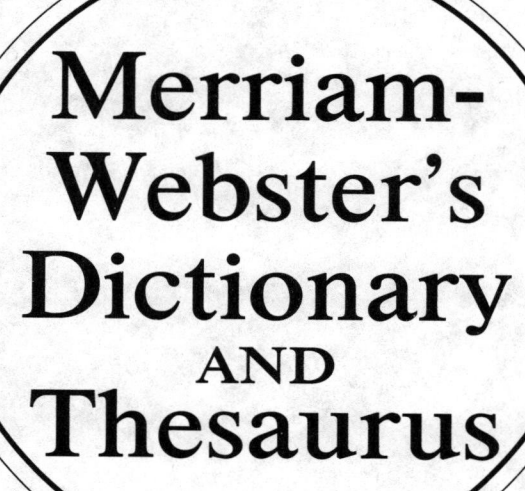

Merriam-
Webster's
Dictionary
AND
Thesaurus
®

Merriam-Webster's Dictionary AND Thesaurus

Merriam-Webster, Incorporated
Springfield, Massachusetts

A GENUINE MERRIAM-WEBSTER

The name *Webster* alone is no guarantee of excellence. It is used by a number of publishers and may serve mainly to mislead an unwary buyer.

Merriam-Webster™ is the name you should look for when you consider the purchase of dictionaries or other fine reference books. It carries the reputation of a company that has been publishing since 1831 and is your assurance of quality and authority.

Copyright © 2020 by Merriam-Webster, Incorporated

Library of Congress Cataloging-in-Publication Data

Names: Merriam-Webster, Inc., editor.
Title: Merriam-Webster's dictionary and thesaurus.
Other titles: Dictionary and thesaurus
Description: Springfield, Massachusetts : Merriam-Webster, Incorporated, 2020.
Identifiers: LCCN 2020002059 | ISBN 9780877793526 (hardcover) | ISBN 9780877797425 (trade paperback)
Subjects: LCSH: English language—Dictionaries. | English language—Synonyms and antonyms—Dictionaries.
Classification: LCC PE1628 .M367 2020 | DDC 423—dc23
LC record available at https://lccn.loc.gov/2020002059

Printed in China

1st printing   XY Printing Co.   Guangzhou   May 2020

PREFACE

Merriam-Webster's Dictionary and Thesaurus combines the functions of a dictionary and a thesaurus in one integrated volume. In this work, the dictionary features of word meanings, pronunciations, and grammatical information are presented along with the synonym and antonym features of a thesaurus. Rather than separating the dictionary and thesaurus into different sections of the book, here the thesaurus material for a word immediately follows its dictionary entry. Presenting the dictionary and thesaurus as a unified whole enables readers and writers to access both kinds of information quickly and to see the relationship between them easily.

The dictionary entries in this book are based on *The Merriam-Webster Dictionary*, our highly popular paperback, and on *Merriam-Webster's Collegiate Dictionary* and the dictionary on our award-winning website, Merriam-Webster.com. The thesaurus entries are drawn from Merriam-Webster's most up-to-date thesauruses. Our editors prepared both the dictionary and thesaurus entries to ensure correspondence between the indicated dictionary senses and the selection of similar and contrasting words offered in the thesaurus lists.

More than 60,000 boldface dictionary entries give coverage to the most frequently used words in the language. The definitions are based on examples of actual word use found in the Merriam-Webster citation files, which now contain more than 100 million words available to us through electronic searching. The thesaurus lists, which follow the definitions, are set off in lightly tinted boxes. They offer more than 160,000 synonyms, antonyms, and related words for the writer interested in finding a more appropriate or more colorful word choice. In the back of the book is a guide to Basic English Punctuation.

The idea for this book came from John M. Morse while he was president of Merriam-Webster, Incorporated. The original volume was years in the making and it drew upon the work and experience of the Merriam-Webster staff of professional lexicographers. Editing was done by Mary W. Cornog, Amy K. Harris Van Vranken, Amy West, Jocelyn W. Franklin, Cynthia S. Ashby, and James G. Lowe, with additional editorial contributions from Daniel B. Brandon, Jennifer N. Cislo, Ilya A. Davidovich, Mary M. Dunn, and E. Louise Langford. Robert D. Copeland was general editor of the project.

The current volume is the result of a significant updating. The editors who worked on the project were Susan L. Brady, who did the primary editing, Daniel B. Brandon, Serenity H. Carr, Sarah S. Carragher, Allison M. DeJordy, Joanne M. Despres, Joshua S. Guenter, Anne E. McDonald, Madeline L. Novak, James L. Rader, Adrienne M. Scholz, Neil S. Serven, Emily A. Vezina, Linda P. Wood, and Paul S. Wood. New material was drawn from the on-going work of Merriam-Webster's full editorial staff.

Merriam-Webster published its first dictionary in 1847 and its first thesaurus in 1976. This book continues Merriam-Webster's long and proud tradition of excellence as the premier American publisher of dictionaries, thesauruses, and other references.

PREFACE

USING THIS BOOK

This volume contains so much information that it is necessary to condense much of it, especially the dictionary material, to accommodate the limitations of the printed page. This section provides information on the conventions used throughout the book, from the styling of entries and pronunciation to how we present information on usage and meaning. An understanding of the information contained in these notes will make the book both easier and more rewarding to use.

ENTRIES

A boldface letter or a combination of such letters, including punctuation marks and diacritics where needed, that is set flush with the left-hand margin of each column of type is a main entry. The main entry may consist of letters set solid, of letters joined by a hyphen or a diagonal, or of letters separated by spaces:

alone . . . *adj*
avant–garde . . . *n*
and/or . . . *conj*
assembly language . . . *n*

The material in lightface type that follows each main entry on the same line and on succeeding indented lines presents information about the main entry.

The main entries follow one another in alphabetical order letter by letter: *bird of prey* follows *birdlime*; *Day of Atonement* follows *daylight saving time*. Main entries containing an Arabic numeral are alphabetized as if the numeral were spelled out: *4-H* comes between *fourfold* and *Four Hundred*; *3-D* comes between *three* and *three-dimensional*. Those that often begin with the abbreviation *St.* in common usage have the abbreviation spelled out: *Saint Valentine's Day*. Main entries that begin with *Mc* are alphabetized just as they are spelled.

***

A pair of guide words is printed at the top of each two-page spread. These guide words indicate the range of entries that fall on those pages.

***

When one main entry has exactly the same written form as another, the two are distinguished by superscript numerals preceding each word:

¹melt . . . *vb*
²melt *n*
¹pine . . . *n*
²pine *vb*

Full words come before parts of words made up of the same letters; solid compounds come before hyphenated compounds; hyphenated compounds come before open compounds; and lowercase entries come before those with an initial capital:

¹su·per . . . *n*
²super *adj*
super- . . . *prefix*

run·down . . . *n*
run–down . . . *adj*
run down *vb*
dutch . . . *adv*
Dutch . . . *n*

The centered dots within entry words indicate division points at which a hyphen may be put at the end of a line of print or writing. Thus the noun *cap·puc·ci·no* may be ended on one line and continued on the next in this manner:

           cap-
puccino

           cappuc-
cino

           cappucci-
no

Centered dots are not shown after a single initial letter or before a single terminal letter because typesetters seldom cut off a single letter:

abyss . . . *n*
flighty . . . *adj*
idea . . . *n*

Centered dots are not usually shown at the second and succeeding homographs unless they differ among themselves:

¹sig·nal . . . *n*
²signal *vb*
³signal *adj*
   but
¹min·ute . . . *n*
²mi·nute . . . *adj*

There are acceptable alternative end-of-line divisions just as there are acceptable variant spellings and pronunciations, but no more than one pattern is shown for any entry in this book.

A double hyphen (=) at the end of a line in this book (as in the definition at **bluebell**) stands for a hyphen that is retained when the word is written as a unit on one line. This kind of fixed hyphen is always represented in boldface words in this book with an en dash, longer than an ordinary hyphen.

***

When a main entry is followed by the word *or* and another spelling, the two spellings are equal variants. Both are standard, and either one may be used according to personal inclination:

ocher *or* ochre

If two variants joined by *or* are out of alphabetical order, they remain equal variants. The one printed first is, however, slightly more common than the second:

¹pol·ly·wog *or* pol·li·wog

When another spelling is joined to the main entry by the word *also*, the spelling after *also* is a secondary variant and occurs less frequently than the first:

ab·sinthe *also* ab·sinth

Secondary variants belong to standard usage and may be used according to personal inclination. Once the word *also* is used to signal a secondary variant, all following secondary variants are joined by *or*:

²wool·ly *also* wool·ie *or* wooly

Variants whose spelling puts them alphabetically more than a column away from the main entry are entered at their own alphabetical places as well as at the main entry:

²gage *var of* GAUGE
. . .
¹gauge *also* gage

The Canadian and British spellings (shown as *or Can and Brit*) appear at main entries for single words (**color** . . . *or Can and Brit* **colour**) and hyphenated compounds (**color-blind** . . . *or Can and Brit* **colour-blind**) and for inflected forms. The user can assume the spelling variations carry through to open compounds with the same initial word and to undefined run-on entries, such as **color blindness** and **colorfastness**. Additionally, there are a number of British spelling variants (not so common in Canada) entered separately, such as **idealise** *chiefly Brit var of* IDEALIZE.

To show all the stylings that are found for English compounds would require space that can be better used for other information. So this dictionary limits itself to a single styling for a compound:

peace·mak·er
pell—mell
boom box

When a compound is widely used and one styling predominates, that styling is shown. When a compound is uncommon or when the evidence indicates that two or three stylings are approximately equal in frequency, the styling shown is based on the comparison of other similar compounds.

A main entry may be followed by one or more derivatives or by a homograph with a different functional label. These are run-on entries. Each is introduced by a long dash, and each has a functional label. They are not defined, however, since their meanings are readily understood from the meaning of the root word:

ab·do·men . . . *n* . . . — ab·dom·i·nal . . . *adj* — ab·dom·i·nal·ly . . . *adv*
seis·mo·graph . . . *n* . . . — seis·mo·graph·ic . . . *adj* — seis·mog·ra·phy . . . *n*

A main entry may be followed by one or more phrases containing the entry word or an inflected form of it. These are also run-on entries. Each is introduced by a long dash but there is no functional label. They are, however, defined since their meanings are more than the sum of the meanings of their elements:

¹set . . . *vb* . . . — set sail : to begin a voyage
¹hand . . . *n* . . . — at hand : near in time . . .

Defined phrases of this sort are run on at the entry defining the first major word in the phrase. When there are variants, however, the run-on appears at the entry defining the first major invariable word in the phrase:

¹seed . . . *n* . . . 1 : the grains of plants used for sowing . . . — go to seed *or* run to seed 1 : to develop seed 2 : DECAY

PRONUNCIATION

The matter between a pair of reversed slashes \ \ following the entry word indicates the pronunciation. The symbols used are explained in the chart at the end of this section.

A hyphen is used in the pronunciation to show syllabic division. These hyphens sometimes coincide with the centered dots in the entry word that indicate end-of-line division, and sometimes they do not:

ab·sen·tee \ˌab-sən-ˈtē\
met·ric \ˈme-trik\

A high-set mark ' indicates major (primary) stress or accent; a low-set mark , indicates minor (secondary) stress or accent:

heart·beat \ˈhärt-ˌbēt\

The stress mark stands at the beginning of the syllable that receives the stress. A syllable with neither a high-set mark nor a low-set mark is unstressed:

¹struc·ture \ˈstrək-chər\

The presence of variant pronunciations indicates that not all educated speakers pronounce words the same way. A second-place variant is not to be regarded as less acceptable than the pronunciation that is given first. It may, in fact, be used by as many educated speakers as the first variant, but the requirements of the printed page are such that one must precede the other:

apri·cot \ˈa-prə-ˌkät, ˈā-\
fore·head \ˈfȯr-əd, ˈfȯr-ˌhed\

Symbols enclosed by parentheses represent elements that are present in the pronunciation of some speakers but are absent from the pronunciation of other speakers, or elements that are present in some but absent from other utterances of the same speaker:

¹**om·ni·bus** \\'äm-ni-(,)bəs\\
ad·di·tion·al \\ə-'di-sh(ə-)nəl\\

Thus, the above parentheses indicate that some people say \\'äm-ni-,bəs\\ and others say \\'äm-ni-bəs\\; some \\ə-'di-shə-nəl\\, others \\ə-'di-shnəl\\.

When a main entry has less than a full pronunciation, the missing part is to be supplied from a pronunciation in a preceding entry or within the same pair of reversed slashes:

cham·pi·on·ship \\-,ship\\
pa·la·ver \\pə-'la-vər, -'lä-\\

The pronunciation of the first three syllables of *championship* is found at the main entry *champion*. The hyphens before and after \\'lä\\ in the pronunciation of *palaver* indicate that both the first and the last parts of the pronunciation are to be taken from the immediately preceding pronunciation.

***

In general, no pronunciation is indicated for open compounds consisting of two or more English words that have own-place entry:

witch doctor *n*

Only the first entry in a sequence of numbered homographs is given a pronunciation if their pronunciations are the same:

¹**re·ward** \\ri-'word\\ *vb*
²**reward** *n*

The absent but implied pronunciation of derivatives and compounds run on after a main entry is a combination of the pronunciation at the main entry and the pronunciation of the other element as given at its alphabetical place in the vocabulary:

— **ab·ject·ness** *n*
— **bungee jumper** *n*

Thus, the pronunciation of *abjectness* is the sum of the pronunciations given at *abject* and *-ness*; that of *bungee jumper*, the sum of the pronunciations of the two elements that make up the phrase.

FUNCTIONAL LABELS

An italic label indicating a part of speech or another functional classification follows the pronunciation or, if no pronunciation is given, the main entry. The eight traditional parts of speech are indicated as follows:

bold . . . *adj*
forth·with . . . *adv*
¹**but** . . . *conj*
ge·sund·heit . . . *interj*
bo·le·ro . . . *n*
²**un·der** . . . *prep*
¹**it** . . . *pron*
¹**slap** . . . *vb*

Other italicized labels used to indicate functional classifications that are not traditional parts of speech include:

AT *abbr*
self- *comb form*
un- . . . *prefix*
-ial *adj suffix*
²**-ly** *adv suffix*
²**-er** . . . *n suffix*
-ize . . . *vb suffix*
Fe *symbol*
may . . . *verbal auxiliary*

Functional labels are sometimes combined:

afloat . . . *adj or adv*

INFLECTED FORMS

NOUNS

The plurals of nouns are shown in this dictionary when suffixation brings about a change of final *-y* to *-i-*, when the noun ends in a consonant plus *-o* or in *-ey*, when the noun ends in *-oo*, when the noun has an irregular plural or an uninflected plural or a foreign plural, when the noun is a compound that pluralizes any element but the last, when a final consonant is doubled, when the noun has variant plurals, and when it is believed that the dictionary user might have reasonable doubts about the spelling of the plural or when the plural is spelled in a way contrary to what is expected:

²**spy** *n, pl* **spies**
si·lo . . . *n, pl* **silos**
val·ley . . . *n, pl* **valleys**

²**shampoo** *n, pl* **shampoos**
mouse . . . *n, pl* **mice**
moose . . . *n, pl* **moose**
cri·te·ri·on . . . *n, pl* **-ria**
son–in–law . . . *n, pl* **sons–in–law**
¹**quiz** . . . *n, pl* **quiz·zes**
¹**fish** . . . *n, pl* **fish** *or* **fish·es**
pi . . . *n, pl* **pis**
³**dry** *n, pl* **drys**

Cutback inflected forms are used when the noun has three or more syllables:

ame·ni·ty . . . *n, pl* **-ties**

The plurals of nouns are usually not shown when the base word is unchanged by suffixation, when the noun is a compound whose second element is readily recognizable as a regular free form entered at its own place, or when the noun is unlikely to occur in the plural:

¹night . . . *n*
fore·foot . . . *n*
mo·nog·a·my . . . *n*

Nouns that are plural in form and that are regularly construed as plural are labeled *n pl*:

munch·ies. . . *n pl*

Nouns that are plural in form but that are not always construed as plurals are appropriately labeled:

lo·gis·tics . . . *n sing or pl* : . . .
me·dia . . . *n, pl* **me·di·as**. . . . *2 sing or pl in*
constr : MASS MEDIA

VERBS

The principal parts of verbs are shown in this dictionary when suffixation brings about a doubling of a final consonant or an elision of a final *-e* or a change of final *-y* to *-i-*, when final *-c* changes to *-ck* in suffixation, when the verb ends in *-ey*, when the inflection is irregular, when there are variant inflected forms, and when it is believed that the dictionary user might have reasonable doubts about the spelling of an inflected form or when the inflected form is spelled in a way contrary to what is expected:

²snag *vb* **snagged; snag·ging**
¹move . . . *vb* **moved; mov·ing**
¹cry . . . *vb* **cried; cry·ing**
¹frol·ic . . . *vb* **frol·icked; frol·ick·ing**
¹sur·vey . . . *vb* **sur·veyed; sur·vey·ing**
¹drive . . . *vb* **drove** . . . **driv·en** . . . **driv·ing**
²bus *vb* **bused** *or* **bussed; bus·ing** *or* **bus·sing**
²visa *vb* **vi·saed** . . . **vi·sa·ing**
²chagrin *vb* **cha·grined** . . . **cha·grin·ing**

The principal parts of a regularly inflected verb are shown when it is desirable to indicate the pronunciation of one of the inflected forms:

learn . . . *vb* **learned** \'lərnd, 'lərnt\; **learn·ing**
¹al·ter \'òl-tər\ *vb* **al·tered; al·ter·ing** \-t(ə-)riŋ\

Cutback inflected forms are usually used when the verb has three or more syllables, when it is a two-syllable word that ends in *-l* and has variant spellings, and when it is a compound whose second element is readily recognized as an irregular verb:

elim·i·nate . . . *vb* **-nat·ed; -nat·ing**
²quarrel *vb* **-reled** *or* **-relled; -rel·ing** *or* **-rel·ling**
¹re·take . . . *vb* **-took** . . . **-tak·en** . . . **-tak·ing**

The principal parts of verbs are usually not shown when the base word is unchanged by suffixation or when the verb is a compound whose second element is readily recognizable as a regular free form entered at its own place:

¹jump . . . *vb*
pre·judge . . . *vb*

Another inflected form of English verbs is the third person singular of the present tense, which is regularly formed by the addition of *-s* or *-es* to the base form of the verb. This inflected form is not shown except at a handful of entries (as *have* and *do*) for which it is in some way unusual.

ADJECTIVES & ADVERBS

The comparative and superlative forms of adjectives and adverbs are shown when suffixation brings about a doubling of a final consonant or an elision of a final *-e* or a change of final *-y* to *-i-*, when the word ends in *-ey*, when the inflection is irregular, and when there are variant inflected forms:

¹red . . . *adj* **red·der; red·dest**
¹tame . . . *adj* **tam·er; tam·est**
¹kind·ly . . . *adj* **kind·li·er; -est**
hors·ey *also* **horsy** . . . *adj* **hors·i·er; -est**
¹good . . . *adj* **bet·ter** . . . **best**
¹far . . . *adv* **far·ther** . . . *or* **fur·ther**
. . . **far·thest** *or* **fur·thest**

The superlative forms of adjectives and adverbs of two or more syllables are usually cut back:

³fancy *adj* **fan·ci·er; -est**
¹ear·ly . . . *adv* **ear·li·er; -est**

The comparative and superlative forms of regularly inflected adjectives and adverbs are shown when it is desirable to indicate the pronunciation of the inflected forms:

¹young \'yəŋ\ *adj* **youn·ger** \'yəŋ-gər\;
youn·gest \'yəŋ-gəst\

The inclusion of inflected forms in *-er* and *-est* at adjective and adverb entries means nothing more about the use of more and most with these adjectives and adverbs than that their comparative and superlative degrees may be expressed in either way: *lazier* or *more lazy*; *laziest* or *most lazy*.

At a few adjective entries only the superlative form is shown:

²mere *adj, superlative* **mer·est**

The absence of the comparative form indicates that there is no evidence of its use.

The comparative and superlative forms of adjectives and adverbs are usually not shown when the base word is unchanged by suffixation, when the inflected forms of the word are identical with those of a preceding homograph, or when the word is a compound whose second element is readily recognizable as a regular free form entered at its own place:

¹**near** . . . *adv*
³**good** *adv*
un·wor·thy . . . *adj*

Inflected forms are not shown at run-in and undefined run-on entries.

CAPITALIZATION

Most entries in this dictionary begin with a lowercase letter. A few of these have an italicized label *often cap*, which indicates that the word is as likely to be capitalized as not and that it is as acceptable with an uppercase initial as it is with one in lowercase. Some entries begin with an uppercase letter, which indicates that the word is usually capitalized. The absence of an initial capital or of an *often cap* label indicates that the word is not ordinarily capitalized:

salm·on . . . *n*
gar·gan·tuan . . . *adj, often cap*
Mo·hawk . . . *n*

The capitalization of entries that are open or hyphenated compounds is similarly indicated by the form of the entry or by an italicized label:

dry goods . . . *n pl*
french fry *n, often cap 1st F*
un–Amer·i·can . . . *adj*
Par·kin·son's disease . . . *n*
lazy Su·san . . . *n*
Jack Frost *n*

A word that is capitalized in some senses and lowercase in others shows variations from the form of the main entry by the use of italicized labels at the appropriate senses:

Trin·i·ty . . . *n* . . . **2** *not cap*
To·ry . . . *n* . . . **3** *often not cap*
ti·tan . . . *n* **1** *cap*
re·nais·sance . . . *n* **1** *cap* . . . **2** *often cap*

ETYMOLOGY

This book gives the etymologies for a number of the vocabulary entries. These etymologies are inside square brackets preceding the definition. Meanings given in Roman type within these brackets are not definitions of the entry, but are meanings of the Middle English, Old English, or non-English words within the brackets.

The etymology gives the language from which words borrowed into English have come. It also gives the form of the word in that language or a representation of the word in our alphabet if the form in that language differs from that in English:

philo·den·dron . . . [NL, fr. Gk, neut. of *philodendros* loving trees]
¹**sav·age** . . . [ME, fr. AF *salvage, savage,* fr. LL *salvaticus,* alter. of L *silvaticus* of the woods, wild, fr. *silva* forest]

An etymology beginning with the name of a language (including ME or OE) and not giving the foreign (or Middle English or Old English) form indicates that this form is the same as the form of the entry word:

le·gume . . . [F]
¹**jour·ney** . . . [ME, fr. OE . . .]

An etymology beginning with the name of a language (including ME or OE) and not giving the foreign (or Middle English or Old English) meaning indicates that this meaning is the same as the meaning expressed in the first definition in the entry:

ug·ly . . . *adj* . . . [ME, fr. ON *uggligr* . . .] **1** : FRIGHTFUL, DIRE

USAGE

Three types of status labels are used in this dictionary—temporal, regional, and stylistic—to signal that a word or a sense of a word is not part of the standard vocabulary of English.

The temporal label *obs* for "obsolete" means that there is no evidence of use since 1755:

³**post** *n* **1** *obs*

The label *obs* is a comment on the word being defined. When a thing, as distinguished from the

word used to designate it, is obsolete, appropriate orientation is usually given in the definition:

cat·a·pult . . . *n* **1** : an ancient military machine for hurling missiles

The temporal label *archaic* means that a word or sense once in common use is found today only sporadically or in special contexts:

¹**mete** . . . *vb* . . . **1** *archaic*
¹**thou** . . . *pron, archaic*

The temporal label *dated* means that a word or sense is not often used today but was used by people in the recent past or by older people:

lu·na·cy . . . *n* . . . 1 *dated*

A word or sense limited in use to a specific region of the U.S. has an appropriate label. The adverb *chiefly* precedes a label when the word has some currency outside the specified region, and a double label is used to indicate considerable currency in each of two specific regions:

²wash *n* . . . 5 *West*
do·gie . . . *n, chiefly West*
crul·ler . . . *n* . . . 2 *Northern & Midland*

Words current in all regions of the U.S. have no label.

A word or sense limited in use to one of the other countries of the English-speaking world has an appropriate regional label:

chem·ist . . . *n* . . . 2 *Brit*
loch . . . *n, Scot*
²wireless *n* . . . 2 *chiefly Brit*

The label *dial* for "dialect" indicates that the pattern of use of a word or sense is too complex for summary labeling: it usually includes several regional varieties of American English or of American and British English:

²mind *vb* 1 *chiefly dial*

The stylistic label *slang* is used with words or senses that are especially appropriate in contexts of extreme informality:

³can . . . *vb* . . . 2 *slang*
²grand *n* . . . *slang*

There is no satisfactory objective test for slang, especially with reference to a word out of context. No word, in fact, is invariably slang, and many standard words can be given slang applications.

The stylistic labels *offensive* and *disparaging* are used for those words or senses that in common use are intended to hurt or that are likely to give offense even when they are used without such an intent:

dumb . . . *adj* 1 *often offensive*
egg·head . . . *n, often disparaging*

Definitions are sometimes followed by verbal illustrations that show a typical use of the word in context. These illustrations are enclosed in angle brackets, and the word being illustrated is usually replaced by a lightface swung dash. The swung dash stands for the boldface entry word, and it may be followed by an italicized suffix:

¹jump . . . *vb* . . . 5 . . . ⟨~ the gun⟩
all–around . . . *adj* 1 . . . ⟨best ~ performance⟩
¹can·on . . . *n* . . . 3 . . . ⟨the ~s of good taste⟩
en·joy . . . *vb* . . . 2 . . . ⟨~ed the concert⟩

The swung dash is not used when the form of the boldface entry word is changed in suffixation, and it is not used for compounds:

²deal *vb* . . . 2 . . . ⟨*dealt* him a blow⟩
drum up *vb* 1 . . . ⟨*drum up* business⟩

Definitions are sometimes followed by usage notes that give supplementary information about such matters as idiom, syntax, and semantic relationship. A usage note is introduced by a lightface dash:

²cry *n* . . . 5 . . . — usu. used in the phrase *a far cry*
²drum *vb* . . . 4 . . . — usu. used with *out*
¹jaw . . . *n* . . . 2 . . . — usu. used in pl.
¹ada·gio . . . *adv or adj* . . . — used as a direction in music
hajji . . . *n* . . . — often used as a title

Sometimes a usage note is used in place of a definition. Some function words (as conjunctions and prepositions) have chiefly grammatical meaning and little or no lexical meaning; most interjections express feelings but are otherwise untranslatable into lexical meaning; and some other words (as honorific titles) are more amenable to comment than to definition:

or . . . *conj* — used as a function word to indicate an alternative
at . . . *prep* 1 — used to indicate a point in time or space
auf Wie·der·seh·en . . . *interj* . . . — used to express farewell
sir . . . *n* . . . 2 — used as a usu. respectful form of address

SENSE DIVISION

A boldface colon is used in this dictionary to introduce a definition:

¹equine . . . *adj* . . . : of or relating to the horse

It is also used to separate two or more definitions of a single sense:

no·ti·fy . . . *vb* . . . 1 : to give notice of : report the occurrence of

Boldface Arabic numerals separate the senses of a word that has more than one sense:

ad·judge . . . *vb* . . . 1 : to decide or rule upon as a judge : JUDGE, ADJUDICATE 2 : to hold or pronounce to be : DEEM 3 : . . .

A particular semantic relationship between senses is sometimes suggested by the use of an italic sense divider (as *esp* or *also*).

The sense divider *esp* (for *especially*) is used to introduce the most common meaning included in the more general preceding definition:

crys·tal . . . *n* . . . 2 : something resembling crystal (as in transparency); *esp* : a clear glass used for table articles

The sense divider *also* is used to introduce a meaning related to the preceding sense by an easily understood extension of that sense:

chi·na . . . *n* : porcelain ware; *also* : domestic pottery in general

The order of senses is generally historical: the sense known to have been first used in English is usually entered first. This is not to be taken to mean, however, that each sense of a multisense word developed from the immediately preceding sense. It is altogether possible that sense 1 of a word has given rise to sense 2 and sense 2 to sense 3, but frequently sense 2 and sense 3 may have developed independently of one another from sense 1.

When an italicized label follows a boldface numeral, the label applies only to that specific numbered sense. It does not apply to any other boldface numbered senses:

¹**craft** . . . *n* . . . **3** *pl usu* **craft**
¹**fa·ther** . . . *n* . . . **2** *cap* . . . **5** *often cap*
dul·ci·mer . . . *n* . . . **2** *or* **dul·ci·more** \-ˌmȯr\
²**lift** *n* . . . **5** *chiefly* Brit

At *craft* the *pl* label applies to sense 3 but to none of the other numbered senses. At *father* the *cap label* applies only to sense 2 and the *often cap* label only to sense 5. At *dulcimer* the variant spelling and pronunciation apply only to sense 2, and the *chiefly Brit* label at *lift* applies only to sense 5.

THESAURUS LISTS

Thesaurus lists follow their dictionary entries set off in a light, tinted box. Every dictionary sense that has a corresponding thesaurus list is marked with a black diamond, and the thesaurus list is likewise indicated.

> **bore·dom** . . . *n* ♦ : the condition of being weary and restless because of dullness
>
> ♦ doldrums, ennui, listlessness, restlessness, tedium, tiredness, weariness; . . .

When there are multiple dictionary senses highlighted, the thesaurus lists are marked with the appropriate dictionary sense numbers in square brackets to make it easy for the user to choose the corresponding list of synonyms.

> **abide** . . . *vb* . . . **1** ♦ : to bear patiently . . . **2 a** ♦ : to continue in a state or place **b** ♦ : to have one's abode . . .
>
> ♦ [1] bear, brook . . . ♦ [2a] continue, endure . . . [2b] dwell, live, reside . . .

A word in the synonym lists following an italic *also* is still comparable to the dictionary word in the indicated sense, but has a somewhat less close relationship than words ahead of it. Semicolons separate additional words into related groups.

> ¹**cloak** . . . *n* . . . **2** ♦ : something that conceals . . .
>
> ♦ curtain, hood, mantle, mask, shroud, veil; *also* cover, screen, shield; facade, face, veneer

Thesaurus entries all show synonyms, and some lists also have common contrasting words (antonyms), which are introduced by a bold italic *Ant*.

> **fer·tile** . . . *adj* **1** ♦ : producing plentifully . . .
>
> ♦ fecund, fruitful, luxuriant, productive, prolific, rich . . . ***Ant*** barren, infertile, sterile, unfruitful, unproductive

CROSS-REFERENCE

Four different kinds of cross-references are used in this book: directional, synonymous, cognate, and inflectional. In each instance the cross-reference is readily recognized by the lightface small capitals in which it is printed.

A cross-reference following a lightface dash and beginning with *see*, *compare*, or *more at* is a directional cross-reference. It directs the user to look elsewhere for further information:

> **ordinal number** . . . *n* . . . —compare CARDINAL NUMBER

A cross-reference following a boldface colon is a synonymous cross-reference. It may stand alone as the only definition for an entry or for a sense of an entry; it may follow an analytical definition; it may be one of two or more synonymous cross-references separated by commas:

> **fact** . . . *n* . . . **1** : DEED . . .
> ²**paper** *adj* . . . **3** : existing only in theory : NOMINAL

A synonymous cross-reference indicates that an entry, a definition at the entry, or a specific sense at the entry cross-referred to can be substituted as a definition for the entry or the sense in which the cross-reference appears.

A cross-reference following an italic *var of* ("variant of") is a cognate cross-reference:

> **pick·a·back** . . . *var of* PIGGYBACK

Occasionally a cognate cross-reference has a limiting label preceding *var of* as an indication that the variant is not standard American English:

> **cosy** *chiefly Brit var of* COZY

A cross-reference following an italic label that identifies an entry as an inflected form (as of a noun or verb) is an inflectional cross-reference:

> **calves** *pl of* CALF
> **woven** *past part of* WEAVE

Inflectional cross-references appear only when the inflected form falls at least a column away from the entry cross-referred to.

COMBINING FORMS, PREFIXES, & SUFFIXES

An entry that begins or ends with a hyphen is an element that forms part of a compound:

-wise . . . *adv comb form* . . . ⟨slant*wise*⟩
ex- . . . *prefix* . . . **2** . . . ⟨*ex*-president⟩
-let . . . *n suffix* **1** . . . ⟨book*let*⟩

Combining forms, prefixes, and suffixes are entered in this dictionary for two reasons: to make understandable the meaning of many undefined run-ons and to make recognizable the meaningful elements of words that are not entered in the dictionary.

LISTS OF UNDEFINED WORDS

Many words that begin with the prefixes or combining forms *anti-, in-, non-, over-, re-, self-, semi-, sub-, super-,* and *un-* are self-explanatory combinations of the prefix or combining form

and a word entered elsewhere in the dictionary, and these words are listed undefined at the bottom of the page or spread following the entry for the prefix.

ABBREVIATIONS & SYMBOLS

Abbreviations and symbols for chemical elements are included as main entries in the vocabulary:

RSVP *abbr* . . . *please reply*
Ca *symbol calcium*

Abbreviations have been normalized to one form. However, there is considerable variation in the use of periods and capitalization (as *vhf, v.h.f, VHF,* and *V.H.F.,* and stylings other than those in this book are often acceptable.

ABBREVIATIONS IN THIS WORK

ab	about	G, Ger	German	ON	Old Norse
abbr	abbreviation	Gk	Greek	OPer	Old Persian
abl	ablative	Gmc	Germanic	orig	originally
acc	accusative	Heb	Hebrew	Per	Persian
A.D.	anno Domini	Hung	Hungarian	perh	perhaps
adj	adjective	imit	imitative	Pg	Portuguese
adv	adverb	imper	imperative	pl	plural
alter	alteration	interj	interjection	Pol	Polish
Am	American	Ir	Irish	pp	past participle
AmerF	American French	irreg	irregular	prep	preposition
AmerInd	American Indian	It, Ital	Italian	pres	present, president
AmerSp	American Spanish	Jp	Japanese	prob	probably
Ant	Antonym(s)	K	Kelvin	pron	pronoun,
Ar	Arabic	L	Latin		pronunciation
B.C.	before Christ	LaF	Louisiana French	prp	present participle
Brit	British	LG	Low German	pseud	pseudonym
C	Celsius	LGk	Late Greek	r	reigned
Calif	California	LHeb	Late Hebrew	Russ	Russian
Can	Canadian	lit	literally	Sc	Scotch, Scots
CanF	Canadian French	LL	Late Latin	Scand	Scandinavian
cap	capital, capitalized	masc	masculine	ScGael	Scottish Gaelic
Celt	Celtic	MD	Middle Dutch	Scot	Scottish
cent	century	ME	Middle English	sing	singular
Chin	Chinese	MexSp	Mexican Spanish	Skt	Sanskrit
comb	combining	MF	Middle French	So	South
compar	comparative	MGk	Middle Greek	Sp	Spanish
conj	conjunction	ML	Medieval Latin	St	Saint
D	Dutch	modif	modification	superl	superlative
Dan	Danish	MS	manuscript	Sw	Swedish
dat	dative	n	noun	trans	translation
dial	dialect	neut	neuter	Turk	Turkish
dim	diminutive	NL	New Latin	US	United States
E	English	No	North	usu	usually
Egypt	Egyptian	Norw	Norwegian	var	variant
Eng	English	n pl	noun plural	vb	verb
esp	especially	obs	obsolete	VL	Vulgar Latin
F	Fahrenheit, French	OE	Old English	W	Welsh
fem	feminine	OF	Old French		
fr	from	OIt	Old Italian		

PRONUNCIATION SYMBOLS

ə	abut, collect, suppose	ȯi	toy
ˈə, ˌə	humdrum	p	pepper, lip
ə	(in əl, ən) battle, cotton; (in lə, mə, rə)	r	rarity
	French table, prisme, titre	s	source, less
ər	operation, further	sh	shy, mission
a	map, patch	t	tie, attack
ā	day, fate	th	thin, ether
ä	bother, cot, father	th	then, either
är	car, heart	ü	boot, few \ˈfyü\
au̇	now, out	u̇	put, pure \ˈpyu̇r\
b	baby, rib	u̇r	boor, tour
ch	chin, catch	ᴜє	French rue, German füllen, fühlen
d	did, adder	v	vivid, give
e	set, red	w	we, away
er	bare, fair	y	yard, cue \ˈkyü\
ē	beat, easy	y	indicates that a preceding \l\, \n\, or
f	fifty, cuff		\w\ is modified by having the tongue
g	go, big		approximate the position for \y\, as in
h	hat, ahead		French digne \dēnʸ\
hw	whale	z	zone, raise
i	tip, banish	zh	vision, pleasure
ir	near, deer	\	slant line used in pairs to mark the
ī	site, buy		beginning and end of a transcription:
j	job, edge		\ˈpen\
k	kin, cook	ˈ	mark at the beginning of a syllable that
k̲	German Bach, Scots loch		has primary (strongest) stress: \ˈshə-fəl-
l	lily, cool		ˌbȯrd\
m	murmur, dim	ˌ	mark at the beginning of a syllable that
n	nine, own		has secondary (next-strongest) stress:
ⁿ	indicates that a preceding vowel is pro-		\ˈshə-fəl-ˌbȯrd\
	nounced through both nose and mouth,	-	mark of a syllable division in pronunci-
	as in French bon \bōⁿ\		ations (the mark of end-of-line division
ŋ	sing, singer, finger, ink		in boldface entries is a centered dot
ō	bone, hollow	( )	indicate that what is symbolized be-
ȯ	saw		tween sometimes occurs and sometimes
ȯr	boar, port		does not occur in the pronunciation of
œ	French bœuf, feu, German Hölle,		the word: **bakery** \ˈbā-k(ə-)rē\ =
	Höhle		\ˈbā-kə-rē, ˈbā-krē\

A

¹a \'ā\ *n, pl* **a's** *or* **as** \'āz\ *often cap* **1** : the 1st letter of the English alphabet **2** : a grade rating a student's work as superior

²a \ə, (')ā\ *indefinite article* : ONE, SOME — used to indicate an unspecified or unidentified individual ⟨there's ∼ man outside⟩

³a *abbr, often cap* **1** absent **2** acre **3** alto **4** answer **5** are **6** area

AA *abbr* **1** Alcoholics Anonymous **2** antiaircraft **3** associate in arts

AAA *abbr* American Automobile Association

A and M *abbr* agricultural and mechanical

A and R *abbr* artists and repertory

aard·vark \'ärd-,värk\ *n* [obs. Afrikaans, fr. Afrikaans *aard* earth + *vark* pig] : a large burrowing African mammal that feeds on ants and termites with its long sticky tongue

¹ab \'ab\ *n* : an abdominal muscle

²ab *abbr* about

AB *abbr* **1** able-bodied seaman **2** airman basic **3** [NL *artium baccalaureus*] bachelor of arts

ABA *abbr* American Bar Association

aback \ə-'bak\ *adv* ♦ : by surprise ⟨taken ∼⟩

♦ suddenly, unaware, unawares — more at UNAWARES

aba·cus \'a-bə-kəs\ *n, pl* **aba·ci** \-,sī, -,kē\ *or* **aba·cus·es** : an instrument for making calculations by sliding counters along rods or grooves

¹abaft \ə-'baft\ *prep* : to the rear of

²abaft *adv* : toward or at the stern : AFT

ab·a·lo·ne \,a-bə-'lō-nē, 'a-bə-,\ *n* : any of a genus of large edible sea mollusks with a flattened slightly spiral shell with holes along the edge

¹aban·don \ə-'ban-dən\ *vb* [ME *abandounen*, fr. AF *abanduner*, fr. (*mettre*) *a bandun* to hand over, put in someone's control] ♦ : to give up completely : FORSAKE, DESERT

♦ desert, forsake, maroon, quit; *also* relinquish, retreat (from), take off (from), vacate, withdraw (from)

²abandon *n* ♦ : a thorough yielding to natural impulses

♦ abandonment, ease, lightheartedness, naturalness, spontaneity, unrestraint; *also* ardor, enthusiasm, exuberance, fervor, spirit, warmth, zeal *Ant* constraint, restraint

aban·doned \ə-'ban-dənd\ *adj* **1** : morally unrestrained **2** ♦ : given up : FORSAKEN

♦ derelict, deserted, forsaken; *also* ignored, neglected, unattended, untended

aban·don·ment \ə-'ban-dən-mənt\ *n* **1** ♦ : the act of abandoning **2** ♦ : freedom from restraint

♦ [1] dereliction, desertion — more at DERELICTION
♦ [2] abandon, ease, lightheartedness, naturalness, spontaneity, unrestraint — more at ABANDON

abase \ə-'bās\ *vb* **abased; abas·ing** ♦ : to lower in rank, office, prestige, or esteem : HUMBLE, DEGRADE — **abasement** *n*

♦ debase, degrade, demean, demoralize, humble, subvert, warp — more at DEBASE

abash \ə-'bash\ *vb* ♦ : to destroy the composure of : EMBARRASS

♦ confound, confuse, discomfit, disconcert, discountenance, embarrass, faze, fluster, mortify, rattle — more at EMBARRASS

abash·ment \ə-'bash-mənt\ *n* ♦ : the quality or state of being abashed

♦ confusion, discomfiture, embarrassment, fluster, mortification — more at EMBARRASSMENT

abate \ə-'bāt\ *vb* **abat·ed; abat·ing** **1** : to put an end to ⟨∼ a nuisance⟩ **2** ♦ : to decrease in amount, number, or degree

♦ decline, decrease, diminish, dwindle, ebb, fall, lessen, recede, subside, taper, wane — more at DECREASE

abate·ment \ə-'bāt-mənt\ *n* **1** ♦ : an amount of taking away; *esp* : a deduction from a tax **2** ♦ : an amount abated or lessened

♦ [1] deduction, discount, reduction — more at DEDUCTION ♦ [1, 2] decline, decrease, decrement, diminution, drop, fall, loss, reduction, shrinkage — more at DECREASE

ab·at·toir \'a-bə-,twär\ *n* [F] : SLAUGHTERHOUSE

ab·ba·cy \'a-bə-sē\ *n, pl* **-cies** : the office or term of office of an abbot or abbess

ab·bé \a-'bā, 'a-,\ *n* : a member of the French secular clergy — used as a title

ab·bess \'a-bəs\ *n* : the superior of a convent for nuns

ab·bey \'a-bē\ *n, pl* **abbeys** **1** ♦ : a house for persons and esp. monks under religious vows : MONASTERY **2** : CONVENT **3** : an abbey church

♦ cloister, friary, monastery, priory — more at MONASTERY

ab·bot \'a-bət\ *n* [ME *abbod*, fr. OE, fr. LL *abbat-, abbas*, fr. LGk *abbas*, fr. Aramaic *abbā* father] : the superior of a monastery for men

abbr *abbr* abbreviation

ab·bre·vi·ate \ə-'brē-vē-,āt\ *vb* **-at·ed; -at·ing** ♦ : to make briefer : SHORTEN, CURTAIL; *esp* : to reduce to an abbreviation

♦ abridge, curtail, cut back, shorten — more at SHORTEN

ab·bre·vi·a·tion \ə-,brē-vē-'ā-shən\ *n* **1** ♦ : the act or result of abbreviating : ABRIDGMENT **2** : a shortened form of a word or phrase used for brevity esp. in writing

♦ abridgment, condensation, digest — more at ABRIDGMENT

¹ABC \,ā-(,)bē-'sē\ *n, pl* **ABC's** *or* **ABCs** \-'sēz\ **1** : ALPHABET — usu. used in pl. **2** : RUDIMENTS — usu. used in pl.

²ABC *abbr* American Broadcasting Company

Ab·di·as \ab-'dī-əs\ *n* : OBADIAH

ab·di·cate \'ab-di-,kāt\ *vb* **-cat·ed; -cat·ing** ♦ : to give up (as a throne) formally — **ab·di·ca·tion** \,ab-di-'kā-shən\ *n*

♦ abnegate, cede, relinquish, renounce, resign, step down, surrender; *also* abjure, disavow, disclaim, disown, deny, waive

ab·do·men \'ab-də-mən, ab-'dō-\ *n* **1** ♦ : the cavity in or area of the body between the chest and the pelvis **2** : the part of the body posterior to the thorax in an arthropod — **ab·dom·i·nal** \ab-'dä-mən-ᵊl\ *adj* — **ab·dom·i·nal·ly** *adv*

♦ belly, gut, solar plexus, stomach, tummy — more at STOMACH

ab·duct \ab-'dəkt\ *vb* : to take away (a person) by force : KIDNAP — **ab·duc·tion** \-'dək-shən\ *n* — **ab·duc·tor** \-tər\ *n*

abeam \ə-'bēm\ *adv or adj* : on a line at right angles to a ship's keel

abed \ə-'bed\ *adv or adj* : in bed

Abe·na·ki \,a-bə-'nä-kē\ *n, pl* **Abenaki** *or* **Abenakis** : a member of a group of American Indian peoples of northern New England and southern Quebec

ab·er·rant \a-'ber-ənt\ *adj* **1** ♦ : departing from the right or normal way **2** ♦ : departing from the usual or natural type : ATYPICAL

♦ [1] abnormal, anomalous, deviant, irregular, unnatural — more at DEVIANT ♦ [2] abnormal, atypical, exceptional, extraordinary, freak, odd, peculiar, uncommon, uncustomary, unique, unusual, unwonted — more at EXCEPTIONAL

ab·er·ra·tion \ˌa-bə-ˈrā-shən\ *n* **1** : deviation esp. from a moral standard or normal state **2** : failure of a mirror or lens to produce exact point-to-point correspondence between an object and its image **3** ♦ : unsoundness of mind : DERANGEMENT

  ♦ dementia, derangement, insanity, lunacy, madness, mania — more at INSANITY

abet \ə-ˈbet\ *vb* **abet·ted; abet·ting** [ME *abetten*, fr. AF *abeter*, fr. *beter* to bait] **1** ♦ : to actively second and encourage (as in wrongdoing) : INCITE **2** ♦ : to assist or support in the achievement of a purpose

  ♦ [1, 2] ferment, foment, incite, instigate, provoke, raise, stir, whip — more at INCITE ♦ [2] aid, assist, back, help, prop, support — more at HELP

abet·tor *also* **abet·ter** \-ˈbe-tər\ *n* ♦ : one that abets

  ♦ accessory, accomplice, cohort, confederate — more at ACCOMPLICE ♦ ally, backer, confederate, supporter, sympathizer — more at ALLY

abey·ance \ə-ˈbā-əns\ *n* ♦ : a condition of suspended activity

  ♦ doldrums, dormancy, latency, quiescence, suspension; *also* inaction, inertia, inertness, motionlessness *Ant* continuance, continuation

ab·hor \əb-ˈhȯr, ab-\ *vb* **ab·horred; ab·hor·ring** [ME *abhorren*, fr. L *abhorrēre*, fr. *ab-* + *horrēre* to shudder] ♦ : to regard with extreme dislike : LOATHE, DETEST

  ♦ abominate, despise, detest, execrate, hate, loathe — more at HATE

ab·hor·rence \-əns\ *n* **1** ♦ : the feeling of one who abhors **2** ♦ : one that is abhorred

  ♦ [1] abomination, execration, hate, hatred, loathing — more at HATE ♦ [2] abomination, anathema, antipathy, aversion, bête noire, hate — more at HATE

ab·hor·rent \-ənt\ *adj* ♦ : causing or deserving strong dislike : LOATHSOME

  ♦ abominable, appalling, hideous, horrible, horrid, offensive, repellent, repugnant, repulsive, revolting, shocking — more at OFFENSIVE

abid·ance \ə-ˈbī-dən(t)s\ *n* ♦ : an act or state of abiding

  ♦ ceaselessness, continuance, continuation, duration, endurance, persistence, subsistence — more at CONTINUATION

abide \ə-ˈbīd\ *vb* **abode** \-ˈbōd\ *or* **abid·ed; abid·ing** **1** ♦ : to bear patiently : ENDURE **2 a** ♦ : to continue in a state or place **b** ♦ : to have one's abode — **abide by** : to conform or acquiesce to ⟨*abide by* the law⟩

  ♦ [1] bear, brook, countenance, endure, meet, stand, stick out, stomach, support, sustain, take, tolerate — more at BEAR ♦ [2a] continue, endure, hold, keep up, last, persist, run on — more at CONTINUE ♦ [2b] dwell, live, reside — more at LIVE

abid·ing \ə-ˈbī-diŋ\ *adj* ♦ : lasting and unchanging : ENDURING, CONTINUING ⟨an ∼ interest in nature⟩

  ♦ ageless, continuing, dateless, enduring, eternal, everlasting, immortal, imperishable, lasting, perennial, perpetual, timeless, undying; *also* ceaseless, endless, permanent; changeless, constant, stable, stationary, steady, unchanging, unvarying

abil·i·ty \ə-ˈbi-lə-tē\ *n, pl* **-ties** ♦ : the quality of being able

  ♦ capability, capacity, competence, faculty; *also* aptitude, aptness, endowment, facility, gift, knack, talent *Ant* inability, incapability, incapacity, incompetence, ineptitude

-ability *also* **-ibility** *n suffix* : capacity, fitness, or tendency to act or be acted on in a (specified) way ⟨flamm*ability*⟩

ab·ject \ˈab-jekt, ab-ˈjekt\ *adj* : low in spirit or hope : CRINGING — **ab·jec·tion** \ab-ˈjek-shən\ *n* — **ab·ject·ly** *adv* — **ab·ject·ness** *n*

ab·jure \ab-ˈju̇r\ *vb* **ab·jured; ab·jur·ing** **1** ♦ : to renounce

solemnly : RECANT **2** : to abstain from — **ab·ju·ra·tion** \ˌab-jə-ˈrā-shən\ *n*

  ♦ recant, renounce, retract, take back, unsay, withdraw; *also* deny, contradict, disavow, disclaim, disown, gainsay, negate, negative, repudiate *Ant* adhere (to)

abl *abbr* ablative

ab·late \a-ˈblāt\ *vb* **ab·lat·ed; ab·lat·ing** : to remove or become removed esp. by cutting, abrading, or vaporizing

ab·la·tion \a-ˈblā-shən\ *n* **1** : surgical cutting and removal **2** : loss of a part (as the outside of a nose cone) by melting or vaporization

ab·la·tive \ˈab-lə-tiv\ *adj* : of, relating to, or constituting a grammatical case (as in Latin) expressing typically the relation of separation and source — **ablative** *n*

ablaze \ə-ˈblāz\ *adj or adv* **1** ♦ : being on fire : BLAZING **2** ♦ : radiant with light

  ♦ [1] afire, burning, fiery; *also* aglow, alight, flaring, glowing, live, smoldering ♦ [2] alight, bright, light — more at BRIGHT

able \ˈā-bəl\ *adj* **abler** \-b(ə-)lər\; **ablest** \-b(ə-)ləst\ [ME, fr. AF, fr. L *habilis* apt, fr. *habēre* to hold, possess] **1** ♦ : having sufficient power, skill, or resources to accomplish an object **2** ♦ : marked by skill or efficiency

  ♦ [1, 2] capable, competent, fit, good, qualified, suitable — more at COMPETENT

-able *also* **-ible** *adj suffix* **1** : capable of, fit for, or worthy of (being so acted upon or toward) ⟨break*able*⟩ ⟨collect*ible*⟩ **2** : tending, given, or liable to ⟨knowledge*able*⟩ ⟨perish*able*⟩

able–bod·ied \ˌā-bəl-ˈbä-dēd\ *adj* ♦ : having a sound strong body

  ♦ chipper, fit, hale, healthy, hearty, robust, sound, well, whole, wholesome — more at HEALTHY

abloom \ə-ˈblüm\ *adj* : BLOOMING

ab·lu·tion \ə-ˈblü-shən, a-\ *n* : the washing of one's body or part of it

ably \ˈā-blē\ *adv* ♦ : in an able manner

  ♦ adeptly, expertly, masterfully, proficiently, skillfully, well — more at WELL

ABM \ˌā-(ˌ)bē-ˈem\ *n, pl* **ABM's** *or* **ABMs** : ANTIBALLISTIC MISSILE

ab·ne·gate \ˈab-ni-ˌgāt\ *vb* **-gat·ed; -gat·ing** **1** : DENY, RENOUNCE **2** ♦ : to give up (as a right or privilege) : SURRENDER, RELINQUISH

  ♦ abdicate, cede, relinquish, renounce, resign, step down, surrender — more at ABDICATE

ab·ne·ga·tion \ˌab-ni-ˈgā-shən\ *n* ♦ : restraint or denial of desire or self-interest

  ♦ renouncement, renunciation, repudiation, self-denial — more at RENUNCIATION

ab·nor·mal \ab-ˈnȯr-məl\ *adj* ♦ : deviating from the normal or average — **ab·nor·mal·ly** *adv*

  ♦ aberrant, exceptional, extraordinary, rare, singular, uncommon, uncustomary, unique, unusual — more at EXCEPTIONAL ♦ aberrant, anomalous, atypical, deviant, irregular, unnatural — more at DEVIANT

ab·nor·mal·i·ty \ˌab-nȯr-ˈma-lə-tē\ *n* ♦ : something abnormal

  ♦ freak, monster, monstrosity — more at FREAK

¹aboard \ə-ˈbȯrd\ *adv* **1** : ALONGSIDE **2** : on, onto, or within a car, ship, or aircraft **3** : in or into a group or association ⟨welcome new workers ∼⟩

²aboard *prep* : ON, ONTO, WITHIN

abode \ə-ˈbōd\ *n* **1** : STAY, SOJOURN **2** ♦ : the place where one abides : HOME, RESIDENCE

  ♦ domicile, dwelling, home, house, lodging, quarters, residence — more at HOME

abol·ish \ə-ˈbä-lish\ *vb* ♦ : to do away with : ANNUL — **ab·o·li·tion** \ˌa-bə-ˈli-shən\ *n*

  ♦ abrogate, annul, cancel, dissolve, invalidate, negate, nullify, quash, repeal, rescind, void; *also* countermand, override, overrule, overturn, veto; retract, reverse, revoke, suspend, withdraw

ab·o·li·tion·ism \ˌa-bə-ˈli-shə-ˌni-zəm\ n : advocacy of the abolition of slavery — **ab·o·li·tion·ist** \-ˈli-sh(ə-)nist\ n or adj

A–bomb \ˈā-ˌbäm\ n : ATOMIC BOMB — **A–bomb** vb

abom·i·na·ble \ə-ˈbä-mə-nə-bəl\ adj ♦ : worthy of or causing disgust or hatred : ODIOUS

♦ abhorrent, appalling, awful, horrible, horrid, odious, offensive, repellent, repugnant, repulsive, revolting

abominable snow·man \-ˈsnō-mən, -ˌman\ n, often cap A&S : a mysterious creature with human or apelike characteristics reported to exist in the high Himalayas

abom·i·nate \ə-ˈbä-mə-ˌnāt\ vb **-nat·ed; -nat·ing** [L abominari, lit., to deprecate as an ill omen, fr. ab- away + omen omen] ♦ : to hate or loathe intensely : LOATHE, DETEST

♦ abhor, despise, detest, execrate, hate, loathe — more at HATE

abom·i·na·tion \ə-ˌbä-mə-ˈnā-shən\ n **1** ♦ : something abominable **2** ♦ : extreme disgust and hatred : LOATHING

♦ [1] abhorrence, anathema, antipathy, aversion, bête noire, hate — more at HATE ♦ [2] abhorrence, execration, hate, hatred, loathing — more at HATE

ab·orig·i·nal \ˌa-bə-ˈri-jə-nəl\ adj ♦ : being the first or earliest known of its kind present in a region : INDIGENOUS

♦ born, endemic, indigenous, native — more at NATIVE

ab·orig·i·ne \ˌa-bə-ˈri-jə-nē\ n : a member of the original race of inhabitants of a region : NATIVE

aborn·ing \ə-ˈbȯr-niŋ\ adv : while being born or produced

¹**abort** \ə-ˈbȯrt\ vb **1** : to cause or undergo abortion **2** ♦ : to terminate prematurely ⟨∼ a spaceflight⟩

♦ call, call off, cancel, drop, recall, repeal, rescind, revoke — more at CANCEL

²**abort** n : the premature termination of a mission of or a procedure relating to an aircraft or spacecraft

abor·tion \ə-ˈbȯr-shən\ n **1** : the spontaneous or induced termination of a pregnancy after, accompanied by, resulting in, or closely followed by the death of the embryo or fetus **2** ♦ : arrest of development (as of a part or process); also : a result of such arrest

♦ calling, cancellation, recall, repeal, rescission, revocation — more at CANCELLATION

abor·tion·ist \-sh(ə-)nist\ n : one who induces abortions

abor·tive \ə-ˈbȯr-tiv\ adj ♦ : not successful

♦ fruitless, futile, ineffective, unproductive, unsuccessful — more at FUTILE

abound \ə-ˈbau̇nd\ vb **1** ♦ : to be plentiful : TEEM **2** : to be fully supplied

♦ brim, bulge, burst, crawl, swarm, teem

¹**about** \ə-ˈbau̇t\ adv **1** ♦ : reasonably close to; also : on the verge of ⟨∼ to join the army⟩ **2** : on all sides **3** : in the vicinity : NEARBY **4** ♦ : in the opposite direction

♦ [1] almost, most, much, near, nearly, next to, nigh, practically, some, virtually, well-nigh — more at ALMOST ♦ [4] around, back, round — more at AROUND

²**about** prep **1** : on every side of **2** ♦ : near to **3** ♦ : relating to : CONCERNING **4** ♦ : over or in different parts of

♦ [2] around, by, near, next to — more at AROUND ♦ [3] apropos of, concerning, of, on, regarding, respecting, toward; also as to, over ♦ [4] around, over, round, through, throughout — more at AROUND

about–face \-ˈfās\ n : a reversal of direction or attitude — **about–face** vb

¹**above** \ə-ˈbəv\ adv **1** : in the sky; also : in or to heaven **2** ♦ : in or to a higher place; also : higher on the same page or on a preceding page

♦ aloft, over, overhead, skyward *Ant* below, beneath, under

²**above** prep **1** : in or to a higher place than : OVER ⟨storm clouds ∼ the bay⟩ **2** : superior to ⟨he thought her far ∼ him⟩ **3** : more than : EXCEEDING **4** : as distinct from ⟨∼ the noise⟩

above·board \-ˌbȯrd\ adv or adj : without concealment or deception : OPENLY

abp abbr archbishop

abr abbr abridged; abridgment

ab·ra·ca·dab·ra \ˌa-brə-kə-ˈda-brə\ n **1** ♦ : a magical charm or incantation against calamity **2** ♦ : unintelligible or meaningless language : GIBBERISH

♦ [1, 2] bewitchment, charm, conjuration, enchantment, incantation, spell — more at SPELL

abrade \ə-ˈbrād\ vb **abrad·ed; abrad·ing 1 a** ♦ : to wear away by friction **b** ♦ : to irritate or roughen by rubbing **2** : to wear down in spirit : IRRITATE

♦ [1a] chafe, erode, fray, fret, gall, rub, wear; also file, gnaw, grate, graze, grind, nibble, rasp, sandblast, sandpaper, scour, scrape, scuff, shave ♦ [1b] graze, scrape, scratch, scuff — more at SCRAPE

abra·sion \ə-ˈbrā-zhən\ n [ML abrasion-, abrasio, fr. L abradere] : an abraded area of the skin or mucous membrane

¹**abra·sive** \ə-ˈbrā-siv\ n : a substance (as pumice) for abrading, smoothing, or polishing

²**abrasive** adj : tending to abrade : causing irritation ⟨∼ relationships⟩ — **abra·sive·ly** adv — **abra·sive·ness** n

abreast \ə-ˈbrest\ adv or adj **1** : side by side **2** ♦ : up to a standard or level esp. of knowledge

♦ conversant, familiar, informed, knowledgeable, up, up-to-date, versed — more at FAMILIAR

abridge \ə-ˈbrij\ vb **abridged; abridg·ing** [ME abregen, fr. AF abreger, fr. LL abbreviare, fr. L ad to + brevis short] ♦ : to lessen in length or extent : SHORTEN

♦ abbreviate, curtail, cut back, shorten — more at SHORTEN

abridg·ment or **abridge·ment** \ə-ˈbrij-mənt\ n ♦ : a shortened form of a work

♦ abbreviation, condensation, digest; also abstract, brief, outline, overview, précis, recap, recapitulation, résumé, review, sketch, sum, summary, summation, syllabus, synopsis, survey, wrap-up

abroad \ə-ˈbrȯd\ adv or adj **1** : over a wide area **2** : away from one's home **3** : outside one's country

ab·ro·gate \ˈa-brə-ˌgāt\ vb **-gat·ed; -gat·ing** ♦ : to abolish by authoritative action : ANNUL — **ab·ro·ga·tion** \ˌa-brə-ˈgā-shən\ n

♦ abolish, annul, cancel, dissolve, invalidate, negate, nullify, quash, repeal, rescind, void — more at ABOLISH

abrupt \ə-ˈbrəpt\ adj **1** : broken or as if broken off **2** : SUDDEN, HASTY **3** ♦ : so quick as to seem rude **4** : DISCONNECTED **5** : STEEP

♦ bluff, blunt, brusque, curt, snippy — more at BLUNT

abrupt·ly \-lē\ adv : in an abrupt manner

abs abbr absolute

ab·scess \ˈab-ˌses\ n, pl **ab·scess·es** [L abscessus, lit., act of going away, fr. abscedere to go away, fr. abs-, ab- away + cedere to go] : a localized collection of pus surrounded by inflamed tissue — **ab·scessed** \-ˌsest\ adj

ab·scis·sa \ab-ˈsi-sə\ n, pl **abscissas** also **ab·scis·sae** \-ˈsi-(ˌ)sē\ : the horizontal coordinate of a point in a plane coordinate system obtained by measuring parallel to the x-axis

ab·scis·sion \ab-ˈsi-zhən\ n **1** : the act or process of cutting off **2** : the natural separation of flowers, fruits, or leaves from plants — **ab·scise** \ab-ˈsīz\ vb

ab·scond \ab-ˈskänd\ vb ♦ : to depart secretly and hide oneself

♦ clear out, escape, flee, fly, get out, lam, run away, run off — more at ESCAPE

ab·sence \ˈab-səns\ n **1** : the state or time of being absent **2** ♦ : failure to be present where needed, wanted, or normally expected : WANT, LACK **3** : INATTENTION

♦ lack, need, want — more at NEED

¹**ab·sent** \ˈab-sənt\ adj **1** ♦ : not present **2** ♦ : to be deficient or missing : LACKING **3** : not paying attention : INATTENTIVE

♦ [1] away, missing, out; *also* AWOL, truant *Ant* here, present ♦ [2] missing, nonexistent, wanting; *also* dead, departed, extinct, lost, perished, vanished *Ant* existent, present

²**ab·sent** \ab-'sent\ *vb* : to keep (oneself) away

³**ab·sent** \'ab-sənt\ *prep* : in the absence of : WITHOUT

ab·sen·tee \ˌab-sən-'tē\ *n* : one that is absent or keeps away

absentee ballot *n* : a ballot submitted (as by mail) in advance of an election by a voter who is unable to be present at the polls

ab·sen·tee·ism \ˌab-sən-'tē-ˌi-zəm\ *n* : chronic absence (as from work or school)

ab·sent·mind·ed \ˌab-sənt-'mīn-dəd\ *adj* ♦ : unaware of one's surroundings or actions : INATTENTIVE — **ab·sent·mind·ed·ly** *adv* — **ab·sent·mind·ed·ness** *n*

♦ abstracted, preoccupied; *also* absorbed, dreaming, dreamy, distracted, engrossed, faraway, intent, pensive, rapt *Ant* alert

ab·sinthe *also* **ab·sinth** \'ab-ˌsinth\ *n* [F] : a liqueur flavored esp. with wormwood and anise

ab·so·lute \'ab-sə-ˌlüt, ˌab-sə-'lüt\ *adj* **1** ♦ : free from imperfection or mixture **2** ♦ : free from control, restriction, or qualification **3** : lacking grammatical connection with any other word in a sentence ⟨~ construction⟩ **4** : not disputable : POSITIVE ⟨~ proof⟩ **5** : relating to the fundamental units of length, mass, and time **6** : FUNDAMENTAL, ULTIMATE

♦ [1] faultless, flawless, ideal, impeccable, letter-perfect, perfect, unblemished — more at PERFECT ♦ [1] fine, neat, plain, pure, refined, straight, unadulterated, undiluted, unmixed — more at PURE ♦ [2] autocratic, despotic, dictatorial, tyrannical, tyrannous; *also* authoritarian, totalitarian *Ant* limited ♦ [2] complete, consummate, perfect, total, unequivocal, unqualified, utter; *also* authentic, classic, genuine, real, veritable ♦ [4] clear, conclusive, decisive, definitive, positive — more at CONCLUSIVE

ab·so·lute·ly \-lē\ *adv* ♦ : in an absolute manner or condition

♦ all, altogether, clean, completely, entirely, fully, quite, totally, utterly, wholly — more at ALL

absolute pitch *n* **1** : the position of a tone in a standard scale independently determined by its rate of vibration **2** : the ability to sing a note asked for or to name a note heard

absolute value *n* : a nonnegative number equal to a given real number with any negative sign removed

absolute zero *n* : a theoretical temperature marked by a complete absence of heat and motion and equivalent to exactly -273.15°C or -459.67°F

ab·so·lu·tion \ˌab-sə-'lü-shən\ *n* ♦ : the act of absolving; *esp* : a remission of sins pronounced by a priest in the sacrament of reconciliation

♦ amnesty, forgiveness, pardon, remission — more at PARDON

ab·so·lut·ism \'ab-sə-ˌlü-ˌti-zəm\ *n* **1** : the theory that a ruler or government should have unlimited power **2** : government by an absolute ruler or authority

ab·solve \əb-'zälv, -'sälv\ *vb* **ab·solved; ab·solv·ing** ♦ : to set free from an obligation or the consequences of guilt

♦ acquit, clear, exculpate, exonerate, vindicate — more at EXCULPATE

ab·sorb \əb-'sȯrb, -'zȯrb\ *vb* **1** : to take in and make part of an existent whole **2** ♦ : to suck up or take in in the manner of a sponge **3** ♦ : to engage (one's attention) : ENGROSS **4** : to receive without recoil or echo ⟨a ceiling that ~s sound⟩ **5** : ASSUME, BEAR ⟨~ all costs⟩ **6** : to transform (radiant energy) into a different form usu. with a resulting rise in temperature

♦ [2] drink, imbibe, soak, sponge, suck; *also* gulp, guzzle, quaff, sip, slurp, swallow, swig, swill ♦ [3] busy, engage, engross, enthrall, fascinate, grip, immerse, interest, intrigue, involve, occupy — more at ENGAGE

ab·sorbed \əb-'sȯrbd, -'zȯrbd\ *adj* ♦ : obliviously engaged or occupied

♦ attentive, engrossed, intent, observant, rapt — more at ATTENTIVE

ab·sor·bent *also* **ab·sor·bant** \əb-'sȯr-bənt, -'zȯr-\ *adj* : able to absorb ⟨~ cotton⟩ — **ab·sor·ben·cy** \-bən-sē\ *n* — **absorbent** *also* **absorbant** *n*

ab·sorb·ing \əb-'sȯrb-iŋ, -'zȯrb-iŋ\ *adj* ♦ : fully taking attention : ENGROSSING — **ab·sorb·ing·ly** *adv*

♦ engaging, engrossing, enthralling, fascinating, interesting, intriguing — more at INTERESTING

ab·sorp·tion \əb-'sȯrp-shən, -'zȯrp-\ *n* **1** : a process of absorbing or being absorbed **2** ♦ : concentration of attention — **ab·sorp·tive** \-tiv\ *adj*

♦ attention, concentration — more at ATTENTION

ab·stain \əb-'stān\ *vb* **1** ♦ : to refrain from an action or practice **2** : to choose not to vote — **ab·stain·er** *n* — **ab·sten·tion** \-'sten-chən\ *n*

♦ forbear, forgo, keep, refrain — more at FORBEAR

ab·ste·mi·ous \ab-'stē-mē-əs\ *adj* ♦ : sparing in use of food or drink : TEMPERATE — **ab·ste·mi·ous·ly** *adv* — **ab·ste·mi·ous·ness** *n*

♦ abstinent, sober, temperate; *also* ascetic, austere; disciplined, self-controlled, self-governed *Ant* self-indulgent

ab·sti·nence \'ab-stə-nəns\ *n* : voluntary refraining esp. from eating certain foods, drinking liquor, or engaging in sexual intercourse

ab·sti·nent \'ab-stə-nənt\ *adj* [ME, from MF, from L *abstinent-, abstinens*, present participle of *abstinēre* to abstain] ♦ : practicing abstinence

♦ abstemious, sober, temperate — more at ABSTEMIOUS

abstr *abbr* abstract

¹**ab·stract** \ab-'strakt, 'ab-ˌstrakt\ *adj* **1** : considered apart from a particular instance **2** : expressing a quality apart from an object ⟨*whiteness* is an ~ word⟩ **3** : having only intrinsic form with little or no pictorial representation ⟨~ painting⟩ — **ab·stract·ly** *adv* — **ab·stract·ness** *n*

²**ab·stract** \'ab-ˌstrakt; 2 *also* ab-'strakt\ *n* **1** ♦ : a summary of points (as of a writing) : SUMMARY, EPITOME **2** : an abstract thing or state

♦ digest, encapsulation, epitome, outline, précis, recapitulation, résumé (*or* resume), roundup, sum, summary, synopsis, wrap-up — more at SUMMARY

³**ab·stract** \ab-'strakt, 'ab-ˌstrakt; 2 *usu* 'ab-ˌstrakt\ *vb* **1** : REMOVE, SEPARATE **2** ♦ : to make an abstract of : SUMMARIZE **3** : to draw away the attention of **4** : STEAL — **ab·stract·ed·ly** \ab-'strak-təd-lē, 'ab-ˌstrak-\ *adv*

♦ digest, encapsulate, epitomize, outline, recapitulate, sum up, summarize, wrap up — more at SUMMARIZE

ab·stract·ed \ab-'strak-təd, 'ab-ˌstrak-\ *adj* ♦ : lost in thought and unaware of one's surroundings or actions

♦ absentminded, preoccupied — more at ABSENTMINDED

abstract expressionism *n* : art that expresses the artist's attitudes and emotions through abstract forms — **abstract expressionist** *n*

ab·strac·tion \ab-'strak-shən\ *n* **1** : the act of abstracting : the state of being abstracted **2** : an abstract idea **3** : an abstract work of art

ab·struse \ab-'strüs\ *adj* ♦ : hard to understand : RECONDITE — **ab·struse·ly** *adv* — **ab·struse·ness** *n*

♦ deep, esoteric, profound — more at PROFOUND

ab·surd \əb-'sərd, -'zərd\ *adj* [MF *absurde*, fr. L *absurdus*, fr. *ab-* from + *surdus* deaf, stupid] ♦ : ridiculously unreasonable, unsound, or incongruous — **ab·surd·ly** *adv*

♦ bizarre, crazy, fanciful, fantastic, foolish, insane, nonsensical, preposterous, unreal, wild — more at FANTASTIC ♦ comical, derisive, farcical, laughable, ludicrous, preposterous, ridiculous, risible, silly — more at RIDICULOUS

ab·sur·di·ty \-'sər-də-tē, -'zər-\ *n* **1** ♦ : the quality or state of being absurd **2** ♦ : something that is absurd

♦ [1] craziness, daftness, fatuity, folly, foolishness, inanity, insanity, silliness, zaniness ♦ [2] fatuity, folly, foolery, foolishness, idiocy, inanity, madness, stupidity

abun·dance \ə-'bən-dəns\ *n* ♦ : an ample quantity

♦ deal, gobs, heap, loads, lot, pile, plenty, quantity, scads — more at LOT ♦ plenty, superabundance, wealth — more at PLENTY

abun·dant \ə-'bən-dənt\ *adj* [ME, fr. AF, fr. L *abundant-, abundans*, prp. of *abundare* to abound, fr. *ab-* from + *unda* wave] ♦ : more than enough : amply sufficient — **abun·dance** \-dəns\ *n* — **abun·dant·ly** *adv*

♦ ample, bountiful, comfortable, generous, liberal, plentiful — more at PLENTIFUL

¹**abuse** \ə-'byüs\ *n* 1 : a corrupt practice 2 ♦ : incorrect or improper use : MISUSE ⟨drug ∼⟩ 3 ♦ : coarse and insulting speech ⟨verbal ∼⟩ 4 : MISTREATMENT ⟨child ∼⟩

♦ [2] misuse, perversion — more at MISUSE ♦ [3] fulmination, invective, vitriol, vituperation; *also* blasphemy, curse, execration, imprecation, malediction, profanity

²**abuse** \ə-'byüz\ *vb* **abused; abus·ing** 1 ♦ : to put to a wrong use : MISUSE 2 ♦ : to use so as to injure or damage : MISTREAT 3 ♦ : to attack in words 4 : to use to excess ⟨∼ alcohol⟩ — **abus·er** *n* — **abu·sive·ness** *n*

♦ [1] misapply, misuse, pervert, profane, prostitute — more at MISAPPLY ♦ [1] capitalize, cash in, exploit, impose, play, use — more at EXPLOIT ♦ [2] ill-treat, maltreat, manhandle, mishandle, mistreat, misuse; *also* molest, outrage, violate ♦ [3] assail, attack, belabor, blast, castigate, excoriate, jump, lambaste, slam, vituperate — more at ATTACK

abu·sive \ə-'byü-siv\ *adj* ♦ : characterized by or serving for abuse — **abu·sive·ly** *adv*

♦ opprobrious, scurrilous; *also* affronting, offending, offensive, outrageous, outraging; coarse, crude, dirty, filthy, foul, gross, indecent, nasty, obscene, vulgar; defamatory, libelous (*or* libellous), scandalous, slanderous; hateful, malevolent, malicious, spiteful

abut \ə-'bət\ *vb* **abut·ted; abut·ting** ♦ : to touch along a border : border on

♦ adjoin, border (on), flank, fringe, join, skirt, touch, verge (on) — more at ADJOIN

abut·ment \ə-'bət-mənt\ *n* : the part of a structure (as a bridge) that supports weight or withstands lateral pressure

abut·ter \ə-'bə-tər\ *n* : one that abuts; *esp* : the owner of a contiguous property

abys·mal \ə-'biz-məl\ *adj* 1 : immeasurably deep : BOTTOMLESS 2 : absolutely wretched ⟨∼ living conditions of the poor⟩ — **abys·mal·ly** *adv*

abyss \ə-'bis\ *n* 1 : the bottomless pit in old accounts of the universe 2 : an immeasurable depth

abys·sal \ə-'bi-səl\ *adj* : of or relating to the bottom waters of the ocean depths

ac *abbr* account

-ac *n suffix* : one affected with ⟨hypochondri*ac*⟩

Ac *symbol* actinium

AC *abbr* 1 air-conditioning 2 alternating current 3 [L *ante Christum*] before Christ 4 [L *ante cibum*] before meals 5 area code

aca·cia \ə-'kā-shə\ *n* : any of numerous leguminous trees or shrubs with round white or yellow flower clusters and often fernlike leaves

acad *abbr* academic; academy

ac·a·deme \'a-kə-‚dēm, ‚a-kə-'\ *n* : SCHOOL; *also* : academic environment

¹**ac·a·dem·ic** \‚a-kə-'de-mik\ *n* : a person who is academic in background, outlook, or methods

²**academic** *adj* 1 ♦ : of, relating to, or associated with schools or colleges 2 : literary or general rather than technical 3 : theoretical rather than practical — **ac·a·dem·i·cal·ly** \-mi-k(ə-)lē\ *adv*

♦ educational, scholarly, scholastic; *also* bookish, pedantic, professorial *Ant* nonacademic, unacademic

ac·a·de·mi·cian \‚a-kə-də-'mi-shən, ə-‚ka-də-\ *n* 1 : a member of a society of scholars or artists 2 : ACADEMIC

ac·a·dem·i·cism \‚a-kə-'de-mə-‚si-zəm\ *also* **acad·e·mism** \ə-'ka-də-‚mi-zəm\ *n* 1 : a formal academic quality 2 : purely speculative thinking

acad·e·my \ə-'ka-də-mē\ *n, pl* **-mies** [Gk *Akadēmeia*, school of philosophy founded by Plato, fr. *Akadēmeia*, gymnasium where Plato taught, fr. *Akadēmos* Greek mythological hero] 1 : a school usu. above the elementary level; *esp* : a private high school 2 : a society of scholars or artists

acan·thus \ə-'kan-thəs\ *n, pl* **acanthus** 1 : any of a genus of prickly herbs of the Mediterranean region 2 : an ornamentation (as on a column) representing the leaves of the acanthus

a cap·pel·la *also* **a ca·pel·la** \‚ä-kə-'pe-lə\ *adv or adj* [It *a cappella* in chapel style] : without instrumental accompaniment

acc *abbr* accusative

ac·cede \ak-'sēd\ *vb* **ac·ced·ed; ac·ced·ing** 1 : to become a party to an agreement 2 ♦ : to express approval 3 : to enter upon an office

♦ acquiesce, agree, assent, come round, consent, subscribe (to); *also* adopt, embrace, espouse; abide, bear (with), endure, stand, suffer, tolerate; yield *Ant* dissent

ac·cel·er·ate \ik-'se-lə-‚rāt, ak-\ *vb* **-at·ed; -at·ing** 1 : to bring about earlier 2 ♦ : to speed up : QUICKEN — **ac·cel·er·a·tion** \-‚se-lə-'rā-shən\ *n*

♦ hasten, hurry, quicken, rush, speed (up), step up, whisk — more at HURRY

ac·cel·er·a·tor \ik-'se-lə-‚rā-tər, ak-\ *n* 1 : one that accelerates 2 : a pedal for controlling the speed of a motor-vehicle engine 3 : an apparatus for imparting high velocities to charged particles

ac·cel·er·om·e·ter \ik-‚se-lə-'rä-mə-tər, ak-\ *n* : an instrument for measuring acceleration or vibrations

¹**ac·cent** \'ak-‚sent, ak-'sent\ *vb* ♦ : to give prominence to : STRESS, EMPHASIZE

♦ accentuate, emphasize, feature, highlight, play, point, stress, underline, underscore — more at EMPHASIZE

²**ac·cent** \'ak-‚sent\ *n* 1 : a distinctive manner of pronunciation ⟨a foreign ∼⟩ 2 : prominence given to one syllable of a word esp. by stress 3 : a mark (as ´, `, ˆ) over a vowel used usu. to indicate a difference in pronunciation from a vowel not so marked 4 ♦ : special concern or attention : EMPHASIS — **ac·cen·tu·al** \ak-'sen-chə-wəl\ *adj*

♦ accentuation, emphasis, stress, weight — more at EMPHASIS

ac·cen·tu·ate \ak-'sen-chə-‚wāt\ *vb* **-at·ed; -at·ing** ♦ : to give prominence to : ACCENT

♦ accent, emphasize, feature, highlight, play, point, stress, underline, underscore — more at EMPHASIZE

ac·cen·tu·a·tion \-‚sen-chə-'wā-shən\ *n* ♦ : the act or the result of accentuating

♦ accent, emphasis, stress, weight — more at EMPHASIS

ac·cept \ik-'sept, ak-\ *vb* 1 : to receive with consent 2 ♦ : to make a favorable response to 3 ♦ : to recognize as true 4 ♦ : to assume an obligation

♦ [2] approve, care, countenance, favor (*or* favour), OK, subscribe ♦ [3] believe, credit, swallow, trust — more at BELIEVE ♦ [4] assume, bear, shoulder, take over, undertake — more at ASSUME

ac·cept·able \ik-'sep-tə-bəl, ak-\ *adj* ♦ : capable or worthy of being accepted — **ac·cept·abil·i·ty** \-'bi-lə-tē, ak-\ *n*

♦ adequate, all right, decent, fine, OK, passable, respectable, satisfactory, tolerable — more at ADEQUATE

ac·cep·tance \ik-'sep-təns, ak-\ *n* 1 : the act of accepting 2 : the state of being accepted or acceptable 3 : an accepted bill of exchange

ac·cep·ta·tion \‚ak-‚sep-'tā-shən\ *n* : the generally understood meaning of a word

¹**ac·cess** \'ak-‚ses\ *n* 1 ♦ : capacity to enter or approach 2 ♦ : a way of approach : ENTRANCE

♦ admission, doorway, entrance, entrée, entry, gateway — more at ENTRANCE

²**access** *vb* ♦ : to get at : gain access to

♦ enter, penetrate, pierce, probe

ac·ces·si·ble \ik-ˈse-sə-bəl, ak-, ek-\ *adj* **1** ♦ : capable of being reached ⟨∼ by train⟩ **2** ♦ : capable of being used, seen, or known : OBTAINABLE ⟨∼ information⟩ — **ac·ces·si·bil·i·ty** \-ˌse-sə-ˈbi-lə-tē\ *n*

♦ [1] convenient, handy, reachable — more at CONVENIENT ♦ [2] acquirable, attainable, available, obtainable, procurable — more at AVAILABLE

ac·ces·sion \ik-ˈse-shən, ak-\ *n* **1** : increase by something added **2** : something added **3** : the act of coming to a high office or position

¹**ac·ces·so·ry** *also* **ac·ces·sa·ry** \ik-ˈse-sə-rē, ak-\ *n, pl* **-ries** **1** ♦ : a person who though not present abets or assists in the commission of an offense **2** ♦ : something helpful but not essential

♦ [1] abettor, accomplice, cohort, confederate — more at ACCOMPLICE ♦ [2] accoutrement (*or* accouterment), adjunct, appendage, attachment; *also* accompaniment, additive, complement, supplement

²**accessory** *adj* ♦ : aiding or contributing in a secondary way

♦ auxiliary, peripheral, supplementary — more at AUXILIARY

ac·ci·dent \ˈak-sə-dənt\ *n* **1** ♦ : an esp. unfortunate event occurring by chance or unintentionally **2** ♦ : lack of intention or necessity : CHANCE ⟨met by ∼⟩ **3** : a nonessential property

♦ [1] casualty, mishap; *also* calamity, cataclysm, catastrophe, cropper, deathblow, disaster, tragedy ♦ [2] chance, circumstance, hazard, luck — more at CHANCE

¹**ac·ci·den·tal** \ˌak-sə-ˈdent-ᵊl\ *adj* **1** ♦ : happening unexpectedly or by chance **2** : happening without intent or through carelessness — **ac·ci·den·tal·ly** \-ˈdent-tə-lē\ *also* **ac·ci·dent·ly** \-ˈdent-lē\ *adv*

♦ casual, chance, fluky, fortuitous, incidental, unintended, unintentional, unplanned, unpremeditated, unwitting; *also* coincidental *Ant* deliberate, intended, intentional, planned, premeditated

²**accidental** *n* : a musical note foreign to a key indicated by a signature

¹**ac·claim** \ə-ˈklām\ *vb* **1** ♦ : to express a favorable judgment of : APPLAUD, PRAISE **2** : to declare by acclamation

♦ applaud, cheer, crack up, hail, laud, praise, salute, tout; *also* ballyhoo *Ant* knock, pan, slam

²**acclaim** *n* ♦ : the act of acclaiming

♦ accolade, credit, distinction, glory, homage, honor (*or* honour), laurels — more at GLORY

ac·cla·ma·tion \ˌa-klə-ˈmā-shən\ *n* **1** ♦ : loud eager expression of approval, praise, or assent **2** : an overwhelming affirmative vote by shouting or applause rather than by ballot

♦ applause, ovation — more at APPLAUSE

ac·cli·mate \ˈa-klə-ˌmāt, ə-ˈklī-mət\ *vb* **-mat·ed; -mat·ing** ♦ : to accustom or become accustomed to a new environment or situation — **ac·cli·ma·tion** \ˌa-klə-ˈmā-shən, -ˌklī-\ *n*

♦ accommodate, adapt, adjust, condition, conform, fit, shape — more at ADAPT

ac·cli·ma·tize \ə-ˈklī-mə-ˌtīz\ *vb* **-tized; -tiz·ing** : ACCLIMATE — **ac·cli·ma·ti·za·tion** \-ˌklī-mə-tə-ˈzā-shən\ *n*

ac·cliv·i·ty \ə-ˈkli-və-tē\ *n, pl* **-ties** : an ascending slope

ac·co·lade \ˈa-kə-ˌlād\ *n* [F, fr. *accoler* to embrace, ultim. fr. L *ad-* to + *collum* neck] ♦ : an expression of praise

♦ citation, commendation, encomium, eulogy, homage, paean, panegyric, salutation, tribute — more at ENCOMIUM ♦ acclaim, credit, distinction, glory, homage, honor (*or* honour), laurels — more at GLORY

ac·com·mo·date \ə-ˈkä-mə-ˌdāt\ *vb* **-dat·ed; -dat·ing** **1** ♦ : to make fit or suitable : ADAPT, ADJUST **2** ♦ : to bring into agreement or concord : HARMONIZE, RECONCILE **3** : to provide with something needed **4** ♦ : to hold without crowding **5** : to undergo visual accommodation

♦ [1] acclimate, adapt, adjust, condition, conform, fit, shape — more at ADAPT ♦ [2] conciliate, conform, coordinate, harmonize, key, reconcile — more at HARMONIZE ♦ [4] fit, hold, take; *also* carry, contain, seat

accommodating *adj* ♦ : willing to please : OBLIGING

♦ friendly, indulgent, obliging; *also* helpful, solicitous; considerate, thoughtful; agreeable, amenable, complaisant, gracious; lenient, overindulgent, permissive

ac·com·mo·da·tion \ə-ˌkä-mə-ˈdā-shən\ *n* **1** : something supplied to satisfy a need; *esp* : LODGINGS — usu. used in pl. **2** ♦ : the act of accommodating **3** : the automatic adjustment of the eye for seeing at different distances

♦ compromise, concession, give-and-take, negotiation — more at CONCESSION

ac·com·pa·ni·ment \ə-ˈkəm-pə-nē-mənt, -ˈkəmp-nē-\ *n* : something that accompanies another; *esp* : subordinate music to support a principal voice or instrument

ac·com·pa·ny \-nē\ *vb* **-nied; -ny·ing** **1** ♦ : to go or occur with : ATTEND **2** : to play an accompaniment for — **ac·com·pa·nist** \-nist\ *n*

♦ attend, convoy, escort, squire; *also* associate, consort, pal (around), team (up)

ac·com·plice \ə-ˈkäm-pləs, -ˈkəm-\ *n* ♦ : an associate in crime

♦ abettor, accessory, cohort, confederate; *also* collaborator, conspirator, informant, informer

ac·com·plish \ə-ˈkäm-plish, -ˈkəm-\ *vb* ♦ : to bring to completion — **ac·com·plish·er** *n*

♦ achieve, carry out, commit, compass, do, execute, follow through, fulfill, make, perform — more at PERFORM

ac·com·plished *adj* **1** ♦ : marked by proficiency : EXPERT, SKILLED **2** : established beyond doubt

♦ ace, adept, crack, experienced, expert, master, masterful, masterly, practiced, proficient, seasoned, skilled, skillful — more at EXPERIENCED

ac·com·plish·ment \ə-ˈkäm-plish-mənt, -ˈkəm-\ *n* **1** ♦ : the act of accomplishing : COMPLETION **2** ♦ : something completed or effected : ACHIEVEMENT **3** : an acquired excellence or skill

♦ [1] achievement, actuality, attainment, consummation, fruition, fulfillment, realization — more at FRUITION ♦ [2] achievement, attainment, coup, success, triumph; *also* conquest, gain, victory, win

¹**ac·cord** \ə-ˈkȯrd\ *vb* [ME, fr. AF *acorder*, fr. VL **accordare*, fr. L *ad-* to + *cord-, cor* heart] **1** ♦ : to grant or give esp. as appropriate, due, or earned : GRANT **2** ♦ : to be consistent or in harmony : AGREE, HARMONIZE — **ac·cor·dant** \-ˈkȯrd-ᵊnt\ *adj*

♦ [1] award, confer, grant — more at CONFER ♦ [2] agree, coincide, comport, conform, correspond, fit, go, harmonize — more at CHECK

²**accord** *n* **1** ♦ : the act or fact of agreeing or being in harmony : AGREEMENT, HARMONY **2** ♦ : willingness to act ⟨gave of their own ∼⟩

♦ [1] agreement, conformity, consonance, harmony, tune — more at CONFORMITY ♦ [1] agreement, concurrence, consensus, unanimity — more at AGREEMENT ♦ [1] agreement, bargain, compact, contract, convention, covenant, deal, pact, settlement, understanding — more at AGREEMENT ♦ [2] choice, free will, option, self-determination, volition, will — more at FREE WILL

ac·cor·dance \ə-ˈkȯrd-ᵊns\ *n* **1** : the act or fact of agreeing or being in harmony : ACCORD **2** : the act of granting

ac·cord·ing·ly \ə-ˈkȯr-diŋ-lē\ *adv* **1** : in accordance **2** ♦ : as a result : CONSEQUENTLY, SO

♦ consequently, ergo, hence, so, therefore, thus, wherefore — more at THEREFORE

according to *prep* **1** : in conformity with ⟨paid *according to* ability⟩ **2** : as stated or attested by ⟨*according to* you⟩

¹**ac·cor·di·on** \ə-ˈkȯr-dē-ən\ *n* [G *Akkordion*, fr. *Akkord* chord] : a portable keyboard instrument with a bellows and reeds — **ac·cor·di·on·ist** \-ə-nist\ *n*

²**accordion** *adj* : folding like the bellows of an accordion ⟨∼ pleats⟩

ac·cost \ə-ˈkȯst\ *vb* [MF *accoster*, ultim. fr. L *ad-* to + *costa* rib, side] : to approach and speak to esp. aggressively

¹**ac·count** \ə-ˈkaȯnt\ *n* **1** ♦ : a statement of business transactions **2** : a formal business arrangement for regular dealings or services ⟨an advertising ∼⟩ ⟨an e-mail ∼⟩ **3** : a statement of reasons, causes, or motives **4** : value or importance esp. as attributed by others **5** ♦ : a sum of money deposited in a bank and subject to withdrawal by the depositor **6** ♦ : a description of facts, conditions, or events — **on account of** : BECAUSE OF — **on no account** : under no circumstances — **on one's own account** : on one's own behalf

♦ [1] bill, check, invoice, statement, tab — more at BILL ♦ [5] budget, deposit, fund, kitty, nest egg, pool — more at FUND ♦ [6] chronicle, history, narrative, record, report, story; *also* version

²**account** *vb* **1** ♦ : to think of as : CONSIDER ⟨I ∼ him lucky⟩ **2** ♦ : to give an explanation — used with *for*

♦ [1] call, consider, count, esteem, hold, rate, reckon, regard, take — more at CONSIDER ♦ *usu* account for [2] explain, rationalize — more at EXPLAIN

ac·count·able \ə-ˈkaȯn-tə-bəl\ *adj* **1** ♦ : subject to giving an account : ANSWERABLE, RESPONSIBLE **2** : EXPLICABLE — **ac·count·abil·i·ty** \-ˌkaȯn-tə-ˈbi-lə-tē\ *n*

♦ answerable, liable, responsible — more at RESPONSIBLE

ac·coun·tant \ə-ˈkaȯnt-ᵊnt\ *n* : a person skilled in accounting — **ac·coun·tan·cy** \-ᵊn-sē\ *n*

account executive *n* : a business executive in charge of a client's account

ac·count·ing \ə-ˈkaȯn-tiŋ\ *n* : the art or system of keeping and analyzing financial records

ac·cou·tre *or* **ac·cou·ter** \ə-ˈkü-tər\ *vb* **-cou·tred** *or* **-cou·tered; -cou·tring** *or* **-cou·ter·ing** \-ˈkü-t(ə-)riŋ\ ♦ : to provide with equipment or furnishings : EQUIP, OUTFIT

♦ equip, fit, furnish, outfit, rig, supply — more at FURNISH

ac·cou·tre·ment *or* **ac·cou·ter·ment** \ə-ˈkü-trə-mənt, -ˈkü-tər-\ *n* [F] **1** ♦ : an accessory item — usu. used in pl. **2** : an identifying characteristic

♦ accessory, adjunct, appendage, attachment — more at ACCESSORY ♦ *usu* accoutrements apparatus, equipment, gear, matériel, outfit, paraphernalia, tackle — more at EQUIPMENT

ac·cred·it \ə-ˈkre-dət\ *vb* **1** ♦ : to endorse or approve officially **2** ♦ : to explain by indicating a cause : CREDIT — **ac·cred·i·ta·tion** \-ˌkre-də-ˈtā-shən\ *n*

♦ [1] authorize, certify, commission, empower, enable, invest, license, qualify — more at AUTHORIZE ♦ [2] ascribe, attribute, credit, impute — more at CREDIT

ac·cre·tion \ə-ˈkrē-shən\ *n* **1** : growth or enlargement esp. by addition from without **2** ♦ : a product of accretion

♦ addition, augmentation, boost, expansion, gain, increase, increment, plus, proliferation, raise, rise, supplement — more at INCREASE

ac·cru·al \ə-ˈkrü-əl\ *n* : something that accrues or has accrued

ac·crue \ə-ˈkrü\ *vb* **ac·crued; ac·cru·ing** **1** : to come by way of increase **2** : to be added by periodic growth

acct *abbr* account; accountant

ac·cul·tur·a·tion \ə-ˌkəl-chə-ˈrā-shən\ *n* : cultural modification of an individual or group by borrowing and adapting traits from another culture

ac·cu·mu·late \ə-ˈkyü-myə-ˌlāt\ *vb* **-lat·ed; -lat·ing** [L *accumulare*, fr. *ad-* to + *cumulare* to heap up] ♦ : to gather or pile up — **ac·cu·mu·la·tive** \-ˈkyü-myə-lə-tiv\ *adj* — **ac·cu·mu·la·tor** \-ˈkyü-myə-ˌlā-tər\ *n*

♦ appreciate, build, increase, mount, multiply, proliferate, rise — more at INCREASE ♦ amass, assemble, collect, gather, group, lump, pile, round up

ac·cu·mu·la·tion \-ˌkyü-myə-ˈlā-shən\ *n* **1** ♦ : something that has accumulated or has been accumulated **2** : the action or process of accumulating

♦ assemblage, collection, gathering; *also* agglomerate, assortment, conglomerate, conglomeration, hodgepodge, jumble, medley, mélange, mix, mixture, motley, potpourri

ac·cu·ra·cy \-rə-sē\ *n* ♦ : the quality, state, or degree of being accurate

♦ closeness, delicacy, exactness, fineness, precision, veracity — more at PRECISION

ac·cu·rate \ˈa-kyə-rət\ *adj* **1** ♦ : free from error : EXACT, PRECISE **2** ♦ : conforming exactly to truth or to a standard — **ac·cu·rate·ness** *n*

♦ [1] close, delicate, exact, fine, mathematical, pinpoint, precise, rigorous — more at PRECISE ♦ [2] correct, exact, precise, proper, right, so, true — more at CORRECT

ac·cu·rate·ly \ˈa-kyə-rət-lē\ *adv* ♦ : in an accurate manner

♦ exactly, just, precisely, right, sharp, squarely — more at EXACTLY

ac·cursed \ə-ˈkərst, -ˈkər-səd\ *or* **ac·curst** \ə-ˈkərst\ *adj* **1** : being under a curse **2** : DAMNABLE, EXECRABLE

ac·cus·al \ə-ˈkyü-zəl\ *n* : ACCUSATION

ac·cu·sa·tive \ə-ˈkyü-zə-tiv\ *adj* : of, relating to, or being a grammatical case marking the direct object of a verb or the object of a preposition — **accusative** *n*

ac·cu·sa·to·ry \ə-ˈkyü-zə-ˌtȯr-ē\ *adj* : expressing accusation ⟨an ∼ tone⟩

ac·cuse \ə-ˈkyüz\ *vb* **ac·cused; ac·cus·ing** ♦ : to charge with an offense : BLAME — **ac·cu·sa·tion** \ˌa-kyə-ˈzā-shən\ *n* — **ac·cus·er** *n*

♦ charge, incriminate, indict; *also* blame, castigate, censure, condemn, criticize, damn, denounce, fault, impugn, reproach, reprobate *Ant* absolve, acquit, clear, exculpate, exonerate, vindicate

ac·cused \ə-ˈkyüzd\ *n, pl* **accused** : the defendant in a criminal case

ac·cus·tom \ə-ˈkəs-təm\ *vb* ♦ : to make familiar with through use or experience

♦ acquaint, familiarize, initiate, introduce, orient — more at ACQUAINT

ac·cus·tomed \ə-ˈkəs-təmd\ *adj* **1** : USUAL, CUSTOMARY **2** ♦ : being in the habit or custom

♦ given, used, wont; *also* apt, inclined, liable, prone *Ant* unaccustomed, unused

¹**ace** \ˈās\ *n* [ME *as* a die face marked with one spot, fr. AF, fr. L, unit, a copper coin] **1** : a playing card bearing a single large pip in its center **2** : a very small amount or degree **3** : a point (as in tennis) won on a serve that goes untouched **4** : a golf score of one stroke on a hole **5** : a combat pilot who has downed five or more enemy planes **6** ♦ : one that excels in knowledge or skill

♦ authority, crackerjack, expert, maestro, master, virtuoso, whiz, wizard — more at EXPERT

²**ace** *vb* **aced; ac·ing** **1** : to score an ace against (an opponent) or on (a golf hole) **2** : to defeat decisively

³**ace** *adj* ♦ : of first or high rank or quality ⟨an ∼ mechanic⟩

♦ accomplished, adept, crack, experienced, expert, master, skilled, skillful — more at EXPERIENCED

ACE in·hib·i·tor \ˌā-ˌsē-ˈē-in-ˈhi-bə-tər, ˈās-\ *n* : any of a group of drugs that lower blood pressure by relaxing the arteries

acer·bic \ə-'sər-bik, a-\ *adj* : acid in temper, mood, or tone

acer·bi·ty \ə-'sər-bə-tē\ *n, pl* **-ties** : SOURNESS, BITTERNESS

acet·amin·o·phen \ə-ˌsē-tə-'mi-nə-fən\ *n* : a crystalline compound used in chemical synthesis and in medicine to relieve pain and fever

ac·e·tate \'a-sə-ˌtāt\ *n* **1** : a salt or ester of acetic acid **2** : a textile fiber made from cellulose and acetic acid; *also* : a fabric or plastic made of this fiber

ace·tic acid \ə-'sē-tik-\ *n* : a colorless pungent liquid acid that is the chief acid of vinegar and is used esp. in making chemical compounds

ac·e·tone \'a-sə-ˌtōn\ *n* : a volatile flammable fragrant liquid compound used in making other chemical compounds and as a solvent

ace·tyl·cho·line \ə-ˌsēt-ᵊl-'kō-ˌlēn\ *n* : a compound that is released at nerve endings of the autonomic nervous system and is active in the transmission of nerve impulses

acet·y·lene \ə-'set-ᵊl-ən, -ᵊl-ˌēn\ *n* : a colorless flammable gas used as a fuel (as in welding and soldering)

ace·tyl·sal·i·cyl·ic acid \ə-ˌsēt-ᵊl-ˌsa-lə-ˌsi-lik-\ *n* : ASPIRIN 1

¹ache \'āk\ *vb* **ached; ach·ing 1** ♦ : to suffer a usu. dull persistent pain **2** ♦ : to experience a painful eagerness or yearning : LONG, YEARN ⟨he *ached* for that new car⟩ — **ache** *n*

    ♦ [1] hurt, pain, smart — more at HURT ♦ [2] die, hanker, hunger, itch, long, pant, pine, sigh, thirst, yearn ♦ *usu* ache for [2] crave, desire, die for, hanker for, hunger for, long for, lust (for *or* after), pine for, repine for, thirst for, want, wish for, yearn for — more at DESIRE

²ache *n* ♦ : a usu. dull persistent pain

    ♦ pain, pang, prick, smart, sting, stitch, tingle, twinge — more at PAIN

achiev·able \-'chē-və-bəl\ *adj* ♦ : capable of being achieved

    ♦ attainable, doable, feasible, possible, practicable, realizable, viable, workable — more at POSSIBLE

achieve \ə-'chēv\ *vb* **achieved; achiev·ing** [ME *acheven*, fr. AF *achever* to finish, fr. *a-* to (fr. L *ad-*) + *chef* end, head, fr. L *caput*] **1** ♦ : to carry out successfully : ACCOMPLISH **2** ♦ : to gain by work or effort — **achiev·er** *n*

    ♦ [1] accomplish, carry out, commit, compass, do, execute, follow through, fulfill, make, perform — more at PERFORM ♦ [2] attain, hit, make, score, win; *also* acquire, capture, carry, draw, garner, get, land, make, obtain, procure, realize, secure

achieve·ment \ə-'chēv-mənt\ *n* **1** ♦ : the act of achieving **2** ♦ : a result gained by effort

    ♦ [1] accomplishment, attainment, success ♦ [2] accomplishment, attainment, coup, success, triumph — more at ACCOMPLISHMENT

Achil·les' heel \ə-ˌki-lēz-\ *n* [fr. the story that the Greek warrior Achilles was vulnerable only in the heel] : a vulnerable point

Achil·les tendon \ə-ˌki-lēz-\ *n* : the tendon joining the muscles in the calf of the leg to the bone of the heel

ach·ing *adj* ♦ : afflicted with aches

    ♦ achy, nasty, painful, sore — more at PAINFUL

ach·ro·mat·ic \ˌa-krə-'ma-tik\ *adj* : giving an image almost free from extraneous colors ⟨∼ lens⟩

achy \'ā-kē\ *adj* **ach·i·er; ach·i·est** ♦ : afflicted with aches — **ach·i·ness** *n*

    ♦ aching, nasty, painful, sore — more at PAINFUL

¹ac·id \'a-səd\ *adj* **1** ♦ : sour or biting to the taste **2** : of or relating to an acid **3** ♦ : sharp, biting, or sour in manner, disposition, or nature — **acid·ly** *adv*

    ♦ [1, 3] acidic, sour, tart, vinegary — more at SOUR

²acid *n* **1** : a sour substance **2** : a usu. water-soluble chemical compound that has a sour taste, reacts with a base to form a salt, and reddens litmus **3** : LSD

acid·ic \ə-'si-dik\ *adj* ♦ : sour or biting to the taste; *also* : sharp or sour in manner

    ♦ acid, sour, tart, vinegary — more at SOUR

acid·i·fy \ə-'si-də-ˌfī\ *vb* **-fied; -fy·ing 1** : to make or become

acid 2 : to change into an acid — **acid·i·fi·ca·tion** \-ˌsi-də-fə-'kā-shən\ *n*

acid·i·ty \ə-'si-də-tē\ *n* ♦ : the quality, state, or degree of being acid

    ♦ acrimony, asperity, bitterness, cattiness, tartness, virulence, vitriol — more at ACRIMONY

ac·i·do·sis \ˌa-sə-'dō-səs\ *n, pl* **-do·ses** \-ˌsēz\ : an abnormal state of reduced alkalinity of the blood and body tissues

acid precipitation *n* : precipitation with above normal acidity that is caused esp. by atmospheric pollutants

acid rain *n* : acid precipitation in the form of rain

acid test *n* : a severe or crucial test

acid·u·lous \ə-'si-jə-ləs\ *adj* : somewhat acid or harsh in taste or manner

ack *abbr* acknowledge; acknowledgment

ac·knowl·edge \ik-'nä-lij, ak-\ *vb* **-edged; -edg·ing 1** : to recognize the rights or authority of **2** : to admit as true **3** : to express thanks for; *also* : to report receipt of **4** ♦ : to recognize as genuine or valid

    ♦ admit, agree, allow, concede, confess, grant, own — more at ADMIT

ac·knowl·edg·ment *or* **ac·knowl·edge·ment** \-mənt\ *n* **1** ♦ : the act of acknowledging **2** : recognition or favorable notice of an act or achievement

    ♦ admission, avowal, concession, confession — more at CONFESSION

ACL \ˌā-ˌsē-'el\ *n* : ANTERIOR CRUCIATE LIGAMENT

ACLU *abbr* American Civil Liberties Union

ac·me \'ak-mē\ *n* [Gk *akmē*] ♦ : the highest point

    ♦ apex, climax, crown, culmination, head, height, meridian, peak, pinnacle, summit, tip-top, top, zenith — more at HEIGHT

ac·ne \'ak-nē\ *n* [Gk *aknē*, MS var. of *akmē*, lit., point] : a skin disorder marked by inflammation of skin glands and hair follicles and by pimple formation esp. on the face

ac·o·lyte \'a-kə-ˌlīt\ *n* **1** : one who assists a member of the clergy in a liturgical service **2** : FOLLOWER

ac·o·nite \'a-kə-ˌnīt\ *n* **1** : MONKSHOOD **2** : a drug obtained from a common Old World monkshood

acorn \'ā-ˌkȯrn, -kərn\ *n* : the nut of the oak

acorn squash *n* : an acorn-shaped dark green winter squash with a ridged surface

acous·tic \ə-'kü-stik\ *or* **acous·ti·cal** \-sti-kəl\ *adj* **1** ♦ : of or relating to the sense or organs of hearing, to sound, or to the science of sounds **2** : deadening sound ⟨∼ tile⟩ **3** : operated by or utilizing sound waves — **acous·ti·cal·ly** \-k(ə-)lē\ *adv*

    ♦ auditory, aural, auricular — more at AUDITORY

acous·tics \ə-'kü-stiks\ *n sing or pl* **1** : the science of sound **2** : the qualities in a room that make it easy or hard for a person in it to hear distinctly

ac·quaint \ə-'kwānt\ *vb* [ME, ultim. fr. L *ad-* + *cognoscere* to know] **1** ♦ : to cause to know personally **2** ♦ : to make familiar : to cause to know firsthand

    ♦ [1, 2] accustom, apprise, brief, clue, familiarize, fill in, inform, initiate, introduce, orient

ac·quain·tance \ə-'kwänt-ᵊns\ *n* **1** ♦ : personal knowledge **2** : a person with whom one is acquainted — **ac·quain·tance·ship** *n*

    ♦ cognizance, familiarity; *also* association, experience, exposure, intimacy, involvement *Ant* unfamiliarity

ac·qui·esce \ˌa-kwē-'es\ *vb* **-esced; -esc·ing** ♦ : to accept, comply, or submit without open opposition — **ac·qui·es·cence** \-'es-ᵊns\ *n* — **ac·qui·es·cent·ly** *adv*

    ♦ accede, agree, assent, come round, consent, subscribe (to) — more at ACCEDE

ac·qui·es·cent \-ᵊnt\ *adj* ♦ : inclined to acquiesce

    ♦ passive, resigned, tolerant, unresistant, unresisting, yielding — more at PASSIVE

ac·quir·able \-'kwī-rə-bəl\ *adj* ♦ : capable of being acquired

♦ accessible, attainable, available, obtainable, procurable — more at AVAILABLE

ac·quire \ə-'kwīr\ *vb* **ac·quired; ac·quir·ing** ♦ : to gain possession of

♦ cultivate, develop, form — more at DEVELOP ♦ attain, capture, carry, draw, earn, garner, get, land, make, obtain, procure, realize, secure, win — more at EARN

ac·quired \ə-'kwīrd\ *adj* **1** : gained by or as a result of effort or experience **2** : caused by environmental forces and not passed from parent to offspring in the genes ⟨~ characteristics⟩

acquired immune deficiency syndrome *n* : AIDS

acquired immunodeficiency syndrome *n* : AIDS

ac·quire·ment \ə-'kwī(-ə)r-mənt\ *n* **1** ♦ : something that has been accomplished : ACHIEVEMENT, ACCOMPLISHMENT **2** : the act of acquiring

♦ accomplishment, achievement, attainment, coup, success, triumph — more at ACCOMPLISHMENT

ac·qui·si·tion \ˌa-kwə-'zi-shən\ *n* **1** : ACQUIREMENT **2** : something acquired

ac·quis·i·tive \ə-'kwi-zə-tiv\ *adj* ♦ : eager to acquire : GREEDY — **ac·quis·i·tive·ly** *adv*

♦ avaricious, avid, covetous, grasping, greedy, mercenary, rapacious — more at GREEDY

ac·quis·i·tive·ness \-nəs\ *n* ♦ : the quality or state of being acquisitive

♦ avarice, avidity, covetousness, cupidity, greed, rapaciousness — more at GREED

ac·quit \ə-'kwit\ *vb* **ac·quit·ted; ac·quit·ting** **1** ♦ : to pronounce not guilty **2** ♦ : to conduct (oneself) usu. satisfactorily

♦ [1] absolve, clear, exculpate, exonerate, vindicate — more at EXCULPATE ♦ [2] bear, behave, comport, conduct, demean, deport, quit — more at BEHAVE

ac·quit·tal \ə-'kwit-ᵊl\ *n* ♦ : a setting free from the charge of an offense by verdict, sentence, or other legal process

♦ exculpation, exoneration, vindication; *also* absolution, condonation, forgiveness, pardon, remission; atonement, expiation; cover-up, whitewash *Ant* conviction

acre \'ā-kər\ *n* **1** *pl* : an area of land under individual ownership : ESTATE **2** : a unit of land measure equal to 43,560 square feet

acre·age \'ā-k(ə-)rij\ *n* : area in acres

ac·rid \'a-krəd\ *adj* **1** : sharp and biting in taste or odor **2** ♦ : deeply bitter : marked by incisive sarcasm : CAUSTIC — **acrid·i·ty** \a-'kri-də-tē\ *n* — **ac·rid·ly** *adv*

♦ acrimonious, bitter, hard, rancorous, resentful, sore — more at BITTER ♦ biting, caustic, cutting, mordant, sarcastic, satiric, scathing, sharp — more at SARCASTIC

ac·rid·ness \-nəs\ *n* : the quality or state of being acrid

ac·ri·mo·ni·ous \ˌa-krə-'mō-nē-əs\ *adj* ♦ : caustic, biting, or rancorous esp. in feeling, language, or manner

♦ acrid, bitter, hard, rancorous, resentful, sore — more at BITTER

ac·ri·mo·ni·ous·ness \-nəs\ *n* : the quality or state of being acrimonious

ac·ri·mo·ny \'a-krə-ˌmō-nē\ *n, pl* **-nies** ♦ : harsh or biting sharpness esp. of words, manner, or disposition — **ac·ri·mo·ni·ous·ly** *adv*

♦ acidity, asperity, bitterness, cattiness, tartness, virulence, vitriol; *also* harshness, hostility, relentlessness, severity, sternness, vehemence

ac·ro·bat \'a-krə-ˌbat\ *n* [F *acrobate*, fr. Gk *akrobatēs*, fr. *akros* topmost + *bainein* to go] : a performer of gymnastic feats — **ac·ro·bat·ic** \ˌa-krə-'ba-tik\ *adj* — **ac·ro·bat·i·cal·ly** \-ti-k(ə-)lē\ *adv*

ac·ro·bat·ics \ˌa-krə-'ba-tiks\ *n sing or pl* : the performance of an acrobat

ac·ro·nym \'a-krə-ˌnim\ *n* : a word (as *radar*) formed from the initial letter or letters of each of the successive parts or major parts of a compound term

ac·ro·pho·bia \ˌa-krə-'fō-bē-ə\ *n* : abnormal dread of being at a great height

acrop·o·lis \ə-'krä-pə-ləs\ *n* [Gk *akropolis*, fr. *akros* topmost + *polis* city] : the upper fortified part of an ancient Greek city

¹across \ə-'kròs\ *adv* **1** ♦ : to or on the opposite side **2** : so as to be understandable ⟨get the point ~⟩

♦ over, through

²across *prep* **1** ♦ : to or on the opposite side of ⟨ran ~ the street⟩ **2** : on so as to cross or pass at an angle ⟨a log ~ the road⟩

♦ athwart, over, through; *also* around, round

across–the–board *adj* **1** : placed to win if a competitor wins, places, or shows ⟨an ~ bet⟩ **2** : including all classes or categories ⟨an ~ wage increase⟩

acros·tic \ə-'kròs-tik\ *n* : a composition usu. in verse in which the initial or final letters of the lines taken in order form a word or phrase — **acrostic** *adj*

acryl·ic \ə-'kri-lik\ *n* **1** : ACRYLIC RESIN **2** : a paint in which the vehicle is acrylic resin **3** : a quick-drying synthetic textile fiber

acrylic resin *n* : a glassy thermoplastic used for cast and molded parts or as coatings and adhesives

¹act \'akt\ *n* **1** ♦ : a thing done : DEED **2** ♦ : the formal product of a legislative body : STATUTE; *also* : a decision or determination of a sovereign, a legislative council, or a court of justice **3** : a main division of a play; *also* : an item on a variety program **4** ♦ : an instance of insincere behavior : PRETENSE

♦ [1] action, deed, doing, exploit, feat, thing — more at ACTION ♦ [2] enactment, law, ordinance, statute — more at LAW ♦ [4] airs, facade, front, guise, masquerade, pose, pretense, put-on, semblance, show — more at MASQUERADE

²act *vb* **1** ♦ : to perform by action esp. on the stage; *also* : to make a pretense of : FEIGN, SIMULATE, PRETEND **2** : to take action **3** ♦ : to conduct oneself or behave in a certain manner ⟨how did she ~ toward you⟩ **4** ♦ : to perform a specified function **5** ♦ : to produce an effect

♦ [1] impersonate, perform, play, portray; *also* depict, dramatize, enact, pantomime, render, represent, take on ♦ *usu* **act toward** [3] be, deal, handle, serve, treat, use — more at TREAT ♦ [4] function, perform, serve, work — more at FUNCTION ♦ [5] appear, look, make, seem, sound — more at SEEM ♦ [5] function, operate, perform, take, work; *also* behave, react, respond

³act *abbr* **1** active **2** actual

ACT *abbr* Australian Capital Territory

actg *abbr* acting

ACTH \ˌā-(ˌ)sē-(ˌ)tē-'āch\ *n* : a protein hormone of the pituitary gland that stimulates the adrenal cortex

act·ing \'ak-tiŋ\ *adj* ♦ : doing duty temporarily or for another ⟨~ president⟩

♦ interim, provisional, temporary; *also* alternate, makeshift, proxy, substitute *Ant* long-term, permanent

ac·tin·i·um \ak-'ti-nē-əm\ *n* : a radioactive metallic chemical element

ac·tion \'ak-shən\ *n* **1** ♦ : a legal proceeding **2** : the manner or method of performing **3** : ACTIVITY **4** ♦ : a thing done : ACT, DEED **5** : the accomplishment of a thing usu. over a period of time, in stages, or with the possibility of repetition **6** *pl* ♦ : the deportment and expression of one that acts or speaks : CONDUCT **7** : combat in war : BATTLE **8** : the events of a literary plot **9** : an operating mechanism ⟨the ~ of a gun⟩; *also* : the way it operates ⟨stiff ~⟩

♦ [1] lawsuit, proceeding, suit — more at LAWSUIT ♦ [4] act, deed, doing, exploit, feat, thing; *also* accomplishment, achievement, attainment ♦ *usu* **actions** [6] bearing, behavior (*or* behaviour), comportment, conduct, demeanor (*or* demeanour), deportment — more at BEHAVIOR

ac·tion·able \'ak-sh(ə-)nə-bəl\ *adj* : affording ground for an action or suit at law — **ac·tion·ably** \-blē\ *adv*

action figure *n* : a small-scale figure (as of a superhero) used esp. as a toy

ac·ti·vate \'ak-tə-ˌvāt\ *vb* **-vat·ed; -vat·ing** **1** ♦ : to spur into action; *also* : to make active, reactive, or radioactive **2** : to treat (as carbon) so as to improve adsorptive properties **3** : to set up (a military unit) formally; *also* : to call to active duty — **ac·ti·va·tion** \ˌak-tə-'vā-shən\ *n* — **ac·ti·va·tor** \'ak-tə-ˌvā-tər\ *n*

♦ actuate, crank, drive, move, propel, run, set off, spark, start, touch off, trigger, turn on; *also* charge, electrify, energize, fire, fuel, generate, power, push *Ant* cut, deactivate, kill, shut off, turn off

ac·tive \'ak-tiv\ *adj* **1** : causing or involving action or change **2** : asserting that the grammatical subject performs the action represented by the verb ⟨∼ voice⟩ **3** ♦ : briskly alert and energetic : BRISK, LIVELY **4** ♦ : marked by vigorous activity : BUSY **5** : erupting or likely to erupt ⟨∼ volcano⟩ **6** ♦ : presently in operation or use **7** : tending to progress or to cause degeneration ⟨∼ tuberculosis⟩ — **active** *n* — **ac·tive·ly** *adv* — **ac·tive·ness** *n*

♦ [3] animate, animated, brisk, energetic, lively, spirited, sprightly, springy — more at LIVELY ♦ [4] assiduous, busy, diligent, engaged, laborious, occupied, sedulous, working — more at BUSY ♦ [6] alive, functional, living, on, operational, operative, running, working; *also* effective, effectual *Ant* broken, dead, inactive, inoperative, nonfunctional

ac·tiv·ism \'ak-ti-ˌvi-zəm\ *n* : a doctrine or practice that emphasizes vigorous action for political ends — **ac·tiv·ist** \-vist\ *n or adj*

ac·tiv·i·ty \ak-'ti-və-tē\ *n, pl* **-ties** **1** : the quality or state of being active **2** ♦ : forceful or energetic action **3** : an occupation in which one is engaged

♦ exercise, exertion — more at EXERCISE

ac·tor \'ak-tər\ *n* ♦ : a person who acts (as in a play, movie, television show, etc.)

♦ impersonator, mummer, player, trouper; *also* entertainer, performer

act out *vb* ♦ : to behave badly or in a socially unacceptable often self-defeating manner esp. as a means of venting painful emotions (as fear or frustration)

♦ act up, carry on, misbehave — more at MISBEHAVE

ac·tress \'ak-trəs\ *n* : a woman or girl who is an actor

Acts \'akts\ *or* **Acts of the Apostles** *n* : a book of the New Testament of the Christian Scripture

ac·tu·al \'ak-chə-wəl, -shə-\ *adj* ♦ : really existing : REAL

♦ concrete, existent, factual, real, true, very; *also* attested, authenticated, confirmed, demonstrated, established, proven, substantiated, validated, verified *Ant* hypothetical, ideal, nonexistent, theoretical

ac·tu·al·i·ty \ˌak-chə-'wa-lə-tē, -shə-\ *n* ♦ : the quality or state of being actual

♦ existence, reality, subsistence — more at EXISTENCE ♦ accomplishment, achievement, attainment, consummation, fruition, fulfillment, realization — more at FRUITION

ac·tu·al·ize \'ak-chə-wə-ˌlīz, -shə-\ *vb* ♦ : to become actual — **ac·tu·al·iza·tion** \ˌak-chə-wə-lə-'zā-shən, -shə-\ *n*

♦ begin, commence, get off, launch, open, start — more at BEGIN

ac·tu·al·ly \'ak-chə-wə-lē, -shə-\ *adv* **1** ♦ : in fact or in truth : REALLY **2** ♦ : in point of fact — used to suggest something unexpected

♦ [1] admittedly, frankly, honestly, really, truly, truthfully, verily; *also* absolutely, certainly, indisputably, indubitably, positively, realistically, undoubtedly, unquestionably, veritably ♦ [2] authentically, genuinely, really, veritably, very — more at VERY

ac·tu·ary \'ak-chə-ˌwer-ē, -shə-\ *n, pl* **-ar·ies** : a person who calculates insurance risks and premiums — **ac·tu·ar·i·al** \ˌak-chə-'wer-ē-əl, -shə-\ *adj*

ac·tu·ate \'ak-chə-ˌwāt\ *vb* **-at·ed; -at·ing** **1** ♦ : to put into mechanical action **2** ♦ : to move to action — **ac·tu·a·tion** \ˌak-chə-'wā-shən, -shə-\ *n* — **ac·tu·a·tor** \'ak-chə-ˌwā-tər, -shə-\ *n*

♦ [1] activate, crank, drive, move, propel, run, set off, spark, start, touch off, trigger, turn on — more at ACTIVATE ♦ [2] drive, impel, move, propel, work

act up *vb* **1 a** ♦ : to behave in an unruly, recalcitrant, or capricious manner : MISBEHAVE **b** ♦ : to seek to attract attention by conspicuous behavior **2** : to function improperly

♦ [1a] act out, carry on, misbehave — more at MISBEHAVE ♦ [1b] clown (around), cut up, fool around, monkey, show off, skylark — more at CUT UP

acu·ity \ə-'kyü-ə-tē\ *n, pl* **-ities** ♦ : keenness of perception

♦ acuteness, delicacy, keenness, sensitiveness, sensitivity

acu·men \ə-'kyü-mən\ *n* ♦ : mental keenness and penetration

♦ astuteness, caginess, canniness, hardheadedness, intelligence, keenness, sharpness, shrewdness, wit; *also* discernment, insight, perception, sagaciousness, sagacity, sageness, sapience, wisdom

acu·pres·sure \'a-kyu̇-ˌpre-shər\ *n* : the application of pressure (as with the thumbs or fingertips) to the same discrete points on the body stimulated in acupuncture that is used for its therapeutic effects (as the relief of tension or pain)

acu·punc·ture \-ˌpəŋk-chər\ *n* : an orig. Chinese practice of puncturing the body (as with needles) at specific points to cure disease or relieve pain — **acu·punc·tur·ist** \ˌa-kyu̇-'pəŋk-chə-rist\ *n*

acute \ə-'kyüt\ *adj* **acut·er; acut·est** [ME, fr. L *acutus*, pp. of *acuere* to sharpen, fr. *acus* needle] **1** : SHARP, POINTED **2** : containing less than 90 degrees ⟨an ∼ angle⟩ **3** ♦ : sharply perceptive; *esp* : mentally keen **4 a** ♦ : characterized by sharpness or severity : SEVERE ⟨∼ distress⟩ **b** ♦ : having a sudden onset, sharp rise, and short duration ⟨∼ inflammation⟩ **5** ♦ : high in pitch **6** : of, marked by, or being an accent mark having the form ´ — **acute·ly** *adv* — *n*

♦ [3] delicate, keen, perceptive, sensitive, sharp; *also* accurate, clear, discerning, fine, good, piercing, precise, quick, receptive, sensible, subtle ♦ [4a] agonizing, biting, excruciating, severe, sharp ♦ [4b] critical, dire, imperative, imperious, instant, pressing, urgent; *also* compelling, demanding, extreme, immediate, insistent, intense, overriding *Ant* noncritical ♦ [5] sharp, shrill, squeaky, treble — more at SHRILL

acute·ness \-nəs\ *n* ♦ : the quality or state of being acute

♦ acuity, delicacy, keenness, sensitiveness, sensitivity

acy·clo·vir \(ˌ)ā-'sī-klō-ˌvir\ *n* : a drug used esp. to treat the genital form of herpes simplex

ad \'ad\ *n* : a public notice : ADVERTISEMENT

AD *abbr* **1** after date **2** [L *anno Domini*] in the year of our Lord — often printed in small capitals and often punctuated **3** assistant director **4** athletic director

ad·age \'a-dij\ *n* ♦ : an old familiar saying : PROVERB, MAXIM

♦ aphorism, byword, epigram, maxim, proverb, saying — more at SAYING

¹ada·gio \ə-'dä-j(ē-ˌ)ō, -zh(ē-ˌ)ō\ *adv or adj* [It] : at a slow tempo — used as a direction in music

²adagio *n, pl* **-gios** **1** : an adagio movement **2** : a ballet duet or trio displaying feats of lifting and balancing

¹ad·a·mant \'a-də-mənt, -ˌmant\ *n* [ME, fr. AF, fr. L *adamant-, adamas* hardest metal, diamond, fr. Gk] : a stone believed to be impenetrably hard

²adamant *adj* ♦ : unshakable or insistent esp. in maintaining a position or opinion : INFLEXIBLE, UNYIELDING — **ad·a·mant·ly** *adv*

♦ hard, immovable, implacable, inflexible, pat, rigid, unbending, uncompromising, unrelenting, unyielding

ad·a·man·tine \ˌa-də-'man-ˌtēn, -ˌtīn\ *adj* : rigidly firm : UNYIELDING

Ad·am's apple \'a-dəmz-\ *n* : the projection in front of the neck formed by the largest cartilage of the larynx

adapt \ə-'dapt\ *vb* ♦ : to make suitable or fit (as for a new use or for different conditions) — **ad·ap·ta·tion** \ˌa-ˌdap-'tā-shən\ *n* — **ad·ap·ta·tion·al** \-sh(ə-)nəl\ *adj* — **adap·tive** \ə-'dap-tiv\ *adj* — **ad·ap·tiv·i·ty** \ˌa-ˌdap-'ti-və-tē\ *n*

♦ acclimate, accommodate, adjust, condition, conform, fit, shape; *also* readjust

adapt·able \ə-'dap-tə-bəl\ *adj* ♦ : capable of being or becoming adapted — **adapt·abil·i·ty** \ə-ˌdap-tə-'bi-lə-tē\ *n*

♦ protean, universal, versatile — more at VERSATILE

♦ adjustable, changeable, elastic, flexible, fluid, malleable, variable — more at FLEXIBLE

adapt·er *also* **adap·tor** \ə-'dap-tər\ *n* **1** : one that adapts **2** : a device for connecting two dissimilar parts of an apparatus **3** ♦ : an attachment for adapting an apparatus for uses not orig. intended

♦ *also* **adaptor** accessory, accoutrement (*or* accouterment), adjunct, appendage, attachment, option — more at ACCESSORY

ADC 1 aide-de-camp **2** Aid to Dependent Children

add \'ad\ *vb* **1** ♦ : to join to something else so as to increase in number or amount **2** : to say further ⟨let me ∼ this⟩ **3** ♦ : to combine (numbers) into one sum **4** ♦ : to serve as or make an addition ⟨the TV appearance *added* to his fame⟩ ⟨*added* to her savings⟩

♦ [1] adjoin, annex, append, tack; *also* affix, attach, fasten, fix, graft, hitch, tie *Ant* deduct, remove, subtract, take ♦ [3] foot, sum, total; *also* calculate, cast, cipher, compute, figure, reckon, tally ♦ *usu* **add to** [4] aggrandize, amplify, augment, boost, compound, enlarge, escalate, expand, extend, increase, multiply, raise, swell, up — more at INCREASE

ADD *abbr* attention deficit disorder

ad·dend \'a-ˌdend\ *n* : a number to be added to another

ad·den·dum \ə-'den-dəm\ *n, pl* **-da** \-də\ [L] : something added; *esp* : a supplement to a book

¹**ad·der** \'a-dər\ *n* [ME, alter. (by false division of *a naddre*) of *naddre*, fr. OE *nǣddre*] **1** : a poisonous European viper or a related snake **2** : any of various harmless No. American snakes (as the hognose snake)

²**add·er** \'a-dər\ *n* : one that adds; *esp* : a device that performs addition

¹**ad·dict** \ə-'dikt\ *vb* **1** : to devote or surrender (oneself) to something habitually or excessively **2** : to cause addiction to a substance in (as a person) — **ad·dic·tive** \-'dik-tiv\ *adj*

²**ad·dict** \'a-(ˌ)dikt\ *n* **1** ♦ : one who is addicted esp. to a substance **2** ♦ : an ardent follower, supporter, or enthusiast

♦ [1] doper, fiend, user — more at DOPER ♦ [2] aficionado, buff, bug, devotee, enthusiast, fan, fanatic, fancier, fiend, freak, lover, maniac, nut — more at FAN

ad·dic·tion \ə-'dik-shən\ *n* **1** : the quality or state of being addicted **2** : compulsive need for and use of a habit-forming substance (as heroin, nicotine, or alcohol) characterized by well-defined physiological symptoms upon withdrawal; *also* : persistent compulsive use of a substance known by the user to be harmful

ad·di·tion \ə-'di-shən\ *n* **1** ♦ : the act or process of adding; *also* : something added **2** : the operation of combining numbers to obtain their sum

♦ annex, extension, penthouse — more at ANNEX ♦ accretion, augmentation, boost, expansion, gain, increase, increment, plus, proliferation, raise, rise, supplement — more at INCREASE

ad·di·tion·al \ə-'di-sh(ə-)nəl\ *adj* ♦ : coming by way of addition : ADDED

♦ another, else, farther, further, more, other; *also* accessory, collateral, extraneous, side, supplemental, supplementary

ad·di·tion·al·ly \ə-'di-sh(ə-)nə-lē\ *adv* ♦ : in or by way of addition : FURTHERMORE

♦ again, also, besides, further, furthermore, likewise, more, moreover, then, too, withal, yet

¹**ad·di·tive** \'a-də-tiv\ *adj* **1** : of, relating to, or characterized by addition **2** : produced by addition — **ad·di·tiv·i·ty** \ˌa-də-'ti-və-tē\ *n*

²**additive** *n* : a substance added to another in small quantities to effect a desired change in properties ⟨food ∼s⟩

ad·dle \'ad-ᵊl\ *vb* **ad·dled; ad·dling 1** ♦ : to throw into confusion : MUDDLE **2** : to become rotten ⟨*addled* eggs⟩

♦ baffle, befog, befuddle, bemuse, bewilder, confound, confuse, disorient, muddle, muddy, mystify, perplex, puzzle — more at CONFUSE

addn *abbr* addition

addnl *abbr* additional

add-on \'ad-ˌȯn, -ˌän\ *n* : something (as a feature or accessory) added esp. as an enhancement

¹**ad·dress** \ə-'dres\ *vb* **1** ♦ : to direct the attention of (oneself) **2** : to direct one's remarks to : deliver an address to **3** : to mark directions for delivery on **4** : to identify (as a memory location) by an address

♦ apply, bend, buckle, devote, give — more at APPLY

²**ad·dress** \ə-'dres, 'a-ˌdres\ *n* **1** : skillful management **2** ♦ : a formal speech **3** : the place where a person or organization may be communicated with **4** : the directions for delivery placed on mail; *also* : the designation of a computer account for sending and receiving e-mail **5** : a location (as in a computer's memory) where particular data is stored

♦ declamation, harangue, oration, speech, talk — more at SPEECH

ad·dress·ee \ˌa-ˌdre-'sē, ə-ˌdre-'sē\ *n* : one to whom something is addressed

ad·duce \ə-'düs, -'dyüs\ *vb* **ad·duced; ad·duc·ing** ♦ : to offer as example, reason, or proof — **ad·duc·er** *n*

♦ cite, instance, mention, quote — more at QUOTE

add up *vb* **1** ♦ : to come to the expected total **2** ♦ : to reach in kind or quality — used with *to*

♦ *usu* **add up to** [1] amount (to), come, number, sum, total — more at AMOUNT (TO) ♦ *usu* **add up to** [2] amount, come, correspond, equal — more at AMOUNT (TO)

-ade *n suffix* **1** : act : action ⟨block*ade*⟩ **2** : product; *esp* : sweet drink ⟨lime*ade*⟩

ad·e·nine \'ad-ᵊn-ˌēn\ *n* : one of the purine bases that make up the genetic code of DNA and RNA

ad·e·noid \'ad-ˌnȯid, -ᵊn-ˌȯid\ *n* : an enlarged mass of tissue near the opening of the nose into the throat — usu. used in pl. — **adenoid** *or* **ad·e·noi·dal** \ˌad-'nȯi-dəl, -ᵊn-'ȯi-\ *adj*

aden·o·sine tri·phos·phate \ə-'de-nə-ˌsēn-trī-'fäs-ˌfāt\ *n* : ATP

¹**ad·ept** \'a-ˌdept\ *n* ♦ : a highly skilled or well-trained individual : EXPERT

♦ artist, authority, expert, master, virtuoso, whiz, wizard — more at EXPERT

²**adept** \ə-'dept\ *adj* ♦ : highly skilled : EXPERT

♦ accomplished, ace, crack, experienced, expert, master, masterful, masterly, practiced, proficient, seasoned, skilled, skillful, versed — more at EXPERIENCED

adept·ly \ə-'dep(t)-lē\ *adv* ♦ : in an adept manner

♦ ably, capably, expertly, masterfully, proficiently, skillfully, well — more at WELL

adept·ness \-'dep(t)-nəs\ *n* ♦ : the quality or state of being adept

♦ adroitness, art, artfulness, artifice, artistry, cleverness, craft, cunning, deftness, masterfulness, skill — more at SKILL

ad·e·qua·cy \'a-di-kwə-sē\ *n* : the quality or state of being adequate

ad·e·quate \'a-di-kwət\ *adj* ♦ : equal to or sufficient for a specific requirement — **ad·e·quate·ness** *n*

♦ acceptable, all right, decent, fine, OK, passable, respectable, satisfactory, tolerable; *also* agreeable, bearable, endurable, sufferable *Ant* deficient, inadequate, lacking, unacceptable, unsatisfactory, wanting

ad·e·quate·ly \-lē\ *adv* ♦ : in an adequate manner

♦ enough, satisfactorily — more at ENOUGH

ad·here \ad-'hir\ *vb* **ad·hered; ad·her·ing** **1** ♦ : to give support : maintain loyalty **2** ♦ : to stick fast : CLING

♦ *usu* **adhere to** [1] cling, hew, keep, stick; *also* cleave (to), hang on (to) *Ant* defect (from) ♦ [2] cling, hew, stick — more at STICK

ad·her·ence \-'hir-əns\ *n* ♦ : the act, action, or quality of adhering

♦ adhesion, cohesion — more at ADHESION

¹**ad·her·ent** \-ənt\ *adj* : able or tending to adhere

²**ad·her·ent** *n* ♦ : one that adheres: as **a** : a follower of a leader, party, or profession **b** : a believer in or advocate esp. of a particular idea or church

♦ convert, disciple, follower, partisan, pupil, votary — more at FOLLOWER

ad·he·sion \ad-'hē-zhən\ *n* **1** ♦ : the act or state of adhering **2** : the union of bodily tissues abnormally grown together after inflammation; *also* : the newly formed uniting tissue **3** : the molecular attraction between the surfaces of bodies in contact

♦ adherence, cohesion; *also* agglutination, clumping

¹**ad·he·sive** \-'hē-siv, -ziv\ *adj* **1** ♦ : tending to adhere : STICKY **2** : prepared for adhering

♦ gelatinous, gluey, glutinous, gooey, gummy, sticky, viscid, viscous — more at STICKY

²**adhesive** *n* ♦ : an adhesive substance

♦ cement, glue, size — more at GLUE

adhesive tape *n* : tape coated on one side with an adhesive mixture; *esp* : one used for covering wounds

¹**ad hoc** \'ad-'häk, -'hōk\ *adv* [L, for this] : for the case at hand apart from other applications

²**ad hoc** *adj* : concerned with or formed for a particular purpose ⟨an *ad hoc* committee⟩ ⟨*ad hoc* solutions⟩

adi·a·bat·ic \ˌa-dē-ə-'ba-tik\ *adj* : occurring without loss or gain of heat — **adi·a·bat·i·cal·ly** \-ti-k(ə-)lē\ *adv*

adieu \ə-'dü, -'dyü\ *n, pl* **adieus** *or* **adieux** \ə-'düz, -'dyüz\ ♦ : a wish of well-being at parting : FAREWELL — often used interjectionally

♦ au revoir, bon voyage, farewell, good-bye — more at GOOD-BYE

ad in·fi·ni·tum \ˌad-ˌin-fə-'nī-təm\ *adv or adj* : without end or limit

ad in·ter·im \ad-'in-tə-rəm, -ˌrim\ *adv* : for the intervening time — **ad interim** *adj*

adi·os \ˌa-dē-'ōs, ˌä-\ *interj* [Sp *adiós*, lit., to God] — used to express farewell

adi·pose \'a-də-ˌpōs\ *adj* : of or relating to animal fat : FATTY

adj *abbr* **1** adjective **2** adjutant

ad·ja·cent \ə-'jās-ᵊnt\ *adj* ♦ : situated near or next — **ad·ja·cent·ly** *adv*

♦ adjoining, contiguous, touching; *also* close, closest, immediate, near, nearby, neighboring, nigh *Ant* nonadjacent

ad·jec·tive \'a-jik-tiv\ *n* : a word that typically serves as a modifier of a noun — **ad·jec·ti·val** \ˌa-jik-'tī-vəl\ *adj* — **ad·jec·ti·val·ly** *adv*

ad·join \ə-'join\ *vb* **1** ♦ : to add or attach by joining **2** ♦ : to be situated next to

♦ [1] add, annex, append, tack — more at ADD ♦ [2] abut, border (on), flank, fringe, join, skirt, touch, verge (on); *also* attach (to), communicate (with), connect (with), link (with)

ad·join·ing *adj* ♦ : touching or bounding at a point or line

♦ adjacent, contiguous, touching — more at ADJACENT

ad·journ \ə-'jərn\ *vb* **1** ♦ : to suspend indefinitely or until a stated time **2** : to transfer to another place — **ad·journ·ment** *n*

♦ break off, discontinue, interrupt, recess, suspend

ad·judge \ə-'jəj\ *vb* **ad·judged; ad·judg·ing** **1** : to decide or rule upon as a judge : JUDGE, ADJUDICATE **2** : to hold or pronounce to be : DEEM **3** : to award by judicial decision

ad·ju·di·cate \ə-'jü-di-ˌkāt\ *vb* **-cat·ed; -cat·ing** ♦ : to pass judgment on : to settle judicially — **ad·ju·di·ca·tion** \ə-ˌjü-di-'kā-shən\ *n*

♦ arbitrate, decide, determine, judge, referee, rule, settle, umpire — more at JUDGE

ad·junct \'a-ˌjəŋkt\ *n* ♦ : something joined or added to another but not essentially a part of it

♦ accessory, accoutrement (*or* accouterment), adapter, appendage, attachment — more at ACCESSORY

ad·jure \ə-'jür\ *vb* **ad·jured; ad·jur·ing** : to command solemnly : urge earnestly — **ad·ju·ra·tion** \ˌa-jə-'rā-shən\ *n*

ad·just \ə-'jəst\ *vb* **1** : to bring to agreement : SETTLE **2** ♦ : to cause to conform : ADAPT, FIT **3** : REGULATE ⟨∼ a watch⟩ — **ad·just·er** *also* **ad·jus·tor** \ə-'jəs-tər\ *n* — **ad·just·ment** \ə-'jəst-mənt\ *n*

♦ acclimate, accommodate, adapt, condition, conform, fit, shape — more at ADAPT

ad·just·able \-'jəs-tə-bəl\ *adj* ♦ : capable of being adjusted

♦ adaptable, changeable, elastic, flexible, fluid, malleable, variable — more at FLEXIBLE

ad·ju·tant \'a-jə-tənt\ *n* ♦ : one who assists; *esp* : an officer who assists a commanding officer by handling correspondence and keeping records

ad·ju·vant \'a-jə-vənt\ *n* : one that helps or facilitates; *esp* : something that enhances the effectiveness of medical treatment — **adjuvant** *adj*

¹**ad–lib** \'ad-'lib\ *vb* **ad–libbed; ad–lib·bing** : to improvise (esp. lines or a speech) — **ad–lib** *n*

²**ad–lib** *adj* ♦ : spoken, composed, or performed without preparation

♦ extemporaneous, impromptu, offhand, snap, unplanned, unpremeditated, unprepared, unrehearsed — more at EXTEMPORANEOUS

ad lib \'ad-'lib\ *adv* [NL *ad libitum*] **1** : at one's pleasure **2** : without limit

adm *abbr* administration; administrative

ADM *abbr* admiral

ad·man \'ad-ˌman\ *n* : one who writes, solicits, or places advertisements

admin *abbr* administration; administrative

ad·min·is·ter \əd-'mi-nə-stər\ *vb* **1** ♦ : to manage or supervise the execution, use, or conduct of **2** ♦ : to mete out : DISPENSE **3** : to give ritually or remedially ⟨∼ quinine for malaria⟩ **4** : to perform the office of administrator — **ad·min·is·tra·ble** \-strə-bəl\ *adj* — **ad·min·is·trant** \-strənt\ *n*

♦ [1] apply, enforce, execute, implement — more at ENFORCE ♦ [1] carry on, conduct, control, direct, govern, guide, handle, manage, operate, oversee, regulate, run, superintend, supervise — more at CONDUCT ♦ [2] allocate, apportion, deal, dispense, distribute, mete, parcel, portion, prorate; *also* allot, allow, appropriate, assign, dish (out), divide, measure (out), ration, redistribute, split

ad·min·is·tra·tion \əd-ˌmi-nə-'strā-shən\ *n* **1** : the act or process of administering **2** ♦ : performance of executive duties **3** : the officials directing the government of a country **4** : the term of office of an administrative officer or body — **ad·min·is·tra·tive·ly** *adv*

♦ authority, government, jurisdiction, regime, rule — more at RULE ♦ conduct, control, direction, guidance, management, operation, oversight, regulation, running, superintendence, supervision — more at CONDUCT

ad·min·is·tra·tive \ad-'mi-nə-ˌstrā-tiv\ *adj* : of or relating to administration

ad·min·is·tra·tor \ad-'mi-nə-ˌstrā-tər\ *n* ♦ : one that administers; *esp* : one who settles an intestate estate

♦ director, executive, manager, superintendent, supervisor — more at EXECUTIVE

ad·mi·ra·ble \'ad-m(ə-)rə-bəl\ *adj* ♦ : worthy of admiration : EXCELLENT — **ad·mi·ra·bil·i·ty** \ˌad-m(ə-)rə-'bi-lə-tē\ *n* — **ad·mi·ra·ble·ness** *n* — **ad·mi·ra·bly** \-blē\ *adv*

♦ applaudable, commendable, creditable, excellent, laudable, meritorious, praiseworthy; *also* awesome, distinctive, distinguished, honorable (*or* honourable), noteworthy, noticeable, outstanding, reputable, worthy *Ant* censurable, discreditable, reprehensible

ad·mi·ral \'ad-m(ə-)rəl\ *n* [ME, ultim. fr. Ar *amīr-al-* commander of the (as in *amīr-al-baḥr* commander of the sea)] : a commissioned officer in the navy ranking next below a fleet admiral

ad·mi·ral·ty \'ad-m(ə-)rəl-tē\ *n* **1** *cap* : a British government department formerly having authority over naval affairs **2** : the court having jurisdiction over questions of maritime law

ad·mi·ra·tion \ˌad-mə-'rā-shən\ *n* ♦ : delighted or astonished approval

♦ appreciation, esteem, estimation, favor (*or* favour), regard, respect; *also* acclamation, adoration, approbation, deference, homage, honor (*or* honour), praise, reverence, veneration, worship *Ant* disfavor

ad·mire \əd-'mīr\ *vb* **ad·mired; ad·mir·ing** [MF *admirer*, fr. L *admirari*, fr. *ad-* to + *mirari* to wonder] ♦ : to regard with high esteem — **ad·mir·er** *n* — **ad·mir·ing·ly** \-'mī-riŋ-lē\ *adv*

♦ appreciate, esteem, regard, respect; *also* acclaim, accredit, applaud, approve, commend, compliment, credit, praise

ad·mis·si·ble \əd-'mi-sə-bəl\ *adj* ♦ : that can be or is worthy to be admitted or allowed : ALLOWABLE ⟨~ evidence⟩ — **ad·mis·si·bil·i·ty** \-ˌmi-sə-'bi-lə-tē\ *n*

♦ allowable, permissible, sufferable — more at PERMISSIBLE

ad·mis·sion \əd-'mi-shən\ *n* **1** ♦ : the act of admitting **2** ♦ : the privilege of being admitted **3** : a fee paid for admission **4** : the granting of an argument **5** : the acknowledgment of a fact

♦ [1] acknowledgment, avowal, concession, confession — more at CONFESSION ♦ [2] access, doorway, entrance, entrée, entry, gateway — more at ENTRANCE

ad·mit \əd-'mit\ *vb* **ad·mit·ted; ad·mit·ting** **1** : PERMIT, ALLOW **2** ♦ : to recognize as genuine or valid **3** : to allow to enter

♦ acknowledge, agree, allow, concede, confess, grant, own; *also* disburden, unburden, unload *Ant* deny

ad·mit·tance \əd-'mit-ᵊns\ *n* : permission to enter
ad·mit·ted·ly \əd-'mi-təd-lē\ *adv* **1** : as has been or must be admitted **2** ♦ : it must be admitted

♦ actually, frankly, honestly, indeed, really, truly, truthfully, verily — more at ACTUALLY

ad·mix \ad-'miks\ *vb* : to mix in
ad·mix·ture \ad-'miks-chər\ *n* **1** : something added in mixing **2** ♦ : a product of mixing : MIXTURE

♦ amalgam, blend, combination, composite, compound, fusion, intermixture, mix, mixture — more at BLEND

ad·mon·ish \ad-'mä-nish\ *vb* ♦ : to express warning or disapproval to esp. in a gentle manner — **ad·mon·ish·er** *n* — **ad·mon·ish·ment** *n*

♦ chide, rebuke, reprimand, reproach, reprove

ad·mon·ish·ing \-iŋ\ *adj* ♦ : expressing admonition

♦ admonitory, cautionary, warning — more at CAUTIONARY

ad·mo·ni·tion \ˌad-mə-'ni-shən\ *n* ♦ : counsel or warning against fault or oversight

♦ alarm, alert, caution, notice, warning — more at WARNING

ad·mon·i·to·ry \ad-'mä-nə-ˌtōr-ē\ *adj* ♦ : expressing admonition

♦ admonishing, cautionary, warning — more at CAUTIONARY

ad nau·se·am \ad-'nȯ-zē-əm\ *adv* [L] : to a sickening or excessive degree

ado \ə-'dü\ *n* **1** ♦ : bustling excitement : FUSS **2** : TROUBLE

♦ commotion, disturbance, furor, fuss, hubbub, hullabaloo, pandemonium, tumult, turmoil, uproar — more at COMMOTION

ado·be \ə-'dō-bē\ *n* **1** : sun-dried brick; *also* : clay for making such bricks **2** : a structure made of adobe bricks

ad·o·les·cence \ˌad-ᵊl-'es-ᵊns\ *n* : the process or period of growth between childhood and maturity

¹ad·o·les·cent \-ᵊnt\ *n* : one that is in the state of adolescence

²adolescent *adj* **1** ♦ : of, relating to, or being in adolescence **2** ♦ : emotionally or intellectually immature

♦ [1] immature, juvenile, young, youthful — more at YOUNG ♦ [2] callow, green, immature, inexperienced, juvenile, raw — more at CALLOW

adopt \ə-'däpt\ *vb* **1** : to take (a child of other parents) as one's own child **2** ♦ : to take up and practice or use as one's own **3** : to accept formally and put into effect — **adopt·able** \-'däp-tə-bəl\ *adj* — **adopt·er** *n* — **adop·tion** \-'däp-shən\ *n*

♦ borrow, embrace, take up; *also* domesticate, naturalize

adop·tive \ə-'däp-tiv\ *adj* : made or acquired by adoption ⟨~ father⟩ — **adop·tive·ly** *adv*

ador·able \ə-'dȯr-ə-bəl\ *adj* **1** ♦ : worthy of adoration **2** : extremely charming — **ador·able·ness** *n* — **ador·ably** \-blē\ *adv*

♦ darling, dear, endearing, lovable, precious, sweet, winning — more at LOVABLE

adore \ə-'dȯr\ *vb* **adored; ador·ing** [ME *adouren*, fr. MF *adorer*, fr. L *adorare*, fr. *ad-* to + *orare* to speak, pray] **1** ♦ : to worship or honor as a deity or as divine : WORSHIP **2** ♦ : to regard with loving admiration ⟨~s her family⟩ **3** ♦ : to be extremely fond of often to the point of excess — **ad·o·ra·tion** \ˌa-də-'rā-shən\ *n*

♦ [1] deify, glorify, revere, venerate, worship — more at WORSHIP ♦ [2] cherish, love, worship — more at LOVE ♦ [2] delight, enjoy, fancy, like, love, relish, revel — more at ENJOY ♦ [3] canonize, deify, dote on, idolize, worship — more at IDOLIZE

adorn \ə-'dȯrn\ *vb* ♦ : to enhance the appearance of esp. with ornaments

♦ array, beautify, deck, decorate, do, dress, embellish, enrich, garnish, grace, ornament, trim — more at DECORATE

adorn·ment \-mənt\ *n* ♦ : something that adorns

♦ caparison, decoration, embellishment, frill, garnish, ornament, trim — more at DECORATION

ad·re·nal \ə-'drēn-ᵊl\ *adj* : of, relating to, or being a pair of endocrine organs (**adrenal glands**) that are located near the kidneys and produce several hormones and esp. epinephrine

adren·a·line \ə-'dren-ᵊl-ən\ *n* : EPINEPHRINE

adrift \ə-'drift\ *adv or adj* **1** : afloat without motive power or moorings **2** : without guidance or purpose

adroit \ə-'drȯit\ *adj* [F, fr. OF, fr. *a-* to + *droit* right] ♦ : having or showing skill, cleverness, or resourcefulness in handling situations — **adroit·ly** *adv*

♦ artful, dexterous, masterful, practiced, skillful, virtuoso — more at SKILLFUL

adroit·ness \-nəs\ *n* ♦ : the quality or state of being adroit

♦ cleverness, craft, dexterity, finesse, sleight — more at DEXTERITY ♦ adeptness, art, artfulness, artifice, artistry, cleverness, craft, cunning, deftness, masterfulness, skill — more at SKILL

ad·sorb \ad-'sȯrb, -'zȯrb\ *vb* : to take up (as molecules of gases) and hold on the surface of a solid or liquid — **ad·sorp·tion** \-'sȯrp-shən, -'zȯrp-\ *n*

ad·u·late \'a-jə-ˌlāt\ vb -lat·ed; -lat·ing : to flatter or admire excessively — **ad·u·la·tor** \'a-jə-ˌlā-tər\ n

ad·u·la·tion \ˌa-jə-'lā-shən\ n ♦ : excessive or slavish admiration or flattery

♦ deification, idolatry, worship — more at WORSHIP
♦ blarney, flattery, overpraise — more at FLATTERY

ad·u·la·to·ry \-lə-ˌtōr-ē\ adj ♦ : characterized by or given to adulation

♦ fulsome, unctuous — more at FULSOME

¹adult \ə-'dəlt, 'a-ˌ\ adj [L adultus, pp. of adolescere to grow up, fr. ad- to + alescere to grow] ♦ : fully developed and mature

♦ full-blown, full-fledged, mature, ripe — more at MATURE

²adult n : one that is adult; esp : a human being after an age (as 18) specified by law

adul·ter·ant \ə-'dəl-tə-rənt\ n ♦ : something used to adulterate another

♦ contaminant, defilement, impurity, pollutant — more at IMPURITY

adul·ter·ate \ə-'dəl-tə-ˌrāt\ vb -at·ed; -at·ing [L adulterare, fr. ad- to + alter other] ♦ : to make impure by mixing in a foreign or inferior substance — **adul·ter·a·tion** \-ˌdəl-tə-'rā-shən\ n

♦ dilute, thin, water, weaken; also befoul, contaminate, corrupt, defile, dirty, foul, infect, poison, pollute, soil, spoil, sully, taint Ant enrich, fortify, strengthen

adul·tery \ə-'dəl-t(ə-)rē\ n, pl -ter·ies : sexual unfaithfulness of a married person — **adul·ter·er** \-tər-ər\ n — **adul·ter·ess** \-t(ə-)rəs\ n — **adul·ter·ous** \-t(ə-)rəs\ adj

adult·hood \ə-'dəlt-ˌhůd\ n : the state or time of being an adult

ad·um·brate \'a-dəm-ˌbrāt\ vb -brat·ed; -brat·ing 1 : to foreshadow vaguely : INTIMATE 2 : to suggest or disclose partially 3 : SHADE, OBSCURE — **ad·um·bra·tion** \ˌa-dəm-'brā-shən\ n

adv abbr 1 adverb 2 advertisement

ad va·lor·em \ˌad-və-'lōr-əm\ adj [L, according to the value] : imposed at a percentage of the value ⟨an ad valorem tax⟩

¹ad·vance \əd-'vans\ vb ad·vanced; ad·vanc·ing 1 ♦ : to assist the progress of 2 ♦ : to bring or move forward 3 ♦ : to promote in rank 4 : to make earlier in time 5 ♦ : to bring forward for notice, consideration, or acceptance : PROPOSE 6 : to supply or furnish in expectation of repayment : LEND 7 : to raise in rate : INCREASE

♦ [1] cultivate, encourage, forward, foster, further, nourish, nurture, promote — more at FOSTER ♦ [2] fare, forge, get along, go, march, proceed, progress — more at GO ♦ [3] elevate, promote, raise, upgrade — more at PROMOTE ♦ [5] offer, pose, proffer, propose, propound, suggest, vote — more at PROPOSE

²advance n 1 ♦ : a forward movement 2 ♦ : a progressive step : IMPROVEMENT 3 : a rise esp. in price or value 4 : OFFER — **in advance** : BEFOREHAND

♦ [1] advancement, furtherance, headway, march, onrush, passage, process, procession, progress, progression; also current, drift, flow, flux, stream, way Ant recession, regression, retrogression ♦ [2] advancement, breakthrough, enhancement, improvement, refinement; also amelioration, boost, heightening, increase, melioration, strengthening, upgrade, uplift, upswing, upturn Ant setback

³advance adj : made, sent, or furnished ahead of time ⟨∼ sales⟩

ad·vanced \əd-'vanst\ adj 1 ♦ : far on in time or course ⟨a man ∼ in years⟩ 2 ♦ : being beyond others in progress ⟨a student with ∼ abilities⟩

♦ high, progressive, refined; also full-blown, full-fledged, full-scale Ant backward, low, lower, primitive, retarded, rudimentary, undeveloped

ad·vance·ment \-mənt\ n ♦ : the action of advancing : the state of being advanced

♦ ascent, elevation, promotion, rise, upgrade; also aggrandizement, ennoblement, exaltation, glorification Ant abasement, demotion, downgrade, reduction ♦ breakthrough, enhancement, improvement, refinement; also amelioration, boost, heightening, increase, melioration, strengthening, upgrade, uplift, upswing, upturn Ant setback

ad·van·tage \əd-'van-tij\ n 1 ♦ : superiority of position 2 ♦ : something that promotes well-being : BENEFIT 3 : the 1st point won in tennis after deuce — **ad·van·ta·geous·ly** adv

♦ [1] better, drop, edge, jump, upper hand, vantage; also allowance, head start, lead, margin, odds, start Ant disadvantage, handicap, liability ♦ [2] aid, benefit, boon, help — more at HELP

ad·van·ta·geous \ˌad-van-'tā-jəs\ adj ♦ : giving an advantage

♦ beneficial, favorable (or favourable), helpful, profitable, salutary — more at BENEFICIAL

ad·vent \'ad-ˌvent\ n 1 cap : a penitential period beginning four Sundays before Christmas 2 cap : the coming of Christ 3 : a coming into being or use

ad·ven·ti·tious \ˌad-vən-'ti-shəs\ adj 1 ♦ : coming from another source and not inherent or innate 2 : arising or occurring sporadically or in other than the usual location ⟨∼ buds⟩ — **ad·ven·ti·tious·ly** adv

♦ alien, extraneous, extrinsic, foreign — more at EXTRINSIC

¹ad·ven·ture \əd-'ven-chər\ n 1 : a risky undertaking 2 ♦ : a remarkable and exciting experience

♦ experience, happening, time; also escapade, lark

²adventure vb -ven·tured; -ven·tur·ing \-'ven-ch(ə-)riŋ\ ♦ : to expose to danger or loss : RISK, HAZARD

♦ compromise, gamble with, hazard, imperil, jeopardize, menace, risk, venture

ad·ven·tur·er \əd-'ven-ch(ə-)rər\ n 1 : a person who seeks dangerous or exciting experiences 2 : a person who follows a military career for adventure or profit 3 : a person who tries to gain wealth by questionable means

ad·ven·ture·some \əd-'ven-chər-səm\ adj : inclined to take risks

ad·ven·tur·ess \əd-'ven-ch(ə-)rəs\ n : a woman who seeks dangerous or exciting experiences

ad·ven·tur·ous \-ch(ə-)rəs\ adj ♦ : disposed to seek adventure or to cope with the new and unknown

♦ audacious, bold, daring, enterprising, nervy, venturesome — more at BOLD

ad·verb \'ad-ˌvərb\ n : a word that typically serves as a modifier of a verb, an adjective, or another adverb — **ad·ver·bi·al** \ad-'vər-bē-əl\ adj — **ad·ver·bi·al·ly** adv

¹ad·ver·sary \'ad-vər-ˌser-ē\ n, pl -sar·ies ♦ : one that contends with, opposes, or resists

♦ antagonist, enemy, foe, opponent — more at ENEMY

²adversary adj : involving antagonistic parties or interests

ad·verse \ad-'vərs, 'ad-ˌvərs\ adj 1 : acting against or in a contrary direction 2 ♦ : opposed to one's interests : UNFAVORABLE — **ad·verse·ly** adv

♦ counter, disadvantageous, hostile, inimical, negative, prejudicial, unfavorable (or unfavourable), unfriendly, unsympathetic; also bad, baleful, baneful, evil Ant advantageous, favorable, friendly, positive, sympathetic, well-disposed

ad·ver·si·ty \ad-'vər-sə-tē\ n, pl -ties ♦ : hard times : occurrences of misfortune

♦ knock, misadventure, mischance, misfortune, mishap — more at MISFORTUNE ♦ asperity, difficulty, hardness, hardship, rigor — more at DIFFICULTY

ad·vert \ad-'vərt\ vb ♦ : to call attention in the course of speaking or writing : REFER

♦ cite, instance, mention, name, note, notice, quote, refer (to), specify, touch (on or upon) — more at MENTION

ad·ver·tise \'ad-vər-ˌtīz\ *vb* **-tised; -tis·ing** **1** : INFORM, NO-TIFY **2** ♦ : to call public attention to esp. in order to sell — **ad·ver·tis·er** *n*

♦ announce, blaze, broadcast, declare, enunciate, plac-ard, post, proclaim, promulgate, publicize, publish, sound — more at ANNOUNCE

ad·ver·tise·ment \ˌad-vər-'tīz-mənt; əd-'vər-təs-mənt\ *n* **1** : the act of advertising **2** ♦ : a public notice intended to advertise something

♦ announcement, bulletin, notice, notification, release — more at ANNOUNCEMENT

ad·ver·tis·ing \'ad-vər-ˌtī-ziŋ\ *n* : the business of preparing advertisements

ad·vice \əd-'vīs\ *n* **1** ♦ : recommendation with regard to a course of action : COUNSEL **2** : INFORMATION, REPORT

♦ counsel, guidance, input; *also* recommendation, sug-gestion; hint, pointer, tip; data, feedback, information; answer, solution; advisement, consideration, thought; admonishment, admonition, caution, cautioning, ex-postulation, remonstration, urging, warning; judg-ment (*or* judgement), observation, verdict; assistance, briefing, coaching, direction, instruction, mentoring, priming, prompting, teaching, tutoring; interference, kibitzing, meddling; moralizing, pontificating, preach-ing; exhortation, lecture, lesson, sermon, speech

ad·vis·able \əd-'vī-zə-bəl\ *adj* ♦ : proper to be done : EXPE-DIENT — **ad·vis·abil·i·ty** \-ˌvī-zə-'bi-lə-tē\ *n*

♦ desirable, expedient, judicious, politic, prudent, tacti-cal, wise — more at EXPEDIENT

ad·vise \əd-'vīz\ *vb* **ad·vised; ad·vis·ing** **1 a** : to give ad-vice to : COUNSEL **b** ♦ : to recommend esp. as the best or most expedient act, course, or policy **2** ♦ : to give information or notice to : INFORM **3** ♦ : to take counsel : CONSULT, CONFER

♦ [1b] counsel, suggest; *also* advocate, back, favor, support ♦ [2] acquaint, apprise, brief, clue, enlighten, familiarize, fill in, inform, instruct, tell, wise — more at ENLIGHTEN ♦ [3] confer, consult, counsel, parley, powwow — more at CONFER

ad·vised \əd-'vīzd\ *adj* ♦ : thought out : CONSIDERED ⟨well-*advised*⟩

♦ calculated, deliberate, measured, reasoned, studied, thoughtful, thought-out — more at DELIBERATE

ad·vis·ed·ly \əd-'vī-zəd-lē\ *adv* : with or after forethought or consideration

ad·vise·ment \əd-'vīz-mənt\ *n* **1** ♦ : careful consideration **2** : the act of advising

♦ consideration, debate, deliberation, study, thought — more at CONSIDERATION

ad·vis·er *or* **ad·vi·sor** \-'vī-zər\ *n* : one that gives advice

ad·vi·so·ry \əd-'vi-zə-rē\ *adj* **1** : having or exercising power to advise **2** : containing advice

¹**ad·vo·cate** \'ad-və-kət, -ˌkāt\ *n* [ultim. fr. L *advocare* to summon, fr. *ad-* to + *vocare* to call] **1** ♦ : one who pleads another's cause **2** ♦ : one who argues or pleads for a cause or proposal — **ad·vo·ca·cy** \-və-kə-sē\ *n*

♦ [1] attorney, counsel, lawyer — more at LAWYER ♦ [2] apostle, backer, booster, champion, exponent, friend, promoter, proponent, supporter — more at EX-PONENT

²**ad·vo·cate** \-ˌkāt\ *vb* **-cat·ed; -cat·ing** ♦ : to plead in favor of — **ad·vo·ca·tion** \ˌad-və-'kā-shən\ *n*

♦ back, champion, endorse, patronize, support — more at SUPPORT

advt *abbr* advertisement

adze *also* **adz** \'adz\ *n* : a tool with a curved blade set at right angles to the handle that is used in shaping wood

AEC *abbr* Atomic Energy Commission

ae·gis \'ē-jəs\ *n* **1** ♦ : one that protects : SHIELD **2** : PA-TRONAGE, SPONSORSHIP

♦ armor (*or* armour), cover, defense (*or* defence), guard, protection, safeguard, screen, security, shield, wall, ward — more at DEFENSE

ae·o·li·an harp \ē-'ō-lē-ən-\ *n* : a box with strings that pro-duce musical sounds when the wind blows on them

ae·on *chiefly Brit var of* EON

aer·ate \'a(-ə)r-ˌāt\ *vb* **aer·at·ed; aer·at·ing** **1** : to supply (blood) with oxygen by respiration **2** : to supply, im-pregnate, or combine with a gas and esp. air — **aer·a·tion** \ˌa(-ə)r-'ā-shən\ *n* — **aer·a·tor** \'a(-ə)r-ˌā-tər\ *n*

¹**aer·i·al** \'ar-ē-əl\ *adj* **1** : inhabiting, occurring in, or done in the air **2** : AIRY **3** : of or relating to aircraft

²**aer·i·al** \'ar-ē-əl\ *n* : ANTENNA 2

aer·i·al·ist \'ar-ē-ə-list\ *n* : a performer of feats above the ground esp. on a trapeze

ae·rie \'ar-ē, 'ir-ē\ *n* : a highly placed nest (as of an eagle)

aer·o·bat·ics \ˌar-ə-'ba-tiks\ *n sing or pl* : spectacular flying feats and maneuvers

aer·o·bic \ˌa(-ə)r-'rō-bik\ *adj* **1** : living or active only in the presence of oxygen ⟨∼ bacteria⟩ **2** : involving or increasing oxygen consumption ⟨∼ activity⟩; *also* : of or relating to aerobics — **aer·o·bi·cal·ly** \-bi-k(ə-)lē\ *adv*

aer·o·bics \-biks\ *n sing or pl* : strenuous exercises that produce a marked temporary increase in respiration and heart rate; *also* : a system of physical conditioning in-volving these

aero·drome \'ar-ə-ˌdrōm\ *n, chiefly Brit* : AIRPORT

aero·dy·nam·ics \ˌar-ō-dī-'na-miks\ *n* : the science dealing with the forces acting on bodies in motion in a gas (as air) — **aero·dy·nam·ic** \-mik\ *also* **aero·dy·nam·i·cal** \-mi-kəl\ *adj* — **aero·dy·nam·i·cal·ly** \-mi-k(ə-)lē\ *adv*

aero·naut \'ar-ə-ˌnȯt\ *n* [F *aéronaute*, ultim. fr. Gk *aēr* air + *nautēs* sailor] : one who operates or travels in an airship or balloon

aero·nau·tics \ˌar-ə-'nȯ-tiks\ *n* : the science of aircraft op-eration — **aero·nau·ti·cal** \-ti-kəl\ *also* **aero·nau·tic** \-tik\ *adj*

aero·sol \'ar-ə-ˌsäl, -ˌsȯl\ *n* **1** : a suspension of fine solid or liquid particles in a gas **2** : a substance (as an insecticide) dispensed from a pressurized container as an aerosol

aero·space \'ar-ō-ˌspās\ *n* : the earth's atmosphere and the space beyond — **aerospace** *adj*

aery \'ar-ē\ *adj* **aer·i·er; -est** : having an aerial quality : ETHEREAL

aes·thete \'es-ˌthēt\ *n* : a person having or affecting sensi-tivity to beauty esp. in art

aes·thet·ic \es-'the-tik\ *adj* **1** : of or relating to aesthetics : ARTISTIC **2** : appreciative of the beautiful **3** ♦ : pleasing in appearance : ATTRACTIVE — **aes·thet·i·cal·ly** \-ti-k(ə-)lē\ *adv*

♦ attractive, beautiful, cute, fair, gorgeous, handsome, knockout, lovely, pretty, ravishing, stunning — more at BEAUTIFUL

aes·thet·ics \-tiks\ *n* : a branch of philosophy dealing with the nature, creation, and appreciation of beauty

AF *abbr* **1** air force **2** audio frequency

¹**afar** \ə-'fär\ *adv* : from, at, or to a great distance

²**afar** *n* : a great distance

AFB *abbr* air force base

AFC *abbr* **1** American Football Conference **2** automatic frequency control

AFDC *abbr* Aid to Families with Dependent Children

af·fa·bil·i·ty \ˌa-fə-'bi-lə-tē\ *n* : the quality or state of being affable

af·fa·ble \'a-fə-bəl\ *adj* ♦ : courteous and agreeable esp. in conversation — **af·fa·bly** \'a-fə-blē\ *adv*

♦ agreeable, amiable, genial, good-natured, gracious, nice, sweet, well-disposed — more at AMIABLE ♦ cordial, ge-nial, gracious, hospitable, sociable — more at GRACIOUS

af·fair \ə-'far\ *n* [ME *afere*, fr. AF fr. *afaire*, fr. *a faire* to do] **1** ♦ : something that relates to or involves one : MAT-TER **2 a** ♦ : a procedure, action, or occasion only vaguely specified ⟨the most important social ∼ of the year⟩

b : an object or collection of objects only vaguely specified ⟨their house was a 2-story ∼⟩ **3 ♦** : a romantic or sexual attachment of limited duration

♦ [2a] blowout, event, fete, function, get-together, party — more at PARTY ♦ [2a] circumstance, episode, event, happening, incident, occasion, occurrence, thing — more at EVENT ♦ [3] amour, love affair, romance; also dalliance, entanglement, fling, flirtation; liaison

¹**af·fect** \ə-ˈfekt, a-\ vb **1** : to be fond of using or wearing **2 ♦** : to put on a pretense of : SIMULATE, ASSUME, PRETEND

♦ assume, counterfeit, fake, feign, pretend, profess, put on, sham, simulate — more at FEIGN

²**affect** vb **♦** : to produce an effect on : INFLUENCE

♦ impact, impress, influence, move, strike, sway, tell, touch; also bias, color

af·fec·ta·tion \ˌa-ˌfek-ˈtā-shən\ n **♦** : an attitude or behavior that is assumed by a person but not genuinely felt

♦ pretense, pretension, pretentiousness — more at PRETENSE

af·fect·ed \a-ˈfek-təd\ adj **1 ♦** : given to affectation **2 ♦** : artificially assumed to impress others — **af·fect·ed·ly** adv

♦ [1] grandiose, highfalutin, ostentatious, pompous, pretentious — more at PRETENTIOUS ♦ [2] artificial, assumed, fake, false, feigned, phony, put-on, sham, unnatural — more at ARTIFICIAL

af·fect·ing \a-ˈfek-tiŋ\ adj **♦** : evoking a strong emotional response ⟨an ∼ story⟩ — **af·fect·ing·ly** adv

♦ emotional, impressive, moving, poignant, stirring, touching — more at MOVING

af·fec·tion \ə-ˈfek-shən\ n **1 ♦** : tender attachment **2** : a condition of the living animal or plant body or of one of its parts that impairs normal function : DISEASE — **af·fec·tion·ate·ly** adv

♦ attachment, devotion, fondness, love, passion — more at LOVE

af·fec·tion·ate \-sh(ə-)nət\ adj **1 ♦** : having affection or warm regard : LOVING **2 ♦** : motivated by affection : TENDER

♦ [1, 2] devoted, fond, loving, tender, tenderhearted — more at LOVING

af·fer·ent \ˈa-fə-rənt, -ˌfer-ənt\ adj : bearing or conducting inward toward a more central part and esp. a nerve center (as the brain or spinal cord)

af·fi·ance \ə-ˈfī-əns\ vb **-anced; -anc·ing** : BETROTH, ENGAGE

af·fi·da·vit \ˌa-fə-ˈdā-vət\ n [ML, he has made an oath] : a sworn statement in writing

¹**af·fil·i·ate** \ə-ˈfi-lē-ˌāt\ vb **-at·ed; -at·ing** : to associate as a member or branch

²**af·fil·i·ate** \ə-ˈfi-lē-ət\ n **♦** : an affiliated person or organization

♦ branch, chapter, local — more at CHAPTER

af·fil·i·a·tion \-ˌfi-lē-ˈā-shən\ n **♦** : the act of affiliating : the state or relation of being affiliated

♦ alliance, association, collaboration, confederation, connection, cooperation, hookup, liaison, partnership, relation, relationship, union — more at ASSOCIATION

af·fin·i·ty \ə-ˈfi-nə-tē\ n, pl **-ties 1** : KINSHIP, RELATIONSHIP **2 ♦** : an attraction to or liking for something

♦ bent, devices, disposition, genius, inclination, leaning, partiality, penchant, predilection, predisposition, proclivity, propensity, talent, tendency, turn — more at INCLINATION

af·firm \ə-ˈfərm\ vb **1** : CONFIRM **2 ♦** : to assert positively **3** : to make a solemn and formal declaration or assertion in place of an oath

♦ allege, assert, aver, avouch, avow, claim, contend, declare, insist, maintain, profess, protest, warrant — more at CLAIM

af·fir·ma·tion \ˌa-fər-ˈmā-shən\ n **♦** : something affirmed : a positive assertion

♦ assertion, avowal, claim, declaration, profession, protestation — more at PROTESTATION

¹**af·fir·ma·tive** \ə-ˈfər-mə-tiv\ adj : asserting that the fact is so : POSITIVE

²**affirmative** n **1** : an expression of affirmation or assent **2** : the side that upholds the proposition stated in a debate

affirmative action n : an active effort to improve the employment or educational opportunities of members of minority groups and women

¹**af·fix** \ə-ˈfiks\ vb **1 ♦** : to attach physically ⟨∼ a stamp to a letter⟩ **2** : to attach in any way : ADD ⟨∼ a signature to the document⟩

♦ attach, fasten, fix — more at FASTEN

²**af·fix** \ˈa-ˌfiks\ n : one or more sounds or letters attached to the beginning or end of a word that produce a derivative word or an inflectional form

af·fla·tus \ə-ˈflā-təs\ n : divine inspiration

af·flict \ə-ˈflikt\ vb **♦** : to cause pain and distress to

♦ agonize, bedevil, curse, harrow, martyr, persecute, plague, rack, torment, torture; also assail, attack, beset, set upon

af·flic·tion \-ˈflik-shən\ n **♦** : great suffering

♦ agony, anguish, distress, misery, pain, torment, torture, tribulation, woe — more at DISTRESS

af·flic·tive \ə-ˈflik-tiv\ adj **♦** : causing affliction : DISTRESSING — **af·flic·tive·ly** adv

af·flu·ence \ˈa-ˌflü-ən(t)s, a-ˈflü-\ n : abundant supply; also : WEALTH, RICHES

af·flu·ent \-ənt\ adj **♦** : having a generously sufficient and typically increasing supply of material possessions

♦ flush, loaded, moneyed, opulent, rich, wealthy, well-fixed, well-heeled, well-off, well-to-do — more at RICH

af·ford \ə-ˈfȯrd\ vb **1** : to manage to bear or bear the cost of without serious harm or loss **2** : PROVIDE, FURNISH

af·ford·able \ə-ˈfȯr-də-bəl\ adj **♦** : that can be afforded : of a cost that can be borne without serious harm or loss

♦ cheap, cut-rate, inexpensive, low, popular, reasonable — more at CHEAP

af·for·es·ta·tion \a-ˌfȯr-ə-ˈstā-shən\ n : the act or process of establishing a forest — **af·for·est** \a-ˈfȯr-əst, -ˈfär-\ vb

af·fray \ə-ˈfrā\ n, chiefly Brit : a fight between two or more people in a public place that disturbs the peace : FRAY

af·fright \ə-ˈfrīt\ vb, archaic : to make afraid : FRIGHTEN, ALARM — **affright** n

¹**af·front** \ə-ˈfrənt\ vb **1 ♦** : to insult esp. to the face **2** : CONFRONT

♦ insult, offend, outrage, slight, wound — more at INSULT

²**affront** n **♦** : a deliberate offense

♦ barb, dart, dig, indignity, insult, name, offense, outrage, put-down, sarcasm, slight, slur, wound — more at INSULT

af·ghan \ˈaf-ˌgan\ n **1** cap : a native or inhabitant of Afghanistan **2** : a blanket or shawl of colored wool knitted or crocheted in sections — **Afghan** adj

Afghan hound n : any of a breed of tall slim swift hunting dogs with a coat of silky thick hair and a long silky topknot

afi·cio·na·do \ə-ˌfi-sh(ē-)ə-ˈnä-dō, -sē-ə-\ n, pl **-dos** [Sp, fr. pp. of aficionar to inspire affection] **♦** : a person who likes, knows about, and appreciates a usu. fervently pursued interest or activity : DEVOTEE, FAN

♦ addict, buff, bug, devotee, enthusiast, fan, fanatic, fancier, fiend, freak, lover, maniac, nut — more at FAN

afield \ə-ˈfēld\ adv **1** : to, in, or on the field **2** : away from home **3 ♦** : out of the way : ASTRAY — **afield** adj

♦ amiss, astray, awry, wrong — more at WRONG

afire \ə-ˈfīr\ adj : being on fire : BURNING — **afire** adv

♦ ablaze, burning, fiery — more at ABLAZE

AFL abbr American Football League

aflame \ə-ˈflām\ adj : being on fire — **aflame** adv

AFL–CIO *abbr* American Federation of Labor and Congress of Industrial Organizations

afloat \ə-'flōt\ *adj or adv* **1** : borne on or as if on the water **2** : CIRCULATING ⟨rumors were ∼⟩ **3** : ADRIFT

aflut·ter \ə-'flə-tər\ *adj* **1** : FLUTTERING **2** ♦ : nervously excited

♦ anxious, edgy, jittery, jumpy, nervous, perturbed, tense, uneasy — more at NERVOUS

afoot \ə-'fút\ *adv or adj* **1** : on foot **2** ♦ : in action : in progress

♦ ongoing, proceeding — more at ONGOING

afore·men·tioned \ə-'fōr-'men-chənd\ *adj* : mentioned previously

afore·said \-,sed\ *adj* : said or named before

afore·thought \-,thȯt\ *adj* : PREMEDITATED ⟨with malice ∼⟩

a for·ti·o·ri \,ä-,fȯr-tē-'ōr-ē\ *adv* [NL., lit., from the stronger (argument)] : with even greater reason

afoul \ə-'faúl-əv\ *prep* **1** : in or into conflict with **2** : in or into collision or entanglement with

Afr *abbr* Africa; African

afraid \ə-'frād\ *adj* ♦ : filled with fear or apprehension : FRIGHTENED, FEARFUL

♦ aghast, fearful, scared, terrified; *also* fainthearted, fearsome, shrinking, shy, timid, timorous, tremulous *Ant* fearless, unafraid

A–frame \'ā-,frām\ *n* : a building having triangular front and rear walls with the roof reaching to the ground

afresh \ə-'fresh\ *adv* : from a fresh beginning : ANEW, AGAIN

Af·ri·can \'a-fri-kən\ *n* **1** : a native or inhabitant of Africa **2** : a person of African ancestry — **African** *adj*

African American *n* : an American of African and esp. of black African descent — **African American** *or* **Af·ri·can–Amer·i·can** \-ə-'mer-ə-kən\ *adj*

Af·ri·can·ized bee \'a-frə-kə-,nīzd-\ *n* : a highly aggressive hybrid honeybee accidentally produced from Brazilian and African stocks that has spread from So. America into Mexico and the southern U.S.

Africanized honeybee *n* : AFRICANIZED BEE

African violet *n* : a tropical African plant widely grown indoors for its velvety fleshy leaves and showy purple, pink, or white flowers

Af·ri·kaans \,a-fri-'käns\ *n* : a language developed from 17th century Dutch that is one of the official languages of the Republic of So. Africa

Afro \'a-frō\ *n, pl* **Afros** : a hairstyle of tight curls in a full evenly rounded shape

Af·ro–Amer·i·can \,a-frō-ə-'mer-ə-kən\ *n* : AFRICAN AMERICAN — **Afro–American** *adj*

aft \'aft\ *adv* : near, toward, or in the stern of a ship or the tail of an aircraft

AFT *abbr* American Federation of Teachers

¹af·ter \'af-tər\ *adv* ♦ : following in time or place : AFTERWARD, SUBSEQUENTLY

♦ afterward, later, subsequently, thereafter; *also* next *Ant* before, beforehand, earlier, previously

²after *prep* **1** : behind in place **2** : later than **3** : in pursuit or search of ⟨he's ∼ your job⟩

³after *conj* : following the time when

⁴after *adj* **1** ♦ : later in time **2** : located toward the rear

♦ later, posterior, subsequent — more at SUBSEQUENT

after all *adv* **1** : in spite of considerations or expectations to the contrary : NEVERTHELESS **2** : in view of the circumstances

af·ter·birth \'af-tər-,bərth\ *n* : the placenta and membranes of the fetus that are expelled after childbirth

af·ter·burn·er \-,bər-nər\ *n* : a device incorporated in the tail pipe of a turbojet engine for injecting fuel into the hot exhaust gases and burning it to provide extra thrust

af·ter·care \-,ker\ *n* : the care, nursing, or treatment of a convalescent patient

af·ter·deck \-,dek\ *n* : the rear half of the deck of a ship

af·ter·ef·fect \-ə-,fekt\ *n* : an effect that follows its cause after an interval

af·ter·glow \-,glō\ *n* : a glow remaining where a light has disappeared

af·ter·im·age \-,im-ij\ *n* : a usu. visual sensation continuing after the stimulus causing it has ended

af·ter·life \-,līf\ *n* : an existence after death

♦ eternity, hereafter, immortality — more at ETERNITY

af·ter·math \-,math\ *n* **1** : a second-growth crop esp. of hay **2** ♦ : something produced by a cause or necessarily following from a set of conditions : CONSEQUENCE, EFFECT

♦ consequence, effect, outcome, outgrowth, product, result, resultant, sequence, upshot — more at EFFECT

af·ter·noon \,af-tər-'nün\ *n* : the time between noon and evening

af·ter·shave \'af-tər-,shāv\ *n* : a usu. scented lotion for the face after shaving

af·ter·taste \-,tāst\ *n* : a sensation (as of flavor) continuing after the stimulus causing it has ended

af·ter–tax \'af-tər-'taks\ *adj* : remaining after payment of taxes and esp. of income tax ⟨an ∼ profit⟩

af·ter·thought \-,thȯt\ *n* : a later thought; *also* : something thought of later

af·ter·ward \-wərd\ *or* **af·ter·wards** \-wərdz\ *adv* ♦ : at a later time

♦ after, later, subsequently, thereafter — more at AFTER

Ag *symbol* [L *argentum*] silver

AG *abbr* **1** adjutant general **2** attorney general

again \ə-'gen, -'gin\ *adv* **1** ♦ : once more : ANEW **2** : on the other hand **3** ♦ : in addition : BESIDES

♦ [1] anew, over; *also* always, constantly, continuously, endlessly, ever, evermore, perpetually *Ant* nevermore
♦ [3] additionally, also, besides, further, furthermore, likewise, more, moreover, then, too, withal, yet

against \ə-'genst\ *prep* **1** : in opposition to **2** : directly opposite to : FACING **3** : as defense from **4 a** : in the direction of and into contact with ⟨threw him ∼ the ropes⟩ **b** : in contact with ⟨leaning ∼ the wall⟩

¹aga·pe \ä-'gä-pā, 'ä-gə-,pā\ *n* [LL, fr. Gk *agapē*, lit., love] : unselfish unconditional love for another

²agape \ə-'gāp\ *adj or adv* ♦ : being in a state of wonder or expectation

♦ agog, anticipatory, expectant — more at EXPECTANT

agar \'ä-,gär\ *n* **1** : a jellylike substance extracted from a red alga and used esp. as a gelling and stabilizing agent in foods **2** : a culture medium containing agar

agar–agar \,ä-,gär-'ä-,gär\ *n* : AGAR

ag·ate \'a-gət\ *n* **1** : a striped or clouded quartz **2** : a playing marble of agate or of glass

aga·ve \ə-'gä-vē\ *n* : any of a genus of spiny-leaved plants (as a century plant) related to the amaryllis

agcy *abbr* agency

¹age \'āj\ *n* **1** ♦ : the length of time during which a being or thing has lived or existed **2** : the time of life at which some particular qualification is achieved; *esp* : MAJORITY **3** : the latter part of life **4** ♦ : a long time **5** : a period in history

♦ [1] epoch, era, period, time ♦ [4] cycle, eon (*or* aeon), eternity; *also* infinity

²age *vb* **aged; ag·ing** *or* **age·ing** **1** : to grow old or cause to grow old **2** ♦ : to become or cause to become mature or mellow

♦ develop, grow, grow up, mature, progress, ripen — more at MATURE

-age *n suffix* **1** : aggregate : collection ⟨track*age*⟩ **2** : action : process ⟨haul*age*⟩ **3** : cumulative result of ⟨break*age*⟩ **4** : rate of ⟨dos*age*⟩ **5** : house or place of ⟨orphan*age*⟩ **6** : state : rank ⟨vassal*age*⟩ **7** : fee : charge ⟨post*age*⟩

aged \'ā-jəd *for 1*; 'ājd *for 2*\ *adj* **1** : of advanced age **2** : having attained a specified age ⟨a man ∼ 40 years⟩

age·ism \'ā-ˌji-zəm\ *n* : discrimination against persons of a particular age and esp. the elderly

age·less \'āj-ləs\ *adj* 1 : not growing old or showing the effects of age 2 ♦ : not affected by time : having infinite duration : TIMELESS ⟨~ truths⟩

♦ abiding, continuing, dateless, enduring, eternal, everlasting, immortal, imperishable, lasting, perennial, perpetual, timeless, undying — more at ABIDING

agen·cy \'āj-jən-sē\ *n, pl* **-cies** 1 ♦ : one through which something is accomplished : INSTRUMENTALITY 2 : the office or function of an agent 3 : an establishment doing business for another 4 : an administrative division (as of a government)

♦ agent, instrument, instrumentality, machinery, means, medium, organ, vehicle — more at AGENT

agen·da \ə-'jen-də\ *n* ♦ : a list of things to be done : PROGRAM

♦ calendar, docket, program, schedule, timetable — more at PROGRAM

agen·der \ā-'jen-dər\ *adj* : of, relating to, or being a person whose gender identity is genderless or neutral

agent \'ā-jənt\ *n* 1 : one that acts 2 ♦ : something that produces or is capable of producing an effect : MEANS, INSTRUMENT 3 ♦ : a person acting or doing business for another

♦ [2] agency, instrument, instrumentality, machinery, means, medium, organ, vehicle; *also* determinant, expedient, factor, influence, ingredient, mechanism, tool ♦ [3] attorney, commissary, delegate, deputy, envoy, factor, proxy, representative; *also* ambassador, emissary, foreign minister, legate, minister

Agent Orange *n* : an herbicide widely used in the Vietnam War that is composed of 2,4-D and 2,4,5-T and contains a toxic contaminant

agent pro·vo·ca·teur \'ä-ˌzhäⁿ-prō-ˌvä-kə-'tər, 'ä-jənt-\ *n, pl* **agents provocateurs** \'ä-ˌzhäⁿ-prō-ˌväk-ə-'tər, 'ä-jəntsprō-\ [F] : a person hired to infiltrate a group and incite its members to illegal action

age–old \'āj-'ōld\ *adj* ♦ : having existed for ages : ANCIENT

♦ ancient, antediluvian, antique, dateless, old, venerable — more at ANCIENT

ag·er·a·tum \ˌa-jə-'rä-təm\ *n, pl* **-tum** *also* **-tums** : any of a large genus of tropical American plants that are related to the daisies and have small showy heads of blue or white flowers

Ag·ge·us \a-'gē-əs\ *n* : HAGGAI

¹**ag·glom·er·ate** \ə-'glä-mə-ˌrāt\ *vb* **-at·ed; -at·ing** [L *agglomerare* to heap up, join, fr. *ad-* to + *glomer-, glomus* ball] ♦ : to gather into a mass : CLUSTER

♦ ball, cluster, conglomerate, roll, round, wad — more at WAD

²**ag·glom·er·ate** \-rət\ *n* : rock composed of volcanic fragments

ag·glom·er·a·tion \ə-ˌglä-mə-'rā-shən\ *n* ♦ : a cluster of disparate elements

♦ assortment, clutter, jumble, medley, mélange, miscellany, motley, muddle, variety, welter — more at MISCELLANY

ag·glu·ti·nate \ə-'glüt-ᵊn-ˌāt\ *vb* **-nat·ed; -nat·ing** 1 : to cause to adhere : gather into a group or mass 2 : to cause (as red blood cells or bacteria) to collect into clumps — **ag·glu·ti·na·tion** \-ˌglüt-ᵊn-'ā-shən\ *n*

ag·gran·dise *Brit var of* AGGRANDIZE

ag·gran·dize \ə-'gran-ˌdīz, 'a-grən-\ *vb* **-dized; -diz·ing** 1 ♦ : to make great or greater 2 ♦ : to enhance the power, wealth, position, or reputation of — **ag·gran·dize·ment** \ə-'gran-dəz-mənt, -ˌdīz-; ˌa-grən-'dīz-\ *n*

♦ [1] add, amplify, augment, boost, compound, enlarge, escalate, expand, extend, increase, multiply, raise, swell, up — more at INCREASE ♦ [2] dignify, ennoble, exalt, glorify, magnify — more at EXALT

ag·gra·vate \'a-grə-ˌvāt\ *vb* **-vat·ed; -vat·ing** 1 : to make

more severe : INTENSIFY 2 ♦ : to rouse to displeasure or anger by usu. persistent and often petty goading : IRRITATE

♦ annoy, bother, bug, grate, irk, irritate, nettle, peeve, persecute, pique, put out, rile, vex — more at IRRITATE

aggravating *adj* ♦ : arousing displeasure, impatience, or anger

♦ annoying, bothersome, frustrating, galling, irksome, irritating, pesty, vexatious — more at ANNOYING

ag·gra·va·tion \ˌa-grə-'vā-shən\ *n* ♦ : the act, action, or result of aggravating

♦ annoyance, bother, harassment, vexation — more at ANNOYANCE

¹**ag·gre·gate** \'a-gri-gət\ *adj* : formed by the gathering of units into one mass

²**ag·gre·gate** \-ˌgāt\ *vb* **-gat·ed; -gat·ing** : to collect into one mass

³**ag·gre·gate** \-gət\ *n* 1 : a mass or body of units or parts somewhat loosely associated with one another 2 ♦ : the whole amount

♦ full, sum, total, totality, whole — more at WHOLE

ag·gre·ga·tion \ˌa-gri-'gā-shən\ *n* 1 : a group, body, or mass composed of many distinct parts 2 : the collecting of units or parts into a mass or whole

ag·gres·sion \ə-'gre-shən\ *n* 1 ♦ : an unprovoked attack 2 : the practice of making attacks 3 ♦ : hostile, injurious, or destructive behavior or outlook esp. when caused by frustration

♦ [1] assault, attack, charge, offense (*or* offence), offensive, onset, onslaught, raid, rush, strike — more at ATTACK ♦ [3] aggressiveness, belligerence, fight, militancy, pugnacity, truculence — more at BELLIGERENCE

ag·gres·sive \ə-'gre-siv\ *adj* 1 ♦ : tending toward or exhibiting aggression; *esp* : marked by combative readiness 2 ♦ : marked by driving energy or initiative : ENTERPRISING 3 : more intensive or comprehensive esp. in dosage or extent — **ag·gres·sive·ly** *adv*

♦ [1] argumentative, bellicose, belligerent, combative, contentious, militant, pugnacious, quarrelsome, scrappy, truculent, warlike — more at BELLIGERENT ♦ [2] ambitious, assertive, enterprising, fierce, go-getting, high-pressure, militant, self-assertive; *also* dynamic, energetic, gung ho, hustling, scrappy, strenuous, vigorous *Ant* unaggressive, unambitious, unassertive, unenterprising

ag·gres·sive·ness *n* ♦ : the quality or state of being aggressive

♦ aggression, belligerence, fight, militancy, pugnacity, truculence — more at BELLIGERENCE ♦ ambition, drive, enterprise, go, hustle, initiative — more at ENTERPRISE

ag·gres·sor \-'gre-sər\ *n* : one that commits or practices aggression

ag·grieve \ə-'grēv\ *vb* **ag·grieved; ag·griev·ing** 1 : to cause grief to 2 : to inflict injury on : WRONG

aggrieved *adj* ♦ : troubled or distressed in spirit

♦ discontent, discontented, dissatisfied, malcontent — more at DISCONTENTED

aghast \ə-'gast\ *adj* ♦ : struck with amazement or horror

♦ afraid, terrified — more at AFRAID

ag·ile \'a-jəl\ *adj* ♦ : able to move quickly and easily

♦ graceful, light, lissome, lithe, nimble, spry — more at GRACEFUL

agil·i·ty \ə-'ji-lə-tē\ *n* ♦ : the quality or state of being agile

♦ deftness, dexterity, nimbleness, sleight — more at DEXTERITY

ag·i·tate \'a-jə-ˌtāt\ *vb* **-tat·ed; -tat·ing** 1 ♦ : to move or cause to move with an irregular rapid motion 2 ♦ : to excite and often trouble the mind or feelings of : DISTURB 3 : to discuss earnestly 4 : to attempt to arouse public feeling

♦ [1] convulse, jolt, jounce, quake, quiver, shake, shudder, vibrate, wobble — more at SHAKE ♦ [2] bother, concern, discompose, disquiet, distress, disturb, perturb, unsettle, upset, worry

agitated *adj* ♦ : troubled in mind

♦ feverish, frenzied, heated, hectic, overactive, overwrought — more at FEVERISH

ag·i·ta·tion \ˌa-jə-'tā-shən\ *n* ♦ : the act or state of agitating or being agitated

♦ anxiety, apprehension, care, concern, disquiet, nervousness, perturbation, uneasiness, worry — more at ANXIETY

ag·i·ta·tor \'a-jə-ˌtā-tər\ *n* ♦ : one that agitates

♦ demagogue, firebrand, incendiary, inciter, rabble-rouser; *also* demonstrator, marcher, objector, protester

ag·it·prop \'a-jət-ˌpräp\ *n* [Russ] : political propaganda promulgated esp. through the arts

agleam \ə-'glēm\ *adj* : GLEAMING

aglit·ter \ə-'gli-tər\ *adj* : GLITTERING

aglow \ə-'glō\ *adj* ♦ : glowing esp. with warmth or excitement : GLOWING

♦ beaming, glowing, radiant, sunny — more at RADIANT

ag·nos·tic \ag-'näs-tik\ *adj* [Gk *agnōstos* unknown, unknowable, fr. *a*- un- + *gnōstos* known] : of or relating to the belief that the existence of any ultimate reality (as God) is unknown and prob. unknowable — **agnostic** *n* — **ag·nos·ti·cism** \-'näs-tə-ˌsi-zəm\ *n*

ago \ə-'gō\ *adj or adv* : earlier than the present time

agog \ə-'gäg\ *adj* [MF *en gogues* in mirth] ♦ : full of intense interest or excitement

♦ agape, anticipatory, expectant — more at EXPECTANT ♦ anxious, ardent, athirst, avid, eager, enthusiastic, keen — more at EAGER

a–go–go \ä-'gō-ˌgō\ *adj* [*Whisky à Gogo*, café and disco in Paris, France, fr. F *à gogo* galore] : GO-GO

ag·o·nise *Brit var of* AGONIZE

ag·o·nize \'a-gə-ˌnīz\ *vb* **-nized; -niz·ing** ♦ : to suffer or cause to suffer agony

♦ afflict, bedevil, curse, harrow, martyr, persecute, plague, rack, torment, torture — more at AFFLICT ♦ bleed, feel, grieve, hurt, mourn, sorrow, suffer — more at GRIEVE

agonizing *adj* ♦ : causing agony

♦ bitter, cruel, excruciating, galling, grievous, harrowing, harsh, hurtful, painful, tortuous — more at BITTER

ag·o·niz·ing·ly \-lē\ *adv* ♦ : in a manner that is agonizing

♦ bitterly, grievously, hard, sorrowfully, unhappily, wretchedly — more at HARD

ag·o·ny \'a-gə-nē\ *n, pl* **-nies** [ME *agonie*, fr. L *agonia*, fr. Gk *agōnia* struggle, anguish, fr. *agōn* gathering, contest for a prize] **1** ♦ : extreme pain of mind or body **2** : a strong sudden display (as of joy or delight) : OUTBURST

♦ affliction, anguish, distress, misery, pain, torment, torture, tribulation, woe — more at DISTRESS

ag·o·ra·pho·bia \ˌa-gə-rə-'fō-bē-ə\ *n* : abnormal fear of being in a helpless, embarrassing, or inescapable situation characterized esp. by avoidance of open or public places — **ag·o·ra·pho·bic** \-'fō-bik, -'fä-\ *adj or n*

agr *abbr* agricultural; agriculture

agrar·i·an \ə-'grer-ē-ən\ *adj* **1** : of or relating to land or its ownership ⟨∼ reforms⟩ **2** : of or relating to farmers or farming interests — **agrarian** *n* — **agrar·i·an·ism** *n*

agree \ə-'grē\ *vb* **agreed; agree·ing 1** ♦ : to concur in (as an opinion) : ADMIT, CONCEDE **2** ♦ : to be similar : CORRESPOND **3** ♦ : to express agreement or approval **4** ♦ : to be in harmony **5** : to settle by common consent **6** : to be fitting or healthful : SUIT

♦ [1, 3] acknowledge, admit, allow, concede, confess, grant, own — more at ADMIT ♦ [2] accord, check, coincide, comport, conform, correspond, dovetail, fit, go, harmonize, jibe, square, tally — more at CHECK ♦ [3] accede, acquiesce, assent, consent, subscribe (to) — more at ACCEDE ♦ [4] blend, conform, coordinate, harmonize — more at HARMONIZE

agree·able \ə-'grē-ə-bəl\ *adj* **1** ♦ : pleasing to the mind or senses esp. as according well with one's tastes or needs **2** : ready to consent **3** ♦ : being in harmony

♦ [1] all right, alright, fine, good, OK, palatable, satisfactory — more at SATISFACTORY ♦ [1] congenial, delightful, enjoyable, felicitous, good, pleasant, pleasurable, satisfying ♦ [1] affable, amiable, genial, good-natured, gracious, nice, sweet, well-disposed — more at AMIABLE ♦ [3] amicable, compatible, congenial, harmonious, kindred, unanimous, united — more at HARMONIOUS

agree·able·ness \-nəs\ *n* ♦ : the quality or state of being agreeable

♦ amenity, amiability, geniality, graciousness, niceness, pleasantness, sweetness — more at AMIABILITY

agree·ably \-blē\ *adv* ♦ : in an agreeable manner

♦ delightfully, favorably (*or* favourably), felicitously, gloriously, nicely, pleasantly, pleasingly, satisfyingly, splendidly, well

agree·ment \ə-'grē-mənt\ *n* **1** ♦ : harmony of opinion or action **2** ♦ : mutual understanding or arrangement; *also* : a document containing such an arrangement

♦ [1] accord, conformity, consonance, harmony, tune — more at CONFORMITY ♦ [1] accord, concurrence, consensus, unanimity; *also* accession, assent, consent *Ant* disagreement, dissent ♦ [2] accord, bargain, compact, contract, convention, covenant, deal, pact, settlement, understanding; *also* charter, treaty

ag·ri·busi·ness \'a-grə-ˌbiz-nəs, -nəz\ *n* : an industry engaged in the manufacture and sale of farm equipment and supplies and in the production, processing, storage, and sale of farm commodities

agric *abbr* agricultural; agriculture

ag·ri·cul·tur·al \ˌa-gri-'kəl-ch(ə-)rəl\ *adj* : of, relating to, used in, or concerned with agriculture

ag·ri·cul·ture \'a-gri-ˌkəl-chər\ *n* : the science, art, or practice of cultivating the soil, producing crops, and raising livestock and in varying degrees the preparation and marketing of the resulting products : FARMING, HUSBANDRY

ag·ri·cul·tur·ist \-ch(ə-)rist\ *or* **ag·ri·cul·tur·al·ist** \-ch(ə-)rə-list\ *n* ♦ : one that is trained in or practices agriculture

♦ cultivator, farmer, grower, planter, tiller — more at FARMER

agron·o·mist \ə-'grä-nə-mist\ *n* : one that is trained in or practices agronomy

agron·o·my \ə-'grä-nə-mē\ *n* : a branch of agriculture that deals with the raising of crops and the care of the soil — **ag·ro·nom·ic** \ˌa-grə-'nä-mik\ *adj*

aground \ə-'graund\ *adv or adj* : on or onto the bottom or shore ⟨ran ∼⟩

agt *abbr* agent

ague \'ā-gyü\ *n* : a fever (as malaria) with recurrent chills and sweating

ahead \ə-'hed\ *adv or adj* **1** ♦ : in or toward the front **2** ♦ : into or for the future ⟨plan ∼⟩ **3** : in or toward a more advantageous position **4** ♦ : at or to an earlier time

♦ [1, 2] along, forth, forward, on, onward — more at ALONG ♦ [4] before, beforehand, previously; *also* formerly *Ant* after, afterward, later

ahead of *prep* **1** ♦ : in front or advance of **2** : in excess of : ABOVE

♦ before, ere, of, previous to, prior to, to — more at BEFORE

AHL *abbr* American Hockey League

ahoy \ə-'hȯi\ *interj* — used in hailing ⟨ship ∼⟩

AI *abbr* artificial intelligence

¹aid \'ād\ *vb* ♦ : to provide with what is useful in achieving an end : ASSIST

♦ abet, assist, back, help, prop, support — more at HELP

²aid *n* **1** ♦ : an act or instance of help given : ASSISTANCE **2** ♦ : an assisting person, group, or device : ASSISTANT

♦ [1] assist, assistance, backing, boost, help, lift, support — more at HELP ♦ [2] apprentice, assistant, deputy, helper, helpmate, mate, sidekick — more at HELPER

♦ [2] advantage, benefit, boon, help — more at HELP

AID *abbr* Agency for International Development

aide \'ād\ *n* : a person who acts as an assistant; *esp* : a military officer assisting a superior

aide–de–camp \,ād-di-'kamp, -'käⁿ\ *n, pl* **aides–de–camp** \,ādz-di-\ [F] : AIDE

AIDS \'ādz\ *n* [*acquired immuno deficiency syndrome*] : a serious disease of the human immune system that is characterized by severe reduction in the numbers of helper T cells and increased vulnerability to life-threatening illnesses and that is caused by infection with HIV commonly transmitted in infected blood and in bodily secretions

AIDS–related complex *n* : a group of symptoms (as fever, weight loss, and lymphadenopathy) that is associated with the presence of antibodies to HIV and is followed by the development of AIDS in a certain proportion of cases

AIDS virus *n* : HIV

ai·grette \ā-'gret, 'ā-,\ *n* [F, plume, egret] : a plume or decorative tuft for the head

ail \'āl\ *vb* **1** ♦ : to be the matter with : be trouble to **2** : to be unwell

♦ agitate, bother, concern, discompose, disquiet, distress, disturb, exercise, freak out, perturb, undo, unhinge, unsettle, upset, worry — more at DISTURB

ai·lan·thus \ā-'lan-thəs\ *n* : any of a genus of Asian trees or shrubs with pinnate leaves and ill-scented greenish flowers

ai·le·ron \'ā-lə-,rän\ *n* : a movable part of an airplane wing used in banking

ail·ment \'āl-mənt\ *n* ♦ : a bodily disorder

♦ bug, complaint, complication, condition, disease, disorder, fever, ill, illness, infirmity, malady, sickness, trouble — more at DISEASE

¹aim \'ām\ *vb* [ME, fr. AF *aesmer* & *esmer*; AF *aesmer*, fr. *a*-to (fr. L *ad*-) + *esmer* to estimate, fr. L *aestimare*] **1** : to point a weapon at an object **2** ♦ : to direct one's efforts : ASPIRE **3** ♦ : to direct to or toward a specified object or goal

♦ [2] aspire, contemplate, design, intend, mean, meditate, plan, propose — more at INTEND ♦ [3] bend, cast, direct, head, level, set, train; *also* bear, face

²aim *n* **1** : the pointing of a weapon at an object **2** : the ability to hit a target **3** ♦ : a clearly directed intent or purpose : OBJECT, PURPOSE — **aim·less·ly** *adv* — **aim·less·ness** *n*

♦ ambition, aspiration, design, end, goal, intent, object, objective, plan, purpose — more at GOAL

aim·less \-ləs\ *adj* ♦ : without aim or purpose

♦ arbitrary, desultory, erratic, haphazard, random, scattered, stray — more at RANDOM

AIM *abbr* American Indian Movement

ain't \'ānt\ **1** are not **2** is not **3** am not — though disapproved by many and more common in less educated speech, used in both speech and writing to catch attention and to gain emphasis

Ai·nu \'ī-nü\ *n, pl* **Ainu** *or* **Ainus** **1** : a member of an indigenous people of northern Japan **2** : the language of the Ainu people

¹air \'ar\ *n* **1** : the gaseous mixture surrounding the earth **2** ♦ : a light breeze **3** ♦ : a sweet or agreeable succession or arrangement of sounds : MELODY, TUNE **4** ♦ : the outward appearance of a person or thing : apparent character **5** *usu* **airs** ♦ : an artificial manner **6** : COMPRESSED AIR ⟨~ sprayer⟩ **7** : AIRCRAFT ⟨~ patrol⟩ **8** : AVIATION ⟨~ safety⟩ **9** : the medium of transmission of radio waves; *also* : RADIO, TELEVISION

♦ [2] breath, breeze, puff, waft, zephyr — more at BREEZE ♦ [3] lay, melody, song, strain, tune, warble — more at MELODY ♦ [4] atmosphere, aura, climate, flavor (*or* flavour), mood, note, temper — more at AURA

♦ **airs** [5] act, facade, front, guise, masquerade, pose, pretense, put-on, semblance, show — more at MASQUERADE

²air *vb* **1** : to expose to the air **2** ♦ : to expose to public view or bring to public notice **3** : to broadcast on radio or television

♦ express, give, look, sound, state, vent, voice — more at EXPRESS

air·bag \'er-,bag\ *n* : a bag designed to inflate automatically to protect automobile occupants in case of collision

air·boat \'ar-,bōt\ *n* : a shallow-draft boat driven by an airplane propeller

air·borne \-,bōrn\ *adj* : done or being in the air

air brake *n* **1** : a brake operated by a piston driven by compressed air **2** : a surface projected into the airflow to lower an airplane's speed

air·brush \'ar-,brəsh\ *n* : a device for applying a fine spray (as of paint) by compressed air — **airbrush** *vb*

air–con·di·tion \,ar-kən-'di-shən\ *vb* : to equip with an apparatus for filtering air and controlling its humidity and temperature — **air con·di·tion·er** \-'di-sh(ə-)nər\ *n*

air·craft \'ar-,kraft\ *n, pl* **aircraft** : a vehicle for traveling through the air

aircraft carrier *n* : a warship with a deck on which airplanes can be launched and landed

air·drop \'ar-,dräp\ *n* : delivery of cargo or personnel by parachute from an airplane in flight — **air–drop** *vb*

Aire·dale terrier \'ar-,dāl-\ *n* : any of a breed of large terriers with a hard wiry coat

air·fare \'ar-,far\ *n* : fare for travel by airplane

air·field \-,fēld\ *n* : an area of land from which aircraft operate : AIRPORT

air·flow \-,flō\ *n* : the motion of air relative to a body in it

air·foil \-,foil\ *n* : an airplane surface designed to produce reaction forces from the air through which it moves

air force *n* : the military organization of a nation for air warfare

air·frame \'ar-,frām\ *n* : the structure of an aircraft, rocket, or missile without the power plant

air·freight \-'frāt\ *n* : freight transport by aircraft in volume; *also* : the charge for this service

air gun *n* **1** : a gun operated by compressed air **2** : a hand tool that works by compressed air; *esp* : AIRBRUSH

air·head \'ar-,hed\ *n* : a mindless or stupid person

air lane *n* : AIRWAY 1

air·lift \'ar-,lift\ *n* : transportation (as of supplies or passengers) by aircraft — **airlift** *vb*

air·line \-,līn\ *n* : a transportation system using airplanes

air·lin·er \-,lī-nər\ *n* : a large passenger airplane operated by an airline

air lock *n* : an airtight chamber separating areas of different pressure

air·mail \'ar-,māl\ *n* : the system of transporting mail by aircraft; *also* : mail so transported — **airmail** *vb*

air·man \-mən\ *n* **1** : a civilian or military pilot, aviator, or aviation technician : AVIATOR, PILOT **2** : an enlisted person in the air force ranking next below an airman first class

♦ aviator, flier, pilot — more at PILOT

airman basic *n* : an enlisted person of the lowest rank in the air force

airman first class *n* : an enlisted person in the air force ranking next below a senior airman

air mass *n* : a large horizontally homogeneous body of air

air·mo·bile \'ar-,mō-bəl, -,bēl\ *adj* : of, relating to, or being a military unit whose members are transported to combat areas usu. by helicopter

air·plane \-,plān\ *n* : a powered heavier-than-air aircraft that has fixed wings from which it derives lift

airplane mode *n* : an operating mode for an electronic device (as a smartphone) in which the device does not connect to wireless networks and cannot send or receive communications (as calls) or access the Internet but is usable for other functions

air·play \-ˌplā\ *n* : the playing of a musical recording on the air by a radio station

air pocket *n* : a condition of the atmosphere that causes an airplane to drop suddenly

air police *n* : the military police of an air force

air·port \'ar-ˌpōrt\ *n* : a place from which aircraft operate that usu. has paved runways and a terminal

air raid *n* : an attack by armed airplanes on a surface target

air·ship \'ar-ˌship\ *n* : a lighter-than-air aircraft having propulsion and steering systems

air·sick \-ˌsik\ *adj* : affected with motion sickness associated with flying — **air·sick·ness** *n*

air·space \-ˌspās\ *n* : the space above a nation and under its jurisdiction

air·speed \-ˌspēd\ *n* : the speed of an object (as an airplane) with relation to the surrounding air

air·strip \-ˌstrip\ *n* : a runway without normal airport facilities

air·tight \'ar-'tīt\ *adj* **1** : so tightly sealed that no air can enter or escape **2** : leaving no opening for attack

air–to–air *adj* : launched from one airplane in flight at another; *also* : involving aircraft in flight

air·waves \'ar-ˌwāvz\ *n pl* : AIR 9

air·way \-ˌwā\ *n* **1** : a regular route for airplanes **2** : AIRLINE

air·wor·thy \-ˌwər-ᵗhē\ *adj* : fit for operation in the air ⟨an ∼ plane⟩ — **air·wor·thi·ness** *n*

airy \'ar-ē\ *adj* **air·i·er**; **-est** **1** : high in the air : LOFTY **2** : lacking in reality : EMPTY **3** ♦ : exceptionally light, delicate, or refined **4** : BREEZY

♦ ethereal, fluffy, light; *also* dainty, delicate, downy, feathery, flimsy, insubstantial, tender, wispy **Ant** heavy, leaden

aisle \'īl\ *n* [ME *ile*, fr. AF *ele*, lit., wing, fr. L *ala*] **1** : the side of a church nave separated by piers from the nave proper **2** : a passage between sections of seats

ajar \ə-'jär\ *adj or adv* : partly open

AK *abbr* Alaska

aka *abbr* also known as

AKC *abbr* American Kennel Club

akim·bo \ə-'kim-bō\ *adj or adv* : having the hand on the hip and the elbow turned outward

akin \ə-'kin\ *adj* **1** ♦ : related by blood **2** ♦ : essentially similar or related

♦ [1] kindred, related — more at RELATED ♦ [2] alike, analogous, comparable, correspondent, like, parallel, similar — more at ALIKE

Al *symbol* aluminum

AL *abbr* **1** Alabama **2** American League **3** American Legion

¹-al *adj suffix* : of, relating to, or characterized by ⟨directional⟩

²-al *n suffix* : action : process ⟨rehearsal⟩

Ala *abbr* Alabama

al·a·bas·ter \'a-lə-ˌbas-tər\ *n* **1** : a compact fine-textured usu. white and translucent gypsum often carved into objects (as vases) **2** : a hard translucent calcite

à la carte \ˌa-lə-'kärt, ˌä-\ *adv or adj* [F] : with a separate price for each item on the menu

alac·ri·ty \ə-'la-krə-tē\ *n* ♦ : cheerful readiness

♦ gameness, goodwill, willingness; *also* celerity, quickness, rapidity, speed, swiftness

à la mode \ˌa-lə-'mōd, ˌä-\ *adj* [F, according to the fashion] **1** ♦ : conforming to the custom, fashion, or established mode : STYLISH **2** : topped with ice cream

♦ chic, fashionable, in, modish, sharp, smart, snappy, stylish — more at STYLISH

¹alarm \ə-'lärm\ *also* **ala·rum** \ə-'lär-əm, -'lar-\ *n* [ME *alarme*, fr. MF, fr. OIt *all'arme*, lit., to arms] **1** ♦ : a warning signal or device **2** ♦ : the terror caused by sudden danger

♦ [1] admonition, alert, caution, notice, warning — more at WARNING ♦ [2] anxiety, apprehension, dread,

fear, fright, horror, panic, terror, trepidation — more at FEAR

²alarm *also* **alarum** *vb* **1** : to warn of danger **2** ♦ : to strike with fear : FRIGHTEN

♦ frighten, horrify, panic, scare, shock, spook, startle, terrify, terrorize — more at FRIGHTEN

alarm·ist \ə-'lär-mist\ *n* : a person who alarms others esp. needlessly

alas \ə-'las\ *interj* — used to express unhappiness, pity, or concern

al·ba·core \'al-bə-ˌkōr\ *n, pl* **-core** *or* **-cores** : a large tuna that is a source of canned tuna

Al·ba·nian \al-'bā-nē-ən\ *n* : a native or inhabitant of Albania

al·ba·tross \'al-bə-ˌtros, -ˌträs\ *n, pl* **-tross** *or* **-tross·es** : any of a family of large web-footed seabirds

al·be·do \al-'bē-(ˌ)dō\ *n, pl* **-dos** : the fraction of incident radiation that is reflected by a body or surface

al·be·it \ol-'bē-ət, al-\ *conj* ♦ : even though : ALTHOUGH

♦ although, howbeit, though, when, while — more at ALTHOUGH

al·bi·no \al-'bī-nō\ *n, pl* **-nos** : a person or nonhuman mammal lacking coloring matter in the skin, hair, and eyes — **al·bi·nism** \'al-bə-ˌni-zəm\ *n*

al·bum \'al-bəm\ *n* **1** : a book with blank pages used for making a collection (as of stamps) **2** : one or more recordings (as on tape or disk) produced as a single unit **3** ♦ : a collection usu. in book form of literary selections, musical compositions, or pictures : ANTHOLOGY

♦ anthology, compilation, miscellany — more at ANTHOLOGY

al·bu·men \al-'byü-mən\ *n* **1** : the white of an egg **2** : ALBUMIN

al·bu·min \al-'byü-mən\ *n* : any of numerous water-soluble proteins of blood, milk, egg white, and plant and animal tissues

al·bu·min·ous \al-'byü-mə-nəs\ *adj* : containing or resembling albumen or albumin

alc *abbr* alcohol

al·cal·de \al-'käl-dē\ *n* : the chief administrative and judicial officer of a Spanish or Spanish-American town

al·ca·zar \al-'kä-zər, -'ka-\ *n* [Sp *alcázar*, fr. Ar *al-qaṣr* the castle] : a Spanish fortress or palace

al·che·my \'al-kə-mē\ *n* : medieval chemistry chiefly concerned with efforts to turn base metals into gold — **al·che·mist** \'al-kə-mist\ *n*

al·co·hol \'al-kə-ˌhȯl\ *n* [NL, fr. ML, powdered antimony, fr. Sp, fr. Ar *al-kuḥul* the powdered antimony] **1** : a colorless flammable liquid that is the intoxicating agent in fermented and distilled liquors **2** : any of various carbon compounds similar to alcohol **3** ♦ : beverages containing alcohol

♦ booze, drink, intoxicant, liquor, moonshine, spirits; *also* ale, beer, mead, sake, wine

¹al·co·hol·ic \ˌal-kə-'hȯl-ik, -'hä-\ *adj* **1** : of, relating to, caused by, or containing alcohol **2** : affected with alcoholism — **al·co·hol·i·cal·ly** \-li-k(ə-)lē\ *adv*

²alcoholic *n* ♦ : a person affected with alcoholism

♦ drunk, drunkard, inebriate, soak, sot, souse, tippler — more at DRUNK

al·co·hol·ism \'al-kə-ˌhȯ-ˌli-zəm\ *n* : continued excessive and usu. uncontrollable use of alcoholic drinks; *also* : a complex chronic psychological and nutritional disorder associated with such use

al·cove \'al-ˌkōv\ *n* **1** : a nook or small recess opening off a larger room **2** ♦ : a niche or arched opening (as in a wall)

♦ niche, nook, recess — more at NICHE

ald *abbr* alderman

al·der \'ȯl-dər\ *n* : a tree or shrub related to the birches and growing in wet areas

al·der·man \'ȯl-dər-mən\ *n* : a member of a city legislative body

ale \'āl\ *n* : an alcoholic beverage brewed from malt and hops that is usu. more bitter than beer

ale·a·tor·ic \ˌā-lē-ə-'tòr-ik\ *adj* : characterized by chance or random elements ⟨∼ music⟩

ale·a·to·ry \'ā-lē-ə-ˌtòr-ē\ *adj* : ALEATORIC

alee \ə-'lē\ *adv* : on or toward the lee

ale·house \'āl-ˌhaùs\ *n* : a place where ale is sold to be drunk on the premises

¹alert \ə-'lərt\ *adj* [It *all'erta*, lit., on the ascent] 1 ♦ : watchful against danger 2 ♦ : quick to perceive and act — **alert·ly** *adv*

♦ [1] attentive, awake, vigilant, watchful, wide-awake; *also* alive, aware, conscious, sensitive ♦ [2] brainy, bright, brilliant, clever, intelligent, keen, nimble, quick, quick-witted, sharp, smart — more at INTELLIGENT ♦ [2] expeditious, prompt, quick, ready, willing — more at QUICK

²alert *n* 1 ♦ : a warning signal or device : ALARM 2 : the period during which an alert is in effect

♦ admonition, alarm, caution, notice, warning — more at WARNING

³alert *vb* 1 ♦ : to call to a state of readiness : WARN 2 : to make aware of

♦ caution, forewarn, warn — more at WARN

alert·ness \-nəs\ *n* ♦ : the quality or state of being alert

♦ attentiveness, lookout, vigilance, watch — more at VIGILANCE

Aleut \ˌa-lē-'üt, ə-'lüt\ *n* 1 : a member of a people of the Aleutian and Shumagin islands and the western part of Alaska Peninsula 2 : the language of the Aleuts

ale·wife \'āl-ˌwīf\ *n, pl* **ale·wives** \-ˌwīvz\ : a food fish of the herring family abundant esp. on the Atlantic coast

Al·ex·an·dri·an \ˌa-lig-'zan-drē-ən\ *adj* 1 : of or relating to Alexander the Great 2 : HELLENISTIC

al·ex·an·drine \-'zan-drən\ *n, often cap* : a line of six iambic feet

al·fal·fa \al-'fal-fə\ *n* : a leguminous plant widely grown for hay and forage

al·fres·co \al-'fres-kō\ *adj or adv* [It] : taking place in the open air

alg *abbr* algebra

al·ga \'al-gə\ *n, pl* **al·gae** \'al-(ˌ)jē\ : any of a group of lower plants having chlorophyll but no vascular system and including seaweeds and related freshwater plants — **al·gal** \-gəl\ *adj*

al·ge·bra \'al-jə-brə\ *n* [ML, fr. Ar *al-jabr*] : a branch of mathematics using symbols (as letters) to explore the relationships between numbers and the operations used to work with them — **al·ge·bra·ic** \ˌal-jə-'brā-ik\ *adj* — **al·ge·bra·i·cal·ly** \-'brā-ə-k(ə-)lē\ *adv*

Al·ge·ri·an \al-'jir-ē-ən\ *n* : a native or inhabitant of Algeria — **Algerian** *adj*

Al·gon·quin \al-'gän-kwən, -'gäŋ-\ *n* : a member of an American Indian people of the Ottawa River valley

al·go·rithm \'al-gə-ˌri-t͟həm\ *n* : a procedure for solving a problem esp. in mathematics or computing — **al·go·rith·mic** \ˌal-gə-'rit͟h-mik\ *adj* — **al·go·rith·mi·cal·ly** \-mi-k(ə-)lē\ *adv*

¹ali·as \'ā-lē-əs, 'āl-yəs\ *adv* [L, otherwise, fr. *alius* other] : otherwise called

²alias *n* ♦ : an assumed or additional name

♦ cognomen, nickname — more at NICKNAME

¹al·i·bi \'a-lə-ˌbī\ *n* [L, elsewhere, fr. *alius* other] 1 : a plea offered by an accused person of not having been at the scene of an offense 2 ♦ : an excuse (as for failure)

♦ defense (*or* defence), excuse, justification, plea, reason — more at EXCUSE

²alibi *vb* **-bied; -bi·ing** 1 : to furnish an excuse for 2 : to offer an excuse

¹alien \'ā-lē-ən, 'āl-yən\ *adj* ♦ : belonging or relating to another person, place, or thing : FOREIGN

♦ adventitious, extraneous, extrinsic, foreign — more at EXTRINSIC

²alien *n* 1 : a foreign-born resident who has not been naturalized 2 : EXTRATERRESTRIAL

alien·able \'āl-yə-nə-bəl, 'ā-lē-ə-nə-\ *adj* : transferable to the ownership of another ⟨∼ property⟩

alien·ate \'ā-lē-ə-ˌnāt, 'āl-yə-\ *vb* **-at·ed; -at·ing** 1 ♦ : to make hostile : ESTRANGE 2 : to transfer (property) to another

♦ disaffect, disgruntle, estrange, sour — more at ESTRANGE

alien·ation \ˌā-lē-ə-'nā-shən, ˌāl-yə-\ *n* ♦ : a withdrawing or separation of a person or a person's affections from an object or position of former attachment

♦ disaffection, estrangement — more at ESTRANGEMENT

alien·ist \'ā-lē-ə-nist, 'āl-yə-\ *n* : PSYCHIATRIST

¹alight \ə-'līt\ *vb* **alight·ed** *also* **alit** \ə-'lit\; **alight·ing** 1 : to get down (as from a vehicle) 2 ♦ : to come to rest from the air

♦ land, light, perch, roost, settle

²alight *adj* ♦ : lighted up

♦ ablaze, bright, light — more at BRIGHT

align *also* **aline** \ə-'līn\ *vb* 1 : to bring into line 2 : to array on the side of or against a cause — **align·er** *n* — **align·ment** *also* **aline·ment** *n*

¹alike \ə-'līk\ *adv* ♦ : in the same manner, form, or degree

♦ also, correspondingly, likewise, similarly, so — more at ALSO

²alike *adj* ♦ : exhibiting close resemblance without being identical : LIKE

♦ akin, analogous, comparable, correspondent, like, parallel, similar, such; *also* commensurate, proportionate *Ant* different, dissimilar, diverse, unlike

al·i·ment \'a-lə-mənt\ *n* : NOURISHMENT 1 — **aliment** *vb*

al·i·men·ta·ry \ˌa-lə-'men-t(ə-)rē\ *adj* : of, relating to, or functioning in nourishment or nutrition

alimentary canal *n* : the tube that extends from the mouth to the anus and functions in the digestion and absorption of food and the elimination of residues

al·i·mo·ny \'a-lə-ˌmō-nē\ *n, pl* **-nies** [L *alimonia* sustenance, fr. *alere* to nourish] : an allowance made to one spouse by the other for support pending or after legal separation or divorce

A–line \'ā-ˌlīn\ *adj* : having a flared bottom and a close-fitting top ⟨an ∼ skirt⟩

alive \ə-'līv\ *adj* 1 ♦ : having life 2 ♦ : being in force or operation 3 ♦ : knowing or realizing the existence of ⟨∼ to the danger⟩ 4 : ALERT, BRISK 5 ♦ : marked by much life, animation, or activity : ANIMATED ⟨streets ∼ with traffic⟩ — **alive·ness** *n*

♦ [1] existent, extant, living — more at EXTANT ♦ [1] animate, live, living; *also* active, animated, dynamic, lively, thriving, vibrant, vital, vivacious *Ant* dead, deceased, defunct, lifeless, nonliving ♦ [2] active, functional, living, on, operational, operative, running, working — more at ACTIVE ♦ [3] aware, cognizant, conscious, mindful, sensible, sentient, witting — more at CONSCIOUS ♦ [5] animated, astir, busy, lively, vibrant; *also* abounding, crowded, overflowing, populous, swarming, teeming, thronging *Ant* asleep, dead, inactive, lifeless, sleepy

alk *abbr* alkaline

al·ka·li \'al-kə-ˌlī\ *n, pl* **-lies** *or* **-lis** 1 : a substance (as a hydroxide) that has a bitter taste and neutralizes acids 2 : a mixture of salts in the soil of some dry regions in such amount as to make ordinary farming impossible — **al·ka·line** \-kə-lən, -ˌlīn\ *adj* — **al·ka·lin·i·ty** \ˌal-kə-'li-nə-tē\ *n*

al·ka·loid \'al-kə-ˌlòid\ *n* : any of various usu. basic and bitter organic compounds found esp. in seed plants

al·kane \'al-ˌkān\ *n* : a hydrocarbon in which each carbon atom is bonded to 4 other atoms

al·kyd \'al-kəd\ *n* : any of numerous synthetic resins used esp. for protective coatings and in paint

¹all \'òl\ *adj* 1 ♦ : the whole of 2 : every member of 3 : EV-

ERY ⟨∼ manner of problems⟩ **4** : any whatever ⟨beyond ∼ doubt⟩ **5** : nothing but ⟨∼ ears⟩ **6** : being more than one person or thing ⟨who ∼ is coming⟩

♦ concentrated, entire, undivided, whole — more at WHOLE

²**all** *adv* **1** ♦ : to the full or entire extent : WHOLLY **2** : selected as the best — used in combination ⟨*all*-state champs⟩ **3** : so much ⟨∼ the better for it⟩ **4** : for each side ⟨the score is two ∼⟩

♦ absolutely, clean, completely, entirely, fully, quite, totally, utterly; *also* exhaustively, thoroughly

³**all** *pron* **1** : the whole number, quantity, or amount ⟨∼ of it is gone⟩ **2** : every person or thing ⟨that is ∼⟩

⁴**all** *n* : the whole of one's resources ⟨gave his ∼⟩

Al·lah \'ä-lä, 'a-, ä-'lä\ *n* [Ar *allāh*] : the Being perfect in power, wisdom, and goodness who is worshipped as creator and ruler of the universe — used in Islam

all along *adv* : all the time ⟨knew it *all along*⟩

all–Amer·i·can \,ȯl-ə-'mer-ə-kən\ *adj* **1** : selected as the best in the U.S. **2** : composed wholly of American elements **3** : typical of the U.S. — **all–American** *n*

all–around \,ȯl-ə-'raȯnd\ *adj* **1** ♦ : considered in or encompassing all aspects ⟨best ∼ performance⟩ **2** : competent in many fields : VERSATILE ⟨an ∼ athlete⟩

♦ general, unlimited, unqualified, unrestricted

all around \,ȯl-ə-'raȯnd\ *adv* ♦ : without concentration on one area or aspect

♦ altogether, collectively, overall, together; *also* broadly, generally, liberally, loosely; completely, comprehensively, entirely, exhaustively, fully, thoroughly, wholly

al·lay \ə-'lā\ *vb* **1** ♦ : to subdue or reduce in intensity or severity : ALLEVIATE **2** ♦ : to make quiet : CALM

♦ [1] alleviate, assuage, ease, help, mitigate, mollify, palliate, relieve, soothe — more at HELP ♦ [2] calm, compose, quiet, settle, soothe, still, tranquilize — more at CALM

all clear *n* : a signal that a danger has passed

al·lege \ə-'lej\ *vb* **al·leged; al·leg·ing 1** ♦ : to assert without proof **2** : to offer as a reason — **al·le·ga·tion** \,a-li-'gā-shən\ *n* — **al·leg·ed·ly** \ə-'le-jəd-lē\ *adv*

♦ affirm, assert, aver, avouch, avow, claim, contend, declare, insist, maintain, profess, protest, warrant — more at CLAIM

al·le·giance \ə-'lē-jəns\ *n* **1** : loyalty owed by a citizen to a government **2** ♦ : loyalty to a person or cause

♦ constancy, dedication, devotion, faith, faithfulness, fastness, fealty, fidelity, loyalty, steadfastness — more at FIDELITY

al·le·go·ry \'a-lə-,gȯr-ē\ *n, pl* **-ries** : the expression through symbolism of truths or generalizations about human experience; *also* : an instance (as in a story or painting) of such expression — **al·le·gor·i·cal** \,a-lə-'gȯr-i-kəl\ *adj* — **al·le·gor·i·cal·ly** \-k(ə-)lē\ *adv*

¹**al·le·gro** \ə-'le-grō, -'lā-\ *n, pl* **-gros** : an allegro movement

²**allegro** *adv or adj* [It, merry] : at a brisk lively tempo — used as a direction in music

al·le·lu·ia \,a-lə-'lü-yə\ *interj* : HALLELUJAH

Al·len wrench \'a-lən-\ *n* [*Allen* Manufacturing Company, Hartford, Conn.] : an L-shaped hexagonal metal bar of which either end fits the socket of a screw or bolt

al·ler·gen \'a-lər-jən\ *n* : something that causes allergy — **al·ler·gen·ic** \,a-lər-'je-nik\ *adj*

al·ler·gic \ə-'lər-jik\ *adj* : of, relating to, affected with, or caused by allergy

al·ler·gist \'a-lər-jist\ *n* : a specialist in allergies

al·ler·gy \'a-lər-jē\ *n, pl* **-gies** [G *Allergie*, fr. Gk *allos* other + *ergon* work] **1** : exaggerated or abnormal reaction (as by sneezing) to substances or situations harmless to most people **2** ♦ : a feeling of antipathy or aversion

♦ aversion, disfavor (*or* disfavour), disinclination, dislike — more at DISLIKE

al·le·vi·ate \ə-'lē-vē-,āt\ *vb* **-at·ed; -at·ing** ♦ : to remove or lessen (as suffering) : RELIEVE

♦ allay, assuage, ease, help, mitigate, mollify, palliate, relieve, soothe — more at HELP

al·le·vi·a·tion \ə-,lē-vē-'ā-shən\ *n* ♦ : the action of alleviating or of being alleviated

♦ comfort, ease, relief — more at EASE

al·ley \'a-lē\ *n, pl* **alleys 1** : a garden or park walk **2** : a place for bowling **3** : a narrow passageway esp. between buildings

al·ley–oop \,a-lē-'yüp\ *n* : a basketball play in which a player catches a pass above the basket and immediately dunks the ball

al·ley·way \'a-lē-,wā\ *n* : ALLEY 3

All·hal·lows \ȯl-'ha-lōz\ *n, pl* **Allhallows** : ALL SAINTS' DAY

al·li·ance \ə-'lī-əns\ *n* **1** ♦ : a union to promote common interests **2** ♦ : union by relationship in qualities **3** : a treaty of alliance

♦ [1] bloc, coalition, combination, combine, confederacy, confederation, federation, league, union — more at CONFEDERACY ♦ [2] affiliation, association, collaboration, confederation, connection, cooperation, hookup, liaison, partnership, relation, relationship, union — more at ASSOCIATION

al·li·ga·tor \'a-lə-,gā-tər\ *n* [Sp *el lagarto* the lizard] : either of two large short-legged reptiles resembling crocodiles but having a shorter and broader snout

alligator pear *n* : AVOCADO

al·lit·er·ate \ə-'li-tə-,rāt\ *vb* **-at·ed; -at·ing 1** : to form an alliteration **2** : to arrange so as to make alliteration

al·lit·er·a·tion \ə-,li-tə-'rā-shən\ *n* : the repetition of initial sounds in adjacent words or syllables — **al·lit·er·a·tive** \-'li-tə-,rā-tiv\ *adj*

al·lo·cate \'a-lə-,kāt\ *vb* **-cat·ed; -cat·ing** ♦ : to apportion for a specific purpose or to particular persons or things

♦ administer, apportion, deal, dispense, distribute, mete, parcel, portion, prorate — more at ADMINISTER

♦ allot, allow, apportion, ration — more at ALLOT

al·lo·ca·tion \,a-lə-'kā-shən\ *n* **1** ♦ : the act or action of allocating **2** ♦ : the amount allocated to one sharer

♦ [1] dispensation, distribution, division, issuance — more at DISTRIBUTION ♦ [2] allotment, appropriation, grant, subsidy — more at APPROPRIATION

al·lot \ə-'lät\ *vb* **al·lot·ted; al·lot·ting** ♦ : to distribute as a share

♦ allocate, allow, apportion, ration; *also* deal, dispense, distribute, divide, dole (out), measure, mete (out), parcel (out), portion, prorate, reserve

al·lot·ment \-mənt\ *n* **1** : the act of allotting **2** ♦ : something that is allotted

♦ allocation, appropriation, grant, subsidy — more at APPROPRIATION ♦ allowance, cut, part, portion, proportion, quota, share — more at SHARE

all–out \'ȯl-'aȯt\ *adj* ♦ : marked by thoroughness or zeal : THOROUGHGOING

♦ clean, complete, comprehensive, exhaustive, full-scale, out-and-out, thorough, thoroughgoing, total — more at EXHAUSTIVE

all out *adv* ♦ : with maximum effort

♦ full tilt

all over *adv* : in every place or part : EVERYWHERE

al·low \ə-'laȯ\ *vb* **1** ♦ : to assign as a share ⟨∼ time for rest⟩ **2** : to count as a deduction **3** : to make allowance ⟨∼ for expansion⟩ **4** ♦ : to accept as true, valid, or accurate usu. reluctantly : ADMIT, CONCEDE **5 a** : to give leave for or make possible : PERMIT ⟨∼s the dog to roam⟩ **b** ♦ : to give leave to

♦ [1] allocate, allot, apportion, ration — more at ALLOT ♦ [4] acknowledge, admit, agree, concede, confess, grant, own — more at ADMIT *Ant* ban, enjoin, forbid, prohibit, proscribe, veto ♦ [5b] let, permit, suffer; *also* authorize, commission, empower, license *Ant* enjoin, forbid, prohibit

al·low·able \ə-'laú-ə-bəl\ *adj* ♦ : that may be permitted
♦ admissible, permissible, sufferable — more at PERMISSIBLE

al·low·ance \-əns\ *n* ♦ **1** : an allotted share **2** : money given regularly for expenses **3** ♦ : the act of allowing : PERMISSION **4** : a taking into account of extenuating circumstances
♦ [1] allotment, cut, part, portion, proportion, quota, share — more at SHARE ♦ [3] authorization, clearance, concurrence, consent, leave, license (*or* licence), permission, sanction, sufferance — more at PERMISSION

al·loy \'a-,lói, ə-'lói\ *n* **1** : a substance composed of metals melted together **2** : an admixture that lessens value — **al·loy** \ə-'lói, 'a-,lói\ *vb*

¹all right *adj* **1** ♦ : giving satisfaction : SATISFACTORY **2** ♦ : free from harm or risk **3** : having qualities that tend to give pleasure — often used as a generalized term of approval
♦ [1] acceptable, adequate, decent, fine, OK, passable, respectable, satisfactory, tolerable — more at ADEQUATE ♦ [2] alright, safe, secure — more at SAFE

²all right *adv* **1** ♦ — used interjectionally to express agreement or resignation or to indicate the resumption of a discussion ⟨*all right*, let's go⟩ **2** : beyond doubt **3** ♦ : well enough : SATISFACTORILY
♦ [1] alright, OK, yea, yes — more at YES ♦ [3] adequately, fine, good, nicely, OK, passably, satisfactorily, so-so, tolerably, well — more at WELL

All Saints' Day *n* : a Christian feast on November 1 in honor of all the saints

All Souls' Day *n* : a day of prayer observed by some Christian churches on November 2 for the souls of the faithful departed

all·spice \'ól-,spīs\ *n* : the berry of a West Indian tree related to the European myrtle; *also* : the mildly pungent and aromatic spice made from it

all–star \'ól-,stär\ *n* : a member of a team of star performers — **all–star** *adj*

all–ter·rain vehicle *n* : a small motor vehicle for use on a wide range of terrain

all told *adv* : with everything counted

al·lude \ə-'lüd\ *vb* **al·lud·ed; al·lud·ing** [L *alludere*, lit., to play with] ♦ : to refer indirectly — **al·lu·sion** \-'lü-zhən\ *n* — **al·lu·sive** \-'lü-siv\ *adj* — **al·lu·sive·ly** *adv* — **al·lu·sive·ness** *n*
♦ hint, imply, indicate, infer, insinuate, intimate, suggest — more at HINT

¹al·lure \ə-'lùr\ *vb* **al·lured; al·lur·ing** ♦ : to entice by charm or attraction — **allure** *n* — **al·lur·ing·ly** *adv*
♦ beguile, bewitch, captivate, charm, enchant, fascinate, wile — more at CHARM ♦ beguile, decoy, entice, lead on, lure, seduce, tempt — more at LURE

²allure *n* ♦ : power of attraction or fascination
♦ appeal, attractiveness, captivation, charisma, charm, enchantment, fascination, glamour, magic, magnetism — more at CHARM

alluring *adj* ♦ : marked by allure
♦ attractive, captivating, charming, elfin, engaging, fascinating, fetching, glamorous, magnetic, seductive — more at FASCINATING

al·lu·vi·um \ə-'lü-vē-əm\ *n, pl* **-vi·ums** *or* **-via** \-vē-ə\ : soil material (as clay) deposited by running water — **al·lu·vi·al** \-vē-əl\ *adj or n*

¹al·ly \ə-'lī, 'a-,lī\ *vb* **al·lied; al·ly·ing** ♦ : to enter into an alliance
♦ associate, band, club, confederate, conjoin, cooperate, federate, league, unite; *also* collaborate, gang (up), team (up) *Ant* break up, disband

²al·ly \'a-,lī, ə-'lī\ *n* ♦ : one that is associated with another as a helper
♦ abettor, backer, confederate, supporter, sympathizer; *also* well-wisher

-ally *adv suffix* : ²-LY ⟨specific*ally*⟩

al·ma ma·ter \,al-mə-'mä-tər\ *n* [L, fostering mother] **1** : an educational institute that one has attended **2** : the song or hymn of an alma mater

al·ma·nac \'ól-mə-,nak, 'al-\ *n* **1** : a publication esp. of astronomical and meteorological data **2** : a usu. annual publication of miscellaneous information

al·man·dite \'al-mən-,dīt\ *n* : a deep red garnet

al·mighty \ól-'mī-tē\ *adj* **1** *often cap* : having absolute power over all ⟨*Almighty* God⟩ **2** : relatively unlimited in power — **al·might·i·ness** *n*

Almighty *n* ♦ : the Being worshipped as the creator and ruler of the universe
♦ deity, Jehovah, Supreme Being — more at DEITY

al·mond \'ä-mənd, 'a-; 'al-\ *n* : a small tree related to the peach; *also* : the edible nutlike kernel of its fruit

al·mo·ner \'al-mə-nər, 'ä-mə-\ *n* : a person who distributes alms

al·most \'ól-,mōst, ól-'mōst\ *adv* ♦ : very nearly but not exactly
♦ about, most, much, near, nearly, next to, nigh, practically, some, virtually, well-nigh; *also* appreciably, chiefly, largely, mainly, mostly

alms \'ämz, 'älmz\ *n, pl* **alms** [ME *almesse, almes*, fr. OE *ælmesse, ælms*, fr. L *eleemosyna* alms, fr. Gk *eleēmosynē* pity, alms, fr. *eleēmōn* merciful, fr. *eleos* pity] ♦ : something given freely to relieve the poor
♦ benefaction, beneficence, charity, contribution, donation, philanthropy — more at CONTRIBUTION

alms·house \-,haús\ *n* : POORHOUSE

al·oe \'a-lō\ *n* **1** : any of a large genus of succulent chiefly southern African plants related to the lilies **2** *pl* : the dried juice of the leaves of an aloe used esp. formerly as a laxative

aloft \ə-'lóft\ *adv* **1** ♦ : high in the air **2** : in flight
♦ above, over, overhead, skyward — more at ABOVE

alo·ha \ə-'lō-ə, ä-'lō-hä\ *interj* [Hawaiian] — used to greet or bid farewell

¹alone \ə-'lōn\ *adj* **1** ♦ : separated from others **2** ♦ : not including anyone or anything else : ONLY — **alone** *adv*
♦ [1] lone, lonely, lonesome, solitary, unaccompanied; *also* unattended, unchaperoned *Ant* accompanied ♦ [2] lone, only, singular, sole, solitary, special, unique — more at ONLY

²alone *adv* **1** ♦ : to the exclusion of all else : SOLELY **2** ♦ : without aid or support
♦ [1] exclusively, just, only, simply, solely — more at SOLELY ♦ [2] independently, singly, solely, unaided, unassisted; *also* individually, separately

¹along \ə-'lóŋ\ *prep* **1** : in line with the direction of ⟨sail ∼ the coast⟩ **2** : at a point on or during ⟨stopped ∼ the way⟩

²along *adv* **1** : FORWARD, ON **2** : as a companion ⟨bring her ∼⟩ **3** ♦ : at an advanced point ⟨plans are far ∼⟩
♦ ahead, forth, forward, on, onward; *also* before

along·shore \ə-'lóŋ-'shōr\ *adv or adj* : along the shore or coast

¹along·side \-,sīd\ *adv* : along or by the side

²alongside *prep* **1** : along or by the side of **2** : in association with

alongside of *prep* : ALONGSIDE

aloof \ə-'lüf\ *adj* ♦ : removed or distant physically or emotionally — **aloof·ness** *n*
♦ antisocial, cold, cool, detached, distant, frosty, remote, standoffish, unsociable — more at COOL

al·o·pe·cia \,a-lə-'pē-sh(ē-)ə\ *n* : BALDNESS

aloud \ə-'laúd\ *adv* : with the speaking voice

alp \'alp\ *n* : a high rugged mountain

al·paca \al-'pa-kə\ *n* : a domesticated mammal esp. of Peru that is prob. descended from the vicuña; *also* : its woolly hair or cloth made from this

al·pha \'al-fə\ *n* **1** : the 1st letter of the Greek alphabet — A or α **2** : something first : BEGINNING

al·pha·bet \\'al-fə-,bet\ *n* : the set of letters or characters used in writing a language

al·pha·bet·i·cal \,al-fə-'be-ti-kəl\ *or* **al·pha·bet·ic** \-'be-tik\ *adj* **1** : arranged in the order of the letters of the alphabet **2** : of or employing an alphabet — **al·pha·bet·i·cal·ly** \-ti-k(ə-)lē\ *adv*

al·pha·bet·ize \'al-fə-bə-,tīz\ *vb* **-ized; -iz·ing** : to arrange in alphabetical order — **al·pha·bet·iz·er** *n*

al·pha·nu·mer·ic \,al-fə-nù-'mer-ik, -nyù-\ *adj* : consisting of letters and numbers and often other symbols ⟨an ∼ code⟩; *also* : being a character in an alphanumeric system

alpha particle *n* : a positively charged particle identical with the nucleus of a helium atom that is ejected at high speed in certain radioactive transformations

alpha rhythm *n* : ALPHA WAVE

alpha wave *n* : an electrical rhythm of the brain often associated with a state of wakeful relaxation

Al·pine \'al-,pīn\ *adj* **1** : relating to, located in, or resembling the Alps mountains **2** *often not cap* : of, relating to, or growing on upland slopes above timberline **3** : of or relating to competitive ski events consisting of slalom and downhill racing

al·ready \òl-'re-dē\ *adv* : by this time : PREVIOUSLY

¹al·right \òl-'rīt\ *adv* : very well : ALL RIGHT — used interjectionally to express agreement or resignation or to indicate the resumption of a discussion ⟨alright, let's go⟩

²alright *adj* **1** ♦ : giving satisfaction : SATISFACTORY **2** ♦ : free from harm or risk **3** ♦ : having qualities that tend to give pleasure — often used as a generalized term of approval

  ♦ [1] agreeable, all right, fine, good, OK, palatable, satisfactory — more at SATISFACTORY ♦ [2] all right, safe, secure — more at SAFE ♦ [3] OK, yea, yes — more at YES

al·so \'òl-sō\ *adv* **1** ♦ : in like manner : LIKEWISE **2** ♦ : in addition : TOO

  ♦ [1] alike, correspondingly, likewise, similarly, so; *also* equally **Ant** differently, otherwise ♦ [2] additionally, again, besides, further, furthermore, likewise, more, moreover, then, too, withal, yet

al·so-ran \-,ran\ *n* **1** : a horse or dog that finishes out of the money in a race **2** : a contestant that does not win

alt *abbr* **1** alternate **2** altitude

Alta *abbr* Alberta

al·tar \'òl-tər\ *n* **1** : a structure on which sacrifices are offered or incense is burned **2** : a table used as a center of ritual or worship

altar server *n* : a boy or girl who assists the celebrant at a church service

¹al·ter \'òl-tər\ *vb* **al·tered; al·ter·ing** \-t(ə-)riŋ\ **1** ♦ : to make or become different **2** : to remove the sex organs of

  ♦ change, make over, modify, recast, redo, refashion, remake, remodel, revamp, revise, rework, vary — more at CHANGE

²alter *abbr* alteration

al·ter·a·tion \,òl-tə-'rā-shən\ *n* ♦ : the act, process, or result of altering

  ♦ change, difference, modification, revise, revision, variation — more at CHANGE

al·ter·ca·tion \,òl-tər-'kā-shən\ *n* ♦ : a noisy or angry dispute

  ♦ argument, disagreement, dispute, fight, hassle, misunderstanding, quarrel, row, scrap, spat, squabble, wrangle — more at ARGUMENT

al·ter ego \,òl-tər-'ē-gō\ *n* [L, lit., second I] : a second self; *esp* : a trusted friend

¹al·ter·nate \'òl-tər-nət, 'al-\ *adj* **1** : arranged or succeeding by turns **2** : every other **3** : being an alternative ⟨an ∼ route⟩ — **al·ter·nate·ly** *adv*

²al·ter·nate \-,nāt\ *vb* **-nat·ed; -nat·ing** : to occur or cause to occur by turns — **al·ter·na·tion** \,òl-tər-'nā-shən, ,al-\ *n*

³alternate *n* : SUBSTITUTE

alternating current *n* : an electric current that reverses its direction at regular intervals

¹al·ter·na·tive \òl-'tər-nə-tiv, al-\ *adj* : offering a choice

²alternative *n* ♦ : an opportunity for deciding between two or more courses or propositions

  ♦ choice, discretion, option, pick, preference, way — more at CHOICE

alternative medicine *n* : any of various systems of healing (as homeopathy) not typically practiced in conventional Western medicine

al·ter·na·tor \'òl-tər-,nā-tər, 'al-\ *n* : an electric generator for producing alternating current

al·though *also* **al·tho** \òl-'thō\ *conj* ♦ : in spite of the fact that : even though

  ♦ albeit, howbeit, though, when, while; *also* but, whereas

al·tim·e·ter \al-'ti-mə-tər, 'al-tə-,mē-tər\ *n* : an instrument for measuring altitude

al·ti·tude \'al-tə-,tüd, -,tyüd\ *n* **1** : angular distance above the horizon **2** ♦ : vertical distance : HEIGHT **3** : the perpendicular distance in a geometric figure from the vertex to the base, from the vertex of an angle to the side opposite, or from the base to a parallel side or face

  ♦ elevation, height — more at HEIGHT

al·to \'al-tō\ *n, pl* **altos** [It, lit., high, fr. L *altus*] : the lower female voice part in a 4-part chorus; *also* : a singer having this voice or part

¹al·to·geth·er \,òl-tə-'ge-thər\ *adv* **1** ♦ : to the full or entire extent : WHOLLY **2** ♦ : in all **3** ♦ : on the whole

  ♦ [1] absolutely, all, clean, completely, dead, entirely, fast, flat, full, fully, perfectly, quite, thoroughly, well, wholly — more at FULLY ♦ [2] all around, collectively, overall, together — more at ALL AROUND ♦ [3] chiefly, generally, largely, mainly, mostly, overall, predominantly, primarily, principally; *also* considerably, greatly, significantly, substantially

²altogether *n* : NUDE ⟨posed in the ∼⟩

al·tru·ism \'al-trù-,i-zəm\ *n* [F *altruisme*, fr. *autrui* other people, fr. OF, oblique case form of *autre* other, fr. L *alter*] : unselfish interest in the welfare of others — **al·tru·ist** \-ist\ *n* — **al·tru·is·ti·cal·ly** \-ti-k(ə-)lē\ *adv*

al·tru·is·tic \,al-trù-'is-tik\ *adj* ♦ : relating to or given to altruism

  ♦ beneficent, benevolent, charitable, humanitarian, philanthropic — more at CHARITABLE

al·um \'a-ləm\ *n* : either of two colorless crystalline aluminum-containing compounds used esp. as an emetic or as an astringent and styptic

alu·mi·na \ə-'lü-mə-nə\ *n* : the oxide of aluminum occurring in nature as corundum and in bauxite

al·u·min·i·um \,al-yə-'mi-nē-əm\ *n, chiefly Brit* : ALUMINUM

alu·mi·nize \ə-'lü-mə-,nīz\ *vb* **-nized; -niz·ing** : to treat with aluminum

alu·mi·num \ə-'lü-mə-nəm\ *n* : a silver-white malleable ductile light metallic element that is the most abundant metal in the earth's crust

alum·na \ə-'ləm-nə\ *n, pl* **-nae** \-,nē\ : a woman or girl who is a graduate or former student of a college or school

alum·nus \ə-'ləm-nəs\ *n, pl* **-ni** \-,nī\ [L, foster son, pupil, fr. *alere* to nourish] : a graduate or former student of a college or school

al·ways \'òl-wēz, -wəz, -,(,)wāz\ *adv* **1** ♦ : at all times : INVARIABLY **2** ♦ : for a limitless time : FOREVER

  ♦ [1] constantly, continually, ever, forever, incessantly, invariably, perpetually, unfailingly; *also* commonly, frequently, oft, often, oftentimes, repeatedly **Ant** ne'er, never ♦ [2] eternally, ever, everlastingly, forever, permanently, perpetually — more at EVER

Alz·hei·mer's disease \'älts-,hī-mərz-, 'alts-\ *n* : a degenerative brain disease characterized esp. by progressive mental deterioration and memory loss

am *pres 1st sing of* BE

¹Am *abbr* America; American

²Am *symbol* americium

¹AM \'ā-,em\ *n* : a broadcasting system using amplitude modulation; *also* : a radio receiver for broadcasts made by such a system

²AM *abbr* **1** ante meridiem — often not cap. and often punctuated **2** [NL *artium magister*] master of arts

AMA *abbr* American Medical Association

amah \'ä-(₁)mä\ *n* : a female servant in eastern Asia; *esp* : a Chinese nurse

amal·gam \ə-'mal-gəm\ *n* **1** : an alloy of mercury with another metal used in making dental cements **2** ♦ : a mixture of different elements

♦ admixture, blend, combination, composite, compound, fusion, intermixture, mix, mixture — more at BLEND

amal·gam·ate \ə-'mal-gə-₁māt\ *vb* **-at·ed; -at·ing** ♦ : to unite or merge into one body

♦ blend, combine, commingle, fuse, incorporate, integrate, intermingle, merge, mingle, mix — more at MIX

amal·ga·ma·tion \-₁mal-gə-'mā-shən\ *n* : the result of amalgamating

aman·u·en·sis \ə-₁man-yə-'wen-səs\ *n, pl* **-en·ses** \-₁sēz\ : one employed to write from dictation or to copy what another has written : SECRETARY

am·a·ranth \'a-mə-₁ranth\ *n* **1** : any of a large genus of coarse herbs sometimes grown for their showy flowers **2** : a flower that never fades

am·a·ran·thine \₁a-mə-'ran-thən, -₁thīn\ *adj* **1** : relating to or resembling an amaranth **2** : UNDYING

am·a·ryl·lis \₁a-mə-'ri-ləs\ *n* : any of various plants related to the lilies; *esp* : any of several African herbs having bulbs and grown for their clusters of large showy flowers

amass \ə-'mas\ *vb* ♦ : to collect into a mass : ACCUMULATE

♦ accumulate, assemble, collect, concentrate, garner, gather, group, lump, pick up, round up, scrape — more at GATHER

¹am·a·teur \'a-mə-(₁)tər, -₁tùr, -₁tyùr, -₁chùr, -chər\ *n* [F, fr. L *amator* lover, fr. *amare* to love] **1** : a person who engages in a pursuit for pleasure and not as a profession **2** : a person who is not expert — **am·a·teur·ism** \'a-mə-(₁)tər-i-zəm, -₁tùr-, -₁tyùr-, -₁chùr-, -chər-\ *n*

²amateur *adj* ♦ : engaged in or performed by or as if by an amateur

♦ amateurish, inexperienced, inexpert, nonprofessional, unprofessional, unskilled, unskillful — more at AMATEURISH

am·a·teur·ish \₁a-mə-'tər-ish, -'tùr-, -'tyùr-, -'chùr-, -'chər-\ *adj* ♦ : having the characteristics of an amateur : lacking professional finish

♦ amateur, inexperienced, inexpert, nonprofessional, unprofessional, unskilled, unskillful; *also* primitive, self-taught, unprepared, unqualified, unschooled, untaught, untrained, untutored *Ant* ace, expert, masterful, professional

am·a·tive \'a-mə-tiv\ *adj* : indicative of love : AMOROUS — **am·a·tive·ly** *adv* — **am·a·tive·ness** *n*

am·a·to·ry \'a-mə-₁tȯr-ē\ *adj* ♦ : of or expressing sexual love

♦ amorous, erotic, sexy — more at EROTIC

amaze \ə-'māz\ *vb* **amazed; amaz·ing** ♦ : to fill with wonder : ASTOUND — **amaz·ing·ly** *adv*

♦ astonish, astound, bowl, dumbfound, flabbergast, floor, shock, startle, stun, stupefy, surprise — more at SURPRISE

amazed *adj* ♦ : filled with wonder or astonishment

♦ awestruck, stunned, thunderstruck — more at THUNDERSTRUCK

amaze·ment \-mənt\ *n* ♦ : the quality or state of being amazed

♦ admiration, astonishment, awe, wonder, wonderment — more at WONDER

amazing *adj* ♦ : causing amazement, great wonder, or surprise

♦ astonishing, astounding, eye-opening, shocking, startling, stunning, surprising — more at SURPRISING

♦ astonishing, astounding, awesome, fabulous, marvelous (*or* marvellous), miraculous, surprising, wonderful — more at MARVELOUS

am·a·zon \'a-mə-₁zän, -zən\ *n* **1** *cap* : a member of a race of female warriors of Greek mythology **2** : a tall strong often masculine woman — **am·a·zo·ni·an** \₁a-mə-'zō-nē-ən\ *adj, often cap*

amb *abbr* ambassador

am·bas·sa·dor \am-'ba-sə-dər\ *n* ♦ : a representative esp. of a government — **am·bas·sa·do·ri·al** \-₁ba-sə-'dȯr-ē-əl\ *adj* — **am·bas·sa·dor·ship** *n*

♦ delegate, emissary, envoy, legate, minister, representative; *also* agent, attaché, consul, deputy, diplomat, foreign minister, nuncio, procurator, proxy

am·ber \'am-bər\ *n* : a yellowish or brownish fossil resin used esp. for ornamental objects; *also* : the color of this resin

Amber Alert *n* : a widely publicized bulletin that alerts the public to a recently abducted or missing child

am·ber·gris \'am-bər-₁gris, -₁grēs\ *n* : a waxy substance from the sperm whale used in making perfumes

am·bi·dex·trous \₁am-bi-'dek-strəs\ *adj* : using both hands with equal ease — **am·bi·dex·trous·ly** *adv*

am·bi·ence *or* **am·bi·ance** \'am-bē-əns, äⁿ-'byäⁿs\ *n* : a pervading atmosphere

am·bi·ent \'am-bē-ənt\ *adj* : existing on all sides

am·bi·gu·i·ty \₁am-bə-'gyü-ə-tē\ *n* ♦ : the quality or state of being ambiguous

♦ darkness, murkiness, obscurity, opacity — more at OBSCURITY

am·big·u·ous \am-'bi-gyə-wəs\ *adj* ♦ : capable of being understood in more than one way — **am·big·u·ous·ly** *adv*

♦ cryptic, enigmatic, equivocal, mysterious, nebulous, obscure — more at OBSCURE

am·bi·tion \am-'bi-shən\ *n* [ME, fr. MF or L; MF, fr. L *ambition-, ambitio*, lit., act of soliciting for votes, fr. *ambire* to go around] **1** ♦ : eager desire for success or power **2** ♦ : the object of ambition

♦ [1] aspiration, go-getting; *also* determination, diligence, drive, energy, enterprise, go, hustle, industry, initiative, motivation, push ♦ [2] aim, aspiration, goal, mark, meaning, object, objective, plan, purpose — more at GOAL

am·bi·tious \-shəs\ *adj* ♦ : characterized by ambition — **am·bi·tious·ly** *adv*

♦ go-getting, self-seeking; *also* determined, diligent, driving, dynamic, enterprising, hustling, industrious, motivated, venturesome, venturous

am·biv·a·lence \am-'bi-və-ləns\ *n* : simultaneous attraction toward and repulsion from a person, object, or action — **am·biv·a·lent** \-lənt\ *adj*

¹am·ble \'am-bəl\ *vb* **am·bled; am·bling** \-b(ə-)liŋ\ : to go at an amble

²amble *n* : an easy gait esp. of a horse

am·bro·sia \am-'brō-zh(ē-)ə\ *n* : the food of the Greek and Roman gods

am·bro·sial \-zh(ē-)əl\ *adj* ♦ : pleasing to the senses esp. of taste or smell

♦ aromatic, fragrant, redolent, savory, scented, sweet — more at FRAGRANT ♦ appetizing, delectable, delicious, flavorful (*or* flavourful), luscious, palatable, savory, scrumptious, tasty, toothsome, yummy — more at DELICIOUS

am·bu·lance \'am-byə-ləns\ *n* : a vehicle equipped for carrying the injured or sick

am·bu·lant \'am-byə-lənt\ *adj* : AMBULATORY

¹am·bu·la·to·ry \'am-byə-lə-₁tȯr-ē\ *adj* **1** : of, relating to, or adapted to walking **2** : able to walk or move about

²ambulatory *n, pl* **-ries** : a sheltered place (as in a cloister) for walking

am·bus·cade \'am-bə-₁skäd\ *n* : AMBUSH

¹am·bush \'am-₁bùsh\ *n* ♦ : a trap in which concealed persons wait to attack by surprise

♦ net, snare, trap, web — more at TRAP ♦ surprise, trap; *also* assault, attack, charge, sally

²**am·bush** *vb* ♦ : to attack from an ambush

♦ surprise, waylay; *also* assail, assault, attack, storm, strike

amdt *abbr* amendment

ame·ba, ameboid *var of* AMOEBA, AMOEBOID

ame·lio·rate \ə-'mēl-yə-ˌrāt\ *vb* **-rat·ed; -rat·ing** ♦ : to make or grow better : IMPROVE — **ame·lio·ra·tion** \-ˌmēl-yə-'rā-shən\ *n*

♦ amend, better, enhance, enrich, improve, perfect, refine — more at IMPROVE

amen \(ˌ)ā-'men, (ˌ)ä-\ *interj* — used esp. at the end of prayers to affirm or express approval

ame·na·ble \ə-'mē-nə-bəl, -'me-\ *adj* **1** : ANSWERABLE **2 a** ♦ : readily brought to yield, submit, or cooperate : COMPLIANT **b** ♦ : inclined or favorably disposed in mind : WILLING

♦ [2a] compliant, conformable, docile, obedient, submissive, tractable — more at OBEDIENT ♦ [2b] disposed, game, glad, inclined, ready, willing — more at WILLING

amend \ə-'mend\ *vb* **1** ♦ : to change for the better : IMPROVE **2** : to alter formally in phraseology — **amend·able** \-'men-də-bəl\ *adj*

♦ ameliorate, better, enhance, enrich, improve, perfect, refine — more at IMPROVE ♦ correct, debug, emend, rectify, reform, remedy — more at CORRECT

amend·ment \ə-'mend-mənt\ *n* **1** : the act of amending **2** : the process of amending a parliamentary motion or a constitution; *also* : the alteration so proposed or made

amends \ə-'mendz\ *n sing or pl* : compensation for injury or loss

ame·ni·ty \ə-'me-nə-tē, -'mē-\ *n, pl* **-ties** **1** ♦ : the quality of being pleasant or agreeable : AGREEABLENESS **2** ♦ : a gesture observed in social relationships **3** ♦ : something that serves as a comfort or convenience

♦ [1] agreeableness, amiability, geniality, graciousness, niceness, pleasantness, sweetness — more at AMIABILITY ♦ [2] civility, courtesy, formality, gesture — more at CIVILITY ♦ [3] comfort, extra, frill, indulgence, luxury, superfluity — more at LUXURY

Amer *abbr* America; American

amerce \ə-'mərs\ *vb* **amerced; amerc·ing** **1** : to penalize by a fine determined by the court **2** : PUNISH — **amerce·ment** *n*

Amer·i·can \ə-'mer-ə-kən\ *n* **1** : a native or inhabitant of No. or So. America **2** : a citizen of the U.S. — **American** *adj* — **Amer·i·can·ism** \-ə-kə-ˌni-zəm\ *n* — **Amer·i·can·iza·tion** \-ˌmer-ə-kə-nə-'zā-shən\ *n* — **Amer·i·can·ize** \ə-'mer-ə-kə-ˌnīz\ *vb* — **Amer·i·can·ness** *n*

Amer·i·ca·na \ə-ˌmer-ə-'ka-nə, -'kä-\ *n pl* : materials concerning or characteristic of America, its civilization, or its culture

American Indian *n* : a member of any of the indigenous peoples of No. and So. America except often those distinguished as Eskimos or Inuits

American plan *n* : a hotel plan whereby the daily rates cover the cost of room and three meals

American Sign Language *n* : a sign language for the deaf in which meaning is conveyed by a system of hand gestures and placement

am·er·i·ci·um \ˌam-ə-'rish-ē-əm, -'ris-\ *n* : a radioactive metallic chemical element produced artificially from plutonium

AmerInd *abbr* American Indian

Am·er·in·di·an \ˌa-mə-'rin-dē-ən\ *n* : AMERICAN INDIAN — **Amerindian** *adj*

am·e·thyst \'a-mə-thəst\ *n* [ME *amatiste*, fr. AF & L; AF, fr. L *amethystus*, fr. Gk *amethystos*, lit., remedy against drunkenness, fr. *a-* not + *methyein* to be drunk, fr. *methy* wine] : a gemstone consisting of clear purple or bluish violet quartz

ami·a·bil·i·ty \ˌā-mē-ə-'bi-lə-tē\ *n* ♦ : the quality of being amiable

♦ agreeableness, amenity, geniality, graciousness, niceness, pleasantness, sweetness; *also* complaisance **Ant** disagreeableness, unpleasantness

ami·a·ble \'ā-mē-ə-bəl\ *adj* **1** : pleasing to one's mind or senses : AGREEABLE **2** ♦ : having a friendly and sociable disposition — **ami·a·bly** \'ā-mē-ə-blē\ *adv*

♦ affable, agreeable, genial, good-natured, gracious, nice, sweet, well-disposed; *also* amicable, cordial, friendly, neighborly **Ant** disagreeable, ill-natured, ill-tempered, ungracious, unpleasant

ami·a·ble·ness \-nəs\ *n* : the quality of being amiable

am·i·ca·ble \'a-mi-kə-bəl\ *adj* ♦ : characterized by friendly goodwill — **am·i·ca·bil·i·ty** \ˌa-mi-kə-'bi-lə-tē\ *n* — **am·i·ca·bly** \'a-mi-kə-blē\ *adv*

♦ agreeable, compatible, congenial, harmonious, kindred, unanimous, united — more at HARMONIOUS ♦ companionable, comradely, cordial, friendly, genial, hearty, neighborly, warm, warmhearted — more at FRIENDLY

amid \ə-'mid\ *or* **amidst** \-'midst\ *prep* ♦ : in or into the middle of : AMONG

♦ among, midst, through — more at AMONG

amid·ships \ə-'mid-ˌships\ *adv* : in or near the middle of a ship

ami·no acid \ə-'mē-nō-\ *n* : any of numerous nitrogen-containing acids that include some which are used by cells to build proteins

amir *var of* EMIR

¹**amiss** \ə-'mis\ *adv* **1** ♦ : in a mistaken way : WRONGLY **2** ♦ : off the right path or route : ASTRAY **3** : IMPERFECTLY

♦ [1] erroneously, faultily, improperly, inaptly, incorrectly, mistakenly, wrongly ♦ [2] afield, astray, awry, wrong — more at WRONG

²**amiss** *adj* **1** : WRONG **2** ♦ : out of place under the circumstances **3** ♦ : marked by fault or defect : FAULTY, IMPERFECT

♦ [2] improper, inappropriate, inapt, infelicitous, unbecoming, unfit, unseemly, unsuitable, wrong — more at INAPPROPRIATE ♦ [3] bad, defective, faulty, imperfect — more at FAULTY

am·i·ty \'a-mə-tē\ *n, pl* **-ties** ♦ : the quality or state of being friendly; *esp* : friendly relations between nations

♦ benevolence, cordiality, fellowship, friendliness, friendship, goodwill, kindliness — more at GOODWILL

am·me·ter \'a-ˌmē-tər\ *n* : an instrument for measuring electric current in amperes

am·mo \'a-mō\ *n* : AMMUNITION

am·mo·nia \ə-'mō-nyə\ *n* [NL, fr. L *sal ammoniacus* sal ammoniac (ammonium chloride), lit., salt of Ammon, fr. Gk *ammōniakos* of Ammon, fr. *Ammōn* Ammon, an Egyptian god near one of whose temples it was extracted] **1** : a colorless gaseous compound of nitrogen and hydrogen used in refrigeration and in the making of fertilizers and explosives **2** : a solution (**ammonia water**) of ammonia in water

am·mo·ni·um \ə-'mō-nē-əm\ *n* : an ion or chemical group derived from ammonia by combination with hydrogen

ammonium chloride *n* : a white crystalline volatile salt used in batteries and as an expectorant

am·mu·ni·tion \ˌam-yə-'ni-shən\ *n* **1** : projectiles fired from guns **2** : explosive items used in war **3** : material for use in attack or defense

Amn *abbr* airman

am·ne·sia \am-'nē-zhə\ *n* **1** : abnormal loss of memory **2** : the selective overlooking of events or acts not favorable to one's purpose — **am·ne·si·ac** \-zhē-ˌak, -zē-\ *or* **am·ne·sic** \-zik, -sik\ *adj or n*

am·nes·ty \'am-nə-stē\ *n, pl* **-ties** ♦ : an act granting a pardon to a group of individuals — **amnesty** *vb*

♦ absolution, forgiveness, pardon, remission — more at PARDON

am·nio·cen·te·sis \,am-nē-ō-,sen-'tē-səs\ *n, pl* **-te·ses** \-,sēz\ : the surgical insertion of a hollow needle through the abdominal wall and uterus of a pregnant female esp. to obtain fluid used to check the fetus for chromosomal abnormality and to determine sex

amoe·ba \ə-'mē-bə\ *n, pl* **-bas** *or* **-bae** \-(,)bē\ : any of various tiny one-celled protozoans that lack permanent cell organs and occur esp. in water and soil — **amoe·bic** \-bik\ *adj*

amoe·boid \-,bȯid\ *adj* : resembling an amoeba esp. in moving or readily changing shape

amok \ə-'mək, -'mäk\ *or* **amuck** \-'mək\ *adv* ♦ : in a violent, frenzied, or uncontrolled manner ⟨run ∼⟩

♦ berserk, frantically, harum-scarum, hectically, helter-skelter, madly, pell-mell, wild, wildly — more at HELTER-SKELTER

among \ə-'məŋ\ *also* **amongst** \-'məŋst\ *prep* **1** ♦ : in or through the midst of **2** : in the number, class, or company of **3** : in shares to each of **4** : by common action of

♦ amid, midst, through; *also* between, betwixt

amon·til·la·do \ə-,män-tə-'lä-dō\ *n, pl* **-dos** [Sp] : a medium dry sherry

amor·al \ā-'mȯr-əl\ *adj* **1** : neither moral nor immoral; *esp* : being outside the sphere to which moral judgments apply **2** : lacking moral sensibility — **amor·al·ly** *adv*

am·o·rous \'a-mə-rəs\ *adj* **1** ♦ : strongly moved by love and esp. sexual love **2** : being in love **3** ♦ : of or indicative of love and esp. sexual love — **am·o·rous·ly** *adv* — **am·o·rous·ness** *n*

♦ [1, 3] amatory, erotic, sexy — more at EROTIC

amor·phous \ə-'mȯr-fəs\ *adj* **1** ♦ : having no definite form : FORMLESS **2** : not crystallized

♦ formless, shapeless, unformed, unshaped, unstructured — more at FORMLESS

am·or·tize \'a-mər-,tīz, ə-'mȯr-\ *vb* **-tized; -tiz·ing** : to extinguish (as a mortgage) usu. by payment on the principal at the time of each periodic interest payment — **amor·ti·za·tion** \,a-mər-tə-'zā-shən, ə-,mȯr-\ *n*

¹**amount** \ə-'maunt\ *vb* **1** ♦ : to be equivalent — usu. used with *to* **2** ♦ : to reach a total : add up — usu. used with *to*

♦ *usu* **amount to** [1] add up, come, correspond, equal; *also* approach, match, measure (up), meet, rival, touch
♦ *usu* **amount to** [2] add up, come, number, sum, total; *also* average, equal, measure, reach

²**amount** *n* **1** ♦ : the total number or quantity **2** : a principal sum plus the interest on it

♦ measure, quantity; *also* body, portion

amour \ə-'mur, ä-, a-\ *n* **1** ♦ : a love affair esp. when illicit **2** : LOVER

♦ affair, love affair, romance — more at AFFAIR

amour pro·pre \,a-,mur-'prōprᵊ, ,ä-, -'prȯprᵊ\ *n* [F] : SELF-ESTEEM

¹**amp** \'amp\ *n* : AMPLIFIER; *also* : a unit consisting of an electronic amplifier and a loudspeaker

²**amp** *abbr* ampere

am·per·age \'am-p(ə-)rij\ *n* : the strength of a current of electricity measured in amperes

am·pere \'am-,pir\ *n* : a unit of electric current equivalent to a steady current produced by one volt applied across a resistance of one ohm

am·per·sand \'am-pər-,sand\ *n* [alter. of *and per se and*, spoken form of the phrase *& per se and*, lit., (the character) *&* by itself (stands for the word) *and*] : a character *&* used for the word *and*

am·phet·amine \am-'fe-tə-,mēn, -mən\ *n* : a compound or one of its derivatives that stimulates the central nervous system and is used esp. to treat hyperactive children and to suppress appetite

am·phib·i·an \am-'fi-bē-ən\ *n* **1** : an amphibious organism; *esp* : any of a class of vertebrate animals (as frogs and salamanders) intermediate between fishes and reptiles **2** : an airplane that can land on and take off from either land or water

am·phib·i·ous \am-'fi-bē-əs\ *adj* [Gk *amphibios*, lit., living a double life, fr. *amphi-* on both sides + *bios* mode of life] **1** : able to live both on land and in water **2** : adapted for both land and water **3** : made by joint action of land, sea, and air forces invading from the sea; *also* : trained for such action

am·phi·bole \'am-fə-,bōl\ *n* : any of a group of rock-forming minerals of similar crystal structure

am·phi·the·ater \'am-fə-,thē-ə-tər\ *n* **1** : an oval or circular structure with rising tiers of seats around an arena **2** : a very large auditorium

am·pho·ra \'am-fə-rə\ *n, pl* **-rae** \-,rē\ *or* **-ras** : an ancient Greek jar or vase with two handles that rise almost to the level of the mouth

am·ple \'am-pəl\ *adj* **am·pler** \-plər;\ **am·plest** \-pləst\ **1** ♦ : generous or more than adequate in size, scope, or capacity : CAPACIOUS **2** ♦ : enough to satisfy : ABUNDANT

♦ [1] capacious, commodious, roomy, spacious — more at SPACIOUS ♦ [2] abundant, bountiful, comfortable, generous, liberal, plentiful — more at PLENTIFUL

am·pli·fy \'am-plə-,fī\ *vb* **-fied; -fy·ing** **1** ♦ : to expand by extended treatment **2** ♦ : to increase in magnitude or strength; *esp* : to make louder — **am·pli·fi·ca·tion** \,am-plə-fə-'kā-shən\ *n* — **am·pli·fi·er** \'am-plə-,fī(-ə)r\ *n*

♦ [1] develop, elaborate (on), enlarge (on), expand — more at EXPAND ♦ [2] add, aggrandize, augment, boost, compound, enlarge, escalate, expand, extend, increase, multiply, raise, swell, up — more at INCREASE ♦ [2] beef, boost, consolidate, deepen, enhance, heighten, intensify, magnify, redouble, step up, strengthen — more at INTENSIFY

am·pli·tude \-,tüd, -,tyüd\ *n* **1** : ample extent : FULLNESS **2** ♦ : the extent or range of a quality, property, process, or phenomenon: as : the extent of a vibratory movement (as of a pendulum) or of an oscillation (as of an alternating current or a radio wave)

♦ breadth, compass, extent, range, reach, realm, scope, sweep, width — more at RANGE

amplitude modulation *n* : modulation of the amplitude of a radio carrier wave in accordance with the strength of the signal; *also* : a broadcasting system using such modulation

am·ply \'am-plē\ *adv* ♦ : in an ample manner

♦ bountifully, generously, handsomely, liberally, unstintingly, well — more at WELL

am·poule *or* **am·pule** *also* **am·pul** \'am-,pyül, -,pül\ *n* : a small sealed bulbous glass vessel used to hold a solution for hypodermic injection

am·pu·tate \'am-pyə-,tāt\ *vb* **-tat·ed; -tat·ing** : to cut off ⟨∼ a leg⟩ — **am·pu·ta·tion** \,am-pyə-'tā-shən\ *n*

am·pu·tee \,am-pyə-'tē\ *n* : one who has had a limb amputated

AMSLAN *abbr* American Sign Language

amt *abbr* amount

amuck *var of* AMOK

am·u·let \'am-yə-lət\ *n* ♦ : an ornament worn as a charm against evil

♦ charm, fetish, mascot, talisman — more at CHARM

amuse \ə-'myüz\ *vb* **amused; amus·ing** ♦ : to entertain in a light or playful manner : DIVERT

♦ disport, divert, entertain, regale; *also* absorb, busy, distract, engage, engross, immerse, interest, involve, occupy

amuse·ment \-mənt\ *n* ♦ : pleasurable diversion

♦ distraction, diversion, entertainment — more at ENTERTAINMENT

amus·ing \ə-'myü-ziŋ\ *adj* ♦ : giving amusement

♦ delightful, diverting, enjoyable, entertaining, fun, pleasurable — more at FUN

AM·VETS \'am-,vets\ *abbr* American Veterans (of World War II)

am·y·lase \'a-mə-,lās, -,lāz\ *n* : any of several enzymes that accelerate the breakdown of starch and glycogen

an \ən, (')an\ *indefinite article* : A — used before words beginning with a vowel sound

¹-an *or* **-ian** *also* **-ean** *n suffix* **1** : one that belongs to ⟨Americ*an*⟩ ⟨crustac*ean*⟩ **2** : one skilled in or specializing in ⟨phonetic*ian*⟩

²-an *or* **-ian** *also* **-ean** *adj suffix* **1** : of or belonging to ⟨Americ*an*⟩ **2** : characteristic of : resembling ⟨Shakespear*ean*⟩

AN *abbr* airman (Navy)

an·a·bol·ic steroid \ˌa-nə-'bä-lik-\ *n* : any of a group of synthetic steroid hormones sometimes abused by athletes in training to increase temporarily the size of their muscles

anach·ro·nism \ə-'na-krə-ˌni-zəm\ *n* **1** : the error of placing a person or thing in the wrong period **2** : one that is chronologically out of place — **anach·ro·nis·tic** \ə-ˌna-krə-'nis-tik\ *adj* — **anach·ro·nous** \-'na-krə-nəs\ *adj*

an·a·con·da \ˌa-nə-'kän-də\ *n* : a large So. American snake that suffocates and kills its prey by constriction

anad·ro·mous \ə-'na-drə-məs\ *adj* : ascending rivers from the sea for breeding ⟨∼ fish⟩

an·aer·obe \'a-nə-ˌrōb\ *n* : an anaerobic organism

an·aer·o·bic \ˌa-nə-'rō-bik\ *adj* : living, active, occurring, or existing in the absence of free oxygen

ana·gram \'a-nə-ˌgram\ *n* : a word or phrase made by transposing the letters of another word or phrase

¹anal \'ān-ᵊl\ *adj* **1** : of, relating to, or situated near the anus **2** : of, relating to, or characterized by the stage of psychosexual development in psychoanalytic theory during which one is concerned esp. with feces **3** : of, relating to, or characterized by personality traits (as parsimony and ill humor) considered typical of fixation at the anal stage of development — **anal·ly** *adv*

²anal *abbr* **1** analogy **2** analysis; analytic

an·al·ge·sia \ˌan-ᵊl-'jē-zhə\ *n* : insensibility to pain — **an·al·ge·sic** \-'jē-zik, -sik\ *adj*

an·al·ge·sic \-'jē-zik, -sik\ *n* : an agent for producing analgesia

analog computer \'an-ᵊl-ˌóg-, -ˌäg-\ *n* : a computer that operates with numbers represented by directly measurable quantities (as voltages)

anal·o·gous \ə-'na-lə-gəs\ *adj* ♦ : similar in one or more respects

  ♦ akin, alike, comparable, correspondent, like, parallel, similar, such — more at ALIKE

an·a·logue *or* **an·a·log** \'a-nə-ˌóg, -ˌäg\ *n* **1** : something that is analogous to something else **2** : an organ similar in function to one of another animal or plant but different in structure or origin

anal·o·gy \ə-'na-lə-jē\ *n, pl* **-gies** **1** : inference that if two or more things agree in some respects they will probably agree in others **2** : a likeness in one or more ways between things otherwise unlike — **an·a·log·i·cal** \ˌan-ᵊl-'äji-kəl\ *adj* — **an·a·log·i·cal·ly** \-k(ə-)lē\ *adv*

anal·y·sis \ə-'na-lə-səs\ *n, pl* **-y·ses** \-ˌsēz\ [NL, fr. Gk, fr. *analyein* to break up, fr. *ana-* up + *lyein* to loosen] **1** ♦ : separation of a thing into the parts or elements of which it is composed **2 a** : an examination of a thing to determine its parts or elements **b** ♦ : a statement showing the results of a critical examination **3** : PSYCHOANALYSIS — **an·a·lyst** \'an-ᵊl-ist\ *n* — **an·a·lyt·i·cal·ly** *adv*

  ♦ [1] assay, breakdown, breakup, dissection; *also* assessment, evaluation, examination, inspection, investigation, scrutiny ♦ [2b] comment, commentary, exposition — more at COMMENTARY

an·a·lyt·ic \ˌan-ᵊl-'i-tik\ *or* **an·a·lyt·i·cal** \-ti-kəl\ *adj* ♦ : of or relating to analysis; *esp* : separating something into component parts or constituent elements

  ♦ coherent, good, logical, rational, reasonable, sensible, sober, sound, valid — more at LOGICAL

an·a·lyze \'an-ᵊl-ˌīz\ *vb* **-lyzed; -lyz·ing** ♦ : to make an analysis of

  ♦ anatomize, assay, break down, break up, dissect; *also* assess, evaluate, examine, inspect, investigate, scrutinize

an·a·pest \'a-nə-ˌpest\ *n* : a metrical foot of two unac-

cented syllables followed by one accented syllable — **an·a·pes·tic** \ˌa-nə-'pes-tik\ *adj or n*

an·ar·chic \a-'när-kik\ *adj* ♦ : of, relating to, or advocating anarchy

  ♦ disorderly, lawless, unruly — more at LAWLESS

an·ar·chism \'a-nər-ˌki-zəm\ *n* : the theory that all government is undesirable — **an·ar·chist** \-kist\ *n or adj* — **an·ar·chis·tic** \ˌa-nər-'kis-tik\ *adj*

an·ar·chy \'an-ər-kē\ *n* **1 a** : a social structure without government or law and order **b** : a state of lawlessness or political disorder due to the absence of governmental authority **2** : utter confusion — **an·ar·chi·cal·ly** \-ki-k(ə-)lē\ *adv*

anas·to·mo·sis \ə-ˌnas-tə-'mō-səs\ *n, pl* **-mo·ses** \-ˌsēz\ **1** : the union of parts or branches (as of blood vessels) **2** : NETWORK

anat *abbr* anatomical; anatomy

anath·e·ma \ə-'na-thə-mə\ *n* **1 a** : a person or thing accursed **b** ♦ : one intensely disliked **2** ♦ : a solemn curse

  ♦ [1b] abhorrence, abomination, antipathy, aversion, bête noire, hate — more at HATE ♦ [2] curse, execration, imprecation, malediction — more at CURSE

anath·e·ma·tize \-ˌtīz\ *vb* **-tized; -tiz·ing** : to pronounce an anathema against : CURSE

anat·o·mise *Brit var of* ANATOMIZE

anat·o·mize \ə-'na-tə-ˌmīz\ *vb* **-mized; -miz·ing** **1** : to dissect so as to examine the structure and parts **2** ♦ : to study or determine the nature and relationship of the parts of by analysis : ANALYZE

  ♦ analyze, assay, break down, break up, dissect — more at ANALYZE

anat·o·my \ə-'na-tə-mē\ *n, pl* **-mies** [LL *anatomia* dissection, fr. Gk *anatomē*, fr. *anatemnein* to dissect, fr. *ana-* up + *temnein* to cut] **1** : a branch of science dealing with the structure of organisms **2** : structural makeup esp. of an organism or any of its parts **3** : a separating into parts for detailed study : ANALYSIS — **an·a·tom·ic** \ˌa-nə-'tä-mik\ *or* **an·a·tom·i·cal** \-mi-kəl\ *adj* — **an·a·tom·i·cal·ly** \-mi-k(ə-)lē\ *adv* — **anat·o·mist** \ə-'na-tə-mist\ *n*

anc *abbr* ancient

-ance *n suffix* **1** : action or process ⟨further*ance*⟩ : instance of an action or process ⟨perform*ance*⟩ **2** : quality or state : instance of a quality or state ⟨protuber*ance*⟩ **3** : amount or degree ⟨conduct*ance*⟩

an·ces·tor \'an-ˌses-tər\ *n* [ME *ancestre*, fr. AF, fr. L *antecessor* predecessor, fr. *antecedere* to go before, fr. *ante-* before + *cedere* to go] **1** ♦ : one from whom an individual is descended **2** ♦ : an individual that exhibits the essential features of a later type

  ♦ [1] father, forebear, forefather, grandfather; *also* grandmother, matriarch, patriarch **Ant** descendant ♦ [2] antecedent, forerunner, precursor; *also* archetype, model, original, prototype **Ant** descendant

an·ces·tress \'an-ˌses-trəs\ *n* : a female ancestor

an·ces·try \'an-ˌses-trē\ *n* **1** ♦ : line of descent : LINEAGE **2** : ANCESTORS — **an·ces·tral** \an-'ses-trəl\ *adj*

  ♦ birth, blood, bloodline, breeding, descent, extraction, family tree, genealogy, line, lineage, origin, parentage, pedigree, stock, strain; *also* heredity, succession **Ant** issue, posterity, progeny, seed

¹an·chor \'aŋ-kər\ *n* **1** : a heavy metal device attached to a ship that catches hold of the bottom and holds the ship in place **2** : a broadcaster who reads the news and introduces the reports of other broadcasters : ANCHORPERSON

²anchor *vb* ♦ : to hold or become held in place by or as if by an anchor

  ♦ catch, clamp, fasten, fix, hitch, moor, secure, set

an·chor·age \'aŋ-k(ə-)rij\ *n* ♦ : a place suitable for ships to anchor

  ♦ harbor (*or* harbour), haven, port — more at HARBOR

an·cho·rite \'aŋ-kə-ˌrīt\ *n* ♦ : one that retires from society and lives in solitude : HERMIT

♦ hermit, recluse, solitary — more at RECLUSE

an·chor·man \'aŋ-kər-ˌman\ n **1** : the member of a team who competes last **2** : an anchorperson who is a man

an·chor·per·son \-ˌpər-sən\ n : a broadcaster who reads the news and introduces the reports of other broadcasters

an·chor·wom·an \-ˌwu̇-mən\ n : a woman who anchors a broadcast

an·cho·vy \'an-ˌchō-vē, an-'chō-\ n, pl **-vies** or **-vy** : a small herringlike fish used esp. for sauces and relishes

an·cien ré·gime \ˌäⁿs-yaⁿ-rā-'zhēm\ n **1** : the political and social system of France before the Revolution of 1789 **2** : a system no longer prevailing

¹**an·cient** \'ān-shənt\ adj **1** ♦ : having existed for many years **2** ♦ : belonging to times long past; esp : belonging to the period before the Middle Ages

♦ [1] elderly, geriatric, old, senior — more at ELDERLY ♦ [2] age-old, antediluvian, antique, dateless, hoary, old, venerable; also aging, mature Ant modern, new, recent ♦ [2] early, primal, primeval, primitive — more at EARLY

²**ancient** n **1** : an aged person **2** pl : the peoples of ancient Greece and Rome; esp : the classical authors of Greece and Rome

an·cil·lary \'an-sə-ˌler-ē\ adj **1** : SUBORDINATE, SUBSIDIARY **2** : AUXILIARY, SUPPLEMENTARY — **ancillary** n

-ancy n suffix : quality or state ⟨flamboyancy⟩

and \ənd, (')and\ conj **1** — used to indicate connection or addition esp. of items within the same class or type or to join words or phrases of the same grammatical rank or function **2** — used to join one finite verb to another so that together they are equivalent to an infinitive of purpose ⟨come ∼ see me⟩

¹**an·dan·te** \än-'dän-ˌtā, -tē\ adv or adj [It., lit., going, prp. of andare to go] : moderately slow — used as a direction in music

²**andante** n : an andante movement

and·iron \'an-ˌdī(-ə)rn\ n : one of a pair of metal supports for firewood in a fireplace

and/or \'and-'ȯr\ conj — used to indicate that either and or or may apply ⟨"apples ∼ oranges" means that the possibilities include apples, oranges, or both⟩

An·dor·ran \an-'dȯr-ən\ n : a native or inhabitant of Andorra

an·dro·gen \'an-drə-jən\ n : a male sex hormone

an·drog·y·nous \an-'drä-jə-nəs\ adj **1** : having the characteristics of both male and female **2** : suitable for either sex ⟨∼ clothing⟩

an·droid \'an-ˌdrȯid\ n : a mobile robot usu. with a human form

an·ec·dot·al \ˌa-nik-'dōt-ᵊl\ adj **1** : relating to or consisting of anecdotes **2** : based on reports of an unscientific nature — **an·ec·dot·al·ly** adv

an·ec·dote \'an-ik-ˌdōt\ n, pl **-dotes** also **-dota** \ˌa-nik-'dō-tə\ [F, fr. Gk anekdota unpublished items, fr. a- not + ekdidonai to publish] ♦ : a brief story of an interesting, amusing, or biographical incident

♦ story, tale — more at STORY

ane·mia \ə-'nē-mē-ə\ n **1** : a condition in which blood is deficient in quantity, in red blood cells, or in hemoglobin and which is marked by pallor, weakness, and irregular heart action **2** : lack of vitality — **ane·mic** \ə-'nē-mik\ adj

an·e·mom·e·ter \ˌa-nə-'mä-mə-tər\ n : an instrument for measuring the force or speed of the wind

anem·o·ne \ə-'ne-mə-nē\ n : any of a large genus of herbs related to the buttercups that have showy flowers without petals but with conspicuous often colored sepals

anent \ə-'nent\ prep : CONCERNING

an·es·the·sia or Can and Brit **an·aes·the·sia** \ˌa-nəs-'thē-zhə\ n : loss of bodily sensation

an·es·the·si·ol·o·gy or chiefly Brit **an·aes·the·si·ol·o·gy** \-ˌthē-zē-'ä-lə-jē\ n : a branch of medical science dealing with anesthesia and anesthetics — **an·es·the·si·ol·o·gist** \-jist\ n

¹**an·es·thet·ic** or Can and Brit **an·aes·thet·ic** \ˌa-nəs-'the-tik\ adj : of, relating to, or capable of producing anesthesia

²**anesthetic** or Can and Brit **anaesthetic** n : an agent that produces anesthesia — **anes·the·tist** \ə-'nes-thə-tist\ n — **anes·the·tize** \-thə-ˌtīz\ vb

an·eu·rysm \'an-yə-ˌri-zəm\ n : an abnormal blood-filled bulge of a blood vessel

anew \ə-'nü, -'nyü\ adv **1** ♦ : over again **2** : in a new form

♦ again, over — more at AGAIN

an·gel \'ān-jəl\ n [ME, fr. OE engel & AF angele, both fr. L angelus, fr. Gk angelos, lit., messenger] **1** : a spiritual being superior to humans **2** : an attendant spirit **3** : a winged figure of human form in art **4** ♦ : one that precedes and indicates the approach of another : HARBINGER **5** : a person held to resemble an angel (as in looks or behavior) **6** : a financial backer — **an·gel·ic** \an-'je-lik\ or **an·gel·i·cal** \-li-kəl\ adj — **an·gel·i·cal·ly** \-k(ə-)lē\ adv

♦ forerunner, harbinger, herald, precursor — more at FORERUNNER

an·gel·fish \'ān-jəl-ˌfish\ n : any of several bright-colored tropical fishes that are flattened from side to side

an·gel·i·ca \an-'je-li-kə\ n : a biennial herb related to the carrot whose roots and fruit furnish a flavoring oil

¹**an·ger** \'aŋ-gər\ vb ♦ : to make angry

♦ antagonize, enrage, incense, inflame, infuriate, madden, outrage, rankle, rile, roil; also affront, aggravate, annoy, cross, exasperate, get, irritate, nettle, offend, peeve, pique, provoke, put out, ruffle, vex Ant delight, gratify, please

²**anger** n [ME, affliction, anger, fr. ON angr grief] ♦ : a strong feeling of displeasure

♦ furor, fury, indignation, ire, outrage, rage, spleen, wrath, wrathfulness; also aggravation, annoyance, exasperation, irritation, vexation Ant delight, pleasure

an·gi·na \an-'jī-nə\ n : a disorder (as of the heart) marked by attacks of intense pain; esp : ANGINA PECTORIS — **an·gi·nal** \an-'jīn-ᵊl\ adj

angina pec·to·ris \-'pek-t(ə-)rəs\ n : a heart disease marked by brief attacks of sharp chest pain caused by deficient oxygenation of heart muscles

an·gio·gram \'an-jē-ə-ˌgram\ n : an X-ray photograph made by angiography

an·gi·og·ra·phy \ˌan-jē-'ä-grə-fē\ n : the use of X-rays to make blood vessels visible (as by photography) after injection of a substance opaque to radiation

an·gio·plas·ty \'an-jē-ə-ˌplas-tē\ n : surgical repair of a blood vessel esp. by using an inflatable catheter to unblock arteries clogged by atherosclerotic deposits

an·gio·sperm \-ˌspərm\ n : FLOWERING PLANT

¹**an·gle** \'aŋ-gəl\ n **1** : a sharp projecting corner **2** : the figure formed by the meeting of two lines in a point **3 a** ♦ : a point of view **b** ♦ : the aspect seen from such an angle **4** : a special technique or plan : GIMMICK — **an·gled** adj

♦ [3a] outlook, perspective, point of view, slant, standpoint, viewpoint — more at POINT OF VIEW ♦ [3b] aspect, facet, hand, phase, side — more at ASPECT

²**angle** vb **an·gled; an·gling** \-g(ə-)liŋ\ ♦ : to turn, move, or direct at an angle

♦ cant, cock, heel, incline, lean, list, slant, slope, tilt, tip — more at LEAN

³**angle** vb **an·gled; an·gling** \-g(ə-)liŋ\ : to fish with a hook and line — **an·gler** \-glər\ n

an·gle·worm \'aŋ-gəl-ˌwərm\ n : EARTHWORM

An·gli·can \'aŋ-gli-kən\ adj **1** : of or relating to the established episcopal Church of England **2** : of or relating to England or the English nation — **Anglican** n — **An·gli·can·ism** \-kə-ˌni-zəm\ n

an·gli·cize \'aŋ-glə-ˌsīz\ vb **-cized; -ciz·ing** often cap **1** : to make English (as in habits, speech, character, or outlook) **2** : to borrow (a foreign word or phrase) into English without changing form or spelling and sometimes without changing pronunciation — **an·gli·ci·za·tion** \ˌaŋ-glə-sə-ˈzā-shən\ *n, often cap*

an·gling \-gliŋ\ *n* : the action of one who angles; *esp* : the action or sport of fishing with hook and line

An·glo \ˈaŋ-glō\ *n, pl* **Anglos** : a non-Hispanic white inhabitant of the U.S.; *esp* : one of English origin and descent

An·glo–French \ˌaŋ-glō-ˈfrench\ *n* : the French language used in medieval England

An·glo·phile \ˈaŋ-glə-ˌfīl\ *also* **An·glo·phil** \-ˌfil\ *n* : one who greatly admires England and things English

An·glo·phobe \ˈaŋ-glə-ˌfōb\ *n* : one who is averse to England and things English

An·glo–Sax·on \ˌaŋ-glō-ˈsak-sən\ *n* 1 : a member of any of the Germanic peoples who invaded England in the 5th century A.D. 2 : a member of the English people 3 : the language of the English people before about 1100 — **Anglo–Saxon** *adj*

an·go·ra \aŋ-ˈgōr-ə, an-\ *n* 1 : yarn or cloth made from the hair of an Angora goat or rabbit 2 *cap* : any of a breed of cats, goats, or rabbits with a long silky coat

an·gry \ˈaŋ-grē\ *adj* **an·gri·er; -est** ♦ : feeling or showing anger — **an·gri·ly** \-grə-lē\ *adv*

♦ enraged, furious, irate, sore, wrathful *Ant* delighted, pleased

angst \ˈäŋst\ *n* [G] : a feeling of anxiety

ang·strom \ˈaŋ-strəm\ *n* : a unit of length equal to one ten-billionth of a meter

an·guish \ˈaŋ-gwish\ *n* ♦ : extreme pain or distress esp. of mind

♦ affliction, agony, distress, misery, pain, torment, torture, tribulation, woe — more at DISTRESS ♦ affliction, dolor, grief, heartache, sorrow, woe — more at SORROW

an·guished \-gwisht\ *adj* 1 : suffering anguish ⟨the ∼ martyrs⟩ 2 ♦ : expressing anguish ⟨∼ cries⟩

♦ dolorous, lamentable, mournful, plaintive, sorrowful, sorry, woeful — more at SORROWFUL

an·gu·lar \ˈaŋ-gyə-lər\ *adj* 1 : sharp-cornered 2 : having one or more angles 3 : being thin and bony — **an·gu·lar·i·ty** \ˌaŋ-gyə-ˈlar-ə-tē\ *n*

An·gus \ˈaŋ-gəs\ *n* : any of a breed of usu. black hornless beef cattle originating in Scotland

an·hy·drous \an-ˈhī-drəs\ *adj* : free from water

an·i·line \ˈan-ᵊl-ən\ *n* : an oily poisonous liquid used in making dyes, medicines, and explosives

an·i·mad·vert \ˌa-nə-ˌmad-ˈvərt\ *vb* : to remark critically : express censure — **an·i·mad·ver·sion** \-ˈvər-zhən\ *n*

¹**an·i·mal** \ˈa-nə-məl\ *n* 1 : any of a kingdom of living things typically differing from plants in capacity for active movement, in rapid response to stimulation, and in lack of cellulose cell walls 2 ♦ : a lower animal as distinguished from human beings; *also* : MAMMAL

♦ beast, brute, creature, critter; *also* varmint, vermin

²**animal** *adj* 1 : of, relating to, or derived from animals 2 ♦ : of or relating to the physical as distinguished from the mental or spiritual

♦ bodily, carnal, corporal, fleshly, material, physical, somatic — more at PHYSICAL

an·i·mal·cule \ˌa-nə-ˈmal-kyül\ *n* : a tiny animal usu. invisible to the naked eye

¹**an·i·mate** \ˈa-nə-mət\ *adj* 1 ♦ : having life : ALIVE 2 ♦ : full of vigor and spirit : LIVELY

♦ [1] alive, live, living — more at ALIVE ♦ [2] active, animated, energetic, lively, peppy, perky, spirited, sprightly, springy, vital, vivacious — more at LIVELY

²**an·i·mate** \-ˌmāt\ *vb* **-mat·ed; -mat·ing** 1 : to impart life to 2 ♦ : to give spirit and vigor to 3 : to make appear to move ⟨∼ a cartoon for motion pictures⟩

♦ brace, energize, enliven, fire, invigorate, jazz up, liven up, pep up, quicken, stimulate, vitalize, vivify, zip (up); *also* arouse, awake, awaken, raise, rouse, stir, wake (up) *Ant* damp, dampen, deaden, dull

an·i·mat·ed \-ˌmā-təd\ *adj* 1 ♦ : endowed with life or the qualities of life : ALIVE 2 ♦ : full of movement and activity ⟨an ∼ crowd⟩ 3 ♦ : full of vigor and spirit : LIVELY

♦ [1, 2] alive, astir, busy, lively, vibrant — more at ALIVE ♦ [3] active, animate, energetic, lively, peppy, perky, spirited, sprightly, springy, vital, vivacious — more at LIVELY

an·i·ma·tion \ˌa-nə-ˈmā-shən\ *n* 1 ♦ : the state of being animate or animated : LIVELINESS 2 : a motion picture made from a series of drawings, computer graphics, or stop-motion images simulating motions by means of slight progressive changes

♦ briskness, exuberance, liveliness, lustiness, robustness, sprightliness, vibrancy, vitality — more at VITALITY

an·i·mism \ˈa-nə-ˌmi-zəm\ *n* : attribution of conscious life to objects in and phenomena of nature or to inanimate objects — **an·i·mist** \-mist\ *n* — **an·i·mis·tic** \ˌa-nə-ˈmis-tik\ *adj*

an·i·mos·i·ty \ˌa-nə-ˈmä-sə-tē\ *n, pl* **-ties** ♦ : ill will or resentment tending toward active hostility

♦ antagonism, antipathy, bitterness, enmity, gall, grudge, hostility, rancor — more at ENMITY

an·i·mus \ˈa-nə-məs\ *n* : deep-seated resentment and hostility

an·ion \ˈa-ˌnī-ən, -ˌnī-ˌän\ *n* : a negatively charged ion

an·ise \ˈa-nəs\ *n* : an herb related to the carrot with aromatic seeds (**aniseed** \-sēd\) used in flavoring

an·is·ette \ˌa-nə-ˈset, -ˈzet\ *n* [F] : a usu. colorless sweet liqueur flavored with aniseed

ankh \ˈäŋk\ *n* : a cross having a loop for its upper vertical arm and serving esp. in ancient Egypt as an emblem of life

an·kle \ˈaŋ-kəl\ *n* : the joint or region between the foot and the leg

an·kle·bone \ˈaŋ-kəl-ˌbōn\ *n* : the bone that in human beings bears the weight of the body and with the tibia and fibula forms the ankle joint

an·klet \ˈaŋ-klət\ *n* 1 : something (as an ornament) worn around the ankle 2 : a short sock reaching slightly above the ankle

ann *abbr* 1 annals 2 annual

an·nal·ist \ˈan-ᵊl-ist\ *n* : a writer of annals

an·nals \ˈan-ᵊlz\ *n pl* 1 ♦ : a record of events in chronological order 2 : historical records

♦ chronicle, history, record — more at HISTORY

an·neal \ə-ˈnēl\ *vb* 1 : to make (as glass or steel) less brittle by heating and then cooling 2 : STRENGTHEN, TOUGHEN

¹**an·nex** \ə-ˈneks, ˈa-ˌneks\ *vb* 1 ♦ : to attach as an addition 2 : to incorporate (as a territory) within a political domain — **an·nex·a·tion** \ˌa-ˌnek-ˈsā-shən\ *n*

♦ add, adjoin, append, tack — more at ADD

²**an·nex** \ˈa-ˌneks, -niks\ *n* ♦ : a subsidiary or supplementary structure

♦ addition, extension, penthouse; *also* arm, ell, wing

an·ni·hi·late \ə-ˈnī-ə-ˌlāt\ *vb* **-lat·ed; -lat·ing** ♦ : to destroy completely

♦ blot out, demolish, eradicate, exterminate, liquidate, obliterate, root, rub out, snuff, stamp, wipe out; *also* decimate, destroy, devastate

an·ni·hi·la·tion \-ˌnī-ə-ˈlā-shən\ *n* ♦ : the act of annihilating or state of being annihilated

♦ demolition, desolation, destruction, devastation, havoc, loss, obliteration, ruin, wastage, wreckage — more at DESTRUCTION

an·ni·ver·sa·ry \ˌa-nə-ˈvər-sə-rē\ *n, pl* **-ries** : the annual return of the date of a notable event and esp. a wedding

an·no Do·mi·ni \ˌa-nō-ˈdä-mə-nē, -ˈdō-, -ˌnī\ *adv, often cap A* [ML, in the year of the Lord] — used to indicate that a time division falls within the Christian era

an·no·tate \ˈa-nə-ˌtāt\ *vb* **-tat·ed; -tat·ing** : to furnish with notes — **an·no·ta·tion** \ˌa-nə-ˈtā-shən\ *n* — **an·no·ta·tor** \ˈa-nə-ˌtā-tər\ *n*

an·nounce \ə-ˈnau̇ns\ *vb* **an·nounced; an·nounc·ing** 1 ♦ : to make known publicly 2 : to give notice of the arrival or presence of

♦ advertise, blaze, broadcast, declare, enunciate, placard, post, proclaim, promulgate, publicize, publish, sound; *also* advise, apprise, inform, notify

an·nounce·ment \-mənt\ *n* ♦ : a public notification or declaration

♦ advertisement, bulletin, notice, notification, release; *also* broadside, circular, flier, handbill, handout, bill, billboard, placard, poster, sign

an·nounc·er \ə-'naún-sər\ *n* : a person who introduces radio or television programs, makes commercial announcements, or gives station identification

an·noy \ə-'nói\ *vb* ♦ : to disturb or irritate esp. by repeated acts : VEX — **an·noy·ing·ly** *adv*

♦ aggravate, bother, bug, chafe, exasperate, gall, get, grate, irk, irritate, nettle, peeve, rile, vex — more at IRRITATE

an·noy·ance \ə-'nói-əns\ *n* **1** ♦ : the act of annoying **2** ♦ : the state of being annoyed **3** ♦ : one that is annoying, unpleasant, or obnoxious : NUISANCE

♦ [1] aggravation, disturbance, harassment, vexation; *also* molestation, offense, persecution, provocation, torment, torture ♦ [2] aggravation, bother, exasperation, frustration, vexation; *also* agitation, anger, discomfort, displeasure, distress, disturbance, indignation, ire, outrage, perturbation, resentment ♦ [3] bother, exasperation, frustration, hassle, headache, inconvenience, irritant, nuisance, peeve, pest, problem, thorn; *also* affront, insult, offense

an·noy·ing \-iŋ\ *adj* ♦ : causing vexation

♦ aggravating, bothersome, frustrating, galling, irksome, irritating, pesty, vexatious; *also* burdensome, discomforting, displeasing, disquieting, distressing, importunate, inconveniencing, infuriating, maddening, mischievous, offensive, pesky, troublesome, upsetting, stressful, tiresome, troubling, trying, worrisome

¹**an·nu·al** \'an-yə-wəl\ *adj* **1** : covering the period of a year **2** : occurring once a year : YEARLY **3** : completing the life cycle in one growing season ⟨~ plants⟩ — **an·nu·al·ly** *adv*

²**annual** *n* **1** : a publication appearing once a year **2** : an annual plant

annual ring *n* : the layer of wood produced by a single year's growth of a woody plant

an·nu·i·tant \ə-'nü-ə-tənt, -'nyü-\ *n* : a beneficiary of an annuity

an·nu·i·ty \ə-'nü-ə-tē, -'nyü-\ *n, pl* **-i·ties 1** : an amount payable annually **2** : the right to receive an annual payment

an·nul \ə-'nəl\ *vb* **an·nulled; an·nul·ling 1** ♦ : to make ineffective or inoperative **2** ♦ : to make legally void — **an·nul·ment** *n*

♦ [1, 2] abolish, abrogate, cancel, dissolve, invalidate, negate, nullify, quash, repeal, rescind, void — more at ABOLISH

an·nu·lar \'an-yə-lər\ *adj* : ring-shaped

an·nun·ci·ate \ə-'nən-sē-,āt\ *vb* **-at·ed; -at·ing** : ANNOUNCE

an·nun·ci·a·tion \ə-,nən-sē-'ā-shən\ *n* **1** : ANNOUNCEMENT **2** *cap* : March 25 observed as a church festival commemorating the announcement of the Incarnation

an·nun·ci·a·tor \ə-'nən-sē-,ā-tər\ *n* : one that annunciates; *specif* : a usu. electrically controlled signal board or indicator

an·ode \'a-,nōd\ *n* **1** : the positive electrode of an electrolytic cell **2** : the negative terminal of a battery **3** : the electron-collecting electrode of an electron tube — **an·od·ic** \a-'nä-dik\ *also* **an·od·al** \-'nōd-ºl\ *adj*

an·od·ize \'a-nə-,dīz\ *vb* **-ized; -iz·ing** : to subject (a metal) to electrolytic action as the anode of a cell in order to coat with a protective or decorative film

an·o·dyne \'a-nə-,dīn\ *n* : something that relieves pain : a soothing agent

anoint \ə-'nóint\ *vb* **1** : to apply oil to esp. as a sacred rite **2** : CONSECRATE — **anoint·ment** *n*

anom·a·lous \ə-'nä-mə-ləs\ *adj* ♦ : deviating from a general rule : ABNORMAL

♦ aberrant, abnormal, atypical, deviant, irregular, unnatural — more at DEVIANT

anom·a·ly \ə-'nä-mə-lē\ *n, pl* **-lies** : something anomalous

¹**anon** \ə-'nän\ *adv* ♦ : in the near future

♦ momentarily, presently, shortly, soon — more at SHORTLY

²**anon** *abbr* anonymous; anonymously

an·o·nym·i·ty \,a-nə-'ni-mə-tē\ *n* : the quality or state of being anonymous

anon·y·mous \ə-'nä-nə-məs\ *adj* ♦ : of unknown or undeclared origin or authorship — **anon·y·mous·ly** *adv*

♦ nameless, unbaptized, unchristened, unidentified, unnamed, untitled — more at NAMELESS

anoph·e·les \ə-'nä-fə-,lēz\ *n* [NL, genus name, fr. Gk *anōphelēs* useless, fr. *a-* not + *ophelos* advantage, help] : any of a genus of mosquitoes that includes all mosquitoes which transmit malaria to human beings

an·o·rec·tic \,a-nə-'rek-tik\ *adj* : ANOREXIC — **anorectic** *n*

an·orex·ia \,a-nə-'rek-sē-ə\ *n* **1** : loss of appetite esp. when prolonged **2** : ANOREXIA NERVOSA

anorexia ner·vo·sa \-,nər-'vō-sə\ *n* : a serious disorder in eating behavior marked esp. by a pathological fear of weight gain leading to faulty eating patterns, malnutrition, and usu. excessive weight loss

an·orex·ic \,a-nə-'rek-sik\ *adj* **1** : lacking or causing loss of appetite **2** : affected with or as if with anorexia nervosa — **anorexic** *n*

¹**an·oth·er** \ə-'nə-thər\ *adj* **1** : some other **2** ♦ : being one in addition : one more

♦ additional, else, farther, further, more, other — more at ADDITIONAL

²**another** *pron* **1** : an additional one : one more **2** : one that is different from the first or present one

ans *abbr* answer

¹**an·swer** \'an-sər\ *n* **1** ♦ : something spoken or written in reply to a question **2** : a solution of a problem

♦ comeback, reply, response, retort, return; *also* banter, persiflage, repartee *Ant* inquiry, query, question

²**answer** *vb* **1** ♦ : to speak or write in reply to **2** ♦ : to be or make oneself responsible or accountable ⟨~ for a debt⟩ **3** ♦ : to be in conformity or correspondence ⟨~ed to the description⟩ **4** : to be adequate **5** ♦ : to offer a solution for — **an·swer·er** *n*

♦ [1] rejoin, reply, respond, retort, return; *also* acknowledge, comment, communicate, correspond, react, remark *Ant* inquire, question ♦ [2] comply, fill, fulfill, keep, meet, redeem, satisfy — more at FULFILL ♦ [3] check, coincide, comport, conform, correspond, dovetail, fit, go, harmonize, jibe, square, tally — more at CHECK ♦ [5] break, crack, dope, figure out, puzzle, resolve, riddle, solve, unravel, work, work out — more at SOLVE

an·swer·able \'an-sə-rə-bəl\ *adj* **1** ♦ : subject to taking blame or responsibility **2** : capable of being refuted

♦ accountable, liable, responsible — more at RESPONSIBLE

answering machine *n* : a machine that receives telephone calls by playing a recorded message and usu. by recording messages from callers

answering service *n* : a commercial service that answers telephone calls for its clients

¹**ant** \'ant\ *n* : any of a family of small social insects related to the bees and living in communities usu. in earth or wood

²**ant** *abbr* antonym

Ant *abbr* Antarctica

¹**-ant** *n suffix* **1** : one that performs or promotes (a specified action) ⟨coolant⟩ **2** : thing that is acted upon (in a specified manner) ⟨inhalant⟩

²**-ant** *adj suffix* **1** : performing (a specified action) or being (in a specified condition) ⟨propellant⟩ **2** : promoting (a specified action or process) ⟨expectorant⟩

ant·ac·id \ant-'a-səd\ *n* : an agent that counteracts acidity — **antacid** *adj*

an·tag·o·nism \an-'ta-gə-,ni-zəm\ n   1 ♦ : active opposition or hostility   2 : opposition in physiological action

  ♦ animosity, antipathy, bitterness, enmity, gall, grudge, hostility, rancor — more at ENMITY

an·tag·o·nist \-nist\ n ♦ : one that contends with or opposes another : ADVERSARY, OPPONENT

  ♦ adversary, enemy, foe, opponent — more at ENEMY

an·tag·o·nis·tic \-,ta-gə-'nis-tik\ adj ♦ : marked by or resulting from antagonism

  ♦ hostile, inhospitable, inimical, jaundiced, negative, unfriendly, unsympathetic — more at HOSTILE

an·tag·o·nize \an-'ta-gə-,nīz\ vb -nized; -niz·ing ♦ : to provoke the hostility of

  ♦ anger, enrage, incense, inflame, infuriate, madden, outrage, rankle, rile, roil — more at ANGER

ant·arc·tic \ant-'ärk-tik, -'är-tik\ adj, often cap : of or relating to the south pole or the region near it

antarctic circle n, often cap A&C : the parallel of latitude that is approximately 66½ degrees south of the equator

¹an·te \'an-tē\ n : a poker stake put up before the deal to build the pot; also : an amount paid : PRICE

²ante vb an·ted; an·te·ing   1 : to put up (an ante)   2 : PAY

ant·eat·er \'ant-,ē-tər\ n : any of several mammals (as an aardvark) that feed mostly on ants or termites

an·te·bel·lum \,an-ti-'be-ləm\ adj : existing before a war; esp : existing before the U.S. Civil War of 1861-65

¹an·te·ced·ent \,an-tə-'sēd-ᵊnt\ n   1 : a noun, pronoun, phrase, or clause referred to by a personal or relative pronoun   2 ♦ : a preceding event or cause   3 pl : the significant conditions of one's earlier life   4 a ♦ : one that precedes : PREDECESSOR; esp : a model or stimulus for later developments   b pl : ANCESTORS

  ♦ [2] cause, occasion, reason — more at CAUSE ♦ [4a] ancestor, forerunner, precursor — more at ANCESTOR

²antecedent adj ♦ : earlier in time or order

  ♦ anterior, foregoing, preceding, previous, prior — more at PREVIOUS

an·te·cham·ber \'an-ti-,chām-bər\ n : ANTEROOM

an·te·date \'an-ti-,dāt\ vb   1 : to date (a paper) as of an earlier day than that on which the actual writing or signing is done   2 ♦ : to precede in time

  ♦ forego, precede — more at PRECEDE

an·te·di·lu·vi·an \,an-ti-də-'lü-vē-ən, -dī-\ adj   1 : of the period before the biblical flood   2 ♦ : made, evolved, or developed a long time ago   3 : extremely primitive or outmoded

  ♦ age-old, ancient, antique, dateless, hoary, old, venerable — more at ANCIENT

an·te·lope \'ant-ᵊl-,ōp\ n, pl -lope or -lopes [ME, fabulous heraldic beast, prob. fr. MF antelop savage animal with sawlike horns, fr. ML anthalopus, fr. LGk antholops]   1 : any of various deerlike ruminant mammals that chiefly inhabit Africa and have a slender build and horns extending upward and backward   2 : PRONGHORN

an·te me·ri·di·em \'an-ti-mə-'ri-dē-əm\ adj [L] : being before noon

an·ten·na \an-'te-nə\ n, pl -nae \-(,)nē\ or -nas [ML, fr. L, sail yard]   1 : one of the long slender paired segmented sensory organs on the head of an arthropod (as an insect or crab)   2 pl usu -nas : a metallic device (as a rod or wire) for sending out or receiving radio waves

an·te·pe·nult \,an-ti-'pē-,nəlt\ also **an·te·pen·ul·ti·ma** \-pi-'nəl-tə-mə\ n : the 3d syllable of a word counting from the end — **an·te·pen·ul·ti·mate** \-pi-'nəl-tə-mət\ adj or n

an·te·ri·or \an-'tir-ē-ər\ adj   1 : situated before or toward the front   2 : situated near or nearer to the head   3 ♦ : coming before in time

  ♦ antecedent, foregoing, preceding, previous, prior — more at PREVIOUS

anterior cruciate ligament n : a cross-shaped ligament of the knee that connects the tibia and femur

ante·room \'an-ti-,rüm, -,rùm\ n : a room forming the entrance to another and often used as a waiting room

an·them \'an-thəm\ n   1 ♦ : a sacred vocal composition   2 ♦ : a song or hymn of praise or gladness

  ♦ [1, 2] canticle, carol, chorale, hymn, psalm, spiritual — more at HYMN

an·ther \'an-thər\ n : the part of a stamen of a seed plant that produces and contains pollen

ant·hill \'ant-,hil\ n : a mound thrown up by ants or termites in digging their nest

an·thol·o·gy \an-'thä-lə-jē\ n, pl -gies [NL anthologia collection of epigrams, fr. MGk, fr. Gk, flower gathering, fr. anthos flower + logia collecting, fr. legein to gather] ♦ : a collection of literary selections — **an·thol·o·gist** \-jist\ n — **an·thol·o·gize** \-,jīz\ vb

  ♦ album, compilation, miscellany; also archives

an·thra·cite \'an-thrə-,sīt\ n : a hard glossy coal that burns without much smoke

an·thrax \'an-,thraks\ n : an infectious and usu. fatal bacterial disease of warm-blooded animals (as cattle and sheep) that is transmissible to humans; also : a bacterium causing anthrax

an·thro·po·cen·tric \,an-thrə-pə-'sen-trik\ adj : interpreting or regarding the world in terms of human values and experiences

an·thro·poid \'an-thrə-,pòid\ n   1 : any of several large tailless apes (as a gorilla)   2 : a person resembling an ape — **anthropoid** adj

an·thro·pol·o·gy \,an-thrə-'pä-lə-jē\ n : the science of human beings and esp. of their physical characteristics, their origin and the distribution of races, their environment and social relations, and their culture — **an·thro·po·log·i·cal** \-pə-'lä-ji-kəl\ adj — **an·thro·pol·o·gist** \-'pä-lə-jist\ n

an·thro·po·mor·phism \,an-thrə-pə-'mòr-,fi-zəm\ n : an interpretation of what is not human or personal in terms of human or personal characteristics : HUMANIZATION — **an·thro·po·mor·phic** \-fik\ adj

an·ti \'an-,tī, -tē\ n, pl antis : one who is opposed

anti- \,an-ti, -tē, -,tī\ or **ant-** or **anth-** prefix   1 : opposite in kind, position, or action   2 : opposing : hostile toward   3 : counteractive   4 : preventive of : curative of

an·ti·abor·tion \,an-tē-ə-'bòr-shən, ,an-,tī-\ adj : opposed to abortion

an·ti·bal·lis·tic missile \,an-ti-bə-'lis-tik-, ,an-,tī-\ n : a missile for intercepting and destroying ballistic missiles

an·ti·bi·ot·ic \-bī-'ä-tik, -bē-\ n : a substance produced by or derived by chemical alteration of a substance produced by a microorganism (as a fungus or bacterium) that in dilute solution inhibits or kills another microorganism — **antibiotic** adj

an·ti·body \'an-ti-,bä-dē\ n : any of a large number of proteins of high molecular weight produced normally by specialized B cells after stimulation by an antigen and acting specifically against the antigen in an immune response

¹an·tic \'an-tik\ n ♦ : an often wildly playful or funny act or action

  ♦ caper, escapade, frolic, monkeyshine, practical joke, prank, trick — more at PRANK

²antic adj [It antico ancient thing or person, fr. antico ancient, fr. L antiquus]   1 archaic : GROTESQUE   2 a ♦ : characterized by clownish extravagance or absurdity   b ♦ : whimsically gay : PLAYFUL

  ♦ [2a] comic, comical, droll, farcical, funny, hilarious, humorous, hysterical, laughable, ludicrous, ridiculous, riotous — more at FUNNY ♦ [2b] coltish, elfish, fay, frisky, frolicsome, playful, sportive — more at PLAYFUL

an·ti·can·cer \,an-ti-'kan-sər, ,an-,tī-\ adj : used against or tending to arrest cancer ⟨∼ drugs⟩

An·ti·christ \'an-ti-,krīst\ n   1 : one who denies or opposes Christ   2 : a false Christ

an·tic·i·pate \an-'ti-sə-,pāt\ vb -pat·ed; -pat·ing   1 ♦ : to foresee and provide for beforehand **2 ♦** : to look forward to — **an·tic·i·pa·tion** \-,ti-sə-'pā-shən\ *n*

♦ [1] divine, foreknow, foresee — more at FORESEE
♦ [2] await, expect, hope, watch — more at EXPECT

an·tic·i·pa·to·ry \-'ti-sə-pə-,tōr-ē\ *adj* ♦ : characterized by anticipation

♦ agape, agog, expectant — more at EXPECTANT

an·ti·cli·max \,an-ti-'klī-,maks\ *n* : something closing a series that is strikingly less important than what has preceded it — **an·ti·cli·mac·tic** \-klī-'mak-tik\ *adj*

an·ti·cline \'an-ti-,klīn\ *n* : an arch of layers of rock in the earth's crust

an·ti·co·ag·u·lant \,an-ti-kō-'a-gyə-lənt\ *n* : a substance that hinders the clotting of blood — **anticoagulant** *adj*

an·ti·cy·clone \,an-ti-'sī-,klōn\ *n* : a system of winds that rotates about a center of high atmospheric pressure — **an·ti·cy·clon·ic** \-sī-'klä-nik\ *adj*

¹an·ti·de·pres·sant \,an-ti-di-'pres-ᵊnt, ,an-,tī-\ *adj* : used or tending to relieve or prevent depression ⟨∼ drugs⟩

²antidepressant *n* : an antidepressant drug

an·ti·dote \'an-ti-,dōt\ *n* : a remedy to counteract the effects of poison

an·ti·drug \'an-,tī-,drəg\ *adj* : acting against or opposing illicit drugs

an·ti·fer·til·i·ty \,an-ti-fər-'ti-lə-tē\ *adj* : tending to reduce or destroy fertility : CONTRACEPTIVE ⟨∼ agents⟩

an·ti·freeze \'an-ti-,frēz\ *n* : a substance added to a liquid to lower its freezing temperature

an·ti·gen \'an-ti-jən\ *n* : any substance (as a toxin or an enzyme) foreign to the body that induces an immune response — **an·ti·gen·ic** \,an-ti-'je-nik\ *adj* — **an·ti·ge·nic·i·ty** \-jə-'ni-sə-tē\ *n*

an·ti·grav·i·ty \,an-ti-'gra-və-tē, ,an-,tī-\ *adj* : reducing or canceling the effect of gravity

an·ti·he·ro \'an-ti-,hē-rō, 'an-,tī-\ *n* : a protagonist who is notably lacking in heroic qualities (as courage)

an·ti·his·ta·mine \,an-ti-'his-tə-,mēn, ,an-,tī-, -mən\ *n* : any of various drugs used in treating allergies and colds

an·ti·hy·per·ten·sive \-,hī-pər-'ten-siv\ *n* : a substance that is effective against high blood pressure — **antihypertensive** *adj*

an·ti·in·flam·ma·to·ry \-in-'fla-mə-,tōr-ē\ *adj* : counteracting inflammation — **anti–inflammatory** *n*

an·ti·in·tel·lec·tu·al \-,int-ᵊl-'ek-chə-wəl\ *adj* : opposing or hostile to intellectuals or to an intellectual view or approach

an·ti·lock \'an-ti-,läk, 'an-,tī-\ *adj* : being a braking system designed to prevent the wheels from locking

an·ti·log·a·rithm \,an-ti-'lo·gə-,ri-thəm, ,an-,tī-, -'lä-\ *n* : the number corresponding to a given logarithm

an·ti·ma·cas·sar \,an-ti-mə-'ka-sər\ *n* : a cover to protect the back or arms of furniture

an·ti·mat·ter \'an-ti-,ma-tər, 'an-,tī-\ *n* : matter composed of antiparticles

an·ti·mo·ny \'an-tə-,mō-nē\ *n* : a brittle silvery white metallic chemical element used esp. in alloys

an·ti·neu·tron \,an-ti-'nü-,trän, ,an-,tī-, -'nyü-\ *n* : the antiparticle of the neutron

an·ti·no·mi·an \,an-ti-'nō-mē-ən\ *n* : one who denies the validity of moral laws

an·tin·o·my \an-'ti-nə-mē\ *n, pl* **-mies** : a contradiction between two seemingly true statements

an·ti·nov·el \'an-ti-,nä-vəl, 'an-,tī-\ *n* : a work of fiction that lacks all or most of the traditional features of the novel

an·ti·nu·cle·ar \,an-ti-'nü-klē-ər, -'nyü-\ *adj* : opposing the use or production of nuclear power plants

an·ti·ox·i·dant \,an-tē-'äk-sə-dənt, ,an-,tī-\ *n* : a substance that inhibits oxidation — **antioxidant** *adj*

an·ti·par·ti·cle \'an-ti-,pär-ti-kəl, 'an-,tī-\ *n* : a subatomic particle identical to another subatomic particle in mass but opposite to it in electric and magnetic properties

an·ti·pas·to \,an-ti-'pas-tō, ,än-ti-'päs-\ *n, pl* **-ti** \-(,)tē\ : any of various typically Italian hors d'oeuvres

an·ti·pa·thet·ic \,an-ti-pə-'the-tik\ *adj* : having an aversion to or dislike of

an·tip·a·thy \an-'ti-pə-thē\ *n, pl* **-thies 1 ♦** : settled aversion or dislike **2 ♦** : an object of aversion

♦ [1] animosity, antagonism, bitterness, enmity, gall, grudge, hostility, rancor — more at ENMITY ♦ [2] abhorrence, abomination, anathema, aversion, bête noire, hate — more at HATE

an·ti·per·son·nel \,an-ti-,pərs-ᵊn-'el, ,an-,tī-\ *adj* : designed for use against military personnel ⟨∼ mine⟩

an·ti·per·spi·rant \-'pər-spə-rənt\ *n* : a preparation used to check perspiration

an·tiph·o·nal \an-'ti-fən-ᵊl\ *adj* : performed by two alternating groups — **an·tiph·o·nal·ly** *adv*

an·tip·o·dal \an-'ti-pəd-ᵊl\ *adj* ♦ : diametrically opposite or opposed to

♦ antithetical, contradictory, contrary, diametric, opposite, polar — more at OPPOSITE

an·ti·pode \'an-tə-,pōd\ *n, pl* **an·tip·o·des** \an-'ti-pə-,dēz\ [ME *antipodes*, pl., persons dwelling at opposite points on the globe, fr. L, fr. Gk, fr. pl. of *antipod-, antipous* with feet opposite, fr. *anti-* against + *pod-, pous* foot] **1** : the parts of the earth diametrically opposite — usu. used in pl. **2 ♦** : the exact opposite or contrary

♦ antithesis, contrary, negative, opposite, reverse — more at OPPOSITE

an·tip·o·de·an \(,)an-,ti-pə-'dē-ən\ *adj* : diametrically opposite or opposed to

an·ti·pol·lu·tion \,an-ti-pə-'lü-shən\ *adj* : designed to prevent, reduce, or eliminate pollution ⟨∼ laws⟩

an·ti·pope \'an-ti-,pōp\ *n* : one elected or claiming to be pope in opposition to the pope canonically chosen

an·ti·pro·ton \,an-ti-'prō-,tän\ *n* : the antiparticle of the proton

an·ti·quar·i·an \,an-tə-'kwer-ē-ən\ *adj* **1** : of or relating to antiquities **2** : dealing in old books — **antiquarian** *n* — **an·ti·quar·i·an·ism** *n*

an·ti·quary \'an-tə-,kwer-ē\ *n, pl* **-quar·ies** : a person who collects or studies antiquities

an·ti·quat·ed \'an-tə-,kwā-təd\ *adj* ♦ : outmoded or discredited by reason of age : OUT-OF-DATE

♦ archaic, dated, obsolete, outdated, outmoded, outworn, passé — more at OBSOLETE

¹an·tique \an-'tēk\ *n* : an object made in a bygone period

²antique *adj* **1 ♦** : belonging to antiquity **2 ♦** : being in the style or fashion of former times : OLD-FASHIONED **3** : of a bygone period or period

♦ [1] age-old, ancient, antediluvian, dateless, hoary, old, venerable — more at ANCIENT ♦ [2] old-fashioned, old-time, quaint — more at OLD-FASHIONED

³antique *vb* **-tiqued; -tiqu·ing 1** : to finish or refinish in antique style : give an appearance of age to **2** : to shop around for antiques — **an·tiqu·er** *n*

an·tiq·ui·ty \an-'ti-kwə-tē\ *n, pl* **-ties 1** : ancient times **2** : great age **3** *pl* : relics of ancient times **4** *pl* : matters relating to ancient culture

antis *pl of* ANTI

an·ti–Sem·i·tism \,an-ti-'se-mə-,ti-zəm, ,an-,tī-\ *n* : hostility

---

List of self-explanatory words with the prefix *anti-*

antiaging	antiapartheid	anticlerical	antidemocratic
anti–AIDS	antibacterial	anticolonial	antiestablishment
antiaircraft	anticapitalist	anticommunism	antifascist
antialcohol	anti–Catholic	anticommunist	antigovernment
anti–American	anticholesterol		

toward Jews as a religious or social minority — **an·ti–Se·mit·ic** \-sə-'mi-tik\ *adj*

an·ti·sep·tic \,an-tə-'sep-tik\ *adj* **1** : killing or checking the growth of germs that cause decay or infection **2** : scrupulously clean : ASEPTIC — **antiseptic** *n* — **an·ti·sep·ti·cal·ly** *adv*

an·ti·se·rum \'an-ti-,sir-əm, 'an-,tī-\ *n* : a serum containing antibodies

an·ti·so·cial \,an-ti-'sō-shəl\ *adj* **1** ◆ : disliking the society of others **2** : contrary or hostile to the well-being of society ⟨crime is ∼⟩ — **an·ti·so·cial·ly** *adv*

◆ aloof, cold, cool, detached, distant, frosty, remote, standoffish, unsociable — more at COOL

an·tith·e·sis \an-'ti-thə-səs\ *n, pl* **-e·ses** \-,sēz\ **1** : the opposition or contrast of ideas **2** ◆ : the direct opposite

◆ antipode, contrary, negative, opposite, reverse — more at OPPOSITE

an·ti·thet·i·cal \,an-tə-'the-ti-kəl\ *also* **an·ti·thet·ic** \-tik\ *adj* ◆ : constituting or marked by antithesis — **an·ti·thet·i·cal·ly** \-ti-k(ə-)lē\ *adv*

◆ antipodal, contradictory, contrary, diametric, opposite, polar — more at OPPOSITE

an·ti·tox·in \,an-ti-'täk-sən\ *n* : an antibody that is able to neutralize a particular toxin or disease-causing agent; *also* : an antiserum containing an antitoxin

an·ti·trust \,an-ti-'trəst\ *adj* : of or relating to legislation against trusts; *also* : consisting of laws to protect trade and commerce from unlawful restraints and monopolies or unfair business practices

an·ti·ven·in \-'ve-nən\ *n* : an antitoxin to a venom; *also* : a serum containing such antitoxin

ant·ler \'ant-lər\ *n* [ME *aunteler*, fr. AF *antiler*, fr. VL **anteocularis* located before the eye, fr. L *ante-* before + *oculus* eye] : one of the paired deciduous solid bone processes on the head of a deer; *also* : a branch of this — **ant·lered** \-lərd\ *adj*

ant lion *n* : any of various insects having a long-jawed larva that digs a conical pit in which it lies in wait for insects (as ants) on which it feeds

an·to·nym \'an-tə-,nim\ *n* : a word of opposite meaning

anus \'ā-nəs\ *n* [L] : the lower or posterior opening of the alimentary canal

an·vil \'an-vəl\ *n* **1** : a heavy iron block on which metal is shaped **2** : INCUS

anx·i·ety \aŋ-'zī-ə-tē\ *n, pl* **-et·ies** **1** ◆ : painful uneasiness of mind usu. over an anticipated ill **2** : abnormal apprehension and fear often accompanied by physiological signs (as sweating and increased pulse), by doubt about the nature and reality of the threat itself, and by self-doubt

◆ agitation, apprehension, care, concern, disquiet, nervousness, perturbation, uneasiness, worry; *also* strain, stress, tension

anx·ious \'aŋk-shəs\ *adj* **1** ◆ : uneasy in mind : WORRIED ⟨∼ parents⟩ **2** ◆ : characterized by, resulting from, or causing anxiety ⟨an ∼ night⟩ **3** : earnestly wishing : EAGER — **anx·ious·ly** *adv*

◆ [1, 2] distressful, nervous, restless, tense, unsettling, upsetting, worrisome — more at NERVOUS

¹**any** \'e-nē\ *adj* **1** : one chosen at random **2** : of whatever number or quantity

²**any** *pron* **1** : any one or ones ⟨take ∼ of the books you like⟩ **2** : any amount ⟨∼ of the money not used is to be returned⟩

³**any** *adv* : to any extent or degree : AT ALL ⟨could not walk ∼ farther⟩

any·body \-,bä-dē, -bə-\ *pron* : ANYONE

any·how \-,haů\ *adv* **1** : in any way **2** : in spite of that; *also* : in any case

any·more \,e-nē-'mȯr\ *adv* **1** : any longer **2** ◆ : at the present time

◆ now, nowadays, presently, right now, today — more at NOW

any·one \'e-nē-(,)wən\ *pron* : any person

any·place \-,plās\ *adv* : ANYWHERE

any·thing \-,thiŋ\ *pron* : any thing whatever

any·time \'e-nē-,tīm\ *adv* : at any time whatever

any·way \-,wā\ *adv* : in spite of that : ANYHOW

any·where \-,hwer\ *adv* : in or to any place

any·wise \-,wīz\ *adv* : in any way whatever

A–OK \,ā-ō-'kā\ *adv or adj* : very definitely OK

A1 \'ā-'wən\ *adj* ◆ : of the finest quality

◆ excellent, fabulous, fine, grand, great, prime, sensational, splendid, superb, superior, unsurpassed, wonderful — more at EXCELLENT

aor·ta \ā-'ȯr-tə\ *n, pl* **-tas** *or* **-tae** \-tē\ : the main artery that carries blood from the heart — **aor·tic** \-tik\ *adj*

ap *abbr* **1** apostle **2** apothecaries'

AP *abbr* **1** American plan **2** Associated Press

apace \ə-'pās\ *adv* ◆ : at a quick pace : SWIFTLY

◆ briskly, fast, hastily, pronto, quick, quickly, rapidly, speedily, swift, swiftly — more at FAST

Apache \ə-'pa-chē\ *n, pl* **Apache** *or* **Apach·es** \-'pa-chēz, -'pa-shəz\ : a member of an American Indian people of the southwestern U.S.; *also* : any of the languages of the Apache people — **Apach·e·an** \ə-'pa-chē-ən\ *adj or n*

apart \ə-'pärt\ *adv* **1** : separately in place or time **2** : ASIDE **3** : in two or more parts : to pieces

apart·heid \ə-'pär-,tāt, -,tīt\ *n* [Afrikaans] : a policy of racial segregation practiced in the Republic of So. Africa

apart·ment \ə-'pärt-mənt\ *n* : a room or set of rooms occupied as a dwelling; *also* : a building divided into individual dwelling units

ap·a·thet·ic \,a-pə-'the-tik\ *adj* ◆ : having or showing apathy

◆ casual, disinterested, indifferent, insouciant, nonchalant, perfunctory, unconcerned, uncurious, uninterested — more at INDIFFERENT

ap·a·thy \'a-pə-thē\ *n* **1** ◆ : lack of emotion **2** ◆ : lack of interest : INDIFFERENCE — **ap·a·thet·i·cal·ly** \-ti-k(ə-)lē\ *adv*

◆ [1] impassivity, numbness, phlegm, stupor; *also* callousness, coldness, coolness, hardness, insensitivity, obduracy *Ant* emotion, feeling, sensibility ◆ [2] disinterestedness, disregard, indifference, insouciance, nonchalance — more at INDIFFERENCE

ap·a·tite \'a-pə-,tīt\ *n* : any of a group of minerals that are phosphates of calcium and occur esp. in phosphate rock and in bones and teeth

apato·sau·rus \ə-,pa-tə-'sȯr-əs\ *n* : any of a genus of very large 4-footed plant-eating dinosaurs of the Jurassic : BRONTOSAURUS

APB *abbr* all points bulletin

¹**ape** \'āp\ *n* **1** : any of the larger tailless primates (as a baboon or gorilla); *also* : MONKEY **2** : MIMIC, IMITATOR; *also* : a large uncouth person

²**ape** *vb* **aped; ap·ing** ◆ : to copy closely but often clumsily and ineptly : IMITATE, MIMIC

◆ copy, emulate, imitate, mime, mimic — more at IMITATE

ape–man \'āp-,man\ *n* : a primate intermediate in character between Homo sapiens and the higher apes

---

List of self-explanatory words with the prefix *anti-* (continued)

anti–imperialism	antimalarial	antislavery	antitank
anti–imperialist	antimicrobial	antispasmodic	antitumor
antiknock	antinausea	antistatic	antiviral
antilabor	antipoverty	antisubmarine	antiwar

aper·çu \ȧ-per-sū̄ē, ˌa-pər-'sü\ *n, pl* **aperçus** \-sū̄ē(z), -'süz\ : an immediate impression; *esp* : INSIGHT

aper·i·tif \ȧ-ˌä-ˌper-ə-'tēf\ *n* : an alcoholic drink taken as an appetizer

ap·er·ture \'a-pər-ˌchùr, -chər\ *n*² ♦ : an opening or open space : OPENING, HOLE

    ♦ hole, opening, orifice, perforation — more at HOLE

apex \'ā-ˌpeks\ *n, pl* **apex·es** *or* **api·ces** \'ā-pə-ˌsēz, 'a-\ **1** ♦ : the highest point : PEAK **2** ♦ : the narrowed or pointed end

    ♦ [1] acme, climax, crown, culmination, head, height, meridian, peak, pinnacle, summit, tip-top, top, zenith — more at HEIGHT ♦ [2] cusp, end, pike, point, tip — more at POINT

apha·sia \ə-'fā-zh(ē-)ə\ *n* : loss or impairment of the power to use or comprehend words — **apha·sic** \-zik\ *adj or n*

aph·elion \a-'fēl-yən\ *n, pl* **-elia** \-yə\ [NL, fr. *apo-* away from + Gk *hēlios* sun] : the point in an object's orbit most distant from the sun

aphid \'ā-fəd\ *n* : any of numerous small insects that suck the juices of plants

aphis \'ā-fəs, 'a-\ *n, pl* **aphi·des** \-fə-ˌdēz\ : APHID

aph·o·rism \'a-fə-ˌri-zəm\ *n* ♦ : a short saying stating a general truth or sentiment : MAXIM

    ♦ adage, byword, epigram, maxim, proverb, saying — more at SAYING

aph·o·ris·tic \ˌa-fə-'ris-tik\ *adj* : of, resembling, or characterized by aphorisms

aph·ro·di·si·ac \ˌa-frə-'di-zē-ˌak, -'dē-zē-\ *n* : an agent that excites sexual desire — **aphrodisiac** *adj*

api·ary \'ā-pē-ˌer-ē\ *n, pl* **-ar·ies** : a place where bees are kept — **api·a·rist** \-pē-ə-rist\ *n*

api·cal \'ā-pi-kəl, 'a-\ *adj* : of, relating to, or situated at an apex — **api·cal·ly** \-k(ə-)lē\ *adv*

apiece \ə-'pēs\ *adv* : for each one

aplen·ty \ə-'plen-tē\ *adj* : being in plenty or abundance

aplomb \ə-'pläm, -'pləm\ *n* [F, lit., perpendicularity, fr. MF, fr. *a plomb*, lit., according to the plummet] ♦ : complete composure or self-assurance

    ♦ calmness, composure, coolness, equanimity, placidity, self-possession, serenity, tranquility — more at EQUANIMITY ♦ confidence, self-assurance, self-confidence, self-esteem — more at CONFIDENCE

APO *abbr* army post office

Apoc *abbr* **1** Apocalypse **2** Apocrypha

apoc·a·lypse \ə-'pä-kə-ˌlips\ *n* **1** : a writing prophesying a cataclysm in which evil forces are destroyed **2** *cap* : a book of the New Testament of the Christian Scripture — **apoc·a·lyp·tic** \-ˌpä-kə-'lip-tik\ *also* **apoc·a·lyp·ti·cal** \-ti-kəl\ *adj*

Apoc·ry·pha \ə-'pä-krə-fə\ *n* **1** *not cap* : writings of dubious authenticity **2** : books included in the Septuagint and Vulgate but excluded from the Jewish and Protestant canons of the Old Testament **3** : early Christian writings not included in the New Testament

apoc·ry·phal \-fəl\ *adj* **1** : not canonical : SPURIOUS **2** *often cap* : of or resembling the Apocrypha — **apoc·ry·phal·ly** *adv* — **apoc·ry·phal·ness** *n*

apo·gee \'a-pə-(ˌ)jē\ *n* [F *apogée*, fr. NL *apogaeum*, fr. Gk *apogaion*, fr. *apo* away from + *gē, gaia* earth] : the point at which an orbiting object is farthest from the body being orbited

apo·lit·i·cal \ˌā-pə-'li-ti-kəl\ *adj* **1** : having an aversion for or no interest in political affairs **2** : having no political significance — **apo·lit·i·cal·ly** \-k(ə-)lē\ *adv*

apol·o·get·ic \ə-ˌpä-lə-'je-tik\ *adj* ♦ : expressing apology — **apol·o·get·i·cal·ly** \-ti-k(ə-)lē\ *adv*

    ♦ contrite, penitent, regretful, remorseful, repentant, rueful, sorry — more at CONTRITE

ap·o·lo·gia \ˌa-pə-'lō-j(ē-)ə\ *n* : APOLOGY; *esp* : an argument in support or justification

apol·o·gise *Brit var of* APOLOGIZE

apol·o·gize \ə-'pä-lə-ˌjīz\ *vb* **-gized; -giz·ing** : to make an apology : express regret — **apol·o·gist** \-jist\ *n*

apol·o·gy \ə-'pä-lə-jē\ *n, pl* **-gies** **1** : a formal justification : DEFENSE **2** : an expression of regret for a wrong

ap·o·plexy \'a-pə-ˌplek-sē\ *n* : STROKE **3** — **ap·o·plec·tic** \ˌa-pə-'plek-tik\ *adj*

aport \ə-'pōrt\ *adv* : on or toward the left side of a ship

apos·ta·sy \ə-'päs-tə-sē\ *n, pl* **-sies** : a renunciation or abandonment of a former loyalty (as to a religion)

apos·tate \ə-'päs-ˌtāt, -tət\ *n* ♦ : one who commits apostasy — **apostate** *adj*

    ♦ betrayer, double-crosser, quisling, recreant, traitor, turncoat — more at TRAITOR

a pos·te·ri·o·ri \ˌä-pō-ˌstir-ē-'ōr-ē\ *adj* [L, lit., from the latter] : relating to or derived by reasoning from observed facts — **a posteriori** *adv*

apos·tle \ə-'pä-səl\ *n* **1** : one of the group composed of Jesus' 12 original disciples and Paul **2** : the first prominent missionary to a region or group **3 a** : a person who initiates or first advocates a great reform **b** ♦ : an ardent supporter — **apos·tle·ship** *n*

    ♦ advocate, backer, booster, champion, exponent, friend, promoter, proponent, supporter — more at EXPONENT

ap·os·tol·ic \ˌa-pə-'stä-lik\ *adj* **1** : of or relating to an apostle or to the New Testament apostles **2** : of or relating to a succession of spiritual authority from the apostles **3** : PAPAL ⟨~ authority⟩

¹apos·tro·phe \ə-'päs-trə-(ˌ)fē\ *n* : the rhetorical addressing of a usu. absent person or a usu. personified thing (as in "O grave, where is thy victory?")

²apostrophe *n* : a punctuation mark ' used esp. to indicate the possessive case or the omission of a letter or figure

apos·tro·phise *Brit var of* APOSTROPHIZE

apos·tro·phize \ə-'päs-trə-ˌfīz\ *vb* **-phized; -phiz·ing** : to address as if present or capable of understanding

apothecaries' weight *n* : a system of weights based on the troy pound and ounce and used chiefly by pharmacists

apoth·e·cary \ə-'pä-thə-ˌker-ē\ *n, pl* **-car·ies** [ME *apothecarie*, fr. ML *apothecarius*, fr. LL, shopkeeper, fr. L *apotheca* storehouse, fr. Gk *apothēkē*, fr. *apotithenai* to put away] : one who prepares and sells drugs or compounds for medicinal purposes : DRUGGIST

ap·o·thegm \'a-pə-ˌthem\ *or Can and Brit* **ap·o·phthegm** *n* : APHORISM

apo·the·o·sis \ə-ˌpä-thē-'ō-səs, ˌa-pə-'thē-ə-səs\ *n, pl* **-o·ses** \-ˌsēz\ **1** : DEIFICATION **2** : the perfect example

app *abbr* **1** apparatus **2** appendix

ap·pall *also* **ap·pal** \ə-'pól\ *vb* **ap·palled; ap·pall·ing** ♦ : to overcome with consternation, shock, or dismay

    ♦ bowl, floor, jolt, shake up, shock — more at SHOCK

ap·pall·ing *adj* ♦ : inspiring horror, dismay, or disgust

    ♦ abhorrent, abominable, awful, distasteful, horrible, horrid, nauseating, noisome, obnoxious, odious, offensive, repellent, revolting — more at OFFENSIVE ♦ astonishing, awful, dreadful, frightful, ghastly, hideous, horrible, horrid, shocking, terrible — more at HORRIBLE

Ap·pa·loo·sa \ˌa-pə-'lü-sə\ *n* : any of a breed of saddle horses developed in western No. America and usu. having a white or solid-colored coat with small spots

ap·pa·nage \'a-pə-nij\ *n* **1** : provision (as a grant of land) made by a sovereign or legislative body for dependent members of the royal family **2** : something that is attached or associated in a natural or necessary way : a natural adjunct

ap·pa·ra·tus \ˌa-pə-'ra-təs, -'rā-\ *n, pl* **-tus·es** *or* **-tus** [L] **1** ♦ : a set of materials or equipment for a particular use **2** : a complex machine or device : MECHANISM **3** : the organization of a political party or underground movement

    ♦ accoutrements (*or* accouterments), equipment, gear, matériel, outfit, paraphernalia, tackle — more at EQUIPMENT

¹**ap·par·el** \ə-'par-əl\ *vb* **-eled** *or* **-elled; -el·ing** *or* **-el·ling** **1 :** to put clothes on : CLOTHE **2 :** ADORN

²**apparel** *n* ♦ **:** personal attire : CLOTHING, DRESS

  ♦ attire, clothing, dress, duds, raiment, wear — more at CLOTHING

ap·par·ent \ə-'par-ənt\ *adj* **1** ♦ **:** open to view : VISIBLE **2** ♦ **:** clear or manifest to the understanding : EVIDENT, OBVIOUS **3** ♦ **:** appearing as real or true : SEEMING

  ♦ [1] observable, visible, visual — more at VISIBLE
  ♦ [2] clear, distinct, evident, manifest, obvious, plain, transparent, unambiguous, unequivocal, unmistakable — more at CLEAR ♦ [3] assumed, evident, ostensible, reputed, seeming, supposed; *also* external, outward, visible

ap·par·ent·ly \-lē\ *adv* ♦ **:** it seems apparent

  ♦ evidently, ostensibly, presumably, seemingly, supposedly; *also* externally, outwardly, visibly

ap·pa·ri·tion \ˌa-pə-'ri-shən\ *n* ♦ **:** a supernatural appearance : GHOST

  ♦ bogey, ghost, phantasm, phantom, poltergeist, shade, shadow, specter, spirit, spook, vision, wraith — more at GHOST

¹**ap·peal** \ə-'pēl\ *n* **1** ♦ **:** an earnest plea **2** ♦ **:** the power of arousing a sympathetic response

  ♦ [1] cry, entreaty, petition, plea, prayer, solicitation, suit, supplication — more at PLEA ♦ [2] allure, attractiveness, captivation, charisma, charm, enchantment, fascination, glamour, magic, magnetism — more at CHARM

²**appeal** *vb* **1 :** to take steps to have (a case) reheard in a higher court **2** ♦ **:** to plead for help, corroboration, or decision **3 :** to arouse a sympathetic response

  ♦ *usu* **appeal to** beg, beseech, entreat, implore, importune, petition, plead, pray, solicit, supplicate — more at BEG

ap·pear \ə-'pir\ *vb* **1** ♦ **:** to become visible **2 :** to come formally before an authority **3** ♦ **:** to have an outward aspect : SEEM **4 :** to become evident **5 :** to come before the public

  ♦ [1] come out, materialize, show up, turn up; *also* reappear, resurface *Ant* disappear, clear, dissolve, evaporate, fade, go (away), melt (away), vanish ♦ [3] act, look, make, seem, sound — more at SEEM

ap·pear·ance \ə-'pir-əns\ *n* **1** ♦ **:** outward aspect : LOOK **2 :** the act of appearing **3 :** PHENOMENON

  ♦ aspect, look, mien, presence; *also* air, attitude, bearing, behavior, comportment, demeanor (*or* demeanour), deportment, manner, poise, pose ♦ face, guise, name, semblance, show; *also* affectation, display, fiction, imposture, pose, pretense, simulation

ap·pease \ə-'pēz\ *vb* **ap·peased; ap·peas·ing** **1 :** to cause to subside : ALLAY **2** ♦ **:** to bring to a state of peace or quiet : PACIFY, CONCILIATE; *esp* : to buy off by concessions — **ap·peas·able** \-'pē-zə-bəl\ *adj* — **ap·pease·ment** *n* — **ap·peas·er** *n*

  ♦ conciliate, disarm, mollify, pacify, placate, propitiate — more at PACIFY

ap·pel·lant \ə-'pe-lənt\ *n* **:** one who appeals esp. from a judicial decision

ap·pel·late \ə-'pe-lət\ *adj* **:** having power to review decisions of a lower court

ap·pel·la·tion \ˌa-pə-'lā-shən\ *n* ♦ **:** an identifying name or title : NAME, DESIGNATION

  ♦ cognomen, denotation, designation, handle, name, title — more at NAME

ap·pel·lee \ˌa-pə-'lē\ *n* **:** one against whom an appeal is taken

ap·pend \ə-'pend\ *vb* ♦ **:** to attach esp. as something additional

  ♦ add, adjoin, annex, tack — more at ADD

ap·pend·age \ə-'pen-dij\ *n* **1** ♦ **:** something appended to a principal or greater thing **2 :** a projecting part of the body (as an antenna) esp. when paired with one on each side

  ♦ accessory, accoutrement (*or* accouterment), adjunct, attachment — more at ACCESSORY

ap·pen·dec·to·my \ˌa-pən-'dek-tə-mē\ *n, pl* **-mies :** surgical removal of the intestinal appendix

ap·pen·di·ci·tis \ə-ˌpen-də-'sī-təs\ *n* **:** inflammation of the intestinal appendix

ap·pen·dix \ə-'pen-diks\ *n, pl* **-dix·es** *or* **-di·ces** \-də-ˌsēz\ [L] **1 :** supplementary matter added at the end of a book **2 :** a narrow blind tube usu. about three or four inches long that extends from the cecum in the lower right-hand part of the abdomen

ap·per·tain \ˌa-pər-'tān\ *vb* ♦ **:** to belong or be connected as a rightful part or privilege

  ♦ apply, bear, pertain, refer, relate — more at APPLY

ap·pe·tite \'a-pə-ˌtīt\ *n* [ME *apetit*, fr. AF, fr. L *appetitus*, fr. *appetere* to strive after, fr. *ad-* to + *petere* to go to] **1** ♦ **:** natural desire for satisfying some want or need esp. for food **2** ♦ **:** individual preference : TASTE

  ♦ [1] craving, desire, drive, hankering, hunger, itch, thirst, urge, yen — more at DESIRE ♦ [2] fancy, favor (*or* favour), fondness, like, liking, love, partiality, preference, relish, shine, taste, use — more at LIKING

ap·pe·tiz·er \'a-pə-ˌtī-zər\ *n* **:** a food or drink taken just before a meal to stimulate the appetite

ap·pe·tiz·ing \-zin\ *adj* ♦ **:** tempting to the appetite — **ap·pe·tiz·ing·ly** *adv*

  ♦ delectable, delicious, flavorful (*or* flavourful), palatable, tasty, toothsome — more at DELICIOUS

appl *abbr* applied

ap·plaud \ə-'plȯd\ *vb* ♦ **:** to show approval esp. by clapping

  ♦ acclaim, cheer, hail, laud, praise, salute, tout — more at ACCLAIM

ap·plaud·able \ə-'plȯ-də-bəl\ *adj* ♦ **:** worthy of being applauded

  ♦ admirable, commendable, creditable, laudable, meritorious, praiseworthy — more at ADMIRABLE

ap·plause \ə-'plȯz\ *n* ♦ **:** approval publicly expressed (as by clapping)

  ♦ acclamation, ovation; *also* clapping *Ant* hissing

ap·ple \'a-pəl\ *n* **:** a rounded fruit with firm white flesh and a seedy core; *also* : a tree that bears this fruit

ap·ple·jack \-ˌjak\ *n* **:** a liquor distilled from fermented cider

ap·plet \'a-plət\ *n* **:** a short computer program esp. for performing a simple specific task

ap·pli·ance \ə-'plī-əns\ *n* **1 :** an instrument or device designed for a particular use or function **2 :** a piece of household equipment (as a stove or toaster) operated by gas or electricity

ap·pli·ca·bil·i·ty \ˌa-pli-kə-'bi-lə-tē, ə-ˌpli-kə-\ *n* ♦ **:** the quality or state of being applicable

  ♦ bearing, connection, pertinence, relevance — more at PERTINENCE

ap·pli·ca·ble \'a-pli-kə-bəl, ə-'pli-kə-\ *adj* ♦ **:** capable of being applied

  ♦ functional, practicable, practical, serviceable, usable, useful, workable, working — more at PRACTICAL ♦ appropriate, apt, felicitous, fit, fitting, good, happy, meet, proper, right, suitable — more at FIT ♦ apposite, apropos, germane, material, pertinent, pointed, relative, relevant — more at PERTINENT

ap·pli·cant \'a-pli-kənt\ *n* ♦ **:** one who applies

  ♦ aspirant, campaigner, candidate, contender, hopeful, prospect, seeker — more at CANDIDATE

ap·pli·ca·tion \ˌa-plə-'kā-shən\ *n* **1** ♦ **:** the act of applying **2 :** assiduous attention **3 :** REQUEST; *also* : a form used in making a request **4 :** something placed or spread on a surface **5 :** capacity for use **6 :** a program (as a word processor) that performs one of a computer's major tasks

♦ employment, exercise, operation, play, use — more at USE

ap·pli·ca·tor \'a-plə-ˌkā-tər\ *n* : a device for applying a substance (as medicine or polish)

ap·plied \ə-'plīd\ *adj* : put to practical use ⟨∼ art⟩

ap·pli·qué \ˌa-plə-'kā\ *n* [F] : a fabric decoration cut out and fastened to a larger piece of material — **appliqué** *vb*

ap·ply \ə-'plī\ *vb* **ap·plied; ap·ply·ing 1 a ♦** : to put to practical use **b ♦** : to bring into action **c** : to lay or spread on **d ♦** : to put into operation or effect **2** : to place in contact : put or spread on a surface **3 ♦** : to employ with close attention **4 ♦** : to have reference or connection **5** : to submit a request

♦ [1a, 1b] employ, exercise, exploit, harness, operate, use, utilize — more at USE ♦ [1d] administer, enforce, execute, implement — more at ENFORCE ♦ [3] address, bend, buckle, devote, give; *also* readdress, reapply ♦ [4] appertain, bear, pertain, refer, relate; *also* affect, concern, interest, involve, touch

ap·point \ə-'point\ *vb* **1 ♦** : to fix or set officially ⟨∼ a day for trial⟩ **2 ♦** : to name officially **3** : to fit out : EQUIP

♦ [1] designate, fix, name, set; *also* adopt, assign, choose, determine, establish, opt (for), pick, prefer, select, settle, single (out), specify ♦ [2] assign, attach, commission, constitute, designate, detail, name; *also* authorize, delegate, depute, deputize, inaugurate, induct, install, instate, invest, ordain

ap·poin·tee \ə-ˌpoin-'tē, ˌa-\ *n* : a person appointed

ap·point·ive \ə-'poin-tiv\ *adj* : subject to appointment

ap·point·ment \ə-'point-mənt\ *n* **1** : the act of appointing **2 ♦** : an arrangement for a meeting **3** *pl* : articles of furniture for the interior of a building : FURNISHINGS **4 ♦** : a nonelective office or position

♦ [2] date, engagement, rendezvous, tryst — more at ENGAGEMENT ♦ *usu* **appointments** [4] billet, capacity, function, job, place, position, post, situation — more at JOB ♦ [4] assignment, commission, designation; *also* billet, job, office, place, position, situation, spot, station *Ant* discharge, dismissal, expulsion, firing

ap·por·tion \ə-'pōr-shən\ *vb* **♦** : to distribute proportionately

♦ allocate, allot, allow, ration — more at ALLOT ♦ administer, allocate, deal, dispense, distribute, mete, parcel, portion, prorate — more at ADMINISTER

ap·por·tion·ment \-mənt\ *n* : an act or result of apportioning

ap·po·site \'a-pə-zət\ *adj* **♦** : highly pertinent or appropriate : RELEVANT — **ap·po·site·ly** *adv* — **ap·po·site·ness** *n*

♦ applicable, apropos, germane, material, pertinent, pointed, relative, relevant — more at PERTINENT

ap·po·si·tion \ˌa-pə-'zi-shən\ *n* : a grammatical construction in which a noun or pronoun is followed by another that has the same referent (as *the poet* and *Burns* in "a biography of the poet Burns")

ap·pos·i·tive \ə-'pä-zə-tiv, a-\ *adj* : of, relating to, or standing in grammatical apposition — **appositive** *n*

ap·prais·al \ə-'prā-zəl\ *n* **♦** : an act or instance of appraising

♦ assessment, estimate, estimation, evaluation, judgment (*or* judgement) — more at ESTIMATION

ap·praise \ə-'prāz\ *vb* **ap·praised; ap·prais·ing 1** : to set a value on **2 ♦** : to evaluate the worth, significance, or status of — **ap·prais·er** *n*

♦ assess, estimate, evaluate, rate, set, value — more at ESTIMATE

ap·pre·cia·ble \ə-'prē-shə-bəl\ *adj* **♦** : large enough to be recognized and measured — **ap·pre·cia·bly** *adv*

♦ detectable, discernible, distinguishable, palpable, perceptible, sensible — more at PERCEPTIBLE

ap·pre·ci·ate \ə-'prē-shē-ˌāt\ *vb* **-at·ed; -at·ing 1 ♦** : to value justly **2 ♦** : to judge with understanding : be fully aware of **3** : to be grateful for **4 ♦** : to increase in value

♦ [1] cherish, prize, treasure, value ♦ [1] admire, esteem, regard, respect — more at ADMIRE ♦ [2] apprehend, catch, catch on (to), comprehend, get, grasp, make, make out, perceive, see, seize, understand — more at COMPREHEND ♦ [4] accumulate, build, expand, increase, mount, multiply, proliferate, rise — more at INCREASE

ap·pre·ci·a·tion \ə-ˌprē-shē-'ā-shən\ *n* **1 a ♦** : an opinion or estimate formed by discerning and comparing; *esp* : a favorable critical estimate **b** : sensitive awareness **2 ♦** : an expression of admiration, approval, or gratitude

♦ [1a] admiration, esteem, estimation, favor (*or* favour), regard, respect — more at ADMIRATION ♦ [1a] apprehension, comprehension, grasp, grip, perception, understanding — more at COMPREHENSION ♦ [2] gratefulness, gratitude, thanks — more at THANKS

ap·pre·cia·tive \ə-'prē-shə-tiv, -shē-ˌā-\ *adj* **♦** : having or showing appreciation — **ap·pre·cia·tive·ly** *adv*

♦ complimentary, favorable (*or* favourable), friendly, good, positive — more at FAVORABLE ♦ grateful, obliged, thankful — more at GRATEFUL

ap·pre·hend \ˌa-pri-'hend\ *vb* **1 ♦** : to take or keep in custody by authority of law : ARREST **2** : to become aware of **3** : to look forward to with dread **4 ♦** : to grasp with the understanding : UNDERSTAND

♦ [1] arrest, nab, pick up, restrain, seize — more at ARREST ♦ [4] appreciate, catch, catch on (to), comprehend, get, grasp, make, make out, perceive, see, seize, understand — more at COMPREHEND

ap·pre·hen·sion \ˌa-pri-'hen-chən\ *n* **1 a** : the act or power of perceiving or comprehending **b ♦** : the result of apprehending mentally **2** : seizure by legal process **3 ♦** : suspicion or fear esp. of future evil

♦ [1b] appreciation, comprehension, grasp, grip, perception, understanding — more at COMPREHENSION ♦ [3] agitation, anxiety, care, concern, disquiet, nervousness, perturbation, uneasiness, worry — more at ANXIETY

ap·pre·hen·sive \-'hen-siv\ *adj* : viewing the future with anxiety — **ap·pre·hen·sive·ly** *adv* — *n*

ap·pre·hen·sive·ness \-nəs\ *n* : the quality or state of being apprehensive

¹**ap·pren·tice** \ə-'pren-təs\ *n* **1 ♦** : a person learning a craft under a skilled worker **2** : BEGINNER — **ap·pren·tice·ship** *n*

♦ aid, assistant, helper — more at HELPER

²**apprentice** *vb* **-ticed; -tic·ing** : to bind or set at work as an apprentice

ap·prise \ə-'prīz\ *vb* **ap·prised; ap·pris·ing ♦** : to give notice to : INFORM

♦ acquaint, advise, brief, clue, enlighten, familiarize, fill in, inform, instruct, tell, wise — more at ENLIGHTEN

¹**ap·proach** \ə-'prōch\ *vb* **1 ♦** : to move nearer to **2 ♦** : to be almost the same as **3** : to make advances to esp. for the purpose of creating a desired result **4** : to take preliminary steps toward — **ap·proach·able** *adj*

♦ [1] advance, close, come, come, near; *also* arrive, attain, come, gain, hit, land, make, reach, show up, turn up *Ant* back (up *or* away), recede, retire, retreat, withdraw ♦ [2] approximate, compare, measure up, stack up — more at APPROXIMATE

²**approach** *n* **1 ♦** : a means of access : AVENUE **2 a** : the taking of preliminary steps toward a particular purpose **b ♦** : a particular manner of taking steps toward an end

♦ [1] avenue, passage, path, route, way — more at PASSAGE ♦ [2b] fashion, form, manner, method, strategy, style, system, tack, tactics, technique, way — more at METHOD

ap·pro·ba·tion \ˌa-prə-'bā-shən\ *n* **♦** : an act of commending : APPROVAL

♦ approval, blessing, favor (*or* favour), imprimatur, OK — more at APPROVAL

¹**ap·pro·pri·ate** \ə-'prō-prē-ˌāt\ *vb* **-at·ed; -at·ing** **1** ♦ : to take possession of **2** : to set apart for a particular use

♦ arrogate, commandeer, preempt, usurp; *also* annex, claim, confiscate, expropriate, preoccupy, sequester

²**ap·pro·pri·ate** \ə-'prō-prē-ət\ *adj* ♦ : fitted to a purpose or use

♦ applicable, apt, felicitous, fit, fitting, good, happy, meet, proper, right, suitable — more at FIT

ap·pro·pri·ate·ly \-lē\ *adv* ♦ : in an appropriate manner

♦ correctly, fittingly, happily, properly, rightly, suitably — more at PROPERLY

ap·pro·pri·ate·ness \-nəs\ *n* ♦ : the quality or state of being appropriate

♦ aptness, fitness, rightness, suitability; *also* agreeableness, compatibility, congruity, harmoniousness *Ant* inaptness, infelicity, unfitness

ap·pro·pri·a·tion \ə-ˌprō-prē-'ā-shən\ *n* ♦ : something (as money) set aside by formal action for a specific use

♦ allocation, allotment, grant, subsidy; *also* advance, allowance, benefit, endowment, fund, stipend, trust

ap·prov·al \ə-'prü-vəl\ *n* ♦ : an act of approving — **on approval** : subject to a prospective buyer's acceptance or refusal

♦ approbation, blessing, favor (*or* favour), imprimatur, OK; *also* backing, endorsement, sanction, support *Ant* disapprobation, disapproval, disfavor

ap·prove \ə-'prüv\ *vb* **ap·proved; ap·prov·ing** **1** ♦ : to have or express a favorable opinion of **2** ♦ : to accept as satisfactory : RATIFY

♦ [1] authorize, clear, OK, ratify, sanction, warrant; *also* accept, acknowledge, affirm, confirm *Ant* decline, deny, disallow, disapprove, negative, reject, turn down ♦ *usu* **approve of** [2] accept, care, countenance, favor (*or* favour), OK, subscribe; *also* acclaim, applaud, laud, praise, salute *Ant* disapprove (of), discountenance, disfavor, frown (on *or* upon)

approx *abbr* approximate; approximately

¹**ap·prox·i·mate** \ə-'präk-sə-mət\ *adj* ♦ : nearly correct or exact — **ap·prox·i·mate·ly** *adv*

♦ comparative, near, relative — more at COMPARATIVE

²**ap·prox·i·mate** \-ˌmāt\ *vb* **-mat·ed; -mat·ing** ♦ : to come near : APPROACH — **ap·prox·i·ma·tion** \ə-ˌpräk-sə-'mā-shən\ *n*

♦ approach, compare, measure up, stack up; *also* add up (to), amount (to), come (to)

appt *abbr* appoint; appointed; appointment

ap·pur·te·nance \ə-'pərt-nəns, -ᵊn-əns\ *n* : something that belongs to or goes with another thing — **ap·pur·te·nant** \ə-'pərt-nənt, -ᵊn-ənt\ *adj*

Apr *abbr* April

APR *abbr* annual percentage rate

apri·cot \'a-prə-ˌkät, 'ā-\ *n* [alter. of earlier *abrecock*, ultim. fr. Ar *al-birqūq*, ultim. fr. L (*persicum*) *praecox*, lit., early-ripening (peach)] : an oval orange-colored fruit resembling the related peach and plum in flavor; *also* : a tree bearing apricots

April \'ā-prəl\ *n* [ME, fr. AF & L; AF *avrill*, fr. L *Aprilis*] : the 4th month of the year

a pri·o·ri \ˌä-prē-'ōr-ē\ *adj* [L, from the former] **1** : characterized by or derived by reasoning from self-evident propositions **2** : independent of experience — **a priori** *adv*

apron \'ā-prən\ *n* [ME, alter. (fr. misdivision of *a napron*) of *napron*, fr. MF *naperon*, dim. of *nape* cloth, modif. of L *mappa* napkin] **1** : a garment tied over the front of the body to protect the clothes **2** : a paved area for parking or handling airplanes — **aproned** *adj*

¹**ap·ro·pos** \ˌa-prə-'pō, 'a-prə-ˌpō\ *adv* [F *à propos*, lit., to the purpose] **1** : OPPORTUNELY **2** : in passing : INCIDENTALLY

²**apropos** *adj* ♦ : being to the point

♦ applicable, apposite, germane, material, pertinent, pointed, relative, relevant — more at PERTINENT

apropos of *prep* ♦ : with regard to

♦ about, concerning, of, on, regarding, respecting, toward — more at ABOUT

apse \'aps\ *n* : a projecting usu. semicircular and vaulted part of a building (as a church)

¹**apt** \'apt\ *adj* **1** ♦ : well adapted : SUITABLE **2** ♦ : having an habitual tendency **3** : quick to learn — **apt·ly** *adv*

♦ [1] applicable, appropriate, felicitous, fit, fitting, good, happy, meet, proper, right, suitable — more at FIT ♦ [2] given, inclined, prone — more at PRONE

²**apt** *abbr* **1** apartment **2** aptitude

ap·ti·tude \'ap-tə-ˌtüd, -ˌtyüd\ *n* **1** ♦ : natural ability : TALENT **2** : capacity for learning **3** : APPROPRIATENESS

♦ endowment, faculty, flair, genius, gift, knack, talent — more at TALENT

apt·ness \'apt-nəs\ *n* ♦ : the quality or state of being apt

♦ proneness, propensity, tendency, way — more at TENDENCY ♦ appropriateness, fitness, rightness, suitability — more at APPROPRIATENESS

aqua \'ä-kwə, 'ä-\ *n* : a light greenish blue color

aqua·cul·ture *also* **aqui·cul·ture** \'a-kwə-ˌkəl-chər, 'ä-\ *n* : the cultivation of aquatic plants or animals (as fish or shellfish) for human use

aqua·ma·rine \ˌa-kwə-mə-'rēn, ˌä-\ *n* **1** : a bluish green gem **2** : a pale blue to light greenish blue

aqua·naut \'a-kwə-ˌnòt, 'ä-\ *n* : a person who lives in an underwater shelter for an extended period

aqua·plane \-ˌplān\ *n* : a board towed behind a motorboat and ridden by a person standing on it — **aquaplane** *vb*

aqua re·gia \ˌa-kwə-'rē-j(ē-)ə\ *n* [NL, lit., royal water] : a mixture of nitric and hydrochloric acids that dissolves gold or platinum

aquar·i·um \ə-'kwar-ē-əm\ *n, pl* **-i·ums** *or* **-ia** \-ē-ə\ **1** : a container (as a glass tank) in which living aquatic animals or plants are kept **2** : a place where aquatic animals and plants are exhibited

Aquar·i·us \ə-'kwar-ē-əs\ *n* [L, lit., water carrier] **1** : a zodiacal constellation between Capricorn and Pisces usu. pictured as a man pouring water **2** : the 11th sign of the zodiac in astrology; *also* : one born under this sign

¹**aquat·ic** \ə-'kwä-tik, -'kwa-\ *adj* **1** : growing or living in or frequenting water **2** : performed in or on water

²**aquatic** *n* : an aquatic animal or plant

aqua·vit \'ä-kwə-ˌvēt\ *n* : a clear liquor flavored with caraway seeds

aqua vi·tae \ˌa-kwə-'vī-tē, ˌä-\ *n* [ME, fr. ML, lit., water of life] : a strong alcoholic liquor (as brandy)

aq·ue·duct \'a-kwə-ˌdəkt\ *n* **1** ♦ : a conduit for carrying running water **2** : a structure carrying a canal over a river or hollow **3** : a passage in a bodily part

♦ canal, channel, conduit, flume, raceway, watercourse — more at CHANNEL

aque·ous \'ā-kwē-əs, 'a-\ *adj* **1** : WATERY **2** : made of, by, or with water

aqueous humor *n* : a clear fluid occupying the space between the lens and the cornea of the eye

aqui·fer \'a-kwə-fər, 'ä-\ *n* : a water-bearing stratum of permeable rock, sand, or gravel

aq·ui·line \'a-kwə-ˌlīn, -lən\ *adj* **1** : of or resembling an eagle **2** : hooked like an eagle's beak ⟨an ∼ nose⟩

ar *abbr* arrival; arrive

Ar *symbol* argon

AR *abbr* Arkansas

-ar *adj suffix* **1** : of or relating to ⟨molecul*ar*⟩ : being ⟨spectacul*ar*⟩ **2** : resembling ⟨oracul*ar*⟩

Ar·ab \'ar-əb\ *n* **1** : a member of a Semitic people of the Arabian peninsula in southwestern Asia **2** : a member of an Arabic-speaking people — **Arab** *adj* — **Ara·bi·an** \ə-'rā-bē-ən\ *adj or n*

ar·a·besque \ˌar-ə-'besk\ *n* : a design of interlacing lines forming figures of flowers, foliage, and sometimes animals — **arabesque** *adj*

¹Ar·a·bic \'ar-ə-bik\ *n* : a Semitic language of southwestern Asia and northern Africa

²Arabic *adj* **1** : of or relating to the Arabs, Arabic, or the Arabian peninsula in southwestern Asia **2** : expressed in or making use of Arabic numerals

Arabic numeral *n* : any of the number symbols 0, 1, 2, 3, 4, 5, 6, 7, 8, 9

ar·a·ble \'ar-ə-bəl\ *adj* : fit for or used for the growing of crops

arach·nid \ə-'rak-nəd\ *n* : any of a class of usu. 8-legged arthropods comprising the spiders, scorpions, mites, and ticks — **arachnid** *adj*

Ar·a·ma·ic \ar-ə-'mā-ik\ *n* : an ancient Semitic language

ar·a·mid \'ar-ə-məd, -ˌmid\ *n* : any of several light but very strong heat-resistant synthetic materials used esp. in textiles and plastics

Arap·a·ho *or* **Arap·a·hoe** \ə-'ra-pə-ˌhō\ *n, pl* **-ho** *or* **-hos** *or* **-hoe** *or* **-hoes** : a member of an American Indian people of the western U.S.

ar·bi·ter \'är-bə-tər\ *n* ♦ : one having power to decide a dispute

♦ arbitrator, judge, referee, umpire — more at JUDGE ♦ arbitrator, broker, go-between, intercessor, intermediary, mediator, middleman, peacemaker — more at MEDIATOR

ar·bi·trage \'är-bə-ˌträzh\ *n* [F, fr. MF, arbitration] : the purchase and sale of the same or equivalent securities in different markets in order to profit from price discrepancies

ar·bi·tra·geur \ˌär-bə-(ˌ)trä-'zhər\ *or* **ar·bi·trag·er** \'är-bə-ˌträ-zhər\ *n* : one who practices arbitrage

ar·bit·ra·ment \är-'bi-trə-mənt\ *n* **1** : the act of deciding a dispute **2** : the judgment given by an arbitrator

ar·bi·trary \'är-bə-ˌtrer-ē\ *adj* **1** ♦ : marked by or resulting from the unrestrained and often tyrannical exercise of power **2** ♦ : determined by will or caprice : selected at random — **ar·bi·trari·ly** \ˌär-bə-'trer-ə-lē\ *adv* — **ar·bi·trari·ness** \'är-bə-ˌtrer-ē-nəs\ *n*

♦ [1] dictatorial, high-handed, imperious, peremptory, willful; *also* arrogant, commanding, demanding, dominant, domineering, haughty, imperative, lordly, masterful, overbearing, presumptuous ♦ [2] aimless, desultory, erratic, haphazard, random, scattered, stray — more at RANDOM

ar·bi·trate \'är-bə-ˌtrāt\ *vb* **-trat·ed; -trat·ing** **1** : to act as arbitrator **2** ♦ : to act on as arbitrator **3** : to submit for decision to an arbitrator — **ar·bi·tra·tion** \ˌär-bə-'trā-shən\ *n*

♦ adjudicate, decide, determine, judge, referee, rule, settle, umpire — more at JUDGE

ar·bi·tra·tor \'är-bə-ˌtrā-tər\ *n* ♦ : one chosen to settle differences between two parties in a controversy

♦ arbiter, judge, referee, umpire — more at JUDGE ♦ arbiter, broker, go-between, intercessor, intermediary, mediator, middleman, peacemaker — more at MEDIATOR

ar·bor *or Can and Brit* **ar·bour** \'är-bər\ *n* [ME *erber, herber* garden, fr. AF, fr. *herbe* herb, grass] : a shelter formed of or covered with vines or branches

ar·bo·re·al \är-'bōr-ē-əl\ *adj* **1** : of, relating to, or resembling a tree **2** : living in trees ⟨~ monkeys⟩

ar·bo·re·tum \ˌär-bə-'rē-təm\ *n, pl* **-retums** *or* **-re·ta** \-tə\ [L, plantation of trees, fr. *arbor* tree] : a place where trees and plants are grown for scientific and educational purposes

ar·bor·vi·tae \ˌär-bər-'vī-tē\ *n* : any of various evergreen trees and shrubs with scalelike leaves that are related to the cypresses

ar·bu·tus \är-'byü-təs\ *n* : TRAILING ARBUTUS

¹arc \'ärk\ *n* **1** : a sustained luminous discharge of electricity (as between two electrodes) **2** ♦ : a continuous portion of a curved line (as part of the circumference of a circle)

♦ arch, bend, bow, crook, curve — more at BEND

²arc *vb* **arced** \'ärkt\; **arc·ing** \'är-kiŋ\ **1** : to form an electric arc **2** ♦ : to follow an arc-shaped course

♦ bend, bow, crook, curve, hook, round, sweep, swerve, wheel — more at CURVE

ARC *abbr* **1** AIDS-related complex **2** American Red Cross

ar·cade \är-'kād\ *n* **1** : an arched or covered passageway; *esp* : one lined with shops **2** : a row of arches with their supporting columns **3** : an amusement center having coin-operated games

ar·cane \är-'kān\ *adj* : SECRET, MYSTERIOUS

¹arch \'ärch\ *n* **1** : a curved structure spanning an opening (as a door) **2** : something resembling an arch **3** : ARCHWAY

♦ arc, bend, bow, crook, curve — more at BEND

²arch *vb* **1** : to cover with an arch **2** : to form or bend into an arch

³arch *adj* **1** ♦ : most important : CHIEF **2** ♦ : impertinently bold and impudent — **arch·ly** *adv* — **arch·ness** *n*

♦ [1] chief, dominant, foremost, key, main, predominant, primary, principal — more at FOREMOST ♦ [2] bold, brash, cheeky, cocky, fresh, impertinent, impudent, insolent, nervy, sassy, saucy — more at NERVY

⁴arch *abbr* architect; architectural; architecture

ar·chae·ol·o·gy *or* **ar·che·ol·o·gy** \ˌär-kē-'ä-lə-jē\ *n* : the study of past human life as revealed by relics left by ancient peoples — **ar·chae·o·log·i·cal** \-ə-'lä-ji-kəl\ *adj* — **ar·chae·ol·o·gist** \-'ä-lə-jist\ *n*

ar·cha·ic \är-'kā-ik\ *adj* **1** : having the characteristics of the language of the past and surviving chiefly in specialized uses ⟨~ words⟩ **2** ♦ : belonging to an earlier time : ANTIQUATED — **ar·cha·i·cal·ly** \-i-k(ə-)lē\ *adv*

♦ antiquated, dated, obsolete, outdated, outmoded, outworn, passé — more at OBSOLETE

arch·an·gel \'är-ˌkān-jəl\ *n* : a chief angel

arch·bish·op \ärch-'bi-shəp\ *n* : a bishop of high rank

arch·bish·op·ric \-shə-(ˌ)prik\ *n* : the jurisdiction or office of an archbishop

arch·con·ser·va·tive \(ˌ)ärch-kən-'sər-və-tiv\ *n* : an extreme conservative — **archconservative** *adj*

arch·dea·con \-'dē-kən\ *n* : a church official who assists a diocesan bishop in ceremonial or administrative functions

arch·di·o·cese \-'dī-ə-səs, -ˌsēz\ *n* : the diocese of an archbishop

arch·duke \-'dük, -'dyük\ *n* **1** : a sovereign prince **2** : a prince of the imperial family of Austria

Ar·che·an \är-'kē-ən\ *adj* : of, relating to, or being the earliest eon of geologic history — **Archean** *n*

arch·en·e·my \ˌärch-'e-nə-mē\ *n, pl* **-mies** : a principal enemy

Ar·cheo·zo·ic \ˌär-kē-ə-'zō-ik\ *adj* : ARCHEAN — **Archeozoic** *n*

ar·chery \'är-chə-rē\ *n* : the art or practice of shooting with bow and arrows — **ar·cher** \'är-chər\ *n*

ar·che·type \'är-ki-ˌtīp\ *n* : the original pattern or model of all things of the same type

arch·fiend \ˌärch-'fēnd\ *n* : a chief fiend; *esp* : SATAN

ar·chi·epis·co·pal \ˌär-kē-ə-'pis-kə-pəl\ *adj* : of or relating to an archbishop

ar·chi·man·drite \ˌär-kə-'man-ˌdrīt\ *n* : a dignitary in an Eastern church ranking below a bishop

ar·chi·pel·a·go \ˌär-kə-'pe-lə-ˌgō, ˌär-chə-\ *n, pl* **-goes** *or* **-gos** : a group of islands

ar·chi·tect \'är-kə-ˌtekt\ *n* **1** : a person who plans buildings and oversees their construction **2** : a person who designs and guides a plan or undertaking

ar·chi·tec·ture \'är-kə-ˌtek-chər\ *n* **1** : the art or science of planning and building structures **2** : a method or style of building **3** : the manner in which the elements (as of a design) are arranged or organized — **ar·chi·tec·tur·al** \ˌär-kə-'tek-chə-rəl, -'tek-shrəl\ *adj* — **ar·chi·tec·tur·al·ly** *adv*

ar·chi·trave \'är-kə-ˌtrāv\ *n* : the supporting horizontal member just above the columns in a building in the classical style of architecture

ar·chive \'är-ˌkīv\ *n* : a place for keeping public records; *also* : public records — often used in pl.

ar·chi·vist \'är-kə-vist, -ˌkī-\ *n* : a person in charge of archives

ar·chon \'är-ˌkän, -kən\ *n* : a chief magistrate of ancient Athens

arch·way \'ärch-ˌwā\ *n* : a passageway under an arch; *also* : an arch over a passage

arc lamp *n* : a gas-filled electric lamp that produces light when a current arcs between incandescent electrodes

¹**arc·tic** \'ärk-tik, 'är-tik\ *adj* [ME *artik*, fr. L *arcticus*, fr. Gk *arktikos*, fr. *arktos* bear, Ursa Major, north] **1** *often cap* : of or relating to the north pole or the region near it **2** ♦ : bitter cold : FRIGID

♦ bitter, cold, freezing, frigid, frosty, glacial, icy, polar

²**arc·tic** \'är-tik, 'ärk-tik\ *n* : a rubber overshoe that reaches to the ankle or above

arctic circle *n, often cap A&C* : the parallel of latitude that is approximately 66½ degrees north of the equator

-ard *also* **-art** *n suffix* : one that is characterized by performing some action, possessing some quality, or being associated with some thing esp. conspicuously or excessively ⟨brag*art*⟩ ⟨dull*ard*⟩

ar·dent \'är-dᵊnt\ *adj* **1** ♦ : characterized by warmth of feeling typically expressed in eager zealous support or activity **2** : FIERY, HOT **3** : GLOWING — **ar·dent·ly** *adv*

♦ burning, charged, emotional, fervent, fiery, impassioned, passionate, vehement — more at FERVENT
♦ avid, eager, enthusiastic, gung ho, hot, hungry, keen — more at EAGER

ar·dor *or Can and Brit* **ar·dour** \'är-dər\ *n* **1 a** ♦ : warmth of feeling **b** ♦ : eagerness and ardent interest in pursuit of something **2** : sexual excitement

♦ [1a] emotion, fervency, fervor, heat, intensity, passion, vehemence, warmth; *also* histrionics, mawkishness, melodrama, sentimentality **Ant** impassivity
♦ [1b] avidity, eagerness, enthusiasm, excitement, hunger, impatience, keenness, thirst — more at EAGERNESS

ar·du·ous \'är-jə-wəs, -dyü-wəs\ *adj* **1** ♦ : hard to accomplish or achieve : DIFFICULT **2** ♦ : marked by great labor or effort — **ar·du·ous·ness** *n*

♦ [1, 2] demanding, difficult, exacting, formidable, grueling, hard, laborious, strenuous, toilsome, tough — more at HARD

ar·du·ous·ly \-lē\ *adv* : in an arduous manner

¹**are** *pres 2d sing or pres pl of* BE

²**are** \'är\ *n* : a metric measure equal to 100 square meters

ar·ea \'ar-ē-ə\ *n* **1** : a flat surface or space **2** : the amount of surface included (as within the lines of a geometric figure) **3** ♦ : range or extent of some thing or concept : FIELD **4** ♦ : any particular extent of space or surface : REGION

♦ [3] arena, demesne, department, discipline, domain, field, line, province, realm, specialty, sphere — more at FIELD ♦ [4] demesne, field, region, zone — more at REGION

area code *n* : a 3-digit number that identifies each telephone service area in a country (as the U.S. or Canada)

are·na \ə-'rē-nə\ *n* [L *harena, arena* sand, sandy place] **1** ♦ : an enclosed area used for public entertainment **2** ♦ : a sphere of activity or competition

♦ [1] hall, theater — more at HALL ♦ [2] area, demesne, department, discipline, domain, field, line, province, realm, specialty, sphere — more at FIELD

Ar·gen·tine \'är-jən-ˌtēn, -ˌtīn\ *or* **Ar·gen·tin·ean** *or* **Ar·gen·tin·i·an** \ˌär-jən-'ti-nē-ən\ *n* : a native or inhabitant of Argentina — **Argentine** *or* **Argentinean** *or* **Argentinian** *adj*

ar·gen·tite \'är-jən-ˌtīt\ *n* : a dark gray mineral that is an important ore of silver

ar·gon \'är-ˌgän\ *n* [Gk, neut. of *argos* idle, lazy, fr. *a-* not + *ergon* work; fr. its relative inertness] : a colorless odorless gaseous chemical element found in the air and used for filling electric lamps

ar·go·sy \'är-gə-sē\ *n, pl* **-sies** **1** : a large merchant ship **2** : FLEET

ar·got \'är-gət, -ˌgō\ *n* ♦ : the language of a particular group or class

♦ cant, jargon, language, lingo, slang, terminology, vocabulary — more at TERMINOLOGY

ar·gu·able \'är-gyü-ə-bəl\ *adj* ♦ : open to argument, dispute, or question

♦ debatable, disputable, doubtful, moot, questionable — more at DEBATABLE

ar·gu·ably \'är-gyü-(ə-)blē\ *adv* : it can be argued

ar·gue \'är-gyü\ *vb* **ar·gued; ar·gu·ing** **1** ♦ : to give reasons for or against something **2** ♦ : to contend in words : DISPUTE ⟨*argued* about money⟩ **3** ♦ : to consider the pros and cons of **4** ♦ : to persuade by giving reasons

♦ [1] assert, contend, maintain, plead, reason; *also* claim, insist ♦ [2] bicker, brawl, dispute, fall out, fight, hassle, quarrel, row, scrap, spat, squabble, wrangle; *also* challenge, dare, defy ♦ [3] chew over, debate, discuss, dispute, hash, moot, talk over — more at DISCUSS ♦ [4] convince, get, induce, move, persuade, prevail, satisfy, talk, win — more at PERSUADE

ar·gu·er \'är-gyə-wər\ *n* ♦ : one who argues

♦ debater, disputant, disputer — more at DISPUTANT

ar·gu·ment \'är-gyə-mənt\ *n* **1** ♦ : a reason offered in proof **2** ♦ : discourse intended to persuade **3** ♦ : a usu. verbal conflict : QUARREL

♦ [1] assertion, contention, thesis — more at CONTENTION ♦ [1] case, defense (*or* defence), explanation, rationale, reason — more at REASON ♦ [2] colloquy, conference, deliberation, discourse, discussion, give-and-take, parley, talk — more at DISCUSSION ♦ [3] altercation, bicker, brawl, disagreement, dispute, fight, hassle, misunderstanding, quarrel, row, scrap, spat, squabble, wrangle; *also* clash, run-in, skirmish, tussle

ar·gu·men·ta·tion \ˌär-gyə-mən-'tā-shən\ *n* : the art of formal discussion

ar·gu·men·ta·tive \ˌär-gyə-'men-tə-tiv\ *adj* ♦ : inclined to argue

♦ contentious, disputatious, quarrelsome, scrappy; *also* bellicose, belligerent, combative, pugnacious, truculent

ar·gyle *also* **ar·gyll** \'är-ˌgīl\ *n, often cap* : a geometric knitting pattern of varicolored diamonds on a single background color; *also* : a sock knit in this pattern

aria \'är-ē-ə\ *n* : an accompanied elaborate vocal solo forming part of a larger work

ar·id \'ar-əd\ *adj* : very dry; *esp* ♦ : having insufficient rainfall to support agriculture — **arid·i·ty** \ə-'ri-də-tē\ *n*

♦ dry, sere, thirsty — more at DRY

Ar·i·es \'ar-ˌēz, -ē-ˌēz\ *n* [L, lit., ram] **1** : a zodiacal constellation between Pisces and Taurus pictured as a ram **2** : the 1st sign of the zodiac in astrology; *also* : one born under this sign

aright \ə-'rīt\ *adv* : RIGHT, CORRECTLY

arise \ə-'rīz\ *vb* **arose** \-'rōz\; **aris·en** \-'riz-ᵊn\; **aris·ing** \-'rī-ziŋ\ **1** : to get up **2 a** ♦ : to originate from a source **b** ♦ : to come into being or to attention **3** ♦ : to move upward : ASCEND

♦ [2a] begin, commence, dawn, form, materialize, originate, spring, start — more at BEGIN ♦ [2b] crop, emerge, materialize, spring, surface; *also* appear, come out, show up, turn up ♦ [3] ascend, climb, lift, mount, rise, soar, up — more at ASCEND

ar·is·toc·ra·cy \ˌar-ə-'stä-krə-sē\ *n, pl* **-cies** **1** : government by a noble or privileged class; *also* : a state so governed **2** : the governing class of an aristocracy **3** : UPPER CLASS

aris·to·crat \ə-'ris-tə-ˌkrat\ *n* ♦ : a member of an aristocracy

♦ gentleman, grandee, noble, patrician — more at GEN-TLEMAN

aris·to·crat·ic \ə-ˌris-tə-'kra-tik\ *adj* ♦ : belonging to, having the qualities of, or favoring aristocracy

♦ genteel, gentle, grand, highborn, noble, patrician, wellborn — more at NOBLE

arith *abbr* arithmetic; arithmetical

arith·me·tic \ə-'rith-mə-ˌtik\ *n* **1** ♦ : a branch of mathematics that deals with computations usu. with nonnegative real numbers **2** ♦ : the process or an act of computing or calculating : COMPUTATION, CALCULATION — **ar·ith·met·ic** \ˌar-ith-'me-tik\ *or* **ar·ith·met·i·cal** \-ti-kəl\ *adj* — **ar·ith·met·i·cal·ly** \-ti-k(ə-)lē\ *adv* — **arith·me·ti·cian** \ə-ˌrith-mə-'ti-shən\ *n*

♦ calculation, computation, reckoning — more at CAL-CULATION

arithmetic mean *n* : the sum of a set of numbers divided by the number of numbers in the set

Ariz *abbr* Arizona

ark \'ärk\ *n* **1** : a boat held to resemble that of Noah's at the time of the Flood **2** : the sacred chest in a synagogue representing to Hebrews the presence of God; *also* : the repository for the scrolls of the Torah

Ark *abbr* Arkansas

¹**arm** \'ärm\ *n* [ME, fr. OE *earm*] **1** : a human upper limb and esp. the part between the shoulder and wrist; *also* : a corresponding limb of a 2-footed vertebrate **2** : something resembling an arm in shape or position ⟨an ∼ of land⟩ ⟨an ∼ of a chair⟩ **3** ♦ : the power, authority, or resources wielded (as by an individual or group) ⟨the ∼ of the law⟩ — **armed** \'ärmd\ *adj* — **arm·less** *adj*

♦ authority, clutch, command, control, dominion, grip, hold, mastery, power, sway — more at POWER

²**arm** *vb* [ME, fr. AF *armer*, fr. L *armare*, fr. *arma* weapons, tools] : to furnish with weapons

³**arm** *n* **1** ♦ : a means (as a weapon) of offense or defense; *esp* : FIREARM **2** : a branch of the military forces **3** *pl* : the hereditary heraldic devices of a family

♦ firearm, gun, piece — more at GUN

ar·ma·da \är-'mä-də, -'mā-\ *n* **1** : a fleet of warships **2** ♦ : a large force or group usu. of moving things ⟨an ∼ of trailers⟩

♦ caravan, cavalcade, fleet, motorcade, train — more at FLEET

ar·ma·dil·lo \ˌär-mə-'di-lō\ *n, pl* **-los** [Sp, fr. dim. of *armado* armed one] : any of several small burrowing mammals with the head and body protected by an armor of bony plates

Ar·ma·ged·don \ˌär-mə-'ged-ᵊn\ *n* : a final conclusive battle between the forces of good and evil; *also* : the site or time of this

ar·ma·ment \'är-mə-mənt\ *n* **1** : military strength **2** : arms and equipment (as of a tank or combat unit) **3** : the process of preparing for war

ar·ma·ture \'är-mə-ˌchùr, -chər\ *n* **1** : a protective covering or structure (as the spines of a cactus) **2** : the rotating part of an electric generator or motor; *also* : the movable part in an electromagnetic device (as a loudspeaker)

arm·chair \'ärm-ˌcher\ *n* : a chair with armrests

armed forces *n pl* ♦ : the combined military, naval, and air forces of a nation

♦ military, services, troops; *also* GI's, men-at-arms, rank and file, soldiery

Ar·me·nian \är-'mē-nē-ən\ *n* : a native or inhabitant of Armenia

arm·ful \'ärm-ˌfùl\ *n, pl* **armfuls** *or* **arms·ful** \'ärmz-ˌfùl\ : as much as the arm or arms can hold

arm·hole \'ärm-ˌhōl\ *n* : an opening for the arm in a garment

ar·mi·stice \'är-mə-stəs\ *n* : temporary suspension of hostilities by mutual agreement : TRUCE

arm·let \'ärm-lət\ *n* : a band worn around the upper arm

ar·mor *or Can and Brit* **ar·mour** \'är-mər\ *n* **1** ♦ : protective covering **2** ♦ : a quality or circumstance that affords protection **3** : armored forces and vehicles — **ar·mored** \-mərd\ *adj*

♦ [1] capsule, case, casing, cocoon, cover, housing, husk, jacket, pod, sheath, shell — more at CASE
♦ [2] aegis, cover, defense (*or* defence), guard, protection, safeguard, screen, security, shield, wall, ward — more at DEFENSE

ar·mor·er \'är-mər-ər\ *or Can and Brit* **ar·mour·er** *n* **1** : a person who makes arms and armor **2** : a person who services firearms

ar·mo·ri·al \är-'mōr-ē-əl\ *or Can and Brit* **ar·mou·ri·al** *adj* : of or bearing heraldic arms

ar·mory \'är-mə-rē\ *or Can and Brit* **ar·moury** *n, pl* **ar·mor·ies** *or* **ar·mour·ies** **1** ♦ : a place where arms are stored **2** : a factory where arms are made

♦ arsenal, depot, dump, magazine; *also* fort, fortress, stronghold

arm·pit \'ärm-ˌpit\ *n* : the hollow under the junction of the arm and shoulder

arm·rest \-ˌrest\ *n* : a support for the arm

ar·my \'är-mē\ *n, pl* **armies** **1** ♦ : a body of armed personnel organized for war **2** *often cap* : the complete military organization of a country for land warfare **3** ♦ : a great number ⟨an ∼ of birds⟩ **4** : a body of persons organized to advance a cause

♦ [1] battalion, host, legion; *also* infantry, ranks, regulars, troops, troopers ♦ [3] crowd, crush, drove, flock, horde, host, legion, mob, multitude, press, swarm, throng — more at CROWD

army ant *n* : any of various nomadic social ants

ar·my·worm \'är-mē-ˌwərm\ *n* : any of numerous moths whose larvae move about destroying crops

aro·ma \ə-'rō-mə\ *n* ♦ : a usu. pleasing odor : FRAGRANCE

♦ bouquet, fragrance, incense, perfume, redolence, scent, spice — more at FRAGRANCE

aro·ma·ther·a·py \ə-ˌrō-mə-'ther-ə-pē\ *n* : massage with a preparation of fragrant oils extracted from herbs, flowers, and fruits

ar·o·mat·ic \ˌar-ə-'ma-tik\ *adj* ♦ : of, relating to, or having aroma

♦ ambrosial, fragrant, redolent, savory, scented, sweet — more at FRAGRANT

arose *past of* ARISE

¹**around** \ə-'raùnd\ *adv* **1** : in a circle or in circumference ⟨a tree five feet ∼⟩ **2** : in or along a circuit ⟨the road goes ∼ by the lake⟩ **3** : on all sides ⟨nothing for miles ∼⟩ **4** ♦ : at all times : throughout the extent ⟨mild weather the year ∼⟩ **4** ♦ : in or near one's present place or situation : NEARBY ⟨wait ∼ awhile⟩ **5** : from one place to another ⟨travels ∼ on business⟩ **6** ♦ : in an opposite direction ⟨turn ∼⟩

♦ [3b] over, round, through, throughout ♦ [4] by, close, hard, in, near, nearby, nigh — more at NEAR
♦ [6] about, back, round; *also* backward, behind, down, downward, rearward

²**around** *prep* **1 a** : on all sides of : SURROUNDING ⟨trees ∼ the house⟩ **b** : so as to encircle or enclose ⟨go ∼ the world⟩ **2** : to or on another side of ⟨∼ the corner⟩ **3** ♦ : at, within, or to a short distance or time : NEAR ⟨stayed right ∼ home⟩ **4** ♦ : here and there in or throughout ⟨barnstorming ∼ the country⟩

♦ [3] about, by, near, next to; *also* alongside, beside
♦ [4] about, over, round, through, throughout; *also* on

arouse \ə-'raùz\ *vb* **aroused**; **arous·ing** **1** ♦ : to awaken from sleep **2** ♦ : to stir up — **arous·al** \-'raù-zəl\ *n*

♦ [1] awake, rouse, wake ♦ [2] encourage, excite, fire, incite, instigate, move, pique, provoke, stimulate, stir

ar·peg·gio \är-'pe-jē-ˌō, -'pe-jō\ *n, pl* **-gios** [It fr. *arpeggiare* to play on the harp, fr. *arpa* harp] : a chord whose notes are performed in succession and not simultaneously

arr *abbr* **1** arranged **2** arrival; arrive

ar·raign \ə-'rān\ *vb* **1** : to call before a court to answer to an indictment **2** : to accuse of wrong or imperfection — **ar·raign·ment** *n*

ar·range \ə-'rānj\ *vb* **ar·ranged; ar·rang·ing** **1** ♦ : to put in order **2** : to make preparations for **3** : to adapt (a musical composition) to voices or instruments other than those for which it was orig. written **4** ♦ : to come to an agreement about : SETTLE — **ar·rang·er** *n*

♦ [1] array, classify, codify, dispose, draw up, marshal, order, organize, range, systematize — more at ORDER ♦ [4] decide, fix, set, settle; *also* agree, contract, pledge, promise

ar·range·ment \-mənt\ *n* **1 a** ♦ : the state of being arranged : the act of arranging **2** : something arranged: as **a** ♦ : a preparatory act or measure **b** : an adaptation of a musical composition **c** : an informal agreement or settlement **3** : something made by arranging parts or things together ⟨a floral ∼⟩

♦ [1a] composition, configuration, design, form, format, layout, makeup, pattern — more at COMPOSITION ♦ [1a] array, disposal, disposition, distribution, order, sequence, setup — more at ORDER ♦ [2a] blueprint, design, game, plan, project, system — more at PLAN

ar·rant \'ar-ənt\ *adj* : being notoriously without moderation : EXTREME

ar·ras \'ar-əs\ *n, pl* **arras** **1** : TAPESTRY **2** : a wall hanging or screen of tapestry

¹ar·ray \ə-'rā\ *vb* **1** ♦ : to dress or decorate esp. splendidly **2** ♦ : to arrange in order

♦ [1] adorn, beautify, clothe, deck, decorate, do, dress, embellish, enrich, garnish, ornament, trim — more at DECORATE ♦ [2] arrange, classify, codify, dispose, draw up, marshal, order, organize, range, systematize — more at ORDER

²array *n* **1** : a regular arrangement **2** ♦ : rich apparel **3** ♦ : an imposing group

♦ [1] arrangement, disposal, disposition, distribution, order, sequence, setup — more at ORDER ♦ [2] attire, best, bravery, caparison, feather, finery, frippery, full dress, gaiety, regalia — more at FINERY ♦ [3] assemblage, block, collection, group, lot

ar·rears \ə-'rirz\ *n pl* **1** : a state of being behind in the discharge of obligations ⟨in ∼ with the rent⟩ **2** : overdue debts

¹ar·rest \ə-'rest\ *vb* **1** ♦ : to bring to a stop **2** ♦ : to take into legal custody **3** ♦ : to catch suddenly and engagingly ⟨∼ attention⟩

♦ [1] catch, check, draw up, fetch up, halt, hold up, stall, stay, still, stop — more at HALT ♦ [2] apprehend, nab, pick up, restrain, seize; *also* bag, capture, catch, collar, get, grab, grapple, hook, land, nail, snare, snatch, trap *Ant* discharge ♦ [3] enchant, enthrall, fascinate, grip, hypnotize, mesmerize — more at ENTHRALL

²arrest *n* **1** : the act of stopping; *also* : the state of being stopped **2** : the taking into custody by legal authority

ar·riv·al \ə-'rī-vəl\ *n* **1** : the act of arriving **2** : one that arrives

ar·rive \ə-'rīv\ *vb* **ar·rived; ar·riv·ing** **1** ♦ : to reach a destination **2** : to make an appearance ⟨the guests have *arrived*⟩ **3** : to attain success — **arrive at** : to reach by effort or thought ⟨*arrived at* a decision⟩

♦ come, land, show up, turn up — more at COME

ar·ro·gance \'ar-ə-gəns\ *n* ♦ : an attitude of superiority that shows itself in an overbearing manner or in presumptuous claims or assumptions

♦ haughtiness, loftiness, pretense, pretension, pretentiousness, self-importance, superiority; *also* authoritativeness, dominance, high-handedness *Ant* humility, modesty

ar·ro·gant \'ar-ə-gənt\ *adj* ♦ : offensively exaggerating one's own importance — **ar·ro·gant·ly** *adv*

♦ cavalier, haughty, highfalutin, high-handed, high-hat, imperious, important, lofty, overweening, peremptory, pompous, presumptuous, pretentious, supercilious;

also authoritarian, bossy, dominant, dominating, domineering, magisterial, pontificating *Ant* humble, modest

ar·ro·gate \-ˌgāt\ *vb* **-gat·ed; -gat·ing** ♦ : to claim or seize without justification as one's right — **ar·ro·ga·tion** \ˌar-ə-'gā-shən\ *n*

♦ appropriate, commandeer, preempt, usurp — more at APPROPRIATE

ar·row \'ar-ō\ *n* **1** : a missile shot from a bow and usu. having a slender shaft, a pointed head, and feathers at the butt **2** : a pointed mark used to indicate direction

ar·row·head \'ar-ō-ˌhed\ *n* : the pointed end of an arrow

ar·row·root \-ˌrüt, -ˌrut\ *n* : an edible starch from the roots of any of several tropical American plants; *also* : a plant yielding arrowroot

ar·royo \ə-'rói-ə, -ō\ *n, pl* **-royos** [Sp] **1** : a watercourse in a dry region **2** : a water-carved gully or channel

ar·se·nal \'ärs-nəl, 'ärs-ᵊn-əl\ *n* [ultim. fr. Ar *dār ṣināʿa* house of manufacture] **1** ♦ : a place for making and storing arms and military equipment **2** : STORE, REPERTORY

♦ armory, depot, dump, magazine — more at ARMORY

ar·se·nic \'ärs-nik, 'ärs-ᵊn-ik\ *n* **1** : a solid brittle poisonous chemical element of grayish metallic luster **2** : a very poisonous oxygen compound of arsenic used in making insecticides

ar·son \'ärs-ᵊn\ *n* : the willful or malicious burning of property — **ar·son·ist** \-ist\ *n*

¹art \'ärt\ *n* **1** : skill acquired by experience or study **2** : a branch of learning; *esp* : one of the humanities **3** : an occupation requiring knowledge or skill **4** ♦ : the use of skill and imagination in the production of things of beauty; *also* : works so produced **5** : ARTFULNESS

♦ adeptness, adroitness, artfulness, artifice, artistry, cleverness, craft, cunning, deftness, masterfulness, skill — more at SKILL

²art *abbr* **1** article **2** artificial **3** artillery

ar·te·ri·al \är-'tir-ē-əl\ *adj* **1** : of or relating to an artery; *also* : relating to or being the oxygenated blood found in most arteries **2** : of, relating to, or being a route for through traffic

ar·te·ri·ole \är-'tir-ē-ˌōl\ *n* : one of the small terminal branches of an artery that ends in capillaries — **ar·te·ri·o·lar** \-ˌtir-ē-'ō-lər\ *adj*

ar·te·rio·scle·ro·sis \är-ˌtir-ē-ō-sklə-'rō-səs\ *n* : a chronic disease in which arterial walls are abnormally thickened and hardened — **ar·te·rio·scle·rot·ic** \-'rä-tik\ *adj or n*

ar·tery \'är-tə-rē\ *n, pl* **-ter·ies** **1** : one of the tubular vessels that carry blood from the heart **2** ♦ : a main channel of transportation or communication

♦ avenue, highway, road, route, thoroughfare, turnpike, way — more at WAY

ar·te·sian well \är-'tē-zhən-\ *n* : a well from which the water flows to the surface by natural pressure; *also* : a deep well

art·ful \'ärt-fəl\ *adj* **1** ♦ : performed with or showing art or skill ⟨an ∼ performance on the violin⟩ **2 a** ♦ : using or characterized by art and skill ⟨an ∼ writer⟩ **b** ♦ : adroit in attaining an end usu. by deceptive or indirect means : CRAFTY — **art·ful·ly** *adv*

♦ [1] adroit, dexterous, masterful, practiced, skillful, virtuoso — more at SKILLFUL ♦ [2a] clever, creative, imaginative, ingenious — more at CLEVER ♦ [2b] cagey, crafty, cunning, devious, foxy, guileful, slick, sly, subtle, wily; *also* astute, cute, facile, glib, sharp, shrewd *Ant* artless, ingenuous

art·ful·ness \-nəs\ *n* ♦ : the quality or state of being artful

♦ artifice, caginess, canniness, craft, craftiness, cunning, guile, slyness, wiliness — more at CUNNING ♦ adeptness, adroitness, art, artifice, artistry, cleverness, craft, cunning, deftness, masterfulness, skill — more at SKILL

ar·thri·tis \är-'thrī-təs\ *n, pl* **-thri·ti·des** \-'thri-tə-ˌdēz\ : inflammation of the joints — **ar·thrit·ic** \-'thri-tik\ *adj or n*

ar·thro·pod \'är-thrə-ˌpäd\ *n* : any of a phylum of invertebrate animals comprising those (as insects, spiders, or crabs) with segmented bodies and jointed limbs — **ar-thropod** *adj*

ar-thros-co-py \är-'thräs-kə-pē\ *n, pl* **-pies** : visual examination of the interior of a joint (as the knee) with a special surgical instrument; *also* : joint surgery using arthroscopy — **ar-thro-scope** \'är-thrə-ˌskōp\ *n* — **ar-thro-scop-ic** \ˌär-thrə-'skä-pik\ *adj*

ar-ti-choke \'är-tə-ˌchōk\ *n* [It dial. *articiocco*, ultim. fr. Ar *al-khurshūf*] : a tall herb related to the daisies; *also* : its edible flower head

ar-ti-cle \'är-ti-kəl\ *n* [ME, fr. AF, fr. L *articulus* joint, division, dim. of *artus* joint, limb] **1** : a distinct part of a written document **2** ♦ : a nonfictional prose composition forming an independent part of a publication **3** : a word (as *an, the*) used with a noun to limit or give definiteness to its application **4** : a member of a class of things; *esp* : COMMODITY

♦ composition, essay, paper, theme — more at ESSAY

ar-tic-u-lar \är-'ti-kyə-lər\ *adj* : of or relating to a joint

¹ar-tic-u-late \är-'ti-kyə-lət\ *adj* **1** : divided into meaningful parts : INTELLIGIBLE **2** ♦ : able to speak; *also* : expressing oneself readily and effectively **3** : JOINTED — **ar-tic-u-late-ly** *adv* — *n*

♦ eloquent, fluent, well-spoken; *also* facile, glib, voluble *Ant* inarticulate

²ar-tic-u-late \-ˌlāt\ *vb* **-lat-ed; -lat-ing** **1 a** ♦ : to give clear and effective utterance to ⟨~ their grievances⟩ **b** : to utter distinctly ⟨~ each note in the musical phrase⟩ **2** : to unite by or as if by joints

♦ clothe, couch, express, formulate, phrase, put, say, state, word — more at PHRASE

ar-tic-u-late-ness \-nəs\ *n* ♦ : the quality or state of being articulate

♦ eloquence, poetry, rhetoric — more at ELOQUENCE

ar-tic-u-la-tion \-ˌti-kyə-'lā-shən\ *n* **1** ♦ : the act of giving utterance or expression **2** : the act or manner of articulating sounds

♦ expression, formulation, statement, utterance, voice — more at EXPRESSION

ar-ti-fact \'är-tə-ˌfakt\ *n* : something made or modified by humans usu. for a purpose; *esp* : an object remaining from another time or culture ⟨prehistoric ~s⟩

ar-ti-fice \'är-tə-fəs\ *n* **1 a** ♦ : clever or artful skill **b** : an ingenious device **2 a** ♦ : an artful stratagem : TRICK **b** ♦ : false or insincere behavior

♦ [1a] adeptness, adroitness, art, artfulness, artistry, cleverness, craft, cunning, deftness, masterfulness, skill — more at SKILL ♦ [2a] device, dodge, gimmick, jig, ploy, scheme, sleight, stratagem, trick, wile — more at TRICK ♦ [2b] craft, craftiness, crookedness, cunning, deceit, deceitfulness, dishonesty, dissimulation, double-dealing, duplicity, guile, wiliness — more at DECEIT

ar-ti-fi-cer \är-'ti-fə-sər, 'är-tə-fə-sər\ *n* ♦ : a skilled worker

♦ artisan, craftsman, handicrafter — more at ARTISAN

ar-ti-fi-cial \ˌär-tə-'fi-shəl\ *adj* **1** ♦ : produced by art rather than nature; *also* : made by humans to imitate nature **2** ♦ : not genuine : FEIGNED — **ar-ti-fi-ci-al-i-ty** \-ˌfi-shē-'a-lə-tē\ *n* — **ar-ti-fi-cial-ly** *adv* — **ar-ti-fi-cial-ness** *n*

♦ [1] fake, faux, imitation, mock, sham, synthetic — more at IMITATION ♦ [2] affected, assumed, bogus, contrived, false, feigned, insincere, mechanical, phony, put-on, spurious, unnatural; *also* automatic, canned, concocted, fabricated, labored, manufactured, unauthentic, unreal, unrealistic *Ant* genuine, natural, spontaneous, unfeigned, unforced

artificial insemination *n* : introduction of semen into the uterus or oviduct by other than natural means

artificial intelligence *n* : the capability of a machine and esp. a computer to imitate intelligent human behavior

artificial respiration *n* : the rhythmic forcing of air into and out of the lungs of a person whose breathing has stopped

ar-til-lery \är-'ti-lə-rē\ *n, pl* **-ler-ies** **1** : crew-served

mounted firearms (as guns) **2** : a branch of the army armed with artillery — **ar-til-ler-ist** \-rist\ *n*

ar-ti-san \'är-tə-zən, -sən\ *n* ♦ : a skilled manual worker

♦ artificer, craftsman, handicrafter; *also* artist, maker

art-ist \'är-tist\ *n* **1** : one who practices an imaginative art; *esp* : one who creates objects of beauty **2** : ARTISTE **3** ♦ : one who is adept at something

♦ adept, authority, expert, master, virtuoso, whiz, wizard — more at EXPERT

ar-tiste \är-'tēst\ *n* : a skilled public performer

ar-tis-tic \är-'tis-tik\ *adj* **1** : of, relating to, or characteristic of art or artists **2** : showing taste and skill — **ar-tis-ti-cal-ly** \-ti-k(ə-)lē\ *adv*

art-ist-ry \'är-tə-strē\ *n* ♦ : artistic quality or ability

♦ adeptness, adroitness, art, artfulness, artifice, cleverness, craft, cunning, deftness, masterfulness, skill — more at SKILL

art-less \'ärt-ləs\ *adj* **1** : lacking art or skill **2 a** ♦ : made without skill : CRUDE **b** : free from artificiality : NATURAL **3** ♦ : free from guile : SINCERE

♦ [2a] clumsy, crude, rough, rude, unrefined — more at RUDE ♦ [3] genuine, honest, ingenuous, innocent, naive, natural, real, simple, sincere, true, unaffected, unpretentious

art-less-ly \-lē\ *adv* ♦ : in an artless manner

♦ ingenuously, naively, naturally, unaffectedly — more at NATURALLY

art-less-ness \-nəs\ *n* ♦ : the quality or state of being artless

♦ greenness, ingenuousness, innocence, naïveté, naturalness, simplicity, unworldliness — more at NAÏVETÉ

art nou-veau \ˌär-nü-'vō, ˌärt-\ *n, often cap A&N* [F, lit., new art] : a late 19th century design style characterized by sinuous lines and leaf-shaped forms

arty \'är-tē\ *adj* **art-i-er; -est** : showily or pretentiously artistic — **art-i-ly** \'ärt-ᵊl-ē\ *adv* — **art-i-ness** *n*

ar-um \'ar-əm\ *n* : any of a family of plants (as the jack=in-the-pulpit or a skunk cabbage) with flowers in a fleshy enclosed spike

ARV *abbr* American Revised Version

¹-ary *n suffix* : thing or person belonging to or connected with ⟨function*ary*⟩

²-ary *adj suffix* : of, relating to, or connected with ⟨budget*ary*⟩

Ary-an \'ar-ē-ən, 'er-; 'är-yən\ *adj* **1** : INDO-EUROPEAN **2** : NORDIC — **Aryan** *n*

¹as \əz, (ˌ)az\ *adv* **1** : to the same degree or amount : EQUALLY ⟨~ green as grass⟩ **2** : for instance ⟨various trees, ~ oak or pine⟩ **3** : when considered in a specified relation ⟨my opinion ~ distinguished from his⟩

²as *conj* **1** : in the same amount or degree in which ⟨green ~ grass⟩ **2** : in the same way that ⟨farmed ~ his father before him had farmed⟩ **3** : WHILE, WHEN ⟨spoke to me ~ I was leaving⟩ **4** : THOUGH ⟨improbable ~ it seems⟩ **5** : SINCE, BECAUSE ⟨~ I'm not wanted, I'll go⟩ **6** : that the result is ⟨so guilty ~ to leave no doubt⟩

³as *pron* **1** : THAT — used after *same* or *such* ⟨it's the same price ~ before⟩ **2** : a fact that ⟨he's rich, ~ you know⟩

⁴as *prep* : in the capacity or character of ⟨this will serve ~ a substitute⟩

As *symbol* arsenic

AS *abbr* **1** American Samoa **2** Anglo-Saxon **3** associate in science

asa-fet-i-da *or* **asa-foe-ti-da** \ˌa-sə-'fi-tə-dē, -'fe-tə-də\ *n* : an ill-smelling plant gum formerly used in medicine

ASAP *abbr* as soon as possible

as-bes-tos \as-'bes-təs, az-\ *n* : a noncombustible grayish mineral that occurs in fibrous form and has been used as a fireproof material

as-cend \ə-'send\ *vb* **1** ♦ : to move upward : MOUNT, CLIMB **2** : to succeed to : OCCUPY ⟨he ~ed the throne⟩

♦ arise, climb, lift, mount, rise, soar, up; *also* boost, elevate, raise, uplift, upraise *Ant* decline, descend, dip, drop, fall (off)

as·cen·dan·cy *also* **as·cen·den·cy** \ə-'sen-dən-sē\ *n* ♦ : controlling influence

♦ dominance, dominion, predominance, preeminence, supremacy — more at SUPREMACY

¹**as·cen·dant** *also* **as·cen·dent** \ə-'sen-dənt\ *n* : a dominant position

²**ascendant** *also* **ascendent** *adj* **1** : moving upward **2** : DOMINANT

as·cen·sion \ə-'sen-chən\ *n* : the act or process of ascending

Ascension Day *n* : the Thursday 40 days after Easter observed in commemoration of Christ's ascension into heaven

as·cent \ə-'sent\ *n* **1 a** ♦ : the act of mounting upward : CLIMB **b** : an upward slope or rising grade **2** ♦ : an advance in social status or reputation

♦ [1a] climb, rise, soar; *also* boost, hike, increase, raise *Ant* descent, dip, drop, fall ♦ [2] advancement, elevation, promotion, rise, upgrade — more at ADVANCEMENT

as·cer·tain \ˌas-ər-'tān\ *vb* ♦ : to learn with certainty — **as·cer·tain·able** *adj*

♦ catch on, discover, find out, hear, learn, realize, see — more at DISCOVER ♦ detect, determine, discover, ferret out, find, hit on, locate, track down — more at FIND

as·cet·ic \ə-'se-tik\ *adj* : practicing self-denial esp. for spiritual reasons : AUSTERE — **ascetic** *n* — **as·cet·i·cism** \-'se-tə-ˌsi-zəm\ *n*

ASCII \'as-kē\ *n* [*A*merican *S*tandard *C*ode for *I*nformation *I*nterchange] : a computer code for representing alphanumeric information

ascor·bic acid \ə-'skȯr-bik-\ *n* : VITAMIN C

as·cot \'as-kət, -ˌkät\ *n* [*Ascot* Heath, racetrack near Ascot, England] : a broad neck scarf that is looped under the chin

as·cribe \ə-'skrīb\ *vb* **as·cribed; as·crib·ing** ♦ : to refer to a supposed cause, source, or author : ATTRIBUTE — **as·crib·able** *adj* — **as·crip·tion** \-'skrip-shən\ *n*

♦ accredit, attribute, credit, impute — more at CREDIT

asep·tic \ā-'sep-tik\ *adj* ♦ : free or freed from disease-causing germs

♦ hygienic, sanitary, sterile — more at SANITARY

asex·u·al \ā-'sek-shə-wəl\ *adj* **1** : lacking sex or functional sex organs **2** : occurring or formed without the production and union of two kinds of germ cells ⟨∼ reproduction⟩ **3** : devoid of sexuality **4** : neither male nor female — **asex·u·al·ly** *adv*

as for *prep* : with regard to : CONCERNING ⟨*as for* the others, they were late⟩

¹**ash** \'ash\ *n* **1** : any of a genus of trees related to the olive and having winged seeds and bark with grooves and ridges **2** : the tough elastic wood of an ash

²**ash** *n* **1** : the solid matter left when material is burned **2** : fine mineral particles from a volcano **3** *pl* : the remains of the dead human body after cremation or disintegration

ashamed \ə-'shāmd\ *adj* **1** ♦ : feeling shame **2** : restrained by anticipation of shame ⟨∼ to say anything⟩ — **asham·ed·ly** \-'shā-məd-lē\ *adv*

♦ contrite, guilty, hangdog, penitent, remorseful, repentant, shamefaced — more at GUILTY

ash·en \'a-shən\ *adj* ♦ : resembling ashes (as in color); *esp* : deadly pale

♦ cadaverous, livid, lurid, pale, pasty, peaked — more at PALE

ash·lar \'ash-lər\ *n* : hewn or squared stone; *also* : masonry of such stone

ashore \ə-'shȯr\ *adv* : on or to the shore

as how *conj* : THAT ⟨allowed *as how* she was glad to be here⟩

ash·ram \'äsh-rəm\ *n* : a religious retreat esp. of a Hindu sage

ash·tray \'ash-ˌtrā\ *n* : a receptacle for tobacco ashes

Ash Wednesday *n* : the 1st day of Lent

ashy \'a-shē\ *adj* **ash·i·er; -est** : resembling ashes (as in color); *esp* : deadly pale : ASHEN

Asian \'ā-zhən\ *adj* : of, relating to, or characteristic of the continent of Asia or its people — **Asian** *n*

¹**aside** \ə-'sīd\ *adv* **1** : to or toward the side ⟨stepped ∼⟩ **2** : out of the way : AWAY ⟨put ∼ some savings⟩

²**aside** *n* : an actor's words heard by the audience but supposedly not by other characters on stage

aside from *prep* **1** : BESIDES ⟨*aside from* being pretty, she's intelligent⟩ **2** ♦ : with the exception of ⟨*aside from* one D his grades are excellent⟩

♦ bar, barring, besides, but, except, outside (of), save

as if *conj* **1** : as it would be if ⟨it's *as if* nothing had changed⟩ **2** : as one would if ⟨he acts *as if* he'd never been away⟩ **3** : THAT ⟨it seems *as if* nothing ever happens around here⟩

as·i·nine \'as-ᵊn-ˌīn\ *adj* [L *asininus*, fr. *asinus* ass] ♦ : extremely or utterly foolish

♦ absurd, crazy, cuckoo, fatuous, foolish, mad, nonsensical, nutty, senseless, silly, stupid — more at FOOLISH

as·i·nin·i·ty \ˌa-sə-'ni-nə-tē\ *n* **1** ♦ : the quality or state of being asinine **2** : something that is asinine

♦ craziness, daftness, folly, foolishness, inanity, insanity, lunacy, madness, silliness

ask \'ask\ *vb* **asked** \'askt\; **ask·ing** **1** ♦ : to call on for an answer **2** : UTTER ⟨∼ a question⟩ **3** : to make a request of ⟨∼ him for help⟩ **4** ♦ : to make a request for ⟨∼ help of her⟩ **5** ♦ : to set as a price ⟨∼ed $800 for the car⟩ **6** : to increase the likelihood of : INVITE

♦ [1] inquire of, interrogate, query, question, quiz; *also* cross-examine, examine, grill, pump *Ant* answer, reply, respond ♦ *usu* **ask for** [4] call, plead, quest, request, seek, solicit, sue; *also* apply (for), beg (for), clamor (for) (*or* clamour (for)), urge ♦ [5] charge, command, demand — more at CHARGE

askance \ə-'skans\ *adv* **1** : with a side glance **2** ♦ : with distrust

♦ distrustfully, dubiously, mistrustfully, suspiciously; *also* hesitantly *Ant* trustfully

askew \ə-'skyü\ *adj* ♦ : being out of line : AWRY — **askew** *adv*

♦ awry, cockeyed, crooked, listing, lopsided, slantwise, uneven — more at AWRY

ASL *abbr* American Sign Language

¹**aslant** \ə-'slant\ *adv or adj* : in a slanting direction

²**aslant** *prep* : over or across in a slanting direction

asleep \ə-'slēp\ *adv or adj* **1** ♦ : in or into a state of sleep **2** : DEAD **3** ♦ : lacking sensation : NUMB **4** : INACTIVE

♦ [1] dormant; *also* drowsy, nodding, sleepy, slumberous, somnolent *Ant* awake, wakeful, wide-awake ♦ [3] dead, numb, unfeeling — more at NUMB

as long as *conj* **1** : provided that ⟨do as you like *as long as* you get home on time⟩ **2** : INASMUCH AS, SINCE ⟨*as long as* you're up, turn on the light⟩

aso·cial \(ˌ)ā-'sō-shəl\ *adj* : ANTISOCIAL

as of *prep* : AT, DURING, FROM, ON ⟨takes effect *as of* July 1⟩

asp \'asp\ *n* : a small poisonous African snake

as·par·a·gus \ə-'spar-ə-gəs\ *n* : a tall branching perennial herb related to the lilies; *also* : its edible young stalks

as·par·tame \as-'pär-ˌtām\ *n* : a crystalline low-calorie sweetener

ASPCA *abbr* American Society for the Prevention of Cruelty to Animals

as·pect \'as-ˌpekt\ *n* **1** : a position facing a particular direction **2** ♦ : a particular appearance or countenance : APPEARANCE, LOOK **3** ♦ : a particular status or phase in which something appears or may be regarded

♦ [2] appearance, look, mien, presence — more at APPEARANCE ♦ [3] angle, facet, hand, phase, side; *also* air, appearance, character, color, complexion, condition, face, look, semblance, shape, state, visage

as·pen \'as-pən\ *n* : any of several poplars with leaves that flutter in the slightest breeze

as per \'az-ˌpər\ *prep* : in accordance with ⟨*as per* instructions⟩

as·per·i·ty \a-'sper-ə-tē\ *n, pl* **-ties** **1** ♦ : a characteristic making for hardship : RIGOR **2** : ROUGHNESS **3** ♦ : harshness of manner or temper

♦ [1] adversity, difficulty, hardness, hardship, rigor — more at DIFFICULTY ♦ [3] acidity, acrimony, bitterness, cattiness, tartness, virulence, vitriol — more at ACRIMONY

as·per·sion \ə-'spər-zhən\ *n* : a slanderous or defamatory remark

as·phalt \'as-ˌfȯlt\ *also* **as·phal·tum** \as-'fȯl-təm\ *n* : a dark substance found in natural beds or obtained as a residue in petroleum refining and used esp. in paving streets

asphalt jungle *n* : a big city or a specified part of a big city

as·pho·del \'as-fə-ˌdel\ *n* : any of several Old World herbs related to the lilies and bearing flowers in long erect spikes

as·phyx·ia \as-'fik-sē-ə\ *n* : a lack of oxygen or excess of carbon dioxide in the body usu. caused by interruption of breathing and causing unconsciousness

as·phyx·i·ate \-sē-ˌāt\ *vb* **-at·ed; -at·ing** : SUFFOCATE — **as·phyx·i·a·tion** \-ˌfik-sē-'ā-shən\ *n*

as·pic \'as-pik\ *n* [F, lit., asp] : a savory meat jelly

as·pi·rant \'as-pə-rənt, ə-'spī-rənt\ *n* ♦ : one who aspires

♦ applicant, campaigner, candidate, contender, hopeful, prospect, seeker — more at CANDIDATE

¹as·pi·rate \'as-pə-rət\ *n* **1** : an independent sound \h\ or a character (as the letter *h*) representing it **2** : a consonant having aspiration as its final component

²as·pi·rate \'as-pə-ˌrāt\ *vb* **-rat·ed; -rat·ing** : to draw, remove, or take up or into by suction

as·pi·ra·tion \ˌas-pə-'rā-shən\ *n* **1** : the pronunciation or addition of an aspirate; *also* : the aspirate or its symbol **2** : a drawing of something in, out, up, or through by or as if by suction **3 a** : a strong desire to achieve something noble **b** ♦ : an object of strong desire

♦ aim, ambition, design, dream, end, goal, intent, object, objective, purpose — more at GOAL

as·pire \ə-'spīr\ *vb* **as·pired; as·pir·ing** **1** ♦ : to seek to attain or accomplish a particular goal **2** : to rise aloft

♦ aim, contemplate, design, intend, plan, propose — more at INTEND

as·pi·rin \'as-pə-rən\ *n, pl* **aspirin** *or* **aspirins** **1** : a white crystalline drug used to relieve pain and fever **2** : a tablet of aspirin

as regards *also* **as respects** *prep* : in regard to : with respect to

ass \'as\ *n* **1** ♦ : any of several long-eared mammals smaller than the related horses; *esp* : one of Africa ancestral to the donkey **2** *impolite* : a foolish or unlikeable person

♦ donkey, jackass — more at DONKEY

as·sail \ə-'sāl\ *vb* ♦ : to attack violently with blows or words — **as·sail·able** *adj* — **as·sail·ant** *n*

♦ abuse, attack, belabor, blast, castigate, excoriate, jump, lambaste, slam, vituperate — more at ATTACK ♦ assault, attack, beset, charge, descend, jump, pounce (on *or* upon), raid, rush, storm, strike — more at ATTACK

as·sas·sin \ə-'sas-ᵊn\ *n* [ML *assassinus*, fr. Ar *ḥashshāshīn*, pl. of *ḥashshāsh* worthless person, lit., hashish-user, fr. *hashīsh* hashish] : a murderer esp. for hire or fanatical reasons

as·sas·si·nate \ə-'sas-ᵊn-ˌāt\ *vb* **-nat·ed; -nat·ing** : to murder by sudden or secret attack — **as·sas·si·na·tion** \-ˌsas-ᵊn-'ā-shən\ *n*

¹as·sault \ə-'sȯlt\ *n* **1** ♦ : a violent attack **2** : an unlawful attempt or threat to do harm to another

♦ aggression, attack, charge, descent, offense (*or* offence), offensive, onset, onslaught, raid, rush, strike — more at ATTACK

²assault *vb* ♦ : to make an assault on

♦ assail, attack, beset, charge, descend, jump, pounce (on *or* upon), raid, rush, storm, strike — more at ATTACK

assault rifle *n* : a military automatic rifle with a large-capacity magazine

¹as·say \'a-ˌsā, a-'sā\ *n* ♦ : analysis to determine the quantity of one or more components present in a sample (as of an ore or drug)

♦ analysis, breakdown, breakup, dissection — more at ANALYSIS

²as·say \a-'sā, 'a-ˌsā\ *vb* **1** ♦ : to make an attempt at : TRY **2** ♦ : to subject (as an ore or drug) to an assay **3** : JUDGE 3

♦ [1] attempt, endeavor (*or* endeavour), essay, seek, strive, try — more at ATTEMPT ♦ [2] analyze, anatomize, break down, break up, dissect — more at ANALYZE

as·sem·blage \ə-'sem-blij, 3 & 4 *also* ˌas-ˌäm-'bläzh\ *n* **1** ♦ : a collection of persons or things **2** : the act of assembling **3** : an artistic composition made from scraps, junk, and odds and ends **4** : the art of making assemblages

♦ assembly, conference, congregation, convocation, gathering, meeting, muster — more at GATHERING ♦ accumulation, array, bunch, collection, group, lot, package, parcel

as·sem·ble \ə-'sem-bəl\ *vb* **-bled; -bling** **1** ♦ : to collect into one place **2** ♦ : to fit together the parts of **3** ♦ : to meet together : CONVENE

♦ [1] accumulate, amass, collect, concentrate, garner, gather, group, lump, pick up, round up, scrape — more at GATHER ♦ [2] build, construct, erect, fabricate, make, make up, piece, put up, raise, rear, set up — more at BUILD ♦ [3] cluster, collect, concentrate, conglomerate, congregate, convene, forgather, gather, meet, rendezvous; *also* affiliate, ally, associate, band (together), club, collaborate, confederate, conjoin, consolidate, cooperate, consort, couple, federate, gang (up), join, merge, unite *Ant* break up, disband, disperse, split up

as·sem·bly \ə-'sem-blē\ *n, pl* **-blies** **1** ♦ : a gathering of persons : MEETING **2** *cap* : a legislative body; *esp* : the lower house of a legislature **3** : a signal for troops to assemble **4** : the fitting together of parts (as of a machine)

♦ assemblage, conference, congregation, convocation, gathering, meeting, muster — more at GATHERING

assembly language *n* : a computer language consisting of mnemonic codes corresponding to machine-language instructions

assembly line *n* : an arrangement of machines, equipment, and workers in which work passes from operation to operation in a direct line

as·sem·bly·man \ə-'sem-blē-mən\ *n* : a member of an assembly

as·sem·bly·wom·an \-ˌwu̇-mən\ *n* : a woman who is a member of an assembly

as·sent \ə-'sent\ *vb* ♦ : to join with others in agreement : AGREE — **assent** *n*

♦ accede, acquiesce, agree, come round, consent, subscribe (to) — more at ACCEDE

as·sert \ə-'sərt\ *vb* **1** ♦ : to state positively **2** : to demonstrate the existence of

♦ affirm, aver, avouch, avow, declare, lay down, profess; *also* advance, advertise, boost, plug, promote, publicize ♦ argue, contend, maintain, plead, reason — more at ARGUE ♦ allege, aver, avouch, avow, claim, contend, declare, insist, maintain, profess, protest, warrant — more at CLAIM

as·ser·tion \ə-'sər-shən\ *n* ♦ : a positive statement

♦ argument, contention, thesis — more at CONTENTION ♦ affirmation, avowal, claim, declaration, profession, protestation — more at PROTESTATION

as·ser·tive \ə-'sər-tiv\ *adj* ♦ : disposed to or characterized by bold or confident assertion

♦ aggressive, dynamic, emphatic, energetic, forceful, resounding, strenuous, vehement, vigorous — more at EMPHATIC

as·ser·tive·ness \-nəs\ *n* ♦ : the quality or state of being assertive

♦ emphasis, fierceness, intensity, vehemence — more at VEHEMENCE

as·sess \ə-'ses\ *vb* **1** ♦ : to fix the rate or amount of **2** ♦ : to impose (as a tax) at a specified rate **3** : to evaluate for taxation **4** ♦ : to determine the importance, size, or value of ⟨~ the problem⟩ — **as·ses·sor** \-'se-sər\ *n*

♦ [1, 2] charge, exact, fine, impose, lay, levy, put — more at IMPOSE ♦ [4] appraise, estimate, evaluate, rate, set, value — more at ESTIMATE

as·sess·ment \-mənt\ *n* **1** ♦ : the action or an instance of assessing : APPRAISAL **2** ♦ : the amount assessed

♦ [1] appraisal, estimate, estimation, evaluation, reckoning, valuation — more at ESTIMATE ♦ [2] duty, impost, levy, tax — more at TAX

as·set \'a-ˌset\ *n* **1** *pl* ♦ : the entire property of a person or company that may be used to pay debts **2** : ADVANTAGE, RESOURCE

♦ capital, fortune, means, opulence, riches, substance, wealth, wherewithal — more at WEALTH

as·sev·er·ate \ə-'se-və-ˌrāt\ *vb* **-at·ed; -at·ing** : to assert earnestly — **as·sev·er·a·tion** \-ˌse-və-'rā-shən\ *n*

as·si·du·i·ty \ˌa-sə-'dü-ə-tē, -'dyü-\ *n* ♦ : the quality or state of being assiduous

♦ diligence, industry — more at DILIGENCE

as·sid·u·ous \ə-'si-jə-wəs\ *adj* ♦ : marked by careful unremitting attention or persistent application : DILIGENT

♦ active, busy, diligent, engaged, laborious, occupied, sedulous, working — more at BUSY

as·sid·u·ous·ly \ə-'si-jə-wəs-lē\ *adv* : in an assiduous manner
as·sid·u·ous·ness \-nəs\ *n* : the quality or state of being assiduous

as·sign \ə-'sīn\ *vb* **1** ♦ : to transfer (property) to another **2** ♦ : to appoint to or as a duty ⟨~ a lesson⟩ **3** : FIX, SPECIFY ⟨~ a limit⟩ **4** : ASCRIBE ⟨~ a reason⟩ — **as·sign·able** *adj*

♦ [1] cede, deed, make over, transfer — more at TRANSFER ♦ [2] appoint, attach, commission, constitute, designate, detail, name — more at APPOINT

as·sig·na·tion \ˌa-sig-'nā-shən\ *n* : an appointment for a meeting; *esp* : TRYST

assigned risk *n* : a poor risk (as an accident-prone motorist) that an insurance company is forced to insure by state law

as·sign·ment \ə-'sīn-mənt\ *n* **1** : the act of assigning **2** ♦ : something assigned

♦ chore, duty, job, stint, task — more at CHORE ♦ charge, job, mission, operation, post — more at MISSION

as·sim·i·late \ə-'si-mə-ˌlāt\ *vb* **-lat·ed; -lat·ing** **1** ♦ : to take up and absorb as nourishment; *also* : to absorb into a cultural tradition **2** : COMPREHEND **3** : to make or become similar — **as·sim·i·la·tion** \-ˌsi-mə-'lā-shən\ *n*

♦ embody, incorporate, integrate — more at EMBODY

¹**as·sist** \ə-'sist\ *vb* ♦ : to give support or aid : HELP

♦ abet, aid, back, help, prop, support — more at HELP

²**assist** *n* **1** ♦ : an act of assistance **2** : the action of a player who enables a teammate to make a putout (as in baseball) or score a goal (as in hockey)

♦ aid, assistance, backing, boost, help, lift, support — more at HELP

as·sis·tance \-'sis-təns\ *n* ♦ : the act of assisting or the help supplied

♦ aid, assist, backing, boost, help, lift, support — more at HELP

as·sis·tant \ə-'sis-tənt\ *n* ♦ : a person who assists : HELPER

♦ aid, apprentice, deputy, helper, helpmate, mate, sidekick — more at HELPER

as·sist·ed living \ə-'sis-təd-\ *n* : a system of housing and limited care for senior citizens who need assistance with daily activities but do not require care in a nursing home

as·size \ə-'sīz\ *n* [ME *assise*, fr. AF, session, legal action, fr. *asseer, asseoir* to seat, fr. VL *assedēre*, fr. L *assidēre* to sit beside] **1** : a judicial inquest **2** *pl* : the former regular sessions of superior courts in English counties

assn *abbr* association

assoc *abbr* associate; associated; association

¹**as·so·ci·ate** \ə-'sō-shē-ˌāt, -sē-\ *vb* **-at·ed; -at·ing** **1** ♦ : to join in companionship or partnership **2** ♦ : to connect in thought

♦ [1] ally, band, club, confederate, conjoin, cooperate, federate, league, unite — more at ALLY ♦ [1] chum, consort, fraternize, hang around, hobnob, pal; *also* affiliate, ally, attach, band, bond, club, collaborate, confederate, conjoin, connect, cooperate, couple, gang, get along, group, hook, interrelate, join, knot, league, link, mingle, mix, rally, relate, side, socialize, team, tie, wed ♦ [2] connect, correlate, identify, link, relate; *also* compare, equate, liken

²**as·so·ciate** \-shē-ət, -sē-; -shət\ *n* **1** : a fellow worker : PARTNER **2** ♦ : one that accompanies another : COMPANION **3** *often cap* : a degree conferred esp. by a junior college ⟨~ in arts⟩ — **associate** *adj*

♦ cohort, companion, comrade, crony, fellow, mate; *also* colleague, coworker, equal, peer

as·so·ci·a·tion \ə-ˌsō-shē-'ā-shən, -sē-\ *n* **1 a** : the act of associating **b** ♦ : the state of being associated **2** ♦ : an organization of persons : SOCIETY

♦ [1b] affiliation, alliance, collaboration, confederation, connection, cooperation, hookup, liaison, partnership, relation, relationship, union; *also* business, dealings, interaction *Ant* dissociation ♦ [2] brotherhood, club, college, congress, council, fellowship, fraternity, guild, institute, institution, league, order, organization, society; *also* collective, commune, community, cooperative

as·so·cia·tive \ə-'sō-shē-ˌā-tiv, -sē-; -shə-tiv\ *adj* : of, relating to, or involved in association esp. of ideas or images

as·so·nance \'a-sə-nəns\ *n* : repetition of vowels esp. as an alternative to rhyme in verse — **as·so·nant** \-nənt\ *adj or n*

as soon as *conj* : immediately at or shortly after the time that ⟨we'll start *as soon as* they arrive⟩

as·sort \ə-'sȯrt\ *vb* **1** ♦ : to distribute into like groups : CLASSIFY **2** : HARMONIZE

♦ break down, categorize, class, classify, grade, group, peg, place, range, rank, separate, sort — more at CLASSIFY

as·sort·ed \-'sȯr-təd\ *adj* ♦ : consisting of various kinds

♦ heterogeneous, miscellaneous, mixed, motley, varied — more at MISCELLANEOUS

as·sort·ment \-'sȯrt-mənt\ *n* **1 a** : the act of assorting **b** ♦ : the state of being assorted **2** ♦ : a collection of assorted things or persons

♦ [1b] diversity, variety — more at VARIETY ♦ [2] clutter, jumble, medley, mélange, miscellany, motley, muddle, variety, welter — more at MISCELLANY

asst *abbr* assistant

as·suage \ə-'swāj\ *vb* **as·suaged; as·suag·ing** **1** ♦ : to make (as pain or grief) less : EASE **2** ♦ : to put an end to by satisfying

♦ [1] allay, alleviate, ease, help, mitigate, mollify, palliate, relieve, soothe — more at HELP ♦ [2] quench, sate, satiate, satisfy

as·sume \ə-'süm\ *vb* **as·sumed; as·sum·ing** **1** ♦ : to take upon oneself **2** ♦ : to pretend to have or be **3** ♦ : to take as granted or true though not proved

♦ [1] accept, bear, shoulder, take over, undertake; *also* adopt, embrace *Ant* disavow, disclaim, disown,

repudiate ♦ [2] affect, counterfeit, fake, feign, pretend, profess, put on, sham, simulate — more at FEIGN
♦ [3] postulate, premise, presume, presuppose, suppose; *also* accept, believe, credit, swallow

as·sumed \ə-'sümd\ *adj* **1 ♦ :** not real or genuine ⟨an ∼ cheerfulness⟩ ⟨a ∼ name⟩ **2 ♦ :** taken for granted : SUPPOSED

♦ [1] affected, artificial, bogus, contrived, fake, false, feigned, phony, put-on, sham — more at ARTIFICIAL
♦ [2] apparent, evident, ostensible, reputed, seeming, supposed — more at APPARENT

as·sump·tion \ə-'səmp-shən\ *n* **1 :** the taking up of a person into heaven **2** *cap* **:** August 15 observed in commemoration of the Assumption of the Virgin Mary **3 :** a taking upon oneself **4 :** PRETENSION **5 a :** an assuming that something is true **b ♦ :** a fact or statement taken for granted : SUPPOSITION

♦ postulate, premise, presumption, supposition; *also* hypothesis, proposition, theory, thesis

as·sur·ance \ə-'shùr-əns\ *n* **1 :** PLEDGE **2** *chiefly Brit* **:** INSURANCE **3 :** the state of being assured: as **a :** SECURITY **b ♦ :** a being certain in the mind **c ♦ :** confidence of mind or manner; *also* **:** excessive self-confidence

♦ [3b] certainty, certitude, confidence, conviction, positiveness, sureness — more at CONFIDENCE
♦ [3c] aplomb, confidence, self-assurance, self-confidence, self-esteem — more at CONFIDENCE

as·sure \ə-'shùr\ *vb* **as·sured; as·sur·ing 1 ♦ :** to make safe **2 :** to give confidence to **3 :** to state confidently to **4 :** to make certain the coming or attainment of

♦ cinch, ensure, guarantee, guaranty, insure, secure — more at ENSURE

¹as·sured \ə-'shùrd\ *adj* **1 ♦ :** sure of oneself **2 ♦ :** satisfied as to the certainty or truth of a matter

♦ [1] confident, secure, self-assured, self-confident — more at CONFIDENT ♦ [2] certain, clear, cocksure, confident, doubtless, positive, sanguine, sure — more at CERTAIN

²assured *n, pl* **assured** *or* **assureds** **:** INSURED
as·ta·tine \'as-tə-,tēn\ *n* **:** an unstable radioactive chemical element
as·ter \'as-tər\ *n* **:** any of various mostly fall-blooming leafy-stemmed composite herbs with daisylike purple, white, pink, or yellow flower heads
as·ter·isk \'as-tə-,risk\ *n* [L *asteriscus*, fr. Gk *asteriskos*, lit., little star, dim. of *astēr* star] **:** a character * used as a reference mark or as an indication of the omission of letters or words
astern \ə-'stərn\ *adv or adj* **1 :** in, at, or toward the stern **2 :** BACKWARD
as·ter·oid \'as-tə-,ròid\ *n* **:** any of the numerous small celestial bodies found esp. between Mars and Jupiter
asth·ma \'az-mə\ *n* **:** a chronic lung disorder marked by recurrent episodes of labored breathing, a feeling of tightness in the chest, and coughing — **asth·mat·ic** \az-'ma-tik\ *adj or n*
as though *conj* **:** as it would be or as one would do if **:** AS IF
astig·ma·tism \ə-'stig-mə-,ti-zəm\ *n* **:** a defect in a lens or an eye causing improper focusing — **as·tig·mat·ic** \,as-tig-'ma-tik\ *adj*
astir \ə-'stər\ *adj* **1 ♦ :** exhibiting activity **2 :** being out of bed

♦ alive, animated, busy, lively, vibrant — more at ALIVE

as to *prep* **1 :** ABOUT, CONCERNING ⟨uncertain *as to* what went on⟩ **2 :** ACCORDING TO ⟨graded *as to* size⟩
as·ton·ish \ə-'stä-nish\ *vb* **♦ :** to strike with sudden and usu. great wonder **:** AMAZE

♦ amaze, astound, bowl, dumbfound, flabbergast, floor, shock, stun, stupefy, surprise — more at SURPRISE

as·ton·ish·ing \-iŋ\ *adj* **♦ :** causing astonishment **:** SURPRISING — **as·ton·ish·ing·ly** *adv*

♦ amazing, astounding, eye-opening, shocking, startling, stunning, surprising — more at SURPRISING
as·ton·ish·ment \-mənt\ *n* **♦ :** the state of being astonished

♦ amazement, awe, wonder, wonderment — more at WONDER
as·tound \ə-'staùnd\ *vb* **♦ :** to fill with bewilderment or wonder — **as·tound·ing·ly** *adv*

♦ amaze, astonish, bowl, dumbfound, flabbergast, floor, shock, startle, stun, stupefy, surprise — more at SURPRISE
as·tound·ing \-iŋ\ *adj* **♦ :** causing astonishment or amazement

♦ amazing, astonishing, awesome, fabulous, marvelous (*or* marvellous), prodigious, stunning, stupendous, surprising, wonderful — more at MARVELOUS
¹astrad·dle \ə-'strad-ᵊl\ *adv* **:** on or above and extending onto both sides
²astraddle *prep* **:** ASTRIDE
as·tra·khan \'as-trə-kən, -,kan\ *n, often cap* **1 :** karakul of Russian origin **2 :** a cloth with a usu. wool, curled, and looped pile resembling karakul
as·tral \'as-trəl\ *adj* **♦ :** of, relating to, or coming from the stars

♦ star, starry, stellar — more at STELLAR
astray \ə-'strā\ *adv or adj* **1 ♦ :** off the right path or route **2 :** into error

♦ afield, amiss, awry, wrong — more at WRONG
¹astride \ə-'strīd\ *adv* **1 :** with one leg on each side **2 :** with legs apart
²astride *prep* **:** with one leg on each side of
¹as·trin·gent \ə-'strin-jənt\ *adj* **:** able or tending to shrink body tissues — **as·trin·gen·cy** \-jən-sē\ *n*
²astringent *n* **:** an astringent agent or substance
astrol *abbr* astrologer; astrology
as·tro·labe \'as-trə-,lāb\ *n* **:** an instrument formerly used for observing the positions of celestial bodies
as·trol·o·gy \ə-'strä-lə-jē\ *n* **:** divination based on the supposed influence of the stars upon human events — **as·trol·o·ger** \-jər\ *n* — **as·tro·log·i·cal** \,as-trə-'lä-ji-kəl\ *adj*
astron *abbr* astronomer; astronomy
as·tro·naut \'as-trə-,nòt\ *n* **:** a traveler in a spacecraft
as·tro·nau·tics \as-trə-'nò-tiks\ *n* **:** the science of the construction and operation of spacecraft — **as·tro·nau·tic** \-tik\ *or* **as·tro·nau·ti·cal** \-ti-kəl\ *adj*
as·tro·nom·i·cal \,as-trə-'nä-mi-kəl\ *also* **as·tro·nom·ic** \-mik\ *adj* **1 :** of or relating to astronomy **2 ♦ :** extremely large ⟨an ∼ amount of money⟩

♦ colossal, enormous, giant, gigantic, ginormous, huge, prodigious, titanic, tremendous, whopping — more at HUGE
astronomical unit *n* **:** a unit of length used in astronomy equal to the mean distance of the earth from the sun or about 93 million miles (150 million kilometers)
as·tron·o·my \ə-'strä-nə-mē\ *n, pl* **-mies :** the science of objects and matter beyond the earth's atmosphere — **as·tron·o·mer** \-mər\ *n*
as·tro·phys·ics \,as-trə-'fi-ziks\ *n* **:** astronomy dealing esp. with the physical properties and dynamic processes of celestial objects — **as·tro·phys·i·cal** \-zi-kəl\ *adj* — **as·tro·phys·i·cist** \-'fi-zə-sist\ *n*
as·tute \ə-'stüt, -'styüt, a-\ *adj* [L *astutus*, fr. *astus* craft] **♦ :** shrewdly discerning; *also* **:** WILY — **as·tute·ly** *adv*

♦ canny, hardheaded, knowing, sharp, shrewd, smart, wily — more at SHREWD
as·tute·ness *n* **♦ :** the quality or state of being astute

♦ acumen, caginess, canniness, hardheadedness, intelligence, keenness, sharpness, shrewdness, wit — more at ACUMEN
asun·der \ə-'sən-dər\ *adv or adj* **1 :** into separate pieces ⟨torn ∼⟩ **2 :** separated in position from each other
ASV *abbr* American Standard Version

¹as well as *conj* : and in addition : and moreover ⟨brave *as well as* loyal⟩

²as well as *prep* : in addition to : BESIDES ⟨the coach, *as well as* the team, is ready⟩

asy·lum \ə-'sī-ləm\ *n* [ME, fr. L, fr. Gk *asylon*, neut. of *asylos* inviolable, fr. *a-* not + *sylon* right of seizure] 1 ♦ : a place of refuge 2 : protection given to esp. political fugitives 3 : an institution for the care of the needy or sick and esp. of the insane

♦ haven, refuge, retreat, sanctuary, shelter — more at SHELTER

asym·met·ri·cal \ˌā-sə-'me-tri-kəl\ *or* **asym·met·ric** \-trik\ *adj* : not symmetrical — **asym·me·try** \(ˌ)ā-'si-mə-trē\ *n*

as·ymp·tote \'a-səmp-ˌtōt\ *n* : a straight line that is associated with a curve and tends to approximate it along an infinite branch — **as·ymp·tot·ic** \ˌa-səmp-'tä-tik\ *adj* — **as·ymp·tot·i·cal·ly** \-ti-k(ə-)lē\ *adv*

at \ət, (')at\ *prep* 1 — used to indicate a point in time or space ⟨be here ∼ 3 o'clock⟩ 2 — used to indicate a goal ⟨swung ∼ the ball⟩ 3 — used to indicate position or condition ⟨∼ rest⟩ 4 — used to indicate means, cause, or manner ⟨sold ∼ auction⟩

At *symbol* astatine

AT *abbr* automatic transmission

at all *adv* : in any way : in any circumstances ⟨not *at all* likely⟩

at·a·vism \'a-tə-ˌvi-zəm\ *n* : appearance in an individual of a character typical of an ancestral form; *also* : such an individual or character — **at·a·vis·tic** \ˌa-tə-'vis-tik\ *adj*

atax·ia \ə-'tak-sē-ə\ *n* : an inability to coordinate muscular movements

ate *past of* EAT

¹-ate *n suffix* 1 : one acted upon (in a specified way) ⟨distill*ate*⟩ 2 : chemical compound or complex derived from a (specified) compound or element ⟨acet*ate*⟩

²-ate *n suffix* 1 : office : function : rank : group of persons holding a (specified) office or rank ⟨episcop*ate*⟩ 2 : state : dominion : jurisdiction ⟨emir*ate*⟩

³-ate *adj suffix* 1 : acted on (in a specified way) : being in a (specified) state ⟨temper*ate*⟩ ⟨degener*ate*⟩ 2 : marked by having ⟨vertebr*ate*⟩

⁴-ate *vb suffix* 1 : cause to be modified or affected by ⟨pollin*ate*⟩ : cause to become ⟨activ*ate*⟩ 2 : furnish with ⟨aer*ate*⟩

ate·lier \ˌat-əl-'yā\ *n* 1 : an artist's or designer's studio 2 : WORKSHOP

athe·ist \'ā-thē-ist\ *n* : one who denies the existence of God — **athe·ism** \-ˌi-zəm\ *n* — **athe·is·tic** \ˌā-thē-'is-tik\ *adj*

ath·e·nae·um *or* **ath·e·ne·um** \ˌa-thə-'nē-əm\ *n* : LIBRARY 1

ath·ero·scle·ro·sis \ˌa-thə-rō-sklə-'rō-səs\ *n* : arteriosclerosis characterized by the deposition of fatty substances in and the hardening of the inner layer of the arteries — **ath·ero·scle·rot·ic** \-'rä-tik\ *adj*

athirst \ə-'thərst\ *adj* 1 *archaic* : THIRSTY 2 ♦ : having a strong eager desire

♦ eager, enthusiastic, gung ho, keen, raring — more at EAGER

ath·lete \'ath-ˌlēt\ *n* [ME, fr. L *athleta*, fr. Gk *athlētēs*, fr. *athlein* to contend for a prize, fr. *athlon* prize, contest] : a person who is trained to compete in athletics

athlete's foot *n* : ringworm of the feet

ath·let·ic \ath-'le-tik\ *adj* 1 : of or relating to athletes or athletics 2 : VIGOROUS, ACTIVE 3 : STURDY, MUSCULAR

ath·let·ics \ath-'le-tiks\ *n sing or pl* : exercises and games requiring physical skill, strength, and endurance

athletic supporter *n* : an elastic pouch used to support the male genitals and worn esp. during athletic activity

¹athwart \ə-'thwȯrt\ *prep* 1 ♦ : to or on the opposite side of : ACROSS 2 : in opposition to

♦ across, over, through — more at ACROSS

²athwart *adv* ♦ : obliquely across

♦ crosswise, obliquely, transversely — more at CROSSWISE

atilt \ə-'tilt\ *adv or adj* 1 : in a tilted position 2 : with lance in hand

-ation *n suffix* : action or process ⟨flirt*ation*⟩ : something connected with an action or process ⟨discolor*ation*⟩

Atl *abbr* Atlantic

at·las \'at-ləs\ *n* : a book of maps

atm *abbr* atmosphere; atmospheric

ATM *n* : a computerized electronic machine that performs basic banking functions

at·mo·sphere \'at-mə-ˌsfir\ *n* 1 : the gaseous envelope of a celestial body; *esp* : the mass of air surrounding the earth 2 ♦ : a surrounding influence or environment 3 : a unit of pressure equal to the pressure of air at sea level or about 14.7 pounds per square inch (10 newtons per square centimeter) 4 : a dominant effect — **at·mo·spher·ic** \ˌat-mə-'sfir-ik, -'sfer-\ *adj* — **at·mo·spher·i·cal·ly** \-i-k(ə-)lē\ *adv*

♦ air, aura, climate, flavor (*or* flavour), mood, note, temper — more at AURA ♦ climate, environment, environs, medium, milieu, setting, surroundings — more at ENVIRONMENT

at·mo·spher·ics \ˌat-mə-'sfir-iks, -'sfer-\ *n pl* : radio noise from atmospheric electrical phenomena

atoll \'a-ˌtȯl, -ˌtäl, 'ā-\ *n* : a coral island consisting of a reef surrounding a lagoon

at·om \'a-təm\ *n* [ME, fr. L *atomus*, fr. Gk *atomos*, fr. *atomos* indivisible, fr. *a-* not + *temnein* to cut] 1 ♦ : a tiny particle : BIT 2 : the smallest particle of a chemical element that can exist alone or in combination

♦ bit, grain, granule, molecule, particle

atom·ic \ə-'tä-mik\ *adj* 1 : of or relating to atoms; *also* : NUCLEAR 2 ⟨∼ energy⟩ 2 ♦ : extremely small

♦ infinitesimal, microscopic, miniature, minute, tiny — more at TINY

atomic bomb *n* : a very destructive bomb utilizing the energy released by splitting the atom

atomic clock *n* : a very precise clock regulated by the natural vibration of atoms or molecules (as of cesium)

atomic number *n* : the number of protons in the nucleus of an element

atomic weight *n* : the mass of one atom of an element

at·om·ise, at·om·is·er *Brit var of* ATOMIZE, ATOMIZER

at·om·ize \'a-tə-ˌmīz\ *vb* **-ized; -iz·ing** ♦ : to reduce to minute particles

♦ crush, grind, powder, pulverize — more at POWDER

at·om·iz·er \'a-tə-ˌmī-zər\ *n* : a device for dispensing a liquid (as perfume) as a mist

atom smasher *n* : ACCELERATOR 3

aton·al \ā-'tōn-əl\ *adj* : marked by avoidance of traditional musical tonality — **ato·nal·i·ty** \ˌā-tō-'na-lə-tē\ *n* — **aton·al·ly** \ā-'tōn-əl-ē\ *adv*

atone \ə-'tōn\ *vb* **atoned; aton·ing** 1 : to make amends 2 : EXPIATE ⟨∼ for sins⟩

atone·ment \ə-'tōn-mənt\ *n* 1 : the reconciliation of God and humankind through the death of Jesus Christ 2 : reparation for an offense : SATISFACTION

¹atop \ə-'täp\ *prep* : on top of

²atop *adv or adj* : on, to, or at the top

ATP \ˌā-ˌtē-'pē\ *n* [adenosine*tri*phosphate] : a compound that occurs widely in living tissue and supplies energy for many cellular processes by undergoing enzymatic hydrolysis

atri·um \'ā-trē-əm\ *n, pl* **atria** \-trē-ə\ *also* **atri·ums** 1 : the central room of a Roman house; *also* : an open patio or court in the center of a building (as a hotel) 2 : an anatomical cavity or passage; *esp* : one of the chambers of the heart that receives blood from the veins — **atri·al** \-əl\ *adj*

atro·cious \ə-'trō-shəs\ *adj* 1 : savagely brutal, cruel, or wicked 2 ♦ : inspiring horror, dismay, or disgust : APPALLING 3 ♦ : utterly revolting 4 ♦ : of very poor quality — **atro·cious·ly** *adv*

♦ [2, 3] appalling, awful, dreadful, frightful, ghastly, hideous, horrible, horrid, shocking, terrible — more at

HORRIBLE ♦ [4] awful, execrable, lousy, punk, rotten, terrible, wretched — more at WRETCHED

atro·cious·ness \-nəs\ *n* ♦ : the quality or state of being atrocious

♦ atrocity, frightfulness, hideousness, horror, monstrosity, repulsiveness — more at HORROR

atroc·i·ty \ə-'trä-sə-tē\ *n, pl* **-ties** 1 ♦ : the quality or state of being atrocious : ATROCIOUSNESS 2 : an atrocious act or object ⟨the *atrocities* of war⟩

♦ atrociousness, depravity, enormity, heinousness, monstrosity, vileness, wickedness — more at ENORMITY

at·ro·phy \'a-trə-fē\ *n, pl* **-phies** : decrease in size or wasting away of a bodily part or tissue — **atrophy** *vb*

at·ro·pine \'a-trə-,pēn\ *n* : a drug from belladonna and related plants used esp. to relieve spasms and to dilate the pupil of the eye

att *abbr* 1 attached 2 attention 3 attorney

at·tach \ə-'tach\ *vb* 1 : to seize legally in order to force payment of a debt 2 ♦ : to assign (an individual or unit in the military) temporarily 3 : to bind by personal ties 4 ♦ : to make fast (as by tying or gluing) : FASTEN 5 : to be fastened or connected

♦ [2] appoint, assign, commission, constitute, designate, detail, name — more at APPOINT ♦ [4] affix, fasten, fix — more at FASTEN

at·ta·ché \,a-tə-'shā, ,a-,ta-, ə-,ta-\ *n* [F] : a technical expert on the diplomatic staff of an ambassador

at·ta·ché case \ə-'ta-shā-, ,a-tə-'shā-\ *n* : a small thin suitcase used esp. for carrying business papers; *also* : BRIEFCASE

at·tach·ment \ə-'tach-mənt\ *n* 1 : legal seizure of property 2 ♦ : connection by ties of affection and regard 3 : a device attached to a machine or implement 4 : a connection by which one thing is attached to another 5 : a document or file included with an electronic message

♦ affection, devotion, fondness, love, passion — more at LOVE

¹at·tack \ə-'tak\ *vb* 1 ♦ : to set upon with force or words : ASSAIL 2 : to set to work on

♦ assail, assault, beset, charge, descend, jump, pounce (on *or* upon), raid, rush, storm, strike; *also* gang (up on), mob, swarm ♦ abuse, assail, belabor, blast, castigate, excoriate, jump, lambaste, slam, vituperate; *also* berate, harangue, harass, harry, revile, scold

²attack *n* 1 ♦ : the act or action of attacking with physical force or unfriendly words 2 ♦ : a fit of sickness

♦ [1] aggression, assault, charge, descent, offense (*or* offence), offensive, onset, onslaught, raid, rush, strike; *also* ambuscade, ambush ♦ [2] bout, case, fit, seizure, siege, spell; *also* relapse, recurrence

at·tain \ə-'tān\ *vb* 1 ♦ : to reach as an end : ACHIEVE ⟨∼ a goal⟩ 2 : to come to as the end of a progression or course of movement ⟨∼ the top of the hill⟩ ⟨∼ a ripe old age⟩ — **at·tain·abil·i·ty** \-'tā-nə-'bi-lə-tē\ *n*

♦ achieve, hit, make, score, win — more at ACHIEVE

at·tain·able \ə-'tā-nə-bəl\ *adj* ♦ : capable of being attained

♦ achievable, doable, feasible, possible, practicable, realizable, viable, workable — more at POSSIBLE ♦ accessible, acquirable, available, obtainable, procurable — more at AVAILABLE

at·tain·der \ə-'tān-dər\ *n* : extinction of the civil rights of a person upon sentence of death or outlawry

at·tain·ment \ə-'tān-mənt\ *n* 1 ♦ : the act of attaining : the condition of being attained 2 ♦ : something that has been accomplished : ACCOMPLISHMENT

♦ [1] accomplishment, actuality, consummation, fruition, fulfillment, realization — more at FRUITION ♦ [2] accomplishment, achievement, coup, success, triumph — more at ACCOMPLISHMENT

at·tar \'a-tər\ *n* [Pers 'aṭir perfumed, fr. Ar., fr. 'iṭr perfume] : a fragrant floral oil

¹at·tempt \ə-'tempt\ *vb* ♦ : to make an effort toward

♦ assay, endeavor (*or* endeavour), essay, seek, strive, try; *also* fight, strain, struggle, toil, trouble, work

²attempt *n* ♦ : the act or an instance of attempting

♦ bid, crack, endeavor (*or* endeavour), essay, fling, go, pass, shot, stab, trial, try, whack, whirl; *also* struggle, undertaking

at·tend \ə-'tend\ *vb* 1 ♦ : to look after : TEND 2 ♦ : to go or stay with as a companion, nurse, or servant 3 : to be present at 4 : to apply oneself 5 ♦ : to pay attention 6 : to direct one's attention

♦ [1] care, mind, oversee, superintend, supervise, tend — more at TEND ♦ [2] accompany, convoy, escort, squire — more at ACCOMPANY ♦ [5] hark, hear, heed, listen, mind — more at LISTEN

at·ten·dance \ə-'ten-dəns\ *n* 1 : the act or fact of attending 2 : the number of persons present; *also* : the number of times a person attends

¹at·ten·dant \ə-'ten-dənt\ *n* ♦ : one that attends another to render a service

♦ companion, escort, guard, guide — more at ESCORT

²attendant *adj* ♦ : accompanying or following as a consequence or result ⟨∼ circumstances⟩

♦ consequent, consequential, due, resultant — more at RESULTANT ♦ coincident, concomitant, concurrent — more at COINCIDENT

at·ten·tion \ə-'ten-chən\ *n* 1 ♦ : the act or state of attending esp. through applying the mind to an object of sense or thought 2 : CONSIDERATION 3 : an act of courtesy 4 : a position of readiness assumed on command by a soldier

♦ absorption, concentration; *also* fixation, obsession, preoccupation *Ant* inattention ♦ awareness, cognizance, ear, eye, heed, notice, observance, observation; *also* advisement, care, concern, consideration, regard, watch

attention deficit disorder *n* : a behavioral syndrome esp. of children that is marked by hyperactivity, impulsive behavior, and inattention

attention–deficit/hyperactivity disorder *n* : ATTENTION DEFICIT DISORDER

at·ten·tive \ə-'ten-tiv\ *adj* 1 ♦ : regarding with care or attention : OBSERVANT 2 ♦ : heedful of the comfort of others — **at·ten·tive·ly** *adv*

♦ [1] absorbed, engrossed, intent, observant, rapt; *also* interested, intrigued, involved *Ant* distracted, inattentive, unfocused, unobservant ♦ [1] alert, awake, vigilant, watchful, wide-awake — more at ALERT ♦ [2] considerate, kind, solicitous, thoughtful — more at THOUGHTFUL

at·ten·tive·ness \-nəs\ *n* ♦ : the quality or state of being attentive

♦ alertness, lookout, vigilance, watch — more at VIGILANCE

at·ten·u·ate \ə-'ten-yə-,wāt\ *vb* **-at·ed; -at·ing** 1 : to make or become thin 2 : WEAKEN — **attenuate** \-wət\ *adj* — **at·ten·u·a·tion** \-,ten-yə-'wā-shən\ *n*

at·test \ə-'test\ *vb* 1 ♦ : to certify as genuine by signing as a witness 2 : MANIFEST 3 ♦ : to bear witness : TESTIFY

♦ [1] authenticate, avouch, certify, testify, vouch, witness — more at CERTIFY ♦ [3] depose, swear, testify, witness — more at TESTIFY

at·tes·ta·tion \,a-,tes-'tā-shən\ *n* 1 : the act of attesting 2 ♦ : the proof or evidence by which something is attested

♦ confirmation, corroboration, documentation, evidence, proof, substantiation, testament, testimony, validation, witness — more at PROOF

at·tic \'a-tik\ *n* : the space or room in a building immediately below the roof

¹at·tire \ə-'tīr\ *vb* **at·tired; at·tir·ing** ♦ : to put garments on : DRESS, ARRAY

♦ apparel, array, clothe, deck, dress, garb, rig, suit — more at CLOTHE

²attire *n* ♦ : garments in general : DRESS, CLOTHES

♦ apparel, clothing, dress, duds, raiment, wear — more at CLOTHING

at·ti·tude \'a-tə-ˌtüd, -ˌtyüd\ *n* **1** : POSTURE **2** : a mental position or feeling with regard to a fact or state **3** : the position of something in relation to something else **4** : a cocky, arrogant, or hostile manner

at·ti·tu·di·nise *Brit var of* ATTITUDINIZE

at·ti·tu·di·nize \ˌa-tə-'tüd-ᵊn-ˌiz, -'tyüd-\ *vb* **-nized; -niz·ing** : to assume an affected mental attitude : POSE

attn *abbr* attention

at·tor·ney \ə-'tər-nē\ *n, pl* **-neys** ♦ : one who is legally appointed to transact business on another's behalf; *esp* : one whose profession is to conduct lawsuits for clients or to advise as to legal rights and obligations in other matters : LAWYER

♦ commissary, delegate, deputy, envoy, factor, proxy, representative; *also* ambassador, emissary, foreign minister, legate, minister ♦ advocate, counsel, lawyer — more at LAWYER

attorney general *n, pl* **attorneys general** *or* **attorney generals** : the chief legal representative and adviser of a nation or state

at·tract \ə-'trakt\ *vb* **1** : to draw to or toward oneself : cause to approach **2** : to draw by emotional or aesthetic appeal

at·trac·tant \ə-'trak-tənt\ *n* : a substance (as a pheromone) used to attract insects or other animals

at·trac·tion \ə-'trak-shən\ *n* **1** : the act or power of attracting; *esp* : personal charm **2** ♦ : an attractive quality, object, or feature **3** : a force tending to draw particles together

♦ draw, lodestone, magnet — more at MAGNET

at·trac·tive \ə-'trak-tiv\ *adj* **1** ♦ : having or relating to the power to attract **2** ♦ : arousing interest or pleasure — **at·trac·tive·ly** *adv*

♦ [1] alluring, captivating, charming, elfin, engaging, fascinating, fetching, glamorous, magnetic, seductive — more at FASCINATING ♦ [2] beautiful, cute, handsome, lovely, pretty — more at BEAUTIFUL

at·trac·tive·ness \-nəs\ *n* ♦ : the state or quality of being attractive

♦ allure, appeal, captivation, charisma, charm, enchantment, fascination, glamour, magic, magnetism — more at CHARM ♦ beauty, comeliness, handsomeness, looks, loveliness, prettiness — more at BEAUTY

attrib *abbr* attributive

¹at·tri·bute \'a-trə-ˌbyüt\ *n* **1** ♦ : an inherent characteristic **2** : a word ascribing a quality; *esp* : ADJECTIVE

♦ character, characteristic, feature, mark, peculiarity, point, property, quality, trait — more at CHARACTERISTIC

²at·trib·ute \ə-'tri-ˌbyüt, -byət\ *vb* **-ut·ed; -ut·ing** **1** ♦ : to explain as to cause or origin ⟨∼ the illness to fatigue⟩ **2** : to regard as a characteristic — **at·trib·ut·able** *adj* — **at·tri·bu·tion** \ˌa-trə-'byü-shən\ *n*

♦ accredit, ascribe, credit, impute — more at CREDIT

at·trib·u·tive \ə-'trib-yə-tiv\ *adj* : joined directly to a modified noun without a linking verb ⟨red in red hair is an ∼ adjective⟩ — **attributive** *n*

at·tri·tion \ə-'tri-shən\ *n* **1** : the act of wearing away by or as if by rubbing **2** : the act of weakening or exhausting by constant harassment, abuse, or attack **3** : a reduction in numbers as a result of resignation, retirement, or death

at·tune \ə-'tün, -'tyün\ *vb* : to bring into harmony : TUNE — **at·tune·ment** *n*

atty *abbr* attorney

ATV *abbr* all-terrain vehicle

atyp·i·cal \ā-'ti-pi-kəl\ *adj* ♦ : not typical — **atyp·i·cal·ly** \-k(ə-)lē\ *adv*

♦ aberrant, abnormal, exceptional, extraordinary, irregular, odd, peculiar, uncommon, uncustomary, unique, unusual, unwonted — more at EXCEPTIONAL

Au *symbol* [L *aurum*] gold

au·burn \'ò-bərn\ *adj* : reddish brown — **auburn** *n*

au cou·rant \ˌō-kú-'räⁿ\ *adj* [F, lit., in the current] : UP-TO-DATE, STYLISH

¹auc·tion \'òk-shən\ *n* [L *auction-, auctio,* fr. *augēre* to increase] : public sale of property to the highest bidder

²auction *vb* **auc·tioned; auc·tion·ing** \-shə-niŋ\ : to sell at auction

auc·tion·eer \ˌòk-shə-'nir\ *n* : an agent who conducts an auction

aud *abbr* audit; auditor

au·da·cious \ò-'dā-shəs\ *adj* **1** ♦ : intrepidly daring **2** : contemptuous of law, religion, or decorum : INSOLENT — **au·da·cious·ly** *adv* — **au·da·cious·ness** *n*

♦ adventurous, bold, daring, enterprising, gutsy, hardy, nervy, venturesome — more at BOLD

au·dac·i·ty \ò-'da-sə-tē\ *n* ♦ : the quality or state of being audacious; *also* : the quality of being bold to the point of rudeness

♦ brass, brazenness, cheek, chutzpah, effrontery, gall, nerve, presumption, sauce, sauciness, temerity — more at EFFRONTERY

¹au·di·ble \'ò-də-bəl\ *adj* : capable of being heard — **au·di·bil·i·ty** \ˌò-də-'bi-lə-tē\ *n* — **au·di·bly** \'ò-də-blē\ *adv*

²audible *n* : a play called at the line of scrimmage

au·di·ence \'ò-dē-əns\ *n* **1** : a formal interview **2** : an opportunity of being heard **3** : an assembly of listeners or spectators

¹au·dio \'ò-dē-ˌō\ *adj* **1** : of or relating to frequencies (as of radio waves) corresponding to those of audible sound waves **2** : of or relating to sound or its reproduction and esp. high-fidelity reproduction **3** : relating to or used in the transmission or reception of sound

²audio *n* **1** : the transmission, reception, or reproduction of sound **2** : the section of television or motion-picture equipment that deals with sound

au·dio·book \'ò-dē-ō-ˌbúk\ *n* : a recording of a book or magazine being read aloud

au·di·ol·o·gy \ˌò-dē-'ä-lə-jē\ *n* : a branch of science dealing with hearing and esp. with the treatment of individuals having trouble with hearing — **au·di·o·log·i·cal** \-ə-'lä-ji-kəl\ *adj* — **au·di·ol·o·gist** \-'ä-lə-jist\ *n*

au·dio·phile \'ò-dē-ō-ˌfīl\ *n* : one who is enthusiastic about high-fidelity sound reproduction

au·dio·tape \'ò-dē-ō-ˌtāp\ *n* : a tape recording of sound

au·dio·vi·su·al \ˌò-dē-ō-'vi-zhə-wəl\ *adj* : of, relating to, or making use of both hearing and sight

au·dio·vi·su·als \-wəlz\ *n pl* : audiovisual teaching materials (as videotapes)

¹au·dit \'ò-dət\ *n* **1** : a formal examination and verification of financial accounts **2** ♦ : a methodical examination and review

♦ check, checkup, examination, inspection, review, scan, scrutiny, survey — more at INSPECTION

²audit *vb* **1** ♦ : to perform an audit on or for **2** : to attend (a course) without expecting formal credit

♦ check, examine, inspect, review, scan, scrutinize, survey — more at INSPECT

¹au·di·tion \ò-'di-shən\ *n* : HEARING; *esp* : a trial performance to appraise an entertainer's merits

²audition *vb* **-tioned; -tion·ing** \-'di-shə-niŋ\ : to give an audition to; *also* : to give a trial performance

au·di·tor \'ò-də-tər\ *n* **1** : LISTENER **2** : a person who audits

au·di·to·ri·um \ˌò-də-'tòr-ē-əm\ *n, pl* **-riums** *or* **-ria** \-rē-ə\ **1** : the part of a public building where an audience sits **2** : a hall or building used for public gatherings

au·di·to·ry \'ò-də-ˌtòr-ē\ *adj* ♦ : of or relating to hearing or to the sense or organs of hearing

♦ acoustic, aural, auricular; *also* audible, clear, discernible, distinct, distinguishable, heard, perceptible

auditory tube *n* : EUSTACHIAN TUBE

auf Wie·der·seh·en \aúf-'vē-dər-ˌzān\ *interj* [G] — used to express farewell

Aug *abbr* August

au·ger \'ȯ-gər\ *n* ♦ : a tool for boring

aught \'ȯt, 'ät\ *n* ♦ : the arithmetical symbol 0 denoting the absence of all magnitude or quantity : ZERO, CIPHER

♦ cipher, naught, nil, nothing, zero, zip — more at ZERO

aug·ment \ȯg-'ment\ *vb* ♦ : to make greater, more numerous, larger, or more intense : ENLARGE, INCREASE

♦ add, aggrandize, amplify, boost, compound, enlarge, escalate, expand, extend, increase, multiply, raise, swell, up — more at INCREASE

aug·men·ta·tion \ˌȯg-mən-'tā-shən\ *n* **1 a** : the act or process of augmenting **b** : the state of being augmented **2** ♦ : something that augments : ADDITION

♦ accretion, addition, boost, expansion, gain, increase, increment, plus, proliferation, raise, rise, supplement — more at INCREASE

au gra·tin \ō-'grat-ᵊn, ȯ-, -'grät-\ *adj* [F, lit., with the burnt scrapings from the pan] : covered with bread crumbs or grated cheese and browned

¹au·gur \'ȯ-gər\ *n* ♦ : one held to foretell events by omens : DIVINER, SOOTHSAYER

♦ diviner, forecaster, fortune-teller, futurist, prognosticator, prophet, seer, soothsayer — more at PROPHET

²augur *vb* **1** ♦ : to foretell esp. from omens **2** ♦ : to give promise of : show potential for a good outcome

♦ [1] forecast, foretell, predict, presage, prognosticate, prophesy — more at FORETELL ♦ [2] bode, promise — more at BODE

au·gu·ry \'ȯ-gyə-rē, -gə-\ *n, pl* **-ries 1** : divination from omens **2** ♦ : an occurrence or phenomenon believed to portend a future event : OMEN, PORTENT

♦ auspice, foreboding, omen, portent, presage — more at OMEN

au·gust \ȯ-'gəst\ *adj* ♦ : marked by majestic dignity or grandeur — **au·gust·ly** *adv*

♦ dignified, grand, imposing, magnificent, majestic, regal, royal, splendid, stately

Au·gust \'ȯ-gəst\ *n* [ME, fr. OE, fr. L *Augustus*, fr. *Augustus* Caesar] : the 8th month of the year

au·gust·ness \-nəs\ *n* ♦ : the quality or state of being august

♦ grandeur, grandness, magnificence, majesty, nobility, nobleness, stateliness — more at MAGNIFICENCE

au jus \ō-'zhü, -'zhüs, -'jüs; ō-zhǖ\ *adj* [F] : served in the juice obtained from roasting

auk \'ȯk\ *n* : any of several stocky black-and-white diving seabirds that breed in colder parts of the northern hemisphere

auld \'ȯl, 'ȯld, 'äl, 'äld\ *adj, chiefly Scot* : OLD

aunt \'ant, 'änt\ *n* **1** : the sister of one's father or mother **2** : the wife of one's uncle or aunt

au pair \'ō-'par\ *n* [F, on even terms] : a usu. young foreign person who does domestic work for a family in return for room and board and to learn the family's language

au·ra \'ȯr-ə\ *n* **1** ♦ : a distinctive atmosphere surrounding a given source **2** : a luminous radiation

♦ air, atmosphere, climate, flavor (*or* flavour), mood, note, temper; *also* feel, feeling, sensation, sense, spirit

au·ral \'ȯr-əl\ *adj* ♦ : of or relating to the ear or to the sense of hearing

♦ acoustic, auditory, auricular — more at AUDITORY

au·re·ole \'ȯr-ē-ˌōl\ *or* **au·re·o·la** \ȯ-'rē-ə-lə\ *n* : HALO, NIMBUS

au re·voir \ˌō-rə-'vwär\ *n* [F, lit., till seeing again] ♦ : a concluding remark or gesture at parting : GOOD-BYE

♦ adieu, bon voyage, farewell, good-bye — more at GOOD-BYE

au·ri·cle \'ȯr-i-kəl\ *n* : an atrium of the heart

au·ric·u·lar \ȯ-'ri-kyə-lər\ *adj* **1** : told privately ⟨~ confession⟩ **2** ♦ : known or recognized by the sense of hearing

♦ acoustic, auditory, aural — more at AUDITORY

au·ro·ra \ə-'rȯr-ə\ *n, pl* **auroras** *or* **au·ro·rae** \-(ˌ)ē\ **1** ♦ : the first appearance of light in the morning followed by sunrise **2** : a luminous phenomenon of streamers or arches of light appearing in the upper atmosphere esp. of a planet's polar regions — **au·ro·ral** \-əl\ *adj*

♦ cockcrow, dawn, morning, sunrise — more at DAWN

aurora aus·tra·lis \-ȯ-'strā-ləs\ *n* : an aurora that occurs in earth's southern hemisphere

aurora bo·re·al·is \-ˌbȯr-ē-'a-ləs\ *n* : an aurora that occurs in earth's northern hemisphere

AUS *abbr* Army of the United States

aus·pice \'ȯ-spəs\ *n, pl* **aus·pic·es** \-spə-səz, -ˌsēz\ [L *auspicium*, fr. *auspic-, auspex* diviner by birds, fr. *avis* bird + *specere* to look, look at] **1** : observation of birds by an augur **2** *pl* : kindly patronage and protection **3** ♦ : a prophetic sign or omen

♦ augury, foreboding, omen, portent, presage — more at OMEN

aus·pi·cious \ȯ-'spi-shəs\ *adj* **1** ♦ : promising success : PROPITIOUS **2** : FORTUNATE, PROSPEROUS — **aus·pi·cious·ly** *adv* — **aus·pi·cious·ness** *n*

♦ bright, encouraging, heartening, hopeful, likely, promising, propitious, rosy, upbeat — more at HOPEFUL

aus·tere \ȯ-'stir\ *adj* **1** ♦ : stern and cold in appearance or manner : STERN, SEVERE **2** : ABSTEMIOUS **3** : UNADORNED ⟨~ style⟩ — **aus·tere·ly** *adv* — **aus·ter·i·ty** \-'ster-ə-tē\ *n*

♦ authoritarian, flinty, hard, harsh, heavy-handed, ramrod, rigid, rigorous, severe, stern, strict — more at SEVERE

aus·tral \'ȯs-trəl\ *adj* : SOUTHERN

Aus·tra·lian \ȯ-'strāl-yən\ *n* : a native or inhabitant of Australia — **Australian** *adj*

Aus·tri·an \'ȯ-strē-ən\ *n* : a native or inhabitant of Austria — **Austrian** *adj*

Aus·tro·ne·sian \ˌȯs-trə-'nē-zhən\ *adj* : of, relating to, or constituting a family of languages spoken in the area extending from Madagascar eastward through the Malay Peninsula to Hawaii and Easter Island

auth *abbr* **1** authentic **2** author **3** authorized

au·then·tic \ə-'then-tik, ȯ-\ *adj* ♦ : not false or imitation — **au·then·tic·i·ty** \ˌȯ-ˌthen-'ti-sə-tē\ *n*

♦ bona fide, genuine, real, right, true; *also* actual, historical, original *Ant* bogus, counterfeit, fake, false, mock, phony, pseudo, sham, spurious, unauthentic, unreal ♦ accurate, exact, faithful, precise, right, strict, true, veracious — more at FAITHFUL

au·then·ti·cal·ly \-ti-k(ə-)lē\ *adv* ♦ : in actual fact

♦ actually, genuinely, really, veritably, very — more at VERY

au·then·ti·cate \ə-'then-ti-ˌkāt, ȯ-\ *vb* **-cat·ed; -cat·ing** ♦ : to prove genuine — **au·then·ti·ca·tion** \-ˌthen-ti-'kā-shən\ *n*

♦ attest, avouch, certify, testify, vouch, witness — more at CERTIFY

au·thor \'ȯ-thər\ *n* [ME *auctour*, fr. AF *auctor, autor,* fr. L *auctor* originator, author, fr. *augēre* to increase] **1** ♦ : one that originates or creates **2** : one that writes or composes a literary work

♦ creator, father, founder, originator — more at FATHER

au·thor·ess \'ȯ-thə-rəs\ *n* : a woman or girl who is an author

au·tho·ri·sa·tion, au·tho·rise *Brit var of* AUTHORIZATION, AUTHORIZE

au·thor·i·tar·i·an \ȯ-ˌthär-ə-'ter-ē-ən, ə-, -ˌthȯr-\ *adj* **1** ♦ : characterized by or favoring the principle of blind obedience to authority **2** : characterized by or favoring concentration of political power in an authority not responsible to the people — **authoritarian** *n*

♦ autocratic, bossy, despotic, dictatorial, domineering, imperious, masterful, overbearing, peremptory, tyrannical, tyrannous — more at BOSSY ♦ austere, flinty, hard, harsh, heavy-handed, ramrod, rigid, rigorous, severe, stern, strict — more at SEVERE

au·thor·i·ta·tive \ə-'thär-ə-ˌtā-tiv, ȯ-, -'thȯr-\ *adj* ♦ : supported by, proceeding from, or being an authority — **au·thor·i·ta·tive·ly** *adv* — **au·thor·i·ta·tive·ness** *n*

♦ forceful, influential, weighty — more at INFLUENTIAL

au·thor·i·ty \ə-'thär-ə-tē, ȯ-, -'thȯr-\ *n, pl* **-ties** **1** : a citation used in support of a statement or in defense of an action; *also* : the source of such a citation **2** ♦ : one appealed to as an expert **3** ♦ : power to influence thought or behavior **4** : freedom granted : RIGHT **5 a** : persons in command **b** ♦ : the office, authority, or function of governing : GOVERNMENT **6** ♦ : convincing force

♦ [2] ace, adept, expert, master, scholar, virtuoso, whiz, wizard — more at EXPERT ♦ [3] clout, influence, pull, sway, weight — more at INFLUENCE ♦ [5b] administration, government, jurisdiction, regime, rule — more at RULE ♦ [6] arm, clutch, command, control, dominion, grip, hold, mastery, power, sway — more at POWER

au·tho·ri·za·tion \ˌȯ-thə-rə-'zā-shən\ *n* ♦ : the act of authorizing

♦ allowance, clearance, concurrence, consent, leave, license (*or* licence), permission, sanction, sufferance — more at PERMISSION ♦ commission, delegation, license (*or* licence), mandate — more at COMMISSION

au·tho·rize \'ȯ-thə-ˌrīz\ *vb* **-rized; -riz·ing** **1** ♦ : to establish by or as if by authority : SANCTION **2** ♦ : to invest esp. with legal authority

♦ [1] approve, clear, OK, ratify, sanction, warrant — more at APPROVE ♦ [2] accredit, certify, commission, empower, enable, invest, license, qualify

au·tho·rized \'ȯ-thə-ˌrīzd\ *adj* : sanctioned by authority

au·thor·ship \'ȯ-thər-ˌship\ *n* **1** : the state of being an author **2** : the source of a piece of writing, music, or art

au·tism \'ȯ-ˌti-zəm\ *n* : a disorder that appears by age three and is characterized esp. by impaired ability to communicate with others and form normal social relationships and by repetitive patterns of behavior — **au·tis·tic** \ȯ-'tis-tik\ *adj or n*

¹**au·to** \'ȯ-tō\ *n, pl* **autos** : a usu. 4-wheeled automotive vehicle designed for passenger transportation : AUTOMOBILE

²**auto** *abbr* automatic

au·to·bahn \'ȯ-tō-ˌbän, 'au̇-\ *n* : a German, Swiss, or Austrian expressway

au·to·bi·og·ra·phy \ˌȯ-tə-bī-'ä-grə-fē\ *n* : the biography of a person narrated by that person — **au·to·bi·og·ra·pher** \-fər\ *n* — **au·to·bi·o·graph·i·cal** \-ˌbī-ə-'gra-fi-kəl\ *adj* — **au·to·bi·o·graph·i·cal·ly** \-k(ə-)lē\ *adv*

au·toch·tho·nous \ȯ-'täk-thə-nəs\ *adj* : INDIGENOUS, NATIVE

au·to·clave \'ȯ-tō-ˌklāv\ *n* : an apparatus (as for sterilizing) using superheated high-pressure steam

au·to·cor·rect \'ȯ-tō-kə-'rekt\ *n* : a computer feature that attempts to correct the spelling of a word as the user types — **autocorrect** *vb*

au·toc·ra·cy \ȯ-'tä-krə-sē\ *n, pl* **-cies** ♦ : government by one person having unlimited power

♦ despotism, dictatorship, totalitarianism, tyranny — more at DESPOTISM

au·to·crat \'ȯ-tə-ˌkrat\ *n* **1** ♦ : a person (as a monarch) ruling with unlimited authority **2** : one who has undisputed influence or power

♦ [1] monarch, ruler, sovereign — more at MONARCH ♦ [2] despot, dictator, oppressor, tyrant — more at DESPOT

au·to·crat·ic \ˌȯ-tə-'kra-tik\ *adj* **1** : of, relating to, or being an autocracy **2** ♦ : characteristic of or resembling an autocrat : DESPOTIC — **au·to·crat·i·cal·ly** \-ti-k(ə-)lē\ *adv*

♦ absolute, despotic, dictatorial, tyrannical, tyrannous — more at ABSOLUTE ♦ authoritarian, bossy, domineering, imperious, masterful, overbearing, peremptory — more at BOSSY

¹**au·to·graph** \'ȯ-tə-ˌgraf\ *n* **1** : an original manuscript **2** : a person's signature written by hand

²**autograph** *vb* : to write one's signature on

au·to·im·mune \ˌȯ-tō-i-'myün\ *adj* : of, relating to, or caused by antibodies or lymphocytes that attack molecules, cells, or tissues of the organism producing them ⟨∼ diseases⟩ — **au·to·im·mu·ni·ty** \-i-'myü-nə-tē\ *n*

au·to·mate \'ȯ-tə-ˌmāt\ *vb* **-mat·ed; -mat·ing** **1** : to operate automatically using mechanical or electronic devices **2** : to convert to automatic operation — **au·to·ma·tion** \ȯ-tə-'mā-shən\ *n*

automated teller machine *n* : a computer terminal allowing access to one's own bank accounts

¹**au·to·mat·ic** \ˌȯ-tə-'ma-tik\ *adj* **1** ♦ : largely or wholly involuntary **2** ♦ : made so that certain parts act in a desired manner at the proper time : SELF-ACTING — **au·to·mat·i·cal·ly** \-ti-k(ə-)lē\ *adv*

♦ [1] involuntary, mechanical, spontaneous; *also* conditioned, natural, reactive, reflex, simple, subliminal, unconscious, unforced ♦ [2] laborsaving (*or* laboursaving), robotic, self-acting — more at LABORSAVING

²**automatic** *n* **1** : an automatic device; *esp* : an automatic firearm **2** : an automobile with an automatic transmission

au·tom·a·ton \ȯ-'tä-mə-tən, -ˌtän\ *n, pl* **-atons** *or* **-a·ta** \-ə-tə, -ə-ˌtä\ **1** : an automatic machine; *esp* : ROBOT **2** : an individual who acts mechanically

au·to·mo·bile \'ȯ-tə-mō-ˌbēl, ˌȯ-tə-mə-'bēl\ *n* ♦ : a usu. 4-wheeled automotive vehicle for conveying passengers

♦ car, machine, motor vehicle — more at CAR

au·to·mo·tive \ˌȯ-tə-'mō-tiv\ *adj* **1** : of or relating to automobiles, trucks, or buses **2** : SELF-PROPELLED

au·to·nom·ic nervous system \ˌȯ-tə-'nä-mik-\ *n* : a part of the vertebrate nervous system that governs involuntary actions and that consists of the sympathetic nervous system and the parasympathetic nervous system

au·ton·o·mous \ȯ-'tä-nə-məs\ *adj* ♦ : having the right or power of self-government — **au·ton·o·mous·ly** *adv*

♦ free, independent, self-governing, separate, sovereign — more at FREE

au·ton·o·my \-mē\ *n* ♦ : the quality or state of being independent, free, and self-directing

♦ freedom, independence, liberty, self-government, sovereignty — more at FREEDOM

au·top·sy \'ȯ-ˌtäp-sē, 'ȯ-təp-\ *n, pl* **-sies** [Gk *autopsia* act of seeing with one's own eyes, fr. *autos* self + *opsis* sight] : examination of a dead body usu. with dissection sufficient to determine the cause of death or extent of change produced by disease — **autopsy** *vb*

au·tumn \'ȯ-təm\ *n* : the season between summer and winter — **au·tum·nal** \ȯ-'təm-nəl\ *adj*

aux *abbr* auxiliary

¹**aux·il·ia·ry** \ȯg-'zil-yə-rē, -'zi-lə-rē\ *adj* **1** ♦ : providing help **2** : functioning in a subsidiary capacity **3** : accompanying a verb form to express person, number, mood, or tense ⟨∼ verbs⟩

♦ accessory, peripheral, supplementary; *also* backup, makeshift, substitute *Ant* chief, main, principal

²**auxiliary** *n, pl* **-ries** **1** : an auxiliary person, group, or device **2** : an auxiliary verb

aux·in \'ȯk-sən\ *n* : a plant hormone that stimulates growth in length

av *abbr* **1** avenue **2** average **3** avoirdupois

AV *abbr* **1** ad valorem **2** audiovisual **3** Authorized Version

¹**avail** \ə-'vāl\ *vb* ♦ : to produce or result in as a benefit or advantage

♦ benefit, profit, serve — more at BENEFIT

²**avail** *n* ♦ : advantage toward attainment of a goal or purpose : USE ⟨effort was of no ∼⟩

♦ account, service, use, utility — more at USE

avail·able \ə-'vā-lə-bəl\ *adj* **1** ♦ : present or ready for immediate use : USABLE **2** ♦ : capable of being reached : ACCESSIBLE **3** : free and able to do something ⟨∼ to meet⟩ **4** : qualified or willing to do something ⟨∼ workers⟩ — **avail·abil·i·ty** \-ˌvā-lə-'bi-lə-tē\ *n*

♦ [1] fit, functional, operable, practicable, serviceable, usable, useful — more at USABLE ♦ [2] accessible, acquirable, attainable, obtainable, procurable; *also* purchasable *Ant* inaccessible, unattainable, unavailable, unobtainable

av·a·lanche \'a-və-ˌlanch\ *n* : a mass of snow, ice, earth, or rock sliding down a mountainside

avant–garde \ˌä-ˌvän-'gärd, -ˌvänt-\ *n* [F, vanguard] : those esp. in the arts who create or apply new or experimental ideas and techniques — **avant–garde** *adj*

av·a·rice \'a-və-rəs\ *n* ♦ : excessive desire for wealth : GREED

♦ acquisitiveness, avidity, covetousness, cupidity, greed, rapaciousness — more at GREED

av·a·ri·cious \ˌa-və-'ri-shəs\ *adj* ♦ : excessively acquisitive

♦ acquisitive, avid, covetous, grasping, greedy, mercenary, rapacious — more at GREEDY

avast \ə-'vast\ *vb imper* — a nautical command to stop or cease

av·a·tar \'a-və-ˌtär\ *n* [Skt *avatāra* descent] 1 : INCARNATION 2 : an electronic image that represents and may be manipulated by a computer user (as in a game)

avaunt \ə-'vȯnt\ *adv* : AWAY, HENCE

avdp *abbr* avoirdupois

ave *abbr* avenue

Ave Ma·ria \ˌä-ˌvä-mə-'rē-ə\ *n* : HAIL MARY 1

avenge *vb* **avenged; aveng·ing** ♦ : to take vengeance for

♦ requite, retaliate, revenge; *also* castigate, fix, get, penalize, punish, scourge

aveng·er \ə-'ven-jər\ *n* ♦ : one that avenges

♦ castigator, nemesis, scourge — more at NEMESIS

av·e·nue \'a-və-ˌnü, -ˌnyü\ *n* 1 ♦ : a way or route to a place or goal : PATH 2 ♦ : a broad street

♦ [1, 2] approach, passage, path, route, way — more at PASSAGE ♦ [2] artery, road, route, street, way — more at WAY

aver \ə-'vər\ *vb* **averred; aver·ring** 1 a : to verify or prove to be true in pleading a cause b ♦ : to allege or assert in pleading 2 ♦ : to declare positively

♦ [1b, 2] affirm, allege, assert, avouch, avow, claim, contend, declare, insist, maintain, profess, protest, warrant — more at CLAIM

¹**av·er·age** \'a-və-rij, 'a-vrij\ *n* [earlier, proportionally distributed charge for damage at sea, modif. of MF *avarie* damage to ship or cargo, fr. It *avaria*, fr. Ar *'awārīyah* damaged merchandise] 1 : ARITHMETIC MEAN 2 a : an estimation of or approximation to an arithmetic mean b ♦ : a level (as of intelligence) typical of a group, class, or series 3 : a ratio of successful tries to total tries esp. in athletics ⟨batting ~ of .303⟩

♦ norm, normal, par, standard; *also* commonplace, mean, median, middle, ordinary, rule, run, status quo, usual

²**average** *adj* 1 : equaling or approximating an arithmetic mean 2 ♦ : being about midway between extremes 3 ♦ : not out of the ordinary

♦ [2] intermediate, median, medium, middle, moderate, modest — more at MIDDLE ♦ [3] common, commonplace, everyday, normal, ordinary, routine, run-of-the-mill, standard, typical, usual — more at ORDINARY

³**average** *vb* **av·er·aged; av·er·ag·ing** 1 : to be at or come to an average 2 : to be, do, or get usu. 3 : to find the average of

averse \ə-'vərs\ *adj* : having an active feeling of dislike or reluctance ⟨~ to exercise⟩

aver·sion \ə-'vər-zhən\ *n* 1 ♦ : a feeling of repugnance for something with a desire to avoid it 2 : something decidedly disliked

♦ disgust, distaste, loathing, nausea, repugnance, repulsion, revulsion — more at DISGUST ♦ allergy, disfavor (*or* disfavour), disinclination, dislike — more at DISLIKE

avert \ə-'vərt\ *vb* 1 : to turn aside or away ⟨~ the eyes⟩ 2 ♦ : to ward off

♦ forestall, help, obviate, preclude, prevent — more at PREVENT

avg *abbr* average

avi·an \'ā-vē-ən\ *adj* [L *avis* bird] : of, relating to, or derived from birds

avi·ary \'ā-vē-ˌer-ē\ *n, pl* **-ar·ies** : a place for keeping birds confined

avi·a·tion \ˌā-vē-'ā-shən, ˌa-\ *n* 1 : the operation of heavier-than-air aircraft 2 : aircraft manufacture, development, and design

avi·a·tor \'ā-vē-ˌā-tər, 'ā-\ *n* ♦ : an airplane pilot

♦ airman, flier, pilot — more at PILOT

avi·a·trix \ˌā-vē-'ā-triks, ˌa-\ *n, pl* **-trix·es** \-trik-səz\ *or* **-tri·ces** \-trə-ˌsēz\ : a woman who is an aviator

av·id \'a-vəd\ *adj* 1 ♦ : desirous to the point of greed : GREEDY 2 ♦ : enthusiastic in pursuit of an interest — **av·id·ly** *adv* — **av·id·ness** *n*

♦ [1] acquisitive, avaricious, covetous, grasping, greedy, mercenary, rapacious — more at GREEDY ♦ [2] ardent, eager, enthusiastic, keen, nuts, raring — more at EAGER

avid·i·ty \ə-'vi-də-tē, a-\ *n* ♦ : the quality or state of being avid

♦ acquisitiveness, avarice, covetousness, cupidity, greed, rapaciousness — more at GREED ♦ eagerness, enthusiasm, excitement, keenness, thirst — more at EAGERNESS

avi·on·ics \ˌā-vē-'ä-niks, ˌa-\ *n pl* : electronics designed for use in aerospace vehicles — **avi·on·ic** \-nik\ *adj*

av·o·ca·do \ˌa-və-'kä-dō, ˌä-\ *n, pl* **-dos** *also* **-does** [modif. of Sp *aguacate*, fr. Nahuatl *āhuacatl*, avocado, testicle] : a pulpy green to purple nutty-flavored edible fruit of a tropical American tree; *also* : this tree

av·o·ca·tion \ˌa-və-'kā-shən\ *n* : HOBBY

av·o·cet \'a-və-ˌset\ *n* : any of several long-legged shorebirds with webbed feet and slender upward-curving bills

avoid \ə-'vȯid\ *vb* 1 ♦ : to keep away from : SHUN 2 : to prevent the occurrence of 3 : to refrain from — **avoid·able** *adj* — **avoid·ably** *adv*

♦ dodge, duck, elude, escape, eschew, evade, shake, shirk, shun — more at ESCAPE

avoid·ance \-ᵊns\ *n* ♦ : an act or practice of avoiding or withdrawing from something

♦ cop-out, escape, evasion, out — more at ESCAPE

av·oir·du·pois \ˌa-vər-də-'pȯiz\ *n* [ME *avoir de pois* goods sold by weight, fr. AF, lit., goods of weight] 1 : AVOIRDUPOIS WEIGHT 2 : WEIGHT, HEAVINESS; *esp* : personal weight

avoirdupois weight *n* : a system of weights based on a pound of 16 ounces and an ounce of 16 drams (28 grams)

avouch \ə-'vau̇ch\ *vb* 1 ♦ : to declare positively : AVER 2 ♦ : to maintain as just or true : vouch for

♦ [1] affirm, allege, assert, aver, avow, claim, contend, declare, insist, maintain, profess, protest, warrant — more at CLAIM ♦ [2] attest, authenticate, certify, testify, vouch, witness — more at CERTIFY

avow \ə-'vau̇\ *vb* ♦ : to declare openly

♦ affirm, allege, assert, aver, avouch, claim, contend, declare, insist, maintain, profess, protest, warrant — more at CLAIM

avow·al \-'vau̇(-ə)l\ *n* ♦ : an open declaration or acknowledgment

♦ acknowledgment, admission, concession, confession — more at CONFESSION ♦ affirmation, assertion, claim, declaration, profession, protestation — more at PROTESTATION

avun·cu·lar \ə-'vəŋ-kyə-lər\ *adj* : of, relating to, or resembling an uncle

await \ə-'wāt\ *vb* ♦ : to wait for : EXPECT

♦ anticipate, expect, hope, watch — more at EXPECT ♦ bide, hold on, stay, wait — more at WAIT

¹**awake** \ə-'wāk\ vb **awoke** \-'wōk\ also **awaked** \-'wākt\; **awo·ken** \-'wō-kən\ or **awaked** also **awoke**; **awak·ing** ♦ : to bring back to consciousness : wake up

♦ arouse, rouse, wake

²**awake** adj ♦ : fully conscious, alert, and aware

♦ sleepless, wakeful, wide-awake — more at WAKEFUL
♦ alert, attentive, vigilant, watchful, wide-awake — more at ALERT

awak·en \ə-'wā-kən\ vb **awak·ened**; **awak·en·ing** \-'wā-kə-niŋ\ : to bring back to consciousness : wake up

¹**award** \ə-'word\ vb **1** : to give by judicial decision 〈∼ damages〉 **2** ♦ : to confer or bestow as being deserved, earned, or needed

♦ accord, confer, grant — more at CONFER

²**award** n **1** : a final decision : JUDGMENT **2** ♦ : something awarded : PRIZE

♦ decoration, distinction, honor (or honour), plume, prize; also badge, crown, cup, laurel, medal, order, ribbon, trophy

aware \ə-'war\ adj ♦ : having perception or knowledge : CONSCIOUS

♦ alive, cognizant, conscious, mindful, sensible, sentient, witting — more at CONSCIOUS

aware·ness \-nəs\ n ♦ : the quality or state of being aware

♦ attention, cognizance, ear, eye, heed, notice, observance, observation — more at ATTENTION

awash \ə-'wosh, -'wäsh\ adj **1** : washed by waves or tide **2** : AFLOAT **3** : covered with water : FLOODED

¹**away** \ə-'wā\ adv **1** : from this or that place 〈go ∼〉 **2** : out of the way **3** : in another direction 〈turn ∼〉 **4** : out of existence 〈fade ∼〉 **5** : from one's possession 〈give ∼〉 **6** : without interruption 〈chatter ∼〉 **7** : at a distance in space or time 〈far ∼〉 〈∼ back in 1910〉

²**away** adj **1** ♦ : absent from a place : ABSENT **2** ♦ : distant in space or time 〈a lake 10 miles ∼〉

♦ [1] absent, missing, out — more at ABSENT ♦ [2] distant, far, far-off, remote — more at DISTANT

¹**awe** \'o\ n **1** ♦ : an emotion variously combining dread, veneration, and wonder that is inspired by authority or by the sacred or sublime **2** : respectful fear inspired by authority

♦ admiration, amazement, astonishment, wonder, wonderment — more at WONDER

²**awe** vb **awed**; **aw·ing** : to inspire with awe

aweigh \ə-'wā\ adj : just clear of the bottom 〈anchors ∼〉

awe·some \'o-səm\ adj **1** : expressive of awe **2** ♦ : inspiring awe

♦ amazing, astonishing, astounding, marvelous (or marvellous), stunning, surprising, wonderful — more at MARVELOUS

awe·struck \-,strək\ also **awe·strick·en** \-,stri-kən\ adj ♦ : filled with awe

♦ amazed, stunned, thunderstruck — more at THUNDERSTRUCK

aw·ful \'o-fəl\ adj **1** : inspiring awe **2** ♦ : extremely disagreeable, unpleasant, or shoddy **3** : very great 〈an ∼ lot of money〉

♦ appalling, dreadful, frightful, ghastly, grisly, gruesome, hideous, horrible, horrid, repellent, repugnant, repulsive, revolting, shocking, terrible — more at HORRIBLE ♦ atrocious, execrable, lousy, punk, rotten, wretched — more at WRETCHED

aw·ful·ly \'o-fə-lē\ adv : to a great degree : VERY

awhile \ə-'hwīl\ adv : for a while

awhirl \ə-'hwərl\ adj : being in a whirl

awk·ward \'o-kwərd\ adj **1** ♦ : lacking dexterity or skill (as in the use of hands) **2** ♦ : lacking ease or grace (as of movement or expression) **3** ♦ : difficult to explain : EMBARRASSING **4** ♦ : difficult to deal with — **awk·ward·ly** adv — **awk·ward·ness** n

♦ [1, 2] clumsy, gauche, gawky, graceless, inelegant, stiff, stilted, uncomfortable, uneasy, ungainly, ungraceful, wooden Ant graceful, suave, urbane ♦ [3] disconcerting, embarrassing, uncomfortable; also confusing, difficult, disagreeable, impossible, inconvenient, intolerable, troublesome, unpleasant, unwieldy ♦ [4] clumsy, cranky, cumbersome, ungainly, unhandy, unwieldy — more at CUMBERSOME

awl \'ol\ n : a pointed instrument for making small holes

aw·ning \'o-niŋ\ n : a rooflike cover (as of canvas) extended over or in front of a place as a shelter

AWOL \'ā-,wol, ,ā-,də-bəl-yü-,ō-'el\ n : a person who is absent without leave — **AWOL** adj or adv

awry \ə-'rī\ adv or adj **1** ♦ : in a turned or twisted position or direction : ASKEW **2** ♦ : off the correct or expected course : AMISS 〈the plans went ∼〉

♦ [1] askew, cockeyed, crooked, listing, lopsided, slantwise, uneven; also asymmetrical, unbalanced, unsymmetrical Ant even, level, straight ♦ [2] afield, amiss, astray, wrong — more at WRONG

ax or **axe** \'aks\ n : a chopping or cutting tool with an edged head fitted parallel to a handle

ax·i·al \'ak-sē-əl\ adj **1** : of, relating to, or functioning as an axis **2** : situated around, in the direction of, on, or along an axis — **ax·i·al·ly** adv

ax·i·om \'ak-sē-əm\ n [L axioma, fr. Gk axiōma, lit., something worthy, fr. axioun to think worthy, fr. axios worth, worthy] **1** : a statement generally accepted as true : MAXIM **2** : a proposition regarded as a self-evident truth — **ax·i·om·at·ic** \,ak-sē-ə-'ma-tik\ adj — **ax·i·om·at·i·cal·ly** \-ti-k(ə-)lē\ adv

ax·is \'ak-səs\ n, pl **ax·es** \-,sēz\ **1** : a straight line around which a body rotates **2** : a straight line or structure with respect to which a body or figure is symmetrical **3** : one of the reference lines of a system of coordinates **4** : an alliance between major powers

ax·le \'ak-səl\ n : a shaft on which a wheel revolves

ayah \'ī-ə\ n [Hindi & Urdu āyā, fr. Pg aia, fr. L avia grandmother] : a nurse or maid native to India

aya·tol·lah \,ī-ə-'tō-lə\ n [Pers āyatollāh, lit., sign of God, fr. Ar aya sign, miracle + allāh God] : an Islamic religious leader — used as a title of respect

¹**aye** also **ay** \'ā\ adv : for a limitless time : ALWAYS, EVER

²**aye** also **ay** \'ī\ adv : YES — used as a function word to express assent or agreement

³**aye** also **ay** \'ī\ n, pl **ayes** : an affirmative vote

AZ abbr Arizona

aza·lea \ə-'zāl-yə\ n : any of numerous rhododendrons with funnel-shaped blossoms and usu. deciduous leaves

az·i·do·thy·mi·dine \ə-,zi-dō-'thī-mə-,dēn\ n : AZT

az·i·muth \'a-zə-məth\ n : horizontal direction expressed as an angular distance from a fixed point

AZT \,ā-(,)zē-'tē\ n : an antiviral drug used to treat AIDS

Az·tec \'az-,tek\ n : a member of a Nahuatl-speaking people that founded the Mexican empire and were conquered by Hernan Cortes in 1519 — **Az·tec·an** adj

azure \'a-zhər\ n : the blue of the clear sky — **azure** adj

¹b \'bē\ *n, pl* **b's** *or* **bs** \'bēz\ *often cap* **1** : the 2d letter of the English alphabet **2** : a grade rating a student's work as good

²b *abbr, often cap* **1** bachelor **2** bass **3** bishop **4** book **5** born

B *symbol* boron

Ba *symbol* barium

BA *abbr* **1** bachelor of arts **2** batting average

bab·bitt \'ba-bət\ *n* : an alloy used for lining bearings; *esp* : one containing tin, copper, and antimony

¹bab·ble \'ba-bəl\ *vb* **bab·bled; bab·bling 1 ♦** : to talk enthusiastically or excessively **2 ♦** : to utter meaningless sounds

♦ chatter, drivel, gabble, gibber, jabber, prattle, sputter; *also* gab, jaw, patter, prate, rattle, run on

²babble *n* **1** : foolish or idle talk **2 ♦** : continuous meaningless vocal sounds : a murmur or a continuity of confused sounds

♦ gabble, gibberish, gobbledygook, hogwash, nonsense, piffle, prattle — more at GIBBERISH

bab·bler \-b(ə-)lər\ *n* : one that babbles

babe \'bāb\ *n* **1** : an extremely young child : BABY **2** *slang* : GIRL, WOMAN **3** *slang* : a person who is physically attractive

ba·bel \'bā-bəl, 'ba-\ *n, often cap* [fr. the Tower of *Babel*, Gen 11:4–9] : a place or scene of noise and confusion; *also* : a confused sound

ba·boon \ba-'bün\ *n* [ME *babewin*, fr. MF *babouin*, fr. *baboue* grimace] : any of several large apes of Asia and Africa with doglike muzzles

ba·bush·ka \bə-'büsh-kə, -'bùsh-\ *n* [Russ, grandmother, dim. of *baba* old woman] **♦** : a kerchief for the head

♦ bandanna, do-rag, kerchief, mantilla — more at BANDANNA

¹ba·by \'bā-bē\ *n, pl* **babies 1 ♦** : a very young child : INFANT **2** : the youngest or smallest of a group **3** : a childish person — **baby** *adj* — **ba·by·hood** *n*

♦ child, infant, newborn; *also* cherub

²baby *vb* **ba·bied; ba·by·ing ♦** : to tend or treat often with excessive care

♦ coddle, mollycoddle, nurse, pamper, spoil; *also* cater (to), humor, indulge *Ant* abuse, ill-treat, ill-use, maltreat, mishandle, mistreat, misuse

baby boom *n* : a marked rise in birthrate — **baby boom·er** \-'bü-mər\ *n*

ba·by·ish *adj* **♦** : resembling a baby : CHILDISH, INFANTILE

♦ childish, immature, infantile, juvenile, kiddish — more at CHILDISH

baby's breath *n* : any of a genus of herbs that are related to the pinks and have small delicate flowers

ba·by·sit \'bā-bē-ˌsit\ *vb* **-sat** \-ˌsat\; **-sit·ting** : to care for children usu. during a short absence of the parents

ba·by·sit·ter *n* : a person usu. hired for relatively short periods of time to take care of a child or children while the parents are away from the home

bac·ca·lau·re·ate \ˌba-kə-'lor-ē-ət\ *n* **1** : the degree of bachelor conferred by colleges and universities **2** : a sermon delivered to a graduating class

bac·ca·rat \ˌbä-kə-'rä, ˌba-\ *n* : a card game in which three hands are dealt and players may bet either or both hands against the dealer's

bac·cha·nal \'ba-kən-ᵊl, ˌba-kə-'nal, ˌbä-kə-'näl\ *n* **1** : ORGY **2** : REVELER

bac·cha·na·lia \ˌba-kə-'nāl-yə\ *n, pl* **bacchanalia** : a drunken orgy — **bac·cha·na·lian** \-'nāl-yən\ *adj or n*

bach·e·lor \'ba-chə-lər\ *n* **1** : a person who has received the usu. lowest degree conferred by a 4-year college **2** : an unmarried man — **bach·e·lor·hood** *n*

bach·e·lor·ette \ˌba-chə-lə-'ret\ *n* : a young unmarried woman

bachelor's button *n* : a European plant related to the daisies and having blue, pink, or white flower heads

ba·cil·lus \bə-'si-ləs\ *n, pl* **-li** \-ˌlī\ [NL, fr. ML, small staff, dim. of L *baculus* staff] : any of numerous rod=shaped bacteria; *also* : a disease-producing bacterium — **bac·il·lary** \'ba-sə-ˌler-ē\ *adj*

¹back \'bak\ *n* **1** : the rear or dorsal part of the human body; *also* : the corresponding part of a lower animal **2** : the part or surface opposite the front **3** : a player in the backfield in football — **back·less** \-ləs\ *adj*

²back *adv* **1 ♦** : to, toward, or at the rear **2** : AGO **3** : so as to be restrained or delayed **4 ♦** : to, toward, or in a former place or state **5** : in return or reply

♦ [1, 4] about, around, round — more at AROUND

³back *adj* **1 ♦** : located at or in the back **2** : OVERDUE **3** : moving or operating backward **4** : not current

♦ hind, hindmost, posterior, rear *Ant* anterior, fore, forward, front

⁴back *vb* **1 ♦** : to assist by material, moral, or financial assistance : SUPPORT **2** : to go or cause to go backward or in reverse **3** : to furnish with a back : form the back of

♦ advocate, champion, endorse, patronize, support — more at SUPPORT ♦ abet, aid, assist, help, prop, support — more at HELP

back·ache \'ba-ˌkāk\ *n* : a pain in the lower back

back away *vb* **♦** : to move away (as from a stand on an issue or from a commitment)

♦ fall back, recede, retire, retreat, withdraw — more at RETREAT

back–bench·er \-'ben-chər\ *n* : a rank-and-file member of a British legislature

back·bite \-ˌbīt\ *vb* **-bit** \-ˌbit\; **-bit·ten** \-ˌbit-ᵊn\; **-bit·ing** \-ˌbī-tiŋ\ : to say mean or spiteful things about someone who is absent — **back·bit·er** *n*

back·board \-ˌbord\ *n* : a board placed at or serving as the back of something

back·bone \-ˌbōn\ *n* **1 ♦** : the bony column in the back of a vertebrate that is the chief support of the trunk and consists of a jointed series of vertebrae enclosing and protecting the spinal cord **2 ♦** : firm resolute character

♦ [1] spine, vertebral column — more at SPINE
♦ [2] fiber (*or* fibre), fortitude, grit, guts, pluck, spunk — more at FORTITUDE

back down *vb* **♦** : to withdraw from a commitment or position

♦ cop out, renege — more at RENEGE

back·drop \'bak-ˌdräp\ *n* **1** : a painted cloth hung across the rear of a stage **2** : the scenery or ground behind something : BACKGROUND

back·er \'ba-kər\ *n* **♦** : one that supports

♦ advocate, apostle, booster, champion, exponent, friend, promoter, proponent, supporter — more at EXPONENT ♦ guarantor, patron, sponsor, surety — more at SPONSOR

back·field \-ˌfēld\ *n* : the football players whose positions are behind the line

¹back·fire \-ˌfīr\ *n* : a loud noise caused by the improperly timed explosion of fuel in the cylinder of an internal combustion engine

²backfire *vb* **1** : to make or undergo a backfire **2** : to have a result opposite to what was intended

back·gam·mon \ˈbak-ˌga-mən\ *n* : a game played with pieces on a double board in which the moves are determined by throwing dice

back·ground \ˈbak-ˌgraůnd\ *n* **1** : the scenery behind something **2** : the setting within which something takes place; *also* : the sum of a person's experience, training, and understanding

back·hand \ˈbak-ˌhand\ *n* : a stroke (as in tennis) made with the back of the hand turned in the direction of movement; *also* : the side on which such a stroke is made — **back·hand** *vb*

back·hand·ed \ˈbak-ˈhan-dəd\ *adj* **1** : not straightforward and open : characterized by wiliness and trickery; *esp* : SARCASTIC ⟨a ~ compliment⟩ **2** : using or made with a backhand ⟨a ~ catch⟩

back·hoe \ˈbak-ˌhō\ *n* : an excavating machine having a bucket that is drawn toward the machine

back·ing \ˈba-kiŋ\ *n* **1** : something forming a back **2** ♦ : the act or process of supporting : AID; *also* : a body of supporters

♦ aid, assist, assistance, boost, help, lift, support — more at HELP

back·lash \ˈbak-ˌlash\ *n* **1** : a sudden violent backward movement or reaction **2** : a strong adverse reaction

¹back·log \-ˌlȯg, -ˌläg\ *n* **1** : a large log at the back of a hearth fire **2** : an accumulation of tasks unperformed or materials not processed

²backlog *vb* : to accumulate in reserve

back of *prep* : in or to a place or situation to the rear of : BEHIND

back off *vb* : to withdraw from a commitment or position : BACK DOWN

back out *vb* : to withdraw esp. from a commitment or contest

¹back·pack \ˈbak-ˌpak\ *n* : a camping pack supported by a frame and carried on the back

²backpack *vb* : to hike with a backpack — **back·pack·er** *n*

back·ped·al \ˈbak-ˌped-ᵊl\ *vb* : RETREAT

back·rest \-ˌrest\ *n* : a rest for the back

back·side \-ˌsīd\ *n* ♦ : the seat of the body : BUTTOCKS

♦ bottom, butt, buttocks, posterior, rear, rump, seat — more at BUTTOCKS

back·slap \-ˌslap\ *vb* : to display excessive cordiality — **back·slap·per** *n*

back·slide \-ˌslīd\ *vb* **-slid** \-ˌslid\; **-slid** *or* **-slid·den** \-ˌslid-ᵊn\; **-slid·ing** \-ˌslī-diŋ\ : to lapse morally or in religious practice

back·slid·er *n* : one that backslides ⟨a ~ who pleads his former righteousness⟩

back·spin \-ˌspin\ *n* : a backward rotary motion of a ball

¹back·stage \ˈbak-ˌstāj\ *adj* **1** : relating to or occurring in the area behind a stage **2** : of or relating to the private lives of theater people **3** : of or relating to the inner working or operation

²back·stage \ˈbak-ˈstāj\ *adv* **1** : in or to a backstage area **2** : SECRETLY

back·stairs \-ˌsatrz\ *adj* : SECRET, FURTIVE; *also* : SORDID, SCANDALOUS

¹back·stop \-ˌstäp\ *n* : something serving as a stop behind something else; *esp* : a screen or fence to keep a ball from leaving the field of play

²backstop *vb* **1** : SUPPORT **2** : to serve as a backstop to

back·stretch \ˈbak-ˈstrech\ *n* : the side opposite the homestretch on a racecourse

back·stroke \-ˌstrōk\ *n* : a swimming stroke executed on the back

back talk *n* ♦ : impudent, insolent, or argumentative replies

♦ cheek, impertinence, impudence, insolence, sauce; *also* comeback, rejoinder, retort, riposte, wisecrack

back·track \ˈbak-ˌtrak\ *vb* **1** : to retrace one's course **2** : to reverse a position or stand

back·up \-ˌəp\ *n* **1** ♦ : one that serves as a substitute or

alternative **2** ♦ : an accumulation caused by a stoppage in the flow ⟨traffic ~⟩

♦ [1] pinch hitter, relief, replacement, reserve, stand-in, sub, substitute — more at SUBSTITUTE ♦ [2] bottleneck, jam, snarl

¹back·ward \ˈbak-wərd\ *or* **back·wards** \-wərdz\ *adv* **1** : toward the back **2** : with the back foremost **3** : in a reverse or contrary direction or way **4** : toward the past; *also* : toward a worse state

²backward *adj* **1** : directed, turned, or done backward **2** : DIFFIDENT, SHY **3** : slow in development or learning — **back·ward·ly** *adv* — **back·ward·ness** *n*

back·wash \ˈbak-ˌwȯsh, -ˌwäsh\ *n* : a backward flow or movement (as of water or air) produced by a propelling force (as the motion of oars)

back·wa·ter \-ˌwȯ-tər, -ˌwä-\ *n* **1** : water held or turned back in its course **2** : an isolated or backward place or condition

back·woods \-ˈwůdz\ *n pl* **1** ♦ : wooded or partly cleared areas far from cities **2** ♦ : a remote or isolated place

♦ [1, 2] bush, frontier, hinterland, sticks, up-country — more at FRONTIER

ba·con \ˈbā-kən\ *n* : salted and smoked meat from the sides or back of a pig

bac·te·ri·cid·al \bak-ˌtir-ə-ˈsīd-ᵊl\ *adj* : destroying bacteria — **bac·te·ri·cide** \-ˈtir-ə-ˌsīd\ *n*

bac·te·ri·ol·o·gy \bak-ˌtir-ē-ˈä-lə-jē\ *n* **1** : a science dealing with bacteria **2** : bacterial life and phenomena — **bac·te·ri·o·log·ic** \-ə-ˈlä-jik\ *or* **bac·te·ri·o·log·i·cal** \-ə-ˈlä-ji-kəl\ *adj* — **bac·te·ri·ol·o·gist** \-ˈä-lə-jist\ *n*

bac·te·rio·phage \bak-ˈtir-ē-ə-ˌfāj\ *n* : any of various viruses that attack specific bacteria

bac·te·ri·um \bak-ˈtir-ē-əm\ *n, pl* **-ria** \-ē-ə\ [NL, fr. Gk *baktērion* staff] : any of a group of single-celled microorganisms including some that are disease producers and others that are valued esp. for their chemical effects (as fermentation) — **bac·te·ri·al** \-ē-əl\ *adj*

bad \ˈbad\ *adj* **worse** \ˈwərs\; **worst** \ˈwərst\ **1** ♦ : below standard : POOR; *also* : UNFAVORABLE ⟨a ~ report⟩ **2** ♦ : having deteriorated because of spoiling **3 a** ♦ : morally unacceptable or reprehensible : EVIL **b** : not well-behaved : NAUGHTY **4 a** ♦ : causing discomfort : DISAGREEABLE ⟨a ~ taste⟩ **b** ♦ : causing harm : HARMFUL **5** : having a defect : FAULTY ⟨~ wiring⟩; *also* : not valid ⟨a ~ check⟩ **6** : being in poor health : UNWELL, ILL **7** : full of regret : SORRY

♦ [1] deficient, inferior, lousy, off, poor, substandard, unacceptable, unsatisfactory, wanting, wretched, wrong; *also* defective, faulty *Ant* acceptable, satisfactory ♦ [2] putrid, rotten — more at ROTTEN ♦ [3a] black, evil, immoral, iniquitous, nefarious, sinful, unethical, unsavory, vile, villainous, wicked; *also* base, contemptible, despicable, dirty, disreputable, evil-minded, ignoble, ill, infernal, low, mean *Ant* ethical, good, moral, right, righteous, virtuous ♦ [4a] disagreeable, distasteful, nasty, rotten, sour, unpleasant — more at UNPLEASANT ♦ [4b] adverse, baleful, baneful, damaging, deleterious, detrimental, evil, harmful, hurtful, ill, injurious, mischievous, noxious, pernicious, prejudicial — more at HARMFUL

bade *past and past part of* BID

badge \ˈbaj\ *n* : a device or token usu. worn as a sign of status

¹bad·ger \ˈba-jər\ *n* : any of several sturdy burrowing mammals with long claws on their forefeet

²badger *vb* : to harass or annoy persistently

ba·di·nage \ˌbad-ᵊn-ˈäzh\ *n* [F] : playful talk back and forth : BANTER

bad·land \ˈbad-ˌland\ *n* : a region marked by intricate erosional sculpturing and scanty vegetation — usu. used in pl.

bad·ly *adv* : in a bad manner ⟨played ~⟩

bad·min·ton \ˈbad-ˌmint-ᵊn\ *n* : a court game played with light rackets and a shuttlecock volleyed over a net

bad–mouth \'bad-ˌmaůth\ *vb* : to criticize severely
bad·ness *n* : the quality or state of being bad
Bae·de·ker \'bā-di-kər, 'be-\ *n* : GUIDEBOOK
¹**baf·fle** \'ba-fəl\ *vb* **baf·fled; baf·fling** \-fə-liŋ\ **1 ♦** : to interfere with or slow the progress of : FRUSTRATE, THWART **2 ♦** : to cause to be mentally confused : PERPLEX

♦ [1] balk, checkmate, foil, frustrate, thwart — more at FRUSTRATE ♦ [2] addle, befog, befuddle, bemuse, bewilder, confound, confuse, disorient, muddle, muddy, mystify, perplex, puzzle — more at CONFUSE

²**baffle** *n* : a device (as a wall or screen) to deflect, check, or regulate flow (as of liquid or sound) — **baf·fled** \'ba-fəld\ *adj*
baf·fle·ment *n* ♦ : the state of being baffled

♦ bewilderment, confusion, distraction, muddle, mystification, perplexity, puzzlement, whirl — more at CONFUSION

¹**bag** \'bag\ *n* ♦ : a flexible usu. closable container (as for storing or carrying)

♦ handbag, pocketbook, purse — more at PURSE

²**bag** *vb* **bagged; bag·ging 1** : to expand from internal pressure : BULGE **2** : to put in a bag **3 ♦** : to get possession of; *esp* : to take in hunting

♦ capture, catch, get, grab, nab, seize, snare, trap — more at CATCH

ba·gasse \bə-'gas\ *n* [F] : plant residue (as of sugarcane) left after a product (as juice) has been extracted
bag·a·telle \ˌba-gə-'tel\ *n* [F] : TRIFLE
ba·gel \'bā-gəl\ *n* [Yiddish *beygl*] : a hard glazed doughnut-shaped roll
bag·gage \'ba-gij\ *n* **1** : the traveling bags and personal belongings of a traveler : LUGGAGE **2** : things that get in the way
bag·gie \'ba-gē\ *n* : a usu. small clear plastic bag
bag·gies \'ba-gēz\ *n pl* : baggy pants or shorts
bag·gy \'ba-gē\ *adj* **bag·gi·er; -est** : puffed out or hanging like a bag ⟨a ∼ sweater⟩ — **bag·gi·ly** \-gə-lē\ *adv* — **bag·gi·ness** \-gē-nəs\ *n*
bag·man \'bag-mən\ *n* : a person who collects or distributes illicitly gained money on behalf of another
ba·gnio \'ban-yō\ *n, pl* **bagnios** [It *bagno*, lit., public bath] : BROTHEL
bag·pipe \'bag-ˌpīp\ *n* : a musical wind instrument consisting of a bag, a tube with valves, and sounding pipes — often used in pl.
ba·guette \ba-'get\ *n* [F, lit., rod] **1** : a gem having the shape of a narrow rectangle; *also* : the shape itself **2** : a long thin loaf of French bread
Ba·ha·mi·an \bə-'hä-mē-ən, -'hä-\ *n* : a native or inhabitant of the Bahama Islands
¹**bail** \'bāl\ *n* : a container for ladling water out of a boat
²**bail** *vb* : to dip and throw water from a boat — **bail·er** *n*
³**bail** *n* : security given to guarantee a prisoner's appearance when legally required; *also* : one giving such security or the release secured
⁴**bail** *vb* : to release under bail; *also* : to procure the release of by giving bail — **bail·able** \'bā-lə-bəl\ *adj*
⁵**bail** *n* : the arched handle (as of a pail or kettle)
bai·liff \'bā-ləf\ *n* **1** : an aide of a British sheriff who serves writs and makes arrests; *also* : a minor officer of a U.S. court **2** : an estate or farm manager esp. in Britain : STEWARD
bai·li·wick \'bā-li-ˌwik\ *n* : one's special province or domain
bail·out \'bā-ˌlaůt\ *n* : a rescue from financial distress
bairn \'barn\ *n, chiefly Scot* : CHILD
¹**bait** \'bāt\ *vb* **1 ♦** : to persecute by continued attacks **2** : to harass with dogs usu. for sport ⟨∼ a bear⟩ **3** : to furnish (as a hook) with bait **4** : ALLURE, ENTICE **5** : to give food and drink to (as an animal)

♦ bug, hassle, heckle, needle, ride, taunt, tease — more at TEASE

²**bait** *n* **1** : a lure for catching animals (as fish) **2** : an inducement to pleasure or gain : LURE, TEMPTATION
baize \'bāz\ *n* : a coarse feltlike fabric
¹**bake** \'bāk\ *vb* **baked; bak·ing 1** : to cook or become cooked in dry heat esp. in an oven **2** : to dry and harden by heat ⟨∼ bricks⟩ — **bak·er** *n*
²**bake** *n* : a social gathering featuring baked food
baker's dozen *n* : THIRTEEN
bak·ery \'bā-k(ə-)rē\ *n, pl* **-er·ies** : a place for baking or selling baked goods
bake sale *n* : a fund-raising event at which usu. homemade foods are sold
bake·shop \'bāk-ˌshäp\ *n* : BAKERY
baking powder *n* : a powder that consists of a carbonate, an acid, and a starch and that makes the dough rise in baking cakes and biscuits
baking soda *n* : SODIUM BICARBONATE
bak·sheesh \'bak-ˌshēsh\ *n* : payment (as a tip or bribe) to expedite service
bal *abbr* balance
bal·a·lai·ka \ˌba-lə-'lī-kə\ *n* [Russ] : a triangular 3-stringed instrument of Russian origin played by plucking or strumming
¹**bal·ance** \'ba-ləns\ *n* [ME, fr. AF, fr. VL *bilancia*, fr. LL *bilanc-, bilanx* having two scalepans, fr. L *bi* two + *lanc-, lanx* plate] **1** : a weighing device : SCALE **2 ♦** : a weight, force, or influence counteracting the effect of another **3** : an oscillating wheel used to regulate a timepiece **4 ♦** : a state of equilibrium **5 ♦** : a remaining group, part, or trace : REST; *esp* : an amount in excess esp. on the credit side of an account **6** : mental and emotional steadiness **7 ♦** : an aesthetically pleasing integration of elements

♦ [2] canceler, counterbalance, counterweight, offset ♦ [4] equilibrium, equipoise, poise *Ant* imbalance ♦ [5] leavings, leftovers, odds and ends, remainder, remains, remnant, residue, rest — more at REMAINDER ♦ [7] coherence, consonance, harmony, proportion, symmetry, symphony, unity — more at HARMONY

²**balance** *vb* **bal·anced; bal·anc·ing 1** : to compute the balance of an account **2 ♦** : to arrange so that one set of elements equals another; *also* : to equal or equalize in weight, number, or proportions **3** : WEIGH **4** : to bring or come to a state or position of balance; *also* : to bring into harmony or proportion

♦ equalize, equate, even, level — more at EQUALIZE

bal·anced \-lənst\ *adj* ♦ : being in a state of balance (as physically, emotionally, or aesthetically)

♦ clearheaded, lucid, normal, right, sane, stable — more at SANE ♦ congruous, consonant, harmonious — more at HARMONIOUS

bal·co·ny \'bal-kə-nē\ *n, pl* **-nies 1** : a platform projecting from the side of a building and enclosed by a railing **2** : a gallery inside a building
bald \'bold\ *adj* **1 ♦** : lacking a natural or usual covering (as of hair) **2 ♦** : lacking embellishment or decoration : PLAIN **3** : having little or no tread ⟨∼ tires⟩ **4** : not disguised ⟨∼ hate⟩ — **bald·ly** *adv* — **bald·ness** *n*

♦ [1] bare, exposed, naked, open, uncovered — more at NAKED ♦ [2] plain, simple, unadorned, undecorated, unvarnished — more at PLAIN

bal·da·chin \'bol-də-kən, 'bal-\ *or* **bal·da·chi·no** \ˌbal-də-'kē-nō\ *n, pl* **-chins** *or* **-chinos** : a canopylike structure over an altar
bald cypress *n* : either of two large swamp trees of the southern U.S. with hard red wood
bald eagle *n* : an eagle of No. America that when mature has white head and neck feathers and a white tail
bal·der·dash \'bol-dər-ˌdash\ *n* : NONSENSE
bald·ing \'bol-diŋ\ *adj* : getting bald
bal·dric \'bol-drik\ *n* : a belt worn over the shoulder to carry a sword or bugle
¹**bale** \'bāl\ *n* : a large or closely packed bundle
²**bale** *vb* **baled; bal·ing** : to pack in a bale — **bal·er** *n*

ba·leen \bə-'lēn\ *n* : a horny substance attached in plates to the upper jaw of some large whales (**baleen whales**)

bale·ful \'bāl-fəl\ *adj* **1** ♦ : likely to cause or capable of producing harm or death **2** ♦ : foreboding or foreshadowing evil : OMINOUS

♦ [1] adverse, bad, baneful, damaging, deleterious, detrimental, evil, harmful, hurtful, pernicious — more at HARMFUL ♦ [2] dire, foreboding, menacing, ominous, portentous, sinister — more at OMINOUS

¹balk \'bȯk\ *n* **1** ♦ : something that makes movement or progress more difficult : HINDRANCE **2** : an illegal motion of the pitcher in baseball while in position

²balk *vb* **1** ♦ : to hinder the passage, progress, or accomplishment of : THWART **2** : to stop short and refuse to go on **3** : to commit a balk in sports

♦ baffle, beat, checkmate, foil, frustrate, thwart — more at FRUSTRATE

balky \'bȯ-kē\ *adj* : refusing or likely to refuse to proceed, act, or function as directed or expected ⟨a ∼ mule⟩

¹ball \'bȯl\ *n* **1** ♦ : a rounded body or mass (as at the base of the thumb or for use as a missile or in a game) **2** : a game played with a ball **3** : a pitched baseball that misses the strike zone and is not swung at by the batter **4** : a hit or thrown ball in various games ⟨foul ∼⟩ — **on the ball** : COMPETENT, KNOWLEDGEABLE, ALERT

♦ orb, sphere

²ball *vb* ♦ : to form into a ball

♦ agglomerate, conglomerate, roll, round, wad — more at WAD

³ball *n* ♦ : a large formal dance

♦ dance, formal, prom — more at DANCE

bal·lad \'ba-ləd\ *n* **1** : a narrative poem of strongly marked rhythm suitable for singing **2** : a simple song : AIR **3** : a slow romantic song

bal·lad·eer \,ba-lə-'dir\ *n* : a singer of ballads

¹bal·last \'ba-ləst\ *n* **1** : heavy material used to stabilize a ship or control a balloon's ascent **2** : crushed stone laid in a railroad bed or used in making concrete

²ballast *vb* : to provide with ballast

ball bearing *n* : a bearing in which the revolving part turns upon steel balls that roll easily in a groove; *also* : one of the balls in such a bearing

ball·car·ri·er \'bȯl-,kar-ē-ər\ *n* : the football player carrying the ball in an offensive play

bal·le·ri·na \,ba-lə-'rē-nə\ *n* : a woman or girl who is a ballet dancer

bal·let \'ba-,lā, ba-'lā\ *n* **1** : dancing in which fixed poses and steps are combined with light flowing movements often to convey a story; *also* : a theatrical art form using ballet dancing **2** : a company of ballet dancers

bal·let·o·mane \ba-'le-tə-,mān\ *n* : a devotee of ballet

bal·lis·tic missile \bə-'lis-tik-\ *n* : a missile that is guided during ascent and that falls freely during descent

bal·lis·tics \-tiks\ *n sing or pl* **1** : the science of the motion of projectiles (as bullets) in flight **2** : the flight characteristics of a projectile — **ballistic** *adj*

¹bal·loon \bə-'lün\ *n* **1** : a bag filled with gas or heated air so as to rise and float in the atmosphere **2** : a toy consisting of an inflatable bag — **bal·loon·ist** *n*

²balloon *vb* **1** ♦ : to swell or puff out **2** : to travel in a balloon **3** ♦ : to increase rapidly

♦ [1, 3] appreciate, build, burgeon, enlarge, escalate, expand, increase, mushroom, rise, swell, wax — more at INCREASE ♦ [1] belly, bulge, overhang, poke, project, protrude, start, stick out — more at BULGE

¹bal·lot \'ba-lət\ *n* [It *ballotta* small ball used in secret voting, fr. It dial., dim. of *balla* ball] **1** : a piece of paper used to cast a vote **2** : the action or a system of voting; *also* : the right to vote

²ballot *vb* : to decide by ballot : VOTE

¹ball·park \'bȯl-,park\ *n* : a park in which ball games are played

²ballpark *adj* : approximately correct ⟨∼ estimate⟩

ball·point \'bȯl-,pȯint\ *n* : a pen whose writing point is a small rotating metal ball that inks itself from an inner container

ball·room \'bȯl-,rüm, -,ru̇m\ *n* : a large room for dances

¹bal·ly·hoo \'ba-lē-,hü\ *n, pl* **-hoos** : extravagant statements and claims made for publicity

²ballyhoo *vb* **bal·ly·hoo·ed; bal·ly·hoo·ing; bal·ly·hoos** ♦ : to drum up interest in by means of ballyhoo : PUBLICIZE

♦ boast, plug, promote, publicize, tout — more at PUBLICIZE

balm \'bäm, 'bȧlm\ *n* **1** : a fragrant healing or soothing lotion or ointment **2** : any of several spicy fragrant herbs of the mint family **3** : something that comforts or soothes

balm·i·ness \'bä-mē-nəs, 'bȧl-\ *n* ♦ : the quality or state of being balmy

♦ absurdity, asininity, craziness, daftness, fatuity, folly, foolishness, inanity, insanity, lunacy, madness, silliness, simplicity, zaniness

balmy \'bä-mē, 'bȧl-\ *adj* **balm·i·er; -est** **1 a** ♦ : gently soothing : MILD **b** ♦ : being pleasant and not too cool or too hot **2 a** ♦ : disordered in mind **b** ♦ : lacking in judgment : FOOLISH

♦ [1a] benign, bland, delicate, gentle, light, mellow, mild, soft, soothing, tender — more at GENTLE ♦ [1b] clement, equable, gentle, mild, moderate, temperate — more at CLEMENT ♦ [2a, 2b] absurd, crazy, cuckoo, fatuous, foolish, mad, nonsensical, nutty, senseless, silly, stupid — more at FOOLISH

ba·lo·ney \bə-'lō-nē\ *n* : NONSENSE

bal·sa \'bȯl-sə\ *n* : the extremely light strong wood of a tropical American tree; *also* : the tree

bal·sam \'bȯl-səm\ *n* **1** : a fragrant aromatic and usu. resinous substance oozing from various plants; *also* : a preparation containing or smelling like balsam **2** : a balsam-yielding tree (as balsam fir) **3** : a common garden ornamental plant — **bal·sam·ic** \bȯl-'sa-mik\ *adj*

balsam fir *n* : a resinous American evergreen tree that is widely used for pulpwood and as a Christmas tree

balsamic vinegar *n* : an aged Italian vinegar made from white grapes

Bal·ti·more oriole \'bȯl-tə-,mȯr-\ *n* : a common American oriole in which the male is brightly colored with orange, black, and white

bal·us·ter \'ba-lə-stər\ *n* [F *balustre*, fr. It *balaustro*, fr. *balaustra* wild pomegranate flower, fr. L *balaustium*; fr. its shape] : an upright support for a rail (as of a staircase)

bal·us·trade \'ba-lə-,strād\ *n* : a row of balusters topped by a rail

bam·boo \bam-'bü\ *n, pl* **bamboos** : any of various woody mostly tall tropical grasses including some with strong hollow stems used for building, furniture, or utensils

bamboo curtain *n, often cap B&C* : a political, military, and ideological barrier in eastern Asia

bam·boo·zle \bam-'bü-zəl\ *vb* **-boo·zled; -boo·zling** : TRICK, HOODWINK

¹ban \'ban\ *vb* **banned; ban·ning** ♦ : to hinder or prevent by authority

♦ bar, enjoin, forbid, interdict, outlaw, prohibit, proscribe — more at FORBID

²ban *n* **1** : CURSE **2** ♦ : a legal or formal prohibition ⟨∼ remarks⟩

♦ embargo, interdict, interdiction, prohibition, proscription, veto — more at PROHIBITION

ba·nal \bə-'näl, -'nal; 'bān-ᵊl\ *adj* [F] ♦ : lacking originality, freshness, or novelty : COMMONPLACE, TRITE

♦ commonplace, hackneyed, musty, stale, stereotyped, threadbare, tired, trite — more at STALE

ba·nal·i·ty \bā-'na-lə-tē\ *n* ♦ : something banal : COMMONPLACE

♦ cliché, commonplace, platitude, shibboleth — more at COMMONPLACE

ba·nana \bə-'na-nə\ *n* : a treelike tropical plant bearing thick clusters of yellow or reddish finger-shaped fruit; *also* : this fruit

¹**band** \'band\ *n* **1** ♦ : something that binds, ties, or goes around **2** ♦ : a strip or stripe that can be distinguished (as by color or texture) from nearby matter **3** : a range of wavelengths (as in radio)

♦ [1] bond, chain, fetter, irons, ligature, manacle, shackle — more at BOND ♦ [2] circle, hoop, ring, round — more at RING ♦ [2] bar, streak, stripe — more at STRIPE

²**band** *vb* **1** ♦ : to tie up, finish, or enclose with a band **2** ♦ : to gather together or unite esp. for some common end — often used with *together* **3** : to furnish or decorate with a band — **band·er** *n*

♦ [1] belt, gird, girdle, wrap — more at GIRD ♦ [1] bind, gird, tie, truss — more at TIE ♦ *often* **band together** [2] ally, associate, club, confederate, conjoin, cooperate, federate, league, unite — more at ALLY

³**band** *n* ♦ : a group of persons, animals, or things; *esp* : a group of musicians organized for playing together

♦ company, crew, gang, outfit, party, squad, team — more at GANG

¹**ban·dage** \'ban-dij\ *n* : a strip of material used esp. in dressing wounds

²**bandage** *vb* **ban·daged; ban·dag·ing** : to dress or cover with a bandage

ban·dan·na *or* **ban·dana** \ban-'da-nə\ *n* ♦ : a large colored figured handkerchief

♦ babushka, do-rag, kerchief, mantilla; *also* shawl

B and B *abbr* bed-and-breakfast

band·box \'band-,bäks\ *n* : a usu. cylindrical box for carrying clothing

band·ed \'ban-dəd\ *adj* : having or marked with bands

ban·de·role *or* **ban·de·rol** \'ban-də-,rōl\ *n* : a long narrow forked flag or streamer

ban·dit \'ban-dət\ *n* [It *bandito*, fr. *bandire* to banish] **1** *pl also* **ban·dit·ti** \ban-'di-tē\ : an outlaw who lives by plunder; *esp* : a member of a band of marauders **2** : ROBBER — **ban·dit·ry** \'ban-də-trē\ *n*

ban·do·lier *or* **ban·do·leer** \,ban-də-'lir\ *n* : a belt slung over the shoulder esp. to carry ammunition

band saw *n* : a saw in the form of an endless steel belt running over pulleys

band·stand \'band-,stand\ *n* : a usu. roofed platform on which a band or orchestra performs outdoors

b and w *abbr* black and white

band·wag·on \'band-,wa-gən\ *n* **1** : a wagon carrying musicians in a parade **2** ♦ : a movement that attracts growing support ⟨a political ∼⟩

♦ campaign, cause, crusade, drive, movement — more at CAMPAIGN

¹**ban·dy** \'ban-dē\ *vb* **ban·died; ban·dy·ing** **1** : to exchange (as blows or quips) esp. in rapid succession **2** : to use in a glib or offhand way

²**bandy** *adj* : curved outward ⟨∼ legs⟩

bane \'bān\ *n* **1** ♦ : a substance that through its chemical action usu. kills, injures, or impairs an organism : POISON **2** : WOE, HARM; *also* : a source of this

♦ poison, toxin, venom — more at POISON

bane·ful \'bān-fəl\ *adj* ♦ : productive of destruction or woe : seriously harmful

♦ bad, baleful, damaging, deleterious, harmful, hurtful, injurious, noxious, pernicious — more at HARMFUL

¹**bang** \'baŋ\ *vb* **1** ♦ : to knock against something with a forceful jolt : BUMP ⟨fell and ∼ed his knee⟩ **2** ♦ : to strike, thrust, or move vigorously and often with a loud noise

♦ [1, 2] bash, bump, collide, crash, hit, impact, knock, smash, strike — more at HIT

²**bang** *n* **1** : a resounding blow **2** ♦ : a sudden loud noise **3** ♦ : a sudden wave of emotion ⟨I get a ∼ out of all this⟩

♦ [2] blast, boom, clap, crack, crash, pop, report, slam, smash — more at CLAP ♦ [3] exhilaration, kick, thrill, titillation — more at THRILL

³**bang** *adv* : DIRECTLY, RIGHT

⁴**bang** *n* : a fringe of hair cut short (as across the forehead) — usu. used in pl.

⁵**bang** *vb* : to cut a bang in

Ban·gla·deshi \,bäŋ-glə-'de-shē\ *n* : a native or inhabitant of Bangladesh — **Bangladeshi** *adj*

ban·gle \'baŋ-gəl\ *n* : an ornamental band or chain worn around the wrist; *also* : a loose-hanging ornament

bang–up \'baŋ-,əp\ *adj* ♦ : being of the very best kind : FIRST-RATE, EXCELLENT ⟨a ∼ job⟩

♦ A1, banner, excellent, fabulous, fine, grand, great, prime, sensational, splendid, superb, superior, unsurpassed, wonderful — more at EXCELLENT

ban·ish \'ba-nish\ *vb* **1** ♦ : to require by authority to leave a country **2** ♦ : to drive out : EXPEL

♦ [1] deport, displace, exile, expatriate, transport; *also* dismiss, eject, eliminate, evict, exclude, expel, oust, throw out ♦ [2] boot (out), bounce, cast, drum, eject, expel, oust, rout, run off, throw out — more at EJECT

ban·ish·ment *n* ♦ : a legal expulsion from a country

♦ deportation, displacement, exile, expulsion — more at EXILE

ban·is·ter \'ba-nə-stər\ *n* **1** : an upright often vase-shaped support for a rail **2** : a handrail with its supporting posts **3** : HANDRAIL

ban·jo \'ban-,jō\ *n, pl* **banjos** *also* **banjoes** : a musical instrument with a long neck, a drumlike body, and usu. five strings — **ban·jo·ist** \-ist\ *n*

¹**bank** \'baŋk\ *n* **1** ♦ : a piled-up mass (as of cloud or earth) **2** : an undersea elevation **3** : rising ground bordering a lake, river, or sea **4** : the sideways slope of a surface along a curve or of a vehicle as it rounds a curve

♦ bar, drift, mound; *also* snowbank, snowdrift

²**bank** *vb* **1** : to form a bank about **2** : to cover (as a fire) with fuel to keep inactive **3** : to build (a curve) with the roadbed or track inclined laterally upward from the inside edge **4** : to pile or heap in a bank; *also* : to arrange in a tier **5** : to incline (an airplane) laterally

³**bank** *n* [ME, fr. MF or It; MF *banque*, fr. It *banca*, lit., bench] **1** : an establishment concerned esp. with the custody, loan, exchange, or issue of money, the extension of credit, and the transmission of funds **2** : a stock of or a place for holding something in reserve ⟨a blood ∼⟩

⁴**bank** *vb* **1** : to conduct the business of a bank **2** : to deposit money or have an account in a bank — **bank·er** *n* — **bank·ing** *n*

⁵**bank** *n* : a group of objects arranged close together (as in a row or tier) ⟨a ∼ of file drawers⟩

bank·book \'baŋk-,bùk\ *n* : the depositor's book in which a bank records deposits and withdrawals

bank·card \-,kärd\ *n* : a credit card issued by a bank

bank·note \-,nōt\ *n* : a promissory note issued by a bank and circulating as money

bank·roll \-,rōl\ *n* : supply of money : FUNDS

¹**bank·rupt** \'baŋ-(,)krəpt\ *n* [modif. of MF *banquerote* bankruptcy, fr. It *bancarotta*, fr. *banca* bank + *rotta* broken] : an insolvent person; *esp* : one whose property is turned over by court action to a trustee to be handled for the benefit of his or her creditors

²**bankrupt** *adj* **1** : reduced to financial ruin; *esp* : legally declared a bankrupt **2** : wholly lacking in or deprived of some essential ⟨morally ∼⟩ — **bank·rupt·cy** \'baŋ-(,)krəpt-sē\ *n*

³**bankrupt** *vb* : to reduce to bankruptcy

¹**ban·ner** \'ba-nər\ *n* **1** ♦ : a piece of cloth attached to a staff and used by a leader as his or her standard **2** ♦ : a usu. rectangular piece of fabric of distinctive design that is used as a symbol (as of a nation), as a signaling device, or as a decoration : FLAG **3** : an advertisement that runs usu. across the top of a Web page

♦ [1, 2] colors (*or* colours), ensign, flag, jack, pennant, standard, streamer — more at FLAG

²**ban·ner** *adj* ♦ : distinguished from all others esp. in excellence ⟨a ~ year⟩

♦ A1, boss, excellent, grand, great, stellar, superior, unsurpassed — more at EXCELLENT

ban·nock \'ba-nək\ *n* : a flat oatmeal or barley cake usu. cooked on a griddle

banns \'banz\ *n pl* : public announcement esp. in church of a proposed marriage

¹**ban·quet** \'baŋ-kwət\ *n* [MF, fr. It *banchetto*, fr. dim. of *banca* bench] ♦ : a ceremonial dinner

♦ dinner, feast, feed, spread — more at FEAST

²**banquet** *vb* : to partake of or treat with a banquet

ban·quette \baŋ-'ket\ *n* : a long upholstered bench esp. along a wall

ban·shee \'ban-shē\ *n* [Ir *bean sídhe* & ScGael *bean sìth*, lit., woman of fairyland] : a female spirit in Gaelic folklore whose wailing warns a family that one of them will soon die

ban·tam \'ban-təm\ *n* **1** : any of numerous small domestic fowls that are often miniatures of standard breeds **2** : a small but pugnacious person

¹**ban·ter** \'ban-tər\ *vb* : to speak to in a witty and teasing manner

²**banter** *n* ♦ : good-natured witty joking

♦ chaff, persiflage, raillery, repartee; *also* barb, crack, dig, gag, jest, joke, quip, sally, wisecrack, witticism

Ban·tu \'ban-,tü\ *n, pl* **Bantu** *or* **Bantus** **1** : a member of a group of African peoples of central and southern Africa **2** : a group of African languages spoken by the Bantu

Ban·tu·stan \,ban-tu-'stan, ,bän-tü-'stän\ *n* : an all-black enclave formerly in the Republic of So. Africa with a limited degree of self-government

ban·yan \'ban-yən\ *n* [earlier *banyan* Hindu merchant, fr. Hindi *baniyā*; fr. a merchant's pagoda erected under a tree of the species in Iran] : a large tropical Asian tree whose aerial roots grow downward to the ground and form new trunks

ban·zai \bän-'zī\ *n* : a Japanese cheer or cry of triumph

bao·bab \'baù-,bab, 'bā-ə-\ *n* : a tropical African tree with a short swollen trunk and sour edible gourdlike fruits

bap·tism \'bap-,ti-zəm\ *n* **1** : a Christian sacrament signifying spiritual rebirth and symbolized by the ritual use of water **2** : an act, experience, or ordeal by which one is purified, sanctified, initiated, or named — **bap·tis·mal** \bap-'tiz-məl\ *adj*

baptismal name *n* : GIVEN NAME

Bap·tist \'bap-tist\ *n* : a member of any of several Protestant denominations emphasizing baptism by immersion of believers only

bap·tis·tery *or* **bap·tis·try** \'bap-tə-strē\ *n, pl* **-ter·ies** *or* **-tries** : a place esp. in a church used for baptism

bap·tize \bap-'tīz, 'bap-,tīz\ *vb* **bap·tized; bap·tiz·ing** [ME, fr. AF *baptiser*, fr. L *baptizare*, fr. Gk *baptizein* to dip, baptize, fr. *baptein* to dip] **1 a** : to administer baptism to **b** : to give a name to : CHRISTEN **2 a** : to purify esp. by an ordeal **b** ♦ : to induct into membership by or as if by special rites : INITIATE

♦ inaugurate, induct, initiate, install, invest — more at INSTALL

¹**bar** \'bär\ *n* **1** : a long narrow piece of material (as wood or metal) used esp. for a lever, fastening, or support **2 a** ♦ : something that blocks or is intended to block passage : OBSTACLE **b** : a submerged or partly submerged bank (as of sand) along a shore or in a river often obstructing navigation **3 a** : the railing in a law court at which prisoners are stationed **b** : the legal profession or the whole body of lawyers **4** ♦ : a stripe, band, or line much longer than wide **5** ♦ : a counter at which food or esp. drink is served; *also* : BARROOM **6** : a vertical line across the musical staff

♦ [2a] block, encumbrance, hindrance, inhibition, obstacle — more at ENCUMBRANCE ♦ [4] band, streak,

stripe — more at STRIPE ♦ [5] barroom, café, pub, public house, saloon, tavern — more at BARROOM

²**bar** *vb* **barred; bar·ring 1** : to fasten, confine, or obstruct with or as if with a bar or bars **2** : to mark with bars : STRIPE **3** ♦ : to shut or keep out : EXCLUDE **4** ♦ : to command against : FORBID

♦ [3] ban, count out, debar, eliminate, except, exclude, rule out — more at EXCLUDE ♦ [4] ban, enjoin, forbid, interdict, outlaw, prohibit, proscribe — more at FORBID

³**bar** *prep* ♦ : with the exclusion or exception of : EXCEPT

♦ aside from, barring, besides, but, except, outside (of), save

⁴**bar** *abbr* barometer; barometric

Bar *abbr* Baruch

barb \'bärb\ *n* **1** : a sharp projection extending backward (as from the point of an arrow) **2** ♦ : a biting critical remark — **barbed** \'bärbd\ *adj*

♦ affront, dart, dig, indignity, insult, name, offense, outrage, put-down, sarcasm, slight, slur, wound — more at INSULT

¹**bar·bar·ian** \bär-'ber-ē-ən\ *adj* **1** : of, relating to, or being a land, culture, or people alien to and usu. believed to be inferior to another's **2** : lacking refinement, learning, or artistic or literary culture

²**barbarian** *n* : one that is barbarian

bar·bar·ic \bär-'bar-ik\ *adj* **1** : BARBARIAN **2** : marked by a lack of restraint : WILD **3** : mercilessly harsh or cruel : BARBAROUS ⟨a ~ crime⟩

bar·ba·rism \'bär-bə-,ri-zəm\ *n* **1** : the social condition of barbarians; *also* : the use or display of barbarian or barbarous acts, attitudes, or ideas **2** : a word or expression that offends standards of correctness or purity

bar·bar·i·ty \bär-'bar-ə-tē\ *n* ♦ : barbarous cruelty

♦ brutality, cruelty, inhumanity, sadism, savagery, viciousness, wantonness — more at CRUELTY

bar·ba·rous \'bär-bə-rəs\ *adj* **1** ♦ : lacking culture or refinement **2** : using linguistic barbarisms **3** ♦ : mercilessly harsh or cruel — **bar·ba·rous·ly** *adv*

♦ [1] heathen, heathenish, Neanderthal, rude, savage, uncivil, uncivilized, uncultivated, wild — more at SAVAGE ♦ [3] brutal, cruel, heartless, inhumane, sadistic, savage, vicious — more at CRUEL

¹**bar·be·cue** \'bär-bi-,kyü\ *n* : a social gathering at which barbecued food is served

²**barbecue** *vb* **-cued; -cu·ing 1** : to cook over hot coals or on a revolving spit **2** : to cook in a highly seasoned vinegar sauce

bar·bell \'bär-,bel\ *n* : a bar with adjustable weights attached to each end used for exercise and in weight lifting

bar·ber \'bär-bər\ *n* [ME, fr. AF *barbour*, fr. *barbe* beard, fr. L *barba*] : one whose business is cutting and dressing hair and shaving and trimming beards

bar·ber·ry \'bär-,ber-ē\ *n* : any of a genus of spiny shrubs bearing yellow flowers and oblong red berries

bar·bi·tu·rate \bär-'bi-chə-rət\ *n* : any of various compounds (as a salt or ester) formed from an organic acid (**bar·bi·tu·ric acid** \,bär-bə-'tùr-ik-, -'tyùr-\); *esp* : one used as a sedative or hypnotic

bar·ca·role *or* **bar·ca·rolle** \'bär-kə-,rōl\ *n* : a Venetian boat song characterized by a beat suggesting a rowing rhythm; *also* : a piece of music imitating this

bar chart *n* : BAR GRAPH

bar·code \'bär-,kōd\ *n* : a set of printed and variously spaced bars and sometimes numerals that is designed to be scanned to identify the object it labels — **bar–cod·ed** \'bär-,kō-dəd\ *adj* — **bar coding** *n*

bard \'bärd\ *n* ♦ : one who writes poetry : a maker of verses : POET

♦ minstrel, poet, versifier — more at POET

bard·ic \'bär-dik\ *adj* ♦ : being, belonging, or relating to a bard or the poetry of a bard

♦ lyric, lyrical, poetic — more at POETIC

¹**bare** \'bar\ *adj* **bar·er; bar·est 1 ♦** : devoid of customary or natural covering : NAKED **2** : open to view : UNCONCEALED, EXPOSED **3 ♦** : containing nothing : EMPTY ⟨the cupboard was ∼⟩ **4** : leaving nothing to spare : MERE **5 ♦** : lacking ornament : PLAIN, UNADORNED

♦ [1] bald, exposed, naked, nude, open, uncovered — more at NAKED ♦ [3] blank, devoid, empty, stark, vacant, void — more at EMPTY ♦ [5] bald, naked, plain, simple, unadorned, undecorated, unvarnished — more at PLAIN

²**bare** *vb* **bared; bar·ing ♦** : to make or lay bare : UNCOVER

♦ disclose, discover, divulge, expose, reveal, spill, tell, uncover, unmask, unveil — more at REVEAL

bare·back \-ˌbak\ *or* **bare·backed** \-'bakt\ *adv or adj* : without a saddle

bare·faced \-'fāst\ *adj* **1** : having the face uncovered; *esp* : BEARDLESS **2** : not concealed : OPEN — **bare·faced·ly** \-'fā-səd-lē, -'fāst-lē\ *adv*

bare·foot \-ˌfu̇t\ *or* **bare·foot·ed** \-'fu̇-təd\ *adv or adj* : with bare feet

bare–hand·ed \-'han-dəd\ *adv or adj* **1** : without gloves **2** : without tools or weapons

bare·head·ed \-'he-dəd\ *adv or adj* : without a hat

bare·ly \'bar-lē\ *adv* **1** : PLAINLY, MEAGERLY **2 ♦** : by a narrow margin : only just ⟨∼ enough money⟩

♦ hardly, just, marginally, scarcely, slightly — more at JUST

bare·ness *n* : the quality or state of being bare

barf \'bärf\ *vb* [origin unknown] **♦** : to discharge the contents of the stomach through the mouth : VOMIT

♦ gag, heave, hurl, puke, retch, spit up, throw up, vomit — more at VOMIT

bar·fly \'bär-ˌflī\ *n* : a drinker who frequents bars

¹**bar·gain** \'bär-gən\ *n* **1 ♦** : an agreement between parties settling a transaction **2 ♦** : an advantageous purchase **3** : a transaction, situation, or event regarded in the light of its results

♦ [1] accord, agreement, compact, contract, convention, covenant, deal, pact, settlement, understanding — more at AGREEMENT ♦ [2] buy, deal, steal; *also* markdown

²**bargain** *vb* **1 ♦** : to negotiate over the terms of an agreement; *also* : to come to terms **2** : BARTER

♦ chaffer, deal, dicker, haggle, negotiate, palter; *also* argue, bicker, clash, quibble, squabble, wrangle

bar·gain–base·ment \'bär-gən-'bās-mənt\ *adj* : markedly inexpensive

¹**barge** \'bärj\ *n* **1** : a broad flat-bottomed boat usu. moved by towing **2** : a motorboat supplied to a flagship (as for an admiral) **3** : a ceremonial boat elegantly furnished — **barge·man** \-mən\ *n*

²**barge** *vb* **barged; barg·ing 1** : to carry by barge **2** : to move or thrust oneself clumsily or rudely

bar graph *n* : a graphic technique for comparing amounts by rectangles whose lengths are proportional to the amounts they represent

ba·ris·ta \bə-'rēs-tə\ *n* : a person who makes and serves coffee to the public

bari·tone \'bar-ə-ˌtōn\ *n* [F *baryton* or It *baritono*, fr. Gk *barytonos* deep sounding, fr. *barys* heavy + *tonos* tone] : a male singing voice between bass and tenor; *also* : a person having this voice

bar·i·um \'bar-ē-əm\ *n* : a silver-white metallic chemical element that occurs only in combination

¹**bark** \'bärk\ *vb* **1** : to make the short loud cry of a dog **2** : to speak or utter in a curt loud tone : SNAP

²**bark** *n* : the sound made by a barking dog

³**bark** *n* : the tough corky outer covering of a woody stem or root

⁴**bark** *vb* **1 ♦** : to strip the bark from **2 ♦** : to rub the skin from

♦ [1, 2] flay, hull, husk, peel, shell, skin — more at PEEL

⁵**bark** *n* : a ship of three or more masts with the aft mast fore-and-aft rigged and the others square-rigged

bar·keep \'bär-ˌkēp\ *also* **bar·keep·er** \-ˌkē-pər\ *n* : BARTENDER

bark·er \'bär-kər\ *n* : a person who stands at the entrance esp. to a show and tries to attract customers to it

bar·ley \'bär-lē\ *n* : a cereal grass with seeds used as food and in making malt liquors; *also* : its seed

bar mitz·vah \bär-'mits-və\ *n, often cap B&M* [Heb *bar miṣwāh*, lit., son of the (divine) law] **1** : a Jewish boy who reaches his 13th birthday and assumes religious responsibilities **2** : the ceremony recognizing a boy as a bar mitzvah

barn \'bärn\ *n* [ME *bern*, fr. OE *bereærn*, fr. *bere* barley + *ærn* house, store] : a building used esp. for storing hay and grain and for housing livestock or farm equipment

bar·na·cle \'bär-ni-kəl\ *n* : any of numerous small marine crustaceans free-swimming when young but permanently fixed (as to rocks, whales, or ships) when adult

barn·storm \'bärn-ˌstȯrm\ *vb* : to travel through the country making brief stops to entertain (as with shows or flying stunts) or to campaign for political office

barn·yard \-ˌyärd\ *n* : a usu. fenced area adjoining a barn

baro·graph \'bar-ə-ˌgraf\ *n* : a recording barometer

ba·rom·e·ter \bə-'räm-ə-tər\ *n* : an instrument for measuring atmospheric pressure — **baro·met·ric** \ˌbar-ə-'me-trik\ *adj*

bar·on \'bar-ən\ *n* **1** : a member of the lowest grade of the British peerage **2 ♦** : a man who possesses great power or influence in some field of activity — **bar·ony** \'bar-ə-nē\ *n*

♦ czar, king, magnate, mogul, prince, tycoon — more at MAGNATE

bar·on·age \'bar-ə-nij\ *n* : PEERAGE

bar·on·ess \'bar-ə-nəs\ *n* **1** : the wife or widow of a baron **2** : a woman holding a baronial title in her own right

bar·on·et \'bar-ə-nət\ *n* : the holder of a rank of honor below a baron but above a knight — **bar·on·et·cy** \-sē\ *n*

ba·ro·ni·al \bə-'rō-nē-əl\ *adj* **1** : of or relating to a baron or the baronage **2 ♦** : generous or more than adequate in size, scope, or capacity : STATELY

♦ grand, grandiose, imposing, magnificent, majestic, monumental, stately — more at GRAND

ba·roque \bə-'rōk, -'räk\ *adj* : marked by the use of complex forms, bold ornamentation, and the juxtapositioning of contrasting elements

ba·rouche \bə-'rüsh\ *n* [G *Barutsche*, fr. It *biroccio*, ultim. fr. LL *birotus* two-wheeled, fr. L *bi-* two + *rota* wheel] : a 4-wheeled carriage with a high driver's seat in front and a folding top

bar·racks \'bar-əks\ *n sing or pl* : a building or group of buildings for lodging soldiers

bar·ra·cu·da \ˌbar-ə-'kü-də\ *n, pl* **-da** *or* **-das** : any of several large slender predaceous sea fishes including some used for food

bar·rage \bə-'räzh, -'räj\ *n* **1** : a heavy concentration of fire (as of artillery) **2 ♦** : vigorous or rapid outpouring of many things at once

♦ bombardment, cannonade, fusillade, hail, salvo, shower, storm, volley; *also* broadside, burst, outburst; deluge, flood, flood tide, flush, gush, inundation, outflow, outpouring, overflow, spate, surge, torrent

barred \'bärd\ *adj* : marked by or divided off by bars : STRIPED

¹**bar·rel** \'bar-əl\ *n* **1 ♦** : a round bulging cask with flat ends of equal diameter **2 a** : the amount contained in a barrel **b ♦** : a great quantity **3** : a drum or cylindrical part ⟨gun ∼⟩ — **bar·reled** \-əld\ *adj*

♦ [1] cask, hogshead, keg, pipe, puncheon — more at CASK ♦ [2b] abundance, deal, gobs, heap, loads, lot, pile, plenty, quantity, scads — more at LOT

²**barrel** *vb* **-reled** *or* **-relled; -rel·ing** *or* **-rel·ling 1** : to pack in a barrel **2 ♦** : to travel at high speed

♦ dash, fly, hurry, hurtle, rush, speed, tear, zip, zoom — more at HURRY

bar·rel·head \-ˌhed\ *n* : the flat end of a barrel — **on the**

barrelhead : asking for or granting no credit ⟨paid cash *on the barrelhead*⟩

barrel roll *n* : an airplane maneuver in which a complete revolution about the longitudinal axis is made

¹**bar·ren** \'bar-ən\ *adj* **1** ♦ : not producing fruit, spores, or offspring : STERILE **2 a** : not productive ⟨a ∼ scheme⟩ **b** ♦ : producing little or no vegetation : DESOLATE **3** : lacking interest or charm **4** : DULL, STUPID — **bar·ren·ness** \-nəs\ *n*

♦ **[1]** impotent, infertile, sterile — more at STERILE
♦ **[2b]** infertile, poor, stark, unproductive, waste; *also* bleak, dead, desolate, inhospitable, lifeless *Ant* fertile, fruitful, lush, luxuriant, productive, rich

²**barren** *n* ♦ : a tract of barren land

♦ desert, desolation, waste, wasteland — more at WASTELAND

bar·rette \bä-'ret, bə-\ *n* : a clasp or bar for holding the hair in place

¹**bar·ri·cade** \'bar-ə-ˌkād, ˌbar-ə-'kād\ *vb* **-cad·ed; -cad·ing** **1** : to block, obstruct, or fortify with a barricade **2** ♦ : to prevent access to by means of a barricade

♦ besiege, block, cut off, dam, encircle, surround

²**barricade** *n* [F, fr. MF, fr. *barriquer* to barricade, fr. *barrique* barrel] **1** : a hastily thrown-up obstruction or fortification **2** : something that impedes progress or achievement : BARRIER

bar·ri·er \'bar-ē-ər\ *n* ♦ : something that separates, demarcates, or serves as a barricade ⟨racial ∼s⟩ ⟨traffic ∼s⟩

♦ fence, hedge, wall; *also* bar, encumbrance, handicap, hindrance, hurdle, impediment, obstacle, obstruction, roadblock, stop

barrier island *n* : a long broad sandy island lying parallel to a shore

barrier reef *n* : a coral reef roughly parallel to a shore and separated from it by a lagoon

bar·ring \'bär-iŋ\ *prep* ♦ : excluding by exception

♦ aside from, bar, besides, but, except, outside (of), save

bar·rio \'bär-ē-ˌō, 'bar-\ *n, pl* **-ri·os** **1** : a district of a city or town in a Spanish-speaking country **2** : a Spanish-speaking quarter in a U.S. city

bar·ris·ter \'bar-ə-stər\ *n* : a British counselor admitted to plead in the higher courts

bar·room \'bär-ˌrüm, -ˌrùm\ *n* ♦ : a room or establishment whose main feature is a bar for the sale of liquor

♦ bar, café, pub, public house, saloon, tavern; *also* cabaret, dive, joint, nightclub, speakeasy

¹**bar·row** \'bar-ō\ *n* : a large burial mound of earth and stones

²**barrow** *n* **1** : WHEELBARROW **2** : a cart with a boxlike body and two shafts for pushing it

Bart *abbr* baronet

bar·tend·er \'bär-ˌten-dər\ *n* : a person who serves liquor at a bar

¹**bar·ter** \'bär-tər\ *vb* : to trade by exchange of goods — **bar·ter·er** *n*

²**barter** *n* **1** ♦ : the act or practice of carrying on trade by bartering **2** : the thing given in exchange in bartering

♦ commutation, exchange, swap, trade, truck — more at EXCHANGE

Ba·ruch \'bär-ˌük, bə-'rük\ *n* : homiletic book included in the Roman Catholic canon of the Old Testament and in the Protestant Apocrypha

bas·al \'bā-səl\ *adj* **1** : situated at or forming the base **2** : BASIC

basal metabolism *n* : the turnover of energy in a fasting and resting organism using energy solely to maintain vital cellular activity, respiration, and circulation as measured by the rate at which heat is given off

ba·salt \bə-'sòlt, 'bā-ˌsòlt\ *n* : a dark fine-grained igneous rock — **ba·sal·tic** \bə-'sòl-tik\ *adj*

¹**base** \'bās\ *n, pl* **bas·es** \'bā-səz\ **1 a** ♦ : the lowest part or

place : BOTTOM **b** ♦ : the physical or philosophical foundation upon which something is based **2** : a side or face on which a geometrical figure stands; *also* : the length of a base **3** ♦ : a main ingredient or fundamental part **4** : the point of beginning an act or operation **5** : a place on which a force depends for supplies **6** : a number (as 5 in 5⁷) that is raised to a power; *esp* : a number that when raised to a power equal to the logarithm of a number yields the number itself ⟨the logarithm of 100 to ∼ 10 is 2 since $10^2 = 100$⟩ **7** : the number of units in a given digit's place of a number system that is required to give the numeral 1 in the next higher place ⟨the decimal system uses a ∼ of 10⟩; *also* : such a system using an indicated base ⟨convert from ∼ 10 to ∼ 2⟩ **8** : any of the four stations at the corners of a baseball diamond **9** : a chemical compound (as lime or ammonia) that reacts with an acid to form a salt, has a bitter taste, and turns litmus blue — **base·man** \'bās-mən\ *n*

♦ **[1a]** bottom, foot — more at BOTTOM ♦ **[1b]** basis, bedrock, cornerstone, footing, foundation, ground, groundwork, keystone, underpinning — more at CORNERSTONE ♦ **[3]** center (*or* centre), core, cynosure, eye, focus, heart, hub, mecca, nucleus, seat — more at CENTER

²**base** *vb* **based; bas·ing** **1** ♦ : to form or serve as a base for **2** : ESTABLISH

♦ ground, rest; *also* establish, found

³**base** *adj* **1** : of inferior quality : DEBASED, ALLOYED **2** ♦ : characterized by baseness, lowness, or meanness : CONTEMPTIBLE, IGNOBLE **3** : MENIAL, DEGRADING **4** : of little value — **base·ly** *adv* — **base·ness** *n*

♦ contemptible, despicable, detestable, dirty, dishonorable (*or* dishonourable), ignoble, low, mean, snide, sordid, vile, wretched — more at IGNOBLE

base·ball \'bās-ˌbòl\ *n* : a game played with a bat and ball by two teams on a field with four bases arranged in a diamond; *also* : the ball used in this game

base·board \-ˌbòrd\ *n* : a line of boards or molding covering the joint of a wall and the adjoining floor

base·born \-'bòrn\ *adj* **1** : MEAN, IGNOBLE **2** : of humble birth **3** : of illegitimate birth

base exchange *n* : a post exchange at a naval or air force base

base hit *n* : a hit in baseball that enables the batter to reach base safely with no error made and no base runner forced out

BASE jumping \'bās-\ *n* [building, *a*ntenna, *s*pan, *e*arth] : the activity of parachuting from a high structure or cliff

base·less \-ləs\ *adj* ♦ : having no base or basis : GROUNDLESS

♦ groundless, invalid, unfounded, unreasonable, unsubstantiated, unsupported, unwarranted; *also* illogical, irrational, nonlogical, unconscionable, unsound *Ant* reasonable, reasoned, substantiated, valid, well-founded

base·line \'bās-ˌlīn\ *n* **1** : a line serving as a basis esp. to calculate or locate something **2** : the area within which a baseball player must keep when running between bases

base·ment \-mənt\ *n* **1** : the part of a building that is wholly or partly below ground level **2** : the lowest or fundamental part of something

base on balls : an advance to first base awarded a baseball player who during a turn at bat takes four pitches that are balls

base runner *n* : a baseball player who is on base or is attempting to reach a base

¹**bash** \'bash\ *vb* **1** ♦ : to strike violently : HIT **2** : to smash by a blow **3** ♦ : to attack physically or verbally

♦ **[1]** bang, collide, crash, hit, ram, slam, smash, strike
♦ **[3]** bat, batter, beat, hammer, lambaste, pelt, pound, thrash

²**bash** *n* **1** : a heavy blow **2** : a festive social gathering : PARTY

bash·ful \'bash-fəl\ *adj* ♦ : inclined to shrink from public attention — **bash·ful·ness** *n*

♦ coy, demure, diffident, introverted, modest, retiring, sheepish, shy — more at SHY

ba·sic \'bā-sik\ *adj* **1** ♦ : of, relating to, or forming the base or essence : FUNDAMENTAL **2** : of, relating to, or having the character of a chemical base — **ba·sic·i·ty** \bā-'si-sə-tē\ *n*

♦ elemental, elementary, essential, fundamental, rudimentary, underlying — more at ELEMENTARY

BA·SIC \'bā-sik\ *n* [*B*eginner's *A*ll-purpose *S*ymbolic *In*struction *C*ode] : a simplified language for programming a computer

ba·si·cal·ly \'bā-si-k(ə-)lē\ *adv* **1** : at a basic level **2** ♦ : for the most part **3** : in a basic manner

♦ altogether, chiefly, generally, largely, mainly, mostly, overall, predominantly, primarily, principally — more at CHIEFLY

ba·sil \'bā-zəl, 'ba-, -səl\ *n* : any of several mints with fragrant leaves used in cooking

ba·sil·i·ca \bə-'si-li-kə, -'zi-\ *n* [L, fr. Gk *basilikē*, fr. fem. of *basilikos* royal, fr. *basileus* king] **1** : an early Christian church building consisting of nave and aisles with clerestory and apse **2** : a Roman Catholic church given ceremonial privileges

bas·i·lisk \'ba-sə-,lisk, 'ba-zə-\ *n* [ME, fr. L *basiliscus*, fr. Gk *basiliskos*, fr. dim. of *basileus* king] : a legendary reptile with fatal breath and glance

ba·sin \'bās-ᵊn\ *n* **1** : an open usu. circular vessel with sloping sides for holding liquid (as water) **2** : a hollow or enclosed place containing water; *also* : the region drained by a river

ba·sis \'bā-səs\ *n, pl* **ba·ses** \-,sēz\ **1** : the lowest part or place : FOUNDATION **2** ♦ : a fundamental principle

♦ base, bedrock, cornerstone, footing, foundation, ground, groundwork, keystone, underpinning — more at CORNERSTONE

bask \'bask\ *vb* **1** ♦ : to lie or relax in comfortable warmth **2** : to enjoy something warmly comforting ⟨~*ing* in his friends' admiration⟩

♦ loll, lounge, relax, repose, rest — more at REST

bas·ket \'bas-kət\ *n* : a container made of woven material (as twigs or grasses); *also* : any of various lightweight usu. wood containers — **bas·ket·ful** *n*

bas·ket·ball \-,bȯl\ *n* : a game played on a court by two teams who try to throw an inflated ball through a raised goal; *also* : the ball used in this game

basket case *n* **1** : a person who has all four limbs amputated **2** : a person who is mentally incapacitated or worn out (as from nervous tension)

basket weave *n* : a textile weave resembling the checkered pattern of a plaited basket

basmati rice \,bäz-'mä-tē-\ *n* : an aromatic long-grain rice originating in southern Asia

bas mitzvah *var of* BAT MITZVAH

Basque \'bask\ *n* **1** : a member of a people inhabiting a region bordering on the Bay of Biscay in northern Spain and southwestern France **2** : the language of the Basque people — **Basque** *adj*

bas–re·lief \,bä-ri-'lēf\ *n* [F] : a sculpture in relief with the design raised very slightly from the background

¹**bass** \'bas\ *n, pl* **bass** *or* **bass·es** : any of numerous sport and food bony fishes (as a striped bass)

²**bass** \'bās\ *adj* ♦ : of low pitch

♦ deep, low, throaty — more at DEEP

³**bass** \'bās\ *n* **1** : a deep sound or tone **2** : the lower half of the musical pitch range **3** : the lowest part in a 4-part chorus; *also* : a singer having this voice or part

bas·set hound \'ba-sət-\ *n* : any of an old breed of short-legged hunting dogs of French origin having long ears and a short smooth coat

bas·si·net \,ba-sə-'net\ *n* : a baby's bed that resembles a basket and often has a hood over one end

bas·so \'ba-sō, 'bä-\ *n, pl* **bassos** *or* **bas·si** \'bä-,sē\ [It] : a bass singer

bas·soon \bə-'sün\ *n* : a musical wind instrument lower in pitch than the oboe

bass·wood \'bas-,wȯd\ *n* : any of several New World lindens or their wood

bast \'bast\ *n* : BAST FIBER

¹**bas·tard** \'bas-tərd\ *n* **1** : an illegitimate child **2** : an offensive or disagreeable person

²**bastard** *adj* **1** : not recognized as lawful offspring : ILLEGITIMATE **2** : of an inferior or nontypical kind, size, or form; *also* : SPURIOUS — **bas·tardy** *n*

bas·tard·ise *Brit var of* BASTARDIZE

bas·tard·ize \'bas-tər-,dīz\ *vb* **-ized; -iz·ing** : to reduce from a higher to a lower state : DEBASE

¹**baste** \'bāst\ *vb* **bast·ed; bast·ing** : to sew with long stitches so as to keep temporarily in place

²**baste** *vb* **bast·ed; bast·ing** : to moisten (as meat) at intervals with liquid while cooking

bast fiber *n* : a strong woody plant fiber obtained chiefly from phloem and used esp. in making ropes

bas·ti·na·do \,bas-tə-'nā-dō, -'nä-\ *or* **bas·ti·nade** \,bas-tə-'nād, -'näd\ *n, pl* **-na·does** *or* **-nades** **1** : a blow or beating esp. with a stick **2** : a punishment consisting of beating the soles of the feet

bas·tion \'bas-chən\ *n* **1** : a projecting part of a fortification **2** ♦ : a fortified position

♦ citadel, fastness, fort, fortification, fortress, hold, stronghold — more at FORT

¹**bat** \'bat\ *n* **1** ♦ : a stout stick : CLUB **2** ♦ : a sharp blow **3** : an implement (as of wood) used to hit a ball (as in baseball) **4** : a turn at batting — usu. used with *at*

♦ [1] billy club, bludgeon, club, cudgel, staff, truncheon — more at CLUB ♦ [2] belt, blow, box, clout, hit, punch, slug, wallop, whack — more at BLOW

²**bat** *vb* **bat·ted; bat·ting** : to hit with or as if with a bat

³**bat** *n* : any of an order of night-flying mammals with fore-limbs modified to form wings

⁴**bat** *vb* **bat·ted; bat·ting** : WINK, BLINK

batch \'bach\ *n* **1** : a quantity (as of bread) baked at one time **2** : a quantity of material for use at one time or produced at one operation **3** ♦ : a quantity (as of persons or things) considered as a group

♦ array, assemblage, block, bunch, collection, group, set

bate \'bāt\ *vb* **bat·ed; bat·ing** : MODERATE, REDUCE

bath \'bath, 'båth\ *n, pl* **baths** \'bathz, 'baths, 'båthz, 'båths\ **1** : a washing of the body **2** : water for washing the body **3** : a liquid in which objects are immersed so that it can act on them **4** : a room containing a bathtub or shower and usu. a sink and toilet : BATHROOM **5** : a financial loss ⟨took a ~ in the market⟩

bathe \'bāth\ *vb* **bathed; bath·ing** **1** ♦ : to wash in liquid and esp. water; *also* : to apply water or a medicated liquid to ⟨*bathed* her eyes⟩ **2** : to take a bath; *also* : to take a swim **3** ♦ : to wash along, over, or against so as to wet **4** : to suffuse with or as if with light — **bath·er** *n*

♦ [1, 3] douse, drench, soak, sop, souse, wash, water, wet — more at WET

bath·house \'bath-,haus, 'båth-\ *n* **1** : a building equipped for bathing **2** : a building containing dressing rooms for bathers

bathing suit *n* : SWIMSUIT

ba·thos \'bā-,thäs\ *n* [Gk, lit., depth] **1** : the sudden appearance of the commonplace in otherwise elevated matter or style **2** : insincere or overdone pathos — **ba·thet·ic** \bə-'the-tik\ *adj*

bath·robe \'bath-,rōb, 'båth-\ *n* : a loose often absorbent robe worn before and after a bath or as a dressing gown

bath·room \-,rüm, -,rum\ *n* ♦ : a room containing a bathtub or shower and usu. a sink and toilet

♦ lavatory, toilet — more at TOILET

bathroom tissue *n* : TOILET PAPER

bath·tub \-,təb\ *n* : a usu. fixed tub for bathing

ba·tik \bə-'tēk, 'ba-tik\ *n* [Javanese *baṭik*] **1** : an Indonesian method of hand-printing textiles by coating with wax the parts not to be dyed; *also* : a design so executed **2** : a fabric printed by batik

ba·tiste \bə-'tēst\ *n* : a fine sheer fabric of plain weave

bat·man \'bat-mən\ *n* : an orderly of a British military officer

bat mitz·vah \bät-'mits-və\ *also* **bas mitzvah** \bäs-\ *n, often cap B&M* [Heb *bath miṣwāh*, lit., daughter of the (divine) law] **1** : a Jewish girl who at 12 or more years of age assumes religious responsibilities **2** : the ceremony recognizing a girl as a bat mitzvah

ba·ton \bə-'tän\ *n* : STAFF, ROD; *esp* : a stick with which the leader directs an orchestra or band

bats·man \'bats-mən\ *n* : a batter esp. in cricket

bat·tal·ion \bə-'tal-yən\ *n* **1** ♦ : a large body of troops organized to act together : ARMY **2** : a military unit composed of a headquarters and two or more units (as companies)

♦ army, host, legion — more at ARMY

¹bat·ten \'bat-ᵊn\ *vb* **1** : to grow or make fat **2** : THRIVE
²batten *n* : a strip of wood used esp. to seal or strengthen a joint
³batten *vb* : to fasten with or as if with battens

¹bat·ter \'ba-tər\ *vb* ♦ : to beat or damage with repeated blows

♦ bash, beat, bludgeon, club, pound, thrash, thump, wallop — more at BEAT

²batter *n* : a soft mixture (as for cake) basically of flour and liquid
³batter *n* : one that bats; *esp* : the player whose turn it is to bat

battering ram *n* **1** : an ancient military machine for battering down walls **2** : a heavy metal bar with handles used to batter down doors

bat·tery \'ba-tə-rē\ *n, pl* **-ter·ies** **1** : BEATING; *esp* : unlawful beating or use of force on a person **2** : a grouping of artillery pieces for tactical purposes; *also* : the guns of a warship **3** : a group of electric cells for furnishing electric current; *also* : a single electric cell ⟨a flashlight ∼⟩ **4** : a number of similar items grouped or used as a unit ⟨a ∼ of tests⟩ **5** : the pitcher and catcher of a baseball team

bat·ting \'ba-tiŋ\ *n* : layers or sheets of cotton or wool (as for lining quilts)

¹bat·tle \'bat-ᵊl\ *n* [ME *batel*, fr. AF *bataille* battle, battalion, fr. LL *battalia* combat, alter. of *battualia* fencing exercises, fr. L *battuere* to beat] **1** : a general military engagement **2** ♦ : an extended contest, struggle, or controversy

♦ fight, fray, scrabble, struggle — more at STRUGGLE
♦ combat, conflict, confrontation, contest, duel, rivalry, struggle, tug-of-war, warfare — more at CONTEST

²battle *vb* **bat·tled; bat·tling** **1** ♦ : to engage in battle : FIGHT **2** ♦ : to contend with full strength, vigor, skill, or resources

♦ [1] clash, combat, fight, scrimmage, skirmish, war — more at FIGHT ♦ [2] combat, contend, counter, fight, oppose — more at FIGHT

bat·tle–ax \'bat-ᵊl-ˌaks\ *n* **1** : a long-handled ax formerly used as a weapon **2** : an angry and domineering woman

battle fatigue *n* : COMBAT FATIGUE

bat·tle·field \'bat-ᵊl-ˌfēld\ *n* : a place where a battle is fought

bat·tle·ment \-mənt\ *n* : a decorative or defensive parapet on top of a wall

bat·tle·ship \-ˌship\ *n* : a warship of the most heavily armed and armored class

bat·tle·wag·on \-ˌwa-gən\ *n* : BATTLESHIP

bat·ty \'ba-tē\ *adj* **bat·ti·er; -est** : disordered in mind : CRAZY

bau·ble \'bȯ-bəl\ *n* ♦ : a small ornament (as a jewel or ring) : TRINKET

♦ curiosity, gewgaw, knickknack, novelty, tchotchke, trinket — more at KNICKKNACK

baud \'bȯd, *Brit* 'bōd\ *n, pl* **baud** *also* **bauds** : a unit of data transmission speed

baux·ite \'bȯk-ˌsīt\ *n* : a clayey mixture that is the chief ore of aluminum

bawd \'bȯd\ *n* **1** : MADAM 2 **2** : PROSTITUTE

bawd·i·ness \-dē-nəs\ *n* ♦ : the quality or state of being bawdy ⟨his ribaldry and ∼⟩

♦ coarseness, indecency, lewdness, nastiness, obscenity, ribaldry, smut, vulgarity — more at OBSCENITY

bawdy \'bȯ-dē\ *adj* **bawd·i·er; -est** ♦ : offensive to morality or virtue : LEWD — **bawd·i·ly** \'bȯd-ᵊl-ē\ *adv*

♦ coarse, crude, indecent, obscene, smutty, unprintable, vulgar ♦ lewd, racy, ribald, risqué, spicy, suggestive — more at SUGGESTIVE

¹bawl \'bȯl\ *vb* ♦ : to cry or cry out loudly; *also* : to scold harshly

♦ blubber, cry, sob, weep — more at CRY ♦ call, cry, holler, shout, vociferate, yell — more at CALL

²bawl *n* : a long loud cry : BELLOW

bawl out *vb* ♦ : to reprimand loudly or severely

♦ admonish, chide, lecture, rail (at *or* against), rate, rebuke, reprimand, scold — more at SCOLD

¹bay \'bā\ *adj* : reddish brown
²bay *n* **1** : a bay-colored animal **2** : a reddish brown color
³bay *n* **1** : a section or compartment of a building or vehicle **2** : a compartment projecting outward from the wall of a building and containing a window (**bay window**)
⁴bay *vb* ♦ : to bark with deep long tones

♦ howl, keen, wail, yowl — more at HOWL

⁵bay *n* **1** : the position of one unable to escape and forced to face danger **2** : a baying of dogs
⁶bay *n* ♦ : an inlet of a body of water (as the sea) usu. smaller than a gulf

♦ bight, cove, estuary, firth, fjord, gulf, inlet — more at GULF

⁷bay *n* : the European laurel; *also* : a shrub or tree resembling this

bay·ber·ry \'bā-ˌber-ē\ *n* : a hardy deciduous shrub of coastal eastern No. America bearing small hard berries coated with a white wax used for candles; *also* : its fruit

bay leaf *n* : the dried leaf of the European laurel used in cooking

¹bay·o·net \'bā-ə-nət, ˌbā-ə-'net\ *n* : a daggerlike weapon made to fit on the muzzle end of a rifle
²bayonet *vb* **-net·ed** *also* **-net·ted; -net·ing** *also* **-net·ting** : to use or stab with a bayonet

bay·ou \'bī-yü, -ō\ *n* [Louisiana French, fr. Choctaw *bayuk*] : a marshy or sluggish body of water

bay rum *n* : a fragrant liquid used esp. as a cologne or aftershave lotion

ba·zaar \bə-'zär\ *n* **1** : a group of shops : MARKETPLACE **2** : a fair for the sale of articles usu. for charity

ba·zoo·ka \bə-'zü-kə\ *n* [*bazooka* (a crude musical instrument made of pipes and a funnel)] : a weapon consisting of a tube that launches a rocket able to pierce armor

¹BB \'bē-(ˌ)bē\ *n* : a small round shot pellet
²BB *abbr* base on balls

BBB *abbr* Better Business Bureau

BBC *abbr* British Broadcasting Corporation

bbl *abbr* barrel; barrels

BC *abbr* **1** before Christ — often printed in small capitals and often punctuated **2** British Columbia

¹bcc \ˌbē-ˌsē-'sē\ *vb* **1** : to send a blind carbon copy to **2** : to send as a blind carbon copy

²bcc *abbr* blind carbon copy

B cell *n* [*bone-marrow-derived cell*] : any of the lymphocytes that secrete antibodies when mature

B complex *n* : VITAMIN B COMPLEX

bd *abbr* **1** board **2** bound

bdl *or* **bdle** *abbr* bundle

bdrm *abbr* bedroom

be \'bē\ *vb, past 1st & 3d sing* **was** \'wəz, 'wäz\; *2d sing* **were** \'wər\; *pl* **were**; *past subjunctive* **were**; *past part* **been** \'bin\; *pres part* **be·ing** \'bē-iŋ\; *pres 1st sing* **am** \əm,

'am**; *2d sing* **are **ər, 'är\; *3d sing* **is \'iz, əz\; *pl* **are**; *pres subjunctive* **be** **1** : to equal in meaning or symbolically ⟨God *is* love⟩; *also* : to have a specified qualification or relationship ⟨leaves *are* green⟩ ⟨this fish *is* a trout⟩ **2 a ♦** : to have objective existence ⟨I think, therefore I *am*⟩ **b ♦** : to have or occupy a particular place ⟨here *is* your pen⟩ **3** : to take place : OCCUR ⟨the meeting *is* tonight⟩ **4** — used with the past participle of transitive verbs as a passive voice auxiliary ⟨the door *was* opened⟩ **5** — used as the auxiliary of the present participle in expressing continuous action ⟨he *is* sleeping⟩ **6** — used as an auxiliary with the past participle of some intransitive verbs to form archaic perfect tenses **7** — used as an auxiliary with *to* and the infinitive to express futurity, prearrangement, or obligation ⟨you *are* to come when called⟩

♦ [2a] breathe, exist, live, subsist; *also* abide, continue, endure, last, lead, persist, survive *Ant* depart, die, expire, pass away, perish, succumb **♦ [2b]** lie, sit, stand

Be *symbol* beryllium

¹beach \'bēch\ *n* : a sandy or gravelly part of the shore of an ocean or lake

²beach *vb* : to run or drive ashore

beach buggy *n* : DUNE BUGGY

beach·comb·er \'bēch-ˌkō-mər\ *n* : a person who searches along a shore for something of use or value

beach·head \'bēch-ˌhed\ *n* : a small area on an enemy-held shore occupied in the initial stages of an invasion

bea·con \'bē-kən\ *n* **1** : a signal fire **2** : a guiding or warning signal (as a lighthouse) **3** : a radio transmitter emitting signals for guidance of aircraft

¹bead \'bēd\ *n* [ME *bede* prayer, prayer bead, fr. OE *bed*, *gebed* prayer] **1** *pl* : a series of prayers and meditations made with a rosary **2** : a small piece of material pierced for threading on a line (as in a rosary) **3** : a small globular body **4** : a narrow projecting rim or band — **bead·ing** *n* — **beady** *adj*

²bead *vb* : to form into a bead

bea·dle \'bēd-ᵊl\ *n* : a usu. English parish officer whose duties include keeping order in church

bea·gle \'bē-gəl\ *n* : a small short-legged smooth-coated hound

beak \'bēk\ *n* : the bill of a bird and esp. of a bird of prey; *also* : a pointed projecting part — **beaked \'**bēkt\ *adj*

bea·ker \'bē-kər\ *n* **1** : a large widemouthed drinking cup **2** : a widemouthed thin-walled laboratory vessel

¹beam \'bēm\ *n* **1** : a large long piece of timber or metal **2** : the bar of a balance from which the scales hang **3** : the breadth of a ship at its widest part **4** : a ray or shaft of light **5** : a collection of nearly parallel rays (as X-rays) or particles (as electrons) **6** : a constant radio signal transmitted for the guidance of pilots; *also* : the course indicated by this signal

²beam *vb* **1** : to send out light **2** : to aim (a broadcast) by directional antennas **3** : to smile with joy

beam·ing *adj* **1 ♦** : marked by, emitting, or reflecting strong or clear rays of light **2 ♦** : marked by or expressive of extreme and unreserved joy, happiness, or satisfaction

♦ [1] bright, brilliant, incandescent, luminous, shiny — more at BRIGHT **♦ [2]** aglow, glowing, radiant, sunny — more at RADIANT

¹bean \'bēn\ *n* : the edible seed borne in pods by some leguminous plants; *also* : a plant or a pod bearing these

²bean *vb* : to strike on the head with an object

bean·bag \'bēn-ˌbag\ *n* : a cloth bag partially filled typically with dried beans and used as a toy

bean·ball \'bēn-ˌbȯl\ *n* : a pitch thrown at a batter's head

bean curd *n* : TOFU

bean·ie \'bē-nē\ *n* : a small round tight-fitting skullcap

beano \'bē-nō\ *n, pl* **beanos** : BINGO

¹bear \'bar\ *n, pl* **bears 1** *or pl* **bear** : any of a family of large heavy mammals with shaggy hair and small tails **2 ♦** : a gruff or sullen person **3** : one who sells (as securities) in expectation of a price decline

♦ complainer, crab, crank, curmudgeon, grouch, grumbler, whiner — more at GROUCH

²bear *vb* **bore \'**bōr\; **borne \'**bōrn\ *also* **born \'**bȯrn\; **bear·ing 1 ♦** : to move while supporting : CARRY **2** : to be equipped with **3** : to give as testimony ⟨∼ witness to the facts of the case⟩ **4** : to give birth to; *also* : PRODUCE, YIELD ⟨a tree that ∼s regularly⟩ **5 a ♦** : to support (as a weight or structure) ⟨*bore* the weight on piles⟩ **b ♦** : to accept or allow oneself to be subject to : take on or endure ⟨∼ pain⟩ **6** : to go in an indicated direction ⟨∼ to the right⟩ **7** : to manage the actions of (oneself) in a particular way : CONDUCT **8 ♦** : to hold in the mind or emotions **9** : to exert pressure or influence **10 ♦** : to have relevance or a valid connection : PERTAIN — often used with *on* or *upon* ⟨facts ∼*ing* on the question⟩ — **bear·er** *n*

♦ [1] carry, cart, convey, ferry, haul, lug, pack, tote, transport — more at CARRY **♦ [5a]** bolster, brace, buttress, carry, prop, shore, stay, support, uphold — more at SUPPORT **♦ [5b]** accept, assume, shoulder, take over, undertake — more at ASSUME **♦ [5b]** abide, brook, countenance, endure, meet, stand, stick out, stomach, support, sustain, take, tolerate; *also* accept, allow, permit, suffer, swallow **♦ [8]** cherish, entertain, harbor (*or* harbour), have, hold, nurse — more at HARBOR **♦** *usu* **bear on [10]** appertain, apply, pertain, refer, relate — more at APPLY

bear·able *adj* **♦** : capable of being borne

♦ endurable, sufferable, supportable, sustainable, tolerable; *also* livable *Ant* insufferable, insupportable, intolerable, unbearable, unendurable, unsupportable

¹beard \'bird\ *n* **1** : the hair that grows on the face of a man **2** : a growth of bristly hairs (as on a goat's chin) — **beard·ed \'**bir-dəd\ *adj* — **beard·less** *adj*

²beard *vb* **♦** : to confront boldly

♦ brave, brazen, confront, dare, defy, face — more at FACE

bear down *vb* : to exert full strength and concentrated attention — **bear down on ♦** : to weigh heavily on

♦ *usu* **bear down on** depress, press, shove, weigh — more at PRESS

bear·ing \'bar-iŋ\ *n* **1 ♦** : manner of carrying oneself : COMPORTMENT **2** : a supporting object, purpose, or point **3** : a machine part in which another part (as an axle or pin) turns **4** : an emblem in a coat of arms **5** : the position or direction of one point with respect to another or to the compass; *also* : a determination of position **6** *pl* : comprehension of one's situation **7 ♦** : connection with or influence on something; *also* : SIGNIFICANCE

♦ [1] actions, behavior (*or* behaviour), comportment, conduct, demeanor (*or* demeanour), deportment — more at BEHAVIOR **♦ [7]** applicability, pertinence, relevance, significance — more at PERTINENCE **♦ [7]** association, connection, linkage, relation, relationship — more at CONNECTION

bear·ish *adj* **1 ♦** : resembling a bear in build or in roughness, gruffness, or surliness ⟨a ∼ man⟩ **2** : marked by, tending to cause, or fearful of falling prices (as in a stock market)

♦ bilious, cantankerous, disagreeable, dyspeptic, ill-humored, ill-tempered, ornery, splenetic, surly — more at ILL-TEMPERED

bear market *n* : a market in which securities or commodities are persistently falling in value

bear out *vb* **♦** : to give new assurance of the validity of : CONFIRM, SUBSTANTIATE ⟨a theory *borne out* by data⟩

♦ confirm, corroborate, substantiate, support, validate, verify, vindicate — more at CONFIRM

bear·skin \'bar-ˌskin\ *n* : an article made of the skin of a bear

beast \'bēst\ *n* **1 ♦** : any of a kingdom of living things typically differing from plants in capacity for active movement, in rapid response to stimulation, and in lack of cellulose cell walls : ANIMAL; *esp* : a 4-footed mammal **2** ♦ : a contemptible person

    ♦ [1] animal, creature, critter ♦ [2] brute, devil, fiend, monster, savage, villain — more at FIEND

¹beast·ly \'bēst-lē\ *adj* **beast·li·er; -est 1** : BESTIAL **2** : ABOMINABLE, DISAGREEABLE — **beast·li·ness** \-nəs\ *n*
²beastly *adv* : to a high degree : VERY, EXCEEDINGLY
¹beat \'bēt\ *vb* **beat; beat·en** \'bēt-ᵊn\ *or* **beat; beat·ing 1** ♦ : to strike repeatedly **2** : TREAD **3** ♦ : to affect or alter by beating ⟨~ metal into sheets⟩ **4** : to sound (as an alarm) on a drum **5 a** ♦ : to get the better of : OVERCOME **b** ♦ : to become better, greater, or stronger than : SURPASS **6** : to act or arrive before ⟨~ his brother home⟩ **7** : to beat or vibrate rhythmically : THROB **8** : to flap or thrash at vigorously **9** : to glare or strike with oppressive intensity ⟨the sun ~ down on the caravan⟩

    ♦ [1] bash, bat, batter, club, drub, pound, thrash, thump, wallop, whale, whip; *also* assail, attack, box, bust, cane, chop, clobber, clout, crack, cudgel, cuff, hit, horsewhip, knock, lam, lash, lay on, paste, punch, slap, smack, smash, sock, spank, swat, swipe, thwack, whack ♦ [3] forge, hammer, pound — more at HAMMER ♦ [5a] best, conquer, crush, defeat, lick, overcome, prevail, rout, skunk, subdue, thrash, triumph, trounce, wallop, whip; *also* nose out **Ant** lose (to) ♦ [5b] better, eclipse, excel, outdistance, outdo, outshine, outstrip, surpass, top, transcend — more at SURPASS

²beat *n* **1 a** : a single stroke or blow esp. of a series **b** ♦ : a rhythmic throbbing, contraction and expansion, or vibration : PULSATION **2** ♦ : a rhythmic stress in poetry or music or the rhythmic effect of these **3** : a regularly traversed course

    ♦ [1b] palpitation, pulsation, pulse, throb — more at PULSATION ♦ [2] cadence, measure, meter (*or* metre), rhythm — more at RHYTHM

³beat *adj* **1** ♦ : consumed entirely : EXHAUSTED **2** : of or relating to beatniks

    ♦ bushed, dead, drained, exhausted, prostrate, spent, weary, worn-out — more at WEARY

⁴beat *n* : BEATNIK
beat·er *n* : one that beats
be·atif·ic \ˌbē-ə-'ti-fik\ *adj* : giving or indicative of great joy or bliss
be·at·i·fy \bē-'a-tə-ˌfī\ *vb* **-fied; -fy·ing 1** : to make supremely happy **2** : to declare to have attained the blessedness of heaven and authorize the title "Blessed" for — **be·at·i·fi·ca·tion** \-ˌa-tə-fə-'kā-shən\ *n*
be·at·i·tude \bē-'a-tə-ˌtüd, -ˌtyüd\ *n* **1** : a state of utmost bliss **2** : any of the declarations made in the Sermon on the Mount (Mt 5:3–12) beginning "Blessed are"
beat·nik \'bēt-nik\ *n* : a person who rejects the mores of established society and indulges in exotic philosophizing and self-expression
beau \'bō\ *n, pl* **beaux** \'bōz\ *or* **beaus** [F, fr. *beau* beautiful, fr. L *bellus* pretty] **1** : a man of fashion : DANDY **2** ♦ : a male romantic companion : BOYFRIEND

    ♦ boyfriend, fellow, man, swain — more at BOYFRIEND

beau geste \bō-'zhest\ *n, pl* **beaux gestes** *or* **beau gestes** \bō-'zhest\ : a graceful or magnanimous gesture
beau ide·al \ˌbō-ī-'dē(-ə)l\ *n, pl* **beau ideals** [F] ♦ : the perfect type or model

    ♦ classic, epitome, exemplar, ideal, model, nonpareil, paragon, perfection, quintessence — more at QUINTESSENCE

Beau·jo·lais \ˌbō-zhō-'lā\ *n* : a French red table wine
beau monde \bō-'mänd, -'mōⁿd\ *n, pl* **beau mondes** \-'mänz, -'mändz\ *or* **beaux mondes** \bō-'mōⁿd\ [F] : the world of high society and fashion
beau·te·ous \'byü-tē-əs\ *adj* : having beauty : BEAUTIFUL — **beau·te·ous·ly** *adv*

beau·ti·cian \byü-'ti-shən\ *n* : COSMETOLOGIST
beau·ti·ful \'byü-ti-fəl\ *adj* ♦ : characterized by beauty : LOVELY — **beau·ti·ful·ly** \-f(ə-)lē\ *adv*

    ♦ attractive, cute, fair, gorgeous, handsome, knockout, lovely, pretty, ravishing, stunning; *also* alluring, appealing, charming, delightful, glamorous, prepossessing **Ant** homely, plain, ugly, unattractive, unhandsome, unlovely

beau·ti·ful·ness \'byü-ti-fəl-nəs\ *n* ♦ : the quality or state of being beautiful
beautiful people *n pl, often cap B&P* : wealthy or famous people whose lifestyle is usu. expensive and well-publicized
beau·ti·fy \'byü-tə-ˌfī\ *vb* **-fied; -fy·ing** ♦ : to make more beautiful — **beau·ti·fi·ca·tion** \ˌbyü-tə-fə-'kā-shən\ *n* — **beau·ti·fi·er** *n*

    ♦ adorn, bedeck, deck, decorate, embellish, enrich, garnish, grace, ornament, trim — more at DECORATE

beau·ty \'byü-tē\ *n, pl* **beauties 1** ♦ : qualities that give pleasure to the senses or exalt the mind : LOVELINESS **2** ♦ : a beautiful person or thing; *esp* : a beautiful woman **3** ♦ : an extreme or egregious example or instance

    ♦ [1] attractiveness, comeliness, handsomeness, looks, loveliness, prettiness; *also* allure, appeal, attraction, glamour **Ant** homeliness, plainness, ugliness ♦ [2] enchantress, fox, goddess, knockout, queen; *also* belle, charmer, honey ♦ [3] crackerjack, dandy, jim-dandy, knockout, pip — more at JIM-DANDY

beauty shop *n* : an establishment where hairdressing, facials, and manicures are done
beaux arts \bō-'zär\ *n pl* [F] : FINE ARTS
bea·ver \'bē-vər\ *n, pl* **beavers** : a large fur-bearing herbivorous rodent that builds dams and underwater houses of mud and sticks; *also* : its fur
be·calm \bi-'käm, -'kälm\ *vb* : to keep (as a ship) motionless by lack of wind
be·cause \bi-'kóz, -'kəz\ *conj* ♦ : for the reason that

    ♦ for, now, since, whereas — more at SINCE

because of *prep* ♦ : by reason of

    ♦ due to, owing to, through, with

beck \'bek\ *n* : a beckoning gesture; *also* : SUMMONS
beck·on \'be-kən\ *vb* : to summon or signal esp. by a nod or gesture; *also* : ATTRACT
be·cloud \bi-'klaúd\ *vb* ♦ : to prevent clear perception or realization of

    ♦ befog, blur, cloud, darken, dim, fog, haze, mist, obscure, overcast, overshadow, shroud — more at CLOUD

be·come \bi-'kəm\ *vb* **-came** \-'kām\; **-come; -com·ing 1** ♦ : to come to be ⟨~ tired⟩ **2** : to suit or be suitable to ⟨her dress ~s her⟩

    ♦ come, get, go, grow, run, turn, wax; *also* alter, change, metamorphose, modify, mutate, transfigure, transform, transmute

be·com·ing *adj* : adapted to a use or purpose : SUITABLE, FIT; *also* : ATTRACTIVE — **be·com·ing·ly** *adv*
¹bed \'bed\ *n* **1** ♦ : an article of furniture to sleep on **2** : a plot of ground prepared for plants **3** : an underlying base or support : BOTTOM **4** : LAYER, STRATUM

    ♦ bunk, pad, sack; *also* bedstead, mattress, pallet

²bed *vb* **bed·ded; bed·ding 1** : to put or go to bed **2** : to fix in a foundation : EMBED **3** : to plant in beds **4** : to lay or lie flat or in layers
bed–and–breakfast *n* : an establishment offering lodging and breakfast
be·daub \bi-'dób\ *vb* : to spread or daub over a surface : SMEAR
be·daz·zle \bi-'da-zəl\ *vb* : to confuse by or as if by a strong light; *also* : FASCINATE — **be·daz·zle·ment** *n*
bed·bug \'bed-ˌbəg\ *n* : a wingless bloodsucking bug infesting houses and esp. beds
bed·clothes \'bed-ˌklōthz\ *n pl* : BEDDING 1

bed·ding \'be-diŋ\ *n* **1** : materials for making up a bed **2** : FOUNDATION

be·deck \bi-'dek\ *vb* ♦ : to furnish with something ornamental : ADORN

♦ adorn, array, beautify, deck, decorate, do, dress, embellish, enrich, garnish, grace, ornament, trim — more at DECORATE

be·dev·il \bi-'de-vəl\ *vb* **1** ♦ : to cause distress : TORMENT **2** : CONFUSE, MUDDLE

♦ afflict, agonize, curse, harrow, martyr, persecute, plague, rack, torment, torture — more at AFFLICT

be·dew \bi-'dü, -'dyü\ *vb* : to wet with or as if with dew

bed·fast \'bed-ˌfast\ *adj* : BEDRIDDEN

bed·fel·low \-ˌfe-lō\ *n* **1** : one sharing the bed of another **2** : a close associate : ALLY

be·di·zen \bi-'dīz-ᵊn, -'diz-\ *vb* : to dress or adorn with showy or vulgar finery

bed·lam \'bed-ləm\ *n* [*Bedlam*, popular name for the Hospital of St. Mary of Bethlehem, London, an insane asylum, fr. ME *Bedlem* Bethlehem] **1** *often cap* : an insane asylum **2** ♦ : a scene of uproar and confusion

♦ circus, hell, madhouse — more at MADHOUSE

bed·ou·in *or* **bed·u·in** \'be-də-wən\ *n, pl* **bedouin** *or* **bedouins** *or* **beduin** *or* **beduins** *often cap* [ME *Bedoyne*, fr. MF *bedoïn*, fr. Ar *badawī* desert dweller] : a nomadic Arab of the Arabian, Syrian, or northern African deserts

bed·pan \'bed-ˌpan\ *n* : a shallow vessel used by a bedridden person for urination or defecation

bed·post \-ˌpōst\ *n* : the post of a bed

be·drag·gled \bi-'dra-gəld\ *adj* : soiled and disordered as if by being drenched

bed·rid·den \'bed-ˌrid-ᵊn\ *adj* : kept in bed by illness or weakness

¹bed·rock \-'räk\ *n* **1** : the solid rock underlying surface materials (as soil) **2** ♦ : the bottom of something considered as its foundation

♦ base, basis, cornerstone, footing, foundation, ground, groundwork, keystone, underpinning — more at CORNERSTONE

²bedrock *adj* : solidly fundamental, basic, or reliable ⟨traditional ∼ values⟩

bed·roll \'bed-ˌrōl\ *n* : bedding rolled up for carrying

bed·room \-ˌrüm, -ˌrùm\ *n* : a room containing a bed and used esp. for sleeping

bed·side \-ˌsīd\ *n* : the place beside a bed esp. of a sick or dying person

bed·sore \-ˌsōr\ *n* : an ulceration of tissue deprived of adequate blood supply by prolonged pressure

bed·spread \-ˌspred\ *n* ♦ : a usu. ornamental cloth cover for a bed

♦ counterpane, spread — more at COUNTERPANE

bed·stead \-ˌsted\ *n* : the framework of a bed

bed·time \-ˌtīm\ *n* : time for going to bed

bed·wet·ting \-ˌwe-tiŋ\ *n* : involuntary discharge of urine esp. in bed during sleep — **bed·wet·ter** *n*

¹bee \'bē\ *n* : any of numerous 4-winged insects (as honeybees or bumblebees) that feed on nectar and pollen and that sometimes produce honey or have a painful sting

²bee *n* : a gathering of people for a specific purpose ⟨quilting ∼⟩

beech \'bēch\ *n, pl* **beech·es** *or* **beech** : any of a genus of deciduous hardwood trees with smooth gray bark and small sweet triangular nuts; *also* : the wood of a beech — **beech·en** \'bē-chən\ *adj*

beech·nut \'bēch-ˌnət\ *n* : the nut of a beech

¹beef \'bēf\ *n, pl* **beefs** \'bēfs\ *or* **beeves** \'bēvz\ **1** : the flesh of a steer, cow, or bull; *also* : the dressed carcass of a beef animal **2** : a steer, cow, or bull esp. when fattened for food **3** : MUSCLE, BRAWN **4** *pl* **beefs** ♦ : expression of grief, pain, or dissatisfaction : COMPLAINT

♦ complaint, fuss, grievance, gripe, grumble, murmur, plaint, squawk — more at COMPLAINT

²beef *vb* **1** ♦ : to increase or add substance, strength, or power to : STRENGTHEN — usu. used with *up* **2** ♦ : to express grief, pain, or discontent : COMPLAIN

♦ *usu.* **beef up** [1] fortify, harden, strengthen, toughen — more at STRENGTHEN ♦ *usu.* **beef up** [1] amplify, boost, consolidate, deepen, enhance, heighten, intensify, magnify, redouble, step up — more at INTENSIFY ♦ [2] bellyache, carp, complain, crab, gripe, grouse, growl, grumble, kick, moan, squawk, wail, whine — more at COMPLAIN

beef·eat·er \'bē-ˌfē-tər\ *n* : a yeoman of the guard of an English monarch

beef·steak \-ˌstāk\ *n* : a slice of beef suitable for broiling or frying

beefy \'bē-fē\ *adj* **beef·i·er; -est** ♦ : heavily and powerfully built : BRAWNY ⟨a ∼ wrestler⟩

♦ brawny, burly, husky — more at HUSKY

bee·hive \'bē-ˌhīv\ *n* : HIVE 1, 3

bee·keep·er \-ˌkē-pər\ *n* : a person who raises bees — **bee·keep·ing** *n*

bee·line \-ˌlīn\ *n* : a straight direct course

been *past part of* BE

beep·er \'bē-pər\ *n* : a small radio receiver that beeps when signaled to alert the person carrying it

beer \'bir\ *n* : an alcoholic beverage brewed from malt and hops — **beery** *adj*

bees·wax \'bēz-ˌwaks\ *n* : WAX 1

beet \'bēt\ *n* : a garden plant with edible leaves and a thick sweet root used as a vegetable, as a source of sugar, or as forage; *also* : its root

¹bee·tle \'bēt-ᵊl\ *n* : any of an order of insects having four wings of which the stiff outer pair covers the membranous inner pair when not in flight

²beetle *vb* **bee·tled; bee·tling** ♦ : to jut out : PROJECT

♦ bulge, overhang, poke, project, protrude, stick out — more at BULGE

be·fall \bi-'fȯl\ *vb* **-fell** \-'fel\; **-fall·en** \-'fȯ-lən\; **-fall·ing** ♦ : to happen to : OCCUR

♦ be, betide, chance, come, go, happen, occur, pass, transpire — more at HAPPEN

be·fit \bi-'fit\ *vb* ♦ : to be suitable to

♦ do, fit, go, serve, suit — more at DO

be·fog \bi-'fȯg, -'fäg\ *vb* **1** ♦ : to make dark, dim, or indistinct : OBSCURE **2** ♦ : to make mentally unclear or uncertain : CONFUSE

♦ [1] becloud, blur, cloud, darken, dim, fog, haze, mist, obscure, overcast, overshadow, shroud — more at CLOUD ♦ [2] addle, baffle, befuddle, bemuse, bewilder, confound, confuse, disorient, muddle, muddy, mystify, perplex, puzzle — more at CONFUSE

¹be·fore \bi-'fōr\ *adv or adj* **1** : in front **2** ♦ : at an earlier time : PREVIOUSLY

♦ ahead, beforehand, previously — more at AHEAD

²before *prep* **1** : in front of ⟨stood ∼ him⟩ **2** ♦ : earlier than ⟨got there ∼ me⟩ **3** : in a more important category than ⟨put quality ∼ quantity⟩

♦ ahead of, ere, of, previous to, prior to, to; *also* till, until **Ant** after, following

³before *conj* **1** : earlier than the time that ⟨she started ∼ I did⟩ **2** : more willingly than ⟨he'd starve ∼ he'd steal⟩

be·fore·hand \bi-'fōr-ˌhand\ *adv or adj* ♦ : in advance

♦ ahead, before, early, previously — more at AHEAD

be·foul \bi-'faùl\ *vb* ♦ : to make foul (as with dirt or waste)

♦ begrime, besmirch, blacken, dirty, muddy, smirch, soil, stain — more at DIRTY ♦ contaminate, defile, foul, poison, pollute, taint — more at CONTAMINATE

be·friend \bi-'frend\ *vb* : to act as friend to

be·fud·dle \bi-'fəd-ᵊl\ *vb* ♦ : to muddle or stupefy with or as if with drink : CONFUSE

♦ addle, baffle, befog, bemuse, bewilder, confound, confuse, disorient, muddle, muddy, mystify, perplex, puzzle — more at CONFUSE

beg \'beg\ vb **begged; beg·ging 1** ♦ : to ask as a charity; also : ENTREAT **2** : EVADE; also : assume as established, settled, or proved ⟨∼ the question⟩

♦ appeal, beseech, entreat, implore, importune, petition, plead, pray, solicit, supplicate; also sponge

be·get \bi-'get\ vb **-got** \-'gät\; **-got·ten** \-'gät-ᵊn\ or **-got; -get·ting** ♦ : to become the father of : SIRE

♦ father, get, produce, sire — more at FATHER

¹**beg·gar** \'be-gər\ n : one that begs; esp : a person who begs as a way of life

²**beggar** vb : IMPOVERISH

beg·gar·ly \'be-gər-lē\ adj **1** : contemptibly mean or inadequate **2** : marked by unrelieved poverty ⟨a ∼ life⟩

beg·gary \'be-gə-rē\ n ♦ : extreme poverty

♦ destitution, impecuniousness, impoverishment, indigence, need, pauperism, penury, poverty, want — more at POVERTY

be·gin \bi-'gin\ vb **be·gan** \-'gan\; **be·gun** \-'gən\; **be·gin·ning 1** ♦ : to do the first part of an action : COMMENCE **2** ♦ : to come into being : ARISE; also : FOUND ⟨they began the movement⟩ **3** : ORIGINATE, INVENT

♦ [1] commence, embark (on or upon), enter, get off, launch, open, start, strike; also create, generate, inaugurate, initiate, innovate, invent, originate **Ant** conclude, end, finish, terminate ♦ [2] arise, commence, dawn, form, found, materialize, originate, spring, start; also be, breathe, exist, live, subsist **Ant** cease, end, stop

be·gin·ner n ♦ : one that begins something; esp : an inexperienced person

♦ fledgling, freshman, greenhorn, neophyte, newcomer, novice, recruit, rookie, tenderfoot, tyro; also apprentice, cub **Ant** old-timer, vet, veteran

be·gin·ning \bi-'gi-niŋ, bē-\ n ♦ : the point at which something starts : START

♦ birth, commencement, dawn, genesis, launch, morning, onset, outset, start, threshold; also creation, inauguration, initiation, institution **Ant** close, conclusion, end, ending

beg off vb : to ask to be excused from something

be·gone \bi-'gȯn\ vb : to go away : DEPART — used esp. in the imperative

be·go·nia \bi-'gō-nyə\ n : any of a genus of tropical herbs widely grown for their showy leaves and waxy flowers

be·grime \bi-'grīm\ vb **be·grimed; be·grim·ing** ♦ : to make dirty

♦ befoul, besmirch, blacken, dirty, foul, grime, mire, muddy, smirch, soil, stain — more at DIRTY

be·grudge \bi-'grəj\ vb **1** : to give or concede reluctantly **2** : to be reluctant to grant or allow

be·guile \-'gīl\ vb **be·guiled; be·guil·ing 1** ♦ : to lead by deception **2** : to while away **3** ♦ : to engage the interest of by guile

♦ [1] deceive, dupe, fool, hoax, misinform, mislead, take in, trick — more at DECEIVE ♦ [1] decoy, entice, lead on, lure, seduce, tempt — more at LURE ♦ [3] bewitch, captivate, charm, enchant, fascinate, wile — more at CHARM

be·guine \bi-'gēn\ n [AmerF béguine, fr. F béguin flirtation] : a vigorous popular dance of the islands of Saint Lucia and Martinique

be·gum \'bā-gəm, 'bē-\ n : a Muslim woman of high rank

be·half \bi-'haf, -'háf\ n : BENEFIT, SUPPORT, DEFENSE

be·have \bi-'hāv\ vb **be·haved; be·hav·ing 1** ♦ : to bear, comport, or conduct oneself in a particular and esp. a proper way **2** : to act, function, or react in a particular way

♦ acquit, bear, comport, conduct, demean, deport, quit; also check, collect, compose, constrain, contain, control, curb, handle, inhibit, quiet, repress, restrain

be·hav·ior \bi-'hā-vyər\ or Can and Brit **be·hav·iour** n ♦ : way of behaving; esp : personal conduct — **be·hav·ior·al** \-vyə-rəl\ adj

♦ actions, bearing, comportment, conduct, demeanor (or demeanour), deportment; also etiquette, form, manners, mores

be·hav·ior·ism or Can and Brit **be·hav·iour·ism** \bi-'hā-vyə-,ri-zəm\ n : a school of psychology concerned with the objective evidence of behavior without reference to conscious experience

be·head \bi-'hed\ vb : to remove the head from

be·he·moth \bi-'hē-məth, 'bē-ə-,mäth\ n **1** : a huge powerful animal described in Job 40:15–24 **2** ♦ : something of monstrous size or power

♦ blockbuster, colossus, giant, jumbo, leviathan, mammoth, monster, titan, whale, whopper — more at GIANT

be·hest \bi-'hest\ n **1** ♦ : an authoritative order : COMMAND **2** : an urgent prompting

♦ charge, command, commandment, decree, dictate, direction, directive, edict, instruction, order, word — more at COMMAND

¹**be·hind** \bi-'hīnd\ adv or adj **1** : BACK, BACKWARD ⟨look ∼⟩ **2** ♦ : later in time : LATE

♦ belated, delinquent, late, overdue, tardy — more at LATE

²**behind** prep **1** : in or to a place or situation in back of or to the rear of ⟨look ∼ you⟩ ⟨the staff stayed ∼ the troops⟩ **2** : inferior to (as in rank) : BELOW ⟨three games ∼ the first-place team⟩ **3** : in support of : SUPPORTING ⟨we're ∼ you all the way⟩ **4** — used as a function word to indicate backwardness, delay, or deficiency ⟨∼ the times⟩

be·hind·hand \bi-'hīnd-,hand\ adj : being in arrears

be·hold \bi-'hōld\ vb **-held** \-'held\; **-hold·ing 1** ♦ : to have in sight : SEE **2** — used imperatively to direct the attention — **be·hold·er** n

♦ descry, discern, distinguish, espy, eye, look, note, notice, observe, perceive, regard, remark, see, sight, spy, view, witness — more at SEE

be·hold·en \bi-'hōl-dən\ adj ♦ : owing gratitude or recognition to another : OBLIGATED, INDEBTED

♦ indebted, obligated, obliged; also appreciative, grateful, thankful

be·hoof \bi-'hüf\ n : ADVANTAGE, PROFIT

be·hoove \bi-'hüv\ vb **be·hooved; be·hoov·ing** : to be necessary, proper, or advantageous for

beige \'bāzh\ n : a pale dull yellowish brown — **beige** adj

be·ing \'bē-iŋ\ n **1 a** : EXISTENCE **b** ♦ : something that actually exists **2** : the qualities or constitution of an existent thing **3** ♦ : a living thing; esp : PERSON

♦ [1b] entity, individual, object, substance, thing — more at ENTITY ♦ [3] body, creature, human, individual, man, mortal, person — more at HUMAN

be·la·bor of Can and Brit **be·la·bour** \bi-'lā-bər\ vb ♦ : to assail (as with words) tiresomely or at length

♦ abuse, assail, attack, blast, castigate, excoriate, jump, lambaste, slam, vituperate — more at ATTACK

be·lat·ed \bi-'lā-təd\ adj ♦ : delayed beyond the usual time : LATE ⟨∼ birthday wishes⟩

♦ behind, delinquent, late, overdue, tardy — more at LATE

be·lay \bi-'lā\ vb **1** : to wind (a rope) around a pin or cleat in order to hold secure **2** : QUIT, STOP — used in the imperative

belch \'belch\ vb **1** : to expel (gas) from the stomach through the mouth **2** ♦ : to gush forth ⟨a volcano ∼ing lava⟩ — **belch** n

♦ disgorge, eject, erupt, expel, jet, spew, spout, spurt — more at ERUPT

bel·dam or **bel·dame** \'bel-dəm\ n [ME beldam grandmother, fr. AF bel beautiful + ME dam lady, mother] : an old woman

be·lea·guer \bi-'lē-gər\ *vb* **1** : to surround with armed forces : BESIEGE **2** : HARASS ⟨~ed parents⟩

bel·fry \'bel-frē\ *n, pl* **belfries** : a tower for a bell (as on a church); *also* : the part of the tower in which the bell hangs

Belg *abbr* Belgian; Belgium

Bel·gian \'bel-jən\ *n* : a native or inhabitant of Belgium — **Belgian** *adj*

Belgian waffle *n* : a waffle with large depressions and often served with fruit topping

be·lie \bi-'lī\ *vb* **-lied; -ly·ing** **1** : to give a false impression of : MISREPRESENT **2** ♦ : to show (something) to be false **3** : to run counter to
   ♦ confute, disprove, rebut, refute — more at DISPROVE

be·lief \bə-'lēf\ *n* **1** : CONFIDENCE, TRUST **2** ♦ : something (as a tenet or creed) believed
   ♦ conviction, eye, feeling, judgment (*or* judgement), mind, notion, opinion, persuasion, sentiment, verdict, view — more at OPINION ♦ credence, credit, faith; *also* axiom, law, precept, principle, tenet *Ant* disbelief, discredit, doubt, unbelief

be·liev·able \-'lē-və-bəl\ *adj* ♦ : capable of being believed esp. as within the range of known possibility or probability
   ♦ credible, likely, plausible, probable; *also* acceptable, conceivable, imaginable, possible, practical, reasonable *Ant* implausible, improbable, incredible, unbelievable, unlikely

be·lieve \bə-'lēv\ *vb* **be·lieved; be·liev·ing** **1** : to have religious convictions **2** ♦ : to have a firm conviction about something : accept as true **3** ♦ : to hold as an opinion : SUPPOSE — **be·liev·er** *n*
   ♦ [2] accept, credit, swallow, trust; *also* account, accredit, understand *Ant* disbelieve, discredit, reject
   ♦ [3] consider, deem, feel, figure, guess, hold, imagine, suppose, think; *also* esteem, regard, view

be·like \bi-'līk\ *adv, archaic* : PROBABLY

be·lit·tle \bi-'lit-ºl\ *vb* **-lit·tled; -lit·tling** **1** : to make seem little or less **2** ♦ : to speak slightingly about : DISPARAGE
   ♦ cry down, decry, deprecate, depreciate, diminish, discount, disparage, minimize, put down, write off — more at DECRY

¹**bell** \'bel\ *n* **1** : a hollow metallic device that makes a ringing sound when struck **2** : the sounding or stroke of a bell (as on shipboard to tell the time); *also* : time so indicated **3** : something with the flared form of a bell

²**bell** *vb* : to provide with a bell

bel·la·don·na \,be-lə-'dä-nə\ *n* [It., lit., beautiful lady] : a medicinal extract (as atropine) from a poisonous European herb related to the potato; *also* : this herb

bell–bot·toms \'bel-'bä-təmz\ *n pl* : pants with wide flaring bottoms — **bell–bottom** *adj*

bell·boy \'bel-,bói\ *n* : BELLHOP

belle \'bel\ *n* : an attractive and popular girl or woman

belles let·tres \bel-'letrª\ *n pl* [F] : literature that is an end in itself and not practical or purely informative — **bel·le·tris·tic** \,be-lə-'tris-tik\ *adj*

bell·hop \'bel-,häp\ *n* : a hotel or club employee who takes guests to rooms, carries luggage, and runs errands

bel·li·cose \'be-li-,kōs\ *adj* ♦ : favoring or inclined to start quarrels or wars : WARLIKE, PUGNACIOUS
   ♦ aggressive, argumentative, belligerent, combative, contentious, discordant, disputatious, militant, pugnacious, quarrelsome, scrappy, truculent, warlike — more at BELLIGERENT

bel·li·cos·i·ty \,be-li-'kä-sə-tē\ *n* : showy or extreme combativeness or aggressiveness

bel·lig·er·ence \-rəns\ *n* ♦ : an aggressive or truculent attitude, atmosphere, or disposition
   ♦ aggression, aggressiveness, fight, militancy, pugnacity, truculence; *also* antagonism, fierceness, hostility, unfriendliness *Ant* pacifism

bel·lig·er·en·cy \bə-'li-jə-rən-sē\ *n* **1** : the status of a nation engaged in war **2** : BELLIGERENCE, TRUCULENCE

bel·lig·er·ent \-rənt\ *adj* **1** : waging war **2** ♦ : inclined to or exhibiting assertiveness, hostility, or combativeness : TRUCULENT — **belligerent** *n*
   ♦ aggressive, argumentative, bellicose, combative, contentious, discordant, disputatious, militant, pugnacious, quarrelsome, scrappy, truculent, warlike; *also* antagonistic, fierce, hostile *Ant* nonbelligerent, pacific, peaceable, peaceful

bel·low \'be-lō\ *vb* **1** : to make the deep hollow sound characteristic of a bull **2** ♦ : to shout in a deep voice — **bellow** *n*
   ♦ boom, growl, roar, thunder — more at ROAR

bel·lows \-lōz, -ləz\ *n sing or pl* : a closed device with sides that can be spread apart and then pressed together to draw in air and expel it through a tube

bell·weth·er \'bel-'we-thər, -,we-\ *n* : one that takes the lead or initiative

¹**bel·ly** \'be-lē\ *n, pl* **bellies** [ME *bely* bellows, belly, fr. OE *belg* bag, skin] **1** ♦ : the part of the body between the thorax and the pelvis : ABDOMEN **2** : the underpart of an animal's body
   ♦ abdomen, gut, solar plexus, stomach, tummy — more at STOMACH

²**belly** *vb* **bel·lied; bel·ly·ing** ♦ : to swell or fill beyond a point : BULGE
   ♦ billow, bulge, overhang, protrude, start, stick out — more at BULGE

¹**bel·ly·ache** \'be-lē-,āk\ *n* : pain in the abdomen

²**bellyache** *vb* ♦ : to find fault : COMPLAIN
   ♦ beef, carp, complain, crab, croak, fuss, gripe, grouse, growl, grumble, kick, moan, murmur, mutter, repine, squawk, wail, whine — more at COMPLAIN

bel·ly·ach·er \'be-lē-,ā-kər\ *n* ♦ : one who bellyaches
   ♦ bear, complainer, crab, crank, curmudgeon, grouch, grumbler, whiner — more at GROUCH

belly button *n* : the human navel

belly dance *n* : a usu. solo dance emphasizing movement of the belly — **belly dance** *vb* — **belly dancer** *n*

belly laugh *n* : a deep hearty laugh

be·long \bi-'lón\ *vb* **1** : to be suitable or appropriate; *also* : to be properly situated ⟨shoes ~ in the closet⟩ **2** : to be the property ⟨this ~s to me⟩; *also* : to be attached (as through birth or membership) ⟨~ to a club⟩ **3** : to form an attribute or part ⟨this wheel ~s to the cart⟩ **4** : to be classified ⟨whales ~ among the mammals⟩

be·long·ings \-'lón-inz\ *n pl* ♦ : moveable property : EFFECTS, POSSESSIONS
   ♦ chattels, effects, holdings, paraphernalia, possessions, things — more at POSSESSION

¹**be·loved** \bi-'ləvd, -'lə-vəd\ *adj* ♦ : dearly loved
   ♦ darling, dear, favorite (*or* favourite), loved, pet, precious, special, sweet

²**beloved** *n* : one who is loved; *esp* : SWEETHEART

¹**be·low** \bi-'lō\ *adv* **1** : in or to a lower place or rank **2** : on earth **3** : in hell
   ♦ down, downward, over — more at DOWN ♦ beneath, under; *also* beside, near, nearby *Ant* up

²**below** *prep* **1** : lower than **2** : inferior to (as in rank)

be·low·decks \bi-,lō-'deks, -'lō-,deks\ *adv* : inside the superstructure of a boat or down to a lower deck

¹**belt** \'belt\ *n* **1** ♦ : a strip (as of leather) worn about the waist **2** : a flexible continuous band to communicate motion or convey material **3** ♦ : a region marked by some distinctive feature; *esp* : one suited to a particular crop
   ♦ [1] cincture, cummerbund, girdle, sash; *also* band, waistband ♦ [3] land, region, tract, zone — more at REGION

²**belt** *vb* **1** ♦ : to encircle or secure with a belt **2** : to beat with or as if with a belt **3** : to mark with an encircling band **4** : to sing loudly

♦ band, gird, girdle, wrap — more at GIRD

³**belt** *n* 1 ♦ : a jarring blow : WHACK 2 : DRINK ⟨a ∼ of whiskey⟩

♦ bat, blow, box, clout, hit, punch, slug, thump, wallop, whack — more at BLOW

belt–tightening *n* : a reduction in spending

belt·way \'belt-,wā\ *n* : a highway around a city

be·lu·ga \bə-'lü-gə\ *n* [Russ] 1 : a large white sturgeon of the Black Sea, Caspian Sea, and their tributaries that is a source of caviar; *also* : caviar from beluga roe 2 : a whale of arctic and subarctic waters that is white when mature

bel·ve·dere \'bel-və-,dir\ *n* [It., lit., beautiful view] : a structure (as a summerhouse) designed to command a view

be·mire \bi-'mīr\ *vb* : to cover or soil with or sink in mire

be·moan \bi-'mōn\ *vb* ♦ : to express deep grief or distress over : LAMENT, DEPLORE

♦ bewail, deplore, grieve, lament, mourn, wail — more at LAMENT

be·muse \bi-'myüz\ *vb* ♦ : to make confused : BEWILDER

♦ addle, baffle, befog, befuddle, bewilder, confound, confuse, disorient, muddle, muddy, mystify, perplex, puzzle — more at CONFUSE

¹**bench** \'bench\ *n* 1 : a long seat for two or more persons 2 : the seat of a judge in court; *also* : the office or dignity of a judge 3 a : COURT b ♦ : the persons who sit as judges 4 : a table for holding work and tools ⟨a carpenter's ∼⟩

♦ court, judge, justice, magistrate — more at JUDGE

²**bench** *vb* 1 : to furnish with benches 2 : to seat on a bench 3 : to remove from or keep out of a game

bench mark *n* 1 : a mark on a permanent object serving as an elevation reference in topographical surveys 2 *usu* **bench·mark** : a point of reference for measurement; *also* : STANDARD

bench press *n* : a press in weight lifting performed by a lifter lying on a bench — **bench–press** *vb*

bench warrant *n* : a warrant issued by a presiding judge or by a court against a person guilty of contempt or indicted for a crime

¹**bend** \'bend\ *vb* **bent** \'bent\; **bend·ing** 1 : to draw (as a bow) taut 2 ♦ : to curve or cause a change of shape in ⟨∼ a bar⟩ 3 : to make fast : SECURE 4 : DEFLECT 5 ♦ : to turn in a certain direction ⟨*bent* his steps toward town⟩ 6 ♦ : to direct strenuously or with interest : APPLY ⟨*bent* themselves to the task⟩ 7 : SUBDUE 8 : to curve downward 9 : YIELD, SUBMIT

♦ [2] arc, arch, bow, crook, curve, hook, round, sweep, swerve, wheel — more at CURVE ♦ [5] aim, cast, direct, head, level, set, train — more at AIM ♦ [6] address, apply, buckle, devote, give — more at APPLY

²**bend** *n* 1 : an act or process of bending 2 ♦ : something bent; *esp* : CURVE 3 *pl* : a painful and sometimes fatal disorder caused by release of gas bubbles in the tissues upon too rapid decrease in air pressure after a stay in a compressed atmosphere

♦ angle, arc, arch, bow, crook, curve, turn, wind; *also* kink, warp *Ant* straight line

³**bend** *n* : a knot by which a rope is fastened (as to another rope)

bend·er \'ben-dər\ *n* : SPREE

¹**be·neath** \bi-'nēth\ *adv* ♦ : in or to a lower position : BELOW

♦ below, under — more at BELOW

²**beneath** *prep* 1 : in or to a lower position than : BELOW, UNDER ⟨stood ∼ a tree⟩ 2 : unworthy of ⟨considered such behavior ∼ her⟩ 3 : concealed by

bene·dic·tion \,be-nə-'dik-shən\ *n* : the invocation of a blessing esp. at the close of a public worship service

ben·e·fac·tion \-'fak-shən\ *n* ♦ : a charitable donation

♦ alms, beneficence, charity, contribution, donation, philanthropy — more at CONTRIBUTION

ben·e·fac·tor \'ben-ə-,fak-tər\ *n* : one that confers a benefit and esp. a benefaction

ben·e·fac·tress \-,fak-trəs\ *n* : a woman who is a benefactor

ben·e·fice \'be-nə-fəs\ *n* : an ecclesiastical office to which the revenue from an endowment is attached

be·nef·i·cence \bə-'ne-fə-səns\ *n* 1 : beneficent quality 2 ♦ : a benefit conferred : BENEFACTION

♦ alms, benefaction, charity, contribution, donation, philanthropy — more at CONTRIBUTION

be·nef·i·cent \-sənt\ *adj* 1 ♦ : doing or producing good (as by acts of kindness or charity) 2 : BENEFICIAL

♦ benevolent, compassionate, good-hearted, humane, kind, kindly, sympathetic, tender, tenderhearted, warmhearted — more at HUMANE ♦ altruistic, benevolent, charitable, humanitarian, philanthropic — more at CHARITABLE

ben·e·fi·cial \,be-nə-'fi-shəl\ *adj* ♦ : being of benefit or help : HELPFUL — **ben·e·fi·cial·ly** *adv*

♦ advantageous, favorable (*or* favourable), helpful, profitable, salutary; *also* gratifying, rewarding, satisfying *Ant* disadvantageous, unfavorable, unhelpful

ben·e·fi·cia·ry \,be-nə-'fi-shē-,er-ē, -'fi-shə-rē\ *n, pl* **-ries** : one that receives a benefit (as the income of a trust or the proceeds of an insurance)

¹**ben·e·fit** \'be-nə-,fit\ *n* 1 ♦ : something that promotes well-being : ADVANTAGE ⟨the ∼s of exercise⟩ 2 a ♦ : a useful aid b : material aid provided or due (as in sickness or unemployment) as a right 3 : a performance or event to raise funds

♦ advantage, aid, boon, help — more at HELP

²**benefit** *vb* **-fit·ed** \-,fi-təd\ *also* **-fit·ted; -fit·ing** *also* **-fit·ting** 1 ♦ : to be useful or profitable to 2 : to receive benefit

♦ avail, profit, serve; *also* succeed, work (for)

be·nev·o·lence \bə-'ne-və-ləns\ *n* 1 ♦ : charitable nature 2 : an act of kindness : CHARITY — **be·nev·o·lent·ly** *adv*

♦ amity, cordiality, fellowship, friendliness, friendship, goodwill, kindliness — more at GOODWILL

be·nev·o·lent \-lənt\ *adj* ♦ : marked by or disposed to doing good

♦ beneficent, compassionate, good-hearted, humane, kind, kindly, sympathetic, tender, tenderhearted, warmhearted — more at HUMANE ♦ altruistic, beneficent, charitable, humanitarian, philanthropic — more at CHARITABLE

be·night·ed \bi-'nī-təd\ *adj* 1 : overtaken by darkness or night 2 : living in ignorance

be·nign \bi-'nīn\ *adj* [ME *benigne*, fr. AF, fr. L *benignus*] 1 ♦ : of a gentle disposition; *also* : showing kindness 2 : of a mild kind; *esp* : not malignant ⟨∼ tumors⟩ — **be·nig·ni·ty** \-'nig-nə-tē\ *n*

♦ balmy, bland, delicate, gentle, light, mellow, mild, soft, soothing, tender — more at GENTLE

be·nig·nant \-'nig-nənt\ *adj* : having a kind and gentle nature

ben·i·son \'be-nə-sən, -zən\ *n* : a prayer that blesses : BLESSING, BENEDICTION

bent \'bent\ *n* 1 ♦ : strong inclination or interest 2 : power of endurance

♦ affinity, devices, disposition, genius, inclination, leaning, partiality, penchant, predilection, predisposition, proclivity, propensity, talent, tendency, turn — more at INCLINATION

ben·thic \'ben-thik\ *adj* : of, relating to, or occurring at the bottom of a body of water

ben·ton·ite \'bent-³n-,īt\ *n* : an absorptive clay used esp. as a filler (as in paper)

bent·wood \'bent-,wud\ *adj* : made of wood bent into shape ⟨a ∼ rocker⟩

be·numb \bi-'nəm\ *vb* 1 : to make inactive : DULL, DEADEN 2 : to make numb esp. by cold

ben·zene \'ben-,zēn\ *n* : a colorless volatile flammable liquid hydrocarbon used in organic synthesis and as a solvent

ben·zine \\'ben-₁zēn\\ *n* : any of various flammable petroleum distillates used as solvents or as motor fuels

ben·zo·ate \\'ben-zə-₁wāt\\ *n* : a salt or ester of benzoic acid

ben·zo·ic acid \\ben-'zō-ik-\\ *n* : a white crystalline acid used as a preservative and antiseptic and in synthesizing chemicals

ben·zo·in \\'ben-zə-wən, -₁zóin\\ *n* : a balsamlike resin from trees of southern Asia used esp. in medicine and perfumes

be·queath \\bi-'kwēth, -'kwēth\\ *vb* [ME *bequethen*, fr. OE *becwethan*, fr. *be-* + *cwethan* to say] **1** : to leave by will **2** : to hand down

be·quest \\bi-'kwest\\ *n* **1** : the action of bequeathing **2** ♦ : something bequeathed : LEGACY

♦ birthright, heritage, inheritance, legacy — more at INHERITANCE

be·rate \\-'rāt\\ *vb* ♦ : to scold harshly

♦ admonish, chide, lecture, rail (at *or* against), rate, rebuke, reprimand, scold — more at SCOLD

Ber·ber \\'bər-bər\\ *n* : a member of any of various peoples living in northern Africa west of Tripoli

ber·ceuse \\ber-'sœz, -'süz\\ *n, pl* **berceuses** *same or* -'sü-zəz\\ [F, fr. *bercer* to rock] **1** : LULLABY **2** : a musical composition that resembles a lullaby

¹be·reaved \\bi-'rēvd\\ *adj* : grieving the death of a loved one ⟨her ∼ family⟩ — **be·reave·ment** *n*

²bereaved *n, pl* **bereaved** : one who is bereaved

be·reft \\-'reft\\ *adj* **1** ♦ : deprived of or lacking something — usu. used with *of* **2** : grieving the death of a loved one : BEREAVED

♦ destitute, devoid, void — more at DEVOID

be·ret \\bə-'rā\\ *n* : a round soft cap with no visor

berg \\'bərg\\ *n* : ICEBERG

beri·beri \\₁ber-ē-'ber-ē\\ *n* : a deficiency disease marked by weakness, wasting, and nerve damage and caused by lack of thiamine

berke·li·um \\'bər-klē-əm\\ *n* : an artificially prepared radioactive chemical element

berm \\'bərm\\ *n* : a narrow shelf or path at the top or bottom of a slope; *also* : a mound or bank of earth

Ber·mu·das \\bər-'myü-dəz\\ *n pl* : BERMUDA SHORTS

Bermuda shorts *n pl* : knee-length walking shorts

ber·ry \\'ber-ē\\ *n, pl* **berries 1** : a small pulpy fruit (as a strawberry) **2** : a simple fruit (as a grape, tomato, or banana) with the wall of the ripened ovary thick and pulpy **3** : the dry seed of some plants (as coffee)

¹ber·serk \\bər-'sərk, -'zərk\\ *adj* [ON *berserkr* warrior frenzied in battle, prob. fr. *ber-* bear + *serkr* shirt] : FRENZIED, CRAZED

²berserk *adv* ♦ : in a berserk manner

♦ amok, frantically, harum-scarum, hectically, helter‐skelter, madly, pell-mell, wild, wildly — more at HELTER‐SKELTER

¹berth \\'bərth\\ *n* **1** : adequate distance esp. for a ship to maneuver **2** : the place where a ship is anchored or a vehicle rests **3** : ACCOMMODATIONS **4** : an employment for which one has been hired : JOB, POSITION

²berth *vb* **1** : to bring or come into a berth **2** : to allot a berth to

ber·yl \\'ber-əl\\ *n* : a hard silicate mineral occurring as green, yellow, pink, or white crystals

be·ryl·li·um \\bə-'ri-lē-əm\\ *n* : a light strong metallic chemical element used as a hardener in alloys

be·seech \\bi-'sēch\\ *vb* **-sought** \\-'sòt\\ *or* **-seeched; -seech·ing** ♦ : to beg earnestly or urgently : ENTREAT

♦ appeal, beg, entreat, implore, importune, petition, plead, pray, solicit, supplicate — more at BEG

be·seem \\bi-'sēm\\ *vb, archaic* : BEFIT

be·set \\-'set\\ *vb* **-set; -set·ting 1** : TROUBLE, HARASS **2 a** ♦ : to set upon : ASSAIL ⟨∼ by wild dogs⟩ **b** : SURROUND

♦ assail, assault, attack, charge, descend, jump, pounce (on *or* upon), raid, rush, storm, strike — more at ATTACK

be·set·ting *adj* : persistently present

¹be·side \\bi-'sīd\\ *prep* **1** : by the side of ⟨sit ∼ me⟩ **2** : BESIDES: as **a** : other than **b** : together with **3** : not relevant to

²beside *adv, archaic* : BESIDES

¹be·sides \\bi-'sīdz\\ *prep* **1** ♦ : other than **2** : together with

♦ aside from, bar, barring, but, except, outside (of), save

²besides *adv* **1** : as well : ALSO **2** ♦ : in addition to what precedes : MOREOVER

♦ additionally, again, also, further, furthermore, likewise, more, moreover, then, too, withal, yet

be·siege \\bi-'sēj\\ *vb* **1** ♦ : to lay siege to **2** : to press with requests — **be·sieg·er** *n*

♦ barricade, block, cut off, dam, encircle, surround

be·smear \\-'smir\\ *vb* : to spread with something oily, thick, or sticky : SMEAR

be·smirch \\-'smərch\\ *vb* ♦ : to make soiled or tarnished : SMIRCH, SOIL

♦ befoul, begrime, blacken, dirty, foul, grime, mire, muddy, smirch, soil, stain — more at DIRTY

be·som \\'bē-zəm\\ *n* : BROOM

be·sot \\bi-'sät\\ *vb* **be·sot·ted; be·sot·ting 1** : INFATUATE **2** : to make dull esp. by drinking

be·spat·ter \\-'spa-tər\\ *vb* : to splash with or as if with a liquid : SPATTER

be·speak \\bi-'spēk\\ *vb* **-spoke** \\-'spōk\\; **-spo·ken** \\-'spō-kən\\; **-speak·ing 1** : to hire, engage, or claim beforehand : PREARRANGE **2** : ADDRESS **3** : REQUEST **4** ♦ : to be a sign or indication of ⟨∼s considerable practice⟩ **5** : FORETELL

♦ betray, demonstrate, display, evince, expose, give away, manifest, reveal, show — more at SHOW

be·sprin·kle \\-'sprin-kəl\\ *vb* : SPRINKLE

¹best \\'best\\ *adj, superlative of* GOOD **1** : excelling all others ⟨the ∼ student⟩ **2** : most productive (as of good or satisfaction) **3** : LARGEST, MOST

²best *adv, superlative of* WELL **1** : in the best way **2** : MOST

³best *n* **1** ♦ : something that is best **2** ♦ : best clothes ⟨Sunday ∼⟩

♦ [1] choice, cream, elect, elite, fat, flower, pick, prime — more at ELITE ♦ [2] array, bravery, caparison, feather, finery, frippery, full dress, gaiety, regalia — more at FINERY

⁴best *vb* ♦ : to get the better of

♦ beat, defeat, master, overcome, prevail, triumph, trounce, wallop, whip, win

best friend *n* : one's closest and dearest friend

bes·tial \\'bes-chəl\\ *adj* **1** : of or relating to beasts **2** : resembling a beast esp. in brutality or lack of intelligence

bes·ti·al·i·ty \\₁bes-chē-'a-lə-tē, ₁bēs-\\ *n, pl* **-ties 1** : the condition or status of a lower animal **2** : display or gratification of bestial traits or impulses

bes·ti·ary \\'bes-chē-₁er-ē\\ *n, pl* **-ar·ies** : a medieval allegorical or moralizing work on the appearance and habits of animals

best·ie \\'be-stē\\ *n* : BEST FRIEND

be·stir \\bi-'stər\\ *vb* : to rouse to action

best man *n* : the principal groomsman at a wedding

be·stow \\bi-'stō\\ *vb* **1** : PUT, PLACE, STOW **2** ♦ : to present as a gift

♦ contribute, donate, give, present — more at GIVE

be·stow·al *n* ♦ : something bestowed or given

♦ donation, freebie, gift, lagniappe, present — more at GIFT

be·stride \\bi-'strīd\\ *vb* **-strode** \\-'strōd\\; **-strid·den** \\-'strid-ᵊn\\; **-strid·ing** : to ride, sit, or stand astride

¹bet \\'bet\\ *n* **1 a** : something that is wagered, risked, or pledged usu. between two parties on the outcome of a contest **b** : the making of such a bet **2** : OPTION ⟨the back road is your best ∼⟩

²bet *vb* **bet** *also* **bet·ted; bet·ting 1** ♦ : to stake on the outcome of an issue or a contest ⟨∼ $2 on the race⟩ **2** : to make a bet with **3** : to lay a bet

♦ gamble, go, lay, stake, wager; *also* bid, offer

³**bet** *abbr* between

be·ta \'bā-tə\ *n* **1** : the 2d letter of the Greek alphabet — B or β **2** : a nearly complete version of a new product (as computer software)

beta–block·er \-,blä-kər\ *n* : any of a group of drugs that decrease the rate and force of heart contractions and lower high blood pressure

be·ta–car·o·tene \-'kar-ə-,tēn\ *n* : an isomer of carotene found in dark green and dark yellow vegetables and fruits

be·take \bi-'tāk\ *vb* **-took** \-'tůk\; **-tak·en** \-'tā-kən\; **-tak·ing** : to cause (oneself) to go

beta particle *n* : a high-speed electron; *esp* : one emitted by a radioactive nucleus

beta ray *n* **1** : BETA PARTICLE **2** : a stream of beta particles

beta test *n* : a field test of the beta version of a product prior to commercial release

be·tel \'bēt-ᵊl\ *n* : a climbing pepper whose leaves are chewed together with lime and betel nut as a stimulant esp. by southern Asians

betel nut *n* : the astringent seed of an Asian palm that is chewed with betel leaves

bête noire \,bet-'nwär, ,bāt-\ *n, pl* **bêtes noires** *same or* -'nwärz\ [F, lit., black beast] ♦ : a person or thing strongly disliked, avoided, or feared

♦ bogey, bugbear, hobgoblin, ogre — more at BOGEY ♦ abhorrence, abomination, anathema, antipathy, aversion, hate — more at HATE

beth·el \'be-thəl\ *n* [Heb *bēth'ēl* house of God] : a place of worship esp. for seamen

be·tide \bi-'tīd\ *vb* ♦ : to happen to

♦ be, befall, chance, come, go, happen, occur, pass, transpire — more at HAPPEN

be·times \bi-'tīmz\ *adv* : in good time : EARLY

be·to·ken \bi-'tō-kən\ *vb* **1** : PRESAGE **2** ♦ : to give evidence of

♦ display, disport, exhibit, expose, flash, flaunt, parade, show, show off, sport, strut, unveil — more at SHOW

be·tray \bi-'trā\ *vb* **1** : to lead astray; *esp* : SEDUCE **2** : to deliver to an enemy **3** : ABANDON **4** : to prove unfaithful to **5** ♦ : to reveal unintentionally; *also* : SHOW

♦ bespeak, demonstrate, display, evince, expose, give away, manifest, reveal, show — more at SHOW

be·tray·al *n* ♦ : the act of betraying or fact of being betrayed

♦ disloyalty, double cross, faithlessness, falseness, falsity, infidelity, perfidy, treachery, treason, unfaithfulness; *also* abandonment, desertion

be·tray·er *n* ♦ : one who betrays (something or someone)

♦ blabbermouth, informer, rat, snitch, stool pigeon, tattler, tattletale — more at INFORMER ♦ apostate, double-crosser, quisling, recreant, traitor, turncoat — more at TRAITOR

be·troth \bi-'trōth, -'trôth\ *vb* : to promise to marry

be·troth·al *n* ♦ : the act of betrothing or fact of being betrothed; *also* : a mutual promise or contract for a future marriage

♦ engagement, espousal, troth — more at ENGAGEMENT

be·trothed *n* ♦ : the person to whom one is betrothed

♦ intended; *also* admirer, beau, beloved, boyfriend, darling, dear, favorite, fellow, flame, girlfriend, honey, love, lover, steady, swain, sweet, sweetheart, valentine

¹**bet·ter** \'be-tər\ *adj, comparative of* GOOD **1** : greater than half **2** : improved in health **3** : more attractive, favorable, or commendable **4** : more advantageous or effective **5** : improved in accuracy or performance

²**better** *vb* **1** ♦ : to make or become better **2** ♦ : to surpass in excellence : EXCEL

♦ [1] ameliorate, amend, enhance, enrich, improve, perfect, refine — more at IMPROVE ♦ [2] beat, eclipse, excel, outdistance, outdo, outshine, outstrip, surpass, top, transcend — more at SURPASS

³**better** *adv, comparative of* WELL **1** : in a superior manner **2** : to a higher or greater degree; *also* : MORE

⁴**better** *n* **1** : something better; *also* : a superior esp. in merit or rank **2** : superiority of position or condition : ADVANTAGE

⁵**better** *verbal auxiliary* : had better ⟨you ~ hurry⟩

better half *n* ♦ : the person to whom another is married : SPOUSE

♦ consort, mate, partner, spouse — more at SPOUSE

bet·ter·ment \'be-tər-mənt\ *n* : IMPROVEMENT

bet·tor *or* **bet·ter** \'be-tər\ *n* : one that bets

¹**be·tween** \bi-'twēn\ *prep* **1** : by the common action of ⟨earned $10,000 ~ the two of them⟩ **2** : in the interval separating ⟨an alley ~ two buildings⟩; *also* : in intermediate relation to **3** : in point of comparison of ⟨choose ~ two cars⟩

²**between** *adv* : in an intervening space or interval

be·twixt \bi-'twikst\ *adv or prep* : BETWEEN

¹**bev·el** \'be-vəl\ *n* **1** : a device for adjusting the slant of the surfaces of a piece of work **2** : the angle or slant that one surface or line makes with another when not at right angles

²**bevel** *vb* **-eled** *or* **-elled**; **-el·ing** *or* **-el·ling** **1** : to cut or shape to a bevel **2** : INCLINE, SLANT

bev·er·age \'bev-rij\ *n* ♦ : a drinkable liquid

♦ drink, libation, quencher — more at DRINK

bevy \'be-vē\ *n, pl* **bev·ies** **1** : a large group or collection **2** : a group of animals and esp. quail together

be·wail \bi-'wāl\ *vb* ♦ : to express deep sorrow for usu. by wailing and lamentation

♦ bemoan, deplore, grieve, lament, mourn, wail — more at LAMENT

be·ware \-'war\ *vb* ♦ : to be on one's guard : be wary of

♦ *usu* beware of guard (against), mind, watch out (for); *also* attend, heed, mark, note, notice

be·wil·der \bi-'wil-dər\ *vb* ♦ : to perplex or confuse esp. by complexity or variety

♦ addle, baffle, befog, befuddle, bemuse, confound, confuse, disorient, muddle, muddy, mystify, perplex, puzzle — more at CONFUSE

be·wil·der·ment *n* **1** ♦ : the quality or state of being bewildered **2** : a bewildering tangle or confusion

♦ bafflement, confusion, distraction, muddle, mystification, perplexity, puzzlement, whirl — more at CONFUSION

be·witch \-'wich\ *vb* **1** ♦ : to affect by witchcraft **2** ♦ : to attract as if by the power of witchcraft : CHARM, FASCINATE

♦ [1] charm, enchant, hex, spell; *also* curse, jinx, possess ♦ [2] allure, beguile, captivate, charm, enchant, fascinate, wile — more at CHARM

be·witch·ment *n* **1** ♦ : the act or power of bewitching; *also* : a spell that bewitches **2** : the state of being bewitched

♦ charm, conjuration, enchantment, incantation, spell — more at SPELL ♦ enchantment, magic, necromancy, sorcery, witchcraft, wizardry — more at MAGIC

bey \'bā\ *n* **1** : a former Turkish provincial governor **2** : the former native ruler of Tunis or Tunisia

¹**be·yond** \bē-'änd\ *adv* **1** ♦ : on or to the farther side **2** : BESIDES

♦ farther, further, yonder — more at FARTHER

²**beyond** *prep* **1** : at a greater distance than **2** ♦ : past the reach or sphere of **3** : BESIDES

♦ outside, without; *also* except **Ant** within

be·zel \'bē-zəl, 'be-\ *n* **1** : a rim that holds a transparent covering (as on a watch) **2** : the faceted part of a cut gem that rises above the setting

bf *abbr* boldface

BFF *abbr* best friends forever

BG *or* **B Gen** *abbr* brigadier general

Bh *symbol* bohrium

bhang \'baŋ\ *n* [Hindi *bhāṅg*] : a mildly intoxicating preparation of the leaves and flowering tops of uncultivated hemp
Bi *symbol* bismuth
BIA *abbr* Bureau of Indian Affairs
bi·an·nu·al \(,)bī-'an-yə-wəl\ *adj* : occurring twice a year — **bi·an·nu·al·ly** *adv*
¹**bi·as** \'bī-əs\ *n* **1** : a line diagonal to the grain of a fabric **2** ♦ : a personal and sometimes unreasoned judgment : PREJUDICE

♦ favor (*or* favour), partiality, partisanship, prejudice; *also* favoritism, nepotism *Ant* impartiality, neutrality, objectivity

²**bias** *adv* : on the bias : DIAGONALLY
³**bias** *vb* **bi·ased** *or* **bi·assed**; **bi·as·ing** *or* **bi·as·sing** : to give a settled and often prejudiced outlook to : PREJUDICE
bi·ased *adj* ♦ : exhibiting or characterized by bias

♦ one-sided, partial, partisan, prejudiced — more at PARTIAL

bi·ath·lon \bī-'ath-lən, -,län\ *n* : a composite athletic contest consisting of cross-country skiing and target shooting with a rifle
¹**bib** \'bib\ *n* : a cloth or plastic shield tied under the chin to protect the clothes while eating
²**bib** *abbr* Bible; biblical
bi·be·lot \'bē-bə-,lō\ *n, pl* **bibelots** *same or* -,lōz\ : a small household ornament or decorative object
bi·ble \'bī-bəl\ *n* [ME, fr. OF, fr. ML *biblia*, fr. Gk, pl. of *biblion* book, dim. of *byblos* papyrus, book, fr. *Byblos*, ancient Phoenician city from which papyrus was exported] **1** *cap* : the sacred scriptures of Christians comprising the Old and New Testaments **2** *cap* : the sacred scriptures of Judaism; *also* : those of some other religion **3** : a publication that is considered authoritative for its subject — **bib·li·cal** \'bi-bli-kəl\ *adj*
bib·li·og·ra·phy \,bi-blē-'ä-grə-fē\ *n, pl* **-phies** **1** : the history or description of writings or publications **2** : a list of writings (as on a subject or of an author) — **bib·li·og·ra·pher** \-fər\ *n* — **bib·lio·graph·ic** \-ə-'gra-fik\ *also* **bib·lio·graph·i·cal** \-fi-kəl\ *adj*
bib·lio·phile \'bi-blē-ə-,fīl\ *n* : a lover of books
bib·u·lous \'bi-byə-ləs\ *adj* **1** : highly absorbent **2** : fond of alcoholic beverages
bi·cam·er·al \'bī-'ka-mə-rəl\ *adj* : having or consisting of two legislative branches
bicarb \(,)bī-'kärb, 'bī-,\ *n* : SODIUM BICARBONATE
bi·car·bon·ate \(,)bī-'kär-bə-,nāt, -nət\ *n* : an acid carbonate
bi·cen·te·na·ry \,bī-sen-'te-nə-rē, bī-'sent-ᵊn-,er-ē\ *n* : BICENTENNIAL
bi·cen·ten·ni·al \,bī-sen-'te-nē-əl\ *n* : a 200th anniversary or its celebration — **bicentennial** *adj*
bi·ceps \'bī-,seps\ *n, pl* **biceps** *also* **bicepses** [NL, fr. L, two-headed, fr. *bi-* two + *caput* head] : a muscle (as in the front of the upper arm) having two points of origin
¹**bick·er** \'bi-kər\ *n* : petulant quarreling : ALTERCATION
²**bicker** *vb* ♦ : to engage in a petty quarrel

♦ argue, brawl, dispute, fall out, fight, hassle, quarrel, row, scrap, spat, squabble, wrangle — more at ARGUE

bick·er·er \'bi-kə-rər\ *n* : one who bickers
bi·coast·al \bī-'kōst-ᵊl\ *adj* : living or working on both the East and West coasts of the U.S.
bi·con·cave \,bī-(,)kän-'kāv, (,)bī-'kän-,kāv\ *adj* : concave on both sides
bi·con·vex \,bī-(,)kän-'veks, (,)bī-'kän-,veks\ *adj* : convex on both sides
bi·cus·pid \bī-'kəs-pəd\ *n* : PREMOLAR
¹**bi·cy·cle** \'bī-,si-kəl\ *n* : a light 2-wheeled vehicle with a steering handle, saddle, and pedals
²**bicycle** *vb* **-cy·cled**; **-cy·cling** \-,si-k(ə-)liŋ, -,sī-\ : to ride a bicycle — **bi·cy·cler** \-k(ə-)lər\ *n* — **bi·cy·clist** \-k(ə-)list\ *n*
¹**bid** \'bid\ *vb* **bade** \'bad, 'bād\ *or* **bid**; **bid·den** \'bid-ᵊn\ *or* **bid** *also* **bade**; **bid·ding** **1** ♦ : to issue an order to : COMMAND, ORDER **2** : INVITE **3** : to give expression to **4** : to make a bid : OFFER — **bid·der** *n*

♦ boss, charge, command, direct, enjoin, instruct, order, tell — more at COMMAND

²**bid** *n* **1** : the act of one who bids; *also* : an offer for something **2** : INVITATION **3** : an announcement in a card game of what a player proposes to accomplish **4** ♦ : an attempt to win or gain ⟨a ~ for mayor⟩

♦ attempt, crack, endeavor (*or* endeavour), essay, fling, go, pass, shot, stab, trial, try, whack, whirl — more at ATTEMPT

bid·da·ble \'bi-də-bəl\ *adj* **1** : OBEDIENT, DOCILE **2** : capable of being bid
bid·dy \'bi-dē\ *n, pl* **biddies** : HEN; *also* : a young chicken
bide \'bīd\ *vb* **bode** \'bōd\ *or* **bid·ed**; **bid·ed**; **bid·ing** **1** : to wait for **2** ♦ : to wait awhile : TARRY **3** : DWELL

♦ await, hold on, stay, tarry, wait — more at WAIT

bi·det \bi-'dā\ *n* : a bathroom fixture used esp. for bathing the external genitals and the posterior parts of the body
bi·di·rec·tion·al \,bī-də-'rek-sh(ə-)nəl\ *adj* : involving, moving, or taking place in two usu. opposite directions — **bi·di·rec·tion·al·ly** *adv*
bi·en·ni·al \bī-'e-nē-əl\ *adj* **1** : taking place once in two years **2** : lasting two years **3** : producing leaves the first year and fruiting and dying the second year — **biennial** *n* — **bi·en·ni·al·ly** *adv*
bi·en·ni·um \bī-'e-nē-əm\ *n, pl* **-niums** *or* **-nia** \-ə\ [L, fr. *bi-* two + *annus* year] : a period of two years
bier \'bir\ *n* : a stand bearing a coffin or corpse
bi·fo·cal \'bī-,fō-kəl\ *adj* : having two focal lengths
bifocals \-kəlz\ *n pl* : eyeglasses with lenses that have one part that corrects for near vision and one for distant vision
bi·fur·cate \'bī-fər-,kāt, bī-'fər-\ *vb* **-cat·ed**; **-cat·ing** : to divide into two branches or parts — **bi·fur·ca·tion** \,bī-fər-'kā-shən\ *n*
big \'big\ *adj* **big·ger**; **big·gest** **1** ♦ : large in size, amount, or scope **2** : PREGNANT; *also* : SWELLING **3** ♦ : of great importance or significance : IMPORTANT **4** : POPULAR

♦ [1] bumper, considerable, goodly, grand, great, large, sizable, substantial, voluminous — more at LARGE
♦ [3] consequential, eventful, important, major, material, meaningful, momentous, significant, substantial, weighty — more at IMPORTANT

big·a·my \'bi-gə-mē\ *n* : the act of marrying one person while still legally married to another — **big·a·mist** \-mist\ *n* — **big·a·mous** \-məs\ *adj*
big bang theory *n* : a theory in astronomy: the universe originated in an explosion (**big bang**) from a single point of nearly infinite energy density
big brother *n* **1** : an older brother **2** : a man who serves as a friend, father figure, or role model for a boy **3** *cap both Bs* : the leader of an authoritarian state or movement **4** : a powerful government organization that watches people and controls their actions
Big Dipper *n* : the seven principal stars of Ursa Major in a form resembling a dipper
big·foot \'big-,fut\ *n* : SASQUATCH
big·horn \'big-,hòrn\ *n, pl* **bighorn** *or* **bighorns** : a wild sheep of mountainous western No. America
bight \'bīt\ *n* **1** : a curve in a coast; *also* : the bay formed by such a curve **2** : a slack part in a rope

♦ bay, cove, estuary, fjord, gulf, inlet — more at GULF

big leaguer *n* ♦ : one who operates at the top rank of an activity or enterprise

♦ big shot, bigwig, kingpin, nabob, nawab, wheel — more at BIG SHOT

big–name \'big-'nām\ *adj* : widely popular ⟨a ~ performer⟩ — **big name** *n*
big·ness *n* ♦ : quality or state of being big

♦ grandness, greatness, largeness — more at LARGENESS

big·ot \'bi-gət\ *n* : one intolerantly devoted to his or her own prejudices or opinions — **big·ot·ry** \-trē\ *n*
big·ot·ed \-gə-təd\ *adj* ♦ : obstinately and blindly attached to some creed, opinion, or practice

♦ intolerant, narrow, narrow-minded, prejudiced — more at INTOLERANT

big shot \'big-ˌshät\ *n* ♦ : an important person

♦ big leaguer, bigwig, kingpin, nabob, nawab, wheel; *also* baron, czar (*also* tsar *or* tzar), king, lion, magnate, mogul, prince, princess, queen, tycoon; VIP *Ant* lightweight, nobody, nonentity, nothing, shrimp, twerp, whippersnapper, zero, zilch

big sister *n* **1** : an older sister **2** : a woman who serves as a friend, mother figure, and role model for a girl

big time \-ˌtīm\ *n* **1** : a high-paying vaudeville circuit requiring only two performances a day **2** : the top rank of an activity or enterprise — **big–tim·er** *n*

big top *n* **1** : the main tent of a circus **2** : CIRCUS

big·wig \'big-ˌwig\ *n* ♦ : an important person

♦ big shot, big leaguer, kingpin, nabob, nawab, wheel — more at BIG SHOT

bike \'bīk\ *n* **1** : BICYCLE **2** : MOTORCYCLE

bik·er *n* : MOTORCYCLIST; *esp* : one who is a member of an organized gang

bike·way \'bīk-ˌwā\ *n* : a thoroughfare for bicycles

bi·ki·ni \bə-'kē-nē\ *n* [F, fr. *Bikini*, atoll in the Marshall Islands] : a woman's brief 2-piece bathing suit

bi·lat·er·al \bī-'la-tə-rəl\ *adj* **1** : having or involving two sides **2** : affecting reciprocally two sides or parties — **bi·lat·er·al·ly** *adv*

bile \'bīl\ *n* **1** : a bitter greenish fluid secreted by the liver that aids in the digestion of fats **2** ♦ : an ill-humored mood

♦ acidity, acrimony, asperity, bitterness, cattiness, tartness, virulence, vitriol — more at ACRIMONY

bilge \'bilj\ *n* **1** : the part of a ship that lies between the bottom and the point where the sides go straight up **2** : stale or worthless remarks or ideas

bi·lin·gual \bī-'liŋ-gwəl\ *adj* : expressed in, knowing, or using two languages

bil·ious \'bil-yəs\ *adj* **1** : marked by or suffering from disordered liver function **2** ♦ : of or indicative of a peevish ill-natured disposition : ILL-TEMPERED ⟨a ~ disposition⟩

♦ bearish, cantankerous, disagreeable, dyspeptic, ill-humored, ill-tempered, ornery, splenetic, surly — more at ILL-TEMPERED

bil·ious·ness *n* ♦ : an ill-natured disposition

♦ grumpiness, irritability, peevishness, perverseness, perversity

bilk \'bilk\ *vb* : CHEAT, SWINDLE

¹**bill** \'bil\ *n* **1** : the jaws of a bird together with their horny covering; *also* : a mouth structure (as of a turtle) resembling these **2** : the visor of a cap or hood — **billed** \'bild\ *adj*

²**bill** *vb* : to caress fondly

³**bill** *n* **1** ♦ : an itemized statement of particulars; *also* : INVOICE **2** : a written document or note **3** ♦ : a printed advertisement (as a poster) announcing an event **4** : a draft of a law presented to a legislature for enactment **5** : a written statement of a legal wrong suffered or of some breach of law **6** : a piece of paper money

♦ [1] account, check, invoice, statement, tab; *also* receipt, reckoning ♦ [3] placard, poster — more at POSTER

⁴**bill** *vb* **1** : to enter in or prepare a bill; *also* : to submit a bill or account to **2** : to advertise by bills or posters

bill·board \-ˌbȯrd\ *n* : a flat surface on which advertising bills are posted

¹**bil·let** \'bi-lət\ *n* **1** : an order requiring a person to provide lodging for a soldier; *also* : quarters assigned by or as if by such an order **2** ♦ : a regular paying position : APPOINTMENT

♦ appointment, capacity, function, job, place, position, post, situation — more at JOB

²**billet** *vb* ♦ : to assign lodging to by billet

♦ accommodate, chamber, domicile, harbor (*or* harbour), house, lodge, put up, quarter, roof, shelter, take in — more at HOUSE

bil·let–doux \ˌbi-lā-'dü\ *n*, *pl* **billets–doux** *same or* -'düz\ [F *billet doux*, lit., sweet letter] : a love letter

bill·fold \'bil-ˌfōld\ *n* : WALLET

bil·liards \'bil-yərdz\ *n* : any of several games played on an oblong table by driving balls against each other or into pockets with a cue

bil·lings·gate \'bi-liŋz-ˌgāt, *Brit usu* -git\ *n* [*Billingsgate*, old gate and fish market, London, England] : coarsely abusive language

bil·lion \'bil-yən\ *n* **1** : a thousand millions **2** *Brit* : a million millions — **billion** *adj* — **bil·lionth** \-yənth\ *adj or n*

¹**bil·low** \'bi-lō\ *n* **1** ♦ : a moving ridge or swell on the surface of a liquid : WAVE; *esp* : a great wave **2** : a rolling mass (as of fog or flame) like a great wave — **bil·lowy** \'bi-lə-wē\ *adj*

♦ surge, swell, wave — more at WAVE

²**billow** *vb* **1** : to rise and roll in waves **2** ♦ : to swell out ⟨~ing sails⟩

♦ balloon, beetle, belly, bulge, overhang, poke, project, protrude, start, stick out — more at BULGE

bil·ly \'bi-lē\ *n*, *pl* **billies** : a heavy usu. wooden club : BILLY CLUB

billy club *n* ♦ : a heavy usu. wooden club; *esp* : a police officer's club

♦ bat, bludgeon, club, cudgel, nightstick, staff, truncheon — more at CLUB

bil·ly goat \'bi-lē-\ *n* : a male goat

bi·met·al \'bī-ˌmet-ᵊl\ *adj* : BIMETALLIC — **bimetal** *n*

bi·me·tal·lic \ˌbī-mə-'ta-lik\ *adj* : made of two different metals — often used of devices having a bonded expansive part — **bimetallic** *n*

bi·met·al·lism \bī-'met-ᵊl-ˌi-zəm\ *n* : the use of two metals at fixed ratios to form a standard of value for a monetary system

¹**bi·month·ly** \bī-'mənth-lē\ *adj* **1** : occurring every two months **2** : occurring twice a month : SEMIMONTHLY — **bimonthly** *adv*

²**bimonthly** *n* : a bimonthly publication

bin \'bin\ *n* ♦ : a box, crib, or enclosure used for storage

♦ box, caddy, case, casket, chest, locker, trunk — more at CHEST

bi·na·ry \'bī-nə-rē, -ˌner-ē\ *adj* **1** ♦ : consisting of two things or parts **2** : relating to, being, or belonging to a system of numbers having 2 as its base ⟨the ~ digits 0 and 1⟩ **3** : involving a choice between or condition of two alternatives only (as on-off, yes-no) — **binary** *n*

♦ bipartite, double, dual, duplex, twin — more at DOUBLE

binary star *n* : a system of two stars revolving around each other

bin·au·ral \bī-'nȯr-əl\ *adj* : of or relating to sound reproduction involving the use of two separated microphones and two transmission channels to achieve a stereophonic effect

bind \'bīnd\ *vb* **bound** \'baùnd\; **bind·ing** **1 a** : to make secure by tying **b** : to restrain as if by tying **2** : to put under an obligation; *also* : to constrain with legal authority **3** : to dress or cover with a bandage **4** ♦ : to unite into a mass **5** : to compel as if by a pledge ⟨a handshake ~s the deal⟩ **6** : to strengthen or decorate with a band **7** : to fasten together and enclose in a cover ⟨~ books⟩ **8** : to exert a tying, restraining, or compelling effect — **bind·er** *n*

♦ band, gird, tie, truss — more at TIE

bind·ing \'bīn-diŋ\ *n* : something (as a ski fastening, a book cover, or an edging fabric) used to bind

¹**binge** \'binj\ *n* ♦ : an unrestrained and often excessive indulgence : SPREE

♦ fling, frolic, gambol, lark, revel, rollick, romp — more at FLING

²**binge** *vb* **binged**; **binge·ing** *or* **bing·ing** : to go on a binge and esp. an eating binge — **bing·er** *n*

bin·go \'biŋ-gō\ *n*, *pl* **bingos** : a game of chance played with cards having numbered squares corresponding to numbered balls drawn at random and won by covering five squares in a row

bin·na·cle \'bi-ni-kəl\ *n* [alter. of ME *bitakle*, fr. Pg or Sp; Pg *bitácola* & Sp *bitácula*, fr. L *habitaculum* dwelling place, fr. *habitare* to inhabit] : a container holding a ship's compass

¹**bin·oc·u·lar** \bī-'nä-kyə-lər, bə-\ *adj* : of, relating to, or adapted to the use of both eyes — **bin·oc·u·lar·ly** *adv*

²**bin·oc·u·lar** \bə-'nä-kyə-lər, bī-\ *n* **1** : a binocular optical instrument (as a microscope) **2** : a handheld optical instrument composed of two telescopes and a focusing device — usu. used in pl.

bi·no·mi·al \bī-'nō-mē-əl\ *n* **1** : a mathematical expression consisting of two terms connected by the sign plus (+) or minus (−) **2** : a biological species name consisting of two terms — **binomial** *adj*

bio·chem·is·try \,bī-ō-'ke-mə-strē\ *n* : chemistry that deals with the chemical compounds and processes occurring in living things — **bio·chem·i·cal** \-mi-kəl\ *adj or n* — **bio·chem·ist** \-mist\ *n*

bio·de·grad·able \-di-'grā-də-bəl\ *adj* : capable of being broken down esp. into innocuous products by the actions of living things (as microorganisms) ⟨a ∼ detergent⟩ — **bio·de·grad·abil·i·ty** \-,grā-də-'bi-lə-tē\ *n* — **bio·deg·ra·da·tion** \-,de-grə-'dā-shən\ *n* — **bio·de·grade** \-di-'grād\ *vb*

bio·di·ver·si·ty \-də-'vər-sə-tē, -dī-\ *n* : biological diversity in an environment as indicated by numbers of different species of plants and animals

bio·en·gi·neer·ing *n* **1** : the application of engineering principles to medicine and biology **2** : GENETIC ENGINEERING

bio·eth·ics \-'e-thiks\ *n* : the ethics of biological research and its applications esp. in medicine — **bio·eth·i·cal** \-'e-thi-kəl\ *adj* — **bio·eth·i·cist** \-'e-thə-sist\ *n*

bio·feed·back \-'fēd-,bak\ *n* : the technique of making unconscious or involuntary bodily processes (as heartbeats or brain waves) objectively perceptible to the senses (as by use of an oscilloscope) in order to manipulate them by conscious mental control

biog *abbr* biographer; biographical; biography

bio·ge·og·ra·phy \,bī-ō-jē-'ä-grə-fē\ *n* : a science that deals with the geographical distribution of plants and animals — **bio·ge·og·ra·pher** *n*

bi·og·ra·phy \bī-'ä-grə-fē, bē-\ *n, pl* **-phies** : a written history of a person's life; *also* : such writings in general — **bi·og·ra·pher** *n* — **bi·o·graph·i·cal** \,bī-ə-'gra-fi-kəl\ *also* **bi·o·graph·ic** \-fik\ *adj*

biol *abbr* biologic; biological; biologist; biology

bi·o·log·i·cal \,bī-ə-'lä-ji-kəl\ *also* **bi·o·log·ic** \-jik\ *adj* **1** : of, relating to, or produced by biology or life and living processes **2** : related by direct genetic relationship rather than by adoption or marriage ⟨∼ parents⟩ — **bi·o·log·i·cal·ly** \-ji-k(ə-)lē\ *adv*

biological clock *n* : an inherent timing mechanism in a living system that is inferred to exist in order to explain the timing of various physiological and behavioral states and processes

biological warfare *n* : warfare in which harmful living organisms (**biological weapons**) are used against an enemy esp. to cause large-scale death and disease

bi·ol·o·gy \bī-'ä-lə-jē\ *n* [G *Biologie*, fr. Gk *bios* mode of life + *logos* word, discourse] **1** : a science that deals with living beings and life processes **2** : the life processes of an organism or group — **bi·ol·o·gist** \bī-'ä-lə-jist\ *n*

bio·mass \'bī-ō-,mas\ *n* **1** : the amount of living matter (as in a unit area) **2** : plant materials and animal waste used esp. as fuel

bio·med·i·cal \,bī-ō-'me-di-kəl\ *adj* : of, relating to, or involving biological, medical, and physical science

bi·on·ic \bī-'ä-nik\ *adj* : having normal biological capability or performance enhanced by or as if by electronic or mechanical devices

bio·phys·ics \,bī-ō-'fi-ziks\ *n* : a branch of science concerned with the application of physical principles and

methods to biological problems — **bio·phys·i·cal** \-zi-kəl\ *adj* — **bio·phys·i·cist** \-'fi-zə-sist\ *n*

bi·op·sy \'bī-,äp-sē\ *n, pl* **-sies** : the removal of tissue, cells, or fluids from the living body for examination — **biopsy** *vb*

bio·rhythm \'bī-ō-,ri-thəm\ *n* : an innately determined rhythmic biological process (as sleep); *also* : the internal mechanism controlling such a process

bio·sphere \'bī-ə-,sfir\ *n* **1** : the part of the world in which life can exist **2** : living beings together with their environment

bio·tech \'bī-ō-,tek\ *n* : BIOTECHNOLOGY

bio·tech·nol·o·gy \,bī-ō-tek-'nä-lə-jē\ *n* : biological science when applied esp. in genetic engineering and recombinant DNA technology

bio·ter·ror·ism \-'ter-ər-,i-zəm\ *n* : terrorism involving the use of biological weapons

bi·ot·ic \bī-'ä-tik\ *adj* : of or relating to life; *esp* : caused by living beings

bi·o·tin \'bī-ə-tən\ *n* : a vitamin of the vitamin B complex found esp. in yeast, liver, and egg yolk and active in growth promotion

bi·o·tite \'bī-ə-,tīt\ *n* : a dark mica containing iron, magnesium, potassium, and aluminum

bi·par·ti·san \bī-'pär-tə-zən\ *adj* : marked by or involving cooperation, agreement, and compromise between two major political parties — **bi·par·ti·san·ship** \-,ship\ *n*

bi·par·tite \-'pär-,tīt\ *adj* **1** ♦ : being in two parts **2** : shared by two ⟨∼ treaty⟩

♦ binary, double, dual, duplex, twin — more at DOUBLE

bi·ped \'bī-,ped\ *n* : a 2-footed animal — **bi·ped·al** \(,)bī-'ped-ᵊl\ *adj*

bi·plane \'bī-,plān\ *n* : an aircraft with two wings placed one above the other

bi·po·lar \bī-'pō-lər\ *adj* : having or involving the use of two poles — **bi·po·lar·i·ty** \,bī-pō-'lar-ə-tē\ *n*

bipolar disorder *n* : any of several psychological disorders of mood characterized by usu. alternating episodes of depression and mania

bi·ra·cial \bī-'rā-shəl\ *adj* : of, relating to, or involving members of two races

¹**birch** \'bərch\ *n* **1** : any of a genus of mostly short-lived deciduous shrubs and trees with membranous outer bark and pale close-grained wood; *also* : this wood **2** : a birch rod or bundle of twigs for flogging — **birch** *or* **birch·en** \'bər-chən\ *adj*

²**birch** *vb* : to beat with or as if with a birch : WHIP

¹**bird** \'bərd\ *n* : any of a class of warm-blooded egg-laying vertebrates having the body feathered and the forelimbs modified to form wings

²**bird** *vb* : to observe or identify wild birds in their native habitat — **bird·er** *n*

bird·bath \'bərd-,bath, -,bàth\ *n* : a usu. ornamental basin set up for birds to bathe in

bird·house \-,haủs\ *n* : an artificial nesting place for birds; *also* : AVIARY

bird·ie \'bər-dē\ *n* : a score of one under par on a hole in golf

bird·lime \-,līm\ *n* : a sticky substance smeared on twigs to snare small birds

bird of prey : a carnivorous bird (as a hawk, falcon, or vulture) that feeds wholly or chiefly on meat taken by hunting or on carrion

bird·seed \'bərd-,sēd\ *n* : a mixture of small seeds (as of hemp or millet) used for feeding birds

bird's-eye \'bərdz-,ī\ *adj* **1** : marked with spots resembling birds' eyes ⟨∼ maple⟩ **2 a** : seen from above as if by a flying bird ⟨∼ view⟩ **b** ♦ : having or involving a bird's-eye view : CURSORY

♦ broad, cursory, general, nonspecific, overall — more at GENERAL

bi·ret·ta \bə-'re-tə\ *n* : a square cap with three ridges on top worn esp. by Roman Catholic clergymen

birth \'bərth\ *n* **1** : the act or fact of being born or of bringing forth young **2** ♦ : descent in a line from a common progenitor : LINEAGE **3** ♦ : rise, beginning, or derivation from a source

♦ [2] ancestry, blood, bloodline, breeding, descent, extraction, family tree, genealogy, line, lineage, origin, parentage, pedigree, stock, strain — more at ANCESTRY ♦ [3] beginning, commencement, dawn, genesis, launch, morning, onset, outset, start, threshold — more at BEGINNING

birth canal *n* : the channel formed by the cervix, vagina, and vulva through which the fetus passes during birth
birth control *n* : control of the number of children born esp. by preventing or lessening the frequency of conception
birth•day \'bərth-ˌdā\ *n* : the day or anniversary of one's birth
birth defect *n* : a physical or biochemical defect present at birth and inherited or environmentally induced
birth•mark \'bərth-ˌmärk\ *n* : an unusual mark or blemish on the skin at birth
birth•place \-ˌplās\ *n* ♦ : place of birth or origin

♦ cradle, home; *also* fatherland, motherland

birth•rate \-ˌrāt\ *n* : the number of births per number of individuals in a given area or group during a given time
birth•right \-ˌrīt\ *n* ♦ : a right, privilege, or possession to which one is entitled by birth

♦ prerogative, right — more at RIGHT

birth•stone \-ˌstōn\ *n* : a gemstone associated symbolically with the month of one's birth
bis•cuit \'bis-kət\ *n* [ME *bisquite*, fr. AF *besquit*, fr. (*pain*) *besquit* twice-cooked bread] **1** : a crisp flat cake; *esp, Brit* : CRACKER **2** : a small quick bread made from dough that has been rolled and cut or dropped from a spoon
bi•sect \'bī-ˌsekt\ *vb* : to divide into two usu. equal parts; *also* : CROSS, INTERSECT — **bi•sec•tion** \'bī-ˌsek-shən\ *n* — **bi•sec•tor** \-tər\ *n*
bi•sex•u•al \bī-'sek-shə-wəl\ *adj* **1** : possessing characters of both sexes **2** : having sexual or romantic attraction to both sexes **3** : of, relating to, or involving both sexes — **bisexual** *n* — **bi•sex•u•al•i•ty** \ˌbī-ˌsek-shə-'wal-ə-tē\ *n*
bish•op \'bi-shəp\ *n* [ME *bisshop*, fr. OE *bisceop*, fr. LL *episcopus*, fr. Gk *episkopos*, lit., overseer, fr. *epi-* on, over + *skeptesthai* to look] **1** : a member of the clergy ranking above a priest and typically governing a diocese **2** : any of various Protestant church officials who superintend other clergy **3** : a chess piece that can move diagonally across any number of adjoining unoccupied squares
bish•op•ric \'bi-shə-prik\ *n* **1** : DIOCESE **2** : the office of bishop
bis•muth \'biz-məth\ *n* : a heavy brittle grayish white metallic chemical element used in alloys and medicine
bi•son \'bīs-ᵊn, 'bīz-\ *n, pl* **bison** : BUFFALO 2
bisque \'bisk\ *n* : a thick cream soup
bis•tro \'bēs-trō, 'bis-\ *n, pl* **bistros** [F] **1** : a small or unpretentious restaurant **2** : BAR; *also* : NIGHTCLUB
¹**bit** \'bit\ *n* **1** : the biting or cutting edge or part of a tool **2** : the part of a bridle that is placed in a horse's mouth
²**bit** *n* **1 a** : a morsel of food **b** ♦ : a small piece or quantity of something **2** : a small coin; *also* : a unit of value equal to 12½ cents **3** : something small or trivial **4** ♦ : an indefinite usu. small degree or extent ⟨a ~ tired⟩

♦ [1b] ace, crumb, dab, hint, lick, little, mite, nip, particle, shred, speck, spot, touch, trace — more at PARTICLE ♦ [4] space, spell, stretch, while — more at WHILE

³**bit** *n* [*binary digit*] : a unit of computer information equivalent to the result of a choice between two alternatives; *also* : its physical representation
¹**bitch** \'bich\ *n* **1** : a female canine; *esp* : a female dog **2** *often offensive* : a malicious, spiteful, and domineering woman **3** *informal* : something difficult or unpleasant
²**bitch** *vb* : COMPLAIN
¹**bite** \'bīt\ *vb* **bit** \'bit\; **bit•ten** \'bit-ᵊn\ *also* **bit**; **bit•ing** \'bī-tiŋ\ **1** ♦ : to grip with teeth or jaws; *also* : to wound or sting with or as if with fangs **2** : to cut or pierce with

or as if with an edged instrument **3** : to cause to smart or sting **4** ♦ : to eat away by degrees as if by gnawing : CORRODE **5** : to take bait

♦ *usu* **bite on** [1] champ, chew, chomp, crunch, gnaw, nibble; *also* lap, lick, munch ♦ *usu* **bite at** [4] corrode, eat, erode, fret — more at EAT

²**bite** *n* **1** : the act or manner of biting **2** ♦ : a small amount of food **3 a** : a wound made by biting **b** ♦ : a penetrating effect or sensation

♦ [2] morsel, mouthful, nibble, taste, tidbit — more at MORSEL ♦ [3b] bitterness, harshness, pungency, sharpness, tartness

bit•ing \'bī-tiŋ\ *adj* ♦ : having the power to bite so as to cause physical or mental discomfort ⟨a ~ wind⟩; *esp* : able to grip and impress deeply ⟨a ~ wit⟩

♦ bitter, cutting, keen, penetrating, piercing, raw, sharp — more at CUTTING ♦ acute, agonizing, excruciating, sharp, smart — more at SHARP ♦ acrid, caustic, cutting, mordant, pungent, sarcastic, satiric, scathing, sharp, tart — more at SARCASTIC

bit•mapped \'bit-ˌmapt\ *adj* : of, relating to, or being a digital image or display for which an array of binary data specifies the value of each pixel — **bit•map** \-ˌmap\ *n*
bit•ter \'bi-tər\ *adj* **1** : being or inducing the one of the basic taste sensations that is acrid, astringent, or disagreeable and is suggestive of hops **2** ♦ : marked by intensity or severity (as of distress or hatred) **3** ♦ : extremely harsh or cruel **4** ♦ : intensely unpleasant esp. in coldness or rawness

♦ [2] acrid, acrimonious, hard, rancorous, resentful, sore; *also* disaffected, discontented, disgruntled, malcontent ♦ [3] agonizing, galling, harrowing, harsh, hurtful, painful, tortuous; *also* insufferable, insupportable, intolerable, unacceptable, unbearable, unendurable, unsupportable *Ant* gratifying, pleasing, sweet ♦ [3] brutal, burdensome, grim, hard, harsh, heavy, onerous, oppressive, severe, stiff, tough, trying — more at HARSH ♦ [4] arctic, cold, freezing, frigid, frosty, glacial, icy, polar, raw, wintry — more at COLD

bit•ter•ly *adv* ♦ : in a bitter manner

♦ hard, sadly, sorrowfully, unhappily, wretchedly — more at HARD

bit•tern \'bi-tərn\ *n* : any of various small or medium-sized herons
bit•ter•ness *n* ♦ : the quality or state of being bitter; *also* : something bitter

♦ animosity, antagonism, antipathy, enmity, gall, grudge, hostility, rancor — more at ENMITY ♦ bite, harshness, pungency, sharpness, tartness

bit•ters \'bi-tərz\ *n sing or pl* : a usu. alcoholic solution of bitter and often aromatic plant products used in mixing drinks and as a mild tonic
¹**bit•ter•sweet** \'bi-tər-ˌswēt\ *n* **1** : a poisonous nightshade with purple flowers and orange-red berries **2** : a woody vine with yellow capsules that open when ripe and disclose scarlet seed coverings
²**bittersweet** *adj* : being at once both bitter and sweet
bi•tu•mi•nous coal \bə-'tü-mə-nəs-, bī-, -'tyü-\ *n* : a coal that when heated yields considerable volatile waste matter
bi•valve \'bī-ˌvalv\ *n* : any of a class of mollusks (as clams or scallops) with a shell composed of two separate parts that open and shut — **bivalve** *adj*
¹**biv•ouac** \'bi-və-ˌwak\ *n* [F, fr. LG *biwacht*, fr. *bi* at + *wacht* guard] ♦ : a temporary encampment or shelter

♦ camp, encampment — more at CAMP

²**bivouac** *vb* **-ouacked; -ouack•ing** : to form a bivouac : CAMP
¹**bi•week•ly** \ˌbī-'wē-klē\ *adj* **1** : occurring twice a week **2** : occurring every two weeks : FORTNIGHTLY — **biweekly** *adv*
²**biweekly** *n* : a biweekly publication
bi•year•ly \-'yir-lē\ *adj* **1** : BIANNUAL **2** : BIENNIAL

bi·zarre \bə-'zär\ *adj* : strikingly out of the ordinary: as **a** ♦ : odd, extravagant, or eccentric in style or mode **b** ♦ : involving sensational contrasts or incongruities : FANTASTIC — **bi·zarre·ly** *adv*

 ♦ [a] curious, far-out, funny, odd, outlandish, peculiar, quaint, queer, quirky, screwy, strange, weird ♦ [b] absurd, crazy, fanciful, fantastic, foolish, insane, nonsensical, preposterous, unreal, wild — more at FANTASTIC

bi·zar·ro \bə-'zär-ō\ *adj* : characterized by a bizarre, fantastic, or unconventional approach ⟨a ∼ movie⟩

bk *abbr* **1** bank **2** book

Bk *symbol* berkelium

bkg *abbr* banking

bkgd *abbr* background

bks *abbr* barracks

bkt *abbr* **1** basket **2** bracket

bl *abbr* **1** bale **2** barrel **3** blue

blab \'blab\ *vb* **blabbed; blab·bing 1** ♦ : to talk idly or thoughtlessly **2** : to reveal a secret esp. by indiscreet chatter : TATTLE, GOSSIP

 ♦ chat, converse, gab, jaw, palaver, patter, prattle, rattle, talk, visit — more at CHAT

blab·ber·mouth \'bla-bər-ˌmau̇th\ *n* ♦ : a person who talks too much; *esp* : TATTLETALE

 ♦ betrayer, informer, rat, snitch, stool pigeon, tattler, tattletale — more at INFORMER

blab·by \'bla-bē\ *adj* : given to talking

¹**black** \'blak\ *adj* **1** ♦ : of the color black; *also* : very dark **2** : having dark skin, hair, and eyes **3** : of or relating to any of various population groups having dark pigmentation of the skin **4** : of or relating to African American people or their culture **5** : SOILED, DIRTY **6** : lacking light ⟨a ∼ night⟩ **7** ♦ : thoroughly sinister or evil : WICKED ⟨∼ magic⟩ **8** ♦ : very sad, gloomy, or calamitous : DISMAL ⟨a ∼ outlook⟩ **9** : SULLEN ⟨a ∼ mood⟩ — **black·ish** *adj* — **black·ly** *adv*

 ♦ [1] ebony, raven; *also* dark, dusky, inky *Ant* white ♦ [7] bad, evil, immoral, iniquitous, nefarious, rotten, sinful, unethical, unsavory, vicious, vile, villainous, wicked, wrong ♦ [8] bleak, dark, dismal, dreary, gloomy, gray (*or* grey), somber (*or* sombre), wretched — more at GLOOMY

²**black** *n* **1** : a black pigment or dye; *also* : something (as clothing) that is black **2** : the characteristic color of soot or coal **3** : a person belonging to any of various population groups having dark pigmentation of the skin **4** : AFRICAN AMERICAN

³**black** *vb* : BLACKEN

⁴**black** *n* ♦ : total or nearly total absence of light

 ♦ dark, darkness, dusk, gloaming, gloom, murk, night, semidarkness, shade, shadows, twilight — more at DARK

black–and–blue \ˌbla-kən-'blü\ *adj* : darkly discolored from blood effused by bruising

black·ball \'blak-ˌbȯl\ *vb* **1** ♦ : to vote against; *esp* : to exclude from membership by casting a negative vote **2** : OSTRACIZE — **black·ball** *n*

 ♦ kill, negative, veto — more at NEGATIVE

black bass *n* : any of several freshwater sunfishes native to eastern and central No. America

black bear *n* : a usu. black-furred bear of the North American forests

¹**black belt** \'blak-ˌbelt\ *n, often cap both Bs* : an area densely populated by black people

²**black belt** \-'belt\ *n* : one who holds the rating of expert (as in judo or karate); *also* : the rating itself

black·ber·ry \-ˌber-ē\ *n* : the usu. black or purple juicy but seedy edible fruit of various brambles; *also* : a plant bearing this fruit

black·bird \-ˌbərd\ *n* : any of various birds (as the red-winged blackbird) of which the male is largely or wholly black

black·board \-ˌbȯrd\ *n* : a smooth usu. dark surface used for writing or drawing on with chalk

black·body \-'bä-dē\ *n* : a body or surface that completely absorbs incident radiation with no reflection

black box *n* **1** : a usu. complicated electronic device whose components and workings are unknown or mysterious to the user **2** : a device used in aircraft to record cockpit conversations and flight data

black death *n* : an epidemic of bacterial plague and esp. bubonic plague that spread rapidly in Europe and Asia in the 14th century

black·en \'bla-kən\ *vb* **black·ened; black·en·ing 1** ♦ : to make or become black or dark **2** ♦ : to speak evil of : DEFAME

 ♦ [1] becloud, cloud, darken, dim, obscure, overcast, overshadow, shadow ♦ [1] befoul, begrime, besmirch, dirty, muddy, smirch, soil, stain — more at DIRTY ♦ [2] defame, libel, malign, slander, smear, traduce, vilify — more at SLANDER

black·ened *adj* : coated with spices and quickly seared in a very hot skillet ⟨∼ swordfish⟩

black eye *n* : a discoloration of the skin around the eye from bruising

black–eyed Su·san \ˌblak-ˌīd-'süz-ᵊn\ *n* : a coarse No. American plant that is related to the daisies and has deep yellow to orange flower heads with dark conical centers

Black·foot \'blak-ˌfu̇t\ *n, pl* **Black·feet** *or* **Blackfoot** : a member of an American Indian people of Montana, Alberta, and Saskatchewan

black·guard \'bla-gərd, -ˌgärd\ *n* : SCOUNDREL, RASCAL

black·head \'blak-ˌhed\ *n* : a small usu. dark oily mass plugging the outlet of a skin gland

black hole *n* : a hypothetical celestial object with a gravitational field so strong that light cannot escape from it

black ice *n* : a thin layer of ice on a paved road that is very difficult to see

black·ing \'bla-kiŋ\ *n* : a substance applied to something to make it black

¹**black·jack** \'blak-ˌjak\ *n* **1** : a leather-covered club with a flexible handle **2** : a card game in which the object is to be dealt cards having a higher count than the dealer but not exceeding 21

²**blackjack** *vb* : to hit with or as if with a blackjack

black light *n* : invisible ultraviolet light

black·list \'blak-ˌlist\ *n* : a list of persons who are disapproved of and are to be punished or boycotted — **blacklist** *vb*

black·mail \'blak-ˌmāl\ *n* : extortion by threats esp. of public exposure; *also* : something so extorted — **blackmail** *vb*

black·mail·er *n* : one who blackmails another

black market *n* : illicit trade in goods; *also* : a place where such trade is carried on

Black Mass *n* : a travesty of the Christian mass ascribed to worshipers of Satan

Black Muslim *n* : a member of a chiefly black group that professes Islamic religious belief

black nationalist *n, often cap B&N* : a member of a group of militant black people who advocate separatism from white people and the formation of self-governing black communities — **black nationalism** *n, often cap B&N*

black·ness *n* : the quality or state of being black

black·out \'bla-ˌkau̇t\ *n* **1** : a period of darkness due to electrical power failure **2** ♦ : a transitory loss or dulling of vision or consciousness **3** : the prohibition or restriction of the telecasting of a sports event

 ♦ faint, knockout, swoon — more at FAINT

black out *vb* ♦ : to temporarily lose vision, consciousness, or memory

 ♦ faint, pass out, swoon — more at FAINT

black pepper *n* : a spice that consists of the dried berry of a pepper plant that is ground with the black husk still on

black power *n* : the mobilization of the political and economic power of black Americans esp. to compel respect for their rights and improve their condition

black sheep *n* : a member of a group who is disreputable or who is not regarded favorably

black·smith \\'blak-ˌsmith\\ *n* : a smith who forges iron — **black·smith·ing** *n*

black·thorn \\-ˌthȯrn\\ *n* : a European thorny plum

black–tie \\'blak-'tī\\ *adj* : characterized by or requiring semiformal evening clothes consisting of a usu. black tie and tuxedo for men and a formal dress for women

black·top \\'blak-ˌtäp\\ *n* : a dark tarry material (as asphalt) used esp. for surfacing roads — **blacktop** *vb*

black widow *n* : a venomous New World spider having the female black with an hourglass-shaped red mark on the underside of the abdomen

blad·der \\'bla-dər\\ *n* : a sac in which liquid or gas is stored; *esp* : one in a vertebrate into which urine passes from the kidneys

blade \\'blād\\ *n* 1 : a leaf of a plant and esp. of a grass; *also* : the flat part of a leaf as distinguished from its stalk 2 : something (as the flat part of an oar or an arm of a propeller) resembling the blade of a leaf 3 : the cutting part of an instrument or tool 4 : a weapon (as a cutlass or rapier) with a long blade for cutting or thrusting that is often used as a symbol of honor or authority : SWORD; *also* : SWORDSMAN 5 : a dashing fellow ⟨a gay ∼⟩ 6 : the runner of an ice skate — **blad·ed** \\'blā-dəd\\ *adj*

blain \\'blān\\ *n* : an inflammatory swelling or sore

blam·able *adj* ♦ : deserving blame

♦ blameworthy, censurable, culpable, reprehensible — more at BLAMEWORTHY

¹blame \\'blām\\ *vb* **blamed; blam·ing** [ME, fr. AF *blamer, blasmer,* fr. L *blasphemare* to blaspheme, fr. Gk *blasphēmein*] 1 ♦ : to find fault with 2 : to hold responsible or responsible for

♦ censure, condemn, criticize, denounce, fault, knock, pan, reprehend — more at CRITICIZE

²blame *n* 1 : CENSURE, REPROOF 2 ♦ : responsibility for fault or error

♦ culpability, fault, guilt, rap; *also* regret, remorse, self-reproach, shame *Ant* blamelessness

blame·less *adj* ♦ : free from blame or fault — **blame·less·ly** *adv* — **blame·less·ness** *n*

♦ clear, faultless, guiltless, impeccable, innocent, irreproachable — more at INNOCENT

blame·wor·thy \\-ˌwər-thē\\ *adj* ♦ : deserving blame — **blame·wor·thi·ness** *n*

♦ blamable, censurable, culpable, reprehensible; *also* bad, guilty, sinful, wicked *Ant* blameless, faultless, impeccable, irreproachable

blanch \\'blanch\\ *vb* ♦ : to make or become white or pale : BLEACH

♦ bleach, blench, dull, fade, pale, wash out, whiten — more at PALE

blanc·mange \\blə-'mänj, -'mäⁿzh\\ *n* [ME *blancmanger,* fr. MF *blanc manger,* lit., white food] : a dessert made from gelatin or a starchy substance and milk usu. sweetened and flavored

bland \\'bland\\ *adj* 1 : smooth in manner : SUAVE 2 ♦ : gently soothing ⟨a ∼ diet⟩; *also* : INSIPID — **bland·ly** *adv* — **bland·ness** *n*

♦ balmy, benign, delicate, gentle, insipid, light, mellow, mild, soft, soothing, tender — more at GENTLE

blan·dish·ment \\'blan-dish-mənt\\ *n* : flattering or coaxing speech or action : CAJOLERY

¹blank \\'blaŋk\\ *adj* 1 a : showing or causing an appearance of dazed dismay b ♦ : lacking expression 2 ♦ : free from writing or marks; *also* : having spaces to be filled in 3 : DULL, EMPTY ⟨∼ moments⟩ 4 : ABSOLUTE, DOWNRIGHT ⟨a ∼ refusal⟩ 5 : not shaped in final form — **blank·ly** *adv*

♦ [1b] deadpan, expressionless, impassive, inexpressive, stolid, vacant; *also* dull, empty, vacuous, vapid *Ant* demonstrative, expressive ♦ [2] bare, devoid, empty, stark, vacant, void — more at EMPTY

²blank *n* 1 ♦ : an empty space 2 ♦ : a form with spaces for the entry of data 3 : an unfinished form (as of a key) 4 : a cartridge with propellant and a seal but no projectile

♦ [1] blankness, emptiness, vacancy, vacuity, void — more at VACANCY ♦ [2] document, form, paper — more at FORM

³blank *vb* 1 : to cover or close up : OBSCURE 2 : to keep from scoring

blank check *n* 1 : a signed check with the amount unspecified 2 : complete freedom of action

¹blan·ket \\'blaŋ-kət\\ *n* 1 : a heavy woven often woolen covering 2 ♦ : a covering layer ⟨a ∼ of snow⟩

♦ cloak, curtain, hood, mantle, mask, shroud, veil — more at CLOAK

²blanket *vb* 1 ♦ : to cover with or as if with a blanket 2 ♦ : to cover so as to obscure, interrupt, suppress, or extinguish

♦ [1] carpet, coat, cover, overlay, overlie, overspread — more at COVER ♦ [2] blot out, cloak, conceal, cover, curtain, enshroud, hide, mask, obscure, occlude, occult, screen, shroud, veil — more at HIDE

³blanket *adj* ♦ : covering a group or class ⟨∼ insurance⟩; *also* : applicable in all instances ⟨∼ rules⟩

♦ common, general, generic, global, overall, universal — more at GENERAL

blank·ness *n* ♦ : the quality or state of being blank

♦ blank, emptiness, vacancy, vacuity, void — more at VACANCY

blank verse *n* : unrhymed iambic pentameter

blare \\'blar\\ *vb* **blared; blar·ing** : to sound loud and harsh; *also* : to proclaim loudly — **blare** *n*

blar·ney \\'blär-nē\\ *n* [*Blarney stone,* a stone in Blarney Castle, near Cork, Ireland, held to bestow skill in flattery on those who kiss it] ♦ : skillful flattery : BLANDISHMENT

♦ adulation, flattery, overpraise — more at FLATTERY

bla·sé \\blä-'zā\\ *adj* [F] : apathetic to pleasure or excitement as a result of excessive indulgence; *also* : SOPHISTICATED

blas·pheme \\blas-'fēm, 'blas-ˌ\\ *vb* **blas·phemed; blas·phem·ing** 1 : to speak of or address with irreverence 2 : to utter blasphemy — **blas·phem·er** *n*

blas·phe·mous \\-məs\\ *adj* ♦ : impiously irreverent

♦ irreverent, profane, sacrilegious

blas·phe·my \\'blas-fə-mē\\ *n, pl* **-mies** 1 ♦ : the act of expressing lack of reverence for God 2 ♦ : irreverence toward something considered sacred

♦ [1, 2] defilement, desecration, impiety, irreverence, sacrilege; *also* cursing, profanity, swearing *Ant* adoration, glorification, worship

¹blast \\'blast\\ *n* 1 ♦ : a violent gust of wind; *also* : its effect 2 : sound made by a wind instrument 3 : a current of air forced at high pressure through a hole in a furnace (**blast furnace**) 4 : a sudden withering esp. of plants : BLIGHT 5 ♦ : an explosion or violent detonation; *also* : the often destructive shock wave of an explosion

♦ [1] blow, flurry, gust, williwaw — more at GUST ♦ [5] detonation, eruption, explosion — more at EXPLOSION

²blast *vb* 1 ♦ : to make a vigorous attack 2 a : to use an explosive b ♦ : to discharge or propel something by means of an explosive : SHOOT 3 ♦ : to shatter by or as if by an explosive

♦ [1] abuse, assail, attack, belabor, castigate, excoriate, jump, lambaste, slam, vituperate — more at ATTACK ♦ [2b] discharge, fire, loose, shoot — more at SHOOT ♦ [3] blow up, burst, demolish, explode, pop, shatter, smash; *also* dynamite

blast off *vb* : TAKE OFF 4 — used esp. of rocket-propelled vehicles — **blast·off** \\'blast-ˌȯf\\ *n*

bla·tant \\'blāt-^ənt\\ *adj* ♦ : offensively obtrusive : vulgarly showy — **bla·tan·cy** \\-^ən-sē\\ *n* — **bla·tant·ly** *adv*

♦ conspicuous, egregious, flagrant, glaring, gross, obvious, patent, prominent, pronounced, rank, striking — more at EGREGIOUS

blath·er \'bla-<u>th</u>ər\ *vb* : to talk foolishly at length — **blather** *n*

blath·er·skite \'bla-<u>th</u>ər-ˌskīt\ *n* : a person who blathers

¹**blaze** \'blāz\ *n* **1** : FIRE **2** ♦ : intense direct light often accompanied by heat ⟨the ∼ of TV lights⟩ **3** : something (as a dazzling display or sudden outburst) suggesting fire ⟨a ∼ of autumn leaves⟩

♦ flare, fluorescence, glare, gleam, glow, illumination, incandescence, light, luminescence, radiance, shine — more at LIGHT

²**blaze** *vb* **blazed; blaz·ing 1** ♦ : to burn brightly; *also* : to flare up **2** ♦ : to be conspicuously bright

♦ [1] burn, flame, flare, glow — more at BURN ♦ [1, 2] beat, burn, flame, flare, glare — more at GLARE

³**blaze** *vb* **blazed; blaz·ing** ♦ : to make public or conspicuous

♦ advertise, announce, broadcast, declare, enunciate, flash, herald, placard, post, proclaim, promulgate, publicize, publish, sound — more at ANNOUNCE

⁴**blaze** *n* **1** : a usu. white stripe on the face of an animal **2** : a trail marker; *esp* : one made on a tree

⁵**blaze** *vb* **blazed; blaz·ing** : to mark (as a tree or trail) with blazes

blaz·er \'blā-zər\ *n* : a sports jacket often with notched collar and pockets that are stitched on

¹**bla·zon** \'blā-ᵊn\ *n* **1** : COAT OF ARMS **2** : ostentatious display

²**blazon** *vb* **1** : to publish widely : PROCLAIM **2** : DECK, ADORN

bldg *abbr* building

bldr *abbr* builder

¹**bleach** \'blēch\ *vb* ♦ : to make or become white : BLANCH

♦ blanch, blench, dull, fade, pale, wash out, whiten — more at PALE

²**bleach** *n* : a preparation used in bleaching

bleach·ers \'blē-chərz\ *n sing or pl* : a usu. uncovered stand of tiered seats for spectators

bleak \'blēk\ *adj* **1** ♦ : desolately barren and often windswept **2** ♦ : lacking warm or cheering qualities — **bleak·ish** *adj* — **bleak·ly** *adv*

♦ [1] dirty, foul, inclement, nasty, raw, rough, squally, stormy, tempestuous, turbulent — more at FOUL ♦ [2] dark, dismal, dreary, gloomy, gray (*or* grey), somber (*or* sombre), wretched — more at GLOOMY

bleak·ness *n* ♦ : the quality or state of being bleak

♦ bite, bitterness, chill, nip, rawness, sharpness — more at CHILL

blear \'blir\ *adj* : dim with water or tears ⟨∼ eyes⟩

bleary \'blir-ē\ *adj* **1** : dull or dimmed esp. from fatigue or sleep **2** ♦ : poorly outlined or defined

♦ dim, faint, foggy, fuzzy, hazy, indefinite, indistinct, unclear, undefined, undetermined — more at FAINT

bleat \'blēt\ *n* : the cry of a sheep or goat or a sound like it — **bleat** *vb*

bleed \'blēd\ *vb* **bled** \'bled\; **bleed·ing 1** : to lose or shed blood **2 a** : to be wounded **b** ♦ : to feel pain or distress **3 a** ♦ : to flow or ooze from a wounded surface **b** ♦ : to draw fluid from esp. in a controlled manner ⟨∼ steam from the pipes⟩ ⟨∼ a tire⟩ **4** : to extort money from

♦ [2b] agonize, feel, grieve, hurt, mourn, sorrow, suffer — more at GRIEVE ♦ [3a] exude, ooze, percolate, seep, strain, sweat, weep — more at EXUDE ♦ [3b] drain, draw, pump, siphon, tap — more at DRAIN

bleed·er \'blē-dər\ *n* : one that bleeds; *esp* : HEMOPHILIAC

bleeding heart *n* **1** : a garden plant related to the poppies that has usu. deep pink drooping heart-shaped flowers **2** *disparaging* : a person who shows extreme sympathy esp. for an object of alleged persecution

¹**blem·ish** \'ble-mish\ *vb* ♦ : to spoil by a flaw : MAR

♦ mar, poison, spoil, stain, taint, tarnish, touch, vitiate — more at TAINT

²**blemish** *n* ♦ : a noticeable flaw

♦ defect, deformity, disfigurement, fault, flaw, imperfection, mark, pockmark, scar; *also* abnormality, distortion, irregularity, malformation

¹**blench** \'blench\ *vb* [ME, to deceive, blench, fr. OE *blencan* to deceive] ♦ : to draw back or turn aside from lack of courage : FLINCH, QUAIL

♦ flinch, quail, recoil, shrink, wince — more at FLINCH

²**blench** *vb* ♦ : to grow or make pale

♦ blanch, bleach, dull, fade, pale, wash out, whiten — more at PALE

¹**blend** \'blend\ *vb* **blend·ed; blend·ing 1** ♦ : to mix thoroughly **2** : to prepare (as coffee) by mixing different varieties **3** ♦ : to combine into an integrated whole **4** : to produce a harmonious effect : HARMONIZE — **blend·er** *n*

♦ amalgamate, commingle, fuse, incorporate, intermingle, merge, mingle, mix *Ant* break down, break up, separate

²**blend** *n* ♦ : a product of blending

♦ admixture, amalgam, combination, composite, compound, fusion, intermixture, mix, mixture; *also* coalescence, concoction, incorporation, intermingling, mingling

bless \'bles\ *vb* **blessed** \'blest\ *also* **blest** \'blest\; **bless·ing** [ME, fr. OE *blētsian*, fr. *blōd* blood; fr. the use of blood in consecration] **1** ♦ : to consecrate by religious rite or word **2** : to sanctify with the sign of the cross **3** : to invoke divine care for **4** ♦ : to give glory to : PRAISE, GLORIFY **5** : to confer happiness upon

♦ [1] consecrate, hallow, sanctify; *also* cleanse, purify ♦ [4] extol, glorify, laud, magnify, praise — more at PRAISE

bless·ed \'ble-səd\ *also* **blest** \'blest\ *adj* **1 a** ♦ : held in reverence **b** ♦ : venerated as or as if sacred : HOLY **2** : BEATIFIED **3** : DELIGHTFUL — **bless·ed·ly** *adv*

♦ [1a] hallowed, holy, sacred, sacrosanct, sanctified — more at HOLY ♦ [1b] divine, godlike, heavenly, holy — more at HOLY

bless·ed·ness *n* ♦ : the quality or state of being blessed

♦ bliss, felicity, gladness, happiness, joy — more at HAPPINESS ♦ devoutness, godliness, holiness, piety, sainthood, sanctity — more at HOLINESS

bless·ing \'ble-siŋ\ *n* **1 a** ♦ : the act or words of one who blesses **b** ♦ : acknowledgment and acceptance or support of something : APPROVAL ⟨gave their ∼ to the proposal⟩ **2** ♦ : a thing conducive to happiness **3** : grace said at a meal

♦ [1a] consecration, sanctification — more at CONSECRATION ♦ [1b] approbation, approval, favor (*or* favour), imprimatur, OK — more at APPROVAL ♦ [2] benefit, boon, felicity, godsend, good, manna, windfall; *also* bonus, extra, lagniappe *Ant* affliction, bane, curse, evil, plague, scourge

blew *past of* BLOW

¹**blight** \'blīt\ *n* **1** : a plant disease or injury marked by withering; *also* : an organism causing a blight **2** : an impairing or frustrating influence; *also* : a deteriorated condition ⟨urban ∼⟩

²**blight** *vb* : to affect with or suffer from blight

blimp \'blimp\ *n* : a nonrigid airship

¹**blind** \'blīnd\ *adj* **1** : lacking or grossly deficient in ability to see; *also* : intended for blind persons **2** : not based on reason, evidence, or knowledge ⟨∼ chance⟩ **3** : not intelligently controlled or directed ⟨∼ chance⟩ **4** : performed solely by using aircraft instruments ⟨a ∼ landing⟩ **5** : hard to discern or make out : HIDDEN ⟨a ∼ seam⟩ **6** : lacking an opening or outlet ⟨a ∼ alley⟩ — **blind·ly** *adv* — **blind·ness** \'blīnd-nəs\ *n*

²**blind** *vb* **1** : to make blind **2** : to overpower with brightness : DAZZLE **3** : DARKEN; *also* : HIDE

³**blind** *n* **1** : something (as a shutter) to hinder vision or keep out light **2** : a place of concealment : SUBTERFUGE

blind carbon copy *n* : a copy of a message (such as an

e-mail) that is sent without the knowledge of the other recipients

blind date *n* : a date between persons who have not previously met; *also* : either of these persons

blind·er \'blīn-dər\ *n* : either of two flaps on a horse's bridle to prevent it from seeing to the side

blind·fold \'blīnd-ˌfōld\ *vb* : to cover the eyes of with or as if with a bandage — **blindfold** *n*

¹**blink** \'bliŋk\ *vb* **1** : to close and open the eyes involuntarily : WINK **2** ♦ : to shine dimly or intermittently : TWINKLE **3** : EVADE, IGNORE — often used with *at* **4** ♦ : to cease resistance : YIELD

♦ [2] flash, twinkle, wink; *also* flicker, glance, glimmer, glint, glisten, glister, glitter, scintillate, shimmer, sparkle ♦ [4] bow, budge, capitulate, concede, give in, knuckle under, quit, submit, succumb, surrender, yield — more at YIELD

²**blink** *n* **1** : GLIMMER, SPARKLE **2** : a usu. involuntary shutting and opening of the eye

blink·er \'bliŋ-kər\ *n* : a blinking light used as a signal

blin·tze \'blint-sə\ *or* **blintz** \'blints\ *n* [Yiddish *blintse*] : a thin rolled pancake with a filling usu. of cream cheese

blip \'blip\ *n* **1** : a spot on a radar screen **2** : ABERRATION 1

bliss \'blis\ *n* ♦ : complete happiness : JOY

♦ blessedness, felicity, gladness, happiness, joy — more at HAPPINESS

bliss·ful \-fəl\ *adj* ♦ : full of, marked by, or causing bliss — **bliss·ful·ly** *adv*

♦ delighted, glad, happy, joyful, pleased — more at GLAD

¹**blis·ter** \'blis-tər\ *n* **1** : a raised area of skin containing watery fluid; *also* : an agent that causes blisters **2** : something (as a raised spot in paint) suggesting a blister **3** : a disease of plants marked by large swollen patches on the leaves

²**blister** *vb* : to develop a blister; *also* : to cause blisters

blithe \'blīth, 'blīth\ *adj* **blith·er; blith·est** ♦ : happily lighthearted — **blithe·ly** *adv*

♦ bright, buoyant, cheerful, cheery, chipper, gay, lightsome, sunny, upbeat — more at CHEERFUL ♦ boon, festive, gay, gleeful, jocund, jolly, jovial, merry, mirthful, sunny — more at MERRY

blithe·some \-səm\ *adj* : full of gaiety or high spirits

¹**blitz** \'blits\ *n* **1** : an intensive series of air raids **2** : a fast intensive campaign **3** : a rush of the passer by the defensive linebackers in football

²**blitz** *vb* ♦ : to subject to a blitz; *esp* : to damage by a blitz

♦ bombard, shell — more at BOMBARD

blitz·krieg \-ˌkrēg\ *n* [G, fr. *Blitz* lightning + *Krieg* war] ♦ : a sudden violent enemy attack

♦ aggression, assault, attack, charge, descent, offense (*or* offence), offensive, onset, onslaught, raid, rush, strike — more at ATTACK

bliz·zard \'bli-zərd\ *n* : a long severe snowstorm

blk *abbr* **1** black **2** block

bloat \'blōt\ *vb* : to swell by or as if by filling with water or air

blob \'bläb\ *n* ♦ : a small lump or drop of a thick consistency

♦ chunk, clod, clump, glob, gob, hunk, lump, nub, wad — more at LUMP

bloc \'bläk\ *n* [F, lit., block] ♦ : a combination of individuals or groups (as nations) working for a common purpose

♦ body, coalition, combination, combine, faction, party, sect, set, side, wing — more at FACTION ♦ alliance, coalition, combination, combine, confederacy, confederation, federation, league, union — more at CONFEDERACY

¹**block** \'bläk\ *n* **1** : a solid piece of substantial material (as wood or stone) **2** ♦ : something that impedes progress or achievement : HINDRANCE, OBSTRUCTION; *also* : interruption of normal function of body or mind ⟨heart ∼⟩ **3** : a frame enclosing one or more pulleys and having a

hook or strap by which it may be attached **4** : a piece of material with a hand-cut design on its surface from which copies are to be made **5** : a large building divided into separate units (as apartments or offices) **6** : a row of houses or shops **7** : a city square; *also* : the distance along one of the sides of such a square **8** ♦ : a quantity of things considered as a unit ⟨a ∼ of seats⟩

♦ [2] bar, clog, crimp, drag, embarrassment, hindrance, let, obstacle, stop, stumbling block — more at OBSTACLE ♦ [8] array, assemblage, batch, bunch, cluster, collection, group, package, set, suite

²**block** *vb* **1** ♦ : to make unsuitable for passage or progress by obstruction : OBSTRUCT **2** : to outline roughly ⟨∼ out a design⟩ **3** : to provide or support with a block ⟨∼ up a wheel⟩ — **block·er** *n*

♦ dam, fill, pack, plug, stop, stuff — more at FILL ♦ choke, clog, close (off), congest, dam, jam, obstruct, plug (up), stop (up), stuff — more at CLOG

¹**block·ade** \blä-'kād\ *n* : the isolation of a place usu. by troops or ships

²**blockade** *vb* : to subject to or isolate with a blockade — **block·ad·er** *n*

block·age \'blä-kij\ *n* : an act or instance of obstructing : the state of being blocked

block·bust·er \'bläk-ˌbəs-tər\ *n* ♦ : one that is very large, successful, or violent ⟨a ∼ of a movie⟩

♦ hit, smash, success, winner — more at HIT ♦ behemoth, colossus, giant, jumbo, leviathan, mammoth, monster, titan, whale, whopper — more at GIANT

block·head \'bläk-ˌhed\ *n* ♦ : a slow-witted or stupid person : DOLT, DUNCE

♦ dope, dummy, idiot, imbecile, jackass, moron, numskull — more at IDIOT

block·house \-ˌhaús\ *n* : a small strong building used as a shelter (as from enemy fire) or observation post

blog \'blòg, 'bläg\ *n* [short for *Weblog*] : a website containing one's reflections, opinions, and comments; *also* : the contents of such a site — **blog** *vb* — **blog·ger** *n* — **blog·ging** *n*

¹**blond** *or* **blonde** \'bländ\ *adj* **1** : fair in complexion **2** ♦ : of a light or bleached color ⟨∼ mahogany⟩ — **blond·ish** \'blän-dish\ *adj*

♦ fair, flaxen, golden, sandy, straw; *also* gold, light, white *Ant* dark

²**blond** *or* **blonde** *n* : a person having blond hair

blood \'bləd\ *n* **1** : a usu. red liquid that circulates in the heart, arteries, and veins of animals **2** : LIFEBLOOD; *also* : LIFE **3** ♦ : human stock or lineage **4 a** : relationship by descent from a common ancestor **b** ♦ : persons related by means of a common ancestor : KINDRED **5** : the taking of life **6** : TEMPER, PASSION **7** : DANDY 1 — **blood·less** *adj*

♦ [3] ancestry, birth, bloodline, breeding, descent, extraction, family tree, genealogy, line, lineage, origin, parentage, pedigree, stock, strain — more at ANCESTRY ♦ [4b] clan, family, folks, house, kin, kindred, kinfolk, line, lineage, people, race, stock, tribe

blood bank *n* : a place where blood or plasma is stored

blood·bath \'bləd-ˌbath, -ˌbäth\ *n* : MASSACRE

blood count *n* : the determination of the number of blood cells in a specific volume of blood; *also* : the number of cells so determined

blood·cur·dling \'bləd-kərd-liŋ, -ˌkər-dᵊl-iŋ\ *adj* : arousing fright or horror

blood·ed \'blə-dəd\ *adj* **1** : having blood of a specified kind ⟨warm-*blooded* animals⟩ **2** : entirely or largely purebred ⟨∼ horses⟩

blood group *n* : one of the classes into which human beings can be separated by the presence or absence in their blood of specific antigens

blood·hound \'bləd-ˌhaùnd\ *n* : any of a breed of large powerful hounds with long drooping ears, a wrinkled face, and keen sense of smell

blood·let·ting \-₁le-tiŋ\ *n* 1 : PHLEBOTOMY 2 : BLOODSHED
blood·line \-₁līn\ *n* ♦ : a sequence of direct ancestors esp. in a pedigree

♦ ancestry, birth, blood, breeding, descent, extraction, family tree, genealogy, line, lineage, origin, parentage, pedigree, stock, strain — more at ANCESTRY

blood·mo·bile \-mō-₁bēl\ *n* : a motor vehicle equipped for collecting blood from donors
blood poisoning *n* : invasion of the bloodstream by virulent microorganisms from a focus of infection accompanied esp. by chills, fever, and prostration
blood pressure *n* : pressure of the blood on the walls of blood vessels and esp. arteries
blood·root \'blǝd-₁rüt, -₁rut\ *n* : a plant related to the poppy that has a red root and sap, a solitary leaf, and a white flower in early spring
blood·shed \-₁shed\ *n* : wounding or taking of life : CARNAGE, SLAUGHTER
blood·shot \-₁shät\ *adj* : inflamed to redness ⟨∼ eyes⟩
blood·stain \-₁stān\ *n* : a discoloration caused by blood
blood·stained \-₁stānd\ *adj* : stained with blood; *also* : involved with slaughter
blood·stone \-₁stōn\ *n* : a green quartz sprinkled with red spots
blood·stream \-₁strēm\ *n* : the flowing blood in a circulatory system
blood·suck·er \-₁sǝ-kǝr\ *n* : an animal that sucks blood; *esp* : LEECH — **blood·suck·ing** *adj*
blood test *n* : a test of the blood; *esp* : one for syphilis
blood·thirsty \'blǝd-₁thǝr-stē\ *adj* ♦ : eager to shed blood — **blood·thirst·i·ly** \-₁thǝr-stǝ-lē\ *adv* — **blood·thirst·i·ness** \-stē-nǝs\ *n*

♦ bloody, homicidal, murderous, sanguinary, sanguine; *also* barbaric, barbarous, cruel, heartless, inhumane, sadistic, savage, vicious, wanton

blood type *n* : BLOOD GROUP — **blood–typ·ing** *n*
blood vessel *n* : a vessel (as a vein or artery) in which blood circulates in the body
bloody *adj* 1 : containing or made up of blood; *also* : smeared or stained with blood 2 ♦ : accompanied by or involving bloodshed

♦ bloodthirsty, homicidal, murderous, sanguinary, sanguine — more at BLOODTHIRSTY

Bloody Mary \-'mer-ē\ *n, pl* **Bloody Marys** : a drink made essentially of vodka and tomato juice
¹**bloom** \'blüm\ *n* 1 : the part of a seed plant that normally bears reproductive organs : FLOWER 1; *also* : flowers or amount of flowers (as of a plant) 2 : the period or state of flowering 3 ♦ : a state or time of beauty and vigor 4 : a powdery coating esp. on fruits and leaves 5 : rosy color; *also* : an appearance of freshness or health — **bloomy** *adj*

♦ blossom, flower, flush, heyday, prime; *also* acme, apex, climax, meridian, peak, pinnacle, summit, zenith

²**bloom** *vb* 1 ♦ : to produce or yield flowers 2 : MATURE 3 : to glow esp. with healthy color

♦ blossom, blow, burgeon, flower, unfold; *also* leaf, leave

bloo·mers \'blü-mǝrz\ *n pl* [Amelia *Bloomer* †1894 Am. reformer] : a woman's garment of short loose trousers gathered at the knee
bloop·er \'blü-pǝr\ *n* 1 : a fly ball hit barely beyond a baseball infield 2 : an embarrassing public blunder
¹**blos·som** \'blä-sǝm\ *n* 1 : the flower of a plant 2 ♦ : the period or state of flowering 3 : a peak period or stage of development

♦ bloom, flower, flush, heyday, prime — more at BLOOM

²**blossom** *vb* ♦ : to produce or yield flowers : BLOOM, FLOWER

♦ bloom, blow, burgeon, flower, unfold — more at BLOOM

¹**blot** \'blät\ *n* 1 : SPOT, STAIN ⟨ink ∼s⟩ 2 ♦ : a mark of reproach : moral flaw or blemish ⟨a ∼ on her record⟩

♦ brand, smirch, spot, stain, stigma, taint — more at STAIN

²**blot** *vb* **blot·ted; blot·ting** 1 : SPOT, STAIN 2 : OBSCURE, ECLIPSE 3 *obs* : MAR; *esp* : DISGRACE 4 : to dry or remove with or as if with an absorbing material 5 : to make a blot
¹**blotch** \'bläch\ *n* : a usu. large and irregular spot or mark (as of ink or color) — **blotchy** *adj*
²**blotch** *vb* ♦ : to mark or mar with blotches

♦ mottle, spot

blot out *vb* 1 ♦ : to make obscure, insignificant, or inconsequential ⟨∼ out the sun⟩ 2 ♦ : to destroy completely

♦ [1] blanket, cloak, conceal, cover, curtain, enshroud, hide, mask, obscure, occlude, occult, screen, shroud, veil — more at HIDE ♦ [2] annihilate, demolish, destroy, exterminate, extinguish, obliterate, pulverize, ruin, smash, waste, wipe out, wreck — more at DESTROY

blot·ter \'blä-tǝr\ *n* 1 : a piece of blotting paper 2 : a book for preliminary records (as of sales or arrests)
blot·ting paper *n* : a spongy paper used to absorb ink
blouse \'blaùs, 'blaùz\ *n* 1 : a loose outer garment like a smock 2 : a usu. loose garment reaching from the neck to about the waist
¹**blow** \'blō\ *vb* **blew** \'blü\; **blown** \'blōn\; **blow·ing** 1 : to move forcibly ⟨the wind *blew*⟩ 2 : to send forth a current of gas (as air) 3 : to act on with a current of gas or vapor; *esp* : to drive with such a current 4 : to sound or cause to sound ⟨∼ a horn⟩ 5 ♦ : to breathe quickly or in a labored manner ; PANT, GASP; *also* : to expel moist air in breathing ⟨the whale *blew*⟩ 6 : BOAST; *also* : BLUSTER 7 : MELT — used of an electrical fuse 8 : to shape or form by blown or injected air ⟨∼ glass⟩ 9 : to shatter or destroy by or as if by explosion 10 : to make breathless by exertion 11 ♦ : to spend recklessly 12 : to foul up hopelessly ⟨*blew* her lines⟩ — **blow·er** *n*

♦ [5] gasp, pant, puff, wheeze — more at GASP ♦ [11] dissipate, fritter, lavish, misspend, run through, spend, squander, throw away, waste — more at WASTE

²**blow** *n* 1 : a usu. strong blowing of air : GALE 2 : BOASTING, BRAG 3 : an act or instance of blowing
³**blow** *vb* **blew** \'blü\; **blown** \'blōn\; **blow·ing** : to produce or yield flowers : FLOWER, BLOOM
⁴**blow** *n* 1 ♦ : a forcible stroke 2 : COMBAT ⟨come to ∼s⟩ 3 : a severe and usu. unexpected calamity

♦ bat, belt, box, clout, hit, punch, slug, thump, wallop, whack; *also* flick, jab, poke, roundhouse, stab

blow–by–blow *adj* : minutely detailed ⟨∼ account⟩
blow–dry \-₁drī\ *vb* : to dry and usu. style hair with a blow-dryer
blow–dry·er \-₁drī(-ǝ)r\ *n* : a handheld hair dryer
blow·fly \'blō-₁flī\ *n* : any of a family of dipteran flies (as a bluebottle) that deposit their eggs or maggots on meat or in wounds
blow·gun \-₁gǝn\ *n* : a tube from which an arrow or a dart may be shot by the force of the breath
blow·out \'blō-₁aùt\ *n* 1 ♦ : a festive social affair 2 : a bursting of something (as a tire) because of pressure of the contents (as air)

♦ affair, event, fete, function, get-together, party — more at PARTY

blow·sy *also* **blow·zy** \'blaù-zē\ *adj* : DISHEVELED, SLOVENLY
blow·torch \'blō-₁tòrch\ *n* : a small portable burner whose flame is made hotter by a blast of air or oxygen
blow·up \'blō-₁ǝp\ *n* 1 : EXPLOSION 2 ♦ : an outburst of temper 3 : a photographic enlargement

♦ dudgeon, explosion, fireworks, fit, huff, scene, tantrum — more at TANTRUM

blow up *vb* 1 ♦ : to rend apart, shatter, or destroy by or as if by explosion 2 ♦ : to lose self-control; *esp* : to become violently angry 3 ♦ : to undergo or be destroyed by an explosion

♦ [1, 3] blast, burst, demolish, detonate, explode, pop, shatter, smash — more at BLAST ♦ [2] flare, flip, fulminate, rant, vituperate *Ant* calm (down)

blowy \'blō-ē\ *adj* ♦ : marked by strong wind : WINDY

♦ blustery, breezy, gusty, windy — more at WINDY

BLT \ˌbē-ˌel-'tē\ *n* : a bacon, lettuce, and tomato sandwich

¹**blub·ber** \'blə-bər\ *vb* ♦ : to cry noisily

♦ bawl, cry, sob, weep — more at CRY

²**blubber** *n* **1** : the fat of large sea mammals (as whales) **2** : a noisy crying

¹**blud·geon** \'blə-jən\ *n* ♦ : a short often loaded club

♦ bat, billy club, club, cudgel, staff, truncheon — more at CLUB

²**bludgeon** *vb* ♦ : to strike with or as if with a bludgeon

♦ bash, bat, batter, beat, club, pound — more at BEAT

¹**blue** \'blü\ *adj* **blu·er; blu·est** [ME, fr. AF *blef, blew*, of Gmc origin] **1** : of the color blue; *also* : BLUISH **2** ♦ : low in spirits : MELANCHOLY; *also* : DEPRESSING **3** : PURITANICAL **4** : INDECENT **5** : tending to support Democratic candidates ⟨a ∼ state⟩ — **blue·ness** *n*

♦ depressed, down, downcast, glum, low, melancholy, miserable, sad, unhappy

²**blue** *n* **1** : a color between green and violet in the spectrum : the color of the clear daytime sky **2** ♦ : something (as clothing or the sky or ocean) that is blue

♦ high, sky — more at SKY ♦ brine, deep, ocean, sea — more at OCEAN

blue baby *n* : a baby with bluish skin due to faulty circulation caused by a heart defect

blue·bell \-ˌbel\ *n* : any of various plants with blue bell-shaped flowers

blue·ber·ry \'blü-ˌber-ē, -bə-rē\ *n* : the edible blue or blackish berry of various shrubs of the heath family; *also* : one of these shrubs

blue·bird \-ˌbərd\ *n* : any of several small No. American thrushes that are blue above and reddish-brown or pale blue below

blue·bon·net \'blü-ˌbä-nət\ *n* : either of two low-growing annual lupines of Texas with silky foliage and blue flowers

blue·bot·tle \'blü-ˌbät-ᵊl\ *n* : any of several blowflies with iridescent blue bodies or abdomens

blue cheese *n* : cheese having veins of greenish blue mold

blue–col·lar \'blü-'kä-lər\ *adj* : of, relating to, or being the class of workers whose duties call for work clothes

blue·fish \-ˌfish\ *n* : a marine sport and food fish bluish above and silvery below

blue·grass \-ˌgras\ *n* **1** : KENTUCKY BLUEGRASS **2** : country music played on stringed instruments having free improvisation and close harmonies

blue jay \-ˌjā\ *n* : a crested bright blue No. American jay

blue jeans *n pl* : pants usu. made of blue denim

blue·nose \'blü-ˌnōz\ *n* : a person who advocates a rigorous moral code

blue·point \-ˌpȯint\ *n* : a small oyster typically from the south shore of Long Island, New York

¹**blue·print** \-ˌprint\ *n* **1** : a photographic print in white on a blue ground used esp. for copying mechanical drawings and architects' plans **2** ♦ : a detailed plan of action

♦ arrangement, design, game, plan, project, scheme, strategy, system — more at PLAN

²**blueprint** *vb* **1** : to make a blueprint of **2** ♦ : to work out (as a program or plan) in detail

♦ arrange, calculate, chart, design, frame, lay out, map, plan, project, scheme — more at PLAN

blues \'blüz\ *n pl* **1** ♦ : low spirits : MELANCHOLY **2** : music in a style marked by recurrent minor intervals and melancholy lyrics

♦ dejection, depression, doldrums, dumps, melancholy, sadness — more at SADNESS

blue screen *n* : a cinematic technique in which a subject is filmed in front of a blue background so as to allow the creation of a composite with other footage

blue-stock·ing \'blü-ˌstä-kiŋ\ *n* : a woman having intellectual interests

blu·et \'blü-ət\ *n* : a low No. American herb with dainty bluish flowers

blue whale *n* : a very large baleen whale that may reach a weight of 150 tons (135 metric tons) and a length of 100 feet (30 meters)

¹**bluff** \'bləf\ *adj* **1** : having a broad flattened front **2** : rising steeply with a broad flat front **3** : good-naturedly frank and outspoken

²**bluff** *n* ♦ : a high steep bank : CLIFF

♦ cliff, crag, escarpment, palisade, precipice, scarp — more at CLIFF

³**bluff** *vb* ♦ : to frighten or deceive by pretense or a mere show of strength

♦ deceive, dupe, fool, gull, misinform, mislead, trick — more at DECEIVE

⁴**bluff** *n* : an act or instance of bluffing; *also* : one who bluffs

blu·ing *or* **blue·ing** \'blü-iŋ\ *n* : a preparation used in laundering to counteract yellowing of white fabrics

blu·ish \'blü-ish\ *adj* : somewhat blue

¹**blun·der** \'blən-dər\ *vb* **1** ♦ : to move clumsily or unsteadily **2** : to make a stupid or needless mistake

♦ flounder, limp, lumber, plod, stumble — more at FLOUNDER

²**blunder** *n* ♦ : an avoidable and usu. serious mistake

♦ error, fault, flub, fumble, goof, lapse, miscue, misstep, mistake, oversight, slip, stumble — more at ERROR

blun·der·buss \'blən-dər-ˌbəs\ *n* [obs. D *donderbus*, fr. D *donder* thunder + obs. D *bus* gun] : an obsolete short-barreled firearm with a flaring muzzle

¹**blunt** \'blənt\ *adj* **1** ♦ : not sharp : DULL **2** ♦ : lacking in tact : BLUFF — **blunt·ly** *adv* — **blunt·ness** *n*

♦ [1] dull, obtuse — more at DULL ♦ [2] abrupt, brusque, curt, snippy; *also* gruff, rough, short *Ant* circuitous, mealymouthed

²**blunt** *vb* ♦ : to make or become less sharp, definite, or forceful

♦ dampen, deaden, dull, numb — more at DULL

¹**blur** \'blər\ *n* **1** : a smear or stain that obscures **2** : something vaguely perceived; *esp* : something moving too quickly to be clearly perceived

²**blur** *vb* **blurred; blur·ring** ♦ : to make dim, imperfect, or confused : CLOUD, OBSCURE ⟨*blurred* vision⟩

♦ becloud, befog, cloud, confuse, dim, fog, haze, mist, obscure, shroud — more at CLOUD

blurb \'blərb\ *n* : a short publicity notice (as on a book jacket)

blur·ry \'blər-ē\ *adj* ♦ : lacking definition or focus

♦ bleary, dim, faint, foggy, fuzzy, hazy, indefinite, indistinct, indistinguishable, misty, murky, nebulous, obscure, opaque, shadowy, unclear, undefined, undetermined, vague — more at FAINT

blurt \'blərt\ *vb* ♦ : to utter suddenly and impulsively

♦ *usu* blurt out bolt, cry, ejaculate, spout

¹**blush** \'bləsh\ *n* **1** : a reddening of the face (as from modesty or confusion) : FLUSH **2** : a cosmetic used to tint the face pink — **blush·ful** *adj*

²**blush** *vb* ♦ : to become red in the face esp. from shame, modesty, or confusion

♦ bloom, color (*or* colour), crimson, flush, glow, redden; *also* rouge

¹**blus·ter** \'bləs-tər\ *vb* **1** : to blow in stormy noisy gusts **2** ♦ : to talk or act with noisy swaggering threats

♦ fulminate, rant, rave, spout — more at RANT

²**bluster** *n* **1** : a violent boisterous blowing **2** ♦ : violent commotion **3** ♦ : loudly boastful or threatening speech

♦ [2] cacophony, clamor (*or* clamour), din, noise, racket, roar — more at NOISE ♦ [3] bombast, brag, gas, grandiloquence, rant — more at BOMBAST

blus·tery \-tə-rē\ *adj* ♦ : blowing boisterously ⟨a ∼ day⟩
♦ blowy, breezy, gusty, windy — more at WINDY

blvd *abbr* boulevard

B lymphocyte *n* : B CELL

BM *abbr* bowel movement

B movie *n* : a cheaply produced motion picture

BO *abbr* **1** best offer **2** body odor **3** box office **4** branch office

boa \'bō-ə\ *n* **1** : a large snake (as the **boa con·stric·tor** \-kən-'strik-tər\ or the related anaconda) that suffocates and kills its prey by constriction **2** : a fluffy scarf usu. of fur or feathers

boar \'bōr\ *n* : a male swine; *also* : WILD BOAR

¹board \'bōrd\ *n* **1** : the side of a ship **2** : a thin flat length of sawed lumber; *also* : material (as cardboard) or a piece of material formed as a thin flat firm sheet **3** *pl* : a theater stage as representing the acting profession **4 a** : a table spread with a meal **b** : daily meals esp. when furnished for pay **5** : a table at which a council or magistrates sit **6** : a group or association of persons organized for a special responsibility (as the management of a business or institution); *also* : an organized commercial exchange **7** : a sheet of insulating material carrying circuit elements and inserted in an electronic device

²board *vb* **1** : to go or put aboard ⟨∼ a boat⟩ **2** : to cover with boards **3** ♦ : to provide or be provided with meals and often lodging
♦ accommodate, billet, bunk, domicile, house, lodge, put up, quarter

board·er *n* ♦ : one that boards; *esp* : one that is provided with regular meals or regular meals and lodging
♦ lodger, renter, roomer, tenant — more at TENANT

board game *n* : a game (such as checkers, chess, or backgammon) played by placing or moving pieces on a board

board·ing·house \'bōr-diŋ-,haủs\ *n* : a house at which persons are boarded

board·walk \'bōrd-,wȯk\ *n* : a promenade (as of planking) along a beach

¹boast \'bōst\ *vb* **1** ♦ : to praise oneself **2** ♦ : to mention or assert with excessive pride **3** : to prize as a possession; *also* : HAVE ⟨the house ∼s a fireplace⟩ — **boast·ful** \-fəl\ *adj* — **boast·ful·ly** *adv*
♦ [1, 2] brag, crow, plume, swagger; *also* puff (up)

²boast *n* **1** : the act or an instance of boasting **2** ♦ : a cause for pride
♦ credit, glory, honor (*or* honour), jewel, pride, treasure — more at GLORY

boast·er \'bō-stər\ *n* ♦ : one who boasts
♦ brag, braggadocio, braggart, bragger — more at BRAGGART

¹boat \'bōt\ *n* ♦ : a small vessel for travel on water; *also* : SHIP
♦ bottom, craft, ship, vessel; *also* canoe, catamaran, catboat, cockleshell, coracle, dinghy, dory, dugout, flatboat, float, gondola, houseboat, ironclad, kayak, launch, longboat, motorboat, outrigger, pontoon, punt, raft, rowboat, sail, sampan, scow, scull, shallop, shell, sloop, tender, umiak

²boat *vb* : to go by boat

boat·er \'bō-tər\ *n* **1** : one that travels in a boat **2** : a stiff straw hat

boat·load \'bōt-,lōd\ *n* ♦ : an indefinitely large number
♦ abundance, deal, gobs, heap, loads, lot, pile, plenty, quantity, scads — more at LOT

boat·man \'bōt-mən\ *n* : a man who operates, works on, or deals in boats

boat people *n pl* : refugees fleeing by boat

boat·swain \'bōs-ᵊn\ *n* : a subordinate officer of a ship in charge of the hull and related equipment

¹bob \'bäb\ *vb* **bobbed; bob·bing 1** ♦ : to move up and down jerkily or repeatedly **2** : to emerge, arise, or appear suddenly or unexpectedly
♦ bobble, jog, jounce, nod, pump, seesaw — more at NOD

²bob *n* : a bobbing movement

³bob *n* **1** : a knob, knot, twist, or curl esp. of ribbons, yarn, or hair **2** : a short haircut of a woman or child **3** : FLOAT 2 **4** : a weight hanging from a line

⁴bob *vb* **bobbed; bob·bing** : to cut hair in a bob

⁵bob *n, pl* **bob** *slang Brit* : SHILLING

bob·bin \'bä-bən\ *n* : a cylinder or spindle for holding or dispensing thread (as in a sewing machine)

bob·ble \'bä-bəl\ *vb* **bob·bled; bob·bling 1** ♦ : to move up and down in a short quick movement **2** ♦ : to make awkward attempts to do or find something; *also* : FUMBLE ⟨the catcher *bobbled* the ball⟩ — **bobble** *n*
♦ [1] bob, jog, jounce, nod, pump, seesaw — more at NOD ♦ [2] botch, bungle, butcher, flub, foul up, fumble, mangle, mess up, screw up — more at BOTCH

bob·by \'bä-bē\ *n, pl* **bobbies** [*Bobby*, nickname for Sir *Robert* Peel, who organized the London police force] *Brit* : a police officer

bobby pin *n* : a flat wire hairpin with prongs that press close together

bob·cat \'bäb-,kat\ *n* : a small usu. rusty-colored No. American lynx

bob·o·link \'bä-bə-,liŋk\ *n* : an American migratory songbird related to the meadowlarks

bob·sled \'bäb-,sled\ *n* **1** : a short sled usu. used as one of a joined pair **2** : a racing sled with two pairs of runners, a steering wheel, and a hand brake — **bobsled** *vb*

bob·white \(,)bäb-'hwīt\ *n* : any of a genus of quail; *esp* : a popular game bird of eastern and central No. America

boc·cie *or* **boc·ci** *or* **boc·ce** \'bä-chē\ *n* : Italian lawn bowling played on a long narrow court

bock \'bäk\ *n* : a strong dark beer usu. sold in early spring

bod \'bäd\ *n* : BODY

¹bode \'bōd\ *vb* **bod·ed; bod·ing** ♦ : to indicate by signs : PRESAGE
♦ augur, promise; *also* forecast, foretell, predict, presage, prognosticate, prophesy

²bode *past of* BIDE

bo·de·ga \bō-'dā-gə\ *n* [Sp, fr. L *apotheca* storehouse] : a store specializing in Hispanic groceries

bod·ice \'bä-dəs\ *n* [alter. of *bodies*, pl. of *body*] : the usu. close-fitting part of a dress above the waist

bodi·less \'bä-di-ləs\ *adj* ♦ : lacking a body or material form
♦ immaterial, incorporeal, insubstantial, nonmaterial, nonphysical, spiritual, unsubstantial — more at IMMATERIAL

¹bodi·ly \'bäd-ᵊl-ē\ *adj* ♦ : of or relating to the body ⟨∼ contact⟩
♦ animal, carnal, corporal, fleshly, material, physical, somatic — more at PHYSICAL

²bodily *adv* **1** : in the flesh **2** : as a whole ⟨lifted the crate up ∼⟩

bod·kin \'bäd-kən\ *n* **1** : DAGGER **2** : a pointed implement for punching holes in cloth **3** : a blunt needle for drawing tape or ribbon through a loop or hem

body \'bä-dē\ *n, pl* **bod·ies 1** : the physical whole of a living or dead organism; *also* : the trunk or main mass of an organism as distinguished from its appendages **2** ♦ : a human being : PERSON **3** ♦ : the main part of something **4** : a mass of matter distinct from other masses **5** ♦ : a group of persons or things **6** : VISCOSITY, FIRMNESS **7** : richness of flavor — used esp. of wines — **bod·ied** \'bä-dēd\ *adj*
♦ [2] being, creature, human, individual, man, mortal, person — more at HUMAN ♦ [3] bulk, core, generality, main, mass, staple, weight; *also* majority ♦ [5] array, batch, bunch, cluster, crop, group, huddle, knot, lot, parcel, party

body·build·ing \'bä-dē-,bil-diŋ\ *n* : a developing of the body through exercise and diet — **body·build·er** \-dər\ *n*

body English *n* : bodily motions made in a usu. unconscious effort to influence the movement of a propelled object (as a ball)

body·guard \'bä-dē-ˌgärd\ *n* : a personal guard; *also* : RET-INUE

body language *n* : body movements or postures inter-preted as a means of communication

body stocking *n* : a sheer close-fitting one-piece garment for the torso that often has sleeves and legs

body·work \'bä-dē-ˌwərk\ *n* : the making or repairing of vehicle bodies

Boer \'bȯr, 'bu̇r\ *n* [D, lit., farmer] : a South African of Dutch or Huguenot descent

¹bog \'bäg, 'bȯg\ *n* ♦ : wet, spongy, poorly drained, and usu. acid ground — **bog·gy** *adj*

♦ fen, marsh, mire, morass, slough, swamp — more at SWAMP

²bog *vb* **bogged; bog·ging** : to sink into or as if into a bog

bo·gey *also* **bo·gie** *or* **bo·gy** \'bu̇-gē, 'bō- *for 1;* 'bō- *for 2*\ *n, pl* **bogeys** *also* **bogies** **1 a** ♦ : a visible disembodied spirit : SPECTER **b** ♦ : a source of fear or annoyance **2** : a score of one over par on a hole in golf

♦ [1a] apparition, ghost, phantasm, phantom, pol-tergeist, shade, shadow, specter, spirit, spook, vision, wraith — more at GHOST ♦ [1b] bête noire, bugbear, hobgoblin, ogre; *also* apparition, ghost, phantasm, phan-tom, poltergeist, shade, specter, spirit, spook, wraith

bo·gey·man \'bu̇-gē-ˌman, 'bō-, 'bu̇-\ *n* : an imaginary monster used in threatening children

bog·gle \'bä-gəl\ *vb* **bog·gled; bog·gling** : to overwhelm or be overwhelmed with fright or amazement

bo·gus \'bō-gəs\ *adj* ♦ : not genuine : SHAM

♦ counterfeit, fake, false, inauthentic, phony, sham, spurious, unauthentic — more at COUNTERFEIT ♦ arti-ficial, fake, faux, imitation, mock, sham, synthetic — more at IMITATION

Bo·he·mi·an \bō-'hē-mē-ən\ *n* **1** : a native or inhabitant of Bohemia **2** *often not cap* : VAGABOND, WANDERER **3** *of-ten not cap* ♦ : a person (as a writer or artist) living an unconventional life — **bohemian** *adj, often cap*

♦ deviant, individualist, loner, maverick, nonconform-ist — more at NONCONFORMIST

bohr·i·um \'bȯr-ē-əm\ *n* : an artifically produced radioac-tive chemical element

¹boil \'bȯil\ *n* : an inflamed swollen bump on the skin re-sulting from an infected hair follicle

²boil *vb* **1 a** : to heat or become heated to a temperature (**boil·ing point**) at which vapor is formed and rises in bub-bles ⟨water ∼*s* and changes to steam⟩ **b** ♦ : to act on or be acted on by a boiling liquid ⟨∼ eggs⟩ **2** ♦ : to be in a state of seething agitation **3** ♦ : to churn violently as if boiling

♦ [1b] coddle, stew; *also* scald ♦ [2, 3] burn, churn, fume, rage, seethe, steam; *also* fulminate, rant, rave

³boil *n* : the act or state of boiling

boil·er \'bȯi-lər\ *n* **1** : a container in which something is boiled **2** : a strong vessel used in making steam **3** : a tank holding hot water

boil·er·mak·er \'bȯi-lər-ˌmā-kər\ *n* : whiskey with a beer chaser

boil·ing *adj* ♦ : intensely agitated ⟨∼ with anger⟩

♦ angry, furious, irate, mad, rabid, sore — more at AN-GRY

bois·ter·ous \'bȯi-st(ə-)rəs\ *adj* ♦ : noisily turbulent or ex-uberant — **bois·ter·ous·ly** *adv*

♦ rambunctious, raucous, rowdy; *also* rampageous, riotous, stormy, tempestuous, turbulent, violent *Ant* orderly

bok choy \'bäk-'chȯi\ *n* : a Chinese vegetable related to the mustards that forms a loose head of green leaves with long thick white stalks

bo·la \'bō-lə\ *or* **bo·las** \-ləs\ *n, pl* **bolas** \-ləz\ *also* **bo·las·es** [AmerSp *bolas*, fr. Sp *bola* ball] : a cord with weights at-tached to the ends

bold \'bōld\ *adj* **1** ♦ : fearless before danger **2** ♦ : over-stepping due bounds : IMPUDENT **3** : marked by great and continuous steepness : STEEP **4** : ADVENTUROUS, FREE ⟨a ∼ thinker⟩ **5** ♦ : standing out prominently **6** : being set in boldface — **bold·ly** *adv* — **bold·ness** \'bōld-nəs\ *n*

♦ [1] adventurous, audacious, daring, enterprising, gutsy, hardy, nervy, venturesome; *also* brash, daredevil, foolhardy, heedless, hotheaded, impetuous, imprudent, impulsive, incautious, madcap, overbold, overconfi-dent, rash, reckless, spirited, thoughtless, wild *Ant* un-adventurous, unenterprising ♦ [2] arch, brash, brazen, cheeky, cocky, fresh, impertinent, impudent, insolent, nervy, sassy, saucy — more at NERVY ♦ [2] familiar, forward, free, immodest, presumptuous — more at PRESUMPTUOUS ♦ [5] catchy, conspicuous, emphatic, marked, noticeable, prominent, pronounced, remark-able, striking — more at NOTICEABLE

bold·face \'bōld-ˌfās\ *n* : a heavy-faced type; *also* : printing in boldface — **bold–faced** \-'fāst\ *adj*

bole \'bōl\ *n* : the trunk of a tree

bo·le·ro \bə-'ler-ō\ *n, pl* **-ros** **1** : a Spanish dance or its music **2** : a short loose jacket open at the front

Bo·liv·i·an \bə-'li-vē-ən\ *n* : a native or inhabitant of Bo-livia — **Bolivian** *adj*

boll \'bōl\ *n* : a seed pod (as of cotton)

boll weevil *n* : a small grayish weevil that infests the cotton plant both as a larva and as an adult

boll·worm \'bōl-ˌwərm\ *n* : any of several moths and esp. the corn earworm whose larvae feed on cotton bolls

bo·lo·gna \bə-'lō-nē\ *n* [short for *Bologna sausage*, fr. *Bo-logna*, Italy] : a large smoked sausage of beef, veal, and pork

Bol·she·vik \'bōl-shə-ˌvik\ *n, pl* **Bolsheviks** *also* **Bol·she·vi·ki** \ˌbōl-shə-'vi-kē\ [Russ *bol'shevik*, fr. *bol'shiĭ* larger] **1** : a member of the party that seized power in Russia in the revolution of November 1917 **2** : COMMUNIST — **Bol-shevik** *adj*

bol·she·vism \'bōl-shə-ˌvi-zəm\ *n, often cap* : the doctrine or program of the Bolsheviks advocating violent over-throw of capitalism

¹bol·ster \'bōl-stər\ *n* : a long pillow or cushion

²bolster *vb* ♦ : to support with or as if with a bolster; *also* : REINFORCE

♦ bear, brace, buttress, carry, prop, shore, stay, sup-port, uphold — more at SUPPORT

¹bolt \'bōlt\ *n* **1** : a missile (as an arrow) for a crossbow or catapult **2** : a flash of lightning : THUNDERBOLT **3** : a sliding bar used to fasten a door **4** : a roll of cloth or wallpaper of specified length **5** : a rod with a head at one end and a screw thread at the other used with a nut to fasten objects together **6** : a metal cylinder that drives the cartridge into the chamber of a firearm

²bolt *vb* **1 a** ♦ : to move suddenly (as in fright or hurry) : START **b** ♦ : to rush off or away (as in fleeing) ⟨he ∼*ed* out of the room⟩ **2** : to break away (as from association) ⟨∼ from a political platform⟩ **3** : to produce seed pre-maturely **4** : to secure or fasten with a bolt **5** : to swal-low hastily or without chewing **6** ♦ : to say impulsively

♦ [1a] jump, start, startle — more at START ♦ [1b] break, flee, fly, retreat, run, run away, run off — more at RUN ♦ [6] blurt, cry, ejaculate, spout

³bolt *n* : an act of bolting

bo·lus \'bō-ləs\ *n* **1** : a large pill **2** : a soft mass of chewed food

¹bomb \'bäm\ *n* **1** : a fused explosive device designed to detonate under specified conditions (as impact) **2** : an aerosol or foam dispenser (as of insecticide) : SPRAY CAN **3** : a long pass in football **4** ♦ : one that has failed : FAIL-URE, FLOP

♦ bummer, bust, catastrophe, debacle, dud, failure, fi-asco, fizzle, flop, lemon, loser, miss, turkey, washout — more at FAILURE

²bomb *vb* **1** : to attack with bombs **2** : to fail utterly

bom·bard \bäm-'bärd\ vb 1 ♦ : to attack esp. with artillery or bombers 2 : to assail persistently 3 : to subject to the impact of rapidly moving particles (as electrons)

♦ blitz, shell; also rake, strafe

bom·bar·dier \,bäm-bər-'dir\ n : a bomber-crew member who releases the bombs

bom·bard·ment n ♦ : the act or an instance of bombarding or the state of being bombarded

♦ barrage, cannonade, fusillade, hail, salvo, shower, storm, volley — more at BARRAGE

bom·bast \'bäm-,bast\ n [ME, cotton padding, fr. MF bombace, fr. ML bombax cotton, alter. of L bombyx silkworm, silk, fr. Gk] ♦ : pretentious wordy speech or writing — **bom·bas·ti·cal·ly** \-ti-k(ə-)lē\ adv

♦ bluster, brag, gas, grandiloquence, rant, rhetoric

bom·bas·tic \bäm-'bas-tik\ adj ♦ : marked by or given to bombast

♦ gaseous, grandiloquent, oratorical, rhetorical, windy — more at RHETORICAL

bom·ba·zine \,bäm-bə-'zēn\ n 1 : a twilled fabric with silk warp and worsted filling 2 : a silk fabric in twill weave dyed black

bomb·er \'bä-mər\ n : one that bombs; esp : an airplane for dropping bombs

bomb·proof \'bäm-,prüf\ adj : safe against the explosive force of bombs

bomb·shell \'bäm-,shel\ n 1 : BOMB 1 2 ♦ : one that stuns, amazes, or completely upsets

♦ bolt, jar, jolt, surprise — more at SURPRISE

bona fide \'bō-nə-,fīd, 'bä-; ,bō-nə-'fī-dē, -də\ adj [L, in good faith] 1 : made in good faith ⟨a bona fide agreement⟩ 2 ♦ : neither specious nor counterfeit : GENUINE, REAL ⟨a bona fide bargain⟩

♦ authentic, genuine, real, right, true — more at AUTHENTIC

bo·nan·za \bə-'nan-zə\ n [Sp, lit., calm sea, fr. ML bonacia, alter. of L malacia, fr. Gk malakia, lit., softness, fr. malakos soft] : something yielding a rich return

bon·bon \'bän-,bän\ n : a candy with a creamy center and a soft covering (as of chocolate)

¹bond \'bänd\ n 1 ♦ : something that binds or restrains : FETTER 2 ♦ : a binding or uniting force or tie ⟨~s of friendship⟩ 3 ♦ : an agreement or obligation often made binding by a pledge of money or goods 4 : a person who acts as surety for another 5 : an interest-bearing certificate of public or private indebtedness 6 : the state of goods subject to supervision pending payment of taxes or duties due

♦ [1] band, chain, fetter, irons, ligature, manacle, shackle; also confinement, constraint, curb, hamper, hindrance, restraint, restriction ♦ [2] cement, knot, ligature, link, tie; also attachment, connection, entanglement, fastening, joint, linkage ♦ [3] contract, covenant, guarantee, guaranty, surety, warranty — more at GUARANTEE

²bond vb 1 : to assure payment of duties or taxes on (goods) by giving a bond 2 : to insure against losses caused by the acts of ⟨~ a bank teller⟩ 3 : to make or become firmly united as if by bonds ⟨~ iron to copper⟩ 4 : to form a close relationship ⟨gave them a chance to ~ with their father⟩

bond·age \'bän-dij\ n ♦ : a state of being bound usu. by compulsion : SLAVERY, SERVITUDE

♦ enslavement, servitude, slavery, thrall, yoke — more at SLAVERY

bond·hold·er \'bänd-,hōl-dər\ n : one that owns a government or corporation bond

bond·ing n 1 : the formation of a close personal relationship esp. through frequent or constant association 2 : the attaching of a material (as porcelain) to a tooth surface esp. for cosmetic purposes

bond·man \'bänd-mən\ n ♦ : a person held in servitude as the chattel of another : SLAVE

♦ chattel, slave, thrall — more at SLAVE

¹bonds·man \'bändz-mən\ n : SURETY 3

²bondsman n ♦ : one who is bound to another as a servant or slave

♦ bondman, chattel, slave, thrall — more at SLAVE

bond·wom·an \'bänd-,wù-mən\ n : a female slave

¹bone \'bōn\ n 1 : a hard largely calcareous tissue forming most of the skeleton of a vertebrate animal; also : one of the pieces of bone making up a vertebrate skeleton 2 : a hard animal substance (as ivory or baleen) similar to true bone 3 : something made of bone — **bone·less** adj — **bony** also **bon·ey** \'bō-nē\ adj

²bone vb boned; bon·ing : to free from bones ⟨~ a chicken⟩

bone black n : the black carbon residue from calcined bones used esp. as a pigment

bone meal n : crushed or ground bone used esp. as fertilizer or feed

bon·er \'bō-nər\ n : a stupid and ridiculous blunder

bone up vb 1 : to try to master necessary information quickly 2 : to refresh one's memory ⟨boned up on the speech before giving it⟩

bon·fire \'bän-,fīr\ n [ME bonefire a fire of bones, fr. bon bone + fire] : a large fire built in the open air

bon·go \'bän-gō\ n, pl bongos also bongoes [AmerSp bongó] : one of a pair of small tuned drums played with the hands

bon·ho·mie \,bä-nə-'mē\ n [F bonhomie, fr. bonhomme good-natured man, fr. bon good + homme man] : good-natured easy friendliness

bo·ni·to \bə-'nē-tō\ n, pl -tos or -to : any of several medium-sized tunas

bon mot \bōⁿ-'mō\ n, pl bons mots \same\ or bon mots \same or -'mōz\ [F, lit., good word] : a clever remark

bon·net \'bä-nət\ n : a covering (as a cap) for the head; esp : a hat for a woman or infant tied under the chin

bon·ny \'bä-nē\ adj bon·ni·er; -est chiefly Brit ♦ : very pleasing to look at : ATTRACTIVE; also : FINE, EXCELLENT

♦ attractive, beautiful, cute, fair, gorgeous, handsome, knockout, lovely, pretty, ravishing, stunning — more at BEAUTIFUL

bon·sai \bōn-'sī\ n, pl bonsai [Jp] : a potted plant (as a tree) dwarfed by special methods of culture; also : the art of growing such a plant

bo·nus \'bō-nəs\ n ♦ : something in addition to what is expected

♦ dividend, extra, lagniappe, perquisite, tip; also fillip

bon vi·vant \,bän-vē-'vänt, ,bōⁿ-vē-'väⁿ\ n, pl bons vivants \,bän-vē-'vänts, ,bōⁿ-vē-'väⁿ\ or bon vivants \same\ [F, lit., good liver] : a person having cultivated, refined, and sociable tastes esp. in food and drink

bon voy·age \,bōⁿ-,vòi-'äzh, ,bän-; ,bōⁿ-,vwä-'yäzh\ n ♦ : a wish of well-being at parting : FAREWELL — often used as an interjection

♦ adieu, au revoir, farewell, good-bye — more at GOOD-BYE

bony fish n : any of a very large group of fishes (as a salmon or marlin) with a bony rather than a cartilaginous skeleton

bonze \'bänz\ n : a Buddhist monk

boo \'bü\ n, pl boos ♦ : a shout of disapproval or contempt — **boo** vb

♦ catcall, hiss, hoot, jeer, raspberry, snort — more at CATCALL

boo·by \'bü-bē\ n, pl boobies ♦ : an awkward foolish person : DOPE

♦ dope, fool, goose, jackass, nitwit, nut, simpleton, turkey — more at FOOL

booby hatch n : an insane asylum

booby prize n : an award for the poorest performance in a contest

booby trap n ♦ : a trap for the unwary; esp : a concealed explosive device set to go off when some harmless-looking object is touched — **booby–trap** vb

♦ catch, pitfall, snag — more at PITFALL ♦ explosive

boo·dle \'büd-ᵊl\ *n* **1** : bribe money **2** : a large amount of money

¹book \'bu̇k\ *n* **1** : a set of sheets bound into a volume **2** : a long written or printed narrative or record **3** : a major division of a long literary work **4** *cap* : BIBLE — **in one's book** : in one's opinion

²book *vb* **1** : to engage, reserve, or schedule by or as if by writing in a book ⟨~ seats on a plane⟩ **2** : to enter charges against in a police register

book·case \-,kās\ *n* : a piece of furniture consisting of shelves to hold books

book·end \-,end\ *n* : a support to hold up a row of books

book·ie \'bu̇-kē\ *n* : BOOKMAKER

book·ish \'bu̇-kish\ *adj* **1** : fond of books and reading **2 a** : inclined to rely unduly on book knowledge **b** *of words* ♦ : literary and formal as opposed to colloquial and informal

♦ erudite, learned, literary; *also* academic, pedantic, scholastic *Ant* colloquial, nonliterary

book·keep·er \'bu̇k-,kē-pər\ *n* : one who records the accounts or transactions of a business — **book·keep·ing** *n*

book·let \'bu̇k-lət\ *n* ♦ : a little book; *esp* : PAMPHLET

♦ brochure, circular, folder, leaflet, pamphlet — more at PAMPHLET

book·mak·er \'bu̇k-,mā-kər\ *n* : one who determines odds and receives and pays off bets — **book·mak·ing** *n*

book·mark \-,märk\ *or* **book·mark·er** \-,mär-kər\ *n* **1** : a marker for finding a place in a book **2** : a shortcut to a previously viewed location (as on a website) on a computer

book·mo·bile \'bu̇k-mō-,bēl\ *n* : a truck that serves as a traveling library

book off *vi, chiefly Can* : to notify an employer that one is not reporting for work (as because of sickness)

book·plate \'bu̇k-,plāt\ *n* : a label pasted in a book to show who owns it

book·sell·er \'bu̇k-,se-lər\ *n* : one who sells books; *esp* : the proprietor of a bookstore

book·shelf \-,shelf\ *n* : a shelf for books

book·worm \'bu̇k-,wərm\ *n* : a person unusually devoted to reading and study

¹boom \'büm\ *vb* **1** : to make a deep hollow sound **2** : to grow or cause to grow rapidly esp. in value, esteem, or importance

²boom *n* **1** ♦ : a booming sound or cry **2** : a rapid expansion or increase esp. of economic activity

♦ bang, blast, clap, crack, crash, pop, report, slam, smash, snap, thwack, whack — more at CLAP

³boom *n* [D, tree, beam] **1** : a long spar used to extend the bottom of a sail **2** : a line of floating timbers used to obstruct passage or catch floating objects **3** : a beam projecting from the upright pole of a derrick to support or guide the object lifted **4** : a long supporting pole or arm (as for a microphone)

boom box *n* : a large portable radio and often CD or tape player

boo·mer·ang \'bü-mə-,raŋ\ *n* [Dharuk (an Australian aboriginal language) *bumarinʸ*] : a bent or angular club that can be so thrown as to return near the starting point

boom·ing *adj* **1** ♦ : making a loud deep sound ⟨his ~ voice⟩ **2** : forcefully or powerfully executed ⟨hit a ~ serve⟩

♦ clamorous (*or* clamourous), loud, resounding, roaring, sonorous, stentorian, thunderous — more at LOUD

¹boon \'bün\ *n* [ME *bone* prayer, request, the favor requested, fr. ON *bōn* request] **1** ♦ : something that promotes well-being; *also* : useful aid **2** ♦ : something given or granted as a favor

♦ [1] advantage, aid, benefit, help — more at HELP ♦ [1] benefit, blessing, felicity, godsend, good, manna, windfall — more at BLESSING ♦ [2] courtesy, favor (*or* favour), grace, indulgence, kindness, mercy, service, turn

²boon *adj* [ME *bon*, fr. AF, good] ♦ : enjoying companionship and the pleasures of feasting and drinking ⟨a ~ companion⟩

♦ companionable, convivial, extroverted, gregarious, outgoing, sociable, social — more at CONVIVIAL

boon·docks \'bün-,däks\ *n pl* [Tagalog (language of the Philippines) *bundok* mountain] **1** : rough country filled with dense brush **2** : a rural area

boon·dog·gle \'bün-,dä-gəl, -,dȯ-\ *n* : a useless or wasteful project or activity

boor \'bu̇r\ *n* **1** : YOKEL **2** ♦ : a rude or insensitive person

♦ beast, churl, clown, creep, cretin, cur, heel, jerk, joker, louse, lout, skunk, slob, snake — more at JERK

boor·ish *adj* ♦ : having the qualities or behavior of a boor

♦ churlish, clownish, loutish, uncouth — more at CLOWNISH

¹boost \'büst\ *vb* **1** ♦ : to push up from below **2** ♦ : to make or become greater : INCREASE, RAISE ⟨~ prices⟩ **3** : to enthusiastically promote or support (a cause) ⟨voted a bonus to ~ morale⟩

♦ [1] crane, elevate, heave, heft, heighten, hike, hoist, jack, lift, pick up, raise, up, uphold — more at RAISE ♦ [2] add, aggrandize, amplify, augment, compound, enlarge, escalate, expand, extend, increase, multiply, raise, swell, up — more at INCREASE ♦ [2] amplify, beef, consolidate, deepen, enhance, heighten, intensify, magnify, redouble, step up, strengthen — more at INTENSIFY

²boost *n* **1** : a push upward **2** ♦ : an act that brings help or encouragement **3** ♦ : an increase in amount

♦ [2] aid, assist, assistance, backing, help, lift, support — more at HELP ♦ [3] accretion, addition, augmentation, expansion, gain, increase, increment, plus, proliferation, raise, rise, supplement — more at INCREASE

boost·er *n* ♦ : one that boosts; *esp* : an enthusiastic supporter

♦ advocate, apostle, backer, champion, exponent, friend, promoter, proponent, supporter — more at EXPONENT

¹boot \'bu̇t\ *n, chiefly dial* : something to equalize a trade — **to boot** : BESIDES

²boot *vb, archaic* : AVAIL, PROFIT

³boot *n* **1** : a covering for the foot and leg **2** : a protective sheath (as of a flower) **3** *Brit* : an automobile trunk **4** : KICK; *also* : a discharge from employment **5** : a navy or marine corps trainee

⁴boot *vb* **1** : KICK **2** ♦ : to eject or discharge summarily — often used with *out* **3** *of a computer* : to start or make ready for operation

♦ *usu* **boot out** banish, bounce, cast, chase, dismiss, drum, eject, expel, oust, rout, run off, throw out — more at EJECT

boot·black \'bu̇t-,blak\ *n* : a person who shines shoes

boot camp *n* **1** : a navy or marine corps training camp **2** : a facility with a rigorous disciplinary program for young offenders

boo·tee *or* **boo·tie** \'bü-tē\ *n* : an infant's knitted or crocheted sock

booth \'büth\ *n, pl* **booths** \'büthz, 'büths\ **1** : a small enclosed stall (as at a fair) **2** : a small enclosure giving privacy for a person ⟨voting ~⟩ ⟨telephone ~⟩ **3** : a restaurant accommodation having a table between backed benches

boot·leg \'bu̇t-,leg\ *vb* : to make, transport, or sell (as liquor) illegally — **boot·leg** *adj or n* — **boot·leg·ger** *n*

boot·less \'bu̇t-ləs\ *adj* ♦ : producing no gain, good, or result : USELESS — **boot·less·ly** *adv* — **boot·less·ness** *n*

♦ fruitless, futile, ineffective, unproductive, unsuccessful — more at FUTILE

¹boo·ty \'bü-tē\ *n, pl* **booties** ♦ : plunder taken (as in war) : SPOIL

♦ loot, plunder, spoil, swag — more at LOOT

²**booty** \'bü-tē\ *n, pl* **booties** *slang* : BUTTOCK 2
¹**booze** \'büz\ *vb* **boozed; booz·ing** : to drink liquor to excess — **booz·er** *n*
²**booze** *n* ♦ : intoxicating liquor — **boozy** *adj*
　♦ alcohol, drink, intoxicant, liquor, moonshine, spirits — more at ALCOHOL
¹**bop** \'bäp\ *vb* **bopped; bop·ping** : to reach with a blow : HIT, SOCK
²**bop** *n* : a blow esp. with the fist or a club
BOQ *abbr* bachelor officers' quarters
bor *abbr* borough
bo·rate \'bōr-ˌāt\ *n* : a salt or ester of boric acid
bo·rax \'bōr-ˌaks\ *n* : a crystalline borate of sodium that occurs as a mineral and is used as a flux and cleanser
bor·del·lo \bȯr-'de-lō\ *n, pl* **-los** [It] : BROTHEL
¹**bor·der** \'bȯr-dər\ *n* 1 ♦ : an outer part or edge   2 ♦ : something that marks or fixes a limit : BOUNDARY
　♦ [1] borderland, frontier, march; *also* backwater, backwoods, hinterland, up-country ♦ [2] bound, boundary, circumference, compass, confines, edge, end, fringe, margin, perimeter, periphery, rim, skirt, verge; *also* crest, hem, lip
²**border** *vb* **bor·dered; bor·der·ing** 1 ♦ : to put a border on   2 ♦ : to touch at the edge or boundary : ADJOIN   3 : to approach the nature of a specified thing : VERGE ⟨∼s on the ridiculous⟩
　♦ *usu* **border on** [1] bound, fringe, margin, rim, skirt; *also* edge, hem, trim ♦ *usu* **border on** [2] abut, adjoin, flank, fringe, join, skirt, touch, verge (on) — more at ADJOIN
border collie *n, often cap B* : any of a British breed of medium-sized long-haired sheepdogs
bor·der·land \'bȯr-dər-ˌland\ *n* 1 ♦ : territory at or near a border   2 : an outlying or intermediate region often not clearly defined
　♦ border, frontier, march — more at FRONTIER
bor·der·line \-ˌlīn\ *adj* : being in an intermediate position or state; *esp* : not quite up to what is standard or expected ⟨∼ intelligence⟩
¹**bore** \'bōr\ *vb* **bored; bor·ing** 1 ♦ : to make a hole in with or as if with a drill   2 : to make (as a well) by boring or digging away material — **bor·er** *n*
　♦ drill, hole, perforate, pierce, punch, puncture — more at PERFORATE
²**bore** *n* 1 : a hole made by or as if by boring   2 : a cylindrical cavity   3 : the diameter of a hole or tube; *esp* : the interior diameter of a gun barrel or engine cylinder
³**bore** *past of* BEAR
⁴**bore** *n* : a tidal flood with a high abrupt front
⁵**bore** *n* : one that causes boredom
⁶**bore** *vb* **bored; bor·ing** ♦ : to weary with tedious dullness
　♦ jade, tire, weary; *also* pall **Ant** absorb, engage, engross, grip, interest, intrigue
bo·re·al \'bōr-ē-əl\ *adj* : of, relating to, or located in northern regions
bore·dom \'bōr-dəm\ *n* ♦ : the condition of being weary and restless because of dullness
　♦ doldrums, ennui, listlessness, restlessness, tedium, tiredness, weariness; *also* cheerlessness, melancholy
bo·ric acid \'bōr-ik-\ *n* : a white crystalline weak acid that contains boron and is used esp. as an antiseptic
born \'bȯrn\ *adj* 1 : brought into life by birth   2 ♦ : belonging by birth : NATIVE ⟨American-*born*⟩   3 : having special natural abilities or character from birth ⟨a ∼ leader⟩
　♦ aboriginal, endemic, indigenous, native — more at NATIVE
born–again *adj* : having experienced a revival of a personal faith or conviction ⟨∼ believer⟩ ⟨∼ liberal⟩
borne *past part of* BEAR
bo·ron \'bōr-ˌän\ *n* : a chemical element that occurs in nature only in combination (as in borax)

bor·ough \'bər-ō\ *n* [ME *burgh*, fr. OE *burg* fortified town] 1 : a British town that sends one or more members to Parliament; *also* : an incorporated British urban area   2 : an incorporated town or village in some U.S. states; *also* : any of the five political divisions of New York City   3 : a civil division of the state of Alaska corresponding to a county in most other states
bor·row \'bär-ō\ *vb* 1 : to take or receive (something) temporarily and with intent to return   2 ♦ : to take into possession or use from another source ⟨∼ a metaphor⟩
　♦ adopt, embrace, take up — more at ADOPT
borscht \'bȯrsht\ *or* **borsch** \'bȯrsh\ *n* [Yiddish *borsht* & Ukrainian & Russ *borshch*] : a soup made mainly from beets
bosh \'bäsh\ *n* [Turk *boş* empty] : foolish talk or action : NONSENSE
bosky \'bäs-kē\ *adj* : covered with trees or shrubs
¹**bos·om** \'bu̇-zəm, 'bü-\ *n* 1 : the front of the human chest; *esp* : the female breasts   2 : the seat of secret thoughts and feelings   3 : the part of a garment covering the breast — **bos·omed** \-zəmd\ *adj*
²**bosom** *adj* ♦ : closely acquainted : INTIMATE
　♦ chummy, close, familiar, friendly, intimate, thick — more at FAMILIAR
¹**boss** \'bäs, 'bȯs\ *n* : a knoblike ornament : STUD
²**boss** *vb* : to ornament with bosses
³**boss** \'bȯs\ *n* 1 ♦ : one (as a foreman or manager) exercising control or supervision   2 : a politician who controls votes or dictates policies
　♦ captain, chief, foreman, head, headman, helmsman, kingpin, leader, master, taskmaster; *also* administrator, commander, director, executive, general, manager, overseer, principal, standard-bearer, straw boss, superintendent, superior, supervisor
⁴**boss** \'bȯs\ *vb* 1 ♦ : to act as a boss : SUPERVISE   2 ♦ : to give usu. arbitrary orders to — usu. used with *around*
　♦ [1] captain, head, oversee, superintend, supervise; *also* command, control, direct, guide, manage, order, run, shepherd, show, steer ♦ *usu* **boss around** [2] bid, charge, command, direct, enjoin, instruct, order, tell — more at COMMAND
⁴**boss** *adj, slang* ♦ : very good of its kind : EXCELLENT, FIRST-RATE
　♦ A1, bang-up, banner, excellent, fabulous, fine, grand, great, prime, sensational, splendid, superb, superior, unsurpassed, wonderful — more at EXCELLENT
bossy *adj* ♦ : inclined to issue orders
　♦ authoritarian, autocratic, despotic, dictatorial, domineering, imperious, masterful, overbearing, peremptory, tyrannical, tyrannous; *also* arrogant, disdainful, haughty, lofty, lordly, proud, supercilious, superior
bosun *var of* BOATSWAIN
¹**bot** \'bät\ *n* 1 : ROBOT   2 : a computer program that performs automatic, repetitive, and sometimes harmful tasks   3 : a computer program or character that mimics human actions
²**bot** *abbr* botanical; botanist; botany
bot·a·ny \'bät-ᵊn-ē, 'bät-nē\ *n, pl* **-nies** 1 : a branch of biology dealing with plants and plant life   2 : plant life (as of a given region); *also* : the biology of a plant or plant group — **bo·tan·i·cal** \bə-'ta-ni-kəl\ *adj* — **bot·a·nist** \'bät-ᵊn-ist, 'bät-nist\ *n* — **bot·a·nize** \-ᵊn-ˌīz\ *vb*
botch \'bäch\ *vb* ♦ : to foul up hopelessly : BUNGLE — **botch** *n*
　♦ bobble, bungle, butcher, flub, foul up, fumble, mangle, mess up, screw up; *also* blunder, goof (up), gum (up)
¹**both** \'bōth\ *pron* : both ones : the one as well as the other
²**both** *conj* — used as a function word to indicate and stress the inclusion of each of two or more things specified by coordinated words, phrases, or clauses ⟨∼ New York and London⟩
³**both** *adj* : being the two : including the one and the other

¹**both·er** \'bä-<u>th</u>ər\ *vb* **1 a ♦** : to annoy esp. by petty provocation **b ♦** : to intrude upon : PESTER **2 a ♦** : to become concerned : become mentally troubled **b ♦** : to cause to be anxious or concerned

♦ [1a] aggravate, annoy, bug, chafe, exasperate, gall, get, grate, irk, irritate, nettle, peeve, persecute, pique, put out, rasp, rile, vex — more at IRRITATE **♦** [1b] bug, disturb, intrude, pester; *also* inconvenience, trouble **♦** [2a] fear, fret, stew, sweat, trouble, worry — more at WORRY **♦** [2b] concern, discompose, disquiet, distress, disturb, perturb, unsettle, upset, worry — more at DISTURB

²**bother** *n* **1 a** : a state of petty discomfort, annoyance, or worry **b ♦** : something that causes petty annoyance or worry **2 ♦** : needless bustle or excitement

♦ [1b] aggravation, annoyance, exasperation, frustration, hassle, headache, inconvenience, irritant, nuisance, peeve, pest, problem, thorn, vexation — more at ANNOYANCE **♦** [2] bustle, commotion, disturbance, furor, fuss, pother, stew, stir

both·er·some \-səm\ *adj* **♦** : causing bother

♦ aggravating, annoying, frustrating, galling, irksome, irritating, pesty, vexatious — more at ANNOYING

¹**bot·tle** \'bät-ᵊl\ *n* **1** : a container (as of glass) with a narrow neck and usu. no handles **2** : the quantity held by a bottle **3** : intoxicating liquor

²**bottle** *vb* **bot·tled; bot·tling 1** : to confine as if in a bottle : RESTRAIN **2** : to put into a bottle

bot·tle·neck \'bät-ᵊl-ˌnek\ *n* **1** : a narrow passage or point of congestion **2 ♦** : something that obstructs or impedes

♦ backup, jam, snarl

¹**bot·tom** \'bä-təm\ *n* **1 a ♦** : an under or supporting surface **b ♦** : the seat of the body : BUTTOCKS **2** : the surface on which a body of water lies **3 ♦** : the lowest part or place; *also* : an inferior position ⟨start at the ∼⟩ **4** : BOTTOMLAND **5 a** : the part of a ship's hull lying below the water **b ♦** : a craft for traveling on water : BOAT — **bottom** *adj* — **bot·tom·less** *adj*

♦ [1a] underbelly, underside; *also* belly, sole *Ant* face, top **♦** [1b] backside, butt, buttocks, posterior, rear, rump, seat — more at BUTTOCKS **♦** [3] base, foot; *also* basis, bed, bedrock, foundation, ground, groundwork, keystone, seat, underpinning *Ant* head, top **♦** [5b] boat, craft, ship, vessel — more at BOAT

²**bottom** *vb* **1** : to furnish with a bottom **2** : to reach the bottom **3** : to reach a low point before rebounding — usu. used with *out*

bot·tom·land \'bä-təm-ˌland\ *n* : low land along a river

bottom line *n* **1** : the essential point : CRUX **2** : the final result : OUTCOME

bot·u·lism \'bä-chə-ˌli-zəm\ *n* : an acute paralytic disease caused by a bacterial toxin (**bot·u·li·num toxin** \ˌbä-chə-ˌlī-nəm-\) esp. in tainted food

bou·doir \'bü-ˌdwär, 'bu-, ˌbü-ˈ, ˌbu-ˈ\ *n* [F, fr. *bouder* to pout] : a woman's dressing room or bedroom

bouf·fant \bü-ˈfänt, 'bü-ˌfänt\ *adj* [F] : puffed out ⟨∼ hairdos⟩

bough \'baù\ *n* : a usu. large or main branch of a tree

bought *past and past part of* BUY

bouil·la·baisse \ˌbü-yə-ˈbäs\ *n* [F] : a highly seasoned fish stew made with at least two kinds of fish

bouil·lon \'bü-ˌyän; 'bùl-ˌyän, -yən\ *n* : a clear soup made usu. from beef

boul·der \'bōl-dər\ *n* : a large detached rounded or worn mass of rock — **boul·dered** \-dərd\ *adj*

bou·le·vard \'bù-lə-ˌvärd, 'bü-\ *n* [F, modif. of MD *bolwerc* bulwark] : a broad often landscaped thoroughfare

¹**bounce** \'baùns\ *vb* **bounced; bounc·ing 1** : to cause to rebound ⟨∼ a ball⟩ **2 ♦** : to rebound after striking **3 ♦** : to expel hastily from a place **4** : to issue (a check) on an account having insufficient funds **5 ♦** : to recover quickly from a blow or defeat — usu. used with *back*

♦ [2] carom, glance, rebound, ricochet, skim, skip — more at GLANCE **♦** [3] banish, boot (out), cast,

chase, dismiss, drum, eject, expel, oust, rout, run off, throw out — more at EJECT **♦** *usu* **bounce back** [5] rally, rebound, recover, snap back

²**bounce** *n* **♦** : the quality or state of being lively — **bouncy** \'baùn-sē\ *adj*

♦ dash, drive, esprit, pep, punch, snap, spirit, verve, vim, zing, zip — more at SPIRIT

bounc·er \'baùn-sər\ *n* : a person employed in a public place to remove disorderly persons

¹**bound** \'baùnd\ *adj* **♦** : intending to go ⟨homeward ∼⟩

♦ decisive, determined, firm, intent, purposeful, resolute, set, single-minded — more at DETERMINED

²**bound** *n* : something that limits or restrains : LIMIT, BOUNDARY

³**bound** *vb* **1 ♦** : to set limits to **2 ♦** : to form the boundary of **3** : to name the boundaries of

♦ [1] circumscribe, define, delimit, demarcate, limit, mark, terminate — more at LIMIT **♦** [2] border, fringe, margin, rim, skirt — more at BORDER

⁴**bound** *past and past part of* BIND

⁵**bound** *adj* **1** : constrained by or as if by bonds : CONFINED, OBLIGED **2** : enclosed in a binding or cover **3 ♦** : firmly decided : RESOLVED, DETERMINED; *also* : SURE

♦ decisive, determined, firm, intent, purposeful, resolute, set, single-minded — more at DETERMINED

⁶**bound** *n* **1 ♦** : the act or an instance of leaping into the air : JUMP **2** : REBOUND, BOUNCE

♦ hop, jump, leap, spring, vault — more at JUMP

⁷**bound** *vb* : to move by leaping : SPRING, BOUNCE

bound·ary \'baùn-drē\ *n, pl* **-aries ♦** : something that marks or fixes a limit (as of territory)

♦ bound, ceiling, confines, end, extent, limit, limitation, line, termination — more at LIMIT **♦** border, bound, circumference, compass, confines, edge, end, fringe, margin, perimeter, periphery, rim, skirt, verge — more at BORDER

bound·en \'baùn-dən\ *adj* : BINDING

bound·less *adj* **♦** : having no boundaries — **bound·less·ness** *n*

♦ endless, illimitable, immeasurable, indefinite, infinite, limitless, measureless, unbounded, unfathomable, unlimited — more at INFINITE

boun·te·ous \'baùn-tē-əs\ *adj* **1** : bestowing gifts or favors freely : GENEROUS **2** : more than enough : ABUNDANT — **boun·te·ous·ly** *adv* — **boun·te·ous·ness** *n*

boun·ti·ful \'baùn-ti-fəl\ *adj* **1 ♦** : giving freely **2 ♦** : given or provided abundantly : PLENTIFUL

♦ [1] charitable, free, generous, liberal, munificent, openhanded, unselfish, unsparing — more at GENEROUS **♦** [2] abundant, ample, comfortable, generous, liberal, plentiful — more at PLENTIFUL

boun·ti·ful·ly *adv* **♦** : in a bountiful degree

♦ generously, handsomely, liberally, well — more at WELL

boun·ti·ful·ness *n* : the quality or state of being bountiful

boun·ty \'baùn-tē\ *n, pl* **bounties** [ME *bounte* goodness, fr. AF *bunté*, fr. L *bonitas*, fr. *bonus* good] **1 ♦** : liberality in giving : GENEROSITY **2** : something given liberally **3** : a reward, premium, or subsidy given usu. for doing something

♦ generosity, liberality, philanthropy, unselfishness — more at LIBERALITY

bou·quet \bō-ˈkā, bü-\ *n* [F, fr. MF, thicket, bunch of flowers, fr. OF (dial. of Normandy and Picardy) *bosquet* thicket, fr. *bosc* forest] **1** : flowers picked and fastened together in a bunch **2 ♦** : a distinctive aroma (as of wine)

♦ aroma, fragrance, incense, perfume, redolence, scent, spice — more at FRAGRANCE

bour·bon \'bər-bən\ *n* : a whiskey distilled from a corn mash

bour·geois \'bùrzh-ˌwä, bùrzh-ˈwä\ *n, pl* **bourgeois** *same or* -ˌwäz, -ˈwäz\ [MF, fr. OF *burgeis* townsman, fr. *burc, borg* town, fr. L *burgus* fortified place, of Gmc origin] : a middle-class person — **bourgeois** *adj*

bour·geoi·sie \ˌbúrzh-ˌwä-'zē\ n : a social order dominated by bourgeois

bourne also **bourn** \'bōrn, 'búrn\ : BOUNDARY; also : DESTINATION

bourse \'búrs\ n : a European stock exchange

bout \'baút\ n 1 ♦ : an athletic match : CONTEST 2 a ♦ : a fit of sickness : ATTACK ⟨a ∼ of measles⟩ b : OUTBREAK 3 : SESSION

♦ [1] competition, contest, event, game, match, meet, tournament — more at GAME ♦ [2a] attack, case, fit, seizure, siege, spell — more at ATTACK

bou·tique \bü-'tēk\ n : a small fashionable specialty shop

bou·ton·niere \ˌbüt-ᵊn-'iər\ n : a flower or bouquet worn in a buttonhole

¹bo·vine \'bō-ˌvīn, -ˌvēn\ adj 1 : of or relating to bovines 2 : having qualities (as placidity or dullness) characteristic of oxen or cows

²bovine n : any of a group of mammals including oxen, buffalo, and their close relatives

bovine spon·gi·form encephalopathy \-'spən-ji-ˌfórm-\ : MAD COW DISEASE

¹bow \'baú\ vb 1 ♦ : to give oneself over to the will or authority of another : YIELD 2 : to bend the head or body (as in submission, courtesy, or assent)

♦ blink, budge, capitulate, concede, give in, knuckle under, quit, submit, succumb, surrender, yield — more at YIELD

²bow n : an act or posture of bowing

³bow \'bō\ n 1 a ♦ : something bent into a simple curve : BEND, ARCH b : RAINBOW 2 : a weapon for shooting arrows; also : ARCHER 3 : a knot formed by doubling a line into two or more loops 4 : a wooden rod strung with horsehairs for playing an instrument of the violin family

♦ angle, arc, arch, bend, crook, curve, turn, wind — more at BEND

⁴bow \'bō\ vb 1 : to bend into a curve 2 : to play (an instrument) with a bow

⁵bow \'baú\ n : the forward part of a ship — **bow** adj

bowd·ler·ise Brit var of BOWDLERIZE

bowd·ler·ize \'bōd-lə-ˌrīz, 'baúd-\ vb -ized; -iz·ing : to expurgate by omitting parts considered vulgar

bow·el \'baú(-ə)l\ n 1 : INTESTINE; also : one of the divisions of the intestine — usu. used in pl. 2 pl : the inmost parts ⟨the ∼s of the earth⟩

bowel movement n : an act of passing usu. solid waste through the rectum and anus; also : STOOL 4

bow·er \'baú(-ə)r\ n : a shelter of boughs or vines : ARBOR

¹bowl \'bōl\ n 1 : a concave vessel used to hold liquids 2 : a drinking vessel 3 ♦ : a bowl-shaped part or structure; esp : an athletic stadium — **bowl·ful** \-ˌfúl\ n

♦ circus, coliseum, stadium — more at STADIUM

²bowl n 1 : a ball for rolling on a level surface in bowling 2 : a cast of the ball in bowling

³bowl vb 1 : to play a game of bowling; also : to roll a ball in bowling 2 ♦ : to travel (as in a vehicle) rapidly and smoothly 3 ♦ : to strike or knock down with a moving object

♦ [2] breeze, coast, drift, flow, glide, roll, sail, skim, slide, slip, stream, sweep, whisk — more at FLOW ♦ usu **bowl down** [3] down, drop, fell, floor, knock, level

bow·legged \'bō-ˌle-gəd\ adj : having legs that bow outward at or below the knee — **bow·leg** \'bō-ˌleg\ n

¹bowl·er \'bō-lər\ n : a person who bowls

²bowl·er \'bō-lər\ n : DERBY 3

bow·line \'bō-lən, -ˌlīn\ n : a knot used to form a loop that neither slips nor jams

bowl·ing \'bō-liŋ\ n : any of various games in which balls are rolled on a green or alley at an object or a group of objects; esp : TENPINS

bowl over vb ♦ : to overwhelm with surprise; also : to make a vivid impression on

♦ amaze, astonish, astound, dumbfound, flabbergast, floor, shock, startle, stun, stupefy, surprise — more at SURPRISE

bow·man \'bō-mən\ n : ARCHER

bow·sprit \'baú-ˌsprit\ n : a spar projecting forward from the prow of a ship

bow·string \'bō-ˌstriŋ\ n : the cord connecting the two ends of a shooting bow

¹box \'bäks\ n, pl **box** or **box·es** : an evergreen shrub or small tree used esp. for hedges

²box n 1 ♦ : a rigid typically rectangular receptacle often with a cover; also : the quantity held by a box 2 : a small compartment (as for a group of theater patrons); also : a boxlike receptacle or division 3 : any of six spaces on a baseball diamond where the batter, pitcher, coaches, and catcher stand 4 : a difficult situation : PREDICAMENT

♦ caddy, case, casket, chest, locker, trunk — more at CHEST

³box vb : to enclose in or as if in a box

⁴box n ♦ : a punch or slap esp. on the ear

♦ belt, blow, buffet, hit, punch, slug — more at BLOW

⁵box vb 1 : to strike with the hand 2 : to engage in boxing with

box·car \'bäks-ˌkär\ n : a roofed freight car usu. with sliding doors in the sides

box cutter n : a small cutting tool with a retractable razor blade

¹box·er \'bäk-sər\ n 1 ♦ : a person who engages in boxing 2 pl : BOXER SHORTS

♦ fighter, prizefighter, pugilist; also featherweight, heavyweight, lightweight, middleweight, welterweight

²boxer n : any of a German breed of compact medium-sized dogs with a short usu. fawn or brindled coat

boxer shorts n pl : men's loose-fitting shorts worn as underwear

box·ing \'bäk-siŋ\ n : the sport of fighting with the fists

box office n : an office (as in a theater) where admission tickets are sold

box turtle n : any of several No. American land turtles able to withdraw completely into their shell

box·wood \'bäks-ˌwúd\ n : the tough hard wood of the box; also : a box tree or shrub

boy \'bói\ n 1 : a male child : YOUTH 2 : SON — **boy·hood** \-ˌhúd\ n — **boy·ish** adj — **boy·ish·ly** adv — **boy·ish·ness** n

♦ lad, nipper, shaver, stripling, youth; also adolescent, juvenile, kid, minor, moppet, teenager, youngster

boy·cott \'bói-ˌkät\ vb [Charles C. Boycott †1897 Eng. land agent in Ireland who was ostracized for refusing to reduce rents] : to refrain from having any dealings with — **boycott** n

boy·friend \'bói-ˌfrend\ n 1 : a male friend 2 ♦ : a frequent or regular male companion in a romantic or sexual relationship

♦ beau, fellow, man, swain; also admirer, crush, steady

Boy Scout n : a member of any of various national scouting programs (as the Boy Scouts of America)

boy·sen·ber·ry \'bóiz-ᵊn-ˌber-ē, 'bóis-\ n : a large bramble fruit with a raspberry flavor; also : the hybrid plant bearing it developed by crossing blackberries and raspberries

bo·zo \'bō-ˌzō\ n, pl **bozos** : a foolish or incompetent person

bp abbr 1 bishop 2 birthplace

BP abbr 1 batting practice 2 blood pressure 3 boiling point

bpl abbr birthplace

BPOE abbr Benevolent and Protective Order of Elks

br abbr 1 branch 2 brass 3 brown

¹Br abbr Britain; British

²Br symbol bromine

BR abbr bedroom

bra \'brä\ n : BRASSIERE

¹brace \'brās\ vb **braced**; **brac·ing** 1 archaic : to make fast : BIND 2 : to tighten preparatory to use; also : to get ready for : prepare oneself 3 ♦ : to restore strength and activity to : INVIGORATE 4 ♦ : to furnish or support with a brace; also : STRENGTHEN 5 : to set firmly 6 ♦ : to gain courage or confidence

♦ [3] animate, energize, enliven, fire, invigorate, jazz up, liven up, pep up, quicken, stimulate, vitalize, vivify, zip (up) — more at ANIMATE ♦ [4] bear, bolster, buttress, carry, prop, shore, stay, strengthen, support, uphold — more at SUPPORT ♦ [6] forearm, fortify, nerve, psych (up), ready, steel — more at FORTIFY

²**brace** n, pl **brac·es** 1 or pl **brace** ♦ : two of a kind ⟨a ~ of dogs⟩ 2 : a crank-shaped device for turning a bit 3 ♦ : something (as a tie, prop, or clamp) that distributes, directs, or resists pressure or weight 4 pl : SUSPENDERS 5 : an appliance for supporting a body part (as the shoulders) 6 pl : a dental appliance used to exert pressure to straighten misaligned teeth 7 : one of two marks { } used to connect words or items to be considered together

♦ [1] couple, duo, pair, twain, twosome — more at PAIR ♦ [3] bulwark, buttress, mount, shore, stay, support, underpinning — more at SUPPORT

brace·let \'brā-slət\ n [ME, fr. MF, dim. of bras arm, fr. L bracchium, fr. Gk brachiōn] 1 : an ornamental band or chain worn around the wrist 2 : something (as handcuffs) resembling a bracelet

bra·ce·ro \brä-'ser-ō\ n, pl **-ros** : a Mexican laborer admitted to the U.S. esp. for seasonal farm work

brac·ing adj ♦ : giving strength, vigor, or freshness

♦ invigorating, refreshing, restorative, stimulative, tonic — more at TONIC

brack·en \'bra-kən\ n : a large coarse fern; also : a growth of such ferns

¹**brack·et** \'bra-kət\ n 1 : a projecting framework or arm designed to support weight; also : a shelf on such framework 2 : one of a pair of punctuation marks [ ] used esp. to enclose interpolated matter 3 ♦ : a continuous section of a series; esp : one of a graded series of income groups

♦ category, class, division, family, grade, group, kind, order, set, species, type — more at CLASS

²**bracket** vb 1 : to furnish or fasten with brackets 2 a : to place within brackets b : to separate or group with or as if with brackets

brack·ish \'bra-kish\ adj : somewhat salty — **brack·ish·ness** n

bract \'brakt\ n : an often modified leaf on or at the base of a flower stalk

brad \'brad\ n : a slender nail with a small head

brae \'brā\ n, chiefly Scot : a hillside esp. along a river

¹**brag** \'brag\ vb **bragged; brag·ging** ♦ : to talk or assert boastfully — **brag·ger** n

♦ boast, crow, plume, swagger — more at BOAST

²**brag** n 1 ♦ : arrogant talk or manner 2 : one who brags : BRAGGART

♦ bluster, bombast, braggadocio, gas, grandiloquence, hot air, rant — more at BOMBAST

brag·ga·do·cio \,bra-gə-'dō-shē-,ō, -sē-, -chē-\ n, pl **-cios** 1 ♦ : one who brags : BRAGGART 2 ♦ : empty boasting 3 : arrogant pretension : COCKINESS

♦ [1] braggart, boaster, bragger — more at BRAGGART
♦ [2] bluster, bombast, brag, gas, grandiloquence, hot air, rant — more at BOMBAST

brag·gart \'bra-gərt\ n ♦ : one who brags

♦ boaster, braggadocio, bragger; also blusterer, magpie, windbag

brag·ger \'bra-gər\ n ♦ : one who brags

♦ braggart, boaster, braggadocio — more at BRAGGART

Brah·man or **Brah·min** \'brä-mən for 1; 'brā-, 'brä-, 'bra- for 2\ n 1 : a Hindu of the highest caste traditionally assigned to the priesthood 2 : any of a breed of large vigorous humped cattle developed in the southern U.S. from Indian stock 3 usu **Brahmin** : a person of high social standing and cultivated intellect and taste

Brah·man·ism \'brä-mə-,ni-zəm\ n : orthodox Hinduism

¹**braid** \'brād\ vb 1 : to form (strands) into a braid : PLAIT; also : to make from braids 2 : to ornament with braid

²**braid** n 1 ♦ : a length of braided hair 2 ♦ : a cord or ribbon of three or more interwoven strands

♦ [1, 2] lace, plait; also stripe

braille \'brāl\ n, often cap : a system of writing for the blind that uses characters made up of raised dots

¹**brain** \'brān\ n 1 : the part of the vertebrate central nervous system enclosed in the skull and continuous with the spinal cord that is composed of neurons and supporting structures and is the center of thought and nervous system control; also : a centralized mass of nerve tissue in an invertebrate 2 a ♦ : INTELLECT, INTELLIGENCE — often used in pl. b ♦ : a very intelligent or intellectual person — **brained** \'brānd\ adj

♦ often **brains** [2a] gray matter (or grey matter), intellect, intelligence, reason, sense — more at INTELLIGENCE ♦ [2b] genius, intellect, thinker, whiz, wizard — more at GENIUS

²**brain** vb 1 : to kill by smashing the skull 2 : to hit on the head

brain·child \'brān-,chīld\ n : a product of one's creative imagination

brain death n : final cessation of activity in the central nervous system esp. as indicated by a flat electroencephalogram — **brain–dead** \-,ded\ adj

brain drain n : the departure of educated or professional people from one country, sector, or field to another usu. for better pay or living conditions

brain·less adj : lacking intelligence

brain·storm \-,stórm\ n : a sudden inspiration or idea — **brainstorm** vb

brain·teas·er \-,tē-zər\ n : a challenging puzzle

brain·wash·ing \'brān-,wò-shiŋ, -,wä-\ n 1 : a forcible indoctrination to induce someone to give up basic political, social, or religious beliefs and attitudes and to accept contrasting regimented ideas 2 : persuasion by propaganda or salesmanship — **brain·wash** vb

brain wave n 1 : BRAINSTORM 2 : rhythmic fluctuations of voltage between parts of the brain; also : a current produced by brain waves

brainy adj ♦ : having or showing a well-developed intellect

♦ alert, bright, brilliant, clever, intelligent, keen, nimble, quick, quick-witted, sharp, smart — more at INTELLIGENT

braise \'brāz\ vb **braised; brais·ing** : to cook (meat) slowly in fat and little moisture in a closed pot

¹**brake** \'brāk\ n : a common bracken fern

²**brake** n ♦ : rough or wet land heavily overgrown (as with thickets or reeds)

♦ brushwood, chaparral, coppice, covert, thicket — more at THICKET

³**brake** n : a device for slowing or stopping motion esp. by friction — **brake·less** adj

⁴**brake** vb **braked; brak·ing** 1 ♦ : to slow or stop by or as if by a brake 2 : to apply a brake

♦ decelerate, retard, slow — more at SLOW

brake·man \'brāk-mən\ n : a train crew member who inspects the train and assists the conductor

bram·ble \'bram-bəl\ n : any of a large genus of prickly shrubs (as a blackberry) related to the roses; also : any rough prickly shrub or vine

bram·bly \-b(ə-)lē\ adj ♦ : like or full of brambles

♦ prickly, scratchy, thorny — more at SCRATCHY

bran \'bran\ n : the edible broken husks of cereal grain sifted from flour or meal

¹**branch** \'branch\ n [ME, fr. AF branche, fr. LL branca paw] 1 : a natural subdivision (as a bough or twig) of a plant stem 2 : a division (as of an antler or a river) related to a whole like a plant branch to its stem 3 : a discrete element of a complex system: as a ♦ : a separate but dependent part of a central organization ⟨the executive ~⟩ b : a division of a family descended from one ancestor — **branched** \'brancht\ adj

♦ affiliate, chapter, local — more at CHAPTER

²**branch** *vb* **1** : to develop branches **2** ♦ : to spring out (as from a main stem) : DIVERGE **3** : to extend activities ⟨the business is ∼*ing* out⟩

♦ diverge, fan, radiate — more at RADIATE ♦ *usu* **branch out** diverge, divide, fork, separate — more at SEPARATE

¹**brand** \'brand\ *n* **1** : a piece of charred or burning wood **2 a** : a mark made (as by burning) usu. to identify **b** ♦ : a mark of disgrace : STIGMA **3** : a class of goods identified as the product of a particular firm or producer **4** : a distinctive kind ⟨my own ∼ of humor⟩

♦ blot, smirch, spot, stain, stigma, taint — more at STAIN

²**brand** *vb* **1** : to mark with a brand **2** : STIGMATIZE

bran·dish \'bran-dish\ *vb* : to shake or wave menacingly

brand–new \'bran-'nü, -'nyü\ *adj* ♦ : conspicuously new and unused

♦ fresh, pristine, virgin — more at FRESH ♦ new, spick=and-span, unused — more at NEW

bran·dy \'bran-dē\ *n, pl* **brandies** [short for *brandywine*, fr. D *brandewijn*, fr. MD *brantwijn*, fr. *brant* distilled + *wijn* wine] : a liquor distilled from wine or fermented fruit juice — **brandy** *vb*

brash \'brash\ *adj* **1** ♦ : prone to act in a rash, impetuous manner **2** ♦ : aggressively self-assertive — **brash·ly** *adv* — **brash·ness** *n*

♦ [1] foolhardy, madcap, overbold, overconfident, reckless — more at FOOLHARDY ♦ [2] arch, bold, brazen, cheeky, cocky, fresh, impertinent, impudent, insolent, nervy, sassy, saucy — more at NERVY

brass \'bras\ *n* **1** : an alloy of copper and zinc; *also* : an object of brass **2** ♦ : brazen self-assurance **3** : persons of high rank (as in the military)

♦ audacity, brazenness, cheek, chutzpah, effrontery, gall, nerve, presumption, sauce, sauciness, temerity — more at EFFRONTERY

bras·siere \brə-'zir\ *n* : a woman's close-fitting undergarment designed to support the breasts

brassy *adj* : shamelessly bold

brat \'brat\ *n* **1** *disparaging* : an ill-behaved child **2** : a child of a career military person — **brat·ti·ness** *n* — **brat·ty** *adj*

bra·va·do \brə-'vä-dō\ *n, pl* **-does** *or* **-dos** **1** : blustering swaggering conduct **2** : a show of bravery

¹**brave** \'brāv\ *adj* **brav·er; brav·est** [MF, fr. It & Sp *bravo* courageous, wild, prob. fr. L *barbarus* barbarous] **1** ♦ : showing courage **2** : EXCELLENT, SPLENDID — **brave·ly** *adv*

♦ courageous, dauntless, doughty, fearless, gallant, greathearted, heroic, intrepid, lionhearted, manful, stalwart, stout, undaunted, valiant, valorous; *also* determined, firm, game, plucky, resolute, undeterred, undismayed, unflinching, unswerving *Ant* cowardly, craven, fainthearted, fearful, pusillanimous, timorous

²**brave** *vb* **braved; brav·ing** ♦ : to face or endure bravely

♦ beard, brazen, confront, dare, defy, face — more at FACE

³**brave** *n* : an American Indian warrior

brav·ery \'brā-və-rē\ *n, pl* **-er·ies** **1** ♦ : the quality or state of being brave : COURAGE **2** : fine clothes; *also* : showy display

♦ courage, daring, fearlessness, gallantry, guts, hardihood, heart, heroism, nerve, stoutness, valor — more at COURAGE

bra·vo \'brä-vō\ *n, pl* **bravos** : a shout of approval — often used as an interjection in applauding

bra·vu·ra \brə-'vyùr-ə, -'vùr-\ *n* **1** : a florid brilliant musical style **2** : self-assured brilliant performance — **bra·vura** *adj*

¹**brawl** \'bròl\ *n* ♦ : a noisy quarrel — **brawl·er** *n*

♦ altercation, argument, disagreement, dispute, fight, quarrel, row, wrangle — more at ARGUMENT ♦ fracas,

fray, free-for-all, melee, row; *also* battle, clash, combat, conflict, contest, fight, fisticuffs, scrap, scrimmage, scuffle, struggle, tussle

²**brawl** *vb* ♦ : to quarrel or fight noisily

♦ argue, bicker, dispute, fall out, fight, hassle, quarrel, row, scrap, spat, squabble, wrangle — more at ARGUE

brawn \'bròn\ *n* : strong muscles; *also* : muscular strength — **brawn·i·ness** *n*

brawny *adj* ♦ : having well-developed muscles

♦ muscular, rugged, sinewy, stalwart, stout, strong — more at STRONG

bray \'brā\ *n* : the characteristic harsh cry of a donkey — **bray** *vb*

braze \'brāz\ *vb* **brazed; braz·ing** : to solder with an alloy (as brass) that melts at a lower temperature than the metals being joined — **braz·er** *n*

¹**bra·zen** \'brāz-ᵊn\ *adj* **1** : made of brass **2** : sounding harsh and loud **3** : of the color of brass **4** ♦ : marked by contemptuous boldness — **bra·zen·ly** *adv*

♦ arch, bold, brash, cheeky, cocky, fresh, impertinent, impudent, insolent, nervy, sassy, saucy — more at NERVY

²**brazen** *vb* ♦ : to face boldly or defiantly

♦ beard, brave, confront, dare, defy, face — more at FACE

bra·zen·ness *n* ♦ : the quality or state of being brazen

♦ discourtesy, disrespect, impertinence, impudence, incivility, insolence, rudeness — more at DISCOURTESY ♦ audacity, brass, cheek, chutzpah, effrontery, gall, nerve, presumption, sauce, sauciness, temerity — more at EFFRONTERY

¹**bra·zier** \'brā-zhər\ *n* : a worker in brass

²**brazier** *n* **1** : a vessel holding burning coals (as for heating) **2** : a device on which food is grilled

Bra·zil·ian \brə-'zil-yən\ *n* : a native or inhabitant of Brazil — **Brazilian** *adj*

Bra·zil nut \brə-'zil-\ *n* : a triangular oily edible nut borne in large capsules by a tall So. American tree; *also* : the tree

¹**breach** \'brēch\ *n* **1** ♦ : a breaking of a law, obligation, tie (as of friendship), or standard (as of conduct) **2** ♦ : an interruption or opening made by or as if by breaking through

♦ [1] infraction, infringement, offense, transgression, trespass, violation *Ant* observance ♦ [2] break, discontinuity, gap, gulf, hole, interval, opening, rent, rift, separation — more at GAP

²**breach** *vb* **1** : to make a breach in **2** : to leap out of water ⟨whales ∼*ing*⟩ **3** ♦ : to fail to keep or honor : violate a trust ⟨∼*ed* the agreement⟩

♦ break, transgress, violate — more at VIOLATE

¹**bread** \'bred\ *n* **1** : baked food made basically of flour or meal **2** : a substance with food value : FOOD

²**bread** *vb* : to cover with bread crumbs before cooking

bread·bas·ket \'bred-,bas-kət\ *n* : a major cereal-producing region

bread·fruit \-,früt\ *n* : a round usu. seedless fruit resembling bread in color and texture when baked; *also* : a tall tropical tree related to the mulberry and bearing breadfruit

bread·stuff \-,stəf\ *n* : GRAIN, FLOUR

breadth \'bredth, 'bretth\ *n* **1 a** : distance from side to side : WIDTH **b** ♦ : a wide expanse **2** ♦ : comprehensive quality : SCOPE ⟨∼ of knowledge⟩

♦ [1b] expanse, extent, reach, spread, stretch — more at EXPANSE ♦ [2] amplitude, compass, extent, range, reach, realm, scope, sweep, width — more at RANGE

bread·win·ner \'bred-,wi-nər\ *n* : a member of a family whose wages supply its livelihood

¹**break** \'brāk\ *vb* **broke** \'brōk\; **bro·ken** \'brō-kən\; **break·ing** **1** ♦ : to separate into parts usu. suddenly or violently : come or force apart **2** ♦ : to violate a command or law : TRANS-

GRESS ⟨∼ a law⟩ **3** : to force a way into, out of, or through **4 a** : to disrupt the order or unity of ⟨∼ ranks⟩ ⟨∼ up a gang⟩ **b** : to cause the destruction or loss of effectiveness of; *also* : to bring to submission or helplessness **5** : EXCEED, SURPASS ⟨∼ a record⟩ **6 a** : to cause to suffer financial ruin **b ♦** : to reduce in rank ⟨*broken* from sergeant to private⟩ **7 a** : to make known **b ♦** : to find an explanation or solution for; *also* : to discover the essentials of (a code or cipher system) **8 a ♦** : to stop or bring to an end suddenly : HALT **b** : to act or change abruptly (as a course or activity) **9** : to come esp. suddenly into being or notice ⟨as day ∼s⟩ **10 ♦** : to fail under stress **11** : HAPPEN, DEVELOP **12 ♦** : to escape with sudden forceful effort

♦ [1] bust, fracture, fragment; *also* blast, blow up, burst, detonate, explode ♦ [2] breach, transgress, violate — more at VIOLATE ♦ [6b] bust, degrade, demote, downgrade, reduce — more at DEMOTE ♦ [7b] answer, crack, decode, dope, figure out, puzzle, resolve, riddle, solve, unravel, work, work out — more at SOLVE ♦ [8a] break off, cease, cut, desist, discontinue, drop, end, halt, knock off, lay off, leave off, quit, shut off, stop — more at STOP ♦ [10] break down, conk, crash, cut out, die, fail, stall — more at FAIL ♦ [12] bolt, flee, fly, retreat, run, run away, run off — more at RUN

²**break** *n* **1** : an act of breaking **2 ♦** : a result of breaking; *esp* : an interruption of strength or continuity ⟨coffee ∼⟩ ⟨a ∼ in the wall⟩ **3** : a stroke of good luck

♦ breach, discontinuity, gap, gulf, hole, interval, opening, rent, rift, separation — more at GAP ♦ breath, breather, recess, respite; *also* time-out

break·able *adj* ♦ : capable of being broken — **breakable** *n*

♦ delicate, fragile, frail — more at FRAGILE

break·age \'brā-kij\ *n* **1** : the action of breaking **2** : articles or amount broken **3** : loss due to things broken

break·down \'brāk-ˌdaùn\ *n* **1** : functional failure; *esp* : a physical, mental, or nervous collapse **2** : DISINTEGRATION **3 ♦** : the process of decomposing : DECOMPOSITION **4** : division into categories : ANALYSIS

♦ [3] corruption, decay, decomposition, putrefaction, rot, spoilage — more at CORRUPTION ♦ [4] analysis, assay, dissection — more at ANALYSIS

break down *vb* **1 ♦** : to stop functioning because of breakage or wear **2 ♦** : to divide into parts or categories **3 ♦** : to undergo decomposition **4 ♦** : to succumb to mental or emotional stress

♦ [1] break, conk, crash, cut out, die, fail, stall — more at FAIL ♦ [2] assort, categorize, class, classify, grade, group, peg, place, range, rank, separate, sort — more at CLASSIFY ♦ [3] corrupt, decay, decompose, disintegrate, molder, putrefy, rot, spoil — more at DECAY ♦ [4] crack, flip, freak — more at CRACK

break·er \'brā-kər\ *n* **1** : one that breaks **2** : a wave that breaks into foam (as against the shore)

break·fast \'brek-fəst\ *n* : the first meal of the day — **breakfast** *vb*

break in *vb* **1** : to enter a building by force **2 ♦** : to hinder by speaking when another is speaking : INTERRUPT; *also* : INTRUDE **3** : TRAIN — **break–in** \'brāk-ˌin\ *n*

♦ chime in, cut in, interpose, interrupt, intrude — more at INTERRUPT

break·neck \'brāk-'nek\ *adj* ♦ : very fast or dangerous ⟨∼ speed⟩

♦ breathless, dizzy, fast, fleet, lightning, rapid, rattling, speedy, swift — more at FAST

break off *vb* ♦ : to stop abruptly : bring or come to an end

♦ break, cease, cut, desist, discontinue, drop, end, halt, knock off, lay off, leave off, quit, shut off, stop — more at STOP

break out *vb* **1 ♦** : to develop or erupt suddenly or with force **2** : to develop a skin rash

♦ burst, erupt, explode, flame, flare, go off — more at ERUPT

break·through \'brāk-ˌthrü\ *n* **1** : an act or instance of breaking through an obstruction or defensive line **2 ♦** : a sudden advance in knowledge or technique

♦ advance, advancement, enhancement, improvement, refinement — more at ADVANCE

break·up \-ˌəp\ *n* **1 ♦** : the act or process of dissolving : DISSOLUTION **2** : a division into smaller units

♦ dissolution, division, partition, schism, separation, split — more at SEPARATION

break up *vb* **1 ♦** : to cease to exist as a unified whole **2 ♦** : to break into pieces

♦ [1] disband, disperse, dissolve — more at DISBAND ♦ [2] disconnect, disjoint, dissever, dissociate, disunite, divide, divorce, part, resolve, separate, sever, split, sunder, unyoke — more at SEPARATE

break·wa·ter \'brāk-ˌwȯ-tər, -ˌwä-\ *n* : a structure protecting a harbor or beach from the force of waves

bream \'brim, 'brēm\ *n, pl* **bream** *or* **breams** : any of various small freshwater sunfishes

breast \'brest\ *n* **1** : either of the pair of mammary glands extending from the front of the chest esp. in pubescent and adult human females **2** : the front part of the body between the neck and the abdomen **3** : the seat of emotion and thought

breast·bone \'brest-ˌbōn\ *n* : STERNUM

breast–feed \-ˌfēd\ *vb* : to feed (a baby) from a mother's breast rather than from a bottle

breast·plate \-ˌplāt\ *n* : a metal plate of armor for the breast

breast·stroke \-ˌstrōk\ *n* : a swimming stroke executed by extending both arms forward and then sweeping them back with palms out while kicking backward and outward with both legs

breast·work \-ˌwərk\ *n* : a temporary fortification

breath \'breth\ *n* **1 a** : the act or power of breathing **b ♦** : opportunity or time to breathe; *esp* : a pause in an activity **2 ♦** : a slight breeze **3** : air inhaled or exhaled in breathing **4** : spoken sound **5** : SPIRIT — **breath·less·ly** *adv* — **breath·less·ness** *n* — **breathy** \'bre-thē\ *adj*

♦ [1b] break, breather, pause, recess, respite — more at BREAK ♦ [2] air, breeze, puff, waft, zephyr — more at BREEZE

breathe \'brēth\ *vb* **breathed; breath·ing** **1** : to inhale and exhale **2 ♦** : to be alive : LIVE **3** : to halt for rest **4** : to utter softly or secretly — **breath·able** *adj*

♦ be, exist, live, subsist — more at BE

breath·er \'brē-thər\ *n* **1** : one that breathes **2 ♦** : a short rest

♦ break, breath, recess, respite — more at BREAK

breath·less *adj* **1 a** : panting or gasping for breath **b ♦** : not breathing : not alive **2 ♦** : very rapid or strenuous **3 ♦** : oppressive because of no fresh air or breeze

♦ [1b] dead, deceased, defunct, gone, late, lifeless — more at DEAD ♦ [2] breakneck, brisk, dizzy, fast, fleet, hasty, lightning, nippy, quick, rapid, rattling, snappy, speedy, swift — more at FAST ♦ [3] close, stuffy — more at STUFFY

breath·tak·ing \'breth-ˌtā-kiŋ\ *adj* **1** : making one out of breath **2 ♦** : producing excitement : EXCITING, THRILLING ⟨∼ beauty⟩ — **breath·tak·ing·ly** *adv*

♦ electric, exciting, exhilarating, rousing, stirring, thrilling — more at EXCITING

brec·cia \'bre-chē-ə, -chə\ *n* : a rock consisting of sharp fragments held in fine-grained material

breech \'brēch\ *n* **1** *usu* **breech·es** *usu* 'bri-chəz\ ♦ : trousers ending near the knee; *also* : PANTS **2** : the hind end of the body : BUTTOCKS, RUMP **3** : the part of a firearm at the rear of the barrel

♦ britches, pantaloons, pants, slacks, trousers — more at PANTS

¹**breed** \'brēd\ *vb* **bred** \'bred\; **breed·ing** **1** : BEGET; *also* : ORIGINATE **2 ♦** : to propagate sexually; *also* : MATE **3 ♦** : to bring (a person) to maturity through nurturing

care and education : BRING UP **4** : to produce (fission-able material) from material that is not fissionable — **breed·er** *n*

♦ [2] mate, multiply, procreate, propagate, reproduce — more at PROCREATE ♦ [3] bring up, foster, raise, rear — more at BRING UP

²**breed** *n* **1** : a strain of similar and presumably related plants or animals usu. developed in domestication **2** ♦ : a group, set, or kind sharing common attributes : SORT, CLASS

♦ class, description, feather, ilk, kind, like, manner, nature, order, sort, species, type — more at SORT

breed·ing *n* **1** ♦ : line of descent : ANCESTRY **2** : training in polite social interaction **3** : sexual propagation of plants or animals

♦ ancestry, birth, blood, bloodline, descent, extraction, family tree, genealogy, line, lineage, origin, parentage, pedigree, stock, strain — more at ANCESTRY

¹**breeze** \'brēz\ *n* **1** ♦ : a light wind **2** ♦ : something easily done : CINCH, SNAP — **breeze·less** *adj*

♦ [1] air, breath, puff, waft, zephyr; *also* draft, whiff ♦ [2] child's play, cinch, picnic, pushover, snap — more at CINCH

²**breeze** *vb* **breezed; breez·ing** ♦ : to progress quickly and easily; *also* : to move swiftly and airily

♦ bowl, coast, drift, flow, glide, roll, sail, skim, slide, slip, stream, sweep, whisk — more at FLOW ♦ dash, fly, hasten, hurry, run, rush, speed, whirl, zip, zoom — more at HURRY

breeze·way \'brēz-ˌwā\ *n* : a roofed open passage connecting two buildings (as a house and garage)

breezy \'brē-zē\ *adj* **1** ♦ : swept by breezes **2** ♦ : briskly informal — **breez·i·ly** \'brē-zə-lē\ *adv* — **breez·i·ness** \-zē-nəs\ *n*

♦ [1] blowy, blustery, gusty, windy — more at WINDY ♦ [2] affable, easygoing, happy-go-lucky, laid-back — more at EASYGOING

breth·ren \'breth-rən, 'bre-thə-; 'bre-thərn\ *pl of* BROTHER — used esp. in formal or solemn address

Brethren *n pl* : members of one of several Protestant denominations originating chiefly in a German religious movement and stressing personal religious experience

bre·via·ry \'brē-vyə-rē, -vē-ˌer-ē\ *n, pl* **-ries** *often cap* : a book of prayers, hymns, psalms, and readings used by Roman Catholic priests

brev·i·ty \'bre-və-tē\ *n, pl* **-ties** **1** ♦ : shortness or conciseness of expression **2** ♦ : shortness of duration

♦ [1, 2] briefness, conciseness, shortness; *also* abbreviation, abridgment, compression, condensation, contraction, curtailment

brew \'brü\ *vb* **1** : to prepare (as beer) by steeping, boiling, and fermenting **2** : to prepare (as tea) by steeping in hot water — **brew** *n* — **brew·er** *n* — **brew·ery** \'brü-ə-rē, 'brù(-ə)r-ē\ *n*

¹**briar** *also* **brier** \'brī-ər\ *n* : a plant (as a bramble or rose) with a thorny or prickly usu. woody stem

²**briar** *n* : a tobacco pipe made from the root or stem of a European heath

brib·able *adj* ♦ : capable of being bribed

♦ corruptible, purchasable, venal — more at VENAL

¹**bribe** \'brīb\ *n* [ME, morsel given to a beggar, bribe, fr. AF, morsel] : something (as money or a favor) given or promised to a person to influence conduct

²**bribe** *vb* **bribed; brib·ing** : to influence by offering a bribe — **brib·er** *n* — **brib·ery** \'brī-bə-rē\ *n*

bric–a–brac \'bri-kə-ˌbrak\ *n pl* [F] : small ornamental articles

¹**brick** \'brik\ *n* : a block molded from moist clay and hardened by heat used esp. for building

²**brick** *vb* : to close, cover, or pave with bricks

brick·bat \'brik-ˌbat\ *n* **1** : a piece of a hard material (as a brick) esp. when thrown as a missile **2** : an uncomplimentary remark

brick·lay·er \'brik-ˌlā-ər\ *n* : a person who builds or paves with bricks — **brick·lay·ing** *n*

¹**brid·al** \'brīd-ᵊl\ *n* [ME *bridale*, fr. OE *brȳdealu*, fr. *brȳd* bride + *ealu* ale] : a marriage festival or ceremony : WEDDING

²**bridal** *adj* : of or relating to a bride or a wedding

bride \'brīd\ *n* : a woman just married or about to be married

bride·groom \'brīd-ˌgrüm, -ˌgrùm\ *n* : a man just married or about to be married

brides·maid \'brīdz-ˌmād\ *n* : a woman who attends a bride at her wedding

¹**bridge** \'brij\ *n* **1** : a structure built over a depression or obstacle for use as a passageway **2** : something (as the upper part of the nose) resembling a bridge in form or function **3** : a curved piece raising the strings of a musical instrument **4** : the forward part of a ship's superstructure from which it is navigated **5** : an artificial replacement for missing teeth

²**bridge** *vb* **bridged; bridg·ing** : to build a bridge over — **bridge·able** *adj*

³**bridge** *n* : a card game for four players developed from whist

bridge·head \-ˌhed\ *n* : an advanced position seized in enemy territory

bridge·work \-ˌwərk\ *n* : dental bridges

¹**bri·dle** \'brīd-ᵊl\ *n* **1** : headgear with which a horse is controlled **2** : CURB, RESTRAINT

²**bridle** *vb* **bri·dled; bri·dling** **1 a** : to put a bridle on **b** ♦ : to restrain with or as if with a bridle **2** : to show hostility or scorn usu. by tossing the head

♦ check, constrain, contain, control, curb, govern, inhibit, regulate, rein, restrain, tame

Brie \'brē\ *n* : a soft cheese with a whitish rind and a pale yellow interior

¹**brief** \'brēf\ *adj* **1** ♦ : short in duration or extent **2** ♦ : marked by brevity of expression or statement : CONCISE; *also* : CURT — **brief·ly** *adv*

♦ [1] little, short, short-lived — more at SHORT ♦ [2] compact, compendious, concise, crisp, curt, epigrammatic, laconic, pithy, succinct, summary, terse — more at CONCISE

²**brief** *n* **1** : a concise statement or document; *esp* : one summarizing a law client's case or a legal argument **2** *pl* : short snug underpants

³**brief** *vb* ♦ : to give instructions or information to

♦ acquaint, advise, apprise, clue, enlighten, familiarize, fill in, inform, instruct, tell, wise — more at ENLIGHTEN

brief·case \'brēf-ˌkās\ *n* : a flat flexible case for carrying papers

brief·ness *n* ♦ : the quality or state of being brief

♦ brevity, conciseness, shortness — more at BREVITY ♦ brevity, compactness, conciseness, crispness, succinctness, terseness — more at SUCCINCTNESS

bri·er *var of* BRIAR

¹**brig** \'brig\ *n* : a 2-masted square-rigged sailing ship

²**brig** *n* ♦ : the place of confinement for offenders on a naval ship

♦ hoosegow, jail, jug, lockup, pen, penitentiary, prison, stockade — more at JAIL

³**brig** *abbr* brigade

bri·gade \bri-'gād\ *n* **1** : a military unit composed of a headquarters, one or more units of infantry or armored forces, and supporting units **2** : a group organized for a particular purpose (as fire fighting)

brig·a·dier general \ˌbri-gə-ˌdir-\ *n* : a commissioned officer (as in the army) ranking next below a major general

brig·and \'bri-gənd\ *n* : BANDIT — **brig·and·age** \-gən-dij\ *n*

brig·an·tine \'bri-gən-ˌtēn\ *n* : a 2-masted square-rigged ship with a fore-and-aft mainsail

Brig Gen *abbr* brigadier general

bright \'brīt\ *adj* **1** ♦ : radiating or reflecting light **2** : ILLUSTRIOUS, GLORIOUS **3 a** ♦ : having a cheerful nature **b** ♦ : mentally quick and resourceful : INTELLIGENT,

CLEVER ⟨a ∼ student⟩ **4** ♦ : conducive to cheer — **bright** adv — **bright·ly** adv

♦ [1] beaming, brilliant, effulgent, glowing, incandescent, lambent, lucent, lucid, luminous, lustrous, radiant, refulgent, shiny; also blazing, burning, fiery **Ant** dim, dull, lackluster ♦ [1] ablaze, alight, light; also floodlit, highlighted, spotlighted **Ant** blackened, dark, darkened, darkling, dimmed, dusky ♦ [3a] blithe, buoyant, cheerful, cheery, chipper, gay, lightsome, sunny, upbeat — more at CHEERFUL ♦ [3b] alert, brainy, brilliant, clever, intelligent, keen, nimble, quick, quick-witted, sharp, smart — more at INTELLIGENT ♦ [4] auspicious, encouraging, fair, golden, heartening, hopeful, likely, promising, propitious, rosy, upbeat — more at HOPEFUL

bright·en \'brīt-ᵊn\ vb : to make or become bright or brighter — **bright·en·er** n

bright·ness n : the state or quality of being bright

bril·liance \-yəns\ n ♦ : the quality or state of being brilliant

♦ augustness, glory, grandeur, grandness, magnificence, majesty, nobility, nobleness, resplendence, splendor, stateliness — more at MAGNIFICENCE ♦ dazzle, effulgence, illumination, lightness, lucidity, luminosity, radiance, refulgence, splendor; also blaze, flare, flicker, light **Ant** blackness, dark, darkness, duskiness

bril·lian·cy \-yən-sē\ n : the quality or state of being brilliant

¹**bril·liant** \'bril-yənt\ adj [F brillant, prp. of briller to shine, fr. It brillare] **1** ♦ : very bright **2** STRIKING, DISTINCTIVE **3** ♦ : very intelligent — **bril·liant·ly** adv

♦ [1] beaming, bright, effulgent, glowing, incandescent, lambent, lucent, lucid, luminous, lustrous, radiant, refulgent, shiny — more at BRIGHT ♦ [3] alert, brainy, bright, clever, intelligent, keen, nimble, quick, quick-witted, sharp, smart — more at INTELLIGENT

²**brilliant** n : a gem cut in a particular form with many facets

¹**brim** \'brim\ n **1** : an upper or outer margin : EDGE, RIM **2** : the projecting rim of a hat — **brim·less** adj

²**brim** vb **brimmed; brim·ming** ♦ : to be or become full often to overflowing

♦ abound, bulge, burst, crawl, swarm, teem — more at ABOUND

brim·ful \-'fùl\ adj ♦ : full to the brim

♦ chock-full, crowded, fat, fraught, full, loaded, packed, replete — more at FULL

brim·stone \'brim-,stōn\ n : SULFUR

brin·dled \'brin-d²ld\ adj : having dark streaks or flecks on a gray or tawny ground ⟨a ∼ Great Dane⟩

brine \'brīn\ n **1** : water saturated with salt **2** ♦ : the water of a sea or salt lake : OCEAN

♦ blue, deep, ocean, sea — more at OCEAN

bring \'briŋ\ vb **brought** \'brȯt\; **bring·ing** \'briŋ-iŋ\ **1** : to cause to come with one **2** : INDUCE, PERSUADE, LEAD **3** : PRODUCE, EFFECT **4** ♦ : to sell for ⟨∼ a good price⟩ — **bring·er** n

♦ cost, fetch, go, sell — more at COST

bring about vb ♦ : to cause to take place

♦ cause, create, effect, effectuate, generate, induce, make, produce, prompt, result, work, yield — more at EFFECT

bring up vb **1** ♦ : to give a parent's fostering care to **2** : to come or bring to a sudden halt **3** ♦ : to call to notice

♦ [1] breed, foster, raise, rear; also father, mother ♦ [3] broach, introduce, moot, raise — more at INTRODUCE

brink \'briŋk\ n **1** : an edge at the top of a steep place **2** : the point of onset

briny \'brī-nē\ adj ♦ : of, relating to, or resembling brine or the sea — **brin·i·ness** n

♦ saline, salty — more at SALTY

brio \'brē-ō\ n : VIVACITY, SPIRIT

bri·quette or **bri·quet** \bri-'ket\ n : a compacted often brick-shaped mass of fine material ⟨a charcoal ∼⟩

bris also **briss** \'bris\ n : the Jewish rite of circumcision

brisk \'brisk\ adj **1** ♦ : keenly alert : LIVELY **2** : INVIGORATING **3** : acting or capable of acting with speed

♦ active, animate, animated, energetic, jaunty, lively, peppy, perky, pert, spirited, sprightly, springy, vital, vivacious — more at LIVELY

bris·ket \'bris-kət\ n : the breast or lower chest of a quadruped; also : a cut of beef from the brisket

brisk·ly adv ♦ : in a brisk manner

♦ apace, fast, hastily, pronto, quick, quickly, rapidly, speedily, swift, swiftly — more at FAST

brisk·ness n ♦ : the quality or state of being brisk

♦ animation, exuberance, liveliness, lustiness, robustness, sprightliness, vibrancy, vitality — more at VITALITY

bris·ling \'briz-liŋ, 'bris-\ n : SPRAT

¹**bris·tle** \'bri-səl\ n : a short stiff coarse hair — **bris·tle·like** \'bri-səl-,līk\ adj

²**bristle** vb **bris·tled; bris·tling** **1** : to stand stiffly erect **2** : to show angry defiance **3** : to appear as if covered with bristles

bris·tly adj : consisting of or like bristles

Brit abbr Britain; British

Bri·tan·nic \bri-'ta-nik\ adj : BRITISH

britch·es \'bri-chəz\ n pl ♦ : an outer garment covering each leg separately from waist to ankle : BREECHES, TROUSERS

♦ breeches, pantaloons, pants, slacks, trousers — more at PANTS

Brit·ish \'bri-tish\ n pl : the people of Great Britain or the Commonwealth — **British** adj — **Brit·ish·ness** n

British thermal unit n : the quantity of heat needed to raise the temperature of one pound of water one degree Fahrenheit

Brit·on \'brit-ᵊn\ n **1** : a member of a people inhabiting Britain before the Anglo-Saxon invasion **2** : a native or inhabitant of Great Britain

brit·tle \'brit-ᵊl\ adj **brit·tler; brit·tlest** ♦ : easily broken — **brit·tle·ness** n

♦ crisp, crumbly, flaky, friable, short — more at CRISP

bro \'brō\ n, pl **bros** **1** : BROTHER 1 **2** : SOUL BROTHER

¹**broach** \'brōch\ n : a pointed tool

²**broach** vb **1** : to pierce (as a cask) in order to draw the contents **2** ♦ : to introduce as a topic of conversation

♦ bring up, introduce, moot, raise — more at INTRODUCE

¹**broad** \'brȯd\ adj **1** : having a specified extension from side to side : WIDE **2** ♦ : extending far and wide **3** : CLEAR, OPEN **4** ♦ : easily understood : OBVIOUS ⟨a ∼ hint⟩ **5** : COARSE, CRUDE ⟨∼ stories⟩ **6** : tolerant in outlook **7** : GENERAL **8** ♦ : dealing with main or essential points — **broad·ness** n

♦ [2] expansive, extended, extensive, far-flung, far-reaching, wide, widespread — more at EXTENSIVE ♦ [4] apparent, clear, clear-cut, distinct, evident, lucid, manifest, obvious, palpable, patent, perspicuous, plain, transparent, unambiguous, unequivocal, unmistakable — more at CLEAR ♦ [8] bird's-eye, general, nonspecific, overall — more at GENERAL

²**broad** n, slang, often offensive : WOMAN

broad·band \'brȯd-,band\ n : a system of high-speed telecommunications in which a frequency range is divided into multiple independent channels for simultaneous transmission of signals

¹**broad·cast** \'brȯd-,kast\ vb **broadcast** also **broad·cast·ed; broad·cast·ing** **1** : to scatter or sow broadcast **2** ♦ : to make widely known **3** : to transmit a broadcast — **broad·cast·er** n

♦ circulate, disseminate, propagate, spread, strew — more at SPREAD ♦ advertise, announce, blaze, declare, enunciate, placard, post, proclaim, promulgate, publicize, publish, sound — more at ANNOUNCE

²**broadcast** *adv* : to or over a wide area

³**broadcast** *n* **1** : the transmission of sound or images by radio or television **2** : a single radio or television program

broad·cloth \-ˌklȯth\ *n* **1** : a smooth dense woolen cloth **2** : a fine soft cloth of cotton, silk, or synthetic fiber

broad·en \'brȯd-ᵊn\ *vb* : WIDEN

broad·loom \-ˌlüm\ *adj* : woven on a wide loom esp. in a solid color

broad·ly *adv* ♦ : in a broad manner; *esp* : to a great extent
♦ considerably, greatly, largely, much, sizably

broad–mind·ed \-'mīn-dəd\ *adj* ♦ : tolerant of varied opinions — **broad–mind·ed·ly** *adv* — **broad–mind·ed·ness** *n*
♦ liberal, nonorthodox, nontraditional, open-minded, progressive, radical, unconventional, unorthodox — more at LIBERAL

¹**broad·side** \-ˌsīd\ *n* **1** : a sheet of paper printed usu. on one side (as an advertisement) **2** : all of the guns on one side of a ship; *also* : their simultaneous firing **3** : a volley of abuse or denunciation

²**broadside** *adv* **1** : with one side forward : SIDEWAYS **2** : from the side ⟨the car was hit ∼⟩

broad–spectrum *adj* : effective against a wide range of organisms ⟨∼ antibiotics⟩

broad·sword \'brȯd-ˌsȯrd\ *n* : a broad-bladed sword

broad·tail \-ˌtāl\ *n* : a karakul esp. with flat and wavy fur

bro·cade \brō-'kād\ *n* : a usu. silk fabric with a raised design

broc·co·li \'brä-kə-lē\ *n* [It, pl. of *broccolo* flowering top of a cabbage, dim. of *brocco* small nail, sprout, fr. L *broccus* projecting] : the stems and immature usu. green or purple flower heads of either of two garden vegetable plants closely related to the cabbage; *also* : either of the plants

bro·chette \brō-'shet\ *n* : SKEWER

bro·chure \brō-'shur\ *n* [F, fr. *brocher* to sew, fr. MF, to prick, fr. OF *brochier*, fr. *broche* pointed tool] ♦ : an unbound printed publication with no cover or with a paper cover : PAMPHLET, BOOKLET
♦ booklet, circular, folder, leaflet, pamphlet — more at PAMPHLET

bro·gan \'brō-gən, brō-'gan\ *n* : a heavy shoe

brogue \'brōg\ *n* : a dialect or regional pronunciation; *esp* : an Irish accent

broil \'brȯil\ *vb* : to cook by exposure to radiant heat : GRILL — **broil** *n*

broil·er \'brȯi-lər\ *n* **1** : a utensil for broiling **2** : a young chicken fit for broiling

broil·ing *adj* ♦ : extremely hot
♦ burning, fiery, hot, red-hot, scorching, sultry, torrid — more at HOT

¹**broke** \'brōk\ *past of* BREAK

²**broke** *adj* ♦ : having no money or assets : PENNILESS
♦ destitute, impecunious, indigent, needy, penniless, penurious, poor, poverty-stricken — more at POOR

¹**bro·ken** \'brō-kən\ *past part of* BREAK

²**broken** *adj* **1** : SHATTERED **2 a** : having gaps or breaks : INTERRUPTED, DISRUPTED **b** ♦ : being irregular, interrupted, or full of obstacles **3** : SUBDUED, CRUSHED **4** : BANKRUPT **5** : imperfectly spoken ⟨∼ English⟩ — **bro·ken·ly** *adv*
♦ bumpy, coarse, irregular, jagged, lumpy, pebbly, ragged, rough, rugged, uneven — more at UNEVEN

bro·ken·heart·ed \ˌbrō-kən-'här-təd\ *adj* ♦ : overcome by grief or despair
♦ depressed, despondent, disconsolate, heartsick, miserable, mournful, sad, sorrowful, unhappy, wretched — more at SAD

bro·ker \'brō-kər\ *n* ♦ : an agent who negotiates contracts of purchase and sale — **broker** *vb*
♦ arbiter, arbitrator, go-between, intercessor, intermediary, mediator, middleman, peacemaker — more at MEDIATOR

bro·ker·age \'brō-kə-rij\ *n* **1** : the business of a broker **2** : the fee or commission charged by a broker

bro·mance \'brō-mans\ *n* : a close nonsexual friendship between men — **bro·man·tic** \brō-'man-tik\ *adj*

bro·mide \'brō-ˌmīd\ *n* : a compound of bromine and another element or chemical group including some (as potassium bromide) used as sedatives

bro·mid·ic \brō-'mi-dik\ *adj* : TRITE, UNORIGINAL

bro·mine \'brō-ˌmēn\ *n* [F *brome* bromine, fr. Gk *brōmos* stink] : a deep red liquid corrosive chemical element that gives off an irritating vapor

bronc \'bräŋk\ *n* : an unbroken or partly broken range horse of western No. America; *also* : MUSTANG

bron·chi·al \'bräŋ-kē-əl\ *adj* : of, relating to, or affecting the bronchi or their branches

bron·chi·tis \brän-'kī-təs, bräŋ-\ *n* : inflammation of the bronchi and their branches — **bron·chit·ic** \-'ki-tik\ *adj*

bron·chus \'bräŋ-kəs\ *n, pl* **bron·chi** \'bräŋ-ˌkī, -ˌkē\ : either of the main divisions of the windpipe each leading to a lung

bron·co \'bräŋ-kō\ *n, pl* **broncos** [MexSp, fr. Sp, rough, wild] : BRONC

bron·to·sau·rus \ˌbrän-tə-'sȯr-əs\ *also* **bron·to·saur** \'brän-tə-ˌsȯr\ *n* [NL, fr. Gk *brontē* thunder + *sauros* lizard] : any of a genus of very large 4-footed plant-eating dinosaurs of the Jurassic : APATOSAURUS

Bronx cheer \'bräŋks-\ *n* : RASPBERRY 2

¹**bronze** \'bränz\ *vb* **bronzed; bronz·ing** : to give the appearance of bronze to

²**bronze** *n* **1** : an alloy of copper and tin and sometimes other elements; *also* : something made of bronze **2** : a yellowish brown color — **bronzy** \'brän-zē\ *adj*

brooch \'brōch, 'brüch\ *n* : an ornamental clasp or pin

¹**brood** \'brüd\ *n* : a family of young animals or children and esp. of birds

²**brood** *adj* : kept for breeding ⟨a ∼ mare⟩

³**brood** *vb* **1** ♦ : to sit on eggs to hatch them; *also* : to shelter (hatched young) with the wings **2** : to think anxiously or gloomily about something — **brood·ing·ly** *adv*
♦ hatch, incubate, set, sit — more at SET

brood·er \'brü-dər\ *n* **1** : one that broods **2** : a heated structure for raising young birds

¹**brook** \'bruk\ *n* ♦ : a small natural stream
♦ creek, rill, rivulet, streamlet — more at CREEK

²**brook** *vb* ♦ : to stand for : TOLERATE, BEAR
♦ abide, bear, countenance, endure, meet, stand, stick out, stomach, support, sustain, take, tolerate — more at BEAR

brook·let \'bruk-lət\ *n* : a small brook

brook trout *n* : a common speckled cold-water char of No. America

broom \'brüm, 'brum\ *n* **1** : any of several shrubs of the legume family with long slender branches and usu. yellow flowers **2** : an implement with a long handle (**broom·stick** \-ˌstik\) used for sweeping

bros *pl of* BRO

broth \'brȯth\ *n, pl* **broths** \'brȯths, 'brȯthz\ **1** : liquid in which meat or sometimes vegetable food has been cooked **2** : a fluid culture medium

broth·el \'brä-thəl, 'brȯ-\ *n* : a house of prostitution

broth·er \'brə-thər\ *n, pl* **brothers** *also* **breth·ren** \'breth-rən, 'bre-thə-; 'bre-thərn\ **1** : a male having one or both parents in common with another individual **2** : a man who is a religious but not a priest **3** : KINSMAN; *also* : SOUL BROTHER — **broth·er·li·ness** \-lē-nəs\ *n* — **broth·er·ly** *adj*

broth·er·hood \'brə-thər-ˌhud\ *n* **1** : the state of being brothers or a brother **2** ♦ : an association (as a labor union or monastic society) for a particular purpose : FRATERNITY **3** : the whole body of persons in a business or profession
♦ association, club, college, congress, council, fellowship, fraternity, guild, institute, institution, league, order, organization, society — more at ASSOCIATION

broth·er–in–law \'brə-thə-rən-ˌlȯ, 'brə-thərn-ˌlȯ\ *n, pl* **brothers–in–law** \'brə-thər-zən-\ : the brother of one's spouse; *also* : the husband of one's sibling or of one's spouse's sibling

brougham \'brü-(ə)m, 'brō(-ə)m\ *n* : a light closed horse-drawn carriage with the driver outside in front

brought *past and past part of* BRING

brou·ha·ha \'brü-ˌhä-ˌhä\ *n* : HUBBUB, UPROAR

brow \'braù\ *n* **1** : the eyebrow or the ridge on which it grows; *also* : FOREHEAD **2** : the projecting upper part of a steep place

brow·beat \'braù-ˌbēt\ *vb* **-beat; -beat·en** \-ˈbēt-ᵊn\ *or* **-beat; -beat·ing** ♦ : to intimidate by sternness or arrogance

  ♦ bully, cow, hector, intimidate — more at INTIMIDATE

¹brown \'braùn\ *adj* : of the color brown; *also* : of dark or tanned complexion

²brown *n* : a color like that of coffee or chocolate that is a blend of red and yellow darkened by black — **brown·ish** *adj*

³brown *vb* : to make or become brown

brown bag·ging \-ˈba-giŋ\ *n* : the practice of carrying one's lunch usu. in a brown bag — **brown bag·ger** *n*

brown bear *n* : any of various large typically brown-furred bears including the grizzly bear

brown·ie \'braù-nē\ *n* **1** ♦ : a legendary cheerful elf who performs good deeds at night **2** *cap* : a member of a program of the Girl Scouts for girls in the first through third grades **3** : a small square or rectangle of chocolate cake

  ♦ dwarf, elf, fairy, fay, gnome, hobgoblin, leprechaun, pixie, puck, troll

brown·nose \'braùn-ˌnōz\ *vb, disparaging* : to ingratiate oneself with — **brownnose** *n*

brown·out \'braù-ˌnaùt\ *n* : a period of reduced voltage of electricity caused esp. by high demand and resulting in reduced illumination

brown rice *n* : hulled but unpolished rice that retains most of the bran layers

brown·stone \'braùn-ˌstōn\ *n* : a dwelling faced with reddish brown sandstone

¹browse \'braùz\ *vb* **browsed; brows·ing** **1** ♦ : to feed on browse; *also* : GRAZE **2** ♦ : to read or look over something in a casual way **3** : to access (as the World Wide Web) with a browser

  ♦ [1] forage, graze, pasture — more at GRAZE ♦ [2] dip, glance, glimpse, peek, skim — more at GLANCE

²browse *n* : tender shoots, twigs, and leaves fit for food for cattle

brows·er \'braù-zər\ *n* : a computer program for accessing sites or information on a network (as the World Wide Web)

bru·in \'brü-ən\ *n* : BEAR

¹bruise \'brüz\ *vb* **bruised; bruis·ing** **1** : to inflict a bruise on; *also* : to become bruised **2** : to break down (as leaves or berries) by pounding

²bruise *n* : a surface injury to flesh : CONTUSION

bruis·er \'brü-zər\ *n* : a big husky man

bruit \'brüt\ *vb* : to make widely known by common report

brunch \'brənch\ *n* : a meal that combines a late breakfast and an early lunch

bru·net *or* **bru·nette** \brü-ˈnet\ *adj* [F *brunet*, masc., *brunette*, fem., brownish, fr. OF, fr. *brun* brown, of Gmc origin] : having brown or black hair and usu. a relatively dark complexion — **brunet** *or* **brunette** *n*

brunt \'brənt\ *n* : the main shock, force, or stress esp. of an attack; *also* : the greater burden

bru·schet·ta \brü-ˈshe-tə, -ˈske-\ *n* : an appetizer of grilled bread with toppings

¹brush \'brəsh\ *n* **1** : BRUSHWOOD **2** : scrub vegetation or land covered with it

²brush *n* **1** : a device composed of bristles set in a handle and used esp. for cleaning or painting **2** : a bushy tail (as of a fox) **3** : an electrical conductor that makes contact between a stationary and a moving part (as of a motor) **4** : a quick light touch in passing

³brush *vb* **1** : to treat (as in cleaning or painting) with a

brush **2 a** : to remove with or as if with a brush **b** ♦ : to dismiss in an offhand manner — usu. used with *aside* or *off* **3** ♦ : to touch gently in passing

  ♦ *usu* brush aside *or* brush off [2b] condone, disregard, excuse, gloss over, ignore, pardon, pass over, shrug off, wink at — more at EXCUSE ♦ [3] graze, kiss, nick, shave, skim; *also* bump, contact, scrape, strike, sweep, swipe, touch

⁴brush *n* ♦ : a brief encounter or skirmish : SKIRMISH

  ♦ encounter, run-in, scrape, skirmish — more at ENCOUNTER

brush–off \'brəsh-ˌȯf\ *n* ♦ : a curt offhand dismissal

  ♦ cold shoulder, rebuff, repulse, snub — more at COLD SHOULDER

brush up *vb* : to renew one's skill

brush·wood \'brəsh-ˌwùd\ *n* **1** : small branches of wood esp. when cut **2** ♦ : a thicket of shrubs and small trees

  ♦ brake, chaparral, coppice, covert, thicket — more at THICKET

brusque \'brəsk\ *adj* [F *brusque*, fr. It *brusco*, fr. ML *bruscus* a plant with stiff twigs used for brooms] ♦ : blunt in manner or speech often to the point of ungracious harshness : CURT, BLUNT, ABRUPT — **brusque·ly** *adv*

  ♦ abrupt, blunt, curt, snippy — more at BLUNT

brus·sels sprout \'brəs-əlz-\ *n, often cap B* : one of the edible small heads borne on the stalk of a plant closely related to the cabbage; *also, pl* : this plant

bru·tal \'brüt-ᵊl\ *adj* **1** ♦ : befitting a brute : CRUEL **2** ♦ : physically discomforting : HARSH, SEVERE ⟨~ weather⟩ **3** : unpleasantly accurate — **bru·tal·ly** *adv*

  ♦ [1] barbarous, cruel, heartless, inhumane, sadistic, savage, vicious, wanton — more at CRUEL ♦ [2] bitter, burdensome, cruel, excruciating, grievous, grim, hard, harsh, heavy, inhuman, murderous, onerous, oppressive, rough, rugged, severe, stiff, tough, trying — more at HARSH

bru·tal·ise *Brit var of* BRUTALIZE

bru·tal·i·ty \brü-ˈta-lə-tē\ *n* ♦ : the quality or state of being brutal

  ♦ barbarity, cruelty, inhumanity, sadism, savagery, viciousness, wantonness — more at CRUELTY

bru·tal·ize \'brüt-ᵊl-ˌīz\ *vb* **-ized; -iz·ing** **1** : to make brutal **2** : to treat brutally

¹brute \'brüt\ *adj* [ME, fr. MF *brut* rough, fr. L *brutus* brutish, lit., heavy] **1** : of or relating to beasts **2** : BRUTAL **3** : UNREASONING; *also* : purely physical ⟨~ strength⟩

²brute *n* **1** ♦ : a 4-footed animal : BEAST **2** ♦ : a brutal person

  ♦ [1] animal, beast, creature, critter — more at ANIMAL ♦ [2] beast, devil, fiend, monster, savage, villain

brut·ish \'brü-tish\ *adj* **1** : BRUTE 1 **2** : strongly sensual; *also* : showing little intelligence

BS *abbr* bachelor of science

BSA *abbr* Boy Scouts of America

bskt *abbr* basket

Bt *abbr* baronet

btry *abbr* battery

Btu *abbr* British thermal unit

bu *abbr* bushel

¹bub·ble \'bə-bəl\ *n* **1** : a globule of gas in a liquid **2** : a thin film of liquid filled with gas **3** : something lacking firmness or solidity

²bubble *vb* **bub·bled; bub·bling** : to form, rise in, or give off bubbles

bub·bly *adj* ♦ : full of or showing good spirits

  ♦ buoyant, effervescent, exuberant, frolicsome, high-spirited, vivacious — more at EXUBERANT

bub·kes \'bəp-kəs, 'bùp-\ *n pl* [Yiddish] : the least amount ⟨didn't win ~⟩

bu·bo \'bü-bō, 'byü-\ *n, pl* **buboes** : an inflammatory swelling of a lymph gland

bu·bon·ic plague \ˌbü-ˈbä-nik-, byü-\ *n* : plague caused by a bacterium transmitted to human beings by flea bites and marked esp. by chills and fever and by buboes usu. in the groin

buc·ca·neer \,bə-kə-'nir\ *n* ♦ : any of the freebooters preying on Spanish ships and settlements esp. in 17th century West Indies; *broadly* : PIRATE

♦ corsair, freebooter, pirate, rover — more at PIRATE

¹buck \'bək\ *n, pl* **bucks** **1** *or pl* **buck** : a male animal (as a deer or antelope) **2 a** ♦ : a male human being **b** ♦ : a man with unusual consideration for personal appearance : DANDY **3** : DOLLAR

♦ [2a] chap, dude, fellow, gent, gentleman, guy, hombre, jack, joker, lad, male, man — more at MAN ♦ [2b] dandy, dude, fop, gallant — more at DANDY

²buck *vb* **1** ♦ : to spring with an arching leap ⟨a ~*ing* horse⟩ **2** : to charge against something; *also* : to strive for advancement sometimes without regard to ethical behavior **3** ♦ : to offer resistance to

♦ [1] hitch, jerk, jolt, twitch — more at JERK ♦ [3] defy, fight, oppose, repel, resist, withstand — more at RESIST

buck·board \-,bōrd\ *n* : a 4-wheeled horse-drawn wagon with a floor of long springy boards

buck·et \'bə-kət\ *n* **1** : a cylindrical open-top container with a handle : PAIL **2 a** : an object resembling a bucket in collecting, scooping, or carrying something **b** : as much as a bucket will hold; *broadly* ♦ : a large quantity — usu. used in pl. ⟨has *buckets* of money⟩ — **buck·et·ful** *n*

♦ usu **buckets** abundance, deal, gobs, heap, loads, lot, pile, plenty, quantity, scads — more at LOT

bucket list *n* [from the phrase *kick the bucket* (to die)] : a list of things one has not done but wants to do before dying

bucket seat *n* : a low separate seat for one person (as in an automobile)

buck·eye \'bə-,kī\ *n* : any of various trees or shrubs related to the horse chestnut; *also* : the large nutlike seed of such a shrub or tree

buck fever *n* : nervous excitement of an inexperienced hunter at the sight of game

¹buck·le \'bə-kəl\ *n* : a clasp (as on a belt) for two loose ends

²buckle *vb* **buck·led; buck·ling** **1** : to fasten with a buckle **2** ♦ : to apply oneself with vigor **3** : to crumple up : BEND, COLLAPSE

♦ address, apply, bend, devote, give — more at APPLY

³buckle *n* : BEND, FOLD, KINK

buck·ler \'bə-klər\ *n* : SHIELD

buck·ram \'bə-krəm\ *n* : a coarse stiff cloth used esp. for binding books

buck·saw \'bək-,sò\ *n* : a saw set in a usu. H-shaped frame for sawing wood

buck·shot \'bək-,shät\ *n* : lead shot that is from .24 to .33 inch (about 6.1 to 8.4 millimeters) in diameter

buck·skin \-,skin\ *n* **1** : the skin of a buck **2** : a soft usu. suede-finished leather — **buckskin** *adj*

buck·tooth \-'tüth\ *n* : a large projecting front tooth — **buck–toothed** \-'tütht\ *adj*

buck·wheat \-,hwēt\ *n* : either of two plants grown for their triangular seeds which are used as a cereal grain; *also* : these seeds

bu·col·ic \byü-'kä-lik\ *adj* [L *bucolicus*, fr. Gk *boukolikos*, fr. *boukolos* cowherd] ♦ : relating to or typical of rural life and esp. shepherds or herdsmen : PASTORAL

♦ country, pastoral, rural, rustic — more at RURAL

¹bud \'bəd\ *n* **1** : an undeveloped plant shoot (as of a leaf or a flower); *also* : a partly opened flower **2** : an asexual reproductive structure that detaches from the parent and forms a new individual **3** : something not yet fully developed ⟨nipped in the ~⟩

²bud *vb* **bud·ded; bud·ding** **1** : to form or put forth buds; *also* : to reproduce by asexual buds **2** : to be or develop like a bud **3** : to reproduce a desired variety (as of peach) by inserting a bud in a plant of a different variety

Bud·dhism \'bü-,di-zəm, 'bù-\ *n* : a religion of eastern and

central Asia growing out of the teachings of Gautama Buddha — **Bud·dhist** \'bü-dist, 'bù-\ *n or adj*

bud·dy \'bə-dē\ *n, pl* **buddies** **1** ♦ : one associated with another esp. in an action; *also* : FRIEND **2** : FELLOW

♦ chum, comrade, crony, familiar, friend, intimate, pal — more at FRIEND

budge \'bəj\ *vb* **budged; budg·ing** **1** ♦ : to change the place, position, or direction of : MOVE, SHIFT **2** ♦ : to give up resistance : YIELD

♦ [1] dislocate, displace, disturb, move, remove, shift, transfer — more at MOVE ♦ [2] blink, bow, capitulate, concede, give in, knuckle under, quit, submit, succumb, surrender, yield — more at YIELD

bud·ger·i·gar \'bə-jə-rē-,gar\ *n* : a small brightly colored Australian parrot often kept as a pet

¹bud·get \'bə-jət\ *n* [ME *bowgette*, fr. MF *bougette*, dim. of *bouge* leather bag, fr. L *bulga*] **1** ♦ : a store or supply accumulated or available **2** : a financial report containing estimates of income and expenses; *also* : a plan for coordinating income and expenses **3** ♦ : the amount of money available for a particular use — **bud·get·ary** \'bə-jə-,ter-ē\ *adj*

♦ [1, 3] account, deposit, fund, kitty, nest egg, pool, supply — more at FUND

²budget *vb* **1** : to allow for in a budget **2** : to draw up a budget

³budget *adj* : INEXPENSIVE

bud·gie \'bə-jē\ *n* : BUDGERIGAR

¹buff \'bəf\ *n* **1** : a yellow to orange yellow color **2** ♦ : one who is ardently attached to a cause, object, or pursuit : FAN, ENTHUSIAST

♦ addict, aficionado, bug, devotee, enthusiast, fan, fanatic, fancier, fiend, freak, lover, maniac, nut — more at FAN

²buff *adj* : of the color buff

³buff *vb* ♦ : to make smooth and glossy usu. by friction

♦ burnish, dress, gloss, grind, polish, rub, shine, smooth — more at POLISH

buf·fa·lo \'bə-fə-,lō\ *n, pl* **-lo** *or* **-loes** *also* **-los** **1** : WATER BUFFALO **2** : a large shaggy-maned No. American wild bovine mammal that has short horns and heavy forequarters with a large muscular hump

¹buf·fer \'bə-fər\ *n* ♦ : something or someone that protects or shields (as from physical damage or a financial blow)

♦ bumper, cushion, fender, pad — more at CUSHION

²buffer *n* : one that buffs

¹buf·fet \'bə-fət\ *n* : a blow esp. with the hand : SLAP

²buffet *vb* **1 a** : to strike with the hand **b** ♦ : to pound repeatedly **2** : to struggle against or on

♦ bash, bat, batter, beat, hammer, pound, thump — more at BEAT

³buf·fet \(,)bə-'fā, bü-\ *n* **1** : piece of dining-room furniture having compartments and shelves for holding articles of table service : SIDEBOARD **2** : a counter for refreshments; *also* : a meal at which people serve themselves informally

buff leather *n* : a strong supple oil-tanned leather

buf·foon \(,)bə-'fün\ *n* [MF *bouffon*, fr. It *buffone*] ♦ : a ludicrous figure : CLOWN — **buf·foon·ery** \-'fü-nə-rē\ *n*

♦ clown, harlequin, zany — more at CLOWN

¹bug \'bəg\ *n* **1** : an insect or other creeping or crawling invertebrate animal; *esp* : an insect pest (as a bedbug) **2** : any of an order of insects with sucking mouthparts and incomplete metamorphosis that includes many plant pests **3** : an unexpected flaw or imperfection ⟨a ~ in a computer program⟩ **4 a** : a disease-producing germ **b** ♦ : a disease caused by a germ **5** : a concealed listening device **6** ♦ : one who is ardently attached to a cause, object, or pursuit — **bug·gy** \'bə-gē\ *adj*

♦ [4b] ailment, complaint, complication, condition, disease, disorder, fever, ill, illness, infirmity, malady, sickness, trouble — more at DISEASE ♦ [6] addict, aficionado, buff, devotee, enthusiast, fan, fanatic, fancier, fiend, freak, lover, maniac, nut — more at FAN

²bug *vb* **bugged; bug·ging** **1** ♦ : to annoy esp. by petty provocation **2** : to plant a concealed microphone in

◆ bait, hassle, heckle, needle, ride, taunt, tease — more at TEASE ◆ aggravate, annoy, bother, chafe, exasperate, gall, get, grate, irk, irritate, nettle, peeve, persecute, pique, put out, rasp, rile, vex — more at IRRITATE

³**bug** *vb* **bugged; bug·ging** *of the eyes* : PROTRUDE, BULGE

bug·a·boo \'bə-gə-ˌbü\ *n, pl* **-boos** : an imaginary object of fear : BOGEY

bug·bear \'bəg-ˌbar\ *n* ◆ : an imaginary object of fear : BOGEY; *also* : a source of dread

◆ bête noire, bogey, hobgoblin, ogre — more at BOGEY

bug·gy \'bə-gē\ *n, pl* **buggies** **1** : a light horse-drawn carriage **2** : a carriage for a baby

bu·gle \'byü-gəl\ *n* [ME, buffalo, instrument made of buffalo horn, bugle, fr. AF, fr. L *buculus*, dim. of *bos* head of cattle] : a valveless brass instrument resembling a trumpet and used esp. for military calls — **bu·gler** *n*

bug out *vb* : to depart in a hurry; *also* : to flee in panic

¹**build** \'bild\ *vb* **built** \'bilt\; **build·ing** **1 a** ◆ : to form or have formed by ordering and uniting materials ⟨~ a house⟩ **b** ◆ : to develop or bring into being esp. according to a set plan **2** ◆ : to produce or create gradually ⟨~ an argument on facts⟩ **3** ◆ : to become progressively greater : INCREASE, ENLARGE; *also* : ENHANCE **4** : to engage in building — **build·er** *n*

◆ [1a, 1b] assemble, construct, erect, fabricate, make, make up, piece, put up, raise, rear, set up; *also* fashion, forge, frame, manufacture, mold, produce, shape *Ant* disassemble, dismantle, take down ◆ *usu* **build up** [2] carve, forge, grind, hammer, work out ◆ *usu* **build up** [3] accumulate, appreciate, balloon, burgeon, enhance, enlarge, escalate, expand, increase, mount, multiply, mushroom, proliferate, rise, snowball, swell, wax — more at INCREASE

²**build** *n* ◆ : form or mode of structure; *esp* : PHYSIQUE

◆ constitution, figure, form, frame, physique, shape — more at PHYSIQUE

build·ing \'bil-diŋ\ *n* **1** : a usu. roofed and walled structure (as a house) for permanent use **2** : the art or business of constructing buildings

building block *n* ◆ : a unit of construction or composition

◆ component, constituent, element, factor, ingredient, member — more at ELEMENT

build·up \'bil-ˌdəp\ *n* : the act or process of building up; *also* : something produced by this

built-in \'bil-'tin\ *adj* **1** : forming an integral part of a structure **2** : INHERENT

bulb \'bəlb\ *n* **1** : an underground resting stage of a plant (as a lily or an onion) consisting of a short stem base bearing one or more buds enclosed in overlapping leaves; *also* : a fleshy plant structure (as a tuber) resembling a bulb **2** : a plant having or growing from a bulb **3** : a rounded more or less bulb-shaped object or part (as for an electric lamp) — **bul·bous** \'bəl-bəs\ *adj*

Bul·gar·i·an \ˌbəl-'gar-ē-ən, bùl-\ *n* : a native or inhabitant of Bulgaria — **Bulgarian** *adj*

¹**bulge** \'bəlj\ *vb* **bulged; bulg·ing** ◆ : to become or cause to become protuberant

◆ balloon, beetle, belly, billow, overhang, poke, project, protrude, start, stick out; *also* dome

²**bulge** *n* ◆ : a swelling projecting part

◆ overhang, projection, protrusion; *also* dome *Ant* concavity, dent, depression, hollow, indentation, pit

bu·li·mia \bü-'lē-mē-ə, byü-, -'li-\ *n* **1** : an abnormal and constant craving for food **2** : a serious eating disorder chiefly of females that is characterized by compulsive overeating usu. followed by self-induced vomiting or laxative or diuretic abuse — **bu·lim·ic** \-'lē-mik, -'li-\ *adj or n*

¹**bulk** \'bəlk\ *n* **1** : MAGNITUDE, VOLUME **2** : material that forms a mass in the intestine; *esp* : FIBER 2 **3** : a large mass **4** ◆ : the major portion

◆ body, core, generality, main, mass, staple, weight — more at BODY

²**bulk** *vb* **1** : to cause to swell or bulge **2** : to appear as a factor : LOOM

bulk·head \'bəlk-ˌhed\ *n* **1** : a partition separating compartments **2** : a structure built to cover a shaft or a cellar stairway

bulky \'bəl-kē\ *adj* **bulk·i·er; -est** : having bulk; *esp* : being large and unwieldy

¹**bull** \'bùl\ *n* **1** : a male bovine animal; *also* : a usu. adult male of various large animals (as the moose, elephant, or whale) **2** : one who buys securities or commodities in expectation of a price increase — **bull·ish** *adj*

²**bull** *adj* **1** : of, relating to, or suggestive of a bull : MALE **2** : large of its kind

³**bull** *n* [ME *bulle*, fr. ML *bulla*, fr. L, bubble, amulet] **1** : a papal letter **2** : DECREE

⁴**bull** *n, slang* : NONSENSE

⁵**bull** *abbr* bulletin

¹**bull·dog** \'bùl-ˌdòg\ *n* : any of a breed of compact muscular short-haired dogs of English origin

²**bulldog** *vb* : to throw (a steer) by seizing the horns and twisting the neck

bull·doze \-ˌdōz\ *vb* **1** : to move, clear, or level with a tractor-driven machine (**bull·doz·er**) having a broad blade for pushing **2** ◆ : to force as if by using a bulldozer

◆ elbow, muscle, press, push — more at PRESS

bul·let \'bù-lət\ *n* [MF *boulette* small ball & *boulet* missile, dims. of *boule* ball, fr. L *bulla* bubble] : a missile to be shot from a firearm

bul·le·tin \'bù-lət-ᵊn\ *n* **1** ◆ : a brief public report intended for immediate release on a matter of public interest **2** : a periodical publication (as of a college) — **bulletin** *vb*

◆ advertisement, announcement, notice, notification, release — more at ANNOUNCEMENT

bulletin board *n* **1** : a board (as of cork) for posting notices **2** : a public forum on a computer network in which users write or read messages or download files

bul·let·proof \'bù-lət-ˌprüf\ *adj* **1** : impenetrable to bullets; *also* : INVINCIBLE **2** : not subject to corrections, alteration, or modification

bull·fight \'bùl-ˌfīt\ *n* : a spectacle in which people ceremonially fight with and usu. kill bulls in an arena — **bull·fight·er** *n*

bull·frog \-ˌfròg, -ˌfräg\ *n* : a large deep-voiced frog

bull·head \-ˌhed\ *n* : any of several common freshwater catfishes of the U.S.

bull·head·ed \-'he-dəd\ *adj* : stupidly stubborn : HEADSTRONG

bull·head·ed·ness \-'he-dəd-nəs\ *n* ◆ : the quality or state of being bullheaded

◆ hardheadedness, mulishness, obduracy, obstinacy, peevishness, persistence, pertinacity, self-will, stubbornness, tenacity — more at OBSTINACY

bul·lion \'bùl-yən\ *n* : gold or silver esp. in bars or ingots

bull market *n* : a market in which securities or commodities are persistently rising in value

bull·ock \'bù-lək\ *n* : a young bull; *also* : STEER

bull pen *n* : a place on a baseball field where pitchers warm up; *also* : the relief pitchers of a baseball team

bull session *n* : an informal discussion

bull's-eye \'bùl-ˌzī\ *n, pl* **bull's-eyes** : the center of a target; *also* : a shot that hits the bull's-eye

¹**bul·ly** \'bù-lē\ *n, pl* **bullies** ◆ : a person habitually cruel to others who are weaker

◆ gangster, goon, hood, hoodlum, mobster, mug, punk, rowdy, ruffian, thug, tough — more at HOODLUM

²**bully** *adj* : EXCELLENT, FIRST-RATE — often used interjectionally

³**bully** *vb* **bul·lied; bul·ly·ing** ◆ : to behave as a bully toward — **bul·ly·ing** *n*

◆ browbeat, cow, hector, intimidate — more at INTIMIDATE

bul·rush \'bùl-ˌrəsh\ *n* : any of several large rushes or sedges of wetlands

bul·wark \'bùl-(,)wərk, -,wȯrk; 'bəl-(,)wərk\ *n* 1 : a wall-like defensive structure 2 ♦ : a strong support or protection

♦ brace, buttress, mount, shore, stay, support, underpinning — more at SUPPORT

¹bum \'bəm\ *adj* 1 : of poor quality ⟨∼ advice⟩ 2 : DISABLED ⟨a ∼ knee⟩

²bum *vb* **bummed; bum·ming** 1 : to spend time unemployed and wandering; *also* : LOAF 2 : to obtain by begging

³bum *n* 1 : LOAFER 2 : a person who is devoted to a recreational activity ⟨a ski ∼⟩ 3 ♦ : a person who has no job and wanders from place to place : VAGRANT, TRAMP

♦ hobo, tramp, vagabond, vagrant — more at TRAMP

bum·ble·bee \'bəm-bəl-,bē\ *n* : any of numerous large hairy social bees

bum·mer \'bə-mər\ *n* 1 : an unpleasant experience 2 ♦ : something that fails or disappoints : FAILURE

♦ bust, catastrophe, debacle, dud, failure, fiasco, fizzle, flop, lemon, loser, turkey, washout — more at FAILURE

¹bump \'bəmp\ *n* 1 ♦ : a local bulge; *esp* : a swelling of tissue 2 ♦ : a sudden forceful blow or impact

♦ [1] knot, lump, nodule, swelling; *also* growth, tumor, wart ♦ [2] collision, concussion, crash, impact, jar, jolt, shock, smash, strike, wallop — more at IMPACT

²bump *vb* 1 : to strike or knock forcibly; *also* : to move by or as if by bumping 2 ♦ : to collide with

♦ bang, bash, collide, crash, hit, impact, knock, ram, slam, smash, strike, swipe, thud — more at HIT

¹bum·per \'bəm-pər\ *n* 1 : a cup or glass filled to the brim 2 : something unusually large

²bumper *adj* ♦ : unusually large

♦ big, grand, great, large, outsize, oversize, whopping — more at LARGE

³bump·er \'bəm-pər\ *n* ♦ : a device for absorbing shock or preventing damage; *esp* : a usu. metal bar at either end of an automobile

♦ buffer, cushion, fender, pad — more at CUSHION

bump·kin \'bəmp-kən\ *n* ♦ : an awkward and unsophisticated country person

♦ clodhopper, hick, rustic, yokel — more at HICK

bump·tious \'bəmp-shəs\ *adj* : obtusely and often noisily self-assertive

bumpy *adj* ♦ : having or covered with bumps; *also* : marked by bumps or jolts

♦ broken, coarse, irregular, jagged, lumpy, pebbly, ragged, rough, rugged, uneven — more at UNEVEN

bun \'bən\ *n* : a sweet or plain round roll

¹bunch \'bənch\ *n* 1 : SWELLING 2 ♦ : a number of things of the same kind — **bunchy** *adj*

♦ array, assemblage, batch, block, clump, cluster, collection, group, huddle, knot, lot, package, parcel, set, suite

²bunch *vb* ♦ : to form into a group or bunch

♦ cluster, crowd, huddle, press — more at PRESS

bun·co *or* **bun·ko** \'bəŋ-kō\ *n, pl* **buncos** *or* **bunkos** : a swindling scheme — **bunco** *vb*

¹bun·dle \'bən-d°l\ *n* 1 ♦ : several items bunched and fastened together; *also* : something wrapped for carrying 2 : a considerable amount : LOT 3 : a small band of mostly parallel nerve or muscle fibers

♦ pack, package, parcel — more at PACKAGE

²bundle *vb* **bun·dled; bun·dling** : to gather or tie in a bundle

bun·dling \'bənd-(ə-)liŋ\ *n* : a former custom of a courting couple's occupying the same bed without undressing

bung \'bəŋ\ *n* : the stopper in the bunghole of a cask

bun·ga·low \'bəŋ-gə-,lō\ *n* [Hindi & Urdu *baṅglā*, lit., (house) in the Bengal style] : a one-storied house with a low-pitched roof

bun·gee cord \'bən-jē-\ *n* : a long elastic cord used esp. as a fastening or shock-absorbing device

bungee jump *vb* : to jump for sport from a height (as from a bridge) while attached to a sturdy bungee cord — **bungee jumper** *n*

bung·hole \'bəŋ-,hōl\ *n* : a hole for emptying or filling a cask

bun·gle \'bəŋ-gəl\ *vb* **bun·gled; bun·gling** ♦ : to do badly : BOTCH — **bungle** *n* — **bun·gler** *n*

♦ bobble, botch, butcher, flub, foul up, fumble, mangle, mess up, screw up — more at BOTCH

bun·ion \'bən-yən\ *n* : an inflamed swelling of the first joint of the big toe

¹bunk \'bəŋk\ *n* ♦ : an article of furniture to sleep on : BED; *esp* : a built-in bed that is often one of a tier

♦ bed, pad, sack — more at BED

²bunk *n* ♦ : insincere or foolish talk : BUNKUM, NONSENSE

♦ claptrap, drivel, folly, foolishness, fudge, hogwash, humbug, nonsense, piffle, rot, silliness, slush, stupidity, trash — more at NONSENSE

bunk bed *n* : one of two single beds usu. placed one above the other

bun·ker \'bəŋ-kər\ *n* 1 : a bin or compartment for storage (as for coal on a ship) 2 : a protective embankment or dugout 3 : a sand trap or embankment constituting a hazard on a golf course

bun·kum *or* **bun·combe** \'bəŋ-kəm\ *n* [*Buncombe* County, N.C.; fr. a remark made by its congressman, who defended an irrelevant speech by claiming that he was speaking to Buncombe] : insincere or foolish talk

bun·ny \'bə-nē\ *n, pl* **bun·nies** : RABBIT

Bun·sen burner \'bən-sən-\ *n* : a gas burner usu. consisting of a straight tube with air holes at the bottom

¹bunt \'bənt\ *vb* 1 : ¹BUTT 2 : to push or tap a baseball lightly without swinging the bat

²bunt *n* : an act or instance of bunting; *also* : a bunted ball

¹bun·ting \'bən-tiŋ\ *n* : any of numerous small stout-billed finches

²bunting *n* : a thin fabric used esp. for flags; *also* : FLAGS

¹buoy \'bü-ē, 'bȯi\ *n* 1 : a floating object anchored in water to mark something (as a channel) 2 : a float consisting of a ring of buoyant material to support a person who has fallen into the water

²buoy *vb* 1 : to mark by a buoy 2 : to keep afloat 3 ♦ : to raise the spirits of — usu. used with *up*

♦ *usu* **buoy up** cheer, comfort, embolden, encourage, hearten, inspire, steel — more at ENCOURAGE

buoy·an·cy \'bȯi-ən-sē, 'bü-yən-\ *n* 1 : the tendency of a body to float or rise when submerged in a fluid 2 : the power of a fluid to exert an upward force on a body placed in it 3 : resilience of spirit

buoy·ant \-ənt, -yənt\ *adj* : having buoyancy: as **a** : capable of floating **b** ♦ : having or inducing high spirits

♦ blithe, bright, cheerful, cheery, chipper, gay, lightsome, sunny, upbeat — more at CHEERFUL ♦ bubbly, effervescent, exuberant, frolicsome, high-spirited, vivacious — more at EXUBERANT

¹bur \'bər\ *var of* BURR

²bur *abbr* bureau

¹bur·den \'bərd-°n\ *n* 1 **a** ♦ : something that is carried : LOAD **b** ♦ : a duty or obligation one must take care of : RESPONSIBILITY 2 : something oppressive : ENCUMBRANCE 3 : goods or merchandise loaded to be conveyed : CARGO; *also* : capacity for cargo

♦ [1a, 3] cargo, freight, haul, lading, load, payload, weight — more at LOAD ♦ [1b] charge, commitment, duty, need, obligation, responsibility — more at OBLIGATION

²burden *vb* ♦ : to encumber or oppress with something heavy, laborious, or disheartening

♦ depress, oppress, sadden — more at DEPRESS ♦ encumber, load, lumber, saddle, weight — more at LOAD

³burden *n* 1 ♦ : a phrase or verse recurring regularly in a poem or song : REFRAIN, CHORUS 2 : a main theme or idea : GIST

♦ chorus, refrain — more at CHORUS

bur·den·some \-səm\ *adj* ♦ : imposing or constituting a burden

♦ grim, hard, harsh, heavy, oppressive, rough, rugged, severe, stiff, tough, trying — more at HARSH ♦ arduous, challenging, demanding, exacting, grueling, laborious, onerous, taxing, toilsome — more at DEMANDING

bur·dock \'bər-ˌdäk\ *n* : any of a genus of coarse composite herbs with globe-shaped flower heads surrounded by prickly bracts

bu·reau \'byur-ō\ *n, pl* **bureaus** *also* **bu·reaux** \-ōz\ [F, desk, cloth covering for desks, fr. OF *burel* woolen cloth, ultim. fr. L *burra* shaggy cloth] **1** : a chest of drawers **2** ♦ : an administrative unit (as of a government department) **3** : a branch of a publication or wire service in an important news center

♦ department, desk, division, office — more at DIVISION

bu·reau·cra·cy \byu-'rä-krə-sē\ *n, pl* **-cies 1** : a body of appointive government officials **2** : government marked by specialization of functions under fixed rules and a hierarchy of authority; *also* : an unwieldy administrative system burdened with excessive complexity and lack of flexibility

bu·reau·crat \'byur-ə-ˌkrat\ *n* : a member of a bureaucracy — **bu·reau·crat·ic** \ˌbyur-ə-'kra-tik\ *adj*

bur·geon \'bər-jən\ *vb* **1** ♦ : to put forth fresh growth (as from buds) **2** ♦ : to grow and expand rapidly

♦ [1] bloom, blossom, blow, flower, unfold — more at BLOOM ♦ [2] accumulate, appreciate, balloon, build, enlarge, escalate, expand, increase, mount, multiply, mushroom, proliferate, rise, snowball, swell, wax — more at INCREASE ♦ [2] flourish, prosper, thrive — more at THRIVE

burgh \'bər-ō\ *n* : a Scottish town

bur·gher \'bər-gər\ *n* **1** ♦ : an inhabitant of a borough or a town **2** : a prosperous solid citizen

♦ townie; *also* denizen, dweller, inhabitant, occupant, national, native, resident

bur·glar·ize \'bər-glə-ˌrīz\ *vb* ♦ : to break into and steal from; *also* : to commit burglary

♦ rip off, rob, steal — more at ROB

bur·glary \'bər-glə-rē\ *n, pl* **-glar·ies** : forcible entry into a building esp. at night with the intent to commit a crime (as theft) — **bur·glar** \-glər\ *n*

bur·gle \'bər-gəl\ *vb* **bur·gled; bur·gling** : to commit burglary on

bur·go·mas·ter \'bər-gə-ˌmas-tər\ *n* : the chief magistrate of a town in some European countries

bur·gun·dy \'bər-gən-dē\ *n, pl* **-dies** *often cap* **1** : a red or white table wine from the Burgundy region of France **2** : an American red table wine

buri·al \'ber-ē-əl\ *n* ♦ : the act or process of burying

♦ entombment, interment, sepulture; *also* funeral *Ant* exhumation, unearthing

bur·ka *or* **bur·qa** \'bur-kə\ *n* : a loose garment that covers the face and body and is worn in public by certain Muslim women

burl \'bərl\ *n* : a hard woody often flattened hemispherical outgrowth on a tree

bur·lap \'bər-ˌlap\ *n* : a coarse fabric usu. of jute or hemp used esp. for bags

¹**bur·lesque** \(ˌ)bər-'lesk\ *n* [*burlesque*, adj., comic, droll, fr. F, fr. It *burlesco*, fr. *burla* joke, fr. Sp] **1** ♦ : a witty or derisive literary or dramatic imitative work **2** : broadly : humorous theatrical entertainment consisting of several items (as songs, skits, or dances)

♦ caricature, parody, spoof, takeoff — more at PARODY

²**burlesque** *vb* **bur·lesqued; bur·lesqu·ing** ♦ : to make ludicrous by burlesque

♦ caricature, imitate, mimic, mock, parody, take off, travesty — more at MIMIC

bur·ly \'bər-lē\ *adj* **bur·li·er; -est** ♦ : strongly and heavily built : HUSKY

♦ beefy, brawny, husky — more at HUSKY

Bur·mese \ˌbər-'mēz, -'mēs\ *n, pl* **Burmese** : a native or inhabitant of Burma (Myanmar) — **Burmese** *adj*

¹**burn** \'bərn\ *vb* **burned** \'bərnd, 'bərnt\ *or* **burnt** \'bərnt\; **burn·ing 1** ♦ : to be on fire **2** ♦ : to feel or look as if on fire **3** : to alter or become altered by or as if by the action of fire or heat **4** ♦ : to use as fuel ⟨~ coal⟩; *also* : to destroy by fire ⟨~ trash⟩ **5** : to cause or make by fire ⟨~ a hole⟩; *also* : to affect as if by heat **6** ♦ : to become emotionally excited or agitated **7** : to record (as music or data) on by means of a laser ⟨~ a CD⟩

♦ [1, 2] blaze, flame, flare, glow; *also* fire, ignite, kindle ♦ [4] fire, ignite, inflame, kindle, light; *also* char, scorch *Ant* douse, extinguish, put out, quench, snuff (out) ♦ [6] boil, fume, rage, seethe, steam — more at BOIL

²**burn** *n* : an injury or effect produced by or as if by burning

burn·er \'bər-nər\ *n* : the part of a fuel-burning or heat-producing device where the flame or heat is produced

burn·ing \'bər-niŋ\ *adj* **1 a** ♦ : being on fire **b** ♦ : affecting with or as if with heat **2** ♦ : existing in an extreme degree ⟨a ~ desire⟩

♦ [1a] ablaze, afire, fiery — more at ABLAZE ♦ [1b] broiling, fiery, hot, red-hot, scorching, sultry, torrid — more at HOT ♦ [2] ardent, charged, emotional, fervent, hot-blooded, impassioned, passionate, red-hot, vehement — more at FERVENT

bur·nish \'bər-nish\ *vb* ♦ : to make shiny esp. by rubbing : POLISH — **bur·nish·er** *n* — **bur·nish·ing** *adj or n*

♦ buff, dress, gloss, grind, polish, rub, shine, smooth — more at POLISH

bur·noose *or* **bur·nous** \(ˌ)bər-'nüs\ *n* : a hooded cloak worn esp. by Arabs

burn·out \'bər-ˌnaut\ *n* **1** : the cessation of operation of a jet or rocket engine **2** ♦ : exhaustion of one's physical or emotional strength; *also* : a person suffering from burnout

♦ collapse, exhaustion, fatigue, lassitude, prostration, tiredness, weariness — more at FATIGUE

burn out *vb* **1** : to drive out or destroy the property of by fire **2** ♦ : to cause to fail, wear out, or become exhausted esp. from overwork or overuse; *also* : to suffer burnout

♦ do in, drain, exhaust, fag, fatigue, tire, tucker, wash out, wear, wear out, weary — more at EXHAUST

burp \'bərp\ *n* : an act of belching — **burp** *vb*

burp gun *n* : a small submachine gun

burr \'bər\ *n* **1** *usu* **bur** : a rough or prickly envelope of a fruit; *also* : a plant that bears burs **2** : roughness left in cutting or shaping metal **3** : WHIR — **bur·ry** *adj*

bur·ri·to \bə-'rē-tō\ *n* [AmerSp, fr. Sp, little donkey, dim. of *burro*] : a flour tortilla rolled around a filling and baked

bur·ro \'bər-ō, 'bur-\ *n, pl* **burros** [Sp] : a usu. small donkey

¹**bur·row** \'bər-ō\ *n* ♦ : a hole in the ground made by an animal (as a rabbit)

♦ den, hole, lair, lodge — more at DEN

²**burrow** *vb* **1** : to form by tunneling; *also* : to make a burrow **2** : to progress by or as if by digging — **bur·row·er** *n*

bur·sar \'bər-sər\ *n* : a treasurer esp. of a college

bur·si·tis \(ˌ)bər-'sī-təs\ *n* : inflammation of the serous sac (**bur·sa** \'bər-sə\) of a joint (as the elbow or shoulder)

¹**burst** \'bərst\ *vb* **burst** *or* **burst·ed; burst·ing 1** ♦ : to fly apart or into pieces : to cause to burst **2** : to show one's feelings suddenly; *also* : PLUNGE ⟨~ into song⟩ **3** ♦ : to enter or emerge suddenly **4** : to be filled to the breaking point

♦ [1] blast, blow up, demolish, explode, pop, shatter, smash — more at BLAST ♦ *usu* **burst forth** [3] break out, erupt, explode, flame, flare, go off — more at ERUPT

²**burst** *n* **1 a** ♦ : a sudden outbreak : SPURT **b** ♦ : a vehement outburst (as of emotion) **2** : EXPLOSION **3** : result of bursting

♦ [1a] flare, flare-up, flash, flurry, flutter, outbreak, outburst, spurt — more at OUTBREAK ♦ [1b] agony, eruption, explosion, fit, flare, flare-up, flash, flush, gale, gush, gust, outburst, paroxysm, spasm, storm — more at OUTBURST

Bu·run·di·an \bu̇-'rün-dē-ən\ *n* : a native or inhabitant of Burundi

bury \'ber-ē\ *vb* **bur·ied; bury·ing** **1** : to deposit in the earth; *also* : to inter with funeral ceremonies **2 ♦** : to conceal from view or in obscurity : HIDE **3** : SUBMERGE, ENGROSS — usu. used with *in*

♦ cache, conceal, ensconce, hide, secrete — more at HIDE

¹bus \'bəs\ *n, pl* **bus·es** *or* **bus·ses** [short for *omnibus*, fr. F, fr. L, for all, dat. pl. of *omnis* all] : a large motor vehicle for carrying passengers

²bus *vb* **bused** *or* **bussed; bus·ing** *or* **bus·sing** **1** : to travel or transport by bus **2** : to work as a busboy

³bus *abbr* business

bus·boy \'bəs-ˌbȯi\ *n* : a waiter's helper

bus·by \'bəz-bē\ *n, pl* **busbies** : a military full-dress fur hat

bush \'bu̇sh\ *n* **1** : SHRUB **2 ♦** : rough uncleared country **3** : a thick tuft ⟨a ∼ of hair⟩ — **bushy** *adj*

♦ backwoods, frontier, hinterland, sticks, up-country — more at FRONTIER

bushed \'bu̇sht\ *adj* ♦ : drained of strength and energy : TIRED, EXHAUSTED

♦ beat, dead, drained, effete, jaded, limp, prostrate, spent, tired, weary, worn-out — more at WEARY

bush·el \'bu̇-shəl\ *n* **1** : a measure of dry capacity equal to 4 pecks **2 ♦** : a large quantity

♦ abundance, deal, gobs, heap, loads, lot, pile, plenty, quantity, scads — more at LOT

bush·ing \'bu̇-shiŋ\ *n* : a usu. removable cylindrical lining for an opening of a mechanical part to limit the size of the opening, resist wear, or serve as a guide

bush·mas·ter \'bu̇sh-ˌmas-tər\ *n* : a large venomous tropical American pit viper

bush·whack \-ˌhwak\ *vb* **1** : AMBUSH **2** : to clear a path through esp. by chopping down bushes and branches — **bush·whack·er** *n*

busi·ly \'bi-zə-lē\ *adv* : in a busy manner

busi·ness \'biz-nəs, -nəz\ *n* **1** : OCCUPATION; *also* : TASK, MISSION **2 a ♦** : a commercial or industrial enterprise **b ♦** : the dealings and transactions involved in buying and selling : TRADE ⟨∼ is good⟩ **3** : a subject under consideration : AFFAIR, MATTER **4** : personal concern

♦ [2a] company, concern, enterprise, establishment, firm, house, outfit — more at ENTERPRISE ♦ [2b] commerce, marketplace, trade, traffic — more at COMMERCE

busi·ness·man \-ˌman\ *n* : a man engaged in business esp. as an executive

busi·ness·per·son \-ˌpərs-ᵊn\ *n* : a businessman or businesswoman

busi·ness·wom·an \-ˌwu̇-mən\ *n* : a woman engaged in business esp. as an executive

bus·kin \'bəs-kən\ *n* **1** : a laced boot reaching halfway to the knee **2** : tragic drama

buss \'bəs\ *n* : KISS — **buss** *vb*

¹bust \'bəst\ *n* [F *buste*, fr. It *busto*, fr. L *bustum* tomb] **1** : sculpture representing the upper part of the human figure **2** : the part of the human torso between the neck and the waist; *esp* : the breasts of a woman

²bust *vb* **bust·ed** *also* **bust; bust·ing** **1 ♦** : to break or smash esp. with force; *also* : BURST **2 ♦** : to ruin financially **3** : TAME **4 ♦** : to reduce to a lower grade or rank : DEMOTE **5** *slang* : ARREST; *also* : RAID **6 ♦** : to strike heavily with or as if with the fist or a bat

♦ [1] break, burst, fracture, fragment — more at BREAK ♦ [2] ruin ♦ [4] break, degrade, demote, downgrade, reduce — more at DEMOTE ♦ [6] bash, bat, clobber, clout, hammer, hit, pound, punch, slug, strike, thump

³bust *n* **1** : a drinking session **2 ♦** : a complete failure

: FLOP **3** : a business depression **4** : a quick blow with or as if with the fist : PUNCH, SOCK **5** *slang* : a police raid; *also* : ARREST

♦ bummer, catastrophe, debacle, dud, failure, fiasco, fizzle, flop, lemon, loser, turkey, washout — more at FAILURE

¹bus·tle \'bə-səl\ *vb* **bus·tled; bus·tling** : to move or work in a brisk busy manner

²bustle *n* ♦ : briskly energetic activity

♦ commotion, disturbance, furor, hubbub, hullabaloo, pandemonium, tumult, turmoil — more at COMMOTION

³bustle *n* : a pad or frame worn to support the fullness at the back of a woman's skirt

¹busy \'bi-zē\ *adj* **busi·er; -est** **1 ♦** : engaged in action : not idle **2** : being in use ⟨∼ telephones⟩ **3 ♦** : full of activity ⟨∼ streets⟩ **4** : full of distracting detail ⟨a ∼ design⟩

♦ [1] active, assiduous, diligent, engaged, laborious, occupied, sedulous, working; *also* absorbed, concentrating, focused, engrossed, immersed, intent, preoccupied ♦ [3] alive, animated, astir, lively, vibrant — more at ALIVE

²busy *vb* **bus·ied; busy·ing** ♦ : to make or keep busy : OCCUPY

♦ absorb, engage, engross, enthrall, fascinate, grip, immerse, interest, intrigue, involve, occupy — more at ENGAGE

busy·body \'bi-zē-ˌbä-dē\ *n* ♦ : an officious or inquisitive person : MEDDLER

♦ interloper, intruder, kibitzer, meddler; *also* peeper, snoop, spy

busy·work \-ˌwərk\ *n* : work that appears productive but only keeps one occupied

¹but \'bət\ *conj* **1** ♦ : except for the fact ⟨would have protested ∼ that he was afraid⟩ **2** : THAT ⟨there's no doubt ∼ he won⟩ **3** : without the certainty that ⟨never rains ∼ it pours⟩ **4** : on the contrary ⟨not one, ∼ two job offers⟩ **5** : YET ⟨poor ∼ proud⟩ **6** : with the exception of ⟨none ∼ the strongest attempt it⟩

♦ except, only, yet — more at EXCEPT

²but *prep* ♦ : other than : EXCEPT ⟨this letter is nothing ∼ an insult⟩; *also* : with the exception of ⟨no one here ∼ me⟩

♦ aside from, bar, barring, besides, except, outside (of), save

³but *adv* **1** ♦ : being nothing more than **2** ♦ : to the contrary

♦ [1] just, merely, only, simply — more at JUST ♦ [2] howbeit, however, nevertheless, nonetheless, notwithstanding, still, though, withal, yet — more at HOWEVER

bu·tane \'byü-ˌtān\ *n* : either of two gaseous hydrocarbons used as a fuel

butch \'bu̇ch\ *adj* : notably masculine in appearance or manner

¹butch·er \'bu̇-chər\ *n* [ME *bocher*, fr. AF, fr. *buc* he-goat] **1** : one who slaughters animals or dresses their flesh; *also* : a dealer in meat **2** : one that kills brutally or needlessly **3** : one that botches

²butcher *vb* **1** : to slaughter and dress for meat ⟨∼ hogs⟩ **2** : to kill barbarously **3 ♦** : to foul up hopelessly : BOTCH ⟨the singer ∼ed the song⟩

♦ [2] massacre, slaughter — more at MASSACRE ♦ [3] bobble, botch, bungle, flub, foul up, fumble, mangle, mess up, screw up — more at BOTCH

butch·ery \-chə-rē\ *n* **1** : the preparation of meat for sale **2 ♦** : cruel and ruthless slaughter of human beings

♦ carnage, massacre, slaughter — more at MASSACRE

but·ler \'bət-lər\ *n* [ME *buteler*, fr. AF *butiller*, fr. OF *botele* bottle] : the chief male servant of a household

¹butt \'bət\ *vb* : to strike with the head or horns

²**butt** *n* : a blow or thrust with the head or horns
³**butt** *n* : a large cask
⁴**butt** *n* **1** : TARGET **2** ♦ : an object of abuse or ridicule **3** ♦ : the seat of the body : BUTTOCKS

♦ [2] laughingstock, mark, mock, mockery, target — more at LAUGHINGSTOCK ♦ [3] backside, bottom, buttocks, posterior, rear, rump, seat — more at BUTTOCKS

⁵**butt** *n* **1** : a large, thicker, or bottom end of something **2** : BUTTOCKS
⁶**butt** *vb* **1** : ABUT **2** : to place or join edge to edge without overlapping
butte \'byüt\ *n* : an isolated steep hill
¹**but·ter** \'bə-tər\ *n* [ME, fr. OE *butere*, fr. L *butyrum* butter, fr. Gk *boutyron*, fr. *bous* cow + *tyros* cheese] **1** : a solid edible emulsion of fat obtained from cream by churning **2** : a substance resembling butter — **but·tery** *adj*
²**butter** *vb* : to spread with or as if with butter
but·ter–and–eggs \ˌbə-tə-rə-'negz\ *n sing or pl* : a common perennial herb related to the snapdragon that has showy yellow and orange flowers
butter bean *n* **1** : LIMA BEAN **2** : WAX BEAN **3** : a green shell bean
butter cream *n* : a sweet butter-based mixture used esp. as a filling or frosting
but·ter·cup \'bə-tər-ˌkəp\ *n* : any of a genus of herbs having usu. yellow flowers with five petals and sepals
but·ter·fat \-ˌfat\ *n* : the natural fat of milk and chief constituent of butter
but·ter·fin·gered \-ˌfiŋ-gərd\ *adj* : likely to let things fall or slip through the fingers — **but·ter·fin·gers** \-gərz\ *n sing or pl*
but·ter·fly \-ˌflī\ *n* : any of a group of slender day-flying insects with broad often brightly-colored wings
but·ter·milk \-ˌmilk\ *n* : the liquid remaining after butter is churned
but·ter·nut \-ˌnət\ *n* : the sweet egg-shaped nut of an American tree related to the walnut; *also* : this tree
butternut squash *n* : a smooth buff-colored cylindrical winter squash
but·ter·scotch \-ˌskäch\ *n* : a candy made from brown sugar, corn syrup, and water; *also* : the flavor of such candy
butt in *vb* ♦ : to meddle in the affairs of others

♦ interfere, intrude, meddle, mess, nose, obtrude, poke, pry, snoop — more at INTERFERE

but·tock \'bə-tək\ *n* **1** : the back of a hip that forms one of the fleshy parts on which a person sits **2** *usu* **but·tocks** ♦ : the seat of the body : RUMP

♦ **buttocks** backside, bottom, butt, posterior, rear, rump, seat

¹**but·ton** \'bət-ᵊn\ *n* **1** : a small knob secured to an article (as of clothing) and used as a fastener by passing it through a buttonhole or loop **2** : something that resembles a button **3** : PUSH BUTTON **4** : a hidden sensitivity that can be manipulated to produce a desired response ⟨he is constantly pushing my ∼s⟩ **5** : a usu. box-shaped computer icon that when clicked initiates a software function
²**button** *vb* : to close or fasten with or as if with buttons
¹**but·ton·hole** \'bət-ᵊn-ˌhōl\ *n* : a slit or loop for a button to pass through
²**buttonhole** *vb* : to detain in conversation by or as if by holding on to the outer garments of
¹**but·tress** \'bə-trəs\ *n* [ME *butres*, fr. AF (*arche*) *boteraz* thrusting (arch), ultim. fr. *buter* to thrust] **1** : a projecting structure to support a wall **2** ♦ : something that supports or strengthens : SUPPORT

♦ dependence, mainstay, pillar, reliance, standby, support — more at DEPENDENCE ♦ brace, bulwark, mount, shore, stay, support, underpinning — more at SUPPORT

²**buttress** *vb* ♦ : to furnish or shore up with a buttress : SUPPORT

♦ bear, bolster, brace, carry, prop, shore, stay, support, uphold — more at SUPPORT

bux·om \'bək-səm\ *adj* : healthily plump; *esp* : full-bosomed
¹**buy** \'bī\ *vb* **bought** \'bȯt\; **buy·ing** **1** ♦ : to obtain for a price : PURCHASE; *also* : BRIBE **2** : to accept as true — **buy·er** *n*

♦ acquire, get, obtain, pick up, procure, purchase, secure, take

²**buy** *n* **1** : PURCHASE 1, 2 **2** ♦ : an exceptional value : BARGAIN

♦ bargain, deal, steal — more at BARGAIN

¹**buzz** \'bəz\ *vb* **1** : to make a buzz **2** ♦ : to fly fast and close to

♦ drone, hum, whir, whish, whiz, zip, zoom — more at WHIR

²**buzz** *n* **1** ♦ : a low humming sound **2** : RUMOR, GOSSIP

♦ drone, hum, purr, whir, whiz, zoom — more at HUM

buz·zard \'bə-zərd\ *n* : any of various usu. large birds of prey and esp. the turkey vulture
buzz·er \'bə-zər\ *n* : a device that signals with a buzzing sound
buzz saw *n* : CIRCULAR SAW
buzz·word \'bəz-ˌwərd\ *n* : a voguish word or phrase often from technical jargon
BV *abbr* Blessed Virgin
BVM *abbr* Blessed Virgin Mary
BWI *abbr* British West Indies
bx *abbr* box
BX *abbr* base exchange
¹**by** \'bī, bə\ *prep* **1** ♦ : in proximity to : NEAR ⟨stood ∼ the window⟩ **2** : through or through the medium of ⟨left ∼ the door⟩ **3** : into the vicinity of and beyond : PAST ⟨drove ∼ the house⟩ **4** : DURING, AT ⟨studied ∼ night⟩ **5** : no later than ⟨get here ∼ 3 p.m.⟩ **6** ♦ : through the means or direct agency of ⟨∼ force⟩ **7** : in conformity with; *also* : ACCORDING TO ⟨did it ∼ the book⟩ **8** : with respect to ⟨a vet ∼ profession⟩ **9** : to the amount or extent of ⟨won ∼ a nose⟩ **10** — used to express relationship in multiplication, in division, and in measurements ⟨divide *a* ∼ *b*⟩ ⟨multiply ∼ 6⟩ ⟨15 feet ∼ 20 feet⟩

♦ [1] about, around, near, next to — more at AROUND ♦ [6] per, through, with

²**by** \'bī\ *adv* **1 a** ♦ : near at hand **b** : at or to another's house : IN ⟨stop ∼⟩ **2** : PAST **3** : ASIDE, APART

♦ around, close, hard, in, near, nearby, nigh — more at NEAR

bye \'bī\ *n* : a position of a participant in a tournament who advances to the next round without playing
by–elec·tion *also* **bye–elec·tion** \'bī-ə-ˌlek-shən\ *n* : a special election held between regular elections in order to fill a vacancy
by·gone \'bī-ˌgȯn\ *adj* ♦ : gone by — **bygone** *n*

♦ dead, defunct, extinct, gone — more at EXTINCT

by·law *or* **bye·law** \'bī-ˌlȯ\ *n* : a rule adopted by an organization for managing its internal affairs
by–line \'bī-ˌlīn\ *n* : a line at the beginning of a news story or magazine article giving the writer's name
BYO *abbr* bring your own
BYOB *abbr* bring your own beer; bring your own booze; bring your own bottle
¹**by·pass** \'bī-ˌpas\ *n* : a passage to one side or around a blocked or congested area; *also* : a surgical procedure establishing this ⟨a coronary ∼⟩
²**bypass** *vb* ♦ : to avoid by means of a bypass

♦ circumvent, detour, skirt — more at DETOUR

by·path \-ˌpath, -ˌpáth\ *n* : BYWAY
by·play \'bī-ˌplā\ *n* : action engaged in on the side (as of a stage) while the main action proceeds
by–prod·uct \-ˌprä-(ˌ)dəkt\ *n* : a sometimes unexpected product or result produced in addition to the main product or result
by·stand·er \-ˌstan-dər\ *n* : one present but not participating

byte \\'bīt\ *n* : a group of 8 bits that a computer processes as a unit

by·way \\'bī-ˌwā\ *n* 1 : a little-traveled side road 2 : a secondary aspect

by·word \-ˌwərd\ *n* 1 ♦ : a proverbial saying : PROVERB 2 : one that is noteworthy or notorious

♦ adage, aphorism, epigram, maxim, proverb, saying — more at SAYING

Byz·an·tine \\'biz-ᵊn-ˌtēn, 'bī-, -ˌtīn; bə-'zan-, bī-\ *adj* 1 : of, relating to, or characteristic of the ancient city of Byzantium or the Byzantine Empire 2 *often not cap* : intricately involved and often devious

¹**c** \\'sē\ *n, pl* **c's** *or* **cs** \\'sēz\ *often cap* 1 : the 3d letter of the English alphabet 2 *slang* : a sum of $100 3 : a grade rating a student's work as fair

²**c** *abbr, often cap* 1 calorie 2 carat 3 Celsius 4 cent 5 centigrade 6 centimeter 7 century 8 chapter 9 circa 10 cocaine 11 copyright

C *symbol* carbon

ca *abbr* circa

Ca *symbol* calcium

CA *abbr* 1 California 2 chartered accountant 3 chief accountant 4 chronological age

cab \\'kab\ *n* 1 : a light closed horse-drawn carriage 2 : an automobile available on call to carry a passenger for a fare determined by a running meter or a flat rate : TAXICAB 3 : the covered compartment for the engineer and controls of a locomotive; *also* : a similar compartment (as on a truck)

CAB *abbr* Civil Aeronautics Board

ca·bal \kə-'bäl, -'bal\ *n* [F *cabale*, fr. ML *cabbala* cabala, fr. Heb *qabbālāh*, lit., received (lore)] ♦ : a secret group of plotters or political conspirators

♦ conspiracy, gang, mob, ring, syndicate — more at RING

cabala *var of* KABBALAH

ca·bana \kə-'ban-yə, -'ba-nə\ *n* : a shelter at a beach or swimming pool

cab·a·ret \ˌka-bə-'rā\ *n* : a place of entertainment open at night usu. serving food and liquor and often having a floor show : NIGHTCLUB

cab·bage \\'ka-bij\ *n* [ME *caboche*, fr. MF dial., lit., head, noggin] : a vegetable related to the mustard with a dense head of leaves

cab·bie *or* **cab·by** \\'ka-bē\ *n, pl* **cabbies** : a driver of a cab

cab·er·net sau·vi·gnon \ˌka-bər-'nä-sō-vē-'nyōⁿ\ *n* : a dry red wine made from a single variety of black grape

cab·in \\'ka-bən\ *n* 1 : a private room on a ship; *also* : a compartment below deck on a boat for passengers or crew 2 : the passenger or cargo compartment of a vehicle (as an airplane or automobile) 3 ♦ : a small simple one-story house

♦ camp, cottage, hut, hutch, shack, shanty — more at SHACK

cabin boy *n* : a boy working as a servant on a ship

cabin class *n* : a class of accommodations on a passenger ship superior to tourist class and inferior to first class

cabin cruiser *n* : CRUISER 3

cab·i·net \\'kab-nit\ *n* 1 ♦ : a case or cupboard for holding or displaying articles 2 : the advisory council of a head of state (as a president or sovereign)

♦ buffet, closet, cupboard, hutch, locker, sideboard; *also* bookcase, secretary; shelving; console

cab·i·net·mak·er \-ˌmā-kər\ *n* : a woodworker who makes fine furniture — **cab·i·net·mak·ing** *n*

cab·i·net·work \-ˌwərk\ *n* : the finished work of a cabinetmaker

¹**ca·ble** \\'kā-bəl\ *n* 1 ♦ : a very strong rope, wire, or chain 2 : a bundle of insulated wires usu. twisted around a central core 3 : CABLEGRAM 4 : CABLE TELEVISION

♦ cord, lace, line, rope, string, wire — more at CORD

²**cable** *vb* **ca·bled; ca·bling** : to telegraph by cable

cable car *n* : a vehicle moved by an endless cable

ca·ble·cast \\'kā-bəl-ˌkast\ *n* : a cable television transmission — **cablecast** *vb*

ca·ble·gram \\'kā-bəl-ˌgram\ *n* : a message sent by a submarine telegraph cable

cable modem *n* : a modem for connecting a computer to a network over a cable television line

cable television *n* : a system of television reception in which signals from distant stations are sent by cable to the receivers of paying subscribers

cab·o·chon \\'ka-bə-ˌshän\ *n* : a gem or bead cut in convex form and highly polished but not given facets; *also* : this style of cutting — **cabochon** *adv*

ca·boose \kə-'büs\ *n* : a car usu. at the rear of a freight train for the use of the train crew and railroad workers

cab·ri·o·let \ˌka-brē-ə-'lā\ *n* [F] 1 : a light 2-wheeled one-horse carriage 2 : a convertible coupe

cab·stand \\'kab-ˌstand\ *n* : a place where cabs wait for passengers

ca·cao \kə-'kaù, -'kā-ō\ *n, pl* **cacaos** [Sp, fr. Nahuatl *cacahuatl*] : a So. American tree whose seeds (**cacao beans**) are the source of cocoa and chocolate; *also* : its dried fatty seeds

cac·cia·to·re \ˌkä-chə-'tȯr-ē\ *adj* [It] : cooked with tomatoes and herbs ⟨chicken ∼⟩

¹**cache** \\'kash\ *n* [F] 1 : a hiding place esp. for preserving provisions 2 ♦ : something hidden or stored in a cache

♦ deposit, hoard, reserve, stash, stockpile, store — more at STORE

²**cache** *vb* ♦ : to place, hide, or store in a cache

♦ bury, conceal, ensconce, hide, secrete — more at HIDE

ca·chet \ka-'shā\ *n* [F] 1 : a seal used esp. as a mark of official approval 2 : a feature or quality conferring prestige; *also* : PRESTIGE 3 : a design, inscription, or advertisement printed or stamped on mail

¹**cack·le** \\'ka-kəl\ *vb* **cack·led; cack·ling** 1 : to make the sharp broken cry characteristic of a hen 2 : to laugh or chatter noisily

²**cackle** *n* ♦ : the action or noise of cackling

♦ chortle, laugh, laughter, snicker, titter — more at LAUGH

cack·ler *n* : one that cackles

ca·coph·o·nous \ka-'kä-fə-nəs\ *adj* ♦ : marked by cacophony

♦ discordant, dissonant, inharmonious, unmelodious, unmusical — more at DISSONANT

ca·coph·o·ny \ka-'kä-fə-nē\ *n, pl* **-nies** ♦ : harsh or discordant sound

♦ bluster, clamor (*or* clamour), din, noise, racket, roar — more at NOISE

cac·tus \\'kak-təs\ *n, pl* **cac·ti** \-ˌtī\ *or* **cac·tus·es** *also* **cactus** : any of a large family of drought-resistant flowering plants with succulent stems and with leaves replaced by scales or prickles

cad \\'kad\ *n* : a man who deliberately disregards another's feelings — **cad·dish** \'ka-dish\ *adj* — **cad·dish·ly** *adv* — **cad·dish·ness** *n*

ca·dav·er \kə-'da-vər\ *n* : a dead body esp. of a human being

ca·dav·er·ous \kə-'da-və-rəs\ *adj* ♦ : suggesting a corpse esp. in gauntness or pallor — **ca·dav·er·ous·ly** *adv*

♦ ashen, livid, lurid, pale, pasty, peaked — more at PALE ♦ gaunt, haggard, skeletal, wasted

cad·die *or* **cad·dy** \'ka-dē\ *n, pl* **caddies** [Sc, errand boy, modif. of F *cadet* military cadet] : a person who assists a golfer esp. by carrying the clubs — **caddie** *or* **caddy** *vb*

cad·dy \'ka-dē\ *n, pl* **caddies** [Malay *kati* a unit of weight] ♦ : a small box, can, or chest; *esp* : one to keep tea in

♦ box, case, casket, chest, locker, trunk — more at CHEST

ca·dence \'kād-ᵊns\ *n* ♦ : the measure or beat of a rhythmical flow : RHYTHM

♦ beat, measure, meter (*or* metre), rhythm — more at RHYTHM

ca·denced \-ᵊnst\ *adj* ♦ : marked by cadence

♦ measured, metrical, rhythmic — more at RHYTHMIC

ca·den·za \kə-'den-zə\ *n* [It] : a brilliant sometimes improvised passage usu. toward the close of a musical composition

ca·det \kə-'det\ *n* [F, fr. Occitan (Gascony) *capdet* chief, fr. L *capitellum*, fr. L *caput* head] 1 : a younger son or brother 2 : a student in a service academy

Ca·dette \kə-'det\ *n* : a member of a Girl Scout program for girls in sixth through ninth grades

cadge \'kaj\ *vb* **cadged; cadg·ing** : SPONGE, BEG ⟨~ a free meal⟩ — **cadg·er** *n*

cad·mi·um \'kad-mē-əm\ *n* : a bluish-white metallic chemical element used esp. in protective platings

cad·re \'ka-ˌdrā, 'kä-, -ˌdrē\ *n* [F] 1 : FRAMEWORK 2 : a central unit esp. of trained personnel able to assume control and train others 3 : a group of indoctrinated leaders active in promoting the interests of a revolutionary party

ca·du·ceus \kə-'dü-sē-əs, -'dyü-, -shəs\ *n, pl* **-cei** \-sē-ˌī\ [L] 1 : the staff of a herald; *esp* : a representation of a staff with two entwined snakes and two wings at the top 2 : an insignia bearing a caduceus and symbolizing a physician

cae·cum *var of* CECUM

Cae·sar \'sē-zər\ *n* 1 : any of the Roman emperors succeeding Augustus Caesar — used as a title 2 *often not cap* : a powerful ruler : AUTOCRAT, DICTATOR; *also* : the civil or temporal power

caesarean *var of* CESAREAN

cae·sura \si-'zhùr-ə\ *n, pl* **-suras** *or* **-su·rae** \-'zhùr-ˌ(ˌ)ē\ : a break in the flow of sound usu. in the middle of a line of verse

ca·fé \ka-'fā\ *n* [F, lit., coffee] 1 : a usu. small and informal establishment serving various refreshments (as coffee) : RESTAURANT 2 ♦ : a room or establishment whose main feature is a bar for the sale of liquor : BARROOM 3 ♦ : a place of entertainment open at night usu. serving food and liquor and providing music and space for dancing and often having a floor show : NIGHTCLUB

♦ [2] bar, barroom, pub, public house, saloon, tavern — more at BARROOM ♦ [3] disco, discotheque, nightclub — more at NIGHTCLUB

ca·fé au lait \(ˌ)ka-ˌfā-ō-'lā\ *n* : coffee with hot milk in about equal parts

caf·e·te·ria \ˌka-fə-'tir-ē-ə\ *n* [AmerSp *cafetería* coffeehouse] : a restaurant in which the customers serve themselves or are served at a counter

caf·fein·at·ed \'ka-fə-ˌnā-təd\ *adj* 1 : stimulated by or as if by caffeine 2 : containing caffeine

caf·feine \ka-'fēn, 'ka-ˌfēn\ *n* : a stimulating alkaloid found esp. in coffee and tea

caf·fe lat·te \'kä-fā-'lä-tā\ *n* [It] : espresso mixed with hot or steamed milk

caf·tan \kaf-'tan, 'kaf-ˌtan\ *n* [Russ *kaftan*, fr. Turk, fr. Pers *qaftān*] : an ankle-length garment with long sleeves worn in countries of the eastern Mediterranean

¹**cage** \'kāj\ *n* 1 ♦ : an openwork enclosure for confining an animal 2 : something resembling a cage

♦ coop, corral, pen, pound; *also* fence; cote, fold; aquarium, terrarium

²**cage** *vb* **caged; cag·ing** : to put or keep in or as if in a cage

ca·gey *also* **ca·gy** \'kā-jē\ *adj* **cag·i·er; -est** 1 : wary of being trapped or deceived : SHREWD 2 ♦ : marked by cleverness — **ca·gi·ly** \-jə-lē\ *adv*

♦ artful, crafty, cunning, devious, foxy, guileful, slick, sly, subtle, wily — more at ARTFUL

ca·gi·ness \-jē-nəs\ *n* ♦ : skill in devising or using indirect or subtle methods

♦ artfulness, artifice, canniness, craft, craftiness, cunning, guile, slyness, wiliness — more at CUNNING

CAGS *abbr* Certificate of Advanced Graduate Study

ca·hoot \kə-'hüt\ *n* : PARTNERSHIP, LEAGUE — usu. used in pl. ⟨officials in ~s with the underworld⟩

cai·man \'kā-mən; kā-'man, kī-\ *n* : any of several Central and So. American reptiles closely related to alligators and crocodiles

cairn \'karn\ *n* : a heap of stones serving as a memorial or a landmark

cais·son \'kā-ˌsän, 'kās-ᵊn\ *n* 1 : a usu. 2-wheeled vehicle for artillery ammunition 2 : a watertight chamber used in underwater construction work or as a foundation

caisson disease *n* : ²BEND 2

cai·tiff \'kā-təf\ *adj* [ME *caitif*, fr. AF *caitif, chaitif* wretched, despicable, fr. L *captivus* captive] : being base, cowardly, or despicable — **caitiff** *n*

ca·jole \kə-'jōl\ *vb* **ca·joled; ca·jol·ing** [F *cajoler*] ♦ : to persuade or coax esp. with flattery or false promises — **ca·jole·ment** *n* — **ca·jol·ery** \-'jō-lə-rē\ *n*

♦ coax, wheedle — more at COAX

Ca·jun \'kā-jən\ *n* : a Louisianan descended from French-speaking immigrants from Acadia (Nova Scotia) — **Cajun** *adj*

¹**cake** \'kāk\ *n* 1 : a baked or fried breadlike food usu. in a small flat shape 2 : a sweet baked food made from batter or dough usu. containing flour, sugar, or shortening, and a leaven (as baking powder) 3 : a hardened or compacted substance ⟨a ~ of soap⟩ 4 : something easily done ⟨the quiz was ~⟩

²**cake** *vb* **caked; cak·ing** 1 : to cover or overlay with or as if with a crust : ENCRUST 2 : to form or harden into a cake

cake·walk \'kāk-ˌwòk\ *n* 1 : a stage dance typically involving a high prance with backward tilt 2 : a one-sided contest or an easy task

cal *abbr* 1 calendar 2 caliber

Cal *abbr* 1 California 2 calorie

cal·a·bash \'ka-lə-ˌbash\ *n* : the fruit of a gourd; *also* : a utensil made from its hard shell

cal·a·boose \'ka-lə-ˌbüs\ *n* [Sp *calabozo* dungeon] : JAIL

ca·la·di·um \kə-'lā-dē-əm\ *n* : any of a genus of tropical American ornamental plants related to the arums

cal·a·mari \ˌkä-lə-'mär-ē\ *n* [It] : squid used as food

cal·a·mine \'ka-lə-ˌmīn\ *n* : a lotion of oxides of zinc and iron

ca·lam·i·tous \-təs\ *adj* ♦ : being, causing, or accompanied by calamity — **ca·lam·i·tous·ly** *adv* — **ca·lam·i·tous·ness** *n*

♦ cataclysmic, catastrophic, destructive, disastrous, fatal, fateful, ruinous, unfortunate — more at FATAL

ca·lam·i·ty \kə-'la-mə-tē\ *n, pl* **-ties** 1 : great distress or misfortune 2 ♦ : an event causing great harm or loss and affliction : DISASTER

♦ cataclysm, catastrophe, debacle, disaster, tragedy — more at DISASTER

calc *abbr* calculate; calculated

cal·car·e·ous \kal-'kar-ē-əs\ *adj* : resembling calcium carbonate in hardness; *also* : containing calcium or calcium carbonate

cal·cif·er·ous \kal-'si-fə-rəs\ *adj* : producing or containing calcium carbonate

cal·ci·fy \'kal-sə-ˌfī\ *vb* **-fied; -fy·ing** : to make or become calcareous — **cal·ci·fi·ca·tion** \ˌkal-sə-fə-'kā-shən\ *n*

cal·ci·mine \'kal-sə-ˌmīn\ *n* : a thin water paint used esp. on plastered surfaces — **calcimine** *vb*

cal·cine \kal-'sīn\ *vb* **cal·cined; cal·cin·ing** : to heat to a high temperature but without fusing to drive off volatile matter and often to reduce to powder — **cal·ci·na·tion** \ˌkal-sə-'nā-shən\ *n*

cal·cite \'kal-ˌsīt\ *n* : a crystalline mineral consisting of calcium carbonate — **cal·cit·ic** \kal-'si-tik\ *adj*

cal·ci·um \'kal-sē-əm\ *n* : a silver-white soft metallic chemical element occurring only in combination

calcium carbonate *n* : a substance found in nature as limestone and marble and in plant ashes, bones, and shells

cal·cu·late \'kal-kyə-ˌlāt\ *vb* **-lat·ed; -lat·ing** [L *calculare*, fr. *calculus* pebble (used in reckoning)] **1** ♦ : to determine by mathematical processes : COMPUTE **2** ♦ : to reckon by exercise of practical judgment : ESTIMATE **3** ♦ : to design or adapt for a purpose by forethought or careful plan **4** : COUNT, RELY — **cal·cu·la·ble** \-lə-bəl\ *adj* — **cal·cu·la·tor** \-ˌlā-tər\ *n*

♦ [1] compute, figure, reckon, work out; *also* conjecture, estimate, guess, judge, suppose; add up, sum, tally, total; add, cipher, divide, multiply, subtract; calibrate, gauge, measure, scale; ascertain, discover, dope (out), figure out, find out; recompute, refigure ♦ [2] call, conjecture, estimate, figure, gauge, guess, judge, make, place, put, reckon, suppose — more at ESTIMATE ♦ [3] arrange, blueprint, chart, design, frame, lay out, map, plan, project, scheme — more at PLAN

cal·cu·lat·ed \-ˌlā-təd\ *adj* **1** ♦ : undertaken after estimating the probability of success or failure ⟨a ∼ risk⟩ **2** ♦ : planned purposefully : DELIBERATE

♦ [1, 2] advised, deliberate, measured, reasoned, studied, thoughtful, thought-out — more at DELIBERATE

cal·cu·lat·ing \-ˌlā-tiṇ\ *adj* : marked by shrewd consideration esp. of self-interest — **cal·cu·lat·ing·ly** *adv*

cal·cu·la·tion \ˌkal-kyə-'lā-shən\ *n* **1** ♦ : the process or an act of calculating **2** : the result of an act of calculating **3** : studied care; *also* : cold heartless planning to promote self-interest

♦ arithmetic, computation, reckoning; *also* mathematics; addition, division, multiplication, subtraction; appraisal, assessment, estimation, evaluation, judgment

cal·cu·lus \'kal-kyə-ləs\ *n, pl* **-li** \-ˌlī\ *also* **-lus·es** [L, pebble (used in reckoning)] **1** : a method of computation or calculation in a special notation (as of logic) **2** : a branch of mathematics concerned with the rate of change of functions and with methods of finding lengths, areas, and volumes **3** : a concretion usu. of mineral salts esp. in hollow organs or ducts

cal·de·ra \kal-'der-ə, kȯl-, -'dir-\ *n* [Sp, lit., cauldron] : a large crater usu. formed by the collapse of a volcanic cone

cal·dron *var of* CAULDRON

¹cal·en·dar \'ka-lən-dər\ *n* **1** : an arrangement of time into days, weeks, months, and years; *also* : a sheet or folder containing such an arrangement for a period **2** ♦ : an orderly list

♦ agenda, docket, program, schedule, timetable — more at PROGRAM

²calendar *vb* : to enter in a calendar

¹cal·en·der \'ka-lən-dər\ *vb* : to press (as cloth or paper) between rollers or plates so as to make smooth or glossy or to thin into sheets

²calender *n* : a machine for calendering

ca·lends \'ka-ləndz, 'kā-\ *n sing or pl* : the first day of the ancient Roman month

ca·len·du·la \kə-'len-jə-lə\ *n* : any of a genus of yellow-flowered herbs related to the daisies

¹calf \'kaf, 'kȧf\ *n, pl* **calves** \'kavz, 'kȧvz\ **1** : the young of the domestic cow; *also* : the young of various large mammals (as the elephant or whale) **2** : CALFSKIN

²calf *n, pl* **calves** \'kavz, 'kȧvz\ : the fleshy back of the leg below the knee

calf·skin \'kaf-ˌskin, 'kȧf-\ *n* : leather made of the skin of a calf

cal·i·ber *or Can and Brit* **cal·i·bre** \'ka-lə-bər\ *n* [MF *calibre*, fr. It *calibro*, fr. Ar *qālib* shoemaker's last] **1** ♦ : degree of mental capacity, excellence, or importance **2** : the diameter of a projectile **3** : the diameter of the bore of a gun

♦ grade, quality, rate — more at QUALITY

cal·i·brate \'ka-lə-ˌbrāt\ *vb* **-brat·ed; -brat·ing** : to adjust precisely

cal·i·bra·tion \ˌka-lə-'brā-shən\ *n* : a set of graduated marks indicating values or positions — usu. used in pl.

cal·i·co \'ka-li-ˌkō\ *n, pl* **-coes** *or* **-cos** **1** : printed cotton fabric **2** : a mottled or spotted animal — **calico** *adj*

Calif *abbr* California

Cal·i·for·nia poppy \ˌka-lə-'fȯr-nyə-\ *n* : a widely cultivated herb with usu. yellow or orange flowers that is related to the poppies

cal·i·for·ni·um \ˌka-lə-'fȯr-nē-əm\ *n* : an artificially prepared radioactive chemical element

cal·i·per \'ka-lə-pər\ *n* **1** : any of various instruments having two arms, legs, or jaws used esp. to measure diameter or thickness — usu. used in pl. **2** : a device for pressing a frictional material against the sides of a rotating wheel or disk

ca·liph \'kā-ləf, 'ka-\ *n* : a successor of Muhammad as head of Islam — used as a title — **ca·liph·ate** \-lə-ˌfāt, -fət\ *n*

cal·is·then·ics \ˌka-ləs-'the-niks\ *n sing or pl* [Gk *kalos* beautiful +*sthenos* strength] : bodily exercises usu. done without apparatus — **cal·is·then·ic** *adj*

calk \'kȯk\ *var of* CAULK

¹call \'kȯl\ *vb* **1 a** ♦ : to speak in a loud distinct voice so as to be heard at a distance esp. in order to attract the attention of, summon, or make a request of another : SHOUT, CRY **b** : to utter a characteristic note or cry **2** : to utter in a loud clear voice **3** : to announce authoritatively **4** ♦ : to invite or command (a group) to meet : SUMMON **5** ♦ : to make a request or demand ⟨∼ for an investigation⟩ **6** : to halt (a baseball game or other public event) because of unsuitable conditions (as rain or darkness) **7** : to demand payment of (a loan); *also* : to demand surrender of (as a bond) for redemption **8** ♦ : to get or try to get in communication by telephone **9** ♦ : to make a brief stop or visit at a place ⟨*called* on a friend⟩ **10 a** ♦ : to speak of or address by name : give a name to **b** : regard as or characterize as of a certain kind : describe as **11** ♦ : to estimate or consider for practical purposes ⟨∼ it ten miles⟩ **12** : to temporarily transfer control of computer processing to (as a subroutine or procedure)

♦ [1a] bawl, cry, holler, shout, vociferate, yell; *also* bellow, roar; whoop; scream, screech, shriek, shrill, squeak, squeal; caterwaul, howl, wail, yawp, yowl ♦ [4] assemble, convene, convoke, muster, summon — more at CONVOKE ♦ [5] ask, insist, plead, press, quest, request, seek, solicit, sue ♦ [5] claim, clamor (*or* clamour), command, demand, enjoin, exact, insist, press, quest, stipulate (for) — more at DEMAND ♦ [8] dial, telephone; *also* buzz ♦ [9] drop (by *or* in), pop (in), stop (by *or* in), visit; *also* look up, see; frequent, hang around (in), hang out (at), haunt, resort (to) ♦ [10a] baptize, christen, denominate, designate, dub, entitle, label, name, style, term, title — more at NAME ♦ [11] calculate, conjecture, estimate, figure, gauge, guess, judge, make, place, put, reckon, suppose — more at ESTIMATE

²call *n* **1** : SHOUT **2** : the cry of an animal (as a bird) **3** : a request or a command to come or assemble : INVITATION, SUMMONS **4 a** ♦ : a calling on another for something due or supposed to be due : CLAIM **b** : an instance of asking for something : REQUEST **5** : a brief usu. formal visit **6** : an act of calling on the telephone : DECISION ⟨a tough ∼⟩ **8** : a temporary transfer of control of computer processing to a particular set of instructions

♦ claim, pretense, pretension, right — more at CLAIM

cal·la lily \'ka-lə-\ n : a plant related to the arums and grown for its large white lilylike bract that surrounds a fleshy spike of small yellow flowers

call·back \'kȯl-ˌbak\ n : a calling back; esp : RECALL 5

call–board \-ˌbȯrd\ n : a board for posting notices (as of rehearsal calls)

call down vb : REPRIMAND

call·er n ♦ : one that calls : a person who makes a brief visit

♦ guest, visitor

call girl n : a prostitute with whom appointments are made by phone

cal·lig·ra·phy \kə-'li-grə-fē\ n : artistic or elegant handwriting; also : the art of producing such writing — **cal·lig·ra·pher** \-fər\ n

call–in \'kȯl-ˌin\ adj : allowing listeners to engage in broadcast telephone conversations ⟨a ∼ show⟩

call in vb 1 : to order to return or be returned 2 : to summon to one's aid 3 : to report by telephone

call·ing \'kȯ-liŋ\ n 1 : a strong inner impulse toward a particular course of action 2 ♦ : the activity in which one customarily engages as an occupation

♦ employment, line, occupation, profession, trade, vocation, work — more at OCCUPATION

cal·li·ope \kə-'lī-ə-(ˌ)pē, 'ka-lē-ˌōp\ n [fr. Calliope, chief of the Muses, fr. L, fr. Gk Kalliopē] : a keyboard musical instrument similar to an organ and made up of a series of whistles

call number n : a combination of characters assigned to a library book to indicate its place on a shelf

call off vb ♦ : to give up (an undertaking or planned activity) : CANCEL

♦ abort, cancel, drop, recall, repeal, rescind, revoke — more at CANCEL

cal·los·i·ty \ka-'lä-sə-tē\ n, pl **-ties** 1 : the quality or state of being callous 2 : CALLUS 1

¹**cal·lous** \'ka-ləs\ adj 1 : being thickened and hardened ⟨∼ skin⟩ 2 ♦ : feeling no emotion or sympathy — **cal·lous·ly** adv — **cal·lous·ness** n

♦ hard, heartless, inhuman, inhumane, pitiless, soulless, unfeeling, unsympathetic — more at HARD

²**callous** vb : to make callous

cal·low \'ka-lō\ adj [ME calu bald, fr. OE] ♦ : lacking adult sophistication ⟨a ∼ youth⟩ — **cal·low·ness** n

♦ adolescent, green, immature, inexperienced, juvenile, raw; also babyish, childish, infantile; boyish, girlish, maidenly, virginal, youthful; ingenuous, innocent, naive (or naïve); unseasoned, untrained, untried Ant adult, experienced, grown-up, mature, ripe

call–up \'kȯl-ˌəp\ n : an order to report for active military service

call up vb : to summon for active military duty

cal·lus \'ka-ləs\ n 1 : a callous area on skin or bark 2 : tissue that is converted into bone in the healing of a bone fracture — **callus** vb

call–waiting n : a telephone service by which during a call in progress an incoming call is signaled (as by a click)

¹**calm** \'käm, 'kälm\ n 1 ♦ : a period or a condition free from storms, high winds, or rough water 2 : complete or almost complete absence of wind 3 ♦ : a state of tranquility

♦ [1, 3] calmness, hush, peace, placidity, quiet, quietness, repose, serenity, still, stillness, tranquility; also lull, pause, respite; silence; comity, concord, harmony Ant bustle, commotion, hubbub, hurly-burly, pandemonium, tumult, turmoil, uproar

²**calm** vb 1 ♦ : to make or become calm 2 ♦ : to make peaceful : induce quietude and repose in instead of agitation, passion, or excitement — often used with down

♦ [1, 2] allay, compose, quiet, settle, soothe, still, tranquilize; also alleviate, assuage, ease, mitigate, relieve;

appease, conciliate, mollify, pacify, placate; lull, relax, stupefy Ant agitate, discompose, disquiet, disturb, perturb, upset ♦ [2] collect, compose, control, settle — more at COLLECT ♦ usu **calm down** [2] cool (off or down), hush, quiet, settle (down) — more at QUIET

³**calm** adj 1 ♦ : marked by calm : STILL 2 ♦ : free from agitation, excitement, or disturbance ⟨a ∼ manner⟩

♦ [1, 2] collected, composed, cool, placid, self-possessed, serene, still, tranquil, undisturbed, unperturbed, unruffled, unshaken, untroubled, unworried; also imperturbable, nerveless, unflappable, unshakable; disciplined, self-contained; affable, breezy, easygoing, happy-go-lucky, laid-back; carefree, nonchalant, unconcerned; assured, confident, self-assured; aloof, detached, dispassionate, indifferent; impassive, phlegmatic, stolid Ant agitated, discomposed, disturbed, perturbed, upset ♦ [1, 2] halcyon, hushed, peaceful, placid, quiet, serene, still, tranquil, untroubled; also calming, pacific, restful, soothing; inactive, inert, quiescent, reposing, resting; smooth, unruffled; clear, cloudless, fair, sunny, sunshiny Ant agitated, angry, stormy, turbulent

calm·ly adv ♦ : in a calm manner : with calm

♦ quiet, quietly, still — more at STILL

calm·ness n ♦ : the quality or state of being calm

♦ aplomb, composure, coolness, equanimity, placidity, self-possession, serenity, tranquility — more at EQUANIMITY

cal·o·mel \'ka-lə-məl, -ˌmel\ n : a chloride of mercury used esp. as a fungicide

ca·lor·ic \kə-'lȯ-rik\ adj 1 : of or relating to heat 2 : of, relating to, or containing calories

cal·o·rie also **cal·o·ry** \'ka-lə-rē\ n, pl **-ries** : a unit for measuring heat; esp : one for measuring the value of foods for producing heat and energy in the human body equivalent to the amount of heat required to raise the temperature of one kilogram of water one degree Celsius

cal·o·rim·e·ter \ˌka-lə-'ri-mə-tər\ n : an apparatus for measuring quantities of heat — **cal·o·rim·e·try** \-trē\ n

cal·u·met \'kal-yə-ˌmet, -mət\ n : an American Indian ceremonial pipe

ca·lum·ni·ate \kə-'ləm-nē-ˌāt\ vb **-at·ed; -at·ing** : to make false and malicious statements about — **ca·lum·ni·a·tion** \-ˌləm-nē-'ā-shən\ n — **ca·lum·ni·a·tor** \-'ləm-nē-ˌā-tər\ n

cal·um·ny \'ka-ləm-nē\ n, pl **-nies** : false and malicious accusation — **ca·lum·ni·ous** \kə-'ləm-nē-əs\ adj

calve \'kav, 'käv\ vb **calved; calv·ing** : to give birth to a calf

calves pl of CALF

Cal·vin·ism \'kal-və-ˌni-zəm\ n : the theological system of John Calvin and his followers — **Cal·vin·ist** \-nist\ n or adj — **Cal·vin·is·tic** \ˌkal-və-'nis-tik\ adj

ca·lyp·so \kə-'lip-sō\ n, pl **-sos** : a style of music originating in the British West Indies and having lyrics that usu. satirize local personalities and events

ca·lyx \'kā-liks, 'ka-\ n, pl **ca·lyx·es** or **ca·ly·ces** \'kā-lə-ˌsēz, 'ka-\ : the usu. green or leaflike outer part of a flower consisting of sepals

cal·zo·ne \kal-'zōn, -'zō-nē\ n : a baked or fried turnover of pizza dough stuffed with cheese and various fillings

¹**cam** \'kam\ n : a rotating or sliding piece in a mechanical linkage by which rotary motion is transformed into linear motion or vice versa

²**cam** n : CAMERA

ca·ma·ra·de·rie \ˌkäm-'rä-də-rē, ˌkam-, -'ra-\ n [F] ♦ : friendly feeling and goodwill among comrades

♦ companionship, company, comradeship, fellowship, society — more at COMPANIONSHIP

cam·bi·um \'kam-bē-əm\ n, pl **-bi·ums** or **-bia** \-bē-ə\ : a thin cellular layer between xylem and phloem of most higher plants from which new tissues develop — **cam·bi·al** \-əl\ adj

Cam·bo·di·an \kam-'bō-dē-ən\ n : a native or inhabitant of Cambodia — **Cambodian** adj

Cam·bri·an \'kam-brē-ən, 'kām-\ *adj* : of, relating to, or being the earliest period of the Paleozoic era — **Cambrian** *n*

cam·bric \'kām-brik\ *n* : a fine thin white linen or cotton fabric

cam·cord·er \'kam-ˌkȯr-dər\ *n* : a small portable video camera and recorder

came *past of* COME

cam·el \'ka-məl\ *n* : either of two large hoofed cud-chewing mammals used esp. in desert regions of Asia and Africa for carrying and riding

camel hair *also* **camel's hair** *n* **1** : the hair of a camel or a substitute for it **2** : cloth made of camel hair or of camel hair and wool

ca·mel·lia \kə-'mēl-yə\ *n* : any of a genus of shrubs and trees related to the tea plant and grown in warm regions and greenhouses for their showy roselike flowers

Cam·em·bert \'ka-məm-ˌber\ *n* : a soft cheese with a grayish rind and yellow interior

cam·eo \'ka-mē-ˌō\ *n, pl* **-eos 1** : a gem carved in relief; *also* : a small medallion with a profiled head in relief **2** : a brief appearance esp. by a well-known actor in a play or movie

cam·era \'kam-rə, 'ka-mər-ə\ *n* : a device with a lightproof chamber fitted with a lens through which the image of an object is projected onto a surface for recording (as on film) or for conversion into electrical signals (as for television broadcast) — **cam·era·man** \-ˌman, -mən\ *n* — **cam·era·wom·an** *n*

Cam·er·oo·ni·an \ˌka-mə-'rü-nē-ən\ *n* : a native or inhabitant of the Republic of Cameroon or the Cameroons region — **Cameroonian** *adj*

cam·i·sole \'ka-mə-ˌsōl\ *n* : a short sleeveless garment for women

camomile *var of* CHAMOMILE

¹cam·ou·flage \'ka-mə-ˌfläzh, -ˌfläj\ *n* [F] **1** : the disguising of military equipment with paint, nets, or foliage; *also* : the disguise itself **2** ♦ : concealment by means of disguise **3** : deceptive behavior

♦ disguise, guise — more at DISGUISE

²camouflage *vb* ♦ : to conceal or disguise by camouflage

♦ cloak, disguise, dress up, mask — more at DISGUISE

¹camp \'kamp\ *n* **1** : a place where tents or buildings are erected for usu. temporary shelter; *also* : a building in such a place for occasional use **2** : a collection of tents or other shelters **3** : a program offering recreational activities (as boating and hiking) for a limited time ⟨summer ∼⟩ **4** : a body of persons encamped **5** : a training session for athletes outside of the regular season

♦ cabin, chalet, cottage, lodge — more at COTTAGE

♦ bivouac, encampment; *also* barracks; colony, plantation, settlement; concentration camp, prison camp

²camp *vb* **1** : to make or occupy a camp **2** : to live in a camp or outdoors

³camp *n* **1** : exaggerated effeminate mannerisms **2** : something so outrageous, inappropriate, or theatrical as to be considered amusing — **camp** *adj* — **camp·i·ly** \'kam-pə-lē\ *adv* — **camp·i·ness** \-pē-nəs\ *n* — **campy** \-pē\ *adj*

⁴camp *vb* : to engage in camp : exhibit the qualities of camp

cam·paign \kam-'pān\ *n* **1** : a series of military operations forming one distinct stage in a war **2** ♦ : a series of activities designed to bring about a particular result ⟨advertising ∼⟩ — **campaign** *vb*

♦ bandwagon, cause, crusade, drive, movement; *also* attack, march, offensive

cam·paign·er *n* ♦ : one that goes on, engages in, or conducts a campaign

♦ applicant, aspirant, candidate, contender, hopeful, prospect, seeker — more at CANDIDATE

cam·pa·ni·le \ˌkam-pə-'nē-lē\ *n, pl* **-ni·les** *or* **-ni·li** \-'nē-lē\ : a usu. freestanding bell tower

cam·pa·nol·o·gy \ˌkam-pə-'nä-lə-jē\ *n* : the art of bell ringing — **cam·pa·nol·o·gist** \-jist\ *n*

camp·er \'kam-pər\ *n* **1** : one who camps **2** ♦ : a portable

dwelling (as a specially equipped vehicle) for use during casual travel and camping

♦ caravan, motor home, trailer; *also* van

Camp Fire Girl *n* : a member of a national organization of girls from ages 5 to 18

camp follower *n* **1** : a civilian (as a prostitute) who follows a military unit to attend or exploit its personnel **2** : a follower of a group who is not an adherent; *esp* : a politician who joins a movement solely for personal gain

camp·ground \-ˌgrau̇nd\ *n* : the area or place used for a camp, for camping, or for a camp meeting

cam·phor \'kam-fər\ *n* : a gummy volatile aromatic compound obtained from an evergreen Asian tree (**camphor tree**) and used esp. in medicine

camp meeting *n* : a series of evangelistic meetings usu. held outdoors

camp·o·ree \ˌkam-pə-'rē\ *n* : a gathering of Boy Scouts or Girl Scouts from a given geographic area

camp·site \-ˌsīt\ *n* : a place suitable for or used as the site of a camp

cam·pus \'kam-pəs\ *n* [L, plain] : the grounds and buildings of a college or school; *also* : grounds resembling a campus ⟨hospital ∼⟩

cam·shaft \'kam-ˌshaft\ *n* : a shaft to which a cam is fastened

¹can \kən, 'kan\ *vb, past* **could** \kəd, 'ku̇d\ *pres sing & pl* **can 1** : be able to **2** : may perhaps ⟨∼ he still be alive⟩ **3** : be permitted by conscience or feeling to ⟨you ∼ hardly blame her⟩ **4** : have permission to ⟨you ∼ go now⟩

²can \'kan\ *n* **1** ♦ : a usu. cylindrical container or receptacle ⟨garbage ∼⟩ ⟨coffee ∼⟩ **2** : JAIL **3** : TOILET

♦ canister, drum, tin; *also* tube

³can \'kan\ *vb* **canned**; **can·ning 1** : to put in a can : preserve by sealing in airtight cans or jars **2** *slang* : to discharge from employment **3** *slang* : to put a stop or an end to — **can·ner** *n*

Can *or* **Canad** *abbr* Canada; Canadian

Canada Day *n* : July 1 observed as a legal holiday in commemoration of the proclamation of dominion status in 1867

Can·a·da goose \'ka-nə-də-\ *n* : a common wild goose of No. America

Ca·na·di·an \kə-'nā-dē-ən\ *n* : a native or inhabitant of Canada — **Canadian** *adj*

Canadian football *n* : a game resembling American football that is played on a turfed field between two teams of 12 players each

ca·naille \kə-'nī, -'näl\ *n* [F, fr. It *canaglia*, fr. *cane* dog] : RABBLE, RIFFRAFF

ca·nal \kə-'nal\ *n* **1** : a tubular passage in the body : DUCT **2** ♦ : an artificial waterway (as for boats or irrigation)

♦ aqueduct, channel, conduit, flume, raceway, watercourse — more at CHANNEL

can·a·lize \'kan-ᵊl-ˌīz\ *vb* **-lized**; **-liz·ing 1** : to provide with a canal or make into or like a channel **2** : to provide with an outlet; *esp* : to direct into preferred channels — **ca·nal·i·za·tion** \ˌkan-ᵊl-ə-'zā-shən\ *n*

can·a·pé \'ka-nə-pē, -ˌpā\ *n* [F, lit., sofa, fr. ML *canopeum*, *canapeum* mosquito net] : a piece of bread or toast or a cracker topped with a savory food

ca·nard \kə-'närd\ *n* : a false or unfounded report or story

ca·nary \kə-'ner-ē\ *n, pl* **ca·nar·ies** [fr. the *Canary* Islands] **1** : a usu. sweet wine similar to Madeira **2** : a usu. yellow or greenish finch often kept in a cage as a pet

ca·nas·ta \kə-'nas-tə\ *n* [Sp, lit., basket] : rummy played with two full decks of cards plus four jokers

canc *abbr* canceled

can·can \'kan-ˌkan\ *n* : a woman's dance of French origin characterized by high kicking

¹can·cel \'kan-səl\ *vb* **-celed** *or* **-celled**; **-cel·ing** *or* **-cel·ling** [ME *cancellen*, fr. AF *canceller*, *chanceller*, fr. LL *cancellare*, fr. L, to make like a lattice, fr. *cancelli* lattice] **1** ♦ : to destroy the force or validity of ⟨∼ a magazine subscription⟩ **2** ♦ : to match in force or effect : OFF-SET — often used with *out* **3** : to cross out : DELETE **4** : to remove (a common divisor) from a numerator and denominator; *also* : to remove (equivalents) on opposite sides of an equation or account **5** : to mark (a postage stamp or check) so that it cannot be reused **6** : to neutralize each other's strength or effect

♦ [1] abort, call off, drop, recall, repeal, rescind, revoke; *also* abrogate, annul, invalidate, nullify, void, write off; recant, retract, take back, withdraw; countermand, reverse; end, halt, stop, terminate; give up, relinquish, surrender **Ant** continue, keep ♦ *often* **cancel out** [2] annul, compensate, correct, counteract, counterbalance, make up, neutralize, offset — more at OFFSET

²**cancel** *n* **1** : CANCELLATION **2** : a deleted part
can·cel·er *or* **can·cel·ler** *n* ♦ : a force or influence that cancels out or offsets an opposing force

♦ balance, counterbalance, counterweight, equipoise, offset

can·cel·la·tion \ˌkan-sə-'lā-shən\ *n* ♦ : the act or an instance of canceling : the calling off of an arrangement

♦ abortion, calling, recall, repeal, rescission, revocation; *also* annulment, invalidation, neutralization, nullification; abolition, ending, halting, stopping, termination; giving up, relinquishment, surrender **Ant** continuation

can·cer \'kan-sər\ *n* [L, lit., crab] **1** *cap* : a zodiacal constellation between Gemini and Leo usu. pictured as a crab **2** *cap* : the 4th sign of the zodiac in astrology; *also* : one born under this sign **3** : a malignant tumor that tends to spread in the body; *also* : an abnormal state marked by such tumors **4** : a malignant evil that spreads destructively — **can·cer·ous** \-sə-rəs\ *adj* — **can·cer·ous·ly** *adv*
can·de·la·bra \ˌkan-də-'lä-brə, -'la-\ *n* : an ornamental branched candlestick or lamp with several lights
can·de·la·brum \-brəm\ *n, pl* **-bra** *also* **-brums** : CANDELABRA
can·did \'kan-dəd\ *adj* **1** ♦ : marked by honest sincere expression : FRANK, STRAIGHTFORWARD **2** : relating to photography of subjects acting naturally or spontaneously without being posed — **can·did·ly** *adv*

♦ direct, forthright, foursquare, frank, honest, open, outspoken, plain, straight, straightforward, unguarded, unreserved — more at FRANK

can·di·da·cy \'kan-də-də-sē\ *n, pl* **-cies** : the state of being a candidate
can·di·date \'kan-də-ˌdāt, 'ka-nə-, -dət\ *n* [L *candidatus*, fr. *candidatus* clothed in white, fr. *candidus* white; fr. the white toga worn by office seekers in ancient Rome] ♦ : one who seeks or is proposed for an office, honor, or membership

♦ applicant, aspirant, campaigner, contender, hopeful, prospect, seeker; *also* entrant, competitor, contestant; also-ran, dark horse, favorite, finisher, has-been, runner-up; nominee; claimant, pretender

can·di·da·ture \'kan-də-də-ˌchùr, 'ka-nə-\ *n, chiefly Brit* : CANDIDACY
can·did·ness \'kan-dəd-nəs\ *n* ♦ : the quality or state of being candid

♦ candor (*or* candour), directness, forthrightness, frankness, openness, outspokenness, plainness — more at CANDOR

can·died \'kan-dēd\ *adj* : preserved in or encrusted with sugar
¹**can·dle** \'kan-dᵊl\ *n* : a usu. slender mass of tallow or wax molded around a wick that is burned to give light
²**candle** *vb* **can·dled; can·dling** : to examine (as eggs) by holding between the eye and a light — **can·dler** *n*
can·dle·light \'kan-dᵊl-līt\ *n* **1** : the light of a candle; *also* : any soft artificial light **2** : the time when candles are lit : TWILIGHT
can·dle·lit \-ˌlit\ *adj* : illuminated by candlelight ⟨a ∼ dinner⟩

Can·dle·mas \'kan-dᵊl-məs\ *n* : February 2 observed as a church festival in commemoration of the presentation of Christ in the temple
can·dle·stick \-ˌstik\ *n* : a holder with a socket for a candle
can·dle·wick \-ˌwik\ *n* : a soft cotton yarn; *also* : embroidery made with this yarn usu. in tufts
can·dor \'kan-dər\ *or Can and Brit* **can·dour** *n* ♦ : unreserved, honest, or sincere expression : FRANKNESS

♦ candidness, directness, forthrightness, frankness, openness, plainness; *also* earnestness, sincerity, sobriety; artlessness, genuineness, naïveté, simplicity; bluntness; freedom, license, unrestraint **Ant** dissembling, pretense

C and W *abbr* country and western
¹**can·dy** \'kan-dē\ *n, pl* **candies** [ME *sugre candy*, fr. MF *sucre candi*, fr. OF *sucre* sugar + Ar *qandī* candied, fr. *qand* crystallized sugar] **1** : a confection made from sugar often with flavoring and filling **2** : something that appeals in a light or frivolous way
²**candy** *vb* **can·died; can·dy·ing** : to encrust in sugar often by cooking in a syrup
candy floss *n, Can and Brit* : COTTON CANDY
candy strip·er \-'strī-pər\ *n* : a teenage volunteer worker at a hospital
¹**cane** \'kān\ *n* **1** : a slender hollow or pithy stem (as of a reed or bramble) **2** : a tall woody grass or reed (as sugarcane) **3 a** : a walking stick **b** : a rod for flogging
²**cane** *vb* **caned; can·ing** **1** : to beat with a cane **2** : to weave or make with cane — **can·er** *n*
cane·brake \'kān-ˌbrāk\ *n* : a thicket of cane
¹**ca·nine** \'kā-ˌnīn\ *n* **1** : a pointed tooth between the outer incisor and the first premolar **2** : a canine mammal (as a domestic dog)
²**canine** *adj* [L *caninus*, fr. *canis* dog] : of or relating to dogs or to the family to which they belong
can·is·ter \'ka-nə-stər\ *n* ♦ : an often cylindrical container

♦ can, drum, tin — more at CAN

can·ker \'kaŋ-kər\ *n* : a spreading sore that eats into tissue — **can·ker·ous** \-kə-rəs\ *adj*
can·ker·worm \-ˌwərm\ *n* : either of two moths and esp. their larvae that are pests of fruit and shade trees
can·na \'ka-nə\ *n* : any of a genus of tropical herbs with large leaves and racemes of bright-colored flowers
can·na·bis \'ka-nə-bəs\ *n* : any of the psychoactive preparations (as marijuana) or chemicals (as THC) derived from hemp; *also* : HEMP
canned \'kand\ *adj* : prepared in standardized form for general use or wide distribution
can·nery \'ka-nə-rē\ *n, pl* **-ner·ies** : a factory for the canning of foods
can·ni·bal \'ka-nə-bəl\ *n* [NL *Canibalis* a member of a Caribbean Indian people, fr. Sp *Caníbal*] : one that eats the flesh of its own kind — **can·ni·bal·ism** \-bə-ˌli-zəm\ *n* — **can·ni·bal·is·tic** \-bə-'lis-tik\ *adj*
can·ni·bal·ise *Brit var of* CANNIBALIZE
can·ni·bal·ize \'ka-nə-bə-ˌlīz\ *vb* **-ized; -iz·ing** **1** : to take usable parts from (as an inoperative machine) to construct or repair another machine **2** : to practice cannibalism
can·ni·ness \'ka-nē-nəs\ *n* ♦ : skill in devising or using indirect or subtle methods

♦ artfulness, artifice, caginess, craft, craftiness, cunning, guile, slyness, wiliness — more at CUNNING ♦ acumen, astuteness, caginess, hardheadedness, intelligence, keenness, sharpness, shrewdness, wit — more at ACUMEN

can·non \'ka-nən\ *n, pl* **cannons** *or* **cannon** [ME *canon*, fr. AF, fr. It *cannone*, lit., large tube, fr. *canna* reed, tube, fr. L, cane, reed] : a large heavy gun; *esp* : one mounted on a carriage
can·non·ade \ˌka-nə-'nād\ *n* **1** : a heavy fire of artillery **2** ♦ : an attack (as with words) likened to artillery fire : BOMBARDMENT — **cannonade** *vb*

♦ barrage, bombardment, fusillade, hail, salvo, shower, storm, volley — more at BARRAGE

can·non·ball \'ka-nən-ˌból\ *n* : a usu. round solid missile for a cannon

can·non·eer \ˌka-nə-'nir\ *n* : an artillery gunner

can·not \'ka-ˌnät, kə-'nät\ : can not — **cannot but** : to be unable to do otherwise than ⟨we *cannot but* wonder why⟩

can·nu·la \'kan-yə-lə\ *n, pl* **-las** *or* **-lae** \-ˌlē\ : a small tube for insertion into a body cavity or into a duct or vessel

can·ny \'ka-nē\ *adj* **can·ni·er; -est** ♦ : marked by clever discerning awareness : SHREWD ⟨a *canny* lawyer⟩ — **can·ni·ly** \'kan-ᵊl-ē\ *adv*

♦ astute, hardheaded, knowing, sharp, shrewd, smart — more at SHREWD

ca·noe \kə-'nü\ *n* : a light narrow boat with sharp ends and curved sides that is usu. propelled by paddles — **canoe** *vb* — **ca·noe·ist** *n*

ca·no·la \kə-'nō-lə\ *n* : a rape plant producing seeds that are low in a toxic acid and yield an edible oil (**canola oil**) high in monounsaturated fatty acids; *also* : this oil

¹**can·on** \'ka-nən\ *n* **1** : a regulation decreed by a church council; *also* : a provision of canon law **2** : an official or authoritative list (as of works of literature) **3** : an accepted principle ⟨the ∼s of good taste⟩

²**canon** *n* : a member of the clergy on the staff of a cathedral

ca·non·i·cal \kə-'nä-ni-kəl\ *adj* **1** : of, relating to, or forming a canon **2** : conforming to a general rule or acceptable procedure : ORTHODOX **3** : of or relating to a canon of a cathedral — **ca·non·i·cal·ly** \-k(ə-)lē\ *adv*

can·on·ize \'ka-nə-ˌnīz\ *vb* **can·on·ized** \-ˌnīzd\; **can·on·iz·ing 1** : to declare (a deceased person) an officially recognized saint **2** ♦ : to treat as illustrious, preeminent, or sacred — **can·on·i·za·tion** \ˌka-nə-nə-'zā-shən\ *n*

♦ adore, deify, dote on, idolize, worship — more at IDOLIZE

canon law *n* : the law governing a church

can·o·py \'ka-nə-pē\ *n, pl* **-pies** [ME *canope*, fr. ML *canopeum* mosquito net, fr. L *conopeum*, fr. Gk *kōnōpion*, fr. *kōnōps* mosquito] **1** : an overhanging cover, shelter, or shade **2** : the uppermost spreading layer of a forest **3** : a transparent cover for an airplane cockpit **4** : the fabric part of a parachute — **canopy** *vb*

♦ ceiling, roof, tent; *also* screen, shade, shelter, shield, sunshade; canvas, fly

¹**cant** \'kant\ *vb* ♦ : to give a slant to

♦ angle, cock, heel, incline, lean, list, slant, slope, tilt, tip — more at LEAN

²**cant** *n* **1** : an oblique or slanting surface **2** ♦ : upward or downward slant or inclination or degree of slope : TILT, SLANT

♦ diagonal, grade, inclination, incline, lean, pitch, slant, slope, tilt, upgrade — more at SLANT

³**cant** *vb* **1** : to beg in a whining manner **2** : to talk hypocritically

⁴**cant** *n* **1** ♦ : the special idiom of a profession or trade : JARGON **2** ♦ : insincere speech; *esp* : insincerely pious words or statements

♦ [1] argot, jargon, language, lingo, slang, terminology, vocabulary — more at TERMINOLOGY ♦ [2] dissimulation, hypocrisy, insincerity, piety — more at HYPOCRISY

Cant *abbr* Canticle of Canticles

can·ta·bi·le \kän-'tä-bə-ˌlā\ *adv or adj* [It] : in a singing manner — used as a direction in music

can·ta·loupe *also* **can·ta·loup** \'kant-ᵊl-ˌōp\ *n* : MUSKMELON; *esp* : one with orange flesh and rough skin

can·tan·ker·ous \kan-'taŋ-kə-rəs\ *adj* : marked by ill humor, irritability, and determination to disagree : ILL-NATURED — **can·tan·ker·ous·ly** *adv* — **can·tan·ker·ous·ness** *n*

♦ bearish, bilious, disagreeable, dyspeptic, ill-humored, ill-tempered, ornery, splenetic, surly — more at ILL-TEMPERED

can·ta·ta \kən-'tä-tə\ *n* [It] : a choral composition usu. sung to instrumental accompaniment

canted *adj* ♦ : placed at an incline or given a degree of cant : SLANTED

♦ diagonal, inclined, listing, oblique, slantwise — more at DIAGONAL

can·teen \kan-'tēn\ *n* [F *cantine* bottle case, canteen (store), fr. It *cantina* wine cellar] **1** : a flask for carrying liquids **2** : a place of recreation and entertainment for military personnel **3** : a small cafeteria or counter at which snacks are served

can·ter \'kan-tər\ *n* : a horse's 3-beat gait resembling but smoother and slower than a gallop — **canter** *vb*

Can·ter·bury bell \'kant-ər-ˌber-ē-\ *n* : any of several plants related to the bluebell that are cultivated for their showy flowers

can·ti·cle \'kan-ti-kəl\ *n* **1** : SONG **2** ♦ : any of several liturgical songs taken from the Bible

♦ anthem, carol, chorale, hymn, psalm, spiritual — more at HYMN

Canticle of Canticles *n* : SONG OF SONGS

¹**can·ti·le·ver** \'kant-ᵊl-ˌē-vər\ *n* : a projecting beam or structure supported only at one end; *also* : either of a pair of such structures projecting toward each other so that when joined they form a bridge

²**cantilever** *vb* **1** : to support by a cantilever ⟨a ∼ed shelf⟩ **2** : to build as a cantilever **3** : to project as a cantilever

can·tle \'kant-ᵊl\ *n* : the upwardly projecting rear part of a saddle

can·to \'kan-ˌtō\ *n, pl* **cantos** [It, fr. L *cantus* song] : one of the major divisions of a long poem

can·ton \'kant-ᵊn, 'kan-ˌtän\ *n* : a small territorial division of a country; *esp* : one of the political divisions of Switzerland — **can·ton·al** \'kant-ᵊn-əl, kan-'tän-ᵊl\ *adj*

can·ton·ment \kan-'tōn-mənt, -'tän-\ *n* : usu. temporary quarters for troops

can·tor \'kan-tər\ *n* **1** : a choir leader **2** : a synagogue official who sings liturgical music and leads the congregation in prayer

Ca·nuck \kə-'nək *sometimes* -'núk\ *n* [origin unknown] : a Canadian and esp. a French Canadian

can·vas *also* **can·vass** \'kan-vəs\ *n* **1** : a strong cloth formerly much used for making tents and sails **2** : a set of sails **3** : a group of tents **4** : a piece of cloth prepared as a surface for painting; *also* : a painting on this surface **5** : the canvas-covered floor of a boxing or wrestling ring

can·vas·back \'kan-vəs-ˌbak\ *n* : a No. American wild duck with red head and gray back

¹**can·vass** *also* **can·vas** \'kan-vəs\ *vb* **can·vassed; can·vassing** ♦ : to go through (a district) or to (persons) to solicit votes or orders for goods or to determine public opinion or sentiment — **can·vass·er** *n*

♦ poll, solicit, survey; *also* interrogate, interview, question; feel (out), sound (out)

²**canvass** *n* : an act or instance of canvassing

can·yon \'kan-yən\ *n* ♦ : a deep narrow valley with high steep sides

♦ defile, flume, gap, gorge, gulch, notch, pass, ravine; *also* abyss, chasm, cirque, cleft, crevasse, crevice, fissure; dale, glen, hollow, vale, valley; basin, floodplain, plain; arroyo, coulee, gully, gutter

¹**cap** \'kap\ *n* **1** ♦ : a covering for the head esp. with a visor and no brim **2** ♦ : something that serves as a cover or protection esp. for a tip, knob, or end ⟨a bottle ∼⟩ **3** : a container holding an explosive charge **4** : an upper limit (as on expenditures)

♦ [1] hat, headgear — more at HAT ♦ [2] cover, lid, top — more at COVER

²**cap** *vb* **capped; cap·ping 1** : to provide or protect with a cap **2** : to form a cap over : CROWN ⟨snow-*capped* mountains⟩ **3** : OUTDO, SURPASS **4** ♦ : to provide a culminating event for : CLIMAX — often used with *off*

♦ *often* **cap off** climax, crown — more at CROWN

³**cap** *abbr* **1** capacity **2** capital **3** capitalize; capitalized

CAP *abbr* Civil Air Patrol
ca·pa·bil·i·ty \ˌkā-pə-ˈbi-lə-tē\ *n* **1 ♦** : the quality or state of being capable physically, intellectually, morally, or legally **2 ♦** : natural talent or acquired proficiency esp. in a particular work or activity

♦ [1] ability, capacity, competence, faculty — more at ABILITY ♦ [2] credentials, qualification, stuff — more at QUALIFICATION

ca·pa·ble \ˈkā-pə-bəl\ *adj* **♦** : having ability, capacity, or power to do something : ABLE, COMPETENT

♦ able, competent, fit, good, qualified, suitable — more at COMPETENT

ca·pa·bly *adv* **♦** : in a capable manner

♦ ably, adeptly, expertly, masterfully, proficiently, skillfully, well — more at WELL

ca·pa·cious \kə-ˈpā-shəs\ *adj* **♦** : able to contain much — **ca·pa·cious·ly** *adv* — **ca·pa·cious·ness** *n*

♦ ample, commodious, roomy, spacious — more at SPACIOUS

ca·pac·i·tance \kə-ˈpa-sə-təns\ *n* : the property of an electric nonconductor that permits the storage of energy
ca·pac·i·tor \kə-ˈpa-sə-tər\ *n* : an electronic circuit device for temporary storage of electrical energy
¹ca·pac·i·ty \kə-ˈpa-sə-tē\ *n, pl* **-ties** **1** : legal qualification or fitness **2** : the ability to contain, receive, or accommodate **3** : the maximum amount or number that can be contained **4 ♦** : an individual's mental or physical ability and skill in doing something : ABILITY **5 ♦** : position or character assigned or assumed ⟨is happy to serve in any ∼⟩

♦ [4] ability, capability, competence, faculty — more at ABILITY ♦ [5] appointment, billet, function, job, place, position, post, situation — more at JOB ♦ [5] function, job, part, place, position, purpose, role, task, work — more at ROLE

²capacity *adj* : equaling maximum capacity ⟨a ∼ crowd⟩
cap–a–pie *or* **cap–à–pie** \ˌka-pə-ˈpē\ *adv* [MF] : from head to foot : at all points
¹ca·par·i·son \kə-ˈpar-ə-sən\ *n* **1** : an ornamental covering for a horse **2 ♦** : rich clothing

♦ array, best, bravery, feather, finery, frippery, full dress, gaiety, regalia — more at FINERY

²caparison *vb* : to dress richly
¹cape \ˈkāp\ *n* **1 ♦** : a point of land jutting out into water **2** *often cap* : CAPE COD COTTAGE

♦ headland, peninsula, point, promontory, spit; *also* breakwater, jetty

²cape *n* : a sleeveless garment hanging from the neck over the shoulders
Cape Cod cottage \ˈkāp-ˈkäd-\ *n* : a compact rectangular dwelling of one or one-and-a-half stories usu. with a steep gable roof
¹ca·per \ˈkā-pər\ *n* : the flower bud or young berry of a Mediterranean shrub pickled for use as a relish; *also* : this shrub
²caper *vb* **ca·pered; ca·per·ing ♦** : to leap about in a playful manner

♦ cavort, disport, frisk, frolic, gambol, lark, rollick, romp, sport — more at FROLIC

³caper *n* **1** : a frolicsome leap **2 ♦** : a capricious escapade **3** : an illegal or questionable act

♦ antic, escapade, frolic, monkeyshine, practical joke, prank, trick — more at PRANK

cape·skin \ˈkāp-ˌskin\ *n* : a light flexible leather made from sheepskins
Cape Verd·ean \-ˈvər-dē-ən\ *n* : a native or inhabitant of the Republic of Cape Verde
cap·ful \ˈkap-ˌfu̇l\ *n, pl* **cap·fuls** *also* **caps·ful** \ˈkaps-\ : as much as a cap will hold
cap·il·lar·i·ty \ˌka-pə-ˈlar-ə-tē\ *n, pl* **-ties** : the action by which the surface of a liquid where it is in contact with a solid (as in a slender tube) is raised or lowered depending

on the relative attraction of the molecules of the liquid for each other and for those of the solid
¹cap·il·lary \ˈka-pə-ˌler-ē\ *adj* **1** : resembling a hair **2** : having a very small bore ⟨∼ tube⟩ **3** : of or relating to capillaries or to capillarity
²capillary *n, pl* **-lar·ies** : any of the tiny thin-walled blood vessels that carry blood between the smallest arteries and their corresponding veins
¹cap·i·tal \ˈka-pət-ᵊl\ *n* : the top part or piece of an architectural column
²capital *adj* **1** : conforming to the series A, B, C rather than a, b, c ⟨∼ letters⟩ ⟨∼ G⟩ **2** : punishable by death ⟨a ∼ crime⟩ **3** : most serious ⟨a ∼ error⟩ **4** : first in importance or position : CHIEF; *also* : being the seat of government ⟨the ∼ city⟩ **5** : of or relating to capital ⟨∼ expenditures⟩; *esp* : relating to or being assets that add to the long-term net worth of a corporation **6** : of the first order of size, importance, or quality : FIRST-RATE, EXCELLENT
³capital *n* **1 ♦** : accumulated wealth esp. as used to produce more wealth **2** : the total face value of shares of stock issued by a company **3** : persons holding capital **4** : ADVANTAGE, GAIN **5** : a letter larger than the ordinary small letter and often different in form **6 a** : the capital city of a state, province, or country **b** : a city preeminent in some activity ⟨the fashion ∼⟩

♦ assets, fortune, means, opulence, riches, substance, wealth, wherewithal — more at WEALTH

capital gain *n* : the increase in value of an asset (as stock or real estate) between the time it is bought and the time it is sold
capital goods *n pl* : machinery, tools, factories, and commodities used in the production of goods
cap·i·tal·ise *Brit var of* CAPITALIZE
cap·i·tal·ism \ˈka-pət-ᵊl-ˌi-zəm\ *n* : an economic system characterized by private or corporate ownership of capital goods and by prices, production, and distribution of goods that are determined mainly by competition in a free market
¹cap·i·tal·ist \-ist\ *n* **1** : a person who has capital esp. invested in business **2** : a person of great wealth : PLUTOCRAT **3** : a believer in capitalism
²capitalist *or* **cap·i·tal·is·tic** \ˌka-pət-ᵊl-ˈis-tik\ *adj* **1** : owning capital **2** : practicing or advocating capitalism **3** : marked by capitalism — **cap·i·tal·is·ti·cal·ly** \-ti-k(ə-)lē\ *adv*
cap·i·tal·iza·tion \ˌka-pət-ᵊl-ə-ˈzā-shən\ *n* **1** : the act or process of capitalizing **2** : the total amount of money used as capital in a business
cap·i·tal·ize *or Brit* **cap·i·tal·ise** \ˈka-pət-ᵊl-ˌīz\ *vb* **-ized; -iz·ing** **1** : to write or print with an initial capital or in capitals **2** : to convert into or use as capital **3 ♦** : to supply capital for **4 ♦** : to gain by turning something to advantage ⟨∼ on an opponent's mistake⟩

♦ [3] endow, finance, fund, stake, subsidize, underwrite — more at FINANCE ♦ *usu* **capitalize on** [4] abuse, cash in, exploit, impose, play, use — more at EXPLOIT

cap·i·tal·ly \ˈka-pət-ᵊl-ē\ *adv* : ADMIRABLY, EXCELLENTLY
cap·i·ta·tion \ˌka-pə-ˈtā-shən\ *n* : a direct uniform tax levied on each person
cap·i·tol \ˈka-pət-ᵊl\ *n* : the building in which a legislature holds its sessions
ca·pit·u·late \kə-ˈpi-chə-ˌlāt\ *vb* **-lat·ed; -lat·ing** **1 ♦** : to surrender esp. on conditions agreed upon **2 ♦** : to cease resisting

♦ [1, 2] blink, bow, budge, concede, give in, give up, knuckle under, quit, submit, succumb, surrender, yield — more at YIELD

ca·pit·u·la·tion \-ˌpi-chə-ˈlā-shən\ *n* **1 ♦** : the act of surrendering or yielding **2** : the terms of surrender

♦ relinquishment, submission, surrender — more at SURRENDER

cap·let \ˈka-plət\ *n* : a capsule-shaped medicinal tablet

ca·pon \'kā-ˌpän, -pən\ *n* : a castrated male chicken

cap·puc·ci·no \ˌka-pə-'chē-nō, ˌkä-\ *n* [It., lit., Capuchin; fr. the likeness of its color to that of a Capuchin's habit] : espresso mixed with foamy hot milk or cream and often flavored with cinnamon

ca·pric·cio \kə-'prē-chē-ˌō, -chō\ *n, pl* **-cios** [It., lit., whim, prank] : an instrumental piece in free form usu. lively in tempo and brilliant in style

ca·price \kə-'prēs\ *n* [F, fr. It *capriccio*] **1** ♦ : a sudden whim or fancy **2** : an inclination to do things impulsively **3** : CAPRICCIO

♦ fancy, freak, notion, vagary, whim — more at WHIM

ca·pri·cious \-'pri-shəs\ *adj* **1** ♦ : marked or guided by a sudden whim or fancy **2** ♦ : not guided by steady judgment or purpose — **ca·pri·cious·ly** *adv* — **ca·pri·cious·ness** *n*

♦ [1] impulsive, whimsical — more at WHIMSICAL
♦ [2] changeable, fickle, fluid, inconstant, mercurial, mutable, temperamental, uncertain, unpredictable, unsettled, unstable, unsteady, variable, volatile — more at FICKLE

Cap·ri·corn \'ka-pri-ˌkȯrn\ *n* **1** : a zodiacal constellation between Sagittarius and Aquarius usu. pictured as a goat **2** : the 10th sign of the zodiac in astrology; *also* : one born under this sign

cap·ri·ole \'ka-prē-ˌōl\ *n* : ³CAPER 1; *also* : an upward leap of a horse with a backward kick at the height of the leap — **capriole** *vb*

caps *abbr* **1** capitals **2** capsule

cap·sa·i·cin \kap-'sā-ə-sən\ *n* : a colorless compound found in various capsicums that gives hot peppers their hotness

cap·si·cum \'kap-si-kəm\ *n* : PEPPER 1

cap·size \'kap-ˌsīz, kap-'sīz\ *vb* **cap·sized; cap·siz·ing** : to turn over : UPSET, OVERTURN

cap·stan \'kap-stən, -ˌstan\ *n* **1** : a machine for moving or raising heavy weights that consists of a vertical drum which can be rotated and around which cable is turned **2** : a rotating shaft that drives recorder tape

cap·su·lar \'kap-sə-lər\ *adj* : of, relating to, or resembling a capsule

cap·su·lat·ed \-ˌlā-təd\ *adj* : enclosed in a capsule

¹cap·sule \'kap-səl, -sül\ *n* **1 a** : a membrane or sac enclosing a body part (as of a joint) **b** ♦ : a surrounding saclike structure that protects something held inside **2** : a case bearing spores or seeds **3** ♦ : a gelatin shell for packaging something (as a drug or vitamins) **4** : a small pressurized compartment or vehicle (as for space flight)

♦ [1b] armor, case, casing, cocoon, cover, housing, husk, jacket, pod, sheath, shell — more at CASE
♦ [3] pill, tablet

²capsule *adj* **1** ♦ : very brief **2** : very compact

♦ brief, compact, compendious, concise, crisp, epigrammatic, laconic, pithy, succinct, summary, terse — more at CONCISE

Capt *abbr* captain

¹cap·tain \'kap-tən\ *n* **1** ♦ : a commander of a body of troops **2** : a commissioned officer in the army, air force, or marine corps ranking next below a major **3** : an officer in charge of a ship **4** : a commissioned officer in the navy ranking next below a rear admiral or a commodore **5** ♦ : one who leads or supervises (as a sports team or work crew) **6** : a dominant figure — **cap·tain·cy** *n*

♦ [1] commander — more at COMMANDER ♦ [5] boss, chief, foreman, head, headman, helmsman, kingpin, leader, master, taskmaster — more at BOSS

²captain *vb* ♦ : to be or fill the role of captain ⟨~ed the football team⟩

♦ boss, head, oversee, superintend, supervise — more at BOSS ♦ boss, command, control, govern, preside, rule — more at GOVERN ♦ boss, command, dominate, head, lead, spearhead — more at LEAD

cap·tion \'kap-shən\ *n* **1** : a heading esp. of an article or

document : TITLE **2** : the explanatory matter accompanying an illustration **3** : a motion-picture subtitle — **cap·tion** *vb*

cap·tious \'kap-shəs\ *adj* ♦ : marked by an inclination to find fault — **cap·tious·ly** *adv* — **cap·tious·ness** *n*

♦ carping, critical, hypercritical, overcritical — more at CRITICAL

cap·ti·vate \'kap-tə-ˌvāt\ *vb* **-vat·ed; -vat·ing** ♦ : to attract and hold irresistibly by some special charm or art — **cap·ti·va·tor** \'kap-tə-ˌvā-tər\ *n*

♦ allure, beguile, bewitch, charm, enchant, fascinate, wile — more at CHARM

cap·ti·vat·ing *adj* ♦ : having the ability to captivate : CHARMING

♦ alluring, attractive, charming, elfin, engaging, fascinating, fetching, glamorous, magnetic, seductive — more at FASCINATING

cap·ti·va·tion \ˌkap-tə-'vā-shən\ *n* ♦ : the action or power of influencing and dominating by some special charm or irresistible appeal

♦ allure, appeal, attractiveness, charisma, charm, enchantment, fascination, glamour, magic, magnetism — more at CHARM

¹cap·tive \'kap-tiv\ *adj* **1** : made prisoner esp. in war **2** : kept within bounds : CONFINED **3** : held under control

²captive *n* ♦ : one captured and held prisoner

♦ capture, internee, prisoner; *also* convict, jailbird; parolee *Ant* captor

cap·tiv·i·ty \kap-'ti-və-tē\ *n* ♦ : state or condition of being held captive esp. in war

♦ confinement, imprisonment, incarceration, internment — more at INTERNMENT

cap·tor \'kap-tər\ *n* : one that captures

¹cap·ture \'kap-chər\ *n* **1** : the act of capturing **2** : one that has been captured

²capture *vb* **cap·tured; cap·tur·ing 1 a** ♦ : to take, seize, or catch esp. as captive or prize by effort or skill **b** : to take control of esp. by force ⟨~ the city⟩ **c** ♦ : to gain or win esp. through effort **2** : to preserve in a relatively permanent form

♦ [1a] bag, catch, collar, corral, get, grab, grapple, hook, land, nab, seize, snare, trap — more at CATCH ♦ [1c] acquire, attain, carry, draw, earn, gain, garner, get, land, make, obtain, procure, realize, secure, win — more at EARN

Ca·pu·chin \'ka-pyə-shən\ *n* : a member of an austere branch of the order of St. Francis of Assisi engaged in missionary work and preaching

car \'kär\ *n* **1** ♦ : a vehicle moving on wheels **2** : the compartment of an elevator **3** : the part of a balloon or airship that carries passengers or equipment

♦ automobile, machine, motor vehicle; *also* bus, coach, minibus; beach buggy, brougham, compact, convertible, coupe, dune buggy, fastback, hardtop, hatchback, hot rod, jeep, limousine, roadster, sedan, sports car, station wagon, stock car, subcompact, van; flivver, jalopy

car·a·cole \'kar-ə-ˌkōl\ *n* : a half turn to right or left executed by a mounted horse — **caracole** *vb*

car·a·cul \'kar-ə-ˌkəl\ *n* : the pelt of a karakul lamb after the curl begins to loosen

ca·rafe \kə-'raf, -'räf\ *n* **1** : a bottle with a flaring lip used esp. to hold wine **2** : a usu. glass pitcher for pouring coffee

car·am·bo·la \ˌkar-əm-'bō-lə\ *n* **1** : a five-angled green to yellow edible tropical fruit of star-shaped cross section **2** : a tropical Asian tree widely cultivated for carambolas

car·a·mel \'kar-ə-məl, 'kär-məl\ *n* **1** : an amorphous substance obtained by heating sugar and used for flavoring and coloring **2** : a firm chewy candy

car·a·pace \'kar-ə-ˌpās\ *n* : a protective case or shell on the back of some animals (as turtles or crabs)

¹carat *var of* KARAT

²**car·at** \'kar-ət\ n : a unit of weight for precious stones equal to 200 milligrams

car·a·van \'kar-ə-,van\ n 1 : a group of travelers journeying together through desert or hostile regions 2 ♦ : a group of vehicles traveling in a file 3 ♦ : a covered wagon or motortruck equipped as traveling living quarters

♦ [2] armada, cavalcade, fleet, motorcade, train — more at FLEET ♦ [3] camper, motor home, trailer — more at CAMPER

car·a·van·sa·ry \,kar-ə-'van-sə-rē\ or **car·a·van·se·rai** \-sə-,rī\ n, pl **-ries** or **-rais** or **-rai** [Pers kārvānsarāī, fr. kārvān caravan + sarāī palace, inn] 1 : an inn in eastern countries where caravans rest at night 2 : an establishment that provides lodging and usu. meals for the public : HOTEL, INN

car·a·vel \'kar-ə-,vel\ n : a small 15th and 16th century ship with a broad bow, high narrow poop, and usu. three masts

car·a·way \'kar-ə-,wā\ n : an aromatic herb related to the carrot with fruits (**caraway seed**) used in seasoning and medicine; also : its fruit

car·bide \'kär-,bīd\ n : a compound of carbon with another element

car·bine \'kär-,bēn, -,bīn\ n : a short-barreled lightweight rifle

car·bo·hy·drate \,kär-bō-'hī-,drāt, -drət\ n : any of various compounds composed of carbon, hydrogen, and oxygen (as sugars and starches)

car·bol·ic acid \,kär-'bä-lik-\ n : PHENOL

car·bon \'kär-bən\ n 1 : a nonmetallic chemical element occurring in nature esp. as diamond and graphite and as a constituent of coal, petroleum, and limestone 2 : a sheet of carbon paper; also : CARBON COPY 1 — **car·bon·less** \-ləs\ adj

car·bo·na·ceous \,kär-bə-'nā-shəs\ adj : relating to, containing, or composed of carbon

¹**car·bon·ate** \'kär-bə-,nāt, -nət\ n : a salt or ester of carbonic acid

²**car·bon·ate** \-,nāt\ vb **-at·ed; -at·ing** : to combine or infuse with carbon dioxide ⟨carbonated beverages⟩ — **car·bon·ation** \,kär-bə-'nā-shən\ n

carbon black n : any of various black substances consisting chiefly of carbon and used esp. as pigments

carbon copy n 1 : a copy made by carbon paper 2 ♦ : one that strongly resembles or closely corresponds to another : DUPLICATE

♦ counterpart, double, duplicate, duplication, facsimile, image, likeness, match, picture, replica, ringer, spit — more at IMAGE

carbon dating n : the determination of the age of old material (as an archaeological specimen) by its content of carbon 14

carbon dioxide n : a heavy colorless gas that does not support combustion and is formed in animal respiration and in the combustion and decomposition of organic substances

carbon footprint n : the amount of carbon dioxide emitted by something in a given period

carbon 14 n : a heavy radioactive form of carbon used esp. in dating archaeological materials

car·bon·ic acid \kär-'bä-nik-\ n : a weak acid that decomposes readily into water and carbon dioxide

car·bon·if·er·ous \,kär-bə-'ni-fə-rəs\ adj 1 : producing or containing carbon or coal 2 cap : of, relating to, or being the period of the Paleozoic era between the Devonian and the Permian — **Carboniferous** n

carbon monoxide n : a colorless odorless very poisonous gas formed by the incomplete burning of carbon

carbon paper n : a thin paper coated with a pigment and used for making copies

carbon tet·ra·chlo·ride \-,te-trə-'klōr-,īd\ n : a colorless nonflammable toxic liquid used esp. as a solvent

carbon 12 n : the most abundant isotope of carbon having

a nucleus of 6 protons and 6 neutrons and used as a standard for measurements of atomic weight

car·boy \'kär-,bói\ n [Pers qarāba, fr. Ar qarrāba demijohn] : a large container for liquids

car·bun·cle \'kär-,bən-kəl\ n : a painful inflammation of the skin and underlying tissue that discharges pus from several openings

car·bu·re·tor \'kär-bə-,rā-tər, -byə-\ n : an apparatus for premixing vaporized fuel and air and supplying the mixture to an internal combustion engine

car·cass \'kär-kəs\ n : a dead body; esp : one of an animal dressed for food

car·cin·o·gen \kär-'si-nə-jən\ n : an agent causing or inciting cancer — **car·ci·no·gen·ic** \,kärs-³n-ō-'je-nik\ adj — **car·ci·no·ge·nic·i·ty** \-jə-³ni-sə-tē\ n

car·ci·no·ma \,kärs-³n-'ō-mə\ n, pl **-mas** also **-ma·ta** \-tə\ : a malignant tumor of epithelial origin — **car·ci·no·ma·tous** \-təs\ adj

¹**card** \'kärd\ vb : to comb with a card : cleanse and untangle before spinning — **card·er** n

²**card** n : an instrument for combing fibers (as wool or cotton)

³**card** n 1 : PLAYING CARD 2 pl : a game played with playing cards; also : card playing 3 : an emotional issue used to one's advantage (as in a political campaign) 4 ♦ : a usu. clownishly amusing person : WAG 5 : a flat stiff usu. small piece of paper, cardboard, or plastic often bearing pictures or information 6 : PROGRAM; esp : a sports program

♦ comedian, comic, humorist, jester, joker, wag, wit — more at HUMORIST

⁴**card** vb 1 : to list or schedule on a card 2 : SCORE 3 : to ask for identification (as at a bar)

⁵**card** abbr cardinal

car·da·mom \'kär-də-məm\ n : the aromatic capsular fruit of an East Indian herb related to the ginger whose seeds are used as a spice or condiment and in medicine; also : this plant

card·board \'kärd-,bōrd\ n : a material thicker than paper and made from cellulose fiber

card–car·ry·ing \'kärd-,kar-ē-iŋ\ adj : being a regularly enrolled member of an organization (as a political party)

card catalog n : a catalog (as of books) in which the entries are arranged systematically on cards

car·di·ac \'kär-dē-,ak\ adj [L cardiacus, fr. Gk kardiakos, fr. kardia heart] 1 : of, relating to, or located near the heart 2 : of, relating to, or affected with heart disease

car·di·gan \'kär-di-gən\ n : a sweater or jacket usu. without a collar and with a full-length opening in the front

¹**car·di·nal** \'kärd-nəl, 'kär-d³n-əl\ n 1 : an ecclesiastical official of the Roman Catholic Church ranking next below the pope 2 : a crested No. American finch that is nearly completely red in the male

²**cardinal** adj [ME, fr. LL cardinalis, fr. L serving as a hinge, fr. cardo hinge] 1 ♦ : of basic importance : CHIEF, MAIN, PRIMARY 2 : very serious ⟨a ∼ sin⟩ — **car·di·nal·ly** adv

♦ arch, central, chief, dominant, first, foremost, grand, key, main, paramount, predominant, preeminent, premier, primary, principal, sovereign, supreme — more at FOREMOST

car·di·nal·ate \'kärd-nə-lət, 'kär-d³n-ə-let, -,lāt\ n : the office, rank, or dignity of a cardinal

cardinal flower n : a No. American plant that bears a spike of brilliant red flowers

cardinal number n : a number (as 1, 5, 82, 357) that is used in simple counting and answers the question "how many?"

cardinal point n : one of the four principal compass points north, south, east, and west

car·dio \'kär-dē-ō\ adj : CARDIOVASCULAR 2

car·di·ol·o·gy \,kär-dē-'ä-lə-jē\ n : the study of the heart and its action and diseases — **car·di·ol·o·gist** \-jist\ n

car·dio·pul·mo·nary resuscitation \‚kär-dē-ō-'púl-mə-‚ner-ē-\ *n* : a procedure to restore normal breathing after cardiac arrest that includes the clearance of air passages to the lungs, mouth-to-mouth method of artificial respiration, and heart massage by the exertion of pressure on the chest

car·dio·vas·cu·lar \-'vas-kyə-lər\ *adj* **1** : of or relating to the heart and blood vessels **2** : causing a temporary increase in heart rate ⟨a ~ workout⟩

card·sharp·er \'kärd-‚shär-pər\ *or* **card·sharp** \-‚shärp\ *n* : a cheater at cards

¹care \'ker\ *n* **1** : a disquieted state of uncertainty and responsibility : ANXIETY **2** ♦ : painstaking or watchful attention **3** ♦ : responsibility for the care of another ⟨under a doctor's ~⟩ **4** : a person or thing that is an object of attention, anxiety, or solicitude

♦ [2] alertness, carefulness, caution, circumspection, heedfulness — more at CAUTION ♦ [2] carefulness, heed, heedfulness, pains, scrupulousness; *also* exactness, meticulousness, particularity; dutifulness, responsibility; bother, effort, trouble; alertness, vigilance, watchfulness *Ant* carelessness, heedlessness ♦ [3] custody, guardianship, keeping, safekeeping, trust, ward — more at CUSTODY ♦ [3] charge, guidance, headship, oversight, regulation, superintendence, supervision — more at SUPERVISION

²care *vb* **cared; car·ing** **1** : to feel trouble or anxiety **2** : to feel interest or concern ⟨~ about freedom⟩ **3** ♦ : to give care — usu. used with *for* ⟨~ for the sick⟩ **4 a** ♦ : to have a liking, fondness, taste, or inclination **b** : have regard or respect **5** : to be concerned about ⟨nobody ~s what I do⟩ **6** : to have or express a wish for — usu. used with *for*

♦ *usu* care for [3] aid, minister, mother, nurse — more at NURSE ♦ *usu* care for [3] attend, mind, oversee, superintend, supervise, tend — more at TEND ♦ *usu* care for [4a] accept, approve, countenance, favor (*or* favour), OK, subscribe

CARE *abbr* Cooperative for American Relief to Everywhere

ca·reen \kə-'rēn\ *vb* **1** : to put (a ship or boat) on a beach esp. in order to clean or repair its hull **2** ♦ : to sway from side to side **3** : CAREER

♦ lurch, pitch, rock, roll, seesaw, sway, toss, wobble — more at ROCK

¹ca·reer \kə-'rir\ *n* [MF *carrière*, fr. Old Occitan *carriera* street, fr. ML *carraria* road for vehicles, fr. L *carrus* car] **1** : COURSE, PASSAGE; *also* : speed in a course ⟨ran at full ~⟩ **2** : an occupation or profession followed as a life's work

²career *vb* ♦ : to go at top speed esp. in a headlong manner

♦ barrel, bowl, fly, hurry, hurtle, pelt, race, rocket, rush, shoot, speed, tear, zip, zoom — more at HURRY

care·free \'ker-‚frē\ *adj* ♦ : free from care or worry

♦ careless, cavalier, easygoing, gay, happy-go-lucky, insouciant, lighthearted, unconcerned; *also* breezy, nonchalant; casual, informal, laid-back, relaxed; heedless, irresponsible, lackadaisical, negligent, reckless *Ant* careworn

care·ful \-fəl\ *adj* **care·ful·er; care·ful·est** **1** ♦ : using or taking care **2** ♦ : marked by solicitude, caution, or prudence — **care·ful·ly** *adv*

♦ [1] conscientious, fussy, meticulous, painstaking — more at PAINSTAKING ♦ [2] alert, cautious, circumspect, considerate, gingerly, guarded, heedful, safe, wary; *also* attentive, chary, observant, vigilant, watchful; foresighted, provident; cagey, noncommittal; calculating, scheming, shrewd; considerate, thoughtful; deliberate, slow *Ant* careless, heedless, incautious, unguarded, unsafe, unwary

care·ful·ness *n* ♦ : the quality of being careful : close or steady attention (as to a task)

♦ alertness, care, caution, circumspection, heedfulness — more at CAUTION

care·giv·er \-‚gi-vər\ *n* : a person who provides direct care (as for children, the disabled, or the chronically ill)

care·less \-ləs\ *adj* **1** : free from care : UNTROUBLED **2** ♦ : having no concern or interest ⟨~ of the consequences⟩ **3** ♦ : not taking care esp. to avoid danger or harm **4 a** ♦ : not taking ordinary or proper care **b** : not showing or receiving care — **care·less·ly** *adv*

♦ [2, 3] heedless, mindless, unguarded, unsafe, unwary; *also* bold, impetuous, rash, reckless; inattentive, unobservant; blithe, inconsiderate, thoughtless; absentminded, forgetful, unmindful; lax, neglectful, negligent, remiss; imprudent, indiscreet, injudicious; inadvertent, unintentional, unplanned *Ant* alert, cautious, circumspect, gingerly, guarded, heedful, safe, wary ♦ [4a] derelict, lax, negligent, remiss, slack — more at NEGLIGENT

care·less·ness *n* ♦ : failure to exercise the care that a reasonably prudent person would in like circumstances

♦ dereliction, heedlessness, laxness, negligence, remissness, slackness — more at NEGLIGENCE

¹ca·ress \kə-'res\ *n* : a tender or loving touch or embrace

²caress *vb* ♦ : to touch or stroke tenderly or lovingly — **ca·ress·er** *n*

♦ fondle, love, pat, pet, stroke — more at FONDLE

car·et \'kar-ət\ *n* [L, there is lacking, fr. *carēre* to lack, be without] : a mark ^ used to indicate the place where something is to be inserted

care·tak·er \'ker-‚tā-kər\ *n* **1** ♦ : one in charge usu. as occupant in place of an absent owner **2** : one temporarily fulfilling the functions of an office

♦ custodian, guardian, janitor, keeper, warden, watchman — more at CUSTODIAN

care·worn \-‚wörn\ *adj* : showing the effects of grief or anxiety

car·fare \'kär-‚far\ *n* : passenger fare (as on a streetcar or bus)

car·go \'kär-gō\ *n, pl* **cargoes** *or* **cargos** ♦ : the goods carried in a ship, airplane, or vehicle : FREIGHT

♦ freight, load, payload, shipment; *also* consignment; bale, bundle, packet; manifest burden, freight, haul, lading, load, payload, weight — more at LOAD

Ca·rib·be·an \‚kar-ə-'bē-ən, kə-'ri-bē-ən\ *adj* : of or relating to the eastern and southern West Indies or the Caribbean Sea

car·i·bou \'kar-ə-‚bü\ *n, pl* **caribou** *or* **caribous** : a large circumpolar gregarious deer of northern taiga and tundra that usu. has palmate antlers in both sexes — used esp. for one of the New World

¹car·i·ca·ture \'kar-i-kə-‚chúr\ *n* **1** ♦ : distorted representation to produce a ridiculous effect **2** ♦ : a representation esp. in literature or art having the qualities of caricature — **car·i·ca·tur·ist** \-ist\ *n*

♦ [1] farce, joke, mockery, parody, sham, travesty — more at MOCKERY ♦ [2] burlesque, parody, spoof, takeoff — more at PARODY

²caricature *vb* ♦ : to make or draw a caricature of : represent in caricature

♦ burlesque, imitate, mimic, mock, parody, take off, travesty — more at MIMIC

car·ies \'kar-ēz\ *n, pl* **caries** : tooth decay

car·il·lon \'kar-ə-‚län\ *n* : a set of tuned bells sounded by hammers controlled from a keyboard

car·i·ous \'kar-ē-əs\ *adj* : affected with caries

car·jack·ing \'kär-ja-kiŋ\ *n* : the theft of an automobile by force or intimidation — **car·jack·er** *n*

car·load \'kär-‚lōd\ *n* : a load that fills a car

car·mi·na·tive \kär-'mi-nə-tiv\ *adj* : expelling gas from the alimentary canal — **carminative** *n*

car·mine \'kär-mən, -‚mīn\ *n* : a vivid red

car·nage \'kär-nij\ *n* ♦ : great destruction of life : SLAUGHTER

♦ butchery, massacre, slaughter — more at MASSACRE

car·nal \'kärn-ᵊl\ *adj* [ME, fr. LL *carnalis*, fr. L *carn-, caro* flesh] **1 ♦** : of or relating to the body **2 ♦** : relating to or given to sensual pleasures and appetites **3 ♦** : of or relating to this world : earthly rather than heavenly or spiritual — **car·nal·i·ty** \kär-'na-lə-tē\ *n* — **car·nal·ly** *adv*

♦ [1] animal, bodily, corporal, fleshly, material, physical, somatic — more at PHYSICAL **♦ [2]** fleshly, luscious, sensual, sensuous, voluptuous — more at SENSUAL **♦ [3]** earthly, fleshly, material, mundane, temporal, terrestrial, worldly — more at EARTHLY

car·na·tion \kär-'nā-shən\ *n* : a cultivated pink of any of numerous usu. double-flowered varieties derived from an Old World species

car·nau·ba wax \kär-'nȯ-bə-, -'naů-; ˌkär-nə-'ü-bə-\ *n* : a brittle yellowish wax from a Brazilian palm that is used esp. in polishes

car·ne·lian \kär-'nēl-yən\ *n* : a hard tough reddish quartz used as a gem

car·ni·val \'kär-nə-vəl\ *n* [It *carnevale*, alter. of *carnelevare*, lit., removal of meat] **1** : a festival of merrymaking just before Lent **2** : a boisterous merrymaking **3** : a traveling enterprise offering amusements **4 ♦** : an organized program of entertainment

♦ celebration, festival, festivity, fete, fiesta, gala, jubilee — more at FESTIVAL

car·niv·o·ra \kär-'ni-və-rə\ *n pl* : carnivorous mammals
car·ni·vore \'kär-nə-ˌvȯr\ *n* : a flesh-eating animal; *esp* : any of an order of mammals (as dogs, cats, bears, minks, and seals) feeding mostly on animal flesh
car·niv·o·rous \kär-'ni-və-rəs\ *adj* **1** : feeding on animal tissues **2** : of or relating to the carnivores — **car·niv·o·rous·ly** *adv* — **car·niv·o·rous·ness** *n*
car·ny *or* **car·ney** *or* **car·nie** \'kär-nē\ *n, pl* **carnies** *or* **car·neys 1** : CARNIVAL 3 **2** : one who works with a carnival
¹**car·ol** \'kar-əl\ *n* **♦** : a song of joy or devotion

♦ anthem, canticle, chorale, hymn, psalm, spiritual — more at HYMN

²**carol** *vb* : to sing esp. in a cheerful manner
car·ol·er *or* **car·ol·ler** *n* **♦** : one that carols

♦ singer, songster, vocalist, voice — more at SINGER

¹**car·om** \'kar-əm\ *n* **1** : a shot in billiards in which the cue ball strikes two other balls **2** : a rebounding esp. at an angle
²**carom** *vb* **♦** : to strike and rebound

♦ bounce, glance, rebound, ricochet, skim, skip — more at GLANCE

car·o·tene \'kar-ə-ˌtēn\ *n* : any of several orange to red pigments (as beta-carotene) formed esp. in plants and used as a source of vitamin A
ca·rot·en·oid \kə-'rä-tə-ˌnȯid\ *n* : any of various usu. yellow to red pigments (as carotenes) found widely in plants and animals
ca·rot·id \kə-'rä-təd\ *adj* : of, relating to, or being the chief artery or pair of arteries that pass up the neck and supply the head — **carotid** *n*
ca·rous·al \kə-'raů-zəl\ *n* : a period of heavy drinking : CAROUSE
ca·rouse \kə-'raůz\ *n* [MF *carrousse*, fr. *carous*, adv., all out (in *boire carous* to empty the cup), fr. G *garaus*] : a drunken revel — **carouse** *vb* — **ca·rous·er** *n*
car·ou·sel \ˌkar-ə-'sel, 'kar-ə-ˌsel\ *n* **1** : MERRY-GO-ROUND **2** : a circular conveyor ⟨a baggage ∼⟩
¹**carp** \'kärp\ *vb* **♦** : to find fault — **carp** *n*

♦ beef, bellyache, cavil, complain, crab, croak, fuss, gripe, grouse, growl, grumble, kick, moan, squawk, wail, whine — more at COMPLAIN

²**carp** *n, pl* **carp** *or* **carps** : a large variable Asian freshwater fish of sluggish waters often raised for food
¹**car·pal** \'kär-pəl\ *adj* : relating to the wrist or the bones of the wrist
²**carpal** *n* : a carpal element or bone
carpal tunnel syndrome *n* : a condition characterized esp. by weakness, pain, and disturbances of sensation (as

numbness) in the hand and fingers and caused by compression of a nerve in the wrist
car park *n, chiefly Can and Brit* : a lot or garage for parking
car·pe di·em \ˌkär-pe-'dē-ˌem, -'dī-\ *n* [L, lit., pluck the day] : enjoyment of the present without concern for the future
car·pel \'kär-pəl\ *n* : one of the highly modified leaves that together form the ovary of a flower of a seed plant
car·pen·ter \'kär-pən-tər\ *n* : one who builds or repairs wooden structures — **carpenter** *vb* — **car·pen·try** \-trē\ *n*
carp·er *n* **♦** : an excessive faultfinder

♦ castigator, caviler, censurer, critic, faultfinder, nitpicker, railer, scold — more at CRITIC

¹**car·pet** \'kär-pət\ *n* : a heavy fabric used as a floor covering
²**carpet** *vb* **♦** : to cover with or as if with a carpet

♦ blanket, coat, cover, overlay, overlie, overspread — more at COVER

car·pet·bag \-ˌbag\ *n* : a traveling bag common in the 19th century
car·pet·bag·ger \-ˌba-gər\ *n* : a Northerner in the South after the American Civil War usu. seeking private gain under the reconstruction governments
car·pet·ing \'kär-pə-tiŋ\ *n* : material for carpets; *also* : CARPETS
carping *adj* **♦** : marked by or inclined to querulous and often perverse criticism

♦ captious, critical, hypercritical, overcritical — more at CRITICAL

car pool *n* : an arrangement in which a group of people commute together by car; *also* : a group having this arrangement — **car·pool** \-ˌpül\ *vb*
car·port \'kär-ˌpȯrt\ *n* : an open-sided automobile shelter
car·pus \'kär-pəs\ *n* : the wrist or its bones
car·ra·geen·an *or* **car·ra·geen·in** \ˌkar-ə-'gē-nən\ *n* : a colloid extracted esp. from a dark purple branching seaweed and used in foods esp. to stabilize and thicken them
car·rel \'kar-əl\ *n* : a table often partitioned or enclosed for individual study in a library
car·riage \'kar-ij\ *n* **1** : the act of carrying **2** : manner of holding the body **3** : a wheeled vehicle **4** *Brit* : a railway passenger coach **5** : a movable part of a machine for supporting some other moving part ⟨a typewriter ∼⟩
carriage trade *n* : trade from well-to-do or upper-class people
car·ri·er \'kar-ē-ər\ *n* **1** : one that carries **2** : a person or organization in the transportation business **3** : AIRCRAFT CARRIER **4** : one whose system carries the causative agents of a disease but who is immune to the disease **5** : an individual having a gene for a trait or condition that is not expressed outwardly **6** : an electromagnetic wave whose amplitude or frequency is varied in order to convey a radio or television signal
carrier pigeon *n* : a pigeon used esp. to carry messages
car·ri·on \'ker-ē-ən\ *n* : dead and decaying flesh
car·rot \'ker-ət\ *n* : the elongated usu. orange root of a common garden plant that is eaten as a vegetable; *also* : this plant
carrousel *var of* CAROUSEL
¹**car·ry** \'ka-rē, 'ker-ē\ *vb* **car·ried; car·ry·ing** [ME *carien*, fr. AF *carier*, fr. *carre* vehicle, fr. L *carrus*] **1 ♦** : to move while supporting : TRANSPORT, CONVEY **2** : to influence by mental or emotional appeal **3** : to get possession or control of : CAPTURE, WIN **4** : to transfer from one place to another ⟨∼ a number in adding⟩ **5** : to have or wear on one's person; *also* : to bear within one **6 ♦** : to have within or as part of itself : INVOLVE, INCLUDE **7** : to hold or bear (oneself) in a specified way **8** : to keep in stock for sale **9 ♦** : to sustain the weight or burden of : SUPPORT **10** : to prolong in space, time, or degree **11** : to keep on one's books as a debtor **12** : to succeed in (an election) **13** : to win adoption (as in a legislature) **14 a** : to present to the public for use or as entertainment **b** : PUBLISH, PRINT **15** : to reach or penetrate to a distance

♦ [1] bear, cart, convey, ferry, haul, lug, pack, tote, transport; *also* deliver, hand over, transfer; forward, send, ship, transmit; bring, fetch, take; move, remove, shift ♦ [6] comprehend, contain, embrace, encompass, entail, include, involve, number, take in — more at IN-CLUDE ♦ [9] bear, bolster, brace, buttress, prop, shore, stay, support, uphold — more at SUPPORT

²**carry** *n* **1** : the range of a gun or projectile or of a struck or thrown ball **2** : PORTAGE **3** : an act or method of carrying ⟨fireman's ∼⟩

car·ry·all \'kar-ē-,ȯl\ *n* ♦ : a large bag or carrying case

♦ grip, handbag, portmanteau, suitcase, traveling bag — more at TRAVELING BAG

carry away *vb* ♦ : to arouse to a high and often excessive degree of emotion

♦ enrapture, enthrall, entrance, ravish, transport — more at ENTRANCE

carrying charge *n* : a charge added to the price of merchandise sold on the installment plan

car·ry-on *n* : a piece of luggage suitable for being carried aboard an airplane by a passenger — **carry-on** *adj*

carry on *vb* **1** ♦ : to have the direction of : CONDUCT, MANAGE **2** ♦ : to behave in a foolish, excited, or improper manner **3** : to continue in spite of hindrance or discouragement

♦ [1] administer, conduct, control, direct, govern, guide, handle, manage, operate, oversee, regulate, run, superintend, supervise — more at CONDUCT ♦ [2] act out, act up, misbehave — more at MISBEHAVE

carry out *vb* **1** ♦ : to bring to a successful conclusion **2** : to put into execution

♦ accomplish, achieve, commit, compass, do, execute, follow through, fulfill, make, perform — more at PER-FORM

car·sick \'kär-,sik\ *adj* : affected with motion sickness esp. in an automobile — **car sickness** *n*

¹**cart** \'kärt\ *n* **1** : a heavy 2-wheeled wagon **2** : a small wheeled vehicle

²**cart** *vb* ♦ : to convey in or as if in a cart — **cart·er** *n*

♦ bear, carry, convey, ferry, haul, lug, pack, tote, transport — more at CARRY

cart·age \'kär-tij\ *n* : the act of or rate charged for carting

carte blanche \'kärt-'blänsh\ *n*, *pl* **cartes blanches** *same or* -'blän-shəz\ [F, lit., blank document] : full discretionary power

car·tel \kär-'tel\ *n* ♦ : a combination of independent business enterprises designed to limit competition

♦ combination, combine, syndicate, trust; *also* chain, conglomerate, multinational; association, organization, pool

car·ti·lage \'kär-tə-lij\ *n* : a usu. translucent somewhat elastic tissue that composes most of the skeleton of young vertebrate embryos and later is mostly converted to bone in higher vertebrates — **car·ti·lag·i·nous** \,kärt-ᵊl-'a-jə-nəs\ *adj*

cartilaginous fish *n* : any of a class of fishes (as a shark or ray) having the skeleton wholly or largely composed of cartilage

car·tog·ra·phy \kär-'tä-grə-fē\ *n* : the making of maps — **car·tog·ra·pher** *n* — **car·to·graph·ic** \,kär-tə-'gra-fik\ *adj*

car·ton \'kärt-ᵊn\ *n* : a cardboard box or container

car·toon \kär-'tün\ *n* **1** ♦ : a preparatory sketch (as for a painting) **2** : a drawing intended as humor, caricature, or satire **3** ♦ : a group of cartoons or drawings arranged in a narrative sequence : COMIC STRIP — **cartoon** *vb* — **car·toon·ist** *n*

♦ [1] delineation, drawing, sketch — more at DRAWING
♦ [3] comic strip — more at COMIC STRIP

car·tridge \'kär-trij\ *n* **1** : a tube containing a complete charge for a firearm **2** : a container of material for insertion into an apparatus **3** : a small case containing a phonograph needle and transducer that is attached to a

tonearm **4** : a case containing a magnetic tape or disk **5** : a case for holding integrated circuits containing a computer program

cart·wheel \'kärt-,hwēl\ *n* **1** : a large coin (as a silver dollar) **2** : a lateral handspring with arms and legs extended

carve \kärv\ *vb* **carved; carv·ing 1** : to cut with care or precision : shape by cutting **2** ♦ : to cut or hew out esp. with some effort : make or get by or as if by cutting — often used with *out* ⟨∼ out a fortune⟩ **3** : to slice and serve meat at table — **carv·er** *n*

♦ usu **carve out** build, forge, grind, hammer, work out

cary·at·id \,kar-ē-'a-təd\ *n*, *pl* **-ids** *or* **-i·des** \-'a-tə-,dēz\ : a sculptured draped female figure used as an architectural column

CAS *abbr* certificate of advanced study

ca·sa·ba \kə-'sä-bə\ *n* : any of several muskmelons with a yellow rind and sweet flesh

¹**cas·cade** \,kas-'kād\ *n* **1** : a steep usu. small waterfall **2** : something arranged in a series or succession of stages so that each stage derives from or acts upon the product of the preceding

²**cas·cade** *vb* **cas·cad·ed; cas·cad·ing** : to fall, pass, or connect in or as if in a cascade ⟨water *cascaded* over the rocks⟩

cas·cara \kas-'kar-ə\ *n* : the dried bark of a small Pacific coastal tree of the U.S. and southern Canada used as a laxative; *also* : this tree

¹**case** \'kās\ *n* [ME *cas*, fr. AF, fr. L *casus* fall, chance, fr. *cadere* to fall] **1 a** ♦ : a set of circumstances or conditions **b** ♦ : a set of circumstances constituting a problem : a matter for consideration or decision **2** : an inflectional form of a noun, pronoun, or adjective indicating its grammatical relation to other words; *also* : such a relation whether indicated by inflection or not **3** : what actually exists or happens : FACT **4** : a suit or action in law : CAUSE **5** ♦ : a convincing argument **6 a** : an instance of disease or injury **b** : a sick individual esp. when awaiting medical care or treatment : PATIENT **7** ♦ : an instance or example of a particular type : INSTANCE, EXAMPLE — **in case** : as a precaution — **in case of** : in the event of

♦ [1a] contingency, event, eventuality, possibility — more at EVENT ♦ [1b] knot, matter, problem, trouble — more at PROBLEM ♦ [5] argument, defense (*or* defence), explanation, rationale, reason — more at REASON ♦ [7] example, exemplar, illustration, instance, representative, sample, specimen — more at EXAMPLE

²**case** *n* [ME *cas*, fr. AF *case, chase*, fr. L *capsa*] **1** ♦ : a box or container for holding something; *also* : a box with its contents **2** ♦ : an outer covering **3** : a divided tray for holding printing type **4** : CASING 2

♦ [1] box, caddy, casket, chest, locker, trunk — more at CHEST ♦ [2] armor, capsule, casing, cocoon, cover, housing, husk, jacket, pod, sheath, shell; *also* bark, crust; mail, plate, plating, shield; hide, skin; envelope, wrapper; backing, coating, facing

³**case** *vb* **cased; cas·ing 1** : to enclose in or cover with a case **2** : to inspect esp. with intent to rob

ca·sein \'kā-,sēn, kā-'\ *n* : any of several phosphorus-containing proteins occurring in or produced from milk

case·ment \'kās-mənt\ *n* : a window that opens like a door

case·work \-,wərk\ *n* : social work that involves the individual person or family — **case·work·er** *n*

¹**cash** \'kash\ *n* [MF or It; MF *casse* money box, fr. It *cassa*, fr. L *capsa* chest, case] **1** : ready money **2** ♦ : money or its equivalent paid at the time of purchase or delivery

♦ currency, dough, lucre, money, pelf, tender — more at MONEY

²**cash** *vb* : to pay or obtain cash for

ca·shew \'ka-shü, kə-'shü\ *n* : an edible kidney-shaped nut of a tropical American tree related to the sumacs; *also* : this tree

¹**ca·shier** \ka-'shir\ *vb* ♦ : to dismiss from service; *esp* : to dismiss in disgrace

♦ dismiss, fire, remove, retire, sack — more at DISMISS

²**cash·ier** \ka-'shir\ *n* **1** : a bank official responsible for moneys received and paid out **2** : a person who receives and records payments

cashier's check *n* : a check drawn by a bank upon its own funds and signed by its cashier

cash in *vb* **1** : to convert into cash ⟨*cash in* bonds⟩ **2** : to settle accounts and withdraw from a gambling game or business deal **3** ♦ : to obtain advantage or financial profit — often used with *on* ⟨*cash in* on a best seller⟩

♦ *usu* **cash in on** abuse, capitalize, exploit, impose, play, use — more at EXPLOIT

cash·less \'kash-ləs\ *adj* : relying on monetary transactions that use electronic means rather than cash

cash·mere \'kazh-ˌmir, 'kash-\ *n* : fine wool from the undercoat of an Indian goat (**cashmere goat**) or a yarn spun of this; *also* : a soft twilled fabric orig. woven from this yarn

cash out *vb* : to convert noncash assets into cash

cash register *n* : a business machine that usu. has a money drawer, indicates each sale, and records the money received

cash–strapped \'kash-ˌstrapt\ *adj* : lacking sufficient money

cas·ing \'kā-siŋ\ *n* **1** ♦ : something that encases **2** : the frame of a door or window

♦ armor, capsule, case, cocoon, cover, housing, husk, jacket, pod, sheath, shell — more at CASE

ca·si·no \kə-'sē-nō\ *n, pl* **-nos** [It, fr. *casa* house] **1** : a building or room for social amusements; *esp* : one used for gambling **2** *also* **cas·si·no** : a card game in which players win cards by matching those on the table

cask \'kask\ *n* ♦ : a barrel-shaped container usu. for liquids; *also* : the quantity held by such a container

♦ barrel, hogshead, keg, pipe, puncheon; *also* tub, vat; can, drum

cas·ket \'kas-kət\ *n* **1** ♦ : a small chest or box (as for jewels) **2** : a usu. fancy coffin for burying a corpse : COFFIN

♦ box, caddy, case, chest, locker, trunk — more at CHEST

casque \'kask\ *n* : HELMET

cas·sa·va \kə-'sä-və\ *n* : any of several tropical spurges with rootstocks yielding a nutritious starch from which tapioca is prepared; *also* : the rootstock or its starch

cas·se·role \'ka-sə-ˌrōl\ *n* **1** : a dish in which food may be baked and served **2** : food cooked and served in a casserole

cas·sette *also* **ca·sette** \kə-'set\ *n* **1** : a lightproof container for photographic plates or film **2** : a plastic case containing magnetic tape

cas·sia \'ka-shə\ *n* **1** : a coarse cinnamon bark **2** : any of a genus of leguminous herbs, shrubs, and trees of warm regions including several which yield senna

cas·sit·er·ite \kə-'si-tə-ˌrīt\ *n* : a dark mineral that is the chief tin ore

cas·sock \'ka-sək\ *n* : an ankle-length garment worn esp. by Roman Catholic and Anglican clergy

cas·so·wary \'ka-sə-ˌwer-ē\ *n, pl* **-war·ies** : any of a genus of large flightless birds closely related to the emu

¹**cast** \'kast\ *vb* **cast; cast·ing** **1** ♦ : to cause to move or send forth by throwing : THROW, FLING **2** ♦ : to point, extend, or project in a specified line or course : DIRECT ⟨~ a glance⟩ **3** : to deposit (a ballot) formally **4** ♦ : to throw off, out, or away : DISCARD, SHED **5** : COMPUTE; *esp* : to add up **6** : to assign the parts of (a play) to actors; *also* : to assign to a role or part **7 a** : to shape (a substance) by pouring it in liquid or plastic form into a mold and letting it harden without pressure **b** ♦ : to give form to : establish or create in a particular form ⟨the book is ~ in the form of an autobiography⟩ **8** : to make (as a knot or stitch) by looping or catching up

♦ [1] catapult, chuck, dash, fire, fling, heave, hurl, hurtle, launch, peg, pelt, pitch, sling, throw, toss—more

at THROW ♦ [2] aim, bend, direct, head, level, set, train — more at AIM ♦ [4] discard, ditch, dump, fling, jettison, junk, lose, reject, scrap, shed, shuck, slough, throw away, throw out, unload — more at DISCARD ♦ [7b] compose, craft, draft, draw, formulate, frame, prepare — more at COMPOSE

²**cast** *n* **1** : THROW, FLING **2** : a throw of dice **3** : the set of actors in a dramatic production **4** : something formed in or as if in a mold; *also* : a rigid surgical dressing (as for protecting and supporting a fractured bone) **5** ♦ : a slight change in the appearance of a substance by a trace of some added hue : a trace of a particular quality : TINGE, HUE **6 a** : a turning of the eye in a particular direction **b** ♦ : a physical form or character : SHAPE **c** ♦ : facial aspect or vocal intonation as indicative of feeling : LOOK **7** : something thrown out or off, shed, or expelled ⟨worm ~s⟩ **8** : a forecast or conjecture concerning future events or conditions

♦ [5] color (*or* colour), hue, shade, tinge, tint, tone — more at COLOR ♦ [6b] configuration, conformation, figure, form, geometry, shape ♦ [6c] countenance, expression, face, look, visage — more at LOOK

cast about *vb* ♦ : to seek here and there : look around

♦ cast around, forage, hunt, pursue, quest, search (for *or* out), seek — more at SEEK

cas·ta·net \ˌkas-tə-'net\ *n* [Sp *castañeta*, fr. *castaña* chestnut, fr. L *castanea*] : a rhythm instrument consisting of two small wooden, ivory, or plastic shells held in the hand and clicked together

cast around *vb* ♦ : to look around : SEEK

♦ cast about, forage, hunt, pursue, quest, search (for *or* out), seek — more at SEEK

¹**cast·away** \'kas-tə-ˌwā\ *adj* **1** : thrown away : REJECTED **2** : cast adrift or ashore as a survivor of a shipwreck

²**castaway** *n* ♦ : one who has been cast away, cast off, or rejected

♦ outcast, reject — more at OUTCAST

caste \'kast\ *n* [Pg *casta*, lit., race, lineage, fr. fem. of *casto* pure, chaste, fr. L *castus*] **1** : one of the hereditary social classes in Hinduism **2** ♦ : a division of a society based on wealth, inherited rank, or occupation **3** : social position : PRESTIGE **4** : a system of rigid social stratification

♦ class, estate, folk, order, stratum — more at CLASS

cas·tel·lat·ed \'kas-tə-ˌlā-təd\ *adj* : having battlements like a castle

cast·er \'kas-tər\ *n* **1** *or* **cas·tor** : a small container to hold salt or pepper at the table **2** : a small wheel that turns freely and is used to support and move furniture, trucks, and equipment

cas·ti·gate \'kas-tə-ˌgāt\ *vb* **-gat·ed; -gat·ing** ♦ : to punish or criticize severely

♦ admonish, chide, lecture, rail (at *or* against), rate, rebuke, reprimand, scold — more at SCOLD ♦ chasten, chastise, correct, discipline, penalize, punish — more at PUNISH

cas·ti·ga·tion \ˌkas-tə-'gā-shən\ *n* ♦ : severe punishment or criticism

♦ chastisement, correction, desert, discipline, nemesis, penalty, punishment, wrath — more at PUNISHMENT

cas·ti·ga·tor \'kas-tə-ˌgā-tər\ *n* ♦ : one that castigates

♦ carper, caviler, censurer, critic, faultfinder, nitpicker, railer, scold — more at CRITIC

cast·ing \'kas-tiŋ\ *n* **1** : CAST 7 **2** : something cast in a mold

casting vote *n* : a deciding vote cast by a presiding officer to break a tie

cast iron *n* : a hard brittle alloy of iron, carbon, and silicon cast in a mold

cas·tle \'ka-səl\ *n* **1** : a large fortified building or set of buildings **2** ♦ : a large or imposing house **3** : ³ROOK

♦ estate, hall, manor, mansion, palace, villa — more at MANSION

cast–off \'kas-ˌtóf\ *adj* : thrown away or aside — **cast·off** *n*
cas·tor oil \'kas-tər-\ *n* : a thick yellowish oil extracted from the poisonous seeds of an herb (**castor–oil plant**) and used as a lubricant and purgative
cast out *vb* ♦ : to banish, expel, or drive away (as from a former home or country)

♦ banish, boot (out), bounce, chase, dismiss, drum, eject, expel, oust, rout, run off, throw out — more at EJECT

cas·trate \'kas-ˌtrāt\ *vb* **cas·trat·ed; cas·trat·ing** : to deprive of sex glands and esp. testes — **cas·tra·tion** \kas-'trā-shən\ *n* — **cas·tra·tor** \-ər\ *n*
ca·su·al \'ka-zhə-wəl\ *adj* **1** ♦ : resulting from or occurring by chance **2** ♦ : occurring without regularity : OCCASIONAL **3** ♦ : feeling or showing little concern : NONCHALANT **4** ♦ : designed for informal use ⟨∼ clothing⟩ — **ca·su·al·ly** *adv*

♦ [1] accidental, chance, fluky, fortuitous, incidental, unintended, unintentional, unplanned, unpremeditated, unwitting — more at ACCIDENTAL ♦ [2] choppy, discontinuous, erratic, fitful, intermittent, irregular, occasional, spasmodic, sporadic, spotty, unsteady — more at FITFUL ♦ [3] apathetic, disinterested, indifferent, insouciant, nonchalant, perfunctory, unconcerned, uncurious, uninterested — more at INDIFFERENT ♦ [4] everyday, informal, workaday; *also* sporty **Ant** dressy, formal

ca·su·al·ness *n* : the quality, state, or fact of being casual or disinterested
ca·su·al·ty \'ka-zhəl-tē, 'ka-zhə-wəl-\ *n, pl* **-ties** **1** ♦ : a serious or fatal accident **2** : a military person lost through death, injury, sickness, or capture or through being missing in action **3** ♦ : a person or thing injured, lost, or destroyed

♦ [1] accident, mishap — more at ACCIDENT ♦ [3] fatality, loss, victim; *also* failure, loser

ca·su·ist·ry \'ka-zhə-wə-strē\ *n, pl* **-ries** : specious argument : RATIONALIZATION — **ca·su·ist** \-wist\ *n* — **ca·su·is·tic** \ˌka-zhə-'wis-tik\ *or* **ca·su·is·ti·cal** \-ti-kəl\ *adj*
ca·sus bel·li \ˌkä-səs-'be-ˌlē, ˌkä-səs-'be-ˌlī\ *n, pl* **ca·sus belli** \ˌkä-ˌsüs-, ˌkä-\ [NL, occasion of war] : a cause or pretext for a declaration of war
¹**cat** \'kat\ *n* **1** ♦ : a carnivorous mammal long domesticated as a pet and for catching rats and mice **2** : any of a family of animals (as the lion, lynx, or leopard) including the domestic cat **3** : a spiteful woman **4** : GUY

♦ feline, kitty, puss; *also* mouser; kit, kitten, tabby, tomcat

²**cat** *abbr* catalog
ca·tab·o·lism \kə-'ta-bə-ˌli-zəm\ *n* : destructive metabolism involving the release of energy and resulting in the breakdown of complex materials — **cat·a·bol·ic** \ˌka-tə-'bä-lik\ *adj*
cat·a·clysm \'ka-tə-ˌkli-zəm\ *n* **1** ♦ : a surging flood of water : DELUGE **2** ♦ : a violent change or upheaval

♦ [1] cataract, deluge, flood, inundation, overflow, spate, torrent — more at FLOOD ♦ [2] calamity, catastrophe, debacle, disaster, tragedy — more at DISASTER ♦ [2] convulsion, paroxysm, storm, tempest, tumult, upheaval, uproar — more at CONVULSION

cat·a·clys·mic \ˌka-tə-'kliz-mik\ *or* **cat·a·clys·mal** \-'kliz-məl\ *adj* ♦ : of, relating to, or having the characteristics of a cataclysm ⟨a ∼ nuclear war⟩

♦ calamitous, catastrophic, destructive, devastating, disastrous, fatal, fateful, ruinous, unfortunate — more at FATAL

cat·a·comb \'ka-tə-ˌkōm\ *n* : an underground burial place with galleries and recesses for tombs
cat·a·falque \'ka-tə-ˌfalk, -ˌfólk, -ˌfók\ *n* : an ornamental structure sometimes used in solemn funerals to hold the body
cat·a·lep·sy \'ka-tə-ˌlep-sē\ *n, pl* **-sies** : a trancelike nervous condition characterized esp. by loss of voluntary motion — **cat·a·lep·tic** \ˌka-tə-'lep-tik\ *adj or n*

¹**cat·a·log** *or* **cat·a·logue** \'kat-ˀl-ˌóg\ *n* **1** ♦ : a simple series of items (as the names of persons or objects) : LIST, REGISTER **2** : a systematic list of items with descriptive details; *also* : a book containing such a list

♦ checklist, list, listing, menu, register, registry, roll, roster, schedule, table — more at LIST

²**catalog** *or* **catalogue** *vb* **-loged** *or* **-logued; -log·ing** *or* **-logu·ing** **1** : to make a catalog of **2** ♦ : to enter in a catalog — **cat·a·log·er** *or* **cat·a·logu·er** *n*

♦ enroll, enter, index, inscribe, list, put down, record, register, schedule, slate — more at LIST

ca·tal·pa \kə-'tal-pə\ *n* : any of a genus of broad-leaved trees with showy flowers and long slim pods
ca·tal·y·sis \kə-'ta-lə-səs\ *n, pl* **-y·ses** \-ˌsēz\ : a change and esp. increase in the rate of a chemical reaction brought about by a substance (**cat·a·lyst** \'kat-ˀl-ist\) that is itself unchanged at the end of the reaction — **cat·a·lyt·ic** \ˌkat-ˀl-'i-tik\ *adj* — **cat·a·lyt·i·cal·ly** \-ti-k(ə-)lē\ *adv*
catalytic converter *n* : an automobile exhaust-system component in which a catalyst changes harmful gases into mostly harmless products
cat·a·lyze \'kat-ˀl-ˌīz\ *vb* **-lyzed; -lyz·ing** : to bring about the catalysis of (a chemical reaction)
cat·a·ma·ran \ˌka-tə-mə-'ran\ *n* [Tamil (a language of southern India) *kaṭṭumaram*, fr. *kaṭṭu* to tie + *maram* tree] : a boat with twin hulls
cat·a·mount \'ka-tə-ˌmaùnt\ *n* : a large powerful tawny= brown cat : COUGAR; *also* : LYNX
¹**cat·a·pult** \'ka-tə-ˌpəlt, -ˌpúlt\ *n* **1** : an ancient military machine for hurling missiles **2** : a device for launching an airplane (as from an aircraft carrier)
²**catapult** *vb* ♦ : to throw or launch by or as if by a catapult

♦ cast, chuck, dash, fire, fling, heave, hurl, hurtle, launch, peg, pelt, pitch, sling, throw, toss — more at THROW

cat·a·ract \'ka-tə-ˌrakt\ *n* **1** : a cloudiness of the lens of the eye obstructing vision **2 a** : a large waterfall; *also* : steep rapids in a river **b** ♦ : an overwhelming downpour or rush

♦ cataclysm, deluge, flood, inundation, overflow, spate, torrent — more at FLOOD

ca·tarrh \kə-'tär\ *n* : inflammation of a mucous membrane esp. of the nose and throat — **ca·tarrh·al** \-əl\ *adj*
ca·tas·tro·phe \kə-'tas-trə-(ˌ)fē\ *n* [Gk *katastrophē*, fr. *katastrephein* to overturn, fr. *kata-* down + *strephein* to turn] **1** ♦ : a great disaster or misfortune **2** : utter failure

♦ calamity, cataclysm, debacle, disaster, tragedy — more at DISASTER

cat·a·stroph·ic \ˌka-tə-'strä-fik\ *adj* ♦ : of, relating to, resembling, or resulting in catastrophe — **cat·a·stroph·i·cal·ly** \-fi-k(ə-)lē\ *adv*

♦ calamitous, cataclysmic, destructive, disastrous, fatal, fateful, ruinous, unfortunate — more at FATAL

cat·a·ton·ic \ˌka-tə-'tä-nik\ *adj* : of, relating to, or marked by schizophrenia characterized esp. by stupor, negativism, rigidity, purposeless excitement, and bizarre posturing — **catatonic** *n*
cat·bird \'kat-ˌbərd\ *n* : an American songbird with a cat-like mewing call
cat·boat \'kat-ˌbōt\ *n* : a single-masted sailboat with a single large sail extended by a long boom
cat·call \-ˌkól\ *n* ♦ : a loud cry made esp. to express disapproval — **catcall** *vb*

♦ boo, hiss, hoot, jeer, raspberry; *also* sneer, taunt; whistle **Ant** cheer

¹**catch** \'kach, 'kech\ *vb* **caught** \'kót\; **catch·ing** [ME *cacchen*, fr. AF *cacher, chacher, chacer* to hunt, ultim. fr. L *captare* to chase] **1** : to capture esp. after pursuit **2** ♦ : to capture, take, or entangle in or as if in a snare : TRAP **3** : to discover unexpectedly ⟨*caught* in the act⟩ **4** : to become suddenly aware of **5** : to take hold of : SNATCH ⟨∼ at a straw⟩ **6** ♦ : stop or interrupt the progress or

course of **7** : to get entangled **8 ♦** : to become affected with or by ⟨∼ fire⟩ ⟨∼ cold⟩ **9 a ♦** : to seize and hold firmly **b** : to cause to be seized and held **10** : OVERTAKE **11** : to be in time for ⟨∼ a train⟩ **12** : to take in and retain ⟨didn't ∼ your name⟩ **13** : to look at or listen to ⟨∼ a TV show⟩

♦ [2, 9a] bag, capture, collar, corral, get, grab, grapple, hook, land, nab, seize, snare, trap; *also* lasso, rope; apprehend, arrest, detain; clasp, clutch, grasp, grip, hold, secure; ensnare, entangle, entrap; abduct, kidnap, spirit (away *or* off) *Ant* miss ♦ [6] arrest, check, draw up, fetch up, halt, hold up, stall, stay, still, stop — more at HALT ♦ [8] come down, contract, get, sicken, take — more at CONTRACT

²**catch** *n* **1 a** : something caught **b ♦** : the total quantity caught at one time ⟨a good ∼ of fish⟩ **2** : the act of catching; *also* : a game consisting of throwing and catching a ball **3** : something that catches or checks or holds immovable ⟨a door ∼⟩ **4 ♦** : one that is worth catching or acquiring esp. as a mate **5** : FRAGMENT, SNATCH **6 ♦** : a concealed difficulty or complication

♦ [1b] haul, take, yield — more at HAUL ♦ [4] gem, jewel, pearl, plum, prize, treasure — more at PRIZE ♦ [6] booby trap, pitfall, snag — more at PITFALL

catch·all \'ka-ˌchȯl, 'ke-\ *n* : something to hold a variety of odds and ends
catch–as–catch–can *adj* : using any means available
catch·er \'ka-chər, 'ke-\ *n* : one that catches; *esp* : a player positioned behind home plate in baseball
catch·ing *adj* **1 ♦** : communicable by infection : CONTAGIOUS ⟨the flu is ∼⟩ **2 ♦** : spreading or capable of spreading rapidly to others ⟨their enthusiasm was ∼⟩

♦ [1, 2] communicable, contagious, transmittable — more at CONTAGIOUS ♦ [2] contagious, infectious — more at CONTAGIOUS

catch·ment \'kach-mənt, 'kech-\ *n* **1** : something that catches water **2** : the action of catching water
catch on *vb* **1 a ♦** : to become aware : LEARN **b ♦** : to grasp the meaning of : UNDERSTAND **2** : to become popular

♦ [1a] ascertain, discover, find out, hear, learn, realize, see — more at DISCOVER ♦ *usu* **catch on to** [1b] appreciate, apprehend, catch, comprehend, get, grasp, make, make out, perceive, see, seize, understand — more at COMPREHEND

catch·pen·ny \'kach-ˌpe-nē, 'kech-\ *adj* : using sensationalism or cheapness for appeal ⟨a ∼ newspaper⟩
catch·phrase \-ˌfrāz\ *n* : a word or expression frequently used to represent or characterize a person, group, idea, or point of view
catch–22 \-ˌtwen-tē-'tü\ *n, pl* **catch–22's** *or* **catch–22s** *often cap* C [fr. *Catch-22*, a paradoxical rule found in the novel *Catch-22* (1961) by Joseph Heller] : a problematic situation for which the only solution is denied by a circumstance inherent in the problem or by a rule; *also* : the circumstance or rule that denies a solution
catchup *var of* KETCHUP
catch up *vb* : to travel or work fast enough to overtake or complete
catch·word \'kach-ˌwərd, 'kech-\ *n* **1** : GUIDE WORD **2** : CATCHPHRASE
catchy \'ka-chē, 'ke-\ *adj* **catch·i·er; -est 1 ♦** : likely to catch the interest or attention **2 ♦** : requiring skill or caution (as in doing or handling) : TRICKY

♦ [1] bold, conspicuous, emphatic, marked, noticeable, prominent, pronounced, remarkable, striking — more at NOTICEABLE ♦ [2] delicate, difficult, knotty, problematic, spiny, thorny, ticklish, touchy, tough, tricky — more at TRICKY

cat·e·chism \'ka-tə-ˌki-zəm\ *n* : a summary or test (as of religious doctrine) usu. in the form of questions and answers — **cat·e·chist** \-ˌkist\ *n* — **cat·e·chize** \-ˌkīz\ *vb*

cat·e·chu·men \ˌka-tə-'kyü-mən\ *n* : a religious convert receiving training before baptism
cat·e·gor·i·cal \ˌka-tə-'gȯr-i-kəl\ *adj* **1** : not modified or restricted : ABSOLUTE, UNQUALIFIED ⟨a ∼ denial⟩ **2** : of, relating to, or constituting a category — **cat·e·gor·i·cal·ly** \-i-k(ə-)lē\ *adv*
cat·e·go·rise *Brit var of* CATEGORIZE
cat·e·go·rize \'ka-ti-gə-ˌrīz\ *vb* **-rized; -riz·ing ♦** : to put into a category : CLASSIFY — **cat·e·go·ri·za·tion** \ˌka-ti-gə-rə-'zā-shən\ *n*

♦ assort, break down, class, classify, grade, group, peg, place, range, rank, separate, sort — more at CLASSIFY

cat·e·go·ry \'ka-tə-ˌgȯr-ē\ *n, pl* **-ries ♦** : a division within a system of classification; *esp* : CLASS, GROUP, KIND

♦ bracket, class, division, family, grade, group, kind, order, set, species, type — more at CLASS

ca·ter \'kā-tər\ *vb* [obs. *cater* buyer of provisions, fr. ME *catour*, short for *acatour*, fr. AF, fr. *acater*, *achater* to buy] **1 ♦** : to provide a supply of food **2 ♦** : to supply what is wanted — **ca·ter·er** *n*

♦ [1] board, feed, provision — more at FEED ♦ *usu* **cater to** [2] gratify, humor (*or* humour), indulge — more at INDULGE

catercorner *or* **cater–cornered** *var of* KITTY-CORNER
cat·er·pil·lar \'ka-tər-ˌpi-lər\ *n* [ME *catyrpel*, fr. OF *catepelose*, lit., hairy cat] : a wormlike often hairy insect larva esp. of a butterfly or moth
cat·er·waul \'ka-tər-ˌwȯl\ *vb* : to make a harsh cry — **caterwaul** *n*
cat·fish \'kat-ˌfish\ *n* : any of an order of chiefly freshwater stout-bodied fishes with slender tactile processes around the mouth
cat·gut \-ˌgət\ *n* : a tough cord made usu. from sheep intestines
ca·thar·sis \kə-'thär-səs\ *n, pl* **ca·thar·ses** \-ˌsēz\ **1** : an act of purging or purification **2** : elimination of a complex by bringing it to consciousness and affording it expression
¹**ca·thar·tic** \kə-'thär-tik\ *adj* : of, relating to, or producing catharsis
²**cathartic** *n* : PURGATIVE
ca·the·dral \kə-'thē-drəl\ *n* : the principal church of a diocese
cath·e·ter \'ka-thə-tər\ *n* : a tube for insertion into a bodily passage or cavity usu. for injecting or drawing off material or for keeping a passage open
cath·e·ter·i·za·tion \ˌka-thə-tə-rə-'zā-shən\ *n* : the use of or introduction of a catheter — **cath·e·ter·ize** \'ka-thə-tə-ˌrīz\ *vb*
cath·ode \'ka-ˌthōd\ *n* **1** : the negative electrode of an electrolytic cell **2** : the positive terminal of a battery **3** : the electron-emitting electrode of an electron tube — **cath·od·al** \'ka-ˌthō-dᵊl\ *adj* — **ca·thod·ic** \ka-'thä-dik\ *adj*
cathode–ray tube *n* : a vacuum tube in which a beam of electrons is projected on a fluorescent screen to produce a luminous spot
cath·o·lic \'kath-lik, 'ka-thə-\ *adj* [ME *catholik* relating to the church universal, ultim. fr. Gk *katholikos* universal, general, fr. *katholou* in general] **1** *cap* : of or relating to Catholics and esp. Roman Catholics **2** : GENERAL, UNIVERSAL
Cath·o·lic \'kath-lik, 'ka-thə-\ *n* : a member of a church claiming historical continuity from the ancient undivided Christian church; *esp* : a member of the Roman Catholic Church — **Ca·thol·i·cism** \kə-'thä-lə-ˌsi-zəm\ *n*
cath·o·lic·i·ty \ˌka-thə-'li-sə-tē\ *n, pl* **-ties 1** *cap* : the character of being in conformity with a Catholic church **2** : liberality of sentiments or views **3** : comprehensive range
cat·ion \'kat-ˌī-ən\ *n* : the ion in an electrolyte that migrates to the cathode; *also* : a positively charged ion
cat·kin \'kat-kən\ *n* : a long flower cluster (as of a willow) bearing crowded flowers and prominent bracts
cat·like \-ˌlīk\ *adj* : resembling a cat or its behavior; *esp* : STEALTHY

¹**cat·nap** \-ₘnap\ *n* ♦ : a very short light nap

♦ doze, drowse, forty winks, nap, siesta, snooze, wink — more at NAP

²**catnap** *vb* : to sleep for a short period of time

cat·nip \-ₘnip\ *n* : an aromatic mint that is esp. attractive to cats

cat–o'–nine–tails \ₘka-tə-ˈnīn-ₘtālz\ *n, pl* **cat–o'–nine–tails** : a whip made of usu. nine knotted cords fastened to a handle

CAT scan \ˈkat-\ *n* [*computerized axial tomography*] : an image made by computed tomography

CAT scanner *n* : a medical instrument consisting of integrated X-ray and computing equipment that is used to make CAT scans

cat's cradle *n* : a game played with a string looped on the fingers in such a way as to resemble a small cradle

cat's–eye \ˈkats-ₘī\ *n, pl* **cat's–eyes** : any of various iridescent gems

cat's–paw \-ₘpȯ\ *n, pl* **cat's–paws** : a person used by another as a tool

cat·tail \ˈkat-ₘtāl\ *n* : any of a genus of tall reedlike marsh plants with furry brown spikes of tiny flowers

cat·ti·ly \ˈka-tᵊl-ē\ *adv* : in a catty manner

cat·ti·ness *n* ♦ : the quality or state of being catty

♦ acidity, acrimony, asperity, bitterness, tartness, virulence, vitriol — more at ACRIMONY ♦ despite, hatefulness, malice, malignity, meanness, nastiness, spite, spleen, venom, viciousness — more at MALICE

cat·tle \ˈkat-ᵊl\ *n pl* : LIVESTOCK; *esp* : domestic bovines (as cows, bulls, or calves) — **cat·tle·man** \-mən, -ₘman\ *n*

cat·ty \ˈka-tē\ *adj* **cat·ti·er; -est** ♦ : slyly spiteful

♦ cruel, hateful, malevolent, malicious, malign, malignant, mean, nasty, spiteful, virulent — more at HATEFUL

catty–corner *or* **catty–cornered** *var of* KITTY-CORNER

CATV *abbr* community antenna television

cat·walk \ˈkat-ₘwȯk\ *n* : a narrow walk (as along a bridge)

Cau·ca·sian \kȯ-ˈkā-zhən\ *adj* : of or relating to the white race of humankind — **Caucasian** *n* — **Cau·ca·soid** \ˈkȯ-kə-ₘsȯid\ *adj or n*

cau·cus \ˈkȯ-kəs\ *n* : a meeting of a group of persons belonging to the same political party or faction usu. to decide upon policies and candidates — **caucus** *vb*

cau·dal \ˈkȯ-dᵊl\ *adj* : of, relating to, or located near the tail or the hind end of the body — **cau·dal·ly** *adv*

cau·di·llo \kaü-ˈthē-(ₘ)yō, -ˈthēl-\ *n, pl* **-llos** : a Spanish or Latin-American military dictator

caught \ˈkȯt\ *past and past part of* CATCH

caul \ˈkȯl\ *n* : the inner fetal membrane of higher vertebrates esp. when covering the head at birth

caul·dron \ˈkȯl-drən\ *n* : a large kettle

cau·li·flow·er \ˈkȯ-li-ₘflaü(-ə)r\ *n* [It *cavolfiore*, fr. *cavolo* cabbage + *fiore* flower] : a garden plant closely related to cabbage and grown for its compact edible head of undeveloped flowers; *also* : this head used as a vegetable

cauliflower ear *n* : an ear deformed from injury and excessive growth of scar tissue

¹**caulk** \ˈkȯk\ *vb* [ME, fr. AF *cauker, calcher* to trample, fr. L *calcare*, fr. *calx* heel] : to stop up and make tight against leakage (as a boat or its seams) — **caulk·er** *n*

²**caulk** *also* **caulk·ing** *n* : material used to caulk

caus·al \ˈkȯ-zəl\ *adj* **1** : expressing or indicating cause **2** : relating to or acting as a cause — **cau·sal·i·ty** \kȯ-ˈza-lə-tē\ *n* — **caus·al·ly** *adv*

cau·sa·tion \kȯ-ˈzā-shən\ *n* **1** : the act or process of causing **2** : the means by which an effect is produced

¹**cause** \ˈkȯz\ *n* **1** : REASON, MOTIVE **2 a** ♦ : something that brings about a result **b** ♦ : a person or thing that is the agent of bringing something about **3** : a suit or action in court : CASE **4** : a question or matter to be decided **5** : a principle or movement earnestly supported — **cause·less** *adj*

♦ [2a] bandwagon, campaign, crusade, drive, movement — more at CAMPAIGN ♦ [2a, 2b] antecedent,

occasion, reason; *also* consideration, determinant, factor; impetus, incentive, inspiration, instigation, stimulus; mother, origin, root, source, spring *Ant* aftereffect, aftermath, consequence, corollary, development, effect, fate, fruit, issue, outcome, outgrowth, product, result, resultant, sequel, sequence, upshot

²**cause** *vb* **caused; caus·ing** ♦ : to be the cause or occasion of — **caus·a·tive** \ˈkȯ-zə-tiv\ *adj* — **caus·er** *n*

♦ bring about, create, effect, effectuate, generate, induce, make, produce, prompt, result, work, yield — more at EFFECT

cause cé·lè·bre \ₘkȯz-sā-ˈlebrᵊ, ₘkȯz-\ *n, pl* **causes célèbres** *same*\ [F, lit., celebrated case] **1** : a legal case that excites widespread interest **2** : a notorious person, thing, incident, or episode

cau·se·rie \ₘkȯz-ˈrē, ₘkō-zə-\ *n* [F] **1** : an informal conversation : CHAT **2** : a short informal essay

cause·way \ˈkȯz-ₘwā\ *n* : a raised way or road across wet ground or water

¹**caus·tic** \ˈkȯ-stik\ *adj* **1** : CORROSIVE **2** ♦ : marked by incisive sarcasm : SHARP ⟨∼ wit⟩

♦ acrid, biting, cutting, mordant, pungent, sarcastic, satiric, scathing, sharp, tart — more at SARCASTIC

²**caustic** *n* **1** : a substance that burns or destroys organic tissue by chemical action **2** : SODIUM HYDROXIDE

cau·ter·ize \ˈkȯ-tə-ₘrīz\ *vb* **-ized; -iz·ing** : to burn or sear usu. to prevent infection or bleeding — **cau·ter·i·za·tion** \ₘkȯ-tə-rə-ˈzā-shən\ *n*

¹**cau·tion** \ˈkȯ-shən\ *n* **1** ♦ : a warning or reminder of possible danger or risk : ADMONITION, WARNING **2** ♦ : prudent forethought to minimize risk **3** ♦ : one that astonishes

♦ [1] admonition, alarm, alert, notice, warning — more at WARNING ♦ [2] alertness, care, carefulness, circumspection, heedfulness; *also* attentiveness, vigilance, watchfulness; foresight, foresightedness, providence; calculation, canniness, deliberateness, deliberation, shrewdness *Ant* carelessness, heedlessness, recklessness ♦ [3] flash, marvel, miracle, phenomenon, portent, prodigy, sensation, wonder — more at WONDER

²**caution** *vb* ♦ : to advise caution to

♦ alert, forewarn, warn — more at WARN

cau·tion·ary \-shə-ₘner-ē\ *adj* ♦ : having the characteristics of or serving as a caution

♦ admonishing, admonitory, warning; *also* advisory, counseling; punishing, punitive

cau·tious \ˈkȯ-shəs\ *adj* ♦ : marked by or given to caution : CAREFUL — **cau·tious·ly** *adv*

♦ alert, careful, circumspect, considerate, gingerly, guarded, heedful, safe, wary — more at CAREFUL

cau·tious·ness *n* : the quality or state of being cautious

cav *abbr* **1** cavalry **2** cavity

cav·al·cade \ₘka-vəl-ˈkād\ *n* **1 a** : a procession of riders or carriages **b** ♦ : a procession of vehicles **2** : a dramatic sequence or procession

♦ armada, caravan, fleet, motorcade, train — more at FLEET

¹**cav·a·lier** \ₘka-və-ˈlir\ *n* [MF, fr. It *cavaliere*, fr. Old Occitan *cavalier*, fr. LL *caballarius* horseman, fr. L *caballus* horse] **1** : a mounted soldier : KNIGHT **2** *cap* : an adherent of Charles I of England **3** : a man who is esp. attentive to women : GALLANT

²**cavalier** *adj* **1** : DEBONAIR **2** ♦ : marked by or given to offhand dismissal of important matters **3** ♦ : marked by lofty disregard of others' interests or feelings : HAUGHTY — **cav·a·lier·ly** *adv*

♦ [2, 3] arrogant, haughty, highfalutin, high-handed, high-hat, imperious, important, lofty, lordly, masterful, overweening, peremptory, pompous, presumptuous, pretentious, supercilious, superior, uppity — more at ARROGANT

cav·al·ry \ˈka-vəl-rē\ *n, pl* **-ries** : troops mounted on horseback or moving in motor vehicles — **cav·al·ry·man** \-mən, -ˌman\ *n*

¹cave \'kāv\ *n* : a natural underground chamber open to the surface

²cave *vb* **caved; cav·ing** **1** ♦ : to collapse or cause to collapse — usu. used with *in* **2** : to cease to resist : SUBMIT — usu. used with *in*

  ♦ *usu* **cave in** collapse, crumple, give, go, yield — more at COLLAPSE

ca·ve·at \'ka-vē-ˌät, -ˌat; 'kä-vē-ˌät\ *n* [L, let him beware] : WARNING

caveat emp·tor \-'emp-tər, -ˌtȯr\ *n* [NL, let the buyer beware] : a principle in commerce: without a warranty the buyer takes a risk

cave–in \'kā-ˌvin\ *n* **1** : the action of caving in **2** : a place where earth has caved in

cave·man \'kāv-ˌman\ *n* **1** : a cave dweller esp. of the Stone Age **2** : a man who acts in a rough or crude manner

cav·ern \'ka-vərn\ *n* : a natural underground chamber or series of chambers open to the surface : CAVE; *esp* : one of large or unknown size — **cav·ern·ous** *adj* — **cav·ern·ous·ly** *adv*

cav·i·ar *also* **cav·i·are** \'ka-vē-ˌär, 'kä-\ *n* : the salted roe of a large fish (as sturgeon) used as an appetizer

cav·il \'ka-vəl\ *vb* **-iled** *or* **-illed; -il·ing** *or* **-il·ling** ♦ : to make frivolous objections or raise trivial objections to — **cavil** *n*

  ♦ carp, fuss, quibble — more at QUIBBLE

cav·il·er *or* **cav·il·ler** *n* ♦ : a person who complains and criticizes for trivial reasons

  ♦ carper, castigator, censurer, critic, faultfinder, nitpicker, railer, scold — more at CRITIC

cav·ing \'kā-viŋ\ *n* : the sport of exploring caves : SPELUNKING

cav·i·ta·tion \ˌka-və-'tā-shən\ *n* : the formation of partial vacuums in a liquid by a swiftly moving solid body (as a propeller) or by high-intensity sound waves

cav·i·ty \'ka-və-tē\ *n, pl* **-ties** **1** ♦ : an unfilled space within a mass : a hollow place **2** : an area of decay in a tooth

  ♦ concavity, dent, depression, hole, hollow, indentation, pit, recess — more at HOLE

ca·vort \kə-'vȯrt\ *vb* ♦ : to bound, prance, or frisk about : CAPER

  ♦ caper, disport, frisk, frolic, gambol, lark, rollick, romp, sport — more at FROLIC

ca·vy \'kā-vē\ *n, pl* **cavies** : GUINEA PIG 1

caw \'kȯ\ *vb* : to utter the harsh call of the crow or a similar cry — **caw** *n*

cay \'kē, 'kā\ *n* ♦ : a small area of land surrounded by water : KEY

  ♦ island, isle, key

cay·enne pepper \ˌkī-'en-, ˌkā-\ *n* : a condiment consisting of ground dried fruits or seeds of a hot pepper

cayman *var of* CAIMAN

Ca·yu·ga \kā-'ü-gə, kī-\ *n, pl* **Cayuga** *or* **Cayugas** : a member of an American Indian people of New York

Cay·use \'kī-ˌyüs, kī-'\ *n* **1** *pl* **Cayuse** *or* **Cayuses** : a member of an American Indian people of Oregon and Washington **2** *pl* **cayuses,** *not cap, West* : a native range horse

Cb *symbol* columbium

CB \'sē-'bē\ *n* : CITIZENS BAND; *also* : the radio set used for citizens-band communications

CBC *abbr* Canadian Broadcasting Corporation

CBD *abbr* cash before delivery

CBS *abbr* Columbia Broadcasting System

CBW *abbr* chemical and biological warfare

¹cc \ˌsē-'sē\ *vb* **cc'd; cc'ing** : to send a copy of an e-mail, letter, etc., to someone ⟨~ an e-mail to a coworker⟩ ⟨~ me on your reply⟩

²cc *abbr* cubic centimeter

CC *abbr* **1** carbon copy **2** community college **3** country club

CCD \ˌsē-ˌsē-'dē\ *n* : CHARGE-COUPLED DEVICE

CCTV *abbr* closed-circuit television

CCU *abbr* **1** cardiac care unit **2** coronary care unit **3** critical care unit

ccw *abbr* counterclockwise

cd *abbr* cord

Cd *symbol* cadmium

¹CD \ˌsē-'dē\ *n* : CERTIFICATE OF DEPOSIT

²CD *n* : a small optical disk usu. containing recorded music or computer data; *also* : the content of a CD

³CD *abbr* Civil Defense

CDR *abbr* commander

CD–ROM \ˌsē-ˌdē-'räm\ *n* : a CD containing computer data that cannot be altered

CDT *abbr* central daylight (saving) time

Ce *symbol* cerium

CE *abbr* **1** chemical engineer **2** civil engineer **3** Corps of Engineers

cease \'sēs\ *vb* **ceased; ceas·ing** ♦ : to come or bring to an end : STOP

  ♦ break off, break up, close, conclude, desist, die, discontinue, end, expire, finish, halt, quit, stop, terminate; *also* lay off (of), refrain (from); knock off; break down, conk (out), cut out, stall; pause, stay, suspend *Ant* continue, hang on, persist

cease–fire \'sēs-'fī(-ə)r\ *n* : a suspension of active hostilities

cease·less \'sēs-ləs\ *adj* ♦ : being without pause or stop : continuing without interruption — **cease·less·ly** *adv*

  ♦ continual, continuous, incessant, unbroken, unceasing, uninterrupted — more at CONTINUOUS ♦ dateless, deathless, endless, eternal, everlasting, immortal, permanent, perpetual, undying, unending — more at EVERLASTING

cease·less·ness *n* ♦ : the quality or state of being ceaseless

  ♦ abidance, continuance, duration, endurance, persistence, subsistence — more at CONTINUATION

ce·cum *also* **cae·cum** \'sē-kəm\ *n, pl* **ce·ca** \-kə\ : the blind pouch at the beginning of the large intestine into which the small intestine opens — **ce·cal** *also* **cae·cal** \-kəl\ *adj*

ce·dar \'sē-dər\ *n* : any of numerous coniferous trees (as a juniper) noted for their fragrant durable wood; *also* : this wood

cede \'sēd\ *vb* **ced·ed; ced·ing** **1** ♦ : to yield or give up **2** ♦ : to transfer (as property) to another : ASSIGN, TRANSFER — **ced·er** *n*

  ♦ [1] deliver, give up, hand over, leave, relinquish, render, surrender, turn over, yield — more at SURRENDER ♦ [2] alienate, assign, deed, make over, transfer — more at TRANSFER

ce·dil·la \si-'di-lə\ *n* : a mark placed under the letter *c* (as ç) to show that the *c* is to be pronounced like *s*

ceil·ing \'sē-liŋ\ *n* **1** : the overhead inside lining of a room **2** ♦ : something thought of as an overhanging shelter or canopy **3** : the height above the ground of the base of the lowest layer of clouds when over half of the sky is obscured **4** : the greatest height at which an airplane can operate efficiently **5** ♦ : a prescribed upper limit ⟨price ~⟩

  ♦ [2] canopy, roof, tent — more at CANOPY ♦ [5] bound, boundary, confines, end, extent, limit, limitation, line, termination — more at LIMIT

cel·an·dine \'se-lən-ˌdīn, -ˌdēn\ *n* : a yellow-flowered herb related to the poppies

cel·e·brant \-brənt\ *n* ♦ : one who celebrates

  ♦ merrymaker, reveler, roisterer; *also* carouser, wassailer; cutup *Ant* killjoy

cel·e·brate \'se-lə-ˌbrāt\ *vb* **-brat·ed; -brat·ing** **1** ♦ : to perform (as a sacrament) with appropriate rites **2** ♦ : to honor (as a holiday) by solemn ceremonies or by refraining from ordinary business **3** : to observe a notable occasion with festivities **4** : EXTOL — **cel·e·bra·to·ry** \-brə-ˌtȯr-ē, -ˌtȯr-; ˌse-lə-'brā-tə-rē\ *adj*

♦ [1, 2] commemorate, keep, observe — more at KEEP

cel·e·brat·ed *adj* ♦ : widely known and often referred to

♦ famed, famous, noted, notorious, prominent, renowned, star, well-known — more at FAMOUS

cel·e·bra·tion \ˌse-lə-'brā-shən\ *n* ♦ : the act or process of celebrating

♦ carnival, festival, festivity, fete, fiesta, gala, jubilee — more at FESTIVAL

cel·e·bra·tor \'se-lə-brā-tər\ *n* : one that celebrates

ce·leb·ri·ty \sə-'le-brə-tē\ *n, pl* **-ties 1** ♦ : the state of being celebrated **2** ♦ : a celebrated person

♦ [1] fame, notoriety, renown — more at FAME
♦ [2] figure, light, luminary, notable, personage, personality, somebody, standout, star, superstar, VIP; *also* favorite, hero, idol; demigod, dignitary, eminence, immortal, pillar, worthy; baron, big shot, bigwig, magnate, mogul, nabob *Ant* nobody

ce·ler·i·ty \sə-'ler-ə-tē\ *n* ♦ : rapidity of motion or action : SPEED, RAPIDITY

♦ fastness, fleetness, haste, hurry, quickness, rapidity, speed, swiftness, velocity — more at SPEED

cel·ery \'se-lə-rē\ *n, pl* **-er·ies** : a European herb related to the carrot and widely grown for the crisp edible stems of its leaves

celery cabbage *n* : CHINESE CABBAGE 2

ce·les·ta \sə-'les-tə\ *or* **ce·leste** \sə-'lest\ *n* : a keyboard instrument with hammers that strike steel plates

ce·les·tial \sə-'les-chəl\ *adj* **1** ♦ : of, relating to, or suggesting heaven or divinity : HEAVENLY **2** : of or relating to the sky ⟨~ bodies⟩ — **ce·les·tial·ly** *adv*

♦ Elysian, empyrean, heavenly, supernal; *also* ethereal, supernatural, transcendent, transcendental, unearthly, unworldly; angelic, beatific, blissful; utopian; cosmic, stellar *Ant* hellish, infernal

celestial navigation *n* : navigation by observation of the positions of stars

celestial sphere *n* : an imaginary sphere of infinite radius against which the celestial bodies appear to be projected

cel·i·ba·cy \'se-lə-bə-sē\ *n* **1** : the state of being unmarried; *esp* : abstention by vow from marriage **2** : abstention from sexual intercourse

cel·i·bate \'se-lə-bət\ *n* : one who lives in celibacy — **celibate** *adj*

cell \'sel\ *n* **1 a** ♦ : a small room (as in a convent or prison) usu. for one person **b** ♦ : a small compartment, cavity, or bounded space **2** : a tiny mass of protoplasm that usu. contains a nucleus, is enclosed by a membrane, and forms the smallest structural unit of living matter capable of functioning independently **3** : a container holding an electrolyte either for generating electricity or for use in electrolysis **4** : a single unit in a device for converting radiant energy into electrical energy — **celled** \'seld\ *adj*

♦ [1a] chamber, closet, room — more at ROOM ♦ [1a, 1b] bay, chamber, compartment, cubicle, room — more at COMPARTMENT

cel·lar \'se-lər\ *n* **1** : the part of a building that is wholly or partly below ground level : BASEMENT **2** : the lowest position (as in an athletic league) **3** : a stock of wines

cel·lar·ette *or* **cel·lar·et** \ˌse-lə-'ret\ *n* : a case or cabinet for a few bottles of wine or liquor

cell body *n* : the nucleus-containing central part of a neuron

cel·lo \'che-lō\ *n, pl* **cellos** : a bass member of the violin family tuned an octave below the viola — **cel·list** \-list\ *n*

cel·lo·phane \'se-lə-ˌfān\ *n* ♦ : a thin transparent material made from cellulose and used as a wrapping

cell phone *n* : a portable cordless telephone for use in a cellular system

cel·lu·lar \'sel-yə-lər\ *adj* **1** : of, relating to, or consisting of cells **2** : of, relating to, or being a radiotelephone system in which a geographical area is divided into small sections each served by a transmitter of limited range

cel·lu·lite \'sel-yə-ˌlīt\ *n* : deposits of lumpy fat within connective tissue (as in the thighs, hips, and buttocks)

cel·lu·lose \'sel-yə-ˌlōs\ *n* : a complex carbohydrate of the cell walls of plants used esp. in making paper or rayon — **cel·lu·los·ic** \ˌsel-yə-'lō-sik\ *adj or n*

Cel·si·us \'sel-sē-əs\ *adj* : relating to or having a scale for measuring temperature on which the interval between the triple point and the boiling point of water is divided into 99.99 degrees with 0.01° being the triple point and 100.00° the boiling point

Celt \'kelt, 'selt\ *n* : a member of any of a group of peoples (as the Irish or Welsh) of western Europe — **Celt·ic** *adj*

cem·ba·lo \'chem-bə-ˌlō\ *n, pl* **-ba·li** \-ˌlē\ *or* **-balos** [It] : HARPSICHORD

¹ce·ment \si-'ment\ *n* **1** : a powder that is produced from a burned mixture chiefly of clay and limestone and that is used in mortar and concrete; *also* : CONCRETE **2 a** ♦ : a binding element or substance (as glue, paste, or plaster) **b** ♦ : something serving to unite firmly **3** : CEMENTUM; *also* : a substance for filling cavities in teeth

♦ [2a] adhesive, glue, size — more at GLUE ♦ [2b] bond, knot, ligature, link, tie — more at BOND

²cement *vb* **1** : to unite by or as if by cement **2** : to cover with concrete — **ce·ment·er** *n*

ce·men·tum \si-'men-təm\ *n* : a specialized external bony layer covering the dentin of the part of a tooth normally within the gum

cem·e·tery \'se-mə-ˌter-ē\ *n, pl* **-ter·ies** [ME *cimitery*, fr. AF *cimiterie*, fr. LL *coemeterium*, fr. Gk *koimētērion* sleeping chamber, burial place, fr. *koiman* to put to sleep] : a burial ground : GRAVEYARD

cen·o·bite \'se-nə-ˌbīt\ *n* : a member of a religious group living together in a monastic community — **cen·o·bit·ic** \ˌse-nə-'bi-tik\ *adj*

ceno·taph \'se-nə-ˌtaf\ *n* [F *cénotaphe*, fr. L *cenotaphium*, fr. Gk *kenotaphion*, fr. *kenos* empty + *taphos* tomb] : a tomb or a monument erected in honor of a person whose body is elsewhere

Ce·no·zo·ic \ˌsē-nə-'zō-ik, ˌse-\ *adj* : of, relating to, or being the era of geologic history that extends from about 65 million years ago to the present — **Cenozoic** *n*

cen·ser \'sen-sər\ *n* : a vessel for burning incense (as in a religious ritual)

¹cen·sor \'sen-sər\ *n* **1** : one of two early Roman magistrates whose duties included taking the census **2** : an official who inspects printed matter or sometimes motion pictures with power to suppress anything objectionable — **cen·so·ri·al** \sen-'sōr-ē-əl\ *adj*

²censor *vb* : to subject to censorship

cen·so·ri·ous \sen-'sōr-ē-əs\ *adj* : marked by or given to censure : CRITICAL — **cen·so·ri·ous·ly** *adv* — **cen·so·ri·ous·ness** *n*

cen·sor·ship \'sen-sər-ˌship\ *n* **1** : the action of a censor esp. in stopping the transmission or publication of matter considered objectionable **2** : the office of a Roman censor

cen·sur·able *adj* ♦ : deserving or open to censure

♦ blamable, blameworthy, culpable, reprehensible — more at BLAMEWORTHY ♦ objectionable, obnoxious, offensive, reprehensible — more at OBJECTIONABLE

¹cen·sure \'sen-chər\ *n* **1** : the act of blaming or condemning sternly **2** ♦ : an official reprimand

♦ denunciation, rebuke, reprimand, reproach, reproof, stricture; *also* admonishment, admonition, castigation, chastisement, punishment; criticism, deprecation, depreciation, disparagement *Ant* citation, commendation, endorsement

²censure *vb* **cen·sured; cen·sur·ing** ♦ : to find fault with and criticize as blameworthy

♦ condemn, damn, decry, denounce, reprehend, reprobate — more at CONDEMN ♦ blame, condemn, criticize, denounce, fault, knock, pan, reprehend — more at CRITICIZE ♦ condemn, denounce, rebuke, reprimand, reproach, reprove; *also* admonish, castigate, chastise, punish; belittle, criticize, deprecate, depreciate, disparage *Ant* cite, commend, endorse

cen·sur·er *n* ♦ : one that censures

♦ carper, castigator, caviler, critic, faultfinder, nitpicker, railer, scold — more at CRITIC

cen·sus \'sen-səs\ *n* **1** : a periodic governmental count of population **2** : COUNT, TALLY — **cen·sus** *vb*

¹cent \'sent\ *n* [MF, hundred, fr. L *centum*] **1** : a monetary unit equal to ¹⁄₁₀₀ of a basic unit of value (as of a dollar) **2** : a coin, token, or note representing one cent

²cent *abbr* **1** centigrade **2** central **3** century

cen·taur \'sen-ˌtȯr\ *n* : any of a race of creatures in Greek mythology half human and half horse

cen·te·nar·i·an \ˌsent-ᵊn-'er-ē-ən\ *n* : a person who is 100 or more years old

cen·te·na·ry \sen-'te-nə-rē, 'sent-ᵊn-ˌer-ē\ *n, pl* **-ries** : CENTENNIAL — **centenary** *adj*

cen·ten·ni·al \sen-'te-nē-əl\ *n* : a 100th anniversary or its celebration — **centennial** *adj*

¹cen·ter *or Can and Brit* **cen·tre** \'sen-tər\ *n* **1** ♦ : the point that is equally distant from all points on the circumference of a circle or surface of a sphere; *also* : MIDDLE **2** ♦ : the point about which an activity concentrates or from which something originates **3** : a region of concentrated population **4** : a middle part **5** *often cap* : political figures holding moderate views esp. between those of conservatives and liberals **6** : a player occupying a middle position (as in football or basketball)

♦ [1] core, midpoint, midst; *also* inside, interior *Ant* perimeter, periphery ♦ [2] base, core, cynosure, eye, focus, heart, hub, mecca, nucleus, seat; *also* kernel, nub, pith; deep, thick; essence, quintessence, soul; attraction, lodestone, magnet

²center *or Can and Brit* **cen·tre** *vb* centered *or* centred; centering *or* centring **1** ♦ : to place or fix at or around a center or central area **2** ♦ : to give a central focus or basis : CONCENTRATE **3** : to have a center : FOCUS

♦ centralize, concentrate, consolidate, unify, unite — more at CENTRALIZE

cen·ter·board *or Can and Brit* **cen·tre·board** \'sen-tər-ˌbȯrd\ *n* : a retractable keel used esp. in sailboats

cen·ter·piece \-ˌpēs\ *or Can and Brit* **cen·tre·piece** *n* **1** : an object in a central position; *esp* : an adornment in the center of a table **2** : one that is of central importance or interest in a larger whole ⟨the ∼ of the speech⟩

cen·tes·i·mal \sen-'te-sə-məl\ *adj* : marked by or relating to division into hundredths

cen·ti·grade \'sen-tə-ˌgrād, 'sän-\ *adj* : relating to, conforming to, or having a thermometer scale on which the interval between the freezing and boiling points of water is divided into 100 degrees with 0° representing the freezing point and 100° the boiling point ⟨10° ∼⟩

cen·ti·gram \-ˌgram\ *n* : a metric unit of measure equal to ¹⁄₁₀₀ gram

cen·ti·li·ter \'sen-ti-ˌlē-tər\ *or Can and Brit* **cen·ti·li·tre** *n* : a metric unit of measure equal to ¹⁄₁₀₀ liter

cen·ti·me·ter \'sen-tə-ˌmē-tər, 'sän-\ *or Can and Brit* **cen·ti·me·tre** *n* : a metric unit of measure equal to ¹⁄₁₀₀ meter

centimeter–gram–second *adj* : of, relating to, or being a system of units based on the centimeter as the unit of length, the gram as the unit of mass, and the second as the unit of time

cen·ti·pede \'sen-tə-ˌpēd\ *n* [L *centipeda*, fr. *centum* hundred + *pes* foot] : any of a class of long flattened segmented arthropods with one pair of legs on each segment except the first which has a pair of poison fangs

¹cen·tral \'sen-trəl\ *adj* **1** : constituting a center **2** ♦ : belonging to the center as the most important part : PRINCIPAL **3** : situated at, in, or near the center **4** : centrally placed and superseding separate units ⟨∼ heating⟩ — **cen·tral·ly** *adv*

♦ arch, cardinal, chief, dominant, first, foremost, grand, key, main, paramount, predominant, preeminent, premier, primary, principal, sovereign, supreme — more at FOREMOST

²central *n* : a central controlling office

cen·tral·ise *Brit var of* CENTRALIZE

cen·tral·ize \'sen-trə-ˌlīz\ *vb* **-ized; -iz·ing** ♦ : to bring to a central point or under central control — **cen·tral·i·za·tion** \ˌsen-trə-lə-'zā-shən\ *n* — **cen·tral·iz·er** \'sen-trə-ˌlī-zər\ *n*

♦ center (*or* centre), concentrate, consolidate, unify, unite; *also* coordinate, harmonize, integrate, orchestrate; blend, coalesce, combine, fuse, incorporate, merge; conjoin, join, link; assemble, collect, gather; reunify, reunite *Ant* decentralize, spread (out)

central nervous system *n* : the part of the nervous system which integrates nervous function and activity and which in vertebrates consists of the brain and spinal cord

cen·tre *Can and Brit var of* CENTER

cen·trif·u·gal \sen-'tri-fyə-gəl, -fi-\ *adj* [NL *centrifugus*, fr. *centr-* center + L *fugere* to flee] **1** : proceeding or acting in a direction away from a center or axis **2** : using or acting by centrifugal force

centrifugal force *n* : the apparent force felt by an object moving in a curved path and acting outward from a center of rotation

cen·tri·fuge \'sen-trə-ˌfyüj\ *n* : a machine using centrifugal force (as for separating substances of different densities or for removing moisture)

cen·trip·e·tal \sen-'tri-pət-ᵊl\ *adj* [NL *centripetus*, fr. *centr-* center + L *petere* to seek] : proceeding or acting in a direction toward a center or axis

centripetal force *n* : the force needed to keep an object revolving about a point moving in a circular path

cen·trist \'sen-trist\ *n* **1** *often cap* : a member of a center party **2** : one who holds moderate views

cen·tu·ri·on \sen-'tùr-ē-ən, -'tyùr-\ *n* : an officer commanding a Roman century

cen·tu·ry \'sen-chə-rē\ *n, pl* **-ries** **1** : a subdivision of a Roman legion **2** : a group or sequence of 100 like things **3** : a period of 100 years

century plant *n* : a Mexican agave maturing and flowering only once in many years and then dying

CEO \ˌsē-(ˌ)ē-'ō\ *n* : the executive with the chief decision-making authority in an organization or business

ce·phal·ic \sə-'fa-lik\ *adj* **1** : of or relating to the head **2** : directed toward or situated on or in or near the head

ce·ram·ic \sə-'ra-mik\ *n* **1** *pl* : the art or process of making articles from a nonmetallic mineral (as clay) by firing **2** : a product produced by ceramics — **ceramic** *adj*

ce·ra·mist \sə-'ra-mist\ *or* **ce·ram·i·cist** \sə-'ra-mə-sist\ *n* : one who engages in ceramics

¹ce·re·al \'sir-ē-əl\ *adj* [L *cerealis*, fr. *Ceres*, the Roman goddess of agriculture] : relating to grain or to the plants that produce it; *also* : made of grain

²cereal *n* **1** : a grass (as wheat) yielding grain suitable for food; *also* : its grain **2** : a food and esp. a breakfast food prepared from the grain of a cereal

cer·e·bel·lum \ˌser-ə-'be-ləm\ *n, pl* **-bellums** *or* **-bel·la** \-lə\ [ML, fr. L, dim. of *cerebrum* brain] : a part of the brain that projects over the medulla and is concerned esp. with coordination of muscular action and with bodily balance — **cer·e·bel·lar** \-lər\ *adj*

ce·re·bral \sə-'rē-brəl, 'ser-ə-\ *adj* **1** ♦ : of or relating to the brain, intellect, or cerebrum **2** ♦ : appealing to or involving the intellect — **ce·re·bral·ly** *adv*

♦ [1, 2] inner, intellectual, mental, psychological — more at MENTAL

cerebral cortex *n* : the surface layer of gray matter of the cerebrum that functions chiefly in coordination of sensory and motor information

cerebral palsy *n* : a disorder caused by brain damage usu. before, during, or shortly after birth and marked esp. by defective muscle control

cer·e·brate \'ser-ə-₁brāt\ vb **-brat·ed; -brat·ing** : THINK — **cer·e·bra·tion** \₁ser-ə-'brā-shən\ n

ce·re·brum \sə-'rē-brəm, 'ser-ə-\ n, pl **-brums** or **-bra** \-brə\ [L, brain] : the enlarged front and upper part of the brain that contains the higher nervous centers

cere·ment \'ser-ə-mənt, 'sir-mənt\ n : a shroud for the dead

¹cer·e·mo·ni·al \₁ser-ə-'mō-nē-əl\ adj **1** ♦ : of, relating to, or forming a ceremony **2** : stressing careful attention to form and detail — **cer·e·mo·ni·al·ly** adv

♦ ceremonious, conventional, formal, orthodox, regular, routine — more at FORMAL

²ceremonial n : a ceremonial act or system : RITUAL, FORM

cer·e·mo·ni·ous \₁ser-ə-'mō-nē-əs\ adj **1** : devoted to forms and ceremony **2** : of, relating to, or constituting a ceremony : CEREMONIAL **3** ♦ : according to formal usage or procedure **4** ♦ : marked by ceremony — **cer·e·mo·ni·ous·ly** adv — **cer·e·mo·ni·ous·ness** n

♦ [3, 4] correct, decorous, formal, proper, starchy; also sober, solemn, stately; chivalrous, courtly, gallant; genteel, polished, refined; civil, courteous, polite, red-carpet **Ant** casual, easygoing, informal, laid-back

cer·e·mo·ny \'ser-ə-₁mō-nē\ n, pl **-nies 1** ♦ : a formal act or series of acts prescribed by law, ritual, or convention **2** : a conventional act of politeness **3** : a mere outward form with no deeper significance **4** : FORMALITY

♦ ceremonial, form, formality, observance, rite, ritual, solemnity — more at RITE

ce·re·us \'sir-ē-əs\ n : any of various cacti of the western U.S. and tropical America

ce·rise \sə-'rēs\ n [F, lit., cherry] : a moderate red color

ce·ri·um \'sir-ē-əm\ n : a malleable metallic chemical element used esp. in alloys

cer·met \'sər-₁met\ n : a strong alloy of a heat-resistant compound and a metal used esp. for turbine blades

cert abbr certificate; certification; certified; certify

¹cer·tain \'sərt-ᵊn\ adj **1** ♦ : not subject to change or fluctuation : FIXED, SETTLED **2** ♦ : of a specific but unspecified character ⟨~ people in authority⟩ **3 a** : capable of being depended on : DEPENDABLE, RELIABLE **b** ♦ : incapable of failing **4** : INDISPUTABLE, UNDENIABLE **5** ♦ : assured in mind or action ⟨I am ~ that I am right⟩ **6** : INEVITABLE

♦ [1] determinate, final, firm, fixed, flat, frozen, hard, hard-and-fast, set, settled, stable — more at FIXED ♦ [2] anonymous, one, some, unidentified, unnamed, unspecified; also particular, specific ♦ [3b] sure, surefire, unfailing ♦ [5] assured, clear, cocksure, confident, doubtless, positive, sanguine, sure; also self-assured, self-confident; decisive, resolute, unfaltering, unhesitating, unwavering **Ant** doubtful, dubious, uncertain, unsure

²certain pron : certain ones

cer·tain·ly adv **1** ♦ : in a manner that is certain : with certainty **2** : it is certain that

♦ definitely, doubtless, incontestably, indeed, indisputably, really, surely, truly, undeniably, undoubtedly, unquestionably — more at INDEED

cer·tain·ty \-tē\ n, pl **-ties 1** : something that is certain **2** ♦ : the quality or state of being certain

♦ assurance, certitude, confidence, conviction, positiveness, sureness — more at CONFIDENCE

cer·tif·i·cate \sər-'ti-fi-kət\ n **1** : a document testifying to the truth of a fact **2** : a document testifying that one has fulfilled certain requirements (as of a course or school) **3** : a document giving evidence of ownership or debt ⟨a stock ~⟩

certificate of deposit : a money-market bond redeemable without penalty only on maturity

cer·ti·fi·ca·tion \₁sər-tə-fə-'kā-shən\ n **1** : the act of certifying : the state of being certified **2** : a certified statement

certified mail n : first class mail for which proof of delivery may be secured but no indemnity value is claimed

certified public accountant n : an accountant who has met

the requirements of a state law and has been granted a certificate

cer·ti·fy \'sər-tə-₁fī\ vb **-fied; -fy·ing 1** ♦ : to attest as being true **2** : to endorse officially **3** : to guarantee (a bank check) as good by a statement to that effect stamped on its face **4** ♦ : to provide with a usu. professional certificate or license — **cer·ti·fi·able** \-ə-bəl\ adj — **cer·ti·fi·ably** \-blē\ adv — **cer·ti·fi·er** n

♦ [1] attest, authenticate, avouch, testify, vouch, witness; also guarantee, warrant; affirm, assert, aver, avow, profess ♦ [4] accredit, authorize, commission, empower, enable, invest, license, qualify — more at AUTHORIZE

cer·ti·tude \'sər-tə-₁tüd, -₁tyüd\ n ♦ : the state of being or feeling certain

♦ assurance, certainty, confidence, conviction, positiveness, sureness — more at CONFIDENCE

ce·ru·le·an \sə-'rü-lē-ən\ adj : AZURE

ce·ru·men \sə-'rü-mən\ n : EARWAX

cer·vi·cal \'sər-vi-kəl\ adj : of or relating to a neck or cervix

cervical cap n : a contraceptive device in the form of a thimble-shaped molded cap that fits over the uterine cervix and blocks sperm from entering the uterus

cer·vix \'sər-viks\ n, pl **cer·vi·ces** \-və-₁sēz\ or **cer·vix·es 1** : NECK; esp : the back part of the neck **2** : a constricted portion of an organ or part; esp : the narrow outer end of the uterus

ce·sar·e·an or **cae·sar·e·an** also **ce·sar·i·an** \si-'zar-ē-ən\ n, often cap : CESAREAN SECTION — **cesarean** or **caesarean** also **cesarian** adj, often cap

cesarean section also **caesarean section** n, often cap C [fr. the legendary association of such a delivery with the Roman cognomen Caesar] : surgical incision of the walls of the abdomen and uterus for delivery of offspring

ce·si·um \'sē-zē-əm\ n : a silver-white soft ductile chemical element

ces·sa·tion \se-'sā-shən\ n ♦ : a temporary or final ceasing (as of action)

♦ close, closure, conclusion, end, ending, expiration, finish, halt, lapse, shutdown, stop, stoppage, termination — more at END

ces·sion \'se-shən\ n : a yielding (as of rights) to another

cess·pool \'ses-₁pül\ n : an underground pit or tank for receiving household sewage

ce·ta·cean \si-'tā-shən\ n : any of an order of aquatic mostly marine mammals that includes whales, porpoises, dolphins, and related forms — **cetacean** adj

cf abbr [L confer] compare

Cf symbol californium

CF abbr cystic fibrosis

CFC abbr chlorofluorocarbon

CFL abbr compact fluorescent lamp; compact fluorescent light bulb

CFO abbr chief financial officer

cg abbr centigram

CG abbr **1** coast guard **2** commanding general

cgs abbr centimeter-gram-second

ch abbr **1** chain **2** champion **3** chapter **4** church

CH abbr **1** clearinghouse **2** courthouse **3** customhouse

Cha·blis \sha-'blē, shə-, shä-; 'sha-₁blē\ n, pl **Cha·blis** \-'blēz, -(₁)blēz\ **1** : a dry sharp white Burgundy wine **2** : a white California wine

cha–cha \'chä-₁chä\ n : a fast rhythmic ballroom dance of Latin American origin

Chad·ian \'cha-dē-ən\ n : a native or inhabitant of Chad — **Chadian** adj

chafe \'chāf\ vb **chafed; chaf·ing 1** ♦ : to bring trouble or distress to : cause agitation or anxiety to : IRRITATE, VEX **2** : FRET **3** : to warm by rubbing **4** ♦ : to rub so as to wear away **5** ♦ : to make sore by rubbing

♦ [1] aggravate, annoy, bother, bug, exasperate, gall, get, grate, irk, irritate, nettle, peeve, persecute, pique, put out, rasp, rile, vex — more at IRRITATE ◆ [4] abrade, erode, fray, fret, gall, rub, wear — more at ABRADE ◆ [5] abrade, gall, irritate; *also* graze, scrape, scratch; burn, inflame; flay, peel, skin

cha·fer \'chā-fər\ *n* : any of various scarab beetles

¹chaff \'chaf\ *n* **1** : debris (as husks) separated from grain in threshing **2** ◆ : something relatively worthless

◆ deadwood, dust, garbage, junk, litter, refuse, riffraff, rubbish, scrap, trash, waste — more at GARBAGE

²chaff *n* ◆ : light jesting talk : BANTER

◆ banter, persiflage, raillery, repartee — more at BANTER

³chaff *vb* ◆ : to tease good-naturedly

◆ jive, josh, kid, rally, razz, rib, ride, roast, tease — more at TEASE

chaf·fer \'cha-fər\ *vb* ◆ : to discuss terms : haggle esp. over a price — **chaf·fer·er** *n*

◆ bargain, deal, dicker, haggle, negotiate, palter — more at BARGAIN

chaf·finch \'cha-,finch\ *n* : a common European finch with a cheerful song

chaffy *adj* ◆ : of little importance or worth

◆ empty, junky, no-good, null, valueless, worthless — more at WORTHLESS

chaf·ing dish \'chā-fiŋ-\ *n* : a utensil for cooking food at the table

¹cha·grin \shə-'grin\ *n* : mental uneasiness or annoyance caused by failure, disappointment, or humiliation

²chagrin *vb* **cha·grined** \-'grind\; **cha·grin·ing** : to cause to feel chagrin

¹chain \'chān\ *n* [ME *cheyne*, fr. AF *chaene*, fr. L *catena*] **1** : a flexible series of connected links **2** : a chainlike surveying instrument; *also* : a unit of length equal to 66 feet (about 20 meters) **3** ◆ : something that confines, restrains, or secures : BOND, FETTER **4** ◆ : a series of things linked, connected, or associated together ⟨a ∼ of events⟩ ⟨a mountain ∼⟩

◆ [3] band, bond, fetter, irons, ligature, manacle, shackle — more at BOND ◆ [4] progression, sequence, string, train; *also* chain reaction; belt, circle, cycle; continuum, gamut, scale, spectrum; flow, river, stream; file, line, queue, row, succession

²chain *vb* **1** ◆ : to fasten, bind, or connect with a chain; *also* : FETTER **2** ◆ : to join together so as to make a chain

◆ [1] bind, enchain, fetter, handcuff, manacle, shackle, trammel ◆ [2] compound, connect, couple, hitch, hook, join, link, yoke — more at CONNECT

chain gang *n* : a gang of convicts chained together

chain letter *n* : a letter sent to several persons with a request that each send copies to an equal number of persons

chain mail *n* : flexible armor of interlocking metal rings

chain reaction *n* **1** : a series of events in which each event initiates the succeeding one **2** : a chemical or nuclear reaction yielding products that cause further reactions of the same kind

chain saw *n* : a portable power saw that has teeth linked together to form an endless chain — **chain·saw** \'chān-,so\ *vb*

chain–smoke \'chān-'smōk\ *vb* : to smoke esp. cigarettes continuously

chain store *n* : any of numerous stores under the same ownership that sell the same lines of goods

¹chair \'cher\ *n* [ME *chaiere*, fr. AF, fr. L *cathedra*, fr. Gk *kathedra*, fr. *kata-* down + *hedra* seat] **1** : a seat with a back for one person **2** : ELECTRIC CHAIR **3** ◆ : an official seat or a seat of authority, state, or dignity; *also* : an office or position of authority or dignity **4** : the presiding officer of a meeting or event : CHAIRMAN

◆ head, headship, helm, rein — more at HEAD

²chair *vb* : to act as chairman of

chair·lift \'cher-,lift\ *n* : a motor-driven conveyor for skiers consisting of seats hung from a moving cable

chair·man \-mən\ *n* ◆ : the presiding officer of a meeting or of a committee — **chair·man·ship** *n*

◆ chair, moderator, president, speaker

chair·per·son \-,pər-sən\ *n* : the presiding officer of a meeting or assembly : CHAIRMAN

chair·wom·an \-,wu̇-mən\ *n* : a woman who serves as chairman

chaise \'shāz\ *n* : a 2-wheeled horse-drawn carriage with a folding top

chaise longue \'shāz-'loŋ\ *n, pl* **chaise longues** *same or* -'loŋz\ [F, lit., long chair] : a long reclining chair

chaise lounge \-'laùnj\ *n* : CHAISE LONGUE

chal·ced·o·ny \kal-'sed-ᵊn-ē\ *n, pl* **-nies** : a translucent pale blue or gray quartz

chal·co·py·rite \,kal-kə-'pī-,rīt\ *n* : a yellow mineral constituting an important ore of copper

cha·let \sha-'lā\ *n* **1** : a herdsman's cabin in the Swiss mountains **2 a** : a building in the style of a Swiss cottage with a wide roof overhang **b** ◆ : a cottage or house in chalet style

◆ cabin, camp, cottage, lodge — more at COTTAGE

chal·ice \'cha-ləs\ *n* : a drinking cup; *esp* : the eucharistic cup

¹chalk \'chok\ *n* **1** : a soft limestone **2** : chalk or chalky material esp. when used as a crayon — **chalky** *adj*

²chalk *vb* **1** : to rub or mark with chalk **2** : to record with or as if with chalk — usu. used with *up*

chalk·board \'chok-,bòrd\ *n* : BLACKBOARD

chalk up *vb* **1** : ASCRIBE, CREDIT **2** : ATTAIN, ACHIEVE

¹chal·lenge \'cha-lənj\ *vb* **chal·lenged; chal·leng·ing** [ME *chalengen* to accuse, fr. OF *chalengier*, fr. L *calumniari* to accuse falsely, fr. *calumnia* calumny] **1** : to order to halt and prove identity **2** ◆ : to dispute esp. as being unjust, invalid, or untrue : to take exception to : DISPUTE **3** ◆ : to issue an invitation to compete against one esp. in single combat : DARE, DEFY

◆ [2] contest, dispute, query, question; *also* doubt, mistrust; kick (about), object (to), protest; combat, fight, oppose, resist *Ant* accept, believe, embrace, swallow ◆ [3] dare, defy; *also* beard, brave, brazen, breast, confront, face

²challenge *n* **1** : a summons to a duel **2** : an invitation to compete in a sport **3** ◆ : a calling to account or into question **4** : an exception taken to a juror **5** : a sentry's command to halt and prove identity **6** : a stimulating or interesting task or problem

◆ complaint, demur, expostulation, fuss, kick, objection, protest, question, remonstrance — more at OBJECTION

challenged *adj* : presented with difficulties (as by a disability) : DISABLED

chal·leng·er *n* ◆ : one that challenges; *specif* : a contender for a championship (as boxing)

◆ competition, competitor, contender, contestant, rival — more at COMPETITOR

challenging *adj* ◆ : arousing competitive interest, thought, or action ⟨a ∼ course of study⟩

◆ arduous, burdensome, demanding, exacting, grueling, laborious, onerous, taxing, toilsome — more at DEMANDING

chal·lis \'sha-lē\ *n, pl* **chal·lises** \-lēz\ : a lightweight clothing fabric of wool, cotton, or synthetic yarns

cham·ber \'chām-bər\ *n* **1** ◆ : a partitioned part of the inside of a building : ROOM **2** ◆ : an enclosed space or cavity **3** : a hall for meetings of a legislative body **4** : a judge's consultation room — usu. used in pl. **5** : a legislative or judicial body; *also* : a council for a business purpose **6** : the part of a firearm that holds the cartridge or powder charge during firing — **cham·bered** \-bərd\ *adj*

◆ [1, 2] bay, cabin, cell, compartment, cubicle — more at COMPARTMENT

cham·ber·lain \'chām-bər-lən\ *n* **1** : a chief officer in the household of a king or nobleman **2** : TREASURER

cham·ber·maid \-,mād\ *n* : a maid who takes care of bedrooms

chamber music *n* : music intended for performance by a few musicians before a small audience

cham·bray \'sham-,brā\ *n* : a lightweight clothing fabric of white and colored threads

cha·me·leon \kə-'mēl-yən\ *n* [ME *camelion*, fr. MF, fr. L *chamaeleon*, fr. Gk *chamaileōn*, fr. *chamai* on the ground + *leōn* lion] : a small lizard whose skin changes color esp. according to its surroundings

¹cham·fer \'cham-fər\ *vb* 1 : to cut a furrow in (as a column) : GROOVE 2 : to make a chamfer on : BEVEL

²chamfer *n* : a beveled edge

cham·ois \'sha-mē\ *n, pl* **cham·ois** *same or* -mēz\ 1 : a small goatlike antelope of Europe and the Caucasus region of Russia 2 *also* **cham·my** \'sha-mē\ : a soft leather made esp. from the skin of the sheep or goat 3 : a cotton fabric made in imitation of chamois leather

cham·o·mile \'ka-mə-,mīl, -,mēl\ *n* : any of a genus of strong-scented herbs related to the daisies and having flower heads that yield a bitter substance used esp. in tonics and teas

¹champ \'champ, 'chämp\ *vb* 1 : to chew noisily 2 : to show impatience of delay or restraint

²champ \'champ\ *n* ♦ : a winner of first prize or first place in competition : CHAMPION; *also* : one who shows marked superiority

♦ champion, victor, winner — more at CHAMPION

cham·pagne \sham-'pān\ *n* : a white effervescent wine

¹cham·pi·on \'cham-pē-ən\ *n* 1 ♦ : a militant advocate or defender 2 ♦ : one that wins first prize or place in a contest 3 : one that is acknowledged to be better than all others

♦ [1] advocate, apostle, backer, booster, exponent, friend, promoter, proponent, supporter — more at EXPONENT ♦ [2] champ, victor, winner; *also* finalist, semifinalist; medalist, prizewinner; star, superstar

²champion *vb* ♦ : to protect or fight for as a champion

♦ advocate, back, endorse, patronize, support — more at SUPPORT

cham·pi·on·ship \-,ship\ *n* 1 : the position or title of a champion 2 : the act of championing : DEFENSE 3 : a contest held to determine a champion

¹chance \'chans\ *n* 1 : something that happens without apparent cause 2 ♦ : the unpredictable element in existence : LUCK 3 ♦ : a situation favoring some purpose : OPPORTUNITY 4 ♦ : the likelihood of a particular outcome in an uncertain situation : PROBABILITY 5 ♦ : a gamble or risk taken in hopes of a favorable outcome with a real possibility of loss 6 : a raffle ticket — **by chance** : in the haphazard course of events

♦ [2] accident, circumstance, hazard, luck; *also* randomness, uncertainty; fluke; destiny, doom, fate, fortune, lot; danger, peril, risk ♦ [3] occasion, opening, opportunity, room — more at OPPORTUNITY ♦ [4] odds, percentage, probability — more at PROBABILITY ♦ [5] enterprise, flier, gamble, speculation, venture — more at GAMBLE

²chance *vb* **chanced; chanc·ing** 1 ♦ : to take place by chance : HAPPEN 2 ♦ : to encounter or discover by chance — used with *upon* 3 : to leave the outcome of to chance 4 ♦ : to accept the risk of

♦ [1] be, befall, betide, come, go, happen, occur, pass, transpire — more at HAPPEN ♦ *usu* **chance upon** [2] encounter, find, happen (on *or* upon), hit, meet, stumble ♦ [4] gamble, hazard, risk, venture — more at RISK

³chance *adj* ♦ : happening, experienced, or encountered by chance, without forethought, plan, or intention

♦ accidental, casual, fluky, fortuitous, incidental, unintended, unintentional, unplanned, unpremeditated, unwitting — more at ACCIDENTAL

chan·cel \'chan-səl\ *n* : the part of a church including the altar and choir

chan·cel·lery *or* **chan·cel·lory** \'chan-sə-lə-rē\ *n, pl* **-ler·ies** *or* **-lor·ies** 1 : the position or office of a chancellor 2 : the building or room where a chancellor works 3 : the office or staff of an embassy or consulate

chan·cel·lor \'chan-sə-lər\ *n* 1 : a high state official in various countries 2 : the head of a university 3 : a judge in the equity court in various states of the U.S. 4 : the chief minister of state in some European countries — **chan·cel·lor·ship** *n*

chan·cery \'chan-sə-rē\ *n, pl* **-cer·ies** 1 : any of various courts of equity in the U.S. and Britain 2 : a record office for public or diplomatic archives 3 : a chancellor's court or office 4 : the office of an embassy

chan·cre \'shan-kər\ *n* [F, fr. OF, fr. L *cancer*] : a primary sore or ulcer at the site of entry of an infective agent (as of syphilis)

chan·croid \'chan-,krȯid\ *n* : a sexually transmitted disease caused by a bacterium and characterized by chancres that differ from those of syphilis in lacking hardened margins

chancy \'chan-sē\ *adj* **chanc·i·er; -est** 1 *Scot* : AUSPICIOUS 2 : RISKY

chan·de·lier \,shan-də-'lir\ *n* : a branched lighting fixture suspended from a ceiling

chan·dler \'chand-lər\ *n* [ME *chandeler* a maker or seller of candles, fr. AF, fr. *chandele* candle, fr. L *candela*] : a dealer in provisions and supplies of a specified kind ⟨ship's ∼⟩ — **chan·dlery** *n*

¹change \'chānj\ *vb* **changed; chang·ing** 1 ♦ : to make or become different : ALTER 2 ♦ : to replace with another 3 : to give or receive an equivalent sum in notes or coins of usu. smaller denominations or of another currency 4 : to put fresh clothes or covering on ⟨∼ a bed⟩ 5 : to put on different clothes 6 ♦ : to switch to or with another : EXCHANGE ⟨neither liked his seat so they ∼ed with each other⟩ — **chang·er** *n*

♦ [1] alter, make over, modify, recast, redo, refashion, remake, remodel, revamp, revise, rework, vary; *also* deform, metamorphose, mutate; revolutionize, transfigure, transform, transmute; commute, convert, exchange *Ant* fix, freeze, set, stabilize ♦ [1] fluctuate, mutate, shift, vary; *also* metamorphose, transmute; better, improve; deteriorate, worsen; seesaw, teeter, vacillate, waver *Ant* stabilize ♦ [2, 6] commute, exchange, shift, substitute, swap, switch, trade; *also* interchange; displace, replace, supersede; cede, surrender, yield

²change *n* 1 ♦ : the act, process, or result of changing 2 : a fresh set of clothes 3 : money given in exchange for other money of higher denomination 4 : money returned when a payment exceeds the sum due 5 : coins esp. of small denominations

♦ alteration, difference, modification, revise, revision, variation; *also* amendment, correction, rectification; conversion, deformation, distortion, metamorphosis, mutation, transfiguration, transformation; fluctuation, oscillation, shift; displacement, replacement, substitution; adjustment, modulation, regulation *Ant* fixation, stabilization

change·able *adj* 1 ♦ : subject to change ⟨∼ plans⟩ 2 ♦ : able or apt to vary ⟨∼ weather⟩

♦ [1] adaptable, adjustable, elastic, flexible, fluid, malleable, variable — more at FLEXIBLE ♦ [2] capricious, fickle, fluid, inconstant, mercurial, mutable, temperamental, uncertain, unpredictable, unsettled, unstable, unsteady, variable, volatile — more at FICKLE

change·ful *adj* : notably variable : UNCERTAIN

change·ling \'chānj-liŋ\ *n* : a child secretly exchanged for another in infancy

change·over \'chānj-,ō-vər\ *n* ♦ : the action of changing over : CONVERSION

♦ conversion, metamorphosis, transfiguration, transformation — more at CONVERSION

change ringing *n* : the art or practice of ringing a set of tuned bells in continually varying order

¹**chan·nel** \'chan-ᵊl\ *n* **1** : the bed of a stream **2** : the deeper part of a waterway **3** ♦ : a comparatively narrow passageway connecting two large bodies of water : STRAIT **4** : a means of passage or transmission **5** : a range of frequencies of sufficient width for a single radio or television transmission **6** ♦ : a usu. tubular enclosed passage : CONDUIT **7** ♦ : a long gutter, groove, or furrow usu. for the passage of water

  ♦ [3] narrows, sound, strait; *also* arm, bay, gulf, inlet; roads, roadstead; reach, stretch ♦ [6] conduit, duct, leader, line, penstock, pipe, tube — more at PIPE ♦ [6, 7] aqueduct, canal, conduit, flume, raceway, watercourse; *also* millrace, millstream; river, rivulet, stream

²**channel** *vb* **-neled** *or* **-nelled; -neling** *or* **-nel·ling** **1** : to make a channel in **2** ♦ : to direct into or through a channel

  ♦ conduct, direct, funnel, pipe, siphon; *also* carry, convey, transmit; concentrate, consolidate, focus

chan·nel·ize \'chan-ᵊl-ˌīz\ *vb* **-ized; -iz·ing** : to direct through or into a channel or restricted area : CHANNEL — **chan·nel·iza·tion** \ˌchan-ᵊl-ə-'zā-shən\ *n*

chan·son \shän-'sōⁿ\ *n, pl* **chan·sons** *same or* -'sōⁿz\ : SONG; *esp* : a cabaret song

¹**chant** \'chant\ *vb* **1** ♦ : to make melodic sounds with the voice : SING; *esp* : to sing a chant **2** : to utter or recite in the manner of a chant **3** : to celebrate or praise in song — **chant·er** *n*

  ♦ carol, descant, sing, vocalize — more at SING

²**chant** *n* **1** : a repetitive melody in which several words are sung to one tone : SONG; *esp* : a liturgical melody **2** : a manner of singing or speaking in musical monotones

chan·te·relle \ˌshan-tə-'rel\ *n* : a fragrant edible mushroom

chan·teuse \shäⁿ-'tərz, shan-'tüz\ *n, pl* **chan·teuses** *same or* -'tər-zəz, -'tü-zəz\ [F] : a woman who is a concert or nightclub singer

chan·tey *or* **chan·ty** \'shan-tē, 'chan-\ *n, pl* **chanteys** *or* **chanties** : a song sung by sailors in rhythm with their work

chan·ti·cleer \ˌchan-tə-'klir, ˌshan-\ *n* : ROOSTER

Chanukah *var of* HANUKKAH

cha·os \'kā-ˌäs\ *n* **1** *often cap* : the confused unorganized state existing before the creation of distinct forms **2** : the inherent unpredictability in the behavior of a natural system (as the atmosphere or the beating heart) **3** ♦ : a state of utter confusion or disorder

  ♦ confusion, disarray, disorder, disorganization, havoc, hell, jumble, mess, muddle, shambles; *also* anarchy, lawlessness, misrule; knot, snarl, tangle; labyrinth, maze, web; maelstrom, storm; clutter, litter, shuffle; hodgepodge, medley, miscellany, motley *Ant* order, orderliness

chaos theory *n* : a branch of mathematical and physical theory concerned with chaotic systems

cha·ot·ic \kā-'ä-tik\ *adj* ♦ : completely confused or disordered — **cha·ot·i·cal·ly** \-ti-k(ə-)lē\ *adv*

  ♦ confused, disheveled, disordered, messy, muddled, sloppy, unkempt, untidy — more at MESSY

¹**chap** \'chap\ *vb* **chapped; chap·ping** : to dry and crack open usu. from wind and cold ⟨*chapped* lips⟩

²**chap** *n* : a jaw with its fleshy covering — usu. used in pl.

³**chap** *n* ♦ : an adult male individual : FELLOW

  ♦ buck, dude, fellow, gent, gentleman, guy, hombre, jack, joker, lad, male, man — more at MAN

⁴**chap** *abbr* chapter

chap·ar·ral \ˌsha-pə-'ral\ *n* **1** ♦ : a dense impenetrable thicket of shrubs or dwarf trees **2** : an ecological community esp. of southern California composed of shrubby plants

  ♦ brake, brushwood, coppice, covert, thicket — more at THICKET

chap·book \'chap-ˌbùk\ *n* : a small book of ballads, tales, or tracts

cha·peau \sha-'pō\ *n, pl* **cha·peaus** \-'pōz\ *or* **cha·peaux** \-'pō, -'pōz\ [MF] : HAT

cha·pel \'cha-pəl\ *n* [ME, fr. AF *chapele*, fr. ML *cappella*, fr. LL *cappa* cloak; fr. the cloak of St. Martin of Tours preserved as a sacred relic in a chapel built for that purpose] **1** : a private or subordinate place of worship **2** : an assembly at an educational institution usu. including devotional exercises **3** : a place of worship used by a Christian group other than an established church

¹**chap·er·one** *or* **chap·er·on** \'sha-pə-ˌrōn\ *n* [F *chaperon*, lit., hood, fr. MF, head covering, fr. *chape* cape, fr. LL *cappa*] **1** : a person (as a matron) who accompanies young unmarried women in public for propriety **2** : an older person who accompanies young people at a social gathering to ensure proper behavior

²**chaperone** *or* **chaperon** *vb* **-oned; -on·ing** **1** ♦ : to attend upon : ESCORT **2** ♦ : to act as a chaperone to or for ⟨∼ a dance⟩ — **chap·er·on·age** \-ˌrō-nij\ *n*

  ♦ [1, 2] accompany, attend, convoy, escort, squire — more at ACCOMPANY

chap·fall·en \'chap-ˌfò-lən, 'chäp-\ *adj* **1** : having the lower jaw hanging loosely **2** : DEJECTED, DEPRESSED

chap·lain \'cha-plən\ *n* **1** : a member of the clergy officially attached to a special group (as the army) **2** : a person chosen to conduct religious exercises (as for a club) — **chap·lain·cy** \-sē\ *n*

chap·let \'cha-plət\ *n* **1** : a wreath for the head **2** : a string of beads : NECKLACE

chap·man \'chap-mən\ *n, Brit* : an itinerant dealer : PEDDLER

chaps \'shaps, 'chaps\ *n pl* [MexSp *chaparreras*] : leather leggings resembling trousers without a seat that are worn esp. by western ranch hands

chap·ter \'chap-tər\ *n* **1** : a main division of a book **2** : a body of canons (as of a cathedral) **3** ♦ : a local branch of an organization

  ♦ affiliate, branch, local; *also* arm, division, wing; offshoot; lodge, post

¹**char** \'chär\ *n, pl* **char** *or* **chars** : any of a genus of trouts (as the common brook trout) with small scales

²**char** *vb* **charred; char·ring** **1** : to burn or become burned to charcoal **2** ♦ : to burn slightly or partly : SCORCH

  ♦ scorch, sear, singe — more at SCORCH

³**char** *vb* **charred; char·ring** : to work as a cleaning woman

char·ac·ter \'kar-ik-tər\ *n* [ME *caracter*, fr. MF *caractère*, fr. L *character* mark, distinctive quality, fr. Gk *charaktēr*, fr. *charassein* to scratch, engrave] **1** : a graphic symbol (as a letter) used in writing or printing **2** : a symbol that represents information; *also* : a representation of such a character that may be accepted by a computer **3** : a distinguishing feature : ATTRIBUTE **4** ♦ : the complex of mental and ethical traits marking a person or a group **5** ♦ : a person marked by conspicuous often peculiar traits **6** : one of the persons in a novel or play **7** ♦ : reputation esp. when good : good name **7** : REPUTATION **8** ♦ : moral excellence

  ♦ [4] complexion, constitution, genius, identity, nature, personality, tone — more at NATURE ♦ [5] crackpot, crank, eccentric, kook, nut, oddball, screwball, weirdo — more at ECCENTRIC ♦ [7] mark, name, note, report, reputation — more at REPUTATION ♦ [8] decency, goodness, honesty, honor (*or* honour), integrity, morality, probity, rectitude, righteousness, uprightness, virtue — more at MORALITY

¹**char·ac·ter·is·tic** \ˌkar-ik-tə-'ris-tik\ *n* ♦ : a distinguishing trait, quality, or property

  ♦ attribute, character, feature, mark, peculiarity, point, property, quality, trait; *also* badge, indication, sign; emblem, symbol, token; excellence, merit, virtue; individuality, singularity, uniqueness

²**characteristic** *adj* ♦ : serving to mark individual character — **char·ac·ter·is·ti·cal·ly** \-ti-k(ə-)lē\ *adv*

♦ classic, distinct, distinctive, individual, peculiar, proper, symptomatic, typical; *also* idiosyncratic; identifiable, pronounced, unmistakable; general, generic; common, normal, regular, usual; particular, special, specific; model, paradigmatic **Ant** atypical, nontypical

char·ac·ter·ize \'kar-ik-tə-ˌrīz\ *vb* **-ized; -iz·ing** **1** ♦ : to describe the character of **2** : to be a characteristic of — **char·ac·ter·iza·tion** \ˌkar-ik-tə-rə-'zā-shən\ *n*

♦ define, depict, describe, portray, represent; *also* categorize, classify, pigeonhole, type; identify, indicate, name, specify; distinguish, individualize, mark, particularize, stamp

cha·rades \shə-'rādz\ *n sing or pl* : a game in which some of the players try to guess a word or phrase from the actions of another player who may not speak

char·coal \'chär-ˌkōl\ *n* **1** : a porous carbon prepared from vegetable or animal substances **2** : a piece of fine charcoal used in drawing; *also* : a drawing made with charcoal

chard \'chärd\ *n* : SWISS CHARD

char·don·nay \ˌshard-ᵊn-'ā\ *n, often cap* [F] : a dry white wine made from a single variety of white grape

¹**charge** \'chärj\ *n* **1** : a quantity (as of fuel or ammunition) required to fill something to capacity **2** : a store or accumulation of force **3** : an excess or deficiency of electrons in a body **4** : THRILL, KICK **5** ♦ : a task or duty imposed **6** : a person or thing committed to the care of another : CARE **7** ♦ : control of the acts, workings, or disposition of something **8 a** ♦ : a direction or order calling for compliance **b** : instructions from a judge to a jury **9** ♦ : the price demanded for something : COST, PRICE; *also* : a debit to an account **10** ♦ : a formal assertion of illegality : INDICTMENT **11** : a violent rush forward (as to attack) : ATTACK, ASSAULT

♦ [5] assignment, job, mission, operation, post — more at MISSION ♦ [7] care, guidance, headship, oversight, regulation, superintendence, supervision — more at SUPERVISION ♦ [8a] behest, command, commandment, decree, dictate, direction, directive, edict, instruction, order, word — more at COMMAND ♦ [9] cost, fee, figure, price — more at PRICE ♦ [10] complaint, count, indictment, rap; *also* accusation, allegation, arraignment, impeachment; implication, innuendo, insinuation; censure, denunciation; incrimination

²**charge** *vb* **charged; charg·ing** **1** : to load or fill to capacity **2** : to give an electric charge to; *also* : to restore the activity of (a storage battery) by means of an electric current **3** ♦ : to impose a task or responsibility on **4** : to command, instruct, or exhort with authority : COMMAND, ORDER ⟨I ∼ you not to go⟩ **5** : to make an assertion against esp. by ascribing guilt or blame : ACCUSE **6** ♦ : to rush against : rush forward in assault **7** ♦ : to make liable for payment; *also* : to record a debt or liability against **8** ♦ : to fix as a price — **charge·able** *adj*

♦ [3] assign, commission, entrust, trust — more at ENTRUST ♦ [6] assail, assault, attack, beset, descend, jump, pounce (on *or* upon), raid, rush, storm, strike — more at ATTACK ♦ [7] assess, exact, fine, impose, lay, levy, put — more at IMPOSE ♦ [8] ask, command, demand; *also* overcharge, undercharge; bring, fetch, sell (for); discount, mark down, mark up; assess, price, value

charge–coupled device *n* : a semiconductor device used esp. as an optical sensor

charged \'chärjd\ *adj* **1** ♦ : possessing or showing strong emotion **2** : capable of arousing strong emotion; *also* : EXCITING

♦ ardent, burning, emotional, fervent, fiery, hot‑blooded, impassioned, passionate, red-hot, vehement — more at FERVENT

char·gé d'af·faires \shär-ˌzhā-də-'far\ *n, pl* **chargés d'affaires** \-ˌzhā-, -ˌzhāz-\ [F] : a diplomat who substitutes for an ambassador or minister

¹**char·ger** \'chär-jər\ *n* : a large platter

²**charg·er** *n* **1** : a device or a worker that charges something **2** : WARHORSE

char·i·ness \'cher-ē-nəs\ *n* : the quality or state of being chary

char·i·ot \'char-ē-ət\ *n* : a 2-wheeled horse-drawn vehicle of ancient times used esp. in war and in races — **char·i·o·teer** \ˌchar-ē-ə-'tir\ *n*

cha·ris·ma \kə-'riz-mə\ *n* ♦ : a personal quality of leadership arousing popular loyalty or enthusiasm — **char·is·mat·ic** \ˌkar-əz-'ma-tik\ *adj*

♦ allure, appeal, attractiveness, captivation, charm, enchantment, fascination, glamour, magic, magnetism — more at CHARM

char·i·ta·ble \'char-ə-tə-bəl\ *adj* **1** ♦ : liberal in giving to needy people **2** ♦ : merciful or lenient in judging others — **char·i·ta·ble·ness** *n* — **char·i·ta·bly** \-blē\ *adv*

♦ [1] bountiful, free, generous, liberal, munificent, openhanded, unselfish, unsparing — more at GENEROUS ♦ [2] altruistic, beneficent, benevolent, humanitarian, philanthropic; *also* selfless, self-sacrificing; bounteous, bountiful, free, generous, greathearted, handsome, liberal, magnanimous, munificent, openhanded, unselfish, unsparing; compassionate, humane, kind **Ant** self-centered, selfish

char·i·ty \'char-ə-tē\ *n, pl* **-ties** **1** : a disposition to goodwill, kindliness, and sympathy **2** ♦ : an act or feeling of generosity **3** ♦ : the giving of aid to the poor; *also* : ALMS **4** : an institution engaged in relief of the poor **5** : leniency in judging others

♦ [2, 3] alms, benefaction, beneficence, contribution, donation, philanthropy — more at CONTRIBUTION

char·la·tan \'shär-lə-tən\ *n* ♦ : a person making usu. showy pretenses to knowledge or ability : FRAUD

♦ fake, fraud, hoaxer, humbug, mountebank, phony, pretender, quack

Charles·ton \'chärl-stən\ *n* : a lively dance in which the knees are swung in and out and the heels are turned sharply outward on each step

char·ley horse \'chär-lē-ˌhòrs\ *n* : a muscular pain, cramping, or stiffness from a strain or bruise

¹**charm** \'chärm\ *n* [ME *charme,* fr. AF, fr. L *carmen* song, fr. *canere* to sing] **1** ♦ : a practice or expression believed to have magic power **2** ♦ : something worn about the person to ward off evil or bring good fortune : AMULET **3** : a trait that fascinates or allures **4** ♦ : physical grace or attraction **5** : a small ornament worn on a bracelet or chain **6** : a quark with a charge of +²/₃ and a measured energy of approximately 1.5 billion electron volts

♦ [1] bewitchment, conjuration, enchantment, incantation, spell — more at SPELL ♦ [2] amulet, fetish, mascot, talisman; *also* emblem, symbol, token, totem **Ant** hoodoo, jinx ♦ [4] allure, appeal, attractiveness, captivation, charisma, enchantment, fascination, glamour, magic, magnetism; *also* attraction, call, lure, seduction; agreeableness, desirableness, niceness, pleasantness, sweetness **Ant** repulsion, repulsiveness

²**charm** *vb* **1** ♦ : to affect by or as if by a magic spell **2** : to protect by or as if by charms **3** : to please, soothe, or delight by compelling attraction : FASCINATE, ENCHANT ⟨∼s customers with his suave manner⟩ — **charm·er** *n*

♦ allure, beguile, bewitch, captivate, enchant, fascinate, wile; *also* disarm, draw, entice, lure, pull, seduce, tempt; delight, gratify, please; arrest, enrapture, enthrall, entrance; appeal (to), interest, intrigue; beckon, court, invite, solicit, woo ♦ bewitch, enchant, hex, spell — more at BEWITCH

charmed \'chärmd\ *adj* : extremely lucky or prosperous ⟨a ∼ life⟩

charm·er *n* **1** : one that charms : ENCHANTER, MAGICIAN **2** : one that pleases, intrigues, or fascinates

charm·ing \'chär-miŋ\ *adj* ♦ : marked by compelling attraction or appeal — **charm·ing·ly** *adv*

♦ alluring, attractive, captivating, elfin, engaging, fascinating, fetching, glamorous, magnetic, seductive — more at FASCINATING

char·nel house \'chärn-ᵊl-\ *n* : a building or chamber in which bodies or bones are deposited

¹chart \'chärt\ *n* **1** : an outline map detailing certain geographical aspects of an area : MAP **2** : a sheet giving information in the form of a table, list, or diagram; *also* : GRAPH

²chart *vb* **1** : to make a chart of **2** ♦ : to lay out a plan for : PLAN

♦ arrange, blueprint, calculate, design, frame, lay out, map, plan, project, scheme — more at PLAN

¹char·ter \'chär-tər\ *n* **1** : an official document granting rights or privileges (as to a colony, town, or college) from a sovereign or a governing body **2** : CONSTITUTION **3** : a written instrument from a society creating a branch **4** : a mercantile lease of a ship

²charter *vb* **1** : to grant a charter to **2** *Brit* : CERTIFY ⟨~ed engineer⟩ **3** : to hire, rent, or lease for temporary use — **char·ter·er** *n*

charter member *n* : an original member of an organization

char·treuse \shär-'trüz, -'trüs\ *n* : a brilliant yellow green

char·wom·an \'chär-ˌwu̇-mən\ *n* : a cleaning woman esp. in large buildings

chary \'char-ē\ *adj* **chari·er; -est** [ME, sorrowful, dear, fr. OE *cearig* sorrowful, fr. *caru* sorrow] **1** : CAUTIOUS, CIRCUMSPECT **2** : SPARING — **char·i·ly** \-ə-lē\ *adv*

¹chase \'chās\ *n* **1 a** ♦ : the act of chasing : PURSUIT **b** : HUNTING **2** : something pursued : QUARRY **3** : a tract of unenclosed land used as a game preserve

♦ following, pursuit, tracing — more at PURSUIT

²chase *vb* **chased; chas·ing 1** ♦ : to follow rapidly : PURSUE **2** : to pursue for food or in sport : HUNT **3** : to seek out ⟨*chasing* down clues⟩ **4** ♦ : to cause to depart or flee : drive away **5** : RUSH, HASTEN

♦ [1] dog, follow, hound, pursue, shadow, tag, tail, trace, track, trail — more at FOLLOW ♦ [4] banish, boot (out), bounce, dismiss, drum, eject, expel, oust, rout, run off — more at EJECT

³chase *vb* **chased; chas·ing** : to decorate (a metal surface) by embossing or engraving

⁴chase *n* : FURROW, GROOVE

chas·er \'chā-sər\ *n* **1** : one that chases **2** : a mild drink (as beer) taken after hard liquor

chasm \'ka-zəm\ *n* : a deep cleft in the surface (as of a planet) : GORGE 2

chas·sis \'cha-sē, 'sha-sē\ *n, pl* **chas·sis** \-sēz\ : the supporting frame of a structure (as an automobile or television set)

chaste \'chāst\ *adj* **chast·er; chast·est 1** ♦ : innocent of unlawful sexual intercourse : VIRTUOUS, PURE **2** : CELIBATE **3** ♦ : pure in thought : MODEST **4** : severe or simple in design

♦ [1, 3] clean, decent, immaculate, modest, pure, virtuous; *also* spotless, stainless, unblemished, undefiled, unsoiled, unspotted, unstained, unsullied, untainted, untarnished; decorous, proper, seemly; cultivated, refined, tasteful; harmless, innocent, innocuous, inoffensive *Ant* immodest, impure, indecent, unchaste, unclean

chaste·ly *adv* ♦ : in a chaste manner

♦ modestly, purely, righteously, virtuously — more at PURELY

chas·ten \'chās-ᵊn\ *vb* **1** ♦ : to correct through punishment or suffering : DISCIPLINE **2** : PURIFY — **chas·ten·er** *n*

♦ castigate, chastise, correct, discipline, penalize, punish — more at PUNISH

chaste·ness *n* : the state or quality of being chaste

chas·tise \chas-'tīz\ *vb* **chas·tised; chas·tis·ing** [ME *chastisen*, alter. of *chasten*] **1** ♦ : to punish esp. bodily **2** ♦ : to censure severely : CASTIGATE

♦ [1, 2] castigate, chasten, correct, discipline, penalize, punish — more at PUNISH

chas·tise·ment \-mənt, 'chas-təz-\ *n* ♦ : the action, an act, or the means of chastising; *esp* : PUNISHMENT

♦ castigation, correction, desert, discipline, nemesis, penalty, punishment, wrath — more at PUNISHMENT

chas·ti·ty \'chas-tə-tē\ *n* ♦ : the quality or state of being chaste; *esp* : sexual purity

♦ modesty, purity; *also* goodness, righteousness; morality, probity, rectitude; decency, decorum, propriety *Ant* immodesty, impurity, unchastity

cha·su·ble \'cha-zə-bəl, -sə-\ *n* : the outer vestment of the priest at mass

¹chat \'chat\ *n* **1** ♦ : light familiar informal talk **2** : online discussion in a chat room — **chat** *vb*

♦ chatter, chitchat, gabfest, gossip, palaver, rap, talk; *also* colloquy, conference, discourse, parley, powwow, symposium; debate, dialogue, exchange, give-and-take

²chat *vb* ♦ : to talk in a light and familiar manner

♦ converse, gab, jaw, palaver, patter, prattle, rattle, talk, visit; *also* gossip, tattle; descant, discuss, expatiate ♦ *usu* chat with speak, talk

châ·teau \sha-'tō\ *n, pl* **châ·teaus** \-'tōz\ *or* **châ·teaux** \-'tō, -'tōz\ [F, fr. OF *chastel*, fr. L *castellum* castle, dim. of *castra* camp] **1** : a feudal castle in France **2** : a large country house **3** : a French vineyard estate

chat·e·laine \'shat-ᵊl-ˌān\ *n* **1** : the mistress of a chateau **2** : a clasp or hook for a watch, purse, or keys

chat room *n* : a real-time online interactive discussion group

chat·tel \'chat-ᵊl\ *n* **1** ♦ : an item of tangible property other than real estate **2** : a person held in servitude : SLAVE, BONDMAN

♦ *usu* chattels effects, holdings, paraphernalia, possessions, things — more at POSSESSION

¹chat·ter \'cha-tər\ *vb* **1** ♦ : to utter speechlike but meaningless sounds **2** ♦ : to talk idly, incessantly, or fast **3** : to click repeatedly or uncontrollably

♦ [1] babble, drivel, gabble, gibber, jabber, prattle, sputter — more at BABBLE ♦ [2] chat, converse, gab, jaw, palaver, patter, prattle, rattle, talk, visit — more at CHAT

²chatter *n* : idle talk

chat·ter·box \'cha-tər-ˌbäks\ *n* ♦ : one who talks incessantly

♦ jabberer, magpie, talker; *also* gossip, tattler, tattletale

chat·ter·er *n* : a person who rambles on and on

chat·ty \'cha-tē\ *adj* **chat·ti·er; -est 1** ♦ : fond of chatting : TALKATIVE ⟨a ~ neighbor⟩ **2** ♦ : having the style and manner of light familiar conversation ⟨a ~ letter⟩ — **chat·ti·ly** \-tə-lē\ *adv* — **chat·ti·ness** \-tē-nəs\ *n*

♦ [1] conversational, gabby, garrulous, loquacious, talkative — more at TALKATIVE ♦ [2] colloquial, conversational, newsy; *also* casual, familiar, informal, intimate; digressive, discursive, rambling; communicative, expansive, garrulous, talkative *Ant* bookish, literary

¹chauf·feur \'shō-fər, shō-'fər\ *n* [F, lit., stoker, fr. *chauffer* to heat] : a person employed to drive an automobile

²chauffeur *vb* **chauf·feured; chauf·feur·ing 1** : to do the work of a chauffeur **2** : to transport in the manner of a chauffeur

chau·vin·ism \'shō-və-ˌni-zəm\ *n* [F *chauvinisme*, fr. Nicolas *Chauvin*, fictional soldier of excessive patriotism and devotion to Napoleon] **1** : excessive or blind patriotism **2** : an attitude of superiority toward members of the opposite sex — **chau·vin·is·tic** \ˌshō-və-'nis-tik\ *adj* — **chau·vin·is·ti·cal·ly** \-ti-k(ə-)lē\ *adv*

chau·vin·ist *n or adj* : one who practices chauvinism

cheap \'chēp\ *adj* **1** ♦ : of small cost : INEXPENSIVE **2** : costing little effort to obtain **3** ♦ : of inferior quality or worth : SHODDY **4** : worthy of scorn **5** : not generous or liberal in using, giving, or spending : STINGY — **cheap** *adv* — **cheap·ly** *adv*

♦ [1] cut-rate, inexpensive, low, reasonable; *also* moderate, popular; discounted, lowered, reduced; wholesale

Ant costly, dear, expensive, high, premium ♦ [3] bad, bum, coarse, common, cut-rate, execrable, inferior, junky, lousy, mediocre, miserable, poor, rotten, second-rate, shoddy, sleazy, terrible, trashy, wretched; *also* useless, valueless, worthless; flashy, garish, gaudy, meretricious, showy, tawdry; seedy, shabby, tacky; counterfeit, fake, phony, sham *Ant* excellent, fine, first-rate, good, superior, top-notch

cheap·en \'chē-pən\ *vb* **1** ♦ : to make or become cheap or cheaper in price or value **2** : to make tawdry

♦ depreciate, depress, mark down, write off — more at DEPRECIATE

cheap·ness *n* ♦ : the quality or state of being cheap

♦ closeness, miserliness, parsimony, stinginess, tightness — more at PARSIMONY

cheap·skate \'chēp-₁skāt\ *n* ♦ : a miserly or stingy person; *esp* : one who tries to avoid paying a fair share of costs

♦ miser, niggard, skinflint, tightwad — more at MISER

¹cheat \'chēt\ *vb* **1** ♦ : to deprive of something through fraud or deceit **2** : to practice fraud or trickery **3** : to violate rules (as of a game) dishonestly — **cheat·er** *n*

♦ bleed, chisel, cozen, defraud, fleece, hustle, mulct, rook, shortchange, skin, squeeze, stick, sting, swindle, victimize — more at FLEECE

²cheat *n* **1** : the act of deceiving : FRAUD, DECEPTION **2** ♦ : one that cheats : a dishonest person

♦ dodger, hoaxer, shark, sharper, swindler, trickster — more at TRICKSTER

¹check \'chek\ *n* **1** : exposure of a chess king to an attack **2** : a sudden stoppage of progress **3** : a sudden pause or break **4** ♦ : something that stops or restrains **5** : a standard for testing or evaluation **6** ♦ : a strict or close inspection : a study of by close examination : EXAMINATION **7** : the act of testing or verifying **8** *or Can and Brit* **cheque** : a written order directing a bank to pay money as instructed : DRAFT **9** : a ticket or token showing ownership or identity **10** ♦ : a slip indicating an amount due **11** : a pattern in squares; *also* : a fabric in such a pattern **12** : a mark typically ✓ placed beside an item to show that it has been noted **13** : CRACK, SPLIT

♦ [4] condition, constraint, curb, fetter, limitation, restraint, restriction — more at RESTRICTION ♦ [6] audit, checkup, examination, inspection, review, scan, scrutiny, survey — more at INSPECTION ♦ [10] account, bill, invoice, statement, tab — more at BILL

²check *vb* **1** : to put (a chess king) in check **2** ♦ : to slow down or stop **3** ♦ : to restrain the action or force of : CURB **4** : to compare with a source, original, or authority : VERIFY — often used with *out* **5** ♦ : to inspect or test for satisfactory condition **6** : to mark with a check as examined **7** : to consign for shipment for one holding a passenger ticket **8** : to mark into squares **9** : to leave or accept for safekeeping in a checkroom **10** : to prove to be consistent or truthful **11** : CRACK, SPLIT **12** ♦ : to correspond often detail for detail

♦ [2] arrest, catch, draw up, fetch up, halt, hold up, stall, stay, still, stop — more at HALT ♦ [3] bridle, constrain, contain, control, curb, govern, inhibit, regulate, rein, restrain, tame — more at CONTROL ♦ *usu* **check out** [5] audit, examine, inspect, review, scan, scrutinize, survey — more at INSPECT ♦ [12] accord, agree, answer, coincide, comport, conform, correspond, dovetail, fit, go, harmonize, jibe, square, tally; *also* equal, match, parallel *Ant* differ (from), disagree (with)

check·book \'chek-₁buk\ *n* : a book containing blank checks
¹check·er \'che-kər\ *n* : a piece in the game of checkers
²checker *vb* **1** : to variegate with different colors or shades **2** : to vary with contrasting elements ⟨a ∼ed career⟩ **3** : to mark into squares
³checker *n* : one that checks; *esp* : one who checks out purchases in a supermarket

check·er·ber·ry \'che-kər-₁ber-ē\ *n* : WINTERGREEN 1; *also* : the spicy red fruit of this plant
check·er·board \-₁bȯrd\ *n* : a board of 64 squares of alternate colors used in various games
check·ered \'che-kərd\ *adj* : marked by inconsistent fortune or recurring problems ⟨his ∼ past⟩
check·ers \'che-kərz\ *n* : a game for two played on a checkerboard with each player having 12 pieces
check in *vb* : to report one's presence or arrival (as at a hotel)
check·list \'chek-₁list\ *n* **1** ♦ : a list of things to be checked or done **2** ♦ : a comprehensive list

♦ [1, 2] catalog, list, listing, menu, register, registry, roll, roster, schedule, table — more at LIST

check·mate \'chek-₁māt\ *vb* [ME *chekmaten*, fr. *chekmate*, interj. used to announce checkmate, fr. MF *eschec mat*, fr. Ar *shāh māt*, fr. Per, lit., the king is left unable to escape] **1** ♦ : to thwart completely : FRUSTRATE **2** : to attack (an opponent's king) in chess so that escape is impossible — **checkmate** *n*

♦ baffle, balk, beat, foil, frustrate, thwart — more at FRUSTRATE

check·off \'che-₁kȯf\ *n* : the deduction of union dues from a worker's paycheck by the employer
check·out \'che-₁kaut\ *n* **1** : the action or an instance of checking out **2** : a counter at which checking out is done **3** : the process of examining and testing something as to readiness for intended use
check out *vb* **1** : to settle one's account (as at a hotel) and leave **2** : to total or have totaled the cost of purchases in a store and to make or receive payment for them
check·point \'chek-₁pȯint\ *n* : a point at which a check is performed
check·room \-₁rüm, -₁rum\ *n* : a room at which baggage, parcels, or clothing is left for safekeeping
checks and balances *n pl* : a system allowing each branch of a government to restrict the actions of another branch (as by a veto)
check·up \'che-₁kəp\ *n* ♦ : the act of checking something or someone : EXAMINATION; *esp* : a general physical examination

♦ audit, check, examination, inspection, review, scan, scrutiny, survey — more at INSPECTION

ched·dar \'che-dər\ *n, often cap* : a hard mild to sharp white or yellow cheese of smooth texture
cheek \'chēk\ *n* **1** : the fleshy side part of the face **2** ♦ : insolent boldness and self-assurance : IMPUDENCE, AUDACITY **3** : BUTTOCK 1 — **cheeked** \'chēkt\ *adj*

♦ audacity, brass, brazenness, chutzpah, effrontery, gall, impertinence, impudence, nerve, presumption, sauce, sauciness, temerity — more at EFFRONTERY

cheek·bone \'chēk-₁bōn\ *n* : the bone or bony ridge below the eye
cheek·i·ness \-kē-nəs\ *n* : insolence or impudence of speech or behavior
cheeky \'chē-kē\ *adj* **cheek·i·er; -est** ♦ : insolently bold : IMPUDENT, SAUCY — **cheek·i·ly** \-kə-lē\ *adv*

♦ arch, bold, brash, brazen, cocky, fresh, impertinent, impudent, insolent, nervy, sassy, saucy — more at NERVY

cheep \'chēp\ *vb* ♦ : to utter faint shrill sounds : PEEP — **cheep** *n*

♦ chirp, peep, pipe, tweet, twitter — more at CHIRP

¹cheer \'chir\ *n* [ME *chere* face, cheer, fr. AF, face, fr. ML *cara*, prob. fr. Gk *kara* head, face] **1** ♦ : state of mind or heart : SPIRIT **2** ♦ : lightness of mind and feeling **3** : hospitable entertainment : WELCOME **4** : food and drink for a feast **5** : something that gladdens **6** : a shout of applause or encouragement

♦ [1] frame, humor (*or* humour), mode, mood, spirit, temper — more at MOOD ♦ [2] comfort, consolation, relief, solace — more at COMFORT ♦ [2] cheerfulness, cheeriness, glee, hilarity, joviality, merriment, mirth — more at MIRTH

²**cheer** *vb* **1** ♦ : to give hope or courage to : COMFORT — usu. used with *up* **2** : to make glad **3** : to urge on esp. by shouts **4** ♦ : to applaud or show approval of esp. with shouts **5** : to grow or be cheerful — usu. used with *up* — **cheer·er** *n*

♦ *usu* **cheer up** [1] buoy (up), comfort, embolden, encourage, hearten, inspire, steel — more at ENCOURAGE ♦ [4] acclaim, applaud, crack up, hail, laud, praise, salute, tout — more at ACCLAIM

cheer·ful \'chir-fəl\ *adj* **1** ♦ : having or showing good spirits **2** ♦ : conducive to good spirits : pleasant and bright

♦ [1] blithe, bright, buoyant, cheery, chipper, gay, lightsome, sunny, upbeat; *also* hopeful, sanguine; jaunty, lively, perky, sprightly, vivacious; carefree, careless, cavalier, easygoing, happy-go-lucky, insouciant, lighthearted, unconcerned; boon, jolly, jovial, merry, mirthful; glad, happy, pleased *Ant* dour, gloomy, glum, morose, saturnine, sulky, sullen ♦ [2] bright, cheery, gay, glad; *also* gladdening, heartening, heartwarming; gleaming, radiant, sparkling *Ant* bleak, cheerless, dark, depressing, dismal, dreary, gloomy, gray

cheer·ful·ly *adv* ♦ : in a cheerful manner

♦ gaily, happily, heartily, jovially, merrily, mirthfully — more at GAILY

cheer·ful·ness *n* ♦ : the quality or state of being cheerful

♦ cheer, cheeriness, glee, hilarity, joviality, merriment, mirth — more at MIRTH

cheer·i·ness \-ē-nəs\ *n* ♦ : the quality or state of being cheery

♦ cheer, cheerfulness, glee, hilarity, joviality, merriment, mirth, mirthfulness — more at MIRTH

cheer·lead·er \'chir-,lē-dər\ *n* : a person who directs organized cheering esp. at a sports event

cheer·less \'chir-ləs\ *adj* : lacking qualities that cheer : BLEAK, DISPIRITING — **cheer·less·ly** *adv* — **cheer·less·ness** *n*

cheery \'chir-ē\ *adj* **cheer·i·er; -est** **1** ♦ : marked by cheerfulness or good spirits : CHEERFUL **2** ♦ : causing or suggesting cheerfulness ⟨~ music⟩ — **cheer·i·ly** \-ə-lē\ *adv*

♦ [1] blithe, bright, buoyant, cheerful, chipper, gay, lightsome, sunny, upbeat — more at CHEERFUL ♦ [2] bright, cheerful, gay, glad — more at CHEERFUL

cheese \'chēz\ *n* : the curd of milk usu. pressed into cakes and cured for use as food

cheese·burg·er \-,bər-gər\ *n* : a hamburger topped with cheese

cheese·cake \-,kāk\ *n* **1** : a dessert consisting of a creamy filling usu. containing cheese baked in a shell **2** : photographs of shapely scantily clad women

cheese·cloth \-,klȯth\ *n* : a lightweight coarse cotton gauze

cheese·par·ing \-,par-iŋ\ *n* : miserly economizing — **cheeseparing** *adj*

cheese·steak \-,stāk\ *n* : a sandwich of thinly sliced beef topped with melted cheese

cheesy \'chē-zē\ *adj* **chees·i·er; -est** **1** : resembling, suggesting, or containing cheese **2** : CHEAP 3

chee·tah \'chē-tə\ *n* [Hindu *cītā* leopard, fr. Skt *citraka*, fr. *citra* bright, variegated] : a large long-legged swift-moving spotted cat of Africa and formerly Asia

chef \'shef\ *n* **1** : a cook who manages the kitchen (as of a restaurant) **2** : a person who prepares food for eating : COOK

chef d'oeu·vre \shā-'dœvrᵊ\ *n, pl* **chefs d'oeuvre** *same*\ : MASTERPIECE

chem *abbr* chemical; chemist; chemistry

¹**chem·i·cal** \'ke-mi-kəl\ *adj* **1** : of, relating to, used in, or produced by chemistry **2** : acting or operated or produced by chemicals — **chem·i·cal·ly** \-k(ə-)lē\ *adv*

²**chemical** *n* : a substance obtained by a chemical process or used for producing a chemical effect

chemical engineering *n* : engineering dealing with the industrial application of chemistry

chemical warfare *n* : warfare using incendiary mixtures, smokes, or irritant, burning, or asphyxiating gases

chemical weapon *n* : a weapon used in chemical warfare

che·mise \shə-'mēz\ *n* **1** : a woman's one-piece undergarment **2** : a loose straight-hanging dress

chem·ist \'ke-mist\ *n* **1** : one trained in chemistry **2** *Brit* : PHARMACIST

chem·is·try \'ke-mə-strē\ *n, pl* **-tries** **1** : the science that deals with the composition, structure, and properties of substances and of the changes they undergo **2** : chemical composition or properties ⟨the ~ of gasoline⟩ **3** : a strong mutual attraction; *also* : harmonious interaction among people (as on a team)

che·mo \'kē-mō\ *n* : CHEMOTHERAPY

che·mo·ther·a·py \,kē-mō-'ther-ə-pē\ *n* : the use of chemicals in the treatment or control of disease — **che·mo·ther·a·peu·tic** \-,ther-ə-'pyü-tik\ *adj*

che·nille \shə-'nēl\ *n* [F, lit., caterpillar, fr. OF, fr. L *canicula*, dim. of *canis* dog] : a fabric with a deep fuzzy pile often used for bedspreads and rugs

cheque *Can and Brit var of* ¹CHECK 8

cher·ish \'cher-ish\ *vb* **1** ♦ : to hold dear : feel or treat with care and affection **2** ♦ : to keep deeply in mind — **cher·ish·able** *adj* — **cher·ish·er** *n*

♦ [1] adore, love, worship — more at LOVE ♦ [1] appreciate, love, prize, treasure, value — more at LOVE ♦ [2] bear, entertain, harbor (*or* harbour), have, hold, nurse — more at HARBOR

Cher·o·kee \'cher-ə-(,)kē\ *n, pl* **Cherokee** *or* **Cherokees** : a member of an American Indian people orig. of Tennessee and No. Carolina; *also* : their language

che·root \shə-'rüt\ *n* : a cigar cut square at both ends

cher·ry \'cher-ē\ *n, pl* **cherries** [ME *chery*, fr. AF *cherise*, *cirice* (taken as a pl.), fr. LL *ceresia*, fr. L *cerasus* cherry tree, fr. Gk *kerasos*] **1** : the small fleshy pale yellow to deep blackish red fruit of a tree related to the roses; *also* : the tree or its wood **2** : a moderate red

chert \'chərt, 'chat\ *n* : a rock resembling flint and consisting essentially of fine crystalline quartz and fibrous chalcedony — **cherty** *adj*

cher·ub \'cher-əb\ *n* **1** *pl* **cher·u·bim** \'cher-ə-,bim\ : an angel of the 2d highest rank **2** *pl* **cherubs** : a chubby rosy person — **che·ru·bic** \chə-'rü-bik\ *adj*

chess \'ches\ *n* : a game for two played on a chessboard with each player having 16 pieces — **chess·man** \-,man, -mən\ *n*

chess·board \'ches-,bȯrd\ *n* : a checkerboard used in the game of chess

chest \'chest\ *n* **1** ♦ : a box, case, or boxlike receptacle for storage or shipping **2** : the part of the body enclosed by the ribs and sternum — **chest·ed** \'ches-təd\ *adj* — **chest·ful** \'chest-,fül\ *n*

♦ box, caddy, case, casket, locker, trunk; *also* footlocker; safe

ches·ter·field \'ches-tər-,fēld\ *n* **1** : an overcoat with a velvet collar **2** : a large sofa usu. with upright armrests

chest·nut \'ches-(,)nət\ *n* **1** : the edible nut of any of a genus of trees related to the beech and oaks; *also* : this tree **2** : a grayish to reddish brown **3** : an old joke or story

che·val glass \shə-'val-\ *n* : a full-length mirror that may be tilted in a frame

che·va·lier \,she-və-'lir, shə-'val-,yā\ *n* : a member of one of various orders of knighthood or of merit

chev·i·ot \'she-vē-ət\ *n, often cap* **1** : a twilled fabric with a rough nap **2** : a sturdy soft-finished cotton fabric

chev·ron \'she-vrən\ *n* : a sleeve badge of one or more V-shaped or inverted V-shaped stripes worn to indicate rank or service (as in the armed forces)

¹**chew** \'chü\ *vb* ♦ : to crush, grind, or gnaw (as food) with the teeth — **chew·able** *adj* — **chew·er** *n* — **chew on** : to think about : PONDER ⟨*chew on* the proposals⟩ — **chew the fat** : to make conversation : CHAT

♦ bite, champ, chomp, crunch, gnaw, nibble

²**chew** *n* **1** : an act of chewing **2** : something for chewing

chew out *vb* ◆ : to bawl out : to criticize severely

◆ admonish, chide, lecture, rail (at *or* against), rate, rebuke, reprimand, scold — more at SCOLD

chew over *vb* ◆ : to meditate on : think about reflectively

◆ cogitate, consider, contemplate, debate, deliberate, entertain, meditate, mull, ponder, question, ruminate, study, think, weigh — more at PONDER

chewy \'chü-ē\ *adj* : requiring much chewing ⟨∼ candy⟩

Chey·enne \shī-'an, -'en\ *n, pl* **Cheyenne** *or* **Cheyennes** [AmerF, fr. Dakota *šahíyena*] : a member of an American Indian people of the western plains of the U.S.; *also* : their language

chg *abbr* 1 change 2 charge

chi \'kī\ *n* : the 22d letter of the Greek alphabet — X or χ

Chi·an·ti \kē-'än-tē, -'an-\ *n* : a dry usu. red wine

chiar·oscu·ro \kē-,är-ə-'skur̄-ō, -'skyur̄-\ *n, pl* **-ros** [It, fr. *chiaro* clear, light + *oscuro* obscure, dark] 1 : pictorial representation in terms of light and shade without regard to color 2 : the arrangement or treatment of light and dark parts in a pictorial work of art

¹**chic** \'shēk\ *n* : STYLISHNESS

²**chic** *adj* ◆ : cleverly stylish : SMART; *also* : currently fashionable

◆ à la mode, fashionable, in, modish, sharp, smart, snappy, stylish — more at STYLISH

Chi·ca·na \chi-'kä-nə, *also* shi-\ *n* : an American woman or girl of Mexican descent — **Chicana** *adj*

chi·cane \shi-'kän\ *n* : CHICANERY

chi·ca·nery \-'ka-nə-rē\ *n, pl* **-ner·ies** ◆ : deception by artful subterfuge or sophistry : TRICKERY

◆ artifice, hanky-panky, subterfuge, trickery, wile — more at TRICKERY

Chi·ca·no \chi-'kä-nō\ *n, pl* **-nos** : an American of Mexican descent — **Chicano** *adj*

chi·chi \'shē-(,)shē, 'chē-(,)chē\ *adj* [F] 1 : SHOWY, FRILLY 2 : ARTY, PRECIOUS 3 : CHIC ⟨a ∼ restaurant⟩ — **chichi** *n*

chick \'chik\ *n* 1 : a young chicken; *also* : a young bird 2 *sometimes offensive* : a young woman

chick·a·dee \'chi-kə-(,)dē\ *n* : any of several small grayish American birds with black or brown caps

Chick·a·saw \'chi-kə-,sò\ *n, pl* **Chickasaw** *or* **Chickasaws** : a member of an American Indian people of Mississippi and Alabama

¹**chick·en** \'chi-kən\ *n* 1 : a common domestic fowl esp. when young; *also* : its flesh used as food 2 ◆ : one who is easily frightened and easily daunted : COWARD

◆ coward, craven, dastard, poltroon, recreant, sissy — more at COWARD

²**chicken** *adj* 1 ◆ : being or behaving like a coward : COWARDLY 2 *slang* : insistent on petty esp. military discipline

◆ cowardly, craven, dastardly, pusillanimous, recreant, spineless, yellow — more at COWARDLY

chicken feed *n, slang* : an insignificant sum of money

chick·en-heart·ed \,chi-kən-'här-təd\ *adj* : being or behaving like a coward : COWARDLY

chicken out *vb* : to lose one's courage

chicken pox *n* : an acute contagious virus disease esp. of children characterized by a low fever and vesicles

chicken wire *n* : a light wire netting of hexagonal mesh

chick·pea \'chik-,pē\ *n* : an Asian herb of the legume family cultivated for its short pods with one or two edible seeds; *also* : its seed

chick·weed \'chik-,wēd\ *n* : any of several low-growing small-leaved weeds related to the pinks

chi·cle \'chi-kəl\ *n* : a gum from the latex of a tropical tree used as the chief ingredient of chewing gum

chic·o·ry \'chi-kə-rē\ *n, pl* **-ries** : a usu. blue-flowered herb related to the daisies and grown for its root and for use in salads; *also* : its dried ground root used to flavor or adulterate coffee

chide \'chīd\ *vb* **chid** \'chid\ *or* **chid·ed** \'chī-dəd\; **chid** *or*

chid·den \'chid-³n\ *or* **chided; chid·ing** ◆ : to speak disapprovingly to

◆ admonish, rebuke, reprimand, reproach, reprove admonish, lecture, rail (at *or* against), rate, rebuke, scold — more at SCOLD

¹**chief** \'chēf\ *adj* 1 ◆ : highest in rank 2 ◆ : most important

◆ [1] first, foremost, head, high, lead, preeminent, premier, primary, prime, principal, supreme — more at HEAD ◆ [2] arch, cardinal, central, dominant, first, foremost, grand, key, main, paramount, predominant — more at FOREMOST

²**chief** *n* 1 ◆ : the leader of a body or organization : HEAD 2 : the principal or most valuable part — **chief·dom** *n*

◆ boss, captain, foreman, head, headman, helmsman, kingpin, leader, master, taskmaster — more at BOSS

chief·ly *adv* ◆ : for the most part : most importantly

◆ altogether, basically, generally, largely, mainly, mostly, overall, predominantly, primarily, principally; *also* nearly, practically, virtually; approximately, broadly, roughly; commonly, frequently, normally, ordinarily, usually; incompletely, partially, partly

chief master sergeant *n* : a noncommissioned officer of the highest rank in the air force

chief petty officer *n* : an enlisted person in the navy ranking next below a senior chief petty officer

chief·tain \'chēf-tən\ *n* : a chief esp. of a band, tribe, or clan — **chief·tain·cy** \-sē\ *n* — **chief·tain·ship** *n*

chief warrant officer *n* : a warrant officer of senior rank

chif·fon \shi-'fän, 'shi-,\ *n* [F, lit., rag, fr. *chiffe* old rag] : a sheer fabric esp. of silk

chif·fo·nier \,shi-fə-'nir\ *n* : a high narrow chest of drawers

chig·ger \'chi-gər\ *n* : a bloodsucking larval mite that causes intense itching

chi·gnon \'shēn-,yän\ *n* [F, fr. MF *chaignon* chain, collar, nape] : a knot of hair worn at the back of the head

Chi·hua·hua \chə-'wä-,wä\ *n* : any of a breed of very small large-eared dogs that originated in Mexico

chil·blain \'chil-,blān\ *n* : a sore or inflamed swelling (as on the feet or hands) caused by exposure to cold

child \'chīld\ *n, pl* **chil·dren** \'chil-drən\ 1 ◆ : an unborn or recently born person 2 ◆ : a young person between the periods of infancy and youth 3 : a male or female offspring : SON, DAUGHTER 4 : one strongly influenced by another or by a place or state of affairs — **child·less** *adj* — **child·less·ness** *n* — **child·like** *adj*

◆ [1] baby, infant, newborn — more at BABY ◆ [2] cub, juvenile, kid, youngster, youth; *also* adolescent, minor; schoolboy, schoolgirl; moppet, nestling, toddler, tot, tyke; brat, imp, squirt, urchin, whippersnapper; cherub; preteen, subteen, teenager; nipper, lad, shaver, stripling; hoyden, tomboy *Ant* adult, grown-up

child·bear·ing \'chīld-,bar-iŋ\ *n* : of or relating to the process of conceiving, being pregnant with, and giving birth to children : CHILDBIRTH — **childbearing** *adj*

child·birth \-,bərth\ *n* ◆ : the act or process of giving birth to offspring

◆ delivery, labor (*or* labour); *also* pains; pregnancy; abortion, miscarriage; cesarean section

child·hood \-,hud\ *n* : the state or period of being a child

child·ish *adj* ◆ : marked by or suggestive of immaturity and lack of poise — **child·ish·ly** *adv* — **child·ish·ness** *n*

◆ adolescent, babyish, immature, infantile, juvenile, kiddish; *also* boyish, girlish; childlike, innocent, naive, simple, unsophisticated *Ant* adult, grown-up, mature

¹**child·proof** \-,prüf\ *adj* 1 : made to prevent opening or use by children ⟨∼ lighters⟩ 2 : made safe for children

²**childproof** *vb* : to make childproof ⟨∼ a house⟩

child's play *n* 1 ◆ : an extremely simple task or act 2 : something that is insignificant

◆ breeze, cinch, picnic, pushover, snap — more at CINCH

Chil·ean \'chi-lē-ən, chə-'lā-ən\ *n* : a native or inhabitant of Chile — **Chilean** *adj*

chili *or* **chile** *or* **chil·li** \'chi-lē\ *n, pl* **chil·ies** *or* **chil·es** *or* **chil·lies** **1** : a pungent pepper related to the tomato **2** : a thick sauce of meat and chilies **3** : CHILI CON CARNE

chili con car·ne \ˌchi-lē-ˌkän-'kär-nē\ *n* [AmerSp *chile con carne* chili with meat] : a spiced stew of ground beef and chili peppers or chili powder usu. with beans

chili powder *n* : a seasoning made of ground chili peppers and other spices

chili sauce *n* : a spiced tomato sauce usu. made with red and green peppers

¹chill \'chil\ *n* **1** : a feeling of coldness accompanied by shivering **2** ♦ : moderate coldness **3** : a check to enthusiasm or warmth of feeling

♦ bite, bitterness, bleakness, nip, rawness, sharpness; *also* briskness, crispness; coldness, frigidity, iciness; cold, freeze, snap

²chill *adj* **1** : moderately cold **2** : affected by a penetrating cold : benumbed or shivering with cold : COLD, RAW **3** : cool in manner or feeling : lacking warmth : UNFRIENDLY ⟨a ∼ reception⟩ **4** : DEPRESSING, DISPIRITING

³chill *vb* **1** : to make or become cold or chilly **2** : to make cool esp. without freezing — **chill·er** *n*

chill·i·ness *n* : the quality or state of being chilly

chill·ing \'chi-liŋ\ *adj* : gravely disturbing or frightening ⟨a ∼ scene⟩

chill out *vb, slang* ♦ : to calm down : RELAX

♦ de-stress, relax, unwind — more at RELAX

chilly \'chi-lē\ *adj* **chill·i·er; -est** **1** ♦ : noticeably cold **2** : unpleasantly affected by cold **3** ♦ : lacking warmth of feeling

♦ [1] bitter, bleak, chill, nippy, raw, sharp; *also* brisk, crisp; arctic, cold, freezing, frigid, frosty, icy ♦ [3] chill, cold, cold-blooded, cool, frigid, frosty, glacial, icy, unfriendly, unsympathetic, wintry — more at COLD

¹chime \'chīm\ *n* **1** : a set of bells musically tuned **2** : the sound of a set of bells — usu. used in pl. **3** : a musical sound suggesting bells

²chime *vb* **chimed; chim·ing** **1** ♦ : to make bell-like sounds **2** : to indicate (as the time of day) by chiming **3** : to be or act in accord : be in harmony

♦ knell, peal, ring, toll — more at RING

chime in *vb* ♦ : to break into or join in a conversation

♦ break, cut in, interpose, interrupt, intrude — more at INTERRUPT

chi·me·ra \kī-'mir-ə, kə-\ *n* [L *chimaera,* fr. Gk *chimaira* she-goat, chimera] **1** : an imaginary monster made up of incongruous parts **2 a** ♦ : an illusion or fabrication of the mind **b** : an impossible dream

♦ conceit, daydream, delusion, dream, fancy, fantasy, figment, hallucination, illusion, phantasm, pipe dream, unreality, vision

chi·me·ri·cal \ki-'mer-i-kəl\ *also* **chi·me·ric** \-ik\ *adj* **1** ♦ : existing only as the product of unchecked imagination : fantastically visionary or improbable **2** : given to fantastic schemes

♦ fabulous, fanciful, fantastic, fictitious, imaginary, made-up, mythical, phantom, pretend, unreal — more at IMAGINARY

chim·ney \'chim-nē\ *n, pl* **chimneys** **1** : a vertical structure extending above the roof of a building for carrying off smoke **2** : a glass tube around a lamp flame

chimp \'chimp\ *n* : CHIMPANZEE

chim·pan·zee \ˌchim-ˌpan-'zē, chim-'pan-zē\ *n* : an African ape related to the much larger gorilla

¹chin \'chin\ *n* : the part of the face below the lower lip including the prominence of the lower jaw — **chin·less** *adj*

²chin *vb* **chinned; chin·ning** : to raise (oneself) while hanging by the hands until the chin is level with the support

chi·na \'chī-nə\ *n* : porcelain ware; *also* : domestic pottery in general

Chi·na·town \-ˌtaùn\ *n* : the Chinese quarter of a city

chinch bug \'chinch-\ *n* : a small black and white bug destructive to cereal grasses

chin·chil·la \chin-'chi-lə\ *n* **1** : either of two small So. American rodents with soft pearl-gray fur; *also* : this fur **2** : a heavy long-napped woolen cloth

chine \'chīn\ *n* : the back or spine of an animal or human : BACKBONE, SPINE; *also* : a cut of meat including all or part of the backbone

Chi·nese \chī-'nēz, -'nēs\ *n, pl* **Chinese** **1** : a native or inhabitant of China **2** : any of a group of related languages of China — **Chinese** *adj*

Chinese cabbage *n* **1** : BOK CHOY **2** : an Asian garden plant related to the cabbage and widely grown in the U.S. for its tight elongate cylindrical heads of pale green to cream-colored leaves

Chinese checkers *n* : a game in which each player in turn transfers a set of marbles from a home point to the opposite point of a pitted 6-pointed star

Chinese gooseberry *n* : a subtropical vine that bears kiwifruit; *also* : KIWIFRUIT

Chinese lantern *n* : a collapsible translucent cover for a light

¹chink \'chiŋk\ *n* ♦ : a small crack or fissure

♦ cleft, crack, cranny, crevice, fissure, rift, split — more at CRACK

²chink *vb* : to fill the chinks of : stop up

³chink *n* : a slight sharp metallic sound

⁴chink *vb* ♦ : to make a slight sharp metallic sound

♦ jingle, tinkle — more at JINGLE

chi·no \'chē-nō\ *n, pl* **chinos** **1** : a usu. khaki cotton twill **2** *pl* : an article of clothing made of chino

Chi·nook \shə-'nùk, chə-, -'nük\ *n, pl* **Chinook** *or* **Chinooks** : a member of an American Indian people of Oregon

chintz \'chints\ *n* : a usu. glazed printed cotton cloth

chintzy \'chint-sē\ *adj* **chintz·i·er; -est** **1** : decorated with or as if with chintz **2** : GAUDY, CHEAP **3** : STINGY

chin–up \'chi-ˌnəp\ *n* : the act of chinning oneself

¹chip \'chip\ *n* **1** ♦ : a small usu. thin and flat piece (as of wood) cut or broken off **2** : a thin crisp morsel of food **3** : a counter used in games (as poker) **4** *pl* : something generally accepted as a means of payment : MONEY **5** ♦ : a flaw left after a chip is removed **6** : INTEGRATED CIRCUIT **7** : a very small slice of silicon containing electronic circuits

♦ [1] flake, splinter; *also* bit, disk, fragment, particle, scrap, shard; shiver, smithereens; shred, tatter; clipping, paring, shaving; leaf, sheet, slice; chunk, hunk, lump, slab ♦ [5] hack, indentation, nick, notch — more at NOTCH

²chip *vb* **chipped; chip·ping** **1** : to cut or break chips from **2** : to break off in small pieces at the edges **3** : to play a chip shot

chip in *vb* ♦ : to give money or assistance to an enterprise : CONTRIBUTE

♦ contribute, kick in, pitch in — more at CONTRIBUTE

chip·munk \'chip-ˌməŋk\ *n* [earlier *chitmunk,* prob. fr. Ojibwa *ačitamo·n** red squirrel] : any of a genus of small striped No. American and Asian rodents closely related to the squirrels and marmots

chi·pot·le \chə-'pōt-lā\ *n* : a smoked and usu. dried jalapeño pepper

chipped beef \'chipt-\ *n* : smoked dried beef sliced thin

¹chip·per \'chi-pər\ *n* : one that chips

²chipper *adj* **1** ♦ : being high in spirits : CHEERFUL **2** ♦ : being in good health : being in a state of physical well-being

♦ [1] blithe, bright, buoyant, cheerful, cheery, gay, lightsome, sunny, upbeat — more at CHEERFUL ♦ [2] able-bodied, fit, hale, healthy, hearty, robust, sound, well, whole, wholesome — more at HEALTHY

Chip·pe·wa \'chi-pə-ˌwò, -ˌwä, -ˌwā, -wə\ *n, pl* **Chippewa** *or* **Chippewas** : OJIBWA

chip shot *n* : a short usu. low shot to the green in golf

chi·rog·ra·phy \kī-'rä-grə-fē\ *n* : HANDWRITING, PENMAN-SHIP — **chi·ro·graph·ic** \ˌkī-rə-'gra-fik\ *adj*

chi·rop·o·dy \kə-'rä-pə-dē, shə-\ *n* : PODIATRY — **chi·rop·o·dist** \-dist\ *n*

chi·ro·prac·tic \'kī-rə-ˌprak-tik\ *n* : a system of therapy based esp. on manipulation of body structures — **chi·ro·prac·tor** \-tər\ *n*

¹**chirp** \'chərp\ *n* : a short sharp sound characteristic of a small bird or cricket

²**chirp** *vb* ♦ : to make a usu. repetitive short sharp sound

   ♦ cheep, peep, pipe, tweet, twitter; *also* cackle, chatter, jabber; sing, trill, warble

¹**chis·el** \'chi-zəl\ *n* : a metal tool with a sharpened edge at one end used to chip, carve, or cut into a solid material (as wood or stone)

²**chisel** *vb* **-eled** *or* **-elled; -el·ing** *or* **-el·ling** **1** : to work with or as if with a chisel **2 a** ♦ : to obtain something from by unfair practices : CHEAT **b** : to obtain by shrewd often unfair methods — **chis·el·er** *n*

   ♦ bleed, cheat, cozen, defraud, fleece, hustle, mulct, rook, shortchange, skin, squeeze, stick, sting, swindle, victimize — more at FLEECE

¹**chit** \'chit\ *n* [ME *chitte* kitten, cub] **1** : CHILD **2** : a pert young woman

²**chit** *n* [Hindi *ciṭṭhī* letter, note] : a signed voucher for a small debt

chit·chat \'chit-ˌchat\ *n* ♦ : casual or trifling conversation — **chitchat** *vb*

   ♦ chat, chatter, gabfest, gossip, palaver, rap, talk — more at CHAT

chi·tin \'kīt-ᵊn\ *n* : a sugar polymer that forms part of the hard outer integument esp. of insects — **chi·tin·ous** *adj*

chit·ter·lings *or* **chit·lins** \'chit-lənz\ *n pl* : the intestines of hogs esp. when prepared as food

chiv·al·ric \shə-'val-rik\ *adj* : relating to chivalry : CHIVALROUS

chiv·al·rous \'shi-vəl-rəs\ *adj* **1** : of or relating to chivalry **2** ♦ : marked by honor, courtesy, and generosity **3** : marked by gracious courtesy esp. to women — **chiv·al·rous·ly** *adv* — **chiv·al·rous·ness** *n*

   ♦ gallant, great, greathearted, high, high-minded, lofty, lordly, magnanimous, noble, sublime — more at NOBLE

chiv·al·ry \'shi-vəl-rē\ *n, pl* **-ries** **1** : mounted men-at-arms **2** : the system or practices of knighthood **3** : the spirit or character of the ideal knight

chive \'chīv\ *n* : an herb related to the onion that has leaves used for flavoring

chla·myd·ia \klə-'mi-dē-ə\ *n, pl* **-i·ae** \-dē-ˌē\ **1** : any of a genus of bacteria that cause various diseases of the eye and urogenital tract **2** : a disease or infection caused by chlamydiae

chlo·ral hydrate \'klȯr-əl-\ *n* : a white crystalline compound used as a hypnotic and sedative

chlor·dane \'klȯr-ˌdān\ *n* : a highly chlorinated persistent insecticide

chlo·ride \'klȯr-ˌīd\ *n* : a compound of chlorine with another element or group

chlo·ri·nate \'klȯr-ə-ˌnāt\ *vb* **-nat·ed; -nat·ing** : to treat or combine with chlorine or a chlorine compound — **chlo·ri·na·tion** \ˌklȯr-ə-'nā-shən\ *n* — **chlo·ri·na·tor** \'klȯr-ə-ˌnā-tər\ *n*

chlo·rine \'klȯr-ˌēn\ *n* : a nonmetallic chemical element that is found alone as a strong-smelling greenish yellow irritating gas and is used as a bleach, oxidizing agent, and disinfectant

chlo·rite \'klȯr-ˌīt\ *n* : a usu. green mineral found with and resembling mica

chlo·ro·flu·o·ro·car·bon \ˌklȯr-ə-ˌflȯr-ə-ˌkär-bən, -'flu̇r-\ *n* : any of several gaseous compounds that contain carbon, chlorine, fluorine, and sometimes hydrogen and are used esp. as solvents, refrigerants, and aerosol propellants

¹**chlo·ro·form** \'klȯr-ə-ˌfȯrm\ *n* : a colorless heavy fluid with etherlike odor used as a solvent and anesthetic

²**chloroform** *vb* : to treat with chloroform to produce anesthesia or death

chlo·ro·phyll \-ˌfil\ *n* : the green coloring matter of plants that functions in photosynthesis

chm *abbr* chairman

chock \'chäk\ *n* : a wedge for steadying something or for blocking the movement of a wheel — **chock** *vb*

chock·a·block \'chä-kə-ˌbläk\ *adj* : very full : CROWDED

chock–full *or* **chock·ful** \'chək-'ful, 'chäk-\ *adj* ♦ : full to the limit : CRAMMED

   ♦ brimful, crowded, fat, fraught, full, loaded, packed, replete — more at FULL

choc·o·late \'chä-k(ə-)lət, 'chȯ-\ *n* [Sp, fr. Nahuatl *chocolātl*] **1** : a food prepared from ground roasted cacao beans; *also* : a drink prepared from this **2** : a candy made of or with a coating of chocolate **3** : a dark brown color — **choc·o·laty** *or* **choc·o·lat·ey** \-k(ə-)lə-tē\ *adj*

Choc·taw \'chäk-ˌtȯ\ *n, pl* **Choctaw** *or* **Choctaws** : a member of an American Indian people of Mississippi, Alabama, and Louisiana; *also* : their language

¹**choice** \'chȯis\ *n* **1** ♦ : the act of choosing : SELECTION **2** ♦ : the power or opportunity of choosing : OPTION **3** ♦ : the best part **4** : a person or thing selected **5** : a variety offered for selection

   ♦ [1] election, selection — more at SELECTION ♦ [2] alternative, discretion, option, pick, preference, way; *also* say, voice, vote; inclination, liking, partiality, penchant, predilection, proclivity, propensity, tendency; discernment, judgment, perspicacity ♦ [3] best, cream, elect, elite, fat, flower, pick, prime — more at ELITE

²**choice** *adj* **choic·er; choic·est** **1** : worthy of being chosen **2** : selected with care **3** ♦ : of high quality

   ♦ dainty, delicate, elegant, exquisite, rare, select; *also* elite, exclusive; excellent, outstanding, premium, prime, superior

choir \'kwī(-ə)r\ *n* **1** ♦ : an organized company of singers (as in a church service) **2** : the part of a church occupied by the singers or by the clergy

   ♦ chorale, chorus — more at CHORUS

choir·boy \'kwī(-ə)r-ˌbȯi\ *n* : a boy member of a church choir

choir·mas·ter \-ˌmas-tər\ *n* : the director of a choir (as in a church)

¹**choke** \'chōk\ *vb* **choked; chok·ing** **1** ♦ : to hinder breathing (as by obstructing the trachea) : STRANGLE **2** : to check the growth or action of **3** ♦ : to obstruct by filling up or clogging : CLOG, OBSTRUCT **4** : to enrich the fuel mixture of (a motor) by restricting the carburetor air intake **5** : to perform badly in a critical situation

   ♦ [1] smother, stifle, strangle, suffocate — more at SMOTHER ♦ [1] garrote, strangle, throttle; *also* asphyxiate, smother, suffocate ♦ [3] block, clog, close (off), congest, dam, jam, obstruct, plug (up), stop (up), stuff — more at CLOG

²**choke** *n* **1** : the act of choking **2** : a narrowing in size toward the muzzle in the bore of a gun **3** : a valve for choking a gasoline engine

chok·er \'chō-kər\ *n* : something (as a necklace) worn tightly around the neck

cho·ler \'kä-lər, 'kō-\ *n* : a tendency toward anger : IRASCIBILITY

chol·era \'kä-lə-rə\ *n* : any of several bacterial diseases usu. marked by severe vomiting and dysentery

chol·er·ic \'kä-lə-rik, kə-'ler-ik\ *adj* **1** ♦ : easily moved to often unreasonable or excessive anger : hot-tempered **2** : ANGRY, IRATE

   ♦ crabby, cranky, cross, crotchety, grouchy, grumpy, irascible, irritable, peevish, perverse, petulant, short-tempered, snappish, snappy, snippy, testy, waspish — more at IRRITABLE

cho·les·ter·ol \kə-'les-tə-ˌrȯl\ *n* : a physiologically important waxy steroid alcohol found in animal tissues and in high concentrations implicated as a cause of arteriosclerosis

chomp \\'chämp, 'chómp\ *vb* ♦ : to chew or bite on something heavily

♦ bite, champ, chew, crunch, gnaw, nibble

choose \\'chüz\ *vb* **chose** \\'chōz\; **cho·sen** \\'chōz-³n\; **choos·ing** \chü-ziŋ\ **1** ♦ : to select esp. after consideration **2** ♦ : to make a final choice or judgment about : DECIDE **3** : to have a preference for — **choos·er** *n*

♦ [1] cull, elect, handpick, name, opt, pick, prefer, select, single, take; *also* appoint, designate, nominate, tab; accept, adopt, embrace, espouse *Ant* decline, refuse, reject, turn down ♦ [2] conclude, decide, determine, figure, opt, resolve — more at DECIDE

choosy *or* **choos·ey** \\'chü-zē\ *adj* **choos·i·er; -est** ♦ : very particular in making choices

♦ demanding, exacting, particular, picky, selective — more at SELECTIVE

¹chop \\'chäp\ *vb* **chopped; chop·ping 1** ♦ : to cut or sever usu. by repeated blows **2** ♦ : to cut into small pieces : MINCE **3** : to strike (a ball) with a short quick downward stroke

♦ [1] cut, fell, hew — more at FELL ♦ [2] hash, mince; *also* chip, grind, mash, puree, slice

²chop *n* **1** : a sharp downward blow or stroke **2** : a small cut of meat often including part of a rib **3** : a short abrupt motion (as of a wave)

³chop *n* **1** : an official seal or stamp **2** : a mark on goods to indicate quality or kind; *also* : QUALITY, GRADE

chop·house \\'chäp-,haùs\ *n* : RESTAURANT

chop·per \\'chä-pər\ *n* **1** : one that chops **2** *pl, slang* : TEETH **3** : HELICOPTER

chop·pi·ness \\'chä-pē-nəs\ *n* : the quality or state of being choppy

¹chop·py \\'chä-pē\ *adj* **chop·pi·er; -est 1** : rough with small waves ⟨a ～ sea⟩ **2** ♦ : interrupted by ups and downs : moving along with fits and starts **3** ♦ : lacking orderly continuity, arrangement, or relevance : DISCONNECTED ⟨short ～ sentences⟩ — **chop·pi·ly** \-pə-lē\ *adv*

♦ [2] casual, discontinuous, erratic, fitful, intermittent, irregular, occasional, spasmodic, sporadic, spotty, unsteady — more at FITFUL ♦ [3] disconnected, disjointed, unconnected — more at INCOHERENT

²choppy *adj* **chop·pi·er; -est** : CHANGEABLE, VARIABLE ⟨a ～ wind⟩

chops \\'chäps\ *n pl* **1** : the fleshy covering of the jaws **2** : expertise in a particular field or activity ⟨acting ～⟩

chop·stick \\'chäp-,stik\ *n* : one of a pair of sticks used chiefly in Asian countries for lifting food to the mouth

chop su·ey \chäp-'sü-ē\ *n, pl* **chop sueys** : a dish made of vegetables (as bean sprouts, bamboo shoots, water chestnuts, onions, mushrooms) and meat or fish and served with rice

cho·ral \\'kōr-əl\ *adj* : of, relating to, or sung by a choir or chorus or in chorus — **cho·ral·ly** *adv*

cho·rale \kə-'ral, -'räl\ *n* **1** ♦ : a hymn or psalm sung in church; *also* : a harmonization of a traditional melody **2** : a group formed to sing church music : CHORUS, CHOIR

♦ anthem, canticle, carol, hymn, psalm, spiritual — more at HYMN

¹chord \\'kòrd\ *n* [alter. of ME *cord*, short for *accord*] : three or more musical tones sounded simultaneously

²chord *n* **1** : CORD 2 **2** : a straight line joining two points on a curve

chore \\'chōr\ *n* [ME *char* turn, piece of work, fr. OE *chierr*] **1** *pl* : the daily light work of a household or farm **2** ♦ : a routine task or job **3** : a difficult or disagreeable task

♦ assignment, duty, job, stint, task; *also* endeavor, enterprise, project, undertaking; care, charge, commission, responsibility; function, mission, office; errand; circuit, round, route

cho·rea \kə-'rē-ə\ *n* : a nervous disorder marked by spasmodic uncontrolled movements

cho·re·og·ra·phy \,kōr-ē-'ä-grə-fē\ *n, pl* **-phies** : the art of composing and arranging dances and esp. ballets — **cho·re·o·graph** \\'kōr-ē-ə-,graf\ *vb* — **cho·re·og·ra·pher** \,kōr-ē-'ä-grə-fər\ *n* — **cho·re·o·graph·ic** \,kōr-ē-ə-'grafik\ *adj* — **cho·re·o·graph·i·cal·ly** \-fi-k(ə-)lē\ *adv*

cho·ris·ter \\'kōr-ə-stər\ *n* : a singer in a choir

¹chor·tle \\'chòrt-³l\ *vb* **chor·tled; chor·tling** : to laugh or chuckle esp. in satisfaction or exultation

²chortle *n* ♦ : a sound expressive of pleasure or exultation

♦ cackle, laugh, laughter, snicker, titter — more at LAUGH

¹chorus \\'kōr-əs\ *n* **1** ♦ : an organized company of singers : CHOIR **2** : a group of dancers and singers (as in a musical comedy) **3** : a part of a song repeated at intervals **4** : a composition to be sung by a chorus; *also* : group singing **5** : sounds uttered by a number of persons or animals together ⟨a ～ of boos⟩

♦ choir, chorale; *also* ensemble; minstrelsy

²chorus *vb* : to sing or utter in chorus

chose *past of* CHOOSE

cho·sen \\'chōz-³n\ *adj* ♦ : selected or marked for special favor or privilege

♦ elect, select — more at SELECT

¹chow \\'chaù\ *n* ♦ : material that is taken or absorbed into the body in order to sustain growth and to furnish energy : FOOD

♦ fare, food, grub, meat, provender, provisions, viands, victuals — more at FOOD

²chow *vb* : EAT — often used with *down*

³chow *n* : CHOW CHOW

chow·chow \\'chaù-,chaù\ *n* : chopped mixed pickles in mustard sauce

chow chow \\'chaù-,chaù\ *n* : any of a breed of thick-coated straight-legged muscular dogs of Chinese origin with a blue-black tongue and a short tail curled close to the back

chow·der \\'chaù-dər\ *n* : a soup or stew made from seafood or vegetables and containing milk or tomatoes

chow mein \\'chaù-'mān\ *n* : a seasoned stew of shredded or diced meat, mushrooms, and vegetables that is usu. served with fried noodles

chrism \\'kri-zəm\ *n* : consecrated oil used esp. in baptism, confirmation, and ordination

Christ \\'krīst\ *n* [ME *Crist*, fr. OE, fr. L *Christus*, fr. Gk *Christos*, lit., anointed] : Jesus esp. as the Messiah — **Christ·like** *adj* — **Christ·ly** *adj*

chris·ten \\'kris-³n\ *vb* **1** : BAPTIZE **2** ♦ : to name at baptism **3** ♦ : to name or dedicate (as a ship) by a ceremony suggestive of baptism — **chris·ten·ing** *n*

♦ [2, 3] baptize, call, denominate, designate, dub, entitle, label, name, style, term, title — more at NAME

Chris·ten·dom \\'kris-³n-dəm\ *n* **1** : CHRISTIANITY **2** : the part of the world in which Christianity prevails

¹Chris·tian \\'kris-chən\ *n* : an adherent of Christianity

²Christian *adj* **1** : of or relating to Christianity **2** : based on or conforming with Christianity **3** : of or relating to a Christian **4** : professing Christianity

Chris·ti·an·ia \,kris-chē-'a-nē-ə, ,kris-tē-\ *n* : CHRISTIE

Chris·ti·an·i·ty \,kris-chē-'a-nə-tē\ *n* : the religion derived from Jesus Christ, based on the Bible as sacred scripture, and professed by Christians

Chris·tian·ize \\'kris-chə-,nīz\ *vb* **-ized; -iz·ing** : to make Christian

Christian name *n* : a name that precedes one's surname : GIVEN NAME

Christian Science *n* : a religion and system of healing founded by Mary Baker Eddy and taught by the Church of Christ, Scientist — **Christian Scientist** *n*

chris·tie *or* **chris·ty** \\'kris-tē\ *n, pl* **christies** : a skiing turn made by shifting body weight forward and skidding into a turn with parallel skis

Christ·mas \\'kris-məs\ *n* : December 25 celebrated as a church festival in commemoration of the birth of Christ and observed as a legal holiday

Christmas club *n* : a savings account in which regular deposits are made to provide money for Christmas shopping

Christ·mas·tide \'kris-məs-ˌtīd\ *n* ♦ : the season of Christmas

  ♦ Christmastime, Noel, yuletide — more at YULETIDE

Christ·mas·time \-ˌtīm\ *n* ♦ : the Christmas season

  ♦ Christmastide, Noel, yuletide — more at YULETIDE

chro·mat·ic \krō-'ma-tik\ *adj* **1** : of or relating to color **2** : proceeding by half steps of the musical scale — **chro·mat·i·cism** \-tə-ˌsi-zəm\ *n*

chro·mato·graph \krō-'ma-tə-ˌgraf\ *n* : an instrument used in chromatography

chro·ma·tog·ra·phy \ˌkrō-mə-'tä-grə-fē\ *n* : the separation of a complex mixture into its component compounds as a result of the different rates at which the compounds travel through or over a stationary substance due to differing affinities for the substance — **chro·mato·graph·ic** \krō-ˌma-tə-'gra-fik\ *adj* — **chro·mato·graph·i·cal·ly** \-fi-k(ə-)lē\ *adv*

chrome \'krōm\ *n* **1** : CHROMIUM **2** : a chromium pigment **3** : something plated with an alloy of chromium

chro·mi·um \'krō-mē-əm\ *n* : a bluish white metallic element used esp. in alloys and chrome plating

chro·mo·some \'krō-mə-ˌsōm, -ˌzōm\ *n* [G *Chromosom*, fr. Gk *chrōma* color, pigment + *sōma* body] : any of the rod-shaped or threadlike DNA-containing structures of cellular organisms that contain most or all of the genes of the organism — **chro·mo·som·al** \ˌkrō-mə-'sō-məl, -'zō-\ *adj*

chro·mo·sphere \'krō-mə-ˌsfir\ *n* : the lower part of a star's atmosphere

chron *abbr* **1** chronicle **2** chronological; chronology

Chron *abbr* Chronicles

chron·ic \'krä-nik\ *adj* **1** : marked by long duration or frequent recurrence ⟨a ~ disease⟩ **2** ♦ : being such habitually : HABITUAL ⟨a ~ grumbler⟩ — **chron·i·cal·ly** \-ni-k(ə-)lē\ *adv*

  ♦ confirmed, habitual, inveterate — more at HABITUAL

chronic fatigue syndrome *n* : a disorder of unknown cause that is characterized by persistent profound fatigue

¹chron·i·cle \'krä-ni-kəl\ *n* ♦ : an account of events arranged in the order of time : HISTORY, NARRATIVE

  ♦ account, history, narrative, record, report, story — more at ACCOUNT

²chronicle *vb* **-cled; -cling** : to record in or as if in a chronicle

chron·i·cler *n* : a writer or compiler of a chronicle

Chronicles *n* : either of two books of the Jewish and Christian Scripture

chro·no·graph \'krä-nə-ˌgraf\ *n* : an instrument for measuring and recording time intervals with accuracy — **chro·no·graph·ic** \ˌkrä-nə-'gra-fik\ *adj* — **chro·nog·ra·phy** \krə-'nä-grə-fē\ *n*

chro·nol·o·gy \krə-'nä-lə-jē\ *n, pl* **-gies** **1** : the science that deals with measuring time and dating events **2** : a chronological list or table **3** : arrangement of events in the order of their occurrence — **chron·o·log·i·cal** \ˌkrän-ᵊl-'ä-ji-kəl\ *adj* — **chron·o·log·i·cal·ly** \-k(ə-)lē\ *adv* — **chro·nol·o·gist** \krə-'nä-lə-jist\ *n*

chro·nom·e·ter \krə-'nä-mə-tər\ *n* : a very accurate timepiece

chrys·a·lid \'kri-sə-ləd\ *n* : CHRYSALIS

chrys·a·lis \'kri-sə-ləs\ *n, pl* **chry·sal·i·des** \kri-'sa-lə-ˌdēz\ *or* **chrys·a·lis·es** : an insect pupa in a firm case without a cocoon

chry·san·the·mum \kri-'san-thə-məm\ *n* [L, fr. Gk *chrysanthemon*, fr. *chrysos* gold + *anthemon* flower] : any of various plants related to the daisies including some grown for their showy flowers or for medicinal products or insecticides; *also* : a flower of a chrysanthemum

chub \'chəb\ *n, pl* **chub** *or* **chubs** : any of various small freshwater fishes related to the carp

chub·bi·ness *n* : the quality or state of being chubby

chub·by \'chə-bē\ *adj* **chub·bi·er; -est** ♦ : short, thick, and well-rounded : PLUMP

  ♦ corpulent, fat, fleshy, full, gross, obese, overweight, plump, portly, rotund, round — more at FAT

¹chuck \'chək\ *vb* **1** : to give a pat or tap **2** ♦ : to throw with a short action of the arm or hand : TOSS **3** : DISCARD; *also* : EJECT **4** : to have done with

  ♦ cast, catapult, dash, fire, fling, heave, hurl, hurtle, launch, peg, pelt, pitch, sling, throw, toss — more at THROW

²chuck *n* **1** : a light pat under the chin **2** : TOSS

³chuck *n* **1** : a cut of beef including most of the neck and the parts around the shoulder blade and the first three ribs **2** : a device for holding work or a tool in a machine (as a lathe)

chuck·hole \'chək-ˌhōl\ *n* : POTHOLE

¹chuck·le \'chə-kəl\ *vb* **chuck·led; chuck·ling** : to laugh in a quiet hardly audible manner

²chuckle *n* : a quiet hardly audible laugh

chuck wagon *n* : a wagon equipped with a stove and food supplies

¹chug \'chəg\ *n* : a dull explosive sound made by or as if by a laboring engine

²chug *vb* **chugged; chug·ging** : to move or go with chugs

chuk·ka \'chə-kə\ *n* : a usu. ankle-length leather boot

chuk·ker \'chə-kər\ *also* **chuk·ka** \'chə-kə\ *n* : a playing period of a polo game

¹chum \'chəm\ *n* ♦ : a close friend

  ♦ buddy, comrade, crony, familiar, friend, intimate, pal — more at FRIEND

²chum *vb* **chummed; chum·ming** **1** : to room together **2** ♦ : to be a close friend

  ♦ associate, consort, fraternize, hang around, hobnob, pal — more at ASSOCIATE

chum·mi·ness \-mē-nəs\ *n* : the quality or state of being chummy

chum·my \'chə-mē\ *adj* **chum·mi·er; -est** ♦ : quite friendly : INTIMATE — **chum·mi·ly** \-mə-lē\ *adv* — **chum·mi·ness** \-mē-nəs\ *n*

  ♦ bosom, close, familiar, friendly, intimate, thick — more at FAMILIAR

chump \'chəmp\ *n* : stupid lout : FOOL, BLOCKHEAD

chunk \'chəŋk\ *n* **1** ♦ : a short thick piece **2** : a sizable amount

  ♦ blob, clod, clump, glob, gob, hunk, lump, nub, wad — more at LUMP

chunky \'chəŋ-kē\ *adj* **chunk·i·er; -est** **1** ♦ : compact, sturdy, and thick in build : STOCKY **2** : containing chunks

  ♦ dumpy, heavyset, squat, stocky, stout, stubby, stumpy, thickset — more at STOCKY

church \'chərch\ *n* [ME *chirche*, fr. OE *cirice*, ultim. fr. LGk *kyriakon*, fr. Gk, neut. of *kyriakos* of the lord, fr. *kyrios* lord, master] **1** : a building for public and esp. Christian worship **2** *often cap* : the whole body of Christians **3** : DENOMINATION **4** : a group of persons assembled for worship : CONGREGATION **5** : public divine worship

church·go·er \'chərch-ˌgō(-ə)r\ *n* : one who habitually attends church — **church·go·ing** *adj or n*

church·less \'chərch-ləs\ *adj* : not affiliated with a church

church·man \'chərch-mən\ *n* **1** : CLERGYMAN **2** : a member of a church

church·war·den \'chərch-ˌwȯrd-ᵊn\ *n* : WARDEN 5

church·yard \-ˌyärd\ *n* : a yard that belongs to a church and is often used as a burial ground

churl \'chərl\ *n* **1** : a medieval peasant **2** : RUSTIC **3** ♦ : a rude ill-bred person — **churl·ish** *adj* — **churl·ish·ly** *adv* — **churl·ish·ness** *n*

  ♦ beast, boor, clown, creep, cretin, cur, heel, jerk, joker, louse, lout, skunk, slob, snake — more at JERK

churl·ish *adj* ♦ : marked by a lack of civility or graciousness — **churl·ish·ly** *adv* — **churl·ish·ness** *n*

  ♦ boorish, clownish, loutish, uncouth — more at CLOWNISH

¹churn \'chərn\ *n* : a container in which milk or cream is violently agitated in making butter

²churn *vb* **1** : to stir in a churn; *also* : to make (butter) by such stirring **2 ♦** : to stir or shake around esp. violently **3 ♦** : to experience violent motion or agitation

♦ [2] agitate, stir, swirl, whirl — more at STIR ♦ [3] boil, roil, seethe — more at SEETHE

churn out *vb* : to produce mechanically or in large quantity

chute \'shüt\ *n* **1** : an inclined surface, trough, or passage down or through which something may pass ⟨a coal ∼⟩ ⟨a mail ∼⟩ **2** : PARACHUTE

chut·ney \'chət-nē\ *n, pl* **chutneys** : a thick sauce containing fruits, vinegar, sugar, and spices

chutz·pah \'hut-spə, 'kut-, -(ˌ)spä\ *n* ♦ : supreme self-confidence

♦ audacity, brass, brazenness, cheek, effrontery, gall, nerve, presumption, sauce, sauciness, temerity — more at EFFRONTERY

CIA *abbr* Central Intelligence Agency

cía *abbr* [Sp *compañía*] company

cia·bat·ta \chə-'bä-tə\ *n* [It, lit., slipper] : a flat bread with a moist interior and a crispy crust

ciao \'chau̇\ *interj* — used to express greeting or farewell

ci·ca·da \sə-'kä-də\ *n* : any of a family of stout-bodied insects related to the aphids and having wide blunt heads and large transparent wings

ci·ca·trix \'si-kə-ˌtriks\ *n, pl* **ci·ca·tri·ces** \ˌsi-kə-'trī-ˌsēz\ [L] : a scar resulting from formation and contraction of fibrous tissue in a wound

ci·ce·ro·ne \ˌsi-sə-'rō-nē, ˌchē-chə-\ *n, pl* **-ni** \-(ˌ)nē\ : a guide who conducts sightseers

CID *abbr* Criminal Investigation Department

ci·der \'sī-dər\ *n* : juice pressed from fruit (as apples) and used as a beverage, vinegar, or flavoring

cie *abbr* [F *compagnie*] company

ci·gar \si-'gär\ *n* [Sp *cigarro*] : a roll of tobacco for smoking

cig·a·rette \ˌsi-gə-'ret, 'si-gə-ˌret\ *n* [F, dim. of *cigare* cigar] : a slender roll of cut tobacco enclosed in paper for smoking

cig·a·ril·lo \ˌsi-gə-'ri-lō, -'rē-ō\ *n, pl* **-los** [Sp] **1** : a very small cigar **2** : a cigarette wrapped in tobacco rather than paper

ci·lan·tro \si-'län-trō, -'lan-\ *n* : leaves of coriander used as a flavoring or garnish; *also* : the coriander plant

cil·i·ate \'si-lē-ˌāt\ *n* : any of a group of protozoans characterized by cilia

cil·i·um \'si-lē-əm\ *n, pl* **-ia** \-lē-ə\ **1** : a minute short hairlike process; *esp* : one of a cell **2** : EYELASH

C in C *abbr* commander in chief

¹cinch \'sinch\ *n* **1** : a girth for a pack or saddle **2 ♦** : a thing done with ease

♦ breeze, child's play, picnic, pushover, snap; *also* nothing **Ant** chore, headache, labor

²cinch *vb* ♦ : to make certain : ASSURE

♦ assure, ensure, guarantee, guaranty, insure, secure — more at ENSURE

cin·cho·na \sin-'kō-nə\ *n* : any of a genus of So. American trees related to the madder; *also* : the bitter quinine-containing bark of a cinchona

cinc·ture \'sink-chər\ *n* ♦ : an article of dress encircling the body usu. at the waist : BELT, SASH

♦ belt, cummerbund, girdle, sash — more at BELT

cin·der \'sin-dər\ *n* **1** : SLAG **2** *pl* : ASHES **3** : a hot piece of partly burned wood or coal **4** : a fragment of lava from an erupting volcano — **cinder** *vb* — **cin·dery** *adj*

cinder block *n* : a building block made of cement and coal cinders

cin·e·ma \'si-nə-mə\ *n* **1** : a motion-picture theater **2** : the film industry : MOVIES — **cin·e·mat·ic** \ˌsi-nə-'ma-tik\ *adj*

cin·e·ma·theque \ˌsi-nə-mə-'tek\ *n* : a small movie house specializing in avant-garde films

cin·e·ma·tog·ra·phy \ˌsi-nə-mə-'tä-grə-fē\ *n* : motion-

picture photography — **cin·e·ma·tog·ra·pher** *n* — **cin·e·mat·o·graph·ic** \-ˌma-tə-'gra-fik\ *adj*

cin·e·plex \'si-nə-ˌpleks\ *n* : a complex that houses several movie theaters

cin·er·ar·i·um \ˌsi-nə-'rer-ē-əm\ *n, pl* **-ia** \-ē-ə\ : a place to receive the ashes of the cremated dead — **cin·er·ary** \'si-nə-ˌrer-ē\ *adj*

cin·na·bar \'si-nə-ˌbär\ *n* : a red mineral that is the only important ore of mercury

cin·na·mon \'si-nə-mən\ *n* : a spice prepared from the highly aromatic bark of any of several trees related to the true laurel; *also* : a tree that yields cinnamon

cinque·foil \'sink-ˌfȯil, 'sank-\ *n* : any of a genus of plants related to the roses with leaves having five lobes

¹ci·pher \'sī-fər\ *n* [ME, fr. MF *cifre*, fr. ML *cifra*, fr. Ar *ṣifr* empty, zero] **1 ♦** : the symbol 0 denoting the absence of all magnitude or quantity : ZERO, NAUGHT **2** : a method of secret writing

♦ aught, naught, nil, nothing, zero, zip — more at ZERO

²cipher *vb* : to compute arithmetically

cir *or* **circ** *abbr* circular

cir·ca \'sər-kə\ *prep* : ABOUT ⟨∼ 1600⟩

cir·ca·di·an \ˌsər-'kā-dē-ən, ˌsər-kə-'dī-ən\ *adj* : being, having, characterized by, or occurring in approximately 24-hour intervals (as of biological activity)

¹cir·cle \'sər-kəl\ *n* **1 ♦** : a closed curve every point of which is equally distant from a fixed point within it **2 ♦** : something circular **3** : an area of action or influence **4** : a series ending at its starting point : CYCLE **5** ♦ : a group bound by a common tie

♦ [1, 2] band, hoop, ring, round — more at RING ♦ [5] clan, clique, coterie, crowd, fold, gang, ring, set — more at GANG

²circle *vb* **cir·cled; cir·cling 1 ♦** : to enclose in a circle **2 ♦** : to move or revolve around; *also* : to move in a circle

♦ [1] encircle, enclose, encompass, ring, surround — more at SURROUND ♦ [2] circumnavigate, coil, compass, encircle, girdle, loop, orbit, ring, round — more at ENCIRCLE

cir·clet \'sər-klət\ *n* : a small circle; *esp* : a circular ornament

cir·cuit \'sər-kət\ *n* **1** : a boundary around an enclosed space **2** : a course around a periphery **3** : a regular tour (as by a judge) around an assigned territory **4** : the complete path of an electric current; *also* : an assemblage of electronic components **5** : LEAGUE; *also* : a chain of theaters — **cir·cuit·al** \-ᵊl\ *adj*

circuit breaker *n* : a switch that automatically interrupts an electric circuit under an abnormal condition

circuit court *n* : a court that sits at two or more places within one judicial district

cir·cu·i·tous \ˌsər-'kyü-ə-təs\ *adj* **1 ♦** : having a circular or winding course **2 ♦** : not being forthright or direct in language or action

♦ [1] circular, indirect, roundabout — more at INDIRECT ♦ [2] diffuse, long-winded, prolix, rambling, verbose, windy, wordy — more at WORDY

cir·cuit·ry \'sər-kə-trē\ *n, pl* **-ries** : the plan or the components of an electric circuit

cir·cu·ity \ˌsər-'kyü-ə-tē\ *n, pl* **-ities** : INDIRECTION

¹cir·cu·lar \'sər-kyə-lər\ *adj* **1** : having the form of a circle : ROUND **2** : moving in or around a circle **3 ♦** : not forthright or direct in language or action : CIRCUITOUS **4** : intended for circulation ⟨a ∼ letter⟩ — **cir·cu·lar·i·ty** \ˌsər-kyə-'lar-ə-tē\ *n*

♦ circuitous, indirect, roundabout — more at INDIRECT

²circular *n* ♦ : a paper (as a leaflet) intended for wide distribution

♦ booklet, brochure, folder, leaflet, pamphlet — more at PAMPHLET

cir·cu·lar·ise *Brit var of* CIRCULARIZE

cir·cu·lar·ize \'sər-kyə-lə-ˌrīz\ *vb* **-ized; -iz·ing 1** : to send circulars to **2** : to poll by questionnaire

circular saw *n* : a power saw with a round cutting blade

cir·cu·late \'sər-kyə-ˌlāt\ *vb* -**lat·ed; -lat·ing** **1** : to move or cause to move in a circle, circuit, or orbit **2 ♦** : to pass from place to place or from person to person **3 ♦** : to become well-known or widespread — **cir·cu·la·tion** \ˌsər-kyə-'lā-shən\ *n*

♦ [2, 3] broadcast, disseminate, propagate, spread, strew — more at SPREAD

cir·cu·la·to·ry \'sər-kyə-lə-ˌtōr-ē\ *adj* : of or relating to circulation or the circulatory system

circulatory system *n* : the system of blood, blood vessels, lymphatic vessels, and heart concerned with the circulation of the blood and lymph

cir·cum·am·bu·late \ˌsər-kəm-'am-byə-ˌlāt\ *vb* -**lat·ed; -lat·ing** : to circle on foot esp. as part of a ritual

cir·cum·cise \'sər-kəm-ˌsīz\ *vb* -**cised; -cis·ing** [ME, fr. L *circumcisus*, pp. of *circumcidere*, lit., to cut around, fr. *circum* around + *caedere* to cut] : to cut off the foreskin of — **cir·cum·ci·sion** \ˌsər-kəm-'si-zhən\ *n*

cir·cum·fer·ence \sər-'kəm-f(ə-)rəns\ *n* **1** : the perimeter of a circle **2 ♦** : the external boundary or surface of a figure or object

♦ border, bound, boundary, compass, confines, edge, end, fringe, margin, perimeter, periphery, rim, skirt, verge — more at BORDER

cir·cum·flex \'sər-kəm-ˌfleks\ *n* : the mark ˆ over a vowel

cir·cum·lo·cu·tion \ˌsər-kəm-lō-'kyü-shən\ *n ♦* : the use of an unnecessarily large number of words to express an idea

♦ prolixity, redundancy, verbiage, wordiness — more at VERBIAGE

cir·cum·lu·nar \-'lü-nər\ *adj* : revolving about or surrounding the moon

cir·cum·nav·i·gate \-'na-və-ˌgāt\ *vb ♦* : to go completely around (as the earth) esp. by water — **cir·cum·nav·i·ga·tion** \-ˌna-və-'gā-shən\ *n*

♦ circle, coil, compass, encircle, girdle, loop, orbit, ring, round — more at ENCIRCLE

cir·cum·po·lar \-'pō-lər\ *adj* **1** : continually visible above the horizon ⟨a ∼ star⟩ **2** : surrounding or found near a pole of the earth

cir·cum·scribe \'sər-kəm-ˌskrīb\ *vb* **1 ♦** : to constrict the range or activity of **2** : to draw a line around — **cir·cum·scrip·tion** \ˌsər-kəm-'skrip-shən\ *n*

♦ check, confine, control, curb, inhibit, limit, restrain, restrict ♦ bound, define, delimit, demarcate, limit, mark, terminate — more at LIMIT

cir·cum·spect \'sər-kəm-ˌspekt\ *adj ♦* : careful to consider all circumstances and consequences : PRUDENT — **cir·cum·spec·tion** \ˌsər-kəm-'spek-shən\ *n*

♦ alert, careful, cautious, considerate, gingerly, guarded, heedful, prudent, safe, wary — more at CAREFUL

cir·cum·spec·tion \ˌsər-kəm-'spek-shən\ *n ♦* : careful consideration to minimize risk

♦ alertness, care, carefulness, caution, heedfulness — more at CAUTION

cir·cum·stance \'sər-kəm-ˌstans\ *n* **1** : a condition, fact, or event accompanying, conditioning, or determining another **2** : surrounding conditions **3 a ♦** : an inevitable and often adverse end : FATE **b ♦** : something that happens unpredictably : CHANCE **4** *pl* : situation with regard to wealth **5** : CEREMONY ⟨pomp and ∼⟩

♦ [3a] destiny, doom, fate, fortune, lot, portion — more at FATE ♦ [3b] accident, chance, hazard, luck — more at CHANCE

cir·cum·stan·tial \ˌsər-kəm-'stan-chəl\ *adj* **1** : consisting of or depending on circumstances **2** : INCIDENTAL **3 ♦** : containing full details — **cir·cum·stan·tial·ly** *adv*

♦ detailed, elaborate, full, minute, thorough — more at DETAILED

cir·cum·vent \ˌsər-kəm-'vent\ *vb* **1 a ♦** : to go around : make a full circuit around or bypass without going through **b ♦** : to manage to get around esp. by ingenuity

or stratagem **2** : to check or defeat esp. by stratagem — **cir·cum·ven·tion** \-'vent-shən\ *n*

♦ [1a, 1b] dodge, sidestep, skirt; *also* avoid, duck, elude, escape, eschew, evade, shake, shun; disobey, disregard, flout, ignore *Ant* comply (with), follow, keep, obey, observe ♦ [1a, 1b] bypass, detour, skirt — more at DETOUR

cir·cus \'sər-kəs\ *n* **1 ♦** : a large arena enclosed by tiers of seats on three or all four sides and used esp. for sports or spectacles **2** : a usu. traveling show that features feats of physical skill, wild animal acts, and performances by clowns **3** : a circus performance; *also* : the equipment, livestock, and personnel of a circus **4 ♦** : something suggestive of a circus (as in frenzied activity or razzle-dazzle) ⟨a media ∼⟩

♦ [1] bowl, coliseum, stadium — more at STADIUM ♦ [4] bedlam, hell, madhouse — more at MADHOUSE

cirque \'sərk\ *n* : a deep steep-walled mountain basin usu. forming the blunt end of a valley

cir·rho·sis \sə-'rō-səs\ *n, pl* -**rho·ses** \-ˌsēz\ [NL, fr. Gk *kirrhos* orange-colored] : fibrosis of the liver — **cir·rhot·ic** \-'rä-tik\ *adj or n*

cir·rus \'sir-əs\ *n, pl* **cir·ri** \'sir-ˌī\ : a wispy white cloud usu. of minute ice crystals at high altitudes

cis \'sis\ *adj* : CISGENDER

cis·gen·der \(ˌ)sis-'jen-dər\ *also* **cis·gen·dered** \-dərd\ *adj* : of, relating to, or being a person whose gender identity corresponds with the sex the person had or was identified as having at birth

cis·lu·nar \(ˌ)sis-'lü-nər\ *adj* : lying between the earth and the moon or the moon's orbit

cis·tern \'sis-tərn\ *n* : an often underground tank for storing water

cit *abbr* **1** citation; cited **2** citizen

cit·a·del \'si-tə-dəl, -ˌdel\ *n* **1 ♦** : a fortress commanding a city **2 ♦** : a place of security or survival : STRONGHOLD

♦ [1, 2] bastion, fastness, fort, fortification, fortress, hold, stronghold

ci·ta·tion \sī-'tā-shən\ *n* **1** : an official summons to appear (as before a court) **2 a** : something that is quoted **b** : a passage referred to or given as an example : QUOTATION **3 ♦** : a formal statement of the achievements of a person; *also* : a specific reference in a military dispatch to meritorious performance of duty

♦ accolade, commendation, encomium, eulogy, homage, paean, panegyric, salutation, tribute — more at ENCOMIUM

cite \'sīt\ *vb* **cit·ed; cit·ing** **1** : to summon to appear before a court **2 ♦** : to quote by way of example, authority, or proof : QUOTE **3** : to refer to esp. in commendation or praise **4 ♦** : to bring forward or call to another's attention esp. as an example

♦ [2] advert (to), instance, mention, name, note, notice, quote, refer (to), specify, touch (*on* or *upon*) — more at MENTION ♦ [4] adduce, instance, mention, quote

cit·i·fied \'si-ti-ˌfīd\ *adj* : of, relating to, or characterized by an urban style of living

cit·i·zen \'si-tə-zən\ *n* **1** : an inhabitant of a city or town **2** : a person who owes allegiance to a government and is entitled to its protection — **cit·i·zen·ship** *n*

cit·i·zen·ry \-rē\ *n, pl* -**ries** : a whole body of citizens

citizens band *n* : a range of radio frequencies set aside for private radio communications

cit·ric acid \'si-trik-\ *n* : a sour organic acid obtained from lemon and lime juices or by fermentation of sugars and used as a flavoring

cit·ron \'si-trən\ *n* **1** : the oval lemonlike fruit of an Asian citrus tree; *also* : the tree **2** : a small hard-fleshed watermelon used esp. in pickles and preserves

cit·ro·nel·la \ˌsi-trə-'ne-lə\ *n* : a lemon-scented oil obtained from a fragrant grass of southern Asia and used in perfumes and as an insect repellent

cit·rus \'si-trəs\ *n, pl* **citrus** *or* **cit·rus·es** : any of a genus of often thorny evergreen trees or shrubs grown for their fruits (as the orange, lemon, lime, and grapefruit); *also* : the fruit

city \\'si-tē\ *n, pl* **cit·ies** [ME *citie* large or small town, fr. OF *cité*, fr. ML *civitas*, fr. L, citizenship, state, city of Rome, fr. *civis* citizen] **1 ♦** : an inhabited place larger or more important than a town **2** : a municipality in the U.S. governed under a charter granted by the state; *also* : an incorporated municipal unit of the highest class in Canada

♦ metropolis, municipality

city manager *n* : an official employed by an elected council to direct the administration of a city government

city–state \\'si-tē-ˌstāt\ *n* : an autonomous state consisting of a city and surrounding territory

civ *abbr* **1** civil; civilian **2** civilization

civ·et \\'si-vət\ *n* : a yellowish strong-smelling substance obtained from a catlike mammal (**civet cat**) of Africa or Asia and used in making perfumes

civ·ic \\'si-vik\ *adj* : of or relating to a city, citizenship, or civil affairs

civ·ics \-viks\ *n* : a social science dealing with the rights and duties of citizens

civ·il \\'si-vəl\ *adj* **1 ♦** : of or relating to citizens or to the state as a political body **2 ♦** : adequate in courtesy and politeness : COURTEOUS, POLITE **3** : of or relating to legal proceedings in connection with private rights and obligations ⟨the ∼ code⟩ **4** : of or relating to the general population : not military or ecclesiastical

♦ [1] national, public, state — more at NATIONAL **♦** [2] courteous, genteel, gracious, mannerly, polite, well-bred — more at POLITE

civil defense *n* : protective measures and emergency relief activities conducted by civilians in case of enemy attack or natural disaster

civil disobedience *n* : refusal to obey governmental commands esp. as a nonviolent means of protest

civil engineer *n* : an engineer whose training or occupation is in the design and construction esp. of public works (as roads or harbors) — **civil engineering** *n*

ci·vil·ian \sə-'vil-yən\ *n* : a person not on active duty in a military, police, or fire-fighting force

ci·vil·i·ty \sə-'vi-lə-tē\ *n, pl* **-ties** **1 ♦** : civilized conduct : POLITENESS, COURTESY **2 ♦** : a polite act or expression

♦ [1] courtesy, gentility, graciousness, mannerliness, politeness — more at POLITENESS **♦** [2] amenity, courtesy, formality, gesture; *also* ceremony, observance, rite, ritual; etiquette, manners; greetings, regards, respects; favor, grace, kindness

civ·i·li·za·tion \ˌsi-və-lə-'zā-shən\ *n* **1 ♦** : a relatively high level of cultural and technological development **2 ♦** : the culture characteristic of a time or place — **civ·i·li·za·tion·al** \-shə-nᵊl\ *adj*

♦ [1] cultivation, culture, polish, refinement — more at CULTURE **♦** [2] culture, life, lifestyle, society; *also* customs, manners, mores; folklore, heritage, tradition

civ·i·lize \\'si-və-ˌlīz\ *vb* **-lized; -liz·ing** **1** : to raise from a primitive state to an advanced and ordered stage of cultural development **2** : REFINE

civ·i·lized *adj* **1** : characteristic of a state of civilization **2 ♦** : characterized by taste, refinement, or restraint

♦ cultivated, cultured, genteel, polished, refined — more at CULTIVATED

civil liberty *n* : freedom from arbitrary governmental interference specifically by denial of governmental power — usu. used in pl.

civ·il·ly \\'si-vəl-lē\ *adv* **1** : in terms of civil rights, matters, or law ⟨∼ dead⟩ **2** : in a civil manner : POLITELY

civil rights *n pl* : the nonpolitical rights of a citizen; *esp* : those guaranteed by the 13th and 14th amendments to the Constitution and by acts of Congress

civil servant *n* : a member of a civil service

civil service *n* : the administrative service of a government

civil war *n* : a war between opposing groups of citizens of the same country

civ·vies \\'si-vēz\ *n pl* : civilian clothes as distinguished from a military uniform

CJ *abbr* chief justice

ck *abbr* **1** cask **2** check

cl *abbr* **1** centiliter **2** class

Cl *symbol* chlorine

¹clack \\'klak\ *vb* **1** : CHATTER, PRATTLE **2** : to make an abrupt striking sound or series of sounds

²clack *n* **1** : rapid continuous talk : CHATTER **2** : a sound of clacking ⟨the ∼ of a typewriter⟩

clad \\'klad\ *adj* **1** : CLOTHED, COVERED **2** : being or consisting of coins made of outer layers of one metal bonded to a core of a different metal

¹claim \\'klām\ *vb* [ME, fr. AF *claimer, clamer*, fr. L *clamare* to cry out, shout] **1 ♦** : to ask for esp. as a right **2** : to call for : REQUIRE **3 ♦** : to state as a fact : MAINTAIN

♦ [1] call, clamor (*or* clamour), command, demand, enjoin, exact, insist, press, quest, stipulate (for) — more at DEMAND **♦** [3] affirm, allege, assert, aver, avouch, avow, contend, declare, insist, maintain, profess, protest, warrant; *also* announce, broadcast, proclaim; argue, rationalize, reason; confirm, justify, vindicate; defend, support, uphold *Ant* deny, gainsay

²claim *n* **1 ♦** : a demand for something due or believed to be due **2 ♦** : a right to something usu. in another's possession **3 ♦** : an assertion open to challenge **4 ♦** : something claimed (as a tract of land)

♦ [1] demand, dun, requisition — more at DEMAND **♦** [2] call, pretense, pretension, right; *also* birthright, prerogative; favor, privilege; refusal **♦** [3] affirmation, assertion, avowal, declaration, profession, protestation — more at PROTESTATION **♦** [4] interest, share, stake — more at INTEREST

claim·ant \\'klā-mənt\ *n* : a person making a claim

clair·voy·ance \-əns\ *n* : the power or faculty of discerning objects not present to the senses

clair·voy·ant \klar-'vȯi-ənt\ *adj* [F, fr. *clair* clear + *voyant* seeing] **1** : unusually perceptive **2** : having the power of discerning objects not present to the senses — **clairvoyant** *n*

clam \\'klam\ *n* **1** : any of numerous bivalve mollusks including many that are edible **2** : DOLLAR

clam·bake \-ˌbāk\ *n* : a party or gathering (as at the seashore) at which food is cooked usu. on heated rocks covered by seaweed

clam·ber \\'klam-bər\ *vb* : to climb awkwardly — **clam·ber·er** *n*

clam·my \\'kla-mē\ *adj* **clam·mi·er; -est** : being damp, soft, sticky, and usu. cool — **clam·mi·ness** *n*

¹clam·or *or Can and Brit* **clam·our** *n* **1 ♦** : a noisy shouting **2 ♦** : a loud continuous noise **3** : insistent public expression (as of support or protest)

♦ [1] howl, hubbub, hue and cry, hullabaloo, noise, outcry, roar, tumult, uproar; *also* clangor, din, jangle, racket **♦** [2] bluster, cacophony, din, noise, racket, roar — more at NOISE

²clamor *or Can and Brit* **clamour** *vb* **♦** : to appeal, demand, or protest by sustained noisy outcry : to become loudly insistent — usu. used with *for*

♦ *usu* **clamor for** call, claim, demand, enjoin, exact, insist, press, quest, stipulate (for) — more at DEMAND

clam·or·ous *or Can and Brit* **clamorous** *adj* **1 ♦** : marked by confused din or outcry **2 ♦** : full of noise : noisily insistent

♦ [1] blatant, obstreperous, vociferous — more at VOCIFEROUS **♦** [2] booming, deafening, earsplitting, loud, piercing, resounding, ringing, roaring, sonorous, stentorian, thunderous — more at LOUD

¹clamp \\'klamp\ *n* : a device that holds or presses parts together firmly

²clamp *vb* **♦** : to fasten with or as if with a clamp

♦ anchor, fasten, fix, hitch, moor, secure, set

clamp down *vb* ♦ : to impose restrictions : become repressive — **clamp·down** \'klamp-ˌdau̇n\ *n*

♦ *usu* **clamp down on** crack down, crush, put down, quash, quell, repress, silence, snuff, squash, squelch, subdue, suppress — more at QUELL

clam·shell \'klam-ˌshel\ *n* **1** : the shell of a clam **2** : a bucket or grapnel (as on a dredge) having two hinged jaws

clam up *vb* ♦ : to become silent

♦ hush, pipe down, quiet (down), shut up — more at SHUT UP

clan \'klan\ *n* [ME, fr. ScGael *clann* offspring, clan, fr. Old Irish *cland* plant, offspring, fr. L *planta* plant] **1** ♦ : a group of people tracing descent from a common ancestor **2** ♦ : a group united by a common interest or common characteristics — **clan·nish** *n* — **clan·nish·ness** *n*

♦ [1] blood, family, folks, house, kin, kindred, kinfolk, line, lineage, people, race, stock, tribe ♦ [2] circle, clique, coterie, crowd, fold, gang, ring, set — more at GANG

clan·des·tine \klan-'des-tən\ *adj* ♦ : held in or conducted with secrecy

♦ covert, furtive, hugger-mugger, private, secret, sneak, sneaky, stealthy, surreptitious, undercover, underground, underhanded — more at SECRET

clang \'klaŋ\ *n* ♦ : a loud metallic ringing sound — **clang** *vb*

♦ clash; *also* chime, peel, ring; clink, jangle, jingle, tinkle; clap, clop, crack, crash

clan·gor *or Can and Brit* **clan·gour** \'klaŋ-ər, -gər\ *n* : a loud deeply resounding sound made esp. by metal objects struck together

clank \'klaŋk\ *n* : a sharp brief metallic ringing sound — **clank** *vb*

clan·nish *n* : tending to associate only with a select group of similar background or status — **clan·nish·ness** *n*

¹**clap** \'klap\ *vb* **clapped; clap·ping** **1** : to strike noisily **2** : APPLAUD

²**clap** *n* **1** ♦ : a loud noisy crash **2** : a sudden sometimes resounding blow or stroke **3** : the noise made by clapping the hands

♦ bang, blast, boom, crack, crash, pop, report, slam, smash, snap, thwack, whack; *also* clang, clangor, clank, clash; knock, rap, tap; clamor, howl, hubbub, hue and cry, hullabaloo, outcry, roar, tumult, uproar

³**clap** *n* : GONORRHEA

clap·board \'kla-bərd, -ˌbȯrd; 'klap-ˌbȯrd\ *n* : a narrow board thicker at one edge than the other used for siding — **clap·board** *vb*

clap·per \'kla-pər\ *n* : one that claps; *esp* : the tongue of a bell

clap·trap \'klap-ˌtrap\ *n* ♦ : pretentious nonsense

♦ bunk, drivel, fiddlesticks, folly, foolishness, fudge, hogwash, humbug, nonsense, piffle, rot, silliness, slush, stupidity, trash — more at NONSENSE

claque \'klak\ *n* [F, fr. *claquer* to clap] **1** : a group hired to applaud at a performance **2** : a group of sycophants

clar·et \'klar-ət\ *n* [ME, fr. AF (*vin*) *claret* clear wine] : a dry red wine

clar·i·fi·ca·tion \ˌklar-ə-fə-'kā-shən\ *n* ♦ : the act or process of clarifying; *also* : something that clarifies

♦ construction, elucidation, explanation, explication, exposition, illumination, illustration, interpretation — more at EXPLANATION

clar·i·fy \'klar-ə-ˌfī\ *vb* **-fied; -fy·ing** ♦ : to make or become clear

♦ clear (up), construe, demonstrate, elucidate, explain, explicate, expound, illuminate, illustrate, interpret, spell out — more at EXPLAIN ♦ clear, distill, filter, purify; *also* process, refine; clean, cleanse, purge; extract, leach; screen, sieve, sift

clar·i·net \ˌklar-ə-'net\ *n* : a single-reed woodwind instrument in the form of a cylindrical tube with a moderately flaring end — **clar·i·net·ist** *or* **clar·i·net·tist** \-'ne-tist\ *n*

clar·i·on \'klar-ē-ən\ *adj* : brilliantly clear ⟨a ∼ call⟩

clar·i·ty \'klar-ə-tē\ *n* ♦ : the quality or state of being clear : LUCIDITY

♦ explicitness, lucidity, perspicuity, simplicity — more at SIMPLICITY

¹**clash** \'klash\ *vb* **1** : to make or cause to make a clash **2** ♦ : to be incompatible **3** ♦ : to come into conflict

♦ [2] collide, conflict, jar; *also* mismatch; battle, combat, fight, war (against); chafe, gall, grate, jangle; differ, disagree *Ant* blend, harmonize, match ♦ *usu* **clash with** [3] battle, combat, fight, scrimmage, skirmish, war — more at FIGHT

²**clash** *n* **1** ♦ : a noisy usu. metallic sound of collision **2** ♦ : a hostile encounter; *also* : a conflict of opinion

♦ [1] clang — more at CLANG ♦ [2] battle, combat, conflict, contest, fight, fracas, fray, hassle, scrap, scrimmage, scuffle, skirmish, struggle, tussle — more at FIGHT

¹**clasp** \'klasp\ *n* **1** : a device (as a hook) for holding objects or parts together **2** : a holding or enveloping with or as if with the hands or arms : EMBRACE, GRASP

²**clasp** *vb* ♦ : to enclose and hold with the arms or hands

♦ caress, embrace, enfold, grasp, hug — more at EMBRACE ♦ grasp, grip, hold, take — more at TAKE

¹**class** \'klas\ *n* [F *classe*, fr. L *classis* group called to military service, fleet, class] **1** : a group of students meeting regularly in a course; *also* : a group graduating together **2** : a course of instruction; *also* : the period when such a course is taught **3 a** ♦ : social rank; *esp* : high social rank **b** ♦ : high quality : ELEGANCE **4** ♦ : a group of the same general status or nature; *esp* : a major category in biological classification that is above the order and below the phylum **5** ♦ : a division or rating based on grade or quality — **class·less** *adj*

♦ [3a] caste, estate, folk, order, place, position, rank, standing, status, stratum; *also* bracket, level, tier; place, grouping, hierarchy, stratification; clan, family, people, race, tribe ♦ [3b] elegance, grace, handsomeness, majesty, refinement, stateliness — more at ELEGANCE ♦ [4] breed, description, feather, ilk, kind, like, manner, nature, order, sort, species, type — more at SORT ♦ [5] bracket, category, division, family, grade, group, kind, order, set, species, type; *also* description, feather, ilk, nature, sort; branch, section, subdivision, subgroup, variety; breed, race; classification, heading, label, rubric, title

²**class** *vb* ♦ : to arrange in classes : CLASSIFY

♦ assort, break down, categorize, classify, grade, group, peg, place, range, rank, separate, sort — more at CLASSIFY

class action *n* : a legal action undertaken in behalf of the plaintiffs and all others having an identical interest in the alleged wrong

¹**clas·sic** \'kla-sik\ *adj* **1** ♦ : serving as a standard of excellence; *also* : TRADITIONAL **2** : CLASSICAL 2 **3** : notable esp. as the best example **4** : AUTHENTIC **5** ♦ : typical or regarded as typical : ideally illustrative

♦ [1] model, paradigmatic, quintessential, traditional — more at MODEL ♦ [5] characteristic, distinct, distinctive, individual, peculiar, proper, symptomatic, typical — more at CHARACTERISTIC

²**classic** *n* **1** : a work of enduring excellence and esp. of ancient Greece or Rome; *also* : its author **2** ♦ : a typical or perfect example **3** : a traditional event

♦ beau ideal, epitome, exemplar, ideal, perfection, quintessence — more at QUINTESSENCE

clas·si·cal \'kla-si-kəl\ *adj* **1** : CLASSIC **2** : of or relating to the ancient Greek and Roman classics **3** : of or relating to a form or system of primary significance before modern times ⟨∼ economics⟩ **4** : concerned with a general study of the arts and sciences **5** ♦ : handed down (as beliefs or customs) by example from one generation to another — **clas·si·cal·ly** \-k(ə-)lē\ *adv*

♦ conventional, customary, traditional — more at TRA-DITIONAL

clas·si·cism \'kla-sə-ˌsi-zəm\ n **1** : the principles or style of the literature or art of ancient Greece and Rome **2** : adherence to traditional standards believed to be universally valid — **clas·si·cist** \-sist\ n

clas·si·fi·ca·tion \ˌkla-sə-fə-'kā-shən\ n ♦ : a group of the same general status or nature : CLASS, CATEGORY

♦ bracket, category, class, division, family, grade, group, kind, order, rank, set, species, type — more at CLASS

clas·si·fied \'kla-sə-ˌfīd\ adj : withheld from general circulation for reasons of national security

clas·si·fieds \-ˌfīdz\ n pl : advertisements grouped by subject

clas·si·fy \'kla-sə-ˌfī\ vb **-fied; -fy·ing** ♦ : to arrange in or assign to classes — **clas·si·fi·able** adj — **clas·si·fi·ca·tion** \ˌkla-sə-fə-'kā-shən\ n — **clas·si·fi·er** n

♦ arrange, array, codify, dispose, draw up, marshal, order, organize, range, systematize — more at ORDER ♦ assort, break down, categorize, class, grade, group, peg, place, range, rank, separate, sort; also arrange, order, organize, systematize; alphabetize, catalog, codify, file, index, list; pigeonhole, shelve; distinguish, identify, recognize; cull, screen, sift, winnow

class·less \'klas-ləs\ adj ♦ : having the qualities or behavior of a boor : BOORISH

♦ boorish, churlish, clownish, loutish, uncouth — more at CLOWNISH

class·mate \'klas-ˌmāt\ n : a member of the same class (as in a college)

class·room \-ˌrüm, -ˌrùm\ n : a place where classes meet

classy \'kla-sē\ adj **class·i·er; -est** : ELEGANT, STYLISH — **class·i·ness** n

¹clat·ter \'kla-tər\ n **1** : a rattling sound ⟨the ∼ of dishes⟩ **2** : an agitated disturbance or noisy confusion

²clatter vb : to make a rattling sound

clause \'klòz\ n **1** : a group of words having its own subject and predicate but forming only part of a compound or complex sentence **2** : a separate part of an article or document

claus·tro·pho·bia \ˌklò-strə-'fō-bē-ə\ n : abnormal dread of being in closed or narrow spaces — **claus·tro·pho·bic** \-bik\ adj

clav·i·chord \'kla-və-ˌkòrd\ n : an early keyboard instrument in use before the piano

clav·i·cle \'kla-vi-kəl\ n [F clavicule, fr. NL clavicula, fr. L, dim. of L clavis key] : COLLARBONE

cla·vier \klə-'vir; 'klā-vē-ər\ n **1** : the keyboard of a musical instrument **2** : an early keyboard instrument

¹claw \'klò\ n **1** : a sharp usu. curved nail on the toe of an animal **2** : a sharp curved process (as on the foot of an insect); also : a pincerlike organ at the end of a limb of some arthropods (as a lobster) — **clawed** \'klòd\ adj

²claw vb : to rake, seize, or dig with or as if with claws

clay \'klā\ n **1** : an earthy material that is plastic when moist but hard when fired and is used in making pottery; also : finely divided soil consisting largely of such clay **2** : EARTH, MUD **3** : a plastic substance used for modeling **4** : the mortal human body — **clay·ey** \'klā-ē\ adj

clay·more \'klā-ˌmòr\ n : a large 2-edged sword formerly used by Scottish Highlanders

clay pigeon n : a saucer-shaped target thrown from a trap in trapshooting

¹clean \'klēn\ adj **1** ♦ : free from dirt or disease **2 a** ♦ : free from moral taint or corruption : PURE **b** ♦ : observing the rules : FAIR **3** ♦ : so decisive and complete as to leave no loose ends or uncertainty : THOROUGH ⟨made a ∼ break with the past⟩ **4** : TRIM ⟨a ship with ∼ lines⟩; also : EVEN **5** : habitually neat — **clean·ly** \'klēn-lē\ adv — **clean·ness** \'klēn-nəs\ n

♦ [1] immaculate, spick-and-span, spotless, stainless, unsoiled, unsullied; also pure, undefiled, unpolluted, untainted, wholesome; cleanly, hygienic, sanitary;

bleached, cleansed, purified, whitened; milky, snowy, white; flawless, unblemished; bright, shiny, sparkling **Ant** dirty, filthy, foul, grubby, soiled, spotted, stained, sullied, unclean ♦ [2a] chaste, decent, immaculate, modest, pure — more at CHASTE ♦ [2b] fair, legal, sportsmanlike ♦ [3] all-out, complete, comprehensive, exhaustive, full-scale, out-and-out, thorough, thoroughgoing, total — more at EXHAUSTIVE

²clean adv ♦ : all the way : COMPLETELY

♦ absolutely, all, altogether, completely, entirely, fully, quite, totally, utterly, wholly

³clean vb **1** ♦ : to make or become clean **2** ♦ : to remove the entrails from **3** ♦ : to exhaust the stock of — usu. used with out

♦ [2] draw, eviscerate, gut — more at GUT ♦ usu **clean out** [3] consume, deplete, drain, exhaust, expend, spend, use up — more at DEPLETE

clean–cut \'klēn-'kət\ adj **1** : cut so that the surface or edge is smooth and even **2** : sharply defined or outlined **3** : giving an effect of wholesomeness

clean·er n ♦ : a preparation for cleaning

♦ detergent, soap; also disinfectant, purifier, solvent

clean·ly \'klen-lē\ adj **clean·li·er; -est** **1** : careful to keep clean **2** : habitually kept clean — **clean·li·ness** n

clean room \'klēn-ˌrüm, -ˌrùm\ n : an uncontaminated room maintained for the manufacture or assembly of objects (as precision parts)

cleanse \'klenz\ vb **cleansed; cleans·ing 1** : to make clean **2** : to rid of impurities by or as if by washing

cleans·er vb : a preparation (as a scouring powder or a skin cream) used for cleaning

cleans·ing n : the action or an act of cleansing esp. morally or spiritually

¹clean·up \'klē-ˌnəp\ n **1** : an act or instance of cleaning **2** : a very large profit

²cleanup adj : being 4th in the batting order of a baseball team

clean up vb **1** : to make a spectacular business profit **2** : rid of debasing or harmful features or elements

¹clear \'klir\ adj [ME clere, fr. AF cler, fr. L clarus] **1 a** : shining brightly : entirely light **b** : UNTROUBLED, SERENE **2** ♦ : having the sky free from clouds : CLOUDLESS **3 a** : CLEAN, PURE **b** ♦ : easily seen through : TRANSPARENT **4 a** ♦ : easily heard, seen, or understood **b** : easy to perceive or determine with certainty **5 a** : capable of sharp discernment **b** : free from doubt **6** ♦ : free from guile or guilt : INNOCENT **7** ♦ : free from restriction, obstruction, or entanglement — **clear** adv — **clear·ly** \'klir-lē\ adv — **clear·ness** n

♦ [2] cloudless, fair, sunny, sunshiny, unclouded — more at FAIR ♦ [3b] limpid, liquid, lucent, pellucid, transparent; also colorless, uncolored; lucid, translucent; crystal, crystalline, glassy, sparkling; bright, brilliant, effulgent, luminous **Ant** cloudy, opaque ♦ [4a] apparent, broad, clear-cut, distinct, evident, lucid, manifest, obvious, palpable, patent, perspicuous, plain, transparent, unambiguous, unequivocal, unmistakable; also comprehensible, decipherable, fathomable, intelligible, knowable, understandable; self-evident, self-explanatory; simple; overt, undisguised; appreciable, perceptible, recognizable, sensible, tangible; discernible, noticeable, observable, visible **Ant** dark, enigmatic, indistinct, mysterious, obscure, unclear; ambiguous, equivocal ♦ [6] blameless, faultless, guiltless, impeccable, innocent, irreproachable — more at INNOCENT ♦ [7] free, open, unobstructed — more at OPEN

²clear vb **1** ♦ : to make or become clear **2** : to go away : DISPERSE **3 a** ♦ : to free from accusation or blame **b** ♦ : to accept officially as satisfactory **c** : to certify as trustworthy **4** ♦ : to explain or make understandable — often used with up **5** : to get free from obstruction **6** ♦ : to make clear or free from debt or obligation : SETTLE **7** : NET **8** : to get rid of : REMOVE ⟨∼ed snow off the roof⟩ **9 a ♦** : to free (as from contact or entanglement) : DISENTANGLE **b** : to jump or go by without touching; *also* : PASS

♦ [1] clarify, distill, filter, purify — more at CLARIFY **♦ [3a]** absolve, acquit, exculpate, exonerate, vindicate — more at EXCULPATE **♦ [3b]** approve, authorize, OK, ratify, sanction, warrant — more at APPROVE **♦** *usu* **clear up [4]** clarify, construe, demonstrate, elucidate, explain, explicate, expound, illuminate, illustrate, interpret, spell out — more at EXPLAIN **♦ [6]** discharge, foot, liquidate, pay, pay off, quit, recompense, settle, spring, stand — more at PAY **♦ [9a]** disengage, disentangle, extricate, free, liberate, release, untangle — more at EXTRICATE

³clear *n* : a clear space or part

clear·ance \'klir-əns\ *n* **1** : an act or process of clearing **2** : the distance by which one object clears another **3 ♦** : certification as clear of objection : AUTHORIZATION

♦ allowance, authorization, concurrence, consent, leave, license (*or* licence), permission, sanction, sufferance — more at PERMISSION

clear–cut \'klir-'kət\ *adj* **1** : sharply outlined : DISTINCT **2 ♦** : free from ambiguity or uncertainty : DEFINITE, UNEQUIVOCAL

♦ definite, definitive, explicit, express, specific, unambiguous, unequivocal — more at EXPLICIT

clear·head·ed \-'he-dəd\ *adj* **♦** : having a clear understanding : able to think clearly

♦ balanced, lucid, normal, right, sane, stable — more at SANE

clear·ing \'klir-iŋ\ *n* **1** : a tract of land cleared of wood and brush **2** : the passage of checks and claims through a clearinghouse **3** : the act or process of becoming clear

clear·ing·house \-,haùs\ *n* : an institution maintained by banks for making an exchange of checks and claims held by each bank against other banks; *also* : an informal channel for information or assistance

clear out *vb* **1 ♦** : to drive out or away usu. by force **2 ♦** : to go away or run from : DEPART

♦ [1] disband, disperse, dissipate, scatter — more at SCATTER **♦ [2]** abscond, escape, flee, fly, get out, lam, run away, run off — more at ESCAPE **♦ [2]** depart, exit, get off, go, move, pull, quit, sally, shove, take off — more at GO

cleat \'klēt\ *n* : a piece of wood or metal fastened on or projecting from something to give strength, provide a grip, or prevent slipping

cleav·age \'klē-vij\ *n* **1** : a splitting apart : SPLIT **2** : the depression between a woman's breasts esp. when exposed by a low-cut neckline

¹cleave \'klēv\ *vb* **cleaved** \'klēvd\ *or* **clove** \'klōv\; **cleaved**; **cleav·ing** : to adhere firmly and closely or loyally and unwaveringly : ADHERE, CLING

²cleave *vb* **cleaved** \'klēvd\ *also* **cleft** \'kleft\ *or* **clove** \'klōv\; **cleaved** *also* **cleft** *or* **clo·ven** \'klō-vən\; **cleav·ing** **1** : to divide by force : split asunder **2** : DIVIDE

cleav·er \'klē-vər\ *n* : a heavy chopping knife for cutting meat

clef \'klef\ *n* : a sign placed on the staff in music to show what pitch is represented by each line and space

cleft \'kleft\ *n* **♦** : a space or opening made by or as if by splitting : FISSURE, CRACK

♦ chink, crack, cranny, crevice, fissure, rift, split — more at CRACK

cleft palate *n* : a split in the roof of the mouth that appears as a birth defect

clem·a·tis \'kle-mə-təs; kli-'ma-təs\ *n* : any of a genus of vines or herbs related to the buttercups that have showy usu. white or purple flowers

clem·en·cy \'kle-mən-sē\ *n, pl* **-cies** **1 ♦** : disposition to be merciful **2** : mildness of weather

♦ charity, leniency, mercy, quarter — more at MERCY

clem·ent \'kle-mənt\ *adj* **1** : MERCIFUL, LENIENT **2 ♦** : not severe in temperature : TEMPERATE, MILD

♦ balmy, equable, gentle, mild, moderate, temperate; *also* clear, cloudless, fair, sunny, sunshiny; calm, halcyon, peaceful, placid, tranquil; delightful, fine, pleasant *Ant* harsh, inclement, intemperate, severe

clem·en·tine \'kle-mən-,tēn\ *n* : a small citrus fruit that is probably a hybrid between a tangerine and an orange

clench \'klench\ *vb* **1** : CLINCH 1 **2 ♦** : to hold fast : CLUTCH **3** : to set or close tightly

♦ cling, clutch, grip, hang on, hold, hold on — more at HOLD

clere·sto·ry \'klir-,stōr-ē\ *n* : an outside wall of a room or building that rises above an adjoining roof and contains windows

cler·gy \'klər-jē\ *n* : a body of religious officials authorized to conduct services

cler·gy·man \-mən\ *n* **♦** : a member of the clergy

♦ divine, ecclesiastic, father, minister, preacher, priest, reverend; *also* evangelist, missionary; deaconess, priestess; dean, pastor, rector, vicar; chaplain, confessor; canon, curate; friar, mendicant, monastic, monk, religious *Ant* layman

cler·ic \'kler-ik\ *n* : a member of the clergy

cler·i·cal \'kler-i-kəl\ *adj* **1 ♦** : of or relating to the clergy ⟨∼ vestments⟩ **2** : of or relating to a clerk

♦ ministerial, pastoral, priestly, sacerdotal; *also* evangelical, missionary; apostolic, canonical, episcopal, papal, patriarchal, pontifical; ecclesiastic, ecclesiastical; divine, holy, religious, sacramental; rabbinic *Ant* lay, nonclerical

cler·i·cal·ism \'kler-i-kə-,li-zəm\ *n* : a policy of maintaining or increasing the power of a religious hierarchy

clerk \'klərk, *Brit* 'klärk\ *n* **1** : CLERIC **2 a ♦** : an official responsible for correspondence, records, and accounts **b** : a person employed to perform general office work **3** : a store salesperson — **clerk** *vb* — **clerk·ship** *n*

♦ register, registrar, scribe; *also* archivist, bookkeeper, recorder; annalist, chronicler

clev·er \'kle-vər\ *adj* **1 ♦** : showing skill or resourcefulness **2 ♦** : marked by wit or ingenuity — **clev·er·ly** *adv*

♦ [1] alert, brainy, bright, intelligent, keen, nimble, quick, quick-witted, sharp, smart — more at INTELLIGENT **♦ [1]** adroit, artful, creative, deft, imaginative, ingenious, innovative *Ant* uncreative, unimaginative **♦ [2]** facetious, humorous, jocular, smart, witty — more at WITTY

clev·er·ness *n* **♦** : the quality of being clever

♦ adeptness, adroitness, art, artfulness, artifice, artistry, craft, cunning, deftness, masterfulness, skill — more at SKILL

clev·is \'kle-vəs\ *n* : a U-shaped shackle used for fastening

¹clew \'klü\ *n* **1** : CLUE **2** : a metal loop on a lower corner of a sail

²clew *vb* : to haul (a sail) up or down by ropes through the clews

cli·ché \kli-'shā\ *n* [F] **♦** : a trite phrase or expression — **cli·chéd** \-'shād\ *adj*

♦ banality, commonplace, platitude, shibboleth — more at COMMONPLACE

¹click \'klik\ *vb* **1** : to make or cause to make a click **2** : to fit together : hit it off **3 ♦** : to function or operate smoothly or successfully **4** : to select or make a selection on a computer by pressing a button on a control device (as a mouse) — **click·able** \'kli-kə-bəl\ *adj*

♦ deliver, go over, pan out, succeed, work out — more at SUCCEED

²click *n* : a slight sharp noise

click·er \'kli-kər\ *n* : a remote control device (as for a television)

cli·ent \'klī-ənt\ *n* **1** : DEPENDENT **2** : a person who engages the professional services of another; *also* : PATRON,

CUSTOMER 3 : a computer in a network that uses the services (as access to files) provided by a server

cli·en·tele \‚klī-ən-'tel, ‚klē-\ n : a body of clients and esp. customers

cliff \'klif\ n ♦ : a high steep face of rock, earth, or ice

♦ bluff, crag, escarpment, palisade, precipice, scarp; also tor; bulwark, embankment

cliff–hang·er \-‚haŋ-ər\ n 1 : an adventure serial or melodrama usu. presented in installments each of which ends in suspense 2 : a contest whose outcome is in doubt up to the very end

cli·mac·ter·ic \klī-'mak-tə-rik\ n 1 : a major turning point or critical stage 2 : MENOPAUSE; also : a corresponding period in the male

cli·mate \'klī-mət\ n [ME climat, fr. MF, fr. LL clima, fr. Gk klima inclination, latitude, climate, fr. klinein to lean] 1 : a region having specific climatic conditions 2 : the average weather conditions at a place over a period of years 3 : the prevailing set of conditions (as temperature and humidity) indoors 4 ♦ : a prevailing atmosphere or environment ⟨the ∼ of opinion⟩ — cli·mat·ic \klī-'ma-tik\ adj — cli·mat·i·cal·ly \-ti-k(ə-)lē\ adv

♦ air, atmosphere, aura, flavor (or flavour), mood, note, temper — more at AURA ♦ atmosphere, environment, environs, medium, milieu, setting, surroundings — more at ENVIRONMENT

cli·ma·tol·o·gy \‚klī-mə-'tä-lə-jē\ n : the science that deals with climates — cli·ma·to·log·i·cal \-mət-ᵊl-'ä-ji-kəl\ adj — cli·ma·to·log·i·cal·ly \-k(ə-)lē\ adv — cli·ma·tol·o·gist \-mə-'tä-lə-jist\ n

¹cli·max \'klī-‚maks\ n [L, fr. Gk klimax ladder, fr. klinein to lean] 1 : a series of ideas or statements so arranged that they increase in force and power from the first to the last; also : the last member of such a series 2 ♦ : the highest point ⟨the ∼ of her career⟩ 3 : ORGASM — cli·mac·tic \klī-'mak-tik\ adj

♦ acme, apex, crown, culmination, head, height, meridian, peak, pinnacle, summit, tip-top, top, zenith — more at HEIGHT

²climax vb : to come or bring to a climax : provide a culminating event for

¹climb \'klīm\ vb 1 ♦ : to rise to a higher point 2 ♦ : to go up or down esp. by use of hands and feet; also : to ascend in growing — climb·er n

♦ [1, 2] arise, ascend, lift, mount, rise, soar, up — more at ASCEND

²climb n 1 : a place where climbing is necessary 2 ♦ : the act of climbing : ascent by climbing

♦ ascent, rise, soar — more at ASCENT

clime \'klīm\ n : CLIMATE ⟨prefers a warmer ∼⟩

¹clinch \'klinch\ vb 1 : to turn over or flatten the end of something sticking out ⟨∼ a nail⟩; also : to fasten by clinching 2 : to make final : SETTLE ⟨∼ a deal⟩ 3 : to hold fast or firmly

²clinch n 1 : a fastening by means of a clinched nail, rivet, or bolt 2 : an act or instance of clinching in boxing

clinch·er \'klin-chər\ n : one that clinches; esp : a decisive fact, argument, act, or remark

cling \'kliŋ\ vb clung \'kləŋ\; cling·ing 1 a ♦ : to adhere as if glued b ♦ : to hold or hold on tightly 2 : to have a strong emotional attachment 3 ♦ : to give support or maintain loyalty

♦ [1a] adhere, hew, stick — more at STICK ♦ usu cling to [1b] clench, clutch, grip, hang on, hold, hold on — more at HOLD ♦ usu cling to [3] adhere, hew, keep, stick

cling·stone \'kliŋ-‚stōn\ n : any of various fruits (as some peaches) whose flesh adheres strongly to the pit

clin·ic \'kli-nik\ n 1 : a medical class in which patients are examined and discussed 2 : a group meeting for teaching a certain skill and working on individual problems ⟨a reading ∼⟩ 3 : a facility (as of a hospital) for diagnosis and treatment of outpatients

clin·i·cal \'kli-ni-kəl\ adj 1 : of, relating to, or typical of a clinic; esp : involving direct observation of the patient 2 : scientifically dispassionate — clin·i·cal·ly \-k(ə-)lē\ adv

cli·ni·cian \kli-'ni-shən\ n : a person qualified in the clinical practice of medicine, psychiatry, or psychology as distinguished from one specializing in laboratory or research techniques or in theory

¹clink \'kliŋk\ vb : to make or cause to make a sharp short metallic sound

²clink n : a clinking sound

clin·ker \'kliŋ-kər\ n : stony matter fused together : SLAG

¹clip \'klip\ vb clipped; clip·ping : to fasten with a clip

²clip n 1 : a device that grips, clasps, or hooks 2 : a cartridge holder for a rifle

³clip vb clipped; clip·ping 1 ♦ : to cut or cut off with shears 2 : CURTAIL, DIMINISH 3 : HIT, PUNCH 4 : to illegally block (an opponent) in football

♦ bob, crop, cut, cut back, dock, lop, nip, prune, shave, shear, trim; also manicure, mow; abbreviate, abridge, shorten

⁴clip n 1 : a 2-bladed instrument for cutting esp. the nails 2 : a sharp blow 3 : a rapid pace ⟨moving at a good ∼⟩

clip·board \'klip-‚bōrd\ n : a small writing board with a spring clip at the top for holding papers

clip joint n, slang : an establishment (as a nightclub) that makes a practice of defrauding its customers

clip·per \'kli-pər\ n 1 : an implement for clipping esp. the hair or nails — usu. used in pl. 2 : a fast sailing ship

clip·ping \'kli-piŋ\ n : a piece clipped from something (as a newspaper)

clique \'klēk, 'klik\ n [F] ♦ : a small exclusive group of people : COTERIE — cliqu·ey \'klē-kē, 'kli-\ adj — cliqu·ish \-kish\ adj

♦ circle, clan, community, coterie, crowd, fold, gang, ring, set — more at GANG

cli·to·ris \'kli-tə-rəs\ n, pl cli·to·ris·es : a small erectile organ at the anterior or ventral part of the vulva homologous to the penis — cli·to·ral \-rəl\ adj

clk abbr clerk

clo abbr clothing

¹cloak \'klōk\ n 1 : a loose outer garment 2 ♦ : something that conceals

♦ curtain, hood, mantle, mask, shroud, veil; also cover, screen, shield; facade, face, veneer

²cloak vb ♦ : to cover or hide with a cloak

♦ blanket, blot out, conceal, cover, curtain, enshroud, hide, mask, obscure, occult, screen, shroud, veil — more at HIDE

cloak–and–dagger adj : involving or suggestive of espionage

clob·ber \'klä-bər\ vb 1 : to pound mercilessly 2 : to hit with force 3 ♦ : to defeat overwhelmingly

♦ drub, rout, skunk, thrash, trim, trounce, wallop, whip

cloche \'klōsh\ n [F, lit., bell] : a woman's small close-fitting hat

¹clock \'kläk\ n : a timepiece not intended to be carried on the person

²clock vb 1 : to time (a person or a performance) by a timing device 2 : to register (as speed) on a mechanical recording device — clock·er n

³clock n : an ornamental figure on a stocking or sock

clock·wise \'kläk-‚wīz\ adv : in the direction in which the hands of a clock move — clockwise adj

clock·work \-‚wərk\ n 1 : the machinery that runs a mechanical device (as a clock or toy) 2 : the precision or regularity associated with a clock

clod \'kläd\ n 1 ♦ : a lump esp. of earth or clay 2 ♦ : a dull or insensitive person

♦ [1] blob, chunk, clump, glob, gob, hunk, lump, nub, wad — more at LUMP ♦ [2] hulk, lout, lubber, lug, oaf — more at OAF

clod·hop·per \-‚hä-pər\ n 1 ♦ : an uncouth rustic 2 : a large heavy shoe

♦ bumpkin, hick, rustic, yokel — more at HICK

¹clog \'kläg\ n 1 a : a weight attached to an animal to impede motion b : something that shackles or impedes 2 : a thick-soled shoe

²clog vb clogged; clog·ging 1 a : to impede with a clog : HINDER b ♦ : to halt or slow the progress, operation, or growth of : ENCUMBER 2 ♦ : to obstruct passage through 3 : to become filled with extraneous matter

♦ [1b] encumber, hamper, hinder, hold up, impede, inhibit, interfere with, obstruct, tie up — more at HAMPER ♦ [2] block, choke, close (off), congest, dam, jam, obstruct, plug (up), stop (up), stuff; also bung, fill, pack; flood, glut, inundate, overwhelm, swamp Ant clear, free, open (up), unclog

clois·son·né \,klȯiz-ᵊn-'ā\ adj : a colored decoration made of enamels poured into the divided areas in a design outlined with wire or metal strips

¹clois·ter \'klȯi-stər\ n [ME cloistre, fr. OF, fr. ML claustrum, fr. L, bar, bolt, fr. claudere to close] 1 ♦ : a monastic establishment 2 : a covered usu. colonnaded passage on the side of a court — clois·tral \-strəl\ adj

♦ abbey, friary, monastery, priory — more at MONASTERY

²cloister vb : to shut away from the world

clois·tered \'klȯi-stərd\ adj 1 : being or living in or as if in a cloister 2 ♦ : providing shelter from contact with the outside world

♦ covert, isolated, quiet, remote, secluded, secret — more at SECLUDED

clone \'klōn\ n [Gk klōn twig, slip] 1 : the collection of genetically identical cells or organisms produced asexually from a single ancestral cell or organism; also : an individual grown from a single cell and genetically identical to it ⟨a sheep ∼⟩ 2 : a group of replicas of a biological molecule (as DNA) 3 : one that appears to be a copy of an original form — clon·al \'klō-nᵊl\ adj — clone vb

clop \'kläp\ n : a sound made by or as if by a hoof or wooden shoe against pavement — clop vb

¹close \'klōz\ vb closed; clos·ing 1 : to bar passage through : SHUT 2 : to suspend the operations (as of a school) 3 ♦ : to bring or come to an end or period : END, TERMINATE 4 : to bring together the parts or edges of; also : to fill up 5 ♦ : to come near or approach close 6 : GRAPPLE ⟨∼ with the enemy⟩ 7 : to enter into an agreement — clos·able or close·able adj

♦ [3] conclude, end, finish, round, terminate, wind up, wrap up; also climax, crown; complete, consummate, perfect; halt, stop, suspend Ant begin, commence, inaugurate, open, start ♦ [5] approach, near — more at APPROACH

²close \'klōz\ n ♦ : a coming or bringing of something to a conclusion or an end : CONCLUSION, END

♦ conclusion, consummation, end, ending, finale, finis, finish, windup — more at FINALE ♦ cessation, closure, conclusion, end, ending, expiration, finish, halt, lapse, shutdown, stop, stoppage, termination — more at END

³close \'klōs\ n ♦ : an enclosed space

♦ court, courtyard, quadrangle, yard — more at COURT

⁴close \'klōs\ adj clos·er; clos·est 1 : having no openings : CLOSED 2 : narrowly restricting or restricted 3 : limited to a privileged class 4 a : SECLUDED b ♦ : marked by a disposition to secrecy or extreme discreetness about divulging information : SECRETIVE 5 : RIGOROUS 6 ♦ : hot and stuffy : causing a sensation of being slightly smothered or stifled 7 : not generous in giving or spending : STINGY 8 ♦ : having little space between items or units 9 : fitting tightly; also : SHORT ⟨∼ haircut⟩ 10 ♦ : being near in time, space, effect, or degree : NEAR 11 ♦ : marked by a warm friendship developing through long association : INTIMATE ⟨∼ friends⟩ 12 : very precise and attentive to details : ACCURATE 13 ♦ : decided by a narrow margin ⟨a ∼ game⟩ — close·ly adv

♦ [4b] closemouthed, dark, reticent, secretive, uncommunicative — more at SECRETIVE ♦ [6] breathless, stuffy — more at STUFFY ♦ [8] compact, crowded, dense, packed, serried, thick, tight; also airtight, snug; compacted, compressed, condensed; firm, hard, solid; impenetrable, impermeable, impervious Ant loose, uncrowded ♦ [10] immediate, near, nearby, nigh; also abutting, adjacent, adjoining, contiguous; approaching, coming, forthcoming, oncoming, upcoming Ant distant, far, faraway, far-off, remote ♦ [11] bosom, chummy, familiar, friendly, intimate, thick — more at FAMILIAR ♦ [13] narrow, neck and neck, nip and tuck, tight; also crowded

⁵close adv ♦ : in proximity of space or time

♦ around, by, hard, in, near, nearby, nigh — more at NEAR

closed–cir·cuit \'klōzd-'sər-kət\ adj : used in, shown on, or being a television installation in which the signal is transmitted by wire to a limited number of receivers

closed shop n : an establishment having only members of a labor union on the payroll

close·fist·ed \'klōz-'fis-təd, 'klōs-\ adj : not openhanded or liberal esp. in giving : STINGY

close–knit \'klōs-'nit\ adj : closely bound together by social, cultural, economic, or political ties

close·mouthed \'klōz-'maüthd, 'klōs-'maütht\ adj 1 ♦ : cautious or reticent in speaking 2 ♦ : disposed to secrecy about one's personal affairs

♦ [1] laconic, reserved, reticent, silent, taciturn, uncommunicative — more at SILENT ♦ [2] close, dark, reticent, secretive, uncommunicative — more at SECRETIVE

close·ness n ♦ : the quality or state of being close

♦ familiarity, intimacy, nearness — more at FAMILIARITY ♦ contiguity, immediacy, nearness, proximity — more at PROXIMITY

close·out \'klō-,zaüt\ n : a sale of a business's entire stock at low prices

close out vb 1 : to dispose of by a closeout 2 : to dispose of a business : SELL OUT

¹clos·et \'klä-zət, 'klȯ-\ n 1 ♦ : a small room for privacy 2 ♦ : a small compartment for household utensils or clothing 3 : a state or condition of secrecy ⟨came out of the ∼⟩

♦ [1] cell, chamber, room — more at ROOM ♦ [2] buffet, cabinet, cupboard, hutch, locker, sideboard — more at CABINET

²closet vb 1 : to shut up in or as if in a closet 2 : to take into a private room for an interview

close–up \'klō-,səp\ n 1 : a photograph or movie shot taken at close range 2 : an intimate view or examination

clo·sure \'klō-zhər\ n 1 ♦ : an act of closing : the condition of being closed 2 : a bringing to a point of completion 3 : something that closes 4 : CLOTURE

♦ cessation, close, conclusion, end, ending, expiration, finish, halt, lapse, shutdown, stop, stoppage, termination — more at END

¹clot \'klät\ n : a mass formed by a portion of liquid (as blood) thickening and sticking together

²clot vb ♦ : to become a clot

♦ coagulate, congeal, gel, jell, set — more at COAGULATE

cloth \'klȯth\ n, pl cloths \'klȯthz, 'klȯths\ 1 : a pliable fabric made usu. by weaving or knitting natural or synthetic fibers and filaments 2 : TABLECLOTH 3 : distinctive dress of the clergy; also : CLERGY

clothe \'klōth\ vb clothed or clad \'klad\; cloth·ing 1 ♦ : to provide with clothes : cover with clothes : DRESS 2 ♦ : to express by suitably significant language

♦ [1] apparel, array, attire, caparison, deck, dress, garb, invest, rig, suit; also cloak, mantle; drape, swaddle, swathe; accoutre, equip, furnish, outfit Ant disrobe, strip, unclothe, undress ♦ [2] articulate, couch, express, formulate, phrase, put, say, state, word

clothes \'klōthz, 'klōz\ n pl 1 : covering for the human

body or garments in general : CLOTHING **2** : BED-
CLOTHES

clothes‧horse \-‚hȯrs\ *n* **1** : a frame on which to hang
clothes **2** : a conspicuously dressy person

clothes‧line \-‚līn\ *n* : a rope or cord on which clothes are
hung to dry

clothes moth *n* : any of several small pale moths whose
larvae eat wool, fur, and feathers

clothes‧pin \'klōthz-‚pin, 'klōz-\ *n* : a device for fastening
clothes on a line

clothes‧press \-‚pres\ *n* : a receptacle for clothes

cloth‧ier \'klōth-yər, 'klō-thē-ər\ *n* : a maker or seller of
clothing

cloth‧ing \'klō-thiŋ\ *n* ♦ : garments in general

♦ apparel, attire, dress, duds, raiment, wear; *also* garment, vestment; array, bravery, finery; rags, tatters;
costume, garb, getup, guise, outfit, rig, wardrobe; hab-
erdashery

clo‧ture \'klō-chər\ *n* : the closing or limitation (as by calling for a vote) of debate in a legislative body

¹cloud \'klau̇d\ *n* [ME, rock, cloud, fr. OE *clūd*] **1** : a visible mass of particles of condensed vapor (as water or
ice) suspended in the atmosphere **2** : a usu. visible mass
of minute airborne particles; *also* : a mass of obscuring
matter in interstellar space **3** : CROWD, SWARM ⟨a ∼ of
mosquitoes⟩ **4** : something having a dark or threatening
aspect ⟨a ∼ of suspicion⟩ **5** : something that obscures
or blemishes ⟨a ∼ of ambiguity⟩ **6** : the computers and
networks that support cloud computing — **cloud‧i‧ness**
\'klau̇-dē-nəs\ *n*

²cloud *vb* ♦ : to darken or hide with or as if with a cloud
: OBSCURE **2** ♦ : to make unclear or confused : CONFUSE
3 : TAINT, SULLY

♦ [1] becloud, befog, blur, darken, dim, fog, haze, mist,
obscure, overshadow, shroud; *also* blot out, conceal,
hide, screen, shade; camouflage, cloak, cover, curtain,
disguise, mask, veil; distort, falsify, garble, misrepresent
Ant brighten, illuminate, illumine, lighten ♦ [2] becloud, befog, blur, confuse, fog, muddy — more at
CONFUSE

cloud‧burst \-‚bərst\ *n* ♦ : a sudden heavy rainfall

♦ deluge, downpour, rain, rainstorm, storm, wet —
more at RAIN

cloud computing *n* : the practice of storing regularly used
computer data on multiple servers that can be accessed
through the Internet

cloud‧less *adj* ♦ : free from any cloud

♦ clear, fair, sunny, sunshiny, unclouded — more at
FAIR

cloud‧let \-lət\ *n* : a small cloud

cloud nine *n* : a feeling of extreme well-being or elation —
usu. used with *on*

cloudy *adj* **1** ♦ : having a cloudy or overcast sky
2 ♦ : dimmed or dulled as if by clouds **3** ♦ : having visible material in suspension : MURKY

♦ [1] dull, hazy, heavy, overcast — more at OVERCAST
♦ [2] foggy, hazy, misty, murky, smoggy, soupy —
more at HAZY ♦ [3] muddy, murky, turbid; *also* dingy,
filmy, hazy, unfiltered; opaque *Ant* clear

¹clout \'klau̇t\ *n* **1** ♦ : a blow esp. with the hand **2** ♦ : the
power to sway people : special influence

♦ [1] bat, belt, blow, box, hit, punch, slug, thump, wallop, whack — more at BLOW ♦ [2] authority, influence,
pull, sway, weight — more at INFLUENCE

²clout *vb* : to hit forcefully

¹clove \'klōv\ *n* : one of the small bulbs that grows at the
base of the scales of a large bulb ⟨a ∼ of garlic⟩

²clove *past of* CLEAVE

³clove *n* [ME *clowe*, fr. AF *clou (de girofle)*, lit., nail of
clove, fr. L *clavus* nail] : the dried flower bud of an East
Indian tree used esp. as a spice

clo‧ven \'klō-vən\ *past part of* CLEAVE

cloven foot *n* : CLOVEN HOOF — **cloven–foot‧ed** \-'fu̇-təd\ *adj*

cloven hoof *n* : a foot (as of a sheep) with the front part divided into two parts — **cloven–hoofed** \-'hu̇ft, -'hu̇vd\ *adj*

clo‧ver \'klō-vər\ *n* : any of a genus of leguminous herbs
with usu. 3-parted leaves and dense flower heads

clo‧ver‧leaf \-‚lēf\ *n, pl* **cloverleafs** \-‚lēfs\ *or* **clo‧ver‧leaves**
\-‚lēvz\ : an interchange between two major highways
that from above resembles a four-leaf clover

¹clown \'klau̇n\ *n* **1** ♦ : a rude ill-bred person : BOOR
2 ♦ : a fool or comedian in an entertainment (as a circus)

♦ [1] beast, boor, churl, creep, cretin, cur, heel, jerk,
joker, louse, lout, skunk, slob, snake — more at JERK
♦ [2] buffoon, harlequin, zany; *also* cutup, madcap;
fool, jester, motley; mime, mummer; comedian, comedienne, comic, joker, wag

²clown *vb* ♦ : to act like a clown ⟨always ∼*ing* around⟩

♦ *usu* **clown around** act up, cut up, fool around, monkey, show off, skylark — more at CUT UP

clown‧ish *adj* ♦ : resembling or befitting a clown (as in
ignorance and lack of sophistication) — **clown‧ish‧ly** *adv*
— **clown‧ish‧ness** *n*

♦ boorish, churlish, loutish, uncouth; *also* coarse, ill=
bred, uncultivated, unpolished, unrefined; tasteless,
vulgar; beastly, bestial; doltish, oafish, stupid; discourteous, impolite, rude, uncivil *Ant* cultivated, polished,
refined, well-bred; courtly, genteel, gentlemanly, ladylike; civil, courteous, polite

cloy \'klȯi\ *vb* : to disgust or nauseate with excess of something orig. pleasing — **cloy‧ing‧ly** *adv*

clr *abbr* clear

¹club \'kləb\ *n* **1** ♦ : a heavy wooden stick or staff used as
a weapon; *also* : BAT **2** : any of a suit of playing cards
marked with a black figure resembling a clover leaf
3 a ♦ : a group of persons associated for a common purpose **b** : the meeting place of a group or association

♦ [1] bat, billy club, bludgeon, cudgel, nightstick, staff,
truncheon; *also* blackjack, mace; birch, switch; hammer, mallet, maul; walking stick ♦ [3a] association,
brotherhood, college, congress, council, fellowship,
fraternity, guild, institute, institution, league, order, organization, society — more at ASSOCIATION

²club *vb* **clubbed**; **club‧bing** **1** : to strike with a club
2 ♦ : to unite or combine for a common cause

♦ ally, associate, band, confederate, conjoin, cooperate,
federate, league, unite — more at ALLY

club‧foot \'kləb-'fu̇t\ *n* : a misshapen foot twisted out of
position from birth; *also* : this deformed condition —
club‧foot‧ed \-'fu̇-təd\ *adj*

club‧house \'kləb-‚hau̇s\ *n* **1** : a house occupied by a club
2 : locker rooms used by an athletic team **3** : a building
at a golf course with locker rooms and usu. a pro shop
and a restaurant

club sandwich *n* : a sandwich of three slices of bread with
two layers of meat (as turkey) and lettuce, tomato, and
mayonnaise

club soda *n* : SODA WATER

cluck \'klək\ *n* : the call of a hen esp. to her chicks —
cluck *vb*

¹clue \'klü\ *n* **1** ♦ : something that guides through an intricate procedure or maze; *esp* : a piece of evidence leading
to the solution of a problem **2** ♦ : an indication that
properly interpreted may lead to full understanding of
something : IDEA, NOTION ⟨has no ∼ what he's doing⟩

♦ [1, 2] cue, hint, idea, indication, inkling, intimation,
lead, notion, suggestion — more at HINT

²clue *vb* **clued**; **clue‧ing** *or* **clu‧ing** **1** : to provide with a clue
2 ♦ : to give information to ⟨∼ me in⟩

♦ *usu* **clue in** acquaint, advise, apprise, brief, enlighten,
familiarize, fill in, inform, instruct, tell, wise — more
at ENLIGHTEN

¹clump \'kləmp\ *n* **1** ♦ : a group of things clustered together **2** ♦ : a compact mass **3** : a heavy tramping sound

♦ array, assemblage, bank, batch, block, bunch, cluster, collection, group, huddle, knot, lot, package, parcel, set, suite

²**clump** *vb* : to tread clumsily and noisily

clum·sy \'kləm-zē\ *adj* **clum·si·er; -est 1** ♦ : lacking dexterity, nimbleness, or grace **2** ♦ : not tactful or subtle ⟨a ∼ attempt at a joke⟩ **3** ♦ : awkward or inefficient in use or construction — UNWIELDY — **clum·si·ly** \-zə-lē\ *adv* — **clum·si·ness** \-zē-nəs\ *n*

♦ [1] awkward, gawky, graceless, heavy-handed, lubberly, lumpish, ungainly, unhandy; *also* butterfingered, uncoordinated; oafish; bungling, gauche, inept, inexpert, maladroit, unskilled, unskillful; cumbersome, unwieldy *Ant* deft, dexterous, graceful, handy ♦ [2] awkward, inept, inexpert, maladroit ♦ [3] awkward, cranky, cumbersome, ungainly, unhandy, unwieldy — more at CUMBERSOME

clung *past and past part of* CLING

clunk·er \'kləŋ-kər\ *n* **1** : a dilapidated automobile **2** : a notable failure

¹**clus·ter** \'kləs-tər\ *n* ♦ : a number of similar things that occur together : GROUP, BUNCH

♦ array, assemblage, bank, batch, block, bunch, clump, collection, group, huddle, knot, lot, package, parcel, set, suite

²**cluster** *vb* ♦ : to grow or gather in a cluster

♦ assemble, collect, concentrate, conglomerate, congregate, convene, forgather, gather, meet, rendezvous — more at ASSEMBLE ♦ bunch, crowd, huddle, press — more at PRESS

¹**clutch** \'kləch\ *vb* ♦ : to grasp with or as if with the hand

♦ clench, cling, grip, hang on, hold, hold on — more at HOLD

²**clutch** *n* **1 a** : the claws or a hand in the act of grasping **b** ♦ : an often cruel or unrelenting control, power, or possession : CONTROL, POWER **2** : a device for gripping an object **3** : a coupling used to connect and disconnect a driving and a driven part of a mechanism; *also* : a lever or pedal operating such a coupling **4** ♦ : a crucial situation

♦ [1b] arm, authority, command, control, dominion, grip, hold, mastery, power, sway — more at POWER ♦ [4] crisis, crunch, emergency, head, juncture — more at EMERGENCY

³**clutch** *adj* : made, done, or successful in a crucial situation

⁴**clutch** *n* **1** : a nest or batch of eggs; *also* : a brood of chicks **2** : GROUP, BUNCH

¹**clut·ter** \'klə-tər\ *vb* : to fill or cover with a disorderly scattering of things

²**clutter** *n* ♦ : a crowded mass

♦ assortment, jumble, medley, mélange, miscellany, motley, muddle, variety, welter — more at MISCELLANY

cm *abbr* centimeter

Cm *symbol* curium

CM *abbr* [Commonwealth of the Northern Mariana Islands] Northern Mariana Islands

cmdr *abbr* commander

cml *abbr* commercial

CMSgt *abbr* chief master sergeant

Cn *symbol* copernicium

CNO *abbr* chief of naval operations

CNS *abbr* central nervous system

co *abbr* **1** company **2** county

Co *symbol* cobalt

CO *abbr* **1** Colorado **2** commanding officer **3** conscientious objector

c/o *abbr* care of

¹**coach** \'kōch\ *n* [MF *coche*, ultim. fr. Hung *kocsi (szekér)*, lit., (wagon) of Kocs (town in Hungary)] **1** : a large closed 4-wheeled carriage with an elevated outside front seat for the driver **2** : a railroad passenger car esp. for day travel **3** : BUS **4 a** : a private tutor **b** : one who instructs or trains; *esp* : one who instructs players in a sport ⟨a soccer ∼⟩

²**coach** *vb* ♦ : to instruct, direct, or prompt as a coach

♦ counsel, guide, lead, mentor, pilot, shepherd, show, tutor — more at GUIDE

coach·man \-mən\ *n* : a man who drives a coach or carriage

co·ad·ju·tor \ˌkō-ə-ˈjü-tər, kō-ˈa-jə-tər\ *n* : one who works together with another : ASSISTANT; *esp* : an assistant bishop having the right of succession

co·ag·u·lant \kō-ˈa-gyə-lənt\ *n* : something that produces coagulation

co·ag·u·late \-ˌlāt\ *vb* **-lat·ed; -lat·ing** ♦ : to cause to become viscous or thickened into a coherent mass : CLOT — **co·ag·u·la·tion** \kō-ˌa-gyə-ˈlā-shən\ *n*

♦ clot, congeal, gel, jell, set; *also* concrete, firm (up), freeze, harden, solidify, stiffen; condense, thicken; curdle, lump (up)

¹**coal** \'kōl\ *n* **1** : EMBER **2** : a black solid combustible mineral used as fuel

²**coal** *vb* **1** : to supply with coal **2** : to take in coal

co·a·lesce \ˌkō-ə-ˈles\ *vb* **co·a·lesced; co·a·lesc·ing 1** : to grow together **2** ♦ : to unite into a whole : FUSE — **co·a·les·cence** \-ˈles-ᵊn(t)s\ *n*

♦ associate, combine, conjoin, connect, couple, fuse, join, link, marry, unify, unite — more at UNITE

coal·field \'kōl-ˌfēld\ *n* : a region rich in coal deposits

coal gas *n* : gas from coal; *esp* : gas distilled from bituminous coal and used for heating

co·a·li·tion \ˌkō-ə-ˈli-shən\ *n* **1** : UNION **2** ♦ : a temporary alliance of distinct parties, persons, or states for a common purpose — **co·a·li·tion·ist** *n*

♦ alliance, bloc, combination, combine, confederacy, confederation, federation, league, union — more at CONFEDERACY ♦ bloc, body, combination, combine, faction, party, sect, set, side, wing

coal oil *n* : KEROSENE

coal tar *n* : tar distilled from bituminous coal and used in dyes and drugs

co·an·chor \'kō-ˈaŋ-kər\ *n* : a newscaster who shares the duties of head broadcaster

coarse \'kòrs\ *adj* **coars·er; coars·est 1** ♦ : of ordinary or inferior quality **2** ♦ : composed of large parts or particles ⟨∼ sand⟩ **3** ♦ : crude or unrefined in taste, manners, or language : CRUDE ⟨∼ manners⟩ **4** : harsh or rough in tone or texture : ROUGH, HARSH — **coarse·ly** *adv*

♦ [1] bad, bum, cheap, common, cut-rate, inferior, junky, lousy, mediocre, poor, second-rate, shoddy, sleazy, trashy — more at CHEAP ♦ [2] grainy, granular; *also* rough; unfiltered, unrefined; gravelly, gritty, sandy; pebbly, rocky, stony; lumpy, mealy *Ant* dusty, fine, floury, powdery ♦ [3] common, crass, crude, gross, illbred, low, rough, rude, tasteless, uncouth, uncultivated, uncultured, unpolished, unrefined, vulgar; *also* boorish, churlish, clownish, loutish, ungentlemanly; clumsy, lubberly, lumpish, oafish; inconsiderate, thoughtless; countrified, provincial, rustic; graceless, inelegant, tacky *Ant* cultivated, cultured, genteel, polished, refined, smooth, tasteful, well-bred

coars·en \'kòr-sᵊn\ *vb* : to make or become coarse

coarse·ness *n* ♦ : the quality or state of being coarse

♦ grossness, indelicacy, lowness, rudeness, vulgarity — more at VULGARITY

¹**coast** \'kōst\ *n* [ME *cost*, fr. AF *coste*, fr. L *costa* rib, side] **1** : SEASHORE **2** : a slide down a slope **3** : the immediate area of view — used in the phrase *the coast is clear* — **coast·al** *adj*

²**coast** *vb* **1** : to sail along the shore **2** ♦ : to move (as downhill on a sled) without effort

♦ bowl, breeze, drift, flow, glide, roll, sail, skim, slide, slip, stream, sweep, whisk — more at FLOW

coast·er *n* **1** : one that coasts **2** : a shallow container or a plate or mat to protect a surface

coaster brake *n* : a brake in the hub of the rear wheel of a bicycle

coast guard *n* : a military force employed in guarding or patrolling a coast — coast·guards·man \'kōst-ˌgärdz-mən\ *n*

coast·line \'kōst-ˌlīn\ *n* : the outline or shape of a coast

¹coat \'kōt\ *n* 1 : an outer garment for the upper part of the body 2 ♦ : an external growth (as of fur or feathers) on an animal 3 : a covering layer ⟨a ~ of paint⟩ — coat·ed \'kō-təd\ *adj*

♦ fleece, fur, hair, pelage, pile, wool

²coat *vb* ♦ : to cover usu. with a finishing or protective coat or layer

♦ blanket, carpet, cover, overlay, overlie, overspread — more at COVER

coat·ing \'kō-tiŋ\ *n* : COAT, COVERING

coat of arms : a shield or similar device for displaying the insignia of a family or group

co·au·thor \'kō-'ȯ-thər\ *n* : a joint or associate author — coauthor *vb*

coax \'kōks\ *vb* ♦ : to gain by gentle urging or flattery : WHEEDLE

♦ cajole, wheedle; *also* adulate, flatter, overpraise; compliment, praise; beguile, charm, woo; beg, importune, urge; bug, nag, pester

co·ax·i·al \'kō-'ak-sē-əl\ *adj* : having coincident axes — co·ax·i·al·ly *adv*

coaxial cable *n* : a cable that consists of a tube of electrically conducting material surrounding a central conductor

cob \'käb\ 1 : a male swan 2 : CORNCOB 3 : a short-legged stocky horse

co·balt \'kō-ˌbȯlt\ *n* [G *Kobalt*, alter. of *Kobold*, lit., goblin; fr. its occurrence in silver ore, believed to be due to goblins] : a tough shiny silver-white magnetic metallic chemical element found with iron and nickel

cob·ble \'kä-bəl\ *vb* cob·bled; cob·bling : to make or put together roughly or hastily — often used with *together* or *up* ⟨~ together a solution⟩

cob·bler \'kä-blər\ *n* 1 : a mender or maker of shoes 2 : a deep-dish fruit pie with a thick crust

cob·ble·stone \'kä-bəl-ˌstōn\ *n* : a naturally rounded stone larger than a pebble and smaller than a boulder

co·bra \'kō-brə\ *n* [Pg *cobra (de capello)*, lit., hooded snake] : any of several venomous snakes of Asia and Africa that when excited expand the skin of the neck into a broad hood

cob·web \'käb-ˌweb\ *n* [ME *coppeweb*, fr. *coppe* spider, fr. OE ātor *coppe*] 1 : SPIDERWEB; *also* : a thread spun by a spider or insect larva 2 : something flimsy or entangling — cob·web·by \-ˌwe-bē\ *adj*

co·caine \kō-'kān, 'kō-ˌkān\ *n* : a drug obtained from the leaves of a So. American shrub (co·ca \'kō-kə\) that can result in severe psychological dependence and is sometimes used in medicine as a local anesthetic and illegally as a stimulant of the central nervous system

coc·cus \'kä-kəs\ *n, pl* coc·ci \'käk-ˌsī\ : a spherical bacterium

coc·cyx \'käk-siks\ *n, pl* coc·cy·ges \'käk-sə-ˌjēz\ *also* coc·cyx·es \'käk-sik-səz\ : the end of the spinal column beyond the sacrum esp. in humans

co·chi·neal \'kä-chə-ˌnēl\ *n* : a red dye made from the dried bodies of females of a tropical American insect (cochineal insect)

co·chlea \'kō-klē-ə, 'kä-\ *n, pl* co·chle·as *or* co·chle·ae \-klē-ˌē, -ˌī\ : the usu. spiral part of the inner ear containing nerve endings which carry information about sound to the brain — co·chle·ar \-klē-ər\ *adj*

¹cock \'käk\ *n* 1 : the adult male of a bird and esp. of the common domestic chicken 2 ♦ : a device (as a faucet or valve) for regulating the flow of a liquid : VALVE, FAUCET 3 : LEADER 4 a : the hammer of a firearm b : the position of the hammer when ready for firing

♦ faucet, gate, spigot, tap, valve — more at FAUCET

²cock *vb* 1 : to draw back the hammer of a firearm 2 : to

set or draw back in readiness for some action ⟨~ your arm to throw⟩ 3 ♦ : to turn or tilt usu. to one side

♦ angle, cant, heel, incline, lean, list, slant, slope, tilt, tip — more at LEAN

³cock *n* ♦ : the act of tilting : the state or position of being tilted

♦ bend, inclination, list, slant, tilt, tip — more at TILT

⁴cock *n* : a small pile (as of hay)

cock·ade \kä-'kād\ *n* : an ornament worn on the hat as a badge

cock·a·tiel \ˌkä-kə-'tēl\ *n* : a small crested gray parrot often kept as a cage bird

cock·a·too \'kä-kə-ˌtü\ *n, pl* -toos [D *kaketoe*, fr. Malay *kakatua*] : any of various large noisy crested parrots chiefly of Australia

cock·a·trice \'kä-kə-trəs, -ˌtrīs\ *n* : a legendary serpent with a deadly glance

cock·crow \'käk-ˌkrō\ *n* ♦ : the first appearance of light in the morning followed by sunrise : DAWN

♦ aurora, dawn, morning, sunrise — more at DAWN

cocked hat \'käkt-\ *n* : a hat with the brim turned up on two or three sides

cock·er·el \'kä-kə-rəl\ *n* : a young male domestic chicken

cock·er spaniel \'kä-kər-\ *n* [*cocking* woodcock hunting] : any of a breed of small spaniels with long ears, square muzzle, and silky coat

cock·eyed \'kä-'kīd\ *adj* 1 ♦ : turned or tilted to one side 2 : slightly crazy : FOOLISH

♦ askew, awry, crooked, listing, lopsided, slantwise, uneven — more at AWRY

cock·fight \'käk-ˌfīt\ *n* : a contest of gamecocks usu. fitted with metal spurs

¹cock·le \'kä-kəl\ *n* : any of several weedy plants related to the pinks

²cockle *n* : a bivalve mollusk with a heart-shaped shell

cock·le·shell \-ˌshel\ *n* 1 : the shell of a cockle 2 : a light flimsy boat

cock·ney \'käk-nē\ *n, pl* cockneys : a native of London and esp. of the East End of London; *also* : the dialect of a cockney

cock·pit \'käk-ˌpit\ *n* 1 : a pit for cockfights 2 : a space or compartment in a vehicle from which it is steered, piloted, or driven

cock·roach \'käk-ˌrōch\ *n* [Sp *cucaracha*] : any of an order or suborder of active nocturnal insects including some which infest houses and ships

cock·sure \'käk-'shùr\ *adj* 1 ♦ : perfectly sure : CERTAIN 2 : COCKY

♦ assured, certain, clear, confident, doubtless, positive, sanguine, sure — more at CERTAIN

cock·tail \'käk-ˌtāl\ *n* 1 : an iced drink made of liquor and flavoring ingredients 2 : an appetizer (as tomato juice) served as a first course of a meal

cocky \'kä-kē\ *adj* cock·i·er; -est ♦ : boldly and brashly self-confident — cock·i·ly \-kə-lē\ *adv* — cock·i·ness \-kē-nəs\ *n*

♦ arch, bold, brash, brazen, cheeky, fresh, impertinent, impudent, insolent, nervy, sassy, saucy — more at NERVY

co·coa \'kō-kō\ *n* 1 : CACAO 2 : chocolate deprived of some of its fat and powdered; *also* : a drink made of this heated with water or milk

cocoa butter *n* : a pale vegetable fat obtained from cacao beans

co·co·nut \'kō-kə-(ˌ)nət\ *n* : a large edible nut produced by a tall tropical palm (coconut palm)

co·coon \kə-'kün\ *n* 1 : a case usu. of silk formed by some insect larvae for protection during the pupal stage 2 ♦ : something suggesting a cocoon esp. in providing protection or in producing isolation

♦ armor, capsule, case, casing, cover, housing, husk, jacket, pod, sheath, shell — more at CASE

cod \\'käd\\ *n, pl* **cod** *also* **cods** : a bottom-dwelling bony fish of the No. Atlantic that is an important food fish; *also* : a related fish of the Pacific Ocean

COD *abbr* **1** cash on delivery **2** collect on delivery

co·da \\'kō-də\\ *n* : a closing section in a musical composition that is formally distinct from the main structure

cod·dle \\'käd-ᵊl\\ *vb* **cod·dled; cod·dling** **1** : to cook slowly in water below the boiling point **2** ♦ : to treat with extreme or excessive care or kindness : PAMPER

♦ baby, mollycoddle, nurse, pamper, spoil — more at BABY

¹**code** \\'kōd\\ *n* [ME, fr. MF, fr. L *caudex, codex* trunk of a tree, document formed orig. from wooden tablets] **1** : a systematic statement of a body of law **2** : a system of principles or rules ⟨moral ∼⟩ **3** : a system of signals **4** : a system of symbols (as in secret communication) with special meanings **5** : GENETIC CODE

²**code** *vb* **cod·ed; cod·ing** : to put into the form or symbols of a code

co·deine \\'kō-,dēn\\ *n* : a narcotic drug obtained from opium and used esp. as an analgesic and cough suppressant

co·dex \\'kō-,deks\\ *n, pl* **co·di·ces** \\'kō-də-,sēz, 'kä-\\ : a manuscript book (as of the Scriptures or classics)

cod·fish \\'käd-,fish\\ *n* : COD

cod·ger \\'kä-jər\\ *n* : an odd or cranky and usu. elderly fellow

cod·i·cil \\'kä-də-səl, -,sil\\ *n* : a legal instrument modifying an earlier will

cod·i·fy \\'kä-də-,fī, 'kō-\\ *vb* **-fied; -fy·ing** ♦ : to arrange in a systematic form — **cod·i·fi·ca·tion** \\,kä-də-fə-'kä-shən, ,kō-\\ *n*

♦ arrange, array, classify, dispose, draw up, marshal, order, organize, range, systematize — more at ORDER

co·ed \\'kō-,ed\\ *n* : a female student in a coeducational institution — **coed** *adj*

co·ed·u·ca·tion \\,kō-,e-jə-'kä-shən\\ *n* : the education of male and female students at the same institution — **co·ed·u·ca·tion·al** \\-shə-nəl\\ *adj* — **co·ed·u·ca·tion·al·ly** *adv*

co·ef·fi·cient \\,kō-ə-'fi-shənt\\ *n* **1** : a constant factor as distinguished from a variable in a mathematical term **2** : a number that serves as a measure of some property (as of a substance, device, or process)

coe·len·ter·ate \\si-'len-tə-,rāt, -rət\\ *n* : any of a phylum of radially symmetrical invertebrate animals including the corals, sea anemones, and jellyfishes

co·equal \\kō-'ē-kwəl\\ *adj* : equal with another — **coequal** *n* — **co·equal·i·ty** \\,kō-ē-'kwä-lə-tē\\ *n* — **co·equal·ly** *adv*

co·erce \\kō-'ərs\\ *vb* **co·erced; co·erc·ing** **1** : RESTRAIN, REPRESS **2** ♦ : to compel to an act or choice **3** : ENFORCE — **co·er·cive** \\-'ər-siv\\ *adj*

♦ compel, constrain, drive, force, make, muscle, obligate, oblige, press, pressure — more at FORCE

co·er·cion \\-'ər-zhən, -shən\\ *n* ♦ : the act, process, or power of coercing

♦ compulsion, constraint, duress, force, pressure — more at FORCE

¹**co·e·val** \\kō-'ē-vəl\\ *adj* ♦ : of the same age

♦ concurrent, contemporary, simultaneous, synchronous — more at CONTEMPORARY

²**coeval** *n* : one of the same age

co·ex·ist \\,kō-ig-'zist\\ *vb* **1** : to exist together or at the same time **2** : to live in peace with each other

co·ex·is·tence \\-'zis-təns\\ *n* : the quality or state of coexisting

co·ex·ten·sive \\,kō-ik-'sten-siv\\ *adj* : having the same scope or extent in space or time

C of C *abbr* Chamber of Commerce

cof·fee \\'ko-fē\\ *n* [It & Turk; It *caffè*, fr. Turk *kahve*, fr. Ar *qahwa*] : a drink made from the roasted and ground seeds of a fruit of a tropical shrub or tree; *also* : these seeds **(coffee beans)** or a plant producing them

cof·fee·house \\-,haús\\ *n* : a place where refreshments (as coffee) are sold

coffee klatch \\-,klach\\ *n* : KAFFEEKLATSCH

cof·fee·pot \\-,pät\\ *n* : a pot for brewing or serving coffee

coffee shop *n* : a small restaurant

coffee table *n* : a low table customarily placed in front of a sofa

cof·fer \\'ko-fər\\ *n* : a chest or box used esp. for valuables

cof·fer·dam \\-,dam\\ *n* : a watertight enclosure from which water is pumped to expose the bottom of a body of water and permit construction

cof·fin \\'ko-fən\\ *n* : a box or chest for a corpse to be buried in

C of S *abbr* chief of staff

¹**cog** \\'käg\\ *n* : a tooth on the rim of a wheel or gear — **cogged** \\'kägd\\ *adj*

²**cog** *abbr* cognate

co·gen·cy \\-jən-sē\\ *n* ♦ : the quality or state of being cogent

♦ effectiveness, force, impact, persuasiveness, pertinence, punch, relevance, soundness, strength **Ant** ineffectiveness

co·gen·er·a·tion \\,kō-je-nə-'rā-shən\\ *n* : the simultaneous generation of electricity and heat from the same fuel

co·gent \\'kō-jənt\\ *adj* ♦ : having power to compel or constrain : CONVINCING

♦ compelling, conclusive, convincing, decisive, effective, forceful, persuasive, pertinent, relevant, satisfying, sound, strong, telling, valid; *also* well-founded; important, significant, weighty; material **Ant** inconclusive, indecisive, ineffective, unconvincing

cog·i·tate \\'kä-jə-,tāt\\ *vb* **-tat·ed; -tat·ing** ♦ : to ponder or meditate on usu. intently : THINK, PONDER — **cog·i·ta·tion** \\,kä-jə-'tā-shən\\ *n* — **cog·i·ta·tive** \\'kä-jə-,tā-tiv\\ *adj*

♦ chew over, consider, contemplate, debate, deliberate, entertain, meditate, mull, ponder, question, ruminate, study, think, weigh — more at PONDER

co·gnac \\'kōn-,yak\\ *n* : a French brandy

cog·nate \\'käg-,nāt\\ *adj* **1** : of the same or similar nature **2** : RELATED; *esp* : related by descent from the same ancestral language — **cognate** *n*

cog·ni·tive \\'käg-nə-tiv\\ *adj* : of, relating to, or being conscious intellectual activity (as thinking, remembering, reasoning, or using language) — **cog·ni·tion** \\käg-'ni-shən\\ *n* — **cog·ni·tive·ly** *adv*

cog·ni·zance \\'käg-nə-zəns\\ *n* **1** ♦ : apprehension by the mind : AWARENESS **2** : NOTICE, HEED **3** : particular knowledge : conscious recognition

♦ attention, awareness, ear, eye, heed, notice, observance, observation — more at ATTENTION

cog·ni·zant \\'käg-nə-zənt\\ *adj* ♦ : knowledgeable of something esp. through personal experience

♦ alive, aware, conscious, mindful, sensible, sentient, witting — more at CONSCIOUS

cog·no·men \\käg-'nō-mən, 'käg-nə-\\ *n, pl* **cognomens** *or* **cog·no·mi·na** \\käg-'nä-mə-nə, -'nō-\\ ♦ : a word or phrase that constitutes the distinctive designation of a person or thing : NAME; *esp* : NICKNAME

♦ alias, nickname — more at NICKNAME ♦ appellation, denotation, designation, handle, name, title — more at NAME

co·gno·scen·te \\,kän-yə-'shen-tē\\ *n, pl* **-scen·ti** \\-tē\\ [obs. It] : CONNOISSEUR

cog·wheel \\'käg-,hwēl\\ *n* : a wheel with cogs or teeth

co·hab·it \\kō-'ha-bət\\ *vb* : to live together as a couple — **co·hab·i·ta·tion** \\-,ha-bə-'tā-shən\\ *n*

co·here \\kō-'hir\\ *vb* **co·hered; co·her·ing** **1** : to stick together **2** : to become united in principles, relationships, or interests

co·her·ence \\-əns\\ *n* ♦ : the quality or state of being coherent

♦ balance, consonance, harmony, proportion, symmetry, symphony, unity — more at HARMONY

co·her·ent \kō-'hir-ənt\ *adj* 1 : having the quality of cohering 2 ♦ : logically consistent — **co·her·ent·ly** *adv*

♦ analytic, good, logical, rational, reasonable, sensible, sober, sound, valid — more at LOGICAL

co·he·sion \kō-'hē-zhən\ *n* 1 ♦ : a sticking together 2 : molecular attraction by which the particles of a body are united — **co·he·sive** \-siv\ *adj* — **co·he·sive·ly** *adv* — **co·he·sive·ness** *n*

♦ adherence, adhesion — more at ADHESION

co·ho \'kō-ˌhō\ *n, pl* **cohos** *or* **coho** : a rather small Pacific salmon with light-colored flesh

co·hort \'kō-ˌhȯrt\ *n* 1 : a group of warriors or followers 2 ♦ : one that keeps company with another : COMPANION, ACCOMPLICE

♦ accomplice, associate, companion, comrade, crony, fellow, mate — more at ASSOCIATE

coif \'kȯif; *2 usu* 'kwäf\ *n* 1 : a close-fitting hat 2 : COIFFURE

coif·feur \kwä-'fər\ *n* [F] : HAIRDRESSER

coif·feuse \kwä-'fərz, -'fəz, -'füz, -'fyüz\ *n* : a female hairdresser

coif·fure \kwä-'fyùr\ *n* : a manner of arranging the hair

¹**coil** \'kȯil\ *vb* ♦ : to wind in a spiral shape

♦ curl, entwine, spiral, twine, twist, wind — more at WIND

²**coil** *n* : a series of rings or loops (as of coiled rope, wire, or pipe) : RING, LOOP

¹**coin** \'kȯin\ *n* [ME, wedge, corner, image on a coin, fr. AF *coing*, fr. L *cuneus* wedge] 1 : a piece of metal issued by government authority as money 2 : metal money

²**coin** *vb* 1 : to make (a coin) esp. by stamping : MINT 2 : CREATE, INVENT ⟨~ a phrase⟩ — **coin·er** *n*

coin·age \'kȯi-nij\ *n* 1 : the act or process of coining 2 a ♦ : something that has been coined   b : COINS

♦ concoction, contrivance, creation, innovation, invention, wrinkle — more at INVENTION

co·in·cide \ˌkō-ən-'sīd, 'kō-ən-ˌsīd\ *vb* **-cid·ed; -cid·ing** 1 : to occupy the same place in space or time 2 ♦ : to correspond or agree exactly

♦ accord, agree, answer, check, comport, conform, correspond, dovetail, fit, go, harmonize, jibe, square, tally — more at CHECK

co·in·ci·dence \kō-'in-sə-dəns\ *n* 1 : exact agreement 2 : occurrence together apparently without reason; *also* : an event that so occurs

co·in·ci·dent \-sə-dənt\ *adj* 1 : of similar nature 2 ♦ : occupying the same space or time

♦ attendant, concomitant, concurrent; *also* contemporaneous, contemporary, simultaneous, synchronous; associated, collateral, connected, related; consequent, resultant, resulting; ensuing, following, subsequent; accidental, casual, chance, fluky, fortuitous, freak, incident, incidental

co·in·ci·den·tal \kō-ˌin-sə-'dent-ᵊl\ *adj* : occurring or existing at the same time

co·i·tus \'kō-ə-təs\ *n* [L, fr. *coire* to come together] : physical union of male and female genitalia : SEXUAL INTERCOURSE — **co·i·tal** \-ᵊl\ *adj*

¹**coke** \'kōk\ *n* : a hard gray porous fuel made by heating soft coal to drive off most of its volatile material

²**coke** *n* : COCAINE

¹**col** *abbr* 1 colonial; colony 2 column

²**col** *or* **coll** *abbr* 1 collect, collected, collection 2 college, collegiate

Col *abbr* 1 colonel 2 Colorado 3 Colossians

COL *abbr* 1 colonel 2 cost of living

co·la \'kō-lə\ *n* : a carbonated soft drink usu. containing sugar, caffeine, caramel, and special flavoring

col·an·der \'kə-lən-dər, 'kä-\ *n* : a perforated utensil for draining food

¹**cold** \'kōld\ *adj* 1 ♦ : having a low or decidedly subnormal temperature 2 ♦ : lacking warmth of feeling 3 : suf-

fering or uncomfortable from lack of warmth 4 : giving the appearance of being dead : UNCONSCIOUS — **cold·ly** *adv* — **cold·ness** *n* — **in cold blood** : with premeditation : DELIBERATELY

♦ [1] arctic, bitter, chill, chilly, cool, freezing, frigid, frosty, glacial, icy, nippy, polar, raw, snappy, wintry; *also* subfreezing, subzero; cutting, keen, penetrating, piercing, sharp; bracing, brisk, crisp, invigorating, rigorous; chilled, cooled, frosted, frozen, iced, refrigerated, unheated *Ant* broiling, burning, fiery, hot, piping hot, red-hot, roasting, scalding, scorching, searing, sultry, summery, sweltering, torrid, tropical, warm, warming ♦ [2] aloof, antisocial, cool, detached, distant, frosty, remote, standoffish, unsociable — more at COOL ♦ [2] chill, chilly, cold-blooded, cool, frigid, frosty, glacial, icy, unfriendly, unsympathetic, wintry; *also* heartless, pitiless, unfeeling; reserved, soulless, undemonstrative, unemotional, unresponsive; apathetic, indifferent, unenthusiastic, uninterested; aloof, detached, impersonal *Ant* cordial, friendly, genial, hearty, sympathetic, warm, warm-blooded, warmhearted

²**cold** *n* 1 a : a condition marked by low temperature b : cold weather 2 : a chilly feeling 3 : a bodily disorder popularly associated with chilling; *esp* : COMMON COLD

³**cold** *adv* 1 : TOTALLY, FINALLY ⟨stopped them ~⟩ 2 : without notice or preparation ⟨performed the song ~⟩

cold–blood·ed \'kōld-'blə-dəd\ *adj* 1 ♦ : lacking normal human feelings 2 : having a body temperature not internally regulated but close to that of the environment 3 : sensitive to cold

♦ callous, hard, heartless, inhuman, inhumane, pitiless, soulless, unfeeling, unsympathetic — more at HARD
♦ apathetic, impassive, phlegmatic, stoic, stolid, unemotional — more at IMPASSIVE

cold feet *n pl* : doubt or fear that prevents action

cold front *n* : an advancing edge of a cold air mass

cold shoulder *n* ♦ : cold or unsympathetic behavior — **cold–shoul·der** *vb*

♦ brush-off, rebuff, repulse, snub; *also* dismissal, rejection; banishment, ostracism

cold sore *n* : a group of fluid-filled blisters appearing in or about the mouth in the oral form of herpes simplex

cold sweat *n* : concurrent perspiration and chill usu. associated with fear, pain, or shock

¹**cold turkey** *n* : abrupt complete cessation of the use of an addictive drug

²**cold turkey** *adv* 1 : without a period of adjustment 2 : without preparation

cold war *n* : a conflict characterized by the use of means short of sustained overt military action

cole·slaw \'kōl-ˌslo\ *n* [D *koolsla*, fr. *kool* cabbage + *sla* salad] : a salad made of raw cabbage

col·ic \'kä-lik\ *n* 1 : sharp sudden abdominal pain 2 : a condition marked by recurrent episodes of crying and irritability in an otherwise healthy infant — **col·icky** \'kä-li-kē\ *adj*

col·i·se·um \ˌkä-lə-'sē-əm\ *n* ♦ : a large structure esp. for athletic contests

♦ bowl, circus, stadium — more at STADIUM

co·li·tis \kō-'lī-təs\ *n* : inflammation of the colon

col·lab·o·rate \kə-'la-bə-ˌrāt\ *vb* **-rat·ed; -rat·ing** 1 ♦ : to work jointly with others (as in writing a book) 2 : to cooperate with an enemy force occupying one's country — **col·lab·o·ra·tive** \-'la-bə-ˌrā-tiv, -b(ə-)rə-\ *adj* — **col·lab·o·ra·tor** \-'la-bə-ˌrā-tər\ *n*

♦ concert, cooperate, join, team — more at COOPERATE

col·lab·o·ra·tion \-ˌla-bə-'rā-shən\ *n* ♦ : the act of collaborating or a situation marked by collaborating

♦ affiliation, alliance, association, confederation, connection, cooperation, hookup, liaison, partnership, relation, relationship, union — more at ASSOCIATION ♦ cooperation, coordination, teamwork — more at TEAMWORK

col·lage \kə-ˈläzh\ n [F, lit., gluing] : an artistic composition of fragments (as of printed matter) pasted on a surface

col·la·gen \ˈkä-lə-jən\ n : any of a group of fibrous proteins widely found in vertebrate connective tissue

¹col·lapse \kə-ˈlaps\ vb **col·lapsed; col·laps·ing** 1 ♦ : to fall or shrink together abruptly 2 : to break down completely : DISINTEGRATE; also : to fall in : give way 3 a : to break down physically or mentally; esp : to fall helpless or unconscious b : to suddenly lose force, significance, effectiveness, or worth 4 : to fold down compactly — **col·laps·ible** adj

♦ cave in, crumple, give, go, yield; also deflate, flatten, melt; break, break down, conk (out), crash, die, fail, give out, stall; burst, shatter, smash; crack, pop, snap

²collapse n ♦ : sudden failure : a failure to function

♦ burnout, exhaustion, fatigue, lassitude, prostration, tiredness, weariness — more at FATIGUE ♦ crash, cropper, defeat, failure, fizzle, nonsuccess — more at FAILURE

¹col·lar \ˈkä-lər\ n 1 : a band, strip, or chain worn around the neck or the neckline of a garment 2 : something resembling a collar — **col·lar·less** adj

²collar vb 1 : to seize by the collar 2 ♦ : to take or seize by or as if by a sudden motion or grasp : GRAB 3 ♦ : to take or get control of

♦ [2, 3] bag, capture, catch, corral, get, grab, grapple, hook, land, nab, seize, snare, trap — more at CATCH

col·lar·bone \-ˌbōn\ n : the bone of the shoulder that joins the breastbone and the shoulder blade

col·lard \ˈkä-lərd\ n : a stalked smooth-leaved kale — usu. used in pl.

col·late \kə-ˈlāt; ˈkä-ˌlāt, ˈkō-\ vb **col·lat·ed; col·lat·ing** 1 : to compare (as two texts) carefully and critically 2 : to assemble in proper order

¹col·lat·er·al \kə-ˈla-tə-rəl\ adj 1 : associated but of secondary importance 2 : descended from the same ancestors but not in the same line 3 : PARALLEL 4 : of, relating to, or being collateral used as security; also : secured by collateral

²collateral n : property (as stocks) used as security for the repayment of a loan

col·la·tion \kä-ˈlā-shən, kō-\ n 1 : a light meal 2 : the act, process, or result of collating

col·league \ˈkä-ˌlēg\ n : an associate esp. in a profession

¹col·lect \ˈkä-likt, -ˌlekt\ n : a short prayer comprising an invocation, petition, and conclusion

²col·lect \kə-ˈlekt\ vb 1 a ♦ : to bring or come together into one body or place : GATHER b : to gather or exact from a number of persons or sources 2 ♦ : to gain control of ⟨∼ his thoughts⟩ 3 : to receive payment of 4 ♦ : to form a layer, heap, or mass — **col·lect·ible** or **col·lect·able** adj or n — **col·lec·tor** \-ˈlek-tər\ n

♦ [1a] accumulate, amass, assemble, concentrate, garner, gather, group, lump, pick up, round up, scrape — more at GATHER ♦ [2] calm, compose, control, settle; also allay, lull, quiet, soothe, still, tranquilize ♦ [4] accumulate, conglomerate, gather, heap, pile up; also bank, drift, ridge

³col·lect \kə-ˈlekt\ adv or adj : to be paid for by the receiver

col·lect·ed \kə-ˈlek-təd\ adj ♦ : possessed of calmness and composure often through concentrated effort : SELF=POSSESSED, CALM

♦ calm, composed, cool, placid, self-possessed, serene, tranquil, undisturbed, unperturbed, unshaken, untroubled, unworried — more at CALM

col·lec·tion \kə-ˈlek-shən\ n 1 : the act or process of collecting ⟨garbage ∼⟩ 2 ♦ : something collected ⟨a stamp ∼⟩ 3 ♦ : a number of individuals or objects brought together as a unit : GROUP

♦ [2, 3] accumulation, assemblage, gathering — more at ACCUMULATION ♦ [3] array, assemblage, bank, batch, block, bunch, clump, cluster, group, huddle, knot, lot, package, parcel, set, suite

¹col·lec·tive \kə-ˈlek-tiv\ adj 1 : of, relating to, or denoting a group of individuals considered as a whole 2 ♦ : involving all members of a group as distinct from its individuals 3 ♦ : shared or assumed by all members of the group

♦ [2, 3] common, communal, concerted, conjoint, joint, mutual, public, united; also cooperative, reciprocal, symbiotic; mass, popular; general, generic, universal Ant individual, single, sole

²collective n 1 : GROUP 2 : a cooperative unit or organization

collective bargaining n : negotiation between an employer and a labor union

col·lec·tive·ly \kə-ˈlek-tiv-lē\ adv ♦ : in a collective sense or manner

♦ all around, altogether, overall, together — more at ALL AROUND

col·lec·tiv·ise chiefly Brit var of COLLECTIVIZE

col·lec·tiv·ism \kə-ˈlek-ti-ˌvi-zəm\ n : a political or economic theory advocating collective control esp. over production and distribution

col·lec·tiv·ize \-ˌvīz\ vb **-ized; -iz·ing** : to organize under collective control — **col·lec·tiv·i·za·tion** \-ˌlek-ti-və-ˈzā-shən\ n

col·leen \kä-ˈlēn, ˈkä-ˌlēn\ n : an Irish girl

col·lege \ˈkä-lij\ n [ME, endowed body of clergy or scholars, fr. AF, fr. L collegium society, fr. collega colleague, fr. com- with + legare to depute] 1 : a building used for an educational or religious purpose 2 : an institution of higher learning or division of a university granting a bachelor's degree; also : an institution offering instruction esp. in a vocational or technical field ⟨barber ∼⟩ 3 ♦ : an organized body of persons having common interests or duties ⟨∼ of cardinals⟩ — **col·le·giate** \kə-ˈlē-jət\ adj

♦ association, brotherhood, club, congress, council, fellowship, fraternity, guild, institute, institution, league, order, organization, society — more at ASSOCIATION

col·le·gi·al·i·ty \kə-ˌlē-jē-ˈa-lə-tē\ n : the relationship of colleagues

col·le·gian \kə-ˈlē-jən\ n : a college student or recent college graduate

col·le·gi·um \kə-ˈle-gē-əm, -ˈlā-\ n, pl **-gia** \-gē-ə\ or **-giums** : a group in which each member has approximately equal power

col·lide \kə-ˈlīd\ vb **col·lid·ed; col·lid·ing** 1 ♦ : to come together with solid impact 2 ♦ : to come into conflict : CLASH

♦ [1] bang, bash, bump, crash, hit, impact, knock, ram, slam, smash, strike, swipe, thud — more at HIT
♦ [2] clash, conflict, jar — more at CLASH

col·lid·er \kə-ˈlī-dər\ n : a particle accelerator in which two beams of particles are made to collide

col·lie \ˈkä-lē\ n : any of a breed of large dogs developed in Scotland for herding sheep that occur in rough-coated and smooth-coated varieties

col·lier \ˈkäl-yər\ n 1 : a coal miner 2 : a ship for carrying coal

col·liery \ˈkäl-yə-rē\ n, pl **-lier·ies** : a coal mine and its associated buildings

col·li·mate \ˈkä-lə-ˌmāt\ vb **-mat·ed; -mat·ing** : to make (as light rays) parallel

col·li·sion \kə-ˈli-zhən\ n ♦ : an act or instance of colliding

♦ bump, concussion, crash, impact, jar, jolt, shock, smash, strike, wallop — more at IMPACT ♦ crack-up, crash, smash, wreck — more at CRASH

col·lo·ca·tion \ˌkä-lə-ˈkā-shən\ n : the act or result of placing or arranging together; esp : a noticeable arrangement or conjoining of linguistic elements (as words)

col·loid \ˈkä-ˌlȯid\ n : a substance in the form of submicroscopic particles that when in solution or suspension do not settle out; also : such a substance together with the medium in which it is dispersed — **col·loi·dal** \kə-ˈlȯid-ᵊl\ adj

colloq *abbr* colloquial

col·lo·qui·al \kə-'lō-kwē-əl\ *adj* ♦ : of, relating to, or characteristic of conversation and esp. of familiar and informal conversation

♦ conversational, informal, nonliterary, vernacular, vulgar; *also* nonstandard, substandard, uneducated; slang, slangy *Ant* bookish, formal, learned, literary

col·lo·qui·al·ism \-'lō-kwē-ə-ˌli-zəm\ *n* : a colloquial expression

col·lo·qui·um \kə-'lō-kwē-əm\ *n, pl* **-qui·ums** *or* **-quia** \-ə\ : CONFERENCE, SEMINAR

col·lo·quy \'kä-lə-kwē\ *n, pl* **-quies** ♦ : a usu. formal conversation or conference

♦ forum, panel, parley, powwow, seminar, symposium — more at FORUM ♦ argument, conference, deliberation, discourse, discussion, give-and-take, parley, talk — more at DISCUSSION

col·lu·sion \kə-'lü-zhən\ *n* ♦ : secret agreement or cooperation for an illegal or deceitful purpose — **col·lu·sive** \-siv\ *adj*

♦ connivance, conspiracy; *also* chicanery, foul play, skulduggery (*or* skullduggery); double-dealing, duplicity; cover-up, frame-up; intrigue, plot, scheme

Colo *abbr* Colorado

co·logne \kə-'lōn\ *n* [*Cologne*, Germany] : a perfumed liquid — **co·logned** \-'lōnd\ *adj*

Co·lom·bi·an \kə-'ləm-bē-ən\ *n* : a native or inhabitant of Colombia — **Colombian** *adj*

¹co·lon \'kō-lən\ *n, pl* **colons** *or* **co·la** \-lə\ : the part of the large intestine extending from the cecum to the rectum — **co·lon·ic** \kō-'lä-nik\ *adj*

²colon *n, pl* **colons** : a punctuation mark : used esp. to direct attention to following matter (as in a list)

col·o·nel \'kərn-ᵊl\ *n* [alter. of *coronel*, fr. MF, fr. It *colonnello* column of soldiers, colonel, ultim. fr. L *columna*] : a commissioned officer (as in the army) ranking next below a brigadier general

¹co·lo·nial \kə-'lō-nē-əl\ *adj* 1 : of, relating to, or characteristic of a colony; *also* : possessing or composed of colonies 2 *often cap* : of or relating to the original 13 colonies forming the U.S.

²colonial *n* : a member or inhabitant of a colony

co·lo·nial·ism \-ə-ˌli-zəm\ *n* : control by one power over a dependent area or people; *also* : a policy advocating or based on such control — **co·lo·nial·ist** \-list\ *n or adj*

col·o·nise *Brit var of* COLONIZE

col·o·nist \'kä-lə-nist\ *n* 1 ♦ : a member or inhabitant of a colony : COLONIAL 2 ♦ : one that colonizes or settles in a new country

♦ [1, 2] frontiersman, homesteader, pioneer, settler — more at FRONTIERSMAN

col·o·nize \'kä-lə-ˌnīz\ *vb* **-nized; -niz·ing** 1 : to establish a colony in or on 2 : SETTLE — **col·o·ni·za·tion** \ˌkä-lə-nə-'zā-shən\ *n*

col·o·niz·er *n* : one that colonizes or settles in a new country

col·on·nade \ˌkä-lə-'nād\ *n* : an evenly spaced row of columns usu. supporting the base of a roof structure

co·nos·co·py \ˌkō-lə-'näs-kə-pē\ *n, pl* **-pies** : endoscopic examination of the colon — **co·lon·o·scope** \kō-'lä-nə-ˌskōp\ *n*

col·o·ny \'kä-lə-nē\ *n, pl* **-nies** 1 : a body of people living in a new territory; *also* : the territory inhabited by these people 2 : a localized population of organisms ⟨a ∼ of bees⟩ 3 : a group with common interests situated in close association ⟨a writers' ∼⟩; *also* : the area occupied by such a group

col·o·phon \'kä-lə-fən, -ˌfän\ *n* 1 : an inscription placed at the end of a book with facts relative to its production 2 : a distinctive symbol used by a printer or publisher

¹col·or *or Can and Brit* **col·our** \'kə-lər\ *n* 1 ♦ : a phenomenon of light (as red or blue) or visual perception that enables one to differentiate otherwise identical objects; *also*

: a hue as contrasted with black, white, or gray 2 : APPEARANCE 3 : complexion tint 4 *pl* ♦ : an identifying badge, pennant, or flag; *also* : military service ⟨a call to the ∼s⟩ 5 : VIVIDNESS, INTEREST 6 ♦ : something used to give color

♦ [1] cast, hue, shade, tinge, tint, tone; *also* primary color; brightness, saturation, value; coloration, coloring ♦ *usu* **colors** [4] banner, ensign, flag, jack, pennant, standard, streamer — more at FLAG ♦ [6] dye, pigment, stain — more at PIGMENT

²color *or Can and Brit* **colour** *vb* 1 a ♦ : to give color to b ♦ : to change the color of (as by dyeing, staining, or painting) 2 ♦ : to become red in the face : BLUSH 3 ♦ : to give a false or misleading representation of the facts

♦ [1a, 1b] dye, paint, stain, tinge, tint; *also* brighten, lighten; darken, tone (down); daub ♦ [2] bloom, blush, crimson, flush, glow, redden — more at BLUSH ♦ [3] distort, falsify, garble, misinterpret, misrepresent, misstate, pervert, twist, warp — more at GARBLE ♦ [3] elaborate, embroider, exaggerate, magnify, pad, stretch — more at EMBROIDER

Col·o·ra·do potato beetle \ˌkä-lə-'ra-dō-, -'rä-\ *n* : a black-and-yellow striped beetle that feeds on the leaves of the potato

col·or·ation \ˌkə-lə-'rā-shən\ *n* : use or arrangement of colors

col·or·a·tu·ra \ˌkə-lə-rə-'tür-ə, -'tyùr-\ *n* 1 : elaborate ornamentation in vocal music 2 : a soprano specializing in coloratura

col·or–blind *or Can and Brit* **col·our–blind** \'kə-lər-ˌblīnd\ *adj* 1 : partially or totally unable to distinguish one or more chromatic colors 2 : not influenced by differences of race — **col·or blind·ness** *n*

col·ored *or Can and Brit* **col·oured** \'kə-lərd\ *adj* 1 : having color 2 : SLANTED, BIASED

col·or·fast *or Can and Brit* **col·our·fast** \'kə-lər-ˌfast\ *adj* : having color that does not fade or run — **col·or·fast·ness** *n*

col·or·ful *or Can and Brit* **col·our·ful** *adj* ♦ : having striking colors

♦ multicolored (*or* multicoloured), variegated; *also* brave, bright, brilliant, gay; flashy, garish, gaudy, loud, showy; deep, rich, unbleached *Ant* colorless; monochromatic

col·or·ize *or Can* **col·our·ize** *or Brit* **-ise** \'kə-lə-ˌrīz\ *vb* **-ized; -iz·ing** : to add color to by means of a computer — **col·or·iza·tion** \ˌkə-lə-rə-'zā-shən\ *n*

col·or·less *or Can and Brit* **col·our·less** *adj* ♦ : lacking color

♦ uncolored (*or* uncoloured), unpainted, white; *also* clear, limpid, liquid, lucent, pellucid, transparent; bleached, faded, washed; dull, faint, gray, neutral, pale, pallid *Ant* colored, dyed, painted, stained, tinged, tinted

co·los·sal \kə-'lä-səl\ *adj* ♦ : of very great size or degree

♦ astronomical, enormous, giant, gigantic, ginormous, grand, huge, mammoth, massive, monumental, tremendous

Co·los·sians \kə-'lä-shənz\ *n* : a book of the New Testament of Christian Scripture

co·los·sus \kə-'lä-səs\ *n, pl* **co·los·si** \-ˌsī\ [L] 1 : a gigantic statue 2 : something of great size or scope

♦ behemoth, blockbuster, giant, jumbo, leviathan, mammoth, monster, titan, whale, whopper — more at GIANT

col·our *Can and Brit var of* COLOR

col·por·teur \'käl-ˌpōr-tər\ *n* [F] : a peddler of religious books

colt \'kōlt\ *n* 1 : FOAL; *also* : a young male horse, ass, or zebra 2 : a young untried person

colt·ish *adj* ♦ : full of play : inclined to friskiness or liveliness

♦ antic, elfish, fay, frisky, frolicsome, playful, sportive — more at PLAYFUL

col·um·bine \'kä-ləm-ˌbīn\ n [ME, fr. AF, fr. ML *colum-bina*, fr. L, fem. of *columbinus* dovelike, fr. *columba* dove] : any of a genus of plants with showy spurred flowers that are related to the buttercups

co·lum·bi·um \kə-'ləm-bē-əm\ n : NIOBIUM

Columbus Day \kə-'ləm-bəs-\ n : the 2d Monday in October or formerly October 12 observed as a legal holiday in many states in commemoration of the landing of Columbus in the Bahamas in 1492

col·umn \'kä-ləm\ n 1 : one of two or more vertical sections of a printed page; *also* : one in a usu. regular series of articles (as in a newspaper) 2 ♦ : a supporting pillar; *esp* : one consisting of a usu. round shaft, a capital, and a base 3 : something resembling a column ⟨a ～ of water⟩ 4 ♦ : a long row (as of soldiers) — **co·lum·nar** \kə-'ləm-nər\ adj

♦ [2] pier, pillar, post, stanchion — more at PILLAR ♦ [4] cue, file, line, queue, range, string, train — more at LINE

col·um·nist \'kä-ləm-nist\ n : a person who writes a newspaper or magazine column

com abbr 1 comedy; comic 2 comma 3 commercial organization

co·ma \'kō-mə\ n : a state of deep unconsciousness caused by disease, injury, or poison — **co·ma·tose** \'kō-mə-ˌtōs, 'kä-\ adj

Co·man·che \kə-'man-chē\ n, pl **Comanche** or **Comanches** : a member of an American Indian people ranging from Wyoming and Nebraska south into New Mexico and Texas

¹comb \'kōm\ n 1 : a toothed instrument for arranging the hair or for separating and cleaning textile fibers 2 : a fleshy crest on the head of a fowl 3 : HONEYCOMB — **combed** \'kōmd\ adj

²comb vb 1 : to draw a comb through for the purpose of arranging or cleaning 2 : to pass across with a scraping or raking action 3 : to eliminate (as with a comb) by a thorough going-over 4 : to search or examine systematically

³comb abbr combination; combining

¹com·bat \'käm-ˌbat\ n ♦ : a fight or contest between individuals or groups

♦ battle, conflict, confrontation, contest, duel, face-off, rivalry, struggle, tug-of-war, warfare — more at CONTEST ♦ battle, clash, conflict, contest, fight, fracas, fray, hassle, scrap, scrimmage, scuffle, skirmish, struggle, tussle — more at FIGHT

²combat \kəm-'bat, 'käm-ˌbat\ vb **-bat·ed** or **-bat·ted**; **-bat·ing** or **-bat·ting** 1 ♦ : to fight with : FIGHT, CONTEND 2 ♦ : to struggle against : OPPOSE 3 : to engage in battle during war — **com·bat·ant** \kəm-'bat-ᵊnt, 'käm-bə-tənt\ n

♦ battle, contend, counter, fight, oppose — more at FIGHT

combat fatigue n : a traumatic psychological reaction occurring under wartime conditions (as combat) that cause intense stress

com·bat·ive \kəm-'ba-tiv\ adj ♦ : marked by eagerness to fight or contend

♦ aggressive, argumentative, bellicose, belligerent, contentious, discordant, disputatious, militant, pugnacious, quarrelsome, scrappy, truculent, warlike — more at BELLIGERENT

comb·er \'kō-mər\ n 1 : one that combs 2 : a long curling wave of the sea

com·bi·na·tion \ˌkäm-bə-'nā-shən\ n 1 a ♦ : a result or product of combining b ♦ : an alliance of individuals, corporations, or states united to achieve a social, political, or economic end c ♦ : two or more persons working as a team 2 : a sequence of letters or numbers chosen in setting a lock 3 a ♦ : the act or process of combining b : the quality or state of being combined

♦ [1a] admixture, amalgam, blend, composite, compound, fusion, intermixture, mix, mixture — more at BLEND ♦ [1b] alliance, bloc, coalition, combine, confederacy, confederation, federation, league, union—

more at CONFEDERACY ♦ [1b, 1c] bloc, body, coalition, combine, faction, party, sect, set, side, wing ♦ [3a] connection, consolidation, coupling, junction, unification, union — more at UNION

¹com·bine \kəm-'bīn\ vb **com·bined**; **com·bin·ing** 1 ♦ : to become one : UNITE 2 ♦ : to cause (as two or more things or ideas) to mix together

♦ [1] associate, coalesce, conjoin, connect, couple, fuse, join, link, marry, unify, unite — more at UNITE ♦ [2] amalgamate, blend, commingle, fuse, incorporate, integrate, intermingle, merge, mingle, mix — more at MIX

²com·bine \'käm-ˌbīn\ n 1 ♦ : a combination esp. of business or political interests 2 : a machine that harvests and threshes grain while moving over a field

♦ alliance, bloc, coalition, combination, confederacy, confederation, federation, league, union — more at CONFEDERACY ♦ cartel, combination, syndicate, trust — more at CARTEL ♦ bloc, body, coalition, combination, faction, party, sect, set, side, wing

comb·ings \'kō-miŋz\ n pl : loose hairs or fibers removed by a comb

combining form n : a linguistic form that occurs only in compounds or derivatives

com·bo \'käm-bō\ n, pl **combos** : a small jazz or dance band

com·bus·ti·ble \kəm-'bəs-tə-bəl\ adj ♦ : capable of being burned — **com·bus·ti·bil·i·ty** \-ˌbəs-tə-'bi-lə-tē\ n — **combustible** n

♦ flammable, ignitable, inflammable; *also* explosive, incendiary *Ant* fireproof, incombustible, noncombustible, nonflammable, noninflammable

com·bus·tion \kəm-'bəs-chən\ n 1 : an act or instance of burning 2 : slow oxidation (as in the animal body)

comdg abbr commanding

comdr abbr commander

comdt abbr commandant

come \'kəm\ vb **came** \'kām\; **come**; **com·ing** \'kə-miŋ\ 1 ♦ : to move toward something : APPROACH 2 ♦ : to arrive at a particular place, end, result, or conclusion : ARRIVE 3 : to reach the point of being or becoming ⟨～ to a boil⟩ 4 a ♦ : to reach a total : add up : AMOUNT ⟨the bill came to $10⟩ b ♦ : to be equal or nearly equal in or at the end 5 ♦ : to come to pass : take place 6 : ORIGINATE, ARISE 7 : to be available 8 : REACH, EXTEND — **come across** 1 : to make a specified impression ⟨came across as rude⟩ 2 : to find esp. by chance ⟨came across an intriguing story⟩ — **come clean** : CONFESS — **come into** : ACQUIRE, ACHIEVE — **come of age** : MATURE — **come to grips with** : to meet or deal with frankly — **come to pass** : HAPPEN — **come to terms** : to reach an agreement

♦ [1] advance, approach, near; *also* drop (in), enter, pop (in) *Ant* go, retreat, withdraw ♦ [2] arrive, land, show up, turn up; *also* hit, make, reach; pull (in), touch down; debark, disembark; barge (in), breeze (in), burst (in or into), waltz (in) *Ant* go ♦ *usu* **come to** [4a, 4b] add up, amount, equal, number, sum, total — more at AMOUNT (TO) ♦ [5] be, befall, betide, chance, go, happen, occur, pass, transpire — more at HAPPEN

come around vb 1 : to come round 2 ♦ : to recover consciousness

♦ come round, come to, revive — more at COME TO

come·back \'kəm-ˌbak\ n 1 ♦ : a sharp or witty reply : RETORT 2 ♦ : a return to a former position or condition — **come back** vb

♦ [1] repartee, retort, riposte — more at RETORT ♦ [1] answer, reply, response, retort, return — more at ANSWER ♦ [2] convalescence, rally, recovery, recuperation, rehabilitation — more at CONVALESCENCE

come by vb ♦ : to make a brief visit

♦ call, drop (by or in), pop (in), stop (by or in), visit — more at CALL

co·me·di·an \kə-'mē-dē-ən\ n 1 : an actor in comedy 2 ♦ : a comic person; *esp* : an entertainer specializing in comedy

♦ card, comic, humorist, jester, joker, wag, wit — more at HUMORIST

co·me·di·enne \-ˌmē-dē-'en\ *n* : a woman who is a comedian

come·down \'kəm-ˌdaún\ *n* ♦ : a descent in rank or dignity

♦ decline, descent, down, downfall, fall; *also* breakdown, collapse, crash, meltdown, ruin, undoing; defeat, disappointment, reversal, setback; bottom, nadir *Ant* aggrandizement, ascent, exaltation, rise, up

come down *vb* **1** : to lose or fall in estate or condition **2 a** : to pass by tradition **b** : to pass from a usu. high source **3** : to reduce itself : AMOUNT ⟨it *comes down* to this⟩ **4** ♦ : to become ill ⟨*come down* with measles⟩

♦ catch, contract, get, sicken, take — more at CONTRACT

com·e·dy \'kä-mə-dē\ *n, pl* **-dies** [ME, narrative that ends happily, fr. ML *comoedia*, fr. L, play with a happy ending, fr. Gk *kōmōidia*, fr. *kōmos* revel + *aeidein* to sing] **1** : a light amusing play with a happy ending **2** : a literary work treating a comic theme or written in a comic style **3** ♦ : humorous entertainment — **co·me·dic** \kə-'mē-dik\ *adj*

♦ farce, humor (*or* humour), slapstick; *also* burlesque, parody, satire; banter, persiflage, wit; foolery, fun, horseplay, monkeyshines, shenanigans

come·li·ness *n* ♦ : the condition of being comely esp. with respect to grace or beauty of external form

♦ attractiveness, beauty, handsomeness, looks, loveliness, prettiness — more at BEAUTY

come·ly \'kəm-lē\ *adj* **come·li·er; -est** : having a pleasing appearance : ATTRACTIVE, HANDSOME

come off *vb* : SUCCEED

come-on \'kə-ˌmòn, -ˌmän\ *n* : INDUCEMENT, LURE

come out *vb* **1 a** ♦ : to come into view **b** ♦ : to become public **2** : to declare oneself **3** ♦ : to turn out in an outcome : end up : TURN OUT **5** ⟨everything *came out* all right⟩ — **come out with** : SAY 1

♦ [1a] appear, materialize, show up, turn up — more at APPEAR ♦ [1b] get out, leak out, out, spread — more at GET OUT ♦ [3] pan out, prove, turn out; *also* develop, emerge, evolve, play out, unfold, work out

com·er \'kə-mər\ *n* **1** : one that comes ⟨all ~s⟩ **2** : a promising beginner

come round *vb* **1** : to change direction **2** ♦ : to recover consciousness **3** ♦ : to accede to a particular opinion or course of action

♦ [2] come around, come to, revive — more at COME TO ♦ [3] accede, acquiesce, agree, assent, consent, subscribe (to) — more at ACCEDE

¹co·mes·ti·ble \kə-'mes-tə-bəl\ *adj* : EDIBLE

²comestible *n* : FOOD — usu. used in pl.

com·et \'kä-mət\ *n* [ME *comete*, fr. OE *cometa*, fr. L, fr. Gk *komētēs*, lit., long-haired, fr. *komē* hair] : a small bright celestial body that develops a long tail when near the sun

come to *vb* ♦ : to regain consciousness

♦ come around, come round, revive; *also* rally, recover; awake, awaken, wake up

come-up·pance \kə-'mə-pəns\ *n* : a deserved rebuke or penalty

com·fit \'kəm-fət\ *n* : a candied fruit or nut

¹com·fort \'kəm-fərt\ *vb* **1** ♦ : to give strength and hope to **2** ♦ : to ease the grief or trouble of : CONSOLE

♦ [1] buoy (up), cheer, embolden, encourage, hearten, inspire, steel — more at ENCOURAGE ♦ [2] assure, cheer, console, reassure, solace, soothe; *also* commiserate, condole, sympathize; boost, buoy (up), elevate, lift, uplift; allay, alleviate, assuage, relieve; calm, quiet, relax, tranquilize *Ant* distress, torment, torture, trouble

²comfort *n* **1** : the act or an instance of consoling : the state of being consoled **2** ♦ : freedom from pain, trouble, or anxiety **3** ♦ : something that consoles : something that gives freedom or ease **4** ♦ : one that gives or brings comfort ⟨all the ~s of home⟩

♦ [2] alleviation, ease, relief — more at EASE ♦ [2] cheer, consolation, relief, solace; *also* encouragement, inspiration, uplift; assurance, reassurance; alleviation, mitigation; contentment, gladness, happiness; commiseration, empathy, sympathy ♦ [3, 4] amenity, convenience, luxury; *also* extra; benefit, help, service; delight, indulgence, joy, pleasure *Ant* burden, millstone, weight

com·fort·able \'kəm-fər-tə-bəl, 'kəmf-tər-\ *adj* **1** ♦ : providing comfort or security **2** ♦ : feeling at ease **3** ♦ : affording an ease with money and a secure way of living without great wealth — **com·fort·ably** \-blē\ *adv*

♦ [1] easy, snug, soft; *also* relaxing, reposeful, restful; genial, hospitable, inviting, pleasant; commodious, roomy, spacious; homely, homey, homey *Ant* uncomfortable ♦ [2] content, contented, peaceful, pleased, relaxed, untroubled *Ant* uncomfortable ♦ [3] abundant, ample, bountiful, generous, liberal, plentiful — more at PLENTIFUL

com·fort·er \'kəm-fər-tər\ *n* **1** : one that comforts **2** : QUILT

comforting *adj* ♦ : providing or intended to provide comfort

♦ encouraging, gratifying, heartening, heartwarming, rewarding, satisfying — more at HEARTWARMING ♦ dreamy, narcotic, sedative, soothing — more at SOOTHING

com·fy \'kəm-fē\ *adj* : COMFORTABLE

¹com·ic \'kä-mik\ *adj* **1** : relating to comedy or comic strips **2** : provoking laughter or amusement

²comic *n* **1** ♦ : a comical individual esp. a professional entertainer who uses any of various physical or verbal means to be amusing : COMEDIAN **2** *pl* : the part of a newspaper devoted to comic strips

♦ card, comedian, humorist, jester, joker, wag, wit — more at HUMORIST

com·i·cal *adj* ♦ : causing laughter

♦ antic, comic, droll, farcical, funny, hilarious, humorous, hysterical, laughable, ludicrous, ridiculous, riotous, risible, screaming, uproarious — more at FUNNY ♦ absurd, derisive, farcical, laughable, ludicrous, preposterous, ridiculous, risible, silly — more at RIDICULOUS

comic book *n* : a magazine containing sequences of comic strips

comic strip *n* ♦ : a group of cartoons in narrative sequence

♦ cartoon; *also* comic book, funny paper(s); animated cartoon, animation; caricature

coming \'kə-miŋ\ *adj* **1** ♦ : immediately due in sequence or development : APPROACHING, NEXT **2** : gaining importance

♦ forthcoming, imminent, impending, oncoming, pending — more at FORTHCOMING ♦ following, next, succeeding — more at NEXT

co·mi·ty \'kä-mə-tē, 'kō-\ *n, pl* **-ties** : friendly civility : COURTESY

coml *abbr* commercial

comm *abbr* **1** command; commander **2** commerce; commercial **3** commission; commissioner **4** committee **5** common **6** commonwealth

com·ma \'kä-mə\ *n* : a punctuation mark, used esp. as a mark of separation within the sentence

¹com·mand \kə-'mand\ *vb* **1** ♦ : to direct authoritatively : ORDER **2** ♦ : to exercise a dominating influence over : have command of **3** : to overlook from a strategic position **4** ♦ : to demand or receive as one's due ⟨~s a high fee⟩

♦ [1] bid, boss, charge, direct, enjoin, instruct, order, tell; *also* ask, petition, request; beg, beseech, entreat; advise, counsel, warn; appoint, assign, authorize, commission; oversee, superintend, supervise; conduct, control, lead, manage; coerce, compel, constrain, force, oblige, require *Ant* mind, obey ♦ [2] boss, captain, control, govern, preside, rule — more at GOVERN ♦ [2] dominate, head, lead, spearhead — more at LEAD ♦ [4] ask, charge, demand — more at CHARGE

²**command** *n* **1** ♦ : an order given **2 a** ♦ : ability to control : MASTERY **b** : facility in use ⟨a good ∼ of French⟩ **3** : the act of commanding **4** : a signal that actuates a device (as a computer); *also* : the activation of a device by means of a signal **5 a** : a body of troops under a commander **b** : an area or position that one commands **6** : a position of highest authority

♦ [1] behest, charge, commandment, decree, dictate, direction, directive, edict, instruction, order, word; *also* demand, requirement; injunction, mandate; law, precept, rule; ordinance, regulation, statute ♦ [2a] arm, authority, clutch, control, dominion, grip, hold, mastery, power, sway — more at POWER

com·man·dant \ˈkä-mən-ˌdant, -ˌdänt\ *n* : an officer in command

com·man·deer \ˌkä-mən-ˈdir\ *vb* ♦ : to take possession of by force

♦ appropriate, arrogate, preempt, usurp — more at APPROPRIATE

com·mand·er \kə-ˈman-dər\ *n* **1 a** ♦ : one in an official position of command or control **b** ♦ : an officer commanding an army or subdivision of an army **2** : a commissioned officer in the navy ranking next below a captain

♦ [1a, 1b] captain; *also* commissioned officer

com·mand·ment \kə-ˈmand-mənt\ *n* ♦ : something that is commanded : COMMAND, ORDER; *esp* : any of the Ten Commandments

♦ behest, charge, command, decree, dictate, direction, directive, edict, instruction, order, word — more at COMMAND

command module *n* : a space vehicle module designed to carry the crew and reentry equipment

com·man·do \kə-ˈman-dō\ *n, pl* **-dos** *or* **-does** : a member of a military unit trained for surprise raids

command sergeant major *n* : a noncommissioned officer in the army ranking above a sergeant major

com·mem·o·rate \kə-ˈme-mə-ˌrāt\ *vb* **-rat·ed; -rat·ing 1** : to call or recall to mind **2** : to serve as a memorial of **3** ♦ : to mark by some ceremony or observation : OBSERVE — **com·mem·o·ra·tion** \-ˌme-mə-ˈrā-shən\ *n*

♦ celebrate, keep, observe — more at KEEP

com·mem·o·ra·tive \kə-ˈmem-rə-tiv, -ˈme-mə-ˌrā-tiv\ *adj* : intended to commemorate an event

com·mence \kə-ˈmens\ *vb* **com·menced; com·menc·ing** ♦ : to have or make a beginning : BEGIN, START

♦ arise, begin, dawn, form, materialize, originate, spring, start — more at BEGIN ♦ begin, embark (on *or* upon), enter, get off, launch, open, start, strike — more at BEGIN

com·mence·ment \-mənt\ *n* **1** ♦ : the act or time of a beginning **2** : the graduation exercises of a school or college

♦ beginning, birth, dawn, genesis, launch, morning, onset, outset, start, threshold — more at BEGINNING

com·mend \kə-ˈmend\ *vb* **1** ♦ : to entrust for care or preservation **2** : RECOMMEND **3** : PRAISE — **com·mend·ably** \-blē\ *adv* — **com·men·da·tion** \ˌkä-mən-ˈdā-shən, -ˌmen-\ *n* — **com·mend·er** *n*

♦ commit, consign, delegate, deliver, entrust, give, hand over, leave, pass, transfer, transmit, trust, turn over, vest — more at GIVE

com·mend·able \-ˈmen-də-bəl\ *adj* ♦ : worthy of being commended

♦ admirable, creditable, laudable, meritorious, praiseworthy — more at ADMIRABLE

com·men·da·tion \ˌkä-mən-ˈdā-shən, -ˌmen-\ *n* ♦ : the act of commending : the expression of approval

♦ accolade, citation, encomium, eulogy, homage, paean, panegyric, salutation, tribute — more at ENCOMIUM

com·men·su·ra·ble \kə-ˈmen-sə-rə-bəl\ *adj* : having a common measure or a common divisor

com·men·su·rate \kə-ˈmen-sə-rət, -ˈmen-chə-\ *adj* : equal in measure or extent; *also* : PROPORTIONAL, CORRESPONDING ⟨a job ∼ with her abilities⟩

¹**com·ment** \ˈkä-ˌment\ *n* **1** ♦ : an expression of opinion **2** ♦ : an explanatory, illustrative, or critical note or observation : REMARK

♦ note, observation, reflection, remark — more at REMARK

²**comment** *vb* ♦ : to explain or interpret something by comment : OBSERVE — **com·men·ter** *n*

♦ note, observe, opine, remark — more at REMARK

com·men·tary \ˈkä-mən-ˌter-ē\ *n, pl* **-tar·ies** ♦ : a systematic series of comments

♦ analysis, comment, exposition; *also* annotation, explication; note, observation, remark; report, review, write-up

com·men·ta·tor \-ˌtā-tər\ *n* : one who comments; *esp* : a person who discusses news events on radio or television

com·merce \ˈkä-(ˌ)mərs\ *n* ♦ : the buying and selling of commodities : TRADE

♦ business, marketplace, trade, traffic; *also* free trade; dealings; merchandising, retailing, wholesaling; bartering

¹**com·mer·cial** \kə-ˈmər-shəl\ *adj* **1** : having to do with commerce **2** : designed for profit or for mass appeal — **com·mer·cial·ly** *adv*

²**commercial** *n* : an advertisement broadcast on radio or television

com·mer·cial·ise *Brit var of* COMMERCIALIZE

com·mer·cial·ism \kə-ˈmər-shə-ˌli-zəm\ *n* **1** : a spirit, method, or practice characteristic of business **2** : excessive emphasis on profit

com·mer·cial·ize *or Brit* **com·mer·cial·ise** \-ˌlīz\ *vb* **-ized; -iz·ing 1** : to manage on a business basis for profit **2** : to exploit for profit

com·mi·na·tion \ˌkä-mə-ˈnā-shən\ *n* : DENUNCIATION — **com·mi·na·to·ry** \ˈkä-mə-nə-ˌtōr-ē\ *adj*

com·min·gle \kə-ˈmiŋ-gəl\ *vb* ♦ : to mingle or mix together : MINGLE, BLEND

♦ amalgamate, blend, combine, fuse, incorporate, integrate, intermingle, merge, mingle, mix — more at MIX

com·mis·er·ate \kə-ˈmi-zə-ˌrāt\ *vb* **-at·ed; -at·ing** ♦ : to feel or express pity : SYMPATHIZE

♦ bleed, feel, pity, sympathize — more at PITY

com·mis·er·a·tion \-ˌmi-zə-ˈrā-shən\ *n* ♦ : the act of commiserating : the feeling or showing of sorrow or the expression of condolence for the wants or distresses of another

♦ charity, compassion, feeling, heart, humanity, kindliness, kindness, mercy, pity, sympathy — more at HEART

com·mis·sar \ˈkä-mə-ˌsär\ *n* [Russ *komissar*] : a Communist party official

com·mis·sar·i·at \ˌkä-mə-ˈser-ē-ət\ *n* **1** : a system for supplying troops with food **2** : a department headed by a commissar

com·mis·sary \ˈkä-mə-ˌser-ē\ *n, pl* **-sar·ies 1** : a store for equipment and provisions esp. for military personnel **2** ♦ : one delegated by a superior to execute a duty or an office

♦ agent, attorney, delegate, deputy, envoy, factor, proxy, representative — more at AGENT

¹**com·mis·sion** \kə-ˈmi-shən\ *n* **1** ♦ : a warrant granting certain powers and imposing certain duties; *also* : the fact of granting these powers or duties **2** : a certificate conferring military rank and authority **3** ♦ : authority to act as agent for another; *also* : something to be done by an agent **4** : a body of persons charged with performing a duty **5** ♦ : the doing of some act; *also* : the thing done **6** : the allowance made to an agent for transacting business for another

♦ [1] authorization, delegation, license (*or* licence), mandate; *also* commendation, consignment; fostering, promotion; commanding, directing, ordering

♦ [3] appointment, assignment, designation — more at APPOINTMENT ♦ [5] accomplishment, achievement, discharge, enactment, execution, fulfillment, implementation, performance; *also* dispatch, expedition; administration, direction, handling, management; application, operation, practice **Ant** nonfulfillment, nonperformance

²**commission** *vb* **1** ♦ : to give a commission to **2** : to order to be made **3** : to put (a ship) into a state of readiness for service

♦ assign, charge, entrust, trust — more at ENTRUST ♦ accredit, authorize, certify, delegate, empower, enable, invest, license, qualify — more at AUTHORIZE ♦ appoint, assign, attach, constitute, designate, detail, name — more at APPOINT

commissioned officer *n* : an officer of the armed forces holding rank by a commission from the president

com·mis·sion·er \kə-'mi-shə-nər\ *n* **1** : a member of a commission **2** : an official in charge of a department of public service **3** : the administrative head of a professional sport — **com·mis·sion·er·ship** *n*

com·mit \kə-'mit\ *vb* **com·mit·ted; com·mit·ting 1 a** : to put into charge or trust : ENTRUST **b** ♦ : to put into a place for disposal or safekeeping **2** ♦ : to put in a prison or mental institution **3** : TRANSFER, CONSIGN **4** ♦ : to carry into action ⟨∼ a crime⟩ **5** ♦ : to pledge or assign to some particular course or use — **com·mit·tal** *n*

♦ [1b] commend, consign, delegate, deliver, entrust, give, hand over, leave, pass, transfer, transmit, trust, turn over, vest — more at GIVE ♦ [2] confine, immure, imprison, jail — more at IMPRISON ♦ [4] accomplish, achieve, carry out, compass, do, execute, follow through, fulfill, make, perform — more at PERFORM ♦ [5] engage, pledge, troth — more at PLEDGE

com·mit·ment *n* ♦ : an agreement or pledge to do something in the future

♦ burden, charge, duty, need, obligation, responsibility — more at OBLIGATION

com·mit·tee \kə-'mi-tē\ *n* : a body of persons selected to consider and act or report on some matter — **com·mit·tee·man** \-mən\ *n* — **com·mit·tee·wom·an** \-ˌwù-mən\ *n*

commo *abbr* commodore

com·mode \kə-'mōd\ *n* [F, fr. *commode*, adj., suitable, convenient, fr. L *commodus*, fr. *com-* with + *modus* measure] **1** : a movable washstand with cupboard below **2** : TOILET **3**

com·mo·di·ous \kə-'mō-dē-əs\ *adj* ♦ : comfortably spacious : ROOMY

♦ ample, capacious, roomy, spacious — more at SPACIOUS

com·mod·i·ty \kə-'mä-də-tē\ *n, pl* **-ties 1** : a product of agriculture or mining **2** ♦ : an article of commerce — often used in pl. **3** : something useful or valued ⟨that valuable ∼ patience⟩

♦ *usu* **commodities** merchandise, wares — more at MERCHANDISE

com·mo·dore \'kä-mə-ˌdōr\ *n* **1** : a commissioned officer in the navy ranking next below a rear admiral **2** : an officer commanding a group of merchant ships **3** : the chief officer of a yacht club

¹**com·mon** \'kä-mən\ *adj* **1** ♦ : belonging to or serving the community : PUBLIC **2** ♦ : shared by a number in a group **3** ♦ : widely or generally known, found, or observed : FAMILIAR ⟨∼ knowledge⟩ **4** : VERNACULAR **3** ⟨∼ names of plants⟩ **5** ♦ : not above the average esp. in social status **6** ♦ : lacking refinement : COARSE **7** ♦ : falling below ordinary standards

♦ [1] blanket, general, generic, global, overall, public, universal — more at GENERAL ♦ [2] collective, communal, concerted, conjoint, joint, mutual, public, united — more at COLLECTIVE ♦ [3] commonplace, customary, everyday, familiar, frequent, normal, ordinary,

regular, routine, standard, usual **Ant** extraordinary, infrequent, rare, uncommon, unfamiliar, unusual ♦ [5] humble, ignoble, inferior, low, lowly, mean, plebeian, vulgar — more at IGNOBLE ♦ [6] coarse, crass, crude, gross, ill-bred, low, rough, rude, tasteless, uncouth, uncultivated, uncultured, unpolished, unrefined, vulgar — more at COARSE ♦ [7] fair, indifferent, mediocre, medium, middling, ordinary, passable, run-of-the-mill, second-rate, so-so — more at MEDIOCRE

²**common** *n* **1** *pl* : the common people **2** *pl* : a dining hall **3** *pl, cap* : the lower house of the British and Canadian parliaments **4** : a piece of land subject to common use — **in common** : shared together

com·mon·al·ty \'kä-mən-ᵊl-tē\ *n, pl* **-ties** : the common people

common cold *n* : a contagious respiratory disease caused by a virus and characterized by a sore, swollen, and inflamed nose and throat, usu. by much mucus, and by coughing and sneezing

common denominator *n* **1** : a common multiple of the denominators of a group of fractions **2** : a common trait or theme

common divisor *n* : a number or expression that divides two or more numbers or expressions without remainder

com·mon·er \'kä-mə-nər\ *n* ♦ : one of the common people : a person having no rank of nobility

♦ *usu* **commoners** herd, masses, mob, people, plebeians, populace, rank and file — more at MASSES

common fraction *n* : a fraction (as ½ or ¾) in which the numerator and denominator are both integers and are separated by a horizontal or slanted line

common law *n* : a group of legal practices and traditions based on judges' decisions and social customs and usu. having the same force as laws passed by legislative bodies

common logarithm *n* : a logarithm whose base is 10

com·mon·ly *adv* ♦ : as a general thing : often in the usual course of events

♦ generally, ordinarily, typically, usually — more at NATURALLY

common market *n* : an economic association formed to remove trade barriers among members

common multiple *n* : a multiple of each of two or more numbers or expressions

¹**com·mon·place** \'kä-mən-ˌplās\ *n* ♦ : something that is ordinary or trite

♦ banality, cliché, platitude, shibboleth; *also* inanity; generality, generalization, simplification; adage, proverb, saw, saying; old wives' tale, stereotype

²**commonplace** *adj* ♦ : commonly found or seen : ORDINARY

♦ average, common, everyday, normal, ordinary, prosaic, routine, run-of-the-mill, standard, unexceptional, unremarkable, usual, workaday — more at ORDINARY

common sense *n* ♦ : ordinary good sense and judgment — **com·mon·sen·si·cal** \'kä-mən-'sen-si-kəl\ *adj*

♦ horse sense, sense, wisdom, wit; *also* street smarts; foresight, judgment, prudence; brains, gray matter, intelligence; practicality, rationality; acumen, discernment, insight

com·mon·weal \'kä-mən-ˌwēl\ *n* **1** *archaic* : COMMONWEALTH **2** : the general welfare

com·mon·wealth \-ˌwelth\ *n* **1** ♦ : the body of people politically organized into a state **2** : a state esp. conceived as a body politic founded on law and united by compact or by tacit agreement of the people for the common good; *also* : an association or federation of autonomous states

♦ country, land, nation, sovereignty, state — more at NATION

com·mo·tion \kə-'mō-shən\ *n* **1** ♦ : violent or sharp disturbance : noisy, unruly, or tumultuous stir **2** : mental excitement, uncertainty, or confusion

♦ disturbance, furor, fuss, hubbub, hullabaloo, pandemonium, tumult, turmoil, uproar; *also* cacophony, clamor, din, howl, hue and cry, outcry, noise, racket, roar; disorder, unrest, upheaval; eruption, flare-up, flurry, outbreak, outburst; brawl, fracas, fray, hassle, melee, scuffle; dither, fever, fret, lather, tizzy

com·mu·nal \kə-'myün-ªl, 'käm-yən-ªl\ *adj* **1** : of or relating to a commune or community **2** : marked by collective ownership and use of property **3** ♦ : shared or used in common

♦ collective, common, concerted, conjoint, joint, mutual, public, united — more at COLLECTIVE

¹**com·mune** \kə-'myün\ *vb* **com·muned; com·mun·ing** : to communicate intimately

²**com·mune** \'käm-ˌyün; kə-'myün\ *n* **1** : the smallest administrative district in some European countries **2** : a community organized on a communal basis

com·mu·ni·ca·ble \kə-'myü-ni-kə-bəl\ *adj* ♦ : capable of being communicated ⟨∼ diseases⟩ — **com·mu·ni·ca·bil·i·ty** \-ˌmyü-ni-kə-'bi-lə-tē\ *n*

♦ catching, contagious, transmittable — more at CONTAGIOUS

com·mu·ni·cant \-'myü-ni-kənt\ *n* **1** : a church member entitled to receive Communion **2** : one that communicates; *esp* : INFORMANT

com·mu·ni·cate \kə-'myü-nə-ˌkāt\ *vb* **-cat·ed; -cat·ing** **1** : to make known **2** ♦ : to pass from one to another : TRANSMIT **3** : to receive Communion **4** : to be in communication **5** : JOIN, CONNECT — **com·mu·ni·ca·tor** \-ˌkā-tər\ *n*

♦ convey, impart, spread, transfer, transfuse, transmit; *also* deliver, hand over, surrender, turn over; broadcast, diffuse, disseminate, propagate; contaminate, infect, poison

com·mu·ni·ca·tion \kə-ˌmyü-nə-'kā- shən\ *n* **1** : an act of transmitting **2** : information communicated : a verbal or written message **3** : exchange of information or opinions **4** : a means of communicating — **com·mu·ni·ca·tive** \-'myü-nə-ˌkā-tiv, -ni-kə-tiv\ *adj*

com·mu·nion \kə-'myü-nyən\ *n* **1** : a sharing of something with others **2** *cap* : a Christian sacrament in which bread and wine are consumed as the substance or symbols of Christ's body and blood in commemoration of the death of Christ **3** : intimate fellowship or rapport **4** : a body of Christians having a common faith and discipline

com·mu·ni·qué \kə-'myü-nə-ˌkā, -ˌmyü-nə-'kā\ *n* ♦ : a brief public report intended for immediate release on a matter of public interest : BULLETIN

♦ advertisement, announcement, bulletin, notice, notification, release — more at ANNOUNCEMENT

com·mu·nism \'käm-yə-ˌni-zəm\ *n* **1** : social organization in which goods are held in common **2** : a theory of social organization advocating common ownership of means of production and a distribution of products of industry based on need **3** *cap* : a political doctrine based on revolutionary Marxist socialism that was the official ideology of the U.S.S.R. and some other countries; *also* : a system of government in which one party controls state-owned means of production — **com·mu·nist** \-nist\ *n or adj, often cap* — **com·mu·nis·tic** \ˌkäm-yə-'nis-tik\ *adj, often cap*

com·mu·ni·ty \kə-'myü-nə-tē\ *n, pl* **-ties** **1** : a body of people living in the same place under the same laws; *also* : a natural population of plants and animals that interact ecologically and live in one place (as a pond) **2** : society at large **3** : joint ownership **4** ♦ : common character : SIMILARITY, LIKENESS **5** : the people with common interests living in a particular area **6** ♦ : a body of persons of common and esp. professional interests scattered through a larger society

♦ [4] correspondence, likeness, parallelism, resemblance, similarity, similitude — more at SIMILARITY
♦ [6] brotherhood, corps, fellowship, fraternity — more at CORPS

community college *n* : a 2-year government-supported college that offers an associate degree

community property *n* : property held jointly by a married couple

com·mu·ta·tion \ˌkäm-yə-'tā-shən\ *n* ♦ : substitution of one form of payment or penalty for another

♦ barter, exchange, swap, trade, truck — more at EXCHANGE

com·mu·ta·tive \'käm-yə-ˌtā-tiv, kə-'myü-tə-\ *adj* : of, having, or being the property that the result obtained using a mathematical operation on any two elements of a set does not differ with the order in which the elements are used ⟨$a \times b = b \times a$ because multiplication is ∼⟩ — **com·mu·ta·tiv·i·ty** \kə-ˌmyü-tə-'ti-və-tē, ˌkäm-yə-tə-\ *n*

com·mu·ta·tor \'käm-yə-ˌtā-tər\ *n* : a device (as on a generator or motor) for changing the direction of electric current

¹**com·mute** \kə-'myüt\ *vb* **com·mut·ed; com·mut·ing** **1** ♦ : to give in exchange for another : EXCHANGE **2** : to revoke (a sentence) and impose a milder penalty **3** : to travel back and forth regularly — **com·mut·er** *n*

♦ change, exchange, shift, substitute, swap, switch, trade — more at CHANGE

²**commute** *n* : a trip made in commuting

comp *abbr* **1** comparative; compare **2** compensation **3** compiled; compiler **4** composition; compositor **5** compound **6** comprehensive **7** comptroller

¹**com·pact** \kəm-'pakt, 'käm-ˌpakt\ *adj* **1** ♦ : having a dense structure or parts or units closely packed or joined : SOLID, DENSE **2** ♦ : not diffuse or verbose : BRIEF, SUCCINCT **3** ♦ : occupying a small volume by efficient use of space ⟨a ∼ formation of troops⟩

♦ [1] dense, firm, hard, rigid, solid, stiff, unyielding — more at FIRM ♦ [2] brief, compendious, concise, crisp, epigrammatic, laconic, pithy, succinct, summary, terse — more at CONCISE ♦ [3] close, crowded, dense, packed, serried, thick, tight — more at CLOSE

²**compact** *vb* **1** ♦ : to pack together : COMPRESS **2** : to knit or draw together : CONSOLIDATE — **com·pac·tor** \kəm-'pak-tər, 'käm-ˌpak-\ *n*

♦ compress, condense, constrict, contract, squeeze — more at COMPRESS

³**com·pact** \'käm-ˌpakt\ *n* **1** : a small case for cosmetics **2** : a small automobile

⁴**com·pact** \'käm-ˌpakt\ *n* ♦ : an agreement or covenant between two or more parties

♦ accord, agreement, bargain, contract, convention, covenant, deal, pact, settlement, understanding — more at AGREEMENT

com·pact disc \'käm-ˌpakt-\ *n* : CD

com·pact·ly *adv* ♦ : in a compact manner

♦ concisely, crisply, laconically, shortly, succinctly, summarily, tersely — more at SHORTLY

com·pact·ness *n* ♦ : the quality or state of being compact

♦ brevity, briefness, conciseness, crispness, succinctness, terseness — more at SUCCINCTNESS

com·pa·dre \kəm-'pä-drā\ *n* ♦ : a close friend : BUDDY

♦ buddy, chum, comrade, crony, familiar, friend, intimate, pal — more at FRIEND

¹**com·pan·ion** \kəm-'pan-yən\ *n* [ME *compainoun*, fr. AF *cumpaing, cumpaignun*, fr. LL *companion-, compartio*, fr. L *com-* together + *panis* bread] **1 a** ♦ : one that accompanies another : COMRADE **b** ♦ : an intimate friend or associate **2** ♦ : one that is closely connected with something similar

♦ [1a, 1b] associate, cohort, comrade, crony, fellow, mate — more at ASSOCIATE ♦ [2] half, match, mate, twin — more at MATE

²**companion** *n* : COMPANIONWAY

com·pan·ion·able *adj* ♦ : marked by, conducive to, or suggestive of companionship

♦ amicable, comradely, cordial, friendly, genial, hearty, neighborly, warm, warmhearted — more at FRIENDLY

♦ boon, convivial, extroverted, gregarious, outgoing, sociable, social — more at CONVIVIAL

com·pan·ion·ship *n* ♦ : the fellowship existing among companions : COMPANY

♦ camaraderie, company, comradeship, fellowship, society; *also* amity, benevolence, cordiality, friendliness, friendship, goodwill, kindliness, civility, comity, concord, harmony, rapport; charity, generosity; affinity, compassion, empathy, sympathy; chumminess, familiarity, inseparability, intimacy, nearness; affection, devotion, fondness, love

com·pan·ion·way *n* : a ship's stairway from one deck to another

com·pa·ny \'kəm-pə-nē\ *n, pl* **-nies** **1** ♦ : association with another or others : FELLOWSHIP; *also* : COMPANIONS **2** : GUESTS **3** ♦ : a group of persons or things **4** : an infantry unit consisting of two or more platoons and normally commanded by a captain **5** : a group of musical or dramatic performers **6** : the officers and crew of a ship **7** ♦ : an association of persons for carrying on a business

♦ [1] camaraderie, companionship, comradeship, fellowship, society — more at COMPANIONSHIP ♦ [3] band, crew, gang, outfit, party, squad, team — more at GANG ♦ [7] business, concern, enterprise, establishment, firm, house, outfit — more at ENTERPRISE

com·pa·ra·ble \'käm-pə-rə-bəl, -prə-\ *adj* ♦ : capable of being compared — **com·pa·ra·bil·i·ty** \ˌkäm-pə-rə-'bi-lə-tē\ *n*

♦ akin, alike, analogous, correspondent, like, parallel, similar, such — more at ALIKE

¹com·par·a·tive \kəm-'par-ə-tiv\ *adj* **1** : of, relating to, or constituting the degree of grammatical comparison that denotes increase in quality, quantity, or relation **2** ♦ : considered as if in comparison to something else as a standard not quite attained : RELATIVE ⟨a ∼ stranger⟩ — **com·par·a·tive·ly** *adv*

♦ approximate, near, relative; *also* alike, comparable, similar; equal, equivalent *Ant* absolute, complete, downright, out-and-out, outright, perfect, pure, unqualified

²comparative *n* : the comparative degree or form in a language

¹com·pare \kəm-'par\ *vb* **com·pared; com·par·ing** **1** ♦ : to represent as similar : LIKEN **2 a** : to examine for likenesses and differences **b** ♦ : to view in relation to **3** : to inflect or modify (an adjective or adverb) according to the degrees of comparison

♦ [1] bracket, equate, liken; *also* associate, connect, couple, link; allude, refer, relate; equal, match, parallel *Ant* contrast ♦ *usu* **compare with** [2b] approach, approximate, measure up, stack up — more at APPROXIMATE

²compare *n* : the possibility of comparing ⟨beauty beyond ∼⟩

com·par·i·son \kəm-'par-ə-sən\ *n* **1** : the act of comparing **2** : change in the form of an adjective or adverb to show different levels of quality, quantity, or relation

com·part·ment \kəm-'pärt-mənt\ *n* **1** : a separate division **2** ♦ : a part of an enclosed space

♦ bay, cabin, cell, chamber, cubicle; *also* cubbyhole, pigeonhole; alcove, niche, nook, recess; cabinet, drawer; cavity, hole, hollow; booth, crib, stall; crypt, vault

com·part·men·tal·ise *Brit var of* COMPARTMENTALIZE

com·part·men·tal·ize \kəm-ˌpärt-'ment-ᵊl-ˌīz\ *vb* **-ized; -iz·ing** : to separate into compartments

¹com·pass \'kəm-pəs, 'käm-\ *vb* [ME, fr. OF *compasser* to measure, fr. (assumed) VL *compassare* to pace off, fr. L *com-* + *passus* pace] **1** : CONTRIVE, PLOT **2** ♦ : to lie around : ENCIRCLE **3** ♦ : to bring about : ACHIEVE

♦ [2] circle, circumnavigate, coil, encircle, girdle, loop, orbit, ring, round — more at ENCIRCLE ♦ [3] accomplish, achieve, carry out, commit, do, execute, follow through, fulfill, make, perform — more at PERFORM

²compass *n* **1** ♦ : an often rounded or curved boundary limit : BOUNDARY, CIRCUMFERENCE **2** : an enclosed space **3** ♦ : range or limit of perception, knowledge, interest, or concern : RANGE, SCOPE **4** : a device for determining direction by means of a magnetic needle swinging freely and pointing to the magnetic north; *also* : a nonmagnetic device that indicates direction **5** : an instrument for drawing circles or transferring measurements consisting of two legs joined by a pivot

♦ [1] border, bound, boundary, circumference, confines, edge, end, fringe, margin, perimeter, periphery, rim, skirt, verge — more at BORDER ♦ [3] amplitude, breadth, extent, range, reach, realm, scope, sweep, width — more at RANGE

com·pas·sion \kəm-'pa-shən\ *n* ♦ : sympathetic feeling : PITY, MERCY

♦ charity, commiseration, feeling, heart, humanity, kindliness, kindness, mercy, pity, sympathy

com·pas·sion·ate \-shə-nət\ *adj* ♦ : having or showing compassion — **com·pas·sion·ate·ly** *adv*

♦ beneficent, benevolent, good-hearted, humane, kind, kindly, sympathetic, tender, tenderhearted, warmhearted — more at HUMANE

com·pat·i·bil·i·ty \-ˌpa-tə-'bi-lə-tē\ *n* ♦ : the quality or state of being compatible

♦ concord, harmony, peace — more at HARMONY

com·pat·i·ble \kəm-'pa-tə-bəl\ *adj* ♦ : able to exist or act together harmoniously ⟨∼ colors⟩ ⟨∼ drugs⟩

♦ agreeable, amicable, congenial, harmonious, kindred, unanimous, united — more at HARMONIOUS ♦ conformable (to), congruous, consistent, consonant, correspondent, harmonious — more at CONSISTENT

com·pa·tri·ot \kəm-'pā-trē-ət, -ˌät\ *n* : a fellow countryman

com·peer \'käm-ˌpir\ *n* : EQUAL, PEER

com·pel \kəm-'pel\ *vb* **com·pelled; com·pel·ling** ♦ : to drive or urge with force

♦ coerce, constrain, drive, force, make, muscle, obligate, oblige, press, pressure — more at FORCE

compelling *adj* **1** : demanding and holding one's attention ⟨a ∼ novel⟩ **2** ♦ : tending to convince or convert by or as if by forcefulness of evidence

♦ cogent, conclusive, convincing, decisive, effective, forceful, persuasive, satisfying, strong, telling — more at COGENT

com·pen·di·ous \kəm-'pen-dē-əs\ *adj* **1** ♦ : marked by brief expression of a comprehensive matter : concise and comprehensive **2** ♦ : covering completely or broadly : COMPREHENSIVE

♦ [1] brief, compact, concise, crisp, epigrammatic, laconic, pithy, succinct, summary, terse — more at CONCISE ♦ [2] complete, comprehensive, encyclopedic, full, global, inclusive, omnibus, panoramic, universal — more at ENCYCLOPEDIC

com·pen·di·um \kəm-'pen-dē-əm\ *n, pl* **-di·ums** *or* **-dia** \-ə\ **1** : a brief summary of a larger work or of a field of knowledge **2** : COLLECTION

com·pen·sate \'käm-pən-ˌsāt\ *vb* **-sat·ed; -sat·ing** **1 a** : to be equivalent to **b** ♦ : to make up for : COUNTERBALANCE **2** ♦ : to make an appropriate and usu. counterbalancing payment to : PAY, REMUNERATE — **com·pen·sa·to·ry** \kəm-'pen-sə-ˌtōr-ē\ *adj*

♦ *usu* **compensate for** [1b] annul, cancel, correct, counteract, counterbalance, make up, neutralize, offset — more at OFFSET ♦ [2] indemnify, pay, recompense, recoup, remunerate, requite; *also* refund, reimburse, repay; redress, remedy, repair

com·pen·sa·tion \ˌkäm-pən-'sā-shən\ *n* **1** ♦ : the act or action of making up, making good, or counterbalancing : rendering equal **2** ♦ : something that constitutes an equivalent or recompense

♦ [1] disbursement, payment, remittance, remuneration — more at PAYMENT ♦ [2] damages, indemnity, quittance, recompense, redress, remuneration, reparation, requital, restitution, satisfaction; *also* amends, atonement, expiation; refund, reimbursement, repayment; adjustment, settlement; punishment, reprisal, retaliation ♦ [2] consideration, pay, payment, remittance, remuneration, requital — more at PAYMENT

com·pete \kəm-ˈpēt\ vb **com·pet·ed; com·pet·ing** ♦ : to seek or strive for something (as a position, possession, reward) for which others are also contending : CONTEND, VIE

♦ battle, contend, fight, race, vie; also challenge, engage, play; jockey, maneuver; go out, try out; train, work

com·pe·tence \ˈkäm-pə-təns\ n **1** : adequate means for subsistence **2** ♦ : the quality or state of being functionally adequate or of having sufficient knowledge, judgment, skill, or strength : ABILITY

♦ ability, capability, capacity, faculty — more at ABILITY

com·pe·ten·cy \-tən-sē\ n, pl **-cies** : the quality or state of being competent

com·pe·tent \-tənt\ adj ♦ : having requisite or adequate ability or qualities : CAPABLE, FIT, QUALIFIED

♦ able, capable, fit, good, qualified, suitable; also accomplished, ace, adept, experienced, expert, master, masterful, masterly, practiced, proficient, seasoned, skilled, skillful, veteran; prepared, schooled, trained **Ant** incompetent, inept, poor, unfit, unqualified

com·pe·ti·tion \ˌkäm-pə-ˈti-shən\ n **1** : the act of competing : RIVALRY **2 a** ♦ : a contest between rivals : CONTEST, MATCH **b** : one that competes; also : one's competitors — **com·pet·i·tive** \kəm-ˈpe-tə-tiv\ adj — **com·pet·i·tive·ly** adv — **com·pet·i·tive·ness** n

♦ bout, contest, event, game, match, meet, tournament — more at GAME

com·pet·i·tor \kəm-ˈpe-tə-tər\ n ♦ : one that competes : RIVAL

♦ challenger, competition, contender, contestant, rival; also finalist, semifinalist; entrant, player; adversary, antagonist, opponent

com·pi·la·tion \ˌkäm-pə-ˈlā-shən\ n ♦ : something that is a product of the putting together of two or more items

♦ album, anthology, miscellany — more at ANTHOLOGY

com·pile \kəm-ˈpīl\ vb **com·piled; com·pil·ing** [ME, fr. MF compiler, fr. L compilare to plunder] **1** : to compose out of materials from other documents **2** : to collect and edit into a volume **3** : to translate (a computer program) with a compiler **4** : to build up gradually ⟨∼ a record of four wins and two losses⟩

com·pil·er \kəm-ˈpī-lər\ n **1** : one that compiles **2** : a computer program that translates any program correctly written in a specific programming language into machine language

com·pla·cence \kəm-ˈplās-ᵊns\ n ♦ : the quality or state of being self-satisfied

♦ conceit, ego, egotism, pride, self-conceit, self-esteem, self-importance, self-satisfaction, smugness, vainglory, vanity; also assurance, confidence, self-assurance, self-confidence; egoism, self-centeredness, selfishness; self-respect **Ant** humbleness, humility, modesty

com·pla·cen·cy \-ᵊn-sē\ n, pl **-cies** **1** : SATISFACTION **2** : the quality or state of being self-satisfied

com·pla·cent \-ᵊnt\ adj ♦ : marked by complacency : SELF-SATISFIED — **com·pla·cent·ly** adv

♦ conceited, egotistic, important, overweening, pompous, prideful, proud, self-important, self-satisfied, smug, stuck-up, vain — more at CONCEITED

com·plain \kəm-ˈplān\ vb **1** ♦ : to express grief, pain, or discontent **2** : to make a formal accusation

♦ beef, bellyache, carp, crab, croak, fuss, gripe, grouse, growl, grumble, kick, moan, murmur, mutter, repine, squawk, wail, whine; also object (to); protest, quarrel (with); cavil, quibble; fret, stew, worry; blubber, cry, sob; bemoan, bewail, deplore, lament **Ant** rejoice

com·plain·ant n **1** : the party who makes the complaint in a legal action or proceeding : **2** : one who complains

com·plain·er n ♦ : one that complains

♦ bear, crab, crank, curmudgeon, grouch, grumbler, whiner — more at GROUCH

com·plaint \kəm-ˈplānt\ n **1** ♦ : expression of grief, pain, or dissatisfaction **2** ♦ : a bodily ailment or disease **3** ♦ : a formal accusation against a person

♦ [1] challenge, demur, expostulation, fuss, kick, objection, protest, question, remonstrance — more at OBJECTION ♦ [1] beef, fuss, grievance, gripe, grumble, murmur, plaint, squawk; also challenge, demur, expostulation, kick, objection, protest, quibble, remonstrance ♦ [2] ailment, complication, condition, disease, disorder, fever, ill, illness, infirmity, malady, sickness, trouble — more at DISEASE ♦ [3] charge, count, indictment, rap — more at CHARGE

com·plai·sance \kəm-ˈplās-ᵊns, ˌkäm-plā-ˈzans\ n [F] : disposition to please — **com·plai·sant** \-ᵊnt, -ˈzant\ adj

com·pleat \kəm-ˈplēt\ adj : PROFICIENT

com·plect·ed \kəm-ˈplek-təd\ adj : having a specified facial complexion ⟨dark-*complected*⟩

¹com·ple·ment \ˈkäm-plə-mənt\ n **1 a** : something that fills up or completes **b** : the full quantity, number, or amount that makes a thing complete **2** : an added word by which a predicate is made complete **3** : a group of proteins in blood that combines with antibodies to destroy antigens

²com·ple·ment \-ˌment\ vb : to be complementary to : fill out

com·ple·men·ta·ry \ˌkäm-plə-ˈmen-t(ə-)rē\ adj : serving to fill out or complete : being complements of each other

complementary medicine n : ALTERNATIVE MEDICINE

¹com·plete \kəm-ˈplēt\ adj **com·plet·er; -est** **1** : having all parts or elements **2** ♦ : brought to an end **3** ♦ : fully carried out **4** : fully realized : carried to the ultimate : ABSOLUTE **2** ⟨∼ silence⟩ — **com·plete·ness** n — **com·ple·tion** \-ˈplē-shən\ n

♦ [1] compendious, comprehensive, encyclopedic, full, global, inclusive, omnibus, panoramic, universal — more at ENCYCLOPEDIC ♦ [1] comprehensive, entire, full, grand, intact, integral, perfect, plenary, total, whole; also unabridged, uncut, undiminished; all-out, exhaustive, extensive; full-blown, full-fledged, full-scale **Ant** imperfect, incomplete, partial ♦ [2] done, down, over, through, up; also accomplished, achieved, attained, compassed, realized; dead, defunct, extinct, obsolete; expired **Ant** continuing, incomplete, ongoing, unfinished ♦ [3] all-out, clean, comprehensive, exhaustive, full-scale, out-and-out, thorough, thoroughgoing, total — more at EXHAUSTIVE

²complete vb **com·plet·ed; com·plet·ing** **1** ♦ : to bring to an end and esp. into a perfected state : FINISH **2** ♦ : to make whole or perfect ⟨the hat ∼s the outfit⟩

♦ [1, 2] consummate, finalize, finish, perfect — more at FINISH

com·plete·ly adv **1** ♦ : so as to be complete : FULLY **2** ♦ : to a complete degree

♦ [1, 2] altogether, dead, entirely, fast, flat, full, fully, perfectly, quite, thoroughly, well, wholly — more at FULLY

¹com·plex \ˈkäm-ˌpleks\ n **1** : a whole made up of or involving intricately interrelated elements **2** : a group of repressed desires and memories that exert a dominating influence on one's personality and behavior ⟨a guilt ∼⟩ **3** ♦ : a building or group of buildings housing related units

♦ establishment, facility, installation — more at FACILITY

²com·plex \käm-ˈpleks, ˈkäm-ˌpleks\ adj **1** ♦ : composed of two or more parts **2** : consisting of a main clause and one or more subordinate clauses ⟨∼ sentence⟩ **3** ♦ : hard to separate, analyze, solve, or do **4** ♦ : marked by an involvement of many parts, aspects, or details necessitating careful study or attention — **com·plex·ly** adv

♦ [1, 4] complicated, convoluted, elaborate, intricate, involved, knotty, sophisticated; also composite, compound, heterogeneous, mixed, multifarious, varied; challenging, difficult, tough; impenetrable, incomprehensible, inexplicable, unfathomable, unintelligible *Ant* plain, simple ♦ [3] complicated, detailed, elaborate, fancy, intricate, involved, sophisticated

complex fraction *n* : a fraction with a fraction or mixed number in the numerator or denominator or both

com·plex·ion \kəm-ˈplek-shən\ *n* 1 : the hue or appearance of the skin esp. of the face 2 ♦ : overall aspect or character — **com·plex·ioned** \-shənd\ *adj*

♦ character, constitution, genius, nature, personality, tone — more at NATURE

com·plex·i·ty \käm-ˈplek-sə-tē\ *n* 1 ♦ : something complex 2 ♦ : the quality or state of being complex

♦ [1] complication, difficulty, intricacy — more at COMPLICATION ♦ [2] elaborateness, intricacy, sophistication; *also* diversity; impenetrability *Ant* plainness, simpleness, simplicity

complex number *n* : a number of the form $a + b\sqrt{-1}$ where a and b are real numbers

com·pli·ance \kəm-ˈplī-əns\ *n* 1 ♦ : the act of complying to a demand or proposal 2 ♦ : a disposition to yield

♦ [1] conformity, obedience, observance, submission, subordination — more at OBEDIENCE ♦ [2] deference, docility, obedience; *also* amiability, complaisance; servility, subservience, subserviency; conformity; receptiveness, receptivity; humoring, indulgence; acceptance, acquiescence, assent, consent; capitulation, submission, surrender; affability, amicability, congeniality, cordiality, friendliness, geniality, sociability *Ant* defiance, disobedience, recalcitrance

com·pli·ant \-ənt\ *adj* ♦ : ready or disposed to comply

♦ amenable, conformable, docile, obedient, submissive, tractable — more at OBEDIENT

com·pli·cate \ˈkäm-plə-ˌkāt\ *vb* **-cat·ed; -cat·ing** : to make or become complex or intricate

com·pli·cat·ed \ˈkäm-plə-ˌkā-təd\ *adj* 1 ♦ : consisting of parts intricately combined 2 : difficult to analyze, understand, or explain 3 : not simple or easy to fabricate or comprehend ⟨a ∼ issue⟩ — **com·pli·cat·ed·ly** *adv*

♦ complex, convoluted, detailed, elaborate, intricate, involved, knotty, sophisticated — more at COMPLEX

com·pli·ca·tion \ˌkäm-plə-ˈkā-shən\ *n* 1 a : the quality or state of being complicated b ♦ : a complex feature 2 ♦ : a disease or condition that develops during and affects the course of a primary disease or condition

♦ [1b] complexity, difficulty, intricacy; *also* aftereffect, ramification, side effect; subtlety, technicality; annoyance, bother, headache, inconvenience, matter, trouble ♦ [2] ailment, bug, complaint, condition, disease, disorder, fever, ill, illness, infirmity, malady, sickness, trouble — more at DISEASE

com·plic·i·ty \kəm-ˈpli-sə-tē\ *n, pl* **-ties** : the state of being an accomplice

¹**com·pli·ment** \ˈkäm-plə-ment\ *n* 1 : an expression of approval or admiration; *esp* : a flattering remark 2 *pl* ♦ : best wishes : REGARDS

♦ *usu* **compliments** greetings, regards, respects; *also* approval, blessing, endorsement; acknowledgement, citation, commendation; adulation, flattery, praise

²**com·pli·ment** \-ˌment\ *vb* : to pay a compliment to

com·pli·men·ta·ry \ˌkäm-plə-ˈmen-t(ə-)rē\ *adj* 1 ♦ : containing or expressing a compliment 2 ♦ : given free as a courtesy ⟨∼ ticket⟩

♦ [1] appreciative, favorable (*or* favourable), friendly, good, positive — more at FAVORABLE ♦ [2] free, gratuitous — more at FREE

com·ply \kəm-ˈplī\ *vb* **com·plied; com·ply·ing** ♦ : to conform, submit, or adapt (as to a regulation or to another's wishes) as required or requested

♦ *usu* **comply with** conform, follow, mind, obey, observe — more at OBEY ♦ *usu* **comply with** answer, fill, fulfill, keep, meet, redeem, satisfy — more at FULFILL

¹**com·po·nent** \kəm-ˈpō-nənt, ˈkäm-ˌpō-\ *n* ♦ : a component part

♦ constituent, element, factor, ingredient, member — more at ELEMENT

²**component** *adj* : serving to form a part of : CONSTITUENT

com·port \kəm-ˈpōrt\ *vb* 1 ♦ : to be fitting : AGREE, ACCORD 2 ♦ : to behave in a manner conformable to what is right, proper, or expected : CONDUCT

♦ [1] accord, agree, answer, check, coincide, conform, correspond, dovetail, fit, go, harmonize, jibe, square, tally — more at CHECK ♦ [2] acquit, bear, behave, conduct, demean, deport, quit — more at BEHAVE

com·port·ment *n* ♦ : manner of bearing : DEMEANOR

♦ actions, bearing, behavior (*or* behaviour), conduct, demeanor (*or* demeanour), deportment — more at BEHAVIOR

com·pose \kəm-ˈpōz\ *vb* **com·posed; com·pos·ing** 1 a : to form by putting together b ♦ : to form the substance of 2 ♦ : to produce (as pages of type) by composition 3 : ADJUST, ARRANGE 4 ♦ : to free from agitation : CALM, QUIET 5 : to practice composition ⟨∼ music⟩

♦ [1b] comprise, constitute, form, make up — more at CONSTITUTE ♦ [2] cast, craft, draft, draw, formulate, frame, prepare; *also* fabricate, fashion, form, mold, sculpture, shape; couch, express, phrase, state, verbalize, word; author, pen, write; conceive, concoct, devise; build, construct, make; assemble, compound, piece (together) ♦ [4] allay, calm, quiet, settle, soothe, still, tranquilize — more at CALM ♦ [4] calm, collect, control, settle — more at COLLECT

composed *adj* ♦ : free from agitation

♦ calm, collected, cool, placid, self-possessed, serene, tranquil, undisturbed, unperturbed, unshaken, untroubled, unworried — more at CALM

com·pos·er *n* : one that composes : a person who writes music

¹**com·pos·ite** \käm-ˈpä-zət\ *adj* 1 : made up of distinct parts or elements 2 : of, relating to, or being a large family of flowering plants (as a daisy or aster) that bear many small flowers united into compact heads resembling single flowers

²**composite** *n* 1 ♦ : something composite 2 : a plant of the composite family

♦ admixture, amalgam, blend, combination, compound, fusion, intermixture, mix, mixture — more at BLEND

com·po·si·tion \ˌkäm-pə-ˈzi-shən\ *n* 1 a : the act or process of composing b ♦ : arrangement esp. in artistic form 2 : the arrangement or production of type for printing 3 : general makeup 4 : a product of mixing various elements or ingredients 5 a ♦ : a literary, musical, or artistic product b ♦ : a brief piece of writing : ESSAY

♦ [1b] arrangement, configuration, design, form, format, layout, makeup, pattern; *also* motif, theme ♦ [5a] opus, piece, work; *also* classic, magnum opus, masterpiece, pièce de résistance, showpiece; model, outline, sketch; étude ♦ [5b] article, essay, paper, theme — more at ESSAY

com·pos·i·tor \kəm-ˈpä-zə-tər\ *n* : one who sets type

com·post \ˈkäm-ˌpōst\ *n* : a fertilizing material consisting largely of decayed organic matter

com·po·sure \kəm-ˈpō-zhər\ *n* ♦ : a calmness or repose esp. of mind, bearing, or appearance : CALMNESS, SELF-POSSESSION

♦ aplomb, calmness, coolness, equanimity, placidity, self-possession, serenity, tranquility — more at EQUANIMITY

com·pote \ˈkäm-ˌpōt\ *n* 1 : fruits cooked in syrup 2 : a bowl (as of glass) usu. with a base and stem for serving esp. fruit or compote

¹**com·pound** \käm-ˈpaund, ˈkäm-ˌ\ *vb* [ME *compounen*, fr. AF **cumpundre*, fr. L *componere*, fr. *com-* together + *ponere* to put] 1 ♦ : to put together (parts) so as to form

a whole : COMBINE **2** : to form by combining parts ⟨∼ a medicine⟩ **3** : SETTLE ⟨∼ a dispute⟩; *also* : to refrain from prosecuting (an offense) in return for a consideration **4 a** : to increase (as interest) by an amount that can itself vary **b ♦** : to add to

♦ [1] chain, combine, connect, couple, hitch, hook, join, link, yoke — more at CONNECT ♦ [4b] add, aggrandize, amplify, augment, boost, enlarge, escalate, expand, extend, increase, multiply, raise, swell, up — more at INCREASE

²com·pound \'käm-ˌpaúnd\ *adj* **1** : made up of individual parts **2** : composed of united similar parts esp. of a kind usu. independent ⟨a ∼ plant ovary⟩ **3** : formed by the combination of two or more otherwise independent elements ⟨∼ sentence⟩

³com·pound \'käm-ˌpaúnd\ *n* **1** : a word consisting of parts that are words **2 ♦** : something formed from a union of elements or parts; *esp* : a distinct substance formed by the union of two or more chemical elements

♦ admixture, amalgam, blend, combination, composite, fusion, intermixture, mix, mixture — more at BLEND

⁴com·pound \'käm-ˌpaúnd\ *n* [by folk etymology fr. Malay *kampung* group of buildings, village] : an enclosure containing buildings

compound interest *n* : interest computed on the sum of an original principal and accrued interest

com·pre·hend \ˌkäm-pri-'hend\ *vb* **1 ♦** : to grasp the nature, significance, or meaning of : UNDERSTAND **2 ♦** : to contain or hold within a total scope, significance, or amount : INCLUDE — **com·pre·hen·si·ble** \-'hen-sə-bəl\ *adj*

♦ [1] appreciate, apprehend, catch, catch on (to), get, grasp, make, make out, perceive, see, seize, understand; *also* absorb, assimilate, digest, take in; know, realize, sense; fathom, penetrate *Ant* miss ♦ [2] carry, contain, embrace, encompass, entail, include, involve, number, take in — more at INCLUDE

com·pre·hen·sion \-'hen-chən\ *n* ♦ : knowledge gained by comprehending

♦ appreciation, apprehension, grasp, grip, perception, understanding; *also* absorption, assimilation, uptake; conception, visualization; awareness, consciousness, realization

com·pre·hen·sive \-siv\ *adj* ♦ : covering completely or broadly : covering all possibilities — **com·pre·hen·sive·ly** *adv* — **com·pre·hen·sive·ness** *n*

♦ compendious, complete, encyclopedic, full, global, inclusive, omnibus, panoramic, universal — more at ENCYCLOPEDIC ♦ complete, entire, full, grand, intact, integral, perfect, plenary, total, whole — more at COMPLETE

¹com·press \kəm-'pres\ *vb* **1 ♦** : to press or squeeze together **2 ♦** : to reduce in size, quantity, or volume as if by squeezing — **com·pres·sor** \-'pre-sər\ *n*

♦ [1] condense, constrict, contract, shrink — more at CONTRACT ♦ [2] compact, condense, constrict, contract, squeeze; *also* cram, crowd; jam, jam-pack, pack; abbreviate, abridge, curtail, shorten; downsize, shrink; concentrate, consolidate; simplify, streamline; decrease, diminish, lessen *Ant* expand, open, outspread

²com·press \'käm-ˌpres\ *n* : a folded pad or cloth used to press upon a body part

compressed air *n* : air under pressure greater than that of the atmosphere

com·pres·sion \-'pre-shən\ *n* **1 ♦** : the act or process of compressing **2** : the process of compressing the fuel mixture in an internal combustion engine **3** : conversion (as of data) in order to reduce the space occupied or the bandwidth required

♦ condensation, constriction, contraction; *also* abbreviation, abridgment, curtailment, shortening; concentration, consolidation; simplification; decreasing, lessening *Ant* expansion

com·prise \kəm-'prīz\ *vb* **com·prised; com·pris·ing** **1** : IN-

CLUDE, CONTAIN **2** : to consist of : to be made up of **3 ♦** : to make up : COMPOSE, CONSTITUTE

♦ compose, constitute, form, make up — more at CONSTITUTE

¹com·pro·mise \'käm-prə-ˌmīz\ *n* ♦ : a settlement of differences reached by mutual concessions

♦ accommodation, concession, give-and-take, negotiation — more at CONCESSION

²compromise *vb* **-mised; -mis·ing** **1** : to settle by compromise **2 a** : to expose to suspicion or loss of reputation **b ♦** : to put in jeopardy : endanger by some act that cannot be recalled

♦ adventure, gamble with, hazard, imperil, jeopardize, menace, risk, venture

comp·trol·ler \kən-'trō-lər, 'kämp-ˌtrō-\ *n* : an official who audits and supervises expenditures and accounts

com·pul·sion \kəm-'pəl-shən\ *n* **1 ♦** : an act of compelling **2** : a force that compels **3** : an irresistible persistent impulse to perform an act

♦ coercion, constraint, duress, force, pressure — more at FORCE

com·pul·sive \-siv\ *adj* : of, having to do with, caused by, or suggestive of psychological compulsion or obsession

com·pul·so·ry \-sə-rē\ *adj* ♦ : demanded, directed, or designated by authority

♦ imperative, incumbent, involuntary, mandatory, necessary, nonelective, obligatory, peremptory — more at MANDATORY

com·punc·tion \kəm-'pəŋk-shən\ *n* ♦ : anxiety arising from guilt

♦ misgiving, qualm, scruple — more at QUALM

com·pu·ta·tion \ˌkäm-pyù-'tā-shən\ *n* ♦ : the act or action of computing — **com·pu·ta·tion·al** *adj*

♦ arithmetic, calculation, reckoning — more at CALCULATION

com·pute \kəm-'pyüt\ *vb* **com·put·ed; com·put·ing** ♦ : to determine or ascertain esp. by mathematical means : arrive at an answer to or sum for : CALCULATE, RECKON

♦ calculate, figure, reckon, work out — more at CALCULATE

computed tomography *n* : radiography in which a three-dimensional image of a body structure is constructed by computer from a series of plane cross-sectional images made along an axis

com·put·er \kəm-'pyü-tər\ *n* : a programmable electronic device that can store, retrieve, and process data

com·put·er·ise *chiefly Brit var of* COMPUTERIZE

com·put·er·ize \kəm-'pyü-tə-ˌrīz\ *vb* **-ized; -iz·ing** **1** : to carry out, control, or produce by means of a computer **2** : to provide with computers **3** : to store in a computer; *also* : put into a form that a computer can use — **com·put·er·iza·tion** \-ˌpyü-tə-rə-'zā-shən\ *n*

computerized axial tomography *n* : COMPUTED TOMOGRAPHY

com·rade \'käm-ˌrad\ *n* [MF *comarade* group sleeping in one room, roommate, companion, fr. Sp *camarada*, fr. *câmara* room, fr. LL *camera*] ♦ : an intimate friend or associate : COMPANION, ASSOCIATE

♦ associate, cohort, companion, crony, fellow, mate — more at ASSOCIATE ♦ buddy, chum, crony, familiar, friend, intimate, pal — more at FRIEND

com·rade·ly *adj* ♦ : of or like a comrade or partner

♦ amicable, companionable, cordial, friendly, genial, hearty, neighborly, warm, warmhearted — more at FRIENDLY

com·rade·ship *n* ♦ : association as comrades

♦ camaraderie, companionship, company, fellowship, society — more at COMPANIONSHIP

¹con \'kän\ *vb* **conned; con·ning** **1** : to commit to memory by vocal or mental repetition : MEMORIZE **2** : STUDY

²con *adv* : in opposition : AGAINST

³**con** *n* : an opposing argument, person, or position ⟨pros and ∼*s*⟩
⁴**con** *vb* **conned; con·ning** 1 : SWINDLE 2 : PERSUADE, CAJOLE
⁵**con** *n* : CONVICT
conc *abbr* concentrated
con·cat·e·nate \kän-'ka-tə-ˌnāt\ *vb* **-nat·ed; -nat·ing** : to link together in a series or chain — **con·cat·e·na·tion** \(ˌ)kän-ˌka-tə-'nā-shən\ *n*
con·cave \kän-'kāv, 'kän-ˌ\ *adj* ♦ : curved or rounded inward like the inside of a bowl
   ♦ depressed, hollow, sunken — more at HOLLOW
con·cav·i·ty \kän-'ka-və-tē\ *n* ♦ : a concave line, surface, or space
   ♦ cavity, dent, depression, hole, hollow, indentation, pit, recess — more at HOLE
con·ceal \kən-'sēl\ *vb* ♦ : to place out of sight : HIDE
   ♦ bury, cache, ensconce, hide, secrete — more at HIDE
con·ceal·ment *n* 1 ♦ : the act or practice of concealing 2 ♦ : a hiding place
   ♦ [1] secretion; *also* burial, burying, entombment, interment, interring **Ant** display, exhibition, exposure, parading, showing ♦ [2] covert, den, hideout, lair, nest — more at HIDEOUT
con·cede \kən-'sēd\ *vb* **con·ced·ed; con·ced·ing** 1 ♦ : to admit to be true 2 ♦ : to make concession : GRANT, YIELD
   ♦ [1] acknowledge, admit, agree, allow, confess, grant, own — more at ADMIT ♦ [2] blink, bow, budge, capitulate, give in, grant, knuckle under, quit, submit, succumb, surrender, yield — more at YIELD
con·ceit \kən-'sēt\ *n* 1 ♦ : excessively high opinion of one's self or ability 2 : an elaborate or strained metaphor 3 ♦ : a fanciful idea
   ♦ [1] complacence, ego, egotism, pride, self-conceit, self-esteem, self-importance, self-satisfaction, smugness, vainglory, vanity ♦ [3] chimera, daydream, delusion, dream, fancy, fantasy, figment, hallucination, illusion, phantasm, pipe dream, unreality, vision
con·ceit·ed *adj* ♦ : having or showing an excessively high opinion of oneself — **con·ceit·ed·ly** *adv* — **con·ceit·ed·ness** *n*
   ♦ complacent, egotistic, important, overweening, pompous, prideful, proud, self-important, self-satisfied, smug, stuck-up, vain; *also* boastful, braggart, bragging; arrogant, cavalier, disdainful, haughty, lordly, self-assertive, snobbish, supercilious, superior, uppity; domineering, high-handed, imperious; highfalutin, pretentious; overconfident, presumptuous; confident, self-assured, self-confident; self-centered, selfish **Ant** humble, modest
con·ceiv·ably \-blē\ *adv* ♦ : it may be conceived : POSSIBLY
   ♦ maybe, perchance, perhaps, possibly — more at PERHAPS
con·ceive \kən-'sēv\ *vb* **con·ceived; con·ceiv·ing** 1 : to become pregnant or pregnant with ⟨∼ a child⟩ 2 ♦ : to form an idea of : IMAGINE — **con·ceiv·able** \-'sē-və-bəl\ *adj*
   ♦ dream, envisage, fancy, imagine, picture, vision, visualize — more at IMAGINE
con·cel·e·brant \kən-'se-lə-brənt\ *n* : one that jointly participates in celebrating the Eucharist
¹**con·cen·trate** \'kän-sən-ˌtrāt\ *vb* **-trat·ed; -trat·ing** 1 ♦ : to gather into one body, mass, or force 2 : to make less dilute 3 ♦ : to fix one's powers, efforts, or attentions
   ♦ [1] center (*or* centre), centralize, consolidate, unify, unite — more at CENTRALIZE ♦ [1] accumulate, amass, assemble, collect, garner, gather, group, lump, pick up, round up, scrape ♦ [3] fasten, focus, rivet, train; *also* aim, direct, level, point, zero (in on); attend, heed, mind
²**concentrate** *n* : something concentrated

concentrated *adj* 1 ♦ : rich in respect to a particular or essential element 2 ♦ : not scattered or dispersed
   ♦ [1] full, full-bodied, potent, rich, robust, strong — more at FULL-BODIED ♦ [2] all, entire, undivided, whole — more at WHOLE
con·cen·tra·tion \ˌkän-sən-'trā-shən\ *n* 1 ♦ : the act or process of concentrating : the state of being concentrated; *esp* : direction of attention on a single object 2 : the amount of a component in a given area or volume
   ♦ absorption, attention — more at ATTENTION
concentration camp *n* : a camp where persons (as prisoners of war or political prisoners) are confined
con·cen·tric \kən-'sen-trik\ *adj* 1 : having a common center ⟨∼ circles⟩ 2 : COAXIAL
¹**con·cept** \'kän-ˌsept\ *n* ♦ : something conceived in the mind : THOUGHT, NOTION, IDEA
   ♦ idea, image, impression, notion, picture, thought — more at IDEA
²**concept** *adj* 1 : organized around a main idea or theme ⟨a ∼ album⟩ 2 : created to illustrate a concept ⟨a ∼ car⟩
con·cep·tion \kən-'sep-shən\ *n* 1 : the process of conceiving or being conceived 2 : the power to form or understand ideas or concepts 3 : a general idea : CONCEPT 4 : the originating of something
con·cep·tu·al \kən-'sep-chə-wəl\ *adj* : of, relating to, or consisting of concepts — **con·cep·tu·al·ly** *adv*
con·cep·tu·al·ise *Brit var of* CONCEPTUALIZE
con·cep·tu·al·ize \-'sep-chə-wə-ˌlīz\ *vb* **-ized; -iz·ing** : to form a conception of
¹**con·cern** \kən-'sərn\ *vb* 1 ♦ : to relate to : be about ⟨the novel ∼*s* three soldiers⟩ 2 ♦ : to be the business of : INVOLVE 3 : ENGAGE, OCCUPY 4 ♦ : to be a care, trouble, or distress to
   ♦ [1] cover, deal, pertain, treat; *also* appertain (to), bear (on *or* upon), refer (to), relate (to); allude (to), glance (upon), mention, touch (upon); offer, present; contain, embrace, encompass, entail, include, incorporate ♦ [2] affect, interest, involve, touch; *also* apply (to), relate (to); embroil, ensnare, entangle, implicate ♦ [4] agitate, bother, discompose, disquiet, distress, disturb, exercise, freak out, perturb, undo, unhinge, unsettle, upset, worry
²**concern** *n* 1 ♦ : an uneasy state of blended interest, uncertainty, and apprehension : ANXIETY 2 : AFFAIR, MATTER 3 ♦ : a business organization
   ♦ [1] agitation, anxiety, apprehension, care, disquiet, nervousness, perturbation, uneasiness, worry — more at ANXIETY ♦ [3] business, company, enterprise, establishment, firm, house, outfit — more at ENTERPRISE
con·cerned *adj* 1 : ANXIOUS, UNEASY 2 : INVOLVED
con·cern·ing *prep* ♦ : relating to : REGARDING
   ♦ about, apropos of, of, on, regarding, respecting, toward — more at ABOUT
con·cern·ment \kən-'sərn-mənt\ *n* 1 : something in which one is concerned 2 : IMPORTANCE, CONSEQUENCE
¹**con·cert** \'kän-(ˌ)sərt\ *n* 1 : agreement in a plan or design 2 : a concerted action 3 : a public performance (as of music)
²**con·cert** \kən-'sərt\ *vb* 1 ♦ : to plan together 2 ♦ : to settle or adjust by conferring and reaching an agreement
   ♦ [1] collaborate, cooperate, join, team — more at CO-OPERATE ♦ [2] arrange, conclude, negotiate — more at NEGOTIATE
con·cert·ed \kən-'sər-təd\ *adj* 1 : mutually agreed on 2 ♦ : performed in unison
   ♦ collective, common, communal, conjoint, joint, mutual, public, united — more at COLLECTIVE
con·cer·ti·na \ˌkän-sər-'tē-nə\ *n* : an instrument of the accordion family
concertina wire *n* : a coiled wire with sharp points for use as an obstacle
con·cert·mas·ter \'kän-sərt-ˌmas-tər\ *or* **con·cert·meis·ter**

\-ˌmī-stər\ *n* : the leader of the first violins of an orchestra and assistant to the conductor

con·cer·to \kən-'cher-tō\ *n, pl* **-ti** \-(ˌ)tē\ *or* **-tos** [It] : a piece for one or more solo instruments and orchestra in three movements

con·ces·sion \kən-'se-shən\ *n* **1** ♦ : an act of conceding or yielding **2** ♦ : something yielded **3** : a grant by a government of land or of a right to use it **4** : a grant of a portion of premises for some specific purpose; *also* : the activities or enterprise carried on — **con·ces·sion·ary** \-'se-shə-ˌner-ē\ *adj*

♦ [1] acknowledgment, admission, avowal, confession — more at CONFESSION ♦ [1, 2] accommodation, compromise, give-and-take, negotiation; *also* arrangement, bargain, deal, understanding; agreement, settlement

con·ces·sion·aire \kən-ˌse-shə-'nar, -'ner\ *n* : one that owns or operates a concession

conch \'käŋk, 'känch\ *n, pl* **conchs** \'käŋks\ *or* **conch·es** \'kän-chəz\ : a large spiral-shelled marine gastropod mollusk; *also* : its shell

con·cierge \kōⁿ-'syerzh\ *n, pl* **con·cierges** *same or* -'syer-zhəz\ [F] **1** : a resident in an apartment building who performs services for the tenants **2** : a usu. multilingual hotel staff member who usu. handles mail and reservations

con·cil·i·ate \kən-'si-lē-ˌāt\ *vb* **-at·ed; -at·ing** **1** ♦ : to bring into agreement : RECONCILE **2** : to gain the goodwill of — **con·cil·i·a·tion** \-ˌsi-lē-'ā-shən\ *n*

♦ accommodate, conform, coordinate, harmonize, key, reconcile — more at HARMONIZE

con·cil·ia·to·ry \-'si-lē-ə-ˌtōr-ē\ *adj* ♦ : tending to conciliate

♦ pacific, propitiatory — more at PACIFIC

con·cise \kən-'sīs\ *adj* ♦ : expressing much in few words : BRIEF

♦ brief, compact, compendious, crisp, epigrammatic, laconic, pithy, succinct, summary, terse; *also* abrupt, blunt, brusque, curt, short, snippy; abbreviated, abridged, condensed, shortened; meaty, substantial; meaningful, significant *Ant* diffuse, long-winded, prolix, rambling, verbose, wordy

con·cise·ly *adv* ♦ : in a concise manner

♦ compactly, crisply, laconically, shortly, succinctly, summarily, tersely — more at SHORTLY

con·cise·ness *n* ♦ : the quality or state of being concise

♦ brevity, briefness, compactness, crispness, succinctness, terseness — more at SUCCINCTNESS

con·clave \'kän-ˌklāv\ *n* [ME, fr. ML, fr. L, room that can be locked, fr. *com-* together + *clavis* key] : a private gathering; *also* : CONVENTION

con·clude \kən-'klüd\ *vb* **con·clud·ed; con·clud·ing** **1** ♦ : to bring or come to a close : END **2 a** ♦ : to reach as a logically necessary end by reasoning : JUDGE **b** ♦ : to make a decision about : DECIDE **3** : to bring about as a result

♦ [1] close, end, finish, round, terminate, wind up, wrap up — more at CLOSE ♦ [2a] deduce, extrapolate, gather, infer, judge, reason, understand — more at INFER ♦ [2b] choose, decide, determine, figure, opt, resolve — more at DECIDE

con·clu·sion \kən-'klü-zhən\ *n* **1** ♦ : the logical consequence of a reasoning process **2** ♦ : the last part of anything : END **3** ♦ : a final decision or settlement : OUTCOME, RESULT

♦ [1, 3] aftermath, consequence, corollary, development, effect, issue, outcome, outgrowth, product, result, resultant, sequence, upshot — more at EFFECT ♦ [2] close, consummation, end, ending, finale, finis, finish, windup — more at FINALE

con·clu·sive \-siv\ *adj* ♦ : putting an end to debate or question esp. by reason of irrefutability — **con·clu·sive·ly** *adv*

♦ absolute, clear, decisive, definitive; *also* incontestable, incontrovertible, indisputable, indubitable, irrefutable, undeniable, unquestionable; unchallenged, uncontested, undisputed; unambiguous, unequivocal; certain, definite, positive, sure *Ant* inconclusive, indecisive, unclear

con·clu·sive·ness *adj* ♦ : the quality or state of being conclusive

♦ authority, cogency, effectiveness, force, persuasion, persuasiveness — more at COGENCY

con·coct \kən-'käkt, kän-\ *vb* **1** : to prepare by combining raw materials **2 a** ♦ : to formulate by thought **b** : to put together usu. for the purposes of deception : DEVISE

♦ contrive, cook up, devise, fabricate, invent, make up, manufacture, think up — more at INVENT

con·coc·tion \-'käk-shən\ *n* **1** ♦ : something that is concocted (as a food or scheme) **2** : something that suggests origin by concoction (as by mingling of diverse elements)

♦ coinage, contrivance, creation, innovation, invention, wrinkle — more at INVENTION

¹con·com·i·tant \-'kä-mə-tənt\ *adj* ♦ : accompanying esp. in a subordinate or incidental way

♦ attendant, coincident, concurrent — more at COINCIDENT

²concomitant *n* : something that accompanies or is collaterally connected with something else

con·cord \'kän-ˌkȯrd, 'käŋ-\ *n* ♦ : a state of agreement : HARMONY

♦ compatibility, harmony, peace — more at HARMONY

con·cor·dance \kən-'kȯr-dⁿns\ *n* **1** : an alphabetical index of words in a book or in an author's works with the passages in which they occur **2** : AGREEMENT, COVENANT

con·cor·dant \-dⁿnt\ *adj* ♦ : marked by accord in sentiment or action : HARMONIOUS

♦ compatible, conformable (to), congruous, consistent, consonant, correspondent, harmonious — more at CONSISTENT

con·cor·dat \kən-'kȯr-ˌdat\ *n* : CONCORDANCE 2

con·course \'kän-ˌkȯrs\ *n* **1** : a spontaneous coming together : GATHERING **2** : an open space or hall (as in a bus terminal) where crowds gather

¹con·crete \kän-'krēt, 'kän-ˌkrēt\ *adj* **1** : naming a real thing or class of things : not abstract **2** ♦ : not theoretical : ACTUAL **3** : made of or relating to concrete **4** ♦ : formed by coalition of particles into one solid mass

♦ [2] actual, existent, factual, real, true, very — more at ACTUAL ♦ [4] material, physical, substantial — more at MATERIAL

²con·crete \'kän-ˌkrēt, kän-'krēt\ *vb* **con·cret·ed; con·cret·ing** **1** : to form into a solid mass : SOLIDIFY **2** : to cover with concrete

³con·crete \'kän-ˌkrēt, kän-'krēt\ *n* : a hard building material made by mixing cement, sand, and gravel with water

con·cre·tion \kän-'krē-shən\ *n* : a hard mass esp. when formed abnormally in the body

con·cu·bine \'käŋ-kyù-ˌbīn\ *n* [ME, fr. MF, fr. L *concubina*, fr. *com-* with + *cubare* to lie] : a woman who is not legally a wife but lives with a man and sometimes has a recognized position in his household; *also* : MISTRESS — **con·cu·bi·nage** \kän-'kyü-bə-nij\ *n*

con·cu·pis·cence \kän-'kyü-pə-səns\ *n* : ardent sexual desire : LUST

con·cur \kən-'kər\ *vb* **con·curred; con·cur·ring** **1** : to act together **2** : to express agreement : AGREE **3** : to happen together : COINCIDE

con·cur·rence \-'kər-əns\ *n* **1** ♦ : agreement in action or opinion **2** : occurrence together

♦ accord, agreement, consensus, unanimity — more at AGREEMENT

con·cur·rent \-'kər-ənt\ *adj* **1** ♦ : happening or operating at the same time **2** : joint and equal in authority

♦ coeval, contemporary, simultaneous, synchronous — more at CONTEMPORARY ♦ attendant, coincident, concomitant — more at COINCIDENT

con·cus·sion \kən-'kə-shən\ *n* 1 ♦ : a hard blow or collision; *also* : bodily injury (as to the brain) resulting from a sudden jar 2 : AGITATION, SHAKING

♦ bump, collision, crash, impact, jar, jolt, shock, smash, strike, wallop — more at IMPACT

con·demn \kən-'dem\ *vb* 1 ♦ : to declare to be wrong, reprehensible, or evil 2 : to pronounce guilty 3 ♦ : to sentence judicially 4 ♦ : to pronounce unfit for use or consumption ⟨∼ a building⟩ 5 : to declare forfeited or taken for public use 6 ♦ : to pronounce judgment on the faults of — **con·dem·na·tion** \kən-dem-'nā-shən\ *n*

♦ [1] censure, damn, decry, denounce, reprehend, reprobate; *also* attack, blast, criticize, knock, pan, slam; belittle, deprecate, disparage; doom, sentence; convict; blacklist, excommunicate, ostracize; rebuke, reprimand, reproach; admonish, chide, reprove; lambaste, scold, upbraid *Ant* bless ♦ [3] damn, doom, sentence — more at SENTENCE ♦ [4] censure, denounce, rebuke, reprimand, reproach, reprove — more at CENSURE ♦ [6] blame, censure, criticize, denounce, fault, knock, pan, reprehend — more at CRITICIZE

con·den·sate \'kän-dən-,sāt, kən-'den-\ *n* : a product of condensation

con·den·sa·tion \kän-den-'sā-shən\ *n* 1 ♦ : the act or process of condensing 2 ♦ : abridgment and usu. compression of a literary work

♦ [1] compression, constriction, contraction — more at COMPRESSION ♦ [2] abbreviation, digest

con·dense \kən-'dens\ *vb* **con·densed; con·dens·ing** 1 ♦ : to make or become more compact or dense : compress or concentrate into a smaller scope or volume 2 : to change from vapor to liquid

♦ compact, compress, constrict, contract, squeeze — more at COMPRESS

con·densed *adj* : reduced to a more compact form

con·dens·er \kən-'den-sər\ *n* 1 : one that condenses 2 : CAPACITOR

con·de·scend \kän-di-'send\ *vb* 1 : to descend to a less formal or dignified level 2 : to assume an air of superiority — **con·de·scend·ing·ly** \-'sen-diŋ-lē\ *adv* — **con·de·scen·sion** \-'sen-chən\ *n*

con·dign \kən-'dīn, 'kän-,dīn\ *adj* : DESERVED, APPROPRIATE ⟨∼ punishment⟩

con·di·ment \'kän-də-mənt\ *n* : something used to make food savory; *esp* : a pungent seasoning (as pepper)

¹**con·di·tion** \kən-'di-shən\ *n* 1 ♦ : something essential to the occurrence of some other thing 2 ♦ : state of being 3 : social status 4 *pl* : state of affairs : CIRCUMSTANCES 5 : a bodily state in which something is wrong ⟨a heart ∼⟩ 6 ♦ : a state of health, fitness, or working order ⟨in good ∼⟩ 7 ♦ : a restricting or modifying factor

♦ [1] essential, must, necessity, provision, proviso, qualification, requirement, stipulation ♦ [2, 6] estate, fettle, form, order, repair, shape, trim; *also* practice; kilter; pass, phase, stage ♦ [7] check, constraint, curb, fetter, limitation, restraint, restriction — more at RESTRICTION

²**condition** *vb* 1 ♦ : to put into proper condition for action or use 2 ♦ : to adapt, modify, or mold to respond in a particular way 3 : to modify so that an act or response previously associated with one stimulus becomes associated with another

♦ [1, 2] acclimate, accommodate, adapt, adjust, conform, fit, shape — more at ADAPT

con·di·tion·al \kən-'di-shə-nəl\ *adj* ♦ : containing, implying, or depending on a condition — **con·di·tion·al·ly** *adv*

♦ contingent, dependent, subject — more at DEPENDENT

con·di·tioned *adj* : determined or established by conditioning

con·di·tion·er \-'di-shə-nər\ *n* : a preparation used to improve the condition of hair

con·do \'kän-(,)dō\ *n* : CONDOMINIUM 3

con·dole \kən-'dōl\ *vb* **con·doled; con·dol·ing** : to express sympathetic sorrow — **con·do·lence** \kən-'dō-ləns\ *n*

con·dom \'kän-dəm, 'kən-\ *n* : a usu. rubber sheath worn over the penis (as to prevent pregnancy or venereal infection during sexual intercourse)

con·do·min·i·um \kän-də-'mi-nē-əm\ *n, pl* **-ums** 1 : joint sovereignty (as by two or more nations) 2 : a politically dependent territory under condominium 3 : individual ownership of a unit (as an apartment) in a multiunit structure; *also* : a unit so owned

con·done \kən-'dōn\ *vb* **con·doned; con·don·ing** ♦ : to overlook or forgive esp. by treating (an offense) as harmless or trivial — **con·do·na·tion** \kän-də-'nā-shən\ *n*

♦ disregard, excuse, gloss over, ignore, pardon, pass over, shrug off, wink at — more at EXCUSE

con·dor \'kän-dər, -,dȯr\ *n* [Sp *cóndor*, fr. Quechua (a So. American Indian language) *kuntur*] : a very large American vulture of the high Andes; *also* : a related nearly extinct vulture of southern California

con·duce \kən-'düs, -'dyüs\ *vb* **con·duced; con·duc·ing** : to lead or contribute to a particular result — **con·du·cive** *adj*

¹**con·duct** \'kän-(,)dəkt\ *n* 1 ♦ : the act, manner, or process of carrying on : MANAGEMENT, DIRECTION 2 ♦ : a mode or standard of personal behavior esp. as based on moral principles : BEHAVIOR

♦ [1] administration, control, direction, government, guidance, management, operation, oversight, regulation, running, superintendence, supervision; *also* care, custody, guardianship, protection, tutelage; engineering, machination, manipulation ♦ [2] actions, bearing, behavior (*or* behaviour), comportment, demeanor (*or* demeanour), deportment — more at BEHAVIOR

²**con·duct** \kən-'dəkt\ *vb* 1 ♦ : to bring by or as if by leading : GUIDE 2 ♦ : to direct or take part in the operation or management of : MANAGE, DIRECT 3 ♦ : to convey in a channel 4 ♦ : to cause (oneself) to act or behave in a particular and esp. in a controlled manner : BEHAVE — **con·duc·tion** \-'dək-shən\ *n*

♦ [1] direct, guide, lead, marshal, pilot, route, show, steer, usher — more at LEAD ♦ [2] administer, carry on, control, direct, govern, guide, handle, manage, operate, oversee, regulate, run, superintend, supervise; *also* care (for), keep, mind, tend, watch; lead, pilot, steer; guard, protect, safeguard ♦ [3] channel, direct, funnel, pipe, siphon — more at CHANNEL ♦ [4] acquit, bear, behave, comport, demean, deport, quit — more at BEHAVE

con·duc·tance \kən-'dək-təns\ *n* : the readiness with which a conductor transmits an electric current

con·duc·tive \kən-'dək-tiv\ *adj* : having the power to conduct (as heat or electricity) — **con·duc·tiv·i·ty** \kän-,dək-'ti-və-tē\ *n*

con·duc·tor \kən-'dək-tər\ *n* 1 : one that conducts; *esp* : a material that permits an electric current to flow easily 2 : a collector of fares in a public conveyance 3 : the leader of a musical ensemble

con·duit \'kän-,dü-ət, ,dyü-, -dwət\ *n* 1 ♦ : a natural or artificial channel through which something (as a fluid) is conveyed 2 : a tube or trough for protecting electric wires or cables 3 : a means of transmitting or distributing

♦ channel, duct, leader, line, penstock, pipe, tube — more at PIPE ♦ aqueduct, canal, channel, flume, raceway, watercourse — more at CHANNEL

con·dyle \'kän-,dīl, -d°l\ *n* : an articular prominence of a bone — **con·dy·lar** \-də-lər\ *adj*

cone \'kōn\ *n* 1 : the scaly fruit of trees of the pine family 2 : a solid figure formed by rotating a right triangle about one of its legs 3 : a solid figure that slopes evenly to a point from a usu. circular base 4 : any of the conical light-sensitive receptor cells of the retina that function in color vision 5 : something shaped like a cone

Con·es·to·ga wagon \ˌkä-nə-'stō-gə-\ *n* : a broad-wheeled covered wagon used esp. for transporting freight across the prairies

co·ney \'kō-nē\ *n, pl* **coneys** **1** : RABBIT; *also* : its fur **2** : PIKA

conf *abbr* **1** conference **2** confidential

con·fab \'kän-ˌfab, kən-'fab\ *n* : CONFABULATION 1

con·fab·u·la·tion \kən-ˌfab-yə-'lā-shən\ *n* **1** : CHAT; *also* : CONFERENCE **2** : a filling in of gaps in memory by fabrication

con·fec·tion \kən-'fek-shən\ *n* : a fancy dish or sweet; *also* : CANDY

con·fec·tion·er \-sh(ə-)nər\ *n* : a maker of or dealer in confections

con·fec·tion·ery \-shə-ˌner-ē\ *n, pl* **-er·ies** **1** : sweet foods **2** : a confectioner's place of business

Confed *abbr* Confederate

con·fed·er·a·cy \kən-'fe-də-rə-sē\ *n, pl* **-cies** **1** ♦ : a league or compact for mutual support or common action : LEAGUE, ALLIANCE **2** *cap* : the 11 southern states that seceded from the U.S. in 1860 and 1861

♦ alliance, bloc, coalition, combination, combine, confederation, federation, league, union; *also* cabal, conspiracy; cartel, syndicate, trust; faction, side, wing; association, group, organization; affiliation, cooperative, partnership

¹con·fed·er·ate \kən-'fe-də-rət\ *adj* **1** : united in a league : ALLIED **2** *cap* : of or relating to the Confederacy

²confederate *n* **1** ♦ : one that is associated with another as a helper **2** *cap* : an adherent of the Confederacy

♦ abettor, accessory, accomplice, cohort — more at ACCOMPLICE ♦ abettor, ally, backer, supporter, sympathizer — more at ALLY

³con·fed·er·ate \-'fe-də-ˌrāt\ *vb* **-at·ed; -at·ing** ♦ : to unite in a confederacy

♦ ally, associate, band, club, conjoin, cooperate, federate, league, unite — more at ALLY

con·fed·er·a·tion \kən-ˌfe-də-'rā-shən\ *n* **1** : an act of confederating : ALLIANCE **2** ♦ : as association of parties for mutual assistance : LEAGUE

♦ alliance, bloc, coalition, combination, combine, confederacy, federation, league, union — more at CONFEDERACY

con·fer \kən-'fər\ *vb* **con·ferred; con·fer·ring** **1** ♦ : to give or grant from or as if from a position of superiority : BESTOW **2** ♦ : to exchange views : CONSULT — **con·fer·ee** \ˌkän-fə-'rē\ *n*

♦ [1] accord, award, bestow, give, grant; *also* contribute, donate, present; furnish, provide, supply; extend, offer, proffer; allocate, appropriate, assign ♦ [2] advise, consult, counsel, parley; *also* debate, deliberate, discuss, hash (over); coach, guide, tutor; recommend, suggest; direct, refer (to)

con·fer·ence \'kän-f(ə-)rəns\ *n* **1 a** ♦ : an interchange of views **b** ♦ : a meeting for an exchange of views **2** : an association of athletic teams

♦ [1a] argument, colloquy, deliberation, discourse, discussion, give-and-take, parley, talk — more at DISCUSSION ♦ [1b] assembly, congress, convention, convocation, council, gathering, get-together, huddle, meeting, powwow, seminar — more at MEETING

con·fer·enc·ing \'kän-f(ə-)rən-siŋ\ *n* : the holding of conferences esp. by means of electronic devices

con·fess \kən-'fes\ *vb* **1** ♦ : to tell or make known (as something wrong or damaging to oneself) **2** : to acknowledge one's sins to God or to a priest **3** : to receive the confession of (a penitent)

♦ acknowledge, admit, agree, allow, concede, grant, own — more at ADMIT

con·fessed·ly \-'fe-səd-lē\ *adv* : by confession : ADMITTEDLY

con·fes·sion \-'fe-shən\ *n* **1** ♦ : an act of confessing (as in the sacrament of penance) **2** ♦ : an acknowledgment of guilt **3** : a formal statement of religious beliefs **4** : a religious body having a common creed — **con·fes·sion·al** *adj*

♦ [1, 2] acknowledgment, admission, avowal, concession; *also* allowance; betrayal, disclosure, revelation; announcement, declaration, proclamation; contrition, regret, remorse, repentance

con·fes·sion·al \-'fe-shə-nəl\ *n* : a place where a priest hears confessions

con·fes·sor \kən-'fe-sər\ *n* **1** : one that confesses **2** : a priest who hears confessions

con·fet·ti \kən-'fe-tē\ *n* [It, pl. of *confetto* sweetmeat, fr. ML *confectum*, fr. L, neut. of *confectus*, pp. of *conficere* to prepare] : bits of colored paper or ribbon for throwing (as at weddings)

con·fi·dant \'kän-fə-ˌdänt, -ˌdant\ *n* : one to whom secrets are confided

con·fi·dante \-ˌdänt, -ˌdant\ *n* : CONFIDANT; *esp* : one who is a woman

con·fide \kən-'fīd\ *vb* **con·fid·ed; con·fid·ing** **1** : to have or show faith : TRUST ⟨~ in a friend⟩ **2** : to tell confidentially ⟨~ a secret⟩ **3** : ENTRUST

¹con·fi·dence \'kän-fə-dəns\ *n* **1** : faith or belief that one will act in a right, proper, or effective way : TRUST **2** ♦ : a feeling or consciousness of one's powers or of reliance on one's circumstances : SELF-ASSURANCE **3** ♦ : a state of trust or intimacy **4** : a communication made in confidence : SECRET **2** **5** ♦ : the quality or state of being certain : CERTITUDE

♦ [2] aplomb, assurance, self-assurance, self-confidence, self-esteem; *also* cockiness, complacence, complacency, conceit, ego, egotism, overconfidence, pride, self-conceit, self-importance, self-satisfaction, smugness, vainglory, vanity; calmness, composure, coolness, equanimity; self-possession *Ant* diffidence, self-doubt

♦ [3] credence, faith, stock, trust — more at TRUST

♦ [5] assurance, certainty, certitude, conviction, positiveness, sureness; *also* dogmatism; decisiveness, firmness, resolution *Ant* doubt, incertitude, uncertainty

²confidence *adj* : of or relating to swindling by false promises ⟨a ~ game⟩

con·fi·dent \-dənt\ *adj* **1** ♦ : full of conviction : CERTAIN **2** ♦ : having or showing assurance and self-reliance — **con·fi·dent·ly** *adv*

♦ [1] assured, certain, clear, cocksure, doubtless, positive, sanguine, sure — more at CERTAIN ♦ [2] assured, secure, self-assured, self-confident; *also* hopeful, rosy, sanguine, upbeat; complacent, conceited, egoistic, egotistic, important, overweening, pompous, prideful, proud, self-important, self-satisfied, smug, stuck-up, vain, vainglorious; calm, collected, composed, cool, placid, self-possessed, serene, tranquil, undisturbed, unperturbed *Ant* diffident, insecure

con·fi·den·tial \ˌkän-fə-'den-shəl\ *adj* **1** ♦ : known only to a limited few : SECRET, PRIVATE **2** : entrusted with confidences ⟨~ clerk⟩ — **con·fi·den·tial·ly** \-'den-shə-lē\ *adv*

♦ hushed, inside, intimate, private, secret — more at PRIVATE

con·fig·u·ra·tion \kən-ˌfi-gyə-'rā-shən\ *n* ♦ : relative arrangement of parts or elements : SHAPE

♦ arrangement, composition, design, form, format, layout, makeup, pattern, shape — more at COMPOSITION

con·fig·ure \kən-'fi-gyər\ *vb* **-ured; -ur·ing** : to set up for operation esp. in a particular way

con·fine \kən-'fīn\ *vb* **con·fined; con·fin·ing** **1** ♦ : to hold within a location; *also* : IMPRISON **2** ♦ : to keep within limits ⟨will ~ my remarks to one subject⟩ — **con·fin·er** *n*

♦ [1] commit, immure, imprison, jail — more at IMPRISON ♦ [2] check, circumscribe, control, curb, inhibit, limit, restrain, restrict

con·fine·ment *n* ♦ : an act of confining : the state of being confined

♦ captivity, imprisonment, incarceration, internment — more at INTERNMENT

con·fines \'kän-ˌfīnz\ *n pl* ♦ : something (as borders or walls) that encloses : something that restrains

♦ boundary, ceiling, end, extent, limit, limitation, line, termination — more at LIMIT ♦ border, boundary, circumference, compass, edge, end, fringe, margin, perimeter, periphery, rim, skirt, verge — more at BORDER

con·firm \kən-'fərm\ *vb* **1** : to give approval to : RATIFY **2** : to make firm or firmer **3** : to administer the rite of confirmation to **4** ♦ : to give new assurance of the validity of : VERIFY, CORROBORATE

♦ bear out, corroborate, substantiate, support, validate, verify, vindicate; *also* attest, authenticate, avouch, certify, testify (to), vouch (for), witness; guarantee, warrant; affirm, assert, aver, avow, profess *Ant* disprove, rebut, refute

con·fir·ma·tion \ˌkän-fər-'mā-shən\ *n* **1** : a religious ceremony admitting a person to full membership in a church or synagogue **2** ♦ : an act of ratifying or corroborating; *also* : PROOF

♦ attestation, corroboration, documentation, evidence, proof, substantiation, testament, testimony, validation, witness — more at PROOF

con·fir·ma·to·ry \-'fər-mə-ˌtōr-ē\ *adj* ♦ : serving to confirm

♦ corroborative — more at CORROBORATIVE

confirmed *adj* **1** ♦ : marked by long continuance and likely to persist **2** ♦ : fixed in habit and unlikely to change

♦ [1] deep-rooted, deep-seated, inveterate, settled — more at INVETERATE ♦ [2] chronic, habitual, inveterate — more at HABITUAL

con·fis·cate \'kän-fə-ˌskāt\ *vb* **-cat·ed; -cat·ing** [L *confiscare,* fr. *com-* with + *fiscus* treasury] : to take possession of by or as if by public authority — **con·fis·ca·tion** \ˌkän-fə-'skā-shən\ *n* — **con·fis·ca·to·ry** \kən-'fis-kə-ˌtōr-ē\ *adj*

con·fit \kōn-'fē\ *n* : a garnish of fruit or vegetables cooked in a seasoned liquid

con·fla·gra·tion \ˌkän-flə-'grā-shən\ *n* ♦ : FIRE; *esp* : a large disastrous fire

♦ fire, holocaust, inferno — more at FIRE

¹con·flict \'kän-ˌflikt\ *n* **1** ♦ : prolonged fighting esp. with weapons : WAR **2** ♦ : a clash between hostile or opposing elements, ideas, or forces

♦ [1] battle, clash, combat, contest, fight, fracas, fray, hassle, scrap, scrimmage, scuffle, skirmish, struggle, war, warfare ♦ [1, 2] battle, combat, confrontation, contest, duel, face-off, rivalry, struggle, tug-of-war, warfare — more at CONTEST ♦ [2] discord, dissension, dissent, disunity, friction, schism, strife, variance, war, warfare — more at DISCORD

²con·flict \kən-'flikt\ *vb* ♦ : to show opposition or irreconcilability : CLASH

♦ clash, collide, jar — more at CLASH

con·flu·ence \'kän-ˌflü-əns, kən-'flü-\ *n* **1** ♦ : a coming together at one point **2** : the meeting or place of meeting of two or more streams — **con·flu·ent** \-ənt\ *adj*

♦ conjunction, convergence, meeting — more at CONVERGENCE

con·flux \'kän-ˌfləks\ *n* : CONFLUENCE

con·form \kən-'fȯrm\ *vb* **1 a** : to be similar or identical **b** ♦ : to be in agreement or harmony : AGREE **2** ♦ : to be obedient or compliant — usu. used with *to; also* : COMPLY **3** ♦ : to make like : shape to fit — **con·form·ist** \-'fȯr-mist\ *adj*

♦ [1b] accord, agree, answer, check, coincide, comport, correspond, dovetail, fit, go, harmonize, jibe, square, tally — more at CHECK ♦ *usu* **conform to** [2] comply, follow, mind, obey, observe — more at OBEY ♦ [3] acclimate, accommodate, adapt, adjust, condition, fit, shape — more at ADAPT

con·form·able *adj* **1** ♦ : corresponding or consistent in form or character **2** ♦ : giving compliance or obedience

♦ *usu* **conformable to** [1] compatible, congruous, consistent, consonant, correspondent, harmonious — more at CONSISTENT ♦ [2] amenable, compliant, docile, obedient, submissive, tractable — more at OBEDIENT

con·for·mance \kən-'fȯr-məns\ *n* : CONFORMITY

con·for·ma·tion \ˌkän-fȯr-'mā-shən\ *n* ♦ : formation of something by appropriate arrangement of parts or elements : an assembling into a whole

♦ arrangement, configuration, format, layout, setup

con·for·mi·ty \kən-'fȯr-mə-tē\ *n, pl* **-ties** **1** ♦ : correspondence in form, manner, or character : HARMONY, AGREEMENT **2** ♦ : action in accordance with some specified standard or authority : COMPLIANCE, OBEDIENCE

♦ [1] accord, agreement, consonance, harmony, tune; *also* assimilation, integration; oneness, solidarity, togetherness; affinity, empathy, sympathy *Ant* conflict, disagreement ♦ [2] compliance, obedience, observance, submission, subordination — more at OBEDIENCE

con·found \kən-'faùnd, kän-\ *vb* **1** ♦ : to throw (a person) into confusion or perplexity **2** ♦ : to put to shame : CONFUSE 2

♦ [1] addle, baffle, befog, befuddle, bemuse, bewilder, confuse, disorient, muddle, muddy, mystify, perplex, puzzle — more at CONFUSE ♦ [2] abash, confuse, discomfit, disconcert, discountenance, embarrass, faze, fluster, mortify, rattle — more at EMBARRASS

con·fra·ter·ni·ty \ˌkän-frə-'tər-nə-tē\ *n* : a society devoted esp. to a religious or charitable cause

con·frere \'kän-ˌfrer, 'kōⁿ-\ *n* : COLLEAGUE, COMRADE

con·front \kən-'frənt\ *vb* **1 a** ♦ : to face esp. in challenge **b** ♦ : to deal unflinchingly with ⟨~ed the issue⟩ **2** : to cause to face or meet

♦ [1a, 1b] beard, brave, brazen, dare, defy, face — more at FACE

con·fron·ta·tion \ˌkän-frən-'tā-shən\ *n* ♦ : the act of confronting : the state of being confronted — **con·fron·ta·tion·al** \-shə-nᵊl\ *adj*

♦ battle, combat, conflict, contest, duel, face-off, rivalry, struggle, tug-of-war, warfare — more at CONTEST

Con·fu·cian \kən-'fyü-shən\ *adj* : of or relating to the Chinese philosopher Confucius or his teachings — **Con·fu·cian·ism** \-shə-ˌni-zəm\ *n*

con·fuse \kən-'fyüz\ *vb* **con·fused; con·fus·ing** **1 a** ♦ : to make mentally unclear or uncertain **b** ♦ : to disturb the composure of **2** : to mix up : JUMBLE **3** ♦ : to fail to make clear or distinct — **con·fus·ed·ly** \-'fyü-zəd-lē\ *adv*

♦ [1a] addle, baffle, befog, befuddle, bemuse, bewilder, confound, disorient, muddle, muddy, mystify, perplex, puzzle; *also* stick, stump; abash, discomfit, disconcert, discountenance, embarrass, faze, fluster, mortify, nonplus, rattle; agitate, bother, chagrin, discomfort, discompose, dismay, disquiet, distress, disturb, perturb, stun, unhinge, unsettle, upset; deceive, misguide, mislead ♦ [1b] abash, confound, discomfit, disconcert, discountenance, embarrass, faze, fluster, mortify, rattle — more at EMBARRASS ♦ [3] becloud, befog, blur, cloud, fog, muddy; *also* complicate, perplex; entangle, snarl, tangle; disorder, jumble, mess (up), mix (up) *Ant* clarify

confused *adj* **1** ♦ : being perplexed or disconcerted **2** ♦ : being disordered or mixed up

♦ [1] dizzy, stunned — more at DIZZY ♦ [2] chaotic, disheveled, disordered, messy, muddled, sloppy, unkempt, untidy — more at MESSY

con·fu·sion \-'fyü-zhən\ *n* **1** : an act or instance of confusing **2** : the quality or state of being confused **3** ♦ : a confused mass or mixture

♦ [2] bafflement, bewilderment, distraction, muddle, mystification, perplexity, puzzlement, whirl; *also* abashment, discomfiture, embarrassment, fluster, mortification; agitation, chagrin, discomfort, dismay, disquiet, distress, disturbance, perturbation, upset ♦ [3] chaos, disarray, disorder, disorganization, havoc, hell, jumble, mess, muddle, shambles — more at CHAOS

con·fu·ta·tion \ˌkän-fyù-'tā-shən\ *n* ♦ : something (as an argument or statement) that refutes

♦ rebuttal, refutation *Ant* proof

con·fute \kən-'fyüt\ *vb* **con·fut·ed; con·fut·ing** ♦ : to overwhelm by argument : refute conclusively

♦ belie, disprove, rebut, refute — more at DISPROVE

cong *abbr* congress; congressional

con·ga \'käŋ-gə\ *n* : a Cuban dance of African origin performed by a group usu. in single file

con·geal \kən-'jēl\ *vb* **1** ♦ : to change from a fluid to a solid state by or as if by cold : FREEZE **2** ♦ : to make or become hard or thick

♦ [1] clot, coagulate, gel, jell, set — more at COAGULATE ♦ [1, 2] concrete, firm, freeze, harden, set, solidify — more at HARDEN

con·gee \'kän-jē\ *n* : porridge made from rice

con·ge·ner \'kän-jə-nər\ *n* : one related to another; *esp* : a plant or animal of the same taxonomic genus as another — **con·ge·ner·ic** \ˌkän-jə-'ner-ik\ *adj*

con·ge·nial \kən-'jē-nyəl\ *adj* **1** ♦ : having the same nature, disposition, or tastes : KINDRED **2** ♦ : agreeably suited to one's nature, tastes, or outlook : AGREEABLE — **con·ge·ni·al·i·ty** \-ˌjē-nē-'a-lə-tē\ *n* — **con·ge·nial·ly** *adv*

♦ [1] agreeable, amicable, compatible, harmonious, kindred, unanimous, united — more at HARMONIOUS ♦ [2] agreeable, delectable, delicious, delightful, dreamy, felicitous, good, grateful, gratifying, nice, palatable, pleasant, pleasurable, satisfying

con·gen·i·tal \kən-'je-nə-t°l\ *adj* : existing at or dating from birth

con·ger eel \'kän-gər-\ *n* : a large edible marine eel of the Atlantic

con·ge·ries \'kän-jə-(ˌ)rēz\ *n, pl* **congeries** : AGGREGATION, COLLECTION

con·gest \kən-'jest\ *vb* **1** : to cause excessive fullness of the blood vessels of (as a lung) **2** ♦ : to obstruct by overcrowding **3** : to concentrate in a small or narrow space — **con·ges·tion** \-'jes-chən\ *n* — **con·ges·tive** \-'jes-tiv\ *adj*

♦ block, choke, clog, close (off), dam, jam, obstruct, plug (up), stop (up), stuff — more at CLOG

congestive heart failure *n* : heart failure in which the heart is unable to keep enough blood circulating in the tissues or is unable to pump out the blood returned to it by the veins

¹con·glom·er·ate \kən-'glä-mə-rət\ *adj* [L *conglomerare* to roll together, fr. *com-* together + *glomerare* to wind into a ball, fr. *glomer-, glomus* ball] : made up of parts from various sources

²con·glom·er·ate \-ˌrāt\ *vb* **-at·ed; -at·ing** ♦ : to gather into a mass : form a coherent whole — **con·glom·er·a·tion** \-ˌglä-mə-'rā-shən\ *n*

♦ accumulate, collect, gather, heap, pile up — more at COLLECT

³con·glom·er·ate \-rət\ *n* **1** : a mass formed of fragments from various sources; *esp* : a rock composed of fragments varying from pebbles to boulders held together by a cementing material **2** : a widely diversified corporation

Con·go·lese \ˌkäŋ-gə-'lēz, -'lēs\ *n* : a native or inhabitant of Congo — **Congolese** *adj*

con·grat·u·late \kən-'gra-chə-ˌlāt\ *vb* **-lat·ed; -lat·ing** : to express sympathetic pleasure to on account of success or good fortune : FELICITATE — **con·grat·u·la·to·ry** \-'gra-chə-lə-ˌtōr-ē\ *adj*

con·grat·u·la·tion \-ˌgra-chə-'lā-shən\ *n* **1** : the act of congratulating **2** : a congratulatory expression — usu. used in pl.

con·gre·gate \'käŋ-gri-ˌgāt\ *vb* **-gat·ed; -gat·ing** [ME, fr. L

congregatus, pp. of *congregare*, fr. *com-* together + *greg-, grex* flock] ♦ : to collect into a group or crowd : ASSEMBLE

♦ assemble, cluster, collect, concentrate, conglomerate, convene, forgather, gather, meet, rendezvous — more at ASSEMBLE

con·gre·ga·tion \ˌkäŋ-gri-'gā-shən\ *n* **1** ♦ : an assembly of persons met esp. for worship; *also* : a group that habitually so meets **2** : a religious community or order **3** : the act or an instance of congregating

♦ assemblage, assembly, conference, convocation, gathering, meeting, muster — more at GATHERING

con·gre·ga·tion·al \-shə-nəl\ *adj* **1** : of or relating to a congregation **2** *cap* : observing the faith and practice of certain Protestant churches which recognize the independence of each congregation in church matters — **con·gre·ga·tion·al·ism** \-nə-ˌli-zəm\ *n, often cap* — **con·gre·ga·tion·al·ist** \-list\ *n, often cap*

con·gress \'käŋ-grəs\ *n* **1** ♦ : an assembly esp. of delegates for discussion and usu. action on some question **2** : the body of senators and representatives constituting a nation's legislature **3** : the body of persons coming together for a common purpose — **con·gres·sio·nal** \kən-'gre-shə-nəl\ *adj*

♦ assembly, conference, convention, convocation, council, gathering, get-together, huddle, meeting, powwow, seminar — more at MEETING

con·gress·man \'käŋ-grəs-mən\ *n* : a member of a congress

con·gress·wom·an \-ˌwù-mən\ *n* : a woman who is a member of a congress

con·gru·ence \kən-'grü-əns, 'käŋ-grü-\ *n* : the quality of agreeing or coinciding : CONGRUITY — **con·gru·ent** \kən-'grü-ənt, 'käŋ-grü-\ *adj*

con·gru·en·cy \-sē\ *n, pl* **-cies** : CONGRUENCE

con·gru·ity \kän-'grü-ə-tē\ *n, pl* **-ities** : correspondence between things

con·gru·ous \'käŋ-grü-əs\ *adj* ♦ : being in agreement, harmony, or correspondence

♦ balanced, consonant, harmonious — more at HARMONIOUS ♦ compatible, conformable (to), consistent, consonant, correspondent, harmonious — more at CONSISTENT

con·ic \'kä-nik\ *adj* **1** : of or relating to a cone **2** : CONICAL

con·i·cal \'kä-ni-kəl\ *adj* : resembling a cone esp. in shape

co·ni·fer \'kä-nə-fər, 'kō-\ *n* : any of an order of shrubs or trees (as the pines) that usu. are evergreen and bear cones — **co·nif·er·ous** \kō-'ni-fə-rəs\ *adj*

conj *abbr* conjunction

con·jec·tur·al \-chə-rəl\ *adj* ♦ : of the nature of or involving or based on conjecture

♦ hypothetical, speculative, theoretical — more at THEORETICAL

¹con·jec·ture \kən-'jek-chər\ *n* **1** ♦ : a conclusion deduced by surmise or guesswork : GUESS, SURMISE **2** ♦ : inference from defective or presumptive evidence

♦ [1, 2] guess, supposition, surmise; *also* hypothesis, theory, thesis; speculation; hunch, intuition; belief, faith ♦ [2] hypothesis, proposition, supposition, theory — more at THEORY

²conjecture *vb* ♦ : to arrive at or deduce by conjecture : GUESS

♦ calculate, call, estimate, figure, gauge, guess, judge, make, place, put, reckon, suppose — more at ESTIMATE ♦ assume, guess, presume, speculate, suppose, surmise, suspect — more at GUESS

con·join \kən-'jòin\ *vb* ♦ : to join together — **con·joint** \-'jòint\ *adj*

♦ associate, coalesce, combine, connect, couple, fuse, join, link, marry, unify, unite — more at UNITE

con·joint \-'jòint\ *adj* ♦ : related to, made up of, or carried on by two or more in combination

♦ collective, common, communal, concerted, joint, mutual, public, united — more at COLLECTIVE

con·ju·gal \'kän-ji-gəl\ *adj* ♦ : of or relating to marriage
: MATRIMONIAL

♦ connubial, marital, matrimonial, nuptial — more at
MARITAL

¹**con·ju·gate** \'kän-ji-gət, -jə-ˌgāt\ *adj* **1** : united esp. in
pairs : COUPLED **2** : of kindred origin and meaning ⟨*sing*
and *song* are ~⟩ — **con·ju·gate·ly** *adv*

²**con·ju·gate** \-jə-ˌgāt\ *vb* **-gat·ed; -gat·ing** **1** : INFLECT ⟨~ a
verb⟩ **2** : to join together : COUPLE

con·ju·ga·tion \ˌkän-jə-'gā-shən\ *n* **1** : an arrangement of
the inflectional forms of a verb **2** : the act of conjugating
: the state of being conjugated

con·junct \kän-'jəŋkt\ *adj* : JOINED, UNITED

con·junc·tion \kən-'jəŋk-shən\ *n* **1** ♦ : the act or an instance of conjoining : the state of being combined **2** : occurrence at the same time **3** : a word that joins together
sentences, clauses, phrases, or words

♦ confluence, convergence, meeting — more at CON-
VERGENCE

con·junc·ti·va \ˌkän-ˌjəŋk-'tī-və\ *n, pl* **-vas** *or* **-vae** \-(ˌ)vē\
: the mucous membrane lining the inner surface of the
eyelids and continuing over the forepart of the eyeball

con·junc·tive \kən-'jəŋk-tiv\ *adj* **1** : CONNECTIVE
2 : CONJUNCT **3** : being or functioning like a conjunction

con·junc·ti·vi·tis \kən-ˌjəŋk-ti-'vī-təs\ *n* : inflammation of
the conjunctiva

con·junc·ture \kən-'jəŋk-chər\ *n* **1** : CONJUNCTION,
UNION **2** : JUNCTURE 3

con·jun·to \kōn-'hün-tō\ *n* : Mexican-American music influenced by the music of German immigrants to Texas

con·ju·ra·tion \ˌkän-jù-'rā-shən, ˌkən-\ *n* ♦ : a magic expression used in conjuring

♦ bewitchment, charm, enchantment, incantation, spell
— more at SPELL

con·jure \'kän-jər, 'kən-** *for 1, 2;* kən-'jùr *for 3*\ *vb* **con-
jured; con·jur·ing** **1** : to implore earnestly or solemnly
2 : to practice magic; *esp* : to summon (as a devil) by
sorcery **3** : to practice sleight of hand **4 a** : to summon
by or as if by invocation or incantation **b** : to affect or
effect by or as if by magic

con·jur·er *or* **con·ju·ror** \'kän-jər-ər, 'kən-\ *n* **1** ♦ : one that
practices magic arts : WIZARD **2** ♦ : one that performs
feats of sleight of hand and illusion : MAGICIAN

♦ [1] enchanter, magician, necromancer, sorcerer, voodoo, witch, wizard — more at MAGICIAN ♦ [2] illusionist, magician, trickster

conk \'käŋk\ *vb* ♦ : to become inoperative or ineffective
: BREAK DOWN; *esp* : STALL ⟨the motor ~ed out⟩

♦ break, break down, crash, cut out, die, fail, stall —
more at FAIL

Conn *abbr* Connecticut

con·nect \kə-'nekt\ *vb* **1** ♦ : to join or fasten together in a
single relationship often by something intervening : JOIN,
LINK **2** ♦ : to associate in one's mind **3** : to establish
a communications connection ⟨~ to the Internet⟩ —
con·nect·able *adj* — **con·nec·tor** *n*

♦ [1] chain, compound, couple, hitch, hook, join,
link, yoke; *also* dovetail; concatenate, string; cement,
coalesce, combine, fuse, unite *Ant* disconnect, disjoin,
separate, unchain, uncouple, unhitch, unyoke ♦ [2] associate, correlate, identify, link, relate — more at AS-
SOCIATE

con·nec·tion \kə-'nek-shən\ *n* **1 a** ♦ : the act of connecting : a coming into or being put in contact : JUNCTION,
UNION **b** ♦ : the state of being connected or linked
c ♦ : the place where a connection occurs **2** ♦ : logical
relationship; *esp* : relation of a word to other words in a
sentence **3** : family relationship **4** : something that connects or the point of the connecting **5** : a person related
by blood or marriage **6** ♦ : relationship in social affairs
or in business **7** : a set or group of persons connected or
associated together in a common interest; *esp* : a religious
denomination

♦ [1a] combination, consolidation, coupling, junction,
unification, union — more at UNION ♦ [1b] association,
bearing, kinship, liaison, linkage, relation, relationship;
also correlation, interrelation; pertinence, relevance;
bond, link, tie; affiliation, alliance, union; likeness, resemblance, similarity ♦ [1c] coupling, joint, junction,
juncture — more at JOINT ♦ [2] applicability, bearing,
pertinence, relevance — more at PERTINENCE ♦ [6] affiliation, alliance, association, collaboration, confederation, cooperation, hookup, liaison, partnership, relation,
relationship, union — more at ASSOCIATION

¹**con·nec·tive** \kə-'nek-tiv\ *adj* : serving to connect —
con·nec·tiv·i·ty \ˌkä-ˌnek-'ti-və-tē\ *n*

²**connective** *n* : a word (as a conjunction) that connects
words or word groups

connective tissue *n* : a tissue (as bone or cartilage) that
forms a supporting framework for the body or its parts

con·nex·ion *chiefly Brit var of* CONNECTION

con·ning tower \'kä-niŋ-\ *n* : a raised structure on the deck
of a submarine

con·nip·tion \kə-'nip-shən\ *n* : a fit of rage, hysteria, or
alarm

con·niv·ance *n* ♦ : knowledge of and active or passive consent to wrongdoing

♦ collusion, conspiracy — more at COLLUSION

con·nive \kə-'nīv\ *vb* **con·nived; con·niv·ing** [F or L; F
conniver, fr. L *conivēre* to close the eyes, connive] **1** : to
pretend ignorance of something one ought to oppose
as wrong **2** : to cooperate secretly : give secret aid —
con·niv·er *n*

con·nois·seur \ˌkä-nə-'sər\ *n* : a critical judge in matters
of art or taste

con·no·ta·tion \ˌkä-nə-'tā-shən\ *n* : a meaning in addition
to or apart from the thing explicitly named or described
by a word

con·no·ta·tive \'kä-nə-ˌtā-tiv, kə-'nō-tə-\ *adj* **1** : connoting
or tending to connote **2** : relating to connotation

con·note \kə-'nōt\ *vb* **con·not·ed; con·not·ing** : to suggest
or mean as a connotation

con·nu·bi·al \kə-'nü-bē-əl, -'nyü-\ *adj* ♦ : of or relating to
the married state : CONJUGAL

♦ conjugal, marital, matrimonial, nuptial — more at
MARITAL

con·quer \'käŋ-kər\ *vb* **1** ♦ : to gain by force of arms
: WIN **2** ♦ : to get the better of : OVERCOME

♦ [1] prevail, triumph, win — more at WIN ♦ [2] beat,
crush, defeat, dominate, overcome, overpower, subdue,
subject, vanquish

con·quer·or \-ər\ *n* ♦ : one that conquers

♦ master, victor, winner — more at VICTOR

con·quest \'kän-ˌkwest, 'käŋ-\ *n* **1** ♦ : an act of conquering **2** : something conquered

♦ domination, subjection; *also* triumph, victory, winning; beating, defeat, drubbing, licking, trouncing; enslavement

con·quis·ta·dor \kȯn-'kēs-tə-ˌdȯr, kän-'kwis-\ *n, pl* **-do·res**
\-ˌkēs-tə-'dȯr-ēz, -ˌkwis-\ *or* **-dors** : CONQUEROR; *esp* : a
leader in the Spanish conquest of the Americas in the
16th century

cons *abbr* consonant

con·san·guin·i·ty \ˌkän-ˌsan-'gwi-nə-tē, -ˌsaŋ-\ *n, pl* **-ties**
: blood relationship — **con·san·guin·e·ous** \-nē-əs\ *adj*

con·science \'kän-chəns\ *n* : consciousness of the moral
right and wrong of one's own acts or motives — **con-
science·less** *adj*

con·sci·en·tious \ˌkän-chē-'en-chəs\ *adj* **1** ♦ : guided by
one's own sense of right and wrong **2** ♦ : marked by or
done with exact or thoughtful attention — **con·sci·en-
tious·ly** *adv*

♦ [1] ethical, honest, honorable (*or* honourable),
just, moral, principled, scrupulous; *also* good, righteous, upright, virtuous; dutiful, observant, respectful;

overconscientious; reliable, trustworthy, trusty *Ant* cutthroat, dishonest, dishonorable, immoral, unethical, unjust, unprincipled, unscrupulous ♦ [2] careful, fussy, meticulous, painstaking — more at PAINSTAKING

conscientious objector *n* : a person who refuses to serve in the armed forces or to bear arms on moral or religious grounds

¹**con·scious** \'kän-chəs\ *adj* **1** ♦ : perceiving, apprehending, or noticing with a degree of controlled thought or observation : AWARE **2** : known or felt by one's inner self **3** : mentally awake or alert : not asleep or unconscious **4** : INTENTIONAL — **con·scious·ness** *n*

  ♦ alive, aware, cognizant, mindful, sensible, sentient, witting; *also* attentive, heedful, observant, regardful, vigilant, watchful *Ant* insensible, unaware, unconscious, unmindful

²**conscious** *n* : the upper level of mental life of which a person is aware : CONSCIOUSNESS

con·scious·ly *adv* ♦ : in a conscious manner

  ♦ deliberately, intentionally, knowingly, purposely, willfully — more at INTENTIONALLY

¹**con·script** \kən-'skript\ *vb* : to enroll by compulsion for military or naval service — **con·scrip·tion** \kən-'skrip-shən\ *n*

²**conscript** \'kän-ˌskript\ *n* : a conscripted person (as a military recruit)

con·se·crate \'kän-sə-ˌkrāt\ *vb* **-crat·ed; -crat·ing** [ME, fr. L *consecratus*, pp. of *consecrare*, fr. *com-* together + *sacrare* to set aside as sacred, fr. *sacer* sacred] **1** : to induct (as a bishop) into an office with a religious rite **2** ♦ : to make or declare sacred ⟨∼ a church⟩ **3** ♦ : to devote solemnly to a purpose

  ♦ [2] bless, hallow, sanctify — more at BLESS ♦ [3] allocate, dedicate, devote, earmark, reserve, save — more at DEVOTE

con·se·cra·tion \ˌkän-sə-'krā-shən\ *n* ♦ : the act or ceremony of consecrating

  ♦ blessing, sanctification; *also* dedication

con·sec·u·tive \kən-'se-kyə-tiv\ *adj* ♦ : following in regular order : SUCCESSIVE — **con·sec·u·tive·ly** *adv*

  ♦ sequential, successive; *also* serial; constant, continuous, uninterrupted; ensuing, following, later, next, subsequent

con·sen·su·al \kən-'sen-chə-wəl\ *adj* : involving or based on mutual consent

con·sen·sus \kən-'sen-səs\ *n* **1** ♦ : agreement in opinion, testimony, or belief **2** : collective opinion

  ♦ accord, agreement, concurrence, unanimity — more at AGREEMENT

¹**con·sent** \kən-'sent\ *vb* ♦ : to give assent or approval

  ♦ accede, acquiesce, agree, assent, come round, subscribe (to) — more at ACCEDE

²**consent** *n* ♦ : approval or acceptance of something done or proposed by another

  ♦ allowance, authorization, clearance, concurrence, leave, license (*or* licence), permission, sanction, sufferance — more at PERMISSION

con·se·quence \'kän-sə-ˌkwens\ *n* **1** ♦ : something produced by a cause or necessarily following from a set of conditions : RESULT **2** ♦ : importance with respect to power to produce an effect

  ♦ [1] aftermath, conclusion, corollary, development, effect, issue, outcome, outgrowth, product, result, resultant, sequence, upshot — more at EFFECT ♦ [2] import, magnitude, moment, significance, weight

con·se·quent \-kwənt, -ˌkwent\ *adj* ♦ : following as a result or effect

  ♦ attendant, consequential, due, resultant — more at RESULTANT

con·se·quen·tial \ˌkän-sə-'kwen-chəl\ *adj* **1** ♦ : having significant consequences : IMPORTANT **2** : showing self-importance **3** : following as a result

  ♦ big, eventful, important, major, material, meaningful, momentous, significant, substantial, weighty — more at IMPORTANT

con·se·quent·ly \'kän-sə-ˌkwent-lē, -kwənt-\ *adv* ♦ : as a result : ACCORDINGLY

  ♦ accordingly, ergo, hence, so, therefore, thus, wherefore — more at THEREFORE

con·ser·van·cy \kən-'sər-vən-sē\ *n, pl* **-cies** : an organization or area designated to conserve natural resources

con·ser·va·tion \ˌkän-sər-'vā-shən\ *n* ♦ : a careful preservation and protection of something : PRESERVATION; *esp* : planned management of natural resources

  ♦ maintenance, preservation, upkeep — more at MAINTENANCE

con·ser·va·tion·ist \-shə-nist\ *n* : a person who advocates conservation esp. of natural resources

con·ser·va·tism \kən-'sər-və-ˌti-zəm\ *n* : disposition to keep to established ways : opposition to change

¹**con·ser·va·tive** \kən-'sər-və-tiv\ *adj* **1** : PRESERVATIVE **2** ♦ : disposed to maintain existing views, conditions, or institutions **3** : MODERATE, CAUTIOUS **4** ♦ : marked by or relating to traditional norms of taste, elegance, style, or manners — **con·ser·va·tive·ly** *adv*

  ♦ [2] old-fashioned, orthodox, reactionary, traditional; *also* conventional; faithful, loyal, steadfast, true-blue *Ant* liberal, nonorthodox, nontraditional, progressive, unorthodox ♦ [4] muted, quiet, restrained, subdued, unpretentious — more at QUIET

²**conservative** *n* : a person who is conservative esp. in politics

  ♦ reactionary, rightist, Tory; *also* conformist *Ant* leftist, liberal, progressive

con·ser·va·tor \kən-'sər-və-tər, 'kän-sər-ˌvā-\ *n* **1** : PROTECTOR, GUARDIAN **2** : one named by a court to protect the interests of an incompetent (as a child)

con·ser·va·to·ry \kən-'sər-və-ˌtōr-ē\ *n, pl* **-ries** **1** : a greenhouse for growing or displaying plants **2** : a place of instruction in one of the fine arts (as music)

¹**con·serve** \kən-'sərv\ *vb* **con·served; con·serv·ing** ♦ : to keep from losing or wasting : preserve in a sound state

  ♦ keep up, maintain, preserve, save — more at MAINTAIN

²**con·serve** \'kän-ˌsərv\ *n* **1** : CONFECTION; *esp* : a candied fruit **2** : PRESERVE; *esp* : one prepared from a mixture of fruits

con·sid·er \kən-'si-dər\ *vb* [ME, fr. AF *considerer*, fr. L *considerare* to observe, think about, fr. *com-* together + *sider-, sidus* heavenly body] **1** ♦ : to reflect on : think about with a degree of care or caution **2** ♦ : to be of the opinion : REGARD **3** ♦ : to think of : come to view, judge, or classify — **con·sid·ered** *adj*

  ♦ [1] chew over, cogitate, contemplate, debate, deliberate, entertain, meditate, mull, ponder, question, ruminate, study, think, weigh — more at PONDER ♦ [2, 3] account, count, esteem, hold, rate, reckon, regard, take; *also* believe, feel, sense, think; conceive, fancy, imagine

con·sid·er·able \-'si-dər-ə-bəl, -'si-drə-bəl\ *adj* **1** : worthy of consideration : of consequence or distinction **2** ♦ : large in extent, amount, or degree

  ♦ good, goodly, healthy, respectable, significant, sizable, substantial, tidy; *also* big, colossal, enormous, gigantic, great, huge, immense, mammoth *Ant* inconsiderable, insignificant, insubstantial

con·sid·er·ably \-blē\ *adv* ♦ : to a notable extent or degree

  ♦ broadly, greatly, hugely, largely, massively, monstrously, much, sizably, stupendously, tremendously, utterly, vastly — more at GREATLY

con·sid·er·ate \kən-'si-də-rət\ *adj* **1** ♦ : observant of the rights and feelings of others **2** ♦ : marked by or given to careful consideration

♦ [1] attentive, kind, solicitous, thoughtful — more at THOUGHTFUL ♦ [2] alert, careful, cautious, circumspect, gingerly, guarded, heedful, safe, wary — more at CAREFUL

con·sid·er·ation \kən-ˌsi-də-'rā-shən\ n 1 ♦ : careful thought : DELIBERATION 2 : a matter taken into account 3 : thoughtful attention 4 : JUDGMENT, OPINION 5 ♦ : something given as recompense

♦ [1] debate, deliberation, thought; *also* cogitation, contemplation, meditation, pondering, rumination; introspection, reflection; agonizing, hesitation, indecision ♦ [5] compensation, pay, payment, recompense, remittance, remuneration, requital — more at PAYMENT

con·sid·er·ing *prep* : in view of : taking into account

con·sign \kən-'sīn\ vb 1 ♦ : to give over to another's charge, custody, or care : ENTRUST, COMMIT 2 : to deliver formally 3 : to send (goods) to an agent for sale — **con·sign·ee** \ˌkän-sə-'nē, -ˌsī-; kən-ˌsī-\ n — **con·sign·or** \ˌkän-sə-'nȯr, -ˌsī-; kən-ˌsī-\ n

♦ commend, commit, delegate, deliver, entrust, give, hand over, leave, pass, transfer, transmit, trust, turn over, vest — more at GIVE

con·sign·ment \kən-'sīn-mənt\ n : something consigned esp. in a single shipment

con·sist \kən-'sist\ vb 1 : to be inherent : LIE — usu. used with *in* 2 : to be composed or made up — usu. used with *of*

con·sis·tence \kən-'sis-təns\ n : CONSISTENCY

con·sis·ten·cy \-tən-sē\ n, pl **-cies** 1 : COHESIVENESS, FIRMNESS 2 : agreement or harmony in parts or of different things 3 : UNIFORMITY ⟨~ of behavior⟩ 4 ♦ : degree of firmness, density, viscosity, or resistance to movement or separation of constituent particles

♦ thickness, viscosity; *also* compactness, firmness, solidity

con·sis·tent \-tənt\ adj ♦ : marked by agreement

♦ compatible, conformable (to), congruous, consonant, correspondent, harmonious; *also* appropriate, fitting, meet, suitable **Ant** conflicting, incompatible, incongruous, inconsistent, inharmonious

con·sis·tent·ly adv : in a consistent manner

con·sis·to·ry \kən-'sis-tə-rē\ n, pl **-ries** : a solemn assembly (as of Roman Catholic cardinals)

consol abbr consolidated

con·so·la·tion \ˌkän-sə-'lā-shən\ n ♦ : the act or an instance of consoling : the state of being consoled

♦ cheer, comfort, relief, solace — more at COMFORT ♦ comforting, solace; *also* commiseration, condolence, sympathy; counseling

¹**con·sole** \'kän-ˌsōl\ n [F] 1 : the desklike part of an organ at which the organist sits 2 : the combination of displays and controls of a device or system 3 : a cabinet for a radio or television set resting directly on the floor 4 : a small storage cabinet between bucket seats in an automobile

²**con·sole** \kən-'sōl\ vb **con·soled; con·sol·ing** ♦ : to soothe the grief of : COMFORT, SOLACE — **con·so·la·to·ry** \kən-'sō-lə-ˌtōr-ē, -'sä-\ adj

♦ assure, cheer, comfort, reassure, solace, soothe — more at COMFORT

con·sol·i·date \kən-'sä-lə-ˌdāt\ vb **-dat·ed; -dat·ing** 1 ♦ : to unite or become united into one whole : COMBINE 2 : to make stronger or more secure 3 ♦ : to form into a compact mass

♦ [1, 3] center (*or* centre), centralize, combine, compact, concentrate, unify, unite — more at CENTRALIZE

con·sol·i·da·tion \-ˌsä-lə-'dā-shən\ n ♦ : the act or process of consolidating : the state of being consolidated

♦ combination, connection, coupling, junction, unification, union — more at UNION

con·som·mé \ˌkän-sə-'mā\ n [F] : a clear soup made from well-seasoned stock

con·so·nance \'kän-sə-nəns\ n 1 ♦ : harmony or agreement among components 2 : repetition of consonants esp. as an alternative to rhyme in verse

♦ balance, coherence, harmony, proportion, symmetry, symphony, unity — more at HARMONY

¹**con·so·nant** \-nənt\ adj ♦ : having consonance, harmony, or agreement — **con·so·nant·ly** adv

♦ compatible, conformable (to), congruous, consistent, correspondent, harmonious — more at CONSISTENT

²**consonant** n 1 : a speech sound (as p, g, n, l, s, r) characterized by constriction or closure at one or more points in the breath channel 2 : a letter other than a, e, i, o, and u — **con·so·nan·tal** \ˌkän-sə-'nant-ᵊl\ adj

¹**con·sort** \'kän-ˌsȯrt\ n 1 : a ship accompanying another 2 : a wife or husband : SPOUSE, MATE

²**con·sort** \kən-'sȯrt\ vb 1 ♦ : to spend time in the company of 2 : ACCORD, HARMONIZE

♦ associate, chum, fraternize, hang around, hobnob, pal — more at ASSOCIATE

con·sor·tium \kən-'sȯr-shəm; -shē-əm, -tē-\ n, pl **-sor·tia** \-shə-; -shē-ə, -tē-\ [L, fellowship] : an agreement or combination (as of companies) formed to undertake a large enterprise

con·spec·tus \kən-'spek-təs\ n 1 : a brief survey or summary 2 : SUMMARY

con·spic·u·ous \kən-'spi-kyə-wəs\ adj 1 ♦ : obvious to the eye or mind : PROMINENT 2 ♦ : attracting attention : STRIKING 3 ♦ : marked by a noticeable violation of good taste — **con·spic·u·ous·ly** adv

♦ [1, 2] bold, catchy, emphatic, marked, noticeable, prominent, pronounced, remarkable, striking — more at NOTICEABLE ♦ [3] blatant, egregious, flagrant, glaring, gross, obvious, patent, prominent, pronounced, rank, striking — more at EGREGIOUS

con·spir·a·cy \kən-'spir-ə-sē\ n, pl **-cies** 1 ♦ : an agreement among conspirators : PLOT 2 ♦ : a group of conspirators

♦ [1] design, intrigue, machination, plot, scheme — more at PLOT ♦ [2] cabal, gang, mob, ring, syndicate — more at RING

con·spir·a·tor \kən-'spir-ə-tər\ n : one that conspires — **con·spir·a·to·ri·al** \-ˌspir-ə-'tōr-ē-əl\ adj

con·spire \kən-'spīr\ vb **con·spired; con·spir·ing** [ME, fr. MF *conspirer*, fr. L *conspirare* to be in harmony, conspire, fr. *com-* with + *spirare* to breathe] ♦ : to plan secretly an unlawful act : PLOT

♦ contrive, intrigue, machinate, plot, scheme — more at PLOT

const abbr 1 constant 2 constitution; constitutional

con·sta·ble \'kän-stə-bəl, 'kən-\ n [ME *conestable*, fr. OF, fr. LL *comes stabuli*, lit., officer of the stable] ♦ : a public officer responsible for keeping the peace

♦ cop, officer, police officer — more at OFFICER

con·stab·u·lary \kən-'sta-byə-ˌler-ē\ n, pl **-lar·ies** 1 : the police of a particular district or country 2 : a police force organized like the military

con·stan·cy \'kän-stən-sē\ n, pl **-cies** 1 ♦ : firmness of mind 2 ♦ : a state of being constant or unchanging

♦ [1] allegiance, dedication, devotion, faith, faithfulness, fastness, fealty, fidelity, loyalty, steadfastness — more at FIDELITY ♦ [2] fixedness, immutability, stability, steadiness; *also* consistency, regularity, sameness, uniformity; durability, permanence **Ant** instability, mutability, unsteadiness, variability

¹**con·stant** \-stənt\ adj 1 ♦ : marked by firm steadfast resolution or faithfulness : STEADFAST, FAITHFUL 2 ♦ : fixed and invariable : remaining unchanged : UNCHANGING 3 ♦ : continually recurring : REGULAR

♦ [1] devoted, faithful, fast, good, loyal, pious, staunch, steadfast, steady, true, true-blue — more at FAITHFUL ♦ [2] stable, stationary, steady, unchanging, unvarying; *also* fast, fixed, hard-and-fast, immutable, inflexible, invariable, unalterable, unchangeable; established, set, settled; durable, enduring, lasting, permanent *Ant* changeful, changing, fluctuating, inconstant, varying, unstable, unsteady ♦ [3] frequent, habitual, periodic, regular, repeated, steady

²**constant** *n* : something unchanging

con·stant·ly *adv* ♦ : with regular occurrence

♦ continually, frequently, often, repeatedly — more at OFTEN ♦ always, continually, ever, forever, incessantly, invariably, perpetually, unfailingly — more at ALWAYS

con·stel·la·tion \ˌkän-stə-ˈlā-shən\ *n* : any of 88 groups of stars forming patterns

con·ster·na·tion \ˌkän-stər-ˈnā-shən\ *n* : amazement or dismay that hinders or throws into confusion

con·sti·pa·tion \ˌkän-stə-ˈpā-shən\ *n* : abnormally difficult or infrequent bowel movements — **con·sti·pate** \ˈkän-stə-ˌpāt\ *vb*

con·stit·u·en·cy \kən-ˈsti-chə-wən-sē\ *n, pl* **-cies** : a body of constituents; *also* : an electoral district

¹**con·stit·u·ent** \-wənt\ *n* 1 : a person entitled to vote for a representative for a district 2 ♦ : a component part

♦ component, element, factor, ingredient, member — more at ELEMENT

²**constituent** *adj* 1 : COMPONENT 2 : having power to create a government or frame or amend a constitution

con·sti·tute \ˈkän-stə-ˌtüt, -ˌtyüt\ *vb* **-tut·ed; -tut·ing** 1 ♦ : to appoint to an office or duty 2 ♦ : to set up : ESTABLISH ⟨∼ a law⟩ 3 ♦ : to make up (the element or elements of which a thing, person, or idea is made up) : COMPOSE

♦ [1] appoint, assign, attach, commission, designate, detail, name — more at APPOINT ♦ [2] establish, found, inaugurate, initiate, innovate, institute, introduce, launch, pioneer, set up, start — more at FOUND ♦ [3] compose, comprise, form, make up; *also* embody, incorporate, integrate; complement, complete, supplement; fill out, flesh (out)

con·sti·tu·tion \ˌkän-stə-ˈtü-shən, -ˈtyü-\ *n* 1 : an established law or custom 2 ♦ : the physical makeup of the individual 3 ♦ : the structure, composition, or makeup of something ⟨∼ of the sun⟩ 4 : the basic law in a politically organized body; *also* : a document containing such law

♦ [2] build, figure, form, frame, physique, shape — more at PHYSIQUE ♦ [3] character, complexion, genius, nature, personality, tone — more at NATURE

¹**con·sti·tu·tion·al** \-shə-nəl\ *adj* 1 : of or relating to the constitution of body or mind 2 : being in accord with the constitution of a state or society; *also* : of or relating to such a constitution

²**constitutional** *n* : an exercise (as a walk) taken for one's health

con·sti·tu·tion·al·i·ty \-ˌtü-shə-ˈna-lə-tē, -ˌtyü-\ *n* : the quality or state of being constitutional

con·sti·tu·tion·al·ly *adv* ♦ : with respect to mental or spiritual makeup : with respect to bodily makeup

♦ inherently, innately, intrinsically, naturally — more at NATURALLY

con·sti·tu·tive \ˈkän-stə-ˌtü-tiv, -ˌtyü-; kən-ˈsti-chə-tiv\ *adj* 1 : CONSTRUCTIVE 2 : CONSTITUENT, ESSENTIAL

constr *abbr* construction

con·strain \kən-ˈstrān\ *vb* 1 ♦ : to force by imposed stricture, restriction, or limitation : COMPEL 2 : CONFINE 3 ♦ : to withhold or restrain by force

♦ [1] coerce, compel, drive, force, make, muscle, obligate, oblige, press, pressure — more at FORCE ♦ [3] bridle, check, contain, control, curb, govern, inhibit, regulate, rein, restrain, tame — more at CONTROL

con·straint \-ˈstränt\ *n* 1 a : the state of being checked, restricted, or compelled to avoid or perform some action : COMPULSION b ♦ : the act or action of using force or threat of force to prevent or condition an action c ♦ : a constraining condition, agency, or force : RESTRAINT 2 ♦ : repression of one's natural feelings

♦ [1b] coercion, compulsion, duress, force, pressure — more at FORCE ♦ [1c] check, condition, curb, fetter, limitation, restraint, restriction — more at RESTRICTION ♦ [2] reserve, restraint, self-control — more at RESERVE

con·strict \kən-ˈstrikt\ *vb* 1 ♦ : to draw together : SQUEEZE 2 ♦ : to become constricted — **con·stric·tion** \-ˈstrik-shən\ *n* — **con·stric·tive** \-ˈstrik-tiv\ *adj*

♦ [1, 2] compact, compress, condense, contract, squeeze — more at COMPRESS

con·stric·tion \-ˈstrik-shən\ *n* ♦ : the act or product of constricting

♦ compression, condensation, contraction — more at COMPRESSION

con·stric·tor \kən-ˈstrik-tər\ *n* : a snake that coils around and compresses its prey

con·struct \kən-ˈstrəkt\ *vb* ♦ : to make or form by combining or arranging parts or elements : BUILD, MAKE — **con·struc·tor** \-ˈstrək-tər\ *n*

♦ assemble, build, erect, fabricate, make, make up, piece, put up, raise, rear, set up — more at BUILD

con·struc·tion \kən-ˈstrək-shən\ *n* 1 ♦ : the act or result of construing, interpreting, or explaining 2 a : the art, process, or manner of building b : something built, created, or established : STRUCTURE 3 : syntactical arrangement of words in a sentence

♦ clarification, elucidation, explanation, explication, exposition, illumination, illustration, interpretation — more at EXPLANATION

con·struc·tion·ist \-shə-nist\ *n* : a person who construes a legal document (as the U.S. Constitution) in a specific way ⟨a strict ∼⟩

con·struc·tive \-tiv\ *adj* : of or relating to construction or creation

con·strue \kən-ˈstrü\ *vb* **con·strued; con·stru·ing** 1 : to analyze the mutual relations of words in a sentence; *also* : TRANSLATE 2 ♦ : to understand or explain the sense or intention of usu. in a particular way or with respect to a given set of circumstances : EXPLAIN, INTERPRET — **con·stru·able** *adj*

♦ clarify, clear (up), demonstrate, elucidate, explain, explicate, expound, illuminate, illustrate, interpret, spell out — more at EXPLAIN

con·sub·stan·ti·a·tion \ˌkän-səb-ˌstan-chē-ˈā-shən\ *n* : the actual substantial presence and combination of the body and blood of Christ with the eucharistic bread and wine

con·sul \ˈkän-səl\ *n* 1 : a chief magistrate of the Roman republic 2 : a government official who resides in a foreign country to care for the commercial interests of the appointing government's citizens — **con·sul·ar** \-sə-lər\ *adj* — **con·sul·ate** \-lət\ *n* — **con·sul·ship** *n*

con·sult \kən-ˈsəlt\ *vb* 1 : to ask the advice or opinion of 2 ♦ : to deliberate together : CONFER — **con·sul·ta·tion** \ˌkän-səl-ˈtā-shən\ *n*

♦ advise, confer, counsel, parley, powwow — more at CONFER

con·sul·tant \-ᵊnt\ *n* : one who gives professional advice or services

con·sume \kən-ˈsüm\ *vb* **con·sumed; con·sum·ing** 1 : to do away with completely ⟨*consumed* by fire⟩ 2 a : to spend wastefully b ♦ : to use up 3 : to eat up : DEVOUR 4 : to absorb the attention of : ENGROSS 5 : to utilize as a customer — **con·sum·able** *adj* — **con·sum·er** *n*

♦ clean, deplete, drain, exhaust, expend, spend, use up — more at DEPLETE

con·sum·er·ism \kən-ˈsü-mə-ˌri-zəm\ *n* : the promotion of consumers' interests (as against false advertising)

consumer price index *n* : an index measuring the change in the cost of widely purchased goods and services from the cost in some base period

¹**con·sum·mate** \ˈkän-sə-mət, kən-ˈsə-\ *adj* 1 : complete in

every detail : PERFECT **2 ♦** : extremely skilled and accomplished **3 ♦** : of the highest degree

♦ [2] accomplished, adept, crack, crackerjack, expert, good, great, master, masterful, masterly, proficient, skilled, skillful, virtuoso — more at PROFICIENT ♦ [3] maximum, most, nth, paramount, supreme, top, ultimate, utmost — more at ULTIMATE

²con·sum·mate \'kän-sə-ˌmāt\ vb -mat·ed; -mat·ing ♦ : to make complete : FINISH

♦ complete, finalize, finish, perfect — more at FINISH

con·sum·ma·tion \ˌkän-sə-'mā-shən\ n ♦ : the ultimate end

♦ close, conclusion, end, ending, finale, finis, finish, windup — more at FINALE ♦ accomplishment, achievement, actuality, attainment, fruition, fulfillment, realization — more at FRUITION

con·sump·tion \kən-'səmp-shən\ n **1** : progressive bodily wasting away; also : TUBERCULOSIS **2** : the act of consuming or using up **3** : the use of economic goods

¹con·sump·tive \-'səmp-tiv\ adj **1** : tending to consume **2** : relating to or affected with consumption

²consumptive n : a person who has consumption

cont abbr **1** containing **2** contents **3** continent; continental **4** continued **5** control

¹con·tact \'kän-ˌtakt\ n **1** : a touching or meeting of bodies **2** : association or relationship (as in physical or mental or business or social meeting or communication) : CONNECTION **3** : a person serving as a go-between or source of information **4** : CONTACT LENS

²contact vb **1** : to come or bring into contact : TOUCH **2** : to get in communication with

contact lens n : a thin lens fitting over the cornea usu. to correct vision

con·ta·gion \kən-'tā-jən\ n [ME, fr. L contagio, fr. contingere to have contact with, pollute, fr. com together + tangere to touch] **1** : a contagious disease; also : the transmission of such a disease **2** : a disease-producing agent (as a virus) **3** : transmission of an influence on the mind or emotions

con·ta·gious \-jəs\ adj **1** ♦ : able to be passed by contact between individuals ⟨colds are ∼⟩ ⟨∼ disease⟩; also : capable of passing on a contagious disease **2** ♦ : communicated or transmitted like a contagious disease; esp : exciting similar emotion or conduct in others

♦ [1] catching, communicable, transmittable; also infectious, infective ♦ [2] catching, infectious; also irresistible, overpowering, overwhelming; fetching, inviting, winning

con·tain \kən-'tān\ vb **1** ♦ : to keep within limits : hold back or hold down **2** : to have within : HOLD **3** ♦ : to consist of wholly or in part : COMPRISE, INCLUDE — con·tain·able \-'tā-nə-bəl\ adj — con·tain·ment n

♦ [1] bridle, check, constrain, control, curb, govern, inhibit, regulate, rein, restrain, tame — more at CONTROL ♦ [3] carry, comprehend, comprise, embrace, encompass, entail, include, involve, number, take in — more at INCLUDE

con·tain·er \kən-'tā-nər\ n ♦ : a receptacle (as a box or jar) for holding goods; esp : one for shipment of goods

♦ holder, receptacle, vessel; also cartridge; bin, box, carton, case, crate; bag, pocket, sack; cooler, warmer

con·tam·i·nant \kən-'ta-mə-nənt\ n ♦ : something that contaminates

♦ adulterant, defilement, impurity, pollutant — more at IMPURITY

con·tam·i·nate \kən-'ta-mə-ˌnāt\ vb -nat·ed; -nat·ing ♦ : to soil, stain, or infect by contact or association — con·tam·i·na·tion \-ˌta-mə-'nā-shən\ n

♦ befoul, defile, foul, poison, pollute, taint; also infect; besmirch, dirty, soil, sully; corrupt, rot, spoil; adulterate, doctor; dilute, water (down) Ant decontaminate, purify

contd abbr continued

con·temn \kən-'tem\ vb : to view or treat with contempt : DESPISE

con·tem·plate \'kän-təm-ˌplāt\ vb -plat·ed; -plat·ing [L contemplari, fr. com- with + templum space marked out for observation of auguries] **1** ♦ : to view or consider with continued attention **2** ♦ : to view as contingent or probable or as an end or intention : INTEND

♦ [1] chew over, cogitate, consider, debate, deliberate, entertain, meditate, mull, ponder, question, ruminate, study, think, weigh — more at PONDER ♦ [2] aim, aspire, design, intend, mean, meditate, plan, propose — more at INTEND

con·tem·pla·tion \ˌkän-təm-'plā-shən\ n : an act of considering with attention

con·tem·pla·tive \kən-'tem-plə-tiv, 'kän-təm-ˌplā-\ adj ♦ : marked by or given to contemplation

♦ meditative, melancholy, pensive, reflective, ruminant, thoughtful; also introspective, retrospective; earnest, serious, sober, somber; analytical, logical, rational; deliberate, purposeful Ant unreflective

con·tem·po·ra·ne·ous \kən-ˌtem-pə-'rā-nē-əs\ adj : existing, occurring, or originating during the same time : CONTEMPORARY

¹con·tem·po·rary \kən-'tem-pə-ˌrer-ē\ adj **1** ♦ : occurring or existing at the same time **2** ♦ : marked by characteristics of the present period

♦ [1] coeval, concurrent, simultaneous, synchronous; also accompanying, attendant, attending, coincident, concomitant ♦ [2] current, hot, mod, modern, new, newfangled, red-hot, space-age, ultramodern, up-to-date — more at MODERN

²contemporary n : one of the same or nearly the same age as another

con·tempt \kən-'tempt\ n **1** ♦ : the act of despising : the state of mind of one who despises **2** : the state of being despised **3** : disobedience to or open disrespect of a court or legislature

♦ despite, disdain, scorn; also abhorrence, abomination, execration, hate, hatred, loathing; cattiness, hatefulness, malevolence, malice, malignancy, malignity, meanness, spite, spitefulness; aversion, disgust, distaste, horror, odium, repugnance, repulsion, revulsion; animosity, antagonism, antipathy, bitterness, enmity, grudge, hostility, jealousy, pique, resentment; bile, jaundice, rancor, spleen, venom, virulence, vitriol Ant admiration, esteem, regard, respect

con·tempt·ible \kən-'temp-tə-bəl\ adj ♦ : deserving contempt : DESPICABLE — con·tempt·ibly \-blē\ adv

♦ base, despicable, detestable, dirty, dishonorable (or dishonourable), ignoble, low, mean, snide, sordid, vile, wretched — more at IGNOBLE ♦ despicable, lousy, nasty, pitiful, scabby, scurvy, sorry, wretched; also abhorrent, abominable, detestable, execrable, hateful, loathsome, odious; disgusting, repugnant, repulsive; disgraceful, dishonorable, shameful; base, ignoble, low, mean; shabby, sordid, squalid, vile; cowardly, craven, dastardly Ant admirable

con·temp·tu·ous \-'temp-chə-wəs\ adj ♦ : manifesting, feeling, or expressing contempt — con·temp·tu·ous·ly adv

♦ degrading, derogatory, disdainful, scornful, uncomplimentary — more at DEROGATORY

con·tend \kən-'tend\ vb **1** ♦ : to strive or vie in contest or rivalry or against difficulties — often used with with **2** : to strive in debate : ARGUE **3** ♦ : to affirm in or as if in argument : MAINTAIN, ASSERT

♦ [1] battle, compete, fight, race, vie — more at COMPETE ♦ usu contend with [1] cope with, grapple with, handle, manage, maneuver (or manoeuvre), negotiate, swing, treat — more at HANDLE ♦ [3] affirm, allege, argue, assert, aver, avouch, avow, claim, declare, insist, maintain, profess, protest, warrant — more at CLAIM

con·tend·er n ♦ : one that contends

♦ applicant, aspirant, campaigner, candidate, hopeful, prospect, seeker — more at CANDIDATE ♦ challenger, competition, competitor, contestant, rival — more at COMPETITOR

¹**con·tent** \kən-'tent\ *adj* ♦ : having desires limited to whatever one has : SATISFIED

♦ contented, happy, pleased; *also* delighted, glad, joyful, joyous, jubilant; ecstatic, elated, enraptured, euphoric, overjoyed, rapturous, thrilled; appeased, mollified, pacified, placated *Ant* discontent, discontented, displeased, dissatisfied, malcontent, unhappy

²**content** *vb* ♦ : to appease the desires of : SATISFY; *esp* : to limit (oneself) in requirements or actions

♦ delight, gladden, gratify, please, rejoice, satisfy, suit, warm — more at PLEASE

³**content** *n* : the quality or state of being contented : CONTENTMENT

⁴**con·tent** \'kän-ˌtent\ *n* 1 : something contained ⟨~s of a room⟩ 2 ♦ : subject matter or topics treated (as in a book) 3 : material (as text or music) offered by a website 4 : essential meaning or significance 5 : the amount of material contained 6 : the ability to hold, receive, or accommodate

♦ matter, motif, question, subject, theme, topic — more at MATTER

con·tent·ed \kən-'ten-təd\ *adj* ♦ : easy in mind : satisfied esp. with one's lot in life — **con·tent·ed·ly** *adv*

♦ content, happy, pleased — more at CONTENT

con·tent·ed·ness *n* ♦ : the quality or state of being contented

♦ content, contentment, gratification, happiness, pleasure, satisfaction

con·ten·tion \kən-'ten-chən\ *n* 1 : CONTEST, STRIFE 2 ♦ : an idea or point for which a person argues

♦ argument, assertion, thesis; *also* hypothesis, theory; proposal, proposition; assumption, presupposition, supposition; position, stand

con·ten·tious \-chəs\ *adj* ♦ : exhibiting an often perverse and wearisome tendency to quarrels and disputes — **con·ten·tious·ly** *adv*

♦ argumentative, disputatious, quarrelsome, scrappy — more at ARGUMENTATIVE

con·tent·ment \kən-'tent-mənt\ *n* ♦ : ease of mind : SATISFACTION

♦ delectation, delight, enjoyment, gladness, gratification, pleasure, relish, satisfaction — more at PLEASURE

con·ter·mi·nous \kän-'tər-mə-nəs\ *adj* : having the same or a common boundary — **con·ter·mi·nous·ly** *adv*

¹**con·test** \kən-'test\ *vb* 1 : to engage in a struggle or competition : COMPETE, VIE 2 ♦ : to make the subject of dispute, contention, or litigation : CHALLENGE, DISPUTE

♦ challenge, dispute, query, question — more at CHALLENGE

²**con·test** \'kän-ˌtest\ *n* ♦ : a struggle for superiority or victory

♦ bout, competition, event, game, match, meet, tournament — more at GAME ♦ battle, combat, conflict, confrontation, duel, face-off, rivalry, struggle, tug-of-war, warfare; *also* showdown; contention, discord, friction, strife; controversy, debate, disagreement

con·tes·tant \-'tes-tənt\ *n* ♦ : one that participates in a contest

♦ challenger, competition, competitor, contender, rival — more at COMPETITOR

con·text \'kän-ˌtekst\ *n* [ME, fr. L *contextus* connection of words, coherence, fr. *contexere* to weave together] : the parts of a discourse that surround a word or passage and help to explain its meaning; *also* : the circumstances surrounding an act or event — **con·tex·tu·al·ly** *adv*

con·ti·gu·i·ty \ˌkän-tə-'gyü-ə-tē\ *n* ♦ : the quality or state of being contiguous

♦ closeness, immediacy, nearness, proximity — more at PROXIMITY

con·tig·u·ous \kən-'ti-gyə-wəs\ *adj* ♦ : being in contact : TOUCHING; *also* : ADJOINING

♦ adjacent, adjoining, touching — more at ADJACENT

con·ti·nence \'känt-ᵊn-əns\ *n* 1 : SELF-RESTRAINT; *esp* : a refraining from sexual intercourse 2 : the ability to retain urine or feces voluntarily

¹**con·ti·nent** \'känt-ᵊn-ənt\ *adj* : exercising continence

²**continent** *n* 1 : any of the great divisions of land on the globe 2 *cap* : the continent of Europe

¹**con·ti·nen·tal** \ˌkän-tə-'nent-ᵊl\ *adj* 1 : of or relating to a continent; *esp, often cap* : of or relating to the continent of Europe 2 *often cap* : of or relating to the colonies later forming the U.S. 3 : of or relating to cuisine based on classical European cooking

²**continental** *n* 1 *often cap* : a soldier in the Continental army 2 : EUROPEAN

continental drift *n* : a hypothetical slow movement of the continents over a fluid layer deep within the earth

continental shelf *n* : a shallow submarine plain forming a border to a continent

continental slope *n* : a usu. steep slope from a continental shelf to the ocean floor

con·tin·gen·cy \kən-'tin-jən-sē\ *n, pl* **-cies** ♦ : a chance or possible event

♦ case, event, eventuality, possibility — more at EVENT

¹**con·tin·gent** \-jənt\ *adj* 1 : liable but not certain to happen : POSSIBLE 2 : happening by chance : not planned 3 ♦ : dependent on something that may or may not occur — used with *on* or *upon*

♦ *usu* **contingent on** *or* **contingent upon** conditional, dependent, subject — more at DEPENDENT

²**contingent** *n* : a quota (as of troops) supplied from an area or group

con·tin·u·al \kən-'tin-yə-wəl\ *adj* 1 ♦ : continuing indefinitely in time without interruption : CONTINUOUS, UNBROKEN 2 ♦ : steadily recurring

♦ [1] ceaseless, continuous, incessant, unbroken, unceasing, uninterrupted — more at CONTINUOUS
♦ [2] intermittent, periodic, recurrent

con·tin·u·al·ly *adv* ♦ : in a continual way : in an unceasing or regular way

♦ always, constantly, ever, forever, incessantly, invariably, perpetually, unfailingly — more at ALWAYS

con·tin·u·ance \-yə-wəns\ *n* 1 : unbroken succession 2 : the extent of continuing : DURATION 3 : adjournment of legal proceedings

♦ continuation, duration, endurance, persistence, subsistence — more at CONTINUATION

con·tin·u·a·tion \kən-ˌtin-yə-'wā-shən\ *n* 1 ♦ : extension or prolongation of a state or activity 2 : resumption after an interruption; *also* : something that carries on after a pause or break

♦ continuance, duration, endurance, persistence, subsistence; *also* elongation, extension, lengthening, prolongation *Ant* ending, termination

con·tin·ue \kən-'tin-yü\ *vb* **-tin·ued; -tinu·ing** 1 : to maintain without interruption 2 ♦ : to remain in existence : ENDURE, LAST 3 : to remain in a place or condition 4 ♦ : to resume (as a story) after an intermission 5 : EXTEND; *also* : to persist in 6 : to allow to remain 7 : to keep (a legal case) on the calendar or undecided

♦ [2] abide, endure, hold, keep up, last, persist, run on; *also* linger, remain, stay, stick around, tarry *Ant* cease, desist, discontinue, quit, stop ♦ [4] renew, reopen, restart, resume — more at RESUME

con·tin·u·ing *adj* ♦ : needing no renewal : ENDURING

♦ abiding, ageless, dateless, enduring, eternal, everlasting, immortal, imperishable, lasting, perennial, perpetual, timeless, undying — more at ABIDING

con·ti·nu·i·ty \ˌkän-tə-'nü-ə-tē, -'nyü-\ *n, pl* **-ties** **1** : the state of being continuous **2** : something that has or provides continuity
con·tin·u·ous \kən-'tin-yə-wəs\ *adj* ♦ : continuing without interruption — **con·tin·u·ous·ly** *adv*

♦ ceaseless, continual, incessant, unbroken, unceasing, uninterrupted; *also* endless, eternal, everlasting, interminable, perpetual, unending; constant, stable, steady, unchanging, unvarying *Ant* noncontinuous

con·tin·u·um \-yə-wəm\ *n, pl* **-ua** \-yə-wə\ *also* **-u·ums** : something that is the same throughout or consists of a series of variations or of a sequence of things in regular order
con·tort \kən-'tòrt\ *vb* ♦ : to twist out of shape

♦ deform, distort, screw, warp; *also* deface, disfigure; wrench, wrest, wring; coil, curl, twine, wind, wreathe

con·tor·tion \-'tòr-shən\ *n* ♦ : a twisting into abnormal or grotesque shape

♦ deformation, distortion; *also* defacement, disfigurement

con·tor·tion·ist \-'tòr-shə-nist\ *n* : an acrobat able to twist the body into unusual postures
con·tour \'kän-ˌtùr\ *n* [F, fr. It *contorno* fr. *contornare* to round off, fr. ML, to turn around, fr. L *com-* together + *tornare* to turn on a lathe, fr. *tornus* lathe] **1** ♦ : an outline esp. of a curving or irregular figure : OUTLINE **2** : SHAPE, FORM — often used in pl. ⟨the ∼s of a statue⟩

♦ outline, silhouette — more at OUTLINE

contr *abbr* contract; contraction
con·tra·band \'kän-trə-ˌband\ *n* : goods legally prohibited in trade; *also* : smuggled goods
con·tra·cep·tion \ˌkän-trə-'sep-shən\ *n* : intentional prevention of conception and pregnancy — **con·tra·cep·tive** \-'sep-tive\ *adj or n*
¹**con·tract** \'kän-ˌtrakt\ *n* **1** ♦ : a binding agreement **2** : an undertaking to win a specified number of tricks in bridge — **con·trac·tu·al** \kən-'trak-chə-wəl\ *adj* — **con·trac·tu·al·ly** *adv*

♦ bond, covenant, guarantee, guaranty, surety, warranty — more at GUARANTEE ♦ accord, agreement, bargain, compact, convention, covenant, deal, pact, settlement, understanding — more at AGREEMENT

²**con·tract** \kən-'trakt, *2 usu* 'kän-ˌtrakt\ *vb* **1** ♦ : to become affected with ⟨∼ a disease⟩ **2** : to establish or undertake by contract **3 a** ♦ : to reduce to smaller size by or as if by squeezing or forcing together : SHRINK, LESSEN; *esp* : to draw together esp. so as to shorten ⟨∼ a muscle⟩ **b** ♦ : to become reduced in size or volume **4** : to shorten (a word) by omitting letters or sounds in the middle — **con·tract·ible** \kən-'trak-tə-bəl, 'kän-ˌ\ *adj* — **con·trac·tor** \'kän-ˌtrak-tər, kən-'trak-\ *n*

♦ [1] catch, come down, get, sicken, take; *also* break out (with); die (from), succumb (to); fail, sink, weaken ♦ [3a, 3b] compress, condense, constrict, lessen, shrink; *also* collapse, deflate; dry (up), shrivel, wither; decrease, diminish, dwindle; recede, retreat, withdraw *Ant* expand, swell

con·trac·tile \kən-'trakt-ᵊl\ *adj* : able to contract — **con·trac·til·i·ty** \ˌkän-ˌtrak-'ti-lə-tē\ *n*
con·trac·tion \kən-'trak-shən\ *n* ♦ : the action or process of contracting

♦ compression, condensation, constriction — more at COMPRESSION

con·tra·dict \ˌkän-trə-'dikt\ *vb* ♦ : to assert the contrary of : deny the truth of

♦ deny, disallow, disavow, disclaim, gainsay, negate, negative, reject, repudiate — more at DENY

con·tra·dic·tion \-'dik-shən\ *n* ♦ : the act or an instance of contradicting

♦ denial, disallowance, disavowal, disclaimer, negation, rejection, repudiation — more at DENIAL

con·tra·dic·to·ry \-'dik-tə-rē\ *adj* ♦ : involving, causing, or constituting a contradiction

♦ antipodal, antithetical, contrary, diametric, opposite, polar — more at OPPOSITE

con·tra·dis·tinc·tion \ˌkän-trə-dis-'tiŋk-shən\ *n* : distinction by contrast
con·trail \'kän-ˌtrāl\ *n* : a streak of condensed water vapor created by an airplane or rocket at high altitudes
con·tra·in·di·cate \ˌkän-trə-'in-də-ˌkāt\ *vb* : to make (a treatment or procedure) inadvisable — **con·tra·in·di·ca·tion** \-ˌin-də-'kā-shən\ *n*
con·tral·to \kən-'tral-tō\ *n, pl* **-tos** : the lowest female voice; *also* : a singer having such a voice
con·trap·tion \kən-'trap-shən\ *n* ♦ : something devised or contrived : CONTRIVANCE

♦ contrivance, gadget, gimmick, gizmo, jigger — more at GADGET

con·tra·pun·tal \ˌkän-trə-'pənt-ᵊl\ *adj* : of or relating to counterpoint
con·tra·ri·ety \ˌkän-trə-'rī-ə-tē\ *n, pl* **-eties** : the state of being contrary : DISAGREEMENT, INCONSISTENCY
con·trari·wise \'kän-ˌtrer-ē-ˌwīz, kən-'trer-\ *adv* **1** : on the contrary **2** : VICE VERSA
con·trary \'kän-ˌtrer-ē; *4 often* kən-'trer-ē\ *adj* **1** ♦ : opposite in nature or position **2** : COUNTER, OPPOSED **3** : UNFAVORABLE — used of wind or weather **4** ♦ : unwilling to accept control or advice — **con·trari·ly** \-ˌtrer-ə-lē, -'trer-\ *adv* — **con·trar·i·ness** \'kän-ˌtrer-ē-nəs, -'trer-\ *n* — **con·trary** *n is* 'kän-ˌtrer-ē, *adv is like adj*\ *n or adv*

♦ [1] antipodal, antithetical, contradictory, diametric, opposite, polar — more at OPPOSITE ♦ [4] defiant, disobedient, froward, intractable, rebellious, recalcitrant, refractory, unruly, untoward, wayward, willful — more at DISOBEDIENT

¹**con·trast** \kən-'trast\ *vb* [F *contraster*, fr. MF, to oppose, resist, fr. VL *contrastare, fr. L contra-* against + *stare* to stand] **1** : to show differences when compared **2** : to compare in such a way as to show differences
²**con·trast** \'kän-ˌtrast\ *n* **1** : diversity of adjacent parts in color, emotion, tone, or brightness ⟨the ∼ of a photograph⟩ **2** ♦ : unlikeness as shown when things are compared : DIFFERENCE

♦ difference, disagreement, discrepancy, disparity, distinction, diversity, unlikeness — more at DIFFERENCE

con·tra·vene \ˌkän-trə-'vēn\ *vb* **-vened; -ven·ing** **1** : to go or act contrary to ⟨∼ a law⟩ **2** : CONTRADICT
con·tre·temps \'kän-trə-ˌtäⁿ, kōⁿ-trə-'täⁿ\ *n, pl* **con·tre·temps** \-ˌtäⁿ, -ˌtäⁿz\ [F] : an inopportune or embarrassing occurrence
contrib *abbr* contribution; contributor
con·trib·ute \kən-'tri-byət\ *vb* **-ut·ed; -ut·ing** **1** ♦ : to give along with others (as to a fund) **2** : HELP, ASSIST — **con·trib·u·tor** \kən-'tri-byə-tər\ *n* — **con·trib·u·to·ry** \-byə-ˌtòr-ē\ *adj*

♦ bestow, chip in, donate, give, kick in, pitch in, present

con·tri·bu·tion \ˌkän-trə-'byü-shən\ *n* **1** : the act of contributing **2** ♦ : the thing contributed

♦ alms, benefaction, beneficence, charity, donation, philanthropy; *also* offering, tithe; bequest, endowment, legacy; aid, assistance, relief, welfare; grant, subsidy

con·trite \'kän-ˌtrīt, kən-'trīt\ *adj* ♦ : feeling or showing sorrow and remorse for a sin or shortcoming : PENITENT, REPENTANT — **con·trite·ly** *adv*

♦ apologetic, penitent, regretful, remorseful, repentant, rueful, sorry; *also* sad, grieving, mournful, sorrowful, woeful *Ant* impenitent, remorseless, unapologetic, unrepentant

con·tri·tion \kən-'tri-shən\ *n* ♦ : the state of being contrite

♦ guilt, penitence, remorse, repentance, self-reproach, shame — more at GUILT

con·triv·ance \kən-'trī-vəns\ *n* **1** ♦ : a mechanical de-

vice; *broadly* : something contrived, invented, or devised
2 : SCHEME, PLAN **3** : the act or faculty of contriving
: the state of being contrived

♦ contraption, creation, gadget, gimmick, gizmo, invention, jigger — more at GADGET

con·trive \kən-'trīv\ *vb* **con·trived; con·triv·ing 1** ♦ : to form or create in an artistic or ingenious manner : PLAN, DEVISE **2** ♦ : to make devices : form plans, schemes, or designs **3** : to bring about with difficulty

♦ [1] concoct, cook up, devise, fabricate, invent, make up, manufacture, plan, think up — more at INVENT
♦ [2] conspire, intrigue, machinate, plot, scheme — more at PLOT

con·trived \-'trīvd\ *adj* ♦ : lacking in natural or spontaneous quality

♦ affected, artificial, assumed, bogus, factitious, fake, false, feigned, mechanical, mock, phony, put-on, sham, spurious, unnatural — more at ARTIFICIAL

con·triv·er *n* : one that contrives

¹con·trol \kən-'trōl\ *vb* **con·trolled; con·trol·ling** [ME *countrollen* to verify, fr. AF *countrerouler*, fr. *countreroule* copy of an account, audit, fr. ML *contrarotulus*, fr. L *contra* against + ML *rotulus* roll] **1** ♦ : to exercise restraining or directing influence over : REGULATE **2** ♦ : to have power over : RULE

♦ [1] bridle, check, constrain, contain, curb, govern, inhibit, regulate, rein, restrain, tame; *also* bottle (up), repress, suppress; arrest, interrupt, stop; block, hinder, impede, obstruct; gag, muzzle, silence ♦ [1] check, circumscribe, confine, curb, inhibit, limit, restrain, restrict — more at LIMIT ♦ [2] boss, captain, command, govern, preside, rule — more at GOVERN ♦ [2] administer, carry on, conduct, direct, govern, guide, handle, manage, operate, oversee, regulate, run, superintend, supervise — more at CONDUCT

²control *n* **1** ♦ : power to direct or regulate **2** : the condition of being restrained, checked, or controlled; *also* : RESERVE, RESTRAINT **3** : a device for regulating a mechanism

♦ arm, authority, clutch, command, dominion, grip, hold, mastery, power, sway — more at POWER

con·trol·ler \kən-'trō-lər, 'kän-ˌtrō-lər\ *n* **1** : COMPTROLLER **2** : one that controls

con·tro·ver·sy \'kän-trə-ˌvər-sē\ *n, pl* **-sies 1** ♦ : a clash of opposing views **2** : strife through expression of opposing views or claims : DISPUTE — **con·tro·ver·sial** \ˌkän-trə-ˌvər-shəl, -sē-əl\ *adj*

♦ difference, disagreement, dispute, dissension

con·tro·vert \'kän-trə-ˌvərt, ˌkän-trə-'vərt\ *vb* : DENY, CONTRADICT — **con·tro·vert·ible** *adj*

con·tu·ma·cious \ˌkän-tü-'mā-shəs, -tyü-\ *adj* : stubbornly disobedient — **con·tu·ma·cy** \kən-'tü-mə-sē, -'tyü-; 'kän-tyə-\ *n* — **con·tu·ma·cious·ly** *adv*

con·tu·me·ly \kən-'tü-mə-lē, -'tyü-; 'kän-tə-ˌmē-lē, -tyə-\ *n, pl* **-lies** : contemptuous treatment : INSULT

con·tu·sion \kən-'tü-zhən, -'tyü-\ *n* : BRUISE — **con·tuse** \-'tüz, -'tyüz\ *vb*

co·nun·drum \kə-'nən-drəm\ *n* ♦ : an intricate and difficult problem : RIDDLE

♦ enigma, mystery, mystification, puzzle, puzzlement, riddle, secret — more at MYSTERY

conv *abbr* **1** convention **2** convertible

con·va·lesce \ˌkän-və-'les\ *vb* **-lesced; -lesc·ing** ♦ : to recover health gradually — **con·va·les·cent** \-ᵊnt\ *adj or n*

♦ gain, heal, mend, rally, recover, recuperate, snap back; *also* come round, come to, revive; cheer (up), perk (up); survive; recruit

con·va·les·cence \-ᵊns\ *n* ♦ : gradual recovery of health and strength after disease

♦ comeback, rally, recovery, recuperation, rehabilitation; *also* resuscitation, revival; survival

con·vec·tion \kən-'vek-shən\ *n* : circulatory motion in a fluid due to warmer portions rising and cooler denser portions sinking; *also* : the transfer of heat by such motion — **con·vec·tion·al** \-shə-nəl\ *adj* — **con·vec·tive** \-'vek-tiv\ *adj*

convection oven *n* : an oven with a fan that circulates hot air uniformly and continuously around the food

con·vene \kən-'vēn\ *vb* **con·vened; con·ven·ing 1** ♦ : to come together, meet, or assemble in a group or body : ASSEMBLE, MEET **2** ♦ : to cause (persons) to assemble in a group or body : call or gather together

♦ [1] assemble, cluster, collect, concentrate, conglomerate, congregate, forgather, gather, meet, rendezvous — more at ASSEMBLE ♦ [2] assemble, call, convoke, muster, summon — more at CONVOKE

con·ve·nience \kən-'vē-nyəns\ *n* **1** : SUITABLENESS **2** : a laborsaving device **3** : a suitable time ⟨at your ∼⟩ **4** ♦ : personal comfort : EASE

♦ amenity, comfort, luxury — more at COMFORT

convenience store *n* : a small market that is open long hours

con·ve·nient \-nyənt\ *adj* **1** : suited to personal comfort or ease **2** ♦ : placed near at hand — **con·ve·nient·ly** *adv*

♦ accessible, handy, reachable; *also* close, near, nigh; abutting, adjacent, adjoining **Ant** inaccessible, inconvenient, unhandy, unreachable

con·vent \'kän-vənt, -ˌvent\ *n* [ME *covent*, fr. OF, fr. ML *conventus*, fr. L, assembly, fr. *convenire* to come together] : a local community or house of a religious order esp. of nuns — **con·ven·tu·al** \kän-'ven-chə-wəl\ *adj*

con·ven·ti·cle \kən-'ven-ti-kəl\ *n* : MEETING; *esp* : a secret meeting for worship

con·ven·tion \kən-'ven-chən\ *n* **1** ♦ : an agreement esp. between states on a matter of common concern **2** : MEETING, ASSEMBLY **3** ♦ : an assembly of delegates convened for some purpose **4** : generally accepted custom, practice, or belief

♦ [1] accord, agreement, bargain, compact, contract, covenant, deal, pact, settlement, understanding — more at AGREEMENT ♦ [3] assembly, conference, congress, convocation, council, gathering, get-together, huddle, meeting, powwow, seminar — more at MEETING

con·ven·tion·al \-chə-nəl\ *adj* **1** ♦ : sanctioned by general custom **2** : COMMONPLACE, ORDINARY — **con·ven·tion·al·i·ty** \-ˌven-chə-'na-lə-tē\ *n* — **con·ven·tion·al·ize** \-'ven-chə-nə-ˌlīz\ *vb* — **con·ven·tion·al·ly** *adv*

♦ current, customary, popular, standard, stock, usual — more at CURRENT ♦ classical, customary, traditional — more at TRADITIONAL

con·verge \kən-'vərj\ *vb* **con·verged; con·verg·ing** : to approach one common center or single point — **con·ver·gent** \-jənt\ *adj*

con·ver·gence \kən-'vər-jəns\ *n* ♦ : the act of converging

♦ confluence, conjunction, meeting; *also* joining, juncture, merging, union **Ant** divergence

con·ver·sant \kən-'vərs-ᵊnt\ *adj* ♦ : having knowledge and experience — used with *with*

♦ *usu* conversant with abreast, familiar, informed, knowledgeable, up, up-to-date, versed — more at FAMILIAR

con·ver·sa·tion \ˌkän-vər-'sā-shən\ *n* ♦ : an informal talking together — **con·ver·sa·tion·al·ly** *adv*

♦ colloquy, dialogue, discourse, discussion, exchange; *also* banter, cross fire, give-and-take, repartee; conference, parley, powwow; babble, chat, chatter, chitchat, gabfest, gossip, palaver, prate, prattle, rap, small talk; symposium; debate, deliberation

con·ver·sa·tion·al \-shə-nəl\ *adj* **1** ♦ : inclined to converse : fond of or given to conversation **2** ♦ : of, for, characteristic of, or suited to conversation or oral communication

♦ [1] chatty, gabby, garrulous, loquacious, talkative — more at TALKATIVE ♦ [2] colloquial, informal, nonliterary, vernacular, vulgar — more at COLLOQUIAL

con·ver·sa·tion·al·ist \-shə-nᵊl-ist\ *n* : a person who converses a great deal or who excels in conversation

¹con·verse \'kän-ˌvərs\ *n* : CONVERSATION

²con·verse \kən-'vərs\ *vb* **con·versed; con·vers·ing** : to engage in conversation

³con·verse \'kän-ˌvərs\ *n* : a statement related to another statement by having its hypothesis and conclusion or its subject and predicate reversed or interchanged

⁴con·verse \kən-'vərs, 'kän-ˌvers\ *adj* : reversed in order or relation — **con·verse·ly** *adv*

con·ver·sion \kən-'vər-zhən\ *n* **1 ♦** : a change in nature or form **2** : an experience associated with a decisive adoption of religion

♦ changeover, metamorphosis, transfiguration, transformation; *also* shift, transition; adjustment, alteration, modification; redoing, remaking, remodeling, revamping, revision, reworking, variation; deformation, disfigurement, distortion, mutation, transmutation; displacement, replacement, substitution

¹con·vert \kən-'vərt\ *vb* **1** : to turn from one belief or party to another **2 ♦** : to change from one form or function to another : TRANSFORM **3** : MISAPPROPRIATE **4** : EXCHANGE — **con·vert·er** *or* **con·ver·tor** \-'vər-tər\ *n*

♦ make over, metamorphose, transfigure, transform; *also* adjust, alter, modify; redo, refashion, remake, remodel, revamp, revise, rework, vary; deform, disfigure, distort, mutate, transmute; displace, replace, substitute, supplant

²con·vert \'kän-ˌvərt\ *n* **♦** : one that is converted

♦ adherent, disciple, follower, partisan, pupil, votary — more at FOLLOWER

¹con·vert·ible \kən-'vər-tə-bəl\ *adj* : capable of being converted

²convertible *n* : an automobile with a top that may be lowered or removed

con·vex \kän-'veks, 'kän-ˌveks\ *adj* : curved or rounded like the exterior of a sphere or circle — **con·vex·i·ty** \kän-'vek-sə-tē\ *n*

con·vey \kən-'vā\ *vb* **1 ♦** : to bear from one place to another : CARRY, TRANSPORT **2 ♦** : to transfer or deliver (as property) to another : TRANSMIT, TRANSFER — **con·vey·or** *also* **con·vey·er** \-ər\ *n*

♦ [1] bear, carry, cart, ferry, haul, lug, pack, tote, transport — more at CARRY ♦ [2] communicate, impart, spread, transfer, transfuse, transmit — more at COMMUNICATE

con·vey·ance \-'vā-əns\ *n* **1** : the act of conveying **2** : a legal paper transferring ownership of property **3 ♦** : a means of transport : VEHICLE

♦ transport, vehicle; *also* carrier, hauler, mover; transit

¹con·vict \kən-'vikt\ *vb* : to prove or find guilty

²con·vict \'kän-ˌvikt\ *n* : a person serving a prison sentence

con·vic·tion \kən-'vik-shən\ *n* **1** : the act of convicting esp. in a court **2 ♦** : the state of being convinced **3 ♦** : a strong persuasion or belief

♦ [2] assurance, certainty, certitude, confidence, positiveness, sureness — more at CONFIDENCE ♦ [3] belief, eye, feeling, judgment (*or* judgement), mind, notion, opinion, persuasion, sentiment, verdict, view — more at OPINION

con·vince \kən-'vins\ *vb* **con·vinced; con·vinc·ing ♦** : to bring (as by argument) to belief or action — **con·vinc·ing·ly** *adv*

♦ argue, get, induce, move, persuade, prevail, satisfy, talk, win — more at PERSUADE

con·vinc·ing *adj* **♦** : satisfying or assuring by argument or proof

♦ cogent, compelling, conclusive, decisive, effective, forceful, persuasive, satisfying, strong, telling — more at COGENT

con·viv·ial \kən-'vi-vē-əl\ *adj* [LL *convivialis*, fr. L *convivium* banquet, fr. *com-* together + *vivere* to live] **♦** : enjoying companionship and the pleasures of feasting and drinking — **con·viv·ial·ly** *adv*

♦ boon, companionable, extroverted, gregarious, outgoing, sociable, social; *also* cordial, friendly, hospitable; affable, genial, gracious; animated, lively, sprightly, vivacious; communicative, expansive, garrulous, talkative **Ant** antisocial, introverted, unsociable

con·viv·i·al·i·ty \-ˌvi-vē-'a-lə-tē\ *n* **♦** : convivial activities or behavior

♦ festivity, gaiety, jollification, merriment, merrymaking, revelry — more at MERRYMAKING

con·vo·ca·tion \ˌkän-və-'kā-shən\ *n* **1 a** : a ceremonial assembly (as of the clergy) **b ♦** : an assembly of persons convoked **2** : the act of convoking

♦ assemblage, assembly, conference, congregation, gathering, meeting, muster — more at GATHERING

con·voke \kən-'vōk\ *vb* **con·voked; con·vok·ing ♦** : to call together to a meeting

♦ assemble, call, convene, muster, summon; *also* amass, collect, gather, group, round up

con·vo·lut·ed \'kän-və-ˌlü-təd\ *adj* **1** : folded in curved or tortuous windings **2 ♦** : marked by extreme and often needless or excessive complexity : INVOLVED, INTRICATE

♦ complex, complicated, elaborate, intricate, involved, knotty, sophisticated — more at COMPLEX

con·vo·lu·tion \ˌkän-və-'lü-shən\ *n* : a tortuous or sinuous structure; *esp* : one of the ridges of the brain

¹con·voy \'kän-ˌvȯi, kən-'vȯi\ *vb* **♦** : to accompany for protection

♦ accompany, attend, escort, squire — more at ACCOMPANY

²con·voy \'kän-ˌvȯi\ *n* **1** : one that convoys; *esp* : a protective escort (as for ships) **2** : the act of convoying **3** : a group of moving vehicles

con·vulse \kən-'vəls\ *vb* **con·vulsed; con·vuls·ing ♦** : to agitate violently

♦ agitate, jolt, jounce, quake, quiver, shake, shudder, vibrate, wobble — more at SHAKE

con·vul·sion \kən-'vəl-shən\ *n* **1** : an abnormal and violent involuntary contraction or series of contractions of muscle **2 ♦** : a violent disturbance

♦ cataclysm, paroxysm, storm, tempest, tumult, upheaval, uproar; *also* overthrow, overturn, revolution, subversion, upset; fit, seizure, spasm; eruption, flare-up, outbreak, outburst; commotion, furor, fuss, hubbub, hullabaloo, row, ruckus, stew, turmoil; quaking, rocking, shaking, trembling

con·vul·sive \-siv\ *adj* **♦** : resembling a convulsion in being violent, sudden, frantic, or spasmodic — **con·vul·sive·ly** *adv*

♦ stormy, tempestuous, tumultuous; *also* fitful, spasmodic, sporadic

cony *var of* CONEY

coo \'kü\ *n* : a soft low sound made by doves or pigeons; *also* : a sound like this — **coo** *vb*

COO *abbr* chief operating officer

¹cook \'kuk\ *n* : a person who prepares food for eating

²cook *vb* **1** : to prepare food for eating **2** : to subject to heat or fire **3 ♦** : to devise by thinking : FABRICATE — usu. used with *up* — **cook·er** *n* — **cook·ware** \-ˌwar\ *n*

♦ *usu* **cook up** concoct, contrive, devise, fabricate, invent, make up, manufacture, think up — more at INVENT

cook·book \-ˌbuk\ *n* : a book of cooking directions and recipes

cook·ery \'ku-kə-rē\ *n, pl* **-er·ies** : the art or practice of cooking

cook·ie *or* **cooky** \'ku-kē\ *n, pl* **cook·ies** [D *koekje*, dim. of *koek* cake] **1** : a small sweet flat cake **2** *cookie* : a file containing information about a website user created and read by a website server and stored on the user's computer

cookie–cutter *adj* : marked by a lack of originality or distinction ⟨~ malls⟩

cook·out \'kůk-ˌaůt\ *n* : an outing at which a meal is cooked and served in the open

¹**cool** \'kül\ *adj* **1** : moderately cold **2** ♦ : not excited : CALM **3** ♦ : not friendly **4** : IMPUDENT **5** : protecting from heat **6** *slang* : very good — **cool·ly** *adv*

   ♦ [2] calm, collected, composed, placid, self-possessed, serene, tranquil, undisturbed, unperturbed, unshaken, untroubled, unworried — more at CALM ♦ [3] aloof, antisocial, chilly, cold, detached, distant, frosty, remote, standoffish, unfriendly, unsociable; *also* introverted, reserved, withdrawn; misanthropic; apathetic, indifferent, unconcerned; disinterested, incurious, uninterested; reticent, silent, taciturn; diffident, shy, timid *Ant* cordial, friendly, sociable, warm

²**cool** *vb* ♦ : to make or become cool : lose or cause to lose heat, warmth, or passion — sometimes used with *off* or *down*

   ♦ *sometimes* **cool off** *or* **cool down** calm (down), hush, quiet, settle (down) — more at QUIET

³**cool** *n* **1** : a cool time or place **2** : INDIFFERENCE; *also* : SELF-ASSURANCE, COMPOSURE ⟨kept his ~⟩

cool·ant \'kü-lənt\ *n* : a usu. fluid cooling agent

cool·er \'kü-lər\ *n* **1** : a container for keeping food or drink cool **2** : JAIL, PRISON **3** : a tall iced drink

coo·lie \'kü-lē\ *n* [Hindi & Urdu *qulī*] *usu offensive* : an unskilled laborer usu. in or from the Far East

cool·ness *n* ♦ : the quality or state of being cool

   ♦ aplomb, calmness, composure, equanimity, placidity, self-possession, serenity, tranquility — more at EQUANIMITY

coon \'kün\ *n* : RACCOON

coon·hound \-ˌhaůnd\ *n* : a sporting dog trained to hunt raccoons

coon·skin \-ˌskin\ *n* : the pelt of a raccoon; *also* : something (as a cap) made of this

¹**coop** \'küp, 'kůp\ *n* ♦ : a small enclosure or building usu. for poultry

   ♦ cage, corral, pen, pound — more at CAGE

²**coop** *vb* ♦ : to confine in or as if in a coop — usu. used with *up*

   ♦ *usu* **coop up** cage, closet, corral, encase, enclose, envelop, fence, hedge, hem, house, immure, pen, wall — more at ENCLOSE

co–op \'kō-ˌäp\ *n* : COOPERATIVE

coo·per \'kü-pər, 'ků-\ *n* : one who makes or repairs barrels or casks — **cooper** *vb* — **coo·per·age** \-pə-rij\ *n*

co·op·er·ate \kō-'ä-pə-ˌrāt\ *vb* ♦ : to act jointly with another or others — **co·op·er·a·tor** \-'ä-pə-ˌrā-tər\ *n*

   ♦ affiliate, ally, associate, band, collaborate, combine, concert, confederate, join, league, team, unite

co·op·er·a·tion \-ˌä-pə-'rā-shən\ *n* ♦ : the act of cooperating : a condition marked by cooperating

   ♦ collaboration, coordination, teamwork — more at TEAMWORK

¹**co·op·er·a·tive** \kō-'ä-prə-tiv, -'ä-pə-ˌrā-\ *adj* **1** : willing to work with others **2** : of or relating to an association formed to enable its members to buy or sell to better advantage by eliminating middlemen's profits **3** ♦ : marked by cooperation

   ♦ collective, common, communal, concerted, conjoint, joint, mutual, public, united — more at COLLECTIVE

²**cooperative** *n* : a cooperative association

co–opt \kō-'äpt\ *vb* **1** : to choose or elect as a colleague **2** : ABSORB, ASSIMILATE; *also* : TAKE OVER

¹**co·or·di·nate** \kō-'órd-ᵊn-ət\ *adj* **1** : equal in rank or order **2** : of equal rank in a compound sentence ⟨~ clause⟩ **3** : joining words or word groups of the same rank — **co·or·di·nate·ly** *adv*

²**co·or·di·nate** \-'órd-ᵊn-ˌāt\ *vb* **-nat·ed; -nat·ing 1** ♦ : to make or become coordinate **2** ♦ : to work or act together harmoniously — **co·or·di·na·tor** \-'órd-ᵊn-ˌā-tər\ *n*

   ♦ accommodate, agree, blend, conciliate, conform, harmonize, key, reconcile — more at HARMONIZE

³**co·or·di·nate** \-'órd-ᵊn-ət\ *n* **1** : one of a set of numbers used in specifying the location of a point on a surface or in space **2** *pl* : articles (as of clothing) designed to be used together and to attain their effect through pleasing contrast **3** ♦ : one who is of equal rank, authority, or importance with another

   ♦ counterpart, equal, equivalent, fellow, like, match, parallel, peer, rival — more at EQUAL

co·or·di·na·tion \-ˌórd-ᵊn-'ā-shən\ *n* ♦ : the harmonious functioning of parts for effective results

   ♦ collaboration, cooperation, teamwork — more at TEAMWORK

coot \'küt\ *n* **1** : a dark-colored ducklike bird related to the rails **2** : any of several No. American sea ducks **3** : a harmless simple person

coo·tie \'kü-tē\ *n* : a body louse

¹**cop** \'käp\ *n* ♦ : a member of a police force : POLICE OFFICER

   ♦ constable, officer, police officer — more at OFFICER

²**cop** *vb* **1** *slang* : to take surreptitiously ⟨~ a glance⟩ **2** *slang* : ADMIT — used with *to* ⟨~ to the charges⟩ **3** : to take up and practice or use : ADOPT ⟨~ an attitude⟩

co–pay \'kō-ˌpā\ *n* : CO-PAYMENT

co–pay·ment \'kō-ˌpā-mənt, ˌkō-'\ *n* : a fixed fee required of a patient by a health insurer (as an HMO) at the time of each outpatient service or filling of a prescription

¹**cope** \'kōp\ *n* : a long cloaklike ecclesiastical vestment

²**cope** *vb* **coped; cop·ing** ♦ : to struggle to overcome problems or difficulties — usu. used with *with*

   ♦ do, fare, get along, make out, manage, shift — more at GET ALONG ♦ *usu* **cope with** contend with, grapple with, handle, manage, maneuver (*or* manoeuvre), negotiate, swing, treat — more at HANDLE

co·per·nic·i·um \ˌkō-pər-'ni-sē-əm\ *n* : a short-lived artificially produced radioactive element

copi·er \'kä-pē-ər\ *n* : one that copies; *esp* : a machine for making copies

co·pi·lot \'kō-ˌpī-lət\ *n* : an assistant pilot of an aircraft or spacecraft

cop·ing \'kō-piŋ\ *n* : the top layer of a wall

co·pi·ous \'kō-pē-əs\ *adj* ♦ : present in large quantity : LAVISH — **co·pi·ous·ly** *adv* — **co·pi·ous·ness** *n*

   ♦ lavish, profuse, riotous — more at PROFUSE

cop–out \'käp-ˌaůt\ *n* ♦ : an excuse for copping out; *also* : an act of copping out

   ♦ avoidance, escape, evasion, out — more at ESCAPE

cop out *vb* ♦ : to back out (as of an unwanted responsibility)

   ♦ back down, renege — more at RENEGE

cop·per \'kä-pər\ *n* **1** : a malleable reddish metallic chemical element that is one of the best conductors of heat and electricity **2** : a coin or token made of copper — **cop·pery** *adj*

cop·per·head \'kä-pər-ˌhed\ *n* : a largely coppery brown pit viper esp. of the eastern and central U.S.

cop·pice \'kä-pəs\ *n* ♦ : a thicket, grove, or growth of small trees : THICKET

   ♦ brake, brushwood, chaparral, covert, thicket — more at THICKET

co·pra \'kō-prə\ *n* : dried coconut meat yielding coconut oil

copse \'käps\ *n* : a thicket, grove, or growth of small trees : THICKET

cop·ter \'käp-tər\ *n* : HELICOPTER

cop·u·la \'kä-pyə-lə\ *n* : LINKING VERB — **cop·u·la·tive** \-lə-tiv, -ˌlā-\ *adj*

cop·u·late \'kä-pyə-ˌlāt\ *vb* **-lat·ed; -lat·ing** : to engage in sexual intercourse — **cop·u·la·to·ry** \'kä-pyə-lə-ˌtōr-ē\ *adj*

cop·u·la·tion \ˌkä-pyə-'lā-shən\ *n* ♦ : sexual union

   ♦ intercourse, sexual intercourse — more at SEXUAL INTERCOURSE

¹copy \'kä-pē\ *n, pl* **cop·ies** **1** ♦ : an imitation or reproduction of an original work **2** : material to be set in type

♦ carbon copy, duplicate, duplication, facsimile, imitation, replica, replication, reproduction; *also* counterfeit, fake, forgery, phony, sham; dummy, mock-up, simulation; reconstruction, re-creation; image, likeness, semblance, shadow; impression, imprint, print *Ant* original

²copy *vb* **cop·ied; copy·ing** **1** ♦ : to make a copy of **2** ♦ : to attempt to resemble : IMITATE — **copy·ist** *n*

♦ [1] duplicate, imitate, replicate, reproduce; *also* counterfeit, fake, forge; simulate; reconstruct *Ant* originate ♦ [2] ape, emulate, imitate, mime, mimic — more at IMITATE

copy·book \'kä-pē-,bůk\ *n* : a book formerly used to teach handwriting containing examples to be copied

copy·boy \-,bȯi\ *n* : a person who carries copy and runs errands (as in a newspaper office)

copy·cat \-,kat\ *n* : a slavish imitator

copy·desk \-,desk\ *n* : the desk at which newspaper copy is edited

copy editor *n* : one who edits newspaper copy and writes headlines; *also* : one who reads and corrects manuscript copy in a publishing house

copy·read·er \-,rē-dər\ *n* : COPY EDITOR

¹copy·right \-,rīt\ *n* : the sole right to reproduce, publish, and sell a literary or artistic work

²copyright *vb* : to secure a copyright on

copy·writ·er \'kä-pē-,rī-tər\ *n* : a writer of advertising copy

co·quet *or* **co·quette** \kō-'ket\ *vb* **co·quet·ted; co·quet·ting** : FLIRT — **co·quet·ry** \'kō-kə-trē, kō-'ke-trē\ *n*

co·quette \kō-'ket\ *n* [F, fem. of *coquet*, flirtatious man, dim. of *coq* cock] : FLIRT

co·quett·ish *adj* ♦ : having the air or nature of a coquette

♦ coy, demure, kittenish — more at COY

cor *abbr* corner

Cor *abbr* Corinthians

cor·a·cle \'kȯr-ə-kəl\ *n* [W *corwgl*] : a boat made of a frame covered usu. with hide or tarpaulin

cor·al \'kȯr-əl\ *n* **1** : a stony or horny material that forms the skeleton of colonies of tiny sea polyps and includes a red form used in jewelry; *also* : a coral-forming polyp or polyp colony **2** : a deep pink color — **coral** *adj*

coral snake *n* : any of several venomous chiefly tropical New World snakes brilliantly banded in red, black, and yellow or white

cor·bel \'kȯr-bəl\ *n* : a bracket-shaped architectural member that projects from a wall and supports a weight

¹cord \'kȯrd\ *n* **1** ♦ : a usu. heavy string consisting of several strands woven or twisted together **2** : a long slender anatomical structure (as a tendon or nerve) **3** : a small flexible insulated electrical cable used to connect an appliance with a receptacle **4** : a cubic measure used esp. for firewood and equal to a stack 4×4×8 feet **5** : a rib or ridge on cloth

♦ cable, lace, line, rope, string, wire; *also* guy, lanyard, stay

²cord *vb* **1** : to tie or furnish with a cord **2** : to pile (wood) in cords

cord·age \'kȯr-dij\ *n* : ROPES, CORDS; *esp* : ropes in the rigging of a ship

¹cor·dial \'kȯr-jəl\ *adj* [ME, fr. ML *cordialis*, fr. L *cord-, cor* heart] ♦ : warmly receptive or welcoming — **cor·dial·ly** *adv*

♦ amicable, companionable, comradely, friendly, genial, hearty, neighborly, warm, warmhearted — more at FRIENDLY ♦ affable, genial, gracious, hospitable, sociable — more at GRACIOUS

²cordial *n* **1** : a stimulating medicine or drink **2** : LIQUEUR

cor·di·al·i·ty \,kȯr-jē-'a-lə-tē, kȯr-'ja-\ *n* ♦ : sincere affection and kindness

♦ amity, benevolence, fellowship, friendliness, friendship, goodwill, kindliness — more at GOODWILL

cor·dil·le·ra \,kȯr-dəl-'yer-ə, -də-'ler-\ *n* [Sp] : a series of parallel mountain ranges

cord·less \'kȯrd-ləs\ *adj* : having no cord; *esp* : powered by a battery ⟨a ~ phone⟩ — **cord·less** *n*

cor·don \'kȯrd-ᵊn\ *n* **1** : an ornamental cord or ribbon **2** : an encircling line (as of troops or police) — **cordon** *vb*

cor·do·van \'kȯr-də-vən\ *n* : a soft fine-grained leather

cor·du·roy \'kȯr-də-,rȯi\ *n, pl* **-roys** : a heavy ribbed fabric; *also, pl* : trousers of this material

cord·wain·er \'kȯrd-,wā-nər\ *n* : SHOEMAKER

¹core \'kȯr\ *n* **1 a** : the central usu. inedible part of some fruits (as the apple) **b** ♦ : an inmost part of something **2** ♦ : the essential meaning : GIST **3** ♦ : a central or most important part distinct from the enveloping part

♦ [1b, 2] crux, gist, heart, nub, pith, pivot — more at CRUX ♦ [3] base, center (*or* centre), cynosure, eye, focus, heart, hub, mecca, nucleus, seat — more at CENTER ♦ [3] body, bulk, generality, main, mass — more at BODY ♦ [3] center (*or* centre), midpoint — more at CENTER

²core *vb* **cored; cor·ing** : to take out the core of — **cor·er** *n*

CORE \'kȯr\ *abbr* Congress of Racial Equality

co·re·op·sis \,kȯr-ē-'äp-səs\ *n, pl* **coreopsis** : any of a genus of widely cultivated composite herbs with showy often yellow flower heads

co·re·spon·dent \,kō-ri-'spän-dənt\ *n* : a person named as guilty of adultery with the defendant in a divorce suit

co·ri·an·der \'kȯr-ē-,an-dər\ *n* : an herb related to the carrot; *also* : its aromatic dried fruit used as a flavoring

Cor·in·thi·ans \kə-'rin-thē-ənz\ *n* : either of two letters written by St. Paul to the Christians of Corinth and included as books in the New Testament

¹cork \'kȯrk\ *n* **1** : the tough elastic bark of a European oak (**cork oak**) used esp. for stoppers and insulation; *also* : a stopper of this **2** : a tissue of a woody plant making up most of the bark — **corky** *adj*

²cork *vb* : to furnish with or stop up with cork or a cork

cork·screw \'kȯrk-,skrü\ *n* : a device for drawing corks from bottles

corm \'kȯrm\ *n* : a solid bulblike underground part of a stem (as of the crocus or gladiolus)

cor·mo·rant \'kȯr-mə-rənt, -,rant\ *n* [ME *cormeraunt*, fr. MF *cormorant*, fr. OF *cormareng*, fr. *corp* raven + *marenc* of the sea, fr. L *marinus*] : any of a family of dark-colored water birds with a long neck, hooked bill, and distensible throat pouch

¹corn \'kȯrn\ *n* **1** *Brit* : the seeds of a cereal grass and esp. of the chief cereal crop of a region (as wheat in Britain); *also* : a cereal grass **2 a** : a tall widely cultivated cereal grass grown for its large ears of starchy seeds **b** : the typically yellow or whitish seeds of corn esp. used as a food **c** : an ear of corn

²corn *vb* : to salt (as beef) in brine and preservatives

³corn *n* : a local hardening and thickening of skin (as on a toe)

¹corn·ball \'kȯrn-,bȯl\ *n* : an unsophisticated person; *also* : something corny

²cornball *adj* : CORNY

corn bread *n* : bread made with cornmeal

corn·cob \-,käb\ *n* : the woody core on which the kernels of corn are arranged

corn·crib \-,krib\ *n* : a crib for storing ears of corn

cor·nea \'kȯr-nē-ə\ *n* : the transparent part of the coat of the eyeball covering the iris and the pupil — **cor·ne·al** *adj*

corn ear·worm \-'ir-,wərm\ *n* : a moth whose larva is destructive esp. to corn

¹cor·ner \'kȯr-nər\ *n* [ME, fr. OF *cornere*, fr. *corne* horn, corner, fr. L *cornu* horn, point] **1** : the point or angle formed by the meeting of lines, edges, or sides **2** ♦ : the place where two streets come together **3** : a quiet secluded place **4** ♦ : a position from which retreat or escape is impossible **5** : control of enough of the available supply (as of a commodity) to permit manipulation of the price — **cor·nered** *adj* — **around the corner** : ready to take place : about to happen ⟨has a birthday just *around the corner*⟩

♦ [2] crossing, crossroad, intersection — more at CROSSROAD ♦ [4] fix, hole, jam, pickle, predicament, spot — more at PREDICAMENT

²**cor·ner** *vb* 1 : to drive into a corner 2 : to get a corner on ⟨~ the wheat market⟩ 3 : to turn a corner

cor·ner·stone \ˈkȯr-nər-ˌstōn\ *n* 1 : a stone forming part of a corner in a wall; *esp* : such a stone laid at a formal ceremony 2 ♦ : something of basic importance

♦ base, basis, bedrock, footing, foundation, ground, groundwork, keystone, underpinning; *also* center, core, eye, focus, heart, hub, nucleus, seat; kernel, nut, pith; essence, quintessence, soul

cor·net \kȯr-ˈnet\ *n* : a brass band instrument resembling the trumpet

corn flour *n, Brit* : CORNSTARCH

corn·flow·er \ˈkȯrn-ˌflau̇(-ə)r\ *n* : BACHELOR'S BUTTON

cor·nice \ˈkȯr-nəs\ *n* : the horizontal projecting part crowning the wall of a building

corn·meal \ˈkȯrn-ˌmēl\ *n* : meal ground from corn

corn·row \-ˌrō\ *n* : a section of hair braided flat to the scalp in rows — **cornrow** *vb*

corn·stalk \-ˌstȯk\ *n* : a stalk of corn

corn·starch \-ˌstärch\ *n* : a starch made from corn and used in cookery as a thickening agent

corn syrup *n* : a sweet syrup obtained from cornstarch

cor·nu·co·pia \ˌkȯr-nə-ˈkō-pē-ə, -nyə-\ *n* [LL, fr. L *cornu copiae* horn of plenty] : a horn-shaped container filled with fruits and grain emblematic of abundance

corny \ˈkȯr-nē\ *adj* **corn·i·er; -est** ♦ : tiresomely simple or sentimental

♦ maudlin, mawkish, mushy, saccharine, sappy, schmaltzy, sentimental; *also* dreamy, moonstruck, nostalgic; flat, insipid, tasteless, vapid *Ant* unsentimental

co·rol·la \kə-ˈrä-lə, -ˈrō-\ *n* : the petals of a flower

cor·ol·lary \ˈkȯr-ə-ˌler-ē\ *n, pl* **-lar·ies** 1 : a deduction from a proposition already proved true 2 ♦ : something that naturally follows : CONSEQUENCE, RESULT

♦ aftermath, conclusion, consequence, development, effect, issue, outcome, outgrowth, product, result, resultant, sequence, upshot — more at EFFECT

co·ro·na \kə-ˈrō-nə\ *n* 1 : a colored circle often seen around and close to a luminous body (as the sun or moon) 2 : the outermost part of the atmosphere of a star (as the sun) — **co·ro·nal** \ˈkȯr-ən-ᵊl, kə-ˈrōn-ᵊl\ *adj*

cor·o·nal \ˈkȯr-ən-ᵊl\ *n* : a circlet for the head

¹**cor·o·nary** \ˈkȯr-ə-ˌner-ē\ *adj* : of or relating to the heart or its blood vessels

²**coronary** *n, pl* **-nar·ies** 1 : a coronary blood vessel 2 : CORONARY THROMBOSIS; *also* : HEART ATTACK

coronary thrombosis *n* : the blocking by a thrombus of one of the arteries supplying the heart tissues

cor·o·na·tion \ˌkȯr-ə-ˈnā-shən\ *n* : the act or ceremony of crowning a monarch

cor·o·ner \ˈkȯr-ə-nər\ *n* [ME, an officer of the crown, fr. AF, fr. *corone* crown, fr. L *corona*] : a public official who investigates causes of deaths possibly not due to natural causes

cor·o·net \ˌkȯr-ə-ˈnet\ *n* 1 : a small crown 2 : an ornamental band worn around the temples

corp *abbr* 1 corporal 2 corporation

¹**cor·po·ral** \ˈkȯr-p(ə-)rəl\ *adj* ♦ : of or relating to the body ⟨~ punishment⟩

♦ animal, bodily, carnal, fleshly, material, physical, somatic — more at PHYSICAL

²**corporal** *n* : a noncommissioned officer (as in the army) ranking next below a sergeant

cor·po·rate \ˈkȯr-p(ə-)rət\ *adj* 1 : INCORPORATED; *also* : belonging to an incorporated body 2 : combined into one body

cor·po·ra·tion \ˌkȯr-pə-ˈrā-shən\ *n* 1 : the municipal authorities of a town or city 2 : a legal creation authorized to act with the rights and liabilities of a person ⟨a business ~⟩

cor·po·rat·ize \ˈkȯr-pə-rə-ˌtīz\ *vb* **-ized; -iz·ing** : to subject to corporate control ⟨~ education⟩

cor·po·re·al \kȯr-ˈpȯr-ē-əl\ *adj* 1 : having, consisting of, or relating to a physical material body : PHYSICAL, MATERIAL 2 *archaic* : BODILY — **cor·po·re·al·i·ty** \kȯr-ˌpȯr-ē-ˈa-lə-tē\ *n* — **cor·po·re·al·ly** *adv*

corps \ˈkȯr\ *n, pl* **corps** \ˈkȯrz\ [F, fr. OF *cors*, fr. L *corpus* body] 1 : an organized subdivision of a country's military forces 2 ♦ : a group acting under common direction

♦ brotherhood, community, fellowship, fraternity; *also* calling, profession; association, club, federation, guild, organization, society

corpse \ˈkȯrps\ *n* : a dead body

corps·man \ˈkȯr-mən, ˈkȯrz-\ *n* : an enlisted person trained to give first aid

cor·pu·lence \ˈkȯr-pyə-ləns\ *n* ♦ : excessive fatness : OBESITY

♦ fatness, grossness, obesity, plumpness; *also* heaviness; huskiness, stoutness; brawniness *Ant* leanness, thinness

cor·pu·lent \-lənt\ *adj* ♦ : having a large bulky body : OBESE

♦ chubby, fat, fleshy, full, gross, obese, overweight, plump, portly, rotund, round — more at FAT

cor·pus \ˈkȯr-pəs\ *n, pl* **cor·po·ra** \-pə-rə\ [ME, fr. L] 1 : BODY; *esp* : CORPSE 2 : a body of writings or works

cor·pus·cle \ˈkȯr-pə-səl, -ˌpə-\ *n* 1 : a minute particle 2 : a living cell (as in blood or cartilage) not aggregated into continuous tissues — **cor·pus·cu·lar** \kȯr-ˈpəs-kyə-lər\ *adj*

cor·pus de·lic·ti \ˌkȯr-pəs-di-ˈlik-ˌtī, -tē\ *n, pl* **corpora delicti** [NL, lit., body of the crime] 1 : the substantial fact proving that a crime has been committed 2 : the body of a victim of murder

corr *abbr* 1 correct; corrected; correction 2 correspondence; correspondent; corresponding

¹**cor·ral** \kə-ˈral\ *n* [Sp] 1 ♦ : an enclosure for confining or capturing animals 2 : an enclosure of wagons for defending a camp

♦ cage, coop, pen, pound

²**corral** *vb* **corralled; corralling** 1 ♦ : to enclose in a corral 2 ♦ : to gain or regain control of

♦ [1] cage, closet, coop up, encase, enclose, envelop, fence, hedge, hem, house, immure, pen, wall — more at ENCLOSE ♦ [2] bag, capture, catch, collar, get, grab, grapple, hook, land, nab, seize, snare, trap — more at CATCH

¹**cor·rect** \kə-ˈrekt\ *vb* 1 ♦ : to make right 2 ♦ : to punish (as a child) with a view to reforming or improving : CHASTISE 3 ♦ : to counteract the activity or effect of — **cor·rect·able** \-ˈrek-tə-bəl\ *adj*

♦ [1] amend, debug, emend, rectify, reform, remedy; *also* redraft, redraw, restyle, revise, rework, rewrite; redress, right; ameliorate, better, improve; perfect, polish, touch up; fix, mend, repair; adjust, modulate, regulate; alter, change, modify ♦ [2] castigate, chasten, chastise, discipline, penalize, punish — more at PUNISH ♦ [3] annul, cancel, compensate, counteract, counterbalance, make up, neutralize, offset — more at OFFSET

²**correct** *adj* 1 ♦ : conforming to a conventional standard 2 ♦ : agreeing with fact or truth 3 : conforming to the standards of a specific ideology ⟨environmentally ~⟩ — **cor·rect·ness** *n*

♦ [1] decent, decorous, genteel, nice, polite, proper, respectable, seemly — more at PROPER ♦ [2] accurate, exact, precise, proper, right, so, true; *also* legitimate, logical, valid; errorless, faultless, flawless, impeccable, letter-perfect, perfect; rigorous, strict, stringent *Ant* false, improper, inaccurate, incorrect, inexact, untrue, wrong

cor·rec·tion \-'rek-shən\ *n* **1** ♦ : the action or an instance of correcting **2** ♦ : a reproving or punishing of faults or deviations from proper actions

♦ [1, 2] castigation, chastisement, desert, discipline, nemesis, penalty, punishment, wrath — more at PUNISHMENT

cor·rec·tion·al \-'rek-sh(ə-)nəl\ *adj* : of or relating to correction

cor·rec·tive \-'rek-tiv\ *adj* ♦ : tending to correct

♦ disciplinary, penal, punitive — more at PUNITIVE ♦ reformative, remedial; *also* curative, medicinal, therapeutic; reparative, restorative; beneficial, helpful, salutary, wholesome

cor·rect·ly *adv* ♦ : in a correct manner

♦ appropriately, fittingly, happily, properly, rightly, suitably — more at PROPERLY

cor·re·late \'kȯr-ə-ˌlāt\ *vb* **-lat·ed; -lat·ing** ♦ : to connect in a systematic way : establish the mutual relations of — **cor·re·late** \-lət, -ˌlāt\ *n* — **cor·re·la·tion** \ˌkȯr-ə-'lā-shən\ *n*

♦ associate, connect, identify, link, relate — more at ASSOCIATE

cor·rel·a·tive \kə-'re-lə-tiv\ *adj* **1** : reciprocally related **2** : regularly used together (as *either* and *or*) — **correlative** *n* — **cor·rel·a·tive·ly** *adv*

cor·re·spond \ˌkȯr-ə-'spänd\ *vb* **1** ♦ : to be in agreement **2** : to communicate by letter **3** ♦ : to compare closely — usu. used with *to* or *with*

♦ [1] accord, agree, answer, check, coincide, comport, conform, dovetail, fit, go, harmonize, jibe, square, tally — more at CHECK ♦ *usu* **correspond to** [3] equal, match, parallel — more at MATCH

cor·re·spon·dence \-'spän-dəns\ *n* **1** ♦ : agreement between particular things **2** : communication by letters; *also* : the letters exchanged

♦ community, likeness, parallelism, resemblance, similarity, similitude — more at SIMILARITY

¹cor·re·spon·dent \-dənt\ *adj* **1** ♦ : having or participating in the same relationship (as kind, degree, position, correspondence, or function) : SIMILAR **2** ♦ : of a kind appropriate to the situation — used with *with* or *to*

♦ [1] akin, alike, analogous, comparable, like, parallel, similar, such — more at ALIKE ♦ *usu* **correspondent with** *or* **correspondent to** [2] compatible, conformable (to), congruous, consistent, consonant, harmonious — more at CONSISTENT

²correspondent *n* **1** : something that corresponds **2** : a person with whom one communicates by letter **3** ♦ : a person employed to contribute news regularly from a place

♦ journalist, newsman, reporter — more at REPORTER

cor·re·spond·ing·ly *adv* ♦ : in a corresponding manner

♦ alike, also, likewise, similarly, so — more at ALSO

cor·ri·dor \'kȯr-ə-dər, -ˌdȯr\ *n* **1** ♦ : a passageway into which compartments or rooms open (as in a hotel or school) **2** : a narrow strip of land esp. through foreign-held territory **3** : a densely populated strip of land including two or more major cities

♦ gallery, hall, hallway, passage — more at HALL

cor·ri·gen·dum \ˌkȯr-ə-'jen-dəm\ *n, pl* **-da** \-də\ [L] : an error in a printed work discovered after printing and shown with its correction on a separate sheet

cor·ri·gi·ble \'kȯr-ə-jə-bəl\ *adj* : CORRECTABLE

cor·rob·o·rate \kə-'rä-bə-ˌrāt\ *vb* **-rat·ed; -rat·ing** [L *corroborare*, fr. *robur* strength] ♦ : to support with evidence : CONFIRM

♦ bear out, confirm, substantiate, support, validate, verify, vindicate — more at CONFIRM

cor·rob·o·ra·tion \-ˌrä-bə-'rā-shən\ *n* ♦ : something that corroborates

♦ attestation, confirmation, documentation, evidence, proof, substantiation, testament, testimony, validation, witness — more at PROOF

cor·rob·o·ra·tive \-'rä-bə-ˌrā-tiv, -'rä-brə-\ *adj* ♦ : serving or tending to corroborate

♦ confirmatory; *also* auxiliary, supplementary; beneficial, helpful **Ant** confuting, disproving, refuting

cor·rob·o·ra·to·ry \-'rä-bə-rə-ˌtōr-ē\ *adj* : serving or tending to corroborate

cor·rode \kə-'rōd\ *vb* **cor·rod·ed; cor·rod·ing** ♦ : to wear or be worn away gradually (as by chemical action) — **cor·ro·sion** \-'rō-zhən\ *n* — **cor·ro·sive** \-'rō-siv\ *adj or n*

♦ bite, eat, erode, fret — more at EAT

cor·ru·gate \'kȯr-ə-ˌgāt\ *vb* **-gat·ed; -gat·ing** : to form into wrinkles or ridges and grooves — **cor·ru·gat·ed** *adj* — **cor·ru·ga·tion** \ˌkȯr-ə-'gā-shən\ *n*

¹cor·rupt \kə-'rəpt\ *vb* **1 a** ♦ : to make evil : DEPRAVE **b** : BRIBE **2** ♦ : to undergo decomposition from the action of bacteria or fungi : ROT, SPOIL

♦ [1a] debase, degrade, demean, demoralize, humble, subvert, warp — more at DEBASE ♦ [2] break down, decay, decompose, disintegrate, molder, putrefy, rot, spoil — more at DECAY

²corrupt *adj* ♦ : morally degenerate; *also* : characterized by improper conduct ⟨∼ officials⟩

♦ debauched, decadent, degenerate, dissolute, perverse, perverted, reprobate; *also* crooked, cutthroat, dishonest, unethical, unprincipled, unscrupulous; contaminated, spoiled, tainted; bad, evil, immoral, iniquitous, nefarious, sinful, vicious, wicked

cor·rupt·ible *adj* ♦ : capable of being corrupted

♦ bribable, purchasable, venal — more at VENAL

cor·rup·tion \-'rəp-shən\ *n* **1** ♦ : impairment of integrity, virtue, or moral principle **2** ♦ : the process of rotting

♦ [1] debasement, debauchery, decadence, degeneracy, degeneration, degradation, demoralization, depravity, dissipation, dissoluteness, perversion; *also* evil, immorality, sinfulness, wickedness ♦ [2] breakdown, decay, decomposition, putrefaction, rot, spoilage; *also* crumbling, disintegration, dissolution; curdling, fermentation, moldering, souring

cor·sage \kȯr-'säzh, -'säj\ *n* [F, bust, bodice, fr. OF, bust, fr. *cors* body, fr. L *corpus*] **1** : the waist or bodice of a dress **2** : a bouquet to be worn or carried

cor·sair \'kȯr-ˌsar\ *n* ♦ : one who commits or practices piracy : PIRATE

♦ buccaneer, freebooter, pirate, rover — more at PIRATE

cor·set \'kȯr-sət\ *n* : a stiffened undergarment worn for support or to give shape to the waist and hips

cor·tege *also* **cor·tÈge** \kȯr-'tezh, 'kȯr-ˌtezh\ *n* [F] **1** : PROCESSION; *esp* : a funeral procession **2** ♦ : a train of attendants

♦ following, retinue, suite, train; *also* crew, personnel, staff; assistant, attendant, helper, retainer

cor·tex \'kȯr-ˌteks\ *n, pl* **cor·ti·ces** \'kȯr-tə-ˌsēz\ *or* **cor·tex·es** : an outer or covering layer of an organism or one of its parts ⟨the adrenal ∼⟩ ⟨∼ of a plant stem⟩; *esp* : CEREBRAL CORTEX — **cor·ti·cal** \'kȯr-ti-kəl\ *adj*

cor·ti·co·ste·roid \ˌkȯr-ti-kō-'stir-ˌȯid, -'ster-\ *n* : any of various steroids made in the adrenal cortex and used medically as anti-inflammatory agents

cor·ti·sone \'kȯr-tə-ˌsōn, -ˌzōn\ *n* : an adrenal hormone used in treating rheumatoid arthritis

co·run·dum \kə-'rən-dəm\ *n* : a very hard aluminum-containing mineral used as an abrasive or as a gem

cor·us·cate \'kȯr-ə-ˌskāt\ *vb* **-cat·ed; -cat·ing** : FLASH, SPARKLE — **cor·us·ca·tion** \ˌkȯr-ə-'skā-shən\ *n*

cor·vette \kȯr-'vet\ *n* **1** : a naval sailing ship smaller than a frigate **2** : an armed escort ship smaller than a destroyer

co·ry·za \kə-'rī-zə\ *n* : an inflammatory disorder of the upper respiratory tract; *esp* : COMMON COLD

cos *abbr* cosine

COS *abbr* **1** cash on shipment **2** chief of staff

co·sig·na·to·ry \kō-'sig-nə-ˌtōr-ē\ *n* : a joint signer

co·sign·er \'kō-ˌsī-nər\ *n* : COSIGNATORY; *esp* : a joint signer of a promissory note

co·sine \'kō-ˌsīn\ *n* : the trigonometric function that is the ratio between the side next to an acute angle in a right triangle and the hypotenuse

¹cos·met·ic \käz-'me-tik\ *adj* [Gk *kosmētikos* skilled in adornment, fr. *kosmein* to arrange, adorn, fr. *kosmos* order, ornament, universe] **1** : intended to beautify the hair or complexion **2** : correcting physical defects esp. to improve appearance ⟨~ dentistry⟩ **3** : SUPERFICIAL

²cosmetic *n* : a cosmetic preparation

cos·me·tol·o·gist \ˌkäz-mə-'tä-lə-jist\ *n* : one who gives beauty treatments — **cos·me·tol·o·gy** \-jē\ *n*

cos·mic \'käz-mik\ *also* **cos·mi·cal** \-mi-kəl\ *adj* **1** : of or relating to the cosmos **2** : characterized by greatness esp. in extent, intensity, or comprehensiveness : VAST, GRAND — **cos·mi·cal·ly** *adv*

cosmic ray *n* : a stream of very penetrating atomic nuclei that enter the earth's atmosphere from outer space

cos·mog·o·ny \käz-'mä-gə-nē\ *n, pl* **-nies** : the origin or creation of the world or universe

cos·mol·o·gy \-'mä-lə-jē\ *n, pl* **-gies** : a branch of astronomy dealing with the origin and structure of the universe — **cos·mo·log·i·cal** \ˌkäz-mə-'lä-ji-kəl\ *adj* — **cos·mol·o·gist** \käz-'mä-lə-jist\ *n*

cos·mo·naut \'käz-mə-ˌnȯt\ *n* : a Soviet or Russian astronaut

cos·mo·pol·i·tan \ˌkäz-mə-'pä-lət-ᵊn\ *adj* ♦ : belonging to all the world : not local — **cosmopolitan** *n*

♦ smart, sophisticated, worldly, worldly-wise — more at WORLDLY-WISE

cos·mos \'käz-məs, *1 also* -ˌmōs, -ˌmäs\ **1** ♦ : the whole body of things and phenomena observed or postulated : UNIVERSE **2** : a tall garden herb related to the daisies

♦ creation, macrocosm, nature, universe, world — more at UNIVERSE

co·spon·sor \'kō-ˌspän-sər, -'spän-\ *n* : a joint sponsor — **cosponsor** *vb*

Cos·sack \'kä-ˌsak, -sək\ *n* [Pol & Ukrainian *kozak*, of Turkic origin] : a member of one of several autonomous communities drawn from various ethnic groups in southern Russia; *also* : a mounted soldier from one of these communities

¹cost \'kȯst\ *n* **1** ♦ : the amount paid or charged for something **2** : the loss or penalty incurred in gaining something ⟨knowledge is gained at the ~ of innocence⟩ **3** *pl* : expenses incurred in a lawsuit — **at all costs** : regardless of consequences ⟨win *at all costs*⟩

♦ disbursement, expenditure, expense, outgo, outlay — more at EXPENSE ♦ charge, fee, figure, price — more at PRICE

²cost *vb* **cost; cost·ing 1** : to require a specified amount in payment **2** : to cause to pay, suffer, or lose **3** ♦ : to have a price of

♦ bring, fetch, go, sell; *also* amount (to), come (to), total; command, exact; ask, demand

co–star \'kō-ˌstär\ *n* : one of two leading players in a motion picture or play — **co–star** *vb*

Cos·ta Ri·can \ˌkäs-tə-'rē-kən\ *n* : a native or inhabitant of Costa Rica — **Costa Rican** *adj*

cos·tive \'käs-tiv\ *adj* : affected with or causing constipation

cost·ly \'kȯst-lē\ *adj* **cost·li·er; -est 1** ♦ : of great cost or value : not cheap **2** : done at great expense or sacrifice ⟨a ~ error⟩ — **cost·li·ness** *n*

♦ dear, expensive, high, precious, valuable; *also* exorbitant, extravagant, prohibitive, steep, stiff, unreasonable; invaluable, priceless **Ant** cheap, inexpensive

cos·tume \'käs-ˌtüm, -ˌtyüm\ *n* [F, fr. It, custom, dress, fr. L *consuetudo* custom] **1** : the style of attire characteristic of a period or country **2** : an outfit worn to create the appearance characteristic of a particular period, person, place, or thing ⟨Halloween ~s⟩ — **cos·tum·er** \'käs-ˌtü-mər, -ˌtyü-\ *n*

costume jewelry *n* : inexpensive jewelry

cosy *chiefly Brit var of* COZY

¹cot \'kät\ *n* : a small house : COTTAGE

²cot *n* : a small often collapsible bed

cote \'kōt, 'kät\ *n* : a small shed or coop (as for sheep or doves)

co·te·rie \'kō-tə-ˌrē, ˌkō-tə-'rē\ *n* [F] ♦ : an intimate often exclusive group of persons with a common interest

♦ circle, clan, clique, crowd, fold, gang, ring, set — more at GANG

co·ter·mi·nous \ˌkō-'tər-mə-nəs\ *adj* : having the same scope or duration

co·til·lion \kō-'til-yən, kə-\ *n* : a formal ball

cot·tage \'kä-tij\ *n* ♦ : a small house — **cot·tag·er** *n*

♦ cabin, camp, chalet, lodge; *also* bungalow, cot; hut, shack, shanty

cottage cheese *n* : a soft uncured cheese made from soured skim milk

cot·ter *or* **cot·tar** \'kä-tər\ *n* : a peasant or farm laborer occupying a cottage and often a small holding

cotter pin *n* : a metal strip bent into a pin whose ends can be spread apart after insertion through a hole or slot

cot·ton \'kä-tᵊn\ *n* [ME *coton*, fr. AF *cotun*, fr. Ar *quṭun*] **1** : a soft fibrous usu. white substance composed of hairs attached to the seeds of various tropical plants related to the mallow; *also* : this plant **2** : thread or cloth made of cotton

cotton candy *n* : a candy made of spun sugar

cot·ton·mouth \'kät-ᵊn-ˌmau̇th\ *n* : WATER MOCCASIN

cot·ton·seed \-ˌsēd\ *n* : the seed of the cotton plant yielding a protein-rich meal and a fatty oil (**cottonseed oil**) used esp. in cooking

cot·ton·tail \-ˌtāl\ *n* : a No. American rabbit with a white-tufted tail

cot·ton·wood \-ˌwu̇d\ *n* : a poplar having seeds with cottony hairs

cot·tony *adj* ♦ : resembling cotton in appearance or character

♦ downy, satiny, silken, soft, velvety — more at SOFT

cot·y·le·don \ˌkä-tə-'lēd-ᵊn\ *n* : the first leaf or one of the first pair or whorl of leaves developed by a seed plant

¹couch \'kau̇ch\ *vb* **1** : to lie or place on a couch **2** ♦ : to phrase in a specified manner

♦ articulate, clothe, express, formulate, phrase, put, say, state, word — more at PHRASE

²couch *n* ♦ : a piece of furniture (as a bed or sofa) that one can sit or lie on

♦ davenport, divan, lounge, settee, sofa; *also* love seat; day bed, sofa bed; bench

couch·ant \'kau̇-chənt\ *adj* : lying down with the head raised ⟨coat of arms with lion ~⟩

couch potato *n* : one who spends a great deal of time watching television

cou·gar \'kü-gər\ *n, pl* **cougars** *also* **cougar** [F *couguar*, fr. NL *cuguacuarana*, modif. of Tupi (a Brazilian Indian language) *siwasuarána*, fr. *siwasú* deer + *-rana* resembling] ♦ : a large powerful tawny brown wild American cat

♦ mountain lion, panther

cough \'kȯf\ *vb* : to force air from the lungs with short sharp noises; *also* : to expel by coughing — **cough** *n*

could \kəd, 'ku̇d\ *past of* CAN — used as an auxiliary in the past or as a polite or less forceful alternative to *can* in the present

cou·lee \'kü-lē\ *n* **1** : a small stream **2** : a dry streambed **3** : GULLY

cou·lomb \'kü-ˌläm, -ˌlōm\ *n* : a unit of electric charge equal to the electricity transferred by a current of one ampere in one second

coun·cil \'kau̇n-səl\ *n* **1** ♦ : an assembly or meeting for consultation, advice, or discussion **2** : an official body of lawmakers ⟨city ~⟩ **3** ♦ : an association of persons for some common object usu. jointly supported and meeting periodically — **coun·cil·lor** *or* **coun·cil·or** \-sə-lər\

— **coun·cil·man** \-səl-mən\ *n* — **coun·cil·wom·an** \-,wù-mən\ *n*

♦ [1] assembly, conference, congress, convention, convocation, gathering, get-together, huddle, meeting, powwow, seminar — more at MEETING ♦ [3] association, brotherhood, club, college, congress, fellowship, fraternity, guild, institute, institution, league, order, organization, society — more at ASSOCIATION

¹**coun·sel** \'kaùn-səl\ *n* 1 : ADVICE 2 : a plan of action 3 : deliberation together 4 *pl* counsel ♦ : one who gives professional advice or services : LAWYER

♦ advocate, attorney, lawyer — more at LAWYER

²**counsel** *vb* **-seled** *or* **-selled; -sel·ing** *or* **-sel·ling** 1 ♦ : to give advice to 2 ♦ : to ask the advice or opinion of : CONSULT

♦ [1] coach, guide, lead, mentor, pilot, shepherd, show, tutor — more at GUIDE ♦ [2] advise, confer, consult, parley — more at CONFER

coun·sel·or *or* **coun·sel·lor** \'kaùn-sə-lər\ *n* 1 : a person who gives advice or counseling : ADVISER 2 : one that gives advice in law and manages cases for clients in court : LAWYER 3 : one who has supervisory duties at a summer camp

¹**count** \'kaùnt\ *vb* [ME, fr. AF *cunter, counter,* fr. L *computare,* fr. *com-* with + *putare* to consider] 1 ♦ : to name or indicate one by one in order to find the total number 2 : to recite numbers in order 3 ♦ : to take into account : CONSIDER, ACCOUNT 4 ♦ : to rely or depend on someone or something : RELY — used with *on* ⟨you can ∼ on me⟩ 5 ♦ : to be of value or account 6 ♦ : to exclude by or as if by counting — used with *out* ⟨∼ him *out*⟩ 7 : to include by or as if by counting — used with *in* ⟨∼ me *in*⟩ — **count·able** *adj*

♦ [1] enumerate, number, tell; *also* add (up), tally, total; calculate, compute, reckon, table, tabulate; check, mark, tick (off) ♦ [3] account, consider, esteem, hold, rate, reckon, regard, take — more at CONSIDER ♦ *usu* **count on** [4] depend, lean, reckon, rely — more at DEPEND ♦ [5] import, matter, mean, signify, weigh — more at MATTER ♦ *usu* **count out** [6] ban, bar, debar, eliminate, except, exclude, rule out — more at EXCLUDE

²**count** *n* 1 : the act of counting; *also* : the total obtained by counting 2 ♦ : a particular charge in an indictment or legal declaration

♦ charge, complaint, indictment, rap — more at CHARGE

³**count** *n* [ME, fr. AF *cunte,* fr. LL *comes,* fr. L, companion, one of the imperial court, fr. *com-* with + *ire* to go] : a European nobleman whose rank corresponds to that of a British earl

count·down \'kaùnt-,daùn\ *n* : a backward counting in fixed units (as seconds) to indicate the time remaining before an event (as the launching of a rocket) — **count down** *vb*

¹**coun·te·nance** \'kaùnt-ᵊn-əns\ *n* 1 ♦ : the human face 2 : FAVOR, APPROVAL 3 ♦ : the expression of the face

♦ [1] face, mug, visage ♦ [3] cast, expression, face, look, visage — more at LOOK

²**countenance** *vb* **-nanced; -nanc·ing** ♦ : to extend approval or toleration to : SANCTION, TOLERATE

♦ accept, approve, care, favor (*or* favour), OK, sanction, subscribe ♦ abide, bear, brook, endure, meet, stand, stick out, stomach, support, sustain, take, tolerate — more at BEAR

¹**coun·ter** \'kaùn-tər\ *n* 1 : a piece (as of metal or plastic) used in reckoning or in games 2 : a level surface over which business is transacted, food is served, or work is conducted

²**count·er** *n* : a device for recording a number or amount

³**coun·ter** *vb* ♦ : to act in opposition to

♦ battle, combat, contend, fight, oppose — more at FIGHT

⁴**coun·ter** *adv* : in an opposite direction : CONTRARY

⁵**coun·ter** *n* 1 : OPPOSITE, CONTRARY 2 : an answering or offsetting force or blow

⁶**coun·ter** *adj* : marked by or tending toward or in an opposite direction or effect : CONTRARY, OPPOSITE

coun·ter·act \,kaùn-tər-'akt\ *vb* ♦ : to lessen the force of : OFFSET — **coun·ter·ac·tive** \-'ak-tiv\ *adj*

♦ annul, cancel, compensate, correct, counterbalance, make up, neutralize, offset — more at OFFSET

coun·ter·at·tack \'kaùn-tər-ə-,tak\ *n* : an attack made to oppose an enemy's attack — **counterattack** *vb*

¹**coun·ter·bal·ance** \'kaùn-tər-,ba-ləns\ *n* ♦ : a weight or influence that balances another

♦ balance, canceler, counterweight, equipoise, offset

²**counterbalance** \,kaùn-tər-'ba-ləns\ *vb* : to oppose with equal weight or influence

coun·ter·claim \'kaùn-tər-,klām\ *n* : an opposing claim esp. in law

coun·ter·clock·wise \,kaùn-tər-'kläk-,wīz\ *adv* : in a direction opposite to that in which the hands of a clock rotate — **counterclockwise** *adj*

coun·ter·cul·ture \'kaùn-tər-,kəl-chər\ *n* : a culture esp. of the young with values and mores that run counter to those of established society

coun·ter·es·pi·o·nage \,kaùn-tər-'es-pē-ə-,näzh, -nij\ *n* : activities intended to discover and defeat enemy espionage

¹**coun·ter·feit** \'kaùn-tər-,fit\ *adj* 1 : not genuine or real 2 ♦ : made in imitation of something else with intent to deceive

♦ bogus, fake, false, inauthentic, phony, sham, spurious, unauthentic; *also* artificial, factitious, imitation, man-made, mock, substitute, synthetic; fabricated, manufactured; deceptive, delusive, misleading *Ant* authentic, bona fide, genuine, real

²**counterfeit** *vb* 1 : to copy or imitate in order to deceive 2 ♦ : to imitate or feign esp. with intent to deceive : PRETEND, FEIGN — **coun·ter·feit·er** *n*

♦ affect, assume, fake, feign, pretend, profess, put on, sham, simulate — more at FEIGN

³**counterfeit** *n* ♦ : something counterfeit : FORGERY

♦ fake, forgery, hoax, humbug, phony, sham — more at FAKE

coun·ter·in·sur·gen·cy \,kaùn-tər-in-'sər-jən-sē\ *n* : military activity designed to deal with insurgents

coun·ter·in·tel·li·gence \-in-'te-lə-jəns\ *n* : organized activities of an intelligence service designed to counter the activities of an enemy's intelligence service

coun·ter·in·tu·i·tive \-in-'tü-ə-tiv, -'tyü-\ *adj* : contrary to what would intuitively be expected

coun·ter·man \'kaùn-tər-,man, -mən\ *n* : one who tends a counter

coun·ter·mand \'kaùn-ər-,mand\ *vb* : to withdraw (an order already given) by a contrary order

coun·ter·mea·sure \-,me-zhər\ *n* : an action or device designed to counter another

coun·ter·of·fen·sive \-ə-,fen-siv\ *n* : a large-scale counterattack

coun·ter·pane \-,pān\ *n* ♦ : a usu. ornamental cloth cover for a bed : BEDSPREAD

♦ bedspread, spread; *also* comforter, puff, quilt; bedclothes, bedding

coun·ter·part \-,pärt\ *n* ♦ : a person or thing very closely like or corresponding to another person or thing

♦ coordinate, equal, equivalent, fellow, like, match, parallel, peer, rival — more at EQUAL ♦ carbon copy, double, duplicate, duplication, facsimile, image, likeness, match, picture, replica, ringer, spit — more at IMAGE

coun·ter·point \-,pòint\ *n* : music in which one melody is accompanied by one or more other melodies all woven into a harmonious whole

coun·ter·poise \-,pòiz\ *n* : a force or influence that offsets or checks an opposing force : COUNTERBALANCE

coun·ter·rev·o·lu·tion \,kaùn-tər-,re-və-'lü-shən\ *n* : a revolution opposed to a current or earlier one — **coun·ter·rev·o·lu·tion·ary** \-shə-,ner-ē\ *adj or n*

coun·ter·sign \'kau̇n-tər-ˌsīn\ *n* **1** : a confirmatory signature added to a writing already signed by another person **2** : a military secret signal that must be given by a person who wishes to pass a guard — **countersign** *vb*

coun·ter·sink \-ˌsiŋk\ *vb* **-sunk** \-ˌsəŋk\; **-sink·ing** **1** : to form a funnel-shaped enlargement at the outer end of a drilled hole **2** : to set the head of (as a screw) at or below the surface — **countersink** *n*

coun·ter·spy \-ˌspī\ *n* : a spy engaged in counterespionage

coun·ter·ten·or \-ˌte-nər\ *n* : a tenor with an unusually high range

coun·ter·vail \ˌkau̇n-tər-'vāl\ *vb* : COUNTERACT

coun·ter·weight \'kau̇n-tər-ˌwāt\ *n* ♦ : a force or influence that offsets or checks an opposing force : COUNTERBALANCE

♦ balance, canceler, counterbalance, equipoise, offset

count·ess \'kau̇n-təs\ *n* **1** : the wife or widow of a count or an earl **2** : a woman holding the rank of a count or an earl in her own right

count·ing·house \'kau̇n-tiŋ-ˌhau̇s\ *n* : a building or office for keeping books and conducting business

count·less \'kau̇nt-ləs\ *adj* ♦ : too numerous to be counted : INNUMERABLE

♦ innumerable, numberless, uncountable, unnumbered, untold; *also* endless, infinite, unlimited, vast; many, multitudinous, numerous *Ant* countable

coun·tri·fied *also* **coun·try·fied** \'kən-tri-ˌfīd\ *adj* **1** : RURAL, RUSTIC **2** : UNSOPHISTICATED **3** : played or sung in the manner of country music

¹**coun·try** \'kən-trē\ *n, pl* **countries** [ME *contree*, fr. AF *cuntree*, *contré*, fr. ML *contrata*, fr. L *contra* against, on the opposite side] **1** : REGION, DISTRICT **2** ♦ : the land of a person's birth, residence, or citizenship : FATHERLAND **3** ♦ : a nation or its territory **4** : rural regions as opposed to towns and cities **5** : COUNTRY MUSIC

♦ [2] fatherland, home, homeland, motherland, sod; *also* community, neighborhood ♦ [3] commonwealth, land, nation, sovereignty, state — more at NATION

²**country** *adj* **1** ♦ : of, relating to, or characteristic of the country : RURAL **2** : of or relating to country music ⟨a ~ singer⟩

♦ bucolic, pastoral, rural, rustic — more at RURAL

country and western *n* : COUNTRY MUSIC

country club *n* : a suburban club for social life and recreation; *esp* : one having a golf course — **country–club** *adj*

coun·try–dance \'kən-trē-ˌdans\ *n* : an English dance in which partners face each other esp. in rows

coun·try·man \'kən-trē-mən, *2 often* -ˌman\ *n* **1** : an inhabitant of a specified country **2** : COMPATRIOT **3** : one raised or living in the country : RUSTIC

country music *n* : music derived from or imitating the folk style of the southern U.S. or of the Western cowboy

coun·try·side \'kən-trē-ˌsīd\ *n* : a rural area or its people

coun·ty \'kau̇n-tē\ *n, pl* **counties** **1** : the domain of a count **2** : a territorial division of a country or state for purposes of local government

coup \'kü\ *n, pl* **coups** \'küz\ [F, blow, stroke] **1** ♦ : a highly successful stroke, action, plan, or stratagem **2** : COUP D'ÉTAT

♦ accomplishment, achievement, attainment, success, triumph — more at ACCOMPLISHMENT

coup de grace \ˌkü-də-'gräs\ *n, pl* **coups de grace** *same*\ [F *coup de grâce*, lit., stroke of mercy] : DEATHBLOW; *also* : a final decisive stroke or event

coup d'état \ˌkü-də-'tä\ *n, pl* **coups d'état** *same*\ [F, lit., stroke of state] : a sudden violent overthrow of a government by a small group

cou·pé *or* **coupe** \kü-'pā, *2 often* 'küp\ *n* [F *coupé*, fr. *couper* to cut] **1** : a closed horse-drawn carriage for two persons inside with an outside seat for the driver **2** *usu* **coupe** : a 2-door automobile with an enclosed body

¹**cou·ple** \'kə-pəl\ *n* **1** : two persons closely associated; *esp* : two persons married, engaged, or otherwise romantically paired **2** ♦ : two of the same kind considered together : PAIR **3** : BOND, TIE **4** : an indefinite small number : FEW ⟨a ~ of days ago⟩

♦ brace, duo, pair, twain, twosome — more at PAIR

²**couple** *vb* **cou·pled**; **cou·pling** ♦ : to link together

♦ associate, combine, conjoin, connect, hitch, hook, join, link, marry, unify, unite, yoke — more at UNITE

cou·plet \'kə-plət\ *n* : two successive rhyming lines of verse

cou·pling \'kə-pliŋ (*usual for 2*), -pə-liŋ\ *n* **1** ♦ : the act of bringing or coming together : CONNECTION; *also* : the point at which things are connected **2** : a device for connecting two parts or things

♦ combination, connection, consolidation, junction, unification, union — more at UNION

cou·pon \'kü-ˌpän, 'kyü-\ *n* **1** : a statement attached to a bond showing interest due and designed to be cut off and presented for payment **2** : a form surrendered in order to obtain an article, service, or accommodation **3** : a printed document or slip used to submit orders or inquiries or to obtain a discount on merchandise or services

cour·age \'kər-ij\ *n* ♦ : ability to conquer fear or despair : BRAVERY, VALOR

♦ bravery, daring, fearlessness, gallantry, guts, hardihood, heart, heroism, nerve, stoutness, valor; *also* backbone, fiber, fortitude, grit, gumption, mettle, pluck, spunk; determination, perseverance, resolution; endurance, stamina, tenacity; audacity, boldness, brazenness, cheek, effrontery, gall, temerity *Ant* cowardice

cou·ra·geous \kə-'rā-jəs\ *adj* ♦ : having or characterized by courage — **cou·ra·geous·ly** *adv*

♦ brave, dauntless, doughty, fearless, gallant, greathearted, heroic, intrepid, lionhearted, manful, stalwart, stout, undaunted, valiant, valorous — more at BRAVE

cou·ri·er \'kur-ē-ər, 'kər-ē-\ *n* : one who bears messages or information esp. for the diplomatic or military services

♦ go-between, messenger, page, runner — more at MESSENGER

¹**course** \'kōrs\ *n* **1 a** : the act or action of moving in a path from point to point : PROGRESS, PASSAGE **b** ♦ : direction of progress **2** : the ground or path over which something moves **3 a** ♦ : method of procedure **b** : CONDUCT, BEHAVIOR **4** ♦ : an ordered series of acts or proceedings : sequence of events **5** : a series of instruction periods dealing with a subject **6** : the series of studies leading to graduation from a school or college **7** : the part of a meal served at one time — **of course** : as might be expected

♦ [1b] line, path, route, track, way — more at PATH
♦ [3a] line, policy, procedure, program; *also* blueprint, design, plan, scheme, strategy; intent, intention, purpose; approach, direction, path, pathway, tack
♦ [4] operation, procedure, proceeding, process — more at PROCESS

²**course** *vb* **coursed**; **cours·ing** **1** : to hunt with dogs **2** ♦ : to run or go speedily

♦ barrel, career, dash, fly, hurry, pelt, race, rip, rocket, run, rush, shoot, speed, tear, zip, zoom — more at HURRY

cours·er \'kōr-sər\ *n* : a swift or spirited horse

¹**court** \'kōrt\ *n* [ME, fr. AF, fr. L *cohort-, cohors* enclosure, group, retinue, cohort] **1** : the residence of a sovereign or similar dignitary **2** : a sovereign's formal assembly of officials and advisers as a governing power **3** : an assembly of the retinue of a sovereign **4** ♦ : an open space enclosed by a building or buildings **5** : a space walled or marked off for playing a game (as tennis or basketball) **6** : the place where justice is administered; *also* : a judicial body or a meeting of a judicial body **7** : attention intended to win favor **8** ♦ : a judge or judges in session

♦ [4] close, courtyard, quadrangle, yard; *also* place, plaza, square; deck, terrace ♦ [8] bench, judge, justice, magistrate — more at JUDGE

²**court** *vb* **1** : to try to gain the favor of **2** ♦ : to seek to gain or achieve : WOO **3** : ATTRACT, TEMPT

♦ ask, woo; *also* angle (for), fish (for); hunt, search, seek

cour·te·ous \'kər-tē-əs\ *adj* ♦ : marked by respect for others : CIVIL, POLITE

♦ civil, genteel, gracious, mannerly, polite, well-bred — more at POLITE

cour·te·ous·ly *adv* ♦ : in a courteous manner

♦ kindly, nicely, thoughtfully, well — more at WELL

cour·te·san \'kȯr-tə-zən, -,zan\ *n* : PROSTITUTE

cour·te·sy \'kər-tə-sē\ *n, pl* **-sies** 1 ♦ : courteous behavior 2 ♦ : a favor courteously performed

♦ [1] amenity, civility, formality, gesture — more at CIVILITY ♦ [1] civility, gentility, graciousness, mannerliness, politeness — more at POLITENESS ♦ [2] boon, favor (*or* favour), grace, indulgence, kindness, mercy, service, turn

court·house \'kȯrt-,haůs\ *n* : a building in which courts of law are held or county offices are located

court·ier \'kȯr-tē-ər\ *n* : a person in attendance at a royal court

court·li·ness *n* ♦ : the quality of being courtly

♦ class, elegance, grace, gracefulness, handsomeness, majesty, refinement, stateliness — more at ELEGANCE

court·ly \'kȯrt-lē\ *adj* **court·li·er; -est** : of a quality befitting the court : REFINED, ELEGANT

court–mar·tial \'kȯrt-,mär-shəl\ *n, pl* **courts–martial** : a military or naval court for trial of offenses against military or naval law; *also* : a trial by this court — **court–martial** *vb*

court·room \-,rüm, -,rům\ *n* : a room in which a court of law is held

court·ship \-,ship\ *n* : the act of courting : the act of wooing

court·yard \-,yärd\ *n* ♦ : an enclosure next to a building

♦ close, court, quadrangle, yard — more at COURT

cous·cous \'küs-,küs\ *n* : a No. African dish of steamed semolina usu. served with meat or vegetables; *also* : the semolina itself

cous·in \'kə-zən\ *n* [ME *cosin*, fr. AF, fr. L *consobrinus*, fr. *com-* with + *sobrinus* second cousin, fr. *soror* sister] : a child of one's uncle or aunt

cou·ture \kü-'tůr, -'tœ̄r\ *n* [F] : the business of designing fashionable custom-made women's clothing; *also* : the designers and establishments engaged in this business

cou·tu·ri·er \kü-'tůr-ē-ər, -ē-,ā\ *n* [F, dressmaker] : the owner of an establishment engaged in couture

cove \'kōv\ *n* ♦ : a small sheltered inlet or bay

♦ bay, bight, estuary, fjord, gulf, inlet — more at GULF

co·ven \'kə-vən\ *n* : an assembly or band of witches

¹**cov·e·nant** \'kə-və-nənt\ *n* ♦ : a formal binding agreement : COMPACT

♦ accord, agreement, bargain, compact, contract, convention, deal, pact, settlement, understanding — more at AGREEMENT ♦ bond, contract, guarantee, surety, warranty — more at GUARANTEE

²**cov·e·nant** \-nənt, -,nant\ *vb* ♦ : to promise by a covenant

♦ pledge, promise, swear, vow — more at PROMISE

¹**cov·er** \'kə-vər\ *vb* 1 : to bring or hold within range of a firearm 2 ♦ : to afford protection or security to : PROTECT, SHIELD 3 ♦ : to hide from sight or knowledge : HIDE, CONCEAL 4 ♦ : to place something over or upon 5 : INCLUDE, COMPRISE 6 : to have as one's field of activity ⟨one salesman ∼s the state⟩ 7 : to buy (stocks) in order to have them for delivery on a previous short sale 8 ♦ : to deal with 9 ♦ : to pass over 10 ♦ : to act as a substitute or replacement during an absence

♦ [2] defend, guard, protect, safeguard, screen, secure, shield, ward — more at DEFEND ♦ [3] blanket, blot out, cloak, conceal, curtain, enshroud, hide, mask, obscure, occult, screen, shroud, veil — more at HIDE ♦ [4] blanket, carpet, coat, overlay, overlie, overspread; *also* : enclose, enshroud, envelop, mantle, shawl, shroud, swathe, wrap; cloak, clothe, curtain, veil; circle, encircle, encompass ♦ [8] concern, deal, pertain, treat — more at

CONCERN ♦ [9] crisscross, cross, cut, follow, go, pass, proceed, travel, traverse — more at TRAVERSE ♦ [10] fill in, pinch-hit, stand in, sub, substitute, take over; *also* understudy; relieve, spell; double (as)

²**cover** *n* 1 ♦ : something that protects or shelters 2 ♦ : a movable cover for the opening of a hollow container : LID, TOP 3 : CASE, BINDING 4 : TABLECLOTH 5 : a cloth used on a bed 6 : SCREEN, DISGUISE 7 : an envelope or wrapper for mail

♦ [1] aegis, armor, defense (*or* defence), guard, protection, safeguard, screen, security, shield, wall, ward — more at DEFENSE ♦ [1] armor, capsule, case, casing, cocoon, housing, husk, jacket, pod, sheath, shell — more at CASE ♦ [2] cap, lid, top; *also* dome, hood, roof; capsule, case, casing, covering, housing, jacket, sheath, shell

cov·er·age \'kə-və-rij\ *n* 1 : the act or fact of covering 2 : the total group covered : SCOPE

cov·er·all \'kə-vər-,ȯl\ *n* : a one-piece outer garment worn to protect one's clothes — usu. used in pl.

cover charge *n* : a charge made by a restaurant or nightclub in addition to the charge for food and drink

cover crop *n* : a crop planted to prevent soil erosion and to provide humus

cov·er·ing *n* : something that covers or conceals

cov·er·let \'kə-vər-lət\ *n* : a usu. ornamental cloth cover for a bed : BEDSPREAD

¹**co·vert** \'kō-,vərt, 'kə-vərt\ *adj* 1 ♦ : not openly shown, engaged in, or avowed : SECRET 2 : SHELTERED — **co·vert·ly** *adv*

♦ cloistered, isolated, quiet, remote, secluded, secret — more at SECLUDED ♦ clandestine, furtive, hugger-mugger, private, secret, sneak, sneaky, stealthy, surreptitious, undercover, underground, underhanded — more at SECRET

²**co·vert** \'kə-vərt, 'kō-\ *n* 1 ♦ : a secret or sheltered place; *esp* : a thicket sheltering game 2 : a feather covering the bases of the quills of the wings and tail of a bird

♦ concealment, den, hideout, lair, nest — more at HIDEOUT ♦ brake, brushwood, chaparral, coppice, thicket — more at THICKET

cov·er–up \'kə-vər-,əp\ *n* 1 : a device for masking or concealing 2 : a usu. concerted effort to keep an illegal or unethical act or situation from being made public

cov·et \'kə-vət\ *vb* ♦ : to desire enviously (what belongs to another)

♦ ache for, crave, desire, die for, hanker for, hunger for, long for, lust (for *or* after), pine for, repine for, thirst for, want, wish for, yearn for — more at DESIRE

cov·et·ous *adj* ♦ : marked by inordinate desire for wealth or possessions or for another's possessions

♦ acquisitive, avaricious, avid, grasping, greedy, mercenary, rapacious — more at GREEDY

cov·et·ous·ness *n* ♦ : the state of being covetous

♦ acquisitiveness, avarice, avidity, cupidity, greed, rapaciousness — more at GREED

cov·ey \'kə-vē\ *n, pl* **coveys** [ME, fr. AF *covee* sitting (of a hen), fr. *cover* to sit on, brood over, fr. L *cubare* to lie] 1 : a bird with her brood of young 2 : a small flock (as of quail)

¹**cow** \'kaů\ *n* 1 : the mature female of cattle or of an animal (as the moose, elephant, or whale) of which the male is called *bull* 2 : any domestic bovine animal irrespective of sex or age

²**cow** *vb* ♦ : to destroy the resolve or courage of : INTIMIDATE

♦ browbeat, bully, hector, intimidate — more at INTIMIDATE

cow·ard \'kaů-(ə)rd\ *n* [ME, fr. OF *coart*, fr. *coe* tail, fr. L *cauda*] ♦ : one who lacks courage or shows shameful fear or timidity — **coward** *adj* — **cow·ard·ice** \'kaů-ər-dəs\ *n*

♦ chicken, craven, dastard, poltroon, recreant, sissy; *also* defeatist, quitter; pushover, weakling, wimp; snake, sneak *Ant* hero, stalwart, valiant

cow·ard·ly *adv or adj* ♦ : being, resembling, or befitting a coward

♦ chicken, craven, dastardly, pusillanimous, recreant, spineless, yellow; *also* diffident, fainthearted, fearful, timid, timorous; afraid, frightened, scared; careful, cautious, wary; bashful, coy, shy; feeble, soft, weak *Ant* brave, courageous, daring, dauntless, doughty, fearless, gallant, greathearted, gutsy, hardy, heroic, intrepid, lionhearted, stalwart, stout, valiant, valorous

cow·bird \'kaủ-ˌbərd\ *n* : a small No. American blackbird that lays its eggs in the nests of other birds

cow·boy \-ˌbȯi\ *n* : one (as a mounted ranch hand) who tends cattle or horses

cow·er \'kaủ(-ə)r\ *vb* ♦ : to shrink or crouch down from fear or cold : QUAIL

♦ cringe, grovel, quail; *also* flinch, recoil, shrink; blanch, blench, whiten; fawn, kowtow, toady

cow·girl \'kaủ-ˌgərl\ *n* : a girl or woman who tends cattle or horses

cow·hand \'kaủ-ˌhand\ *n* : one who tends cattle or horses : COWBOY

cow·hide \-ˌhīd\ *n* **1** : the hide of a cow; *also* : leather made from it **2** : a coarse whip of braided rawhide

cowl \'kaủl\ *n* : a monk's hood

cow·lick \'kaủ-ˌlik\ *n* : a turned-up tuft of hair that resists control

cowl·ing \'kaủ-liŋ\ *n* : a usu. metal covering for the engine or another part of an airplane

cow·man \'kaủ-mən, -ˌman\ *n* : one who tends cattle or horses : COWBOY; *also* : a cattle owner or rancher

co·work·er \'kō-ˌwər-kər\ *n* : a fellow worker

cow·poke \'kaủ-ˌpōk\ *n* : one who tends cattle or horses : COWBOY

cow pony *n* : a strong and agile horse trained for herding cattle

cow·pox \'kaủ-ˌpäks\ *n* : a mild disease of the cow that when communicated to humans protects against smallpox

cow·punch·er \-ˌpən-chər\ *n* : one who tends cattle or horses : COWBOY

cow·slip \'kaủ-ˌslip\ *n* **1** : a yellow-flowered European primrose **2** : MARSH MARIGOLD

cox·comb \'käks-ˌkōm\ *n* : a conceited foolish person : FOP

cox·swain \'käk-sən, -ˌswān\ *n* : the steersman of a ship's boat or a racing shell

coy \'kȯi\ *adj* [ME, quiet, shy, fr. AF *quei, quoi, koi* quiet, fr. L *quietus*] **1** ♦ : shrinking from contact or familiarity : BASHFUL, SHY **2** ♦ : marked by artful playfulness : COQUETTISH — **coy·ly** *adv* — **coy·ness** *n*

♦ [1] bashful, demure, diffident, introverted, modest, retiring, sheepish, shy — more at SHY ♦ [2] coquettish, demure, kittenish; *also* flirtatious; goody-goody, overmodest, priggish, prim, prudish

coy·ote \'kī-ˌōt, kī-'ō-tē\ *n, pl* **coyotes** *or* **coyote** : a mammal of No. America smaller than the related wolves

coy·pu \'kȯi-pü\ *n* : NUTRIA 2

coz·en \'kəz-ᵊn\ *vb* ♦ : to deceive, win over, or induce to do something by artful coaxing and wheedling or shrewd trickery — **coz·en·age** \-ij\ *n* — **coz·en·er** *n*

♦ beguile, bluff, deceive, delude, dupe, fool, gull, have, hoax, hoodwink, humbug, misinform, mislead, string along, take in, trick — more at DECEIVE ♦ bleed, cheat, chisel, defraud, fleece, hustle, mulct, rook, shortchange, skin, squeeze, stick, sting, swindle, victimize — more at FLEECE

¹co·zy \'kō-zē\ *adj* **co·zi·er; -est** : enjoying or affording warmth and ease : SNUG, COMFORTABLE — **co·zi·ly** \-zə-lē\ *adv* — **co·zi·ness** \-zē-nəs\ *n*

²cozy *n, pl* **co·zies** : a padded covering for a vessel (as a teapot) to keep the contents hot

cp *abbr* **1** compare **2** coupon

CP *abbr* **1** cerebral palsy **2** chemically pure **3** command post **4** communist party

CPA *abbr* certified public accountant

CPB *abbr* Corporation for Public Broadcasting

cpd *abbr* compound

CPI *abbr* consumer price index

Cpl *abbr* corporal

CPO *abbr* chief petty officer

CPOM *abbr* master chief petty officer

CPOS *abbr* senior chief petty officer

CPR *abbr* cardiopulmonary resuscitation

CPT *abbr* captain

CPU \ˌsē-ˌpē-'yü\ *n* [central *p*rocessing *u*nit] : the part of a computer that performs its basic operations, manages its components, and exchanges data with memory or peripherals

CQ *abbr* charge of quarters

cr *abbr* credit; creditor

Cr *symbol* chromium

¹crab \'krab\ *n* : any of various crustaceans with a short broad shell and small abdomen

²crab *n* ♦ : an ill-natured person

♦ bear, complainer, crank, grouch, grumbler, whiner — more at GROUCH

³crab *vb* **crabbed; crab·bing** ♦ : to complain about peevishly : COMPLAIN, GROUSE

♦ beef, bellyache, carp, complain, croak, fuss, gripe, grouse, growl, grumble, kick, moan, murmur, mutter, repine, squawk, wail, whine — more at COMPLAIN

crab apple *n* : a small often highly colored sour apple; *also* : a tree that produces crab apples

crab·bed \'kra-bəd\ *adj* **1** : MOROSE, PEEVISH **2** : CRAMPED, IRREGULAR

crab·by \'kra-bē\ *adj* **crab·bi·er; -est** ♦ : marked by typically transitory bad temper : CROSS

♦ choleric, cranky, cross, crotchety, grouchy, grumpy, irascible, irritable, peevish, perverse, petulant, short=tempered, snappish, snappy, snippy, testy, waspish — more at IRRITABLE

crab·grass \'krab-ˌgras\ *n* : a weedy grass with creeping or sprawling stems that root freely at the nodes

crab louse *n* : a louse infesting the pubic region in humans

¹crack \'krak\ *vb* **1** : to break with a sharp sudden sound **2** : to break with or without completely separating into parts **3** : to fail in tone or become harsh ⟨her voice ~*ed*⟩ **4** : to subject (as a petroleum oil) to heat for breaking down into lighter products (as gasoline) **5** : to strike with a sharp noise **6** ♦ : to puzzle out and expose, solve, or reveal the mystery of **7** ♦ : to lose control or effectiveness under pressure

♦ [6] answer, break, decode, dope, figure out, puzzle, resolve, riddle, solve, unravel, work, work out — more at SOLVE ♦ [7] break, flip, freak

²crack *n* **1** ♦ : a sudden sharp noise **2** ♦ : a witty or sharp remark **3** ♦ : a narrow break or opening : FISSURE **4** ♦ : a sharp blow **5** ♦ : an attempt or opportunity to do something **6** : a potent form of cocaine in small chips used illicitly for smoking

♦ [1] bang, blast, boom, clap, crash, pop, report, slam, smash, snap, thwack, whack — more at CLAP ♦ [2] gag, jest, joke, laugh, pleasantry, quip, sally, waggery, wisecrack, witticism — more at JOKE ♦ [3] chink, cleft, cranny, crevice, fissure, rift, split; *also* craze, hairline; fracture, rupture; breach, gap, opening; cut, gash, incision, slit ♦ [4] bat, belt, blow, box, clout, hit, punch, slug, thump, wallop, whack — more at BLOW ♦ [5] attempt, bid, endeavor (*or* endeavour), essay, fling, go, pass, shot, stab, trial, try, whack, whirl — more at ATTEMPT

³crack *adj* ♦ : extremely proficient

♦ accomplished, adept, consummate, crackerjack, expert, good, great, master, masterful, masterly, proficient, skilled, skillful, virtuoso — more at PROFICIENT

crack·down \'krak-ˌdaún\ *n* : an act or instance of taking positive disciplinary action ⟨a ~ on gambling⟩

crack down *vb* ♦ : to take positive regulatory or disciplinary action — used with *on*

♦ *usu* **crack down on** clamp down, crush, put down, quash, quell, repress, silence, snuff, squash, squelch, subdue, suppress — more at QUELL

cracked *adj* ♦ : mentally disturbed

♦ balmy, crazy, deranged, insane, loco, lunatic, mad, nuts, nutty, screwy, unsound — more at INSANE

crack·er \'kra-kər\ *n* **1** : FIRECRACKER **2** : a dry thin crispy baked bread product made of flour and water

¹**crack·er·jack** \-ˌjak\ *n* ♦ : a person or thing of marked excellence

♦ ace, adept, artist, authority, expert, maestro, master, scholar, shark, virtuoso, whiz, wizard — more at EXPERT

²**crackerjack** *adj* ♦ : of striking ability or excellence

♦ accomplished, adept, consummate, crack, expert, good, great, master, masterful, masterly, proficient, skilled, skillful, virtuoso — more at PROFICIENT

crack·le \'kra-kəl\ *vb* **crack·led**; **crack·ling 1** : to make small sharp snapping noises **2** : to develop fine cracks in a surface — **crackle** *n* — **crack·ly** \-k(ə-)lē\ *adj*

crack·pot \'krak-ˌpät\ *n* ♦ : an eccentric person

♦ character, crank, eccentric, kook, nut, oddball, screwball, weirdo — more at ECCENTRIC

crack–up \'krak-ˌəp\ *n* **1** ♦ : a wrecking or smashing esp. of a vehicle : CRASH, WRECK **2** : BREAKDOWN

♦ collision, crash, smash, wreck — more at CRASH

crack up *vb* **1** ♦ : to express a favorable judgment of : PRAISE ⟨isn't all it's *cracked up* to be⟩ **2** : to laugh or cause to laugh out loud **3** : to crash a vehicle

♦ acclaim, applaud, cheer, hail, laud, praise, salute, tout — more at ACCLAIM

¹**cra·dle** \'krād-ᵊl\ *n* **1** : a baby's bed or cot **2** : a framework or support (as for a telephone receiver) **3** : INFANCY ⟨from ~ to the grave⟩ **4** ♦ : a place of origin

♦ birthplace, home — more at BIRTHPLACE

²**cradle** *vb* **cra·dled**; **cra·dling 1** : to place in or as if in a cradle **2** : SHELTER, REAR

¹**craft** \'kraft\ *n* **1 a** ♦ : skill in planning, making, or executing **b** ♦ : an occupation requiring special skill **2** ♦ : skill in deceiving to gain an end : CUNNING, GUILE **3** *pl usu* **craft** ♦ : a boat esp. of small size; *also* : AIRCRAFT, SPACECRAFT

♦ [1a] adeptness, adroitness, art, artfulness, artifice, artistry, cleverness, cunning, deftness, masterfulness, skill — more at SKILL ♦ [1b] handicraft, trade; *also* art, skill; calling, occupation, profession, vocation ♦ [2] artfulness, artifice, caginess, canniness, craftiness, cunning, guile, slyness, wiliness — more at CUNNING ♦ [3] boat, bottom, vessel — more at BOAT

²**craft** *vb* ♦ : to make or produce with care, skill, or ingenuity — **craft·er** *n*

♦ cast, compose, draft, draw, formulate, frame, prepare — more at COMPOSE

craft·i·ness \-tē-nəs\ *n* ♦ : the quality or state of being crafty

♦ artfulness, artifice, caginess, canniness, craft, cunning, guile, slyness, wiliness — more at CUNNING

crafts·man \'krafts-mən\ *n* ♦ : a skilled artisan — **crafts·man·ship** *n*

♦ artificer, artisan, handicrafter — more at ARTISAN

crafty \'kraf-tē\ *adj* **craft·i·er**; **-est** ♦ : adept in the use of subtlety and cunning : CUNNING, SUBTLE — **craft·i·ly** \-tə-lē\ *adv*

♦ artful, cagey, cunning, devious, foxy, guileful, slick, sly, subtle, wily — more at ARTFUL

crag \'krag\ *n* ♦ : a steep rugged cliff or rock

♦ bluff, cliff, escarpment, palisade, precipice, scarp — more at CLIFF

crag·gy *adj* ♦ : having a broken, uneven, or bumpy surface

♦ broken, jagged, ragged, scraggly — more at RAGGED

cram \'kram\ *vb* **crammed**; **cram·ming 1** ♦ : to pack in tight : JAM **2** : to eat greedily **3** : to study rapidly under pressure for an examination

♦ crowd, jam, ram, sandwich, squeeze, stuff, wedge — more at CROWD ♦ charge, fill, heap, jam, jam-pack, load, pack, stuff — more at FILL

¹**cramp** \'kramp\ *n* **1** ♦ : a sudden painful contraction of muscle **2** : sharp abdominal pain — usu. used in pl.

♦ spasm; *also* contraction, jerk, stitch, twinge, twitch

²**cramp** *vb* **1** : to affect with a cramp or cramps **2** ♦ : to restrain from free action : HAMPER

♦ encumber, hamper, hinder, hold up, impede, inhibit, interfere with, obstruct, tie up — more at HAMPER

cran·ber·ry \'kran-ˌber-ē, -bə-rē\ *n* : the red acid berry of any of several trailing plants related to the heaths; *also* : one of these plants

¹**crane** \'krān\ *n* **1** : any of a family of tall wading birds related to the rails; *also* : any of several herons **2** : a machine for lifting and carrying heavy objects

²**crane** *vb* **craned**; **cran·ing 1** : to stretch one's neck to see better **2** ♦ : to raise or lift by or as if by a crane

♦ boost, elevate, heave, heft, heighten, hike, hoist, jack, lift, pick up, raise, up, uphold — more at RAISE

crane fly *n* : any of a family of long-legged slender dipteran flies that resemble large mosquitoes but do not bite

cranial nerve *n* : any of the nerves that arise in pairs from the lower surface of the brain and pass through openings in the skull to the periphery of the body

cra·ni·um \'krā-nē-əm\ *n, pl* **-ni·ums** *or* **-nia** \-ə-\ : SKULL; *esp* : the part enclosing the brain — **cra·ni·al** \-əl\ *adj*

¹**crank** \'kraŋk\ *n* **1** : a bent part of an axle or shaft or an arm at right angles to the end of a shaft by which circular motion is imparted to or received from it **2** ♦ : an eccentric person **3** ♦ : a bad-tempered person : GROUCH

♦ [2] character, crackpot, eccentric, kook, nut, oddball, screwball, weirdo — more at ECCENTRIC ♦ [3] bear, complainer, crab, curmudgeon, grouch, grumbler, whiner — more at GROUCH

²**crank** *vb* ♦ : to start or operate by or as if by turning a crank — usu. used with *up*

♦ *usu* **crank up** activate, actuate, drive, move, propel, run, set off, spark, start, touch off, trigger, turn on — more at ACTIVATE

crank·case \'kraŋk-ˌkās\ *n* : the housing of a crankshaft

crank out *vb* : to produce in a mechanical manner

crank·shaft \'kraŋk-ˌshaft\ *n* : a shaft turning or driven by a crank

cranky \'kraŋ-kē\ *adj* **crank·i·er**; **-est 1** ♦ : given to fretful fussiness : IRRITABLE **2** ♦ : operating uncertainly or imperfectly

♦ [1] choleric, crabby, cross, crotchety, fussy, grouchy, grumpy, irascible, irritable, peevish, perverse, petulant, short-tempered, snappish, snappy, snippy, testy, waspish — more at IRRITABLE ♦ [2] awkward, clumsy, cumbersome, ungainly, unhandy, unwieldy — more at CUMBERSOME

cran·ny \'kra-nē\ *n, pl* **crannies** ♦ : a small break or slit : CREVICE, CHINK

♦ chink, cleft, crack, crevice, fissure, rift, split — more at CRACK

craps \'kraps\ *n* : a gambling game played with two dice

crap·shoot·er \'krap-ˌshü-tər\ *n* : a person who plays craps

¹**crash** \'krash\ *vb* **1** ♦ : to break noisily : SMASH **2** : to damage an airplane in landing **3** : to enter or attend without invitation or without paying ⟨~ a party⟩ **4** : to decline suddenly and steeply **5** ♦ : to suffer a sudden major failure usu. with loss of data ⟨my computer ~ed⟩

♦ [1] bang, bash, bump, collide, hit, impact, knock, ram, slam, smash, strike, swipe, thud — more at HIT ♦ [5] break, break down, conk, cut out, die, fail, stall — more at FAIL

²**crash** n 1 ♦ : a loud sound (as of things smashing) 2 ♦ : an instance of crashing ⟨a plane ∼⟩; also : COLLISION 3 ♦ : a sudden failure (as of a business)

♦ [1] bang, blast, boom, clap, crack, pop, report, slam, smash, snap, thwack, whack — more at CLAP ♦ [2] collision, crack-up, smash, wreck; also accident; destruction, ruin ♦ [3] collapse, cropper, defeat, failure, fizzle, nonsuccess — more at FAILURE

³**crash** adj : marked by concerted effort over the shortest possible time

⁴**crash** n : coarse linen fabric used for towels and draperies

crash–land \'krash-ˌland\ vb : to land an aircraft or spacecraft under emergency conditions usu. with damage to the craft — **crash landing** n

crass \'kras\ adj ♦ : coarse in nature or behavior : GROSS — **crass·ly** adv

♦ coarse, common, crude, gross, ill-bred, low, rough, rude, tasteless, uncouth, uncultivated, uncultured, unpolished, unrefined, vulgar — more at COARSE

crate \'krāt\ n : a container often of wooden slats — **crate** vb

cra·ter \'krā-tər\ n [L, mixing bowl, crater, fr. Gk kratēr, fr. kerannynai to mix] 1 : the depression around the opening of a volcano 2 : a depression formed by the impact of a meteorite or by the explosion of a bomb or shell

cra·vat \krə-'vat\ n : NECKTIE

crave \'krāv\ vb **craved; crav·ing** 1 : to ask for earnestly : BEG 2 ♦ : to long for : DESIRE

♦ ache for, covet, desire, die for, hanker for, hunger for, long for, lust (for or after), pine for, repine for, thirst for, want, wish for, yearn for — more at DESIRE

¹**cra·ven** \'krā-vən\ adj ♦ : lacking the least bit of courage : contemptibly fainthearted

♦ chicken, cowardly, dastardly, pusillanimous, recreant, spineless, yellow — more at COWARDLY

²**craven** n : an avowed coward

crav·ing \'krā-viŋ\ n ♦ : an urgent or abnormal desire

♦ appetite, desire, drive, hankering, hunger, itch, longing, lust, passion, thirst, urge, yearning, yen — more at DESIRE

craw·fish \'krȯ-ˌfish\ n 1 : CRAYFISH 1 2 : SPINY LOBSTER

¹**crawl** \'krȯl\ vb 1 ♦ : to move slowly by drawing the body along the ground 2 ♦ : to advance feebly, cautiously, or slowly 3 ♦ : to be swarming with or feel as if swarming with creeping things ⟨a place ∼ing with ants⟩ ⟨her flesh ∼ed⟩

♦ [1] creep, grovel, slither, snake, worm; also crouch, squat; slide; edge, inch, nose ♦ [2] creep, drag, inch, plod, poke; also lumber, shamble, shuffle, tramp, trudge Ant fly, race, speed, whiz, zip ♦ [3] abound, brim, bulge, burst, swarm, teem — more at ABOUND

²**crawl** n 1 : a very slow pace 2 : a prone speed swimming stroke

cray·fish \'krā-ˌfish\ n 1 : any of numerous freshwater crustaceans usu. much smaller than the related lobsters 2 : SPINY LOBSTER

cray·on \'krā-ˌän, -ən\ n : a stick of chalk or wax used for writing, drawing, or coloring; also : a drawing made with such material — **crayon** vb

¹**craze** \'krāz\ vb **crazed; craz·ing** [ME crasen to crush, craze, of Scand origin] ♦ : to make or become insane

♦ derange, madden, unhinge; also agitate, bother, confuse, discompose, disquiet, distract, disturb, perturb, unsettle, upset; annoy, irritate, vex

²**craze** n ♦ : an exaggerated and often transient enthusiasm : FAD

♦ fad, mode, rage, style, trend, vogue — more at FAD

cra·zi·ness \-zē-nəs\ n ♦ : the quality or state of being crazy

♦ absurdity, asininity, balminess, daftness, fatuity, folly, foolishness, inanity, insanity, lunacy, madness, silliness, simplicity, zaniness

cra·zy \'krā-zē\ adj **cra·zi·er; -est** 1 ♦ : mentally disordered : INSANE 2 ♦ : not characterized by common sense : wildly impractical; also : ERRATIC 3 ♦ : distracted with desire or excitement 4 ♦ : absurdly fond — usu. used with about or over — **cra·zi·ly** \-zə-lē\ adv

♦ [1, 2] absurd, cuckoo, fatuous, foolish, mad, nonsensical, nutty, senseless, silly, stupid — more at FOOLISH ♦ [3] agog, anxious, ardent, athirst, avid, eager, enthusiastic, gung ho, hot, hungry, keen, nuts, raring, solicitous, thirsty, voracious — more at EAGER ♦ usu crazy about or crazy over [4] mad, nuts

CRC abbr Civil Rights Commission

creak \'krēk\ vb : to make a prolonged squeaking or grating sound — **creak** n — **creaky** adj

¹**cream** \'krēm\ n 1 : the yellowish fat-rich part of milk 2 : a thick smooth sauce, confection, or cosmetic 3 ♦ : the choicest part 4 : a pale yellow color — **creamy** adj

♦ best, choice, elect, elite, fat, flower, pick, prime — more at ELITE

²**cream** vb 1 : to prepare with a cream sauce 2 : to beat or blend into creamy consistency 3 : to defeat decisively

cream cheese n : a cheese made from whole milk enriched with cream

cream·ery \'krē-mə-rē\ n, pl **-er·ies** : an establishment where butter and cheese are made or milk and cream are prepared for sale

¹**crease** \'krēs\ n ♦ : a mark or line made by or as if by folding

♦ crimp, crinkle, furrow, wrinkle — more at WRINKLE

²**crease** vb : to become creased

cre·ate \krē-'āt\ vb **cre·at·ed; cre·at·ing** ♦ : to bring into being : cause to exist

♦ bring about, cause, effect, effectuate, generate, induce, make, produce, prompt, result, work, yield — more at EFFECT ♦ engender, generate, induce, make, produce, spawn — more at GENERATE

cre·a·tion \krē-'ā-shən\ n 1 : the act of creating or producing ⟨∼ of the world⟩ 2 ♦ : something that is created 3 ♦ : all created things : WORLD

♦ [2] coinage, concoction, contrivance, innovation, invention, wrinkle — more at INVENTION ♦ [3] cosmos, macrocosm, nature, universe, world — more at UNIVERSE

cre·a·tion·ism \krē-'ā-shə-ˌni-zəm\ n : a doctrine or theory holding that matter, the various forms of life, and the world were created by God out of nothing — **cre·a·tion·ist** \-nist\ n or adj

cre·a·tive \-'ā-tiv\ adj ♦ : marked by the ability or power to create — **cre·a·tive·ness** n

♦ artful, clever, imaginative, ingenious, innovative, inventive, original; also gifted, inspired, talented; resourceful; fecund, fertile, fruitful, productive, prolific Ant uncreative, unimaginative, unoriginal

cre·a·tiv·i·ty \ˌkrē-(ˌ)ā-'ti-və-tē\ n ♦ : the ability to create

♦ ingenuity, invention, inventiveness, originality; also resourcefulness; fecundity, fertility, fruitfulness, productiveness, productivity; freshness, newness, novelty; genius, inspiration, talent

cre·a·tor \krē-'ā-tər\ n 1 ♦ : one that creates : MAKER, AUTHOR 2 cap : GOD 1

♦ author, father, founder, originator — more at FATHER

crea·ture \'krē-chər\ n 1 ♦ : a lower animal 2 ♦ : a human being

♦ [1] animal, beast, brute, critter — more at ANIMAL ♦ [2] being, body, human, individual, man, mortal, person — more at HUMAN

crèche \'kresh\ n [F, manger, crib, fr. OF creche, of Gmc origin] : a representation of the Nativity scene

cre·dence \'krēd-ᵊns\ n ♦ : mental acceptance as true or real

♦ confidence, faith, stock, trust — more at TRUST ♦ belief, credit, faith — more at BELIEF

cre·den·tial \kri-'den-chəl\ *n* ♦ : something that gives a basis for credit or confidence — used in pl.

♦ *usu* **credentials** capability, qualification, stuff — more at QUALIFICATION

cre·den·za \kri-'den-zə\ *n* [It, lit., belief, confidence] : a sideboard, buffet, or bookcase usu. without legs

cred·i·ble \'kre-də-bəl\ *adj* ♦ : offering reasonable grounds for being believed : BELIEVABLE — **cred·i·bil·i·ty** \ˌkre-də-'bi-lə-tē\ *n*

♦ believable, likely, plausible, probable — more at BELIEVABLE

¹**cred·it** \'kre-dət\ *vb* **1** ♦ : to trust in the truth of : BELIEVE **2** ♦ : to give credit to

♦ [1] accept, believe, swallow, trust — more at BELIEVE ♦ [2] accredit, ascribe, attribute, impute; *also* blame, pin (on); associate, connect, link

²**credit** *n* [MF, fr. It *credito*, fr. L *creditum* something entrusted to another, loan, fr. *credere* to believe, entrust] **1** : the balance (as in a bank) in a person's favor **2** : time given for payment for goods sold on trust **3** : an accounting entry of payment received **4** ♦ : reliance on the truth or reality of something : BELIEF, FAITH **5** : financial trustworthiness **6** ♦ : good name **7** ♦ : a source of honor or distinction **8** : a unit of academic work

♦ [4] belief, credence, faith — more at BELIEF ♦ [6] acclaim, accolade, distinction, glory, homage, honor (*or* honour), laurels — more at GLORY ♦ [7] boast, glory, honor (*or* honour), jewel, pride, treasure — more at GLORY

cred·it·able \'kre-də-tə-bəl\ *adj* ♦ : worthy of esteem or praise ⟨a ∼ performance⟩ — **cred·it·ably** \-blē\ *adv*

♦ admirable, commendable, laudable, meritorious, praiseworthy — more at ADMIRABLE

credit card *n* : a card authorizing purchases on credit

cred·i·tor \'kre-də-tər\ *n* : a person to whom money is owed

cre·do \'krē-dō, 'krā-\ *n, pl* **credos** [ME, fr. L, I believe] **1** : a set of fundamental beliefs : CREED **2** : a guiding principle

cred·u·lous \'kre-jə-ləs\ *adj* : inclined to believe esp. on slight evidence — **cre·du·li·ty** \kri-'dü-lə-tē, -'dyü-\ *n* — **cred·u·lous·ly** *adv*

Cree \'krē\ *n, pl* **Cree** *or* **Crees** : a member of an American Indian people of Canada

creed \'krēd\ *n* [ME *crede*, fr. OE *crēda*, fr. L *credo* I believe, first word of the Apostles' and Nicene Creeds] **1** ♦ : a statement of the essential beliefs of a religious faith; *also* : the body of such beliefs **2** ♦ : a guiding principle

♦ [1] cult, faith, persuasion, religion — more at RELIGION ♦ [2] doctrine, gospel, ideology, philosophy; *also* manifesto

creek \'krēk, 'krik\ *n* **1** *chiefly Brit* : a small inlet **2** ♦ : a stream smaller than a river

♦ brook, rill, rivulet, streamlet; *also* freshet, runoff; river, stream, watercourse, waterway; canal, race, millrace, millstream

Creek \'krēk\ *n* : a member of an American Indian people of Alabama, Georgia, and Florida

creel \'krēl\ *n* : a wicker basket esp. for carrying fish

¹**creep** \'krēp\ *vb* **crept** \'krept\; **creep·ing** **1** ♦ : to move along with the body prone and close to the ground : CRAWL **2** : to feel as though insects were crawling on the skin **3** : to grow over a surface like ivy **4** ♦ : to go very slowly **5** : to enter, advance, or progress gradually so as to be almost unnoticed ⟨the cost of living keeps ∼*ing* up⟩ — **creep·er** *n*

♦ [1] crawl, grovel, slither, snake, worm — more at CRAWL ♦ [4] crawl, drag, inch, plod, poke — more at CRAWL

²**creep** *n* ♦ : an unpleasant or obnoxious person

♦ beast, boor, churl, clown, cretin, cur, heel, jerk, joker, louse, lout, skunk, slob, snake — more at JERK

creep·ing \'krē-piŋ\ *adj* ♦ : developing or advancing by imperceptible degrees

♦ dilatory, laggard, languid, poky, slow, sluggish, tardy — more at SLOW

creepy \'krē-pē\ *adj* **creep·i·er; -est** ♦ : having or producing a nervous shivery fear

♦ eerie, haunting, spooky, uncanny, unearthly, weird — more at EERIE

cre·mate \'krē-ˌmāt\ *vb* **cre·mat·ed; cre·mat·ing** : to reduce (a dead body) to ashes with fire — **cre·ma·tion** \kri-'mā-shən\ *n*

cre·ma·to·ry \'krē-mə-ˌtōr-ē, 'krē-\ *n, pl* **-ries** : a furnace for cremating; *also* : a structure containing such a furnace

crème \'krem, 'krēm\ *n, pl* **crèmes** *same or* 'kremz, 'krēmz\ [F, lit., cream] : a sweet liqueur

cren·el·lat·ed *or* **cren·el·at·ed** \'kren-ᵊl-ˌā-təd\ *adj* : having battlements — **cren·el·la·tion** \ˌkren-ᵊl-'ā-shən\ *n*

Cre·ole \'krē-ˌōl\ *n* **1** : a descendant of early French or Spanish settlers of the U.S. Gulf states preserving their speech and culture; *also* : a person of mixed French or Spanish and black descent speaking a dialect of French or Spanish **2** *not cap* : a language that has evolved from a pidgin but serves as the native language of a speech community

cre·o·sote \'krē-ə-ˌsōt\ *n* : an oily liquid obtained by distillation of coal tar and used in preserving wood

crepe *or* **crêpe** \'krāp\ *n* : a light crinkled fabric of any of various fibers

crêpe su·zette \ˌkrāp-sù-'zet\ *n, pl* **crêpes suzette** *same or* ˌkrāps-\ *or* **crêpe suzettes** \-sù-'zets\ *often cap S* : a thin folded or rolled pancake in a hot orange-butter sauce that is sprinkled with a liqueur and set ablaze for serving

cre·pus·cu·lar \kri-'pəs-kyə-lər\ *adj* **1** : of, relating to, or resembling twilight **2** : occurring or active during twilight ⟨∼ insects⟩

cre·scen·do \krə-'shen-dō\ *adv or adj* [It] : increasing in loudness — used as a direction in music — **crescendo** *n*

cres·cent \'kres-ᵊnt\ *n* [ME *cressant*, fr. AF fr. prp. of *crestre* to grow, increase, fr. L *crescere*] : the moon at any stage between new moon and first quarter and between last quarter and new moon; *also* : something shaped like the figure of the crescent moon with a convex and a concave edge — **cres·cen·tic** \kre-'sen-tik\ *adj*

cress \'kres\ *n* : any of several salad plants related to the mustards

¹**crest** \'krest\ *n* **1** : a tuft or process on the head of an animal (as a bird) **2** : a heraldic device **3** : an upper part, edge, or limit ⟨the ∼ of a hill⟩ — **crest·ed** \'kres-təd\ *adj* — **crest·less** *adj*

²**crest** *vb* **1** : CROWN **2** : to reach the crest of **3** : to rise to a crest

crest·fall·en \'krest-ˌfȯ-lən\ *adj* : feeling shame or humiliation; *also* : feeling low in spirit : DISPIRITED, DEJECTED

Cre·ta·ceous \kri-'tā-shəs\ *adj* : of, relating to, or being the latest period of the Mesozoic era marked by great increase in flowering plants, diversification of mammals, and extinction of the dinosaurs — **Cretaceous** *n*

cre·tin \'krēt-ᵊn\ *n* [F *crétin*, fr. F dial. *cretin*, lit., wretch, innocent victim, fr. L *christianus* Christian] **1** *often offensive* : one affected with cretinism **2** ♦ : a stupid, vulgar, or insensitive person

♦ blockhead, dope, dummy, idiot, imbecile, jackass, moron, numskull — more at IDIOT

cre·tin·ism \-ˌi-zəm\ *n* : a usu. congenital condition characterized by physical stunting and intellectual disability

cre·tonne \'krē-ˌtän\ *n* : a strong unglazed cotton cloth for curtains and upholstery

cre·vasse \kri-'vas\ *n* : a deep fissure esp. in a glacier

crev·ice \'kre-vəs\ *n* ♦ : a narrow fissure

♦ chink, cleft, crack, cranny, fissure, rift, split — more at CRACK

¹**crew** \'krü\ *chiefly Can and Brit past of* CROW

²**crew** *n* [ME *crue*, fr. MF, a reinforcement, lit., increase, fr. *croistre* to grow, fr. L *crescere*] **1** ♦ : a body of people trained to work together for certain purposes **2** : a group

of people who operate a ship, train, aircraft, or spacecraft **3** : the rowers and coxswain of a racing shell; *also* : the sport of rowing engaged in by a crew — **crew·man** \-mən\ *n*

♦ band, company, gang, outfit, party, squad, team — more at GANG

crew cut *n* : a very short bristly haircut

crew·el \'krü-əl\ *n* : slackly twisted worsted yarn used for embroidery — **crew·el·work** \-,wərk\ *n*

¹**crib** \'krib\ *n* **1** : a manger for feeding animals **2** : a child's bedstead with high sides **3** : a building or bin for storage (as of grain) **4** : something used for cheating in an exam

²**crib** *vb* **cribbed; crib·bing** **1** : to put in a crib **2** : STEAL, PLAGIARIZE — **crib·ber** *n*

crib·bage \'kri-bij\ *n* : a card game usu. played by two players and scored on a board (**cribbage board**)

crib death *n* : SUDDEN INFANT DEATH SYNDROME

crick \'krik\ *n* : a painful spasm of muscles (as of the neck)

¹**crick·et** \'kri-kət\ *n* [ME *criket*, fr. AF, of imit. origin] : any of a family of leaping insects related to the grasshoppers and noted for the chirping noises of the male

²**cricket** *n* [MF *criquet* goal stake in a bowling game] : a game played with a bat and ball by two teams on a field centering upon two wickets each defended by a batsman

cri·er \'krī-(-ə)r\ *n* : one who calls out proclamations and announcements

crime \'krīm\ *n* **1** ♦ : a serious offense against the public law **2** ♦ : something reprehensible, foolish, or disgraceful

♦ [1] error, malefaction, misdeed, misdoing, offense, sin, transgression, violation, wrongdoing — more at OFFENSE ♦ [2] disgrace, outrage, pity, scandal, shame, sin

¹**crim·i·nal** \'kri-mən-ᵊl\ *adj* **1** ♦ : involving or being a crime **2** : relating to crime or its punishment — **crim·i·nal·i·ty** \,kri-mə-'na-lə-tē\ *n* — **crim·i·nal·ly** *adv*

♦ illegal, illegitimate, illicit, unlawful, wrongful — more at ILLEGAL

²**criminal** *n* ♦ : one who has committed a crime

♦ crook, culprit, felon, lawbreaker, malefactor, offender; *also* desperado, outlaw; *also* convict, jailbird; perpetrator; evildoer, sinner, transgressor, trespasser, wrongdoer; gangster, gunman, hoodlum, mobster, racketeer, thug; backslider, repeater

crim·i·nol·o·gy \,kri-mə-'nä-lə-jē\ *n* : the scientific study of crime and criminals — **crim·i·nol·o·gist** \,kri-mə-'nä-lə-jist\ *n*

¹**crimp** \'krimp\ *vb* : to cause to become crinkled, wavy, or bent

²**crimp** *n* **1** : something (as a curl in hair) produced by or as if by crimping **2** ♦ : a bend or crease formed in something **3** ♦ : something that cramps or inhibits

♦ [2] crease, crinkle, furrow, wrinkle — more at WRINKLE ♦ [3] bar, block, encumbrance, hindrance, inhibition, obstacle — more at ENCUMBRANCE

¹**crim·son** \'krim-zən\ *n* : a deep purplish red color — **crimson** *adj*

²**crimson** *vb* ♦ : to make or become crimson

♦ bloom, blush, color (*or* colour), flush, glow, redden — more at BLUSH

cringe \'krinj\ *vb* **cringed; cring·ing** ♦ : to shrink in fear : COWER

♦ cower, grovel, quail — more at COWER

¹**crin·kle** \'kriŋ-kəl\ *vb* **crin·kled; crin·kling** ♦ : to form many short bends or curves; *also* : WRINKLE — **crin·kly** \-kə-lē\ *adj*

♦ crease, furrow, rumple, wrinkle — more at WRINKLE

²**crinkle** *n* : a line, mark, or ridge made by or as if by folding a pliable substance

crin·o·line \'kri-nᵊl-ən\ *n* **1** : an open-weave cloth used for stiffening and lining **2** : a full stiff skirt or underskirt made of crinoline

¹**crip·ple** \'kri-pəl\ *n* : one that is disabled or deficient in a specified manner ⟨a social ~⟩

²**cripple** *vb* **crip·pled; crip·pling** **1** ♦ : to make lame **2** ♦ : to make useless or imperfect

♦ [1] disable, lame, maim, mutilate — more at MAIM ♦ [2] blemish, break, damage, deface, disfigure, flaw, harm, hurt, injure, mar, spoil, vitiate — more at DAMAGE ♦ [2] disable, hamstring, immobilize, incapacitate, paralyze, prostrate — more at PARALYZE

cri·sis \'krī-səs\ *n, pl* **cri·ses** \-,sēz\ [ME, fr. L, fr. Gk *krisis*, lit., decision, fr. *krinein* to decide] **1** : the turning point for better or worse in an acute disease or fever **2** ♦ : a decisive or critical moment

♦ clutch, crunch, emergency, head, juncture — more at EMERGENCY

crisp \'krisp\ *adj* **1** : CURLY, WAVY **2** ♦ : easily crumbled : BRITTLE **3** : FIRM, FRESH ⟨~ lettuce⟩ **4** ♦ : being sharp and clear; *also* : concise and to the point **5** : LIVELY, SPARKLING **6** : FROSTY, SNAPPY; *also* : INVIGORATING **7** ♦ : noticeably neat — **crisp** *vb*

♦ [2] brittle, crumbly, flaky, friable; *also* crunchy; breakable, delicate, fragile ♦ [4] brief, compact, compendious, concise, epigrammatic, laconic, pithy, succinct, summary, terse — more at CONCISE ♦ [7] neat, orderly, shipshape, snug, tidy, trim, uncluttered — more at NEAT

crisp·ly *adv* ♦ : in a crisp manner

♦ compactly, concisely, laconically, shortly, succinctly, summarily, tersely — more at SHORTLY

crisp·ness *n* ♦ : the quality or state of being crisp

♦ brevity, briefness, compactness, conciseness, succinctness, terseness — more at SUCCINCTNESS

crispy *adj* : easily crumbled

¹**criss·cross** \'kris-,krȯs\ *vb* **1** : to mark with crossed lines **2** ♦ : to go or pass back and forth through or over

♦ cover, cross, cut, follow, go, pass, proceed, travel, traverse — more at TRAVERSE

²**crisscross** *adj* : marked or characterized by crisscrossing — **crisscross** *adv*

³**crisscross** *n* : a pattern formed by crossed lines

crit *abbr* critical; criticism

cri·te·ri·on \krī-'tir-ē-ən\ *n, pl* **-ria** \-ē-ə\ ♦ : a standard on which a judgment may be based

♦ grade, mark, measure, par, standard, touchstone, yardstick — more at STANDARD

crit·ic \'kri-tik\ *n* **1** : a person who judges literary or artistic works **2** ♦ : one inclined to find fault

♦ carper, castigator, caviler, censurer, faultfinder, nitpicker, railer, scold; *also* detractor; pettifogger, quibbler; complainer, crybaby, whiner

crit·i·cal \'kri-ti-kəl\ *adj* **1** : being or relating to a condition or disease involving danger of death **2** ♦ : being a crisis **3** ♦ : inclined to criticize **4** : relating to criticism or critics **5** : requiring careful judgment **6** : UNCERTAIN **7** ♦ : marked by or indicative of significant worth or consequence — **crit·i·cal·ly** \-k(ə-)lē\ *adv*

♦ [2] acute, dire, imperative, imperious, instant, pressing, urgent — more at ACUTE ♦ [3] captious, carping, hypercritical, overcritical; *also* discerning, discriminating, judicious; demanding, exacting, fastidious, finicky, fussy, particular *Ant* uncritical ♦ [7] crucial, key, pivotal, vital — more at CRUCIAL

crit·i·cise *Brit var of* CRITICIZE

crit·i·cism \'kri-tə-,si-zəm\ *n* **1** : the act of criticizing; *esp* : CENSURE **2** : a judgment or review **3** : the art of judging works of literature or art

crit·i·cize \'kri-tə-,sīz\ *vb* **-cized; -ciz·ing** **1** : to judge as a critic : EVALUATE **2** ♦ : to find fault : express criticism

♦ blame, censure, condemn, denounce, fault, knock, pan, reprehend; *also* assail, attack, blast, slam, slash; beef, bellyache, carp, complain, crab, croak, fuss, gripe, grouse, growl, grumble, kick, moan, murmur, mutter, repine, squawk, wail, whine, yammer; admonish, chide, rebuke, reprimand, reproach, reprove; berate, castigate, crucify, excoriate, flay, lambaste, lash, pillory, scold, upbraid; bad-mouth, belittle, disparage, put down *Ant* extol, laud, praise

cri·tique \krə-'tēk\ *n* : a critical estimate or discussion

crit·ter \'kri-tər\ *n* ♦ : a lower animal : CREATURE

♦ animal, beast, brute, creature — more at ANIMAL

¹**croak** \'krōk\ *n* : a hoarse harsh cry (as of a frog)

²**croak** *vb* ♦ : to mutter in discontent

♦ beef, bellyache, carp, complain, crab, fuss, gripe, grouse, growl, grumble, kick, moan, murmur, mutter, repine, squawk, wail, whine — more at COMPLAIN

Croat \'krō-,at\ *n* : CROATIAN

Cro·atian \krō-'ā-shən\ *n* : a native or inhabitant of Croatia — **Croatian** *adj*

cro·chet \krō-'shā\ *n* [F, hook, crochet, fr. MF, dim. of *croche* hook] : needlework done with a single thread and hooked needle — **crochet** *vb*

crock \'kräk\ *n* : a thick earthenware pot or jar

crock·ery \'krä-kə-rē\ *n* : EARTHENWARE

croc·o·dile \'krä-kə-,dīl\ *n* [ME & L; ME *cocodrille*, fr. OF, fr. ML *cocodrillus*, alter. of L *crocodilus*, fr. Gk *krokodilos* lizard, crocodile, fr. *krokē* shingle, pebble + *drillos* worm] : any of several thick-skinned long-bodied carnivorous reptiles of tropical and subtropical waters

cro·cus \'krō-kəs\ *n, pl* **cro·cus·es** *also* **crocus** *or* **cro·ci** \-,kī\ : any of a large genus of low herbs related to the irises and having brightly colored flowers borne singly in early spring

Crohn's disease \'krōnz\ *n* : a chronic inflammatory disease of the gastrointestinal tract and esp. the ileum

crois·sant \krȯ-'sänt, krwä-'säⁿ\ *n, pl* **croissants** *same or* -'sänts, -'säⁿz\ : a rich crescent-shaped roll

Cro–Ma·gnon \krō-'mag-nən, -'man-yən\ *n* : any of a tall erect human race known from skeletal remains found chiefly in southern France and usu. classified as the same species as present-day human beings — **Cro–Magnon** *adj*

crone \'krōn\ *n* ♦ : a withered old woman : HAG

♦ hag, witch; *also* grandam (*or* grandame), harpy, shrew, virago

cro·ny \'krō-nē\ *n, pl* **cronies** ♦ : a close friend esp. of long standing

♦ associate, cohort, companion, comrade, fellow, mate — more at ASSOCIATE ♦ buddy, chum, comrade, familiar, friend, intimate, pal — more at FRIEND

¹**crook** \'krȯk\ *vb* ♦ : to curve or bend sharply

♦ arc, arch, bend, bow, curve, hook, round, sweep, swerve, wheel — more at CURVE

²**crook** *n* 1 : a bent or curved implement 2 : a bent or curved part; *also* : BEND, CURVE 3 : a person who engages in fraudulent or criminal practices : SWINDLER, THIEF

crook·ed \'krȯ-kəd\ *adj* 1 ♦ : having a crook 2 ♦ : characterized by lack of truth, honesty, or trustworthiness : DISHONEST — **crook·ed·ly** *adv*

♦ [1] devious, serpentine, sinuous, tortuous, winding; *also* zigzag, zigzagging; circling, coiled, coiling, spiral, spiraling, swirling; circuitous, indirect, roundabout; meandering, rambling, wandering *Ant* straight, straightaway ♦ [2] deceptive, dishonest, fast, fraudulent, shady, sharp, shifty, underhanded — more at DISHONEST

crook·ed·ness *n* ♦ : the quality or state of being crooked

♦ artifice, craft, craftiness, cunning, deceit, deceitfulness, dishonesty, dissimulation, double-dealing, duplicity, guile, wiliness — more at DECEIT

croon \'krün\ *vb* : to sing or hum in a gentle murmuring voice — **croon·er** *n*

¹**crop** \'kräp\ *n* 1 : the handle of a whip; *also* : a short riding whip 2 : a pouch in the throat of many birds and insects where food is received 3 : something that can be harvested; *also* : the yield at harvest 4 : two or more figures forming a complete unit in a composition

²**crop** *vb* **cropped; crop·ping** 1 ♦ : to remove the tips of : cut off short; *also* : TRIM 2 : to feed on by cropping 3 a : to devote (land) to crops b ♦ : to grow as a crop : yield a crop 4 ♦ : to appear unexpectedly — often used with *up*

♦ [1] bob, clip, cut, cut back, dock, lop, nip, prune, shave, shear, trim — more at CLIP ♦ [3b] cultivate, grow, promote, raise, rear, tend — more at GROW ♦ *usu* **crop up** [4] arise, emerge, materialize, spring, surface — more at ARISE

crop duster *n* : a person who uses an airplane to spray crops with insecticidal dusts; *also* : an airplane so used

crop·land \-,land\ *n* : land devoted to the production of plant crops

¹**crop·per** \'krä-pər\ *n* : a raiser of crops; *esp* : SHARECROPPER

²**cropper** *n* ♦ : a sudden or violent failure or collapse

♦ collapse, crash, defeat, failure, fizzle, nonsuccess — more at FAILURE

cro·quet \krō-'kā\ *n* : a game in which mallets are used to drive wooden balls through a series of wickets set out on a lawn

cro·quette \krō-'ket\ *n* [F] : a small often rounded mass of minced meat, fish, or vegetables fried in deep fat

cro·sier \'krō-zhər\ *n* : a staff carried by bishops and abbots

¹**cross** \'krȯs\ *n* 1 : a structure consisting of an upright beam and a crossbar used esp. by the ancient Romans for execution 2 : a figure of the cross on which Christ was crucified used as a Christian symbol 3 : a hybridizing of unlike individuals or strains; *also* : a product of this 4 : a punch delivered with a circular motion over an opponent's lead 5 ♦ : an affliction that tries one's virtue, steadfastness, or patience

♦ gauntlet, ordeal, trial — more at TRIAL

²**cross** *vb* 1 : to lie or place across; *also* : INTERSECT 2 : to cancel by marking a cross on or by lining through 3 : THWART, OBSTRUCT 4 ♦ : to go or extend across : TRAVERSE 5 : HYBRIDIZE 6 : to meet and pass on the way

♦ cover, crisscross, cut, follow, go, pass, proceed, travel, traverse — more at TRAVERSE

³**cross** *adj* 1 : lying across 2 : CONTRARY, OPPOSED 3 ♦ : marked by bad temper 4 : HYBRID — **cross·ly** *adv*

♦ choleric, crabby, cranky, crotchety, grouchy, grumpy, irascible, irritable, peevish, perverse, petulant, short-tempered, snappish, snappy, snippy, testy, waspish — more at IRRITABLE

cross·bar \'krȯs-,bär\ *n* : a transverse bar or piece

cross·bow \-,bō\ *n* : a short bow mounted crosswise at the end of a wooden stock that shoots short arrows

cross·breed \'krȯs-,brēd, -'brēd\ *vb* **-bred** \-'bred\; **-breed·ing** : HYBRIDIZE

cross–coun·try \-'kən-trē\ *adj* 1 : extending or moving across a country 2 : proceeding over the countryside (as fields and woods) and not by roads 3 : of or relating to racing or skiing over the countryside instead of over a track or run — **cross–country** *adv*

cross–cur·rent \-'kər-ənt\ *n* 1 : a current running counter to another 2 : a conflicting tendency — usu. used in pl.

¹**cross–cut** \-,kət\ *vb* : to cut or saw crosswise esp. of the grain of wood

²**crosscut** *adj* 1 : made or used for crosscutting ⟨a ∼ saw⟩ 2 : cut across the grain

³**crosscut** *n* : something that cuts through transversely

cross–ex·am·ine \,krȯ-sig-'za-mən\ *vb* : to examine with questions to check the answers to previous questions — **cross–ex·am·i·na·tion** \-,za-mə-'nā-shən\ *n*

cross–eyed \'krȯ-,sīd\ *adj* : having one or both eyes turned inward toward the nose

cross–fer·til·i·za·tion \-,fərt-ᵊl-ə-'zā-shən\ *n* 1 : fertilization between sex cells produced by separate individuals or sometimes by individuals of different kinds; *also* : CROSS-POLLINATION 2 : a broadening or productive interchange (as between cultures) — **cross–fer·til·ize** \-'fərt-ᵊl-,īz\ *vb*

cross fire *n* **1** : crossing lines of fire in combat **2** : rapid or angry interchange

cross·hair \'krȯs-ˌhar\ *n* : a fine wire or thread in the eyepiece of an optical instrument used as a reference line

cross·hatch \'krȯs-ˌhach\ *vb* : to mark with two series of parallel lines that intersect — **cross–hatch·ing** *n*

cross·ing \'krȯ-siŋ\ *n* **1** : a place or structure for crossing something (as a river) **2** ◆ : a point of intersection (as of a street and a railroad track) **3** ◆ : the act or action of crossing

◆ [2] corner, crossroad, intersection — more at CROSSROAD ◆ [3] cruise, passage, sail, voyage — more at SAIL

cross·over \'krȯs-ˌō-vər\ *n* **1** : CROSSING **2** : a member of a political party who votes in the primary of the other party **3** : a broadening of the popular appeal of an artist (as a musician) by a change in the artist's style, genre, or medium **4** : an instance of breaking into another category

cross over *vb* : to achieve broader popularity by a change of medium or style

cross·piece \'krȯs-ˌpēs\ *n* : a horizontal member

cross–pol·li·na·tion \ˌkrȯs-ˌpä-lə-'nā- shən\ *n* : transfer of pollen from one flower to the stigma of another — **cross–pol·li·nate** \'krȯs-'pä-lə-ˌnāt\ *vb*

cross–pur·pose \'krȯs-'pər-pəs\ *n* : a purpose contrary to another purpose ⟨working at *cross-purposes*⟩

cross–ques·tion \-'kwes-chən\ *vb* : CROSS-EXAMINE — **cross–question** *n*

cross–re·fer \ˌkrȯs-ri-'fər\ *vb* : to refer by a notation or direction from one place to another (as in a book or list) — **cross–ref·er·ence** \'krȯs-'re-frəns\ *n*

cross·road \'krȯs-ˌrōd\ *n* **1** : a road that crosses a main road or runs between main roads **2** ◆ : a place where roads meet — usu. used in pl. **3** : a crucial point where a decision must be made

◆ *usu* **crossroads** corner, crossing, intersection; *also* overpass, underpass

cross section *n* **1** : a section cut across something; *also* : a representation made by or as if by such cutting **2** : a number of persons or things selected from a group that show the general nature of the whole group — **cross–sec·tion·al** *adj*

cross·walk \'krȯs-ˌwȯk\ *n* : a marked path for pedestrians crossing a street

cross·ways \-ˌwāz\ *adv* : so as to cross something : CROSSWISE

cross·wind \-ˌwind\ *n* : a wind not parallel to a course (as of an airplane)

cross·wise \-ˌwīz\ *adv* ◆ : so as to cross something — **crosswise** *adj*

◆ athwart, obliquely, transversely

cross·word \'krȯs-ˌwərd\ *n* : a puzzle in which words are put into a pattern of numbered squares in answer to clues

cros·ti·ni \krȯ-'stē-nē\ *n pl* : small slices of toasted bread served with a topping

crotch \'kräch\ *n* : an angle formed by the parting of two legs, branches, or members

crotch·et \'krä-chət\ *n* **1** : an odd notion : WHIM **2** ◆ : a highly individual and usu. eccentric opinion or preference

◆ eccentricity, idiosyncrasy, mannerism, oddity, peculiarity, quirk, singularity, trick — more at IDIOSYNCRASY

crotch·ety *adj* ◆ : given to crotchets : subject to whims, crankiness, or ill temper

◆ choleric, crabby, cranky, cross, grouchy, grumpy, irascible, irritable, peevish, perverse, petulant, short-tempered, snappish, snappy, snippy, testy, waspish — more at IRRITABLE

crouch \'kraúch\ *vb* **1** ◆ : to stoop or bend low **2** : CRINGE, COWER — **crouch** *n*

◆ huddle, hunch, squat; *also* curl up

croup \'krüp\ *n* : laryngitis esp. of infants marked by a hoarse ringing cough and difficult breathing — **croupy** *adj*

crou·pi·er \'krü-pē-ər, -pē-ˌā\ *n* [F, lit., rider on the rump of a horse, fr. *croupe* rump] : an employee of a gambling casino who collects and pays bets at a gaming table

crou·ton \'krü-ˌtän\ *n* [F *croûton*, dim. of *croûte* crust] : a small cube of bread toasted or fried crisp

¹crow \'krō\ *n* **1** : any of various large glossy black birds related to the jays **2** *cap* : a member of an American Indian people of a region in Montana and Wyoming; *also* : the language of the Crow people

²crow *vb* **1** : to make the loud shrill sound characteristic of the cock **2** ◆ : to utter a sound expressive of pleasure **3** ◆ : to exult gloatingly esp. over the distress of another : EXULT **4** ◆ : to brag exultantly or blatantly : BRAG, BOAST

◆ [2, 3] delight, exult, glory, joy, rejoice, triumph — more at EXULT ◆ [4] boast, brag, plume, swagger — more at BOAST

³crow *n* : the cry of the cock

crow·bar \'krō-ˌbär\ *n* : a metal bar usu. wedge-shaped at the end for use as a pry or lever

¹crowd \'kraúd\ *vb* **1** ◆ : to press close **2** ◆ : to gather in numbers : THRONG **3** ◆ : to press, force, or thrust into a small space : CRAM, STUFF

◆ [1, 3] cram, jam, ram, sandwich, squeeze, stuff, wedge; *also* fill, heap, jam-pack, load, pack ◆ [2] flock, mob, swarm, throng; *also* beset, infest, invade, overrun; clog, dam, obstruct, plug (up)

²crowd *n* **1** ◆ : a large number of people gathered together at random : THRONG **2** ◆ : a group of people having something (as a habit, interest, or occupation) in common

◆ [1] army, crush, drove, flock, horde, host, legion, mob, multitude, press, swarm, throng; *also* masses, rabble, riffraff; gaggle, herd; heap, mountain, pile ◆ [2] circle, clan, clique, coterie, fold, gang, ring, set — more at GANG

crowd·ed *adj* **1** ◆ : filled with numerous things or people often overly compacted or concentrated **2** ◆ : pressed together

◆ [1] brimful, chock-full, fat, fraught, full, loaded, packed, replete — more at FULL ◆ [2] close, compact, dense, packed, serried, thick, tight — more at CLOSE

crowd·fund·ing \'kraúd-ˌfən-diŋ\ *n* : the practice of obtaining funding (as for a business) by seeking contributions from a large group of people esp. from the online community

crowd·sourc·ing \'kraúd-ˌsȯr-siŋ\ *n* : the practice of obtaining needed services, ideas, or content by seeking contributions from a large group of people and esp. from the online community

¹crown \'kraún\ *n* **1** : a mark of victory or honor; *esp* : the title of a champion in a sport **2** : a royal headdress **3** : the top of the head **4** ◆ : the highest part (as of a tree or tooth) **5** *often cap* : sovereign power; *also* : MONARCH **6** : a formerly used British silver coin — **crowned** \'kraúnd\ *adj*

◆ acme, apex, climax, culmination, head, height, meridian, peak, pinnacle, summit, tip-top, top, zenith — more at HEIGHT

²crown *vb* **1** : to place a crown on **2** : HONOR **3** : TOP, SURMOUNT **4** : to fit (a tooth) with an artificial crown

crown vetch *n* : a European leguminous herb with umbels of pink-and-white flowers and sharp-angled pods

crow's–foot \'krōz-ˌfút\ *n, pl* **crow's–feet** \-ˌfēt\ : any of the wrinkles around the outer corners of the eyes — usu. used in pl.

crow's nest *n* : a partly enclosed platform high on a ship's mast for use as a lookout

crozier *var of* CROSIER

¹CRT \ˌsē-(ˌ)är-'tē\ *n, pl* **CRTs** *or* **CRT's** : CATHODE-RAY

TUBE; *also* : a display device incorporating a cathode-ray tube

²**CRT** *abbr* carrier route

cru·cial \'krü-shəl\ *adj* **1** ♦ : important or essential as resolving a crisis : DECISIVE **2** : IMPORTANT, SIGNIFICANT

♦ critical, decisive, essential, indispensable, key, necessary, pivotal, pressing, requisite, urgent, vital

cru·ci·ate \'krü-shē-ˌāt\ *adj* : CRUCIFORM

cru·ci·ble \'krü-sə-bəl\ *n* **1** : a heat-resistant container in which material can be subjected to great heat **2** : a severe test

cru·ci·fix \'krü-sə-ˌfiks\ *n* : a representation of Christ on the cross

cru·ci·fix·ion \ˌkrü-sə-'fik-shən\ *n* **1** *cap* : the crucifying of Christ **2** : the act of crucifying

cru·ci·form \'krü-sə-ˌfórm\ *adj* : shaped like a cross

cru·ci·fy \'krü-sə-ˌfī\ *vb* **-fied; -fy·ing 1** : to put to death by nailing or binding the hands and feet to a cross **2** : MORTIFY 1 **3** : TORTURE, PERSECUTE

¹**crude** \'krüd\ *adj* **crud·er; crud·est 1** ♦ : not refined : RAW ⟨~ oil⟩ ⟨~ statistics⟩ **2** ♦ : lacking grace, taste, tact, or polish **3** ♦ : rough or inexpert in plan or execution — **crude·ly** *adv* — **cru·di·ty** \'krü-də-tē\ *n*

♦ [1] native, natural, raw, undressed, unprocessed, unrefined, untreated; *also* undeveloped; unfinished, unpolished; unbaked, uncooked; impure, unfiltered *Ant* processed, refined, treated ♦ [2] coarse, common, crass, gross, ill-bred, low, rough, rude, tasteless, uncouth, uncultivated, uncultured, unpolished, unrefined, vulgar — more at COARSE ♦ [3] artless, clumsy, rough, rude, unrefined — more at RUDE

²**crude** *n* : unrefined petroleum

cru·el \'krü-əl\ *adj* **cru·el·er** *or* **cru·el·ler; cru·el·est** *or* **cru·el·lest** [ME, fr. AF, fr. L *crudelis,* fr. *crudus* crude] **1** ♦ : causing pain and suffering to others **2** ♦ : extremely painful — **cru·el·ly** *adv*

♦ [1] barbarous, brutal, heartless, inhumane, sadistic, savage, vicious, wanton; *also* cutthroat, merciless, pitiless, ruthless; fell, ferocious, grim; bloodthirsty, murderous, sanguinary, sanguine; catty, hateful, malevolent, malicious, malign, malignant, mean, nasty, spiteful *Ant* benign, benignant, compassionate, good= hearted, humane, kind, kindhearted, sympathetic, tenderhearted ♦ [2] agonizing, bitter, excruciating, galling, grievous, harrowing, harsh, hurtful, painful, tortuous — more at BITTER

cru·el·ty \-tē\ *n* ♦ : the quality or state of being cruel

♦ barbarity, brutality, inhumanity, sadism, savagery, viciousness, wantonness; *also* ruthlessness; ferocity, fierceness; bloodthirstiness; cattiness, hatefulness, malevolence, malignity, meanness, nastiness, spitefulness *Ant* benignity, compassion, humanity, kindness, sympathy

cru·et \'krü-ət\ *n* : a small usu. glass bottle for vinegar, oil, or sauce

¹**cruise** \'krüz\ *vb* **cruised; cruis·ing** [D *kruisen* to make a cross, cruise] **1** : to sail about touching at a series of ports **2** : to travel for pleasure **3** : to travel about the streets at random **4** : to travel at the most efficient operating speed ⟨the airplane's *cruising* speed⟩

²**cruise** *n* ♦ : an act or an instance of cruising; *esp* : a tour by ship

♦ crossing, passage, sail, voyage — more at SAIL

cruis·er \'krü-zər\ *n* **1** : SQUAD CAR **2** : a large fast moderately armored and gunned warship **3** : a motorboat equipped for living aboard

crul·ler \'krə-lər\ *n* **1** : a small sweet cake in the form of a twisted strip fried in deep fat **2** *Northern & Midland* : an unraised doughnut

¹**crumb** \'krəm\ *n* **1** ♦ : a small fragment **2** ♦ : a small piece or quantity of some material thing

♦ atom, bit, fleck, flyspeck, grain, granule, molecule, morsel, mote, particle, patch, scrap, scruple, speck, tittle

²**crumb** *vb* **1** : to break into crumbs **2** : to cover with crumbs

crum·ble \'krəm-bəl\ *vb* **crum·bled; crum·bling 1** : to break into small pieces : DISINTEGRATE **2** : to break down completely

crum·bly *adj* ♦ : easily crumbled

♦ brittle, crisp, flaky, friable — more at CRISP

crum·my \'krə-mē\ *adj* **crum·mi·er; -est** ♦ : very poor or inferior : LOUSY

♦ bad, deficient, inferior, lousy, off, poor, punk, rotten, substandard, unacceptable, unsatisfactory, wanting, wretched, wrong — more at BAD

crum·pet \'krəm-pət\ *n* : a small round unsweetened bread cooked on a griddle

crum·ple \'krəm-pəl\ *vb* **crum·pled; crum·pling 1** ♦ : to crush together : RUMPLE **2** ♦ : fall into a jumbled or flattened mass through the force of external pressure : COLLAPSE

♦ [1] crinkle, rumple, wrinkle; *also* corrugate, crease, crimp, fold, furrow, pleat; ripple, ruffle; disarrange, jumble, mess (up), muss (up) *Ant* iron out, smooth ♦ [2] cave in, collapse, give, go, yield — more at COLLAPSE

¹**crunch** \'krənch\ *vb* **1** ♦ : to chew with a grinding noise **2** ♦ : to grind or press with a crushing noise

♦ *usu* **crunch on** [1] bite, champ, chew, chomp, gnaw, nibble ♦ [2] gnash, grate, grind, grit, scrape — more at GRIND

²**crunch** *n* **1** : an act of or a sound made by crunching **2** ♦ : a tight or critical situation — **crunchy** *adj*

♦ clutch, crisis, emergency, head, juncture — more at EMERGENCY

cru·sade \krü-'sād\ *n* **1** *cap* : any of the expeditions in the 11th, 12th, and 13th centuries undertaken by Christian countries to take the Holy Land from the Muslims **2** ♦ : a reforming enterprise undertaken with zeal — **crusade** *vb*

♦ bandwagon, campaign, cause, drive, movement — more at CAMPAIGN

cru·sad·er *n* ♦ : one engaged in a crusade

♦ fanatic, militant, partisan, zealot — more at ZEALOT

cruse \'krüz, 'krüs\ *n* : a jar for water or oil

¹**crush** \'krəsh\ *vb* **1** ♦ : to squeeze out of shape **2** : HUG, EMBRACE **3** ♦ : to grind or pound to small bits **4** ♦ : to suppress or overwhelm as if by pressure or weight : SUPPRESS **5** ♦ : to subdue completely

♦ [1] mash, squash; *also* press, squeeze; beat, pound, powder, pulverize ♦ [3] atomize, grind, powder, pulverize — more at POWDER ♦ [4, 5] clamp down, crack down, put down, quash, quell, repress, silence, snuff, squash, squelch, subdue, suppress — more at QUELL ♦ [4, 5] carry away, devastate, floor, oppress, overcome, overpower, overwhelm, prostrate, snow under, swamp — more at OVERWHELM

²**crush** *n* **1** : an act of crushing **2** ♦ : a violent crowding **3** : INFATUATION

♦ army, crowd, drove, flock, horde, host, legion, mob, multitude, press, swarm, throng — more at CROWD

crust \'krəst\ *n* **1** : the outside part of bread; *also* : a piece of old dry bread **2** : the cover of a pie **3** : a hard surface layer — **crust·al** *adj*

crus·ta·cean \ˌkrəs-'tā-shən\ *n* : any of a large class of mostly aquatic arthropods (as lobsters or crabs) having a firm crustlike shell — **crustacean** *adj*

crusty *adj* **crust·i·er; -est 1** : having or being a crust **2** : giving an effect of surly incivility in address or disposition : CROSS, GRUMPY

crutch \'krəch\ *n* : a supporting device; *esp* : a support fitting under the armpit for use by the disabled in walking

crux \'krəks, 'krúks\ *n, pl* **crux·es 1** : a puzzling or difficult problem **2** ♦ : a crucial point

♦ core, gist, heart, nub, pith, pivot; *also* course, direction, drift, tenor; body, essence, substance

¹cry \'krī\ *vb* **cried; cry·ing 1 ♦** : to call out : SHOUT **2** : to proclaim publicly : ADVERTISE **3 ♦** : to shed tears often noisily : WEEP **4 ♦** : to protest or complain loudly or vigorously — often used with *out*

  ♦ **[1]** bawl, call, holler, shout, vociferate, yell — more at CALL ♦ **[3]** bawl, blubber, sob, weep; *also* grieve, keen, lament, mourn; howl, scream, squall, wail, yowl; whimper, whine; sniffle, snivel; groan, moan, sigh ♦ *usu* **cry out [4]** blurt, bolt, ejaculate, spout

²cry *n, pl* **cries 1 ♦** : a loud outcry **2 ♦** : an earnest plea : APPEAL, ENTREATY **3** : a fit of weeping **4** : the characteristic sound uttered by an animal **5** : DISTANCE — usu. used in the phrase *a far cry* **6 ♦** : a loud shout **7 ♦** : a word or motto that embodies a principle or guide to action of an individual or group

  ♦ **[1, 6]** holler, hoot, howl, shout, whoop, yell, yowl — more at SHOUT ♦ **[2]** appeal, entreaty, petition, plea, prayer, solicitation, suit, supplication — more at PLEA ♦ **[7]** shibboleth, slogan, watchword — more at SLOGAN

cry·ba·by \'krī-ˌbā-bē\ *n* **♦** : one who cries or complains easily or often

  ♦ complainer, grumbler, whiner; *also* malcontent; carper, critic, faultfinder, nitpicker; weeper

cry down *vb* **♦** : to lower in rank or reputation

  ♦ belittle, decry, deprecate, depreciate, diminish, discount, disparage, minimize, put down, write off — more at DECRY

cryo·gen·ic \ˌkrī-ə-'je-nik\ *adj* : of or relating to the production of very low temperatures; *also* : involving the use of a very low temperature — **cryo·gen·i·cal·ly** \-ni-k(ə-)lē\ *adv*
cryo·gen·ics \-niks\ *n* : a branch of physics that relates to the production and effects of very low temperatures
cryo·lite \'krī-ə-ˌlīt\ *n* : a usu. white mineral used in making aluminum
crypt \'kript\ *n* : a chamber wholly or partly underground
cryp·tic \'krip-tik\ *adj* **1 ♦** : meant to be puzzling or mysterious **2 ♦** : having or seeming to have a hidden or ambiguous meaning

  ♦ ambiguous, dark, darkling, deep, enigmatic, equivocal, inscrutable, murky, mysterious, mystic, nebulous, obscure, occult — more at OBSCURE

cryp·to·gram \'krip-tə-ˌgram\ *n* : a communication in cipher or code
cryp·tog·ra·phy \krip-'tä-grə-fē\ *n* : the coding and decoding of secret messages — **cryp·tog·ra·pher** \-fər\ *n*
crys·tal \'krist-ᵊl\ *n* [ME *cristal*, fr. AF, fr. L *crystallum*, fr. Gk *krystallos* ice, crystal] **1** : transparent quartz **2** : something resembling crystal (as in transparency); *esp* : a clear glass used for table articles **3** : a body that is formed by solidification of a substance and has a regular repeating arrangement of atoms and often of external plane faces ⟨a salt ∼⟩ **4** : the transparent cover of a watch dial
crystal clear *adj* : perfectly or transparently clear
crys·tal·line \'kris-tə-lən\ *adj* **1** : made of or resembling crystal **2** : very clear or sparkling
crys·tal·lise *Brit var of* CRYSTALLIZE
crys·tal·lize \'kris-tə-ˌlīz\ *vb* **-lized; -liz·ing 1** : to assume or cause to assume a crystalline form **2 ♦** : to take or cause to take a definite form — **crys·tal·li·za·tion** \ˌkris-tə-lə-'zā-shən\ *n*

  ♦ form, jell, shape, solidify

crys·tal·log·ra·phy \ˌkris-tə-'lä-grə-fē\ *n* : the science dealing with the forms and structures of crystals — **crys·tal·log·ra·pher** *n*
cs *abbr* case; cases
Cs *symbol* cesium
CS *abbr* **1** civil service **2** county seat
CSA *abbr* Confederate States of America
C–section \'sē-ˌsek-shən\ *n* : CESAREAN SECTION
CSM *abbr* command sergeant major
CST *abbr* central standard time

ct *abbr* **1** carat **2** cent **3** count **4** county **5** court
CT *abbr* **1** central time **2** Connecticut
ctn *abbr* carton
ctr *abbr* **1** center **2** counter
CT scan \ˌsē-'tē-\ *n* : CAT SCAN
cu *abbr* cubic
Cu *symbol* [L *cuprum*] copper
cub \'kəb\ *n* **1** : a young individual of some animals (as a fox, bear, or lion) **2 ♦** : a young person

  ♦ child, juvenile, kid, kiddo, moppet, whelp, youngster, youth — more at CHILD

Cu·ban \'kyü-bən\ *n* : a native or inhabitant of Cuba — **Cuban** *adj*
Cuban sandwich \'kyü-bən-\ *n* : a usu. grilled and pressed sandwich served on a long split roll
cub·by·hole \'kə-bē-ˌhōl\ *n* : a snug place (as for storing things)
¹cube \'kyüb\ *n* **1** : a solid having 6 equal square sides **2** : the product obtained by taking a number 3 times as a factor ⟨27 is the ∼ of 3⟩
²cube *vb* **cubed; cub·ing 1** : to raise to the third power **2** : to form into a cube **3** : to cut into cubes
cube root *n* : a number whose cube is a given number
cu·bic \'kyü-bik\ *also* **cu·bi·cal** *adj* **1** : having the form of a cube **2** : being the volume of a cube whose edge is a specified unit **3** : having length, width, and height
cu·bi·cle \'kyü-bi-kəl\ *n* **♦** : a small separate space (as for sleeping or studying)

  ♦ bay, cabin, cell, chamber, compartment — more at COMPARTMENT

cubic measure *n* : a unit (as cubic inch) for measuring volume
cubic zir·co·nia \-ˌzər-'kō-nē-ə\ *also* **cubic zirconium** *n* : a synthetic gemstone resembling a diamond made from an oxide of zirconium
cub·ism \'kyü-ˌbi-zəm\ *n* : a style of art characterized by the abstraction of natural forms into fragmented geometric shapes — **cub·ist** \-bist\ *n or adj*
cu·bit \'kyü-bət\ *n* : an ancient unit of length equal to about 18 inches (46 centimeters)
Cub Scout *n* : a member of the program of the Boy Scouts for boys in the first through fifth grades in school
cuck·old \'kə-kəld, 'kú-\ *n* : a man whose wife is unfaithful — **cuckold** *vb*
¹cuck·oo \'kü-kü, 'kú-\ *n, pl* **cuckoos** : a largely grayish brown European bird that lays its eggs in the nests of other birds for them to hatch
²cuckoo *n* : a silly or foolish person
³cuckoo *adj* **♦** : being one that is silly or foolish

  ♦ absurd, crazy, fatuous, foolish, mad, nonsensical, nutty, senseless, silly, stupid — more at FOOLISH

cu·cum·ber \'kyü-(ˌ)kəm-bər\ *n* : the long fleshy many-seeded fruit of a vine of the gourd family that is grown as a garden vegetable; *also* : this vine
cud \'kəd\ *n* : food brought up into the mouth by some animals (as cows) from the rumen to be chewed again
cud·dle \'kəd-ᵊl\ *vb* **cud·dled; cud·dling 1 ♦** : to lie close : SNUGGLE **2 ♦** : to hold close for warmth or comfort or in affection

  ♦ nestle, nuzzle, snug, snuggle — more at NUZZLE

cud·gel \'kə-jəl\ *n* **♦** : a short heavy club — **cudgel** *vb*

  ♦ bat, billy club, bludgeon, club, staff, truncheon — more at CLUB

¹cue \'kyü\ *n* **1** : a word, phrase, or action in a play serving as a signal for the next actor to speak or act **2 ♦** : a hint, intimation, or suggestion as to what course of action to take or when to take it : HINT — **cue** *vb*

  ♦ clue, hint, indication, inkling, intimation, lead, suggestion — more at HINT

²cue *n* : a tapered rod for striking the balls in billiards or pool
³cue *n* : a waiting line esp. of persons or vehicles
cue ball *n* : the ball a player strikes with a cue in billiards or pool

¹cuff \'kəf\ *n* **1** : a part (as of a sleeve or glove) encircling the wrist **2** : the folded hem of a trouser leg

²cuff *vb* : to strike esp. with the open hand : SLAP

³cuff *n* : to strike esp. with or as if with the palm of the hand

cui·sine \kwi-'zēn\ *n* : style of cooking; *also* : the food prepared

cuke \'kyük\ *n* : CUCUMBER

cul–de–sac \ˌkəl-di-'sak, ˌkúl-\ *n, pl* **culs–de–sac** *same or* ˌkəlz-, ˌkúlz-\ *also* **cul–de–sacs** \ˌkəl-də-'saks, ˌkúl-\ [F, lit., bottom of the bag] : a street or passage closed at one end

cu·li·nary \'kə-lə-ˌner-ē, 'kyü-\ *adj* : of or relating to the kitchen or cookery

¹cull \'kəl\ *vb* **1** ♦ : to pick out from a group **2** : to reduce or control the size of something (as a herd) by removal (as by hunting or slaughter) of esp. weak or sick individuals ⟨∼*ing* a herd of cattle⟩

    ♦ choose, elect, handpick, name, opt, pick, prefer, select, single, take — more at CHOOSE

²cull *n* ♦ : something rejected from a group or lot as worthless or inferior

    ♦ discard, reject, rejection; *also* second, throwaway

cul·mi·nate \'kəl-mə-ˌnāt\ *vb* **-nat·ed; -nat·ing** : to reach the highest point

cul·mi·na·tion \ˌkəl-mə-'nā-shən\ *n* ♦ : culminating position

    ♦ acme, apex, climax, crown, head, height, meridian, peak, pinnacle, summit, tip-top, top, zenith — more at HEIGHT

cu·lotte \'kü-ˌlät, ˌkyü-, kù-ˌlät, kyù-\ *n* [F, breeches, fr. dim. of *cul* backside] : a divided skirt; *also* : a garment having a divided skirt — often used in pl.

cul·pa·bil·i·ty \ˌkəl-pə-'bi-lə-tē\ *n* ♦ : the quality or state of being culpable

    ♦ blame, fault, guilt, rap — more at BLAME

cul·pa·ble \'kəl-pə-bəl\ *adj* ♦ : deserving blame

    ♦ blamable, blameworthy, censurable, reprehensible — more at BLAMEWORTHY

cul·prit \'kəl-prət\ *n* [AF *cul.* (abbr. of *culpable* guilty) + *prest, prit* ready (i.e., to prove it), fr. L *praestus*] ♦ : one accused or guilty of a crime

    ♦ criminal, crook, felon, lawbreaker, malefactor, offender — more at CRIMINAL

cult \'kəlt\ *n* **1** : formal religious veneration **2** ♦ : a religious system or its adherents **3** : faddish devotion; *also* : a group of persons showing such devotion — **cult·ish** \'kəl-tish\ *adj* — **cult·ist** \-tist\ *n*

    ♦ creed, faith, persuasion, religion — more at RELIGION

cul·ti·va·ble \'kəl-tə-və-bəl\ *adj* : capable of being cultivated

cul·ti·var \'kəl-tə-ˌvär, -ˌver\ *n* : a plant variety originating and persisting under cultivation

cul·ti·vate \'kəl-tə-ˌvāt\ *vb* **-vat·ed; -vat·ing** **1** ♦ : to prepare for the raising of crops **2** ♦ : to foster the growth of by tilling or by labor and care ⟨∼ vegetables⟩ **3** ♦ : to improve by labor, care, or study **4** : to help forward : ENCOURAGE, FURTHER ⟨∼ the arts⟩ **5** : to seek the friendship of

    ♦ [1] farm, tend — more at FARM ♦ [2] advance, encourage, forward, foster, further, nourish, nurture, promote — more at FOSTER ♦ [3] crop, grow, promote, raise, rear, tend — more at GROW

cul·ti·vat·ed \'kəl-tə-ˌvāt-əd\ *adj* ♦ : having an education; *esp* : trained in the arts and social graces

    ♦ civilized, cultured, genteel, polished, refined; *also* cerebral, highbrow, intellectual; educated, erudite, knowledgeable, learned, literate, scholarly, well-read; civil, courteous, mannerly, polite, well-bred; cosmopolitan, sophisticated, urbane *Ant* philistine, uncivilized, uncultured, unpolished, unrefined

cul·ti·va·tion \ˌkəl-tə-'vā-shən\ *n* ♦ : enlightenment and excellence of taste acquired by intellectual and aesthetic training

    ♦ civilization, culture, polish, refinement — more at CULTURE

cul·ti·va·tor \'kəl-tə-ˌvā-tər\ *n* ♦ : one that cultivates

    ♦ agriculturist, farmer, grower, planter, tiller — more at FARMER

cul·ture \'kəl-chər\ *n* **1** : TILLAGE, CULTIVATION **2** : the act of developing by education and training **3** ♦ : refinement of intellectual and artistic taste **4** ♦ : the customary beliefs, social forms, and material traits of a racial, religious, or social group — **cul·tur·al** \'kəl-chə-rəl\ *adj* — **cul·tur·al·ly** *adv*

    ♦ [3] civilization, cultivation, polish, refinement; *also* education, erudition, learning, literacy, scholarship; sophistication, urbanity; breeding, gentility, manners; class, elegance, grace, taste; civility, courtesy, politeness ♦ [4] civilization, life, lifestyle, society — more at CIVILIZATION

cul·tured \-chərd\ *adj* ♦ : having an education; *esp* : having an education beyond the average

    ♦ civilized, cultivated, genteel, polished, refined — more at CULTIVATED

cul·vert \'kəl-vərt\ *n* : a drain crossing under a road or railroad

cum *abbr* cumulative

cum·ber \'kəm-bər\ *vb* : to weigh down : BURDEN, HINDER

cum·ber·some \'kəm-bər-səm\ *adj* ♦ : hard to handle or manage because of size or weight

    ♦ awkward, clumsy, cranky, ungainly, unhandy, unwieldy; *also* uncontrollable, unmanageable; bulky, heavy, massive; impracticable, impractical *Ant* handy

cum·brous \'kəm-brəs\ *adj* : unwieldy because of heaviness and bulk : CUMBERSOME — **cum·brous·ly** *adv* — **cum·brous·ness** *n*

cum·in \'kə-mən, 'kyü-\ *n* : the seedlike fruit of a small annual herb related to the carrot that is used as a spice; *also* : this herb

cum·mer·bund \'kə-mər-ˌbənd, 'kəm-bər-\ *n* [Hindi *kamarband*, fr. Per, fr. *kamar* waist + *band* band] ♦ : a broad sash worn as a waistband

    ♦ belt, cincture, girdle, sash — more at BELT

cu·mu·la·tive \'kyü-myə-lə-tiv, -ˌlā-\ *adj* : increasing in force or value by successive additions

cu·mu·lo·nim·bus \ˌkyü-myə-lō-'nim-bəs\ *n* : an anvil-shaped cumulus cloud extending to great heights

cu·mu·lus \'kyü-myə-ləs\ *n, pl* **-li** \-ˌlī, -ˌlē\ : a massive cloud having a flat base and rounded outlines

cu·ne·i·form \kyù-'nē-ə-ˌfòrm\ *adj* **1** : wedge-shaped **2** : composed of wedge-shaped characters

cun·ni·lin·gus \ˌkə-ni-'liŋ-gəs\ *also* **cun·ni·linc·tus** \-'liŋk-təs\ *n* : oral stimulation of the vulva or clitoris

¹cun·ning \'kə-niŋ\ *adj* **1** ♦ : dexterous or crafty in the use of special resources (as skill or knowledge) or in attaining an end : DEXTEROUS **2** ♦ : marked by wiliness and trickery **3** : CUTE — **cun·ning·ly** *adv*

    ♦ [1] clever, deft, dexterous, handy — more at DEXTEROUS ♦ [2] artful, cagey, crafty, devious, foxy, guileful, slick, sly, subtle, wily — more at ARTFUL

²cunning *n* **1** ♦ : skill in planning, making, or executing : SKILL **2** ♦ : skill in deceiving to gain an end

    ♦ [1] adeptness, adroitness, art, artfulness, artifice, artistry, cleverness, craft, deftness, masterfulness, skill — more at SKILL ♦ [2] artfulness, artifice, caginess, canniness, craft, craftiness, guile, slyness, wiliness; *also* calculation, care, design; savvy, sharpness, shrewdness; cleverness, ingeniousness, ingenuity, inventiveness; ease, facility, finesse; deceitfulness, duplicity

¹cup \'kəp\ *n* **1** : a small bowl-shaped drinking vessel **2** : the contents of a cup **3** : the consecrated wine of the Communion **4** : something resembling a cup : a small bowl or hollow **5** : a half pint — **cup·ful** *n* — **cup·like** \-ˌlīk\ *adj*

²cup *vb* **cupped; cup·ping** : to curve into the shape of a cup

cup·board \'kə-bərd\ *n* ♦ : a small closet with shelves for food or dishes

♦ buffet, cabinet, closet, hutch, locker, sideboard — more at CABINET

cup·cake \'kəp-ˌkāk\ *n* : a small cake baked in a cuplike mold

cu·pid \'kyü-pəd\ *n* : a winged naked figure of an infant often with a bow and arrow that represents the god Cupid

cu·pid·i·ty \kyú-'pi-də-tē\ *n, pl* **-ties** ♦ : excessive desire for money

♦ acquisitiveness, avarice, avidity, covetousness, greed, rapaciousness — more at GREED

cu·po·la \'kyü-pə-lə, -ˌlō\ *n* : a small structure on top of a roof or building

¹**cur** \'kər\ *n* 1 : a mongrel dog 2 ♦ : a surly or cowardly fellow

♦ beast, boor, churl, clown, creep, cretin, heel, jerk, joker, louse, lout, skunk, slob, snake — more at JERK

²**cur** *abbr* 1 currency 2 current

cu·rate \'kyür-ət\ *n* 1 : a member of the clergy who is in charge of a parish 2 : a member of the clergy who assists a rector or vicar — **cu·ra·cy** \-ə-sē\ *n*

cu·ra·tive \-ə-tiv\ *adj* : relating to or used in the cure of diseases — **curative** *n*

cu·ra·tor \'kyür-ˌā-tər, kyú-'rā-\ *n* : CUSTODIAN; *esp* : one in charge of a place of exhibit (as a museum or zoo)

¹**curb** \'kərb\ *n* 1 : a bit that exerts pressure on a horse's jaws 2 ♦ : one that arrests, limits, or restrains : CHECK, RESTRAINT 3 : a raised edging (as of stone or concrete) along a paved street

♦ check, condition, constraint, fetter, limitation, restraint, restriction — more at RESTRICTION

²**curb** *vb* ♦ : to hold in or back : RESTRAIN

♦ bridle, check, constrain, contain, control, govern, inhibit, regulate, rein, restrain, tame — more at CONTROL

curb·ing \'kər-biŋ\ *n* 1 : the material for a curb 2 : CURB

curd \'kərd\ *n* : the thick protein-rich part of coagulated milk

cur·dle \'kərd-³l\ *vb* **cur·dled; cur·dling** : to form curds; *also* : SPOIL, SOUR

¹**cure** \'kyür\ *n* 1 : spiritual care 2 : recovery or relief from disease 3 ♦ : a curative agent : REMEDY 4 : a course or period of treatment

♦ drug, medicine, pharmaceutical, remedy, specific — more at MEDICINE

²**cure** *vb* **cured; cur·ing** 1 ♦ : to restore to health : HEAL; *also* : to become cured 2 : to process for storage or use ⟨∼ bacon⟩ — **cur·able** *adj*

♦ heal, mend, rehabilitate — more at HEAL

cu·ré \kyú-'rā\ *n* [F] : a parish priest

cure-all \'kyür-ˌól\ *n* : a remedy for all ills : PANACEA

cu·ret·tage \ˌkyür-ə-'täzh\ *n* : a surgical scraping or cleaning of a body part (as the uterus)

cur·few \'kər-ˌfyü\ *n* [ME, fr. MF *covrefeu*, signal given to bank the hearth fire, curfew, fr. *covrir* to cover + *feu* fire, fr. L *focus* hearth] : a regulation that specified persons (as children) be off the streets at a set hour of the evening; *also* : the sounding of a signal (as a bell) at this hour

cu·ria \'kyür-ē-ə, 'kúr-\ *n, pl* **cu·ri·ae** \'kyür-ē-ˌē, 'kúr-ē-ˌī\ *often cap* : the body of congregations, tribunals, and offices through which the pope governs the Roman Catholic Church

cu·rie \'kyür-ē\ *n* : a unit of radioactivity equal to 37 billion disintegrations per second

cu·rio \'kyür-ē-ˌō\ *n, pl* **cu·ri·os** : an object or article valued because it is strange or rare

cu·ri·os·i·ty \ˌkyür-ē-'ä-sə-tē\ *n* 1 ♦ : one that arouses interest esp. for uncommon or exotic characteristics 2 ♦ : an unusual knickknack

♦ [1] exotic, oddity, rarity; *also* marvel, prodigy, wonder; abnormality, anomaly, freak, monster, monstrosity; malformation, mutant, mutation ♦ [2] bauble, gewgaw, knickknack, novelty, tchotchke, trinket — more at KNICKKNACK

cu·ri·ous \'kyúr-ē-əs\ *adj* 1 ♦ : having a desire to investigate and learn 2 ♦ : exciting attention as strange, novel, or unexpected : STRANGE, UNUSUAL, ODD

♦ [1] inquisitive, nosy, prying; *also* interfering, intrusive, meddlesome, meddling, obtrusive, officious; inquisitorial; concerned, interested *Ant* incurious, uncurious ♦ [2] extraordinary, funny, odd, peculiar, rare, singular, strange, unaccustomed, uncommon, uncustomary, unique, unusual, weird — more at UNUSUAL

cu·ri·ous·ly *adv* 1 : in a curious manner 2 : as is curious

cu·ri·um \'kyúr-ē-əm\ *n* : a metallic radioactive element produced artificially

¹**curl** \'kərl\ *vb* 1 : to form into ringlets 2 ♦ : to move or progress in curves or spirals : COIL — **curl·er** *n*

♦ coil, entwine, spiral, twine, twist, wind — more at WIND

²**curl** *n* 1 : a lock of hair that coils : RINGLET 2 : something having a spiral or twisted form — **curly** *adj*

cur·lew \'kər-lü, 'kərl-yü\ *n, pl* **curlews** *or* **curlew** : any of various long-legged brownish birds that have a down-curved bill and are related to the sandpipers and snipes

curli·cue \'kər-li-ˌkyü\ *n* : a fancifully curved or spiral figure

curl up *vb* ♦ : to arrange oneself in or as if in a ball or curl

♦ nestle, snug, snuggle — more at SNUGGLE

cur·mud·geon \(ˌ)kər-'mə-jən\ *n* ♦ : a crusty, ill-tempered, and usu. old man

♦ bear, complainer, crab, crank, grouch, grumbler, whiner — more at GROUCH

cur·rant \'kər-ənt\ *n* 1 : a small seedless raisin 2 : the acid berry of a shrub related to the gooseberry; *also* : this plant

cur·ren·cy \'kər-ən-sē\ *n, pl* **-cies** 1 : general use or acceptance 2 ♦ : something that is in circulation as a medium of exchange : MONEY

♦ cash, dough, lucre, money, pelf, tender — more at MONEY

¹**cur·rent** \'kər-ənt\ *adj* 1 ♦ : occurring in or belonging to the present 2 : used as a medium of exchange 3 ♦ : generally accepted or practiced

♦ [1] contemporary, hot, mod, modern, new, newfangled, red-hot, space-age, ultramodern, up-to-date — more at MODERN ♦ [3] conventional, customary, popular, standard, stock, usual; *also* average, common, everyday, normal, ordinary; regular, routine; ubiquitous, universal, widespread; accustomed, wonted; fashionable, in, modish, stylish *Ant* nonstandard, unconventional, unpopular, unusual

²**current** *n* 1 : the part of a body of fluid moving continuously in a certain direction; *also* : the swiftest part of a stream 2 : a flow of electric charge; *also* : the rate of such flow 3 ♦ : a tendency or course of events that is usu. the result of an interplay of forces

♦ drift, leaning, run, tendency, tide, trend, wind — more at TREND

cur·ric·u·lum \kə-'ri-kyə-ləm\ *n, pl* **-la** \-lə\ *also* **-lums** [L, running, course, fr. *currere* to run] : the courses offered by an educational institution

¹**cur·ry** \'kər-ē\ *vb* **cur·ried; cur·ry·ing** 1 : to clean the coat of (a horse) with a currycomb 2 : to treat (tanned leather) esp. by incorporating oil or grease — **curry favor** : to seek to gain favor by flattery or attention

²**cur·ry** *n, pl* **cur·ries** : a powder of pungent spices used in cooking; *also* : a food seasoned with curry

cur·ry·comb \-ˌkōm\ *n* : a comb used esp. to curry horses — **currycomb** *vb*

¹**curse** \'kərs\ *n* 1 ♦ : a prayer for harm to come upon one 2 : something that is cursed 3 : evil or misfortune coming as if in response to a curse

♦ anathema, execration, imprecation, malediction; *also* censure, damnation, denunciation; hex, spell *Ant* benediction, benison, blessing

²**curse** *vb* **cursed; curs·ing** 1 : to call on divine power to

send injury upon **2** : BLASPHEME **3** ♦ : to bring great evil upon : AFFLICT

♦ afflict, agonize, bedevil, harrow, martyr, persecute, plague, rack, torment, torture — more at AFFLICT

cur·sive \'kər-siv\ *adj* : written with the strokes of the letters joined together and the angles rounded

cur·sor \'kər-sər\ *n* : a visual cue (as a pointer) on a computer screen that indicates position (as for data entry)

cur·so·ri·ly \-rə-lē\ *adj* ♦ : in a cursory manner

♦ hastily, headlong, hurriedly, pell-mell, precipitately, rashly — more at HASTILY

cur·so·ry \'kər-sə-rē\ *adj* ♦ : rapidly and often superficially done : HASTY

♦ hasty, headlong, pell-mell, precipitate, precipitous, rash — more at HASTY

curt \'kərt\ *adj* ♦ : rudely short or abrupt — **curt·ly** *adv* — **curt·ness** *n*

♦ abrupt, bluff, blunt, brusque, snippy — more at BLUNT

cur·tail \(ˌ)kər-'tāl\ *vb* ♦ : to cut off the end of : SHORTEN — **cur·tail·ment** *n*

♦ abbreviate, abridge, cut back, shorten — more at SHORTEN

¹cur·tain \'kərt-ᵊn\ *n* **1** : a hanging screen that can be drawn back esp. at a window **2** : the screen between the stage and auditorium of a theater

²curtain *vb* ♦ : to veil with or as if with a curtain

♦ blanket, blot out, cloak, conceal, cover, enshroud, hide, mask, obscure, occult, screen, shroud, veil — more at HIDE

curt·sy *also* **curt·sey** \'kərt-sē\ *n, pl* **curtsies** *or* **curtseys** : a courteous bow made by women chiefly by bending the knees — **curtsy** *also* **curtsey** *vb*

cur·va·ceous *also* **cur·va·cious** \ˌkər-'vā-shəs\ *adj* : having curves suggestive of a well-proportioned feminine figure

cur·va·ture \'kər-və-ˌchùr\ *n* **1** : a measure or amount of curving : BEND **2** : curved part

¹curve \'kərv\ *vb* **curved**; **curv·ing** ♦ : to bend from a straight line or course

♦ arc, arch, bend, bow, crook, hook, round, sweep, swerve, wheel; *also* circle, coil, curl, loop, spiral; turn, twist, wind; deviate, veer *Ant* straighten

²curve *n* **1** : a line esp. when curved **2** ♦ : something that bends or curves without angles ⟨a ∼ in the road⟩ **3** : a baseball pitch thrown so that it swerves esp. downward and to one side — **curvy** \'kər-vē\ *adj*

♦ angle, arc, arch, bend, bow, crook, turn, wind — more at BEND

cur·vet \(ˌ)kər-'vet\ *n* : a prancing leap of a horse — **curvet** *vb*

¹cush·ion \'kù-shən\ *n* [ME *cusshin*, fr. AF *cussin, quissin*, fr. VL *coxinus*, fr. L *coxa* hip] **1** : a soft pillow or pad to rest on or against **2** : the springy pad inside the rim of a billiard table **3** ♦ : something soft that prevents discomfort or protects against injury

♦ buffer, bumper, fender, pad; *also* baffle, muffler; padding; safeguard, shield

²cushion *vb* **1** : to provide (as a seat) with a cushion **2** ♦ : to soften or lessen the force or shock of

♦ buffer, gentle, soften; *also* baffle, dampen, deaden, dull; moderate, modulate, temper; allay, alleviate, assuage, ease; lighten, mitigate, relieve

cusp \'kəsp\ *n* ♦ : a pointed end or part (as of a tooth)

♦ apex, end, pike, point, tip — more at POINT

cus·pid \'kəs-pəd\ *n* : a canine tooth

cus·pi·dor \'kəs-pə-ˌdòr\ *n* : SPITTOON

cus·tard \'kəs-tərd\ *n* : a sweetened cooked mixture of milk and eggs

cus·to·di·al \ˌkəs-'tō-dē-əl\ *adj* : marked by watching and protecting rather than seeking to cure ⟨∼ care⟩

cus·to·di·an \ˌkəs-'tō-dē-ən\ *n* ♦ : one that protects and maintains; *esp* : one who has custody (as of a building)

♦ caretaker, guardian, janitor, keeper, warden, watchman; *also* curator; sexton; steward ♦ defender, defense (*or* defence), guard, protection, protector — more at PROTECTOR

cus·to·dy \'kəs-tə-dē\ *n, pl* **-dies** ♦ : immediate charge and control

♦ care, guardianship, keeping, safekeeping, trust, ward; *also* control, governorship, management, superintendence, supervision

¹cus·tom \'kəs-təm\ *n* **1** ♦ : habitual course of action : recognized usage **2** *pl* : taxes levied on imports **3** : business patronage

♦ fashion, habit, pattern, practice, trick, way, wont — more at HABIT

²custom *adj* **1** : made to personal order **2** : doing work only on order

cus·tom·ary \'kəs-tə-ˌmer-ē\ *adj* **1** ♦ : based on or established by custom **2** ♦ : commonly practiced or observed — **cus·tom·ar·i·ly** *adv*

♦ [1] classical, conventional, traditional — more at TRADITIONAL ♦ [2] conventional, current, popular, standard, stock, usual — more at CURRENT

cus·tom–built \'kəs-təm-'bilt\ *adj* : built to individual order

cus·tom·er \'kəs-tə-mər\ *n* **1** ♦ : one that purchases a commodity or service; *esp* : a regular or frequent buyer **2** : an individual usu. having some specified distinctive trait

♦ guest, patron; *also* consumer, user; buyer, purchaser; prospect, shopper, window-shopper

cus·tom·house \'kəs-təm-ˌhaùs\ *n* : the building where customs are paid

cus·tom·ise *Brit var of* CUSTOMIZE

cus·tom·ize \'kəs-tə-ˌmīz\ *vb* **-ized**; **-iz·ing** : to build, fit, or alter according to individual specifications

cus·tom–made \'kəs-təm-'mād\ *adj* ♦ : made to individual order

♦ custom, tailored; *also* particular, special, specialized; handcrafted, handmade *Ant* mass-produced, ready-made

¹cut \'kət\ *vb* **cut**; **cut·ting** **1** ♦ : to penetrate or divide with a sharp edge : CLEAVE, GASH; *also* : to experience the growth of (a tooth) through the gum **2** : to hurt the feelings of **3** : to strike sharply **4** ♦ : to diminish or reduce by or as if by paring : SHORTEN, REDUCE **5** : to remove by severing or paring **6** : INTERSECT, CROSS **7** : to divide into parts **8 a** : to go quickly or change direction abruptly **b** : to veer from a direct line **9** : to cause to stop **10** ♦ : to proceed obliquely from a straight course — often used with *across* **11** : to remove (text, etc.) from a computer document for pasting elsewhere

♦ [1] rip, slash, slice, slit; *also* saw; rive, split; pierce, stab; bruise, hack, lacerate, mangle; rend, tear; butcher, carve, dissect; chop, dice, mince; amputate, cut off, sever ♦ [4] bob, clip, crop, cut back, dock, lop, nip, prune, reduce, shave, shear, shorten, trim — more at CLIP ♦ *usu* **cut across** [10] cover, crisscross, cross, follow, go, pass, proceed, travel, traverse — more at TRAVERSE

²cut *n* **1** : something made by cutting : GASH, CLEFT **2** ♦ : a portion belonging to, due to, or contributed by an individual or group : SHARE **3** : a segment or section of a meat carcass **4** : an excavated channel or roadway **5** : a sharp stroke or blow **6** : REDUCTION ⟨∼ in wages⟩ **7** : the shape or manner in which a thing is cut **8** ♦ : a grade or step

♦ [2] allotment, allowance, part, portion, proportion, quota, share — more at SHARE ♦ [8] degree, grade, inch, notch, peg, phase, point, stage, step — more at DEGREE

cut–and–dried \ˌkət-ᵊn-'drīd\ *also* **cut–and–dry** \-'drī\ *adj* : according to a plan, set procedure, or formula

cu·ta·ne·ous \kyù-'tā-nē-əs\ *adj* : of, relating to, or affecting the skin

cut·back \'kət-ˌbak\ *n* **1** : something cut back **2** : REDUCTION

cut back *vb* **1** ♦ : to shorten by cutting **2** ♦ : to remake in a smaller size

♦ [1] bob, clip, crop, cut, dock, lop, nip, prune, shave, shear, trim — more at CLIP ♦ [2] abbreviate, abridge, curtail, shorten — more at SHORTEN

cut down *vb* ♦ : to strike to the ground with or as if with a sharp blow
♦ chop, fell, hew — more at FELL

cute \'kyüt\ *adj* **cut·er; cut·est** [short for *acute*] **1** : CLEVER, SHREWD **2** ♦ : daintily attractive : PRETTY
♦ attractive, beautiful, bonny, fair, pretty — more at BEAUTIFUL

cu·ti·cle \'kyü-ti-kəl\ *n* **1** : an outer layer (as of skin or a leaf) **2** : dead or horny epidermis esp. around a finger-nail — **cu·tic·u·lar** \kyù-'ti-kyə-lər\ *adj*

cut in *vb* **1** ♦ : to thrust oneself between others **2** : to interrupt a dancing couple and take one as one's partner
♦ break, chime in, interpose, interrupt, intrude — more at INTERRUPT

cut·lass \'kət-ləs\ *n* : a short heavy curved sword

cut·ler \'kət-lər\ *n* [ME, fr. AF *cuteler*, fr. LL *cultellarius*, fr. L *cultellus* knife] : one who makes, deals in, or repairs cutlery

cut·lery \'kət-lə-rē\ *n* : edged or cutting tools; *esp* : implements for cutting and eating food

cut·let \'kət-lət\ *n* **1** : a slice of meat (as veal) for broiling or frying **2** ♦ : a flat croquette of chopped meat or fish
♦ fritter, patty

cut·off \'kət-ˌȯf\ *n* **1** : the channel formed when a stream cuts through the neck of an oxbow; *also* : SHORTCUT **2** : a device for cutting off **3** *pl* : shorts orig. made from jeans with the legs cut off at the knees or higher

cut off *vb* ♦ : to set apart from others
♦ insulate, isolate, seclude, segregate, separate, seques-ter — more at ISOLATE

cut·out \'kət-ˌaüt\ *n* : something cut out or prepared for cutting out from something else ⟨a page of animal ∼s⟩

¹cut out *vb* **1** : to determine or assign through necessity ⟨had her work *cut out* for her⟩ **2** : DISCONNECT **3** ♦ : to cease operating ⟨the engine *cut out*⟩ **4** : ELIMINATE ⟨*cut out* unnecessary expense⟩ **5** : to put an end to
♦ break, break down, conk, crash, die, fail, stall — more at FAIL

cut–rate \'kət-ˈrāt\ *adj* **1** ♦ : relating to or dealing in goods sold at reduced rates **2** ♦ : of second or inferior quality or value
♦ [1] cheap, low, reasonable — more at CHEAP
♦ [2] bad, bum, cheap, coarse, common, execrable, in-ferior, junky, lousy, mediocre, miserable, poor, rotten, second-rate, shoddy, sleazy, terrible, trashy, wretched — more at CHEAP

cut·ter \'kə-tər\ *n* **1** : a tool or a machine for cutting **2** : a ship's boat for carrying stores and passengers **3** : a small armed vessel in government service **4** : a light sleigh

¹cut·throat \'kət-ˌthrōt\ *n* : MURDERER

²cutthroat *adj* **1** : MURDEROUS, CRUEL **2** ♦ : marked by unprincipled practices ⟨∼ competition⟩
♦ immoral, Machiavellian, unconscionable, unethical, unprincipled, unscrupulous

cutthroat trout *n* : a large American trout with a red mark under the jaw

¹cut·ting \'kə-tiŋ\ *n* : a piece of a plant able to grow into a new plant

²cutting *adj* **1** ♦ : made for cutting, severing, or divid-ing : SHARP, EDGED **2** ♦ : marked by piercing cold **3** ♦ : likely to hurt the feelings : SARCASTIC ⟨a ∼ remark⟩
♦ [1] edgy, ground, keen, sharp — more at SHARP
♦ [2] biting, bitter, keen, penetrating, piercing, raw, sharp; *also* brisk, invigorating, nippy, snappy; prickly, tingling; caustic, corrosive ♦ [3] acrid, biting, caustic, mordant, pungent, sarcastic, satiric, scathing, sharp, tart — more at SARCASTIC

cut·tle·fish \'kə-tᵊl-ˌfish\ *n* : any of various marine mol-lusks having eight arms and two usu. longer tentacles and an internal shell (**cut·tle·bone** \-ˌbōn\) composed of calcium compounds

cut·up \'kət-ˌəp\ *n* : a person who clowns or acts boister-ously

cut up *vb* ♦ : to behave in a comic, boisterous, or unruly manner
♦ act up, clown, fool, monkey, show off, skylark; *also* carry on, misbehave; roughhouse; caper, cavort, dis-port, frisk, frolic, gambol, lark, rollick, romp; carouse, revel, wassail

cut·worm \-ˌwərm\ *n* : any of various smooth-bodied moth larvae that feed on plants at night

cw *abbr* clockwise

CWO *abbr* **1** cash with order **2** chief warrant officer

cwt *abbr* hundredweight

-cy \sē\ *n suffix* **1** : action : practice ⟨mendican*cy*⟩ **2** : rank : office ⟨chaplain*cy*⟩ **3** : body : class ⟨constitu-en*cy*⟩ **4** : state : quality ⟨accura*cy*⟩

cy·an \'sī-ˌan, -ən\ *n* : a greenish blue color

cy·a·nide \'sī-ə-ˌnīd, -nəd\ *n* : a poisonous compound of carbon and nitrogen with another element (as potas-sium)

cy·ber \'sī-bər\ *adj* : of, relating to, or involving computers or computer networks

cyber- *comb form* : computer : computer network

cy·ber·at·tack \'sī-bər-ə-ˌtak\ *n* : an attempt to gain illegal access to a computer or computer system for the purpose of causing damage or harm

cy·ber·bul·ly·ing \-ˌbù-lē-iŋ\ *n* : the electronic posting of mean-spirited messages about a person

cy·ber·ca·fe \'sī-bər-ka-ˈfā\ *n* : a small restaurant offering use of computers with Internet access

cy·ber·crime \-ˌkrīm\ *n* : criminal activity (as fraud or theft) committed using a computer

cy·ber·net·ics \ˌsī-bər-ˈne-tiks\ *n* : the science of commu-nication and control theory that is concerned esp. with the comparative study of automatic control systems — **cy·ber·net·ic** *adj*

cy·ber·punk \'sī-bər-ˌpəŋk\ *n* **1** : science fiction dealing with computer-dominated future societies **2** : HACKER **3**

cy·ber·se·cu·ri·ty \-si-ˌkyùr-ə-tē\ *n* : protection of a com-puter or computer system against unauthorized access or attack

cy·ber·sex \'sī-bər-ˌseks\ *n* **1** : online sex-oriented conver-sations **2** : sex-oriented material available on a computer

cy·ber·space \'sī-bər-ˌspās\ *n* : the online world of com-puter networks

cy·ber·ter·ror·ism \-ˌter-ər-ˌi-zəm\ *n* : terrorist activities in-tended to damage or disrupt computer systems

cy·cla·men \'sī-klə-mən\ *n* : any of a genus of plants re-lated to the primroses and grown for their showy nodding flowers

¹cy·cle \'sī-kəl\ *n* **1** : a period of time occupied by a se-ries of events that repeat themselves regularly and in the same order **2** : a recurring round of operations or events **3** : one complete occurrence of a periodic process (as a vibration or current alternation) **4** : a circular or spiral arrangement **5** ♦ : a long period of time : AGE **6** : BICY-CLE **7** : MOTORCYCLE — **cy·clic** \'sī-klik, 'si-\ *or* **cy·cli·cal** \-kli-kəl\ *adj* — **cy·cli·cal·ly** \-k(ə-)lē\ *also* **cy·clic·ly** *adv*
♦ age, eon (*or* aeon), eternity — more at AGE

²cycle *vb* **cy·cled; cy·cling** : to ride a cycle — **cy·clist** \'sī-klist, -kə-list\ *n*

cy·clone \'sī-ˌklōn\ *n* **1** : a storm or system of winds that rotates about a center of low atmospheric pressure and advances at 20 to 30 miles (about 30 to 50 kilometers) an hour **2** : TORNADO — **cy·clon·ic** \sī-ˈklä-nik\ *adj*

cy·clo·pe·dia *or* **cy·clo·pae·dia** \ˌsī-klə-ˈpē-dē-ə\ *n* : ENCY-CLOPEDIA

cy·clo·tron \'sī-klə-ˌträn\ *n* : a device for giving high speed to charged particles by magnetic and electric fields

cyg·net \'sig-nət\ *n* : a young swan

cyl *abbr* cylinder

cyl·in·der \'si-lən-dər\ *n* : the solid figure formed by turn-ing a rectangle about one side as an axis; *also* : a body or space of this form ⟨an engine ∼⟩ ⟨a bullet in the ∼ of a revolver⟩ — **cy·lin·dri·cal** \sə-'lin-dri-kəl\ *adj*

cyn·ic \'si-nik\ *n* : one who attributes all actions to selfish motives — **cyn·i·cal** \-ni-kəl\ *adj* — **cyn·i·cal·ly** \-k(ə-)lē\ *adv* — **cyn·i·cism** \si-nə-,si-zəm\ *n*

cy·no·sure \'sī-nə-,shùr, 'si-\ *n* [MF & L; MF, Ursa Minor, guide, fr. L *cynosura* Ursa Minor, fr. Gk *kynosoura*, fr. *kynos oura* dog's tail] : a center of attraction or attention

♦ base, center (*or* centre), core, eye, focus, heart, hub, mecca, nucleus, seat — more at CENTER

CYO *abbr* Catholic Youth Organization

cy·pher *chiefly Brit var of* CIPHER

cy·press \'sī-prəs\ *n* **1** : any of a genus of scaly-leaved evergreen trees and shrubs **2** : BALD CYPRESS **3** : the wood of a cypress

Cyp·ri·ot \'si-prē-ət, -,ät\ *or* **Cyp·ri·ote** \-,ōt, -ət\ *n* : a native or inhabitant of Cyprus — **Cypriot** *adj*

cyst \'sist\ *n* : an abnormal closed bodily sac usu. containing liquid — **cys·tic** \'sis-tik\ *adj*

cystic fibrosis *n* : a common hereditary disease marked

esp. by deficiency of pancreatic enzymes, by respiratory symptoms, and by excessive loss of salt in the sweat

cy·tol·o·gy \sī-'tä-lə-jē\ *n* : a branch of biology dealing with cells — **cy·to·log·i·cal** \,sīt-ªl-'ä-ji-kəl\ *or* **cy·to·log·ic** \-jik\ *adj* — **cy·tol·o·gist** \sī-'tä-lə-jist\ *n*

cy·to·plasm \'sī-tə-,pla-zəm\ *n* : the protoplasm of a cell that lies external to the nucleus — **cy·to·plas·mic** \,sī-tə-'plaz-mik\ *adj*

cy·to·sine \'sī-tə-,sēn\ *n* : a chemical base that is a pyrimidine coding genetic information in DNA and RNA

CZ *abbr* **1** Canal Zone **2** cubic zirconia

czar \'zär, 'tsär\ *n* [NL, fr. Russ *tsar'*, ultim. fr. L *Caesar* Caesar] **1** : the ruler of Russia until 1917 **2** ♦ : one having great authority — **czar·ist** \-ist\ *n or adj*

♦ baron, king, magnate, mogul, prince, tycoon — more at MAGNATE

cza·ri·na \zä-'rē-nə\ *n* : the wife of a czar

Czech \'chek\ *n* **1** : a native or inhabitant of Czechoslovakia or the Czech Republic **2** : the language of the Czechs — **Czech** *adj*

¹d \'dē\ *n, pl* **d's** *or* **ds** \'dēz\ *often cap* **1** : the 4th letter of the English alphabet **2** : a grade rating a student's work as poor

²d *abbr, often cap* **1** date **2** daughter **3** day **4** dead **5** deceased **6** degree **7** Democrat **8** [L *denarius, denarii*] penny; pence **9** depart; departure **10** diameter

D *symbol* deuterium

DA *abbr* **1** deposit account **2** district attorney **3** don't answer

¹dab \'dab\ *n* **1 a** ♦ : a sudden blow or thrust : POKE **b** : PECK **2** ♦ : a small amount **3** : a gentle touch or stroke : PAT **4** : DAUB

♦ [1a] dig, jab, poke — more at POKE ♦ [2] bit, hint, lick, little, particle, spot, touch — more at PARTICLE

²dab *vb* **dabbed; dab·bing 1** : to strike or touch gently : PAT **2** : to apply lightly or irregularly : DAUB — **dab·ber** *n*

dab·ble \'da-bəl\ *vb* **dab·bled; dab·bling 1** : to wet by splashing : SPATTER **2** : to paddle or play in or as if in water **3** : to work or involve oneself without serious effort — **dab·bler** *n*

da ca·po \dä-'kä-(,)pō\ *adv or adj* [It] : from the beginning — used as a direction in music to repeat

dace \'dās\ *n, pl* **dace** : any of various small No. American freshwater fishes related to the carp

da·cha \'dä-chə\ *n* [Russ] : a Russian country house

dachs·hund \'däks-,hùnt\ *n, pl* **dachshunds** [G, fr. *Dachs* badger + *Hund* dog] : any of a breed of long-bodied short-legged dogs of German origin

dac·tyl \'dakt-ªl\ *n* [ME *dactile*, fr. L *dactylus*, fr. Gk *dakty-los*, lit., finger; fr. the fact that the three syllables have the first one longest like the joints of the finger] : a metrical foot of one accented syllable followed by two unaccented syllables — **dac·tyl·ic** \dak-'ti-lik\ *adj or n*

dad \'dad\ *n* : a male parent : FATHER 1

Da·da \'dä-(,)dä\ *n* : a movement in art and literature based on deliberate irrationality and negation of traditional artistic values — **da·da·ism** \-,i-zəm\ *n, often cap* — **da·da·ist** \-,ist\ *n or adj, often cap*

dad·dy \'da-dē\ *n, pl* **daddies** ♦ : a male human parent : FATHER 1

♦ father, papa, pop — more at FATHER

dad·dy long·legs \,da-dē-'lȯŋ-,legz\ *n, pl* **daddy longlegs** : any of an order of arachnids resembling the true spiders but having small rounded bodies and long slender legs

daemon *var of* DEMON

daf·fo·dil \'da-fə-,dil\ *n* : any of various bulbous herbs with usu. large flowers having a trumpetlike center

daf·fy \'da-fē\ *adj* **daf·fi·er; -est** : exhibiting or indicative of a lack of common sense or sound judgment : FOOLISH **2** : disordered in mind : INSANE

daft \'daft\ *adj* **1** ♦ : exhibiting or indicative of a lack of common sense or sound judgment : FOOLISH **2** ♦ : disordered in mind : INSANE

♦ [1] absurd, crazy, cuckoo, fatuous, foolish, mad, nonsensical, nutty, senseless, silly, stupid — more at FOOLISH ♦ [2] cracked, crazy, deranged, insane, loco, lunatic, mad, maniacal, nuts, nutty, screwy, unsound — more at INSANE

daft·ness \-nəs\ *n* ♦ : the quality or state of being daft

♦ absurdity, asininity, balminess, craziness, fatuity, folly, foolishness, inanity, insanity, lunacy, madness, silliness, simplicity, zaniness

dag *abbr* dekagram

dag·ger \'da-gər\ *n* **1** : a sharp pointed knife for stabbing **2** : a character † used as a reference mark or to indicate a death date

da·guerre·o·type \də-'ger-(ē-)ə-,tīp\ *n* : an early photograph produced on a silver or a silver-covered copper plate

dahl·ia \'dal-yə, 'däl-\ *n* : any of a genus of tuberous herbs related to the daisies and having showy flowers

¹dai·ly \'dā-lē\ *adj* **1** : occurring, done, or used every day or every weekday **2** : of or relating to every day ⟨∼ visitors⟩ **3** : computed in terms of one day ⟨∼ wages⟩ — **dai·li·ness** \-lē-nəs\ *n* — **daily** *adv*

²daily *n, pl* **dailies** : a newspaper published every weekday

daily double *n* : a system of betting on races in which the bettor must pick the winners of two stipulated races in order to win

dain·ti·ness \'dān-tē-nəs\ *n* ♦ : the quality or state of being dainty

♦ delicacy, fineness, fragility — more at DELICACY

¹dain·ty \'dān-tē\ *n, pl* **dainties** [ME *deinte*, fr. OF *deintié*, fr. L *dignitas* dignity, worth] ♦ : something delicious or pleasing to the taste : DELICACY

♦ delicacy, goody, tidbit, treat — more at DELICACY

²dainty *adj* **dain·ti·er; -est 1** ♦ : pleasing to taste **2** : delicately pretty **3 ♦ :** marked by fastidious discrimination or finicky taste — **dain·ti·ly** \-ti-lē\ *adv*

   ♦ **[1]** choice, delicate, elegant, exquisite, rare, select — more at CHOICE ♦ **[3]** choosy, delicate, demanding, exacting, fastidious, finicky, fussy, nice, old-maidish, particular, picky — more at FINICKY

dai·qui·ri \'dī-kə-rē, 'da-kə-rē\ *n* [*Daiquirí*, Cuba] **:** a cocktail made of usu. rum, lime juice, and sugar

dairy \'der-ē\ *n, pl* **dair·ies** [ME *deyerie*, fr. *deye* dairymaid, fr. OE *dǣge* kneader of bread] **1 :** CREAMERY **2 :** a farm specializing in milk production **3 :** food made primarily of or from milk

dairy·ing \'der-ē-in\ *n* **:** the business of operating a dairy

dairy·maid \-,mād\ *n* **:** a woman employed in a dairy

dairy·man \-mən, -,man\ *n* **:** a person who operates a dairy farm or works in a dairy

da·is \'dā-əs\ *n* ♦ **:** a raised platform usu. above the floor of a hall or large room

   ♦ platform, podium, rostrum, stage, stand — more at PLATFORM

dai·sy \'dā-zē\ *n, pl* **daisies** [ME *dayeseye*, fr. OE *dǣgesēage*, fr. *dǣg* day + *ēage* eye] **:** any of numerous composite plants having flower heads in which the marginal flowers resemble petals

dai·sy–chain \-,chān\ *vb* **:** to link (as computer components) together in series — **daisy chain** *n*

daisy wheel *n* **:** a disk with spokes bearing type that serves as the printing element of an electric typewriter or printer; *also* **:** a printer that uses such a disk

Da·ko·ta \də-'kō-tə\ *n, pl* **Dakotas** *also* **Dakota :** a member of an American Indian people of the northern Mississippi valley; *also* **:** their language

dal *abbr* dekaliter

dale \'dāl\ *n* ♦ **:** a long depression between ranges of hills or mountains **:** VALLEY

   ♦ hollow, valley — more at VALLEY

dal·li·ance \'da-lē-əns\ *n* ♦ **:** an act of dallying

   ♦ frolic, fun, play, relaxation, sport — more at PLAY

dal·ly \'da-lē\ *vb* **dal·lied; dal·ly·ing 1 ♦ :** to act playfully; *esp* **:** to play amorously **2 ♦ :** to waste time **3 :** to move slowly **:** LINGER

   ♦ **[1]** disport, frolic, play, recreate, rollick, sport — more at PLAY ♦ **[2]** dawdle, dillydally, hang around, hang out, idle, loaf, loll, lounge — more at IDLE

dal·ma·tian \dal-'mā-shən\ *n, often cap* **:** any of a breed of medium-sized dogs having a white short-haired coat with many black or brown spots

¹dam \'dam\ *n* **:** the female parent of an animal and esp. of a domestic animal

²dam *n* ♦ **:** a barrier (as across a stream) to stop the flow of water

   ♦ dike, embankment, levee; *also* breakwater, jetty, seawall; breastwork, bulwark, earthwork, rampart; canal, channel, ditch, gutter, trough; lock; barricade, barrier, block; floodgate, sluice

³dam *vb* **1 :** to provide or restrain with a dam **2 ♦ :** to stop up **:** BLOCK

   ♦ block, choke, clog, close (off), congest, jam, obstruct, plug (up), stop (up), stuff — more at CLOG

⁴dam *abbr* dekameter

¹dam·age \'da-mij\ *n* **1 ♦ :** loss or harm due to injury to persons, property, or reputation **2** *pl* ♦ **:** compensation in money imposed by law for loss or injury ⟨sued for ∼s⟩

   ♦ **[1]** detriment, harm, hurt, injury — more at INJURY ♦ *usu* **damages [2]** fine, forfeit, mulct, penalty — more at FINE ♦ *usu* **damages [2]** compensation, indemnity, quittance, recompense, redress, remuneration, reparation, requital, restitution, satisfaction — more at COMPENSATION

²damage *vb* **dam·aged; dam·ag·ing** ♦ **:** to cause damage to

   ♦ blemish, break, cripple, deface, disfigure, flaw, harm, hurt, injure, mar, spoil, vitiate; *also* enfeeble, undermine,

weaken; erode, scour, wash out, wear (away); blight, tarnish; dent, dint; botch, gum (up); lacerate, wound; maim, mangle, mutilate, torment, torture; annihilate, crush, dash, decimate, demolish, destroy, devastate, pulverize, raze, ruin, scourge, shatter, smash, tear down, waste, wipe out, wreck *Ant* fix, mend, patch, rebuild, recondition, reconstruct, renovate, repair, revamp

dam·ag·ing *adj* ♦ **:** causing or able to cause damage

   ♦ adverse, bad, baleful, baneful, deleterious, detrimental, evil, harmful, hurtful, ill, injurious, mischievous, noxious, pernicious, prejudicial — more at HARMFUL

dam·a·scene \'da-mə-,sēn\ *vb* **-scened; -scen·ing :** to ornament (as iron or steel) with wavy patterns or with inlaid work of precious metals

dam·ask \'da-məsk\ *n* **1 :** a firm lustrous reversible figured fabric used for household linen **2 :** a tough steel having decorative wavy lines

dame \'dām\ *n* **1 ♦ :** a woman of rank, station, or authority **2 ♦ :** an elderly woman **3 :** WOMAN

   ♦ **[1]** gentlewoman, lady, noblewoman — more at GENTLEWOMAN ♦ **[2]** dowager, matriarch, matron — more at MATRIARCH

damn \'dam\ *vb* [ME *dampnen*, fr. OF *dampner*, fr. L *damnare*, fr. *damnum* damage, loss, fine] **1 :** to condemn to a punishment or fate; *esp* **:** to condemn esp. to hell **2 ♦ :** to condemn as invalid, illegal, immoral, bad, or harmful **3 :** CURSE — **damned** *adj*

   ♦ censure, condemn, decry, denounce, reprehend, reprobate — more at CONDEMN

dam·na·ble \'dam-nə-bəl\ *adj* **1 :** liable to or deserving punishment **2 :** DETESTABLE ⟨∼ weather⟩ — **dam·na·bly** \-blē\ *adv*

dam·na·tion \dam-'nā-shən\ *n* **1 :** the act of damning **2 :** the state of being damned

¹damp \'damp\ *n* **1 :** a noxious gas **2 :** the small amount of liquid that causes dampness **:** MOISTURE

²damp *vb* **:** to check or diminish the activity or vigor of **:** DAMPEN

³damp *adj* **:** MOIST

damp·en \'dam-pən\ *vb* **1 ♦ :** to check or diminish in activity or vigor **2 :** to make or become damp

   ♦ blunt, deaden, dull, numb — more at DULL

damp·er \'dam-pər\ *n* **1 :** a dulling or deadening influence ⟨put a ∼ on the party⟩ **2 :** one that damps; *esp* **:** a valve or movable plate (as in the flue of a stove, furnace, or fireplace) to regulate the draft

damp·ness \'damp-nəs\ *n* **:** the quality or state of being damp

dam·sel \'dam-zəl\ *n* **:** a young woman **:** MAIDEN

dam·sel·fly \-,flī\ *n* **:** any of a group of insects that are closely related to the dragonflies but fold their wings above the body when at rest

dam·son \'dam-zən\ *n* **:** a plum with acid purple fruit; *also* **:** its fruit

Dan *abbr* Daniel

¹dance \'dans\ *vb* **danced; danc·ing 1 ♦ :** to glide, step, or move through a set series of movements usu. to music **2 ♦ :** to move quickly up and down or about **3 :** to perform or take part in as a dancer — **danc·er** *n*

   ♦ **[1]** foot, step; *also* prance, strut, trip; gavotte, jig, jitterbug, jive, mambo, polka, tango, waltz; tread ♦ **[2]** dart, flit, flutter, zip — more at FLIT

²dance *n* **1 :** an act or instance of dancing **2 ♦ :** a social gathering for dancing **3 :** a piece of music (as a waltz) by which dancing may be guided **4 :** the art of dancing

   ♦ ball, formal, hop, prom; *also* blowout, celebration, event, festival, festivity, fete, gala, masquerade, mixer, party, reception, soiree

D & C *n* [dilation *and* curettage] **:** a surgical procedure that involves stretching the cervix and scraping the inside walls of the uterus (as to test for cancer or to perform an abortion)

dan·de·li·on \'dan-də-ˌlī-ən, -dē-\ *n* [ME *dendelyoun*, fr. AF *dent de lion*, lit., lion's tooth] : any of a genus of common yellow-flowered composite herbs

dan·der \'dan-dər\ *n* : ANGER, TEMPER

dan·di·fy \'dan-di-ˌfī\ *vb* -**fied**; -**fy·ing** : to cause to resemble a dandy

dan·dle \'dand-ᵊl\ *vb* **dan·dled**; **dan·dling** 1 : to move up and down in one's arms or on one's knee in affectionate play 2 : to treat with extreme or excessive care and attention

dan·druff \'dan-drəf\ *n* : scaly white or grayish flakes of dead skin cells that come off the scalp — **dan·druffy** \-drə-fē\ *adj*

¹**dan·dy** \'dan-dē\ *n, pl* **dandies** 1 ♦ : a man unduly attentive to personal appearance 2 ♦ : something excellent in its class

♦ [1] buck, dude, fop, gallant; *also* coxcomb, popinjay; blade, cavalier; swell; clotheshorse ♦ [2] beauty, crackerjack, jim-dandy, knockout, pip — more at JIM-DANDY

²**dandy** *adj* **dan·di·er**; -**est** : very good : FIRST-RATE

Dane \'dān\ *n* 1 : a native or inhabitant of Denmark 2 : GREAT DANE

dan·ger \'dān-jər\ *n* [ME *daunger* control, resistance, peril, fr. AF *dangier*, fr. VL *dominiarium*, fr. L *dominium* ownership] 1 ♦ : exposure or liability to injury, harm, or evil 2 ♦ : something that may cause injury or harm

♦ [1] distress, jeopardy, peril, risk, trouble; *also* exposure, liability, vulnerability; precariousness, threat *Ant* safety, security ♦ [2] hazard, menace, peril, pitfall, risk, threat, trouble; *also* snare, trap

dan·ger·ous \'dān-jə-rəs\ *adj* 1 ♦ : exposing to or involving danger : HAZARDOUS 2 : able or likely to inflict injury — **dan·ger·ous·ly** *adv*

♦ grave, grievous, hazardous, menacing, parlous, perilous, risky, serious, unhealthy, unsafe, venturesome; *also* insecure, precarious, treacherous, uncertain; chance, haphazard, random; distressing, sickening, unpleasant, ugly, wicked; adverse, bad, baleful, baneful, deleterious, detrimental, evil, harmful, hurtful, ill, inimical, injurious, malignant, nasty, noxious, pernicious, pestilent; deadly, deathly, destructive, dire, fatal, fateful, fell, killer, lethal, mortal, murderous *Ant* harmless, innocent, innocuous, safe

dan·gle \'daŋ-gəl\ *vb* **dan·gled**; **dan·gling** 1 ♦ : to hang loosely esp. with a swinging motion : SWING 2 : to be a hanger-on or dependent 3 : to be left without proper grammatical connection in a sentence 4 : to keep hanging uncertainly 5 : to offer as an inducement

♦ hang, sling, suspend, swing — more at HANG

Dan·iel \'dan-yəl\ *n* : a book of Jewish and Christian Scripture

Dan·ish \'dā-nish\ *n* 1 : the language of the Danes 2 *pl* **Danish** : a piece of Danish pastry — **Danish** *adj*

Danish pastry *n* : a pastry made of a rich yeast-raised dough

dank \'daŋk\ *adj* : disagreeably wet or moist : DAMP — **dank·ness** *n*

dan·seuse \dāⁿ-'sərz, -'səz; dän-'süz\ *n* [F] : a female ballet dancer

dap·per \'da-pər\ *adj* 1 ♦ : neat and trim in style or appearance : SPRUCE 2 : being alert and lively in movement and manners : JAUNTY

♦ natty, sharp, smart, spruce — more at SMART

dap·ple \'da-pəl\ *vb* **dap·pled**; **dap·pling** ♦ : to mark with different-colored spots

♦ blotch, dot, fleck, freckle, mottle, pepper, speck, spot, sprinkle, stipple — more at SPOT

dap·pled *adj* ♦ : marked with small spots or patches contrasting with the background

♦ mottled, piebald, pied, spotted — more at PIED ♦ mottled, spotted, spotty, variegated — more at SPOTTED

DAR *abbr* Daughters of the American Revolution

¹**dare** \'der\ *vb* **dared**; **dar·ing** 1 : to have sufficient courage : be bold enough to 2 ♦ : to challenge to perform an action esp. as a proof of courage 3 ♦ : to confront boldly

♦ [2] challenge, defy — more at CHALLENGE ♦ [3] beard, brave, brazen, confront, defy, face — more at FACE

²**dare** *n* : an act or instance of daring : CHALLENGE

dare·dev·il \-ˌde-vəl\ *n* ♦ : a recklessly bold person — **dare·devil** *adj*

♦ devil, madcap; *also* cutup, show-off

¹**daring** \'der-iŋ\ *adj* ♦ : venturesomely bold in action or thought — **dar·ing·ly** *adv*

♦ adventurous, audacious, bold, enterprising, gutsy, hardy, nervy, venturesome — more at BOLD

²**dar·ing** *n* ♦ : venturesome boldness

♦ bravery, courage, fearlessness, gallantry, guts, hardihood, heart, heroism, nerve, stoutness, valor — more at COURAGE

¹**dark** \'därk\ *adj* 1 ♦ : being without light or without much light 2 : not light in color ⟨a ~ suit⟩ 3 a : showing or causing gloom or depression : GLOOMY b ♦ : lacking knowledge or culture 4 ♦ : not clear to the understanding 5 *often cap* : being a period of stagnation or decline ⟨the *Dark* Ages⟩ 6 : tending to keep secrets or to act secretly : SECRETIVE — **dark·ly** *adv*

♦ [1] darkling, dim, dusky, gloomy, murky, obscure, somber (*or* sombre); *also* sunless; cloudy, dull, dulled, lackluster; shadowy, shady; gray, leaden, pale *Ant* bright, brightened, brilliant, illuminated, illumined, light, lighted, lucent, lucid, luminous ♦ [3b] ignorant, illiterate, simple, uneducated, unlearned, untaught — more at IGNORANT ♦ [4] ambiguous, cryptic, darkling, deep, enigmatic, equivocal, inscrutable, murky, mysterious, mystic, nebulous, obscure, occult — more at OBSCURE

²**dark** *n* 1 a ♦ : a place or time of little or no light b ♦ : absence of light : DARKNESS; *esp* : NIGHT 2 : a dark or deep color — **in the dark** 1 : in secrecy 2 : in ignorance ⟨kept *in the dark* about the plans⟩

♦ darkness, dusk, gloaming, gloom, murk, night, semidarkness, shade, shadows, twilight; *also* blackout, brownout; dullness; cloudiness, haziness, mistiness, murkiness; dimness, faintness, gloominess, grayness, paleness *Ant* blaze, brightness, brilliance, day, daylight, glare, glow, light, lightness

dark·en \'där-kən\ *vb* 1 a ♦ : to make or grow dark or darker b ♦ : to make or become less clear : DIM 3 : BESMIRCH, TARNISH 4 ♦ : to make or become gloomy or forbidding

♦ [1a, 1b] becloud, befog, blur, cloud, dim, fog, haze, mist, obscure, overcast, overshadow, shroud — more at CLOUD ♦ [4] gloom, glower, lower; *also* frown, scowl; glare, stare; brood, mope, pout, sulk; anger, fume, rage, steam, intimidate, menace, threaten *Ant* brighten, cheer (up), lighten, perk (up)

dark horse *n* : a contestant or a political figure whose abilities and chances as a contender are not known

dark·ling \'där-kliŋ\ *adj* 1 : DARK: as a : devoid or partially devoid of light b ♦ : not clear to the understanding : MYSTERIOUS 2 : done or taking place in the dark

♦ ambiguous, cryptic, dark, deep, enigmatic, equivocal, inscrutable, murky, mysterious, mystic, nebulous, obscure, occult — more at OBSCURE

dark·ness \-nəs\ *n* ♦ : the quality or state of being dark

♦ dark, dusk, gloaming, gloom, murk, night, semidarkness, shade, shadows, twilight — more at DARK ♦ ambiguity, murkiness, obscurity, opacity — more at OBSCURITY

dark·room \'därk-ˌrüm, -ˌrům\ *n* : a lightproof room in which photographic materials are processed

¹**dar·ling** \'där-liŋ\ *n* 1 ♦ : a dearly loved person 2 ♦ : one that is treated or regarded with special favor or liking : FAVORITE

♦ [1] beloved, dear, flame, honey, love, sweet, sweetheart — more at SWEETHEART ♦ [2] favorite (or favourite), minion, pet, preference — more at FAVORITE

²**darling** adj **1** ♦ : dearly loved : FAVORITE **2** ♦ : very pleasing : CHARMING

♦ [1] adorable, dear, endearing, lovable, precious, sweet, winning — more at LOVABLE ♦ [2] agreeable, charming, delectable, delicious, delightful, enjoyable, heavenly, luscious, pleasurable

darm·stadt·i·um \ˌdärm-ˈsta-tē-əm\ n : a short-lived radioactive chemical element produced artificially

¹**darn** \ˈdärn\ vb : to mend with interlacing stitches — **darn·er** n

²**darn** or **darned** \ˈdärnd\ adv : VERY, EXTREMELY ⟨a ∼ good job⟩

darning needle n **1** : a needle for darning **2** : DRAGONFLY

¹**dart** \ˈdärt\ n **1** : a small missile with a point on one end and feathers on the other; also, pl : a game in which darts are thrown at a target **2** ♦ : something causing a sudden pain or distress **3** : a stitched tapering fold in a garment **4** : a quick movement

♦ affront, barb, dig, indignity, insult, name, offense, outrage, put-down, sarcasm, slight, slur, wound — more at INSULT

²**dart** vb **1** : to throw with a sudden movement **2** ♦ : to thrust or move suddenly or rapidly **3** : to shoot with a dart containing a usu. tranquilizing drug

♦ dance, flit, flutter, zip — more at FLIT

dart·er \ˈdär-tər\ n : any of numerous small No. American freshwater fishes related to the perches

Dar·win·ism \ˈdär-wə-ˌni-zəm\ n : a theory explaining the origin and continued existence of new species of plants and animals by means of natural selection acting on chance variations — **Dar·win·ist** \-nist\ n or adj

¹**dash** \ˈdash\ vb **1** : SMASH **2** ♦ : to knock, hurl, or thrust violently **3** : to soil or stain with splashed liquid : SPLASH **4** : RUIN **5** : DEPRESS, SADDEN **6** : to perform or finish hastily **7** ♦ : to move with sudden speed : move rapidly

♦ [2] cast, catapult, chuck, fire, fling, heave, hurl, hurtle, launch, peg, pelt, pitch, sling, throw, toss — more at THROW ♦ [7] career, course, fly, hasten, hurry, race, rip, rocket, run, rush, shoot, speed, tear, zip, zoom — more at HURRY

²**dash** n **1** : a sudden burst or splash **2** : a stroke of a pen **3** : a punctuation mark — that is used esp. to indicate a break in the thought or structure of a sentence **4** : a small addition ⟨a ∼ of salt⟩ **5** : flashy showiness **6** ♦ : animation in style and action **7** : a sudden rush or attempt ⟨made a ∼ for the door⟩ **8** : a short foot race **9** : DASHBOARD

♦ energy, life, pep, vigor (or vigour), vim, vitality — more at VIGOR

dash·board \-ˌbȯrd\ n : a panel in an automobile or aircraft below the windshield usu. containing dials and controls

dash·er \ˈda-shər\ n : a device (as in a churn) for agitating something

da·shi·ki \də-ˈshē-kē\ also **dai·shi·ki** \dī-\ n [modif. of Yoruba (an African language) dàńṣíkí] : a usu. brightly colored loose-fitting pullover garment

dash·ing \ˈda-shin\ adj **1** : marked by vigorous action **2** : marked by smartness esp. in dress and manners

das·tard \ˈdas-tərd\ n **1** ♦ : one who shows disgraceful fear or timidity : COWARD **2** : a person who acts treacherously

♦ chicken, coward, craven, poltroon, recreant, sissy — more at COWARD

das·tard·ly \-lē\ adj ♦ : showing disgraceful fear or timidity : COWARDLY

♦ chicken, cowardly, craven, pusillanimous, recreant, spineless, yellow — more at COWARDLY

dat abbr dative

da·ta \ˈdā-tə, ˈda-, ˈdä-\ n sing or pl [L, pl. of datum] : factual information (as measurements or statistics) used as a basis for reasoning, discussion, or calculation

da·ta·base \-ˌbās\ n : a usu. large collection of data organized esp. for rapid search and retrieval (as by a computer) — **database** vb

data processing n : the action or process of supplying a computer with information and having the computer use it to produce a desired result

¹**date** \ˈdāt\ n [ME, fr. AF, ultim. fr. L dactylus, fr. Gk daktylos, lit., finger] : the oblong edible fruit of a tall palm; also : this palm

²**date** n [ME, fr. AF, fr. LL data, fr. data (as in data Romae given at Rome), fem. of L datus, pp. of dare to give] **1** : the day, month, or year of an event **2** : a statement giving the time of execution or making (as of a coin or check) **3** ♦ : the period to which something belongs **4** ♦ : an appointment to meet at a specified time; esp : a social engagement between two persons that often has a romantic character **5** : a person with whom one has a usu. romantic date — **to date** : up to the present moment

♦ [3] duration, life, lifetime, run, standing, time — more at DURATION ♦ [4] appointment, engagement, rendezvous, tryst — more at ENGAGEMENT

³**date** vb **dat·ed; dat·ing** **1** : to record the date of or on **2** : to determine, mark, or reveal the date, age, or period of **3** : to make or have a date with **4** : ORIGINATE ⟨∼s from ancient times⟩ **5** : EXTEND ⟨dating back to childhood⟩ **6** : to show qualities typical of a past period

dat·ed \ˈdā-təd\ adj **1** : provided with a date **2** ♦ : no longer acceptable, stylish, current, or usable

♦ antiquated, archaic, obsolete, outdated, outmoded, outworn, passé — more at OBSOLETE

date·less \ˈdāt-ləs\ adj **1** : being or seeming to be without end : ENDLESS **2** : having no date **3** ♦ : too ancient to be dated **4** : not limited or affected by time : TIMELESS

♦ age-old, ancient, antediluvian, antique, hoary, old, venerable — more at ANCIENT

date·line \ˈdāt-ˌlīn\ n : a line in a publication giving the date and place of composition or issue — **dateline** vb

date rape n : rape committed by the victim's date

da·tive \ˈdā-tiv\ adj : of, relating to, or constituting a grammatical case marking typically the indirect object of a verb — **dative** n

da·tum \ˈdā-təm, ˈda-, ˈdä-\ n, pl **da·ta** \-tə\ or **datums** : a single piece of data : FACT

dau abbr daughter

¹**daub** \ˈdȯb\ vb **1** ♦ : to cover or smear with something sticky or dirty **2** : to apply paint or color crudely — **daub·er** n

♦ smear; also coat, paint, plaster

²**daub** n **1** : something daubed on : SMEAR **2** : a crude picture

daugh·ter \ˈdȯ-tər\ n **1** : a female offspring esp. of human beings **2** : a female adopted child **3** : a human female descendant — **daughter** adj — **daugh·ter·less** \-ləs\ adj

daugh·ter-in-law \ˈdȯ-tə-rən-ˌlȯ\ n, pl **daugh·ters-in-law** \-tər-zən-\ : the wife of one's son or daughter

daunt \ˈdȯnt\ vb [ME, fr. AF danter, daunter, fr. L domitare to tame] ♦ : to lessen the courage of

♦ demoralize, discourage, dishearten, dismay, dispirit, unman, unnerve — more at DISCOURAGE

daunt·ing \ˈdȯn-tiŋ\ adj : tending to overwhelm or intimidate ⟨a ∼ task⟩

daunt·less \-ləs\ adj ♦ : marked by courageous resolution : FEARLESS — **daunt·less·ly** adv

♦ brave, courageous, doughty, fearless, gallant, greathearted, heroic, intrepid, lionhearted, manful, stalwart, stout, undaunted, valiant, valorous — more at BRAVE

dau·phin \ˈdȯ-fən\ n, often cap : the eldest son of a king of France

DAV abbr Disabled American Veterans

dav·en·port \ˈda-vən-ˌpȯrt\ n ♦ : a large upholstered sofa

♦ couch, divan, lounge, settee, sofa — more at COUCH

da·vit \ˈdā-vət, ˈda-\ n : a small crane on a ship used in pairs esp. to raise or lower boats

daw·dle \'dȯd-ᵊl\ *vb* **daw·dled; daw·dling** **1** ♦ : to spend time wastefully or idly **2** ♦ : to move lackadaisically — **daw·dler** *n*

♦ [1] dally, dillydally, hang around, hang out, idle, loaf, loll, lounge — more at IDLE ♦ [2] crawl, creep, dally, delay, dillydally, drag, lag, linger, loiter, poke, tarry — more at DELAY

¹**dawn** \'dȯn\ *vb* **1** : to begin to grow light as the sun rises **2** ♦ : to begin to appear or develop **3** : to begin to be understood ⟨the solution ∼ed on him⟩

♦ arise, begin, commence, form, materialize, originate, spring, start — more at BEGIN

²**dawn** *n* **1** ♦ : the first appearance of light in the morning **2** ♦ : a first appearance : BEGINNING ⟨the ∼ of a new era⟩

♦ [1] aurora, cockcrow, morning, sunrise; *also* daytime, light; twilight; forenoon *Ant* nightfall, sundown, sunset ♦ [2] beginning, birth, commencement, genesis, launch, morning, onset, outset, start, threshold — more at BEGINNING

day \'dā\ *n* **1** : the period of light between one night and the next; *also* : DAYLIGHT, DAYTIME **2** : the period of rotation of a planet (as earth) or a moon on its axis **3** : a period of 24 hours beginning at midnight **4** : a specified day or date ⟨wedding ∼⟩ **5** : a specified time or period : AGE ⟨in olden ∼s⟩ **6** : the conflict or contention of the day **7** : the time set apart by usage or law for work ⟨the 8-hour ∼⟩

day·bed \'dā-ˌbed\ *n* : a couch that can be converted into a bed

day·book \-ˌbu̇k\ *n* : DIARY, JOURNAL

day·break \-ˌbrāk\ *n* : the first appearance of light in the morning followed by sunrise : DAWN

day care *n* : supervision of and care for children or disabled adults provided during the day; *also* : a program offering day care

day·dream \'dā-ˌdrēm\ *n* ♦ : a pleasant reverie — **daydream** *vb*

♦ chimera, conceit, delusion, dream, fancy, fantasy, figment, hallucination, illusion, phantasm, pipe dream, unreality, vision

day·light \'dā-ˌlīt\ *n* **1** : the light of day **2** : the time during which there is daylight : DAYTIME **3** : the first appearance of light in the morning followed by sunrise : DAWN **4** : understanding of something that has been obscure **5** *pl* : CONSCIOUSNESS; *also* : WITS **6** : a perceptible space, gap, or difference

daylight saving time *n* : time usu. one hour ahead of standard time

Day of Atonement : YOM KIPPUR

day school *n* : a private school without boarding facilities

day student *n* : a student who attends regular classes at a college or preparatory school but does not live there

day·time \'dā-ˌtīm\ *n* : the period of daylight

¹**daze** \'dāz\ *vb* **dazed; daz·ing** **1** : to stupefy esp. by a blow **2** : to dazzle with light : DAZZLE — **da·zed·ly** \'dā-zəd-lē\ *adv*

²**daze** *n* ♦ : the state of being dazed

♦ fog, haze, muddle, spin — more at HAZE

¹**daz·zle** \'da-zəl\ *vb* **daz·zled; daz·zling** **1** ♦ : to overpower with light **2** : to impress greatly or confound with brilliance

♦ daze; *also* confuse, overpower, overwhelm, stun

²**dazzle** *n* ♦ : the action of dazzling

♦ brilliance, effulgence, illumination, lightness, lucidity, luminosity, radiance, refulgence, splendor — more at BRILLIANCE

dB *abbr* decibel

Db *symbol* dubnium

d/b/a *abbr* doing business as

dbl *or* **dble** *abbr* double

DC *abbr* **1** [It *da capo*] from the beginning **2** direct current **3** District of Columbia **4** doctor of chiropractic

DD *abbr* **1** days after date **2** demand draft **3** dishonorable discharge **4** doctor of divinity

D–day *n* [*D*, abbr. for *day*] : a day set for launching an operation (as an invasion)

DDS *abbr* doctor of dental surgery

DDT \ˌdē-(ˌ)dē-'tē\ *n* : a persistent insecticide poisonous to many higher animals

DE *abbr* Delaware

dea·con \'dē-kən\ *n* [ME *dekene*, fr. OE *dēacon*, fr. LL *diaconus*, fr. Gk *diakonos*, lit., servant] : a subordinate officer in a Christian church

dea·con·ess \'dē-kə-nəs\ *n* : a woman chosen to assist in the church ministry

de·ac·ti·vate \dē-'ak-tə-ˌvāt\ *vb* ♦ : to make inactive or ineffective

♦ kill, shut off, turn off; *also* dismantle, mothball, phase out *Ant* activate, actuate, crank (up), drive, move, propel, run, set off, spark, start, touch off, trigger, turn on

¹**dead** \'ded\ *adj* **1** ♦ : deprived of life : LIFELESS **2** : having the appearance of death : DEATHLIKE ⟨in a ∼ faint⟩ **3** : lacking power to move, feel, or respond : NUMB **4** ♦ : very tired **5** : UNRESPONSIVE **6** : EXTINGUISHED ⟨∼ coals⟩ **7** : INANIMATE, INERT **8** ♦ : no longer active or functioning ⟨a ∼ battery⟩ **9** : lacking power, significance, or effect ⟨a ∼ custom⟩ **10** ♦ : no longer in use ⟨a ∼ language⟩ **11** : lacking in gaiety or animation ⟨a ∼ party⟩ **12** : QUIET, IDLE, UNPRODUCTIVE ⟨∼ capital⟩ **13** : lacking elasticity ⟨a ∼ tennis ball⟩ **14** : not circulating : STAGNANT ⟨∼ air⟩ **15** : lacking warmth, vigor, or taste ⟨∼ wine⟩ **16** : absolutely uniform ⟨∼ level⟩ **17** : UNERRING, EXACT ⟨a ∼ shot⟩ **18** : ABRUPT ⟨a ∼ stop⟩ **19** : having no exceptions or restrictions : COMPLETE ⟨a ∼ loss⟩

♦ [1] breathless, deceased, defunct, gone, late, lifeless; *also* extinct; dying, fading, moribund; stillborn; finished, lapsed, terminated; barren, desert; inanimate, insensate, nonliving *Ant* alive, breathing, living ♦ [4] beat, bushed, drained, effete, jaded, limp, prostrate, spent, tired, weary, worn-out — more at WEARY ♦ [8] dormant, fallow, free, idle, inactive, inert, inoperative, latent, off, vacant — more at INACTIVE ♦ [10] bygone, defunct, extinct, gone — more at EXTINCT

²**dead** *n, pl* **dead** **1** : one that is dead — usu. used collectively ⟨the living and the ∼⟩ **2** : the time of greatest quiet ⟨the ∼ of the night⟩

³**dead** *adv* **1** ♦ : in an absolute manner or condition ⟨∼ right⟩ **2** : in a sudden and complete manner ⟨stopped ∼⟩ **3** : in a direct manner : DIRECTLY ⟨∼ ahead⟩

♦ altogether, completely, entirely, fast, flat, full, fully, perfectly, quite, thoroughly, well, wholly — more at FULLY

dead·beat \-ˌbēt\ *n* : a person who persistently fails to pay personal debts or expenses

dead duck *n* : GONER

dead·en \'de-ᵊn\ *vb* **1** ♦ : to impair in vigor or sensation : BLUNT ⟨∼ pain⟩ **2** : to lessen the luster or spirit of **3** : to make (as a wall) soundproof

♦ blunt, dampen, dull, numb — more at DULL

dead end *n* **1** : an end (as of a street) without an exit **2** : a position, situation, or course of action that leads to nothing further — **dead–end** \ˌded-ˌend\ *adj*

dead heat *n* ♦ : a contest in which two or more contestants tie (as by crossing the finish line simultaneously)

♦ draw, stalemate, standoff, tie — more at TIE

dead horse *n* : an exhausted topic or issue

dead letter *n* **1** : something that has lost its force or authority without being formally abolished **2** : a letter that cannot be delivered or returned

dead·line \'ded-ˌlīn\ *n* : a date or time before which something must be done

dead·lock \'ded-ˌläk\ *n* **1** ♦ : a stoppage of action because neither faction in a struggle will give in **2** : a tie score — **deadlock** *vb*

♦ halt, impasse, stalemate, standstill — more at IMPASSE

¹**dead·ly** \'ded-lē\ *adj* **dead·li·er; -est** **1** ♦ : likely to cause or capable of causing death **2** : HOSTILE, IMPLACABLE

3 : very accurate : UNERRING 4 : tending to deprive of force or vitality ⟨a ~ habit⟩ 5 : suggestive of death 6 : very great : EXTREME — **dead·li·ness** n

♦ baleful, deathly, fatal, fell, lethal, mortal, murderous, pestilent, vital; also baneful, destructive, harmful, noxious, pernicious; poisonous, toxic, virulent; dangerous, grave, grievous, hazardous, menacing, parlous, perilous; risky, serious, threatening, ugly, unhealthy, unsound; capital; bloody, internecine, sanguinary, sanguine *Ant* healthful, healthy, nonfatal, nonlethal, wholesome

²**deadly** adv 1 : suggesting death ⟨~ pale⟩ 2 : to a high degree : EXTREMELY ⟨~ dull⟩

deadly sin n : one of seven sins of pride, covetousness, lust, anger, gluttony, envy, and sloth held to be fatal to spiritual progress

dead meat n : one that is doomed

¹**dead·pan** \'ded-ˌpan\ adj ♦ : marked by an impassive manner or expression — **deadpan** vb — **deadpan** adv

♦ blank, expressionless, impassive, inexpressive, stolid, vacant — more at BLANK

²**deadpan** n : a completely expressionless face

dead reckoning n : the determination of the position of a ship or aircraft solely from the record of the direction and distance of its course

dead·weight \'ded-'wāt\ n 1 : the unrelieved weight of an inert mass 2 : a ship's load including the weight of cargo, fuel, crew, and passengers

dead·wood \-ˌwu̇d\ n 1 : wood dead on the tree 2 ♦ : useless personnel or material

♦ chaff, dust, garbage, junk, litter, refuse, riffraff, rubbish, scrap, trash, waste — more at GARBAGE

deaf \'def\ adj 1 : unable to hear 2 : unwilling to hear or listen ⟨~ to all suggestions⟩ — **deaf·ness** n

deaf·en \'de-fən\ vb : to make deaf

deaf·en·ing \-iŋ\ adj ♦ : very loud

♦ booming, clamorous (or clamourous), earsplitting, loud, piercing, resounding, ringing, roaring, sonorous, stentorian, thunderous — more at LOUD

deaf–mute \'def-ˌmyüt\ n, often offensive : a deaf person who cannot speak

¹**deal** \'dēl\ n 1 : a usu. large or indefinite quantity or degree ⟨a great ~ of support⟩ 2 : the act or right of distributing cards to players in a card game; also : HAND

²**deal** vb dealt \'delt\; **deal·ing** 1 a ♦ : to give as one's portion : DISTRIBUTE b : to distribute playing cards to players in a game 2 : ADMINISTER, DELIVER ⟨dealt him a blow⟩ 3 ♦ : to concern itself : TREAT ⟨the book ~s with crime⟩ 4 : to take action in regard to something ⟨~ with offenders⟩ 5 a : TRADE b ♦ : to sell or distribute something as a business ⟨~ in used cars⟩ 6 : to reach a state of acceptance ⟨~ with her child's death⟩ 7 : to engage in bargaining

♦ [1a] administer, allocate, apportion, dispense, distribute, mete, parcel, portion, prorate — more at ADMINISTER ♦ [3] concern, cover, pertain, treat — more at CONCERN ♦ [5b] market, merchandise, put up, retail, sell, vend

³**deal** n 1 ♦ : an act of buying and selling : TRANSACTION 2 : treatment received ⟨a raw ~⟩ 3 ♦ : an often secret agreement or arrangement for mutual advantage 4 ♦ : something acquired by or as if by bargaining; esp : an advantageous purchase : BARGAIN

♦ [1] sale, trade, transaction — more at SALE ♦ [3] accord, agreement, bargain, compact, contract, convention, covenant, pact, settlement, understanding — more at AGREEMENT ♦ [4] bargain, buy, steal — more at BARGAIN

⁴**deal** n : wood or a board of fir or pine

deal·er \'dē-lər\ n ♦ : one that deals; esp : a person who makes a business of buying and selling goods

♦ merchant, trader, trafficker — more at MERCHANT ♦ seller, vendor — more at VENDOR

deal·er·ship \'dē-lər-ˌship\ n : an authorized sales agency

deal·ing \'dē-liŋ\ n 1 : a way of acting or of doing business 2 pl ♦ : friendly or business transactions

♦ usu **dealings** intercourse, relations

dean \'dēn\ n [ME deen, fr. MF deien, fr. LL decanus, lit., chief of ten, fr. Gk dekanos, fr. deka ten] 1 : a clergyman who is head of a group of canons or of joint pastors of a church 2 : the head of a division, faculty, college, or school of a university 3 : a college or secondary school administrator in charge of counseling and disciplining students 4 ♦ : the senior member of a body or group ⟨the ~ of a diplomatic corps⟩ — **dean·ship** n

♦ elder, senior; also better, superior *Ant* baby

dean·ery \'dē-nə-rē\ n, pl **-er·ies** : the office, jurisdiction, or official residence of a clerical dean

¹**dear** \'dir\ adj 1 ♦ : highly valued : PRECIOUS 2 : AFFECTIONATE, FOND 3 ♦ : high in price : EXPENSIVE 4 : HEARTFELT — **dear·ly** adv — **dear·ness** n

♦ [1] beloved, darling, favorite (or favourite), loved, pet, precious, special, sweet ♦ [3] costly, expensive, high, precious, valuable — more at COSTLY

²**dear** n ♦ : a loved one : DARLING

♦ beloved, darling, honey, love, sweet, sweetheart — more at SWEETHEART

Dear John \-'jän\ n : a letter (as to a soldier) in which a woman breaks off a marital or romantic relationship

dearth \'dərth\ n 1 ♦ : scarcity that makes dear : FAMINE 2 ♦ : an inadequate supply : LACK

♦ deficiency, deficit, failure, famine, inadequacy, insufficiency, lack, paucity, poverty, scantiness, scarcity, shortage, want — more at DEFICIENCY

death \'deth\ n 1 ♦ : the end of life 2 : the cause of loss of life 3 : the state of being dead 4 ♦ : the passing or destruction of something inanimate 5 : SLAUGHTER

♦ [1] decease, demise, doom, end, passing, quietus; also casualty, fatality; martyrdom, self-destruction, suicide; annihilation, destruction, ending, expiration, extermination, ruin *Ant* birth ♦ [4] demise, expiration, termination; also dispersion, dissolution; shutdown; decease, doom, end, ending, passing, quietus; suicide; annihilation, destruction, ruin *Ant* beginning, creation, start

death·bed \-ˌbed\ n 1 : the bed in which a person dies 2 : the last hours of life

death·blow \-ˌblō\ n : a destructive or killing stroke or event

death grip n : an extremely tight grip or hold

death·less \-ləs\ adj ♦ : not subject to death or destruction : IMMORTAL ⟨~ fame⟩

♦ ceaseless, dateless, endless, eternal, everlasting, immortal, permanent, perpetual, undying, unending — more at EVERLASTING

death·like \-līk\ adj : of, relating to, or suggestive of death : DEATHLY

death·ly \-lē\ adj 1 ♦ : causing death : FATAL 2 ♦ : of, relating to, or suggesting death ⟨a ~ pallor⟩ — **deathly** adv

♦ [1] baleful, deadly, fatal, fell, lethal, mortal, murderous, pestilent, vital — more at DEADLY ♦ [2] dead, mortal; also ghostly, phantom, spectral; inactive, inert, inoperative, lifeless, quiescent, still; macabre; baleful, fatal, fateful, fell, killer, lethal, murderous, pestilent

death rattle n : a sound produced by air passing through mucus in the lungs and air passages of a dying person

death's–head \'deths-ˌhed\ n : a human skull emblematic of death

death·watch \'deth-ˌwäch\ n : a vigil kept over the dead or dying

deb \'deb\ n : DEBUTANTE

de·ba·cle \di-'bä-kəl, -'ba-\ also **dé·bâ·cle** \same or dā-'bäk\ n [F débâcle] 1 ♦ : a great disaster 2 ♦ : a complete failure : FIASCO ⟨a financial ~⟩

♦ [1] calamity, cataclysm, catastrophe, disaster, tragedy — more at DISASTER ♦ [2] bummer, bust, catastrophe, dud, failure, fiasco, fizzle, flop, lemon, loser, turkey, washout — more at FAILURE

de·bar \di-'bär\ *vb* ♦ : to bar from having or doing something

♦ ban, bar, count out, eliminate, except, exclude, rule out — more at EXCLUDE

de·bark \di-'bärk\ *vb* : DISEMBARK — **de·bar·ka·tion** \ˌdē-ˌbär-'kā-shən\ *n*

de·base \di-'bās\ *vb* ♦ : to lower in character, quality, or value

♦ abase, corrupt, debauch, degrade, demean, demoralize, deprave, pervert, poison, profane, prostitute, subvert, vitiate, warp; *also* disgrace, humble, humiliate; blemish, damage, harm, hurt, impair, mar, ruin, spoil, stain, tarnish, wreck *Ant* elevate, ennoble, uplift ♦ discredit, disgrace, dishonor (*or* dishonour), humble, humiliate, lower, shame, smirch, take down — more at HUMBLE

de·base·ment \-mənt\ *n* **1** ♦ : the act or process of debasing **2** : the state of being debased

♦ corruption, debauchery, decadence, degeneracy, degeneration, degradation, demoralization, depravity, dissipation, dissoluteness, perversion — more at CORRUPTION

de·bat·able \di-'bā-tə-bəl\ *adj* ♦ : open to dispute : giving reason for being doubted, questioned, or challenged

♦ arguable, disputable, doubtful, moot, questionable; *also* controversial, debated, disputed; dubious, inconclusive, indecisive, problematic, uncertain; academic, hypothetical, speculative, theoretical; ambiguous, equivocal *Ant* incontestable, incontrovertible, indisputable, indubitable, undeniable, unquestionable doubtful, equivocal, problematic, questionable, suspect, suspicious — more at DOUBTFUL

¹**de·bate** \di-'bāt\ *n* **1** ♦ : a contention by words or arguments **2** : consideration of or reflection upon a problem ⟨after a moment of ∼, she went forward⟩

♦ [1] controversy, disagreement, dissension ♦ [2] consideration, deliberation, thought — more at CONSIDERATION

²**debate** *vb* **de·bat·ed; de·bat·ing 1** ♦ : to discuss a question by considering opposed arguments **2** : to take part in a debate **3** ♦ : to reflect upon (a question or problem)

♦ [1] argue, chew over, discuss, dispute, hash, moot, talk over — more at DISCUSS ♦ [3] chew over, cogitate, consider, contemplate, deliberate, entertain, meditate, mull, ponder, question, ruminate, study, think, weigh — more at PONDER

de·bat·er \-'bā-tər\ *n* ♦ : one that debates

♦ arguer, contender, disputant, disputer — more at DISPUTANT

de·bauch \di-'bȯch\ *vb* ♦ : to lead away from virtue or excellence : CORRUPT

♦ debase, degrade, demean, demoralize, humble, subvert, warp — more at DEBASE

de·bauched \-'bȯcht\ *adj* ♦ : having or showing looseness in morals or conduct

♦ corrupt, decadent, degenerate, dissolute, perverse, perverted, reprobate — more at CORRUPT

de·bauch·ery \-'bȯ-chə-rē\ *n* ♦ : extreme indulgence in sensuality

♦ corruption, debasement, decadence, degeneracy, degeneration, degradation, demoralization, depravity, dissipation, dissoluteness, perversion — more at CORRUPTION ♦ corruption, depravity, immorality, iniquity, licentiousness, sin, vice — more at VICE

de·ben·ture \di-'ben-chər\ *n* : BOND; *esp* : one secured by the general credit of the issuer rather than a lien on particular assets

de·bil·i·tate \di-'bi-lə-ˌtāt\ *vb* **-tat·ed; -tat·ing** ♦ : to impair the health or strength of

♦ enervate, enfeeble, prostrate, sap, soften, tire, waste, weaken — more at WEAKEN

de·bil·i·ty \di-'bi-lə-tē\ *n, pl* **-ties** ♦ : an infirm or weakened state

♦ delicacy, enfeeblement, faintness, feebleness, frailty, infirmity, languor, lowness, weakness — more at WEAKNESS

¹**deb·it** \'de-bət\ *vb* : to enter as a debit : charge with or as a debit

²**debit** *n* **1** : an entry in an account showing money paid out or owed **2** : DISADVANTAGE, SHORTCOMING

debit card *n* : a card by which money may be withdrawn or the cost of purchases paid directly from the holder's bank account

deb·o·nair \ˌde-bə-'nar\ *adj* [ME *debonere,* fr. AF *deboneire,* fr. *de bon aire* of good family or nature] **1** ♦ : smoothly gracious and sophisticated : SUAVE **2** : LIGHTHEARTED

♦ smooth, sophisticated, suave, urbane — more at SUAVE

de·bouch \di-'bau̇ch, -'büsh\ *vb* [F *déboucher,* fr. *dé-* out of + *bouche* mouth] : to come out into an open area : EMERGE

de·brief \di-'brēf\ *vb* **1** : to question (as a pilot back from a mission) in order to obtain useful information **2** : to review carefully upon completion

de·bris \də-'brē, dā-; 'dā-ˌbrē\ *n, pl* **debris** \-'brēz, -ˌbrēz\ **1** ♦ : the remains of something broken down or destroyed **2** : an accumulation of rock fragments **3** : RUBBISH

♦ remains, rubble, ruins, wreck, wreckage — more at REMAINS

debt \'det\ *n* **1** : an offense against religious or moral law : SIN **2** : something owed : OBLIGATION **3** : a condition of owing

debt·or \'de-tər\ *n* **1** : one guilty of neglect or violation of duty **2** : one that owes a debt

de·bug \(ˌ)dē-'bəg\ *vb* ♦ : to eliminate errors in

♦ amend, correct, emend, rectify, reform, remedy — more at CORRECT

de·bunk \dē-'bəŋk\ *vb* ♦ : to expose the sham or falseness of ⟨∼ a legend⟩

♦ expose, show up, uncloak, uncover, unmask — more at EXPOSE

¹**de·but** \'dā-ˌbyü, dā-'byü\ *n* **1** : a first appearance **2** : a formal entrance into society

²**debut** *vb* : to make a debut; *also* : INTRODUCE

deb·u·tante \'de-byü-ˌtänt\ *n* : a young woman making her formal entrance into society

dec *abbr* **1** deceased **2** decrease

Dec *abbr* December

de·cade \'de-ˌkād, de-'kād\ *n* : a period of 10 years

dec·a·dence \'de-kə-dəns, di-'kād-ᵊns\ *n* **1** ♦ : the process of becoming decadent : the quality or state of being decadent **2** ♦ : a period of decline

♦ [1, 2] corruption, debasement, debauchery, degeneracy, degeneration, degradation, demoralization, depravity, dissipation, dissoluteness, perversion — more at CORRUPTION

¹**dec·a·dent** \'de-kə-dənt, di-'kād-ᵊnt\ *adj* **1** ♦ : marked by decay or decline **2** ♦ : characterized by or appealing to self-indulgence

♦ [1] degenerate, effete, overripe — more at EFFETE
♦ [1, 2] corrupt, debauched, degenerate, dissolute, perverse, perverted, reprobate — more at CORRUPT

²**decadent** *n* ♦ : one that is decadent

♦ degenerate, libertine, pervert, profligate — more at DEGENERATE

de·caf \'dē-ˌkaf\ *n* : decaffeinated coffee

de·caf·fein·at·ed \(ˌ)dē-'ka-fə-nā-təd\ *adj* : having the caffeine removed ⟨∼ coffee⟩

deca·gon \'de-kə-ˌgän\ *n* : a plane polygon of 10 angles and 10 sides

de·cal \'dē-ˌkal\ *n* : a picture, design, or label made to be transferred (as to glass) from specially prepared paper

Deca·logue \'de-kə-ˌlȯg\ *n* : TEN COMMANDMENTS

de·camp \di-'kamp\ *vb* **1** : to break up a camp **2** : to depart suddenly

de·cant \di-'kant\ *vb* : to pour (as wine) gently from one vessel into another

de·cant·er \di-'kan-tər\ *n* : an ornamental glass bottle for serving wine

de·cap·i·tate \di-'ka-pə-ˌtāt\ *vb* **-tat·ed; -tat·ing** : BEHEAD — **de·cap·i·ta·tion** \-ˌka-pə-'tā-shən\ *n* — **de·cap·i·ta·tor** \-'ka-pə-ˌtā-tər\ *n*

deca·syl·lab·ic \ˌde-kə-sə-'la-bik\ *adj* : having or composed of verses having 10 syllables — **decasyllabic** *n*

de·cath·lon \di-'kath-lən, -ˌlän\ *n* : a 10-event athletic contest

¹de·cay \di-'kā\ *vb* **1** ♦ : to decline from a sound or prosperous condition **2** ♦ : to cause or undergo decomposition ⟨radium ∼s slowly⟩; *esp* : to break down while spoiling : ROT

♦ [1] decline, degenerate, descend, deteriorate, ebb, rot, sink, worsen — more at DETERIORATE ♦ [2] break down, corrupt, decompose, disintegrate, molder, putrefy, rot, spoil; *also* sour, turn; contaminate, defile, pollute, taint; curdle, ferment; crumble, degenerate, deteriorate

²decay *n* **1** ♦ : gradual decline in strength, soundness, or prosperity or in degree of excellence or perfection **2** ♦ : the process of rotting : the state of being rotten

♦ [1] decline, degeneration, deterioration — more at DECLINE ♦ [2] breakdown, corruption, decomposition, putrefaction, rot, spoilage — more at CORRUPTION

decd *abbr* deceased

de·cease \di-'sēs\ *n* ♦ : a permanent cessation of all vital functions : DEATH

♦ death, demise, doom, end, passing, quietus — more at DEATH

¹de·ceased \-'sēst\ *adj* ♦ : no longer alive; *esp* : recently dead

♦ breathless, dead, defunct, gone, late, lifeless — more at DEAD

²deceased *n, pl* **deceased** : a dead person

de·ce·dent \di-'sēd-ᵊnt\ *n* : a deceased person

de·ceit \di-'sēt\ *n* **1** : the act or practice of deceiving : DECEPTION **2** : an attempt or device to deceive : TRICK **3** ♦ : the quality of being deceitful : DECEITFULNESS

♦ artifice, craft, craftiness, crookedness, cunning, deceitfulness, dishonesty, dissimulation, double-dealing, duplicity, guile, wiliness; *also* equivocation, prevarication; chicanery, skulduggery, subterfuge, trickery; hypocrisy, insincerity; shrewdness; underhandedness, unscrupulousness; furtiveness, secrecy, oiliness, slipperiness, slyness, smoothness *Ant* artlessness, forthrightness, good faith, guilelessness, sincerity

de·ceit·ful \-fəl\ *adj* **1** ♦ : practicing or tending to practice deceit **2** ♦ : tending or having power to deceive : DECEPTIVE ⟨a ∼ answer⟩ — **de·ceit·ful·ly** *adv*

♦ [1] crooked, dishonest, double-dealing, false, fraudulent — more at FRAUDULENT ♦ [2] deceptive, delusive, fallacious, false, misleading, specious — more at DECEPTIVE

de·ceit·ful·ness \-nəs\ *n* ♦ : the quality or state of being deceitful

♦ artifice, craft, craftiness, crookedness, cunning, deceit, dishonesty, dissimulation, double-dealing, duplicity, guile, wiliness — more at DECEIT

de·ceive \di-'sēv\ *vb* **de·ceived; de·ceiv·ing** **1** ♦ : to cause to believe an untruth **2** : to use or practice deceit — **de·ceiv·er** *n*

♦ beguile, bluff, cozen, delude, dupe, fool, gull, have, hoax, hoodwink, humbug, misinform, mislead, string along, take in, trick; *also* cheat, chisel, defraud, fleece, hustle, rook, swindle *Ant* undeceive

de·cel·er·ate \dē-'se-lə-ˌrāt\ *vb* **-at·ed; -at·ing** ♦ : to slow down

♦ brake, retard, slow — more at SLOW

De·cem·ber \di-'sem-bər\ *n* [ME *Decembre*, fr. OF, fr. L *December* (tenth month), fr. *decem* ten] : the 12th month of the year

de·cen·cy \'dēs-ᵊn-sē\ *n, pl* **-cies** **1** ♦ : the quality or state of being decent : PROPRIETY **2** ♦ : conformity to standards of taste, propriety, or quality **3** : a standard of propriety — usu. used in pl.

♦ [1] decorum, form, propriety; *also* civility, courtesy, politeness; dignity, grace, refinement; discretion, prudence; correctness, fitness, rightness; attention, attentiveness, care, carefulness; goodness, high-mindedness, honesty, morality, probity, rectitude, righteousness, uprightness, virtue *Ant* impropriety, indecency ♦ [2] character, goodness, honesty, honor (*or* honour), integrity, morality, probity, rectitude, righteousness, uprightness, virtue — more at MORALITY

de·cen·ni·al \di-'se-nē-əl\ *adj* **1** : consisting of 10 years **2** : happening every 10 years ⟨∼ census⟩

de·cent \'dē-sᵊnt\ *adj* **1** ♦ : conforming to standards of propriety, good taste, or morality **2** : modestly clothed **3** ♦ : free from immodesty or obscenity **4** ♦ : ADEQUATE ⟨∼ housing⟩ — **de·cent·ly** *adv*

♦ [1] ethical, good, honest, honorable (*or* honourable), just, moral, right, righteous, straight, upright, virtuous — more at GOOD ♦ [1] correct, decorous, genteel, nice, polite, proper, respectable, seemly — more at PROPER ♦ [3] chaste, clean, immaculate, modest, pure — more at CHASTE ♦ [4] acceptable, adequate, all right, fine, OK, passable, respectable, satisfactory, tolerable — more at ADEQUATE

de·cen·tral·i·za·tion \dē-ˌsen-trə-lə-'zā-shən\ *n* **1** : the distribution of powers from a central authority to regional and local authorities **2** : the redistribution of population and industry from urban centers to outlying areas — **de·cen·tral·ize** \-'sen-trə-ˌlīz\ *vb*

de·cep·tion \di-'sep-shən\ *n* **1** : the act of deceiving **2** : the fact or condition of being deceived **3** : FRAUD, TRICK

de·cep·tive \di-'sep-tiv\ *adj* ♦ : tending or having power to deceive — **de·cep·tive·ly** *adv* — **de·cep·tive·ness** *n*

♦ deceitful, delusive, fallacious, false, misleading, specious; *also* devious, guileful, shady, shifty, sly, sneaking, sneaky, trick, tricky, underhand, underhanded; inaccurate, incorrect, wrong; bewildering, confounding, distracting, perplexing, puzzling; crooked, dishonest, double-dealing, faithless, fraudulent, fast, knavish; lying, mendacious, untrustworthy, untruthful; insidious, perfidious, treacherous; artificial, backhanded, feigned, hypocritical, insincere, left-handed, two-faced *Ant* aboveboard, forthright, straightforward

deci·bel \'de-sə-ˌbel, -bəl\ *n* : a unit for measuring the relative loudness of sounds

de·cide \di-'sīd\ *vb* **de·cid·ed; de·cid·ing** [ME, fr. MF *decider*, fr. L *decidere*, lit., to cut off, fr. *de-* off + *caedere* to cut] **1** ♦ : to arrive at a solution that ends uncertainty or dispute about **2** : to bring to a definitive end ⟨one blow *decided* the fight⟩ **3** : to induce to come to a choice **4** ♦ : to make a choice or judgment

♦ [1] arrange, fix, set, settle — more at ARRANGE ♦ [4] choose, conclude, determine, figure, opt, resolve; *also* decree, rule; cull, elect, handpick, pick, prefer, select, single (out), take ♦ [4] adjudicate, arbitrate, determine, judge, referee, rule, settle, umpire — more at JUDGE

de·cid·ed \di-'sī-dəd\ *adj* **1** : UNQUESTIONABLE **2** : FIRM, DETERMINED — **de·cid·ed·ly** *adv*

de·cid·u·ous \di-'si-jə-wəs\ *adj* **1** : falling off or out usu. at the end of a period of growth or function ⟨∼ leaves⟩ ⟨a ∼ tooth⟩ **2** : having deciduous parts ⟨∼ trees⟩

deci·gram \'de-sə-ˌgram\ *n* : a metric unit of measure equal to ¹⁄₁₀ gram

deci·li·ter \-ˌlē-tər\ *n* : a metric unit of measure equal to ¹⁄₁₀ liter

¹dec·i·mal \'de-sə-məl\ *adj* : based on the number 10 : reckoning by tens

²decimal *n* : any number expressed in base 10; *esp* : DECIMAL FRACTION

decimal fraction *n* : a fraction or mixed number in which the denominator is a power of 10 and that is usu. expressed with a decimal point ⟨the *decimal fraction* .25 is equivalent to the common fraction ²⁵⁄₁₀₀⟩

decimal place *n* : the position of a digit as counted to the right of the decimal point in a decimal fraction

decimal point *n* : a period, centered dot, or in some countries a comma at the left of a decimal fraction (as .678) less than one or between a whole number and a decimal fraction in a mixed number (as 3.678)

dec·i·mate \'de-sə-ˌmāt\ *vb* **-mat·ed; -mat·ing** **1** ♦ : to take or destroy the 10th part of **2** : to cause great destruction or harm to

dec·i·me·ter \'de-sə-ˌmē-tər\ *n* : a metric unit of measure equal to ¹⁄₁₀ meter

de·ci·pher \di-'sī-fər\ *vb* **1** : to convert (as a coded message) into intelligible form : DECODE **2** : to make out the meaning of despite indistinctness — **de·ci·pher·able** *adj*

de·ci·sion \di-'si-zhən\ *n* **1** ♦ : the act or result of deciding **2** ♦ : promptness and firmness in deciding

♦ [1] conclusion, determination, diagnosis, judgment (*or* judgement), opinion, resolution, verdict; *also* decree, mandate, order; say-so; doom, finding, ruling, sentence; choice, option, selection ♦ [2] decisiveness, determination, firmness, granite, resolution, resolve — more at DETERMINATION

de·ci·sive \-'sī-siv\ *adj* **1** : having the power to decide ⟨the ~ vote⟩ **2** ♦ : marked by firm determination : RESOLUTE **3** ♦ : not questionable : CONCLUSIVE ⟨a ~ victory⟩ — **de·ci·sive·ly** *adv*

♦ [2] bound, determined, firm, intent, purposeful, resolute, set, single-minded — more at DETERMINED ♦ [3] absolute, clear, conclusive, definitive — more at CONCLUSIVE

de·ci·sive·ness \-nəs\ *n* ♦ : the quality or state of being decisive

♦ decision, determination, firmness, granite, resolution, resolve — more at DETERMINATION

¹deck \'dek\ *n* **1** : a floorlike platform of a ship; *also* : something resembling the deck of a ship **2** : a pack of playing cards

²deck *vb* **1** ♦ : to clothe in a striking or elegant manner : ARRAY **2** ♦ : to furnish with something ornamental : DECORATE **3** : to furnish with a deck **4** : KNOCK DOWN, FLOOR

♦ [1] apparel, array, attire, caparison, clothe, dress, garb, invest, rig, suit — more at CLOTHE ♦ [2] adorn, array, beautify, bedeck, decorate, do, dress, embellish, enrich, garnish, grace, ornament, trim — more at DECORATE

deck·hand \'dek-ˌhand\ *n* : a sailor who performs manual duties

de·claim \di-'klām\ *vb* ♦ : to speak or deliver in the manner of a formal speech — **de·clam·a·to·ry** \di-'kla-mə-ˌtōr-ē\ *adj*

♦ descant, discourse, harangue, lecture, orate, speak, talk — more at TALK

dec·la·ma·tion \ˌde-klə-'mā-shən\ *n* ♦ : the act or art of declaiming

♦ address, harangue, oration, speech, talk — more at SPEECH

dec·la·ra·tion \ˌde-klə-'rā-shən\ *n* **1** ♦ : the act of declaring **2** : something that is declared

♦ affirmation, assertion, avowal, claim, profession, protestation

de·clar·a·tive \di-'klar-ə-tiv\ *adj* : making a declaration ⟨~ sentence⟩

de·clare \di-'klar\ *vb* **de·clared; de·clar·ing** **1** ♦ : to make known formally, officially, or explicitly : ANNOUNCE ⟨~ war⟩ **2** ♦ : to state emphatically : AFFIRM **3** : to make a full statement of — **de·clar·a·to·ry** \di-'klar-ə-ˌtōr-ē\ *adj* — **de·clar·er** *n*

♦ [1] advertise, announce, blaze, broadcast, enunciate, placard, post, proclaim, promulgate, publicize, publish,

sound — more at ANNOUNCE ♦ [2] affirm, allege, assert, aver, avouch, avow, claim, contend, insist, maintain, profess, protest, warrant — more at CLAIM

de·clas·si·fy \dē-'kla-sə-ˌfī\ *vb* : to remove the security classification of — **de·clas·si·fi·ca·tion** \-ˌkla-sə-fə-'kā-shən\ *n*

de·clen·sion \di-'klen-chən\ *n* **1** : the inflectional forms of a noun, pronoun, or adjective **2** : a falling off or away esp. from a standard or a high point of development **3** : a bending or sloping downward

¹de·cline \di-'klīn\ *vb* **de·clined; de·clin·ing** **1** ♦ : to slope downward : DESCEND **2** : DROOP **3** : WANE **4** ♦ : to tend toward an inferior state or weaker condition **5** ♦ : to withhold consent; *also* : REFUSE **6** : INFLECT 2 ⟨~ a noun⟩ — **de·clin·able** *adj* — **dec·li·na·tion** \ˌde-klə-'nā-shən\ *n*

♦ [1] descend, dip, drop, fall, lower, plummet, plunge, sink, tumble — more at DROP ♦ [4] decay, degenerate, descend, deteriorate, ebb, rot, sink, worsen — more at DETERIORATE ♦ [5] disallow, disapprove, negative, refuse, reject, repudiate, spurn, turn down; *also* overrule, veto; forbid, prohibit, proscribe; dismiss; abstain, forbear, refrain; deny, dispute, gainsay; balk, stick; abjure, renounce; avoid, bypass, detour *Ant* accept, agree (to), approve

²decline *n* **1** ♦ : a gradual sinking and wasting away **2** ♦ : a change to a lower state or level **3** : the time when something is approaching its end **4** : a descending slope

♦ [1] decay, degeneration, deterioration; *also* atrophy; exhaustion; flagging, limping; relapse, setback *Ant* improvement, recovery, revitalization ♦ [2] degradation, fall; *also* decay, rotting, spoiling; breakup, crumbling, decomposition, disintegration, dissolution; destruction, havoc, ruin, ruination *Ant* ascent, rise, upswing

de·cliv·i·ty \di-'kli-və-tē\ *n, pl* **-ties** : a steep downward slope

de·code \dē-'kōd\ *vb* ♦ : to convert (a coded message) into ordinary language — **de·cod·er** *n*

♦ break, crack; *also* render, translate; dope (out), puzzle (out), figure out, solve, unravel, work, work out *Ant* cipher, code, encode

dé·col·le·tage \dā-ˌkä-lə-'täzh\ *n* : the low-cut neckline of a dress

dé·col·le·té \dā-ˌkäl-'tā\ *adj* [F] **1** : wearing a strapless or low-necked gown **2** : having a low-cut neckline

de·com·mis·sion \ˌdē-kə-'mi-shən\ *vb* : to remove from service

de·com·pose \ˌdē-kəm-'pōz\ *vb* **1** : to separate into constituent parts **2** ♦ : to break down in decay : ROT

♦ break down, corrupt, decay, disintegrate, molder, putrefy, rot, spoil — more at DECAY

de·com·po·si·tion \dē-ˌkäm-pə-'zi-shən\ *n* ♦ : the act or process of decomposing

♦ breakdown, corruption, decay, putrefaction, rot, spoilage — more at CORRUPTION

de·com·press \ˌdē-kəm-'pres\ *vb* : to release from pressure or compression — **de·com·pres·sion** \-'pre-shən\ *n*

de·con·ges·tant \ˌdē-kən-'jes-tənt\ *n* : an agent that relieves congestion (as of mucous membranes)

de·con·struc·tion \ˌdē-kən-'strək-shən\ *n* : the analysis of something (as language or literature) by the separation and individual examination of its basic elements — **de·con·struct** \-'strəkt\ *vb*

de·con·tam·i·nate \ˌdē-kən-'ta-mə-ˌnāt\ *vb* : to rid of contamination (as radioactive material) — **de·con·tam·i·na·tion** \-ˌta-mə-'nā-shən\ *n*

de·con·trol \ˌdē-kən-'trōl\ *vb* : to end control of ⟨~ prices⟩ — **decontrol** *n*

de·cor *or* **dé·cor** \dā-'kȯr, 'dā-ˌkȯr\ *n* : DECORATION; *esp* : the style and layout of interior furnishings

dec·o·rate \'de-kə-ˌrāt\ *vb* **-rat·ed; -rat·ing** **1** ♦ : to furnish with something ornamental ⟨~ a room⟩ **2** : to award a mark of honor (as a medal) to

♦ adorn, array, beautify, bedeck, deck, do, dress, embellish, enrich, garnish, grace, ornament, trim; *also* doll up, dress up, trick (out); brighten, freshen, spruce (up); boss, chase, emboss; embroider, figure, flounce, fringe, garland, hang, lace, wreathe; gild, paint; redecorate, redo *Ant* blemish, deface, disfigure, mar, scar, spoil

dec·o·ra·tion \ˌde-kə-ˈrā-shən\ *n* **1** : the act or process of decorating **2** ♦ : something that adorns, enriches, or beautifies : ORNAMENT **3** ♦ : a badge of honor

♦ [2] adornment, caparison, embellishment, frill, garnish, ornament, trim; *also* finery, frippery; flounce, flourish, furbelow, ruffle; enhancement, enrichment, improvement; embroidery, fancywork; gilt, glitter; design, figure, pattern; furnishings, regalia, trappings ♦ [3] award, distinction, honor (*or* honour), plume, prize — more at AWARD

dec·o·ra·tive \ˈde-kə-rə-tiv\ *adj* : serving to decorate : ORNAMENTAL

dec·o·ra·tor \ˈde-kə-ˌrā-tər\ *n* : one that decorates; *esp* : a person who designs or executes interiors and their furnishings

dec·o·rous \ˈde-kə-rəs, di-ˈkōr-əs\ *adj* ♦ : marked by propriety and good taste : PROPER

♦ correct, decent, genteel, nice, polite, proper, respectable, seemly — more at PROPER

de·co·rum \di-ˈkōr-əm\ *n* [L] **1** ♦ : conformity to accepted standards of conduct **2** : ORDERLINESS

♦ decency, form, propriety — more at DECENCY

¹de·coy \ˈdē-ˌkȯi, di-ˈkȯi\ *n* [prob. fr. D *de kooi*, lit., the cage] **1** : something that lures or entices; *esp* : an artificial bird used to attract live birds within shot **2** : something used to draw attention away from another

²de·coy \di-ˈkȯi, ˈdē-ˌkȯi\ *vb* ♦ : to lure by or as if by a decoy : ENTICE

♦ allure, beguile, entice, lead on, lure, seduce, tempt — more at LURE

¹de·crease \di-ˈkrēs\ *vb* **de·creased; de·creas·ing** ♦ : to grow or cause to grow less : DIMINISH

♦ abate, decline, de-escalate, die, diminish, dwindle, ebb, fall, lessen, let up, lower, moderate, recede, relent, shrink, subside, taper, wane; *also* compress, condense, constrict, contract; evaporate, fade (away), give out, melt (away), peter (out), vanish; slacken, slow (down); alleviate, ease, relax; flag, sink, weaken; cave (in), collapse, deflate, give out *Ant* accumulate, balloon, build, burgeon, enlarge, escalate, expand, grow, increase, intensify, mount, mushroom, pick up, rise, snowball, soar, swell, wax

²de·crease \ˈdē-ˌkrēs\ *n* **1** : the process of decreasing **2** ♦ : an amount of diminution : REDUCTION

♦ abatement, decline, decrement, diminution, drop, fall, loss, reduction, shrinkage; *also* dent, depression; slip, slump; curtailment, cut, cutback *Ant* boost, enlargement, gain, increase, increment, raise, rise

¹de·cree \di-ˈkrē\ *n* **1** ♦ : an order usu. having the force of law : EDICT **2** : a judicial decision

♦ behest, charge, command, commandment, dictate, direction, directive, edict, instruction, order, word

²decree *vb* **de·creed; de·cree·ing** **1** ♦ : to direct authoritatively : COMMAND **2** : to determine or order judicially

♦ command, dictate, direct, ordain, order — more at COMMAND

dec·re·ment \ˈde-krə-mənt\ *n* **1** : gradual decrease **2** ♦ : the quantity lost by diminution or waste

♦ abatement, decline, decrease, diminution, drop, fall, loss, reduction, shrinkage — more at DECREASE

de·crep·it \di-ˈkre-pət\ *adj* : broken down with age : WORN-OUT — **de·crep·i·tude** \-pə-ˌtüd, -ˌtyüd\ *n*

de·cre·scen·do \ˌdā-krə-ˈshen-dō\ *adv or adj* : with a decrease in volume — used as a direction in music

de·crim·i·nal·ize \dē-ˈkri-mən-ᵊl-ˌīz\ *vb* : to remove or reduce the criminal status of

de·cry \di-ˈkrī\ *vb* ♦ : to express strong disapproval of

♦ belittle, cry down, deprecate, depreciate, diminish, discount, disparage, minimize, put down, write off;

also abuse, scold; disapprove (of), dislike; censure, condemn, criticize, denounce, reprehend, reprobate; defame, malign, slander, traduce, vilify; discredit, disgrace *Ant* acclaim, applaud, exalt, extol, glorify, laud, magnify, praise

ded·i·cate \ˈde-di-ˌkāt\ *vb* **-cat·ed; -cat·ing** **1** : to devote to the worship of a divine being esp. with sacred rites **2** ♦ : to set apart for a definite purpose **3** : to inscribe or address as a compliment — **ded·i·ca·tor** \ˈde-di-ˌkā-tər\ *n* — **ded·i·ca·to·ry** \-kə-ˌtōr-ē\ *adj*

♦ allocate, consecrate, devote, earmark, reserve, save — more at DEVOTE

ded·i·ca·tion \ˌde-di-ˈkā-shən\ *n* **1** : an act or rite of dedicating esp. to a sacred use **2** : a setting aside for a particular purpose **3** ♦ : self-sacrificing devotion

♦ allegiance, constancy, devotion, faith, faithfulness, fastness, fealty, fidelity, loyalty, steadfastness — more at FIDELITY

de·duce \di-ˈdüs, -ˈdyüs\ *vb* **de·duced; de·duc·ing** **1** ♦ : to derive by reasoning : INFER **2** : to trace the course of

♦ conclude, extrapolate, gather, infer, judge, reason, understand — more at INFER

de·duct \di-ˈdəkt\ *vb* : SUBTRACT — **de·duct·ible** *adj*

de·duc·tion \di-ˈdək-shən\ *n* **1** : an act of taking away : SUBTRACTION **2** ♦ : something that is or may be subtracted **3** : the deriving of a conclusion by reasoning : the conclusion so reached — **de·duc·tive** \-ˈdək-tiv\ *adj* — **de·duc·tive·ly** *adv*

♦ abatement, discount, reduction; *also* kickback, rebate; dent, depreciation; decline, decrement, diminution, drop, fall, loss; forfeit, forfeiture, penalty *Ant* accession, addition

¹deed \ˈdēd\ *n* **1** ♦ : something done **2** ♦ : a usu. illustrious act or action : FEAT **3** : a document containing some legal transfer, bargain, or contract

♦ exploit, feat, thing

²deed *vb* ♦ : to convey or transfer by deed

♦ alienate, assign, cede, make over, transfer — more at TRANSFER

dee·jay \ˈdē-ˌjā\ *n* : DISC JOCKEY

deem \ˈdēm\ *vb* ♦ : to come to think or judge

♦ believe, consider, feel, figure, guess, hold, imagine, suppose, think — more at BELIEVE

de–em·pha·size \dē-ˈem-fə-ˌsīz\ *vb* : to reduce in relative importance; *also* : to attach little importance to — **de–em·pha·sis** \-səs\ *n*

¹deep \ˈdēp\ *adj* **1** : extending far down, back, within, or outward **2** : having a specified extension downward or backward **3** ♦ : difficult to understand; *also* : MYSTERIOUS ⟨a ~ dark secret⟩ **4** : WISE **5** : ENGROSSED, INVOLVED ⟨~ in thought⟩ **6** ♦ : characterized by profundity of feeling or quality : INTENSE ⟨~ grief⟩ ⟨~ sleep⟩ **7** : dark and rich in color ⟨a ~ red⟩ **8** ♦ : having a low musical pitch or range ⟨a ~ voice⟩ **9** : situated well within **10** : covered, enclosed, or filled often to a specified degree — **deep·ly** *adv*

♦ [3] ambiguous, cryptic, dark, darkling, enigmatic, equivocal, inscrutable, murky, mysterious, mystic, nebulous, obscure, occult — more at OBSCURE ♦ [6] explosive, exquisite, fearful, ferocious, fierce, furious, hard, heavy, intense, profound, terrible, vehement, vicious, violent — more at INTENSE ♦ [8] bass, low, throaty; *also* gruff, hoarse, husky, rough *Ant* acute, high, piping, sharp, shrill, treble

²deep *adv* **1** : DEEPLY **2** : far on : LATE ⟨~ in the night⟩

³deep *n* **1** ♦ : an extremely deep place or part; *esp* : the whole body of salt water that covers nearly three fourths of the surface of the earth : OCEAN **2** ♦ : the middle or most intense part ⟨the ~ of winter⟩

♦ [1] blue, brine, ocean, sea — more at OCEAN ♦ [2] depth, height, middle, midst, thick — more at THICK

deep·en \'dē-pən\ *vb* ♦ : to make or become deep or deeper

♦ amplify, beef, boost, consolidate, enhance, heighten, intensify, magnify, redouble, step up, strengthen — more at INTENSIFY

deep–freeze \'dēp-'frēz\ *vb* **-froze** \-'frōz\; **-fro·zen** \-'frōz-ᵊn\; **-freez·ing** : QUICK-FREEZE

deep–fry *vb* : to cook in enough oil to cover the food being fried

deep pocket *n* **1** : one having substantial financial resources **2** *pl* : substantial financial resources

deep–root·ed \'dēp-'rü-təd, -'rü-\ *adj* ♦ : deeply implanted or established

♦ confirmed, deep-seated, inveterate, settled — more at INVETERATE

deep–sea \'dēp-'sē\ *adj* : of, relating to, or occurring in the deeper parts of the sea ⟨~ fishing⟩

deep–seat·ed \'dēp-'sē-təd\ *adj* **1** : situated far below the surface **2** ♦ : firmly established ⟨~ convictions⟩

♦ confirmed, deep-rooted, inveterate, settled — more at INVETERATE

deer \'dir\ *n, pl* **deer** [ME, deer, animal, fr. OE *dēor* beast] : any of numerous ruminant mammals with cloven hoofs and usu. antlers esp. in the males

deer·fly \-ˌflī\ *n* : any of numerous small horseflies

deer·skin \-ˌskin\ *n* : leather made from the skin of a deer; *also* : a garment of such leather

deer tick *n* : a tick that transmits the bacterium causing Lyme disease

de–es·ca·late \dē-'es-kə-ˌlāt\ *vb* ♦ : to decrease in extent, volume, or scope — **de–es·ca·la·tion** \-ˌes-kə-'lā-shən\ *n*

♦ abate, decline, decrease, die, diminish, dwindle, ebb, fall, lessen, let up, lower, moderate, recede, relent, shrink, subside, taper, wane — more at DECREASE

deet \'dēt\ *n, often all cap* : a colorless oily liquid insect and tick repellent

def *abbr* **1** defendant **2** definite **3** definition

de·face \di-'fās\ *vb* ♦ : to destroy or mar the appearance of — **de·face·ment** *n* — **de·fac·er** *n*

♦ blemish, break, cripple, damage, disfigure, flaw, harm, hurt, injure, mar, spoil, vitiate — more at DAMAGE

de fac·to \di-'fak-tō, dā-\ *adj or adv* **1** : actually existing ⟨*de facto* segregation⟩ **2** : actually exercising power ⟨*de facto* government⟩

de·fal·ca·tion \ˌdē-ˌfal-'kā-shən, -ˌfȯl-; ˌde-fəl-\ *n* : EMBEZZLEMENT

def·a·ma·tion \ˌde-fə-'mā-shən\ *n* ♦ : the act of defaming another

♦ libel, slander, vilification — more at SLANDER

de·fam·a·to·ry \di-'fa-mə-ˌtōr-ē\ *adj* ♦ : containing defamation : injurious to reputation

♦ libelous, scandalous, slanderous — more at LIBELOUS

de·fame \di-'fām\ *vb* **de·famed; de·fam·ing** ♦ : to injure or destroy the reputation of by libel or slander

♦ blacken, libel, malign, slander, smear, traduce, vilify — more at SLANDER

de·fault \di-'fȯlt\ *n* **1** ♦ : failure to do something required by duty or law; *also* : failure to appear for a legal proceeding **2** : failure to compete in or to finish an appointed contest ⟨lose a race by ~⟩ **3** : a choice made without active consideration due to lack of viable alternatives **4** : a selection made automatically by a computer in the absence of a choice by the user — **default** *vb* — **de·fault·er** *n*

♦ delinquency, dereliction, failure, neglect, negligence, oversight — more at FAILURE

¹de·feat \di-'fēt\ *vb* **1** : FRUSTRATE, NULLIFY **2** ♦ : to win victory over : BEAT

♦ beat, conquer, master, overcome, prevail, rout, subdue, surmount, triumph, win — more at BEAT

²defeat *n* **1** ♦ : frustration by nullification or by prevention of success : the state or face of being defeated ⟨the bill suffered ~ in the Senate⟩ **2** : an overthrow of an army in battle **3** ♦ : loss of a contest

♦ [1] collapse, crash, cropper, failure, fizzle, nonsuccess — more at FAILURE ♦ [3] loss, rout, shellacking; *also* collapse, debacle, failure, fizzle, flop, nonsuccess, setback, upset, washout; lurch, shutout *Ant* success, triumph, victory, win

de·feat·ism \-'fē-ˌti-zəm\ *n* : acceptance of or resignation to defeat — **de·feat·ist** \-tist\ *n*

defeatist *adj* ♦ : characterized by defeatism

♦ despairing, hopeless, pessimistic — more at PESSIMISTIC

def·e·cate \'de-fi-ˌkāt\ *vb* **-cat·ed; -cat·ing** **1** : to free from impurity or corruption **2** : to discharge feces from the bowels — **def·e·ca·tion** \ˌde-fi-'kā-shən\ *n*

¹de·fect \'dē-ˌfekt, di-'fekt\ *n* ♦ : an imperfection that impairs worth or utility : BLEMISH

♦ blemish, deformity, disfigurement, fault, flaw, imperfection, mark, pockmark, scar — more at BLEMISH

²de·fect \di-'fekt\ *vb* : to desert a cause or party esp. in order to espouse another — **de·fec·tion** \-'fek-shən\ *n*

de·fec·tive \di-'fek-tiv\ *adj* ♦ : imperfect in form or function : FAULTY — **defective** *n*

♦ bad, faulty, imperfect — more at FAULTY

de·fec·tor \di-'fek-tər\ *n* ♦ : one that defects

♦ deserter, recreant, renegade — more at RENEGADE

de·fence *Can and Brit var of* DEFENSE

de·fend \di-'fend\ *vb* [ME, fr. OF *defendre*, fr. L *defendere*, fr. *de-* from + *-fendere* to strike] **1** ♦ : to repel danger or attack from **2** : to act as attorney for **3** : to oppose the claim of another in a lawsuit : CONTEST **4** ♦ : to maintain against opposition ⟨~ an idea⟩

♦ [1] cover, guard, protect, safeguard, screen, secure, shield, ward; *also* avert, prevent; fend (off), oppose, resist, withstand; battle, contend, fight, war; conserve, keep, preserve, save; buffer, palisade, picket, wall *Ant* assail, assault, attack ♦ [4] justify, maintain, support, uphold — more at MAINTAIN

de·fen·dant \di-'fen-dənt\ *n* : a person required to make answer in a legal action or suit

de·fend·er \di-'fen-dər\ *n* ♦ : one that defends

♦ custodian, defense (*or* defence), guard, protection, protector — more at PROTECTOR

de·fense *or Can and Brit* **de·fence** \di-'fens\ *n* **1** : the act of defending : resistance against attack **2** ♦ : means, method, or capability of defending **3** ♦ : an argument in support or justification **4** : the answer made by the defendant in a legal action **5** : a defending party, group, or team

♦ [2] aegis, armor, cover, guard, protection, safeguard, screen, security, shield, wall, ward; *also* arm, armament, munitions, weapon, weaponry; fastness, fort, fortress, palisade, stronghold ♦ [3] alibi, excuse, justification, plea, reason — more at EXCUSE

de·fense·less *or Can and Brit* **de·fence·less** \-ləs\ *adj* ♦ : being without defense

♦ exposed, helpless, susceptible, undefended, unguarded, unprotected, unresistant, vulnerable — more at HELPLESS

defense mechanism *n* : an often unconscious mental process (as repression) that assists in reaching compromise solutions to personal problems

de·fen·si·ble \di-'fen(t)-si-bəl\ *adj* ♦ : capable of being defended

♦ justifiable, maintainable, supportable, sustainable, tenable — more at TENABLE

¹de·fen·sive \di-'fen-siv\ *adj* **1** : serving or intended to defend or protect **2** : of or relating to the attempt to keep an opponent from scoring (as in a game) — **de·fen·sive·ly** *adv* — **de·fen·sive·ness** *n*

²defensive *n* : a defensive position

¹de·fer \di-'fər\ *vb* **de·ferred; de·fer·ring** [ME *deferren, differ-ren*, fr. MF *differer*, fr. L *differre* to postpone, be different] ◆ : to put off to a later time : POSTPONE

◆ delay, hold up, postpone, put off, shelve — more at POSTPONE

²defer *vb* **deferred; deferring** [ME *deferren, differen*, fr. MF *deferer, defferer*, fr. LL *deferre*, fr. L, to bring down, bring, fr. *de-* down + *ferre* to carry] : to submit or yield to the opinion or wishes of another

def·er·ence \'de-fər-əns\ *n* ◆ : courteous, respectful, or in-gratiating regard for another's wishes

◆ compliance, docility, obedience — more at COMPLIANCE

def·er·en·tial \ˌde-fə-'ren-chəl\ *adj* ◆ : showing or express-ing deference

◆ dutiful, regardful, respectful — more at RESPECTFUL

de·fer·ment \di-'fər-mənt\ *n* : the act of delaying; *esp* : offi-cial postponement of military service

de·fi·ance \di-'fī-əns\ *n* **1** ◆ : the act or an instance of defying **2** : disposition to resist or contend

◆ disobedience, insubordination, rebelliousness, recal-citrance, refractoriness, unruliness — more at DISOBE-DIENCE

de·fi·ant \-ənt\ *adj* ◆ : full of defiance — **de·fi·ant·ly** *adv*

◆ contrary, disobedient, froward, intractable, rebel-lious, recalcitrant, refractory, unruly, untoward, way-ward, willful — more at DISOBEDIENT

de·fi·bril·la·tor \dē-'fi-brə-ˌlā-tər\ *n* : an electronic device that applies an electric shock to restore the rhythm of a fibrillating heart — **de·fi·bril·late** \-ˌlāt\ *vb* — **de·fi·bril·la-tion** \-ˌfi-brə-'lā-shən\ *n*

de·fi·cien·cy \di-'fi-shən-sē\ *n* ◆ : the quality or state of being deficient

◆ dearth, deficit, failure, famine, inadequacy, insuf-ficiency, lack, paucity, poverty, scantiness, scarcity, shortage, want; *also* absence, omission; meagerness; necessity, need, privation *Ant* abundance, adequacy, amplitude, plenitude, plenty, sufficiency

deficiency disease *n* : a disease (as scurvy or beriberi) caused by a lack of essential dietary elements and esp. a vitamin or mineral

de·fi·cient \di-'fi-shənt\ *adj* ◆ : lacking in something neces-sary; *also* : not up to a normal standard

◆ inadequate, insufficient, scarce, short, shy, wanting — more at SHORT ◆ bad, inferior, lousy, off, poor, punk, rotten, substandard, unacceptable, unsatisfac-tory, wanting, wretched, wrong — more at BAD

def·i·cit \'de-fə-sət\ *n* ◆ : a deficiency in amount; *esp* : an excess of expenditures over revenue

◆ dearth, deficiency, failure, famine, inadequacy, in-sufficiency, lack, paucity, poverty, scantiness, scarcity, shortage, want — more at DEFICIENCY

¹de·file \di-'fīl\ *vb* **de·filed; de·fil·ing 1** ◆ : to corrupt the purity or perfection of **2** ◆ : to make physically unclean esp. with something unpleasant or contaminating **3** : to violate the chastity of **4** ◆ : to violate the sanctity of : DESECRATE **5** : DISHONOR

◆ [1, 2] befoul, contaminate, foul, poison, pollute, taint — more at CONTAMINATE ◆ [4] desecrate, profane, vi-olate — more at DESECRATE

²de·file \di-'fīl, 'dē-ˌfīl\ *n* ◆ : a narrow passage or gorge

◆ canyon, flume, gap, gorge, gulch, notch, pass, ravine — more at CANYON

de·file·ment \-mənt\ *n* **1** ◆ : the act of defiling or state of being defiled **2** ◆ : something that defiles

◆ [1] blasphemy, desecration, impiety, irreverence, sacrilege — more at BLASPHEMY ◆ [2] adulterant, con-taminant, impurity, pollutant — more at IMPURITY

de·fine \di-'fīn\ *vb* **de·fined; de·fin·ing 1** : to set forth the meaning of ⟨∼ a word⟩ **2** ◆ : to fix or mark the limits of **3** ◆ : to clarify in outline or character — **de·fin·able** *adj* — **de·fin·er** *n*

◆ [2] bound, circumscribe, delimit, demarcate, limit, mark, terminate — more at LIMIT ◆ [3] delineate, outline, silhouette, sketch, trace — more at OUTLINE ◆ [3] characterize, depict, describe, portray, represent — more at CHARACTERIZE

def·i·nite \'de-fə-nət\ *adj* **1** ◆ : having distinct lim-its **2** ◆ : clear in meaning **3** : typically designating an identified or immediately identifiable person or thing — **def·i·nite·ness** *n*

◆ [1] determinate, finite, limited, measured, narrow, restricted — more at LIMITED ◆ [2] clear-cut, defini-tive, explicit, express, specific, unambiguous, unequiv-ocal — more at EXPLICIT

def·i·nite·ly \-lē\ *adv* ◆ : in a definite way or manner

◆ certainly, doubtless, incontestably, indeed, indisput-ably, really, surely, truly, undeniably, undoubtedly, un-questionably — more at INDEED

def·i·ni·tion \ˌde-fə-'ni-shən\ *n* **1** : an act of determining or settling **2** : a statement of the meaning of a word or word group; *also* : the action or process of defining **3** : the ac-tion or the power of making definite and clear : CLARITY, DISTINCTNESS

de·fin·i·tive \di-'fi-nə-tiv\ *adj* **1** ◆ : serving to provide a final solution or to end a situation : DECISIVE **2** : author-itative and apparently exhaustive **3** ◆ : serving to define or specify precisely

◆ [1] absolute, clear, conclusive, decisive — more at CONCLUSIVE ◆ [3] clear-cut, definite, explicit, express, specific, unambiguous, unequivocal — more at EXPLICIT

de·flate \di-'flāt\ *vb* **de·flat·ed; de·flat·ing 1** : to release air or gas from **2** : to reduce in size, importance, or effec-tiveness; *also* : to reduce from a state of inflation **3** : to become deflated

de·fla·tion \-'flā-shən\ *n* **1** : an act or instance of deflating : the state of being deflated **2** : reduction in the volume of available money or credit resulting in a decline of the general price level

de·flect \di-'flekt\ *vb* ◆ : to turn aside — **de·flec·tion** \-'flek-shən\ *n*

◆ divert, swerve, swing, turn, veer, wheel, whip — more at TURN

de·flo·ra·tion \ˌde-flə-'rā-shən\ *n* : rupture of the hymen

de·flow·er \dē-'flaů(-ə)r\ *vb* : to deprive of virginity

de·fog \dē-'fóg, -'fäg\ *vb* : to remove fog or condensed moisture from — **de·fog·ger** *n*

de·fo·li·ant \dē-'fō-lē-ənt\ *n* : a chemical spray or dust used to defoliate plants

de·fo·li·ate \-ˌāt\ *vb* : to deprive of leaves esp. prematurely — **de·fo·li·a·tion** \dē-ˌfō-lē-'ā-shən\ *n* — **de·fo·li·a·tor** \dē-'fō-lē-ˌā-tər\ *n*

de·for·es·ta·tion \dē-ˌfór-ə-'stā-shən\ *n* : the action or process of clearing an area of forests; *also* : the state of having been cleared of forests — **de·for·est** \(ˌ)dē-'fór-əst, -'fär-\ *vb*

de·form \di-'fórm\ *vb* **1** : DISFIGURE, DEFACE **2** ◆ : to make or become misshapen or changed in shape

◆ contort, distort, screw, warp — more at CONTORT

de·for·ma·tion \ˌdē-fór-'mā-shən, ˌde-fər-\ *n* ◆ : the action of deforming

◆ contortion, distortion — more at CONTORTION

de·formed *adj* ◆ : distorted or unshapely in form

◆ distorted, malformed, misshapen, monstrous, shape-less — more at MALFORMED

de·for·mi·ty \di-'fór-mə-tē\ *n, pl* **-ties 1** : the state of being deformed **2** ◆ : a physical blemish or distortion

◆ blemish, defect, disfigurement, fault, flaw, imperfec-tion, mark, pockmark, scar — more at BLEMISH

de·fraud \di-'fród\ *vb* ◆ : to deprive of something by de-ception or fraud : CHEAT

◆ bleed, cheat, chisel, cozen, fleece, hustle, mulct, rook, shortchange, skin, squeeze, stick, sting, swindle, victimize — more at FLEECE

de·fray \di-'frā\ *vb* : to provide for the payment of : PAY — **de·fray·al** *n*

de·frock \(ˌ)dē-'fräk\ *vb* : to deprive (as a priest) of the right to exercise the functions of office

de·frost \di-'frȯst\ *vb* **1** : to thaw out **2** : to free from ice — **de·frost·er** *n*

deft \'deft\ *adj* ♦ : characterized by facility and skill — **deft·ly** *adv*

♦ clever, cunning, dexterous, handy — more at DEXTEROUS

deft·ness \-nəs\ *n* ♦ : the quality or state of being deft

♦ agility, dexterity, nimbleness, sleight — more at DEXTERITY ♦ adeptness, adroitness, art, artfulness, artifice, artistry, cleverness, craft, cunning, masterfulness, skill — more at SKILL

de·funct \di-'fəŋkt\ *adj* ♦ : no longer living, existing, or functioning

♦ bygone, dead, extinct, gone — more at EXTINCT

de·fuse \dē-'fyüz\ *vb* **1** : to remove the fuse from (as a bomb) **2** : to make less harmful, potent, or tense

de·fy \di-'fī\ *vb* **de·fied; de·fy·ing** [ME, to renounce faith in, challenge, fr. AF *desfier, defier*, fr. *de-* from + *fier* to entrust, ultim. fr. L *fidere* to trust] **1** ♦ : to challenge to do something considered impossible : DARE **2** ♦ : to refuse boldly to obey or to yield to ⟨~ the law⟩ **3** ♦ : to resist attempts at : WITHSTAND ⟨a scene that *defies* description⟩

♦ [1] challenge, dare — more at CHALLENGE ♦ [2] beard, brave, brazen, confront, dare, face — more at FACE ♦ [3] buck, fight, oppose, repel, resist, withstand — more at RESIST

deg *abbr* degree

de·gas \dē-'gas\ *vb* : to remove gas from

de·gen·er·a·cy \di-'je-nə-rə-sē\ *n, pl* **-cies 1** : the state of being degenerate **2** ♦ : the process of becoming degenerate **3** : PERVERSION

♦ corruption, debasement, debauchery, decadence, degeneration, degradation, demoralization, depravity, dissipation, dissoluteness, perversion — more at CORRUPTION

¹**de·gen·er·ate** \di-'je-nə-rət\ *adj* ♦ : fallen or deteriorated from a former, higher, or normal condition — **de·gen·er·a·tive** \-'je-nə-ˌrā-tiv\ *adj*

♦ corrupt, debauched, decadent, dissolute, perverse, perverted, reprobate — more at CORRUPT

²**de·gen·er·ate** \di-'je-nə-ˌrāt\ *vb* ♦ : to undergo deterioration (as in morality, intelligence, structure, or function)

♦ decay, decline, descend, deteriorate, ebb, rot, sink, worsen — more at DETERIORATE

³**de·gen·er·ate** \-rət\ *n* ♦ : a degenerate person; *esp* : a sexual pervert

♦ decadent, libertine, pervert, profligate; *also* delinquent, derelict, incorrigible; blackguard, cad, heel, knave, rascal, miscreant, reprobate, rogue, scoundrel, villain; playboy, satyr

de·gen·er·a·tion \di-ˌje-nə-'rā-shən\ *n* ♦ : the process of passing from a higher to a lower type

♦ decay, decline, deterioration — more at DECLINE ♦ corruption, debasement, debauchery, decadence, degeneracy, degradation, demoralization, depravity, dissipation, dissoluteness, perversion — more at CORRUPTION

de·grad·able \di-'grā-də-bəl\ *adj* : capable of being chemically degraded

deg·ra·da·tion \ˌde-grə-'dā-shən\ *n* **1** : the act or process of degrading **2 a** ♦ : decline to a low, destitute, or demoralized state **b** ♦ : moral or intellectual decadence

♦ [2a] decline, fall — more at DECLINE ♦ [2b] corruption, debasement, debauchery, decadence, degeneracy, degeneration, demoralization, depravity, dissipation, dissoluteness, perversion — more at CORRUPTION

de·grade \di-'grād\ *vb* **1** ♦ : to reduce from a higher to a lower rank or degree **2 a** ♦ : to bring to low esteem or into disrepute **b** ♦ : to drag down in moral or intellectual character : DEBASE **3** : DECOMPOSE

♦ [1] break, bust, demote, downgrade, reduce — more at DEMOTE ♦ [2a] abase, debase, demean, discredit, disgrace, dishonor (*or* dishonour), humble, humiliate, lower, shame, smirch, take down — more at HUMBLE ♦ [2b] debase, demean, demoralize, humble, subvert, warp — more at DEBASE

de·grad·ing *adj* ♦ : that degrades

♦ contemptuous, derogatory, disdainful, scornful, uncomplimentary — more at DEROGATORY

de·gree \di-'grē\ *n* [ME, fr. AF *degré*, fr. VL **degradus*, fr. L *de-* down + *gradus* step, grade] **1** ♦ : a step in a series **2** ♦ : a rank or grade of official, ecclesiastical, or social position; *also* : the civil condition of a person **3** : the extent, intensity, or scope of something esp. as measured by a graded series **4** : one of the forms or sets of forms used in the comparison of an adjective or adverb **5** : a title conferred upon students by a college, university, or professional school on completion of a program of study **6** : a line or space of the musical staff; *also* : a note or tone of a musical scale **7** : a unit of measure for angles that is equal to an angle with its vertex at the center of a circle and its sides cutting off ¹⁄₃₆₀ of the circumference; *also* : a unit of measure for arcs of a circle that is equal to the amount of arc extending ¹⁄₃₆₀ of the circumference **8** : any of various units for measuring temperature

♦ [1] cut, grade, inch, notch, peg, phase, point, stage, step; *also* amount, measure, plane; decrement, increment ♦ [2] footing, level, place, position, rank, situation, standing, station, status — more at RANK

de·horn \dē-'hȯrn\ *vb* : to deprive of horns

de·hu·man·ize \dē-'hyü-mə-ˌnīz\ *vb* ♦ : to deprive of human qualities, personality, or spirit — **de·hu·man·i·za·tion** \ˌdē-ˌhyü-mə-nə-'zā-shən\ *n*

de·hu·mid·i·fy \ˌdē-hyü-'mi-də-ˌfī\ *vb* ♦ : to remove moisture from (as the air) — **de·hu·mid·i·fi·er** *n*

de·hy·drate \dē-'hī-ˌdrāt\ *vb* ♦ : to remove water from; *also* : to lose liquid — **de·hy·dra·tion** \ˌdē-hī-'drā-shən\ *n*

♦ dry, parch, sear — more at DRY

de·hy·dro·ge·na·tion \ˌdē-(ˌ)hī-ˌdrä-jə-'nā-shən, -drə-\ *n* : the removal of hydrogen from a chemical compound — **de·hy·dro·ge·nate** \ˌdē-(ˌ)hī-'drä-jə-ˌnāt, dē-'hī-drə-jə-\ *vb*

de·ice \dē-'īs\ *vb* : to keep free or rid of ice ⟨~ a plane⟩ — **de·ic·er** *n*

de·i·fi·ca·tion \ˌdē-ə-fə-'kā-shən\ *n* ♦ : the act or an instance of deifying

♦ adulation, idolatry, worship — more at WORSHIP

de·i·fy \'dē-ə-ˌfī\ *vb* **-fied; -fy·ing 1 a** : to make a god of **b** ♦ : to treat as an object of worship **2** ♦ : to glorify as of supreme worth; *also* : WORSHIP

♦ [1b] adore, canonize, dote on, idolize, worship — more at IDOLIZE ♦ [2] adore, glorify, revere, venerate, worship — more at WORSHIP

deign \'dān\ *vb* [ME, fr. AF *deigner*, fr. L *dignare, dignari*, fr. *dignus* worthy] : CONDESCEND

de·ion·ize \dē-'ī-ə-ˌnīz\ *vb* : to remove ions from

de·ism \'dē-ˌi-zəm\ *n, often cap* : a system of thought advocating natural religion based on human morality and reason rather than divine revelation — **de·ist** \'dē-ist\ *n, often cap* — **de·is·tic** \dē-'is-tik\ *adj*

de·i·ty \'dē-ə-tē, 'dā-\ *n, pl* **-ties 1** ♦ : the quality or state of being divine : DIVINITY **2** *cap* ♦ : the Being worshipped as the creator and ruler of the universe : GOD **1 3** : a god or goddess

♦ [1] divinity, godhead — more at DIVINITY ♦ **Deity** [2] Almighty, Jehovah, Supreme Being

dé·jà vu \ˌdā-ˌzhä-'vü\ *n* [F, adj., already seen] : the feeling that one has seen or heard something before

de·ject·ed \di-'jek-təd\ *adj* ♦ : low in spirits : SAD — **de·ject·ed·ly** *adv*

♦ bad, blue, depressed, despondent, disconsolate, down, forlorn, gloomy, glum, low, melancholy, miserable, mournful, sad, unhappy

de·jec·tion \di-'jek-shən\ n ♦ : lowness of spirits

♦ blues, depression, desolation, despondency, doldrums, dumps, forlornness, gloom, heartsickness, melancholy, sadness — more at SADNESS

de ju·re \dē-'jùr-ē\ adv or adj [ML] : by legal right

deka·gram \'de-kə-ˌgram\ n : a metric unit of measure equal to 10 grams

deka·li·ter \-ˌlē-tər\ n : a metric unit of measure equal to 10 liters

deka·me·ter \-ˌmē-tər\ n : a metric unit of measure equal to 10 meters

del abbr delegate; delegation

Del abbr Delaware

Del·a·ware \'de-lə-ˌwar\ n, pl **Delaware** or **Delawares** : a member of an American Indian people orig. of the Delaware valley; also : their language

¹de·lay \di-'lā\ n 1 : the act of delaying : the state of being delayed 2 : the time for which something is delayed

²delay vb 1 ♦ : to put off to a later time : POSTPONE 2 ♦ : to stop, detain, or hinder for a time 3 ♦ : to move or act slowly

♦ [1] defer, hold up, postpone, put off, shelve — more at POSTPONE ♦ [2] encumber, hamper, hinder, hold up, impede, inhibit, interfere with, obstruct, tie up — more at HAMPER ♦ [3] crawl, creep, dally, dawdle, dillydally, drag, lag, linger, loiter, poke, tarry; also hang around, hang out, idle, loaf, loll, lounge; amble, ease, inch, lumber, plod, saunter, shuffle, stagger, stroll; decelerate, slow (down or up); filibuster, procrastinate, stall, temporize Ant hurry, run, rush, speed

de·lec·ta·ble \di-'lek-tə-bəl\ adj 1 ♦ : highly pleasing : DELIGHTFUL 2 ♦ : very pleasing to the taste or smell : DELICIOUS

♦ [1] agreeable, congenial, delicious, delightful, dreamy, felicitous, good, grateful, gratifying, nice, palatable, pleasant, pleasurable, satisfying ♦ [2] ambrosial, appetizing, delicious, flavorful (or flavourful), luscious, palatable, savory, scrumptious, tasty, toothsome, yummy — more at DELICIOUS

de·lec·ta·tion \ˌdē-ˌlek-'tā-shən\ n 1 ♦ : a high degree of gratification 2 ♦ : something that gives great pleasure : DELIGHT

♦ contentment, delight, enjoyment, gladness, gratification, pleasure, relish, satisfaction — more at PLEASURE

¹del·e·gate \'de-li-gət, -ˌgāt\ n 1 ♦ : a person acting for another 2 : a member of the lower house of the legislature of Maryland, Virginia, or West Virginia

♦ ambassador, emissary, envoy, legate, minister, representative — more at AMBASSADOR ♦ agent, attorney, commissary, deputy, envoy, factor, proxy, representative — more at AGENT

²del·e·gate \-ˌgāt\ vb **-gat·ed; -gat·ing** 1 : to assign (as responsibility or power to act or make decisions) to another ⟨~ authority⟩ 2 ♦ : to appoint as one's delegate

♦ commission, deputize; also assign, charge; appoint, designate, name, nominate

del·e·ga·tion \ˌde-li-'gā-shən\ n 1 ♦ : the act of delegating 2 : one or more persons chosen to represent others

♦ authorization, commission, license (or licence), mandate — more at COMMISSION

de·lete \di-'lēt\ vb **de·let·ed; de·let·ing** [L deletus, pp. of delēre to wipe out, destroy] : to eliminate esp. by blotting out, cutting out, or erasing — **de·le·tion** \-'lē-shən\ n

del·e·te·ri·ous \ˌde-lə-'tir-ē-əs\ adj ♦ : harmful often in a subtle or unexpected way : NOXIOUS

♦ adverse, bad, baleful, baneful, damaging, detrimental, evil, harmful, hurtful, ill, injurious, mischievous, noxious, pernicious, prejudicial — more at HARMFUL

delft \'delft\ n 1 : a Dutch pottery with an opaque white glaze and predominantly blue decoration 2 : glazed pottery esp. when blue and white

delft·ware \-ˌwer\ n : DELFT

deli \'de-lē\ n, pl **del·is** : DELICATESSEN

¹de·lib·er·ate \di-'li-bə-ˌrāt\ vb **-at·ed; -at·ing** ♦ : to consider carefully — **de·lib·er·a·tive** \-'li-bə-ˌrā-tiv, -brə-tiv\ adj — **de·lib·er·a·tive·ly** adv

♦ chew over, cogitate, consider, contemplate, debate, entertain, meditate, mull, ponder, question, ruminate, study, think, weigh — more at PONDER

²de·lib·er·ate \di-'li-bə-rət, -'li-brət\ adj [L deliberare to consider carefully, fr. libra scale, pound] 1 ♦ : determined after careful thought 2 ♦ : done or said intentionally 3 : UNHURRIED, SLOW — **de·lib·er·ate·ness** n

♦ [1] advised, calculated, measured, reasoned, studied, thoughtful, thought-out; also aforethought, premeditated; educated, informed; intentional, purposeful; designed, intended, planned, projected; careful, meticulous; foresighted, provident, prudent Ant casual ♦ [2] freewill, intentional, purposeful, voluntary, willful, willing; also intended, planned; conscious; considered, reasoned; premeditated; optional, volunteer Ant coerced, forced, involuntary, unintentional

de·lib·er·ate·ly \-lē\ adv ♦ : in a deliberate manner

♦ consciously, intentionally, knowingly, purposely, willfully — more at INTENTIONALLY

de·lib·er·a·tion \di-ˌli-bə-'rā-shən\ n 1 ♦ : the act of deliberating 2 : the quality or state of being deliberate

♦ consideration, debate, thought — more at CONSIDERATION ♦ argument, colloquy, conference, discourse, discussion, give-and-take, parley, talk — more at DISCUSSION

del·i·ca·cy \'de-li-kə-sē\ n, pl **-cies** 1 ♦ : something pleasing to eat and considered rare or luxurious 2 a ♦ : the quality or state of being dainty : FINENESS b : the quality or state of being frail : FRAILTY 3 : nicety or expressiveness of touch 4 a : precise perception and discrimination b ♦ : extreme sensitivity and precision 5 : sensibility in feeling or conduct; also : SQUEAMISHNESS 6 : the quality or state of requiring delicate handling

♦ [1] dainty, goody, tidbit, treat; also candy, dessert, junket, morsel, sweet, sweetmeat ♦ [2a] daintiness, fineness, fragility; also flimsiness Ant coarseness, crudity, roughness, rudeness ♦ [4b] accuracy, closeness, exactness, fineness, precision, veracity — more at PRECISION

del·i·cate \'de-li-kət\ adj 1 : pleasing to the senses of taste or smell esp. in a mild or subtle way 2 ♦ : marked by daintiness or charm : EXQUISITE 3 a : difficult to please : FASTIDIOUS b : SQUEAMISH 4 a ♦ : easily damaged : FRAGILE b : not robust in health or constitution : SICKLY 5 ♦ : requiring skill or tact 6 ♦ : marked by care, skill, or tact 7 ♦ : marked by minute precision : very sensitive — **del·i·cate·ly** adv

♦ [1] dainty, exquisite, gentle, mild, refined, subtle; also choice, elegant, extraordinary, incomparable, peerless, preeminent, prime, rare, select, superior, superlative, supreme, transcendent, unsurpassed; picked, selected; fine, fragile, frail Ant robust, strong, sturdy ♦ [2] choice, dainty, elegant, exquisite, rare, select — more at CHOICE ♦ [4a] breakable, fragile, frail — more at FRAGILE ♦ [5] catchy, difficult, knotty, problematic, spiny, thorny, ticklish, touchy, tough, tricky — more at TRICKY ♦ [6] exact, fine, minute, nice, refined, subtle — more at FINE ♦ [7] acute, keen, perceptive, sensitive, sharp — more at ACUTE

del·i·ca·tes·sen \ˌde-li-kə-'tes-ᵊn\ n pl [G, pl. of Delicatessen delicacy, fr. F délicatesse] 1 : ready-to-eat food products (as cooked meats and prepared salads) 2 sing, pl **delicatessens** : a store where delicatessen are sold

de·li·cious \di-'li-shəs\ adj 1 : affording great pleasure : DELIGHTFUL 2 ♦ : appealing to one of the bodily senses esp. of taste or smell

♦ ambrosial, appetizing, delectable, flavorful (or flavourful), luscious, palatable, savory, scrumptious, tasty, toothsome, yummy; also digestible, eatable, edible; delightful, heavenly, pleasing; agreeable, gratifying, pleasant; satisfying; choice, dainty, delicate, exquisite, rare *Ant* flat, flavorless, insipid, stale, tasteless, unappetizing, unpalatable

de·li·cious·ly \-lē\ *adv* **1** : in a delicious manner **2** : so as to produce delight

de·li·cious·ness \-nəs\ *n* ♦ : the quality or state of being delicious

♦ lusciousness, palatability, savor, tastiness

¹de·light \di-ˈlīt\ *n* **1** ♦ : great pleasure or satisfaction **2** ♦ : something that gives great pleasure

♦ [1] delectation, joy, kick, manna, pleasure, treat; *also* amusement, diversion, entertainment, fun; comfort, relief, solace; gratification, indulgence; ambrosia ♦ [1, 2] contentment, delectation, enjoyment, gladness, gratification, pleasure, relish, satisfaction — more at PLEASURE

²delight *vb* **1** ♦ : to take great pleasure **2** ♦ : to satisfy greatly : PLEASE

♦ [1] crow, exult, glory, joy, rejoice, triumph — more at EXULT ♦ *usu* **delight in** [1] adore, dig, enjoy, fancy, groove, like, love, relish, revel — more at ENJOY ♦ [2] content, gladden, gratify, please, rejoice, satisfy, suit, warm — more at PLEASE

de·light·ed *adj* ♦ : highly pleased : GRATIFIED — **de·light·ed·ly** *adv*

♦ blissful, glad, happy, joyful, pleased — more at GLAD

de·light·ful \-fəl\ *adj* ♦ : affording great pleasure and satisfaction

♦ agreeable, congenial, delectable, delicious, dreamy, felicitous, good, grateful, gratifying, nice, palatable, pleasant, pleasurable, satisfying ♦ amusing, diverting, enjoyable, entertaining, fun, pleasurable — more at FUN

de·light·ful·ly \-fə-lē\ *adv* ♦ : in a delightful manner

♦ agreeably, favorably (*or* favourably), felicitously, gloriously, nicely, pleasantly, pleasingly, satisfyingly, splendidly, well

de·lim·it \di-ˈli-mət\ *vb* ♦ : to mark the limits of

♦ bound, circumscribe, define, demarcate, limit, mark, terminate — more at LIMIT

de·lin·eate \di-ˈli-nē-ˌāt\ *vb* **-eat·ed; -eat·ing** **1** ♦ : to mark the outline of : SKETCH **2** ♦ : to picture in words : DESCRIBE

♦ [1] define, outline, silhouette, sketch, trace — more at OUTLINE ♦ [2] depict, describe, draw, image, paint, picture, portray, sketch — more at DESCRIBE

de·lin·ea·tion \di-ˌli-nē-ˈā-shən\ *n* **1** : the act of delineating **2** ♦ : something made by delineating

♦ cartoon, drawing, sketch — more at DRAWING ♦ depiction, description, picture, portrait, portrayal, sketch — more at DESCRIPTION

de·lin·quen·cy \di-ˈliŋ-kwən-sē\ *n, pl* **-cies** ♦ : the quality or state of being delinquent

♦ default, dereliction, failure, neglect, negligence, oversight — more at FAILURE

¹de·lin·quent \-kwənt\ *n* : a delinquent person

²delinquent *adj* **1** : offending by neglect or violation of duty or of law **2** ♦ : being overdue in payment

♦ behind, belated, late, overdue, tardy — more at LATE

del·i·quesce \ˌde-li-ˈkwes\ *vb* **-quesced; -quesc·ing** ♦ : to dissolve or melt away — **del·i·ques·cent** \-ˈkwes-ᵊnt\ *adj*

♦ flux, fuse, liquefy, melt, run, thaw — more at LIQUEFY

de·lir·i·ous \-ē-əs\ *adj* **1** : of, relating to, or characteristic of delirium **2** ♦ : affected with or marked by delirium — **de·lir·i·ous·ly** *adv*

♦ feverish, fierce, frantic, frenetic, frenzied, furious, mad, rabid, violent, wild — more at FURIOUS

de·lir·i·um \di-ˈlir-ē-əm\ *n* [L, fr. *delirare* to be crazy, lit., to leave the furrow (in plowing), fr. *de-* from + *lira* furrow] **1** : mental disturbance marked by confusion, disordered speech, and hallucinations **2** ♦ : frenzied excitement

♦ agitation, distraction, frenzy, furor, fury, hysteria, rage, rampage, uproar — more at FRENZY

delirium tre·mens \-ˈtrē-mənz, -ˈtre-\ *n* : a violent delirium with tremors that is induced by excessive and prolonged use of alcoholic liquors

de·liv·er \di-ˈli-vər\ *vb* **-ered; -er·ing** **1** ♦ : to set free : rescue from actual or feared evil : SAVE **2** ♦ : to take and hand over to or leave for another : TRANSFER ⟨∼ a letter⟩ **3** : to assist in giving birth or at the birth of; *also* : to give birth to **4** : UTTER, COMMUNICATE **5** : to send to an intended target or destination **6** ♦ : to produce the promised, desired, or expected results — **de·liv·er·able** \-ˈli-v(ə-)rə-bəl\ *adj*

♦ [1] rescue, save — more at SAVE ♦ [2] commend, commit, consign, entrust, give, hand over, leave, pass, transfer, transmit, trust, turn over, vest — more at GIVE ♦ [6] click, go over, pan out, succeed, work out — more at SUCCEED

de·liv·er·ance \di-ˈli-v(ə-)rən(t)s\ *n* **1** : the act of delivering someone or something : the state of being delivered **2** : something delivered; *esp* : an opinion or decision (as the verdict of a jury) expressed publicly

♦ rescue, salvation — more at SALVATION

de·liv·er·er \-ər\ *n* ♦ : one that delivers

♦ redeemer, rescuer, savior — more at SAVIOR

de·liv·ery \di-ˈli-və-rē\ *n, pl* **-er·ies** ♦ : the act or manner of delivering something; *also* : something delivered — **de·liv·ery·man** \-ˌman\ *n*

♦ discharge, quietus, quittance, release — more at RELEASE ♦ childbirth, labor (*or* labour) — more at CHILDBIRTH

dell \ˈdel\ *n* : a small secluded valley

de·louse \dē-ˈlaůs\ *vb* : to remove lice from

del·phin·i·um \del-ˈfi-nē-əm\ *n* : any of a genus of mostly perennial herbs related to the buttercups with tall branching spikes of irregular flowers

del·ta \ˈdel-tə\ *n* **1** : the 4th letter of the Greek alphabet — Δ or δ **2** : something shaped like a capital Δ; *esp* : the triangular silt-formed land at the mouth of a river — **del·ta·ic** \del-ˈtā-ik\ *adj*

del·toid \ˈdel-ˌtȯid\ *n* : a large triangular muscle that covers the shoulder joint and raises the arm laterally

de·lude \di-ˈlüd\ *vb* **de·lud·ed; de·lud·ing** ♦ : to mislead the mind or judgment of : DECEIVE

♦ beguile, bluff, cozen, deceive, dupe, fool, gull, have, hoax, hoodwink, humbug, misinform, mislead, string along, take in, trick — more at DECEIVE

¹del·uge \ˈdel-yüj\ *n* **1** ♦ : a flooding of land by water **2** ♦ : a drenching rain **3** : a great amount or number

♦ [1] cataclysm, cataract, flood, inundation, overflow, spate, torrent — more at FLOOD ♦ [2] cloudburst, downpour, rain, rainstorm, storm, wet — more at RAIN

²deluge *vb* **del·uged; del·ug·ing** **1** ♦ : to overflow with water : INUNDATE **2** : to overwhelm as if with a deluge

♦ drown, engulf, flood, inundate, overflow, overwhelm, submerge, swamp — more at FLOOD

de·lu·sion \di-ˈlü-zhən\ *n* ♦ : a deluding or being deluded; *esp* : a persistent false psychotic belief — **de·lu·sion·al** \-ˈlü-zhə-nəl\ *adj*

♦ chimera, conceit, daydream, dream, fancy, fantasy, figment, hallucination, illusion, phantasm, pipe dream, unreality, vision

de·lu·sive \di-ˈlü-siv\ *adj* **1** ♦ : likely to delude **2** : constituting a delusion

♦ deceitful, deceptive, fallacious, false, misleading, specious — more at DECEPTIVE

de·luxe \di-ˈlůks, -ˈləks, -ˈlüks\ *adj* ♦ : notably luxurious or elegant

♦ lavish, luxuriant, luxurious, opulent, palatial, plush, sumptuous — more at LUXURIOUS

delve \ˈdelv\ *vb* **delved; delv·ing** **1** : to dig or labor with or as if with a spade **2** ♦ : to seek laboriously for information

♦ *usu* **delve into** dig, explore, go, inquire into, investigate, look, probe, research — more at EXPLORE

dely *abbr* delivery

Dem *abbr* Democrat; Democratic

de·mag·ne·tize \dē-'mag-nə-ˌtīz\ *vb* : to cause to lose magnetic properties — **de·mag·ne·ti·za·tion** \dē-ˌmag-nə-tə-'zā-shən\ *n*

dem·a·gogue *also* **dem·a·gog** \'de-mə-ˌgäg\ *n* [Gk *dēmagōgos*, fr. *dēmos* people + *agōgos* leading, fr. *agein* to lead] ♦ : a person who appeals to the emotions and prejudices of people esp. in order to gain political power — **dem·a·gogu·ery** \-ˌgä-gə-rē\ *n* — **dem·a·gogy** \-ˌgä-gē, -ˌgä-jē\ *n*

♦ agitator, firebrand, incendiary, inciter, rabble-rouser — more at AGITATOR

¹de·mand \di-'mand\ *n* **1** ♦ : an act of demanding; *also* : something claimed as due or just **2** : the ability and desire to buy goods or services; *also* : the quantity of goods wanted at a stated price **3** : a seeking or being sought after : urgent need **4** ♦ : a pressing need or requirement

♦ [1] claim, dun, requisition; *also* desire, request, want, wish; drive, need, requirement, stipulation; basic, essential, must; imposition; condition, provision ♦ [4] condition, essential, must, necessity, need, requirement, requisite — more at ESSENTIAL

²demand *vb* **1** ♦ : to ask for with authority : claim as due or just **2** : to ask earnestly or in the manner of a command **3** ♦ : to call for as useful or necessary : REQUIRE ⟨a patient who ∼s constant care⟩

♦ [1] call, claim, clamor (*or* clamour), command, enjoin, exact, insist, press, quest, stipulate (for); *also* ask, plead (for), request, want; cry (for), necessitate, need, require, take, warrant; requisition; impose; badger, dun, hound ♦ [3] necessitate, need, require, take, want, warrant — more at NEED

de·mand·ing *adj* **1** ♦ : requiring much time, effort, or attention **2** ♦ : difficult in making demands

♦ [1] arduous, burdensome, challenging, exacting, grueling, laborious, onerous, taxing, toilsome; *also* difficult, formidable, hard, herculean, rough, rugged, stiff, strenuous, tough; oppressive, trying; rigid, rigorous, severe, stern, strict, stringent *Ant* light, undemanding ♦ [2] choosy, dainty, delicate, exacting, fastidious, finicky, fussy, nice, old-maidish, particular, picky — more at FINICKY

de·mar·cate \di-'mär-ˌkāt, 'dē-ˌmär-\ *vb* **-cat·ed; -cat·ing** **1** ♦ : to fix or define the limits of : DELIMIT **2** : to set apart : DISTINGUISH

♦ bound, circumscribe, define, delimit, limit, mark, terminate — more at LIMIT

de·mar·ca·tion \ˌdē-ˌmär-'kā-shən\ *n* ♦ : the act or process of demarcating; *also* : the result of demarcating

♦ discrimination, distinction, separation — more at SEPARATION

dé·marche *or* **de·marche** \dā-'märsh\ *n* : a course of action : MANEUVER

¹de·mean \di-'mēn\ *vb* **de·meaned; de·mean·ing** ♦ : to behave or conduct (oneself) usu. in a proper manner

♦ acquit, bear, behave, comport, conduct, deport, quit — more at BEHAVE

²demean *vb* **de·meaned; de·mean·ing** ♦ : to lower in character, status, or reputation : DEGRADE

♦ debase, degrade, demoralize, humble, subvert, warp — more at DEBASE

de·mean·or *or Can and Brit* **de·mean·our** \di-'mē-nər\ *n* ♦ : behavior toward others : BEARING

♦ actions, bearing, behavior (*or* behaviour), comportment, conduct, deportment — more at BEHAVIOR

de·ment·ed \di-'men-təd\ *adj* : disordered in mind : INSANE — **de·ment·ed·ly** *adv*

de·men·tia \di-'men-chə\ *n* **1** : deterioration of cognitive functioning (as in Alzheimer's disease) **2** ♦ : a deranged state of the mind : INSANITY

♦ aberration, derangement, insanity, lunacy, madness, mania — more at INSANITY

de·mer·it \di-'mer-ət\ *n* **1** ♦ : a quality that deserves blame or lacks merit : FAULT **2** : a mark placed against a person's record for some fault or offense

♦ failing, fault, foible, frailty, shortcoming, vice, weakness — more at FAULT

de·mesne \di-'mān, -'mēn\ *n* **1** : manorial land actually possessed by the lord and not held by free tenants **2 a** ♦ : the land attached to a mansion **b** : ESTATE **3** ♦ : an indeterminate geographic area : REGION **4** : a sphere of knowledge, influence, or activity : REALM

♦ [2a] grounds, park, premises, yard ♦ [3] area, field, region, zone — more at REGION

demi·god \'de-mi-ˌgäd\ *n* : a mythological being with more power than a mortal but less than a god

demi·john \'de-mi-ˌjän\ *n* [F *dame-jeanne*, lit., Lady Jane] : a large narrow-necked bottle usu. enclosed in wickerwork

de·mil·i·ta·rize \dē-'mi-lə-tə-ˌrīz\ *vb* : to strip of military forces, weapons, or fortifications — **de·mil·i·tar·i·za·tion** \dē-ˌmi-lə-tə-rə-'zā-shən\ *n*

demi·mon·daine \ˌde-mi-ˌmän-'dān\ *n* : a woman of the demimonde

demi·monde \'de-mi-ˌmänd\ *n* [F *demi-monde*, fr. *demi-* half + *monde* world] **1** : a class of women on the fringes of respectable society supported by wealthy lovers **2** : a distinct isolated group having low reputation or prestige

de·min·er·al·ize \dē-'mi-nə-rə-ˌlīz\ *vb* : to remove the mineral matter from — **de·min·er·al·i·za·tion** \-ˌmi-nə-rə-lə-'zā-shən\ *n*

de·mise \di-'mīz\ *n* **1** : LEASE **2** : transfer of sovereignty to a successor ⟨∼ of the crown⟩ **3 a** ♦ : a permanent cessation of all vital functions : DEATH **b** ♦ : a cessation of existence or activity **4** : loss of status

♦ [3a] death, expiration, termination — more at DEATH ♦ [3b] death, decease, doom, end, passing, quietus — more at DEATH

demi·tasse \'de-mi-ˌtas\ *n* : a small cup of black coffee; *also* : the cup used to serve it

demo \'de-mō\ *n, pl* **dem·os** **1** : DEMONSTRATION **2** : a product used to show performance or merits to prospective buyers **3** : a recording used to show off a song or performer

de·mo·bi·lize \di-'mō-bə-ˌlīz, dē-\ *vb* **1** : DISBAND **2** : to discharge from military service — **de·mo·bi·li·za·tion** \di-ˌmō-bə-lə-'zā-shən, dē-\ *n*

de·moc·ra·cy \di-'mä-krə-sē\ *n, pl* **-cies** [MF *democratie*, fr. LL *democratia*, fr. Gk *dēmokratia*, fr. *dēmos* people + *kratos* strength, power] **1** : government by the people; *esp* : rule of the majority **2** : a government in which the supreme power is held by the people **3** : a political unit that has a democratic government **4** *cap* : the principles and policies of the Democratic party in the U.S. **5** : the common people esp. when constituting the source of political authority **6** : the absence of hereditary or arbitrary class distinctions or privileges

dem·o·crat \'de-mə-ˌkrat\ *n* **1** : one who believes in or practices democracy **2** *cap* : a member of the Democratic party of the U.S.

dem·o·crat·ic \ˌde-mə-'kra-tik\ *adj* **1** ♦ : of, relating to, or favoring democracy **2** *often cap* : of or relating to one of the two major political parties in the U.S. associated in modern times with policies of broad social reform and internationalism **3** : relating to or appealing to the common people ⟨∼ art⟩ **4** : not snobbish — **dem·o·crat·i·cal·ly** \-ti-k(ə-)lē\ *adv*

♦ popular, republican, self-governing; *also* representative, libertarian *Ant* undemocratic

de·moc·ra·tize \di-'mä-krə-ˌtīz\ *vb* **-tized; -tiz·ing** : to make democratic

dé·mo·dé \ˌdā-mō-'dā\ *adj* [F] : no longer fashionable : OUT-OF-DATE

de·mo·graph·ics \ˌde-mə-'gra-fiks, ˌdē-\ *n pl* : the statistical characteristics of human populations

de·mog·ra·phy \di-'mä-grə-fē\ *n* : the statistical study of human populations and esp. their size and distribution and the number of births and deaths — **de·mog·ra·pher** \-fər\ *n* — **de·mo·graph·ic** \ˌde-mə-'gra-fik, ˌdē-\ *adj* — **de·mo·graph·i·cal·ly** \-fi-k(ə-)lē\ *adv*

dem·oi·selle \ˌdem-wə-'zel\ *n* [F] : a young woman

de·mol·ish \di-'mä-lish\ *vb* **1** ♦ : to destroy to the ground : RAZE **2** ♦ : to break to pieces : SMASH **3** ♦ : to put an end to

♦ [1, 3] annihilate, blot out, desolate, destroy, devastate, do in, exterminate, extinguish, obliterate, pulverize, ruin, shatter, smash, tear down, waste, wipe out, wreck — more at DESTROY ♦ [2] blast, blow up, burst, explode, pop, shatter, smash — more at BLAST

de·mo·li·tion \ˌde-mə-'li-shən, ˌdē-\ *n* ♦ : the act of demolishing; *esp* : destruction by means of explosives

♦ annihilation, desolation, destruction, devastation, havoc, loss, obliteration, ruin, wastage, wreckage — more at DESTRUCTION

de·mon *or* **dae·mon** \'dē-mən\ *n* **1** ♦ : an evil spirit : DEVIL **2** *usu* **daemon** : an attendant power or spirit **3** : one that has unusual drive or effectiveness

♦ devil, fiend, ghoul, imp; *also* apparition, bogey, familiar, ghost, phantasm, phantom, poltergeist, shade, shadow, specter, spirit, spook, vision, wraith; brownie, dwarf, elf, faerie, fairy, fay, gnome, goblin, gremlin, hobgoblin, leprechaun, pixie, puck, sprite, troll; monster, ogre

de·mon·e·tize \dē-'mä-nə-ˌtīz, -'mä-\ *vb* : to stop using as money or as a monetary standard ⟨~ silver⟩ — **de·mon·e·ti·za·tion** \dē-ˌmä-nə-tə-'zā-shən, -ˌmə-\ *n*

de·mo·ni·ac \di-'mō-nē-ˌak\ *also* **de·mo·ni·a·cal** \ˌdē-mə-'nī-ə-kəl\ *adj* **1** : possessed or influenced by a demon **2** : of, relating to, or suggestive of a demon : DEVILISH

de·mon·ic \di-'mä-nik\ *also* **de·mon·i·cal** \-ni-kəl\ *adj* ♦ : of, relating to, or suggestive of a demon : FIENDISH

♦ devilish, diabolical, fiendish, satanic — more at FIENDISH

de·mon·ize \'dē-mə-ˌnīz\ *vb* **-ized; -iz·ing 1** : to convert into a demon **2** : to characterize or treat as evil or harmful

de·mon·ol·o·gy \ˌdē-mə-'nä-lə-jē\ *n* **1** : the study of demons **2** : belief in demons

de·mon·stra·ble \di-'män-strə-bəl\ *adj* **1** ♦ : capable of being demonstrated **2** : APPARENT, EVIDENT — **de·mon·stra·bly** \-blē\ *adv*

♦ provable, supportable, sustainable, verifiable — more at VERIFIABLE

dem·on·strate \'de-mən-ˌstrāt\ *vb* **-strat·ed; -strat·ing 1** ♦ : to show clearly **2** ♦ : to prove or make clear by reasoning or evidence **3** ♦ : to explain esp. with many examples **4** : to show publicly ⟨~ a new car⟩ **5** : to make a public display ⟨~ in protest⟩ — **dem·on·stra·tor** \'de-mən-ˌstrā-tər\ *n*

♦ [1] establish, prove, show, substantiate — more at ESTABLISH ♦ [2] document, establish, prove, substantiate, validate — more at PROVE ♦ [3] clarify, clear (up), construe, elucidate, explain, explicate, expound, illuminate, illustrate, interpret, spell out — more at EXPLAIN

dem·on·stra·tion \ˌde-mən-'strā-shən\ *n* **1** : an act, process, or means of demonstrating to the intelligence **2** ♦ : an outward expression or display

♦ display, exhibition, show — more at SHOW

¹de·mon·stra·tive \di-'män-strə-tiv\ *adj* **1** : demonstrating as real or true **2** : characterized by demonstration **3** : pointing out the one referred to and distinguishing it

from others of the same class ⟨~ pronoun⟩ **4** ♦ : marked by display of feeling : EFFUSIVE — **de·mon·stra·tive·ly** *adv* — **de·mon·stra·tive·ness** *n*

♦ effusive, emotional, uninhibited, unreserved, unrestrained; *also* dramatic, histrionic, melodramatic, theatrical; communicative, expansive; extroverted, outgoing; affectionate, loving, passionate, warm; blunt, candid, frank, outspoken, plain *Ant* inhibited, reserved, restrained, undemonstrative, unemotional

²demonstrative *n* : a demonstrative word and esp. a pronoun

de·mor·al·i·za·tion \di-ˌmȯr-ə-lə-'zā-shən\ *n* ♦ : the act or process of demoralizing : a demoralized state

♦ corruption, debasement, debauchery, decadence, degeneracy, degeneration, degradation, depravity, dissipation, dissoluteness, perversion — more at CORRUPTION ♦ despair, despondency, discouragement, dismay — more at DISCOURAGEMENT

de·mor·al·ize \di-'mȯr-ə-ˌlīz\ *vb* **1** ♦ : to corrupt in morals **2** ♦ : to weaken in discipline or spirit

♦ [1] debase, degrade, demean, humble, subvert, warp — more at DEBASE ♦ [2] daunt, discourage, dishearten, dismay, dispirit, unman, unnerve — more at DISCOURAGE

de·mote \di-'mōt\ *vb* **de·mot·ed; de·mot·ing** ♦ : to reduce to a lower grade or rank — **de·mo·tion** \-'mō-shən\ *n*

♦ break, bust, degrade, downgrade, reduce; *also* dismiss, fire, lay off, sack; abase, debase, demean, humble, humiliate, lower *Ant* advance, elevate, promote, raise

de·mot·ic \di-'mä-tik\ *adj* : COMMON, POPULAR

¹de·mur \di-'mər\ *vb* **de·murred; de·mur·ring** [ME *demuren, demeren* to linger, fr. AF *demurer, demoerer,* fr. L *demorari,* fr. *morari* to linger, fr. *mora* delay] ♦ : to take exception : OBJECT

♦ kick, object, protest, remonstrate — more at OBJECT

²demur *n* **1** : hesitation (as in doing or accepting) usu. based on doubt of the acceptability of something offered or proposed **2** ♦ : the act or an instance of objecting — **de·mur·ral** \-əl\ *n*

♦ challenge, complaint, expostulation, fuss, kick, objection, protest, question, remonstrance — more at OBJECTION

de·mure \di-'myu̇r\ *adj* **1** ♦ : quietly modest **2** ♦ : affectedly modest, reserved, or serious — **de·mure·ly** *adv*

♦ [1] humble, lowly, meek, modest, retiring, shy, unassuming, unpretentious — more at HUMBLE ♦ [2] coquettish, coy, kittenish — more at COY

de·mur·rer \di-'mər-ər\ *n* : a claim by the defendant in a legal action that the plaintiff does not have sufficient grounds to proceed

den \'den\ *n* **1** ♦ : the lair of a wild usu. predatory animal **2** ♦ : a refuge or place for hiding : HIDEOUT ⟨a robber's ~⟩; *also* : a place like a hideout or a center of secret activity ⟨opium ~⟩ ⟨a ~ of iniquity⟩ **3** : a cozy private little room

♦ [1] burrow, hole, lair, lodge; *also* nest ♦ [2] concealment, covert, hideout, lair, nest — more at HIDEOUT

Den *abbr* Denmark

de·na·ture \dē-'nā-chər\ *vb* **de·na·tured; de·na·tur·ing** : to remove or change the natural qualities of; *esp* : to make (alcohol) unfit for drinking

den·drol·o·gy \den-'drä-lə-jē\ *n* : the study of trees — **den·drol·o·gist** \-jist\ *n*

den·gue \'deŋ-gē, -ˌgā\ *n* [Sp] : an acute infectious disease characterized by headache, severe joint pain, and rash

de·ni·al \di-'nī-əl\ *n* **1** ♦ : rejection of a request **2** ♦ : refusal to admit the truth of a statement or charge; *also* : assertion that something alleged is false **3** : DISAVOWAL **4** : restriction on one's own activity or desires

♦ [1] disallowance, nay, no, refusal, rejection; *also* decline, rebuff, repudiation; negative *Ant* allowance, grant ♦ [2] contradiction, disallowance, disavowal, disclaimer, negation, rejection, repudiation; *also* disproof, rebuttal, refutation; negative *Ant* acknowledgment, admission, avowal, confirmation

de·nier \'den-yər\ *n* : a unit of fineness for yarn

den·i·grate \'de-ni-ˌgrāt\ *vb* **-grat·ed; -grat·ing** [L *denigrare*, fr. *nigrare* to blacken, fr. *niger* black] : to cast aspersions on : DEFAME — **den·i·gra·tion** \ˌde-ni-'grā-shən\ *n*

den·im \'de-nəm\ *n* [F *(serge) de Nîmes* serge of Nîmes, France] **1** : a firm durable twilled usu. cotton fabric woven with colored warp and white filling threads **2** *pl* : overalls or pants of usu. blue denim

den·i·zen \'de-nə-zən\ *n* ♦ : one that occupies a particular place regularly, routinely, or for a period of time : INHABITANT

♦ dweller, inhabitant, occupant, resident — more at INHABITANT

de·nom·i·nate \di-'nä-mə-ˌnāt\ *vb* ♦ : to assign a name to : DESIGNATE

♦ baptize, call, christen, designate, dub, entitle, label, name, style, term, title — more at NAME

de·nom·i·na·tion \di-ˌnä-mə-'nā-shən\ *n* **1** : an act of denominating **2** : a value or size of a series of related values (as of money) **3** : a word or phrase that constitutes the distinctive designation of a person or thing : NAME; *esp* : a general name for a category **4** : a religious organization uniting local congregations in a single body — **de·nom·i·na·tion·al** \-shə-nəl\ *adj*

de·nom·i·na·tor \di-'nä-mə-ˌnā-tər\ *n* : the part of a fraction that is below the line indicating division

de·no·ta·tion \ˌdē-nō-'tā-shən\ *n* **1** : an act or process of denoting **2** ♦ : the thing one conveys or intends to convey esp. by language; *esp* : a direct specific meaning as distinct from an implied or associated idea **3** ♦ : a denoting term : NAME

♦ [2] drift, import, intent, meaning, purport, sense, significance, signification — more at MEANING ♦ [3] appellation, cognomen, designation, handle, name, title — more at NAME

de·no·ta·tive \'dē-nō-ˌtā-tiv, di-'nō-tə-tiv\ *adj* **1** ♦ : denoting or tending to denote **2** : relating to denotation

♦ indicative, significant, telltale — more at INDICATIVE

de·note \di-'nōt\ *vb* **1** : to mark out plainly : INDICATE **2** : to make known **3** ♦ : to serve as a linguistic expression of the notion of : MEAN

♦ express, import, mean, signify, spell — more at MEAN

de·noue·ment \ˌdā-ˌnü-'mäⁿ\ *n* [F *dénouement*, lit., untying] : the final outcome of the dramatic complications in a literary work

de·nounce \di-'nauns\ *vb* **de·nounced; de·nounc·ing** **1** ♦ : to pronounce esp. publicly to be blameworthy or evil **2** : to inform against : ACCUSE **3** : to announce formally the termination of (as a treaty) — **de·nounce·ment** *n*

♦ censure, condemn, damn, decry, reprehend, reprobate — more at CONDEMN ♦ blame, criticize, fault, knock, pan — more at CRITICIZE

de no·vo \di-'nō-vō\ *adv or adj* [L] : over again : ANEW

dense \'dens\ *adj* **dens·er; dens·est** **1** ♦ : marked by compactness or crowding together of parts : THICK ⟨∼ forest⟩ ⟨a ∼ fog⟩ **2** ♦ : slow to understand : STUPID — **dense·ly** *adv*

♦ [1] close, compact, crowded, packed, serried, thick, tight — more at CLOSE ♦ [2] dull, dumb, obtuse, simple, slow, stupid, thick

dense·ness \-nəs\ *n* ♦ : the quality or state of being dense

♦ dopiness, obtuseness, stupidity

den·si·ty \'den-sə-tē\ *n, pl* **-ties** **1** : the quality or state of being dense **2** : the quantity of something per unit volume, unit area, or unit length

dent \'dent\ *n* **1** ♦ : a small depressed place made by a blow or by pressure **2** : an impression or weakening effect made usu. against resistance **3** : initial progress — **dent** *vb*

♦ cavity, concavity, depression, hole, hollow, indentation, pit, recess — more at HOLE

den·tal \'dent-ᵊl\ *adj* : of or relating to teeth or dentistry — **den·tal·ly** *adv*

dental floss *n* : a thread used to clean between the teeth

dental hygienist *n* : a person licensed to clean and examine teeth

den·tate \'den-ˌtāt\ *adj* : having pointed projections : NOTCHED

den·ti·frice \'den-tə-frəs\ *n* [ME *dentifricie*, fr. L *dentifricium*, fr. *dent-, dens* tooth + *fricare* to rub] : a powder, paste, or liquid for cleaning the teeth

den·tin \'dent-ᵊn\ *or* **den·tine** \'den-ˌtēn, den-'tēn\ *n* : a calcareous material like bone but harder and denser that composes the principal mass of a tooth

den·tist \'den-tist\ *n* : a person licensed in the care, treatment, and replacement of teeth — **den·tist·ry** *n*

den·ti·tion \den-'ti-shən\ *n* : the number, kind, and arrangement of teeth (as of a person or animal); *also* : TEETH

den·ture \'den-chər\ *n* : a set of teeth; *esp* : a partial or complete set of false teeth

de·nude \di-'nüd, -'nyüd\ *vb* **de·nud·ed; de·nud·ing** : to strip the covering from — **de·nu·da·tion** \ˌdē-nü-'dā-shən, -nyü-\ *n*

de·nun·ci·a·tion \di-ˌnən-sē-'ā-shən\ *n* ♦ : the act of denouncing; *esp* : a public condemnation

♦ censure, rebuke, reprimand, reproach, reproof, stricture — more at CENSURE

de·ny \di-'nī\ *vb* **de·nied; de·ny·ing** **1** ♦ : to declare untrue **2** ♦ : to refuse to recognize or acknowledge : DISAVOW **3** ♦ : to refuse to grant ⟨∼ a request⟩ **4** : to reject as false ⟨∼ a theory⟩

♦ [1] contradict, disallow, disavow, disclaim, gainsay, negate, negative, reject, repudiate; *also* disown, renounce; challenge, confute, disprove, rebut, refute; disagree (with), dispute *Ant* acknowledge, admit, allow, avow, concede, confirm, own ♦ [3] decline, disallow, refuse, reject, withhold; *also* rebuff, repel, spurn; check, constrain, hold, keep, restrain, restrict *Ant* allow, concede, grant, let, permit

de·o·dar \'dē-ə-ˌdär\ *n* [Hindi & Urdu *devadār, deodār*, fr. Skt *devadāru*, fr. *deva* god + *dāru* wood] : a Himalayan cedar

de·odor·ant \dē-'ō-də-rənt\ *n* : a preparation that destroys or masks unpleasant odors

de·odor·ize \dē-'ō-də-ˌrīz\ *vb* : to eliminate the offensive odor of

de·ox·i·dize \dē-'äk-sə-ˌdīz\ *vb* : to remove oxygen from

de·oxy·ri·bo·nu·cle·ic acid \dē-'äk-si-ˌrī-bō-nü-ˌklē-ik-, -nyü-\ *n* : DNA

de·oxy·ri·bose \dē-ˌäk-si-'rī-ˌbōs\ *n* : a sugar with five carbon and four oxygen atoms in each molecule that is part of DNA

dep *abbr* **1** depart; departure **2** deposit **3** deputy

de·part \di-'pärt\ *vb* **1** ♦ : to go away : go away from **2** : to cease living : DIE **3** : to turn aside : DEVIATE

♦ clear out, exit, get off, go, move, pull, quit, sally, shove, take off — more at GO

de·part·ment \di-'pärt-mənt\ *n* **1** ♦ : a distinct sphere or category esp. of an activity or attribute **2** ♦ : a functional or territorial division (as of a government, business, or college) — **de·part·men·tal** \di-ˌpärt-'ment-ᵊl, ˌdē-\ *adj* — **de·part·men·tal·ly** *adv*

♦ [1] area, arena, demesne, discipline, domain, field, line, province, realm, specialty, sphere — more at FIELD ♦ [2] bureau, desk, division, office — more at DIVISION

department store *n* : a store having separate sections for a wide variety of goods

de·par·ture \di-'pär-chər\ *n* **1** ♦ : the act of going away **2** : a starting out (as on a journey) **3** : DIVERGENCE

♦ exit, farewell, leave-taking, parting; *also* flight, retirement, retreat, running away, withdrawal; emigration, evacuation, exodus; egress; abandonment, forsaking, relinquishment *Ant* arrival

de·pend \di-'pend\ *vb* **1 ♦** : to be determined, based, or contingent ⟨life ∼s on food⟩ **2 ♦** : to place reliance or trust ⟨you can ∼ on me⟩ **3** : to be dependent esp. for financial support **4** : to hang down ⟨a vine ∼*ing* from a tree⟩

♦ [1] base, hang, rest; *also* establish, found, stay; ground ♦ [2] count, lean, reckon, rely; *also* commit, confide, entrust, trust

de·pend·abil·i·ty \di-ˌpen-də-'bi-lə-tē\ *n* ♦ : the quality or state of being dependable

♦ reliability, solidity, sureness, trustworthiness — more at RELIABILITY

de·pend·able \di-'pen-də-bəl\ *adj* ♦ : capable of being depended on : RELIABLE

♦ good, reliable, responsible, safe, solid, steady, sure, tried, true, trustworthy; *also* constant, devoted, faithful, fast, loyal, staunch, steadfast; honest, sincere; infallible, unerring; firm, sound, strong; effective, telling; attested, authenticated, confirmed, proven, valid, validated, verified; blameless, irreproachable, unimpeachable, unquestionable *Ant* irresponsible, undependable, unreliable, untrustworthy

de·pen·dence *also* **de·pen·dance** \di-'pen-dəns\ *n* **1** : the quality or state of being dependent; *esp* : the quality or state of being influenced by or subject to another **2** : RELIANCE, TRUST **3 ♦** : something on which one relies **4** : drug addiction; *also* : HABITUATION 2

♦ buttress, mainstay, pillar, reliance, standby, support; *also* backbone, spine; crutch, prop, stay

de·pen·den·cy \-dən-sē\ *n, pl* **-cies** **1** : DEPENDENCE **2** : a territory under the jurisdiction of a nation but not formally annexed by it

¹de·pen·dent \-dənt\ *adj* **1 ♦** : hanging down **2 a ♦** : determined or conditioned by another **b** : affected with drug dependence **3** : relying on another for support **4** : subject to another's jurisdiction **5** : SUBORDINATE 4

♦ [1] pendulous ♦ [2a] conditional, contingent, subject; *also* liable, open, susceptible; iffy, tentative, uncertain *Ant* independent

²dependent *also* **de·pen·dant** \-dənt\ *n* : one that is dependent; *esp* : a person who relies on another for support

de·pict \di-'pikt\ *vb* **1 ♦** : to represent by a picture **2 ♦** : to describe in words

♦ [1] image, picture, portray, represent — more at PICTURE ♦ [2] delineate, describe, draw, image, paint, picture, portray, sketch — more at DESCRIBE

de·pic·tion \di-'pik-shən\ *n* ♦ : a descriptive statement

♦ delineation, description, picture, portrait, portrayal, sketch — more at DESCRIPTION

de·pil·a·to·ry \di-'pi-lə-ˌtōr-ē\ *n, pl* **-ries** : a preparation for removing hair, wool, or bristles

de·plane \dē-'plān\ *vb* : to get out of an airplane

de·plete \di-'plēt\ *vb* **de·plet·ed; de·plet·ing** ♦ : to exhaust esp. of strength or resources — **de·ple·tion** \-'plē-shən\ *n*

♦ clean, consume, drain, exhaust, expend, spend, use up; *also* decrease, diminish, lessen, reduce; eat, use; bankrupt, impoverish; cripple, debilitate, disable, enfeeble, sap, undermine, weaken; dry up, empty; dissipate, squander, waste *Ant* renew, replace

de·plor·able \di-'plōr-ə-bəl\ *adj* **1 ♦** : that is to be regretted or lamented : LAMENTABLE **2** : deserving censure or contempt : WRETCHED — **de·plor·ably** *adv*

♦ distressful, grievous, heartbreaking, lamentable, regrettable, unfortunate, woeful — more at REGRETTABLE

de·plore \-'plōr\ *vb* **de·plored; de·plor·ing** **1 ♦** : to feel or express grief for **2 ♦** : to regret strongly **3** : to consider unfortunate or deserving of disapproval

♦ [1] bemoan, bewail, grieve, lament, mourn, wail — more at LAMENT ♦ [2] bemoan, lament, regret, repent, rue — more at REGRET

de·ploy \di-'plȯi\ *vb* : to spread out (as troops or ships) in order for battle — **de·ploy·ment** \-mənt\ *n*

de·po·nent \di-'pō-nənt\ *n* : one who gives evidence

de·pop·u·late \dē-'pä-pyə-ˌlāt\ *vb* : to reduce greatly the population of — **de·pop·u·la·tion** \-ˌpä-pyə-'lā-shən\ *n*

de·port \di-'pōrt\ *vb* **1 ♦** : to behave or comport (oneself) esp. in accord with a code : CONDUCT **2 ♦** : to send out of the country : BANISH

♦ [1] acquit, bear, behave, comport, conduct, demean, quit — more at BEHAVE ♦ [2] banish, displace, exile, expatriate, transport — more at BANISH

de·por·ta·tion \ˌdē-ˌpōr-'tā-shən\ *n* ♦ : an act or instance of deporting

♦ banishment, displacement, exile, expulsion — more at EXILE

de·port·ment \di-'pōrt-mənt\ *n* ♦ : the manner in which one conducts oneself : BEHAVIOR

♦ actions, bearing, behavior (*or* behaviour), comportment, conduct, demeanor (*or* demeanour) — more at BEHAVIOR

de·pose \di-'pōz\ *vb* **de·posed; de·pos·ing** **1 ♦** : to remove from high office (as of king) **2 ♦** : to testify under oath or by affidavit

♦ [1] oust; *also* discharge, dismiss; overthrow, subvert, topple, usurp; eject, throw out *Ant* crown, enthrone, throne ♦ [2] attest, swear, testify, witness — more at TESTIFY

¹de·pos·it \di-'pä-zət\ *vb* **de·pos·it·ed** \-zə-təd\; **de·pos·it·ing** **1 ♦** : to place for safekeeping or as a pledge; *esp* : to put money in a bank **2 ♦** : to lay down : PLACE **3** : to let fall or sink ⟨silt ∼*ed* by a flood⟩ — **de·pos·i·tor** \-zə-tər\ *n*

♦ [1] bank, cache, lay away, store; *also* hoard, reserve, salt away, save, squirrel (away), stash, stow; invest *Ant* withdraw ♦ [2] dispose, fix, lay, place, position, put, set, set up, stick — more at PLACE

²deposit *n* **1** : the state of being deposited ⟨money on ∼⟩ **2 ♦** : something placed for safekeeping; *esp* : money deposited in a bank **3** : money given as a pledge **4** : an act of depositing **5 ♦** : something laid down ⟨a ∼ of silt⟩ **6** : a natural accumulation (as of a mineral)

♦ [2] cache, hoard, reserve, store — more at STORE ♦ [2] account, budget, fund, kitty, nest egg, pool — more at FUND ♦ [5] dregs, grounds, lees, precipitate, sediment; *also* dross, slag, waste

de·po·si·tion \ˌde-pə-'zi-shən, ˌdē-\ *n* **1** : an act of removing from a position of authority **2** : TESTIMONY **3** : the process of depositing **4** : something deposited : DEPOSIT

de·pos·i·to·ry \di-'pä-zə-ˌtōr-ē\ *n, pl* **-ries** ♦ : a place where something is deposited esp. for safekeeping

♦ repository, storage, storehouse, warehouse — more at STOREHOUSE

de·pot *1, 2 usu* 'de-pō, *3 usu* 'dē-\ *n* **1** : a place for storing goods or motor vehicles : STOREHOUSE **2 ♦** : a place where military supplies or replacements are kept or assembled **3** : a building for railroad or bus passengers

♦ armory, arsenal, dump, magazine — more at ARMORY

depr *abbr* depreciation

de·prave \di-'prāv\ *vb* **de·praved; de·prav·ing** [ME, fr. MF *depraver*, fr. L *depravare* to pervert, fr. *pravus* crooked, bad] ♦ : to make bad : CORRUPT

♦ debase, degrade, demean, demoralize, humble, subvert, warp — more at DEBASE

de·praved *adj* : marked by corruption or evil

de·prav·i·ty \di-'pra-və-tē\ *n* **1 ♦** : a corrupt act or practice **2 ♦** : the quality or state of being depraved

♦ [1] corruption, debasement, debauchery, decadence, degeneracy, degeneration, degradation, demoralization, dissipation, dissoluteness, perversion — more at CORRUPTION ♦ [1] immorality, iniquity, licentiousness, sin, vice — more at VICE ♦ [2] atrociousness, atrocity, enormity, heinousness, monstrosity, vileness, wickedness — more at ENORMITY

dep·re·cate \'de-pri-ˌkāt\ *vb* **-cat·ed; -cat·ing** [L *deprecari* to avert by prayer, fr. *precari* to pray] **1** ♦ : to express disapproval of **2** ♦ : to speak slightingly of : BELITTLE

♦ [1] disapprove, discountenance, disfavor (*or* disfavour), dislike, frown, reprove ♦ [2] belittle, cry down, decry, depreciate, diminish, discount, disparage, minimize, put down, write off — more at DECRY

dep·re·ca·tion \ˌde-pri-'kā-shən\ *n* ♦ : an act of deprecating

♦ disapproval, disfavor (*or* disfavour), dislike, displeasure — more at DISAPPROVAL

dep·re·ca·to·ry \'de-pri-kə-ˌtōr-ē\ *adj* **1** : APOLOGETIC **2** : serving to deprecate : DISAPPROVING

de·pre·ci·ate \di-'prē-shē-ˌāt\ *vb* **-at·ed; -at·ing** [ME, fr. LL *depreciatus*, pp. of *depretiare*, fr. L *pretium* price] **1** : to speak slightingly of : DISPARAGE **2** ♦ : to lessen in price or value

♦ cheapen, depress, mark down, write off; *also* underrate, undervalue; abate, abridge, compress, contract, de-escalate, deflate, diminish, dwindle, lessen, lower, moderate, reduce, shrink *Ant* appreciate, mark up

de·pre·ci·a·tion \di-ˌprē-shē-'ā-shən\ *n* ♦ : the act of reducing in value or esteem

♦ deprecation, detraction, disparagement, put-down; *also* aspersion, backbiting, defamation, libel, slander, vilification; derision, mockery, ridicule; abuse, invective, vituperation; censure, denunciation *Ant* aggrandizement, ennoblement, exaltation, glorification, magnification

dep·re·da·tion \ˌde-prə-'dā-shən\ *n* : a laying waste or plundering — **dep·re·date** \'de-prə-ˌdāt\ *vb*

de·press \di-'pres\ *vb* **1** ♦ : to press down : cause to sink to a lower position **2** : to lessen the activity or force of **3** ♦ : to make sad : SADDEN **4** ♦ : to lessen in price or value — **de·pres·sor** \-'pre-sər\ *n*

♦ [1] bear, press, shove, weigh — more at PRESS ♦ [3] burden, oppress, sadden; *also* ail, distress, trouble; afflict, torment, torture; discourage, dishearten, dispirit; bother, disturb, disquiet, perturb, upset *Ant* brighten, buoy, cheer, gladden ♦ [4] cheapen, depreciate, mark down, write off — more at DEPRECIATE

de·pres·sant \di-'pres-ᵊnt\ *n* : one that depresses; *esp* : a chemical substance (as a drug) that reduces bodily functional activity — **depressant** *adj*

de·pressed *adj* **1** ♦ : low in spirits; *also* : affected with psychological depression **2** ♦ : having the central part lower than the margin **3** : suffering from economic depression

♦ [1] bad, blue, down, gloomy, glum, low, melancholy, miserable, mournful, sad, sorrowful, sorry, unhappy ♦ [2] concave, hollow, sunken — more at HOLLOW

de·press·ing *adj* ♦ : that depresses; *esp* : causing emotional depression

♦ bleak, dark, dismal, dreary, gloomy, gray (*or* grey), somber (*or* sombre), wretched — more at GLOOMY

de·pres·sion \di-'pre-shən\ *n* **1** : an act of depressing : a state of being depressed **2** : a pressing down : LOWERING **3** ♦ : a state of feeling sad **4** ♦ : a psychological disorder marked esp. by sadness, inactivity, difficulty in thinking and concentration, and feelings of dejection **5** ♦ : a depressed area or part **6** : a period of low general economic activity with widespread unemployment

♦ [3] blues, dejection, desolation, despondency, doldrums, dumps, forlornness, gloom, heartsickness, melancholy, sadness — more at SADNESS ♦ [5] cavity, concavity, dent, hole, hollow, indentation, pit, recess — more at HOLE

¹**de·pres·sive** \di-'pre-siv\ *adj* **1** : tending to depress **2** : characterized or affected by psychological depression

²**depressive** *n* : a person affected with or prone to psychological depression

de·pres·sur·ize \(ˌ)dē-'pre-shə-ˌrīz\ *vb* : to release pressure from

dep·ri·va·tion \ˌde-prə-'vā-shən\ *n* **1** : an act or instance of depriving : LOSS **2** : PRIVATION 2

de·prive \di-'prīv\ *vb* **de·prived; de·priv·ing** **1** : to take something away from **2** : to stop from having something

deprived *adj* : marked by deprivation esp. of the necessities of life

de·pro·gram \(ˌ)dē-'prō-ˌgram, -grəm\ *vb* : to dissuade from convictions usu. of a religious nature often by coercive means

dept *abbr* department

depth \'depth\ *n, pl* **depths** \'depths\ **1** : something that is deep; *esp* : the deep part of a body of water **2** : a part that is far from the outside or surface; *also* : the middle or innermost part **3** : ABYSS **4** ♦ : a profound or intense state ⟨the ∼s of reflection⟩; *also* : the worst part ⟨during the ∼s of the depression⟩ **5** : a reprehensibly low condition **6** : the distance from top to bottom or from front to back **7** : the quality of being deep **8** : the degree of intensity

♦ deep, height, middle, midst, thick — more at THICK

depth charge *n* : an explosive device for use underwater esp. against submarines

dep·u·ta·tion \ˌde-pyə-'tā-shən\ *n* **1** : the act of appointing a deputy **2** : DELEGATION

de·pute \di-'pyüt\ *vb* **de·put·ed; de·put·ing** : to appoint as one's representative : DELEGATE

dep·u·tize \'de-pyə-ˌtīz\ *vb* **-tized; -tiz·ing** ♦ : to appoint or act as deputy

♦ commission, delegate — more at DELEGATE

dep·u·ty \'de-pyə-tē\ *n, pl* **-ties** **1** ♦ : a person appointed to act for or in place of another **2** : a second in command or assistant who usu. takes charge when his or her superior is absent **3** : a member of a lower house of a legislative assembly

♦ agent, attorney, commissary, delegate, envoy, factor, proxy, representative — more at AGENT

der *or* **deriv** *abbr* derivation; derivative

de·rail \di-'rāl\ *vb* : to leave or cause to leave the rails — **de·rail·ment** *n*

de·rail·leur \di-'rā-lər\ *n* [F *dérailleur*] : a device for shifting gears on a bicycle by moving the chain from one set of exposed gears to another

de·range \di-'rānj\ *vb* **de·ranged; de·rang·ing** **1** : to disturb the arrangement or order of : DISARRANGE **2** ♦ : to make insane

♦ craze, madden, unhinge — more at CRAZE

deranged *adj* ♦ : mentally disordered

♦ crazy, insane, lunatic, mad, maniacal, mental, unsound — more at INSANE

de·range·ment \-mənt\ *n* ♦ : the state of being deranged

♦ aberration, dementia, insanity, lunacy, madness, mania — more at INSANITY

der·by \'dər-bē, *Brit* 'där-\ *n, pl* **derbies** **1** : a horse race usu. for three-year-olds held annually **2** : a race or contest open to all **3** : a stiff felt hat with dome-shaped crown and narrow brim

de·re·cho \də-'rā-chō\ *n, pl* **-chos** : a complex of thunderstorms with powerful winds

de·reg·u·la·tion \(ˌ)dē-ˌre-gyü-'lā-shən\ *n* : the act of removing restrictions or regulations — **de·reg·u·late** \-'re-gyü-ˌlāt\ *vb*

¹**der·e·lict** \'der-ə-ˌlikt\ *adj* **1** ♦ : abandoned by the owner or occupant **2** ♦ : failing to exercise the care expected : NEGLIGENT ⟨∼ in his duty⟩

♦ [1] abandoned, deserted, forsaken — more at ABANDONED ♦ [2] careless, lax, negligent, remiss, slack — more at NEGLIGENT

²**derelict** *n* **1** : something voluntarily abandoned; *esp* : a ship abandoned on the high seas **2** : a destitute homeless social misfit : VAGRANT, BUM

der·e·lic·tion \ˌder-ə-'lik-shən\ *n* **1** ♦ : the act of abandoning : the state of being abandoned **2** ♦ : a failure in duty

♦ [1] abandonment, desertion; *also* defection; discard, dumping, jettison *Ant* reclamation ♦ [2] default, delinquency, failure, neglect, negligence, oversight — more at FAILURE

de·ride \di-'rīd\ *vb* **de·rid·ed; de·rid·ing** [L *deridēre*, fr. *ridēre* to laugh] ♦ : to laugh at scornfully : RIDICULE

♦ gibe, jeer, laugh, mock, ridicule, scout — more at RIDICULE

de ri·gueur \də-rē-'gər\ *adj* [F] : prescribed or required by fashion, etiquette, or custom : PROPER

de·ri·sion \də-'ri-zhən\ *n* **1** : RIDICULE **2** : an object of ridicule or scorn

de·ri·sive \də-'rī-siv\ *adj* ♦ : expressing or causing derision — **de·ri·sive·ly** *adv* — **de·ri·sive·ness** *n*

♦ absurd, comical, farcical, laughable, ludicrous, preposterous, ridiculous, risible, silly — more at RIDICULOUS

de·ri·so·ry \də-'rī-sə-rē\ *adj* : worthy of derision

der·i·va·tion \ˌder-ə-'vā-shən\ *n* **1** : the formation of a word from an earlier word or root; *also* : an act of ascertaining or stating the derivation of a word **2** : ETYMOLOGY **3** : SOURCE, ORIGIN; *also* : DESCENT **4** : an act or process of deriving

de·riv·a·tive \di-'ri-və-tiv\ *n* **1** : a word formed by derivation **2** ♦ : something derived — **derivative** *adj*

♦ offshoot, outgrowth, spin-off; *also* descendant; aftermath, consequence, result; aftereffect, side effect; copy, duplicate, facsimile, replica, reproduction *Ant* origin, root, source

de·rive \di-'rīv\ *vb* **de·rived; de·riv·ing** [ME, fr. AF *deriver*, fr. L *derivare*, lit., to draw off (water), fr. *de-* from + *rivus* stream] **1** : to receive or obtain from a source **2** : to obtain from a parent substance **3** ♦ : to come to as a conclusion from facts or premises : INFER, DEDUCE **4** : to trace the derivation of **5** : to come from a certain source

♦ conclude, deduce, extrapolate, gather, infer, judge, reason, understand — more at INFER

der·mal \'dər-məl\ *adj* : of or relating to the skin : CUTANEOUS

der·ma·ti·tis \ˌdər-mə-'tī-təs\ *n, pl* **-ti·tis·es** *or* **-ti·ti·des** \-'ti-tə-ˌdēz\ : inflammation of the skin

der·ma·tol·o·gy \-'tä-lə-jē\ *n* : a branch of medical science dealing with the structure, functions, and diseases of the skin — **der·ma·tol·o·gist** \-jist\ *n*

der·mis \'dər-məs\ *n* : the sensitive vascular inner layer of the skin

der·o·gate \'der-ə-ˌgāt\ *vb* **-gat·ed; -gat·ing** **1** : to cause to seem inferior : DISPARAGE **2** : DETRACT — **der·o·ga·tion** \ˌder-ə-'gā-shən\ *n* — **de·rog·a·tive** \di-'rä-gə-tiv\ *adj*

de·rog·a·to·ry \di-'rä-gə-ˌtōr-ē\ *adj* ♦ : intended to lower the reputation of a person or thing : DISPARAGING — **de·rog·a·to·ri·ly** \-ˌrä-gə-'tōr-ə-lē\ *adv*

♦ contemptuous, degrading, disdainful, scornful, uncomplimentary; *also* defamatory, insulting, libelous, maligning, slandering, slanderous, vilifying; abusive, opprobrious, scurrilous; malevolent, malicious, spiteful *Ant* complimentary

der·rick \'der-ik\ *n* [obs. *derrick* hangman, gallows, fr. *Derick*, name of 17th cent. Eng. hangman] **1** : a hoisting apparatus : CRANE **2** : a framework over a drill hole (as for oil) for supporting machinery

der·ri·ere *or* **der·ri·ère** \ˌder-ē-'er\ *n* : BUTTOCKS

der·ring-do \ˌder-iŋ-'dü\ *n* : DARING

der·rin·ger \'der-ən-jər\ *n* : a short-barreled pocket pistol

der·vish \'dər-vish\ *n* [Turk *derviş*, lit., beggar, fr. Pers *darvīsh*] : a member of a Muslim religious order noted for devotional exercises (as bodily movements leading to a trance)

de·sal·i·nate \dē-'sa-lə-ˌnāt\ *vb* **-nat·ed; -nat·ing** : DESALT — **de·sal·i·na·tion** \-ˌsa-lə-'nā-shən\ *n*

de·sal·i·nize \dē-'sa-lə-ˌnīz\ *vb* **-nized; -niz·ing** : DESALT — **de·sal·i·ni·za·tion** \-ˌsa-lə-nə-'zā-shən\ *n*

de·salt \dē-'sȯlt\ *vb* : to remove salt from ⟨∼ seawater⟩ — **de·salt·er** *n*

des·cant \'des-ˌkant\ *vb* **1** ♦ : to sing or play part music : SING **2** : to discourse or write at length

♦ carol, chant, sing, vocalize — more at SING

de·scend \di-'send\ *vb* **1** ♦ : to pass from a higher to a lower place or level : pass, move, or climb down or down along **2** : DERIVE ⟨∼ed from royalty⟩ **3** : to pass by inheritance or transmission **4** ♦ : to incline, lead, or extend downward **5** ♦ : to swoop down or appear suddenly (as in an attack)

♦ [1, 4] decline, dip, drop, fall, plunge; *also* cant, incline, lean, list, recline, slant, slope, tilt, tip *Ant* ascend, climb, rise ♦ [5] assail, assault, attack, beset, charge, jump, pounce (on *or* upon), raid, rush, storm, strike — more at ATTACK

¹de·scen·dant *also* **de·scen·dent** \di-'sen-dənt\ *adj* **1** : moving or directed downward **2** : proceeding from an ancestor or source

²descendant *also* **descendent** *n* **1** : one descended from another or from a common stock **2** : one deriving directly from a precursor or prototype

de·scent \di-'sent\ *n* **1** ♦ : derivation from an ancestor : LINEAGE **2** ♦ : the act or process of descending **3** : SLOPE **4** : a descending way (as a downgrade) **5** ♦ : a sudden hostile raid or assault **6** ♦ : a downward step (as in station or value) : DECLINE

♦ [1] ancestry, birth, blood, bloodline, breeding, extraction, family tree, genealogy, line, lineage, origin, parentage, pedigree, stock, strain — more at ANCESTRY ♦ [2] dip, dive, down, drop, fall, plunge; *also* comedown, downfall, downgrade; sinking *Ant* ascent, climb, rise, upswing, upturn ♦ [5] aggression, assault, attack, charge, offense (*or* offence), offensive, onset, onslaught, raid, rush, strike — more at ATTACK ♦ [6] comedown, decline, down, downfall, fall — more at COMEDOWN

de·scribe \di-'skrīb\ *vb* **de·scribed; de·scrib·ing** **1 a** ♦ : to represent or give an account of in words **b** ♦ : to communicate an account of salient identifying features of **2** : to trace the outline of — **de·scrib·able** *adj*

♦ delineate, depict, draw, image, narrate, paint, picture, portray, recount, sketch; *also* characterize, qualify, represent; demonstrate, illustrate; narrate, recite, recount, relate; display, exhibit, show; hint, suggest; draft, outline

de·scrip·tion \di-'skrip-shən\ *n* **1** ♦ : an account of something; *esp* : an account that presents a picture to a person who reads or hears it **2** ♦ : kind or character esp. as determined by prominent features : SORT — **de·scrip·tive** \-'skrip-tiv\ *adj*

♦ [1] delineation, depiction, picture, portrait, portrayal, sketch; *also* account, chronicle, narrative, report, story, tale; demonstration, exemplification, illustration ♦ [2] breed, class, feather, ilk, kind, like, manner, nature, order, sort, species, type — more at SORT

de·scry \di-'skrī\ *vb* **de·scried; de·scry·ing** **1** ♦ : to catch sight of **2** : to discover by observation or investigation

♦ behold, discern, distinguish, espy, eye, look, note, notice, observe, perceive, regard, remark, see, sight, spy, view, witness — more at SEE

des·e·crate \'de-si-ˌkrāt\ *vb* **-crat·ed; -crat·ing** ♦ : to violate the sanctity of : PROFANE

♦ defile, profane, violate; *also* blaspheme, curse, swear; befoul, contaminate, foul, pollute; affront, insult, offend; crush, decimate, demolish, destroy, devastate, ravage, raze, ruin, waste, wreck; despoil, loot, pillage, plunder, raid, ransack, rob, sack, spoil, strip

des·e·cra·tion \ˌde-si-'krā-shən\ *n* ♦ : an act or instance of desecrating

♦ blasphemy, defilement, impiety, irreverence, sacrilege — more at BLASPHEMY

de·seg·re·gate \dē-'se-gri-ˌgāt\ *vb* : to eliminate segregation in; *esp* : to free of any law or practice requiring isolation on the basis of race — **de·seg·re·ga·tion** \-ˌse-gri-'gā-shən\ *n*

de·sen·si·tize \dē-'sen-sə-ˌtīz\ *vb* : to make (a sensitized or hypersensitive individual) insensitive or nonreactive to a sensitizing agent — **de·sen·si·ti·za·tion** \-ˌsen-sə-tə-ˈzā-shən\ *n*

¹**des·ert** \ˈde-zərt\ *n* ♦ : dry land with few plants and little rainfall

♦ barren, desolation, waste, wasteland — more at WASTELAND

²**des·ert** \ˈde-zərt\ *adj* : of, relating to, or resembling a desert; *esp* : being barren and without life ⟨a ∼ island⟩

³**de·sert** \di-ˈzərt\ *n* **1** : the quality or fact of deserving reward or punishment **2** ♦ : a just reward or punishment

♦ castigation, chastisement, correction, discipline, nemesis, penalty, punishment, wrath — more at PUNISHMENT

⁴**de·sert** \di-ˈzərt\ *vb* **1** ♦ : to withdraw from and leave esp. permanently **2** ♦ : to leave in the lurch : ABANDON

♦ [1, 2] abandon, forsake, maroon, quit — more at ABANDON

de·sert·ed \di-ˈzər-təd\ *adj* ♦ : left without the accustomed occupants, company, or support

♦ abandoned, derelict, forsaken — more at ABANDONED

de·sert·er \di-ˈzər-tər\ *n* ♦ : one who forsakes a duty or cause

♦ defector, recreant, renegade — more at RENEGADE

de·ser·tion \di-ˈzər-shən\ *n* ♦ : an act of deserting

♦ abandonment, dereliction — more at DERELICTION

de·serve \di-ˈzərv\ *vb* **de·served; de·serv·ing** ♦ : to be worthy of : MERIT

♦ earn, merit, rate

de·serv·ed·ly \-ˈzər-vəd-lē\ *adv* : according to merit : JUSTLY **deserving** *adj* ♦ : meriting honor or esteem

♦ good, meritorious, worthy — more at WORTHY

des·ic·cate \ˈde-si-ˌkāt\ *vb* **-cat·ed; -cat·ing** : DRY, DEHYDRATE — **des·ic·ca·tion** \ˌde-si-ˈkā-shən\ *n* — **des·ic·ca·tor** \ˈde-si-ˌkā-tər\ *n*

de·sid·er·a·tum \di-ˌsi-də-ˈrä-təm, -ˌzi-, -ˈrā-\ *n, pl* **-ta** \-tə\ [L] : something desired as essential

¹**de·sign** \di-ˈzīn\ *vb* **1** ♦ : to conceive and plan out in the mind **2** ♦ : to have as a purpose : INTEND **3** : to devise for a specific function or end **4** : to make a pattern or sketch of **5** : to conceive and draw the plans for

♦ [1] arrange, blueprint, calculate, chart, frame, lay out, map, plan, project, scheme — more at PLAN
♦ [2] aim, aspire, contemplate, intend, mean, meditate, plan, propose — more at INTEND

²**design** *n* **1** ♦ : a particular purpose : deliberate planning **2** ♦ : a mental project or scheme : PLAN **3** ♦ : a secret project or scheme : PLOT **4** *pl* : aggressive or evil intent — used with *on* or *against* **5** : a preliminary sketch or plan **6** : an underlying scheme that governs functioning, developing, or unfolding : MOTIF **7** ♦ : the arrangement of elements or details in a product or a work of art **8** ♦ : a decorative pattern **9** : the art of executing designs

♦ [1] arrangement, blueprint, game, plan, project, scheme, strategy, system — more at PLAN ♦ [2] aim, ambition, aspiration, dream, end, goal, intent, mark, meaning, object, objective, plan, pretension, purpose, thing — more at GOAL ♦ [3] conspiracy, intrigue, machination, plot, scheme — more at PLOT ♦ [7] arrangement, composition, configuration, form, format, layout, makeup, pattern — more at COMPOSITION ♦ [8] figure, motif, motive, pattern — more at PATTERN

¹**des·ig·nate** \ˈde-zig-ˌnāt, -nət\ *adj* : chosen but not yet installed ⟨ambassador ∼⟩

²**des·ig·nate** \-ˌnāt\ *vb* **-nat·ed; -nat·ing 1** ♦ : to appoint and set apart for a special purpose **2** : to mark or point out : INDICATE; *also* : SPECIFY, STIPULATE **3** ♦ : to call by a name or title

♦ [1] appoint, assign, attach, commission, constitute, detail, name — more at APPOINT ♦ [3] baptize, call, christen, denominate, dub, entitle, label, name, style, term, title — more at NAME

designated driver *n* : a person chosen to abstain from alcohol so as to transport others safely

designated hitter *n* : a baseball player designated at the start of the game to bat in place of the pitcher without causing the pitcher to be removed from the game

des·ig·na·tion \ˌde-zig-ˈnā-shən\ *n* **1** : the act of indicating or identifying **2** ♦ : appointment to or selection for an office, post, or service **3** ♦ : a distinguishing name, sign, or title

♦ [2] appointment, assignment, commission — more at APPOINTMENT ♦ [3] appellation, cognomen, denotation, handle, name, title — more at NAME

de·sign·er \di-ˈzī-nər\ *n* ♦ : one that designs: as **a** : one who creates plans for a project or structure **b** : one who designs and manufactures a new product style or design; *esp* : one who designs and manufactures high-fashion clothing — **designer** *adj*

♦ developer, innovator, inventor, originator — more at INVENTOR

designer drug *n* : a synthetic version of an illicit drug that has been chemically altered to avoid its prohibition

de·sign·ing \di-ˈzī-niŋ\ *adj* ♦ : adept in the use of subtlety and cunning : CRAFTY, SCHEMING

♦ artful, cagey, crafty, cunning, devious, foxy, guileful, scheming, slick, sly, subtle, wily — more at ARTFUL

de·sir·able \di-ˈzī-rə-bəl\ *adj* **1** : PLEASING, ATTRACTIVE **2** ♦ : worth seeking or doing as advantageous, beneficial, or wise : ADVISABLE ⟨∼ legislation⟩ — **de·sir·abil·i·ty** \-ˌzī-rə-ˈbi-lə-tē\ *n* — **de·sir·able·ness** *n*

♦ advisable, expedient, judicious, politic, prudent, tactical, wise — more at EXPEDIENT

¹**de·sire** \di-ˈzīr\ *vb* **de·sired; de·sir·ing** [ME, fr. AF *desirer*, fr. L *desiderare*, fr. *sider-, sidus* heavenly body] **1** ♦ : to long or hope for : exhibit or feel desire for **2** : REQUEST

♦ ache for, covet, crave, die for, hanker for, hunger for, long for, lust (for *or* after), pine for, repine for, thirst for, want, wish for, yearn for; *also* delight (in), enjoy, fancy, like, relish

²**desire** *n* **1** ♦ : a strong wish : LONGING **2** : sexual urge or appetite **3** : a usu. formal request for action **4** : something desired

♦ appetite, craving, drive, hankering, hunger, itch, longing, lust, passion, thirst, urge, yearning, yen; *also* compulsion, impulse, urge, will, zeal; liking, love, taste; eagerness, impatience; wish, want; necessity, need, requirement; avarice, cupidity, greed, rapacity

de·sir·ous \di-ˈzīr-əs\ *adj* : impelled or governed by desire

de·sist \di-ˈzist, -ˈsist\ *vb* ♦ : to cease to proceed, act, or continue

♦ *usu* **desist from** break, break off, cease, cut, discontinue, drop, end, halt, knock off, layoff, leave off, quit, shut off, stop — more at STOP

desk \ˈdesk\ *n* [ME *deske*, fr. ML *desca*, fr. OIt *desco* table, fr. L *discus* dish, disc] **1** : a table, frame, or case esp. for writing and reading **2** : a counter, stand, or booth at which a person performs duties **3** ♦ : a specialized division of an organization (as a newspaper) ⟨city ∼⟩

♦ bureau, department, division, office — more at DIVISION

desk·top publishing \ˈdesk-ˌtäp-\ *n* : the production of printed matter by means of a microcomputer

¹**des·o·late** \ˈde-sə-lət, -zə-\ *adj* **1** : DESERTED, ABANDONED **2** ♦ : joyless, disconsolate, and sorrowful through or as if through separation from a loved one : LONELY **3** : DILAPIDATED **4** : BARREN, LIFELESS **5** ♦ : devoid of warmth, comfort, or hope : CHEERLESS — **des·o·late·ly** *adv* — **des·o·late·ness** *n*

♦ [2] forlorn, lonely, lonesome — more at LONESOME
♦ [5] bleak, dark, dismal, dreary, gloomy, gray (*or* grey), somber (*or* sombre), wretched — more at GLOOMY

²**des·o·late** \-ˌlāt\ *vb* **-lat·ed; -lat·ing** : to make desolate : de-

stroy the activity, vitality, or sound condition or contentment of : make wretched

des·o·la·tion \ˌde-sə-ˈlā-shən, -zə-\ *n* **1** ♦ : the action of desolating : state of being desolated **2** : the quality or state of being sad : SADNESS **3** : LONELINESS **4** ♦ : a condition of neglect leading to confusion and disintegration or of natural barrenness and bleakness **5** ♦ : barren wasteland

♦ [1] annihilation, demolition, destruction, devastation, havoc, loss, obliteration, ruin, wastage, wreckage — more at DESTRUCTION ♦ [4] dilapidation, disrepair, neglect — more at NEGLECT ♦ [5] barren, desert, waste, wasteland — more at WASTELAND

des·oxy·ri·bo·nu·cle·ic acid \de-ˌzäk-sē-ˈrī-bō-nù-ˌklē-ik-, -nyù-\ *n* : DNA

¹de·spair \di-ˈspar\ *vb* : to lose all hope or confidence

²despair *n* **1** ♦ : utter destruction of hope **2** : a cause of hopelessness

♦ desperation, despondency, forlornness, hopelessness; *also* blues, depression, dejection, desolation, doldrums, dolor, dumps, gloom, melancholy, oppression, sadness, sorrow, unhappiness; cynicism, pessimism; acceptance, resignation *Ant* hope, hopefulness

de·spair·ing *adj* ♦ : given to, arising from, or marked by despair : having no hope — **de·spair·ing·ly** *adv*

♦ defeatist, hopeless, pessimistic — more at PESSIMISTIC

des·per·a·do \ˌdes-pə-ˈrä-dō, -ˈrā-\ *n, pl* **-does** *or* **-dos** : a bold or reckless criminal

des·per·ate \ˈdes-pə-rət, -prət\ *adj* **1** : being beyond or almost beyond hope : causing despair **2** : RASH ⟨a ~ attempt⟩ **3** : extremely intense — **des·per·ate·ly** *adv* — **des·per·ate·ness** *n*

des·per·a·tion \ˌdes-pə-ˈrā-shən\ *n* **1** ♦ : a loss of hope and surrender to despair **2** : a state of hopelessness leading to rashness

♦ despair, despondency, forlornness, hopelessness — more at DESPAIR

de·spi·ca·ble \di-ˈspi-kə-bəl, ˈdes-pi-\ *adj* ♦ : deserving to be despised — **de·spi·ca·bly** \-blē\ *adv*

♦ contemptible, lousy, nasty, pitiful, scabby, scurvy, sorry, wretched — more at CONTEMPTIBLE ♦ base, contemptible, detestable, dirty, dishonorable (*or* dishonourable), ignoble, low, mean, snide, sordid, vile, wretched — more at IGNOBLE

de·spise \di-ˈspīz\ *vb* **de·spised; de·spis·ing** **1** ♦ : to look down on with contempt or aversion : DETEST **2** ♦ : to regard as negligible, worthless, or distasteful

♦ [1] abhor, abominate, detest, execrate, hate, loathe — more at HATE ♦ [2] disregard, flout, scorn — more at SCORN

¹de·spite \di-ˈspīt\ *prep* ♦ : in spite of

♦ notwithstanding, regardless of, with

²despite *n* : the act of despising : CONTEMPT

de·spoil \di-ˈspȯil\ *vb* ♦ : to strip of belongings, possessions, or value — **de·spoil·er** *n* — **de·spoil·ment** *n*

♦ loot, maraud, pillage, plunder, ransack, sack, strip — more at RANSACK

de·spo·li·a·tion \di-ˌspō-lē-ˈā-shən\ *n* : the act of plundering : the state of being despoiled

¹de·spond \di-ˈspänd\ *vb* : to become discouraged or disheartened

²despond *n* : DESPONDENCY

de·spon·den·cy \-ˈspän-dən-sē\ *n* ♦ : the state of being despondent

♦ blues, dejection, depression, desolation, doldrums, dumps, forlornness, gloom, heartsickness, melancholy, sadness — more at SADNESS ♦ despair, desperation, forlornness, hopelessness — more at DESPAIR

de·spon·dent \-dənt\ *adj* ♦ : feeling or showing extreme discouragement, dejection, or depression — **de·spon·dent·ly** *adv*

♦ brokenhearted, dejected, depressed, disconsolate, heartsick, miserable, sad, wretched — more at SAD

des·pot \ˈdes-pət, -ˌpät\ *n* [MF *despote*, fr. Gk *despotēs* master, lord, autocrat] **1** : a ruler with absolute power and authority **2** ♦ : a person exercising power tyrannically

♦ autocrat, dictator, oppressor, tyrant; *also* dominator, master, overlord, ruler; king, lord, monarch, prince, queen, sovereign; baron, czar, magnate, mogul, tycoon; authoritarian, disciplinarian, martinet

des·pot·ic \des-ˈpä-tik\ *adj* ♦ : of, relating to, or characteristic of a despot

♦ authoritarian, autocratic, bossy, dictatorial, domineering, imperious, masterful, overbearing, peremptory, tyrannical, tyrannous — more at BOSSY

des·po·tism \ˈdes-pə-ˌti-zəm\ *n* ♦ : a system of government in which the ruler has unlimited power

♦ autocracy, dictatorship, totalitarianism, tyranny; *also* monarchy; fascism; domination, oppression

des·sert \di-ˈzərt\ *n* : a course of sweet food, fruit, or cheese served at the close of a meal

des·ti·na·tion \ˌdes-tə-ˈnā-shən\ *n* **1** : a purpose for which something is destined **2** : an act of appointing, setting aside for a purpose, or predetermining **3** : a place to which one is journeying or to which something is sent

des·tine \ˈdes-tən\ *vb* **des·tined; des·tin·ing** **1** : to settle in advance **2** ♦ : to designate, assign, or dedicate in advance **3** : to direct or set apart for a specific purpose or place

♦ doom, foredoom, foreordain, ordain, predestine; *also* forecast, foretell, predict, prognosticate, prophesy; preconceive, prejudge; condemn, sentence

des·ti·ny \ˈdes-tə-nē\ *n, pl* **-nies** **1** ♦ : something to which a person or thing is destined : FATE **2** : a predetermined course of events

♦ circumstance, doom, fate, fortune, lot, portion — more at FATE

des·ti·tute \ˈdes-tə-ˌtüt, -ˌtyüt\ *adj* **1** : lacking something needed or desirable **2** ♦ : suffering extreme poverty

♦ broke, devoid, impecunious, indigent, needy, penniless, penurious, poor, poverty-stricken — more at POOR

des·ti·tu·tion \ˌdes-tə-ˈtü-shən, -ˈtyü-\ *n* ♦ : the state of being destitute

♦ beggary, impecuniousness, impoverishment, indigence, need, pauperism, penury, poverty, want — more at POVERTY

de–stress \ˈdē-ˈstres\ *vb* ♦ : to release bodily or mental tension : UNWIND

♦ chill out, relax, unwind — more at RELAX

de·stroy \di-ˈstrȯi\ *vb* **1** ♦ : to put an end to : RUIN **2** ♦ : to deprive of life : KILL

♦ [1] annihilate, blot out, demolish, desolate, devastate, do in, exterminate, extinguish, obliterate, pulverize, ruin, shatter, smash, tear down, waste, wipe out, wreck; *also* gut; beat, best, clobber, conquer, crush, defeat, lick, master, overcome, prevail (over), stamp (out), subdue, surmount, thrash, triumph (over), win (against); blow up, break, damage, deface, disintegrate, dynamite, mangle, mar, mutilate, spoil, vitiate; erode, scour, wash out, wear (away); dismantle, undo; eradicate, remove, rub out; despoil, loot, pillage, plunder, ravage, sack, vandalize; assassinate, butcher, cut down, dispatch, execute, kill, massacre, murder, slaughter, slay, zap *Ant* build, construct, erect, put up, raise ♦ [2] dispatch, do in, fell, kill, slay — more at KILL

de·stroy·er \di-ˈstrȯi-ər\ *n* **1** : one that destroys **2** : a small speedy warship

de·struc·ti·ble \di-ˈstrək-tə-bəl\ *adj* : capable of being destroyed — **de·struc·ti·bil·i·ty** \-ˌstrək-tə-ˈbi-lə-tē\ *n*

de·struc·tion \di-ˈstrək-shən\ *n* **1** : the state or fact of being destroyed : RUIN **2** : the action or process of destroying something **3** : a destroying agency

♦ annihilation, demolition, desolation, devastation, havoc, loss, obliteration, ruin, wastage, wreckage; *also* depredation, despoliation, despoilment; breakup, disintegration, dissolution; assassination, execution, killing, massacre, slaughter *Ant* building, construction, erection, raising

de·struc·tive \di-'strək-tiv\ *adj* **1** ♦ : causing destruction : RUINOUS **2** ♦ : designed or tending to destroy — **de·struc·tive·ly** *adv* — **de·struc·tive·ness** *n*

♦ calamitous, devastating, disastrous, ruinous; *also* deadly, fatal, lethal, mortal, vital; deleterious, detrimental, harmful, pernicious *Ant* constructive

de·sue·tude \'de-swi-ˌtüd, -ˌtyüd\ *n* : DISUSE
des·ul·to·ry \'de-səl-ˌtōr-ē\ *adj* ♦ : passing aimlessly from one thing or subject to another

♦ aimless, arbitrary, erratic, haphazard, random, scattered, stray — more at RANDOM

det *abbr* **1** detached; detachment **2** detail
de·tach \di-'tach\ *vb* **1** : to separate esp. from a larger mass **2** : DISENGAGE, WITHDRAW — **de·tach·able** *adj*
de·tached \di-'tacht\ *adj* **1** ♦ : not joined or connected : SEPARATE **2** ♦ : exhibiting an aloof objectivity ⟨a ∼ attitude⟩

♦ [1] disconnected, discrete, freestanding, separate, single, unattached, unconnected — more at SEPARATE
♦ [2] aloof, antisocial, cold, cool, distant, frosty, remote, standoffish, unsociable — more at COOL

de·tach·ment \di-'tach-mənt\ *n* **1** : SEPARATION **2** : the dispatching of a body of troops or part of a fleet from the main body for special service; *also* : the portion so dispatched **3** : a small permanent military unit of special composition **4** : indifference to worldly concerns : ALOOFNESS **5** ♦ : freedom from bias or prejudice : IMPARTIALITY

♦ disinterestedness, impartiality, neutrality, objectivity; *also* fairness; apathy, indifference, unconcern; broad-mindedness, tolerance *Ant* bias, favor, favoritism, partiality, partisanship, prejudice

¹de·tail \di-'tāl, 'dē-ˌtāl\ *n* [F *détail*, fr. OF *detail* slice, piece, fr. *detaillier* to cut in pieces, fr. *taillier* to cut] **1** : a dealing with something item by item ⟨go into ∼⟩ **2** ♦ : a part of a whole ⟨the ∼s of a story⟩ **3** : selection (as of soldiers) for special duty; *also* : the persons thus selected

♦ fact, particular, point — more at FACT

²detail *vb* **1** ♦ : to report minutely and distinctly **2** ♦ : to assign to a special duty

♦ [1] enumerate, itemize, list, numerate, rehearse, tick (off) — more at ENUMERATE ♦ [2] appoint, assign, attach, commission, constitute, designate, name — more at APPOINT

de·tailed \di-'tāld, 'dē-ˌtāld\ *adj* ♦ : marked by abundant detail

♦ circumstantial, elaborate, full, minute, thorough; *also* enumerated, itemized, listed; delineated, specific, specified; abundant, copious; comprehensive, exhausting, exhaustive, thoroughgoing; accurate, exact, precise; complete, entire, replete; distinct, explicit, precise, sharp; inclusive, mapped (out); descriptive, graphic, picturesque, vivid *Ant* compendious, summary complex, complicated, elaborate, fancy, intricate, involved, sophisticated — more at ELABORATE

de·tail·ing \'dē-ˌtāl-iŋ\ *n* : the meticulous cleaning and refurbishing of an automobile
de·tain \di-'tān\ *vb* **1** : to hold in or as if in custody **2** : STOP, DELAY
de·tect \di-'tekt\ *vb* ♦ : to discover the nature, existence, presence, or fact of — **de·tec·tor** \-'tek-tər\ *n*

♦ determine, dig up, discover, ferret out, find, hit on, locate, track down — more at FIND

de·tect·able \di-tek-tə-bəl\ *adj* ♦ : capable of being detected
♦ appreciable, discernible, distinguishable, palpabie, perceptible, sensible — more at PERCEPTIBLE

de·tec·tion \di-'tek-shən\ *n* ♦ : the act of detecting
♦ discovery, finding — more at DISCOVERY

¹de·tec·tive \di-'tek-tiv\ *adj* **1** : fitted or used for detection **2** : of or relating to detectives
²detective *n* ♦ : a person employed or engaged in detecting lawbreakers or getting information that is not readily accessible

♦ investigator, operative, shadow, sleuth, tail

dé·tente *or* **de·tente** \dā-'tänt\ *n* [F] : a relaxation of strained relations or tensions (as between nations)
de·ten·tion \di-'ten-chən\ *n* **1** : the act or fact of detaining : CONFINEMENT; *esp* : a period of temporary custody prior to disposition by a court **2** : a forced delay
de·ter \di-'tər\ *vb* **de·terred; de·ter·ring** [L *deterrēre*, fr. *terrēre* to frighten] **1** ♦ : to turn aside, discourage, or prevent from acting (as by fear) **2** : INHIBIT

♦ discourage, dissuade, inhibit — more at DISCOURAGE

de·ter·gent \di-'tər-jənt\ *n* ♦ : a cleansing agent; *esp* : a chemical product similar to soap in its cleaning ability

♦ cleaner, soap — more at CLEANER

de·te·ri·o·rate \di-'tir-ē-ə-ˌrāt\ *vb* **-rat·ed; -rat·ing** ♦ : to make or become worse in quality or condition

♦ decay, decline, degenerate, descend, ebb, rot, sink, worsen; *also* recede, wane; decompose, degrade, disintegrate; sour, spoil; lessen, lower, reduce; debilitate, undermine, weaken *Ant* ameliorate, improve, meliorate

de·te·ri·o·ra·tion \di-ˌtir-ē-ə-'rā-shən\ *n* ♦ : the action or process of deteriorating

♦ decay, decline, degeneration — more at DECLINE

de·ter·min·able \-'tər-mə-nə-bəl\ *adj* : capable of being determined; *esp* : ASCERTAINABLE
de·ter·mi·nant \-mə-nənt\ *n* **1** : something that determines or conditions **2** : GENE
de·ter·mi·nate \di-'tər-mə-nət\ *adj* **1** ♦ : having fixed limits : DEFINITE **2** ♦ : definitely settled — **de·ter·mi·nate·ness** *n*

♦ [1] definite, finite, limited, measured, narrow, restricted — more at LIMITED ♦ [2] certain, final, firm, fixed, flat, frozen, hard, hard-and-fast, set, settled, stable — more at FIXED

de·ter·mi·na·tion \di-ˌtər-mə-'nā-shən\ *n* **1 a** : the act of coming to a decision **b** ♦ : the decision or conclusion reached **2** : a fixing of the extent, position, or character of something **3** : accurate measurement (as of length or volume) **4** ♦ : firm or fixed purpose

♦ [1b] conclusion, decision, deliverance, diagnosis, judgment (*or* judgement), opinion, resolution, verdict — more at DECISION ♦ [4] decision, decisiveness, firmness, granite, resolution, resolve; *also* doggedness, obstinacy, perseverance, persistence, stubbornness, tenacity; backbone, fortitude, grit, pluck *Ant* hesitation, indecision, irresolution, vacillation

de·ter·mine \di-'tər-mən\ *vb* **-mined; -min·ing** **1** ♦ : to fix conclusively or authoritatively **2** ♦ : to come to a decision : RESOLVE **3** : to fix the form or character of beforehand : ORDAIN; *also* : REGULATE **4** : to find out the limits, nature, dimensions, or scope of ⟨∼ a position at sea⟩ **5** : to find out or come to a decision about by investigation, reasoning, or calculation **6** : to bring about as a result

♦ [1] adjudicate, arbitrate, decide, judge, referee, rule, settle, umpire — more at JUDGE ♦ [2] choose, conclude, decide, figure, opt, resolve — more at DECIDE

de·ter·mined \-'tər-mənd\ *adj* **1** ♦ : firmly resolved **2** ♦ : characterized by or showing determination — **de·ter·mined·ness** \-mənd-nəs\ *n*

♦ [1] bound, decisive, firm, intent, purposeful, resolute, set, single-minded; *also* certain, cocksure, positive, sure; earnest, serious; steady, unfaltering, unhesitating, unswerving, unwavering *Ant* faltering, hesitant, indecisive, irresolute, undetermined, unresolved, vacillating, wavering ♦ [2] dogged, grim, implacable, relentless, unflinching, unrelenting, unyielding — more at UNYIELDING

de·ter·mined·ly \di-'tər-mənd-lē, -mə-nəd-lē\ *adv* ♦ : in a determined manner

♦ diligently, hard, hardly, laboriously, mightily, slavishly, strenuously, tirelessly — more at HARD

de·ter·min·ism \di-'tər-mə-ˌni-zəm\ *n* : a doctrine that acts of the will, natural events, or social changes are determined by preceding events or natural causes — **de·ter·min·ist** \-nist\ *n or adj*

de·ter·rence \di-'tər-əns\ *n* : the inhibition of criminal behavior by fear esp. of punishment

de·ter·rent \-ənt\ *adj* 1 : serving to deter ⟨the law's ~ effect⟩ 2 : relating to deterrence — **deterrent** *n*

de·test \di-'test\ *vb* [L *detestari*, lit., to curse while calling a deity to witness, fr. *de-* from + *testari* to call to witness] ♦ : to feel intense and often violent antipathy toward : LOATHE — **de·tes·ta·tion** \ˌdē-ˌtes-'tā-shən\ *n*

♦ abhor, abominate, despise, execrate, hate, loathe — more at HATE

de·test·able \di-'tes-tə-bəl\ *adj* ♦ : arousing or meriting intense dislike

♦ base, contemptible, despicable, dirty, dishonorable (*or* dishonourable), ignoble, low, mean, snide, sordid, vile, wretched — more at IGNOBLE

de·throne \di-'thrōn\ *vb* : to remove from a throne : DEPOSE — **de·throne·ment** *n*

det·o·nate \'det-ᵊn-ˌāt\ *vb* **-nat·ed; -nat·ing** ♦ : to explode or cause to explode with violence

♦ blow up, burst, explode, go off, pop — more at EXPLODE

det·o·na·tion \ˌdet-ᵊn-'ā-shən\ *n* ♦ : the action or process of detonating

♦ blast, eruption, explosion — more at EXPLOSION

det·o·na·tor \'det-ᵊn-ˌā-tər\ *n* : a device for detonating an explosive

¹**de·tour** \'dē-ˌtùr\ *n* : an indirect way replacing part of a route

²**detour** *vb* ♦ : to go by detour

♦ bypass, circumvent, skirt; *also* circumnavigate; avoid, dodge, duck, elude, escape, eschew, evade, shake, shun deviate, sheer, swerve, swing, turn, turn off, veer — more at TURN

de·tox \'dē-ˌtäks, di-'täks\ *n* : detoxification from an intoxicating or addictive substance — **detox** *vb*

de·tox·i·fy \dē-'täk-sə-ˌfī\ *vb* **-fied; -fy·ing** 1 : to remove a poison or toxin or the effect of such from 2 : to free (someone) from an intoxicating or addictive substance or from dependence on it — **de·tox·i·fi·ca·tion** \dē-ˌtäk-sə-fə-'kā-shən\ *n*

de·tract \di-'trakt\ *vb* 1 : to take away or diminish the value or effect of something 2 : DIVERT — **de·trac·tor** \-'trak-tər\ *n*

de·trac·tion \di-'trak-shən\ *n* ♦ : a lessening of reputation or esteem esp. by envious, malicious, or petty criticism

♦ deprecation, depreciation, disparagement, put=down — more at DEPRECIATION

de·train \dē-'trān\ *vb* : to leave or cause to leave a railroad train

det·ri·ment \'de-trə-mənt\ *n* 1 : hurt, damage, or loss sustained 2 ♦ : a cause of injury or damage

♦ damage, harm, hurt, injury — more at INJURY

det·ri·men·tal \ˌde-trə-'men-ᵊl\ *adj* ♦ : obviously harmful — **det·ri·men·tal·ly** *adv*

♦ adverse, bad, baleful, baneful, damaging, deleterious, evil, harmful, hurtful, ill, injurious, mischievous, noxious, pernicious, prejudicial — more at HARMFUL

de·tri·tus \di-'trī-təs\ *n, pl* **de·tri·tus** : fragments resulting from disintegration (as of rocks) : DEBRIS

deuce \'düs, 'dyüs\ *n* 1 : a two in cards or dice 2 : a tie in a tennis game with both sides at 40 3 : DEVIL — used chiefly as a mild oath

Deut *abbr* Deuteronomy

deu·te·ri·um \dü-'tir-ē-əm, dyü-\ *n* : an isotope of hydrogen that has twice the mass of ordinary hydrogen

Deu·ter·on·o·my \ˌdü-tə-'rä-nə-mē, ˌdyü-\ *n* : a book of Jewish and Christian Scripture

deut·sche mark \'dòi-chə-ˌmärk\ *n* : a former monetary unit of Germany

dev *abbr* deviation

de·val·ue \dē-'val-yü\ *vb* : to reduce the international exchange value of ⟨~ a currency⟩ — **de·val·u·a·tion** \-ˌval-yə-'wā-shən\ *n*

dev·as·tate \'de-və-ˌstāt\ *vb* **-tat·ed; -tat·ing** 1 ♦ : to bring to ruin 2 ♦ : to reduce to chaos or helplessness

♦ [1] destroy, ravage, ruin, scourge — more at RAVAGE ♦ [2] carry away, crush, floor, oppress, overcome, overpower, overwhelm, prostrate, snow under, swamp — more at OVERWHELM

devastating *adj* ♦ : serving, tending, or having the power to devastate

♦ calamitous, destructive, disastrous, ruinous — more at DESTRUCTIVE

dev·as·ta·tion \ˌde-və-'stā-shən\ *n* ♦ : the action of devastating or state of being devastated

♦ annihilation, demolition, desolation, destruction, havoc, loss, obliteration, ruin, wastage, wreckage — more at DESTRUCTION

de·vel·op \di-'ve-ləp\ *vb* 1 ♦ : to unfold gradually or in detail 2 : to place (exposed photographic material) in chemicals to produce a visible image 3 : to bring out the possibilities of 4 : to make more available or usable ⟨~ land⟩ 5 ♦ : to acquire gradually ⟨~ a taste for olives⟩ 6 ♦ : to go through a natural process of growth, differentiation, or evolution 7 : to come into being gradually

♦ [1] amplify, elaborate (on), enlarge (on), expand — more at EXPAND ♦ [5] acquire, cultivate, form; *also* gain, get, obtain; achieve, attain, reach; foster, nourish, nurture, promote *Ant* lose ♦ [6] age, grow, grow up, mature, progress, ripen — more at MATURE

de·vel·op·er \-lə-pər\ *n* ♦ : one that develops something new

♦ designer, innovator, inventor, originator — more at INVENTOR

de·vel·op·ment \-ləp-mənt\ *n* ♦ : the act, process, or result of developing — **de·vel·op·men·tal** \-ˌve-ləp-'ment-ᵊl\ *adj* — **de·vel·op·men·tal·ly** \-tᵊl-ē\ *adv*

♦ elaboration, evolution, expansion, growth, maturation, progress, progression; *also* advancement, betterment, improvement, perfection, refinement *Ant* regression, retrogression aftermath, conclusion, consequence, corollary, effect, issue, outcome, outgrowth, product, result, resultant, sequence, upshot — more at EFFECT

¹**de·vi·ant** \'dē-vē-ənt\ *adj* ♦ : deviating esp. from some accepted norm ⟨~ behavior⟩ — **de·vi·ance** \-əns\ *n* — **de·vi·an·cy** \-ən-sē\ *n*

♦ aberrant, abnormal, anomalous, atypical, irregular, unnatural; *also* extraordinary, preternatural; rare, uncommon, uncustomary, unusual, unwonted; odd, peculiar, strange, weird *Ant* natural, normal, regular, standard, typical

²**deviant** *n* ♦ : one that is deviant

♦ bohemian, individualist, loner, maverick, nonconformist — more at NONCONFORMIST

de·vi·ate \'dē-vē-ˌāt\ *vb* **-at·ed; -at·ing** [LL *deviare*, fr. L *de-* from + *via* way] ♦ : to turn aside from a course, standard, principle, or topic — **de·vi·ate** \-vē-ət, -vē-ˌāt\ *n* — **de·vi·a·tion** \ˌdē-vē-'ā-shən\ *n*

♦ detour, sheer, swerve, swing, turn, turn off, veer — more at TURN

de·vice \di-'vīs\ *n* 1 ♦ : a scheme to deceive : STRATAGEM 2 ♦ : a piece of equipment or a mechanism for a special purpose 3 ♦ : a particular disposition of mind or character : INCLINATION — used in pl. ⟨left to my own ~s⟩ 4 : an emblematic design

♦ [1] artifice, dodge, gimmick, jig, ploy, scheme, sleight, stratagem, trick, wile — more at TRICK ♦ [2] implement, instrument, tool, utensil — more at IMPLEMENT *usu* **devices** ♦ [3] affinity, bent, disposition, genius, inclination, leaning, partiality, penchant, predilection, predisposition, proclivity, propensity, talent, tendency, turn — more at INCLINATION

¹dev·il \'de-vəl\ n [ME *devel*, fr. OE *dēofol*, fr. LL *diabolus*, fr. Gk *diabolos*, lit., slanderer, fr. *diaballein* to throw across, slander, fr. *dia-* across + *ballein* to throw] **1** *often cap* : the personal supreme spirit of evil **2** ♦ : an evil spirit : DEMON **3** ♦ : a wicked person **4 a** ♦ : an energetic, reckless, or dashing person **b** ♦ : a person prone to mischief **5** : an individual human : FELLOW ⟨poor ~⟩ ⟨lucky ~⟩

♦ [2] demon, fiend, ghoul, imp — more at DEMON ♦ [3] beast, evildoer, fiend, no-good, reprobate, rogue, varlet, villain, wretch — more at VILLAIN ♦ [4a] daredevil, madcap — more at DAREDEVIL ♦ [4b] hellion, imp, mischief, monkey, rapscallion, rascal, rogue, scamp, urchin — more at SCAMP

²devil vb -iled or -illed; -il·ing or -il·ling **1** : to season highly ⟨~ed eggs⟩ **2** : TEASE, ANNOY

dev·il·ish \'de-və-lish\ adj **1** ♦ : befitting a devil : EVIL; *also* : MISCHIEVOUS **2** : exceeding the ordinary, usual, or expected : EXTREME

♦ demonic, diabolical, evil, fiendish, satanic — more at FIENDISH ♦ impish, knavish, mischievous, rascally, roguish, sly, waggish, wicked — more at MISCHIEVOUS

dev·il·ish·ly \-lē\ adv ♦ : in a devilish manner

♦ excessively, inordinately, monstrously, overly, overmuch, too — more at TOO

dev·il·ish·ness \-nəs\ n ♦ : the quality or state of being devilish

♦ impishness, knavery, mischief, mischievousness, rascality, shenanigans, waggery, wickedness — more at MISCHIEF

dev·il·ment \'de-vəl-mənt, -,ment\ n : MISCHIEF
dev·il·ry \-rē\ or dev·il·try \-trē\ n, pl -il·ries or -il·tries **1** : action performed with the help of the devil **2** : action that annoys or irritates : MISCHIEF

de·vi·ous \'dē-vē-əs\ adj **1** ♦ : deviating from a straight line **2** : ERRANT 3 **3 a** : deviating from a right, accepted, or common course **b** ♦ : not straightforward : CUNNING ⟨a ~ politician⟩; *also* : tending or having power to deceive ⟨a ~ trick⟩

♦ [1] crooked, serpentine, sinuous, tortuous, winding — more at CROOKED ♦ [3b] artful, cagey, crafty, cunning, foxy, guileful, slick, sly, subtle, wily — more at ARTFUL

¹de·vise \di-'vīz\ vb de·vised; de·vis·ing [ME, fr. AF *deviser* to divide, distinguish, invent, fr. VL *divisare*, fr. L *dividere* to divide] **1** ♦ : to form in the mind by new combinations or applications of ideas or principles : INVENT **2** : PLOT **3** : to give (real estate) by will

♦ concoct, contrive, cook up, fabricate, invent, make up, manufacture, think up — more at INVENT

²devise n **1** : a disposing of real property by will **2** : a will or clause of a will disposing of real property **3** : property given by will

de·vi·tal·ize \dē-'vīt-²l-,īz\ vb : to deprive of life or vitality

de·void \di-'vȯid\ adj ♦ : being without : VOID ⟨a book ~ of interest⟩

♦ bare, blank, empty, stark, vacant, void — more at EMPTY ♦ bereft, destitute, empty, void; *also* bare, barren, blank, stark, vacant, wanting; deficient, fragmentary, incomplete, partial; absent, missing *Ant* replete

de·voir \də-'vwär\ n **1** : DUTY **2** : a formal act of civility or respect

de·volve \di-'välv\ vb de·volved; de·volv·ing : to pass (as

rights or responsibility) from one to another usu. by succession or transmission — dev·o·lu·tion \,de-və-'lü-shən, ,dē-\ n

De·vo·ni·an \di-'vō-nē-ən\ adj : of, relating to, or being the period of the Paleozoic era between the Silurian and the Mississippian — **Devonian** n

de·vote \di-'vōt\ vb de·vot·ed; de·vot·ing **1** ♦ : to commit to wholly or chiefly ⟨~s herself to serving the poor⟩ **2** ♦ : to set apart for a special purpose : DEDICATE

♦ [1] address, apply, bend, buckle, give — more at APPLY ♦ [2] allocate, consecrate, dedicate, earmark, reserve, save; *also* hallow, sanctify; commit, confide, consign, entrust

de·vot·ed \-'vō-təd\ adj ♦ : characterized by loyalty and devotion : FAITHFUL

♦ constant, faithful, fast, good, loyal, pious, staunch, steadfast, steady, true, true-blue — more at FAITHFUL

dev·o·tee \,de-və-'tē, -'tā\ n ♦ : an ardent follower, supporter, or enthusiast

♦ addict, aficionado, buff, bug, enthusiast, fan, fanatic, fancier, fiend, freak, lover, maniac, nut — more at FAN

de·vo·tion \di-'vō-shən\ n **1** ♦ : religious fervor **2** : an act of prayer or private worship — usu. used in pl. **3** : a religious exercise for private use **4** ♦ : the fact or state of being dedicated and loyal ⟨~ to the cause⟩; *also* : the act of devoting

♦ [1] faith, piety, religion — more at FAITH ♦ [4] allegiance, constancy, dedication, faith, faithfulness, fastness, fealty, fidelity, loyalty, steadfastness — more at FIDELITY ♦ [4] affection, attachment, fondness, love, passion — more at LOVE

de·vo·tion·al \-shə-nəl\ adj ♦ : of, relating to, or characterized by devotion

♦ religious, sacred, spiritual — more at RELIGIOUS

de·vour \di-'vaȯr\ vb **1** ♦ : to eat up greedily or ravenously **2** : WASTE, ANNIHILATE **3** : to enjoy avidly ⟨~ a book⟩ — de·vour·er n

♦ bolt, gobble, gorge, gormandize, gulp, scarf — more at GOBBLE

de·vout \di-'vaȯt\ adj **1** ♦ : devoted to religion : PIOUS **2** : expressing devotion or piety **3** : EARNEST, SERIOUS — de·vout·ly adv

♦ faithful, godly, holy, pious, religious, sainted, saintly — more at HOLY

de·vout·ness \-nəs\ n ♦ : the quality or state of being devout

♦ blessedness, godliness, holiness, piety, sainthood, sanctity — more at HOLINESS

dew \'dü, 'dyü\ n : moisture that condenses on the surfaces of cool bodies at night — **dewy** adj

dew·ber·ry \'dü-,ber-ē, 'dyü-\ n : any of several sweet edible berries related to and resembling blackberries; *also* : a trailing bramble bearing these

dew·claw \-,klȯ\ n : a digit on the foot of a mammal that does not reach the ground; *also* : its claw or hoof

dew·lap \-,lap\ n : loose skin hanging under the neck of an animal

dew point n : the temperature at which the moisture in the air begins to condense

dex·ter·i·ty \dek-'ster-ə-tē\ n, pl -ties **1** ♦ : quickness and skill in managing any complicated or difficult affair **2** ♦ : readiness and grace in physical activity; *esp* : skill and ease in using the hands

♦ [1] adroitness, cleverness, craft, finesse, sleight; *also* ability, prowess, talent; competence, efficiency, expertise, know-how, proficiency; ingeniousness, ingenuity, resourcefulness ♦ [2] agility, deftness, nimbleness, sleight; *also* coordination *Ant* awkwardness, clumsiness

dex·ter·ous also dex·trous \'dek-strəs\ adj **1** : CLEVER **2** ♦ : done with skillfulness **3** ♦ : skillful and competent with the hands — dex·ter·ous·ly adv

♦ [2] adroit, artful, masterful, practiced, skillful, virtuoso — more at SKILLFUL ♦ [3] clever, cunning, deft, handy; *also* agile, flexible, graceful, limber, lissome, lithe, nimble, spry; coordinated; adept, competent, expert, masterful, masterly, proficient, skilled, skillful; double-jointed *Ant* butterfingered, heavy-handed, unhandy

dex·trose \'dek-ˌstrōs\ *n* : the naturally occurring form of glucose found in plants and blood

DFC *abbr* Distinguished Flying Cross

dg *abbr* decigram

DG *abbr* 1 [LL *Dei gratia*] by the grace of God 2 director general

DH \ˌdē-'āch\ *n* : DESIGNATED HITTER

dhow \'daů\ *n* : an Arab sailing ship usu. having a long overhang forward and a high poop

DI *abbr* drill instructor

dia *abbr* diameter

di·a·be·tes \ˌdī-ə-'bē-tēz, -təs\ *n* : an abnormal state marked by passage of excessive amounts of urine; *esp* : one (**diabetes mel·li·tus** \-'me-lə-təs\) characterized by deficient insulin, by excess sugar in the blood and urine, and by thirst, hunger, and loss of weight — **di·a·bet·ic** \-'be-tik\ *adj or n*

di·a·bol·i·cal \ˌdī-ə-'bä-li-kəl\ *or* **di·a·bol·ic** \-lik\ *adj* ♦ : of, relating to, or characteristic of the devil : DEVILISH — **di·a·bol·i·cal·ly** \-k(ə-)lē\ *adv*

   ♦ demonic, devilish, fiendish, satanic — more at FIENDISH

di·a·bol·i·cal·ness \ˌdī-ə-'bä-li-kəl-nəs\ *n* : the quality or state of being diabolical

di·a·crit·ic \ˌdī-ə-'kri-tik\ *n* : a mark accompanying a letter and indicating a sound value different from that of the same letter when unmarked — **di·a·crit·i·cal** \-ti-kəl\ *adj*

di·a·dem \'dī-ə-ˌdem\ *n* : CROWN; *esp* : a royal headband

di·aer·e·sis *or* **di·er·e·sis** \dī-'er-ə-səs\ *n, pl* **-e·ses** \-ˌsēz\ : a mark ¨ placed over a vowel to show that it is pronounced in a separate syllable (as in *naïve*)

diag *abbr* 1 diagonal 2 diagram

di·ag·no·sis \ˌdī-ig-'nō-səs\ *n, pl* **-no·ses** \-ˌsēz\ 1 : the art or act of identifying a disease from its signs and symptoms; *also* : the decision reached by diagnosis 2 a : investigation or analysis of the cause or nature of a condition, situation, or problem b ♦ : a statement or conclusion from an investigation or analysis — **di·ag·nose** \'dī-ig-ˌnōs\ *vb* — **di·ag·nos·tic** \ˌdī-ig-'näs-tik\ *adj* — **di·ag·nos·ti·cian** \-ˌnäs-'ti-shən\ *n*

   ♦ conclusion, decision, deliverance, determination, judgment (*or* judgement), opinion, resolution, verdict — more at DECISION

¹di·ag·o·nal \dī-'a-gə-nəl\ *adj* 1 : extending from one corner to the opposite corner in a 4-sided figure 2 ♦ : running in a slanting direction ⟨~ stripes⟩ 3 : having slanting markings or parts ⟨a ~ weave⟩ — **di·ag·o·nal·ly** *adv*

   ♦ canted, inclined, listing, oblique, slantwise

²diagonal *n* 1 : a diagonal line or plane 2 : a diagonal row, pattern, or direction 3 : a mark / used esp. to mean "or," "and or," or "per"

¹di·a·gram \'dī-ə-ˌgram\ *n* ♦ : a design and esp. a drawing that makes something easier to understand — **di·a·gram·ma·ble** \-ˌgra-mə-bəl\ *adj* — **di·a·gram·mat·ic** \ˌdī-ə-grə-'ma-tik\ *adj* — **di·a·gram·mat·i·cal·ly** \-ti-k(ə-)lē\ *adv*

   ♦ figure, graphic, illustration, plate — more at ILLUSTRATION

²diagram *vb* **-grammed** *or* **-gramed** \-ˌgramd\; **-gram·ming** *or* **-gram·ing** : to represent by a diagram

¹di·al \'dī-(-ə)l\ *n* [ME *dyal*, fr. ML *dialis* clock wheel revolving daily, fr. L *dies* day] 1 : the face of a sundial 2 : the face of a timepiece 3 : a face with a pointer and numbers that indicate something ⟨the ~ of a gauge⟩ 4 : a device used for making electrical connections or for regulating operation (as of a radio)

²dial *vb* **di·aled** *or* **di·alled**; **di·al·ing** *or* **di·al·ling** 1 : to manipulate a dial so as to operate or select 2 ♦ : to make a telephone call or connection

   ♦ call, telephone — more at CALL

³dial *abbr* dialect

di·a·lect \'dī-ə-ˌlekt\ *n* ♦ : a regional variety of a language

   ♦ argot, cant, jargon, language, lingo, patois, patter, slang, vocabulary; *also* idiom, parlance, pidgin, speech, tongue, vernacular

di·a·lec·tic \ˌdī-ə-'lek-tik\ *n* : the process or art of reasoning by discussion of conflicting ideas; *also* : the tension between opposing elements — **di·a·lec·ti·cal** \-ti-kəl\ *adj*

dialog box *n* : a window on a computer screen for choosing options or inputting information

di·a·logue \'dī-ə-ˌlóg\ *also* **di·a·log** *n* 1 ♦ : a conversation between two or more parties 2 : the parts of a literary or dramatic work that represent conversation

   ♦ colloquy, conversation, discourse, discussion, exchange — more at CONVERSATION

di·al·y·sis \dī-'a-lə-səs\ *n, pl* **-y·ses** \-ˌsēz\ 1 : the separation of substances from solution by means of their unequal diffusion through semipermeable membranes 2 : the medical procedure of removing blood from an artery, purifying it by dialysis, and returning it to a vein

diam *abbr* diameter

di·am·e·ter \dī-'a-mə-tər\ *n* [ME *diametre*, fr. MF, fr. L *diametros*, fr. Gk, fr. *dia-* through + *metron* measure] 1 : a straight line passing through the center of a figure or body; *esp* : one that divides a circle in half 2 : the length of a diameter

di·a·met·ric \ˌdī-ə-'me-trik\ *or* **di·a·met·ri·cal** \-tri-kəl\ *adj* 1 : of, relating to, or constituting a diameter 2 ♦ : completely opposed or opposite — **di·a·met·ri·cal·ly** \-k(ə-)lē\ *adv*

   ♦ antipodal, antithetical, contradictory, contrary, opposite, polar — more at OPPOSITE

di·a·mond \'dī-mənd, 'dī-ə-\ *n* 1 : a hard brilliant mineral that consists of crystalline carbon and is used as a gem 2 : a flat figure having four equal sides, two acute angles, and two obtuse angles 3 : any of a suit of playing cards marked with a red diamond 4 : INFIELD; *also* : the entire playing field in baseball

di·a·mond·back rattlesnake \-ˌbak-\ *n* : either of two large and deadly rattlesnakes of the southern U.S.

di·an·thus \dī-'an-thəs\ *n* : ¹PINK 1

di·a·pa·son \ˌdī-ə-'pāz-ᵊn, -'pās-\ *n* 1 : the organ stop governing the flue pipes that form the primary basis of organ tone 2 : the entire range of musical tones

¹di·a·per \'dī-pər, 'dī-ə-\ *n* 1 : a cotton or linen fabric woven in a simple geometric pattern 2 : a garment for a baby drawn up between the legs and fastened about the waist

²diaper *vb* 1 : to ornament with diaper designs 2 : to put a diaper on

di·aph·a·nous \dī-'a-fə-nəs\ *adj* : of so fine a texture as to be transparent

di·a·pho·ret·ic \ˌdī-ə-fə-'re-tik\ *adj* : having the power to increase perspiration — **diaphoretic** *n*

di·a·phragm \'dī-ə-ˌfram\ *n* 1 : a sheet of muscle between the chest and abdominal cavities of a mammal 2 : a vibrating disk (as in a microphone) 3 : a cup-shaped device usu. of thin rubber fitted over the uterine cervix to act as a mechanical contraceptive barrier — **di·a·phrag·mat·ic** \ˌdī-ə-frag-'ma-tik, -ˌfrag-\ *adj*

di·a·rist \'dī-ə-rist\ *n* : one who keeps a diary

di·ar·rhea *or chiefly Brit* **di·ar·rhoea** \ˌdī-ə-'rē-ə\ *n* [ME *diaria*, fr. LL *diarrhoea*, fr. Gk *diarrhoia*, fr. *diarrhein* to flow through, fr. *dia-* through + *rhein* to flow] : abnormally frequent and watery bowel movements

di·a·ry \'dī-ə-rē\ *n, pl* **-ries** : a daily record esp. of personal experiences; *also* : a book used as a diary

di·as·po·ra \dī-'as-pə-rə\ *n* 1 *cap* : the settling of scattered colonies of Jews outside Palestine after the Babylonian exile 2 *cap* : the Jews living outside Palestine or modern Israel 3 : the migration or scattering of a people away from an ancestral homeland

di·as·to·le \dī-'as-tə-(,)lē\ *n* : the stretching of the chambers of the heart during which they fill with blood — **di·a·stol·ic** \,dī-ə-'stä-lik\ *adj*

dia·ther·my \'dī-ə-,thər-mē\ *n* : the generation of heat in tissue by electric currents for medical purposes

di·a·tom \'dī-ə-,täm\ *n* : any of a class of planktonic one-celled or colonial algae with skeletons of silica

di·atom·ic \,dī-ə-'tä-mik\ *adj* : having two atoms in the molecule

di·a·tribe \'dī-ə-,trīb\ *n* ♦ : biting or abusive speech or writing

♦ harangue, rant, tirade — more at TIRADE

di·az·e·pam \dī-'a-zə-,pam\ *n* : a tranquilizer used esp. to relieve anxiety, tension, and muscle spasms

dib·ble \'di-bəl\ *n* : a pointed hand tool for making holes (as for planting bulbs) in the ground — **dibble** *vb*

¹**dice** \'dīs\ *n, pl* **dice** : DIE 1

²**dice** *vb* **diced; dic·ing** 1 : to cut into small cubes ⟨~ carrots⟩ 2 : to play games with dice

di·chot·o·my \dī-'kä-tə-mē\ *n, pl* **-mies** : a division or the process of dividing into two esp. mutually exclusive or contradictory groups — **di·chot·o·mous** \-məs\ *adj*

dick·er \'di-kər\ *vb* ♦ : to negotiate over the terms of a purchase, agreement, or contract : BARGAIN

♦ bargain, chaffer, deal, haggle, negotiate, palter — more at BARGAIN

dick·ey *or* **dicky** \'di-kē\ *n, pl* **dickeys** *or* **dick·ies** : a small fabric insert worn to fill in the neckline

di·cot·y·le·don \,dī-,kät-ᵊl-'ēd-ᵊn\ *n* : any of a group of seed plants having an embryo with two cotyledons — **di·cot·y·le·don·ous** *adj*

dict *abbr* dictionary

¹**dic·tate** \'dik-,tāt\ *vb* **dic·tat·ed; dic·tat·ing** 1 : to speak or read for a person to transcribe or for a machine to record 2 : to issue as an order : COMMAND — **dic·ta·tion** \dik-'tā-shən\ *n*

²**dic·tate** \'dik-,tāt\ *n* ♦ : an authoritative rule, prescription, or injunction : COMMAND ⟨the ~s of conscience⟩

♦ behest, charge, command, commandment, decree, direction, directive, edict, instruction, order, word — more at COMMAND

dic·ta·tor \'dik-,tā-tər\ *n* 1 ♦ : a person ruling absolutely and often brutally and oppressively 2 : one that dictates

♦ autocrat, despot, oppressor, tyrant — more at DESPOT

dic·ta·to·ri·al \,dik-tə-'tōr-ē-əl\ *adj* ♦ : of, relating to, or characteristic of a dictator or a dictatorship

♦ arbitrary, authoritarian, autocratic, bossy, despotic, domineering, imperious, masterful, overbearing, peremptory, tyrannical, tyrannous — more at BOSSY

dic·ta·tor·ship \dik-'tā-tər-,ship, 'dik-,tā-\ *n* 1 : the office of a dictator 2 : autocratic rule, control, or leadership 3 ♦ : a government or country in which absolute power is held by a dictator or a small clique

♦ autocracy, despotism, totalitarianism, tyranny — more at DESPOTISM

dic·tion \'dik-shən\ *n* 1 ♦ : choice of words esp. with regard to correctness, clearness, or effectiveness : WORDING 2 : ENUNCIATION

♦ language, phraseology, phrasing, wording — more at WORDING

dic·tio·nary \'dik-shə-,ner-ē\ *n, pl* **-nar·ies** : a reference book containing words usu. alphabetically arranged along with information about their forms, pronunciations, functions, etymologies, meanings, and syntactical and idiomatic uses

dic·tum \'dik-təm\ *n, pl* **dic·ta** \-tə\ *also* **dictums** : a noteworthy, formal, or authoritative statement or observation

did *past of* DO

di·dac·tic \dī-'dak-tik\ *adj* 1 : intended to instruct, inform, or teach a moral lesson 2 : making moral observations

di·do \'dī-dō\ *n, pl* **didoes** *or* **didos** : a mischievous act : PRANK

¹**die** \'dī\ *vb* **died; dy·ing** \'dī-iŋ\ [ME *dien*, fr. or akin to ON *deyja* to die] 1 ♦ : to cease living : EXPIRE 2 ♦ : to pass out of existence ⟨a *dying* race⟩ 3 ♦ : to disappear or subside gradually ⟨the wind *died* down⟩ 4 ♦ : to long keenly — usu. used with *to* or *for* ⟨*dying* to go⟩ ⟨*dying* for a snack⟩ 5 : to cease functioning : STOP ⟨the motor *died*⟩

♦ [1] depart, expire, pass, pass away, perish, succumb; *also* disappear, fade *Ant* breathe, live ♦ [2] break off, break up, cease, close, conclude, discontinue, elapse, end, expire, finish, halt, lapse, leave off, let up, pass, quit, stop, terminate, wind up — more at CEASE ♦ *usu* **die down** [3] abate, decline, decrease, de-escalate, diminish, dwindle, ebb, fall, lessen, let up, lower, moderate, recede, relent, shrink, subside, taper, wane — more at DECREASE ♦ *usu* **die for** [4] ache for, crave, desire, hanker for, hunger for, long for, lust ⟨for *or* after⟩, pine for, repine for, thirst for, want, wish for, yearn for — more at DESIRE

²**die** \'dī\ *n* [ME *dee*, fr. AF *dé*] 1 *pl* **dice** \'dīs\ : a small cube marked on each face with one to six spots and used usu. in pairs in games and gambling 2 *pl* **dies** \'dīz\ : a device used to shape, finish, or impress an object

die·hard \'dī-,härd\ *n* : one who is strongly devoted or determined

dieresis *var of* DIAERESIS

die·sel \'dē-zəl, -səl\ *n* 1 : DIESEL ENGINE 2 : a vehicle driven by a diesel engine 3 : DIESEL FUEL

diesel engine *n* : an internal combustion engine in whose cylinders air is compressed to a temperature sufficiently high to ignite the fuel

diesel fuel *n* : a heavy mineral oil used as fuel in diesel engines

die·sel·ing \'dē-zə-liŋ\ *n* : the continued operation of an internal combustion engine after the ignition has been turned off

¹**di·et** \'dī-ət\ *n* [ME *diete*, fr. AF, fr. L *diaeta*, fr. Gk *diaita*, lit., manner of living, fr. *diaitasthai* to lead one's life] 1 : food and drink regularly consumed : FARE 2 : an allowance of food prescribed for a special reason (as to lose weight) — **di·e·tary** \-ə-,ter-ē\ *adj or n*

²**diet** *vb* : to eat or cause to eat or drink less or according to a prescribed rule — **di·et·er** *n*

dietary supplement *n* : a product taken orally that contains ingredients (as vitamins or amino acids) intended to supplement one's diet

di·e·tet·ics \,dī-ə-'te-tiks\ *n sing or pl* : the science or art of applying the principles of nutrition to diet — **di·e·tet·ic** *adj*

di·e·ti·tian *or* **di·e·ti·cian** \,dī-ə-'ti-shən\ *n* : a specialist in dietetics

dif *or* **diff** *abbr* difference

dif·fer \'di-fər\ *vb* **dif·fered; dif·fer·ing** 1 : to be unlike 2 : VARY 3 : DISAGREE

dif·fer·ence \'di-frəns, 'di-fə-rəns\ *n* 1 ♦ : the quality or state of being different : UNLIKENESS ⟨~ in their looks⟩ 2 : distinction or discrimination in preference 3 ♦ : disagreement in opinion; *also* : an instance or cause of disagreement ⟨unable to settle their ~s⟩ 4 : the amount by which one number or quantity differs from another

♦ [1] contrast, disagreement, discrepancy, disparity, distinction, diversity, unlikeness; *also* deviance, divergence; change, modification, variation; conflict, discord, dissension, dissent, dissidence, disunity, friction, strife; variability, variance; incompatibility, incongruity; disproportion *Ant* community, likeness, resemblance, sameness, similarity ♦ [3] controversy, disagreement, dispute, dissension

dif·fer·ent \'di-frənt, 'di-fə-rənt\ *adj* 1 ♦ : unlike in nature or quality 2 ♦ : not the same ⟨~ age groups⟩; *also* : VARIOUS ⟨~ members of the club⟩ 3 : ANOTHER ⟨try a ~ channel⟩ 4 : UNUSUAL, SPECIAL ⟨a quite ~ style⟩

♦ disparate, dissimilar, distinct, distinctive, distinguishable, diverse, other, unalike, unlike; *also* divers, miscellaneous, several, sundry, variant, varied; individual, particular, peculiar, single; unequal; disproportionate *Ant* alike, indistinguishable, like, parallel, same, similar

¹dif·fer·en·tial \ˌdi-fə-'ren-chəl\ *adj* : showing, creating, or relating to a difference

²differential *n* 1 : the amount or degree by which things differ 2 : DIFFERENTIAL GEAR

differential gear *n* : an arrangement of gears in an automobile that allows one wheel to turn faster than another (as in rounding curves)

dif·fer·en·ti·ate \ˌdi-fə-'ren-chē-ˌāt\ *vb* -at·ed; -at·ing 1 : to make or become different 2 : to attain a specialized adult form and function during development 3 ♦ : to recognize or state the difference ⟨∼ between them⟩ — dif·fer·en·ti·a·tion \-ˌren-chē-'ā-shən\ *n*

♦ discern, discriminate, distinguish, separate — more at DISTINGUISH

dif·fer·ent·ly \-lē\ *adv* ♦ : in a different manner

♦ else, other, otherwise — more at OTHERWISE

dif·fi·cult \'di-fi-(ˌ)kəlt\ *adj* 1 ♦ : hard to do or make 2 ♦ : hard to understand or deal with ⟨∼ reading⟩ ⟨a ∼ child⟩

♦ [1] arduous, demanding, exacting, formidable, grueling, hard, herculean, laborious, murderous, rough, stiff, strenuous, tall, toilsome, tough — more at HARD ♦ [2] catchy, delicate, knotty, problematic, spiny, thorny, ticklish, touchy, tough, tricky — more at TRICKY

dif·fi·cul·ty \-(ˌ)kəl-tē\ *n, pl* -ties [ME *difficulte*, fr. AF *difficulté*, fr. L *difficilis* not easy, fr. *dis-* not + *facilis* easy] 1 : difficult nature ⟨the ∼ of a task⟩ 2 : DISAGREEMENT ⟨settled their *difficulties*⟩ 3 ♦ : something that is difficult or serves to impede ⟨overcome *difficulties*⟩ 4 : an instance of trouble ⟨in financial *difficulties*⟩

♦ adversity, asperity, hardness, hardship, rigor; *also* discomfort, inconvenience, nuisance; affliction, trial, tribulation; knock, misfortune, mishap, tragedy; bar, catch, check, clog, crimp, embarrassment, handicap, hindrance, hitch, hurdle, impediment, interference, let, manacle, obstacle, obstruction, rub, shackle, snag, stop, trammel; block, chain, deterrent, encumbrance, fetter, inhibition; hump complexity, complication, intricacy — more at COMPLICATION

dif·fi·dent \'di-fə-dənt\ *adj* 1 ♦ : lacking confidence 2 : RESERVED 1 — dif·fi·dence \-dəns\ *n* — dif·fi·dent·ly *adv*

♦ bashful, coy, demure, introverted, modest, retiring, sheepish, shy — more at SHY

dif·frac·tion \di-'frak-shən\ *n* : the bending or spreading of waves (as of light) esp. when passing through narrow slits

¹dif·fuse \di-'fyüs\ *adj* 1 ♦ : being at once verbose and ill-organized ⟨∼ writing⟩ 2 : not concentrated or localized ⟨∼ light⟩

♦ circuitous, long-winded, prolix, rambling, verbose, windy, wordy — more at WORDY

²dif·fuse \di-'fyüz\ *vb* dif·fused; dif·fus·ing 1 : to pour out or spread widely 2 : to undergo or cause to undergo diffusion 3 : to break up light by diffusion

dif·fu·sion \di-'fyü-zhən\ *n* 1 : a diffusing or a being diffused 2 : movement of particles (as of a gas) from a region of high to one of lower concentration 3 : the reflection of light from a rough surface or the passage of light through a translucent material

¹dig \'dig\ *vb* dug \'dəg\; dig·ging 1 : to turn up the soil (as with a spade) 2 : to hollow out or form by removing earth ⟨∼ a hole⟩ 3 a : to uncover or seek by turning up earth ⟨∼ potatoes⟩ b ♦ : to penetrate below the surface in search of something hidden or buried — used with *into* c ♦ : to advance by or as if by removing or pushing aside material ⟨∼ through the toy box⟩ 4 ♦ : to come upon by searching or effort : DISCOVER ⟨∼ up information⟩ 5 : POKE, THRUST ⟨∼ a person in the ribs⟩ 6 : to work hard 7 a : UNDERSTAND, APPRECIATE b ♦ : to feel attraction toward or take pleasure in : LIKE

♦ *usu* dig into [3b] delve, explore, go, inquire into, investigate, look, probe, research — more at EXPLORE ♦ *usu* dig through [3c] dredge, hunt, rake, ransack, rifle, rummage, scour, search — more at SEARCH ♦ *usu* dig up [4] detect, determine, discover, ferret out, find, hit on, locate, track down — more at FIND ♦ [7b] adore, delight, enjoy, fancy, groove, like, love, relish, revel — more at ENJOY

²dig *n* 1 a : a quick thrust : POKE b ♦ : a cutting remark 2 *pl* : living accommodations

♦ affront, barb, dart, indignity, insult, name, offense, outrage, put-down, sarcasm, slight, slur, wound — more at INSULT

³dig *abbr* digest

¹di·gest \'dī-ˌjest\ *n* ♦ : a summation or condensation of a body of information; *esp* : a summarized or shortened version esp. of a literary work

♦ abbreviation, condensation ♦ abstract, encapsulation, epitome, outline, précis, recapitulation, résumé (*or* resume), roundup, sum, summary, synopsis, wrap-up — more at SUMMARY

²di·gest \dī-'jest, də-\ *vb* 1 : to think over and arrange in the mind 2 : to convert (food) into simpler forms that can be absorbed by the body 3 ♦ : to compress into a short summary — di·gest·ibil·i·ty \-ˌjes-tə-'bi-lə-tē\ *n* — di·gest·ible *adj* — di·ges·tion \-'jes-chən\ *n* — di·ges·tive \-'jes-tiv\ *adj*

♦ abstract, encapsulate, epitomize, outline, recapitulate, sum up, summarize, wrap up — more at SUMMARIZE

di·ges·tif \ˌdē-zhes-'tēf\ *n* : an alcoholic drink taken after a meal

dig in *vb* 1 : to take a defensive stand esp. by digging trenches 2 : to firmly set to work 3 : to begin eating

dig·it \'di-jət\ *n* [ME, fr. L *digitus* finger, toe] 1 ♦ : any of the Arabic numerals 1 to 9 and usu. the symbol 0 2 : FINGER, TOE

♦ figure, integer, number, numeral, whole number — more at NUMBER

dig·i·tal \'di-jə-t³l\ *adj* 1 : of, relating to, or done with a finger or toe 2 : of, relating to, or using calculation by numerical methods or by discrete units 3 : relating to or employing communications signals in the form of binary digits ⟨a ∼ broadcast⟩ 4 : providing a readout in numerical digits ⟨a ∼ watch⟩ 5 : ELECTRONIC; *also* : characterized by computerized technology ⟨the ∼ age⟩ — dig·i·tal·ly *adv*

digital camera *n* : a camera that records images as digital data instead of on film

dig·i·tal·is \ˌdi-jə-'ta-ləs\ *n* : a drug from the common foxglove that is a powerful heart stimulant; *also* : FOXGLOVE

digital versatile disc *n* : DVD

digital video disc *n* : DVD

dig·ni·fied \'dig-nə-ˌfīd\ *adj* ♦ : showing or expressing dignity

♦ august, imposing, solemn, staid, stately; *also* decorous, formal, proper, seemly; grim, sober, somber; aristocratic, lordly, majestic, noble *Ant* flighty, frivolous, giddy, goofy, silly, undignified

dig·ni·fy \-ˌfī\ *vb* -fied; -fy·ing ♦ : to give dignity, distinction, or attention to

♦ aggrandize, ennoble, exalt, glorify, magnify — more at EXALT

dig·ni·tary \'dig-nə-ˌter-ē\ *n, pl* -tar·ies : a person of high position or honor

dig·ni·ty \'dig-nə-tē\ *n, pl* -ties 1 : the quality or state of being worthy, honored, or esteemed 2 : high rank, office, or position 3 : formal reserve of manner, language, or appearance

di·graph \'dī-ˌgraf\ *n* : a group of two successive letters whose phonetic value is a single sound (as *ea* in *bread*)

di·gress \dī-'gres, də-\ *vb* : to turn aside esp. from the main subject or argument — di·gres·sion \dī-'gre-shən\ *n*

di·gres·sive \dī-'gre-siv\ *adj* ♦ : characterized by digressions

♦ desultory, discursive, rambling — more at DISCURSIVE

Di·jon mustard \'dē-ˌzhän-, di-'zhän-\ *n* : a mustard made from dark mustard seeds, white wine, and spices

dike \'dīk\ *n* **1** ♦ : an artificial watercourse : DITCH **2** ♦ : a bank of earth constructed to control water : LEVEE

♦ [1] ditch, gutter, trench — more at DITCH ♦ [2] dam, embankment, levee — more at DAM

dil *abbr* dilute

di·lap·i·dat·ed \də-'la-pə-ˌdā-təd\ *adj* ♦ : fallen into partial ruin or decay

♦ grungy, mean, neglected, ratty, seedy, shabby — more at SHABBY

di·lap·i·da·tion \də-ˌla-pə-'dā-shən\ *n* ♦ : the act of dilapidating or the state of being dilapidated

♦ desolation, disrepair, neglect — more at NEGLECT

di·late \dī-'lāt, 'dī-ˌlāt\ *vb* **di·lat·ed; di·lat·ing** : SWELL, DISTEND, EXPAND — **dil·a·ta·tion** \ˌdi-lə-'tā-shən\ *n* — **di·la·tion** \dī-'lā-shən\ *n*

dil·a·to·ry \'di-lə-ˌtȯr-ē\ *adj* **1** : DELAYING **2** ♦ : characterized by procrastination : TARDY

♦ creeping, laggard, languid, poky, slow, sluggish, tardy — more at SLOW

di·lem·ma \də-'le-mə\ *n* **1** : a usu. undesirable or unpleasant choice; *also* : a situation involving such a choice **2** : PREDICAMENT

dil·et·tante \ˌdi-lə-'tänt, -'tant\ *n, pl* **-tantes** *or* **-tan·ti** \-'tän-tē, -'tan-\ [It, fr. prp. of *dilettare* to delight, fr. L *dilectare*] : a person having a superficial interest in an art or a branch of knowledge

dil·i·gence \'di-lə-jəns\ *n* ♦ : persevering application

♦ assiduity, industry; *also* application, concentration; doggedness, perseverance, persistence, tenacity, tirelessness

dil·i·gent \'di-lə-jənt\ *adj* ♦ : characterized by steady, earnest, and energetic effort

♦ active, assiduous, busy, engaged, laborious, occupied, sedulous, working — more at BUSY

dil·i·gent·ly \-lē\ *adv* ♦ : in a diligent manner

♦ determinedly, hard, laboriously, strenuously, tirelessly — more at HARD

dill \'dil\ *n* : an herb related to the carrot with aromatic leaves and seeds used as seasoning and in pickles

dil·ly \'di-lē\ *n, pl* **dil·lies** : one that is remarkable or outstanding

dil·ly·dal·ly \'di-lē-ˌda-lē\ *vb* ♦ : to waste time by loitering or delaying

♦ crawl, creep, dally, dawdle, delay, drag, lag, linger, loiter, poke, tarry — more at DELAY

¹di·lute \dī-'lüt, də-\ *vb* **di·lut·ed; di·lut·ing** ♦ : to lessen the consistency or strength of by mixing with something else — **di·lu·tion** \-'lü-shən\ *n*

♦ adulterate, thin, water, weaken — more at ADULTERATE

²dilute *adj* ♦ : having the consistency or strength of lessened by mixing with something else

♦ impure, polluted — more at IMPURE ♦ thin, watery, weak — more at WEAK

¹dim \'dim\ *adj* **dim·mer; dim·mest** **1** ♦ : lacking brilliance or luster : DULL **2** ♦ : not bright or distinct : OBSCURE **3** : not seeing or understanding clearly **4** ♦ : perceived by the senses or mind indistinctly or weakly — **dim·ly** *adv* — **dim·ness** *n*

♦ [1] dull, flat, lusterless ♦ [2] dark, darkling, dusky, gloomy, murky, obscure, somber (*or* sombre) — more at DARK ♦ [4] bleary, faint, foggy, fuzzy, hazy, indefinite, indistinct, indistinguishable, murky, nebulous, obscure, opaque, shadowy, unclear, undefined, undetermined, vague — more at FAINT

²dim *vb* **dimmed; dim·ming** **1** ♦ : to make or become dim or lusterless **2** ♦ : to reduce the light from

♦ becloud, befog, blur, cloud, darken, fog, haze, mist, obscure, overcast, overshadow, shroud — more at CLOUD

³dim *abbr* **1** dimension **2** diminished **3** diminutive

dime \'dīm\ *n* [ME, tenth part, tithe, fr. AF *disme, dime*, fr. L *decima*, fr. fem. of *decimus* tenth, fr. *decem* ten] : a U.S. or Canadian coin worth ten cents

di·men·sion \də-'men-chən, dī-\ *n* **1** : the physical property of length, breadth, or thickness; *also* : a measure of this **2 a** ♦ : the quality of spatial extension : EXTENT **b** : the range over which or the degree to which something extends : SCOPE — usu. used in pl. — **di·men·sion·al** \-'men-chə-nəl\ *adj* — **di·men·sion·al·i·ty** \-ˌmen-chə-'na-lə-tē\ *n*

♦ extent, magnitude, measure, measurement, proportion, size — more at SIZE

di·min·ish \də-'mi-nish\ *vb* **1** : to make less or cause to appear less **2** ♦ : to lessen the authority, dignity, or reputation of : BELITTLE **3** ♦ : to become gradually less (as in size or importance) : DWINDLE **4** ♦ : to diminish gradually : TAPER

♦ [2] belittle, cry down, decry, deprecate, depreciate, discount, disparage, minimize, put down, write off — more at DECRY ♦ [3, 4] abate, decline, decrease, de-escalate, die, dwindle, ebb, fall, lessen, let up, lower, moderate, recede, relent, shrink, subside, taper, wane

di·min·u·en·do \də-ˌmin-yə-'wen-dō\ *adv or adj* : DECRESCENDO

dim·i·nu·tion \ˌdi-mə-'nü-shən, -'nyü-\ *n* ♦ : the act, process, or an instance of diminishing

♦ abatement, decline, decrease, decrement, drop, fall, loss, reduction, shrinkage — more at DECREASE

¹di·min·u·tive \də-'min-yə-tiv\ *n* **1** : a diminutive word or affix ⟨the word "kitchenette" is a ∼⟩ **2** : a diminutive individual

²diminutive *adj* **1** : indicating small size and sometimes the state or quality of being lovable, pitiable, or contemptible ⟨the ∼ suffixes *-ette* and *-ling*⟩ **2** : extremely small : TINY

dim·i·ty \'di-mə-tē\ *n, pl* **-ties** : a thin usu. corded cotton fabric

dim·mer \'di-mər\ *n* : a device for controlling the amount of light from an electric lighting unit

di·mor·phic \(ˌ)dī-'mȯr-fik\ *adj* : occurring in two distinct forms — **di·mor·phism** \-ˌfi-zəm\ *n*

¹dim·ple \'dim-pəl\ *n* : a small depression esp. in the cheek or chin

²dimple *vb* **dim·pled; dim·pling** : to form dimples (as in smiling)

din \'din\ *n* ♦ : a loud confused mixture of noises

♦ bluster, cacophony, clamor (*or* clamour), noise, racket, roar — more at NOISE

dine \'dīn\ *vb* **dined; din·ing** [ME, fr. AF *disner, diner* to eat, have a meal, fr. VL *disjejunare* to break one's fast, ultim. fr. L *jejunus* fasting] **1** ♦ : to eat dinner **2** ♦ : to give a dinner to

♦ [1] eat, fare, feed; *also* banquet, feast, fete; board, mess; breakfast, lunch, sup; picnic ♦ [2] banquet, feast, junket, regale — more at FEAST

din·er \'dī-nər\ *n* **1** : one that dines **2** : a railroad dining car **3** ♦ : a restaurant usu. resembling a dining car

♦ café, grill, restaurant — more at RESTAURANT

di·nette \dī-'net\ *n* : an alcove or small room used for dining

ding \'diŋ\ *vb* : to cause minor damage to a surface — **ding** *n*

din·ghy \'diŋ-ē\ *n, pl* **dinghies** **1** : a small boat **2** : LIFE RAFT

din·gi·ness \'din-jē-nəs\ *n* ♦ : the quality or state of being dingy

♦ dirtiness, filthiness, foulness, grubbiness, nastiness, uncleanliness — more at DIRTINESS

din·gle \'diŋ-gəl\ *n* : a small wooded valley

din·go \'diŋ-gō\ *n, pl* **dingoes** : a reddish brown wild dog of Australia

din·gus \'diŋ-gəs, -əs\ *n* : DOODAD

din·gy \'din-jē\ *adj* **din·gi·er; -est** **1** : not clean or pure : DIRTY **2** : SHABBY

dink \'diŋk\ *n, often all cap* [*double income, no kids*] : a couple with two incomes and no children; *also* : a member of such a couple

din·ky \'diŋ-kē\ *adj* **din·ki·er; -est** : overly or unattractively small

din·ner \'di-nər\ *n* **1** : the main meal of the day **2** ♦ : a formal banquet

♦ banquet, feast, feed, spread — more at FEAST

din·ner·ware \'di-nər-,war\ *n* : tableware other than flatware

di·no \'dī-nō\ *n, pl* **dinos** : DINOSAUR

di·no·fla·gel·late \,dī-nō-'fla-jə-lət, -,lāt\ *n* : any of an order of planktonic plantlike unicellular flagellates of which some cause red tide

di·no·saur \'dī-nə-,sȯr\ *n* [ultim. fr. Gk *deinos* terrifying + *sauros* lizard] : any of a group of extinct long-tailed Mesozoic reptiles often of huge size

dint \'dint\ *n* **1** : FORCE ⟨by ∼ of sheer grit⟩ **2** : a depression or hollow made by a blow or by pressure : DENT

di·o·cese \'dī-ə-səs, -,sēz, -,sēs\ *n, pl* **-ces·es** \-sə-səz, -,sē-zəz, -,sē-səz\ : the territorial jurisdiction of a bishop — **di·oc·e·san** \dī-'ä-sə-sən, ,dī-ə-'sēz-ᵊn\ *adj or n*

di·ode \'dī-,ōd\ *n* : an electronic device with two electrodes or terminals used esp. as a rectifier

di·ox·in \dī-'äk-sən\ *n* : a persistent toxic hydrocarbon that occurs esp. as a by-product of industrial processes and waste incineration

¹dip \'dip\ *vb* **dipped; dip·ping** **1** ♦ : to plunge temporarily or partially under the surface (as of a liquid) **2** : to thrust in a way to suggest immersion **3** ♦ : to scoop up or out : LADLE **4** : to lower and then raise quickly ⟨∼ a flag in salute⟩ **5** ♦ : to drop or slope down esp. suddenly ⟨the moon *dipped* below the crest⟩ **6** ♦ : to decrease moderately and usu. temporarily ⟨prices *dipped*⟩ **7** : to reach inside or as if inside or below a surface ⟨*dipped* into their savings⟩ **8** ♦ : to examine or read something casually or superficially ⟨∼ into a book⟩

♦ [1] douse, duck, dunk, immerse, souse, submerge; *also* drench, flood, soak, wet; plunge, thrust ♦ [3] ladle, scoop, spoon; *also* bail; deplete, drain, eliminate, exhaust; bleed, draw (off); dish; draw, siphon ♦ [5, 6] decline, descend, drop, fall, lower, plummet, plunge, sink, tumble — more at DROP ♦ [8] browse, glance, glimpse, peek, skim — more at GLANCE

²dip *n* **1** : an act of dipping; *esp* : a short swim **2** ♦ : inclination downward : DROP **3** : something obtained by or used in dipping **4** : a sauce or soft mixture into which food may be dipped **5** : a liquid into which something may be dipped (as for cleansing or coloring)

♦ descent, dive, down, drop, fall, plunge — more at DESCENT

diph·the·ria \dif-'thir-ē-ə\ *n* : an acute contagious bacterial disease marked by fever and by coating of the air passages with a membrane that interferes with breathing

diph·thong \'dif-,thȯŋ\ *n* : two vowel sounds joined in one syllable to form one speech sound (as *ou* in *out*)

dip·loid \'di-,plȯid\ *adj* : having two haploid sets of chromosomes ⟨∼ somatic cells⟩ — **diploid** *n*

di·plo·ma \də-'plō-mə\ *n, pl* **diplomas** : an official record of graduation from or of a degree conferred by a school

di·plo·ma·cy \də-'plō-mə-sē\ *n* **1** : the art and practice of conducting negotiations between nations **2** : TACT

dip·lo·mat \'di-plə-,mat\ *n* : one employed or skilled in diplomacy — **dip·lo·mat·ic** \,di-plə-'ma-tik\ *adj*

di·plo·ma·tist \də-'plō-mə-tist\ *n* : DIPLOMAT

dip·per \'di-pər\ *n* **1** : any of a genus of birds that are related to the thrushes and are skilled in diving **2** : something (as a ladle or scoop) that dips or is used for dipping **3** *cap* : BIG DIPPER **4** *cap* : LITTLE DIPPER

dip·so·ma·nia \,dip-sə-'mā-nē-ə\ *n* : an uncontrollable craving for alcoholic liquors — **dip·so·ma·ni·ac** \-nē-,ak\ *n*

dip·stick \'dip-,stik\ *n* : a graduated rod for indicating depth

dip·ter·an \'dip-tə-rən\ *adj* : of, relating to, or being a fly (sense 2) — **dipteran** *n* — **dip·ter·ous** \-rəs\ *adj*

dir *abbr* **1** direction **2** director

dire \'dīr\ *adj* **dir·er; dir·est** **1** ♦ : very horrible : DREADFUL **2** ♦ : warning of disaster **3** : EXTREME **4** ♦ : demanding immediate action to fend off disastrous consequences

♦ [1] dreadful, fearful, fearsome, forbidding, formidable, frightful, hair-raising, horrible, redoubtable, scary, shocking, terrible, terrifying — more at FEARFUL ♦ [2] baleful, foreboding, menacing, ominous, portentous, sinister — more at OMINOUS ♦ [4] acute, critical, imperative, imperious, instant, pressing, urgent — more at ACUTE

¹di·rect \də-'rekt, dī-\ *vb* **1** : ADDRESS ⟨∼ a letter⟩; *also* : to impart orally : AIM ⟨∼ a remark to the gallery⟩ **2** ♦ : to regulate the activities or course of : guide the supervision, organizing, or performance of **3** ♦ : to cause to turn, move, or point or to follow a certain course **4** : to point, extend, or project in a specified line or course **5** ♦ : to request or instruct with authority **6** ♦ : to show or point out the way

♦ [2] administer, carry on, conduct, control, govern, guide, handle, manage, operate, oversee, regulate, run, superintend, supervise — more at CONDUCT ♦ [3] aim, bend, cast, head, level, set, train — more at AIM ♦ [5] command, decree, dictate, ordain, order ♦ [5] bid, boss, charge, command, enjoin, instruct, order, tell — more at COMMAND ♦ [6] conduct, guide, lead, marshal, pilot, route, show, steer, usher — more at LEAD

²direct *adj* **1** ♦ : stemming immediately from a source ⟨∼ result⟩ **2** : being or passing in a straight line of descent : LINEAL ⟨∼ ancestor⟩ **3** : leading from one point to another in time or space without turn or stop : STRAIGHT **4** ♦ : free from evasiveness or obscurity : STRAIGHTFORWARD ⟨a ∼ manner⟩ **5** : operating without an intervening agency or step ⟨∼ action⟩ **6** : effected by the action of the people or the electorate and not by representatives ⟨∼ democracy⟩ **7** : consisting of or reproducing the exact words of a speaker or writer

♦ [1] firsthand, immediate, primary; *also* clinical *Ant* indirect, secondhand ♦ [4] candid, forthright, foursquare, frank, honest, open, outspoken, plain, straight, straightforward, unguarded, unreserved — more at FRANK

³direct *adv* ♦ : in a direct way

♦ dead, directly, due, plump, right, straight — more at DIRECTLY

direct broadcast satellite *n* : a television broadcasting system in which satellite transmissions are received at the viewing location

direct current *n* : an electric current flowing in one direction only

direct deposit *n* : a method of payment in which money is transferred to the payee's account without the use of checks or cash

di·rec·tion \də-'rek-shən, dī-\ *n* **1** ♦ : guidance or supervision of action or conduct : MANAGEMENT **2** : an explicit instruction : COMMAND **3** : the course or line along which something moves, lies, or points **4** : TENDENCY, TREND — **di·rec·tion·al** \-shə-nəl\ *adj*

♦ administration, conduct, control, government, guidance, management, operation, oversight, regulation, running, superintendence, supervision — more at CONDUCT

di·rec·tive \də-'rek-tiv, dī-\ *n* ♦ : something that directs and usu. impels toward an action or goal; *esp* : an order issued by a high-level body or official

♦ decree, edict, fiat, ruling — more at EDICT ♦ behest, charge, command, commandment, decree, dictate, direction, edict, instruction, order, word — more at COMMAND

di·rect·ly \-lē\ *adv* 1 ♦ : in a direct manner 2 ♦ : without delay

♦ [1] dead, direct, due, plump, right, straight *Ant* indirectly ♦ [2] forthwith, immediately, instantly, now, promptly, pronto, right away, right now — more at IMMEDIATELY

direct mail *n* : printed matter used for soliciting business or contributions and mailed direct to individuals

di·rect·ness \-nəs\ *n* 1 : the character of being accurate in course or aim 2 ♦ : strict pertinence : FORTHRIGHTNESS

♦ candor (*or* candour), forthrightness, frankness, openness, plainness — more at CANDOR

di·rec·tor \də-'rek-tər, dī-\ *n* 1 ♦ : one that directs : MANAGER 2 : one of a group of persons who direct the affairs of an organized body — **di·rec·tor·ship** *n*

♦ administrator, executive, manager, superintendent, supervisor — more at EXECUTIVE

di·rec·tor·ate \-tə-rət\ *n* 1 : the office or position of director 2 : a board of directors; *also* : membership on such a board 3 : an executive staff

di·rec·to·ri·al \də-ˌrek-'tōr-ē-əl\ *adj* ♦ : serving to direct

♦ executive, managerial, supervisory — more at EXECUTIVE

director's cut *n* : a version of a motion picture that is edited according to the director's wishes

di·rec·to·ry \-tə-rē\ *n, pl* **-ries** : an alphabetical or classified list esp. of names and addresses

dire·ful \'dīr-fəl\ *adj* 1 : causing great and oppressive fear : DREADFUL ⟨a ∼ disease⟩ 2 : OMINOUS

dirge \'dərj\ *n* ♦ : a song of lamentation; *also* : a slow mournful piece of music

♦ elegy, lament, requiem, threnody — more at LAMENT

di·ri·gi·ble \'dir-ə-jə-bəl, də-'ri-jə-\ *n* : AIRSHIP

dirk \'dərk\ *n* : DAGGER 1

dirndl \'dərnd-ᵊl\ *n* [short for G *Dirndlkleid*, fr. G dial. *Dirndl* girl + G *Kleid* dress] : a full skirt with a tight waistband

dirt \'dərt\ *n* 1 ♦ : a filthy or soiling substance (as mud, dust, or grime) 2 ♦ : loose or packed earth : SOIL 3 : moral uncleanness 4 : scandalous gossip 5 : embarrassing or incriminating information

♦ [1] filth, grime, muck, smut, soil — more at FILTH
♦ [2] earth, ground, soil; *also* clay, dust, gravel, humus, loam, loess, marl, mud, sand, silt, subsoil, topsoil

dirt·i·ness \'dər-tē-nəs\ *n* ♦ : the quality or state of being dirty

♦ dinginess, filthiness, foulness, grubbiness, nastiness, uncleanliness; *also* impurity; shabbiness; squalor *Ant* cleanliness

¹**dirty** \'dər-tē\ *adj* **dirt·i·er; -est** 1 ♦ : not clean : SOILED 2 ♦ : morally unclean or corrupt : INDECENT ⟨∼ jokes⟩ 3 a ♦ : lacking honor : BASE ⟨a ∼ trick⟩ b ♦ : not characteristic of or exhibiting good sportsmanship 4 ♦ : relating to, characterized by, or indicative of a storm ⟨∼ weather⟩ 5 : not clear in color : DULL ⟨a ∼ red⟩ — **dirty** *adv*

♦ [1] dusty, filthy, foul, grubby, grungy, mucky, muddy, nasty, smutty, sordid, unclean; *also* contaminated, defiled, impure, polluted, tainted; uncleaned, unsanitary, unsterile, unwashed; discolored; bedraggled; chaotic, cluttered, confused, disarranged, disheveled, disordered, jumbled, littered, messed, messy, muddled, mussed, mussy, rumpled, scruffy, sloppy, slovenly, unkempt, untidy; shabby, sleazy, squalid; smutty, sooty *Ant* clean, cleanly, immaculate, spick-and-span, spotless, stainless, unsoiled, unstained, unsullied ♦ [2] bawdy, coarse, crude, filthy, foul, gross, indecent, lascivious, lewd,

nasty, obscene, pornographic, ribald, smutty, unprintable, vulgar, wanton — more at OBSCENE ♦ [3a] base, contemptible, despicable, detestable, dishonorable (*or* dishonourable), ignoble, low, mean, snide, sordid, vile, wretched — more at IGNOBLE ♦ [3b] foul, illegal, unfair, unsportsmanlike ♦ [4] bleak, foul, inclement, nasty, raw, rough, squally, stormy, tempestuous, turbulent — more at FOUL

²**dirty** *vb* **dirt·ied; dirty·ing** ♦ : to make or become dirty

♦ befoul, begrime, besmirch, blacken, foul, grime, mire, muddy, smirch, soil, stain; *also* contaminate, defile, pollute, taint; discolor; confuse, disarrange, disarray, dishevel, disorder, jumble, mess, muddle *Ant* clean, cleanse

dis·able \di-'sā-bəl\ *vb* **dis·abled; dis·abling** 1 : to disqualify legally 2 ♦ : to make unable to perform by or as if by illness, injury, or malfunction — **dis·abil·i·ty** \ˌdi-sə-'bi-lə-tē\ *n*

♦ cripple, hamstring, immobilize, incapacitate, paralyze, prostrate — more at PARALYZE

dis·abled *adj* : incapacitated by illness, injury, or wounds; *also* : physically or mentally impaired

dis·abuse \ˌdi-sə-'byüz\ *vb* : to free from error, fallacy, or misconception

dis·ad·van·tage \ˌdi-səd-'van-tij\ *n* 1 : loss or damage esp. to reputation or finances 2 a : an unfavorable, inferior, or prejudicial condition b ♦ : a quality or circumstance that makes achievement unusually difficult : HANDICAP

♦ drawback, handicap, liability, minus, penalty, strike; *also* detriment, disability, impairment; failing, shortcoming; bar, catch, check, clog, crimp, embarrassment, hindrance, hitch, hurdle, impediment, interference, let, manacle, obstacle, obstruction, rub, shackle, stop, trammel *Ant* advantage, asset, edge, plus

dis·ad·van·taged \-tijd\ *adj* : lacking in basic resources or conditions believed necessary for an equal position in society

dis·ad·van·ta·geous \di-ˌsad-ˌvan-'tā-jəs, -vən-\ *adj* ♦ : constituting a disadvantage

♦ adverse, counter, hostile, inimical, negative, prejudicial, unfavorable (*or* unfavourable), unfriendly, unsympathetic — more at ADVERSE

dis·af·fect \ˌdi-sə-'fekt\ *vb* ♦ : to alienate the affection or loyalty of

♦ alienate, disgruntle, estrange, sour — more at ESTRANGE ♦ discontent, disgruntle, displease, dissatisfy — more at DISCONTENT

dis·af·fec·tion \ˌdi-sə-'fek-shən\ *n* ♦ : alienation of affection

♦ alienation, estrangement — more at ESTRANGEMENT

dis·agree \ˌdi-sə-'grē\ *vb* 1 : to fail to agree 2 : to differ in opinion 3 : to cause discomfort or distress ⟨fried foods ∼ with her⟩

dis·agree·able \-ə-bəl\ *adj* 1 ♦ : causing discomfort : UNPLEASANT 2 ♦ : marked by ill temper : ILL-TEMPERED — **dis·agree·able·ness** *n* — **dis·agree·ably** \-blē\ *adv*

♦ [1] bad, distasteful, nasty, rotten, sour, uncongenial, unlovely, unpleasant, unwelcome — more at UNPLEASANT ♦ [2] bearish, bilious, cantankerous, dyspeptic, ill-humored, ill-tempered, ornery, splenetic, surly — more at ILL-TEMPERED

dis·agree·ment \-mənt\ *n* 1 ♦ : the act or instance of disagreeing 2 a ♦ : the state of being at variance : DISPARITY b ♦ : a usu. verbal conflict between antagonists : QUARREL

♦ [1] controversy, difference, dispute, dissension; *also* clash, collision, conflict, discord, strife; debate, discussion; altercation, argument, bicker, falling-out, fight, quarrel *Ant* accord, agreement, harmony ♦ [2a] contrast, difference, discrepancy, disparity, distinction, diversity, unlikeness — more at DIFFERENCE ♦ [2b] altercation, argument, bicker, brawl, dispute, fight, hassle, misunderstanding, quarrel, row, scrap, spat, squabble, wrangle — more at ARGUMENT

dis·al·low \ˌdi-sə-ˈlaů\ *vb* **1** ♦ : to deny the force, truth, or validity of : REJECT ⟨~ a claim⟩ **2** ♦ : to refuse to allow

♦ contradict, deny, disavow, disclaim, gainsay, negate, negative, reject, repudiate — more at DENY

dis·al·low·ance \ˌdi-sə-ˈlaů-ən(t)s\ *n* ♦ : the act of disallowing

♦ contradiction, denial, disavowal, disclaimer, negation, rejection, repudiation — more at DENIAL

dis·ap·pear \ˌdi-sə-ˈpir\ *vb* **1** ♦ : to pass out of sight **2** : to cease to be : become lost — **dis·ap·pear·ance** *n*

♦ dissolve, evaporate, fade, flee, go, melt, vanish; *also* clear, dissipate *Ant* appear, materialize

dis·ap·point \ˌdi-sə-ˈpóint\ *vb* ♦ : to fail to fulfill the expectation or hope of

♦ cheat, dissatisfy, fail, let down; *also* discontent, disgruntle, displease; disenchant, disillusion *Ant* satisfy

dis·ap·point·ment \-mənt\ *n* ♦ : the act or an instance of disappointing : the state or emotion of being disappointed

♦ dismay, dissatisfaction, frustration, letdown; *also* disenchantment, disillusionment; blues, dejection, depression, desolateness, desolation, despondency, distress, doldrums, dolor, dumps, gloom, gloominess, melancholy, oppression, sadness, sorrow, unhappiness; alarm, concern, consternation; chagrin, discomfiture *Ant* contentment, gratification, satisfaction

dis·ap·pro·ba·tion \di-ˌsa-prə-ˈbā-shən\ *n* : the act or state of disapproving : the state of being disapproved : DISAPPROVAL

dis·ap·prov·al \ˌdi-sə-ˈprü-vəl\ *n* ♦ : the act or state of disapproving : the state of being disapproved

♦ deprecation, disfavor (*or* disfavour), dislike, displeasure; *also* blame, censure, criticism, denunciation, dressing down, opprobrium, reproach, reprobation; antagonism, antipathy, hostility; disparagement, opposition *Ant* approbation, approval, favor

dis·ap·prove \-ˈprüv\ *vb* **1** ♦ : to pass unfavorable judgment on **2** : to feel or express disapproval ⟨~s of smoking⟩ **3** ♦ : to refuse approval to : REJECT — **dis·ap·prov·ing·ly** \-ˈprü-viŋ-lē\ *adv*

♦ *usu* disapprove of [1] deprecate, discountenance, disfavor (*or* disfavour), dislike, frown, reprove; *also* blame, censure, condemn, criticize, denounce, reprehend, reprobate; chide, rebuke, reproach, scold *Ant* approve, favor, like ♦ [3] decline, disallow, negative, refuse, reject, repudiate, spurn, turn down — more at DECLINE

dis·arm \di-ˈsärm\ *vb* **1** : to take arms or weapons from **2** : to reduce the size and strength of the armed forces of a country **3** ♦ : to make harmless, peaceable, or friendly : win over ⟨a ~*ing* smile⟩ — **dis·ar·ma·ment** \-ˈsär-mə-mənt\ *n*

♦ appease, conciliate, mollify, pacify, placate, propitiate — more at PACIFY

dis·ar·range \ˌdi-sə-ˈrānj\ *vb* : to disturb the arrangement or order of

dis·ar·range·ment \-mənt\ *n* : the act of disarranging or the state of being disarranged

dis·ar·ray \-ˈrā\ *n* **1** ♦ : a lack of order or sequence : DISORDER **2** : disorderly or careless dress

♦ chaos, confusion, disorder, disorganization, havoc, hell, jumble, mess, muddle, shambles — more at CHAOS

dis·as·sem·ble \ˌdi-sə-ˈsem-bəl\ *vb* ♦ : to take apart

♦ dismantle, knock down, strike, take down; *also* detach, disengage; disconnect, divide, disjoin, disunite, separate *Ant* assemble, construct, put together

dis·as·so·ci·ate \-ˈsō-shē-ˌāt, -sē-\ *vb* : to detach from association

di·sas·ter \di-ˈzas-tər, -ˈsas-\ *n* [MF *desastre*, fr. It *disastro*, fr. *astro* star, fr. L *astrum*] ♦ : a sudden or great misfortune — **di·sas·trous·ly** *adv*

♦ calamity, cataclysm, catastrophe, debacle, tragedy; *also* collapse, crash, meltdown; convulsion, paroxysm, upheaval; accident, casualty, fatality; misadventure, mischance, misfortune, mishap, woe; bummer, downer

di·sas·trous \di-ˈzas-trəs\ *adj* ♦ : attended by or causing suffering or disaster

♦ calamitous, catastrophic, destructive, fatal, fateful, ruinous, unfortunate — more at FATAL

dis·avow \ˌdi-sə-ˈvaů\ *vb* **1** ♦ : to deny responsibility for : REPUDIATE **2** ♦ : to refuse to acknowledge or accept : DISCLAIM

♦ [1, 2] contradict, deny, disallow, disclaim, gainsay, negate, negative, reject, repudiate — more at DENY

dis·avow·al \ˌdi-sə-ˈvaů-əl\ *n* ♦ : the act or an instance of disavowing

♦ contradiction, denial, disallowance, disclaimer, negation, rejection, repudiation — more at DENIAL

dis·band \dis-ˈband\ *vb* ♦ : to break up the organization of : DISPERSE

♦ break up, disperse, dissolve *Ant* band, join, unite

dis·bar \dis-ˈbär\ *vb* : to expel from the legal profession — **dis·bar·ment** *n*

dis·be·lieve \ˌdis-bə-ˈlēv\ *vb* **1** : to hold not worthy of belief : not believe **2** : to withhold or reject belief — **dis·be·lief** \-ˈlēf\ *n*

dis·be·liev·er \ˌdis-bə-ˈlē-vər\ *n* ♦ : one that is not a believer

♦ doubter, questioner, skeptic, unbeliever — more at SKEPTIC

dis·bur·den \dis-ˈbər-ᵊn\ *vb* ♦ : to rid of a burden

♦ clear, disencumber, free, relieve, rid, unburden — more at RID

dis·burse \dis-ˈbərs\ *vb* **dis·bursed; dis·burs·ing 1** ♦ : to pay out : EXPEND **2** : DISTRIBUTE

♦ expend, give, lay out, pay, spend — more at SPEND

dis·burse·ment \-mənt\ *n* **1** ♦ : the act of disbursing **2** ♦ : funds paid out

♦ [1] compensation, payment, remittance, remuneration — more at PAYMENT ♦ [2] cost, expenditure, expense, outgo, outlay — more at EXPENSE

¹disc *var of* DISK

²disc *abbr* discount

¹dis·card \dis-ˈkärd, ˈdis-ˌkärd\ *vb* **1** : to let go a playing card from one's hand; *also* : to play (a card) from a suit other than a trump but different from the one led **2** ♦ : to get rid of as unwanted

♦ cast, ditch, dump, fling, jettison, junk, lose, reject, scrap, shed, shuck, slough, throw away, throw out, unload; *also* abandon, desert, forsake; dismiss; abolish, annihilate, eliminate, eradicate, expunge, exterminate, extinguish, extirpate, liquidate, remove, root (out), stamp (out), wipe out

²dis·card \ˈdis-ˌkärd\ *n* ♦ : one that is cast off or rejected

♦ cull, reject, rejection — more at CULL

disc brake *n* : a brake that operates by the friction of a pair of plates pressing against the sides of a rotating disc

dis·cern \di-ˈsərn, -ˈzərn\ *vb* **1** ♦ : to detect with the eyes : DISTINGUISH **2** ♦ : to recognize or identify as separate and distinct : DISCRIMINATE **3** ♦ : to come to know or recognize mentally ⟨~ right from wrong⟩

♦ [1] behold, descry, distinguish, espy, eye, look, note, notice, observe, perceive, regard, remark, see, sight, spy, view, witness — more at SEE ♦ [2] differentiate, discriminate, distinguish, separate — more at DISTINGUISH

dis·cern·ible \di-ˈsər-nə-bəl, -ˈzər-\ *n* ♦ : capable of being discerned

♦ appreciable, detectable, distinguishable, palpable, perceptible, sensible — more at PERCEPTIBLE

dis·cern·ing *adj* ♦ : revealing insight and understanding

♦ insightful, perceptive, sagacious, sage, sapient, wise — more at WISE

dis·cern·ment \-mənt\ *n* ♦ : the ability to grasp and comprehend what is obscure

♦ insight, perception, sagacity, sapience, wisdom — more at WISDOM

¹dis·charge \dis-'chärj, 'dis-ˌchärj\ *vb* **1** ♦ : to relieve of a charge, load, or burden : UNLOAD; *esp* : to remove the electrical energy from ⟨~ a storage battery⟩ **2** ♦ : to let or put off ⟨~ passengers⟩ **3** ♦ : to drive (as an arrow or bullet) forward quickly or forcibly : SHOOT **4** : to set free ⟨~ a prisoner⟩ **5** ♦ : to give outlet or vent to ⟨~ emotions⟩ ⟨~ fumes⟩ **6** : to dismiss from service or employment, service, or duty ⟨~ a soldier⟩ **7** ♦ : to get rid of by paying or doing ⟨~ a debt⟩ **8** : to give forth fluid ⟨the river ~s into the ocean⟩

♦ [1, 2] disburden, disencumber, unburden, unload — more at UNLOAD ♦ [3] blast, fire, loose, shoot — more at SHOOT ♦ [5] cast, emit, exhale, expel, issue, release, shoot, vent — more at EMIT ♦ [7] clear, foot, liquidate, pay, pay off, quit, recompense, settle, spring, stand — more at PAY

²dis·charge \'dis-ˌchärj, dis-'chärj\ *n* **1** ♦ : the act of discharging, unloading, releasing, or relieving **2** : something that discharges; *esp* : a certification of release or payment **3** : a firing off (as of a gun) **4** : a flowing out (as of blood from a wound); *also* : something that is emitted ⟨a purulent ~⟩ **5** ♦ : release or dismissal esp. from an office or employment; *also* : complete separation from military service **6** : a flow of electricity (as through a gas)

♦ [1] delivery, quietus, quittance, release — more at RELEASE ♦ [5] dismissal, layoff — more at LAYOFF

dis·ci·ple \di-'sī-pəl\ *n* [ultim. fr. LL *discipulus* follower of Jesus in his lifetime, fr. L, pupil] **1** ♦ : one who accepts and helps to spread the teachings of another; *also* : a convinced adherent **2** *cap* : a member of the Disciples of Christ

♦ adherent, convert, follower, partisan, pupil, votary — more at FOLLOWER

dis·ci·pli·nar·i·an \ˌdi-sə-plə-'ner-ē-ən\ *n* : one who enforces order

dis·ci·plin·ary \'di-sə-plə-ˌner-ē\ *adj* ♦ : of or relating to discipline; *also* : CORRECTIVE ⟨take ~ action⟩

♦ corrective, penal, punitive — more at PUNITIVE

¹dis·ci·pline \'di-sə-plən\ *n* **1** : suffering, pain, or loss that serves as retribution : PUNISHMENT **2** ♦ : a field of study **3** : training that corrects, molds, or perfects **4** : control gained by obedience or training : orderly conduct **5** : a system of rules governing conduct

♦ area, arena, demesne, department, domain, field, line, province, realm, specialty, sphere — more at FIELD

²discipline *vb* **-plined; -plin·ing 1** ♦ : to punish or penalize for the sake of discipline : PUNISH **2** : to train or develop by instruction and exercise esp. in self-control **3** : to bring under control ⟨~ troops⟩; *also* : to impose order upon

♦ castigate, chasten, chastise, correct, penalize, punish — more at PUNISH

disc jockey *or* **disk jockey** *n* : an announcer of a radio show of popular recorded music

dis·claim \dis-'klām\ *vb* **1** ♦ : to declare untrue : DENY **2** ♦ : to refuse to admit or acknowledge : DISAVOW

♦ disavow, disown, repudiate; *also* contradict, deny, disallow, gainsay, negate, negative, refuse, reject; challenge, confute, criticize, disprove, rebut, refute; dispute, question *Ant* acknowledge, avow, claim, own, recognize

dis·claim·er \dis-'klā-mər\ *n* **1** : a denial or disavowal of legal claim; *also* : a writing that embodies a legal disclaimer **2** ♦ : a refusal to acknowledge or accept

♦ contradiction, denial, disallowance, disavowal, negation, rejection, repudiation — more at DENIAL

dis·close \dis-'klōz\ *vb* **1** : to expose to view **2** ♦ : to make known or public — **dis·clo·sure** \-'klō-zhər\ *n*

♦ bare, discover, divulge, expose, reveal, spill, tell, unbosom, uncloak, uncover, unmask, unveil — more at REVEAL

dis·co \'dis-kō\ *n, pl* **discos 1** ♦ : a nightclub for dancing to live or recorded music **2** : popular dance music characterized by hypnotic rhythm, repetitive lyrics, and electronically produced sounds

♦ café, discotheque, nightclub — more at NIGHTCLUB

dis·col·or *or Can and Brit* **dis·col·our** \dis-'kə-lər\ *vb* : to alter or change in hue or color esp. for the worse — **dis·col·or·ation** \-ˌkə-lə-'rā-shən\ *n*

dis·com·bob·u·late \ˌdis-kəm-'bä-byù-ˌlāt\ *vb* **-lat·ed; -lat·ing** ♦ : to disturb the composure of : CONFUSE

♦ addle, baffle, befog, befuddle, bemuse, bewilder, confound, confuse, disorient, muddle, muddy, mystify, perplex, puzzle — more at CONFUSE

dis·com·fit \dis-'kəm-fət, *esp Southern* ˌdis-kəm-'fit\ *vb* ♦ : to put into a state of perplexity and embarrassment

♦ abash, confound, confuse, disconcert, discountenance, embarrass, faze, fluster, mortify, rattle — more at EMBARRASS

dis·com·fi·ture \dis-'kəm-fə-ˌchùr\ *n* ♦ : the act of discomfiting : the state of being discomfited

♦ abashment, confusion, embarrassment, fluster, mortification — more at EMBARRASSMENT

¹dis·com·fort \dis-'kəm-fərt\ *vb* : to make uncomfortable or uneasy

²discomfort *n* : mental or physical uneasiness

dis·com·mode \ˌdis-kə-'mōd\ *vb* **-mod·ed; -mod·ing** ♦ : to cause inconvenience to : TROUBLE

♦ disoblige, disturb, inconvenience, trouble — more at INCONVENIENCE

dis·com·pose \-kəm-'pōz\ *vb* **1** ♦ : to destroy the composure of : AGITATE **2** : to disturb the order of : DISARRANGE — **dis·com·po·sure** \-'pō-zhər\ *n*

♦ agitate, bother, concern, disquiet, distress, disturb, exercise, freak out, perturb, undo, unhinge, unsettle, upset, worry

dis·con·cert \ˌdis-kən-'sərt\ *vb* ♦ : to disturb the composure of : CONFUSE ⟨the bad news ~ed us⟩

♦ abash, confound, confuse, discomfit, discountenance, embarrass, faze, fluster, mortify, rattle — more at EMBARRASS

dis·con·cert·ing *adj* ♦ : causing loss of composure or self-possession

♦ awkward, embarrassing, uncomfortable — more at AWKWARD

dis·con·nect \ˌdis-kə-'nekt\ *vb* ♦ : to undo the connection of — **dis·con·nec·tion** \-'nek-shən\ *n*

♦ break up, disjoint, dissever, dissociate, disunite, divide, divorce, part, resolve, separate, sever, split, sunder, unyoke — more at SEPARATE

dis·con·nect·ed *adj* **1** ♦ : not connected : SEPARATE **2** ♦ : lacking orderly continuity, arrangement, or relevance — INCOHERENT — **dis·con·nect·ed·ly** *adv* — **dis·con·nect·ed·ness** *n*

♦ [1] detached, discrete, freestanding, separate, single, unattached, unconnected — more at SEPARATE ♦ [2] disjointed, incoherent, unconnected — more at INCOHERENT

dis·con·so·late \dis-'kän-sə-lət\ *adj* **1** : CHEERLESS **2** ♦ : hopelessly sad — **dis·con·so·late·ly** *adv*

♦ brokenhearted, despondent, forlorn, heartsick, miserable, sad, unhappy, wretched — more at SAD

¹dis·con·tent \ˌdis-kən-'tent\ *n* ♦ : uneasiness of mind : DISSATISFACTION

♦ displeasure, disquiet, dissatisfaction; *also* bitterness, resentment; perturbation, uneasiness; blues, dejection, depression, desolateness, desolation, despondency, doldrums, dolor, dumps; misery, sadness, sorrow, unhappiness, wretchedness *Ant* contentedness, contentment, pleasure, satisfaction

²dis·content *vb* ♦ : to make dissatisfied or displeased

♦ disaffect, disgruntle, displease, dissatisfy; *also* alienate, estrange; agitate, discompose, disturb, disquiet, perturb, upset; annoy, irk, irritate, nettle, peeve; depress, sadden *Ant* content, gratify, please, satisfy

dis·con·tent·ed *adj* ♦ : expressing or showing lack of satisfaction

♦ aggrieved, discontent, dissatisfied, malcontent; *also* disappointed, frustrated, unfulfilled; disquieted, disturbed, perturbed, upset; dejected, depressed, despairing, despondent, disconsolate, doleful, down, downcast, downhearted, forlorn, hangdog, inconsolable, joyless, miserable, mournful, sad, sorrowful, unhappy *Ant* content, contented, gratified, pleased, satisfied

dis·con·tin·u·ance \ˌdis-kən-ˈtin-yə-wəns\ *n* : the act or an instance of discontinuing

dis·con·tin·ue \ˌdis-kən-ˈtin-yü\ *vb* 1 ♦ : to break the continuity of : cease to operate, use, or take 2 ♦ : to come or bring to an end

♦ [1, 2] break, break off, cease, cut, desist, drop, end, halt, knock off, lay off, leave off, quit, shut off, stop — more at STOP

dis·con·ti·nu·i·ty \dis-ˌkän-tə-ˈnü-ə-tē, -ˈnyü-\ *n* 1 : lack of continuity or cohesion 2 ♦ : a break in continuity : GAP

♦ gap, hiatus, interim, interlude, intermission, interruption, interval — more at GAP

dis·con·tin·u·ous \ˌdis-kən-ˈtin-yə-wəs\ *adj* ♦ : not continuous

♦ casual, choppy, erratic, fitful, intermittent, irregular, occasional, spasmodic, sporadic, spotty, unsteady — more at FITFUL

dis·cord \ˈdis-ˌkȯrd\ *n* 1 ♦ : lack of agreement or harmony : DISSENSION 2 : a harsh combination of musical sounds 3 : a harsh or unpleasant sound

♦ conflict, dissent, disunity, friction, schism, strife, variance, war, warfare; *also* clash, collision, competition, contention; altercation, argument, bicker, brawl, debate, disagreement, dispute, falling-out, fight, hassle, jar, quarrel, row, run-in, scrap, spat, squabble, tiff, wrangle; incompatibility, incongruity, inconsistency; animosity, antagonism, antipathy, enmity, hostility, ill will, rancor *Ant* accord, agreement, concord, concordance, harmony, peace

dis·cor·dant \dis-ˈkȯrd-ᵊnt\ *adj* 1 a ♦ : being at variance ⟨~ opinions⟩ b : apt or disposed to quarrel in an often petty manner : QUARRELSOME 2 ♦ : relating to a discord ⟨a ~ tone⟩ — dis·cor·dant·ly *adv*

♦ [1a] discrepant, incompatible, incongruous, inharmonious ♦ [2] dissonant, inharmonious, unmelodious, unmusical — more at DISSONANT

dis·co·theque *or* discothèque \ˈdis-kə-ˌtek\ *n* ♦ : a nightclub for dancing to live or recorded music : DISCO 1

♦ café, disco, nightclub — more at NIGHTCLUB

¹dis·count \ˈdis-ˌkaunt\ *n* 1 ♦ : a reduction made from a regular or list price 2 ♦ : a deduction of interest in advance when lending money

♦ [1, 2] abatement, deduction, reduction — more at DEDUCTION

²dis·count \ˈdis-ˌkaunt, dis-ˈkaunt\ *vb* 1 : to deduct from the amount of a bill, debt, or charge usu. for cash or prompt payment; *also* : to sell or offer for sale at a discount 2 : to lend money after deducting the discount ⟨~ a note⟩ 3 a : DISREGARD b ♦ : to minimize the importance of 4 : to make allowance for bias or exaggeration 5 : to take into account (as a future event) in present calculations — dis·count·able *adj* — dis·count·er *n*

♦ belittle, cry down, decry, deprecate, depreciate, diminish, disparage, minimize, put down, write off — more at DECRY

³dis·count \ˈdis-ˌkaunt\ *adj* : selling goods or services at a discount; *also* : sold at or reflecting a discount

dis·coun·te·nance \dis-ˈkaunt-ᵊn-ənts\ *vb* 1 ♦ : to disturb the composure of : DISCONCERT 2 ♦ : to look with disfavor on

♦ [1] abash, confound, confuse, discomfit, disconcert, embarrass, faze, fluster, mortify, rattle — more at EMBARRASS ♦ [2] deprecate, disapprove, disfavor (*or* disfavour), dislike, frown, reprove

dis·cour·age \dis-ˈkər-ij\ *vb* -aged; -ag·ing 1 ♦ : to deprive of courage or confidence : DISHEARTEN 2 : to hinder by disfavoring 3 ♦ : to dissuade or attempt to dissuade — dis·cour·ag·ing·ly *adv*

♦ [1] daunt, demoralize, dishearten, dismay, dispirit, unman, unnerve; *also* browbeat, bully, cow, intimidate; depress, sadden, weigh; afflict, try; damp, dampen, deaden; distress, trouble; bother, irk, vex, worry; debilitate, enfeeble, undermine, weaken; frighten, horrify, scare *Ant* embolden, encourage, hearten, nerve, steel ♦ [3] deter, dissuade, inhibit; *also* divert *Ant* encourage, persuade

dis·cour·age·ment \-mənt\ *n* ♦ : the act of discouraging : the state of being discouraged

♦ demoralization, despair, despondency, dismay; *also* blues, dejection, depression, dumps, gloom, melancholy; defeatism, pessimism, resignation *Ant* encouragement

¹dis·course \ˈdis-ˌkōrs\ *n* [ME *discours*, fr. ML & LL *discursus*; ML, argument, fr. LL, conversation, fr. L, act of running about, fr. *discurrere* to run about, fr. *currere* to run] 1 ♦ : verbal interchange of ideas 2 : formal and usu. extended expression of thought on a subject

♦ colloquy, conversation, dialogue, discussion, exchange — more at CONVERSATION

²dis·course \dis-ˈkōrs\ *vb* dis·coursed; dis·cours·ing 1 ♦ : to express oneself in esp. oral discourse 2 : TALK, CONVERSE

♦ declaim, descant, harangue, lecture, orate, speak, talk — more at TALK

dis·cour·te·ous \(ˌ)dis-ˈkər-tē-əs\ *adj* ♦ : lacking courtesy : RUDE — dis·cour·te·ous·ly *adv*

♦ ill-bred, ill-mannered, impertinent, impolite, inconsiderate, rude, thoughtless, uncivil, ungracious, unmannerly — more at IMPOLITE

dis·cour·te·sy \-ˈkər-tə-sē\ *n* ♦ : the quality or state of being rude : RUDENESS; *also* : a rude act

♦ brazenness, disrespect, impertinence, impudence, incivility, insolence, rudeness; *also* audacity, boldness, sauciness; churlishness, clownishness, vulgarity; bluntness, curtness, sharpness; disagreeableness, grumpiness, sullenness, surliness; impropriety, incorrectness, indecency, unfitness; arrogance, conceit, presumption, pretense, pretension, pretentiousness *Ant* civility, consideration, courtesy, genteelness, gentility, graciousness, politeness, thoughtfulness

dis·cov·er \dis-ˈkə-vər\ *vb* 1 ♦ : to make known or visible 2 a ♦ : to obtain sight or knowledge of for the first time b ♦ : to learn by study, observation, or search : FIND OUT — dis·cov·er·er *n*

♦ [1] bare, disclose, divulge, expose, reveal, spill, tell, unbosom, uncloak, uncover, unmask, unveil — more at REVEAL ♦ [2a] ascertain, catch on, find out, hear, learn, realize, see; *also* hit (on *or* upon), tumble (to); descry, detect, encounter, espy, spot; dope (out), figure out, puzzle (out); discern, note, observe, perceive; divine ♦ [2b] detect, determine, dig up, ferret out, find, hit on, locate, track down — more at FIND

dis·cov·ery \dis-ˈkə-və-rē\ *n, pl* -er·ies 1 ♦ : the act or process of discovering 2 : something discovered 3 : the disclosure usu. before a civil trial of pertinent facts or documents

♦ detection, finding; *also* disclosure, exposure, revelation, uncovering, unveiling; creation, invention; exploration; rediscovery

¹dis·cred·it \(ˌ)dis-'kre-dət\ *vb* **1** : DISBELIEVE **2** : to cause disbelief in the accuracy or authority of **3** ♦ : to deprive of good repute : DISGRACE

♦ abase, debase, degrade, demean, disgrace, dishonor (*or* dishonour), humble, humiliate, lower, shame, smirch, take down — more at HUMBLE

²discredit *n* **1** ♦ : loss of reputation **2** : lack or loss of belief or confidence

♦ disgrace, dishonor (*or* dishonour), disrepute, ignominy, infamy, odium, opprobrium, reproach, shame — more at DISGRACE

dis·cred·it·able \-tə-bəl\ *adj* ♦ : not reputable or decent : injurious to a reputation for decency

♦ disgraceful, dishonorable (*or* dishonourable), disreputable, ignominious, infamous, notorious, shameful — more at DISREPUTABLE

dis·creet \dis-'krēt\ *adj* : showing good judgment; *esp* : capable of observing prudent silence — **dis·creet·ly** *adv*
dis·crep·an·cy \dis-'kre-pən-sē\ *n, pl* **-cies** **1** ♦ : the quality or state of being discrepant : DIFFERENCE **2** : an instance of being discrepant

♦ contrast, difference, disagreement, disparity, distinction, diversity, unlikeness — more at DIFFERENCE

dis·crep·ant \-pənt\ *adj* [ME *discrepaunt*, fr. L *discrepans*, prp. of *discrepare* to sound discordantly, fr. *crepare* to rattle, creak] ♦ : being at variance

♦ discordant, incompatible, incongruous, inharmonious

dis·crete \dis-'krēt, 'dis-ˌkrēt\ *adj* **1** ♦ : individually distinct **2** : NONCONTINUOUS

♦ detached, disconnected, freestanding, separate, single, unattached, unconnected — more at SEPARATE

dis·cre·tion \dis-'kre-shən\ *n* **1** ♦ : the quality of being discreet : PRUDENCE **2** ♦ : individual choice or judgment **3** : power of free decision or latitude of choice

♦ [1] common sense, horse sense, prudence — more at PRUDENCE ♦ [2] alternative, choice, option, pick, preference, way — more at CHOICE

dis·cre·tion·ary \-'kre-shə-ˌner-ē\ *adj* **1** ♦ : left to discretion : exercised at one's own discretion **2** : available for discretionary use

♦ elective, optional, voluntary — more at OPTIONAL

dis·crim·i·nate \dis-'kri-mə-ˌnāt\ *vb* **-nat·ed; -nat·ing** **1** ♦ : to recognize or give expression to a difference : DISTINGUISH **2** : to make a difference in treatment on a basis other than individual merit

♦ differentiate, discern, distinguish, separate — more at DISTINGUISH

dis·crim·i·nat·ing *adj* : marked by discrimination; *esp* : DISCERNING, JUDICIOUS
dis·crim·i·na·tion \dis-ˌkri-mə-'nā-shən\ *n* **1 a** : the quality or power of finely distinguishing **b** ♦ : recognition, perception, or identification esp. of differences **2 a** : the act, practice, or an instance of discriminating categorically rather than individually **b** : prejudiced or prejudicial outlook, action, or treatment

♦ demarcation, distinction, separation — more at SEPARATION

dis·crim·i·na·to·ry \dis-'kri-mə-nə-ˌtȯr-ē\ *adj* : marked by esp. unjust discrimination ⟨∼ treatment⟩
dis·cur·sive \dis-'kər-siv\ *adj* ♦ : moving from topic to topic without order : RAMBLING ⟨a ∼ speech⟩ — **dis·cur·sive·ly** *adv* — **dis·cur·sive·ness** *n*

♦ desultory, digressive, rambling; *also* circuitous, deviating, devious, roundabout

dis·cus \'dis-kəs\ *n, pl* **dis·cus·es** : a disk that is hurled for distance in a track-and-field contest
dis·cuss \di-'skəs\ *vb* [ME, fr. AF *discusser*, fr. L *discussus*, pp. of *discutere* to disperse, fr. *dis-* apart + *quatere* to

shake] **1** ♦ : to argue or consider carefully by presenting the various sides **2** : to talk about

♦ argue, chew over, debate, dispute, hash, moot, talk over; *also* descant (on), lecture (on *or* about), speak (about), talk (about); broach, introduce; forge, hammer (out), thrash (out); consider, deliberate, weigh; reason (with)

dis·cus·sant \di-'skəs-ᵊnt\ *n* : one who takes part in a formal discussion
dis·cus·sion \di-'skə-shən\ *n* ♦ : consideration of a question in open and usu. informal debate

♦ argument, colloquy, conference, deliberation, discourse, give-and-take, parley, talk; *also* debate, dialogue; forum, meeting, powwow, seminar, symposium; chat, rap

¹dis·dain \dis-'dān\ *n* ♦ : a feeling of contempt for someone or something regarded as unworthy or inferior : SCORN

♦ contempt, despite, scorn — more at CONTEMPT

²disdain *vb* **1** ♦ : to look on with scorn **2** : to reject or refrain from because of disdain ⟨∼ed gambling⟩

♦ high-hat, scorn, slight, sniff at, snub — more at SCORN

dis·dain·ful \dis-'dān-fəl\ *adj* ♦ : full of or expressing disdain — **dis·dain·ful·ly** *adv*

♦ haughty, highfalutin, lofty, lordly, prideful, proud, superior — more at PROUD ♦ contemptuous, degrading, derogatory, scornful, uncomplimentary — more at DEROGATORY

dis·ease \di-'zēz\ *n* ♦ : an abnormal bodily condition that impairs normal functioning and can usu. be recognized by signs and symptoms : SICKNESS — **dis·eased** \-'zēzd\ *adj*

♦ ailment, bug, complaint, complication, condition, disorder, fever, ill, illness, infirmity, malady, sickness, trouble; *also* contagion, contagious disease; infection, infectious disease; deficiency disease; attack, bout, fit, spell; debility, decrepitude, feebleness, lameness, weakness; malaise, matter; pest, pestilence, plague *Ant* health, wellness

dis·em·bark \ˌdi-səm-'bärk\ *vb* ♦ : to go or put ashore from a ship — **dis·em·bar·ka·tion** \di-ˌsem-ˌbär-'kā-shən\ *n*

♦ dock, land, moor, tie up

dis·em·body \ˌdi-səm-'bä-dē\ *vb* : to deprive of bodily existence
dis·em·bow·el \-'baù-əl\ *vb* : to take out the bowels of : EVISCERATE — **dis·em·bow·el·ment** *n*
dis·em·pow·er \ˌdis-im-'paù-(-ə)r\ *vb* : to deprive of power, authority, or influence
dis·en·chant \ˌdis-ᵊn-'chant\ *vb* ♦ : to free from illusion : DISILLUSION — **dis·en·chant·ment** *n*

♦ disillusion, undeceive — more at DISILLUSION

dis·en·chant·ed \-'chan-təd\ *adj* : DISAPPOINTED, DISSATISFIED
dis·en·cum·ber \ˌdis-ᵊn-'kəm-bər\ *vb* ♦ : to free from something that burdens

♦ disburden, discharge, unburden, unload — more at UNLOAD

dis·en·fran·chise \ˌdis-in-'fran-ˌchīz\ *vb* : to deprive of a franchise, a legal right, or a privilege; *esp* : to deprive of the right to vote — **dis·en·fran·chise·ment** *n*
dis·en·gage \ˌdis-ᵊn-'gāj\ *vb* ♦ : to release from something that engages or involves : EXTRICATE ⟨∼ from a harness⟩ ⟨∼ the clutch⟩ — **dis·en·gage·ment** *n*

♦ clear, disentangle, extricate, free, liberate, release, untangle — more at EXTRICATE

dis·en·gaged \-'gājd\ *adj* : IMPARTIAL, DETACHED ⟨a ∼ observer⟩
dis·en·tan·gle \ˌdis-ᵊn-'taŋ-gəl\ *vb* ♦ : to free from entanglement

♦ unravel, untangle, untwine — more at UNRAVEL

dis·equi·lib·ri·um \di-ˌsē-kwə-'li-brē-əm\ *n* : loss or lack of equilibrium

dis·es·tab·lish \ˌdi-sə-'sta-blish\ *vb* : to end the establishment of; *esp* : to deprive of the status of an established church — **dis·es·tab·lish·ment** *n*

dis·es·teem \ˌdi-sə-'stēm\ *n* : lack of esteem : DISFAVOR, DISREPUTE

dis·fa·vor *or Can and Brit* **dis·fa·vour** \(ˌ)dis-'fā-vər\ *n* 1 ♦ : a feeling of aversion or disapproval : DISLIKE 2 : the state or fact of being no longer favored

♦ aversion, disinclination, dislike — more at DISLIKE
♦ deprecation, disapproval, dislike, displeasure — more at DISAPPROVAL

dis·fig·ure \dis-'fi-gyər\ *vb* ♦ : to spoil the appearance of ⟨*disfigured* by a scar⟩

♦ blemish, break, cripple, damage, deface, flaw, harm, hurt, injure, mar, spoil, vitiate — more at DAMAGE

dis·fig·ure·ment \-mənt\ *n* 1 : the act of disfiguring or the state of being disfigured 2 ♦ : something that disfigures

♦ blemish, defect, deformity, fault, flaw, imperfection, mark, pockmark, scar — more at BLEMISH

dis·fran·chise \dis-'fran-ˌchīz\ *vb* : DISENFRANCHISE — **dis·fran·chise·ment** *n*

disfunction *var of* DYSFUNCTION

dis·gorge \-'górj\ *vb* 1 : to discharge by the throat and mouth : VOMIT 2 ♦ : to discharge forcefully or confusedly

♦ belch, eject, erupt, expel, jet, spew, spout, spurt — more at ERUPT

¹**dis·grace** \di-'skrās, dis-'grās\ *vb* ♦ : to bring reproach or shame to

♦ abase, debase, degrade, demean, discredit, dishonor (*or* dishonour), humble, humiliate, lower, shame, smirch, take down — more at HUMBLE

²**disgrace** *n* 1 a ♦ : the condition of one fallen from grace or honor : SHAME b ♦ : a source of shame 2 : the condition of being out of favor : loss of respect

♦ [1a] discredit, dishonor (*or* dishonour), disrepute, ignominy, infamy, odium, opprobrium, reproach, shame; *also* contempt, disdain, scorn; deprecation, disapprobation, disapproval, disfavor; abasement, debasement, debasing, degradation, humbling, humiliation; blot, brand, slur, smirch, spot, stain, stigma *Ant* esteem, honor, respect ♦ [1b] dishonor, reflection, reproach, scandal; *also* smirch, spot, stain, stigma *Ant* credit, honor

dis·grace·ful \-fəl\ *adj* ♦ : bringing or involving disgrace — **dis·grace·ful·ly** *adv*

♦ discreditable, dishonorable (*or* dishonourable), disreputable, ignominious, infamous, notorious, shameful — more at DISREPUTABLE

dis·grun·tle \dis-'grənt-ᵊl\ *vb* **dis·grun·tled; dis·grun·tling** ♦ : to put in bad humor — usu. used as a participial adjective ⟨a *disgruntled* employee⟩

♦ alienate, disaffect, estrange, sour — more at ESTRANGE ♦ disaffect, discontent, displease, dissatisfy — more at DISCONTENT

¹**dis·guise** \dis-'gīz\ *vb* **dis·guised; dis·guis·ing** 1 ♦ : to change the appearance of to conceal the identity or to resemble another 2 : HIDE, CONCEAL

♦ camouflage, cloak, dress up, mask; *also* blanket, blot out, conceal, cover, curtain, enshroud, hide, obscure, occult, screen, shroud, veil; affect, assume, counterfeit, dissemble, dissimulate, feign, pose, pretend, sham, simulate

²**disguise** *n* 1 ♦ : clothing put on to conceal one's identity or counterfeit another's 2 : an outward appearance that hides what something really is

♦ camouflage, guise; *also* domino, mask, veil, vizard; dress, getup, outfit, rig; coloring, cosmetic, makeup, paint

¹**dis·gust** \dis-'gəst\ *n* ♦ : marked aversion aroused by something highly distasteful : REPUGNANCE — **dis·gust·ful** \-fəl\ *adj*

♦ distaste, loathing, nausea, repugnance, repulsion, revulsion; *also* abhorrence, abomination, execration, hate, hatred; disapproval, disfavor, disinclination, dislike, disliking, displeasure

²**disgust** *vb* ♦ : to provoke to loathing, repugnance, or aversion : be offensive to — **dis·gust·ing** \-'gəs-tiŋ\ *adj* — **dis·gust·ing·ly** *adv*

♦ nauseate, repel, repulse, revolt, sicken, turn off; *also* displease, distress; appall, horrify; affront, insult, offend, outrage, shock

dis·gust·ed *adj* ♦ : affected by disgust — **dis·gust·ed·ly** *adv*

♦ sick, squeamish — more at SICK

¹**dish** \'dish\ *n* [ME, fr. OE *disc* plate, fr. L *discus* quoit, disk, dish, fr. Gk *diskos*, fr. *dikein* to throw] 1 : a vessel used for serving food 2 : the food served in a dish ⟨a ∼ of berries⟩ 3 : food prepared in a particular way 4 : something resembling a dish esp. in being shallow and concave 5 : SATELLITE DISH 6 : GOSSIP 2

²**dish** *vb* 1 : to put into a dish 2 : to make concave like a dish 3 : GOSSIP

dis·ha·bille \ˌdi-sə-'bēl\ *n* [F *déshabillé*] : the state of being dressed in a casual or careless manner

dis·har·mo·ny \(ˌ)dis-'här-mə-nē\ *n* : lack of harmony — **dis·har·mo·ni·ous** \ˌdis-(ˌ)här-'mō-nē-əs\ *adj*

dish·cloth \'dish-ˌklóth\ *n* : a cloth for washing dishes

dis·heart·en \dis-'härt-ᵊn\ *vb* ♦ : to cause to lose spirit or morale : DISCOURAGE

♦ daunt, demoralize, discourage, dismay, dispirit, unman, unnerve — more at DISCOURAGE

dished \'disht\ *adj* : CONCAVE

di·shev·el \di-'she-vəl\ *vb* **-shev·eled** *or* **-shev·elled; -shev·el·ing** *or* **-shev·el·ling** [ME *discheveled* bareheaded, with disordered hair, fr. AF *deschevelé*, fr. *des-* apart + *chevoil* hair, fr. L *capillus*] ♦ : to throw into disorder or disarray

♦ derange, disarray, disorder, disrupt, disturb, mess, mix, muddle, rumple, upset — more at DISORDER

di·shev·eled *or* **di·shev·elled** *adj* ♦ : marked by disorder or disarray

♦ disordered, messy, muddled, unkempt, untidy — more at MESSY

dis·hon·est \di-'sä-nəst\ *adj* ♦ : not honest — **dis·hon·est·ly** *adv*

♦ lying, mendacious; *also* erroneous, fallacious, false, misleading; double-dealing, hypocritical, two-faced *Ant* honest, truthful, veracious ♦ crooked, deceptive, fast, fraudulent, shady, sharp, shifty, underhanded; *also* unconscionable, unethical, unprincipled, unscrupulous; deceiving, deceitful, deluding, delusive; artful, cunning; devious, furtive, sneaking, sneaky, tricky; insidious, perfidious, treacherous *Ant* aboveboard, honest, straight

dis·hon·es·ty \di-'sä-nə-stē\ *n* ♦ : lack of honesty or integrity

♦ artifice, craft, craftiness, crookedness, cunning, deceit, deceitfulness, dissimulation, double-dealing, duplicity, guile, wiliness — more at DECEIT

¹**dis·hon·or** *or Can and Brit* **dis·hon·our** \di-'sä-nər\ *vb* 1 ♦ : to bring reproach or shame on : DISGRACE 2 : to refuse to accept or pay ⟨∼ a check⟩

♦ abase, debase, degrade, demean, discredit, disgrace, humble, humiliate, lower, shame, smirch, take down — more at HUMBLE

²**dishonor** *or Can and Brit* **dishonour** *n* 1 : lack or loss of honor 2 ♦ : the state of one who has lost honor or prestige : SHAME 3 ♦ : a cause of disgrace 4 : the act of dishonoring a negotiable instrument when presented for payment

♦ [2] discredit, disgrace, disrepute, ignominy, infamy, odium, opprobrium, reproach, shame — more at DISGRACE ♦ [3] disgrace, reflection, reproach, scandal — more at DISGRACE

dis·hon·or·able *or Can and Brit* **dis·hon·our·able** \di-ˈsä-nə-rə-bəl\ *adj* ♦ : lacking honor — **dis·hon·or·ably** \-blē\ *adv*

♦ base, contemptible, despicable, detestable, dirty, ignoble, low, mean, snide, sordid, vile, wretched — more at IGNOBLE ♦ discreditable, disgraceful, disreputable, ignominious, infamous, notorious, shameful — more at DISREPUTABLE

dish out *vb* : to give freely

dish·rag \ˈdish-ˌrag\ *n* : DISHCLOTH

dish·wash·er \-ˌwȯ-shər, -ˌwä-\ *n* : a person or machine that washes dishes

dish·wa·ter \-ˌwȯ-tər, -ˌwä-\ *n* : water used for washing dishes

dis·il·lu·sion \ˌdi-sə-ˈlü-zhən\ *vb* ♦ : to leave without illusion or naive faith and trust — **dis·il·lu·sion·ment** *n*

♦ disenchant, undeceive; *also* debunk, expose, show up, uncloak, uncover, unmask; disclose, divulge, tell, unveil

dis·il·lu·sioned *adj* : DISAPPOINTED, DISSATISFIED

dis·in·cli·na·tion \di-ˌsin-klə-ˈnā-shən\ *n* ♦ : a preference for avoiding something : slight aversion

♦ hesitancy, reluctance, reticence — more at RELUCTANCE

dis·in·cline \ˌdis-ᵊn-ˈklīn\ *vb* : to make unwilling

dis·in·clined *adj* : unwilling because of dislike or disapproval

dis·in·fect \ˌdis-ᵊn-ˈfekt\ *vb* : to cleanse of infection-causing germs — **dis·in·fec·tant** \-ˈfek-tənt\ *n* — **dis·in·fec·tion** \-ˈfek-shən\ *n*

dis·in·for·ma·tion \-ˌin-fər-ˈmā-shən\ *n* : false information deliberately and often covertly spread

dis·in·gen·u·ous \ˌdis-ᵊn-ˈjen-yə-wəs\ *adj* : lacking in candor; *also* : giving a false appearance of simple frankness

dis·in·her·it \ˌdis-ᵊn-ˈher-ət\ *vb* : to deprive of the right to inherit

dis·in·te·grate \di-ˈsin-tə-ˌgrāt\ *vb* **1** ♦ : to break or decompose into constituent parts or small particles **2** : to destroy the unity or integrity of — **dis·in·te·gra·tion** \-ˌsin-tə-ˈgrā-shən\ *n*

♦ break down, corrupt, decay, decompose, molder, putrefy, rot, spoil — more at DECAY

dis·in·ter \ˌdis-ᵊn-ˈtər\ *vb* **1** : to take from the grave or tomb **2** : UNEARTH

dis·in·ter·est·ed \(ˌ)dis-ˈin-tə-rəs-təd, -ˌres-\ *adj* **1** ♦ : not interested **2** ♦ : free from selfish motive or interest : UNBIASED

♦ [1] apathetic, casual, indifferent, insouciant, nonchalant, perfunctory, unconcerned, uncurious, uninterested — more at INDIFFERENT ♦ [2] dispassionate, equal, equitable, fair, impartial, just, nonpartisan, objective, square, unbiased, unprejudiced — more at FAIR

dis·in·ter·est·ed·ness \(ˌ)dis-ˈin-tə-rəs-təd-nəs, -ˌres-\ *n* ♦ : the quality or state of being objective or impartial

♦ detachment, impartiality, neutrality, objectivity — more at DETACHMENT

dis·join \(ˌ)dis-ˈjȯin\ *vb* : to end the joining of : SEPARATE

dis·joint \(ˌ)dis-ˈjȯint\ *vb* **1** : to disturb the orderly arrangement of **2** ♦ : to separate at the joints

♦ break up, disconnect, dissever, dissociate, disunite, divide, divorce, part, resolve, separate, sever, split, sunder, unyoke — more at SEPARATE

dis·joint·ed *adj* **1** ♦ : lacking coherence or orderly sequence **2** : separated at or as if at the joint

♦ disconnected, incoherent, unconnected — more at INCOHERENT

disk *or* **disc** \ˈdisk\ *n* **1** : something round and flat; *esp* : a flat rounded anatomical structure (as the central part of the flower head of a composite plant or a pad of cartilage between vertebrae) **2** *usu disc* : a phonograph record **3** : a round flat plate coated with a magnetic substance on which data for a computer is stored **4** *usu disc* : OPTICAL DISK

disk drive *n* : a device for accessing or storing data on a magnetic disk

dis·kette \ˌdis-ˈket\ *n* : FLOPPY DISK

disk jockey *var of* DISC JOCKEY

¹**dis·like** \(ˌ)dis-ˈlīk\ *n* ♦ : a feeling of aversion or disapproval

♦ deprecation, disapproval, disfavor (*or* disfavour), displeasure — more at DISAPPROVAL ♦ aversion, disfavor (*or* disfavour), disinclination; *also* disgust, distaste, loathing, nausea, repugnance, repulsion, revulsion; abomination, antipathy, detestation, hate, hatred; deprecation, disapproval, displeasure, dissatisfaction; jaundice **Ant** appetite, fondness, like, liking, partiality, preference, taste

²**dislike** *vb* ♦ : to regard with dislike : DISAPPROVE

♦ deprecate, disapprove, discountenance, disfavor (*or* disfavour), frown, reprove

dis·lo·cate \ˈdis-lō-ˌkāt, dis-ˈlō-\ *vb* **1** ♦ : to put out of place; *esp* : to displace (a bone or joint) from normal connections ⟨∼ a shoulder⟩ **2** : to force a change in the usual status, relationship, or order of : DISRUPT

♦ budge, displace, disturb, move, remove, shift, transfer — more at MOVE

dis·lo·ca·tion \ˌdis-(ˌ)lō-ˈkā-shən\ *n* ♦ : the act of dislocating : the state of being dislocated

♦ disruption, disturbance, upset — more at UPSET

dis·lodge \(ˌ)dis-ˈläj\ *vb* : to force out of a place esp. of rest, hiding, or defense

dis·loy·al \(ˌ)dis-ˈlȯi-əl\ *adj* ♦ : lacking in loyalty

♦ faithless, false, fickle, inconstant, loose, perfidious, recreant, traitorous, treacherous, unfaithful, untrue — more at FAITHLESS

dis·loy·al·ty \(ˌ)dis-ˈlȯi-əl-tē\ *n* ♦ : lack of loyalty

♦ betrayal, double cross, faithlessness, falseness, falsity, infidelity, perfidy, treachery, treason, unfaithfulness — more at BETRAYAL

dis·mal \ˈdiz-məl\ *adj* [ME, fr. *dismal*, n., days marked as unlucky in medieval calendars, fr. AF, fr ML *dies mali*, lit., evil days] **1** ♦ : showing or causing gloom or depression **2** : lacking merit ⟨a ∼ performance⟩ — **dis·mal·ly** *adv*

♦ bleak, dark, dreary, gloomy, gray (*or* grey), somber (*or* sombre), wretched — more at GLOOMY

dis·man·tle \(ˌ)dis-ˈmant-ᵊl\ *vb* **-tled; -tling** **1** ♦ : to take apart **2** : to strip of furniture and equipment — **dis·man·tle·ment** *n*

♦ disassemble, knock down, strike, take down — more at DISASSEMBLE

¹**dis·may** \dis-ˈmā\ *vb* ♦ : to cause to lose courage or resolution from alarm or fear : DAUNT — **dis·may·ing·ly** *adv*

♦ daunt, demoralize, discourage, dishearten, dispirit, unman, unnerve — more at DISCOURAGE

²**dismay** *n* **1** ♦ : sudden loss of courage or resolution from alarm or fear **2** ♦ : sudden disappointment

♦ [1] demoralization, despair, despondency, discouragement — more at DISCOURAGEMENT ♦ [2] disappointment, dissatisfaction, frustration, letdown — more at DISAPPOINTMENT

dis·mem·ber \dis-ˈmem-bər\ *vb* **1** : to cut off or separate the limbs or parts of **2** : to break up or tear into pieces — **dis·mem·ber·ment** *n*

dis·miss \dis-ˈmis\ *vb* **1** ♦ : to send away **2** ♦ : to dismiss from service or employment **3** : to put aside or out of mind **4** : to put out of judicial consideration ⟨∼ed all charges⟩ — **dis·mis·sive** \-ˈmi-siv\ *adj* — **dis·mis·sive·ly** *adv*

♦ [1] banish, boot (out), bounce, cast, chase, drum, eject, expel, oust, rout, run off, throw out — more at EJECT ♦ [2] cashier, fire, remove, retire, sack; *also* downsize, furlough, lay off; boot (out), bounce **Ant** employ, hire

dis·miss·al \-ˈmi-səl\ *n* ♦ : the act of dismissing : the fact or state of being dismissed

♦ discharge, layoff — more at LAYOFF

dis·mount \dis-'maunt\ *vb* **1** : to get down from something (as a horse or bicycle) **2** : UNHORSE **3** : DISASSEMBLE

dis·obe·di·ence \ˌdi-sə-'bē-dē-əns\ *n* ♦ : neglect or refusal to obey

♦ defiance, insubordination, rebelliousness, recalcitrance, refractoriness, unruliness; *also* disrespect, impudence, insolence, rudeness; doggedness, hardheadedness, mulishness, obstinacy, pertinacity, perversity, stubbornness; mischievousness, naughtiness *Ant* compliance, docility, obedience

dis·obe·di·ent \-ənt\ *adj* ♦ : refusing or neglecting to obey

♦ contrary, defiant, froward, intractable, rebellious, recalcitrant, refractory, unruly, untoward, wayward, willful; *also* insurgent, mutinous; dogged, hardheaded, headstrong, mulish, obdurate, obstinate, peevish, pertinacious, pigheaded, stubborn, unyielding; obstreperous, uncontrollable, unmanageable, wild; perverse, resistant, wrongheaded; bad, disorderly, errant, misbehaving, mischievous, monkeying, naughty; undisciplined; dissident, nonconforming, nonconformist; disrespectful, ill-mannered, ill-natured, impolite, impudent, insolent, ornery, rude, uncouth *Ant* amenable, compliant, docile, obedient, tractable

dis·obey \ˌdi-sə-'bā\ *vb* : to fail to obey : be disobedient

dis·oblige \ˌdi-sə-'blīj\ *vb* **1** : to go counter to the wishes of **2** ♦ : to subject to inconvenience

♦ discommode, disturb, inconvenience, trouble — more at INCONVENIENCE

¹**dis·or·der** \di-'sȯr-dər\ *vb* **1** ♦ : to disturb the order of **2** : to disturb the regular or normal functions of

♦ confuse, derange, disarray, discompose, dishevel, dislocate, disrupt, disturb, jumble, mess, mix, muddle, rumple, scramble, shuffle, tumble, upset; *also* embroil, entangle, snarl, tangle; agitate, stir (up), unsettle *Ant* arrange, array, draw up, marshal, order, organize, range, regulate, straighten (up), tidy

²**disorder** *n* **1** ♦ : lack of order : CONFUSION **2** : breach of the peace or public order : TUMULT **3** ♦ : an abnormal physical or mental condition : AILMENT

♦ [1] chaos, confusion, disarray, disorganization, havoc, hell, jumble, mess, muddle, shambles — more at CHAOS ♦ [3] ailment, bug, complaint, condition, disease, fever, ill, illness, infirmity, malady, sickness, trouble — more at DISEASE

dis·or·dered *adj* **1** : marked by disorder **2** : not functioning in a normal orderly healthy way

♦ chaotic, confused, disheveled, messy, muddled, sloppy, unkempt, untidy — more at MESSY

dis·or·der·ly \-lē\ *adj* **1** : offensive to public order **2** : marked by disorder ⟨a ∼ desk⟩ — **dis·or·der·li·ness** *n*

♦ anarchic, lawless, unruly — more at LAWLESS

dis·or·ga·ni·za·tion \di-ˌsȯr-gə-nə-'zā-shən\ *n* ♦ : the act of disorganizing or the quality or state of being disorganized

♦ chaos, confusion, disarray, disorder, havoc, hell, jumble, mess, muddle, shambles — more at CHAOS

dis·or·ga·nize \di-'sȯr-gə-ˌnīz\ *vb* : to break up the regular system of : throw into disorder

dis·ori·ent \di-'sȯr-ē-ˌent\ *vb* ♦ : to cause to be confused or lost — **dis·ori·en·ta·tion** \di-ˌsȯr-ē-ən-'tā-shən\ *n*

♦ addle, baffle, befog, befuddle, bemuse, bewilder, confound, confuse, muddle, muddy, mystify, perplex, puzzle — more at CONFUSE

dis·own \di-'sōn\ *vb* ♦ : to repudiate any connection or identification with : DISCLAIM ⟨her parents ∼ed her⟩

♦ disavow, disclaim, repudiate — more at DISCLAIM

dis·par·age \di-'spar-ij\ *vb* **-aged; -ag·ing** [ME to degrade by marriage below one's class, disparage, fr. AF *desparager* to marry below one's class, fr. *parage* equality, lineage, fr. *per* peer] **1** : to lower in rank or reputation : DEGRADE **2** ♦ : to depreciate by indirect means (as invidious comparison) : BELITTLE — **dis·par·ag·ing·ly** *adv*

♦ belittle, cry down, decry, deprecate, depreciate, diminish, discount, minimize, put down, write off — more at DECRY

dis·par·age·ment \-mənt\ *n* ♦ : diminution of esteem or standing

♦ deprecation, depreciation, detraction, put-down — more at DEPRECIATION

dis·pa·rate \'dis-pə-rət, dis-'par-ət\ *adj* ♦ : distinct in quality or character

♦ different, dissimilar, distinct, distinctive, distinguishable, diverse, other, unalike, unlike — more at DIFFERENT

dis·par·i·ty \di-'spar-ə-tē\ *n* ♦ : the state of being disparate

♦ contrast, difference, disagreement, discrepancy, distinction, diversity, unlikeness — more at DIFFERENCE

dis·pas·sion·ate \(ˌ)dis-'pa-shə-nət\ *adj* ♦ : not influenced by strong feeling : IMPARTIAL — **dis·pas·sion** \-'pa-shən\ *n* — **dis·pas·sion·ate·ly** *adv*

♦ disinterested, equal, equitable, fair, impartial, just, nonpartisan, objective, square, unbiased, unprejudiced — more at FAIR

¹**dis·patch** \di-'spach\ *vb* **1** ♦ : to send off or away with promptness or speed esp. on official business **2** ♦ : to put to death **3** : to attend to rapidly or efficiently **4** : DEFEAT — **dis·patch·er** *n*

♦ [1] consign, pack, send, ship, transfer, transmit, transport — more at SEND ♦ [2] do in, execute, kill, liquidate, murder, slay — more at MURDER

²**dis·patch** \di-'spach, 'dis-ˌpach\ *n* **1** ♦ : a message sent with speed **2** : a news item sent in by a correspondent to a newspaper **3** : the act of dispatching; *esp* : SHIPMENT **4** : the act of putting to death **5** : promptness and efficiency in performing a task

♦ letter, memorandum, missive, note — more at LETTER

dis·pel \di-'spel\ *vb* **dis·pelled; dis·pel·ling** : to drive away by scattering : DISSIPATE ⟨∼ a rumor⟩

dis·pens·able \di-'spen-sə-bəl\ *adj* : capable of being dispensed with

dis·pen·sa·ry \di-'spen-sə-rē\ *n, pl* **-ries** : a place where medicine or medical or dental aid is dispensed

dis·pen·sa·tion \ˌdis-pən-'sā-shən\ *n* **1** : a system of rules for ordering affairs **2** : a particular arrangement or provision esp. of nature **3** : an exemption from a rule or from a vow or oath **4** ♦ : the act of dispensing **5** : something dispensed or distributed

♦ allocation, distribution, division, issuance — more at DISTRIBUTION

dis·pense \di-'spens\ *vb* **dis·pensed; dis·pens·ing** **1** ♦ : to portion out **2** : ADMINISTER ⟨∼ justice⟩ **3** : EXEMPT **4** : to make up and give out (remedies) — **dis·pens·er** *n* — **dispense with** **1** : SUSPEND **2** : to do without

♦ administer, allocate, apportion, deal, distribute, mete, parcel, portion, prorate — more at ADMINISTER

dis·per·sal \-'spər-səl\ *n* : the act or result of dispersing

dis·perse \di-'spərs\ *vb* **dis·persed; dis·pers·ing** ♦ : to break up and scatter about

♦ clear out, disband, dissipate, scatter — more at SCATTER ♦ break up, disband, dissolve — more at DISBAND

dis·per·sion \-'spər-zhən\ *n* : the act or process of dispersing : the state of being dispersed

dis·pir·it \dis-'pir-ət\ *vb* ♦ : to deprive of morale or enthusiasm : DISCOURAGE

♦ daunt, demoralize, discourage, dishearten, dismay, unman, unnerve — more at DISCOURAGE

dis·place \dis-'plās\ *vb* **1** ♦ : to remove from the usual or proper place; *esp* : to expel or force to flee from home or native land ⟨*displaced* persons⟩ **2** : to move out of position ⟨water *displaced* by a floating object⟩ **3** ♦ : to take the place of : REPLACE

♦ [1] budge, dislocate, disturb, move, remove, shift, transfer — more at MOVE ♦ [1] banish, deport, exile, expatriate, transport — more at BANISH ♦ [3] replace, substitute, supersede, supplant — more at REPLACE

dis·place·ment \-mənt\ *n* **1** ♦ : the act of displacing : the state of being displaced **2** : the volume or weight of a fluid (as water) displaced by a floating body (as a ship) **3** : the difference between the initial position of an object and a later position

♦ banishment, deportation, exile, expulsion — more at EXILE

¹**dis·play** \di-'splā\ *vb* ♦ : to present to view : make evident

♦ disport, exhibit, expose, flash, flaunt, parade, show, show off, sport, strut, unveil — more at SHOW

²**display** *n* **1** ♦ : a displaying of something **2** : an electronic device (as a cathode-ray tube) that gives information in visual form; *also* : the visual information

♦ demonstration, exhibition, show — more at SHOW
♦ exhibit, exhibition, exposition, fair, show — more at EXHIBITION

dis·please \(ˌ)dis-'plēz\ *vb* **1** ♦ : to arouse the disapproval and dislike of **2** : to be offensive to : give displeasure

♦ disaffect, discontent, disgruntle, dissatisfy — more at DISCONTENT

dis·plea·sure \-'ple-zhər\ *n* ♦ : a feeling of dislike and irritation : a display of disapproval

♦ deprecation, disapproval, disfavor (*or* disfavour), dislike — more at DISAPPROVAL

dis·port \di-'spōrt\ *vb* **1** ♦ : to entertain or occupy in a light, playful, or pleasant manner : AMUSE **2** ♦ : to amuse oneself in light or lively fashion : FROLIC **3** : to make evident : DISPLAY

♦ [1] amuse, divert, entertain, regale — more at AMUSE
♦ [2] caper, cavort, frisk, frolic, gambol, lark, rollick, romp, sport — more at FROLIC

dis·pos·able \di-'spō-zə-bəl\ *adj* **1** : remaining after deduction of taxes ⟨~ income⟩ **2** : designed to be used once and then thrown away ⟨~ diapers⟩ — **disposable** *n*
dis·pos·al \di-'spō-zəl\ *n* **1** : CONTROL, COMMAND **2** ♦ : an orderly arrangement **3** ♦ : a getting rid of **4** : MANAGEMENT, ADMINISTRATION **5** : presenting or bestowing something ⟨~ of favors⟩ **6** : a device used to reduce waste matter (as by grinding)

♦ [2] arrangement, array, disposition, distribution, order, sequence, setup — more at ORDER ♦ [3] disposition, dumping, jettison, removal, riddance; *also* clearance, clearing; demolition, destruction

dis·pose \di-'spōz\ *vb* **dis·posed; dis·pos·ing** **1** : to give a tendency to : INCLINE ⟨*disposed* to accept⟩ **2** ♦ : to put in place ⟨troops *disposed* for withdrawal⟩ **3** : SETTLE — **dis·pos·er** *n* — **dispose of 1** : to transfer to the control of another **2** : to get rid of **3** : to deal with conclusively

♦ deposit, fix, lay, place, position, put, set, set up, stick — more at PLACE ♦ arrange, array, classify, codify, draw up, marshal, order, organize, range, systematize — more at ORDER

dis·posed *adj* ♦ : having a particular temperament, disposition, or tendency : being in a particular frame of mind

♦ amenable, game, glad, inclined, ready, willing — more at WILLING

dis·po·si·tion \ˌdis-pə-'zi-shən\ *n* **1** : the act or power of disposing : DISPOSAL **2** : RELINQUISHMENT **3** ♦ : orderly arrangement **4** ♦ : prevailing tendency, mood, or inclination **5** : natural attitude toward things ⟨a cheerful ~⟩

♦ [3] arrangement, array, disposal, distribution, order, sequence, setup — more at ORDER ♦ [4] affinity, bent, devices, genius, inclination, leaning, partiality, penchant, predilection, predisposition, proclivity, propensity, talent, tendency, turn — more at INCLINATION ♦ [4] grain, nature, temper, temperament; *also* cheer, frame, humor, mode, mood; attitude, outlook, perspective, point of view, standpoint, viewpoint; emotion, feeling, heart, passion, sentiment; strain; belief,

conviction, mind, opinion, persuasion; expression, tone, vein; character, individuality, personality; responsiveness, sensibility, sensitiveness, sensitivity

dis·pos·sess \ˌdis-pə-'zes\ *vb* : to put out of possession or occupancy — **dis·pos·ses·sion** \-'ze-shən\ *n*
dis·praise \(ˌ)dis-'prāz\ *vb* : DISPARAGE — **dispraise** *n* — **dis·prais·er** *n*
dis·proof \(ˌ)dis-'prüf\ *n* : evidence that disproves
dis·pro·por·tion \ˌdis-prə-'pōr-shən\ *n* : lack of proportion, symmetry, or proper relation — **dis·pro·por·tion·ate** \-shə-nət\ *adj*
dis·prove \(ˌ)dis-'prüv\ *vb* ♦ : to prove to be false or wrong

♦ belie, confute, rebut, refute; *also* overthrow, overturn ***Ant*** confirm, prove, verify

dis·put·able \di-'spyü-tə-bəl, 'dis-pyə-tə-bəl\ *adj* ♦ : capable of being disputed or contested

♦ arguable, debatable, doubtful, moot, questionable — more at DEBATABLE

dis·pu·tant \di-'spyüt-ᵊnt, 'dis-pyə-tənt\ *n* ♦ : one that is engaged in a dispute

♦ arguer, contender, debater, disputer; *also* advocate, defendant, plaintiff, pleader; nitpicker, pettifogger, quibbler

dis·pu·ta·tion \ˌdis-pyu̇-'tā-shən\ *n* **1** : the action of disputing : DEBATE **2** : an oral defense of an academic thesis
dis·pu·ta·tious \-shəs\ *adj* ♦ : inclined to dispute : ARGUMENTATIVE

♦ argumentative, contentious, quarrelsome, scrappy — more at ARGUMENTATIVE

¹**dis·pute** \di-'spyüt\ *vb* **dis·put·ed; dis·put·ing** **1** ♦ : to engage in argument : ARGUE **2** : WRANGLE **3** ♦ : to question the truth or rightness of **4** : to struggle against or over : OPPOSE

♦ [1] argue, chew over, debate, discuss, hash, moot, talk over — more at DISCUSS ♦ [3] challenge, contest, query, question — more at CHALLENGE

²**dispute** *n* **1** ♦ : verbal controversy **2** ♦ : a usu. verbal conflict between antagonists : QUARREL

♦ [1] controversy, difference, disagreement, dissension
♦ [2] altercation, argument, bicker, brawl, disagreement, fight, hassle, misunderstanding, quarrel, row, scrap, spat, squabble, wrangle — more at ARGUMENT

dis·put·er *n* ♦ : one that disputes

♦ arguer, contender, debater, disputant — more at DISPUTANT

dis·qual·i·fy \(ˌ)dis-'kwä-lə-ˌfī\ *vb* : to make or declare unfit or not qualified — **dis·qual·i·fi·ca·tion** \-ˌkwä-lə-fə-'kā-shən\ *n*
¹**dis·qui·et** \(ˌ)dis-'kwī-ət\ *vb* ♦ : to make uneasy or restless : DISTURB ⟨was ~ed by the news⟩

♦ agitate, bother, concern, discompose, distress, disturb, exercise, freak out, perturb, undo, unhinge, unsettle, upset, worry

²**disquiet** *n* ♦ : lack of peace or tranquility

♦ agitation, anxiety, apprehension, care, concern, nervousness, perturbation, uneasiness, worry — more at ANXIETY

dis·qui·etude \(ˌ)dis-'kwī-ə-ˌtüd, -ˌtyüd\ *n* : AGITATION, ANXIETY
dis·qui·si·tion \ˌdis-kwə-'zi-shən\ *n* : a formal inquiry or discussion
¹**dis·re·gard** \ˌdis-ri-'gärd\ *vb* ♦ : to pay no attention to : treat as unworthy of notice or regard

♦ forget, ignore, neglect, overlook, pass over, slight, slur — more at NEGLECT ♦ condone, excuse, gloss over, ignore, pardon, pass over, shrug off, wink at — more at EXCUSE

²**disregard** *n* ♦ : the act of disregarding : the state of being disregarded — **dis·re·gard·ful** *adj*

♦ apathy, disinterestedness, indifference, insouciance, nonchalance — more at INDIFFERENCE

dis·re·pair \ˌdis-ri-ˈpar\ *n* ♦ : the state of being in need of repair

♦ desolation, dilapidation, neglect — more at NEGLECT

dis·rep·u·ta·ble \dis-ˈre-pyù-tə-bəl\ *adj* ♦ : having a bad reputation

♦ discreditable, disgraceful, dishonorable (*or* dishonourable), ignominious, infamous, notorious, shameful; *also* bad, immoral, seamy, shady, sordid, unethical, unsavory, wicked; base, contemptible, despicable, detestable, dirty, low, mean, vile, wretched *Ant* honorable, reputable, respectable

dis·re·pute \ˌdis-ri-ˈpyüt\ *n* ♦ : lack or decline of reputation : a state of being held in low esteem

♦ discredit, disgrace, dishonor (*or* dishonour), ignominy, infamy, odium, opprobrium, reproach, shame — more at DISGRACE

dis·re·spect \ˌdis-ri-ˈspekt\ *n* ♦ : lack of respect : DISCOURTESY

♦ brazenness, discourtesy, impertinence, impudence, incivility, insolence, rudeness — more at DISCOURTESY

dis·re·spect·ful \ˌdis-ri-ˈspekt-fəl\ *adj* ♦ : lacking proper respect in speech or action

♦ discourteous, ill-bred, ill-mannered, impertinent, impolite, inconsiderate, rude, thoughtless, uncivil, ungracious, unmannerly — more at IMPOLITE

dis·robe \dis-ˈrōb\ *vb* : to strip of clothing or covering : UNDRESS

dis·rupt \dis-ˈrəpt\ *vb* 1 : to break apart 2 ♦ : to throw into disorder 3 : INTERRUPT — **dis·rup·tive** \-ˈrəp-tiv\ *adj*

♦ discompose, disorder, disturb, upset — more at DISORDER

dis·rup·tion \-ˈrəp-shən\ *n* ♦ : the act or process of disrupting : the state of being disrupted

♦ dislocation, disturbance, upset — more at UPSET

dis·sat·is·fac·tion \ˌdi-ˌsa-təs-ˈfak-shən\ *n* ♦ : the quality or state of being dissatisfied

♦ disappointment, dismay, frustration, letdown — more at DISAPPOINTMENT

dis·sat·is·fied \-ˈfīd\ *adj* ♦ : expressing or showing lack of satisfaction : not pleased or satisfied

♦ aggrieved, discontent, discontented, malcontent — more at DISCONTENTED

dis·sat·is·fy \di-ˈsa-təs-ˌfī\ *vb* ♦ : to fail to satisfy

♦ disappoint, fail, let down — more at DISAPPOINT

dis·sect \di-ˈsekt\ *vb* 1 ♦ : to divide into parts esp. for examination and study 2 ♦ : to analyze and interpret minutely — **dis·sec·tor** \-ˈsek-tər\ *n*

♦ analyze, anatomize, assay, break down, break up — more at ANALYZE

dis·sect·ed *adj* : cut deeply into narrow lobes ⟨a ∼ leaf⟩

dis·sec·tion \-ˈsek-shən\ *n* ♦ : the act or process of dissecting : the state of being dissected

♦ analysis, assay, breakdown, breakup — more at ANALYSIS

dis·sem·ble \di-ˈsem-bəl\ *vb* **-bled; -bling** 1 ♦ : to hide under or put on a false appearance : conceal facts, intentions, or feelings under some pretense 2 : SIMULATE — **dis·sem·bler** *n*

♦ dissimulate, let on, pretend

dis·sem·i·nate \di-ˈse-mə-ˌnāt\ *vb* **-nat·ed; -nat·ing** ♦ : to spread abroad as if sowing seed ⟨∼ ideas⟩ — **dis·sem·i·na·tion** \-ˌse-mə-ˈnā-shən\ *n*

♦ broadcast, circulate, propagate, spread, strew — more at SPREAD

dis·sen·sion \di-ˈsen-chən\ *n* ♦ : disagreement in opinion

♦ controversy, difference, disagreement, dispute

¹dis·sent \di-ˈsent\ *vb* 1 : to withhold assent 2 : to differ in opinion

²dissent *n* 1 a ♦ : difference of opinion; *esp* : religious nonconformity b ♦ : contentious quarreling 2 : a written statement in which a justice disagrees with the opinion of the majority

♦ [1a] heresy, heterodoxy, nonconformity — more at HERESY ♦ [1a, 1b] conflict, discord, disunity, friction, schism, strife, variance, war, warfare — more at DISCORD

dis·sent·er \di-ˈsen-tər\ *n* 1 ♦ : one that dissents 2 *cap* : an English Nonconformist

♦ dissident, heretic, nonconformist — more at HERETIC

dis·ser·ta·tion \ˌdi-sər-ˈtā-shən\ *n* : an extended usu. written treatment of a subject; *esp* : one submitted for a doctorate

dis·ser·vice \di-ˈsər-vəs\ *n* ♦ : ill service : INJURY

♦ injury, injustice, raw deal, wrong; *also* insult, offense, outrage; complaint, grievance *Ant* justice

dis·sev·er \di-ˈse-vər\ *vb* ♦ : to set or keep apart : SEPARATE

♦ break up, disconnect, disjoint, dissociate, disunite, divide, divorce, part, resolve, separate, sever, split, sunder, unyoke — more at SEPARATE

dis·si·dence \ˈdi-sə-dəns\ *n* : difference of opinion : DISSENT

¹dis·si·dent \-dənt\ *adj* [L *dissidens*, prp. of *dissidēre* to sit apart, disagree, fr. *dis-* apart + *sedēre* to sit] ♦ : disagreeing esp. with an established religious or political system, organization, or belief

♦ heretical, heterodox, nonconforming, nonconformist, nonorthodox, unconventional, unorthodox — more at HERETICAL

²dissident *n* : one that is dissident

dis·sim·i·lar \di-ˈsi-mə-lər\ *adj* ♦ : not like : UNLIKE

♦ different, disparate, distinct, distinctive, distinguishable, diverse, other, unalike, unlike — more at DIFFERENT

dis·sim·i·lar·i·ty \di-ˌsi-mə-ˈlar-ə-tē\ *n* : the quality or state of being dissimilar

dis·sim·u·late \di-ˈsi-mya-ˌlāt\ *vb* ♦ : to hide under a false appearance : DISSEMBLE

♦ dissemble, let on, pretend

dis·sim·u·la·tion \di-ˌsi-mya-ˈlā-shən\ *n* ♦ : the act of dissembling or the fact of being dissembled

♦ artifice, craft, craftiness, crookedness, cunning, deceit, deceitfulness, dishonesty, double-dealing, duplicity, guile, wiliness — more at DECEIT

dis·si·pate \ˈdi-sə-ˌpāt\ *vb* **-pat·ed; -pat·ing** 1 ♦ : to break up and drive off : DISPERSE ⟨the breeze *dissipated* the fog⟩ 2 ♦ : to spend or use up wastefully or foolishly : SQUANDER 3 : to break up and vanish 4 : to be dissolute; *esp* : to drink alcoholic beverages to excess — **dis·si·pat·ed** *adj*

♦ [1] clear out, disband, disperse, scatter — more at SCATTER ♦ [2] blow, fritter, lavish, misspend, run through, spend, squander, throw away, waste — more at WASTE

dis·si·pa·tion \ˌdi-sə-ˈpā-shən\ *n* 1 : the action or process of dissipating : the state of being dissipated 2 ♦ : self=indulgence and intemperate living

♦ corruption, debasement, debauchery, decadence, degeneracy, degeneration, degradation, demoralization, depravity, dissoluteness, perversion — more at CORRUPTION

dis·so·ci·ate \di-ˈsō-shē-ˌāt\ *vb* **-at·ed; -at·ing** ♦ : to set or keep apart : DISCONNECT — **dis·so·ci·a·tion** \di-ˌsō-shē-ˈā-shən\ *n* — **dis·so·cia·tive** \di-ˈsō-shē-ˌā-tiv\ *adj*

♦ break up, disconnect, disjoint, dissever, disunite, divide, divorce, part, resolve, separate, sever, split, sunder, unyoke — more at SEPARATE

dis·so·lute \ˈdi-sə-ˌlüt\ *adj* ♦ : loose in morals or conduct — **dis·so·lute·ly** *adv*

♦ corrupt, debauched, decadent, degenerate, perverse, perverted, reprobate — more at CORRUPT

dis·so·lute·ness \-nəs\ *n* ♦ : the quality or state of being dissolute

♦ corruption, debasement, debauchery, decadence, degeneracy, degeneration, degradation, demoralization, depravity, dissipation, perversion — more at CORRUPTION

dis·so·lu·tion \ˌdi-sə-ˈlü-shən\ n 1 : the action or process of dissolving 2 ♦ : separation of a thing into its parts 3 : DECAY; also : DEATH 4 : the termination or breaking up of (as an assembly)

♦ breakup, division, partition, schism, separation, split — more at SEPARATION

dis·solve \di-ˈzälv\ vb 1 ♦ : to separate into component parts 2 : to pass or cause to pass into solution ⟨sugar ∼s in water⟩ 3 ♦ : to bring or come to an end ⟨∼ parliament⟩ ⟨the organization dissolved⟩ 4 : to waste or fade away ⟨his courage dissolved⟩ 5 : to be overcome emotionally ⟨∼ in tears⟩ 6 : to resolve itself as if by dissolution 7 ♦ : to disperse or disappear or cause to disperse or disappear

♦ [1] break up, disband, disperse — more at DISBAND
♦ [3] abolish, abrogate, annul, cancel, invalidate, negate, nullify, quash, repeal, rescind, void — more at ABOLISH ♦ [7] disappear, evaporate, fade, flee, go, melt, vanish — more at DISAPPEAR

dis·so·nance \ˈdi-sə-nəns\ n : DISCORD
dis·so·nant \-nənt\ adj ♦ : marked by dissonance : DISCORDANT

♦ discordant, inharmonious, unmelodious, unmusical; also blaring, clashing, grating, harsh, jangling, jarring, metallic, raucous, scratching, screeching, shrill, squeaky, strident; disagreeable, unpleasant, unpleasing; atonal Ant harmonious, harmonizing, melodious, musical

dis·suade \di-ˈswād\ vb **dis·suad·ed; dis·suad·ing** ♦ : to advise against a course of action : persuade or try to persuade not to do something — **dis·sua·sion** \-ˈswā-zhən\ n — **dis·sua·sive** \-ˈswā-siv\ adj

♦ deter, discourage, inhibit — more at DISCOURAGE

dist abbr 1 distance 2 district
¹**dis·taff** \ˈdis-ˌtaf\ n, pl **distaffs** \-ˌtafs, -ˌtavz\ [ME distaf, fr. OE distæf, fr. dis- bunch of flax + stæf stick, staff] 1 : a staff for holding the flax, tow, or wool in spinning 2 : a woman's work or domain 3 : the female branch or side of a family
²**distaff** adj 1 : MATERNAL 2 2 : FEMALE 1
dis·tal \ˈdist-ᵊl\ adj 1 : situated away from the point of attachment or origin esp. on the body 2 : of, relating to, or being the surface of a tooth that is farthest from the middle of the front of the jaw — **dis·tal·ly** adv
¹**dis·tance** \ˈdis-təns\ n 1 ♦ : measure of separation in space or time 2 : EXPANSE 3 : the full length ⟨go the ∼⟩ 4 : spatial remoteness 5 : COLDNESS, RESERVE 6 : DIFFERENCE, DISPARITY 7 : a distant point

♦ lead, length, remove, spread, stretch, way; also altitude, area, breadth, depth, height, rise, space, volume, width; extension, extent; cast, range, reach, scope, shot, sweep, throw; drop, fall, flight, haul; berth, clearance

²**distance** vb **dis·tanced; dis·tanc·ing** : to leave far behind : OUTSTRIP
³**distance** adj : taking place via electronic media linking instructors and students ⟨∼ learning⟩
dis·tant \ˈdis-tənt\ adj 1 : separate in space : AWAY 2 ♦ : situated at a great distance : FAR-OFF 3 : far apart or behind 4 : not close in relationship ⟨a ∼ cousin⟩ 5 : different in kind 6 ♦ : reserved or aloof in personal relationship : COLD ⟨∼ politeness⟩ 7 : going a long distance — **dis·tant·ly** adv — **dis·tant·ness** n

♦ [2] away, far, far-off, remote; also apart, isolated, obscure, outlying, out-of-the-way, retired, secluded, secret, sequestered Ant close, near, nearby, nigh
♦ [6] aloof, antisocial, cold, cool, detached, frosty, remote, standoffish, unsociable — more at COOL

dis·taste \ˌ(ˌ)dis-ˈtāst\ n ♦ : a settled dislike

♦ disgust, loathing, nausea, repugnance, repulsion — more at DISGUST

dis·taste·ful \-fəl\ adj 1 ♦ : objectionable because inappropriate, unethical, or offensive to taste 2 ♦ : unpleasant to the sense of taste ⟨∼ fruit⟩

♦ [1] bad, disagreeable, nasty, offensive, rotten, sour, uncongenial, unlovely, unpleasant, unwelcome — more at UNPLEASANT ♦ [2] unappetizing, unsavory; also abominable, awful, bad, filthy, foul, horrible, loathsome, nasty, nauseating, noisome, obnoxious, offensive, repellent, repugnant, repulsive, revolting, shocking, sickening; bland, flat, flavorless, insipid, tasteless Ant appetizing, delectable, delicious, palatable, savory, tasty

dis·tem·per \ˌ(ˌ)dis-ˈtem-pər\ n : a bodily disorder usu. of a domestic animal; esp : a contagious often fatal virus disease of dogs
dis·tend \di-ˈstend\ vb : EXPAND, SWELL — **dis·ten·si·ble** \-ˈsten-sə-bəl\ adj — **dis·ten·sion** or **dis·ten·tion** \-chən\ n
dis·tich \ˈdis-(ˌ)tik\ n : a unit of two lines of poetry
dis·till also **dis·til** \di-ˈstil\ vb **dis·tilled; dis·till·ing** 1 : to fall or let fall in drops 2 ♦ : to obtain or purify by distillation — **dis·till·er** n — **dis·till·ery** \-ˈsti-lə-rē\ n

♦ clarify, clear, filter, purify — more at CLARIFY

dis·til·late \ˈdis-tə-ˌlāt, -lət\ n : a liquid product condensed from vapor during distillation
dis·til·la·tion \ˌdis-tə-ˈlā-shən\ n : the process of purifying a liquid by successive evaporation and condensation
dis·tinct \di-ˈstiŋkt\ adj 1 : distinguishable to the eye or mind as discrete : SEPARATE 2 ♦ : presenting a clear unmistakable impression — **dis·tinct·ly** adv

♦ apparent, broad, clear, clear-cut, evident, lucid, manifest, obvious, palpable, patent, perspicuous, plain, transparent, unambiguous, unequivocal, unmistakable — more at CLEAR

dis·tinc·tion \di-ˈstiŋk-shən\ n 1 ♦ : the distinguishing of a difference; also : the difference distinguished 2 : something that distinguishes 3 ♦ : special honor or recognition 4 ♦ : the quality or state of being distinguished or worthy

♦ [1] contrast, difference, disagreement, discrepancy, disparity, diversity, unlikeness — more at DIFFERENCE ♦ [1] demarcation, discrimination, separation — more at SEPARATION ♦ [3] acclaim, accolade, award, credit, glory, homage, honor (or honour), laurels — more at GLORY ♦ [4] excellence, merit, value, virtue — more at EXCELLENCE

dis·tinc·tive \di-ˈstiŋk-tiv\ adj 1 a ♦ : serving to distinguish b ♦ : set apart from others 2 ♦ : having or giving style or distinction — **dis·tinc·tive·ly** adv

♦ [1a, 2] characteristic, classic, distinct, individual, peculiar, proper, symptomatic, typical — more at CHARACTERISTIC ♦ [1b] different, disparate, dissimilar, distinct, distinguishable, diverse, other, unalike, unlike — more at DIFFERENT

dis·tinc·tive·ness \-nəs\ n : the quality or state of being distinctive
dis·tinct·ness \-nəs\ n : the quality or state of being distinct
dis·tin·guish \di-ˈstiŋ-gwish\ vb [alter. of ME distinguen, fr. AF distinguer, fr. L distinguere, lit., to separate by pricking] 1 ♦ : to recognize by some mark or characteristic 2 ♦ : to hear or see clearly : DISCERN 3 ♦ : to make distinctions ⟨∼ between right and wrong⟩ 4 ♦ : to give prominence or distinction to; also : to take special notice of

♦ [1] behold, descry, discern, espy, eye, look, note, notice, observe, perceive, regard, remark, see, sight, spy, view, witness — more at SEE ♦ [2, 3] differentiate, discern, discriminate, separate; also comprehend, grasp, know, understand; divide, part, sever; demarcate, mark (off), set off Ant confuse, mistake, mix (up)

dis·tin·guish·able \di-ˈstiŋ-gwi-shə-bəl\ adj ♦ : capable of being distinguished

♦ appreciable, detectable, discernible, palpable, perceptible, sensible — more at PERCEPTIBLE

dis·tin·guished \-gwisht\ *adj* **1** ♦ : marked by eminence or excellence **2** : befitting an eminent person

♦ eminent, illustrious, noble, notable, noteworthy, outstanding, preeminent, prestigious, signal, star, superior — more at EMINENT

dis·tort \di-'stórt\ *vb* **1** ♦ : to twist out of the true meaning **2** ♦ : to twist out of a natural, normal, or original shape or condition **3** : to cause to be perceived unnaturally

♦ [1] color (*or* colour), falsify, garble, misinterpret, misrepresent, misstate, pervert, twist, warp — more at GARBLE
♦ [2] contort, deform, screw, warp — more at CONTORT

distorted *adj* ♦ : twisted or deformed in shape or condition

♦ deformed, malformed, misshapen, monstrous, shapeless — more at MALFORMED

dis·tor·tion \di-'stòr-shən\ *n* **1** ♦ : the act of distorting **2** : the quality or state of being distorted : a product of distorting

♦ contortion, deformation — more at CONTORTION

distr *abbr* distribute; distribution

dis·tract \di-'strakt\ *vb* **1** : to draw (the attention or mind) to a different object : DIVERT **2** : to stir up or confuse with conflicting emotions or motives

dis·tract·ed \di-'strakt-əd\ *adj* ♦ : mentally confused, troubled, or remote

♦ absent, absentminded, abstracted, preoccupied — more at ABSENTMINDED

dis·trac·tion \-'strak-shən\ *n* **1** ♦ : the act of distracting or the state of being distracted; *esp* : mental confusion ⟨driven to ∼⟩ **2** ♦ : something that distracts; *esp* : AMUSEMENT ⟨a harmless ∼⟩

♦ [1] bafflement, bewilderment, confusion, muddle, mystification, perplexity, puzzlement, whirl — more at CONFUSION ♦ [2] amusement, diversion, entertainment — more at ENTERTAINMENT

dis·trait \di-'strā\ *adj* : apprehensively divided or withdrawn in attention

dis·traught \di-'stròt\ *adj* **1** ♦ : agitated with doubt or mental conflict **2** : INSANE

♦ agitated, delirious, frantic, frenzied, hysterical — more at FRANTIC

¹dis·tress \di-'stres\ *n* **1** ♦ : suffering of body or mind : PAIN **2** : TROUBLE, MISFORTUNE **3** ♦ : a condition of danger or desperate need

♦ [1] affliction, agony, anguish, misery, pain, torment, torture, tribulation, woe; *also* discomfort; cross, crucible, trial; heartbreak, sadness, sorrow, unhappiness; emergency, pinch; asperity, difficulty, hardship, rigor; ache, hurt, pang, smarting, soreness, stitch, throe, twinge; danger, jeopardy, trouble ♦ [3] danger, jeopardy, peril, risk, trouble — more at DANGER

²distress *vb* **1** : to subject to great strain or difficulties **2** ♦ : to cause to worry or be troubled : UPSET

♦ agitate, bother, concern, discompose, disquiet, disturb, exercise, freak out, perturb, undo, unhinge, unsettle, upset, worry

dis·tress·ed \-'strest\ *adj* : experiencing economic decline or difficulty

dis·tress·ful \-fəl\ *adj* ♦ : causing distress : full of distress

♦ anxious, nervous, restless, tense, unsettling, upsetting, worrisome — more at NERVOUS

dis·trib·ute \di-'stri-byüt\ *vb* **-ut·ed; -ut·ing** **1** ♦ : to divide among several or many **2** : to spread out : SCATTER; *also* : DELIVER **3** : CLASSIFY

♦ administer, allocate, apportion, deal, dispense, mete, parcel, portion, prorate — more at ADMINISTER

dis·tri·bu·tion \dis-trə-'byü-shən\ *n* **1** ♦ : the act or process of distributing **2** ♦ : the position, arrangement, or frequency of occurrence (as of the members of a group) over an area or throughout a space or unit of time

♦ [1] allocation, dispensation, division, issuance; *also* disbursement; reapportionment, redistribution

♦ [2] arrangement, array, disposal, disposition, order, sequence, setup — more at ORDER

dis·trib·u·tive \di-'stri-byu-tiv\ *adj* **1** : of or relating to distribution **2** : of, having, or being the property of producing the same value when an operation is carried out on a whole expression and when it is carried out on each part of an expression with the results then collected together ⟨$a(b + c) = ab + ac$ because multiplication is ∼⟩ — **dis·trib·u·tive·ly** *adv*

dis·trib·u·tor \di-'stri-byù-tər\ *n* **1** : one that distributes **2** : one that markets goods **3** : a device for directing current to the spark plugs of an engine

dis·trict \'dis-(,)trikt\ *n* **1** ♦ : a fixed territorial division (as for administrative or electoral purposes) **2** ♦ : an area, region, or section with a distinguishing character

♦ neighborhood (*or* neighbourhood), quarter, section; *also* belt, zone; department, division, part; precinct, ward; area, locality, place, region; barrio, enclave, ghetto

district attorney *n* : the prosecuting attorney of a judicial district

¹dis·trust \dis-'trəst\ *n* ♦ : a lack or absence of trust

♦ doubt, incertitude, misgiving, mistrust, skepticism, suspicion, uncertainty — more at DOUBT

²distrust *vb* ♦ : to hold as untrustworthy or unreliable

♦ doubt, mistrust, question, suspect; *also* disbelieve, discount, discredit, negate *Ant* trust

dis·trust·ful \-fəl\ *adj* ♦ : having or showing distrust

♦ incredulous, leery, mistrustful, skeptical, suspicious — more at SKEPTICAL ♦ doubtful, dubious, mistrustful, skeptical, suspicious, uncertain, undecided, unsettled, unsure — more at DOUBTFUL

dis·trust·ful·ly \-fə-lē\ *adv* ♦ : in a distrustful manner

♦ askance, dubiously, mistrustfully, suspiciously — more at ASKANCE

dis·turb \di-'stərb\ *vb* **1** : to interfere with : INTERRUPT **2** ♦ : to alter the position or arrangement of; *also* : to upset the natural and esp. the ecological balance of **3** ♦ : to destroy the tranquility or composure of : make uneasy **4** : to throw into disorder **5** ♦ : to put to inconvenience — **dis·turb·er** *n* — **dis·turb·ing·ly** \-'stər-biŋ-lē\ *adv*

♦ [2] budge, dislocate, displace, move, remove, shift, transfer — more at MOVE ♦ [3] agitate, bother, concern, discompose, disquiet, distress, exercise, freak out, perturb, undo, unhinge, unsettle, upset, worry; *also* aggravate, anger, annoy, bug, chafe, exasperate, fret, gall, get, grate, harass, harry, irk, irritate, nettle, peeve, pester, pique, put out, rile, vex; bedevil, haunt, plague; abash, confound, confuse, discomfit, disconcert, discountenance, embarrass, faze, fluster, mortify, nonplus, rattle; daunt, demoralize, discourage, dishearten, dismay, dispirit *Ant* calm, compose, quiet, settle, soothe, tranquilize ♦ [5] discommode, disoblige, inconvenience, trouble — more at INCONVENIENCE

dis·tur·bance \-'stər-bəns\ *n* ♦ : the act of disturbing : the state of being disturbed

♦ dislocation, disruption, upset — more at UPSET
♦ commotion, furor, fuss, hubbub

dis·turbed \-'stərbd\ *adj* : showing symptoms of emotional illness

dis·unite \,dis-yü-'nīt\ *vb* ♦ : to destroy the unity of : DIVIDE

♦ break up, disconnect, disjoint, dissever, dissociate, divide, divorce, part, resolve, separate, sever, split, sunder, unyoke — more at SEPARATE

dis·uni·ty \dis-'yü-nə-tē\ *n* ♦ : lack of unity; *esp* : DISSENSION

♦ conflict, discord, dissent, friction, schism, strife, variance, war, warfare — more at DISCORD

dis·use \-'yüs\ *n* : a cessation of use or practice

dis·used \-'yüzd\ *adj* : no longer used or occupied

¹ditch \'dich\ *n* ♦ : a long narrow channel or trench dug in the earth

♦ dike, gutter, trench; *also* culvert, drain, draw, gully, ravine; drill, furrow

²ditch *vb* **1** : to enclose with a ditch; *also* : to dig a ditch in **2** ♦ : to get rid of : DISCARD **3** : to make a forced landing of an airplane on water

♦ cast, discard, dump, fling, jettison, junk, lose, reject, scrap, shed, shuck, slough, throw away, throw out, unload — more at DISCARD

dith·er \'di-thər\ *n* ♦ : a highly nervous, excited, or agitated state

♦ fluster, fret, fuss, huff, lather, pother, stew, tizzy, twitter — more at FRET

dit·sy *or* **dit·zy** \'dit-sē\ *adj* **dits·i·er** *or* **ditz·i·er; -est** : eccentrically silly, giddy, or inane

dit·to \'di-tō\ *n, pl* **dittos** [It *ditto, detto,* pp. of *dire* to say, fr. L *dicere*] **1** : a thing mentioned previously or above — used to avoid repeating a word **2** : a mark " or " used as a symbol for the word *ditto*

dit·ty \'di-tē\ *n, pl* **ditties** : a short simple song

ditz·y *or* **dits·y** \'dit-sē\ *adj* **ditz·i·er** *or* **dits·i·er; -est** : eccentrically silly, giddy, or inane

di·uret·ic \ˌdī-yə-'re-tik\ *adj* : tending to increase urine flow — **diuretic** *n*

di·ur·nal \dī-'ərn-ᵊl\ *adj* **1** : DAILY **2** : of, relating to, occurring, or active in the daytime

div *abbr* **1** divided **2** dividend **3** division **4** divorced

di·va \'dē-və\ *n, pl* **divas** *or* **di·ve** \-ˌvä\ [It, lit., goddess, fr. L, fem. of *divus* divine, god] **1** : PRIMA DONNA **2** : a usu. glamorous and successful female performer or personality ⟨the current ∼ of the popular music world⟩

di·va·gate \'dī-və-ˌgāt\ *vb* **-gat·ed; -gat·ing** : to wander or stray from a course or subject : DIVERGE — **di·va·ga·tion** \ˌdī-və-'gā-shən\ *n*

di·van \'dī-ˌvan, di-'van\ *n* ♦ : a large couch usu. without back or arms often designed for use as a bed

♦ couch, davenport, lounge, settee, sofa — more at COUCH

¹dive \'dīv\ *vb* **dived** \'dīvd\ *or* **dove** \'dōv\; **dived; div·ing** **1** ♦ : to plunge into water headfirst **2** : SUBMERGE **3** : to come or drop down precipitously **4** : to descend in an airplane at a steep angle **5** : to plunge into some matter or activity **6** : DART, LUNGE — **div·er** *n*

♦ pitch, plunge, sound; *also* dip, immerse, submerge

²dive *n* **1** ♦ : the act or an instance of diving **2** ♦ : a sharp decline **3** : a disreputable bar or place of amusement

♦ descent, dip, down, drop, fall, plunge — more at DESCENT

di·verge \də-'vərj, dī-\ *vb* **di·verged; di·verg·ing** **1** ♦ : to move or extend in different directions from a common point : draw apart **2** : to differ in character, form, or opinion **3** : DEVIATE **4** : DEFLECT — **di·ver·gence** \-'vər-jəns\ *n* — **di·ver·gent** \-jənt\ *adj*

♦ branch, fan, radiate — more at RADIATE ♦ branch, divide, fork, separate — more at SEPARATE

di·vers \'dī-vərz\ *adj* : of differing kinds : VARIOUS

di·verse \dī-'vərs, də-, 'dī-ˌvərs\ *adj* **1** ♦ : differing from one another : UNLIKE **2** : composed of distinct forms or qualities — **di·verse·ly** *adv*

♦ different, disparate, dissimilar, distinct, distinctive, distinguishable, other, unalike, unlike — more at DIFFERENT

di·ver·si·fy \də-'vər-sə-ˌfī, dī-\ *vb* **-fied; -fy·ing** : to make different or various in form or quality — **di·ver·si·fi·ca·tion** \-ˌvər-sə-fə-'kā-shən\ *n*

di·ver·sion \də-'vər-zhən, dī-\ *n* **1** : a turning aside from a course, activity, or use : DEVIATION **2** ♦ : something that diverts or amuses

♦ delight, entertainment, fun, pleasure — more at FUN
♦ amusement, distraction, entertainment — more at ENTERTAINMENT

di·ver·si·ty \də-'vər-sə-tē, dī-\ *n, pl* **-ties** **1** ♦ : the condition of being diverse **2** : an instance of being diverse

♦ assortment, variety — more at VARIETY ♦ contrast, difference, disagreement, discrepancy, disparity, distinction, unlikeness — more at DIFFERENCE

di·vert \də-'vərt, dī-\ *vb* **1** ♦ : to turn from a course or purpose : DEFLECT **2** : DISTRACT **3** ♦ : to give pleasure to esp. by distracting the attention from what burdens or distresses : ENTERTAIN

♦ [1] deflect, swerve, swing, turn, veer, wheel, whip — more at TURN ♦ [3] amuse, disport, entertain, regale — more at AMUSE

di·vert·ing \də-'vər-tiŋ, dī-\ *adj* ♦ : providing amusement or entertainment

♦ amusing, delightful, enjoyable, entertaining, fun, pleasurable — more at FUN

di·vest \dī-'vest, də-\ *vb* **1** : to deprive or dispossess esp. of property, authority, or rights **2** : to strip esp. of clothing, ornament, or equipment

¹di·vide \də-'vīd\ *vb* **di·vid·ed; di·vid·ing** **1 a** : to separate into two or more parts, areas, or groups **b** : CLASSIFY **2** : CLEAVE, PART **3** : DISTRIBUTE, APPORTION **4** : to possess or make use of in common : share in **5** ♦ : to cause to be separate, distinct, or apart from one another **6** : to separate into opposing sides or parties **7** : to mark divisions on **8** : to subject to or use in mathematical division; *also* : to be used as a divisor with respect to **9** ♦ : to branch out

♦ [5] break up, disconnect, disjoint, dissever, dissociate, disunite, divorce, part, resolve, separate, sever, split, sunder, unyoke — more at SEPARATE ♦ [9] branch, diverge, fork, separate — more at SEPARATE

²divide *n* : WATERSHED 1

div·i·dend \'di-və-ˌdend\ *n* **1** : an individual share of something distributed **2** ♦ : something in addition to what is expected or strictly due : BONUS **3** : a number to be divided **4** : a sum or fund to be divided or distributed

♦ bonus, extra, lagniappe, perquisite, tip — more at BONUS

di·vid·er \də-'vī-dər\ *n* **1** : one that divides (as a partition) ⟨room ∼⟩ **2** *pl* : COMPASS 5

div·i·na·tion \ˌdi-və-'nā-shən\ *n* **1** : the art or practice of using omens or magic powers to foretell the future **2** : unusual insight or intuitive perception

¹di·vine \də-'vīn\ *adj* **di·vin·er; -est** **1** ♦ : of, relating to, or being God or a god **2** : supremely good : SUPERB; *also* : HEAVENLY — **di·vine·ly** *adv*

♦ blessed, godlike, heavenly, holy — more at HOLY

²divine *n* **1** : a member of the clergy : CLERGYMAN **2** : THEOLOGIAN

³divine *vb* **di·vined; di·vin·ing** **1** : INFER, CONJECTURE **2** ♦ : to predict with assurance or on the basis of mystic knowledge **3** : DOWSE

♦ anticipate, foreknow, foresee — more at FORESEE

di·vin·er \də-'vī-nər\ *n* ♦ : a person who practices divination

♦ augur, forecaster, fortune-teller, futurist, prognosticator, prophet, seer, soothsayer — more at PROPHET

divining rod *n* : a forked rod believed to reveal the presence of water or minerals by dipping downward when held over a vein

di·vin·i·ty \də-'vi-nə-tē\ *n, pl* **-ties** **1** : THEOLOGY **2** ♦ : the quality or state of being divine **3** : a divine being; *esp* : GOD 1

♦ deity, godhead

di·vis·i·ble \də-'vi-zə-bəl\ *adj* : capable of being divided — **di·vis·i·bil·i·ty** \-ˌvi-zə-'bi-lə-tē\ *n*

di·vi·sion \də-'vi-zhən\ *n* **1 a** ♦ : the act or process of dividing : SEPARATION **b** ♦ : the act, process, or an instance of distributing among a number : DISTRIBUTION **2** ♦ : one of the parts or groupings into which a whole is divided **3** : DISAGREEMENT, DISUNITY **4** : something that divides or separates **5** : the mathematical operation of finding how many times one number is contained in another **6** : a large self-contained military unit **7** ♦ : an administrative or operating unit of a governmental, business, or educational organization — **di·vi·sion·al** \-'vi-zhə-nəl\ adj

♦ [1a] breakup, dissolution, partition, schism, separation, split — more at SEPARATION ♦ [1b] allocation, dispensation, distribution, issuance — more at DISTRIBUTION ♦ [2] bracket, category, class, family, grade, group, kind, order, set, species, type — more at CLASS ♦ [7] bureau, department, desk, office

di·vi·sive \də-'vī-siv, -'vi-ziv\ adj : creating disunity or dissension — **di·vi·sive·ly** adv — **di·vi·sive·ness** n
di·vi·sor \də-'vī-zər\ n : the number by which a dividend is divided
¹**di·vorce** \də-'vōrs\ n 1 : an act or instance of legally dissolving a marriage 2 : SEPARATION, SEVERANCE — **di·vorce·ment** n
²**divorce** vb 1 : to end marriage with (one's spouse) by divorce ⟨*divorced* his wife⟩ 2 : to dissolve the marriage contract between ⟨they were *divorced* last year⟩ 3 ♦ : to make or keep separate

♦ break up, disconnect, disjoint, dissever, dissociate, disunite, divide, part, resolve, separate, sever, split, sunder, unyoke — more at SEPARATE

di·vor·cé \də-,vōr-'sā\ n [F] : a divorced man
di·vor·cée \də-,vōr-'sā, -'sē\ n : a divorced woman
div·ot \'di-vət\ n : a piece of turf dug from a golf fairway in making a stroke
di·vulge \də-'vəlj, dī-\ vb **di·vulged**; **di·vulg·ing** ♦ : to make known (as a confidence or secret) : REVEAL

♦ bare, disclose, discover, expose, reveal, spill, tell, unbosom, uncloak, uncover, unmask, unveil — more at REVEAL

Dix·ie·land \'dik-sē-,land\ n : jazz music in duple time played in a style developed in New Orleans
diz·zy \'di-zē\ adj **diz·zi·er**; **-est** [ME *disy*, fr. OE *dysig* stupid] 1 : FOOLISH, SILLY 2 ♦ : having a sensation of whirling : GIDDY 3 a : causing or caused by giddiness b ♦ : confusing or feeling confused mentally 4 ♦ : extremely rapid — **diz·zi·ly** \-zə-lē\ adv — **diz·zi·ness** \-zē-nəs\ n

♦ [2] giddy, light-headed; *also* faint, weak; addled, befuddled, confused, dazed ♦ [3b] confused, stunned; *also* senseless, unconscious **Ant** clearheaded ♦ [4] breakneck, breathless, brisk, fast, fleet, hasty, lightning, nippy, quick, rapid, rattling, snappy, speedy, swift — more at FAST

DJ n, *often not cap* : DISC JOCKEY
dk abbr 1 dark 2 deck 3 dock
dl abbr deciliter
DLitt or **DLit** abbr [NL *doctor litterarum*] doctor of letters; doctor of literature
DLO abbr dead letter office
dm abbr decimeter
DMD abbr [NL *dentariae medicinae doctor*] doctor of dental medicine
DMZ abbr demilitarized zone
dn abbr down
DNA \,dē-(,)en-'ā\ n : any of various nucleic acids that are usu. the molecular basis of heredity and are localized esp. in cell nuclei
DNR abbr do not resuscitate
¹**do** \'dü\ vb **did** \'did\; **done** \'dən\; **do·ing**; **does** \'dəz\ 1 ♦ : to bring to pass : ACCOMPLISH 2 : ACT, BEHAVE ⟨~ as I say⟩ 3 : to be active or busy ⟨up and ~*ing*⟩ 4 : HAPPEN ⟨what's ~*ing*?⟩ 5 : to be engaged in the study or practice of : work at ⟨he *does* tailoring⟩ 6 : COOK ⟨steak *done* rare⟩ 7 : to put in order (as by cleaning or arranging) ⟨~ the dishes⟩ 8 : to furnish with something ornamental : DECORATE ⟨*did* the hall in blue⟩ 9 : GET ALONG ⟨~ well in school⟩ 10 ♦ : to deal with something successfully : MANAGE 11 : RENDER ⟨sleep will ~ you good⟩ 12 : to bring to an end : FINISH ⟨when he had *done*⟩ 13 : EXERT ⟨*did* my best⟩ 14 : PRODUCE ⟨*did* a poem⟩ 15 : to play the part of 16 : CHEAT ⟨*did* him out of his share⟩ 17 : TRAVERSE, TOUR 18 : TRAVEL 19 : to spend or serve out a period of time ⟨*did* ten years in prison⟩ 20 ♦ : to serve the needs of 21 ♦ : to be fitting or proper 22 : USE ⟨doesn't ~ drugs⟩ 23 — used as an auxiliary verb (1) before the subject in an interrogative sentence ⟨*does* he work?⟩ and after some adverbs ⟨never *did* she say so⟩, (2) in a negative statement ⟨I *don't* know⟩, (3) for emphasis ⟨you ~ know⟩, and (4) as a substitute for a preceding predicate ⟨he works harder than I ~⟩ — **do away with** 1 : to put an end to 2 : DESTROY, KILL — **do by** : to deal with : TREAT ⟨*did* right *by* her⟩ — **do for** : to bring about the death or ruin of — **do the trick** : to produce a desired result

♦ [1] accomplish, achieve, carry out, commit, compass, execute, follow through, make, perform — more at PERFORM ♦ [10] cope, fare, get along, make out, manage, shift — more at GET ALONG ♦ [20, 21] befit, fit, go, serve, suit; *also* satisfy, suffice; function, work

²**do** n 1 : AFFAIR, PARTY 2 : a command or entreaty to do something ⟨list of ~s and don'ts⟩ 3 : HAIRDO
³**do** abbr ditto
DOA abbr dead on arrival
do·able \'dü-ə-bəl\ adj ♦ : that can be done : PRACTICABLE

♦ achievable, attainable, feasible, possible, practicable, realizable, viable, workable — more at POSSIBLE

DOB abbr date of birth
dob·bin \'dä-bən\ n [*Dobbin*, nickname for *Robert*] 1 : a farm horse 2 : a quiet plodding horse
Do·ber·man pin·scher \'dō-bər-mən-'pin-chər\ n : any of a German breed of short-haired medium-sized dogs
¹**doc** \'däk\ n : DOCTOR
²**doc** abbr document
do·cent \'dōs-ᵊnt, dōt-'sent\ n [obs. G (now *Dozent*), fr. L *docens*, prp. of *docēre* to teach] : TEACHER, LECTURER; *also* : a person who leads a guided tour
doc·ile \'dä-səl\ adj [L *docilis*, fr. *docēre* to teach] ♦ : easily taught, led, or managed : TRACTABLE

♦ amenable, compliant, conformable, obedient, submissive, tractable — more at OBEDIENT

do·cil·i·ty \dä-'si-lə-tē\ n ♦ : the quality or state of being docile

♦ compliance, deference, obedience — more at COMPLIANCE

¹**dock** \'däk\ n : any of a genus of coarse weedy herbs related to buckwheat
²**dock** vb 1 : to cut off the end of : cut short 2 : to take away a part of : deduct from ⟨~ a worker's wages⟩
³**dock** n 1 : an artificial basin to receive ships 2 : ²SLIP 2 3 ♦ : a wharf or platform for loading or unloading materials

♦ float, jetty, landing, levee, pier, quay, wharf; *also* berth, mooring, slip; dockyard, marina, shipyard

⁴**dock** vb 1 ♦ : to bring or come into dock 2 : to join (as two spacecraft) mechanically in space

♦ disembark, land, moor, tie up

⁵**dock** n : the place in a court where a prisoner stands or sits during trial
dock·age \'dä-kij\ n : docking facilities
dock·et \'dä-kət\ n 1 : a formal abridged record of the proceedings in a legal action; *also* : a register of such records 2 : a list of legal causes to be tried 3 ♦ : a calendar of matters to be acted on : AGENDA 4 : a label attached to a document containing identification or directions — **docket** vb

♦ agenda, calendar, program, schedule, timetable — more at PROGRAM

dock·hand \'däk-,hand\ n : LONGSHOREMAN
dock·work·er \-,wər-kər\ n : LONGSHOREMAN
dock·yard \-,yärd\ n : SHIPYARD
¹**doc·tor** \'däk-tər\ n [ME *doctour* teacher, doctor, fr. AF & ML; AF, fr. ML *doctor*, fr. L, teacher, fr. *docēre* to teach] 1 : a person holding one of the highest academic degrees

(as a PhD) conferred by a university **2** : a person skilled in healing arts; *esp* : one (as a physician, dentist, or veterinarian) academically and legally qualified to practice **3** : a person who restores or repairs things — **doc·tor·al** \-tə-rəl\ *adj*

²**doctor** *vb* **1** : to give medical treatment to **2** : to practice medicine **3** ♦ : to restore to good condition : REPAIR **4** : to adapt or modify for a desired end **5** : to alter deceptively

♦ fix, mend, patch, recondition, renovate, repair, revamp — more at MEND

doc·tor·ate \'däk-tə-rət\ *n* : the degree, title, or rank of a doctor

doc·tri·naire \,däk-trə-'nar\ *n* [F] : one who attempts to put an abstract theory into effect without regard to practical difficulties — **doctrinaire** *adj*

doc·trine \'däk-trən\ *n* **1** : something that is taught **2** ♦ : a principle or position or the body of principles in a branch of knowledge or system of belief — **doc·tri·nal** \-trən-ᵊl\ *adj*

♦ creed, gospel, ideology, philosophy — more at CREED

docu·dra·ma \'dä-kyə-,drä-mə, -,dra-\ *n* : a drama for television, motion pictures, or theater that deals freely with historical events

¹**doc·u·ment** \'dä-kyə-mənt\ *n* **1** : a paper that furnishes information, proof, or support of something else **2** : a computer file containing information input by a computer user usu. via a word processor

²**doc·u·ment** \-,ment\ *vb* ♦ : to furnish documentary evidence of — **doc·u·ment·er** *n*

♦ demonstrate, establish, prove, substantiate, validate — more at PROVE

doc·u·men·ta·ry \,dä-kyə-'men-tə-rē\ *adj* **1** : consisting of documents; *also* : being in writing ⟨~ proof⟩ **2 a** : giving a factual presentation in artistic form ⟨a ~ movie⟩ **b** ♦ : of or relating to facts — **documentary** *n*

♦ factual, hard, historical, literal, matter-of-fact, nonfictional, objective, true — more at FACTUAL

doc·u·men·ta·tion \,dä-kyə-mən-'tä-shən\ *n* **1** : the act or an instance of furnishing or authenticating with documents **2 a** : the provision of documents in substantiation **b** ♦ : documentary evidence

♦ attestation, confirmation, corroboration, evidence, proof, substantiation, testament, testimony, validation, witness — more at PROOF

DOD *abbr* Department of Defense

¹**dod·der** \'dä-dər\ *n* : any of a genus of leafless parasitic twining vines that are highly deficient in chlorophyll

²**dodder** *vb* **dod·dered; dod·der·ing** **1** : to tremble or shake usu. from age **2** ♦ : to progress feebly and unsteadily

♦ careen, lurch, reel, stagger, teeter, totter — more at STAGGER

¹**dodge** \'däj\ *n* **1** : an act of evading by sudden bodily movement **2** ♦ : an artful device to evade, deceive, or trick **3** : EXPEDIENT

♦ artifice, device, gimmick, jig, ploy, scheme, sleight, stratagem, trick, wile — more at TRICK

²**dodge** *vb* **dodged; dodg·ing** **1** ♦ : to evade usu. by trickery **2** ♦ : to move suddenly aside; *also* : to avoid or evade by so doing

♦ [1] avoid, duck, elude, escape, eschew, evade, shake, shirk, shun — more at ESCAPE ♦ [2] duck, sidestep; *also* avoid, elude, escape, evade, parry, shirk, skirt; deflect, turn; slide, slip

dodg·er \'dä-jər\ *n* ♦ : one that dodges; *esp* : one who uses tricky devices

♦ cheat, hoaxer, shark, sharper, swindler, trickster — more at TRICKSTER

do·do \'dō-dō\ *n, pl* **dodoes** *or* **dodos** [Pg *doudo*, fr. *doudo* silly, stupid] **1** : an extinct heavy flightless bird of the island of Mauritius related to the pigeons and larger than a turkey **2** ♦ : one hopelessly behind the times **3** ♦ : a stupid person

♦ [2] antediluvian, fogy, fossil, fuddy-duddy, reactionary — more at FOGY ♦ [3] blockhead, dope, dummy, idiot, imbecile, jackass, moron, numskull — more at IDIOT

doe \'dō\ *n, pl* **does** *or* **doe** : an adult female of various mammals (as a deer, rabbit, or kangaroo) of which the male is called *buck*

DOE *abbr* Department of Energy

do·er \'dü-ər\ *n* : one that does

does *pres 3d sing of* DO *pl of* DOE

doff \'däf\ *vb* [ME, fr. *don* to do + *of* off] **1** : to take off (the hat) in greeting or as a sign of respect **2** : to rid oneself of **3** ♦ : to remove (an article of wear) from the body

♦ peel, put off, remove, take off — more at REMOVE

¹**dog** \'dȯg\ *n* **1** : a flesh-eating domestic mammal related to the wolves; *esp* : a male of this animal **2** : a worthless or contemptible person **3** : FELLOW, CHAP ⟨you lucky ~⟩ **4** : a mechanical device for holding something **5** : uncharacteristic or affected stylishness or dignity ⟨put on the ~⟩ **6** *pl* : RUIN ⟨gone to the ~s⟩

²**dog** *vb* **dogged; dog·ging** **1** ♦ : to hunt or track like a hound **2** : to worry as if by pursuit with dogs : PLAGUE

♦ chase, follow, hound, pursue, shadow, tag, tail, trace, track, trail — more at FOLLOW

dog·bane \'dȯg-,bān\ *n* : any of a genus of mostly poisonous herbs with milky juice and often showy flowers

dog·cart \-,kärt\ *n* : a light one-horse carriage with two seats back to back

dog·catch·er \-,ka-chər, -,ke-\ *n* : a community official assigned to catch and dispose of stray dogs

dog-ear \'dȯg-,ir\ *n* : the turned-down corner of a leaf of a book — **dog-ear** *vb*

dog-eared \'dȯg-,ird\ *adj* : ill-kept : SHABBY

dog·fight \'dȯg-,fīt\ *n* : a fight between fighter planes at close range

dog·fish \-,fish\ *n* : any of various small usu. bottom-dwelling sharks

dog·ged \'dȯ-gəd\ *adj* ♦ : stubbornly determined — **dog·ged·ly** *adv*

♦ insistent, patient, persevering, persistent, pertinacious, tenacious — more at PERSISTENT ♦ determined, grim, implacable, relentless, unflinching, unrelenting, unyielding — more at UNYIELDING

dog·ged·ness \-nəs\ *n* : the quality or state of being dogged

dog·ger·el \'dȯ-gə-rəl\ *n* : verse that is loosely styled and irregular in measure esp. for comic effect

dog·gie bag *or* **doggy bag** \'dȯ-gē-\ *n* : a container for carrying home leftover food from a restaurant meal

¹**dog·gy** *or* **dog·gie** \'dȯ-gē\ *n, pl* **doggies** : a usu. small dog

²**dog·gy** *adj* **dog·gi·er; -est** : of or resembling a dog ⟨a ~ odor⟩

dog·house \'dȯg-,haus\ *n* : a shelter for a dog — **in the doghouse** : in a state of disfavor

do·gie \'dō-gē\ *n, chiefly West* : a motherless calf in a range herd

dog·leg \'dȯg-,leg\ *n* : a sharp bend or angle (as in a road or a golf fairway) — **dogleg** *vb*

dog·ma \'dȯg-mə\ *n, pl* **dogmas** *also* **dog·ma·ta** \-mə-tə\ [L, fr. Gk, fr. *dokein* to think, have an opinion] **1** : a tenet or code of tenets **2** : a doctrine or body of doctrines formally proclaimed by a church

dog·ma·tism \'dȯg-mə-,ti-zəm\ *n* : positiveness in stating matters of opinion esp. when unwarranted or arrogant — **dog·mat·ic** \dȯg-'ma-tik\ *adj* — **dog·mat·i·cal·ly** \-ti-k(ə-)lē\ *adv*

do-good·er \'dü-,gu̇-dər\ *n* : an earnest often naive humanitarian or reformer

dog·tooth violet \'dȯg-,tüth-\ *n* : any of a genus of small spring-flowering bulbous herbs related to the lilies

dog·trot \'dȯg-,trät\ *n* : a gentle trot — **dogtrot** *vb*

dog·wood \'dȯg-,wud\ *n* : any of a genus of trees and shrubs having heads of small flowers often with showy white, pink, or red bracts

doi·ly \'dȯi-lē\ *n, pl* **doilies** : a small often decorative mat

do in *vb* **1** : to bring about the defeat or destruction of

: RUIN **2** ♦ : to deprive of life : KILL **3** ♦ : to tire extremely or completely : EXHAUST ⟨the climb *did* him *in*⟩ **4** : CHEAT

♦ [2] destroy, dispatch, fell, kill, slay — more at KILL ♦ [3] burn out, drain, exhaust, fag, fatigue, tire, tucker, wash out, wear, wear out, weary — more at EXHAUST

do·ing \'dü-iŋ\ *n* **1** ♦ : the act or result of performing, executing, or creating ⟨to achieve those plans will take some ∼⟩ **2** **do·ings** \'dü-iŋz\ *pl* : things that go on or occur ⟨the daily ∼s in the market⟩

♦ deed, exploit, feat, thing

do–it–yourself *n* : the activity of doing or making something without professional training or help — **do–it–your·self·er** *n*

dol *abbr* dollar

dol·drums \'dōl-drəmz, 'däl-\ *n pl* **1** ♦ : a spell of listlessness or despondency **2** *often cap* : a part of the ocean near the equator known for calms **3** : a state or period of inactivity, stagnation, or slump

♦ blues, dejection, depression, desolation, despondency, dumps, forlornness, gloom, heartsickness, melancholy, sadness — more at SADNESS ♦ boredom, ennui, listlessness, restlessness, tedium, tiredness, weariness — more at BOREDOM

¹dole \'dōl\ *n* **1** ♦ : a distribution esp. of food, money, or clothing to the needy; *also* : something so distributed **2** : a grant of government funds to the unemployed

♦ charity, philanthropy — more at CHARITY

²dole *vb* **doled; dol·ing** : to give or distribute as a charity — usu. used with *out*

dole·ful \'dōl-fəl\ *adj* : full of grief : SAD — **dole·ful·ly** *adv*

dole out *vb* **1** ♦ : to give or deliver in small portions **2** : to give or dispense freely : DISH OUT

♦ administer, allocate, apportion, deal, dispense, distribute, mete, parcel, portion, prorate — more at ADMINISTER

doll \'däl, 'dȯl\ *n* **1** : a small figure of a human being used esp. as a child's plaything **2** ♦ : a pretty woman **3** : an attractive person — **doll·ish** \'dä-lish, 'dȯ-\ *adj*

♦ girl, lass, maid, maiden, miss — more at GIRL

dol·lar \'dä-lər\ *n* [Dutch or LG *daler*, fr. G *Taler*, short for *Joachimstaler*, fr. Sankt *Joachimsthal*, Bohemia, where talers were first made] **1** : a basic monetary unit of any of several countries (as the U.S., Canada, Australia, and Singapore) **2** : a coin, note, or token representing one dollar

dol·lop \'dä-ləp\ *n* **1** : LUMP, GLOB **2** : PORTION 1 — **dol·lop** *vb*

doll up *vb* **1** : to dress elegantly or extravagantly **2** : to make more attractive **3** : to get dolled up

dol·ly \'dä-lē\ *n, pl* **dollies** : a small cart or wheeled platform (as for a television or movie camera)

dol·men \'dōl-mən, 'däl-\ *n* : a prehistoric monument consisting of two or more upright stones supporting a horizontal stone slab

do·lo·mite \'dō-lə-ˌmīt, 'dä-\ *n* : a mineral found in broad layers as a compact limestone

do·lor *or Can and Brit* **do·lour** \'dō-lər, 'dä-\ *n* : mental suffering or anguish : SORROW

♦ affliction, anguish, grief, heartache, sorrow, woe — more at SORROW

do·lor·ous \'dō-lə-rəs, 'dä-\ *adj* ♦ : causing, marked by, or expressing misery or grief — **do·lor·ous·ly** *adv*

♦ funeral, lugubrious, mournful, plaintive, regretful, rueful, sorrowful, weeping, woeful — more at MOURNFUL

dol·phin \'däl-fən\ *n* **1** : any of various small whales with conical teeth and an elongated beaklike snout **2** : either of two active food fishes of tropical and temperate seas

dolt \'dōlt\ *n* ♦ : a stupid individual

♦ blockhead, dope, dummy, idiot, imbecile, jackass, moron, numskull — more at IDIOT

dolt·ish \'dōl-tish\ *adj* : like a dolt : STUPID

dolt·ish·ness \-nəs\ *n* : the quality or state of being doltish : STUPIDITY

dom *abbr* **1** domestic **2** dominant **3** dominion

-dom *n suffix* **1** : dignity : office ⟨duke*dom*⟩ **2** : realm : jurisdiction ⟨king*dom*⟩ **3** : state or fact of being ⟨free*dom*⟩ **4** : those having a (specified) office, occupation, interest, or character ⟨official*dom*⟩

do·main \dō-'mān\ *n* **1** : complete and absolute ownership of land **2** : land completely owned **3** : a territory over which dominion is exercised **4** ♦ : a sphere of knowledge, influence, or activity ⟨the ∼ of science⟩ **5** : a subdivision of the Internet made up of computers whose URLs share a characteristic abbreviation (as *com* or *gov*)

♦ area, arena, demesne, department, discipline, field, line, province, realm, specialty, sphere — more at FIELD

domain name *n* : a sequence of characters (as MerriamWebster.com) that specifies a group of online resources and forms part of its URL

dome \'dōm\ *n* **1** : a large hemispherical roof or ceiling **2** : a structure or natural formation that resembles the dome of a building **3** : a roofed sports stadium — **dome** *vb*

¹do·mes·tic \də-'mes-tik\ *adj* **1** : living near or about human habitations **2** : reduced from a state of native wildness esp. so as to be tractable and useful to humans : DOMESTICATED **3** : relating and limited to one's own country or the country under consideration **4** : of or relating to the household or the family **5** : devoted to home duties and pleasures **6** : INDIGENOUS — **do·mes·ti·cal·ly** \-ti-k(ə-)lē\ *adv*

²domestic *n* ♦ : a household servant

♦ girl, housemaid, maid, maidservant — more at MAID

do·mes·ti·cate \də-'mes-ti-ˌkāt\ *vb* **-cat·ed; -cat·ing** : to adapt to life in association with and to the use of humans — **do·mes·ti·ca·tion** \-ˌmes-ti-'kā-shən\ *n*

do·mes·tic·i·ty \ˌdō-ˌmes-'ti-sə-tē, də-\ *n, pl* **-ties** **1** : the quality or state of being domestic or domesticated **2** : domestic activities or life

domestic violence *n* : the inflicting of injury by one family or household member on another

¹dom·i·cile \'dä-mə-ˌsīl, 'dō-; 'dä-mə-səl\ *n* ♦ : a dwelling place : HOME — **dom·i·cil·i·ary** \ˌdä-mə-'si-lē-ˌer-ē, ˌdō-\ *adj*

♦ abode, dwelling, home, house, lodging, quarters, residence — more at HOME

²domicile *vb* ♦ : to establish in or provide with a domicile

♦ accommodate, billet, chamber, harbor (*or* harbour), house, lodge, put up, quarter, roof, shelter, take in — more at HOUSE

dom·i·nance \'dä-mə-nəns\ *n* **1** ♦ : dominant position esp. in a social hierarchy **2** : the property of one of a pair of alleles or traits that suppresses expression of the other when both are present

♦ ascendancy, dominion, predominance, preeminence, supremacy — more at SUPREMACY

¹dom·i·nant \-nənt\ *adj* **1** ♦ : controlling or prevailing over all others **2** : overlooking from a high position **3** : exhibiting genetic dominance

♦ arch, cardinal, central, chief, first, foremost, grand, key, main, paramount, predominant, preeminent, premier, primary, principal, sovereign, supreme — more at FOREMOST

²dominant *n* : a dominant gene or trait

dom·i·nate \'dä-mə-ˌnāt\ *vb* **-nat·ed; -nat·ing** **1** ♦ : to exert control, direction, or influence on **2** ♦ : to have a commanding position or controlling power over **3** : to rise high above in a position suggesting power to dominate — **dom·i·na·tor** \-ˌnā-tər\ *n*

♦ [1] conquer, overpower, subdue, subject, vanquish — more at CONQUER ♦ [2] boss, captain, command, head, lead, spearhead — more at LEAD

dom·i·na·tion \ˌdä-mə-'nā-shən\ *n* **1** : supremacy or pre-eminence over another **2** ♦ : exercise of mastery, ruling power, or preponderant influence

♦ conquest, subjection — more at CONQUEST

dom·i·na·trix \ˌdä-mə-'nā-triks\ *n, pl* **-tri·ces** \-'nā-trə-ˌsēz, -nə-'trī-sēz\ : a woman who dominates her partner in a sexual encounter; *also* : a dominating woman

dom·i·neer \ˌdä-mə-'nir\ *vb* **1** : to rule in an arrogant manner **2** : to be overbearing

dom·i·neer·ing \-'nir-iŋ\ *adj* ♦ : inclined to exercise arbitrary and overbearing control over others

♦ authoritarian, autocratic, bossy, despotic, dictatorial, imperious, masterful, overbearing, peremptory, tyrannical, tyrannous — more at BOSSY

do·mi·nie *1 usu* 'dä-mə-nē, *2 usu* 'dō-\ *n* **1** *chiefly Scot* : SCHOOLMASTER **2** : a member of the clergy : CLERGYMAN

do·min·ion \də-'min-yən\ *n* **1** : DOMAIN **2** ♦ : supreme authority **3** *often cap* : a self-governing nation of the Commonwealth

♦ ascendancy, dominance, predominance, preeminence, supremacy — more at SUPREMACY

dom·i·no \'dä-mə-ˌnō\ *n, pl* **-noes** *or* **-nos** **1** : a long loose hooded cloak usu. worn with a half mask as a masquerade costume **2** : a flat rectangular block used as a piece in a game (**dominoes**)

¹don \'dän\ *vb* **donned; don·ning** [ME, fr. *don* to do + *on*] ♦ : to put on (as clothes)

♦ put on, slip, throw — more at PUT ON

²don *n* [Sp, fr. L *dominus* lord, master] **1** : a Spanish nobleman or gentleman — used as a title prefixed to the first name **2** : a head, tutor, or fellow in an English university

do·ña \'dō-nyə\ *n* : a Spanish woman of rank — used as a title prefixed to the first name

do·nate \'dō-ˌnāt\ *vb* **do·nat·ed; do·nat·ing** **1** ♦ : to make a gift of : CONTRIBUTE **2** : to make a donation

♦ bestow, contribute, give, present — more at GIVE

do·na·tion \dō-'nā-shən\ *n* **1** : the making of a gift esp. to a charity **2** ♦ : a free contribution

♦ alms, benefaction, beneficence, charity, contribution, philanthropy — more at CONTRIBUTION ♦ bestowal, freebie, gift, lagniappe, largesse, present — more at GIFT

¹done \'dən\ *past part of* DO

²done *adj* **1** : doomed to failure, defeat, or death **2** ♦ : gone by : OVER ⟨when day is ∼⟩ **3** : cooked sufficiently **4** : conformable to social convention

♦ complete, down, over, through, up — more at COMPLETE

done deal *n* : FAIT ACCOMPLI

don·key \'däŋ-kē, 'dəŋ-\ *n, pl* **donkeys** **1** ♦ : a sturdy and patient domestic mammal classified with the asses **2** : a stupid or obstinate person

♦ ass, jackass; *also* jack, jenny; mule; pack animal

don·ny·brook \'dä-nē-ˌbruk\ *n, often cap* [*Donnybrook* Fair, annual Irish event known for its brawls] : an uproarious brawl

do·nor \'dō-nər\ *n* : one that gives, donates, or presents

donut *var of* DOUGHNUT

doo·dad \'dü-ˌdad\ *n* : an often small article whose common name is unknown or forgotten

doo·dle \'dü-d²l\ *vb* **doo·dled; doo·dling** : to draw or scribble aimlessly while occupied with something else — **doodle** *n* — **doo·dler** *n*

¹doom \'düm\ *n* **1** ♦ : a judicial decision; *esp* : a judicial condemnation or sentence **2** : something to which a person or thing is destined : DESTINY **3 a** : RUIN **b** : a permanent cessation of all vital functions : DEATH

♦ [1] finding, holding, judgment (*or* judgement), ruling, sentence — more at SENTENCE ♦ [2] circumstance, destiny, fate, fortune, lot, portion — more at FATE

²doom *vb* **1** ♦ : to give judgment against : CONDEMN **2** ♦ : to fix the fate of : DESTINE

♦ [1] condemn, damn, sentence — more at SENTENCE ♦ [2] destine, foredoom, foreordain, ordain, predestine — more at DESTINE

dooms·day \'dümz-ˌdā\ *n* : JUDGMENT DAY

door \'dōr\ *n* **1** ♦ : a usu. swinging or sliding barrier by which an entry is closed and opened; *also* : a similar part of a piece of furniture **2** ♦ : the opening that a door closes : DOORWAY **3** : a means of access or participation : OPPORTUNITY

♦ [1] gate, hatch, portal; *also* French door, lattice, portcullis, postern, trapdoor, wicket ♦ [2] doorway, entrance, gate, gateway, way; *also* hatch, hatchway

door·keep·er \-ˌkē-pər\ *n* ♦ : a person who tends a door

♦ gatekeeper, janitor

door·knob \-ˌnäb\ *n* : a knob that when turned releases a door latch

door·man \-ˌman, -mən\ *n* : a usu. uniformed attendant at the door of a building (as a hotel)

door·mat \-ˌmat\ *n* : a mat placed before or inside a door for wiping dirt from the shoes

door·plate \-ˌplāt\ *n* : a nameplate on a door

door·step \-ˌstep\ *n* : a step or series of steps before an outer door

door·way \-ˌwā\ *n* **1** ♦ : the opening that a door closes **2** ♦ : a means of access or participation

♦ [1] door, entrance, gate, gateway, way — more at DOOR ♦ [2] access, admission, entrance, entrée, gateway — more at ENTRANCE

do·pa \'dō-pə\ *n* : a form of an amino acid that is used esp. in the treatment of Parkinson's disease

do·pa·mine \'dō-pə-ˌmēn\ *n* : an organic compound that occurs esp. as a neurotransmitter in the brain

¹dope \'dōp\ *n* **1** : a preparation for giving a desired quality **2** : an illicit, habit-forming, or narcotic drug; *esp* : MARIJUANA **3** ♦ : a stupid person **4** ♦ : information esp. from a reliable source

♦ [3] blockhead, dummy, idiot, imbecile, jackass, moron, numskull — more at IDIOT ♦ [4] lowdown, scoop, tip; *also* dirt, gossip, rumor, story; hint, pointer; information, intelligence, news, tidings, word

²dope *vb* **doped; dop·ing** **1** : to treat with dope; *esp* : to give a narcotic to **2** ♦ : to find a solution, explanation, or answer for : FIGURE OUT — usu. used with *out* **3** : to take dope

♦ *usu* **dope out** answer, break, crack, figure out, puzzle, resolve, riddle, solve, unravel, work, work out — more at SOLVE

dop·er *n* ♦ : an habitual or frequent drug user

♦ addict, fiend, user; *also* pothead

dop·ey *also* **dopy** \'dō-pē\ *adj* **dop·i·er; -est** **1** : dulled by alcohol or a narcotic **2** : SLUGGISH **3** : slow of mind : STUPID; *also* : complacently or inanely foolish

dop·i·ness \-nəs\ *n* ♦ : the quality or state of being dopey

♦ denseness, foolishness, imbecility, mindlessness, obtuseness, stupidity, vacuity — more at STUPIDITY

doping *n* : the use of a substance or technique to illegally improve athletic performance

Dopp·ler effect \'dä-plər-\ *n* : a change in the frequency at which waves (as of sound) reach an observer from a source in motion with respect to the observer

do-rag \'dü-ˌrag\ *n* ♦ : a kerchief worn esp. to cover the hair

♦ babushka, bandanna, kerchief, mantilla — more at BANDANNA

dork \'dork\ *n, slang* : NERD; *also* : JERK 2

dorm \'dorm\ *n* : DORMITORY

dor·man·cy \-mən-sē\ *n* ♦ : the quality or state of being dormant

♦ abeyance, doldrums, latency, quiescence, suspension — more at ABEYANCE ♦ idleness, inaction, inactivity, inertness, quiescence — more at INACTION

dor·mant \'dor-mənt\ *adj* **1** ♦ : marked by a suspension of activity **2** ♦ : sleeping or drowsing

♦ [1] dead, fallow, free, idle, inactive, inert, inoperative, latent, off, vacant — more at INACTIVE ♦ [2] asleep — more at ASLEEP

dor·mer \'dȯr-mər\ *n* [MF *dormeor* dormitory, fr. L *dormitorium*, fr. *dormire* to sleep] : a window built upright in a sloping roof; *also* : the roofed structure containing such a window

dor·mi·to·ry \'dȯr-mə-ˌtȯr-ē\ *n, pl* **-ries** 1 : a room for sleeping; *esp* : a large room containing a number of beds 2 : a residence hall providing sleeping rooms

dor·mouse \'dȯr-ˌmau̇s\ *n* : any of numerous Old World rodents that resemble small squirrels

dor·sal \'dȯr-səl\ *adj* : of, relating to, or located near or on the surface of the body that in humans is the back but in most other animals is the upper surface — **dor·sal·ly** *adv*

do·ry \'dȯr-ē\ *n, pl* **dories** : a flat-bottomed boat with high flaring sides and a sharp bow

DOS *abbr* disk operating system

¹**dose** \'dōs\ *n* [ME, fr. MF, fr. LL *dosis*, fr. Gk, lit., act of giving, fr. *didonai* to give] 1 : a measured quantity (as of medicine) to be taken or administered at one time 2 : the quantity of radiation administered or absorbed — **dos·age** \'dō-sij\ *n*

²**dose** *vb* **dosed; dos·ing** 1 : to give in doses 2 : to give medicine to

do·sim·e·ter \dō-'si-mə-tər\ *n* : a device for measuring doses of radiations (as X-rays) — **do·sim·e·try** \-mə-trē\ *n*

dos·sier \'dȯs-ˌyā, 'dȯ-sē-ˌā\ *n* [F, bundle of documents labeled on the back, dossier, fr. *dos* back, fr. OF, fr. L *dorsum*] : a file containing detailed records on a particular person or subject

¹**dot** \'dät\ *n* 1 ♦ : a small spot : SPECK 2 : a small round mark 3 : a precise point esp. in time ⟨be here on the ∼⟩

♦ blotch, fleck, mottle, patch, point, speck, spot — more at SPOT

²**dot** *vb* **dot·ted; dot·ting** 1 : to mark with a dot ⟨∼ an *i*⟩ 2 ♦ : to cover with or as if with dots — **dot·ter** *n*

♦ blotch, dapple, fleck, freckle, mottle, pepper, speck, spot, sprinkle, stipple — more at SPOT

DOT *abbr* Department of Transportation

dot·age \'dō-tij\ *n* : feebleness of mind esp. in old age : SENILITY

dot·ard \-tərd\ *n* : a person in dotage

dot–com \'dät-ˌkäm\ *n* : a company that markets its products or services usu. exclusively via a website

dote \'dōt\ *vb* **dot·ed; dot·ing** 1 : to be feebleminded esp. from old age 2 ♦ : to be lavish or excessive in one's attention, affection, or fondness ⟨*doted* on her niece⟩

♦ *usu* dote on adore, canonize, deify, idolize, worship — more at IDOLIZE

dot matrix *n* : a rectangular arrangement of dots from which alphanumeric characters can be formed (as by a computer printer)

Dou·ay Version \dü-'ā-\ *n* : an English translation of the Vulgate used by Roman Catholics

¹**dou·ble** \'də-bəl\ *adj* [ME, fr. AF, fr. L *duplus*, fr. *duo* two + *-plus* multiplied by] 1 : TWOFOLD, DUAL 2 ♦ : consisting of two members or parts 3 : being twice as great or as many 4 : folded in two 5 : having more than one whorl of petals ⟨∼ roses⟩

♦ binary, bipartite, dual, duplex, twin; *also* mated, paired *Ant* single

²**double** *vb* **dou·bled; dou·bling** 1 : to make, be, or become twice as great or as many 2 : to make a call in bridge that increases the trick values and penalties of (an opponent's bid) 3 : FOLD 4 : CLENCH 5 : to be or cause to be bent over 6 : to take the place of another 7 : to hit a double 8 : to turn sharply and suddenly; *esp* : to turn back on one's course

³**double** *adv* 1 : DOUBLY 2 : two together

⁴**double** *n* 1 : something twice another in size, strength, speed, quantity, or value 2 : a base hit that enables the batter to reach second base 3 ♦ : one that is the counterpart of another : DUPLICATE; *esp* : a person who closely

resembles another 4 : UNDERSTUDY, SUBSTITUTE 5 : a sharp turn : REVERSAL 6 : FOLD 7 : a combined bet placed on two different contests 8 *pl* : a game between two pairs of players 9 : an act of doubling in a card game

♦ carbon copy, counterpart, duplicate, duplication, facsimile, image, likeness, match, picture, replica, ringer, spit — more at IMAGE

double bond *n* : a chemical bond in which two atoms in a molecule share two pairs of electrons

double cross *n* ♦ : an act of betraying or cheating esp. an associate — **dou·ble-cross** \ˌdə-bəl-'krȯs\ *vb*

♦ betrayal, disloyalty, faithlessness, falseness, falsity, infidelity, perfidy, treachery, treason, unfaithfulness — more at BETRAYAL

dou·ble–cross·er *n* ♦ : one that double-crosses

♦ apostate, betrayer, quisling, recreant, traitor, turncoat — more at TRAITOR

¹**dou·ble–deal·ing** \ˌdə-bəl-'dē-liŋ\ *n* ♦ : action contradictory to a professed attitude : DUPLICITY — **dou·ble–deal·er** \-'dē-lər\ *n*

♦ artifice, craft, craftiness, crookedness, cunning, deceit, deceitfulness, dishonesty, dissimulation, duplicity, guile, wiliness — more at DECEIT

²**double–dealing** *adj* ♦ : given to or marked by duplicity

♦ crooked, deceitful, dishonest, false, fraudulent — more at FRAUDULENT

dou·ble–deck·er \-'de-kər\ *n* : something having two decks, levels, or layers — **dou·ble–deck** \-ˌdek\ *or* **dou·ble–decked** \-ˌdekt\ *adj*

dou·ble–dig·it \ˌdə-bəl-'di-jət\ *adj* : amounting to 10 percent or more

dou·ble–dip \-'dip\ *vb* 1 : to obtain money from two sources at the same time or by two separate accounting methods; *esp* : to draw a pension from one government department while working for another 2 : to repeat the action of dipping a chip or other snack into a shared dipping sauce or mixture after taking a bite — **dou·ble–dip·per** *n* — **dou·ble–dip·ping** *n*

double down *vb* : to become more tenacious, zealous, or resolute

dou·ble en·ten·dre \ˌdüb°l-än-'tänd, ˌdə-bəl-, -'tänd-rᵊ\ *n, pl* **double entendres** *same or* -'tän-drəz\ [obs. F, lit., double meaning] : a word or expression capable of two interpretations with one usu. risqué

dou·ble·head·er \ˌdə-bəl-'he-dər\ *n* : two games played consecutively on the same day

double helix *n* : a helix or spiral consisting of two strands (as of DNA) in the surface of a cylinder which coil around its axis

dou·ble–hung \ˌdə-bəl-'həŋ\ *adj, of a window* : having an upper and a lower sash that can slide past each other

dou·ble–joint·ed \-'jȯin-təd\ *adj* : having a joint that permits an exceptional degree of freedom of motion of the parts joined ⟨a ∼ finger⟩

dou·ble–park \ˌdə-bəl-'pärk\ *vb* : to park a vehicle beside a row of vehicles already parked parallel to the curb

double play *n* : a play in baseball by which two players are put out

double pneumonia *n* : pneumonia affecting both lungs

double standard *n* : a set of principles that applies differently and usu. more rigorously to one group of people or circumstances than to another

dou·blet \'də-blət\ *n* 1 : a man's close-fitting jacket worn in Europe esp. in the 16th century 2 : one of two similar or identical things

dou·ble take \'də-bəl-ˌtāk\ *n* : a delayed reaction to a surprising or significant situation after an initial failure to notice anything unusual

dou·ble–talk \-'tȯk\ *n* ♦ : language that appears to be meaningful but in fact is a mixture of sense and nonsense

♦ babble, bunk, claptrap, drivel, fudge, gabble, gibberish, gobbledygook, hogwash, jabber, jabberwocky, jazz, moonshine, mumbo jumbo, nonsense, piffle, prattle — more at GIBBERISH

double up *vb* : to share accommodations designed for one

double whammy *n* : a combination of two usu. adverse forces, circumstances, or effects

dou·bloon \,də-'blün\ *n* : a former gold coin of Spain and Spanish America

dou·bly \'də-blē\ *adv* 1 : in a twofold manner 2 : to twice the degree

¹**doubt** \'daüt\ *vb* 1 : to be uncertain about 2 ♦ : to lack confidence in : DISTRUST 3 : to consider unlikely

♦ distrust, mistrust, question, suspect — more at DISTRUST

²**doubt** *n* 1 : uncertainty of belief or opinion 2 : a condition causing uncertainty, hesitation, or suspense ⟨the outcome was in ∼⟩ 3 ♦ : a lack of confidence : DISTRUST 4 : an inclination not to believe or accept

♦ distrust, incertitude, misgiving, mistrust, skepticism, suspicion, uncertainty; *also* disbelief, incredulity, unbelief; anxiety, concern; compunction, qualm, scruple **Ant** assurance, belief, certainty, certitude, confidence, conviction, sureness, surety, trust

doubt·able \'daü-tə-bəl\ *adj* : capable of being doubted : QUESTIONABLE

doubt·er \'daü-tər\ *n* ♦ : one that doubts

♦ disbeliever, questioner, skeptic, unbeliever — more at SKEPTIC

doubt·ful \'daüt-fəl\ *adj* 1 ♦ : giving rise to doubt : open to question 2 a : lacking a definite opinion, conviction, or determination b : uncertain in outcome ⟨company's future is ∼⟩ 3 ♦ : marked by qualities that raise doubts about worth, honesty, or validity — **doubt·ful·ness** *n*

♦ [1, 3] debatable, disputable, dubious, equivocal, fishy, problematic, questionable, shady, shaky, suspect, suspicious; *also* moot; ambiguous, open, unclear; uncertain, undecided, undetermined; flimsy, improbable, unlikely **Ant** certain, incontestable, indisputable, indubitable, sure, undeniable, undoubted, unquestionable ♦ [3] distrustful, dubious, mistrustful, skeptical, suspicious, uncertain, undecided, unsettled, unsure; *also* diffident, insecure; hesitant, indecisive, irresolute, vacillating, wavering **Ant** certain, convinced, positive, sure

doubt·ful·ly \-fə-lē\ *adv* : in a doubtful manner

¹**doubt·less** \'daüt-ləs\ *adv* 1 ♦ : without doubt 2 : without much doubt : PROBABLY

♦ certainly, definitely, incontestably, indeed, indisputably, really, surely, truly, undeniably, undoubtedly, unquestionably — more at INDEED

²**doubtless** *adj* ♦ : free from doubt : CERTAIN — **doubt·less·ly** *adv*

♦ assured, certain, clear, cocksure, confident, positive, sanguine, sure — more at CERTAIN

douche \'düsh\ *n* [F] 1 : a jet of fluid (as water) directed against a part or into a cavity of the body; *also* : a cleansing with a douche 2 : a device for giving douches — **douche** *vb*

dough \'dō\ *n* 1 : a mixture that consists of flour or meal and a liquid (as milk or water) and is stiff enough to knead or roll 2 : something resembling dough esp. in consistency 3 ♦ : something generally accepted as a medium of exchange, a measure of value, or a means of payment : MONEY — **doughy** \'dō-ē\ *adj*

♦ cash, currency, lucre, money, pelf, tender — more at MONEY

dough·boy \-,böi\ *n* : an American infantryman esp. in World War I

dough·nut *also* **do·nut** \-(,)nət\ *n* : a small usu. ring-shaped cake fried in fat

dough·ty \'daü-tē\ *adj* **dough·ti·er; -est** ♦ : marked by fearless resolution : VALIANT

♦ brave, courageous, dauntless, fearless, gallant, greathearted, heroic, intrepid, lionhearted, manful, stalwart, stout, undaunted, valiant, valorous — more at BRAVE

Doug·las fir \'də-gləs-\ *n* : a tall evergreen timber tree of the western U.S.

dou·la \'dü-lə\ *n* : a person trained to provide assistance to a mother before, during, and just after childbirth

do up *vb* 1 : to prepare (as by cleaning) for use 2 : to wrap up 3 : CLOTHE, DECORATE 4 : FASTEN

dour \'daü(-ə)r, 'dür\ *adj* [ME, fr. L *durus* hard] 1 ♦ : marked by harsh sternness or severity 2 : OBSTINATE 3 : SULLEN — **dour·ly** *adv*

♦ austere, fierce, flinty, forbidding, grim, gruff, rough, rugged, severe, stark, steely, stern — more at GRIM

douse \'daüs, 'daüz\ *vb* **doused; dous·ing** 1 ♦ : to plunge into water 2 ♦ : to throw a liquid on : DRENCH 3 ♦ : to cause to cease burning : EXTINGUISH

♦ [1] dip, duck, dunk, immerse, souse, submerge — more at DIP ♦ [2] bathe, drench, soak, sop, souse, wash, water, wet — more at WET ♦ [3] extinguish, put out, quench, snuff — more at EXTINGUISH

¹**dove** \'dəv\ *n* 1 : any of numerous pigeons; *esp* : a small wild pigeon 2 : an advocate of peace or of a peaceful policy 3 ♦ : a gentle woman or child — **dov·ish** \'də-vish\ *adj*

♦ angel, innocent, lamb, sheep — more at LAMB

²**dove** \'dōv\ *past of* DIVE

¹**dove·tail** \'dəv-,tāl\ *n* : something that resembles a dove's tail; *esp* : a flaring tenon and a mortise into which it fits tightly

²**dovetail** *vb* 1 : to join by means of dovetails 2 ♦ : to fit skillfully together to form a whole ⟨our plans ∼ nicely⟩

♦ accord, agree, answer, check, coincide, comport, conform, correspond, fit, go, harmonize, jibe, square, tally — more at CHECK

dow·a·ger \'daü-i-jər\ *n* 1 : a widow owning property or a title from her deceased husband 2 ♦ : a dignified elderly woman

♦ dame, matriarch, matron — more at MATRIARCH

dowdy \'daü-dē\ *adj* **dowd·i·er; -est** 1 ♦ : lacking neatness and charm : UNTIDY 2 ♦ : lacking smartness or taste

♦ [1] frowsy, sloppy, slovenly, unkempt, untidy — more at SLOPPY ♦ [2] inelegant, tacky, tasteless, trashy, unfashionable, unstylish — more at TACKY

dow·el \'daü(-ə)l\ *n* 1 : a pin used for fastening together two pieces of wood 2 : a round rod (as of wood) — **dowel** *vb*

¹**dow·er** \'daü(-ə)r\ *n* [ME *dowere*, fr. AF *dower, douaire*, fr. ML *dotarium*, fr. L *dot-, dos* gift, marriage portion] 1 : the part of a deceased husband's real estate which the law gives for life to his widow 2 : DOWRY

²**dower** *vb* : to supply with a dower or dowry : ENDOW

dow·itch·er \'daü-i-chər\ *n* : any of several long-billed wading birds related to the sandpipers

¹**down** \'daün\ *adv* [ME *doun*, fr. OE *dūne*, short for *adūne*, of *dūne*, lit., from (the) hill] 1 ♦ : toward or in a lower physical position 2 : to a lying or sitting position 3 : toward or to the ground, floor, or bottom 4 : as a down payment ⟨paid $5 ∼⟩ 5 : on paper ⟨put ∼ what he says⟩ 6 : in a direction that is the opposite of up 7 : SOUTH 8 : to or in a lower or worse condition or status 9 : from a past time 10 : to or in a state of less activity 11 : into defeat ⟨voted the motion ∼⟩

♦ below, downward, over; *also* facedown; low; downgrade, downhill, downstairs **Ant** up, upward, upwardly

²**down** *prep* : down in, on, along, or through : toward the bottom of

³**down** *vb* 1 ♦ : to go or cause to go or come down 2 : DEFEAT 3 : to cause (a football) to be out of play

♦ bowl, drop, fell, floor, knock, level

⁴**down** *adj* 1 : occupying a low position; *esp* : lying on the ground 2 ♦ : directed or going downward 3 : being in a state of reduced or low activity 4 : low in spirits : DEJECTED 5 ♦ : affected with disease or ill health : SICK ⟨∼ with a cold⟩ 6 : arrived at or brought to an end : DONE

7 : completely mastered ⟨got her lines ∼⟩   **8** : being on record ⟨you're ∼ for two tickets⟩

  ♦ [2] downcast, downward — more at DOWNCAST

  ♦ [5] bad, ill, indisposed, peaked, punk, sick, unhealthy, unsound, unwell — more at SICK

⁵down *n*   **1** ♦ : a low or falling period (as in activity, emotional life, or fortunes)   **2** : one of a series of attempts to advance a football   **3** : an instance of putting down   **4** : a quark with a charge of -⅓ that is one of the constituents of the proton and neutron

  ♦ comedown, decline, descent, downfall, fall — more at COMEDOWN

⁶down *n* ♦ : a rolling usu. treeless upland with sparse soil — usu. used in pl.

  ♦ *usu* **downs** grassland, plain, prairie, savanna, steppe, veld — more at PLAIN

⁷down *n*   **1** : a covering of soft fluffy feathers; *also* : such feathers   **2** ♦ : a downlike covering or material

  ♦ floss, fluff, fur, fuzz, lint, nap, pile — more at FUZZ

down·beat \ˈdau̇n-ˌbēt\ *n* : the downward stroke of a conductor indicating the principally accented note of a measure of music

down·burst \-ˌbərst\ *n* : a powerful downdraft usu. associated with a thunderstorm that is a hazard for low-flying aircraft; *also* : MICROBURST

down·cast \-ˌkast\ *adj*   **1** : low in spirit : DEJECTED   **2** ♦ : directed down ⟨a ∼ glance⟩

  ♦ down, downward

down·draft \-ˌdraft\ *n* : a downward current of gas (as air)

down·er \ˈdau̇-nər\ *n*   **1** : a depressant drug; *esp* : BARBITURATE   **2** : someone or something depressing

down·fall \ˈdau̇n-ˌfȯl\ *n*   **1** ♦ : a sudden fall (as from high rank)   **2** : something that causes a downfall — **down·fall·en** \-ˌfȯ-lən\ *adj*

  ♦ comedown, decline, descent, down, fall — more at COMEDOWN

¹down·grade \ˈdau̇n-ˌgrād\ *n*   **1** : a downward slope (as of a road)   **2** : a decline toward a worse condition

²downgrade *vb* ♦ : to lower in quality, value, extent, or status

  ♦ break, bust, degrade, demote, reduce — more at DEMOTE

down·heart·ed \-ˈhär-təd\ *adj* : low in spirit : DEJECTED

¹down·hill \ˈdau̇n-ˈhil\ *adv* : toward the bottom of a hill — **downhill** \-ˌhil\ *adj*

²down·hill \-ˌhil\ *n* : the sport of skiing downhill usu. in a race against time

¹down·load \ˈdau̇n-ˌlōd\ *n* : an act or instance of downloading something; *also* : the item downloaded

²download *vb* : to transfer (data) from a computer to another device — **down·load·able** \-ˌlō-də-bəl\ *adj*

down payment *n* : a part of the full price paid at the time of purchase or delivery with the balance to be paid later

down·play \ˈdau̇n-ˌplā\ *vb* : DE-EMPHASIZE ⟨∼ed the allegations⟩

down·pour \ˈdau̇n-ˌpōr\ *n* ♦ : a heavy rain

  ♦ cloudburst, deluge, rain, rainstorm, storm, wet — more at RAIN

down·range \-ˈrānj\ *adv* : away from a launching site

¹down·right \-ˌrīt\ *adv* : THOROUGHLY

²downright *adj*   **1** : being completely or exactly what is stated : ABSOLUTE ⟨a ∼ lie⟩   **2** : abrupt in speech or manner : BLUNT ⟨a ∼ man⟩

down·shift \-ˌshift\ *vb* : to shift an automotive vehicle into a lower gear

down·size \-ˌsīz\ *vb* ♦ : to reduce or undergo reduction in size or numbers

  ♦ abate, decrease, de-escalate, diminish, dwindle, lessen, lower, reduce

down·spout \-ˌspau̇t\ *n* : a vertical pipe used to drain rainwater from a roof

Down's syndrome \ˈdau̇nz-\ *or* **Down syndrome** \ˈdau̇n-\

n : a congenital condition characterized esp. by developmental delays, impairment of cognitive functioning, upward slanting eyes, a flattened nasal bridge, broad hands with short fingers, decreased muscle tone, and the presence of an extra chromosome

down·stage \ˈdau̇n-ˈstāj\ *adv or adj* : toward or at the front of a theatrical stage

down·stairs \-ˈstarz\ *adv* : on or to a lower floor and esp. the main or ground floor — **down·stairs** \-ˌstarz\ *adj or n*

down·stream \-ˈstrēm\ *adv or adj* : in the direction of flow of a stream

down·stroke \-ˌstrōk\ *n* : a downward stroke

down·swing \-ˌswiŋ\ *n*   **1** : a swing downward   **2** : DOWNTURN

down-to-earth *adj* ♦ : having or showing concern for fact or reality and rejection of the impractical and visionary

  ♦ earthy, hardheaded, matter-of-fact, practical, pragmatic, realistic — more at REALISTIC

down·town \ˈdau̇n-ˌtau̇n\ *n* : the main business district of a town or city — **downtown** \ˈdau̇n-ˈtau̇n\ *adj or adv*

down·trod·den \ˈdau̇n-ˈträ-dᵊn\ *adj* : suffering oppression

down·turn \-ˌtərn\ *n* : a downward turn esp. in economic activity

¹down·ward \ˈdau̇n-wərd\ *or* **down·wards** \-wərdz\ *adv*   **1** ♦ : from a higher to a lower place or condition   **2** : from an earlier time   **3** : from an ancestor or predecessor

  ♦ below, down, over — more at DOWN

²downward *adj* ♦ : directed toward or situated in a lower place or condition

  ♦ down, downcast — more at DOWNCAST

down·wind \ˈdau̇n-ˈwind\ *adv or adj* : in the direction that the wind is blowing

downy \ˈdau̇-nē\ *adj* **down·i·er; -est** ♦ : resembling or covered with down

  ♦ cottony, satiny, silken, soft, velvety — more at SOFT

downy mildew *n* : any of various parasitic fungi producing whitish masses esp. on the underside of plant leaves; *also* : a plant disease caused by downy mildew

downy woodpecker *n* : a small black-and-white woodpecker of No. America

dow·ry \ˈdau̇r-ē\ *n, pl* **dowries** [ME *dowarie*, fr. AF, alter. of *dower, douaire* dower] : the property that a woman brings to her husband in marriage

dowse \ˈdau̇z\ *vb* **dowsed; dows·ing** : to use a divining rod esp. to find water — **dows·er** *n*

dox·ol·o·gy \däk-ˈsä-lə-jē\ *n, pl* **-gies** : a usu. short hymn of praise to God

doy·en \ˈdȯi-ən, ˈdwä-ˌyaⁿ\ *n* : the senior or most experienced person in a group

doy·enne \dȯi-ˈyen, dwä-ˈyen\ *n* : a woman who is a doyen

doy·ley *chiefly Brit var of* DOILY

doz *abbr* dozen

¹doze \ˈdōz\ *vb* **dozed; doz·ing** ♦ : to sleep lightly

  ♦ catnap, drowse, nap, slumber, snooze — more at NAP

²doze *n* ♦ : a light sleep

  ♦ catnap, drowse, forty winks, nap, siesta, snooze, wink — more at NAP

doz·en \ˈdə-zᵊn\ *n, pl* **dozens** *or* **dozen** [ME *dozeine*, fr. AF *duzeine*, fr. *duze* twelve, fr. L *duodecim*, fr. *duo* two + *decem* ten] : a group of twelve — **doz·enth** \-zᵊnth\ *adj*

¹DP \ˌdē-ˈpē\ *n, pl* **DP's** *or* **DPs**   **1** : a displaced person   **2** : DOUBLE PLAY

²DP *abbr* data processing

dpt *abbr* department

DPT *abbr* diphtheria-pertussis-tetanus (vaccines)

dr *abbr*   **1** debtor   **2** dram   **3** drive   **4** drum

Dr *abbr* doctor

DR *abbr*   **1** dead reckoning   **2** dining room

drab \ˈdrab\ *adj* **drab·ber; drab·best**   **1** : being of a light olive-brown color   **2** ♦ : characterized by dullness and monotony — **drab·ly** *adv* — **drab·ness** *n*

♦ dreary, dry, dull, monotonous, uninteresting

dra·co·ni·an \drā-'kō-nē-ən, drə-\ *adj, often cap* : CRUEL; *also* : SEVERE

¹**draft** \'draft, 'dráft\ *n* **1** : the act of drawing or hauling **2 a** : the act or an instance of drinking or inhaling **b** ♦ : the portion drunk or inhaled in one such act **3** : DOSE, POTION **4** : DELINEATION, PLAN, DESIGN; *also* : a preliminary sketch, outline, or version ⟨a rough ∼ of a speech⟩ **5** : the act of drawing (as from a cask); *also* : a portion of liquid so drawn **6** : the depth of water a ship draws esp. when loaded **7** : a system for or act of selecting persons (as for compulsory military service or sports teams); *also* : the persons so selected **8** : an order for the payment of money drawn by one person or bank on another **9** : a heavy demand : STRAIN **10** : a current of air; *also* : a device to regulate air supply (as in a stove) — **on draft** : ready to be drawn from a receptacle ⟨beer *on draft*⟩

♦ drag, drink, nip, quaff, shot, slug, snort, swallow, swig — more at DRINK

²**draft** *adj* **1** : used or adapted for drawing loads ⟨∼ horses⟩ **2** : being or having been on draft ⟨∼ beer⟩

³**draft** *vb* **1** : to select usu. on a compulsory basis; *esp* : to conscript for military service **2** : to draw the preliminary sketch, version, or plan of **3** ♦ : to put into written form : COMPOSE **4** : to draw off or away — **draft·ee** \draf-'tē, dráf-\ *n*

♦ cast, compose, craft, draw, formulate, frame, prepare — more at COMPOSE

draft·ee \draf-'tē, dráf-\ *n* : a person who is drafted

drafts·man \'draft-smən, 'dráft-\ *n* : a person who draws plans (as for buildings or machinery)

drafty \'draf-tē, 'dráf-\ *adj* **draft·i·er; -est** : exposed to or abounding in drafts of air

¹**drag** \'drag\ *n* **1** : a device pulled along under water for detecting or gathering **2** : something (as a harrow or sledge) that is dragged along over a surface **3 a** : the act or an instance of dragging **b** : a draft of liquid **4** ♦ : something that hinders progress; *also* : something boring **5** : an open way for vehicles, persons, and animals : STREET ⟨the main ∼⟩ **6** : clothing typical of one sex worn by a member of the opposite sex

♦ bar, block, clog, crimp, embarrassment, hindrance, let, obstacle, stop, stumbling block — more at OBSTACLE

²**drag** *vb* **dragged; drag·ging** **1** ♦ : to draw slowly or heavily : HAUL **2** ♦ : to move with painful or undue slowness or difficulty **3** : to force into or out of some situation, condition, or course of action **4** : PROTRACT ⟨∼ a story out⟩ **5** : to hang or lag behind **6** : to explore, search, or fish with a drag **7** : to trail along on the ground **8** : DRAW, PUFF ⟨∼ on a cigarette⟩ **9** : to move (items on a computer screen) esp. by using a mouse — **drag·ger** *n* — **drag one's feet** *also* **drag one's heels** : to act slowly or with hesitation

♦ [1] draw, hale, haul, lug, pull, tow, tug — more at PULL ♦ [2] crawl, creep, dally, dawdle, delay, dillydally, lag, linger, loiter, poke, tarry — more at DELAY

drag·net \-ˌnet\ *n* **1** : NET, TRAWL **2** : a network of planned actions for pursuing and catching ⟨a police ∼⟩

drag·o·man \'dra-gə-mən\ *n, pl* **-mans** *or* **-men** \-mən\ : an interpreter employed esp. in the Near East

drag·on \'dra-gən\ *n* [ME, fr. AF *dragun*, fr. L *dracon-, draco* serpent, dragon, fr. Gk *drakōn* serpent] : a fabulous animal usu. represented as a huge winged scaly serpent with a crested head and large claws

drag·on·fly \-ˌflī\ *n* : any of a group of large harmless 4-winged insects that hold the wings horizontal and unfolded in repose

¹**dra·goon** \drə-'gün, dra-\ *n* [F *dragon* dragon, dragoon, fr. MF] : a heavily armed mounted soldier

²**dragoon** *vb* : to force or attempt to force into submission : COERCE

drag race *n* : an acceleration contest between vehicles — **drag racer** *n*

drag·ster \'drag-stər\ *n* : a usu. high-powered vehicle used in a drag race

drag strip *n* : a site for drag races

¹**drain** \'drān\ *vb* **1** : to draw off or flow off gradually or completely **2** ♦ : to exhaust physically or emotionally **3** : to make or become gradually dry or empty **4** ♦ : to carry away the surface water of : discharge surface or surplus water **5** ♦ : to deplete or empty by or as if by drawing off by degrees or in increments : EXHAUST — **drain·er** *n*

♦ [2] burn out, do in, exhaust, fag, fatigue, tire, tucker, wash out, wear, wear out, weary — more at EXHAUST ♦ [4] bleed, draw off, pump, siphon, tap; *also* milk; suck; clear, empty, evacuate, exhaust, vacate, void *Ant* fill ♦ [5] clean, consume, deplete, exhaust, expend, spend, use up — more at DEPLETE

²**drain** *n* **1** : a means (as a channel or sewer) of draining **2** : the act of draining **3** : a gradual outflow; *also* : something causing an outflow ⟨a ∼ on our savings⟩

drain·age \'drā-nij\ *n* **1** : the act or process of draining; *also* : something that is drained off **2** : a means for draining : DRAIN, SEWER **3** : an area drained

drained *adj* ♦ : exhausted physically or emotionally

♦ beat, bushed, dead, effete, jaded, limp, prostrate, spent, tired, weary, worn-out — more at WEARY

drain·pipe \'drān-ˌpīp\ *n* : a pipe for drainage

drake \'drāk\ *n* : a male duck

dram \'dram\ *n* **1** : a unit of measure equal to ¹⁄₁₆ ounce **2** : FLUID DRAM **3** : a small drink

dra·ma \'drä-mə, 'dra-\ *n* [LL, fr. Gk, deed, drama, fr. *dran* to do, act] **1 a** : a literary composition designed for theatrical presentation **b** : a play, movie, or television production with a serious tone or subject **2** : dramatic art, literature, or affairs **3** : a series of events involving conflicting forces — **dra·ma·tist** \'dra-mə-tist, 'drä-\ *n*

dra·mat·ic \drə-'ma-tik\ *adj* **1** : of or relating to the drama **2 a** ♦ : suitable to or characteristic of the drama **b** ♦ : striking in appearance or effect — **dra·mat·i·cal·ly** \-ti-k(ə-)lē\ *adv*

♦ [2a] histrionic, melodramatic, theatrical; *also* affected, emotional, sensational ♦ [2b] catchy, conspicuous, flamboyant, showy, striking — more at SHOWY

dram·a·ti·sa·tion, dra·ma·tise *Brit var of* DRAMATIZATION, DRAMATIZE

dra·ma·tize \'dra-mə-ˌtīz, 'drä-\ *vb* **-tized; -tiz·ing** **1** : to adapt for or be suitable for theatrical presentation **2** : to present or represent in a dramatic manner — **dram·a·ti·za·tion** \ˌdra-mə-tə-'zā-shən, ˌdrä-\ *n*

dra·me·dy \'drä-mə-dē, 'dra-\ *n* : a comedy having dramatic moments

drank *past and past part of* DRINK

¹**drape** \'drāp\ *vb* **draped; drap·ing** **1** : to cover or adorn with or as if with folds of cloth **2** : to cause to hang or stretch out loosely or carelessly **3** : to arrange or become arranged in flowing lines or folds

²**drape** *n* **1** : CURTAIN **2** : arrangement in or of folds **3** : the cut or hang of clothing

drap·er \'drā-pər\ *n, chiefly Brit* : a dealer in cloth and sometimes in clothing and dry goods

drap·ery \'drā-pə-rē\ *n, pl* **-er·ies** **1** *Brit* : DRY GOODS **2** : a decorative fabric esp. when hung loosely and in folds; *also* : hangings of heavy fabric used as a curtain

dras·tic \'dras-tik\ *adj* : HARSH, RIGOROUS, SEVERE ⟨∼ punishment⟩ — **dras·ti·cal·ly** \-ti-k(ə-)lē\ *adv*

draught \'dráft,\ **draughty** \'dráf-tē\ *chiefly Brit var of* DRAFT, DRAFTY

draughts \'dráfts\ *n, Brit* : CHECKERS

¹**draw** \'dró\ *vb* **drew** \'drü\; **drawn** \'drón\; **draw·ing** **1** ♦ : to cause to move toward a force exerted **2** : to cause to go in a certain direction ⟨*drew* him aside⟩ **3** : to move or go steadily or gradually ⟨night ∼s near⟩ **4** : ATTRACT, ENTICE **5** : PROVOKE, ROUSE ⟨*drew* enemy fire⟩ **6** : INHALE ⟨∼ a deep breath⟩ **7** : to bring or pull out

⟨*drew* a gun⟩ **8** : to cause to come out of a container ⟨∼ water for a bath⟩ **9** : to take out the entrails of : EVISCERATE **10** : to require (a specified depth) to float in **11** : ACCUMULATE, GAIN ⟨∼*ing* interest⟩ **12** : to take money from a place of deposit : WITHDRAW **13 ♦** : to receive regularly ⟨∼ a salary⟩ **14** : to take (cards) from a stack or the dealer **15** : to receive or take at random ⟨∼ a winning number⟩ **16** : to bend (a bow) by pulling back the string **17** : WRINKLE, SHRINK **18** : to change shape by or as if by pulling or stretching ⟨a face *drawn* with sorrow⟩ **19** : to leave (a contest) undecided : TIE **20 ♦** : to give a portrayal of : DELINEATE **21** : to write out in due form : DRAFT ⟨∼ up a will⟩ **22** : FORMULATE ⟨∼ comparisons⟩ **23** : INFER ⟨∼ a conclusion⟩ **24** : to spread or elongate (metal) by hammering or by pulling through dies **25** : to produce or allow a draft or current of air ⟨the chimney ∼s well⟩ **26** : to swell out in a wind ⟨all sails ∼*ing*⟩ — **draw the line** *or* **draw a line** : to fix an arbitrary boundary usu. between two things

  ♦ [1] drag, hale, haul, lug, pull, tow, tug — more at PULL **♦ [13]** acquire, attain, capture, carry, earn, gain, garner, get, land, make, obtain, procure, realize, secure, win — more at EARN **♦ [20]** delineate, depict, describe, image, paint, picture, portray, sketch — more at DESCRIBE

²draw *n* **1 ♦** : the act, process, or result of drawing **2** : a lot or chance drawn at random **3 ♦** : a contest left undecided or deadlocked : TIE **4 ♦** : one that draws attention or patronage

  ♦ [1] haul, jerk, pluck, pull, tug, wrench — more at PULL **♦ [3]** dead heat, stalemate, standoff, tie — more at TIE **♦ [4]** attraction, lodestone, magnet — more at MAGNET

draw·back \ˈdrȯ-ˌbak\ *n* **♦** : an unfavorable, inferior, or prejudicial condition : DISADVANTAGE

  ♦ disadvantage, handicap, liability, minus, penalty, strike — more at DISADVANTAGE

draw·bridge \-ˌbrij\ *n* : a bridge made to be raised, lowered, or turned to permit or deny passage

draw·er \ˈdrȯr, ˈdrȯ-ər\ *n* **1** : one that draws **2** *pl* : an undergarment for the lower part of the body **3** : a sliding boxlike compartment (as in a table or desk)

draw·ing \ˈdrȯ-iŋ\ *n* **1** : an act or instance of drawing; *esp* : an occasion when something is decided by drawing lots ⟨tonight's lottery ∼⟩ **2** : the act or art of making a figure, plan, or sketch by means of lines **3 ♦** : a representation made by drawing : SKETCH

  ♦ cartoon, delineation, sketch; *also* outline, silhouette; caricature, doodle, illustration; depiction, image, likeness, portrait, representation; engraving, etching; blueprint

drawing card *n* : DRAW 4

drawing room *n* : a formal reception room

drawl \ˈdrȯl\ *vb* : to speak or utter slowly with vowels greatly prolonged — **drawl** *n*

draw off *vb* **♦** : to remove esp. from an environment or container

  ♦ bleed, drain, pump, siphon, tap — more at DRAIN

draw on *vb* : to draw nearer : APPROACH ⟨night *draws on*⟩

draw out *vb* **1 ♦** : to extend beyond a minimum in time : PROLONG **2** : to cause to speak freely

  ♦ elongate, extend, lengthen, prolong, protract, stretch — more at EXTEND

draw·string \ˈdrȯ-ˌstriŋ\ *n* : a string, cord, or tape for use in closing a bag or controlling fullness in garments or curtains

draw up *vb* **1 ♦** : to prepare a draft or version of **2** : to pull oneself erect **3 ♦** : to bring or come to a stop **4 ♦** : to bring (as troops) into array

  ♦ [1] cast, compose, craft, draft, formulate, frame, prepare — more at COMPOSE **♦ [3]** arrest, catch, check, fetch up, halt, hold up, stall, stay, still, stop — more at HALT **♦ [4]** arrange, array, classify, codify, dispose,

marshal, order, organize, range, systematize — more at ORDER

dray \ˈdrā\ *n* : a strong low cart for carrying heavy loads

¹dread \ˈdred\ *vb* **1** : to fear greatly **2** : to feel extreme reluctance to meet or face

²dread *n* **♦** : great fear esp. of some harm to come

  ♦ alarm, anxiety, apprehension, fear, fright, horror, panic, terror, trepidation — more at FEAR

³dread *adj* **1** : causing great fear or anxiety ⟨a ∼ disease⟩ **2** : inspiring awe

dread·ful \ˈdred-fəl\ *adj* **1 ♦** : inspiring dread or awe : FRIGHTENING **2 ♦** : extremely distasteful, unpleasant, or shocking ⟨a ∼ accident⟩ — **dread·ful·ly** *adv*

  ♦ [1] dire, fearful, fearsome, forbidding, formidable, frightful, hair-raising, horrible, redoubtable, scary, shocking, terrible, terrifying — more at FEARFUL **♦ [2]** appalling, atrocious, awful, frightful, ghastly, grisly, gruesome, hideous, horrible, horrid, lurid, macabre, monstrous, nightmarish, shocking, terrible — more at HORRIBLE

dread·locks \ˈdred-ˌläks\ *n pl* : long braids of hair over the entire head

dread·nought \ˈdred-ˌnȯt\ *n* : BATTLESHIP

¹dream \ˈdrēm\ *n* [ME *dreem*, fr. OE *drēam* noise, joy, and ON *draumr* dream] **1** : a series of thoughts, images, or emotions occurring during sleep **2 ♦** : a dreamlike vision **3 ♦** : something notable for its beauty, excellence, or enjoyable quality **4 a ♦** : a strongly desired goal or purpose **b** : IDEAL — **dream·like** \-ˌlīk\ *adj*

  ♦ [2] chimera, conceit, daydream, delusion, fancy, fantasy, figment, hallucination, illusion, phantasm, pipe dream, unreality, vision **♦ [3]** beauty, enchantress, fox, goddess, knockout, queen — more at BEAUTY **♦ [4a]** aim, ambition, aspiration, design, end, goal, intent, mark, meaning, object, objective, plan, pretension, purpose, thing — more at GOAL

²dream \ˈdrēm\ *vb* **dreamed** \ˈdremt, ˈdrēmd\ *or* **dreamt** \ˈdremt\; **dream·ing** **1** : to have a dream of **2** : to indulge in daydreams or fantasies : pass (time) in reverie or inaction **3 ♦** : to consider as a possibility : IMAGINE

  ♦ conceive, envisage, fancy, imagine, picture, vision, visualize — more at IMAGINE

dream·boat \ˈdrēm-ˌbōt\ *n, slang* : something highly desirable; *esp* : a very attractive person

dream·er \ˈdrē-mər\ *n* **1** : one that dreams **2 ♦** : one who lives in a world of fancy and imagination **3 ♦** : one who has ideas or conceives projects regarded as impractical

  ♦ idealist, romantic, utopian, visionary — more at IDEALIST

dream·land \ˈdrēm-ˌland\ *n* : an unreal delightful country that exists in imagination or in dreams

dream up *vb* : INVENT, CONCOCT

dream·world \-ˌwərld\ *n* : a world of illusion or fantasy

dreamy \ˈdrē-mē\ *adj* **♦** : quiet and soothing; *also* : pleasant

  ♦ comforting, narcotic, sedative, soothing — more at SOOTHING **♦** agreeable, congenial, delectable, delicious, delightful, felicitous, good, grateful, gratifying, nice, palatable, pleasant, pleasurable, satisfying

drear \ˈdrir\ *adj* : DREARY

drea·ry \ˈdrir-ē\ *adj* **drea·ri·er; -est** [ME *drery*, fr. OE *drēorig* sad, bloody, fr. *drēor* gore] **1** : feeling, displaying, or reflecting listlessness or discouragement **2 ♦** : having nothing likely to provide cheer, comfort, or interest — **drea·ri·ly** \-ə-lē\ *adv*

  ♦ bleak, dark, dismal, gloomy, gray (*or* grey), somber (*or* sombre), wretched — more at GLOOMY

¹dredge \ˈdrej\ *vb* **dredged; dredg·ing** **♦** : to gather or search with or as if with a dredge; *esp* : to bring to light or gather up by deep searching — often used with *up* — **dredg·er** *n*

  ♦ dig, hunt, rake, ransack, rifle, rummage, scour, search — more at SEARCH **♦** *often* **dredge up** detect, determine, dig up, discover, ferret out, find, hit on, locate, track down — more at FIND

²dredge *n* : a machine or barge for removing earth or silt

³dredge *vb* **dredged; dredg·ing** : to coat (food) by sprinkling (as with flour)

dregs \'dregz\ *n pl* **1** ♦ : the matter that settles to the bottom of a liquid : SEDIMENT **2** : the most undesirable part ⟨the ∼ of humanity⟩

♦ deposit, grounds, lees, precipitate, sediment — more at DEPOSIT

drench \'drench\ *vb* ♦ : to wet thoroughly

♦ bathe, douse, soak, sop, souse, wash, water, wet — more at WET

¹dress \'dres\ *vb* [ME, fr. AF *drescer* to direct, put right, fr. VL **directiare*, fr. L *directus* direct] **1** : to make or set straight : ALIGN **2** : to prepare for use; *esp* : BUTCHER **3** ♦ : to add decorative details or accessories to : EMBELLISH ⟨∼ a store window⟩ **4** ♦ : to put clothes on : CLOTHE; *also* : to put on or wear formal or fancy clothes **5** : to apply dressings or medicine to **6** : to arrange (the hair) by combing, brushing, or curling **7** : to apply fertilizer to **8** ♦ : to put through a finishing process : SMOOTH ⟨∼ leather⟩

♦ [3] adorn, array, beautify, bedeck, deck, decorate, do, embellish, enrich, garnish, grace, ornament, trim — more at DECORATE ♦ [4] apparel, array, attire, caparison, clothe, deck, garb, invest, rig, suit — more at CLOTHE ♦ [8] buff, burnish, gloss, grind, polish, rub, shine, smooth — more at POLISH

²dress *n* **1** ♦ : personal attire : CLOTHING **2** : a garment usu. consisting of a one-piece bodice and skirt **3** ♦ : covering, adornment, or appearance appropriate or peculiar to a particular time — **dress·mak·er** \-,mā-kər\ *n* — **dress·mak·ing** \-,mā-kiŋ\ *n*

♦ [1] apparel, attire, clothing, duds, raiment, wear — more at CLOTHING ♦ [3] garb, getup, guise, outfit — more at OUTFIT

³dress *adj* : suitable for a formal occasion; *also* : requiring formal dress

dres·sage \drə-'säzh\ *n* [F] : the execution by a trained horse of complex movements in response to barely perceptible signals from its rider

dress down *vb* ♦ : to scold severely

♦ admonish, chide, lecture, rail (at *or* against), rate, rebuke, reprimand, scold — more at SCOLD

¹dress·er \'dre-sər\ *n* : a chest of drawers or bureau with a mirror

²dresser *n* : one that dresses

dress·ing \'dre-siŋ\ *n* **1** : the act or process of one who dresses **2** : a sauce for adding to a dish (as a salad) **3** : a seasoned mixture usu. used as stuffing **4** : material used to cover an injury

dressing gown *n* : a loose robe worn esp. while dressing or resting

dress rehearsal *n* : a full rehearsal of a play or other show done with all its costumes, scenery, lighting, etc., shortly before the first performance

dress up *vb* **1** : to change the customary dress or appearance of **2** ♦ : furnish with a false appearance

♦ camouflage, cloak, disguise, mask — more at DISGUISE

dressy \'dre-sē\ *adj* **dress·i·er; -est** **1** : showy in dress **2** : STYLISH, SMART

drew *past of* DRAW

¹drib·ble \'dri-bəl\ *vb* **drib·bled; drib·bling** **1** ♦ : to fall or flow in drops : TRICKLE **2** ♦ : to let saliva trickle from the corner of the mouth : DROOL **3** : to propel by successive slight taps or bounces

♦ [1] gurgle, lap, plash, ripple, slosh, splash, trickle, wash — more at GURGLE ♦ [2] drivel, drool, salivate, slaver, slobber — more at DROOL

²dribble *n* **1** : a small trickling stream or flow **2** : a drizzling shower **3** : the dribbling of a ball or puck

drib·let \'dri-blət\ *n* **1** : a trifling amount **2** ♦ : a drop of liquid

♦ blob, drip, drop, droplet, glob — more at DROP

dri·er *or* **dry·er** \'drī-ər\ *n* **1** : a substance that speeds drying (as of paint or ink) **2** *usu* **dryer** : a device for drying

¹drift \'drift\ *n* **1** ♦ : the motion or course of something drifting; *also* : a gradual shift of position **2** ♦ : a mass of matter (as snow or sand) piled up esp. by wind **3** : earth, gravel, and rock deposited by a glacier **4** ♦ : a general underlying design or tendency : MEANING ⟨if you catch my ∼⟩

♦ [1] current, leaning, run, tendency, tide, trend, wind — more at TREND ♦ [2] bank, bar, mound — more at BANK ♦ [4] denotation, import, intent, meaning, purport, sense, significance, signification — more at MEANING

²drift *vb* **1** ♦ : to float or be driven along by or as if by a current of water or air; *also* : to move along smoothly as if drifting on a current of water or air **2** : to become piled up by wind or water

♦ float, glide, hang, hover, poise, ride, sail, waft — more at FLOAT

drift·er \'drif-tər\ *n* ♦ : a person without aim, ambition, or initiative

♦ nomad, rambler, rover, stroller, vagabond, wanderer — more at NOMAD

drift net *n* : a fishing net often miles in extent arranged to drift with the tide or current

drift·wood \'drift-,wùd\ *n* : wood drifted or floated by water

¹drill \'dril\ *n* **1** : a tool for boring holes **2** : the training of soldiers in marching and the handling of arms **3** ♦ : a regularly practiced exercise

♦ exercise, practice, routine, training, workout — more at EXERCISE

²drill *vb* **1** : to instruct and exercise by repetition **2** : to train in or practice military drill **3** ♦ : to bore or drive a hole in **4** : to shoot with or as if with a gun — **drill·er** *n*

♦ bore, hole, perforate, pierce, punch, puncture — more at PERFORATE

³drill *n* **1** : a shallow furrow or trench in which seed is sown **2** : an agricultural implement for making furrows and dropping seed into them

⁴drill *n* : a firm cotton twilled fabric

drill·mas·ter \'dril-,mas-tər\ *n* : an instructor in military drill

drill press *n* : an upright drilling machine in which the drill is pressed to the work usu. by a hand lever

drily *var of* DRYLY

¹drink \'driŋk\ *vb* **drank** \'draŋk\; **drunk** \'drəŋk\ *or* **drank**; **drink·ing** **1** ♦ : to swallow liquid : IMBIBE **2** ♦ : to take in or suck up : ABSORB **3** : to take in through the senses ⟨∼ in the beautiful scenery⟩ **4** : to give or join in a toast **5** : to drink alcoholic beverages esp. to excess — **drink·able** *adj* — **drink·er** *n*

♦ [1] guzzle, imbibe, quaff, sup, swig, toss; *also* lap, lick; consume, down, mouth (down); tipple; toast, wine ♦ [2] absorb, imbibe, soak, sponge, suck — more at ABSORB

²drink *n* **1 a** ♦ : a liquid suitable for swallowing : BEVERAGE **b** ♦ : an alcoholic beverage **2** ♦ : a draft or portion of liquid **3** : excessive consumption of alcoholic beverages

♦ [1a] beverage, libation, quencher; *also* potion; pop, soda, soda pop, soft drink; alcohol, brew, intoxicant, liquor, spirits ♦ [1b] alcohol, booze, intoxicant, liquor, moonshine, spirits — more at ALCOHOL ♦ [2] draft, drag, nip, quaff, shot, slug, snort, swallow, swig

¹drip \'drip\ *vb* **dripped; drip·ping** **1** : to fall or let fall in drops **2** : to let fall drops of moisture or liquid ⟨a *dripping* faucet⟩ **3** : to overflow with or as if with moisture

²drip *n* **1** : a falling in drops **2** ♦ : liquid that falls, overflows, or is extruded in drops **3** : the sound made by or as if by falling drops

♦ blob, driblet, drop, droplet, glob — more at DROP

¹**drive** \'drīv\ *vb* **drove** \'drōv\; **driv·en** \'dri-vən\; **driv·ing** **1** ♦ : to urge, push, or force onward **2** : to carry through strongly ⟨~ a bargain⟩ **3** ♦ : to set or keep in motion or operation **4** : to direct the movement or course of **5** : to convey in a vehicle **6** : to bring into a specified condition ⟨the noise ~s me crazy⟩ **7** ♦ : to exert inescapable or coercive pressure on : FORCE ⟨*driven* by hunger to steal⟩ **8** : to project, inject, or impress forcefully ⟨*drove* the lesson home⟩ **9** : to produce by opening a way ⟨~ a well⟩ **10** : to progress with strong momentum ⟨a *driving* rain⟩ **11** : to propel an object of play (as a golf ball) by a hard blow — **driv·er** *n*

♦ [1] propel, push, shove, thrust — more at PUSH ♦ [1] herd, punch, run; *also* shepherd; wrangle; egg, exhort, goad, prick, prod, spur, urge ♦ [3] activate, actuate, crank, move, propel, run, set off, spark, start, touch off, trigger, turn on — more at ACTIVATE ♦ [7] coerce, compel, constrain, force, make, muscle, obligate, oblige, press, pressure — more at FORCE

²**drive** *n* **1** : a trip in a carriage or automobile **2** : a driving or collecting of animals ⟨a cattle ~⟩ **3** : the guiding of logs downstream to a mill **4** : the act of driving a ball; *also* : the flight of a ball **5** : DRIVEWAY **6** : a public road for driving (as in a park) **7** : the state of being hurried and under pressure **8** ♦ : a strong systematic group effort ⟨membership ~⟩ **9** : the apparatus by which motion is imparted to a machine **10** : an offensive or aggressive move : a military attack **11 a** ♦ : an urgent, basic, or instinctual need **b** ♦ : an impelling culturally acquired concern, interest, or longing **12** ♦ : dynamic quality **13** : a device for reading and writing on magnetic media (as magnetic tape or disks)

♦ [8] bandwagon, campaign, cause, crusade, movement — more at CAMPAIGN ♦ [11a, 11b] appetite, craving, desire, hankering, hunger, itch, longing, lust, passion, thirst, urge, yearning, yen — more at DESIRE ♦ [12] aggressiveness, ambition, enterprise, go, hustle, initiative — more at ENTERPRISE

drive–in \'drī-,vin\ *adj* : accommodating patrons while they remain in their automobiles — **drive–in** *n*

¹**driv·el** \'dri-vəl\ *vb* **-eled** *or* **-elled**; **-el·ing** *or* **-el·ling** **1** : to let saliva dribble from the mouth : DROOL **2** ♦ : to talk or utter stupidly, carelessly, or in an infantile way — **driv·el·er** *n*

♦ babble, chatter, gabble, gibber, jabber, prattle, sputter — more at BABBLE

²**drivel** *n* ♦ : language, conduct, or an idea that is absurd or contrary to good sense : NONSENSE

♦ bunk, claptrap, fiddlesticks, folly, foolishness, fudge, hogwash, humbug, nonsense, piffle, rot, silliness, slush, stupidity, trash — more at NONSENSE

drive·shaft \'drīv-,shaft\ *n* : a shaft that transmits mechanical power

drive–through *also* **drive–thru** \'drīv-,thrü\ *adj* : designed for the service of patrons remaining in their automobiles — **drive–through** *also* **drive–thru** *n*

drive·way \-,wā\ *n* : a short private road leading from the street to a house, garage, or parking lot

¹**driz·zle** \'dri-zəl\ *n* : a fine misty rain

²**drizzle** *vb* **driz·zled**; **driz·zling** : to rain in very small drops

drogue \'drōg\ *n* : a small parachute for slowing down or stabilizing something (as a space capsule)

droid \'droid\ *n* : ANDROID

droll \'drōl\ *adj* [F *drêole*, fr. *drêole* scamp, fr. MF *drolle*, fr. MD, imp] ♦ : having a humorous, whimsical, or odd quality ⟨a ~ expression⟩ — **droll·ery** \'drō-lə-rē\ *n* — **drol·ly** *adv*

♦ antic, comic, comical, farcical, funny, hilarious, humorous, hysterical, laughable, ludicrous, riotous, risible, screaming, uproarious — more at FUNNY

drom·e·dary \'drä-mə-,der-ē\ *n, pl* **-dar·ies** [ME *dromedarie*, fr. MF *dromedaire*, fr. LL *dromedarius*, fr. L *dromad-, dromas*, fr. Gk, running] : CAMEL; *esp* : a domesticated one-humped camel of western Asia and northern Africa

¹**drone** \'drōn\ *n* **1** : a male honeybee **2** : one that lives on the labors of others : PARASITE **3** : an unmanned aircraft or ship guided by remote control **4** : one whose work is menial or monotonous

²**drone** *vb* **droned**; **dron·ing** ♦ : to sound with a low dull monotonous murmuring sound; *also* : speak monotonously

♦ buzz, hum, whir, whish, whiz, zip, zoom — more at WHIR

³**drone** *n* ♦ : a deep monotonous sound

♦ buzz, hum, purr, whir, whiz, zoom — more at HUM

drool \'drül\ *vb* **1** ♦ : to let liquid flow from the mouth **2** : to talk foolishly

♦ dribble, drivel, salivate, slaver, slobber; *also* water; expectorate, spit; foam, froth; sputter

¹**droop** \'drüp\ *vb* **1** ♦ : to hang or incline downward **2** : to sink gradually **3** ♦ : to become depressed or weakened : LANGUISH

♦ [1] flag, hang, loll, sag, wilt; *also* slouch, slump; collapse, drop, fall, sink, subside ♦ [3] decay, fail, flag, go, lag, languish, sag, waste, weaken, wilt — more at WEAKEN

²**droop** *n* ♦ : the condition or appearance of drooping — **droopy** *adj*

♦ sag, slack, slackness — more at SAG

droopy \'drü-pē\ *adj* **1** : low in spirits **2** ♦ : drooping or tending to droop

♦ pendulous ♦ flaccid, floppy, lank, limp, slack, yielding — more at LIMP

¹**drop** \'dräp\ *n* **1** ♦ : the quantity of fluid that falls in one spherical mass **2** *pl* : a dose of medicine measured by drops **3** : a small quantity of drink **4** : the smallest practical unit of liquid measure **5** : something (as a pendant or a small round candy) that resembles a liquid drop **6** ♦ : the act or an instance of dropping : FALL **7** ♦ : a decline in quantity or quality **8** : a descent by parachute **9** : the distance through which something drops **10** : a slot into which something is to be dropped **11** : something that drops or has dropped **12** ♦ : an advantage or superiority over an opponent — usu. used in the phrase *get the drop on*

♦ [1] blob, driblet, drip, droplet, glob; *also* raindrop, tear; spatter; dribble, trickle ♦ [6] descent, dip, dive, down, fall, plunge — more at DESCENT ♦ [7] abatement, decline, decrease, decrement, diminution, fall, loss, reduction, shrinkage — more at DECREASE ♦ [12] advantage, better, edge, jump, upper hand, vantage — more at ADVANTAGE

²**drop** *vb* **dropped**; **drop·ping** **1** : to fall or let fall in drops **2** : to let fall : LOWER ⟨~ a glove⟩ ⟨*dropped* his voice⟩ **3** : SEND ⟨~ me a note⟩ **4** : to let go : DISMISS ⟨~ the subject⟩ **5** : to knock down : cause to fall **6** ♦ : to go lower : become less ⟨prices *dropped*⟩ **7** : to come or go unexpectedly or informally ⟨~ in to call⟩ **8** : to pass from one state into a less active one ⟨~ off to sleep⟩ **9** ♦ : to move downward or with a current **10** ♦ : to desist from : QUIT **11** : to give birth to — **drop back** : to move toward the rear — **drop behind** : to fail to keep up

♦ [6] decline, descend, dip, fall, lower, plummet, plunge, sink, tumble; *also* decrease, diminish, lessen; recede, retreat *Ant* arise, lift, rise, soar ♦ [9] decline, descend, dip, fall, plunge — more at DESCEND ♦ [10] discontinue, give up, knock off, lay off, quit — more at QUIT

drop by *vb* ♦ : to pay a brief casual visit

♦ **drop by** *or* **drop in** call, pop (in), stop (by *or* in), visit — more at CALL

drop in *vb* : to pay an unexpected or casual visit

♦ call, pop (in), stop (by *or* in), visit — more at CALL

drop·kick \-'kik\ *n* : a kick made by dropping a ball to the ground and kicking it at the moment it starts to rebound — **drop–kick** *vb*

drop·let \'drä-plət\ *n* ♦ : a tiny drop

♦ blob, driblet, drip, drop, glob — more at DROP

drop–off \'dräp-,óf\ *n* **1** : a steep or perpendicular descent **2** : a marked decline ⟨a ∼ in attendance⟩

drop off *vb* : to fall asleep

drop out *vb* : to withdraw from participation or membership; *esp* : to leave school before graduation — **drop·out** \'dräp-,aút\ *n*

drop·per \'drä-pər\ *n* **1** : one that drops **2** : a short glass tube with a rubber bulb used to measure out liquids by drops

drop·pings *n pl* ♦ : the feces of an animal : DUNG

♦ dung, slops, waste; *also* stool; dunghill, guano, manure, muck; spoor; sewage

drop·sy \'dräp-sē\ *n* [ME *dropesie*, short for *ydropesie*, fr. OF, fr. L *hydropisis*, fr. Gk *hydrōps*, fr. *hydōr* water] : EDEMA — **drop·si·cal** \-si-kəl\ *adj*

dross \'dräs\ *n* **1** : the scum that forms on the surface of a molten metal **2** : waste matter : REFUSE

drought \'draút\ *also* **drouth** \'draúth\ *n* : a long spell of dry weather

¹**drove** \'drōv\ *n* **1** : a group of animals driven or moving in a body **2** ♦ : a large number : CROWD — usu. used in pl. ⟨tourists arriving in ∼s⟩

♦ *usu* **droves** army, crowd, crush, flock, horde, host, legion, mob, multitude, press, swarm, throng — more at CROWD

²**drove** *past of* DRIVE

drov·er \'drō-vər\ *n* : one that drives domestic animals usu. to market

drown \'draún\ *vb* **drowned** \'draúnd\; **drown·ing** **1** : to suffocate by submersion esp. in water **2** : to become drowned **3** ♦ : to cover with water; *also* : to soak, drench, or cover with a liquid **4** : to cause to be muted (as a sound) by a loud noise **5** : OVERPOWER, OVERWHELM

♦ deluge, engulf, flood, inundate, overflow, overwhelm, submerge, swamp — more at FLOOD ♦ drench, impregnate, saturate, soak, sop, souse, steep — more at SOAK

¹**drowse** \'draúz\ *vb* **drowsed**; **drows·ing** ♦ : to fall into a light slumber : DOZE

♦ catnap, doze, nap, slumber, snooze — more at NAP

²**drowse** *n* ♦ : the act or an instance of drowsing

♦ catnap, doze, forty winks, nap, siesta, snooze, wink — more at NAP

drowsy \'draú-zē\ *adj* **drows·i·er; -est** **1** ♦ : ready to fall asleep **2** ♦ : making one sleepy — **drows·i·ly** \-zə-lē\ *adv* — **drows·i·ness** \-zē-nəs\ *n*

♦ [1] sleepy, slumberous — more at SLEEPY ♦ [2] hypnotic, narcotic, opiate, slumberous — more at HYPNOTIC

drub \'drəb\ *vb* **drubbed**; **drub·bing** **1** ♦ : to beat severely **2** ♦ : to defeat decisively

♦ [1] bash, bat, batter, beat, pound — more at BEAT ♦ [2] clobber, rout, skunk, thrash, trim, trounce, wallop, whip

¹**drudge** \'drəj\ *vb* **drudged**; **drudg·ing** ♦ : to do hard, menial, or monotonous work

♦ endeavor (*or* endeavour), fag, grub, hustle, labor (*or* labour), peg, plod, plug, slave, slog, strain, strive, struggle, sweat, toil, work — more at LABOR

²**drudge** *n* ♦ : one whose work is menial or routine and boring

♦ fag, peon, slave, toiler, worker — more at SLAVE

drudg·ery \'drə-jə-rē\ *n* ♦ : dull, irksome, and fatiguing work

♦ grind, labor (*or* labour), slavery, sweat, toil, travail — more at TOIL

¹**drug** \'drəg\ *n* **1** ♦ : a substance used as or in medicine **2** : a substance (as heroin or marijuana) that can cause addiction, habituation, or a marked change in mental status

♦ cure, medicine, pharmaceutical, remedy, specific — more at MEDICINE

²**drug** *vb* **drugged**; **drug·ging** : to affect with or as if with drugs; *esp* : to stupefy with a narcotic

drug·gist \'drə-gist\ *n* : a dealer in drugs and medicines; *also* : PHARMACIST

drug·store \'drəg-,stōr\ *n* : a retail shop where medicines and miscellaneous articles are sold

dru·id \'drü-əd\ *n, often cap* : one of an ancient Celtic priesthood appearing in Irish, Welsh, and Christian legends as magicians and wizards

¹**drum** \'drəm\ *n* **1** : a percussion instrument usu. consisting of a hollow cylinder with a skin or plastic head stretched over one or both ends that is beaten with the hands or with a stick **2** : the sound of a drum; *also* : a similar sound **3** ♦ : a drum-shaped object

♦ can, canister, tin — more at CAN

²**drum** *vb* **drummed**; **drum·ming** **1** : to beat a drum **2** : to sound rhythmically : THROB, BEAT **3** : to summon or enlist by or as if by beating a drum ⟨*drummed* into service⟩ **4** ♦ : to dismiss ignominiously : EXPEL — usu. used with *out* **5** : to drive or force by steady effort ⟨∼ the facts into memory⟩ **6** ♦ : to strike or tap repeatedly so as to produce rhythmic sounds

♦ [4] banish, boot (out), bounce, cast, chase, dismiss, eject, expel, oust, rout, run off, throw out — more at EJECT ♦ [6] beat, rap, tap — more at TAP

drum·beat \'drəm-,bēt\ *n* : a stroke on a drum or its sound

drum major *n* : the leader of a marching band

drum ma·jor·ette \-,mā-jə-'rət\ *n* : a girl or woman who leads a marching band; *also* : a baton twirler who accompanies a marching band

drum·mer \'drə-mər\ *n* **1** : one that plays a drum **2** : a traveling salesman

drum·stick \'drəm-,stik\ *n* **1** : a stick for beating a drum **2** : the lower segment of a fowl's leg

drum up *vb* **1** : to bring about by persistent effort ⟨*drum up* business⟩ **2** : INVENT, ORIGINATE ⟨*drum up* a new method⟩

¹**drunk** *past part of* DRINK

²**drunk** \'drəŋk\ *adj* **1** ♦ : having the faculties impaired by alcohol ⟨∼ drivers⟩ **2** : dominated by an intense feeling ⟨∼ with power⟩ **3** : of, relating to, or caused by intoxication

♦ high, inebriate, intoxicated, tipsy; *also* maudlin; befuddled, stupefied; debauched, dissipated, dissolute *Ant* sober

³**drunk** *n* **1** : a period of excessive drinking **2** ♦ : a drunken person

♦ inebriate, soak, sot, souse, tippler; *also* alcoholic, substance abuser; drinker

drunk·ard \'drəŋ-kərd\ *n* : one who is habitually drunk

♦ inebriate, soak, sot, souse, tippler — more at DRUNK

drunk·en \'drəŋ-kən\ *adj* **1** : being under the influence of alcohol : DRUNK **2** : given to habitual excessive use of alcohol **3** : of, relating to, or resulting from intoxication ⟨a ∼ brawl⟩ **4** : unsteady or lurching as if from intoxication — **drunk·en·ly** *adv* — **drunk·en·ness** *n*

drupe \'drüp\ *n* : a partly fleshy fruit (as a plum or cherry) having one seed enclosed in a hard inner shell

¹**dry** \'drī\ *adj* **dri·er** \'drī-ər\; **dri·est** \-əst\ **1** : free or freed from water or liquid ⟨∼ fruits⟩; *also* : not being in or under water **2** ♦ : characterized by lack of water or moisture ⟨∼ climate⟩ **3** : lacking freshness : STALE **4** : devoid of natural moisture ⟨∼ THIRSTY **5** : no longer liquid or sticky ⟨the ink is ∼⟩ **6** : not giving milk ⟨a ∼ cow⟩ **7** : marked by the absence of alcoholic beverages **8** : prohibiting the making or distributing of alcoholic beverages **9** : not sweet ⟨∼ wine⟩ **10** : solid as opposed to liquid ⟨∼ groceries⟩ **11** : containing or employing no liquid **12 a** : not showing or communicating warmth, enthusiasm, or tender feeling : SEVERE

b : causing weariness or lack of interest : UNINTEREST-ING **13** : not productive **14** : marked by a matter-of-fact, ironic, or terse manner of expression 〈~ humor〉 — **dry·ly** *or* **dri·ly** *adv* — **dry·ness** *n*

  ♦ arid, sere, thirsty; *also* baked, dehydrated, parched *Ant* damp, dank, humid, moist, wet

²**dry** *vb* **dried; dry·ing** ♦ : to make or become dry

  ♦ dehydrate, parch, sear; *also* dehumidify; evaporate; shrivel, wither *Ant* hydrate, wet

³**dry** *n, pl* **drys** : PROHIBITIONIST

dry·ad \'drī-əd, -ˌad\ *n* : WOOD NYMPH

dry cell *n* : a battery whose contents are not spillable

dry–clean \'drī-ˌklēn\ *vb* : to clean (fabrics) chiefly with solvents other than water — **dry cleaning** *n*

dry dock \'drī-ˌdäk\ *n* : a dock that can be kept dry during ship construction or repair

dryer *var of* DRIER

dry farm·ing *n* : farming without irrigation in areas of limited rainfall — **dry–farm** *vb* — **dry farm·er** *n*

dry goods \'drī-ˌgu̇dz\ *n pl* : cloth goods (as fabrics, ribbon, and ready-to-wear clothing)

dry ice *n* : solid carbon dioxide

dry measure *n* : a series of units of capacity for dry commodities

dry rot *n* : decay of timber in which fungi consume the wood's cellulose

dry run *n* ♦ : a practice exercise : REHEARSAL

  ♦ practice, rehearsal, trial — more at REHEARSAL

dry·wall \'drī-ˌwȯl\ *n* : a wallboard consisting of fiberboard, paper, or felt over a plaster core

Ds *symbol* darmstadtium

DSC *abbr* **1** Distinguished Service Cross **2** doctor of surgical chiropody

DSM *abbr* Distinguished Service Medal

DST *abbr* daylight saving time

DTP *abbr* diphtheria, tetanus, pertussis (vaccines)

d.t.'s \ˌdē-'tēz\ *n pl, often cap D&T* : DELIRIUM TREMENS

du·al \'dü-əl, 'dyü-\ *adj* **1** ♦ : consisting of two parts or elements or having two like parts : DOUBLE **2** : having a double character or nature — **du·al·ism** \-ə-ˌli-zəm\ *n* — **du·al·i·ty** \dü-'a-lə-tē, dyü-\ *n*

  ♦ binary, bipartite, double, duplex, twin — more at DOUBLE

du·ath·lon \dü-'ath-lən, -ˌlän, dyü-\ *n* : a long-distance race involving running and bicycling — **du·ath·lete** \-ˌlēt\ *n*

¹**dub** \'dəb\ *vb* **dubbed; dub·bing** **1** : to confer knighthood upon **2** ♦ : to call by a distinctive title, epithet, or nickname : NAME

  ♦ baptize, call, christen, denominate, designate, entitle, label, name, style, term, title — more at NAME

²**dub** *n* : a clumsy person : DUFFER

³**dub** *vb* **dubbed; dub·bing** : to add (sound effects) to a motion picture or to a radio or television production

du·bi·ety \dü-'bī-ə-tē, dyü-\ *n, pl* **-eties** **1** : UNCERTAINTY **2** : a matter of doubt

du·bi·ous \'dü-bē-əs, 'dyü-\ *adj* **1** ♦ : of doubtful promise or outcome **2** ♦ : questionable or suspect as to true nature or quality : QUESTIONABLE **3** ♦ : feeling doubt — **du·bi·ous·ness** *n*

  ♦ [1] doubtful, flimsy, improbable, questionable, unlikely — more at IMPROBABLE ♦ [2] debatable, disputable, doubtful, equivocal, fishy, problematic, questionable, shady, shaky, suspect, suspicious — more at DOUBTFUL ♦ [3] distrustful, doubtful, mistrustful, skeptical, suspicious, uncertain, undecided, unsettled, unsure — more at DOUBTFUL

du·bi·ous·ly \-lē\ *adv* ♦ : in a manner expressive of doubt, hesitation, or suspicion

  ♦ askance, distrustfully, mistrustfully, suspiciously — more at ASKANCE

dub·ni·um \'düb-nē-əm, 'dəb-\ *n* : a short-lived radioactive chemical element produced artificially

du·cal \'dü-kəl, 'dyü-\ *adj* : of or relating to a duke or dukedom

duc·at \'də-kət\ *n* : a gold coin formerly used in various European countries

duch·ess \'də-chəs\ *n* **1** : the wife or widow of a duke **2** : a woman holding the rank of duke in her own right

duchy \'də-chē\ *n, pl* **duch·ies** : the territory of a duke or duchess : DUKEDOM

¹**duck** \'dək\ *n, pl* **ducks** : any of various swimming birds related to but smaller than geese and swans

²**duck** *vb* **1** ♦ : to thrust or plunge under water **2 a** : to lower the head or body suddenly : BOW **b** ♦ : to make a sudden movement in a new direction : DODGE **3** ♦ : to evade a duty, question, or responsibility 〈~ the issue〉

  ♦ [1] dip, douse, dunk, immerse, souse, submerge — more at DIP ♦ [2b] dodge, sidestep — more at DODGE ♦ [3] avoid, dodge, elude, escape, eschew, evade, shake, shirk, shun — more at ESCAPE

³**duck** *n* **1** : a durable closely woven usu. cotton fabric **2** *pl* : light clothes made of duck

duck·bill \'dək-ˌbil\ *n* : PLATYPUS

duck·ling \-liŋ\ *n* : a young duck

duck·pin \-ˌpin\ *n* **1** : a small bowling pin shorter and wider in the middle than a tenpin **2** *pl but sing in constr* : a bowling game using duckpins

duck sauce *n* : a thick sweet sauce made with fruits and seasonings and used in Chinese cuisine

duct \'dəkt\ *n* **1** : a tube or canal for conveying a bodily fluid **2** ♦ : a pipe or tube through which a fluid (as air) flows — **duct·less** *adj*

  ♦ channel, conduit, leader, line, penstock, pipe, tube — more at PIPE

duc·tile \'dək-tᵊl\ *adj* **1** : capable of being drawn out into wire or thread **2** : easily led : DOCILE — **duc·til·i·ty** \ˌdək-'ti-lə-tē\ *n*

ductless gland *n* : an endocrine gland

duct tape *n* : a cloth adhesive tape orig. designed for sealing certain ducts and joints — **duct–tape** *vb*

dud \'dəd\ *n* **1** *pl* ♦ : personal attire : CLOTHING **2** ♦ : one that fails completely; *also* : a bomb or missile that fails to explode

  ♦ **duds** ♦ [1] apparel, attire, clothing, dress, raiment, wear — more at CLOTHING ♦ [2] bummer, bust, catastrophe, debacle, failure, fiasco, fizzle, flop, lemon, loser, turkey, washout — more at FAILURE

dude \'düd, 'dyüd\ *n* **1** ♦ : a man who gives exaggerated attention to personal appearance : DANDY **2** : a city dweller; *esp* : an Easterner in the West **3** ♦ : a male human : GUY — sometimes used as an informal form of address

  ♦ [1] buck, dandy, fop, gallant — more at DANDY ♦ [3] buck, chap, fellow, gent, gentleman, guy, hombre, jack, joker, lad, male, man — more at MAN

dude ranch *n* : a vacation resort offering activities (as horseback riding) typical of western ranches

dud·geon \'də-jən\ *n* ♦ : a fit or state of indignation 〈in high ~〉

  ♦ huff, offense, peeve, pique, resentment, umbrage — more at PIQUE

¹**due** \'dü, 'dyü\ *adj* [ME, fr. AF *deu*, pp. of *dever* to owe, fr. L *debēre*] **1** : owed or owing as a debt **2** : owed or owing as a right **3** : APPROPRIATE, FITTING **4** : SUFFICIENT, ADEQUATE **5** ♦ : being in accordance with some established rule, law, or principle 〈~ process of law〉 **6** : capable of being attributed — used with *to* 〈~ to negligence〉 **7** : PAYABLE 〈a bill ~ today〉 **8** : SCHEDULED 〈~ to arrive soon〉

  ♦ [5] just, right — more at JUST ♦ *usu* **due to** [6] attendant, consequent, consequential, resultant — more at RESULTANT

²**due** *n* **1** : something that rightfully belongs to one 〈give everyone their ~〉 **2** : DEBT **3** *pl* : FEES, CHARGES

³**due** *adv* ♦ : in a direct manner : DIRECTLY 〈~ north〉

♦ dead, direct, directly, plump, right, straight — more at DIRECTLY

du·el \'dü-əl, 'dyü-\ n 1 : a combat between two persons; esp : one fought with weapons in the presence of witnesses 2 ♦ : a conflict between antagonistic persons, ideas, or forces; also : a hard-fought contest between two opponents — **duel** vb — **du·el·ist** \-ə-list\ n

♦ battle, combat, conflict, confrontation, contest, face-off, rivalry, struggle, tug-of-war, warfare — more at CONTEST

du·en·de \dü-'en-dā\ n [Sp dial., charm, fr. Sp, ghost, goblin, fr. duen de casa, prob. fr. dueño de casa owner of a house] : the power to attract through personal magnetism and charm

du·en·na \dü-'e-nə, dyü-\ n 1 : an elderly woman in charge of the younger ladies in a Spanish or Portuguese family 2 : CHAPERONE

du·et \dü-'et, dyü-\ n : a musical composition for two performers

due to prep ♦ : as a result of : BECAUSE OF

♦ because of, owing to, through, with — more at BECAUSE OF

duf·fel bag \'də-fəl-\ n : a large cylindrical bag for personal belongings

duf·fer \'də-fər\ n : an incompetent or clumsy person

dug past and past part of DIG

dug·out \'dəg-,au̇t\ n 1 : a boat made by hollowing out a log 2 : a shelter dug in the ground 3 : a low shelter facing a baseball diamond that contains the players' bench

DUI n : the act or crime of driving while under the influence of alcohol

duke \'dük, 'dyük\ n 1 : a sovereign ruler of a continental European duchy 2 : a nobleman of the highest rank; esp : a member of the highest grade of the British peerage 3 slang : FIST 1 ⟨put up your ∼s⟩ — **duke·dom** n

dul·cet \'dəl-sət\ adj 1 : pleasing to the ear 2 : AGREEABLE, SOOTHING

dul·ci·mer \'dəl-sə-mər\ n 1 : a stringed instrument of trapezoidal shape played with light hammers held in the hands 2 or **dul·ci·more** \-,mȯr\ : an American folk instrument with three or four strings that is held on the lap and played by plucking or strumming

¹dull \'dəl\ adj 1 : mentally slow : STUPID 2 : slow in perception or sensibility 3 : LISTLESS 4 : slow in action : SLUGGISH ⟨a ∼ market⟩ 5 : lacking in force or intensity; also : not resonant or ringing 6 ♦ : lacking sharpness of edge or point : BLUNT 7 ♦ : lacking brilliance or luster 8 ♦ : low in saturation and lightness ⟨∼ color⟩ 9 : overcast with clouds : CLOUDY 10 ♦ : causing weariness or lack of interest : UNINTERESTING — **dul·ly** adv

♦ [6] blunt, obtuse; also rounded Ant keen, pointed, sharp, whetted ♦ [7] dim, flat, lusterless ♦ [8] light, pale, pastel, washed-out — more at PALE ♦ [10] dry, flat, monotonous, uninteresting, weary

²dull vb ♦ : to make or become dull

♦ blunt, dampen, deaden, numb; also muffle, mute, tone (down); decrease, diminish, lessen, let up (on), reduce, subdue; debilitate, enfeeble, weaken; dwindle, recede, subside, taper (off), wane; alleviate, ease, lighten; abate, moderate Ant sharpen, whet

dull·ard \'də-lərd\ n : a stupid person

dull·ness also **dul·ness** \'dəl-nəs\ n : the quality or state of being dull

du·ly \'dü-lē, 'dyü-\ adv : in a due manner or time

dumb \'dəm\ adj 1 often offensive : lacking the power of speech 2 ♦ : making no utterance : SILENT 3 ♦ : not having or showing intelligence : STUPID — **dumb·ly** adv

♦ [2] mum, mute, silent, speechless, uncommunicative — more at SILENT ♦ [3] mindless, senseless, simple, stupid, unintelligent — more at STUPID

dumb·bell \'dəm-,bel\ n 1 : a bar with weights at the end used for exercise 2 : one who is stupid : DUMMY

dumb down vb : to lower the level of difficulty or intellectual content of

dumb·found also **dum·found** \,dəm-'fau̇nd\ vb ♦ : to confound briefly and usu. with astonishment : ASTONISH

♦ amaze, astonish, astound, bowl, flabbergast, floor, shock, startle, stun, stupefy, surprise — more at SURPRISE

dumb·wait·er \'dəm-,wā-tər\ n : a small elevator for conveying food and dishes from one floor to another

dum·my \'də-mē\ n, pl **dummies** 1 ♦ : a stupid person 2 dated, offensive : a person who cannot speak 3 : the exposed hand in bridge played by the declarer in addition to that player's own hand; also : a bridge player whose hand is a dummy 4 a : an imitative substitute for something b ♦ : a form representing the human figure used esp. for displaying clothes : MANNEQUIN 5 : one seeming to act alone but really acting for another 6 : a mock-up of matter to be reproduced esp. by printing

♦ [1] blockhead, dope, idiot, imbecile, jackass, moron, numskull — more at IDIOT ♦ [4b] figure, form, manikin, mannequin — more at MANNEQUIN

¹dump \'dəmp\ vb 1 : to let fall in a pile 2 ♦ : to get rid of unceremoniously

♦ cast, discard, ditch, fling, jettison, junk, lose, reject, scrap, shed, shuck, slough, throw away, throw out, unload — more at DISCARD

²dump n 1 : a place for dumping something (as refuse) 2 a : a reserve supply b ♦ : a place where reserve supplies are kept ⟨an ammunition ∼⟩ 3 : a messy or objectionable place

♦ armory, arsenal, depot, magazine — more at ARMORY

dump·ing \'dəm-piŋ\ n ♦ : the act of one that dumps; esp : the selling of goods in quantity at below market price

♦ disposal, disposition, jettison, removal, riddance — more at DISPOSAL

dump·ling \'dəm-pliŋ\ n 1 : a small mass of boiled or steamed dough 2 : a dessert of fruit baked in biscuit dough

dumps \'dəmps\ n pl ♦ : a gloomy state of mind : low spirits ⟨in the ∼⟩

♦ blues, dejection, depression, desolation, despondency, doldrums, forlornness, gloom, heartsickness, melancholy, sadness — more at SADNESS

dump·ster \'dəmp-stər\ n, often cap : a large trash receptacle

dump truck n : a truck for transporting and dumping bulk material

dumpy \'dəm-pē\ adj **dump·i·er; -est** 1 ♦ : short and thick in build 2 : SHABBY

♦ chunky, heavyset, squat, stocky, stout, stubby, stumpy, thickset — more at STOCKY

¹dun \'dən\ n : a brownish dark gray

²dun vb **dunned; dun·ning** 1 : to make persistent demands for payment 2 : PLAGUE, PESTER — **dun** n

³dun n ♦ : an urgent request

♦ claim, demand, requisition — more at DEMAND

dunce \'dəns\ n [John Duns Scotus, whose once accepted writings were ridiculed in the 16th cent.] ♦ : a slow stupid person

♦ blockhead, dope, dummy, idiot, imbecile, jackass, moron, numskull — more at IDIOT

dun·der·head \'dən-dər-,hed\ n : DUNCE, BLOCKHEAD

dune \'dün, 'dyün\ n : a hill or ridge of sand piled up by the wind

dune buggy n : a motor vehicle with oversize tires for use on sand

¹dung \'dəŋ\ n ♦ : the feces of an animal : MANURE

♦ droppings, slops, waste — more at DROPPINGS

²dung vb : to dress (land) with dung

dun·ga·ree \,dəŋ-gə-'rē\ n 1 : a heavy coarse cotton twill; esp : blue denim 2 pl : clothes made of blue denim

dun·geon \\'dən-jən\\ *n* [ME *dongeoun* fortress, prison, fr. AF *donjun*, fr. VL **domnion-, *domnio* keep, mastery, fr. L *dominus* lord] : a dark prison commonly underground

dung·hill \\'dəŋ-ˌhil\\ *n* : a manure pile

dunk \\'dəŋk\\ *vb* **1** ♦ : to dip or submerge temporarily in liquid **2** : to submerge oneself in water **3** : to shoot a basketball into the basket from above the rim

♦ dip, douse, duck, immerse, souse, submerge — more at DIP

duo \\'dü-(ˌ)ō, 'dyü-\\ *n, pl* **du·os 1** : DUET **2** ♦ : two similar or associated things : PAIR

♦ brace, couple, pair, twain, twosome — more at PAIR

duo·dec·i·mal \\ˌdü-ə-'de-sə-məl, ˌdyü-\\ *adj* : of, relating to, or being a system of numbers with a base of 12

du·o·de·num \\ˌdü-ə-'dē-nəm, ˌdyü-, dú-'äd-ᵊn-əm, dyü-\\ *n, pl* **-de·na** \\-'dē-nə, -ᵊn-ə\\ *or* **-denums** : the first part of the small intestine extending from the stomach to the jejunum — **du·o·de·nal** \\-'dēn-ᵊl, -ᵊn-əl\\ *adj*

dup *abbr* **1** duplex **2** duplicate

¹dupe \\'düp, 'dyüp\\ *n* ♦ : one who is easily deceived or cheated

♦ gull, pigeon, sap, sucker, tool; *also* victim; schlemiel; butt, derision, laughingstock, mark, mock, mockery; booby, dodo, fool, goose, half-wit, jackass, lunatic, monkey, nincompoop, ninny, nitwit, simpleton, turkey; pushover; loser

²dupe *vb* **duped; dup·ing** ♦ : to make a dupe of : DECEIVE

♦ beguile, bluff, cozen, deceive, delude, fool, gull, have, hoax, hoodwink, humbug, misinform, mislead, string along, take in, trick — more at DECEIVE

du·ple \\'dü-pəl, 'dyü-\\ *adj* : having two beats or a multiple of two beats to the measure ⟨~ time⟩

¹du·plex \\'dü-ˌpleks, 'dyü-\\ *adj* ♦ : having two principal elements or parts : DOUBLE

♦ binary, bipartite, double, dual, twin — more at DOUBLE

²duplex *n* : something duplex; *esp* : a 2-family house

¹du·pli·cate \\'dü-pli-kət, 'dyü-\\ *adj* **1** : consisting of or existing in two corresponding or identical parts or examples **2** ♦ : being the same as another

♦ equal, even, identical, indistinguishable, same — more at SAME

²du·pli·cate \\'dü-pli-ˌkāt, 'dyü-\\ *vb* **-cat·ed; -cat·ing 1** : to make double or twofold **2** ♦ : to make a copy of

♦ copy, imitate, replicate, reproduce — more at COPY

³du·pli·cate \\-kət\\ *n* ♦ : a thing that exactly resembles another in appearance, pattern, or content : COPY

♦ carbon copy, copy, duplication, facsimile, imitation, replica, replication, reproduction — more at COPY

du·pli·ca·tion \\ˌdü-pli-'kā-shən, ˌdyü-\\ *n* **1** : the act or process of duplicating **2** ♦ : a thing that exactly resembles another in appearance, pattern, or content

♦ carbon copy, counterpart, double, duplicate, facsimile, image, likeness, match, picture, replica, ringer, spit — more at IMAGE

du·pli·ca·tor \\'dü-pli-ˌkā-tər, 'dyü-\\ *n* : COPIER

du·plic·i·ty \\dú-'pli-sə-tē, dyü-\\ *n, pl* **-ties** ♦ : the disguising of true intentions by deceptive words or action — **du·plic·i·tous** \\-təs\\ *adj* — **du·plic·i·tous·ly** *adv*

♦ artifice, craft, craftiness, crookedness, cunning, deceit, deceitfulness, dishonesty, dissimulation, double-dealing, guile, wiliness — more at DECEIT

du·ra·bil·i·ty \\ˌdúr-ə-'bi-lə-tē, ˌdyúr-\\ *n* ♦ : the quality or state of being durable

♦ endurance, persistence

du·ra·ble \\'dúr-ə-bəl, 'dyúr-\\ *adj* : able to exist for a long time without significant deterioration of qualities or capabilities ⟨~ goods⟩

du·rance \\'dúr-əns, 'dyúr-\\ *n* : restraint by or as if by physical force ⟨held in ~ vile⟩

du·ra·tion \\dú-'rā-shən, dyü-\\ *n* **1** ♦ : continuance in time **2** ♦ : the time during which something exists or lasts

♦ [1] continuance, continuation, endurance, persistence, subsistence — more at CONTINUATION ♦ [2] date, life, lifetime, run, standing, time; *also* spell, stretch; span, tenure, term; hitch, tour, turn

du·ress \\dú-'res, dyú-\\ *n* ♦ : compulsion by threat ⟨confession made under ~⟩

♦ coercion, compulsion, constraint, force, pressure — more at FORCE

dur·ing \\'dúr-iŋ, 'dyúr-\\ *prep* **1** ♦ : throughout the duration of ⟨swims every day ~ the summer⟩ **2** : at some point in ⟨broke in ~ the night⟩

♦ over, through, throughout

dusk \\'dəsk\\ *n* **1** ♦ : the darker part of twilight esp. at night **2** : partial darkness

♦ evening, gloaming, nightfall, sundown, sunset, twilight; *also* dark, darkness, night, nighttime *Ant* aurora, cockcrow, dawn, dawning, daybreak, daylight, morn, morning, sunrise, sunup

dusky \\'dəs-kē\\ *adj* **dusk·i·er; -est 1** : somewhat dark in color **2** ♦ : marked by slight or deficient light — **dusk·i·ness** *n*

♦ dark, darkling, dim, gloomy, murky, obscure, somber (*or* sombre) — more at DARK

¹dust \\'dəst\\ *n* **1** : fine particles of matter **2** : the particles into which something disintegrates **3** ♦ : something worthless **4** ♦ : the surface of the ground — **dust·less** *adj*

♦ [3] chaff, deadwood, garbage, junk, litter, refuse, riffraff, rubbish, scrap, trash, waste — more at GARBAGE ♦ [4] dirt, earth, ground, land, soil — more at EARTH

²dust *vb* **1** : to make free of or remove dust **2** : to sprinkle with fine particles **3** : to sprinkle in the form of dust

dust bowl *n* : a region suffering from long droughts and dust storms

dust devil *n* : a small whirlwind containing sand or dust

dust·er \\'dəs-tər\\ *n* **1** : one that removes dust **2** : a dress-length housecoat **3** : one that scatters fine particles; *esp* : a device for applying insecticides to crops

dust·pan \\'dəst-ˌpan\\ *n* : a flat-ended pan for sweepings

dust storm *n* : a violent wind carrying dust across a dry region

dusty \\'dəs-tē\\ *adj* **1** ♦ : consisting of dust : POWDERY **2** : covered or abounding with dust

♦ fine, floury, powdery — more at FINE

dutch \\'dəch\\ *adv, often cap* : with each person paying his or her own way ⟨go ~⟩

Dutch \\'dəch\\ *n* **1** Dutch *pl* : the people of the Netherlands **2** : the language of the Netherlands — **Dutch** *adj* — **Dutch·man** \\-mən\\ *n*

Dutch elm disease *n* : a fungus disease of elms characterized by yellowing of the foliage, defoliation, and death

dutch treat *n, often cap D* : an entertainment (as a meal) for which each person pays his or her own way — **dutch treat** *adv, often cap D*

du·te·ous \\'dü-tē-əs, 'dyü-\\ *adj* : DUTIFUL, OBEDIENT

du·ti·able \\'dü-tē-ə-bəl, 'dyü-\\ *adj* : subject to a duty ⟨~ imports⟩

du·ti·ful \\'dü-ti-fəl, 'dyü-\\ *adj* **1** : motivated by a sense of duty ⟨a ~ son⟩ **2** ♦ : coming from or showing a sense of duty ⟨~ affection⟩ — **du·ti·ful·ly** *adv* — **du·ti·ful·ness** *n*

♦ deferential, regardful, respectful — more at RESPECTFUL

du·ty \\'dü-tē, 'dyü-\\ *n, pl* **duties 1** ♦ : conduct or action required by one's occupation or position; *also* : obligatory tasks, conduct, or functions required by order or usage **2** : assigned service or business; *esp* : active military service **3** ♦ : a moral or legal obligation **4** ♦ : a charge usu. of money imposed by authority on persons or property for public purposes : TAX **5** : the service required (as of a machine) : USE ⟨a heavy-*duty* tire⟩

♦ [1] assignment, chore, job, stint, task — more at CHORE ♦ [3] burden, charge, commitment, need, obligation, responsibility — more at OBLIGATION ♦ [4] assessment, impost, levy, tax — more at TAX

DV *abbr* **1** [L *Deo volente*] God willing **2** Douay Version

DVD \ˌdē-ˌvē-'dē\ *n* [*d*igital *v*ideo *d*isk] : a high-capacity optical disk format; *also* : an optical disk using such a format

DVM *abbr* doctor of veterinary medicine

DVR \ˌdē-ˌvē-'är\ *n* [*d*igital *v*ideo *r*ecorder] : a device that records and plays back television programs

¹dwarf \'dwȯrf\ *n, pl* **dwarfs** \'dwȯrfs\ *also* **dwarves** \'dwȯrvz\ **1** : a person of unusually small stature **2** ♦ : an animal or plant that is much below normal size **3** ♦ : a small legendary manlike being who is usu. misshapen and ugly and skilled as a craftsman

♦ [2] midget, mite, peewee, pygmy, runt; *also* mini, miniature *Ant* behemoth, colossus, giant, jumbo, leviathan, mammoth, monster, titan ♦ [3] brownie, elf, fairy, fay, gnome, hobgoblin, leprechaun, pixie, puck, troll

²dwarf *vb* **1** : to restrict the growth or development of : STUNT **2** : to cause to appear smaller ⟨*dwarfed* by comparison⟩

³dwarf *adj* : characterized by smallness or insignificance of size, proportion, scope, strength, or power

dwarf·ish \'dwȯr-fish\ *adj* ♦ : of or like a dwarf

♦ dwarf, fine, little, pocket, pygmy, slight, small, undersized — more at SMALL

dwarf planet *n* : a spherical celestial body that orbits the sun but is too small to disturb other objects from its orbit

dwell \'dwel\ *vb* **dwelt** \'dwelt\ *or* **dwelled** \'dweld, 'dwelt\; **dwell·ing** [ME, fr. OE *dwellan* to go astray, hinder] **1** ♦ : to remain for a time : ABIDE **2** ♦ : to live as a resident : RESIDE **3** : to keep the attention directed **4** : to write or speak insistently — used with *on* or *upon*

♦ [1] abide, hang around, remain, stay, stick around, tarry — more at STAY ♦ [2] abide, live, reside — more at LIVE

dwell·er \'dwe-lər\ *n* ♦ : one that dwells : INHABITANT

♦ denizen, inhabitant, occupant, resident — more at INHABITANT

dwell·ing \'dwe-liŋ\ *n* ♦ : a shelter (as a house) in which people live : RESIDENCE

♦ abode, domicile, home, house, lodging, quarters, residence — more at HOME

DWI \ˌdē-ˌdəb-əl-(ˌ)yü-'ī\ *n* [*d*riving *w*hile *i*ntoxicated] : DUI

dwin·dle \'dwin-dᵊl\ *vb* **dwin·dled; dwin·dling** ♦ : to make or become steadily less

♦ abate, decline, decrease, de-escalate, die, diminish, ebb, fall, lessen, let up, lower, moderate, recede, relent, shrink, subside, taper, wane — more at DECREASE

dwt *abbr* pennyweight

Dy *symbol* dysprosium

dyb·buk \'di-bək\ *n, pl* **dyb·bu·kim** \ˌdi-bu̇-'kēm\ *also* **dyb·buks** : a wandering soul believed in Jewish folklore to enter and possess a person

¹dye \'dī\ *n* **1** : color produced by dyeing **2** ♦ : material used for coloring or staining

♦ color (*or* colour), pigment, stain — more at PIGMENT

²dye *vb* **dyed; dye·ing 1** ♦ : to impart a new color to esp. by impregnating with a dye **2** : to take up or impart color in dyeing — **dy·er** \'dī(-ə)r\ *n*

♦ color (*or* colour), paint, stain, tinge, tint — more at COLOR

dye·stuff \'dī-ˌstəf\ *n* : material used for coloring or staining : DYE

dying *pres part of* DIE

dy·nam·ic \dī-'na-mik\ *also* **dy·nam·i·cal** \-mi-kəl\ *adj* **1** : of or relating to physical force producing motion **2** ♦ : operating with or marked by vigor or effect : ENERGETIC

♦ energetic, flush, lusty, peppy, robust, strenuous, vigorous, vital — more at VIGOROUS ♦ aggressive, assertive, emphatic, forceful, resounding, vehement — more at EMPHATIC

dy·nam·i·cal·ly \dī-'na-mi-kə-lē\ *adv* ♦ : in a dynamic manner

♦ energetically, firmly, forcefully, forcibly, hard, mightily, powerfully, stiffly, stoutly, strenuously, strongly, sturdily, vigorously — more at HARD

¹dy·na·mite \'dī-nə-ˌmīt\ *n* **1** : an explosive made of nitroglycerin absorbed in a porous material; *also* : an explosive made without nitroglycerin **2** : one that has a powerful effect ⟨a ~ player⟩

²dynamite *vb* **-mit·ed; -mit·ing** : to blow up with dynamite

³dynamite *adj* : TERRIFIC, WONDERFUL

dy·na·mo \'dī-nə-ˌmō\ *n, pl* **-mos 1** : an electrical generator **2** : a forceful energetic individual

dy·na·mom·e·ter \ˌdī-nə-'mä-mə-tər\ *n* : an instrument for measuring mechanical power (as of an engine)

dy·nas·ty \'dī-nəs-tē, -ˌnas-\ *n, pl* **-ties 1** : a succession of rulers of the same family **2** : a powerful group or family that maintains its position for a long time — **dy·nas·tic** \dī-'nas-tik\ *adj*

dys·en·tery \'dis-ᵊn-ˌter-ē\ *n, pl* **-ter·ies** : a disease marked by diarrhea with blood and mucus in the feces; *also* : DIARRHEA

dys·func·tion *also* **dis·func·tion** \dis-'fəŋk-shən\ *n* **1** : impaired or abnormal functioning ⟨liver ~⟩ **2** : abnormal or unhealthy behavior within a group ⟨family ~⟩ — **dys·func·tion·al** \-shə-nəl\ *adj*

dys·lex·ia \dis-'lek-sē-ə\ *n* : a learning disability marked by difficulty in reading, writing, and spelling — **dys·lex·ic** \-sik\ *adj or n*

dys·pep·sia \dis-'pep-shə, -sē-ə\ *n* : INDIGESTION — **dys·pep·tic** \-'pep-tik\ *n*

dys·pep·tic *adj* ♦ : having or showing ill humor

♦ bearish, bilious, cantankerous, disagreeable, ill-humored, ill-tempered, ornery, splenetic, surly — more at ILL-TEMPERED

dys·pla·sia \dis-'plā-zh(ē-)ə\ *n* : abnormal growth or development

dys·pro·si·um \dis-'prō-zē-əm\ *n* : a metallic chemical element that forms highly magnetic compounds

dys·to·pia \dis-'tō-pē-ə\ *n* : an imaginary place where people lead dehumanized and often fearful lives; *also* : a work of literature about such a place — **dys·to·pi·an** \-ən\ *adj*

dys·tro·phy \'dis-trə-fē\ *n, pl* **-phies** : a disorder involving atrophy of muscular tissue; *esp* : MUSCULAR DYSTROPHY

dz *abbr* dozen

¹e \ˈē\ *n, pl* **e's** *or* **es** \ˈēz\ *often cap* **1** : the 5th letter of the English alphabet **2** : the base of the system of natural logarithms having the approximate value 2.71828 **3** : a grade rating a student's work as poor or failing

²e *abbr, often cap* **1** east; eastern **2** error **3** excellent

e- *comb form* : electronic ⟨*e-commerce*⟩

ea *abbr* each

¹each \ˈēch\ *adj* : being one of the class named ⟨∼ player⟩

²each *pron* : every individual one

³each *adv* : to or for each : APIECE ⟨cost five cents ∼⟩

each other *pron* : each of two or more in reciprocal action or relation ⟨looked at *each other*⟩

ea·ger \ˈē-gər\ *adj* ♦ : marked by urgent or enthusiastic desire or interest ⟨∼ to learn⟩ — **ea·ger·ly** *adv*

♦ avid, enthusiastic, hungry, keen, raring, thirsty; *also* engaged, interested; hung up, obsessed; ambitious, covetous, craving, hankering, longing, pining; restive, restless; disposed, inclined, ready, willing *Ant* apathetic, indifferent

ea·ger·ness *n* ♦ : the quality or state of being eager; *also* : an act or instance of being eager

♦ alacrity, ambition, appetite, ardor, avidity, enthusiasm, excitement, hunger, impatience, keenness, quickness, thirst *Ant* apathy, indifference

¹ea·gle \ˈē-gəl\ *n* **1** : a large bird of prey related to the hawks **2** : a score of two under par on a hole in golf

²eagle *vb* **ea·gled; ea·gling** : to score an eagle on a golf hole

ea·glet \ˈē-glət\ *n* : a young eagle

-ean — see -an

E and OE *abbr* errors and omissions excepted

¹ear \ˈir\ *n* **1** : the organ of hearing; *also* : the outer part of this in a vertebrate **2** : something resembling a mammal's ear in shape, position, or function **3** : an ability to understand and appreciate something heard ⟨a good ∼ for music⟩ **4** ♦ : sympathetic attention

♦ attention, awareness, cognizance, eye, heed, notice, observance, observation — more at ATTENTION

²ear *n* : the fruiting spike of a cereal (as wheat or corn)

ear·ache \-ˌāk\ *n* : an ache or pain in the ear

ear·drum \-ˌdrəm\ *n* : a thin membrane that receives and transmits sound waves in the ear

eared \ˈird\ *adj* : having ears esp. of a specified kind or number ⟨a long-*eared* dog⟩

ear·ful \ˈir-ˌfu̇l\ *n* : a verbal outpouring (as of news, gossip, anger, or complaint)

earl \ˈərl\ *n* [ME *erl*, fr. OE *eorl* warrior, nobleman] : a member of the British peerage ranking below a marquess and above a viscount — **earl·dom** \-dəm\ *n*

ear·lobe \ˈir-ˌlōb\ *n* : the pendent part of the ear

¹ear·ly \ˈər-lē\ *adv* **ear·li·er; -est** ♦ : at an early time

♦ beforehand, precociously, prematurely, unseasonably; *also* immediately, promptly, punctually *Ant* late

²early *adj* **ear·li·er; -est** **1** ♦ : of, relating to, or occurring near the beginning; *also* : ANCIENT, PRIMITIVE **2** ♦ : occurring before the usual time ⟨an ∼ breakfast⟩; *also* : occurring in the near future

♦ [1] ancient, primal, primeval, primitive; *also* aged, antediluvian, antiquated, antique, hoary *Ant* late ♦ [2] precocious, premature, unseasonable, untimely; *also* unanticipated, unexpected; abrupt, sudden *Ant* late

¹ear·mark \ˈir-ˌmärk\ *n* : an identification mark (as on the ear of an animal); *also* : a distinguishing mark ⟨∼s of poverty⟩

²earmark *vb* **1** : to mark with an earmark **2** ♦ : to designate for a specific purpose

♦ allocate, consecrate, dedicate, devote, reserve, save — more at DEVOTE

ear·muff \-ˌməf\ *n* : one of a pair of ear coverings worn to protect against cold

earn \ˈərn\ *vb* **1** ♦ : to receive as a return for service **2** ♦ : to make or come to be duly worthy of : DESERVE, MERIT — **earn·er** *n*

♦ [1] acquire, attain, draw, gain, garner, get, land, make, secure, win; *also* clear, net; accomplish, achieve, notch (up); score; accumulate, draw, rack up; catch, pick up; occupy, take over; reacquire, recapture, regain, remake *Ant* forfeit, lose ♦ [2] deserve, merit, rate; *also* entitle, qualify

earned run *n* : a run in baseball that scores without benefit of an error before the fielding team has had a chance to make the third putout of the inning

earned run average *n* : the average number of earned runs per game scored against a pitcher in baseball

¹ear·nest \ˈər-nəst\ *n* ♦ : an intensely serious state of mind ⟨spoke in ∼⟩

♦ earnestness, gravity, intentness, seriousness, sobriety, solemnity — more at EARNESTNESS

²earnest *adj* **1** ♦ : seriously intent and sober ⟨an ∼ face⟩ ⟨an ∼ attempt⟩ **2** ♦ : marked by importance : GRAVE — **ear·nest·ly** *adv*

♦ [1, 2] grave, humorless (*or* humourless), serious, severe, sober, solemn, staid, unsmiling, weighty — more at SERIOUS

³earnest *n* **1** : something of value given by a buyer to a seller to bind a bargain **2** : PLEDGE

ear·nest·ness *n* ♦ : intent and serious state or quality (as of mind)

♦ gravity, intentness, seriousness, sobriety, solemnity; *also* deliberation, determination, firmness, resolve *Ant* frivolity, levity, lightheartedness

earn·ings \ˈər-niŋz\ *n pl* **1** ♦ : something (as wages) earned **2** ♦ : the balance of revenue after deduction of costs and expenses

♦ [1] income, proceeds, profit, return, revenue, yield — more at INCOME ♦ [2] gain, lucre, net, payoff, proceeds, profit, return — more at PROFIT

ear·phone \ˈir-ˌfōn\ *n* : a device that reproduces sound and is worn over or in the ear

ear·piece \-ˌpēs\ *n* : a part of an instrument which is placed against or in the ear; *esp* : EARPHONE

ear·plug \-ˌpləg\ *n* : a protective device for insertion into the opening of the ear

ear·ring \-ˌriŋ\ *n* : an ornament for the earlobe

ear·shot \-ˌshät\ *n* ♦ : range of hearing

♦ hail, hearing, sound

ear·split·ting \-ˌspli-tiŋ\ *adj* ♦ : intolerably loud or shrill

♦ booming, clamorous (*or* clamourous), deafening, loud, piercing, roaring, thunderous — more at LOUD

earth \ˈərth\ *n* **1** ♦ : the fragmental material composing part of the surface of the globe : SOIL, DIRT **2** ♦ : areas of land as distinguished from sea and air : LAND, GROUND **3** *often cap* ♦ : the planet on which we live that is 3d in order from the sun

♦ [1, 2] dirt, dust, ground, land, soil; *also* continent, landmass ♦ [3] planet, world; *also* cosmos, creation, universe; orb, sphere; macrocosm, microcosm

earth·en \ˈər-thən\ *adj* : made of earth or baked clay

earth·en·ware \-ˌwar\ *n* : slightly porous opaque pottery fired at low heat

earth·ling \'ərth-liŋ\ *n* : an inhabitant of the earth
earth·ly \'ərth-lē\ *adj* ♦ : characteristic of or belonging to this earth; *also* : relating to the human race's actual life on this earth — **earth·li·ness** *n*

♦ material, mundane, temporal, terrestrial, worldly; *also* physical *Ant* heavenly, nontemporal

earth·quake \-ˌkwāk\ *n* : a shaking or trembling of a portion of the earth
earth science *n* : any of the sciences (as geology or meteorology) that deal with the earth or one of its parts
earth·shak·ing \'ərth-ˌshā-kiŋ\ *adj* : of great importance : MOMENTOUS
earth·ward \-wərd\ *also* **earth·wards** \-wərdz\ *adv* : toward the earth
earth·work \'ərth-ˌwərk\ *n* : an embankment or fortification of earth
earth·worm \-ˌwərm\ *n* : a long segmented worm found in damp soil
earthy \'ər-thē\ *adj* **earth·i·er; -est** **1** : of, relating to, or consisting of earth; *also* : suggesting earth ⟨~ flavors⟩ **2** ♦ : not theoretical or ideal : PRACTICAL **3** : COARSE, GROSS — **earth·i·ness** *n*

♦ down-to-earth, hardheaded, matter-of-fact, practical, pragmatic, realistic — more at REALISTIC

ear·wax \'ir-ˌwaks\ *n* : the yellow waxy secretion from the ear
ear·wig \-ˌwig\ *n* : any of numerous insects with slender many-jointed antennae and a pair of appendages resembling forceps at the end of the body
¹ease \'ēz\ *n* **1** ♦ : comfort of body or mind : freedom from pain, discomfort, or concern **2** : naturalness of manner **3** ♦ : freedom from difficulty or effort

♦ [1] alleviation, comfort, decrease, relief; *also* calming, salving, soothing ♦ [3] leisure, relaxation, repose, rest — more at REST

²ease *vb* **eased; eas·ing** **1** ♦ : to relieve from distress **2** ♦ : to lessen the pressure or tension of **3** ♦ : to make or become less difficult ⟨~ credit⟩

♦ [1] allay, alleviate, assuage, help, mitigate, mollify, palliate, relieve, soothe — more at HELP ♦ [2] loosen, relax, slack, slacken — more at SLACKEN ♦ [3] assist, facilitate, further, hasten, help, improve, loosen, promote; *also* aid, smooth, speed; advance, unclog *Ant* complicate

ea·sel \'ē-zəl\ *n* [Dutch *ezel*, lit., ass] : a frame for supporting something (as an artist's canvas)
eas·i·ly \'ē-zə-lē\ *adv* ♦ : in an easy manner : without difficulty

♦ effortlessly, fluently, freely, handily, lightly, painlessly, readily, smoothly; *also* ably, adeptly, adroitly, proficiently, skillfully *Ant* arduously, laboriously

¹east \'ēst\ *adv* : to or toward the east
²east *adj* **1** : situated toward or at the east **2** : coming from the east
³east *n* **1** : the general direction of sunrise **2** : the compass point directly opposite to west **3** *cap* : regions or countries east of a specified or implied point — **east·er·ly** \'ē-stər-lē\ *adv or adj* — **east·ward** *adv or adj* — **east·wards** *adv*
Eas·ter \'ē-stər\ *n* : a church feast observed on a Sunday in March or April in commemoration of Christ's resurrection
east·ern \'ē-stərn\ *adj* **1** *often cap* : of, relating to, or characteristic of a region designated East **2** *cap* : of, relating to, or being the Christian churches originating in the Church of the Eastern Roman Empire **3** : lying toward or coming from the east — **East·ern·er** *n*
easy \'ē-zē\ *adj* **eas·i·er; -est** **1** ♦ : marked by ease ⟨an ~ life⟩; *esp* : not causing distress or difficulty ⟨~ tasks⟩ **2** : MILD, LENIENT ⟨be ~ on him⟩ **3** : GRADUAL ⟨an ~ slope⟩ **4** : free from pain, trouble, or worry ⟨felt ~⟩ **5** : LEISURELY ⟨an ~ pace⟩ **6** : NATURAL ⟨an ~ manner⟩ **7** ♦ : giving ease, comfort, or relaxation : COMFORTABLE ⟨an ~ chair⟩ **8** ♦ : readily taken advantage of — **eas·i·ness** \-zē-nəs\ *n*

♦ [1] effortless, facile, fluent, fluid, light, painless, ready, simple, smooth, snap, soft; *also* apparent, clear, distinct, evident, manifest, obvious, plain; clear-cut, straightforward *Ant* arduous, difficult, hard, labored ♦ [7] comfortable, snug, soft — more at COMFORTABLE ♦ [8] gullible, susceptible

easy·go·ing \ˌē-zē-'gō-iŋ\ *adj* ♦ : relaxed and casual in style or manner

♦ affable, breezy, carefree, happy-go-lucky, informal, laid-back *Ant* uptight flexible, lax, loose, relaxed, slack, unrestrained, unrestricted; *also* careless, heedless, negligent, slipshod, sloppy, slovenly, unfussy *Ant* rigorous carefree, careless, cavalier, gay, happy-go-lucky, insouciant, lighthearted, unconcerned — more at CAREFREE

eat \'ēt\ *vb* **ate** \'āt\; **eat·en** \'ēt-ᵊn\; **eat·ing** **1** ♦ : to take in as food : take food **2** : to use up : DEVOUR **3** ♦ : to consume gradually : CORRODE — **eat·able** *adj or n* — **eat·er** *n*

♦ [1] dine, fare, feed — more at DINE ♦ [3] bite, corrode, erode, fret; *also* break down, break up, decompose, disintegrate, dissolve; destroy, ruin, wreck

eat·ery \'ē-tə-rē\ *n, pl* **-er·ies** : LUNCHEONETTE, RESTAURANT
eaves \'ēvz\ *n pl* : the overhanging lower edge of a roof
eaves·drop \'ēvz-ˌdräp\ *vb* : to listen secretly — **eaves·drop·per** *n*
¹ebb \'eb\ *n* **1** : the flowing back from shore of water brought in by the tide **2** : a point or state of decline
²ebb *vb* **1** : to recede from the flood **2** ♦ : to fall from a higher to a lower level or from a better to a worse state : DECLINE ⟨his fortunes ~ed⟩

♦ abate, decline, decrease, diminish, dwindle, fall, lessen, recede, subside, taper — more at DECREASE

EBCDIC \'eb-sə-ˌdik\ *n* [*extended binary coded decimal interchange code*] : a computer code for representing alphanumeric information
Ebo·la \ē-bō-lə\ *n* : an often fatal hemorrhagic fever caused by a virus (**Ebola virus**) of African origin
¹eb·o·ny \'e-bə-nē\ *n, pl* **-nies** : a hard heavy wood of Old World tropical trees related to the persimmon
²ebony *adj* **1** : made of or resembling ebony **2** ♦ : of the color black

♦ black, raven — more at BLACK

e-book \'ē-ˌbůk\ *n* : a book in digital form for displaying on a computer screen or a handheld device
ebul·lient \i-'bůl-yənt, -'bəl-\ *adj* **1** : BOILING, AGITATED **2** : EXUBERANT — **ebul·lience** \-yəns\ *n*
EC *abbr* European Community
¹ec·cen·tric \ik-'sen-trik\ *adj* **1** : deviating from a usual or accepted pattern **2** : deviating from a circular path ⟨~ orbits⟩ **3** : set with axis or support off center ⟨an ~ cam⟩; *also* : being off center — **ec·cen·tri·cal·ly** \-tri-k(ə-)lē\ *adv*
²eccentric *n* ♦ : an eccentric person

♦ character, crackpot, crank, kook, nut, oddball, screwball, weirdo; *also* bohemian, maverick, nonconformist

ec·cen·tric·i·ty \ˌek-ˌsen-'tri-sə-tē\ *n* ♦ : the quality or state of being eccentric; *also* : odd or whimsical behavior

♦ crotchet, idiosyncrasy, mannerism, oddity, peculiarity, quirk, singularity, trick — more at IDIOSYNCRASY

Eccles *abbr* Ecclesiastes
Ec·cle·si·as·tes \i-ˌklē-zē-'as-tēz\ *n* : a book of wisdom literature in canonical Jewish and Christian Scripture
ec·cle·si·as·tic \i-ˌklē-zē-'as-tik\ *n* ♦ : a member of the clergy : CLERGYMAN

♦ clergyman, divine, father, minister, preacher, priest, reverend — more at CLERGYMAN

ec·cle·si·as·ti·cal \-ti-kəl\ *or* **ec·cle·si·as·tic** \-tik\ *adj* : of or relating to a church esp. as an institution ⟨~ art⟩ — **ec·cle·si·as·ti·cal·ly** \-ti-k(ə-)lē\ *adv*
Ec·cle·si·as·ti·cus \i-ˌklē-zē-'as-ti-kəs\ *n* : a didactic book included in the Protestant Apocrypha and as Sirach in the Roman Catholic canon of the Old Testament
Ecclus *abbr* Ecclesiasticus

ECG *abbr* electrocardiogram

ech•e•lon \'e-shə-ˌlän\ *n* [F *échelon*, lit., rung of a ladder] **1** : a steplike arrangement (as of troops or airplanes) **2** ♦ : a level (as of authority or responsibility) within an organization

♦ degree, footing, level, place, position, rank, situation, standing, station, status — more at RANK

ech•i•na•cea \ˌe-ki-'nä-sē-ə, -shə\ *n* : the dried root of three composite herbs that is used primarily in herbal remedies to boost the immune system; *also* : any of these herbs

echi•no•derm \i-'kī-nə-ˌdərm\ *n* : any of a phylum of marine animals (as starfishes and sea urchins) having similar body parts (as the arms of a starfish) arranged around a central axis and often having a calcium-containing outer skeleton

¹echo \'e-kō\ *n, pl* **ech•oes** *also* **ech•os** **1** : repetition of a sound caused by a reflection of the sound waves; *also* : the reflection of a radar signal by an object **2** : one who closely imitates or repeats another's words, ideas, or acts — **echo•ic** \e-'ko-ik\ *adj*

²echo *vb* ♦ : to produce an echo; *also* : to repeat or imitate (as a sound)

♦ repeat, resonate, resound, reverberate — more at REVERBERATE

echo•lo•ca•tion \ˌe-ko-lō-'kā-shən\ *n* : a process for locating distant or invisible objects by sound waves reflected back to the sender (as a bat) from the objects

echt \'ekt\ *adj* [G] : TRUE, GENUINE ⟨an ∼ New Yorker⟩

éclair \ā-'klar\ *n* [F, lit., lightning] : an oblong shell of light pastry with whipped cream or custard filling

éclat \ā-'klä\ *n* [F] **1** : a dazzling effect or success **2** : ACCLAIM

eclec•tic \e-'klek-tik\ *adj* **1** : selecting or made up of what seems best of varied sources **2** ♦ : composed of elements drawn from various sources; *also* : consisting of dissimilar ingredients or constituents — **eclectic** *n* — **eclec•ti•cism** \-'klek-tə-ˌsi-zəm\ *n*

♦ assorted, heterogeneous, miscellaneous, mixed, motley, varied — more at MISCELLANEOUS

¹eclipse \i-'klips\ *n* **1** : the total or partial obscuring of one celestial body by another; *also* : a passing into the shadow of a celestial body **2** : a falling into obscurity or decline ⟨a career in ∼⟩

²eclipse *vb* **eclipsed; eclips•ing** **1** : to cause an eclipse of **2** ♦ : to go beyond in accomplishment : SURPASS

♦ beat, better, excel, outdistance, outdo, outshine, outstrip, surpass, top, transcend — more at SURPASS

eclip•tic \i-'klip-tik\ *n* : the great circle of the celestial sphere that is the apparent path of the sun

ec•logue \'ek-ˌlȯg, -ˌläg\ *n* : a pastoral poem

ECM *abbr* European Common Market

ecol *abbr* ecological; ecology

E. coli \ˌē-'kō-ˌlī\ *n, pl* **E. coli** : a rod-shaped bacterium that sometimes causes intestinal illness

ecol•o•gy \i-'kä-lə-jē, e-\ *n, pl* **-gies** [G *Ökologie*, fr. Gk *oikos* house + *logos* word] **1** : a branch of science concerned with the relationships between organisms and their environment **2** : the pattern of relations between one or more organisms and the environment — **eco•log•i•cal** \ˌē-kə-'lä-ji-kəl, ˌe-\ *also* **eco•log•ic** \-jik\ *adj* — **eco•log•i•cal•ly** \-ji-k(ə-)lē\ *adv* — **ecol•o•gist** \i-'kä-lə-jist, e-\ *n*

e–com•merce \'ē-ˌkä-(ˌ)mərs\ *n* : commerce conducted via the Internet

econ *abbr* economics; economist; economy

eco•nom•ic \ˌe-kə-'nä-mik, ˌē-\ *adj* : of or relating to the production, distribution, and consumption of goods and services

eco•nom•i•cal \-'nä-mi-kəl\ *adj* **1** ♦ : marked by careful use of resources : THRIFTY **2** : operating with little waste or at a saving — **eco•nom•i•cal•ly** \-k(ə-)lē\ *adv*

♦ frugal, provident, sparing, thrifty — more at FRUGAL

eco•nom•ics \ˌe-kə-'nä-miks, ˌē-\ *n sing or pl* : a social science dealing with the production, distribution, and consumption of goods and services — **econ•o•mist** \i-'kä-nə-mist\ *n*

econ•o•mise *Brit var of* ECONOMIZE

econ•o•mize \i-'kä-nə-ˌmīz\ *vb* **-mized; -miz•ing** ♦ : to practice economy : be frugal — **econ•o•miz•er** *n*

♦ save, scrimp, skimp; *also* conserve, husband, manage; scrape; cut back, cut down, retrench *Ant* waste

¹econ•o•my \i-'kä-nə-mē\ *n, pl* **-mies** [MF *yconomie*, fr. ML *oeconomia*, fr. Gk *oikonomia*, fr. *oikonomos* household manager, fr. *oikos* house + *nemein* to manage] **1** ♦ : thrifty and efficient use of resources; *also* : an instance of this **2** : manner of arrangement or functioning : ORGANIZATION **3** : an economic system ⟨a money ∼⟩

♦ frugality, husbandry, providence, thrift; *also* conservation, saving; miserliness, stinginess; discretion, prudence *Ant* wastefulness

²economy *adj* : ECONOMICAL ⟨∼ cars⟩

eco•sys•tem \'ē-kō-ˌsis-təm, 'e-\ *n* : the complex of an ecological community and its environment functioning as a unit in nature

eco•tour•ism \ˌē-kō-'tu̇r-ˌi-zəm, ˌe-\ *n* : the touring of natural habitats in a manner meant to minimize ecological impact — **eco•tour•ist** \-'tu̇r-ist\ *n*

ecru \'e-krü, 'ā-\ *n* [F *écru*, lit., unbleached] : BEIGE — **ecru** *adj*

ec•sta•sy \'ek-stə-sē\ *n, pl* **-sies** **1** ♦ : extreme and usu. rapturous emotional excitement **2** *often cap* : an illicit drug with hallucinogenic properties that is chemically related to amphetamine

♦ elation, euphoria, exhilaration, heaven, intoxication, paradise, rapture, rhapsody, transport; *also* exaltation; bliss, delight, enchantment, gladness, happiness, joy, pleasure; reverie, trance; inspiration; fervor, frenzy, madness, passion *Ant* depression

ec•stat•ic \ek-'sta-tik, ik-\ *adj* ♦ : of, relating to, or marked by ecstasy — **ec•stat•i•cal•ly** \-ti-k(ə-)lē\ *adv*

♦ elated, euphoric, intoxicated, rapturous, rhapsodic; *also* exultant, jubilant, triumphant; enthusiastic, excited, gung ho, thrilled; blissful, delighted, glad, gratified, happy, joyful, joyous, pleased, satisfied, tickled *Ant* depressed

Ecua *abbr* Ecuador

Ec•ua•dor•an \ˌe-kwə-'dȯr-ən\ *or* **Ec•ua•dor•ean** *or* **Ec•ua•dor•ian** \-ē-ən\ *n* : a native or inhabitant of Ecuador — **Ecuadorean** *or* **Ecuadorian** *adj*

ec•u•men•i•cal \ˌe-kyu̇-'me-ni-kəl\ *adj* : general in extent or influence; *esp* : promoting or tending toward worldwide Christian unity — **ec•u•men•i•cal•ly** \-k(ə-)lē\ *adv*

ec•ze•ma \ig-'zē-mə, 'eg-zə-mə, 'ek-sə-\ *n* : an itching skin inflammation with oozing and then crusted lesions — **ec•zem•a•tous** \ig-'ze-mə-təs\ *adj*

ed *abbr* **1** edited; edition; editor **2** education

¹-ed \d *after a vowel or* b, g, j, l, m, n, ŋ, r, th, v, z, zh; əd, after d, t; t *after other sounds*\ *vb suffix or adj suffix* **1** — used to form the past participle of regular weak verbs ⟨end*ed*⟩ ⟨fad*ed*⟩ ⟨tri*ed*⟩ ⟨patt*ed*⟩ **2** : having : characterized by ⟨cultur*ed*⟩ ⟨2-legg*ed*⟩; *also* : having the characteristics of ⟨bigot*ed*⟩

²-ed *vb suffix* — used to form the past tense of regular weak verbs ⟨judg*ed*⟩ ⟨deni*ed*⟩ ⟨dropp*ed*⟩

Edam \'ē-dəm, -ˌdam\ *n* : a yellow Dutch pressed cheese made in balls

ed•a•ma•me \ˌe-də-'mä-mā\ *n* [Jp, fr. *eda* branch + *mame* bean] : immature green soybeans usu. in the pod

ed•dy \'e-dē\ *n, pl* **eddies** : WHIRLPOOL — **eddy** *vb*

edel•weiss \'ād-ºl-ˌwīs, -ˌvīs\ *n* [G, fr. *edel* noble + *weiss* white] : a small perennial woolly composite herb that grows high in the Alps

ede•ma \i-'dē-mə\ *n* : abnormal accumulation of watery fluid in connective tissue or in a serous cavity — **edem•a•tous** \-'de-mə-təs\ *adj*

Eden \'ēd-ºn\ *n* ♦ : a place or state of bliss or delight : PARADISE

♦ Elysium, heaven, paradise, utopia — more at PAR-ADISE

¹edge \'ej\ n 1 : the cutting side of a blade 2 : a noticeably harsh or sharp quality; *also* : FORCE, EFFECTIVENESS 3 ♦ : the line where something begins or ends; *also* : the area adjoining such an edge 4 ♦ : a favorable margin : ADVANTAGE — edged \'ejd\ *adj*

♦ [3] border, bound, boundary, fringe, margin, perimeter, periphery, rim, skirt, verge — more at BORDER
♦ [4] advantage, better, drop, jump, upper hand, vantage — more at ADVANTAGE

²edge *vb* edged; edg•ing 1 ♦ : to give or form an edge 2 : to move or force gradually ⟨~ into a crowd⟩ 3 : to defeat by a small margin ⟨*edged* out her opponent⟩ — edg•er *n*

♦ grind, hone, sharpen, strop, whet — more at SHARPEN

edge•wise \'ej-ˌwīz\ *adv* : SIDEWAYS
edg•ing \'e-jiŋ\ *n* : something that forms an edge or border ⟨a lace ~⟩
edgy \'e-jē\ *adj* edg•i•er; -est 1 ♦ : having an edge : SHARP ⟨an ~ tone⟩ 2 ♦ : being on edge : TENSE, NERVOUS 3 : having a bold, provocative, or unconventional quality — edg•i•ness *n*

♦ [1] cutting, ground, keen, sharp — more at SHARP
♦ [2] aflutter, anxious, jittery, jumpy, nervous, nervy, tense, troubled, upset, worried — more at NERVOUS

ed•i•ble \'e-də-bəl\ *adj* : fit or safe to be eaten — ed•i•bil•i•ty \ˌe-də-'bi-lə-tē\ *n* — edible *n*
edict \'ē-ˌdikt\ *n* ♦ : a proclamation having the force of law; *also* : ORDER, DECREE

♦ decree, directive, fiat, order, ruling; *also* call, decision, judgment; announcement, declaration, dictum, manifesto, proclamation, pronouncement; canon, encyclical

ed•i•fi•ca•tion \ˌe-də-fə-'kā-shən\ *n* : instruction and improvement esp. in morality
ed•i•fice \'e-də-fəs\ *n* : a usu. large building
ed•i•fy \'e-də-ˌfī\ *vb* ♦ : to instruct and improve esp. in moral and religious knowledge

♦ educate, enlighten, nurture — more at ENLIGHTEN

ed•it \'e-dət\ *vb* 1 ♦ : to revise, assemble, or prepare for publication or release (as a motion picture) 2 : to direct the publication and policies of (as a newspaper) 3 : DELETE — ed•i•tor \'e-də-tər\ *n* — ed•i•tor•ship *n* — ed•i•tress \-trəs\ *n*

♦ redraft, revamp, revise, rework; *also* amend, correct, emend, rectify

edi•tion \i-'di-shən\ *n* 1 : the form in which a text is published 2 : the total number of copies (as of a book) published at one time 3 : VERSION

¹ed•i•to•ri•al \ˌe-də-'tōr-ē-əl\ *adj* 1 : of or relating to an editor or editing 2 : being or resembling an editorial — ed•i•to•ri•al•ly *adv*

²editorial *n* : an article (as in a newspaper) giving the views of the editors or publishers; *also* : an expression of opinion resembling an editorial ⟨a television ~⟩
ed•i•to•ri•al•ize \ˌe-də-'tōr-ē-ə-ˌlīz\ *vb* -ized; -iz•ing 1 : to express an opinion in an editorial 2 : to introduce opinions into factual reporting 3 : to express an opinion — ed•i•to•ri•al•i•za•tion \-ˌtōr-ē-ə-lə-'zā-shən\ *n* — ed•i•to•ri•al•iz•er *n*
EDP *abbr* electronic data processing
EDT *abbr* Eastern daylight (saving) time
educ *abbr* education; educational
ed•u•ca•ble \'e-jə-kə-bəl\ *adj* : capable of being educated
ed•u•cate \'e-jə-ˌkāt\ *vb* -cat•ed; -cat•ing [ME, to rear, fr. L *educatus*, pp. of *educare*, fr. *educere* to lead forth, draw out] 1 ♦ : to provide with schooling 2 ♦ : to develop mentally and morally; *also* : to provide with information

♦ [1] indoctrinate, instruct, school, teach, train, tutor — more at TEACH ♦ [2] edify, enlighten, nurture — more at ENLIGHTEN

educated *adj* ♦ : having an education; *esp* : having an education beyond the average

♦ erudite, knowledgeable, learned, literate, scholarly, well-read; *also* civilized, cultivated, cultured; cerebral, highbrow, intellectual; polished, refined, well-bred; academic, bookish, didactic, pedantic, professorial; instructed, schooled, skilled, trained; homeschooled, self-educated, self-taught; briefed, enlightened, informed, versed *Ant* ignorant, illiterate, uneducated

ed•u•ca•tion \ˌe-jə-'kā-shən\ *n* 1 ♦ : the action or process of educating or being educated; *also* : the knowledge and development resulting from an educational process 2 : a field of study dealing with methods of teaching and learning

♦ instruction, teaching, training, tutelage; *also* coaching, conditioning, cultivation, preparation ♦ erudition, knowledge, learning, scholarship, science; *also* culture, edification, enlightenment; literacy, reading; pedantry

ed•u•ca•tion•al \-shə-nəl\ *adj* ♦ : of, relating to, or concerned with education; *also* : serving to further education — ed•u•ca•tion•al•ly *adv*

♦ informative, instructive — more at INFORMATIVE

educational television *n* : PUBLIC TELEVISION
ed•u•ca•tor \-ˌkā-tər\ *n* ♦ : one skilled in teaching

♦ instructor, pedagogue, schoolteacher, teacher — more at TEACHER

educe \i-'düs, -'dyüs\ *vb* educed; educ•ing 1 : to bring out (as something latent) : ELICIT, EVOKE 2 : DEDUCE
ed•u•tain•ment \ˌe-jə-'tān-mənt\ *n* : entertainment that is designed to be educational
¹-ee \'ē, (ˌ)ē\ *n suffix* 1 : one that receives or benefits from (a specified action or thing) ⟨grantee⟩ ⟨patentee⟩ 2 : a person who does (a specified action) ⟨escapee⟩
²-ee *n suffix* 1 : a particular esp. small kind of ⟨bootee⟩ 2 : one resembling or suggestive of ⟨goatee⟩
EE *abbr* electrical engineer
EEC *abbr* European Economic Community
EEG *abbr* 1 electroencephalogram 2 electroencephalograph
eel \'ēl\ *n* : any of numerous snakelike bony fishes with a smooth slimy skin
EEO *abbr* equal employment opportunity
ee•rie *also* ee•ry \'ir-ē\ *adj* ee•ri•er; -est ♦ : so mysterious, strange, or unexpected as to send a chill up the spine : WEIRD, UNCANNY — ee•ri•ly \'ir-ə-lē\ *adv*

♦ creepy, haunting, odd, spooky, strange, uncanny, unearthly, weird; *also* ghostly, spectral

eff *abbr* efficiency
ef•face \i-'fās, e-\ *vb* ef•faced; ef•fac•ing : to obliterate or obscure by or as if by rubbing out — ef•face•able *adj* — ef•face•ment *n*
¹ef•fect \i-'fekt\ *n* 1 : MEANING, INTENT 2 ♦ : something that inevitably follows an antecedent : RESULT 3 : APPEARANCE 4 ♦ : power to bring about a result : INFLUENCE 5 *pl* ♦ : movable property : GOODS, POSSESSIONS 6 : the quality or state of being operative : OPERATION

♦ [2] aftermath, conclusion, consequence, issue, outcome, outgrowth, product, result, upshot; *also* ramification; denouement, repercussion; conclusion, end; by-product, side effect *Ant* antecedent, cause, occasion, reason ♦ [4] impact, influence, mark, repercussion, sway; *also* authority, clout, prestige, weight ♦ *usu* effects ♦ [5] belongings, chattels, holdings, paraphernalia, possessions, things — more at POSSESSION

²effect *vb* ♦ : to cause to happen ⟨~ repairs⟩ ⟨~ changes⟩

♦ bring about, cause, create, effectuate, generate, induce, make, produce, prompt, result; *also* decide, determine; advance, encourage, forward, foster, promote; enact, render, turn out

ef•fec•tive \i-'fek-tiv\ *adj* 1 ♦ : producing a decisive or desired effect; *also* : marked by the quality of being influential or exerting positive influence ⟨an ~ presentation⟩

2 : IMPRESSIVE, STRIKING   3 : ready for service or action
4 : being in effect — **ef·fec·tive·ly** *adv*

 ♦ convincing, decisive, effectual, efficacious, efficient, forceful, fruitful, persuasive, potent, productive; *also* adequate, capable, competent **Ant** ineffective, ineffectual, inefficient, fruitless, unproductive

ef·fec·tive·ness *n* ♦ : the quality or state of being effective; *also* : power to be effective

 ♦ efficacy, efficiency, force, impact, productiveness — more at EFFICACY

ef·fec·tu·al \i-'fek-chə-wəl\ *adj* ♦ : producing an intended effect — **ef·fec·tu·al·ly** *adv*

 ♦ effective, efficacious, efficient, fruitful, potent, productive — more at EFFECTIVE

ef·fec·tu·ate \i-'fek-chə-₁wāt\ *vb* **-at·ed; -at·ing** ♦ : to cause to come into being : BRING ABOUT, EFFECT

 ♦ bring about, cause, create, effect, generate, induce, make, produce, prompt, result, work, yield — more at EFFECT

ef·fem·i·nate \ə-'fe-mə-nət\ *adj* ♦ : marked by qualities more typical of women than men — **ef·fem·i·na·cy** \-nə-sē\ *n*

 ♦ feminine, girlish, unmanly, womanly **Ant** manly, mannish, masculine

ef·fen·di \e-'fen-dē\ *n* [Turk *efendi* master, fr. ModGk *aphentēs*, alter. of Gk *authentēs*] : a man of property, authority, or education in an eastern Mediterranean country

ef·fer·ent \'e-fə-rənt\ *adj* : bearing or conducting outward from a more central part ⟨∼ nerves⟩

ef·fer·vesce \₁e-fər-'ves\ *vb* **-vesced; -vesc·ing** 1 : to bubble and hiss as gas escapes   2 : to show liveliness or exhilaration — **ef·fer·ves·cence** \-'ve-s³ns\ *n*

ef·fer·ves·cent \-³nt\ *adj* ♦ : impossible or difficult to restrain or suppress — **ef·fer·ves·cent·ly** *adv*

 ♦ bubbly, buoyant, exuberant, frolicsome, high-spirited, vivacious — more at EXUBERANT

ef·fete \e-'fēt\ *adj* 1 ♦ : having lost character, vitality, or strength; *also* : DECADENT   2 : EFFEMINATE

 ♦ decadent, degenerate, soft, weak; *also* decaying, declining, dying, failing

ef·fi·ca·cious \₁e-fə-'kā-shəs\ *adj* ♦ : producing an intended effect ⟨∼ remedies⟩

 ♦ effective, effectual, efficient, fruitful, potent, productive — more at EFFECTIVE

ef·fi·ca·cy \'e-fi-kə-sē\ *n* ♦ : the power to produce an effect

 ♦ effectiveness, efficiency, productiveness; *also* ability, capability, capacity **Ant** ineffectiveness, inefficiency

ef·fi·cien·cy \-shən-sē\ *n* ♦ : the quality or degree of being efficient; *also* : efficient operation

 ♦ effectiveness, efficacy, productiveness — more at EFFICACY

ef·fi·cient \i-'fi-shənt\ *adj* ♦ : productive of desired effects esp. without waste — **ef·fi·cient·ly** *adv*

 ♦ effective, effectual, efficacious, fruitful, potent, productive — more at EFFECTIVE

ef·fi·gy \'e-fə-jē\ *n, pl* **-gies** : IMAGE; *esp* : a crude figure of a hated person

ef·flo·res·cence \₁e-flə-'res-³ns\ *n* 1 : the period or state of flowering   2 : the action or process of developing   3 : fullness of development : FLOWERING

ef·flu·ence \'e-₁flü-əns\ *n* : something that flows out

ef·flu·ent \'e-₁flü-ənt\ *n* : something that flows out; *esp* : a fluid (as sewage) discharged as waste — **effluent** *adj*

ef·flu·vi·um \e-'flü-vē-əm\ *n, pl* **-via** \-vē-ə\ *also* **-vi·ums** [L, outflow]   1 : a usu. unpleasant emanation   2 : a by-product usu. in the form of waste

ef·fort \'e-fərt\ *n* 1 ♦ : hard work : EXERTION; *also* : a product of effort   2 : active or applied force

 ♦ exertion, expenditure, labor (*or* labour), pains, sweat, trouble, work; *also* toil, travail

ef·fort·less *adj* ♦ : showing or requiring little or no effort

 ♦ easy, facile, fluent, fluid, light, painless, ready, smooth, snap — more at EASY

ef·fort·less·ly *adv* ♦ : in an effortless manner

 ♦ easily, fluently, freely, handily, lightly, painlessly, readily, smoothly — more at EASILY

ef·fron·tery \i-'frən-tə-rē\ *n, pl* **-ter·ies** ♦ : shameless and offensive boldness

 ♦ audacity, brass, brazenness, cheek, chutzpah, gall, nerve, presumption, temerity; *also* arrogance, cockiness, overconfidence; impertinence, impudence, insolence, rudeness

ef·ful·gence \i-'fül-jəns, -'fəl-\ *n* ♦ : radiant splendor : BRILLIANCE

 ♦ brilliance, dazzle, illumination, luminosity, radiance, splendor — more at BRILLIANCE

ef·ful·gent \-jənt\ *adj* ♦ : extremely radiant

 ♦ beaming, bright, brilliant, glowing, incandescent, luminous, lustrous, radiant — more at BRIGHT

ef·fu·sion \i-'fyü-zhən, e-\ *n* : a gushing forth; *also* : unrestrained utterance — **ef·fuse** \-'fyüz, e-\ *vb*

ef·fu·sive \i-'fyü-siv, e-\ *adj* ♦ : marked by the expression of great or excessive emotion or enthusiasm — **ef·fu·sive·ly** *adv*

 ♦ demonstrative, emotional, uninhibited, unreserved, unrestrained — more at DEMONSTRATIVE

eft \'eft\ *n* : NEWT

EFT *or* **EFTS** *abbr* electronic funds transfer (system)

e.g. *abbr* [L *exempli gratia*] for example

Eg *abbr* Egypt; Egyptian

egal·i·tar·i·an·ism \i-₁ga-lə-'ter-ē-ə-₁ni-zəm\ *n* : a belief in human equality esp. in social, political, and economic affairs — **egal·i·tar·i·an** *adj or n*

¹egg \'eg\ *vb* [ME, fr. ON *eggja*; akin to OE *ecg* edge] ♦ : to urge to action — usu. used with *on*

 ♦ *usu* **egg on** encourage, exhort, goad, press, prod, prompt, urge — more at URGE

²egg *n* [ME *egge*, fr. ON *egg*; akin to OE *ǣg* egg, L *ovum*] 1 : a rounded usu. hard-shelled reproductive body esp. of birds and reptiles from which the young hatches; *also* : the egg of the common domestic chicken as an article of food   2 : a germ cell produced by a female

egg-beat·er \'eg-₁bē-tər\ *n* : a hand-operated kitchen utensil for beating, stirring, or whipping

egg cell *n* : EGG 2

egg·head \-₁hed\ *n, often disparaging* : an intellectual person : INTELLECTUAL, HIGHBROW

egg·nog \-₁näg\ *n* : a drink consisting of eggs beaten with sugar, milk or cream, and often alcoholic liquor

egg·plant \-₁plant\ *n* : the edible usu. large and purplish fruit of a plant related to the potato; *also* : the plant

egg roll *n* : a thin egg-dough casing filled with minced vegetables and often bits of meat and usu. deep-fried

egg·shell \'eg-₁shel\ *n* : the hard exterior covering of an egg

egis *var of* AEGIS

eg·lan·tine \'e-glən-₁tīn, -₁tēn\ *n* : SWEETBRIER

ego \'ē-gō\ *n, pl* **egos** [L, I]   1 : the self as distinguished from others   2 : the one of the three divisions of the psyche in psychoanalytic theory that is the organized conscious mediator between the person and reality   3 ♦ : an exaggerated sense of self-importance; *also* : a confidence and satisfaction in oneself

 ♦ complacence, conceit, pride, self-importance, self-regard, self-respect, self-satisfaction, smugness, vainglory, vanity — more at COMPLACENCE

ego·cen·tric \₁ē-gō-'sen-trik\ *adj* ♦ : concerned or overly concerned with the self; *esp* : SELF-CENTERED

 ♦ egotistic, selfish, self-seeking; *also* complacent, conceited, self-important, self-indulgent, self-satisfied, smug, vain **Ant** selfless

ego·ism \'ē-gō-₁i-zəm\ *n* 1 : a doctrine holding self-interest to be the motive or the valid end of action **2 ♦** : excessive concern for oneself with or without exaggerated feelings of self-importance — **ego·ist** \-ist\ *n*

♦ egotism, self-centeredness, self-interest, selfishness, self-regard; *also* conceit, self-importance, self-indulgence, self-satisfaction *Ant* selflessness

ego·is·tic \ˌē-gō-ˈtis-tik\ *adj* : having an exaggerated sense of self-importance — **ego·is·ti·cal·ly** *adv*

ego·tism \ˈē-gə-ˌti-zəm\ *n* **1** : the practice of talking about oneself too much **2 ♦** : an exaggerated sense of self= importance : CONCEIT — **ego·tist** \-tist\ *n*

♦ complacence, conceit, pride, self-esteem, self-importance, self-satisfaction, smugness, vainglory, vanity — more at COMPLACENCE

ego·tis·tic \ˌē-gə-ˈtis-tik\ *or* **ego·tis·ti·cal** \-ti-kəl\ *adj* **♦** : an exaggerated sense of self-importance — **ego·tis·ti·cal·ly** *adv*

♦ complacent, conceited, important, prideful, proud, self-important, self-satisfied, smug, stuck-up, vain — more at CONCEITED

ego trip *n* : an act that enhances and satisfies one's ego

egre·gious \i-ˈgrē-jəs\ *adj* [L *egregius* outstanding, fr. *ex, e* out of + *greg-, grex* flock, herd] **♦** : notably bad : FLAGRANT — **egre·gious·ly** *adv* — **egre·gious·ness** *n*

♦ blatant, flagrant, glaring, gross, obvious, patent, pronounced, rank, striking; *also* salient; atrocious, awful, deplorable

egress \ˈē-ˌgres\ *n* **♦** : a way out : EXIT

♦ exit, issue, outlet — more at EXIT

egret \ˈē-grət, i-ˈgret\ *n* : any of various herons that bear long plumes during the breeding season

Egyp·tian \i-ˈjip-shən\ *n* **1** : a native or inhabitant of Egypt **2** : the language of the ancient Egyptians from earliest times to about the 3d century A.D. — **Egyptian** *adj*

ei·der \ˈī-dər\ *n* : any of several northern sea ducks that yield a soft down

ei·der·down \-ˌdau̇n\ *n* **1** : the down of the eider **2** : a comforter filled with eiderdown

ei·do·lon \ī-ˈdō-lən\ *n, pl* **-lons** *or* **-la** \-lə\ **1** : PHANTOM **2** : IDEAL

eight \ˈāt\ *n* **1** : one more than seven **2** : the 8th in a set or series **3** : something having eight units — **eight** *adj or pron* — **eighth** \ˈātth\ *adj or adv or n*

eight ball *n* : a black pool ball numbered 8 — **behind the eight ball** : in a highly disadvantageous position

eigh·teen \ˈāt-ˈtēn\ *n* : one more than 17 — **eighteen** *adj or pron* — **eigh·teenth** \-ˈtēnth\ *adj or n*

eighty \ˈā-tē\ *n, pl* **eight·ies** : eight times 10 — **eight·i·eth** \ˈā-tē-əth\ *adj or n* — **eighty** *adj or pron*

ein·stei·ni·um \īn-ˈstī-nē-əm\ *n* : an artificially produced radioactive element

¹ei·ther \ˈē-thər, ˈī-\ *adj* **1** : being the one and the other of two : EACH ⟨trees on ∼ side⟩ **2** : being the one or the other of two ⟨take ∼ road⟩

²either *pron* : the one or the other

³either *conj* — used as a function word before the first of two or more words or word groups of which the last is preceded by *or* to indicate that they represent alternatives ⟨a statement is ∼ true or false⟩

ejac·u·late \i-ˈja-kyə-ˌlāt\ *vb* **-lat·ed; -lat·ing** **1** : to eject a fluid (as semen) **2 ♦** : to utter suddenly : EXCLAIM — **ejac·u·la·to·ry** \-ˈja-kyə-lə-ˌtōr-ē\ *adj*

♦ blurt, bolt, cry, spout

ejac·u·la·tion \i-ˌja-kyə-ˈlā-shən\ *n* : something ejaculated *esp* **♦** : a short sudden emotional utterance

♦ cry, exclamation, interjection — more at EXCLAMATION

eject \i-ˈjekt\ *vb* **♦** : to drive or throw out or off — **ejec·tion** \-ˈjek-shən\ *n*

♦ banish, boot (out), bounce, cast, expel, oust, rout, run off, throw out ♦ belch, disgorge, erupt, jet, spew, spout, spurt — more at ERUPT

eke \ˈēk\ *vb* **eked; ek·ing** **♦** : to gain, supplement, or extend usu. with effort — usu. used with *out* ⟨∼ out a living⟩

♦ *usu* **eke out** scrape, squeeze, wrest, wring; *also* acquire, earn, gain, obtain, procure, secure

EKG *abbr* [G *Elektrokardiogramm*] electrocardiogram; electrocardiograph

el *abbr* elevation

¹elab·o·rate \i-ˈla-bə-rət, -ˈla-brət\ *adj* **1 ♦** : planned or carried out with great care **2 ♦** : being complex and usu. ornate — **elab·o·rate·ly** *adv*

♦ [1, 2] complex, complicated, detailed, fancy, intricate, involved, sophisticated; *also* elegant, grand, ornate, magnificent, splendid *Ant* simple

²elab·o·rate \i-ˈla-bə-ˌrāt\ *vb* **-rat·ed; -rat·ing 1** : to build up from simpler ingredients **2 ♦** : to work out in detail : develop fully

♦ *usu* **elaborate on** amplify, develop, embellish, enlarge (on), expand — more at EXPAND

elab·o·rate·ness *n* **♦** : the state or quality of being elaborate

♦ complexity, intricacy, sophistication — more at COMPLEXITY

elab·o·ra·tion \-ˌla-bə-ˈrā-shən\ *n* **1 ♦** : the act or process of elaborating **2** : something produced by elaborating

♦ development, evolution, expansion, growth, progress, progression — more at DEVELOPMENT

élan \ā-ˈläⁿ\ *n* [F] : ARDOR, SPIRIT

eland \ˈē-lənd, -ˌland\ *n, pl* **eland** *also* **elands** [Afrikaans] : either of two large African antelopes with spirally twisted horns in both sexes

elapse \i-ˈlaps\ *vb* **elapsed; elaps·ing** **♦** : to slip by : PASS

♦ cease, end, expire, finish, pass, quit, stop, terminate, wind up — more at CEASE

¹elas·tic \i-ˈlas-tik\ *adj* **1 ♦** : capable of recovering size and shape after deformation : SPRINGY **2 ♦** : capable of ready change or easy expansion or contraction : FLEXIBLE; *also* ADAPTABLE — **elas·tic·i·ty** \-ˌlas-ˈti-sə-tē, ˌē-ˌlas-\ *n*

♦ [1] flexible, resilient, rubbery, springy, stretch, supple; *also* adaptable, ductile, malleable, plastic, pliable, pliant *Ant* inelastic, inflexible, rigid, stiff ♦ [2] adaptable, adjustable, changeable, flexible, fluid, malleable, variable — more at FLEXIBLE

²elastic *n* **1** : elastic material **2** : a rubber band

elate \i-ˈlāt\ *vb* **elat·ed; elat·ing** **♦** : to fill with joy

♦ elevate, enrapture, exhilarate, transport; *also* excite, inspire, stimulate, uplift *Ant* depress

elated *adj* **♦** : marked by high spirits

♦ ecstatic, euphoric, intoxicated, rapturous, rhapsodic — more at ECSTATIC

ela·tion \-ˈlā-shən\ *n* **♦** : the quality or state of being elated

♦ ecstasy, euphoria, exhilaration, heaven, intoxication, paradise, rapture, rhapsody, transport — more at ECSTASY

¹el·bow \ˈel-ˌbō\ *n* [ME *elbowe*, fr. OE *elboga*, fr. *el-* (akin to *eln* ell) + *boga* bow] **1** : the joint of the arm; *also* : the outer curve of the bent arm **2** : a bend or joint resembling an elbow in shape

²elbow *vb* **♦** : to push aside with the elbow; *also* : to make one's way by elbowing

♦ bulldoze, muscle, press, push — more at PRESS

elbow room \ˈel-ˌbō-ˌrüm, -ˌru̇m\ *n* : enough space for work or operation

¹el·der \ˈel-dər\ *n* : ELDERBERRY 2

²elder *adj* **1** : being the older one **2** : EARLIER, FORMER **3** : of higher rank

³elder *n* **1 ♦** : an older individual : SENIOR **2 ♦** : one having authority by reason of age and experience **3** : a church officer

♦ [1] ancient, golden-ager, oldster, senior citizen — more at SENIOR CITIZEN ♦ [2] dean, senior — more at DEAN

el·der·ber·ry \ˈel-dər-ˌber-ē\ *n* **1** : the edible black or red fruit of a shrub or tree related to the honeysuckle and bearing flat clusters of small white or pink flowers **2** : a tree or shrub bearing elderberries

el·der·ly \'el-dər-lē\ *adj* **1** ♦ : rather old; *esp* : past middle age **2** : of, relating to, or characteristic of later life

♦ ancient, geriatric, old, senior; *also* pensioned, retired, superannuated *Ant* young, youthful

el·dest \'el-dəst\ *adj* : of the greatest age

El Do·ra·do \,el-də-'rä-dō, -'rä-\ *n* [Sp, lit., the gilded one] : a place of vast riches, abundance, or opportunity

elec *abbr* electric; electrical; electricity

¹elect \i-'lekt\ *adj* **1** ♦ : carefully selected : CHOSEN **2** : elected but not yet installed in office ⟨the president-*elect*⟩

♦ chosen, select — more at SELECT

²elect *n, pl* **elect** **1** : a selected person **2** *pl* ♦ : a select or exclusive group

♦ best, choice, cream, elite, fat, flower, pick, prime — more at ELITE

³elect *vb* **1** : to select by vote (as for office or membership) **2** ♦ : to select or choose esp. by preference : PICK

♦ choose, cull, handpick, name, opt, pick, prefer, select, single, take — more at CHOOSE

elec·tion \i-'lek-shən\ *n* **1** ♦ : an act or process of electing **2** : the fact of being elected

♦ choice, selection — more at SELECTION

elec·tion·eer \i-,lek-shə-'nir\ *vb* : to work for the election of a candidate or party

¹elec·tive \i-'lek-tiv\ *adj* **1** : chosen or filled by election **2** ♦ : permitting a choice : OPTIONAL

♦ discretionary, optional, voluntary — more at OPTIONAL

²elective *n* : an elective course or subject of study

elec·tor \i-'lek-tər\ *n* **1** : one qualified to vote in an election **2** : one elected to an electoral college — **elec·tor·al** \i-'lek-tə-rəl\ *adj*

electoral college *n* : a body of electors who elect the president and vice president of the U.S.

elec·tor·ate \i-'lek-tə-rət\ *n* : a body of persons entitled to vote

elec·tric \i-'lek-trik\ *adj* [NL *electricus* produced from amber by friction, electric, fr. ML, of amber, fr. L *electrum* amber, fr. Gk *ēlektron*] **1** *or* **elec·tri·cal** \-tri-kəl\ : of, relating to, operated by, or produced by electricity **2** ♦ : exciting as if by electric shock : ELECTRIFYING, THRILLING; *also* : charged with strong emotion — **elec·tri·cal·ly** *adv*

♦ breathtaking, exciting, exhilarating, rousing, stirring, thrilling — more at EXCITING

electrical storm *n* : THUNDERSTORM

electric chair *n* : a chair used to carry out the death penalty by electrocution

electric eye *n* : PHOTOELECTRIC CELL

elec·tri·cian \i-,lek-'tri-shən\ *n* : a person who installs, operates, or repairs electrical equipment

elec·tric·i·ty \i-,lek-'tri-sə-tē\ *n, pl* **-ties** **1** : a form of energy that occurs naturally (as in lightning) or is produced (as in a generator) and that is expressed in terms of the movement and interaction of electrons **2** : electric current

elec·tri·fy \i-'lek-trə-,fī\ *vb* **-fied; -fy·ing** **1** : to charge with electricity **2** : to equip for use of electric power **3** ♦ : to excite intensely or suddenly : THRILL — **elec·tri·fi·ca·tion** \i-,lek-trə-fə-'kā-shən\ *n*

♦ excite, exhilarate, galvanize, intoxicate, thrill, titillate, turn on — more at THRILL

elec·tro·car·dio·gram \i-,lek-trō-'kär-dē-ə-,gram\ *n* : the tracing made by an electrocardiograph

elec·tro·car·dio·graph \-,graf\ *n* : a device for recording the changes of electrical potential occurring during the heartbeat — **elec·tro·car·dio·graph·ic** \-,kär-dē-ə-'gra-fik\ *adj* — **elec·tro·car·dio·g·ra·phy** \-dē-'ä-grə-fē\ *n*

elec·tro·chem·is·try \-'ke-mə-strē\ *n* : a branch of chemistry that deals with the relation of electricity to chemical changes — **elec·tro·chem·i·cal** \-'ke-mi-kəl\ *adj*

elec·tro·cute \i-'lek-trə-,kyüt\ *vb* **-cut·ed; -cut·ing** **1** : to

kill (a criminal) by electricity **2** : to kill by electric shock — **elec·tro·cu·tion** \-,lek-trə-'kyü-shən\ *n*

elec·trode \i-'lek-,trōd\ *n* : a conductor used to establish electrical contact with a nonmetallic part of a circuit

elec·tro·en·ceph·a·lo·gram \i-,lek-trō-in-'se-fə-lə-,gram\ *n* : the tracing made by an electroencephalograph

elec·tro·en·ceph·a·lo·graph \-,graf\ *n* : an apparatus for detecting and recording brain waves — **elec·tro·en·ceph·a·lo·graph·ic** \-,se-fə-lə-'gra-fik\ *adj* — **elec·tro·en·ceph·a·log·ra·phy** \-'lä-grə-fē\ *n*

elec·trol·o·gist \i-,lek-'trä-lə-jist\ *n* : one that uses electrical means to remove hair, warts, moles, and birthmarks from the body

elec·trol·y·sis \i-,lek-'trä-lə-səs\ *n* **1** : the production of chemical changes by passage of an electric current through an electrolyte **2** : the destruction of hair roots with an electric current — **elec·tro·lyt·ic** \-trə-'li-tik\ *adj*

elec·tro·lyte \i-'lek-trə-,līt\ *n* : a nonmetallic electric conductor in which current is carried by the movement of ions; *also* : a substance whose solution or molten form is such a conductor

elec·tro·mag·net \i-,lek-trō-'mag-nət\ *n* : a core of magnetic material (as iron) surrounded by a coil of wire through which an electric current is passed to magnetize the core

elec·tro·mag·net·ic \-mag-'ne-tik\ *adj* : of, relating to, or produced by electromagnetism — **elec·tro·mag·net·i·cal·ly** *adv*

electromagnetic radiation *n* : energy in the form of electromagnetic waves; *also* : a series of electromagnetic waves

electromagnetic wave *n* : a wave (as a radio wave, an X-ray, or a wave of visible light) that consists of associated electric and magnetic effects and that travels at the speed of light

elec·tro·mag·ne·tism \i-,lek-trō-'mag-nə-,ti-zəm\ *n* **1** : magnetism developed by a current of electricity **2** : a natural force responsible for interactions between charged particles which result from their charge

elec·tro·mo·tive force \i-,lek-trə-'mō-tiv-\ *n* : the potential difference derived from an electrical source per unit quantity of electricity passing through the source

elec·tron \i-'lek-,trän\ *n* : a negatively charged elementary particle

elec·tron·ic \i-,lek-'trä-nik\ *adj* **1** : of or relating to electrons or electronics **2** : involving a computer — **elec·tron·i·cal·ly** \-ni-k(ə-)lē\ *adv*

electronic mail *n* : E-MAIL

elec·tron·ics \i-,lek-'trä-niks\ *n* **1** : the physics of electrons and electronic devices **2** : electronic components, devices, or equipment

electron microscope *n* : an instrument in which a beam of electrons is used to produce an enlarged image of a minute object

electron tube *n* : a device in which electrical conduction by electrons takes place within a sealed container and which is used for the controlled flow of electrons

electron volt *n* : a unit of energy equal to 1.60×10^{-19} joule

elec·tro·pho·re·sis \i-,lek-trə-fə-'rē-səs\ *n* : the movement of suspended particles through a medium (as paper or gel) by an electromotive force — **elec·tro·pho·ret·ic** \-'re-tik\ *adj*

elec·tro·plate \i-'lek-trə-,plāt\ *vb* : to coat (as with metal) by electrolysis

elec·tro·shock therapy \i-'lek-trō-,shäk-\ *n* : the treatment of mental illness by applying electric current to the head and inducing convulsions

elec·tro·stat·ics \i-,lek-trə-'sta-tiks\ *n* : physics dealing with the interactions of stationary electric charges

el·ee·mos·y·nary \,e-li-'mäs-ᵊn-,er-ē\ *adj* : CHARITABLE

el·e·gance \'e-li-gəns\ *n* **1 a** ♦ : refined gracefulness **b** ♦ : tasteful richness (as of design) **2** : something marked by elegance — **el·e·gant·ly** *adv*

♦ [1a, 1b] class, grace, handsomeness, majesty, refinement, stateliness; *also* grandeur, lavishness, magnificence, ornateness, richness, splendor

el·e·gant \-gənt\ *adj* ♦ : marked by elegance; *also* : of a high grade or quality

♦ graceful, handsome, majestic, refined, stately, tasteful; *also* grand, lavish, luxurious, magnificent, ornate, rich, splendid; polished, sophisticated; classic, exquisite; fashionable, posh, smart, stylish *Ant* graceless, inelegant, tasteless, unhandsome choice, dainty, delicate, exquisite, rare, select — more at CHOICE

ele·giac \ˌe-lə-ˈjī-ək, -ˌak\ *adj* : of or relating to an elegy

el·e·gy \ˈe-lə-jē\ *n, pl* **-gies** ♦ : a song, poem, or speech expressing grief for one who is dead; *also* : a reflective poem usu. melancholy in tone

♦ dirge, lament, requiem, threnody — more at LAMENT

elem *abbr* elementary

el·e·ment \ˈe-lə-mənt\ *n* **1** *pl* : weather conditions; *esp* : severe weather ⟨boards exposed to the ∼s⟩ **2** : natural environment ⟨in her ∼⟩ **3** ♦ : a constituent part **4** *pl* ♦ : the simplest principles (as of an art or science) : RUDIMENTS **5** : a member of a mathematical set **6** : any of more than 100 fundamental substances that consist of atoms of only one kind

♦ [3] component, constituent, factor, ingredient, member; *also* detail, item, particular, point *Ant* whole *usu* **elements** ♦ [4] essentials, principles, rudiments; *also* ropes; precept, rule; basis, foundation, groundwork; nitty-gritty; introduction, preface; outline, summary

el·e·men·tal \ˌe-lə-ˈment-ᵊl\ *adj* ♦ : of, relating to, or being an element

♦ basic, elementary, essential, fundamental, rudimentary, underlying — more at ELEMENTARY

el·e·men·ta·ry \ˌe-lə-ˈmen-trē, -tə-rē\ *adj* **1** ♦ : of, relating to, or dealing with the simplest elements or principles of something : RUDIMENTARY **2** : of, relating to, or teaching the basic subjects of education

♦ basic, elemental, essential, fundamental, rudimentary, underlying; *also* primal, primary, prime *Ant* advanced

elementary particle *n* : a subatomic particle of matter and energy that does not appear to be made up of other smaller particles

elementary school *n* : a school usu. including the first six or the first eight grades

el·e·phant \ˈe-lə-fənt\ *n, pl* **elephants** *also* **elephant** : any of a family of huge thickset nearly hairless mammals that have the snout lengthened into a trunk and two long curving tusks of upper incisor ivory tusks

el·e·phan·ti·a·sis \ˌe-lə-fən-ˈtī-ə-səs\ *n, pl* **-a·ses** \-ˌsēz\ : enlargement and thickening of tissues in response esp. to infection by minute parasitic worms

el·e·phan·tine \ˌe-lə-ˈfan-ˌtēn, -ˌtīn, ˈe-lə-fən-\ *adj* **1** ♦ : of great size or strength **2** : CLUMSY, PONDEROUS

♦ enormous, giant, gigantic, ginormous, huge, jumbo, mammoth, monumental, titanic, tremendous, vast, whopping — more at HUGE

elev *abbr* elevation

el·e·vate \ˈe-lə-ˌvāt\ *vb* **-vat·ed; -vat·ing** **1** ♦ : to lift up : RAISE **2** ♦ : to raise in rank or status **3** ♦ : to raise the spirits of : ELATE

♦ [1] boost, hike, hoist, jack, lift, raise ♦ [2] advance, promote, raise, upgrade — more at PROMOTE ♦ [3] elate, enrapture, exhilarate, transport — more at ELATE

el·e·va·tion \ˌe-lə-ˈvā-shən\ *n* **1** : the height to which something is raised (as above sea level) **2** ♦ : a lifting up **3** ♦ : something (as a hill or swelling) that is elevated

♦ [2] advancement, ascent, promotion, rise, upgrade — more at ADVANCEMENT ♦ [3] eminence, height, highland, hill, mound, prominence, rise — more at HEIGHT

el·e·va·tor \ˈe-lə-ˌvā-tər\ *n* **1** : a cage or platform for conveying people or things from one level to another **2** : a building for storing and discharging grain **3** : a movable surface on an airplane to produce motion up or down

elev·en \i-ˈle-vən\ *n* **1** : one more than 10 **2** : the 11th in a set or series **3** : something having 11 units; *esp* : a football team — **eleven** *adj or pron* — **elev·enth** \-vənth\ *adj or n*

elf \ˈelf\ *n, pl* **elves** \ˈelvz\ ♦ : a mischievous fairy

♦ brownie, dwarf, fairy, fay, gnome, hobgoblin, leprechaun, pixie, puck, troll

ELF *abbr* extremely low frequency

elf·in \ˈel-fən\ *adj* **1** : of, relating to, or resembling an elf **2** ♦ : having an otherworldly or magical quality or charm

♦ alluring, attractive, charming, engaging, fascinating, fetching — more at FASCINATING

elf·ish \ˈel-fish\ *adj* ♦ : of, relating to, or like an elf; *also* : irresponsibly playful

♦ antic, coltish, fay, frisky, frolicsome, playful, sportive — more at PLAYFUL

elic·it \i-ˈli-sət\ *vb* ♦ : to draw out or forth

♦ evoke, raise

elide \i-ˈlīd\ *vb* **elid·ed; elid·ing** : to suppress or alter by elision

el·i·gi·ble \ˈe-lə-jə-bəl\ *adj* : qualified to participate or to be chosen — **el·i·gi·bil·i·ty** \ˌe-lə-jə-ˈbi-lə-tē\ *n* — **eligible** *n*

elim·i·nate \i-ˈli-mə-ˌnāt\ *vb* **-nat·ed; -nat·ing** [L *eliminatus*, pp. of *eliminare*, fr. *limen* threshold] **1** : REMOVE, ERADICATE **2** : to pass (wastes) from the body **3** : to leave out **4** ♦ : to bar from participation, enjoyment, consideration, or inclusion — **elim·i·na·tion** \-ˌli-mə-ˈnā-shən\ *n*

♦ ban, bar, count out, debar, except, exclude, rule out — more at EXCLUDE

eli·sion \i-ˈli-zhən\ *n* : the omission of a final or initial sound or a word; *esp* : the omission of an unstressed vowel or syllable in a verse to achieve a uniform rhythm

elite \ā-ˈlēt, ē-\ *n* [F *élite*] **1** ♦ : the choice part; *also* : a superior group **2** : a typewriter type providing 12 characters to the inch — **elite** *adj*

♦ best, choice, cream, elect, fat, flower, pick, prime; *also* aristocracy, upper class

elit·ism \-ˈlē-ˌti-zəm\ *n* : leadership or rule by an elite; *also* : advocacy of such elitism — **elit·ist** \-tist\ *n or adj*

elix·ir \i-ˈlik-sər\ *n* [ME, fr. ML, fr. Ar *al-iksīr* the elixir, fr. *al* the + *iksīr* elixir] **1** : a substance held capable of prolonging life indefinitely; *also* : PANACEA **2** : a sweetened alcoholic medicinal solution

Eliz·a·be·than \i-ˌli-zə-ˈbē-thən\ *adj* : of, relating to, or characteristic of Elizabeth I of England or her times

elk \ˈelk\ *n, pl* **elk** *or* **elks** **1** : MOOSE — used for one of the Old World **2** : a large gregarious deer of No. America, Europe, Asia, and northwestern Africa with curved antlers having many branches

ell *n* : an extension at right angles to a building

el·lipse \i-ˈlips, e-\ *n* : a closed curve of oval shape

el·lip·sis \i-ˈlip-səs, e-\ *n, pl* **el·lip·ses** \-ˌsēz\ **1** : omission from an expression of a word clearly implied **2** : marks (as . . .) to show omission

el·lip·soid \i-ˈlip-ˌsȯid, e-\ *n* : a surface all plane sections of which are circles or ellipses — **el·lip·soi·dal** \-ˌlip-ˈsȯid-ᵊl\ *also* **ellipsoid** *adj*

el·lip·ti·cal \i-ˈlip-ti-kəl, e-\ *or* **el·lip·tic** \-tik\ *adj* **1** : of, relating to, or shaped like an ellipse **2** : of, relating to, or marked by ellipsis — **el·lip·ti·cal·ly** \-ti-k(ə-)lē\ *adv*

elm \ˈelm\ *n* : any of a genus of large trees that have toothed leaves and nearly circular one-seeded winged fruits and are often grown as shade trees; *also* : the wood of an elm

El Ni·ño \el-ˈnē-nyō\ *n* : a flow of unusually warm Pacific Ocean water moving toward and along the west coast of So. America

el·o·cu·tion \ˌe-lə-ˈkyü-shən\ *n* : the art of effective public speaking — **el·o·cu·tion·ist** \-shə-nist\ *n*

elon·gate \i-ˈlȯŋ-ˌgāt\ *vb* **-gat·ed; -gat·ing** ♦ : to make or grow longer

♦ draw out, extend, lengthen, prolong, protract, stretch — more at EXTEND

elon·ga·tion \(ˌ)ē-ˌlȯŋ-ˈgā-shən\ *n* ♦ : the state of being elongated or lengthened; *also* : the process of growing or increasing in length

♦ extension, prolongation — more at EXTENSION

elope \i-'lōp\ *vb* **eloped; elop·ing** : to run away esp. to be married — **elope·ment** *n* — **elop·er** *n*

el·o·quence \-kwəns\ *n* ♦ : forceful and persuasive expression; *also* : the art or power of using such expression

♦ articulateness, persuasiveness, poetry, power, rhetoric; *also* expression, expressiveness

el·o·quent \'e-lə-kwənt\ *adj* **1** ♦ : having or showing clear and forceful expression ⟨an ∼ speaker⟩ **2** ♦ : clearly showing some feeling or meaning — **el·o·quent·ly** *adv*

♦ [1] articulate, fluent, well-spoken — more at ARTICULATE ♦ [2] expressive, meaning, meaningful, pregnant, significant, suggestive — more at EXPRESSIVE

¹**else** \'els\ *adv* **1** ♦ : in a different or additional manner or place or at a different or additional time ⟨where ∼ can we meet⟩ **2** : if not ⟨obey or ∼ you'll be sorry⟩

♦ differently, other, otherwise — more at OTHERWISE

²**else** *adj* ♦ : being another : OTHER; *esp* : being in addition ⟨what ∼ do you want⟩

♦ additional, another, farther, further, more, other — more at ADDITIONAL

else·where \-,hwer\ *adv* : in or to another place

elu·ci·date \i-'lü-sə-,dāt\ *vb* **-dat·ed; -dat·ing** ♦ : to make clear usu. by explanation

♦ clarify, clear (up), demonstrate, explain, explicate, expound, illuminate, illustrate, interpret, spell out — more at EXPLAIN

elu·ci·da·tion \-,lü-sə-'dā-shən\ *n* ♦ : the act, process, or means of elucidating

♦ clarification, explanation, explication, exposition, illumination, illustration, interpretation — more at EXPLANATION

elude \ē-'lüd\ *vb* **elud·ed; elud·ing** **1** ♦ : to avoid adroitly : EVADE **2** : to escape the notice of

♦ avoid, dodge, duck, escape, eschew, evade, shake, shirk, shun — more at ESCAPE

elu·sive \ē-'lü-siv\ *adj* ♦ : tending to elude : EVASIVE ⟨the solution remains ∼⟩ — **elu·sive·ly** *adv* — **elu·sive·ness** *n*

♦ evasive, fugitive, slippery; *also* cagey, shifty

el·ver \'el-vər\ *n* [alter. of *eelfare* migration of eels] : a young eel

elves *pl of* ELF

Ely·sian \-'li-zhən\ *adj* ♦ : of or relating to Elysium; *esp* : full of bliss or delight

♦ celestial, empyrean, heavenly, supernal — more at CELESTIAL

Ely·si·um \i-'li-zhē-əm, -zē-\ *n, pl* **-si·ums** *or* **-sia** \-zhē-ə, -zē-\ ♦ : a place or state of bliss or delight : PARADISE

♦ Eden, heaven, paradise, utopia — more at PARADISE

em \'em\ *n* : a length approximately the width of the letter *M*

EM *abbr* **1** electromagnetic **2** electron microscope **3** enlisted man

ema·ci·ate \i-'mā-shē-,āt\ *vb* **-at·ed; -at·ing** : to become or cause to become very thin — **ema·ci·a·tion** \-,mā-shē-'ā-shən, -sē-\ *n*

e–mail *or* **email** \'ē-,māl\ *n* **1** : a system for transmitting messages between computers on a network **2** : a message or messages sent and received through an e-mail system — **e–mail** *or* **email** *vb*

em·a·nate \'e-mə-,nāt\ *vb* **-nat·ed; -nat·ing** : to come out from a source — **em·a·na·tion** \,e-mə-'nā-shən\ *n*

eman·ci·pate \i-'man-sə-,pāt\ *vb* **-pat·ed; -pat·ing** ♦ : to set free — **eman·ci·pa·tor** \-'man-sə-,pā-tər\ *n*

♦ discharge, enfranchise, free, liberate, loose, loosen, manumit, release, spring, unbind, unchain, unfetter — more at FREE

eman·ci·pa·tion \-,man-sə-'pā-shən\ *n* ♦ : the act or process of emancipating

♦ enfranchisement, liberation, manumission — more at LIBERATION

emas·cu·late \i-'mas-kyù-,lāt\ *vb* **-lat·ed; -lat·ing** **1** : to deprive of virility : CASTRATE **2** : to deprive of strength or spirit : WEAKEN — **emas·cu·la·tion** \-,mas-kyù-'lā-shən\ *n*

em·balm \im-'bäm, -'bälm\ *vb* : to treat (a corpse) so as to protect from decay — **em·balm·er** *n*

em·bank·ment \im-'baŋk-mənt\ *n* ♦ : a raised structure (as of earth) to hold back water or carry a roadway

♦ dam, dike, levee — more at DAM

em·bar·go \im-'bär-gō\ *n, pl* **-goes** [Sp, fr. *embargar* to bar] ♦ : a prohibition on commerce — **embargo** *vb*

♦ ban, interdict, interdiction, prohibition, proscription, veto — more at PROHIBITION

em·bark \im-'bärk\ *vb* **1** : to put or go on board a ship or airplane **2** ♦ : to make a start — **em·bar·ka·tion** \,em-,bär-'kā-shən\ *n*

♦ begin, commence, enter, launch, open, start — more at BEGIN

em·bar·rass \im-'bar-əs\ *vb* **1** : CONFUSE, DISCONCERT **2** : to involve in financial difficulties **3** ♦ : to cause to experience self-conscious distress **4** ♦ : to hamper or impede the movement or freedom of movement of : HINDER, IMPEDE — **em·bar·rass·ing·ly** *adv*

♦ [3] abash, confound, confuse, discomfit, disconcert, discountenance, faze, fluster, mortify, rattle; *also* agitate, bother, disquiet, distress, disturb, perturb, unhinge, unsettle, upset ♦ [4] encumber, hamper, hinder, hold up, impede, inhibit, interfere with, obstruct, tie up — more at HAMPER

em·bar·rass·ing *adj* ♦ : causing embarrassment

♦ awkward, disconcerting, uncomfortable — more at AWKWARD

em·bar·rass·ment *n* **1** : something that embarrasses; *esp* : a burden that impedes action or renders it difficult **2** : the state of being embarrassed: as **a** ♦ : confusion or disturbance of mind **b** ♦ : difficulty in making progress or functioning (as from lack of resources or from disease)

♦ [2a] abashment, confusion, discomfiture, fluster, mortification; *also* agitation, bother, chagrin, discomfort, discomposure, dismay, disquiet, distress, disturbance, perturbation, uneasiness, upset ♦ [2b] bar, block, encumbrance, hindrance, inhibition, obstacle — more at ENCUMBRANCE

em·bas·sy \'em-bə-sē\ *n, pl* **-sies** **1** : a group of representatives headed by an ambassador **2** : the function, position, or mission of an ambassador **3** : the official residence and offices of an ambassador

em·bat·tle \im-'bat-ᵊl\ *vb* : to arrange in order for battle; *also* : FORTIFY

em·bat·tled *adj* **1** : engaged in battle, conflict, or controversy **2** : being a site of battle, conflict, or controversy **3** : characterized by conflict or controversy

em·bed \im-'bed\ *vb* **em·bed·ded; em·bed·ding** **1** ♦ : to enclose closely in a surrounding mass **2** : to make something an integral part of

♦ entrench, fix, implant, ingrain, lodge, root — more at ENTRENCH

em·bel·lish \im-'be-lish\ *vb* **1** ♦ : to make beautiful with ornamentation : DECORATE **2** ♦ : to heighten the attractiveness of by adding decorative or fanciful details

♦ [1, 2] adorn, array, beautify, decorate, dress, enrich, garnish, grace, ornament, trim — more at DECORATE ♦ [2] color (*or* colour), elaborate, embroider, exaggerate, magnify, pad, stretch — more at EMBROIDER

em·bel·lish·ment *n* ♦ : the act or process of embellishing; *also* : something serving to embellish

♦ adornment, caparison, decoration, frill, garnish, ornament, trim — more at DECORATION ♦ elaboration, exaggeration, hyperbole, overstatement, padding — more at EXAGGERATION

em·ber \'em-bər\ *n* 1 : a glowing or smoldering fragment from a fire 2 *pl* : the smoldering remains of a fire

em·bez·zle \im-'be-zəl\ *vb* -zled; -zling : to steal (as money) by falsifying records — **em·bez·zle·ment** *n* — **em·bez·zler** *n*

em·bit·ter \im-'bi-tər\ *vb* 1 : to arouse bitter feelings in 2 : to make bitter

em·bla·zon \im-'blāz-ᵊn\ *vb* 1 : to adorn with heraldic devices 2 : to display conspicuously

em·blem \'em-bləm\ *n* ♦ : something (as an object or picture) suggesting another object or an idea : SYMBOL — **em·blem·at·ic** \em-blə-'ma-tik\ *also* **em·blem·at·i·cal** \-ti-kəl\ *adj*

   ♦ hallmark, logo, symbol, trademark; *also* icon; badge, coat of arms, crest, insignia

em·bodi·ment \-di-mənt\ *n* 1 ♦ : a thing in which something (as a soul, idea, principle, or type) is embodied 2 : the act of embodying; *also* : the state of being embodied

   ♦ epitome, incarnation, manifestation, personification; *also* exemplification, incorporation, substantiation; essence, quintessence; archetype, exemplar, model, paradigm, pattern; acme, apex, culmination, peak, pinnacle, summit, zenith

em·body \im-'bä-dē\ *vb* **em·bod·ied**; **em·body·ing** 1 : INCARNATE 2 : to express in definite form 3 ♦ : to incorporate into a system or body 4 ♦ : to represent in human or animal form : PERSONIFY

   ♦ [3] assimilate, incorporate, integrate; *also* amalgamate, blend, combine, commingle, fuse, intermingle, merge, mingle ♦ [4] epitomize, manifest, materialize, personify, substantiate; *also* actualize, realize; symbolize; exemplify, illustrate

em·bold·en \im-'bōl-dən\ *vb* ♦ : to inspire with courage

   ♦ buoy (up), cheer, comfort, encourage, hearten, inspire, steel — more at ENCOURAGE

em·bo·lism \'em-bə-ˌli-zəm\ *n* : the obstruction of a blood vessel by a foreign or abnormal particle

em·bon·point \äⁿ-bōⁿ-'pwaⁿ\ *n* [F] : plumpness of person : STOUTNESS

em·boss \im-'bäs, -'bós\ *vb* : to ornament with raised work

em·bou·chure \'äm-bù-ˌshùr, ˌäm-bù-'shùr\ *n* [F, ultim. fr. *bouche* mouth] : the position and use of the lips, tongue, and teeth in playing a wind instrument

em·bow·er \im-'baù-(ə-)r\ *vb* : to shelter or enclose in a bower

¹**em·brace** \im-'brās\ *vb* **em·braced**; **em·brac·ing** 1 ♦ : to clasp in the arms; *also* : CHERISH, LOVE 2 : to surround or close in 3 ♦ : to take up esp. readily or gladly : ADOPT ⟨*embraced* the cause⟩; *also* : WELCOME ⟨*embraced* the opportunity⟩ 4 ♦ : to take in or include as a part of a whole 5 : to participate in an embrace

   ♦ [1] caress, clasp, enfold, grasp, hug; *also* cradle, grip, hold; encircle, entwine, envelop; fold, lock, twine, wrap; cuddle, fondle, nestle, nuzzle, pat, pet, snuggle, stroke ♦ [3] adopt, borrow, take up — more at ADOPT ♦ [4] carry, comprehend, contain, encompass, entail, include, involve, number, take in — more at INCLUDE

²**embrace** *n* : an encircling with the arms

em·bra·sure \im-'brā-zhər\ *n* 1 : an opening in a wall through which a cannon is fired 2 : a recess of a door or window

em·bro·ca·tion \ˌem-brə-'kā-shən\ *n* : LINIMENT

em·broi·der \im-'bròi-dər\ *vb* 1 : to ornament with or do needlework 2 ♦ : to elaborate with exaggerated detail

   ♦ color (*or* colour), elaborate, embellish, exaggerate, magnify, stretch; *also* amplify, enhance, enlarge (upon), expand, flesh (out)

em·broi·dery \im-'bròi-də-rē\ *n, pl* -der·ies 1 : the forming of decorative designs with needlework 2 : something embroidered

em·broil \im-'bròil\ *vb* 1 : to throw into confusion or disorder 2 : to involve in conflict or difficulties ⟨∼ed in a dispute⟩ — **em·broil·ment** *n*

em·bryo \'em-brē-ˌō\ *n, pl* **embryos** : a living thing in its earliest stages of development — **em·bry·on·ic** \ˌem-brē-'ä-nik\ *adj*

em·bry·ol·o·gy \ˌem-brē-'ä-lə-jē\ *n* : a branch of biology dealing with embryos and their development — **em·bry·o·log·i·cal** \-brē-ə-'lä-ji-kəl\ *adj* — **em·bry·ol·o·gist** \-brē-'ä-lə-jist\ *n*

em·cee \ˌem-'sē\ *n* : MASTER OF CEREMONIES — **emcee** *vb*

emend \ē-'mend\ *vb* ♦ : to correct usu. by altering the text of — **emen·da·tion** \ˌē-ˌmen-'dā-shən\ *n*

   ♦ amend, correct, debug, rectify, reform, remedy — more at CORRECT

emer *abbr* emeritus

¹**em·er·ald** \'em-rəld, 'e-mə-\ *n* : a green beryl prized as a gem

²**emerald** *adj* : brightly or richly green

emerge \i-'mərj\ *vb* **emerged**; **emerg·ing** ♦ : to rise, come forth, or come out into view — **emer·gence** \-'mər-jəns\ *n* — **emer·gent** \-jənt\ *adj*

   ♦ arise, crop, materialize, spring, surface — more at ARISE

emer·gen·cy \i-'mər-jən-sē\ *n, pl* -cies ♦ : an unforeseen event or condition requiring prompt action

   ♦ clutch, crisis, crunch, fix, hole, jam; *also* climax, landmark, milestone, turning point; predicament

emergency room *n* : a hospital room for receiving and treating persons needing immediate medical care

emer·i·ta \i-'mer-ə-tə\ *adj* : EMERITUS — used of a woman

emer·i·tus \i-'mer-ə-təs\ *adj* [L] : retired from active duty ⟨professor ∼⟩

em·ery \'e-mə-rē\ *n, pl* **em·er·ies** : a dark granular mineral consisting primarily of corundum and used as an abrasive

emet·ic \i-'me-tik\ *n* : an agent that induces vomiting — **emetic** *adj*

emf *n* [electromotive force] : POTENTIAL DIFFERENCE

em·i·grant \'mi-grənt\ *n* ♦ : one who emigrates

   ♦ émigré, immigrant, migrant, settler; *also* defector, evacuee, exile, expatriate, refugee

em·i·grate \'e-mə-ˌgrāt\ *vb* -grat·ed; -grat·ing : to leave a place (as a country) to settle elsewhere — **em·i·gra·tion** \ˌe-mə-'grā-shən\ *n*

émi·gré *also* **emi·gré** \'e-mi-ˌgrā, ˌe-mi-'grā\ *n* [F] ♦ : a person who emigrates esp. because of political conditions

   ♦ emigrant, evacuee, exile, expatriate, refugee; *also* alien, fugitive

em·i·nence \'e-mə-nəns\ *n* 1 ♦ : high rank or position; *also* : a person of high rank or attainments 2 ♦ : a lofty place

   ♦ [1] distinction, dominance, preeminence, superiority; *also* celebrity, fame, glory, honor (*or* honour), renown, reputation, repute; authority, greatness, influence, power, weight ♦ [2] elevation, height, highland, hill, mound, prominence, rise — more at HEIGHT

em·i·nent \'e-mə-nənt\ *adj* 1 : CONSPICUOUS, EVIDENT 2 ♦ : exhibiting eminence esp. in standing above others in some quality or position : DISTINGUISHED, PROMINENT — **em·i·nent·ly** *adv*

   ♦ distinguished, illustrious, noble, notable, noteworthy, outstanding, preeminent, prestigious, prominent, superior; *also* celebrated, famed, famous, glorious, honored, renowned, reputable

eminent domain *n* : a right of a government to take private property for public use

emir *or* **amir** \ə-'mir, ā-\ *n* [Ar *amīr* commander] : a ruler, chief, or commander in Islamic countries — **emir·ate** \'e-mər-ət\ *n*

em·is·sary \'e-mə-ˌser-ē\ *n, pl* -sar·ies 1 ♦ : one designated as the agent of another 2 : a secret agent

   ♦ ambassador, delegate, envoy, legate, minister, representative — more at AMBASSADOR

emis·sion \ē-'mi-shən\ *n* : something emitted; *esp* : substances discharged into the air

emit \ē-'mit\ *vb* **emit·ted**; **emit·ting** 1 ♦ : to give off or out ⟨∼ light⟩; *also* : EJECT 2 : EXPRESS, UTTER — **emit·ter** *n*

♦ cast, discharge, eject, exhale, expel, issue, release, shoot, vent

emo·ji \ē-ˈmō-jē\ *n, pl* **emoji** *or* **emo·jis** [Jp, fr. *e* picture + *moji* letter, character] : any of various small images, symbols, or icons used in text fields in electronic communications to express something (as an emotion) without using words

emol·lient \i-ˈmäl-yənt\ *adj* : making soft or supple; *also* : soothing esp. to the skin or mucous membrane — **emol·lient** *n*

emol·u·ment \i-ˈmäl-yə-mənt\ *n* [ME, fr. L *emolumentum* advantage, fr. *emolere* to produce by grinding] ♦ : the product (as salary or fees) of an employment

♦ hire, pay, payment, salary, stipend, wage — more at WAGE

emote \i-ˈmōt\ *vb* **emot·ed; emot·ing** : to give expression to emotion in or as if in a play

emo·ti·con \i-ˈmō-ti-ˌkän\ *n* : a group of keyboard characters (as :-)) that often represents a facial expression and that is used esp. in electronic communications

emo·tion \i-ˈmō-shən\ *n* ♦ : a usu. intense feeling (as of love, hate, or despair)

♦ feeling, passion, sentiment — more at FEELING ♦ ardor, fervency, fervor, heat, intensity, passion, vehemence, warmth — more at ARDOR

emo·tion·al \-shə-nəl\ *adj* **1** ♦ : of or relating to emotion **2** ♦ : dominated by or prone to emotion **3** ♦ : appealing to or arousing emotion **4** ♦ : markedly aroused or agitated in feeling or sensibilities — **emo·tion·al·ly** *adv*

♦ [2] demonstrative, effusive, uninhibited, unreserved, unrestrained — more at DEMONSTRATIVE ♦ [3] affecting, impressive, moving, poignant, stirring, touching — more at MOVING ♦ [4] ardent, burning, charged, fervent, fiery, impassioned, passionate, red-hot, vehement — more at FERVENT

emot·ive \i-ˈmō-tiv\ *adj* **1** : of or relating to the emotions **2** : appealing to or expressing emotion

emp *abbr* emperor; empress

empanel *var of* IMPANEL

em·pa·thy \ˈem-pə-thē\ *n* : the experiencing as one's own of the feelings of another; *also* : the capacity for this — **em·path·ic** \em-ˈpa-thik\ *adj*

em·pen·nage \ˌäm-pə-ˈnäzh, ˌem-\ *n* [F] : the tail assembly of an airplane

em·per·or \ˈem-pər-ər\ *n* : the sovereign male ruler of an empire

em·pha·sis \ˈem-fə-səs\ *n, pl* **-pha·ses** \-ˌsēz\ ♦ : a forcefulness of expression that gives special significance or prominence (as to a syllable in speaking or to a phase of action)

♦ accent, accentuation, stress, weight; *also* attention, concentration, consideration, heed, note, regard

em·pha·sise *Brit var of* EMPHASIZE

em·pha·size \-ˌsīz\ *vb* **-sized; -siz·ing** ♦ : to place emphasis on : STRESS

♦ accent, accentuate, feature, highlight, play, point, stress, underline, underscore; *also* focus, identify, pinpoint, spotlight *Ant* play (down)

em·phat·ic \im-ˈfa-tik, em-\ *adj* **1** ♦ : uttered with emphasis **2** ♦ : attracting special attention ⟨an ∼ refusal⟩ — **em·phat·i·cal·ly** \-ˈti-k(ə-)lē\ *adv*

♦ [1] aggressive, assertive, dynamic, energetic, forceful, resounding, strenuous, vehement, vigorous; *also* decided, insistent, marked, pointed *Ant* unemphatic ♦ [2] bold, catchy, conspicuous, marked, noticeable, prominent, pronounced, remarkable, striking — more at NOTICEABLE

em·phy·se·ma \ˌem-fə-ˈzē-mə, -ˈsē-\ *n* : a condition marked esp. by abnormal expansion of the air spaces of the lungs and often by impairment of heart action

em·pire \ˈem-ˌpī(-ə)r\ *n* **1** : a large state or a group of states under a single sovereign who is usu. an emperor; *also* : something resembling a political empire **2** : imperial sovereignty or dominion

em·pir·i·cal \im-ˈpir-i-kəl\ *also* **em·pir·ic** \-ik\ *adj* : based on observation; *also* : subject to verification by observation or experiment ⟨∼ laws⟩ — **em·pir·i·cal·ly** \-i-k(ə-)lē\ *adv*

em·pir·i·cism \im-ˈpir-ə-ˌsi-zəm, em-\ *n* : the practice of relying on observation and experiment esp. in the natural sciences — **em·pir·i·cist** \-sist\ *n*

em·place·ment \im-ˈplās-mənt\ *n* **1** : a prepared position for weapons or military equipment **2** : PLACEMENT

¹**em·ploy** \im-ˈplȯi\ *vb* **1** ♦ : to make use of **2** ♦ : to use the services of **3** : OCCUPY, DEVOTE — **em·ploy·er** *n*

♦ [1] apply, exercise, exploit, harness, operate, use, utilize — more at USE ♦ [2] engage, hire, retain, take on; *also* recruit, sign on *Ant* discharge, dismiss, fire, sack

²**em·ploy** \im-ˈplȯi; ˈim-ˌplȯi, ˈem-\ *n* ♦ : the state of being employed : EMPLOYMENT

♦ employment, engagement, hire — more at HIRE

em·ploy·ee *also* **em·ploye** \im-ˌplȯi-ˈē, ˌem-; im-ˈplȯi-ˌē, em-\ *n* ♦ : a person who works for another

♦ hand, hireling, jobholder, worker; *also* assistant, cog, flunky, subordinate, underling *Ant* employer

em·ploy·ment \im-ˈplȯi-mənt\ *n* **1** ♦ : activity in which one engages or is employed : OCCUPATION **2** ♦ : the act of employing : the condition of being employed

♦ [1] calling, line, occupation, profession, trade, vocation, work — more at OCCUPATION ♦ [2] application, exercise, operation, play, use — more at USE ♦ [2] employ, engagement, hire — more at HIRE

em·po·ri·um \im-ˈpȯr-ē-əm, em-\ *n, pl* **-ri·ums** *also* **-ria** \-ē-ə\ [L, fr. Gk *emporion*, fr. *emporos* traveler, trader] ♦ : a commercial center; *esp* : a store carrying varied articles

♦ shop, store — more at SHOP

em·pow·er \im-ˈpau̇(-ə)r\ *vb* ♦ : to give authority or power to; *also* : ENABLE — **em·pow·er·ment** \-mənt\ *n*

♦ accredit, authorize, certify, commission, enable, invest, license, qualify — more at AUTHORIZE

em·press \ˈem-prəs\ *n* **1** : the wife or widow of an emperor **2** : a woman who is the sovereign ruler of an empire

emp·ti·ness *n* ♦ : the quality or state of being empty

♦ blank, blankness, vacancy, vacuity, void — more at VACANCY

¹**emp·ty** \ˈemp-tē\ *adj* **emp·ti·er; -est** [ME, fr. OE *ǣmettig* unoccupied, fr. *ǣmetta* leisure] **1** ♦ : containing nothing **2** : UNOCCUPIED, UNINHABITED **3** ♦ : lacking value, force, sense, or purpose **4** ♦ : feeling the need for food

♦ [1] bare, blank, devoid, stark, vacant, void; *also* barren, hollow *Ant* full ♦ [3] meaningless, pointless, senseless, worthless — more at MEANINGLESS ♦ [3] fruitless, futile, ineffective, unproductive, unsuccessful — more at FUTILE ♦ [4] famished, hungry — more at HUNGRY

²**empty** *vb* **emp·tied; emp·ty·ing** **1** : to make or become empty **2** ♦ : to discharge contents; *also* : to remove from what holds or encloses

♦ clear, evacuate, vacate, void; *also* deplete, drain, eliminate, exhaust *Ant* fill, load

³**empty** *n, pl* **empties** : an empty bottle or can

emp·ty–hand·ed \ˌemp-tē-ˈhan-dəd\ *adj* **1** : having or bringing nothing **2** : having acquired or gained nothing

¹**em·py·re·an** \ˌem-ˌpī-ˈrē-ən, -pə-\ *n* **1** : the highest heaven; *also* : FIRMAMENT **2** : an ideal place or state

²**empyrean** *adj* ♦ : of or relating to the empyrean

♦ celestial, Elysian, heavenly, supernal — more at CELESTIAL

EMT \ˌē-(ˌ)em-ˈtē\ *n* [emergency *m*edical *t*echnician] : a specially trained medical technician certified to provide basic medical services before and during transport to a hospital

¹**emu** \ˈē-myü, -mü\ *n* : a swift-running flightless Australian bird smaller than the related ostrich

²**emu** *abbr* electromagnetic unit

em·u·late \ˈem-yü-ˌlāt\ *vb* **-lat·ed; -lat·ing** ♦ : to strive to equal or excel : IMITATE — **em·u·la·tion** \ˌem-yü-ˈlā-shən\ *n* — **em·u·lous** \ˈem-yü-ləs\ *adj*

♦ ape, copy, imitate, mime, mimic — more at IMITATE

emul·si·fi·er \i-'məl-sə-,fī(-ə)r\ *n* : a substance (as a soap) that helps to form and stabilize an emulsion

emul·si·fy \-,fī\ *vb* **-fied; -fy·ing** : to disperse (as an oil) in an emulsion — **emul·si·fi·ca·tion** \i-,məl-sə-fə-'kā-shən\ *n*

emul·sion \i-'məl-shən\ *n* **1** : a mixture of mutually insoluble liquids in which one is dispersed in droplets throughout the other ⟨an ∼ of oil in water⟩ **2** : a light-sensitive coating on photographic film or paper

en \'en\ *n* : a length approximately half the width of the letter *M*

¹-en *also* **-n** *adj suffix* : made of : consisting of ⟨earth*en*⟩

²-en *vb suffix* **1** : become or cause to be ⟨sharp*en*⟩ **2** : cause or come to have ⟨length*en*⟩

en·able \i-'nā-bəl\ *vb* **en·abled; en·abling 1** ♦ : to make able or feasible **2** ♦ : to give legal power, capacity, or sanction to

♦ [1] allow, let, permit; *also* fit, prepare, qualify, ready **Ant** prevent ♦ [2] accredit, authorize, certify, commission, empower, invest, license, qualify — more at AUTHORIZE

en·act \i-'nakt\ *vb* **1** ♦ : to make into law **2** : to act out

♦ lay down, legislate, make, pass; *also* bring about, effect **Ant** repeal, rescind, revoke

en·act·ment *n* ♦ : the act of enacting; *also* : something (as a law) that has been enacted

♦ act, law, ordinance, statute — more at LAW ♦ accomplishment, achievement, commission, discharge, execution, fulfillment, implementation, performance — more at COMMISSION

enam·el \i-'na-məl\ *n* **1** : a glasslike substance used to coat the surface of metal or pottery **2** : the hard outer layer of a tooth **3** : a usu. glossy paint that forms a hard coat — **enamel** *vb*

enam·el·ware \-,wer\ *n* : metal utensils coated with enamel

en·am·or *or Can and Brit* **en·am·our** \i-'na-mər\ *vb* : to inflame with love

en bloc \äⁿ-'bläk\ *adv or adj* : as a whole : in a mass

enc *or* **encl** *abbr* enclosure

en·camp \in-'kamp\ *vb* : to make camp

en·camp·ment *n* ♦ : the place where a group (as a body of troops) is encamped

♦ bivouac, camp — more at CAMP

en·cap·su·late \in-'kap-sə-,lāt\ *vb* **-lat·ed; -lat·ing 1** : to encase or become encased in a capsule **2** ♦ : to give an abstract of : SUMMARIZE

♦ abstract, digest, outline, recapitulate, sum up, summarize, wrap up — more at SUMMARIZE

en·cap·su·la·tion \-,kap-sə-'lā-shən\ *n* ♦ : an act, instance, or result of encapsulating

♦ abstract, digest, outline, précis, résumé (*or* resume), summary, synopsis, wrap-up — more at SUMMARY

en·case \in-'kās\ *vb* ♦ : to enclose in or as if in a case — **en·case·ment** \-'kā-smənt\ *n*

♦ cage, coop up, corral, enclose, fence, hedge, hem, house, pen, wall — more at ENCLOSE

-ence *n suffix* **1** : action or process ⟨emerg*ence*⟩ : instance of an action or process ⟨refer*ence*⟩ **2** : quality or state ⟨depend*ence*⟩

en·ceinte \äⁿn-'sant\ *adj* : PREGNANT 1

en·ceph·a·li·tis \in-,se-fə-'lī-təs\ *n, pl* **-lit·i·des** \-'li-tə-,dēz\ : inflammation of the brain — **en·ceph·a·lit·ic** \-'li-tik\ *adj*

en·ceph·a·lop·a·thy \in-,se-fə-'lä-pə-thē\ *n, pl* **-thies** : a disease of the brain

en·chain \in-'chān\ *vb* ♦ : to bind or hold with or as if with chains : FETTER, CHAIN

♦ bind, chain, fetter, handcuff, manacle, shackle, trammel

en·chant \in-'chant\ *vb* **1** ♦ : to influence by or as if by charms and incantation : BEWITCH **2** ♦ : to attract and move deeply — **en·chant·ing·ly** *adv*

♦ [1] allure, beguile, bewitch, captivate, charm, fascinate, wile — more at CHARM ♦ [2] arrest, enthrall, fascinate, grip, hypnotize, mesmerize — more at ENTHRALL

en·chant·er *n* ♦ : one that enchants

♦ conjurer, magician, necromancer, sorcerer, voodoo, witch, wizard — more at MAGICIAN

en·chant·ment *n* **1** ♦ : the act or art of enchanting; *also* : the quality or state of being enchanted **2** ♦ : something that enchants

♦ [1] allure, appeal, attractiveness, captivation, charisma, charm, fascination, glamour, magic, magnetism — more at CHARM ♦ [2] bewitchment, charm, conjuration, incantation, spell — more at SPELL

en·chant·ress \-'chan-trəs\ *n* **1** ♦ : a woman who practices magic **2** ♦ : a fascinating or beautiful woman

♦ [1] hag, hex, witch — more at WITCH ♦ [2] beauty, fox, goddess, knockout, queen — more at BEAUTY

en·chi·la·da \,en-chə-'lä-də\ *n* : a rolled filled tortilla covered with chili sauce and usu. baked

en·ci·pher \in-'sī-fər, en-\ *vb* : ENCODE

en·cir·cle \in-'sər-kəl\ *vb* ♦ : to pass completely around : SURROUND — **en·cir·cle·ment** *n*

♦ circle, circumnavigate, coil, compass, enclose, encompass, girdle, ring, round, surround

en·clave \'en-,klāv; 'än-,klāv\ *n* : a distinct territorial, cultural, or social unit enclosed within or as if within foreign territory

en·close \in-'klōz\ *vb* **1** ♦ : to shut up or in; *esp* : to surround with a fence **2** : to include along with something else in a parcel or envelope ⟨∼ a check⟩ — **en·clo·sure** \-'klō-zhər\ *n*

♦ cage, coop up, corral, encase, envelop, fence, hedge, hem, pen; *also* bound, confine, contain, limit, restrict circle, encircle, encompass, ring, surround — more at SURROUND

en·code \in-'kōd, en-\ *vb* : to convert (a message) into code

en·co·mi·um \en-'kō-mē-əm\ *n, pl* **-mi·ums** *also* **-mia** \-mē-ə\ ♦ : high or glowing praise

♦ accolade, citation, commendation, eulogy, homage, paean, panegyric, salutation, tribute; *also* award, decoration, honor, prize

en·com·pass \in-'kəm-pəs\ *vb* **1** ♦ : to form a circle about : ENCIRCLE **2** : to enclose or enfold completely with or as if with a covering : ENVELOP, INCLUDE **3** ♦ : to contain or hold within a total scope, significance, or amount

♦ [1] circle, encircle, enclose, ring, surround — more at SURROUND ♦ [3] carry, comprehend, contain, embrace, entail, include, involve, number, take in — more at INCLUDE

en·core \'än-,kȯr\ *n* **1** : a demand for repetition or reappearance **2** : a further performance or appearance demanded by an audience **3** : a second achievement that usu. surpasses the first — **encore** *vb*

¹en·coun·ter \in-'kaȯn-tər\ *vb* **1** ♦ : to meet as an enemy : FIGHT **2** ♦ : to meet usu. unexpectedly

♦ chance, find, happen (on *or* upon), hit, meet, stumble — more at HAPPEN (on *or* upon)

²encounter *n* **1** ♦ : a hostile meeting : COMBAT **2** : a chance meeting **3** : an experience shared with another ⟨a romantic ∼⟩

♦ brush, run-in, scrape, skirmish; *also* argument, fight, quarrel

en·cour·age \in-'kər-ij\ *vb* **-aged; -ag·ing 1** ♦ : to inspire with courage and hope **2** ♦ : to spur on : STIMULATE, INCITE; *also* : to attempt to persuade **3** ♦ : to give help or patronage to : FOSTER

♦ [1] buoy (up), cheer, comfort, embolden, hearten, inspire, steel; *also* animate, enliven, invigorate; provoke, quicken, rally, stimulate, stir **Ant** daunt, discourage, dishearten, dispirit ♦ [2] arouse, excite, fire, incite, instigate, move, pique, provoke, stimulate, stir ♦ [2] egg on, exhort, goad, press, prod, prompt, urge — more at URGE ♦ [3] advance, cultivate, forward, foster, further, nourish, nurture, promote — more at FOSTER

en·cour·age·ment *n* ♦ : the act of encouraging : the state of being encouraged; *also* : something that encourages
  ♦ boost, goad, impetus, impulse, incentive, instigation, motivation, provocation, spur, stimulus

en·cour·ag·ing \-i-jiŋ, -ri-jiŋ\ *adj* ♦ : giving hope or promise — **en·cour·ag·ing·ly** *adv*
  ♦ auspicious, bright, fair, golden, heartening, hopeful, likely, promising, propitious, rosy, upbeat — more at HOPEFUL ♦ comforting, gratifying, heartening, heartwarming, rewarding, satisfying — more at HEARTWARMING

en·croach \in-ˈkrōch\ *vb* [ME *encrochen* to seize, fr. AF *encrocher*, fr. *croche* hook] : to enter gradually or stealthily upon another's property or rights — **en·croach·er** *n* — **en·croach·ment** *n*

en·crust *also* **in·crust** \in-ˈkrəst\ *vb* : to provide with or form a crust

en·crus·ta·tion \(ˌ)in-ˌkrəs-ˈtā-shən, ˌen-\ *var of* INCRUSTATION

en·crypt \in-ˈkript, en-\ *vb* : to change (information) from one form to another esp. to hide its meaning

en·cum·ber \in-ˈkəm-bər\ *vb* **1** ♦ : to weigh down : BURDEN **2** ♦ : to hinder the function or activity of
  ♦ [1] burden, load, lumber, saddle, weight — more at LOAD ♦ [2] hamper, hinder, hobble, hold back, hold up, impede, inhibit, interfere with, obstruct, tie up — more at HAMPER

en·cum·brance \-brəns\ *n* **1** ♦ : something that encumbers **2** : a claim (as a mortgage) against property
  ♦ bar, block, hindrance, inhibition, obstacle; *also* catch, hitch, rub, snag

ency *or* **encyc** *abbr* encyclopedia

-en·cy *n suffix* : quality or state ⟨despond*ency*⟩

¹**en·cyc·li·cal** \in-ˈsi-kli-kəl, en-\ *adj* : addressed to all the individuals of a group

²**encyclical** *n* : an encyclical letter; *esp* : a papal letter to the bishops of the church

en·cy·clo·pe·dia *also* **en·cy·clo·pae·dia** \in-ˌsī-klə-ˈpē-dē-ə\ *n* [ML *encyclopaedia* course of general education, fr. Gk *enkyklios paideia* general education] : a work treating the various branches of learning

en·cy·clo·pe·dic *also* **en·cy·clo·pae·dic** \-ˈpē-dik\ *adj* ♦ : of, relating to, or suggestive of an encyclopedia or its methods of treating or covering a subject
  ♦ compendious, complete, comprehensive, full, global, inclusive, omnibus, panoramic, universal; *also* broad, catholic, extensive, far-reaching, general, overall, sweeping, vast, wide

en·cyst \in-ˈsist, en-\ *vb* : to form or become enclosed in a cyst — **en·cyst·ment** *n*

¹**end** \ˈend\ *n* **1** ♦ : the part of an area that lies at the boundary; *also* : a point which marks the extent or limit of something or at which something ceases to exist **2** ♦ : a ceasing of a course (as of action or activity); *also* : DEATH **3** : the ultimate state; *also* : RESULT, ISSUE **4** ♦ : something incomplete, fragmentary, or undersized : REMNANT **5** ♦ : an outcome worked toward : PURPOSE, OBJECTIVE **6** : a player stationed at the extremity of a line (as in football) **7** : a share, operation, or aspect of an undertaking
  ♦ [1] bound, boundary, ceiling, confines, extent, limit, limitation, line, termination — more at LIMIT ♦ [2] death, decease, demise, doom, passing, quietus — more at DEATH ♦ [2] cessation, close, closure, conclusion, finish, halt, lapse, shutdown, stop, stoppage, termination *Ant* continuation ♦ [4] fag end, leftover, remainder, remnant, scrap — more at SCRAP ♦ [5] aim, ambition, aspiration, goal, intent, mark, meaning, object, objective, plan, purpose — more at GOAL

²**end** *vb* **1** ♦ : to bring or come to an end **2** : DESTROY; *also* : DIE **3** : to form or be at the end of
  ♦ close, conclude, finish, round, terminate, wind up, wrap up — more at CLOSE ♦ break, break off, cease,

cut, desist, discontinue, drop, halt, knock off, layoff, leave off, quit, shut off, stop — more at STOP

en·dan·ger \in-ˈdān-jər\ *vb* ♦ : to bring into danger; *also* : to create danger
  ♦ compromise, gamble with, hazard, imperil, jeopardize, menace, risk, venture

en·dan·gered *adj* : being or relating to an endangered species

endangered species *n* : a species threatened with extinction

en·dear \in-ˈdir\ *vb* : to cause to become beloved or admired

endearing *adj* ♦ : arousing affection, tenderness, or admiration
  ♦ adorable, darling, dear, lovable, precious, sweet, winning — more at LOVABLE

en·dear·ment \-mənt\ *n* : a sign of affection : CARESS

¹**en·deav·or** *or Can and Brit* **en·deav·our** \in-ˈde-vər\ *vb* ♦ : to attempt (as the fulfillment of an obligation) by exertion of effort; *also* : to work with set purpose
  ♦ assay, attempt, essay, seek, strive, try — more at ATTEMPT

²**endeavor** *or Can and Brit* **endeavour** *n* ♦ : serious determined effort; *also* : activity directed toward a goal
  ♦ attempt, bid, crack, essay, fling, go, pass, shot, stab, trial, try, whack, whirl — more at ATTEMPT

en·dem·ic \en-ˈde-mik, in-\ *adj* ♦ : restricted to a particular place ⟨~ plants⟩ ⟨an ~ disease⟩ — **endemic** *n*
  ♦ aboriginal, born, indigenous, native — more at NATIVE

end·ing \ˈen-diŋ\ *n* **1** ♦ : something that forms an end **2** : SUFFIX
  ♦ close, conclusion, consummation, end, finale, finis, finish, windup — more at FINALE

en·dive \ˈen-ˌdīv\ *n* **1** : an herb related to chicory and grown as a salad plant **2** : the blanched shoot of chicory

end·less \ˈend-ləs\ *adj* **1** ♦ : having or seeming to have no end : ETERNAL **2** : united at the ends : CONTINUOUS ⟨an ~ belt⟩ — **end·less·ly** *adv*
  ♦ boundless, illimitable, immeasurable, indefinite, infinite, limitless, measureless, unbounded, unfathomable, unlimited — more at INFINITE ♦ ceaseless, dateless, deathless, eternal, everlasting, immortal, permanent, perpetual, undying, unending — more at EVERLASTING

end·most \-ˌmōst\ *adj* : situated at the very end

end·note \-ˌnōt\ *n* : a note placed at the end of a text

en·do·crine \ˈen-də-krən, -ˌkrīn, -ˌkrēn\ *adj* : producing secretions that are distributed by way of the bloodstream ⟨~ glands⟩ — **endocrine** *n* — **en·do·cri·nol·o·gist** \-kri-ˈnä-lə-jist\ *n* — **en·do·cri·nol·o·gy** \-jē\ *n*

en·dog·e·nous \en-ˈdä-jə-nəs\ *adj* : caused or produced by factors inside the organism or system ⟨~ psychic depression⟩ — **en·dog·e·nous·ly** *adv*

en·do·me·tri·um \ˌen-dō-ˈmē-trē-əm\ *n, pl* **-tria** \-trē-ə\ : the mucous membrane lining the uterus — **en·do·me·tri·al** \-trē-əl\ *adj*

en·dor·phin \en-ˈdȯr-fən\ *n* : any of a group of endogenous morphinelike proteins found esp. in the brain

en·dorse *also* **in·dorse** \in-ˈdȯrs\ *vb* **en·dorsed; en·dors·ing** [ME *endosen*, fr. AF *endosser* to put on, don, write on the back of, fr. *dos* back, fr. L *dorsum*] **1** : to sign one's name on the back of (as a check) **2** ♦ : to express support or approval of publicly and definitely; *esp* : to recommend (as a product) usu. for financial compensation — **en·dorse·ment** *also* **in·dorse·ment** *n*
  ♦ advocate, back, champion, patronize, support — more at SUPPORT

en·do·scope \ˈen-də-ˌskōp\ *n* : an illuminated usu. fiber-optic instrument for visualizing the interior of a hollow organ or part (as the colon or esophagus) — **en·do·scop·ic** \ˌen-də-ˈskä-pik\ *adj* — **en·dos·co·py** \en-ˈdäs-kə-pē\ *n*

en·do·ther·mic \ˌen-də-ˈthər-mik\ *adj* : characterized by or formed with absorption of heat

en·dow \in-'daú\ vb **1** ♦ : to furnish with funds for support ⟨∼ a school⟩ **2** ♦ : to furnish with something freely or naturally ⟨∼ed with intellect⟩

♦ [1] finance, fund, subsidize; *also* establish, found, organize; bequeath, contribute, donate, subscribe, support; award, grant; back, promote, sponsor ♦ [2] invest; *also* equip, provide, supply

en·dow·ment n : something that is endowed: as **a** : the part of an institution's income derived from donations **b** ♦ : natural capacity, power, or ability

♦ aptitude, faculty, flair, genius, gift, knack, talent — more at TALENT

en·due \in-'dü, -'dyü\ vb **en·dued; en·du·ing** : PROVIDE, ENDOW

en·dur·able adj ♦ : capable of being borne or endured

♦ bearable, sufferable, supportable, sustainable, tolerable — more at BEARABLE

en·dur·ance \in-'dùr-əns, -'dyùr-\ n **1** ♦ : continuation in the same state : DURATION **2** : the ability to withstand hardship or stress : FORTITUDE

♦ continuance, continuation, duration, persistence, subsistence — more at CONTINUATION

en·dure \in-'dùr, -'dyùr\ vb **en·dured; en·dur·ing 1** ♦ : to continue in the same state : LAST, PERSIST **2** ♦ : to suffer firmly or patiently : BEAR **3** : TOLERATE

♦ [1] abide, continue, hold, keep up, last, persist, run on — more at CONTINUE ♦ [2] abide, bear, brook, countenance, meet, stand, stick out, stomach, support, sustain, take, tolerate — more at BEAR

enduring adj ♦ : existing or continuing a long while : LASTING

♦ abiding, ageless, continuing, dateless, eternal, everlasting, immortal, imperishable, lasting, perennial, perpetual, timeless, undying — more at ABIDING

end·ways \'end-,wāz\ adv or adj **1** : LENGTHWISE **2** : with the end forward **3** : on end

end·wise \-,wīz\ adv or adj : ENDWAYS

ENE abbr east-northeast

en·e·ma \'e-nə-mə\ n, pl **enemas** also **ene·ma·ta** \,e-nə-'mätə, 'e-nə-mə-tə\ : injection of liquid into the rectum; *also* : material so injected

en·e·my \'e-nə-mē\ n, pl **-mies** [ME enemi, fr. AF, fr. L inimicus, fr. in- not + amicus friend] ♦ : one that attacks or tries to harm another : FOE; *esp* : a military opponent

♦ adversary, antagonist, foe, opponent; *also* assailant, combatant, invader; competitor, rival **Ant** friend

en·er·get·ic \,e-nər-'je-tik\ adj ♦ : marked by energy : ACTIVE, VIGOROUS

♦ active, animated, jaunty, lively, peppy, spirited, sprightly, springy, vigorous, vital, vivacious

en·er·get·i·cal·ly \-ti-k(ə-)lē\ adv ♦ : in an energetic manner

♦ forcefully, powerfully, strongly, sturdily, vigorously — more at HARD

en·er·gise chiefly Brit var of ENERGIZE

en·er·gize \'e-nər-jīz\ vb **-gized; -giz·ing** ♦ : to give energy to

♦ animate, brace, enliven, fire, invigorate, jazz up, liven up, pep up, quicken, stimulate, vitalize, vivify, zip (up) — more at ANIMATE

en·er·gy \'e-nər-jē\ n, pl **-gies 1** : vigorous action : EFFORT **2** ♦ : capacity for action **3** ♦ : capacity for performing work **4** : usable power (as heat or electricity); *also* : the resources for producing such power

♦ [2] force, main, might, muscle, potency, power, strength, vigor (or vigour) — more at POWER ♦ [2, 3] force, main, might, muscle, potency, power, strength, vigor (or vigour) — more at POWER ♦ [3] dash, life, pep, vigor (or vigour), vim, vitality — more at VIGOR

energy level n : one of the stable states of constant energy that may be assumed by a physical system (as the electrons in an atom)

en·er·vate \'e-nər-,vāt\ vb **-vat·ed; -vat·ing** ♦ : to lessen the strength or vigor of : weaken in mind or body — **en·er·vat·ing·ly** \-,vā-tiŋ-lē\ adv — **en·er·va·tion** \,e-nər-'vā-shən\ n

♦ debilitate, enfeeble, prostrate, sap, soften, tire, waste, weaken — more at WEAKEN

en·er·vat·ed \'e-nər-,vāt-əd\ adj ♦ : lacking physical, mental, or moral vigor

♦ lackadaisical, languid, languorous, limp, listless, spiritless — more at LISTLESS

en·fee·ble \in-'fē-bəl\ vb **-bled; -bling** ♦ : to make feeble

♦ debilitate, enervate, prostrate, sap, soften, tire, waste, weaken — more at WEAKEN

en·fee·ble·ment n ♦ : the action of enfeebling; *also* : the quality or state of being enfeebled

♦ debility, delicacy, faintness, feebleness, frailty, infirmity, languor, lowness, weakness — more at WEAKNESS

en·fi·lade \'en-fə-,lād, -,läd\ n : gunfire directed along the length of an enemy battle line — **enfilade** vb

en·fold \in-'fōld\ vb **1** ♦ : to cover with or as if with folds : ENVELOP **2** ♦ : to clasp within the arms : EMBRACE

♦ [1] caress, clasp, embrace, grasp, hug — more at EMBRACE ♦ [2] enclose, encompass, enshroud, envelop, invest, lap, mantle, shroud, swathe, veil, wrap; *also* curtain, drape; encase; swaddle; blanket, overlay, overspread; camouflage, cloak, disguise, mask; circle, encircle, encompass

en·force \in-'fōrs\ vb **1** : COMPEL ⟨∼ obedience by threats⟩ **2** ♦ : to execute effectively ⟨∼ the law⟩ — **en·force·able** adj — **en·force·ment** n

♦ administer, apply, execute, implement; *also* effect, effectuate; discharge, fulfill, render; cite, invoke; enact, legislate; honor, observe; prosecute; promulgate

en·forc·er \in-'fōr-sər\ n : one that enforces; *esp* : an aggressive player (as in ice hockey) known for rough play

en·fran·chise \in-'fran-,chīz\ vb **-chised; -chis·ing 1** ♦ : to set free (as from slavery) **2** : to admit to the rights of citizenship; *also* : to grant the vote to

♦ discharge, emancipate, free, liberate, loose, loosen, manumit, release, spring, unbind, unchain, unfetter — more at FREE

en·fran·chise·ment \-,chīz-mənt, -chəz-\ n : the act or result of enfranchising: as **a** ♦ : the releasing from slavery or custody **b** ♦ : admission to citizenship and its rights

♦ [a] emancipation, liberation, manumission — more at LIBERATION ♦ [b] franchise, suffrage, vote — more at VOTE

eng abbr engine; engineer; engineering

Eng abbr England; English

en·gage \in-'gāj\ vb **en·gaged; en·gag·ing 1** ♦ : to bind (oneself) by a pledge to do something; *esp* : to bind by a pledge to marry **2** ♦ : to use the services of : EMPLOY, HIRE **3** ♦ : to attract and hold esp. by interesting; *also* : to cause to participate **4** : to commence or take part in a venture **5** ♦ : to bring or enter into conflict **6** : to connect or interlock with : MESH; *also* : to cause to mesh

♦ [1] commit, pledge, troth — more at PLEDGE ♦ [2] employ, hire, retain, take on — more at EMPLOY ♦ [3] absorb, busy, engross, enthrall, fascinate, grip, immerse, interest, intrigue, involve, occupy; *also* allure, attract, bewitch, captivate, charm, enchant ♦ [5] battle, encounter, face, meet, take on; *also* contend, fight, oppose

en·gaged \in-'gājd, en-\ adj **1** ♦ : involved in activity **2** : pledged to be married

♦ active, assiduous, busy, diligent, laborious, occupied, sedulous, working — more at BUSY

en·gage·ment \in-'gāj-mənt\ n **1** ♦ : an arrangement to meet or be present at a specified time and place **2** ♦ : a job or period of employment esp. as a performer **3** ♦ : a mutual promise to marry **4** : a hostile encounter

♦ [1] appointment, date, rendezvous, tryst; *also* arrangement; invitation; interview; get-together, meeting; call, visit; schedule ♦ [2] employ, employment, hire — more at HIRE ♦ [3] espousal, troth *Ant* disengagement

en·gag·ing *adj* ♦ : tending to draw favorable attention or interest : ATTRACTIVE — **en·gag·ing·ly** *adv*

♦ alluring, attractive, captivating, charming, fascinating, fetching, glamorous ♦ absorbing, engrossing, enthralling, fascinating, interesting, intriguing — more at INTERESTING

en·gen·der \in-'jen-dər\ *vb* 1 : BEGET 2 ♦ : to cause to exist or to develop : CREATE

♦ create, generate, induce, make, produce, spawn — more at GENERATE

en·gine \'en-jən\ *n* [ME *engin*, fr. OF, fr. L *ingenium* natural disposition, talent] 1 : a mechanical device 2 : a machine for converting energy into mechanical motion 3 : LOCOMOTIVE 4 : software that performs a fundamental function esp. of a larger program — **en·gine·less** *adj*

¹**en·gi·neer** \,en-jə-'nir\ *n* 1 : a member of a military unit specializing in engineering work 2 : a designer or builder of engines 3 : one trained in engineering 4 : one that operates an engine

²**engineer** *vb* 1 : to lay out or manage as an engineer 2 : to guide the course of

en·gi·neer·ing *n* : the practical applications of scientific and mathematical principles

En·glish \'iŋ-glish\ *n* 1 : the language of England, the U.S., and many areas now or formerly under British rule 2 **English** *pl* : the people of England 3 : spin imparted to a ball that is driven or rolled — **English** *adj* — **En·glish·man** \-mən\ *n* — **En·glish·wom·an** \-,wu̇-mən\ *n*

English horn *n* : a woodwind instrument longer than and having a range lower than the oboe

English setter *n* : any of a breed of hunting dogs with a flat silky coat of white or white with color

English sparrow *n* : HOUSE SPARROW

English system *n* : a system of weights and measures in which the foot is the principal unit of length and the pound is the principal unit of weight

engr *abbr* 1 engineer 2 engraved

en·gram \'en-,gram\ *n* : a hypothetical change in neural tissue postulated in order to account for persistence of memory

en·grave \in-'grāv\ *vb* **en·graved; en·grav·ing** 1 ♦ : to produce (as letters or lines) by incising a surface 2 : to cut figures, letters, or designs on for printing; *also* : to print from an engraved plate 3 : PHOTOENGRAVE 4 ♦ : to impress deeply as if with an engraving tool — **en·grav·er** *n*

♦ [1] etch, grave, inscribe; *also* carve, chisel, sculpt, sculpture; chase; score ♦ [4] etch, impress, imprint, ingrain, inscribe; *also* imbue, implant, inculcate, infuse, instill

en·grav·ing \in-'grā-viŋ\ *n* 1 : the art of one who engraves 2 : an engraved plate; *also* : a print made from it

en·gross \in-'grōs\ *vb* ♦ : to take up the whole interest or attention of

♦ absorb, busy, engage, enthrall, fascinate, grip, immerse, interest, intrigue, involve, occupy — more at ENGAGE

en·grossed \in-'grōst\ *adj* ♦ : completely occupied or absorbed

♦ absorbed, attentive, intent, observant, rapt — more at ATTENTIVE

en·gross·ing *adj* ♦ : taking up the time or attention completely

♦ absorbing, engaging, enthralling, fascinating, interesting, intriguing — more at INTERESTING

en·gulf \in-'gəlf\ *vb* ♦ : to flow over and enclose

♦ deluge, drown, flood, inundate, overflow, overwhelm, submerge, swamp — more at FLOOD

en·hance \in-'hans\ *vb* **en·hanced; en·hanc·ing** ♦ : to increase or improve (as in value or desirability)

♦ ameliorate, amend, better, enrich, improve, perfect, refine — more at IMPROVE

en·hance·ment *n* ♦ : the act of enhancing or state of being enhanced

♦ advance, advancement, breakthrough, improvement, refinement — more at ADVANCE

enig·ma \i-'nig-mə\ *n* [L *aenigma*, fr. Gk *ainigma*, fr. *ainissesthai* to speak in riddles, fr. *ainos* fable] ♦ : something obscure or hard to understand

♦ conundrum, mystery, mystification, puzzle, puzzlement, riddle, secret — more at MYSTERY

enig·mat·ic \,en-ig-'ma-tik\ *adj* ♦ : resembling an enigma — **enig·mat·i·cal·ly** \-ti-k(ə-)lē\ *adv*

♦ ambiguous, cryptic, deep, equivocal, inscrutable, murky, mysterious, mystic, nebulous, obscure, occult — more at OBSCURE

en·join \in-'join\ *vb* 1 ♦ : to direct or impose by authoritative order or with urgent warning : COMMAND 2 ♦ : to forbid by authority

♦ [1] call, charge, command, demand, direct, exact, insist, instruct, order, press, stipulate (for) — more at DEMAND ♦ [1, 2] ban, bar, forbid, interdict, outlaw, prohibit, proscribe — more at FORBID

en·joy \in-'joi\ *vb* 1 ♦ : to have for one's benefit or use ⟨~ good health⟩ 2 ♦ : to take pleasure or satisfaction in ⟨~ed the concert⟩

♦ [1] command, have, hold, occupy, own, possess, retain — more at HAVE ♦ [2] adore, delight, dig, fancy, like, love, relish, revel; *also* admire, appreciate, cherish; prize, treasure, value; devour, drink (in), savor; dote (on), idolize; cotton (to), favor, prefer

en·joy·able *adj* ♦ : being a source of pleasure or enjoyment

♦ agreeable, amusing, delectable, delicious, delightful, entertaining, fun, heavenly, luscious, pleasurable

en·joy·ment *n* 1 ♦ : the action or state of enjoying 2 : something that gives keen satisfaction

♦ contentment, delectation, delight, gladness, gratification, pleasure, relish, satisfaction — more at PLEASURE

enl *abbr* 1 enlarged 2 enlisted

en·large \in-'lärj\ *vb* **en·larged; en·larg·ing** 1 ♦ : to make or grow larger 2 ♦ : to give greater scope to; *also* : to speak or write at length : ELABORATE — often used with *on* or *upon* — **en·large·ment** *n*

♦ [1] add, aggrandize, amplify, augment, boost, compound, escalate, expand, extend, increase, multiply, raise, swell, up — more at INCREASE ♦ *usu* **enlarge on** [2] amplify, develop, elaborate (on), expand — more at EXPAND

en·light·en \in-'līt-ᵊn\ *vb* 1 ♦ : to give knowledge to : INSTRUCT, INFORM 2 ♦ : to give spiritual insight to — **en·light·en·ment** *n*

♦ [1] acquaint, advise, apprise, brief, clue, familiarize, fill in, inform, instruct, tell, wise; *also* clarify, clear (up), construe, elucidate, explain, explicate, expound, illuminate, illustrate, interpret, spell out; announce, disclose, report; disabuse, disenchant, disillusion ♦ [2] edify, educate, nurture; *also* elevate, ennoble, lift, uplift; better, improve, transform; exalt, glorify, transfigure

en·list \in-'list\ *vb* 1 : to secure the aid or support of 2 ♦ : to engage for service in the armed forces 3 ♦ : to participate heartily (as in a cause or effort) ⟨~ed in the cause of world peace⟩ — **en·list·ee** \-,lis-'tē\ *n* — **en·list·ment** \-'list-mənt\ *n*

♦ *usu* **enlist in** [2, 3] enroll, enter, join, sign on, sign up — more at ENTER

en·list·ed \in-'lis-təd\ *adj* : of, relating to, or forming the part of a military force below commissioned or warrant officers

enlisted man *n* : a man or woman in the armed forces ranking below a commissioned or warrant officer

en·liv·en \in-'lī-vən\ *vb* ♦ : to give life, action, or spirit to : ANIMATE

♦ animate, brace, energize, fire, invigorate, jazz up, liven up, pep up, quicken, stimulate, vitalize, vivify, zip (up) — more at ANIMATE

en masse \än-'mas\ *adv* [F] : in a body : as a whole

en·mesh \in-'mesh\ *vb* ♦ : to catch or entangle in or as if in meshes

♦ ensnare, entangle, entrap, mesh, snare, tangle, trap — more at ENTANGLE

en·mi·ty \'en-mə-tē\ *n, pl* -ties ♦ : positive, active, and typically mutual hatred or ill will

♦ animosity, antagonism, antipathy, bitterness, gall, grudge, hostility, rancor *Ant* amity

en·no·ble \i-'nō-bəl\ *vb* -bled; -bling ♦ : to raise in rank or status : EXALT; *esp* : to raise to noble rank — **en·no·ble·ment** *n*

♦ aggrandize, dignify, exalt, glorify, magnify — more at EXALT

en·nui \,än-'wē\ *n* [F] ♦ : a feeling of weariness and dissatisfaction : BOREDOM

♦ boredom, doldrums, listlessness, restlessness, tedium, tiredness, weariness — more at BOREDOM

enor·mi·ty \i-'nȯr-mə-tē\ *n, pl* -ties 1 : an outrageous, vicious, or immoral act 2 ♦ : great wickedness 3 ♦ : the quality or state of being huge : IMMENSITY

♦ [2] atrociousness, atrocity, depravity, heinousness, monstrosity, vileness, wickedness; *also* baseness, devilishness; corruption, decadence, degeneracy; immorality; infamy, notoriety ♦ [3] hugeness, immensity, magnitude, massiveness, vastness — more at IMMENSITY

enor·mous \i-'nȯr-məs\ *adj* [L *enormis*, fr. *e, ex* out of + *norma* rule] 1 : exceedingly wicked 2 ♦ : great in size, number, or degree : HUGE — **enor·mous·ly** *adv*

♦ astronomical, colossal, elephantine, giant, gigantic, ginormous, huge, jumbo, mammoth, massive, prodigious, titanic, tremendous, whopping — more at HUGE

¹enough \i-'nəf\ *adj* : SUFFICIENT

²enough *adv* 1 ♦ : in or to a degree or quantity that suffices : SUFFICIENTLY 2 : FULLY, QUITE 3 ♦ : in a tolerable degree

♦ [1] adequately, satisfactorily; *also* decently, fairly, moderately, passably *Ant* inadequately, insufficiently ♦ [3] fairly, kind of, moderately, so-so, somewhat, sort of

³enough *pron* : a sufficient number, quantity, or amount

en·quire \in-'kwī-(ə)r,\ or **en·qui·ry** \'in-,kwī-(ə)r-ē, in-'; 'in-kwə-rē, 'iŋ-\ *chiefly Brit var of* INQUIRE, INQUIRY

en·rage \in-'rāj\ *vb* ♦ : to fill with rage

♦ anger, antagonize, incense, inflame, infuriate, madden, outrage, rankle, rile, roil — more at ANGER

en·raged \in-'rājd\ *adj* ♦ : full of fury or rage

♦ angry, boiling, furious, irate — more at ANGRY

en·rap·ture \in-'rap-chər\ *vb* **en·rap·tured; en·rap·tur·ing** ♦ : to fill with delight

♦ carry away, elate, elevate, enthrall, exhilarate, transport — more at ELATE

en·rich \in-'rich\ *vb* 1 a : to make rich or richer b ♦ : to add to or improve with additions 2 ♦ : to add beauty to : ORNAMENT, ADORN — **en·rich·ment** *n*

♦ [1b] ameliorate, amend, better, enhance, improve, perfect, refine — more at IMPROVE ♦ [2] adorn, array, beautify, bedeck, deck, decorate, do, dress, embellish, garnish, grace, ornament, trim — more at DECORATE

en·roll *or Can and Brit* **en·rol** \in-'rōl\ *vb* **en·rolled; en·roll·ing** 1 ♦ : to enter or register on a roll or list 2 ♦ : to offer (oneself) for enrolling — **en·roll·ment** *n*

♦ [1] inscribe, itemize, list, matriculate, register; *also* catalog, tabulate, tally ♦ [1] catalog, enter, index, inscribe, list, put down, record — more at LIST ♦ [2] enlist, enter, join, sign on, sign up — more at ENTER

en·roll·ment *or chiefly Can and Brit* **en·rol·ment** *n* 1 : the act or process of enrolling (as at enlistment or registration) 2 : the number enrolled

en route \än-'rüt, en-\ *adv or adj* : on or along the way

ENS *abbr* ensign

en·sconce \in-'skäns\ *vb* **en·sconced; en·sconc·ing** 1 ♦ : to place out of sight : CONCEAL 2 ♦ : to settle snugly or securely

♦ [1] bury, cache, conceal, hide, secrete — more at HIDE ♦ [2] install, lodge, perch, roost, settle; *also* curl up; park, plant

en·sem·ble \än-'säm-bəl\ *n* [F, fr. *ensemble* together, fr. L *insimul* at the same time] : a group (as of singers, dancers, or players) or a set (as of clothes) producing a single effect

en·sheathe \in-'shēth\ *vb* : to cover with or as if with a sheath

en·shrine \in-'shrīn\ *vb* 1 : to enclose in or as if in a shrine 2 : to cherish as sacred — **en·shrine·ment** \-mənt\ *n*

en·shroud \in-'shraud\ *vb* ♦ : to cover or enclose with or as if with a shroud : OBSCURE

♦ blanket, blot out, cloak, conceal, cover, curtain, hide, mask, obscure, occult, screen, shroud, veil — more at HIDE

en·sign \'en-sən, *1 also* 'en-,sīn\ *n* 1 ♦ : a flag that is flown (as by a ship) as the symbol of nationality and that may also be flown with a distinctive badge added to its design; *also* : BADGE, EMBLEM 2 : a commissioned officer in the navy ranking next below a lieutenant junior grade

♦ banner, colors (*or* colours), flag, jack, pennant, standard, streamer — more at FLAG

en·slave \in-'slāv\ *vb* : to make a slave of

en·slave·ment *n* 1 : the act or process of enslaving 2 : the state of being enslaved

♦ bondage, servitude, slavery, thrall, yoke — more at SLAVERY

en·snare \in-'snar\ *vb* ♦ : to take in or as if in a snare : TRAP

♦ enmesh, entangle, entrap, mesh, snare, tangle, trap — more at ENTANGLE

en·sue \in-'sü\ *vb* **en·sued; en·su·ing** : to follow in time or as a result ⟨the birds escaped and chaos *ensued*⟩

en·sure \in-'shur\ *vb* **en·sured; en·sur·ing** ♦ : to give security to : INSURE, GUARANTEE

♦ assure, cinch, guarantee, guaranty, insure, secure; *also* attest, certify, vouch, warrant, witness; pledge, promise, swear

en·tail \in-'tāl\ *vb* 1 : to limit the inheritance of (property) to the owner's lineal descendants or to a class thereof 2 ♦ : to include or involve as a necessary step or result — **en·tail·ment** *n*

♦ carry, comprehend, contain, embrace, encompass, include, involve, number, take in — more at INCLUDE

en·tan·gle \in-'taŋ-gəl\ *vb* 1 ♦ : to wrap or twist together : TANGLE; *also* : to make complicated 2 ♦ : to take in or as if in a snare; *also* : to involve in a perplexing or troublesome situation

♦ [1] interlace, intertwine, interweave, knot, snarl, tangle; *also* weave, wind, wreathe; braid, plait ♦ [2] enmesh, ensnare, entrap, mesh, snare, tangle, trap; *also* bag, capture, collar; embroil, implicate, involve, mire *Ant* disentangle

en·tan·gle·ment *n* 1 : the action of entangling : the state of being entangled 2 ♦ : something that entangles, confuses, or ensnares

♦ net, snare, web — more at WEB

en·tente \än-'tänt\ *n* [F] : an understanding providing for joint action; *also* : parties linked by such an entente

en·ter \'en-tər\ *vb* 1 : to go or come in or into 2 ♦ : to become a member of : JOIN ⟨~ the ministry⟩ 3 ♦ : to make a beginning : to begin to consider a subject — usu. used with *into* or *upon* 4 : to take part in : CONTRIBUTE 5 : to go into or upon and take possession 6 ♦ : to set down (as in a list) : REGISTER ⟨~ the data⟩ 7 : to place (a complaint) before a court; *also* : to put on record ⟨∼ a complaint⟩

♦ [2] enlist, enroll, join, sign on, sign up; *also* reenlist, reenter ♦ *usu* **enter into** *or* **enter upon** [3] begin, commence, embark (on *or* upon), get off, launch, open, start, strike — more at BEGIN ♦ [6] catalog, enroll, index, inscribe, list, put down, record, register, schedule, slate — more at LIST

en·ter·i·tis \ˌen-tə-ˈrī-təs\ *n* : intestinal inflammation; *also* : a disease marked by this

en·ter·prise \ˈen-tər-ˌprīz\ *n* **1** ♦ : a project or undertaking that is esp. difficult, complicated, or risky **2** ♦ : readiness for daring action : INITIATIVE **3** ♦ : a business organization

♦ [1] chance, flier, gamble, speculation, venture — more at GAMBLE ♦ [2] aggressiveness, ambition, drive, go, hustle, initiative; *also* gumption, pluck, snap, spirit, spunk, starch; assertiveness, self-reliance; energy, hardihood, pep, vigor, vitality ♦ [3] business, company, concern, establishment, firm, house, outfit; *also* conglomerate, corporation, multinational; association, cartel, chain, combine, syndicate, trust; agency, dealer, outlet

en·ter·pris·ing \-ˌprī-ziŋ\ *adj* ♦ : bold and vigorous in action

♦ adventurous, audacious, bold, daring, gutsy, hardy, nervy, venturesome — more at BOLD

en·ter·tain \ˌen-tər-ˈtān\ *vb* **1** : to treat or receive as a guest **2** ♦ : to provide entertainment for : AMUSE, DIVERT **3** ♦ : to hold in mind; *also* : to receive and take into consideration — **en·ter·tain·er** *n*

♦ [2] amuse, disport, divert, regale — more at AMUSE ♦ [3] consider, contemplate, debate, deliberate, meditate, mull, ponder, question, ruminate, study, think, weigh — more at PONDER

en·ter·tain·ing \-ˈtā-niŋ\ *adj* ♦ : providing entertainment

♦ amusing, delightful, diverting, enjoyable, fun, pleasurable — more at FUN

en·ter·tain·ment *n* **1** ♦ : the act of entertaining **2** ♦ : amusement or diversion provided esp. by performers; *also* : something or someone diverting or engaging

♦ [1] amusement, distraction, diversion; *also* show business; delectation, delight, enjoyment, joy, mirth; performance, presentation, production, show, spectacle ♦ [2] delight, diversion, fun, pleasure — more at FUN

en·thrall *or* **en·thral** \in-ˈthrȯl\ *vb* **en·thralled**; **en·thrall·ing** **1** : ENSLAVE **2** ♦ : to hold the attention of as if under a spell : hold spellbound

♦ arrest, enchant, fascinate, grip, hypnotize, interest, intrigue, involve, mesmerize; *also* enrapture, entrance, thrill; beguile, bewitch, charm

en·thrall·ing *adj* ♦ : capable of holding spellbound : intensely absorbing or interesting

♦ absorbing, engaging, engrossing, fascinating, interesting, intriguing — more at INTERESTING

en·throne \in-ˈthrōn\ *vb* **1** : to seat on or as if on a throne **2** : EXALT

en·thuse \in-ˈthüz, -ˈthyüz\ *vb* **en·thused**; **en·thus·ing** **1** : to make enthusiastic **2** ♦ : to show enthusiasm

♦ fuss, gush, rave, rhapsodize

en·thu·si·asm \in-ˈthü-zē-ˌa-zəm, -ˈthyü-\ *n* [Gk *enthousiasmos*, fr. *enthousiazein* to be inspired, irreg. fr. *entheos* inspired, fr. *theos* god] **1** ♦ : strong warmth of feeling : keen interest : FERVOR **2** ♦ : something that inspires or is pursued or regarded with ardent zeal or fervor

♦ [1] appetite, ardor, avidity, eagerness, excitement, fervor, hunger, impatience, keenness, thirst — more at EAGERNESS ♦ [2] craze, fad, fashion, go, mode, rage, sensation, style, trend, vogue — more at FASHION

en·thu·si·ast \-ˌast, -əst\ *n* ♦ : a person filled with enthusiasm

♦ addict, aficionado, buff, bug, devotee, fan, fancier, lover, nut — more at FAN

en·thu·si·as·tic \in-ˌthü-zē-ˈas-tik, -ˌthyü-\ *adj* ♦ : filled with or marked by enthusiasm — **en·thu·si·as·ti·cal·ly** \-ti-k(ə-)lē\ *adv*

♦ ardent, athirst, avid, eager, gung ho, keen, nuts, raring, thirsty — more at EAGER

en·tice \in-ˈtīs\ *vb* **en·ticed**; **en·tic·ing** ♦ : to attract cunningly or by arousing hope or desire : ALLURE, TEMPT

♦ allure, beguile, decoy, lead on, lure, seduce, tempt — more at LURE

en·tice·ment *n* **1** ♦ : the act of enticing **2** ♦ : something that entices : a means or method of enticing

♦ lure, seduction, solicitation, temptation — more at TEMPTATION

en·tire \in-ˈtī(-ə)r\ *adj* ♦ : having no element or part left out : COMPLETE, WHOLE

♦ complete, comprehensive, full, grand, intact, integral, perfect, plenary, total, undivided, whole — more at COMPLETE

en·tire·ly *adv* ♦ : to the full or entire extent

♦ altogether, completely, dead, fast, flat, full, fully, perfectly, quite, thoroughly, well, wholly — more at FULLY

en·tire·ty \in-ˈtī-rə-tē, -ˈti(-ə)r-tē\ *n, pl* **-ties** **1** : COMPLETENESS **2** : WHOLE, TOTALITY

en·ti·tle \in-ˈtī-t²l\ *vb* **en·ti·tled**; **en·ti·tling** **1** ♦ : to give a title to : DESIGNATE **2** ♦ : to furnish with proper grounds for seeking or claiming something ⟨*entitled* to a fair trial⟩

♦ [1] baptize, call, christen, denominate, designate, dub, label, name, style, term, title — more at NAME ♦ [2] authorize, qualify; *also* empower, enable, license; approve, endorse; allow, let, permit; certify, ratify, sanction, validate *Ant* disqualify

en·ti·tle·ment \in-ˈtīt-²l-mənt\ *n* : a government program providing benefits to members of a specified group

en·ti·ty \ˈen-tə-tē\ *n, pl* **-ties** **1** : EXISTENCE, BEING **2** ♦ : something with separate and real existence

♦ being, individual, object, substance, thing; *also* body; material, matter, stuff

en·tomb \in-ˈtüm\ *vb* : to place in a tomb : BURY

en·tomb·ment *n* ♦ : the act or process of entombing

♦ burial, interment, sepulture — more at BURIAL

en·to·mol·o·gy \ˌen-tə-ˈmä-lə-jē\ *n* : a branch of zoology that deals with insects — **en·to·mo·log·i·cal** \-mə-ˈlä-ji-kəl\ *adj* — **en·to·mol·o·gist** \-jist\ *n*

en·tou·rage \ˌän-tu̇-ˈräzh\ *n* [F] : RETINUE

en·tr'acte \ˈän-ˌtrakt\ *n* [F] **1** : something (as a dance) performed between two acts of a play **2** : the interval between two acts of a play

en·trails \ˈen-ˌtrālz\ *n pl* : the internal organs esp. in the trunk of the body : VISCERA; *esp* : the tubular part of the alimentary canal that extends from the stomach to the anus

¹**en·trance** \ˈen-trəns\ *n* **1** ♦ : permission or right to enter **2** : the act of entering **3** ♦ : a means or place of entry

♦ [1] access, admission, doorway, entrée, entry, gateway ♦ [3] door, doorway, gate, gateway, way — more at DOOR

²**en·trance** \in-ˈtrans\ *vb* **en·tranced**; **en·tranc·ing** ♦ : to carry away with delight, wonder, or rapture

♦ carry away, enrapture, enthrall, ravish, transport; *also* delight, gladden, gratify, please, satisfy; bewitch, captivate, charm, enchant, fascinate; elate, excite, exhilarate, stir

en·trant \ˈen-trənt\ *n* : one that enters esp. as a competitor **en·trap** \in-ˈtrap\ *vb* ♦ : to catch in or as if in a trap : ENSNARE, TRAP — **en·trap·ment** *n*

♦ enmesh, ensnare, entangle, mesh, snare, tangle, trap — more at ENTANGLE

en·treat \in-ˈtrēt\ *vb* ♦ : to ask urgently : BESEECH

♦ appeal, beg, beseech, implore, importune, petition, plead, pray, solicit, supplicate — more at BEG

en·treaty \-'trē-tē\ n ♦ : an act of entreating

♦ appeal, cry, petition, plea, prayer, solicitation, suit, supplication — more at PLEA

en·trée or **en·tree** \'än-ˌtrā\ n [F *entrée*] **1** ♦ : freedom of entry or access **2** : the main course of a meal in the U.S.

♦ access, admission, doorway, entrance, entry, gateway — more at ENTRANCE

en·trench \in-'trench\ vb **1 a** : to place within or surround with a trench esp. for defense **b** ♦ : to establish solidly ⟨~ed customs⟩ **2** : ENCROACH, TRESPASS — **en·trench·ment** n

♦ embed, fix, implant, ingrain, lodge, root; *also* imbue, infuse, instill; establish, place, put, settle, stick *Ant* dislodge, root (out), uproot

en·tre·pre·neur \ˌän-trə-prə-'nər, -'nu̇r, -'nyu̇r\ n [F, fr. OF, fr. *entreprendre* to undertake] : one who organizes and assumes the risk of a business or enterprise — **en·tre·pre·neur·ial** \-'nu̇r-ē-əl, -'nyu̇r-, -'nər-\ adj — **en·tre·pre·neur·ship** \-ˌship\ n

en·tro·py \'en-trə-pē\ n, pl **-pies 1** : the degree of disorder in a system **2** : an ultimate state of inert uniformity

en·trust \in-'trəst\ vb **1** ♦ : to commit something to as a trust **2** ♦ : to commit to another with confidence

♦ [1] assign, charge, commission, trust; *also* confer, impose; commit, consign, delegate, relegate; allocate, allot; authorize, empower, invest ♦ [2] commend, commit, consign, delegate, deliver, give, hand over, leave, pass, transfer, transmit, trust, turn over, vest — more at GIVE

en·try \'en-trē\ n, pl **entries 1** ♦ : a place of entrance; *also* : the act, means, right, or privilege of entering **2** : an entering in a record; *also* : an item so entered **3** : a headword with its definition or identification; *also* : VOCABULARY ENTRY **4** : one entered in a contest

♦ foyer, hall, lobby, vestibule — more at HALL ♦ access, admission, doorway, entrée, entrance, gateway — more at ENTRANCE

en·twine \in-'twīn\ vb ♦ : to twine together or around

♦ coil, curl, spiral, twine, twist, wind — more at WIND

enu·mer·ate \i-'nü-mə-ˌrāt, -'nyü-\ vb **-at·ed; -at·ing 1** ♦ : to determine the number of : COUNT **2** ♦ : to specify one after another : LIST — **enu·mer·a·tion** \-ˌnü-mə-'rā-shən, -ˌnyü-\ n

♦ [1] count, number, tell — more at COUNT ♦ [2] detail, itemize, list, numerate, rehearse, tick (off); *also* outline; tabulate, tally; catalog, inventory; chart, diagram, graph; calculate, compute, estimate, figure, reckon; cite, mention, name

enun·ci·ate \ē-'nən-sē-ˌāt\ vb **-at·ed; -at·ing 1 a** : to state definitely **b** ♦ : to make known publicly : ANNOUNCE, PROCLAIM **2** : to say clearly and effectively : PRONOUNCE, ARTICULATE — **enun·ci·a·tion** \-ˌnən-sē-'ā-shən\ n

♦ advertise, announce, blaze, broadcast, declare, placard, post, proclaim, promulgate, publicize, publish, sound — more at ANNOUNCE

en·ure·sis \ˌen-yu̇-'rē-səs\ n : involuntary discharge of urine : BED-WETTING

env abbr envelope

en·vel·op \in-'ve-ləp\ vb ♦ : to enclose completely with or as if with a covering — **en·vel·op·ment** n

♦ embrace, enclose, encompass, enfold, enshroud, invest, lap, mantle, shroud, swathe, veil, wrap — more at ENFOLD

en·ve·lope \'en-və-ˌlōp, 'än-\ n **1** : a usu. paper container for a letter **2** : WRAPPER, COVERING **3** : a conventionally accepted limit ⟨fashions that push the ~⟩

en·ven·om \in-'ve-nəm\ vb **1** : to make poisonous **2** : EMBITTER

en·vi·able \'en-vē-ə-bəl\ adj : highly desirable — **en·vi·ably** \-blē\ adv

en·vi·ous \'en-vē-əs\ adj ♦ : feeling or showing envy — **en·vi·ous·ly** adv

♦ covetous, jaundiced, jealous, resentful; *also* begrudging, grudging; malicious, petty, spiteful

en·vi·ous·ness n ♦ : the quality or state of being envious

♦ covetousness, envy, jealousy, resentment — more at ENVY

en·vi·ron·ment \in-'vī-rən-mənt, -'vī(-ə)rn-\ n **1** ♦ : the circumstances, objects, or conditions surrounding someone or something : SURROUNDINGS **2** : the whole complex of factors (as soil, climate, and living things) that influence the form and the ability to survive of a plant or animal or ecological community — **en·vi·ron·men·tal** \-ˌvī-rən-'ment-ᵊl, -ˌvī(-ə)rn-\ adj — **en·vi·ron·men·tal·ly** \-t-ᵊl-ē\ adv

♦ atmosphere, climate, environs, medium, milieu, setting, surroundings; *also* backdrop, background, context; element; situation, status; habitat

en·vi·ron·men·tal·ist \-ˌvī-rən-'ment-ᵊl-ist, -ˌvīrn-\ n : a person concerned about environmental quality esp. with respect to control of pollution

en·vi·rons \in-'vī-rənz\ n pl **1** ♦ : the districts around a city **2** ♦ : the circumstances, conditions, or objects by which one is surrounded : SURROUNDINGS; *also* : VICINITY

♦ [1] exurbia, outskirts, suburbia ♦ [2] atmosphere, climate, environment, medium, milieu, setting, surroundings — more at ENVIRONMENT

en·vis·age \in-'vi-zij\ vb **-aged; -ag·ing** ♦ : to have a mental picture of

♦ conceive, dream, fancy, imagine, picture, vision, visualize — more at IMAGINE

en·vi·sion \in-'vi-zhən, en-\ vb : to picture to oneself ⟨~s world peace⟩

en·voy \'en-ˌvȯi, 'än-\ n **1** ♦ : a diplomatic agent **2** ♦ : one who bears a message or does an errand : REPRESENTATIVE

♦ [1] ambassador, delegate, emissary, legate, minister, representative — more at AMBASSADOR ♦ [2] agent, attorney, commissary, delegate, deputy, factor, proxy, representative — more at AGENT

¹**en·vy** \'en-vē\ n, pl **envies** [ME *envie*, fr. OF, fr. L *invidia*, fr. *invidus* envious, fr. *invidēre* to look askance at, envy, fr. *vidēre* to see] ♦ : painful or resentful awareness of another's advantages; *also* : an object of envy

♦ covetousness, enviousness, jealousy, resentment; *also* animosity, enmity, hatred, ill will; malice, spitefulness

²**envy** vb **en·vied; en·vy·ing** : to feel envy toward or on account of

en·zyme \'en-ˌzīm\ n : any of various complex proteins produced by living cells that catalyze specific biochemical reactions at body temperatures — **en·zy·mat·ic** \ˌen-zə-'ma-tik\ adj

Eo·cene \'ē-ə-ˌsēn\ adj : of, relating to, or being the epoch of the Tertiary between the Paleocene and the Oligocene — **Eocene** n

EOE abbr equal opportunity employer

eo·lian \ē-'ō-lē-ən\ adj : borne, deposited, or produced by the wind

EOM abbr end of month

eon \'ē-ən, -ˌän\ n ♦ : an indefinitely long time : AGE

♦ age, cycle, eternity — more at AGE

EP abbr European plan

EPA abbr Environmental Protection Agency

ep·au·let also **ep·au·lette** \ˌe-pə-'let\ n [F *épaulette*, dim. of *épaule* shoulder] : a shoulder ornament esp. on a coat or military uniform

épée \'e-ˌpā, ā-'pā\ n [F] : a fencing or dueling sword

Eph or **Ephes** abbr Ephesians

ephed·rine \i-'fe-drən\ n : a stimulant drug used to treat asthma and nasal congestion

ephem·era \i-'fe-mər-ə\ n pl : collectibles (as posters or tickets) not intended to have lasting value

ephem·er·al \i-'fe-mə-rəl\ *adj* [Gk *ephēmeros* lasting a day, daily, fr. *epi-* on + *hēmera* day] ♦ : lasting a very short time : SHORT-LIVED, TRANSITORY — **ephem·er·al·i·ty** \i-,fe-mə-'ra-lə-tē\ *n*

♦ evanescent, flash, fleeting, impermanent, momentary, short-lived, transient — more at MOMENTARY

Ephe·sians \i-'fē-zhənz\ *n* : a letter addressed to early Christians and included as a book in the New Testament
ep·ic \'e-pik\ *n* : a long poem in elevated style narrating the deeds of a hero — **epic** *adj*
epi·cen·ter *or Can and Brit* **epi·cen·tre** \'e-pi-,sen-tər\ *n* : the point on the earth's surface directly above the point of origin of an earthquake
ep·i·cure \'e-pi-,kyùr\ *n* ♦ : a person with sensitive and discriminating tastes esp. in food and wine

♦ epicurean, gourmand, gourmet

ep·i·cu·re·an \,e-pi-kyù-'rē-ən, -'kyùr-ē-\ *n* ♦ : a person with sensitive and discriminating tastes esp. in food and wine : EPICURE — **epicurean** *adj*

♦ epicure, gourmand, gourmet

¹**ep·i·dem·ic** \,e-pə-'de-mik\ *adj* : affecting many persons at one time ⟨~ disease⟩; *also* : excessively prevalent
²**epidemic** *n* : an epidemic outbreak esp. of disease
ep·i·de·mi·ol·o·gy \,ep-ə-,dē-mē-'ä-lə-jē\ *n* : the study of the incidence, distribution, and control of disease in a population — **ep·i·de·mi·o·log·i·cal** \-,dē-mē-ə-'lä-ji-kəl\ *also* **ep·i·de·mi·o·log·ic** \-jik\ *adj* — **ep·i·de·mi·ol·o·gist** \-'ä-lə-jist\ *n*
epi·der·mis \,e-pə-'dər-məs\ *n* : an outer layer esp. of skin — **epi·der·mal** \-məl\ *adj*
epi·du·ral \,e-pi-'d(y)ùr-əl\ *adj* : administered into the space outside the membrane that envelops the spinal cord ⟨~ anesthesia⟩ — **epidural** *n*
epi·glot·tis \,e-pə-'glä-təs\ *n* : a thin plate of flexible tissue protecting the tracheal opening during swallowing
ep·i·gram \'e-pə-,gram\ *n* 1 : a short often satirical poem 2 ♦ : a terse, sage, or witty often paradoxical saying

♦ adage, aphorism, byword, maxim, proverb, saying — more at SAYING

ep·i·gram·mat·ic \,e-pə-grə-'ma-tik\ *adj* ♦ : of, relating to, or resembling an epigram; *also* : marked by or given to the use of epigrams

♦ brief, compact, compendious, concise, crisp, laconic, pithy, succinct, summary, terse — more at CONCISE

ep·i·lep·sy \'e-pə-,lep-sē\ *n, pl* **-sies** [ultim. fr. Gk *epilēpsia*, fr. *epilambanein* to seize] : a disorder marked by abnormal electrical discharges in the brain and typically manifested by sudden periods of diminished consciousness or by convulsions — **ep·i·lep·tic** \,e-pə-'lep-tik\ *adj or n*
ep·i·logue *also* **epi·log** \'e-pə-,lòg, -,läg\ *n* 1 : a concluding section of a literary work 2 : a speech addressed to the spectators by an actor at the end of a play
epi·neph·rine \,e-pə-'ne-frən\ *n* : an adrenal hormone used medicinally esp. as a heart stimulant, a muscle relaxant, and a vasoconstrictor
epiph·a·ny \i-'pi-fə-nē\ *n, pl* **-nies** 1 *cap* : January 6 observed as a church festival in commemoration of the coming of the Magi to Jesus at Bethlehem 2 : a sudden striking understanding of something
epis·co·pa·cy \i-'pis-kə-pə-sē\ *n, pl* **-cies** 1 : government of a church by bishops 2 : EPISCOPATE
epis·co·pal \i-'pis-kə-pəl\ *adj* 1 : of or relating to a bishop or episcopacy 2 *cap* : of or relating to the Protestant Episcopal Church
Epis·co·pa·lian \i-,pis-kə-'pāl-yən\ *n* : a member of the Protestant Episcopal Church
epis·co·pate \i-'pis-kə-pət, -,pāt\ *n* 1 : the rank, office, or term of a bishop 2 : a body of bishops
ep·i·sode \'e-pə-,sōd\ *n* [Gk *epeisodion*, fr. *epeisodios* coming in besides, fr. *eisodios* coming in, fr. *eis* into + *hodos* road, journey] 1 : a unit of action in a dramatic or literary work 2 ♦ : an incident in a course of events : OCCURRENCE ⟨a feverish ~⟩

♦ affair, circumstance, event, happening, incident, occasion, occurrence, thing — more at EVENT

ep·i·sod·ic \,e-pə-'sä-dik\ *adj* ♦ : made up of separate esp. loosely connected episodes

♦ periodic, serial — more at SERIAL

epis·tle \i-'pi-səl\ *n* 1 *cap* : one of the letters of the New Testament 2 : a direct or personal written or printed message addressed to a person or organization : LETTER; *esp* : a formal or elegant letter — **epis·to·lary** \i-'pis-tə-,ler-ē\ *adj*
ep·i·taph \'e-pə-,taf\ *n* : an inscription in memory of a dead person
ep·i·tha·la·mi·um \,e-pə-thə-'lä-mē-əm\ *or* **ep·i·tha·la·mi·on** \-mē-ən\ *n, pl* **-mi·ums** *or* **-mia** \-mē-ə\ : a song or poem in honor of a bride and bridegroom
ep·i·the·li·um \,e-pə-'thē-lē-əm\ *n, pl* **-lia** \-lē-ə\ : a cellular membrane covering a bodily surface or lining a cavity — **ep·i·the·li·al** \-lē-əl\ *adj*
ep·i·thet \'e-pə-,thet, -thət\ *n* : a characterizing and often abusive word or phrase
epit·o·me \i-'pi-tə-mē\ *n* 1 ♦ : a brief presentation or statement of something : ABSTRACT, SUMMARY 2 ♦ : a typical or ideal example : EMBODIMENT

♦ [1] abstract, digest, encapsulation, outline, précis, recapitulation, résumé (*or* resume), roundup, sum, summary, synopsis, wrap-up — more at SUMMARY
♦ [2] embodiment, exemplar, ideal, incarnation, manifestation, personification, quintessence — more at EMBODIMENT

epit·o·mize \-,mīz\ *vb* 1 ♦ : to make or give an epitome of 2 ♦ : to serve as the typical or ideal example of

♦ [1] abstract, digest, encapsulate, outline, recapitulate, sum up, summarize, wrap up ♦ [2] embody, manifest, materialize, personify — more at EMBODY

ep·och \'e-pək, -,päk\ *n* ♦ : a usu. extended period : ERA, AGE — **ep·och·al** \-pə-kəl, -,pä-\ *adj*

♦ age, era, period, time

ep·onym \'e-pə-,nim\ *n* 1 : one for whom something is or is believed to be named 2 : a name (as of a disease) based on or derived from an eponym — **epon·y·mous** \i-'pä-nə-məs\ *adj*
ep·oxy \i-'päk-sē\ *vb* **ep·ox·ied** *or* **ep·oxyed; ep·oxy·ing** : to glue, fill, or coat with epoxy resin
epoxy resin *n* : a synthetic resin used in coatings and adhesives
ep·si·lon \'ep-sə-län, -lən\ *n* : the 5th letter of the Greek alphabet — E or ϵ
Ep·som salts \'ep-səm-\ *n* : a bitter colorless or white magnesium salt with cathartic properties
eq *abbr* 1 equal 2 equation
equa·ble \'e-kwə-bəl, 'ē-\ *adj* ♦ : showing regular or consistent movement, occurrence, operation, — or character; *esp* : free from unpleasant extremes — **eq·ua·bil·i·ty** \,e-kwə-'bi-lə-tē, ,ē-\ *n* — **eq·ua·bly** \'e-kwə-blē, 'ē-\ *adv*

♦ balmy, clement, gentle, mild, moderate, temperate — more at CLEMENT

¹**equal** \'ē-kwəl\ *adj* 1 ♦ : of the same measure, quantity, value, quality, number, degree, or status as another 2 ♦ : regarding or affecting all objects in the same way : IMPARTIAL ⟨~ justice⟩ 3 : free from extremes 4 : able to cope with a situation or task — **equal·ly** *adv*

♦ [1] duplicate, even, identical, indistinguishable, same — more at SAME ♦ [2] disinterested, dispassionate, equitable, fair, impartial, just, nonpartisan, objective, square, unbiased, unprejudiced — more at FAIR

²**equal** *vb* **equaled** *or* **equalled; equal·ing** *or* **equal·ling** 1 ♦ : to be or become equal to; *also* : to be identical in value to 2 ♦ : to make or produce something equal to

♦ [1, 2] correspond, match, parallel — more at MATCH
♦ [1, 2] add up, amount, come, correspond, meet, rival, tie, touch — more at AMOUNT (TO)

³**equal** *n* ♦ : one that is equal

♦ coordinate, counterpart, equivalent, fellow, like, match, parallel, peer, rival; *also* analogue; double, mate, twin; associate, colleague, companion, partner; competitor

equal·ise, equal·is·er *Brit var of* EQUALIZE, EQUALIZER
equal·i·ty \i-'kwä-lə-tē\ *n* ♦ : the quality or state of being equal

♦ equivalence, par, parity, sameness — more at EQUIV-ALENCE

equal·ize \'ē-kwə-ˌlīz\ *vb* **-ized; -iz·ing** ♦ : to make equal, uniform, or constant — **equal·i·za·tion** \ˌē-kwə-lə-'zā-shən\ *n* — **equal·iz·er** *n*

♦ balance, equate, even, level; *also* accommodate, adjust, compensate, fit; homogenize, normalize, regularize, standardize; democratize

equals sign *or* **equal sign** *n* : a sign = indicating equivalence
equa·nim·i·ty \ˌē-kwə-'ni-mə-tē, ˌe-\ *n, pl* **-ties** ♦ : evenness of mind esp. under stress : COMPOSURE

♦ aplomb, calmness, composure, coolness, placidity, self-possession, serenity, tranquility; *also* assurance, confidence, poise, self-assurance, self-confidence *Ant* agitation, discomposure, perturbation

equate \i-'kwāt\ *vb* **equat·ed; equat·ing** 1 ♦ : to make, treat, or regard as equal or comparable 2 : show the relationship between

♦ balance, equalize, even, level — more at EQUALIZE
♦ bracket, compare, liken — more at COMPARE

equa·tion \i-'kwā-zhən\ *n* 1 : an act of equating : the state of being equated 2 : a usu. formal statement of equivalence esp. of mathematical expressions
equa·tor \i-'kwā-tər, 'ē-\ *n* : an imaginary circle around the earth that is everywhere equally distant from the two poles — **equa·to·ri·al** \ˌē-kwə-'tōr-ē-əl, ˌe-\ *adj*
equer·ry \'e-kwə-rē, i-'kwer-ē\ *n, pl* **-ries** 1 : an officer in charge of the horses of a prince or noble 2 : a personal attendant of a member of the British royal family
¹**eques·tri·an** \i-'kwes-trē-ən\ *adj* : of or relating to horseback riding; *also* : representing a person on horseback ⟨an ∼ statue⟩
²**equestrian** *n* : one who rides a horse
eques·tri·enne \i-ˌkwes-trē-'en\ *n* : a female rider on horseback
equi·dis·tant \ˌē-kwə-'dis-tənt\ *adj* : equally distant
equi·lat·er·al \ˌē-kwə-'la-tə-rəl\ *adj* : having all sides or faces equal ⟨∼ triangles⟩
equi·lib·ri·um \ˌē-kwə-'li-brē-əm, ˌe-\ *n, pl* **-ri·ums** *or* **-ria** \-brē-ə\ 1 : a state of intellectual or emotional balance 2 ♦ : a state of balance between opposing forces or actions

♦ balance, equipoise, poise — more at BALANCE

¹**equine** \'ē-ˌkwīn, 'e-\ *adj* [L *equinus*, fr. *equus* horse] : of or relating to the horse
²**equine** *n* : a member of the family of hoofed mammals consisting of the horses, asses, and zebras and extinct related animals; *specif* : HORSE
equi·noc·tial \ˌē-kwə-'näk-shəl, ˌe-\ *adj* : relating to an equinox
equi·nox \'ē-kwə-ˌnäks, 'e-\ *n* : either of the two times each year when the sun appears directly overhead at the equator and day and night are everywhere of equal length
equip \i-'kwip\ *vb* **equipped; equip·ping** [AF *eskiper* to load on board a ship, outfit, man, of Gmc origin] 1 ♦ : to supply with needed resources 2 ♦ : to make ready : PRE-PARE

♦ [1] accoutre, fit, furnish, outfit, rig, supply — more at FURNISH ♦ [2] fit, prepare, qualify, ready, season — more at QUALIFY

eq·ui·page \'e-kwə-pij\ *n* : a horse-drawn carriage usu. with its servants
equip·ment \i-'kwip-mənt\ *n* 1 ♦ : things used in equipping : OUTFIT 2 : the equipping of a person or thing : the state of being equipped

♦ accoutrements (*or* accouterments), apparatus, gear, matériel, outfit, paraphernalia, tackle; *also* accessories, attachments, fittings; baggage, belongings, impedimenta; appliances, facilities, instruments, machinery, tools; apparel, attire, habiliments, raiment, trappings; battery

equi·poise \'e-kwə-ˌpȯiz, 'ē-\ *n* 1 ♦ : a state of equilibrium : BALANCE 2 ♦ : a weight or force that offsets another : COUNTERBALANCE

♦ [1] balance, equilibrium, poise — more at BALANCE
♦ [2] balance, counterbalance, counterweight, offset

eq·ui·ta·ble \'e-kwə-tə-bəl\ *adj* ♦ : having or exhibiting equity : JUST, FAIR — **eq·ui·ta·bly** \-blē\ *adv*

♦ disinterested, dispassionate, equal, fair, impartial, just, nonpartisan, objective, square, unbiased, unprejudiced — more at FAIR

eq·ui·ta·tion \ˌe-kwə-'tā-shən\ *n* : the act or art of riding on horseback
eq·ui·ty \'e-kwə-tē\ *n, pl* **-ties** 1 : JUSTNESS, IMPARTIALITY 2 : value of a property or of an interest in it in excess of claims against it
equiv *abbr* equivalent
equiv·a·lence \-ləns\ *n* ♦ : the state or property of being equivalent

♦ equality, par, parity, sameness; *also* compatibility, correlation, correspondence; likeness, similarity *Ant* inequality

¹**equiv·a·lent** \i-'kwi-və-lənt\ *adj* : EQUAL; *also* : virtually identical
²**equivalent** *n* ♦ : one that is equivalent (as in value, meaning, or effect)

♦ coordinate, counterpart, equal, fellow, like, match, parallel, peer, rival — more at EQUAL

equiv·o·cal \i-'kwi-və-kəl\ *adj* 1 ♦ : subject to two or more interpretations and usu. used to mislead or confuse : AM-BIGUOUS 2 : UNCERTAIN, UNDECIDED 3 ♦ : of doubtful advantage, genuineness, or morality : SUSPICIOUS, DUBI-OUS ⟨∼ behavior⟩ — **equiv·o·cal·ly** *adv*

♦ [1] ambiguous, cryptic, enigmatic, inscrutable, mysterious, mystic, nebulous, obscure, occult — more at OBSCURE ♦ [3] debatable, disputable, doubtful, dubious, fishy, problematic, questionable, shady, shaky, suspect, suspicious — more at DOUBTFUL

equiv·o·cate \i-'kwi-və-ˌkāt\ *vb* **-cat·ed; -cat·ing** 1 : to use misleading language 2 ♦ : to avoid committing oneself in what one says

♦ fudge, hedge, pussyfoot; *also* dodge, duck, evade, sidestep, skirt; bypass, circumvent; cavil, quibble

equiv·o·ca·tion \-ˌkwi-və-'kā-shən\ *n* : an equivocal state or character; *esp* : the state of having more than one meaning
¹**-er** \ər\ *adj suffix or adv suffix* — used to form the comparative degree of adjectives and adverbs of one or two syllables ⟨hotter⟩ ⟨drier⟩ ⟨sillier⟩ and sometimes of longer ones
²**-er** \ər\ *also* **-ier** \ē-ər, yər\ *or* **-yer** \yər\ *n suffix* 1 : a person occupationally connected with ⟨hatter⟩ ⟨lawyer⟩ 2 : a person or thing belonging to or associated with ⟨old-timer⟩ 3 : a native of : resident of ⟨New Zealander⟩ 4 : one that has ⟨double-decker⟩ 5 : one that produces or yields ⟨porker⟩ 6 : one that does or performs (a specified action) ⟨reporter⟩ 7 : one that is a suitable object of (a specified action) ⟨broiler⟩ 8 : one that is ⟨foreigner⟩
Er *symbol* erbium
ER *abbr* emergency room
era \'ir-ə, 'er-ə, 'ē-rə\ *n* [LL *aera*, fr. L, counters, pl. of *aes* copper, money] 1 : a chronological order or system of notation reckoned from a given date as basis 2 ♦ : a period identified by some special feature 3 : any of the four major divisions of geologic time

♦ age, epoch, period, time

ERA *abbr* 1 earned run average 2 Equal Rights Amendment
erad·i·cate \i-'ra-də-ˌkāt\ *vb* **-cat·ed; -cat·ing** [L *eradicatus*,

pp. of *eradicare*, fr. *e-* out + *radix* root] **1** : to pull up (as a weed) by the roots : UPROOT **2 ♦** : destroy completely : ELIMINATE — **erad·i·ca·ble** \-di-kə-bəl\ *adj* — **erad·i·ca·tion** \-,ra-də-'kā-shən\ *n*

♦ annihilate, blot out, demolish, eliminate, exterminate, liquidate, obliterate, root, rub out, snuff, stamp, wipe out — more at ANNIHILATE

erase \i-'rās\ *vb* **erased; eras·ing** : to rub or scratch out (as written words); *also* : OBLITERATE — **eras·er** *n* — **era·sure** \i-'rā-shər\ *n*

er·bi·um \'ər-bē-əm\ *n* : a rare metallic element found with yttrium

¹ere \,er\ *prep* **♦** : preceding in time : BEFORE

♦ ahead of, before, of, previous to, prior to, to — more at BEFORE

²ere *conj* **♦** : BEFORE

e–read·er \'ē-,rē-dər\ *n* : a handheld electronic device used esp. for reading e-books

¹erect \i-'rekt\ *adj* **1 ♦** : not leaning or lying down : UPRIGHT **2** : being in a state of physiological erection

♦ perpendicular, standing, upright, upstanding, vertical; *also* elevated, lifted, upended, upraised; freestanding *Ant* flat, recumbent

²erect *vb* **1 ♦** : to put up by the fitting together of materials or parts : BUILD **2 ♦** : to fix or set in an upright position **3** : SET UP; *also* : ESTABLISH, DEVELOP

♦ [1] assemble, build, construct, fabricate, make, make up, piece, put up, raise — more at BUILD ♦ [2] pitch, put up, raise, rear, set up; *also* brace, buttress, prop (up), shore (up), support; elevate, hoist, lift

erec·tile \i-'rekt-ᵊl, -'rek-,tīl\ *adj* : capable of becoming erect ⟨~ tissue⟩ ⟨~ feathers of a bird⟩

erec·tion \i-'rek-shən\ *n* **1** : the turgid state of a previously flaccid bodily part when it becomes dilated with blood **2** : CONSTRUCTION ⟨the ~ of a building⟩

ere·long \er-'lȯŋ\ *adv* : before long

er·e·mite \'er-ə-,mīt\ *n* : a religious recluse : HERMIT

er·go \'er-gō, 'ər-\ *adv* [L] **♦** : because of a preceding fact or premise : THEREFORE

♦ accordingly, consequently, hence, so, therefore, thus, wherefore — more at THEREFORE

er·go·nom·ics \,ər-gə-'nä-miks\ *n sing or pl* : an applied science concerned with designing and arranging things people use in order to improve efficiency and safety — **er·go·nom·ic** \-mik\ *adj*

er·got \'er-gət, -,gät\ *n* **1** : a disease of rye and other cereals caused by a fungus; *also* : this fungus **2** : a medicinal compound or preparation derived from an ergot fungus

Er·i·tre·an \,er-ə-'trē-ən, -'trā-\ *n* : a native or inhabitant of Eritrea — **Eritrean** *adj*

er·mine \'ər-mən\ *n, pl* **ermines 1** : any of several weasels with winter fur mostly white; *also* : this white fur **2** : a rank or office whose official robe is ornamented with ermine

erode \i-'rōd\ *vb* **erod·ed; erod·ing ♦** : to diminish or destroy by degrees; *esp* : to gradually eat into or wear away ⟨soil *eroded* by wind and water⟩ — **erod·ible** *also* **erod·able** \-'rō-də-bəl\ *adj*

♦ abrade, bite, chafe, corrode, eat, fray, fret, gall, rub, wear — more at ABRADE

erog·e·nous \i-'rä-jə-nəs\ *adj* **1** : sexually sensitive ⟨~ zones⟩ **2** : of, relating to, or arousing sexual feelings

ero·sion \i-'rō-zhən\ *n* : the process or state of being eroded — **ero·sion·al** \-'rō-zhə-nəl\ *adj* — **ero·sion·al·ly** *adv*

ero·sive \i-'rō-siv\ *adj* : tending to erode — **ero·sive·ness** *n*

erot·ic \i-'rä-tik\ *adj* **♦** : relating to or dealing with sexual love : AMATORY — **erot·i·cal·ly** \-ti-k(ə-)lē\ *adv* — **erot·i·cism** \-tə-,si-zəm\ *n*

♦ amatory, amorous, sexy; *also* carnal, sensual, sensuous; bawdy, lascivious, lewd, lustful, obscene, prurient, spicy

err \'ər, 'er\ *vb* **♦** : to be or do wrong

♦ offend, sin, transgress, trespass — more at OFFEND

er·rand \'er-ənd\ *n* : a short trip taken to do something; *also* : the object or purpose of such a trip

er·rant \'er-ənt\ *adj* **1 ♦** : traveling or given to traveling : WANDERING ⟨an ~ knight⟩ **2** : straying outside proper bounds ⟨a ~ throw⟩ **3 ♦** : deviating from an accepted pattern or standard (as of behavior) ⟨an ~ child⟩

♦ [1] itinerant, nomad, peripatetic, roaming, vagabond, vagrant — more at ITINERANT ♦ [3] bad, contrary, froward, mischievous, naughty — more at NAUGHTY

er·ra·ta \e-'rä-tə\ *n* : a list of corrigenda

er·rat·ic \i-'ra-tik\ *adj* **1** : having no fixed course **2 a ♦** : characterized by lack of consistency, regularity, or uniformity : INCONSISTENT **b** : ECCENTRIC ⟨~ behavior⟩ — **er·rat·i·cal·ly** \-ti-k(ə-)lē\ *adv*

♦ aimless, arbitrary, desultory, haphazard, random, scattered, stray — more at RANDOM ♦ choppy, discontinuous, fitful, intermittent, irregular, occasional, spasmodic, sporadic, spotty, uneven, unsteady — more at FITFUL

er·ra·tum \e-'rä-təm\ *n, pl* **-ta** \-tə\ : CORRIGENDUM

er·ro·ne·ous \i-'rō-nē-əs, e-'rō-\ *adj* **♦** : containing or characterized by error : INCORRECT

♦ false, inaccurate, incorrect, inexact, invalid, off, unsound, untrue, wrong — more at FALSE

er·ro·ne·ous·ly *adv* **♦** : in an erroneous manner

♦ amiss, faultily, improperly, inaptly, incorrectly, mistakenly, wrongly

er·ror \'er-ər\ *n* **1 ♦** : a usu. ignorant or unintentional deviating from accuracy or truth ⟨made an ~ in adding⟩ **2** : a defensive misplay in baseball **3** : the state of one that errs ⟨to be in ~⟩ **4** : a product of mistake ⟨a typographical ~⟩ **5 ♦** : an act or condition of ignorant or imprudent deviation from a code of behavior **6 ♦** : an instance of false belief : a mistaken idea or system of ideas

♦ [1] blunder, fault, flub, fumble, goof, lapse, misstep, mistake, oversight, slip, stumble; *also* foul-up, muff; misapprehension, miscalculation, misconception, misjudgment, misstatement, misunderstanding ♦ [5] crime, malefaction, misdeed, misdoing, offense, sin, transgression, violation, wrongdoing — more at OFFENSE ♦ [6] fallacy, falsehood, falsity, illusion, misconception, untruth — more at FALLACY

er·ror·less *adj* : done, played, or performed without an error

er·satz \'er-,zäts\ *adj* [G *ersatz-*, fr. *Ersatz*, n., substitute] : being usu. an artificial and inferior substitute

erst \'ərst\ *adv, archaic* : ERSTWHILE

¹erst·while \-,hwī(-ə)l\ *adv* : in the past : FORMERLY

²erstwhile *adj* **♦** : having been or existed at some past time : FORMER ⟨~ friends⟩

♦ former, late, old, onetime, past, sometime, whilom — more at FORMER

er·u·dite \'er-ə-,dīt, 'er-yə-\ *adj* **♦** : possessing or displaying erudition

♦ educated, knowledgeable, learned, literate, scholarly, well-read — more at EDUCATED ♦ bookish, learned, literary — more at BOOKISH

er·u·di·tion \,er-ə-'di-shən, ,er-yə-\ *n* **♦** : extensive knowledge acquired chiefly from books : SCHOLARSHIP, LEARNING

♦ education, knowledge, learning, scholarship, science — more at EDUCATION

erupt \i-'rəpt\ *vb* **1 a ♦** : to burst forth : emerge with a sudden often violent rush **b ♦** : to cause to burst forth : force out or release usu. suddenly and violently **2** : to break through a surface ⟨teeth ~ing through the gum⟩ **3** : to break out with or as if with a skin rash — **erup·tive** \-tiv\ *adj*

♦ [1a] break out, burst, explode, flame, flare, go off; *also* burgeon, mushroom, snowball; blow up, detonate, touch off ♦ [1b] belch, disgorge, eject, expel, jet, spew, spout, spurt; *also* gush, pour, stream, surge; emanate, issue, spring; discharge, emit, fire; cast, fling, heave, hurl, launch, pitch, toss

erup·tion \-'rəp-shən\ *n* ♦ : an act, process, or instance of erupting; *also* : a product of erupting (as a skin rash)

♦ agony, burst, explosion, fit, flare, flush, gush, outburst, paroxysm, spasm, storm — more at OUTBURST
♦ blast, detonation, explosion — more at EXPLOSION

-ery *n suffix* **1** : qualities collectively : character : -NESS ⟨snobb*ery*⟩ **2** : art : practice ⟨cook*ery*⟩ **3** : place of doing, keeping, producing, or selling (the thing specified) ⟨fish*ery*⟩ ⟨bak*ery*⟩ **4** : collection : aggregate ⟨fin*ery*⟩ **5** : state or condition ⟨slav*ery*⟩

ery·sip·e·las \ˌer-ə-'si-pə-ləs, ˌir-\ *n* : an acute bacterial disease marked by fever and severe skin inflammation

er·y·the·ma \ˌer-ə-'thē-mə\ *n* : abnormal redness of the skin due to capillary congestion (as in inflammation)

eryth·ro·cyte \i-'ri-thrə-ˌsīt\ *n* : RED BLOOD CELL

Es *symbol* einsteinium

¹-es \əz, iz *after* s, z, sh, ch; z *after* v *or a vowel*\ *n pl suffix* — used to form the pl. of most nouns that end in *s* ⟨glass*es*⟩, *z* ⟨fuzz*es*⟩, *sh* ⟨bush*es*⟩, *ch* ⟨peach*es*⟩, or a final *y* that changes to *i* ⟨lad*ies*⟩ and of some nouns ending in *f* that changes to *v* ⟨loav*es*⟩

²-es *vb suffix* — used to form the third person singular present of most verbs that end in *s* ⟨bless*es*⟩, *z* ⟨fizz*es*⟩, *sh* ⟨hush*es*⟩, *ch* ⟨catch*es*⟩, or a final *y* that changes to *i* ⟨def*ies*⟩

es·ca·late \'es-kə-ˌlāt\ *vb* **-lat·ed; -lat·ing** ♦ : to increase in extent, volume, number, intensity, or scope ⟨the violence *escalated*⟩ — **es·ca·la·tion** \ˌes-kə-'lā-shən\ *n*

♦ accumulate, appreciate, balloon, build, burgeon, enlarge, expand, increase, mount, multiply, mushroom, proliferate, rise, snowball, swell, wax — more at INCREASE

es·ca·la·tor \'es-kə-ˌlā-tər\ *n* : a moving set of stairs

es·ca·pade \'es-kə-ˌpād\ *n* [F, action of escaping] ♦ : a mischievous adventure

♦ antic, caper, frolic, monkeyshine, practical joke, prank, trick — more at PRANK

¹es·cape \is-'kāp\ *vb* **es·caped; es·cap·ing** [ME, fr. OF *escaper*, fr. (assumed) VL *excappare*, fr. L *ex-* out + LL *cappa* head covering, cloak] **1** ♦ : to get free or away **2** : to avoid a threatening evil **3** ♦ : miss or succeed in averting : AVOID 2 ⟨~ injury⟩ ⟨*escaped* punishment⟩ **4** : to fail to be noticed or recallable by : ELUDE ⟨his name ~*s* me⟩ **5** : to be produced or uttered involuntarily by ⟨let a sob ~ him⟩

♦ [1] abscond, clear out, flee, fly, get out, lam, run away, run off; *also* avoid, elude, evade, lose, shun; decamp, depart, exit, leave; disentangle, extricate; emancipate, free, liberate, redeem, release ♦ [3] avoid, dodge, duck, elude, eschew, evade, shake, shirk, shun; *also* miss; avert, deflect, divert, obviate, parry, prevent, ward (off); debar, exclude, preclude; bypass, circumvent, skirt; foil, frustrate, outwit, thwart

²escape *n* **1** ♦ : flight from or avoidance of something unpleasant **2** : LEAKAGE **3** ♦ : a means of escape

♦ [1] avoidance, cop-out, evasion, out; *also* bypassing, circumvention; averting, deflection, prevention
♦ [3] flight, getaway, lam, slip; *also* deliverance, liberation, redemption, release, rescue, salvation

³escape *adj* : providing a means or way of escape

es·cap·ee \is-ˌkā-'pē, ˌes-(ˌ)kā-\ *n* : one that has escaped esp. from prison

escape velocity *n* : the minimum velocity needed by a body (as a rocket) to escape from the gravitational field of a celestial body (as the earth)

es·cap·ism \is-'kā-ˌpi-zəm\ *n* : diversion of the mind to imaginative activity as an escape from routine — **es·cap·ist** \-pist\ *adj or n*

es·car·got \ˌes-ˌkär-'gō\ *n, pl* **-gots** \-'gō(z)\ : a snail prepared for use as food

es·ca·role \'es-kə-ˌrōl\ *n* : ENDIVE 1

es·carp·ment \es-'kärp-mənt\ *n* **1** : a steep slope in front of a fortification **2** ♦ : a long cliff

♦ bluff, cliff, crag, palisade, precipice, scarp — more at CLIFF

es·chew \is-'chü\ *vb* ♦ : to avoid habitually esp. on moral or practical grounds : SHUN, AVOID

♦ avoid, dodge, duck, elude, escape, evade, shake, shirk, shun — more at ESCAPE

¹es·cort \'es-ˌkȯrt\ *n* ♦ : one (as a person or warship) accompanying another esp. as a protection or courtesy

♦ attendant, companion, guard, guide; *also* chaperon, squire; shadow, sidekick; conductor, leader, pilot

²es·cort \is-'kȯrt, es-\ *vb* ♦ : to accompany as an escort

♦ accompany, attend, convoy, squire — more at ACCOMPANY

es·crow \'es-ˌkrō\ *n* : something (as a deed or a sum of money) delivered by one person to another to be delivered to a third party only upon the fulfillment of a condition; *also* : a fund or deposit serving as an escrow

es·cutch·eon \is-'kə-chən\ *n* : the usu. shield-shaped surface on which a coat of arms is shown

Esd *abbr* Esdras

Es·dras \'ez-drəs\ *n* **1** : either of two books of the Roman Catholic canon of the Old Testament: **a** : a narrative book of canonical Jewish and Christian Scripture **b** : narrative and historical book of canonical Jewish and Christian Scripture **2** : either of two uncanonical books of Scripture included in the Protestant Apocrypha

ESE *abbr* east-southeast

Es·ki·mo \'es-kə-ˌmō\ *n* **1** *now sometimes offensive* : a member of a group of peoples of northern Canada, Greenland, Alaska, and eastern Siberia **2** : any of the languages of the Eskimo peoples

Eskimo dog *n* : a sled dog of American origin

ESL *abbr* English as a second language

esoph·a·gus \i-'sä-fə-gəs\ *n, pl* **-gi** \-ˌgī, -ˌjī\ : a muscular tube that leads from the cavity behind the mouth to the stomach — **esoph·a·geal** \-ˌsä-fə-'jē-əl\ *adj*

es·o·ter·ic \ˌe-sə-'ter-ik\ *adj* **1** ♦ : designed for or understood only by the specially initiated; *broadly* : difficult to understand **2** : PRIVATE, SECRET

♦ abstruse, deep, profound — more at PROFOUND

esp *abbr* especially

ESP \ˌē-(ˌ)es-'pē\ *n* : EXTRASENSORY PERCEPTION

es·pa·drille \'es-pə-ˌdril\ *n* [F] : a flat sandal usu. having a fabric upper and a flexible sole

es·pal·ier \is-'pal-yər, -ˌyā\ *n* : a plant (as a fruit tree) trained to grow flat against a support — **espalier** *vb*

es·pe·cial \is-'pe-shəl\ *adj* ♦ : being distinctive : SPECIAL

♦ distinct, express, precise, set, special, specific — more at EXPRESS

es·pe·cial·ly *adv* **1** : in a special manner; *also* : in particular **2** ♦ : in a particularly strong or good way — used as an intensive

♦ extra, extremely, greatly, highly, hugely, mightily, mighty, mortally, most, much, real, right, so, very — more at VERY

Es·pe·ran·to \ˌes-pə-'ran-tō, -'rän-\ *n* : an artificial international language based esp. on words common to the chief European languages

es·pi·o·nage \'es-pē-ə-ˌnäzh, -nij\ *n* [F *espionnage*] : the practice of spying

es·pla·nade \'es-plə-ˌnäd\ *n* : a level open stretch or area; *esp* : one for walking or driving along a shore

es·pous·al \i-'spau̇-zəl\ *n* **1** ♦ : the act of betrothing or fact of being betrothed : BETROTHAL; *also* : WEDDING **2** : a taking up (as of a cause) as a supporter — **es·pouse** \-'spau̇z\ *vb*

♦ marriage, wedding — more at WEDDING ♦ betrothal, engagement, troth — more at ENGAGEMENT

espres·so \e-'spre-sō\ *n, pl* **-sos** : coffee brewed by forcing steam through finely ground darkly roasted coffee beans

es·prit \i-'sprē\ *n* ♦ : sprightly wit

♦ bounce, dash, drive, pep, punch, snap, spirit, verve, vim, zing, zip — more at SPIRIT

es·prit de corps \i-ˌsprē-də-'kȯr\ *n* [F] : the common spirit existing in the members of a group

es·py \i-'spī\ *vb* **es·pied; es·py·ing** ♦ : to catch sight of

♦ discern, eye, notice, observe, perceive, regard, see, sight, spy, view — more at SEE

Esq *or* **Esqr** *abbr* esquire

es·quire \'es-ˌkwī(-ə)r\ *n* [ME, fr. MF *esquier* squire, fr. LL *scutarius*, fr. L *scutum* shield] **1** : a man of the English gentry ranking next below a knight **2** : a candidate for knighthood serving as attendant to a knight **3** — used as a title of courtesy

-ess \əs, ˌes\ *n suffix* : female ⟨author*ess*⟩

¹es·say \e-'sā, 'e-ˌsā\ *vb* ♦ : to make an often tentative or experimental effort to perform : ATTEMPT, TRY

♦ assay, attempt, endeavor (*or* endeavour), seek, strive, try — more at ATTEMPT

²es·say *n* **1** \'e-ˌsā, e-'sā\ ♦ : an initial tentative effort : AT-TEMPT **2** \'e-ˌsā\ ♦ : a literary composition usu. dealing with a subject from a limited or personal point of view — **es·say·ist** \'e-ˌsā-ist\ *n*

♦ [1] attempt, bid, crack, endeavor (*or* endeavour), fling, go, pass, shot, stab, trial, try, whack, whirl — more at ATTEMPT ♦ [2] article, composition, paper, theme; *also* column, commentary, editorial, feature, report, review, write-up; dissertation, thesis; tract, trea-tise; discourse, discussion, exposition, study

es·sence \'es-ᵊns\ *n* **1** ♦ : fundamental nature or quality **2** : a substance distilled or extracted from another sub-stance (as a plant or drug) and having the special qualities of the original substance **3** : PERFUME **4** ♦ : the most significant element or aspect of something ⟨the ~ of the issue⟩

♦ [1, 4] nature, quintessence, soul, stuff, substance; *also* heart, spirit; center, core, keynote, marrow, pith, seat; embodiment, epitome, incarnation, manifestation, personification; aspect, attribute, feature, property; gist, kernel, nub

¹es·sen·tial \i-'sen-chəl\ *adj* **1** ♦ : of, relating to, or consti-tuting an essence ⟨voting is an ~ right of citizenship⟩ ⟨~ oils⟩ **2** ♦ : of the utmost importance : INDISPENSABLE ⟨water is ~ for life⟩; *also* : of, relating to, or forming the base or essence **3** : being a substance that must be obtained from the diet because it is not sufficiently pro-duced by the body ⟨~ amino acids⟩ — **es·sen·tial·ly** *adv*

♦ [1] ingrained, inherent, innate, integral, intrinsic, natural — more at INHERENT ♦ [1] basic, elemental, elementary, fundamental, underlying — more at EL-EMENTARY ♦ [2] imperative, indispensable, integral, necessary, needful, requisite, vital; *also* prerequisite; compulsory, mandatory, obligatory; important, mo-mentous, significant; basic, central, fundamental, key, organic; insistent, persistent, pressing, urgent *Ant* dis-pensable, needless, nonessential

²essential *n* ♦ : something indispensable

♦ condition, demand, must, necessity, need, require-ment, requisite; *also* precondition, prerequisite *Ant* nonessential *usu* **essentials** elements, principles, rudi-ments — more at ELEMENT

est *abbr* **1** established **2** estimate; estimated

EST *abbr* eastern standard time

¹-est \əst, ist\ *adj suffix or adv suffix* — used to form the superlative degree of adjectives and adverbs of one or two syllables ⟨fatt*est*⟩ ⟨lat*est*⟩ ⟨lucki*est*⟩ ⟨often*est*⟩ and less often of longer ones

²-est \əst, ist\ *or* **-st** \st\ *vb suffix* — used to form the ar-chaic second person singular of English verbs (with *thou*) ⟨did*st*⟩

es·tab·lish \i-'sta-blish\ *vb* **1** : to institute permanently ⟨~ a law⟩ **2** ♦ : to bring into existence : FOUND ⟨~ a settlement⟩; *also* : EFFECT **3** : to make firm or stable **4** : to put on a firm basis : SET UP ⟨~ a son in business⟩ **5** ♦ : to gain acceptance or recognition of ⟨the movie ~ed her as a star⟩; *also* : PROVE ⟨~ed his innocence⟩

♦ [2] constitute, effect, found, inaugurate, initiate, innovate, institute, introduce, launch, pioneer, set up, start — more at FOUND ♦ [5] demonstrate, prove, show, substantiate; *also* attest, authenticate, bear out, document, evidence, support, sustain, uphold; confirm, corroborate, justify, validate, verify *Ant* disprove

es·tab·lish·ment \-mənt\ *n* **1** : something established: as **a** ♦ : a permanent civil or military organization **b** ♦ : a public or private institution **2** : a place of residence or business with its furnishings and staff **3** : an established ruling or controlling group ⟨the literary ~⟩ **4** : the act or state of establishing or being established

♦ [1a, 1b] foundation, institute, institution — more at INSTITUTION ♦ [1b] business, company, concern, en-terprise, firm, house, outfit — more at ENTERPRISE

es·tate \i-'stāt\ *n* **1 a** ♦ : mode or condition of being : STATE **b** : social standing : STATUS **2** ♦ : a social or political class ⟨the three ~s of nobility, clergy, and commons⟩ **3** : a person's possessions : FORTUNE **4** ♦ : a landed property

♦ [1a] condition, fettle, form, order, repair, shape, state, trim — more at CONDITION ♦ [2] caste, class, folk, or-der, stratum — more at CLASS ♦ [4] castle, hall, manor, mansion, palace, villa — more at MANSION

¹es·teem \i-'stēm\ *n* ♦ : high regard

♦ admiration, appreciation, estimation, favor (*or* favour), regard, respect — more at ADMIRATION

²esteem *vb* **1** ♦ : to view as : REGARD ⟨was highly ~ed⟩ **2** ♦ : to set a high value on

♦ [1] account, call, consider, count, hold, rate, reckon, regard, take — more at CONSIDER ♦ [2] admire, appre-ciate, regard, respect — more at ADMIRE

es·ter \'es-tər\ *n* : an often fragrant organic compound formed by the reaction of an acid and an alcohol

Esth *abbr* Esther

Es·ther \'es-tər\ *n* : a narrative book of canonical Jewish and Christian Scripture

esthete, esthetic, esthetically, esthetics *var of* AESTHETE, AESTHETIC, AESTHETICALLY, AESTHETICS

es·ti·ma·ble \'es-tə-mə-bəl\ *adj* : worthy of esteem

¹es·ti·mate \'es-tə-ˌmāt\ *vb* **-mat·ed; -mat·ing** **1** ♦ : to give or form an approximation (as of value, size, or cost) **2** : JUDGE, CONCLUDE — **es·ti·ma·tor** \-ˌmā-tər\ *n*

♦ appraise, assess, evaluate, rate, set, value; *also* ad-judge, deem, judge; ascertain, determine, discover, learn; price, prize; decide, settle; assay, analyze, survey, test; reappraise, reassess, reevaluate, revalue calculate, call, conjecture, figure, gauge, guess, judge, make, place, put, reckon, suppose

²es·ti·mate \'es-tə-mət\ *n* **1** ♦ : an opinion or judgment of the nature, character, or quality of a person or thing **2** ♦ : a rough or approximate calculation **3** : a statement of the cost of work to be done

♦ [1] appraisal, assessment, estimation, evaluation, judgment (*or* judgement) — more at ESTIMATION ♦ [2] calculation, computation, measurement, reckon-ing, valuation

es·ti·ma·tion \ˌes-tə-'mā-shən\ *n* **1** ♦ : a view, judgment, or appraisal formed in the mind about a particular matter : JUDGMENT **2** ♦ : the value, amount, or size arrived at in an estimate : ESTIMATE; *also* : the act of estimating something **3** ♦ : high regard : ESTEEM

♦ [1] appraisal, assessment, estimate, evaluation, judg-ment (*or* judgement), reckoning, valuation — more at ES-TIMATE ♦ [2] appraisal, assessment, estimate, evaluation, judgment (*or* judgement); *also* impression, notion, per-ception; confidence, faith, stock, trust ♦ [3] admiration, appreciation, esteem, favor (*or* favour), regard, respect — more at ADMIRATION

es·ti·vate \'es-tə-ˌvāt\ *vb* **-vat·ed; -vat·ing** : to pass the summer in an inactive or resting state ⟨creatures *estivating* in the cool mud⟩ — **es·ti·va·tion** \ˌes-tə-'vā-shən\ *n*

Es·to·nian \e-'stō-nē-ən\ *n* : a native or inhabitant of Estonia — **Estonian** *adj*

es·trange \i-'strānj\ *vb* **es·tranged; es·trang·ing** ♦ : to alienate the affections or confidence of

♦ alienate, disaffect, disgruntle, sour; *also* antagonize, embitter; anger, disunite, divide, separate, sever, sunder; disappoint, disenchant, disillusion *Ant* reconcile

es·trange·ment *n* ♦ : the act of estranging or the condition of being estranged : alienation esp. in friendship

♦ alienation, disaffection; *also* antagonism, division, divorce, schism, separation; disenchantment, disillusionment *Ant* reconciliation

es·tro·gen \'es-trə-jən\ *n* : a steroid (as a sex hormone) that tends to cause estrus and the development of female secondary sex characteristics — **es·tro·gen·ic** \ˌes-trə-'je-nik\ *adj*

estrous cycle *n* : the cycle of changes in the endocrine and reproductive systems of a female mammal from the beginning of one period of estrus to the beginning of the next

es·trus \'es-trəs\ *n* : a periodic state of sexual excitability during which the female of most mammals is willing to mate with the male and is capable of becoming pregnant : HEAT — **es·trous** \-trəs\ *adj*

es·tu·ary \'es-chù-ˌwer-ē\ *n, pl* **-ar·ies** ♦ : an arm of the sea at the mouth of a river

♦ bay, bight, cove, gulf, inlet — more at GULF

ET *abbr* eastern time

eta \'ā-tə\ *n* : the 7th letter of the Greek alphabet — H or η

ETA *abbr* estimated time of arrival

et al. \et-'al\ *abbr* [L *et alii* (masc.), *et aliae* (fem.), or *et alia* (neut.)] and others

etc. *abbr* et cetera

et cet·era \et-'set-ə-rə\ [L] : and others esp. of the same kind — used to imply that other items are to be understood

etch \'ech\ *vb* [D *etsen*, fr. G *ätzen* to etch, corrode, fr. OHG *azzen* to feed] **1** ♦ : to produce (as a design) on a hard material by corroding its surface (as by acid) **2** ♦ : to delineate or impress clearly — **etch·er** *n*

♦ [1] engrave, grave, inscribe — more at ENGRAVE
♦ [2] engrave, impress, imprint, ingrain, inscribe — more at ENGRAVE

etch·ing *n* **1** : the action, process, or art of etching **2** : a design produced on or print made from an etched plate

ETD *abbr* estimated time of departure

eter·nal \i-'tərn-ᵊl\ *adj* ♦ : having infinite duration : EVERLASTING, PERPETUAL

♦ ceaseless, dateless, deathless, endless, everlasting, immortal, permanent, perpetual, undying, unending — more at EVERLASTING

eter·nal·ly *adv* ♦ : throughout eternity

♦ always, ever, everlastingly, forever, permanently, perpetually — more at EVER

eter·ni·ty \i-'tər-nə-tē\ *n, pl* **-ties** **1** : infinite duration **2** ♦ : the state after death : IMMORTALITY **3** ♦ : a seemingly endless or immeasurable time

♦ [2] afterlife, hereafter, immortality; *also* otherworld
♦ [3] age, cycle, eon (*or* aeon) — more at AGE

¹-eth \əth, ith\ *or* **-th** \th\ *vb suffix* — used to form the archaic third person singular present of verbs ⟨do*th*⟩

eth·ane \'e-ˌthān\ *n* : a colorless odorless gaseous hydrocarbon found in natural gas and used esp. as a fuel

eth·a·nol \'e-thə-ˌnȯl\ *n* : ALCOHOL 1

ether \'ē-thər\ *n* **1** : the upper regions of space; *also* : the gaseous element formerly held to fill these regions **2** : a light flammable liquid used as an anesthetic and solvent

ethe·re·al \i-'thir-ē-əl\ *adj* **1** : CELESTIAL, HEAVENLY

2 ♦ : exceptionally delicate : AIRY, DAINTY ⟨∼ flaky pastry⟩ — **ethe·re·al·ly** *adv* — **ethe·re·al·ness** *n*

♦ airy, dainty, fluffy, light — more at AIRY

Ether·net \'ē-thər-ˌnet\ *n* : a computer network architecture for local area networks

eth·i·cal \'e-thi-kəl\ *adj* **1** : of or relating to ethics **2** ♦ : conforming to accepted and esp. professional standards of conduct — **eth·i·cal·ly** *adv*

♦ decent, good, honest, honorable (*or* honourable), just, moral, principled, right, straight, upright, virtuous — more at GOOD ♦ conscientious, honest, honorable (*or* honourable), just, moral, principled, scrupulous — more at CONSCIENTIOUS

eth·ics \'e-thiks\ *n sing or pl* **1** : a discipline dealing with good and evil and with moral duty **2** ♦ : moral principles or practice

♦ morality, morals, principles, standards; *also* customs, etiquette, manners, mores; beliefs, dogma, faith, tenets

Ethi·o·pi·an \ˌē-thē-'ō-pē-ən\ *n* : a native or inhabitant of Ethiopia — **Ethiopian** *adj*

¹eth·nic \'eth-nik\ *adj* [ME, heathen, fr. LL *ethnicus*, fr. Gk *ethnikos* national, gentile, fr. *ethnos* nation, people] : of or relating to races or large groups of people classed according to common traits and customs — **eth·ni·cal·ly** *adv*

²ethnic *n* : a member of a minority ethnic group who retains its customs, language, or social views

eth·nol·o·gy \eth-'nä-lə-jē\ *n* : a science dealing with the races of human beings, their origin, distribution, characteristics, and relations — **eth·no·log·i·cal** \ˌeth-nə-'lä-ji-kəl\ *adj* — **eth·nol·o·gist** \eth-'nä-lə-jist\ *n*

ethol·o·gy \ē-'thä-lə-jē\ *n* : the scientific and objective study of animal behavior — **etho·log·i·cal** \ˌē-thə-'lä-ji-kəl, ˌe-\ *adj* — **ethol·o·gist** \ē-'thä-lə-jist\ *n*

ethos \'ē-ˌthäs\ *n* : the distinguishing character, sentiment, moral nature, or guiding beliefs of a person, group, or institution

ethyl alcohol *n* : ALCOHOL 1

eth·yl·ene \'e-thə-ˌlēn\ *n* : a colorless flammable gas found in coal gas or obtained from petroleum

eti·ol·o·gy \ˌē-tē-'ä-lə-jē\ *n* : the causes of a disease or abnormal condition; *also* : a branch of medicine concerned with the causes and origins of diseases — **eti·o·log·ic** \ˌē-tē-ə-'lä-jik\ *or* **eti·o·log·i·cal** \-ji-kəl\ *adj*

et·i·quette \'e-ti-kət, -ˌket\ *n* [F *étiquette*, lit., label, list] ♦ : the forms prescribed by custom or authority to be observed in social, official, or professional life

♦ manners, mores

Etrus·can \i-'trəs-kən\ *n* **1** : the language of the Etruscans **2** : an inhabitant of ancient Etruria — **Etruscan** *adj*

et seq *abbr* [L *et sequens*] and the following one [L *et sequentes* (masc. & fem. pl.) or *et sequentia* (neut. pl.)] and the following ones

-ette \'et, ˌet, ət, it\ *n suffix* **1** : little one ⟨din*ette*⟩ **2** : female ⟨usher*ette*⟩

étude \'ā-ˌtüd, -ˌtyüd\ *n* [F, lit., study] : a musical composition for practice to develop technical skill

et·y·mol·o·gy \ˌe-tə-'mä-lə-jē\ *n, pl* **-gies** **1** : the history of a linguistic form (as a word) shown by tracing its development and relationships **2** : a branch of linguistics dealing with etymologies — **et·y·mo·log·i·cal** \-mə-'lä-ji-kəl\ *adj* — **et·y·mol·o·gist** \-'mä-lə-jist\ *n*

Eu *symbol* europium

EU *abbr* European Union

eu·ca·lyp·tus \ˌyü-kə-'lip-təs\ *n, pl* **-ti** \-ˌtī\ *or* **-tus·es** : any of a genus of mostly Australian evergreen trees widely grown for shade or their wood, oils, resins, and gums

Eu·cha·rist \'yü-kə-rəst\ *n* : COMMUNION 2 — **eu·cha·ris·tic** \ˌyü-kə-'ris-tik\ *adj, often cap*

¹eu·chre \'yü-kər\ *n* : a card game in which the side naming the trump must take three of five tricks to win

²euchre *vb* **eu·chred; eu·chring** : CHEAT, TRICK

eu·clid·e·an *also* **eu·clid·i·an** \yù-'kli-dē-ən\ *adj, often cap*

: of or relating to the geometry of Euclid or a geometry based on similar axioms

eu·gen·ics \yù-'je-niks\ *n* : a science dealing with the improvement (as by selective breeding) of hereditary qualities esp. of human beings — **eu·gen·ic** \-nik\ *adj*

eu·lo·gy \'yü-lə-jē\ *n, pl* **-gies** 1 ♦ : a speech in praise of some person or thing esp. in honor of a deceased person 2 : high praise — **eu·lo·gis·tic** \,yü-lə-'jis-tik\ *adj* — **eu·lo·gize** \'yü-lə-,jīz\ *vb*

    ♦ accolade, citation, commendation, encomium, homage, paean, panegyric, salutation, tribute — more at ENCOMIUM

eu·nuch \'yü-nək\ *n* : a castrated man

eu·phe·mism \'yü-fə-,mi-zəm\ *n* [Gk *euphēmismos*, fr. *euphēmos* auspicious, sounding good, fr. *eu-* good + *phēmē* speech] : the substitution of a mild or pleasant expression for one offensive or unpleasant; *also* : the expression substituted — **eu·phe·mis·tic** \,yü-fə-'mis-tik\ *adj* — **eu·phe·mis·ti·cal·ly** \-tĭ-k(ə-)lē\ *adv*

eu·pho·ni·ous \yù-'fō-nē-əs\ *adj* ♦ : pleasing to the ear — **eu·pho·ni·ous·ly** *adv*

    ♦ harmonious, lyric, melodious, musical, symphonic, tuneful — more at HARMONIOUS

eu·pho·ny \'yü-fə-nē\ *n, pl* **-nies** : the effect produced by words so combined as to please the ear

eu·pho·ria \yù-'fòr-ē-ə\ *n* ♦ : a marked feeling of well-being or elation

    ♦ ecstasy, elation, exhilaration, heaven, intoxication, paradise, rapture, rhapsody, transport — more at ECSTASY

eu·phor·ic \-'fòr-ik\ *adj* ♦ : characterized by or based on euphoria

    ♦ ecstatic, elated, intoxicated, rapturous, rhapsodic — more at ECSTATIC

Eur *abbr* Europe; European

Eur·asian \yù-'rā-zhən, -shən\ *adj* 1 : of mixed European and Asian origin 2 : of or relating to Europe and Asia — **Eurasian** *n*

eu·re·ka \yù-'rē-kə\ *interj* [Gk *heurēka* I have found, fr. *heuriskein* to find; fr. the exclamation attributed to Archimedes on discovering a method for determining the purity of gold] — used to express triumph on a discovery

eu·ro \'yùr-ō\ *n, pl* **euros** : the common basic monetary unit of most countries of the European Union

Eu·ro–Amer·i·can \,yùr-ō-ə-'mer-ə-kən\ *n* 1 : a person of mixed European and American ancestry 2 : CAUCASIAN

Eu·ro·bond \'yùr-ō-,bänd\ *n* : a bond of a U.S. corporation that is sold outside the U.S. but that is valued and paid for in dollars and yields interest in dollars

Eu·ro·cur·ren·cy \,yùr-ō-'kər-ən-sē\ *n* : moneys (as of the U.S. and Japan) held outside their countries of origin and used in the money markets of Europe

Eu·ro·dol·lar \'yùr-ō-,dä-lər\ *n* : a U.S. dollar held as Eurocurrency

Eu·ro·pe·an \,yùr-ə-'pē-ən\ *n* 1 : a native or inhabitant of Europe 2 : a person of European descent — **European** *adj* — **Eu·ro·pe·an·ize** \-ə-,nīz\ *vb*

European–American *n* : EURO-AMERICAN

Eu·ro·pe·an·ism \yùr-,ō-'pē-ə-ni-zəm\ *n* 1 : allegiance to the traditions, interests, or ideals of Europeans 2 : advocacy of political and economic integration of Europe — **eu·ro·pe·an·ist** \-nist\ *n*

European plan *n* : a hotel plan whereby the daily rates cover only the cost of the room

eu·ro·pi·um \yù-'rō-pē-əm\ *n* : a rare metallic chemical element

eu·sta·chian tube \yù-'stā-shən-\ *n, often cap E* : a tube connecting the inner cavity of the ear with the throat and equalizing air pressure on both sides of the eardrum

eu·tha·na·sia \,yü-thə-'nā-zhə\ *n* [Gk, easy death, fr. *eu-* good + *thanatos* death] : the act or practice of killing or permitting the death of hopelessly sick or injured persons or animals with as little pain as possible for reasons of mercy

EVA *abbr* extravehicular activity

evac·u·ate \i-'va-kyə-,wāt\ *vb* **-at·ed; -at·ing** 1 ♦ : to to make empty : empty out 2 : to discharge wastes from the body 3 : to remove or withdraw from : VACATE — **evac·u·a·tion** \-,va-kyə-'wā-shən\ *n*

    ♦ clear, empty, vacate, void — more at EMPTY

evac·u·ee \i-,va-kyə-'wē\ *n* ♦ : a person removed from a dangerous place

    ♦ émigré, exile, expatriate, refugee — more at ÉMIGRÉ

evade \i-'vād\ *vb* **evad·ed; evad·ing** ♦ : to manage to avoid esp. by dexterity or slyness : ELUDE, ESCAPE

    ♦ avoid, dodge, duck, elude, escape, eschew, shake, shirk, shun — more at ESCAPE

eval·u·ate \i-'val-yù-,wāt\ *vb* **-at·ed; -at·ing** ♦ : to determine or fix the value of : APPRAISE, VALUE; *also* : to determine the significance, worth, or condition of usu. by careful appraisal and study

    ♦ appraise, assess, estimate, rate, set, value — more at ESTIMATE

eval·u·a·tion \-,val-yù-'wā-shən\ *n* ♦ : the act or result of evaluating

    ♦ appraisal, assessment, estimate, estimation, judgment (*or* judgement) — more at ESTIMATION

ev·a·nes·cent \,e-və-'nes-ᵊnt\ *adj* ♦ : tending to vanish like vapor — **ev·a·nes·cence** \-ᵊns\ *n*

    ♦ ephemeral, flash, fleeting, impermanent, momentary, short-lived, transient — more at MOMENTARY

evan·gel·i·cal \,ē-,van-'je-li-kəl, ,e-vən-\ *adj* [LL *evangelium* gospel, fr. Gk *evangelion*, fr. *eu-* good + *angelos* messenger] 1 : of or relating to the Christian gospel esp. as presented in the four Gospels 2 : of or relating to certain Protestant churches emphasizing the authority of Scripture and the importance of preaching as contrasted with ritual 3 : ZEALOUS ⟨~ fervor⟩ — **Evangelical** *n* — **Evan·gel·i·cal·ism** \-kə-,li-zəm\ *n* — **evan·gel·i·cal·ly** *adv*

evan·ge·lism \i-'van-jə-,li-zəm\ *n* 1 : the winning or revival of personal commitments to Christ 2 : militant or crusading zeal — **evan·ge·lis·tic** \-,van-jə-'lis-tik\ *adj* — **evan·ge·lis·ti·cal·ly** *adv*

evan·ge·list \i-'van-jə-list\ *n* 1 *often cap* : the writer of any of the four Gospels 2 : a person who evangelizes; *esp* : a Protestant minister or layman who preaches at special services

evan·ge·lize \i-'van-jə-,līz\ *vb* **-lized; -liz·ing** 1 : to preach the gospel 2 : to convert to Christianity

evap *abbr* evaporate

evap·o·rate \i-'va-pə-,rāt\ *vb* **-rat·ed; -rat·ing** 1 : to pass off or cause to pass off in vapor 2 ♦ : to disappear quickly 3 : to drive out the moisture from (as by heat) — **evap·o·ra·tion** \-,va-pə-'rā-shən\ *n* — **evap·o·ra·tor** \-,rā-tər\ *n*

    ♦ disappear, dissolve, fade, flee, go, melt, vanish — more at DISAPPEAR

evap·o·rite \i-'va-pə-,rīt\ *n* : a sedimentary rock that originates by the evaporation of seawater in an enclosed basin

eva·sion \i-'vā-zhən\ *n* 1 ♦ : a means of evading 2 ♦ : an act or instance of evading ⟨tax ~⟩ — **eva·sive·ness** *n*

    ♦ [1, 2] avoidance, cop-out, escape, out — more at ESCAPE

eva·sive \i-'vā-siv\ *adj* ♦ : tending or intended to evade; *also* : not easily caught

    ♦ elusive, fugitive, slippery — more at ELUSIVE

eve \'ēv\ *n* 1 : EVENING 2 : the period just before some important event

¹even \'ē-vən\ *adj* 1 ♦ : having a horizontal surface : LEVEL, FLAT ⟨~ grounds⟩ 2 : REGULAR, SMOOTH 3 : EQUAL, FAIR 4 : BALANCED; *also* : fully revenged 5 : divisible by two 6 ♦ : having no fraction either lacking or in excess : EXACT ⟨an ~ dollar⟩ — **even·ly** *adv* — **even·ness** *n*

    ♦ [1] flat, flush, level, plane, smooth — more at LEVEL
    ♦ [6] exact, flat, precise, round

²**even** *adv* **1** : EXACTLY, PRECISELY **2** : FULLY, QUITE **3** : at the very time **4** ◆ — used as an intensive to stress the identity or character of something ⟨∼ I know that⟩ ⟨he looked content, ∼ happy⟩ **5** — used as an intensive to emphasize something extreme or highly unlikely ⟨so simple ∼ a child can do it⟩ **6** — used as an intensive to stress the comparative degree ⟨did ∼ better⟩ **7** — used as an intensive to indicate a small or minimum degree ⟨didn't ∼ try⟩

◆ indeed, nay, truly, verily, yea; *also* certainly, decidedly, definitely, positively, really, surely, undeniably, unquestionably

³**even** *vb* ◆ : to make or become even

◆ balance, equalize, equate, level — more at EQUALIZE ◆ level, plane, smooth; *also* clip, crop, pare, prune, shave, trim *Ant* rough, roughen

even·hand·ed \ˌē-vən-ˈhan-dəd\ *adj* ◆ : marked by justice, honesty, and freedom from bias : FAIR, IMPARTIAL ⟨an ∼ assessment⟩ — **even·hand·ed·ly** *adv*

◆ disinterested, dispassionate, equal, equitable, fair, impartial, just, nonpartisan, objective, square, unbiased, unprejudiced — more at FAIR

eve·ning \ˈēv-niŋ\ *n* **1** ◆ : the end of the day and early part of the night **2** *chiefly Southern & Midland* : AFTERNOON

◆ dusk, gloaming, nightfall, sundown, sunset, twilight — more at DUSK

evening primrose *n* : a coarse biennial herb with yellow flowers that open in the evening

evening star *n* : a bright planet (as Venus) seen esp. in the western sky at or after sunset

even·song \ˈē-vən-ˌsȯŋ\ *n, often cap* **1** : VESPERS **2** : evening prayer esp. when sung

event \i-ˈvent\ *n* [MF or L; MF, fr. L *eventus*, fr. *evenire* to happen, fr. *venire* to come] **1** ◆ : something that happens : OCCURRENCE **2** ◆ : a noteworthy happening; *also* : a social occasion or activity **3** ◆ : a postulated outcome, condition, or eventuality : CONTINGENCY ⟨in the ∼ of rain⟩ **4** ◆ : a contest in a program of sports

◆ [1] affair, circumstance, deed, episode, experience, occurrence; *also* achievement, exploit, feat; news, hap, happening, incident, landmark, milestone, occasion, occurrence, page, phenomenon, tidings, turning point; adventure ◆ [2] affair, fete, function, get-together, party — more at PARTY ◆ [3] case, contingency, eventuality, possibility; *also* probability; chance, risk ◆ [4] bout, competition, contest, game, match, meet, tournament — more at GAME

event·ful *adj* **1** : full of or rich in events **2** ◆ : very important

◆ big, consequential, important, major, material, meaningful, momentous, significant, substantial, weighty — more at IMPORTANT

even·tide \ˈē-vən-ˌtīd\ *n* : the time of evening : EVENING

even·tu·al \i-ˈven-chü-wəl\ *adj* ◆ : coming at some later time : ULTIMATE

even·tu·al·i·ty \i-ˌven-chü-ˈwa-lə-tē\ *n, pl* **-ties** ◆ : a possible event or outcome

◆ case, contingency, event, possibility — more at EVENT

even·tu·al·ly *adv* ◆ : at an unspecified later time : in the end

◆ someday, sometime, ultimately, yet — more at YET

even·tu·ate \i-ˈven-chü-ˌwāt\ *vb* **-at·ed; -at·ing** : to result finally

ev·er \ˈe-vər\ *adv* **1** ◆ : at all times : ALWAYS **2** ◆ : at any time **3** : in any way : AT ALL ⟨how can I ∼ thank you⟩

◆ [1] always, eternally, everlastingly, forever, permanently, perpetually; *also* long, perennially *Ant* never, nevermore ◆ [2] always, invariably, unfailingly — more at ALWAYS

ev·er·glade \ˈe-vər-ˌglād\ *n* : a low-lying tract of swampy or marshy land

ev·er·green \-ˌgrēn\ *adj* : having foliage that remains green ⟨most coniferous trees are ∼⟩ — **evergreen** *n*

¹**ev·er·last·ing** \ˌe-vər-ˈlas-tiŋ\ *adj* **1** ◆ : enduring forever : ETERNAL **2** : having or being flowers or foliage that retain form or color for a long time when dried

◆ ceaseless, dateless, deathless, endless, eternal, immortal, permanent, perpetual, undying, unending; *also* durable, enduring, lasting, persistent; imperishable, indestructible; timeless; abiding, steadfast, steady, unfailing, unfaltering *Ant* impermanent, mortal, temporary

²**everlasting** *n* **1** : ETERNITY ⟨from ∼⟩ **2** : a plant with everlasting flowers; *also* : its flower

ev·er·last·ing·ly *adv* ◆ : in an everlasting manner

◆ always, eternally, ever, forever, permanently, perpetually — more at EVER

ev·er·more \ˌe-vər-ˈmȯr\ *adv* : for a limitless time : FOREVER

ev·ery \ˈev-rē\ *adj* [ME *everich, every*, fr. OE *ǣfre ǣlc*, fr. *ǣfre* ever + *ǣlc* each] **1** : being each one of a group **2** : all possible ⟨given ∼ chance⟩; *also* : COMPLETE ⟨have ∼ confidence⟩

ev·ery·body \ˈev-ri-ˌbä-dē, -bə-\ *pron* : every person

ev·ery·day \ˈev-rē-ˌdā\ *adj* ◆ : encountered or used routinely : ORDINARY

◆ average, common, commonplace, customary, familiar, normal, ordinary, prosaic, routine, run-of-the-mill, standard, unexceptional, unremarkable, usual, workaday — more at ORDINARY

ev·ery·one \-(ˌ)wən\ *pron* : every person : EVERYBODY

ev·ery·thing \ˈev-rē-ˌthiŋ\ *pron* **1** : all that exists **2** : all that is relevant

ev·ery·where \ˈev-rē-ˌhwer\ *adv* : in every place or part

evg *abbr* evening

evict \i-ˈvikt\ *vb* **1** : to put (a person) out from a property by legal process **2** : EXPEL — **evic·tion** \-ˈvik-shən\ *n*

¹**ev·i·dence** \ˈe-və-dəns\ *n* **1** : an outward sign **2** ◆ : something that furnishes proof : PROOF, TESTIMONY; *esp* : matter submitted in court to determine the truth of alleged facts

◆ attestation, confirmation, corroboration, documentation, proof, substantiation, testament, testimony, validation, witness — more at PROOF

²**evidence** *vb* : PROVE, EVINCE

ev·i·dent \-dənt\ *adj* ◆ : clear to the vision and understanding

◆ apparent, broad, clear, clear-cut, distinct, lucid, manifest, obvious, palpable, patent, perspicuous, plain, transparent, unambiguous, unequivocal, unmistakable — more at CLEAR

ev·i·dent·ly \ˈe-və-dənt-lē, ˌe-və-ˈdent-\ *adv* **1** : in an evident manner **2** ◆ : on the basis of available evidence ⟨he was born ∼ in Texas⟩

◆ apparently, ostensibly, presumably, seemingly, supposedly — more at APPARENTLY

¹**evil** \ˈē-vəl\ *adj* **evil·er** *or* **evil·ler; evil·est** *or* **evil·lest** **1** ◆ : morally reprehensible : WICKED **2** ◆ : causing or threatening distress or harm : PERNICIOUS — **evil·ly** *adv*

◆ [1] bad, black, immoral, iniquitous, nefarious, rotten, sinful, vicious, vile, villainous, wicked, wrong ◆ [2] bad, damaging, deleterious, detrimental, harmful, hurtful, injurious, noxious, pernicious — more at HARMFUL

²**evil** *n* **1** ◆ : the fact of suffering, misfortune, and wrongdoing; *also* : evil actions or deeds **2** : a source of sorrow, distress, or calamity

◆ bad, ill, immorality, iniquity, sin, villainy, wrong; *also* atrociousness, badness, heinousness, sinfulness, vileness, wickedness; devilry; cancer, decay, rot, squalor; corruption, debauchery, degeneracy, depravity, indecency, perversion; abomination, anathema, taboo *Ant* good, morality, right, virtue

evil·do·er \ˌē-vəl-ˈdü-ər\ *n* ◆ : one who does evil

♦ beast, devil, fiend, no-good, reprobate, rogue, varlet, villain, wretch — more at VILLAIN ♦ malefactor, sinner, wrongdoer; *also* criminal, crook, felon, lawbreaker, miscreant, reprobate, transgressor, villain

evil–mind·ed \-ˈmīn-dəd\ *adj* : having an evil disposition or evil thoughts — **evil–mind·ed·ly** *adv*

evince \i-ˈvins\ *vb* **evinced; evinc·ing** ♦ : to constitute outward evidence of : SHOW, REVEAL

♦ bespeak, betray, demonstrate, display, expose, give away, manifest, reveal, show — more at SHOW

evis·cer·ate \i-ˈvi-sə-ˌrāt\ *vb* **-at·ed; -at·ing** 1 ♦ : to remove the entrails of 2 : to deprive of vital content or force — **evis·cer·a·tion** \-ˌvi-sə-ˈrā-shən\ *n*

♦ clean, draw, gut — more at GUT

evoke \i-ˈvōk\ *vb* **evoked; evok·ing** ♦ : to call forth or up — **evo·ca·tion** \ˌē-vō-ˈkā-shən, ˌe-və-\ *n* — **evoc·a·tive** \i-ˈvä-kə-tiv\ *adj*

♦ elicit, raise

evo·lu·tion \ˌe-və-ˈlü-shən\ *n* 1 : one of a set of prescribed movements (as in a dance) 2 ♦ : a process of change in a particular direction 3 : a theory that the various kinds of plants and animals are descended from other kinds that lived in earlier times and that the differences are due to inherited changes that occurred over many generations — **evo·lu·tion·ary** \-shə-ˌner-ē\ *adj* — **evo·lu·tion·ist** \-shə-nist\ *n*

♦ development, elaboration, expansion, growth, progress, progression — more at DEVELOPMENT

evolve \i-ˈvälv\ *vb* **evolved; evolv·ing** [L *evolvere* to unroll] : to develop or change by or as if by evolution

EW *abbr* enlisted woman

e–waste \ˈē-ˌwāst\ *n* : waste consisting of discarded electronic products

ewe \ˈyü\ *n* : a female sheep

ew·er \ˈyü-ər\ *n* ♦ : a water pitcher

♦ flagon, jug, pitcher — more at PITCHER

¹ex \ˈeks\ *prep* [L] : out of : FROM

²ex *n* : a former spouse

³ex *abbr* 1 example 2 express 3 extra

Ex *abbr* Exodus

ex- \e *also* occurs in this prefix where only i is shown below (as in "express") and ks *sometimes* occurs where only gz is shown (as in "exact")\ *prefix* 1 : out of : outside 2 : former ⟨*ex*-president⟩

ex·ac·er·bate \ig-ˈza-sər-ˌbāt\ *vb* **-bat·ed; -bat·ing** : to make more violent, bitter, or severe ⟨comments that ∼ the dispute⟩ — **ex·ac·er·ba·tion** \-ˌza-sər-ˈbā-shən\ *n*

¹ex·act \ig-ˈzakt\ *vb* 1 ♦ : to demand and force or compel (as payment, surrender, concession, performance, or compliance) 2 : to call for or establish as suitable or necessary — **ex·ac·tion** \-ˈzak-shən\ *n*

♦ call, claim, command, demand, enjoin, extort, insist, press ♦ assess, charge, fine, impose ♦ lay, levy, put — more at IMPOSE

²exact *adj* ♦ : precisely accurate or correct

♦ accurate, correct, precise, proper, right, so, true — more at CORRECT ♦ delicate, fine, minute, nice, refined, subtle — more at FINE

ex·act·ing \ig-ˈzak-tiŋ\ *adj* 1 ♦ : greatly demanding ⟨an ∼ taskmaster⟩ 2 ♦ : requiring close attention and precision

♦ [1] choosy, demanding, fastidious, finicky, particular, picky — more at FINICKY ♦ [1] inflexible, rigid, rigorous, strict, stringent, uncompromising — more at RIGID ♦ [2] arduous, burdensome, challenging, demanding, grueling, laborious, onerous, taxing, toilsome — more at DEMANDING

ex·ac·ti·tude \ig-ˈzak-tə-ˌtüd, -ˌtyüd\ *n* : the quality or state of being exact

ex·act·ly *adv* 1 ♦ : in a manner or measure or to a degree or number that strictly conforms to a fact or condition; *also* : in every respect 2 : quite so : as you say or state — used to express agreement

♦ accurately, just, precisely, right, sharp, squarely, strictly

ex·act·ness *n* ♦ : the quality or an instance of being exact

♦ accuracy, closeness, delicacy, fineness, precision, veracity — more at PRECISION

ex·ag·ger·ate \ig-ˈza-jə-ˌrāt\ *vb* **-at·ed; -at·ing** [L *exaggeratus*, pp. of *exaggerare*, lit., to heap up, fr. *agger* heap] ♦ : to enlarge (as a statement) beyond normal — **ex·ag·ger·at·ed·ly** *adv* — **ex·ag·ger·a·tor** \-ˈza-jə-ˌrā-tər\ *n*

♦ color (*or* colour), elaborate, embellish, embroider, magnify, pad, stretch — more at EMBROIDER

ex·ag·ger·a·tion \-ˌza-jə-ˈrā-shən\ *n* ♦ : the act of exaggerating; *also* : the state or an instance of being exaggerated

♦ elaboration, embellishment, hyperbole, magnification, overstatement, padding; *also* amplification, enhancement; fabrication, misrepresentation; fudging, hedging *Ant* understatement

ex·alt \ig-ˈzȯlt\ *vb* 1 ♦ : to raise up esp. in rank, power, or dignity 2 ♦ : to elevate in estimation : GLORIFY — **ex·al·ta·tion** \ˌeg-ˌzȯl-ˈtā-shən, ˌek-ˌsȯl-\ *n*

♦ [1, 2] aggrandize, dignify, ennoble, glorify, magnify; *also* boost, elevate, lift, promote, raise, upgrade, uplift; heighten, intensify; idealize, sanitize; canonize, deify; acclaim, extol, honor, laud, praise *Ant* abase, debase, degrade, demean, humble, humiliate

ex·am \ig-ˈzam\ *n* : an exercise or a series of exercises designed to examine progress or test qualification : EXAMINATION

ex·am·i·na·tion \-ˌza-mə-ˈnā-shən\ *n* 1 ♦ : the act or process of examining; *also* : the state of being examined 2 ♦ : an exercise designed to examine progress or test qualification or knowledge 3 : a formal interrogation

♦ [1] check, checkup, inspection, review, scan, scrutiny, survey — more at INSPECTION ♦ [1] exploration, inquiry, investigation, probe, research, study — more at INQUIRY ♦ [2] quiz, test; *also* catechism; audition; final; checkup, inspection, review; inquiry, interrogation, investigation, probe, research

ex·am·ine \ig-ˈza-mən\ *vb* **ex·am·ined; ex·am·in·ing** 1 ♦ : to inspect closely 2 ♦ : to attempt to determine or test by questioning

♦ [1] audit, check, inspect, review, scan, scrutinize, survey — more at INSPECT ♦ [2] grill, interrogate, pump, query, question, quiz; *also* debrief; cross-examine; catechize; annoy, harass, hound, pester

ex·am·ple \ig-ˈzam-pəl\ *n* 1 ♦ : something forming a model to be followed or avoided 2 ♦ : a representative sample 3 : a problem to be solved in order to show the application of some rule

♦ case, exemplar, illustration, instance, representative, sample, specimen; *also* cross section; evidence, indication, manifestation, sign

ex·as·per·ate \ig-ˈzas-pə-ˌrāt\ *vb* **-at·ed; -at·ing** ♦ : to excite the anger of : VEX, IRRITATE

♦ aggravate, annoy, bother, bug, grate, irk, irritate, vex — more at IRRITATE

ex·as·per·at·ing *adj* ♦ : causing irritation : ANNOYING

♦ aggravating, annoying, frustrating, irksome, irritating, pesty, vexatious — more at ANNOYING

ex·as·per·a·tion \ig-ˌzas-pə-ˈrā-shən\ *n* ♦ : the state of being exasperated; *also* : the act or source of being exasperated

♦ aggravation, annoyance, bother, frustration, hassle, headache, irritant, nuisance, problem, thorn, vexation — more at ANNOYANCE

exc *abbr* 1 excellent 2 except

ex·ca·vate \ˈek-skə-ˌvāt\ *vb* **-vat·ed; -vat·ing** 1 : to hollow out; *also* : to form by hollowing out 2 : to dig out and remove (as earth) 3 : to reveal to view by digging away a covering — **ex·ca·va·tion** \ˌek-skə-ˈvā-shən\ *n* — **ex·ca·va·tor** \ˈek-skə-ˌvā-tər\ *n*

ex·ceed \ik-'sēd\ *vb* **1** ♦ : to go or be beyond the limit of **2** ♦ : to be greater than or superior to : SURPASS

♦ [1, 2] overreach, overrun, overshoot, overstep, surpass; *also* encroach, entrench, infringe, invade, trespass; overdo, overuse, overwork

ex·ceed·ing \-'sē-diŋ\ *adj* ♦ : exceptional in amount, quality, or degree

♦ aberrant, abnormal, atypical, exceptional, extraordinary, freak, odd, peculiar, phenomenal, rare, singular, uncommon, unaccustomary, unique, unusual, unwonted — more at EXCEPTIONAL

ex·ceed·ing·ly \-'sē-diŋ-lē\ *also* **ex·ceed·ing** *adv* : to an extreme degree : EXTREMELY, VERY

ex·cel \ik-'sel\ *vb* **ex·celled; ex·cel·ling** ♦ : to be superior to : SURPASS, OUTDO

♦ beat, better, eclipse, outdistance, outdo, outshine, outstrip, surpass, top, transcend — more at SURPASS

ex·cel·lence \'ek-sə-ləns\ *n* **1** ♦ : the quality of being excellent **2** ♦ : an excellent or valuable quality : VIRTUE **3** : EXCELLENCY 2

♦ [1] distinction, greatness, preeminence, superiority, supremacy; *also* flawlessness, impeccability, perfection; goodness, value, worth; consequence, importance, notability ♦ [2] distinction, merit, value, virtue; *also* advantage, edge, superiority *Ant* deficiency

ex·cel·len·cy \-lən-sē\ *n, pl* **-cies** **1** : outstanding or valuable quality : EXCELLENCE **2** — used as a title of honor
ex·cel·lent \-lənt\ *adj* ♦ : very good of its kind — **ex·cel·lent·ly** *adv*

♦ A1, bang-up, banner, fabulous, fine, grand, great, marvelous (*or* marvellous), prime, sensational, splendid, superb, superior, unsurpassed, wonderful; *also* better, exceptional, fancy, premium, special *Ant* poor

ex·cel·si·or \ik-'sel-sē-ər\ *n* : fine curled wood shavings used esp. for packing fragile items
¹**ex·cept** \ik-'sept\ *also* **ex·cept·ing** *prep* ♦ : with the exclusion or exception of ⟨daily ∼ Sundays⟩

♦ aside from, bar, barring, besides, but, except for, exclusive of, outside (of), save

²**except** *vb* **1** ♦ : to take or leave out **2** : OBJECT

♦ ban, bar, count out, debar, eliminate, exclude, rule out — more at EXCLUDE

³**except** *also* **excepting** *conj* **1** : UNLESS ⟨∼ you repent⟩ **2** ♦ : were it not that : ONLY ⟨I'd go, ∼ it's too far⟩

♦ but, only, yet

except for *prep* **1** ♦ : with the exception of ⟨everyone was gone *except for* me⟩ **2** : were it not for ⟨*except for* you I would be dead⟩

♦ aside from, bar, barring, besides, but, exclusive of, other than, outside (of), save

ex·cep·tion \ik-'sep-shən\ *n* **1** : the act of excepting **2** : something excepted **3** : OBJECTION
ex·cep·tion·able \ik-'sep-shə-nə-bəl\ *adj* : being likely to cause objection : OBJECTIONABLE
ex·cep·tion·al \ik-'sep-shə-nəl\ *adj* **1** ♦ : forming an exception : UNUSUAL ⟨an ∼ number of rainy days⟩ **2** : SUPERIOR ⟨∼ skill⟩ — **ex·cep·tion·al·ly** *adv*

♦ abnormal, atypical, rare, singular, uncommon, uncustomary, unique, unusual, unwonted; *also* conspicuous, notable, noticeable, outstanding, prominent, remarkable, salient, striking; bizarre, deviant, eccentric, outlandish, quaint, strange, weird; incomprehensible, inconceivable, incredible, unimaginable, unthinkable *Ant* common, customary, normal, ordinary, typical

ex·cerpt \'ek-sərpt, 'eg-ˌzərpt\ *n* : a passage selected or copied : EXTRACT — **excerpt** \ek-'sərpt, eg-'zərpt; 'ek-ˌsərpt, 'eg-ˌzərpt\ *vb*
¹**ex·cess** \ik-'ses, 'ek-ˌses\ *n* **1** ♦ : the state or an instance of surpassing usual, proper, or specified limits : SUPERFLUITY, SURPLUS **2** : the amount by which one quantity exceeds another **3** : INTEMPERANCE; *also* : an instance of intemperance ⟨the dictator's ∼es⟩

♦ fat, overabundance, overflow, superfluity, surfeit, surplus; *also* abundance, bounty, plenty, profusion, sufficiency; overproduction, overstock *Ant* deficiency, deficit, insufficiency

²**excess** *adj* ♦ : more than the usual, proper, or specified amount

♦ extra, spare, superfluous, supernumerary, surplus — more at SPARE

ex·ces·sive \ik-'se-siv\ *adj* ♦ : exceeding what is usual, proper, necessary, or normal

♦ extravagant, extreme, immoderate, inordinate, lavish, overmuch, steep, stiff; *also* boundless, endless, immeasurable, infinite, limitless; intolerable, unbearable, unjustifiable, unwarranted; improper, inappropriate, thick, unseemly *Ant* moderate, modest, reasonable, temperate

ex·ces·sive·ly *adv* ♦ : to an exceptional or even improper degree

♦ inordinately, overly, overmuch, too — more at TOO

exch *abbr* exchange; exchanged
¹**ex·change** \iks-'chānj\ *n* **1** ♦ : the giving or taking of one thing in return for another : TRADE **2** : a substituting of one thing for another **3** : interchange of valuables and esp. of bills of exchange or money of different countries **4** : a place where things and services are exchanged; *esp* : a marketplace for securities **5** : a central office in which telephone lines are connected for communication **6** ♦ : a reciprocal interchange (as of things or ideas); *also* : the act of such an interchange

♦ [1] barter, commutation, swap, trade, truck; *also* replacement, substitution; reciprocation, recompense, requital; bargain, deal, negotiation, transaction; bargaining, dealing, dickering, haggling; logrolling ♦ [6] colloquy, conversation, dialogue, discourse, discussion — more at CONVERSATION

²**exchange** *vb* **ex·changed; ex·chang·ing** ♦ : to transfer in return for some equivalent : SWAP — **ex·change·able** \iks-'chān-jə-bəl\ *adj*

♦ change, commute, shift, substitute, swap, switch, trade — more at CHANGE

ex·che·quer \'eks-ˌche-kər\ *n* [ME *escheker*, fr. AF, chessboard, counting table, office charged with revenue collection, fr. *eschec* check (in chess), chess] : TREASURY; *esp* : a national treasury
ex·cise \'ek-ˌsīz\ *n* : a tax on the manufacture, sale, or consumption of a commodity
ex·ci·sion \ik-'si-zhən\ *n* : removal by or as if by cutting out esp. by surgical means — **ex·cise** \ik-'sīz\ *vb*
ex·cit·able \ik-'sī-tə-bəl\ *adj* ♦ : easily excited — **ex·cit·abil·i·ty** \-ˌsī-tə-'bi-lə-tē\ *n*

♦ flighty, fluttery, high-strung, jittery, jumpy, nervous, skittish, spooky; *also* hot-blooded, mercurial, temperamental, unstable, volatile; anxious, edgy, jumpy, nervy, tense, uptight; emotional, hypersensitive, intense, sensitive, soulful; dramatic, histrionic, melodramatic; irascible, irritable, prickly, testy, touchy *Ant* unflappable

ex·cite \ik-'sīt\ *vb* **ex·cit·ed; ex·cit·ing** **1** ♦ : to stir up the emotions of **2** ♦ : to increase the activity of : STIMULATE — **ex·ci·ta·tion** \ˌek-ˌsī-'tā-shən, ˌek-sə-\ *n* — **ex·cit·ed·ly** *adv* — **ex·cit·ing·ly** *adv*

♦ [1] electrify, exhilarate, galvanize, intoxicate, thrill, titillate, turn on — more at THRILL ♦ [2] arouse, encourage, fire, incite, instigate, move, pique, provoke, stimulate, stir

ex·cite·ment \ik-'sīt-mənt\ *n* **1** ♦ : something that excites or rouses **2** ♦ : the action of exciting : the state of being excited

♦ [1] incitement, instigation, provocation, stimulus — more at PROVOCATION ♦ [2] appetite, ardor, avidity, eagerness, enthusiasm, hunger, impatience, keenness, thirst — more at EAGERNESS

ex·cit·ing *adj* ♦ : producing excitement

♦ breathtaking, electric, exhilarating, rousing, stirring, thrilling; *also* arresting, interesting, intriguing, provocative, tantalizing; absorbing, engrossing, gripping, riveting; moving, poignant, touching; enthralling, fascinating *Ant* unexciting

ex·claim \iks-'klām\ *vb* : to cry out, speak, or utter sharply or vehemently — **ex·clam·a·to·ry** \iks-'kla-mə-ˌtȯr-ē\ *adj*
ex·cla·ma·tion \ˌeks-klə-'mā-shən\ *n* ♦ : a sharp or sudden utterance

♦ cry, ejaculation, interjection; *also* holler, hoot, howl, shout, whoop, yell; scream, screech, shriek, squall, squeak, squeal

exclamation point *n* : a punctuation mark ! used esp. after an interjection or exclamation
ex·clude \iks-'klüd\ *vb* **ex·clud·ed; ex·clud·ing** **1** ♦ : to prevent from using or participating : BAR **2** : to put out : EXPEL — **ex·clu·sion** \-'klü-zhən\ *n*

♦ ban, bar, count out, debar, eliminate, except, rule out; *also* blackball, blacklist, ostracize; banish, deport, exile, expel, oust, throw out; block, hinder, impede, obstruct; cease, discontinue, halt, suspend; deter, stave off, ward (off) *Ant* admit, include

ex·clud·ing *adj* : being prevented from using or participating
ex·clu·sive \iks-'klü-siv\ *adj* **1** : reserved for particular persons **2** : snobbishly aloof; *also* : STYLISH **3** : having no sharer : SOLE ⟨~ rights⟩; *also* : UNDIVIDED — **exclusive** *n* — **ex·clu·sive·ness** *n* — **ex·clu·siv·i·ty** \ˌeks-ˌklü-si-və-tē, iks-, -zi-\ *n*
ex·clu·sive·ly *adv* ♦ : in an exclusive manner

♦ alone, just, only, simply, solely — more at SOLELY

exclusive of *prep* ♦ : not taking into account

♦ aside from, bar, barring, besides, but, except for, other than, outside (of), save

ex·cog·i·tate \ek-'skä-jə-ˌtāt\ *vb* : to think out : DEVISE
ex·com·mu·ni·cate \ˌek-skə-'myü-nə-ˌkāt\ *vb* : to cut off officially from the rites of the church — **ex·com·mu·ni·ca·tion** \-ˌmyü-nə-'kā-shən\ *n*
ex·co·ri·ate \ek-'skȯr-ē-ˌāt\ *vb* **-at·ed; -at·ing** ♦ : to criticize severely

♦ abuse, assail, attack, belabor, blast, castigate, jump, lambaste, slam, vituperate — more at ATTACK

ex·co·ri·a·tion \(ˌ)ek-ˌskȯr-ē-'ā-shən\ *n* ♦ : a harsh and usu. public criticism

♦ denunciation, rebuke, reprimand, reproach, reproof, stricture — more at CENSURE

ex·cre·ment \'ek-skrə-mənt\ *n* : waste discharged from the body and esp. from the alimentary canal; *esp* : FECES — **ex·cre·men·tal** \ˌek-skrə-'ment-ᵊl\ *adj*
ex·cres·cence \ik-'skres-ᵊns\ *n* : OUTGROWTH; *esp* ♦ : an abnormal outgrowth (as a wart)

♦ growth, lump, neoplasm, tumor — more at GROWTH

ex·cre·ta \ik-'skrē-tə\ *n pl* : waste matter separated or eliminated from an organism
ex·crete \ik-'skrēt\ *vb* **ex·cret·ed; ex·cret·ing** : to separate and eliminate wastes from the body esp. in urine or sweat — **ex·cre·tion** \-'skrē-shən\ *n* — **ex·cre·to·ry** \'ek-skrə-ˌtȯr-ē\ *adj*
ex·cru·ci·at·ing \ik-'skrü-shē-ˌā-tiŋ\ *adj* [L *excruciare*, fr. *cruciare* to crucify, fr. *crux* cross] ♦ : intensely painful, distressing, or difficult to bear — **ex·cru·ci·at·ing·ly** *adv*

♦ agonizing, harrowing; *also* acute, exquisite, extreme, fierce, intense, vehement, violent; piercing, sharp, shooting, stabbing, stinging, tearing, tingling

ex·cul·pate \'ek-(ˌ)skəl-ˌpāt\ *vb* **-pat·ed; -pat·ing** ♦ : to clear from alleged fault or guilt

♦ absolve, acquit, clear, exonerate, vindicate; *also* atone (for), expiate; discharge, liberate, redeem, release, unburden; condone, excuse, forgive, pardon, remit; avenge, redress, revenge *Ant* incriminate

ex·cul·pa·tion \ˌek-(ˌ)skəl-'pā-shən\ *n* ♦ : the act or fact of exculpating from alleged fault or crime

♦ acquittal, exoneration, vindication — more at ACQUITTAL

ex·cur·sion \ik-'skər-zhən\ *n* **1 a** : EXPEDITION **b** ♦ : a pleasure trip **2** : deviation from a direct, definite, or proper course : DIGRESSION

♦ jaunt, junket, outing, sally; *also* journey; circuit, tour; expedition, odyssey, safari; detour; hike, peregrination, trek, walk; pilgrimage

ex·cur·sion·ist \-zhə-nist\ *n* ♦ : a person who goes on an excursion

♦ sightseer, tourist, traveler — more at TOURIST

ex·cur·sive \-'skər-siv\ *adj* : constituting or characterized by digression
ex·cus·able *adj* ♦ : capable of or fit for being excused, forgiven, justified, or acquitted of blame

♦ forgivable, pardonable, venial — more at VENIAL

¹ex·cuse \ik-'skyüz\ *vb* **ex·cused; ex·cus·ing** [ME, fr. OF *excuser*, fr. L *excusare*, fr. *causa* cause, explanation] **1 a** : to make excuse for : offer apology for **b** : to try to remove blame from **2** ♦ : to forgive entirely or overlook as of little consequence : PARDON **3** : to release from an obligation **4** : JUSTIFY

♦ disregard, forgive, gloss over, pardon, pass over, shrug off, wink at; *also* explain, justify, rationalize, whitewash; absolve, acquit, clear, exculpate, exonerate, vindicate

²excuse \ik-'skyüs\ *n* **1** : an act of excusing **2** ♦ : something that excuses or is a reason for excusing : JUSTIFICATION

♦ alibi, defense (*or* defence), justification, plea, reason; *also* guise, pretense, pretext, rationale, rationalization; cop-out, out; acknowledgment, apology, atonement, confession

exec *n* : EXECUTIVE
ex·e·cra·ble \'ek-si-krə-bəl\ *adj* **1** : DETESTABLE **2** ♦ : very bad ⟨~ spelling⟩

♦ atrocious, awful, lousy, punk, rotten, terrible, wretched

ex·e·crate \'ek-sə-ˌkrāt\ *vb* **-crat·ed; -crat·ing** [L *exsecratus*, pp. of *exsecrari* to put under a curse, fr. *ex-* out of + *sacer* sacred] ♦ : to denounce as evil or detestable; *also* : DETEST

♦ condemn, damn, denounce; *also* curse, imprecate; abhor, abominate, detest, hate, loathe; berate, lambaste, revile, scold; blame, censure, criticize, rebuke *Ant* bless abhor, abominate, despise, detest, hate, loathe — more at HATE

ex·e·cra·tion \ˌek-sə-'krā-shən\ *n* **1** ♦ : the act of cursing or denouncing; *also* : the curse so uttered **2** : an object of curses : something detested

♦ anathema, curse, imprecation, malediction — more at CURSE

ex·e·cute \'ek-si-ˌkyüt\ *vb* **-cut·ed; -cut·ing** **1** ♦ : to carry out fully : put completely into effect **2** ♦ : to do what is called for by (as a law) **3** ♦ : to put to death esp. in accordance with a legal sentence **4** : to produce by carrying out a design **5** : to do what is needed to give validity to ⟨~ a deed⟩ — **ex·e·cu·tion·er** *n*

♦ [1] accomplish, achieve, carry out, commit, compass, do, follow through, make, perform — more at PERFORM ♦ [1, 2] administer, apply, enforce, implement — more at ENFORCE ♦ [3] dispatch, do in, liquidate, murder, slay — more at MURDER

ex·e·cu·tion \ˌek-si-'kyü-shən\ *n* ♦ : the act or process of executing

♦ accomplishment, achievement, commission, discharge, enactment, fulfillment, implementation, performance, perpetration — more at COMMISSION

¹ex·ec·u·tive \ig-'ze-kyə-tiv\ *adj* **1** ♦ : of or relating to the enforcement of laws and the conduct of affairs **2** : designed for or related to carrying out plans or purposes

♦ directorial, managerial, supervisory; *also* bureaucratic, governmental, ministerial, official, parliamentary; regulatory; authoritarian, despotic, dictatorial

²**executive** *n* 1 : the branch of government with executive duties 2 ♦ : one having administrative or managerial responsibility

♦ administrator, director, manager, superintendent, supervisor; *also* officer, official; commissioner, minister; boss, chief, head, leader, president

ex·ec·u·tor \ig-'ze-kyə-tər\ *n* : the person named in a will to execute it

ex·ec·u·trix \ig-'ze-kyə-,triks\ *n, pl* **ex·ec·u·tri·ces** \-,ze-kyə-'trī-,sēz\ *or* **ex·ec·u·trix·es** \-'ze-kyə-,trik-səz\ : a woman who is an executor

ex·e·ge·sis \,ek-sə-'jē-səs\ *n, pl* **-ge·ses** \-'jē-,sēz\ : explanation or critical interpretation of a text

ex·e·gete \'ek-sə-,jēt\ *n* : one who practices exegesis — **ex·e·get·i·cal** \,ek-sə-'je-ti-kəl\ *adj*

ex·em·plar \ig-'zem-,plär, -plər\ *n* 1 ♦ : one that serves as a model or example; *esp* : an ideal model ⟨an ∼ of courage⟩ 2 ♦ : a typical instance or example

♦ [1] beau ideal, classic, epitome, ideal, model, nonpareil, paragon, perfection, quintessence — more at QUINTESSENCE ♦ [2] case, example, illustration, instance, representative, sample, specimen — more at EXAMPLE

ex·em·pla·ry \ig-'zem-plə-rē\ *adj* : serving as a pattern; *also* : COMMENDABLE

ex·em·pli·fy \ig-'zem-plə-,fī\ *vb* **-fied; -fy·ing** ♦ : to illustrate by example : serve as an example of — **ex·em·pli·fi·ca·tion** \-,zem-plə-fə-'kā-shən\ *n*

♦ illustrate, instance — more at ILLUSTRATE

¹**ex·empt** \ig-'zempt\ *adj* : free from some liability to which others are subject

²**exempt** *vb* : to make exempt : EXCUSE — **ex·emp·tion** \ig-'zemp-shən\ *n*

¹**ex·er·cise** \'ek-sər-,sīz\ *n* 1 ♦ : the act of bringing into play or realizing in action : EMPLOYMENT, USE ⟨∼ of authority⟩ 2 ♦ : exertion made for the sake of training or physical fitness 3 ♦ : a task or problem done to develop skill 4 *pl* : a public exhibition or ceremony

♦ [1] application, employment, operation, play, use — more at USE ♦ [2] activity, exertion; *also* training, workout; toning, trimming; aerobics, calisthenics, isometrics, weight lifting; physical therapy ♦ [3] drill, practice, routine, training, workout; *also* assignment, homework, lesson

²**exercise** *vb* **-cised; -cis·ing** 1 ♦ : to make effective in action; *also* : to bring to bear : EXERT ⟨∼ control⟩ 2 : to train by or engage in exercise 3 : to cause anxiety, alarm, or indignation in : WORRY, DISTRESS — **ex·er·cis·er** *n*

♦ [1] apply, exert, put out, wield — more at EXERT ♦ [1] apply, employ, exploit, harness, operate, use, utilize — more at USE

ex·ert \ig-'zert\ *vb* ♦ : to bring or put into action ⟨∼ influence⟩ ⟨∼ed himself⟩

♦ apply, exercise, put out, wield; *also* employ, use, utilize

ex·er·tion \-'zər-shən\ *n* ♦ : the act or an instance of exerting; *esp* : a laborious or perceptible effort

♦ activity, exercise — more at EXERCISE ♦ effort, labor (*or* labour), pains, sweat, trouble, work — more at EFFORT

ex·fo·li·ate \eks-'fō-lē-,āt\ *vb* **-at·ed; -at·ing** : to cast off in scales, layers, or splinters — **ex·fo·lia·tion** \-,fō-lē-'ā-shən\ *n*

ex·hale \eks-'hāl\ *vb* **ex·haled; ex·hal·ing** 1 ♦ : to breathe out 2 ♦ : to give off or pass off in the form of vapor — **ex·ha·la·tion** \,eks-hə-'lā-shən\ *n*

♦ [1] blow, breathe, expire *Ant* inhale, inspire ♦ [2] cast, discharge, emit, expel, issue, release, shoot, vent — more at EMIT

¹**ex·haust** \ig-'zȯst\ *vb* 1 ♦ : to use up wholly 2 ♦ : to tire or wear out 3 : to draw off or let out completely; *also* : EMPTY 4 : to develop (a subject) completely

♦ [1] clean, consume, deplete, drain, expend, spend, use up — more at DEPLETE ♦ [2] burn out, do in, drain, fag, fatigue, tire, tucker, wash out, wear, wear out, weary; *also* debilitate, enervate, enfeeble, sap, waste, weaken

²**exhaust** *n* 1 : the escape of used vapor or gas from an engine; *also* : the gas that escapes 2 : a system of pipes through which exhaust escapes

ex·haust·ed *adj* : being tired, worn out, or completely used up

♦ bushed, dead, drained, prostrate, spent, weary, worn-out — more at WEARY

ex·haus·tion \ig-'zȯs-chən\ *n* ♦ : extreme weariness : FATIGUE

♦ burnout, collapse, fatigue, lassitude, prostration, tiredness, weariness — more at FATIGUE

ex·haus·tive \ig-'zȯ-stiv\ *adj* ♦ : covering all possibilities : THOROUGH

♦ all-out, clean, complete, comprehensive, full-scale, out-and-out, thorough, thoroughgoing, total; *also* broad, extensive, far-reaching, wide; general, global, inclusive

ex·haus·tive·ly *adv* ♦ : in a thorough or exhaustive manner

♦ completely, fully, minutely, roundly, thoroughly, totally — more at THOROUGHLY

¹**ex·hib·it** \ig-'zi-bət\ *vb* 1 : to display esp. publicly 2 : to present to a court in legal form — **ex·hib·i·tor** \ig-'zi-bə-tər\ *n*

²**exhibit** *n* 1 ♦ : an act or instance of exhibiting; *also* : something exhibited 2 : something produced and identified in court for use as evidence

♦ display, exhibition, exposition, fair, show — more at EXHIBITION

ex·hi·bi·tion \,ek-sə-'bi-shən\ *n* ♦ : an act or instance of exhibiting; *also* : a public showing (as of works of art, objects of manufacture, or athletic skill)

♦ demonstration, display, show — more at SHOW ♦ display, exhibit, exposition, fair, show; *also* demonstration, performance, presentation, production; extravaganza, pageant, spectacle; auction, offering, sale

ex·hi·bi·tion·ism \,ek-sə-'bi-shə-,ni-zəm\ *n* 1 : a perversion marked by a tendency to indecently expose one's genitals 2 : the act or practice of behaving so as to attract attention to oneself — **ex·hi·bi·tion·ist** \-nist\ *n or adj*

ex·hil·a·rate \ig-'zi-lə-,rāt\ *vb* **-rat·ed; -rat·ing** ♦ : to make cheerful and excited

♦ elate, elevate, enrapture, thrill, transport — more at ELATE

exhilarating *adj* ♦ : serving to exhilarate

♦ breathtaking, exciting, rousing, stirring, thrilling — more at EXCITING

ex·hil·a·ra·tion \-,zi-lə-'rā-shən\ *n* 1 : the action of exhilarating 2 ♦ : the feeling or the state of being exhilarated

♦ ecstasy, elation, euphoria, heaven, intoxication, paradise, rapture, rhapsody, thrill, transport — more at ECSTASY

ex·hort \ig-'zȯrt\ *vb* ♦ : to urge, advise, or warn earnestly — **ex·hor·ta·tion** \,ek-,sȯr-'tā-shən, ,eg-,zȯr-, -zər-\ *n*

♦ egg on, encourage, goad, press, prod, prompt, urge — more at URGE

ex·hume \ig-'züm, iks-'hyüm\ *vb* **ex·humed; ex·hum·ing** [ME fr. ML *exhumare*, fr. L *ex* out of + *humus* earth] : DISINTER — **ex·hu·ma·tion** \,eks-hyü-'mā-shən, ,eg-zü-\ *n*

ex·i·gen·cy \'ek-sə-jən-sē, ig-'zi-jən-\ *n, pl* **-cies** 1 *pl* : REQUIREMENTS 2 : urgent need — **ex·i·gent** \'ek-sə-jənt\ *adj*

ex·ig·u·ous \ig-'zi-gyə-wəs\ *adj* : scanty in amount — **ex·i·gu·i·ty** \,eg-zi-'gyü-ə-tē\ *n*

¹**ex·ile** \'eg-,zīl, 'ek-,sīl\ *n* 1 ♦ : the state or a period of forced absence from one's country or home : BANISHMENT; *also* : voluntary absence from one's country or home 2 ♦ : a person driven from his or her native place

♦ [1] banishment, deportation, displacement, expulsion; *also* ostracism; extradition; dispersion, scattering; emigration, migration; evacuation ♦ [2] émigré, evacuee, expatriate, refugee — more at ÉMIGRÉ

²**exile** *vb* **ex·iled; ex·il·ing** ♦ : to expel from one's own country or home : BANISH

♦ banish, deport, displace, expatriate, transport — more at BANISH

ex·ist \ig-'zist\ *vb* **1** : to have being **2** ♦ : to continue to be : LIVE

♦ be, breathe, live, subsist — more at BE

ex·is·tence \ig-'zis-təns\ *n* **1** : continuance in living **2** ♦ : actual or present occurrence ⟨∼ of a state of war⟩ **3** : something existing

♦ actuality, reality, subsistence; *also* genuineness, realness; activity, animation, life; currency, presence, prevalence *Ant* nonexistence

ex·is·tent \-tənt\ *adj* ♦ : having being; *also* : existing now

♦ actual, concrete, factual, real, true, very — more at ACTUAL ♦ alive, extant, living — more at EXTANT

ex·is·ten·tial \,eg-zis-'ten-chəl, ,ek-sis-\ *adj* **1** : of or relating to existence **2** : EMPIRICAL **3** : having being in time and space **4** : of or relating to existentialism or existentialists

ex·is·ten·tial·ism \,eg-zis-'ten-chə-,li-zəm\ *n* : a philosophy centered on individual existence and personal responsibility for acts of free will in the absence of certain knowledge of what is right or wrong — **ex·is·ten·tial·ist** \-list\ *adj or n*

¹**ex·it** \'eg-zət, 'ek-sət\ *n* **1** : a departure from a stage **2** ♦ : a going out or away; *also* : DEATH **3** ♦ : a way out of an enclosed space **4** : a point of departure from an expressway

♦ [2] departure, farewell, leave-taking, parting — more at DEPARTURE ♦ [3] egress, issue, outlet; *also* escape, release; opening, passage, vent *Ant* entrance, entry; ingress

²**exit** *vb* ♦ : to go out or away from

♦ clear out, depart, get off, go, move, pull, quit, sally, shove, take off — more at GO

exo·bi·ol·o·gy \,ek-sō-bī-'ä-lə-jē\ *n* : biology concerned with life originating or existing outside the earth or its atmosphere — **exo·bi·ol·o·gist** \-jist\ *n*

exo·crine gland \'ek-sə-krən-, -,krīn-, -,krēn-\ *n* : a gland (as a salivary gland) that releases a secretion externally by means of a canal or duct

Exod *abbr* Exodus

ex·o·dus \'ek-sə-dəs\ *n* **1** *cap* : the mainly narrative second book of canonical Jewish and Christian Scripture **2** : a mass departure : EMIGRATION

ex of·fi·cio \,ek-sə-'fi-shē-,ō\ *adv or adj* : by virtue of or because of an office ⟨*ex officio* chairman⟩

ex·og·e·nous \ek-'sä-jə-nəs\ *adj* : caused or produced by factors outside the organism or system — **ex·og·e·nous·ly** *adv*

ex·on·er·ate \ig-'zä-nə-,rāt\ *vb* **-at·ed; -at·ing** [ME, fr. L *exoneratus*, pp. of *exonerare* to unburden, fr. *ex-* out + *onus* load] ♦ : to free from blame

♦ absolve, acquit, clear, exculpate, vindicate — more at EXCULPATE

ex·on·er·a·tion \-,zä-nə-'rā-shən\ *n* ♦ : the act or state of exonerating

♦ acquittal, exculpation, vindication — more at ACQUITTAL

exo·plan·et \'ek-sō-,pla-nət\ *n* : a planet orbiting a star that is not our sun

ex·or·bi·tant \ig-'zȯr-bə-tənt\ *adj* ♦ : exceeding what is usual or proper

♦ excessive, extravagant, extreme, immoderate, inordinate, lavish, steep, stiff — more at EXCESSIVE

ex·or·cise \'ek-,sȯr-,sīz, -sər-\ *vb* **-cised; -cis·ing 1** : to get rid of by or as if by solemn command **2** : to free of an evil spirit — **ex·or·cism** \-,si-zəm\ *n* — **ex·or·cist** \-,sist\ *n*

exo·sphere \'ek-sō-,sfir\ *n* : the outermost region of the atmosphere

exo·ther·mic \,ek-sō-'thər-mik\ *adj* : characterized by or formed with evolution of heat

ex·ot·ic \ig-'zä-tik\ *adj* **1** : introduced from another country **2** ♦ : strikingly, excitingly, or mysteriously different or unusual

♦ fantastic, glamorous, marvelous (*or* marvellous), outlandish, romantic, strange; *also* colorful, picturesque, quaint; alien, foreign; distant, faraway, remote; alluring, captivating, fascinating

exp *abbr* **1** expense **2** experiment **3** export **4** express

ex·pand \ik-'spand\ *vb* **1** ♦ : to open up : UNFOLD **2** ♦ : to increase in extent, number, volume, or scope : ENLARGE **3** ♦ : to develop in detail — **ex·pand·er** *n*

♦ [1] extend, fan, flare, open, spread, stretch, unfold ♦ [2] add, aggrandize, amplify, augment, boost, compound, enlarge, escalate, extend, increase, multiply, raise, swell, up — more at INCREASE ♦ [3] amplify, develop, elaborate (on), enlarge (on); *also* add (to), complement, supplement; discourse, expatiate, ramble, run on *Ant* abbreviate, abridge, condense, shorten

ex·panse \ik-'spans\ *n* ♦ : a broad extent (as of land or sea)

♦ breadth, extent, reach, spread, stretch; *also* domain, field, sphere, territory; compass, range, scope, sweep; gamut, scale, spectrum; depth, emptiness, void; distance, extension, latitude, length, span; amplitude, immensity, magnitude

ex·pan·sion \ik-'span-chən\ *n* **1** ♦ : the act or process of expanding **2** : the quality or state of being expanded **3** ♦ : an expanded part or thing

♦ [1] development, elaboration, evolution, growth, progress, progression — more at DEVELOPMENT ♦ [3] accretion, addition, augmentation, boost, gain, increase, increment, plus, proliferation, raise, rise, supplement — more at INCREASE

expansion slot *n* : a socket on a motherboard for a circuit board (**expansion card**) offering additional capabilities

ex·pan·sive \ik-'span-siv\ *adj* **1** : tending to expand or to cause expansion **2** : warmly benevolent, generous, or ready to talk **3** ♦ : of large extent or scope — **ex·pan·sive·ly** *adv* — **ex·pan·sive·ness** *n*

♦ broad, extended, extensive, far-flung, far-reaching, wide, widespread — more at EXTENSIVE

ex par·te \eks-'pär-tē\ *adv or adj* [ML] : from a one-sided point of view

ex·pa·ti·ate \ek-'spā-shē-,āt\ *vb* **-at·ed; -at·ing** : to talk or write at length — **ex·pa·ti·a·tion** \ek-,spā-shē-'ā-shən\ *n*

¹**ex·pa·tri·ate** \ek-'spā-trē-,āt\ *vb* **-at·ed; -at·ing 1** : to leave one's native country to live elsewhere : EXILE **2** ♦ : to drive into exile

♦ banish, deport, displace, exile, transport — more at BANISH

²**ex·pa·tri·ate** \ek-'spā-trē-,āt, -trē-ət\ *adj* : living in a foreign country

³**expatriate** *n* : one who lives in a foreign country; *specif* : one who has renounced his or her native country

ex·pa·tri·a·tion \ek-,spā-trē-'ā-shən\ *n* : the act or action of expatriating

ex·pect \ik-'spekt\ *vb* **1** : SUPPOSE, THINK **2** ♦ : to look forward to : ANTICIPATE **3** : to consider reasonable, due, or necessary **4** : to consider to be obliged

♦ anticipate, await, hope, watch; *also* count (on *or* upon), depend (on *or* upon), rely (on *or* upon); envisage, foresee; assume, presume, presuppose; contemplate, eye, view

ex·pec·tan·cy \-'spek-tən-sē\ *n, pl* **-cies 1** : EXPECTATION **2** : the expected amount (as of years of life)

ex·pec·tant \-tənt\ *adj* ♦ : marked by expectation; *esp* : expecting the birth of a child — **ex·pec·tant·ly** *adv*

♦ agape, agog, anticipatory; *also* alert, vigilant, watchful; anxious, breathless, eager, enthusiastic, raring; impatient, restive, restless

ex·pec·ta·tion \ˌek-ˌspek-'tā-shən\ *n* **1** : the act or state of expecting **2** : prospect of good or bad fortune — usu. used in pl. **3** : something expected

ex·pec·to·rant \ik-'spek-tə-rənt\ *n* : an agent that promotes the discharge or expulsion of mucus from the respiratory tract — **expectorant** *adj*

ex·pec·to·rate \-ˌrāt\ *vb* **-rat·ed; -rat·ing** : SPIT — **ex·pec·to·ra·tion** \-ˌspek-tə-'rā-shən\ *n*

ex·pe·di·ence \ik-'spē-dē-əns\ *n* : EXPEDIENCY

ex·pe·di·en·cy \-ən-sē\ *n, pl* **-cies** **1** : fitness to some end **2** : use of expedient means and methods; *also* : something expedient

¹ex·pe·di·ent \-ənt\ *adj* [ME, fr. AF or L; AF, fr. L *expediens*, prp. of *expedire* to extricate, prepare, be useful, fr. *ex-* out + *ped-, pes* foot] **1** ♦ : adapted for achieving a particular end **2** : marked by concern with what is advantageous; *esp* : governed by self-interest

♦ advisable, desirable, judicious, politic, prudent, tactical, wise; *also* advantageous, beneficial, profitable; useful, utilitarian; feasible, possible, practicable, practical; opportune, seasonable, timely; opportunistic, self-seeking *Ant* imprudent, inadvisable, inexpedient, injudicious, unwise

²expedient *n* ♦ : something expedient; *esp* : a temporary means to an end

♦ measure, move, shift, step — more at MEASURE ♦ recourse, resort, resource — more at RESOURCE

ex·pe·dite \'ek-spə-ˌdīt\ *vb* **-dit·ed; -dit·ing** : to carry out promptly; *also* : to speed up ⟨∼ a lawsuit⟩

ex·pe·dit·er \-ˌdī-tər\ *n* : one that expedites; *esp* : one employed to ensure efficient movement of goods or supplies in a business

ex·pe·di·tion \ˌek-spə-'di-shən\ *n* **1** ♦ : a journey for a particular purpose; *also* : the persons making it **2** : efficient promptness

♦ journey, passage, peregrination, trek, trip — more at JOURNEY

ex·pe·di·tion·ary \-'di-shə-ˌner-ē\ *adj* : of, relating to, or constituting an expedition; *also* : sent on military service abroad

ex·pe·di·tious \-'di-shəs\ *adj* ♦ : marked by or acting with prompt efficiency

♦ alert, prompt, quick, ready, willing — more at QUICK

ex·pel \ik-'spel\ *vb* **ex·pelled; ex·pel·ling** ♦ : to drive or force out

♦ banish, boot (out), bounce, cast, chase, dismiss, drum, eject, oust, rout, run off, throw out — more at EJECT ♦ belch, disgorge, eject, erupt, jet, spew, spout, spurt — more at ERUPT

ex·pend \ik-'spend\ *vb* **1** ♦ : to pay out : SPEND **2** ♦ : to make use of ⟨∼ energy⟩; *also* : USE UP — **ex·pend·able** *adj*

♦ [1] disburse, give, lay out, pay, spend — more at SPEND ♦ [2] clean, consume, deplete, drain, exhaust, spend, use up — more at DEPLETE

ex·pen·di·ture \ik-'spen-di-chər, -ˌchủr\ *n* **1** : the act or process of expending **2** ♦ : something expended

♦ cost, disbursement, expense, outgo, outlay — more at EXPENSE

ex·pense \ik-'spens\ *n* **1** ♦ : something expended to secure a benefit or bring about a result : EXPENDITURE **2** : COST **3** : a cause of expenditure **4** : a loss, detriment, or embarrassment that results from some action or gain ⟨had a laugh at my ∼⟩

♦ cost, disbursement, expenditure, outgo, outlay; *also* overhead; outflow; spending money; charge, price, rate, tab, tariff, toll

ex·pen·sive \ik-'spen-siv\ *adj* ♦ : involving high cost or sacrifice : COSTLY, DEAR

♦ costly, dear, high, precious, valuable — more at COSTLY

ex·pen·sive·ly *adv* ♦ : in an expensive manner

♦ extravagantly, grandly, high, lavishly, luxuriously, opulently, richly — more at HIGH

¹ex·pe·ri·ence \ik-'spir-ē-əns\ *n* **1** : observation of or participation in events resulting in or tending toward knowledge **2** ♦ : knowledge, practice, or skill derived from observation or participation in events; *also* : the length of such participation **3** ♦ : something encountered, undergone, or lived through (as by a person or community)

♦ [2] expertise, know-how, proficiency, savvy; *also* background; command, mastery; acquaintance, familiarity, intimacy *Ant* inexperience ♦ [3] adventure, happening, time — more at ADVENTURE

²experience *vb* **-enced; -enc·ing** **1** : FIND OUT, DISCOVER **2** ♦ : to have experience of : UNDERGO

♦ endure, feel, have, know, see, suffer, sustain, taste, undergo; *also* encounter, meet; accept, receive

ex·pe·ri·enced *adj* ♦ : made capable through experience

♦ accomplished, adept, expert, masterful, masterly, practiced, proficient, seasoned, skilled, skillful, versed; *also* able, capable, competent, fit, good, qualified; educated, prepared, schooled, trained; long-term, old *Ant* amateurish, inexperienced, inexpert, unseasoned, unskilled

¹ex·per·i·ment \ik-'sper-ə-mənt\ *n* ♦ : a controlled procedure carried out to discover, test, or demonstrate something; *also* : the process of testing

♦ test, trial; *also* dry run, shakedown; exercise, practice, rehearsal, workout; crucible, ordeal; attempt, effort, try

²ex·per·i·ment \-ˌment\ *vb* : to make experiments — **ex·per·i·men·ter** *n*

ex·per·i·men·tal \-ˌsper-ə-'ment-ᵊl\ *adj* : of, relating to, or based on experience or experiment; *also* : serving the ends of or used as a means of experimentation — **ex·per·i·men·tal·ly** \-'ment-ᵊl-ē\ *adv*

ex·per·i·men·ta·tion \ik-ˌsper-ə-mən-'tā-shən\ *n* : the act, process, or practice of making experiments; *also* : an instance of experimentation

¹ex·pert \'ek-ˌspərt\ *adj* ♦ : showing special skill or knowledge ⟨∼ advice⟩ — **ex·pert·ness** *n*

♦ accomplished, ace, adept, crack, experienced, master, masterful, masterly, practiced, proficient, seasoned, skilled, skillful, versed — more at EXPERIENCED

²ex·pert \'ek-ˌspərt\ *n* ♦ : an expert person

♦ ace, artist, authority, master, scholar, shark, virtuoso, whiz, wizard; *also* pro, professional; specialist; addict, aficionado, buff, devotee, enthusiast, fan; craftsman, journeyman; jack-of-all-trades *Ant* amateur

ex·per·tise \ˌek-(ˌ)spər-'tēz\ *n* ♦ : the skill of an expert

♦ experience, know-how, proficiency, savvy — more at EXPERIENCE

ex·pert·ly *adv* ♦ : in an expert manner

♦ ably, adeptly, capably, masterfully, proficiently, skillfully, well — more at WELL

expert system *n* : computer software that attempts to mimic the reasoning of a human specialist

ex·pi·ate \'ek-spē-ˌāt\ *vb* **-at·ed; -at·ing** : to give satisfaction for : ATONE ⟨∼ sin⟩ — **ex·pi·a·tion** \ˌek-spē-'ā-shən\ *n*

ex·pi·a·to·ry \'ek-spē-ə-ˌtōr-ē\ *adj* : serving to expiate

ex·pi·ra·tion \ˌek-spə-'rā-shən\ *n* **1** : the last emission of breath; *also* : the act or process of releasing air from the lungs through the nose or mouth **2** ♦ : the fact of coming to an end or the point at which something ends

♦ death, demise, termination — more at DEATH ♦ cessation, close, conclusion, end, ending, finish, shutdown, stop, stoppage, termination — more at END

expiration date *n* **1** : the date after which something is no longer in effect **2** : the date after which a product is expected to decline in quality or effectiveness

ex·pire \ik-'spīr, ek-\ *vb* **ex·pired; ex·pir·ing** **1** ♦ : to breathe one's last breath : DIE **2** ♦ : to come to an end **3** ♦ : to breathe out from or as if from the lungs

♦ [1] decease, depart, die, pass, pass away, perish, succumb — more at DIE ♦ [2] cease, close, conclude, die, discontinue, end, finish, halt, pass, quit, stop, terminate — more at CEASE ♦ [3] blow, breathe, exhale — more at EXHALE

ex·plain \ik-'splān\ vb [ME explanen, fr. L explanare, lit., to make level, fr. planus level, flat] **1** ♦ : to make clear **2** ♦ : to give the reason for — **ex·plan·a·to·ry** \ik-'spla-nə-ˌtōr-ē\ adj

♦ [1] clarify, clear (up), construe, demonstrate, elucidate, explicate, expound, illuminate, illustrate, interpret, spell out; also decipher, decode; analyze, break down; disentangle, undo, unravel, unscramble, untangle; resolve, solve; define, specify Ant obscure ♦ [2] account, rationalize; also condone, excuse, forgive, justify; absolve, acquit, exculpate, exonerate, vindicate

explain away vb : to get rid of by or as if by explanation; also : to minimize the significance of by or as if by explanation

ex·pla·na·tion \ˌek-splə-'nā-shən\ n **1** : the act or process of explaining **2** ♦ : something that explains

♦ clarification, construction, elucidation, explication, exposition, illumination, illustration, interpretation; also paraphrase, restatement, translation; deciphering, decoding; unscrambling; analysis; definition, meaning; demonstration, enactment; justification, rationale, rationalization, reasoning argument, case, defense (or defence), rationale, reason — more at REASON

ex·ple·tive \'ek-splə-tiv\ n : a usu. profane exclamation

ex·pli·ca·ble \ek-'spli-kə-bəl, 'ek-(ˌ)spli-\ adj ♦ : capable of being explained

♦ answerable, resolvable, soluble, solvable — more at SOLVABLE

ex·pli·cate \'ek-splə-ˌkāt\ vb -cat·ed; -cat·ing ♦ : to give a detailed explanation of; esp : to interpret the meaning or sense of

♦ clarify, clear (up), construe, demonstrate, elucidate, explain, expound, illuminate, illustrate, interpret, spell out — more at EXPLAIN

ex·pli·ca·tion \ˌek-spli-'kā-shən\ n **1** : the act or process of explicating **2** ♦ : something that explicates or that results from the act or process of explicating

♦ clarification, construction, elucidation, explanation, exposition, illumination, illustration, interpretation — more at EXPLANATION

ex·plic·it \ik-'spli-sət\ adj ♦ : clearly and precisely expressed ⟨∼ directions⟩ — **ex·plic·it·ly** adv

♦ clear-cut, definite, definitive, express, specific, unambiguous, unequivocal; also declared, stated; categorical, complete, comprehensive, exhaustive, full; certain, sure, unmistakable; clear, distinct, lucid, exact, precise; direct, literal, plain, simple, straightforward; comprehensible, intelligible, understandable Ant implicit, implied, inferred; ambiguous, circuitous

ex·plic·it·ness n ♦ : the quality or state of being explicit

♦ clarity, lucidity, perspicuity, simplicity — more at SIMPLICITY

ex·plode \ik-'splōd\ vb **ex·plod·ed; ex·plod·ing** [L explodere to drive off the stage by clapping, fr. ex- out + plaudere to clap] **1** : DISCREDIT ⟨∼ a belief⟩ **2** ♦ : to burst or cause to burst violently and noisily ⟨∼ a bomb⟩ ⟨the boiler exploded⟩ **3** : to undergo a rapid chemical or nuclear reaction with production of heat and violent expansion of gas ⟨dynamite ∼s⟩ **4** : to give forth a sudden strong and noisy outburst of emotion **5** : to increase rapidly ⟨the city's population exploded⟩ **6** ♦ : to suggest an explosion (as in appearance or effect)

♦ [2] blow up, burst, detonate, go off, pop; also fragment, shatter, smash, splinter; discharge, fire, shoot; balloon, burgeon, mushroom Ant implode ♦ [6] break out, burst, erupt, flame, flare, go off — more at ERUPT

ex·plod·ed adj : showing the parts separated but in correct relationship to each other ⟨an ∼ view of a carburetor⟩

¹**ex·ploit** \'ek-ˌsplȯit\ n ♦ : something that is done; esp : a notable or heroic act

♦ deed, feat, stunt, trick — more at FEAT

²**ex·ploit** \ik-'splȯit\ vb **1** ♦ : to make productive use of : UTILIZE **2** ♦ : to use unfairly for one's own advantage ⟨∼ migrant workers⟩ — **ex·ploi·ta·tion** \ˌek-ˌsplȯi-'tā-shən\ n

♦ [1] apply, employ, exercise, harness, operate, use, utilize — more at USE ♦ [2] abuse, capitalize, cash in, impose, play, use; also manipulate, mistreat; bleed, cheat, fleece, overcharge, skin, soak, stick; commercialize

ex·plo·ra·tion \ˌek-splə-'rā-shən\ n ♦ : the act or an instance of exploring

♦ examination, inquiry, investigation, probe, research, study — more at INQUIRY

ex·plore \ik-'splȯr\ vb **ex·plored; ex·plor·ing 1** ♦ : to look into or travel over thoroughly **2** ♦ : to examine carefully ⟨∼ a wound⟩ — **ex·plor·a·to·ry** \ik-'splȯr-ə-ˌtōr-ē\ adj — **ex·plor·er** n

♦ [1] hunt, probe, prospect, search; also reconnoiter, scout; disclose, discover, reveal, unearth; fathom, plumb, sound ♦ [2] delve, dig, go, inquire into, investigate, look, probe, research; also examine, inspect, sift, study, view; browse, peruse, scan, skim (through), thumb (through)

ex·plo·sion \ik-'splō-zhən\ n ♦ : the act or an instance of exploding

♦ agony, burst, fit, flash, flush, outburst, paroxysm, spasm, storm — more at OUTBURST ♦ blast, detonation, eruption; also discharge, firing, shooting; blowout, flare-up; bang, boom, pop Ant implosion

ex·plo·sive \ik-'splō-siv\ adj **1 a** : relating to or able to cause explosion **b** : characterized by or like an explosion **2** ♦ : tending to explode; also : likely to erupt in or produce hostile reaction or violence ⟨an ∼ temper⟩ — **explosive** n — **ex·plo·sive·ly** adv

♦ ferocious, fierce, furious, hot, rabid, rough, stormy, tempestuous, turbulent, violent, volcanic — more at VIOLENT

ex·po \'ek-ˌspō\ n, pl expos : EXPOSITION 2

ex·po·nent \ik-'spō-nənt, 'ek-ˌspō-\ n **1** : a symbol written above and to the right of a mathematical expression (as ^{3} in a^3) to signify how many times it is to be used as a factor **2** : INTERPRETER, EXPOUNDER **3** ♦ : one that champions, practices, or exemplifies : ADVOCATE — **ex·po·nen·tial** \ˌek-spə-'nen-chəl\ adj — **ex·po·nen·tial·ly** adv

♦ advocate, apostle, backer, booster, champion, friend, promoter, proponent, supporter; also loyalist, partisan, stalwart; adherent, cohort, disciple, follower; expounder, interpreter; cheerleader Ant adversary, antagonist, opponent

ex·po·nen·ti·a·tion \ˌek-spə-ˌnen-chē-'ā-shen\ n : the mathematical operation of raising a quantity to a power

¹**ex·port** \ek-'spȯrt, 'ek-ˌspȯrt\ vb : to send (as merchandise) to foreign countries — **ex·por·ta·tion** \ˌek-ˌspȯr-'tā-shən, -spər-\ n — **ex·port·er** n

²**ex·port** \'ek-ˌspȯrt\ n **1** : something exported esp. for trade **2** : the act of exporting

ex·pose \ik-'spōz\ vb **ex·posed; ex·pos·ing 1** : to deprive of shelter or protection **2** : to submit or subject to an action or influence; esp : to subject (as photographic film) to radiant energy (as light) **3** ♦ : to bring to light; esp : to disclose or reveal the true nature of ⟨∼ a scam⟩ **4** ♦ : to cause to be open to view

♦ [3] bare, disclose, discover, divulge, reveal, spill, tell ♦ [3] debunk, show up, uncloak, uncover, unmask; also discredit, disprove; disclose, divulge, tell, unveil Ant camouflage, cloak, disguise, mask ♦ [4] display, exhibit, show, unveil — more at SHOW

ex·po·sé \ˌek-spō-'zā\ n : an exposure of something discreditable

ex·posed \ik-'spōzd\ adj ♦ : open to view; also : not shielded or protected

♦ liable, open, sensitive, subject, susceptible, unprotected, vulnerable — more at LIABLE ♦ bald, bare, naked, open, uncovered — more at NAKED

ex·po·si·tion \ˌek-spə-'zi-shən\ n 1 ♦ : a setting forth of the meaning or purpose (as of a writing); *also* : discourse designed to convey information 2 ♦ : a public exhibition

♦ [1] clarification, construction, elucidation, explanation, explication, illumination, illustration, interpretation — more at EXPLANATION ♦ [1] analysis, comment, commentary — more at COMMENTARY ♦ [2] display, exhibit, exhibition, fair, show — more at EXHIBITION

ex·pos·i·tor \ik-'spä-zə-tər\ n : one who explains : COMMENTATOR

ex·pos·i·to·ry \ik-'spä-zə-tə-rē\ adj : serving to explain

ex post fac·to \ˌeks-'pōst-ˌfak-tō\ adv or adj : after the fact

ex·pos·tu·late \ik-'späs-chə-ˌlāt\ vb : to reason earnestly with a person esp. in dissuading : REMONSTRATE

ex·pos·tu·la·tion \-ˌspäs-chə-'lā-shən\ n ♦ : an act or an instance of expostulating

♦ challenge, complaint, demur, fuss, kick, objection, protest, question, remonstrance — more at OBJECTION

ex·po·sure \ik-'spō-zhər\ n 1 ♦ : the fact or condition of being exposed 2 : the act or an instance of exposing 3 : the length of time for which a film is exposed 4 : a section of a photographic film for one picture

♦ liability, openness, vulnerability; *also* susceptibility; helplessness, weakness; danger, jeopardy, peril, risk

ex·pound \ik-'spaünd\ vb 1 : STATE 2 ♦ : to explain by setting forth in careful and often elaborate detail : INTERPRET — **ex·pound·er** n

♦ clarify, clear (up), construe, demonstrate, elucidate, explain, explicate, illuminate, illustrate, interpret, spell out — more at EXPLAIN

¹**ex·press** \ik-'spres\ adj 1 ♦ : directly, firmly, and explicitly stated; *also* : EXACT, PRECISE 2 ♦ : of a particular sort : SPECIFIC ⟨this ∼ purpose⟩ 3 : traveling at high speed and esp. with few stops ⟨an ∼ train⟩; *also* : adapted to high speed use ⟨∼ roads⟩ — **ex·press·ly** adv

♦ [1] clear-cut, definite, definitive, explicit, specific, unambiguous, unequivocal — more at EXPLICIT ♦ [1, 2] distinct, especial, exact, precise, set, special, specific; *also* lone, only, separate, single, sole, solitary; distinctive, exclusive, individual, peculiar, unique; limited, restricted; specified *Ant* nonspecific

²**express** adv : by express ⟨ship it ∼⟩

³**express** n 1 : a system for the prompt transportation of goods; *also* : a company operating such a service or the shipments so transported 2 : an express vehicle

⁴**express** vb 1 ♦ : to make known : STATE ⟨∼ regret⟩; *also* : to represent by a sign or symbol 2 ♦ : to squeeze out : extract by pressing 3 : to send by express 4 : to manifest or produce by a genetic process

♦ [1] denote, import, mean, signify, spell — more at MEAN ♦ [1] articulate, clothe, couch, formulate, phrase, put, say, state, word — more at PHRASE ♦ [1] air, give, sound, state, voice; *also* announce, declare, enunciate, proclaim; describe, write, write up; sound off, speak out, speak up; communicate, convey, put across, put over; offer, submit *Ant* stifle, suppress ♦ [2] crush, mash, press, squeeze — more at PRESS

ex·pres·sion \ik-'spre-shən\ n 1 ♦ : an act, process, or instance of representing in a medium (as words) : UTTERANCE 2 : something that represents or symbolizes : SIGN; *esp* : a mathematical symbol or combination of signs and symbols representing a quantity or operation 3 : a significant word or phrase; *also* : manner of expressing (as in writing or music) 4 ♦ : facial aspect or vocal intonation indicative of feeling

♦ [1] articulation, formulation, statement, utterance, voice; *also* outlet, vent; observation, reflection, remark, thought; speech, tongue ♦ [4] cast, countenance, face, look, visage — more at LOOK

ex·pres·sion·ism \ik-'spre-shə-ˌni-zəm\ n : a theory or practice in art of seeking to depict the artist's subjective

responses to objects and events — **ex·pres·sion·ist** \-nist\ n or adj — **ex·pres·sion·is·tic** \-ˌspre-shə-'nis-tik\ adj

ex·pres·sion·less adj ♦ : lacking expression

♦ blank, deadpan, impassive, inexpressive, stolid, vacant — more at BLANK

ex·pres·sive \ik-'spre-siv\ adj 1 : of or relating to expression 2 ♦ : serving to express ⟨an ∼ gesture⟩ — **ex·pres·sive·ly** adv — **ex·pres·sive·ness** n

♦ eloquent, meaning, meaningful, pregnant, significant, suggestive; *also* graphic, pictorial, vivid; evocative, redolent, reminiscent, sententious, weighty; flavorful, rich

ex·press·way \ik-'spres-ˌwā\ n : a divided superhighway with limited access

ex·pro·pri·ate \ek-'sprō-prē-ˌāt\ vb **-at·ed; -at·ing** : to deprive of possession or the right to own — **ex·pro·pri·a·tion** \(ˌ)ek-ˌsprō-prē-'ā-shən\ n

expt abbr experiment

ex·pul·sion \ik-'spəl-shən\ n ♦ : an expelling or being expelled

♦ banishment, deportation, displacement, exile — more at EXILE

ex·punge \ik-'spənj\ vb **ex·punged; ex·pung·ing** [L *expungere* to mark for deletion by dots, fr. *ex-* out + *pungere* to prick] : to efface completely : OBLITERATE

ex·pur·gate \'ek-spər-ˌgāt\ vb **-gat·ed; -gat·ing** : to clear (as a book) of objectionable passages — **ex·pur·ga·tion** \ˌek-spər-'gā-shən\ n

ex·qui·site \ik-'skwi-zət, 'ek-(ˌ)skwi-\ adj [ME *exquisit*, fr. L *exquisitus*, pp. of *exquirere* to search out, fr. *ex* out + *quaerere* to seek] 1 : marked by flawless form or workmanship 2 : keenly appreciative or sensitive 3 ♦ : pleasingly beautiful or delicate 4 : characterized by sharpness or severity : INTENSE ⟨∼ pain⟩

♦ dainty, delicate, refined, subtle — more at DELICATE

ext abbr 1 extension 2 exterior 3 external 4 extra 5 extract

ex·tant \'ek-stənt; ek-'stant\ adj ♦ : currently or actually existing; *esp* : not lost or destroyed

♦ current, ongoing, present — more at PRESENT ♦ alive, existent, living; *also* active, busy, functioning, operating, working *Ant* dead, extinct

ex·tem·po·ra·ne·ous \ek-ˌstem-pə-'rā-nē-əs\ adj ♦ : not planned beforehand : IMPROMPTU — **ex·tem·po·ra·ne·ous·ly** adv

♦ ad-lib, impromptu, informal, offhand, spontaneous, unplanned, unprepared, unrehearsed; *also* casual *Ant* considered, planned, premeditated, prepared, rehearsed

ex·tem·po·rary \ik-'stem-pə-ˌrer-ē\ adj : EXTEMPORANEOUS

ex·tem·po·re \ik-'stem-pə-(ˌ)rē\ adv : EXTEMPORANEOUSLY

ex·tem·po·rise chiefly Brit var of EXTEMPORIZE

ex·tem·po·rize \ik-'stem-pə-ˌrīz\ vb **-rized; -riz·ing** : to do something extemporaneously ⟨∼ a speech⟩

ex·tend \ik-'stend\ vb 1 ♦ : to spread or stretch forth or out (as in reaching) 2 : to exert or cause to exert to full capacity 3 ♦ : to make the offer of : PROFFER ⟨∼ credit⟩ 4 : PROLONG ⟨∼ a note⟩ 5 : to make greater or broader ⟨∼ knowledge⟩ ⟨∼ a business⟩ 6 : to stretch out or reach across a distance, space, or time — **ex·tend·able** also **ex·tend·ible** \-'sten-də-bəl\ adj

♦ [1] expand, fan, flare, open, spread, stretch, unfold ♦ [1] draw out, elongate, lengthen, prolong, protract, stretch; *also* amplify, enlarge, expand, increase; attenuate, thin *Ant* abbreviate, abridge, curtail, cut, cut back, shorten ♦ [3] give, offer, proffer, tender — more at OFFER

ex·tend·ed adj 1 ♦ : drawn out in length esp. of time 2 : fully stretched out 3 ♦ : having wide or considerable extent

♦ [1] far, great, lengthy, long, marathon — more at LONG ♦ [3] broad, expansive, extensive, far-flung, far-reaching, wide, widespread — more at EXTENSIVE

ex·ten·sion \ik-'sten-chən\ n 1 ♦ : an extending or being extended 2 : a program that geographically extends the educational resources of an institution **3 ♦** : an additional part; *also* : an extra telephone connected to a line

♦ elongation, prolongation *Ant* abbreviation, abridgment, curtailment, cutback, shortening ♦ [3] addition, annex, penthouse — more at ANNEX

ex·ten·sive \ik-'sten-siv\ *adj* ♦ : of considerable extent : FAR-REACHING, BROAD ⟨~ training⟩ — **ex·ten·sive·ly** *adv*

♦ broad, expansive, extended, far-flung, far-reaching, wide, widespread; *also* comprehensive, general, global, inclusive; boundless, endless, limitless, unlimited; capacious, commodious, roomy, spacious *Ant* narrow

ex·tent \ik-'stent\ *n* **1** ♦ : the range or space over which something extends ⟨a property of large ~⟩ **2** ♦ : the point or degree to which something extends ⟨to the fullest ~ of the law⟩ ⟨exerting the full ~ of his power⟩

♦ [1] amplitude, breadth, compass, range, reach, realm, scope, sweep, width — more at RANGE ♦ [1] dimension, magnitude, measure, measurement, proportion, size — more at SIZE ♦ [2] bound, boundary, ceiling, confines, end, limit, limitation, line, termination — more at LIMIT

ex·ten·u·ate \ik-'sten-yù-ˌwāt\ *vb* **-at·ed; -at·ing** : to lessen the seriousness of — **ex·ten·u·a·tion** \-ˌsten-yù-'wā-shən\ *n*

¹ex·te·ri·or \ek-'stir-ē-ər\ *adj* **1** ♦ : being on an outside surface : EXTERNAL **2** : suitable for use on an outside surface ⟨~ paint⟩

♦ external, outer, outside, outward — more at OUTER

²exterior *n* ♦ : an exterior part or surface

♦ face, outside, skin, surface, veneer; *also* facade, front, top; cover, covering, facing; appearance, disguise, guise, mask, semblance, show *Ant* inside, interior

ex·ter·mi·nate \ik-'stər-mə-ˌnāt\ *vb* **-nat·ed; -nat·ing** ♦ : to get rid of completely usu. by killing off — **ex·ter·mi·na·tor** \-'stər-mə-ˌnā-tər\ *n*

♦ annihilate, blot out, demolish, eradicate, liquidate, obliterate, root, rub out, snuff, stamp, wipe out — more at ANNIHILATE

ex·ter·mi·na·tion \-ˌstər-mə-'nā-shən\ *n* : the act of exterminating or the condition of being exterminated

¹ex·ter·nal \ek-'stərn-ᵊl\ *adj* **1** : outwardly perceivable; *also* : SUPERFICIAL **2** ♦ : of, relating to, or located on the outside or an outer part **3** : arising or acting from without; *also* : FOREIGN ⟨~ affairs⟩ — **ex·ter·nal·ly** *adv*

♦ exterior, outer, outside, outward — more at OUTER

²external *n* : an external feature

ex·tinct \ik-'stiŋkt\ *adj* **1** : EXTINGUISHED; *also* : no longer active ⟨an ~ volcano⟩ **2** ♦ : no longer existing or in use ⟨dinosaurs are ~⟩ ⟨~ languages⟩

♦ bygone, dead, defunct, gone; *also* nonexistent; obsolete, passé; finished, lapsed, terminated; lost, missing *Ant* alive, existent, existing, extant, living

ex·tinc·tion \ik-'stiŋk-shən\ *n* **1** : the act of making extinct or causing to be extinguished **2** : the condition or fact of being extinct or extinguished; *also* : the process of becoming extinct

ex·tin·guish \ik-'stiŋ-gwish\ *vb* **1** ♦ : to cause to stop burning **2** ♦ : to bring to an end : cause to die out ⟨disease that *extinguished* an entire population⟩ ⟨*extinguishing* the last glimmer of hope⟩ — **ex·tin·guish·able** *adj* — **ex·tin·guish·er** *n*

♦ [1] douse, put out, quench, snuff; *also* choke, smother, suffocate; stamp (out) *Ant* fire, ignite, inflame, kindle ♦ [2] annihilate, blot out, demolish, desolate, destroy, devastate, do in, obliterate, ruin, shatter, smash, wipe out, wreck — more at DESTROY

ex·tir·pate \'ek-stər-ˌpāt\ *vb* **-pat·ed; -pat·ing** [L *exstirpatus*, pp. of *exstirpare*, fr. *ex-* out + *stirps* trunk, root] **1** : to destroy completely ⟨~ a heresy⟩ **2** : UPROOT — **ex·tir·pa·tion** \ˌek-stər-'pā-shən\ *n*

ex·tol *also* **ex·toll** \ik-'stōl\ *vb* **ex·tolled; ex·tol·ling** ♦ : to praise highly : GLORIFY

♦ bless, glorify, laud, magnify, praise — more at PRAISE

ex·tort \ik-'stȯrt\ *vb* [L *extortus*, pp. of *extorquēre* to wrench out, extort, fr. *ex-* out + *torquēre* to twist] ♦ : to obtain by force or improper pressure ⟨~ a bribe⟩ — **ex·tor·tion** \-'stȯr-shən\ *n* — **ex·tor·tion·er** *n*

♦ exact, wrest, wring; *also* bleed, fleece, gouge, milk, skin, squeeze; cheat, racketeer, swindle; coerce, compel, force

ex·tor·tion·ate \ik-'stȯr-shə-nət\ *adj* : EXCESSIVE, EXORBITANT — **ex·tor·tion·ate·ly** *adv*

ex·tor·tion·ist *n* ♦ : one that practices or is given to extortion

♦ racketeer — more at RACKETEER

¹ex·tra \'ek-strə\ *adj* **1** ♦ : more than is due, usual, or necessary **2** : SUPERIOR

♦ excess, spare, superfluous, supernumerary, surplus — more at SPARE

²extra *n* ♦ : one that is extra or additional: as **a** : a special edition of a newspaper **b** : an added charge **c** : an additional worker or performer (as in a motion picture)

♦ amenity, comfort, frill, indulgence, luxury, superfluity — more at LUXURY ♦ bonus, dividend, lagniappe, perquisite, tip — more at BONUS

³extra *adv* ♦ : beyond what is usual

♦ extremely, greatly, highly, hugely, mightily, mighty, mortally, most, much, real, right, so, very — more at VERY

¹ex·tract \ik-'strakt, *esp for 3* 'ek-ˌstrakt\ *vb* **1** ♦ : to draw out; *esp* : to pull out forcibly ⟨~ a tooth⟩ **2** : to withdraw (as a juice or a constituent) by a physical or chemical process **3** : to select for citation : QUOTE — **ex·tract·able** *adj* — **ex·trac·tor** \-tər\ *n*

♦ prize, pry, pull, root, tear, uproot, wrest; *also* remove, take (out), withdraw

²ex·tract \'ek-ˌstrakt\ *n* **1** : EXCERPT, CITATION **2** : a product (as a juice or concentrate) obtained by extracting

ex·trac·tion \ik-'strak-shən\ *n* **1** : the act or process of extracting something **2** ♦ : line of descent

♦ ancestry, birth, descent, line, lineage, origin, parentage — more at ANCESTRY

ex·tra·cur·ric·u·lar \ˌek-strə-kə-'ri-kyə-lər\ *adj* : lying outside the regular curriculum; *esp* : of or relating to school-connected activities (as sports) usu. carrying no academic credit

ex·tra·dite \'ek-strə-ˌdīt\ *vb* **-dit·ed; -dit·ing** : to obtain by or deliver up to extradition

ex·tra·di·tion \ˌek-strə-'di-shən\ *n* : the surrender of an alleged criminal to a different jurisdiction for trial

ex·tra·mar·i·tal \ˌek-strə-'mar-ət-ᵊl\ *adj* : of or relating to sexual intercourse by a married person with someone other than his or her spouse

ex·tra·mu·ral \-'myùr-əl\ *adj* : existing or functioning beyond the bounds of an organized unit

ex·tra·ne·ous \ek-'strā-nē-əs\ *adj* **1** : coming from without **2** ♦ : not forming a vital part; *also* : IRRELEVANT — **ex·tra·ne·ous·ly** *adv*

♦ immaterial, irrelevant — more at IRRELEVANT

ex·tra·net \'ek-strə-ˌnet\ *n* : a network like an intranet but also allowing access by certain outside parties

ex·traor·di·nary \ik-'strȯr-də-ˌner-ē, ˌek-strə-'ȯr-\ *adj* **1** ♦ : notably unusual or exceptional ⟨did ~ work on the project⟩ **2** : employed on special service ⟨an ambassador ~⟩ — **ex·traor·di·nari·ly** \-ˌstrȯr-də-'ner-ə-lē, ˌek-strə-ˌȯr-\ *adv*

♦ atypical, exceptional, phenomenal, rare, uncustomary, unique, unusual — more at EXCEPTIONAL

ex·trap·o·late \ik-'stra-pə-ˌlāt\ *vb* **-lat·ed; -lat·ing** ♦ : to infer (unknown data) from known data — **ex·trap·o·la·tion** \-ˌstra-pə-'lā-shən\ *n*

♦ conclude, deduce, gather, infer, judge, reason, understand — more at INFER

ex·tra·sen·so·ry \ˌek-strə-'sen-sə-rē\ *adj* : not acting or occurring through the known senses

extrasensory perception *n* : perception (as in telepathy) of events external to the self not gained through the senses and not deducible from previous experience

ex·tra·ter·res·tri·al \-tə-'res-trē-əl\ *adj* : originating or existing outside the earth or its atmosphere ⟨∼ life⟩ — **extraterrestrial** *n*

ex·tra·ter·ri·to·ri·al \-ˌter-ə-'tōr-ē-əl\ *adj* : existing or taking place outside the territorial limits of a jurisdiction

ex·tra·ter·ri·to·ri·al·i·ty \-ˌtōr-ē-ˈa-lə-tē\ *n* : exemption from the application or jurisdiction of local law or tribunals ⟨diplomats enjoy ∼⟩

ex·trav·a·gance \-gəns\ *n* ♦ : an instance of excess or prodigality; *specif* : an excessive outlay of money

♦ lavishness, prodigality, wastefulness; *also* bountifulness, generosity, liberality; improvidence, squandering, indulgence, overindulgence, self-indulgence; excess, immoderacy, overkill *Ant* economy, frugality

ex·trav·a·gant \ik-ˈstra-vi-gənt\ *adj* 1 ♦ : exceeding the limits of reason or necessity : EXCESSIVE ⟨∼ claims⟩ 2 ♦ : spending or tending to spend much more than necessary : spending lavishly, recklessly, or wastefully 3 : too costly

♦ [1] excessive, extreme, immoderate, inordinate, lavish, overmuch, steep, stiff — more at EXCESSIVE ♦ [2] prodigal, profligate, spendthrift, thriftless, unthrifty, wasteful — more at PRODIGAL

ex·trav·a·gant·ly *adv* ♦ : in an extravagant manner

♦ expensively, grandly, high, lavishly, luxuriously, opulently, richly — more at HIGH

ex·trav·a·gan·za \ik-ˌstra-və-'gan-zə\ *n* 1 : a literary or musical work marked by extreme freedom of style and structure 2 : a spectacular show

ex·tra·ve·hic·u·lar \ˌek-strə-vē-'hi-kyə-lər\ *adj* : taking place outside a vehicle (as a spacecraft) ⟨∼ activity⟩

¹**ex·treme** \ik-'strēm\ *adj* 1 : very great or intense ⟨∼ cold⟩ 2 : very severe or radical ⟨∼ measures⟩ 3 : going to great lengths or beyond normal limits ⟨politically ∼⟩ 4 ♦ : most remote ⟨the ∼ end⟩ 5 : UTMOST; *also* : MAXIMUM

♦ [3] excessive, immoderate, inordinate, overmuch, unconscionable — more at EXCESSIVE ♦ [3] extremist, fanatic, rabid, radical, revolutionary, ultra; *also* subversive, violent, wild; reactionary *Ant* middle-of-the-road ♦ [4] farthest, furthest, outermost, ultimate, utmost *Ant* inmost, innermost

²**extreme** *n* 1 : something located at one end or the other of a range or series 2 : EXTREMITY 4

ex·treme·ly *adv* ♦ : in an extreme manner : to an extreme extent

♦ extra, greatly, highly, hugely, mightily, mighty, mortally, most, much, real, right, so, very — more at VERY

extremely low frequency *n* : a radio frequency in the lowest range of the radio spectrum

ex·trem·ism \ik-'strē-ˌmi-zəm\ *n* : the quality or state of being extreme; *esp* : advocacy of extreme political measures

¹**ex·trem·ist** \-mist\ *n* ♦ : an adherent or advocate of extremism

♦ radical, revolutionary — more at RADICAL

²**extremist** *adj* ♦ : of, relating to, or favoring extremism or extremists

♦ extreme, fanatic, rabid, radical, revolutionary, ultra — more at EXTREME

ex·trem·i·ty \ik-'stre-mə-tē\ *n, pl* **-ties** 1 ♦ : the most remote part or point 2 : a limb of the body; *esp* : a human hand or foot 3 : the greatest need or danger 4 : the utmost degree; *also* : a drastic or desperate measure

♦ height, limit — more at HEIGHT

ex·tri·cate \'ek-strə-ˌkāt\ *vb* **-cat·ed; -cat·ing** [L *extricatus*, pp. of *extricare*, fr. *ex-* out + *tricae* trifles, perplexities]

♦ : to free from an entanglement or difficulty — **ex·tri·ca·ble** \ik-ˈstri-kə-bəl, ek-; 'ek-(ˌ)stri-\ *adj* — **ex·tri·ca·tion** \ˌek-strə-'kā-shən\ *n*

♦ clear, disengage, disentangle, free, liberate, release, untangle; *also* deliver, redeem, rescue, save; disburden, disencumber, unburden; unravel, unsnarl, untie, untwine *Ant* embroil, entangle

ex·trin·sic \ek-'strin-zik, -sik\ *adj* 1 ♦ : not forming part of or belonging to a thing 2 : EXTERNAL — **ex·trin·si·cal·ly** \-zi-k(ə-)lē, -si-\ *adv*

♦ adventitious, alien, extraneous, foreign; *also* exterior, external, outside; immaterial, inapplicable, insignificant, irrelevant; nonessential, unessential *Ant* inherent, innate, intrinsic

ex·tro·vert *also* **ex·tra·vert** \'ek-strə-ˌvərt\ *n* : a gregarious and unreserved person — **ex·tro·ver·sion** *or* **ex·tra·ver·sion** \ˌek-strə-'vər-zhən\ *n*

ex·tro·vert·ed *also* **ex·tra·vert·ed** *adj* ♦ : having the characteristics of an extrovert : marked by extroversion

♦ boon, companionable, convivial, gregarious, outgoing, sociable, social — more at CONVIVIAL

ex·trude \ik-'strüd\ *vb* **ex·trud·ed; ex·trud·ing** 1 : to force, press, or push out 2 : to shape (as plastic) by forcing through a die — **ex·tru·sion** \-'strü-zhən\ *n* — **ex·trud·er** *n*

ex·u·ber·ance \-rəns\ *n* 1 ♦ : the quality or state of being exuberant 2 : an exuberant act or expression

♦ [1] animation, briskness, liveliness, lustiness, robustness, sprightliness, vibrancy, vitality — more at VITALITY

ex·u·ber·ant \ig-'zü-bə-rənt\ *adj* 1 ♦ : unrestrained in enthusiasm or style 2 : PROFUSE

♦ bubbly, buoyant, effervescent, frolicsome, high-spirited, vivacious; *also* extroverted, outgoing, uninhibited; carefree, insouciant, joyful, lighthearted, lively, sprightly; boisterous, raucous, rollicking, rowdy; giddy, light-headed, silly; ecstatic, euphoric, rapturous; audacious, bold, brash, brazen, impertinent, impudent, insolent, saucy *Ant* sullen

ex·u·ber·ant·ly *adv* ♦ : in an exuberant manner

♦ gaily, jauntily, sprightly — more at GAILY

ex·ude \ig-'züd\ *vb* **ex·ud·ed; ex·ud·ing** [L *exsudare*, fr. *ex-* out + *sudare* to sweat] 1 ♦ : to discharge slowly through pores or cuts : OOZE 2 : to display conspicuously or abundantly ⟨∼s charm⟩ — **ex·u·date** \'ek-sù-ˌdāt, -syù-\ *n* — **ex·u·da·tion** \ˌek-sù-'dā-shən, -syù-\ *n*

♦ bleed, ooze, percolate, seep, strain, sweat, weep; *also* dribble, drip, trickle; discharge, emit, give off, vent; emanate, flow, spring

ex·ult \ig-'zəlt\ *vb* ♦ : to be extremely joyful : REJOICE, GLORY ⟨∼ed in their victory⟩ — **ex·ul·tant·ly** *adv* — **ex·ul·ta·tion** \ˌek-(ˌ)səl-'tā-shən, ˌeg-(ˌ)zəl-\ *n*

♦ crow, delight, glory, joy, rejoice, triumph; *also* gloat; boast, brag; flaunt, parade, show off, strut, swagger

ex·ul·tant \-'zəlt-ᵊnt\ *adj* ♦ : filled with or expressing great joy or triumph

♦ jubilant, rejoicing, triumphant; *also* ecstatic, elated, euphoric, arrogant, boastful, cocky; conquering, victorious, winning

ex·urb \'ek-ˌsərb, 'eg-ˌzərb\ *n* : a region outside a city and its suburbs inhabited chiefly by well-to-do families — **ex·ur·ban** \ek-'sər-bən, eg-'zər-\ *adj*

ex·ur·ban·ite \ek-'sər-bə-ˌnīt; eg-'zər-\ *n* : one who lives in an exurb

ex·ur·bia \ek-'sər-bē-ə, eg-'zer-\ *n* ♦ : the generalized region of exurbs

♦ environs, outskirts, suburbia — more at ENVIRONS

-ey — see -y

¹**eye** \'ī\ *n* 1 : an organ of sight typically consisting in vertebrates of a globular structure that is located in a socket of the skull, is lined with a sensitive retina, and is normally paired 2 : skill or ability dependent upon eyesight : VISION, PERCEPTION; *also* : faculty of discrim-

ination ⟨an ~ for bargains⟩ **3 a ♦ :** a way of looking at or thinking about something **:** JUDGMENT — often used in pl. ⟨in the ~s of the law⟩ **b ♦ :** an attentive or critical observation **4 a :** something having an appearance suggesting an eye ⟨the ~ of a needle⟩ **b :** an undeveloped bud (as on a potato) **5 a :** the calm center of a cyclone **b ♦ :** an important or pivotal point — **eyed** \'īd\ *adj*

♦ [3a] belief, conviction, feeling, judgment (*or* judgement), mind, notion, opinion, persuasion, sentiment, verdict, view — more at OPINION ♦ [3b] cast, gander, glance, glimpse, look, regard, sight, view — more at LOOK ♦ [5b] base, center (*or* centre), core, cynosure, focus, heart, hub, mecca, nucleus, seat — more at CENTER

²**eye** *vb* **eyed; eye·ing** *or* **ey·ing ♦ :** to look at

♦ distinguish, espy, look, note, notice, observe, perceive, regard, remark, see, sight, spy, view, witness — more at SEE

¹**eye·ball** \'ī-ˌbȯl\ *n* **:** the globular capsule of the vertebrate eye
²**eyeball** *vb* **:** to look at intently
eye·brow \-ˌbraù\ *n* **:** the ridge over the eye or the hair growing on it
eye·drop·per \-ˌdrä-pər\ *n* **:** DROPPER 2
eye·glass \-ˌglas\ *n* **♦ :** a lens worn to aid vision; *also, pl* **:** GLASSES

♦ **eyeglasses** glasses, spectacles — more at GLASSES

eye·lash \-ˌlash\ *n* **1 :** the fringe of hair edging the eyelid — usu. used in pl. **2 :** a single hair of the eyelashes
eye·let \-lət\ *n* **1 :** a small hole intended for ornament or for passage of a cord or lace **2 :** a typically metal ring for reinforcing an eyelet **:** GROMMET
eye·lid \-ˌlid\ *n* **:** either of the movable folds of skin and muscle that can be closed over the eyeball

eye·lin·er \-ˌlī-nər\ *n* **:** makeup used to emphasize the contour of the eyes
eye–open·er \-ˌō-pə-nər\ *n* **:** something startling or surprising
eye–open·ing *adj* **♦ :** that which opens the eyes (as with astonishment) **:** surprising or enlightening

♦ amazing, astonishing, astounding, startling, stunning, surprising — more at SURPRISING

eye·piece \-ˌpēs\ *n* **:** the lens or combination of lenses at the eye end of an optical instrument
eye shadow *n* **:** a colored cosmetic applied to the eyelids to accent the eyes
eye·sight \-ˌsīt\ *n* **:** the process, power, or function of seeing **:** SIGHT, VISION
eye·sore \-ˌsōr\ *n* **♦ :** something offensive to view

♦ fright, horror, mess, monstrosity, sight; *also* blot, smear, smudge, spot, stain

eye·strain \-ˌstrān\ *n* **:** weariness or a strained state of the eye
eye·tooth \-ˈtüth\ *n* **:** a canine tooth of the upper jaw
eye·wash \-ˌwȯsh, -ˌwäsh\ *n* **1 :** an eye lotion **2 :** misleading or deceptive statements, actions, or procedures
eye·wit·ness \-ˈwit-nəs\ *n* **:** a person who actually sees something happen
Ez *or* **Ezr** *abbr* Ezra
Ezech *abbr* Ezechiel
Eze·chiel \i-ˈzē-kyəl\ *n* **:** EZEKIEL
Ezek *abbr* Ezekiel
Eze·kiel \i-ˈzē-kyəl\ *n* **:** a book of Jewish and Christian Scripture
e–zine \'ē-ˌzēn\ *n* **:** an online magazine
Ez·ra \'ez-rə\ *n* **:** a book of Jewish and Christian Scripture

¹**f** \'ef\ *n, pl* **f's** *or* **fs** \'efs\ *often cap* **1 :** the 6th letter of the English alphabet **2 :** a grade rating a student's work as failing
²**f** *abbr, often cap* **1** Fahrenheit **2** false **3** family **4** farad **5** female **6** feminine **7** forte **8** French **9** frequency **10** Friday
³**f** *symbol* focal length
F *symbol* fluorine
FAA *abbr* Federal Aviation Administration
fab \'fab\ *adj* **:** FABULOUS
Fa·bi·an \'fā-bē-ən\ *adj* **:** of, relating to, or being a society of socialists organized in England in 1884 to spread socialist principles gradually — **Fabian** *n* — **Fa·bi·an·ism** *n*
fa·ble \'fā-bəl\ *n* **1 :** a legendary story of supernatural happenings **2 :** a narration intended to teach a lesson; *esp* **:** one in which animals speak and act like people **3 :** FALSEHOOD **4 :** the plot, story, or connected series of events forming the theme of a literary work
fa·bled \'fā-bəld\ *adj* **1 :** FICTITIOUS **2 ♦ :** told or celebrated in fable ⟨~ deeds⟩

♦ fabulous, legendary, mythical — more at MYTHICAL

fab·ric \'fa-brik\ *n* [MF *fabrique,* fr. L *fabrica* workshop, structure] **1 :** STRUCTURE, FRAMEWORK ⟨the ~ of society⟩ **2 :** CLOTH; *also* **:** a material that resembles cloth
fab·ri·cate \'fa-bri-ˌkāt\ *vb* **-cat·ed; -cat·ing 1 ♦ :** to think up or imagine **:** concoct mentally **:** INVENT **2 ♦ :** to make up for the sake of deception **3 :** to form, make, or create by combining parts or elements **:** CONSTRUCT ⟨~ tools⟩ **4 ♦ :** to form by art and labor

♦ [1] concoct, contrive, cook up, devise, invent, make up, manufacture, think up — more at INVENT ♦ [2] fib,

lie, prevaricate — more at LIE ♦ [4] fashion, form, frame, make, manufacture, produce — more at MAKE
fab·ri·ca·tion *n* **1 ♦ :** the invention or utterance of something calculated to deceive **2 ♦ :** a product of the imagination

♦ [1] falsehood, fib, lie, story, tale, untruth, whopper — more at LIE ♦ [2] fantasy, fiction, figment, invention — more at FICTION

fab·u·lous \'fa-byə-ləs\ *adj* **1 :** resembling a fable **2 ♦ :** told in or based on fable **3 :** like the contents of fables in being so marvelous, incredible, absurd, extreme, exaggerated, or approaching the impossible **4 :** not real, actual, or historical **5 ♦ :** outstanding or pleasing quality — **fab·u·lous·ly** *adv*

♦ [2] fabled, legendary, mythical — more at MYTHICAL ♦ [5] excellent, grand, great, sensational, splendid, superb, superior, swell, terrific, unsurpassed, wonderful — more at EXCELLENT

fac *abbr* **1** facsimile **2** faculty
fa·cade *also* **fa·çade** \fə-ˈsäd\ *n* [F *façade,* fr. It *facciata,* fr. *faccia* face] **1 :** the principal face or front of a building **2 ♦ :** a false, superficial, or artificial appearance or effect ⟨a ~ of composure⟩ **3 ♦ :** a surface or front

♦ [2] act, airs, front, guise, masquerade, pose, pretense, put-on, semblance, show — more at MASQUERADE ♦ [3] face, front — more at FRONT

¹**face** \'fās\ *n* **1 :** the front part of the head **2 :** PRESENCE ⟨in the ~ of danger⟩ **3 ♦ :** facial expression **:** LOOK ⟨put a sad ~ on⟩ **4 ♦ :** a deliberate or involuntary distortion of the countenance expressive of some feeling **:** GRIMACE ⟨made a ~⟩ **5 :** outward appearance ⟨looks easy on the ~ of it⟩ **6 :** CONFIDENCE; *also* **:** BOLDNESS **7 :** DIGNITY,

PRESTIGE ⟨afraid to lose ∼⟩ **8 ♦** : a front, upper, or outer surface or a surface presented to view or regarded as principal : SURFACE; *esp* : a front, principal, or bounding surface ⟨∼ of a cliff⟩ ⟨the ∼s of a cube⟩ — **faced** \ˈfāst, ˈfā-səd\ *adj*

♦ [3] cast, countenance, expression, look, visage — more at LOOK ♦ [4] frown, grimace, pout, scowl — more at GRIMACE ♦ [8] facade, front — more at FRONT ♦ [8] exterior, outside, skin, surface, veneer — more at EXTERIOR

²**face** *vb* **faced; fac·ing 1 ♦** : to confront brazenly **2** : to line near the edge esp. with a different material; *also* : to cover the front or surface of ⟨∼ a building with marble⟩ **3 ♦** : to meet or bring in direct contact or confrontation ⟨*faced* the problem⟩ **4 ♦** : to stand or sit with the face toward ⟨∼ the sun⟩ **5** : to have the front oriented toward ⟨a house *facing* the park⟩ **6** : to have as or be a prospect ⟨∼ a grim future⟩ **7** : to turn the face or body in a specified direction **8** : to bring directly to the attention of — **face the music** : to meet the unpleasant consequences of one's actions

♦ [1] beard, brave, brazen, confront, dare, defy ♦ [3] battle, encounter, engage, meet, take on — more at ENGAGE ♦ [4] front, look, point

face·down \ˌfās-ˈdau̇n\ *adv* : with the face downward
face·less \-ləs\ *n* **1** : lacking a face **2** : lacking character or individuality
face–lift \ˈfās-ˌlift\ *n* **1** : plastic surgery on the face and neck to remove defects (as wrinkles) typical of aging : a cosmetic surgical operation for removal of facial defects (as wrinkles) typical of aging **2** : MODERNIZATION — **face–lift** *vb*
face–off \ˈfās-ˌȯf\ *n* **1** : a method of beginning play by dropping a ball or puck (as in hockey) between two opposing players each of whom attempts to control it **2 ♦** : the clashing of forces or ideas : CONFRONTATION

♦ battle, combat, conflict, confrontation, contest, duel, rivalry, struggle — more at CONTEST

face off *vb* **♦** : to be or come into opposition or competition

♦ battle, compete, contend, fight, race, vie — more at COMPETE

fac·et \ˈfa-sət\ *n* [F *facette*, dim. of *face*] **1** : a small plane surface of a cut gem **2 ♦** : any of the definable aspects that make up a subject (as of contemplation) or an object (as of consideration) : ASPECT, PHASE

♦ [2] angle, aspect, hand, phase, side — more at ASPECT

fa·ce·tious \fə-ˈsē-shəs\ *adj* **1 ♦** : joking often inappropriately ⟨∼ remarks⟩ **2 ♦** : characterized by pleasantry or levity : exciting laughter : JOCULAR — **fa·ce·tious·ly** *adv*

♦ [1] flip, flippant, pert, smart — more at FLIPPANT ♦ [2] clever, humorous, jocular, smart, witty — more at WITTY

fa·ce·tious·ness *n* **♦** : the quality or state of being facetious

♦ flightiness, flippancy, frivolity, levity, lightness — more at FRIVOLITY

¹**fa·cial** \ˈfā-shəl\ *adj* **1** : of or relating to the face **2** : used to improve the appearance of the face
²**facial** *n* : a facial treatment
fac·ile \ˈfa-səl\ *adj* **1 ♦** : easily accomplished, handled, or attained **2** : SIMPLISTIC **3** : readily manifested and often insincere ⟨∼ prose⟩ **4** : READY, FLUENT ⟨a ∼ writer⟩

♦ easy, effortless, fluent, fluid, light, painless, ready, simple, smooth, snap, soft — more at EASY

fa·cil·i·tate \fə-ˈsi-lə-ˌtāt\ *vb* **-tat·ed; -tat·ing ♦** : to make easier — **fa·cil·i·ta·tion** \-ˌsi-lə-ˈtā-shən\ *n* — **fa·cil·i·ta·tor** \-ˈsi-lə-ˌtā-tər\ *n*

♦ ease, loosen, smooth, unclog — more at EASE

fa·cil·i·ty \fə-ˈsi-lə-tē\ *n, pl* **-ties 1** : the quality of being easily performed **2** : ease in performance : APTITUDE **3** : PLIANCY **4** : something that makes easier an action, operation, or course of conduct; *also* : REST ROOM —

often used in pl. **5 ♦** : something (as a hospital) built or installed for a particular purpose

♦ complex, establishment, installation

fac·ing \ˈfā-sin\ *n* **1** : a lining at the edge esp. of a garment **2** *pl* : the collar, cuffs, and trimmings of a uniform coat **3** : an ornamental or protective layer **4** : material for facing
fac·sim·i·le \fak-ˈsi-mə-lē\ *n* [L *fac simile* make similar] **1 ♦** : an exact copy **2** : a system of transmitting and reproducing printed matter or pictures by means of signals sent over telephone lines

♦ carbon copy, double, duplicate, image, match, replica, reproduction — more at IMAGE

fact \ˈfakt\ *n* **1** : DEED; *esp* : CRIME ⟨accessory after the ∼⟩ **2** : the quality of being actual **3** : something that exists or occurs **4 ♦** : a piece of information — **in fact** : in truth

♦ detail, particular, point

fac·tion \ˈfak-shən\ *n* **♦** : a group or combination (as in a government) acting together within and usu. against a larger body — **fac·tion·al·ism** \-shə-nə-ˌli-zəm\ *n*

♦ bloc, body, coalition, combination, combine, party, sect, set, side, wing

fac·tious \ˈfak-shəs\ *adj* **1** : of, relating to, or caused by faction **2** : inclined to faction or the formation of factions : causing dissension
fac·ti·tious \fak-ˈti-shəs\ *adj* **1 a ♦** : produced by human art, skill, or effort **b ♦** : not natural or real : SHAM ⟨a ∼ display of grief⟩ **2** : not natural or spontaneous

♦ artificial, fake, faux, imitation, mock, sham, synthetic — more at IMITATION

fac·toid \ˈfak-ˌtȯid\ *n* **1** : an invented fact believed to be true because of its appearance in print **2** : a brief usu. trivial fact
¹**fac·tor** \ˈfak-tər\ *n* **1 ♦** : a person that acts or transacts business for another : AGENT **2 ♦** : something that actively contributes to a result ⟨a ∼ in her decision⟩ **3** : GENE **4** : any of the numbers or symbols in mathematics that when multiplied together form a product; *esp* : any of the integers that divide a given integer without a remainder

♦ [1] agent, attorney, delegate, deputy, representative — more at AGENT ♦ [2] component, constituent, element, ingredient, member — more at ELEMENT

²**factor** *vb* **1** : to work as a factor **2** : to find the mathematical factors of and esp. the prime mathematical factors of
¹**fac·to·ri·al** \fak-ˈtȯr-ē-əl\ *adj* : of, relating to, or being a factor
²**factorial** *n* : the product of all the positive integers from 1 to a given integer *n*
fac·to·ry \ˈfak-trē, -tə-rē\ *n, pl* **-ries 1** : a trading post where resident brokers trade **2 ♦** : a building or group of buildings used for manufacturing

♦ mill, plant, shop, works, workshop

fac·to·tum \fak-ˈtō-təm\ *n* [NL, lit., do everything, fr. L *fac* do + *totum* everything] : a person (as a servant) having numerous or varied duties
facts of life : the physiological processes and behavior involved in sex and reproduction
fac·tu·al \ˈfak-chə-wəl\ *adj* **1 ♦** : of or relating to facts **2 ♦** : based on fact — **fac·tu·al·ly** *adv*

♦ [1] actual, concrete, existent, real, true, very — more at ACTUAL ♦ [2] documentary, literal, nonfictional, objective, true

fac·ul·ty \ˈfa-kəl-tē\ *n, pl* **-ties 1 a ♦** : ability to act or do **b ♦** : natural aptitude **2** : one of the powers of the mind or body ⟨the ∼ of hearing⟩ **3** : the teachers in a school or college or one of its divisions

♦ [1a] ability, capability, capacity, competence — more at ABILITY ♦ [1b] aptitude, endowment, flair, genius, gift, knack, talent — more at TALENT

fad \ˈfad\ *n* **♦** : a practice or interest followed for a time with exaggerated zeal : CRAZE — **fad·dist** *n*

♦ craze, mode, rage, style, trend, vogue

fad·dish \\'fa-dish\\ *adj* ♦ : constituting or resembling a fad — **fad·dish·ly** *adv*

♦ fashionable, hot, in, modish, popular, vogue — more at POPULAR

¹**fade** \\'fād\\ *vb* **fad·ed; fad·ing** **1** : WITHER **2** ♦ : to lose or cause to lose freshness or brilliance of color **3** ♦ : to sink away : VANISH **4** : to grow dim or faint

♦ [2] blanch, bleach, blench, dull, pale, wash out, whiten ♦ [3] disappear, dissolve, evaporate, flee, go, melt, vanish — more at DISAPPEAR

²**fade** *n* : a short haircut in which hair on top of the head stands high

FADM *abbr* fleet admiral

fae·cal, fae·ces *chiefly Brit var of* FECAL, FECES

fa·er·ie *also* **fa·ery** \\'fā-rē, 'far-ē\\ *n, pl* **fa·er·ies** **1** : FAIRYLAND **2** : FAIRY

¹**fag** \\'fag\\ *vb* **fagged; fag·ging** **1** : to work hard : DRUDGE **2** : to act as a fag **3** ♦ : to tire by strenuous activity : TIRE, EXHAUST

♦ burn out, do in, drain, exhaust, fatigue, tire, tucker, wash out, wear, wear out, weary — more at EXHAUST

²**fag** *n* ♦ : one who is obliged to do menial work : DRUDGE

♦ drudge, peon, slave, toiler, worker — more at SLAVE

³**fag** *n* : an English public-school boy who acts as servant to another

⁴**fag** *vb* : to act as a fag

⁵**fag** *n* : CIGARETTE

fag end *n* **1** ♦ : a worn, poor, or useless ending or remnant unlikely to afford either pleasure or profit : REMNANT **2** : the extreme end **3** : the last part or coarser end of a web of cloth **4** : the untwisted end of a rope

♦ end, leftover, remainder, remnant, scrap — more at SCRAP

fag·ot *or* **fag·got** \\'fa-gət\\ *n* : a bundle of sticks or twigs

fag·ot·ing *or* **fag·got·ing** *n* : an embroidery produced by tying threads in hourglass-shaped clusters

Fah *or* **Fahr** *abbr* Fahrenheit

Fahr·en·heit \\'far-ən-ˌhīt\\ *adj* : relating to, conforming to, or having a thermometer scale with the boiling point of water at 212 degrees and the freezing point at 32 degrees above zero

fa·ience *or* **fa·ïence** \\fā-'äns\\ *n* [F] : earthenware decorated with opaque colored glazes

¹**fail** \\'fāl\\ *vb* **1** ♦ : to become feeble; *esp* : to decline in health **2** : to die away **3** ♦ : to stop functioning **4** ♦ : to fall short ⟨*~ed* in his duty⟩ **5** : to be or become absent or inadequate **6** ♦ : to be unsuccessful **7** : to become bankrupt **8** ♦ : to disappoint the expectations or trust of **9** : NEGLECT

♦ [1] decay, droop, flag, go, lag, languish, sag, waste, weaken, wilt — more at WEAKEN ♦ [3] break, break down, conk, crash, cut out, die, stall *Ant* start (up) ♦ [4, 8] cheat, disappoint, dissatisfy, let down — more at DISAPPOINT ♦ [6] collapse, flop, flunk, fold, wash out *Ant* succeed

²**fail** *n* : FAILURE ⟨without ~⟩

¹**fail·ing** \\'fā-liŋ\\ *n* ♦ : a usu. slight or insignificant defect in character, conduct, or ability : WEAKNESS, SHORTCOMING

♦ demerit, fault, foible, frailty, shortcoming, vice, weakness — more at FAULT

²**failing** *prep* : in the absence or lack of

faille \\'fī(-ə)l\\ *n* : a somewhat shiny closely woven ribbed fabric (as silk)

fail–safe \\'fāl-ˌsāf\\ *adj* **1** : incorporating a counteractive feature for a possible source of failure **2** : having no chance of failure — **fail–safe** *n*

fail·ure \\'fāl-yər\\ *n* **1** ♦ : a failing or failure to perform **2** : a state of inability to perform a normal function adequately ⟨heart ~⟩; *also* : an abrupt cessation of functioning ⟨a power ~⟩ **3** : a fracturing or giving way under stress **4** ♦ : a lack of success **5** : BANKRUPTCY **6** ♦ : a falling short : DEFICIENCY ⟨crop ~⟩ **7** : DETERIORATION, DECAY **8** ♦ : one that has failed

♦ [1] default, delinquency, dereliction, neglect, negligence, oversight ♦ [4] collapse, crash, cropper, defeat, fizzle, nonsuccess *Ant* accomplishment, achievement, success ♦ [6] dearth, deficiency, deficit, famine, inadequacy, insufficiency, lack, paucity, poverty, scantiness, scarcity, shortage, want — more at DEFICIENCY ♦ [8] bust, catastrophe, debacle, dud, fiasco, fizzle, flop, loser, washout *Ant* hit, smash, success, winner

¹**fain** \\'fān\\ *adj* **1** *archaic* : GLAD; *also* : INCLINED **2** : being obliged or compelled

²**fain** *adv* **1** : with pleasure **2** : by preference

¹**faint** \\'fānt\\ *adj* [ME *faint, feint*, fr. OF, fr. *faindre, feindre* to feign, lose heart] **1** : COWARDLY, SPIRITLESS ⟨~ of heart⟩ **2** : weak, dizzy, and likely to faint **3** ♦ : lacking vigor or strength : FEEBLE ⟨~ praise⟩ **4** ♦ : hardly perceptible : INDISTINCT, DIM — **faint·ly** *adv*

♦ [3] delicate, feeble, frail, infirm, slight, soft, wasted, weak — more at WEAK ♦ [4] bleary, dim, foggy, fuzzy, hazy, indistinct, obscure, opaque, shadowy, unclear, vague *Ant* clear, definite

²**faint** *vb* ♦ : to lose consciousness

♦ black out, pass out, swoon *Ant* come around, come round, come to, revive

³**faint** *n* **1** : the action of fainting **2** ♦ : the condition of one who has fainted

♦ blackout, knockout, swoon

faint·heart·ed \\ˌfānt-'här-təd\\ *adj* ♦ : lacking courage : TIMID

♦ fearful, mousy, shy, skittish, timid — more at SHY

faint·ness *n* ♦ : the quality or state of being faint; *esp* : a loss of strength or near loss of consciousness

♦ debility, feebleness, frailty, infirmity, languor, weakness — more at WEAKNESS

¹**fair** \\'fer\\ *adj* **1** ♦ : pleasing in appearance : BEAUTIFUL **2** : superficially pleasing : SPECIOUS **3** : CLEAN, PURE **4** : CLEAR, LEGIBLE **5** ♦ : not stormy or cloudy **6** ♦ : marked by impartiality and honesty : free from self-interest, prejudice, or favoritism : JUST **7** : conforming with the rules : ALLOWED; *also* : being within the foul lines ⟨~ ball⟩ **8** : open to legitimate pursuit or attack ⟨~ game⟩ **9** : giving promise of success or excellence : PROMISING, LIKELY ⟨a ~ chance of winning⟩ **10** : favorable to a ship's course ⟨a ~ wind⟩ **11** ♦ : light colored **12** ♦ : of middling quality **13** : significant in size ⟨a ~ amount of traffic⟩ — **fair·ness** *n*

♦ [1] attractive, beautiful, cute, handsome, lovely, pretty — more at BEAUTIFUL ♦ [5] clear, cloudless, sunny, sunshiny, unclouded *Ant* bleak, cloudy, overcast, stormy, sunless ♦ [6] disinterested, dispassionate, equal, equitable, impartial, just, nonpartisan, objective, square, unbiased, unprejudiced *Ant* biased, partisan, prejudiced, unequal, unjust ♦ [11] blond, flaxen, golden, sandy, straw — more at BLOND ♦ [12] common, indifferent, mediocre, medium, middling, ordinary, passable, run-of-the-mill, second-rate, so-so — more at MEDIOCRE

²**fair** *adv* **1** : in a fair manner ⟨play ~⟩ **2** *chiefly Brit* : FAIRLY **4**

³**fair** *n* **1** ♦ : a gathering of buyers and sellers at a stated time and place for trade **2** ♦ : a competitive exhibition (as of farm products) **3** ♦ : a sale of assorted articles usu. for a charitable purpose **4** ♦ : an exhibition designed to promote available or planned products or services ⟨a book ~⟩ ⟨a job ~⟩

♦ [1, 2, 3, 4] display, exhibit, exhibition, exposition, show — more at EXHIBITION

fair·ground \\ˌˈgraůnd\\ *n* : an area where outdoor fairs, circuses, or exhibitions are held

fair·ing \\'far-iŋ\\ *n* : a structure for producing a smooth outline and reducing drag (as on an airplane)

fair·ly \'far-lē\ *adv* 1 : HANDSOMELY 2 : in a manner of speaking ⟨~ bursting with pride⟩ 3 : without bias 4 : to a full degree or extent : PLAINLY, DISTINCTLY 5 ♦ : moderately well : SOMEWHAT, RATHER ⟨a ~ easy job⟩

♦ enough, kind of, moderately, pretty, quite, rather, somewhat, sort of, so-so

fair–spo·ken \'far-'spō-kən\ *adj* : pleasant and courteous in speech

fair–trade \-'trād\ *adj* : of, relating to, or being an agreement between a producer and a seller that branded merchandise will be sold at or above a specified price — **fair–trade** *vb*

fair·way \-,wā\ *n* : the mowed part of a golf course between tee and green

fairy \'fer-ē\ *n, pl* **fair·ies** [ME *fairie* fairyland, enchantment, fr. AF *faerie*, fr. *fee* fairy, fr. L *Fata*, goddess of fate, fr. *fatum* fate] ♦ : an imaginary being of folklore and romance usu. having diminutive human form and magic powers — **fairy** *adj*

♦ brownie, dwarf, elf, fay, gnome, hobgoblin, leprechaun, pixie, puck, troll

fairy·land \-,land\ *n* 1 : the land of fairies 2 : a beautiful or charming place

fairy tale *n* 1 : a children's story usu. about mythical beings (as fairies) 2 ♦ : an implausible, incredible, or lying story : a statement designed to delude or mislead : FIB

♦ fabrication, falsehood, falsity, fib, lie, story, untruth

fait ac·com·pli \'fāt-,a-,kōⁿ-'plē\ *n, pl* **faits accomplis** *same or* -'plēz\ [F, accomplished fact] : a thing accomplished and presumably irreversible

faith \'fāth\ *n, pl* **faiths** \'fāths, 'fāthz\ [ME *feith*, fr. OF *feid, foi*, fr. L *fides*] 1 ♦ : allegiance to duty or a person : LOYALTY 2 ♦ : belief and trust in God 3 ♦ : complete trust 4 ♦ : a system of religious beliefs

♦ [1] allegiance, constancy, dedication, devotion, faithfulness, fastness, fealty, fidelity, loyalty, steadfastness — more at FIDELITY ♦ [2] devotion, piety, religion *Ant* atheism, godlessness ♦ [3] confidence, credence, stock, trust — more at TRUST ♦ [4] creed, cult, persuasion, religion — more at RELIGION

faith·ful \-fəl\ *adj* 1 ♦ : true and constant in affection or allegiance 2 ♦ : conforming to the facts or to an original — **faith·ful·ly** *adv*

♦ [1] constant, devoted, loyal, pious, staunch, steadfast, steady, true, true-blue *Ant* disloyal, false, fickle, inconstant, perfidious, traitorous, treacherous ♦ [2] accurate, authentic, exact, precise, right, strict, true, veracious *Ant* false, imprecise, inaccurate, inexact

faith·ful·ness *n* ♦ : the quality or state of being faithful

♦ allegiance, constancy, dedication, devotion, fealty, fidelity, loyalty, steadfastness — more at FIDELITY

faith·less \'fāth-ləs\ *adj* 1 ♦ : false to promises or agreements : DISLOYAL 2 : not to be relied on — **faith·less·ly** *adv*

♦ disloyal, false, fickle, inconstant, perfidious, traitorous, treacherous, unfaithful, untrue *Ant* constant, devoted, loyal, staunch, steadfast, steady, true

faith·less·ness *n* ♦ : the quality or condition of being faithless

♦ betrayal, disloyalty, falsity, infidelity, perfidy, treachery, treason

fa·ji·ta \fə-'hē-tə\ *n* : a marinated strip usu. of beef or chicken grilled or broiled and served usu. with a flour tortilla and savory fillings

¹**fake** \'fāk\ *adj* ♦ : one that is not what it purports to be : SHAM

♦ bogus, counterfeit, false, inauthentic, phony, sham, spurious — more at COUNTERFEIT ♦ artificial, faux, imitation, mock, sham, synthetic — more at IMITATION

²**fake** *n* 1 a ♦ : someone or something that is not genuine b ♦ : one that assumes false identity or title for the purpose of deception 2 : a simulated move in sports (as a pretended pass)

♦ [1a] counterfeit, forgery, hoax, humbug, phony, sham ♦ [1b] charlatan, fraud, hoaxer, humbug, phony, pretender, quack

³**fake** *vb* **faked; fak·ing** 1 : to treat so as to falsify 2 ♦ : to counterfeit or make a counterfeit of in order to deceive 3 : to deceive (an opponent) in a sports contest by making a fake — **fak·er** *n*

♦ affect, assume, counterfeit, feign, pretend, profess, put on, sham, simulate — more at FEIGN

fa·kir \fə-'kir\ *n* [Ar *faqīr*, lit., poor man] 1 : a Muslim mendicant : DERVISH 2 : a wandering Hindu ascetic

fal·con \'fal-kən, 'fȯl-\ *n* 1 : a hawk trained for use in falconry 2 : any of various swift long-winged long-tailed hawks having a notched beak and usu. inhabiting open areas

fal·con·ry \'fal-kən-rē, 'fȯl-\ *n* 1 : the art of training hawks to hunt in cooperation with a person 2 : the sport of hunting with hawks — **fal·con·er** *n*

¹**fall** \'fȯl\ *vb* **fell** \'fel\; **fall·en** \'fȯ-lən\; **fall·ing** 1 ♦ : to descend freely by the force of gravity 2 : to hang freely 3 : to come or go as if by falling ⟨darkness *fell*⟩ 4 : to become uttered 5 ♦ : to lower or become lowered : DROP ⟨her eyes *fell*⟩ 6 ♦ : to leave an erect position suddenly and involuntarily 7 : STUMBLE, STRAY 8 : to drop down wounded or dead esp. in battle 9 ♦ : to become captured ⟨the city *fell* to the enemy⟩ 10 : to suffer ruin, defeat, or failure 11 : to commit an immoral act 12 : to move or extend in a downward direction 13 ♦ : to become quiet or less : SUBSIDE, ABATE 14 : to decline in quality, activity, quantity, or value 15 : to assume a look of shame or dejection ⟨her face *fell*⟩ 16 : to occur at a certain time 17 : to come by chance 18 : DEVOLVE ⟨the duties *fell* to him⟩ 19 : to have the proper place or station ⟨the accent ~s on the first syllable⟩ 20 : to come within the scope of something 21 : to pass from one condition to another ⟨*fell* ill⟩ 22 : to set about heartily or actively ⟨~ to work⟩ — **fall all over oneself** *or* **fall over backward** : to display excessive eagerness — **fall flat** : to produce no response or result — **fall for** 1 : to fall in love with 2 : to become a victim of — **fall foul** : to have a quarrel : CLASH — **fall from grace** : BACKSLIDE — **fall into line** : to comply with a certain course of action — **fall short** 1 : to be deficient 2 : to fail to attain

♦ [1, 5] decline, descend, drop, lower, settle, sink *Ant* rise ♦ [6] slip, stumble, topple, trip, tumble *Ant* get up, rise, stand (up) ♦ [9] capitulate, give up, knuckle under, submit, succumb, surrender *Ant* stand ♦ [13] abate, decline, decrease, diminish, dwindle, ebb, lessen, recede, subside, wane — more at DECREASE

²**fall** *n* 1 ♦ : the act of falling 2 : a falling out, off, or away : DROPPING 3 : AUTUMN 4 : a thing or quantity that falls ⟨a light ~ of snow⟩ ⟨a ~ of 20% in the value of the stock⟩ 5 ♦ : loss of greatness, power, status, influence, or dominion 6 : the surrender or capture of a besieged place 7 : departure from virtue or goodness 8 : SLOPE 9 : WATERFALL — usu. used in pl. 10 ♦ : a decrease in size, quantity, degree, or value ⟨a ~ in price⟩ 11 : the distance which something falls 12 : an act of forcing a wrestler's shoulders to the mat; *also* : a bout of wrestling

♦ [1] descent, dip, dive, down, drop, plunge — more at DESCENT ♦ [1] slip, spill, stumble, tumble ♦ [5] comedown, decline, descent, down, downfall — more at COMEDOWN ♦ [5] decline, degradation — more at DECLINE ♦ [10] decline, decrease, drop, loss, reduction, shrinkage — more at DECREASE

fal·la·cious \fə-'lā-shəs\ *adj* 1 ♦ : embodying a fallacy ⟨a ~ argument⟩ 2 ♦ : tending to deceive or mislead

♦ [1] illogical, invalid, irrational, unsound, weak — more at ILLOGICAL ♦ [2] deceptive, false, misleading, specious — more at DECEPTIVE

fal·la·cy \'fa-lə-sē\ *n, pl* **-cies** 1 ♦ : a false or mistaken idea

2 : an often plausible argument using false or illogical reasoning 3 : erroneous or fallacious character

♦ error, falsehood, falsity, illusion, misconception, myth, untruth *Ant* truth, verity

fall back *vb* ♦ : to give way : RETREAT, RECEDE

♦ back, recede, retire, retreat, withdraw — more at RETREAT

fall guy *n* 1 : one that is easily duped 2 : one who assumes or on whom is placed the blame or responsibility : SCAPEGOAT

fal·li·ble \'fa-lə-bəl\ *adj* 1 : liable to be erroneous 2 : capable of making a mistake — **fal·li·bly** \-blē\ *adv*

fall·ing–out \,fȯ-liŋ-'aůt\ *n, pl* **fallings–out** or **falling–outs** : QUARREL

falling star *n* : METEOR

fal·lo·pi·an tube \fə-'lō-pē-ən-\ *n, often cap F* : either of the pair of anatomical tubes that carry the eggs from the ovary to the uterus

fall·out \'fȯ-,laůt\ *n* 1 : the often radioactive particles that result from a nuclear explosion and descend through the air 2 : a secondary and often lingering effect or result

fall out *vb* ♦ : to have a quarrel : QUARREL

♦ argue, bicker, dispute, quarrel, row, scrap, spat, squabble, wrangle — more at ARGUE

¹**fal·low** \'fa-(,)lō\ *n* : fallow land; *also* : the state or period of being fallow — **fallow** *vb*

²**fallow** *adj* 1 : left without tilling or sowing after plowing 2 ♦ : characterized by a state of creative or recuperative rest or dormancy : DORMANT, INACTIVE ⟨a writer's ~ period⟩

♦ dead, dormant, idle, inactive, inert, inoperative

false \'fȯls\ *adj* **fals·er; fals·est** 1 ♦ : not genuine : artificially made or assumed 2 : intentionally untrue 3 ♦ : adjusted or made so as to deceive ⟨~ scales⟩ 4 a ♦ : tending to mislead : DECEPTIVE ⟨~ promises⟩ b ♦ : assumed or designed to deceive 5 ♦ : not true ⟨~ concepts⟩ 6 ♦ : not faithful or loyal : TREACHEROUS 7 : not essential or permanent ⟨~ front⟩ 8 : inaccurate in pitch 9 : based on mistaken ideas — **false·ly** *adv*

♦ [1] artificial, bogus, fake, imitation, mechanical, mock, phony, sham, synthetic, unnatural ♦ [3, 4b] counterfeit, crooked, deceitful, dishonest, fraudulent, phony, sham, spurious ♦ [4a] deceitful, deceptive, misleading, specious — more at DECEPTIVE ♦ [5] erroneous, inaccurate, incorrect, inexact, untrue, wrong *Ant* accurate, correct, right, sound, true ♦ [6] disloyal, faithless, traitorous, treacherous, unfaithful

false·hood \'fȯls-,hůd\ *n* 1 ♦ : something that is untrue; *esp* : an untrue statement : LIE 2 : absence of truth or accuracy 3 : the practice of lying

♦ error, fallacy, falsity, illusion, misconception, myth, untruth — more at FALLACY ♦ fabrication, fairy tale, falsity, fib, lie, mendacity, prevarication, story, tale, untruth, whopper — more at LIE

false·ness *n* 1 ♦ : the quality or state of being false 2 ♦ : an instance of treachery : an act of perfidy or treason

♦ [1] fallacy, falsity, untruth ♦ [2] betrayal, disloyalty, infidelity, perfidy, treachery, treason, unfaithfulness — more at BETRAYAL

fal·set·to \fȯl-'se-tō\ *n, pl* **-tos** [It., fr. dim. of *falso* false] : an artificially high voice; *esp* : an artificial singing voice that overlaps and extends above the range of the full voice esp. of a tenor

fal·si·fy \'fȯl-sə-,fī\ *vb* **-fied; -fy·ing** 1 : to prove to be false 2 ♦ : to alter so as to deceive 3 : LIE; *also* : MISREPRESENT — **fal·si·fi·able** \,fȯl-sə-'fī-ə-bəl\ *adj* — **fal·si·fi·ca·tion** \,fȯl-sə-fə-'kā-shən\ *n*

♦ color (*or* colour), distort, garble, misinterpret, misrepresent, mistake, pervert, twist, warp — more at GARBLE

fal·si·ty \'fȯl-sə-tē\ *n* 1 ♦ : something false 2 ♦ : the quality or state of being false

♦ [1] fallacy, falsehood, fib, lie, myth, tale, untruth ♦ [2] betrayal, disloyalty, infidelity, perfidy, treachery, treason, unfaithfulness — more at BETRAYAL

fal·ter \'fȯl-tər\ *vb* 1 ♦ : to move unsteadily : TOTTER 2 : to hesitate in speech : STAMMER 3 ♦ : to hesitate in purpose or action : WAVER 4 : to lose effectiveness ⟨a ~ing business⟩ — **fal·ter·ing·ly** *adv*

♦ [1] seesaw, sway, teeter, totter, waver, wobble — more at TEETER ♦ [3] hesitate, shilly-shally, teeter, vacillate, waver — more at HESITATE

fam *abbr* 1 familiar 2 family

fame \'fām\ *n* ♦ : public reputation : RENOWN

♦ celebrity, notoriety, renown *Ant* anonymity, obscurity

famed \'fāmd\ *adj* ♦ : known widely and well

♦ celebrated, famous, noted, prominent, renowned, well-known — more at FAMOUS

fa·mil·ial \fə-'mil-yəl\ *adj* 1 : of, relating to, or suggestive of a family 2 : tending to occur in more members of a family than expected by chance alone ⟨a ~ disorder⟩

¹**fa·mil·iar** \fə-'mil-yər\ *n* 1 ♦ : an intimate associate 2 : a spirit held to attend and serve or guard a person 3 : one who frequents a place

♦ comrade, friend, intimate — more at FRIEND

²**familiar** *adj* 1 ♦ : closely acquainted : INTIMATE 2 : of or relating to a family 3 ♦ : INFORMAL ⟨a ~ style⟩ 4 ♦ : overly free and unrestrained : PRESUMPTUOUS 5 ♦ : frequently seen or experienced ⟨a ~ face⟩ 6 : of everyday occurrence 7 ♦ : having personal or intimate knowledge — often used with *with* — **fa·mil·iar·ly** *adv*

♦ [1] chummy, close, friendly, intimate, thick *Ant* distant ♦ [4] bold, forward, free, immodest, presumptuous — more at PRESUMPTUOUS ♦ [5] common, customary, everyday, frequent, ordinary, routine, usual — more at COMMON ♦ [7] conversant, informed, knowledgeable, up-to-date *Ant* ignorant, unacquainted, unfamiliar, uninformed

fa·mil·iar·ise *Brit var of* FAMILIARIZE

fa·mil·iar·i·ty \fə-,mil-'yar-ə-tē, -,mi-lē-'ar-\ *n, pl* **-ties** 1 ♦ : close friendship : INTIMACY 2 : INFORMALITY 3 ♦ : an unduly bold or forward act or expression : IMPROPRIETY 4 : close acquaintance with something

♦ [1] closeness, intimacy, nearness *Ant* distance ♦ [3] gaffe, impropriety, indiscretion — more at IMPROPRIETY

fa·mil·iar·ize \fə-'mil-yə-,rīz\ *vb* **-ized; -iz·ing** 1 : to make known through experience or repetition : remove strangeness from 2 ♦ : to make (someone) thoroughly acquainted

♦ acquaint, apprise, brief, clue, enlighten, fill in, inform, instruct, tell — more at ENLIGHTEN

fam·i·ly \'fam-lē, 'fa-mə-\ *n, pl* **-lies** [ME *familie*, fr. L *familia* household, fr. *famulus* servant] 1 : a group of individuals living under one roof and under one head : HOUSEHOLD 2 ♦ : a group of persons of common ancestry : CLAN 3 ♦ : a group of things having common characteristics; *esp* : a group of related plants or animals ranking in biological classification above a genus and below an order 4 : a social unit usu. consisting of one or two parents and their children

♦ [2] blood, clan, folks, house, kin, kindred, kinfolk, line, lineage, people, race, stock, tribe ♦ [3] category, class, division, group, kind, set, type — more at CLASS

family planning *n* : planning intended to determine the number and spacing of one's children by using birth control

family tree *n* ♦ : an account or history of the descent of a person, family, or group from an ancestor or ancestors or from older forms : GENEALOGY; *also* : a genealogical diagram

♦ ancestry, bloodline, descent, genealogy, lineage, origin — more at ANCESTRY

fam·ine \'fa-mən\ *n* 1 ♦ : an extreme scarcity of food 2 ♦ : a great shortage

♦ dearth, deficiency, deficit, failure, inadequacy, insufficiency, lack, paucity, poverty, scantiness, scarcity, shortage, want — more at DEFICIENCY

fam·ish \'fa-mish\ *vb* **1** : STARVE **2** : to suffer for lack of something necessary

fam·ished *adj* ♦ : intensely hungry

♦ empty, hungry — more at HUNGRY

fa·mous \'fā-məs\ *adj* **1** ♦ : widely known **2** : honored for achievement **3** : EXCELLENT, FIRST-RATE

♦ celebrated, famed, noted, notorious, prominent, renowned, well-known *Ant* anonymous, obscure, unknown

fa·mous·ly *adv* : SPLENDIDLY, EXCELLENTLY ⟨got along ∼⟩

¹fan \'fan\ *n* : a device (as a hand-waved triangular piece or a mechanism with blades) for producing a current of air

²fan *vb* **fanned; fan·ning** **1** : to drive away the chaff from grain by winnowing **2** : to move (air) with or as if with a fan **3** : to direct a current of air upon ⟨∼ a fire⟩ **4** : to stir up to activity : STIMULATE **5** ♦ : to spread like a fan — often used with *out* **6** : to strike out in baseball

♦ *usu* **fan out** expand, extend, flare, open, radiate, spread, unfold

³fan *n* ♦ : an enthusiastic follower or admirer

♦ addict, aficionado, buff, devotee, enthusiast, fancier, lover

¹fa·nat·ic \fə-'na-tik\ *or* **fa·nat·i·cal** \-ti-kəl\ *adj* [L *fanaticus* inspired by a deity, frenzied, fr. *fanum* temple] ♦ : marked by excessive enthusiasm and often intense uncritical devotion — **fa·nat·i·cism** \-tə-₁si-zəm\ *n*

♦ extreme, extremist, rabid, radical, revolutionary, ultra — more at EXTREME

²fa·nat·ic *n* ♦ : a person who is ardently attached to a cause, object, or pursuit; *esp* : a person exhibiting excessive enthusiasm and intense uncritical devotion usu. toward some controversial matter

♦ crusader, militant, partisan, zealot — more at ZEALOT

fan·ci·er \'fan-sē-ər\ *n* **1** ♦ : one that has a special liking or interest **2** : a person who breeds or grows some kind of animal or plant for points of excellence

♦ aficionado, buff, devotee, enthusiast, fan, lover — more at FAN

fan·ci·ful \'fan-si-fəl\ *adj* **1** ♦ : marked by, existing in, or given to unrestrained imagination or whim rather than reason **2** : curiously made or shaped — **fan·ci·ful·ly** *adv*

♦ fantastic, fictitious, imaginary, made-up, pretend, unreal — more at IMAGINARY

¹fan·cy \'fan-sē\ *vb* **fan·cied; fan·cy·ing** **1** ♦ : to be pleased with esp. on account of external appearance or manners : LIKE **2** ♦ : to form a conception of : IMAGINE **3** : to believe without evidence or certainty **4** : to visualize or interpret as

♦ [1] delight, enjoy, like, love, relish — more at ENJOY
♦ [2] conceive, imagine, picture, visualize

²fancy *n, pl* **fancies** [ME *fantasie, fantsy* imagination, image, preference, fr. AF *fantasie* illusion, fr. L *phantasia*, fr. Gk, appearance, imagination] **1** ♦ : amorous fondness : love or desire; *also* : LOVE **2** ♦ : an opinion or notion formed without much reflection : WHIM, NOTION ⟨a passing ∼⟩ **3** ♦ : an image or representation of something formed in the mind **4** : TASTE, JUDGMENT

♦ [1] favor (*or* favour), fondness, like, liking, love, partiality, preference — more at LIKING ♦ [2] caprice, notion, whim ♦ [3] chimera, conceit, delusion, dream, fantasy, figment, hallucination, illusion, phantasm, pipe dream, unreality, vision

³fancy *adj* **fan·ci·er; -est** **1** : WHIMSICAL **2** : not plain : ornamented and often elegant **3** : of particular excellence **4** : bred esp. for a showy appearance **5** : EXCESSIVE **6** ♦ : executed with technical skill and style — **fan·ci·ly** \'fan-sə-lē\ *adv*

♦ complex, complicated, detailed, elaborate, intricate — more at ELABORATE

fancy dress *n* : a costume (as for a masquerade) chosen to suit a fancy

fan·cy–free \₁fan-sē-'frē\ *adj* : free from amorous attachment; *also* : free to imagine

fan·cy·work \'fan-sē-₁wərk\ *n* : ornamental needlework (as embroidery)

fan·dan·go \fan-'daŋ-gō\ *n, pl* **-gos** **1** : a lively Spanish or Spanish-American dance **2** : TOMFOOLERY

fane \'fān\ *n* **1** : TEMPLE **2** : CHURCH

fan·fare \'fan-₁far\ *n* **1** : a flourish of trumpets **2** : a showy display

fan fiction *n* : stories involving fictional characters that are written by fans

fang \'faŋ\ *n* : a long sharp tooth; *esp* : a grooved or hollow tooth of a venomous snake — **fanged** \'faŋd\ *adj*

fan·light \'fan-₁līt\ *n* : a semicircular window with radiating bars like a fan that is set over a door or window

fan·ny \'fa-nē\ *n, pl* **fannies** : BUTTOCKS

fan·tail \'fan-₁tāl\ *n* **1** : a fan-shaped tail or end **2** : an overhang at the stern of a ship

fan·ta·sia \fan-'tā-zhə, -zhē-ə, -zē-ə; ₁fan-tə-'zē-ə\ *n* : a musical composition free and fanciful in form

fan·ta·sise *chiefly Brit var of* FANTASIZE

fan·ta·size \'fan-tə-₁sīz\ *vb* **-sized; -siz·ing** : IMAGINE, DAYDREAM

fan·tas·tic \fan-'tas-tik\ *also* **fan·tas·ti·cal** \-ti-kəl\ *adj* **1** ♦ : based on fantasy rather than reason : IMAGINARY, UNREAL **2** ♦ : conceived by unrestrained fancy **3** ♦ : exceedingly or unbelievably great **4** ♦ : exhibiting strange, grotesque, inappropriate, or startlingly novel characteristics — **fan·tas·ti·cal·ly** \-ti-k(ə-)lē\ *adv*

♦ [1] fanciful, imaginary, made-up, unreal — more at IMAGINARY ♦ [2] absurd, bizarre, crazy, fanciful, foolish, preposterous, unreal *Ant* realistic, reasonable ♦ [3] inconceivable, incredible, unbelievable, unimaginable ♦ [4] exotic, glamorous, marvelous (*or* marvellous), outlandish, romantic, strange — more at EXOTIC

fan·ta·sy *also* **phan·ta·sy** \'fan-tə-sē\ *n, pl* **-sies** **1** ♦ : the free play of creative imagination as it affects perception and productivity usu. as expressed in an art form or as elicited by projective techniques of formal psychology : IMAGINATION, FANCY **2** ♦ : a product of the imagination : ILLUSION **3** ♦ : a chimerical or fantastic notion — **fantasy** *vb*

♦ [1] creativity, fancy, imagination, invention — more at IMAGINATION ♦ [2, 3] chimera, conceit, delusion, dream, fancy, figment, hallucination, illusion, phantasm, pipe dream, unreality, vision

FAQ \'fak, ₁ef-₁ā-'kyü\ *n* : a document (as on a website) that provides answers to a list of typical user questions

¹far \'fär\ *adv* **far·ther** \-thər\ *or* **fur·ther** \'fər-\; **far·thest** *or* **fur·thest** \-thəst\ **1** : at or to a considerable distance in space or time ⟨∼ from home⟩ **2** : by a broad interval : WIDELY, MUCH ⟨∼ better⟩ **3** : to or at a definite distance, point, or degree ⟨as ∼ as I know⟩ **4** : to an advanced point or extent ⟨go ∼ in his field⟩ **5** : to a great extent — **by far** : by a considerable margin — **far and away** : DECIDEDLY — **so far** : until now

²far *adj* **farther** *or* **further; farthest** *or* **furthest** **1** ♦ : remote in space or time **2** : DIFFERENT **3** : involving a long distance ⟨a ∼ journey⟩ **4** : being the more distant of two ⟨on the ∼ side of the lake⟩

♦ distant, far-off, remote *Ant* close, near, nearby

far·ad \'far-₁ad, -əd\ *n* : a unit of capacitance equal to the capacitance of a capacitor having a potential difference of one volt between its plates when it is charged with one coulomb of electricity

far·away \'fär-ə-₁wā\ *adj* **1** : distant in space or time : DISTANT, REMOTE **2** : DREAMY

farce \'färs\ *n* **1** : a broadly satirical comedy with an improbable plot **2** : the humor characteristic of farce or pretense **3** ♦ : a ridiculous or empty display

♦ [1] comedy, humor (*or* humour), slapstick — more at COMEDY ♦ [3] caricature, joke, mockery, parody, sham, travesty — more at MOCKERY

far·ci·cal \'fär-si-kəl\ *adj* ♦ : of, relating to, or resembling farce

♦ absurd, comical, funny, humorous, laughable, ludicrous, ridiculous, silly

far cry *n* **1** : a long distance **2** : something notably different ⟨a *far cry* from what we expected⟩

¹fare \'far\ *vb* **fared; far·ing** **1** ♦ : to go or travel : GO, TRAVEL **2** ♦ : to get along : make out or turn out : GET ALONG **3** : to consume food : EAT, DINE

♦ [1] advance, go, proceed, progress, travel ♦ [2] cope, do, get along, make out, manage

²fare *n* **1 a** ♦ : a range or stock of food **b** : material provided for use, consumption, or enjoyment ⟨fine theatrical ∼⟩ **2** : the price charged to transport a person **3** : a person paying a fare : PASSENGER

♦ food, provender, provisions, viands, victuals

¹fare·well \far-'wel\ *vb imper* : get along well — used interjectionally to or by one departing

²farewell *n* **1** ♦ : a wish of well-being at parting : GOOD= BYE **2** ♦ : act of departure : LEAVE-TAKING

♦ [1] adieu, au revoir, bon voyage, good-bye — more at GOOD-BYE ♦ [2] departure, leave-taking, parting

³fare·well \'far-,wel\ *adj* : PARTING, FINAL ⟨a ∼ concert⟩

far–fetched \'fär-'fecht\ *adj* : not easily or naturally deduced or introduced : IMPROBABLE ⟨∼ story⟩

far–flung \-'fləŋ\ *adj* ♦ : widely spread or distributed

♦ broad, expansive, extensive, far-reaching, widespread — more at EXTENSIVE

fa·ri·na \fə-'rē-nə\ *n* [L, meal, flour] : a fine meal (as of wheat) used in puddings or as a breakfast cereal

far·i·na·ceous \,far-ə-'nā-shəs\ *adj* **1** : having a mealy texture or surface **2** : containing or rich in starch

¹farm \'färm\ *n* [ME *ferme* rent, lease, fr. AF, fr. *fermer* to fix, rent, fr. L *firmare* to make firm, fr. *firmus* firm] **1** : a tract of land used for raising crops or livestock **2** : a minor-league subsidiary of a major-league team

²farm *vb* ♦ : to use (land) as a farm ⟨∼ed 200 acres⟩; *also* : to raise crops or livestock

♦ cultivate, tend

farm·er *n* ♦ : a person who cultivates land or crops or raises livestock

♦ agriculturist, cultivator, grower, planter, tiller

farm·hand \'färm-,hand\ *n* : a farm laborer

farm·house \-,haus\ *n* : a dwelling on a farm

farm·ing \'fär-miŋ\ *n* : the occupation or business of a person who farms

farm·land \'färm-,land\ *n* : land used or suitable for farming

farm out *vb* : to turn over (as a task) to another

farm·stead \'färm-,sted\ *n* : a farm with its buildings

farm·yard \-,yärd\ *n* : land around or enclosed by farm buildings

far–off \'fär-'of\ *adj* ♦ : remote in time or space : DISTANT

♦ distant, remote — more at DISTANT

fa·rouche \fə-'rüsh\ *adj* [F] **1** : WILD **2** : marked by shyness and lack of polish

far–out \'fär-'aut\ *adj* ♦ : very unconventional ⟨∼ clothes⟩

♦ bizarre, odd, outlandish, outré, peculiar, strange, wacky, weird, wild — more at ODD

far·ra·go \fə-'rä-gō, -'rā-\ *n, pl* **-goes** [L, mixed fodder, mixture] : a confused collection : MIXTURE

far–reach·ing \'fär-'rē-chiŋ\ *adj* ♦ : having a wide range or effect

♦ broad, extensive, widespread — more at EXTENSIVE

far·ri·er \'fer-ē-ər\ *n* [alter. of ME *ferrour*, fr. AF, blacksmith, fr. *ferrer* to shoe (horses)] : a person who shoes horses

¹far·row \'far-ō\ *vb* : to give birth to a litter of pigs

²farrow *n* : a litter of pigs

far·see·ing \'fär-,sē-iŋ\ *adj* **1** : FARSIGHTED 1 **2** : FARSIGHTED 2

far·sight·ed \'fär-,sī-təd\ *adj* **1 a** : seeing or able to see to a great distance **b** ♦ : having foresight : able to anticipate and plan for the future **2** : JUDICIOUS, WISE, SHREWD **3** : affected with an eye condition in which vision is better for distant than near objects — **far·sight·ed·ness** *n*

♦ foresighted, prescient, provident — more at FORESIGHTED

¹far·ther \'fär-thər\ *adv* **1** ♦ : at or to a greater distance or more advanced point **2** : to a greater degree or extent

♦ beyond, further, yonder

²farther *adj* **1** : more distant **2** ♦ : going or extending beyond what exists : ADDITIONAL

♦ additional, another, more

far·ther·most \-,mōst\ *adj* : most remote : FARTHEST

¹far·thest \'fär-thəst\ *adj* ♦ : most distant

♦ extreme, outermost, ultimate, utmost — more at EXTREME

²farthest *adv* **1** : to or at the greatest distance : REMOTEST ⟨hit the ball ∼⟩ **2** : to the most advanced point **3** : by the greatest degree or extent : MOST

fas·cia *1 is usu* 'fā-sh(ē-)ə, *2 is usu* 'fa-\ *n, pl* **-ci·ae** \-shē-,ē\ *or* **-cias** **1** : a flat usu. horizontal part (as a band or board) of or on a building **2** : a sheet of connective tissue covering body structures (as muscles)

fas·ci·cle \'fa-si-kəl\ *n* **1** : a small or slender bundle (as of pine needles or nerve fiber) **2** : one of the divisions of a book published in parts — **fas·ci·cled** \-kəld\ *adj*

fas·ci·nate \'fas-ᵊn-,āt\ *vb* **-nat·ed; -nat·ing** [L *fascinare*, fr. *fascinum* evil spell] **1** : to transfix and hold spellbound by an irresistible power **2 a** ♦ : to have or exercise the power of charming, alluring, or enthralling **b** ♦ : engage and powerfully hold the attention or interest **3** : to be irresistibly attractive

♦ [2a, 2b] allure, beguile, captivate, charm, enchant, enthrall ♦ [2b] engage, engross, grip, interest, intrigue, involve, occupy — more at ENGAGE

fascinating *adj* ♦ : holding the interest as if by a spell

♦ alluring, attractive, captivating, charming, engaging, enthralling, interesting, intriguing **Ant** repellant, repelling, repugnant

fas·ci·na·tion \,fas-ᵊn-'ā-shən\ *n* ♦ : the quality of fascinating : the ability to enthrall

♦ allure, appeal, attractiveness, charisma, charm, enchantment, glamour — more at CHARM

fas·cism \'fa-,shi-zəm\ *n, often cap* : a political philosophy, movement, or regime that exalts nation and often race and stands for a centralized autocratic often militaristic government — **fas·cist** \-shist\ *n or adj, often cap* — **fas·cis·tic** \fa-'shis-tik\ *adj, often cap*

¹fash·ion \'fa-shən\ *n* **1** : the make or form of something **2** ♦ : a distinctive or peculiar and often habitual manner or way : MANNER, WAY **3** ♦ : a prevailing usu. short-lived custom, usage, or style **4** : the prevailing style (as in dress)

♦ [2] custom, habit, manner, pattern, practice, way ♦ [3] craze, enthusiasm, fad, mode, rage, sensation, style, trend, vogue

²fashion *vb* **1** ♦ : to make or construct usu. with the use of imagination and ingenuity **2** : FIT, ADAPT

♦ fabricate, form, frame, make, manufacture, produce — more at MAKE

fash·ion·able \'fa-shə-nə-bəl\ *adj* **1** ♦ : dressing or behaving according to fashion **2** ♦ : of, relating to, or being something in fashion ⟨∼ resorts⟩ — **fash·ion·ably** \-blē\ *adv*

♦ [1] à la mode, chic, in, modish, sharp, smart, snappy, stylish — more at STYLISH ♦ [2] hot, in, popular

¹fast \'fast\ *adj* **1** ♦ : firmly fixed **2** : tightly shut **3** : adhering firmly **4** : STUCK **5** ♦ : firmly loyal : STAUNCH

⟨~ friends⟩ **6 a** ♦ : characterized by quick motion, operation, or effect ⟨a ~ trip⟩ ⟨a ~ track⟩ **b** ♦ : unusually quick and ingenious or cunning in finding or recognizing and profiting by easy and often shady ways of making or acquiring money **7** : indicating ahead of the correct time ⟨the clock is ~⟩ **8** ♦ : not easily disturbed : SOUND ⟨a ~ sleep⟩ **9** : permanently dyed; *also* : being proof against fading ⟨colors ~ to sunlight⟩ **10** : DISSIPATED, WILD ⟨a ~ crowd⟩ **11** : sexually promiscuous

♦ [1, 8] firm, secure, set, snug, sound, stable, tight — more at TIGHT ♦ [5] constant, devoted, faithful, loyal, staunch, steadfast, steady, true — more at FAITHFUL ♦ [6a] brisk, fleet, hasty, quick, rapid, speedy, swift *Ant* slow ♦ [6b] deceptive, dishonest, shady, sharp, shifty

²fast *adv* **1** ♦ : in a fast manner ⟨stuck ~ in the mud⟩ ⟨~ asleep⟩ **2** ♦ : in a rapid manner : SWIFTLY **3** : RECKLESSLY

♦ [1] completely, entirely, fully, thoroughly, well, wholly — more at FULLY ♦ [2] briskly, hastily, presto, pronto, quick, quickly, rapidly, speedily, swiftly *Ant* slow, slowly

³fast *vb* **1** : to abstain from food **2** : to eat sparingly or abstain from some foods

⁴fast *n* **1** : the act or practice of fasting **2** : a time of fasting

fast·back \'fast-ˌbak\ *n* : an automobile having a roof with a long slope to the rear

fast·ball \-ˌbȯl\ *n* : a baseball pitch thrown at full speed

fas·ten \'fas-ᵊn\ *vb* **1** ♦ : to attach or join by or as if by pinning, tying, or nailing **2** ♦ : to make fast : fix securely **3** : to become fixed or joined **4** ♦ : to focus attention ⟨~ed onto the newest trends⟩ — **fas·ten·er** *n*

♦ [1, 2] attach, fix, secure, tie; *also* adhere, bolt, clamp, clasp, clinch, clip, glue, hang, harness, lace, lash, latch, nail, paste, pin, rivet, screw, staple, stick, strap, tack, tie, yoke; connect, join, link, unite; reattach, refix *Ant* detach, loose, loosen, undo ♦ [4] concentrate, focus, rivet, train — more at CONCENTRATE

fas·ten·ing *n* : something that fastens : FASTENER

fast–food \ˌfast-'füd\ *adj* : specializing in food that is prepared and served quickly ⟨a ~ restaurant⟩

fast–for·ward \-'fȯr-wərd\ *n* **1** : a function of an electronic device that advances a recording rapidly **2** : a state of rapid advancement — **fast–forward** *vb*

fas·tid·i·ous \fa-'sti-dē-əs\ *adj* **1** ♦ : overly difficult to please **2** ♦ : showing a meticulous or demanding attitude ⟨~ workmanship⟩ — **fas·tid·i·ous·ly** *adv* — **fas·tid·i·ous·ness** *n*

♦ [1, 2] choosy, demanding, exacting, finicky, fussy, particular, picky — more at FINICKY

fast·ness \'fast-nəs\ *n* **1 a** : the quality or state of being fast **b** : fixed attachment **c** ♦ : the quality or state of being swift **2** ♦ : a fortified or secure place : STRONGHOLD

♦ [1c] celerity, fleetness, haste, hurry, quickness, rapidity, speed, swiftness, velocity — more at SPEED ♦ [2] bastion, citadel, fort, fortification, fortress, stronghold — more at FORT

fast–talk \'fast-ˌtȯk\ *vb* : to influence by persuasive and usu. deceptive talk

fast–track \'fast-ˌtrak\ *vb* ♦ : to speed up the processing or production of

♦ accelerate, hasten, hurry, quicken, rush, speed (up), whisk — more at HURRY

fast track *n* : a course leading to rapid advancement or success

¹fat \'fat\ *adj* **fat·ter; fat·test 1** ♦ : notable for having an unusual amount of fat : PLUMP, OBESE **2** : OILY, GREASY **3** ♦ : well filled out : unusually large **4** ♦ : well furnished, filled, or stocked : ABUNDANT **5** ♦ : richly rewarding **6** ♦ : having the quality or power of producing esp. in abundance

♦ [1] chubby, corpulent, obese, overweight, plump, portly, rotund, round *Ant* lean, slender, slim, spare, thin

♦ [3] broad, thick, wide — more at WIDE ♦ [4] abundant, chock-full, full, packed, replete — more at FULL ♦ [5] gainful, lucrative, profitable, remunerative — more at PROFITABLE ♦ [6] fertile, fruitful, productive, prolific, rich — more at FERTILE

²fat *n* **1** : animal tissue rich in greasy or oily matter **2** : any of various energy-rich esters that occur naturally in animal fats and in plants and are soluble in organic solvents (as ether) but not in water **3** ♦ : the best or richest portion ⟨lived on the ~ of the land⟩ **4** : OBESITY **5** ♦ : something in excess or expendable

♦ [3] best, choice, elite, pick, prime — more at ELITE ♦ [5] excess, overflow, surfeit, surplus — more at EXCESS

fa·tal \'fāt-ᵊl\ *adj* **1** : FATEFUL ⟨that ~ day⟩ **2** ♦ : causing death or ruin ⟨a ~ mistake⟩ — **fa·tal·ly** *adv*

♦ deadly, deathly, lethal, mortal, murderous, pestilent — more at DEADLY ♦ calamitous, catastrophic, destructive, disastrous, fateful, ruinous

fa·tal·ism \-ˌi-zəm\ *n* : the belief that events are determined by fate — **fa·tal·ist** \-ist\ *n* — **fa·tal·is·tic** \ˌfāt-ᵊl-'is-tik\ *adj* — **fa·tal·is·ti·cal·ly** \-ti-k(ə-)lē\ *adv*

fa·tal·i·ty \fā-'ta-lə-tē, fə-\ *n, pl* **-ties 1** ♦ : DEADLINESS **2** : FATE **3 a** : death resulting from a disaster or accident **b** ♦ : one who suffers a death from a disaster or accident

♦ casualty, loss, victim — more at CASUALTY

fat·back \'fat-ˌbak\ *n* : a fatty strip from the back of the hog usu. cured by salting and drying

fat cat *n* **1** : a wealthy contributor to a political campaign **2** : a wealthy privileged person

fate \'fāt\ *n* [ME, fr. MF or L; MF, fr. L *fatum*, lit., what has been spoken, fr. *fari* to speak] **1** ♦ : the cause or will that is held to determine events : DESTINY **2** ♦ : LOT, FORTUNE **3** : DISASTER; *esp* : DEATH **4** : ultimate lot or disposition : final outcome **5** *cap, pl* : the three goddesses of classical mythology who determine the course of human life

♦ [1, 2] circumstance, destiny, doom, fortune, lot

fat·ed \'fā-təd\ *adj* : decreed, controlled, or marked by fate

fate·ful \'fāt-fəl\ *adj* **1** : OMINOUS, PROPHETIC **2** : IMPORTANT, DECISIVE **3** ♦ : bringing on adverse fate : DESTRUCTIVE **4** : determined by fate — **fate·ful·ly** *adv*

♦ calamitous, catastrophic, destructive, disastrous, fatal, ruinous

fath *abbr* fathom

fat·head \'fat-ˌhed\ *n* ♦ : a stupid person — **fat·head·ed** \-'he-dəd\ *adj*

♦ blockhead, dope, dummy, idiot, imbecile, jackass, moron, numskull — more at IDIOT

¹fa·ther \'fä-thər\ *n* **1** ♦ : a male parent **2** *cap* : God esp. as the first person of the Trinity **3** ♦ : a male ancestor more remote than a parent : FOREFATHER **4** : one deserving the respect and love given to a father **5** *often cap* : an early Christian writer accepted by the church as an authoritative witness to its teaching and practice **6** ♦ : one that originates or institutes : ORIGINATOR ⟨the ~ of modern radio⟩; *also* : SOURCE **7** ♦ : a priest of the regular clergy : PRIEST — used esp. as a title **8** : one of the leading men ⟨city ~s⟩ — **fa·ther·hood** \-ˌhud\ *n* — **fa·ther·less** *adj* — **fa·ther·ly** *adj*

♦ [1] daddy, papa, pop ♦ [3] ancestor, forefather, grandfather — more at ANCESTOR ♦ [6] author, creator, founder, originator; *also* contriver, designer, innovator, inventor, spawner; builder, maker, producer; developer, pioneer, researcher; organizer, promoter; inspiration, inspirer ♦ [7] clergyman, minister, preacher, priest, reverend — more at CLERGYMAN

²father *vb* **1** ♦ : to make oneself the father of : BEGET **2** : to be the founder, producer, or author of **3** : to treat or care for as a father

♦ beget, get, produce, sire; *also* breed, multiply, procreate, propagate, reproduce, spawn; bear, engender, generate

father–in–law \'fä-<u>th</u>ə-rən-,lȯ\ *n, pl* **fa·thers–in–law** \-<u>th</u>ər-zən-\ : the father of one's spouse

fa·ther·land \'fä-<u>th</u>ər-,land\ *n* 1 : the native land of one's ancestors 2 ♦ : one's native land

♦ country, home, homeland — more at COUNTRY

¹**fath·om** \'fa-<u>th</u>əm\ *n* [ME *fadme*, fr. OE *fæthm* length of the outstretched arms] : a unit of length equal to 6 feet (about 1.8 meters) used esp. for measuring the depth of water

²**fathom** *vb* 1 : to measure by a sounding line 2 : PROBE 3 : to penetrate and come to understand ⟨∼ the problem⟩ — **fath·om·able** \'fa-<u>th</u>ə-mə-bəl\ *adj*

fath·om·less \'fa-<u>th</u>əm-ləs\ *adj* : incapable of being fathomed

¹**fa·tigue** \fə-'tēg\ *n* [F] 1 : manual or menial work performed by military personnel 2 *pl* : the uniform or work clothing worn on fatigue and in the field 3 ♦ : weariness from labor or stress 4 : the tendency of a material to break under repeated stress

♦ burnout, collapse, exhaustion, lassitude, prostration, tiredness, weariness; *also* enervation, faintness, feebleness, weakness; languor, lethargy, listlessness; sluggishness, slumber, stupor, torpor; apathy, inertia, passivity **Ant** refreshment, rejuvenation, revitalization

²**fatigue** *vb* **fa·tigued; fa·tigu·ing** ♦ : to weary with labor or exertion : WEARY, TIRE

♦ burn out, do in, drain, exhaust, tire, wear out, weary — more at EXHAUST

fat·ness *n* ♦ : the quality or state of being fat or rich in fats : fullness of flesh

♦ corpulence, obesity, plumpness — more at CORPULENCE

fat·ten \'fat-ᵊn\ *vb* : to make or grow fat

Fat Tuesday *n* : MARDI GRAS

¹**fat·ty** \'fa-tē\ *adj* **fat·ti·er; -est** 1 : containing fat esp. in unusual amounts 2 : GREASY

²**fatty** *n, pl* **fat·ties** *offensive* : an overweight person

fatty acid *n* : any of numerous acids that contain only carbon, hydrogen, and oxygen and that occur naturally in fats and various oils

fa·tu·ity \fə-'tü-ə-tē, -'tyü-\ *n, pl* **-ities** 1 ♦ : something foolish or stupid 2 ♦ : the quality or state of being stupid

♦ [1] absurdity, folly, foolery, foolishness, idiocy, inanity, madness, stupidity ♦ [2] absurdity, foolishness, inanity, insanity, lunacy, madness, silliness, simplicity, stupidity

fat·u·ous \'fa-chú-wəs\ *adj* ♦ : marked by lack of intelligence and rational consideration — **fat·u·ous·ly** *adv*

♦ dense, dull, dumb, obtuse, stupid, unintelligent, vacuous, witless — more at STUPID

fau·bourg \fō-'bùr\ *n* 1 : a suburb esp. of a French city 2 : a city quarter

fau·ces \'fȯ-,sēz\ *n pl* [L, throat] : the narrow passage located between the soft palate and the base of the tongue that joins the mouth to the pharynx

fau·cet \'fȯ-sət, 'fä-\ *n* ♦ : a fixture for drawing off a liquid (as from a pipe)

♦ cock, gate, spigot, tap, valve

¹**fault** \'fȯlt\ *n* 1 ♦ : a weakness in character : FAILING 2 ♦ : a physical or intellectual imperfection or impairment : IMPERFECTION, DEFECT 3 : an error esp. in service in a net or racket game 4 ♦ : a failure to do what is right : an unintentional error : MISTAKE 5 ♦ : responsibility for something wrong 6 : a fracture in the earth's crust accompanied by a displacement of one side relative to the other

♦ [1] demerit, failing, foible, frailty, shortcoming, vice, weakness; *also* blot, spot, stain; blemish, deficiency, flaw; Achilles' heel; corruption, depravity, evil, immorality, sinfulness, wickedness **Ant** merit, virtue ♦ [2] blemish, defect, flaw, imperfection — more at BLEMISH ♦ [4] blunder, error, fumble, goof, misstep, mistake, oversight, slip — more at ERROR ♦ [5] blame, culpability, guilt, rap — more at BLAME

²**fault** *vb* 1 : to commit a fault : ERR 2 : to fracture so as to produce a geologic fault 3 ♦ : to find a fault in 4 : to hold responsible or responsible for

♦ blame, condemn, criticize, denounce, knock, pan — more at CRITICIZE

fault·find·er \'fȯlt-,fīn-dər\ *n* ♦ : a person who tends to find fault or complain — **fault·find·ing** *n or adj*

♦ carper, castigator, censurer, critic, nitpicker, scold — more at CRITIC

fault·i·ly \'fȯl-tə-lē\ *adv* ♦ : in a faulty or blamable manner

♦ erroneously, improperly, incorrectly, wrongly

fault·less *adj* ♦ : having no fault : free from defect, imperfection, failing, blemish, or error

♦ flawless, impeccable, perfect, unblemished — more at PERFECT ♦ blameless, innocent, irreproachable — more at INNOCENT

fault·less·ly *adv* ♦ : in a manner having no fault

♦ flawlessly, ideally, impeccably, perfectly — more at PERFECTLY

faulty *adj* ♦ : marked by a fault : having a fault, blemish, or defect

♦ bad, defective, imperfect; *also* fallible; blemished, broken, damaged, defaced, disfigured, impaired, injured, marred, spoiled; deficient, inadequate, incomplete, insufficient, wanting **Ant** faultless, flawless, perfect

faun \'fȯn\ *n* : a Roman god similar to but gentler than a satyr

fau·na \'fȯ-nə\ *n, pl* **faunas** *also* **fau·nae** \-,nē, -,nī\ [NL, fr. L *Fauna*, sister of Faunus (the Roman god of animals)] : animals or animal life esp. of a region, period, or environment — **fau·nal** \-nəl\ *adj*

fau·vism \'fō-,vi-zəm\ *n, often cap* : a movement in painting characterized by vivid colors, free treatment of form, and a vibrant and decorative effect — **fau·vist** \-vist\ *n, often cap*

faux \'fō\ *adj* 1 ♦ : resembling something else that is usu. genuine and of better quality 2 : not sincere ⟨a gesture of ∼ humility⟩

♦ artificial, fake, imitation, mock, sham, synthetic — more at IMITATION

faux pas \'fō-,pä, fō-'\ *n, pl* **faux pas** *same or* -,päz, -'päz\ [F, lit., false step] : BLUNDER; *esp* : a social blunder

fa·va bean \'fä-və-\ *n* : the large flat edible seed of an Old World vetch; *also* : this plant

¹**fa·vor** *or Can and Brit* **fa·vour** \'fā-vər\ *n* 1 ♦ : friendly regard shown toward another esp. by a superior 2 ♦ : the act of approving or the state of being approved of : APPROVAL 3 ♦ : bias in favor : PARTIALITY 4 : POPULARITY 5 : gracious kindness; *also* : an act of such kindness 6 *pl* ♦ : effort in one's behalf : ATTENTION 7 : a token of love (as a ribbon) usu. worn conspicuously 8 : a small gift or decorative item given out at a party 9 : a special privilege 10 : sexual privileges — usu. used in pl. 11 : BEHALF, INTEREST

♦ [1] admiration, appreciation, esteem, estimation, regard, respect — more at ADMIRATION ♦ [2] approbation, approval, blessing, imprimatur, OK — more at APPROVAL ♦ [3] bias, partiality, partisanship, prejudice — more at BIAS ♦ [6] boon, courtesy, grace, indulgence, kindness, mercy, service, turn

²**favor** *or Can and Brit* **favour** *vb* 1 ♦ : to regard or treat with favor 2 : to do a kindness for or oblige esp. with a gift : OBLIGE 3 : ENDOW ⟨∼ed by nature⟩ 4 : to treat gently or carefully : SPARE ⟨∼ a lame leg⟩ 5 ♦ : to show partiality toward : PREFER 6 : SUPPORT, SUSTAIN 7 : FACILITATE ⟨darkness ∼s attack⟩ 8 : RESEMBLE ⟨he ∼s his father⟩

♦ [1] accept, approve, care, countenance, OK, subscribe ♦ [5] lean, like, prefer — more at PREFER

fa·vor·able *or Can and Brit* **fa·vour·able** \'fā-və-rə-bəl\ *adj* 1 ♦ : expressing approval : APPROVING ⟨a ∼ response⟩ 2 ♦ : tending to promote or facilitate : HELPFUL, ADVANTAGEOUS ⟨∼ weather⟩ 3 ♦ : marked by success

♦ [1] appreciative, complimentary, friendly, good, positive; *also* eulogistic, laudatory; respectful; adulatory, worshipful **Ant** adverse, disapproving, negative ♦ [2] advantageous, beneficial, helpful, profitable, salutary — more at BENEFICIAL ♦ [3] auspicious, bright, encouraging, hopeful, promising, propitious; *also* fortunate, happy, lucky, providential; advantageous, beneficial, profitable **Ant** discouraging, inauspicious, unfavorable, unpromising

fa·vor·ably *or Can and Brit* **fa·vour·ably** \-blē\ *adv* ♦ : in a favorable manner

♦ agreeably, nicely, pleasantly, pleasingly, satisfyingly, well

¹**fa·vor·ite** *or Can and Brit* **fa·vour·ite** \'fā-və-rət, -vrət\ *n* **1** ♦ : a person or a thing that is favored above others **2** : a competitor regarded as most likely to win

♦ darling, pet, preference, prize, treasure

²**favorite** *or Can and Brit* **favourite** *adj* ♦ : being a favorite

♦ dear, loved, precious, special

favorite son *n* : a candidate supported by the delegates of his state at a presidential nominating convention

fa·vor·it·ism \'fā-və-rə-ˌti-zəm\ *or Can and Brit* **fa·vour·it·ism** *n* : PARTIALITY, BIAS

¹**fawn** \'fȯn, 'fän\ *vb* **1** : to show affection ⟨a dog ~*ing* on its master⟩ **2** ♦ : to court favor by a cringing or flattering manner

♦ fuss, kowtow, toady; *also* drool, gush, slaver, slobber; endear, ingratiate; court, woo; adulate, idolize, worship; cajole, coax, flatter; cower, cringe, grovel; abase, debase, demean; defer, submit, yield

²**fawn** *n* **1** : a young deer **2** : a light grayish brown — **fawny** \'fȯ-nē, 'fä-\ *adj*

fax \'faks\ *n* **1** : FACSIMILE 2 **2** : a device used to send or receive facsimile communications; *also* : such a communication — **fax** *vb*

¹**fay** \'fā\ *n* ♦ : a mythical being of folklore and romance usu. having diminutive human form and magic powers and given to beneficial or mischievous interference in human affairs

♦ brownie, dwarf, elf, fairy, gnome, hobgoblin, leprechaun, pixie, puck, troll

²**fay** *adj* ♦ : like an elf

♦ antic, elfish, frisky, frolicsome, playful — more at PLAYFUL

faze \'fāz\ *vb* **fazed**; **faz·ing** ♦ : to disturb the composure or courage of

♦ confound, confuse, disconcert, embarrass, fluster, rattle — more at EMBARRASS

FBI *abbr* Federal Bureau of Investigation

FCC *abbr* Federal Communications Commission

FD *abbr* fire department

FDA *abbr* Food and Drug Administration

FDIC *abbr* Federal Deposit Insurance Corporation

Fe *symbol* [L *ferrum*] iron

fe·al·ty \'fēl-tē\ *n, pl* **-ties** ♦ : intense fidelity : LOYALTY, ALLEGIANCE

♦ allegiance, constancy, dedication, devotion, faith, faithfulness, fastness, fidelity, loyalty, steadfastness — more at FIDELITY

¹**fear** \'fir\ *vb* **1** : to have a reverent awe of ⟨~ God⟩ **2** : to be afraid of : have fear ⟨~*s* spiders⟩ **3** ♦ : to be apprehensive

♦ bother, fret, stew, sweat, trouble, worry — more at WORRY

²**fear** *n* **1** ♦ : an unpleasant often strong emotion caused by expectation or awareness of danger; *also* : an instance of or a state marked by this emotion **2** : anxious concern : SOLICITUDE **3** : profound reverence esp. toward God

♦ alarm, anxiety, apprehension, dread, fright, trepidation; *also* phobia; jitters, nervousness, willies; pang, qualm, twinge; agitation, discomposure, disquiet, perturbation;

concern, dismay, worry; cowardice, timidity, timorousness

fear·ful \-fəl\ *adj* **1** ♦ : causing fear **2** ♦ : filled with fear **3** ♦ : showing or caused by fear **4** ♦ : extremely bad, intense, or large ⟨paid a ~ price⟩ — **fear·ful·ly** *adv*

♦ [1] dire, dreadful, fearsome, forbidding, formidable, frightful, hair-raising, horrible, redoubtable, scary, shocking, terrible, terrifying; *also* daunting, disconcerting, discouraging, dismaying, disquieting, distressing, perturbing, startling, threatening, troubling, trying; creepy, eerie, weird; ghastly, gruesome, nightmarish ♦ [2, 3] afraid, scared, skittish, timid — more at AFRAID ♦ [4] deep, fierce, furious, hard, intense, profound, terrible, violent — more at INTENSE

fear·less \-ləs\ *adj* ♦ : free from fear : BRAVE — **fear·less·ly** *adv*

♦ brave, courageous, heroic, intrepid, lionhearted, stalwart, stout, undaunted, valiant

fear·less·ness *n* ♦ : the quality or state of being without fear

♦ bravery, courage, daring, heroism, nerve, stoutness, valor — more at COURAGE

fear·some \-səm\ *adj* **1** ♦ : causing fear **2** : TIMID **3** : INTENSE ⟨~ determination⟩

♦ fearful, formidable, hair-raising, scary, shocking, terrifying — more at FEARFUL

fea·si·ble \'fē-zə-bəl\ *adj* [ME *faisible*, fr. AF *faisable*, fr. *fais-*, stem of *faire* to make, do] **1** ♦ : capable of being done or carried out ⟨a ~ plan⟩ **2** : SUITABLE **3** : REASONABLE, LIKELY — **fea·si·bil·i·ty** \ˌfē-zə-'bi-lə-tē\ *n* — **fea·si·bly** \'fē-zə-blē\ *adv*

♦ achievable, attainable, doable, possible, practicable, viable, workable — more at POSSIBLE

¹**feast** \'fēst\ *n* **1** ♦ : an elaborate meal : BANQUET **2** : ABUNDANCE ⟨a ~ of good books⟩ **3** : FESTIVAL 1

♦ banquet, dinner, feed, spread; *also* chow, repast; blowout, festival, fete, gala, party; festivity; barbecue, clambake, cookout, fry, luau, roast

²**feast** *vb* **1 a** : to take part in a feast **b** ♦ : to give a feast for **2** : to enjoy some unusual pleasure or delight **3** : DELIGHT, GRATIFY

♦ banquet, dine, junket, regale; *also* cater, feed; fete, honor

feat \'fēt\ *n* ♦ : a deed notable esp. for courage : a heroic achievement; *esp* : an act notable for courage, skill, endurance, or ingenuity

♦ deed, exploit, stunt, trick; *also* accomplishment, achievement, coup; adventure; performance

¹**feath·er** \'fe-thər\ *n* **1** : any of the light horny outgrowths that form the external covering of the body of a bird **2** : the vane of an arrow **3** : the entire clothing of feathers of a bird : PLUMAGE **4** ♦ : a group united by common traits or interests ⟨birds of a ~⟩ **5** ♦ : elaborate, showy, or ceremonial dress ⟨in full ~⟩ **6** : CONDITION, MOOD ⟨in fine ~⟩ — **feath·ered** \-thərd\ *adj* — **feath·er·less** *adj* — **a feather in one's cap** : a mark of distinction : HONOR

♦ [4] class, ilk, kind, like, sort, type — more at SORT ♦ [5] array, best, finery, full dress, regalia — more at FINERY

²**feather** *vb* **1** : to furnish with a feather ⟨~ an arrow⟩ **2** : to cover, clothe, line, or adorn with or as if with feathers — **feather one's nest** : to provide for oneself financially esp. while exploiting a position of trust

feath·er·bed·ding \'fe-thər-ˌbe-diŋ\ *n* : the requiring of an employer usu. under a union rule or safety statute to employ more workers than are needed

feath·er·edge \-ˌej\ *n* : a very thin sharp edge

feath·er·weight \-ˌwāt\ *n* : one that is very light in weight; *esp* : a boxer weighing more than 118 but not over 126 pounds

feath·ery *adj* ♦ : light and delicate

♦ airy, light — more at LIGHT

¹**fea·ture** \'fē-chər\ *n* [ME *feture*, fr. AF, fr. L *factura* act of

making, fr. *facere* to make] **1** : the shape or appearance of the face or its parts **2** : a part of the face ⟨his eyes are his best ~⟩ **3 ♦** : a prominent part or characteristic **4** : a special attraction (as in a newspaper) **5** : something offered to the public or advertised as particularly attractive ⟨a car's new ~s⟩ — **fea·ture·less** *adj*

♦ attribute, character, characteristic, mark, peculiarity, point, property, quality, trait — more at CHARACTERISTIC

²feature *vb* **1** : to picture in the mind : IMAGINE **2 ♦** : to give special prominence to ⟨the show ~s new artists⟩ **3** : to play an important part

♦ accent, accentuate, emphasize, highlight, stress, underline, underscore — more at EMPHASIZE

Feb *abbr* February

fe·brile \'fe-ˌbrī(-ə)l\ *adj* : FEVERISH

Feb·ru·ary \'fe-b(y)ə-ˌwer-ē, 'fe-brə-\ *n* [ME *Februarie*, fr. L *Februarius*, fr. *Februa*, pl., feast of purification] : the 2d month of the year

fe·ces \'fē-ˌsēz\ *n pl* : bodily waste discharged from the intestine : EXCREMENT — **fe·cal** \-kəl\ *adj*

feck·less \'fek-ləs\ *adj* **1** : WEAK, INEFFECTIVE ⟨~ behavior⟩ **2** : WORTHLESS, IRRESPONSIBLE

fe·cund \'fe-kənd, 'fē-\ *adj* ♦ : fruitful in offspring or vegetation : FRUITFUL, PROLIFIC ⟨~ fields⟩ — **fe·cun·di·ty** \fi-'kən-də-tē, fe-\ *n*

♦ fat, fertile, fruitful, luxuriant, productive, prolific, rich — more at FERTILE

fed *abbr* federal; federation

fed·er·al \'fe-də-rəl, -drəl\ *adj* **1** : formed by a compact between political units that surrender individual sovereignty to a central authority but retain certain limited powers **2** : of or constituting a form of government in which power is distributed between a central authority and constituent territorial units **3** : of or relating to the central government of a federation **4** *cap* : FEDERALIST **5** *often cap* : of, relating to, or loyal to the federal government or the Union armies of the U.S. in the American Civil War — **fed·er·al·ly** *adv*

Federal *n* : a supporter of the U.S. government in the Civil War; *esp* : a soldier in the federal armies

federal district *n* : a district (as the District of Columbia) set apart as the seat of the central government of a federation

fed·er·al·ism \'fe-də-rə-li-zəm, -drə-\ *n* **1** *often cap* : the distribution of power in an organization (as a government) between a central authority and the constituent units **2** : support or advocacy of federalism **3** *cap* : the principles of the Federalists

fed·er·al·ist \-list\ *n* **1** : an advocate of federalism **2** *often cap* : an advocate of a federal union between the American colonies after the Revolution and of adoption of the U.S. Constitution **3** *cap* : a member of a major political party in the early years of the U.S. favoring a strong centralized national government — **federalist** *adj, often cap*

fed·er·al·ize \'fe-də-rə-ˌlīz, -drə-\ *vb* **-ized; -iz·ing** **1** : to unite in or under a federal system **2** : to bring under the jurisdiction of a federal government

fed·er·ate \'fe-də-ˌrāt\ *vb* **-at·ed; -at·ing** ♦ : to join in a federation

♦ ally, associate, band, club, confederate, conjoin, cooperate, league, unite — more at ALLY

fed·er·a·tion \ˌfe-də-'rā-shən\ *n* **1** : a political or societal entity formed by uniting smaller entities **2** : a federal government **3 ♦** : a union of organizations **4** : the forming of a federal union

♦ alliance, bloc, coalition, combination, combine, confederacy, confederation, league, union — more at CONFEDERACY

fedn *abbr* federation

fe·do·ra \fi-'dōr-ə\ *n* : a low soft felt hat with the crown creased lengthwise

fed up *adj* ♦ : satiated, tired, or disgusted beyond endurance ⟨*fed up* with bureaucracy⟩

♦ jaded, sick, tired, weary — more at WEARY

fee \'fē\ *n* [ME, fr. AF *fé, fief*, of Gmc origin; akin to OE *feoh* cattle, property] **1** : an estate in land held from a feudal lord **2** : an inherited or heritable estate in land **3 ♦** : a fixed charge; *also* : a charge for a service

♦ charge, cost, figure, price — more at PRICE

fee·ble \'fē-bəl\ *adj* **fee·bler** \-bə-lər\; **fee·blest** \-bə-ləst\ [ME *feble*, fr. OF, fr. L *flebilis* lamentable, wretched, fr. *flēre* to weep] **1 ♦** : markedly lacking in strength : FRAIL **2** : INEFFECTIVE, INADEQUATE ⟨a ~ protest⟩ — **fee·bly** \-blē\ *adv*

♦ faint, frail, infirm, wasted, weak

fee·ble-mind·ed \ˌfē-bəl-'mīn-dəd\ *adj* : lacking normal intelligence — **fee·ble·mind·ed·ness** *n*

fee·ble·ness *n* ♦ : the quality or state of being feeble

♦ debility, frailty, weakness

¹feed \'fēd\ *vb* **fed** \'fed\; **feed·ing** **1 ♦** : to give food to; *also* : to give as food **2 a ♦** : to consume food : EAT 1 **b** : to seize and devour prey — used with *on, upon*, or *off* **3** : to furnish what is necessary to the growth or function of **4** : to supply for use or consumption — **feed·er** *n*

♦ [1] board, cater, provision, victual; *also* serve, wait; nourish, nurture; banquet, dine, feast, regale; mess
♦ [2a] dine, eat, fare — more at DINE

²feed *n* **1 a ♦** : a usu. large meal; *esp* : a sumptuous meal **b ♦** : the portion or serving of food eaten at a meal **2** : food for livestock **3** : a mechanism for feeding material to a machine **4** : a continuous series of electronic information updates (as to a blog or social media account)

♦ [1a] banquet, dinner, feast, spread — more at FEAST
♦ [1b] board, chow, meal, mess, repast, table — more at MEAL

feed·back \'fēd-ˌbak\ *n* **1** : the return to the input of a part of the output of a machine, system, or process **2** : response esp. to one in authority about an activity or policy **3** : sound (as whistling) resulting from the retransmission of an amplified or broadcast signal

feed·lot \'fēd-ˌlät\ *n* : land on which cattle are fattened for market

feed·stuff \-ˌstəf\ *n* : FEED 2

¹feel \'fēl\ *vb* **felt** \'felt\; **feel·ing** **1** : to perceive or examine through physical contact : TOUCH, HANDLE **2 ♦** : to undergo passive experience of : EXPERIENCE; *also* : to suffer from **3** : to ascertain by cautious trial ⟨~ out public sentiment⟩ **4 ♦** : to be aware of **5** : to be conscious of an inward impression, state of mind, or physical condition **6 ♦** : to be aware of by instinct or inference : BELIEVE, THINK ⟨say what you ~⟩ **7 ♦** : to search for something with the fingers : GROPE **8** : SEEM ⟨it ~s like spring⟩ **9 ♦** : to have sympathy or pity ⟨I ~ for you⟩

♦ [2] endure, experience, have, know, see, suffer, sustain, taste, undergo — more at EXPERIENCE ♦ [4] perceive, scent, see, sense, smell, taste; *also* discern, observe, view; ascertain, discover, learn; anticipate, expect, foresee [6] believe, consider, deem, figure, guess, hold, imagine, suppose, think — more at BELIEVE ♦ [7] fish, fumble, grope — more at GROPE ♦ *usu* feel for [9] commiserate, pity, sympathize — more at PITY

²feel *n* **1** : the sense of touch **2 ♦** : a sensation experienced through the sense of feeling **3** : the quality of a thing as imparted through touch

♦ [2] feeling, sensation, sense — more at SENSATION

feel·er \'fē-lər\ *n* **1** : one that feels; *esp* : a tactile organ (as on the head of an insect) **2** : a proposal or remark made to find out the views of other people

¹feel·ing \'fē-liŋ\ *n* **1 a** : the sense of touch **b ♦** : a sensation perceived by touch **2 ♦** : a state of mind ⟨a ~ of loneliness⟩ **3** *pl* : general emotional condition : SENSIBILITIES ⟨hurt their ~s⟩ **4 ♦** : often unreasoned opinion or belief : OPINION, BELIEF **5 ♦** : capacity to respond emotionally

♦ [1b] feel, sensation, sense — more at SENSATION
♦ [2] emotion, sentiment; *also* impression, perception,

sense ♦ [4] belief, conviction, eye, judgment (*or* judgement), mind, notion, opinion, persuasion, sentiment, verdict, view — more at OPINION ♦ [5] compassion, heart, humanity, kindness, sympathy — more at HEART

²**feeling** *adj* **1** : having the capacity to feel or respond emotionally : SENSITIVE; *esp* : easily moved emotionally **2** : expressing emotion or sensitivity — **feel·ing·ly** *adv*

feet *pl of* FOOT

feign \'fān\ *vb* **1** ♦ : to give a false appearance of : SHAM ⟨~ illness⟩ **2** : to assert as if true : PRETEND

♦ affect, assume, fake, pretend, put on, sham, simulate; *also* act, dissemble, impersonate, masquerade; forge, imitate; camouflage, conceal, disguise, mask; bluff, feint

feigned \'fānd\ *adj* **1** : not genuine or real **2** ♦ : not genuinely felt

♦ artificial, hypocritical, insincere, two-faced — more at INSINCERE

feint \'fānt\ *n* : something feigned; *esp* : a mock blow or attack intended to distract attention from the real point of attack — **feint** *vb*

feisty \'fī-stē\ *adj* **feist·i·er; -est** : having or showing a lively aggressiveness ⟨a ~ heroine⟩

feld·spar \'feld-ˌspär\ *n* : any of a group of crystalline minerals consisting of silicates of aluminum with another element (as potassium or sodium)

fe·lic·i·tate \fi-'li-sə-ˌtāt\ *vb* **-tat·ed; -tat·ing** : to offer congratulations to : CONGRATULATE ⟨*felicitated* the winner⟩

fe·lic·i·ta·tion \fi-ˌli-sə-'tā-shən\ *n* : the act or an instance of congratulating : CONGRATULATION

fe·lic·i·tous \fi-'li-sə-təs\ *adj* **1** ♦ : suitably expressed : APT **2** ♦ : highly pleasing : affording great pleasure and satisfaction : PLEASANT, DELIGHTFUL

♦ [1] applicable, appropriate, apt, fit, fitting, proper, right, suitable — more at FIT, BECOMING ♦ [2] agreeable, congenial, delightful, pleasant, pleasurable, satisfying

fe·lic·i·tous·ly *adv* ♦ : in a felicitous manner

♦ agreeably, favorably (*or* favourably), nicely, pleasantly, pleasingly, satisfyingly, splendidly, well

fe·lic·i·ty \fi-'li-sə-tē\ *n, pl* **-ties** **1** ♦ : the quality or state of being happy; *esp* : great happiness **2** ♦ : something that causes happiness **3** : a pleasing manner or quality esp. in art or language **4** : an apt expression

♦ [1] blessedness, bliss, gladness, happiness, joy — more at HAPPINESS ♦ [2] benefit, blessing, boon, godsend, good, manna, windfall — more at BLESSING

¹**fe·line** \'fē-ˌlīn\ *adj* [L *felinus,* fr. *felis* cat] **1** : of or relating to cats or their kin **2** : sleekly graceful **3** : SLY, TREACHEROUS **4** : STEALTHY

²**feline** *n* ♦ : a feline animal

♦ cat, kitty, puss — more at CAT

¹**fell** \'fel\ *n* : SKIN, HIDE, PELT

²**fell** *vb* **1 a** ♦ : to cut, beat, or knock down **b** : to deprive of life **2** : to sew (a seam) by folding one raw edge under the other

♦ chop, cut, hew

³**fell** *past of* FALL

⁴**fell** *adj* **1** ♦ : violently hostile or aggressive in temperament : FIERCE **2** ♦ : killing or markedly sickening or destroying : DEADLY — **in one fell swoop** *also* **at one fell swoop** : all at once : with a single effort

♦ [1] ferocious, fierce, grim, savage, vicious — more at FIERCE ♦ [2] deadly, fatal, lethal, mortal, murderous, pestilent, vital — more at DEADLY

fel·lah \'fe-lə, fə-'lä\ *n, pl* **fel·la·hin** *or* **fel·la·heen** \ˌfe-lə-'hēn\ : a peasant or agricultural laborer in Arab countries (as Egypt or Syria)

fel·la·tio \fə-'lä-shē-ˌō\ *also* **fel·la·tion** \-shən\ *n* : oral stimulation of the penis

fel·low \'fe-lō\ *n* [ME *felawe,* fr. OE *fēolaga,* fr. ON *fēlagi,* fr. *fēlag* partnership (fr. *fē* cattle, money) + *lag* act of laying] **1** ♦ : one that accompanies or is in the company of another : one much in the company of another

2 ♦ : an equal in rank, power, or character : EQUAL, PEER **3** : one of a pair : MATE **4** : a member of an incorporated literary or scientific society **5** ♦ : an individual human : an adult male human : MAN **6** ♦ : a frequent, regular, or favorite escort or male companion : BOYFRIEND **7** : a person granted a stipend for advanced study

♦ [1] associate, cohort, companion, comrade, crony, mate — more at ASSOCIATE ♦ [2] equal, like, match, parallel, peer ♦ [5] buck, chap, dude, gent, gentleman, guy, hombre, jack, joker, lad, male, man — more at MAN ♦ [6] beau, boyfriend, man, swain — more at BOYFRIEND

fel·low man \ˌfe-lō-'man\ *n* : a kindred human being

fel·low·ship \'fe-lō-ˌship\ *n* **1** ♦ : the condition of friendly relationship existing among persons **2** ♦ : a community of interest or feeling **3** ♦ : a group with similar interests **4** : the position of a fellow (as of a university) **5** : the stipend granted a fellow

♦ [1] camaraderie, companionship, company, comradeship, society — more at COMPANIONSHIP ♦ [2] brotherhood, community, corps, fraternity — more at CORPS ♦ [3] association, club, college, congress, council, fraternity, league, order, organization, society — more at ASSOCIATION

fellow traveler *n* : a sympathetic supporter of another's cause; *esp* : a person who sympathizes with and often furthers the ideals and program of an organized group (as the Communist party) without joining it

fel·on \'fe-lən\ *n* **1** ♦ : one who has committed a felony **2** : WHITLOW

♦ criminal, crook, culprit, lawbreaker, malefactor, offender — more at CRIMINAL

fe·lo·ni·ous \fə-'lō-nē-əs\ *adj* : of, relating to, or having the nature of a felony

fel·o·ny \'fe-lə-nē\ *n, pl* **-nies** : a serious crime punishable by a heavy sentence

fel·spar *chiefly Brit var of* FELDSPAR

¹**felt** \'felt\ *n* **1** : a cloth made of wool and fur often mixed with natural or synthetic fibers **2** : a material resembling felt

²**felt** *past and past part of* FEEL

fem *abbr* **1** female **2** feminine

FEMA \'fē-mə\ *abbr* Federal Emergency Management Agency

¹**fe·male** \'fē-ˌmāl\ *adj* [ME, alter. of *femel,* fr. MF *femelle,* fr. ML *femella,* fr. L, girl, dim. of *femina* woman] **1** : of, relating to, or being the sex that typically bears young; *also* : PISTILLATE **2** ♦ : of, relating to, or characteristic of girls or women ⟨~ voices⟩

♦ feminine, womanly — more at FEMININE

²**female** *n* : a female individual

¹**fem·i·nine** \'fe-mə-nən\ *adj* **1 a** : of the female sex **b** ♦ : characteristic of or appropriate or unique to women **2** : of, relating to, or constituting the gender that includes most words or grammatical forms referring to females — **fem·i·nin·i·ty** \ˌfe-mə-'ni-nə-tē\ *n*

♦ female, womanly; *also* girlish, unmanly; ladylike *Ant* male, manly, mannish, masculine

²**feminine** *n* : a noun, pronoun, adjective, or inflectional form or class of the feminine gender; *also* : the feminine gender

fem·i·nism \'fe-mə-ˌni-zəm\ *n* **1** : the theory of the political, economic, and social equality of the sexes **2** : organized activity on behalf of women's rights and interests — **fem·i·nist** \-nist\ *n or adj*

femme fa·tale \ˌfem-fə-'tal\ *n, pl* **femmes fa·tales** *same or* -'talz\ [F, lit., disastrous woman] : a seductive woman

fe·mur \'fē-mər\ *n, pl* **fe·murs** *or* **fem·o·ra** \'fe-mə-rə\ : the long leg bone extending from the hip to the knee — **fem·o·ral** \'fe-mə-rəl\ *adj*

fen \'fen\ *n* ♦ : low swampy land

♦ bog, marsh, mire, morass, slough, swamp — more at SWAMP

¹**fence** \'fens\ *n* [ME *fens*, short for *defens* defense] **1 ♦ :** a barrier (as of wood or wire) to prevent escape or entry or to mark a boundary **2 :** a person who receives stolen goods; *also :* a place where stolen goods are disposed of — **on the fence :** in a position of neutrality or indecision

♦ barrier, hedge, wall — more at BARRIER

²**fence** *vb* **fenced; fenc·ing 1 ♦ :** to enclose with a fence **2 :** to keep in or out with a fence **3 :** to practice fencing **4 :** to use tactics of attack and defense esp. in debate — **fenc·er** *n*

♦ *usu* fence in cage, corral, enclose, hedge, pen

fenc·ing *n* **1 :** the art or practice of attack and defense with the foil, épée, or saber **2 :** the fences of a property or region **3 :** material used for building fences

fend \'fend\ *vb* **1 ♦ :** to keep or ward off **:** REPEL **2 :** SHIFT ⟨∼ for yourself⟩

♦ *usu* fend off repel, repulse, stave off — more at REPEL

fend·er \'fen-dər\ *n* **♦ :** a protective device (as a guard over the wheel of an automobile)

♦ buffer, bumper, cushion, pad — more at CUSHION

fen·es·tra·tion \,fe-nə-'strā-shən\ *n* **:** the arrangement and design of windows and doors in a building

Fe·ni·an \'fē-nē-ən\ *n* **:** a member of a secret 19th century Irish and Irish-American organization dedicated to overthrowing British rule in Ireland

fen·nel \'fen-ᵊl\ *n* **:** a garden plant related to the carrot and grown for its aromatic foliage and seeds

FEPC *abbr* Fair Employment Practices Commission

fe·ral \'fir-əl, 'fer-\ *adj* **1 :** SAVAGE **2 ♦ :** not domesticated or cultivated **:** WILD 1 **3 :** having escaped from domestication and become wild

♦ savage, unbroken, undomesticated, untamed, wild — more at WILD

fer–de–lance \'fer-də-'lans\ *n, pl* **fer–de–lance** [F, lit., lance iron, spearhead] **:** a large venomous pit viper of Central and So. America

¹**fer·ment** \fər-'ment\ *vb* **1 :** to cause or undergo fermentation **2 :** to be or cause to be in a state of agitation or intense activity

²**fer·ment** \'fər-,ment\ *n* **1 :** a living organism (as a yeast) causing fermentation by its enzymes; *also :* ENZYME **2 ♦ :** a state of unrest

♦ restlessness, turmoil, uneasiness, unrest — more at UNREST

fer·men·ta·tion \,fər-mən-'tā-shən, -,men-\ *n* **1 :** chemical decomposition of an organic substance (as in the souring of milk or the formation of alcohol from sugar) by enzymatic action in the absence of oxygen often with formation of gas **2 :** FERMENT 2

fer·mi·um \'fer-mē-əm, 'fər-\ *n* **:** an artificially produced radioactive metallic chemical element

fern \'fərn\ *n* **:** any of an order of vascular plants resembling seed plants in having roots, stems, and leaflike fronds but reproducing by spores instead of by flowers and seeds

fern·ery \'fər-nə-rē\ *n, pl* **-er·ies 1 :** a place for growing ferns **2 :** a collection of growing ferns

fe·ro·cious \fə-'rō-shəs\ *adj* **1 ♦ :** exhibiting or given to extreme fierceness and unrestrained violence and brutality **2 ♦ :** extremely intense — **fe·ro·cious·ly** *adv* — **fe·ro·cious·ness** *n*

♦ [1] fell, fierce, grim, savage, vicious — more at FIERCE [2] deep, fearful, heavy, intense, profound

fe·roc·i·ty \fə-'rä-sə-tē\ *n* **:** the quality or state of being ferocious

¹**fer·ret** \'fer-ət\ *n* **:** a partially domesticated usu. white European mammal related to the weasels

²**ferret** *vb* **1 :** to hunt game with ferrets **2 :** to drive out of a hiding place **3 ♦ :** to find and bring to light by searching — usu. used with *out* ⟨∼ out the truth⟩

♦ *usu* ferret out detect, determine, dig up, discover, find, hit on, locate, track down — more at FIND

fer·ric \'fer-ik\ *adj* **:** of, relating to, or containing iron

ferric oxide *n* **:** an oxide of iron found in nature as hematite and as rust and used esp. as a pigment, for polishing, and in magnetic materials

Fer·ris wheel \'fer-əs-\ *n* **:** an amusement device consisting of a large upright power-driven wheel with seats that remain horizontal around its rim

fer·ro·mag·net·ic \,fer-ō-mag-'ne-tik\ *adj* **:** of or relating to substances that are easily magnetized

fer·rous \'fer-əs\ *adj* **:** of, relating to, or containing iron

fer·rule \'fer-əl\ *n* **:** a metal ring or cap around a slender wooden shaft to prevent splitting

¹**fer·ry** \'fer-ē\ *vb* **fer·ried; fer·ry·ing** [ME *ferien*, fr. OE *ferian* to carry, convey] **1 :** to carry by boat across a body of water **2 :** to cross by a ferry **3 ♦ :** to convey from one place to another

♦ bear, carry, convey, haul, transport — more at CARRY

²**ferry** *n, pl* **ferries 1 :** a place where persons or things are ferried **2 :** FERRYBOAT

fer·ry·boat \'fer-ē-,bōt\ *n* **:** a boat used in ferrying

fer·tile \'fərt-ᵊl\ *adj* **1 ♦ :** producing plentifully **:** PRODUCTIVE ⟨∼ soils⟩ ⟨a ∼ mind⟩ **2 :** capable of developing or reproducing ⟨∼ seed⟩ ⟨a ∼ bull⟩ — **fer·til·i·ty** \(,)fər-'ti-lə-tē\ *n*

♦ fecund, fruitful, luxuriant, productive, prolific, rich; *also* bearing, producing, yielding; abounding, abundant, bountiful; copious, plenteous, plentiful; blooming, bursting, swarming, teeming, thriving; creative, inventive, original *Ant* barren, infertile, sterile, unfruitful, unproductive

fer·til·ize \'fərt-ᵊl-,īz\ *vb* **-ized; -iz·ing 1 :** to unite with in the process of fertilization ⟨a sperm ∼s an egg⟩ **2 :** to apply fertilizer to — **fer·til·iza·tion** \,fərt-ᵊl-ə-'zā-shən\ *n*

fer·til·iz·er \-,ī-zər\ *n* **:** material (as manure or a chemical mixture) for enriching land

fer·ule \'fer-əl\ *n* **:** a rod or ruler used to punish children

fer·ven·cy \'fər-vən-sē\ *n, pl* **-cies ♦ :** deep interest in or enthusiasm for something **:** FERVOR

♦ ardor, emotion, fervor, heat, intensity, passion, vehemence, warmth — more at ARDOR

fer·vent \'fər-vənt\ *adj* **1 :** very hot **:** GLOWING **2 ♦ :** marked by great intensity of feeling — **fer·vent·ly** *adv*

♦ ardent, burning, charged, emotional, fiery, hot-blooded, impassioned, passionate, red-hot, vehement *Ant* cold, cool, dispassionate, impassive, unemotional

fer·vid \-vəd\ *adj* **1 :** very hot **2 ♦ :** marked by often extreme fervor **:** ARDENT — **fer·vid·ly** *adv*

♦ ardent, burning, charged, emotional, fervent, fiery, hot-blooded, impassioned, intense, passionate, red-hot, vehement — more at FERVENT

fer·vor *or Can and Brit* **fer·vour** \'fər-vər\ *n* **1 :** intense heat **2 ♦ :** intensity of feeling or expression

♦ ardor, emotion, fervency, heat, intensity, passion, vehemence, warmth — more at ARDOR

fes·cue \'fes-kyü\ *n* **:** any of a genus of tufted perennial grasses

fes·tal \'fest-ᵊl\ *adj* **:** FESTIVE

fester \'fes-tər\ *vb* **1 :** to form pus **2 :** PUTREFY, ROT **3 :** RANKLE

fes·ti·val \'fes-tə-vəl\ *n* **1 ♦ :** a time of celebration marked by special observances; *esp* **:** an occasion marked with religious ceremonies **2 :** a periodic season or program of cultural events or entertainment ⟨a dance ∼⟩

♦ carnival, celebration, festivity, fete, fiesta, gala, jubilee; *also* jollification, merrymaking, revel, revelry; exhibit, exhibition, exposition, fair, show; exercises, honors

fes·tive \'fes-tiv\ *adj* **1 :** of, relating to, or suitable for a feast or festival **2 ♦ :** marked by gaiety, conviviality, or revelry — **fes·tive·ly** *adv*

♦ gay, gleeful, jolly, jovial, merry, mirthful, sunny — more at MERRY

fes·tiv·i·ty \fes-'ti-və-tē\ *n, pl* **-ties 1 ♦ :** a time of celebration marked by special observances **:** FESTIVAL 1 **2 :** the quality or state of being festive **3 ♦ :** festive activity

♦ [1] carnival, celebration, festival, fete, fiesta, gala, jubilee — more at FESTIVAL ♦ [3] conviviality, gaiety, jollification, merriment, merrymaking, revelry — more at MERRYMAKING

¹fes·toon \fes-'tün\ n [F *feston*, fr. It *festone*, fr. *festa* festival] **1** : a decorative chain or strip hanging between two points **2** : a carved, molded, or painted ornament representing a decorative chain

²festoon vb **1** : to hang or form festoons on **2** : to shape into festoons

fe·ta \'fe-tə\ n : a white crumbly Greek cheese made from sheep's or goat's milk

fe·tal \'fēt-ᵊl\ adj : of, relating to, or being a fetus

fetch \'fech\ vb **1** : to go or come after and bring or take back ⟨teach a dog to ~ a stick⟩ **2** ♦ : to have as a price **3** : to cause to come : bring out ⟨~ed tears from the eyes⟩ **4** : to give by striking ⟨~ him a blow⟩

♦ bring, cost, go, sell — more at COST

fetch·ing adj ♦ : tending to win interest or admiration : ATTRACTIVE — **fetch·ing·ly** adv

♦ alluring, attractive, charming, engaging, fascinating

fetch up vb ♦ : to bring to a stop

♦ draw up, halt, hold up, stay, still, stop — more at HALT

¹fete or **fête** \'fāt, 'fet\ n [F *fête*, fr. OF *feste*] **1** ♦ : a festive celebration or entertainment : FESTIVAL **2** ♦ : a large elaborate entertainment or party

♦ [1] carnival, celebration, festival, festivity, fiesta, gala, jubilee — more at FESTIVAL ♦ [2] affair, blowout, event, function, get-together, party — more at PARTY

²fete or **fête** vb **fet·ed** or **fêt·ed**; **fet·ing** or **fêt·ing** **1** : to honor or commemorate with a fete **2** : to pay high honor to

fet·id \'fe-təd\ adj ♦ : having an offensive smell

♦ foul, malodorous, noisome, rank, reeky, smelly, strong — more at MALODOROUS

fe·tish also **fe·tich** \'fe-tish\ n [F & Pg; F *fétiche*, fr. Pg *feitiço*, fr. *feitiço* artificial, false, fr. L *facticius* factitious] **1** ♦ : an object (as an idol or image) believed to have magical powers (as in curing disease) **2** ♦ : an object of unreasoning devotion or concern **3** : an object whose real or fantasied presence is psychologically necessary for sexual gratification

♦ [1] amulet, charm, mascot, talisman — more at CHARM ♦ [2] fixation, mania, obsession, preoccupation, prepossession — more at FIXATION

fe·tish·ism \-ti-ˌshi-zəm\ n **1** : belief in or devotion to fetishes **2** : the pathological transfer of sexual interest and gratification to a fetish — **fe·tish·ist** \-shist\ n — **fe·tish·is·tic** \ˌfe-ti-'shis-tik\ adj

fe·tish·ize \-ti-ˌshīz\ vb **-ized; -iz·ing** : to make a fetish of

fet·lock \'fet-ˌläk\ n : a projection on the back of a horse's leg above the hoof; also : a tuft of hair on this

¹fet·ter \'fe-tər\ n **1** ♦ : a chain or shackle for the feet **2** ♦ : something that confines

♦ [1] band, bond, chain, irons, ligature, manacle, shackle — more at BOND ♦ [2] check, condition, constraint, curb, limitation, restraint, restriction — more at RESTRICTION

²fetter vb **1** ♦ : to put fetters on **2** ♦ : to restrain from motion, action, or progress

♦ [1] bind, chain, enchain, handcuff, manacle, shackle, trammel ♦ [2] delay, encumber, hamper, handicap, hinder, hobble, hold back, impede, inhibit, interfere with, obstruct

fet·tle \'fet-ᵊl\ n ♦ : a state of fitness or order : CONDITION ⟨in fine ~⟩

♦ condition, form, order, repair, shape, trim — more at CONDITION

fe·tus \'fē-təs\ n : an unborn or unhatched vertebrate esp. after its basic structure is laid down; esp : a developing human in the uterus from usu. three months after conception to birth

feud \'fyüd\ n : a prolonged quarrel; esp : a lasting conflict between families or clans marked by violent attacks made for revenge — **feud** vb

feu·dal \'fyü-dᵊl\ adj **1** : of, relating to, or having the characteristics of a medieval fee **2** : of, relating to, or characteristic of feudalism

feu·dal·ism \'fyü-də-ˌli-zəm\ n : a system of political organization prevailing in medieval Europe in which a vassal renders service to a lord and receives protection and land in return; also : a similar political or social system — **feu·dal·is·tic** \ˌfyüd-ᵊl-'is-tik\ adj

¹feu·da·to·ry \'fyü-də-ˌtōr-ē\ adj : owing feudal allegiance

²feudatory n, pl **-ries 1** : FIEF **2** : a person who holds lands by feudal law or usage

fe·ver \'fē-vər\ n **1 a** : a rise in body temperature above the normal **b** ♦ : an abnormal bodily state characterized by increased heat, accelerated pulse, and systemic debility **c** ♦ : a disease of which a high body temperature is a chief symptom **2** : a state of heightened emotion or activity **3** : CRAZE ⟨baseball ~⟩ — **fe·ver·ish·ly** adv

♦ [1b, 1c] ailment, bug, complaint, condition, disease, disorder, ill, illness, infirmity, malady, sickness, trouble — more at DISEASE

fe·ver·ish adj ♦ : marked by intense emotion, activity, or instability

♦ agitated, frenzied, heated, hectic, overactive, overwrought; also fiery, impassioned; high-strung, jittery, jumpy, nervous ♦ delirious, fierce, frantic, frenetic, frenzied, furious, mad, violent, wild — more at FURIOUS

¹few \'fyü\ pron : not many : a small number

²few adj **1** : consisting of or amounting to a small number **2** : not many but some ⟨caught a ~ fish⟩ — **few·ness** n — **few and far between** : RARE 3

³few n **1** ♦ : a small number of units or individuals ⟨a ~ of them⟩ **2** : a special limited number ⟨among the ~⟩

♦ handful, smattering, sprinkle, sprinkling; also minority **Ant** crowd, horde, many

few·er \'fyü-ər\ pron : a smaller number of persons or things

fey \'fā\ adj **1** chiefly Scot : fated to die; also : marked by a foreboding of death or calamity **2** : able to see into the future : VISIONARY **3** : marked by an otherworldly air or attitude **4** : CRAZY, TOUCHED

fez \'fez\ n, pl **fez·zes** also **fez·es** : a round red felt hat that has a flat top and a tassel but no brim

ff abbr **1** folios **2** [following] and the following ones **3** fortissimo

FHA abbr Federal Housing Administration

fi·an·cé \ˌfē-ˌän-'sā\ n [F, fr. MF, fr. pp. of *fiancer* to promise, betroth, fr. OF *fiancier*, fr. *fiance* promise, trust, fr. *fier* to trust, ultim. fr. L *fidere*] : a man engaged to be married

fi·an·cée \ˌfē-ˌän-'sā\ n : a woman engaged to be married

fi·as·co \fē-'as-kō\ n, pl **-coes** [F] ♦ : a complete failure

♦ bust, catastrophe, debacle, failure, flop, washout — more at FAILURE

fi·at \'fē-ət, -ˌat, -ˌät; 'fī-ət, -ˌat\ n [L, let it be done] ♦ : an authoritative and often arbitrary order or decree

♦ decree, directive, edict, ruling — more at EDICT

¹fib \'fib\ n ♦ : a trivial or childish lie

♦ fabrication, falsehood, falsity, lie, story, tale, untruth

²fib vb **fibbed; fib·bing** ♦ : to tell a fib

♦ fabricate, lie, prevaricate — more at LIE

fib·ber n ♦ : one that tells fibs

♦ liar, prevaricator — more at LIAR

fi·ber or Can and Brit **fi·bre** \'fī-bər\ n **1** : a threadlike substance or structure (as a muscle cell or fine root); esp : a natural (as wool or flax) or artificial (as rayon) filament capable of being spun or woven **2** : indigestible material in human food that stimulates the intestine to move its contents along **3** : an element that gives texture or substance **4** ♦ : basic toughness : STRENGTH ⟨moral ~⟩ — **fi·brous** \-brəs\ adj

♦ backbone, fortitude, grit, guts, pluck, spunk — more at FORTITUDE

fi·ber·board *or Can and Brit* **fi·bre·board** \'fī-bər-ˌbōrd\ *n* : a material made by compressing fibers (as of wood) into stiff sheets

fi·ber·fill *or Can and Brit* **fi·bre·fill** \-ˌfil\ *n* : synthetic fibers used as a filling material (as for cushions)

fi·ber·glass *or Can and Brit* **fi·bre·glass** \-ˌglas\ *n* : glass in fibrous form used in making various products (as insulation)

fiber optics *n*   **1** *pl* : thin transparent fibers of glass or plastic that are enclosed by a less refractive material and that transmit light by internal reflection; *also* : a bundle of such fibers used in an instrument   **2** : the technique of the use of fiber optics — **fiber–optic** *adj*

fi·bril \'fī-brəl, 'fi-\ *n* : a small fiber

fi·bril·la·tion \ˌfi-brə-'lā-shən, ˌfī-\ *n* : rapid irregular contractions of the heart muscle fibers resulting in a lack of synchronism between heartbeat and pulse — **fib·ril·late** \'fi-brə-ˌlāt, 'fī-\ *vb*

fi·brin \'fī-brən\ *n* : a white insoluble fibrous protein formed in the clotting of blood

fi·broid \'fī-brȯid, 'fi-\ *adj* : resembling, forming, or consisting of fibrous tissue ⟨~ tumors⟩

fi·bro·my·al·gia \ˌfī-brō-ˌmī-'al-jə\ *n* : any of a group of rheumatic disorders affecting soft tissues (as muscles or tendons)

fi·bro·sis \fī-'brō-səs\ *n* : a condition marked by abnormal increase of fiber-containing tissue

fib·u·la \'fi-byə-lə\ *n, pl* **-lae** \-ˌlē, -ˌlī\ *or* **-las** : the outer and usu. the smaller of the two bones between the knee and ankle — **fib·u·lar** \-lər\ *adj*

FICA *abbr* Federal Insurance Contributions Act

-fication *n comb form* : making : production ⟨simpli*fication*⟩

fiche \'fēsh\ *n, pl* **fiche** : MICROFICHE

fi·chu \'fi-shü\ *n* [F] : a woman's light triangular scarf draped over the shoulders and fastened in front

fick·le \'fi-kəl\ *adj* ♦ : not firm or steadfast in disposition or character : INCONSTANT ⟨~ friends⟩ — **fick·le·ness** *n*

♦ capricious, changeable, inconstant, mercurial, uncertain, unpredictable, unsteady, variable; *also* aimless, erratic, haphazard, irregular, random; hesitating, shilly-shallying, vacillating, wavering; undependable, unreliable, untrustworthy; adaptable, mobile, protean, versatile *Ant* certain, constant, steady, unchangeable disloyal, faithless, false, inconstant, unfaithful, untrue — more at FAITHLESS

fic·tion \'fik-shən\ *n*   **1** ♦ : something (as a story) invented by the imagination   **2** ♦ : fictitious literature (as novels)

♦ [1, 2] fabrication, fantasy, figment, invention; *also* novel, story, tale *Ant* fact

fic·tion·al \'fik-shə-nəl\ *adj* : of, relating to, or characteristic of fiction — **fic·tion·al·ly** *adv*

fic·ti·tious \fik-'ti-shəs\ *adj* ♦ : of, relating to, or characteristic of fiction : IMAGINARY   **2** : FALSE, ASSUMED ⟨a ~ name⟩   **3** : FEIGNED

♦ imaginary, made-up, mythical, pretend, unreal — more at IMAGINARY

¹fid·dle \'fid-ᵊl\ *n* : VIOLIN

²fiddle *vb* **fid·dled; fid·dling**   **1** : to play on a fiddle   **2** ♦ : to move the hands or fingers restlessly   **3** ♦ : to move or act aimlessly or idly — often used with *around*   **4** ♦ : to interest oneself in what is not one's concern — **fid·dler** *n*

♦ [2] fidget, jerk, squirm, twitch, wiggle — more at FIDGET ♦ *usu* fiddle around [3] fool, mess, monkey, play, putter; *also* dally, dawdle, dillydally, hang around, hang out, idle, loaf, loll, lounge; clown (around); tinker ♦ *usu* fiddle with [4] fool, mess, monkey, play, tamper, tinker — more at TAMPER

fid·dle·head \'fid-ᵊl-ˌhed\ *n* : one of the young unfurling fronds of some ferns that are often eaten as greens

fiddler crab *n* : any of a genus of burrowing crabs with one claw much enlarged in the male

fid·dle·stick \'fid-ᵊl-ˌstik\ *n*   **1** *archaic* : a violin bow   **2** *pl* ♦ : language, conduct, or an idea that is absurd or contrary to good sense : NONSENSE — used as an interjection

♦ fiddlesticks foolishness, hogwash, humbug, nonsense, silliness — more at NONSENSE

fi·del·i·ty \fə-'de-lə-tē, fī-\ *n, pl* **-ties**   **1** ♦ : the quality or state of being faithful   **2** : ACCURACY ⟨~ in sound reproduction⟩

♦ allegiance, constancy, dedication, devotion, faith, faithfulness, fastness, fealty, loyalty, steadfastness; *also* affection, attachment, fondness; determination, firmness, resolution; dependability, reliability, trustworthiness *Ant* disloyalty, infidelity, perfidy, treachery

¹fidg·et \'fi-jət\ *n*   **1** : uneasiness or restlessness as shown by nervous movements — usu. used in pl.   **2** : one that fidgets — **fidg·ety** *adj*

²fidget *vb* ♦ : to move or cause to move or act restlessly or nervously

♦ fiddle, jerk, squirm, twitch, wiggle; *also* flit, flutter, twitter; quake, quiver, shake, shiver, tremble; pace

fi·du·cia·ry \fə-'dü-shē-ˌer-ē, -'dyü-, -shə-rē\ *adj*   **1** : involving a confidence or trust   **2** : held or holding in trust for another ⟨~ accounts⟩ — **fiduciary** *n*

fie \'fī\ *interj* — used to express disgust or disapproval

fief \'fēf\ *n* [F, fr. OF] : a feudal estate : FEE

¹field \'fēld\ *n*   **1** ♦ : open country   **2** : a piece of cleared land for cultivation or pasture   **3** : a piece of land yielding some special product   **4** : the place where a battle is fought; *also* : BATTLE   **5** ♦ : an area, division, or sphere of activity ⟨the ~ of science⟩ ⟨sales reps in the ~⟩   **6** : an area for military exercises   **7** : an area for sports   **8** : a background on which something is drawn or projected ⟨a flag with white stars on a ~ of blue⟩   **9** : a region or space in which a given effect (as magnetism) exists   **10** : a particular area (as of a record in a database) in which the same type of information is regularly recorded — **field** *adj*

♦ [1] ground, lot, parcel, plat, plot, tract; *also* grass, green, greensward, lawn; glade, grassland, heath, lea, meadow, moor, pasture ♦ [5] area, arena, department, discipline, domain, line, province, realm, specialty, sphere; *also* study, subject; territory, turf; business, occupation, profession, pursuit, racket, vocation

²field *vb*   **1** : to handle a batted or thrown baseball while on defense   **2** : to put into the field   **3** : to answer satisfactorily ⟨~ a tough question⟩ — **field·er** *n*

field day *n*   **1** : a day devoted to outdoor sports and athletic competition   **2** : a time of extraordinary pleasure or opportunity

field event *n* : a track-and-field event (as weight-throwing) other than a race

field glass *n* : a handheld binocular telescope — usu. used in pl.

field guide *n* : a manual for identifying natural objects, plants, or animals

field hockey *n* : a field game played between two teams of 11 players each whose object is to knock a ball into the opponent's goal with a curved stick

field marshal *n* : an officer (as in the British army) of the highest rank

field–test \-ˌtest\ *vb* : to test (as a new product) in actual situations reflecting intended use — **field test** *n*

fiend \'fēnd\ *n*   **1** : DEVIL 1   **2** ♦ : an infernal being : DEMON   **3** ♦ : an extremely wicked or cruel person   **4** ♦ : a person excessively devoted to a pursuit ⟨a golf ~⟩   **5** ♦ : one who is addicted esp. to a substance : ADDICT ⟨dope ~⟩

♦ [2] demon, devil, ghoul, imp — more at DEMON ♦ [3] beast, devil, evildoer, no-good, reprobate, rogue, varlet, villain, wretch — more at VILLAIN ♦ [4] addict, enthusiast, fan, fanatic, freak, lover, maniac, nut — more at FAN ♦ [5] addict, doper, user — more at DOPER

fiend·ish *adj* ♦ : perversely diabolical — **fiend·ish·ly** *adv*

♦ demonic, devilish, diabolical, satanic; *also* hellish, infernal; baleful, evil, sinister; malevolent, malicious, malignant; heinous, monstrous; barbarous, cruel, ferocious, inhuman, savage, vicious *Ant* angelic

fierce \'firs\ *adj* **fierc·er; fierc·est** **1** ♦ : violently hostile or aggressive in temperament **2** : given to fighting or killing : PUGNACIOUS **3** ♦ : marked by unrestrained zeal or vehemence : INTENSE **4** ♦ : furiously active or determined **5** ♦ : wild or menacing in appearance — **fierce·ly** *adv*

♦ [1] fell, ferocious, grim, savage, vicious; *also* bellicose, belligerent, pugnacious, warlike; contentious, quarrelsome, truculent; menacing, threatening; bestial, brute, inhuman, inhumane; barbaric, uncivilized, wild; heartless, implacable, merciless, pitiless, relentless, ruthless, unrelenting, wanton; bloodthirsty, bloody, murderous; rapacious, ravenous, voracious *Ant* gentle, mild ♦ [3] explosive, ferocious, furious, intense, terrible, vehement, vicious, violent — more at INTENSE ♦ [4] aggressive, ambitious, assertive, enterprising, go-getting, high-pressure, militant, self-assertive — more at AGGRESSIVE ♦ [5] austere, forbidding, grim, rough, rugged, severe, steely, stern — more at GRIM

fierce·ness *n* ♦ : the quality or state of being fierce

♦ aggressiveness, assertiveness, emphasis, intensity, vehemence — more at VEHEMENCE

fi·ery \'fi-ə-rē\ *adj* **fi·er·i·er; -est** **1** : consisting of fire **2** ♦ : on fire : BURNING, BLAZING **3** : FLAMMABLE **4** ♦ : hot like a fire **5** : RED ⟨a ~ sunset⟩ **6** ♦ : full of emotion or spirit **7** : IRRITABLE — **fi·eri·ness** \-rē-nəs\ *n*

♦ [2] ablaze, afire, burning — more at ABLAZE ♦ [4] broiling, burning, hot, torrid — more at HOT ♦ [6] ardent, emotional, fervent, feverish, hot-blooded, impassioned, passionate, red-hot, vehement — more at FERVENT

fi·es·ta \fē-'es-tə\ *n* [Sp] ♦ : a time of celebration marked by special observances : FESTIVAL

♦ carnival, celebration, festival, festivity, fete, gala, jubilee — more at FESTIVAL

fife \'fīf\ *n* [G *Pfeife* pipe, fife] : a small flute

FIFO *abbr* first in, first out

fif·teen \fif-'tēn\ *n* : one more than 14 — **fifteen** *adj or pron* — **fif·teenth** \-'tēnth\ *adj or n*

fifth \'fifth\ *n* **1** : one that is number five in a countable series **2** : one of five equal parts of something **3** : a unit of measure for liquor equal to ⅕ U.S. gallon — **fifth** *adj or adv*

fifth column *n* : a group of secret supporters of a nation's enemy that engage in espionage or sabotage within the country — **fifth columnist** *n*

fifth wheel *n* : one that is unnecessary and often burdensome

fif·ty \'fif-tē\ *n, pl* **fifties** : five times 10 — **fif·ti·eth** \-tē-əth\ *adj or n* — **fifty** *adj or pron*

fif·ty–fif·ty \,fif-tē-'fif-tē\ *adj* **1** : shared equally ⟨a ~ proposition⟩ **2** : half favorable and half unfavorable

¹fig \'fig\ *n* : a soft usu. pear-shaped edible fruit of a tree related to the mulberry; *also* : a tree bearing figs

²fig *abbr* **1** figurative; figuratively **2** figure

¹fight \'fīt\ *vb* **fought** \'fòt\; **fight·ing** **1** ♦ : to contend against another in battle or physical combat **2** : BOX **3** : to put forth a determined effort **4** ♦ : to contend in disagreement or competition **5** ♦ : to attempt to prevent the success or effectiveness of **6** : WAGE ⟨~ a war⟩ **7** : to gain by struggle

♦ [1] battle, clash, combat, scrimmage, skirmish, war; *also* beat, buffet, hit, punch, slug, strike; box, spar; brawl; grapple, scuffle, tussle, wrestle; bump, collide ♦ [4] battle, compete, contend, race, vie — more at COMPETE ♦ [4] argue, brawl, dispute, quarrel, row, scrap, spat, squabble — more at ARGUE ♦ [5] battle, combat, contend, counter, oppose; *also* baffle, foil, frustrate, resist, thwart, withstand; confront, defy, face, meet *Ant* advance, encourage, promote

²fight *n* **1** ♦ : a hostile encounter : BATTLE **2** : a boxing match **3** ♦ : a verbal disagreement **4** ♦ : a struggle for

a goal or an objective **5** ♦ : strength or disposition for fighting ⟨full of ~⟩

♦ [1] battle, clash, combat, conflict, contest, skirmish, struggle; *also* brawl, free-for-all, melee; fisticuffs; confrontation, duel, face-off; altercation, argument, disagreement, quarrel, row, wrangle ♦ [3] argument, brawl, disagreement, dispute, quarrel, row, scrap, spat, squabble — more at ARGUMENT ♦ [4] battle, fray, scrabble, struggle — more at STRUGGLE ♦ [5] aggression, aggressiveness, belligerence, militancy, pugnacity, truculence — more at BELLIGERENCE

fight·er \'fī-tər\ *n* **1** ♦ : one that fights; *esp* : WARRIOR **2** ♦ : one that engages in the sport of boxing : BOXER **3** : a fast maneuverable warplane for destroying enemy aircraft

♦ [1] legionnaire, man-at-arms, regular, serviceman, soldier, warrior — more at SOLDIER ♦ [2] boxer, prizefighter, pugilist — more at BOXER

fig·ment \'fig-mənt\ *n* ♦ : something imagined or made up

♦ chimera, conceit, delusion, dream, fancy, fantasy, hallucination, illusion, phantasm, pipe dream, unreality, vision

fig·u·ra·tion \,fi-gyə-'rā-shən, -gə-\ *n* **1** : FORM, OUTLINE **2** : an act or instance of representation in figures and shapes

fig·u·ra·tive \'fi-gyə-rə-tiv, -gə-\ *adj* **1** : EMBLEMATIC **2** : expressing one thing in terms normally denoting another with which it may be regarded as analogous : SYMBOLIC, METAPHORICAL ⟨~ language⟩ — **fig·u·ra·tive·ly** *adv*

¹fig·ure \'fi-gyər, -gər\ *n* [ME, fr. AF, fr. L *figura*, fr. *fingere* to shape] **1** ♦ : a number symbol : NUMERAL **2** : a written or printed character **3** ♦ : value esp. as expressed in numbers : PRICE **4** : a combination of points, lines, or surfaces in geometry ⟨a circle is a closed plane ~⟩ **5** ♦ : a body apparent chiefly in outline : an object significant or noticeable only in its form : SHAPE, FORM, OUTLINE **6 a** : the graphic representation of a form esp. of a person **b** : a representation of the human figure used esp. for displaying clothes **7** ♦ : a diagram or pictorial illustration of textual matter **8** : an often repetitive pattern or design in a manufactured article (as cloth) or natural product (as wood) : PATTERN, DESIGN **9** : appearance made or impression produced ⟨they cut quite a ~⟩ **10** : a series of movements (as in a dance) **11** ♦ : a prominent personality : PERSONAGE **12** ♦ : the shape of the human body

♦ [1] digit, integer, number, numeral, whole number — more at NUMBER ♦ [3] charge, cost, fee, price — more at PRICE ♦ [5] cast, configuration, form, outline, shape ♦ [7] diagram, graphic, illustration, plate — more at ILLUSTRATION ♦ [11] celebrity, notable, personage, personality — more at CELEBRITY ♦ [12] build, constitution, form, frame, physique, shape — more at PHYSIQUE

²figure *vb* **fig·ured; fig·ur·ing** **1** : to represent by or as if by a figure or outline **2** : to decorate with a pattern **3** : to indicate or represent by numerals **4** ♦ : to think of esp. with regard to taking some action **5** : to be or appear important or conspicuous **6** ♦ : to determine esp. by mathematical means : COMPUTE, CALCULATE ⟨*figured* the cost⟩ **7** : to reckon by exercise of practical judgment **8** ♦ : to take as granted or true

♦ [4] choose, conclude, decide, determine, opt, resolve — more at DECIDE ♦ [6] calculate, compute, reckon, work out — more at CALCULATE ♦ [8] believe, consider, feel, imagine, suppose, think — more at BELIEVE

fig·ure·head \'fi-gyər-,hed, -gər-\ *n* **1** : a figure on the bow of a ship **2** : a head or chief in name only

figure of speech *n* : a form of expression (as a simile or metaphor) that often compares or identifies one thing with another to convey meaning or heighten effect

figure out *vb* **1** : FIND OUT, DISCOVER **2** ♦ : to find a solution, explanation, or answer for : SOLVE

♦ answer, puzzle, resolve, riddle, solve, unravel, work, work out — more at SOLVE

figure skating *n* : skating that includes various jumps, spins, and dance movements

fig·u·rine \ˌfi-gyə-'rēn, -gə-\ *n* : a small carved or molded figure

Fi·ji·an \'fē-jē-ən, fi-'jē-ən\ *n* : a native or inhabitant of the Pacific island country of Fiji — **Fijian** *adj*

fil·a·ment \'fi-lə-mənt\ *n* : a fine thread or threadlike object, part, or process — **fil·a·men·tous** \ˌfi-lə-'men-təs\ *adj*

fil·bert \'fil-bərt\ *n* : the sweet thick-shelled nut of either of two European hazels; *also* : a shrub or small tree bearing filberts

filch \'filch\ *vb* ♦ : to steal furtively

♦ appropriate, pilfer, pocket, steal, swipe, thieve — more at STEAL

¹**file** \'fīl\ *n* : a usu. steel tool with a ridged or toothed surface used esp. for smoothing a hard substance

²**file** *vb* **filed; fil·ing** ♦ : to rub, smooth, or cut away with a file

♦ buff, grind, hone, rasp, rub, sand — more at GRIND

³**file** *vb* **filed; fil·ing** [ME, fr. ML *filare* to string documents on a string or wire, fr. *filum* file of documents, lit., thread, fr. L] **1** : to arrange in order **2** : to enter or record officially or as prescribed by law ⟨~ a lawsuit⟩ **3** : to send (copy) to a newspaper

⁴**file** *n* **1** : a device (as a folder or cabinet) by means of which papers may be kept in order **2** : a collection of papers or publications usu. arranged or classified **3** : a collection of data (as text) treated by a computer as a unit

⁵**file** *n* ♦ : a row of persons, animals, or things arranged one behind the other

♦ column, cue, line, queue, range, string, train — more at LINE

⁶**file** *vb* **filed; fil·ing** ♦ : to march or proceed in file

♦ march, pace, parade, stride — more at MARCH

fi·let mi·gnon \ˌfi-(ˌ)lā-mēn-'yōⁿ, fi-ˌlā-\ *n, pl* **filets mignons** \-(ˌ)lā-mēn-'yōⁿz, -ˌlā-\ [F, lit., dainty fillet] : a thick slice of beef cut from the narrow end of a beef tenderloin

fil·ial \'fi-lē-əl, 'fil-yəl\ *adj* : of, relating to, or befitting a son or daughter

fil·i·bus·ter \'fi-lə-ˌbəs-tər\ *n* [Sp *filibustero*, lit., freebooter] **1** : a military adventurer; *esp* : an American engaged in fomenting 19th century Latin American uprisings **2** : the use of delaying tactics (as extremely long speeches) esp. in a legislative assembly; *also* : an instance of this practice — **filibuster** *vb* — **fil·i·bus·ter·er** *n*

fil·i·gree \'fi-lə-ˌgrē\ *n* [F *filigrane*] : ornamental openwork (as of fine wire) — **fil·i·greed** \-ˌgrēd\ *adj*

fil·ing \'fī-liŋ\ *n* **1** : the act or instance of using a file **2** : a small piece scraped off by a file ⟨iron ~s⟩

Fil·i·pi·no \ˌfi-lə-'pē-nō\ *n, pl* **Filipinos** : a native or inhabitant of the Philippines — **Filipino** *adj*

¹**fill** \'fil\ *vb* **1** ♦ : to make or become full **2** ♦ : to stop up : PLUG ⟨~ a cavity⟩ **3** : FEED, SATIATE **4** ♦ : to carry out the terms of (as a contract) : SATISFY, FULFILL ⟨~ all requirements⟩ **5** : to occupy fully **6** : to spread through ⟨laughter ~ed the room⟩ **7** : OCCUPY ⟨~ the office of president⟩ **8** : to put a person in ⟨~ a vacancy⟩ **9** : to supply as directed ⟨~ a prescription⟩

♦ [1] charge, cram, heap, jam, jam-pack, load, pack, stuff; *also* flood, glut, swamp; crowd, crush, press, ram, shove, squash, squeeze; refill, reload, repack *Ant* empty ♦ [2] block, dam, pack, plug, stop, stuff; *also* choke, clog, obstruct; caulk, chink ♦ [4] answer, comply, fulfill, keep, meet, redeem, satisfy — more at FULFILL

²**fill** *n* **1** : a full supply; *esp* : a quantity that satisfies or satiates **2** : material used esp. for filling a low place

fill·er \'fi-lər\ *n* **1** : one that fills **2** ♦ : a substance added to another substance (as to increase bulk or weight) **3** : a material used for filling cracks and pores in wood before painting

♦ fill, filling, padding, stuffing — more at FILLING

¹**fil·let** \'fi-lət, *in sense 2* fi-'lā, 'fi-(ˌ)lā\ *also* **fi·let** \fi-'lā, 'fi-(ˌ)lā\ *n* [ME *filet*, fr. MF, dim. of *fil* thread] **1** : a narrow band, strip, or ribbon **2** : a piece or slice of boneless meat or fish; *esp* : the tenderloin of beef

²**fil·let** \'fi-lət, *in sense 2 also* fi-'lā, 'fi-(ˌ)lā\ *vb* **1** : to bind or adorn with or as if with a fillet **2** : to cut into fillets

fill in *vb* **1** ♦ : to provide necessary or recent information **2** ♦ : to serve as a temporary substitute

♦ [1] acquaint, brief, enlighten, familiarize, inform, instruct — more at ENLIGHTEN ♦ [2] cover, pinch-hit, stand in, sub, substitute, take over — more at COVER

fill·ing \'fi-liŋ\ *n* **1** ♦ : material used to fill something ⟨a ~ for a tooth⟩ **2** : the yarn interlacing the warp in a fabric **3** : a food mixture used to fill pastry or sandwiches

♦ fill, filler, padding, stuffing; *also* interlining, lining, wadding; cushion

filling station *n* : a retail station for servicing motor vehicles esp. with gasoline and oil

fil·lip \'fi-ləp\ *n* **1** : a blow or gesture made by a flick or snap of the finger across the thumb **2** : something that serves to arouse or excite — **fillip** *vb*

fill-up \'fil-ˌəp\ *n* : an act or instance of filling something

fil·ly \'fi-lē\ *n, pl* **fillies** : a young female horse usu. less than four years old

¹**film** \'film\ *n* **1** : a thin skin or membrane **2** : a thin coating or layer **3** : a flexible strip of chemically treated material used in taking pictures **4** ♦ : a representation (as of a story) by means of motion pictures

♦ motion picture, movie, picture — more at MOVIE

²**film** *vb* **1** : to cover with a film **2** : to make a motion picture of

film·dom \'film-dəm\ *n* : the motion-picture industry

film·og·ra·phy \fil-'mä-grə-fē\ *n, pl* **-phies** : a list of motion pictures featuring the work of a film figure or a particular topic

film·strip \'film-ˌstrip\ *n* : a strip of film bearing a sequence of images for projection as still pictures

filmy *adj* : light, transparent, and fluffy

fils \'fēs\ *n* [F] : SON — used after a family name to distinguish a son from his father

¹**fil·ter** \'fil-tər\ *n* **1** : a porous material through which a fluid is passed to separate out matter in suspension; *also* : a device containing such material **2** : a device for suppressing waves of certain frequencies; *esp* : one (as for a camera) that absorbs light of certain colors **3** : software for sorting or blocking certain online material

²**filter** *vb* **1** ♦ : to remove by means of a filter **2** : to pass through a filter — **fil·ter·able** *also* **fil·tra·ble** \-tə-rə-bəl, -trə-\ *adj* — **fil·tra·tion** \fil-'trā-shən\ *n*

♦ clarify, clear, distill, purify — more at CLARIFY

filth \'filth\ *n* [ME, fr. OE *fӯlth*, fr. *fūl* foul] **1** ♦ : foul matter; *esp* : loathsome dirt or refuse **2** ♦ : moral corruption **3** : something that tends to corrupt or disgust : OBSCENITY

♦ [1] dirt, grime, muck, refuse, smut, soil; *also* scum, sewage, slime, sludge, swill; garbage, trash; soot; dirtiness, filthiness, foulness, grubbiness, nastiness, uncleanliness, uncleanness ♦ [2] coarseness, dirt, grossness, indecency, lewdness, obscenity, smut, vulgarity — more at OBSCENITY

filth·i·ness *n* ♦ : the quality or state of being filthy

♦ dinginess, dirtiness, foulness, grubbiness, nastiness, uncleanliness — more at DIRTINESS

¹**filthy** \'fil-thē\ *adj* **1** ♦ : covered with, having the appearance of, or containing filth : very dirty **2** ♦ : abhorrent to morality or virtue : designed to incite to lust or depravity

♦ [1] dirty, grubby, grungy, mucky, muddy, unclean — more at DIRTY ♦ [2] bawdy, coarse, crude, dirty, gross, indecent, lewd, obscene, pornographic, vulgar — more at OBSCENE

²**filthy** *adv* : VERY, EXTREMELY ⟨~ dirty⟩ ⟨~ rich⟩

fil·trate \'fil-ˌtrāt\ *n* : fluid that has passed through a filter

¹**fin** \'fin\ *n* **1** : one of the thin external processes by which an aquatic animal (as a fish) moves through water **2** : a

fin-shaped part (as on an airplane) 3 : FLIPPER 2 —
finned \'find\ *adj*
²**fin** *abbr* 1 finance; financial 2 finish
fi·na·gle \fə-'nā-gəl\ *vb* **-gled; -gling** 1 ♦ : to obtain by indirect or dishonest means : WANGLE 2 ♦ : to use devious dishonest methods to achieve one's ends — **fi·na·gler** *n*

♦ [1, 2] contrive, finesse, frame, machinate, maneuver, wangle

¹**fi·nal** \'fīn-ᵊl\ *adj* 1 ♦ : not to be altered or undone 2 ♦ : coming at the end : being the last in a series, process, or progress 3 : relating to or occurring at the end or conclusion — **fi·nal·i·ty** \fī-'na-lə-tē, fə-\ *n* — **fi·nal·ly** *adv*

♦ [1] certain, firm, fixed, hard, hard-and-fast, set, settled, stable — more at FIXED ♦ [2] hindmost, last, latter, terminal, ultimate — more at LAST

²**final** *n* 1 : a deciding match or game — usu. used in pl. 2 : the last examination in a course — often used in pl.
fi·na·le \fə-'na-lē, fi-'nä-\ *n* ♦ : the close or end of something; *esp* : the last section of a musical composition

♦ close, conclusion, consummation, end, ending, finis, finish, windup; *also* apex, climax, crescendo, culmination, peak, summit, zenith; aftermath, anticlimax, coda, epilogue, postscript *Ant* beginning, dawn, opening, start

fi·nal·ise *Brit var of* FINALIZE
fi·nal·ist \'fīn-ᵊl-əst\ *n* : a contestant in the finals of a competition
fi·nal·ize \'fīn-ᵊl-ˌīz\ *vb* **-ized; -iz·ing** ♦ : to put in final or finished form

♦ complete, consummate, finish, perfect — more at FINISH

¹**fi·nance** \fə-'nans, 'fī-ˌnans\ *n* [ME, ending, payment, fr. AF, fr. *finer* to end, pay, fr. *fin* end, fr. L *finis* boundary, end] 1 *pl* ♦ : money resources available esp. to a government or business 2 : management of money affairs

♦ *usu* **finances** funds, resources, wherewithal — more at FUND

²**finance** *vb* **fi·nanced; fi·nanc·ing** 1 ♦ : to raise or provide funds for 2 ♦ : to furnish with necessary funds 3 : to sell or supply on credit

♦ [1] capitalize, endow, fund, stake, subsidize, underwrite; *also* grubstake; aid, back, patronize, sponsor, support ♦ [1, 2] endow, fund, subsidize — more at ENDOW

finance company *n* : a company that makes usu. small short-term loans usu. to individuals
fi·nan·cial \fə-'nan-chəl, fī-\ *adj* ♦ : relating to finance or financiers ⟨~ problems⟩ — **fi·nan·cial·ly** *adv*

♦ fiscal, monetary, pecuniary; *also* capitalist, commercial, economic

fi·nan·cials \-shəlz\ *n pl* : financial statistics
fi·nan·cier \ˌfi-nən-'sir, ˌfī-ˌnan-\ *n* 1 : a person skilled in managing public moneys 2 : a person who deals with large-scale finance and investment
finch \'finch\ *n* : any of numerous songbirds with strong conical bills
¹**find** \'fīnd\ *vb* **found** \'faȯnd\; **find·ing** 1 ♦ : to meet with either by chance or by searching or study 2 : to obtain by effort or management ⟨~ time to read⟩ 3 : to arrive at : REACH ⟨the bullet *found* its mark⟩ 4 : EXPERIENCE, FEEL ⟨*found* happiness⟩ 5 : to gain or regain the use of ⟨*found* his voice again⟩ 6 : to determine and make a statement about ⟨~ a verdict⟩

♦ detect, determine, dig up, discover, ferret out, hit on, locate, track down; *also* spot; look for, search (for *or* out), seek *Ant* miss, overlook, pass over

²**find** *n* 1 : an act or instance of finding 2 : something found; *esp* : a valuable item of discovery
find·er \'fīn-dər\ *n* : one that finds; *esp* : VIEWFINDER
fin de siè·cle \ˌfaⁿ-də-sē-'eklᵊ\ *adj* [F, end of century] 1 : of, relating to, or characteristic of the close of the 19th century 2 : of or relating to the end of a century
find·ing \'fīn-diŋ\ *n* 1 ♦ : the act of finding 2 : FIND 2 3 : the result of a judicial proceeding or inquiry

♦ detection, discovery — more at DISCOVERY

find out *vb* ♦ : to learn by study, observation, or search : DISCOVER

♦ ascertain, catch on, discover, hear, learn, realize, see — more at DISCOVER

¹**fine** \'fīn\ *n* ♦ : money exacted as a penalty for an offense

♦ damages, forfeit, mulct, penalty; *also* reparations; award, compensation; indemnity

²**fine** *vb* **fined; fin·ing** ♦ : to impose a fine on : punish by a fine

♦ assess, charge, exact, impose, lay, levy, put — more at IMPOSE

³**fine** *adj* **fin·er; fin·est** 1 ♦ : free from impurity 2 a ♦ : very thin in gauge or texture b ♦ : very small 3 : not coarse 4 : SUBTLE, SENSITIVE ⟨a ~ distinction⟩ 5 ♦ : superior in quality or appearance : eminently good 6 ♦ : very precise or accurate : REFINED 7 ♦ : very well — **fine·ly** *adv*

♦ [1] pure, refined, unadulterated, undiluted — more at PURE ♦ [2a] dusty, floury, powdery; *also* smooth; filtered, pulverized, refined *Ant* coarse, grainy, granular ♦ [2b] narrow, skinny, slender, slim, thin — more at NARROW ♦ [5] A1, excellent, grand, great, heavenly, prime, splendid, superb, superior, unsurpassed, wonderful — more at EXCELLENT ♦ [6] delicate, exact, minute, precise, refined, subtle; *also* petty, piddling, trifling, trivial; fastidious, finicky, fussy, particular *Ant* coarse, inexact, rough ♦ [7] agreeable, all right, alright, good, OK, satisfactory — more at SATISFACTORY

⁴**fine** *adv* 1 ♦ : very well 2 — used to express agreement

♦ all right, good, nicely, OK, satisfactorily, well — more at WELL

fine art *n* : art (as painting, sculpture, or music) concerned esp. with the creation of beautiful objects — usu. used in pl.
fine·ness *n* 1 ♦ : exquisite perfection or elaborateness of form, texture, or construction : superior quality 2 ♦ : delicate, subtle, or sensitive in quality, perception, or discrimination

♦ [1] accuracy, closeness, delicacy, exactness, precision, veracity — more at PRECISION ♦ [2] daintiness, delicacy, fragility — more at DELICACY

fin·ery \'fī-nə-rē\ *n, pl* **-er·ies** 1 : ORNAMENT, DECORATION 2 ♦ : showy clothing and jewels

♦ array, best, feather, frippery, full dress, regalia; *also* apparel, attire, costume, duds, raiment

fine-spun \'fīn-'spən\ *adj* : developed with extremely or excessively fine delicacy or detail
¹**fi·nesse** \fə-'nes\ *n* 1 : refinement or delicacy of workmanship, structure, or texture 2 ♦ : skillful handling of a situation : adroit maneuvering

♦ adroitness, cleverness, craft, dexterity, sleight — more at DEXTERITY

²**finesse** *vb* ♦ : to bring about, direct, or manage by adroit maneuvering

♦ finagle, maneuver, mastermind, negotiate, wangle

fine-tune \'fīn-'tün\ *vb* : to adjust so as to bring to the highest level of performance or effectiveness
fin·fish \'fin-ˌfish\ *n* : FISH 2
¹**fin·ger** \'fiŋ-gər\ *n* 1 : any of the five divisions at the end of the hand; *esp* : one other than the thumb 2 : something that resembles or does the work of a finger 3 : a part of a glove into which a finger is inserted
²**finger** *vb* **fin·gered; fin·ger·ing** 1 : to touch or feel with the fingers : HANDLE 2 : to perform with the fingers or with a certain fingering 3 : to mark the notes of a piece of music as a guide in playing 4 : to point out
fin·ger·board \'fiŋ-gər-ˌbȯrd\ *n* : the part of a stringed instrument against which the fingers press the strings to vary the pitch
finger bowl *n* : a small water bowl for rinsing the fingers at the table
fin·ger·ing \'fiŋ-gə-riŋ\ *n* 1 : handling or touching with the fingers 2 : the act or method of using the fingers in

playing an instrument 3 : the marking of the method of fingering

fin·ger·ling \\'fiŋ-gər-liŋ\ *n* : a small fish

fin·ger·nail \\'fiŋ-gər-ˌnāl\ *n* : the nail of a finger

fin·ger·print \-ˌprint\ *n* : the pattern of marks made by pressing the tip of a finger or thumb on a surface; *esp* : an ink impression of such a pattern taken for the purpose of identification — **fingerprint** *vb*

fin·ger·tip \-ˌtip\ *n* : the tip of a finger

fin·i·al \\'fi-nē-əl\ *n* : an ornamental projection or end (as on a spire)

fin·ick·ing \\'fi-ni-kiŋ\ *adj* : FINICKY

fin·icky \\'fi-ni-kē\ *adj* ♦ : excessively particular in taste or standards 〈a ~ eater〉

♦ choosy, dainty, delicate, demanding, exacting, fastidious, fussy, particular, picky; *also* discerning, discriminating, insightful, knowledgeable; carping, critical; careful, meticulous, punctilious, scrupulous; queasy, squeamish; peevish, petulant, prickly, touchy *Ant* undemanding, unfussy

fi·nis \\'fi-nəs\ *n* 1 : a point that marks the extent of something 2 ♦ : cessation of a course of action, pursuit, or activity : END, CONCLUSION

♦ close, conclusion, consummation, end, ending, finale, finish, windup — more at FINALE

¹**fin·ish** \\'fi-nish\ *vb* 1 ♦ : to come to an end : TERMINATE 2 : to use or dispose of entirely 3 ♦ : to bring to completion 4 : to put a final coat or surface on — **fin·ish·er** *n*

♦ [1] break off, cease, close, conclude, die, end, expire, quit, stop, terminate — more at CEASE ♦ [3] complete, consummate, finalize, perfect; *also* follow through, stick out; accomplish, achieve, effect; discharge, execute, fulfill, perform; machine, polish, refine, round (off *or* out), shine, touch up

²**finish** *n* 1 ♦ : final stage : END, CONCLUSION 2 : something that completes or perfects 3 : the final treatment or coating of a surface

♦ close, conclusion, consummation, end, ending, finale, finis, windup — more at FINALE

fi·nite \\'fī-ˌnīt\ *adj* 1 ♦ : having definite or definable limits; *also* : having a limited nature or existence 2 : being less than some positive integer in number or measure and greater than its negative 3 : showing distinction of grammatical person and number 〈a ~ verb〉

♦ definite, determinate, limited, measured, narrow, restricted — more at LIMITED

fink \\'fiŋk\ *n* 1 : a contemptible person 2 : STRIKEBREAKER 3 : INFORMER

Finn \\'fin\ *n* : a native or inhabitant of Finland

fin·nan had·die \ˌfi-nən-'ha-dē\ *n* : smoked haddock

¹**Finn·ish** \\'fi-nish\ *adj* : of or relating to Finland, the Finns, or Finnish

²**Finnish** *n* : the language of the Finns

fin·ny \\'fi-nē\ *adj* 1 : having or characterized by fins 2 : relating to or being fish

fiord *var of* FJORD

fir \\'fər\ *n* : any of a genus of usu. large evergreen trees related to the pines; *also* : the light soft wood of a fir

¹**fire** \\'fīr\ *n* 1 : the light or heat and esp. the flame of something burning 2 : ENTHUSIASM, ZEAL 3 : fuel that is burning (as in a stove or fireplace) 4 ♦ : destructive burning (as of a house) 5 : the firing of weapons — **fireless** *adj*

♦ conflagration, holocaust, inferno; *also* blaze, flare-up; backfire, bonfire, forest fire, wildfire; arson

²**fire** *vb* **fired; fir·ing** 1 ♦ : to set on fire : set fire to : KINDLE, IGNITE 〈~ a house〉 2 **a** ♦ : to give life or spirit to : STIR, ENLIVEN 〈~ the imagination〉 **b** ♦ : to become irritated : become angry or inflamed with passion 3 ♦ : to dismiss from employment 4 ♦ : to cause to be driven forward with force from a bow, sling, or similar device or from a firearm : SHOOT 〈~ a gun〉 〈~ an ar-

row〉 5 : BAKE 〈*firing* pottery in a kiln〉 6 : to apply fire or fuel to something 〈~ a furnace〉 7 ♦ : to throw with speed or force

♦ [1] burn, ignite, inflame, kindle, light — more at BURN ♦ [2a] animate, brace, energize, enliven, invigorate, jazz up, liven up, pep up, quicken, stimulate, vitalize, vivify, zip (up) — more at ANIMATE ♦ *usu* **fire (up)** [2b] arouse, encourage, excite, incite, instigate, move, pique, provoke, stimulate, stir ♦ [3] cashier, dismiss, remove, retire, sack — more at DISMISS ♦ [4] blast, discharge, loose, shoot — more at SHOOT ♦ [7] dash, fling, heave, hurl, hurtle, launch, pitch, sling, throw, toss — more at THROW

fire ant *n* : either of two small fiercely stinging So. American ants introduced into the southeastern U.S. where they are agricultural pests

fire·arm \\'fī(-ə)r-ˌärm\ *n* ♦ : a weapon (as a pistol) from which a shot is discharged by gunpowder

♦ arm, gun, piece — more at GUN

fire·ball \-ˌbȯl\ *n* 1 : a ball of fire 2 : a very bright meteor 3 : the highly luminous cloud of vapor and dust created by a nuclear explosion 4 : a highly energetic person

fire·boat \-ˌbōt\ *n* : a boat equipped for fighting fires

fire·bomb \-ˌbäm\ *n* : an incendiary bomb — **firebomb** *vb*

fire·box \-ˌbäks\ *n* 1 : a chamber (as of a furnace) that contains a fire 2 : a box containing a fire alarm

fire·brand \-ˌbrand\ *n* 1 : a piece of burning wood 2 ♦ : a person who creates unrest or strife : AGITATOR

♦ agitator, demagogue, incendiary, inciter, rabble-rouser — more at AGITATOR

fire·break \-ˌbrāk\ *n* : a barrier of cleared or plowed land intended to check a forest or grass fire

fire·bug \-ˌbəg\ *n* : a person who deliberately sets destructive fires

fire·crack·er \-ˌkra-kər\ *n* : a paper tube containing an explosive and a fuse and set off to make a noise

fire department *n* : an organization for preventing or extinguishing fires; *also* : its members

fire engine *n* : a motor vehicle with equipment for extinguishing fires

fire escape *n* : a stairway or ladder for escape from a burning building

fire·fight·er \\'fī(-ə)r-ˌfī-tər\ *n* : a person who fights fires; *esp* : a member of a fire department

fire·fly \-ˌflī\ *n* : any of various small night-flying beetles that produce flashes of light for courtship purposes

fire·house \-ˌhau̇s\ *n* : FIRE STATION

fire irons *n pl* : tools for tending a fire esp. in a fireplace

fire·man \\'fī(-ə)r-mən\ *n* 1 : STOKER 2 : FIREFIGHTER

fire off *vb* : to write and send

fire·place \-ˌplās\ *n* 1 : a framed opening made in a chimney to hold an open fire 2 : an outdoor structure of brick or stone for an open fire

fire·plug \-ˌpləg\ *n* : HYDRANT

fire·pow·er \-ˌpau̇(-ə)r\ *n* : the ability to deliver gunfire or warheads on a target

¹**fire·proof** \-'prüf\ *adj* ♦ : resistant to fire

♦ noncombustible, nonflammable, noninflammable

²**fireproof** *vb* : to make fireproof

fire-sale \-ˌsāl\ *adj* : heavily discounted 〈~ prices〉

fire screen *n* : a protective screen before a fireplace

¹**fire·side** \\'fī(-ə)r-ˌsīd\ *n* 1 : a place near the fire or hearth 2 ♦ : one's place of residence : HOME

♦ abode, domicile, dwelling, home, house, lodging — more at HOME

²**fireside** *adj* : having an informal or intimate quality

fire station *n* : a building housing fire engines and usu. firefighters

fire·storm \\'fī(-ə)r-ˌstȯrm\ *n* 1 : a large destructive very hot fire 2 : a sudden or violent outburst 〈~ of criticism〉

fire tower *n* : a tower (as in a forest) from which a watch for fires is kept

fire·trap \'fī(-ə)r-ˌtrap\ *n* : a building or place apt to catch on fire or difficult to escape from in case of fire

fire truck *n* : FIRE ENGINE

fire·wall \-ˌwȯl\ *n* : computer hardware or software for preventing unauthorized access to data

fire·wa·ter \'fī(-ə)r-ˌwȯ-tər, -ˌwä-\ *n* : intoxicating liquor

fire·wood \-ˌwu̇d\ *n* : wood used for fuel

fire·work \-ˌwərk\ *n* **1** : a device designed to produce a striking display by the burning of explosive or flammable materials — usu. used in pl. ⟨a display of ∼s at the end of the festival⟩ **2** ♦ : *pl* a display of temper or intense conflict

♦ *usu* **fireworks** blowup, dudgeon, explosion, fit, huff, scene, tantrum — more at TANTRUM

firing line *n* **1** : a line from which fire is delivered against a target **2** : the forefront of an activity

¹**firm** \'fərm\ *adj* **1** ♦ : securely fixed in place **2** : SOLID, VIGOROUS ⟨a ∼ handshake⟩ **3** ♦ : having a solid or compact texture **4** ♦ : not subject to change or fluctuation : STEADY ⟨∼ prices⟩ **5** ♦ : not easily moved or disturbed : STEADFAST **6** ♦ : indicating firmness or resolution

♦ [1] fast, frozen, secure, set, snug, tight — more at TIGHT ♦ [3] compact, hard, rigid, solid, stiff, unyielding; *also* compacted, compressed, hardened, indurated, tempered; close, dense, heavy, thick, thickset; inelastic, inflexible, ramrod, unbending; compressed, condensed; sturdy, substantial; impenetrable, impermeable, nonporous *Ant* flabby, soft, spongy ♦ [4] certain, fixed, hard, hard-and-fast, set, settled, stable — more at FIXED ♦ [5] fast, sound, stable, stalwart, steady, strong, sturdy — more at STABLE ♦ [6] decisive, determined, intent, purposeful, resolute, set, single-minded — more at DETERMINED

²**firm** *vb* ♦ : to make or become firm

♦ *usu* **firm up** concrete, congeal, freeze, harden, set, solidify — more at HARDEN

³**firm** *n* [G *Firma*, fr. It, signature, ultim. fr. L *firmare* to make firm, confirm] **1** : the name under which a company transacts business **2** : a business partnership of two or more persons **3** ♦ : a business enterprise

♦ business, company, concern, enterprise, establishment, house, outfit — more at ENTERPRISE

fir·ma·ment \'fər-mə-mənt\ *n* : the arch of the sky : HEAVENS

firm·ly *adv* ♦ : in a firm manner

♦ forcefully, forcibly, hard, stoutly, strenuously, strongly, vigorously — more at HARD

firm·ness *n* ♦ : the quality or state of being firm

♦ decision, decisiveness, determination, resolution, resolve, stability, strength — more at DETERMINATION

firm·ware \'firm-ˌwer\ *n* : computer programs contained permanently in a hardware device

¹**first** \'fərst\ *adj* ♦ : preceding all others as in time, order, or importance

♦ chief, dominant, foremost, key, paramount, predominant, primary, principal — more at FOREMOST ♦ initial, original, pioneer, premier; *also* ancient, early, primal, primary, primeval, primitive, primordial; antecedent, preceding, previous *Ant* final, last, terminal, ultimate

²**first** *adv* **1** : before any other **2** : for the first time **3** ♦ : in preference to something else

♦ preferably, rather, readily, soon — more at RATHER

³**first** *n* **1** : number one in a countable series **2** : something that is first **3** : the lowest forward gear in an automotive vehicle **4** : the winning or highest place in a competition or examination

first aid *n* : emergency care or treatment given an injured or ill person

first-born \'fərst-ˈbȯrn\ *adj* : ELDEST — **firstborn** *n*

first class *n* : the best or highest group in a classification — **first–class** *adj or adv*

first-hand \'fərst-ˈhand\ *adj* ♦ : coming from direct personal observation or experience — **firsthand** *adv*

♦ direct, immediate, primary — more at DIRECT

first lady *n*, *often cap F&L* : the wife or hostess of the chief executive of a political unit (as a country)

first lieutenant *n* : a commissioned officer (as in the army) ranking next below a captain

first·ling \'fərst-liŋ\ *n* : one that comes or is produced first

first·ly \-lē\ *adv* ♦ : in the first place : FIRST

♦ first, initially, originally, primarily — more at ORIGINALLY

¹**first–rate** \-ˈrāt\ *adj* ♦ : of the first order of size, importance, or quality

♦ excellent, fabulous, fantastic, great, superb, terrific, wonderful — more at EXCELLENT

²**first–rate** *adv* : very well

first sergeant *n* **1** : a noncommissioned officer serving as the chief assistant to the commander of a military unit **2** : a rank in the army below a sergeant major and in the marine corps below a master gunnery sergeant

first strike *n* : a preemptive nuclear attack

first–string \'fərst-ˈstriŋ\ *adj* : being a regular as distinguished from a substitute — **first–string·er** \-ˈstriŋ-ər\ *n*

firth \'fərth\ *n* [ME, fr. ON *fjǫrthr*] : a narrow arm of the sea : the opening of a river into the sea : ESTUARY

fis·cal \'fis-kəl\ *adj* [L *fiscalis*, fr. *fiscus* basket, treasury] **1** : of or relating to taxation, public revenues, or public debt **2** ♦ : of or relating to financial matters — **fis·cal·ly** *adv*

♦ financial, monetary, pecuniary — more at FINANCIAL

¹**fish** \'fish\ *n*, *pl* **fish** *or* **fish·es** **1** : a water-dwelling animal — usu. used in combination ⟨star*fish*⟩ ⟨shell*fish*⟩ **2** : any of numerous cold-blooded water-breathing vertebrates with fins, gills, and usu. scales that include the bony fishes and usu. the cartilaginous and jawless fishes **3** : the flesh of fish used as food

²**fish** *vb* **1** : to attempt to catch fish **2** : to seek something by roundabout means ⟨∼ for praise⟩ **3** : to search for something underwater **4** ♦ : to engage in a search by groping **5** : to draw forth

♦ feel, fumble, grope — more at GROPE

fish–and–chips *n pl* : fried fish and french fried potatoes

fish·bowl \'fish-ˌbōl\ *n* **1** : a bowl for the keeping of live fish **2** : a place or condition that affords no privacy

fish·er \'fi-shər\ *n* **1** : one that fishes **2** : a dark brown No. American carnivorous mammal related to the weasels

fish·er·man \-mən\ *n* **1** : a person engaged in fishing **2** : a fishing boat

fish·ery \'fi-shə-rē\ *n*, *pl* **-er·ies** **1** : the business of catching fish **2** : a place for catching fish

fish farm *n* : a commercial facility for raising aquatic animals for human food — **fish–farm** *vb*

fish·hook \'fish-ˌhu̇k\ *n* : a usu. barbed hook for catching fish

fish ladder *n* : an arrangement of pools in steps by which fish can pass over a dam in going upstream

fish·net \'fish-ˌnet\ *n* **1** : netting for catching fish **2** : a coarse open-mesh fabric

fish·tail \-ˌtāl\ *vb* : to have the rear end slide from side to side out of control while moving forward

fish·wife \-ˌwīf\ *n* **1** : a woman who sells fish **2** : a vulgar abusive woman

fishy \'fi-shē\ *adj* **fish·i·er**; **-est** **1** : of or resembling fish **2** ♦ : inspiring doubt or suspicion : QUESTIONABLE ⟨the story sounds ∼ to me⟩

♦ debatable, doubtful, problematic, questionable, shady, shaky, suspect, suspicious — more at DOUBTFUL

fis·sion \'fi-shən, -zhən\ *n* [L *fissio*, fr. *findere* to split] **1** : a cleaving into parts **2** : a method of reproduction in which a living cell or body divides into two or more parts each of which grows into a whole new individual **3** : the splitting of an atomic nucleus resulting in the release of large amounts of energy — **fis·sion·able** \'fi-shə-nə-bəl, -zhə-\ *adj*

fis·sure \'fi-shər\ *n* ♦ : a narrow opening or crack

♦ chink, cleft, crack, cranny, crevice, rift, split — more at CRACK

fist \'fist\ *n* **1** : the hand with fingers folded into the palm **2** : INDEX 6

fist bump *n* : a gesture in which two people bump their fists together — **fist–bump** *vb*

fist·ful \'fist-,fùl\ *n* : HANDFUL

fist·i·cuffs \'fis-ti-,kəfs\ *n pl* : a fight with the fists

fist pump *n* : a celebratory gesture in which the fist is raised and lowered quickly and vigorously — **fist–pump** *vb*

fis·tu·la \'fis-chə-lə\ *n, pl* **-las** *or* **-lae** : an abnormal passage leading from an abscess or hollow organ — **fis·tu·lous** \-ləs\ *adj*

¹fit \'fit\ *adj* **fit·ter; fit·test** **1** ♦ : adapted to a purpose **2** : PROPER, RIGHT ⟨a movie ~ for children⟩ **3** ♦ : put into a suitable state : made ready **4** ♦ : physically and mentally sound — **fit·ly** *adv*

> ♦ [1] appropriate, apt, good, happy, proper, right, suitable; *also* just, justified, right; needed, required, requisite; able, capable, competent, qualified, trained; acceptable, adequate, decent, satisfactory, tolerable; correct, decorous, respectable, seemly *Ant* inapplicable, inappropriate, unsuitable, wrong ♦ [1, 3] go, ready, set — more at READY ♦ [3] available, functional, operable, practicable, serviceable, usable, useful — more at US-ABLE ♦ [4] able-bodied, hale, healthy, hearty, robust, sound, well — more at HEALTHY

²fit *n* **1** ♦ : a sudden violent attack (as in epilepsy) **2** ♦ : a sudden outburst

> ♦ [1] attack, bout, case, seizure, siege, spell — more at ATTACK ♦ [2] blowup, dudgeon, explosion, fireworks, huff, outburst, scene, tantrum — more at TANTRUM

³fit *vb* **fit·ted** *also* **fit; fit·ting** **1** ♦ : to be suitable for or to **2** : to be correctly adjusted to or shaped for **3** ♦ : to insert or adjust until correctly in place **4** ♦ : to make a place or room for **5** ♦ : to be in agreement or accord with **6** ♦ : to put into a condition of readiness : PRE-PARE **7** ♦ : to make or adjust to the right shape and size : ADJUST **8** : to supply with something that is adjusted or designed for the use required — usu. used with *out* **9** : to be in harmony or accord : BELONG — **fit·ter** *n*

> ♦ [1] befit, do, go, serve, suit — more at DO ♦ [1, 6] equip, prepare, qualify, ready, season — more at QUALIFY ♦ *usu* fit in *or* fit into [3] inject, insert, insinuate, interject, interpose, introduce — more at INSERT ♦ [4] accommodate, hold, have — more at ACCOMMO-DATE ♦ [5] agree, answer, check, conform, correspond, dovetail, go, harmonize — more at CHECK ♦ [7] accli-mate, accommodate, adapt, adjust, condition, conform, shape — more at ADAPT

⁴fit *n* : the fact, condition, or manner of fitting or being fitted

fit·ful \'fit-fəl\ *adj* ♦ : not regular : INTERMITTENT ⟨~ sleep⟩ — **fit·ful·ly** *adv*

> ♦ erratic, intermittent, irregular, occasional, spasmodic, sporadic, spotty, unsteady; *also* convulsive, sudden, vi-olent; broken, disconnected, fragmentary, interrupted; desultory, haphazard, random; changing, fluctuating, unstable, varying, wavering; changeable, fickle, vari-able *Ant* constant, continuous, regular, steady

fit·ness *n* ♦ : the quality or state of being fit

> ♦ health, robustness, soundness, wellness — more at HEALTH ♦ appropriateness, aptness, rightness, suitabil-ity — more at APPROPRIATENESS

¹fit·ting \'fi-tiŋ\ *adj* ♦ : of a kind appropriate to the situa-tion : APPROPRIATE, SUITABLE ⟨a ~ tribute⟩

> ♦ applicable, appropriate, apt, fit, proper, right, suit-able — more at FIT

²fitting *n* **1** : the action or act of one that fits; *esp* : a trying on of clothes being made or altered **2** : a small often standardized part ⟨a plumbing ~⟩

fit·ting·ly *adv* ♦ : in a fitting manner

> ♦ appropriately, correctly, happily, properly, rightly, suitably — more at PROPERLY

fit·ting·ness *n* : the quality or state of being appropriate to the situation

five \'fīv\ *n* **1** : one more than four **2** : the 5th in a set or series **3** : something having five units; *esp* : a basketball team **4** : a 5-dollar bill — **five** *adj or pron*

¹fix \'fiks\ *vb* **1** : to make firm, stable, or fast **2** : to give a permanent or final form to **3** ♦ : to attach physically : AFFIX, ATTACH **4** : to hold or direct steadily ⟨~es his eyes on the horizon⟩ **5** ♦ : to set or place definitely : SET **6** : ASSIGN ⟨~ the blame⟩ **7** : to set in order : ADJUST **8** : to get ready : PREPARE **9** ♦ : to make whole or sound again **10** : to get even with **11** : to influence by improper or illegal methods ⟨~ a race⟩ **12** ♦ : to assign precisely : settle on : arrange — **fix·er** *n*

> ♦ [3] affix, attach, fasten — more at FASTEN ♦ [5] de-posit, place, position, put, set, set up, stick — more at PLACE ♦ [9] doctor, mend, patch, recondition, reno-vate, repair, revamp — more at MEND ♦ [12] arrange, decide, set, settle — more at ARRANGE

²fix *n* **1** ♦ : a position of difficulty or embarrassment : PREDICAMENT **2** : a determination of position (as of a ship) **3** : an accurate determination or understanding **4** : an act of improper influence **5** : a supply or dose of something (as an addictive drug) strongly desired or craved **6** : something that fixes or restores

> ♦ corner, hole, jam, pickle, predicament, spot — more at PREDICAMENT

fix·a·tion \fik-'sā-shən\ *n* ♦ : an obsessive or unhealthy pre-occupation or attachment — **fix·ate** \'fik-,sāt\ *vb*

> ♦ fetish, mania, obsession, preoccupation, prepossess-sion; *also* complex, hang-up, problem; compulsion, craving, enthusiasm, fascination, infatuation, passion; idiosyncrasy, quirk; penchant, predilection, proclivity

fix·a·tive \'fik-sə-tiv\ *n* : something that stabilizes or sets

fixed \'fikst\ *adj* **1** : securely placed or fastened : STA-TIONARY **2** : not volatile **3** ♦ : not subject to change or fluctuation **4** : INTENT, CONCENTRATED ⟨a ~ stare⟩ **5** : supplied with a definite amount of something needed (as money) — **fixed·ly** \'fik-səd-lē\ *adv*

> ♦ certain, determinate, final, firm, flat, frozen, hard, hard-and-fast, set, settled, stable; *also* nonadjustable, nonnegotiable, unchangeable; constant, steady, un-changing, uniform, unwavering; definite, exact, ex-plicit, specific; stated, stipulated fast, hard-and-fast, immutable, inflexible, unalterable, unchangeable — more at INFLEXIBLE

fixed·ness \'fik-səd-nəs\ *n* ♦ : the quality or state of being fixed

> ♦ constancy, immutability, stability, steadiness — more at CONSTANCY

fix·i·ty \'fik-sə-tē\ *n, pl* **-ties** : the quality or state of being fixed or stable

fix·ture \'fiks-chər\ *n* **1** : something firmly attached as a permanent part of some other thing **2** : a familiar feature in a particular setting; *esp* : a person associated with a place or activity

¹fizz \'fiz\ *vb* ♦ : to make a hissing or sputtering sound

> ♦ hiss, sizzle, swish, whish, whiz

²fizz *n* **1** : a hissing sound **2** : an effervescent beverage

¹fiz·zle \'fi-zəl\ *vb* **fiz·zled; fiz·zling** **1** : FIZZ **2** : to fail after a good start — often used with *out*

²fizzle *n* ♦ : lack of satisfactory performance or effect : FAIL-URE

> ♦ collapse, crash, cropper, defeat, failure, nonsuccess — more at FAILURE

fjord *or* **fiord** \fē-'órd\ *n* [Norw] ♦ : a narrow inlet of the sea between cliffs or steep slopes

> ♦ bay, bight, cove, estuary, gulf, inlet — more at GULF

fl *abbr* **1** [L *floruit*] flourished **2** fluid

Fl *symbol* flerovium

FL *or* **Fla** *abbr* Florida

flab \'flab\ *n* : soft flabby body tissue

flab·ber·gast \'fla-bər-ˌgast\ *vb* ♦ : to overwhelm with shock, surprise, or wonder : ASTOUND

♦ amaze, astonish, astound, bowl, dumbfound, floor, shock, startle, stun, stupefy, surprise — more at SURPRISE

flab·by \'fla-bē\ *adj* **flab·bi·er; -est** ♦ : lacking firmness : FLACCID ⟨~ muscles⟩ — **flab·bi·ness** \-bē-nəs\ *n*

♦ flaccid, mushy, pulpy, soft, spongy — more at SOFT

flac·cid \'flak-səd\ *adj* ♦ : lacking firmness ⟨~ muscles⟩

♦ droopy, floppy, lank, limp, slack, yielding — more at LIMP

¹flag \'flag\ *n* : any of various irises; *esp* : a wild iris

²flag *n* **1** : a usu. rectangular piece of fabric of distinctive design that is used as a symbol (as of a nation) or as a signaling device **2** ♦ : something used like a flag to signal or attract attention **3** : one of the cross strokes of a musical note less than a quarter note in value

♦ banner, colors (*or* colours), ensign, pennant, standard, streamer; *also* bunting; union jack, white flag; semaphore; badge, coat of arms, crest, insignia

³flag *vb* **flagged; flag·ging 1** ♦ : to signal with or as if with a flag; *esp* : to signal to stop ⟨~ a taxi⟩ **2** : to mark or identify with or as if with a flag **3** : to call a penalty on

♦ gesture, motion, signal, wave — more at MOTION

⁴flag *vb* **flagged; flag·ging 1** ♦ : to hang loose or limp **2** ♦ : to become unsteady, feeble, or spiritless **3** : to decline in interest or attraction ⟨the topic *flagged*⟩

♦ [1] droop, hang, loll, sag, wilt — more at DROOP
♦ [2] decay, droop, fail, go, lag, languish, sag, waste, weaken, wilt — more at WEAKEN

⁵flag *n* : a hard flat stone suitable for paving

flag·el·late \'fla-jə-ˌlāt\ *vb* **-lat·ed; -lat·ing** : to punish by whipping — **flag·el·la·tion** \ˌfla-jə-'lā-shən\ *n*

fla·gel·lum \flə-'je-ləm\ *n, pl* **-la** \-lə\ *also* **-lums** : a long whiplike process that is the primary organ of motion of many microorganisms — **fla·gel·lar** \-lər\ *adj*

fla·geo·let \ˌfla-jə-'let, -'lā\ *n* [F] : a small woodwind instrument belonging to the flute class

fla·gi·tious \flə-'ji-shəs\ *adj* : grossly wicked : VILLAINOUS

flag·on \'fla-gən\ *n* ♦ : a container for liquids usu. with a handle, spout, and lid

♦ ewer, jug, pitcher — more at PITCHER

flag·pole \'flag-ˌpōl\ *n* : a pole on which to raise a flag

fla·grant \'flā-grənt\ *adj* [L *flagrans*, prp. of *flagrare* to burn] ♦ : conspicuously bad ⟨~ abuse of power⟩ — **fla·grant·ly** *adv*

♦ blatant, conspicuous, egregious, gross, pronounced, rank, striking — more at EGREGIOUS

fla·gran·te de·lic·to \flə-ˌgran-tē-di-'lik-tō\ *adv* : the act of committing a misdeed — used in the phrase *in flagrante delicto*

flag·ship \'flag-ˌship\ *n* **1** : the ship that carries the commander of a fleet or subdivision thereof and flies the commander's flag **2** : the most important one of a group

flag·staff \-ˌstaf\ *n* : FLAGPOLE

flag·stone \-ˌstōn\ *n* : ⁵FLAG

¹flail \'flāl\ *n* : a tool for threshing grain by hand

²flail *vb* ♦ : to strike or swing with or as if with a flail

♦ flog, hide, lash, switch, thrash, whale, whip

flair \'flar\ *n* [F, lit., sense of smell, fr. OF, odor, fr. *flairier* to give off an odor, fr. VL *flagrare*, alter. of L *fragrare*] **1** ♦ : ability to appreciate or make good use of something : TALENT **2** : a unique style

♦ aptitude, endowment, faculty, genius, gift, knack, talent — more at TALENT

flak \'flak\ *n, pl* **flak** [G, fr. *Fliegerabwehrkanonen*, fr. *Flieger* flyer + *Abwehr* defense + *Kanonen* cannons] **1** : antiaircraft guns or bursting shells fired from them **2** : CRITICISM, OPPOSITION

¹flake \'flāk\ *n* **1** : a small loose mass or bit **2** ♦ : a thin flattened piece or layer : CHIP

♦ chip, splinter — more at CHIP

²flake *vb* **flaked; flak·ing** : to form or separate into flakes

³flake *n* : a markedly eccentric person : ODDBALL — **flak·i·ness** \'flā-kē-nəs\ *n* — **flaky** *adj*

flaky *adj* ♦ : tending to flake

♦ brittle, crisp, crumbly, friable — more at CRISP

flam·beau \'flam-ˌbō\ *n, pl* **flambeaux** \-ˌbōz\ *or* **flambeaus** [F, fr. MF, fr. *flambe* flame] : a flaming torch

flam·boy·ance \flam-'bói-əns\ *n* ♦ : the quality or state of being flamboyant — **flam·boy·an·cy** \-ən-sē\ *n*

♦ flashiness, gaudiness, glitz, ostentation, pretentiousness, showiness, swank — more at OSTENTATION

flam·boy·ant \-ənt\ *adj* ♦ : marked by or given to strikingly elaborate or colorful display or behavior

♦ flashy, garish, gaudy, glitzy, loud, ostentatious, swank, tawdry — more at GAUDY

flam·boy·ant·ly *adv* ♦ : in a flamboyant manner : with flamboyance

♦ flashily, gaily, jauntily, rakishly — more at GAILY

¹flame \'flām\ *n* **1** : the glowing gaseous part of a fire **2** : a state of blazing combustion **3** : a flamelike condition **4** : burning zeal or passion **5** : BRILLIANCE **6** ♦ : a person beloved : SWEETHEART **7** : an angry, hostile, or abusive electronic message

♦ beloved, darling, dear, honey, love, sweet, sweetheart — more at SWEETHEART

²flame *vb* **1** ♦ : to burn with a flame **2** ♦ : to burst or break out violently or passionately **3** ♦ : to shine brightly

♦ [1] blaze, burn, glow — more at BURN ♦ [2] break out, burst, erupt, explode, flare, go off — more at ERUPT ♦ [3] beat, blaze, burn, glare — more at GLARE

fla·men·co \flə-'meŋ-kō\ *n, pl* **-cos** [Sp, fr. *flamenco* of the Gypsies, lit., Flemish, fr. MD *Vlaminc* Fleming] : a vigorous rhythmic dance style of the Spanish Gypsies

flame·throw·er \'flām-ˌthrō-ər\ *n* : a device that expels from a nozzle a burning stream of liquid or semiliquid fuel under pressure

fla·min·go \flə-'miŋ-gō\ *n, pl* **-gos** *also* **-goes** : any of several long-legged long-necked tropical water birds with scarlet wings and a broad bill bent downward

flam·ma·ble \'fla-mə-bəl\ *adj* ♦ : easily ignited and quick-burning — **flam·ma·bil·i·ty** \ˌfla-mə-'bi-lə-tē\ *n* — **flammable** *n*

♦ combustible, ignitable, inflammable — more at COMBUSTIBLE

flan \'flan, 'flän\ *n* **1** : an open pie with a sweet or savory filling **2** : custard baked with a caramel glaze

flange \'flanj\ *n* : a rim used for strengthening or guiding something or for attachment to another object

¹flank \'flaŋk\ *n* **1** : the fleshy part of the side between the ribs and the hip; *also* : the side of a quadruped **2** : SIDE **3** : the right or left of a formation

²flank *vb* **1** : to attack or threaten the flank of **2** ♦ : to be situated on the side of

♦ abut, adjoin, border (on), fringe, join, skirt, touch, verge (on) — more at ADJOIN

flank·er \'flaŋ-kər\ *n* : a football player stationed wide of the formation slightly behind the line of scrimmage as a pass receiver

flan·nel \'flan-ᵊl\ *n* **1** : a soft twilled wool or worsted fabric with a napped surface **2** : a stout cotton fabric napped on one side **3** *pl* : flannel underwear or pants

¹flap \'flap\ *n* **1** : a stroke with something broad : SLAP **2** : something broad, limber, or flat and usu. thin that hangs loose **3** : the motion or sound of something broad and limber as it swings to and fro **4** : a state of excitement or confusion

²flap *vb* **flapped; flap·ping 1** : to beat with something broad and flat : FLING **2** ♦ : to move (as wings) with a beating motion **3** : to sway loosely usu. with a noise of striking

♦ beat, flail, flop, flutter, whip; *also* bang, batter, buffet, knock, pound, smack, spank, thump; flick, flicker, flit; oscillate, sway, swing; undulate, wave; palpitate, pulse, throb

flap·jack \\'flap-,jak\\ *n* ♦ : a flat cake made of thin batter and cooked (as on a griddle) on both sides : PANCAKE

♦ griddle cake, pancake — more at PANCAKE

flap·per \\'fla-pər\\ *n* **1** : one that flaps **2** : a young woman of the 1920s who showed freedom from conventions (as in conduct)

¹**flare** \\'flar\\ *n* **1** ♦ : a blaze of light used esp. to signal or illuminate; *also* : a device for producing such a blaze **2** : an unsteady glaring light **3** ♦ : a sudden outburst (as of sound, excitement, or anger)

♦ [1] blaze, illumination, incandescence, light, luminescence, radiance, shine — more at LIGHT ♦ [3] agony, burst, eruption, explosion, fit, flare-up, flash, outburst, spasm, storm — more at OUTBURST

²**flare** *vb* **flared; flar·ing** **1** ♦ : to flame with a sudden unsteady light **2** ♦ : to spread outward ⟨her skirt *flaring* at the bottom⟩ ⟨a boat with the gunwales *flaring* out⟩ **3** : to become suddenly excited or angry — usu. used with *up* ⟨she ∼s up at the slightest provocation⟩ **4** ♦ : to break out or intensify usu. suddenly or violently — often used with *up* ⟨fighting *flared* up after a 2-week lull⟩

♦ [1] beat, blaze, burn, flame, glare — more at GLARE ♦ *usu* **flare out** [2] expand, extend, fan, open, spread, stretch, unfold ♦ *usu* **flare up** [4] break out, burst, erupt, explode, flame, go off — more at ERUPT

flare–up \\-,əp\\ *n* ♦ : a sudden outburst or intensification

♦ burst, flare, flash, outbreak, outburst, spurt — more at OUTBREAK

¹**flash** \\'flash\\ *vb* **1** : to break forth in or like a sudden flame **2** : to appear or pass suddenly or with great speed **3** ♦ : to send out in or as if in flashes ⟨∼ a message⟩ **4** : to make a sudden display (as of brilliance or feeling) **5** : to gleam or glow intermittently **6** : to fill by a sudden rush of water **7** : to expose to view very briefly ⟨∼ a badge⟩ — **flash·er** *n*

♦ flame, gleam, glimmer, glisten, glitter, shimmer, sparkle, twinkle, wink; *also* beam, radiate, shine; bedazzle, blind, daze, dazzle; blaze, burn, flare, glare, glow

²**flash** *n* **1** : a sudden burst of light **2** : a movement of a flag or light in signaling **3** : a sudden and brilliant burst (as of wit) **4** ♦ : a brief time **5** : SHOW, DISPLAY; *esp* : ostentatious display **6** ♦ : something or someone that attracts notice; *esp* : an outstanding athlete **7** : GLIMPSE, LOOK **8** : a first brief news report **9** : FLASHLIGHT **10** : a device for producing a brief and very bright flash of light for taking photographs **11** : a quick-spreading flame or momentary intense outburst of radiant heat

♦ [4] instant, jiffy, minute, moment, second, shake, twinkling, wink — more at INSTANT ♦ [6] marvel, miracle, phenomenon, prodigy, sensation, wonder — more at WONDER

³**flash** *adj* : of sudden origin and short duration ⟨a ∼ flood⟩

♦ fleeting, momentary, short-lived, transient — more at MOMENTARY

⁴**flash** *adv* : by very brief exposure to an intense agent (as heat or cold) ⟨∼ freeze⟩

flash·back \\'flash-,bak\\ *n* **1** : interruption of the chronological sequence (as of a film or literary work) by an event of earlier occurrence **2** : a past event remembered vividly

flash back *vb* **1** : to vividly remember a past incident **2** : to employ a flashback

flash·bulb \\-,bəlb\\ *n* : an electric bulb that can be used only once to produce a brief and very bright flash of light for taking photographs

flash card *n* : a card bearing words, numbers, or pictures briefly displayed usu. as a learning aid

flash drive *n* : a data storage device that uses flash memory

flash·gun \\-,gən\\ *n* : a device for producing a bright flash of light for photography

flash·i·ly \\-shə-lē\\ *adv* ♦ : in a flashy manner or style

♦ flamboyantly, gaily, jauntily, rakishly — more at GAILY

flash·i·ness \\-shē-nəs\\ *n* ♦ : the quality or state of being flashy

♦ flamboyance, gaudiness, glitz, ostentation, pretentiousness, showiness, swank — more at OSTENTATION

flash·ing \\'fla-shin\\ *n* : sheet metal used in waterproofing (as at the angle between a chimney and a roof)

flash·light \\'flash-,līt\\ *n* : a battery-operated portable electric light

flash memory *n* : a computer memory chip not requiring connection to a power source to retain its data

flashy \\'fla-shē\\ *adj* **flash·i·er; -est** **1** : momentarily dazzling **2** ♦ : superficially attractive or impressive : SHOWY

♦ flamboyant, garish, gaudy, glitzy, loud, ostentatious, showy, swank, tawdry — more at GAUDY

flask \\'flask\\ *n* : a flattened bottle-shaped container ⟨a whiskey ∼⟩

¹**flat** \\'flat\\ *adj* **flat·ter; flat·test** **1** : spread out along a surface; *also* : being or characterized by a horizontal line **2** ♦ : having a smooth, level, or even surface **3** : having a broad smooth surface and little thickness **4** : clearly unmistakable : DOWNRIGHT ⟨a ∼ refusal⟩ **5** : not varying : FIXED ⟨charge a ∼ rate⟩ **6** ♦ : having no fraction either lacking or in excess : EXACT, PRECISE ⟨in four minutes ∼⟩ **7 a** ♦ : lacking in animation, zest, or vigor : DULL, UNINTERESTING **b** ♦ : lacking savor : INSIPID **8** : DEFLATED ⟨a ∼ tire⟩ **9** : lower than the true pitch; *also* : lower by a half step **10** ♦ : free from gloss ⟨a ∼ paint⟩ **11** : lacking depth of characterization — **flat·ly** *adv* — **flat·ness** *n*

♦ [2] even, flush, level, plane, smooth — more at LEVEL ♦ [6] even, exact, precise, round — more at EVEN ♦ [7a] dull, monotonous, uninteresting ♦ [7b] flavorless (*or* flavourless), insipid, tasteless — more at INSIPID ♦ [10] dim, dull, lusterless

²**flat** *n* **1** : a level surface of land : PLAIN **2** : a flat part or surface **3** : a character ♭ that indicates that a specified note is to be lowered by a half step; *also* : the resulting note **4** : something flat **5** : an apartment on one floor **6** : a deflated tire

³**flat** *adv* **1** : FLATLY **2** ♦ : without qualification or reservation : COMPLETELY ⟨∼ broke⟩ **3** : below the true musical pitch

♦ completely, entirely, fully, perfectly, quite, thoroughly, wholly — more at FULLY

⁴**flat** *vb* **flat·ted; flat·ting** **1** : FLATTEN **2** : to lower in pitch esp. by a half step

flat·bed \\'flat-,bed\\ *n* : a truck or trailer with a body in the form of a platform or shallow box

flat·boat \\-,bōt\\ *n* : a flat-bottomed boat used esp. for carrying bulky freight

flat·car \\-,kär\\ *n* : a railroad freight car without sides or roof

flat·fish \\-,fish\\ *n* : any of an order of flattened marine bony fishes with both eyes on the upper side

flat·foot \\-,fút, -'fút\\ *n, pl* **flat·feet** \\-,fēt, -'fēt\\ : a condition in which the arch of the foot is flattened so that the entire sole rests upon the ground — **flat–foot·ed** \\-'fú-təd\\ *adj*

Flat·head \\-,hed\\ *n, pl* **Flatheads** *or* **Flathead** : a member of an American Indian people of Montana

flat·iron \\-,ī(-ə)rn\\ *n* : IRON 3

flat·land \\-,land\\ *n* : land lacking significant variation in elevation

flat–out \\'flat-,aút\\ *adj* **1** : being or going at maximum effort or speed **2** : OUT-AND-OUT, DOWNRIGHT ⟨it was a ∼ lie⟩

flat out *adv* **1** : BLUNTLY, DIRECTLY **2** : at top speed **3** *usu* **flat–out** : to the greatest degree : COMPLETELY ⟨is just *flat-out* confusing⟩

flat–pan·el \\-'pa-nᵊl\\ *adj* : relating to or being a thin flat video display

flat–screen \\-,skrēn\\ *adj* : FLAT-PANEL

flat·ten \\'flat-ᵊn\\ *vb* : to make or become flat

flat·ter \'fla-tər\ vb [ME flateren, fr. AF flater to lap, flatter] **1** ♦ : to praise too much or without sincerity **2** : to represent too favorably ⟨the portrait ∼s him⟩ **3** : to display to advantage **4** : to judge (oneself) favorably or too favorably — **flat·ter·er** n

♦ blarney, overpraise; also cajole, coax, wheedle; fawn, kowtow, toady; idolize, worship; eulogize, extol, laud, praise; applaud, commend, compliment; congratulate, felicitate; drool, gush, slaver, slobber; endear, ingratiate; court, woo

flat·tery \'fla-tə-rē\ n, pl -ter·ies ♦ : flattering speech or attentions : insincere or excessive praise

♦ adulation, blarney, overpraise; also endearments; compliments, greetings, regards, respects; adoration, idolatry, worship; cajolery, endearment; acclaim, applause, commendation, praise

flat·top \'flat-ˌtäp\ n **1** : AIRCRAFT CARRIER **2** : CREW CUT

flat·u·lent \'fla-chə-lənt\ adj **1** : full of gas ⟨a ∼ stomach⟩ **2** : INFLATED, POMPOUS — **flat·u·lence** \-ləns\ n

fla·tus \'flā-təs\ n : gas formed in the intestine or stomach

flat·ware \'flat-ˌwer\ n ♦ : eating and serving utensils

♦ silver, tableware — more at TABLEWARE

flat·worm \-ˌwùrm\ n : any of a phylum of flattened mostly parasitic segmented worms (as trematodes and tapeworms)

flaunt \'flȯnt\ vb **1** ♦ : to display oneself to public notice **2** : to wave or flutter showily **3** : to display ostentatiously or impudently : PARADE — **flaunt** n

♦ display, disport, exhibit, flash, parade, show, show off — more at SHOW

flau·ta \'flaù-tə\ n : a tortilla rolled around a filling and deep-fried

flau·tist \'flȯ-tist, 'flaù-\ n [It flautista] : FLUTIST

¹fla·vor or Can and Brit **fla·vour** \'flā-vər\ n **1** : the quality of something that affects the sense of taste or of taste and smell **2** ♦ : a substance that adds flavor **3** ♦ : characteristic or predominant quality — **fla·vored** \-vərd\ adj — **fla·vor·some** adj

♦ [2] seasoning, spice — more at SEASONING ♦ [3] air, atmosphere, aura, climate, mood, note, temper — more at AURA

²flavor or Can and Brit **flavour** vb ♦ : to give or add flavor to

♦ savor, season, spice — more at SEASON

fla·vor·ful or Can and Brit **flavourful** adj ♦ : full of flavor

♦ appetizing, delectable, delicious, savory, tasty, toothsome, yummy — more at DELICIOUS

fla·vor·ing or Can and Brit **flavouring** n : a substance that flavors : FLAVOR 2

fla·vor·less or Can and Brit **flavourless** adj ♦ : lacking in flavor

♦ flat, insipid, tasteless — more at INSIPID

flaw \'flȯ\ n ♦ : a small often hidden defect — **flaw·less·ness** n

♦ blemish, defect, fault, imperfection, mark — more at BLEMISH

flaw·less adj ♦ : lacking any flaw or imperfection

♦ absolute, faultless, ideal, impeccable, letter-perfect, perfect, unblemished — more at PERFECT

flaw·less·ly \-lē\ adv ♦ : in a flawless manner

♦ faultlessly, ideally, impeccably, perfectly — more at PERFECTLY

flax \'flaks\ n : a fiber that is the source of linen; also : a blue-flowered plant grown for this fiber and its oily seeds

flax·en \'flak-sən\ adj **1** : made of flax **2** ♦ : resembling flax esp. in pale soft straw color

♦ blond, fair, golden, sandy, straw — more at BLOND

flay \'flā\ vb **1** ♦ : to strip off the skin or surface of **2** ♦ : to criticize harshly

♦ [1] bark, hull, husk, peel, shell, skin ♦ [2] admonish, chide, lecture, rail (at or against), rate, rebuke, reprimand, scold — more at SCOLD

fl dr abbr fluid dram

flea \'flē\ n : any of an order of small wingless leaping bloodsucking insects

flea·bane \'flē-ˌbān\ n : any of various plants of the daisy family once believed to drive away fleas

flea–bit·ten \-ˌbit-ᵊn\ adj : bitten by or infested with fleas

flea market n : a usu. open-air market for secondhand articles and antiques

¹fleck \'flek\ vb : to mark in or with spots : STREAK, SPOT

²fleck n **1** ♦ : a small area visibly different (as in color, finish, or material) from the surrounding area : SPOT, MARK **2** ♦ : a small loose mass or bit : PARTICLE

♦ [1] blotch, dapple, dot, mark, speck, spot — more at SPOT ♦ [2] atom, bit, crumb, grain, granule, molecule, particle, speck

fledge \'flej\ vb **fledged; fledg·ing** : to develop the feathers necessary for flying or independent activity

fledg·ling \'flej-liŋ\ n **1** : a young bird with flight feathers newly developed **2** ♦ : an immature or inexperienced person

♦ beginner, greenhorn, neophyte, newcomer, novice, tyro — more at BEGINNER

flee \'flē\ vb **fled** \'fled\; **flee·ing** **1** ♦ : to run away often from danger or evil **2** ♦ : to pass away swiftly from perception

♦ [1] clear out, escape, fly, get out, lam, run away, run off — more at ESCAPE ♦ [2] disappear, dissolve, evaporate, fade, go, melt, vanish — more at DISAPPEAR

¹fleece \'flēs\ n **1** ♦ : the woolly coat of an animal and esp. a sheep **2** : a soft or woolly covering

♦ coat, fur, hair, pelage, pile, wool

²fleece vb **fleeced; fleec·ing** **1** ♦ : to strip of money or property by fraud or extortion **2** ♦ : SHEAR

♦ cheat, defraud, rook, shortchange, skin, squeeze, stick, sting, swindle, victimize; also extort, wrench, wrest, wring; gouge, overcharge, soak; exploit, milk; deceive, dupe, fool, gull, trick; rope (in); betray

fleecy adj ♦ : covered with, made of, or resembling fleece

♦ furry, hairy, unshorn, woolly — more at HAIRY

¹fleet \'flēt\ vb : to pass rapidly

²fleet n [ME flete, fr. OE flēot ship, fr. flēotan to float] **1** : a group of warships under one command **2** ♦ : a group (as of ships, planes, or trucks) under one management

♦ armada, caravan, cavalcade, motorcade, train; also convoy, flotilla, navy; column, cortege, parade, procession

³fleet adj **1** ♦ : swift in motion : SWIFT, NIMBLE **2** : not enduring : FLEETING

♦ breakneck, fast, hasty, lightning, nimble, nippy, quick, rapid, speedy, swift — more at FAST

fleet admiral n : an admiral of the highest rank in the navy

fleet·ing \'flē-tiŋ\ adj ♦ : passing swiftly

♦ ephemeral, evanescent, momentary, short-lived, transient — more at MOMENTARY

fleet·ness n ♦ : the quality or state of being fleet

♦ celerity, fastness, haste, hurry, quickness, rapidity, speed, swiftness, velocity — more at SPEED

Flem·ing \'fle-miŋ\ n : a member of a Germanic people inhabiting chiefly northern Belgium

Flem·ish \'fle-mish\ n **1** : the Dutch language as spoken by the Flemings **2 Flemish** pl : FLEMINGS — **Flemish** adj

fle·ro·vi·um \flə-'trō-vē-əm\ n : a short-lived artifically produced radioactive chemical element

¹flesh \'flesh\ n **1** : the soft parts of an animal's body; esp : muscular tissue **2** : MEAT **3** : the physical nature of humans as distinguished from the soul **4** : human beings; also : living beings **5** : STOCK, KINDRED **6** : fleshy plant tissue (as fruit pulp) — **fleshed** \'flesht\ adj

²flesh vb ♦ : to make fuller or more nearly complete — usu. used with out

♦ usu **flesh out** amplify, develop, elaborate (on), enlarge (on), expand — more at EXPAND

flesh fly *n* : a dipteran fly whose maggots feed on flesh

flesh·ly \'flesh-lē\ *adj* **1** ♦ : of or relating to the flesh or body : CORPOREAL, BODILY **2** ♦ : not spiritual : WORLDLY **3** ♦ : of or relating to bodily appetites : CARNAL, SENSUAL

♦ [1] animal, bodily, carnal, corporal, material, physical, somatic — more at PHYSICAL ♦ [2] carnal, earthly, material, mundane, temporal, terrestrial, worldly — more at EARTHLY ♦ [3] carnal, luscious, sensual, sensuous, voluptuous — more at SENSUAL

flesh·pot \'flesh-ˌpät\ *n* **1** *pl* : bodily comfort : LUXURY **2** : a place of lascivious entertainment — usu. used in pl.

fleshy \'fle-shē\ *adj* **flesh·i·er; -est** **1** : consisting of or resembling animal flesh **2** ♦ : marked by abundant flesh : PLUMP, FAT **3** ♦ : full of juice

♦ [2] chubby, fat, plump, portly, rotund, round — more at FAT ♦ [3] juicy, pulpy, succulent — more at JUICY

flew *past of* ¹FLY

flex \'fleks\ *vb* : to bend esp. repeatedly — **flex** *n*

flex·i·ble \'flek-sə-bəl\ *adj* **1** ♦ : capable of being flexed **2** ♦ : yielding to influence **3** ♦ : readily changed or changing — **flex·i·bil·i·ty** \ˌflek-sə-'bi-lə-tē\ *n*

♦ [1] limber, lissome, lithe, pliable, supple, willowy — more at WILLOWY ♦ [1] elastic, resilient, rubbery, springy, stretch, supple — more at ELASTIC ♦ [2, 3] easygoing, relaxed, unrestrained, unrestricted — more at EASYGOING ♦ [3] adaptable, adjustable, changeable, elastic, fluid, malleable, variable; *also* changing, fluctuating, inconstant, unstable, unsteady *Ant* established, fixed, immutable

flex·or \'flek-sər, -ˌsȯr\ *n* : a muscle serving to bend a body part

flex·ure \'flek-shər\ *n* : TURN, FOLD

flib·ber·ti·gib·bet \ˌfli-bər-tē-'ji-bət\ *n* : a silly flighty person

¹**flick** \'flik\ *n* **1** : a light sharp jerky stroke or movement **2** : a sound produced by a flick **3** : ²FLICKER

²**flick** *vb* **1** : to strike lightly with a quick sharp motion **2** : FLUTTER, FLIT

³**flick** *n* : MOVIE ⟨can't wait to catch the new *flick* at the theater⟩

¹**flick·er** \'fli-kər\ *vb* **1** : to move irregularly or unsteadily : FLUTTER **2** : to burn fitfully or with a fluctuating light — **flick·er·ing·ly** *adv*

²**flicker** *n* **1** : an act of flickering **2** : a sudden brief movement ⟨a ~ of an eyelid⟩ **3** : a momentary stirring ⟨a ~ of interest⟩ **4** : a slight indication : HINT **5** : a wavering light

³**flicker** *n* : a large barred and spotted No. American woodpecker with a brown back that occurs as an eastern form with yellow on the underside of the wings and tail and a western form with red in these areas

flied *past and past part of* ³FLY

fli·er \'flī-ər\ *n* **1** ♦ : one that flies; *esp* : PILOT **2** ♦ : a reckless or speculative undertaking **3** *usu* **fly·er** ♦ : an advertising circular

♦ [1] airman, aviator, pilot — more at PILOT ♦ [2] chance, enterprise, gamble, speculation, venture — more at GAMBLE ♦ *usu* **flyer** [3] circular, leaflet, pamphlet — more at PAMPHLET

¹**flight** \'flīt\ *n* **1** : an act or instance of flying **2** : the ability to fly **3** : a passing through air or space **4** : the distance covered in a flight **5** : swift movement **6** : a trip made by or in an airplane or spacecraft **7** : a group of similar individuals (as birds or airplanes) flying as a unit **8** : a passing (as of the imagination) beyond ordinary limits **9** : a series of stairs from one landing to another — **flight·less** *adj*

²**flight** *n* ♦ : an act or instance of running away

♦ escape, getaway, lam, slip — more at ESCAPE

flight bag *n* **1** : a lightweight traveling bag with zippered outside pockets **2** : a small canvas satchel

flight·i·ness \-tē-nəs\ *n* ♦ : the quality or state of being flighty

♦ facetiousness, flippancy, frivolity, levity, lightness — more at FRIVOLITY

flight line *n* : a parking and servicing area for airplanes

flighty \'flī-tē\ *adj* **flight·i·er; -est** **1** : easily upset : VOLATILE **2** ♦ : easily excited : SKITTISH **3** ♦ : governed or characterized by caprice : CAPRICIOUS, SILLY

♦ [2] excitable, fluttery, high-strung, jittery, jumpy, nervous, skittish, spooky — more at EXCITABLE ♦ [3] capricious, frivolous, giddy, harebrained, scatterbrained, silly — more at GIDDY

flim·flam \'flim-ˌflam\ *n* : DECEPTION, FRAUD — **flim·flam·mery** \-ˌfla-mə-re\ *n*

flim·sy \'flim-zē\ *adj* **flim·si·er; -est** **1** ♦ : lacking strength or substance **2** ♦ : of inferior materials and workmanship **3** ♦ : having little worth or plausibility ⟨a ~ excuse⟩ — **flim·si·ly** \-zə-lē\ *adv* — **flim·si·ness** \-zē-nəs\ *n*

♦ [1, 2] gauzy, insubstantial, unsubstantial; *also* dainty, delicate, fine; feeble, fragile, frail; sheer, transparent *Ant* sturdy, substantial ♦ [3] doubtful, dubious, improbable, questionable, unlikely — more at IMPROBABLE

flinch \'flinch\ *vb* [MF *flenchir* to bend] ♦ : to shrink from or as if from pain : WINCE — **flinch** *n*

♦ blench, quail, recoil, shrink, wince; *also* blanch, pale, whiten; quake, quiver, shake, shudder, tremble; crouch; jerk, start, twitch; recede, retire, retreat, withdraw; falter, hesitate, reel, waver

¹**fling** \'fliŋ\ *vb* **flung** \'fləŋ\; **fling·ing** **1** : to move hastily, brusquely, or violently ⟨*flung* out of the room⟩ **2** : to kick or plunge vigorously **3 a** : to throw with force or recklessness **b** ♦ : to cast as if by throwing **4** : to put suddenly into a state or condition

♦ cast, catapult, chuck, hurl, hurtle, launch, pitch, sling, throw, toss — more at THROW

²**fling** *n* **1** : an act or instance of flinging **2** ♦ : a casual try : ATTEMPT **3** ♦ : a period of self-indulgence

♦ [2] attempt, bid, endeavor (*or* endeavour), essay, go, pass, shot, stab, trial, try, whack, whirl — more at ATTEMPT ♦ [3] frolic, gambol, lark, revel, rollick, romp; *also* caper, escapade, prank; antic; merriment, merrymaking; enjoyment, indulgence, pleasure, self-indulgence; amusement, diversion, entertainment

flint \'flint\ *n* **1** : a hard quartz that produces a spark when struck by steel **2** : an alloy used for producing a spark in lighters

flint glass *n* : heavy glass containing an oxide of lead and used in lenses and prisms

flint·lock \'flint-ˌläk\ *n* **1** : a lock for a gun using a flint to ignite the charge **2** : a firearm fitted with a flintlock

flinty *adj* ♦ : harsh and unyielding : rigorous and stern

♦ austere, authoritarian, hard, harsh, rigorous, severe, stern, strict — more at SEVERE

¹**flip** \'flip\ *vb* **flipped; flip·ping** **1** : to turn by tossing ⟨~ a coin⟩ **2** ♦ : to turn over; *also* : to leaf through **3** : FLICK, JERK ⟨~ a light switch⟩ **4** ♦ : to lose self-control — **flip** *n*

♦ [2] reverse, turn — more at REVERSE ♦ [4] break, crack, freak — more at CRACK

²**flip** *adj* : glib or pert in speech : FLIPPANT

flip·pan·cy \'fli-pən-sē\ *n* ♦ : the quality or state of being flippant

♦ facetiousness, flightiness, frivolity, levity, lightness — more at FRIVOLITY

flip·pant \'fli-pənt\ *adj* ♦ : lacking proper respect or seriousness

♦ facetious, flip, pert, smart; *also* flighty, frivolous; cheeky, cocky, cute, fresh, impertinent, impish, impudent, mischievous, playful, roguish, sassy, saucy, waggish; disrespectful, rude; breezy, casual, glib, inappropriate, thoughtless *Ant* earnest, sincere

flip·per \'fli-pər\ *n* **1** : a broad flat limb (as of a seal) adapted for swimming **2** : a paddlelike shoe used in skin diving

flip side *n* : the reverse and usu. less popular side of a phonograph record

¹flirt \\'flərt\\ *vb* 1 : to move erratically : FLIT 2 : to behave amorously without serious intent 3 : to show casual interest ⟨~*ed* with the idea⟩; *also* : to come close to ⟨~ with danger⟩ — **flir·ta·tion** \\,flər-'tā-shən\\ *n* — **flir·ta·tious** \\-shəs\\ *adj*

²flirt *n* 1 : an act or instance of flirting 2 : a person who flirts

flit \\'flit\\ *vb* **flit·ted; flit·ting** ♦ : to pass or move quickly or abruptly from place to place : DART — **flit** *n*

 ♦ dance, dart, flutter, zip; *also* dash, fly, sail, shoot, speed, sprint, zoom; scamper, scud, scurry, scuttle, skip, skitter; meander, ramble, roam, wander

flitch \\'flich\\ *n* : a side of cured meat; *esp* : a side of bacon

fliv·ver \\'fli-vər\\ *n* : a small cheap usu. old automobile

¹float \\'flōt\\ *n* 1 ♦ : something (as a raft) that floats; *also* : a floating platform anchored near a shoreline for use by swimmers or boats 2 : a cork buoying up the baited end of a fishing line 3 : a hollow ball that floats at the end of a lever in a cistern or tank and regulates the liquid level 4 : a vehicle with a platform to carry an exhibit 5 : a soft drink with ice cream floating in it

 ♦ dock, jetty, landing, levee, pier, quay, wharf — more at DOCK

²float *vb* 1 : to rest on the surface of or be suspended in a fluid 2 ♦ : to move gently on or through a fluid 3 : to cause to float 4 : WANDER 5 : to offer (securities) in order to finance an enterprise 6 : to finance by floating an issue of stocks or bonds 7 : to arrange for ⟨~ a loan⟩ — **float·er** *n*

 ♦ drift, glide, hang, hover, poise, ride, sail, waft; *also* bob, dangle, suspend; buoy; balloon, raft **Ant** settle, sink

¹flock \\'fläk\\ *n* 1 : a group of birds or mammals assembled or herded together 2 : a group of people under the guidance of a leader; *esp* : CONGREGATION 3 ♦ : a large number ⟨a ~ of tourists⟩

 ♦ army, crowd, crush, drove, horde, host, legion, mob, multitude, press, swarm, throng — more at CROWD

²flock *vb* ♦ : to gather or move in a flock ⟨people ~*ed* to the beach⟩

 ♦ crowd, mob, swarm, throng — more at CROWD

floe \\'flō\\ *n* : a flat mass of floating ice

flog \\'fläg\\ *vb* **flogged; flog·ging** 1 ♦ : to beat with or as if with a rod or whip 2 : SELL ⟨~ encyclopedias⟩ — **flog·ger** *n*

 ♦ bash, bat, batter, beat, belt, bludgeon, buffet, club, drub, hammer, hide, lace, lambaste, lick, maul, pelt, pound, thrash, thump, wallop, whale, whip — more at BEAT

¹flood \\'fləd\\ *n* 1 ♦ : a great flow of water over the land 2 : the flowing in of the tide 3 ♦ : an overwhelming volume

 ♦ [1, 3] cataclysm, cataract, deluge, inundation, overflow, spate, torrent; *also* current, river, stream, tide; discharge, flush, gush, outflow, outpouring; flux, inflow, influx; washout; avalanche; cascade, waterfall; excess, glut, overabundance, overage, overkill, overmuch, oversupply, superabundance, superfluity, surfeit, surplus **Ant** drought

²flood *vb* 1 ♦ : to cover or become filled with a flood 2 : to fill abundantly or excessively; *esp* : to supply an excess of fuel to ⟨~*ed* the engine⟩ 3 : to pour forth in a flood — **flood·er** *n*

 ♦ deluge, drown, engulf, inundate, overflow, overwhelm, submerge, swamp; *also* overcome, flow, flush, gush, pour, sluice, spout, spurt, stream; douse, drench **Ant** drain

flood·gate \\'fləd-,gāt\\ *n* : a gate for controlling a body of water : SLUICE

flood·light \\-,līt\\ *n* : a lamp that throws a broad beam of light; *also* : the beam itself — **floodlight** *vb*

flood·plain \\-,plān\\ *n* : a plain along a river or stream subject to periodic flooding

flood tide *n* 1 : a rising tide 2 : an overwhelming quantity 3 : a high point

flood·wa·ter \\'fləd-,wȯ-tər, -,wä-\\ *n* : the water of a flood

¹floor \\'flȯr\\ *n* 1 : the bottom of a room on which one stands 2 : a ground surface 3 : a story of a building 4 : a main level space (as in a legislative chamber) distinguished from a platform or gallery 5 : AUDIENCE 6 : the right to address an assembly 7 : a lower limit ⟨put a ~ under wheat prices⟩ — **floor·ing** *n*

²floor *vb* 1 : to furnish with a floor 2 ♦ : to knock down 3 ♦ : to overwhelm with shock, surprise, or wonder ⟨was ~*ed* by the news⟩ 4 : to press (a vehicle's accelerator) to the floorboard esp. rapidly

 ♦ [2] bowl, down, drop, fell, knock, level ♦ [3] amaze, astonish, astound, bowl, dumbfound, flabbergast, overwhelm, shock, startle, stun, surprise

floor·board \\-,bȯrd\\ *n* 1 : a board in a floor 2 : the floor of an automobile

floor leader *n* : a member of a legislative body who has charge of a party's organization and strategy on the floor

floor show *n* : a series of acts presented in a nightclub

floor·walk·er \\'flȯr-,wȯ-kər\\ *n* : a person employed in a retail store to oversee the sales force and aid customers

floo·zy *or* **floo·zie** \\'flü-zē\\ *n, pl* **floozies** : a usu. young woman of loose morals

¹flop \\'fläp\\ *vb* **flopped; flop·ping** 1 ♦ : to swing or move loosely : FLAP 2 ♦ : to throw oneself down heavily, clumsily, or in a relaxed manner ⟨*flopped* into a chair⟩ 3 ♦ : to fall short of success : FAIL ⟨the show *flopped*⟩ — **flop** *adv* — **flop·per** *n*

 ♦ [1] beat, flail, flap, flutter, whip — more at FLAP
 ♦ [2] plop, plump, plunk; *also* fling, heave, sling, toss; ensconce, install, plant, settle ♦ [3] collapse, fail, flunk, fold, wash out — more at FAIL

²flop *n* ♦ : something that is a failure

 ♦ bust, debacle, dud, failure, fiasco, fizzle, loser, washout — more at FAILURE

flop·house \\'fläp-,haus\\ *n* : a cheap hotel

¹flop·py \\'flä-pē\\ *adj* **flop·pi·er; -est** ♦ : tending to flop; *esp* : soft and flexible — **flop·pi·ly** \\-pə-lē\\ *adv*

 ♦ droopy, flaccid, lank, limp, slack, yielding — more at LIMP

²floppy *n, pl* **flop·pies** : FLOPPY DISK

floppy disk *n* : a thin plastic disk with a magnetic coating on which computer data can be stored

flop sweat *n* : sweat caused by the fear of failing

flo·ra \\'flȯr-ə\\ *n, pl* **floras** *also* **flo·rae** \\-,ē, -,ī\\ [L *Flora*, Roman goddess of flowers] ♦ : plants or plant life esp. of a region or period

 ♦ foliage, green, greenery, herbage, leafage, vegetation, verdure — more at GREENERY

flo·ral \\'flȯr-əl\\ *adj* : of, relating to, or depicting flowers ⟨a ~ design⟩

flo·res·cence \\flȯ-'res-ᵊns, flə-\\ *n* : a state or period of being in bloom or flourishing — **flo·res·cent** \\-ᵊnt\\ *adj*

flor·id \\'flȯr-əd\\ *adj* 1 ♦ : very flowery in style ⟨~ prose⟩ 2 ♦ : tinged with red : RUDDY 3 : marked by emotional or sexual fervor ⟨a ~ love letter⟩

 ♦ [1] flowery, grandiloquent, highfalutin, high-flown — more at FLOWERY ♦ [2] flush, glowing, rosy, ruddy, sanguine — more at RUDDY

flo·rin \\'flȯr-ən\\ *n* 1 : an old gold coin first struck at Florence, Italy, in 1252 2 : a gold coin of a European country patterned after the florin of Florence 3 : any of several modern silver coins issued in Commonwealth countries

flo·rist \\'flȯr-ist\\ *n* : a person who sells flowers or ornamental plants

¹floss \\'fläs\\ *n* 1 : soft thread of silk or mercerized cotton for embroidery 2 : DENTAL FLOSS 3 ♦ : fluffy fibrous material

 ♦ down, fluff, fur, fuzz, lint, nap, pile — more at FUZZ

²floss *vb* : to use dental floss on (one's teeth)

flossy \'flä-sē\ *adj* **floss·i·er; -est** **1** : of, relating to, or having the characteristics of floss **2** : STYLISH, GLAMOROUS — **floss·i·ly** \-sə-lē\ *adv*

flo·ta·tion \flō-'tā-shən\ *n* : the process or an instance of floating

flo·til·la \flō-'ti-lə\ *n* [Sp, dim. of *flota* fleet] : a fleet esp. of small ships

flot·sam \'flät-səm\ *n* : floating wreckage of a ship or its cargo

¹flounce \'flaůns\ *vb* **flounced; flounc·ing** **1** : to move with exaggerated jerky or bouncy motions **2** : to go with sudden determination

²flounce *n* : an act or instance of flouncing — **flouncy** \'flaůn-sē\ *adj*

³flounce *n* ◆ : a strip of fabric attached by one edge; *also* : a wide ruffle

◆ frill, furbelow, ruffle — more at RUFFLE

¹floun·der \'flaůn-dər\ *n, pl* **flounder** *or* **flounders** : FLATFISH; *esp* : any of various important marine food fishes

²flounder *vb* **1** : to struggle to move or obtain footing **2** ◆ : to proceed clumsily ⟨∼ed through the speech⟩

◆ limp, lumber, plod, stumble; *also* shamble, shuffle; wallow, welter; falter, lurch, reel, stagger, sway, teeter, totter; blunder, fumble, muddle

¹flour \'flaůr\ *n* [ME, flower, best of anything, flour, fr. AF *flur* flower] **1** : finely ground and sifted meal of a grain (as wheat); *also* : a fine soft powder

²flour *vb* : to coat with or as if with flour

¹flour·ish \'flar-ish\ *vb* **1** ◆ : to grow luxuriantly : THRIVE, PROSPER **2** : to be in a state of activity or production ⟨∼ed about 1850⟩ **3** ◆ : to reach a height of development or influence **4** : to make bold and sweeping gestures **5** : BRANDISH ⟨∼ed his sword⟩

◆ [1] burgeon, prosper, thrive — more at THRIVE
◆ [3] prosper, succeed, thrive — more at SUCCEED

²flourish *n* **1** : a florid bit of speech or writing; *also* : an ornamental touch or decorative detail **2** : FANFARE **3** : WAVE ⟨with a ∼ of his cane⟩ **4** : showiness in doing something

floury *adj* ◆ : of or resembling flour esp. in fine powdery texture

◆ dusty, fine, powdery — more at FINE

¹flout \'flaůt\ *vb* ◆ : to treat with contemptuous disregard ⟨∼ the law⟩ — **flout·er** *n*

◆ despise, disregard, scorn — more at SCORN

²flout *n* : TAUNT

¹flow \'flō\ *vb* **1** ◆ : to issue or move in a stream **2** : RISE ⟨the tide ebbs and ∼s⟩ **3** : ABOUND **4** ◆ : to proceed smoothly and readily **5** : to have a smooth continuity **6** : to hang loose and billowing **7** : COME, ARISE **8** : MENSTRUATE

◆ [1] pour, roll, run, stream; *also* arise, emanate, issue, spring; course, race, rush; gush, spout, spurt; deluge, engulf, flood, inundate, overflow, swamp; cascade, dribble, drip, gutter, ripple, trickle; flush *Ant* back up
◆ [4] breeze, coast, glide, roll, sail, slide, slip, stream, sweep *Ant* flounder, struggle

²flow *n* **1** : an act of flowing **2** : FLOOD 1, 2 **3** : a smooth uninterrupted movement **4** : STREAM; *also* : a mass of material that has flowed when molten **5** : the quantity that flows in a certain time **6** : MENSTRUATION **7** : a continuous transfer of energy — **flow·age** \'flō-ij\ *n*

flow·chart \'flō-,chärt\ *n* : a symbolic diagram showing step-by-step progression through a procedure

flow diagram *n* : FLOWCHART

¹flow·er \'flaů(-ə)r\ *n* [ME *flour*, fr. AF *flur, flour*, fr. L *flor-, flos*] **1** : a plant shoot modified for reproduction and bearing leaves specialized into floral organs; *esp* : one of a seed plant consisting of a calyx, corolla, stamens, and carpels **2** : a plant cultivated for its blossoms **3** ◆ : the best part or example **4** ◆ : the finest most vigorous period **5** : a state of blooming or flourishing — **flow·ered** \'flaů(-ə)rd\ *adj* — **flow·er·less** *adj* — **flow·er·like** \-,līk\ *adj*

◆ [3] best, choice, cream, elite, pick, prime — more at ELITE ◆ [4] bloom, blossom, flush, heyday, prime — more at BLOOM

²flower *vb* **1** : DEVELOP; *also* : FLOURISH **2** ◆ : to produce flowers : BLOOM

◆ bloom, blossom, blow, burgeon, unfold — more at BLOOM

flower girl *n* : a little girl who carries flowers at a wedding

flower head *n* : a compact cluster of small flowers without stems suggesting a single flower

flowering plant *n* : any of a major group of vascular plants (as magnolias, grasses, or roses) that produce flowers and fruit and have the seeds enclosed in an ovary

flow·er·pot \'flaů(-ə)r-,pät\ *n* : a pot in which to grow plants

flow·ery \'flaů(-ə)r-ē\ *adj* **1** : of, relating to, or resembling flowers **2** ◆ : full of fine words or phrases ⟨a ∼ speech⟩ — **flow·er·i·ly** \-ə-lē\ *adv* — **flow·er·i·ness** \-ē-nəs\ *n*

◆ florid, grandiloquent, highfalutin, high-flown; *also* affected, grandiose, inflated, pompous, pretentious, stilted; excessive, fulsome; boastful, bombastic; elevated, eloquent, lofty

flown \'flōn\ *past part of* **¹FLY**

fl oz *abbr* fluid ounce

flu \'flü\ *n* **1** : INFLUENZA **2** : any of several virus diseases marked esp. by respiratory or intestinal symptoms — **flu-like** \-,līk\ *adj*

¹flub \'fləb\ *vb* **flubbed; flub·bing** ◆ : to make a mess of : BOTCH

◆ bobble, botch, bungle, foul up, fumble, mangle, mess up, screw up

²flub *n* ◆ : a clumsy or stupid failure

◆ blunder, error, fault, fumble, goof, mistake, slip, stumble — more at ERROR

fluc·tu·ate \'flək-chə-,wāt\ *vb* **-at·ed; -at·ing** **1** ◆ : to become wavering, unsteady, irresolute, or undetermined **2** : to move up and down or back and forth — **fluc·tu·a·tion** \,flək-chə-'wā-shən\ *n*

◆ change, mutate, shift, vary — more at CHANGE

flue \'flü\ *n* : a passage (as in a chimney) for directing a current (as of smoke or gases)

flu·ent \'flü-ənt\ *adj* **1** : capable of flowing : FLUID **2** ◆ : ready or facile in speech ⟨∼ in French⟩; *also* : having or showing mastery in a subject or skill **3** ◆ : effortlessly smooth and rapid ⟨∼ speech⟩ — **flu·en·cy** \-ən-sē\ *n*

◆ [2] articulate, eloquent, well-spoken — more at ARTICULATE ◆ [3] easy, effortless, facile, fluid, ready, simple, smooth

flu·ent·ly \-lē\ *adv* ◆ : in a fluent manner

◆ easily, effortlessly, freely, handily, lightly, painlessly, readily, smoothly — more at EASILY

flue pipe *n* : an organ pipe whose tone is produced by an air current striking the beveled opening of the pipe

¹fluff \'fləf\ *n* **1** : ⁷DOWN 1 ⟨∼ from a pillow⟩ **2** ◆ : something fluffy **3** : something inconsequential **4** : BLUNDER; *esp* : an actor's lapse of memory

◆ down, floss, fur, fuzz, lint, nap, pile — more at FUZZ

²fluff *vb* **1** : to make or become fluffy ⟨∼ up a pillow⟩ **2** : to make a mistake

fluffy \'flə-fē\ *adj* **fluff·i·er; -est** **1** : covered with or resembling fluff **2** ◆ : being light and soft or airy **3** : lacking in meaning or substance — **fluff·i·ly** \-fə-lē\ *adv*

◆ airy, ethereal, light — more at AIRY

¹flu·id \'flü-əd\ *adj* **1** ◆ : capable of flowing **2** ◆ : subject to change or movement **3** ◆ : showing a smooth easy style ⟨∼ movements⟩ **4** : available for a different use; *esp* : LIQUID **5** ⟨∼ assets⟩ — **flu·id·i·ty** \flü-'i-də-tē\ *n* — **flu·id·ly** *adv*

◆ [1] fluent, liquid, runny; *also* diluted, thin, watery, weak *Ant* hard, solid ◆ [2] adaptable, adjustable, changeable, elastic, flexible, malleable, variable—more at FLEXIBLE ✦ [3] easy, effortless, facile, fluent, light, ready, smooth

²**fluid** *n* : a substance (as a liquid or gas) tending to flow or take the shape of its container

fluid dram *or* **flu·i·dram** \ˌflü-ə-ˈdram\ *n* : a unit of liquid measure equal to ⅛ fluid ounce

fluid ounce *n* : a unit of liquid measure equal to ¹/₁₆ pint in the U.S. or ¹/₂₀ pint in the U.K.

¹**fluke** \ˈflük\ *n* : any of various trematode flatworms

²**fluke** *n* 1 : the part of an anchor that fastens in the ground 2 : a lobe of a whale's tail

³**fluke** *n* : a stroke of luck

fluky *also* **fluk·ey** \ˈflü-kē\ *adj* 1 ✦ : happening or depending on chance rather than skill 2 : light and uncertain

✦ accidental, casual, chance, fortuitous, incidental, unplanned

flume \ˈflüm\ *n* 1 ✦ : an inclined channel for carrying water 2 ✦ : a ravine or gorge with a stream running through it

✦ [1] aqueduct, canal, channel, conduit, raceway, watercourse — more at CHANNEL ✦ [2] canyon, defile, gap, gorge, gulch, notch, pass, ravine — more at CANYON

flung *past and past part of* FLING

flunk \ˈfləŋk\ *vb* ✦ : to fail esp. in an examination or course — **flunk** *n*

✦ collapse, fail, flop, fold, wash out — more at FAIL

flun·ky *also* **flun·key** *or* **flun·kie** \ˈfləŋ-kē\ *n, pl* **flunkies** *also* **flunkeys** 1 a : a liveried servant b ✦ : one performing menial or miscellaneous duties 2 : YES-MAN

✦ domestic, lackey, menial, retainer, servant, steward — more at SERVANT

fluo·res·cence \flȯ-ˈres-ᵊns\ *n* 1 : luminescence caused by radiation absorption that ceases almost immediately after the incident radiation has stopped 2 ✦ : visible emitted radiation — **fluo·resce** \-ˈres\ *vb* — **fluo·res·cent** \-ˈres-ᵊnt\ *adj*

✦ glow, illumination, incandescence, light, luminescence, radiance, shine — more at LIGHT

fluorescent lamp *n* : a tubular electric lamp in which light is produced by the action of ultraviolet light on a fluorescent material that coats the inner surface of the lamp

fluo·ri·date \ˈflȯr-ə-ˌdāt\ *vb* **-dat·ed; -dat·ing** : to add a fluoride to (as drinking water) to reduce tooth decay — **fluo·ri·da·tion** \ˌflȯr-ə-ˈdā-shən\ *n*

fluo·ride \ˈflȯr-ˌīd\ *n* : a compound of fluorine

fluo·ri·nate \ˈflȯr-ə-ˌnāt\ *vb* **-nat·ed; -nat·ing** : to treat or cause to combine with fluorine or a compound of fluorine — **fluo·ri·na·tion** \ˌflȯr-ə-ˈnā-shən\ *n*

fluo·rine \ˈflȯr-ˌēn, -ən\ *n* : a pale yellowish flammable irritating toxic gaseous chemical element

fluo·rite \ˈflȯr-ˌīt\ *n* : a mineral that consists of the fluoride of calcium used as a flux and in making glass

fluo·ro·car·bon \ˌflȯr-ō-ˈkär-bən\ *n* : a compound containing fluorine and carbon used chiefly as a lubricant, refrigerant, or nonstick coating; *also* : CHLOROFLUOROCARBON

fluo·ro·scope \ˈflȯr-ə-ˌskōp\ *n* : an instrument for observing the internal structure of an opaque object (as the living body) by means of X-rays — **fluo·ro·scop·ic** \ˌflȯr-ə-ˈskä-pik\ *adj* — **fluo·ros·co·py** \-ˈä-skə-pē\ *n*

fluo·ro·sis \ˌflu̇-ˈrō-səs, ˌflȯ-\ *n* : an abnormal condition (as spotting of the teeth) caused by fluorine or its compounds

flu·ox·e·tine \flü-ˈäk-sə-ˌtēn\ *n* : an antidepressant drug that enhances serotonin activity

flur·ry \ˈflər-ē\ *n, pl* **flurries** 1 : a gust of wind 2 : a brief light snowfall 3 : COMMOTION, BUSTLE 4 ✦ : a brief outburst of activity ⟨a ∼ of trading⟩ — **flurry** *vb*

✦ [1] blast, blow, gust, williwaw — more at GUST ✦ [4] burst, flash, outbreak, outburst, spurt — more at OUTBREAK

¹**flush** \ˈfləsh\ *vb* : to cause (a bird) to fly away suddenly

²**flush** *n* : a hand of cards all of the same suit

³**flush** *n* 1 : a sudden flow (as of water) 2 : a surge esp. of emotion ⟨a ∼ of triumph⟩ 3 : a tinge of red : BLUSH 4 ✦ : a fresh and vigorous state ⟨in the ∼ of youth⟩ 5 : a passing sensation of extreme heat

✦ bloom, blossom, flower, heyday, prime — more at BLOOM

⁴**flush** *vb* 1 : to flow and spread suddenly and freely 2 : to glow brightly 3 ✦ : to become red in the face esp. from shame, modesty, or confusion : BLUSH 4 ✦ : to wash out with a rush of fluid 5 : INFLAME, EXCITE ⟨was ∼ed with anger⟩ 6 : to cause to blush

✦ [3] bloom, blush, color (*or* colour), crimson, glow, redden — more at BLUSH ✦ [4] irrigate, rinse, sluice, wash; *also* deluge, engulf, flood, inundate, swamp; flow, gush, rush, stream; douche, hose; drench, saturate, soak; douse, slosh, splash

⁵**flush** *adj* 1 ✦ : of a ruddy healthy color 2 : full of life and vigor 3 ✦ : filled to overflowing 4 ✦ : fully or generously supplied usu. with money : AFFLUENT 5 : readily available : ABUNDANT 6 ✦ : having an unbroken or even surface 7 : directly abutting : immediately adjacent 8 : set even with an edge of a type page or column — **flush·ness** *n*

✦ [1] florid, glowing, rosy, ruddy ✦ [3] fraught, replete, rife, thick ✦ [4] affluent, loaded, moneyed, opulent, rich, wealthy, well-fixed, well-heeled, well-off, well-to-do — more at RICH ✦ [6] even, flat, level, plane, smooth — more at LEVEL

⁶**flush** *adv* 1 : in a flush manner 2 : SQUARELY ⟨a blow ∼ on the chin⟩

⁷**flush** *vb* : to make flush

¹**flus·ter** \ˈfləs-tər\ *vb* ✦ : to put into a state of agitated confusion

✦ abash, confound, confuse, discomfit, disconcert, embarrass, rattle — more at EMBARRASS

²**fluster** *n* ✦ : a state of agitated confusion

✦ abashment, confusion, discomfiture, dither, embarrassment, fret

flute \ˈflüt\ *n* 1 : a hollow pipelike musical instrument 2 : a grooved pleat 3 : GROOVE — **flute** *vb* — **flut·ed** *adj*

flut·ing *n* : fluted decoration

flut·ist \ˈflü-tist\ *n* : a flute player

¹**flut·ter** \ˈflə-tər\ *vb* [ME *floteren* to float, flutter, fr. OE *floterian*, fr. *flotian* to float] 1 : to flap the wings rapidly 2 ✦ : to move with quick wavering or flapping motions 3 : to vibrate in irregular spasms 4 : to move about or behave in an agitated aimless manner

✦ beat, flail, flap, flop, whip — more at FLAP

²**flutter** *n* 1 : an act of fluttering 2 : a state of nervous confusion 3 : a sudden but usu. slight stir : FLURRY

flut·tery \-tə-rē\ *adj* ✦ : given to or characterized by fluttering

✦ excitable, flighty, high-strung, jittery, jumpy, nervous, skittish, spooky — more at EXCITABLE

¹**flux** \ˈfləks\ *n* 1 : an act of flowing 2 : a state of continuous change 3 : a substance used to aid in fusing metals

²**flux** *vb* : to become or cause to become fluid

✦ deliquesce, fuse, liquefy, melt, run, thaw — more at LIQUEFY

¹**fly** \ˈflī\ *vb* **flew** \ˈflü\; **flown** \ˈflōn\; **fly·ing** 1 ✦ : to move in or pass through the air with wings 2 : to move through the air or before the wind 3 : to float or cause to float, wave, or soar in the air 4 ✦ : to take flight : FLEE 5 : to fade and disappear : VANISH 6 ✦ : to move or pass swiftly 7 : to become expended or dissipated rapidly 8 : to operate or travel in an aircraft or spacecraft 9 : to journey over by flying 10 : AVOID, SHUN 11 : to transport by flying

✦ [1] glide, plane, soar, wing; *also* drift, float, hang, hover, waft; coast, cruise, sail, sweep; dart, flit, flutter; catapult, jet, orbit, rocket ✦ [4] abscond, clear out, escape, flee, get out, lam, run away, run off — more at ESCAPE ✦ [6] barrel, bolt, career, course, dash, hasten, hurry, pelt, race, run, rush, speed, tear, zip, zoom — more at HURRY

²fly *n, pl* **flies** **1** : the action or process of flying : FLIGHT **2** *pl* : the space over a theater stage **3** : a garment closing concealed by a fold of cloth **4** : the length of an extended flag from its staff or support **5** : a baseball hit high into the air **6** : the outer canvas of a tent with a double top — **on the fly** : while still in the air

³fly *vb* **flied; fly·ing** : to hit a fly in baseball

⁴fly *n, pl* **flies** **1** : a winged insect — usu. used in combination ⟨butter*fly*⟩ **2** : any of a large order of insects mostly with one pair of functional wings and another pair that if present are reduced to balancing organs and often with larvae without a head, eyes, or legs; *esp* : one (as a housefly) that is large and stout-bodied **3** : a fishhook dressed to suggest an insect

fly·able \'flī-ə-bəl\ *adj* : suitable for flying or being flown

fly ball *n* : ²FLY 5

fly·blown \'flī-,blōn\ *adj* : not pure : TAINTED, CORRUPT

fly·by \-,bī\ *n, pl* **flybys** **1** : a usu. low-altitude flight by an aircraft over a public gathering **2** : a flight of a spacecraft past a celestial body (as Jupiter) close enough to obtain scientific data

fly–by–night \-bī-,nīt\ *adj* **1** : seeking a quick profit usu. by shady acts **2** : TRANSITORY, PASSING

fly casting *n* : the casting of artificial flies in fly-fishing or as a competitive sport

fly·catch·er \-,ka-chər, -,ke-\ *n* : any of various passerine birds that feed on insects caught in flight

flyer *var of* FLIER

fly·fish·ing \'flī-,fi-shiŋ\ *n* : a method of fishing in which an artificial fly is used for bait

flying boat *n* : a seaplane with a hull designed for floating

flying buttress *n* : a projecting arched structure to support a wall or building

flying fish *n* : any of numerous marine bony fishes capable of long gliding flights out of water by spreading their large fins like wings

flying saucer *n* : an unidentified flying object reported to be saucer-shaped or disk-shaped

flying squirrel *n* : either of two small nocturnal No. American squirrels with folds of skin connecting the forelegs and hind legs that enable them to make long gliding leaps

fly·leaf \'flī-,lēf\ *n, pl* **fly·leaves** \-,lēvz\ : a blank leaf at the beginning or end of a book

fly·pa·per \-,pā-pər\ *n* : paper poisoned or coated with a sticky substance for killing or catching flies

fly·speck \-,spek\ *n* **1** : a speck of fly dung **2** ♦ : something small and insignificant

♦ atom, bit, crumb, fleck, grain, particle, speck

fly·way \-,wā\ *n* : an established air route of migratory birds

fly·wheel \-,hwēl\ *n* : a heavy wheel for regulating the speed of machinery

fm *abbr* fathom

Fm *symbol* fermium

FM \'ef-,em\ *n* : a broadcasting system using frequency modulation; *also* : a radio receiver of such a system

fn *abbr* footnote

fo *or* **fol** *abbr* folio

FO *abbr* foreign office

¹foal \'fōl\ *n* : a young horse or related animal; *esp* : one under one year

²foal *vb* : to give birth to a foal

¹foam \'fōm\ *n* **1** ♦ : a mass of bubbles formed on the surface of a liquid : FROTH, SPUME **2** : material (as rubber) in a lightweight cellular form — **foamy** *adj*

♦ froth, head, lather, spume; *also* mousse; mist, spindrift, spray; scum

²foam *vb* : to form foam : FROTH

fob \'fäb\ *n* **1** : a short strap, ribbon, or chain attached esp. to a pocket watch **2** : a small ornament worn on a fob **3** *or* **key fob** : an object attached to a key chain or key ring; *esp* : a small electronic device used typically in place of a key (as to unlock a door) or to remotely work another device

FOB *abbr* free on board

fob off *vb* **1** : to put off with a trick, excuse, or inferior substitute **2** : to pass or offer as genuine **3** : to put aside

FOC *abbr* free of charge

focal length *n* : the distance of a focus from a lens or curved mirror

fo'c'sle *var of* FORECASTLE

¹fo·cus \'fō-kəs\ *n, pl* **fo·ci** \-,sī\ *also* **fo·cus·es** [NL, fr. L, hearth] **1** : a point at which rays (as of light, heat, or sound) meet or diverge or appear to diverge; *esp* : the point at which an image is formed by a mirror, lens, or optical system **2** : FOCAL LENGTH **3** : adjustment (as of eyes or eyeglasses) that gives clear vision **4** ♦ : a central point : CENTER — **fo·cal** \'fō-kəl\ *adj* — **fo·cal·ly** *adv*

♦ base, center (*or* centre), core, heart, hub, nucleus, seat — more at CENTER

²focus *vb* **-cused** *also* **-cussed; -cus·ing** *also* **-cus·sing** **1** : to bring or come to a focus ⟨∼ rays of light⟩ **2** ♦ : to cause to be concentrated ⟨∼ attention on a problem⟩ **3** : to adjust the focus of

♦ concentrate, fasten, rivet, train — more at CONCENTRATE

fod·der \'fä-dər\ *n* **1** : coarse dry food (as cornstalks) for livestock **2** : available material used to supply a heavy demand

foe \'fō\ *n* [ME *fo*, fr. OE *fāh*, fr. *fāh* hostile] ♦ : one who has personal enmity for another : ENEMY

♦ adversary, antagonist, enemy, opponent — more at ENEMY

FOE *abbr* Fraternal Order of Eagles

foehn *or* **föhn** \'fərn, 'fœn, 'fān\ *n* [G *Föhn*] : a warm dry wind blowing down a mountainside

foe·man \'fō-mən\ *n* : FOE

foe·tal, foe·tus *chiefly Brit var of* FETAL, FETUS

¹fog \'fög, 'fäg\ *n* **1** ♦ : fine particles of water suspended in the lower atmosphere **2** ♦ : mental confusion

♦ [1] haze, murk, smog, soup — more at HAZE
♦ [2] daze, haze, muddle, spin — more at HAZE

²fog *vb* **fogged; fog·ging** ♦ : to obscure or be obscured with or as if with fog

♦ blur, cloud, confuse, dim, haze, mist, obscure ♦ becloud, befog, blur, cloud, confuse, muddy — more at CONFUSE

fog·gy \'fö-gē, 'fä-\ *adj* **1 a** : filled or abounding with fog **b** : covered or made opaque by moisture or grime **2** ♦ : blurred or obscured as if by fog

♦ [1b] cloudy, hazy, misty, murky, smoggy, soupy — more at HAZY ♦ [2] bleary, dim, faint, fuzzy, hazy, indefinite, indistinct, murky, obscure, unclear

fog·horn \'fög-,hörn, 'fäg-\ *n* : a horn sounded in a fog to give warning

fo·gy *also* **fo·gey** \'fō-gē\ *n, pl* **fogies** *also* **fogeys** ♦ : a person with old-fashioned ideas ⟨an old ∼⟩

♦ antediluvian, dodo, fossil, fuddy-duddy, reactionary; *also* conservative; old-timer, veteran; old maid *Ant* modern

foi·ble \'föi-bəl\ *n* ♦ : a minor failing or weakness in character or behavior

♦ demerit, failing, fault, frailty, shortcoming, vice, weakness — more at FAULT

foie gras \'fwä-'grä\ *n* [F, lit., fat liver] : the fattened liver of an animal and esp. of a goose usu. served as a pâté

¹foil \'föil\ *vb* [ME, alter. of *fullen* to full cloth, fr. AF *foller*] **1** ♦ : to prevent from attaining an end **2** ♦ : to bring to naught : THWART

♦ [1, 2] baffle, balk, beat, checkmate, frustrate, thwart — more at FRUSTRATE

²foil *n* [ME, leaf, fr. AF *fuille, foille*, fr. L *folia*, pl. of *folium* leaf] **1** : a very thin sheet of metal ⟨aluminum ∼⟩ **2** : one that serves as a contrast to another ⟨acted as a ∼ for a comedian⟩

³foil *n* : a light fencing sword with a flexible blade tapering to a blunt point

foist \'fȯist\ *vb* : to pass off (something false or worthless) as genuine

¹fold \'fōld\ *n* **1** : an enclosure for sheep **2** ♦ : a group of people with a common faith, belief, or interest

♦ body, circle, clan, clique, community, coterie, set — more at GANG

²fold *vb* : to house (sheep) in a fold

³fold *vb* **1** : to lay one part over or against another part **2** : to clasp together **3** : EMBRACE **4** : to bend (as a layer of rock) into folds **5** : to incorporate into a mixture by overturning repeatedly without stirring or beating **6** : to become doubled or pleated **7** ♦ : to fail completely : FAIL, COLLAPSE

♦ collapse, fail, flop, flunk, wash out — more at FAIL

⁴fold *n* **1** : a doubling or folding over **2** : a part doubled or laid over another part

fold·away \'fōl-də-ˌwā\ *adj* : designed to fold out of the way or out of sight

fold·er \'fōl-dər\ *n* **1** : one that folds **2** ♦ : a folded printed circular **3** : a folded cover or large envelope for loose papers **4** : an object in a computer operating system used to organize files or other folders

♦ booklet, brochure, circular, leaflet, pamphlet — more at PAMPHLET

fol·de·rol \'fäl-də-ˌräl\ *n* **1** : a useless trifle **2** : NONSENSE

fold·out \'fōl-ˌdau̇t\ *n* : a folded leaf (as in a magazine) larger in some dimension than the page

fo·liage \'fō-lē-ij\ *n* ♦ : a mass of leaves (as of a plant or forest)

♦ flora, green, greenery, herbage, leafage, vegetation, verdure — more at GREENERY

fo·li·at·ed \'fō-lē-ˌā-təd\ *adj* : composed of or separable into layers

fo·lic acid \ˌfō-lik-\ *n* : a vitamin of the vitamin B complex used esp. to treat nutritional anemias

fo·lio \'fō-lē-ˌō\ *n, pl* **fo·li·os** **1** : a leaf of a book; *also* : a page number **2** : the size of a piece of paper cut two from a sheet **3** : a book printed on folio pages

¹folk \'fōk\ *n, pl* **folk** *or* **folks** **1** : the largest number or most characteristic part of a group of people forming a tribe or nation **2 a** *pl* ♦ : a certain kind, class, or group of people : PEOPLE, PERSONS ⟨country ~⟩ ⟨old ~s⟩ **b** ♦ : people generally **3** *folks pl* ♦ : the persons of one's own family

♦ *usu* **folks** [2a, 2b] humanity, humankind, people, persons, public, society, world — more at PEOPLE ♦ *usu* **folks** [3] blood, clan, family, house, kin, kindred, kinfolk, line, lineage, people, race, stock, tribe

²folk *adj* : of, relating to, or originating among the common people ⟨~ music⟩

folk art *n* : the traditional anonymous art of usu. untrained people

folk·lore \'fōk-ˌlȯr\ *n* ♦ : customs, beliefs, stories, and sayings of a people handed down from generation to generation — **folk·lor·ic** \-ˌlȯr-ik\ *adj* — **folk·lor·ist** \-ist\ *n*

♦ legend, lore, myth, mythology, tradition; *also* information, knowledge, wisdom; anecdote, fable, old wives' tale, tale, yarn

folk mass *n* : a mass in which traditional liturgical music is replaced by folk music

folk·sing·er \'fōk-ˌsiŋ-ər\ *n* : a singer of folk songs — **folk·sing·ing** *n*

folksy \'fōk-sē\ *adj* **folks·i·er; -est** **1** : SOCIABLE, FRIENDLY **2** : informal, casual, or familiar in manner or style

folk·way \'fōk-ˌwā\ *n* : a way of thinking, feeling, or acting common to a given group of people; *esp* : a traditional social custom

fol·li·cle \'fä-li-kəl\ *n* **1** : a small anatomical cavity or gland ⟨a hair ~⟩ **2** : a small fluid-filled cavity in the ovary of a mammal enclosing a developing egg

fol·low \'fä-lō\ *vb* **1** ♦ : to go or come after **2** ♦ : to proceed along **3** : to engage in as a way of life ⟨~ the sea⟩ ⟨~ a profession⟩ **4** ♦ : to be or act in accordance with : to accept as authority : OBEY **5** ♦ : to pursue in an effort to overtake : PURSUE **6** : to come after in order or rank or natural sequence **7** ♦ : to keep one's attention fixed on **8** : to result from **9** : to understand the sense or logic of **10** : to subscribe to the social media feed of — **follow suit** **1** : to play a card of the same suit as the card led **2** : to follow an example set

♦ [1] succeed; *also* displace, replace, supersede, supplant; ensue *Ant* antedate, precede, predate ♦ [2] go, pass, proceed, travel, traverse — more at TRAVERSE ♦ [4] comply, conform, mind, obey, observe — more at OBEY ♦ [5] chase, pursue, tail, trace, track, trail; *also* accompany, chaperon, escort; hunt, search (for), seek; eye, observe, watch *Ant* guide, lead, pilot ♦ [7] heed, listen, mind, note, observe, regard, watch — more at HEED

fol·low·er *n* **1** ♦ : one that follows the opinions or teachings of another **2** : one who subscribes to a feed esp. on social media

♦ adherent, convert, disciple, partisan, pupil, votary; *also* apostle; faithful, loyalist; advocate, backer, champion, supporter; scholar, student; ideologist, sectarian; admirer, cultist, devotee, enthusiast, fan, idolater, worshiper, zealot; flunky, hanger-on, henchman, lackey, satellite, stooge, sycophant, toady, yes-man *Ant* leader

¹fol·low·ing \'fä-lə-wiŋ\ *adj* **1** ♦ : next after : SUCCEEDING ⟨the ~ day⟩ **2** : that immediately follows ⟨trains will leave at the ~ times⟩

♦ coming, next, succeeding — more at NEXT

²following *n* ♦ : a group of followers, adherents, or partisans

♦ cortege, retinue, suite, train — more at CORTEGE

³following *prep* : subsequent to : AFTER

follow through *vb* ♦ : to press on in an activity or process esp. to a conclusion

♦ accomplish, achieve, carry out, commit, compass, do, execute, fulfill, make, perform — more at PERFORM

fol·low–up \'fä-lə-ˌwəp\ *n* : a system or instance of pursuing an initial effort by supplementary action

fol·ly \'fä-lē\ *n, pl* **follies** [ME *folie*, fr. OF, fr. *fol* fool] **1** : lack of good sense **2** ♦ : a foolish act or idea **3** : an excessively costly or unprofitable undertaking

♦ absurdity, fatuity, foolery, foolishness, idiocy, inanity, madness, stupidity

fo·ment \fō-'ment\ *vb* ♦ : to promote the growth or development of : INCITE

♦ abet, ferment, incite, instigate, provoke, raise, stir, whip — more at INCITE

fo·men·ta·tion \ˌfō-mən-'tā-shən, -ˌmen-\ *n* **1** : a hot moist material (as a damp cloth) applied to the body to ease pain **2** : the act of fomenting : INSTIGATION

fond \'fänd\ *adj* [ME, fr. *fonne* fool] **1** : FOOLISH, SILLY ⟨~ pride⟩ **2** : prizing highly : DESIROUS ⟨~ of praise⟩ **3** ♦ : strongly attracted or predisposed ⟨~ of music⟩ **4 a** : foolishly tender : INDULGENT **b** ♦ : feeling or expressing love : LOVING, AFFECTIONATE **5** : CHERISHED, DEAR ⟨his ~est hopes⟩ — **fond·ly** *adv*

♦ [3] inclined, partial; *also* crazy (about *or* over), enamored, enraptured, gone (on), infatuated, mad (about), nuts (about); desirous, eager, enthusiastic, excited, gung ho, keen *Ant* averse, disinclined ♦ [4b] affectionate, devoted, loving, tender, tenderhearted — more at LOVING

fon·dant \'fän-dənt\ *n* : a creamy preparation of sugar used as a basis for candies or icings

fon·dle \'fänd-ᵊl\ *vb* **fon·dled; fon·dling** ♦ : to touch or handle lovingly : CARESS

♦ caress, love, pat, pet, stroke; *also* cuddle, nestle, nose, nuzzle, snuggle; cradle, embrace, enfold, hug; bounce, dandle; knead, massage; baby, coddle, indulge, mollycoddle, pamper, spoil

fond·ness \'fän(d)-nəs\ *n* **1** ♦ : tender affection **2** ♦ : enjoyment of or delight in something that satisfies one's tastes, inclinations, or desires

♦ [1] affection, attachment, devotion, love, passion — more at LOVE ♦ [1, 2] appetite, fancy, favor (or

footnote

favour), like, liking, love, partiality, preference — more at LIKING

fon·due also **fon·du** \fän-'dü, -'dyü\ n [F] : a preparation of melted cheese often flavored with white wine

¹**font** \'fänt\ n 1 : a receptacle for baptismal or holy water 2 : FOUNTAIN, SOURCE

²**font** n : an assortment of printing type of one size and style

food \'füd\ n 1 : material taken into an organism and used for growth, repair, and vital processes and as a source of energy; also : organic material produced by green plants and used by them as food 2 ♦ : nourishment in solid form 3 : something that nourishes, sustains, or supplies ⟨~ for thought⟩

♦ chow, fare, meat, provisions, viands, victuals; also rations; aliment, nutriment; diet, nurture, sustenance; mess, pap; feed, fodder, forage, slop, swill; feast, meal, refreshments, repast, spread; board; dish, plate, serving

food bank n : a usu. nonprofit organization that collects donated food and distributes it to people in need

food·borne \'füd-,bȯrn\ adj : caused by contaminated food ⟨a ~ illness⟩

food chain n 1 : a hierarchical arrangement of organisms in an ecological community such that each uses the next usu. lower member as a food source 2 : a hierarchy based on power or importance

food court n : an area (as within a shopping mall) set apart for food concessions

food poisoning n : a digestive illness caused by bacteria or by chemicals in food

food·stuff \'füd-,stəf\ n : a substance with food value; esp : a specific nutrient (as fat or protein)

¹**fool** \'fül\ n [ME, fr. AF fol, fr. LL follis, fr. L, bellows, bag] 1 ♦ : a person who lacks sense or judgment 2 : JESTER 3 : DUPE 4 : IDIOT

♦ booby, goose, jackass, lunatic, nitwit, nut, simpleton; also daredevil; madman, madwoman; blockhead, cretin, dodo, dolt, dope, dumbbell, dummy, dunce, idiot, imbecile, moron; scatterbrain; butt, dupe, laughingstock, mockery, monkey; chump, loser, schlemiel

²**fool** vb 1 ♦ : to meddle or tamper thoughtlessly or ignorantly 2 ♦ : to speak in jest : JOKE 3 ♦ : to make a fool of : DECEIVE 4 : FRITTER ⟨~ed away his time⟩

♦ [1] fiddle (around), mess, monkey, play, tamper, tinker — more at TAMPER ♦ [2] banter, fun, jest, jive, joke, josh, kid, quip, wisecrack — more at JOKE ♦ [3] deceive, delude, dupe, gull, hoodwink, mislead, take in, trick — more at DECEIVE

fool around vb 1 ♦ : to spend time idly, aimlessly, or frivolously 2 : to engage in casual sexual activity

♦ fiddle (around), monkey, play, trifle

fool·ery \'fü-lə-rē\ n, pl **-er·ies** 1 ♦ : a foolish act, utterance, or belief 2 ♦ : foolish behavior

♦ [1] absurdity, fatuity, folly, foolishness, idiocy, inanity, madness, stupidity ♦ [2] high jinks, horseplay, monkeyshines, shenanigans, tomfoolery — more at HORSEPLAY

fool·har·dy \'fül-,här-dē\ adj ♦ : foolishly daring : RASH — **fool·har·di·ness** \-dē-nəs\ n

♦ brash, madcap, overbold, overconfident, rash, reckless; also adventuresome, adventurous, audacious, bold, daring, venturesome, venturous; brave, courageous, dauntless, fearless, intrepid, lionhearted, undaunted, valiant; hotheaded; impetuous, impulsive, rash; brainless, foolish, harebrained, scatterbrained; careless, heedless, thoughtless; hasty, headlong, precipitate Ant careful, cautious, heedful, prudent

fool·ish \'fü-lish\ adj 1 ♦ : showing or arising from folly or lack of judgment 2 ♦ : ridiculously unreasonable, unsound, or incongruous : ABSURD 3 : ABASHED — **fool·ish·ly** adv

♦ [1] absurd, bizarre, crazy, fanciful, fantastic, insane, nonsensical, preposterous, unreal, wild — more at FANTASTIC ♦ [2] absurd, asinine, crazy, cuckoo, daft,

fatuous, insane, kooky, mad, nonsensical, nutty, preposterous, senseless, silly, stupid; also dumb, idiotic, imbecilic, moronic, fallacious, illogical, invalid, irrational, unreasonable; farcical, laughable, ludicrous, ridiculous Ant judicious, prudent, sensible, sound, wise

fool·ish·ness n 1 ♦ : foolish behavior 2 ♦ : a foolish act or idea

♦ folly, nonsense, piffle, rot, silliness — more at NONSENSE

fool·proof \'fül-,prüf\ adj : so simple or reliable as to leave no opportunity for error, misuse, or failure ⟨a ~ plan⟩

fools·cap \'fül-,skap\ n [fr. the watermark of a fool's cap formerly applied to such paper] : a size of paper typically 16×13 inches

fool's gold n : PYRITE

¹**foot** \'fut\ n, pl **feet** \'fēt\ also **foot** 1 : the end part of a leg below the ankle of a vertebrate animal 2 : a unit of measure equal to 12 inches 3 : a group of syllables forming the basic unit of verse meter 4 : something resembling an animal's foot in position or use 5 ♦ : the lowest part : BOTTOM 6 : the part at the opposite end from the head 7 : the part (as of a stocking) that covers the foot

♦ base, bottom — more at BOTTOM

²**foot** vb 1 ♦ : to tread to music : DANCE 2 ♦ : to go on foot 3 : to add up 4 ♦ : to pay or provide for paying

♦ usu foot it [1] dance, step — more at DANCE ♦ usu foot it [2] leg, pad, step, traipse, tread, walk — more at WALK ♦ [4] clear, discharge, liquidate, pay, recompense, settle, spring, stand — more at PAY

foot·age \'fu-tij\ n 1 : length expressed in feet 2 : the length of film used for a scene; also : the material contained on such footage

foot–and–mouth disease n : an acute contagious viral disease esp. of cattle

foot·ball \'fut-,bȯl\ n 1 : any of several games played by two teams on a rectangular field with goalposts at each end in which the object is to get the ball over the goal line or between goalposts by running, passing, or kicking 2 : the ball used in football

foot·board \-,bȯrd\ n 1 : a narrow platform on which to stand or brace the feet 2 : a board forming the foot of a bed

foot·bridge \-,brij\ n : a bridge for pedestrians

foot·ed \'fu-təd\ adj : having a foot or feet of a specified kind or number ⟨flat-footed⟩ ⟨four-footed⟩

-foot·er \'fu-tər\ comb form : one that is a specified number of feet in height, length, or breadth ⟨a six-footer⟩

foot·fall \'fut-,fȯl\ n : the sound of a footstep

foot·hill \-,hil\ n : a hill at the foot of higher hills or mountains

foot·hold \-,hōld\ n 1 : a hold for the feet : FOOTING 2 : a position usable as a base for further advance

foot·ing n 1 : the placing of one's feet in a stable position 2 : the act of moving on foot 3 : a place or space for standing : FOOTHOLD 4 ♦ : position with respect to one another : STATUS 5 ♦ : an underlying condition or state of affairs : BASIS

♦ [4] degree, level, place, position, rank, situation, standing, station, status — more at RANK ♦ [5] base, basis, bedrock, cornerstone, foundation, ground, groundwork, keystone, underpinning — more at CORNERSTONE

foot·less \'fut-ləs\ adj 1 : having no feet 2 : INEPT, INEFFECTUAL

foot·lights \-,līts\ n pl 1 : a row of lights along the front of a stage floor 2 : the stage as a profession

foo·tling \'füt-liŋ\ adj 1 : INEPT 2 : TRIVIAL

foot·lock·er \'fut-,lä-kər\ n : a small trunk designed to be placed at the foot of a bed (as in a barracks)

foot·loose \-,lüs\ adj ♦ : having no ties : FREE

♦ free, loose, unbound, unconfined, unrestrained — more at FREE

foot·man \-mən\ n : a male servant who attends a carriage or waits on table, admits visitors, and runs errands

foot·note \-,nōt\ n 1 : a note of reference, explanation, or

comment placed usu. at the bottom of a page 2 : COM-
MENTARY

foot·pad \-ˌpad\ *n* : a round somewhat flat foot on the leg
of a spacecraft for distributing weight to minimize sinking into a surface

foot·path \-ˌpath, -ˌpȧth\ *n* ♦ : a narrow path for pedestrians
♦ path, trace, track, trail — more at TRAIL

foot·print \-ˌprint\ *n* 1 : an impression of the foot 2 : the
area on a surface covered by something

foot·race \-ˌrās\ *n* : a race run on foot

foot·rest \-ˌrest\ *n* : a support for the feet

foot·sore \-ˌsōr\ *adj* : having sore or tender feet (as from
much walking)

foot·step \-ˌstep\ *n* 1 : the mark of the foot : TRACK
2 : TREAD 3 : distance covered by a step : PACE 4 : a
step on which to ascend or descend 5 : a way of life,
conduct, or action

foot·stool \-ˌstül\ *n* : a low stool to support the feet

foot·wear \-ˌwar\ *n* : apparel (as shoes or boots) for the feet

foot·work \-ˌwərk\ *n* : the management of the feet (as in
boxing)

fop \ˈfäp\ *n* ♦ : a man who is devoted to or vain about his
appearance or dress : DANDY — **fop·pery** \ˈfä-pə-rē\ *n* —
fop·pish *adj*
♦ buck, dandy, dude, gallant — more at DANDY

¹**for** \fər, ˈfȯr\ *prep* 1 : as a preparation toward ⟨dress ∼
dinner⟩ 2 : toward the purpose or goal of ⟨need time
∼ study⟩ ⟨money ∼ a trip⟩ 3 : so as to reach or attain
⟨run ∼ cover⟩ 4 : as being ⟨took him ∼ a fool⟩ 5 : because of ⟨cry ∼ joy⟩ 6 — used to indicate a recipient ⟨a
letter ∼ you⟩ 7 : in support of ⟨fought ∼ his country⟩
8 : directed at : AFFECTING ⟨a cure ∼ what ails you⟩
9 — used with a noun or pronoun followed by an infinitive to form the equivalent of a noun clause ⟨∼ you to
go would be silly⟩ 10 : in exchange as equal to : so as
to return the value of ⟨a lot of trouble ∼ nothing⟩ ⟨pay
$10 ∼ a hat⟩ 11 : CONCERNING ⟨a stickler ∼ detail⟩
12 : CONSIDERING ⟨tall ∼ her age⟩ 13 : through the
period of ⟨served ∼ three years⟩ 14 : in honor of

²**for** *conj* ♦ : for the reason that : BECAUSE
♦ because, now, since, whereas — more at SINCE

³**for** *abbr* 1 foreign 2 forestry

fora *pl of* FORUM

¹**for·age** \ˈfȯr-ij\ *n* [ME, fr. AF, fr. *fuerre, foer* fodder, straw,
of Gmc origin] 1 : food for animals esp. when taken by
browsing or grazing 2 : a search for food or supplies

²**forage** *vb* **for·aged; for·ag·ing** 1 : to collect forage from
2 : to search for food or supplies 3 : to get by foraging
4 ♦ : to make a search : RUMMAGE
♦ *usu* **forage for** cast about, hunt, pursue, quest, rummage, search (for *or* out), seek — more at SEEK

¹**for·ay** \ˈfȯr-ˌā, fȯ-ˈrā\ *vb* ♦ : to raid esp. in search of plunder
♦ *usu* **foray into** invade, overrun, raid — more at INVADE

²**foray** *n* ♦ : a sudden or irregular incursion for war or spoils
♦ descent, incursion, invasion, irruption, raid — more
at RAID

¹**for·bear** \fȯr-ˈber\ *vb* **-bore** \-ˈbȯr\; **-borne** \-ˈbȯrn\; **-bear·ing**
1 ♦ : to refrain from : ABSTAIN 2 : to be patient
♦ abstain (from), forgo, keep, refrain; *also* avoid, eschew, shun; check, constrain, curb, inhibit; deny, refuse, withhold; buck, combat *Ant* give in (to), succumb
(to), yield (to)

²**forbear** *var of* FOREBEAR

for·bear·ance \-ˈber-əns\ *n* ♦ : the act of forbearing
♦ long-suffering, patience, sufferance, tolerance —
more at PATIENCE

forbearing *adj* ♦ : marked by calm patience
♦ long-suffering, patient, stoic, tolerant, uncomplaining — more at PATIENT

for·bid \fər-ˈbid\ *vb* **-bade** \-ˈbad, -ˈbād\ *also* **-bad** \-ˈbad\;
-bid·den \-ˈbi-dᵊn\; **-bid·ding** 1 ♦ : to command against
: PROHIBIT 2 : HINDER, PREVENT

♦ ban, bar, enjoin, interdict, outlaw, prohibit, proscribe; *also* deter, discourage, dissuade; repress, suppress; halt, preclude, prevent, stop; embargo, exclude,
rule out, shut out; debar, deprive, disallow, reject, veto;
check, curb, inhibit, restrain; block, hinder, impede,
obstruct *Ant* allow, let, permit, suffer

forbidden *adj* ♦ : not allowed : not permitted
♦ impermissible, taboo — more at IMPERMISSIBLE

forbidding *adj* 1 : causing discomfort 2 ♦ : presenting,
suggesting, or constituting a menace
♦ austere, grim, menacing, scary, severe — more at GRIM

¹**force** \ˈfȯrs\ *n* 1 ♦ : strength or energy esp. of an exceptional degree : active power 2 ♦ : capacity to persuade
or convince 3 : military strength; *also, pl* : the whole military strength (as of a nation) 4 ♦ : a body (as of persons
or ships) available for a particular purpose 5 ♦ : violence, compulsion, or constraint used on or against a person or thing : COMPULSION 6 : an influence (as a push or
pull) that causes motion or a change of motion — **in force**
1 : in great numbers 2 : VALID, OPERATIVE
♦ [1] energy, main, might, muscle, potency, power,
strength, vigor (*or* vigour) — more at POWER ♦ [2] cogency, effectiveness, persuasiveness — more at CO-
GENCY ♦ [4] help, personnel, pool, staff; *also* labor,
proletariat, rank and file; band, company, crew, gang,
outfit, party, team; employee, helper, hireling, worker
♦ [5] coercion, compulsion, constraint, duress, pressure;
also browbeating, bullying; fear, intimidation, menace,
sword, terror, terrorism, threat, violence; might, muscle,
strength; hardheadedness, self-will; strain, stress

²**force** *vb* **forced; forc·ing** 1 ♦ : to compel by physical,
moral, or intellectual means : COERCE 2 : to cause
through necessity ⟨*forced* to admit defeat⟩ 3 : to press,
attain to, or effect against resistance or inertia ⟨∼ your
way through⟩ 4 : to raise or accelerate to the utmost
⟨∼ the pace⟩ 5 : to produce with unnatural or unwilling
effort ⟨*forced* a smile⟩ 6 : to hasten (as in growth) by
artificial means
♦ coerce, compel, constrain, drive, make, muscle, obligate, oblige, press, pressure; *also* browbeat, bulldoze,
bully; high-pressure, intimidate, menace, terrorize,
threaten

force·ful \ˈfȯrs-fəl\ *adj* ♦ : possessing or filled with force
— **force·ful·ness** \-nəs\ *n*
♦ cogent, compelling, convincing, decisive, emphatic,
persuasive, strong — more at COGENT ♦ authoritative,
influential, weighty — more at INFLUENTIAL

force·ful·ly \-fə-lē\ *adv* ♦ : in a forceful manner
♦ firmly, forcibly, hard, mightily, powerfully, strongly,
vigorously — more at HARD

for·ceps \ˈfȯr-səps\ *n, pl* **forceps** [L] : a handheld instrument for grasping, holding, or pulling objects esp. for
delicate operations (as by a surgeon)

forc·ible \ˈfȯr-sə-bəl\ *adj* 1 : obtained or done by force
2 : showing force or energy : POWERFUL

forc·i·bly \-blē\ *adv* ♦ : in a forcible manner
♦ energetically, firmly, forcefully, hard, mightily, powerfully, vigorously — more at HARD

¹**ford** \ˈfȯrd\ *n* : a place where a stream may be crossed by
wading

²**ford** *vb* : to cross (a body of water) by wading

¹**fore** \ˈfȯr\ *adv* : in, toward, or adjacent to the front : FOR-
WARD

²**fore** *adj* : being or coming before in time, order, or space

³**fore** *n* : something that occupies a front position

⁴**fore** *interj* — used by a golfer to warn anyone within range
of the probable line of flight of the ball

fore–and–aft \ˌfȯr-ə-ˈnaft\ *adj* : lying, running, or acting
along the length of a structure (as a ship)

¹**fore·arm** \(ˌ)fȯr-ˈärm\ *vb* ♦ : to arm in advance : PREPARE
♦ brace, fortify, nerve, prepare, psych (up), ready,
steel, strengthen — more at FORTIFY

²fore·arm \'fōr-ˌärm\ *n* : the part of the arm between the elbow and the wrist

fore·bear \-ˌbar\ *n* ◆ : one from whom a person is descended and who is usu. more remote in the line of descent than a grandparent : ANCESTOR, FOREFATHER

◆ ancestor, father, forefather, grandfather — more at ANCESTOR

fore·bode \fōr-'bōd\ *vb* 1 : to give promise of 2 : FORETELL, PREDICT

fore·bod·ing *n* ◆ : an omen, prediction, or presentiment esp. of coming evil — **fore·bod·ing·ly** *adv*

◆ omen, portent, premonition, presage, presentiment — more at PREMONITION ◆ alarm, apprehension, dread, misgiving

¹fore·cast \'fōr-ˌkast\ *vb* **-cast** *also* **-cast·ed; -cast·ing** 1 ◆ : to calculate or predict (some future event or condition) : PREDICT ⟨~ weather conditions⟩ 2 ◆ : to indicate as likely to occur

◆ [1, 2] augur, foretell, predict, presage, prognosticate, prophesy — more at FORETELL

²forecast *n* ◆ : a prophecy, estimate, or prediction of a future happening or condition

◆ prediction, prognostication, prophecy

fore·cast·er *n* ◆ : one that forecasts

◆ diviner, fortune-teller, futurist, prognosticator, prophet, seer

fore·cas·tle *or* **fo'c'sle** \'fōk-səl\ *n* 1 : the forward part of the upper deck of a ship 2 : the crew's quarters usu. in a ship's bow

fore·close \fōr-'klōz\ *vb* 1 : to shut out : PRECLUDE 2 : to take legal measures to terminate a mortgage and take possession of the mortgaged property

fore·clo·sure \-'klō-zhər\ *n* : the act of foreclosing; *esp* : the legal procedure of foreclosing a mortgage

fore·doom \fōr-'düm\ *vb* ◆ : to doom beforehand

◆ destine, doom, foreordain, ordain, predestine — more at DESTINE

fore·fa·ther \'fōr-ˌfä-t͟hər\ *n* 1 ◆ : one from whom a person is descended and who is usu. more remote in the line of descent than a grandparent : ANCESTOR 2 : a person of an earlier period and common heritage

◆ ancestor, father, forebear, grandfather — more at ANCESTOR

forefend *var of* FORFEND

fore·fin·ger \-ˌfiŋ-gər\ *n* : INDEX FINGER

fore·foot \-ˌfut\ *n* : either of the front feet of a quadruped; *also* : the front part of the human foot

fore·front \-ˌfrənt\ *n* : the foremost part or place

foregather *var of* FORGATHER

¹fore·go \fōr-'gō\ *vb* **-went** \-'went\; **-gone** \-'gȯn\; **-go·ing** ◆ : to go before : PRECEDE

◆ antedate, precede — more at PRECEDE

²forego *var of* FORGO

fore·go·ing *adj* ◆ : listed, mentioned, or occurring before : PRECEDING

◆ antecedent, anterior, preceding, previous, prior — more at PREVIOUS

fore·gone \'fōr-ˌgȯn\ *adj* : determined in advance ⟨a ~ conclusion⟩

fore·ground \-ˌgrau̇nd\ *n* 1 : the part of a scene or representation that appears nearest to and in front of the spectator 2 : a position of prominence

fore·hand \-ˌhand\ *n* : a stroke (as in tennis) made with the palm of the hand turned in the direction in which the hand is moving; *also* : the side on which such a stroke is made — **forehand** *adj*

fore·hand·ed \(ˌ)fōr-'han-dəd\ *adj* ◆ : mindful of the future : PRUDENT

◆ farsighted, foresighted, prescient, provident, prudent — more at FORESIGHTED

fore·head \'fȯr-əd, 'fōr-ˌhed\ *n* : the part of the face above the eyes

for·eign \'fȯr-ən\ *adj* [ME *forein*, fr. OF, fr. LL *foranus* on the outside, fr. L *foris* outside] 1 : situated outside a place or country and esp. one's own country 2 : born in, belonging to, or characteristic of some place or country other than the one under consideration ⟨~ language⟩ 3 ◆ : not connected, pertinent, or characteristically present 4 : related to or dealing with other nations ⟨~ affairs⟩ 5 : occurring in an abnormal situation in the living body ⟨a ~ body in the eye⟩

◆ alien, extraneous, extrinsic — more at EXTRINSIC

for·eign·er \'fȯr-ə-nər\ *n* : a person belonging to or owing allegiance to a foreign country

foreign minister *n* : a governmental minister for foreign affairs

fore·know \fōr-'nō\ *vb* **-knew** \-'nü, -'nyü\; **-known** \-'nōn\; **-know·ing** ◆ : to have previous knowledge of — **fore·knowl·edge** \'fōr-ˌnä-lij, fōr-'nä-\ *n*

◆ anticipate, divine, foresee — more at FORESEE

fore·la·dy \'fōr-ˌlā-dē\ *n* : FOREWOMAN

fore·leg \-ˌleg\ *n* : a front leg

fore·limb \-ˌlim\ *n* : a front or upper limb (as a wing, arm, fin, or leg)

fore·lock \-ˌläk\ *n* : a lock of hair growing from the front part of the head

fore·man \-mən\ *n* 1 : a spokesperson of a jury 2 ◆ : a person in charge of a group of workers

◆ boss, captain, chief, head, headman, leader, master, taskmaster — more at BOSS

fore·mast \-ˌmast\ *n* : the mast nearest the bow of a ship

fore·most \-ˌmōst\ *adj* ◆ : first in time, place, or order : most important : PREEMINENT — **foremost** *adv*

◆ chief, dominant, first, key, main, predominant, preeminent, primary, principal **Ant** last, least

fore·name \-ˌnām\ *n* : a first name

fore·named \-ˌnāmd\ *adj* : previously named : AFORESAID

fore·noon \-ˌnün\ *n* : MORNING

¹fo·ren·sic \fə-'ren-sik\ *adj* [L *forensis* public, forensic, fr. *forum* forum] 1 : belonging to, used in, or suitable to courts of law or to public speaking or debate 2 : relating to the application of scientific knowledge to legal problems ⟨~ medicine⟩

²forensic *n* 1 : an argumentative exercise 2 *pl* : the art or study of argumentative discourse 3 *pl* : scientific analysis of physical evidence (as from a crime scene)

fore·or·dain \ˌfōr-ȯr-'dān\ *vb* ◆ : to ordain or decree beforehand : PREDESTINE

◆ destine, doom, foredoom, ordain, predestine — more at DESTINE

fore·part \'fōr-ˌpärt\ *n* 1 : the anterior part of something 2 : the earlier part of a period of time

fore·quar·ter \-ˌkwȯr-tər\ *n* : the front half of a lateral half of the body or carcass of a quadruped ⟨a ~ of beef⟩

fore·run·ner \-ˌrə-nər\ *n* 1 ◆ : one that goes before to give notice of the approach of others : HARBINGER 2 ◆ : something belonging to a relatively early developmental period of a contemporary or fully developed object or phenomenon : PREDECESSOR, ANCESTOR

◆ [1] angel, harbinger, herald, precursor ◆ [2] ancestor, antecedent, precursor — more at ANCESTOR

fore·sail \-ˌsāl, -səl\ *n* 1 : the lowest sail on the foremast of a square-rigged ship or schooner 2 : the principal sail forward of the foremast (as of a sloop)

fore·see \fōr-'sē\ *vb* **-saw** \-'sȯ\; **-seen** \-'sēn\; **-see·ing** ◆ : to see or realize beforehand — **fore·see·able** *adj*

◆ anticipate, divine, foreknow

fore·shad·ow \-'sha-dō\ *vb* ◆ : to give a hint or suggestion of beforehand

◆ harbinger, prefigure; *also* anticipate, foreknow, foresee; forecast, foretell, predict, prophesy; forewarn; augur, bode, forebode, presage

fore·short·en \fōr-'shȯrt-ᵊn\ *vb* : to shorten (a detail) in a drawing or painting so that it appears to have depth

fore·sight \'fōr-ˌsīt\ *n* **1** : the act or power of foreseeing **2** ♦ : care or provision for the future : PRUDENCE **3** : an act of looking forward; *also* : a view forward

♦ forethought, prescience, providence, prudence *Ant* improvidence, shortsightedness

fore·sight·ed \-ˌsī-təd\ *adj* ♦ : having foresight — **fore·sight·ed·ness** *n*

♦ farsighted, prescient, provident, prudent *Ant* improvident, shortsighted

fore·skin \-ˌskin\ *n* : a fold of skin enclosing the end of the penis

for·est \'fȯr-əst\ *n* [ME, fr. AF, fr. LL *forestis* (*silva*) un-enclosed (woodland), fr. L *foris* outside] ♦ : a large thick growth of trees and underbrush — **for·est·ed** \'fȯr-ə-stəd\ *adj* — **for·est·land** \'fȯr-əst-ˌland\ *n*

♦ timberland, woodland

fore·stall \fōr-'stȯl\ *vb* ♦ : to keep out, hinder, or prevent by measures taken in advance

♦ avert, help, obviate, preclude, prevent — more at PREVENT

forest ranger *n* : a person in charge of the management and protection of a portion of a forest

for·est·ry \'fȯr-ə-strē\ *n* : the science of growing and caring for forests — **for·est·er** \'fȯr-ə-stər\ *n*

foreswear *var of* FORSWEAR

¹fore·taste \'fōr-ˌtāst\ *n* : an advance indication, warning, or notion ⟨a ∼ of winter⟩

²fore·taste \fōr-'tāst\ *vb* : to taste beforehand : ANTICIPATE

fore·tell \fōr-'tel\ *vb* **-told** \-'tōld\; **-tell·ing** ♦ : to tell of beforehand : PREDICT

♦ augur, forecast, predict, presage, prognosticate, prophesy

fore·thought \'fōr-ˌthȯt\ *n* **1** : PREMEDITATION **2** ♦ : consideration for the future

♦ foresight, prescience, providence — more at FORESIGHT

fore·to·ken \fōr-'tō-kən\ *vb* : to indicate in advance

fore·top \'fōr-ˌtäp\ *n* : a platform near the top of a ship's foremast

for·ev·er \fȯr-'e-vər\ *adv* **1** ♦ : for a limitless time **2** ♦ : at all times : ALWAYS

♦ [1] always, eternally, ever, everlastingly, permanently, perpetually — more at EVER ♦ [2] always, constantly, continually, incessantly, invariably, unfailingly — more at ALWAYS

for·ev·er·more \-ˌe-vər-'mōr\ *adv* : for a limitless time or endless ages : FOREVER

fore·warn \fōr-'wȯrn\ *vb* ♦ : to warn beforehand — **fore·warn·ing** *n*

♦ alert, caution, warn — more at WARN

forewent *past of* FOREGO

fore·wing \'fōr-ˌwiŋ\ *n* : either of the anterior wings of a 4-winged insect

fore·wom·an \'fōr-ˌwu̇-mən\ *n* : a woman who is a foreman

fore·word \-ˌwərd\ *n* ♦ : prefatory comments (as for a book) esp. when written by someone other than the author : PREFACE

♦ introduction, preamble, preface, prologue — more at INTRODUCTION

¹for·feit \'fȯr-fət\ *n* [ME *forfait*, fr. AF, fr. pp. of *forfaire, fors-faire* to commit a crime, forfeit, fr. *fors* outside + *faire* to do] **1** ♦ : something forfeited : PENALTY, FINE **2** : FORFEITURE **3** : something deposited and then redeemed on payment of a fine **4** *pl* : a game in which forfeits are exacted

♦ damages, fine, mulct, penalty — more at FINE

²forfeit *vb* : to lose or lose the right to by some error, offense, or crime

for·fei·ture \'fȯr-fə-ˌchu̇r\ *n* **1** : the act of forfeiting **2** : something forfeited : PENALTY

for·fend \fȯr-'fend\ *vb* **1** : PREVENT **2** : PROTECT, PRESERVE

for·gath·er \fȯr-'ga-thər\ *vb* **1** ♦ : to come together : ASSEMBLE **2** : to meet someone usu. by chance

♦ assemble, collect, congregate, convene, gather, meet, rendezvous — more at ASSEMBLE

¹forge \'fȯrj\ *n* [ME, fr. OF, fr. L *fabrica*, fr. *faber* smith] : a furnace or shop with its furnace where metal is heated and worked

²forge *vb* **forged; forg·ing** **1** ♦ : to form (metal) by heating and hammering **2** ♦ : to form or bring into being esp. by an expenditure of effort : FASHION, SHAPE ⟨∼ an agreement⟩ **3** : to make or imitate falsely esp. with intent to defraud ⟨∼ a signature⟩ — **forg·er** *n*

♦ [1] beat, hammer, pound — more at HAMMER
♦ [2] build, carve, fashion, grind, hammer, shape, work out

³forge *vb* **forged; forg·ing** ♦ : to move ahead steadily but gradually

♦ advance, fare, get along, go, march, proceed, progress — more at GO

forg·ery \'fȯr-jə-rē\ *n* ♦ : something forged

♦ counterfeit, fake, hoax, humbug, phony, sham — more at FAKE

for·get \fər-'get\ *vb* **-got** \-'gät\; **-got·ten** \-'gät-ᵊn\ *or* **-got**; **-get·ting** **1** : to be unable to think of or recall **2** ♦ : to fail to become mindful of at the proper time **3** ♦ : to treat with inattention or disregard : NEGLECT, DISREGARD ⟨*forgot* an old friend⟩ **4** : to give up hope for or expectation of

♦ [2] fail, neglect, omit — more at NEGLECT ♦ [3] disregard, ignore, neglect, overlook, pass over, slight, slur — more at NEGLECT

for·get·ful \-'get-fəl\ *adj* : likely to forget — **for·get·ful·ly** *adv* — **for·get·ful·ness** *n*

for·get–me–not \fər-'get-mē-ˌnät\ *n* : any of a genus of small herbs with bright blue or white flowers

forg·ing *n* : a piece of forged work

for·giv·able *adj* ♦ : being of a kind that can be forgiven

♦ excusable, pardonable, venial — more at VENIAL

for·give \fər-'giv\ *vb* **-gave** \-'gāv\; **-giv·en** \-'gi-vən\; **-giv·ing** **1** : to give up resentment of or claim to requital for **2** : to give up resentment of : PARDON, ABSOLVE **3** : to grant relief from payment of ⟨∼ a debt⟩

for·give·ness *n* ♦ : an act of forgiving or state of being forgiven

♦ absolution, amnesty, pardon, remission — more at PARDON

for·giv·ing *adj* **1** : willing or able to forgive **2** : allowing room for error or weakness ⟨a ∼ recipe⟩

for·go \fȯr-'gō\ *vb* **-went** \-'went\; **-gone** \-'gȯn\; **-go·ing** ♦ : to give up the enjoyment or advantage of : do without

♦ abstain (from), forbear, keep, refrain — more at FORBEAR

¹fork \'fȯrk\ *n* **1** : an implement with two or more prongs for taking up (as in eating), pitching, or digging **2** : a forked part, tool, or piece of equipment **3** : a dividing into branches or a place where something branches; *also* : a branch of such a fork

²fork *vb* **1** ♦ : to divide into two or more branches **2** : to give the form of a fork to ⟨∼*ing* her fingers⟩ **3** : to raise or pitch with a fork ⟨∼ hay⟩ **4** ♦ : to make a disposal or transfer of : PAY — used with *over, out,* or *up*

♦ [1] branch, diverge, divide, separate — more at SEPARATE ♦ *usu* fork over *or* fork out [4] disburse, expend, give, lay out, pay

forked \'fȯrkt, 'fȯr-kəd\ *adj* : having a fork : shaped like a fork ⟨∼ lightning⟩

fork·lift \'fȯrk-ˌlift\ *n* : a machine for lifting heavy objects by means of steel fingers inserted under the load

for·lorn \fər-'lȯrn, fȯr-\ *adj* ♦ : sad and lonely because of isolation or desertion **2** : being in poor condition : WRETCHED **3** : nearly hopeless — **for·lorn·ly** *adv*

♦ desolate, lonely, lonesome, sad — more at LONESOME

for·lorn·ness *n* ♦ : forlorn quality or state

♦ blues, dejection, desolation, melancholy, sadness — more at SADNESS

¹form \\'fȯrm\ *n* **1** : SHAPE, STRUCTURE **2** ♦ : a body esp. of a person : FIGURE **3** : the essential nature of a thing **4** ♦ : an established manner of doing or saying something **5** : FORMULA **6** ♦ : a document with blank spaces for insertion of information ⟨tax ∼⟩ **7** ♦ : conduct regulated by extraneous controls (as of custom or etiquette) : CEREMONY **8** : manner of performing according to recognized standards **9** : a long seat : BENCH **10** ♦ : a model of the human figure used for displaying clothes **11** : MOLD ⟨a ∼ for concrete⟩ **12** : type or plates in a frame ready for printing **13** : one of the different modes of existence, action, or manifestation of a particular thing or substance : MODE, KIND, VARIETY ⟨coal is a ∼ of carbon⟩ **14** : orderly method of arrangement; *also* : a particular kind or instance of such arrangement ⟨the sonnet ∼ in poetry⟩ **15** ♦ : the structural element, plan, or design of a work of art **16** : a bounded surface or volume **17** : a grade in a British school or in some American private schools **18** : RACING FORM **19 a** : known ability to perform **b** ♦ : condition (as of an athlete) suitable for performing **20** : one of the ways in which a word is changed to show difference in use ⟨the plural ∼ of a noun⟩

♦ [2] build, constitution, figure, frame, physique, shape — more at PHYSIQUE ♦ [4] manner, method, style, system, technique, way — more at METHOD ♦ [6] blank, document, paper ♦ [7] ceremonial, ceremony, formality, observance, rite — more at RITE ♦ [10] dummy, figure, mannequin ♦ [15] arrangement, composition, configuration, design, format, layout, makeup, pattern — more at COMPOSITION ♦ [19b] condition, estate, fettle, order, repair, shape, trim — more at CONDITION

²form *vb* **1** ♦ : to give form or shape to : FASHION, MAKE **2** : TRAIN, INSTRUCT **3** ♦ : to serve to make up or constitute : CONSTITUTE, COMPOSE **4** ♦ : to acquire gradually : DEVELOP, ACQUIRE ⟨∼ a habit⟩ **5** : to arrange in order ⟨∼ a battle line⟩ **6** ♦ : to take form : ARISE ⟨clouds are ∼*ing*⟩ **7** : to take a definite form, shape, or arrangement

♦ [1] fabricate, fashion, frame, make, manufacture, produce — more at MAKE ♦ [3] compose, comprise, constitute, make up — more at CONSTITUTE ♦ [4] acquire, cultivate, develop — more at DEVELOP ♦ [6] arise, begin, materialize, originate

¹for·mal \\'fȯr-məl\ *adj* **1** ♦ : according with conventional forms and rules ⟨a ∼ dinner party⟩ **2** : done in due or lawful form ⟨a ∼ contract⟩ **3** ♦ : rigidly ceremonious : CEREMONIOUS ⟨a ∼ manner⟩ **4** ♦ : having the appearance without the substance : NOMINAL — **for·mal·ly** *adv*

♦ [1, 3] ceremonial, ceremonious, conventional, correct, decorous, proper, regular *Ant* informal, irregular, unceremonious ♦ [4] nominal, paper, titular — more at NOMINAL

²formal *n* ♦ : something (as a social event) formal in character

♦ ball, dance, prom — more at DANCE

form·al·de·hyde \fȯr-'mal-də-ˌhīd\ *n* : a colorless pungent gas used in water solution as a preservative and disinfectant

for·mal·ise *chiefly Brit var of* FORMALIZE

for·mal·ism \\'fȯr-mə-ˌli-zəm\ *n* : strict adherence to set forms

for·mal·i·ty \fȯr-'ma-lə-tē\ *n, pl* **-ties** **1** ♦ : compliance with formal or conventional rules **2** : the quality or state of being formal **3** ♦ : an established form that is required or conventional

♦ [1, 3] ceremonial, ceremony, form, observance, rite, ritual, solemnity — more at RITE ♦ [3] amenity, civility, courtesy, gesture — more at CIVILITY

for·mal·ize \\'fȯr-mə-ˌlīz\ *vb* **-ized; -iz·ing** **1** ♦ : to give a certain or definite form to **2** : to make formal; *also* : to give formal status or approval to

♦ homogenize, normalize, regularize, standardize — more at STANDARDIZE

¹for·mat \\'fȯr-ˌmat\ *n* **1** ♦ : the general composition or style of a publication **2** ♦ : the general plan or arrange-

ment of something **3** ♦ : a method of organizing data ⟨various file ∼*s*⟩

♦ arrangement, composition, configuration, design, form, layout, makeup, pattern — more at COMPOSITION

²format *vb* **for·mat·ted; for·mat·ting** : to arrange (as material to be printed) in a particular format — **for·mat·ter** *n*

for·ma·tion \fȯr-'mā-shən\ *n* **1** : an act of giving form to something : DEVELOPMENT **2** : something that is formed **3** : the manner in which a thing is formed : STRUCTURE, SHAPE **4** : an arrangement of persons or things in a prescribed manner or for a certain purpose

for·ma·tive \\'fȯr-mə-tiv\ *adj* **1** : giving or capable of giving form : CONSTRUCTIVE **2** : of, relating to, or characterized by important growth or formation ⟨a child's ∼ years⟩

for·mer \\'fȯr-mər\ *adj* **1** : PREVIOUS, EARLIER **2** : FOREGOING **3** : being first mentioned or in order of two or more things **4** ♦ : having been previously

♦ erstwhile, late, old, onetime, past, sometime

for·mer·ly \-lē\ *adv* : in time past : PREVIOUSLY

form-fit·ting \\'fȯrm-ˌfi-tiŋ\ *adj* : conforming to the outline of the body

for·mi·da·ble \\'fȯr-mə-də-bəl, fȯr-'mi-\ *adj* **1** ♦ : exciting fear, dread, or awe **2** ♦ : imposing serious difficulties — **for·mi·da·bly** \-blē\ *adv*

♦ [1] dreadful, fearful, fearsome, forbidding, frightful, redoubtable, scary ♦ [2] arduous, demanding, difficult, exacting, hard, strenuous, tall, toilsome, tough — more at HARD

form·less *adj* ♦ : having no regular form or shape

♦ amorphous, shapeless, unformed, unshaped, unstructured *Ant* formed, shaped, structured

form letter *n* **1** : a letter on a frequently recurring topic that can be sent to different people at different times **2** : a letter for mass circulation sent out in many printed copies

for·mu·la \\'fȯr-myə-lə\ *n, pl* **-las** *or* **-lae** \-ˌlē, -ˌlī\ **1** : a set form of words for ceremonial use **2** : RECIPE, PRESCRIPTION **3** : a milk mixture or substitute for a baby **4** : a group of symbols or figures joined to express information concisely **5** : a customary or set form or method

for·mu·late \-ˌlāt\ *vb* **-lat·ed; -lat·ing** **1** ♦ : to express in a formula **2** ♦ : to put into a systematized statement or expression ⟨∼ a policy⟩ **3** : to prepare according to a formula

♦ articulate, clothe, couch, express, phrase, put, say, state, word — more at PHRASE ♦ cast, compose, craft, draft, draw, frame, prepare — more at COMPOSE

for·mu·la·tion \ˌfȯr-myə-'lā-shən\ *n* ♦ : an act or the product of formulating

♦ articulation, expression, statement, utterance, voice — more at EXPRESSION

for·ni·ca·tion \ˌfȯr-nə-'kā-shən\ *n* : consensual sexual intercourse between two persons not married to each other — **for·ni·cate** \\'fȯr-nə-ˌkāt\ *vb* — **for·ni·ca·tor** \-ˌkā-tər\ *n*

for·sake \fər-'sāk, fȯr-\ *vb* **for·sook** \-'sùk\; **for·sak·en** \-'sā-kən\; **for·sak·ing** [ME, fr. OE *forsacan,* fr. *sacan* to dispute] ♦ : to renounce or turn away from entirely

♦ abandon, desert, leave, quit — more at LEAVE

forsaken *adj* ♦ : left desolate or empty

♦ abandoned, derelict, deserted — more at ABANDONED

for·swear \fȯr-'swar\ *vb* **-swore** \-'swȯr\; **-sworn** \-'swȯrn\; **-swear·ing** **1** : to swear falsely : commit perjury **2** : to renounce earnestly or under oath **3** : to deny under oath

for·syth·ia \fər-'si-thē-ə\ *n, pl* **-ias** *also* **-ia** : any of a genus of shrubs related to the olive and having yellow bell-shaped flowers appearing before the leaves in early spring

fort \\'fȯrt\ *n* [ME *forte,* fr. MF *fort,* fr. *fort* strong, fr. L *fortis*] ♦ : **1** : a fortified place **2** : a permanent army post

♦ bastion, bulwark, citadel, fastness, fortification, fortress, hold, stronghold

¹forte \\'fȯrt, 'fȯr-ˌtā\ *n* [F *fort,* fr. *fort,* adj., strong] : one's strong point

²for•te \'fȯr-ˌtā\ adv or adj [It, fr. forte strong] : LOUD — used as a direction in music

forth \'fȯrth\ adv 1 ♦ : onward in time, place, or order : FORWARD, ONWARD ⟨from that day ∼⟩ 2 : out into view or notice ⟨put ∼ leaves⟩

♦ ahead, along, forward, on, onward — more at ALONG

forth•com•ing \fȯrth-'kə-miŋ\ adj 1 ♦ : coming or available soon ⟨the ∼ holidays⟩ 2 : marked by openness and candor : OUTGOING

♦ coming, imminent, impending, oncoming, pending
Ant late, recent

forth•right \'fȯrth-ˌrīt\ adj 1 ♦ : free from ambiguity or evasiveness 2 ♦ : going straight to the point ⟨a ∼ answer⟩

♦ candid, direct, frank, honest, open, plain, straight, straightforward, unreserved — more at FRANK

forth•right•ly adv ♦ : in a forthright manner

♦ directly, foursquare, plain, plainly, straight, straightforward

forth•right•ness n ♦ : the quality or state of being forthright

♦ candor (or candour), directness, frankness, openness, plainness — more at CANDOR

forth•with \ˌfȯrth-'with\ adv ♦ : with dispatch : without delay : IMMEDIATELY

♦ directly, immediately, instantly, now, promptly, pronto, right away, right now

for•ti•fi•ca•tion \ˌfȯr-tə-fə-'kā-shən\ n ♦ : something that fortifies, defends, or strengthens; esp : works erected to defend a place or position

♦ bastion, citadel, fastness, fort, fortress, hold, stronghold — more at FORT

for•ti•fy \'fȯr-tə-ˌfī\ vb -fied; -fy•ing 1 : to strengthen by military defenses 2 ♦ : to give physical strength or endurance to 3 ♦ : to add mental or moral strength to : ENCOURAGE 4 : to strengthen or enrich with a material ⟨∼ bread with vitamins⟩

♦ [2] harden, season, steel, strengthen, toughen — more at HARDEN ♦ [3] brace, encourage, forearm, nerve, psych (up), ready, steel, strengthen; also season, toughen; bolster, boost, buoy (up), buttress, prop (up), reinforce, support, sustain

for•tis•si•mo \fȯr-'ti-sə-ˌmō\ adv or adj : very loud — used as a direction in music

for•ti•tude \'fȯr-tə-ˌtüd, -ˌtyüd\ n ♦ : strength of mind that enables one to meet danger or bear pain or adversity with courage

♦ backbone, fiber (or fibre), grit, guts, pluck, spunk; also determination, resoluteness, resolution; bravery, courage, fearlessness, intrepidity; endurance, stamina, tolerance; heart, mettle, spirit; audacity, boldness, brass, cheek, chutzpah, effrontery, hardihood, nerve, temerity

fort•night \'fȯrt-ˌnīt\ n [ME fourtenight, alter. of fourtene night fourteen nights] : two weeks — fort•night•ly \-lē\ adj or adv

for•tress \'fȯr-trəs\ n ♦ : a fortified place : FORT

♦ bastion, citadel, fastness, fort, fortification, hold, stronghold — more at FORT

for•tu•itous \fȯr-'tü-ə-təs, -'tyü-\ adj 1 ♦ : happening by chance ⟨a ∼ discovery⟩ 2 ♦ : producing or resulting in good by chance : FORTUNATE

♦ [1] accidental, casual, chance, fluky, unplanned
♦ [2] fortunate, happy, lucky, providential — more at FORTUNATE

for•tu•ity \-ə-tē\ n, pl -ities 1 : the quality or state of being fortuitous 2 : a chance event or occurrence

for•tu•nate \'fȯr-chə-nət\ adj 1 ♦ : bringing some good thing not foreseen 2 : receiving some unforeseen or unexpected good

♦ fluky, fortuitous, happy, lucky, providential Ant luckless, unfortunate, unhappy, unlucky

for•tu•nate•ly \-lē\ adv 1 : in a fortunate manner 2 : it is fortunate that

for•tune \'fȯr-chən\ n 1 : prosperity attained partly through luck; also : CHANCE, LUCK 2 : what happens to a person : good or bad luck 3 ♦ : a predetermined course of events often held to be an irresistible power or agency : FATE, DESTINY 4 ♦ : abundance of valuable material possessions or resources : RICHES, WEALTH

♦ [3] circumstance, destiny, doom, fate, lot, portion — more at FATE ♦ [4] assets, capital, means, opulence, riches, substance, wealth, wherewithal — more at WEALTH

fortune hunter n : a person who seeks wealth esp. by marriage

for•tune–tell•er \-ˌte-lər\ n ♦ : a person who professes to foretell future events — for•tune–tell•ing n or adj

♦ augur, diviner, forecaster, futurist, prognosticator, prophet, seer, soothsayer — more at PROPHET

for•ty \'fȯr-tē\ n, pl forties : four times 10 — for•ti•eth \'fȯr-tē-əth\ adj or n — forty adj or pron

for•ty–five \-'fīv\ n 1 : a .45 caliber handgun — usu. written .45 2 : a phonograph record designed to be played at 45 revolutions per minute

for•ty–nin•er \-'nī-nər\ n : a person in the rush to California for gold in 1849

forty winks n sing or pl ♦ : a short sleep

♦ catnap, doze, drowse, nap, siesta, snooze, wink — more at NAP

fo•rum \'fȯr-əm\ n, pl forums also fo•ra \-ə\ [L] 1 : the marketplace or central meeting place of an ancient Roman city 2 : a medium (as a publication or online service) of open discussion 3 : COURT 4 ♦ : a public assembly, lecture, or program involving audience or panel discussion

♦ colloquy, panel, parley, powwow, seminar, symposium

¹for•ward \'fȯr-wərd\ adj 1 : being near or at or belonging to the front 2 : EAGER, READY 3 ♦ : lacking modesty or reserve : BOLD 4 : notably advanced or developed : PRECOCIOUS 5 : moving, tending, or leading toward a position in front 6 : EXTREME, RADICAL 7 : of, relating to, or getting ready for the future — for•ward•ness n

♦ bold, familiar, free, immodest, presumptuous — more at PRESUMPTUOUS

²forward adv ♦ : to or toward what is ahead or in front

♦ ahead, along, forth, on, onward — more at ALONG

³forward vb 1 ♦ : to help onward : ADVANCE 2 : to send forward : TRANSMIT 3 : to send or ship onward

♦ advance, cultivate, encourage, foster, further, nourish, nurture, promote — more at FOSTER

⁴forward n : a player who plays at the front of a team's offensive formation near the opponent's goal

for•ward•er \-wər-dər\ n : one that forwards; esp : an agent who forwards goods

for•wards \'fȯr-wərdz\ adv : to or toward what is ahead or in front : FORWARD

forwent past of FORGO

¹fos•sil \'fä-səl\ adj [L fossilis obtained by digging, fr. fodere to dig] 1 : preserved from a past geologic age ⟨∼ plants⟩ 2 : of or relating to fossil fuels

²fossil n 1 : a trace or impression or the remains of a plant or animal of a past geologic age preserved in the earth's crust 2 ♦ : a person whose ideas are out-of-date — fos•sil•ize \'fä-sə-ˌlīz\ vb

♦ antediluvian, dodo, fogy, fuddy-duddy, reactionary — more at FOGY

fossil fuel n : a fuel (as coal or oil) that is formed in the earth from plant or animal remains

¹fos•ter \'fȯs-tər\ adj [ME, fr. OE fōstor-, fr. fōstor food, feeding] : affording, receiving, or sharing nourishment or parental care though not related by blood or legal ties ⟨∼ parent⟩ ⟨∼ child⟩

²foster vb 1 ♦ : to give parental care to 2 ♦ : to promote the growth or development of : ENCOURAGE

♦ [1] breed, bring up, raise, rear — more at BRING UP
♦ [2] advance, cultivate, encourage, forward, further, nourish, nurture, promote **Ant** discourage, frustrate, hinder, inhibit

foster home n : a household in which an orphaned, neglected, or delinquent child is placed for care

fos·ter·ling \-tər-liŋ\ n : a foster child

Fou·cault pendulum \ˌfü-ˈkō-\ n : a device that consists of a heavy weight hung by a long wire and that swings in a constant direction which appears to change showing that the earth rotates

fought past and past part of FIGHT

¹foul \ˈfaú(-ə)l\ adj 1 a ♦ : offensive to the senses b ♦ : clogged with dirt 2 ♦ : arousing or deserving hatred or repugnance : ODIOUS 3 ♦ : abhorrent to morality or virtue : OBSCENE 4 ♦ : being wet and stormy : STORMY ⟨~ weather⟩ 5 : characterized by or manifesting treachery : DISHONORABLE, UNFAIR ⟨by fair means or ~⟩ 6 : marking the bounds of a playing field ⟨~ lines⟩; also : being outside the foul line ⟨~ ball⟩ ⟨~ territory⟩ 7 : containing marked-up corrections 8 : ENTANGLED — **foul·ly** adv

♦ [1a] fetid, malodorous, noisome, rank, reeky, smelly, strong — more at MALODOROUS ♦ [1b] dirty, filthy, muddy, unclean ♦ [2] abhorrent, awful, distasteful, obnoxious, odious, offensive, repellent, repugnant, repulsive ♦ [4] bleak, dirty, inclement, nasty, raw, rough, squally, stormy, tempestuous, turbulent **Ant** clement, fair

²foul n 1 : an entanglement or collision in fishing or sailing 2 : an infraction of the rules in a game or sport; also : a baseball hit outside the foul line

³foul vb 1 ♦ : to make or become foul or filthy 2 : to entangle or become entangled 3 : OBSTRUCT, BLOCK 4 : to collide with 5 : to make or hit a foul

♦ befoul, blacken, contaminate, dirty, muddy, smirch, soil, stain, taint

⁴foul adv : in a foul manner

fou·lard \fù-ˈlärd\ n : a lightweight silk of plain or twill weave usu. decorated with a printed pattern

foul-mouthed \ˈfaú(-ə)l-ˈmaúthd, -ˈmaútht\ adj : given to the use of obscene, profane, or abusive language

foul·ness n ♦ : the quality or state of being foul

♦ dirtiness, filth, filthiness, grossness, nastiness, obscenity, smut, vulgarity — more at OBSCENITY

foul play n 1 : unfair, dishonest, or treacherous conduct or dealing : VIOLENCE 2 : the crime of unlawfully killing a person esp. with malice aforethought : MURDER

foul-up \ˈfaú(-ə)l-ˌəp\ n 1 : a state of being fouled up 2 : a mechanical difficulty

foul up vb 1 ♦ : to spoil by mistakes or poor judgment 2 : to cause a foul-up : BUNGLE

♦ bobble, botch, bungle, butcher, flub, fumble, mangle, mess up, screw up — more at BOTCH

¹found \ˈfaúnd\ past and past part of FIND

²found vb [ME, fr. AF funder, fonder, fr. L fundare, fr. fundus bottom] 1 : to take the first steps in building 2 : to set or ground on something solid : BASE 3 ♦ : to establish (as an institution) often with provision for future maintenance

♦ establish, inaugurate, initiate, institute, introduce, launch, pioneer, set up, start **Ant** close (down), phase out, shut (up)

foun·da·tion \faún-ˈdā-shən\ n 1 : the act of founding 2 ♦ : a basis upon which something stands or is supported ⟨suspicions without ~⟩ 3 a : funds given for the permanent support of an institution or cause : ENDOWMENT b : an endowed institution 4 : supporting structure : BASE 5 : CORSET — **foun·da·tion·al** \-shə-nəl\ adj

♦ [2] base, basis, bedrock, cornerstone, footing, ground, groundwork, keystone, underpinning — more at CORNERSTONE ♦ [3b] establishment, institute, institution — more at INSTITUTION

¹foun·der \ˈfaún-dər\ vb 1 : to make or become lame ⟨the

horse ~ed⟩ 2 : COLLAPSE 3 : SINK ⟨a ~ing ship⟩ 4 : FAIL

²found·er n ♦ : one that founds or establishes

♦ author, creator, father, originator — more at FATHER

found·ling \ˈfaúnd-liŋ\ n : an infant found after its unknown parents have abandoned it

found·ry \ˈfaún-drē\ n, pl foundries : a building or works where metal is cast

fount \ˈfaúnt\ n : SOURCE, FOUNTAIN

foun·tain \ˈfaúnt-ᵊn\ n 1 : a spring of water 2 : SOURCE 3 : an artificial jet of water 4 : a container for liquid that can be drawn off as needed

foun·tain·head \-ˌhed\ n : SOURCE

fountain pen n : a pen with a reservoir that feeds the writing point with ink

four \ˈfōr\ n 1 : one more than three 2 : the 4th in a set or series 3 : something having four units — **four** adj or pron

4x4 also **four–by–four** \ˈfōr-bī-ˌfōr\ n : a four-wheel automobile with four-wheel drive

four–flush \-ˌfləsh\ vb : to make a false claim : BLUFF — **four–flush·er** n

four·fold \-ˌfōld, -ˈfōld\ adj 1 : being four times as great or as many 2 : having four units or members — **four·fold** \-ˈfōld\ adv

4–H \ˈfōr-ˈāch\ adj [fr. the fourfold aim of improving the head, heart, hands, and health] : of or relating to a program set up by the U.S. Department of Agriculture to help young people become productive citizens — **4–H'·er** n

Four Hundred or **400** n : the exclusive social set of a community — used with the

four–in–hand \ˈfōr-ən-ˌhand\ n 1 : a team of four horses driven by one person; also : a vehicle drawn by such a team 2 : a necktie tied in a slipknot with long ends overlapping vertically in front

four–o'clock \ˈfōr-ə-ˌkläk\ n : a garden plant with fragrant yellow, red, or white flowers without petals that open late in the afternoon

four–post·er \ˈfōr-ˈpō-stər\ n : a bed with tall corner posts orig. designed to support curtains or a canopy

four·score \ˈfōr-ˈskōr\ adj : being four times twenty : EIGHTY

four·some \ˈfōr-səm\ n 1 : a group of four persons or things 2 : a golf match between two pairs of partners

¹four·square \-ˈskwer\ adj 1 : SQUARE 2 ♦ : marked by boldness and conviction : FORTHRIGHT

♦ candid, direct, forthright, frank, honest, open, outspoken, plain, straightforward, unreserved — more at FRANK

²foursquare adv ♦ : in a foursquare manner

♦ directly, forthrightly, plain, plainly, straight, straightforward

four·teen \fōr-ˈtēn\ n : one more than 13 — **fourteen** adj or pron — **four·teenth** \-ˈtēnth\ adj or n

fourth \ˈfōrth\ n 1 : one that is number four in a countable series 2 : one of four equal parts of something — **fourth** adj or adv

fourth estate n, often cap F&E : the public press

fourth wall n : an imaginary wall that keeps performers from recognizing or directly addressing their audience

4WD abbr four-wheel drive

four–wheel \ˈfōr-ˌhwēl\ or **four·wheeled** \-ˌhwēld\ adj : acting on or by means of four wheels of a motor vehicle

four–wheel drive n : an automotive drive mechanism that acts on all four wheels of the vehicle; also : a vehicle with such a drive

¹fowl \ˈfaú(-ə)l\ n, pl fowl or fowls 1 : BIRD 2 : a cock or hen of the domestic chicken; also : the flesh of these used as food

²fowl vb : to hunt wildfowl

¹fox \ˈfäks\ n, pl fox·es also fox 1 : any of various flesh-eating mammals related to the wolves but smaller and with shorter legs and a more pointed muzzle; also : the fur of a fox **2** : a clever crafty person **3** *cap* : a member of an American Indian people formerly living in what is now Wisconsin **4** ♦ : a good-looking young woman

♦ beauty, dream, enchantress, knockout, queen — more at BEAUTY

²**fox** *vb* ♦ : to trick by ingenuity or cunning : OUTWIT

♦ outfox, outmaneuver, outsmart, outwit, overreach — more at OUTWIT

fox-glove \'fäks-ˌgləv\ *n* : a common plant related to the snapdragons that is grown for its showy spikes of dotted white or purple tubular flowers and as a source of digitalis
fox-hole \-ˌhōl\ *n* : a pit dug for protection against enemy fire
fox-hound \-ˌhau̇nd\ *n* : any of various large swift powerful hounds used in hunting foxes
fox-ing \'fäk-siŋ\ *n* : brownish spots on old paper
fox terrier *n* : a small lively terrier that occurs in varieties with smooth dense coats or with harsh wiry coats
fox-trot \'fäks-ˌträt\ *n* **1** : a short broken slow trotting gait **2** : a ballroom dance in duple time
foxy \'fäk-sē\ *adj* **fox-i-er; -est** **1** : resembling or suggestive of a fox **2** ♦ : cunningly shrewd : WILY **3** : physically attractive

♦ artful, cagey, crafty, cunning, devious, guileful, slick, sly, subtle, wily — more at ARTFUL

foy-er \'fȯi-ər, 'fȯi-ˌyā\ *n* [F, lit., fireplace, fr. OF *foier*, fr. VL *focarium*, fr. L *focus* hearth] **1** ♦ : an anteroom or lobby esp. of a theater **2** ♦ : an entrance hallway

♦ [1, 2] entry, hall, lobby, vestibule — more at HALL

fpm *abbr* feet per minute
FPO *abbr* fleet post office
fps *abbr* feet per second
fr *abbr* **1** father **2** franc **3** friar **4** from
¹**Fr** *abbr* **1** France; French **2** Friday
²**Fr** *symbol* francium
fra-cas \'frā-kəs, 'fra-\ *n, pl* **fra-cas-es** \-kə-səz\ [F, din, row, fr. It *fracasso*, fr. *fracassare* to shatter] ♦ : a noisy quarrel

♦ brawl, fray, free-for-all, melee, row — more at BRAWL

frack-ing \'fra-kiŋ\ *n* [by shortening fr. (*hydraulic*) *fracturing*] : the injection of fluid into shale beds so as to free up petroleum — **frack** \'frak\ *vb*
frac-tal \'frak-t³l\ *n* : an irregular curve or shape that repeats itself at any scale on which it is examined — **fractal** *adj*
frac-tion \'frak-shən\ *n* **1** : a numerical representation (as ½, ¾, or 3.323) indicating the quotient of two numbers **2** : FRAGMENT **3** : PORTION — **frac-tion-al** \-shə-nəl\ *adj* — **frac-tion-al-ly** *adv*
frac-tious \'frak-shəs\ *adj* **1** : tending to be troublesome : hard to handle or control **2** : QUARRELSOME, IRRITABLE
¹**frac-ture** \'frak-chər\ *n* **1** : a breaking of something and esp. a bone **2** : CRACK, CLEFT
²**fracture** *vb* ♦ : to break or cause to break

♦ break, bust, fragment — more at BREAK

frag-ile \'fra-jəl, -ˌjīl\ *adj* ♦ : easily broken : DELICATE

♦ breakable, delicate, frail *Ant* nonbreakable, strong, sturdy, tough, unbreakable

fra-gil-i-ty \frə-'ji-lə-tē\ *n* ♦ : the quality or state of being fragile

♦ daintiness, delicacy, fineness — more at DELICACY

¹**frag-ment** \'frag-mənt\ *n* ♦ : a part broken off, detached, or incomplete

♦ piece, scrap

²**frag-ment** \-ˌment\ *vb* ♦ : to break into fragments — **frag-men-ta-tion** \ˌfrag-mən-'tā-shən, -ˌmən-\ *n*

♦ break, bust, fracture — more at BREAK

frag-men-tary \'frag-mən-ˌter-ē\ *adj* ♦ : made up of fragments : INCOMPLETE

♦ deficient, halfway, incomplete, partial — more at IN-COMPLETE

fra-grance \-grəns\ *n* ♦ : a sweet or delicate odor

♦ aroma, bouquet, incense, perfume, redolence, scent, spice; *also* odor *Ant* reek, stench, stink

fra-grant \'frā-grənt\ *adj* ♦ : sweet or agreeable in smell — **fra-grant-ly** *adv*

♦ ambrosial, aromatic, redolent, savory, scented; *also* sweet, pungent, spicy; odorous; clean, fresh, pure *Ant* fetid, foul, malodorous, noisome, putrid, smelly, stinking

frail \'frāl\ *adj* [ME, fr. AF *fraile*, fr. L *fragilis* fragile, fr. *frangere* to break] **1** ♦ : morally or physically weak **2** ♦ : easily broken or destroyed : FRAGILE, DELICATE

♦ [1] delicate, feeble, infirm, tender, wasted, weak
♦ [2] breakable, delicate, fragile — more at FRAGILE

frail-ty \'frāl-tē\ *n, pl* **frailties** **1** ♦ : the quality or state of being frail **2** ♦ : a fault due to weakness

♦ [1] debility, delicacy, faintness, feebleness, infirmity, weakness ♦ [2] demerit, failing, fault, foible, shortcoming, vice, weakness — more at FAULT

¹**frame** \'frām\ *vb* **framed; fram-ing** **1** ♦ : to make plans **2** ♦ : to form, make, or create by combining parts or elements : SHAPE, CONSTRUCT **3** ♦ : to give expression to : FORMULATE **4** ♦ : to make a draft of or draw up ⟨∼ a constitution⟩ **5** : to make appear guilty **6** : to fit or adjust for a purpose : ARRANGE **7** : to provide with or enclose in a frame — **fram-er** *n*

♦ [1] arrange, blueprint, calculate, chart, design, lay out, map, plan, project, scheme — more at PLAN
♦ [2] construct, fabricate, fashion, form, make, manufacture, produce, shape — more at MAKE ♦ [3, 4] cast, compose, craft, draft, draw, formulate, prepare — more at COMPOSE

²**frame** *n* **1** : something made of parts fitted and joined together **2** ♦ : the physical makeup of the body **3** ♦ : an arrangement of structural parts that gives form or support **4** : a supporting or enclosing border or open case (as for a window or picture) **5** : one picture of a series (as on a length of film) **6** : FRAME-UP

♦ [2] build, constitution, figure, form, physique, shape — more at PHYSIQUE ♦ [3] configuration, framework, shell, skeleton, structure

³**frame** *adj* : having a wood frame
frame of mind *n* : mental attitude or outlook : MOOD
frame-up \'frā-ˌməp\ *n* **1** : an act or series of actions in which someone is framed **2** : an action that is planned, contrived, or formulated
frame-work \'frām-ˌwərk\ *n* ♦ : a basic supporting part or structure

♦ configuration, frame, shell, skeleton, structure — more at FRAME

franc \'fraŋk\ *n* **1** : any of various former basic monetary units (as of Belgium, France, and Luxembourg) **2** : a basic monetary unit of any of several countries esp. in Africa
fran-chise \'fran-ˌchīz\ *n* [ME, fr. MF, fr. *franchir* to free, fr. OF *franc* free] **1** : a right or license granted to an individual or group ⟨a ∼ to operate a ferry⟩ **2 a** : a constitutional or statutory right or privilege **b** ♦ : the right to vote **3** : the right of membership in a professional sports league; *also* : a team having such membership

♦ enfranchisement, suffrage, vote — more at VOTE

fran-chi-see \ˌfran-ˌchī-'zē, -chə-\ *n* : one granted a franchise
fran-chis-er \'fran-ˌchī-zər\ *n* **1** : FRANCHISEE **2** : FRANCHISOR
fran-chi-sor \ˌfran-ˌchī-'zȯr, -chə-\ *n* : one that grants a franchise
fran-ci-um \'fran-sē-əm\ *n* : a radioactive metallic chemical element
Fran-co-Amer-i-can \ˌfraŋ-kō-ə-'mer-ə-kən\ *n* : an American of French or esp. French-Canadian descent — **Franco-American** *adj*

fran·gi·ble \'fran-jə-bəl\ *adj* : BREAKABLE — **fran·gi·bil·i·ty** \ˌfran-jə-'bi-lə-tē\ *n*

¹frank \'fraŋk\ *adj* ♦ : marked by free, forthright, and sincere expression

♦ candid, direct, forthright, honest, open, outspoken, plain, straight, straightforward *Ant* dissembling

²frank *vb* : to mark (a piece of mail) with an official sign so that it can be mailed free; *also* : to mail free

³frank *n* **1** : the signature or mark on a piece of mail indicating free or paid postage **2** : the privilege of sending mail free

⁴frank *n* : FRANKFURTER

Fran·ken·stein \'fran-kən-ˌstīn\ *n* **1** : a monstrous creation that usu. ruins its originator **2** : a monster in the shape of a man

frank·furt·er \'fraŋk-fər-tər, -ˌfər-\ *or* **frank·furt** \-fərt\ *n* : a seasoned sausage (as of beef or beef and pork)

frank·in·cense \'fran-kən-ˌsens\ *n* : a fragrant resin burned as incense

frank·ly \'fran-klē\ *adv* **1** : in a frank manner **2** ♦ : in truth

♦ actually, honestly, really, truly, truthfully, verily — more at ACTUALLY

frank·ness *n* ♦ : the quality or state of being frank

♦ candor (*or* candour), directness, forthrightness, openness, plainness — more at CANDOR

fran·tic \'fran-tik\ *adj* ♦ : marked by or showing uncontrolled emotion or disordered anxious activity

♦ agitated, distraught, feverish, frenetic, frenzied, hysterical *Ant* collected, composed, self-possessed

fran·ti·cal·ly \-ti-k(ə-)lē\ *adv* ♦ : in a frantic manner

♦ berserk, hectically, helter-skelter, madly, pell-mell, wild, wildly — more at HELTER-SKELTER

frap·pé \fra-'pā\ *or* **frappe** *same or* 'frap\ *n* [F *frappé*, fr. pp. of *frapper* to strike, chill] **1** : an iced or frozen drink **2** : a thick milk shake — **frap·pé** \fra-'pā\ *adj*

fra·ter·nal \frə-'tərn-ᵊl\ *adj* **1** : of, relating to, or involving brothers **2** : of, relating to, or being a fraternity or society **3** : derived from two ova ⟨~ twins⟩ **4** : FRIENDLY, BROTHERLY — **fra·ter·nal·ly** *adv*

fra·ter·ni·ty \frə-'tər-nə-tē\ *n, pl* **-ties** **1** ♦ : a social, honorary, or professional group; *esp* : a men's student organization formed chiefly for social purposes **2** : BROTHERLINESS **3** : persons of the same class, profession, or tastes

♦ association, brotherhood, club, council, fellowship, guild, league, order, organization, society — more at ASSOCIATION

frat·er·nize \'fra-tər-ˌnīz\ *vb* **-nized; -niz·ing** **1** ♦ : to mingle as friends **2** : to associate on close terms with members of a hostile group — **frat·er·ni·za·tion** \ˌfra-tər-nə-'zā-shən\ *n*

♦ associate, chum, consort, hang around, hobnob, pal — more at ASSOCIATE

frat·ri·cide \'fra-trə-ˌsīd\ *n* **1** : one that kills a sibling or countryman **2** : the act of a fratricide — **frat·ri·cid·al** \ˌfra-trə-'sīd-ᵊl\ *adj*

fraud \'frȯd\ *n* **1** : DECEIT, TRICKERY **2** : TRICK **3** ♦ : a person who is not what he or she pretends to be : IMPOSTOR

♦ charlatan, fake, hoaxer, humbug, impostor, mountebank, phony, pretender, quack

fraud·ster \'frȯd-stər\ *n, chiefly Brit* : a person who engages in fraud

fraud·u·lent \'frȯ-jə-lənt\ *adj* ♦ : characterized by, based on, or done by fraud — **fraud·u·lent·ly** *adv*

♦ crooked, deceitful, deceptive, dishonest, double-dealing, false, misleading, specious *Ant* aboveboard, honest, truthful

fraught \'frȯt\ *adj* ♦ : full of or accompanied by something specified ⟨~ with danger⟩

♦ flush, replete, rife

¹fray \'frā\ *n* ♦ : a usu. disorderly or protracted fight, struggle, or dispute : FIGHT, STRUGGLE

♦ battle, clash, combat, conflict, contest, fight, fracas, hassle, struggle

²fray *vb* **1** ♦ : to wear (as an edge of cloth) by rubbing **2** : to separate the threads at the edge of **3** : STRAIN, IRRITATE ⟨~ed nerves⟩

♦ abrade, chafe, erode, fret, gall, rub, wear — more at ABRADE

fraz·zle \'fra-zəl\ *vb* **fraz·zled; fraz·zling** **1** : FRAY **2** : to put in a state of extreme physical or nervous fatigue — **frazzle** *n*

¹freak \'frēk\ *n* **1** ♦ : a sudden and odd or seemingly pointless idea or turn of the mind : a seemingly capricious action or event **2** ♦ : a strange, abnormal, or unusual person or thing **3** *slang* : a person who uses an illicit drug **4** ♦ : an ardent enthusiast — **freaky** \'frē-kē\ *adj*

♦ [1] caprice, fancy, notion, vagary, whim — more at WHIM ♦ [2] abnormality, monster, monstrosity *Ant* average, norm ♦ [4] addict, aficionado, buff, bug, devotee, enthusiast, fan, fanatic, fancier, fiend, lover, maniac, nut — more at FAN

²freak *vb* **1** : to experience the effects (as hallucinations) of taking illicit drugs — often used with *out* **2** ♦ : to distress or become distressed — often used with *out* — **freak–out** \'frē-ˌkau̇t\ *n*

♦ *usu* **freak out** agitate, bother, concern, distress, disturb, exercise, perturb, unsettle, upset, worry

³freak *adj* ♦ : having the character of a freak

♦ aberrant, abnormal, atypical, exceeding, exceptional, extraordinary, odd, peculiar, phenomenal, rare, singular, uncommon, uncustomary, unique, unusual, unwonted — more at EXCEPTIONAL

¹freck·le \'fre-kəl\ *n* : a brownish spot on the skin

²freckle *vb* ♦ : to sprinkle or mark with freckles or small spots

♦ dot, fleck, pepper, speck, spot, sprinkle

¹free \'frē\ *adj* **fre·er; fre·est** **1** ♦ : having liberty **2** ♦ : enjoying political or personal independence; *also* : not subject to or allowing slavery **3** : made or done voluntarily : SPONTANEOUS **4** : relieved from or lacking something unpleasant **5** : not subject to a duty, tax, or charge **6** ♦ : not obstructed : CLEAR **7** : not being used or occupied **8** : not fastened **9** : LAVISH **10** : OPEN, FRANK ⟨a ~ exchange of ideas⟩ **11 a** ♦ : given without charge **b** ♦ : made, done, or given voluntarily or spontaneously **12** : not literal or exact **13** : not restricted by conventional forms **14** ♦ : overly familiar or forward in action or attitude

♦ [1] footloose, loose, unbound, unconfined, unrestrained *Ant* bound, confined, restrained, unfree ♦ [2] autonomous, independent, self-governing, separate, sovereign *Ant* dependent, subject, unfree ♦ [6] clear, open, unobstructed — more at OPEN ♦ [11a] complimentary, gratuitous ♦ [11b] bountiful, charitable, generous, liberal, munificent, openhanded, unselfish, unsparing — more at GENEROUS ♦ [14] bold, familiar, forward, immodest, presumptuous — more at PRESUMPTUOUS

²free *vb* **freed; free·ing** **1** ♦ : to set free **2** ♦ : to relieve or rid of what restrains, confines, restricts, or embarrasses **3** ♦ : to clear from what obstructs or is unneeded : CLEAR

♦ [1, 2] discharge, emancipate, enfranchise, liberate, manumit, release, unchain, unfetter *Ant* bind, confine, enchain, fetter, restrain ♦ [2] clear, disburden, disencumber, relieve, rid, unburden — more at RID ♦ [2, 3] clear, disengage, disentangle, extricate, liberate, release, untangle — more at EXTRICATE ♦ [3] clear, open, unclog, unstop

³free *adv* **1** : FREELY **2** : without charge

free·base \'frē-ˌbās\ *n* : purified cocaine smoked as crack or heated to produce vapors for inhalation — **freebase** *vb*

free·bie *or* **free·bee** \'frē-bē\ *n* ♦ : something given without charge

♦ bestowal, donation, gift, lagniappe, present — more at GIFT

free·board \'frē-ˌbōrd\ *n* : the vertical distance between the waterline and the upper edge of the side of a boat

free·boo·ter \-ˌbü-tər\ *n* [D *vrijbuiter*, fr. *vrijbuit* plunder, fr. *vrij* free + *buit* booty] ♦ : one who commits or practices piracy : PIRATE

♦ buccaneer, corsair, pirate, rover — more at PIRATE

free·born \-'bórn\ *adj* **1** : not born in vassalage or slavery **2** : of, relating to, or befitting one that is freeborn

freed·man \'frēd-mən, -ˌman\ *n* : a person freed from slavery

free·dom \'frē-dəm\ *n* **1** ♦ : the quality or state of being free : INDEPENDENCE · **2** : EXEMPTION, RELEASE **3** : EASE, FACILITY **4** : FRANKNESS **5** : unrestricted use **6** : a political right; *also* : FRANCHISE, PRIVILEGE **7** ♦ : the ability or capacity to act without undue hindrance or restraint

♦ [1] autonomy, independence, liberty, self-government, sovereignty *Ant* dependence, subjection ♦ [7] authorization, latitude, license (*or* licence), run; *also* authority, mandate, power

freedom fighter *n* : a person who takes part in a resistance movement against an oppressive political or social establishment

free enterprise *n* : freedom of private business to operate with little regulation by the government

¹free–for–all \'frē-fə-ˌról\ *adj* ♦ : unrestricted as to entries, participants, or users

♦ open, public, unrestricted — more at OPEN

²free–for–all *n* ♦ : a competition or fight open to all comers and usu. with no rules : BRAWL

♦ brawl, fracas, fray, melee, row — more at BRAWL

free·hand \-ˌhand\ *adj* : done without mechanical aids or devices ⟨a ∼ drawing⟩

free·hold \'frē-ˌhōld\ *n* : ownership of an estate for life usu. with the right to bequeath it to one's heirs; *also* : an estate thus owned — **free·hold·er** *n*

free·lance \-ˌlans\ *n* : one who pursues a profession (as writing) without a long-term commitment to any one employer — **free·lance** *adj or vb*

free–liv·ing \'frē-'li-viŋ\ *adj* **1** : unrestricted in pursuing personal pleasures **2** : being neither parasitic nor symbiotic ⟨∼ organisms⟩

free·load \'frē-ˌlōd\ *vb* : to impose upon another's hospitality — **free·load·er** *n*

free love *n* **1** : the practice of living openly with a sexual partner without marriage **2** : sexual relations without any commitments by either partner

free·ly *adv* ♦ : in a free manner

♦ easily, effortlessly, fluently, handily, lightly, painlessly, readily, smoothly — more at EASILY

free·man \'frē-mən, -ˌman\ *n* **1** : one who has civil or political liberty **2** : one having the full rights of a citizen

Free·ma·son \-ˌmās-ᵊn\ *n* : a member of a secret fraternal society called Free and Accepted Masons — **Free·ma·son·ry** \-rē\ *n*

free radical *n* : an esp. reactive atom or group of atoms with one or more unpaired electrons; *esp* : one that can cause bodily damage (as by altering the chemical structure of cells)

free–range \'frē-ˌrānj\ *adj* : allowed to range and forage with relative freedom ⟨∼ chickens⟩; *also* : produced by free-range animals ⟨∼ eggs⟩

free speech *n* : speech that is protected by the First Amendment to the U.S. Constitution

free spirit *n* : NONCONFORMIST

free·stand·ing \'frē-'stan-diŋ\ *adj* ♦ : standing alone or on its own foundation free of support

♦ detached, disconnected, discrete, separate, single, unattached, unconnected — more at SEPARATE

free·stone \'frē-ˌstōn\ *n* **1** : a stone that may be cut freely without splitting **2** : a fruit stone to which the flesh does not cling; *also* : a fruit (as a peach or cherry) having such a stone

free·think·er \-'thiŋ-kər\ *n* : one who forms opinions on the basis of reason independently of authority; *esp* : one who doubts or denies religious dogma — **free·think·ing** *n or adj*

free trade *n* : trade between nations without restrictions (as high taxes on imports)

free verse *n* : verse whose meter is irregular or whose rhythm is not metrical

free·ware \'frē-ˌwer\ *n* : software that is free or that has a small usu. optional cost

free·way \'frē-ˌwā\ *n* : an expressway without tolls

free·wheel \-'hwēl\ *vb* : to move, live, or play freely or irresponsibly

free·wheel·ing \ˌfrē-'hwē-liŋ\ *adj* : free and loose in form or manner

free–will \'frē-ˌwil\ *adj* ♦ : produced in or by an act of choice

♦ deliberate, intentional, purposeful, voluntary, willful, willing — more at DELIBERATE

free will *n* ♦ : voluntary choice or decision

♦ accord, choice, option, self-determination, volition, will

¹freeze \'frēz\ *vb* **froze** \'frōz\; **fro·zen** \'frōz-ᵊn\; **freez·ing** **1** ♦ : to harden or cause to harden into a solid (as ice) by loss of heat **2** : to withstand freezing **3** : to chill or become chilled with cold **4** : to damage by frost **5** : to adhere solidly by or as if by freezing **6** : to become fixed, motionless, or incapable of speech **7** : to cause to grip tightly **8** : to become clogged with ice **9** : to fix at a certain stage or level

♦ concrete, congeal, firm, harden, set, solidify — more at HARDEN

²freeze *n* **1** : an act or instance of freezing **2** : the state of being frozen **3** : a state of weather marked by low temperature

freeze–dry \'frēz-'drī\ *vb* : to dry in a frozen state under vacuum esp. for preservation — **freeze–dried** *adj*

freez·er \'frē-zər\ *n* : a compartment, device, or room for freezing food or keeping it frozen

freez·ing *adj* ♦ : very cold

♦ arctic, cold, frigid, frosty, glacial, icy, polar, wintry

¹freight \'frāt\ *n* **1** : payment for carrying goods **2** ♦ : something that is loaded for transportation : CARGO **3** : BURDEN **4** : the carrying of goods by a common carrier **5** : a train that carries freight

♦ burden, cargo, haul, lading, load, payload, weight — more at LOAD

²freight *vb* **1** : to load with goods for transportation **2** : BURDEN, CHARGE **3** : to ship or transport by freight

freight·er \'frā-tər\ *n* : a ship or airplane used chiefly to carry freight

French \'french\ *n* **1** : the language of France **2** **French** *pl* : the people of France **3** : strong language — **French** *adj* — **French·man** \-mən\ *n* — **French·wom·an** \-ˌwu̇-mən\ *n*

French Canadian *n* : one of the descendants of French settlers in Lower Canada — **French–Canadian** *adj*

French door *n* : a door with small panes of glass extending the full length

French dressing *n* **1** : a thin salad dressing usu. made of vinegar and oil with spices **2** : a creamy salad dressing flavored with tomatoes

french fry *n, often cap 1st F* : a strip of potato fried in deep fat until brown — **french fry** *vb, often cap 1st F*

French horn *n* : a curved brass instrument with a funnel-shaped mouthpiece and a flaring bell

French press *n* : a coffeepot in which ground beans are infused and then pressed by a plunger

French toast *n* : bread dipped in a mixture of eggs and milk and fried at a low heat

French twist *n* : a woman's hairstyle in which the hair is coiled at the rear and secured in place

fren·e·my \'fre-nə-mē\ *n, pl* **-mies** : one who pretends to be a friend but is actually an enemy

fre·net·ic \fri-'ne-tik\ *adj* ♦ : marked by fast and nervous, disordered, or anxiety-driven activity : FRANTIC — **fre·net·i·cal·ly** \-ti-k(ə-)lē\ *adv*

♦ delirious, feverish, fierce, frantic, frenzied, furious, mad, rabid, violent, wild — more at FURIOUS

fren·zied \'fren-zēd\ *adj* ♦ : feeling or showing great or abnormal excitement or emotional disturbance

♦ delirious, feverish, frantic, frenetic, furious, hectic, hysterical

fren·zy \'fren-zē\ *n, pl* **frenzies** 1 ♦ : temporary madness or a violently agitated state 2 ♦ : intense often disordered activity

♦ [1, 2] agitation, chaos, confusion, disorder, furor, fury, hysteria, rage, rampage, tumult, turmoil, uproar

freq *abbr* frequency; frequent; frequently

fre·quen·cy \'frē-kwən-sē\ *n, pl* **-cies** 1 : the fact or condition of occurring frequently 2 : rate of occurrence 3 : the number of cycles per second of an alternating current 4 : the number of waves (as of sound or electromagnetic energy) that pass a fixed point each second

frequency modulation *n* : variation of the frequency of a carrier wave according to another signal; *also* : FM

¹fre·quent \frē-'kwent, 'frē-kwənt\ *vb* ♦ : to associate with, be in, or resort to habitually

♦ hang around, hang out, haunt, resort, visit *Ant* avoid, shun

²fre·quent \'frē-kwənt\ *adj* 1 ♦ : happening often or at short intervals 2 ♦ : done or happening on a regular or recurring basis

♦ [1] common, commonplace, customary, everyday, familiar, ordinary, routine, usual — more at COMMON ♦ [2] constant, habitual, periodic, regular, repeated, steady — more at REGULAR

fre·quent·er *n* : one that frequents

fre·quent–fli·er \'frē-kwənt-'flī-ər\ *adj* : of, relating to, or being an airline program offering awards for specified numbers of air miles traveled

fre·quent·ly *adv* ♦ : at frequent or short intervals

♦ constantly, continually, often, repeatedly — more at OFTEN

fres·co \'fres-kō\ *n, pl* **frescoes** [It, fr. *fresco* fresh] : the art of painting on fresh plaster; *also* : a painting done by this method

fresh \'fresh\ *adj* 1 : VIGOROUS, REFRESHED 2 : not containing salt 3 : not altered by processing (as freezing or canning) 4 : free from taint : PURE 5 : fairly strong : BRISK ⟨~ breeze⟩ 6 ♦ : not stale, sour, or decayed ⟨~ bread⟩ 7 : not faded 8 ♦ : not worn or rumpled 9 ♦ : experienced, made, or received newly or anew 10 : ADDITIONAL, ANOTHER ⟨made a ~ start⟩ 11 : ORIGINAL, VIVID 12 : INEXPERIENCED 13 : newly come or arrived ⟨~ from school⟩ 14 ♦ : disposed to take liberties : IMPUDENT

♦ [6, 8] brand-new, pristine, virgin; *also* unaltered, unblemished, unbruised, uncontaminated, undamaged, undefiled, unharmed, unhurt, unimpaired, uninjured, unpolluted, unsoiled, unspoiled, unsullied, untainted, untouched, unused, unworn *Ant* [9] new, novel, original, unfamiliar — more at NEW ♦ [14] bold, brash, brazen, cheeky, impudent, insolent, nervy, sassy, saucy — more at NERVY

fresh·en \'fre-shən\ *vb* ♦ : to make, grow, or become fresh

♦ refresh, rejuvenate, renew, restore, revitalize, revive — more at RENEW

fresh·et \'fre-shət\ *n* : an overflowing of a stream (as by heavy rains)

fresh·ly *adv* ♦ : in a fresh manner

♦ just, late, lately, new, newly, now, only, recently — more at NEWLY

fresh·man \'fresh-mən\ *n* 1 : a 1st-year student 2 ♦ : one that begins something; *esp* : an inexperienced person

♦ beginner, greenhorn, neophyte, newcomer, novice, recruit, rookie, tenderfoot, tyro — more at BEGINNER

fresh·ness *n* ♦ : the quality or state of being fresh

♦ newness, novelty, originality — more at NOVELTY

fresh·wa·ter \-,wȯ-tər, -,wä-\ *n* : water that is not salty — **freshwater** *adj*

¹fret \'fret\ *vb* **fret·ted; fret·ting** [ME, to devour, fret, fr. OE *fretan* to devour] 1 : to eat or gnaw into 2 ♦ : to chafe with or as if with friction : RUB 3 : to make by wearing away 4 ♦ : to become irritated : WORRY ⟨*fretted* over his taxes⟩ 5 : GRATE; *also* : AGITATE

♦ [2] abrade, chafe, erode, fray, gall, rub, wear — more at ABRADE ♦ [4] bother, fear, stew, sweat, trouble, worry — more at WORRY

²fret *n* ♦ : an irritated or worried state ⟨in a ~ about the interview⟩

♦ dither, fluster, fuss, huff, lather, pother, stew, tizzy, twitter

³fret *n* : ornamental work esp. of straight lines in symmetrical patterns

⁴fret *n* : one of a series of ridges across the fingerboard of a stringed musical instrument — **fret·ted** *adj*

fret·ful \'fret-fəl\ *adj* : IRRITABLE — **fret·ful·ly** *adv* — **fret·ful·ness** *n*

fret·saw \-,sȯ\ *n* : a narrow-bladed saw used for cutting curved outlines

fret·work \-,wərk\ *n* 1 : decoration consisting of frets 2 : ornamental openwork or work in relief

Fri *abbr* Friday

fri·a·ble \'frī-ə-bəl\ *adj* ♦ : easily crumbled or pulverized ⟨~ soil⟩

♦ brittle, crisp, crumbly, flaky — more at CRISP

fri·ar \'frī-ər\ *n* [ME *frere, fryer,* fr. AF *frere, friere,* lit., brother, fr. L *frater*] : a member of a religious order that orig. lived by alms

fri·ary \'frī-ər-ē\ *n, pl* **-ar·ies** ♦ : a monastery of friars

♦ abbey, cloister, monastery, priory — more at MONASTERY

¹fric·as·see \'fri-kə-,sē, ,fri-kə-'sē\ *n* : a dish made of meat (as chicken) cut into pieces, stewed in stock, and served in sauce

²fricassee *vb* **-seed; -see·ing** : to cook as a fricassee

fric·tion \'frik-shən\ *n* 1 : the rubbing of one body against another 2 : the force that resists motion between bodies in contact 3 ♦ : clash in opinions between persons or groups : DISAGREEMENT — **fric·tion·al** *adj*

♦ conflict, discord, dissent, disunity, schism, strife, variance — more at DISCORD

friction tape *n* : a usu. cloth adhesive tape impregnated with insulating material and used esp. to protect and insulate electrical conductors

Fri·day \'frī-dē, -(,)dā\ *n* : the sixth day of the week

fridge \'frij\ *n* : REFRIGERATOR

fried·cake \'frīd-,kāk\ *n* : DOUGHNUT, CRULLER

fried rice *n* : a dish of boiled or steamed rice that is stir-fried with soy sauce and typically includes egg, meat, and vegetables

¹friend \'frend\ *n* 1 ♦ : one attached to another by respect or affection 2 : ACQUAINTANCE 3 : one who is not hostile 4 ♦ : one who supports or favors something ⟨a ~ of art⟩ 5 *cap* : a member of the Society of Friends : QUAKER — **friend·less** *adj*

♦ [1] buddy, chum, comrade, crony, familiar, intimate, pal *Ant* enemy, foe ♦ [4] advocate, apostle, backer, booster, champion, exponent, promoter, proponent, supporter — more at EXPONENT

²friend *vb* 1 : BEFRIEND 2 : to include (someone) in a list of designated friends on a person's social networking site

friend·li·ness \-lē-nəs\ *n* ♦ : the quality or state of being friendly

♦ amity, benevolence, cordiality, fellowship, friendship, goodwill, kindliness — more at GOODWILL

friend·ly \'fren(d)-lē\ *adj* ♦ : of, relating to, or befitting a friend

♦ appreciative, complimentary, favorable (*or* favourable), good, positive — more at FAVORABLE ♦ amicable, companionable, comradely, cordial, genial, hearty, neighborly, warm, warmhearted *Ant* antagonistic, hostile, unfriendly

friend·ship \-ˌship\ *n* ♦ : the state of being friends

♦ amity, benevolence, cordiality, fellowship, friendliness, goodwill, kindliness — more at GOODWILL

frieze \'frēz\ *n* : an ornamental often sculptured band extending around something (as a building or room)

frig·ate \'fri-gət\ *n* 1 : a square-rigged warship 2 : a warship smaller than a destroyer

fright \'frīt\ *n* 1 ♦ : sudden terror : ALARM 2 ♦ : something that is ugly or shocking

♦ [1] alarm, anxiety, apprehension, dread, fear, horror, panic, terror, trepidation — more at FEAR ♦ [2] eyesore, horror, mess, monstrosity, sight — more at EYESORE

fright·en \'frīt-ᵊn\ *vb* 1 ♦ : to make afraid 2 : to drive away or out by frightening 3 : to become frightened — **fright·en·ing** *adj* — **fright·en·ing·ly** *adv*

♦ alarm, horrify, panic, scare, shock, spook, startle, terrify, terrorize *Ant* reassure

fright·ful \'frīt-fəl\ *adj* 1 ♦ : causing intense fear or alarm : TERRIFYING 2 : startling esp. in being bad or objectionable 3 : EXTREME ⟨~ thirst⟩

♦ fearful, fearsome, forbidding, formidable, hair-raising, scary, shocking, terrifying — more at FEARFUL

fright·ful·ly *adv* ♦ : in a frightful manner

♦ especially, extremely, greatly, highly, hugely, mightily, mighty, mortally, most, much, real, right, so, very — more at VERY

fright·ful·ness *n* ♦ : the quality or state of being frightful

♦ atrociousness, atrocity, hideousness, horror, monstrosity, repulsiveness — more at HORROR

frig·id \'fri-jəd\ *adj* 1 ♦ : intensely cold 2 ♦ : lacking warmth or ardor : INDIFFERENT 3 : abnormally averse to or unable to achieve orgasm during sexual intercourse — used esp. of women — **fri·gid·i·ty** \fri-ˈji-də-tē\ *n*

♦ [1] arctic, bitter, cold, freezing, frosty, glacial, icy, polar, wintry — more at COLD ♦ [2] chill, chilly, cold, cool, frosty, icy, indifferent, unfriendly, wintry

frigid zone *n* : the area or region between the arctic circle and the north pole or between the antarctic circle and the south pole

frill \'fril\ *n* 1 ♦ : a gathered, pleated, or ruffled edging 2 ♦ : something unessential — **frilly** *adj*

♦ [1] flounce, furbelow, ruffle — more at RUFFLE ♦ [2] amenity, comfort, extra, indulgence, luxury, superfluity — more at LUXURY

¹fringe \'frinj\ *n* [ME *frenge*, fr. AF, fr. VL **frimbia*, alter. of L *fimbriae* (pl.)] 1 : an ornamental border consisting of short threads or strips hanging from an edge or band 2 ♦ : something that resembles a fringe : EDGE 3 : something that is additional or secondary to an activity, process, or subject

♦ border, boundary, edge, margin, perimeter, periphery — more at BORDER

²fringe *vb* 1 : to furnish or adorn with a fringe 2 ♦ : to serve as a border or fringe for

♦ border, bound, margin, rim, skirt — more at BORDER

fringe benefit *n* 1 : an employment benefit paid for by an employer without affecting basic wage rates 2 : any additional benefit

frip·pery \'fri-pə-rē\ *n, pl* **-per·ies** [MF *friperie*] 1 a ♦ : dressy or showy clothing and jewels : FINERY b ♦ : something showy, frivolous, or nonessential 2 : pretentious display

♦ [1a] array, best, bravery, caparison, feather, finery, full dress, gaiety, regalia — more at FINERY ♦ [1b] child's play, nothing, trifle, triviality — more at TRIFLE

frisk \'frisk\ *vb* 1 ♦ : to leap, skip, or dance in a lively or playful way : GAMBOL 2 : to search (a person) esp. for concealed weapons by running the hand rapidly over the clothing

♦ caper, cavort, disport, frolic, gambol, lark, rollick, romp, sport — more at FROLIC

frisk·i·ness \-kē-nəs\ *n* ♦ : the quality or state of being inclined to frisk

♦ impishness, mischief, mischievousness, playfulness — more at PLAYFULNESS

frisky \'fris-kē\ *adj* **frisk·i·er; -est** ♦ : inclined to frisk : PLAYFUL — **frisk·i·ly** \-kə-lē\ *adv*

♦ antic, coltish, elfish, fay, frolicsome, playful, sportive — more at PLAYFUL ♦ active, animated, energetic, lively, peppy, perky, spirited, sprightly

¹frit·ter \'fri-tər\ *n* : a small lump of fried batter often containing fruit or meat

²fritter *vb* 1 ♦ : to reduce or waste piecemeal — usu. used with *away* 2 : to break into small fragments

♦ *usu* fritter away blow, dissipate, lavish, misspend, run through, spend, squander, throw away, waste — more at WASTE

fritz \'frits\ *n* : a state of disorder or disrepair — used in the phrase *on the fritz*

fri·vol·i·ty \fri-ˈvä-lə-tē\ *n* ♦ : the quality or state of being frivolous

♦ facetiousness, flightiness, flippancy, levity, lightness *Ant* gravity, seriousness, soberness, sobriety

friv·o·lous \'fri-və-ləs\ *adj* 1 ♦ : of little importance : TRIVIAL 2 ♦ : lacking in seriousness — **friv·o·lous·ly** *adv*

♦ [1] insignificant, little, minor, minute, negligible, slight, small, trifling, trivial, unimportant — more at UNIMPORTANT ♦ [2] flighty, giddy, goofy, harebrained, light-headed, scatterbrained, silly — more at GIDDY

frizz \'friz\ *vb* : to form into small tight curls — **frizz** *n* — **frizzy** *adj*

friz·zies \'fri-zēz\ *n pl* : hair which has become difficult to manage (as due to humidity)

¹friz·zle \'fri-zəl\ *vb* **friz·zled; friz·zling** : FRIZZ, CURL — **frizzle** *n*

²frizzle *vb* **friz·zled; friz·zling** 1 : to fry until crisp and curled 2 : to cook with a sizzling noise

fro \'frō\ *adv* : BACK, AWAY — used in the phrase *to and fro*

frock \'fräk\ *n* 1 : an outer garment worn by monks and friars 2 : an outer garment worn esp. by men 3 : a woman's or girl's dress

frock coat *n* : a man's knee-length usu. double-breasted coat with knee-length skirts

frog \'frȯg, 'fräg\ *n* 1 : any of various largely aquatic smooth-skinned tailless leaping amphibians 2 : an ornamental braiding for fastening the front of a garment by a loop through which a button passes 3 : a condition in the throat causing hoarseness 4 : a small holder (as of metal, glass, or plastic) with perforations or spikes that is placed in a bowl or vase to keep cut flowers in position

frog·man \'frȯg-ˌman, 'fräg-, -mən\ *n* : a swimmer equipped to work underwater for long periods of time

¹frol·ic \'frä-lik\ *vb* **frol·icked; frol·ick·ing** 1 ♦ : to make merry 2 ♦ : to play about happily : ROMP

♦ caper, cavort, disport, frisk, gambol, lark, play, rollick, romp, sport

²frolic *n* 1 ♦ : a playful or mischievous action 2 ♦ : an occasion or scene of fun

♦ [1] dalliance, fun, play, relaxation, sport — more at PLAY ♦ [1] antic, caper, escapade, monkeyshine, practical joke, prank, trick — more at PRANK ♦ [2] binge, fling, gambol, lark, revel, rollick, romp — more at FLING

frol·ic·some \-səm\ *adj* ♦ : full of gaiety

♦ antic, coltish, elfish, fay, frisky, playful, sportive — more at PLAYFUL

from \'frəm, 'främ\ *prep* **1** — used to show a starting point ⟨a letter ⁓ home⟩ **2** — used to show removal or separation ⟨subtract 3 ⁓ 9⟩ **3** — used to show a material, source, or cause ⟨suffering ⁓ a cold⟩

frond \'fränd\ *n* : a usu. large divided leaf esp. of a fern or palm tree

¹front \'frənt\ *n* **1** : FOREHEAD; *also* : the whole face **2** ♦ : external and often feigned appearance **3** : a region of active fighting; *also* : a sphere of activity **4** : a political coalition **5** : the side of a building containing the main entrance **6** ♦ : the forward part or surface **7** : FRONTAGE **8** : a boundary between two dissimilar air masses **9** : a position directly before or ahead of something else **10** : a person, group, or thing used to mask the identity of the actual controlling agent

♦ [2] act, airs, facade, guise, masquerade, pose, pretense, put-on, semblance, show — more at MASQUERADE ♦ [6] facade, face; *also* exterior, outside, skin, surface, veneer *Ant* back, rear, reverse

²front *vb* **1** : to have the principal side adjacent to something **2** : to serve as a front **3** : CONFRONT

front·age \'frən-tij\ *n* **1** : a piece of land lying adjacent (as to a street or the ocean) **2** : the length of a frontage **3** : the front side of a building

front·al \'frənt-ᵊl\ *adj* **1** : of, relating to, or next to the forehead **2** : of, relating to, or directed at the front ⟨a ⁓ attack⟩ — **fron·tal·ly** *adv*

fron·tier \ˌfrən-'tir\ *n* **1** ♦ : a border between two countries **2** ♦ : a region that forms the margin of settled territory **3** : the outer limits of knowledge or achievement ⟨the ⁓s of science⟩

♦ [1] border, borderland, march; *also* no-man's-land ♦ [2] backwoods, bush, hinterland, sticks, up-country; *also* country, countryside

fron·tiers·man \-'tirz-mən\ *n* ♦ : a person who lives or works on a frontier

♦ colonist, homesteader, pioneer, settler; *also* explorer, pathfinder, trailblazer

fron·tis·piece \'frən-tə-ˌspēs\ *n* : an illustration preceding and usu. facing the title page of a book

front man *n* : a person serving as a front or figurehead

front·ward \'frənt-wərd\ *or* **front·wards** \-wərdz\ *adv or adj* : toward the front

¹frost \'frȯst\ *n* **1** : freezing temperature **2** : a covering of tiny ice crystals on a cold surface

²frost *vb* **1** : to cover with frost **2** : to put icing on (as a cake) **3** : to produce a slightly roughened surface on (as glass) **4** : to injure or kill by frost

¹frost·bite \'frȯst-ˌbīt\ *vb* -**bit** \-ˌbit\; -**bit·ten** \-ˌbit-ᵊn\; -**bit·ing** : to injure by frost or frostbite

²frostbite *n* : the freezing or the local effect of a partial freezing of some part of the body

frost heave *n* : an upthrust of pavement caused by freezing of moist soil

frost·ing \'frȯ-stiŋ\ *n* **1** : ICING **2** : dull finish on metal or glass

frosty *adj* **1** ♦ : briskly cold **2** : covered or appearing as if covered with frost **3** ♦ : marked by coolness or extreme reserve in manner

♦ [1] chill, chilly, cold, cool, nippy, raw, snappy, wintry — more at COLD ♦ [3] aloof, antisocial, cold, cool, detached, distant, remote, standoffish, unfriendly, unsociable — more at COOL

froth \'frȯth\ *n, pl* **froths** \'frȯths, 'frȯthz\ [ME, fr. ON *frotha*] **1** ♦ : bubbles formed in or on a liquid **2** : something light or worthless — **frothy** *adj*

♦ foam, head, lather, spume — more at FOAM

frou·frou \'frü-ˌfrü\ *n* [F] **1** : a rustling esp. of a woman's skirts **2** : showy or frilly ornamentation

fro·ward \'frō-wərd\ *adj* ♦ : habitually disposed to disobedience and opposition

♦ contrary, defiant, disobedient, headstrong, intractable, rebellious, unruly, untoward, wayward, willful — more at DISOBEDIENT

¹frown \'fraun\ *vb* **1** : to wrinkle the forehead (as in displeasure or thought) **2** ♦ : to look with disapproval — usu. used with *on* in transitive senses **3** : to express with a frown

♦ glare, gloom, glower, lower, scowl; *also* gape, gaze, ogle, stare; grimace, pout; growl, snarl, sneer *Ant* beam, smile ♦ *usu* **frown on** deprecate, disapprove, discountenance, disfavor (*or* disfavour), dislike, reprove

²frown *n* ♦ : a wrinkling of the brow esp. in a severe, reproving, or stern look

♦ face, grimace, lower, mouth, pout, scowl — more at GRIMACE

frow·sy *or* **frow·zy** \'frau-zē\ *adj* **frow·si·er** *or* **frow·zi·er**; -**est** ♦ : having a slovenly or uncared-for appearance

♦ dowdy, sloppy, slovenly, unkempt, untidy — more at SLOPPY

froze *past of* FREEZE

fro·zen \'frōz-ᵊn\ *adj* **1** : treated, affected, or crusted over by freezing **2** : subject to long and severe cold **3** ♦ : incapable of being changed, moved, or undone ⟨⁓ wages⟩ **4** : not available for present use ⟨⁓ capital⟩ **5** : expressing or characterized by cold unfriendliness

♦ certain, determinate, final, firm, fixed, flat, hard, hard-and-fast, set, settled, stable

FRS *abbr* Federal Reserve System

frt *abbr* freight

fruc·ti·fy \'frək-tə-ˌfī, 'frük-\ *vb* -**fied**; -**fy·ing** **1** : to bear fruit **2** : to make fruitful or productive

fruc·tose \'frək-ˌtōs, 'frük-\ *n* : a very sweet soluble sugar that occurs esp. in fruit juices and honey

fru·gal \'frü-gəl\ *adj* ♦ : characterized by or reflecting economy in the use of resources : ECONOMICAL, THRIFTY — **fru·gal·ly** *adv*

♦ economical, provident, sparing, thrifty; *also* conserving, preserving, saving; forehanded, foresighted, prudent; penny-wise; cheap, close, closefisted, miserly, niggardly, parsimonious, stingy, stinting, tight, tightfisted *Ant* prodigal, wasteful

fru·gal·i·ty \frü-'ga-lə-tē\ *n* ♦ : the quality or state of being frugal

♦ economy, husbandry, providence, thrift — more at ECONOMY

¹fruit \'früt\ *n* [ME, fr. AF *frut, fruit*, fr. L *fructus* fruit, use, fr. *frui* to enjoy, have the use of] **1** : a product of plant growth; *esp* : a usu. edible and sweet reproductive body (as a strawberry or apple) of a seed plant **2** : a product of fertilization in a plant; *esp* : the ripe ovary of a seed plant with its contents and appendages **3** : the effect or consequence of an action or operation — **fruit·ed** \'frü-təd\ *adj*

²fruit *vb* : to bear or cause to bear fruit

fruit·cake \'früt-ˌkāk\ *n* : a rich cake containing nuts, dried or candied fruits, and spices

fruit fly *n* : any of various small dipteran flies whose larvae feed on fruit or decaying vegetable matter

fruit·ful \'früt-fəl\ *adj* **1** ♦ : yielding or producing fruit **2** ♦ : very productive ⟨a ⁓ soil⟩; *also* : bringing results ⟨a ⁓ idea⟩ — **fruit·ful·ly** *adv* — **fruit·ful·ness** *n*

♦ [1] fat, fecund, fertile, luxuriant, productive, prolific, rich — more at FERTILE ♦ [2] effective, effectual, efficacious, efficient, potent, productive — more at EFFECTIVE

fru·ition \frü-'i-shən\ *n* **1** : ENJOYMENT **2** : the state of bearing fruit **3** ♦ : the state of being realized : REALIZATION, ACCOMPLISHMENT

♦ accomplishment, achievement, actuality, attainment, consummation, fulfillment, realization *Ant* naught, nonfulfillment

fruit·less \\'früt-ləs\ *adj* **1** : not bearing fruit **2** ♦ : not successful : UNSUCCESSFUL ⟨a ∼ attempt⟩ — **fruit·less·ly** *adv*

♦ futile, ineffective, unproductive, unsuccessful — more at FUTILE

fruity \\'frü-tē\ *adj* **fruit·i·er; -est** : resembling a fruit esp. in flavor

frumpy \\'frəm-pē\ *adj* **frump·i·er; -est** : DOWDY, DRAB

frus·trate \\'frəs-ˌtrāt\ *vb* **frus·trat·ed; frus·trat·ing** **1** ♦ : to balk or defeat in an endeavor **2** : to induce feelings of insecurity, discouragement, or dissatisfaction in **3** : to bring to nothing — **frus·trat·ing·ly** *adv*

♦ baffle, balk, beat, checkmate, foil, thwart

frus·trat·ing *adj* ♦ : tending to produce or characterized by frustration

♦ aggravating, annoying, bothersome, galling, irksome, irritating, pesty, vexatious — more at ANNOYING

frus·tra·tion \\ˌfrəs-'trā-shən\ *n* **1** ♦ : the state or an instance of being frustrated **2** ♦ : something that frustrates

♦ [1] disappointment, dismay, dissatisfaction, letdown — more at DISAPPOINTMENT ♦ [2] aggravation, annoyance, bother, exasperation, vexation — more at ANNOYANCE

frus·tum \\'frəs-təm\ *n, pl* **frustums** *or* **frus·ta** \-tə\ : the part of a cone or pyramid formed by cutting off the top by a plane parallel to the base

frwy *abbr* freeway

¹fry \\'frī\ *vb* **fried; fry·ing** [ME *frien*, fr. AF *frire*, fr. L *frigere* to roast] **1** : to cook in a pan or on a griddle over heat esp. with the use of fat **2** : to undergo frying

²fry *n, pl* **fries** **1** : a social gathering where fried food is eaten **2** : a dish of something fried; *esp, pl* : FRENCH FRIES

³fry *n, pl* **fry** [ME, fr. AF *frie*, fr. *freier, frier* to rub, spawn, fr. L *fricare* to rub] **1** : recently hatched fishes; *also* : very small adult fishes **2** : members of a group or class ⟨small ∼⟩

fry·er \\'frī-ər\ *n* **1** : something (as a young chicken) suitable for frying **2** : a deep utensil for frying foods

FSLIC *abbr* Federal Savings and Loan Insurance Corporation

ft *abbr* **1** feet; foot **2** fort

FTC *abbr* Federal Trade Commission

FTP \\ˌef-ˌtē-'pē\ *n* [*f*ile *t*ransfer *p*rotocol] : a system for transferring computer files esp. via the Internet — **FTP** *vb*

fuch·sia \\'fyü-shə\ *n* **1** : any of a genus of shrubs related to the evening primrose and grown for their showy nodding often red or purple flowers **2** : a vivid reddish purple color

fud·dle \\'fəd-°l\ *vb* **fud·dled; fud·dling** : MUDDLE, CONFUSE

fud·dy–dud·dy \\'fə-dē-ˌdə-dē\ *n, pl* **-dies** ♦ : one that is old-fashioned, unimaginative, or conservative

♦ antediluvian, dodo, fogy, fossil, reactionary — more at FOGY

¹fudge \\'fəj\ *vb* **fudged; fudg·ing** **1** : to exceed the proper bounds of something **2** : to act dishonestly : CHEAT; *also* : FALSIFY **3** ♦ : to fail to come to grips with

♦ equivocate, hedge, pussyfoot — more at EQUIVOCATE

²fudge *n* **1** ♦ : a piece of foolish nonsense **2** : a soft candy of milk, sugar, butter, and flavoring

♦ bunk, folly, foolishness, hogwash, humbug, nonsense, piffle, rot, silliness — more at NONSENSE

¹fu·el \\'fyü-əl, 'fyül\ *n* : a material used to produce heat or power by burning; *also* : a material from which nuclear energy can be liberated

²fuel *vb* **-eled** *or* **-elled; -el·ing** *or* **-el·ling** : to provide with or take in fuel

fuel cell *n* : a device that continuously changes the chemical energy of a fuel directly into electrical energy

fuel injection *n* : a system for injecting a precise amount of atomized fuel into an internal combustion engine — **fuel–in·ject·ed** \\'fyül-in-ˌjek-təd\ *adj*

¹fu·gi·tive \\'fyü-jə-tiv\ *n* **1** : one who flees or tries to escape **2** : something elusive or hard to find

²fugitive *adj* **1** : running away or trying to escape **2** ♦ : likely to vanish suddenly : not fixed or lasting

♦ ephemeral, evanescent, flash, fleeting, impermanent, momentary, short-lived, transient — more at MOMENTARY

fugue \\'fyüg\ *n* **1** : a musical composition in which different parts successively repeat the theme **2** : a disturbed state of consciousness characterized by acts that are not recalled upon recovery

füh·rer *or* **fueh·rer** \\'fyur-ər, 'fir-\ *n* [G] : LEADER; *esp* : TYRANT

¹-ful \fəl\ *adj suffix, sometimes* **-ful·ler** *sometimes* **-ful·lest** **1** : full of ⟨pride*ful*⟩ **2** : characterized by ⟨peace*ful*⟩ **3** : having the qualities of ⟨master*ful*⟩ **4** : tending, given, or liable to ⟨help*ful*⟩

²-ful \ˌful\ *n suffix* : number or quantity that fills or would fill ⟨room*ful*⟩

ful·crum \\'ful-krəm, 'fəl-\ *n, pl* **ful·crums** *or* **ful·cra** \-krə\ [LL, fr. L, bedpost] : the support on which a lever turns

ful·fill *or* **ful·fil** \ful-'fil\ *vb* **ful·filled; ful·fill·ing** **1** : to put into effect **2** : to bring to an end **3** ♦ : to meet the requirements of : SATISFY ⟨∼ed expectations⟩

♦ [2] accomplish, achieve, carry out, commit, compass, do, execute, follow through, make, perform — more at PERFORM ♦ [3] answer, comply, fill, keep, meet, redeem, satisfy; *also* complete, conclude, finalize, finish; accomplish, achieve, bring about, bring off, effect; discharge, execute, perform *Ant* breach, break, violate

ful·fill·ment *n* ♦ : the act or process of fulfilling

♦ accomplishment, achievement, actuality, attainment, consummation, fruition, realization — more at FRUITION

¹full \\'ful\ *adj* **1** ♦ : containing as much or as many as is possible or normal : FILLED **2** ♦ : complete esp. in detail, number, or duration **3** ♦ : having all the distinguishing characteristics ⟨a ∼ member⟩ **4** ♦ : being at the highest or greatest degree : MAXIMUM **5** : rounded in outline : being full or plump in form ⟨a ∼ figure⟩ **6** : possessing or containing an abundance ⟨∼ of wrinkles⟩ **7** : having an abundance of material ⟨a ∼ skirt⟩ **8** ♦ : satisfied esp. with food or drink **9** : having volume or depth of sound **10** : completely occupied with a thought or plan — **full·ness** *also* **ful·ness** *n*

♦ [1] brimful, crowded, loaded, packed, replete, rife *Ant* bare, empty, stark, vacant ♦ [2] complete, comprehensive, detailed, encyclopedic, inclusive, universal — more at ENCYCLOPEDIC ♦ [3] complete, comprehensive, entire, total, whole — more at COMPLETE ♦ [4] maximum, top, utmost; *also* high *Ant* least, lowest, minimal, minimum ♦ [8] sated, satiate, satiated; *also* glutted, gorged *Ant* empty, hungry, starving

²full *adv* **1** : to a high degree : VERY, EXTREMELY **2** ♦ : to a complete degree : ENTIRELY **3** : STRAIGHT, SQUARELY ⟨hit him ∼ in the face⟩

♦ altogether, completely, entirely, fully, perfectly, quite, thoroughly, well, wholly — more at FULLY

³full *n* **1** : the highest or fullest state or degree **2** : the utmost extent **3** ♦ : the requisite or complete amount

♦ aggregate, sum, total, totality, whole — more at WHOLE

⁴full *vb* : to shrink and thicken (woolen cloth) by moistening, heating, and pressing — **full·er** *n*

full·back \\'ful-ˌbak\ *n* : a football back stationed between the halfbacks

full–blood·ed \\'ful-'blə-dəd\ *adj* ♦ : of unmixed ancestry : PUREBRED

♦ purebred, thoroughbred — more at PUREBRED

full–blown \-'blōn\ *adj* **1** : being at the height of bloom **2** ♦ : fully mature or developed

♦ adult, full-fledged, mature, ripe — more at MATURE

full–bod·ied \-'bä-dēd\ *adj* ♦ : marked by richness and fullness

♦ concentrated, full, potent, rich, robust, strong; *also* heavy; straight, undiluted, unmixed *Ant* light, mild, thin, weak

full dress *n* ♦ : the style of dress worn for ceremonial or formal occasions

♦ array, best, bravery, caparison, feather, finery, frippery, gaiety, regalia — more at FINERY

full–fledged \'fül-'flejd\ *adj* **1** ♦ : fully developed **2** : having attained complete status ⟨a ∼ lawyer⟩

♦ adult, full-blown, mature, ripe — more at MATURE

full house *n* : a poker hand containing three of a kind and a pair

full moon *n* : the moon with its whole disk illuminated

full–on \-ˌón, -ˌän\ *adj* : COMPLETE, FULL-FLEDGED

full–scale \'fül-'skäl\ *adj* **1** : identical to an original in proportion and size ⟨∼ drawing⟩ **2** ♦ : involving full use of available resources ⟨a ∼ revolt⟩

♦ all-out, clean, complete, comprehensive, exhaustive, out-and-out, thorough, thoroughgoing, total — more at EXHAUSTIVE

full–term \-ˌtərm\ *adj* : retained in the uterus for the normal period of gestation before birth ⟨a ∼ baby⟩

full tilt *adv* ♦ : at high speed : with a rush

♦ fast, hastily, posthaste, rapidly, speedily, swiftly — more at FAST

full–time \'fül-'tïm\ *adj or adv* : involving or working a normal or standard schedule

ful·ly \'fü-lē\ *adv* **1** ♦ : in a full manner or degree : COMPLETELY **2** : at least

♦ altogether, chiefly, completely, entirely, generally, largely, mainly, mostly, perfectly, primarily, principally, quite, thoroughly, well, wholly *Ant* partially, partly

ful·mi·nate \'fül-mə-ˌnāt, 'fəl-\ *vb* **-nat·ed; -nat·ing** [ME, fr. ML *fulminatus*, pp. of *fulminare*, fr. L, to strike (of lightning), fr. *fulmen* lightning] ♦ : to utter or send out censure or invective : condemn severely

♦ bluster, rant, rave, spout — more at RANT

ful·mi·na·tion \ˌfül-mə-'nā-shən, ˌfəl-\ *n* ♦ : vehement menace or censure

♦ abuse, invective, vitriol, vituperation — more at ABUSE

ful·some \'fül-səm\ *adj* **1** : COPIOUS, ABUNDANT ⟨∼ detail⟩ **2** : generous in amount or extent ⟨a ∼ victory⟩ **3** ♦ : excessively flattering ⟨∼ praise⟩

♦ adulatory, unctuous

fu·ma·role \'fyü-mə-ˌrōl\ *n* : a hole in a volcanic region from which hot gases issue

fum·ble \'fəm-bəl\ *vb* **fum·bled; fum·bling** **1 a** ♦ : to grope about clumsily **b** : make awkward attempts to do or find something **2** ♦ : to fail to hold, catch, or handle properly

♦ [1a] feel, fish, grope — more at GROPE ♦ [2] bobble, botch, bungle, flub, foul up, mangle, mess up, screw up

²fumble *n* : an act or instance of fumbling

¹fume \'fyüm\ *n* : a usu. irritating smoke, vapor, or gas

²fume *vb* **fumed; fum·ing** **1** : to treat with fumes **2** : to give off fumes **3 a** ♦ : to express anger or annoyance **b** ♦ : to be in a state of excited irritation or anger

♦ [3a] rage, storm — more at RAGE ♦ [3b] boil, burn, rage, seethe, steam — more at BOIL

fu·mi·gant \'fyü-mi-gənt\ *n* : a substance used for fumigation

fu·mi·gate \'fyü-mə-ˌgāt\ *vb* **-gat·ed; -gat·ing** : to treat with fumes to disinfect or destroy pests — **fu·mi·ga·tion** \ˌfyü-mə-'gā-shən\ *n* — **fu·mi·ga·tor** \'fyü-mə-ˌgā-tər\ *n*

¹fun \'fən\ *n* [E dial. *fun* to hoax] **1** ♦ : something that provides amusement or enjoyment **2** : the action or state of enjoying : ENJOYMENT **3** ♦ : a mood for finding or making amusement

♦ [1] delight, diversion, entertainment, pleasure *Ant* bore, bummer, downer, drag ♦ [1] frolic, play, relaxation,

sport — more at PLAY ♦ [3] game, jest, play, sport; *also* facetiousness, flippancy, levity *Ant* earnest

²fun *adj* ♦ : full of fun ⟨a ∼ person⟩ ⟨had a ∼ time⟩

♦ amusing, delightful, diverting, enjoyable, entertaining, pleasurable

¹func·tion \'fəŋk-shən\ *n* **1** ♦ : professional or official position of employment **2** : special purpose **3** ♦ : the particular purpose for which a person or thing is specially fitted or used or for which a thing exists ⟨the ∼ of a hammer⟩; *also* : the natural or proper action of a bodily part in a living thing ⟨the ∼ of the heart⟩ **4** ♦ : a formal ceremony or social affair **5** : a mathematical relationship that assigns to each element of a set one and only one element of the same or another set **6** : a variable (as a quality, trait, or measurement) that depends on and varies with another ⟨height is a ∼ of age in children⟩ **7** : a computer subroutine that performs a calculation with variables provided by a program — **func·tion·al·ly** *adv*

♦ [1] appointment, billet, capacity, job, place, position, post, situation — more at JOB ♦ [3] capacity, job, part, place, position, purpose, role, task, work — more at ROLE ♦ [4] affair, blowout, event, fete, get-together, party — more at PARTY

²function *vb* ♦ : to have or carry on a function

♦ act, perform, serve, work; *also* operate, run; control, direct, manage

func·tion·al \-shə-nəl\ *adj* **1** ♦ : performing or able to perform a regular function **2** : of, connected with, or being a function

♦ active, alive, living, on, operational, operative, running, working — more at ACTIVE ♦ applicable, practicable, practical, serviceable, usable, useful, workable — more at PRACTICAL

func·tion·ary \'fəŋk-shə-ˌner-ē\ *n, pl* **-ar·ies** ♦ : one who performs a certain function; *esp* : one who holds a public office

♦ officeholder, officer, official, public servant — more at OFFICIAL

function word *n* : a word (as a preposition, auxiliary verb, or conjunction) expressing the grammatical relationship between other words

¹fund \'fənd\ *n* [L *fundus* bottom, country estate] **1** ♦ : a sum of money or resources intended for a special purpose ⟨∼ing research⟩ **2** : STORE, SUPPLY **3 a** *pl* ♦ : available money **b** ♦ : an available quantity of material or intangible resources **4** : an organization administering a special fund

♦ [1] account, budget, deposit, kitty, nest egg, pool ♦ *usu* **funds** [3a] finances, pocket, resources, wherewithal ♦ [3b] budget, pool, supply — more at SUPPLY

²fund *vb* **1** ♦ : to provide funds for **2** : to convert (a shortterm obligation) into a long-term interest-bearing debt — **fund·er** *n*

♦ capitalize, endow, finance, stake, subsidize, underwrite — more at FINANCE

fun·da·men·tal \ˌfən-də-'ment-ᵊl\ *adj* **1** : serving as an origin : PRIMARY **2** ♦ : serving as a basis supporting existence or determining essential structure or function : BASIC, ESSENTIAL **3** : RADICAL ⟨∼ change⟩ **4** : of central importance : PRINCIPAL — **fundamental** *n* — **fun·da·men·tal·ly** *adv*

♦ basic, elemental, elementary, essential, rudimentary, underlying — more at ELEMENTARY

fun·da·men·tal·ism \-tə-ˌi-zəm\ *n* **1** *often cap* : a Protestant religious movement emphasizing the literal infallibility of the Bible **2** : a movement or attitude stressing strict adherence to a set of basic principles — **fun·da·men·tal·ist** \-ist\ *adj or n*

¹fu·ner·al \'fyü-nə-rəl\ *adj* **1** : of, relating to, or constituting a funeral **2** ♦ : befitting or suggesting a funeral : FUNEREAL

♦ dolorous, funereal, lugubrious, mournful, plaintive, sorrowful, woeful

²**funeral** *n* : the ceremonies held for a dead person usu. before burial

fu·ner·ary \'fyü-nə-ˌrer-ē\ *adj* : of, used for, or associated with burial ⟨∼ rites⟩

fu·ne·re·al \fyü-'nir-ē-əl\ *adj* **1** : of or relating to a funeral **2 ♦** : suggesting a funeral ⟨a ∼ mood⟩

♦ bleak, dark, dismal, dreary, gloomy, gray (*or* grey), somber (*or* sombre), wretched — more at GLOOMY

fun·gi·cide \'fən-jə-ˌsīd, 'fəŋ-gə-\ *n* : an agent that kills or checks the growth of fungi — **fun·gi·cid·al** \ˌfən-jə-'sīd-ᵊl, ˌfəŋ-gə-\ *adj*

fun·gus \'fəŋ-gəs\ *n, pl* **fun·gi** \'fən-ˌjī, 'fəŋ-ˌgī\ *also* **fun·gus·es** \'fəŋ-gə-səz\ : any of a kingdom of parasitic spore-producing organisms (as molds, mildews, and mushrooms) formerly classified as plants — **fun·gal** \-gəl\ *adj* — **fun·gous** \-gəs\ *adj*

fu·nic·u·lar \fyü-'ni-kyə-lər, fə-\ *n* : a cable railway ascending a mountain

¹**funk** \'fəŋk\ *n* : a strong offensive smell

²**funk** *n* : a depressed state of mind

³**funk** *n* **1** : music that combines elements of rhythm and blues and soul music and that has a strong beat **2** : the quality or state of being funky

funky \'fəŋ-kē\ *adj* **funk·i·er; -est** **1** : having an earthy unsophisticated style and feeling; *esp* : having the style and feeling of older African American music or of funk **2** : odd or quaint in appearance or style ⟨a ∼ restaurant⟩

¹**fun·nel** \'fən-ᵊl\ *n* **1** : a cone-shaped utensil with a tube used for catching and directing a downward flow (as of liquid) **2** : FLUE, SMOKESTACK

²**funnel** *vb* **-neled** *also* **-nelled; -nel·ing** *also* **-nel·ling** **1** : to pass through or as if through a funnel **2 ♦** : to move to a central point or into a central channel

♦ channel, conduct, direct, pipe, siphon — more at CHANNEL

fun·nies \'fə-nēz\ *n pl* : a comic strip or a comic section (as of a newspaper) — used with *the*

¹**fun·ny** \'fə-nē\ *adj* **fun·ni·er; -est** **1 ♦** : affording light mirth and laughter **2 ♦** : seeking or intended to amuse **3 ♦** : differing from the ordinary in a suspicious, perplexing, quaint, or eccentric way : PECULIAR **4** : UNDERHANDED — **funny** *adv*

♦ [1, 2] amusing, antic, comic, comical, droll, farcical, hilarious, humorous, laughable, ludicrous, mirthful, risible *Ant* humorless, lame, uncomic, unfunny ♦ [3] bizarre, curious, odd, peculiar, quaint, queer, quirky, strange, weird

²**funny** *n, pl* **funnies** : a comic strip or a comic section (as of a newspaper)

funny bone *n* : a place at the back of the elbow where a blow easily compresses a nerve and causes a painful tingling sensation

fun·plex \'fən-ˌpleks\ *n* : a center containing various entertainment facilities

¹**fur** \'fər\ *n* **1** : an article of clothing made of or with fur **2 ♦** : the hairy coat of a mammal esp. when fine, soft, and thick **3 ♦** : an animal's coat dressed for use **4** : a coating resembling fur — **fur** *adj* — **furred** \'fərd\ *adj*

♦ [2] coat, fleece, hair, pelage, pile, wool; *also* hide, pelt, skin ♦ [3] hide, pelt, skin — more at HIDE

²**fur** *abbr* furlong

fur·be·low \'fər-bə-ˌlō\ *n* **1 ♦** : a pleated or gathered piece of material **2** : showy trimming

♦ flounce, frill, ruffle — more at RUFFLE

fur·bish \'fər-bish\ *vb* **1** : to make lustrous : POLISH **2** : to give a new look to : RENOVATE

fu·ri·ous \'fyùr-ē-əs\ *adj* **1 ♦** : exhibiting or goaded by anger : indicative of or proceeding from anger **2** : BOISTEROUS **3 ♦** : existing in an extreme degree : INTENSE **4 ♦** : full of activity — **fu·ri·ous·ly** *adv*

♦ [1] angry, enraged, irate — more at ANGRY ♦ [3] deep, ferocious, fierce, hard, heavy, intense, profound,

terrible — more at INTENSE ♦ [4] crazy, delirious, excessive, extreme, feverish, fierce, frantic, frenetic, frenzied, inordinate, insane, intense, irrational, mad, rabid, vehement, violent, wild *Ant* relaxed

furl \'fərl\ *vb* **1** : to wrap or roll (as a sail or a flag) close to or around something **2** : to curl in furls — **furl** *n*

fur·long \'fər-ˌlóŋ\ *n* [ME, fr. OE *furlang*, fr. *furh* furrow + *lang* long] : a unit of distance equal to 220 yards (about 201 meters)

fur·lough \'fər-lō\ *n* [D *verlof*, lit., permission] **1** : a leave of absence from duty granted esp. to a soldier **2** : a leave of absence granted by an employer to an employee — **furlough** *vb*

fur·nace \'fər-nəs\ *n* : an enclosed structure in which heat is produced

fur·nish \'fər-nish\ *vb* **1 ♦** : to provide with what is needed : EQUIP **2 ♦** : to make available for use : SUPPLY, GIVE

♦ [1] accoutre, allocate, allot, assign, bestow, deal, dispense, distribute, donate, equip, fit, give, outfit, present, rig, store, supply ♦ [2] deliver, feed, give, hand, hand over, provide, supply *Ant* hold (back), keep (back), reserve, retain, withhold

fur·nish·ings \-ni-shiŋz\ *n pl* **1** : articles or accessories of dress **2** : an object that tends to increase comfort or utility; *esp* : an article of furniture

fur·ni·ture \'fər-ni-chər\ *n* **1** : equipment that is necessary or desirable **2** : movable articles (as chairs or beds) for a room

fu·ror \'fyùr-ˌór\ *n* **1 ♦** : an angry or maniacal fit : RAGE **2** : a contagious excitement; *esp* : a fashionable craze **3 ♦** : furious or hectic activity : UPROAR

♦ [1] anger, fury, indignation, ire, outrage, rage, spleen, wrath, wrathfulness — more at ANGER ♦ [3] commotion, disturbance, pandemonium, tumult, turmoil, uproar — more at COMMOTION

fu·rore \-ˌór\ *n* [It] **1** : a contagious excitement; *esp* : a fashionable craze **2** : furious or hectic activity : UPROAR

fur·ri·er \'fər-ē-ər\ *n* : one who prepares or deals in fur

fur·ring \'fər-iŋ\ *n* : wood or metal strips applied to a wall or ceiling to form a level surface or an air space

¹**fur·row** \'fər-ō\ *n* **1** : a trench in the earth made by a plow **2 ♦** : a narrow groove or wrinkle

♦ crease, crimp, crinkle, wrinkle — more at WRINKLE

²**furrow** *vb* : to make or form furrows, grooves, wrinkles, or lines

fur·ry \'fər-ē\ *adj* **fur·ri·er; -est** **1 ♦** : resembling or consisting of fur **2 ♦** : covered with fur

♦ [1] fuzzy, hairy, rough, shaggy, woolly — more at HAIRY ♦ [2] fleecy, hairy, hirsute, rough, shaggy, unshorn, woolly — more at HAIRY

¹**fur·ther** \'fər-thər\ *adv* **1 ♦** : at or to a greater distance or more advanced point : FARTHER **2 ♦** : in addition : MOREOVER **3** : to a greater extent or degree

♦ [1] beyond, farther, yonder — more at FARTHER ♦ [2] additionally, again, also, besides, more, moreover, then, too

²**further** *vb* **♦** : to promote or help advance

♦ advance, cultivate, encourage, forward, foster, nourish, nurture, promote — more at FOSTER

³**further** *adj* **1** : FARTHER 1 **2 ♦** : going or extending beyond what exists : ADDITIONAL

♦ additional, another, else, farther, more, other — more at ADDITIONAL

fur·ther·ance \'fər-thə-rəns\ *n* **♦** : the act of furthering

♦ advance, advancement, passage, process, procession, progress, progression — more at ADVANCE

fur·ther·more \'fər-thər-ˌmōr\ *adv* **♦** : in addition to what precedes : BESIDES

♦ additionally, again, also, besides, more, too, withal, yet

fur·ther·most \-ˌmōst\ *adj* : most distant : FARTHEST

fur·thest \'fər-thəst\ *adv or adj* ♦ : to or at the greatest distance in space : FARTHEST

♦ extreme, farthest, outermost, ultimate, utmost — more at EXTREME

fur·tive \'fər-tiv\ *adj* [F or L; F *furtif*, fr. L *furtivus*, fr. *furtum* theft, fr. *fur* thief] ♦ : done by stealth ⟨a ∼ glance⟩ — **fur·tive·ly** *adv* — **fur·tive·ness** *n*

♦ clandestine, covert, secret, sneaky, stealthy, surreptitious, undercover

fu·ry \'fyùr-ē\ *n, pl* **furies** **1** ♦ : intense and often destructive rage **2** : extreme fierceness or violence **3** ♦ : a state of inspired exaltation : FRENZY **4** ♦ : one who resembles an avenging spirit; *esp* : a spiteful woman

♦ [1] anger, furor, indignation, ire, outrage, rage, spleen, wrath, wrathfulness — more at ANGER ♦ [3] agitation, delirium, distraction, frenzy, furor, hysteria, rage, rampage, uproar — more at FRENZY ♦ [4] harpy, shrew, termagant, virago — more at SHREW

furze \'fərz\ *n* : GORSE

¹fuse \'fyüz\ *vb* **fused; fus·ing** **1** ♦ : to reduce to a liquid or plastic state by heat : MELT **2** ♦ : to unite by or as if by melting together — **fus·ible** *adj*

♦ [1] deliquesce, flux, liquefy, melt, run, thaw — more at LIQUEFY ♦ [2] associate, coalesce, combine, couple, join, link, marry, unify, unite — more at UNITE ♦ [2] amalgamate, blend, commingle, merge, mingle — more at MIX

²fuse *n* : an electrical safety device having a metal wire or strip that melts and interrupts the circuit when the current becomes too strong

³fuse *n* **1** : a cord or cable that is set afire to ignite an explosive charge **2** *usu* **fuze** : a mechanical or electrical device for setting off the explosive charge of a projectile, bomb, or torpedo

⁴fuse *also* **fuze** \'fyüz\ *vb* **fused** *or* **fuzed; fus·ing** *or* **fuz·ing** : to equip with a fuse

fu·se·lage \'fyü-sə-ˌläzh, -zə-\ *n* : the central body portion of an aircraft

fu·sil·lade \'fyü-sə-ˌläd, -ˌlȧd\ *n* **1** : a number of shots fired simultaneously or in rapid succession **2** ♦ : something that gives the effect of a fusillade

♦ barrage, bombardment, cannonade, hail, salvo, shower, storm, volley — more at BARRAGE

fu·sion \'fyü-zhən\ *n* **1** : the act or process of melting or making plastic by heat **2** ♦ : union by or as if by melting **3** : the union of light atomic nuclei to form heavier nuclei with the release of huge quantities of energy

♦ [2] admixture, amalgam, blend, combination, composite, compound, intermixture, mix, mixture — more at BLEND

¹fuss \'fəs\ *n* **1** ♦ : needless bustle or excitement : COMMOTION **2** : effusive praise **3** ♦ : a state of agitation **4** ♦ : an act of objecting **5** : DISPUTE

♦ [1] bother, bustle, commotion, furor, hubbub, hullabaloo, pandemonium, stir, tumult, turmoil, uproar — more at COMMOTION ♦ [3] dither, fluster, fret, huff, lather, pother, stew, tizzy, twitter — more at FRET ♦ [4] challenge, complaint, demur, expostulation, kick, objection, protest, question, remonstrance — more at OBJECTION

²fuss *vb* **1** : to make a fuss **2 a** ♦ : to give flattering or doting attention to **b** : to pay close or undue attention to small details **3** ♦ : to express annoyance or complaint

♦ [2a] enthuse, fawn, gush, rave, rhapsodize, slobber — more at GUSH ♦ [3] beef, carp, complain, crab, gripe, grouse, moan, squawk

fuss·bud·get \'fəs-ˌbə-jət\ *n* : one who fusses or is fussy about trifles

fussy \'fə-sē\ *adj* **fuss·i·er; -est** **1** ♦ : nervous or easily upset **2** : overly decorated **3** ♦ : requiring or giving close attention or concern to details or niceties; *also* : overly difficult to please ⟨a ∼ customer⟩ — **fuss·i·ly** \-sə-lē\ *adv* — **fuss·i·ness** \-sē-nəs\ *n*

♦ [1] crabby, cranky, grouchy, grumpy, querulous; *also* fidgety, restive, restless, uneasy; discontented, disgruntled, displeased, displeased; fretful, nervous, worrisome; cantankerous, crotchety, irascible, irritable, ornery *Ant* uncomplaining ♦ [3] choosy, dainty, delicate, demanding, exacting, fastidious, finicky, meticulous, painstaking, particular, picky — more at FINICKY

fus·tian \'fəs-chən\ *n* **1** : a strong usu. cotton fabric **2** : pretentious writing or speech — **fustian** *adj*

fus·ty \'fəs-tē\ *adj* **fus·ti·er; -est** [prob. alter. of ME *foisted*, *foist* musty, fr. *foist* wine cask, fr. AF *fust, fuist* wood, tree trunk, cask] **1** ♦ : saturated with dust and stale odors : MUSTY **2** : OLD-FASHIONED ⟨∼ notions⟩

♦ malodorous, musty, smelly — more at MALODOROUS

fut *abbr* future

fu·tile \'fyüt-ᵊl, 'fyü-ˌtīl\ *adj* **1** ♦ : serving no useful purpose : USELESS, VAIN **2** : FRIVOLOUS, TRIVIAL — **fu·tile·ly** *adv* — **fu·til·i·ty** \fyü-'ti-lə-tē\ *n*

♦ empty, fruitless, hopeless, ineffective, meaningless, pointless, unproductive, unsuccessful, useless, vain *Ant* effective, fruitful, productive, profitable, successful

fu·ton \'fü-ˌtän\ *n* [Jp] : a usu. cotton-filled mattress used on the floor or in a frame as a bed, couch, or chair

¹fu·ture \'fyü-chər\ *adj* **1** : of, relating to, or constituting a verb tense that expresses time yet to come **2** : coming after the present

²future *n* **1** ♦ : time that is to come **2** : what is going to happen **3** : an expectation of advancement or progressive development **4** : the future tense; *also* : a verb form in it

♦ hereafter; *also* eventuality, finality; posterity *Ant* past

fu·tur·ism \'fyü-chə-ˌri-zəm\ *n* : a modern movement in art, music, and literature that tries esp. to express the energy and activity of mechanical processes

fu·tur·ist \'fyü-chə-rist\ *n* : one who studies and predicts the future esp. on the basis of current trends

♦ augur, diviner, forecaster, fortune-teller, prognosticator, prophet, seer, soothsayer — more at PROPHET

fu·tur·is·tic \ˌfyü-chə-'ris-tik\ *adj* : of or relating to the future or to futurism; *also* : very modern

fu·tu·ri·ty \fyù-'tùr-ə-tē, -'tyùr-\ *n, pl* **-ties** **1** : time that is to come : FUTURE **2** : the quality or state of being future **3** *pl* : future events or prospects

fuze *var of* FUSE

fuzz \'fəz\ *n* ♦ : fine light particles or fibers (as of down or fluff)

♦ down, floss, fluff, fur, lint, nap, pile; *also* batting

fuzzy \'fə-zē\ *adj* **fuzz·i·er; -est** **1** ♦ : having or resembling fuzz **2** : lacking in clarity or definition **3** : being or relating to pleasant usu. sentimental emotions ⟨∼ feelings⟩ — **fuzz·i·ness** \-zē-nəs\ *n*

♦ [1] furry, hairy, rough, shaggy, woolly — more at HAIRY ♦ [2] indefinite, unclear, vague — more at VAGUE

fuzzy logic *n* : a system of logic in which a statement can be true, false, or any of a continuum of values in between

fwd *abbr* forward

FWD *abbr* front-wheel drive

FY *abbr* fiscal year

-fy *vb suffix* : make : form into ⟨dandi*fy*⟩

FYI *abbr* for your information

¹g \ˈjē\ *n, pl* **g's** *or* **gs** \ˈjēz\ *often cap* **1** : the 7th letter of the English alphabet **2** : a unit of force equal to the force exerted by gravity on a body at rest and used to indicate the force to which a body is subjected when accelerated **3** *slang* : a sum of $1000

²g *abbr, often cap* **1** game **2** gauge **3** good **4** gram **5** gravity

ga *abbr* gauge

¹Ga *abbr* Georgia

²Ga *symbol* gallium

GA *abbr* **1** general assembly **2** general average **3** general of the army **4** Georgia

gab \ˈgab\ *vb* **gabbed; gab·bing** ♦ : to talk in a rapid or thoughtless manner : CHATTER — **gab** *n*

   ♦ chat, converse, jaw, palaver, patter, prattle, rattle, talk, visit — more at CHAT

gab·ar·dine \ˈga-bər-ˌdēn\ *n* **1** : GABERDINE 1 **2** : a firm durable twilled fabric having diagonal ribs and made of various fibers; *also* : a garment of gabardine

gab·ble \ˈga-bəl\ *vb* **gab·bled; gab·bling** ♦ : to talk fast or foolishly : JABBER, BABBLE — **gab·bler** \-b(ə-)lər\ *n*

   ♦ babble, chatter, drivel, gibber, jabber, prattle, sputter — more at BABBLE

gab·by \ˈga-bē\ *adj* **gab·bi·er; -est** ♦ : pointlessly or annoyingly talkative : GARRULOUS

   ♦ chatty, conversational, garrulous, loquacious, talkative — more at TALKATIVE

gab·er·dine \ˈga-bər-ˌdēn\ *n* **1** : a long loose outer garment worn in medieval times and associated esp. with Jews **2** : GABARDINE 2

gab·fest \ˈgab-ˌfest\ *n* **1** : an informal gathering for general talk **2** ♦ : an extended conversation

   ♦ chat, chatter, chitchat, gossip, palaver, rap, talk — more at CHAT

ga·ble \ˈgā-bəl\ *n* : the vertical triangular end of a building formed by the sides of the roof sloping from the ridge down to the eaves — **ga·bled** \-bəld\ *adj*

Gab·o·nese \ˌga-bə-ˈnēz, -ˈnēs\ *n* : a native or inhabitant of Gabon — **Gabonese** *adj*

gad \ˈgad\ *vb* **gad·ded; gad·ding** ♦ : to be constantly active without specific purpose — usu. used with *about* ⟨*gadded* about Europe for a year⟩ — **gad·der** *n*

   ♦ *usu* **gad about** gallivant, knock, meander, rove, traipse, wander — more at WANDER

gad·about \ˈga-də-ˌbaut\ *n* : a person who flits about in social activity

gad·fly \ˈgad-ˌflī\ *n* **1** : a fly that bites or harasses livestock **2** ♦ : a person who annoys esp. by persistent criticism

   ♦ annoyance, bother, nuisance, persecutor, pest, tease — more at NUISANCE

gad·get \ˈga-jət\ *n* ♦ : an often small mechanical or electronic device with a practical use but often thought of as a novelty : CONTRIVANCE — **gad·get·ry** \ˈga-jə-trē\ *n*

   ♦ contraption, contrivance, gimmick, gizmo, jigger; *also* implement, instrument, tool, utensil; ingenuity, innovation, invention; accessory, adjunct; mechanism, trick

gad·o·lin·i·um \ˌga-də-ˈli-nē-əm\ *n* : a magnetic metallic chemical element

¹Gael \ˈgāl\ *n* : a Celtic inhabitant of Ireland or Scotland

²Gael *abbr* Gaelic

Gael·ic \ˈgā-lik\ *adj* : of or relating to the Gaels or their languages — **Gaelic** *n*

gaff \ˈgaf\ *n* **1** : a spear used in taking fish or turtles; *also* : a metal hook for holding or lifting heavy fish **2** : the

spar supporting the top of a fore-and-aft sail **3** : rough treatment — ABUSE — **gaff** *vb*

gaffe \ˈgaf\ *n* **1** ♦ : a usu. social blunder **2** ♦ : a noticeable mistake

   ♦ [1] familiarity, impropriety, indiscretion — more at IMPROPRIETY ♦ [2] blunder, error, fault, flub, fumble, goof, lapse, miscue, misstep, mistake, oversight, screwup, slip, stumble, trip — more at ERROR

gaf·fer \ˈga-fər\ *n* **1** : an old man **2** : a lighting electrician on a motion-picture or television set

¹gag \ˈgag\ *vb* **gagged; gag·ging** **1** : to restrict use of the mouth with a gag **2** : to prevent from speaking freely **3** ♦ : to retch or cause to retch **4** : OBSTRUCT, CHOKE **5** : BALK **6** : to make quips — **gag·ger** *n*

   ♦ heave, spit up, throw up, vomit — more at VOMIT

²gag *n* **1** : something thrust into the mouth esp. to prevent speech or outcry **2** : an official check or restraint on free speech **3** ♦ : a laugh-provoking remark or act **4** : PRANK, TRICK

   ♦ crack, jest, joke, laugh, pleasantry, quip, sally, waggery, wisecrack, witticism — more at JOKE

¹gage \ˈgāj\ *n* **1** : a token of defiance; *esp* : a glove or cap cast on the ground as a pledge of combat **2** ♦ : something deposited as a pledge of performance : SECURITY

   ♦ guarantee, guaranty, pawn, pledge, security — more at PLEDGE

²gage *var of* GAUGE

gag·gle \ˈga-gəl\ *n* [ME *gagyll,* fr. *gagelen* to cackle] **1** : a flock of geese **2** : an unorganized group

gai·ety \ˈgā-ə-tē\ *n, pl* **-eties** **1** ♦ : festive activity : MERRYMAKING **2** : MERRIMENT **3** ♦ : dressy or showy clothing and jewels : FINERY

   ♦ [1] conviviality, festivity, jollification, merriment, merrymaking, revelry — more at MERRYMAKING ♦ [3] array, best, bravery, caparison, feather, finery, frippery, full dress, regalia — more at FINERY

gai·ly \ˈgā-lē\ *adv* ♦ : in a gay manner ⟨chatting ∼⟩

   ♦ cheerfully, happily, heartily, jovially, merrily, mirthfully; *also* blithely, breezily, brightly; cheerily, gladly; good-naturedly **Ant** bleakly, cheerlessly, darkly, heavily, miserably, morosely, unhappily ♦ exuberantly, jauntily, sprightly; *also* friskily, playfully; briskly, crisply; breezily **Ant** dully, inanimately, sluggishly, tardily ♦ flamboyantly, flashily, jauntily, rakishly; *also* gaudily, loud, loudly, fancily, gallantly, ornately; nattily, neatly, smartly; conspicuously, luridly, strikingly; splendidly **Ant** conservatively, plain, quietly

¹gain \ˈgān\ *n* **1** ♦ : resources or advantage acquired or increased : PROFIT **2** : ACQUISITION, ACCUMULATION **3** ♦ : an increase in amount, magnitude, or degree

   ♦ [1] earnings, lucre, net, payoff, proceeds, profit, return — more at PROFIT ♦ [3] accretion, addition, augmentation, boost, expansion, increase, increment, plus, proliferation, raise, rise, supplement — more at INCREASE

²gain *vb* **1** ♦ : to get possession of usu. by effort, merit, or craft : EARN **2** : WIN ⟨∼ a victory⟩ **3** ♦ : to increase in ⟨∼ momentum⟩ **4** : PERSUADE **5** : to arrive at **6** : ACHIEVE ⟨∼ strength⟩ **7** : to run fast ⟨the watch ∼s a minute a day⟩ **8** : PROFIT **9** : INCREASE **10** ♦ : to improve in health — **gain·er** *n*

   ♦ [1] acquire, attain, capture, carry, draw, earn, garner, get, land, make, obtain, procure, realize, secure, win — more at EARN ♦ [3] build, gather, grow, pick up; *also* accrue, accumulate, amass; excite, stimulate; enhance, enrich, maximize; boost, jack (up), mount, step up *Ant* decrease (in), lose ♦ [10] convalesce, heal, mend, rally, recover, recuperate, snap back — more at CONVALESCE

gain·ful \'gān-fəl\ *adj* ♦ : productive of gain : PROFITABLE — **gain·ful·ly** *adv*

♦ fat, lucrative, profitable, remunerative — more at PROFITABLE

gain·say \ˌgān-'sā\ *vb* **-said** \-'sād, -'sed\; **-say·ing; -says** \-'sāz, -'sez\ [ME *gainsayen,* fr. *gain-* against + *-sayen* to say] 1 ♦ : to declare to be untrue or invalid : DENY 2 : to speak against — **gain·say·er** *n*

♦ contradict, deny, disallow, disavow, disclaim, negate, negative, reject, repudiate — more at DENY

gait \'gāt\ *n* : manner of moving on foot; *also* : a particular pattern or style of such moving — **gait·ed** *adj*

gai·ter \'gā-tər\ *n* 1 : a leg covering reaching from the instep to ankle, mid-calf, or knee 2 : an overshoe with a fabric upper 3 : an ankle-high shoe with elastic gores in the sides

¹**gal** \'gal\ *n* : GIRL, WOMAN
²**gal** *abbr* gallon
Gal *abbr* Galatians
ga·la \'gā-lə, 'ga-, 'gä-\ *n* ♦ : a festive celebration : FESTIVITY — **gala** *adj*

♦ carnival, celebration, festival, festivity, fete, fiesta, jubilee — more at FESTIVAL

ga·lac·tic \gə-'lak-tik\ *adj* : of or relating to a galaxy
Ga·la·tians \gə-'lā-shənz\ *n* : an argumentative letter of St. Paul written to the Christians of Galatia and included as a book in the New Testament
gal·axy \'ga-lək-sē\ *n, pl* **-ax·ies** [ME *galaxie, galaxias,* fr. LL *galaxias,* fr. Gk, fr. *galakt-, gala* milk] 1 *often cap* : MILKY WAY GALAXY — used with *the* 2 : a very large group of stars 3 : an assemblage of brilliant or famous persons or things
gale \'gāl\ *n* 1 : a strong wind 2 ♦ : an emotional outburst ⟨~s of laughter⟩

♦ agony, burst, eruption, explosion, fit, flare, flare-up, flash, flush, gush, gust, outburst, paroxysm, spasm, storm — more at OUTBURST

ga·le·na \gə-'lē-nə\ *n* : a lustrous bluish gray mineral that consists of the sulfide of lead and is the chief ore of lead
¹**gall** \'gȯl\ *n* 1 : BILE 2 : something bitter to endure 3 ♦ : bitterness of spirit : RANCOR 4 ♦ : brazen boldness coupled with impudent assurance and insolence : IMPUDENCE

♦ [3] animosity, antagonism, antipathy, bitterness, enmity, grudge, hostility, rancor — more at ENMITY
♦ [4] audacity, brass, brazenness, cheek, chutzpah, effrontery, impudence, nerve, presumption, sauce, sauciness, temerity — more at EFFRONTERY

²**gall** *n* : a skin sore caused by chafing
³**gall** *vb* 1 ♦ : to make or become sore or worn by rubbing : CHAFE 2 ♦ : to provoke impatience, anger, or displeasure in : VEX

♦ [1] abrade, chafe, erode, fray, fret, rub, wear — more at ABRADE ♦ [2] aggravate, annoy, bother, bug, chafe, exasperate, get, grate, irk, irritate, nettle, peeve, persecute, pique, put out, rasp, rile, vex — more at IRRITATE

⁴**gall** *n* : an abnormal outgrowth of plant tissue usu. due to parasites
¹**gal·lant** \gə-'lant, -'länt; 'ga-lənt\ *n* 1 ♦ : a young man of fashion 2 : a man who shows a marked fondness for the company of women and who is esp. attentive to them 3 : one who courts a woman or seeks to marry her : SUITOR

♦ buck, dandy, dude, fop — more at DANDY

²**gal·lant** \'ga-lənt (*usual for 2, 3, 4*); gə-'lant, -'länt (*usual for 5*)\ *adj* 1 : showy in dress or bearing : SMART 2 : impressive in size or splendor : SPLENDID, STATELY 3 ♦ : full of

energy, animation, or courage : SPIRITED, BRAVE 4 ♦ : nobly chivalrous and often self-sacrificing 5 : polite and attentive to women

♦ [3] brave, courageous, dauntless, doughty, fearless, heroic, intrepid, spirited, stalwart, stout, undaunted, valiant, valorous — more at BRAVE ♦ [4] chivalrous, great, greathearted, high, high-minded, lofty, lordly, magnanimous, noble, sublime — more at NOBLE

gal·lant·ly *adv* ♦ : in a gallant manner

♦ grandly, greatly, heroically, honorably (*or* honourably), magnanimously, nobly — more at GREATLY

gal·lant·ry \'ga-lən-trē\ *n, pl* **-ries** 1 *archaic* : gallant appearance 2 : an act of marked courtesy 3 : courteous attention to a woman 4 ♦ : conspicuous bravery

♦ bravery, courage, daring, fearlessness, guts, hardihood, heart, heroism, nerve, stoutness, valor — more at COURAGE

gall·blad·der \'gȯl-ˌbla-dər\ *n* : a membranous muscular sac attached to the liver and serving to store bile
gal·le·on \'ga-lē-ən\ *n* : a large square-rigged sailing ship formerly used esp. by the Spanish
gal·le·ria \ˌga-lə-'rē-ə\ *n* [It] : a roofed and usu. glass-enclosed promenade or court
gal·lery \'ga-lə-rē\ *n, pl* **-ler·ies** 1 : an outdoor balcony; *also* : PORCH, VERANDA 2 ♦ : a long narrow passage, apartment, or hall 3 : a narrow passage (as one made underground by a miner or through wood by an insect) 4 : a room where works of art are exhibited; *also* : an organization dealing in works of art 5 : a balcony in a theater, auditorium, or church; *esp* : the highest one in a theater 6 : the spectators at a tennis or golf match 7 : a photographer's studio — **gal·ler·ied** \-rēd\ *adj*

♦ corridor, hall, hallway, passage — more at HALL

gal·ley \'ga-lē\ *n, pl* **galleys** 1 : a long low ship propelled esp. by oars and formerly used esp. in the Mediterranean Sea 2 : the kitchen esp. of a ship or airplane 3 : a proof of typeset matter esp. in a single column
Gal·lic \'ga-lik\ *adj* : of or relating to Gaul or France
gal·li·mau·fry \ˌga-lə-'mȯ-frē\ *n, pl* **-fries** [MF *galimafree* stew] : HODGEPODGE
gall·ing \'gȯ-liŋ\ *adj* ♦ : markedly irritating

♦ aggravating, annoying, bothersome, frustrating, irksome, irritating, pesty, vexatious — more at ANNOYING

gal·li·nule \'ga-lə-ˌnül, -ˌnyül\ *n* : any of several aquatic birds related to the rails
gal·li·um \'ga-lē-əm\ *n* : a bluish white metallic chemical element
gal·li·vant \'ga-lə-ˌvant\ *vb* ♦ : to travel, roam, or move about for pleasure

♦ gad, knock, maunder, meander, mope, ramble, range, roam, rove, traipse, wander — more at WANDER

gal·lon \'ga-lən\ *n* : a unit of liquid capacity equal to 231 cubic inches or four quarts
¹**gal·lop** \'ga-ləp\ *vb* 1 : to go or cause to go at a gallop 2 ♦ : to run fast — **gal·lop·er** *n*

♦ dash, jog, run, scamper, sprint, trip — more at RUN

²**gallop** *n* 1 : a bounding gait of a quadruped; *esp* : a fast 3-beat gait of a horse 2 : a ride or run at a gallop
gal·lows \'ga-lōz\ *n, pl* **gallows** *or* **gal·lows·es** : a frame usu. of two upright posts and a crosspiece from which criminals are hanged; *also* : the punishment of hanging
gall·stone \'gȯl-ˌstōn\ *n* : an abnormal concretion occurring in the gallbladder or bile passages
gal·lus·es \'ga-lə-səz\ *n pl* : SUSPENDERS
ga·lore \gə-'lōr\ *adj* [Ir *go leor* enough] : amply supplied : characterized by, constituting, or existing in plenty
ga·losh \gə-'läsh\ *n* : a high overshoe
galv *abbr* galvanized
gal·va·nise *chiefly Brit var of* GALVANIZE
gal·va·nize \'gal-və-ˌnīz\ *vb* **-nized; -niz·ing** 1 ♦ : to stimulate as if by an electric shock 2 : to coat (iron or steel) with zinc — **gal·va·ni·za·tion** \ˌgal-və-nə-'zā-shən\ *n* — **gal·va·niz·er** *n*

♦ electrify, excite, exhilarate, intoxicate, thrill, titillate, turn on — more at THRILL

gal·va·nom·e·ter \ˌgal-və-ˈnä-mə-tər\ n : an instrument for detecting or measuring a small electric current

Gam·bi·an \ˈgam-bē-ən\ n : a native or inhabitant of Gambia — **Gambian** adj

gam·bit \ˈgam-bət\ n [It gambetto, lit., act of tripping someone, fr. gamba leg] 1 : a chess opening in which a player risks one or more minor pieces to gain an advantage in position 2 : a calculated move : STRATAGEM

¹**gam·ble** \ˈgam-bəl\ vb **gam·bled**; **gam·bling** 1 : to play a game for money or property 2 ♦ : to bet on an uncertain outcome : WAGER 3 ♦ : to expose to hazard : VENTURE, HAZARD

♦ [2] bet, go, lay, stake, wager — more at BET ♦ usu **gamble on** [2] chance, hazard, risk, venture — more at RISK ♦ usu **gamble with** [3] adventure, compromise, hazard, imperil, jeopardize, menace, risk, venture

²**gamble** n ♦ : something chancy

♦ chance, enterprise, flier, speculation, venture; also bet, hazard, stake, wager; dark horse, play

¹**gam·bol** \ˈgam-bəl\ vb **-boled** or **-bolled**; **-bol·ing** or **-bol·ling** ♦ : to skip about in play : FRISK

♦ caper, cavort, disport, frisk, frolic, lark, rollick, romp, sport — more at FROLIC

²**gambol** n : a skipping or leaping about in play

gam·brel roof \ˈgam-brəl-\ n : a roof with a lower steeper slope and an upper flatter one on each side

¹**game** \ˈgām\ n 1 : AMUSEMENT, DIVERSION 2 ♦ : often derisive or mocking jesting : SPORT, FUN 3 ♦ : a procedure or strategy for gaining an end : SCHEME, PROJECT 4 : a line of work : PROFESSION 5 ♦ : a physical or mental competition conducted according to rules with the participants in direct opposition to each other : CONTEST 6 : animals hunted for sport or food; also : the flesh of a game animal

♦ [2] fun, jest, play, sport — more at FUN ♦ [3] arrangement, blueprint, design, plan, project, scheme, strategy, system — more at PLAN ♦ [5] bout, competition, contest, event, match, meet, tournament; also athletics, sport; battle, conflict, scrimmage, skirmish, struggle, tug-of-war, tussle; championship, final, nightcap, play-off, semifinal; derby, field day, open; marathon, race; heat, round, run, set; rally, volley; rubber, runoff; dead heat, photo finish, seesaw; classic

²**game** vb **gamed**; **gam·ing** : to play for a stake : GAMBLE
³**game** adj ♦ : having or showing a resolute unyielding spirit; also : willing or ready to proceed — **game·ly** adv

♦ amenable, disposed, glad, inclined, ready, willing — more at WILLING

⁴**game** adj : LAME ⟨a ~ leg⟩

game·cock \ˈgām-ˌkäk\ n : a rooster trained for fighting
game fish n : SPORT FISH
game·keep·er \ˈgām-ˌkē-pər\ n : a person in charge of the breeding and protection of game animals or birds on a private preserve
game·ness n ♦ : the state or quality of being game

♦ alacrity, goodwill, willingness — more at ALACRITY

game·some \ˈgām-səm\ adj : MERRY
game·ster \ˈgām-stər\ n : a person who gambles
gam·ete \ˈga-ˌmēt\ n : a mature germ cell — **ga·met·ic** \gə-ˈme-tik\ adj
game theory n : the analysis of a situation involving conflicting interests (as in business) in terms of gains and losses among opposing players
gam·in \ˈga-mən\ n [F] 1 : a boy who loiters on the streets 2 : GAMINE 2
ga·mine \ga-ˈmēn\ n 1 : a girl who loiters on the streets 2 : a small playfully mischievous girl
gam·ma \ˈga-mə\ n : the 3d letter of the Greek alphabet — Γ or γ
gamma globulin n : a blood protein fraction rich in antibodies; also : a solution of this from human blood donors

that is given to provide immunity against some infectious diseases (as measles)

gamma ray n : a photon emitted by a radioactive substance; also : a high-energy photon — usu. used in pl.
gam·mer \ˈga-mər\ n, archaic : an old woman
gam·mon \ˈga-mən\ n, chiefly Brit : a cured ham or side of bacon
gam·ut \ˈga-mət\ n ♦ : an entire range or series

♦ range, scale, spectrum, spread, stretch — more at RANGE

gamy or **gam·ey** \ˈgā-mē\ adj **gam·i·er**; **-est** 1 : GAME, PLUCKY 2 : having the flavor of game esp. when near tainting ⟨~ meats⟩ 3 : SCANDALOUS; also : DISREPUTABLE — **gam·i·ness** \-mē-nəs\ n

¹**gan·der** \ˈgan-dər\ n : a male goose
²**gander** n ♦ : the act of looking : GLANCE

♦ cast, eye, glance, glimpse, look, peek, peep, regard, sight, view — more at LOOK

¹**gang** \ˈgaŋ\ n 1 : a set of implements or devices arranged to operate together 2 a ♦ : a group of persons working or associated together b ♦ : a group of criminals or young delinquents

♦ [2a] band, company, crew, outfit, party, squad, team; also army, battalion, brigade, corps, troop; force, host, posse, stable, troupe; administration, department, help, personnel, staff ♦ [2a] circle, clan, clique, coterie, crowd, fold, ring, set; also bevy, covey, flock, herd, horde, mob, swarm, throng; club, college, fellowship, guild, league, organization, society; cohort, pack; camp, faction, sect, side, tribe; mess, squad; brotherhood, fraternity, order, sisterhood, sorority; commune; alliance, bloc, coalition, confederation, congress, council, federation, union ♦ [2b] cabal, conspiracy, mob, ring, syndicate — more at RING

²**gang** vb 1 : to attack in a gang — usu. used with up 2 : to form into or move or act as a gang
gang·land \ˈgaŋ-ˌland\ n : the world of organized crime
gan·gling \ˈgaŋ-gliŋ\ adj ♦ : loosely and awkwardly built : LANKY

♦ lanky, rangy, spindly — more at LANKY

gan·gli·on \ˈgaŋ-glē-ən\ n, pl **-glia** \-ə\ also **-gli·ons** : a mass of nerve tissue containing cell bodies of neurons outside the central nervous system; also : NUCLEUS 3 — **gan·gli·on·ic** \ˌgaŋ-glē-ˈä-nik\ adj
gan·gly \ˈgaŋ-glē\ adj : GANGLING
gang·plank \ˈgaŋ-ˌplaŋk\ n : a movable bridge from a ship to the shore
gang·plow \-ˌplau̇\ n : a plow that turns two or more furrows at one time
gan·grene \ˈgaŋ-ˌgrēn, gaŋ-ˈgrēn\ n : the death of soft tissues in a local area of the body due to loss of the blood supply — **gangrene** vb — **gan·gre·nous** \ˈgaŋ-grə-nəs\ adj
gang·ster \ˈgaŋ-stər\ n ♦ : a member of a gang of criminals : RACKETEER

♦ bully, goon, hood, hoodlum, mobster, mug, punk, rowdy, ruffian, thug, tough — more at HOODLUM

gang·way \ˈgaŋ-ˌwā\ n 1 : PASSAGEWAY; also : GANGPLANK 2 : clear passage through a crowd
gan·net \ˈga-nət\ n, pl **gannets** also **gannet** : any of several large fish-eating usu. white and black seabirds that breed chiefly on offshore islands
gantlet var of GAUNTLET
gan·try \ˈgan-trē\ n, pl **gantries** : a frame structure on side supports over or around something
GAO abbr General Accounting Office
gaol \ˈjāl\, **gaol·er** \ˈjā-lər\ chiefly Brit var of JAIL, JAILER
gap \ˈgap\ n 1 : BREACH, CLEFT 2 ♦ : a mountain pass 3 ♦ : a blank space; also : an incomplete or deficient area 4 : a wide difference in character or attitude 5 : a problem caused by a disparity ⟨credibility ~⟩

♦ [2] canyon, defile, flume, gorge, gulch, notch, pass, ravine — more at CANYON ♦ [3] breach, break, gulf, hole, opening, rent, rift, separation; also chink, cleft, crack, cranny, crevice, fissure; notch, slit, slot, split; pore, space; abyss, aperture, cavity, chasm, gape, orifice; fracture, rupture, severance, sundering ♦ [3] discontinuity, hiatus, interim, interlude, intermission, interruption, interval; *also* caesura, pause, space; lapse, suspension; lull, recess, respite, rest **Ant** continuation, continuity

gape \ˈgāp\ *vb* **gaped; gap·ing 1** : to open the mouth wide **2** : to open or part widely **3** ♦ : to stare with mouth open **4** : YAWN — **gape** *n*

   ♦ gawk, gaze, goggle, peer, rubberneck, stare; *also* glare, gloat, glower; eye, observe, watch; leer, ogle

¹gar \ˈgär\ *n* : any of several fishes that have a long body resembling that of a pike and long narrow jaws

²gar *abbr* garage

GAR *abbr* Grand Army of the Republic

¹ga·rage \gə-ˈräzh, -ˈräj\ *n* [F, act of docking, garage, fr. *garer* to dock, fr. MF *garrer*, prob. ultim. fr. ON *vara* to beware, take care] : a shelter or repair shop for automobiles

²garage *vb* **ga·raged; ga·rag·ing** : to keep or put in a garage

garage sale *n* : a sale of used household or personal articles held on the seller's own premises

¹garb \ˈgärb\ *n* **1** ♦ : style of dress **2** : outward form : APPEARANCE

   ♦ dress, getup, guise, outfit — more at OUTFIT

²garb *vb* ♦ : to cover with or as if with clothing

   ♦ apparel, array, attire, caparison, clothe, deck, dress, invest, rig, suit — more at CLOTHE

gar·bage \ˈgär-bij\ *n* **1** : food waste **2** ♦ : unwanted or useless material

   ♦ chaff, deadwood, dust, junk, litter, refuse, riffraff, rubbish, scrap, trash, waste; *also* offal, sewage, slop, swill, wash; debris, detritus, rubble, ruins; odds and ends; flotsam, jetsam; cull, discard, reject, throwaway **Ant** find, prize

gar·bage·man \-ˌman\ *n* : a person who collects and removes garbage

gar·ble \ˈgär-bəl\ *vb* **gar·bled; gar·bling** ♦ : to distort the meaning of ⟨∼ a story⟩

   ♦ color (*or* colour), distort, falsify, misinterpret, misrepresent, misstate, pervert, twist, warp; *also* belie, camouflage, disguise, mask, veil; complicate, confound, confuse, mix up; mystify, obscure, puzzle; equivocate, fib, lie, palter, prevaricate

gar·çon \gär-ˈsōⁿ\ *n, pl* **garçons** *same or* -ˈsoⁿz\ [F, boy, servant] : WAITER

¹gar·den \ˈgär-dᵊn\ *n* **1** : a plot for growing fruits, flowers, or vegetables **2** : a public recreation area; *esp* : one for displaying plants or animals

²garden *vb* : to lay out or work in a garden — **gar·den·er** *n*

gar·de·nia \gär-ˈdē-nyə\ *n* [NL, genus name, fr. Alexander *Garden* †1791 Scot. naturalist] : any of a genus of tropical trees or shrubs that are related to the madder and have fragrant white or yellow flowers; *also* : one of these trees

garden–variety *adj* : COMMONPLACE, ORDINARY

gar·fish \ˈgär-ˌfish\ *n* : GAR

gar·gan·tuan \gär-ˈgan-chə-wən\ *adj, often cap* ♦ : of tremendous size or volume

   ♦ colossal, enormous, giant, ginormous, huge, jumbo, mammoth, massive, prodigious, titanic, tremendous — more at HUGE

gar·gle \ˈgär-gəl\ *vb* **gar·gled; gar·gling** : to rinse the throat with liquid agitated by air forced through it from the lungs — **gargle** *n*

gar·goyle \ˈgär-ˌgȯi(-ə)l\ *n* **1** : a waterspout in the form of a grotesque human or animal figure projecting from the roof or eaves of a building **2** : a grotesquely carved figure

gar·ish \ˈgar-ish\ *adj* **1** : clothed in vivid colors : excessively or disturbingly vivid **2** ♦ : tastelessly showy : FLASHY, GAUDY

   ♦ flamboyant, flashy, gaudy, glitzy, loud, ostentatious, swank, tawdry — more at GAUDY

gar·ish·ness *n* : the quality or state of being garish

¹gar·land \ˈgär-lənd\ *n* : a decorative wreath or rope (as of leaves)

²garland *vb* : to form into or deck with a garland

gar·lic \ˈgär-lik\ *n* [ME *garlek*, fr. OE *gārlēac*, fr. *gār* spear + *lēac* leek] : an herb related to the lilies and grown for its pungent bulbs used in cooking; *also* : its bulb — **gar·licky** \-li-kē\ *adj*

gar·ment \ˈgär-mənt\ *n* : an article of clothing

gar·ner \ˈgär-nər\ *vb* **1** : to gather into storage **2** ♦ : to acquire by effort **3** ♦ : to pick up : ACCUMULATE, COLLECT

   ♦ [2] acquire, attain, capture, carry, draw, earn, gain, get, land, make, obtain, procure, realize, secure, win — more at EARN ♦ [3] accumulate, amass, assemble, collect, concentrate, gather, group, lump, pick up, round up, scrape — more at GATHER

gar·net \ˈgär-nət\ *n* [ME *gernet*, fr. AF *gernete*, fr. *gernet*, dark red, fr. *pume gernete* pomegranate] : a transparent deep red mineral sometimes used as a gem

¹gar·nish \ˈgär-nish\ *vb* **1** ♦ : to furnish with something ornamental : DECORATE, EMBELLISH **2** : to add decorative or savory touches to (food) **3** : GARNISHEE

   ♦ adorn, array, beautify, bedeck, deck, decorate, do, dress, embellish, enrich, grace, ornament, trim — more at DECORATE

²garnish *n* **1** ♦ : something that lends grace or beauty **2** : something (as lemon wedges or parsley) used to garnish food or drink

   ♦ adornment, caparison, decoration, embellishment, frill, ornament, trim — more at DECORATION

gar·nish·ee \ˌgär-nə-ˈshē\ *vb* **-eed; -ee·ing 1** : to serve with a garnishment **2** : to take (as a debtor's wages) by legal authority

gar·nish·ment \ˈgär-nish-mənt\ *n* **1** : GARNISH **2** : a legal warning concerning the attachment of property to satisfy a debt; *also* : the attachment of such property

gar·ni·ture \-ni-chər, -ˌchu̇r\ *n* : EMBELLISHMENT, TRIMMING

gar·ret \ˈgar-ət\ *n* : the part of a house just under the roof : ATTIC

gar·ri·son \ˈgar-ə-sən\ *n* [ME *garisoun* protection, fr. AF *garisun* healing, protection, fr. *garir* to heal, protect, of Gmc origin] **1** : a military post; *esp* : a permanent military installation **2** : the troops stationed at a garrison — **garrison** *vb*

garrison state *n* : a state organized on a primarily military basis

¹gar·rote *or* **ga·rotte** \gə-ˈrät, -ˈrōt\ *n* [Sp *garrote*] **1** : a method of execution by strangulation; *also* : the apparatus used **2** : an implement (as a wire with handles) for strangulation

²garrote *or* **garotte** *vb* ♦ : to strangle with or as if with a garrote

   ♦ choke, strangle, throttle — more at CHOKE

gar·ru·lous \ˈgar-ə-ləs\ *adj* **1** : WORDY **2** ♦ : pointlessly or annoyingly talkative — **gar·ru·li·ty** \gə-ˈrü-lə-tē\ *n* — **gar·ru·lous·ly** *adv* — **gar·ru·lous·ness** *n*

   ♦ chatty, conversational, gabby, loquacious, talkative — more at TALKATIVE

gar·ter \ˈgär-tər\ *n* : a band or strap worn to hold up a stocking or sock

garter snake *n* : any of a genus of harmless American snakes with longitudinal stripes on the back

¹gas \ˈgas\ *n, pl* **gas·es** *also* **gas·ses** [NL, alter. of L *chaos* space, chaos] **1** : a fluid (as hydrogen or air) that tends to expand indefinitely **2** : a gas or mixture of gases used as a fuel or anesthetic **3** : a substance that can be used to produce a poisonous, asphyxiating, or irritant atmosphere **4** : GASOLINE **5** ♦ : empty talk

   ♦ bombast, grandiloquence, hot air, rhetoric, wind — more at RHETORIC

²gas *vb* **gassed; gas·sing 1** : to treat with gas; *also* : to poison with gas **2** : to fill with gasoline ⟨∼ up the car⟩ **3** : to talk idly or garrulously

gas·eous \\'ga-sē-əs, -shəs\\ *adj* **1** : having the form of or being gas **2** ♦ : characterized by many words but little content

♦ bombastic, grandiloquent, oratorical, rhetorical, windy — more at RHETORICAL

¹**gash** \\'gash\\ *n* ♦ : a deep long cut

♦ laceration, rent, rip, slash, slit, tear; *also* abrasion, score, scrape, scratch; injury, wound

²**gash** *vb* : to make a gash in

gas·ket \\'gas-kət\\ *n* : material (as rubber) or a part used to seal a joint

gas·light \\'gas-ˌlīt\\ *n* **1** : light made by burning illuminating gas **2** : a gas flame; *also* : a gas lighting fixture

gas mask *n* : a mask with a chemical air filter used to protect the face and lungs against poison gas

gas·o·line \\'ga-sə-ˌlēn, ˌga-sə-'lēn\\ *n* : a flammable liquid mixture made from petroleum and used esp. as a motor fuel

gasp \\'gasp\\ *vb* **1** : to catch the breath audibly (as with shock) **2** ♦ : to breathe laboriously : PANT **3** : to utter in a gasping manner — **gasp** *n*

♦ blow, pant, puff, wheeze; *also* choke, gulp, huff; exhale, expire

gas·tric \\'gas-trik\\ *adj* : of or relating to the stomach

gastric juice *n* : the acid digestive secretion of the stomach

gas·tri·tis \\gas-'trī-təs\\ *n* : inflammation of the lining of the stomach

gas·tro·en·ter·ol·o·gy \\ˌgas-trō-ˌen-tə-'rä-lə-jē\\ *n* : a branch of medicine concerned with the structure, functions, and diseases of the stomach and intestines — **gas·tro·en·ter·ol·o·gist** \\-jist\\ *n*

gas·tro·in·tes·ti·nal \\ˌgas-trō-in-'tes-tən-ᵊl\\ *adj* : of, relating to, affecting, or including both the stomach and intestine ⟨∼ tract⟩ ⟨∼ distress⟩

gas·tron·o·my \\gas-'trä-nə-mē\\ *n* [F *gastronomie*, fr. Gk *Gastronomia*, title of a 4th cent. B.C. poem, fr. *gastēr* belly + *-nomia* system of laws] : the art of good eating — **gas·tro·nom·ic** \\ˌgas-trə-'nä-mik\\ *also* **gas·tro·nom·i·cal** \\-mi-kəl\\ *adj*

gas·tro·pod \\'gas-trə-ˌpäd\\ *n* : any of a large class of mollusks (as snails and slugs) with a muscular foot and a spiral shell or none — **gastropod** *adj*

gas·works \\'gas-ˌwərks\\ *n sing or pl* : a plant for manufacturing gas

gate \\'gāt\\ *n* **1** ♦ : an opening for passage in a wall or fence **2** : a city or castle entrance often with defensive structures **3** : the frame or door that closes a gate **4** ♦ : a device (as a valve) for controlling the passage of a fluid or signal **5** : the total admission receipts or the number of people at an event

♦ [1] door, hatch, portal — more at DOOR ♦ [1] door, doorway, entrance, way — more at DOOR ♦ [4] cock, faucet, spigot, tap, valve — more at FAUCET

-gate \\ˌgāt\\ *n comb form* [Water*gate*, scandal that resulted in the resignation of President Richard Nixon in 1974] : usu. political scandal often involving the concealment of wrongdoing

gate–crash·er \\'gāt-ˌkra-shər\\ *n* : a person who enters without paying admission or attends without invitation

gat·ed \\'gāt-əd\\ *adj* **1** : having or controlled by a gate **2** : designed to restrict entrance usu. by means of barriers, a private security fence, and a controlled gate ⟨a ∼ community⟩

gate·keep·er \\'gāt-ˌkē-pər\\ *n* ♦ : a person who tends or guards a gate

♦ doorkeeper, janitor — more at DOORKEEPER

gate·post \\-ˌpōst\\ *n* : the post to which a gate is hung or the one against which it closes

gate·way \\-ˌwā\\ *n* **1** : an opening for a gate **2** ♦ : a means of entrance or exit

♦ access, admission, doorway, entrance, entry, entrée — more at ENTRANCE

gateway drug *n* : a drug (as marijuana) whose use is

thought to lead to the use of and dependence on a harder drug

¹**gath·er** \\'ga-thər\\ *vb* **1** ♦ : to bring or come together : COLLECT **2** ♦ : to bring in a crop : PICK, HARVEST **3** ♦ : to pick up little by little **4** : to gain or win by gradual increase : ACCUMULATE ⟨∼ speed⟩ **5** : to summon up ⟨∼ courage to dive⟩ **6** : to draw about or close to something **7** : to pull (fabric) along a line of stitching into puckers **8** ♦ : to reach a conclusion often intuitively from hints or through inferences : DEDUCE, INFER **9** : ASSEMBLE **10** : to swell out and fill with pus **11** : GROW, INCREASE — **gath·er·er** *n*

♦ [1] accumulate, amass, assemble, collect, concentrate, garner, group, lump, pick up, round up, scrape; *also* aggregate, agglomerate, ball, bunch, cluster, huddle; heap, pile, stack; muster, raise, rally; flock, herd, hive, pack, press, swarm, throng, troop; congregate, forgather, meet, rendezvous; affiliate, ally, combine, connect, join, link, merge, unite; arrange, organize, systematize; regather, regroup *Ant* dispel, disperse, dissipate, scatter ♦ [1] assemble, congregate, convene, forgather, meet, rendezvous — more at ASSEMBLE ♦ [2] harvest, pick, reap — more at HARVEST ♦ [3] build, gain, grow, pick up — more at GAIN ♦ [8] conclude, deduce, extrapolate, infer, judge, reason, understand — more at INFER

²**gather** *n* : a puckering in cloth made by gathering

gathering *n* **1** ♦ : a company of persons gathered for deliberation and legislation, worship, or entertainment **2** ♦ : something compiled

♦ [1] assemblage, assembly, conference, congregation, convocation, meeting, muster; *also* aggregation, collection, conglomeration; company, coterie, gang, pack; caucus, forum, market, panel, rally, symposium, synod; crowd, flock, horde, legion, multitude, press, swarm, throng; crush, mob, rabble ♦ [2] accumulation, assemblage, collection — more at ACCUMULATION

GATT \\'gat\\ *abbr* General Agreement on Tariffs and Trade

gauche \\'gōsh\\ *adj* [F, lit., left] **1** ♦ : lacking social experience or grace; *also* : not tactful **2** : crudely made or done

♦ awkward, clumsy, graceless, inelegant, stiff, stilted, uncomfortable, uneasy, ungraceful, wooden — more at AWKWARD

gau·che·rie \\ˌgō-shə-'rē\\ *n* : a tactless or awkward action

gau·cho \\'gau̇-chō\\ *n, pl* **gauchos** : a cowboy of the So. American pampas

gaud \\'gȯd\\ *n* : a small ornament (as a jewel or ring)

gaud·i·ness \\-dē-nəs\\ *n* ♦ : the quality or state of being gaudy

♦ flamboyance, flashiness, glitz, ostentation, pretentiousness, showiness, swank — more at OSTENTATION

gaudy \\'gȯ-dē\\ *adj* **gaud·i·er; -est** **1** ♦ : ostentatiously or tastelessly ornamented **2** : marked by showiness or extravagance — **gaud·i·ly** \\-də-lē\\ *adv*

♦ flamboyant, flashy, garish, glitzy, loud, ostentatious, swank, tawdry; *also* meretricious, pretentious; graceless, inelegant, tacky, tasteless, vulgar; extravagant, fancy, florid, glittery, lurid, ornate, overdone, overwrought *Ant* conservative, quiet, understated

¹**gauge** *also* **gage** \\'gāj\\ *n* **1** : measurement according to some standard or system **2** : DIMENSIONS, SIZE **3** *usu* **gage** : an instrument for measuring, testing, or registering

²**gauge** *also* **gage** *vb* **gauged** *also* **gaged; gaug·ing** *also* **gag·ing** **1** ♦ : to measure precisely the size, dimensions, or other measurable quantity of **2** : to determine the capacity or contents of **3** ♦ : to determine roughly the size, extent, or nature of : ESTIMATE, JUDGE

♦ [1] measure, scale, span — more at MEASURE ♦ [3] calculate, call, conjecture, estimate, figure, guess, judge, make, place, put, reckon, suppose — more at ESTIMATE

gaunt \\'gȯnt\\ *adj* **1** ♦ : excessively thin and angular **2** : BARREN, DESOLATE — **gaunt·ness** *n*

♦ cadaverous, haggard, skeletal, wasted

¹**gaunt·let** \'gȯnt-lət\ *n* **1** : a protective glove **2** : an open challenge (as to combat) **3** : a dress glove extending above the wrist

²**gauntlet** *n* **1** ♦ : a severe trial : ORDEAL **2** : a double file of men armed with weapons (as clubs) with which to strike at an individual who is made to run between them

  ♦ cross, ordeal, trial — more at TRIAL

gauze \'gȯz\ *n* : a very thin often transparent fabric used esp. for draperies and surgical dressings

gauzy *adj* **gauz·i·er; -est** ♦ : made of or resembling gauze; *also* : marked by vagueness, elusiveness, or fuzziness

  ♦ flimsy, insubstantial, sheer, unsubstantial — more at FLIMSY

gave *past of* GIVE

gav·el \'ga-vəl\ *n* : the mallet of a presiding officer or auctioneer

ga·votte \gə-'vät\ *n* : a dance of French peasant origin marked by the raising rather than sliding of the feet

gawk \'gȯk\ *vb* ♦ : to gape or stare stupidly — **gawk·er** *n*

  ♦ gape, gaze, goggle, peer, rubberneck, stare — more at GAPE

gawky \'gȯ-kē\ *adj* **gawk·i·er; -est** ♦ : lacking ease or grace (as of movement or expression) : AWKWARD, CLUMSY — **gawk·i·ly** \-kə-lē\ *adv*

  ♦ awkward, clumsy, graceless, heavy-handed, lubberly, lumpish, ungainly, unhandy — more at CLUMSY

gay \'gā\ *adj* **1** ♦ : happily excited : MERRY **2** ♦ : bright and lively in appearance **3** : brilliant in color **4** : given to social pleasures; *also* : LICENTIOUS **5** : HOMOSEXUAL; *also* : of, relating to, or used by homosexuals

  ♦ [1] active, animate, animated, brisk, energetic, frisky, jaunty, jazzy, lively, peppy, perky, pert, racy, snappy, spirited, sprightly, springy, vital, vivacious — more at LIVELY
  ♦ [1] blithe, boon, festive, gleeful, jocund, jolly, jovial, merry, mirthful, sunny — more at MERRY ♦ [2] bright, cheerful, cheery, glad, upbeat — more at CHEERFUL

gayety, gayly *var of* GAIETY, GAILY

gaz *abbr* gazette

gaze \'gāz\ *vb* **gazed; gaz·ing** ♦ : to fix the eyes in a steady intent look — **gaze** *n* — **gaz·er** *n*

  ♦ gape, gawk, goggle, peer, rubberneck, stare — more at GAPE

ga·ze·bo \gə-'zē-bō\ *n, pl* **-bos** **1** : BELVEDERE **2** : a freestanding roofed structure usu. open on the sides

ga·zelle \gə-'zel\ *n, pl* **gazelles** *also* **gazelle** : any of numerous small swift graceful antelopes

ga·zette \gə-'zet\ *n* **1** : NEWSPAPER **2** : an official journal

gaz·et·teer \ˌga-zə-'tir\ *n* : a geographical dictionary

ga·zil·lion \gə-'zil-yən\ *n* : ZILLION — **gazillion** *adj* — **ga·zil·lionth** \-yənth\ *adj*

gaz·pa·cho \gəz-'pä-(ˌ)chō, gə-'spä-\ *n, pl* **-chos** [Sp] : a spicy soup usu. made from raw vegetables and served cold

GB *abbr* Great Britain

GCA *abbr* ground-controlled approach

gd *abbr* good

Gd *symbol* gadolinium

GDR *abbr* German Democratic Republic

Ge *symbol* germanium

gear \'gir\ *n* **1** : CLOTHING **2** : movable property : GOODS **3** ♦ : the implements used in an operation or activity : EQUIPMENT ⟨fishing ∼⟩ **4** : a mechanism that performs a specific function ⟨steering ∼⟩ **5** : a toothed wheel **6** : working adjustment of gears ⟨in ∼⟩ **7** : an adjustment of transmission gears (as of an automobile or bicycle) that determines speed and direction of travel — **gear** *vb*

  ♦ accoutrements (*or* accouterments), apparatus, equipment, matériel, outfit, paraphernalia, tackle — more at EQUIPMENT

gear·box \'gir-ˌbäks\ *n* : TRANSMISSION 3

gear·shift \-ˌshift\ *n* : a mechanism by which transmission gears are shifted

gear·wheel \-ˌhwēl\ *n* : GEAR 5

gecko \'ge-kō\ *n, pl* **geck·os** *also* **geck·oes** : any of numerous small chiefly tropical insect-eating lizards

GED *abbr* general equivalency diploma

geek \'gēk\ *n* : a person of an intellectual bent who is often disliked — **geeky** *adj*

geese *pl of* GOOSE

gee·zer \'gē-zər\ *n* : an odd or eccentric person usu. of old age

Gei·ger counter \'gī-gər-\ *n* : an electronic instrument for detecting the presence of cosmic rays or radioactive substances

gei·sha \'gā-shə, 'gē-\ *n, pl* **geisha** *or* **geishas** [Jp, fr. *gei* art + *-sha* person] : a Japanese girl or woman who is trained to provide entertaining company for men

¹**gel** \'jel\ *n* : a solid jellylike colloid (as gelatin dessert)

²**gel** *vb* ♦ : to change into or take on the form of a gel

  ♦ clot, coagulate, congeal, jell, set — more at COAGULATE

gel·a·tin *also* **gel·a·tine** \'je-lət-ᵊn\ *n* : glutinous material and esp. protein obtained from animal tissues by boiling and used as a food, in dyeing, and in photography; *also* : an edible jelly formed with gelatin

ge·lat·i·nous \jə-'lat-ᵊn-əs\ *adj* ♦ : resembling gelatin or jelly

  ♦ adhesive, gluey, glutinous, gooey, gummy, sticky, viscid, viscous — more at STICKY

geld \'geld\ *vb* : CASTRATE

geld·ing *n* : a castrated male horse

gel·id \'je-ləd\ *adj* : extremely cold

gem \'jem\ *n* **1** ♦ : a usu. valuable stone cut and polished for ornament **2** : something valued for beauty or perfection ⟨a ∼ of colonial architecture⟩

  ♦ [1] brilliant, gemstone, jewel; *also* birthstone; baguette, cameo, scarab, solitaire; paste, rhinestone, zircon ♦ [2] catch, jewel, pearl, plum, prize, treasure — more at PRIZE

Gem·i·ni \'je-mə-(ˌ)nē, -ˌnī; 'ge-mə-ˌnē\ *n* **1** : a zodiacal constellation between Taurus and Cancer usu. pictured as twins sitting together **2** : the 3d sign of the zodiac in astrology; *also* : one born under this sign

gem·ol·o·gy *or* **gem·mol·o·gy** \je-'mä-lə-jē, jə-\ *n* : the science of gems — **gem·olog·i·cal** \ˌje-mə-'lä-ji-kəl\ *adj* — **gem·ol·o·gist** *also* **gem·mol·o·gist** \je-'mä-lə-jist\ *n*

gem·stone \'jem-ˌstōn\ *n* : a mineral or petrified material that when cut and polished can be used in jewelry

gen *abbr* **1** general **2** genitive

Gen *abbr* Genesis

Gen AF *abbr* general of the air force

gen·darme \'zhän-ˌdärm, 'jän-\ *n* [F, intended as sing. of *gensdarmes*, pl. of *gent d'armes*, lit., armed people] : a member of a body of soldiers esp. in France serving as an armed police force

gen·der \'jen-dər\ *n* [ME *gendre*, fr. AF *genre, gendre*, fr. L *gener-, genus* birth, race, kind, gender] **1** : any of two or more divisions within a grammatical class that determine agreement with and selection of other words or grammatical forms **2** : SEX 1 — **gen·der·less** *adj*

gender identity *n* : a person's internal sense of being male, female, or a combination of male and female, or neither male nor female

gene \'jēn\ *n* : a part of DNA or RNA that contains chemical information needed to make a particular protein (as an enzyme) controlling or influencing an inherited bodily trait (as eye color) or activity or that influences or controls the activity of another gene or genes — **gen·ic** \'jē-nik, 'je-\ *adj*

ge·ne·al·o·gy \ˌjē-nē-'ä-lə-jē, ˌje-, -'a-\ *n, pl* **-gies** ♦ : an ancestral line : PEDIGREE, LINEAGE; *also* : the study of family pedigrees — **ge·ne·a·log·i·cal** \ˌjē-nē-ə-'lä-ji-kəl, ˌje-\ *adj* — **ge·ne·a·log·i·cal·ly** \-k(ə-)lē\ *adv* — **ge·ne·al·o·gist** \ˌjē-nē-'ä-lə-jist, ˌje-; -'a-\ *n*

  ♦ ancestry, birth, blood, bloodline, breeding, descent, extraction, family tree, line, lineage, origin, parentage, pedigree, stock, strain — more at ANCESTRY

genera *pl of* GENUS

¹gen·er·al \'je-nə-rəl, 'jen-rəl\ *adj* **1 ♦** : of or relating to the whole **2** : taken as a whole **3** : relating to or covering all instances **4 ♦** : not special or specialized **5 ♦** : common to many ⟨a ∼ custom⟩ **6** : not limited in meaning : not specific **7** : holding superior rank ⟨inspector ∼⟩

♦ [1] blanket, common, generic, global, overall, universal; *also* broad, collective, comprehensive, extensive, pervasive, sweeping, ubiquitous, wholesale, wide, widespread; complete, full, plenary; planetary, worldwide *Ant* individual, particular **♦** [4] broad, nonspecific, overall, unlimited, wide; *also* comprehensive, inclusive; absolute, boundless, expansive, extensive, infinite, panoramic, sweeping, vast; indeterminate, nebulous, nondescript, vague; nonspecific, unrestricted, unspecified *Ant* delineated, detailed, particularized, specific **♦** [5] characteristic, common, communal, contemporary, current, dominant, everyday, familiar, household, popular, predominant, present, public, rife, typical, universal, usual, well-known, widespread *Ant* uncommon, unpopular

²general *n* **1** : something that involves or is applicable to the whole **2** : a commissioned officer ranking next below a general of the army or a general of the air force **3** : a commissioned officer of the highest rank in the marine corps — **in general** : for the most part

general assembly *n* **1** : a legislative assembly; *esp* : a U.S. state legislature **2** *cap G&A* : the supreme deliberative body of the United Nations

gen·er·al·i·sa·tion, gen·er·al·ise *chiefly Brit var of* GENERALIZATION, GENERALIZE

gen·er·a·lis·si·mo \,je-nə-rə-'li-sə-,mō\ *n, pl* **-mos** [It, fr. *generale* general] : the chief commander of an army

gen·er·al·i·ty \,je-nə-'ra-lə-tē\ *n, pl* **-ties** **1** : the quality or state of being general **2** : a general statement, law, principle, or proposition : GENERALIZATION 2 **3** : a vague or inadequate statement **4 ♦** : the greatest part : BULK

♦ body, bulk, core, main, mass, staple, weight — more at BODY

gen·er·al·i·za·tion \,je-nə-rə-lə-'zā-shən, ,jen-rə-\ *n* **1** : the act or process of generalizing **2** : a general statement, law, principle, or proposition

gen·er·al·ize \'je-nə-rə-līz, 'jen-rə-\ *vb* **-ized; -iz·ing** **1** : to make general **2** : to draw general conclusions from **3** : to reach a general conclusion esp. on the basis of particular instances **4** : to extend throughout the body

gen·er·al·ly \'jen-rə-lē, 'je-nə-\ *adv* **1** : in a general manner **2 ♦** : as a rule

♦ commonly, ordinarily, typically, usually — more at NATURALLY **♦** altogether, basically, chiefly, largely, mainly, mostly, overall, predominantly, primarily, principally — more at CHIEFLY

general of the air force : a commissioned officer of the highest rank in the air force

general of the army : a commissioned officer of the highest rank in the army

general practitioner *n* : a physician or veterinarian whose practice is not limited to a specialty

gen·er·al·ship \'je-nə-rəl-,ship, 'jen-rəl-\ *n* **1** : office or tenure of office of a general **2** : LEADERSHIP **3** : military skill as a high commander

general store *n* : a retail store that carries a wide variety of goods but is not divided into departments

gen·er·ate \'je-nə-,rāt\ *vb* **-at·ed; -at·ing** **♦** : to bring into existence : PRODUCE

♦ create, engender, induce, make, produce, spawn; *also* begin, establish, father, found, inaugurate, initiate, institute, introduce, set, set up; bring about, effect; concoct, contrive, cook (up), design, devise, fabricate, hatch, make up

gen·er·a·tion \,je-nə-'rā-shən\ *n* **1** : a body of living beings constituting a single step in the line of descent from an ancestor; *also* : the average period between generations **2** : PRODUCTION

Generation X *n* : the generation of Americans born in the 1960s and 1970s

gen·er·a·tive \'je-nə-rə-tiv, -,rā-tiv\ *adj* : having the power or function of generating, originating, producing, or reproducing ⟨∼ organs⟩

gen·er·a·tor \'je-nə-,rā-tər\ *n* **1** : one that generates **2** : a machine by which mechanical energy is changed into electrical energy

ge·ner·ic \jə-'ner-ik\ *adj* **1 ♦** : not specific : GENERAL **2** : not protected by a trademark ⟨a ∼ drug⟩ **3** : of or relating to a biological genus — **generic** *n* — **ge·ner·i·cal·ly** \-i-k(ə-)lē\ *adv*

♦ blanket, common, general, global, overall, universal — more at GENERAL

gen·er·os·i·ty \,je-nə-'rä-sə-tē\ *n* **1 ♦** : the quality or fact of being generous **2** : a generous act

♦ bounty, liberality, philanthropy, unselfishness — more at LIBERALITY

gen·er·ous \'je-nə-rəs\ *adj* **1 ♦** : free in giving or sharing **2** : HIGH-MINDED, NOBLE **3 ♦** : marked by abundance or ample proportions : COPIOUS — **gen·er·ous·ness** *n*

♦ [1] bountiful, charitable, free, liberal, munificent, openhanded, unselfish, unsparing; *also* extravagant, handsome, lavish, profuse, unstinting; altruistic, beneficent, benevolent, hospitable, humanitarian, philanthropic; compassionate, good-hearted, greathearted, kindly, magnanimous *Ant* cheap, close, closefisted, miserly, niggardly, parsimonious, penurious, selfish, stingy, tight, tightfisted, uncharitable **♦** [3] abundant, ample, bountiful, comfortable, copious, liberal, plentiful — more at PLENTIFUL

gen·er·ous·ly \'je-nə-rəs-lē\ *adv* **♦** : in a generous manner

♦ bountifully, handsomely, liberally, well — more at WELL

gen·e·sis \'je-nə-səs\ *n, pl* **-e·ses** \-,sēz\ **♦** : the origin or coming into existence of something

♦ beginning, birth, commencement, dawn, launch, morning, onset, outset, start, threshold — more at BEGINNING

Genesis *n* : the mainly narrative first book of canonical Jewish and Christian Scriptures

gene–splic·ing \-,splī-siŋ\ *n* : the process of preparing recombinant DNA

gene therapy *n* : the insertion of normal or altered genes into cells usu. to replace defective genes esp. in the treatment of genetic disorders

ge·net·ic \jə-'ne-tik\ *adj* **1** : of or relating to the origin, development, or causes of something **2 a** : of or relating to genetics **b ♦** : of, relating to, caused by, or controlled by genes — **ge·net·i·cal·ly** \-ti-k(ə-)lē\ *adv*

♦ hereditary, heritable, inborn, inherited — more at HEREDITARY

genetic code *n* : the chemical code that is the basis of genetic inheritance and consists of units of three linked chemical groups in DNA and RNA which specify particular amino acids used to make proteins or which start or stop the process of making proteins

genetic engineering *n* : the alteration of genetic material esp. by cutting up and joining together DNA from one or more species of organism and inserting the result into an organism — **genetically engineered** *adj*

ge·net·ics \jə-'ne-tiks\ *n* : a branch of biology dealing with heredity and variation — **ge·net·i·cist** \-tə-sist\ *n*

ge·nial \'jē-nyəl, 'jē-nē-əl\ *adj* **1** : favorable to growth or comfort ⟨∼ sunshine⟩ **2 ♦** : marked by or diffusing sympathy or friendliness ⟨a ∼ host⟩ — **ge·nial·ly** *adv*

♦ affable, agreeable, amiable, good-natured, gracious, nice, sweet, well-disposed — more at AMIABLE **♦** amicable, companionable, comradely, cordial, friendly, hearty, hospitable, neighborly, sociable, warm, warmhearted — more at FRIENDLY

ge·nial·i·ty \,jē-nē-'a-lə-tē, jēn-'ya-\ *n* **♦** : the quality of being genial; *esp* : warmth of disposition and manners

♦ agreeableness, amenity, amiability, graciousness, niceness, pleasantness, sweetness — more at AMIABILITY

-gen·ic \'je-nik\ *adj comb form* **1** : producing : forming **2** : produced by : formed from **3** : suitable for production or reproduction by (such) a medium

ge·nie \'jē-nē\ *n, pl* **ge·nies** *also* **ge·nii** \-nē-ˌī\ [F *génie*, fr. Ar *jinnīy*] : a supernatural spirit that often takes human form usu. serving the person who calls on it

gen·i·tal \'je-nə-tᵊl\ *adj* **1** : concerned with reproduction ⟨∼ organs⟩ **2** : of, relating to, or characterized by the stage of psychosexual development in psychoanalytic theory in which oral and anal impulses are subordinated to adaptive interpersonal mechanisms — **gen·i·tal·ly** *adv*

gen·i·ta·lia \ˌje-nə-'tāl-yə\ *n pl* : reproductive organs; *esp* : the external genital organs — **gen·i·ta·lic** \-'ta-lik, -'tā-\ *adj*

gen·i·tals \'je-nə-tᵊlz\ *n pl* : GENITALIA

gen·i·tive \'je-nə-tiv\ *adj* : of, relating to, or constituting a grammatical case marking typically a relationship of possessor or source — **genitive** *n*

gen·i·to·uri·nary \ˌje-nə-tō-'yùr-ə-ˌner-ē\ *adj* : of or relating to the genital and urinary organs or functions

ge·nius \'jē-nyəs\ *n, pl* **ge·nius·es** *or* **ge·nii** \-nē-ˌī\ [L, tutelary spirit, natural inclinations, fr. *gignere* to beget] **1** *pl genii* : an attendant spirit of a person or place; *also* : a person who influences another for good or evil **2** ♦ : a strong leaning or inclination **3** ♦ : a peculiar or distinctive character or spirit (as of a nation or a language) **4** *pl usu genii* : SPIRIT, GENIE **5** *pl usu geniuses* ♦ : a single strongly marked capacity or aptitude **6 a** : extraordinary intellectual power **b** ♦ : a person having extraordinary intellectual power

♦ [2] affinity, bent, devices, disposition, inclination, leaning, partiality, penchant, predilection, predisposition, proclivity, propensity, talent, tendency, turn — more at INCLINATION ♦ [3] character, complexion, constitution, nature, personality, tone — more at NATURE ♦ [5] aptitude, endowment, faculty, flair, gift, knack, talent — more at TALENT ♦ [6b] brain, intellect, thinker, whiz, wizard; *also* egghead, highbrow, intellectual; master, virtuoso; ace, crackerjack, natural; sage, savant *Ant* dumbbell, dummy, dunce, idiot, imbecile, moron

genl *abbr* general

geno·cide \'je-nə-ˌsīd\ *n* : the deliberate and systematic destruction of a racial, political, or cultural group

ge·nome \'jē-ˌnōm\ *n* **1** : one haploid set of chromosomes **2** : the genetic material of an organism

ge·no·mics \jē-'nō-miks\ *n* : a branch of biotechnology concerned esp. with investigating and collecting data about the structure and function of all or part of an organism's genome

-genous \jə-nəs\ *adj comb form* **1** : producing : yielding ⟨erog*enous*⟩ **2** : having (such) an origin ⟨endog*enous*⟩

genre \'zhän-rə, 'zhäⁿ-; 'zhäⁿr; 'jän-rə\ *n* **1** : a distinctive type or category esp. of literary composition **2** : a style of painting in which everyday subjects are treated realistically

gens \'jenz, 'gens\ *n, pl* **gen·tes** \'jen-ˌtēz, 'gen-ˌtās\ [L] : a Roman clan embracing the families of the same stock in the male line

gent *n* ♦ : a man of any social class or condition : GENTLEMAN

♦ buck, chap, dude, fellow, gentleman, guy, hombre, jack, joker, lad, male, man — more at MAN

gen·teel \jen-'tēl\ *adj* **1** ♦ : having an aristocratic quality or flavor; *also* : of or relating to the gentry or upper class **2** : ELEGANT, STYLISH **3** ♦ : free from vulgarity or rudeness : POLITE **4** : maintaining the appearance of superior social status **5** : marked by false delicacy, prudery, or affectation — **gen·teel·ly** *adv* — **gen·teel·ness** *n*

♦ [1] aristocratic, gentle, grand, highborn, noble, patrician, wellborn — more at NOBLE ♦ [1] civilized,

cultivated, cultured, polished, refined — more at CULTIVATED ♦ [3] civil, courteous, gracious, mannerly, polite, well-bred — more at POLITE ♦ [3] correct, decent, decorous, nice, polite, proper, respectable, seemly — more at PROPER

gen·tian \'jen-chən\ *n* : any of numerous herbs with opposite leaves and showy usu. blue flowers in the fall

gen·tile \'jen-ˌtī(-ə)l\ *n* [ME, fr. LL *gentilis* heathen, pagan, fr. L *gent-, gens* clan, nation] **1** *often cap* : a person who is not Jewish; *esp* : a Christian as distinguished from a Jew **2** : a person who does not acknowledge the God of the Bible : HEATHEN, PAGAN — **gentile** *adj, often cap*

gen·til·i·ty \jen-'ti-lə-tē\ *n, pl* **-ties** **1** : good birth and family **2** ♦ : the qualities characteristic of a well-bred person **3** : good manners **4** : superior social status shown in manners or mode of life

♦ civility, courtesy, graciousness, mannerliness, politeness — more at POLITENESS

¹gen·tle \'jen-tᵊl\ *adj* **gen·tler** \'jent-lər, -tᵊl-ər\; **gen·tlest** \'jent-ləst, -tᵊl-əst\ **1** ♦ : belonging to a family of high social station **2** : of, relating to, or characteristic of a gentleman **3** : KIND, AMIABLE **4** : TRACTABLE, DOCILE **5** ♦ : not harsh, stern, or violent **6** : SOFT, DELICATE **7** ♦ : marked by moderation : MODERATE — **gen·tle·ness** *n* — **gen·tly** *adv*

♦ [1] aristocratic, genteel, grand, highborn, noble, patrician, wellborn — more at NOBLE ♦ [5] balmy, benign, bland, delicate, light, mellow, mild, soft, soothing, tender; *also* sleek, slick, smooth; calm, pacific, peaceful, placid, quiet, serene, tranquil; clement, compassionate, easy, lenient, merciful; cushioning, softening *Ant* abrasive, caustic, coarse, hard, harsh, rough ♦ [7] balmy, clement, equable, mild, moderate, temperate — more at CLEMENT

²gentle *vb* **gen·tled; gen·tling** **1** : to make or become mild, docile, soft, or moderate **2** : MOLLIFY, PLACATE

gen·tle·folk \'jen-tᵊl-ˌfōk\ *also* **gen·tle·folks** \-ˌfōks\ *n* : persons of good family and breeding

gen·tle·man \-mən\ *n* **1** ♦ : a man of good family **2** : a well-bred man **3** ♦ : an adult male human being : MAN — used in pl. as a form of address — **gen·tle·man·ly** *adj*

♦ [1] aristocrat, grandee, noble, patrician; *also* squire; cavalier, knight; don, seigneur, sheikh; baron, baronet, count, duke, earl, esquire, lord, marquess, marquis, prince, thane, viscount; magnate, mogul, nabob, czar; socialite, swell ♦ [3] buck, chap, dude, fellow, gent, guy, hombre, jack, joker, lad, male, man — more at MAN

gen·tle·wom·an \-ˌwu̇-mən\ *n* **1** ♦ : a woman of good family **2** : a woman attending a lady of rank **3** : a woman with very good manners : LADY

♦ dame, lady, noblewoman; *also* ladyship, madam; baroness, countess, duchess, marchioness; czarina, empress, queen; dowager, matriarch, matron, mistress

gen·tri·fi·ca·tion \ˌjen-trə-fə-'kā-shən\ *n* : the process of renewal accompanying the influx of middle-class people into deteriorating areas that often displaces earlier usu. poorer residents — **gen·tri·fy** \'jen-trə-ˌfī\ *vb*

gen·try \'jen-trē\ *n, pl* **gentries** **1** : people of good birth, breeding, and education : ARISTOCRACY **2** : the class of English people between the nobility and the yeomanry **3** : persons of a designated class

gen·u·flect \'jen-yù-ˌflekt\ *vb* : to bend the knee esp. in worship — **gen·u·flec·tion** \ˌjen-yù-'flek-shən\ *n*

gen·u·ine \'jen-yə-wən\ *adj* **1** ♦ : actually having the reputed or apparent qualities or character : AUTHENTIC, REAL **2** ♦ : free from hypocrisy or pretense : SINCERE, HONEST — **gen·u·ine·ness** *n*

♦ [1] authentic, bona fide, real, right, true — more at AUTHENTIC ♦ [2] artless, honest, ingenuous, innocent, naive, natural, real, simple, sincere, true, unaffected, unpretentious

gen·u·ine·ly *adv* ♦ : in a genuine manner : ACTUALLY

♦ actually, authentically, really, veritably, very — more at VERY

ge·nus \'jē-nəs\ *n, pl* **gen·era** \'je-nə-rə\ [L, birth, race, kind] : a category of biological classification that ranks between the family and the species and contains related species

geo·cen·tric \jē-ō-'sen-trik\ *adj* **1** : relating to or measured from the earth's center **2** : having or relating to the earth as a center

geo·chem·is·try \-'ke-mə-strē\ *n* : a branch of geology that deals with the chemical composition of and chemical changes in the earth — **geo·chem·i·cal** \-mi-kəl\ *adj* — **geo·chem·ist** \-mist\ *n*

ge·ode \'jē-ˌōd\ *n* : a nodule of stone having a cavity lined with mineral matter

¹geo·de·sic \ˌjē-ə-'de-sik\ *adj* : made of light straight structural elements ⟨a ~ dome⟩

²geodesic *n* : the shortest line between two points on a surface

geo·det·ic \ˌjē-ə-'de-tik\ *adj* : of, relating to, or being precise measurement of the earth and its features ⟨a ~ survey⟩

geog *abbr* geographic; geographical; geography

ge·og·ra·phy \jē-'ä-grə-fē\ *n, pl* **-phies** **1** : a science that deals with the natural features of the earth and its climate, products, and inhabitants **2** : the natural features of a region — **ge·og·ra·pher** \-fər\ *n* — **geo·graph·ic** \ˌjē-ə-'gra-fik\ *or* **geo·graph·i·cal** \-fi-kəl\ *adj* — **geo·graph·i·cal·ly** \-fi-k(ə-)lē\ *adv*

geol *abbr* geologic; geological; geology

ge·ol·o·gy \jē-'ä-lə-jē\ *n, pl* **-gies** **1** : a science that deals with the history of the earth and its life esp. as recorded in rocks; *also* : a study of the features of a celestial body (as the moon) **2** : the geologic features of an area — **geo·log·ic** \ˌjē-ə-'lä-jik\ *or* **geo·log·i·cal** \-ji-kəl\ *adj* — **geo·log·i·cal·ly** \-ji-k(ə-)lē\ *adv* — **ge·ol·o·gist** \jē-'ä-lə-jist\ *n*

geom *abbr* geometric; geometrical; geometry

geo·mag·net·ic \ˌjē-ō-mag-'ne-tik\ *adj* : of or relating to the magnetism of the earth — **geo·mag·ne·tism** \-'mag-nə-ˌti-zəm\ *n*

geometric mean *n* : the *n*th root of the product of *n* numbers; *esp* : a number that is the second term of three consecutive terms of a geometric progression ⟨the *geometric mean* of 9 and 4 is 6⟩

geometric progression *n* : a progression (as 1, ½, ¼) in which the ratio of a term to its predecessor is always the same

ge·om·e·try \jē-'ä-mə-trē\ *n, pl* **-tries** [ultim. fr. Gk *geōmetria*, fr. *geōmetrein* to measure the earth, fr. *gē* earth + *metron* measure] **1** : a branch of mathematics dealing with the relations, properties, and measurements of solids, surfaces, lines, points, and angles **2** ♦ : relative arrangement of parts or elements — **ge·om·e·ter** \-tər\ *n* — **ge·o·met·ric** \ˌjē-ə-'me-trik\ *or* **geo·met·ri·cal** \-tri-kəl\ *adj*

♦ cast, configuration, conformation, figure, form, shape

geo·phys·ics \ˌjē-ō-'fi-ziks\ *n* : the physics of the earth — **geo·phys·i·cal** \-zi-kəl\ *adj* — **geo·phys·i·cist** \-zə-sist\ *n*

geo·pol·i·tics \-'pä-lə-ˌtiks\ *n* : a combination of political and geographic factors relating to a state — **geo·po·lit·i·cal** \-pə-'li-ti-kəl\ *adj*

geo·ther·mal \ˌjē-ō-'thər-məl\ *adj* : of, relating to, or using the heat of the earth's interior ⟨~ energy⟩

ger *abbr* gerund

Ger *abbr* German; Germany

ge·ra·ni·um \jə-'rā-nē-əm\ *n* [L, fr. Gk *geranion*, fr. *geranos* crane] : any of a genus of herbs with usu. deeply cut leaves and typically pink, purple, or white flowers; *also* : any of a related genus of herbs that are native to southern Africa and are widely grown for their clusters of showy usu. red, pink, or white flowers

ger·bil *also* **ger·bile** \'jər-bəl\ *n* : any of numerous Old World burrowing desert rodents with long hind legs

ge·ri·at·ric \ˌjer-ē-'a-trik\ *adj* **1** : of or relating to geriatrics

or the process of aging **2** : of, relating to, or appropriate for elderly people **3** ♦ : advanced in years or age : OLD

♦ ancient, elderly, old, senior — more at ELDERLY

ge·ri·at·rics \-triks\ *n* : a branch of medicine dealing with the problems of old age and aging

germ \'jərm\ *n* **1** : a bit of living matter capable of growth and development (as into an organism) **2** : SOURCE, RUDIMENTS **3** : MICROORGANISM; *esp* : one causing disease

Ger·man \'jər-mən\ *n* **1** : a native or inhabitant of Germany **2** : the language of Germany, Austria, and parts of Switzerland — **German** *adj* — **Ger·man·ic** \jər-'ma-nik\ *adj*

ger·mane \jər-'mān\ *adj* [ME *germain*, lit., having the same parents, fr. AF, fr. L *germanus*, fr. *germen* sprout, bud] ♦ : being at once relevant and appropriate

♦ applicable, apposite, apropos, material, pertinent, pointed, relative, relevant — more at PERTINENT

ger·ma·ni·um \jər-'mā-nē-əm\ *n* : a grayish white hard chemical element used esp. in semiconductors

German measles *n sing or pl* : an acute contagious virus disease milder than typical measles but damaging to the fetus when occurring early in pregnancy

German shepherd *n* : any of a breed of intelligent responsive working dogs of German origin often used in police work and as guide dogs for the blind

germ cell *n* : an egg or sperm or one of their antecedent cells

ger·mi·cide \'jər-mə-ˌsīd\ *n* : an agent that destroys germs — **ger·mi·cid·al** \ˌjər-mə-'sīd-ᵊl\ *adj*

ger·mi·nal \'jər-mə-nəl\ *adj* : of or relating to a germ or germ cell; *also* : EMBRYONIC

ger·mi·nate \'jər-mə-ˌnāt\ *vb* **-nat·ed; -nat·ing** **1** : to cause to develop : begin to develop : SPROUT **2** : to come into being : EVOLVE — **ger·mi·na·tion** \ˌjər-mə-'nā-shən\ *n*

ger·on·tol·o·gy \ˌjer-ən-'tä-lə-jē\ *n* : a scientific study of aging and the problems of the aged — **ge·ron·to·log·i·cal** \jə-ˌränt-ᵊl-'ä-ji-kəl\ *adj* — **ger·on·tol·o·gist** \ˌjer-ən-'tä-lə-jist\ *n*

ger·ry·man·der \'jer-ē-ˌman-dər\ *vb* : to divide into election districts so as to give one political party an advantage — **gerrymander** *n*

ger·und \'jer-ənd\ *n* : a word having the characteristics of both verb and noun

ge·sta·po \gə-'stä-pō\ *n, pl* **-pos** [G, fr. *Geheime Staatspolizei*, lit., secret state police] : a usu. terrorist secret-police organization operating against persons suspected of disloyalty

ges·ta·tion \je-'stā-shən\ *n* : PREGNANCY, INCUBATION — **ges·tate** \'jes-ˌtāt\ *vb*

ges·tic·u·late \je-'sti-kyə-ˌlāt\ *vb* **-lat·ed; -lat·ing** : to make gestures esp. when speaking

ges·tic·u·la·tion \-ˌsti-kyə-'lā-shən\ *n* : the act of making gestures; *also* : an expressive gesture made in showing strong feeling or in enforcing an argument

¹ges·ture \'jes-chər\ *n* **1** ♦ : a movement usu. of the body or limbs that expresses or emphasizes an idea, sentiment, or attitude **2** ♦ : something said or done by way of formality or courtesy, as a symbol or token, or for its effect on the attitudes of others — **ges·tur·al** \-chə-rəl\ *adj*

♦ [1] pantomime, sign, signal; *also* beck, flourish, shrug, wave; body language, posture; indication, motion ♦ [2] amenity, civility, courtesy, formality — more at CIVILITY

²gesture *vb* ♦ : to make a gesture; *also* : to express or direct by a gesture

♦ flag, motion, signal, wave — more at MOTION

ge·sund·heit \gə-'zùnt-ˌhīt\ *interj* [G, lit., health] — used to wish good health esp. to one who has just sneezed

¹get \'get\ *vb* **got** \'gät\; **got** *or* **got·ten** \'gät-ᵊn\; **get·ting** **1** ♦ : to gain possession of (as by receiving, acquiring, earning, buying, or winning) : PROCURE, OBTAIN **2** : to succeed in coming or going ⟨got away to the lake⟩ **3** : to cause to come or go ⟨got the car to the station⟩ **4** ♦ : to become the father of : BEGET **5** : to cause to be in a certain condition or position ⟨don't ~ wet⟩ **6** ♦ : to undergo change or development : BECOME ⟨~ sick⟩ **7** : to make ready : PREPARE **8** ♦ : to take possession of : SEIZE **9** : to move emotionally; *also* : IRRITATE **10** : BAFFLE, PUZZLE **11** : KILL **12** : HIT **13** ♦ : to be subjected to ⟨~ the measles⟩ **14** : to receive as punishment **15** ♦ : to find out esp. by calculation **16 a** : HEAR **b** ♦ : to grasp the meaning of : UNDERSTAND **17** : to prevail on : PERSUADE, INDUCE **18** : HAVE ⟨he's *got* no money⟩ **19** : to have as an obligation or necessity ⟨you have *got* to come⟩ **20** : to establish communication with **21** : to be able ⟨finally *got* to go to med school⟩ **22** : to come to be ⟨*got* talking about old times⟩ **23** : to leave at once

♦ [1] acquire, attain, capture, carry, draw, earn, gain, garner, land, make, obtain, procure, realize, secure, win — more at EARN ♦ [4] beget, father, produce, sire — more at FATHER ♦ [6] become, come, go, grow, run, turn, wax — more at BECOME ♦ [8] bag, capture, catch, collar, corral, grab, grapple, hook, land, nab, seize, snare, trap — more at CATCH ♦ [13] catch, come down, contract, sicken, take — more at CONTRACT ♦ [15] detect, determine, dig up, discover, ferret out, find, hit on, locate, track down — more at FIND ♦ [16b] appreciate, apprehend, catch, catch on (to), comprehend, grasp, make, make out, perceive, see, seize, understand — more at COMPREHEND

²**get** \'get\ *n* : OFFSPRING, PROGENY
get across *vb* ♦ : to make clear or convincing

♦ clarify, clear (up), construe, demonstrate, elucidate, explain, explicate, expound, illuminate, illustrate, interpret, spell out — more at EXPLAIN

get along *vb* **1** ♦ : to meet one's needs **2** : to be on friendly terms **3** ♦ : to proceed toward a destination

♦ [1] cope, do, fare, make out, manage, shift; *also* carry on, contrive, fend, handle, scrape (by *or* through), survive; eke out, scrape (out), scrounge, squeeze, wrest, wring; afford, swing ♦ [3] advance, fare, forge, go, march, proceed, progress — more at GO

get around *vb* **1** ♦ : to manage to avoid the intent, effect, or force of something esp. by ingenuity or stratagem : CIRCUMVENT **2** ♦ : to become known or current

♦ [1] circumvent, dodge, shortcut, sidestep, skirt — more at CIRCUMVENT ♦ [2] circulate, come out, get out, leak out, out, spread — more at GET OUT

get·away \'ge-tə-ˌwā\ *n* **1** ♦ : an act or instance of getting away : ESCAPE **2** : START

♦ escape, flight, lam, slip — more at ESCAPE

get by *vb* : to meet one's needs : GET ALONG
get off *vb* ♦ : to go away from; *also* : to do or experience the first stages or actions of ⟨*got off* on the trip early⟩

♦ clear out, depart, exit, go, move, pull, quit, sally, shove, take off — more at GO ♦ begin, commence, embark (on *or* upon), enter, launch, open, start, strike — more at BEGIN

get on *vb* **1** : to proceed toward a destination **2** : to meet one's needs : GET ALONG
get out *vb* **1** ♦ : to become known; *also* : to produce or release for distribution **2** ♦ : to get away (as by flight); *also* : to cause to leave or escape

♦ [1] come out, leak out, out, spread; *also* break, develop, transpire, unfold; circulate, disclose, reveal, spill, tell ♦ [1] issue, print, publish — more at PUBLISH ♦ [2] abscond, clear out, escape, flee, fly, lam, run away, run off — more at ESCAPE

get-to·geth·er \'get-tə-ˌge-thər\ *n* ♦ : an assembly for a common purpose; *esp* : an informal social gathering

♦ assembly, conference, congress, convention, convocation, council, gathering, huddle, meeting, powwow, seminar — more at MEETING

get·up \'get-ˌəp\ *n* **1** ♦ : a clothing ensemble often for a special occasion or activity : OUTFIT, COSTUME **2** : general composition or structure

♦ dress, garb, guise, outfit — more at OUTFIT

get up *vb* **1** : to arise from bed **2** : to rise to one's feet **3** : PREPARE, ORGANIZE **4** : to produce in oneself by effort ⟨*get up* the courage⟩
gew·gaw \'gü-ˌgȯ, 'gyü-\ *n* ♦ : a showy trifle : BAUBLE, TRINKET

♦ bauble, curiosity, knickknack, novelty, tchotchke, trinket — more at KNICKKNACK

gey·ser \'gī-zər\ *n* [Icelandic *Geysir*, hot spring in Iceland] : a spring that intermittently shoots up hot water and steam
g–force \'jē-ˌfȯrs\ *n* : the force of gravity or acceleration on a body
Gha·na·ian \gä-'nā-ən\ *n* : a native or inhabitant of Ghana — **Ghanaian** *adj*
ghast·ly \'gast-lē\ *adj* **ghast·li·er; -est** **1** ♦ : terrifyingly horrible to the senses : SHOCKING **2** : resembling a ghost : DEATHLIKE, PALE

♦ appalling, atrocious, awful, dreadful, frightful, horrible, horrid, nightmarish, shocking, terrible — more at HORRIBLE

ghat \'gȯt\ *n* [Hindi & Urdu *ghāt*] : a broad flight of steps on an Indian riverbank that provides access to the water
gher·kin \'gər-kən\ *n* **1** : a small prickly fruit of a vine related to the cucumber used to make pickles **2** : an immature cucumber
ghet·to \'ge-tō\ *n, pl* **ghettos** *or* **ghettoes** : a quarter of a city in which members of a minority group live because of social, legal, or economic pressure
¹**ghost** \'gōst\ *n* **1** : the seat of life : SOUL **2** ♦ : a disembodied soul; *esp* : the soul of a dead person believed to be an inhabitant of the unseen world or to appear in bodily form to living people **3** : SPIRIT, DEMON **4** : a faint trace ⟨a ~ of a smile⟩ **5** : a false image in a photographic negative or on a television screen — **ghost·ly** *adv*

♦ apparition, bogey, phantasm, phantom, poltergeist, shade, shadow, specter, spirit, spook, vision, wraith; *also* banshee, demon, familiar, genie, imp, incubus, puck; vampire, zombie

²**ghost** *vb* : GHOSTWRITE
ghost·write \-ˌrīt\ *vb* **-wrote** \-ˌrōt\; **-writ·ten** \-ˌri-tᵊn\ : to write for and in the name of another — **ghost·writ·er** *n*
ghoul \'gül\ *n* [Ar *ghūl*] : a legendary evil being that robs graves and feeds on corpses — **ghoul·ish** *adj*

♦ demon, devil, fiend, imp — more at DEMON

GHQ *abbr* general headquarters
gi *abbr* gill
¹**GI** \ˌjē-'ī\ *adj* [galvanized *i*ron; fr. abbr. used in listing such articles as garbage cans, but taken as abbr. for *government issue*] **1** : provided by an official U.S. military supply department ⟨~ shoes⟩ **2** : of, relating to, or characteristic of U.S. military personnel **3** : conforming to military regulations or customs ⟨a ~ haircut⟩
²**GI** *n, pl* **GIs** *or* **GI's** \-'īz\ : a member or former member of the U.S. armed forces; *esp* : an enlisted person
³**GI** *abbr* **1** galvanized iron **2** gastrointestinal **3** general issue **4** government issue
¹**gi·ant** \'jī-ənt\ *n* **1** : a legendary humanlike being of great size and strength **2** ♦ : a living being or thing of extraordinary size or powers

♦ behemoth, blockbuster, colossus, jumbo, leviathan, mammoth, monster, titan, whale, whopper; *also* amazon; bulk, hulk; heavyweight *Ant* dwarf, midget, mini, miniature, peewee, pygmy, runt, shrimp

²**giant** *adj* ♦ : having extremely large size, proportion, or power

♦ astronomical, colossal, enormous, gigantic, ginormous, grand, huge, jumbo, mammoth, massive, monumental, prodigious, titanic, tremendous — more at HUGE

gi·ant·ess \'jī-ən-təs\ *n* : a female giant
giant panda *n* : PANDA 2

gib·ber \'ji-bər\ *vb* ♦ : to speak rapidly, inarticulately, and often foolishly

♦ babble, chatter, drivel, gabble, jabber, prattle, sputter — more at BABBLE

gib·ber·ish \'ji-bə-rish\ *n* ♦ : unintelligible or confused speech or language

♦ babble, bunk, claptrap, drivel, gabble, gobbledygook, hogwash, nonsense, piffle, prattle, rot; *also* abracadabra; chatter, clatter, gab, gibber, prate, tattle, twaddle; double-talk, hocus-pocus, jive; hot air, gas, wind

¹**gib·bet** \'ji-bət\ *n* : GALLOWS

²**gibbet** *vb* 1 : to hang on a gibbet 2 : to expose to public scorn 3 : to execute by hanging

gib·bon \'gi-bən\ *n* : any of several tailless apes of southeastern Asia

gib·bous \'ji-bəs, 'gi-\ *adj* 1 : rounded like the exterior of a sphere or circle 2 : seen with more than half but not all of the apparent disk illuminated ⟨~ moon⟩ 3 : having a hump : HUMPBACKED

gibe *or* **jibe** \'jīb\ *vb* **gibed** *or* **jibed; gib·ing** *or* **jib·ing** ♦ : to utter taunting words : SNEER — **gibe** *or* **jibe** *n*

♦ deride, jeer, laugh, mock, ridicule, scout — more at RIDICULE

gib·lets \'jib-ləts\ *n pl* : the edible viscera of a fowl

Gib·son girl \'gib-sən-\ *adj* : of or relating to a style in women's clothing characterized by high necks, full sleeves, and slender waistlines

gid·dy \'gi-dē\ *adj* **gid·di·er; -est** 1 ♦ : having a whirling sensation in the head with a tendency to fall : DIZZY 2 : causing dizziness 3 ♦ : not serious : FRIVOLOUS, SILLY — **gid·di·ness** \-dē-nəs\ *n*

♦ [1] dizzy, light-headed — more at DIZZY ♦ [3] flighty, frivolous, goofy, harebrained, light-headed, scatterbrained, silly; *also* foolish, fatuous, inane, nonsensical, thoughtless, witless; crazy, daffy, daft, exuberant, flippant, fluttery, light, lighthearted, playful; sappy, shallow, superficial *Ant* earnest, serious, sober

GIF \'gif, 'jif\ *n* [graphic *i*nterchange *f*ormat] : a computer file format for digital images; *also* : the image itself

gift \'gift\ *n* 1 ♦ : a special ability : TALENT 2 ♦ : something given : PRESENT 3 : the act or power of giving

♦ [1] aptitude, endowment, faculty, flair, genius, knack, talent — more at TALENT ♦ [2] bestowal, donation, freebie, lagniappe, present; *also* alms, benefaction, beneficence, benevolence, charity, contribution, dole, generosity, offering, philanthropy; grant, subsidy; remembrance, tribute; bonus, boon, windfall; favor, valentine; gratuity, tip; award, prize, reward; bequest, legacy; sacrifice

gift card *n* : a card entitling the recipient to goods or services of a specified value from the issuer

gift·ed \'gif-təd\ *adj* : TALENTED

¹**gig** \'gig\ *n* 1 : a long light ship's boat 2 : a light 2-wheeled one-horse carriage

²**gig** *n* : a pronged spear for catching fish — **gig** *vb*

³**gig** *n* : a job for a specified time; *esp* : an entertainer's engagement

⁴**gig** *n* : a military demerit — **gig** *vb*

giga·byte \'ji-gə-ˌbīt, 'gi-\ *n* : 1024 megabytes or 1,073,741,824 bytes; *also* : one billion bytes

gi·gan·tic \jī-'gan-tik\ *adj* ♦ : exceeding the usual (as in size or force)

♦ colossal, enormous, giant, ginormous, huge, jumbo, mammoth, massive, prodigious, titanic, tremendous — more at HUGE

¹**gig·gle** \'gi-gəl\ *vb* **gig·gled; gig·gling** : to laugh with repeated short catches of the breath — **gig·gly** \-gə-lē\ *adj*

²**giggle** *n* : the act of giggling

GIGO *abbr* garbage in, garbage out

gig·o·lo \'ji-gə-ˌlō\ *n, pl* **-los** 1 : a man supported by a woman usu. in return for his attentions 2 : a professional dancing partner or male escort

Gi·la monster \'hē-lə-\ *n* : a large orange and black venomous lizard of the southwestern U.S.

¹**gild** \'gild\ *vb* **gild·ed** *or* **gilt** \'gilt\; **gild·ing** 1 : to overlay with or as if with a thin covering of gold 2 : to give an attractive but often deceptive appearance to

²**gild** *var of* GUILD

¹**gill** \'jil\ *n* : a British measure of capacity equal to 5 fluid ounces; *also* : a U.S. measure of capacity equal to 5 fluid ounces

²**gill** \'gil\ *n* : an organ (as of a fish) for obtaining oxygen from water

¹**gilt** \'gilt\ *adj* : of the color of gold

²**gilt** *n* : gold or a substance resembling gold laid on the surface of an object

³**gilt** *n* : a young female swine

¹**gim·crack** \'jim-ˌkrak\ *n* : a showy object of little use or value

²**gimcrack** *adj* : CHEAP, SHODDY

gim·let \'gim-lət\ *n* : a small tool with screw point and cross handle for boring holes

gim·mick \'gi-mik\ *n* 1 ♦ : an ingenious or novel mechanical device : CONTRIVANCE, GADGET 2 : an important feature that is not immediately apparent : CATCH 3 ♦ : a new and ingenious scheme — **gim·micky** \-mi-kē\ *adj*

♦ [1] contraption, contrivance, gadget, gizmo, jigger — more at GADGET ♦ [3] artifice, device, dodge, jig, ploy, scheme, sleight, stratagem, trick, wile — more at TRICK

gim·mick·ry \'gi-mi-krē\ *n, pl* **-ries** : an array of or the use of gimmicks

gimpy \'gim-pē\ *adj* : LAME 1

¹**gin** \'jin\ *n* [ME *gin*, fr. AF, short for *engin* engine] 1 : TRAP, SNARE 2 : a machine to separate seeds from cotton — **gin** *vb*

²**gin** *n* [by shortening & alter. fr. *geneva*, kind of gin] : a liquor distilled from a grain mash and flavored with juniper berries

gin·ger \'jin-jər\ *n* 1 : the pungent aromatic rootstock of a tropical plant used esp. as a spice and in medicine; *also* : the spice or the plant 2 : brisk energy or initiative and high spirits

ginger ale *n* : a carbonated soft drink flavored with ginger

gin·ger·bread \'jin-jər-ˌbred\ *n* 1 : a cake made with molasses and flavored with ginger 2 : lavish or superfluous ornament

gin·ger·ly \'jin-jər-lē\ *adj* ♦ : very cautious or careful — **gingerly** *adv*

♦ alert, careful, cautious, circumspect, considerate, guarded, heedful, safe, wary — more at CAREFUL

gin·ger·snap \-ˌsnap\ *n* : a thin brittle molasses cookie flavored with ginger

ging·ham \'giŋ-əm\ *n* : a cotton cloth that is often marked with a pattern of colored squares

gin·gi·vi·tis \ˌjin-jə-'vī-təs\ *n* : inflammation of the gums

gink·go *also* **ging·ko** \'giŋ-(ˌ)kō\ *n, pl* **ginkgoes** *or* **ginkgos** : a tree of eastern China with fan-shaped leaves often grown as a shade tree

ginkgo bi·lo·ba \-bī-'lō-bə\ *n* : an extract of the leaves of ginkgo that is held to enhance mental functioning

gi·nor·mous \jī-'nór-məs\ *n* ♦ : extremely large : HUGE

♦ colossal, enormous, giant, huge, jumbo, mammoth, massive, prodigious, titanic, tremendous — more at HUGE

gin·seng \'jin-ˌseŋ\ *n* : an aromatic root of a Chinese or No. American herb used esp. in Chinese medicine; *also* : one of these herbs

Gip·sy *chiefly Brit var of* GYPSY

gi·raffe \jə-'raf\ *n, pl* **giraffes** [It *giraffa*, fr. Ar *zirāfah*] : an African ruminant mammal with a very long neck and a short coat with dark blotches

gird \'gərd\ *vb* **gird·ed** *or* **girt** \'gərt\; **gird·ing** 1 ♦ : to encircle or fasten (as a sword) with or as if with a belt 2 : to invest esp. with power or authority 3 : PREPARE, BRACE

♦ band, belt, girdle, wrap; *also* tie up, truss; circle, loop, wind, wreathe; bandage, swathe; chain, cord, enchain, lash, rope, shackle, tape, wire *Ant* unwrap band, bind, tie, truss — more at TIE

gird·er \'gər-dər\ *n* : a horizontal main supporting beam

¹gir·dle \'gər-d²l\ *n* **1** : something (as a belt or sash) that encircles or confines **2** : a woman's supporting undergarment that extends from the waist to below the hips

²girdle *vb* **gir·dled gir·dling** \'gər-d²l-iŋ\ **1** ♦ : to encircle with or as if with a girdle **2** ♦ : to move around

♦ [1] band, belt, gird, wrap — more at GIRD ♦ [2] circle, circumnavigate, coil, compass, encircle, loop, orbit, ring, round — more at ENCIRCLE

girl \'gərl\ *n* **1** : a female child **2** : a young woman **3** : SWEETHEART — **girl·hood** \-,hùd\ *n*

♦ doll, lass, maid, maiden, miss; *also* gamine; hoyden, tomboy; ingenue; belle, deb, debutante, sylph; schoolgirl

girl Friday *n* : a female assistant (as in an office) entrusted with a wide variety of tasks

girl·friend \'gərl-,frend\ *n* **1** : a female friend **2** : a frequent or regular female companion in a romantic or sexual relationship

girl·ish *adj* ♦ : of, relating to, or having the characteristics of a girl or girlhood

♦ effeminate, feminine, unmanly, womanly — more at EFFEMINATE

Girl Scout *n* : a member of any of the scouting programs of the Girl Scouts of the United States of America

girth \'gərth\ *n* **1** : a band around an animal by which something (as a saddle) may be fastened on its back **2** : a measure around something

gist \'jist\ *n* [AF, it lies, fr. *gesir* to lie, ultim. fr. L *jacēre*] ♦ : the main point or part ⟨the ~ of the speech⟩

♦ core, crux, heart, nub, pith, pivot — more at CRUX

git *dial var of* GET

¹give \'giv\ *vb* **gave** \'gāv\; **giv·en** \'gi-vən\; **giv·ing** **1** ♦ : to make a present of **2** : to bestow by formal action **3** : to accord or yield to another **4** ♦ : to yield to force, strain, or pressure **5** ♦ : to put into the possession or keeping of another **6** ♦ : to offer to the action of another : PROFFER **7** : to put into the possession of another : DELIVER **8** ♦ : to present in public performance or to view **9** : PROVIDE ⟨~ a party⟩ **10** : ATTRIBUTE **11** : to make, form, or yield as a product or result ⟨cows ~ milk⟩ **12** : to yield possession of by way of exchange : PAY **13** : to deliver by some bodily action ⟨*gave* me a push⟩ **14** : to offer as a pledge ⟨I ~ you my word⟩ **15** : to apply freely or fully : DEVOTE **16** : to cause to have or receive ⟨~ me time⟩

♦ [1] bestow, contribute, donate, present; *also* chip in, kick in, pitch in; award, confer, dole (out), endow; afford, furnish, provide; lavish, regale; aid, assist, benefit, help; administer, dispense, issue, impart, render; extend, offer, pay, proffer, tender; sacrifice ♦ [4] cave in, collapse, crumple, go, yield — more at COLLAPSE ♦ [5] commend, commit, consign, delegate, deliver, entrust, hand over, leave, pass, transfer, transmit, trust, turn over, vest; *also* confer, grant; assign, deal (out); dispense, disperse, distribute, divide; release, relinquish, submit, surrender, turn in, yield; bequeath, hand down, will; advance, lend, loan; furnish, supply *Ant* hold, keep, retain ♦ [6] extend, offer, proffer, tender — more at OFFER ♦ [8] carry, mount, offer, present, stage — more at PRESENT

²give *n* **1** : capacity or tendency to yield to force or strain **2** : the quality or state of being springy

give–and–take \,giv-ən-'tāk\ *n* **1** ♦ : the practice of making mutual concessions : COMPROMISE **2** ♦ : a usu. good-natured exchange (as of remarks or ideas)

♦ [1] accommodation, compromise, concession, negotiation — more at CONCESSION ♦ [2] argument, colloquy,

conference, deliberation, discourse, discussion, parley, talk — more at DISCUSSION

give·away \'gi-və-,wā\ *n* **1** : an unintentional revelation or betrayal **2** : something given away free; *esp* : PREMIUM

give away *vb* **1** : to make a present of **2** : to deliver (a bride) ceremonially to the bridegroom at a wedding **3** ♦ : to reveal or make known sometimes unintentionally

♦ bespeak, betray, demonstrate, display, evince, expose, manifest, reveal, show — more at SHOW

give in *vb* ♦ : to yield under insistence or entreaty : SUBMIT, SURRENDER

♦ blink, bow, budge, capitulate, concede, knuckle under, quit, submit, succumb, surrender, yield — more at YIELD

¹giv·en \'gi-vən\ *adj* **1** ♦ : having a tendency or inclination : INCLINED ⟨~ to swearing⟩ **2** : SPECIFIED, PARTICULAR ⟨at a ~ time⟩

♦ apt, inclined, prone — more at PRONE ♦ accustomed, used, wont — more at ACCUSTOMED

²given *prep* : CONSIDERING

given name *n* : a name that precedes one's surname

give out *vb* **1** : EMIT **2** : BREAK DOWN **3** : to become exhausted : COLLAPSE

give up *vb* **1** ♦ : to yield control or possession of : SURRENDER **2** : to abandon (oneself) to a feeling, influence, or activity **3** ♦ : to cease doing or attempting something esp. as an admission of defeat : QUIT ⟨*gave up* his job⟩

♦ [1] cede, deliver, hand over, leave, relinquish, render, surrender, turn over, yield — more at SURRENDER ♦ [3] discontinue, drop, knock off, lay off, quit — more at QUIT

giz·mo *also* **gis·mo** \'giz-mō\ *n, pl* **gizmos** *also* **gismos** ♦ : an often small mechanical or electronic device with a practical use but often thought of as a novelty : GADGET

♦ contraption, contrivance, gadget, gimmick, jigger — more at GADGET

giz·zard \'gi-zərd\ *n* : the muscular usu. horny-lined enlargement of the alimentary canal of a bird used for churning and grinding up food

gla·cial \'glā-shəl\ *adj* : suggestive of ice: as **a** ♦ : extremely cold **b** ♦ : devoid of warmth and cordiality **2** : of or relating to glaciers **3** : being or relating to a past period of time when a large part of the earth was covered by glaciers **4** *cap* : PLEISTOCENE **5** : very slow ⟨a ~ pace⟩ — **gla·cial·ly** *adv*

♦ [1a] arctic, bitter, cold, freezing, frigid, polar, raw, wintry — more at COLD ♦ [1b] chill, chilly, cold, cold-blooded, cool, frigid, frosty, icy, unfriendly, unsympathetic, wintry — more at COLD

gla·ci·ate \'glā-shē-,āt\ *vb* **-at·ed; -at·ing** **1** : to subject to glacial action **2** : to produce glacial effects in or on — **gla·ci·a·tion** \,glā-shē-'ā-shən, -sē-\ *n*

gla·cier \'glā-shər\ *n* [F, fr. MF dial. (Savoy), fr. *glace* ice, fr. L *glacies*] : a large body of ice moving slowly down a slope or spreading outward on a land surface

¹glad \'glad\ *adj* **glad·der; glad·dest** **1** ♦ : experiencing pleasure, joy, or delight **2** : PLEASED **3** ♦ : very willing **4** : PLEASANT, JOYFUL **5** ♦ : causing happiness and joy : CHEERFUL — **glad·ly** *adv*

♦ [1] blissful, delighted, happy, joyful, pleased; *also* beaming, blithe, blithesome, buoyant, cheerful, cheery, gay, gladsome, lighthearted, sunny, upbeat, gleeful, jocund, jolly, jovial, laughing, merry, mirthful, smiling; carried away, ecstatic, elated, enraptured, entranced, euphoric, exhilarated, intoxicated, rapturous, rhapsodic; exuberant, exultant, jubilant, rapt, rejoicing, thrilled; hopeful, rosy, sanguine *Ant* displeased, joyless, sad, unhappy, unsatisfied ♦ [3] amenable, disposed, game, inclined, ready, willing — more at WILLING ♦ [5] bright, cheerful, cheery, gay — more at CHEERFUL

²glad *n* : GLADIOLUS

glad·den \'glad-²n\ *vb* ♦ : to make glad

♦ content, delight, gratify, please, rejoice, satisfy, suit, warm — more at PLEASE

glade \'glād\ *n* : a grassy open space surrounded by woods

glad·i·a·tor \'gla-dē-,ā-tər\ *n* **1** ♦ : a person engaged in a fight to the death for public entertainment in ancient Rome **2** : a person engaging in a public fight or controversy; *also* : PRIZEFIGHTER

glad·i·a·to·ri·al \,gla-dē-ə-'tōr-ē-əl\ *adj* **1** : of, relating to, or suggestive of gladiators or the combats of gladiators **2** : inclined toward controversy or contention

glad·i·o·lus \,gla-dē-'ō-ləs\ *n, pl* **-o·li** \-(')ō-(,)lē, -,lī\ *or* **-olus** [L, fr. dim. of *gladius* sword] : any of a genus of chiefly African plants related to the irises and having erect sword-shaped leaves and stalks of bright colored flowers

glad·ness *n* ♦ : the quality or state of being glad

♦ blessedness, bliss, felicity, happiness, joy — more at HAPPINESS ♦ contentment, delectation, delight, enjoyment, gratification, pleasure, relish, satisfaction — more at PLEASURE

glad·some \'glad-səm\ *adj* : giving or showing joy : CHEERFUL

glam \'glam\ *n* : extravagantly showy glamour — **glam** *adj*

glam·or·ise *chiefly Brit var of* GLAMORIZE

glam·or·ize *also* **glam·our·ize** \'gla-mə-,rīz\ *vb* **-ized; -iz·ing** ♦ : to make or look upon as glamorous; *also* : treat as idealized or heroic

♦ dream, glorify, idealize — more at IDEALIZE

glam·or·ous \-mə-rəs\ *adj* ♦ : full of glamour : excitingly attractive

♦ exotic, fantastic, marvelous (*or* marvellous), outlandish, romantic, strange — more at EXOTIC ♦ alluring, attractive, captivating, charming, elfin, engaging, fascinating, fetching, magnetic, seductive — more at FASCINATING

glam·our \'gla-mər\ *n* [Sc *glamour* magic spell, alter. of E *grammar*; fr. the popular association of erudition with occult practices] ♦ : an exciting and often illusory and romantic attractiveness; *esp* : alluring personal attraction

♦ allure, appeal, attractiveness, captivation, charisma, charm, enchantment, fascination, magic, magnetism — more at CHARM

¹glance \'glans\ *vb* **glanced; glanc·ing** **1** ♦ : to strike and fly off to one side **2** ♦ : to flash or gleam with quick intermittent rays of light **3** ♦ : to give a quick look

♦ [1] bounce, carom, rebound, ricochet, skim, skip; *also* brush, graze, nudge, shave, sweep; bump, contact, hit, kiss, touch; sideswipe; reflect ♦ [2] flame, flash, gleam, glimmer, glisten, glitter, scintillate, shimmer, sparkle, twinkle, wink — more at FLASH ♦ [3] browse, dip, glimpse, peek, skim; *also* peep; blink, squint; look over, scan *Ant* stare, gaze

²glance *n* **1** : a quick intermittent flash or gleam **2** : a deflected impact or blow **3** ♦ : a quick look

♦ cast, eye, gander, glimpse, look, peek, peep, regard, sight, view — more at LOOK

gland \'gland\ *n* : a cell or group of cells that prepares and secretes a substance (as saliva or sweat) for further use in or discharge from the body

glan·du·lar \'glan-jə-lər\ *adj* : of, relating to, or involving glands

glans \'glanz\ *n, pl* **glan·des** \'glan-,dēz\ [L, lit., acorn] : a conical vascular body forming the extremity of the penis or clitoris

¹glare \'gler\ *vb* **glared; glar·ing** **1** ♦ : to shine with a harsh dazzling light **2** ♦ : to stare fiercely or angrily

♦ [1] beat, blaze, burn, flame, flare; *also* beam, glow, radiate; flash, glance, gleam, glimmer, glint, glisten, glister, glitter, scintillate, shimmer, sparkle, twinkle; bedazzle, blind, daze, dazzle ♦ [2] frown, gloom, glower, lower, scowl — more at FROWN

²glare *n* **1** : a harsh dazzling light **2** : an angry or fierce stare

glaring *adj* ♦ : very conspicuous ⟨a ∼ error⟩ — **glar·ing·ly** *adv*

♦ blatant, conspicuous, egregious, flagrant, gross, obvious, patent, prominent, pronounced, rank, striking — more at EGREGIOUS

glass \'glas\ *n* **1** : a hard brittle amorphous usu. transparent or translucent material consisting typically of silica **2** : something made of glass; *esp* : TUMBLER 2 **3** *pl* ♦ : a pair of lenses used to correct defects of vision : SPECTACLES **4** : the quantity held by a glass container — **glass** *adj* — **glass·ful** \-,fu̇l\ *n* — **glassy** *adj*

♦ glasses eyeglasses, spectacles; *also* bifocals; monocle, pince-nez; sunglasses; goggles; contact lens

glass·blow·ing \-,blō-iŋ\ *n* : the art of shaping a mass of glass that has been softened by heat by blowing air into it through a tube — **glass·blow·er** *n*

glass·ware \-,wer\ *n* : articles made of glass

glau·co·ma \glau̇-'kō-mə, glȯ-\ *n* : a disease of the eye marked by increased pressure within the eyeball resulting in damage to the retina and gradual loss of vision

¹glaze \'glāz\ *vb* **glazed; glaz·ing** **1** : to furnish (as a window frame) with glass **2** : to apply glaze to

²glaze *n* : a glassy coating or surface

gla·zier \'glā-zhər\ *n* : a person who sets glass in window frames

¹gleam \'glēm\ *n* **1** : a transient subdued or partly obscured light **2 a** ♦ : a small bright light **b** : GLINT **3** : a faint trace ⟨a ∼ of hope⟩

♦ blaze, flare, fluorescence, glare, glow, illumination, incandescence, light, luminescence, radiance, shine — more at LIGHT

²gleam *vb* **1** ♦ : to shine with subdued light or moderate brightness **2** : to appear briefly or faintly

♦ flame, flash, glance, glimmer, glisten, glitter, scintillate, shimmer, sparkle, twinkle, wink — more at FLASH

glean \'glēn\ *vb* **1** : to gather grain left by reapers **2** : to collect little by little or with patient effort ⟨antiques ∼ed from flea markets⟩ — **glean·able** *adj* — **glean·er** *n*

glean·ings \'glē-niŋz\ *n pl* : things acquired by gleaning

glee \'glē\ *n* [ME, fr. OE *glēo* entertainment, music] **1** ♦ : exultant high-spirited joy : HILARITY **2** : a part-song for three usu. male voices

♦ cheer, cheerfulness, hilarity, joviality, merriment, mirth — more at MIRTH

glee club *n* : a chorus organized for singing usu. short choral pieces

glee·ful *adj* ♦ : full of glee

♦ blithe, boon, festive, gay, jocund, jolly, jovial, merry, mirthful, sunny — more at MERRY

glen \'glen\ *n* : a narrow hidden valley

glen·gar·ry \glen-'ga-rē\ *n, pl* **-ries** *often cap* : a woolen cap of Scottish origin

glib \'glib\ *adj* **glib·ber; glib·best** : speaking or spoken with careless ease — **glib·ly** *adv*

glide \'glīd\ *vb* **glid·ed; glid·ing** **1** ♦ : to move smoothly and effortlessly **2** ♦ : to descend gradually without engine power ⟨∼ in an airplane⟩ — **glide** *n*

♦ [1] bowl, breeze, coast, drift, flow, roll, sail, skim, slide, slip, stream, sweep, whisk — more at FLOW ♦ [2] fly, plane, soar, wing — more at FLY

glid·er \'glī-dər\ *n* **1** : one that glides **2** : an aircraft resembling an airplane but having no engine **3** : a porch seat suspended from an upright frame

¹glim·mer \'gli-mər\ *vb* ♦ : to shine faintly or unsteadily

♦ flame, flash, glance, gleam, glisten, glitter, scintillate, shimmer, sparkle, twinkle, wink — more at FLASH

²glimmer *n* **1** : a faint unsteady light **2** : INKLING **3** ♦ : a small amount : HINT

♦ hint, little, mite, particle, touch, trace — more at PARTICLE

¹glimpse \'glimps\ *vb* **glimpsed; glimps·ing** ♦ : to take a brief look : see momentarily or incompletely

♦ browse, dip, glance, peek, skim — more at GLANCE

²glimpse *n* **1** : a faint idea : GLIMMER **2** ♦ : a short hurried look

♦ cast, eye, gander, glance, look, peek, peep, regard, sight, view — more at LOOK

glint \'glint\ *vb* **1** : to shine by reflection : SPARKLE, GLEAM **2** : to appear briefly or faintly — **glint** *n*

glis·san·do \gli-'sän-(ˌ)dō\ *n, pl* **-di** \-(ˌ)dē\ *or* **-dos** : a rapid sliding up or down the musical scale

¹glis·ten \'gli-sⁿn\ *vb* ♦ : to shine by reflection with a soft luster or sparkle

♦ flame, flash, glance, gleam, glimmer, glitter, scintillate, shimmer, sparkle, twinkle, wink — more at FLASH

²glisten *n* : GLITTER, SPARKLE

glis·ter \'glis-tər\ *vb* : to shine by reflection with many small flashes of brilliant light : GLITTER

glitch \'glich\ *n* : MALFUNCTION; *also* : SNAG 2

¹glit·ter \'gli-tər\ *vb* **1** ♦ : to shine with brilliant or metallic luster : SPARKLE **2** ♦ : to shine with strong emotion : FLASH ⟨eyes ~*ing* in anger⟩ **3** : to be brilliantly attractive esp. in a superficial way

♦ flame, flash, glance, gleam, glimmer, glisten, scintillate, shimmer, sparkle, twinkle, wink — more at FLASH

²glitter *n* **1** : sparkling brilliancy, showiness, or attractiveness **2** : small glittering objects used for ornamentation — **glit·tery** \'gli-tə-rē\ *adj*

glitz \'glits\ *n* ♦ : extravagant showiness

♦ flamboyance, flashiness, gaudiness, ostentation, pretentiousness, showiness, swank — more at OSTENTATION

glitzy \'glit-sē\ *adj* ♦ : having glitz

♦ flamboyant, flashy, garish, gaudy, loud, ostentatious, swank, tawdry — more at GAUDY

gloam·ing \'glō-miŋ\ *n* ♦ : the light from the sky between full night and sunrise or between sunset and full night : TWILIGHT, DUSK

♦ dusk, evening, nightfall, sundown, sunset, twilight — more at DUSK

gloat \'glōt\ *vb* : to think about something with triumphant and often malicious delight ⟨~*ing* over their victory⟩

glob \'gläb\ *n* **1** ♦ : a small drop **2** ♦ : a large rounded mass

♦ [1] blob, driblet, drip, drop, droplet — more at DROP
♦ [2] blob, chunk, clod, clump, gob, hunk, lump, nub, wad — more at LUMP

glob·al \'glō-bəl\ *adj* **1** : of, relating to, or involving the entire world : WORLDWIDE **2** ♦ : of, relating to, or applying to a whole : COMPREHENSIVE, GENERAL — **glob·al·ly** *adv*

♦ blanket, common, general, generic, overall, universal — more at GENERAL ♦ compendious, complete, comprehensive, encyclopedic, full, inclusive, omnibus, panoramic, universal — more at ENCYCLOPEDIC

glob·al·i·za·tion \ˌglō-bə-lə-'zā-shən\ *n* : the development of an increasingly integrated global economy

Global Positioning System *n* : GPS

global warming *n* : an increase in the earth's atmospheric and oceanic temperatures due to an increase in the greenhouse effect

globe \'glōb\ *n* **1** : a round body : BALL, SPHERE **2** : the planet on which we live that is third in order from the sun : EARTH; *also* : a spherical representation of the earth

globe–trot·ter \'glōb-ˌträ-tər\ *n* : a person who travels widely — **globe–trot·ting** *n or adj*

glob·u·lar \'glä-byə-lər\ *adj* : having the shape of a globe or globule

glob·ule \'glä-(ˌ)byül\ *n* : a tiny globe or ball esp. of a liquid

glob·u·lin \'glä-byə-lən\ *n* : any of a class of simple proteins insoluble in pure water but soluble in dilute salt solutions that occur widely in plant and animal tissues

glock·en·spiel \'glä-kən-ˌshpēl, -ˌspēl\ *n* [G, fr. *Glocke* bell + *Spiel* play] : a percussion musical instrument consisting of a series of metal bars played with two hammers

gloom \'glüm\ *n* **1** ♦ : partial or total darkness **2** ♦ : lowness of spirits : DEJECTION **3** : an atmosphere of despondency ⟨a ~ fell over the household⟩

♦ [1] dark, darkness, dusk, gloaming, murk, night, semidarkness, shade, shadows, twilight — more at DARK ♦ [2] blues, dejection, depression, doldrums, dumps, melancholy, sadness — more at SADNESS

gloom·i·ness \-mē-nəs\ *n* : the quality or state of being gloomy

gloomy \'glü-mē\ *adj* **gloom·i·er; -est** **1** ♦ : partially or totally dark **2** ♦ : causing gloom; *also* : lacking in promise or hopefulness **3** ♦ : low in spirits — **gloom·i·ly** \'glü-mə-lē\ *adv*

♦ [1] dark, darkling, dim, dusky, murky, obscure, somber (*or* sombre) — more at DARK ♦ [2] bleak, dark, depressing, desolate, dismal, dreary, glum, gray (*or* grey), miserable, murky, somber (*or* sombre); *also* discomfiting, discouraging, disheartening, dismaying, dispiriting, distressful, distressing, upsetting; desperate, hopeless, pessimistic; dour, grim, lowering, menacing, negative, oppressive, threatening *Ant* bright, cheerful, gay, festive, friendly, heartwarming, sunshiny ♦ [3] blue, dejected, depressed, down, downcast, forlorn, glum, low, melancholy, miserable, sad, sorrowful, unhappy — more at SAD

Gloomy Gus \-'gəs\ *n, pl* **Gloomy Gus·es** : a person who is habitually gloomy

glop \'gläp\ *n* : a messy mass or mixture

glo·ri·fy \'glór-ə-ˌfī\ *vb* **-fied; -fy·ing** **1** : to raise to heavenly glory **2** : to light up brilliantly **3** ♦ : to represent as glorious : EXTOL **4** ♦ : to give glory to (as in worship) **5** ♦ : to cause to be or seem to be better than the actual condition **6** ♦ : to make glorious by bestowing honor, praise, or admiration — **glo·ri·fi·ca·tion** \ˌglór-ə-fə-'kā-shən\ *n*

♦ [3] bless, extol, laud, magnify, praise — more at PRAISE ♦ [4] adore, deify, revere, venerate, worship — more at WORSHIP ♦ [5] dream, glamorize, idealize — more at IDEALIZE ♦ [6] aggrandize, dignify, ennoble, exalt, magnify — more at EXALT

glo·ri·ous \'glór-ē-əs\ *adj* **1** : possessing or deserving glory : PRAISEWORTHY **2** : conferring glory **3** ♦ : marked by great beauty or splendor : MAGNIFICENT **4** : DELIGHTFUL, WONDERFUL

♦ august, baronial, gallant, grand, grandiose, heroic, imposing, magnificent, majestic, monumental, noble, proud, regal, royal, splendid, stately — more at GRAND

glo·ri·ous·ly *adv* ♦ : in a glorious manner

♦ agreeably, delightfully, favorably (*or* favourably), felicitously, nicely, pleasantly, pleasingly, satisfyingly, splendidly, well

¹glo·ry \'glór-ē\ *n, pl* **glories** **1** ♦ : praise, honor, or distinction extended by common consent : RENOWN **2** : honor and praise rendered in worship **3** ♦ : something that secures praise or renown **4** : a distinguishing quality or asset **5** ♦ : great beauty and splendor : RESPLENDENCE, MAGNIFICENCE **6** : heavenly bliss **7** : a height of prosperity or achievement

♦ [1] acclaim, accolade, credit, distinction, fame, homage, honor (*or* honour), laurels, praise, renown; *also* compliment, encomium, eulogy, panegyric, toast, tribute; acclamation, ovation, plaudit, rave, rhapsody; citation, commendation, note, recommendation; elevation, exaltation, glorification ♦ [3] boast, credit, honor (*or* honour), jewel, pride, treasure; *also* pièce de résistance, showpiece; attraction, feature, highlight; distinction, excellence, merit, value, virtue ♦ [5] augustness, brilliance, grandeur, grandness, magnificence, majesty, nobility, nobleness, resplendence, splendor, stateliness — more at MAGNIFICENCE

²glory *vb* **glo·ried; glo·ry·ing** ♦ : to rejoice proudly : EXULT

♦ crow, delight, exult, joy, rejoice, triumph — more at EXULT

¹gloss \'gläs, 'glòs\ *n* **1** ♦ : a surface luster or brightness : SHEEN **2** : outward show

♦ luster (*or* lustre), polish, sheen, shine — more at SHINE

²gloss *vb* **1** ♦ : to give a false appearance of acceptableness to ⟨~ over inadequacies⟩ **2** ♦ : to deal with too lightly or not at all — usu. used with *over* ⟨~*ed* over the problem⟩ **3** ♦ : to give a gloss to

♦ *usu* **gloss over** [1] excuse, palliate, whitewash — more at PALLIATE ♦ *usu* **gloss over** [2] condone, disregard, excuse, forgive, ignore, pardon, pass over, shrug off, wink at — more at EXCUSE ♦ [3] buff, burnish, dress, grind, polish, rub, shine, smooth — more at POLISH

³gloss *n* [alter. of *gloze,* fr. ME *glose,* fr. AF, fr. ML *glosa, glossa,* fr. Gk *glōssa, glōtta* tongue, language, unusual word] **1** : an explanatory note (as in the margin of a text) **2** : GLOSSARY **3** : an interlinear translation **4** : a continuous commentary accompanying a text

⁴gloss *vb* : to furnish glosses for

glos·sa·ry \'glä-sə-rē, 'glò-\ *n, pl* **-ries** : a collection of difficult or specialized terms with their meanings — **glos·sar·i·al** \glä-'ser-ē-əl, glò-\ *adj*

glos·so·la·lia \,glä-sə-'lā-lē-ə, ,glò-\ *n* [ultim. fr. Gk *glōssa* tongue, language + *lalia* chatter] : TONGUE 6

¹glossy \'glä-sē, 'glò-\ *adj* **gloss·i·er; -est** ♦ : having a surface luster or brightness — **gloss·i·ly** \-sə-lē\ *adv* — **gloss·i·ness** \-sē-nəs\ *n*

♦ lustrous, polished, satiny, sleek; *also* silken, silky, slick, slippery; glassy, glazed, shellacked, varnished; gleaming, reflective, glittering, shining *Ant* dim, dull, flat, lusterless, matte

²glossy *n, pl* **gloss·ies** : a photograph printed on smooth shiny paper

glot·tis \'glä-təs\ *n, pl* **glot·tis·es** *or* **glot·ti·des** \-tə-,dēz\ : the slitlike opening between the vocal cords in the larynx — **glot·tal** \'glä-t³l\ *adj*

glove \'gləv\ *n* **1** : a covering for the hand having separate sections for each finger **2** : a padded leather covering for the hand for use in a sport

¹glow \'glō\ *vb* **1** ♦ : to shine with or as if with intense heat **2** ♦ : to have a rich warm usu. ruddy color : FLUSH, BLUSH **3** : to feel hot **4** : to show exuberance or elation ⟨~ with pride⟩

♦ [1] blaze, burn, flame — more at BURN ♦ [2] bloom, blush, color (*or* colour), crimson, flush, redden — more at BLUSH

²glow *n* **1** : brightness or warmth of color; *esp* : REDNESS **2** : warmth of feeling or emotion **3** : a sensation of warmth **4** ♦ : light such as is emitted from a heated substance

♦ blaze, flare, fluorescence, glare, gleam, illumination, incandescence, light, luminescence, radiance, shine — more at LIGHT

glow·er \'glau̇(-ə)r\ *vb* ♦ : to stare angrily : SCOWL — **glower** *n*

♦ frown, glare, gloom, lower, scowl — more at FROWN

glowing *adj* **1** ♦ : giving off light esp. because of heat **2** ♦ : marked by a rich warm coloration; *also* : marked by a radiant healthfully ruddy coloration **3** : highly enthusiastic

♦ [1] beaming, bright, brilliant, effulgent, incandescent, lambent, lucent, lucid, luminous, lustrous, radiant, refulgent, shiny — more at BRIGHT ♦ [2] florid, flush, rosy, ruddy, sanguine — more at RUDDY

glow·worm \'glō-,wərm\ *n* : any of various insect larvae or adults that give off light

glox·in·ia \gläk-'si-nē-ə\ *n* : any of a genus of tropical herbs related to the African violets; *esp* : one with showy bell‗ shaped or slipper-shaped flowers

gloze \'glōz\ *vb* **glozed; gloz·ing** : to make appear right or acceptable : GLOSS

glu·cose \'glü-,kōs\ *n* **1** : a form of crystalline sugar; *esp* : DEXTROSE **2** : a sweet light-colored syrup made from cornstarch

glue \'glü\ *n* ♦ : a jellylike protein substance made from animal materials and used for sticking things together; *also* : any of various other strong adhesives — **glue** *vb*

♦ adhesive, cement, size; *also* epoxy, epoxy resin, mucilage; dope, goo, gum

glu·ey \'glü-ē\ *adj* **1** ♦ : having the quality of glue; *also* : resembling or suggestive of glue (as in stickiness or consistency) **2** : daubed, smeared, or covered with glue

♦ adhesive, gelatinous, glutinous, gooey, gummy, sticky, viscid, viscous — more at STICKY

glum \'gləm\ *adj* **glum·mer; glum·mest 1** ♦ : broodingly morose : SULLEN **2** ♦ : having nothing likely to provide cheer, comfort, or interest : DREARY, GLOOMY

♦ [1] moody, morose, sulky, sullen, surly — more at SULKY ♦ [1, 2] bleak, dark, dismal, dreary, gloomy, gray (*or* grey), somber (*or* sombre), wretched — more at GLOOMY

¹glut \'glət\ *vb* **glut·ted; glut·ting 1** : to supply with more than is needed or than can be handled **2** ♦ : to fill esp. with food to satiety : SATIATE

♦ gorge, sate, satiate, stuff, surfeit — more at GORGE

²glut *n* : an excessive supply

glu·ten \'glüt-³n\ *n* : a gluey protein substance that causes dough to be sticky

glu·ti·nous \'glü-tə-nəs\ *adj* ♦ : having the quality of glue : STICKY

♦ adhesive, gelatinous, gluey, gooey, gummy, sticky, viscid, viscous — more at STICKY

glut·ton \'glə-t³n\ *n* : one that eats to excess — **glut·tony** \'glə-tə-nē\ *n*

glut·ton·ous \'glət-³n-əs\ *adj* ♦ : marked by or given to excessive eating or drinking

♦ greedy, hoggish, piggish, rapacious, ravenous, voracious — more at VORACIOUS

glyc·er·in *or* **glyc·er·ine** \'gli-sə-rən\ *n* : GLYCEROL

glyc·er·ol \'gli-sə-,ròl, -,rōl\ *n* : a sweet syrupy alcohol usu. obtained from fats and used esp. as a solvent

gly·co·gen \'glī-kə-jən\ *n* : a white tasteless substance that is the chief storage carbohydrate of animals

gm *abbr* gram

GM *abbr* **1** general manager **2** guided missile

G–man \'jē-,man\ *n* : a special agent of the Federal Bureau of Investigation

GMT *abbr* Greenwich mean time

gnarled \'närld\ *adj* **1** : KNOTTY **2** : GLOOMY, SULLEN

gnash \'nash\ *vb* ♦ : to grind (as teeth) together

♦ crunch, grate, grind, grit, scrape — more at GRIND

gnat \'nat\ *n* : any of various small usu. biting dipteran flies

gnaw \'nò\ *vb* **1** ♦ : to consume, wear away, or make by persistent biting or nibbling **2** : to affect as if by gnawing

♦ *usu* **gnaw on** bite, champ, chew, chomp, crunch, nibble

gnaw·er *n* : one that gnaws

gneiss \'nīs\ *n* : a layered rock similar in composition to granite

gnome \'nōm\ *n* ♦ : a dwarf of folklore who lives inside the earth and guards precious ore or treasure — **gnom·ish** *adj*

♦ brownie, dwarf, elf, fairy, fay, hobgoblin, leprechaun, pixie, puck, troll

GNP *abbr* gross national product

gnu \'nü\ *n, pl* **gnu** *or* **gnus** : WILDEBEEST

¹go \'gō\ *vb* **went** \'went\; **gone** \'gòn, 'gän\; **go·ing; goes** \'gōz\ **1** ♦ : to move on a course : PROCEED ⟨~ slow⟩ **2** ♦ : to move out of or away from a place expressed or implied : LEAVE, DEPART **3** : to take a certain course or follow a certain procedure ⟨reports ∼ through department channels⟩ **4** ♦ : to extend from point to point or in a certain direction : RUN ⟨his land ∼*es* to the river⟩; *also* : LEAD ⟨that door ∼*es* to the cellar⟩ **5** : to be habitually in a certain state ⟨∼*es* armed after dark⟩ **6** : to become lost, consumed, or spent; *also* : DIE **7** : ELAPSE, PASS **8** ♦ : to pass by sale ⟨*went* for a good price⟩ **9** : to become impaired or weakened **10** : to give way under force or pressure **11** : to move along in a specified manner ⟨it *went* well⟩ **12** : to be in general or on an average ⟨cheap, as yachts ∼⟩ **13** : to become esp. as the result of a contest ⟨the decision *went* against him⟩ **14** : to put or subject oneself ⟨∼ to great expense⟩ **15** ♦ : to have recourse to another : RESORT ⟨*went* to court to recover damages⟩ **16** : to begin or maintain an action or motion ⟨here ∼*es*⟩ **17** : to function properly ⟨the clock doesn't ∼⟩ **18** : to be known ⟨∼*es* by an alias⟩ **19** : to be or act in accordance ⟨a good rule to ∼ by⟩ **20** : to come to be applied **21** : to pass by award, assignment, or lot **22** : to contribute to a result ⟨qualities that ∼ to make a hero⟩ **23** : to be about, intending, or expecting something ⟨is ∼*ing* to leave town⟩ **24** : to arrive at a certain state or condition ⟨∼ to sleep⟩ **25** : to come to be ⟨the tire *went* flat⟩ **26** : to be capable of being sung or played ⟨the tune ∼*es* like this⟩ **27** : to be suitable or becoming : HARMONIZE **28** : to be capable of passing, extending, or being contained or inserted ⟨this coat will ∼ in the trunk⟩ **29** : to have a usual or proper place or position : BELONG ⟨these books ∼ on that shelf⟩ **30** : to be capable of being contained in ⟨3 ∼*es* into 6 twice⟩ **31** : to have a tendency ⟨that ∼*es* to show that he is honest⟩ **32** : to be acceptable, satisfactory, or adequate **33** : to empty the bladder or bowels **34** : to proceed along or according to : FOLLOW **35** ♦ : to travel through or along : TRAVERSE **36** : to make a wager or offer of : BET, BID ⟨willing to ∼ $50⟩ **37** : to assume the function or obligation of ⟨∼ bail for a friend⟩ **38** : to participate to the extent of ⟨∼ halves⟩ **39** : WEIGH **40** : ENDURE, TOLERATE **41** : AFFORD ⟨can't ∼ the price⟩ **42** : SAY — used chiefly in oral narration of speech **43** : to engage in ⟨don't ∼ telling everyone⟩ — **go at 1** : ATTACK, ATTEMPT **2** : UNDERTAKE — **go back on 1** : ABANDON **2** : BETRAY **3** : FAIL — **go by the board** : to be discarded — **go for 1** : to pass for or serve as **2** : to try to secure **3** : FAVOR — **go one better** : OUTDO, SURPASS — **go over 1** : EXAMINE **2** : REPEAT **3** : STUDY, REVIEW — **go places** : to be on the way to success — **go steady** : to date one person exclusively — **go to bat for** : DEFEND, CHAMPION — **go to town 1** : to work or act efficiently **2** : to be very successful

♦ [1] advance, fare, forge, get along, march, proceed, progress; *also* accelerate, fast-forward, speed; approach, near; journey, pass, repair, run, travel, wend; actuate, drive, impel, propel, push; do, go off, take out **Ant** remain, stand, stay, stop ♦ [2] clear out, depart, exit, get off, leave, move, pull, quit, sally, shove, take off; *also* set out, start, strike out; abscond, decamp, escape, evacuate, flee, fly, get out, run away, scram, skip; go out, light out, step out; abandon, desert, forsake, vacate; emigrate; remove, retire, retreat, withdraw **Ant** arrive, come, show up, turn up ♦ [4] extend, head, lead, lie, run — more at RUN ♦ *usu* **go for** [8] bring, cost, fetch, sell — more at COST ♦ *usu* **go to** [15] refer, resort, turn ♦ [35] cover, crisscross, cross, cut, follow, pass, proceed, travel, traverse — more at TRAVERSE

²go *n, pl* **goes 1** : the act or manner of going **2** : the height of fashion ⟨boots are all the ∼⟩ **3** : a turn of affairs : OCCURRENCE **4** : active bodily or mental strength or force : ENERGY, VIGOR **5** ♦ : an experimental trial or attempt **6** : a spell of activity — **no go** : USELESS, HOPELESS — **on the go** : constantly active

♦ attempt, bid, crack, endeavor (*or* endeavour), essay, fling, pass, shot, stab, trial, try, whack, whirl — more at ATTEMPT

³go *adj* ♦ : functioning properly

♦ fit, ready, set — more at READY

¹goad \'gōd\ *n* [ME *gode*, fr. OE *gād* spear, goad] **1** : a pointed rod used to urge on an animal **2** ♦ : something that urges

♦ boost, encouragement, impetus, impulse, incentive, incitement, instigation, momentum, motivation, provocation, spur, stimulus, yeast — more at IMPULSE

²goad *vb* ♦ : to incite or rouse as if with a goad

♦ egg on, encourage, exhort, press, prod, prompt, urge — more at URGE

go-ahead \'gō-ə-ˌhed\ *n* : authority to proceed

goal \'gōl\ *n* **1** : the mark set as limit to a race; *also* : an area to be reached safely in children's games **2** ♦ : the end toward which effort is directed : AIM, PURPOSE **3** : an area or object toward which play is directed to score; *also* : a successful attempt to score

♦ aim, ambition, aspiration, design, dream, end, intent, mark, meaning, object, objective, plan, pretension, purpose, thing; *also* plot, project, scheme; desire, hope, wish; destination, terminus

goal·ie \'gō-lē\ *n* : GOALKEEPER

goal·keep·er \'gōl-ˌkē-pər\ *n* : a player who defends the goal in various games

goal·post \-ˌpōst\ *n* : one of the two vertical posts with a crossbar that constitute the goal in various games

goat \'gōt\ *n, pl* **goats** *or* **goat** : any of various hollow-horned ruminant mammals related to the sheep that have backward-curving horns, a short tail, and usu. straight hair

goa·tee \gō-'tē\ *n* : a small trim pointed or tufted beard on a man's chin

goat·herd \'gōt-ˌhərd\ *n* : a person who tends goats

goat·skin \-ˌskin\ *n* : the skin of a goat or a leather made from it

¹gob \'gäb\ *n* **1** ♦ : a piece or mass of indefinite size and shape : LUMP, MASS **2** ♦ : a large amount — usu. used in pl. ⟨∼*s* of money⟩

♦ [1] blob, chunk, clod, clump, glob, hunk, lump, mass, nub, wad — more at LUMP ♦ *usu* **gobs** [2] abundance, deal, heap, loads, lot, pile, plenty, quantity, scads — more at LOT

²gob *n* ♦ : a member of a ship's crew : SAILOR

♦ jack, jack-tar, mariner, sailor, seaman, swab, tar — more at SAILOR

gob·bet \'gä-bət\ *n* : a piece or mass of indefinite size and shape : LUMP, MASS

¹gob·ble \'gä-bəl\ *vb* **gob·bled; gob·bling 1** ♦ : to swallow or eat greedily **2** : to take eagerly : GRAB

♦ bolt, devour, gorge, gormandize, gulp, scarf, scoff, wolf; *also* overeat, swill

²gobble *vb* **gob·bled; gob·bling** : to make the natural guttural noise of a male turkey

gob·ble·dy·gook *also* **gob·ble·de·gook** \'gä-bəl-dē-ˌgùk, -ˌgük\ *n* ♦ : generally unintelligible jargon

♦ babble, gabble, gibberish, hogwash, jabber, jabberwocky, nonsense — more at GIBBERISH

gob·bler \'gä-blər\ *n* : a male turkey

go—be·tween \'gō-bə-ˌtwēn\ *n* ♦ : an intermediate agent : BROKER

♦ arbiter, arbitrator, broker, intercessor, intermediary, mediator, middleman, peacemaker — more at MEDIATOR

gob·let \'gä-blət\ *n* : a drinking glass with a foot and stem

gob·lin \'gä-blən\ *n* : an ugly or grotesque sprite that is mischievous and sometimes evil and malicious

go·by \'gō-bē\ *n, pl* **gobies** *also* **goby** : any of numerous spiny-finned fishes usu. having the pelvic fins united to form a ventral sucking disk

god \'gäd, 'gȯd\ *n* **1** *cap* : the supreme reality; *esp* : the Being worshiped as the creator and ruler of the universe **2** : a being or object believed to have supernatural attributes and powers and to require worship **3** : a thing of supreme value **4** : an extraordinarily attractive person

god·child \'gäd-ˌchīld, 'gód-\ *n* : a person for whom another person stands as sponsor at baptism

god·daugh·ter \-ˌdȯ-tər\ *n* : a female godchild

god·dess \'gä-dəs, 'gó-\ *n* **1** : a female god **2** ♦ : a woman whose charm or beauty arouses adoration

♦ beauty, enchantress, fox, knockout, queen — more at BEAUTY

god·fa·ther \'gäd-ˌfä-thər, 'gód-\ *n* **1** : a man who sponsors a person at baptism **2** : the leader of an organized crime syndicate

god·head \-ˌhed\ *n* **1** ♦ : divine nature or essence **2** *cap* : GOD 1; *also* : the nature of God esp. as existing in three persons

♦ deity, divinity — more at DIVINITY

god·hood \-ˌhu̇d\ *n* : the quality or state of being a god : DIVINITY

god·less \-ləs\ *adj* : not acknowledging a deity or divine law — **god·less·ness** *n*

god·like \-ˌlīk\ *adj* ♦ : resembling or having the qualities of God or a god

♦ blessed, divine, heavenly, holy — more at HOLY

god·li·ness *n* ♦ : the quality or state of living a godly life

♦ blessedness, devoutness, holiness, piety, sainthood, sanctity — more at HOLINESS

god·ly \-lē\ *adj* **god·li·er; -est** **1** : DIVINE **2** ♦ : marked by or showing reverence for deity and devotion to divine worship : PIOUS, DEVOUT

♦ devout, faithful, holy, pious, religious, sainted, saintly — more at HOLY

god·moth·er \-ˌmə-thər\ *n* : a woman who sponsors a person at baptism

god·par·ent \-ˌpar-ənt\ *n* : a sponsor at baptism

god·send \-ˌsend\ *n* ♦ : a desirable or needed thing or event that comes unexpectedly

♦ benefit, blessing, boon, felicity, good, manna, windfall — more at BLESSING

god·son \-ˌsən\ *n* : a male godchild

God·speed \-'spēd\ *n* : a prosperous journey : SUCCESS ⟨bade him ~⟩

go·fer *or* **go·pher** \'gō-fər\ *n* [alter. of *go for*] : an employee whose duties include running errands

go-get·ter \'gō-ˌge-tər\ *n* ♦ : an aggressively enterprising person — *adj or n*

♦ hustler, live wire, powerhouse, self-starter; *also* dasher; doer; he-man

go-get·ting *adj* ♦ : marked by driving forceful energy, ambition, or initiative — **go-getting** *n*

♦ aggressive, ambitious, assertive, enterprising, fierce, high-pressure, militant, self-assertive — more at AGGRESSIVE

gog·gle \'gä-gəl\ *vb* **gog·gled; gog·gling** ♦ : to stare with wide or protuberant eyes

♦ gape, gawk, gaze, peer, rubberneck, stare — more at GAPE

gog·gles \'gä-gəlz\ *n pl* : protective glasses set in a flexible frame that fits snugly against the face

go-go \'gō-ˌgō\ *adj* **1** : related to, being, or employed to entertain in a disco ⟨~ dancers⟩ **2** : aggressively enterprising and energetic ⟨~ entrepreneurs⟩

go·ings-on \ˌgō-iŋ-'zón, -'zän\ *n pl* : ACTIONS, EVENTS

goi·ter *or Can and Brit* **goi·tre** \'gói-tər\ *n* : an abnormally enlarged thyroid gland visible as a swelling at the base of the neck — **goi·trous** \-trəs, -tə-rəs\ *adj*

go-kart \'gō-ˌkärt\ *n* : a small motorized vehicle used esp. for racing

gold \'gōld\ *n* **1** : a malleable yellow metallic chemical element used esp. for coins and jewelry **2** : gold coins; *also* : MONEY **3** : a yellow color

gold·brick \'gōld-ˌbrik\ *n* : a person who shirks assigned work — **goldbrick** *vb*

gold coast *n, often cap G&C* : an exclusive residential district

gold digger *n* : a person who uses charm to extract money or gifts from others

gold·en \'gōl-dən\ *adj* **1** : made of or relating to gold **2** ♦ : having the color of gold; *also* : BLOND **3** : SHINING, LUSTROUS **4** : SUPERB **5** ♦ : marked by success or economic well-being : PROSPEROUS **6** : radiantly youthful and vigorous **7** ♦ : tending to promote or facilitate : FAVORABLE, ADVANTAGEOUS ⟨a ~ opportunity⟩ **8** : rich and full but free from garishness or stridency : MELLOW, RESONANT

♦ [2] blond, fair, flaxen, sandy, straw — more at BLOND
♦ [5] booming, palmy, prosperous, roaring, successful — more at PROSPEROUS ♦ [7] advantageous, auspicious, bright, encouraging, favorable (*or* favourable), heartening, hopeful, promising, propitious — more at FAVORABLE

gold·en–ag·er \'gōl-dən-'ā-jər\ *n* ♦ : an elderly and often retired person usu. engaging in club activities

♦ ancient, elder, oldster, senior citizen — more at SENIOR CITIZEN

golden hamster *n* : a small tawny hamster often kept as a pet

golden handcuffs *n pl* : special benefits offered to an employee as an inducement to continue service

golden handshake *n* : a generous severance agreement given esp. as an inducement to early retirement

golden retriever *n* : any of a breed of retrievers with a flat golden coat

gold·en·rod \'gōl-dən-ˌräd\ *n* : any of numerous herbs related to the daisies that have tall slender stalks with many tiny usu. yellow flower heads

golden years *n pl* : the advanced years in a lifetime

gold·finch \-ˌfinch\ *n* **1** : a small largely red, black, and yellow Old World finch often kept in a cage **2** : any of three small related American finches of which the males usu. become bright yellow and black in summer

gold·fish \-ˌfish\ *n* : a small usu. golden-orange carp often kept as an aquarium or pond fish

gold·smith \-ˌsmith\ *n* : a person who makes or deals in articles of gold

golf \'gälf, 'gólf\ *n* : a game played with a small ball and various clubs on a course having 9 or 18 holes — **golf** *vb* — **golf·er** *n*

-gon \ˌgän\ *n comb form* : figure having (so many) angles ⟨hexagon⟩

go·nad \'gō-ˌnad\ *n* : a sperm- or egg-producing gland : OVARY, TESTIS — **go·nad·al** \gō-'na-dᵊl\ *adj*

go·nad·o·trop·ic \gō-ˌna-də-'trä-pik\ *also* **go·nad·o·tro·phic** \-'trō-fik, -'trä-\ *adj* : acting on or stimulating the gonads

go·nad·o·tro·pin \-'trō-pən\ *also* **go·nad·o·tro·phin** \-fən\ *n* : a gonadotropic hormone

gon·do·la \'gän-də-lə (*usual for 1*), gän-'dō-\ *n* [It. dial. (Venice). prob. fr. MGk *kontoura* small vessel] **1** : a long narrow boat used on the canals of Venice **2** : a railroad car used for hauling loose freight (as coal) **3** : an enclosure beneath an airship or balloon **4** : an enclosed car suspended from a cable and used esp. for transporting skiers

gon·do·lier \ˌgän-də-'lir\ *n* : a person who propels a gondola

¹gone \'gón\ *past part of* GO

²gone *adj* **1** ♦ : no longer alive : DEAD **2** : no longer possessed : LOST, RUINED **3** : SINKING, WEAK **4** : INVOLVED, ABSORBED **5** : INFATUATED **6** : PREGNANT **7** : having existed or taken place in a period before the present : PAST

♦ bygone, dead, deceased, defunct, extinct — more at EXTINCT

gon·er \'gó-nər\ *n* : one whose case is hopeless

gong \'gäŋ, 'gȯŋ\ *n* : a metallic disk that produces a resounding tone when struck

gono·coc·cus \ˌgä-nə-'kä-kəs\ *n, pl* **-coc·ci** \-'käk-ˌsī, -(ˌ)sē, -'kä-ˌkī, -(ˌ)kē\ : a pus-producing bacterium causing gonorrhea — **gono·coc·cal** \-'kä-kəl\ *adj*

gon·or·rhea \ˌgä-nə-'rē-ə\ *n* : a contagious sexually transmitted inflammation of the genital tract caused by the gonococcus — **gon·or·rhe·al** \-'rē-əl\ *adj*

goo \'gü\ *n* 1 : a viscid or sticky substance 2 : sentimental tripe

goo·ber \'gü-bər, 'gü-\ *n, Southern & Midland* : PEANUT

¹**good** \'gu̇d\ *adj* **bet·ter** \'be-tər\; **best** \'best\ 1 ♦ : of a favorable character or tendency 2 : BOUNTIFUL, FERTILE 3 : COMELY, ATTRACTIVE 4 ♦ : adapted to a use or purpose : SUITABLE, FIT 5 : SOUND, WHOLE 6 ♦ : having qualities that tend to give pleasure : AGREEABLE, PLEASANT 7 : SALUTARY, WHOLESOME 8 : of a noticeably large size or quantity : CONSIDERABLE 9 : FULL 10 ♦ : based on excellent reasoning, information, judgment, or grounds 11 : TRUE ⟨holds ∼ for everybody⟩ 12 : legally valid or effectual 13 : sufficient for a specific requirement 14 ♦ : conforming to a standard 15 : DISCRIMINATING 16 : worthy of being commended 17 : KIND 18 : UPPER-CLASS 19 ♦ : having or displaying competence or skill 20 : unswerving in allegiance : LOYAL, CLOSE ⟨a ∼ friend⟩ — **good·ish** *adj* — **good–look·ing** \-'lu̇-kiŋ\ *adj*

♦ [1] appreciative, complimentary, favorable (*or* favourable), friendly, positive — more at FAVORABLE ♦ [4] applicable, appropriate, apt, felicitous, fit, fitting, happy, meet, proper, right, suitable — more at FIT ♦ [6] agreeable, congenial, delightful, felicitous, grateful, gratifying, nice, palatable, pleasant, pleasurable, satisfying ♦ [10] hard, informed, just, logical, rational, reasonable, reasoned, sensible, solid, valid, well-founded; *also* actual, real, true; certain, sure; certified, validated, verified; confirmed, substantiated; cogent, convincing, credible *Ant* baseless, illogical, invalid, unfounded, uninformed, unreasonable, unsound ♦ [14] decent, ethical, honest, honorable (*or* honourable), just, moral, right, straight, virtuous; *also* correct, decorous, proper, seemly; high-minded, noble, principled; commendable, creditable, exemplary, legitimate; esteemed, reputable, respected, upstanding, worthy *Ant* bad, evil, unethical, wrong ♦ [19] accomplished, adept, capable, competent, proficient, skilled, skillful — more at PROFICIENT

²**good** *n* 1 ♦ : something good 2 : GOODNESS 3 ♦ : advancement of prosperity or well-being : BENEFIT, WELFARE ⟨for the ∼ of humankind⟩ 4 : something that has economic utility 5 *pl* : personal property 6 *pl* : CLOTH 7 *pl* : something manufactured or produced for sale : WARES, MERCHANDISE 8 : good persons ⟨the ∼ die young⟩ 9 *pl* : proof of wrongdoing — **for good** : FOREVER, PERMANENTLY — **to the good** : in a position of net gain or profit ⟨$10 *to the good*⟩

♦ [1] blessing, boon, felicity, godsend, manna, windfall — more at BLESSING ♦ [3] benefit, interest, weal, welfare, well-being — more at WELFARE

³**good** *adv* ♦ : in a good or proper manner : WELL

♦ OK, adequately, all right, fine, nicely, passably, satisfactorily, so-so, tolerably, well — more at WELL

good–bye *or* **good–by** \gu̇d-'bī, gə-\ *n* ♦ : a concluding remark at parting

♦ adieu, au revoir, bon voyage, farewell; *also* leave-taking, send-off *Ant* hello

good cholesterol *n* : HDL

good–for–noth·ing \'gu̇d-fər-ˌnə-thiŋ\ *adj* : of no use or value — **good–for–nothing** *n*

Good Friday *n* : the Friday before Easter observed as the anniversary of the crucifixion of Christ

good–heart·ed \-'här-təd\ *adj* ♦ : having a kindly generous disposition

♦ beneficent, benevolent, compassionate, humane, kind, kindly, sympathetic, tender, tenderhearted, warmhearted — more at HUMANE

good·ly \'gu̇d-lē\ *adj* **good·li·er; -est** 1 : of pleasing appearance 2 ♦ : significantly large : CONSIDERABLE

♦ considerable, good, healthy, respectable, significant, sizable, substantial, tidy — more at CONSIDERABLE

good·man \'gu̇d-mən\ *n, archaic* : MR.

good–na·tured \'gu̇d-'nā-chərd\ *adj* ♦ : of a cheerful disposition — **good–na·tured·ly** \-chərd-lē\ *adv*

♦ affable, agreeable, amiable, genial, gracious, nice, sweet, well-disposed — more at AMIABLE

good·ness \-nəs\ *n* ♦ : the quality or state of being good : VIRTUE

♦ character, decency, honesty, honor (*or* honour), integrity, morality, probity, rectitude, righteousness, uprightness, virtue — more at MORALITY

good–tem·pered \-'tem-pərd\ *adj* : not easily angered or upset

good·wife \-ˌwīf\ *n, archaic* : MRS.

good·will \-'wil\ *n* 1 ♦ : kindly feeling of approval and support : BENEVOLENCE 2 : the value of the trade a business has built up over time 3 : cheerful consent 4 ♦ : willing effort

♦ [1] amity, benevolence, cordiality, fellowship, friendliness, friendship, kindliness; *also* camaraderie, community, companionship, comradeship; civility, comity, concord, harmony, rapport; charity, generosity, neighborliness; affinity, communion, empathy, sympathy, tolerance; altruism, philanthropy, selflessness *Ant* ill will, malevolence ♦ [4] alacrity, gameness, willingness — more at ALACRITY

goody *or* **good·ie** \'gu̇-dē\ *n, pl* **good·ies** ♦ : something that is good esp. to eat

♦ dainty, delicacy, tidbit, treat — more at DELICACY

goody–goody \ˌgu̇-dē-'gu̇-dē\ *adj* : affectedly good — **goody–goody** *n*

goo·ey \'gü-ē\ *adj* ♦ : having a sticky or thick quality

♦ adhesive, gelatinous, gluey, glutinous, gummy, sticky, viscid, viscous — more at STICKY

¹**goof** \'güf\ *vb* 1 ♦ : to spend time idly or foolishly — usu. used with *off* 2 : BLUNDER — usu. used with *up*

♦ *usu* goof off dally, dawdle, dillydally, hang around, hang out, idle, loaf, loll, lounge — more at IDLE

²**goof** *n* 1 : a silly or stupid person 2 ♦ : a gross error or mistake resulting usu. from stupidity, ignorance, or carelessness

♦ blunder, error, fault, flub, fumble, lapse, miscue, misstep, mistake, oversight, slip, stumble — more at ERROR

goof·ball \'güf-ˌbȯl\ *n* 1 *slang* : a barbiturate sleeping pill 2 : a goofy person

go off *vb* 1 : to burst forth with sudden violence or noise from internal energy : EXPLODE 2 : to follow a course ⟨the party *went off* well⟩

♦ blow up, burst, detonate, explode, pop — more at EXPLODE

goof–off \'güf-ˌȯf\ *n* : one who evades work or responsibility

goofy \'gü-fē\ *adj* **goof·i·er; -est** ♦ : being crazy, ridiculous, or mildly ludicrous : SILLY — **goof·i·ness** \-fē-nəs\ *n*

♦ flighty, frivolous, giddy, harebrained, light-headed, scatterbrained, silly — more at GIDDY

goo·gle \'gü-gəl\ *vb* **goo·gled; goo·gling** : to use the Google search engine to obtain information on the World Wide Web

goon \'gün\ *n* 1 ♦ : a man hired to terrorize or kill opponents 2 ♦ : a stupid person

♦ [1] bully, gangster, hood, hoodlum, mobster, mug, punk, rowdy, ruffian, thug, tough — more at HOODLUM ♦ [2] blockhead, dope, dummy, idiot, imbecile, jackass, moron, numskull — more at IDIOT

go on *vb* **1** : to continue in a course of action **2** ♦ : to take place : HAPPEN

♦ be, befall, betide, chance, come, happen, occur, pass, transpire — more at HAPPEN

goose \'güs\ *n, pl* **geese** \'gēs\ **1** : any of numerous long=necked web-footed birds related to the swans and ducks; *also* : a female goose as distinguished from a gander **2** ♦ : a foolish person **3** *pl* **goos·es** : a tailor's smoothing iron

♦ booby, fool, half-wit, jackass, lunatic, nitwit, nut, simpleton, turkey — more at FOOL

goose·ber·ry \'güs-₁ber-ē, 'güz-, -bə-rē\ *n* : the acid berry of any of several shrubs related to the currant and used esp. in jams and pies

goose bumps *n pl* : roughening of the skin caused usu. by cold, fear, or a sudden feeling of excitement

goose·flesh \-₁flesh\ *n* : GOOSE BUMPS

goose pimples *n pl* : GOOSE BUMPS

go out *vb* **1** : to become extinguished **2** : to become a candidate ⟨*went out* for the football team⟩

go over *vb* ♦ : to win approval : SUCCEED

♦ click, deliver, pan out, succeed, work out — more at SUCCEED

GOP *abbr* Grand Old Party (Republican)

¹go·pher \'gō-fər\ *n* **1** : a burrowing American land tortoise **2** : any of a family of No. American burrowing rodents with large cheek pouches opening beside the mouth **3** : any of several small ground squirrels of the prairie region of No. America

²gopher *var of* GOFER

¹gore \'gór\ *n* **1** : BLOOD **2** : vivid gruesomeness

²gore *n* : a tapering or triangular piece (as of cloth in a skirt)

³gore *vb* **gored; gor·ing** ♦ : to pierce or wound with something pointed

♦ harpoon, impale, lance, pierce, puncture, skewer, spear, spike, stab, stick, transfix — more at IMPALE

¹gorge \'górj\ *n* **1** : THROAT **2** ♦ : a narrow ravine **3** : a mass of matter that chokes up a passage

♦ canyon, defile, flume, gap, gulch, notch, pass, ravine — more at CANYON

²gorge *vb* **gorged; gorg·ing** ♦ : to eat greedily, hurriedly, or to capacity

♦ glut, sate, stuff, surfeit ♦ bolt, devour, gobble, gormandize, gulp, scarf, scoff, wolf — more at GOBBLE

gor·geous \'gór-jəs\ *adj* ♦ : resplendently beautiful

♦ attractive, beautiful, cute, fair, handsome, knockout, lovely, pretty, ravishing, stunning — more at BEAUTIFUL

Gor·gon·zo·la \₁gór-gən-'zō-lə\ *n* : a blue cheese of Italian origin

go·ril·la \gə-'ri-lə\ *n* [NL, fr. Gk *Gorillai*, a tribe of hairy women in an account of a voyage around Africa] : an African anthropoid ape related to but much larger than the chimpanzee

gor·man·dise *chiefly Brit var of* GORMANDIZE

gor·man·dize \'gór-mən-₁dīz\ *vb* **-dized; -diz·ing** ♦ : to eat ravenously

♦ bolt, devour, gobble, gorge, gulp, scarf, scoff, wolf — more at GOBBLE

gor·man·diz·er \₁dī-zə(r)\ *n* : one who eats gluttonously or ravenously

gorp \'górp\ *n* : a snack consisting of high-calorie food (as raisins and nuts)

gorse \'górs\ *n* : a spiny yellow-flowered European evergreen shrub of the legume family

gory \'gór-ē\ *adj* **gor·i·er; -est** **1** : BLOODSTAINED **2** : HORRIBLE, SENSATIONAL ⟨∼ details⟩

gos·hawk \'gäs-₁hók\ *n* : any of several long-tailed hawks with short rounded wings

gos·ling \'gäz-liŋ, 'góz-\ *n* : a young goose

¹gos·pel \'gäs-pəl\ *n* [ME, fr. OE *gōdspel*, fr. *gōd* good + *spell* message, news] **1** : the teachings of Christ and the

apostles **2** *cap* : any of the first four books of the New Testament **3** ♦ : something accepted as infallible truth

♦ creed, doctrine, ideology, philosophy — more at CREED

²gospel *adj* **1** : of, relating to, or emphasizing the gospel **2** : relating to or being American religious songs associated with evangelism

gos·sa·mer \'gä-sə-mər\ *n* [ME *gossomer*, fr. *gos* goose + *somer* summer] **1** : a film of cobwebs floating in the air **2** : something light, delicate, or tenuous

¹gos·sip \'gä-səp\ *n* **1** : a person who habitually reveals personal or sensational facts **2** : rumor or report of an intimate nature **3** ♦ : an informal conversation

♦ chat, chatter, chitchat, gabfest, palaver, rap, talk — more at CHAT

²gossip *vb* ♦ : to spread gossip

♦ blab, talk, tattle; *also* bandy (about), circulate, noise (about), rumor; disclose, divulge, reveal, tell; hint, imply, insinuate, intimate, let on, suggest; inform, report, snitch, squeal, tip (off); babble, spill; confide

gos·sipy \'gä-sə-pē\ *adj* : characterized by, full of, or given to gossip

got *past and past part of* GET

Goth \'gäth\ *n* : a member of a Germanic people that early in the Christian era overran the Roman Empire

¹Goth·ic \'gä-thik\ *adj* **1** : of or relating to the Goths **2** : of or relating to a style of architecture prevalent in western Europe from the middle 12th to the early 16th century

²Gothic *n* **1** : the Germanic language of the Goths **2** : the Gothic architectural style or decoration

gotten *past part of* GET

Gou·da \'gü-də\ *n* : a mild Dutch milk cheese shaped in balls

¹gouge \'gaúj\ *n* **1** : a rounded troughlike chisel **2** : a hole or groove made with or as if with a gouge

²gouge *vb* **gouged; goug·ing** **1** : to cut holes or grooves in with or as if with a gouge **2** ♦ : to charge too much or too fully

♦ overcharge, soak, sting — more at OVERCHARGE

gou·lash \'gü-₁läsh, -₁lash\ *n* [Hungarian *gulyás*] : a stew made with meat, assorted vegetables, and paprika

go under *vb* : to be overwhelmed, defeated, or destroyed : FAIL

gourd \'górd, 'gúrd\ *n* **1** : any of a family of tendril-bearing vines including the cucumber, squash, and melon **2** : the fruit of a gourd; *esp* : any of various inedible hard=shelled fruits used esp. for ornament or implements

gour·mand \'gúr-₁mänd\ *n* **1** : one who is excessively fond of eating and drinking **2** ♦ : a connoisseur of food and drink : GOURMET

♦ epicure, epicurean, gourmet

gour·met \'gúr-₁mā, gúr-'mā\ *n* [F, fr. MF, alter. of *gromet* boy servant, vintner's assistant] ♦ : a connoisseur of food and drink

♦ epicure, epicurean, gourmand

gout \'gaút\ *n* : a metabolic disease marked by painful inflammation and swelling of the joints — **gouty** *adj*

gov *abbr* **1** government **2** governor

gov·ern \'gə-vərn\ *vb* [ME, fr. AF *governer*, fr. L *gubernare* to steer, govern, fr. Gk *kybernan*] **1** ♦ : to control and direct the making and administration of policy in : RULE **2** ♦ : to prevail or have decisive influence over : CONTROL, DIRECT **3** : DETERMINE, REGULATE **4** ♦ : to hold in check : RESTRAIN

♦ [1] boss, captain, command, control, preside, rule; *also* conduct, direct, head, lead; administer, manage, oversee, regulate, superintend, supervise; dictate, dominate, domineer, lord (it over), master, oppress, reign (over), tyrannize; conquer, subdue, subjugate ♦ [2] administer, carry on, conduct, control, direct, guide, handle, manage, operate, oversee, regulate, run, superintend, supervise — more at CONDUCT ♦ [4] bridle, check, constrain, contain, control, curb, inhibit, regulate, rein, restrain, tame — more at CONTROL

gov·er·nance \-vər-nəns\ *n* : the act or process of governing; *specif* : authoritative direction or control

gov·ern·ess \'gə-vər-nəs\ *n* : a woman who teaches and trains a child esp. in a private home

gov·ern·ment \'gə-vərn-mənt\ *n* **1** ♦ : authoritative direction or control : RULE **2** ♦ : the making of policy **3** : the organization or agency through which a political unit exercises authority **4** : the complex of institutions, laws, and customs through which a political unit is governed **5** : the governing body — **gov·ern·men·tal** \ˌgə-vərn-'ment-°l\ *adj*

  ♦ [1] administration, authority, jurisdiction, regime, rule — more at RULE ♦ [2] conduct, control, direction, guidance, management, operation, oversight, regulation, running, superintendence, supervision — more at CONDUCT

gov·er·nor \'gə-vər-nər\ *n* **1** : one that governs; *esp* : a ruler, chief executive, or head of a political unit (as a state) **2** : an attachment to a machine for automatic control of speed — **gov·er·nor·ship** *n*

govt *abbr* government

¹**gown** \'gaün\ *n* **1** : a loose flowing outer garment **2** : an official robe worn esp. by a judge, clergyman, or teacher **3** : a woman's dress ⟨evening ~s⟩ **4** : a loose robe **5** : an academic community within a town or city

²**gown** *vb* : to dress in or invest with a gown

gp *abbr* group

GP *abbr* general practitioner

GPO *abbr* **1** general post office **2** Government Printing Office

GPS \ˌjē-ˌpē-'es\ *n* [*Global Positioning System*] : a navigation system that uses satellite signals to fix location; *also* : the signal receiver itself

GQ *abbr* general quarters

gr *abbr* **1** grade **2** grain **3** gram **4** gravity **5** gross

¹**grab** \'grab\ *vb* **grabbed; grab·bing** ♦ : to take hastily : SNATCH

  ♦ bag, capture, catch, collar, corral, get, grapple, hook, land, nab, seize, snare, trap — more at CATCH

²**grab** *n* **1** : something grabbed; *also* : an act or instance of grabbing **2** ♦ : an unlawful or unscrupulous seizure

  ♦ rip-off, theft — more at THEFT

¹**grace** \'grās\ *n* **1** : unmerited help given to people by God (as in overcoming temptation) **2** : freedom from sin through divine grace **3** : a virtue coming from God **4** — used as a title for a duke, a duchess, or an archbishop **5** : a short prayer at a meal **6** : a temporary respite (as from the payment of a debt) **7** : APPROVAL, ACCEPTANCE ⟨in his good ~s⟩ **8** : CHARM **9** : ATTRACTIVENESS, BEAUTY **10** ♦ : fitness or proportion of line or expression **11** : ease of movement **12** : a musical trill or ornament **13** ♦ : disposition to or an act or instance of kindness, courtesy, or clemency — **grace·ful·ly** *adv* — **grace·ful·ness** *n*

  ♦ [10] class, elegance, handsomeness, majesty, refinement, stateliness — more at ELEGANCE ♦ [13] boon, courtesy, favor (*or* favour), indulgence, kindness, mercy, service, turn

²**grace** *vb* **graced; grac·ing 1** : HONOR **2** ♦ : to endow with grace : ADORN, EMBELLISH

  ♦ adorn, array, beautify, bedeck, deck, decorate, do, dress, embellish, enrich, garnish, ornament, trim — more at DECORATE

grace·ful \-fəl\ *adj* ♦ : displaying grace in form or action : pleasing or attractive in line, proportion, or movement

  ♦ elegant, handsome, majestic, refined, stately, tasteful — more at ELEGANT ♦ agile, light, lissome, lithe, nimble, spry; *also* flexible, limber, pliable, pliant, supple; adroit, deft, dexterous **Ant** awkward, clumsy, gawky, graceless, lumbering, ungainly, ungraceful

grace·ful·ness *n* : the quality or state of being graceful

grace·less *adj* **1** ♦ : artistically inept or unbeautiful **2** ♦ : lacking a sense of propriety

  ♦ [1] awkward, clumsy, gawky, heavy-handed, lubberly, lumpish, ungainly, unhandy — more at CLUMSY ♦ [1] gauche, inelegant, stiff, stilted, uncomfortable, uneasy, ungraceful, wooden — more at AWKWARD ♦ [2] improper, inappropriate, inapt, infelicitous, unbecoming, unfit, unseemly, unsuitable, wrong — more at INAPPROPRIATE

gra·cious \'grā-shəs\ *adj* **1** ♦ : marked by kindness and courtesy **2** : GRACEFUL **3** : characterized by charm and good taste **4** : MERCIFUL — **gra·cious·ly** *adv*

  ♦ affable, agreeable, amiable, congenial, convivial, cordial, friendly, genial, hospitable, kind, kindly, sociable **Ant** inhospitable, ungracious, unsociable ♦ civil, courteous, genteel, mannerly, polite, well-bred — more at POLITE

gra·cious·ness *n* ♦ : the quality or state of being gracious

  ♦ civility, courtesy, gentility, mannerliness, politeness — more at POLITENESS ♦ agreeableness, amenity, amiability, geniality, niceness, pleasantness, sweetness — more at AMIABILITY

grack·le \'gra-kəl\ *n* : any of several large American blackbirds with glossy iridescent plumage

grad *abbr* graduate; graduated

gra·da·tion \grā-'dā-shən, grə-\ *n* **1** : a series forming successive stages **2** : a step, degree, or stage in a series **3** : an advance by regular degrees **4** : the act or process of grading

¹**grade** \'grād\ *vb* **grad·ed; grad·ing 1** ♦ : to arrange in grades : SORT; *also* : to arrange in a scale or series **2** : to make level or evenly sloping ⟨~ a highway⟩ **3** : to give a grade to ⟨~ a pupil in history⟩ **4** : to assign to a grade

  ♦ assort, break down, categorize, class, classify, group, peg, place, range, rank, rate, separate, sort — more at CLASSIFY

²**grade** *n* [L *gradus* step, degree, fr. *gradi* to step, go] **1** ♦ : a degree or stage in a series, order, or ranking **2** ♦ : a position in a scale of rank, quality, or order **3** ♦ : a class of persons or things of the same rank or quality **4** : a division of the school course representing one year's work; *also* : the pupils in such a division **5** *pl* : the elementary school system **6** : a mark or rating esp. of accomplishment in school **7** ♦ : the degree of slope (as of a road); *also* : SLOPE **8** ♦ : a reference level or starting point used for measuring or calculating

  ♦ [1] cut, degree, inch, notch, peg, phase, point, stage, step — more at DEGREE ♦ [2] caliber (*or* calibre), class, quality, rate — more at QUALITY ♦ [3] bracket, category, class, division, family, group, kind, order, set, species, type — more at CLASS ♦ [7] cant, diagonal, inclination, incline, lean, pitch, slant, slope, tilt, upgrade — more at SLANT ♦ [8] criterion, mark, measure, par, standard, touchstone, yardstick — more at STANDARD

grad·er \'grā-dər\ *n* : a machine for leveling earth

grade school *n* : ELEMENTARY SCHOOL

gra·di·ent \'grā-dē-ənt\ *n* : the rate of regular or graded ascent or descent : SLOPE, GRADE

grad·u·al \'gra-jə-wəl\ *adj* ♦ : proceeding or changing by steps or degrees ⟨~ improvements⟩ — **grad·u·al·ly** *adv*

  ♦ imperceptible, progressive **Ant** sudden

grad·u·al·ism \-wə-ˌli-zəm\ *n* : the policy of approaching a desired end gradually

¹**grad·u·ate** \'gra-jə-wət\ *n* **1** : a holder of an academic degree or diploma **2** : a graduated container for measuring contents

²**graduate** *adj* **1** : holding an academic degree or diploma **2** : of or relating to studies beyond the first or bachelor's degree ⟨~ school⟩

³**grad·u·ate** \'gra-jə-ˌwāt\ *vb* **-at·ed; -at·ing 1** : to grant or receive an academic degree or diploma **2** : to divide into grades, classes, or intervals **3** : to admit to a particular standing or grade

grad·u·a·tion \ˌgra-jə-'wā-shən\ *n* **1** : a mark that graduates something **2** ♦ : arrangement in degrees or ranks **3** : COMMENCEMENT 2

♦ ladder, scale — more at SCALE

graf·fi·ti \grə-'fē-(ˌ)tē\ *n* : unauthorized writing or drawing on a public surface

graf·fi·to \gra-'fē-tō, grə-\ *n, pl* **-ti** \-(ˌ)tē\ : an inscription or drawing made on a public surface (as a wall)

¹**graft** \'graft\ *n* **1** : a grafted plant; *also* : the point of union in this **2** : material (as skin) used in grafting **3** : the getting of money or advantage dishonestly; *also* : the money or advantage so gained

²**graft** *vb* **1** : to insert a shoot from one plant into another so that they join and grow; *also* : to join one thing to another as in plant grafting ⟨∼ skin over a burn⟩ **2** : to get (as money) dishonestly — **graft·er** *n*

gra·ham cracker \'grā-əm-, 'gram-\ *n* : a slightly sweet cracker made chiefly of whole wheat flour

Grail \'grāl\ *n* : the cup or platter used according to medieval legend by Christ at the Last Supper and thereafter the object of knightly quests

grain \'grān\ *n* **1** : a seed or fruit of a cereal grass **2** : seeds or fruits of various food plants and esp. cereal grasses; *also* : a plant (as wheat) producing grain **3** ♦ : a small hard particle **4** : a unit of weight based on the weight of a grain of wheat **5** : TEXTURE; *also* : the arrangement of fibers in wood **6** ♦ : natural disposition — **grained** \'grānd\ *adj*

♦ [3] bit, granule, molecule, particle ♦ [6] disposition, nature, temper, temperament — more at DISPOSITION

grain alcohol *n* : ALCOHOL 1

grainy \'grā-nē\ *adj* **grain·i·er; -est 1** ♦ : resembling or having some characteristic of grain : not smooth or fine **2** : appearing to be composed of grain-like particles ⟨a ∼ photograph⟩

♦ coarse, granular — more at COARSE

¹**gram** \'gram\ *n* [F *gramme*, fr. LL *gramma*, a small weight, fr. Gk *gramma* letter, writing, a small weight, fr. *graphein* to write] : a metric unit of mass and weight equal to ¹⁄₁₀₀₀ kilogram

²**gram** *abbr* grammar; grammatical

-gram \ˌgram\ *n comb form* : drawing : writing : record ⟨tele*gram*⟩

gram·mar \'gra-mər\ *n* **1** : the study of the classes of words, their inflections, and their functions and relations in the sentence **2** : a study of what is to be preferred and what avoided in inflection and syntax **3** : speech or writing evaluated according to its conformity to grammatical rules — **gram·mar·i·an** \grə-'mer-ē-ən, -'mar-\ *n* — **gram·mat·i·cal** \-'ma-ti-kəl\ *adj* — **gram·mat·i·cal·ly** \-k(ə-)lē\ *adv*

grammar school *n* **1** : a secondary school emphasizing Latin and Greek in preparation for college; *also* : a British college preparatory school **2** : a school intermediate between the primary grades and high school **3** : ELEMENTARY SCHOOL

gramme \'gram\ *chiefly Brit var of* GRAM

gram·o·phone \'gra-mə-ˌfōn\ *n* : PHONOGRAPH

gra·na·ry \'grā-nə-rē, 'gra-\ *n, pl* **-ries 1** : a storehouse for grain **2** : a region producing grain in abundance

¹**grand** \'grand\ *adj* **1** ♦ : higher in rank or importance : FOREMOST, CHIEF **2** ♦ : large and striking in size, scope, extent, or conception **3** ♦ : covering or intended to cover all items, costs, or services : COMPLETE ⟨a ∼ total⟩ **4** : MAGNIFICENT, SPLENDID **5** ♦ : showing wealth or high social standing **6** : fine or imposing in appearance or impression : IMPRESSIVE, STATELY **7** : very good : FINE

♦ [1] chief, dominant, first, foremost, key, main, paramount, predominant, preeminent, premier, primary, principal — more at FOREMOST ♦ [2] august, baronial, gallant, glorious, grandiose, heroic, imposing, magnificent, majestic, monumental, noble, proud, regal, royal, splendid, stately; *also* colossal, monstrous, prodigious, stupendous, tremendous; impressive, prepossessing, redoubtable; marvelous, superb, terrific, wonderful; extravagant, lavish, luxurious, opulent, sumptuous *Ant* humble, unheroic, unimposing, unimpressive ♦ [2] big,

considerable, goodly, great, large, outsize, oversize, sizable, substantial ♦ [3] complete, comprehensive, entire, full, intact, integral, perfect, plenary, total, whole — more at COMPLETE ♦ [5] aristocratic, genteel, gentle, highborn, noble, patrician, wellborn — more at NOBLE

²**grand** *n, pl* **grand** *slang* : a thousand dollars

gran·dam \'gran-ˌdam, -dəm\ *or* **gran·dame** \-ˌdām, -dəm\ *n* : an old woman

grand·child \'grand-ˌchī(-ə)ld\ *n* : a child of one's son or daughter

grand·daugh·ter \'gran-ˌdȯ-tər\ *n* : a daughter of one's son or daughter

grande dame \grän-'däm\ *n, pl* **grandes dames** : a usu. elderly woman of great prestige or ability

gran·dee \gran-'dē\ *n* ♦ : a high-ranking Spanish or Portuguese nobleman

♦ aristocrat, gentleman, noble, patrician — more at GENTLEMAN

gran·deur \'gran-jər\ *n* **1** ♦ : the quality or state of being grand : MAGNIFICENCE **2** : something that is grand

♦ augustness, brilliance, glory, grandness, magnificence, majesty, nobility, nobleness, resplendence, splendor, stateliness — more at MAGNIFICENCE

grand·fa·ther \'grand-ˌfä-thər\ *n* ♦ : the father of one's father or mother; *also* : ANCESTOR

♦ ancestor, father, forebear, forefather — more at ANCESTOR

grandfather clock *n* : a tall clock that stands on the floor

gran·dil·o·quence \gran-'di-lə-kwəns\ *n* ♦ : pompous eloquence

♦ bombast, gas, hot air, rhetoric, wind — more at RHETORIC

gran·dil·o·quent \-kwənt\ *adj* ♦ : marked by a lofty, extravagantly colorful, pompous, or bombastic style, manner, or quality esp. in language

♦ florid, flowery, highfalutin, high-flown — more at FLOWERY ♦ bombastic, gaseous, oratorical, rhetorical, windy — more at RHETORICAL

gran·di·ose \'gran-dē-ˌōs, ˌgran-dē-'ōs\ *adj* ♦ : impressive because of uncommon largeness, scope, effect, or grandeur : IMPOSING; *also* : affectedly splendid — **gran·di·ose·ly** *adv*

♦ august, baronial, gallant, glorious, grand, heroic, imposing, magnificent, majestic, monumental, noble, proud, regal, splendid, stately — more at GRAND ♦ affected, highfalutin, ostentatious, pompous, pretentious — more at PRETENTIOUS

gran·di·os·i·ty \ˌgran-dē-'ä-sə-tē\ *n* : the quality or state of being grandiose

grand jury *n* : a jury that examines accusations of crime against persons and makes formal charges on which the persons are later tried

grand·ly \-ndlē, -lī\ *adv* ♦ : in a grand manner

♦ expensively, extravagantly, high, lavishly, luxuriously, opulently, richly — more at HIGH ♦ gallantly, greatly, heroically, honorably (*or* honourably), magnanimously, nobly — more at GREATLY

grand mal \'grän-ˌmäl; 'grand-ˌmal\ *n* [F, lit., great illness] : severe epilepsy

grand·moth·er \'grand-ˌmə-thər\ *n* : the mother of one's father or mother; *also* : a female ancestor

grand·ness \'gran(d)nəs\ *n* ♦ : the quality or state of being grand

♦ augustness, brilliance, glory, grandeur, magnificence, majesty, nobility, nobleness, resplendence, splendor, stateliness — more at MAGNIFICENCE ♦ bigness, greatness, largeness — more at LARGENESS

grand·par·ent \-ˌpar-ənt\ *n* : a parent of one's father or mother

grand piano *n* : a piano with horizontal frame and strings

grand prix \'grän-'prē\ *n, pl* **grand prix** *same or* -'prēz\ *often cap* G&P : a long-distance auto race over a road course

grand slam n 1 : a total victory or success 2 : a home run hit with three runners on base

grand·son \'grand-ˌsən\ n : a son of one's son or daughter

grand·stand \-ˌstand\ n : a usu. roofed stand for spectators at a racecourse or stadium

grange \'grānj\ n 1 : a farm or farmhouse with its various buildings 2 cap : one of the lodges of a national association originally made up of farmers; also : the association itself — **grang·er** \'grān-jər\ n

gran·ite \'gra-nət\ n 1 : a hard granular igneous rock used esp. for building 2 ♦ : unyielding firmness or endurance — **gra·nit·ic** \gra-'ni-tik\ adj

♦ decision, decisiveness, determination, firmness, resolution, resolve — more at DETERMINATION

gran·ite·ware \'gra-nət-ˌwar\ n : ironware with mottled enamel

gra·no·la \grə-'nō-lə\ n : a cereal made of rolled oats and usu. raisins and nuts

¹**grant** \'grant\ vb 1 : to consent to : ALLOW, PERMIT 2 ♦ : to bestow or transfer formally : GIVE 3 ♦ : to admit as true — **grant·er** n — **grant·or** \'gran-tər, -ˌtòr\ n

♦ [2] accord, award, confer, give — more at CONFER
♦ [3] acknowledge, admit, agree, allow, concede, confess, own — more at ADMIT

²**grant** n 1 : the act of granting 2 ♦ : something granted; esp : a gift for a particular purpose ⟨a ∼ for study abroad⟩ 3 : a transfer of property by deed or writing; also : the instrument by which such a transfer is made 4 : the property transferred by grant — **grant·ee** \gran-'tē\ n

♦ allocation, allotment, appropriation, subsidy — more at APPROPRIATION

gran·u·lar \'gra-nyə-lər\ adj ♦ : consisting of or appearing to consist of granules — **gran·u·lar·i·ty** \ˌgra-nyə-'lar-ə-tē\ n

♦ coarse, grainy — more at COARSE

gran·u·late \'gra-nyə-ˌlāt\ vb **-lat·ed; -lat·ing** : to form into grains or crystals — **gran·u·la·tion** \ˌgra-nyə-'lā-shən\ n

gran·ule \'gra-nyül\ n ♦ : a small grain or particle

♦ bit, grain, molecule, particle

grape \'grāp\ n [ME, fr. AF, grape stalk, bunch of grapes, grape, of Gmc origin] 1 : a smooth-skinned juicy edible greenish white, deep red, or purple berry that is the chief source of wine 2 : any of numerous woody vines widely grown for their bunches of grapes

grape·fruit \'grāp-ˌfrüt\ n 1 pl **grapefruit** or **grapefruits** : a large edible yellow-skinned citrus fruit 2 : a tree bearing grapefruit

grape hyacinth n : any of several small bulbous spring-flowering herbs with clusters of usu. blue flowers that are related to the lilies

grape·shot \'grāp-ˌshät\ n : a cluster of small iron balls formerly fired at people from short range by a cannon

grape·vine \-ˌvīn\ n 1 : GRAPE 2 2 : RUMOR; also : an informal means of circulating information or gossip

graph \'graf\ n : a diagram that usu. by means of dots and lines shows change in one variable factor in comparison with one or more other factors — **graph** vb

-graph \ˌgraf\ n comb form 1 : something written ⟨autograph⟩ 2 : instrument for making or transmitting records ⟨seismograph⟩

¹**graph·ic** \'gra-fik\ also **graph·i·cal** \-fi-kəl\ adj 1 : of or relating to the arts (**graphic arts**) of representation, decoration, and printing on flat surfaces 2 : being written, drawn, or engraved 3 : vividly described ⟨∼ details⟩ — **graph·i·cal·ly** \-fi-k(ə-)lē\ adv

²**graphic** n 1 ♦ : a picture, map, or graph used for illustration 2 pl : a pictorial image displayed on a computer screen

♦ diagram, figure, illustration, plate — more at ILLUSTRATION

graphical user interface n : a computer program designed to allow easy user interaction esp. by having graphic menus or icons

graphic design n : the art or practice of using design elements (as typography and images) to convey information or create an effect; also : a product of this art — **graphic designer** n

graph·ics tablet \-fiks-\ n : a computer input device for entering pictorial information by drawing or tracing

graph·ite \'gra-ˌfīt\ n [G Graphit, fr. Gk graphein to write] : a soft black form of carbon used esp. for lead pencils and lubricants

grap·nel \'grap-nəl\ n : a small anchor with usu. four claws used esp. in dragging or grappling operations

¹**grap·ple** \'gra-pəl\ n [MF grappelle, dim. of grape hook] ♦ : the act of grappling

♦ clasp, grasp, grip, hold — more at HOLD

²**grapple** vb **grap·pled; grap·pling** 1 ♦ : to seize or hold with or as if with a hooked implement 2 ♦ : to engage in a hand-to-hand struggle : WRESTLE 3 ♦ : to attempt to deal with something — used with with

♦ [1] bag, capture, catch, collar, corral, get, grab, hook, land, nab, seize, snare, trap — more at CATCH
♦ [2] scuffle, tussle, wrestle — more at WRESTLE ♦ usu **grapple with** [3] contend with, cope with, handle, manage, maneuver (or manoeuvre), negotiate, swing, treat — more at HANDLE

¹**grasp** \'grasp\ vb 1 : to make the motion of seizing 2 : to take or seize firmly 3 ♦ : to enclose and hold with the fingers or arms 4 ♦ : to lay hold of with the mind : COMPREHEND

♦ [3] clasp, grip, hold, take — more at TAKE ♦ [4] appreciate, apprehend, catch, catch on (to), comprehend, get, make, make out, perceive, see, seize, understand — more at COMPREHEND

²**grasp** n 1 : HANDLE 2 : EMBRACE 3 : HOLD, CONTROL 4 : the reach of the arms 5 a ♦ : the act or manner of holding b : the power of seizing and holding 6 ♦ : mental hold or comprehension esp. when broad

♦ [5a] clasp, grapple, grip, hold — more at HOLD
♦ [6] appreciation, apprehension, comprehension, grip, perception, understanding — more at COMPREHENSION

grasp·ing adj ♦ : desiring material possessions urgently and excessively and often to the point of ruthlessness : GREEDY, AVARICIOUS

♦ acquisitive, avaricious, avid, covetous, greedy, mercenary, rapacious — more at GREEDY

grass \'gras\ n 1 : herbage for grazing animals 2 : any of a large family of plants (as wheat, bamboo, or sugarcane) with jointed stems and narrow leaves 3 : grass-covered land 4 : MARIJUANA — **grassy** adj

grass·hop·per \-ˌhä-pər\ n : any of numerous leaping plant-eating insects

grass·land \-ˌland\ n ♦ : land covered naturally or under cultivation with grasses and low-growing herbs

♦ down, plain, prairie, savanna, steppe, veld — more at PLAIN

grass roots n pl : society at the local level as distinguished from the centers of political leadership

¹**grate** \'grāt\ vb **grat·ed; grat·ing** 1 : to pulverize by rubbing against something rough 2 ♦ : to grind or rub against with a rasping noise 3 ♦ : to provoke impatience, anger, or displeasure in : IRRITATE — **grat·er** n — **grat·ing·ly** adv

♦ [2] grind, rasp, scrape, scratch — more at SCRAPE
♦ [3] aggravate, annoy, bother, exasperate, irk, irritate, nettle, peeve, put out, vex — more at IRRITATE

²**grate** n 1 : GRATING 2 : a frame of iron bars for holding fuel while it burns

grate·ful \'grāt-fəl\ adj 1 ♦ : appreciative of benefits received : THANKFUL; also : expressing gratitude 2 : giving pleasure or contentment : PLEASING — **grate·ful·ly** adv

♦ appreciative, obliged, thankful; also beholden, indebted; gratified, pleased Ant thankless, unappreciative, ungrateful

grate·ful·ness n ♦ : the quality or state of being grateful

♦ appreciation, gratitude, thanks — more at THANKS

grat·i·fi·ca·tion \ˌgra-tə-fə-ˈkā-shən\ *n* ♦ : the act of gratifying : the state of being gratified

♦ contentment, delectation, delight, enjoyment, gladness, pleasure, relish, satisfaction — more at PLEASURE

grat·i·fy \ˈgra-tə-ˌfī\ *vb* **-fied; -fy·ing** **1** ♦ : to afford pleasure to **2** ♦ : to give in to

♦ [1] content, delight, gladden, please, rejoice, satisfy, suit, warm — more at PLEASE ♦ [2] cater to, humor (*or* humour), indulge — more at INDULGE

grat·i·fy·ing *adj* ♦ : giving pleasure or satisfaction

♦ agreeable, felicitous, good, grateful, pleasant, pleasurable, satisfying ♦ comforting, encouraging, heartening, heartwarming, rewarding, satisfying — more at HEARTWARMING

grat·ing \ˈgrā-tiŋ\ *n* : a framework with parallel bars or crossbars

gra·tis \ˈgra-təs, ˈgrā-\ *adv or adj* : without charge or recompense : FREE

grat·i·tude \ˈgra-tə-ˌtüd, -ˌtyüd\ *n* ♦ : the state of being grateful : THANKFULNESS

♦ appreciation, gratefulness, thanks — more at THANKS

gra·tu·itous \grə-ˈtü-ə-təs, -ˈtyü-\ *adj* **1** ♦ : done or provided without recompense : FREE **2** : UNWARRANTED

♦ complimentary, free — more at FREE

gra·tu·ity \-ə-tē\ *n, pl* **-ities** : something given voluntarily or beyond obligation usu. for some service : TIP

gra·va·men \grə-ˈvā-mən\ *n, pl* **-va·mens** *or* **-vam·i·na** \-ˈva-mə-nə\ [LL, burden] : the basic or significant part of a grievance or complaint

¹**grave** \ˈgrāv\ *vb* **graved; grav·en** \ˈgrā-vən\ *or* **graved; grav·ing** **1** : to carve or shape with a chisel : SCULPTURE **2** : to carve or cut (as letters or figures) into a hard surface : ENGRAVE

²**grave** *n* : an excavation in the earth as a place of burial; *also* : TOMB

³**grave** \ˈgrāv; *5 also* ˈgräv\ *adj* **1** ♦ : deserving serious consideration **2** ♦ : threatening great harm or danger **3** ♦ : having a serious and dignified quality or demeanor : SOLEMN **4** : drab in color : SOMBER **5** : of, marked by, or being an accent mark having the form ` — **grave·ly** *adv* — **grave·ness** *n*

♦ [1] heavy, serious, weighty — more at SERIOUS ♦ [2] dangerous, grievous, hazardous, menacing, parlous, perilous, risky, serious, unhealthy, unsafe, venturesome — more at DANGEROUS ♦ [3] earnest, humorless (*or* humourless), serious, severe, sober, solemn, staid, unsmiling, weighty — more at SERIOUS

grav·el \ˈgra-vəl\ *n* : pebbles and small pieces of rock larger than grains of sand

grav·el·ly *adj* **1** : of, containing, or covered with gravel **2** ♦ : having a rough or grating sound

♦ coarse, gruff, hoarse, husky, scratchy, throaty — more at HOARSE

Graves' disease \ˈgrāvz-\ *n* : hyperthyroidism characterized by goiter and often protrusion of the eyeballs

grave·stone \ˈgrāv-ˌstōn\ *n* ♦ : a burial monument

♦ headstone, monument, tombstone — more at TOMBSTONE

grave·yard \-ˌyärd\ *n* : CEMETERY

grav·id \ˈgra-vəd\ *adj* [L *gravidus*, fr. *gravis* heavy] : PREGNANT

gra·vi·me·ter \gra-ˈvi-mə-tər, ˈgra-və-ˌmē-\ *n* : a device for measuring variations in a gravitational field

grav·i·tate \ˈgra-və-ˌtāt\ *vb* **-tat·ed; -tat·ing** : to move or tend to move toward something

grav·i·ta·tion \ˌgra-və-ˈtā-shən\ *n* **1** : a natural force of attraction that tends to draw bodies together and that occurs because of the mass of the bodies **2** : the action or process of gravitating — **grav·i·ta·tion·al** \-shə-nəl\ *adj* — **grav·i·ta·tion·al·ly** *adv*

grav·i·ty \ˈgra-və-tē\ *n, pl* **-ties** **1 a** : IMPORTANCE **b** ♦ : the

quality or state of being serious **2** : ²MASS 5 **3** : the gravitational attraction of the mass of a celestial object (as earth) for bodies close to it; *also* : GRAVITATION 1

♦ earnest, earnestness, intentness, seriousness, sobriety, solemnity — more at EARNESTNESS

gra·vure \grə-ˈvyu̇r\ *n* [F] : PHOTOGRAVURE

gra·vy \ˈgrā-vē\ *n, pl* **gravies** **1** : a sauce made from the thickened and seasoned juices of cooked meat **2** : unearned or illicit gain : GRAFT

¹**gray** *or chiefly Can and Brit* **grey** \ˈgrā\ *adj* **1** ♦ : of the color gray; *also* : dull in color **2** : having gray hair **3** ♦ : lacking cheer or brightness in mood, outlook, style, or flavor : CHEERLESS, DISMAL **4** : intermediate in position or character — **gray·ness** *n*

♦ [1] leaden, pewter, silver, silvery, slate, steely; *also* achromatic, neutral; dirty, dull, faded, washed-out; ashen, ashy, chalky, livid, mousy, pale, white, whitish ♦ [3] bleak, dark, dismal, dreary, gloomy, somber (*or* sombre), wretched — more at GLOOMY

²**gray** *or chiefly Can and Brit* **grey** *n* **1** : something of a gray color **2** : a neutral color ranging between black and white

³**gray** *or chiefly Can and Brit* **grey** *vb* : to make or become gray

gray·beard *or chiefly Can and Brit* **greybeard** \ˈgrā-ˌbird\ *n* : an old man

gray·ish *or chiefly Can and Brit* **grey·ish** *adj* : somewhat gray

gray·ling \ˈgrā-liŋ\ *n, pl* **grayling** *also* **graylings** : any of several slender freshwater food and sport fishes related to the trouts

gray matter *n* **1** : the grayish part of nervous tissue consisting mostly of nerve cell bodies **2** ♦ : capacity for knowledge and learning : INTELLIGENCE

♦ brains, intellect, intelligence, reason, sense — more at INTELLIGENCE

gray wolf *n* : a large wolf of northern No. America and Asia that is usu. gray

¹**graze** \ˈgrāz\ *vb* **grazed; graz·ing** [ME *grasen*, fr. OE *grasian*, fr. *græs* grass] **1** ♦ : to feed on herbage or pasture **2** : to feed (livestock) on grass or pasture — **graz·er** *n*

♦ browse, forage, pasture; *also* eat, feed, nibble

²**graze** *vb* **grazed; graz·ing** **1** ♦ : to touch lightly in passing **2** ♦ : to irritate or roughen by rubbing : SCRATCH, ABRADE

♦ [1] brush, kiss, nick, shave, skim — more at BRUSH ♦ [2] abrade, scrape, scratch, scuff — more at SCRAPE

¹**grease** \ˈgrēs\ *n* **1** : rendered animal fat **2** : oily material **3** : a thick lubricant

²**grease** \ˈgrēs, ˈgrēz\ *vb* **greased; greas·ing** ♦ : to smear or lubricate with grease

♦ lubricate, oil, slick, wax — more at LUBRICATE

grease·paint \ˈgrēs-ˌpānt\ *n* : theater makeup

greasy \ˈgrē-sē, -zē\ *adj* **1** : smeared or soiled with grease; *also* : oily in appearance, texture, or manner **2** ♦ : causing or tending to cause something to slide or fall **3** : containing an unusual amount of grease

♦ slick, slippery, slithery — more at SLICK

great \ˈgrāt\ *adj* **1** ♦ : large in size : BIG **2** : ELABORATE, AMPLE **3** : large in number : NUMEROUS **4** : being beyond the average : MIGHTY, INTENSE ⟨a ∼ weight⟩ ⟨in ∼ pain⟩ **5** : EMINENT, GRAND **6** ♦ : long continued ⟨a ∼ while⟩ **7** : MAIN, PRINCIPAL **8** : more distant in a family relationship by one generation ⟨a *great*-grandfather⟩ **9** ♦ : markedly superior in character, quality, or skill ⟨∼ at bridge⟩ **10** ♦ : very good of its kind : EXCELLENT, FINE ⟨had a ∼ time⟩

♦ [1] big, hefty, large, outsize, oversize, sizable, substantial ♦ [6] extended, far, lengthy, long, marathon — more at LONG ♦ [9] accomplished, adept, consummate, crack, crackerjack, expert, good, master, masterful, masterly, proficient, skilled, skillful, virtuoso — more at

PROFICIENT ♦ [10] excellent, fabulous, fine, grand, splendid, superb, superior, swell, terrific, wonderful — more at EXCELLENT

great ape n : any of a family of primates including the gorilla, orangutan, and chimpanzees

great blue heron n : a large crested grayish blue American heron

great circle n : a circle on the surface of a sphere that has the same center as the sphere; *esp* : one on the surface of the earth an arc of which is the shortest travel distance between two points

great·coat \'grāt-ˌkōt\ n : a heavy overcoat

Great Dane n : any of a breed of tall massive powerful smooth-coated dogs

great·er \'grā-tər\ adj, often cap : consisting of a central city together with adjacent areas ⟨the ~ metropolitan area⟩

great·heart·ed \'grāt-'här-təd\ adj 1 ♦ : characterized by bravery : COURAGEOUS 2 : characterized by a noble or forbearing spirit : MAGNANIMOUS

♦ brave, courageous, dauntless, doughty, fearless, gallant, heroic, intrepid, lionhearted, manful, stalwart, stout, undaunted, valiant, valorous — more at BRAVE

great·ly adv 1 ♦ : to a great extent or degree : very much 2 ♦ : in a great manner

♦ [1] broadly, considerably, extremely, highly, hugely, largely, much, sizably, tremendously, very *Ant* slightly ♦ [2] gallantly, grandly, heroically, honorably (*or* honourably), magnanimously, nobly; *also* loftily; magnificently, majestically *Ant* basely, dishonorably, ignobly

great·ness n ♦ : the quality or state of being great

♦ distinction, excellence, preeminence, superiority, supremacy — more at EXCELLENCE ♦ bigness, grandness, largeness — more at LARGENESS

great power n, often cap G&P : one of the nations that figure most decisively in international affairs

great white shark n : a large and dangerous shark of warm seas that has large saw-edged teeth and is whitish below and bluish or brownish above

grebe \'grēb\ n : any of a family of lobe-toed diving birds related to the loons

Gre·cian \'grē-shən\ adj : GREEK

greed \'grēd\ n ♦ : acquisitive or selfish desire beyond reason — **greed·i·ly** \'grē-də-lē\ adv

♦ acquisitiveness, avarice, avidity, covetousness, cupidity, rapaciousness; *also* materialism, possessiveness; appetite, craving, hankering, hunger, itch, longing, lust, passion, ravenousness, thirst, voracity, yearning, yen

greed·i·ness \-dē-nəs\ n : the quality or state of being greedy; *esp* : extreme or excessive desire for wealth or gain

greedy \'grē-dē\ adj 1 ♦ : having a strong desire for food or drink 2 ♦ : marked by greed : having or showing a selfish desire for wealth and possessions

♦ [1] gluttonous, hoggish, piggish, rapacious, ravenous, voracious — more at VORACIOUS ♦ [2] acquisitive, avaricious, avid, covetous, grasping, mercenary, rapacious; *also* materialistic; desirous, eager, itchy, miserly; hoggish, piggish, swinish; devouring, gluttonous, gobbling, insatiable, ravenous, voracious, unquenchable; discontent, discontented, malcontent, unsatisfied; begrudging, grudging, resentful

¹**Greek** \'grēk\ n 1 : a native or inhabitant of Greece 2 : the ancient or modern language of Greece

²**Greek** adj 1 : of, relating to, or characteristic of Greece, the Greeks, or Greek 2 : ORTHODOX 3

¹**green** \'grēn\ adj 1 : of the color green 2 ♦ : covered with verdure; *also* : consisting of green plants or of the leafy parts of plants ⟨a ~ salad⟩ 3 : UNRIPE; *also* : IMMATURE 4 ♦ : having a sickly appearance 5 : not fully processed or treated ⟨~ liquor⟩ ⟨~ hides⟩ 6 ♦ : lacking in training, knowledge, or experience : INEXPERI-

ENCED; *also* : NAIVE 7 : concerned with or supporting environmentalism ⟨~ companies⟩ — **green·ish** adj

♦ [2] leafy, lush, luxuriant, verdant ♦ [4] cadaverous, lurid, pale, pasty, peaked, sallow, sickly — more at SICKLY ♦ [6] adolescent, callow, immature, inexperienced, juvenile, raw — more at CALLOW ♦ [6] ingenuous, innocent, naive, simple, unknowing, unsophisticated, unwary, unworldly — more at NAIVE

²**green** vb : to make or become green

³**green** n 1 : a color between blue and yellow in the spectrum : the color of growing fresh grass or of the emerald 2 : something of a green color 3 : green vegetation; *esp,* pl : leafy herbs or leafy parts of a vegetable ⟨collard ~s⟩ ⟨beet ~s⟩ 4 : a grassy plot; *esp* : a smooth grassy area around the hole into which the ball must be played in golf

green·back \'grēn-ˌbak\ n : a U.S. legal-tender note

green bean n : a kidney bean that is used as a snap bean when the pods are colored green

green·belt \'grēn-ˌbelt\ n : a belt of parks or farmlands around a community

green card n : an identity card attesting the permanent resident status of an alien in the U.S.

green·ery \'grē-nə-rē\ n, pl **-er·ies** ♦ : green foliage or plants

♦ flora, foliage, green, herbage, leafage, vegetation, verdure; *also* grassland, prairie

green–eyed \'grē-'nīd\ adj : JEALOUS

green–gro·cer \'grēn-ˌgrō-sər\ n : a retailer of fresh vegetables and fruit

green·horn \-ˌhȯrn\ n ♦ : an inexperienced person; *also* : NEWCOMER

♦ beginner, fledgling, freshman, neophyte, newcomer, novice, recruit, rookie, tenderfoot, tyro — more at BEGINNER

green·house \-ˌhau̇s\ n : a glass structure for the growing of tender plants

greenhouse effect n : warming of a planet's atmosphere that occurs when the sun's radiation passes through the atmosphere, is absorbed by the planet, and is reradiated as radiation of longer wavelength that can be absorbed by atmospheric gases

green manure n : an herbaceous crop (as clover) plowed under when green to enrich the soil

green·ness n ♦ : the quality or state of being green; *esp* : being unaffectedly simple and candid

♦ artlessness, ingenuousness, innocence, naturalness, naïveté, simplicity, unworldliness — more at NAÏVETÉ

green onion n : a young onion pulled before the bulb has enlarged and used esp. in salads : SCALLION

green pepper n : a sweet pepper before it turns red at maturity

green·room \'grēn-ˌrüm, -ˌru̇m\ n : a room in a theater or concert hall where actors or musicians relax before, between, or after appearances

green·sward \-ˌswȯrd\ n : turf that is green with growing grass

green thumb n : an unusual ability to make plants grow

green·wash·ing \'grēn-ˌwȯ-shiŋ, -ˌwä-\ n : expressions of environmentalist concerns as a cover for products, policies, or activities deleterious to the environment

Green·wich mean time \'gri-nij-, 'gre-, -nich-\ n [*Greenwich,* England] : the time of the meridian of Greenwich used as the basis of worldwide standard time

Greenwich time n : GREENWICH MEAN TIME

green·wood \'grēn-ˌwu̇d\ n : a forest green with foliage

greet \'grēt\ vb 1 : to address with expressions of kind wishes 2 : to meet or react to in a specified manner 3 : to be perceived by — **greet·er** n

greet·ing n 1 ♦ : a salutation on meeting 2 pl ♦ : best wishes : REGARDS

♦ [1] hello, salutation, salute — more at HELLO ♦ **greetings** [2] compliments, regards, respects — more at COMPLIMENT

greeting card *n* : a card that bears a message usu. sent on a special occasion

gre·gar·i·ous \gri-'gar-ē-əs\ *adj* [L *gregarius* of a flock or herd, fr. *greg-, grex* flock, herd] **1 ♦** : marked by or indicating a liking for companionship : SOCIAL, COMPANIONABLE **2** : tending to flock together — **gre·gar·i·ous·ly** *adv* — **gre·gar·i·ous·ness** *n*

  ♦ boon, companionable, convivial, extroverted, outgoing, sociable, social — more at CONVIVIAL

grem·lin \'grem-lən\ *n* : a cause of error or equipment malfunction conceived of as a small gnome

gre·nade \grə-'nād\ *n* [MF, lit., pomegranate, fr. LL *granata*, fr. L, fem. of *granatus* seedy, fr. *granum* grain] : a small bomb that is thrown by hand or launched (as by a rifle)

gren·a·dier \,gre-nə-'dir\ *n* : a member of a European regiment formerly armed with grenades

gren·a·dine \,gre-nə-'dēn, 'gre-nə-,dēn\ *n* : a syrup flavored with pomegranates and used in mixed drinks

grew *past of* GROW

grey *var of* GRAY

grey·hound \'grā-,haund\ *n* : any of a breed of tall slender dogs noted for speed and keen sight

grid \'grid\ *n* **1** : GRATING **2** : a network of conductors for distributing electric power **3** : a network of horizontal and perpendicular lines (as for locating points on a map) **4** : GRIDIRON 2; *also* : FOOTBALL

grid·dle \'grid-ᵊl\ *n* : a flat usu. metal surface for cooking food

griddle cake *n* ♦ : a flat cake made of thin batter and cooked (as on a griddle) on both sides : PANCAKE

  ♦ flapjack, pancake — more at PANCAKE

grid·iron \'grid-,īrn, -,ī-ərn\ *n* **1** : a grate for broiling food **2** : a football field

grid·lock \-,läk\ *n* : a traffic jam in which an intersection is so blocked that vehicles cannot move

grief \'grēf\ *n* **1 ♦** : emotional distress caused by or as if by bereavement; *also* : a cause of such distress **2** : DISASTER ⟨the expedition came to ∼⟩; *also* : MISHAP

  ♦ affliction, anguish, dolor, heartache, sorrow, woe — more at SORROW

griev·ance \'grē-vəns\ *n* **1 ♦** : a cause of distress affording reason for complaint or resistance **2 ♦** : the formal expression of a grievance : COMPLAINT

  ♦ [1] grudge, resentment, score — more at GRUDGE
  ♦ [2] beef, complaint, fuss, gripe, grumble, murmur, plaint, squawk — more at COMPLAINT

grieve \'grēv\ *vb* **grieved; griev·ing** [ME *greven*, fr. OF *grever*, fr. L *gravare* to burden, fr. *gravis* heavy, grave] **1** : to cause grief or sorrow to : DISTRESS **2 ♦** : to feel grief

  ♦ agonize, bleed, feel, hurt, mourn, sorrow, suffer; *also* ache, long (for), pine (away); rack, torment, torture; bemoan, bewail, deplore, lament, rue; bawl, cry, groan, howl, keen, moan, take on, wail, weep, yammer ♦ *usu* **grieve for** bemoan, bewail, deplore, lament, mourn, wail — more at LAMENT

griev·ous \'grē-vəs\ *adj* **1 ♦** : causing or characterized by severe suffering, grief, or sorrow : SEVERE ⟨a ∼ wound⟩ **2 ♦** : unreasonably burdensome or severe : OPPRESSIVE, ONEROUS **3 ♦** : having important or dangerous possible consequences : SERIOUS, GRAVE

  ♦ [1, 2] bitter, brutal, burdensome, cruel, excruciating, grim, hard, harsh, heavy, onerous, oppressive, rough, rugged, severe, stiff, tough, trying — more at HARSH
  ♦ [3] dangerous, grave, hazardous, menacing, parlous, perilous, risky, serious, unhealthy, unsafe, venturesome — more at DANGEROUS

griev·ous·ly *adv* **1 ♦** : in a grievous manner : in a manner characterized by sorrow or grief **2** : to a grievous degree

  ♦ agonizingly, bitterly, hard, hardly, sadly, sorrowfully, unhappily, woefully, wretchedly — more at HARD

¹**grill** \'gril\ *vb* **1** : to broil on a grill; *also* : to fry or toast on a griddle **2 ♦** : to question intensely

  ♦ examine, interrogate, pump, query, question, quiz — more at EXAMINE

²**grill** *n* **1** : a cooking utensil of parallel bars on which food is grilled **2 ♦** : an informal restaurant

  ♦ café, diner, restaurant — more at RESTAURANT

grille *or* **grill** \'gril\ *n* : a grating that forms a barrier or screen

grill·work \'gril-,wərk\ *n* : work constituting or resembling a grille

grim \'grim\ *adj* **grim·mer; grim·mest 1 ♦** : fierce in disposition or action : CRUEL **2 ♦** : harsh and forbidding in appearance **3** : ghastly or repellent in character **4 ♦** : not flinching or shrinking : RELENTLESS — **grim·ly** *adv* — **grim·ness** *n*

  ♦ [1] cruel, fell, ferocious, fierce, savage, vicious — more at FIERCE ♦ [2] austere, dour, fierce, flinty, forbidding, gruff, rough, rugged, severe, stark, steely, stern; *also* bleak, cold, hostile, unfriendly; adamant, determined, firm, resolute, steadfast, unflinching; fixed, hard, immovable, implacable, inflexible, obdurate, rigid, set, stiff, unbending, uncompromising, unyielding; immutable, unchangeable; black, cheerless, dark, gloomy, glum, joyless, moody, morose, sulky, sullen, surly; brooding, grave, melancholy, serious, sober, solemn, somber, unsmiling, weighty *Ant* benign, benignant, gentle, mild, tender ♦ [4] determined, dogged, implacable, relentless, unflinching, unrelenting, unyielding — more at UNYIELDING

¹**gri·mace** \'gri-məs, gri-'mās\ *n* ♦ : a facial expression usu. of disgust or disapproval — **grimace** *vb*

  ♦ face, frown, lower, mouth, pout, scowl; *also* flinch, wince; growl, snarl; simper, smirk; scoff, sneer; glare, glower, look, stare

grime \'grīm\ *n* ♦ : soot, smut, or dirt adhering to or embedded in a surface; *also* : accumulated dirtiness and disorder

  ♦ dirt, filth, muck, smut, soil — more at FILTH

grimy *adj* : full of or covered with grime

grin \'grin\ *vb* **grinned; grin·ning** : to draw back the lips so as to show the teeth esp. in amusement — **grin** *n*

¹**grind** \'grīnd\ *vb* **ground** \'graund\; **grind·ing 1 ♦** : to reduce to small particles **2 ♦** : to wear down, polish, or sharpen by friction **3** : OPPRESS **4 ♦** : to press with a grating noise : GRIT ⟨∼ the teeth⟩ **5** : to operate or produce by turning a crank **6** : DRUDGE; *esp* : to study hard **7** : to move with difficulty or friction ⟨gears ∼ing⟩

  ♦ [1] atomize, crush, powder, pulverize — more at POWDER ♦ [2] buff, burnish, edge, file, hone, plane, polish, rasp, rub, sand, sharpen, whet ♦ [4] crunch, gnash, grate, grit, rasp, scrape, scratch

²**grind** *n* **1 ♦** : dreary monotonous labor, routine, or study **2** : one who works or studies excessively **3 ♦** : the act or sound of grinding

  ♦ [1] drudgery, labor (*or* labour), slavery, sweat, toil, travail — more at TOIL ♦ [3] rasp, scrape, scratch — more at RASP

grind·er \'grīn-dər\ *n* **1** : MOLAR **2** *pl* : TEETH **3** : one that grinds **4 ♦** : a large sandwich on a long split roll : SUBMARINE 2

  ♦ hoagie, poor boy, sub, submarine — more at SUBMARINE

grind out *vb* ♦ : to produce in a mechanical way

  ♦ build, carve, forge, hammer, work out

grind·stone \'grīnd-,stōn\ *n* : a flat circular stone of natural sandstone that revolves on an axle and is used for grinding, shaping, or smoothing

¹**grip** \'grip\ *vb* **gripped; grip·ping 1 ♦** : to seize or hold firmly **2 ♦** : to hold the interest of strongly

  ♦ [1] clasp, clench, cling, clutch, grasp, hang on, hold, hold on — more at HOLD ♦ [2] absorb, busy, engage, engross, enthrall, fascinate, immerse, interest, intrigue, involve, occupy — more at ENGAGE

²**grip** *n* **1** : GRASP; *also* : strength in gripping **2** ♦ : a firm tenacious hold typically giving control, mastery, or understanding **3** ♦ : mental grasp : UNDERSTANDING **4** : a device for gripping **5** ♦ : portable case designed to hold a traveler's clothing and personal articles : TRAVELING BAG

♦ [2] arm, authority, clutch, command, control, dominion, hold, mastery, power, sway — more at POWER ♦ [3] appreciation, apprehension, comprehension, grasp, perception, understanding — more at COMPREHENSION ♦ [5] carryall, handbag, portmanteau, suitcase, traveling bag — more at TRAVELING BAG

¹**gripe** \ˈgrīp\ *vb* **griped; grip·ing 1** : IRRITATE, VEX **2** : to cause or experience spasmodic pains in the bowels **3** ♦ : to complain with grumbling

♦ beef, bellyache, carp, complain, crab, croak, fuss, grouse, growl, grumble, kick, moan, murmur, mutter, repine, squawk, wail, whine — more at COMPLAIN

²**gripe** *n* ♦ : expression of grief, pain, or dissatisfaction

♦ beef, complaint, fuss, grievance, grumble, murmur, plaint, squawk — more at COMPLAINT

grippe \ˈgrip\ *n* : INFLUENZA

gris–gris \ˈgrē-ˌgrē\ *n, pl* **gris–gris** \-ˌgrēz\ [F] : an amulet or incantation used chiefly by people of black African ancestry

gris·ly \ˈgriz-lē\ *adj* **gris·li·er; -est** ♦ : inspiring horror, intense fear, disgust, or distaste : HORRIBLE, GRUESOME

♦ appalling, atrocious, awful, dreadful, frightful, ghastly, gruesome, hideous, horrible, horrid, lurid, macabre, monstrous, nightmarish, shocking, terrible — more at HORRIBLE

grist \ˈgrist\ *n* : grain to be ground or already ground

gris·tle \ˈgri-səl\ *n* : CARTILAGE — **gris·tly** \ˈgris-lē\ *adj*

grist·mill \ˈgrist-ˌmil\ *n* : a mill for grinding grain

¹**grit** \ˈgrit\ *n* **1** : a hard sharp granule (as of sand); *also* : material composed of such granules **2** ♦ : unyielding courage ⟨the pioneers' ∼⟩ — **grit·ty** *adj*

♦ backbone, fiber (*or* fibre), fortitude, guts, pluck, spunk — more at FORTITUDE

²**grit** *vb* **grit·ted; grit·ting** : to give forth a grating sound : GRIND, GRATE

grits \ˈgrits\ *n pl* : coarsely ground hulled grain ⟨hominy ∼⟩

griz·zled \ˈgri-zəld\ *adj* : streaked or mixed with gray

griz·zly \ˈgriz-lē\ *adj* **griz·zli·er; -est** : GRIZZLED

grizzly bear *n* : a large pale-coated bear of western No. America

gro *abbr* gross

groan \ˈgrōn\ *vb* **1** ♦ : to utter a deep moan indicative of pain, grief, or annoyance : MOAN **2** : to make a harsh sound under sudden or prolonged strain ⟨the chair ∼ed under his weight⟩ — **groan** *n*

♦ howl, keen, lament, moan, plaint, wail — more at LAMENT

groat \ˈgrōt\ *n* : an old British coin worth four pennies

gro·cer \ˈgrō-sər\ *n* [ME, fr. AF *groser* wholesaler, fr. *gros* coarse, wholesale, fr. L *grossus* coarse] : a dealer esp. in staple foodstuffs — **gro·cery** \ˈgrōs-rē, ˈgrōsh-, ˈgrō-sə-\ *n*

grog \ˈgräg\ *n* [*Old Grog*, nickname of Edward Vernon †1757 Eng. admiral responsible for diluting the sailors' rum] : alcoholic liquor; *esp* : liquor (as rum) mixed with water

grog·gy \ˈgrä-gē\ *adj* **grog·gi·er; -est** : weak and unsteady on the feet or in action — **grog·gi·ly** \-gə-lē\ *adv* — **grog·gi·ness** \-gē-nəs\ *n*

groin \ˈgroin\ *n* **1** : the juncture of the lower abdomen and inner part of the thigh; *also* : the region of this juncture **2** : the curved line or rib on a ceiling along which two vaults meet

grok \ˈgräk\ *vb* **grokked; grok·king** : to understand profoundly and intuitively

grom·met \ˈgrä-mət, ˈgrə-\ *n* **1** : a ring of rope **2** : an eyelet of firm material to strengthen or protect an opening

¹**groom** \ˈgrüm, ˈgrum\ *n* **1** : a person responsible for the care of horses **2** : BRIDEGROOM

²**groom** *vb* **1** : to clean and care for (an animal) **2** : to make neat or attractive **3** : PREPARE

grooms·man \ˈgrümz-mən, ˈgrumz-\ *n* : a male friend who attends a bridegroom at his wedding

¹**groove** \ˈgrüv\ *n* **1** : a long narrow channel **2** ♦ : a fixed routine

♦ pattern, rote, routine, rut, treadmill — more at ROUTINE

²**groove** *vb* **1** ♦ : to make a groove in; *also* : to form a groove **2** ♦ : to enjoy oneself intensely

♦ [1] score, scribe — more at SCORE ♦ *usu* **groove on** [2] adore, delight, dig, enjoy, fancy, like, love, relish, revel — more at ENJOY

groovy \ˈgrü-vē\ *adj* **groov·i·er; -est 1** : unusually good : EXCELLENT **2** : HIP

grope \ˈgrōp\ *vb* **groped; grop·ing 1** ♦ : to feel about or search for blindly or uncertainly ⟨∼ for the right word⟩ **2** : to feel one's way by groping

♦ feel, fish, fumble; *also* cast about, hunt, look, reach, seek (out); clutch, grab, scrabble, snatch

gros·beak \ˈgrōs-ˌbēk\ *n* : any of several finches of Europe or America with large stout conical bills

gros·grain \ˈgrō-ˌgrān\ *n* [F *gros grain* coarse texture] : a silk or rayon fabric with crosswise cotton ribs

¹**gross** \ˈgrōs\ *adj* **1** ♦ : glaringly noticeable **2** : OUT-AND-OUT, UTTER **3** ♦ : physically large : BIG, BULKY; *esp* : excessively fat **4** : GENERAL, BROAD **5** : consisting of an overall total exclusive of deductions ⟨∼ earnings⟩ **6** : CARNAL, EARTHY ⟨∼ pleasures⟩ **7** ♦ : coarse in nature or behavior : UNREFINED; *also* : crudely vulgar **8** : lacking knowledge — **gross·ly** *adv*

♦ [1] blatant, conspicuous, egregious, flagrant, glaring, obvious, patent, prominent, pronounced, rank, striking — more at EGREGIOUS ♦ [3] chubby, corpulent, fat, fleshy, full, obese, overweight, plump, portly, rotund, round — more at FAT ♦ [7] coarse, common, crass, crude, ill-bred, low, rough, rude, tasteless, uncouth, uncultivated, uncultured, unpolished, unrefined, vulgar — more at COARSE

²**gross** *n* : an overall total exclusive of deductions — **gross** *vb*

³**gross** *n, pl* **gross** : a total of 12 dozen things ⟨a ∼ of pencils⟩

gross domestic product *n* : the gross national product excluding the value of net income earned abroad

gross national product *n* : the total value of the goods and services produced in a nation during a year

gross·ness *n* ♦ : the quality or state of being gross

♦ corpulence, fatness, obesity, plumpness — more at CORPULENCE ♦ coarseness, indelicacy, lowness, rudeness, vulgarity — more at VULGARITY

grot \ˈgrät\ *n* : a natural underground chamber or series of chambers open to the surface : GROTTO

gro·tesque \grō-ˈtesk\ *adj* **1** : FANCIFUL, BIZARRE **2** ♦ : absurdly incongruous **3** ♦ : departing markedly from the natural, the expected, or the typical — **gro·tesque·ly** *adv*

♦ [2] harsh, unaesthetic — more at HARSH ♦ [3] hideous, ugly, unappealing, unattractive

grot·to \ˈgrä-tō\ *n, pl* **grottoes** *also* **grottos 1** : a natural underground chamber or series of chambers open to the surface : CAVE **2** : an artificial cavelike structure

grouch \ˈgrauch\ *n* **1** : a fit of bad temper **2** ♦ : an habitually irritable or complaining person — **grouch** *vb*

♦ bear, complainer, crab, crank, curmudgeon, grumbler, whiner; *also* malcontent, sorehead; killjoy, spoilsport; defeatist, pessimist; faultfinder, kicker, nitpicker, quibbler

grouchy *adj* ♦ : given to grumbling : marked by ill temper

♦ choleric, cross, crotchety, irascible, irritable, peevish, snappy, snippy, testy, waspish — more at IRRITABLE ♦ crabby, cranky, fussy, grumpy, querulous — more at FUSSY

¹ground \'graund\ *n* **1** : the bottom of a body of water **2** *pl* ♦ : sediment at the bottom of a liquid **3** ♦ : a basis for belief, action, or argument **4** : a surrounding area : BACKGROUND **5** ♦ : the surface of the earth; *also* : SOIL **6** : an area with a particular use ⟨fishing ∼s⟩ **7** *pl* ♦ : the area about and belonging to a building **8** : a conductor that makes electrical connection with the earth

♦ **grounds** [2] deposit, dregs, lees, precipitate, sediment — more at DEPOSIT ♦ [3] base, basis, bedrock, cornerstone, footing, foundation, groundwork, keystone, underpinning — more at CORNERSTONE ♦ *usu* **grounds** [3] motive, reason, wherefore, why — more at REASON ♦ [5] dirt, earth, soil — more at DIRT ♦ **grounds** [7] demesne, park, premises, yard; *also* acres, estate, land, lot, parcel, plot, property, real estate, realty; campus; churchyard

²ground *vb* **1** : to bring to or place on the ground **2** : to run or cause to run aground **3** ♦ : to provide a reason or justification for **4** : to furnish with a foundation of knowledge **5** : to connect electrically with a ground **6** : to restrict to the ground; *also* : prohibit from some activity

♦ base, rest — more at BASE

³ground *past and past part of* GRIND

ground ball *n* : a batted baseball that rolls or bounces along the ground

ground cover *n* : low plants that grow over and cover the soil; *also* : a plant suitable for use as ground cover

ground·ed \'graun-dəd\ *adj* : mentally and emotionally stable

ground·er \'graun-dər\ *n* : GROUND BALL

ground·hog \'graund-ˌhȯg, -ˌhäg\ *n* : WOODCHUCK

ground·less \'graun(d)-ləs\ *adj* ♦ : having no ground or foundation

♦ baseless, invalid, unfounded, unreasonable, unsubstantiated, unsupported, unwarranted — more at BASELESS

ground·ling \'graund-liŋ\ *n* : a spectator in the pit of an Elizabethan theater

ground rule *n* **1** : a sports rule adopted to modify play on a particular field, court, or course **2** : a rule of procedure

ground squirrel *n* : any of various burrowing rodents of No. America and Eurasia that are related to the squirrels and live in colonies in open areas

ground swell *n* **1** : a broad deep ocean swell caused by an often distant gale or earthquake **2** *usu* **ground·swell** : a rapid spontaneous growth (as of political opinion)

ground·wa·ter \'graund-ˌwȯ-tər, -ˌwä-\ *n* : water within the earth that supplies wells and springs

ground·work \-ˌwərk\ *n* ♦ : something that forms a foundation or support : BASIS; *also* : preparation made beforehand

♦ base, basis, bedrock, footing, foundation, ground, keystone, underpinning — more at CORNERSTONE

ground zero *n* **1** : the point above, below, or at which a nuclear explosion occurs **2** : the center or origin of rapid, intense, or violent activity

¹group \'grüp\ *n* **1** ♦ : a number of individuals related by a common factor (as physical association, community of interests, or blood) **2** : a combination of atoms commonly found together in a molecule ⟨a methyl ∼⟩

♦ bracket, category, class, division, family, grade, kind, order, set, species, type — more at CLASS

²group *vb* ♦ : to associate in groups

♦ assort, break down, categorize, class, classify, grade, peg, place, range, rank, separate, sort — more at CLASSIFY ♦ accumulate, amass, assemble, collect, concentrate, garner, gather, lump, pick up, round up, scrape — more at GATHER

grou·per \'grü-pər\ *n, pl* **groupers** *also* **grouper** : any of numerous large solitary bottom fishes of warm seas

group home *n* : a residence for persons requiring care or supervision

group·ie \'grü-pē\ *n* : a fan of a rock group who usu. fol-lows the group around on concert tours; *also* : ENTHUSIAST, FAN

group·ing \'grü-piŋ\ *n* **1** : the act or process of combining in groups **2** : a set of objects combined in a group

group therapy *n* : therapy in the presence of a therapist in which several patients discuss their personal problems

groupware \'grüp-ˌwer\ *n* : software that enables users to work jointly via a network on projects or files

¹grouse \'graus\ *n, pl* **grouse** *or* **grouses** : any of numerous ground-dwelling game birds that have feathered legs and are usu. of reddish brown or other protective color

²grouse *vb* **groused; grous·ing** ♦ : to mutter in discontent : COMPLAIN, GRUMBLE

♦ beef, bellyache, carp, complain, crab, fuss, gripe, grumble, kick, moan, squawk, wail, whine — more at COMPLAIN

grout \'graut\ *n* : material (as mortar) used for filling spaces — **grout** *vb*

grove \'grōv\ *n* : a small wood usu. without underbrush

grov·el \'grä-vəl, 'grə-\ *vb* **-eled** *or* **-elled; -el·ing** *or* **-el·ling** **1** ♦ : to creep or lie with the body prostrate in fear or humility **2** : to abase oneself

♦ crawl, creep, slither, snake, worm — more at CRAWL

grow \'grō\ *vb* **grew** \'grü\; **grown** \'grōn\; **grow·ing** **1** ♦ : to spring up and develop to maturity **2** : to be able to grow : THRIVE **3** : to take on some relation through or as if through growth ⟨tree limbs *grown* together⟩ **4** ♦ : to become progressively greater **5** : to develop from a parent source **6** ♦ : to pass into a condition : BECOME **7** : to have an increasing influence **8** ♦ : to cause to grow

♦ [1] age, develop, grow up, mature, progress, ripen — more at MATURE ♦ *usu* **grow in** [4] build, gain, gather, pick up — more at GAIN ♦ [6] become, come, get, go, run, turn, wax — more at BECOME ♦ [8] crop, cultivate, culture, promote, raise, rear, tend; *also* breed, produce, propagate; plant, sow; gather, glean, harvest, reap; germinate, quicken, root, sprout

grow·er *n* **1** : one that grows esp. in a specified way **2** ♦ : a person who grows a specified fruit or other product

♦ agriculturist, cultivator, farmer, planter, tiller — more at FARMER

growing pains *n pl* **1** : pains in the legs of growing children having no known relation to growth **2** : the stresses and strains attending a new project or development

growl \'graul\ *vb* **1** : RUMBLE **2** ♦ : to utter a deep throaty sound **3** : to complain angrily : GRUMBLE — **growl** *n*

♦ bellow, boom, roar, thunder — more at ROAR

grown–up \'grō-ˌnəp\ *adj* : not childish : ADULT — **grown-up** *n*

growth \'grōth\ *n* **1** : stage or condition attained in growing **2** ♦ : a process of growing esp. through progressive development or increase **3 a** : a result or product of growing ⟨a fine ∼ of hair⟩ **b** ♦ : an abnormal mass of tissue (as a tumor)

♦ [2] development, elaboration, evolution, expansion, maturation, progress, progression — more at DEVELOPMENT ♦ [3b] excrescence, lump, neoplasm, tumor; *also* outgrowth; cancer, carcinoma, lymphoma, malignancy, melanoma; cyst, tubercle, wart

growth hormone *n* : a vertebrate hormone that is secreted by the pituitary gland and regulates growth

growth industry *n* : a business, interest, or activity that is increasingly popular, profitable, or trendy

grow up *vb* ♦ : to grow toward or arrive at full stature or physical or mental maturity

♦ age, develop, grow, mature, progress, ripen — more at MATURE

¹grub \'grəb\ *vb* **grubbed; grub·bing** **1** : to clear or root out by digging **2** : to dig in the ground usu. for a hidden object **3** : to search about **4** : to work hard and long

²grub *n* **1** : a soft thick wormlike insect larva ⟨beetle ∼s⟩

2 : DRUDGE; *also* : a slovenly person **3** ♦ : nourishment in solid form : FOOD

♦ chow, fare, food, meat, provender, provisions, viands, victuals — more at FOOD

grub·bi·ness \-bē-nəs\ *n* ♦ : the state of being grubby

♦ dinginess, dirtiness, filthiness, foulness, nastiness, uncleanliness — more at DIRTINESS

grub·by \'grə-bē\ *adj* **grub·bi·er; -est** ♦ : full of or covered with grime : DIRTY, SLOVENLY ⟨∼ clothes⟩

♦ dirty, filthy, foul, grungy, mucky, muddy, slovenly, unclean — more at DIRTY

grub·stake \'grəb-ˌstāk\ *n* : supplies or funds furnished a mining prospector in return for a share in his finds

¹grudge \'grəj\ *vb* **grudged; grudg·ing** : to be reluctant to give : BEGRUDGE

²grudge *n* ♦ : a feeling of deep-seated resentment or ill will

♦ animosity, antagonism, antipathy, bitterness, enmity, gall, hostility, rancor — more at ENMITY ♦ grievance, resentment, score; *also* offense, umbrage; complaint; pique, peeve

gru·el \'grü-əl\ *n* : a thin porridge

gru·el·ing *or* **gru·el·ling** \'grü-liŋ, 'grü-ə-\ *adj* ♦ : requiring extreme effort : EXHAUSTING ⟨a ∼ schedule⟩

♦ arduous, demanding, difficult, exacting, formidable, hard, herculean, laborious, murderous, rough, stiff, strenuous, tall, toilsome, tough — more at HARD

grue·some \'grü-səm\ *adj* [fr. earlier *growsome*, fr. E dial. *grow, grue* to shiver] ♦ : inspiring horror or repulsion

♦ appalling, atrocious, awful, dreadful, frightful, ghastly, grisly, hideous, horrible, horrid, lurid, macabre, monstrous, nightmarish, shocking, terrible — more at HORRIBLE

gruff \'grəf\ *adj* **1** ♦ : rough in speech or manner **2** ♦ : being deep and harsh : HOARSE — **gruff·ly** *adv*

♦ [1] flinty, grim, rough, rugged, severe, stark, steely, stern — more at GRIM ♦ [2] coarse, gravelly, hoarse, husky, scratchy, throaty — more at HOARSE

grum·ble \'grəm-bəl\ *vb* **grum·bled; grum·bling 1** ♦ : to mutter in discontent **2** ♦ : to utter a growl : GROWL, RUMBLE

♦ [1] beef, bellyache, complain, fuss, gripe, grouse, kick, moan, squawk, wail, whine — more at COMPLAIN ♦ [2] growl, lumber, roll, rumble — more at RUMBLE

grum·bler *n* ♦ : one that grumbles

♦ bear, complainer, crab, crank, curmudgeon, grouch, whiner — more at GROUCH

grump·i·ness \-pē-nəs\ *n* ♦ : the quality or state of being grumpy

♦ biliousness, irritability, peevishness, perverseness, perversity

grumpy \'grəm-pē\ *adj* **grump·i·er; -est** ♦ : moodily cross : SURLY — **grump·i·ly** \-pə-lē\ *adv*

♦ choleric, crabby, cranky, cross, crotchety, grouchy, irascible, irritable, peevish, petulant, short-tempered, surly, testy, waspish — more at IRRITABLE

grunge \'grənj\ *n* **1** : one that is grungy **2** : heavy metal rock music expressing alienation and discontent **3** : untidy or tattered clothing typically worn by grunge fans

grun·gy \'grən-jē\ *adj* **grun·gi·er; -est** ♦ : shabby or dirty in character or condition

♦ dirty, grubby, mucky, muddy, unclean — more at DIRTY ♦ dilapidated, mean, neglected, ratty, seedy, shabby — more at SHABBY

grun·ion \'grən-yən\ *n* : a fish of the California coast which comes inshore to spawn at nearly full moon

¹grunt \'grənt\ *n* : a deep throaty sound (as that of a hog)

²grunt *vb* : to utter a grunt; *also* : to utter with a grunt

GSA *abbr* **1** General Services Administration **2** Girl Scouts of America

G suit *n* [*gravity suit*] : a suit for a pilot or astronaut designed to counteract the physiological effects of acceleration

GSUSA *abbr* Girl Scouts of the United States of America

gt *abbr* great

Gt Brit *abbr* Great Britain

gtd *abbr* guaranteed

GU *abbr* Guam

gua·ca·mo·le \ˌgwä-kə-'mō-lē\ *n* [MexSp, fr. Nahuatl *āhuacamōlli*, fr. *āhuacatl* avocado + *mōlli* sauce] : mashed and seasoned avocado

gua·nine \'gwä-ˌnēn\ *n* : a purine base that codes genetic information in the molecular chain of DNA and RNA

gua·no \'gwä-nō\ *n* [Sp, fr. Quechua *wanu* fertilizer, dung] : excrement esp. of seabirds or bats; *also* : a fertilizer composed chiefly of this excrement

¹guar·an·tee \ˌgar-ən-'tē\ *n* **1** : GUARANTOR **2** : GUARANTY 1 **3** ♦ : an agreement by which one person undertakes to secure another in the possession or enjoyment of something **4** : an assurance of the quality of or of the length of use to be expected from a product offered for sale **5** ♦ : something given as security : GUARANTY

♦ [3] bond, contract, covenant, guaranty, surety, warranty; *also* oath, pledge, vow, word; bargain, compact, pact, treaty; assurance, insurance; bail, deposit, pawn, security ♦ [5] gage, guaranty, pawn, pledge, security — more at PLEDGE

²guarantee *vb* **-teed; -tee·ing 1** : to undertake to answer for the debt, failure to perform, or faulty performance of (another) **2** : to undertake an obligation to establish, perform, or continue **3** ♦ : to give security to

♦ assure, cinch, ensure, guaranty, insure, secure — more at ENSURE

guar·an·tor \ˌgar-ən-'tȯr\ *n* ♦ : one who gives a guarantee

♦ backer, patron, sponsor, surety — more at SPONSOR

¹guar·an·ty \'gar-ən-tē\ *n, pl* **-ties 1** : an undertaking to answer for another's failure to pay a debt or perform a duty **2** ♦ : an agreement by which one person undertakes to secure another in the possession or enjoyment of something : GUARANTEE **3** : GUARANTOR **4** ♦ : something given as security : PLEDGE

♦ [2] bond, contract, covenant, guarantee, surety, warranty — more at GUARANTEE ♦ [4] gage, guarantee, pawn, pledge, security — more at PLEDGE

²guaranty *vb* **-tied; -ty·ing** : to give security to : GUARANTEE

¹guard \'gärd\ *n* **1** ♦ : a person or a body of persons on sentinel duty **2** *pl* : troops assigned to protect a sovereign **3** : a defensive position (as in boxing) **4** ♦ : the act or duty of protecting or defending **5** ♦ : one that protects : PROTECTION **6** : a protective or safety device **7** : a football lineman playing between center and tackle; *also* : a basketball player stationed toward the rear — **on guard** : WATCHFUL, ALERT

♦ [1] custodian, guardian, keeper, lookout, picket, sentry, warden, warder, watch, watchman; *also* observer, patrol, spotter, watchdog; bodyguard, convoy, defender, escort ♦ [4] aegis, armor, cover, defense (*or* defence), protection, safeguard, screen, security, shield, wall, ward — more at DEFENSE ♦ [5] custodian, defender, defense (*or* defence), protection, protector — more at PROTECTOR

²guard *vb* **1** ♦ : to protect from danger esp. by watchful attention : DEFEND **2** : to watch over **3** ♦ : to be on guard

♦ [1] cover, defend, protect, safeguard, screen, secure, shield, ward — more at DEFEND ♦ *usu* **guard against** [3] beware (of), mind, watch out (for) — more at BEWARE (OF)

guard·ed \'gär-dəd\ *adj* ♦ : careful to consider all circumstances and possible consequences

♦ alert, careful, cautious, circumspect, considerate, gingerly, heedful, safe, wary — more at CAREFUL

guard·house \'gärd-ˌhau̇s\ *n* **1** : a building occupied by a guard or used as a headquarters by soldiers on guard duty **2** : a military jail

guard·ian \'gär-dē-ən\ *n* **1** ♦ : one that guards : CUSTO-

DIAN **2** ♦ : one who has the care of the person or property of another

♦ caretaker, custodian, janitor, keeper, warden, watchman — more at CUSTODIAN

guard·ian·ship *n* ♦ : supervision or support of one that is smaller and weaker; *specif* : the relationship existing between guardian and ward

♦ care, custody, keeping, safekeeping, trust, ward — more at CUSTODY

guard·room \'gärd-ˌrüm\ *n* **1** : a room used by a military guard while on duty **2** : a room where military prisoners are confined

guards·man \'gärdz-mən\ *n* : a member of a military body called *guard* or *guards*

Gua·te·ma·lan \ˌgwä-tə-'mä-lən\ *n* : a native or inhabitant of Guatemala — **Guatemalan** *adj*

gua·va \'gwä-və\ *n* : the sweet yellow or pink acid fruit of a shrubby tropical American tree used esp. for making jam and jelly; *also* : the tree

gu·ber·na·to·ri·al \ˌgü-bər-nə-'tòr-ē-əl\ *adj* : of or relating to a governor

guer·don \'gərd-ᵊn\ *n* : REWARD, RECOMPENSE

Guern·sey \'gərn-zē\ *n, pl* **Guernseys** : any of a breed of usu. reddish brown and white dairy cattle that produce rich yellowish milk

guer·ril·la *or* **gue·ril·la** \gə-'ri-lə\ *n* [Sp *guerrilla,* fr. dim. of *guerra* war, of Gmc origin] : one who engages in irregular warfare esp. as a member of an independent unit

¹guess \'ges\ *vb* **1** ♦ : to form an opinion from little or no evidence **2** ♦ : to hold as an opinion : BELIEVE, SUPPOSE **3** ♦ : to conjecture correctly about

♦ [1] assume, conjecture, presume, speculate, suppose, surmise, suspect; *also* conclude, deduce, gather, infer; hypothesize, theorize; believe, conceive, expect, imagine, take, think ♦ [2] believe, consider, deem, feel, figure, hold, imagine, suppose, think — more at BELIEVE ♦ [3] calculate, call, conjecture, estimate, figure, gauge, judge, make, place, put, reckon, suppose — more at ESTIMATE

²guess *n* ♦ : a conclusion deduced by surmise or guesswork

♦ conjecture, supposition, surmise — more at CONJECTURE

guest \'gest\ *n* **1** : a person to whom hospitality (as of a house or a club) is extended **2** ♦ : a patron of a commercial establishment (as a hotel) **3** : a person not a regular member of a cast who appears on a program

♦ customer, patron — more at CUSTOMER

guest·house \'gest-ˌhaůs\ *n* : a house run as a boarding house or bed-and-breakfast

guf·faw \(ˌ)gə-'fò\ *n* : a loud burst of laughter — **guf·faw** *vb*

guid·ance \'gīd-ᵊns\ *n* **1** ♦ : the act or process of guiding **2** : the direction provided by a guide : ADVICE

♦ administration, conduct, control, direction, government, management, operation, oversight, regulation, running, superintendence, supervision — more at CONDUCT

¹guide \'gīd\ *n* **1** ♦ : one who leads or directs another's course **2** ♦ : one who shows and explains points of interest **3** : something that provides guiding information; *also* : SIGNPOST **4** : a device to direct the motion of something

♦ [1, 2] attendant, companion, escort, guard — more at ESCORT

²guide *vb* **guid·ed; guid·ing** **1** ♦ : to act as a guide to **2** ♦ : to direct, supervise, or influence usu. to a particular end **3** : to superintend the training of — **guid·able** \'gī-də-bəl\ *adj*

♦ [1] conduct, direct, lead, marshal, pilot, route, show, steer, usher — more at LEAD ♦ [1, 2] administer, carry on, conduct, control, direct, govern, handle, manage, operate, oversee, regulate, run, superintend, supervise — more at CONDUCT ♦ [2] coach, counsel, lead,

mentor, pilot, shepherd, show, tutor; *also* direct, steer; accompany, escort, see; oversee, superintend, supervise; drill, train; brief, enlighten, inform; instruct, school, teach; inculcate, indoctrinate; cultivate, foster, nurture

guide·book \'gīd-ˌbůk\ *n* : a book of information for travelers

guided missile *n* : a missile whose course may be altered during flight

guide dog *n* : a dog trained to lead the blind

guide·line \'gīd-ˌlīn\ *n* : an indication or outline of policy or conduct

guide word *n* : a term at the head of a page of an alphabetical reference work that indicates the alphabetically first or last word on that page

gui·don \'gī-ˌdän, -d³n\ *n* : a small flag (as of a military unit)

guild \'gild\ *n* ♦ : an association of people with common aims and interests; *esp* : a medieval association of merchants or craftsmen — **guild·hall** \-ˌhòl\ *n*

♦ association, brotherhood, club, college, congress, council, fellowship, fraternity, institute, institution, league, order, organization, society — more at ASSOCIATION

guile \'gīl\ *n* ♦ : deceitful cunning : DUPLICITY

♦ artfulness, artifice, caginess, canniness, craft, craftiness, cunning, slyness, wiliness — more at CUNNING ♦ craft, craftiness, crookedness, deceit, deceitfulness, dishonesty, dissimulation, double-dealing, duplicity — more at DECEIT

guile·ful *adj* ♦ : full of guile : characterized by cunning, deceit, or treachery

♦ artful, cagey, crafty, cunning, devious, foxy, slick, sly, subtle, wily — more at ARTFUL

guil·lo·tine \'gi-lə-ˌtēn, ˌgē-ə-'tēn\ *n* [F, fr. Joseph *Guillotin* †1814 Fr. physician] : a machine for beheading persons — **guillotine** *vb*

guilt \'gilt\ *n* **1** : the fact of having committed an offense esp. against the law **2** ♦ : the state of one who has committed an offense esp. consciously **3** ♦ : a feeling of responsibility for wrongdoing

♦ [2] blame, culpability, fault, rap — more at BLAME ♦ [3] contrition, penitence, remorse, repentance, self-reproach, shame; *also* misgiving, qualm, scruple; compunction; blame, fault, responsibility; chagrin, regret

guilt·less *adj* ♦ : free from guilt or evil

♦ blameless, clear, faultless, impeccable, innocent, irreproachable — more at INNOCENT

guilt-trip \'gilt-ˌtrip\ *vb* : to cause feelings of guilt in

guilty \'gil-tē\ *adj* **guilt·i·er; -est** **1** ♦ : having committed a breach of conduct or a crime **2** : suggesting or involving guilt **3** ♦ : aware of or suffering from guilt — **guilt·i·ly** \-tə-lē\ *adv* — **guilt·i·ness** \-tē-nəs\ *n*

♦ [1] accountable, answerable, blamable, blameworthy, censurable, culpable, reprehensible *Ant* blameless, guiltless, innocent ♦ [3] ashamed, contrite, hangdog, penitent, remorseful, repentant, shamefaced; *also* apologetic, sorry; regretful, rueful; penitential; chagrined, embarrassed, sheepish *Ant* impenitent, remorseless, shameless, unashamed, unrepentant

guin·ea \'gi-nē\ *n* **1** : a British gold coin no longer issued worth 21 shillings **2** : a unit of value equal to 21 shillings

guinea fowl *n* : a gray and white spotted West African bird related to the pheasants and widely raised for food; *also* : any of several related birds

guinea hen *n* : a female guinea fowl; *also* : GUINEA FOWL

Guin·ean \'gi-nē-ən\ *n* : a native or inhabitant of Guinea — **Guinean** *adj*

guinea pig *n* **1** : a small stocky short-eared and nearly tailless So. American rodent often kept as a pet or used in lab research **2** : a subject of research or testing

guise \'gīz\ *n* **1** ♦ : a form or style of dress : COSTUME **2** ♦ : external appearance : SEMBLANCE

♦ [1] dress, garb, getup, outfit — more at OUTFIT

♦ [2] appearance, face, name, semblance, show — more at APPEARANCE

gui·tar \gi-'tär\ *n* : a musical instrument with usu. six strings plucked with a pick or with the fingers

gulch \'gəlch\ *n* ♦ : a deep or precipitous cleft : RAVINE

♦ canyon, defile, flume, gap, gorge, notch, pass, ravine — more at CANYON

gulf \'gəlf\ *n* [ME *goulf*, fr. MF *golfe*, fr. It *golfo*, fr. LL *colpus*, fr. Gk *kolpos* bosom, gulf] **1** ♦ : a part of an ocean or sea partly or mostly surrounded by land **2** : ABYSS, CHASM **3** : a wide separation

♦ bay, bight, cove, estuary, fjord, inlet; *also* harbor, port, roadstead; narrow, sound, strait; bayou

¹gull \'gəl\ *n* : any of numerous mostly white or gray long-winged web-footed seabirds

²gull *vb* ♦ : to make a dupe of : DECEIVE

♦ deceive, delude, dupe, fool, misinform, mislead, take in, trick — more at DECEIVE

³gull *n* : a person who is easily deceived or cheated : DUPE

gul·let \'gə-lət\ *n* : ESOPHAGUS; *also* : THROAT

gull·ible \'gə-lə-bəl\ *adj* ♦ : easily duped or cheated

♦ easy, susceptible — more at EASY

gul·ly \'gə-lē\ *n, pl* **gullies** : a trench worn in the earth by and often filled with running water after rains

¹gulp \'gəlp\ *vb* **1** ♦ : to swallow hurriedly or greedily **2** : SUPPRESS ⟨~ down a sob⟩ **3** : to catch the breath as if in taking a long drink

♦ bolt, devour, gobble, gorge, gormandize, scarf, scoff, wolf — more at GOBBLE

²gulp *n* **1** : the act or an instance of gulping **2** : the amount taken in a single large swallow

¹gum \'gəm\ *n* : the oral tissue that surrounds the necks of the teeth

²gum *n* [ME *gomme*, fr. MF, fr. L *cummi, gummi*, fr. Gk *kommi*, fr. Egyptian *qmyt*] **1** : a sticky plant exudate; *esp* : one that hardens on drying **2** : a sticky substance **3** : a preparation usu. of a plant gum sweetened and flavored and used for chewing

gum arabic *n* : a water-soluble gum obtained from several acacias and used esp. in making inks, adhesives, confections, and pharmaceuticals

gum·bo \'gəm-bō\ *n* [AmerF *gombo*, of Bantu origin] : a rich thick soup usu. thickened with okra

gum·drop \'gəm-ˌdräp\ *n* : a candy made usu. from corn syrup with gelatin and coated with sugar crystals

gum·my *adj* ♦ : having a thick or sticky quality; *also* : consisting, containing, or covered with gum

♦ adhesive, gelatinous, gluey, glutinous, gooey, sticky, viscid, viscous — more at STICKY

gump·tion \'gəmp-shən\ *n* **1** : shrewd common sense **2** : ENTERPRISE, INITIATIVE

gum·shoe \'gəm-ˌshü\ *n* : DETECTIVE — **gumshoe** *vb*

¹gun \'gən\ *n* **1** : CANNON **2** ♦ : a portable firearm **3** : a discharge of a gun **4** : something suggesting a gun in shape or function **5** : THROTTLE — **gunned** \'gənd\ *adj*

♦ arm, firearm, piece; *also* handgun, pistol, revolver, six-gun, six-shooter; blunderbuss, flintlock, matchlock, musket, rifle, shotgun; automatic, machine gun, repeater, submachine gun, tommy gun

²gun *vb* **gunned; gun·ning 1** : to hunt with a gun **2** : to hit with a missile (as a bullet) from a gun : SHOOT **3** : to open up the throttle of so as to increase speed

gun·boat \'gən-ˌbōt\ *n* : a small lightly armed ship for use in shallow waters

gun·fight \-ˌfīt\ *n* : a duel with guns — **gun·fight·er** *n*

gun·fire \-ˌfīr\ *n* : the firing of guns

gung ho \'gəŋ-'hō\ *adj* [*Gung ho!*, motto (taken to mean "work together") adopted by certain U.S. marines in World War II, fr. Chin *gōnghé*, short for *Zhōngguó Gōngyè Hézuò Shè* Chinese Industrial Cooperatives Society] ♦ : extremely zealous or enthusiastic

♦ avid, eager, enthusiastic, keen, nuts, raring — more at EAGER

gun·man \-mən\ *n* : a man armed with a gun; *esp* : a professional killer

gun·ner \'gə-nər\ *n* **1** : a soldier or airman who operates or aims a gun **2** : one who hunts with a gun

gun·nery \'gə-nə-rē\ *n* : the use of guns; *esp* : the science of the flight of projectiles and effective use of guns

gunnery sergeant *n* : a noncommissioned officer in the marine corps ranking next below a master sergeant

gun·ny·sack \'gə-nē-ˌsak\ *n* : a sack made of a coarse heavy fabric (as burlap)

gun·point \'gən-ˌpȯint\ *n* : the muzzle of a gun — **at gunpoint** : under a threat of death by being shot

gun·pow·der \-ˌpau̇-dər\ *n* : an explosive powder used in guns and blasting

gun·shot \-ˌshät\ *n* **1** : shot fired from a gun **2** : the range of a gun ⟨within ~⟩

gun-shy \-ˌshī\ *adj* **1** : afraid of a loud noise **2** : markedly distrustful

gun·sling·er \-ˌsliŋ-ər\ *n* : a skilled gunman esp. in the old West

gun·smith \-ˌsmith\ *n* : one who designs, makes, or repairs firearms

gun·wale *also* **gun·nel** \'gən-ᵊl\ *n* : the upper edge of a ship's or boat's side

gup·py \'gə-pē\ *n, pl* **guppies** [R.J.L. *Guppy* †1916 Trinidadian naturalist] : a small brightly colored tropical fish

gur·gle \'gər-gəl\ *vb* **gur·gled; gur·gling 1** : to make a sound like that of an irregularly flowing or gently splashing liquid **2** ♦ : to flow in a broken irregular current — **gurgle** *n*

♦ dribble, lap, plash, ripple, slosh, splash, trickle, wash; *also* eddy, purl, swirl; swash, swish, whish; drip, drop; gush, jet, spout, spurt, squirt, rush *Ant* roll, pour, stream

Gur·kha \'gu̇r-kə, 'gər-\ *n* : a soldier from Nepal in the British or Indian army

gur·ney \'gər-nē\ *n, pl* **gurneys** : a wheeled cot or stretcher

gu·ru \'gu̇r-ü\ *n, pl* **gurus** [ultim. Sanskrit *guru*, fr. *guru*, adj., heavy, venerable] **1** : a personal religious and spiritual teacher in Hinduism **2** : a teacher in matters of fundamental concern **3** ♦ : a person who has knowledge or skills acquired through practice : EXPERT ⟨a fitness ~⟩

♦ ace, adept, artist, authority, crackerjack, expert, hand, hotshot, maestro, master, scholar, shark, virtuoso, whiz, wizard — more at EXPERT

gush \'gəsh\ *vb* **1** ♦ : to issue or pour forth copiously or violently : SPOUT **2** ♦ : to make an effusive display of affection or enthusiasm

♦ [1] jet, pour, rush, spew, spout, spurt, squirt; *also* cascade, issue, run, stream; plash, slosh, splash; surge, swell; flush, sluice; deluge, engulf, flood, inundate, overflow, overwhelm, submerge, swamp *Ant* dribble, drip, drop, trickle ♦ [2] enthuse, fuss, rave, rhapsodize, slobber; *also* dote (on), fawn; emote

gush·er \'gə-shər\ *n* : one that gushes; *esp* : an oil well with a large natural flow

gushy \'gə-shē\ *adj* **gush·i·er; -est** : marked by effusive sentimentality

gus·set \'gə-sət\ *n* : a triangular insert (as in a seam of a sleeve) to give width or strength — **gusset** *vb*

gus·sy up \'gə-sē-\ *vb* **1** : to dress up in best or formal clothes **2** : to make more attractive, glamorous or fancy

¹gust \'gəst\ *n* **1** ♦ : a sudden brief rush of wind **2** : a sudden outburst : SURGE

♦ blast, blow, flurry, williwaw; *also* breeze, zephyr; air, breath, waft; puff, whiff; gale, hurricane, squall, tempest, tornado, windstorm; northeaster, norther, northerly, westerly

²gust *vb* : to blow in gusts ⟨winds ~*ing* up to 40 mph⟩

gus·ta·to·ry \'gəs-tə-ˌtȯr-ē\ *adj* : relating to or associated with the sense of taste

gus·to \'gə-ˌstō\ *n* : enthusiastic and vigorous enjoyment, appreciation, or delight

gusty *adj* ♦ : blowing in gusts

♦ blowy, blustery, breezy, windy — more at WINDY

¹gut \'gət\ *n* **1** *pl* : internal organs of the body : BOWELS, ENTRAILS **2** ♦ : the alimentary canal or a part of it (as the intestine); *also* : BELLY, ABDOMEN **3** *pl* : the inner essential parts **4** *pl* ♦ : fortitude and stamina in coping with what alarms, repels, or discourages : COURAGE, PLUCK

♦ [2] abdomen, belly, solar plexus, stomach, tummy — more at STOMACH ♦ **guts** [4] bravery, courage, daring, fearlessness, hardihood, nerve, stoutness — more at COURAGE ♦ **guts** [4] backbone, fiber (*or* fibre), fortitude, grit, pluck, spunk — more at FORTITUDE

²gut *vb* **gut·ted; gut·ting 1** ♦ : to take out the entrails of : EVISCERATE **2** : to destroy the inside of

♦ clean, draw, eviscerate; *also* bone, dress; cut, excise, extract, remove, withdraw; transplant

gut check *n* : a test of courage, character, or determination

gutsy \'gət-sē\ *adj* **guts·i·er; -est** ♦ : marked by courage and determination

♦ adventurous, audacious, bold, daring, enterprising, hardy, nervy, venturesome — more at BOLD

gut·ter \'gə-tər\ *n* ♦ : a groove or channel for carrying off esp. rainwater

♦ dike, ditch, trench — more at DITCH

gut·ter·snipe \-ˌsnīp\ *n* : a street urchin

gut·tur·al \'gə-tə-rəl\ *adj* **1** : sounded in the throat **2** : being or marked by an utterance that is strange, unpleasant, or disagreeable — **guttural** *n*

gut·ty \'gə-tē\ *adj* **gut·ti·er; -est 1** : GUTSY **2** : having a vigorous challenging quality

gut–wrench·ing \'gət-ˌren-chiŋ\ *adj* : causing emotional anguish

¹guy \'gī\ *n* : a rope, chain, or rod attached to something as a brace or guide

²guy *vb* : to steady or reinforce with a guy

³guy *n* ♦ : an adult male human : MAN, FELLOW; *also, pl* : PERSONS ⟨all the ∼s came⟩

♦ buck, chap, chap, dude, gent, gentleman, hombre, jack, joker, lad, male, man — more at MAN

⁴guy *vb* : to make fun of : RIDICULE

Guy·a·nese \ˌgī-ə-'nēz\ *n, pl* **Guyanese** : a native or inhabitant of Guyana — **Guyanese** *adj*

guz·zle \'gə-zəl\ *vb* **guz·zled; guz·zling** ♦ : to drink greedily

♦ drink, imbibe, quaff, sup, swig, toss — more at DRINK

gym \'jim\ *n* : GYMNASIUM

gym·kha·na \jim-'kä-nə\ *n* **1** : a meet featuring sports contests; *esp* : a contest of automobile-driving skill

gym·na·si·um \for 1 jim-'nä-zē-əm, -zhəm, for 2 gim-'nä-zē-əm\ *n, pl* **-na·si·ums** *or* **-na·sia** \-'nä-zē-ə, -'nä-zhə; -'nä-zē-ə\ [L, exercise ground, school, fr. Gk *gymnasion*, fr. *gymnazein* to exercise naked, fr. *gymnos* naked] **1** : a room or building for indoor sports **2** : a European secondary school that prepares students for the university

gym·nas·tics \jim-'nas-tiks\ *n* : physical exercises designed to demonstrate strength and coordination; *also* : a sport in which individuals perform acrobatic feats mostly on special equipment — **gym·nast** \'jim-ˌnast\ *n* — **gym·nas·tic** *adj*

gym·no·sperm \'jim-nə-ˌspərm\ *n* : any of a class or subdivision of woody vascular seed plants (as conifers) that produce naked seeds not enclosed in an ovary

gyn *or* **gynecol** *abbr* gynecology

gy·nae·col·o·gy *chiefly Brit var of* GYNECOLOGY

gy·ne·col·o·gy \ˌgī-nə-'kä-lə-jē\ *n* : a branch of medicine that deals with the diseases and routine care of the reproduction system of women — **gy·ne·co·log·ic** \-ni-kə-'lä-jik\ *or* **gy·ne·co·log·i·cal** \-ji-kəl\ *adj* — **gy·ne·col·o·gist** \-nə-'kä-lə-jist\ *n*

gy·no·cen·tric \ˌgī-nə-'sen-trik\ *adj* : emphasizing feminine interests or a feminine point of view

¹gyp \'jip\ *n* **1** *now sometimes offensive* : CHEAT, SWINDLER **2** *now sometimes offensive* : FRAUD, SWINDLE

²gyp *vb, now sometimes offensive* : to deprive of something valuable by the use of deceit or fraud

gyp·sum \'jip-səm\ *n* : a calcium-containing mineral used in making plaster of paris

Gyp·sy \'jip-sē\ *n, pl* **Gypsies** [by shortening & alter. fr. *Egyptian*] **1** *sometimes offensive* : a member of a traditionally traveling people coming orig. from India and living chiefly in Europe, Asia, and No. America **2** : the language of the Gypsies

gypsy moth *n* : an Old World moth that was introduced into the U.S. where its caterpillar is a destructive defoliator of many trees

gy·rate \'jī-ˌrāt\ *vb* **gy·rat·ed; gy·rat·ing 1** ♦ : to revolve around a point or axis **2** : to oscillate with or as if with a circular or spiral motion

♦ pirouette, revolve, roll, rotate, spin, turn, twirl, wheel, whirl — more at SPIN

gy·ra·tion \jī-'rā-shən\ *n* : an act or instance of gyrating

♦ pirouette, reel, revolution, roll, rotation, spin, twirl, wheel, whirl — more at SPIN

gyr·fal·con \'jər-ˌfal-kən, -ˌfȯl-\ *n* : an arctic falcon with several color forms that is the largest of all falcons

¹gy·ro \'jī-rō\ *n, pl* **gyros** : GYROSCOPE

²gy·ro \'yē-ˌrō, 'zhir-ō\ *n, pl* **gyros** : a sandwich esp. of lamb and beef, tomato, onion, and yogurt sauce on pita bread

gy·ro·scope \'jī-rō-ˌskōp\ *n* : a wheel or disk mounted to spin rapidly about an axis that is free to turn in various directions

Gy Sgt *abbr* gunnery sergeant

gyve \'jīv, 'gīv\ *n* : FETTER — **gyve** *vb*

¹h \'āch\ *n, pl* **h's** *or* **hs** \'ā-chəz\ *often cap* : the 8th letter of the English alphabet

²h *abbr, often cap* **1** hard; hardness **2** heroin **3** hit **4** husband

H *symbol* hydrogen

¹ha \'hä\ *interj* — used esp. to express surprise or joy

²ha *abbr* hectare

Hab *abbr* Habacuc; Habakkuk

Ha·ba·cuc \'ha-bə-ˌkək, hə-'ba-kək\ *n* : HABAKKUK

Ha·bak·kuk \'ha-bə-ˌkək, hə-'ba-kək\ *n* : a book of the canonical Jewish and Christian Scriptures

ha·ba·ne·ra \ˌhä-bə-'ner-ə\ *n* [Sp (*danza*) *habanera*, lit., dance of Havana] : a Cuban dance in slow time; *also* : the music for this dance

ha·ba·ne·ro *also* **ha·ba·ñe·ro** \ˌ(h)ä-bə-'n(y)er-ō\ *n* : a very hot chili pepper that is usu. orange when mature

ha·be·as cor·pus \'hä-bē-əs-'kȯr-pəs\ *n* [ME, fr. ML, lit., you should have the body (the opening words of the writ)] : a writ issued to bring a party before a court

hab·er·dash·er \'ha-bər-ˌda-shər\ *n* : a dealer in men's clothing and accessories

hab·er·dash·ery \-ˌda-shə-rē\ *n, pl* **-er·ies 1** : goods sold by a haberdasher **2** : a haberdasher's shop

ha·bil·i·ment \hə-'bi-lə-mənt\ *n* **1** *pl* : TRAPPINGS, EQUIP-

MENT **2** : DRESS; *esp* : the dress characteristic of an occupation or occasion — usu. used in pl.

hab·it \'ha-bət\ *n* **1** : DRESS, GARB **2** : BEARING, CONDUCT **3** : PHYSIQUE **4** : mental makeup **5** ♦ : a usual manner of behavior : CUSTOM **6** : a behavior pattern acquired by frequent repetition **7** : ADDICTION **8** : mode of growth or occurrence ⟨trees with a spreading ∼⟩

♦ custom, fashion, pattern, practice, trick, way, wont; *also* addiction; disposition; bent, inclination, proclivity, tendency, turn; convention, form, mode, style; usage; manners, mores; groove, rote, routine, rut; affectation, airs, pose; attribute, characteristic, mark, trait; oddity, peculiarity, quirk, singularity, tic; strangeness, weirdness

hab·it·able \'ha-bə-tə-bəl\ *adj* : capable of being lived in — **hab·it·abil·i·ty** \,ha-bə-tə-'bi-lə-tē\ *n*
hab·i·tat \'ha-bə-,tat\ *n* [L, it inhabits] ♦ : the place or environment where a plant or animal naturally occurs

♦ home, niche, range, territory — more at HOME

hab·i·ta·tion \,ha-bə-'tā-shən\ *n* **1** : OCCUPANCY **2** ♦ : a dwelling place : RESIDENCE **3** : SETTLEMENT

♦ abode, domicile, dwelling, home, house, lodging, quarters, residence — more at HOME

hab·it-form·ing \'ha-bət-,fȯr-miŋ\ *adj* : causing addiction : ADDICTIVE
ha·bit·u·al \hə-'bi-chə-wəl\ *adj* **1** ♦ : having the nature of a habit **2** ♦ : doing, practicing, or acting by force of habit ⟨∼ drunkards⟩ **3** : inherent in an individual — **ha·bit·u·al·ly** *adv* — **ha·bit·u·al·ness** *n*

♦ [1] constant, frequent, periodic, regular, repeated, steady ♦ [2] chronic, confirmed, inveterate; *also* incorrigible, unregenerate; born, natural; persistent, regular, steady, unfailing; addicted; accustomed, habituated, used; deep-rooted, entrenched, inbred, inherent, innate

ha·bit·u·ate \hə-'bi-chə-,wāt\ *vb* **-at·ed; -at·ing 1** : ACCUSTOM **2** : to cause or undergo habituation
ha·bit·u·a·tion \hə-,bi-chə-'wā-shən\ *n* **1** : the process of becoming or state of being accustomed to or dependent on something **2** : psychological dependence on a drug after a period of use
ha·bi·tué *also* **ha·bi·tue** \hə-'bi-chə-,wā\ *n* [F] : one who may be regularly found in or at (as a place of entertainment)
ha·ci·en·da \,hä-sē-,en-də\ *n* **1** : a large estate in a Spanish-speaking country **2** : the main building of a farm or ranch
¹**hack** \'hak\ *vb* **1** : to cut or sever with repeated irregular blows **2** : to cough in a short dry manner **3** : to manage successfully; *also* : TOLERATE **4** : to gain access to a computer or computer system illegally
²**hack** *n* **1** : an implement for hacking **2** : a short dry cough **3** : a hacking blow **4** ♦ : a V-shaped indentation **5** : an act or instance of gaining access to a computer or computer system illegally **6** : a clever tip or technique for doing or improving something

♦ chip, indentation, nick, notch — more at NOTCH

³**hack** *n* **1** : a horse hired or used for varied work **2** : a horse worn out in service **3** : a light easy often 3-gaited saddle horse **4 a** : HACKNEY **b** : an automobile that carries passengers for a fare usu. determined by the distance traveled : TAXICAB **5** : a person who works solely for mercenary reasons; *esp* : a writer working solely for commercial success — **hack** *adj*
⁴**hack** *vb* : to operate a taxicab
hack·er \'ha-kər\ *n* **1** : one that hacks; *also* : a person unskilled at something **2** : an expert at using a computer **3** : a person who illegally gains access to and sometimes tampers with information in a computer system
hack·ie \'ha-kē\ *n* : a taxicab driver
hack·le \'ha-kəl\ *n* **1** : one of the long feathers on the neck or back of a bird **2** *pl* : hairs (as on a dog's neck) that can be erected **3** *pl* : TEMPER, DANDER

hack·man \'hak-mən\ *n* : HACKIE
¹**hack·ney** \'hak-nē\ *n, pl* **hackneys 1** : a horse for riding or driving **2** : a carriage or automobile kept for hire
²**hackney** *vb* : to make trite
hack·neyed \'hak-nēd\ *adj* ♦ : lacking in freshness or originality

♦ banal, commonplace, musty, stale, stereotyped, threadbare, tired, trite — more at STALE

hack·saw \'hak-,sȯ\ *n* : a fine-tooth saw in a frame for cutting metal
hack·work \-,wərk\ *n* : work done on order usu. according to a formula
had *past and past part of* HAVE
had·dock \'ha-dək\ *n, pl* **haddock** *also* **haddocks** : an Atlantic food fish usu. smaller than the related cod
Ha·des \'hā-(,)dēz\ *n* **1** : the abode of the dead in Greek mythology **2** *often not cap* : HELL
hae·ma·tite *chiefly Brit var of* HEMATITE
haf·ni·um \'haf-nē-əm\ *n* : a gray metallic chemical element
haft \'haft\ *n* : the handle of a weapon or tool
hag \'hag\ *n* **1** ♦ : an ugly or evil-looking old woman **2** : a woman that is credited with usu. malignant supernatural powers

♦ crone, witch — more at CRONE

Hag *abbr* Haggai
Hag·gai \'ha-gē-,ī, 'ha-,gī\ *n* : a book of the canonical Jewish and Christian Scriptures
hag·gard \'ha-gərd\ *adj* ♦ : having a worn or emaciated appearance — **hag·gard·ly** *adv* — **hag·gard·ness** *n*

♦ cadaverous, gaunt, skeletal, wasted

hag·gis \'ha-gəs\ *n* : a traditionally Scottish dish made of the heart, liver, and lungs of a sheep or a calf minced with suet, onions, oatmeal, and seasonings
hag·gle \'ha-gəl\ *vb* **hag·gled; hag·gling** ♦ : to argue in bargaining — **hag·gler** *n*

♦ bargain, chaffer, deal, dicker, negotiate, palter — more at BARGAIN

Ha·gi·og·ra·pha \,ha-gē-'ä-grə-fə, ,hā-jē-\ *n pl* : the third part of the Jewish Scriptures
ha·gio·graph·ic \,ha-gē-ə-'gra-fik, ,hā-, -jē-\ *adj* : of or relating to hagiography; *esp* : excessively flattering
ha·gi·og·ra·phy \,ha-gē-'ä-grə-fē, ,hä-jē-\ *n* **1** : biography of saints or venerated persons **2** : idealizing or idolizing biography — **ha·gi·og·ra·pher** \-fər\ *n*
hai·ku \'hī-(,)kü\ *n, pl* **haiku** [Jp] : an unrhymed Japanese verse form of three lines containing usu. 5, 7, and 5 syllables respectively; *also* : a poem in this form
¹**hail** \'hāl\ *n* **1** : precipitation in the form of small lumps of ice **2** ♦ : something that gives the effect of falling hail

♦ rain, shower, storm — more at RAIN ♦ barrage, bombardment, cannonade, fusillade, salvo, shower, storm, volley — more at BARRAGE

²**hail** *vb* **1** : to precipitate hail **2** : to pour down and strike like hail
³**hail** *interj* [ME, fr. ON *heill*, fr. *heill* healthy] — used to express acclamation
⁴**hail** *vb* **1 a** : SALUTE, GREET **b** ♦ : to greet with enthusiastic approval : ACCLAIM **2** : SUMMON

♦ acclaim, applaud, cheer, crack up, laud, praise, salute, tout — more at ACCLAIM

⁵**hail** *n* **1** : an expression of greeting, approval, or praise **2** ♦ : hearing distance

♦ earshot, hearing, sound

Hail Mary *n* **1** : a salutation and prayer to the Virgin Mary **2** : a long forward pass in football thrown as a final attempt to score
hail·stone \'hāl-,stōn\ *n* : a pellet of hail
hail·storm \-,stȯrm\ *n* : a storm accompanied by hail
hair \'har\ *n* **1 a** : a threadlike outgrowth esp. from the skin of a mammal **b** ♦ : a covering or growth of hairs

of an animal or a body part **2 ♦** : a minute distance or amount — **haired** \'hard\ *adj* — **hair·less** *adj*

♦ [1b] coat, fleece, fur, pelage, pile, wool **♦** [2] ace, inch, step, stone's throw; *also* bit, crumb, mite, jot, particle, smidgen, trace, trifle

hair·breadth \'har-ˌbredth\ *or* **hairs·breadth** \'harz-\ *n* **♦** : a very small distance or margin

♦ *or* **hairsbreadth** ace, hair, inch, step, stone's throw — more at HAIR

hair·brush \-ˌbrəsh\ *n* : a brush for the hair
hair·cloth \-ˌklȯth\ *n* : a stiff wiry fabric used esp. for upholstery
hair·cut \-ˌkət\ *n* : the act, process, or style of cutting and shaping the hair
hair·do \-ˌdü\ *n, pl* **hairdos** : a way of wearing the hair
hair·dress·er \-ˌdre-sər\ *n* : one who dresses or cuts hair — **hair·dress·ing** *n*
hair·line \-ˌlīn\ *n* **1** : a very thin line **2** : the outline of the hair on the head
hair·piece \-ˌpēs\ *n* **1** : supplementary hair (as a switch) used in some women's hairdos **2** : TOUPEE
hair·pin \-ˌpin\ *n* **1** : a U-shaped pin to hold the hair in place **2** : a sharp U-shaped turn in a road — **hairpin** *adj*
hair–rais·ing \'har-ˌrā-ziŋ\ *adj* **♦** : causing terror or astonishment

♦ fearful, fearsome, forbidding, formidable, frightful, scary, shocking, terrible, terrifying — more at FEARFUL

hair·split·ter \-ˌspli-tər\ *n* : a person who makes excessively fine distinctions in reasoning — **hair·split·ting** \-ˌspli-tiŋ\ *n*
hair·split·ting *adj* : made or done with extreme care and accuracy
hair·spray \'her-ˌsprā\ *n* : a liquid sprayed onto the hair to hold it in place
hair·style \-ˌstī(-ə)l\ *n* : HAIRDO — **hair·styl·ing** *n*
hair·styl·ist \-ˌstī-list\ *n* : HAIRDRESSER
hair–trigger *adj* : immediately responsive to the slightest stimulus
hairy \'har-ē\ *adj* **hair·i·er; -est 1 ♦** : covered with or as if with hair **2** : tending to cause nervous tension ⟨a few ∼ moments⟩ **3 ♦** : composed of or being like hair — **hair·i·ness** \-ē-nəs\ *n*

♦ [1] fleecy, furry, hirsute, rough, shaggy, unshorn, woolly; *also* bearded, whiskered; downy, fluffy, fuzzy *Ant* bald, hairless, shorn, smooth **♦** [3] furry, fuzzy, rough, shaggy, woolly; *also* downy, fluffy

hairy woodpecker *n* : a common No. American woodpecker with a white back that is larger than the similarly marked downy woodpecker
Hai·tian \'hā-shən\ *n* : a native or inhabitant of Haiti — **Haitian** *adj*
hajj \'haj\ *n* : a pilgrimage to Mecca prescribed as a religious duty for Muslims
hajji \'ha-jē\ *n* : one who has made a pilgrimage to Mecca — often used as a title
hake \'hāk\ *n* : any of several marine food fishes related to the cod
hal·berd \'hal-bərd, 'hȯl-\ *also* **hal·bert** \-bərt\ *n* : a weapon esp. of the 15th and 16th centuries consisting of a battle-ax and pike on a long handle
hal·cy·on \'hal-sē-ən\ *adj* [Gk *halkyōn, alkyōn* a mythical bird believed to nest at sea and to calm the waves] **♦** : marked by calm : PEACEFUL

♦ calm, hushed, peaceful, placid, quiet, serene, still, tranquil, untroubled — more at CALM

¹hale \'hāl\ *adj* **♦** : free from defect, disease, or infirmity

♦ able-bodied, chipper, fit, healthy, hearty, robust, sound, well, whole, wholesome — more at HEALTHY

²hale *vb* **haled; hal·ing 1 ♦** : to exert force upon so as to cause or tend to cause motion toward the force : HAUL, PULL **2** : to compel to go

♦ drag, draw, haul, lug, pull, tow, tug — more at PULL

¹half \'haf, 'håf\ *n, pl* **halves** \'havz, 'håvz\ **1** : either of two equal parts that compose something **2 ♦** : one of a pair

♦ companion, match, mate, twin — more at MATE

²half *adj* **1** : being one of two equal parts **2** : amounting to nearly half **3** : PARTIAL, INCOMPLETE
³half *adv* **1 a** : in an equal part or degree **b** : not completely **2** : by any means : AT ALL
half–and–half \ˌhaf-ᵊn-'haf, ˌhåf-ᵊn-'håf\ *n* : something that is half one thing and half another
half·back \'haf-ˌbak, 'håf-\ *n* **1** : a football back stationed on or near the flank **2** : a player stationed immediately behind the forward line
half–baked \-'bākt\ *adj* **1** : not thoroughly baked **2 ♦** : poorly planned; *also* : lacking common sense

♦ absurd, crazy, cuckoo, fatuous, foolish, mad, nonsensical, nutty, senseless, silly, stupid — more at FOOLISH

half–breed \-ˌbrēd\ *n, often offensive* : one of mixed racial descent — **half–breed** *adj, often offensive*
half brother *n* : a brother related through one parent only
half–caste \'haf-ˌkast, 'håf-\ *n, often offensive* : one of mixed racial descent : HALF-BREED — **half–caste** *adj, often offensive*
half–dol·lar \-'dä-lər\ *n* **1** : a coin representing one half of a dollar **2** : the sum of fifty cents
half–heart·ed \-'här-təd\ *adj* **♦** : lacking spirit or interest — **half·heart·ed·ly** *adv* — **half·heart·ed·ness** *n*

♦ tepid, uneager, unenthusiastic — more at TEPID

half–life \-ˌlīf\ *n* : the time required for half of something (as atoms or a drug) to undergo a process
half–mast \-'mast\ *n* : a point about halfway down from the top of a mast or staff
half note *n* : a musical note equal in time to one half of a whole note
half–pen·ny \'hāp-nē\ *n, pl* **half·pence** \'hā-pəns\ *or* **half·pennies** : a formerly used British coin representing one half of a penny
half–pint \'haf-ˌpīnt, 'håf-\ *adj* : of less than average size — **half–pint** *n*
half sister *n* : a sister related through one parent only
half sole *n* : a shoe sole extending from the shank forward — **half–sole** *vb*
half–staff \'haf-'staf, 'håf-\ *n* : HALF-MAST
half step *n* : a musical interval equivalent to one twelfth of an octave
half·time \'haf-ˌtīm, 'håf-\ *n* : an intermission between halves of a game
half–track \-ˌtrak\ *n* : a motor vehicle propelled by an endless chain-track drive system; *esp* : such a vehicle lightly armored for military use
half–truth \-ˌtrüth\ *n* : a statement that is only partially true; *esp* : one that deliberately mixes truth and falsehood
half·way \-'wā\ *adj* **1 ♦** : midway between two points **2** : of or relating to a part rather than the whole : not general or total : PARTIAL — **halfway** *adv*

♦ intermediary, intermediate, median, medium, middle, midmost — more at MIDDLE

half–wit \-ˌwit\ *n* **♦** : a foolish or imbecilic person

♦ booby, fool, goose, jackass, lunatic, nitwit, nut, simpleton, turkey — more at FOOL **♦** blockhead, dope, dummy, idiot, imbecile, jackass, moron, numskull — more at IDIOT

half–wit·ted \-'wi-təd\ *adj* **1** : exhibiting or indicative of a lack of common sense or sound judgment **2** : mentally deficient — **half–wit·ted·ness** *n*
hal·i·but \'ha-lə-bət\ *n, pl* **halibut** *also* **halibuts** [ME *halybutte*, fr. *haly, holy* holy + *butte* flatfish; fr. its being eaten on holy days] : any of several large edible marine flatfishes
ha·lite \'ha-ˌlīt, 'hā-\ *n* : ROCK SALT
hal·i·to·sis \ˌha-lə-'tō-səs\ *n* : the condition of having fetid breath
hall \'hȯl\ *n* **1** : the residence of a medieval king or noble;

also : the house of a landed proprietor **2** : a large public building **3** : a college or university building; *also* : DORMITORY **4 a ♦** : the entrance room of a building : LOBBY **b ♦** : a corridor or passage in a building **5** : a large room for assembly : AUDITORIUM **6 ♦** : a place used for public entertainment

   ♦ [4a] entry, foyer, lobby, vestibule; *also* antechamber, anteroom, waiting room; doorway, entrance, threshold **♦** [4b] corridor, gallery, hallway, passage; *also* arcade, breezeway, cloister **♦** [6] arena, theater; *also* amphitheater, hippodrome, house, playhouse; ballroom; lyceum; chamber, senate

hal·le·lu·jah \ˌha-lə-ˈlü-yə\ *interj* [Heb *hallĕlūyāh* praise (ye) the Lord] — used to express praise, joy, or thanks
hall·mark \ˈhȯl-ˌmärk\ *n* **1 ♦** : a mark put on an article to indicate origin, purity, or genuineness **2** : a distinguishing characteristic

   ♦ emblem, logo, symbol, trademark — more at EMBLEM

hal·low \ˈha-lō\ *vb* **1 ♦** : to make holy or set apart for holy use **2 ♦** : REVERE

   ♦ bless, consecrate, sanctify — more at BLESS

hal·lowed \ˈha-lōd, -lə-wəd\ *adj* **1 ♦** : made or declared sacred **2 ♦** : regarded as worthy of great honor

   ♦ [1] blessed, holy, sacred, sacrosanct, sanctified — more at HOLY **♦** [2] reverend, venerable — more at VENERABLE

Hal·low·een *also* **Hal·low·e'en** \ˌha-lə-ˈwēn, ˌhä-\ *n* : the evening of October 31 observed esp. by children in merrymaking and masquerading
hal·lu·ci·nate \hə-ˈlüs-ᵊn-ˌāt\ *vb* **-nat·ed; -nat·ing** : to have hallucinations or experience as a hallucination
hal·lu·ci·na·tion \hə-ˌlüs-ᵊn-ˈā-shən\ *n* **1** : perception of objects with no reality due usu. to use of drugs or to disorder of the nervous system **2 ♦** : something perceived by hallucination — **hal·lu·ci·na·to·ry** \-ᵊn-ə-ˌtȯr-ē\ *adj*

   ♦ chimera, conceit, daydream, delusion, dream, fancy, fantasy, figment, illusion, phantasm, pipe dream, unreality, vision

hal·lu·ci·no·gen \hə-ˈlüs-ᵊn-ə-jən\ *n* : a substance that induces hallucinations — **hal·lu·ci·no·gen·ic** \-ˌlüs-ᵊn-ə-ˌje-nik\ *adj or n*
hall·way \ˈhȯl-ˌwā\ *n* **1** : an entrance hall **2 ♦** : a passageway into which compartments or rooms open : CORRIDOR

   ♦ corridor, gallery, hall, passage — more at HALL

ha·lo \ˈhā-lō\ *n, pl* **halos** *or* **haloes** [L *halos*, fr. Gk *halōs* threshing floor, disk, halo] **1** : a circle of light appearing to surround a shining body (as the sun) **2** : the aura of glory surrounding an idealized person or thing
¹**hal·o·gen** \ˈha-lə-jən\ *n* : any of the five elements fluorine, chlorine, bromine, iodine, and astatine
²**halogen** *adj* : containing, using, or being a halogen ⟨a ∼ lamp⟩
¹**halt** \ˈhȯlt\ *adj* : LAME
²**halt** *n* **♦** : a stop in an action or process

   ♦ cessation, close, closure, conclusion, end, ending, expiration, finish, lapse, shutdown, stop, stoppage, termination — more at END

³**halt** *vb* **1** : to stop marching or traveling **2 ♦** : to come or bring to an end : DISCONTINUE

   ♦ break, break off, cease, cut, desist, discontinue, drop, end, knock off, lay off, leave off, quit, shut off, stop — more at STOP **♦** arrest, catch, check, draw up, fetch up, hold up, stall, stay, still, stop; *also* balk, block, blockade, dam, detain, hinder, hold, hold back, impede, obstruct, stem; conclude, end, terminate; call, discontinue, suspend; clamp down, rein (in), squelch, squash, stamp, stanch, stunt, suppress, turn back

¹**hal·ter** \ˈhȯl-tər\ *n* **1** : a rope or strap for leading or tying an animal; *also* : HEADSTALL **2** : NOOSE **3** : a brief blouse held in place by straps around the neck and across the back

²**halter** *vb* **hal·tered; hal·ter·ing** **1** : to catch with or as if with a halter; *also* : to put a halter on (as a horse) **2** : HANG **3** : IMPEDE, RESTRAIN
halt·ing \ˈhȯl-tiŋ\ *adj* : UNCERTAIN, FALTERING — **halt·ing·ly** *adv*
halve \ˈhav, ˈhav\ *vb* **halved; halv·ing** **1** : to divide into two equal parts **2** : to reduce to one half
halv·ers \ˈha-vərz, ˈha-\ *n pl* : half shares : HALVES
halves *pl of* HALF
hal·yard \ˈhal-yərd\ *n* : a rope or tackle for hoisting and lowering (as sails)
¹**ham** \ˈham\ *n* **1** : a buttock with its associated thigh — usu. used in pl. **2** : a cut of meat and esp. pork from the thigh **3** : a showy performer **4** : an operator of an amateur radio station — **ham** *adj*
²**ham** *vb* **hammed; ham·ming** : to overplay a part : OVERACT
ham·burg·er \ˈham-ˌbər-gər\ *or* **ham·burg** \-ˌbərg\ *n* [G *Hamburger* of Hamburg, Germany] **1** : ground beef **2** : a sandwich consisting of a ground-beef patty in a round roll
ham·let \ˈham-lət\ *n* : a small village
¹**ham·mer** \ˈha-mər\ *n* **1** : a hand tool used for pounding; *also* : something resembling a hammer in form or function **2** : the part of a gun whose striking action causes explosion of the charge **3** : a metal sphere hurled for distance in a track-and-field event (**hammer throw**) **4** : ACCELERATOR 2
²**hammer** *vb* **1 ♦** : to beat, drive, or shape with or as if with repeated blows of a hammer : POUND **2** : to produce or bring about as if by repeated blows — usu. used with *out* **3** : to criticize severely

   ♦ beat, forge, pound; *also* chase, fashion, form, knead, mold, model, work; coin, mint, stamp; carve, chisel, hew, sculpt, sculpture

ham·mer·head \ˈha-mər-ˌhed\ *n* **1** : the striking part of a hammer **2** : any of a family of medium-sized sharks with eyes at the ends of lateral extensions of the flattened head
ham·mer·lock \-ˌläk\ *n* : a wrestling hold in which an opponent's arm is held bent behind the back
hammer out *vb* **♦** : to produce or bring about as if by repeated blows

   ♦ build, carve, forge, grind, work out; *also* cobble (together *or* up), create, construct, fabricate, fashion, form, frame, manufacture, model, shape, tailor; conceive, concoct, contrive, cook (up), devise, hatch, invent, originate; bring forth, effect; accomplish, achieve, bring off

ham·mer·toe \-ˌtō\ *n* : a toe deformed by having one or more joints permanently flexed
¹**ham·mock** \ˈha-mək\ *n* [Sp *hamaca*, of AmerInd origin] : a swinging couch hung by cords at each end
²**hammock** *n* : a fertile elevated area of the southern U.S. and esp. Florida with hardwood vegetation and soil rich in humus
¹**ham·per** \ˈham-pər\ *vb* **1 ♦** : to restrict the movement or operation of : IMPEDE **2** : RESTRAIN

   ♦ clog, cramp, delay, embarrass, encumber, fetter, handicap, hinder, hobble, hold back, hold up, impede, inhibit, interfere with, manacle, obstruct, shackle, tie up, trammel; *also* arrest, brake, check, constrain, curb, rein, restrain, snag; bind, chain, handcuff, leash, muzzle, strap, tether, tie; barricade, block, blockade, dam, head (off); plug; balk, choke, hurt, repress, retard, stifle, strangle, straiten, stunt; baffle, foil, frustrate, interrupt, thwart, sabotage; bog (down), confine, hedge (in), hem (in), limit, tie (down) *Ant* aid, assist, facilitate, help

²**hamper** *n* : a large usu. lidded basket
ham·ster \ˈham-stər\ *n* [G, fr. OHG *hamustro*, of Slavic origin] : any of a subfamily of small Old World rodents with large cheek pouches
¹**ham·string** \ˈham-ˌstriŋ\ *n* : any of several muscles at the back of the thigh or tendons at the back of the knee
²**hamstring** *vb* **-strung** \-ˌstrəŋ\; **-string·ing** **1** : to cripple

by cutting the leg tendons **2** ♦ : to make ineffective or powerless

♦ cripple, disable, immobilize, incapacitate, paralyze, prostrate — more at PARALYZE

¹hand \'hand\ *n* **1** : the end of a front limb when modified (as in humans) for grasping **2** ♦ : an indicator or pointer on a dial **3** ♦ : personal possession — usu. used in pl. and in the phrase *in one's hands*; *also* : CONTROL **4** ♦ : a position regarded as opposite to another : SIDE — usu. used in the phrase *on the other hand* **5** : a pledge esp. of betrothal **6** : style of penmanship : HANDWRITING **7** : SKILL, ABILITY; *also* : a significant part **8** : ASSISTANCE; *also* : PARTICIPATION **9** : an outburst of applause **10** : a single round in a card game; *also* : the cards held by a player after a deal **11** ♦ : one employed by another usu. for wages or salary and in a position below the executive level : WORKER, EMPLOYEE; *also* : a member of a ship's crew — **hand·less** *adj* — **at hand** : near in time or place — **on hand** : in present possession or readily available

♦ [2] index, indicator, needle, pointer — more at POINTER ♦ *usu* **hands** [3] control, keeping, possession — more at POSSESSION ♦ [4] angle, aspect, facet, phase, side — more at ASPECT ♦ [11] employee, hireling, jobholder, worker — more at EMPLOYEE

²hand *vb* **1** : to lead, guide, or assist with the hand **2** ♦ : to give, pass, or transmit with the hand ⟨*~ed* her a spoon⟩

♦ deliver, feed, furnish, give, hand over, provide, supply — more at FURNISH ♦ hand over, pass, reach, transfer — more at PASS

hand·bag \'hand-,bag\ *n* ♦ : a bag for carrying small personal articles and money

♦ bag, pocketbook, purse — more at PURSE

hand·ball \-,bȯl\ *n* : a game played by striking a small rubber ball against a wall with the hand
hand·bill \-,bil\ *n* : a small printed sheet for distribution by hand
hand·book \-,bůk\ *n* ♦ : a concise reference book : MANUAL

♦ manual, primer, textbook — more at TEXTBOOK

hand·car \-,kär\ *n* : a small 4-wheeled railroad car propelled by hand or by a small motor
hand·clasp \-,klasp\ *n* : HANDSHAKE
hand·craft \-,kraft\ *vb* : to fashion by manual skill
¹hand·cuff \-,kəf\ *n* : a metal fastening that can be locked around a wrist and is usu. connected with another such fastening — usu. used in pl.
²handcuff *vb* **1** ♦ : to apply handcuffs to : MANACLE **2** ♦ : to hold in check : make ineffective or powerless

♦ [1, 2] bind, chain, enchain, fetter, manacle, shackle, trammel

hand·ed \'han-dəd\ *adj* : having or using such or so many hands ⟨a left-*handed* person⟩ — **hand·ed·ness** *n*
hand·ful \'hand-,fůl\ *n, pl* **hand·fuls** \-,fůlz\ *also* **hands·ful** \'handz-,fůl\ **1** : as much or as many as the hand will grasp **2** ♦ : a small number **3** : as much as one can manage

♦ few, smattering, sprinkle, sprinkling — more at FEW

hand·gun \-,gən\ *n* : a firearm held and fired with one hand
hand·held \'hand-,held\ *adj* : designed for use while being held in the hand — **handheld** *n*
¹hand·i·cap \'han-di-,kap\ *n* [obs. E *handicap*, a game in which forfeits were held in a cap, fr. *hand in cap*] **1** : a contest in which an artificial advantage is given or disadvantage imposed on a contestant to equalize chances of winning; *also* : the advantage given or disadvantage imposed **2** ♦ : a disadvantage that makes achievement difficult

♦ disadvantage, drawback, liability, minus, penalty, strike — more at DISADVANTAGE

²handicap *vb* **-capped; -cap·ping 1** : to give a handicap to **2** ♦ : to put at a disadvantage

♦ encumber, hamper, hinder, hold up, impede, inhibit, interfere with, obstruct, tie up — more at HAMPER

hand·i·capped *adj, sometimes offensive* : having a physical or mental disability
hand·i·cap·per \-,ka-pər\ *n* : a person who predicts the winners in a horse race usu. for a publication
hand·i·craft \'han-di-,kraft\ *n* **1** : manual skill **2** ♦ : an occupation requiring manual skill **3** : the articles fashioned by those engaged in handicraft — **hand·i·crafts·man** \-,krafts-mən\ *n*

♦ craft, trade — more at CRAFT

hand·i·craft·er \'han-di-,kraf-tər\ *n* ♦ : one that engages in a handicraft usu. as a hobby or avocation

♦ artificer, artisan, craftsman — more at ARTISAN

hand·i·ly \'han-də-lē\ *adv* ♦ : in an easy manner : without difficulty

♦ easily, effortlessly, fluently, freely, lightly, painlessly, readily, smoothly — more at EASILY

hand in glove *or* **hand and glove** *adv* : in an extremely close relationship
hand·i·work \'han-di-,wərk\ *n* **1** : work done personally or by the hands **2** ♦ : the product of handiwork

♦ affair, fruit, output, produce, product, thing, work, yield — more at PRODUCT

hand·ker·chief \'haŋ-kər-chəf, -,chēft\ *n, pl* **-chiefs** \-chəfs, -,chēfs\ *also* **-chieves** \-,chēvz\ : a small piece of cloth used for various personal purposes (as the wiping of the face)
¹han·dle \'hand-ᵊl\ *n* **1** : a part (as of a tool) designed to be grasped by the hand **2** : a word or phrase that constitutes the distinctive designation of a person or thing : NAME — **han·dled** \-ᵊld\ *adj* — **off the handle** : into a state of sudden and violent anger — usu. used with *fly*
²handle *vb* **han·dled; han·dling 1** : to touch, hold, or manage with the hands **2** ♦ : to have responsibility for **3** : to deal or trade in **4** : to behave in a certain way when managed or directed ⟨a car that *~s* well⟩ **5** ♦ : to act on or perform a required function with regard to — **han·dler** *n*

♦ [2] contend with, cope with, grapple with, manage, maneuver (or manoeuvre), negotiate, swing, treat; *also* bring off, carry out, pull, swing; command, direct, guide, steer; control, regulate, run *Ant* fumble, muddle (through) ♦ [2] administer, carry on, conduct, control, direct, govern, guide, manage, operate, oversee, regulate, run, superintend, supervise — more at CONDUCT ♦ [5] act, be, deal, serve, treat, use — more at TREAT

han·dle·bar \'hand-ᵊl-,bär\ *n* : a usu. bent bar with a grip at each end (as for steering a bicycle) — usu. used in pl.
hand·made \'hand-'mād\ *adj* : made by hand or by a hand process
hand·maid·en \-,mād-ᵊn\ *also* **hand·maid** \-,mād\ *n* : a female attendant
hand–me–down \-me-,daůn\ *adj* : used by one person after having been used by another — **hand–me–down** *n*
hand·out \'hand-,aůt\ *n* **1** : a portion (as of food) given to a beggar **2** : a piece of printed information for free distribution; *also* : a prepared statement released to the press
hand over *vb* ♦ : to yield control of

♦ cede, deliver, give up, leave, relinquish, render, surrender, turn over, yield — more at SURRENDER ♦ hand, pass, reach, transfer — more at PASS

hand·pick \'hand-'pik\ *vb* ♦ : to select personally ⟨a *~ed* candidate⟩

♦ choose, cull, elect, name, opt, pick, prefer, select, single, take — more at CHOOSE

hand·rail \-,rāl\ *n* : a narrow rail for grasping as a support
hand·saw \-,sȯ\ *n* : a saw designed to be used with one hand
hands down *adv* **1** : with little effort **2** : without question
hand·sel \'han-səl\ *n* **1** : a gift made as a token of good luck **2** : a first installment : earnest money
hand·set \'hand-,set\ *n* : a combined telephone transmitter and receiver mounted on a handle

hand·shake \-ˌshāk\ *n* : a clasping usu. of right hands by two people

hands–off \ˈhandz-ˈȯf\ *adj* : characterized by noninterference

hand·some \ˈhan-səm\ *adj* **hand·som·er; -est** [ME *handsom* easy to manipulate] **1** : moderately large : SIZABLE ⟨a ~ profit⟩ **2** : GENEROUS, LIBERAL **3** ♦ : pleasing and usu. impressive in appearance

♦ attractive, beautiful, fair, gorgeous, knockout, lovely, pretty, ravishing, stunning — more at BEAUTIFUL

hand·some·ly \-lē\ *adv* ♦ : in a handsome manner

♦ bountifully, generously, liberally, well — more at WELL

hand·some·ness \-nəs\ *n* ♦ : the quality or state of being handsome

♦ class, elegance, grace, majesty, refinement, stateliness — more at ELEGANCE ♦ attractiveness, beauty, comeliness, looks, loveliness, prettiness — more at BEAUTY

hands–on \ˈhandz-ˈȯn, -ˈän\ *adj* **1** : being or providing direct practical experience in the operation of something **2** : characterized by active personal involvement ⟨~ management⟩

hand·spring \ˈhand-ˌspriŋ\ *n* : an acrobatic feat in which the body turns in a full circle from a standing position and lands first on the hands and then on the feet

hand·stand \-ˌstand\ *n* : an act of supporting the body on the hands with the trunk and legs balanced in the air

hand–to–hand *adj* : involving physical contact or very close range ⟨~ fighting⟩ — **hand to hand** *adv*

hand–to–mouth *adj* : having or providing nothing to spare

hand·wo·ven \ˈhand-ˌwō-vən\ *adj* : produced on a hand-operated loom

hand·writ·ing \-ˌrī-tiŋ\ *n* **1** ♦ : writing done by hand **2** ♦ : the form of writing peculiar to a person — **hand·writ·ten** \-ˌrit-ᵊn\ *adj*

♦ [1] manuscript, penmanship, script; *also* lettering; shorthand *Ant* print, type ♦ [2] hand, penmanship, script; *also* scratch, scrawl, scribble; backhand, print; autograph, signature

handy \ˈhan-dē\ *adj* **hand·i·er; -est** **1** ♦ : conveniently near **2** : easily used ⟨a ~ tool⟩ **3** ♦ : clever in using the hands : DEXTEROUS — **hand·i·ness** \-dē-nəs\ *n*

♦ [1] accessible, convenient, reachable — more at CONVENIENT ♦ [3] clever, cunning, deft, dexterous — more at DEXTEROUS

handy·man \-ˌman\ *n* **1** : one who does odd jobs **2** : one competent in a variety of small skills or repair work

¹**hang** \ˈhaŋ\ *vb* **hung** \ˈhəŋ\ *also* **hanged; hang·ing** **1** ♦ : to fasten or remain fastened to an elevated point without support from below; *also* : to fasten or be fastened so as to allow free motion on the point of suspension ⟨~ a door⟩ **2** : to suspend by the neck until dead; *also* : to die by hanging **3** : to hold or bear in a suspended or inclined manner : DROOP ⟨*hung* his head in shame⟩ **4** : to fasten to a wall ⟨~ wallpaper⟩ **5** : to prevent (a jury) from coming to a decision **6** : to display (pictures) in a gallery **7** ♦ : to remain stationary in the air **8** ♦ : to be imminent : IMPEND ⟨doom *hung* over the nation⟩ **9** : DEPEND **10** : to take hold for support **11** : to be burdensome **12** : to undergo delay **13** : to incline downward; *also* : to fit or fall from the figure in easy lines **14** : to be raptly attentive **15** : LINGER, LOITER — **hang·er** *n*

♦ [1] dangle, sling, suspend, swing; *also* hook, pin, tack; drape, festoon, garland, string; extend (out), jut, project, stick out; overhang, protrude; cascade, depend, fall ♦ [7] drift, float, glide, hover, poise, ride, sail, waft — more at FLOAT ♦ *usu* hang over [8] hover, menace, overhang, threaten — more at THREATEN

²**hang** *n* **1** : the manner in which a thing hangs **2** : an understanding of something

han·gar \ˈhaŋ-ər\ *n* [F] : a covered and usu. enclosed area for housing and repairing aircraft

hang around *vb* **1** ♦ : to pass time or stay aimlessly in or at **2** ♦ : to spend one's time in company esp. idly

♦ *usu* hang around in [1] frequent, hang out, haunt, resort, visit — more at FREQUENT ♦ [1] abide, dwell, remain, stay, stick around, tarry — more at STAY ♦ [2] associate, chum, consort, fraternize, hobnob, pal — more at ASSOCIATE

hang back *vb* ♦ : to be reluctant

♦ falter, hesitate, shilly-shally, stagger, teeter, vacillate, waver, wobble — more at HESITATE

hang·dog \ˈhaŋ-ˌdȯg\ *adj* **1** ♦ : affected by or showing embarrassment caused by consciousness of a fault : ASHAMED, GUILTY **2** : ABJECT, COWED

♦ ashamed, contrite, guilty, penitent, remorseful, repentant, shamefaced — more at GUILTY

hang·er \ˈhaŋ-ər\ *n* **1** : one that hangs **2** : a device that fits inside or around a garment for hanging from a hook or rod

hang·er–on \ˈhaŋ-ər-ˈȯn, -ˈän\ *n, pl* **hangers–on** ♦ : one who hangs around a person or place esp. for personal gain

♦ leech, parasite, sponge — more at LEECH

hang in *vb* : to persist tenaciously

hang·ing *n* **1** : an execution by strangling or snapping the neck by a suspended noose **2** : something hung

hang·man \ˈhaŋ-mən\ *n* **1** : a public executioner **2** : a game in which players must identify an unknown word by guessing the letters that comprise it within a designated number of chances

hang·nail \-ˌnāl\ *n* : a bit of skin hanging loose at the edge of a fingernail

hang on *vb* **1** : HANG IN **2** : to keep a telephone connection open **3** ♦ : to keep hold onto something

♦ *usu* hang on to hold, keep, reserve, retain, withhold — more at KEEP ♦ *usu* hang on to clench, cling, clutch, grip, hold, hold on — more at HOLD

hang·out \ˈhaŋ-ˌau̇t\ *n* ♦ : a favorite place for spending time

♦ haunt, rendezvous, resort; *also* camp, canteen, club, clubhouse, den, harbor, haven, nest, refuge, retreat

hang out *vb* ♦ : to spend time idly or in loitering around or in a particular place

♦ *usu* hang out at frequent, hang around, haunt, resort, visit — more at FREQUENT ♦ dally, dawdle, dillydally, hang around, idle, loaf, loll, lounge — more at IDLE

hang·over \-ˌō-vər\ *n* **1** : something that remains from what is past **2** : disagreeable physical effects following heavy drinking or the use of drugs

hang–up \ˈhaŋ-ˌəp\ *n* : a source of mental or emotional difficulty

hang up *vb* **1** : to place on a hook or hanger **2** : to end a telephone conversation by breaking the connection **3** : to keep delayed or suspended

hank \ˈhaŋk\ *n* : COIL, LOOP ⟨a ~ of rope⟩

han·ker \ˈhaŋ-kər\ *vb* ♦ : to desire strongly or persistently — often used with *for* or *after*

♦ *usu* hanker for *or* hanker after ache for, covet, crave, desire, die for, hunger for, long for, lust (for *or* after), pine for, repine for, thirst for, want, wish for, yearn for — more at DESIRE

han·ker·ing *n* ♦ : the experience of one that hankers : strong desire

♦ appetite, craving, desire, drive, hunger, itch, longing, lust, passion, thirst, urge, yearning, yen — more at DESIRE

han·kie *or* **han·ky** \ˈhaŋ-kē\ *n, pl* **hankies** : HANDKERCHIEF

han·ky–pan·ky \ˌhaŋ-kē-ˈpaŋ-kē\ *n* **1** ♦ : questionable or underhanded activity **2** : sexual dalliance

♦ artifice, chicanery, subterfuge, trickery, wile — more at TRICKERY

hansel *var of* HANDSEL

han·som \ˈhan-səm\ *n* : a 2-wheeled covered carriage with the driver's seat elevated at the rear

han·ta·virus \ˈhän-tə-ˌvī-rəs, ˈhən-, ˈhan-\ *n* : any of a genus of viruses including some transmitted by rodents that cause pneumonia or hemorrhagic fevers

Ha·nuk·kah \'kä-nə-kə, 'hä-\ *n* [Heb *ḥănukkāh* dedication] : an 8-day Jewish holiday commemorating the rededication of the Temple of Jerusalem after its defilement by Antiochus of Syria

hap \'hap\ *n* **1** : something that happens : HAPPENING **2** : a force which shapes events unpredictably : CHANCE

¹hap·haz·ard \hap-'ha-zərd\ *n* : CHANCE

²haphazard *adj* ♦ : marked by lack of plan or order — **hap·haz·ard·ly** *adv* — **hap·haz·ard·ness** *n*

♦ aimless, arbitrary, desultory, erratic, random, scattered, stray — more at RANDOM

hap·less \'hap-ləs\ *adj* ♦ : having no luck : UNFORTUNATE — **hap·less·ly** *adv* — **hap·less·ness** *n*

♦ ill-fated, ill-starred, luckless, unfortunate, unhappy, unlucky — more at UNLUCKY

hap·loid \'hap-ˌlȯid\ *adj* : having the number of chromosomes characteristic of gametic cells — **haploid** *n*

hap·ly \'hap-lē\ *adv* : by chance

hap·pen \'ha-pən\ *vb* **1** : to occur by chance **2** ♦ : to come into being or occur as an event, process, or result **3** ♦ : to come casually or unexpectedly : CHANCE **2** — used with *on* or *upon*

♦ [2] be, befall, betide, chance, come, go, occur, pass, transpire; *also* arise, develop, materialize, crop (up), spring (up); intervene; fall out, go off, proceed, turn out ♦ *usu* **happen on** *or* **happen upon** [3] chance, encounter, find, hit, meet, stumble; *also* confront, face; discover, turn up

¹hap·pen·ing *n* **1** ♦ : something that happens : OCCURRENCE **2** ♦ : an event that is esp. interesting, entertaining, or important

♦ [1] affair, circumstance, episode, event, incident, occasion, occurrence, thing — more at EVENT ♦ [2] adventure, experience, time — more at ADVENTURE

²happening *adj* **1** : very fashionable **2** : offering much stimulating activity ⟨a ∼ nightclub⟩

hap·pi·ly \'ha-pə-lē\ *adv* **1** : LUCKILY **2** ♦ : in a happy manner or state ⟨lived ∼ ever after⟩ **3** ♦ : in an adequate or fitting manner

♦ [2] cheerfully, gaily, heartily, jovially, merrily, mirthfully — more at GAILY ♦ [3] appropriately, correctly, fittingly, properly, rightly, suitably — more at PROPERLY

hap·pi·ness \'ha-pē-nəs\ *n* **1 a** ♦ : a state of well-being and contentment **b** ♦ : a pleasurable satisfaction **2** : APTNESS

♦ [1a] blessedness, bliss, felicity, gladness, joy; *also* elation, exhilaration, exultation, intoxication; ecstasy, euphoria, heaven, rapture; delectation, delight, enjoyment, pleasure; cheer, cheerfulness, exuberance, gaiety, glee, jollity, joyousness, jubilation, lightheartedness; content, contentedness, gratification, satisfaction *Ant* misery, sadness, unhappiness, wretchedness ♦ [1b] content, contentedness, contentment, gratification, pleasure, satisfaction

hap·py \'ha-pē\ *adj* **hap·pi·er; -est** **1** ♦ : favored by luck or fortune : FORTUNATE **2** ♦ : notably fitting, effective, or well adapted : APT, FELICITOUS **3** : enjoying well-being and contentment **4 a** : PLEASANT **b** ♦ : made pleased, satisfied, or grateful

♦ [1] fluky, fortuitous, fortunate, lucky, providential — more at FORTUNATE ♦ [2] applicable, appropriate, apt, felicitous, fit, fitting, good, meet, proper, right, suitable — more at FIT ♦ [4b] blissful, content, delighted, glad, joyful, pleased — more at GLAD

hap·py–go–lucky \ˌha-pē-gō-'lə-kē\ *adj* ♦ : blithely unconcerned

♦ carefree, careless, cavalier, easygoing, gay, insouciant, lighthearted, unconcerned

happy hour *n* : a period of time when the price of drinks at a bar is reduced

hap·tics \'hap-tiks\ *n* **1** : the use of electronically or mechanically generated movement that a user experiences through the sense of touch as part of an interface (as on a gaming console) **2** : a science concerned with the sense of touch

hara–kiri \ˌhar-i-'kir-ē, -'kar-ē\ *n* [Jp *harakiri*, fr. *hara* belly + *kiri* cutting] : ritual suicide by disembowelment

¹ha·rangue \hə-'raŋ\ *n* **1** ♦ : a ranting speech or writing **2** ♦ : a speech addressed to a public assembly

♦ [1] diatribe, rant, tirade — more at TIRADE ♦ [2] address, declamation, oration, speech, talk — more at SPEECH

²harangue *vb* ♦ : to make a harangue — **ha·rangu·er** *n*

♦ declaim, descant, discourse, lecture, orate, speak, talk — more at TALK

ha·rass \hə-'ras, 'har-əs\ *vb* [F *harasser*, fr. MF, fr. *harer* to set a dog on, fr. OF *hare*, interj. used to incite dogs, of Gmc origin] **1** : EXHAUST, FATIGUE **2** : to worry and impede by repeated raids **3** : to annoy continually

ha·rass·ment \-mənt\ *n* **1** ♦ : the act or an instance of harassing **2** : the condition of being harassed

♦ aggravation, annoyance, disturbance, vexation — more at ANNOYANCE

¹har·bin·ger \'här-bən-jər\ *n* **1** ♦ : one that announces or foreshadows what is coming : PRECURSOR **2** : PORTENT

♦ angel, forerunner, herald, precursor — more at FORERUNNER

²harbinger *vb* ♦ : to be a harbinger of

♦ foreshadow, prefigure — more at FORESHADOW

¹har·bor *or Can and Brit* **har·bour** \'här-bər\ *n* **1** ♦ : a place of security and comfort **2** ♦ : a part of a body of water protected and deep enough to furnish anchorage : PORT

♦ [1] asylum, haven, refuge, retreat, sanctuary, shelter — more at SHELTER ♦ [2] anchorage, haven, port; *also* seaport; roads, roadstead

²harbor *or Can and Brit* **harbour** *vb* **1** : to give or take refuge : SHELTER **2 a** ♦ : to be the home or habitat of **b** : LIVE **3** ♦ : to hold a thought or feeling ⟨∼ a grudge⟩

♦ [2a] accommodate, billet, chamber, domicile, house, lodge, put up, quarter, roof, shelter, take in — more at HOUSE ♦ [3] bear, cherish, entertain, have, hold, nurse; *also* cultivate, foster, nurture, support, sustain; carry, keep, maintain, preserve, remember, retain, treasure; cleave (to), cling (to), hang on (to), stick (to)

har·bor·age *or Can and Brit* **har·bour·age** \'här-bə-rij\ *n* **1** : a place of security and comfort **2** : a part of a body of water protected and deep enough to furnish anchorage : HARBOR

¹hard \'härd\ *adj* **1** ♦ : not easily penetrated : not easily yielding to pressure **2** : high in alcoholic content **3** : containing salts that prevent lathering with soap ⟨∼ water⟩ **4** : stable in value ⟨∼ currency⟩ **5 a** : physically fit **b** ♦ : resistant to stress or disease **6 a** ♦ : not subject to change or revision : FIRM ⟨∼ agreement⟩ **b** ♦ : based on clear fact ⟨∼ evidence⟩ **7** : CLOSE, SEARCHING ⟨∼ look⟩ **8** : free from sentimentality or illusion : REALISTIC ⟨good ∼ sense⟩ **9** ♦ : lacking in responsiveness : OBDURATE, UNFEELING ⟨∼ heart⟩ **10** : difficult to bear ⟨∼ times⟩; *also* : HARSH, SEVERE **11** ♦ : caused or marked by resentment ⟨∼ feelings⟩ **12 a** ♦ : making no concession : STRICT **b** : rigidly firm in will or purpose : UNRELENTING **13** : INCLEMENT ⟨∼ winter⟩ **14** : intense in force, manner, or degree ⟨∼ blow⟩ **15** ♦ : demanding the exertion of considerable effort : ARDUOUS, STRENUOUS ⟨∼ work⟩ **16** : sounding as in *arcing* and *geese* respectively — used of *c* and *g* **17** : TROUBLESOME ⟨∼ problem⟩ **18** : having difficulty in doing something ⟨∼ of hearing⟩ **19** : addictive and gravely detrimental to health ⟨∼ drugs⟩ **20** : of or relating to the natural sciences and esp. the physical sciences

♦ [1] compact, firm, rigid, solid, stiff, unyielding — more at FIRM ♦ [5b] hard-bitten, hardy, rugged, stout, strong, sturdy, tough, vigorous — more at HARDY ♦ [6a] certain, determinate, final, firm, fixed, flat, frozen, hard-and-fast, set, settled, stable — more at FIXED ♦ [6b] documentary, factual, historical, literal, matter-of-fact, nonfictional, objective, true — more at FACTUAL ♦ [9] callous, cold-blooded, heartless, inhuman, inhumane, merciless, obdurate, pitiless, ruthless, soulless, stony, uncharitable, unfeeling, unsparing, unsympathetic; *also* inconsiderate, thoughtless, unfriendly, unloving, unthinking; hard-bitten, grim, harsh, heavy-handed, oppressive, rough, severe, stern, tough, ungentle; abusive, acrimonious, disagreeable, hateful, ill-natured, ill-tempered, malevolent, malicious, mean, rancorous, spiteful, surly, virulent; barbarous, brutal, brutish, bestial, cruel, evil-minded, savage, vicious *Ant* charitable, compassionate, humane, merciful, sensitive, sympathetic, tender, tenderhearted, warm, warmhearted ♦ [11] acrid, acrimonious, bitter, rancorous, resentful, sore — more at BITTER ♦ [12a] austere, authoritarian, flinty, harsh, heavy-handed, ramrod, rigid, rigorous, severe, stern, strict — more at SEVERE ♦ [15] arduous, demanding, difficult, exacting, formidable, grueling, herculean, laborious, murderous, rough, stiff, strenuous, tall, toilsome, tough; *also* abstract, abstruse, complex, complicated, insoluble, intricate, involved, knotty, problematic, recondite, serious, spiny, thorny, ticklish, tricky, stubborn; burdensome, exhausting, labored, onerous, oppressive, problem, sore, stressful, taxing, tight, trying, uphill; annoying, distressing, bothersome, irksome, troublesome, vexatious; grievous, grim, heavy, strict, stringent; brutal, cruel, inhuman, painful *Ant* easy, effortless, facile, simple, soft, undemanding

²hard *adv* 1 a ♦ : with great or utmost effort or energy b ♦ : in a fierce or violent manner 2 a ♦ : in such a manner as to cause hardship, difficulty, or pain b ♦ : with rancor, bitterness, or grief 3 ♦ : close in time or space

♦ [1a] determinedly, diligently, hardly, laboriously, mightily, slavishly, strenuously, tirelessly; *also* actively, briskly, busily, energetically, feverishly, vehemently, vigorously, zealously; continuously, indefatigably, ploddingly, steadily, unrelentingly, unremittingly; ardently, attentively, conscientiously, earnestly, exhaustively, meticulously, painstakingly, seriously, thoroughly ♦ [1b] energetically, firmly, forcefully, forcibly, mightily, powerfully, stiffly, stoutly, strenuously, strongly, sturdily, vigorously; *also* robustly, sharply, vehemently, violently; briskly, crisply, heartily, lustily, vivaciously; decidedly, determinedly, directly, emphatically, fast, fixedly, intensively, intently, resolutely, rigidly, smartly, solidly, soundly, squarely, steadfastly, steadily, surely; aggressively, manfully *Ant* feebly, gently, softly, weakly ♦ [2a] hardly, harshly, ill, oppressively, roughly, severely, sternly, stiffly — more at HARDLY ♦ [2b] agonizingly, bitterly, grievously, hardly, sadly, sorrowfully, unhappily, woefully, wretchedly; *also* abjectly, dejectedly, despondently, blackly, darkly, forlornly, gloomily, miserably; acutely, harshly, keenly, severely, sharply; cruelly, ill *Ant* gladly, happily, joyfully, joyously ♦ [3] around, by, close, in, near, nearby, nigh — more at NEAR

hard-and-fast *adj* ♦ : rigidly binding ⟨a ~ rule⟩

♦ certain, determinate, final, firm, fixed, flat, frozen, hard, set, settled, stable — more at FIXED ♦ fast, fixed, immutable, inflexible, unalterable, unchangeable — more at INFLEXIBLE

hard·back \'härd-ˌbak\ *n* : a hardcover book
hard·ball \-ˌbȯl\ *n* 1 : BASEBALL 2 : forceful uncompromising methods
hard-bit·ten \-'bit-ᵊn\ *adj* ♦ : seasoned or steeled by difficult experience : TOUGH ⟨~ campaigners⟩

♦ hard, hardy, rugged, stout, strong, sturdy, tough, vigorous — more at HARDY
hard-board \-ˌbȯrd\ *n* : a very dense fiberboard
hard-boiled \-'bȯi(-ə)ld\ *adj* 1 : boiled until both white and yolk have solidified ⟨~ eggs⟩ 2 a : lacking sentiment b : HARDHEADED 2
hard-bound \-ˌbaúnd\ *adj* : HARDCOVER
hard copy *n* : a copy of textual or graphic information (as from computer storage) produced on paper
hard-core \'härd-'kȯr\ *adj* 1 : extremely resistant to solution or improvement 2 : being the most determined or dedicated members of a specified group 3 : containing explicit depictions of sex acts — hard core *n*
hard-cov·er \-'kə-vər\ *adj* : having rigid boards on the sides covered in cloth or paper ⟨~ books⟩
hard disk *n* : a sealed rigid metal disk used as a computer storage device
hard-drive *n* : a data-storage device consisting of a drive and one or more hard disks
hard-driv·ing \'härd()-'drī-viŋ\ *adj* ♦ : intensely ambitious, energetic, or hardworking

♦ ambitious, go-getting, self-seeking — more at AMBITIOUS
hard·en \'härd-ᵊn\ *vb* 1 ♦ : to make or become hard or harder 2 : to confirm or become confirmed in disposition or action 3 ♦ : to make hardy or robust — hard·en·er *n*

♦ [1] concrete, congeal, firm, freeze, set, solidify; *also* cake, callus, encrust; coagulate, clot, gel, jell, jelly, stiffen, thicken; calcify, crystallize, ossify, petrify; anneal, temper *Ant* soften ♦ [3] fortify, season, steel, strengthen, toughen; *also* acclimate, acclimatize, adapt, adjust; anneal, temper; invigorate, vitalize; immunize; bolster, boost, brace, buttress, forearm, prop (up), reinforce, support; break in, limber (up), train; accustom, condition, habituate, naturalize *Ant* soften
hard·hack \'härd-ˌhak\ *n* : an American spirea with dense clusters of pink or white flowers and leaves having a hairy rusty yellow underside
hard hat *n* 1 : a protective hat worn esp. by construction workers 2 : a construction worker
hard·head·ed \'härd-'he-dəd\ *adj* 1 ♦ : unreasonably or perversely unyielding : STUBBORN, WILLFUL 2 ♦ : concerned with or involving practical considerations — hard·head·ed·ly *adv*

♦ [1] dogged, headstrong, mulish, obdurate, obstinate, opinionated, peevish, pertinacious, perverse, pigheaded, stubborn, unyielding, willful — more at OBSTINATE ♦ [2] astute, canny, knowing, sharp, shrewd, smart — more at SHREWD ♦ [2] down-to-earth, earthy, matter-of-fact, practical, pragmatic, realistic
hard·head·ed·ness \-nəs\ *n* ♦ : the quality or state of being hardheaded

♦ mulishness, obduracy, obstinacy, peevishness, pertinacity, self-will, stubbornness, tenacity — more at OBSTINACY
hard-heart·ed \-'här-təd\ *adj* : PITILESS, CRUEL — hard-heart·ed·ly *adv* — hard-heart·ed·ness *n*
har·di·hood \'här-dē-ˌhúd\ *n* 1 : resolute courage and fortitude 2 : active bodily or mental strength or force : VIGOR

♦ bravery, courage, daring, fearlessness, gallantry, guts, heart, heroism, nerve, stoutness, valor — more at COURAGE
hard-line \'härd-'līn\ *adj* : advocating or involving a rigidly uncompromising course of action ⟨a ~ conservative⟩ — hard-lin·er \-'lī-nər\ *n*
hard-luck \-ˌlək\ *adj* ♦ : marked by or relating to bad luck ⟨~ losing teams⟩

♦ hapless, ill-fated, ill-starred, luckless, unfortunate, unhappy, unlucky — more at UNLUCKY
hard·ly \'härd-lē\ *adv* 1 : with force 2 a ♦ : in a severe manner : HARSHLY b : with great or excessive grief or

resentment **3 ♦** : with difficulty : by hard work or struggle **4 ♦** : only just : BARELY **5 ♦** : certainly not

♦ [2a] hard, harshly, ill, oppressively, roughly, severely, sternly, stiffly; *also* callously, inhumanly, mercilessly, pitilessly, ruthlessly, uncharitably, unfeelingly, unmercifully, tyrannically; abusively, brutally, savagely, viciously; aggressively, decidedly, determinedly, firmly, grimly, gruffly, resolutely, strongly, toughly **Ant** gently, leniently, lightly, mildly, softly **♦ [3]** determinedly, diligently, hard, laboriously, mightily, slavishly, strenuously, tirelessly — more at HARD **♦ [4]** barely, just, marginally, scarcely, slightly — more at JUST **♦ [5]** no, none, scarcely; *also* near, never, nothing, nowhere, nowise **Ant** absolutely, certainly, completely, definitely, positively, surely

hard·ness \-nəs\ *n* **1 ♦** : the quality or state of being hard **2 ♦** : a condition that makes life difficult, challenging, or uncomfortable

♦ [1] harshness, inflexibility, rigidity, severity, sternness, strictness — more at SEVERITY **♦ [2]** adversity, asperity, difficulty, hardship, rigor — more at DIFFICULTY

hard–nosed \'härd-'nōzd\ *adj* : TOUGH, UNCOMPROMISING; *also* : HARDHEADED 2

hard palate *n* : the bony anterior part of the palate forming the roof of the mouth

hard·pan \'härd-,pan\ *n* : a compact layer in soil that is impenetrable by roots

hard–pressed \-'prest\ *adj* : HARD PUT; *esp* : being under financial strain

hard put *adj* **1** : barely able **2** : faced with difficulty or perplexity

hard rock *n* : rock music marked by a heavy beat, high amplification, and usu. frenzied performances

hard–shell \'härd-,shel\ *adj* : HIDEBOUND, UNCOMPROMISING ⟨a ~ conservative⟩

hard·ship \-,ship\ *n* **1** : SUFFERING, PRIVATION **2 ♦** : something that causes suffering or privation

♦ adversity, asperity, difficulty, hardness, rigor — more at DIFFICULTY

hard·tack \-,tak\ *n* : a saltless hard biscuit, bread, or cracker
hard·top \-,täp\ *n* : an automobile having a permanent rigid top
hard up *adj* **♦** : short of money

♦ broke, destitute, impecunious, impoverished, indigent, needy, penniless, penurious, poor, poverty-stricken — more at POOR

hard·ware \-,war\ *n* **1** : ware (as cutlery or tools) made of metal **2 ♦** : major items of equipment or their components used for a particular purpose **3** : the physical components (as electronic devices) of a vehicle (as a spacecraft) or an apparatus (as a computer)

♦ accoutrements (*or* accouterments), apparatus, equipment, gear, matériel, outfit, paraphernalia, stuff, tackle — more at EQUIPMENT

hard–wired \-,wī(-ə)rd\ *adj* **1** : connected or incorporated by or as if by permanent electrical connections **2** : genetically or innately determined or predisposed ⟨~ reactions⟩ ⟨is ~ to avoid change⟩

hard·wood \-,wùd\ *n* : the wood of a broad-leaved usu. deciduous tree as distinguished from that of a conifer; *also* : such a tree — **hardwood** *adj*
hard·work·ing \-'wər-kiŋ\ *adj* : INDUSTRIOUS
har·dy \'här-dē\ *adj* **har·di·er; -est** **1** : BOLD, BRAVE ⟨~ pioneers⟩ **2 ♦** : intrepidly daring : AUDACIOUS **3 a** : ROBUST **b ♦** : able to withstand adverse conditions ⟨~ shrubs⟩ — **har·di·ly** \-də-lē\ *adv* — **har·di·ness** \-dē-nəs\ *n*

♦ [2] adventurous, audacious, bold, daring, enterprising, gutsy, nervy, venturesome — more at BOLD **♦ [3b]** hard, hard-bitten, rugged, stout, strong, sturdy, tough, vigorous; *also* flinty, leathery, resilient, stalwart; durable, enduring, everlasting, immortal, imperishable,

lasting, permanent, stable, staunch, staying, tenacious, unyielding; prospering, thriving; able-bodied, brawny, muscular; fit, fortified, hale, healthy, husky, lusty, robust, sound, strapping, virile; annealed, seasoned, tempered **Ant** delicate, soft, tender, weak

hare \'har\ *n, pl* **hare** *or* **hares** : any of various swift timid long-eared mammals like the related rabbits but born with open eyes and fur

hare·bell \'har-,bel\ *n* : a slender herb with bright blue bell-shaped flowers

hare·brained \-'brānd\ *adj* : lacking in sense, judgment, or discretion ⟨a ~ scheme⟩ ⟨~ notions⟩

♦ absurd, crazy, cuckoo, fatuous, foolish, mad, nonsensical, nutty, senseless, silly, stupid — more at FOOLISH

hare·lip \-'lip\ *n, sometimes offensive* : a birth defect characterized by one or more clefts in the upper lip

ha·rem \'har-əm\ *n* [Ar *ḥarīm*, lit., something forbidden & *ḥaram*, lit., sanctuary] **1** : a house or part of a house allotted to women in a Muslim household **2** : the women and servants occupying a harem **3** : a group of females associated with one male

hark \'härk\ *vb* **♦** : to pay close attention : LISTEN

♦ attend, hear, heed, listen, mind — more at LISTEN

harken *var of* HEARKEN
har·le·quin \'här-li-kən, -kwən\ *n* **1** *cap* : a character (as in comedy) with a shaved head, masked face, variegated tights, and wooden sword **2 ♦** : a fool or comedian in an entertainment (as a circus) : CLOWN

♦ buffoon, clown, zany — more at CLOWN

har·lot \'här-lət\ *n* : a woman who engages in sexual activities esp. for money : PROSTITUTE

¹harm \'härm\ *n* **1 ♦** : physical or mental damage : INJURY **2** : MISCHIEF, HURT

♦ damage, detriment, hurt, injury — more at INJURY

²harm *vb* **♦** : to cause harm to : INJURE

♦ damage, hurt, injure, wound — more at INJURE

harm·ful \-fəl\ *adj* **♦** : of a kind likely to be damaging — **harm·ful·ly** *adv* — **harm·ful·ness** *n*

♦ adverse, bad, baleful, baneful, damaging, deleterious, detrimental, evil, hurtful, ill, injurious, mischievous, noxious, pernicious, prejudicial; *also* hostile, inimical, unfriendly; contagious, deadly, infectious, pestilent, pestilential, poisonous, venomous; insidious, menacing, ominous, sinister, threatening; dangerous, hazardous, imperiling, parlous, perilous, risky, unsafe, unsound; nasty, noisome, unhealthful, unhealthy, unwholesome; destructive, fatal, lethal, malignant, ruinous **Ant** harmless, innocent, innocuous, inoffensive, safe

harm·less \-ləs\ *adj* **♦** : lacking capacity or intent to injure — **harm·less·ly** *adv* — **harm·less·ness** *n*

♦ innocent, innocuous, safe, white; *also* healthful, healthy, salubrious, wholesome; benign, benignant; sound, trustworthy; gentle, gracious, mild; nonthreatening, painless, unobjectionable; noncorrosive, nondestructive, nonfatal, noninfectious, nonlethal, nonpoisonous, nontoxic, nonvenomous **Ant** adverse, bad, harmful, hurtful, ill, injurious

¹har·mon·ic \här-'mä-nik\ *adj* **1** : of or relating to musical harmony or harmonics **2** : pleasing to the ear — **har·mon·i·cal·ly** \-ni-k(ə-)lē\ *adv*
²harmonic *n* : a musical overtone
har·mon·i·ca \här-'mä-ni-kə\ *n* : a small wind instrument in which the sound is produced by metal reeds
har·mo·ni·ous \här-'mō-nē-əs\ *adj* **1 ♦** : musically concordant **2 ♦** : having the parts agreeably related : CONGRUOUS **3 ♦** : marked by accord in sentiment or action ⟨a ~ relationship⟩ — **har·mo·ni·ous·ly** *adv* — **har·mo·ni·ous·ness** *n*

♦ [1] euphonious, melodious, musical, symphonic, tuneful; *also* blending, chiming, flowing, mellifluous; dulcet, mellow, melodic, sweet; resonant, sonorous; quavering, trilling, warbling; agreeable, appealing, pleasant; cadenced, lyric, lyrical, rhythmic; harmonic, orchestral, polyphonic, tonal *Ant* discordant, dissonant, inharmonious, unmelodious, unmusical ♦ [2] balanced, congruous, consonant; *also* even, proportioned, regular, symmetrical; aesthetic, artistic, becoming, elegant, graceful, tasteful; agreeable, felicitous, pleasant, pleasing, satisfying; compatible, coordinated, correspondent, matched, matching *Ant* incongruous, inharmonious, unbalanced ♦ [3] agreeable, amicable, compatible, congenial, kindred, unanimous, united; *also* pacific, peaceable, peaceful; collaborating, cooperative, symbiotic; noncompeting, noncompetitive, nonconflicting; sympathetic, tolerant, understanding; affable, amiable, cordial, friendly, genial, neighborly; collaborating *Ant* disagreeable, disunited, incompatible, inharmonious, uncongenial

har·mo·nise *chiefly Brit var of* HARMONIZE
har·mo·ni·um \här-ˈmō-nē-əm\ *n* : a keyboard wind instrument in which the wind acts on a set of metal reeds
har·mo·nize \ˈhär-mə-ˌnīz\ *vb* **-nized; -niz·ing** **1** : to play or sing in harmony **2** ♦ : to be in harmony **3** ♦ : to bring into consonance or accord — **har·mo·ni·za·tion** \ˌhär-mə-nə-ˈzā-shən\ *n*

♦ [2, 3] agree, blend, conform, coordinate; *also* balance, correlate, correspond, dovetail, match; meet, parallel; bond, coalesce, cohere, conjoin, fuse, merge, square, tally *Ant* clash, collide, conflict ♦ [3] accommodate, conciliate, conform, coordinate, key, reconcile; *also* adapt, attune, tune; blend, combine, connect, correlate, dovetail, fit, fuse, integrate, join, match, merge, orchestrate, pair, square, suit, synchronize, synthesize, unify, unite; align, arrange, array, balance, equalize, even, order, proportion, regularize, standardize *Ant* alienate, disjoin

har·mo·ny \ˈhär-mə-nē\ *n, pl* **-nies** [ME *armony*, fr. AF *armonie*, fr. L *harmonia*, fr. Gk, joint, harmony, fr. *harmos* joint] **1** : musical agreement of sounds; *esp* : the combination of tones into chords and progressions of chords **2 a** ♦ : a pleasing arrangement of parts **b** ♦ : balanced interrelationship **3** : internal calm

♦ [2a] balance, coherence, consonance, proportion, symmetry, symphony, unity; *also* coordination, correlation, correspondence, equalization, equilibrium, evenness, order, orderliness, regularity, uniformity *Ant* asymmetry, disproportion, disunity, imbalance, incoherence ♦ [2b] compatibility, concord, peace; *also* amity, congeniality, fellowship, fraternization, friendship; collaboration, reciprocity, symbiosis; consensus, unanimity, unity; affinity, connection, empathy, kinship, oneness, rapport, solidarity, sympathy, understanding; serenity, tranquility *Ant* conflict, discord, dissension

¹**har·ness** \ˈhär-nəs\ *n* **1** : the gear other than a yoke of a draft animal **2** : something that resembles a harness
²**harness** *vb* **1** : to put a harness on; *also* : YOKE **2** ♦ : to make use of : UTILIZE

♦ apply, employ, exercise, exploit, operate, use, utilize — more at USE

¹**harp** \ˈhärp\ *n* : a musical instrument consisting of a triangular frame set with strings plucked by the fingers — **harp·ist** \ˈhär-pist\ *n*
²**harp** *vb* **1** : to play on a harp **2** : to dwell on a subject tiresomely — **harp·er** *n*
¹**har·poon** \här-ˈpün\ *n* : a barbed spear used esp. in hunting whales
²**harpoon** *vb* ♦ : to strike or capture with or as if with a harpoon — **har·poon·er** *n*

♦ gore, impale, lance, pierce, puncture, skewer, spear, spike, stab, stick, transfix — more at IMPALE

harp·si·chord \ˈhärp-si-ˌkȯrd\ *n* : a keyboard instrument producing tones by the plucking of its strings with quills or with leather or plastic points
har·py \ˈhär-pē\ *n, pl* **harpies** [L *Harpyia*, a mythical predatory monster having a woman's head and a bird's body,

fr. Gk] **1** : a predatory person : LEECH **2** ♦ : a shrewish woman

♦ fury, shrew, termagant, virago — more at SHREW

har·ri·dan \ˈhar-əd-ᵊn\ *n* : SHREW 2
¹**har·ri·er** \ˈhar-ē-ər\ *n* **1** : any of a breed of medium-sized foxhounds **2** : a runner on a cross-country team
²**harrier** *n* : a slender long-legged hawk
¹**har·row** \ˈhar-ō\ *n* : a cultivating tool that has spikes, spring teeth, or disks and is used esp. to pulverize and smooth the soil
²**harrow** *vb* **1** : to cultivate with a harrow **2** ♦ : to cause distress or suffering to : TORMENT

♦ afflict, agonize, bedevil, curse, martyr, persecute, plague, rack, torment, torture — more at AFFLICT

harrowing *adj* ♦ : acutely distressing or painful

♦ agonizing, bitter, cruel, excruciating, galling, grievous, harsh, hurtful, painful, tortuous — more at BITTER

har·rumph \hə-ˈrəmf\ *vb* : to comment disapprovingly as though clearing the throat
har·ry \ˈhar-ē\ *vb* **har·ried; har·ry·ing** **1** : RAID, PILLAGE **2** : to torment by or as if by constant attack
harsh \ˈhärsh\ *adj* **1** : disagreeably rough **2** ♦ : causing discomfort or pain **3** ♦ : unduly exacting : SEVERE **4** ♦ : lacking in aesthetic appeal or refinement

♦ [2] bitter, brutal, burdensome, cruel, excruciating, grievous, grim, hard, heavy, inhuman, murderous, onerous, oppressive, rough, rugged, severe, stiff, tough, trying; *also* austere, bleak, discomforting, forbidding, hostile, inhospitable, uncomfortable; biting, inclement; intemperate; rigorous, strict, stringent; agonizing, heartbreaking, heartrending, painful, wretched; crushing, grinding, overwhelming, wearing; insufferable, insupportable, intolerable, unbearable, unendurable; harrowing, tortuous; bad, disagreeable, hostile, unpleasant, unfriendly *Ant* easy, light, soft ♦ [3] austere, authoritarian, flinty, hard, heavy-handed, ramrod, rigid, rigorous, severe, stern, strict — more at SEVERE ♦ [4] grotesque, unaesthetic; *also* flashy, garish, gaudy, loud, tawdry; tacky, tasteless, vulgar; inartistic, unartistic; artless, clumsy, crude, graceless, inelegant, rude; uncouth, uncultured, unrefined; disgusting, gross, obscene, repugnant, repulsive, ugly; disagreeable, jolting, unpleasant, unpleasing; blaring, clashing, discordant, dissonant, inharmonious, jangling, raucous, unmelodious, unmusical; bizarre, kinky, odd, outlandish, shocking *Ant* aesthetic

harsh·en \ˈhär-shən\ *vb* : to make or become harsh ⟨~*ed* his voice⟩
harsh·ly \-lē\ *adv* ♦ : in a harsh manner

♦ hard, hardly, ill, oppressively, roughly, severely, sternly, stiffly — more at HARDLY

harsh·ness \-nəs\ *n* ♦ : the quality or state of being harsh

♦ bite, bitterness, pungency, sharpness, tartness ♦ hardness, inflexibility, rigidity, severity, sternness, strictness — more at SEVERITY

hart \ˈhärt\ *n, chiefly Brit* : STAG
¹**har·um–scar·um** \ˌhar-əm-ˈskar-əm\ *adj* ♦ : having or showing a lack of concern for the consequences of one's actions : RECKLESS, IRRESPONSIBLE

♦ daredevil, foolhardy, irresponsible, reckless — more at RECKLESS

²**harum–scarum** *adv* ♦ : in a rash or heedless way

♦ amok, berserk, frantically, hectically, helter-skelter, madly, pell-mell, wild, wildly — more at HELTER-SKELTER

¹**har·vest** \ˈhär-vəst\ *n* **1** : the season for gathering in crops; *also* : the act of gathering in a crop **2** : a mature crop **3** : the product or reward of effort
²**harvest** *vb* **1** ♦ : to gather in a crop : REAP **2** : to gather, hunt, or kill (as deer) for human use or population control — **har·vest·er** *n*

♦ gather, pick, reap; *also* clam, fish, shrimp, seal, whale; accumulate, garner; glean; cut, hay, mow; bag, capture, hunt, net, snare, trap; crop, grow, raise

has *pres 3d sing of* HAVE

has–been \'haz-ˌbin\ *n* : one that has passed the peak of ability, power, effectiveness, or popularity

¹**hash** \'hash\ *vb* [F *hacher*, fr. OF *hachier*, fr. *hache* battle-ax, of Gmc origin] **1** ♦ : to chop into small pieces **2** ♦ : to talk about — often used with *over* or *out* **3** : to make a confused muddle of

♦ [1] chop, mince — more at CHOP ♦ *usu* **hash over** [2] argue, chew over, debate, discuss, dispute, moot, talk over — more at DISCUSS

²**hash** *n* **1** : chopped meat mixed with potatoes and browned **2** ♦ : a mass of things mingled together without order or plan : HODGEPODGE, JUMBLE

♦ assortment, clutter, jumble, medley, mélange, miscellany, motley, muddle, variety, welter — more at MISCELLANY

³**hash** *n* : HASHISH

hash browns *n pl* : boiled potatoes that have been diced, mixed with chopped onions and shortening, and fried

hash·ish \'ha-ˌshēsh, ha-'shēsh\ *n* [Ar *ḥashīsh*] : the intoxicating concentrated resin from the flowering tops of the female hemp plant

hash·tag \'hash-ˌtag\ *n* : a word or phrase preceded by the symbol # that classifies the accompanying text

hasp \'hasp\ *n* : a fastener (as for a door) consisting of a hinged metal strap that fits over a staple and is secured by a pin or padlock

has·si·um \'ha-sē-əm\ *n* : an artificially produced radioactive metallic chemical element

¹**has·sle** \'ha-səl\ *n* **1 a** ♦ : a heated often protracted argument **b** : a violent skirmish : FIGHT **2** ♦ : an annoying or troublesome concern

♦ [1a] altercation, argument, bicker, brawl, disagreement, dispute, fight, misunderstanding, quarrel, row, scrap, spat, squabble, wrangle — more at ARGUMENT ♦ [2] aggravation, annoyance, bother, exasperation, frustration, headache, inconvenience, irritant, nuisance, peeve, pest, problem, thorn — more at ANNOYANCE

²**hassle** *vb* **1** ♦ : to contend or disagree in words **2** : to annoy persistently or acutely

♦ argue, bicker, brawl, dispute, fall out, fight, quarrel, row, scrap, spat, squabble, wrangle — more at ARGUE

has·sock \'ha-sək\ *n* : a cushion that serves as a seat or leg rest; *also* : a cushion to kneel on in prayer

haste \'hāst\ *n* **1** ♦ : rapidity of motion or action : SPEED **2** ♦ : rash or headlong action **3** : excessive eagerness

♦ [1] celerity, fastness, fleetness, hurry, quickness, rapidity, speed, swiftness, velocity — more at SPEED ♦ [2] hurry, hustle, precipitation, rush — more at HURRY

has·ten \'hās-ᵊn\ *vb* **1** : to urge on **2** ♦ : to move or act quickly : HURRY; *also* : to cause to move or act faster

♦ accelerate, hurry, quicken, rush, speed (up), step up, whisk — more at HURRY

hast·i·ly \'hā-stə-lē\ *adv* ♦ : in haste

♦ cursorily, headlong, hurriedly, pell-mell, precipitately, rashly; *also* hotheadedly, impatiently, impetuously, impulsively, recklessly, thoughtlessly; automatically, haphazardly; impromptu, spontaneously; abruptly, suddenly; offhand *Ant* deliberately ♦ apace, briskly, fast, full tilt, posthaste, presto, pronto, quick, quickly, rapidly, soon, speedily, swift, swiftly — more at FAST

hast·i·ness \'hā-stē-nəs\ *n* : the quality or state of being hasty

hasty \'hā-stē\ *adj* ♦ : made, done, or acting in haste

♦ cursory, headlong, pell-mell, precipitate, precipitous, rash; *also* breakneck, breathtaking; heady, hotheaded, headstrong, impatient, impetuous, impulsive, madcap,

reckless; quick, rapid, speedy, swift; impromptu, makeshift, offhand, snap, spontaneous; abrupt, sudden *Ant* deliberate, unhurried

hat \'hat\ *n* ♦ : a covering for the head usu. having a shaped crown and brim

♦ cap, headgear; *also* beret, biretta, boater, bonnet, bowler, derby, fedora, fez, hard hat, helm, helmet, homburg, hood, leghorn, miter, nightcap, panama, pillbox, skullcap, sombrero, sou'wester, sunbonnet, tam-o'-shanter, top hat, toque, turban; coronet, crown, diadem, headband, tiara; coif, babushka, kerchief, mantilla, scarf, shawl, veil, wimple

hat·box \'hat-ˌbäks\ *n* : a round piece of luggage esp. for carrying hats

¹**hatch** \'hach\ *n* **1** ♦ : a small door or opening **2** : a door or cover for access down into a compartment of a ship

♦ door, gate, portal — more at DOOR

²**hatch** *vb* **1 a** : to produce by incubation **b** ♦ : to incubate eggs **2** : to emerge from an egg or pupa; *also* : to give forth young **3** : ORIGINATE — **hatch·ery** \'ha-chə-rē\ *n*

♦ brood, incubate, set, sit — more at SET

hatch·back \'hach-ˌbak\ *n* : an automobile with a rear hatch that opens upward

hatch·et \'ha-chət\ *n* **1** : a short-handled ax with a hammerlike part opposite the blade **2** : TOMAHAWK

hatchet man *n* : a person hired for murder, coercion, or unscrupulous attack

hatch·ing \'ha-chiŋ\ *n* : the engraving or drawing of closely spaced fine lines chiefly to give an effect of shading; *also* : the pattern so created

hatch·way \'hach-ˌwā\ *n* : a hatch giving access usu. by a ladder or stairs

¹**hate** \'hāt\ *n* **1** ♦ : intense hostility and aversion **2** ♦ : an object of hatred

♦ [1] abhorrence, abomination, execration, hatred, loathing; *also* cattiness, despite, hatefulness, malevolence, malice, malignancy, malignity, meanness, spite, spitefulness; aversion, disgust, distaste, horror, odium, repugnance, repulsion, revulsion; animosity, antagonism, antipathy, bitterness, contempt, disdain, enmity, grudge, hostility, jealousy, pique, resentment, scorn; bile, jaundice, rancor, spleen, venom, virulence; *Ant* affection, love, devotion, fondness ♦ [2] abhorrence, abomination, anathema, antipathy, aversion, bête noire; *also* dread, hang-up, horror, phobia; bogey, bugaboo, bugbear; enemy, adversary; annoyance, grievance, hassle, nuisance, peeve *Ant* love

²**hate** *vb* **hat·ed; hat·ing 1** ♦ : to express or feel extreme enmity **2** : to find distasteful — **hat·er** *n*

♦ abhor, abominate, despise, detest, execrate, loathe; *also* deplore, deprecate, disapprove (of), countenance, disdain, disfavor (*or* disfavour), scorn *Ant* love

hate·ful \-fəl\ *adj* ♦ : full of hate : MALICIOUS

♦ catty, cruel, malevolent, malicious, malign, malignant, mean, nasty, spiteful, virulent; *also* devious, scurvy; acrimonious, bitter, envious, jaundiced, jealous, rancorous, resentful; contemptuous, deprecating, disdainful, obnoxious, opprobrious, scornful, snide, unkind, unkindly, unloving; baleful, baneful, evil; harsh, hostile, inimical; acrid, caustic, scathing, venomous *Ant* benevolent, benign, benignant, loving, unmalicious

hate·ful·ly \-fə-lē\ *adv* ♦ : in a hateful manner

♦ maliciously, meanly, nastily, spitefully, viciously, wickedly — more at NASTILY

hate·ful·ness \-nəs\ *n* ♦ : the quality or state of being hateful

♦ cattiness, despite, malice, malignity, meanness, nastiness, spite, spleen, venom, viciousness — more at MALICE

ha·tred \'hā-trəd\ *n* ♦ : intense hostility and aversion : HATE; *also* : prejudiced hostility or animosity

♦ abhorrence, abomination, execration, hate, loathing — more at HATE

hat·ter \'ha-tər\ n : one that makes, sells, or cleans and repairs hats

hau·berk \'hȯ-bərk\ n : a coat of mail

haugh·ti·ness \'hȯ-tē-nəs\ n ♦ : the quality or state of being haughty

♦ arrogance, loftiness, pretense, pretension, pretentiousness, self-importance, superiority — more at ARROGANCE

haugh·ty \'hȯ-tē\ adj **haugh·ti·er; -est** [obs. haught, fr. ME haute, fr. AF halt, haut, lit., high, fr. L altus] ♦ : disdainfully proud — **haugh·ti·ly** \-tə-lē\ adv

♦ disdainful, highfalutin, lofty, lordly, prideful, proud, superior — more at PROUD

¹haul \'hȯl\ vb **1** ♦ : to exert traction on : DRAW, PULL **2** ♦ : to furnish transportation : CART — **haul·er** n

♦ [1] drag, draw, hale, lug, pull, tow, tug — more at PULL ♦ [2] bear, carry, cart, convey, ferry, lug, pack, tote, transport — more at CARRY

²haul n **1** : the act or process of hauling : PULL, TUG **2** ♦ : the result of an effort to obtain, collect, or win **3 a** : the length or course of a transportation route **b** ♦ : a quantity transported : LOAD

♦ [2] catch, take, yield; also bag; earnings, gain, gross, income, net, payoff, proceeds, profit, receipts, return, revenue, winnings; booty, loot, spoils, plunder, swag; appropriation, collection ♦ [3b] burden, cargo, freight, lading, load, payload, weight — more at LOAD

haul·age \'hȯ-lij\ n **1** : the act or process of hauling **2** : a charge for hauling

haunch \'hȯnch\ n **1** : ²HIP **2** : HINDQUARTER 2 — usu. used in pl. **3** : HINDQUARTER 1

¹haunt \'hȯnt\ vb **1** ♦ : to visit often : FREQUENT **2** : to have a disquieting effect on; also : to reappear continually in **3** : to visit or inhabit as a ghost — **haunt·er** n

♦ frequent, hang around, hang out, resort, visit — more at FREQUENT

²haunt \'hȯnt, 2 is usu 'hant\ n **1** ♦ : a place habitually frequented **2** chiefly dial : GHOST

♦ hangout, rendezvous, resort — more at HANGOUT

haunting adj ♦ : having a disquieting effect — **haunt·ing·ly** adv

♦ creepy, eerie, spooky, uncanny, unearthly, weird — more at EERIE

haute cou·ture \ˌōt-kù-'tùr\ n [F] : the establishments or designers that create exclusive and often trend-setting fashions for women; also : the fashions created

haute cui·sine \-kwi-'zēn\ n : artful or elaborate cuisine

hau·teur \hō-'tər, ō-, hȯ-\ n : ARROGANCE, HAUGHTINESS

¹have \'hav, həv, v; in sense 2 before "to" usu 'haf\ vb **had** \'had, həd\; **hav·ing; has** \'haz, həz, in sense 2 before "to" usu 'has\ **1** ♦ : to hold in possession; also : to hold in one's use, service, or regard **2** ♦ : to be compelled or forced — usu. used with an infinitive with to ⟨~ to go now⟩ **3** : to stand in relationship to ⟨has many enemies⟩ **4** : OBTAIN; also : RECEIVE, ACCEPT **5** : to be marked by **6** : SHOW; also : USE, EXERCISE **7 a** ♦ : to experience esp. by submitting to, undergoing, or suffering ⟨~ a cold⟩ **b** : TAKE ⟨~ a look⟩ **8** ♦ : to entertain in the mind ⟨~ an idea⟩ **9** : to cause to **10** : to consent to : ALLOW ⟨I won't ~ you jumping on the bed⟩ **11** : to be competent in **12 a** : to hold in a disadvantageous position **b** ♦ : to take advantage of : TRICK **13** : to give birth to **14** : to partake of **15** — used as an auxiliary with the past participle to form the present perfect, past perfect, or future perfect — **have at** : ATTACK — **have coming** : DESERVE — **have done with** : to be finished with — **have had it** : to have endured all one will permit or can stand — **have to do with** : to have in the way of relation with or effect on

♦ [1] command, enjoy, hold, occupy, own, possess, retain; also keep, reserve, withhold; bear, carry, boast,

show off, sport **Ant** lack, want ♦ usu **have to** [2] must, need, ought, shall, should — more at NEED ♦ [7a] endure, experience, feel, know, see, suffer, sustain, taste, undergo — more at EXPERIENCE ♦ [8] bear, cherish, entertain, harbor (or harbour), hold, nurse — more at HARBOR ♦ [12b] beguile, bluff, cozen, deceive, delude, dupe, fool, gull, hoax, hoodwink, humbug, misinform, mislead, string along, take in, trick — more at DECEIVE

²have \'hav\ n : one that has material wealth

ha·ven \'hā-vən\ n **1** ♦ : a part of a body of water protected and deep enough to furnish anchorage : HARBOR, PORT **2** ♦ : a place of safety **3** : a place offering favorable conditions ⟨a tourist's ~⟩

♦ [1] anchorage, harbor (or harbour), port — more at HARBOR ♦ [2] asylum, refuge, retreat, sanctuary, shelter — more at SHELTER

have–not \'hav-ˌnät, -'nät\ n : one that is poor in material wealth

hav·er·sack \'ha-vər-ˌsak\ n [F havresac, fr. G Habersack bag for oats] : a bag similar to a knapsack but worn over one shoulder

hav·oc \'ha-vək\ n **1** ♦ : wide and general destruction **2** ♦ : great confusion and disorder

♦ [1] annihilation, demolition, desolation, destruction, devastation, loss, obliteration, ruin, wastage, wreckage — more at DESTRUCTION ♦ [2] chaos, confusion, disarray, disorder, disorganization, hell, jumble, mess, muddle, shambles — more at CHAOS

haw \'hȯ\ n : a hawthorn berry; also : HAWTHORN

Ha·wai·ian \hə-'wä-yən\ n : the Polynesian language of Hawaii

¹hawk \'hȯk\ n **1** : any of numerous mostly small or medium-sized day-flying birds of prey (as a falcon or kite) **2** : a supporter of a war or a warlike policy — **hawk·ish** adj

²hawk vb : to offer goods for sale by calling out in the street — **hawk·er** n

³hawk vb : to make a harsh coughing sound in or as if in clearing the throat; also : to raise by hawking

hawk·weed \'hȯk-ˌwēd\ n : any of several plants related to the daisies usu. having yellow flowers

haw·ser \'hȯ-zər\ n : a large rope for towing, mooring, or securing a ship

haw·thorn \'hȯ-ˌthȯrn\ n : any of a genus of spiny spring-flowering shrubs or small trees related to the apple

¹hay \'hā\ n **1** : herbage (as grass) mowed and cured for fodder **2** : REWARD **3** slang : BED ⟨hit the ~⟩ **4** : a small amount of money

²hay vb : to cut, cure, and store for hay

hay·cock \'hā-ˌkäk\ n : a small conical pile of hay

hay fever n : an acute allergic reaction esp. to plant pollen that resembles a cold

hay·loft \'hā-ˌlȯft\ n : a loft for hay

hay·mow \-ˌmaú\ n : a mow of or for hay

hay·rick \-ˌrik\ n : a large sometimes thatched outdoor stack of hay

hay·seed \-ˌsēd\ n, pl **hayseed** or **hayseeds** **1** : clinging bits of straw or chaff from hay **2** : BUMPKIN, YOKEL

hay·stack \-ˌstak\ n : a stack of hay

hay·wire \-ˌwī-(ə)r\ adj : being out of order or control : CRAZY

¹haz·ard \'ha-zərd\ n [ME, a dice game, fr. AF hasard, fr. Sp azar, Ar al-zahr the die] **1** ♦ : a source of danger **2** ♦ : the assumed impersonal purposeless determiner of unaccountable happenings : CHANCE; also : ACCIDENT **3** : an obstacle on a golf course

♦ [1] danger, menace, peril, pitfall, risk, threat, trouble — more at DANGER ♦ [2] accident, chance, circumstance, luck — more at CHANCE

²hazard vb **1** : to expose to possible risk of loss or damage : VENTURE, RISK **2** ♦ : to undertake the risks and dangers of **3** : to offer at the risk of rebuff, rejection, or censure

♦ chance, gamble, risk, venture — more at RISK

haz·ard·ous \\'ha-zər-dəs\\ *adj* ♦ : involving or exposing one to risk (as of loss or harm)

♦ dangerous, grave, grievous, menacing, parlous, perilous, risky, serious, unhealthy, unsafe, venturesome — more at DANGEROUS

¹haze \\'hāz\\ *n* 1 ♦ : fine dust, smoke, or light vapor causing lack of transparency in the air 2 ♦ : vagueness of mind or perception

♦ [1] fog, murk, smog, soup; *also* cloud, fume, miasma, smoke, steam ♦ [2] daze, fog, muddle, spin; *also* reverie, stupor, trance; bewilderment, perplexity, puzzlement; delirium, malaise, paralysis; cloudiness

²haze *vb* : to make or become hazy, dull, or cloudy

³haze *vb* **hazed; haz·ing** : to harass by abusive and humiliating tricks usu. by way of initiation

ha·zel \\'hā-zəl\\ *n* 1 : any of a genus of shrubs or small trees related to the birches and bearing edible brown nuts (**ha·zel·nuts** \\-ˌnəts\\) 2 : a light brown color

hazy \\'hā-zē\\ *adj* **haz·i·er; -est** 1 ♦ : obscured or darkened by haze 2 ♦ : not clearly perceived or understood : VAGUE, INDEFINITE — **haz·i·ly** \\-zə-lē\\ *adv* — **haz·i·ness** \\-zē-nəs\\ *n*

♦ [1] cloudy, foggy, misty, murky, smoggy, soupy; *also* overcast, rainy, stormy, thick; dirty, miry, mucky, muddy, slimy, slushy, turbid; smoky, sooty; filmy, milky, opaque *Ant* clear, cloudless, limpid, pellucid, unclouded ♦ [2] bleary, dim, faint, foggy, fuzzy, indefinite, indistinct, indistinguishable, murky, nebulous, obscure, opaque, shadowy, unclear, undefined, undetermined, vague — more at FAINT

Hb *abbr* hemoglobin

HBM *abbr* Her Britannic Majesty; His Britannic Majesty

H–bomb \\'āch-ˌbäm\\ *n* : HYDROGEN BOMB

HC *abbr* 1 Holy Communion 2 House of Commons

hd *abbr* head

HD *abbr* 1 heavy-duty 2 high definition

hdbk *abbr* handbook

hdkf *abbr* handkerchief

HDL \\ˌāch-(ˌ)dē-'el\\ *n* [*h*igh-*d*ensity *l*ipoprotein] : a cholesterol-poor protein-rich lipoprotein of blood plasma correlated with reduced risk of atherosclerosis

hdwe *abbr* hardware

he \\'hē\\ *pron* 1 : that male one 2 : a person : the person ⟨∼ who hesitates is lost⟩

He *symbol* helium

HE *abbr* 1 Her Excellency 2 His Eminence 3 His Excellency

¹head \\'hed\\ *n* 1 ♦ : the front or upper part of the body containing the brain, the chief sense organs, and the mouth 2 a ♦ : the seat of the intellect : MIND; *also* : mental or emotional control b : natural aptitude 3 : POISE ⟨a level ∼⟩ 4 : the obverse of a coin 5 : a single human being : INDIVIDUAL; *also, pl* head : one of a number (as of cattle) 6 : the end that is upper or higher or opposite the foot; *also* : either end of something (as a drum) whose two ends need not be distinguished 7 : the source of a stream 8 ♦ : a person who leads : LEADER; *also* : a leading element (as of a procession) 9 : a projecting part; *also* : the striking part of a weapon 10 ♦ : the place of leadership or honor 11 : a separate part or topic 12 ♦ : the foam on a fermenting or effervescing liquid 13 : culminating point of action : CRISIS ⟨events came to a ∼⟩ — **head·ed** \\'he-dəd\\ *adj* — **head·less** *adj*

♦ [1] noggin, pate, poll; *also* cranium, crown, scalp, skull ♦ [2a] mind, reason, sanity, wit — more at MIND ♦ [8] boss, captain, chief, foreman, headman, helmsman, kingpin, leader, master, taskmaster — more at BOSS ♦ [10] chair, headship, helm, rein; *also* chieftainship, directorship; forefront, lead, preferment; chairmanship, deanship, dictatorship, governorship, kingship, mastery, presidency, superintendency; dominance, dominion, sovereignty, sway, upper

hand; eminence, height, pedestal, pinnacle, seat, throne, top ♦ [12] foam, froth, lather, spume — more at FOAM

²head *adj* ♦ : most important, consequential, or influential : PRINCIPAL, CHIEF

♦ chief, first, foremost, high, lead, preeminent, premier, primary, prime, principal, supreme; *also* senior; controlling, directing, officiating, overseeing, reigning, ruling, supervisory; paramount, predominant, main, major; dominant, grand, superior, topmost, upmost, upper, uppermost

³head *vb* 1 : to provide with or form a head; *also* : to form the head of 2 ♦ : to act as leader or head to 3 : to get in front of esp. so as to stop; *also* : SURPASS 4 : to put or stand at the head 5 ♦ : to point or proceed in a certain direction

♦ [2] boss, captain, command, dominate, lead, spearhead, supervise — more at LEAD ♦ [5] extend, go, lead, lie, run — more at RUN

head·ache \\'he-ˌdāk\\ *n* 1 : pain in the head 2 ♦ : a vexatious or baffling situation or problem

♦ aggravation, annoyance, bother, exasperation, frustration, hassle, inconvenience, irritant, nuisance, peeve, pest, problem, thorn — more at ANNOYANCE

head·band \\'hed-ˌband\\ *n* : a band worn on or around the head

head·bang·er \\-ˌbaŋ-ər\\ *n* : one who performs or enjoys hard rock

head·board \\-ˌbōrd\\ *n* : a board forming the head (as of a bed)

head cold *n* : a common cold centered in the nasal passages and adjacent mucous tissues

head·dress \\'hed-ˌdres\\ *n* : an often elaborate covering for the head

head·first \\-'fərst\\ *adv* : HEADLONG 1 — **headfirst** *adj*

head·gear \\-ˌgir\\ *n* ♦ : a covering or protective device for the head

♦ cap, hat — more at HAT

head–hunt·ing \\-ˌhən-tiŋ\\ *n* : the practice of seeking out and decapitating enemies and preserving their heads as trophies — **head·hunt·er** \\-tər\\ *n*

head·ing \\'he-diŋ\\ *n* 1 : the compass direction in which the longitudinal axis of a ship or airplane points 2 ♦ : something that forms or serves as a head; *esp* : an inscription, headline, or title standing at the top or beginning (as of a letter or chapter)

♦ title; *also* subhead, subheading, subtitle; guide word, legend; greeting, salutation

head·land \\'hed-lənd, -ˌland\\ *n* ♦ : a high point of land or rock projecting into a body of water : PROMONTORY

♦ cape, peninsula, point, promontory, spit — more at CAPE

head·light \\-ˌlīt\\ *n* : a light mounted on the front of a vehicle to illuminate the road ahead

¹head·line \\-ˌlīn\\ *n* : a head of a newspaper story or article usu. printed in large type

²headline *vb* 1 : to provide with a headline 2 : to publicize highly 3 : to be a leading performer in

head·lock \\-ˌläk\\ *n* : a wrestling hold in which one encircles the opponent's head with one arm

¹head·long \\-'lȯŋ\\ *adv* 1 : with the head foremost 2 ♦ : without deliberation : RASHLY 3 : without delay

♦ cursorily, hastily, hurriedly, pell-mell, precipitately, rashly — more at HASTILY

²head·long \\-ˌlȯŋ\\ *adj* 1 ♦ : lacking in calmness or restraint : PRECIPITATE, RASH 2 : plunging with the head foremost

♦ cursory, hasty, pell-mell, precipitate, precipitous, rash — more at HASTY

head·man \\'hed-'man, -ˌman\\ *n* ♦ : one who is a leader

♦ boss, captain, chief, foreman, head, helmsman, kingpin, leader, master, taskmaster — more at BOSS

head·mas·ter \\-ˌmas-tər\\ *n* : a man who is head of a private school

head·mis·tress \-₁mis-trəs\ *n* : a woman who is head of a private school

head of steam : strong driving force : MOMENTUM

head–on \'hed-'òn, -'än\ *adj* : having the front facing in the direction of initial contact or line of sight ⟨∼ collision⟩ — **head–on** *adv*

head·phone \-₁fōn\ *n* : an earphone held on by a band over the head

head·piece \-₁pēs\ *n* : a covering for the head

head·pin \-₁pin\ *n* : a bowling pin that stands foremost in the arrangement of pins

head·quar·ters \-₁kwòr-tərz\ *n sing or pl* 1 : a place from which a commander exercises command 2 : the administrative center of an enterprise

head·rest \-₁rest\ *n* 1 : a support for the head 2 : a pad at the top of the back of an automobile seat

head·room \-₁rüm, -₁rùm\ *n* : vertical space in which to stand, sit, or move

head–scratcher \-₁skra-chər\ *n* : PUZZLE, MYSTERY

head·set \-₁set\ *n* : a pair of headphones

head·ship \-₁ship\ *n* ♦ : the position, office, or dignity of a head

♦ care, charge, guidance, oversight, regulation, superintendence, supervision — more at SUPERVISION ♦ chair, head, helm, rein — more at HEAD

heads·man \'hedz-mən\ *n* : EXECUTIONER

head·stall \'hed-₁stòl\ *n* : a part of a bridle or halter that encircles the head

head start *n* 1 : an advantage allowed at the start of a race 2 : a favorable or promising beginning

head·stone \-₁stōn\ *n* ♦ : a memorial stone at the head of a grave

♦ gravestone, monument, tombstone — more at TOMBSTONE

head·strong \-₁stròŋ\ *adj* 1 ♦ : not easily restrained 2 ♦ : directed by ungovernable will

♦ [1] froward, intractable, recalcitrant, refractory, uncontrollable, unmanageable, unruly, untoward, wayward, willful — more at UNCONTROLLABLE ♦ [2] dogged, hardheaded, mulish, obdurate, obstinate, opinionated, peevish, pertinacious, perverse, pigheaded, stubborn, unyielding, willful — more at OBSTINATE

heads–up \'hedz-'əp\ *n* : WARNING

head·wait·er \-'wā-tər\ *n* : the head of the dining-room staff of a restaurant or hotel

head·wa·ter \-₁wò-tər, -₁wä-\ *n* : the source of a stream — usu. used in pl.

head·way \-₁wā\ *n* ♦ : forward motion; *also* : PROGRESS

♦ advance, advancement, furtherance, march, onrush, passage, process, procession, progress, progression — more at ADVANCE

head wind *n* : a wind blowing in a direction opposite to a course esp. of a ship or aircraft

head·word \'hed-₁wərd\ *n* 1 : a word or term placed at the beginning 2 : a word qualified by a modifier

head·work \-₁wərk\ *n* : mental work or effort : THINKING

heady \'he-dē\ *adj* **head·i·er; -est** 1 : WILLFUL, RASH; *also* : IMPETUOUS 2 : INTOXICATING ⟨a ∼ wine⟩ 3 : SHREWD

heal \'hēl\ *vb* 1 ♦ : to make or become healthy, sound, or whole 2 ♦ : to restore to health : CURE — **heal·er** *n*

♦ [1] convalesce, gain, mend, rally, recover, recuperate, snap back — more at CONVALESCE ♦ [2] cure, mend, rehabilitate; *also* attend (to), care (for), doctor, minister (to), nurse, treat; fortify, rejuvenate, renew, revive, resuscitate; alleviate, fix, relieve, remedy, repair

health \'helth\ *n* 1 ♦ : sound physical or mental condition; *also* : overall condition of the body ⟨in poor ∼⟩ 2 : WELL-BEING 3 : a toast to someone's health or prosperity

♦ fitness, heartiness, robustness, soundness, wellness, wholeness, wholesomeness; *also* fettle, shape; cleanliness, hygiene; hardiness, lustiness, stamina, ruggedness,

strength, toughness, vigor, vigorousness, vitality; bloom, flush, flushness; activeness, agility, liveliness; weal, welfare, well-being **Ant** illness, sickness, unsoundness

health care *n* : efforts made to maintain or restore health — usu. hyphenated when used attributively

health club *n* : a commercial establishment providing health and fitness facilities and equipment for members

health·ful \'helth-fəl\ *adj* 1 ♦ : beneficial to health 2 : in good health — **health·ful·ly** *adv* — **health·ful·ness** *n*

♦ healthy, restorative, salubrious, salutary, wholesome; *also* corrective, curative, remedial, tonic; advantageous, beneficial, useful; antiseptic, clean, hygienic, sanitary; nonfattening, nonpoisonous, nontoxic **Ant** insalubrious, noxious, unhealthful, unhealthy, unwholesome

health·i·ness \'hel-thē-nəs\ *n* : the quality or state of being healthy

health maintenance organization *n* : HMO

healthy \'hel-thē\ *adj* **health·i·er; -est** 1 ♦ : enjoying or typical of good health : WELL 2 ♦ : evincing or conducive to health 3 a : PROSPEROUS b ♦ : not small or feeble : CONSIDERABLE — **health·i·ly** \-thə-lē\ *adv*

♦ [1] able-bodied, chipper, fit, hale, hearty, robust, sound, well, whole, wholesome; *also* hardy, lusty, rugged, stalwart, strong, sturdy, tough; active, agile, lively, sprightly, spry, vigorous, vital; blooming, clean-cut, flush, thriving; all right, good, right **Ant** ailing, diseased, ill, sick, unfit, unhealthy, unsound, unwell ♦ [2] healthful, restorative, salubrious, salutary, wholesome — more at HEALTHFUL ♦ [3b] considerable, good, goodly, respectable, significant, sizable, substantial, tidy — more at CONSIDERABLE

¹heap \'hēp\ *n* 1 ♦ : a collection of things thrown one on another : PILE 2 ♦ : a great number or large quantity : LOT

♦ [1] cock, hill, mound, mountain, pile, rick, stack — more at PILE ♦ [2] abundance, deal, gobs, loads, lot, pile, plenty, quantity, scads — more at LOT

²heap *vb* 1 ♦ : to throw or lay in a heap : pile or collect in great quantity 2 a ♦ : to give in large quantities b ♦ : to load heavily

♦ [1] accumulate, collect, conglomerate, gather, pile up — more at COLLECT ♦ [1] hill, mound, pile, stack — more at PILE ♦ [2a] lavish, pour, rain, shower — more at RAIN ♦ [2b] charge, cram, fill, jam, jam-pack, load, pack, stuff — more at FILL

hear \'hir\ *vb* **heard** \'hərd\; **hear·ing** 1 : to perceive by the ear 2 ♦ : to gain knowledge of by hearing : LEARN 3 ♦ : to listen to with attention : HEED; *also* : ATTEND 4 : to give a legal hearing to or take testimony from — **hear·er** *n*

♦ [2] ascertain, catch on, discover, find out, learn, realize, see — more at DISCOVER ♦ [3] attend, hark, heed, listen, mind — more at LISTEN

hear·ing *n* 1 : the process, function, or power of perceiving sound; *esp* : the special sense by which noises and tones are received as stimuli 2 ♦ : range of hearing : EARSHOT 3 : opportunity to be heard 4 : a listening to arguments (as in a court); *also* : a session (as of a legislative committee) in which testimony is taken from witnesses

♦ earshot, hail, sound

hear·ken \'här-kən\ *vb* : to give attention : LISTEN

hear·say \'hir-₁sā\ *n* : RUMOR

hearse \'hərs\ *n* : a vehicle for carrying the dead to the grave

heart \'härt\ *n* 1 : a hollow muscular organ that by rhythmic contraction keeps up the circulation of the blood in the body; *also* : something resembling a heart in shape 2 : any of a suit of playing cards marked with a red figure of a heart; *also, pl* : a card game in which the object is to avoid taking tricks containing hearts 3 a : the whole personality b : the emotional or moral as distinguished from the intellectual nature c ♦ : generous disposition

: COMPASSION **4 ♦** : mental or moral strength to venture, persevere, and withstand danger, fear, or difficulty : COURAGE **5 ♦** : one's innermost being **6 a** : CENTER **b ♦** : the essential part **7** : the younger central part of a compact leafy cluster (as of lettuce) **8** : a single human being ⟨dear ∼⟩ — **heart·ed** \'här-təd\ *adj* — **by heart** : by rote or from memory

♦ [3c] charity, commiseration, compassion, feeling, humanity, kindliness, kindness, mercy, pity, sympathy; *also* responsiveness, sensitivity; affection, regard, love; affinity, empathy, rapport; altruism, benevolence, benignity, generosity, goodwill, humanitarianism, philanthropy *Ant* inhumanity ♦ [4] bravery, courage, daring, fearlessness, gallantry, guts, hardihood, heroism, nerve, stoutness, valor — more at COURAGE ♦ [5] core, quick, soul ♦ [6b] core, crux, gist, nub, pith, pivot — more at CRUX

heart·ache \-ˌāk\ *n* ♦ : anguish of mind

♦ affliction, anguish, dolor, grief, sorrow, woe — more at SORROW

heart attack *n* : an acute episode of heart disease due to insufficient blood supply to the heart muscle

heart·beat \'härt-ˌbēt\ *n* : one complete pulsation of the heart

heart·break \-ˌbrāk\ *n* : crushing grief

heart·break·ing \-ˌbrā-kin\ *adj* ♦ : causing extreme sorrow or distress — **heart·break·er** \-ˌbrā-kər\ *n*

♦ depressing, dismal, dreary, melancholy, pathetic, sad, sorry, tearful — more at SAD ♦ deplorable, distressful, grievous, lamentable, regrettable, unfortunate, woeful — more at REGRETTABLE

heart·bro·ken \-ˌbrō-kən\ *adj* : overcome by sorrow

heart·burn \-ˌbərn\ *n* : a burning distress behind the sternum due to the backward flow of acid from the stomach to the esophagus

heart disease *n* : an abnormal organic condition of the heart or of the heart and circulation

heart·en \'härt-ᵊn\ *vb* ♦ : to give heart to : ENCOURAGE, CHEER ⟨were ∼ed by the victory⟩

♦ buoy (up), cheer, comfort, embolden, encourage, inspire, steel — more at ENCOURAGE

heartening *adj* ♦ : tending or serving to hearten, inspire, or give fresh courage

♦ auspicious, bright, encouraging, fair, golden, hopeful, likely, promising, propitious, rosy, upbeat — more at HOPEFUL ♦ comforting, encouraging, gratifying, heartwarming, rewarding, satisfying — more at HEARTWARMING

heart·felt \'härt-ˌfelt\ *adj* : deeply felt : SINCERE ⟨∼ thanks⟩

hearth \'härth\ *n* **1** : an area (as of brick) in front of a fireplace; *also* : the floor of a fireplace **2 ♦** : one's place of residence : HOME

♦ abode, domicile, dwelling, home, house, lodging, quarters, residence — more at HOME

hearth·stone \'härth-ˌstōn\ *n* **1** : stone forming a hearth **2** : one's place of residence : HOME

heart·i·ly \'här-tə-lē\ *adv* ♦ : in a hearty manner

♦ cheerfully, gaily, happily, jovially, merrily, mirthfully — more at GAILY

heart·i·ness \'här-tē-nəs\ *n* ♦ : the quality or state of being hearty

♦ fitness, health, robustness, soundness, wellness, wholeness, wholesomeness — more at HEALTH

heart·less \'härt-ləs\ *adj* ♦ : lacking feeling or affection

♦ callous, hard, inhuman, inhumane, pitiless, soulless, unfeeling, unsympathetic — more at HARD

heart·rend·ing \-ˌren-din\ *adj* : causing extreme sorrow or distress : HEARTBREAKING

heart·sick \-ˌsik\ *adj* ♦ : very despondent

♦ bad, blue, brokenhearted, dejected, depressed, despondent, disconsolate, miserable, mournful, sad, wretched — more at SAD

heart·sick·ness \-nəs\ *n* ♦ : the quality or state of being heartsick

♦ blues, dejection, depression, desolation, despondency, doldrums, dumps, forlornness, gloom, melancholy, sadness — more at SADNESS

heart–stop·ping \-ˌstä-pin\ *adj* : extremely shocking or exciting

heart·strings \-ˌstrinz\ *n pl* : the deepest emotions or affections

heart·throb \-ˌthräb\ *n* **1** : the throb of a heart **2** : sentimental emotion **3** : SWEETHEART **4** : an entertainer noted for his sex appeal

heart–to–heart *adj* : SINCERE, FRANK

heart·warm·ing \'härt-ˌwor-min\ *adj* ♦ : inspiring sympathetic feeling

♦ comforting, encouraging, gratifying, heartening, rewarding, satisfying; *also* affecting, inspiring, moving, poignant, stirring, touching; elevating, uplifting; sympathetic, tender; kind, kindly, loving, warm; exciting, exhilarating, rousing, stimulating, thrilling; pleasing, welcoming *Ant* depressing, discouraging, disheartening, dispiriting

heart·wood \-ˌwud\ *n* : the older harder nonliving and usu. darker wood of the central part of a tree trunk

¹hearty \'här-tē\ *adj* **heart·i·er; -est** **1 a** : giving full support **b ♦** : enthusiastically or exuberantly cordial **2 ♦** : vigorously healthy **3** : ABUNDANT; *also* : NOURISHING ⟨a ∼ soup⟩ **4 ♦** : carried out forcefully and energetically

♦ [1b] amicable, companionable, comradely, cordial, friendly, genial, neighborly, warm, warmhearted — more at FRIENDLY ♦ [2] able-bodied, chipper, fit, hale, healthy, robust, sound, well, whole, wholesome — more at HEALTHY ♦ [4] firm, forceful, lusty, robust, solid, stout, strong, sturdy, vigorous

²hearty *n, pl* **heart·ies** : an enthusiastic jovial fellow; *also* : SAILOR

¹heat \'hēt\ *vb* **1** : to make or become warm or hot **2** : EXCITE — **heat·ed·ly** *adv* — **heat·er** *n*

²heat *n* **1** : a condition of being hot : WARMTH **2** : a form of energy that when added to a body causes the body to rise in temperature, to fuse, to evaporate, or to expand **3** : high temperature **4 a ♦** : intensity of feeling **b** : sexual excitement esp. in a female mammal **5** : a preliminary race for narrowing the competition **6** : pungency of flavor **7** *slang* : POLICE **8** : PRESSURE, COERCION; *also* : ABUSE, CRITICISM

♦ ardor, emotion, fervency, fervor, intensity, passion, vehemence, warmth — more at ARDOR

heat·ed \'hē-təd\ *adj* ♦ : marked by anger or passion

♦ agitated, feverish, frenzied, hectic, overactive, overwrought — more at FEVERISH

heat exchanger *n* : a device (as an automobile radiator) for transferring heat from one fluid to another without allowing them to mix

heat exhaustion *n* : a condition marked by weakness, nausea, dizziness, and profuse sweating resulting from physical exertion in a hot environment

heath \'hēth\ *n* **1** : any of a large family of often evergreen shrubby plants (as a blueberry or heather) of wet acid soils **2** : a tract of wasteland — **heathy** *adj*

¹hea·then \'hē-thən\ *adj* **1** : of or relating to heathens, their religions, or their customs **2 ♦** : not civilized

♦ Neanderthal, barbarous, heathenish, rude, savage, uncivil, uncivilized, uncultivated, wild — more at SAVAGE

²heathen *n, pl* **heathens** *or* **heathen** **1** : an unconverted member of a people or nation that does not acknowledge the God of the Bible **2** : an uncivilized or irreligious person — **hea·then·dom** *n* — **hea·then·ism** *n*

hea·then·ish \'hē-thə-nish\ *adj* ♦ : resembling or characteristic of heathens : BARBAROUS

♦ Neanderthal, barbarous, heathen, rude, savage, uncivil, uncivilized, wild — more at SAVAGE

heath·er \'he-thər\ *n* : a northern and alpine evergreen heath with usu. lavender flowers — **heath·ery** *adj*

heat lightning *n* : flashes of light without thunder ascribed to distant lightning reflected by high clouds

heat·stroke \'hēt-ˌstrōk\ *n* : a disorder marked esp. by high body temperature without sweating and by collapse that follows prolonged exposure to excessive heat

¹**heave** \'hēv\ *vb* **heaved** *or* **hove** \'hōv\; **heav·ing** **1** ♦ : to rise or lift upward **2** ♦ : to propel through the air by a forward motion of the hand and arm : THROW **3** : to rise and fall rhythmically; *also* : PANT **4** : to disgorge the stomach contents through the mouth; *also* : to make an effort to vomit **5** : PULL, PUSH — **heav·er** *n*

♦ [1] boost, heft, hoist, jack; *also* elevate, hike, raise, rear, up, uplift, upraise ♦ [2] cast, catapult, chuck, dash, fire, fling, hurl, hurtle, launch, peg, pelt, pitch, sling, throw, toss — more at THROW

²**heave** *n* **1** : an effort to lift or raise **2** : THROW, CAST **3** : an upward motion **4** *pl* : a chronic lung disease of horses marked by difficult breathing and persistent cough

heav·en \'he-vən\ *n* **1** : FIRMAMENT — usu. used in pl. **2** *often cap* : the abode of the Deity and of the blessed dead; *also* : a spiritual state of everlasting communion with God **3** *cap* : GOD 1 **4** ♦ : a place or condition of supreme happiness — **heav·en·ward** *adv or adj*

♦ Eden, Elysium, paradise, utopia — more at PARADISE
♦ ecstasy, elation, euphoria, exhilaration, intoxication, paradise, rapture, rhapsody, transport — more at ECSTASY

heav·en·ly \-lē\ *adj* **1** ♦ : of or relating to heaven or the heavens **2 a** : suggesting the blessed state of heaven **b** ♦ : highly pleasing

♦ [1] Elysian, celestial, empyrean, supernal — more at CELESTIAL ♦ [2b] agreeable, darling, delectable, delicious, delightful, enjoyable, luscious, pleasurable

heavi·ly \'he-və-lē\ *adv* : to a large degree

¹**heavy** \'he-vē\ *adj* **heavi·er; -est** **1** ♦ : having great weight **2** ♦ : hard to bear **3** : of weighty import : SERIOUS **4** : characterized by intensity of quality : DEEP, PROFOUND **5** : burdened with something oppressive; *also* : PREGNANT **6** : SLUGGISH **7 a** : lacking sparkle or vivacity : DRAB **b** : DOLEFUL **8** : DROWSY **9** : greater than the average of its kind or class **10** : very rich and hard to digest; *also* : not properly raised or leavened **11** : producing goods (as steel) used in the production of other goods **12** ♦ : threatening to rain or snow — **heavi·ness** \-vē-nəs\ *n*

♦ [1] hefty, massive, ponderous, weighty; *also* burdensome, leaden, lumpish; bulky, elephantine, outsize; overweight, top-heavy; solid, substantial **Ant** light, lightweight, weightless ♦ [2] bitter, brutal, burdensome, cruel, excruciating, grievous, grim, hard, harsh, inhuman, murderous, onerous, oppressive, rough, rugged, severe, stiff, tough, trying — more at HARSH ♦ [12] cloudy, dull, hazy, overcast — more at OVERCAST

²**heavy** *n, pl* **heav·ies** **1** : a theatrical role representing a dignified or imposing person **2** : a villain esp. in a story

heavy–du·ty \ˌhe-vē-'dü-tē, -'dyü-\ *adj* : able to withstand unusual strain

heavy–hand·ed \-'han-dəd\ *adj* **1** ♦ : lacking dexterity, nimbleness, or grace : CLUMSY **2** ♦ : unduly exacting : HARSH

♦ [1] awkward, clumsy, gawky, graceless, lubberly, lumpish, ungainly, unhandy — more at CLUMSY ♦ [2] austere, authoritarian, flinty, hard, harsh, ramrod, rigid, rigorous, severe, stern, strict — more at SEVERE

heavy–heart·ed \-'här-təd\ *adj* : SADDENED, DESPONDENT

heavy lifting *n* : a burdensome or laborious duty

heavy metal *n* : energetic and highly amplified electronic rock music

heavy·set \ˌhe-vē-'set\ *adj* ♦ : stocky and compact in build

♦ chunky, dumpy, squat, stocky, stout, stubby, stumpy, thickset — more at STOCKY

heavy water *n* : water enriched in deuterium

heavy·weight \'he-vē-ˌwāt\ *n* : one above average in weight; *esp* : a boxer weighing over 175 pounds

Heb *abbr* Hebrews

He·bra·ism \'hē-brā-ˌi-zəm\ *n* : the thought, spirit, or practice characteristic of the Hebrews — **He·bra·ic** \hi-'brā-ik\ *adj*

He·bra·ist \'hē-ˌbrā-ist\ *n* : a specialist in Hebrew and Hebraic studies

He·brew \'hē-brü\ *n* **1** : the language of the Hebrews **2** : a member of or descendant from a group of Semitic peoples; *esp* : ISRAELITE — **Hebrew** *adj*

He·brews \'hē-(ˌ)brüz\ *n* : a book of the New Testament in Christian Scriptures

hec·a·tomb \'he-kə-ˌtōm\ *n* : an ancient Greek and Roman sacrifice of 100 oxen or cattle

heck·le \'he-kəl\ *vb* **heck·led; heck·ling** ♦ : to harass with questions or gibes

♦ bait, bug, hassle, needle, ride, taunt, tease — more at TEASE

heck·ler \'he-k(ə-)lər\ *n* ♦ : one that heckles

♦ oppressor, persecutor, taunter, tormentor, torturer — more at TORMENTOR

hect·are \'hek-ˌtar\ *n* : a metric measure equal to 10,000 square meters

hec·tic \'hek-tik\ *adj* **1** : being hot and flushed **2** ♦ : filled with excitement, activity, or confusion

♦ agitated, feverish, frenzied, heated, overactive, overwrought — more at FEVERISH

hec·ti·cal·ly \'hek-ti-k(ə-)lē\ *adv* ♦ : in a hectic manner

♦ amok, berserk, frantically, harum-scarum, helter-skelter, madly, pell-mell, wild, wildly — more at HELTER-SKELTER

hec·to·gram \'hek-tə-ˌgram\ *n* : a metric measure equal to 100 grams

hec·to·li·ter \'hek-tə-ˌlē-tər\ *n* : a metric measure equal to 100 liters

hec·to·me·ter \'hek-tə-ˌmē-tər, hek-'tä-mə-tər\ *n* : a metric measure equal to 100 meters

hec·tor \'hek-tər\ *vb* [*hector* bully, fr. *Hector*, champion of Troy in Greek legend] **1** : SWAGGER **2** ♦ : to intimidate by bluster or personal pressure

♦ browbeat, bully, cow, intimidate — more at INTIMIDATE

¹**hedge** \'hej\ *n* **1** : a fence or boundary formed of shrubs or small trees **2** ♦ : something that impedes or separates : BARRIER **3** : a means of protection (as against financial loss)

♦ barrier, fence, wall — more at BARRIER

²**hedge** *vb* **hedged; hedg·ing** **1** ♦ : to enclose or protect with or as if with a hedge **2** : HINDER **3** : to protect oneself financially by a counterbalancing action **4** ♦ : to evade the risk of commitment — **hedg·er** *n*

♦ [1] cage, closet, coop up, corral, encase, enclose, envelop, fence, hem, house, immure, pen, wall — more at ENCLOSE ♦ [4] equivocate, fudge, pussyfoot — more at EQUIVOCATE

hedge·hog \'hej-ˌhȯg, -ˌhäg\ *n* : a small Old World insect-eating mammal covered with spines; *also* : PORCUPINE

hedge·hop \-ˌhäp\ *vb* : to fly an airplane very close to the ground

hedge·row \-ˌrō\ *n* : a row of shrubs or trees bounding or separating fields

he·do·nism \'hēd-ᵊn-ˌi-zəm\ *n* [Gk *hēdonē* pleasure] : the doctrine that pleasure is the chief good in life; *also* : a way of life based on this — **he·do·nist** \-ist\ *n* — **he·do·nis·tic** \ˌhēd-ᵊn-'i-stik\ *adj*

¹**heed** \'hēd\ *vb* ♦ : to pay attention

♦ attend, hark, hear, listen, mind — more at LISTEN
♦ follow, listen, mind, note, observe, regard, watch; *also* consider, contemplate, mull, ponder, weigh; comply

(with), keep, obey, respect; hark (to), hear, hearken (to); mark, notice, see *Ant* disregard, ignore, tune out

²heed *n* ♦ : the act or state of attending or noticing

♦ attention, awareness, cognizance, ear, eye, notice, observance, observation — more at ATTENTION

heed·ful \'hēd-fəl\ *adj* ♦ : taking heed — **heed·ful·ly** *adv*

♦ alert, careful, cautious, circumspect, considerate, gingerly, guarded, safe, wary — more at CAREFUL

heed·ful·ness \-nəs\ *n* ♦ : the quality or state of being heedful

♦ alertness, care, carefulness, caution, circumspection — more at CAUTION ♦ care, carefulness, heed, pains, scrupulousness — more at CARE

heed·less \-ləs\ *adj* ♦ : not taking heed — **heed·less·ly** *adv*

♦ careless, mindless, unguarded, unsafe, unwary — more at CARELESS

heed·less·ness \-ləs-nəs\ *n* ♦ : the quality or state of being heedless

♦ carelessness, dereliction, laxness, negligence, remissness, slackness — more at NEGLIGENCE

¹heel \'hēl\ *n* **1** : the hind part of the foot **2** : one of the crusty ends of a loaf of bread **3** : a solid attachment forming the back of the sole of a shoe **4** : a rear, low, or bottom part **5** ♦ : a contemptible person

♦ beast, boor, churl, clown, creep, cretin, cur, jerk, joker, louse, lout, skunk, slob, snake — more at JERK

²heel *vb* : to tilt to one side : LIST

¹heft \'heft\ *n* : WEIGHT, HEAVINESS

²heft *vb* **1** ♦ : to heave up : HOIST **2** : to test the weight of by lifting

♦ boost, heave, hoist, jack — more at HEAVE

hefty \'hef-tē\ *adj* **heft·i·er; -est 1** : marked by bigness, bulk, and usu. strength **2** ♦ : impressively large **3** ♦ : quite heavy

♦ [2] big, large, outsize, oversize, sizable, substantial — more at LARGE ♦ [3] heavy, massive, ponderous, weighty — more at HEAVY

he·ge·mo·ny \hi-'je-mə-nē\ *n* : preponderant influence or authority over others : DOMINATION

he·gi·ra \hi-'jī-rə\ *n* [the *Hegira*, flight of Muhammad from Mecca in A.D. 622, fr. ML, fr. Ar *hijra*, lit., departure] : a journey esp. when undertaken to escape a dangerous or undesirable environment

heif·er \'he-fər\ *n* : a young cow; *esp* : one that has not had a calf

height \'hīt\ *n* **1** ♦ : the highest or most advanced part or point **2** ♦ : the distance from the bottom to the top of something standing upright **3** : ALTITUDE **4** ♦ : an extent of land rising to a considerable degree above the surrounding country

♦ [1] acme, apex, climax, crown, culmination, head, meridian, peak, pinnacle, summit, tip-top, top, zenith; *also* bloom, flood tide, flower, glory, heyday; high; cap, ceiling, crest, roof; crescendo, extremity, maximum, tip, vertex *Ant* bottom, nadir ♦ [1] extremity, limit; *also* consummation, epitome, quintessence, ultimate ♦ [2] altitude, elevation; *also* rise; highness, loftiness, tallness ♦ [4] elevation, eminence, highland, hill, mound, prominence, rise; *also* alp, mount, mountain, peak; butte, mesa, plateau, table, tableland, cliff, crag, precipice, tor; ridge, sierra; dome; foothill, hillock, knob, knoll; down *Ant* lowland

height·en \'hīt-ᵊn\ *vb* **1** ♦ : to increase in amount or degree **2** ♦ : to make or become high or higher

♦ [1] amplify, beef, boost, consolidate, deepen, enhance, intensify, magnify, redouble, step up, strengthen — more at INTENSIFY ♦ [2] boost, crane, elevate, heave, heft, hike, hoist, jack, lift, pick up, raise, up, uphold — more at RAISE

Heim·lich maneuver \'hīm-lik-\ *n* [Henry J. *Heimlich* *b*1920 Am. surgeon] : the manual application of sudden

upward pressure on the upper abdomen of a choking victim to force a foreign object from the trachea

hei·nous \'hā-nəs\ *adj* [ME, fr. AF *hainus, heinous*, fr. *haine* hate, fr. *hair* to hate] : hatefully or shockingly evil — **hei·nous·ly** *adv*

hei·nous·ness \-nəs\ *n* ♦ : the state or quality of being heinous

♦ atrociousness, atrocity, depravity, enormity, monstrosity, vileness, wickedness — more at ENORMITY

heir \'ar\ *n* : one who inherits or is entitled to inherit property, rank, title, or office — **heir·ship** *n*

heir apparent *n, pl* **heirs apparent** : an heir whose right to succeed (as to a title) cannot be taken away if he or she survives the present holder

heir·ess \'ar-əs\ *n* : a female heir esp. to great wealth

heir·loom \'ar-ˌlüm\ *n* **1** : a piece of personal property that descends by inheritance **2** : something handed on from one generation to another

heir presumptive *n, pl* **heirs presumptive** : an heir whose present right to inherit could be lost through the birth of a nearer relative

heist \'hīst\ *vb* : to commit armed robbery on; *also* : STEAL — **heist** *n*

held *past and past part of* HOLD

he·li·cal \'he-li-kəl, 'hē-\ *adj* ♦ : of, relating to, or having the form of a helix : SPIRAL

♦ spiral, winding — more at SPIRAL

he·li·cop·ter \'he-lə-ˌkäp-tər, 'hē-\ *n* [F *hélicoptère*, fr. Gk *helik-, helix* spiral + *pteron* wing] : an aircraft that is supported in the air by one or more rotors revolving on substantially vertical axes

he·lio·cen·tric \ˌhē-lē-ō-'sen-trik\ *adj* : having or relating to the sun as center

he·lio·sphere \'hē-lē-ə-ˌsfir, -ō-\ *n* : the region in space influenced by the sun or solar wind

he·lio·trope \'hē-lē-ə-ˌtrōp\ *n* [L *heliotropium*, fr. Gk *hēliotropion*, fr. *hēlios* sun + *tropos* turn; fr. its flowers' turning toward the sun] : any of a genus of herbs or shrubs related to the forget-me-not that have small white or purple flowers

he·li·port \'he-lə-ˌpōrt\ *n* : a landing and takeoff place for a helicopter

he·li·um \'hē-lē-əm\ *n* [NL, fr. Gk *hēlios* sun] : a very light nonflammable gaseous chemical element occurring in various natural gases

he·lix \'hē-liks\ *n, pl* **he·li·ces** \'he-lə-ˌsēz, 'hē-\ *also* **he·lix·es** \'hē-lik-səz\ : something spiral in form

hell \'hel\ *n* **1** : a nether world in which the dead continue to exist **2** : the realm of the devil in which the damned suffer everlasting punishment **3** : a place or state of torment or wickedness **4** ♦ : a place or state of turmoil, disorder, or destruction — **hell·ish** *adj*

♦ [3] agony, horror, misery, murder, nightmare, torment, torture; *also* cross, ordeal, trial, tribulation; gall, thorn; bummer, downer, drag *Ant* heaven, paradise ♦ [4] bedlam, circus, madhouse — more at MADHOUSE ♦ [4] chaos, confusion, disarray, disorder, disorganization, havoc, jumble, mess, muddle, shambles — more at CHAOS

hel·la·cious \ˌhe-'lā-shəs\ *adj* **1** : exceptionally powerful or violent ⟨∼ winds⟩ **2** : remarkably good **3** : extremely difficult ⟨a ∼ schedule⟩ **4** : extraordinarily large

hell-bent \'hel-ˌbent\ *adj* ♦ : stubbornly determined

♦ bound, decisive, determined, firm, intent, purposeful, resolute, set, single-minded — more at DETERMINED

hell·cat \-ˌkat\ *n* **1** : WITCH 2 **2** : a violently temperamental person; *esp* : an ill-tempered woman

hel·le·bore \'he-lə-ˌbōr\ *n* **1** : any of a genus of poisonous herbs related to the buttercups; *also* : the dried root of a hellebore **2** : a poisonous plant related to the lilies; *also* : its dried roots used in medicine and insecticides

Hel·lene \'he-ˌlēn\ *n* : GREEK

Hel·le·nism \'he-lə-ˌni-zəm\ *n* : a body of humanistic

and classical ideals associated with ancient Greece —
Hel·len·ic \he-'le-nik\ *adj* — **Hel·le·nist** \'he-lə-nist\ *n*
Hel·le·nis·tic \,he-lə-'nis-tik\ *adj* : of or relating to Greek history, culture, or art after Alexander the Great
hell–for–leather *adv* : at full speed
hell·gram·mite \'hel-grə-,mīt\ *n* : an aquatic insect larva that is used as bait in fishing
hell·hole \'hel-,hōl\ *n* : a place of extreme misery or squalor
hel·lion \'hel-yən\ *n* ♦ : a troublesome or mischievous person

  ♦ devil, imp, mischief, monkey, rapscallion, rascal, rogue, scamp, urchin — more at SCAMP

hel·lo \hə-'lō, he-\ *n, pl* **hellos** ♦ : an expression of greeting — used interjectionally

  ♦ greeting, salutation, salute; *also* amenities, civilities, pleasantries; regards, respects *Ant* adieu, bon voyage, farewell, Godspeed, good-bye

helm \'helm\ *n* **1** : a lever or wheel for steering a ship **2** ♦ : a position of control

  ♦ chair, head, headship, rein — more at HEAD

hel·met \'hel-mət\ *n* : a protective covering for the head
helms·man \'helmz-mən\ *n* ♦ : the person at the helm

  ♦ boss, captain, chief, foreman, head, headman, kingpin, leader, master, taskmaster — more at BOSS

hel·ot \'he-lət\ *n* : SLAVE, SERF
¹**help** \'help\ *vb* **1** ♦ : to give assistance or support to : AID **2** ♦ : to make more pleasant or bearable **3** : to be of use; *also* : PROMOTE **4** : to change for the better **5 a** : to refrain from **b** : to keep from occurring : PREVENT **6** : to serve with food or drink ⟨~ yourself⟩

  ♦ [1] abet, aid, assist, back, prop, support; *also* advance, facilitate, forward, foster, further; champion, endorse, patronize, promote, sponsor; attend, care (for), comfort, minister (to), succor; bolster, boost, buttress, reinforce; advise, counsel, guide, mentor, nurture; deliver, rescue, save; embolden, encourage, hearten; benefit, favor, profit, serve *Ant* hinder ♦ [2] allay, alleviate, assuage, ease, mitigate, mollify, palliate, relieve, soothe; *also* abate, lighten, moderate, soften, temper; cure, heal, remedy; amend, correct, emend, fix, mend, rectify, reform, repair; ameliorate, better, enhance, enrich, improve, meliorate, perfect, refine *Ant* aggravate

²**help** *n* **1 a** ♦ : the act of helping : help given **b** ♦ : a source of aid **2** : REMEDY, RELIEF **3** : one who assists another **4** ♦ : one employed by another usu. for wages or salary and in a position below the executive level — often used collectively

  ♦ [1a] aid, assist, assistance, backing, boost, lift, support; *also* advancement, encouragement, forwarding, furtherance, furthering; benefaction, patronage, promotion, sponsorship; advice, care, counsel, guidance; attendance, attention, service; beneficence, charity, favor, kindness, philanthropy; relief, succor *Ant* hindrance ♦ [1b] advantage, aid, benefit, boon; *also* lift; support, sustenance; blessing, godsend, windfall; recourse, resort, resource; asset *Ant* disadvantage, drawback, hindrance, impediment ♦ [4] force, personnel, pool, staff — more at FORCE

help·er \'hel-pər\ *n* ♦ : one that helps

  ♦ aid, apprentice, assistant, deputy, helpmate, mate, sidekick; *also* attendant, handmaiden, maid, maidservant, scullion, servant; auxiliary, subordinate, underling; employee, hand, help, hireling, laborer, worker

helper T cell *n* : a T cell that participates in the immune response by recognizing foreign antigens and has a protein on its surface to which HIV attaches
help·ful \-fəl\ *adj* ♦ : of service or assistance — **help·ful·ly** *adv* — **help·ful·ness** *n*

  ♦ advantageous, beneficial, favorable (*or* favourable), profitable, salutary — more at BENEFICIAL

help·ing *n* : a portion of food
help·less \-ləs\ *adj* **1** ♦ : lacking protection or support

: DEFENSELESS **2** ♦ : marked by an inability to act or react — **help·less·ly** *adv* — **help·less·ness** *n*

  ♦ [1] defenseless (*or* defenceless), exposed, susceptible, undefended, unguarded, unprotected, unresistant, vulnerable; *also* indefensible, untenable; uncovered, unsafe; overcome, preyed (on *or* upon); passive, resistless, unarmed; feeble, frail, weak; abandoned, marooned *Ant* guarded, invulnerable, protected, resistant, shielded ♦ [2] impotent, powerless, weak — more at POWERLESS

help·mate \'help-,māt\ *n* **1** ♦ : one that helps : HELPER **2** ♦ : a female partner in a marriage : WIFE

  ♦ [1] aid, apprentice, assistant, deputy, helper, mate, sidekick — more at HELPER ♦ [2] lady, old lady, wife — more at WIFE

help·meet \-,mēt\ *n* **1** : one that helps : HELPMATE **2** : a female partner in a marriage : WIFE
hel·ter–skel·ter \,hel-tər-'skel-tər\ *adv* **1** : in undue haste or disorder **2** ♦ : in a haphazard manner

  ♦ amok, berserk, frantically, harum-scarum, hectically, madly, pell-mell, wild, wildly; *also* confusedly, crazily, desperately, feverishly, uncontrollably; heedlessly, hotheadedly, recklessly, wantonly; chaotically, turbulently; aimlessly, haphazardly

helve \'helv\ *n* : a handle of a tool or weapon
Hel·ve·tian \hel-'vē-shən\ *adj* : SWISS — **Helvetian** *n*
¹**hem** \'hem\ *n* **1** : a border of an article (as of cloth) doubled back and stitched down **2** : RIM, MARGIN
²**hem** *vb* **hemmed; hem·ming 1** : to make a hem in sewing; *also* : BORDER, EDGE **2** ♦ : to surround restrictively

  ♦ cage, closet, coop up, corral, encase, enclose, envelop, fence, hedge, house, immure, pen, wall — more at ENCLOSE

he–man \'hē-,man\ *n* : a strong virile man
he·ma·tite \'hē-mə-,tīt\ *n* : a mineral that consists of an oxide of iron and that constitutes an important iron ore
he·ma·tol·o·gy \,hē-mə-'tä-lə-jē\ *n* : a branch of biology that deals with the blood and blood-forming organs — **he·ma·to·log·ic** \-tə-'lä-jik\ *also* **he·ma·to·log·i·cal** \-ji-kəl\ *adj* — **he·ma·tol·o·gist** \-'tä-lə-jist\ *n*
he·ma·to·ma \-'tō-mə\ *n, pl* **mas** *also* **-ma·ta** \-mə-tə\ : a usu. clotted mass of blood forming as a result of a broken blood vessel
heme \'hēm\ *n* : the deep red iron-containing part of hemoglobin
hemi·sphere \'he-mə-,sfir\ *n* **1** : one of the halves of the earth as divided by the equator into northern and southern parts or by a meridian into eastern and western parts **2** : either of two half spheres formed by a plane through the sphere's center — **hemi·spher·ic** \,he-mə-'sfir-ik, -'sfer-\ *or* **hemi·spher·i·cal** \-'sfir-i-kəl, -'sfer-\ *adj*
hem·line \'hem-,līn\ *n* : the line formed by the lower edge of a garment
hem·lock \'hem-,läk\ *n* **1** : any of several poisonous herbs related to the carrot **2** : an evergreen tree related to the pines; *also* : its soft light wood
he·mo·glo·bin \'hē-mə-,glō-bən\ *n* : an iron-containing compound found in red blood cells that carries oxygen from the lungs to the body tissues
he·mo·phil·ia \,hē-mə-'fi-lē-ə\ *n* : a hereditary blood defect usu. of males that slows blood clotting with resulting difficulty in stopping bleeding — **he·mo·phil·i·ac** \-lē-,ak\ *adj or n*
hem·or·rhage \'hem-rij, 'he-mə-\ *n* : a large discharge of blood from the blood vessels — **hemorrhage** *vb* — **hem·or·rhag·ic** \,he-mə-'ra-jik\ *adj*
hem·or·rhoid \'hem-,ròid, 'he-mə-\ *n* : a swollen mass of dilated veins at or just within the anus — usu. used in pl.
hemp \'hemp\ *n* : a tall widely grown Asian herb related to the mulberry that is the source of a tough fiber used in rope and of marijuana and hashish from its flowers and leaves; *also* : the fiber — **hemp·en** \'hem-pən\ *adj*
hem·stitch \'hem-,stich\ *vb* : to embroider (fabric) by

drawing out parallel threads and stitching the exposed threads in groups to form designs

hen \'hen\ *n* : a female chicken esp. over a year old; *also* : a female bird

hence \'hens\ *adv* 1 : AWAY 2 : from this time 3 ♦ : because of a preceding fact or premise : CONSEQUENTLY 4 : from this source or origin

♦ accordingly, consequently, ergo, so, therefore, thus, wherefore — more at THEREFORE

hence·forth \'hens-ˌfōrth\ *adv* : from this point on

hence·for·ward \-'fōr-wərd\ *adv* : HENCEFORTH

hench·man \'hench-mən\ *n* [ME *hengestman* groom, fr. *hengest* stallion] : a trusted follower or supporter

hen·na \'he-nə\ *n* 1 : an Old World tropical shrub with fragrant white flowers; *also* : a reddish brown dye obtained from its leaves and used esp. on hair 2 : the color of henna dye

hen·peck \'hen-ˌpek\ *vb* ♦ : to nag and boss one's husband

♦ hound, nag, needle — more at NAG

hep \'hep\ *adj* : HIP

hep·a·rin \'he-pə-rən\ *n* : a compound found esp. in liver that slows the clotting of blood and is used medically

he·pat·ic \hi-'pa-tik\ *adj* : of, relating to, or associated with the liver

he·pat·i·ca \hi-'pa-ti-kə\ *n* : any of a genus of herbs related to the buttercups that have lobed leaves and delicate white, pink, or bluish flowers

hep·a·ti·tis \ˌhe-pə-'tī-təs\ *n, pl* **-tit·i·des** \-'ti-tə-ˌdēz\ : inflammation of the liver; *also* : a virus disease of which this is a feature

hep·tam·e·ter \hep-'ta-mə-tər\ *n* : a line of verse containing seven metrical feet

hep·tath·lon \hep-'tath-lən, -ˌlän\ *n* : a 7-event athletic contest for women

¹**her** \'hər\ *adj* : of or relating to her or herself

²**her** *pron, objective case of* SHE

¹**her·ald** \'her-əld\ *n* 1 : an official crier or messenger 2 ♦ : one that precedes or foreshadows : HARBINGER 3 : ANNOUNCER 4 : ADVOCATE

♦ angel, forerunner, harbinger, precursor — more at FORERUNNER

²**herald** *vb* 1 : to give notice of 2 : HAIL, GREET; *also* : PUBLICIZE

he·ral·dic \he-'ral-dik, hə-\ *adj* : of or relating to heralds or heraldry

her·ald·ry \'her-əl-drē\ *n, pl* **-ries** 1 : the practice of devising and granting armorial insignia and of tracing genealogies 2 : INSIGNIA 3 : PAGEANTRY

herb \'ərb, 'hərb\ *n* 1 : a seed plant that lacks woody tissue and dies to the ground at the end of a growing season 2 : a plant or plant part valued for medicinal or savory qualities — **her·ba·ceous** \ˌər-'bā-shəs, ˌhər-\ *adj*

herb·age \'ər-bij, 'hər-\ *n* ♦ : green plants esp. when used or fit for grazing

♦ flora, foliage, green, greenery, leafage, vegetation, verdure — more at GREENERY

herb·al \'ər-bəl, 'hər-\ *adj* : of, relating to, utilizing, or made of herbs

herb·al·ist \'ər-bə-list, 'hər-\ *n* 1 : a person who practices healing by the use of herbs 2 : a person who collects or grows herbs

her·bar·i·um \ˌər-'bar-ē-əm, ˌhər-\ *n, pl* **-ia** \-ē-ə\ 1 : a collection of dried plant specimens 2 : a place that houses an herbarium

her·bi·cide \'ər-bə-ˌsīd, 'hər-\ *n* : an agent used to destroy or inhibit plant growth — **her·bi·cid·al** \ˌər-bə-'sīd-ᵊl, ˌhər-\ *adj*

her·biv·o·rous \ˌər-'bi-və-rəs, ˌhər-\ *adj* : feeding on plants — **her·bi·vore** \'ər-bə-ˌvōr, 'hər-\ *n*

her·cu·le·an \ˌhər-kyə-'lē-ən, ˌhər-'kyü-lē-\ *adj, often cap* [*Hercules*, hero of Greek myth renowned for his strength] ♦ : of extraordinary power, size, or difficulty ⟨a ∼ task⟩

♦ arduous, demanding, difficult, exacting, formidable, grueling, hard, laborious, murderous, rough, stiff, strenuous, tall, toilsome, tough — more at HARD

¹**herd** \'hərd\ *n* 1 : a group of animals of one kind kept or living together 2 : a group of people with a common bond 3 ♦ : the undistinguished masses : MOB

♦ commoners, masses, mob, people, plebeians, populace, rank and file — more at MASSES

²**herd** *vb* ♦ : to assemble or move in or as if in a herd — **herd·er** *n*

♦ drive, punch, run — more at DRIVE

herds·man \'hərdz-mən\ *n* : one who manages, breeds, or tends livestock

¹**here** \'hir\ *adv* 1 : in or at this place; *also* : NOW 2 : at or in this point, particular, or case 3 : in the present life or state 4 : to this place

²**here** *n* : this place ⟨get away from ∼⟩

here·abouts \'hir-ə-ˌbaùts\ *or* **here·about** \-ˌbaùt\ *adv* : in this vicinity

¹**here·af·ter** \hir-'af-tər\ *adv* 1 : after this in sequence or in time 2 : in some future time or state

²**hereafter** *n, often cap* 1 : time that is to come : FUTURE 2 ♦ : an existence beyond earthly life

♦ afterlife, eternity, immortality — more at ETERNITY

here·by \hir-'bī\ *adv* : by means of this

he·red·i·tary \hə-'re-də-ˌter-ē\ *adj* 1 ♦ : genetically passed or passable from parent to offspring 2 : passing by inheritance; *also* : having title or possession through inheritance 3 : of a kind established by tradition

♦ genetic, heritable, inborn, inherited; *also* congenital, inbred, inherent, innate, native, natural

he·red·i·ty \-də-tē\ *n* : the characteristics and potentialities genetically derived from one's ancestors; *also* : the passing of these from ancestor to descendant

Her·e·ford \'hər-fərd\ *n* : any of a breed of red-coated beef cattle with white faces and markings

here·in \hir-'in\ *adv* : in this

here·of \-'əv, -'äv\ *adv* : of this

here·on \-'ȯn, -'än\ *adv* : on this

her·e·sy \'her-ə-sē\ *n, pl* **-sies** [ME *heresie*, fr. AF, fr. LL *haeresis*, fr. LGk *hairesis*, fr. Gk, action of taking, choice, sect, fr. *hairein* to take] 1 : adherence to a religious opinion contrary to church dogma 2 : an opinion or doctrine contrary to church dogma 3 ♦ : dissent from a dominant theory, opinion, or practice

♦ dissent, heterodoxy, nonconformity; *also* error, fallacy, falsehood, misconception, myth; apostasy, defection, schism, sectarianism, separatism; deviance, deviation, unconventionality; disagreement, discord, dissension *Ant* conformity, orthodoxy

her·e·tic \'her-ə-ˌtik\ *n* ♦ : one who dissents from an accepted belief or doctrine

♦ dissenter, dissident, nonconformist; *also* apostate, defector, renegade; schismatic, sectarian, separatist; disbeliever, infidel, unbeliever; bohemian, individualist

he·ret·i·cal \hə-'re-ti-kəl\ *adj* ♦ : of, relating to, or characterized by departure from accepted beliefs or standards

♦ dissident, heterodox, nonconforming, nonconformist, nonorthodox, unconventional, unorthodox; *also* nontraditional; apostate, defecting, renegade; schismatic, sectarian, separatist *Ant* conforming, conventional, orthodox

here·to \hir-'tü\ *adv* : to this document

here·to·fore \'hir-tə-ˌfōr\ *adv* ♦ : up to this time

♦ hitherto, yet — more at HITHERTO

here·un·der \hir-'ən-dər\ *adv* : under this or according to this writing

here·un·to \hir-'ən-tü\ *adv* : to this

here·upon \'hir-ə-ˌpȯn, -ˌpän\ *adv* : on this or immediately after this

here·with \hir-'with, -'with\ *adv* 1 : with this 2 : HEREBY

her·i·ta·ble \'her-ə-tə-bəl\ *adj* ♦ : capable of being inherited

♦ genetic, hereditary, inborn, inherited — more at HE-
REDITARY

her·i·tage \'her-ə-tij\ *n* **1** : property that descends to an
heir **2** ♦ : something transmitted by or acquired from a
predecessor : LEGACY **3** : BIRTHRIGHT

♦ bequest, birthright, inheritance, legacy — more at
INHERITANCE

her·maph·ro·dite \(ˌ)hər-'ma-frə-ˌdīt\ *n* : an animal or plant
having both male and female reproductive organs —
hermaphrodite *adj* — **her·maph·ro·dit·ic** \(ˌ)hər-ˌma-frə-
'di-tik\ *adj*

her·met·ic \hər-'me-tik\ *also* **her·met·i·cal** \-ti-kəl\ *adj*
: AIRTIGHT — **her·met·i·cal·ly** \-ti-k(ə-)lē\ *adv*

her·mit \'hər-mət\ *n* [ME *heremite, eremite,* fr. AF, fr. LL
eremita, fr. LGk *erēmītēs,* fr. Gk, adj., living in the desert,
fr. *erēmia* desert, fr. *erēmos* desolate] ♦ : one who lives in
solitude esp. for religious reasons

♦ anchorite, recluse, solitary — more at RECLUSE

her·mit·age \-mə-tij\ *n* **1** : the dwelling of a hermit **2** : a
secluded dwelling

hermit crab *n* : any of numerous crabs that occupy empty
mollusk shells

her·nia \'hər-nē-ə\ *n, pl* **-ni·as** *or* **-ni·ae** \-nē-ˌē, -nē-ˌī\ : a
protrusion of a bodily part (as a loop of intestine) into a
pouch of the weakened wall of a cavity in which it is normally enclosed — **her·ni·ate** \-nē-ˌāt\ *vb* — **her·ni·a·tion**
\ˌhər-nē-'ā-shən\ *n*

he·ro \'hē-rō\ *n, pl* **heroes** **1** : a mythological or legendary
figure of great strength or ability **2** : a person admired
for his or her achievements and qualities **3** : the principal character in a literary or dramatic work **4** *pl usu* **he·**
ros : a large sandwich on a long split roll : SUBMARINE 2

he·ro·ic \hi-'rō-ik\ *adj* **1** : of, relating to, resembling, or
suggesting heroes esp. of antiquity **2** ♦ : exhibiting or
marked by courage and daring **3** ♦ : of impressive size,
power, extent, or effect

♦ [2] brave, courageous, dauntless, doughty, fearless,
gallant, greathearted, intrepid, lionhearted, manful,
stalwart, stout, undaunted, valiant, valorous — more at
BRAVE ♦ [3] august, baronial, gallant, glorious, grand,
grandiose, imposing, magnificent, majestic, monumental, noble, proud, regal, royal, splendid, stately — more
at GRAND

he·ro·i·cal·ly \hi-'rō-i-k(ə-)lē\ *adv* ♦ : in a heroic manner

♦ gallantly, grandly, greatly, honorably (*or* honourably), magnanimously, nobly — more at GREATLY

heroic couplet *n* : a rhyming couplet in iambic pentameter
he·ro·ics \hi-'rō-iks\ *n pl* : heroic or showy behavior
her·o·in \'her-ə-wən\ *n* : an illicit addictive narcotic drug
made from morphine

her·o·ine \'her-ə-wən\ *n* **1** : a woman admired for her
achievements and qualities **2** : the principal female character in a literary or dramatic work

her·o·ism \'her-ə-ˌwi-zəm\ *n* **1** ♦ : heroic conduct **2** : the
qualities of a hero

♦ bravery, courage, daring, fearlessness, gallantry, guts,
hardihood, heart, nerve, stoutness, valor — more at
COURAGE

her·on \'her-ən\ *n, pl* **herons** *also* **heron** : any of various
long-legged long-billed wading birds with soft plumage

her·pes \'hər-pēz\ *n* : any of several virus diseases characterized by the formation of blisters on the skin or mucous
membranes

herpes sim·plex \-'sim-ˌpleks\ *n* : either of two virus diseases marked in one by watery blisters above the waist
(as on the mouth and lips) and in the other on the sex
organs

herpes zos·ter \-'zäs-tər\ *n* : SHINGLES

her·pe·tol·o·gy \ˌhər-pə-'tä-lə-jē\ *n* : a branch of zoology
dealing with reptiles and amphibians — **her·pe·tol·o·gist**
\ˌhər-pə-'tä-lə-jist\ *n*

her·ring \'her-iŋ\ *n, pl* **herring** *or* **herrings** : a valuable nar-
row-bodied food fish of the north Atlantic; *also* : a related
fish of the north Pacific harvested esp. for its roe

her·ring·bone \'her-iŋ-ˌbōn\ *n* : a pattern made up of rows
of parallel lines with adjacent rows slanting in reverse
directions; *also* : a twilled fabric with this pattern

hers \'hərz\ *pron* : one or the ones belonging to her

her·self \hər-'self\ *pron* : SHE, HER — used reflexively, for
emphasis, or in absolute constructions

hertz \'hərts, 'herts\ *n, pl* **hertz** : a unit of frequency equal
to one cycle per second

hes·i·tance \'he-zə-təns\ *n* : HESITANCY

hes·i·tan·cy \'he-zə-tən-sē\ *n* **1** ♦ : the quality or state of
being hesitant **2** ♦ : an act or instance of hesitating

♦ [1] disinclination, reluctance, reticence — more at
RELUCTANCE ♦ [2] hesitation, indecision, irresolution,
vacillation — more at HESITATION

hes·i·tant \'he-zə-tənt\ *adj* ♦ : tending to hesitate — **hes·i·**
tant·ly *adv*

♦ afraid, dubious, indisposed, reluctant; *also* uneager,
unenthusiastic; averse, unwilling; doubtful, faltering,
irresolute, questioning, uncertain, undecided, unsure,
vacillating, wobbly; fainthearted, shy, timid *Ant* disposed, inclined

hes·i·tate \'he-zə-ˌtāt\ *vb* **-tat·ed; -tat·ing** **1** ♦ : to hold back
(as in doubt) **2** : PAUSE

♦ falter, hang back, shilly-shally, stagger, teeter, vacillate, waver, wobble; *also* haw, hem; dally, dawdle,
delay, linger, procrastinate, pause, wait; back down,
chicken (out); consider, debate, deliberate, ponder,
weigh; oscillate; equivocate, hedge, pussyfoot *Ant* dive
(in), plunge (in)

hes·i·ta·tion \ˌhe-zə-'tā-shən\ *n* ♦ : an act or instance of
hesitating

♦ hesitancy, indecision, irresolution, vacillation; *also*
delay, procrastination, waiting; consideration, debate,
deliberation, doubt, incertitude, uncertainty; avoidance, equivocation; aversion, disinclination, indisposition, reluctance; shyness

het·ero·dox \'he-tə-rə-ˌdäks\ *adj* **1** ♦ : differing from an
acknowledged standard **2** ♦ : holding unorthodox opinions

♦ [1, 2] dissident, heretical, nonconforming, nonconformist, nonorthodox, unconventional, unorthodox —
more at HERETICAL

het·ero·doxy \'he-tə-rə-ˌdäk-sē\ *n* ♦ : the quality or state
of being heterodox

♦ dissent, heresy, nonconformity — more at HERESY

het·er·o·ge·neous \ˌhe-tə-rə-'jē-nē-əs, -nyəs\ *adj* ♦ : consisting of dissimilar ingredients or constituents : MIXED
— **het·er·o·ge·ne·ity** \-jə-'nē-ə-tē\ *n* — **het·er·o·ge·neous·ly**
adv

♦ assorted, miscellaneous, mixed, motley, varied —
more at MISCELLANEOUS

het·ero·glos·sia \ˌhe-tə-rō-'glä-sē-ə, -'glö-\ *n* : a diversity of
voices, styles of discourse, or points of view in a literary
work

het·ero·sex·ism \ˌhe-tə-rō-'sek-si-zəm\ *n* : discrimination
or prejudice by heterosexuals against homosexuals

het·ero·sex·u·al \ˌhe-tə-rō-'sek-shə-wəl\ *adj* **1** : of, relating
to, or marked by sexual interest in the opposite sex; *also*
: of, relating to, or involving sexual intercourse between
members of opposite sex **2** : of or relating to different
sexes — **heterosexual** *n* — **het·ero·sex·u·al·i·ty** \-ˌsek-shə-
'wa-lə-tē\ *n*

hew \'hyü\ *vb* **hewed; hewed** *or* **hewn** \'hyün\; **hew·ing**
1 ♦ : to cut or fell with blows (as of an ax) **2** : to give
shape to with or as if with an ax **3** ♦ : to conform or
adhere strictly ⟨∼ to tradition⟩ — **hew·er** *n*

♦ [1] chop, cut, fell — more at FELL ♦ *usu* **hew to**
[3] adhere, cling, stick — more at STICK

HEW *abbr* Department of Health, Education, and Welfare

¹**hex** \'heks\ *vb* **1** : to practice witchcraft **2** : JINX **3** ♦ : to put a hex on

♦ bewitch, charm, enchant, spell — more at BEWITCH

²**hex** *n* **1** ♦ : a person who practices witchcraft : WITCH **2** : SPELL, JINX

♦ enchantress, hag, witch — more at WITCH

³**hex** *adj* : HEXAGONAL

⁴**hex** *abbr* hexagon

hexa·gon \'hek-sə-ˌgän\ *n* [ultim. fr. Gk *hex* six + *gōnia* angle] : a polygon having six angles and six sides — **hex·ag·o·nal** \hek-ˈsa-gən-ᵊl\ *adj*

hex·am·e·ter \hek-ˈsa-mə-tər\ *n* : a line of verse containing six metrical feet

hey \'hā\ *interj* — used esp. to call attention or to express doubt, surprise, or joy

hey·day \'hā-ˌdā\ *n* ♦ : a period of greatest strength, vigor, or prosperity

♦ bloom, blossom, flower, flush, prime — more at BLOOM

hf *abbr* half

Hf *symbol* hafnium

HF *abbr* high frequency

hg *abbr* hectogram

Hg *symbol* [NL *hydrargyrum*, lit., water silver] mercury

hgt *abbr* height

hgwy *abbr* highway

HH *abbr* **1** Her Highness **2** His Highness **3** His Holiness

HHS *abbr* Department of Health and Human Services

HI *abbr* **1** Hawaii **2** humidity index

hi·a·tus \hī-ˈā-təs\ *n* [L, fr. *hiare* to yawn] **1** : a break in an object : GAP **2** ♦ : a lapse in continuity

♦ discontinuity, gap, interim, interlude, intermission, interruption, interval — more at GAP

hi·ba·chi \hi-ˈbä-chē\ *n* [Jp] : a charcoal brazier

hi·ber·nate \'hī-bər-ˌnāt\ *vb* **-nat·ed; -nat·ing** : to pass the winter in a torpid or resting state — **hi·ber·na·tion** \ˌhī-bər-ˈnā-shən\ *n* — **hi·ber·na·tor** \'hī-bər-ˌnā-tər\ *n*

hi·bis·cus \hī-ˈbis-kəs, hə-\ *n* : any of a genus of herbs, shrubs, and trees related to the mallows and noted for large showy flowers

hic·cup *also* **hic·cough** \'hi-(ˌ)kəp\ *n* **1** : a spasmodic breathing movement checked by sudden closing of the glottis accompanied by a peculiar sound; *also, pl* : an attack of hiccuping **2** : a slight irregularity, error, or malfunction **3** : a brief minor interruption or change — **hiccup** *vb*

hick \'hik\ *n* [*Hick*, nickname for *Richard*] ♦ : an awkward provincial person — **hick** *adj*

♦ bumpkin, clodhopper, rustic, yokel; *also* boor, clod, gawk, lout, oaf; greenhorn, tenderfoot; peasant, peon; mountaineer *Ant* cosmopolitan

hick·o·ry \'hi-kə-rē\ *n, pl* **-ries** : any of a genus of No. American hardwood trees related to the walnuts; *also* : the wood of a hickory — **hickory** *adj*

hi·dal·go \hi-ˈdal-gō\ *n, pl* **-gos** *often cap* [Sp, fr. earlier *fijo dalgo*, lit., son of something] : a member of the lower nobility of Spain

hidden tax *n* **1** : a tax ultimately paid by someone other than the person on whom it is formally levied **2** : an economic injustice that reduces one's income or buying power

¹**hide** \'hīd\ *vb* hid \'hid\; **hid·den** \'hid-ᵊn\ *or* hid; **hid·ing** **1** ♦ : to put or remain out of sight **2** : to conceal for shelter or protection; *also* : to seek protection **3** ♦ : to keep secret **4** : to turn away in shame or anger — **hid·er** *n*

♦ [1] bury, cache, conceal, ensconce, secrete; *also* hoard, squirrel (away), stash; entomb, inter *Ant* display, exhibit ♦ [3] blanket, blot out, cloak, conceal, cover, curtain, enshroud, mask, obscure, occult, screen, shroud, veil; *also* camouflage, cover (up), disguise, smother; gild, gloss (over), varnish, whitewash; becloud, befog, cloud, darken, eclipse, overcast, overshadow, shade *Ant* bare,

disclose, display, divulge, expose, reveal, show, uncloak, uncover, unmask, unveil

²**hide** *n* ♦ : the skin of an animal

♦ fur, pelt, skin; *also* badger, beaver, chamois, chinchilla, ermine, fisher, fox, mink, muskrat, otter, Persian lamb, raccoon, sable, seal; bearskin, buckskin, calfskin, coonskin, cowhide, deerskin, goatskin, horsehide, kidskin, lambskin, pigskin, rawhide, sealskin, sharkskin, sheepskin; fleece, mouton; alligator; cordovan, morocco, suede

³**hide** *vb* : to give a beating to

hide-and-seek \ˌhīd-ᵊn-ˈsēk\ *n* : a children's game in which everyone hides from one player who tries to find them

hide·away \'hī-də-ˌwā\ *n* : a place of refuge, retreat, or concealment : HIDEOUT

hide·bound \'hīd-ˌbau̇nd\ *adj* ♦ : being inflexible or conservative

♦ conservative, old-fashioned, orthodox, reactionary, traditional — more at CONSERVATIVE

hid·eous \'hi-dē-əs\ *adj* [ME *hidous*, fr. AF *hidus, hisdos*, fr. *hisde, hide* terror] **1** ♦ : offensive to one of the senses : UGLY **2** ♦ : morally offensive : SHOCKING — **hid·eous·ly** *adv*

♦ [1] grotesque, ugly, unappealing, unattractive, unlovely, unsightly, vile — more at UGLY ♦ [2] appalling, atrocious, awful, dreadful, frightful, ghastly, grisly, gruesome, horrible, horrid, lurid, macabre, monstrous, nightmarish, shocking, terrible — more at HORRIBLE

hid·eous·ness \-nəs\ *n* ♦ : the quality or state of being hideous

♦ atrociousness, atrocity, frightfulness, horror, monstrosity, repulsiveness — more at HORROR

hide·out \'hī-ˌdau̇t\ *n* ♦ : a place of refuge or concealment

♦ concealment, covert, den, lair, nest; *also* blind, cover, nook, recess; hangout, harbor (*or* harbour), haunt, haven, refuge, retreat, shelter

hie \'hī\ *vb* hied; hy·ing *or* hie·ing ♦ : to move or act quickly : HASTEN

♦ accelerate, fast-track, hasten, hurry, quicken, rush, speed, whisk — more at HURRY

hi·er·ar·chy \'hī-ə-ˌrär-kē\ *n, pl* **-chies** **1** : a ruling body of clergy organized into ranks **2** : persons or things arranged in a graded series — **hi·er·ar·chi·cal** \ˌhī-ə-ˈrär-ki-kəl\ *adj* — **hi·er·ar·chi·cal·ly** \-k(ə-)lē\ *adv*

hi·er·o·glyph·ic \ˌhī-ə-rə-ˈgli-fik\ *n* [MF *hieroglyphique*, adj., ultim. fr. Gk *hieroglyphikos*, fr. *hieros* sacred + *glyphein* to carve] **1** : a character in a system of picture writing (as of the ancient Egyptians) **2** : a symbol or sign difficult to decipher

hi-fi \'hī-ˈfī\ *n* **1** : HIGH FIDELITY **2** : equipment for reproduction of sound with high fidelity

¹**hig·gle·dy-pig·gle·dy** \ˌhi-gəl-dē-ˈpi-gəl-dē\ *adv* : in confusion

²**higgledy-piggledy** *adj* ♦ : lacking order

♦ chaotic, disheveled, disordered, disorderly, hugger-mugger, messy, pell-mell, topsy-turvy, unkempt, untidy

¹**high** \'hī\ *adj* **1 a** ♦ : having large extension upward ⟨a ~ wall⟩ **b** : having a specified elevation : TALL ⟨six feet ~⟩ **2** : advanced toward fullness or culmination; *also* : slightly tainted **3** : advanced esp. in complexity ⟨~er mathematics⟩ **4** : long past **5** : SHRILL, SHARP **6** : far from the equator ⟨~ latitudes⟩ **7** : exalted in character **8** ♦ : of greater degree, size, or amount than average ⟨~ in cholesterol⟩ ⟨~ prices⟩ **9** ♦ : of relatively great importance **10** : FORCIBLE, STRONG ⟨~ winds⟩ **11** : showing elation or excitement **12** ♦ : excited or stupefied by alcohol or a drug : INTOXICATED; *also* : excited or stupefied as if by a drug **13** ♦ : dear in price : EXPENSIVE

♦ [1a] lofty, tall, towering; *also* dominant, dominating, eminent, prominent; elevated, lifted, raised, uplifted, upswept; high-rise, statuesque *Ant* low, short, squat ♦ [8] advanced, up; *also* extreme, full, maximized, maximum, peaked, utmost; inflated, over, overflowing, overlarge, oversize, oversized **Ant** down, low ♦ [9] chief, first, foremost, head, lead, preeminent, premier, primary, prime, principal, supreme — more at HEAD ♦ [12] drunk, inebriate, intoxicated, tipsy — more at DRUNK ♦ [13] costly, dear, expensive, precious, valuable — more at COSTLY

²**high** *adv* **1** : at or to a high place or degree **2** ♦ : in a luxurious manner ⟨living ∼⟩

♦ expensively, extravagantly, grandly, lavishly, luxuriously, opulently, richly; *also* imposingly, impressively, magnificently, splendidly; grandiosely, ostentatiously, pretentiously; comfortably, fine; immoderately, indulgently, wantonly, wastefully **Ant** austerely, humbly, modestly, plainly, simply

³**high** *n* **1 a** : an elevated place **b** : the space overhead : SKY **2** : a region of high barometric pressure **3** : a high point or level **4** : the gear of a vehicle giving the highest speed **5** : an excited or stupefied state produced by or as if by a drug

high·ball \'hī-ˌbòl\ *n* : a usu. tall drink of liquor mixed with water or a carbonated beverage

high beam *n* : a vehicle headlight with a long-range focus

high·born \'hī-'bòrn\ *adj* ♦ : of noble birth

♦ aristocratic, genteel, gentle, grand, noble, patrician, wellborn — more at NOBLE

high·boy \-ˌbòi\ *n* : a high chest of drawers mounted on a base with legs

high·bred \-'bred\ *adj* : coming from superior stock

high·brow \-ˌbraù\ *n* ♦ : a person of superior learning or culture — **highbrow** *adj* — **high·brow·ism** \-ˌbraù-ˌi-zəm\ *n*

♦ intellectual, nerd — more at INTELLECTUAL

high-def \'hī-'def\ *also* **hi-def** *adj* : HIGH-DEFINITION — **high-def** *also* **hi-def** *n*

high-definition *adj* : being or relating to a television system with twice as many scan lines per frame as a conventional system — **high definition** *n*

high-density li·po·pro·tein \-ˌlī-pō-'prō-ˌtēn, -ˌli-\ *n* : HDL

high·er-up \ˌhī-ər-'əp\ *n* : a superior officer or official

high-fa·lu·tin \ˌhī-fə-'lüt-ᵊn\ *adj* **1** ♦ : characterized by or reflecting an attitude of self-importance or superciliousness **2** ♦ : expressed in or marked by the use of high-flown bombastic language

♦ [1] disdainful, haughty, lofty, lordly, prideful, proud, superior — more at PROUD ♦ [1, 2] affected, grandiose, ostentatious, pompous, pretentious — more at PRETENTIOUS ♦ [2] florid, flowery, grandiloquent, highflown — more at FLOWERY

high fashion *n* **1** : HIGH STYLE **2** : HAUTE COUTURE

high fidelity *n* : the reproduction of sound or image with a high degree of faithfulness to the original

high five *n* : a slapping of upraised right hands by two people (as in celebration) — **high-five** *vb*

high-flown \'hī-'flōn\ *adj* **1** ♦ : exceedingly or excessively high or favorable **2** ♦ : having an excessively embellished or inflated character

♦ [1] eloquent, formal, lofty, majestic, stately, towering ♦ [2] florid, flowery, grandiloquent, highfalutin — more at FLOWERY

high frequency *n* : a radio frequency between 3 and 30 megahertz

high gear *n* **1** : HIGH 4 **2** : a state of intense or maximum activity

high-hand·ed \'hī-'han-dəd\ *adj* ♦ : having or showing no regard for the rights, concerns, or feelings of others — **high-hand·ed·ly** *adv* — **high-hand·ed·ness** *n*

♦ arbitrary, dictatorial, imperious, peremptory, willful — more at ARBITRARY

¹**high-hat** \-'hat\ *adj* ♦ : assuming an attitude of superiority : SUPERCILIOUS

♦ arrogant, cavalier, haughty, highfalutin, high-handed, imperious, important, lofty, lordly, masterful,

overweening, peremptory, pompous, presumptuous, pretentious, supercilious, superior, uppity — more at ARROGANT

²**high-hat** *vb* ♦ : to treat snobbishly

♦ disdain, scorn, slight, sniff at, snub — more at SCORN

high jinks \'hī-ˌjinks\ *n pl* ♦ : boisterous or rambunctious carryings-on

♦ foolery, horseplay, monkeyshines, roughhouse, shenanigans, tomfoolery — more at HORSEPLAY

high·land \'hī-lənd\ *n* ♦ : elevated or mountainous land

♦ elevation, eminence, height, hill, mound, prominence, rise — more at HEIGHT

high·land·er \-lən-dər\ *n* **1** : an inhabitant of a highland **2** *cap* : an inhabitant of the Scottish Highlands

high-lev·el \'hī-'le-vəl\ *adj* **1** : being of high importance or rank **2** : being or relating to highly concentrated and environmentally hazardous nuclear waste

¹**high·light** \-ˌlīt\ *n* : an event or detail of major importance

²**highlight** *vb* **1** ♦ : to center attention on : EMPHASIZE **2** : to constitute a highlight of

♦ accent, accentuate, emphasize, feature, play, point, stress, underline, underscore — more at EMPHASIZE

high·light·er \-ˌlī-tər\ *n* : a pen with transparent ink used for marking text passages

high·ly \'hī-lē\ *adv* **1** : in or to a high place, level, or rank **2** ♦ : in or to a high degree or amount **3** : with approval : FAVORABLY

♦ especially, extremely, greatly, hugely, mightily, mighty, mortally, most, much, real, right, so, very — more at VERY

high-mind·ed \'hī-'mīn-dəd\ *adj* ♦ : marked by elevated principles and feelings — **high-mind·ed·ness** *n*

♦ chivalrous, gallant, great, greathearted, high, lofty, lordly, magnanimous, noble, sublime — more at NOBLE

high·ness \'hī-nəs\ *n* **1** : the quality or state of being high **2** — used as a title (as for kings)

high-pres·sure \-'pre-shər\ *adj* ♦ : using or involving aggressive and insistent sales techniques

♦ aggressive, ambitious, assertive, enterprising, fierce, go-getting, militant, self-assertive — more at AGGRESSIVE

high-rise \-'rīz\ *adj* : having several stories and being equipped with elevators ⟨∼ apartments⟩; *also* : of or relating to high-rise buildings

high road *n* : HIGHWAY

high school *n* : a school usu. including grades 9 to 12 or 10 to 12

high sea *n* : the open sea outside territorial waters — usu. used in pl.

high-sound·ing \'hī-'saùn-diŋ\ *adj* : POMPOUS, IMPOSING

high-spir·it·ed \-'spir-ə-təd\ *adj* ♦ : characterized by a bold or energetic spirit

♦ bubbly, buoyant, effervescent, exuberant, frolicsome, vivacious — more at EXUBERANT ♦ fiery, mettlesome, peppery, spirited, spunky — more at SPIRITED

high-strung \-'strəŋ\ *adj* ♦ : having an extremely nervous or sensitive temperament

♦ excitable, flighty, fluttery, jittery, jumpy, nervous, skittish, spooky — more at EXCITABLE

high style *n* : the newest in fashion or design

high·tail \'hī-ˌtāl\ *vb* : to retreat at full speed

high tech \-'tek\ *n* : HIGH TECHNOLOGY

high technology *n* : technology involving the use of advanced devices

high-ten·sion \'hī-'ten-chən\ *adj* : having or using a high voltage

high-test \-'test\ *adj* : having a high octane number

high-tick·et \-'ti-kət\ *adj* : EXPENSIVE

high-toned \-'tōnd\ *adj* **1** : high in social, moral, or intellectual quality **2** : PRETENTIOUS, POMPOUS

high·way \'hī-ˌwā\ *n* ♦ : a main direct road

◆ artery, pike, road, thoroughfare, turnpike, way — more at WAY

high·way·man \\'hī-ˌwā-mən\\ *n* : a person who robs travelers on a road

hi·jab \\hē-'jäb, -'jab\\ *n* [Ar *ḥijāb* cover, veil] : the covering for the hair and neck that is worn by Muslim women

hi·jack *also* **high·jack** \\'hī-ˌjak\\ *vb* : to steal esp. by stopping a vehicle on the highway; *also* : to commandeer a flying airplane — **hijack** *n* — **hi·jack·er** *n*

¹hike \\'hīk\\ *vb* **hiked; hik·ing** **1** ◆ : to move or raise with a sudden motion **2** : to take a long walk — **hik·er** *n*

◆ boost, crane, elevate, heave, heft, heighten, hoist, jack, lift, pick up, raise, up, uphold — more at RAISE

²hike *n* **1** : a long walk **2** : RISE, INCREASE

hi·lar·i·ous \\hi-'lar-ē-əs, hī-\\ *adj* ◆ : marked by or providing boisterous merriment — **hi·lar·i·ous·ly** *adv*

◆ antic, comic, comical, droll, farcical, funny, humorous, hysterical, laughable, ludicrous, ridiculous, riotous, risible, screaming, uproarious — more at FUNNY

hi·lar·i·ty \\hi-'lar-ə-tē, hī-\\ *n* ◆ : boisterous and high-spirited merriment or laughter

◆ cheer, cheerfulness, cheeriness, glee, joviality, merriment, mirth — more at MIRTH

hill \\'hil\\ *n* **1** ◆ : a usu. rounded elevation of land **2** ◆ : a little heap or mound (as of earth) — **hilly** *adj*

◆ [1] elevation, eminence, height, highland, mound, prominence, rise — more at HEIGHT ◆ [2] cock, heap, mound, mountain, pile, rick, stack — more at PILE

hill·bil·ly \\'hil-ˌbi-lē\\ *n, pl* **-lies** *often offensive* : a person from a backwoods area

hill·ock \\'hi-lək\\ *n* : a small hill

hill·side \\'hil-ˌsīd\\ *n* : the part of a hill between the summit and the foot

hill·top \\-ˌtäp\\ *n* : the top of a hill

hilt \\'hilt\\ *n* : a handle esp. of a sword or dagger

him \\'him\\ *pron, objective case of* HE

Hi·ma·la·yan \\ˌhi-mə-'lā-ən, hi-'mäl-yən\\ *adj* : of, relating to, or characteristic of the Himalaya mountains or the people living there

him·self \\him-'self\\ *pron* : HE, HIM — used reflexively, for emphasis, or in absolute constructions

¹hind \\'hīnd\\ *n, pl* **hinds** *also* **hind** : a female of a common Eurasian deer

²hind *adj* ◆ : of or forming the part that follows or is behind : REAR

◆ back, hindmost, posterior, rear — more at BACK

¹hin·der \\'hin-dər\\ *vb* **1** ◆ : to impede the progress of **2** : to hold back

◆ encumber, hamper, hold up, impede, inhibit, interfere with, obstruct, tie up — more at HAMPER

²hind·er \\'hīn-dər\\ *adj* : HIND

Hin·di \\'hin-dē\\ *n* : a literary and official language of northern India

hind·most \\'hīnd-ˌmōst\\ *adj* ◆ : farthest to the rear

◆ final, last, latter, terminal, ultimate — more at LAST

hind·quar·ter \\-ˌkwȯr-tər\\ *n* **1** : one side of the back half of the carcass of a quadruped **2** *pl* : the part of the body of a quadruped behind the junction of hind limbs and trunk

hin·drance \\'hin-drəns\\ *n* **1** : the state of being hindered; *also* : the action of hindering **2** ◆ : something that impedes : IMPEDIMENT

◆ bar, block, encumbrance, inhibition, obstacle — more at ENCUMBRANCE

hind·sight \\'hīnd-ˌsīt\\ *n* : understanding of an event after it has happened

Hindu–Arabic *adj* : relating to, being, or composed of Arabic numerals

Hin·du·ism \\'hin-dü-ˌi-zəm\\ *n* : a body of religious beliefs and practices native to India — **Hin·du** *n or adj*

hind wing *n* : either of the posterior wings of a 4-winged insect

¹hinge \\'hinj\\ *n* : a jointed device on which a swinging part (as a door, gate, or lid) turns

²hinge *vb* **hinged; hing·ing** **1** : to attach by or furnish with hinges **2** : to be contingent on a single consideration

¹hint \\'hint\\ *n* **1** ◆ : an indirect or summary suggestion **2** ◆ : a slight indication of the existence, approach, or nature of something : CLUE **3** ◆ : a very small amount

◆ [1, 2] clue, cue, indication, inkling, intimation, lead, suggestion; *also* breath, flicker, glimmer, glimpse, mention, scent, whiff, wind; hunch, idea, inspiration, notion; allusion, implication, innuendo, insinuation; evidence, mark, overtone, pointer, sign, signal, telltale, token; assistance, nod, prompt, tip, tip-off, wink; feeling, foreboding, intuition, premonition, presentiment, suspicion; augury, foretaste, omen, portent, symptom ◆ [3] bit, dab, little, particle, suspicion, touch, trace — more at PARTICLE

²hint *vb* ◆ : to give a hint

◆ allude, imply, indicate, infer, insinuate, intimate, suggest; *also* advert, mention, point, refer, signal, signify; smack (of), smell (of)

hin·ter·land \\'hin-tər-ˌland\\ *n* **1** : a region behind a coast **2** ◆ : a region remote from cities

◆ backwoods, bush, frontier, sticks, up-country — more at FRONTIER

¹hip \\'hip\\ *n* : the fruit of a rose

²hip *n* **1** : the part of the body on either side below the waist consisting of the side of the pelvis and the upper thigh **2** : HIP JOINT

³hip *adj* **hip·per; hip·pest** : keenly aware of or interested in the newest developments or styles — **hip·ness** *n*

⁴hip *vb* **hipped; hip·ping** : TELL, INFORM

hip·bone \\'hip-'bōn, -ˌbōn\\ *n* : the large flaring bone that makes a lateral half of the pelvis in mammals

hip–hop \\'hip-ˌhäp\\ *n* **1** : a subculture esp. of inner-city youths who are devotees of rap music **2** : the stylized rhythmic music that accompanies rap

hip–hug·gers \\'hip-ˌhə-gərz\\ *n pl* : low-slung close-fitting pants that rest on the hips

hip joint *n* : the articulation between the femur and the hipbone

hipped \\'hipt\\ *adj* : having hips esp. of a specified kind ⟨broad-*hipped*⟩

hip·pie *or* **hip·py** \\'hi-pē\\ *n, pl* **hippies** : a usu. young person who rejects established mores and advocates nonviolence; *also* : a long-haired unconventionally dressed young person

hip·po \\'hi-pō\\ *n, pl* **hippos** : HIPPOPOTAMUS

hip·po·drome \\'hi-pə-ˌdrōm\\ *n* : an arena for equestrian performances

hip·po·pot·a·mus \\ˌhi-pə-'pä-tə-məs\\ *n, pl* **-mus·es** *or* **-mi** \\-ˌmī\\ [L, fr. Gk *hippopotamos*, alter. of *hippos potamios*, lit., river horse] : a large thick-skinned aquatic mammal of sub-Saharan Africa that is related to the swine

¹hire \\'hīr\\ *n* **1** : payment for labor or personal services : WAGES **2** ◆ : the state of being hired : EMPLOYMENT **3** : one who is hired

◆ employ, employment, engagement; *also* appointment, assignment, conscription, enlistment, recruitment; incumbency, tenure; occupation, place, position, post, situation, work *Ant* unemployment

²hire *vb* **hired; hir·ing** **1** ◆ : to employ for pay **2** ◆ : to engage the temporary use of for pay **3** : to take employment

◆ [1] employ, engage, retain, take on — more at EMPLOY ◆ [2] engage, lease, let, rent; *also* sublease, sublet; check out; arrange (for), bespeak, book, contract (for), order, reserve, sign up (for)

hire·ling \\'hīr-liŋ\\ *n* ◆ : a hired person; *esp* : one with mercenary motives

◆ employee, hand, jobholder, worker — more at EMPLOYEE

hir·sute \'hər-ˌsüt, 'hir-\ *adj* ♦ : covered with hair or hair-like material : HAIRY

♦ fleecy, furry, hairy, rough, shaggy, unshorn, woolly — more at HAIRY

¹his \'hiz\ *adj* : of or relating to him or himself

²his *pron* : one or the ones belonging to him

His·pan·ic \hi-'spa-nik\ *adj* : of, relating to, or being a person of Latin-American descent living in the U.S. — **Hispanic** *n*

¹hiss \'his\ *vb* : to make a sharp sibilant sound; *also* : to express disapproval of by hissing

²hiss *n* 1 ♦ : a prolonged sibilant sound 2 ♦ : a hiss used to express disapproval

♦ [1] fizz, sizzle, swish, whish, whiz; *also* wheeze, whistle, zip; sibilant ♦ [2] boo, catcall, hoot, jeer, raspberry, snort — more at CATCALL

hissy fit \'hi-sē-\ *n* ♦ : a fit of bad temper : TANTRUM

♦ blowup, explosion, fireworks, fit, huff, scene, tantrum — more at TANTRUM

hist *abbr* historian; historical; history

his·ta·mine \'his-tə-ˌmēn, -mən\ *n* : a compound widespread in animal tissues that plays a major role in allergic reactions (as hay fever)

his·to·gram \'his-tə-ˌgram\ *n* : a representation of statistical data by rectangles whose widths represent class intervals and whose heights usu. represent corresponding frequencies

his·tol·o·gy \his-'tä-lə-jē\ *n, pl* **-gies** 1 : a branch of anatomy dealing with tissue structure 2 : tissue structure or organization — **his·to·log·i·cal** \ˌhis-tə-'lä-ji-kəl\ *or* **his·to·log·ic** \-'lä-jik\ *adj* — **his·tol·o·gist** \-'tä-lə-jist\ *n*

his·to·ri·an \hi-'stör-ē-ən\ *n* : a student or writer of history

his·tor·i·cal \hi-'stör-i-kəl\ *adj* 1 : of, relating to, or having the character of history 2 ♦ : based on history — **his·tor·i·cal·ly** \-k(ə-)lē\ *adv*

♦ documentary, factual, hard, literal, matter-of-fact, nonfictional, objective, true — more at FACTUAL

his·to·ric·i·ty \ˌhis-tə-'ri-sə-tē\ *n* : historical actuality

his·to·ri·og·ra·pher \hi-ˌstör-ē-'ä-grə-fər\ *n* : HISTORIAN

his·to·ry \'his-tə-rē\ *n, pl* **-ries** [ultim. fr. L *historia*, fr. Gk. inquiry, history, fr. *histōr, istōr* knowing, learned] 1 ♦ : a chronological record of significant events often with an explanation of their causes 2 : a branch of knowledge that records and explains past events 3 ♦ : events that form the subject matter of history 4 : an established record ⟨a convict's ∼ of violence⟩ — **his·tor·ic** \hi-'stör-ik\ *adj*

♦ [1] annals, chronicle, record; *also* autobiography, diary, journal, memoir; biography, life; epic, legend, narrative, saga, story, tale; archives, documentation, log, register, report; chronology, genealogy ♦ [1] account, chronicle, narrative, record, report, story — more at ACCOUNT ♦ [3] past, yesteryear, yore — more at PAST

his·tri·on·ic \ˌhis-trē-'ä-nik\ *adj* [LL *histrionicus*, fr. L *histrio* actor] 1 ♦ : deliberately affected 2 : of or relating to actors, acting, or the theater — **his·tri·on·i·cal·ly** \-ni-k(ə-)lē\ *adv*

♦ dramatic, melodramatic, theatrical — more at THEATRICAL

his·tri·on·ics \-niks\ *n pl* 1 : theatrical performances 2 : deliberate display of emotion for effect

¹hit \'hit\ *vb* **hit; hit·ting** 1 ♦ : to reach with a blow : STRIKE; *also* : to arrive with a force like a blow ⟨the storm ∼⟩ 2 ♦ : to make or bring into contact : COLLIDE 3 : to affect detrimentally ⟨was ∼ by the flu⟩ 4 : to make a request of 5 ♦ : to come upon : to discover or meet esp. by chance 6 : to accord with : SUIT 7 ♦ : to reach as an end : ATTAIN 8 : to indulge in often to excess 9 ♦ : to succeed in attaining or coming up with something — often used with *on* or *upon* — **hit·ter** *n*

♦ [1] bang, bash, bat, belt, clout, crack, knock, pound, punch, slug, strike, swat, wallop, whack; *also* batter, beat, buffet, bung, chop, drub, lace, lambaste, lick, mangle, maul, pelt, pepper, pummel, rough; bunt, flick, stroke, tap; bump, butt, jab, jostle, kick, knee, poke, prod, push, shove, stamp; bowl (over), knock (down); cane, club, cudgel, flail, flog, lash, slash, spear, stab, switch, thrash, whip; brain ♦ [2] bang, bash, bump, collide, crash, impact, knock, ram, slam, smash, strike, swipe, thud; *also* bounce, carom, glance, rebound, ricochet, skim, skip; contact, land, touch; brush, graze, kiss, nudge, scrape, shave, sweep; bulldoze, jostle, muscle, press, push ♦ *usu* hit upon [5] chance, encounter, find, happen (on *or* upon), meet, stumble — more at HAPPEN (on *or* upon) ♦ [7] achieve, attain, make, score, win — more at ACHIEVE *often* hit on *or* hit upon ♦ [9] detect, determine, dig up, discover, ferret out, find, locate, track down — more at FIND

²hit *n* 1 ♦ : an act or instance of hitting or being hit 2 ♦ : a great success 3 : BASE HIT 4 : a dose of a drug 5 : a murder committed by a gangster 6 : an instance of connecting to a particular website 7 : a successful match in a search (as of the Internet)

♦ [1] bat, blow, box, clout, punch, slug, thump, wallop, whack — more at BLOW ♦ [2] blockbuster, smash, success, winner; *also* crackerjack, dandy, jim-dandy, pip, prizewinner; gem, jewel, treasure; marvel, phenomenon, sensation, wonder; coup, triumph, victory *Ant* bummer, bust, catastrophe, debacle, dud, failure, fiasco, flop, turkey, washout

¹hitch \'hich\ *vb* 1 ♦ : to move by jerks 2 ♦ : to catch or fasten esp. by a hook or knot 3 : HITCHHIKE

♦ [1] buck, jerk, jolt, twitch — more at JERK ♦ [2] anchor, catch, clamp, fasten, fix, moor, secure, set

²hitch *n* 1 : JERK, PULL 2 : a sudden halt 3 : a connection between something towed and its mover 4 : KNOT 5 ♦ : a delimited period esp. of military service

♦ stint, tenure, term, tour — more at TERM

hitch·hike \'hich-ˌhīk\ *vb* : to travel by securing free rides from passing vehicles — **hitch·hik·er** *n*

¹hith·er \'hi-thər\ *adv* : to this place

²hither *adj* : being on the near or adjacent side

hith·er·to \-ˌtü\ *adv* ♦ : up to this time

♦ heretofore, yet; *also* before, formerly, previously *Ant* henceforth, henceforward, hereafter, thenceforth, thenceforward, thereafter

HIV \ˌāch-(ˌ)ī-'vē\ *n* [*h*uman *i*mmunodeficiency *v*irus] : any of several retroviruses that infect and destroy helper T cells causing the great reduction in their numbers that is diagnostic of AIDS

hive \'hīv\ *n* 1 : a container for housing honeybees 2 : a colony of bees 3 : a place swarming with busy occupants — **hive** *vb*

hives \'hīvz\ *n sing or pl* : an allergic disorder marked by raised itching patches on the skin or mucous membranes

hl *abbr* hectoliter

HL *abbr* House of Lords

hm *abbr* hectometer

HM *abbr* 1 Her Majesty; Her Majesty's 2 His Majesty; His Majesty's

HMO \ˌāch-(ˌ)em-'ō\ *n* [*h*ealth *m*aintenance *o*rganization] : a comprehensive health-care organization financed by periodic fixed payments by voluntarily enrolled individuals and families

HMS *abbr* 1 Her Majesty's ship 2 His Majesty's ship

Ho *symbol* holmium

hoa·gie *also* **hoa·gy** \'hō-gē\ *n, pl* **hoagies** ♦ : a large sandwich on a long split roll : SUBMARINE

♦ grinder, poor boy, sub, submarine — more at SUBMARINE

¹hoard \'hōrd\ *n* ♦ : a hidden accumulation

♦ cache, reserve, stash, stockpile, store; *also* nest egg, treasure; reservoir

²hoard *vb* ♦ : to lay up a hoard — **hoard·er** *n*

♦ cache, lay away, lay up, put by, salt away, stash, stockpile, store; *also* accumulate, amass, assemble, collect, garner, gather, round up; conserve; husband, preserve; bank, deposit, hold, keep, reserve, retain, save, stock, withhold; conceal, ensconce, secrete

hoar·frost \'hōr-ˌfròst\ *n* : FROST 2

hoarse \'hōrs\ *adj* **hoars·er; hoars·est 1** ♦ : rough and harsh in sound **2** : having a grating voice — **hoarse·ly** *adv* — **hoarse·ness** *n*

♦ coarse, gravelly, gruff, husky, scratchy, throaty; *also* guttural; abrasive, cacophonous, discordant, grinding, jarring, rough, scraping, scratching; cawing, raucous, strident; choked, cracked, strained, strangled

hoary \'hōr-ē\ *adj* **hoar·i·er; -est 1** : gray or white with or as if with age **2** ♦ : extremely old : ANCIENT — **hoar·i·ness** \'hōr-ē-nəs\ *n*

♦ age-old, ancient, antediluvian, antique, dateless, old, venerable — more at ANCIENT

¹**hoax** \'hōks\ *vb* ♦ : to trick into believing or accepting as genuine something that is false

♦ beguile, bluff, cozen, deceive, delude, dupe, fool, gull, have, hoodwink, humbug, misinform, mislead, string along, take in, trick — more at DECEIVE

²**hoax** *n* **1** : an act intended to trick or dupe **2** ♦ : something accepted or established by fraud

♦ counterfeit, fake, forgery, humbug, phony, sham — more at FAKE

hoax·er *n* ♦ : one that hoaxes another

♦ cheat, dodger, shark, sharper, swindler, trickster — more at TRICKSTER ♦ charlatan, fake, fraud, humbug, mountebank, phony, pretender, quack

hob \'häb\ *n* : action that annoys or irritates : MISCHIEF — used with *play* and *raise* ⟨always raising ∼⟩

¹**hob·ble** \'hä-bəl\ *vb* **hob·bled; hob·bling 1** : to limp along; *also* : to make lame **2** : to fasten together the legs of (as a horse) to prevent straying : FETTER **3** ♦ : to place under handicap : HAMPER

♦ encumber, hamper, hinder, hold up, impede, inhibit, interfere with, obstruct, tie up — more at HAMPER

²**hobble** *n* **1** : a hobbling movement **2** : something used to hobble an animal

hob·by \'hä-bē\ *n, pl* **hobbies** : a pursuit or interest engaged in for relaxation — **hob·by·ist** \-ist\ *n*

hob·by·horse \'hä-bē-ˌhòrs\ *n* **1** : a stick with a horse's head on which children pretend to ride **2** : a toy horse mounted on rockers **3** : a topic to which one constantly reverts

hob·gob·lin \'häb-ˌgäb-lən\ *n* **1** ♦ : a mischievous goblin **2** ♦ : a source of fear, perplexity, or harassment : BOGEY

♦ [1] brownie, dwarf, elf, fairy, fay, gnome, leprechaun, pixie, puck, troll ♦ [2] bête noire, bogey, bugbear, ogre — more at BOGEY

hob·nail \-ˌnāl\ *n* : a short large-headed nail for studding shoe soles — **hob·nailed** \-ˌnāld\ *adj*

hob·nob \-ˌnäb\ *vb* **hob·nobbed; hob·nob·bing** ♦ : to associate familiarly

♦ associate, chum, consort, fraternize, hang around, pal — more at ASSOCIATE ♦ associate, fraternize, mingle, mix, socialize — more at SOCIALIZE

ho·bo \'hō-bō\ *n, pl* **hoboes** *also* **hobos** ♦ : a homeless and usu. penniless vagabond : TRAMP

♦ bum, tramp, vagabond, vagrant — more at TRAMP

¹**hock** \'häk\ *n* : a joint or region in the hind limb of a quadruped just above the foot and corresponding to the human ankle

²**hock** *n* [D *hok* pen, prison] : PAWN; *also* : DEBT 3 — **hock** *vb*

hock·ey \'hä-kē\ *n* **1** : FIELD HOCKEY **2** : ICE HOCKEY

ho·cus-po·cus \ˌhō-kəs-'pō-kəs\ *n* **1** : SLEIGHT OF HAND **2** : nonsense or sham used to conceal deception

hod \'häd\ *n* : a long-handled carrier for mortar or bricks

hodge·podge \'häj-ˌpäj\ *n* ♦ : a heterogeneous mixture : JUMBLE

♦ assortment, clutter, jumble, medley, mélange, miscellany, motley, muddle, variety, welter — more at MISCELLANY

Hodgkin's disease \'häj-kinz-\ *n* : a neoplastic disease of lymphoid tissue characterized esp. by enlargement of lymph nodes, spleen, and liver

hoe \'hō\ *n* : a long-handled implement with a thin flat blade used esp. for cultivating, weeding, or loosening the earth around plants — **hoe** *vb*

hoe·cake \'hō-ˌkāk\ *n* : a small cornmeal cake

hoe·down \-ˌdaùn\ *n* **1** : SQUARE DANCE **2** : a gathering featuring hoedowns

¹**hog** \'hòg, 'häg\ *n, pl* **hogs** *also* **hog 1** : a domestic swine esp. when grown **2** : a selfish, gluttonous, or filthy person

²**hog** *vb* **hogged; hog·ging** : to take or hold selfishly

ho·gan \'hō-ˌgän\ *n* : a Navajo Indian dwelling usu. made of logs and mud

hog·back \'hòg-ˌbak, 'häg-\ *n* : a ridge with a sharp summit and steep sides

hog·gish \'hò-gish, 'hä-\ *adj* ♦ : grossly selfish, gluttonous, or filthy

♦ gluttonous, greedy, piggish, rapacious, ravenous, voracious — more at VORACIOUS

hog·nose snake \'hòg-ˌnōz-, 'häg-\ *or* **hog·nosed snake** \-ˌnōzd-\ *n* : any of a genus of rather small harmless stout-bodied No. American snakes that seldom bite but hiss wildly and often play dead when disturbed

hogs·head \'hògz-ˌhed, 'hägz-\ *n* ♦ : a large cask or barrel

♦ barrel, cask, keg, pipe, puncheon — more at CASK

hog·tie \'hòg-ˌtī, 'häg-\ *vb* **1** : to tie together the feet of ⟨∼ a calf⟩ **2** : to make helpless

hog·wash \-ˌwòsh, -ˌwäsh\ *n* **1** : SWILL, SLOP **2** ♦ : language, conduct, or an idea that is absurd or contrary to good sense : NONSENSE

♦ bunk, claptrap, drivel, fiddlesticks, folly, foolishness, fudge, humbug, nonsense, piffle, rot, silliness, slush, stupidity, trash — more at NONSENSE

hog–wild \-'wīld\ *adj* : lacking in restraint

hoi pol·loi \ˌhòi-pə-'lòi\ *n pl* [Gk, the many] : the general populace

hoi·sin sauce \'hòi-ˌsin-\ *n* : a thick reddish sauce of soybeans, spices, and garlic used in Asian cookery

¹**hoist** \'hòist\ *vb* ♦ : to raise from a lower to a higher position

♦ boost, crane, elevate, heave, heft, heighten, hike, jack, lift, pick up, raise, up, uphold — more at RAISE

²**hoist** *n* **1** : LIFT **2** : an apparatus for hoisting

hoke \'hōk\ *vb* **hoked; hok·ing** : FAKE — usu. used with *up*

hok·ey \'hō-kē\ *adj* **hok·i·er; -est** : CORNY; *also* : PHONY

ho·kum \'hō-kəm\ *n* : NONSENSE

¹**hold** \'hōld\ *vb* **held** \'held\; **hold·ing 1** ♦ : to have possession or ownership of or have at one's disposal **2** : RESTRAIN **3** ♦ : to have a grasp on **4** : to support, remain, or keep in a particular situation or position **5** : SUSTAIN; *also* : RESERVE **6** : BEAR, COMPORT **7** : to maintain in being or action : PERSIST **8** : to enclose and keep in a container or within bounds : ACCOMMODATE **9 a** ♦ : to have in the mind or express as a judgment, opinion, or belief **b** ♦ : to think of in a particular way : CONSIDER, REGARD **10** : to carry on by concerted action; *also* : CONVOKE **11** : to occupy esp. by appointment or election **12** : to be valid **13** : HALT, PAUSE — **hold forth** : to speak at length — **hold to** : to adhere to : MAINTAIN — **hold with** : to agree with or approve of

♦ [1] hang on, keep, reserve, retain, withhold — more at KEEP ♦ [1] command, enjoy, have, occupy, own, possess, retain — more at HAVE ♦ [3] clench, cling, clutch, grip, hang on, hold on; *also* bear, carry; catch, grapple, nab, seize, snatch, take; feel, finger, handle, paw; clasp, grasp, embrace, hug ♦ [9a] believe, consider, deem, feel, figure, guess, imagine, suppose, think — more at BELIEVE ♦ [9a] bear, cherish, entertain, harbor (or harbour), have, nurse — more at HARBOR ♦ [9b] account, call, consider, count, esteem, rate, reckon, regard, take — more at CONSIDER

²**hold** n 1 ♦ : a fortified place : STRONGHOLD 2 : CONFINEMENT; also : PRISON 3 ♦ : the act or manner of holding : GRIP 4 ♦ : a restraining, dominating, or controlling influence 5 : something that may be grasped as a support 6 : an order or indication that something is to be reserved or delayed — **on hold** : in a temporary state of waiting (as during a phone call); also : in a state of postponement ⟨plans on hold⟩

♦ [1] bastion, citadel, fastness, fort, fortification, fortress, stronghold — more at FORT ♦ [3] clasp, grapple, grasp, grip; also anchorage, leverage, purchase; grab, seizure; foothold, footing, toehold; embrace, hug ♦ [4] arm, authority, clutch, command, control, dominion, grip, mastery, power, sway — more at POWER

³**hold** n 1 : the interior of a ship below decks; esp : a ship's cargo deck 2 : an airplane's cargo compartment

hold back vb ♦ : to hinder the progress or achievement of

♦ encumber, hamper, hinder, hold up, impede, inhibit, interfere with, obstruct, tie up — more at HAMPER

hold·er n 1 ♦ : a person that holds 2 ♦ : a device that holds

♦ [1] owner, possessor, proprietor — more at PROPRIETOR ♦ [2] container, receptacle, vessel — more at CONTAINER

hold·ing n 1 ♦ : land or other property owned — usu. used in pl. 2 ♦ : a ruling of a court esp. on an issue of law

♦ usu **holdings** [1] belongings, chattels, effects, paraphernalia, possessions, things — more at POSSESSION ♦ [2] doom, finding, judgment (or judgement), ruling, sentence — more at SENTENCE

holding pattern n 1 : a course flown by an aircraft waiting to land 2 ♦ : a state of waiting or suspended activity or progress

♦ abeyance, doldrums, dormancy, latency, moratorium, quiescence, suspension — more at ABEYANCE

hold on vb 1 ♦ : to maintain a condition or position : PERSIST 2 ♦ : to maintain a grasp on something 3 ♦ : to await something (as a telephone connection) desired or requested

♦ [1] endure, hold, last, persist ♦ usu **hold on to** [2] clench, cling, clutch, grip, hang on, hold — more at HOLD ♦ [3] await, bide, stay, wait — more at WAIT

hold out vb 1 ♦ : to continue to fight or work 2 : to refuse to come to an agreement — **hold·out** \'hōl-ˌdaùt\ n

♦ hold, keep up, last, prevail, survive; also bear up, carry on, cope, endure, go, hang in, persevere; continue, draw out, hang on, linger, persist, remain, stretch Ant fail, fizzle, give out, go out, peter (out), run out

hold·over \'hōl-ˌdō-vər\ n : one that is held over

hold·up \'hōl-ˌdəp\ n 1 : DELAY 2 : robbery at the point of a gun

hold up vb 1 : to rob at gunpoint 2 ♦ : to stop, delay, or impede the course or advance of 3 : to call attention to 4 ♦ : to continue in the same condition without failing or losing effectiveness or force

♦ [2] arrest, catch, check, draw up, fetch up, halt, stall, stay, still, stop — more at HALT ♦ [2] encumber, hamper, hinder, impede, inhibit, interfere with, obstruct, tie up — more at HAMPER ♦ [4] abide, continue, endure, keep up, last, persist, run on — more at CONTINUE

¹**hole** \'hōl\ n 1 ♦ : an opening into or through something 2 ♦ : a hollow place (as a pit or cave) 3 : the resting or living place of a wild animal : DEN, BURROW 4 : a wretched or dingy place 5 : a unit of play from tee to cup in golf 6 ♦ : an awkward position

♦ [1] breach, break, discontinuity, gap, gulf, interval, opening, rent, rift, separation — more at GAP ♦ [1] aperture, opening, orifice, perforation; also breach, break, chink, cleft, crack, cranny, crevice, cut, fissure, gash, notch, rent, rift, rupture, slash, slit, split; gap, slot, space; exit, mouth, outlet, pore, vent ♦ [2] cavity, concavity, dent, depression, hollow, indentation, pit, recess; also burrow, cave, cavern, ditch, excavation, furrow, groove, trench, trough; basin, bowl, valley; alcove, cleft, niche, nook, opening, recess, socket; chuckhole, crater, posthole, pothole, sinkhole Ant bulge, convexity, protrusion, protuberance ♦ [6] corner, fix, jam, pickle, predicament, spot — more at PREDICAMENT

²**hole** vb ♦ : to make a hole in

♦ bore, drill, perforate, pierce, punch, puncture — more at PERFORATE

hol·i·day \'hä-lə-ˌdā\ n [ME, fr. OE hāligdæg, fr. hālig holy + dæg day] 1 : a day set aside for special religious observance 2 : a day of freedom from work; esp : one in commemoration of an event 3 : VACATION — **holiday** vb

ho·li·ness \'hō-lē-nəs\ n ♦ : the quality or state of being holy — used as a title for various high religious officials

♦ blessedness, devoutness, godliness, piety, sainthood, sanctity; also asceticism, devotion, morality, spirituality; righteousness Ant godlessness, impiety, ungodliness, unholiness

ho·lis·tic \hō-'lis-tik\ adj : relating to or concerned with integrated wholes or complete systems rather than with the analysis or treatment of separate parts ⟨∼ medicine⟩ ⟨∼ ecology⟩

hol·lan·daise \ˌhä-lən-'dāz\ n : a rich sauce made basically of butter, egg yolks, and lemon juice or vinegar

¹**hol·ler** \'hä-lər\ vb : to cry out : SHOUT

²**holler** n ♦ : a loud cry or call

♦ cry, hoot, howl, shout, whoop, yell, yowl — more at SHOUT

¹**hol·low** \'hä-lō\ n 1 : CAVITY, HOLE 2 ♦ : a surface depression

♦ dale, valley — more at VALLEY ♦ cavity, concavity, dent, depression, hole, indentation, pit, recess — more at HOLE

²**hollow** adj **hol·low·er** \'hä-lə-wər\; **hol·low·est** \-lə-wəst\ 1 ♦ : having an indentation or inward curve : CONCAVE, SUNKEN 2 : having a cavity within 3 : lacking in real value, sincerity, or substance; also : FALSE 4 : MUFFLED ⟨a ∼ sound⟩ — **hol·low·ness** n

♦ concave, depressed, sunken; also cavernous, cupped; dimpled, pockmarked; compressed, condensed, contracted, diminished, reduced Ant convex, bulging, protruding, protuberant

³**hollow** vb : to make or become hollow

hol·low·ware or **hol·lo·ware** \'hä-lə-ˌwar\ n : vessels (as bowls or cups) with a significant depth and volume

hol·ly \'hä-lē\ n, pl **hollies** : either of two trees or shrubs with branches of usu. evergreen glossy spiny-margined leaves and red berries

hol·ly·hock \'hä-lē-ˌhäk, -ˌhôk\ n [ME holihoc, fr. holi holy + hoc mallow] : a biennial or perennial herb related to the mallows that is widely grown for its tall stalks of showy flowers

hol·mi·um \'hōl-mē-əm\ n : a metallic chemical element

ho·lo·caust \'hä-lə-ˌkóst, 'hō-\ n 1 ♦ : a thorough destruction esp. by fire 2 often cap : the killing of European Jews by the Nazis during World War II; also : GENOCIDE

♦ conflagration, fire, inferno — more at FIRE

Ho·lo·cene \'hō-lə-ˌsēn\ adj : of, relating to, or being the present geologic epoch — **Holocene** n

ho·lo·gram \'hō-lə-ˌgram, 'hä-\ n : a three-dimensional image produced by an interference pattern of light (as laser light)

ho·lo·graph \'hō-lə-ˌgraf, 'hä-\ n : a document wholly in the handwriting of its author

ho·log·ra·phy \hō-'lä-grə-fē\ n : the process of making a hologram — **ho·lo·graph·ic** \‚hō-lə-'gra-fik, ‚hä-\ adj

Hol·stein \'hōl-‚stēn, -‚stīn\ n : any of a breed of large black-and-white dairy cattle that produce large quantities of comparatively low-fat milk

Hol·stein–Frie·sian \-'frē-zhən\ n : HOLSTEIN

hol·ster \'hōl-stər\ n [D] : a usu. leather case for a firearm

ho·ly \'hō-lē\ adj **ho·li·er; -est** **1 ♦** : worthy of absolute devotion **2 ♦** : to be treated with veneration or the utmost respect : SACRED **3 ♦** : having a divine quality **4 ♦** : devoted to the deity or the work of the deity — **ho·li·ly** \-lə-lē\ adv

> **♦** [1, 2] inviolable, sacred, sacrosanct — more at SACRED **♦** [1, 2] blessed, hallowed, sacred, sacrosanct, sanctified; also adored, glorified, revered, venerated, worshiped; religious, ritual, spiritual **Ant** unconsecrated, unhallowed **♦** [3] blessed, divine, godlike, heavenly; also eternal, everlasting, immortal; almighty, omnipotent, omniscient, supreme **♦** [4] devout, faithful, godly, pious, religious, sainted, saintly; also ascetic, prayerful, reverent, reverential, spiritual, worshipful; beatified, blessed, canonized, venerable; angelic, cherubic; chaste, pure, righteous, virtuous **Ant** faithless, godless, impious, irreligious, ungodly, unholy

Holy Spirit n : the third person of the Christian Trinity

ho·ly·stone \'hō-lē-‚stōn\ n : a soft sandstone used to scrub a ship's wooden decks — **holystone** vb

hom·age \'ä-mij, 'hä-\ n [ME, fr. AF homage, omage, fr. home man, vassal, fr. L homo human being] **♦** : expression of high regard; also : TRIBUTE

> **♦** accolade, citation, commendation, encomium, eulogy, paean, panegyric, salutation, tribute — more at ENCOMIUM **♦** acclaim, accolade, credit, distinction, glory, honor (or honour), laurels — more at GLORY

hom·bre \'äm-brē, 'əm-, -‚brā\ n **♦** : an adult male human : GUY, FELLOW

> **♦** buck, chap, dude, fellow, gent, gentleman, guy, jack, joker, lad, male, man — more at MAN

hom·burg \'häm-‚bərg\ n [Homburg, Germany] : a man's felt hat with a stiff curled brim and a high crown creased lengthwise

¹home \'hōm\ n **1 ♦** : one's residence; also : HOUSE **2** : the social unit formed by a family living together **3** : a congenial environment; also : HABITAT **4 ♦** : a place of origin **5** : the objective in various games **6 ♦** : the place or environment where a plant or animal naturally or normally lives and grows

> **♦** [1] abode, domicile, dwelling, fireside, habitation, hearth, house, lodging, pad, place, quarters, residence, roof; also accommodations, housing, nest, residency, shelter; bungalow, cabin, chalet, cottage; duplex, ranch, town house, tract house, triplex; apartment, condominium, flat, tenement, walk-up; penthouse, salon, suite; barracks, boardinghouse, dorm, dormitory, lodgment; castle, estate, manor, mansion, palace, villa; farmhouse, grange, hacienda, homestead, ranch house; houseboat, mobile home, motor home, trailer; hermitage, manse, parsonage, vicarage; hovel, hut, shack **♦** [4] country, fatherland, homeland, motherland, sod — more at COUNTRY **♦** [6] habitat, niche, range, territory; also element, environment, environs, haunt, locality, milieu, neighborhood, setting, surroundings

²home vb **homed; hom·ing** **1** : to go or return home **2** : to proceed to or toward a source of radiated energy used as a guide

home·body \'hōm-‚bä-dē\ n : one whose life centers on home

home·boy \-‚bȯi\ n **1** slang : a boy or man from one's neighborhood, hometown, or region; also : a male friend **2** slang : a boy or man who is a member of one's peer group; also : a member of one's gang **3** slang : an inner-city youth

home·bred \-'bred\ adj : produced at home : INDIGENOUS

home·com·ing \-‚kə-miŋ\ n **1** : a return home **2** : an annual celebration for alumni at a college or university

home computer n : a small inexpensive microcomputer

home economics n : the theory and practice of homemaking

home-girl \'hōm-gərl\ n **1** slang : a girl or woman from one's neighborhood, hometown, or region; also : a female friend **2** slang : a girl or woman who is a member of one's peer group **3** slang : an inner-city girl or woman

home·grown \'hōm-'grōn\ adj **1** : grown domestically **2** : LOCAL, INDIGENOUS

home·land \-‚land\ n **1 ♦** : native land **2** : an area set aside to be a state for a people of a particular national, cultural, or racial origin

> **♦** country, fatherland, home, motherland, sod — more at COUNTRY

¹home·less \-ləs\ adj : having no home or permanent residence

²homeless n pl : persons esp. in urban areas that have no home

home·ly \'hōm-lē\ adj **home·li·er; -est** **1** : FAMILIAR **2** : unaffectedly natural **3** : lacking beauty or proportion — **home·li·ness** \-lē-nəs\ n

home·made \'hōm-'mād\ adj : made in the home, on the premises, or by one's own efforts

home·mak·er \-‚mā-kər\ n : one who manages a household esp. as a spouse and a parent — **home·mak·ing** \-kiŋ\ n

ho·me·op·a·thy \‚hō-mē-'ä-pə-thē\ n : a system of medical practice that treats disease esp. with minute doses of a remedy that would in larger amounts produce symptoms similar to those of the disease in healthy persons — **ho·meo·path** \'hō-mē-ə-‚path\ n — **ho·meo·path·ic** \‚hō-mē-ə-'pa-thik\ adj

ho·meo·sta·sis \‚hō-mē-ō-'stā-səs\ n : the maintenance of a relatively stable state of equilibrium between interrelated physiological, psychological, or social factors characteristic of an individual or group — **ho·meo·stat·ic** \-'sta-tik\ adj

home page n : the page usu. encountered first on a website that usu. contains hyperlinks to the other pages of the site

home plate n : a slab at the apex of a baseball diamond that a base runner must touch in order to score

hom·er \'hō-mər\ n : HOME RUN — **homer** vb

home·room \'hōm-‚rüm, -‚rùm\ n : a classroom where pupils report at the beginning of each school day

home run n : a hit in baseball that enables the batter to go around all the bases and score a run

home·school \'hōm-‚skül\ vb : to teach school subjects to one's children at home — **home·school·er** \-‚skü-lər\ n

home·sick \'hōm-‚sik\ adj : longing for home and family while absent from them — **home·sick·ness** n

home·spun \-‚spən\ adj **1** : spun or made at home; also : made of a loosely woven usu. woolen or linen fabric **2** : SIMPLE, HOMELY

¹home·stead \-‚sted\ n : the home and land occupied by a family

²homestead vb : to acquire or settle on public land

home·stead·er \-‚ste-dər\ n **♦** : one who seeks, establishes, or possesses a homestead under a homestead law

> **♦** colonist, frontiersman, pioneer, settler — more at FRONTIERSMAN

home·stretch \-'strech\ n **1** : the part of a racecourse between the last curve and the winning post **2 ♦** : a final stage (as of a project)

> **♦** close, conclusion, consummation, end, ending, finale, finis, finish, windup — more at FINALE

home theater n : an entertainment system (as a television with surround sound and a DVD player) for the home

home video n : prerecorded videocassettes or videodiscs for home viewing

¹home·ward \-wərd\ or **home·wards** \-wərdz\ adv : toward home

²**home·ward** *adj* : being or going toward home

home·work \-ˌwərk\ *n* **1** : an assignment given a student to be completed outside the classroom **2** : preparatory reading or research

¹**hom·ey** \'hō-mē\ *adj* **hom·i·er; -est** : characteristic of home

²**homey** *or* **hom·ie** \'hō-mē\ *n, pl* **homeys** *or* **homies** : HOME-BOY

hom·i·cid·al \ˌhä-mə-'sīd-ᵊl\ *adj* ♦ : of, relating to, or tending toward homicide

♦ bloodthirsty, bloody, murderous, sanguinary, sanguine — more at BLOODTHIRSTY

hom·i·cide \'hä-mə-ˌsīd, 'hō-\ *n* [L *homicida* murderer & *homicidium* manslaughter; both fr. *homo* human being + *caedere* to cut, kill] **1** : a person who kills another **2** ♦ : a killing of one human being by another

♦ murder; *also* killing, manslaughter; bloodshed, butchery, carnage, destruction, massacre, slaughter; assassination, execution; euthanasia, mercy killing

hom·i·ly \'hä-mə-lē\ *n, pl* **-lies** : SERMON — **hom·i·let·ic** \ˌhä-mə-'le-tik\ *adj*

homing pigeon *n* : a racing pigeon trained to return home

hom·i·nid \'hä-mə-nəd, -ˌnid\ *n* : any of a family of primate mammals that comprise all living humans and extinct ancestral and related forms — **hominid** *adj*

hom·i·ny \'hä-mə-nē\ *n* : hulled corn with the germ removed

ho·mo·cys·te·ine \ˌhō-mō-'sis-tə-ˌēn\ *n* : an amino acid associated with an increased risk of heart disease when occurring at high levels in the blood

ho·mo·erot·ic \ˌhō-mō-i-'rä-tik\ *adj* : marked by or portraying homosexual desire — **ho·mo·erot·i·cism** \-'rä-tə-ˌsi-zəm\ *n*

ho·mo·ge·neous \ˌhō-mə-'jē-nē-əs, -nyəs\ *adj* : of the same or a similar kind; *also* : of uniform structure — **ho·mo·ge·ne·i·ty** \-jə-'nē-ə-tē\ *n* — **ho·mo·ge·neous·ly** *adv*

ho·mog·e·ni·sa·tion, ho·mog·e·nise *chiefly Brit var of* HOMOGENIZATION, HOMOGENIZE

ho·mog·e·nize \hō-'mä-jə-ˌnīz, hə-\ *vb* **-nized; -niz·ing** **1** ♦ : to make homogeneous **2** : to reduce the particles in (as milk) to uniform size and distribute them evenly throughout the liquid — **ho·mog·e·ni·za·tion** \-ˌmä-jə-nə-'zā-shən\ *n* — **ho·mog·e·niz·er** *n*

♦ formalize, normalize, regularize, standardize — more at STANDARDIZE

ho·mo·graph \'hä-mə-ˌgraf, 'hō-\ *n* : one of two or more words spelled alike but different in origin, meaning, or pronunciation (as the *bow* of a ship, a *bow* and arrow)

ho·mol·o·gy \hō-'mä-lə-jē, hə-\ *n, pl* **-gies** **1** : structural likeness between corresponding parts of different plants or animals due to evolution from a common ancestor **2** : structural likeness between different parts of the same individual — **ho·mol·o·gous** \-'mä-lə-gəs\ *adj*

hom·onym \'hä-mə-ˌnim, 'hō-\ *n* **1** : HOMOPHONE, HOMOGRAPH **2** : one of two or more words spelled and pronounced alike but different in meaning (as *pool* of water and *pool* the game)

ho·mo·pho·bia \ˌhō-mə-'fō-bē-ə\ *n* : irrational fear of, aversion to, or discrimination against homosexuality or homosexuals — **ho·mo·phobe** \'hō-mə-ˌfōb\ *n* — **ho·mo·pho·bic** \-'fō-bik\ *adj*

ho·mo·phone \'hä-mə-ˌfōn, 'hō-\ *n* : one of two or more words (as *to, too, two*) pronounced alike but different in meaning or derivation or spelling

Ho·mo sa·pi·ens \ˌhō-mō-'sā-pē-ənz, -'sa-\ *n* ♦ : the human race : HUMANKIND

♦ humanity, humankind, man, mankind — more at MANKIND

ho·mo·sex·u·al \ˌhō-mō-'sek-shə-wəl\ *adj* : of, relating to, or marked by sexual interest in the same sex as oneself : GAY; *also* : of, relating to, or involving sexual intercourse between members of the same sex — **homosexual** *n* — **ho·mo·sex·u·al·i·ty** \-ˌsek-shə-'wa-lə-tē\ *n*

hon *abbr* honor; honorable; honorary

Hon·du·ran \hän-'dur-ən\ *or* **Hon·du·ra·ne·an** *or* **Hon·du·ra·ni·an** \ˌhan-dü-'rā-nē-ən, -dyù-\ *n* : a native or inhabitant of Honduras — **Honduran** *or* **Honduranean** *or* **Honduranian** *adj*

¹**hone** \'hōn\ *n* : WHETSTONE

²**hone** *vb* **1** ♦ : to sharpen or smooth with a whetstone **2** : to make more acute, intense, or effective — **hon·er** *n*

♦ edge, grind, sharpen, strop, whet — more at SHARPEN

hone in *vb* : to move toward or direct attention to an objective

¹**hon·est** \'ä-nəst\ *adj* [ME, fr. AF, fr. L *honestus* honorable, fr. *honos, honor* honor] **1** ♦ : free from deception : TRUTHFUL; *also* : GENUINE, REAL **2** : REPUTABLE **3** : CREDITABLE **4** ♦ : marked by integrity **5** ♦ : marked by free, forthright, and sincere expression : FRANK

♦ [1] artless, genuine, ingenuous, innocent, naive, natural, real, simple, sincere, true, unaffected, unpretentious ♦ [4] decent, ethical, good, honorable (*or* honourable), just, moral, principled, right, righteous, straight, upright, virtuous — more at GOOD ♦ [4] conscientious, honorable (*or* honourable), just, moral, principled, scrupulous — more at CONSCIENTIOUS ♦ [5] candid, direct, forthright, foursquare, frank, open, outspoken, plain, straight, straightforward, unguarded, unreserved — more at FRANK

²**honest** *adv* : HONESTLY; *also* : with all sincerity ⟨I didn't do it, ~⟩

hon·est·ly \'ä-nəst-lē\ *adv* **1** : in an honest manner **2** ♦ : to be honest ⟨~, I don't know⟩

♦ actually, frankly, really, truly, truthfully, verily — more at ACTUALLY

hon·es·ty \'ä-nə-stē\ *n* **1** ♦ : fairness and straightforwardness of conduct **2** ♦ : adherence to the facts

♦ [1] character, decency, goodness, honor (*or* honour), integrity, morality, probity, rectitude, righteousness, uprightness, virtue — more at MORALITY ♦ [2] integrity, probity, truthfulness, veracity, verity; *also* honor, incorruptibility; candidness, candor (*or* candour), frankness, sincerity; dependability, reliability, reliableness, trustworthiness; accuracy, objectivity; authenticity, correctness, genuineness; credibility **Ant** deceit, deceitfulness, dishonesty, lying, mendacity

hon·ey \'hə-nē\ *n, pl* **honeys** **1** : a sweet sticky substance made by honeybees from the nectar of flowers **2** ♦ : a loved one

♦ beloved, darling, dear, flame, love, sweet, sweetheart — more at SWEETHEART

hon·ey·bee \'hə-nē-ˌbē\ *n* : a social and colonial 4-winged insect often kept in hives for the honey it produces

¹**hon·ey·comb** \-ˌkōm\ *n* : a mass of 6-sided wax cells built by honeybees; *also* : something of similar structure or appearance

²**honeycomb** *vb* : to make or become full of cavities like a honeycomb

hon·ey·dew \-ˌdü, -ˌdyü\ *n* : a sweetish deposit secreted on plants by aphids, scale insects, or fungi

honeydew melon *n* : a smooth-skinned muskmelon with sweet green flesh

honey locust *n* : a tall usu. spiny No. American leguminous tree with hard durable wood and long twisted pods

hon·ey·moon \'hə-nē-ˌmün\ *n* **1** : a period of harmony esp. just after marriage **2** : a holiday taken by a newly married couple — **honeymoon** *vb*

hon·ey·suck·le \'hə-nē-ˌsə-kəl\ *n* : any of a genus of shrubs with fragrant tube-shaped flowers rich in nectar

honk \'häŋk, 'hȯŋk\ *n* : the cry of a goose; *also* : a similar sound (as of a horn) — **honk** *vb* — **honk·er** *n*

hon·ky-tonk \'häŋ-kē-ˌtäŋk, 'hȯŋ-kē-ˌtȯŋk\ *n* : a tawdry nightclub or dance hall — **honky–tonk** *adj*

¹**hon·or** \'ä-nər\ *or Can and Brit* **hon·our** *n* **1** ♦ : good name : REPUTATION; *also* : outward respect **2** ♦ : an exclusive or special right, power, or privilege **3** : a person of superior standing — used esp. as a title **4** : one that brings

respect or fame **5 ♦** : an evidence or symbol of distinction **6** : CHASTITY, PURITY **7 ♦** : a keen sense of ethical conduct : INTEGRITY

♦ [1] boast, credit, glory, jewel, pride, treasure — more at GLORY ♦ [2] boon, concession, privilege — more at PRIVILEGE ♦ [5] acclaim, accolade, credit, distinction, glory, homage, laurels — more at GLORY ♦ [5] award, decoration, distinction, plume, prize — more at AWARD ♦ [7] honesty, integrity, probity, rectitude, righteousness, uprightness; *also* blamelessness, character, decency, fairness, high-mindedness, incorruptibility, justice, morality, nobility, respectability, scrupulousness, virtue *Ant* baseness, lowness

²**honor** *or Can and Brit* **honour** *vb* **1** : to regard or treat with honor **2** : to confer honor on **3** : to fulfill the terms of; *also* : to accept as payment — **hon·or·ee** \ˌä-nə-ˈrē\ *n* — **hon·or·er** *n*

hon·or·able \ˈä-nə-rə-bəl\ *or Can and Brit* **hon·our·able** *adj* **1** : deserving of honor **2** : of great renown **3** : accompanied with marks of honor **4** : doing credit to the possessor **5 ♦** : characterized by integrity — **hon·or·able·ness** *n*

♦ decent, ethical, good, honest, just, moral, right, righteous, straight, upright, virtuous — more at GOOD ♦ decent, ethical, honest, just, noble, principled, respectable, righteous, upright, upstanding; *also* decorous, proper, seemly; blameless, guiltless, irreproachable, unassailable, unimpeachable; chivalrous, high-minded *Ant* base, dishonest, ignoble, low, unethical, unjust, unprincipled, unrighteous conscientious, honest, just, moral, principled, scrupulous — more at CONSCIENTIOUS

hon·or·ably \ˈä-nə-rə-blē\ *or Can and Brit* **hon·our·ably** *adv* **♦** : in an honorable manner

♦ gallantly, grandly, greatly, heroically, magnanimously, nobly — more at GREATLY

hon·o·rar·i·um \ˌä-nə-ˈrer-ē-əm\ *n, pl* **-ia** \-ē-ə\ *also* **-i·ums** : a reward usu. for services on which custom or propriety forbids a price to be set

hon·or·ary \ˈä-nə-ˌrer-ē\ *adj* **1** : having or conferring distinction **2** : conferred in recognition of achievement without the usual prerequisites ⟨∼ degree⟩ **3** : UNPAID, VOLUNTARY — **hon·or·ari·ly** \ˌä-nə-ˈrer-ə-lē\ *adv*

hon·or·if·ic \ˌä-nə-ˈri-fik\ *adj* : conferring or conveying honor ⟨∼ titles⟩

hon·our, hon·our·able *Can and Brit var of* HONOR, HONORABLE

¹**hood** \ˈhu̇d\ *n* **1** : a covering for the head and neck and sometimes the face **2** : an ornamental fold (as at the back of an ecclesiastical vestment) **3 a ♦** : something resembling a hood in form or use **b** : a cover for parts of mechanisms; *esp* : the covering over an automobile engine — **hood·ed** \ˈhu̇-dəd\ *adj*

♦ cloak, curtain, mantle, mask, shroud, veil — more at CLOAK

²**hood** \ˈhu̇d, ˈhüd\ *n* : a brutal ruffian : HOODLUM
³**hood** \ˈhüd\ *n* : an inner-city neighborhood

-hood \ˌhu̇d\ *n suffix* **1** : state : condition : quality : character ⟨boy*hood*⟩ ⟨hardi*hood*⟩ **2** : instance of a (specified) state or quality ⟨false*hood*⟩ **3** : individuals sharing a (specified) state or character ⟨brother*hood*⟩

hood·ie \ˈhu̇-dē\ *n* : a hooded sweatshirt
hood·lum \ˈhüd-ləm, ˈhu̇d-\ *n* **1 ♦** : a brutal ruffian : THUG **2** : a young ruffian or loafer

♦ bully, gangster, goon, hood, mobster, mug, punk, rowdy, ruffian, thug, tough; *also* cutthroat, scoundrel, villain; assassin, bandit, bravo, brigand, criminal, crook, desperado, felon, gunman, highwayman, lawbreaker, mafioso, outlaw, perpetrator, pickpocket, racketeer, robber, swindler, thief

hoo·doo \ˈhü-dü\ *n, pl* **hoodoos** **1** : a body of magical practices traditional esp. among African Americans in the southern U.S. **2** : something that brings bad luck — **hoodoo** *vb*

hood·wink \ˈhu̇d-ˌwiŋk\ *vb* **♦** : to deceive by false appearance

♦ beguile, bluff, cozen, deceive, delude, dupe, fool, gull, have, hoax, humbug, misinform, mislead, string along, take in, trick — more at DECEIVE

hoo·ey \ˈhü-ē\ *n* : NONSENSE
hoof \ˈhu̇f, ˈhüf\ *n, pl* **hooves** \ˈhu̇vz, ˈhüvz\ *or* **hoofs** : a horny covering that protects the ends of the toes of ungulate mammals (as horses or cattle); *also* : a hoofed foot — **hoofed** \ˈhu̇ft, ˈhüft\ *adj*

¹**hook** \ˈhu̇k\ *n* **1** : a curved or bent device for catching, holding, or pulling **2** : something curved or bent like a hook **3** : a flight of a ball (as in golf) that curves in a direction opposite to the dominant hand of the player propelling it **4** : a short punch delivered with a circular motion and with the elbow bent and rigid

²**hook** *vb* **1 ♦** : to form into a hook : CURVE, CROOK **2 a** : to seize or make fast with a hook **b ♦** : to connect by or as if by a hook — often used with *up* **3 ♦** : to take the property of another wrongfully : STEAL **4** : to work as a prostitute

♦ [1] arc, arch, bend, bow, crook, curve, round, sweep, swerve, wheel — more at CURVE ♦ [2b] chain, compound, connect, couple, hitch, join, link, yoke — more at CONNECT ♦ [3] appropriate, filch, misappropriate, nip, pilfer, pocket, purloin, snitch, steal, swipe, thieve — more at STEAL

hoo·kah \ˈhu̇-kə, ˈhü-\ *n* [Ar ḥuqqa bottle of a water pipe] : WATER PIPE
hook·er \ˈhu̇-kər\ *n* **1** : one that hooks **2** : PROSTITUTE
hook·up \ˈhu̇-ˌkəp\ *n* **1 ♦** : a state of cooperation or alliance **2** : an assemblage (as of apparatus or circuits) used for a specific purpose (as in radio)

♦ affiliation, alliance, association, collaboration, confederation, connection, cooperation, liaison, partnership, relation, relationship, union — more at ASSOCIATION

hook up *vb* : to become involved in a working, social, or sexual relationship
hook·worm \ˈhu̇k-ˌwərm\ *n* : any of several parasitic intestinal nematode worms having hooks or plates around the mouth; *also* : infestation with or disease caused by hookworms
hoo·li·gan \ˈhü-li-gən\ *n* **♦** : a brutal person : RUFFIAN, HOODLUM

♦ bully, gangster, goon, homeboy, hood, hoodlum, mobster, mug, punk, rowdy, ruffian, thug, tough — more at hoodlum

hoop \ˈhu̇p, ˈhüp\ *n* **1** : a circular strip used esp. for holding together the staves of a barrel **2** : a circular figure or object : RING **3** : a circle of flexible material for expanding a woman's skirt **4** : BASKETBALL — usu. used in pl.

♦ band, circle, ring, round — more at RING

hoop·la \ˈhüp-ˌlä, ˈhu̇p-\ *n* [F *houp-là*, interj.] : TO-DO; *also* : BALLYHOO
hoop·ster \ˈhüp-stər\ *n* : a basketball player
hoo·ray \hu̇-ˈrā\ *interj* — used to express joy, approval, or encouragement
hoose·gow \ˈhüs-ˌgau̇\ *n* [Sp *juzgado* panel of judges, courtroom] : JAIL
¹**hoot** \ˈhüt\ *vb* **1** : to shout or laugh usu. in contempt **2** : to make the natural throat noise of an owl — **hoot·er** *n*
²**hoot** *n* **1 ♦** : a sound of hooting **2 ♦** : the least bit ⟨don't give a ∼⟩ **3** : something or someone amusing ⟨the play is a real ∼⟩

♦ [1] cry, holler, howl, shout, whoop, yell, yowl — more at SHOUT ♦ [1] boo, catcall, hiss, jeer, raspberry, snort — more at CATCALL ♦ [2] jot, lick, modicum, rap, tittle, whit — more at JOT

hoot·e·nan·ny \ˈhü-tə-ˌna-nē\ *n, pl* **-nies** : a gathering at which folksingers entertain often with the audience joining in

¹**hop** \\'häp\ *vb* **hopped; hop·ping 1** ♦ : to move by a quick springy leap or in a series of leaps **2** : to make a quick trip **3** : to ride on esp. surreptitiously and without authorization

♦ bound, jump, leap, spring, vault — more at JUMP

²**hop** *n* **1** ♦ : a short brisk leap esp. on one leg **2** : a social gathering for dancing : DANCE **3** : a short trip by air

♦ bound, jump, leap, spring, vault — more at JUMP

³**hop** *n* : a vine related to the mulberry whose ripe dried pistillate catkins are used esp. in flavoring malt liquors; *also, pl* : its pistillate catkins

¹**hope** \\'hōp\ *vb* **hoped; hop·ing** ♦ : to desire with expectation of fulfillment ⟨*hopes* for a promotion⟩

♦ *usu* hope for anticipate, await, expect, watch — more at EXPECT

²**hope** *n* **1** : TRUST, RELIANCE **2** : desire accompanied by expectation of fulfillment; *also* : something hoped for **3** : one that gives promise for the future

HOPE *abbr* Health Opportunity for People Everywhere

hope·ful \\'hōp-fəl\ *adj* **1** ♦ : having qualities which inspire hope **2** : full of hope — **hope·ful·ness** *n*

♦ auspicious, bright, encouraging, fair, golden, heartening, likely, promising, propitious, rosy, upbeat; *also* cheering, comforting, reassuring; assured, confident, decisive, doubtless, positive, sure, unhesitating; bullish; favorable, good *Ant* bleak, dark, desperate, discouraging, disheartening, dismal, dreary, gloomy, hopeless, inauspicious, pessimistic, unlikely, unpromising

hope·ful·ly \\'hōp-fə-lē\ *adv* **1** : in a hopeful manner **2** : it is hoped

hope·less \\'hō-pləs\ *adj* **1** ♦ : having no expectation of good or success **2 a** ♦ : incapable of solution, management, or accomplishment : IMPOSSIBLE **b** ♦ : not susceptible to remedy or cure; *also* : incapable of redemption or improvement — **hope·less·ly** *adv*

♦ [1] defeatist, despairing, pessimistic — more at PESSIMISTIC ♦ [2a] impossible, unattainable, unsolvable, unworkable — more at IMPOSSIBLE ♦ [2b] incorrigible, incurable, irredeemable, irremediable, unrecoverable, unredeemable; *also* irreparable, irreversible; unpromising, impenitent, unregenerate, unrepentant *Ant* curable, correctable, reclaimable, recoverable, redeemable, reformable, remediable, retrievable

hope·less·ness \\-nəs\ *n* ♦ : the quality or state of being hopeless

♦ despair, desperation, despondency, forlornness — more at DESPAIR

Ho·pi \\'hō-pē\ *n, pl* **Hopi** *or* **Hopis** : a member of an American Indian people of Arizona; *also* : the language of the Hopi people

hopped–up \\'häpt-'əp\ *adj* **1** : being under the influence of a narcotic; *also* : full of enthusiasm or excitement **2** : having more power than usual ⟨a ~ engine⟩

hop·per \\'hä-pər\ *n* **1** : a usu. immature hopping insect (as a grasshopper) **2** : a usu. funnel-shaped container for delivering material (as grain) **3** : a freight car with hinged doors in a sloping bottom **4** : a box into which a bill to be considered by a legislative body is dropped **5** : a tank holding a liquid and having a device for releasing its contents through a pipe

hop·scotch \\'häp-ˌskäch\ *n* : a child's game in which a player tosses an object (as a stone) into areas of a figure drawn on the ground and hops through the figure to pick up the object

hor *abbr* horizontal

horde \\'hōrd\ *n* ♦ : a teeming crowd or throng : SWARM

♦ army, crowd, crush, drove, flock, host, legion, mob, multitude, press, swarm, throng — more at CROWD

ho·ri·zon \\hə-'rīz-ᵊn\ *n* [ME, fr. LL, fr. Gk *horizont-, horizōn*, fr. prp. of *horizein* to bound, fr. *horos* limit, boundary] **1** : the apparent junction of earth and sky **2** : range of outlook or experience

hor·i·zon·tal \\ˌhȯr-ə-'zänt-ᵊl\ *adj* : parallel to the horizon : LEVEL — **horizontal** *n* — **hor·i·zon·tal·ly** *adv*

hor·mon·al \\hȯr-'mōn-ᵊl\ *adj* : of, relating to, or effected by hormones

hor·mone \\'hȯr-ˌmōn\ *n* [Gk *hormōn*, prp. of *horman* to stir up, fr. *hormē* impulse, assault] : a product of living cells that circulates in body fluids and has a specific effect on the activity of cells remote from its point of origin

horn \\'hȯrn\ *n* **1** : one of the hard projections of bone or keratin on the head of many hoofed mammals **2** : something resembling or suggesting a horn **3** : a brass wind instrument **4** : a usu. electrical device that makes a noise ⟨automobile ~⟩ — **horned** \\'hȯrnd\ *adj* — **horn·less** *adj*

horn·book \\'hȯrn-ˌbu̇k\ *n* **1** : a child's primer consisting of a sheet of parchment or paper protected by a sheet of transparent horn **2** : a rudimentary treatise

horned toad *n* : any of several small harmless insect-eating lizards with spines on the head resembling horns and spiny scales on the body

hor·net \\'hȯr-nət\ *n* : any of the larger social wasps

horn in *vb* : to participate without invitation : INTRUDE

horn·pipe \\'hȯrn-ˌpīp\ *n* : a lively folk dance of the British Isles

horny \\'hȯr-nē\ *adj* **horn·i·er; -est 1** : of or made of horn; *also* : HARD, CALLOUS **2** : having horns **3** : desiring sexual gratification; *also* : excited sexually

ho·rol·o·gy \\hə-'rä-lə-jē\ *n* : the science of measuring time or constructing time-indicating instruments — **hor·o·log·ic** \\ˌhȯr-ə-'lä-jik\ *adj* — **ho·rol·o·gist** \\hə-'rä-lə-jist\ *n*

horo·scope \\'hȯr-ə-ˌskōp\ *n* [ME *horoscopum*, fr. L *horoscopus*, fr. Gk *hōroskopos*, fr. *hōra* hour + *skopos* watcher] **1** : a diagram of the relative positions of planets and signs of the zodiac at a particular time for use by astrologers to foretell events of a person's life **2** : an astrological forecast

hor·ren·dous \\hȯ-'ren-dəs\ *adj* : inspiring horror : DREADFUL, HORRIBLE

hor·ri·ble \\'hȯr-ə-bəl\ *adj* **1** ♦ : marked by or arousing horror **2** ♦ : highly disagreeable ⟨a ~ mistake⟩ — **hor·ri·ble·ness** *n* — **hor·ri·bly** \\-blē\ *adv*

♦ [1] dreadful, fearful, fearsome, hair-raising, scary, terrifying — more at FEARFUL ♦ [2] abhorrent, abominable, distasteful, horrid, obnoxious, odious, offensive, repellent, repugnant, repulsive, revolting, scandalous, ugly — more at OFFENSIVE ♦ [2] appalling, atrocious, awful, dreadful, frightful, ghastly, grisly, gruesome, hideous, horrid, lurid, macabre, monstrous, nightmarish, shocking, terrible; *also* bloodcurdling, dire, direful, fearful, fearsome, forbidding, formidable, frightening, hair-raising, terrifying; abhorrent, deplorable, disagreeable, disgusting, distasteful, loathsome; abominable, evil, foul, heinous, noxious, odious, unspeakable, vile

hor·rid \\'hȯr-əd\ *adj* **1** : inspiring horror : HIDEOUS **2** ♦ : highly disagreeable — **hor·rid·ly** *adv*

♦ abhorrent, abominable, appalling, awful, distasteful, dreadful, horrible, obnoxious, offensive, repugnant, repulsive, revolting, scandalous, shocking, ugly — more at OFFENSIVE

hor·rif·ic \\hȯ-'ri-fik\ *adj* : having the power to horrify ⟨a ~ crime⟩ — **hor·rif·i·cal·ly** \\-fi-k(ə-)lē\ *adv*

hor·ri·fy \\'hȯr-ə-ˌfī\ *vb* **-fied; -fy·ing** ♦ : to cause to feel horror

♦ alarm, frighten, panic, scare, shock, spook, startle, terrify, terrorize — more at FRIGHTEN

hor·ror \\'hȯr-ər\ *n* **1** ♦ : painful and intense fear, dread, or dismay **2** : intense repugnance **3 a** ♦ : something that horrifies **b** : a repulsive or dismal quality or character **4** ♦ : the quality of inspiring horror

♦ [1] alarm, anxiety, apprehension, dread, fear, fright, panic, terror, trepidation — more at FEAR ♦ [3a] agony, hell, misery, murder, nightmare, torment, torture — more at HELL ♦ [4] atrociousness, atrocity, frightfulness, hideousness, monstrosity, repulsiveness; *also* badness, baseness, evil, foulness, heinousness, immorality, iniquity, ungodliness, viciousness, vileness, wickedness; hatefulness; agony, misery, torment, torture

horror story *n* : an account of an unsettling or unfortunate occurrence

hors de com·bat \ˌȯr-də-kōⁿ-ˈbä\ *adv or adj* : in a disabled condition

hors d'oeuvre \ȯr-ˈdərv\ *n, pl* **hors d'oeuvres** *same or* -ˈdərvz\ *also* **hors d'oeuvre** [F *hors-d'oeuvre*, lit., outside of the work] : any of various savory foods usu. served as appetizers

horse \ˈhȯrs\ *n, pl* **hors·es** *also* **horse** 1 : a large solid-hoofed herbivorous mammal domesticated as a draft and saddle animal 2 : a supporting framework usu. with legs — **horse·less** *adj*

¹**horse·back** \ˈhȯrs-ˌbak\ *n* : the back of a horse
²**horseback** *adv* : on horseback

horse chestnut *n* : a large tree with palmate leaves, erect conical clusters of showy flowers, and large glossy brown seeds enclosed in a prickly bur; *also* : its seed

horse·flesh \ˈhȯrs-ˌflesh\ *n* : horses for riding, driving, or racing

horse·fly \-ˌflī\ *n* : any of a family of large dipteran flies with bloodsucking females

horse·hair \-ˌhar\ *n* 1 : the hair of a horse esp. from the mane or tail 2 : cloth made from horsehair

horse·hide \-ˌhīd\ *n* 1 : the dressed or raw hide of a horse 2 : the ball used in baseball

horse latitudes *n pl* : either of two calm regions near 30°N and 30°S latitude

horse·laugh \ˈhȯrs-ˌlaf, -ˌláf\ *n* : a loud boisterous laugh

horse·man \-mən\ *n* 1 : one who rides horseback; *also* : one skilled in managing horses 2 : a breeder or raiser of horses — **horse·man·ship** *n*

horse·play \-ˌplā\ *n* ♦ : rough boisterous play

♦ foolery, high jinks, monkeyshines, roughhouse, shenanigans, tomfoolery; *also* buffoonery, clownishness, foolishness, joking, nonsense, waggery; rowdiness; devilry, impishness, mischief, mischievousness, roguishness, trickery; cavorting, frivolity, frolicking, gamboling, merrymaking, playfulness, revelry, roistering, romping, sporting

horse·play·er \-ər\ *n* : a bettor on horse races

horse·pow·er \ˈhȯrs-ˌpaú(-ə)r\ *n* : a unit of power equal in the U.S. to 746 watts

horse·rad·ish \-ˌra-dish\ *n* : a tall white-flowered herb related to the mustards whose pungent root is used as a condiment; *also* : the pungent condiment

horse sense *n* ♦ : sound and prudent judgment based on a simple perception of the situation or facts

♦ common sense, prudence, sense, wisdom, wit — more at COMMON SENSE

horse·shoe \ˈhȯrs-ˌshü\ *n* 1 : a usu. U-shaped protective metal plate fitted to the rim of a horse's hoof 2 *pl* : a game in which horseshoes are pitched at a fixed object — **horse·shoe** *vb* — **horse·sho·er** *n*

horseshoe crab *n* : any of several marine arthropods with a broad crescent-shaped combined head and thorax

horse·tail \ˈhȯrs-ˌtāl\ *n* : any of a genus of primitive spore-producing plants with hollow jointed stems and leaves reduced to sheaths about the joints

horse·whip \-ˌhwip\ *vb* : to flog with a whip made to be used on a horse

horse·wom·an \-ˌwù-mən\ *n* : a woman skilled in riding horseback or in caring for or managing horses; *also* : a woman who breeds or raises horses

hors·ey *also* **horsy** \ˈhȯr-sē\ *adj* **hors·i·er; -est** 1 : of, relating to, or suggesting a horse 2 : having to do with horses or horse racing

hort *abbr* horticultural; horticulture

hor·ta·tive \ˈhȯr-tə-tiv\ *adj* : giving exhortation

hor·ta·to·ry \ˈhȯr-tə-ˌtōr-ē\ *adj* : HORTATIVE

hor·ti·cul·ture \ˈhȯr-tə-ˌkəl-chər\ *n* : the science and art of growing fruits, vegetables, flowers, and ornamental plants — **hor·ti·cul·tur·al** \ˌhȯr-tə-ˈkəl-chə-rəl\ *adj* — **hor·ti·cul·tur·ist** \-rist\ *n*

Hos *abbr* Hosea

ho·san·na \hō-ˈza-nə, -ˈzä-\ *interj* [Gk *hōsanna*, fr. Heb *hōshīāh-nnā* pray, save (us)!] — used as a cry of acclamation and adoration — **hosanna** *n*

¹**hose** \ˈhōz\ *n, pl* **hose** *or* **hos·es** 1 *pl* **hose** : STOCKING, SOCK; *also* : a close-fitting garment covering the legs and waist 2 : a flexible tube for conveying fluids (as from a faucet)

²**hose** *vb* **hosed; hos·ing** : to spray, water, or wash with a hose ⟨*hosed* off the car⟩

Ho·sea \hō-ˈzā-ə, -ˈzē-\ *n* : a book of the canonical Jewish and Christian Scriptures

ho·siery \ˈhō-zhə-rē, -zə-\ *n* : STOCKINGS, SOCKS

hosp *abbr* hospital

hos·pice \ˈhäs-pəs\ *n* 1 ♦ : a lodging for travelers or for young persons or the underprivileged 2 : a facility or program for caring for dying persons

♦ hotel, inn, lodge, public house, tavern — more at HOTEL

hos·pi·ta·ble \hä-ˈspi-tə-bəl, ˈhäs-(ˌ)pi-\ *adj* 1 ♦ : given to generous and cordial reception of guests 2 : readily receptive — **hos·pi·ta·bly** \-blē\ *adv*

♦ affable, cordial, genial, gracious, sociable — more at GRACIOUS

hos·pi·tal \ˈhäs-ˌpit-ᵊl\ *n* [ME, fr. AF, fr. ML *hospitale* hospice, guest house, fr. neut. of L *hospitalis* of a guest, fr. *hospit-, hospes* guest, host] : an institution where the sick or injured receive medical or surgical care

hos·pi·tal·ise *chiefly Brit var of* HOSPITALIZE

hos·pi·tal·ist \ˈhäs-ˌpit-ᵊl-ist\ *n* : a physician who specializes in providing and managing the care and treatment of hospitalized patients

hos·pi·tal·i·ty \ˌhäs-pə-ˈta-lə-tē\ *n, pl* **-ties** : hospitable treatment, reception, or disposition

hos·pi·tal·ize \ˈhäs-ˌpit-ᵊl-ˌīz\ *vb* **-ized; -iz·ing** : to place in a hospital as a patient — **hos·pi·tal·i·za·tion** \ˌhäs-ˌpit-ᵊl-ə-ˈzā-shən\ *n*

¹**host** \ˈhōst\ *n* [ME, fr. AF *ost*, fr. LL *hostis*, fr. L, stranger, enemy] 1 : a large organized body of armed personnel trained for war esp. on land : ARMY 2 ♦ : a very large number : MULTITUDE ⟨a ∼ of options⟩

♦ army, crowd, crush, drove, flock, horde, legion, mob, multitude, press, swarm, throng — more at CROWD

²**host** *n* [ME *hoste* host, guest, fr. AF, fr. L *hospit-, hospes*] 1 : one who receives or entertains guests 2 : one who talks to guests on a show 3 : an animal or plant on or in which a parasite lives 4 : one into which something (as an organ) is transplanted 5 : SERVER 2 — **host** *vb*

³**host** *n, often cap* [ultim. fr. L *hostia* sacrifice] : the eucharistic bread

hos·tage \ˈhäs-tij\ *n* 1 : a person kept as a pledge pending the fulfillment of an agreement 2 : a person taken by force to secure the taker's demands

hos·tel \ˈhäst-ᵊl\ *n* [ME, fr. AF, fr. ML *hospitale* hospice] 1 : an establishment for the lodging and entertaining of travelers : INN 2 : a supervised lodging for youth — **hos·tel·er** *n*

hos·tel·ry \-rē\ *n, pl* **-ries** : an establishment for the lodging and entertaining of travelers : INN, HOTEL

host·ess \ˈhō-stəs\ *n* 1 : a woman who receives or entertains guests 2 : a woman who talks to guests on a show

hos·tile \ˈhäst-ᵊl, ˈhäs-ˌtīl\ *adj* ♦ : marked by usu. overt antagonism : UNFRIENDLY — **hostile** *n* — **hos·tile·ly** *adv*

♦ antagonistic, inhospitable, inimical, jaundiced, negative, unfriendly, unsympathetic; *also* adverse, bellicose, belligerent, clashing, conflicting, contentious, contrary, opposed, pugnacious, quarrelsome, resisting; antisocial, cold, cool, disagreeable, disapproving, distant, frigid, icy, biased, prejudiced; discourteous, impolite, rude, surly, uncivil, unfavorable, unkind, unpleasant, unsociable; acrimonious, antipathetic, bitter, hateful, malevolent, opprobrious, rancorous, spiteful, unloving, vindictive, virulent *Ant* friendly, hospitable, sympathetic

hos·til·i·ty \hä-'sti-lə-tē\ *n, pl* **-ties** **1** ♦ : an unfriendly state or action **2** *pl* : overt acts of war

♦ animosity, antagonism, antipathy, bitterness, enmity, gall, grudge, rancor — more at ENMITY

hos·tler \'häs-lər, 'äs-\ *n* : one who takes care of horses or mules

hot \'hät\ *adj* **hot·ter; hot·test** **1** ♦ : marked by a high temperature or an uncomfortable degree of body heat **2** : giving a sensation of heat or of burning **3** : ARDENT, FIERY **4** : sexually excited **5** ♦ : marked by enthusiastic or impatient desire or interest : EAGER **6** ♦ : newly made or received **7** : PUNGENT **8** : unusually lucky or favorable ⟨~ dice⟩ **9** : recently and illegally obtained ⟨~ jewels⟩ **10** ♦ : currently popular or in demand **11** ♦ : marked by extreme force or sudden intense activity : VIOLENT — **hot** *adv* — **hot·ly** *adv*

♦ [1] broiling, burning, fiery, red-hot, scorching, sultry, torrid; *also* blazing, glowing, molten, sizzling; heated, warmed; snug, warm; feverish, flushed, inflamed; muggy, steamy, summery, tropical *Ant* arctic, chill, chilled, cold, freezing, frigid, frozen, glacial, iced, icy ♦ [5] agog, anxious, ardent, athirst, avid, crazy, eager, enthusiastic, gung ho, hungry, keen, nuts, raring, solicitous, thirsty, voracious — more at EAGER ♦ [6] contemporary, current, mod, modern, new, newfangled, red-hot, space-age, ultramodern, up-to-date — more at MODERN ♦ [10] fashionable, in, modish, popular, vogue — more at POPULAR ♦ [11] explosive, ferocious, fierce, furious, rabid, rough, stormy, tempestuous, turbulent, violent, volcanic — more at VIOLENT

hot air *n* ♦ : empty talk

♦ bombast, gas, grandiloquence, rhetoric, wind — more at RHETORIC

hot·bed \-ˌbed\ *n* **1** : a glass-covered bed of soil heated (as by fermenting manure) and used esp. for raising seedlings **2** : an environment that favors rapid growth or development

hot–blood·ed \-ˈblə-dəd\ *adj* ♦ : easily roused or excited

♦ ardent, burning, charged, emotional, fervent, fiery, impassioned, passionate, red-hot, vehement — more at FERVENT

hot·box \-ˌbäks\ *n* : a bearing (as of a railroad car) overheated by friction

hot button *n* : an emotional issue or concern that triggers immediate intense reaction

hot·cake \-ˌkāk\ *n* : a flat cake made of thin batter and cooked (as on a griddle) on both sides : PANCAKE

hot dog *n* : a cooked frankfurter usu. served in a long split roll

ho·tel \hō-ˈtel\ *n* [F *hâotel*, fr. OF *hostel*, fr. ML *hospitale* hospice] ♦ : a building where lodging and usu. meals, entertainment, and various personal services are provided for the public

♦ hospice, inn, lodge, public house, tavern; *also* bed=and-breakfast; accommodations, lodgings, rest; motel, resort, spa, youth hostel; camp, campground; dorm, dormitory; boardinghouse, lodging house

hot flash *n* : a sudden brief flushing and sensation of heat usu. associated with menopausal endocrine imbalance

hot·head·ed \'hät-'he-dəd\ *adj* : FIERY, IMPETUOUS ⟨a ~ troublemaker⟩ — **hot·head** \-ˌhed\ *n* — **hot·head·ed·ly** *adv* — **hot·head·ed·ness** *n*

hot·house \-ˌhaus\ *n* : a heated greenhouse esp. for raising tropical plants

hot·line \'hät-ˌlīn\ *n* : a telephone line for emergency use (as between governments or to a counseling service)

hot·ness \-nəs\ *n* : the quality or state of being hot

hot pants *n pl* : very short shorts

hot pepper *n* : a small usu. thin-walled pepper with a pungent taste; *also* : a plant bearing hot peppers

hot plate *n* : a simple portable appliance for heating or for cooking

hot potato *n* : an embarrassing or controversial issue

hot rod *n* : an automobile modified for high speed and fast acceleration — **hot–rod·der** \-ˈrä-dər\ *n*

hots \'häts\ *n pl* : strong sexual desire — usu. used with *the*

hot seat *n* : a position of anxiety or embarrassment

hot·shot \'hät-ˌshät\ *n* ♦ : a showily skillful person

♦ ace, adept, artist, authority, crackerjack, expert, guru, hand, maestro, master, scholar, shark, virtuoso, whiz, wizard — more at EXPERT

hot tub *n* : a large tub of hot water for one or more bathers

hot water *n* : TROUBLE, DIFFICULTY

hot–wire \ˈhät-ˌwī(-ə)r\ *vb* : to start (an automobile) by short-circuiting the ignition system

¹hound \ˈhaund\ *n* **1** : a domestic mammal closely related to the gray wolf; *esp* : any of various hunting dogs that track prey by scent or sight **2** : FAN, ADDICT

²hound *vb* ♦ : to pursue relentlessly

♦ chase, dog, follow, pursue, shadow, tag, tail, trace, track, trail — more at FOLLOW ♦ henpeck, nag, needle — more at NAG

hour \ˈau̇(-ə)r\ *n* **1** : the 24th part of a day : 60 minutes **2** : the time of day **3** : a particular or customary time **4** : a class session — **hour·ly** *adv or adj*

hour·glass \ˈau̇(-ə)r-ˌglas\ *n* : a glass vessel for measuring time in which sand runs from an upper compartment to a lower compartment in an hour

hou·ri \ˈhu̇r-ē\ *n* [F, fr. Pers *hūri*, fr. Ar *ḥūrīya*] : one of the beautiful maidens of the Muslim paradise

¹house \ˈhau̇s\ *n, pl* **hous·es** \ˈhau̇-zəz\ **1** ♦ : a building for human habitation **2** : an animal shelter (as a den or nest) **3** : a building in which something is stored **4 a** : those who dwell under the same roof and compose a family : HOUSEHOLD **b** ♦ : a family including ancestors, descendants, and kindred : FAMILY **5** : a residence for a religious community or for students; *also* : those in residence **6** : a legislative body **7** : a place of business or entertainment **8** ♦ : a business organization **9** : the audience in a theater or concert hall — **house·ful** *n*

♦ [1] abode, domicile, dwelling, home, lodging, quarters, residence — more at HOME ♦ [4b] blood, clan, family, folks, kin, kindred, kinfolk, line, lineage, people, race, stock, tribe ♦ [8] business, company, concern, enterprise, establishment, firm, outfit — more at ENTERPRISE

²house \ˈhau̇z\ *vb* **housed; hous·ing** **1** ♦ : to provide with or take shelter : LODGE **2** ♦ : to encase, enclose, or shelter as if by putting in a house

♦ [1] accommodate, billet, chamber, domicile, harbor (*or* harbour), lodge, put up, quarter, roof, shelter, take in; *also* board, bunk, ensconce, home, roost, secure, stable, tent ♦ [2] cage, closet, coop up, corral, encase, enclose, envelop, fence, hedge, hem, immure, pen, wall — more at ENCLOSE

house·boat \ˈhau̇s-ˌbōt\ *n* : a pleasure boat fitted for use as a dwelling or for leisurely cruising

house·boy \-ˌbȯi\ *n* : a boy or man hired to act as a household servant

house·break \-ˌbrāk\ *vb* **-broke; -bro·ken; -break·ing** : to train (a pet) in excretory habits acceptable in indoor living

house·break·ing \-ˌbrā-kiŋ\ *n* : the act of breaking into a dwelling with the intent of committing a felony

house·clean \-ˌklēn\ *vb* : to clean a house and its furniture — **house·clean·ing** *n*

house·coat \-ˌkōt\ *n* : a woman's often long-skirted informal garment for wear around the house

house·fly \-ˌflī\ *n* : a dipteran fly that is common about human habitations

¹**house·hold** \-ˌhōld\ *n* ♦ : those who dwell as a family under the same roof — **house·hold·er** *n*

♦ house; *also* folks, kin, kindred, kinfolk, kith; brood; nuclear family; clan, community

²**household** *adj* **1** : DOMESTIC **2** ♦ : frequently seen or experienced : FAMILIAR, COMMON ⟨a ∼ name⟩

♦ common, commonplace, customary, everyday, familiar, frequent, ordinary, routine, usual — more at COMMON

house·keep·er \-ˌkē-pər\ *n* : a person employed to take care of a house

house·keep·ing \-ˌkē-piŋ\ *n* : the care and management of a house or institutional property

house·lights \-ˌlīts\ *n pl* : the lights that illuminate the auditorium of a theater

house·maid \-ˌmād\ *n* ♦ : a girl or woman who is a servant employed to do housework

♦ domestic, girl, maid, maidservant — more at MAID

house·moth·er \-ˌmə-thər\ *n* : a woman acting as hostess, chaperone, and often housekeeper in a group residence

House of Commons : the lower house of the British or Canadian parliaments

house·plant \-ˌplant\ *n* : a plant grown or kept indoors

house sparrow *n* : a Eurasian sparrow widely introduced in urban and agricultural areas

house·top \ˈhaus-ˌtäp\ *n* : ROOF

house·wares \-ˌwarz\ *n pl* : small articles of household equipment

house·warm·ing \-ˌwȯr-miŋ\ *n* : a party to celebrate the taking possession of a house or premises

house·wife \-ˌwīf\ *n* : a married woman in charge of a household — **house·wife·ly** *adj* — **house·wif·ery** \-ˌwī-fə-rē\ *n*

house·work \-ˌwərk\ *n* : the work of housekeeping

¹**hous·ing** \ˈhau-ziŋ\ *n* **1** : SHELTER; *also* : dwellings provided for people **2** ♦ : something that covers or protects

♦ armor, capsule, case, casing, cocoon, cover, husk, jacket, pod, sheath, shell — more at CASE

²**housing** *n* : CAPARISON 1

HOV *abbr* high-occupancy vehicle

hove *past and past part of* HEAVE

hov·el \ˈhə-vəl, ˈhä-\ *n* : a small, wretched, and often dirty house : HUT

hov·er \ˈhə-vər, ˈhä-\ *vb* **hov·ered; hov·er·ing** **1 a** : FLUTTER **b** ♦ : to remain suspended over a place or object **2** : to move to and fro **3** ♦ : to be in an uncertain state of uncertainty, irresolution, or suspense

♦ [1b] drift, float, glide, hang, poise, ride, sail, waft — more at FLOAT ♦ [3] hang, menace, overhang, threaten — more at THREATEN

hov·er·craft \-ˌkraft\ *n* : a vehicle that rides on a cushion of air over a surface

¹**how** \ˈhau\ *adv* **1** : in what way or manner ⟨∼ was it done⟩ **2** : with what meaning ⟨∼ do we interpret such behavior⟩ **3** : for what reason ⟨∼ could you have done such a thing⟩ **4** : to what extent or degree ⟨∼ deep is it⟩ **5** : in what state or condition ⟨∼ are you⟩ — **how about** : what do you say to or think of ⟨*how about* coming with me⟩ — **how come** : why is it that

²**how** *conj* **1** : the way or manner in which ⟨remember ∼ they fought⟩ **2** : HOWEVER ⟨do it ∼ you like⟩

¹**how·be·it** \hau-ˈbē-ət\ *conj* ♦ : even though : ALTHOUGH

♦ albeit, although, though, when, while — more at ALTHOUGH

²**howbeit** *adv* ♦ : on the other hand : NEVERTHELESS

♦ but, however, nevertheless, nonetheless, notwithstanding, still, though, withal, yet — more at HOWEVER

how·dah \ˈhau-də\ *n* [Hindi & Urdu *hauda,* fr. Ar *haudaj*] : a seat or covered pavilion on the back of an elephant or camel

¹**how·ev·er** \hau-ˈe-vər\ *conj* : in whatever manner that

²**however** *adv* **1** : to whatever degree; *also* : in whatever manner **2** ♦ : on the other hand

♦ but, howbeit, nevertheless, nonetheless, notwithstanding, still, though, withal, yet; *also* after all, anyhow, regardless

how·it·zer \ˈhau-ət-sər\ *n* : a short cannon that shoots shells at a high angle

¹**howl** \ˈhau-(ə)l\ *vb* **1** ♦ : to emit a loud long doleful sound characteristic of dogs **2** ♦ : to cry loudly

♦ [1] bay, keen, wail, yowl; *also* bawl, caterwaul, squall, yawp, yell, yelp ♦ [2] scream, shriek, shrill, squeal, yell, yelp — more at SCREAM

²**howl** *n* **1** : a loud protracted mournful cry characteristic of dogs **2 a** ♦ : a prolonged cry of distress **b** ♦ : a yell or outcry of disappointment, rage, or protest

♦ [2a] groan, keen, lament, moan, plaint, wail — more at LAMENT ♦ [2b] cry, holler, hoot, shout, whoop, yell, yowl — more at SHOUT ♦ [2b] clamor (*or* clamour), hubbub, hue and cry, hullabaloo, noise, outcry, roar, tumult, uproar — more at CLAMOR

howl·er \ˈhau-lər\ *n* **1** : one that howls **2** : a humorous and ridiculous blunder

howl·ing *adj* **1** : DESOLATE, WILD **2** : very great ⟨a ∼ success⟩

how·so·ev·er \ˌhau-sə-ˈwe-vər\ *adv* : HOWEVER 1

hoy·den \ˈhȯid-ᵊn\ *n* : a girl or woman of saucy, boisterous, or carefree behavior

hp *abbr* horsepower

HP *abbr* high pressure

HPF *abbr* highest possible frequency

HQ *abbr* headquarters

hr *abbr* **1** here **2** hour

HR *abbr* House of Representatives

HRH *abbr* **1** Her Royal Highness **2** His Royal Highness

hrzn *abbr* horizon

Hs *symbol* hassium

HS *abbr* high school

HST *abbr* Hawaiian standard time

ht *abbr* height

HT *abbr* **1** Hawaii time **2** high-tension

HTML \ˌāch-ˌtē-ˌem-ˈel\ *n* [*h*ypertext *m*arkup *l*anguage] : a computer language used to create World Wide Web documents

http *abbr* hypertext transfer protocol

hua·ra·che \wə-ˈrä-chē\ *n* [MexSp] : a sandal with an upper made of interwoven leather strips

hub \ˈhəb\ *n* **1** : the central part of a circular object (as a wheel) **2 a** ♦ : a center of activity **b** : an airport or city through which an airline routes most of its traffic

♦ base, center (*or* centre), core, cynosure, eye, focus, heart, mecca, nucleus, seat — more at CENTER

hub·bub \ˈhə-bəb\ *n* **1** ♦ : a noisy confusion of sound : UPROAR **2** ♦ : a state of tumultuous confusion or excitement : TURMOIL

♦ [1] clamor (*or* clamour), howl, hue and cry, hullabaloo, noise, outcry, roar, tumult, uproar — more at CLAMOR ♦ [2] commotion, disturbance, furor, fuss, pandemonium, tumult, turmoil — more at COMMOTION

hub·cap \ˈhəb-ˌkap\ *n* : a removable metal cap over the end of an axle

hu·bris \ˈhyü-brəs\ *n* : exaggerated pride or self-confidence

huck·le·ber·ry \ˈhə-kəl-ˌber-ē\ *n* **1** : any of a genus of American shrubs of the heath family; *also* : its edible dark blue berry **2** : BLUEBERRY

huck·ster \ˈhək-stər\ *n* : PEDDLER, HAWKER — **huckster** *vb*

HUD *abbr* Department of Housing and Urban Development

¹**hud·dle** \ˈhəd-ᵊl\ *vb* **hud·dled; hud·dling** **1** ♦ : to crowd together **2** : CONFER **3** ♦ : to curl up : CROUCH

♦ [1] bunch, cluster, crowd, press — more at PRESS ♦ [3] crouch, hunch, squat — more at CROUCH

²**huddle** *n* **1** ♦ : a closely packed group **2** ♦ : an assembly for a common purpose : MEETING, CONFERENCE

♦ [1] array, assemblage, bank, batch, block, bunch, clump, cluster, collection, group, knot, lot, package, parcel, set, suite ♦ [2] assembly, conference, congress, convention, convocation, council, gathering, get-together, meeting, powwow, seminar — more at MEETING

hue \'hyü\ *n* **1** ♦ : a phenomenon of light or visual perception that enables one to differentiate otherwise identical objects : COLOR; *also* : gradation of color **2** : the attribute of colors that permits them to be classed as red, yellow, green, blue, or an intermediate color — **hued** \'hyüd\ *adj*

♦ cast, color (*or* colour), shade, tinge, tint, tone — more at COLOR

hue and cry *n* ♦ : a clamor of pursuit or protest

♦ clamor (*or* clamour), howl, hubbub, hullabaloo, noise, outcry, roar, tumult, uproar — more at CLAMOR

huff \'həf\ *n* ♦ : a fit of anger or pique — **huff** *vb* — **huffy** *adj*

♦ dither, fluster, fret, fuss, lather, pother, stew, tizzy, twitter — more at FRET ♦ dudgeon, offense, peeve, pique, resentment, umbrage — more at PIQUE

hug \'həg\ *vb* **hugged**; **hug·ging 1** ♦ : to press tightly esp. in the arms : EMBRACE **2** : to stay close to — **hug** *n*

♦ caress, clasp, embrace, enfold, grasp — more at EMBRACE

huge \'hyüj\ *adj* **hug·er; hug·est** ♦ : very large or extensive

♦ astronomical, colossal, enormous, giant, gigantic, grand, jumbo, mammoth, massive, prodigious, titanic, tremendous, vast, whopping; *also* big, bulky, considerable, extensive, good, goodly, great, gross, handsome, hefty, hulking, major, sizable, substantial, voluminous; august, formidable, grandiose, imposing, lofty, majestic; cavernous, monolithic, overwhelming, staggering, stupendous, towering; boundless, cosmic, immeasurable, infinite *Ant* diminutive, microscopic, minute, teeny, tiny, wee

huge·ly *adv* ♦ : to a great extent or degree

♦ broadly, considerably, greatly, largely, massively, monstrously, much, sizably, stupendously, tremendously, utterly, vastly — more at GREATLY

huge·ness \-nəs\ *n* ♦ : the quality or state of being huge

♦ enormity, immensity, magnitude, massiveness, vastness — more at IMMENSITY

¹**hug·ger–mug·ger** \'hə-gər-ˌmə-gər\ *n* **1** : SECRECY **2** : CONFUSION, MUDDLE

²**hugger–mugger** *adj* **1** ♦ : kept from knowledge or view **2** ♦ : of a confused or disorderly nature

♦ [1] clandestine, covert, furtive, private, secret, sneak, sneaky, stealthy, surreptitious, undercover, underground, underhanded — more at SECRET ♦ [2] chaotic, disheveled, disordered, disorderly, higgledy-piggledy, messy, pell-mell, topsy-turvy, unkempt, untidy

Hu·gue·not \'hyü-gə-ˌnät\ *n* : a French Protestant of the 16th and 17th centuries

hu·la \'hü-lə\ *n* : a sinuous Polynesian dance usu. accompanied by chants

hulk \'həlk\ *n* **1** : a heavy clumsy ship **2** : an old ship unfit for service **3** ♦ : a bulky or unwieldy person or thing

♦ clod, lout, lubber, lug, oaf — more at OAF

hulk·ing \'həl-kiŋ\ *adj* : BURLY, MASSIVE

¹**hull** \'həl\ *n* **1** : the outer covering of a fruit or seed **2** : the frame or body esp. of a ship or boat

²**hull** *vb* ♦ : to remove the hulls of — **hull·er** *n*

♦ bark, flay, husk, peel, shell, skin — more at PEEL

hul·la·ba·loo \'hə-lə-bə-ˌlü\ *n, pl* **-loos** ♦ : a confused noise : UPROAR

♦ clamor (*or* clamour), howl, hubbub, hue and cry, noise, outcry, roar, tumult, uproar — more at CLAMOR

hul·lo \ˌhə-'lō\ *chiefly Brit var of* HELLO

¹**hum** \'həm\ *vb* **hummed; hum·ming 1** : to utter a sound like that of the speech sound m prolonged **2** ♦ : to make the natural noise of an insect in motion or a similar sound : DRONE **3** : to be busily active **4** : to run smoothly **5** : to sing with closed lips

♦ buzz, drone, whir, whish, whiz, zip, zoom — more at WHIR

²**hum** *n* ♦ : the act of humming or the sound made by humming

♦ buzz, drone, purr, whir, whiz, zoom; *also* coo, babble, gurgle, hiss, moan, murmur, rustle, sigh, whisper; whish, zing, zip

¹**hu·man** \'hyü-mən, 'yü-\ *adj* **1** : of, relating to, being, or characteristic of humans **2** : having human form or attributes — **hu·man·ly** *adv* — **hu·man·ness** *n*

²**human** *n* ♦ : any of a species of bipedal primate mammals comprising all living persons and their recent ancestors; *also* : HOMINID

♦ being, body, creature, individual, man, mortal, person, stiff; *also* hominid, Homo sapiens, humanoid; brother, fellow, fellow man, neighbor; celebrity, personage, personality, self, somebody

hu·mane \hyü-'mān, yü-\ *adj* **1** ♦ : marked by compassion, sympathy, or consideration for others **2** : HUMANISTIC — **hu·mane·ly** *adv* — **hu·mane·ness** *n*

♦ beneficent, benevolent, compassionate, good-hearted, kind, kindly, sympathetic, tender, tenderhearted, warmhearted; *also* attentive, considerate, thoughtful; affable, benign, cordial, friendly, gentle, good, good-natured, good-tempered, gracious, mild, nice, pleasant; clement, forbearing, forgiving, lenient, merciful, soft; patient, pitying, tolerant, understanding; altruistic, brotherly, charitable, generous, greathearted, humanitarian, magnanimous, noble, philanthropic, unselfish, unsparing *Ant* barbarous, bestial, brutal, brutish, callous, cold-blooded, cruel, heartless, inhuman, inhumane, insensate, savage, unfeeling, unkind, unkindly, unsympathetic

human immunodeficiency virus *n* : HIV

hu·man·ism \'hyü-mə-ˌni-zəm, 'yü-\ *n* **1** : devotion to the humanities; *also* : the revival of classical letters characteristic of the Renaissance **2** : a doctrine or way of life centered on human interests or values — **hu·man·ist** \-nist\ *n or adj* — **hu·man·is·tic** \ˌhyü-mə-'nis-tik, yü-\ *adj*

¹**hu·man·i·tar·i·an** \hyü-ˌma-nə-'ter-ē-ən, yü-\ *n* : one who practices philanthropy — **hu·man·i·tar·i·an·ism** *n*

²**humanitarian** *adj* ♦ : concerned for or active in the promotion of human welfare

♦ altruistic, beneficent, benevolent, charitable, philanthropic — more at CHARITABLE

hu·man·i·ty \hyü-'ma-nə-tē, yü-\ *n, pl* **-ties 1** ♦ : the quality or state of being human or humane **2** *pl* : the branches of learning dealing with human concerns (as philosophy) as opposed to natural processes (as physics) **3** ♦ : the human race

♦ [1] charity, commiseration, compassion, feeling, heart, kindliness, kindness, mercy, pity, sympathy — more at HEART ♦ [3] folks, humankind, people, persons, public, society, world — more at PEOPLE

hu·man·ize \'hyü-mə-ˌnīz, 'yü-\ *vb* **-ized; -iz·ing** : to make human or humane — **hu·man·iza·tion** \ˌhyü-mə-nə-'zā-shən, ˌyü-\ *n* — **hu·man·iz·er** *n*

hu·man·kind \'hyü-mən-ˌkīnd, 'yü-\ *n* ♦ : the human race

♦ Homo sapiens, humanity, man, mankind — more at MANKIND

hu·man·oid \'hyü-mə-ˌnȯid, 'yü-\ *adj* : having human form or characteristics — **humanoid** *n*

human pap·il·lo·ma·virus \-ˌpa-pə-'lō-mə-ˌvī-rəs\ *n* : any of numerous DNA-containing viruses that cause various human warts

¹**hum·ble** \'həm-bəl\ *adj* **hum·bler** \-bə-lər\; **hum·blest** \-bə-ləst\ [ME, fr. AF, fr. L *humilis* low, humble, fr. *humus*

earth] **1** : not proud or haughty **2 ♦** : not pretentious : UNASSUMING **3 ♦** : ranking low in a hierarchy or scale

♦ [2] demure, lowly, meek, modest, retiring, unassuming, unpretentious; *also* acquiescent, compliant, deferential, resigned, submissive, unaggressive, unassertive, yielding; cowering, cringing, shrinking; ingenuous, naive, plain, simple, unaffected; bashful, diffident, mousy, overmodest, passive, quiet, reserved, shy, subdued, timid, unobtrusive *Ant* arrogant, conceited, presumptuous, proud, self-important ♦ [3] common, ignoble, inferior, low, lowly, mean, plebeian, vulgar — more at IGNOBLE

²**humble** *vb* **hum·bled; hum·bling 1** : to make humble **2 ♦** : to destroy the power or prestige of — **hum·bler** *n*

♦ abase, debase, degrade, demean, discredit, disgrace, dishonor (*or* dishonour), humiliate, lower, shame, smirch, take down; *also* abash, discomfit, discountenance, embarrass, fluster, mortify; belittle, castigate, criticize, decry, depreciate, detract, disparage, minimize, put down, ridicule; bad-mouth, defame, defile, libel, malign, slander; affront, insult; censure, condemn, damn, denounce, reprobate *Ant* aggrandize, elevate, exalt

hum·ble·ness \-nəs\ *n* ♦ : the quality or state of being humble

♦ humility, lowliness, meekness, modesty — more at HUMILITY

hum·bly \'həm-blē\ *adv* ♦ : in a humble manner

♦ lowly, meekly, modestly, sheepishly

¹**hum·bug** \'həm-ˌbəg\ *n* **1 ♦** : something designed to deceive and mislead : HOAX **2 ♦** : language, conduct, or an idea that is absurd or contrary to good sense : NONSENSE **3 ♦** : a willfully false, deceptive, or insincere person

♦ [1] counterfeit, fake, forgery, hoax, phony, sham — more at FAKE ♦ [2] bunk, claptrap, drivel, fiddlesticks, folly, foolishness, fudge, hogwash, nonsense, piffle, rot, silliness, slush, stupidity, trash — more at NONSENSE ♦ [3] charlatan, fake, fraud, hoaxer, mountebank, phony, pretender, quack

²**humbug** *vb* **hum·bugged; hum·bug·ging** ♦ : to cause to accept as true or valid what is false or invalid : DECEIVE

♦ beguile, bluff, cozen, deceive, delude, dupe, fool, gull, have, hoax, hoodwink, misinform, mislead, string along, take in, trick — more at DECEIVE

hum·ding·er \'həm-'diŋ-ər\ *n* : a person or thing of striking excellence

hum·drum \'həm-ˌdrəm\ *adj* ♦ : tediously uniform or unvarying : MONOTONOUS, DULL — **humdrum** *n*

♦ drab, dull, flat, monotonous, ponderous, stuffy, uninteresting

hu·mer·us \'hyü-mə-rəs\ *n, pl* **hu·meri** \'hyü-mə-ˌrī, -ˌrē\ : the long bone extending from shoulder to elbow

hu·mid \'hyü-məd, 'yü-\ *adj* ♦ : containing or characterized by perceptible moisture — **hu·mid·ly** *adv*

♦ muggy, sticky, sultry; *also* summery, sweltering, torrid; subtropical, tropic, tropical; close, heavy, oppressive, smothering, stifling, stuffy, suffocating; clammy, damp, dank, moist; drenched, dripping, soaked, sodden, soggy, sopping, waterlogged, wet *Ant* dry

hu·mid·i·fy \hyü-'mi-də-ˌfī\ *vb* **-fied; -fy·ing** : to make humid — **hu·mid·i·fi·ca·tion** \-ˌmi-də-fə-'kā-shən\ *n* — **hu·mid·i·fi·er** \-'mi-də-ˌfī-ər\ *n*

hu·mid·i·ty \hyü-'mi-də-tē, yü-\ *n, pl* **-ties** : the amount of atmospheric moisture

hu·mi·dor \'hyü-mə-ˌdȯr, 'yü-\ *n* : a case (as for storing cigars) in which the air is kept properly humidified

hu·mil·i·ate \hyü-'mi-lē-ˌāt, yü-\ *vb* **-at·ed; -at·ing** ♦ : to injure the self-respect of — **hu·mil·i·at·ing·ly** *adv* — **hu·mil·i·a·tion** \-ˌmi-lē-'ā-shən\ *n*

♦ abase, debase, degrade, demean, discredit, disgrace, dishonor (*or* dishonour), humble, lower, shame, smirch, take down — more at HUMBLE

hu·mil·i·ty \hyü-'mi-lə-tē, yü-\ *n* ♦ : the quality or state of being humble

♦ humbleness, lowliness, meekness, modesty; *also* acquiescence, compliance, deference, submission; ingenuousness, naïveté; directness, plainness, simpleness; bashfulness, diffidence, passivity, quietness, reserve, reservedness, shyness, timidity *Ant* arrogance, conceit, egoism, egotism, haughtiness, pretense, pretension, pretentiousness, pride, superiority

hum·mer \'hə-mər\ *n* : one that hums

hum·ming·bird \'hə-miŋ-ˌbərd\ *n* : any of a family of tiny brightly colored American birds related to the swifts

hum·mock \'hə-mək\ *n* : a rounded mound : KNOLL — **hum·mocky** \-mə-kē\ *adj*

hum·mus \'hə-məs, 'hu̇-\ *n* [Ar ḥummuṣ chickpeas] : a paste of pureed chickpeas usu. mixed with sesame oil or paste

hu·mon·gous \hyü-'məŋ-gəs, -'mäŋ-\ *adj* [perh. alter. of *huge* + *monstrous*] : extremely large ⟨a ~ stadium⟩

¹**hu·mor** *or Can and Brit* **hu·mour** \'hyü-mər, 'yü-\ *n* **1** : TEMPERAMENT **2 ♦** : a conscious state of mind or predominant emotion : MOOD **3** : WHIM **4** : a quality that appeals to a sense of the ludicrous or incongruous; *also* : a keen perception of the ludicrous or incongruous **5 ♦** : comical or amusing entertainment

♦ [2] cheer, frame, mode, mood, spirit, temper — more at MOOD ♦ [5] comedy, farce, slapstick — more at COMEDY

²**humor** *or Can and Brit* **humour** *vb* ♦ : to comply with the wishes or mood of ⟨~ed their boss⟩

♦ cater to, gratify, indulge — more at INDULGE

hu·mor·ist \'hyü-mə-rist, 'yü-\ *n* ♦ : a person specializing in or noted for humor

♦ card, comedian, comic, jester, joker, wag, wit; *also* comedienne, entertainer; cut up, kidder, practical joker, prankster; clown, buffoon, fool, harlequin, zany; caricaturist, satirist

hu·mor·less *or Can and Brit* **hu·mour·less** \'hyü-mər-ləs, 'yü-\ *adj* **1 ♦** : lacking a sense of humor **2** : lacking humorous characteristics — **hu·mor·less·ly** *adv* — **hu·mor·less·ness** *n*

♦ earnest, grave, serious, severe, sober, solemn, staid, unsmiling, weighty — more at SERIOUS

hu·mor·ous \'hyü-mə-rəs, 'yü-\ *adj* **1 ♦** : full of or characterized by humor **2 ♦** : indicating or expressive of a sense of humor — **hu·mor·ous·ly** *adv*

♦ [1] antic, comic, comical, droll, farcical, funny, hilarious, hysterical, laughable, ludicrous, ridiculous, riotous, risible, screaming, uproarious — more at FUNNY ♦ [2] clever, facetious, jocular, smart, witty — more at WITTY

hu·mor·ous·ness *n* : the quality or state of being humorous

hu·mour *Can and Brit var of* HUMOR

hump \'həmp\ *n* **1** : a rounded protuberance (as on the back of a camel) **2** : a difficult phase or obstacle ⟨over the ~⟩ — **humped** *adj*

hump·back \'həmp-ˌbak, *1 also* -ˈbak\ *n* **1** : HUNCHBACK **2** : HUMPBACK WHALE — **hump·backed** *adj*

humpback whale *n* : a large baleen whale having very long flippers

hu·mus \'hyü-məs, 'yü-\ *n* : the dark organic part of soil formed from decaying matter

Hun \'hən\ *n* : a member of an Asian people that invaded Europe about A.D. 450

¹**hunch** \'hənch\ *vb* **1** : to thrust oneself forward **2 ♦** : to assume or cause to assume a bent or crooked posture

♦ crouch, huddle, squat — more at CROUCH

²**hunch** *n* **1** : PUSH **2** : a strong intuitive feeling about what will happen

hunch·back \'hənch-ˌbak\ *n* : a person with a crooked back; *also* : a back with a hump — **hunch·backed** *adj*

hun·dred \'hən-drəd\ *n, pl* **hundreds** *or* **hundred** : 10 times 10 — **hundred** *adj* — **hun·dredth** \-drədth\ *adj or n*

hun·dred·weight \-ˌwāt\ *n, pl* **hundredweight** *or* **hun·dredweights** : a unit of measurement typically equal to 100 pounds

¹hung *past and past part of* HANG

²hung *adj* : unable to reach a decision or verdict ⟨a ~ jury⟩

Hung *abbr* Hungarian; Hungary

Hun·gar·i·an \ˌhəŋ-ˈger-ē-ən\ *n* **1** : a native or inhabitant of Hungary **2** : the language of the Hungarians — **Hungarian** *adj*

¹hun·ger \ˈhəŋ-gər\ *n* **1** : a craving or urgent need for food **2** ♦ : a strong desire

♦ appetite, craving, desire, drive, hankering, itch, longing, lust, passion, thirst, urge, yearning, yen — more at DESIRE ♦ appetite, ardor, avidity, eagerness, enthusiasm, excitement, impatience, keenness, thirst — more at EAGERNESS

²hunger *vb* **1** : to feel or suffer hunger **2** ♦ : to have an eager desire

♦ ache, die, hanker, itch, long, pant, pine, sigh, thirst, yearn ♦ *usu* **hunger for** ache for, covet, crave, desire, die for, hanker, long for, lust (for *or* after), pine for, repine for, thirst for, want, wish for, yearn for — more at DESIRE

hung·over \ˈhəŋ-ˌō-vər\ *adj* : having a hangover

hun·gry \ˈhəŋ-grē\ *adj* **1** ♦ : feeling hunger **2** ♦ : marked by enthusiastic or impatient desire or interest — **hun·gri·ly** *adv*

♦ [1] empty, famished; *also* rapacious, ravenous, voracious, wolfish; malnourished, undernourished, underfed; gluttonous, gormandizing, greedy, hoggish, insatiable, piggish *Ant* full, satisfied ♦ [2] agog, anxious, ardent, athirst, avid, crazy, eager, enthusiastic, gung ho, hot, keen, nuts, raring, solicitous, thirsty, voracious — more at EAGER

hung up *adj* **1** : DELAYED **2** : ENTHUSIASTIC; *also* : PREOCCUPIED **3** : anxiously nervous

hunk \ˈhəŋk\ *n* **1** ♦ : a large piece **2** : an attractive well-built man — **hunky** *adj*

♦ blob, chunk, clod, clump, glob, gob, lump, nub, wad — more at LUMP

hun·ker \ˈhəŋ-kər\ *vb* **1** : CROUCH, SQUAT — usu. used with *down* **2** : to settle in for a sustained period — used with *down*

hun·ky-do·ry \ˌhəŋ-kē-ˈdōr-ē\ *adj* : quite satisfactory : FINE

¹hunt \ˈhənt\ *vb* **1** : to pursue for food or in sport; *also* : to take part in a hunt **2** ♦ : to try to find : SEEK **3** : to drive or chase esp. by harrying **4** : to traverse or go over in search of prey or quarry **5** ♦ : to find, uncover, or obtain after diligent search — used with *through, up,* or *down* — **hunt·er** *n*

♦ [2] cast about, forage, pursue, quest, search (for *or* out), seek — more at SEEK ♦ *usu* **hunt through** [5] dig, dredge, rake, ransack, rifle, rummage, scour, search — more at SEARCH ♦ *usu* **hunt down** *or* **hunt up** [5] detect, determine, dig up, discover, ferret out, find, hit on, locate, track down — more at FIND

²hunt *n* : an act, practice, or instance of hunting

Hun·ting·ton's disease \ˈhən-tiŋ-tənz-\ *n* : a chorea that usu. begins in middle age and leads to dementia

hunt·ress \ˈhən-trəs\ *n* : a woman who hunts game

hunts·man \ˈhənts-mən\ *n* **1** : HUNTER **2** : a person who manages a hunt and looks after the hounds

hur·dle \ˈhərd-ᵊl\ *n* **1** : a barrier to leap over in a race **2** : something that impedes progress or achievement : OBSTACLE — **hurdle** *vb* — **hur·dler** *n*

hur·dy-gur·dy \ˌhər-dē-ˈgər-dē, ˈhər-dē-ˌgər-dē\ *n, pl* **-gur·dies** : a musical instrument in which the sound is produced by turning a crank

hurl \ˈhərl\ *vb* **1** : to move or cause to move vigorously **2** : to throw down with violence **3 a** ♦ : to throw forcefully : FLING **b** : to throw (a baseball) to a batter : PITCH — **hurl** *n* — **hurl·er** *n*

♦ cast, catapult, chuck, dash, fire, fling, heave, hurtle, launch, peg, pelt, pitch, sling, throw, toss — more at THROW

hur·ly–bur·ly \ˌhər-lē-ˈbər-lē\ *n* : a state of commotion, excitement, or violent disturbance : UPROAR

Hu·ron \ˈhyur-ən, ˈhyur-ˌän\ *n, pl* **Hurons** *or* **Huron** : a member of a confederacy of American Indian peoples formerly living between Georgian Bay and Lake Ontario

hur·rah \hu̇-ˈrȯ, -ˈrä\ *also* **hur·ray** \hu̇-ˈrā\ *interj* — used to express joy, approval, or encouragement

hur·ri·cane \ˈhər-ə-ˌkān\ *n* [Sp *huracán*, of AmerInd origin] : a tropical cyclone with winds of 74 miles (118 kilometers) per hour or greater that is usu. accompanied by rain, thunder, and lightning

hur·ried·ly \ˈhər-əd-lē\ *adv* ♦ : in a hurried manner

♦ cursorily, hastily, headlong, pell-mell, precipitately, rashly — more at HASTILY

¹hur·ry \ˈhər-ē\ *vb* **hur·ried; hur·ry·ing** **1** ♦ : to carry or cause to go with haste **2** : to impel to a greater speed **3** ♦ : to move or act with haste — **hur·ried·ness** *n*

♦ [1, 3] accelerate, hasten, quicken, rush, speed (up), step up, whisk; *also* drive, goad, prod, propel, push, race, spur, stir, urge; advance, aid, dispatch, ease, encourage, expedite, facilitate, forward, further *Ant* decelerate, retard, slow (down) ♦ [3] course, dash, fly, hasten, hurtle, hustle, pelt, race, rocket, run, rush, shoot, speed, step, tear, zip, zoom; *also* dart, flit, scamper, scud, scuffle; stampede, streak, whiz; gallop, jog, sprint; accelerate, quicken; catch up, fast-forward, outrun, outstrip, overtake *Ant* crawl, creep, poke

²hurry *n* ♦ : extreme haste or eagerness

♦ celerity, fastness, fleetness, haste, quickness, rapidity, speed, swiftness, velocity — more at SPEED ♦ haste, hustle, precipitation, rush; *also* bustle, flurry, flutter, scurry, scuttle, stir, whirl; beeline, dash, scramble, stampede; hotheadedness, impetuosity, impulsiveness, rashness; fleetness, quickness, rapidity, speed, swiftness; celerity, dispatch, promptness *Ant* deliberateness, deliberation

¹hurt \ˈhərt\ *vb* **hurt; hurt·ing** **1** ♦ : to feel or cause to feel physical or emotional pain **2** ♦ : to do harm to : DAMAGE **3** : OFFEND **4** : HAMPER **5** : to be in need — usu. used with *for* — **hurt** *adj*

♦ [1] agonize, bleed, feel, grieve, mourn, sorrow, suffer — more at GRIEVE ♦ [1] ache, pain, smart; *also* bleed, bite, burn, chafe, cramp, fester, itch, nag, pinch, pound, rack, sting, swell, throb, tingle, twinge; agonize, suffer ♦ [2] damage, harm, injure, wound — more at INJURE ♦ [2] blemish, break, cripple, damage, deface, disfigure, flaw, harm, injure, mar, spoil, vitiate — more at DAMAGE

²hurt *n* **1** : a bodily injury or wound **2** : SUFFERING **3** ♦ : physical or mental damage : HARM

♦ damage, detriment, harm, injury — more at INJURY

hurt·ful \ˈhərt-fəl\ *adj* ♦ : causing injury, detriment, or suffering — **hurt·ful·ness** *n*

♦ adverse, bad, baleful, baneful, damaging, deleterious, detrimental, evil, harmful, ill, injurious, mischievous, noxious, pernicious, prejudicial — more at HARMFUL

hur·tle \ˈhərt-ᵊl\ *vb* **hur·tled; hur·tling** **1** ♦ : to move rapidly or forcefully **2** : to throw forcefully : HURL, FLING

♦ dash, fly, hasten, hurry, rocket, run, rush, speed, tear, zip, zoom — more at HURRY

¹hus·band \ˈhəz-bənd\ *n* [ME *husbonde,* fr. OE *hūsbonda* master of a house, fr. ON *hūsbōndi,* fr. *hūs* house + *bōndi* householder] : a male partner in a marriage

²husband *vb* : to manage prudently

hus·band·man \ˈhəz-bənd-mən\ *n* : FARMER

hus·band·ry \ˈhəz-bən-drē\ *n* **1** ♦ : the control or judicious use of resources **2** : AGRICULTURE **3** : the production and care of domestic animals

♦ economy, frugality, providence, thrift — more at ECONOMY

¹**hush** \ʹhəsh\ *vb* **1** ♦ : to make or become quiet or calm **2** : SUPPRESS

♦ calm (down), cool (off *or* down), quiet, settle (down) — more at QUIET ♦ mute, quell, settle, silence, still — more at SILENCE

²**hush** *n* ♦ : a silence or calm esp. following noise

♦ calm, calmness, peace, placidity, quiet, quietness, repose, serenity, still, stillness, tranquility — more at CALM

hushed \ʹhəsht\ *adj* **1** ♦ : free of noise or agitation **2** ♦ : marked by secrecy or caution

♦ [1] calm, halcyon, peaceful, placid, quiet, serene, still, tranquil, untroubled — more at CALM ♦ [1] muted, noiseless, quiet, silent, soundless, still — more at SILENCE ♦ [2] confidential, inside, intimate, private, secret — more at PRIVATE

hush–hush \ʹhəsh-ˌhəsh\ *adj* : SECRET, CONFIDENTIAL

¹**husk** \ʹhəsk\ *n* **1** : a usu. thin dry outer covering of a seed or fruit **2** ♦ : an outer layer : SHELL

♦ armor, capsule, case, casing, cocoon, cover, housing, jacket, pod, sheath, shell — more at CASE

²**husk** *vb* ♦ : to strip the husk from — **husk·er** *n*

♦ bark, flay, hull, peel, shell, skin

¹**hus·ky** \ʹhəs-kē\ *adj* **hus·ki·er; -est** ♦ : hoarse with or as if with emotion — **hus·ki·ly** \-kə-lē\ *adv* — **hus·ki·ness** \-kē-nəs\ *n*

♦ coarse, gravelly, gruff, hoarse, scratchy, throaty — more at HOARSE

²**husky** *adj* **1** ♦ : strongly formed or constructed : BURLY **2** : LARGE

♦ beefy, brawny, burly; *also* able-bodied, athletic, heavy, hefty, herculean, mighty, muscle-bound, muscular, powerful, robust, rugged, stalwart, strapping, strong, sturdy; chunky, compact, heavyset, solid, squat, stocky, thickset; dumpy, lumpish, portly, pudgy, stout

³**husky** *n, pl* **huskies** : a heavy-coated working dog of the New World arctic region

hus·sar \(ˌ)hə-ʹzär\ *n* [Hung *huszár*] : a member of any of various European cavalry units

hus·sy \ʹhə-zē, -sē\ *n, pl* **hussies** [alter. of *housewife*] **1** : a lewd or brazen woman **2** : a pert or mischievous girl

hus·tings \ʹhəs-tiŋz\ *n pl* : a place where political campaign speeches are made; *also* : the proceedings in an election campaign

¹**hus·tle** \ʹhə-səl\ *vb* **hus·tled; hus·tling** **1** : JOSTLE, SHOVE **2** : to move or act quickly : HASTEN, HURRY **3** : to work energetically **4** ♦ : to sell something to or obtain something from by energetic and esp. underhanded activity

♦ bleed, cheat, chisel, cozen, defraud, fleece, mulct, rook, shortchange, skin, squeeze, stick, sting, swindle, victimize — more at FLEECE

²**hustle** *n* **1** ♦ : energetic activity **2** ♦ : an act or instance of fraud

♦ [1] haste, hurry, precipitation, rush — more at HURRY ♦ [2] racket, swindle

hus·tler \ʹhəs-lər\ *n* ♦ : one that hustles

♦ go-getter, live wire, powerhouse, self-starter — more at GO-GETTER

hut \ʹhət\ *n* ♦ : an often small and temporary dwelling of simple construction : SHACK

♦ cabin, camp, hutch, shack, shanty — more at SHACK

hutch \ʹhəch\ *n* **1** : a chest or compartment for storage **2** ♦ : a cupboard usu. surmounted with open shelves **3** : a pen or coop for an animal **4** : a small and often temporary dwelling : HUT

♦ buffet, cabinet, closet, cupboard, locker, sideboard — more at CABINET

huz·zah *or* **huz·za** \(ˌ)hə-ʹzä\ *n* : a shout of acclaim — often used interjectionally to express joy or approbation

HV *abbr* **1** high velocity **2** high voltage

HVAC *abbr* heating, ventilating and air-conditioning

hvy *abbr* heavy

HW *abbr* hot water

hwy *abbr* highway

hy·a·cinth \ʹhī-ə-(ˌ)sinth\ *n* : a bulbous Mediterranean herb related to the lilies that is widely grown for its spikes of fragrant bell-shaped flowers

¹**hy·brid** \ʹhī-brəd\ *n* **1** ♦ : an offspring of genetically differing parents (as members of different breeds or species) **2** : one of mixed origin or composition — **hy·brid·i·za·tion** \ˌhī-brə-də-ʹzā-shən\ *n* — **hy·brid·ize** \ʹhī-brə-ˌdīz\ *vb* — **hy·brid·iz·er** *n*

♦ cross, mongrel

²**hybrid** *adj* ♦ : of, relating to, or being a hybrid

♦ mixed, mongrel — more at MIXED

hy·dra \ʹhī-drə\ *n* : any of numerous small tubular freshwater coelenterates that are polyps having at one end a mouth surrounded by tentacles

hy·dran·gea \hī-ʹdrān-jə\ *n* : any of a genus of shrubs related to the currants and grown for their showy clusters of white or tinted flowers

hy·drant \ʹhī-drənt\ *n* : a pipe with a valve and spout at which water may be drawn from a main pipe

hy·drate \ʹhī-ˌdrāt\ *n* : a compound formed by union of water with some other substance — **hydrate** *vb*

hy·drau·lic \hī-ʹdró-lik\ *adj* [ultim. fr. Gk *hydraulis* pipe organ using water pressure, fr. *hydōr* water + *aulos* reed instrument] **1** : operated, moved, or effected by means of water **2** : of or relating to hydraulics **3** : operated by the resistance offered or the pressure transmitted when a quantity of liquid is forced through a small orifice or through a tube **4** : hardening or setting under water

hy·drau·lics \-liks\ *n* : a science that deals with practical applications of liquid (as water) in motion

hydro \ʹhī-drō\ *n* : HYDROPOWER

hy·dro·car·bon \ʹhī-drō-ˌkär-bən\ *n* : an organic compound containing only carbon and hydrogen

hy·dro·ceph·a·lus \ˌhī-drō-ʹse-fə-ləs\ *n* : abnormal increase in the amount of fluid in the cranial cavity accompanied by enlargement of the skull and atrophy of the brain

hy·dro·chlo·ric acid \ˌhī-drə-ʹklōr-ik-\ *n* : a sharp-smelling corrosive acid used in the laboratory and in industry and present in dilute form in gastric juice

hy·dro·dy·nam·ics \ˌhī-drō-dī-ʹna-miks\ *n* : a science that deals with the motion of fluids and the forces acting on moving bodies immersed in fluids — **hy·dro·dy·nam·ic** *adj*

hy·dro·elec·tric \ˌhī-drō-i-ʹlek-trik\ *adj* : of or relating to production of electricity by waterpower — **hy·dro·elec·tric·i·ty** \-ˌlek-ʹtri-sə-tē\ *n*

hy·dro·foil \ʹhī-drə-ˌfói(-ə)l\ *n* : a boat that has fins attached to the bottom by struts for lifting the hull clear of the water to allow faster speeds

hy·dro·gen \ʹhī-drə-jən\ *n* [F *hydrogène*, fr. Gk *hydōr* water + *-genēs* born; fr. the fact that water is generated by its combustion] : a gaseous colorless odorless highly flammable chemical element that is the lightest of the elements — **hy·dro·ge·nous** \hī-ʹdrä-jə-nəs\ *adj*

hy·dro·ge·nate \hī-ʹdrä-jə-ˌnāt, ʹhī-drə-\ *vb* **-nat·ed; -nat·ing** : to combine or treat with hydrogen; *esp* : to add hydrogen to the molecule of — **hy·dro·ge·na·tion** \hī-ˌdrä-jə-ʹnā-shən, ˌhī-drə-\ *n*

hydrogen bomb *n* : a bomb whose violent explosive power is due to the sudden release of atomic energy resulting from the fusion of light nuclei (as of hydrogen atoms)

hydrogen peroxide *n* : an unstable compound of hydrogen and oxygen used esp. as an oxidizing and bleaching agent, an antiseptic, and a propellant

hy·dro·graph·ic \ˌhī-drə-ʹgra-fik\ *adj* : of or relating to the description and study of bodies of water — **hy·drog·ra·pher** *n* — **hy·drog·ra·phy** \hī-ʹdrä-grə-fē\ *n*

hy·drol·o·gy \hī-ʹdrä-lə-jē\ *n* : a science dealing with the properties, distribution, and circulation of water — **hy·dro·log·ic** \ˌhī-drə-ʹlä-jik\ *or* **hy·dro·log·i·cal** \-ji-kəl\ *adj* — **hy·drol·o·gist** \hī-ʹdrä-lə-jist\ *n*

hy·dro·ly·sis \hī-'drä-lə-səs\ *n* : a chemical decomposition involving the addition of the elements of water

hy·drom·e·ter \hī-'drä-mə-tər\ *n* : a floating instrument for determining specific gravities of liquids and hence the strength (as of alcoholic liquors)

hy·dro·pho·bia \,hī-drə-'fō-bē-ə\ *n* [LL, fr. Gk, fr. *hydōr* water + *phobos* fear] : RABIES

hy·dro·phone \'hī-drə-,fōn\ *n* : an underwater listening device

¹hy·dro·plane \'hī-drə-,plān\ *n* 1 : a powerboat designed for racing that skims the surface of the water 2 : SEA-PLANE

²hydroplane *vb* : to skid on a wet road due to loss of contact between the tires and road

hy·dro·pon·ics \,hī-drə-'pä-niks\ *n* : the growing of plants in nutrient solutions — **hy·dro·pon·ic** *adj*

hy·dro·pow·er \'hī-drə-,paủ(-ə)r\ *n* : hydroelectric power

hy·dro·sphere \'hī-drə-,sfir\ *n* : the water (as vapor or lakes) of the earth

hy·dro·stat·ic \,hī-drə-'sta-tik\ *adj* : of or relating to fluids at rest or to the pressures they exert or transmit

hy·dro·ther·a·py \,hī-drə-'ther-ə-pē\ *n* : the use of water esp. externally in the treatment of disease or disability

hy·dro·ther·mal \,hī-drə-'thər-məl\ *adj* : of or relating to hot water

hy·drous \'hī-drəs\ *adj* : containing water

hy·drox·ide \hī-'dräk-,sīd\ *n* 1 : a negatively charged ion consisting of one atom of oxygen and one atom of hydrogen 2 : a compound of hydroxide with an element or group

hy·e·na \hī-'ē-nə\ *n* [ME *hyene*, fr. L *hyaena*, fr. Gk *hyaina*, fr. *hys* hog] : any of several large doglike carnivorous mammals of Asia and Africa

hy·giene \'hī-,jēn\ *n* 1 : a science concerned with establishing and maintaining good health 2 : conditions or practices conducive to health — **hy·gien·i·cal·ly** \-ni-k(ə-)lē\ *adv* — **hy·gien·ist** \hī-'jē-nist, 'hī-,jē-, hī-'je-\ *n*

hy·gien·ic \hī-'je-nik, -'jē-\ *adj* ♦ : having or showing good hygiene

♦ aseptic, sanitary, sterile — more at SANITARY

hy·grom·e·ter \hī-'grä-mə-tər\ *n* : any of several instruments for measuring the humidity of the atmosphere

hy·gro·scop·ic \,hī-grə-'skä-pik\ *adj* : readily taking up and retaining moisture

hying *pres part of* HIE

hy·men \'hī-mən\ *n* : a fold of mucous membrane partly closing the opening of the vagina

hy·me·ne·al \,hī-mə-'nē-əl\ *adj* : NUPTIAL

hymn \'him\ *n* ♦ : a song of praise esp. to God — **hymn** *vb*

♦ anthem, canticle, carol, chorale, psalm, spiritual; *also* dirge, lament, requiem, threnody; hallelujah, paean; mass, oratorio; processional, recessional

hym·nal \'him-nəl\ *n* : a book of hymns

hyp *abbr* hypothesis; hypothetical

¹hype \'hīp\ *vb* hyped; hyp·ing 1 : STIMULATE — usu. used with *up* 2 : INCREASE — **hyped–up** *adj*

²hype *vb* hyped; hyping 1 : DECEIVE 2 : PUBLICIZE

³hype *n* 1 : DECEPTION, PUT-ON 2 : PUBLICITY

hy·per \'hī-pər\ *adj* 1 : HIGH-STRUNG, EXCITABLE 2 : extremely active

hy·per·acid·i·ty \,hī-pər-ə-'si-də-tē\ *n* : the condition of containing excessive acid esp. in the stomach — **hy·per·ac·id** \-'a-səd\ *adj*

hy·per·ac·tive \-'ak-tiv\ *adj* ♦ : excessively or pathologically active — **hy·per·ac·tiv·i·ty** \-,ak-'ti-və-tē\ *n*

♦ agitated, feverish, frenzied, heated, hectic, overactive, overwrought — more at FEVERISH

hy·per·bar·ic \,hī-pər-'bar-ik\ *adj* : of, relating to, or utilizing greater than normal pressure (as of oxygen)

hy·per·bo·la \hī-'pər-bə-lə\ *n, pl* **-las** *or* **-lae** \-(,)lē\ : a curve formed by the intersection of a double right circular cone with a plane that cuts both halves of the cone — **hy·per·bol·ic** \,hī-pər-'bä-lik\ *adj*

hy·per·bo·le \hī-'pər-bə-(,)lē\ *n* ♦ : extravagant exaggeration used as a figure of speech

♦ caricature, elaboration, embellishment, exaggeration, magnification, overstatement, padding — more at EXAGGERATION

hy·per·crit·i·cal \,hī-pər-'kri-ti-kəl\ *adj* ♦ : excessively critical — **hy·per·crit·i·cal·ly** \-k(ə-)lē\ *adv*

♦ captious, carping, critical, overcritical — more at CRITICAL

hy·per·drive \'hī-pər-,drīv\ *n* : a state of extremely heightened activity

hy·per·ex·tend \,hī-pər-ik-'stend\ *vb* : to extend beyond the normal range of motion — **hy·per·ex·ten·sion** \-'sten-shən\ *n*

hy·per·gly·ce·mia \,hī-pər-glī-'sē-mē-ə\ *n* : excess of sugar in the blood — **hy·per·gly·ce·mic** \-mik\ *adj*

hy·per·ki·net·ic \-kə-'ne-tik\ *adj* : characterized by fast-paced or frenetic activity

hy·per·link \'hī-pər-,liŋk\ *n* : a connecting element (as highlighted text) between one place in a hypertext or hypermedia document and another

hy·per·me·dia \'hī-pər-,mē-dē-ə\ *n* : a database format offering direct access to text, sound, or images related to that on display

hy·per·opia \,hī-pə-'rō-pē-ə\ *n* : a condition in which visual images come to focus behind the retina resulting esp. in defective vision for near objects — **hy·per·opic** \-'rō-pik, -'rä-\ *adj*

hy·per·sen·si·tive \-'sen-sə-tiv\ *adj* 1 : excessively or abnormally sensitive 2 : abnormally susceptible physiologically to a specific agent (as a drug) — **hy·per·sen·si·tive·ness** *n* — **hy·per·sen·si·tiv·i·ty** \-,sen-sə-'ti-və-tē\ *n*

hy·per·ten·sion \'hī-pər-,ten-chən\ *n* : high blood pressure — **hy·per·ten·sive** \,hī-pər-'ten-siv\ *adj or n*

hy·per·text \'hī-pər-,tekst\ *n* : a database format in which information related to that on display can be accessed directly from the display

hy·per·thy·roid·ism \,hī-pər-'thī-,rỏi-,di-zəm\ *n* : excessive activity of the thyroid gland; *also* : the resulting bodily condition — **hy·per·thy·roid** \-'thī-,rỏid\ *adj*

hy·per·tro·phy \hī-'pər-trə-fē\ *n, pl* **-phies** : excessive development of a body part — **hy·per·tro·phic** \,hī-pər-'trō-fik\ *adj* — **hypertrophy** *vb*

hy·per·ven·ti·late \,hī-pər-'ven-tə-,lāt\ *vb* : to breathe rapidly and deeply esp. to the point of losing an abnormal amount of carbon dioxide from the blood — **hy·per·ven·ti·la·tion** \-,ven-tə-'lā-shən\ *n*

hy·phen \'hī-fən\ *n* : a punctuation mark - used esp. to divide or to compound words or word parts — **hyphen** *vb*

hy·phen·ate \'hī-fə-,nāt\ *vb* **-at·ed; -at·ing** : to connect or divide with a hyphen — **hy·phen·ation** \,hī-fə-'nā-shən\ *n*

hyp·no·sis \hip-'nō-səs\ *n, pl* **-no·ses** \-,sēz\ : an induced state that resembles sleep and in which the subject is responsive to suggestions of the inducer (**hyp·no·tist** \'hip-nə-tist\) — **hyp·no·tism** \'hip-nə-,ti-zəm\ *n*

¹hyp·not·ic \hip-'nä-tik\ *adj* 1 ♦ : inducing sleep 2 : of or relating to hypnosis or hypnotism 3 : readily holding the attention — **hyp·not·i·cal·ly** \-ti-k(ə-)lē\ *adv*

♦ drowsy, narcotic, opiate, slumberous; *also* depressant, relaxant, sedative, tranquilizing; calming, lulling, quieting, relaxing, restful, settling, soothing; analgesic, anesthetic, benumbing, deadening, dulling; mesmerizing, stupefying *Ant* stimulant

²hypnotic *n* : a sleep-inducing drug

hyp·no·tise *chiefly Brit var of* HYPNOTIZE

hyp·no·tize \'hip-nə-,tīz\ *vb* 1 : to induce hypnosis in 2 ♦ : to dazzle or overcome by or as if by suggestion — **hyp·no·tiz·able** \'hip-nə-,tī-zə-bəl\ *adj*

♦ arrest, enchant, enthrall, fascinate, grip, mesmerize — more at ENTHRALL

hy·po \'hī-pō\ *n, pl* **hypos** : SODIUM THIOSULFATE

hy·po·al·ler·gen·ic \,hī-pō-,a-lər-'je-nik\ *adj* : having little likelihood of causing an allergic response

hy·po·cen·ter \\'hī-pə-ˌsen-tər\ *n* : the point of origin of an earthquake

hy·po·chon·dria \ˌhī-pə-'kän-drē-ə\ *n* [NL, fr. LL, pl., upper abdomen (formerly regarded as the seat of hypochondria), fr. Gk, lit., the parts under the cartilage (of the breastbone), fr. *hypo-* under + *chondros* cartilage] : depression of mind often centered on imaginary physical ailments — **hy·po·chon·dri·ac** \-drē-ˌak\ *adj or n*

hy·poc·ri·sy \hi-'pä-krə-sē\ *n, pl* **-sies** ♦ : a feigning to be what one is not or to believe what one does not; *esp* : the false assumption of an appearance of virtue or religion

♦ cant, dissimulation, insincerity, piety; *also* deception, deceptiveness, dishonesty, falsity, pretense, pretension, pretentiousness, self-satisfaction; duplicity, falseness, shamming; artificiality, oiliness, smoothness *Ant* genuineness, sincerity

hyp·o·crit·i·cal \ˌhī-pə-'kri-ti-kəl\ *adj* ♦ : characterized by hypocrisy; *also* : being a hypocrite — **hyp·o·crite** \'hi-pə-ˌkrit\ *n* — **hyp·o·crit·i·cal·ly** \-k(ə-)lē\ *adv*

♦ artificial, double-dealing, feigned, insincere, left-handed, mealy, mealymouthed, two-faced, unctuous — more at INSINCERE

¹hy·po·der·mic \ˌhī-pə-'dər-mik\ *adj* : administered by or used in making an injection beneath the skin

²hypodermic *n* : a small syringe with a hollow needle for injecting material into or through the skin : HYPODERMIC SYRINGE; *also* : an injection made with this

hypodermic needle *n* **1** : NEEDLE 3 **2** : a small syringe with a hollow needle for injecting material into or through the skin : HYPODERMIC SYRINGE

hypodermic syringe *n* ♦ : a small syringe with a hollow needle for injecting material into or through the skin

♦ needle, syringe — more at NEEDLE

hy·po·gly·ce·mia \ˌhī-pō-glī-'sē-mē-ə\ *n* : abnormal decrease of sugar in the blood — **hy·po·gly·ce·mic** \-mik\ *adj*

hy·pot·e·nuse \hī-'pät-ᵊn-ˌüs, -ˌyüs, -ˌüz, -ˌyüz\ *n* : the side of a triangle having a right angle that is opposite the right angle; *also* : its length

hy·po·thal·a·mus \ˌhī-pō-'tha-lə-məs\ *n* : a part of the brain that lies beneath the thalamus and is a control center for the autonomic nervous system

hy·poth·e·sis \hī-'pä-thə-səs\ *n, pl* **-e·ses** \-ˌsēz\ ♦ : an assumption made esp. in order to test its logical or empirical consequences

♦ conjecture, proposition, supposition, theory — more at THEORY

hy·poth·e·size \-ˌsīz\ *vb* **-sized; -siz·ing** : to adopt as a hypothesis

hy·po·thet·i·cal \ˌhī-pə-'the-ti-kəl\ *adj* ♦ : being or involving a hypothesis — **hy·po·thet·i·cal·ly** \-k(ə-)lē\ *adv*

♦ conjectural, speculative, theoretical — more at THEORETICAL

hy·po·thy·roid·ism \ˌhī-pō-'thī-ˌrȯi-ˌdi-zəm\ *n* : deficient activity of the thyroid gland; *also* : a resultant lowered metabolic rate and general loss of vigor — **hy·po·thy·roid** *adj*

hys·sop \'hi-səp\ *n* : a European mint sometimes used as a potherb

hys·ter·ec·to·my \ˌhis-tə-'rek-tə-mē\ *n, pl* **-mies** : surgical removal of the uterus

hys·te·ria \hi-'ster-ē-ə, -'stir-\ *n* [NL, fr. E *hysteric*, adj., fr. L *hystericus*, fr. Gk *hysterikos*, fr. *hystera* womb; fr. the Greek notion that hysteria was peculiar to women and caused by disturbances in the uterus] **1** : a nervous disorder marked esp. by defective emotional control **2** ♦ : unmanageable fear or outburst of emotion — **hys·ter·ic** \-'ster-ik\ *n* — **hys·ter·i·cal·ly** \-k(ə-)lē\ *adv*

♦ agitation, delirium, distraction, frenzy, furor, fury, rage, rampage, uproar — more at FRENZY

hys·ter·i·cal \-'ster-i-kəl\ *also* **hysteric** *adj* **1** : of, relating to, or marked by hysteria **2** ♦ : exhibiting unrestrained emotionalism

♦ agitated, delirious, distraught, frantic, frenzied — more at FRANTIC

hys·ter·ics \-'ster-iks\ *n pl* : a fit of uncontrollable laughter or crying

Hz *abbr* hertz

¹i \'ī\ *n, pl* **i's** *or* **is** \'īz\ *often cap* : the 9th letter of the English alphabet

²i *abbr, often cap* island; isle

³i *symbol* imaginary unit

¹I \'ī, ə\ *pron* : the one speaking or writing

²I *abbr* interstate

³I *symbol* iodine

Ia *or* **IA** *abbr* Iowa

-ial *adj suffix* : ¹-AL ⟨manor*ial*⟩

iamb \'ī-ˌam\ *or* **iam·bus** \ī-'am-bəs\ *n, pl* **iambs** \'ī-ˌamz\ *or* **iam·bus·es** : a metrical foot of one unaccented syllable followed by one accented syllable — **iam·bic** \ī-'am-bik\ *adj or n*

-i·at·ric \ē-'a-trik\ *also* **-i·at·ri·cal** \-tri-kəl\ *adj comb form* : of or relating to (such) medical treatment or healing ⟨pedi*atric*⟩

-i·at·rics \ē-'a-triks\ *n pl comb form* : medical treatment ⟨pedi*atrics*⟩

ib *or* **ibid** *abbr* ibidem

ibex \'ī-ˌbeks\ *n, pl* **ibex** *or* **ibex·es** [L] : any of several Old World wild goats with large curved horns

ibi·dem \'i-bə-ˌdem, i-'bī-dəm\ *adv* [L] : in the same place

ibis \'ī-bəs\ *n, pl* **ibis** *or* **ibis·es** [L, fr. Gk, fr. Egypt *hbw*] : any of various wading birds related to the herons but having a downwardly curved bill

ibu·pro·fen \ˌī-byü-'prō-fən\ *n* : a nonsteroidal anti-inflammatory drug used to relieve pain and fever

IC \ˌī-'sē\ *n* : INTEGRATED CIRCUIT

¹-ic \ik\ *adj suffix* **1** : of, relating to, or having the form of : being ⟨panoram*ic*⟩ **2** : related to, derived from, or containing ⟨alcohol*ic*⟩ **3** : in the manner of : like that of : characteristic of **4** : associated or dealing with : utilizing ⟨electron*ic*⟩ **5** : characterized by : exhibiting ⟨nostalg*ic*⟩ : affected with ⟨allerg*ic*⟩ **6** : caused by **7** : tending to produce ⟨analges*ic*⟩

²-ic *n suffix* : one having the character or nature of : one belonging to or associated with : one exhibiting or affected by : one that produces

-i·cal \i-kəl\ *adj suffix* : -IC ⟨symmetr*ical*⟩ ⟨geolog*ical*⟩ — **-i·cal·ly** \i-kə-lē, -klē\ *adv suffix*

ICBM \ˌī-ˌsē-(ˌ)bē-'em\ *n, pl* **ICBM's** *or* **ICBMs** \-'emz\ : an intercontinental ballistic missile

ICC *abbr* Interstate Commerce Commission

¹ice \'īs\ *n* **1** : frozen water **2** : a substance resembling ice **3** : a state of coldness (as from formality or reserve) **4** : a flavored frozen dessert; *esp* : one containing no milk or cream

²**ice** *vb* **iced; ic·ing 1** : FREEZE **2** : CHILL **3** : to cover with or as if with icing

ice age *n* : a time of widespread glaciation

ice bag *n* : a waterproof bag to hold ice for local application of cold to the body

ice·berg \'īs-ˌbərg\ *n* : a large floating mass of ice broken off from a glacier

iceberg lettuce *n* : any of various crisp light green lettuces that form a compact head like a cabbage

ice·boat \'īs-ˌbōt\ *n* : a boatlike frame on runners propelled on ice by sails

ice·bound \-ˌbau̇nd\ *adj* : surrounded, obstructed, or covered by ice

ice·box \-ˌbäks\ *n* : REFRIGERATOR

ice·break·er \-ˌbrā-kər\ *n* : a ship equipped to make a channel through ice

ice cap *n* : a glacier forming on relatively level land and flowing outward from its center

ice cream *n* : a frozen food containing sweetened or flavored cream or butterfat

ice hockey *n* : a game in which two teams of ice-skating players try to shoot a puck into the opponent's goal

ice·house \'īs-ˌhau̇s\ *n* : a building in which ice is made or stored

Ice·land·er \-ˌlan-dər, -lən-\ *n* : a native or inhabitant of Iceland

¹**Ice·lan·dic** \īs-ˈlan-dik\ *adj* : of, relating to, or characteristic of Iceland, the Icelanders, or their language

²**Icelandic** *n* : the language of Iceland

ice·man \'īs-ˌman\ *n* : one who sells or delivers ice

ice milk *n* : a sweetened frozen food made of skim milk

ice pick *n* : a hand tool ending in a spike for chipping ice

ice–skate \'īs-ˌskāt\ *vb* : to skate on ice — **ice–skater** *n*

ice storm *n* : a storm in which falling rain freezes on contact

ice water *n* : chilled or iced water esp. for drinking

ich·thy·ol·o·gy \ˌik-thē-ˈä-lə-jē\ *n* : a branch of zoology dealing with fishes — **ich·thy·ol·o·gist** \-jist\ *n*

ici·cle \'ī-ˌsi-kəl\ *n* [ME *isikel*, fr. *is* ice + *ikel* icicle, fr. OE *gicel*] : a hanging mass of ice formed by the freezing of dripping water

ic·ing \'ī-siŋ\ *n* : a sweet usu. creamy mixture used to coat baked goods

ICJ *abbr* International Court of Justice

icky \'i-kē\ *adj* **ick·i·er; -est** : OFFENSIVE, DISTASTEFUL — **ick·i·ness** *n*

icon \'ī-ˌkän\ *n* **1** : IMAGE; *esp* : a religious image painted on a wood panel **2** ♦ : a sign (as a word or graphic symbol) whose form suggests its meaning **3** : a small picture on a computer display that suggests the purpose of an available function

♦ character, sign, symbol — more at CHARACTER

icon·o·clasm \ī-ˈkä-nə-ˌkla-zəm\ *n* : the doctrine, practice, or attitude of an iconoclast

icon·o·clast \-ˌklast\ *n* [ML *iconoclastes*, fr. MGk *eikonoklastēs*, lit., image destroyer, fr. Gk *eikōn* image + *klan* to break] **1** : one who destroys religious images or opposes their veneration **2** : one who attacks cherished beliefs or institutions

-ics \iks\ *n sing or pl suffix* **1** : study : knowledge : skill : practice ⟨linguis*tics*⟩ ⟨electron*ics*⟩ **2** : characteristic actions or activities ⟨acroba*tics*⟩ **3** : characteristic qualities, operations, or phenomena ⟨mechan*ics*⟩

ic·tus \'ik-təs\ *n* : the recurring stress or beat in a rhythmic or metrical series of sounds

ICU *abbr* intensive care unit

icy \'ī-sē\ *adj* **ic·i·er; -est 1** : covered with, abounding in, or consisting of ice **2** ♦ : intensely cold **3** ♦ : being cold and unfriendly — **ic·i·ly** \'ī-sə-lē\ *adv* — **ic·i·ness** \-sē-nəs\ *n*

♦ [2] arctic, bitter, chill, cold, freezing, frigid, frosty, glacial, polar, raw, wintry — more at COLD ♦ [3] chill, chilly, cold, cold-blooded, cool, frigid, frosty, glacial, unfriendly, unsympathetic, wintry — more at COLD

¹**id** \'id\ *n* [L, it] : the part of the psyche in psychoanalytic theory that is completely unconscious and concerned with instinctual needs and drives

²**id** *abbr* idem

¹**ID** \'ī-ˈdē\ *n* : a document with identifying information about an individual whose name appears on it

²**ID** *vb* **ID'd** *or* **IDed; ID'ing** *or* **IDing** : IDENTIFY

³**ID** *abbr* **1** Idaho **2** identification

idea \ī-ˈdē-ə\ *n* **1** : a plan for action : DESIGN **2** ♦ : something (as a thought, concept, sensation, or image) present in the mind **3** : a central meaning or purpose

♦ concept, image, impression, notion, picture, thought; *also* apprehension, premonition, presentiment; chimera, illusion, phantasm; caprice, conceit, fancy, freak, notion, vagary, whim; observation, perception, reflection; assumption, belief, conclusion, conviction; conjecture, guess, hunch, hypothesis, speculation, supposition, surmise, theory; brainstorm, inspiration

¹**ide·al** \ī-ˈdēl\ *adj* **1** : existing only in the mind : IMAGINARY; *also* : lacking practicality **2** ♦ : of or relating to an ideal or to perfection : PERFECT

♦ absolute, faultless, flawless, impeccable, letter-perfect, perfect, unblemished — more at PERFECT

²**ideal** *n* **1** ♦ : a standard of excellence **2** ♦ : one regarded as a model worthy of imitation **3** : GOAL

♦ [1] classic, epitome, exemplar, perfection, quintessence — more at QUINTESSENCE ♦ [2] beau ideal, classic, exemplar, model, nonpareil, paragon; *also* role model; embodiment, epitome, incarnation, manifestation, personification; archetype, example, paradigm, pattern; guideline, principle, rule; gauge, standard, touchstone; essence, quintessence; acme, apex, culmination, peak, pinnacle, summit, zenith

ide·al·ise *chiefly Brit var of* IDEALIZE

ide·al·ism \ī-ˈdē-ə-ˌli-zəm\ *n* : the practice of forming ideals or living under their influence; *also* : an idealized representation — **ide·al·is·tic** \ī-ˌdē-ə-ˈlis-tik\ *adj* — **ide·al·is·ti·cal·ly** \-ti-k(ə-)lē\ *adv*

ide·al·ist \-list\ *n* ♦ : one guided by ideals; *also* : one that places ideals before practical considerations

♦ dreamer, romantic, utopian, visionary; *also* sentimentalist; theorist; perfectionist; thinker *Ant* realist

ide·al·ize \ī-ˈdē-ə-ˌlīz\ *vb* **-ized; -iz·ing** ♦ : to think of or represent as ideal — **ide·al·i·za·tion** \-ˌdē-ə-lə-ˈzā-shən\ *n*

♦ dream, glamorize, glorify; *also* daydream, imagine, romance, theorize

ide·al·ly \ī-ˈdē-lē, -ˈdē-ə-lē\ *adv* **1** : in idea or imagination : MENTALLY **2** ♦ : in agreement with an ideal : PERFECTLY

♦ faultlessly, flawlessly, impeccably, perfectly — more at PERFECTLY

ide·ation \ˌī-dē-ˈā-shən\ *n* : the forming of ideas — **ide·ate** \'ī-dē-ˌāt\ *vb* — **ide·ation·al** \ˌī-dē-ˈā-shə-nəl\ *adj*

idem \'ī-ˌdem, 'ē-, 'i-\ *pron* [L, same] : the same as something previously mentioned

iden·ti·cal \ī-ˈden-ti-kəl\ *adj* **1** ♦ : being the same **2** ♦ : essentially alike

♦ duplicate, equal, even, indistinguishable, same — more at SAME

iden·ti·fi·ca·tion \ī-ˌden-tə-fə-ˈkā-shən\ *n* **1** : an act of identifying : the state of being identified **2** : evidence of identity **3** : an unconscious psychological process by which an individual models thoughts, feelings, and actions after another person or an object

iden·ti·fy \ī-ˈden-tə-ˌfī\ *vb* **-fied; -fy·ing 1** : to regard as identical **2** ♦ : to think of as united (as in spirit, outlook, or principle) : ASSOCIATE **3** ♦ : to establish the identity of **4** : to practice psychological identification — **iden·ti·fi·able** \-ˌden-tə-ˈfī-ə-bəl\ *adj* — **iden·ti·fi·ably** \-blē\ *adv* — **iden·ti·fi·er** \-ˌfī(-ə)r\ *n*

♦ [2] associate, connect, correlate, link, relate — more at ASSOCIATE ♦ [3] distinguish, pinpoint, single; *also* diagnose; find, determine; locate, pick out, place, recognize, spot; check, examine, inspect, investigate, notice, observe, scrutinize; betray, disclose, discover, reveal

iden·ti·ty \ī-'den-tə-tē\ n, pl **-ties** **1** : sameness of essential character **2** ♦ : the distinguishing character or personality of an individual : INDIVIDUALITY **3** : the fact of being the same person or thing as claimed

♦ character, individuality, personality, self-identity — more at INDIVIDUALITY

identity crisis n : psychological conflict esp. in adolescence involving confusion about one's social role and one's personality

identity theft n : the illegal use of someone else's personal information to obtain money or credit

ideo·gram \'ī-dē-ə-ˌgram, 'i-\ n **1** : a picture or symbol used in a system of writing to represent a thing or an idea **2** : a character or symbol used in a system of writing to represent an entire word

ideo·logue also **idea·logue** \'ī-dē-ə-ˌlòg\ n : a partisan advocate or adherent of a particular ideology

ide·ol·o·gy \ˌī-dē-'ä-lə-jē, ˌi-\ also **ide·al·o·gy** \-'ä-lə-jē, -'a-\ n, pl **-gies** **1** ♦ : the body of ideas characteristic of a particular individual, group, or culture **2** : the assertions, theories, and aims that constitute a political, social, and economic program — **ide·o·log·i·cal** \ˌī-dē-ə-'lä-ji-kəl, ˌi-\ adj — **ide·ol·o·gist** \-dē-'ä-lə-jist\ n

♦ creed, doctrine, gospel, philosophy — more at CREED

ides \'īdz\ n sing or pl : the 15th day of March, May, July, or October or the 13th day of any other month in the ancient Roman calendar

id·i·o·cy \'i-dē-ə-sē\ n, pl **-cies** **1** ♦ : something notably stupid or foolish **2** dated, now offensive : extreme mental disability

♦ absurdity, fatuity, folly, foolery, foolishness, inanity, madness, stupidity

id·i·om \'i-dē-əm\ n **1** : the language peculiar to a person or group **2** : the characteristic form or structure of a language **3** : an expression that cannot be understood from the meanings of its separate words (as give way) — **id·i·o·mat·ic** \ˌi-dē-ə-'ma-tik\ adj — **id·i·o·mat·i·cal·ly** \-ti-k(ə-)lē\ adv

id·i·o·path·ic \ˌi-dē-ə-'pa-thik\ adj : arising spontaneously or from an obscure or unknown cause ⟨an ∼ disease⟩

id·i·o·syn·cra·sy \ˌi-dē-ə-'siŋ-krə-sē\ n, pl **-sies** ♦ : personal peculiarity — **id·i·o·syn·crat·ic** \ˌi-dē-ō-sin-'kra-tik\ adj — **id·i·o·syn·crat·i·cal·ly** \-'kra-ti-k(ə-)lē\ adv

♦ crotchet, eccentricity, mannerism, oddity, peculiarity, quirk, singularity, trick; also affectation, airs; attribute, characteristic, property, mark, trait; custom, habit, pattern, practice, way, wont; addiction; abnormality, perversion; disposition, genius, leaning, partiality; bent, inclination, penchant, predilection, predisposition, proclivity, propensity, tendency, turn; attitude, character, humor, identity, individuality, nature, personality, temperament

id·i·ot \'i-dē-ət\ n [ME, fr. AF ydiote, fr. L idiota ignorant person, fr. Gk idiōtēs one in a private station, layman, ignorant person, fr. idios one's own, private] **1** ♦ : a foolish or stupid person **2** dated, now offensive : a person affected with extreme mental disability — **id·i·ot·ic** \ˌi-dē-'ä-tik\ adj — **id·i·ot·i·cal·ly** \-ti-k(ə-)lē\ adv

♦ blockhead, cretin, dodo, dolt, dope, dummy, imbecile, jackass, moron, nitwit, numskull, simpleton; also booby, fool, goose, lunatic, madman, nut, zany; gawk, loser; scatterbrain; beast, boor, cad, churl, clown, creep, cur, heel, jerk, skunk, snake, stinker, villain **Ant** brain, genius

id·i·ot·proof \'i-dē-ət-ˌprüf\ adj : extremely easy to operate or maintain

¹**idle** \'īd-ᵊl\ adj **idler** \'ī-də-lər\; **idlest** \'ī-də-ləst\ **1** : GROUNDLESS, WORTHLESS, USELESS ⟨∼ talk⟩ **2** ♦ : not occupied

or employed : INACTIVE **3** ♦ : lacking in ambition or incentive : LAZY — **idly** \'īd-lē\ adv

♦ [2] dead, dormant, fallow, free, inactive, inert, inoperative, latent, off, vacant — more at INACTIVE

♦ [3] indolent, lazy, shiftless, slothful — more at LAZY

²**idle** vb **idled; idling** **1** ♦ : to spend time doing nothing **2** : to make idle **3** : to run without being connected so that power is not used for useful work

♦ dally, dawdle, dillydally, hang around, hang out, loaf, loll, lounge; also fiddle, fool, mess, monkey, play, potter, putter, trifle; estivate, hibernate; lag, loiter, linger, poke, relax, rest; amble, mosey, saunter, stroll; bum, furlough, goldbrick, malinger

idle·ness n ♦ : the quality or state of being idle (as through lack of worth, occupation, employment, industry)

♦ indolence, inertia, laziness, sloth — more at LAZINESS

♦ dormancy, inaction, inactivity, inertness, quiescence — more at INACTION

idler n ♦ : one that idles or is unoccupied : a lazy person

♦ lazybones, loafer, slouch, slug, sluggard — more at LAZYBONES

idol \'īd-ᵊl\ n **1** : an image worshipped as a god; also : a false god **2** : an object of passionate devotion ⟨a sports ∼⟩

idol·a·ter or **idol·a·tor** \ī-'dä-lə-tər\ n : a worshiper of idols

idol·a·try \-trē\ n, pl **-tries** **1** : the worship of a physical object as a god **2** ♦ : excessive devotion — **idol·a·trous** \-trəs\ adj

♦ adulation, deification, worship — more at WORSHIP

idol·i·za·tion \ˌīd-ᵊl-ə-'zā-shən\ n : the act of idolizing or state of being idolized

idol·ize \'īd-ᵊl-ˌīz\ vb **-ized; -iz·ing** ♦ : to make an idol of

♦ adore, canonize, deify, dote on, worship; also appreciate, cherish, esteem, prize, treasure, value; fancy, favor, like, prefer; regard; respect, revere, venerate; approve, endorse, support

idyll \'īd-ᵊl\ n **1** : a simple work of writing or poetry that describes country life or suggests a peaceful setting **2** ♦ : a lighthearted carefree episode that is a fit subject for an idyll — **idyl·lic** \ī-'di-lik\ adj

♦ binge, fling, frolic, gambol, lark, revel, rollick, romp — more at FLING

i.e. \'ī-'ē\ abbr [L id est] that is

IE abbr industrial engineer

IED abbr improvised explosive device

if \'if\ conj **1** : in the event that ⟨∼ he stays, I leave⟩ **2** : WHETHER ⟨ask ∼ he left⟩ **3** — used as a function word to introduce an exclamation expressing a wish ⟨∼ it would only rain⟩ **4** : even though ⟨an interesting ∼ untenable argument⟩

IF abbr intermediate frequency

if·fy \'i-fē\ adj : full of contingencies or unknown conditions

-i·fy \ə-ˌfī\ vb suffix : -FY

IG abbr inspector general

ig·loo \'i-glü\ n, pl **igloos** [Inuit (an Eskimo language) iglu house] : a house or hut that is often made of blocks of snow in the shape of a dome and that is associated esp. with indigenous peoples of arctic regions

ig·ne·ous \'ig-nē-əs\ adj **1** : FIERY **2** : formed by solidification of molten rock

ig·nit·able \-'nī-tə-bəl\ adj ♦ : capable of being ignited

♦ combustible, flammable, inflammable — more at COMBUSTIBLE

ig·nite \ig-'nīt\ vb **ig·nit·ed; ig·nit·ing** ♦ : to set afire or catch fire

♦ burn, fire, inflame, kindle, light — more at BURN

ig·ni·tion \ig-'ni-shən\ n **1** : a setting on fire **2** : the process or means (as an electric spark) of igniting the fuel mixture in an engine

ig·no·ble \ig-'nō-bəl\ adj **1** ♦ : of common birth **2** ♦ : not honorable : BASE, MEAN — **ig·no·bly** adv

♦ [1] common, humble, inferior, low, lowly, mean, plebeian, vulgar; *also* bourgeois; peasant, plain, poor, simple *Ant* aristocratic, high, highborn, lofty, noble, wellborn ♦ [2] base, contemptible, despicable, detestable, dirty, dishonorable (*or* dishonourable), low, mean, snide, sordid, vile, wretched; *also* bad, black, evil, foul, immoral, iniquitous, wicked, wrong; cruel, nasty, vicious; blamable, blameworthy, censurable, reprehensible; corrupt, debased, debauched, degenerate, depraved, dissolute, perverted; atrocious, villainous; unethical, unprincipled, unscrupulous; discreditable, disgraceful, disreputable, ignominious, shameful *Ant* high, high-minded, honorable, lofty, noble, straight, upright, venerable, virtuous

ig·no·min·i·ous \ˌig-nə-ˈmi-nē-əs\ *adj* **1** ♦ : marked with or characterized by disgrace or shame : DISHONORABLE **2** : DESPICABLE **3** : HUMILIATING, DEGRADING — **ig·no·min·i·ous·ly** *adv*

♦ discreditable, disgraceful, dishonorable (*or* dishonourable), disreputable, infamous, notorious, shameful — more at DISREPUTABLE

ig·no·mi·ny \ˈig-nə-ˌmi-nē, ig-ˈnä-mə-nē\ *n* **1** ♦ : deep personal humiliation and disgrace **2** : disgraceful or dishonorable conduct, quality, or action

♦ discredit, disgrace, dishonor (*or* dishonour), disrepute, infamy, odium, opprobrium, reproach, shame — more at DISGRACE

ig·no·ra·mus \ˌig-nə-ˈrā-məs\ *n* [*Ignoramus*, ignorant lawyer in *Ignoramus* (1615), play by George Ruggle] : an utterly ignorant person

ig·no·rance \ˈig-nə-rəns\ *n* ♦ : the state of being ignorant

♦ obliviousness, unawareness; *also* callowness, greenness, inexperience, innocence, naïveté, rawness, simpleness *Ant* acquaintance, awareness, familiarity

ig·no·rant \ˈig-nə-rənt\ *adj* **1** ♦ : lacking knowledge **2** : resulting from or showing lack of knowledge or intelligence **3** ♦ : not aware : UNAWARE, UNINFORMED — **ig·no·rant·ly** *adv*

♦ [1] dark, illiterate, simple, uneducated, unlearned, untaught; *also* lowbrow, uncultivated, uncultured, callow, green, inexperienced, innocent, naive; unsophisticated; raw, untrained; brainless, dumb, idiotic, imbecilic, moronic, stupid, witless; foolish, senseless, silly *Ant* educated, knowledgeable, literate, schooled ♦ [3] oblivious, unaware, unconscious, uninformed, unknowing, unwitting; *also* uneducated, unschooled, untaught; absent, absentminded, abstracted, heedless, inattentive *Ant* acquainted, aware, cognizant, conscious, conversant, grounded, informed, knowing, mindful, witting

ig·nore \ig-ˈnōr\ *vb* **ig·nored**; **ig·nor·ing** ♦ : to refuse to take notice of

♦ disregard, forget, neglect, overlook, pass over, slight, slur — more at NEGLECT ♦ condone, disregard, excuse, gloss over, pardon, pass over, shrug off, wink at — more at EXCUSE

igua·na \i-ˈgwä-nə\ *n* : any of various large tropical American lizards

ihp *abbr* indicated horsepower

IHS \ˌī-ˌäch-ˈes\ [LL, part transliteration of Gk IHΣ, abbr. for IHΣΟΥΣ *Iēsous* Jesus] — used as a Christian symbol and monogram for *Jesus*

ikon *var of* ICON

IL *abbr* Illinois

il·e·itis \ˌi-lē-ˈī-təs\ *n* : inflammation of the ileum

il·e·um \ˈi-lē-əm\ *n, pl* **il·ea** \-lē-ə\ : the part of the small intestine between the jejunum and the large intestine

il·i·ac \ˈi-lē-ˌak\ *adj* : of, relating to, or located near the ilium

il·i·um \ˈi-lē-əm\ *n* : the uppermost and largest of the three bones making up either side of the pelvis

ilk \ˈilk\ *n* ♦ : a group set up on the basis of any characteristic in common : SORT, KIND

♦ breed, class, description, feather, kind, like, manner, nature, order, sort, species, type — more at SORT

¹ill \ˈil\ *adj* **worse** \ˈwərs\; **worst** \ˈwərst\ **1** ♦ : attended or caused by an evil intent ⟨∼ deeds⟩ **2 a** : not normal or sound ⟨∼ health⟩ **b** ♦ : not in good health : SICK; *also* : feeling nauseated **3** : BAD, UNLUCKY ⟨∼ omen⟩ **4** : not right or proper ⟨∼ manners⟩ **5** : UNFRIENDLY, HOSTILE ⟨∼ feeling⟩

♦ [1] adverse, bad, baleful, baneful, damaging, deleterious, detrimental, evil, harmful, hurtful, injurious, mischievous, noxious, pernicious, prejudicial — more at HARMFUL ♦ [2b] nauseous, queasy, queer, sick, squeamish — more at NAUSEOUS ♦ [2b] bad, down, indisposed, peaked, punk, sick, unhealthy, unsound, unwell — more at SICK

²ill *adv* **worse**; **worst** **1** : with displeasure **2** ♦ : in a harsh manner **3** : probably not : HARDLY ⟨can ∼ afford it⟩ **4** : BADLY, UNLUCKILY **5** : in a faulty way

♦ hard, hardly, harshly, oppressively, roughly, severely, sternly, stiffly — more at HARDLY

³ill *n* **1** ♦ : the reverse of good : EVIL **2** : MISFORTUNE, DISTRESS **3** : AILMENT, SICKNESS; *also* : TROUBLE

♦ bad, evil, immorality, iniquity, sin, villainy, wrong — more at EVIL

⁴ill *abbr* illustrated; illustration; illustrator

Ill *abbr* Illinois

ill–ad·vised \ˌil-əd-ˈvīzd\ *adj* ♦ : not well counseled ⟨∼ efforts⟩ — **ill–ad·vis·ed·ly** \-ˈvī-zəd-lē\ *adv*

♦ imprudent, indiscreet, tactless, unwise — more at INDISCREET

ill–bred \-ˈbred\ *adj* ♦ : showing bad upbringing : IMPOLITE

♦ discourteous, ill-mannered, impertinent, impolite, inconsiderate, rude, thoughtless, uncivil, ungracious, unmannerly — more at IMPOLITE

il·le·gal \il-ˈlē-gəl\ *adj* ♦ : not lawful; *also* : not sanctioned by official rules — **il·le·gal·i·ty** \ˌi-li-ˈga-lə-tē\ *n* — **il·le·gal·ly** *adv*

♦ criminal, illegitimate, illicit, unlawful, wrongful; *also* bad, evil, immoral, shameful, sinful, unethical, wicked, wrong; blameworthy, censurable, reprehensible; banned, barred, disallowed, discouraged, forbidden, interdicted, outlawed, prohibited, proscribed; unauthorized, unlicensed, unsanctioned; corrupt, unprincipled, unscrupulous, villainous *Ant* lawful, legal, legitimate ♦ dirty, foul, unfair, unsportsmanlike

il·leg·i·ble \il-ˈle-jə-bəl\ *adj* ♦ : not legible — **il·leg·i·bil·i·ty** \il-ˌle-jə-ˈbi-lə-tē\ *n* — **il·leg·i·bly** \il-ˈle-jə-blē\ *adv*

il·le·git·i·mate \ˌi-li-ˈji-tə-mət\ *adj* **1** ♦ : born of unmarried parents **2** : ILLOGICAL **3** ♦ : not sanctioned by law : ILLEGAL — **il·le·git·i·ma·cy** \-ˈji-tə-mə-sē\ *n* — **il·le·git·i·mate·ly** *adv*

♦ [1] natural; *also* fatherless, motherless; adopted *Ant* legitimate ♦ [3] criminal, illegal, illicit, unlawful, wrongful — more at ILLEGAL

ill–fat·ed \ˈil-ˈfā-təd\ *adj* ♦ : having or destined to a hapless fate : UNFORTUNATE

♦ hapless, ill-starred, luckless, unfortunate, unhappy, unlucky — more at UNLUCKY

ill–fa·vored \-ˈfā-vərd\ *adj* : unattractive in physical appearance : UGLY

ill–got·ten \-ˈgät-ᵊn\ *adj* : acquired by improper means ⟨∼ gains⟩

ill–hu·mored \-ˈhyü-mərd, -ˈyü-\ *adj* ♦ : irritably sullen and churlish in mood or manner : SURLY

♦ bearish, bilious, cantankerous, disagreeable, dyspeptic, ill-tempered, ornery, splenetic, surly — more at ILL-TEMPERED

ill–lib·er·al \il-ˈli-bə-rəl\ *adj* : not liberal : NARROW, BIGOTED

il·lic·it \il-ˈli-sət\ *adj* ♦ : not permitted : UNLAWFUL — **il·lic·it·ly** *adv*

♦ criminal, illegal, illegitimate, unlawful, wrongful — more at ILLEGAL il·lim·it·able \il-'li-mə-tə-bəl\ adj ♦ : incapable of being limited or bounded : BOUNDLESS, MEASURELESS — il·lim·it·ably \-blē\ adv

♦ boundless, endless, immeasurable, indefinite, infinite, limitless, measureless, unbounded, unfathomable, unlimited — more at INFINITE

Il·li·nois \,i-lə-'nöi also -'nöiz\ n, pl Illinois : a member of an American Indian people of Illinois, Iowa, and Wisconsin

il·lit·er·ate \il-'li-tə-rət\ adj 1 ♦ : having little or no education; esp : unable to read or write 2 : showing a lack of familiarity with the fundamentals of a particular field of knowledge — il·lit·er·a·cy \-'li-tə-rə-sē\ n — illiterate n

♦ dark, ignorant, simple, uneducated, unlearned, untaught — more at IGNORANT

ill–man·nered \'il-'ma-nərd\ adj ♦ : marked by bad manners : RUDE

♦ discourteous, ill-bred, impertinent, impolite, inconsiderate, rude, thoughtless, uncivil, ungracious, unmannerly — more at IMPOLITE

ill–na·tured \-'nā-chərd\ adj : having a bad disposition : CROSS, SURLY — ill–na·tured·ly adv

ill·ness \'il-nəs\ n ♦ : an unhealthy condition of body or mind : SICKNESS; also : a specific disease

♦ ailment, bug, complaint, complication, condition, disease, disorder, fever, infirmity, malady, sickness, trouble — more at DISEASE

il·log·i·cal \il-'lä-ji-kəl\ adj ♦ : lacking sound reasoning; also : SENSELESS — il·log·i·cal·ly \-ji-k(ə-)lē\ adv

♦ fallacious, invalid, irrational, senseless, unreasonable, unsound, weak; also misleading, specious; ill-advised, unconsidered, unreasoned; inconsistent; absurd, asinine, foolish, meaningless, nonsensical, preposterous, silly; odd, peculiar, strange, unusual, weird; insane, nutty, mad, wacky; disordered, disorganized, rambling, random; unconvincing; inexplicable, unaccountable

ill–starred \'il-'stärd\ adj ♦ : having or meeting with misfortune : UNLUCKY

♦ hapless, ill-fated, luckless, unfortunate, unhappy, unlucky — more at UNLUCKY

ill–tem·pered \-'tem-pərd\ adj ♦ : having a bad disposition : CROSS

♦ bearish, bilious, cantankerous, cross, disagreeable, dyspeptic, ill-humored, ornery, splenetic, surly; also choleric, crabby, cranky, crotchety, fussy, grouchy, grumpy, querulous; irascible, irritable, peevish, petulant, snappish, testy, touchy; argumentative, contentious, contrary; angry, indignant, irate, mad, upset, uptight; depressed, dour, glum, morose, sullen Ant amiable, good-natured, good-tempered

ill–treat \-'trēt\ vb ♦ : to treat cruelly or improperly : MALTREAT — ill–treat·ment n

♦ abuse, maltreat, manhandle, mishandle, mistreat, misuse — more at ABUSE

il·lu·mi·nate \i-'lü-mə-,nāt\ vb -nat·ed; -nat·ing 1 ♦ : to supply or brighten with light : light up 2 ♦ : to make clear : ELUCIDATE 3 : to decorate (as a manuscript) with designs or pictures in gold or colors — il·lu·mi·nat·ing·ly adv — il·lu·mi·na·tor \-'lü-mə-,nā-tər\ n

♦ [1] light; also brighten; beam, beat (down), radiate, shine; floodlight; highlight, spotlight; blaze, burn, fire, flame, glare, glow, ignite, incinerate, kindle; bedazzle, blind, daze, dazzle; gleam, glisten, glitter Ant blacken, darken ♦ [2] clarify, clear (up), construe, demonstrate, elucidate, explain, explicate, expound, illustrate, interpret, spell out — more at EXPLAIN

il·lu·mi·na·tion \-,lü-mə-'nā-shən\ n 1 ♦ : the action of illuminating 2 ♦ : the state of being illuminated

♦ [1] blaze, flare, fluorescence, glare, gleam, glow, incandescence, light, luminescence, radiance, shine — more at LIGHT ♦ [2] brilliance, dazzle, effulgence, lightness,

lucidity, luminosity, radiance, refulgence, splendor — more at BRILLIANCE

il·lu·mine \i-'lü-mən\ vb -mined; -min·ing : to make clear or bright : ILLUMINATE

ill–us·age \'il-'yü-sij\ n : harsh, unkind, or abusive treatment

ill–use \-'yüz\ vb : to use badly : MALTREAT, ABUSE

il·lu·sion \i-'lü-zhən\ n [ME, fr. AF, fr. LL illusio, fr. L, action of mocking, fr. illudere to mock at, fr. ludere to play, mock] 1 ♦ : a mistaken idea : MISCONCEPTION 2 ♦ : a misleading visual image; also : HALLUCINATION

♦ [1] error, fallacy, falsehood, falsity, misconception, myth, untruth — more at FALLACY ♦ [2] chimera, conceit, daydream, delusion, dream, fancy, fantasy, figment, hallucination, phantasm, pipe dream, unreality, vision

il·lu·sion·ist \i-'lü-zhə-nist\ n ♦ : one that produces illusions; esp : a sleight-of-hand performer

♦ conjurer, magician, trickster

il·lu·sive \i-'lü-siv\ adj : DECEPTIVE

il·lu·so·ry \i-'lü-sə-rē, -zə-\ adj : DECEPTIVE

illust or illus abbr illustrated; illustration

il·lus·trate \'i-ləs-,trāt\ vb -trat·ed; -trat·ing [L illustrare, fr. lustrare to purify, make bright] 1 ♦ : to explain by use of examples; also : DEMONSTRATE 2 : to provide with pictures or figures that explain or decorate 3 : to serve to explain or decorate — il·lus·tra·tor \'i-lə-,strā-tər\ n

♦ exemplify, instance; also cite, mention, quote; name, specify; analyze, break down; clarify, clear (up); explain, explicate, expound; edify, elucidate, enlighten; illuminate; construe, interpret; simplify, spell out; detail, enumerate, list

il·lus·tra·tion \,i-lə-'strā-shən\ n 1 : the act of illustrating : the condition of being illustrated 2 ♦ : an example or instance that helps make something clear 3 ♦ : a picture or diagram that explains or decorates

♦ [2] clarification, construction, elucidation, explanation, explication, exposition, illumination, interpretation — more at EXPLANATION ♦ [3] diagram, figure, graphic, plate; also drawing, illumination, image, picture; caption, key, legend; depiction, portrait, portrayal, representation; clarification, elucidation, explanation, explication, exposition

il·lus·tra·tive \i-'ləs-trə-tiv, 'i-lə-,strā-\ adj : serving, tending, or designed to illustrate — il·lus·tra·tive·ly adv

il·lus·tri·ous \i-'ləs-trē-əs\ adj ♦ : notably outstanding because of rank or achievement — il·lus·tri·ous·ness n

♦ distinguished, eminent, noble, notable, noteworthy, outstanding, preeminent, prestigious, signal, star, superior — more at EMINENT

ill will n : unfriendly feeling

ILS abbr instrument landing system

¹IM \'ī-'em\ vb IM'd; IM'ing 1 : to send an instant message to 2 : to communicate by instant message

²IM abbr instant message

¹im·age \'i-mij\ n 1 : a likeness or imitation of a person or thing; esp : STATUE 2 : a picture of an object formed by a device (as a mirror or lens) 3 ♦ : a person strikingly like another person ⟨he is the ~ of his father⟩ 4 ♦ : a mental picture or conception : IMPRESSION, IDEA, CONCEPT 5 : a vivid representation or description

♦ [3] carbon copy, counterpart, double, duplicate, duplication, facsimile, likeness, match, picture, replica, ringer, spit; also effigy, portrait, portrayal; companion, counterpart, fellow, mate; equal, equivalent, identical twin; analogue, parallel ♦ [4] concept, idea, impression, notion, picture, thought — more at IDEA

²image vb im·aged; im·ag·ing 1 : to call up a mental picture of 2 ♦ : to describe or portray in words 3 ♦ : to create a representation of 4 : REFLECT, MIRROR 5 : to make appear : PROJECT

♦ [2] delineate, depict, describe, draw, paint, picture, portray, sketch — more at DESCRIBE ♦ [3] depict, picture, portray, represent — more at PICTURE

im·ag·ery \'i-mij-rē\ *n, pl* **-er·ies** 1 : IMAGES; *also* : the art of making images 2 : figurative language 3 : mental images; *esp* : the products of imagination

imag·in·able \i-'ma-jə-nə-bəl\ *adj* : capable of being imagined : CONCEIVABLE — **imag·in·ably** *adv*

imag·i·nary \i-'ma-jə-,ner-ē\ *adj* 1 ♦ : existing only in the imagination 2 : containing or relating to a quantity (**imaginary unit**) that is the positive square root of minus 1 (√−1)

♦ chimerical, fabulous, fanciful, fantastic, fictitious, made-up, mythical, phantom, pretend, unreal; *also* fabled, legendary, romantic; abstract, hypothetical, theoretical; unbelievable, unconvincing, unlikely; conceived, envisaged, pictured, visualized; deceptive, delusive, delusional, hallucinatory, illusory; concocted, fabricated *Ant* actual, existent, existing, real

imaginary number *n* : a complex number (as 2 + 3*i*) with a nonzero term (**imaginary part**) containing the imaginary unit as a factor

imag·i·na·tion \i-,ma-jə-'nā-shən\ *n* 1 ♦ : the act or power of forming a mental image of something not present to the senses or not previously known or experienced 2 : creative ability 3 : RESOURCEFULNESS 4 : a mental image : a creation of the mind

♦ creativity, fancy, fantasy, invention, inventiveness; *also* brainstorm, inspiration; fecundity, fertility; ingenuity, originality; versatility; chimera, daydream, delusion, dream, figment, hallucination, illusion, mirage, phantasm, pipe dream; envisaging, visualization

imag·i·na·tive \i-'ma-jə-nə-tiv, -,nā-\ *adj* ♦ : of, relating to, or characterized by imagination — **imag·i·na·tive·ly** *adv*

♦ creative, ingenious, innovative, inventive, original — more at CREATIVE

imag·ine \i-'ma-jən\ *vb* **imag·ined; imag·in·ing** 1 ♦ : to form a mental picture of something not present 2 ♦ : to hold as an opinion : THINK, GUESS ⟨I ~ it will rain⟩

♦ [1] conceive, dream, envisage, fancy, picture, vision, visualize; *also* daydream; hallucinate; reflect, relive, reminisce; contemplate, meditate, muse, ponder, ruminate; concoct, fabricate, invent, make up, manufacture, plan, project ♦ [2] believe, consider, deem, feel, figure, guess, hold, suppose, think — more at BELIEVE

imag·in·ings \-'maj-niŋz, -'ma-jə-\ *n pl* : products of the imagination

im·ag·ism \'i-mi-ji-zəm\ *n, often cap* : a movement in poetry advocating free verse and the expression of ideas and emotions through clear precise images — **im·ag·ist** \-jist\ *n*

ima·go \i-'mā-gō, -'mä-\ *n, pl* **imagoes** *or* **ima·gi·nes** \-'mā-gə-,nēz, -'mä-\ [NL, fr. L, image] : an insect in its final adult stage — **ima·gi·nal** \i-'mā-gən-ᵊl, -'mä-\ *adj*

im·bal·ance \'im-'ba-ləns\ *n* : lack of balance : the state of being out of equilibrium or out of proportion

im·be·cile \'im-bə-səl, -,sil\ *n* 1 ♦ : a person lacking in judgment or prudence : IDIOT 2 *dated, now offensive* : a person affected with moderate mental disability — **imbecile** *or* **im·be·cil·ic** \,im-bə-'si-lik\ *adj*

♦ blockhead, dope, dummy, idiot, jackass, nitwit, numskull, simpleton — more at IDIOT

im·be·cil·i·ty \,im-bə-'si-lə-tē\ *n* 1 : the quality or state of being imbecile or an imbecile 2 : something that is foolish or nonsensical

imbed *var of* EMBED

im·bibe \im-'bīb\ *vb* **im·bibed; im·bib·ing** 1 : to receive and retain in the mind 2 ♦ : to take through the mouth and esophagus into the stomach : DRINK 3 ♦ : to take in or up : ABSORB — **im·bib·er** *n*

♦ [2] drink, guzzle, quaff, sup, swig, toss — more at DRINK ♦ [3] absorb, drink, soak, sponge, suck — more at ABSORB

im·bri·ca·tion \,im-brə-'kā-shən\ *n* 1 : an overlapping of edges (as of tiles) 2 : a pattern showing imbrication — **im·bri·cate** \'im-bri-kət\ *adj*

im·bro·glio \im-'brōl-yō\ *n, pl* **-glios** [It, fr. *imbrogliare* to entangle] 1 : a confused mass 2 : a complicated situation; *also* : a serious or embarrassing misunderstanding

im·brue \im-'brü\ *vb* **im·brued; im·bru·ing** : STAIN ⟨hands *imbrued* with blood⟩

im·bue \-'byü\ *vb* **im·bued; im·bu·ing** 1 ♦ : to permeate or influence as if by dyeing 2 : to tinge or dye deeply

♦ inculcate, infuse, ingrain, invest, steep, suffuse — more at INFUSE

IMF *abbr* International Monetary Fund

imit *abbr* imitative

im·i·ta·ble \'i-mə-tə-bəl\ *adj* : capable or worthy of being imitated or copied

im·i·tate \'i-mə-,tāt\ *vb* **-tat·ed; -tat·ing** 1 ♦ : to follow as a model 2 : RESEMBLE 3 ♦ : to produce a copy of : REPRODUCE 4 ♦ : to copy or feign esp. with intent to deceive : MIMIC

♦ [1] ape, copy, emulate, mime, mimic; *also* burlesque, caricature, lampoon, mock, parody, travesty; impersonate, perform, play; pantomime ♦ [3] copy, duplicate, replicate, reproduce — more at COPY ♦ [4] burlesque, caricature, mimic, mock, parody, take off, travesty — more at MIMIC

¹**im·i·ta·tion** \,i-mə-'tā-shən\ *n* 1 : an act of imitating 2 ♦ : something produced as a copy 3 : a literary work that reproduces the style of another author

♦ carbon copy, copy, duplicate, duplication, facsimile, replica, replication, reproduction — more at COPY

²**imitation** *adj* ♦ : resembling something else that is usu. genuine and of better quality : not real

♦ artificial, bogus, factitious, fake, false, mimic, mock, sham, substitute, synthetic; *also* dummy, phony; cultured, manufactured; unauthentic; adulterated, doctored, fudged, juggled, manipulated, tampered (with); concocted, fabricated; counterfeit, deceptive, forged, fraudulent, misleading; affected, feigned, pseudo, spurious *Ant* genuine, natural, real

im·i·ta·tive \'i-mə-,tā-tiv\ *adj* 1 ♦ : marked by imitation 2 : inclined to imitate 3 : COUNTERFEIT

♦ mimic, slavish, unoriginal; *also* copied, cribbed, plagiarized; artificial, bogus, factitious, fake, false, imitation, man-made, mock, sham, substitute, synthetic; duplicated, reproduced, transcribed; backup; counterfeit, deceptive, forged, fraudulent, misleading; uninspired *Ant* original

im·i·ta·tor \-,tā-tər\ *n* ♦ : one that imitates

♦ impersonator, impressionist, mimic — more at MIMIC

im·mac·u·late \i-'ma-kyə-lət\ *adj* 1 ♦ : being without stain or blemish : PURE 2 ♦ : spotlessly clean ⟨~ linen⟩ — **im·mac·u·late·ly** *adv*

♦ [1] chaste, clean, decent, modest, pure — more at CHASTE ♦ [2] clean, spick-and-span, spotless, stainless, unsoiled, unsullied — more at CLEAN

im·ma·nent \'i-mə-nənt\ *adj* 1 : INHERENT 2 : being within the limits of experience or knowledge — **im·ma·nence** \-nəns\ *n* — **im·ma·nen·cy** \-nən-sē\ *n*

im·ma·te·ri·al \,i-mə-'tir-ē-əl\ *adj* 1 ♦ : not consisting of matter : SPIRITUAL 2 : of no substantial consequence : UNIMPORTANT, TRIFLING 3 ♦ : not material or essential — **im·ma·te·ri·al·i·ty** \-,tir-ē-'a-lə-tē\ *n*

♦ [1] bodiless, incorporeal, insubstantial, nonmaterial, nonphysical, spiritual, unsubstantial; *also* metaphysical, supernatural; impalpable, insensible, intangible, invisible; airy, diaphanous, ethereal, tenuous, thin, vaporous *Ant* bodily, corporeal, material, physical, substantial ♦ [3] extraneous, irrelevant — more at IRRELEVANT

im·ma·ture \,i-mə-'tür, -'tyür\ *adj* ♦ : lacking complete development : not yet mature ⟨~ behavior⟩ — **im·ma·tu·ri·ty** \-'tür-ə-tē, -'tyür-\ *n*

♦ adolescent, babyish, childish, infantile, juvenile, kiddish — more at CHILDISH ♦ adolescent, callow, green, inexperienced, juvenile, raw — more at CALLOW

im·mea·sur·able \(ˌ)i-ˈme-zhə-rə-bəl\ *adj* ♦ : not capable of being measured : indefinitely extensive — **im·mea·sur·ably** \-blē\ *adv*

♦ boundless, endless, illimitable, indefinite, infinite, limitless, measureless, unbounded, unfathomable, unlimited — more at INFINITE

im·me·di·a·cy \i-ˈmē-dē-ə-sē\ *n, pl* **-cies** **1** ♦ : the quality or state of being immediate **2** : something that is of immediate importance

♦ closeness, contiguity, nearness, proximity — more at PROXIMITY

im·me·di·ate \i-ˈmē-dē-ət\ *adj* **1** ♦ : acting directly and alone : DIRECT ⟨the ∼ cause of death⟩ **2** : being next in line or relation ⟨members of the ∼ family⟩ **3** ♦ : not distant : CLOSE **4** ♦ : made or done at once ⟨an ∼ response⟩ **5** ♦ : near to or related to the present time ⟨the ∼ future⟩

♦ [1] direct, firsthand, primary — more at DIRECT
♦ [3, 5] close, near, nearby, nigh — more at CLOSE
♦ [4] prompt, punctual, timely — more at PROMPT
♦ [4] instant, instantaneous, straightaway — more at INSTANTANEOUS

im·me·di·ate·ly *adv* **1** : in direct connection or relation **2** ♦ : without interval of time

♦ directly, forthwith, instantly, now, promptly, pronto, right away, right now; *also* away, freely; anon, momentarily, shortly, soon; apace, briskly, fast, posthaste, quick, quickly, rapidly, readily, speedily, swift, swiftly; abruptly, presto, suddenly, unexpectedly; hastily, impetuously, impulsively, rashly, recklessly; exactly, opportunely, punctually, seasonably

im·me·mo·ri·al \ˌi-mə-ˈmȯr-ē-əl\ *adj* ♦ : extending beyond the reach of memory, record, or tradition ⟨from time ∼⟩

♦ age-old, ancient, antediluvian, antique, dateless, hoary, old, venerable — more at ANCIENT

im·mense \i-ˈmens\ *adj* [ME, fr. MF, fr. L *immensus* immeasurable, fr. *mensus*, pp. of *metiri* to measure] **1** : very great in size or degree : VAST **2** : EXCELLENT — **im·mense·ly** *adv*

im·men·si·ty \-ˈmen-sə-tē\ *n* **1** ♦ : the quality or state of being immense **2** : something immense

♦ enormity, hugeness, magnitude, massiveness, vastness; *also* bigness, greatness, largeness, voluminousness; grandness; extravagance, immoderacy *Ant* minuteness

im·merse \i-ˈmərs\ *vb* **im·mersed; im·mers·ing** **1** ♦ : to plunge or dip esp. into a fluid **2** ♦ : to take or engage the whole attention of : ENGROSS, ABSORB **3** : to baptize by immersing

♦ [1] dip, douse, duck, dunk, souse, submerge — more at DIP ♦ [2] absorb, busy, engage, engross, enthrall, fascinate, grip, interest, intrigue, involve, occupy — more at ENGAGE

im·mer·sion \-ˈmər-zhən\ *n* : the act of immersing or the state of being immersed; *esp* : absorbing involvement

im·mer·sive \-ˈmər-siv\ *adj* : providing, involving, or characterized by deep absorption or immersion in something

im·mi·grant \ˈi-mi-grənt\ *n* **1** ♦ : a person who immigrates **2** : a plant or animal that becomes established where it did not previously occur

♦ emigrant, émigré, migrant, settler — more at EMIGRANT

im·mi·grate \ˈi-mə-ˌgrāt\ *vb* **-grat·ed; -grat·ing** : to come into a foreign country and take up residence — **im·mi·gra·tion** \ˌi-mə-ˈgrā-shən\ *n*

im·mi·nent \ˈi-mə-nənt\ *adj* ♦ : ready to take place; *esp* : hanging threateningly over one's head ⟨∼ danger⟩ — **im·mi·nence** \-nəns\ *n* — **im·mi·nent·ly** *adv*

♦ coming, forthcoming, impending, oncoming, pending — more at FORTHCOMING ♦ impending, pending; *also* approaching, coming, forthcoming, future, near, nearing, oncoming, upcoming; brewing, gathering; likely, possible, probable; inevitable, unavoidable;

menacing, ominous, portentous; anticipated, awaited, expected, foreseen, predicted

im·mis·ci·ble \(ˌ)i-ˈmi-sə-bəl\ *adj* : incapable of mixing

im·mis·er·a·tion \(ˌ)i-ˌmi-zə-ˈrā-shən\ *n* : IMPOVERISHMENT

im·mo·bile \(ˌ)i-ˈmō-bəl\ *adj* ♦ : incapable of moving or being moved : IMMOVABLE — **im·mo·bil·i·ty** \ˌi-mō-ˈbi-lə-tē\ *n*

♦ immovable, standing, static, stationary, unmovable — more at STATIONARY

im·mo·bi·lize \i-ˈmō-bə-ˌlīz\ *vb* ♦ : to make immobile — **im·mo·bi·li·za·tion** \i-ˌmō-bə-lə-ˈzā-shən\ *n*

♦ cripple, disable, hamstring, incapacitate, paralyze, prostrate — more at PARALYZE

im·mod·er·ate \(ˌ)i-ˈmä-də-rət\ *adj* ♦ : lacking in moderation : EXCESSIVE ⟨∼ drinking⟩ — **im·mod·er·a·cy** \-rə-sē\ *n* — **im·mod·er·ate·ly** *adv*

♦ devilish, excessive, exorbitant, extravagant, extreme, inordinate, lavish, overmuch, overweening, steep, stiff, towering, unconscionable — more at EXCESSIVE

im·mod·est \(ˌ)i-ˈmä-dəst\ *adj* ♦ : not modest ⟨∼ conduct⟩; *specif* : not conforming to the sexual mores of a particular time or place ⟨an ∼ dress⟩ — **im·mod·est·ly** *adv* — **im·mod·es·ty** \-də-stē\ *n*

♦ bold, familiar, forward, free, presumptuous — more at PRESUMPTUOUS

im·mo·late \ˈi-mə-ˌlāt\ *vb* **-lat·ed; -lat·ing** [L *immolare*, to sprinkle with meal before sacrificing, sacrifice, fr. *mola* sacrificial barley cake, lit., millstone] **1** : to offer in sacrifice; *esp* : to kill as a sacrificial victim **2** : to kill or destroy esp. by fire

im·mo·la·tion \ˌi-mə-ˈlā-shən\ *n* **1** : the act of immolating : the state of being immolated **2** : something that is immolated

im·mor·al \(ˌ)i-ˈmȯr-əl\ *adj* ♦ : not moral — **im·mor·al·ly** *adv*

♦ bad, black, evil, iniquitous, nefarious, rotten, sinful, unethical, unsavory, vicious, vile, villainous, wicked, wrong ♦ cutthroat, Machiavellian, unconscionable, unethical, unprincipled, unscrupulous — more at UNPRINCIPLED

im·mo·ral·i·ty \ˌi-mȯ-ˈra-lə-tē, ˌi-mə-\ *n* **1** ♦ : the quality or state of being immoral; *esp* : UNCHASTITY **2** ♦ : an immoral act or practice

♦ [1] bad, evil, ill, iniquity, sin, villainy, wrong — more at EVIL ♦ [2] corruption, debauchery, depravity, iniquity, licentiousness, sin, vice — more at VICE

¹**im·mor·tal** \(ˌ)i-ˈmȯrt-ᵊl\ *adj* **1** ♦ : not mortal : exempt from death ⟨∼ gods⟩ **2** ♦ : destined to be remembered forever ⟨those ∼ words⟩ — **im·mor·tal·ly** *adv*

♦ [1, 2] ceaseless, dateless, deathless, endless, eternal, everlasting, permanent, perpetual, undying, unending — more at EVERLASTING

²**immortal** *n* **1** : one exempt from death **2** *pl, often cap* : the gods in Greek and Roman mythology **3** : a person whose fame is lasting ⟨an ∼ of baseball⟩

im·mor·tal·ise *chiefly Brit var of* IMMORTALIZE

im·mor·tal·i·ty \ˌi-ˌmȯr-ˈta-lə-tē\ *n* ♦ : the quality or state of being immortal; *esp* : unending existence

♦ afterlife, eternity, hereafter — more at ETERNITY

im·mor·tal·ize \i-ˈmȯrt-ᵊl-ˌīz\ *vb* **-ized; -iz·ing** : to make immortal

im·mov·able \(ˌ)i-ˈmü-və-bəl\ *adj* **1** ♦ : firmly fixed, settled, or fastened ⟨∼ mountains⟩ **2** : firm in belief, determination, or adherence : UNYIELDING **3** : IMPASSIVE — **im·mov·abil·i·ty** \-ˌmü-və-ˈbi-lə-tē\ *n* — **im·mov·ably** \-blē\ *adv*

♦ immobile, nonmotile, unbudging, unmovable; *also* motionless, static, stationary, still; fast, fixed, rooted, steadfast, stuck, wedged *Ant* mobile, motile, movable, moving

im·mune \i-ˈmyün\ *adj* **1** : EXEMPT **2** : having a special capacity for resistance (as to a disease) **3** : containing or producing antibodies — **im·mu·ni·ty** \-ˈmyü-nə-tē\ *n*

immune response *n* : a response of the body to an antigen resulting in the formation of antibodies and cells designed to react with the antigen and render it harmless

immune system *n* : the bodily system that protects the body from foreign substances, cells, and tissues by producing the immune response and that includes esp. the thymus, spleen, lymph nodes, and lymphocytes

im·mu·nize \'i-myə-ˌnīz\ *vb* **-nized; -niz·ing** : to make immune — **im·mu·ni·za·tion** \ˌi-myə-nə-'zā-shən\ *n*

im·mu·no·de·fi·cien·cy \ˌi-myə-nō-di-'fi-shən-sē\ *n* : inability to produce the normal number of antibodies or immunologically sensitized cells esp. in response to specific antigens — **im·mu·no·de·fi·cient** \-'fi-shənt\ *adj*

im·mu·no·glob·u·lin \ˌi-myə-nō-'glä-byə-lən\ *n* : ANTIBODY

im·mu·nol·o·gy \ˌi-myə-'nä-lə-jē\ *n* : a science that deals with the immune system, immunity, and the immune response — **im·mu·no·log·ic** \-nə-'lä-jik\ *or* **im·mu·no·log·i·cal** \-ji-kəl\ *adj* — **im·mu·no·log·i·cal·ly** \-ji-k(ə-)lē\ *adv* — **im·mu·nol·o·gist** \-'nä-lə-jist\ *n*

im·mu·no·sup·pres·sion \ˌi-myə-nō-sə-'pre-shən\ *n* : suppression (as by drugs) of natural immune responses — **im·mu·no·sup·press** \-'pres\ *vb* — **im·mu·no·sup·pres·sive** \-'pre-siv\ *adj*

im·mu·no·ther·a·py \-'ther-ə-pē\ *n* : treatment or prevention of disease by attempting to induce immunity

im·mure \i-'myùr\ *vb* **im·mured; im·mur·ing** **1** ♦ : to enclose within or as if within walls; *also* : IMPRISON **2** : to build into a wall; *esp* : to entomb in a wall

♦ cage, closet, coop up, corral, encase, enclose, envelop, fence, hedge, hem, house, pen, wall — more at ENCLOSE
♦ commit, confine, imprison, jail — more at IMPRISON

im·mu·ta·bil·i·ty \-ˌmyü-tə-'bi-lə-tē\ *n* ♦ : the quality or state of being immutable

♦ constancy, fixedness, stability, steadiness — more at CONSTANCY

im·mu·ta·ble \(ˌ)i-'myü-tə-bəl\ *adj* ♦ : not capable of or susceptible to change : UNCHANGEABLE, UNCHANGING — **im·mu·ta·bly** \-'myü-tə-blē\ *adv*

♦ fast, fixed, hard-and-fast, inflexible, unalterable, unchangeable, unchanging — more at INFLEXIBLE

¹imp \'imp\ *n* **1** ♦ : a small demon : FIEND **2** ♦ : a mischievous child

♦ [1] demon, devil, fiend, ghoul — more at DEMON
♦ [2] devil, hellion, mischief, monkey, rapscallion, rascal, rogue, scamp, urchin — more at SCAMP

²imp *abbr* **1** imperative **2** imperfect **3** imperial **4** import; imported

¹im·pact \im-'pakt\ *vb* **1** : to press together **2** ♦ : to have an impact on **3** ♦ : to strike forcefully

♦ [2] affect, impress, influence, move, strike, sway, tell, touch — more at AFFECT ♦ [3] bang, bash, bump, collide, crash, hit, knock, ram, slam, smash, strike, swipe, thud — more at HIT

²im·pact \'im-ˌpakt\ *n* **1** ♦ : a forceful contact, collision, or onset; *also* : the impetus communicated in or as if in a collision **2** ♦ : the force of impression of one thing on another : EFFECT

♦ [1] bump, collision, concussion, crash, jar, jolt, shock, smash, strike, wallop; *also* blow, buffet, hit, knock, punch, rap, slap, thump; bashing, bludgeoning, clobbering, hammering, licking, pounding, pummeling, thrashing; contact, encounter, meeting, touch ♦ [2] effect, influence, mark, repercussion, sway — more at EFFECT

im·pact·ed \im-'pak-təd\ *adj* **1** : packed or wedged in **2** : wedged between the jawbone and another tooth

im·pair \im-'par\ *vb* : to diminish in quantity, value, excellence, or strength : DAMAGE, LESSEN — **im·pair·ment** *n*

im·paired \-'pard\ *adj* : being in a less than perfect or whole condition; *esp* : disabled or functionally defective — often used in combination ⟨hearing-*impaired*⟩

im·pa·la \im-'pa-lə\ *n, pl* **impalas** *or* **impala** : a large brownish African antelope that in the male has slender curved horns with ridges

im·pale \im-'pāl\ *vb* **im·paled; im·pal·ing** ♦ : to pierce with or as if with something pointed — **im·pale·ment** *n*

♦ gore, harpoon, lance, pierce, puncture, skewer, spear, spike, stab, stick, transfix; *also* spindle; perforate; jab, poke, prick, punch, thrust; cut, knife, slice

im·pal·pa·ble \(ˌ)im-'pal-pə-bəl\ *adj* **1** : unable to be felt by touch : INTANGIBLE **2** ♦ : not easily seen or understood — **im·pal·pa·bly** \-blē\ *adv*

♦ imperceptible, inappreciable, indistinguishable — more at IMPERCEPTIBLE

im·pan·el \im-'pan-əl\ *vb* : to enter in or on a panel : ENROLL ⟨∼ a jury⟩

im·part \im-'pärt\ *vb* **1** ♦ : to give from one's store or abundance ⟨the sun ∼s warmth⟩ **2** ♦ : to make known

♦ [1, 2] communicate, convey, spread, transfer, transfuse, transmit — more at COMMUNICATE

im·par·tial \(ˌ)im-'pär-shəl\ *adj* ♦ : not partial : UNBIASED, JUST — **im·par·tial·ly** *adv*

♦ disinterested, dispassionate, equal, equitable, fair, just, nonpartisan, objective, square, unbiased, unprejudiced — more at FAIR

im·par·ti·al·i·ty \-ˌpär-shē-'a-lə-tē\ *n* ♦ : the quality or state of being impartial : freedom from bias or favoritism

♦ detachment, disinterestedness, neutrality, objectivity — more at DETACHMENT

im·pass·able \(ˌ)im-'pa-sə-bəl\ *adj* ♦ : incapable of being passed, traversed, or crossed ⟨∼ roads⟩ — **im·pass·ably** \-blē\ *adv*

♦ impenetrable, impervious

im·passe \'im-ˌpas\ *n* **1** : an impassable road or way **2** ♦ : a predicament from which there is no obvious escape

♦ deadlock, halt, stalemate, standstill; *also* dead end; bottleneck, corner, dilemma, fix, hole, jam, pickle, pinch, plight, predicament, quagmire, quandary, spot; difficulty; problem

im·pas·si·ble \(ˌ)im-'pa-sə-bəl\ *adj* : incapable of feeling : IMPASSIVE

im·pas·sioned \im-'pa-shənd\ *adj* ♦ : filled with passion or zeal : showing great warmth or intensity of feeling

♦ ardent, burning, charged, emotional, fervent, fiery, hot-blooded, passionate, red-hot, vehement — more at FERVENT

im·pas·sive \(ˌ)im-'pa-siv\ *adj* ♦ : showing no signs of feeling, emotion, or interest : EXPRESSIONLESS; *also* : lacking or not feeling emotion — **im·pas·sive·ly** *adv*

♦ blank, deadpan, expressionless, inexpressive, stolid, vacant — more at BLANK ♦ apathetic, cold-blooded, phlegmatic, stoic, stolid, unemotional; *also* cold, cool, dispassionate, unmoved; calm, collected, composed; unflappable; reserved, reticent, taciturn; blank, deadpan, dry, empty, expressionless, inexpressive, vacant, wooden; enigmatic, impenetrable, inscrutable; aloof, detached, unconcerned, unsentimental; impersonal, objective, unresponsive; pitiless, unfeeling; inconsiderate, thoughtless *Ant* demonstrative, emotional, fervent, fervid, hot-blooded, impassioned, passionate

im·pas·siv·i·ty \ˌim-ˌpa-'si-və-tē\ *n* ♦ : the quality or state of being impassive : lack or absence of feeling or expression

♦ apathy, numbness, phlegm, stupor — more at APATHY

im·pas·to \im-'pas-tō, -'päs-\ *n* : the thick application of a pigment to a canvas or panel in painting; *also* : the body of pigment so applied

im·pa·tience \-shəns\ *n* ♦ : the quality or state of being impatient

♦ appetite, ardor, avidity, eagerness, enthusiasm, excitement, hunger, keenness, thirst — more at EAGERNESS

im·pa·tiens \im-'pā-shənz, -shəns\ *n* : any of a genus of herbs with usu. spurred flowers and seed capsules that readily split open

im·pa·tient \(ˌ)im-ˈpā-shənt\ *adj* **1** : not patient : restless or short of temper esp. under irritation, delay, or opposition **2** : INTOLERANT ⟨~ of poverty⟩ **3** : prompted or marked by impatience **4** : eagerly desirous : ANXIOUS — **im·pa·tient·ly** *adv*

im·peach \im-ˈpēch\ *vb* [ME *empechen* to accuse, fr. MF *empeechier* to hinder, fr. LL *impedicare* to fetter, fr. L *pedica* fetter, fr. *ped-, pes* foot] **1** : to charge (a public official) before an authorized tribunal with misconduct in office **2** : to challenge the credibility or validity of **3** : to remove from public office for misconduct — **im·peach·ment** *n*

im·pec·ca·bil·i·ty \(ˌ)im-ˌpe-kə-ˈbi-lə-tē\ *n* : the quality or state of being impeccable

im·pec·ca·ble \(ˌ)im-ˈpe-kə-bəl\ *adj* **1** : not capable of sinning or wrongdoing **2** ♦ : free from fault or blame : FAULTLESS ⟨a man of ~ character⟩

♦ faultless, flawless, irreproachable; *also* accurate, correct, exact, perfect, precise; appropriate, becoming, decorous, fitting, proper, right, seemly; immaculate, unblemished, unmarred, unspoiled; infallible, unerring, unfailing *Ant* censurable, defective, faulty, reproachable ♦ absolute, ideal, letter-perfect, perfect, unblemished — more at PERFECT

im·pec·ca·bly \(ˌ)im-ˈpe-kə-blē\ *adv* ♦ : in an impeccable manner

♦ faultlessly, flawlessly, ideally, perfectly — more at PERFECTLY

im·pe·cu·nious \ˌim-pi-ˈkyü-nyəs, -nē-əs\ *adj* ♦ : having little or no money

♦ broke, destitute, indigent, needy, penniless, penurious, poor, poverty-stricken — more at POOR

im·pe·cu·nious·ness *n* ♦ : the quality or state of being impecunious

♦ beggary, destitution, impoverishment, indigence, need, pauperism, penury, poverty, want — more at POVERTY

im·ped·ance \im-ˈpēd-ᵊns\ *n* : the opposition in an electrical circuit to the flow of an alternating current

im·pede \im-ˈpēd\ *vb* **im·ped·ed; im·ped·ing** [L *impedire*, fr. *ped-, pes* foot] ♦ : to interfere with the progress of

♦ encumber, fetter, hamper, hinder, hold back, hold up, inhibit, interfere with, obstruct — more at HAMPER

im·ped·i·ment \im-ˈpe-də-mənt\ *n* **1** : something that impedes, hinders, or obstructs **2** : a speech defect

im·ped·i·men·ta \im-ˌpe-də-ˈmen-tə\ *n pl* : things that impede

im·pel \im-ˈpel\ *vb* **im·pelled; im·pel·ling** ♦ : to urge or drive forward or on; *also* : PROPEL

♦ actuate, drive, move, propel, work

im·pel·ler *also* **im·pel·lor** \im-ˈpe-lər\ *n* : a rotor esp. in a pump

im·pend \im-ˈpend\ *vb* **1** : to hover or hang over threateningly : MENACE **2** : to be about to occur

impending *adj* ♦ : that is about to occur

♦ coming, forthcoming, imminent, oncoming, pending — more at FORTHCOMING

im·pen·e·tra·ble \(ˌ)im-ˈpe-nə-trə-bəl\ *adj* **1** ♦ : incapable of being penetrated or pierced ⟨an ~ jungle⟩ **2** ♦ : incapable of being comprehended : INSCRUTABLE ⟨an ~ mystery⟩ — **im·pen·e·tra·bil·i·ty** \-ˌpe-nə-trə-ˈbi-lə-tē\ *n* — **im·pen·e·tra·bly** \-ˈpe-nə-trə-blē\ *adv*

♦ [1] impervious, tight — more at TIGHT ♦ [2] cryptic, darkling, deep, enigmatic, inscrutable, mysterious, mystic, occult, uncanny — more at MYSTERIOUS ♦ [2] incomprehensible, unfathomable — more at INCOMPREHENSIBLE

im·pen·i·tent \(ˌ)im-ˈpe-nə-tənt\ *adj* : not penitent : not repenting of sin — **im·pen·i·tence** \-təns\ *n*

im·per·a·tive \im-ˈper-ə-tiv\ *adj* **1** : expressing a command, request, or encouragement ⟨~ sentence⟩ **2** ♦ : having power to restrain, control, or direct **3** ♦ : not to be avoided or evaded — **imperative** *n* — **im·per·a·tive·ly** *adv*

♦ [2] compulsory, incumbent, involuntary, mandatory, necessary, nonelective, obligatory, peremptory — more at MANDATORY ♦ [3] acute, critical, dire, imperious, instant, pressing, urgent — more at ACUTE

im·per·cep·ti·ble \ˌim-pər-ˈsep-tə-bəl\ *adj* ♦ : not perceptible; *esp* : too slight to be perceived ⟨~ changes⟩ — **im·per·cep·ti·bly** \-blē\ *adv*

♦ impalpable, inappreciable, indistinguishable; *also* inaudible, inconspicuous, indistinct, intangible, invisible, unnoticeable, unseen; faint, insignificant, slight, trivial; buried, concealed, covert, disguised, hidden, obscure, shrouded, unapparent, vague *Ant* appreciable, discernible, palpable, perceptible, sensible

im·per·cep·tive \ˌim-pər-ˈsep-tiv\ *adj* : not perceptive

imperf *abbr* imperfect

¹**im·per·fect** \(ˌ)im-ˈpər-fikt\ *adj* **1** ♦ : not perfect esp. by having a fault or a lack **2** : of, relating to, or being a verb tense used to designate a continuing state or an incomplete action esp. in the past — **im·per·fect·ly** *adv*

♦ bad, defective, faulty — more at FAULTY

²**imperfect** *n* : the imperfect tense; *also* : a verb form in it

im·per·fec·tion \ˌim-pər-ˈfek-shən\ *n* **1** : the quality or state of being imperfect **2** ♦ : the quality or aspect which makes something incomplete or defective : FAULT, BLEMISH

♦ blemish, defect, deformity, disfigurement, fault, flaw, mark, pockmark, scar — more at BLEMISH

im·pe·ri·al \im-ˈpir-ē-əl\ *adj* **1** : of, relating to, or befitting an empire or an emperor; *also* : of or relating to the United Kingdom or to the Commonwealth or British Empire **2** : ROYAL, SOVEREIGN; *also* : REGAL, IMPERIOUS **3** ♦ : of unusual size or excellence

♦ august, baronial, gallant, glorious, grand, grandiose, heroic, imposing, magnificent, majestic, monumental, noble, proud, regal, royal, splendid, stately — more at GRAND

im·pe·ri·al·ism \im-ˈpir-ē-ə-ˌli-zəm\ *n* : the policy of seeking to extend the power, dominion, or territories of a nation — **im·pe·ri·al·ist** \-list\ *n or adj* — **im·pe·ri·al·is·tic** \-ˌpir-ē-ə-ˈlis-tik\ *adj* — **im·pe·ri·al·is·ti·cal·ly** \-ti-k(ə-)lē\ *adv*

im·per·il \im-ˈper-əl\ *vb* **-iled** *or* **-illed; -il·ing** *or* **-il·ling** ♦ : to bring into peril : ENDANGER

♦ adventure, compromise, gamble with, hazard, jeopardize, menace, risk, venture

im·pe·ri·ous \im-ˈpir-ē-əs\ *adj* **1** : befitting or characteristic of one of eminent rank or attainments : COMMANDING, LORDLY **2** ♦ : marked by arrogant assurance : DOMINEERING **3** ♦ : intensely compelling : IMPERATIVE, URGENT — **im·pe·ri·ous·ly** *adv*

♦ [2] authoritarian, autocratic, bossy, despotic, dictatorial, domineering, masterful, overbearing, peremptory, tyrannical, tyrannous — more at BOSSY ♦ [2] arbitrary, dictatorial, high-handed, peremptory, willful — more at ARBITRARY ♦ [3] acute, critical, dire, imperative, instant, pressing, urgent — more at ACUTE

im·per·ish·able \(ˌ)im-ˈper-i-shə-bəl\ *adj* : not perishable or subject to decay

im·per·ma·nent \(ˌ)im-ˈpər-mə-nənt\ *adj* ♦ : not permanent — **im·per·ma·nent·ly** *adv*

♦ interim, provisional, short-term, temporary — more at TEMPORARY ♦ ephemeral, evanescent, flash, fleeting, momentary, short-lived, transient — more at MOMENTARY

im·per·me·able \(ˌ)im-ˈpər-mē-ə-bəl\ *adj* : not permitting passage (as of a fluid) through its substance

im·per·mis·si·ble \ˌim-pər-ˈmi-sə-bəl\ *adj* ♦ : not permissible ⟨~ by law⟩

♦ forbidden, taboo; *also* intolerable, unacceptable, unbearable, unendurable; illegal, illegitimate, illicit, improper, inappropriate, unauthorized, unlawful, unlicensed, unmentionable, unseemly, unsuitable; objectionable; disallowed, disapproved, discouraged; refused, rejected, revoked, unsanctioned, vetoed; repressed, suppressed; precluded, prevented, stopped; excluded, ruled out, shut out; blocked, hindered, impeded, obstructed *Ant* allowable, permissible, permissive, sufferable

im·per·son·al \(ˌ)im-ˈpər-sə-nəl\ *adj* **1** : not referring to any particular person or thing **2** : not involving human emotions — **im·per·son·al·i·ty** \-ˌpər-sə-ˈna-lə-tē\ *n* — **im·per·son·al·ly** *adv*

im·per·son·ate \im-ˈpər-sə-ˌnāt\ *vb* **-at·ed; -at·ing ♦** : to assume or act the character of — **im·per·son·a·tion** \-ˌpər-sə-ˈnā-shən\ *n*

♦ act, perform, play, portray — more at ACT **♦** masquerade, play, pose; *also* ape, copy, imitate, mime, mimic, mock, parody, travesty; act, perform, portray

im·per·son·a·tor \-ˈpər-sə-ˌnā-tər\ *n* **♦** : one that impersonates; *esp* : an entertainer who impersonates an individual, a type of person, an animal, or an inanimate object

♦ imitator, impressionist, mimic — more at MIMIC

im·per·ti·nence \(ˌ)im-ˈpərt-ᵊn-əns\ *n* **♦** : the quality or state of being impertinent; *also* : an instance of impertinence

♦ brazenness, discourtesy, disrespect, impudence, incivility, insolence, rudeness — more at DISCOURTESY

im·per·ti·nent \(ˌ)im-ˈpərt-ᵊn-ənt\ *adj* **1** : IRRELEVANT **2 ♦** : not restrained within due or proper bounds ⟨an ∼ reply⟩ — **im·per·ti·nent·ly** *adv*

♦ arch, bold, brash, brazen, cheeky, cocky, fresh, impudent, insolent, nervy, sassy, saucy — more at NERVY **♦** discourteous, ill-bred, ill-mannered, impolite, inconsiderate, rude, thoughtless, uncivil, ungracious, unmannerly — more at IMPOLITE

im·per·turb·able \ˌim-pər-ˈtər-bə-bəl\ *adj* **♦** : marked by extreme calm, impassivity, and steadiness

♦ nerveless, unflappable, unshakable — more at UNFLAPPABLE

im·per·vi·ous \(ˌ)im-ˈpər-vē-əs\ *adj* **1 ♦** : incapable of being penetrated (as by moisture) **2** : not capable of being affected or disturbed ⟨∼ to criticism⟩

♦ impenetrable, tight — more at TIGHT

im·pe·ti·go \ˌim-pə-ˈtē-gō, -ˈtī-\ *n* : a contagious skin disease characterized by vesicles, pustules, and yellowish crusts

im·pet·u·ous \im-ˈpe-chə-wəs\ *adj* **1** : marked by impulsive vehemence ⟨∼ temper⟩ **2** : marked by force and violence ⟨with ∼ speed⟩ — **im·pet·u·os·i·ty** \(ˌ)im-ˌpe-chə-ˈwä-sə-tē\ *n* — **im·pet·u·ous·ly** *adv*

im·pe·tus \ˈim-pə-təs\ *n* [L, assault, impetus, fr. *impetere* to attack, fr. *petere* to go to, seek] **1 ♦** : a driving force : IMPULSE; *also* : INCENTIVE **2** : MOMENTUM

♦ boost, encouragement, goad, impulse, incentive, incitement, instigation, momentum, motivation, provocation, spur, stimulus, yeast — more at IMPULSE

im·pi·e·ty \(ˌ)im-ˈpī-ə-tē\ *n, pl* **-ties** **1** : the quality or state of being impious **2 ♦** : an impious act

♦ blasphemy, defilement, desecration, irreverence, sacrilege — more at BLASPHEMY

im·pinge \im-ˈpinj\ *vb* **im·pinged; im·ping·ing** **1** : to strike or dash esp. with a sharp collision **2** : ENCROACH, INFRINGE — **im·pinge·ment** *n*

im·pi·ous \ˈim-pē-əs, (ˌ)im-ˈpī-\ *adj* : not pious : IRREVERENT, PROFANE

imp·ish \ˈim-pish\ *adj* **♦** : of, relating to, or befitting an imp; *esp* : MISCHIEVOUS — **imp·ish·ly** *adv*

♦ devilish, knavish, mischievous, rascally, roguish, sly, waggish, wicked — more at MISCHIEVOUS

imp·ish·ness *n* **♦** : the quality or state of being impish

♦ friskiness, mischief, mischievousness, playfulness — more at PLAYFULNESS

im·pla·ca·ble \(ˌ)im-ˈpla-kə-bəl, -ˈplā-\ *adj* **♦** : not capable of being appeased, pacified, mitigated, or changed ⟨an ∼ enemy⟩ — **im·pla·ca·bil·i·ty** \-ˌpla-kə-ˈbi-lə-tē, -ˌplā-\ *n* — **im·pla·ca·bly** \-ˈpla-kə-blē\ *adv*

♦ adamant, hard, immovable, inflexible, pat, rigid, unbending, uncompromising, unrelenting, unyielding

im·plant \im-ˈplant\ *vb* **1 ♦** : to set firmly or deeply **2** : to fix in the mind or spirit **3** : to insert in living tissue (as for growth or absorption) — **im·plant** \ˈim-ˌplant\ *n* — **im·plan·ta·tion** \ˌim-ˌplan-ˈtā-shən\ *n*

♦ embed, entrench, fix, ingrain, lodge, root — more at ENTRENCH

im·plau·si·ble \(ˌ)im-ˈplȯ-zə-bəl\ *adj* **♦** : not plausible — **im·plau·si·bil·i·ty** \-ˌplȯ-zə-ˈbi-lə-tē\ *n* — **im·plau·si·bly** \-ˈplȯ-zə-blē\ *adv*

♦ fantastic, inconceivable, incredible, unbelievable, unconvincing, unimaginable, unthinkable — more at INCREDIBLE

¹im·ple·ment \ˈim-plə-mənt\ *n* [ME, fr. AF, fr. ML *implementum* item making a full complement, appurtenance, tool, fr. LL, act of filling up, fr. L *implēre* to fill up] **♦** : a device used in the performance of a task : TOOL, UTENSIL

♦ device, instrument, tool, utensil; *also* apparatus, appliance, mechanism; contraption, contrivance, gadget, gizmo, jigger

²im·ple·ment \-ˌment\ *vb* **1 ♦** : to put into execution or bring to completion **2** : to provide implements for

♦ administer, apply, enforce, execute — more at ENFORCE

im·ple·men·ta·tion \ˌim-plə-mən-ˈtā-shən\ *n* **♦** : the act of implementing or the state of being implemented

♦ accomplishment, achievement, commission, discharge, enactment, execution, fulfillment, performance, perpetration — more at COMMISSION

im·pli·cate \ˈim-plə-ˌkāt\ *vb* **-cat·ed; -cat·ing** **1** : IMPLY **2** : INVOLVE — **im·pli·ca·tion** \ˌim-plə-ˈkā-shən\ *n*

im·plic·it \im-ˈpli-sət\ *adj* **1 ♦** : understood though not directly stated or expressed : IMPLIED; *also* : POTENTIAL **2** : COMPLETE, UNQUESTIONING, ABSOLUTE ⟨∼ faith⟩ — **im·plic·it·ly** *adv*

♦ potential, tacit, unexpressed, unspoken, unvoiced, wordless; *also* inferred; unannounced, undeclared, unsaid, untold; intimated, suggested *Ant* explicit, express, expressed, spoken, stated

im·plode \im-ˈplōd\ *vb* **im·plod·ed; im·plod·ing** **1 ♦** : to burst or collapse inward **2** : SELF-DESTRUCT — **im·plo·sion** \-ˈplō-zhən\ *n* — **im·plo·sive** \-siv\ *adj*

♦ buckle, cave in, collapse, crumple, give, go, yield — more at COLLAPSE

im·plore \im-ˈplȯr\ *vb* **im·plored; im·plor·ing ♦** : to call upon in supplication : BESEECH, ENTREAT

♦ appeal, beg, beseech, entreat, importune, petition, plead, pray, solicit, supplicate — more at BEG

im·ply \im-ˈplī\ *vb* **im·plied; im·ply·ing** **1** : to involve or indicate by inference, association, or necessary consequence rather than by direct statement ⟨war *implies* fighting⟩ **2 ♦** : to express indirectly : hint at

♦ allude, hint, indicate, infer, insinuate, intimate, suggest — more at HINT

im·po·lite \ˌim-pə-ˈlīt\ *adj* **♦** : not polite : RUDE, DISCOURTEOUS

♦ discourteous, ill-bred, ill-mannered, impertinent, inconsiderate, rude, thoughtless, uncivil, ungracious, unmannerly; *also* audacious, bold, bold-faced, brash, brassy, disrespectful, impudent, insolent, saucy, shameless; boorish, churlish, clownish, loutish, uncouth, vulgar; undiplomatic, unsportsmanlike; abrupt, blunt, brusque, crusty, curt, gruff, sharp, snippy; antisocial, crabbed, cross, disagreeable, grumpy, sullen, surly; improper, inappropriate, incorrect, indecent, indecorous, unseemly; arrogant, conceited, presumptuous, pretentious *Ant* civil, considerate, courteous, genteel, gracious, mannerly, polite, thoughtful, well-bred

im·pol·i·tic \(ˌ)im-ˈpä-lə-ˌtik\ *adj* : not politic : UNWISE

im·pon·der·a·ble \(ˌ)im-ˈpän-də-rə-bəl\ *adj* : incapable of being weighed or evaluated with exactness — **imponderable** *n*

¹im·port \im-ˈpōrt\ vb 1 : to bear or convey as meaning or portent : MEAN 2 : to bring (as merchandise) into a place or country from a foreign or external source — im·port·er n

²im·port \ˈim-ˌpōrt\ n 1 : IMPORTANCE, SIGNIFICANCE 2 ♦ : meaning conveyed, professed, or implied : SIGNIFICATION 3 : something (as merchandise) brought in from another country

♦ denotation, drift, intent, meaning, purport, sense, significance, signification — more at MEANING

im·por·tance \im-ˈpȯrt-ᵊns\ n : the quality or state of being important : MOMENT, SIGNIFICANCE

im·por·tant \im-ˈpȯrt-ᵊnt\ adj 1 ♦ : marked by importance : SIGNIFICANT 2 ♦ : giving an impression of self-importance — im·por·tant·ly adv

♦ [1] big, consequential, eventful, major, material, meaningful, momentous, significant, substantial, weighty; also decisive, fatal, fateful, strategic; earnest, grave, serious, sincere; distinctive, exceptional, impressive, outstanding, prominent, remarkable; valuable, worthwhile, worthy; distinguished, eminent, great, illustrious, preeminent, prestigious; famous, notorious, renowned; all-important, critical, crucial Ant insignificant, little, minor, slight, small, trivial, unimportant

♦ [1] influential, mighty, potent, powerful, significant, strong; also senior, top; able, capable, competent, effective, efficient; authoritarian, autocratic, despotic, dictatorial, magisterial, tyrannical; distinguished, dominant, eminent, famous, great, illustrious, notorious, preeminent, prestigious, renowned; dynamic, energetic, forceful, robust, sturdy, tough, vigorous Ant impotent, insignificant, little, powerless, unimportant, weak

♦ [2] complacent, conceited, egotistic, overweening, pompous, prideful, proud, self-important, self-satisfied, smug, stuck-up, vain — more at CONCEITED

im·por·ta·tion \ˌim-ˌpȯr-ˈtā-shən, -pər-\ n 1 : the act or practice of importing 2 : something imported

im·por·tu·nate \im-ˈpȯr-chə-nət\ adj 1 : troublesomely urgent or persistent 2 : BURDENSOME, TROUBLESOME

im·por·tune \ˌim-pər-ˈtün, -ˈtyün; im-ˈpȯr-chən\ vb -tuned; -tun·ing ♦ : to urge or beg with troublesome persistence — im·por·tu·ni·ty \-pər-ˈtü-nə-tē, -ˈtyü-\ n

♦ appeal, beg, beseech, entreat, implore, petition, plead, pray, solicit, supplicate — more at BEG

im·pose \im-ˈpōz\ vb im·posed; im·pos·ing 1 ♦ : to establish or apply by authority ⟨~ a tax⟩; also : to establish by force ⟨imposed a government⟩ 2 : OBTRUDE ⟨imposed herself on others⟩ 3 : to take unwarranted advantage of something ⟨~ on her good nature⟩

♦ assess, charge, exact, fine, lay, levy, put; also dock, mulct, penalize, tax; extort, shake down, wrest, wring; bleed, fleece, gouge, milk, skin, squeeze; coerce, compel, force; inflict, wreak; set Ant remit

im·pos·ing adj ♦ : impressive because of size, bearing, dignity, or grandeur — im·pos·ing·ly adv

♦ august, baronial, gallant, glorious, grand, grandiose, heroic, magnificent, majestic, monumental, noble, proud, regal, royal, splendid, stately — more at GRAND

im·po·si·tion \ˌim-pə-ˈzi-shən\ n : something imposed: as a : an amount levied b : an excessive or uncalled-for requirement or burden

im·pos·si·ble \(ˌ)im-ˈpä-sə-bəl\ adj 1 : incapable of being or of occurring 2 ♦ : enormously difficult : felt to be incapable of being done, attained, or fulfilled 3 : extremely undesirable : UNACCEPTABLE — im·pos·si·bil·i·ty \-ˌpä-sə-ˈbi-lə-tē\ n — im·pos·si·bly \-ˈpä-sə-blē\ adv

♦ hopeless, unattainable, unsolvable, unworkable; also impracticable, impractical; doubtful, dubious, improbable, unlikely; implausible, inconceivable, incredible, unbelievable, unthinkable; futile, useless; absurd, fantastic, outlandish, preposterous, ridiculous Ant achievable, attainable, doable, feasible, possible, realizable, workable

¹im·post \ˈim-ˌpōst\ n ♦ : something imposed or levied : TAX, DUTY

♦ assessment, duty, levy, tax — more at TAX

²impost n : a block, capital, or molding from which an arch springs

im·pos·tor or im·pos·ter \im-ˈpäs-tər\ n : one that assumes an identity or title not one's own in order to deceive

im·pos·ture \im-ˈpäs-chər\ n : DECEPTION; esp : fraudulent impersonation

im·po·tence \-təns\ n ♦ : the quality or state of being impotent

♦ inability, inadequacy, incapability, incompetence, ineptitude — more at INABILITY

im·po·tent \ˈim-pə-tənt\ adj 1 ♦ : lacking in power or strength : deficient in capacity 2 a : unable to copulate b ♦ : failing to produce or incapable of producing offspring : STERILE — im·po·ten·cy \-tən-sē\ n — im·po·tent·ly adv

♦ [1] helpless, powerless, weak — more at POWERLESS
♦ [2b] barren, infertile, sterile — more at STERILE

im·pound \im-ˈpaund\ vb 1 : CONFINE, ENCLOSE ⟨~ stray dogs⟩ 2 : to seize and hold in legal custody 3 : to collect in a reservoir ⟨~ water⟩ — im·pound·ment n

im·pov·er·ish \im-ˈpä-və-rish\ vb : to make poor; also : to deprive of strength, richness, or fertility

impoverished adj 1 : represented by few species or individuals ⟨~ flora and fauna⟩ 2 : deprived of strength, richness, or fertility

im·pov·er·ish·ment n ♦ : the act of impoverishing or the state of being impoverished

♦ beggary, destitution, impecuniousness, indigence, need, pauperism, penury, poverty, want — more at POVERTY

im·prac·ti·ca·ble \(ˌ)im-ˈprak-ti-kə-bəl\ adj : not practicable : incapable of being put into practice or use ⟨an ~ plan⟩

im·prac·ti·cal \(ˌ)im-ˈprak-ti-kəl\ adj 1 : not practical 2 ♦ : incapable of being done by the means available : IMPRACTICABLE

♦ inoperable, unusable, unworkable, useless; also unsuitable; inaccessible, unattainable, unavailable, unobtainable, unreachable; dead, dormant, fallow, free, idle, inactive, inert, inoperative, latent; arrested, interrupted; unrealistic Ant practicable, practical, usable, useful, workable

im·pre·cate \ˈim-pri-ˌkāt\ vb -cat·ed; -cat·ing : CURSE

im·pre·ca·tion \ˌim-pri-ˈkā-shən\ n ♦ : a prayer or invocation for harm or injury to come upon one; also : the act of imprecating

♦ anathema, curse, execration, malediction — more at CURSE

im·pre·cise \ˌim-pri-ˈsīs\ adj ♦ : not precise — im·pre·cise·ly adv — im·pre·cise·ness n — im·pre·ci·sion \-ˈsi-zhən\ n

♦ inaccurate, inexact, loose — more at INEXACT

im·preg·na·ble \im-ˈpreg-nə-bəl\ adj 1 ♦ : incapable of being taken by assault : UNCONQUERABLE 2 : not liable to doubt, attack, or question — im·preg·na·bil·i·ty \(ˌ)im-ˌpreg-nə-ˈbi-lə-tē\ n

♦ indomitable, insurmountable, invincible, invulnerable, unbeatable, unconquerable — more at INVINCIBLE

im·preg·nate \im-ˈpreg-ˌnāt\ vb -nat·ed; -nat·ing 1 : to fertilize or make pregnant 2 ♦ : to cause to be filled, permeated, or saturated — im·preg·na·tion \ˌim-ˌpreg-ˈnā-shən\ n

♦ drench, drown, saturate, soak, sop, souse, steep — more at SOAK

im·pre·sa·rio \ˌim-prə-ˈsär-ē-ˌō\ n, pl -ri·os [It, fr. impresa undertaking, fr. imprendere to undertake] 1 : the manager or conductor of an opera or concert company 2 : one who puts on an entertainment 3 : MANAGER, PRODUCER

¹im·press \im-ˈpres\ vb 1 : to apply with or produce (as a mark) by pressure : IMPRINT 2 : to press, stamp, or print in or upon 3 ♦ : to imprint a vivid impression of (as on

the memory) **4 ♦** : to affect esp. forcibly or deeply — **im·press·ible** *adj*

♦ [3] engrave, etch, imprint, ingrain, inscribe — more at ENGRAVE **♦** [4] affect, impact, influence, move, strike, sway, tell, touch — more at AFFECT

²**im·press** \'im-ˌpres\ *n* **1** : a characteristic or distinctive mark **2** : IMPRESSION, EFFECT **3** : IMPRESSION 2 **4** : an image of something formed by or as if by pressure; *esp* : SEAL **5** : a product of pressure or influence

³**im·press** \im-'pres\ *vb* **1** : to force into naval service **2** : to get the aid or services of by forcible argument or persuasion — **im·press·ment** *n*

im·pres·sion \im-'pre-shən\ *n* **1** : a characteristic trait or feature resulting from influence : IMPRESS **2 ♦** : a stamp, form, or figure made by impressing : IMPRINT **3** : an esp. marked influence or effect on feeling, sense, or mind **4** : a single print or copy (as from type or from an engraved plate or book) **5** : all the copies of a publication (as a book) printed for one issue : PRINTING **6 ♦** : a usu. vague notion or remembrance **7** : an imitation in caricature of a noted personality as a form of entertainment

♦ [2] impress, imprint, print, stamp — more at PRINT **♦** [6] concept, idea, image, notion, picture, thought — more at IDEA

im·pres·sion·able \im-'pre-shə-nə-bəl\ *adj* : capable of being easily impressed : easily molded or influenced

im·pres·sion·ism \im-'pre-shə-ˌni-zəm\ *n, often cap* : a theory or practice in modern art of depicting the natural appearances of objects by dabs or strokes of primary unmixed colors in order to simulate actual reflected light — **im·pres·sion·is·tic** \-ˌpre-shə-'nis-tik\ *adj*

im·pres·sion·ist \im-'pre-shə-nist\ *n* **1** *often cap* : a painter who practices impressionism **2 ♦** : an entertainer who does impressions

♦ imitator, impersonator, mimic — more at MIMIC

im·pres·sive \im-'pre-siv\ *adj* **♦** : making or tending to make a marked impression ⟨an ∼ speech⟩ — **im·pres·sive·ly** *adv* — **im·pres·sive·ness** *n*

♦ affecting, emotional, moving, poignant, stirring, touching — more at MOVING

im·pri·ma·tur \ˌim-prə-'mä-ˌtu̇r\ *n* [NL, let it be printed] **1** : a license to print or publish; *also* : official approval of a publication by a censor **2 ♦** : explicit or official approval, permission, or ratification

♦ approbation, approval, blessing, favor (*or* favour), OK — more at APPROVAL

¹**im·print** \im-'print, 'im-ˌprint\ *vb* **1** : to stamp or mark by or as if by pressure : IMPRESS **2 ♦** : to fix firmly (as on the memory)

♦ engrave, etch, impress, ingrain, inscribe — more at ENGRAVE

²**im·print** \'im-ˌprint\ *n* **1 ♦** : something imprinted or printed; *also* : a mark or depression made by pressure **2** : a publisher's name printed at the foot of a title page **3** : an indelible distinguishing effect or influence

♦ trace, track, trail — more at TRACK **♦** impress, impression, print, stamp — more at PRINT

im·pris·on \im-'priz-ᵊn\ *vb* **♦** : to put in or as if in prison : CONFINE

♦ commit, confine, immure, jail; *also* constrain, limit, restrain, restrict, shut; apprehend, arrest, capture, catch, detain; impress, shanghai; hold, keep; enslave, subjugate *Ant* discharge, free, liberate, release

im·pris·on·ment *n* **♦** : the act of imprisoning or the state of being imprisoned

♦ captivity, confinement, incarceration, internment — more at INTERNMENT

im·prob·a·ble \(ˌ)im-'prä-bə-bəl\ *adj* **♦** : unlikely to be true or to occur — **im·prob·a·bil·i·ty** \-ˌprä-bə-'bi-lə-tē\ *n* — **im·prob·a·bly** \-'prä-bə-blē\ *adv*

♦ doubtful, dubious, flimsy, questionable, unlikely; *also* implausible, impossible, inconceivable, incredible, last, unbelievable, unthinkable; absurd, outlandish, preposterous, ridiculous; outside, remote, slight *Ant* likely, probable

im·promp·tu \im-'prämp-tü, -ˌtyü\ *adj* [F, fr. *impromptu* extemporaneously, fr. L *in promptu* in readiness] **1** : made or done on or as if on the spur of the moment **2 ♦** : composed or uttered without previous preparation : EXTEMPORANEOUS, UNREHEARSED — **impromptu** *adv or n*

♦ ad-lib, extemporaneous, offhand, snap, unplanned, unpremeditated, unprepared, unrehearsed — more at EXTEMPORANEOUS

im·prop·er \(ˌ)im-'prä-pər\ *adj* **1 ♦** : not proper, fit, or suitable **2** : INCORRECT, INACCURATE **3** : not in accord with propriety, modesty, or good manners

♦ inappropriate, inapt, infelicitous, unbecoming, unfit, unseemly, unsuitable, wrong — more at INAPPROPRIATE

improper fraction *n* : a fraction whose numerator is equal to or larger than the denominator

im·prop·er·ly *adv* **♦** : in an improper manner

♦ amiss, erroneously, faultily, inaptly, incorrectly, mistakenly, wrongly

im·pro·pri·e·ty \ˌim-prə-'prī-ə-tē\ *n, pl* -ties **1 ♦** : an improper act or remark; *esp* : an unacceptable use of a word or of language **2 ♦** : the quality or state of being improper

♦ [1] familiarity, gaffe, indiscretion; *also* blunder, error, flub, fumble, goof, lapse, miscue, misstep, mistake, slip, slipup, stumble; discourtesy, incivility, offense; boner, howler; foul-up, muff; misapprehension, miscalculation, misconception, misjudgment, misstatement, misunderstanding *Ant* amenity, civility, courtesy, formality, gesture **♦** [2] incorrectness, indecency; *also* coarseness; imprudence, indiscretion *Ant* appropriateness, correctness, decency, fitness, propriety, rightness, suitability

im·prov \'im-ˌpräv\ *adj* : of, relating to, or being an improvised comedy routine — **improv** *n*

im·prove \im-'prüv\ *vb* **im·proved; im·prov·ing 1 ♦** : to enhance or increase in value or quality **2** : to grow or become better ⟨your work is *improving*⟩ **3** : to make good use of ⟨∼ the time by reading⟩ — **im·prov·able** \-'prü-və-bəl\ *adj*

♦ ameliorate, amend, better, enhance, enrich, perfect, refine; *also* correct, emend, rectify, reform, remedy; help; edit, revise; upgrade; fortify, intensify, strengthen; retouch, touch up *Ant* worsen

im·prove·ment \im-'prüv-mənt\ *n* **1** : the act or process of improving **2** : increased value or excellence of something **3 ♦** : something that adds to the value or appearance of a thing

♦ advance, advancement, breakthrough, enhancement, refinement — more at ADVANCE

im·prov·i·dent \(ˌ)im-'prä-və-dənt\ *adj* : not providing for the future — **im·prov·i·dence** \-dəns\ *n*

im·pro·vise \'im-prə-ˌvīz\ *vb* -vised; -vis·ing [F *improviser*, fr. It *improvvisare*, fr. *improvviso* sudden, fr. L *improvisus*, lit., unforeseen] **1** : to compose, recite, play, or sing on the spur of the moment : EXTEMPORIZE ⟨∼ on the piano⟩ **2** : to make, invent, or arrange offhand ⟨∼ a sail out of shirts⟩ — **im·pro·vi·sa·tion** \im-ˌprä-və-'zā-shən, ˌim-prə-və-\ *n* — **im·pro·vis·er** *or* **im·pro·vi·sor** \ˌim-prə-'vī-zər, 'im-prə-ˌvī-\ *n*

im·pru·dent \(ˌ)im-'prüd-ᵊnt\ *adj* **♦** : not prudent : lacking discretion, wisdom, or good judgment — **im·pru·dence** \-ᵊns\ *n*

♦ ill-advised, indiscreet, tactless, unwise — more at INDISCREET

im·pu·dence \'im-pyu̇-dəns\ *n* **♦** : the quality or state of being impudent; *also* : an impudent remark or act

♦ brazenness, discourtesy, disrespect, impertinence, incivility, insolence, rudeness — more at DISCOURTESY

im·pu·dent \-dənt\ *adj* ✦ : marked by contemptuous boldness or disregard of others — **im·pu·dent·ly** *adv*

✦ arch, bold, brash, brazen, cheeky, cocky, fresh, impertinent, insolent, nervy, sassy, saucy — more at NERVY

im·pugn \im-'pyün\ *vb* [ME, to assail, fr. AF *empugner*, fr. L *inpugnare*, fr. *pugnare* to fight] : to attack by words or arguments : oppose or attack as false or as lacking integrity ⟨~ed his rival's character⟩

im·pulse \'im-ˌpəls\ *n* 1 : a force that starts a body into motion; *also* : the motion produced by such a force 2 ✦ : an arousing of the mind and spirit to some usu. unpremeditated action 3 : NERVE IMPULSE

✦ boost, encouragement, goad, impetus, incentive, incitement, instigation, momentum, motivation, provocation, spur, stimulus, yeast; *also* inducement, invitation; cause, consideration, motive, reason

im·pul·sion \im-'pəl-shən\ *n* 1 : the act of impelling : the state of being impelled 2 : a force that impels 3 : IMPULSE 2; *also* : COMPULSION 3

im·pul·sive \im-'pəl-siv\ *adj* 1 : having the power of or actually driving or impelling 2 ✦ : acting or prone to act on impulse ⟨~ buying⟩ — **im·pul·sive·ly** *adv* — **im·pul·sive·ness** *n*

✦ capricious, whimsical — more at WHIMSICAL

im·pu·ni·ty \im-'pyü-nə-tē\ *n* [MF or L; MF *impunité*, fr. L *impunitas*, fr. *impune* without punishment, fr. *poena* penalty, punishment] : exemption from punishment, harm, or loss

im·pure \(ˌ)im-'pyu̇r\ *adj* 1 : not pure : UNCHASTE, OBSCENE 2 : DIRTY, FOUL 3 ✦ : mixed or impregnated with an extraneous and usu. unwanted substance : ADULTERATED

✦ dilute, polluted; *also* befouled, corrupted, debased, defiled, dirtied, fouled, soiled, spoiled, sullied; blended, commingled, incorporated, intermingled, intermixed, merged, mingled, mixed; coalesced, combined, compounded; cheapened, doctored *Ant* pure, unadulterated, unalloyed, uncontaminated, undiluted, unpolluted, untainted

im·pu·ri·ty \-'pyu̇r-ə-tē\ *n* ✦ : something that is impure or makes something else impure; *also* : the quality or state of being impure

✦ adulterant, contaminant, defilement, pollutant; *also* blot, blotch, spot, stain, taint; dirt, filth, grime; blemish, defect, disfigurement, fault, flaw; abnormality, imperfection, irregularity

im·pute \im-'pyüt\ *vb* **im·put·ed**; **im·put·ing** 1 : to lay the responsibility or blame for often falsely or unjustly 2 ✦ : to credit to a person or a cause : ATTRIBUTE — **im·put·able** \-'pyü-tə-bəl\ *adj* — **im·pu·ta·tion** \ˌim-pyu̇-'tā-shən\ *n*

✦ accredit, ascribe, attribute, credit — more at CREDIT

¹in \'in\ *prep* 1 — used to indicate physical surroundings ⟨swim ~ the lake⟩ 2 : INTO 1 ⟨ran ~ the house⟩ 3 : DURING ⟨~ the summer⟩ 4 : WITH ⟨written ~ pencil⟩ 5 — used to indicate one's situation or state of being ⟨~ luck⟩ ⟨~ love⟩ 6 — used to indicate manner or purpose ⟨~ a hurry⟩ ⟨said ~ reply⟩ 7 : INTO 2 ⟨broke ~ pieces⟩

²in *adv* 1 : to or toward the inside ⟨come ~⟩; *also* : to or toward some destination or place ⟨flew ~ from the South⟩ 2 ✦ : at close quarters : NEAR ⟨the enemy closed ~⟩ 3 : into the midst of something ⟨mix ~ the flour⟩ 4 : to or at its proper place ⟨fit a piece ~⟩ 5 : WITHIN ⟨locked ~⟩ 6 : in vogue or season 7 : in one's presence, possession, or control ⟨the results are ~⟩

✦ around, by, close, hard, near, nearby, nigh — more at NEAR

³in *adj* 1 : located inside or within 2 : that is in position, operation, or power ⟨the ~ party⟩ 3 : directed inward : INCOMING ⟨the ~ train⟩ 4 ✦ : keenly aware of and responsive to what is new and fashionable ⟨the ~ crowd⟩; *also* : extremely fashionable ⟨the ~ thing to do⟩

✦ à la mode, chic, fashionable, modish, popular, sharp, smart, snappy, stylish — more at STYLISH

⁴in *n* 1 : one who is in office or power or on the inside 2 : INFLUENCE, PULL ⟨he has an ~ with the owner⟩

⁵in *abbr* 1 inch 2 inlet

In *symbol* indium

IN *abbr* Indiana

in- \(ˌ)in\ *prefix* : not : absence of : NON-, UN-

in·abil·i·ty \ˌi-nə-'bi-lə-tē\ *n* ✦ : the quality or state of being unable

✦ impotence, inadequacy, incapability, incompetence, ineptitude; *also* inaptitude; ineffectiveness, inefficiency *Ant* ability, adequacy, capability, capacity, competence, potency

in ab·sen·tia \ˌin-ab-'sen-chə, -chē-ə\ *adv* : in one's absence

in·ac·ces·si·ble \ˌi-nik-'se-sə-bəl, (ˌ)i-ˌnak-\ *adj* ✦ : not accessible — **in·ac·ces·si·bil·i·ty** \-ˌse-sə-'bi-lə-tē\ *n*

✦ inconvenient, unapproachable, unattainable, unavailable, unobtainable, unreachable, untouchable; *also* distant, far, faraway, far-off, remote, removed; apart, hidden, isolated, out-of-the-way, secluded *Ant* accessible, approachable, attainable, convenient, obtainable, reachable

in·ac·cu·ra·cy \(ˌ)i-'na-kyə-rə-sē, -k(ə-)rə-sē\ *n, pl* **-cies** 1 : the quality or state of being inaccurate 2 : something (as a statement or act) that is inaccurate

in·ac·cu·rate \-'a-kyə-rət, -k(ə-)rət\ *adj* ✦ : not accurate

✦ erroneous, false, incorrect, inexact, invalid, off, unsound, untrue, wrong — more at FALSE

in·ac·tion \(ˌ)i-'nak-shən\ *n* ✦ : not occupied or employed

✦ dormancy, idleness, inactivity, inertness, quiescence; *also* indolence, languor, lassitude, laziness, lethargy, listlessness, sleepiness, sloth, sluggishness *Ant* action, activeness, activity

in·ac·ti·vate \(ˌ)i-'nak-tə-ˌvāt\ *vb* : to make inactive — **in·ac·ti·va·tion** \(ˌ)i-ˌnak-tə-'vā-shən\ *n*

in·ac·tive \(ˌ)i-'nak-tiv\ *adj* ✦ : not active, energetic, or in use

✦ dull, inert, lethargic, quiescent, sleepy, sluggish, torpid; *also* apathetic, indolent, languorous, lazy, listless, slothful; dormant, inanimate, motionless, sedentary, static, still; dead; dopey, drugged *Ant* active ✦ dead, dormant, fallow, free, idle, inert, inoperative, latent, off, vacant; *also* arrested, interrupted; asleep, lifeless, quiescent, sleepy; inoperable, unusable, unworkable, useless; dead, dull, slow *Ant* active, alive, busy, employed, functioning, on, operating, operative, running, working

in·ac·tiv·i·ty \-ˌnak-'ti-və-tē\ *n* ✦ : the quality or state of being inactive

✦ dormancy, idleness, inaction, inertness, quiescence — more at INACTION

in·ad·e·qua·cy \(ˌ)i-'na-di-kwə-sē\ *n* ✦ : the quality or state of being inadequate or insufficient

✦ dearth, deficiency, deficit, failure, famine, insufficiency, lack, paucity, poverty, scantiness, scarcity, shortage, want — more at DEFICIENCY ✦ impotence, inability, incapability, incompetence, ineptitude — more at INABILITY

in·ad·e·quate \-kwət\ *adj* ✦ : not adequate : INSUFFICIENT — **in·ad·e·quate·ly** *adv* — **in·ad·e·quate·ness** *n*

✦ deficient, insufficient, scarce, short, shy, wanting — more at SHORT

List of self-explanatory words with the prefix in-

in·ad·ver·tent \ˌi-nəd-ˈvərt-ᵊnt\ *adj* **1** : HEEDLESS, INATTENTIVE **2** : not intentional : UNINTENTIONAL — **in·ad·ver·tence** \-ᵊns\ *n* — **in·ad·ver·ten·cy** \-ᵊn-sē\ *n* — **in·ad·ver·tent·ly** *adv*

in·alien·able \(ˌ)i-ˈnāl-yə-nə-bəl, -ˈnā-lē-ə-\ *adj* : incapable of being alienated, surrendered, or transferred ⟨∼ rights⟩ — **in·alien·abil·i·ty** \(ˌ)i-ˌnāl-yə-nə-ˈbi-lə-tē, -ˌnā-lē-ə-\ *n* — **in·alien·ably** *adv*

in·amo·ra·ta \i-ˌnä-mə-ˈrä-tə\ *n* : a woman with whom one is in love

inane \i-ˈnān\ *adj* **inan·er; -est** **1** : EMPTY, INSUBSTANTIAL **2** : lacking significance, meaning, or point

in·an·i·mate \(ˌ)i-ˈna-nə-mət\ *adj* : not animate or animated : lacking the qualities of living things — **in·an·i·mate·ly** *adv* — **in·an·i·mate·ness** *n*

inan·i·ty \i-ˈna-nə-tē\ *n* **1** ♦ : the quality or state of being inane **2** ♦ : something that is inane

♦ [1, 2] absurdity, asininity, balminess, craziness, daftness, fatuity, folly, foolishness, insanity, lunacy, madness, silliness, simplicity, zaniness ♦ [2] absurdity, fatuity, folly, foolery, foolishness, idiocy, madness, stupidity

in·ap·pre·cia·ble \ˌi-nə-ˈprē-shə-bəl\ *adj* ♦ : too small to be perceived — **in·ap·pre·cia·bly** \-blē\ *adv*

♦ impalpable, imperceptible, indistinguishable — more at IMPERCEPTIBLE

in·ap·pro·pri·ate \ˌi-nə-ˈprō-prē-ˌət\ *adj* : not in good taste or suitable for a particular occasion or situation

♦ amiss, graceless, improper, inapt, incongruous, incorrect, indecorous, inept, infelicitous, unapt, unbecoming, unfit, unhappy, unseemly, unsuitable, wrong; *also* inopportune, unfortunate, unseasonable, untimely; bad, naughty; awkward, gauche, ungraceful; unacceptable, unsatisfactory **Ant** appropriate, becoming, befitting, correct, fit, fitting, proper, right, seemly, suitable

in·apt \(ˌ)i-ˈnapt\ *adj* **1** : not suitable ⟨an ∼ analogy⟩ **2** ♦ : inappropriate or incompetent often to an absurd degree : INEPT — **in·apt·ness** *n*

♦ [1, 2] improper, inappropriate, infelicitous, unbecoming, unfit, unseemly, unsuitable, wrong — more at INAPPROPRIATE

in·apt·ly *adv* ♦ : in an inapt manner

♦ amiss, erroneously, faultily, improperly, incorrectly, mistakenly, wrongly

in·ar·tic·u·late \ˌi-när-ˈti-kyə-lət\ *adj* **1** : not understandable as spoken words **2** ♦ : incapable of speech esp. under stress of emotion : MUTE **3** : incapable of being expressed by speech; *also* : UNSPOKEN **4** : not having the power of distinct utterance or effective expression — **in·ar·tic·u·late·ly** *adv*

♦ dumb, mute, speechless, voiceless — more at MUTE

in·as·much as \ˌi-nəz-ˈməch-\ *conj* : seeing that : SINCE

in·at·ten·tion \ˌi-nə-ˈten-chən\ *n* : failure to pay attention : DISREGARD

in·at·ten·tive \-ˈten-tiv\ *adj* : not paying attention : not attentive

¹**in·au·gu·ral** \i-ˈnȯ-gyə-rəl, -gə-\ *adj* **1** : of or relating to an inauguration **2** ♦ : marking a beginning

♦ first, initial, maiden, original, pioneer, premier — more at FIRST

²**inaugural** *n* **1** : an inaugural address **2** : an act of inaugurating : INAUGURATION; *esp* : a ceremonial induction into office

in·au·gu·rate \i-ˈnȯ-gyə-ˌrāt, -gə-\ *vb* **-rat·ed; -rat·ing** **1** ♦ : to introduce into an office with suitable ceremonies : INSTALL **2** : to dedicate ceremoniously **3** ♦ : to bring about the beginning of : INITIATE

♦ [1] baptize, induct, initiate, install, invest — more at INSTALL ♦ [3] constitute, establish, found, initiate,

innovate, institute, introduce, launch, pioneer, set up, start — more at FOUND

in·au·gu·ra·tion \-ˌnȯ-gyə-ˈrā-shən, -gə-\ *n* ♦ : an act of inaugurating; *also* : a ceremonial induction into office

♦ inaugural, induction, installation, investiture — more at INSTALLATION

in·aus·pi·cious \ˌi-ˌnȯ-ˈspi-shəs\ *adj* ♦ : not auspicious

♦ foreboding, ominous, portentous, prophetic

in·au·then·tic \ˌi-nȯ-ˈthen-tik\ *adj* ♦ : not authentic

♦ bogus, counterfeit, fake, false, phony, sham, spurious, unauthentic — more at COUNTERFEIT

in·board \ˈin-ˌbȯrd\ *adv* **1** : inside the hull of a ship **2** : close or closest to the center line of a vehicle or craft — **inboard** *adj*

in·born \ˈin-ˈbȯrn\ *adj* **1** ♦ : present from or as if from birth **2** ♦ : genetically transmitted or transmittable from parent to offspring : HEREDITARY, INHERITED

♦ [1] essential, ingrained, inherent, innate, integral, intrinsic, natural — more at INHERENT ♦ [2] genetic, hereditary, heritable, inherited — more at HEREDITARY

in·bound \ˈin-ˌbau̇nd\ *adj* : inward bound ⟨∼ traffic⟩

in–box \ˈin-ˌbäks\ *n* : a receptacle for incoming interoffice letters; *also* : a computer folder for incoming e-mail

in·bred \ˈin-ˈbred\ *adj* **1** : ingrained in one's nature as deeply as if by heredity **2** : subjected to or produced by inbreeding

in·breed·ing \ˈin-ˌbrē-diŋ\ *n* **1** : the interbreeding of closely related individuals esp. to preserve and fix desirable characters of and to eliminate unfavorable characters from a stock **2** : confinement to a narrow range or a local or limited field of choice — **in·breed** \-ˈbrēd\ *vb*

inc *abbr* **1** incomplete **2** incorporated **3** increase

In·ca \ˈiŋ-kə\ *n* [Sp, fr. Quechua *inka* ruler of the Inca empire] **1** : a noble or a member of the ruling family of an Indian empire of Peru, Bolivia, and Ecuador until the Spanish conquest **2** : a member of any people under Inca influence

in·cal·cu·la·ble \(ˌ)in-ˈkal-kyə-lə-bəl\ *adj* : not capable of being calculated; *esp* : too large or numerous to be calculated ⟨∼ consequences⟩ — **in·cal·cu·la·bly** \-blē\ *adv*

in·can·des·cence \ˌin-kən-ˈdes-ᵊns\ *n* ♦ : the quality or state of being incandescent; *esp* : emission by a hot body of radiation that makes it visible

♦ blaze, flare, fluorescence, glare, gleam, glow, illumination, light, luminescence, radiance, shine — more at LIGHT

in·can·des·cent \ˌin-kən-ˈdes-ᵊnt\ *adj* **1** : glowing with heat **2** ♦ : strikingly bright, radiant, or clear : SHINING, BRILLIANT

♦ beaming, bright, brilliant, effulgent, glowing, lambent, lucent, lucid, luminous, lustrous, radiant, refulgent, shiny — more at BRIGHT

incandescent lamp *n* : a lamp in which an electrically heated filament emits light

in·can·ta·tion \ˌin-ˌkan-ˈtā-shən\ *n* ♦ : a use of spells or verbal charms spoken or sung as a part of a ritual of magic; *also* : a formula of words used in or as if in such a ritual

♦ bewitchment, charm, conjuration, enchantment, spell — more at SPELL

in·ca·pa·bil·i·ty \(ˌ)in-ˌkā-pə-ˈbi-lə-tē\ *n* ♦ : the quality or state of being incapable

♦ impotence, inability, inadequacy, incompetence, ineptitude — more at INABILITY

in·ca·pa·ble \(ˌ)in-ˈkā-pə-bəl\ *adj* ♦ : lacking ability or qualification for a particular purpose; *also* : UNQUALIFIED

List of self-explanatory words with the prefix *in-* **(continued)**

inaptitude	inartistic	inaudibly	incombustible
inarguable	inaudible	incautious	incomprehension

♦ incompetent, inept, inexpert, unfit, unqualified, unskilled, unskillful — more at INCOMPETENT

in·ca·pac·i·tate \ˌin-kə-ˈpa-sə-ˌtāt\ vb **-tat·ed; -tat·ing** ♦ : to make incapable or unfit : DISABLE

♦ cripple, disable, hamstring, immobilize, paralyze, prostrate — more at PARALYZE

in·ca·pac·i·ty \ˌin-kə-ˈpa-sə-tē\ n, pl **-ties** : the quality or state of being incapable

in·car·cer·ate \in-ˈkär-sə-ˌrāt\ vb **-at·ed; -at·ing** : to put in prison : IMPRISON, CONFINE

in·car·cer·a·tion \(ˌ)in-ˌkär-sə-ˈrā-shən\ n ♦ : a confining or state of being confined

♦ captivity, confinement, imprisonment, internment — more at INTERNMENT

in·car·na·dine \in-ˈkär-nə-ˌdīn, -ˌdēn\ vb **-dined; -din·ing** : REDDEN

¹in·car·nate \in-ˈkär-nət, -ˌnāt\ adj **1** : having bodily and esp. human form and substance **2** : PERSONIFIED

²in·car·nate \-ˌnāt\ vb : to make incarnate: as **a** : to give bodily form and substance to **b** : to give a concrete or actual form to

in·car·na·tion \ˌin-ˌkär-ˈnā-shən\ n **1 a** : the embodiment of a deity or spirit in an earthly form **b** ♦ : a concrete or actual form of a quality or concept **2** cap : the union of divine and human natures in Jesus Christ **3** : a person showing a trait or typical character to a marked degree **4** : the act of incarnating : the state of being incarnate

♦ embodiment, epitome, manifestation, personification — more at EMBODIMENT

¹in·cen·di·ary \in-ˈsen-dē-ˌer-ē\ adj **1** : of or relating to a deliberate burning of property **2** : tending to excite or inflame **3** : designed to start fires ⟨an ~ bomb⟩

²incendiary n **1 a** : a person who commits arson **b** : an incendiary agent (as a bomb) **2** ♦ : a person who excites factions, quarrels, or sedition

♦ agitator, demagogue, firebrand, inciter, rabble-rouser — more at AGITATOR

¹in·cense \ˈin-ˌsens\ n **1** : material used to produce a fragrant odor when burned **2** ♦ : the perfume or smoke from some spices and gums when burned

♦ aroma, bouquet, fragrance, perfume, redolence, scent, spice — more at FRAGRANCE

²in·cense \in-ˈsens\ vb **in·censed; in·cens·ing** ♦ : to make extremely angry

♦ anger, antagonize, enrage, inflame, infuriate, madden, outrage, rankle, rile, roil — more at ANGER

in·cen·tive \in-ˈsen-tiv\ n [ME, fr. LL incentivum, fr. incentivus stimulating, fr. L, setting the tune, fr. incinere to play (a tune), fr. canere to sing] ♦ : something that incites or is likely to incite to determination or action

♦ boost, encouragement, goad, impetus, impulse, incitement, instigation, momentum, motivation, provocation, spur, stimulus, yeast — more at IMPULSE

in·cep·tion \in-ˈsep-shən\ n : an act, process, or instance of beginning : COMMENCEMENT

in·cer·ti·tude \(ˌ)in-ˈsər-tə-ˌtüd, -ˌtyüd\ n **1** ♦ : absence of assurance or confidence : UNCERTAINTY, DOUBT **2** : INSECURITY, INSTABILITY

♦ distrust, doubt, misgiving, mistrust, skepticism, suspicion, uncertainty — more at DOUBT

in·ces·sant \(ˌ)in-ˈses-ᵊnt\ adj ♦ : continuing or flowing without interruption ⟨~ rains⟩

♦ ceaseless, continual, continuous, unbroken, unceasing, uninterrupted — more at CONTINUOUS

in·ces·sant·ly adv ♦ : in an unceasing manner or course : without intermission or relief

♦ always, constantly, continually, ever, forever, invariably, perpetually, unfailingly — more at ALWAYS

in·cest \ˈin-ˌsest\ n [ME, fr. L incestus sexual impurity, fr. incestus impure, fr. castus pure] : sexual intercourse between persons so closely related that marriage is illegal — **in·ces·tu·ous** \in-ˈses-chü-wəs\ adj

¹inch \ˈinch\ n [ME, fr. OE ynce, fr. L uncia twelfth part, inch, ounce] **1** : a unit of length equal to ¹⁄₃₆ yard **2** ♦ : a small amount, distance, or degree

♦ ace, hair, step, stone's throw — more at HAIR

²inch vb ♦ : to move by small degrees

♦ crawl, creep, drag, plod, poke — more at CRAWL

in·cho·ate \in-ˈkō-ət, ˈin-kə-ˌwāt\ adj : being only partly in existence or operation : INCOMPLETE ⟨~ yearnings⟩

inch·worm \ˈinch-ˌwərm\ n : LOOPER

in·ci·dence \ˈin-sə-dəns\ n : rate of occurrence or effect

¹in·ci·dent \-dənt\ n **1** ♦ : an occurrence of an action or situation that is a separate unit of experience : HAPPENING **2** : an action likely to lead to grave consequences esp. in diplomatic matters

♦ affair, circumstance, episode, event, happening, occasion, occurrence, thing — more at EVENT

²incident adj **1** : occurring or likely to occur esp. in connection with some other happening **2** : falling or striking on something ⟨~ light rays⟩

¹in·ci·den·tal \ˌin-sə-ˈdent-ᵊl\ adj **1** : subordinate, nonessential, or attendant in position or significance ⟨~ expenses⟩ **2** ♦ : occurring merely by chance or without intention or planning : CASUAL, CHANCE

♦ accidental, casual, chance, fluky, fortuitous, unintended, unintentional, unplanned, unpremeditated, unwitting — more at ACCIDENTAL

²incidental n **1** pl : minor items (as of expense) that are not individually accounted for **2** : something incidental

in·ci·den·tal·ly \ˌin-sə-ˈden-tə-lē, -ˈdent-lē\ adv **1** : in an incidental manner **2** : by the way

in·cin·er·ate \in-ˈsi-nə-ˌrāt\ vb **-at·ed; -at·ing** : to burn to ashes

in·cin·er·a·tor \in-ˈsi-nə-ˌrā-tər\ n : a furnace for burning waste

in·cip·i·ent \in-ˈsi-pē-ənt\ adj : beginning to be or become apparent

in·cise \in-ˈsīz\ vb **in·cised; in·cis·ing** **1** : to cut into **2** : to carve figures, letters, or devices into : ENGRAVE

in·ci·sion \in-ˈsi-zhən\ n : a wound made by something sharp : GASH; esp : a surgical cut

in·ci·sive \in-ˈsī-siv\ adj : impressively direct and decisive — **in·ci·sive·ly** adv

in·ci·sor \in-ˈsī-zər\ n : a front tooth typically adapted for cutting

in·cite \in-ˈsīt\ vb **in·cit·ed; in·cit·ing** ♦ : to arouse to action

♦ abet, ferment, foment, instigate, provoke, raise, stir, whip; also forward, foster, further, promote, sow, stimulate; set off, trigger; excite, galvanize, inflame, inspire, motivate, rouse; activate, energize, quicken, vitalize arouse, encourage, excite, fire, instigate, move, pique, provoke, stimulate, stir

in·cite·ment n ♦ : the act of inciting or the state of being incited

♦ excitement, instigation, provocation, stimulus — more at PROVOCATION

in·cit·er n ♦ : one that incites

♦ agitator, demagogue, firebrand, incendiary, rabble-rouser — more at AGITATOR

in·ci·vil·i·ty \ˌin-sə-ˈvi-lə-tē\ n **1** ♦ : the quality or state of being uncivil : RUDENESS, DISCOURTESY **2** : a rude or discourteous act

---

List of self-explanatory words with the prefix in-

inconclusive	inconsistency	indecipherable	indestructible
incongruent	incoordination	indemonstrable	indeterminable

♦ brazenness, discourtesy, disrespect, impertinence, impudence, insolence, rudeness — more at DISCOURTESY

incl *abbr* include; included; including; inclusive

in·clem·ent \(ˌ)in-ˈkle-mənt\ *adj* ♦ : lacking mildness; *esp* : physically severe : STORMY ⟨∼ weather⟩ — **in·clem·en·cy** \-mən-sē\ *n*

♦ bleak, dirty, foul, nasty, raw, rough, squally, stormy, tempestuous, turbulent — more at FOUL

in·cli·na·tion \ˌin-klə-ˈnā-shən\ *n* **1** ♦ : a particular disposition of mind or character : PROPENSITY; *esp* : LIKING **2** : BOW, NOD ⟨an ∼ of the head⟩ **3** : a tilting of something **4** ♦ : the degree of deviation from the true vertical or horizontal : SLANT, SLOPE

♦ [1] affinity, bent, devices, disposition, genius, leaning, partiality, penchant, predilection, predisposition, proclivity, propensity, talent, tendency, turn; *also* bias, prejudice; aptitude, faculty, flair, gift, knack, talent; addiction, fondness, liking; forte, specialty; convention, custom, habit, pattern, practice, routine, trick, way, wont; oddity, peculiarity, quirk, singularity ♦ [4] cant, diagonal, grade, incline, lean, pitch, slant, slope, tilt, upgrade — more at SLANT

¹**in·cline** \in-ˈklīn\ *vb* **in·clined; in·clin·ing 1** : BOW, BEND **2** ♦ : to be drawn toward an opinion or course of action **3** ♦ : to deviate from the vertical or horizontal : SLOPE **4** : INFLUENCE, PERSUADE — **in·clin·er** *n*

♦ [2] lean, run, tend, trend — more at LEAN ♦ [3] angle, cant, cock, heel, lean, list, slant, slope, tilt, tip — more at LEAN

²**in·cline** \ˈin-ˌklīn\ *n* : an inclined plane : SLOPE

in·clined *adj* **1** ♦ : having inclination, disposition, or tendency **2 a** ♦ : having a leaning or slope **b** ♦ : making an angle with a line or plane

♦ [1] amenable, disposed, game, glad, ready, willing — more at WILLING ♦ [1] apt, given, prone — more at PRONE ♦ [2a, b] canted, diagonal, listing, oblique, slantwise — more at DIAGONAL

inclose, inclosure *var of* ENCLOSE, ENCLOSURE

in·clude \in-ˈklüd\ *vb* **in·clud·ed; in·clud·ing** ♦ : to take in or comprise as a part of a whole ⟨the price ∼s tax⟩ — **in·clu·sion** \in-ˈklü-zhən\ *n*

♦ carry, comprehend, contain, embrace, encompass, entail, involve, number, take in; *also* comprise, consist (of); have, hold, own, possess; admit, receive; compose, constitute, form, make; assimilate, embody, incorporate, integrate **Ant** exclude, omit

in·clu·sive \-ˈklü-siv\ *adj* **1** : comprehending stated limits or extremes **2** ♦ : broad in orientation or scope; *also* : covering or intended to cover all items, costs, or services

♦ compendious, complete, comprehensive, encyclopedic, full, global, omnibus, panoramic, universal — more at ENCYCLOPEDIC

incog *abbr* incognito

¹**in·cog·ni·to** \ˌin-ˌkäg-ˈnē-tō, in-ˈkäg-nə-ˌtō\ *n, pl* **-tos 1** : one appearing or living incognito **2** : the state or disguise of an incognito

²**incognito** *adv or adj* [It, fr. L *incognitus* unknown, fr. *cognoscere* to know] : with one's identity concealed

in·co·her·ent \ˌin-kō-ˈhir-ənt, -ˈher-\ *adj* **1** : not sticking closely or compactly together : LOOSE **2** ♦ : not clearly or logically connected : RAMBLING — **in·co·her·ence** \-əns\ *n* — **in·co·her·ent·ly** *adv*

♦ disconnected, disjointed, rambling, unconnected; *also* baffling, bewildering, confounding, confused, confusing, disordered, disorderly, disorganized, muddled,

perplexing, puzzling; disconcerting, frustrating; fallacious, illogical, inconsistent, invalid, irrational, unsound; asinine, absurd, eccentric, foolish, odd, peculiar, strange, unreasonable, unusual, weird; meaningless, nonsensical, nutty, preposterous, ridiculous, senseless, silly; unconvincing; inexplicable, unaccountable **Ant** coherent, connected

in·come \ˈin-ˌkəm\ *n* ♦ : a gain usu. measured in money that derives from labor, business, or property

♦ earnings, proceeds, profit, return, revenue, yield; *also* killing, windfall; salary, tips, wages; capital finances, funds, money

income tax *n* : a tax on the net income of an individual or business concern

in·com·ing \ˈin-ˌkə-miŋ\ *adj* : coming in ⟨the ∼ tide⟩ ⟨∼ freshmen⟩

in·com·men·su·rate \ˌin-kə-ˈmen-sə-rət, -ˈmen-chə-\ *adj* : not commensurate; *esp* : INADEQUATE

in·com·mode \ˌin-kə-ˈmōd\ *vb* **-mod·ed; -mod·ing** : to give inconvenience or distress to : DISTURB

in·com·mu·ni·ca·ble \ˌin-kə-ˈmyü-ni-kə-bəl\ *adj* : not capable of being communicated or imparted; *also* : UNCOMMUNICATIVE

in·com·mu·ni·ca·do \ˌin-kə-ˌmyü-nə-ˈkä-dō\ *adv or adj* : without means of communication; *also* : in solitary confinement ⟨a prisoner held ∼⟩

in·com·pa·ra·ble \(ˌ)in-ˈkäm-pə-rə-bəl, -prə-\ *adj* **1** ♦ : eminent beyond comparison : MATCHLESS **2** : not suitable for comparison — **in·com·pa·ra·bly** \-blē\ *adv*

♦ inimitable, matchless, nonpareil, only, peerless, unequaled, unmatched, unparalleled, unrivaled, unsurpassed — more at ONLY

in·com·pat·i·ble \ˌin-kəm-ˈpa-tə-bəl\ *adj* ♦ : incapable of or unsuitable for association or use together ⟨∼ colors⟩ ⟨temperamentally ∼⟩ — **in·com·pat·i·bil·i·ty** \ˌin-kəm-ˌpa-tə-ˈbi-lə-tē\ *n*

♦ discordant, discrepant, incongruous, inharmonious

in·com·pe·tence \-təns\ *n* ♦ : the state or fact of being incompetent

♦ impotence, inability, inadequacy, incapability, ineptitude — more at INABILITY

in·com·pe·tent \(ˌ)in-ˈkäm-pə-tənt\ *adj* **1** : not legally qualified **2** ♦ : not competent : lacking sufficient knowledge, skill, or ability — **in·com·pe·ten·cy** \-tən-sē\ *n* — **incompetent** *n*

♦ incapable, inept, inexpert, unfit, unqualified, unskilled, unskillful; *also* ineffective, ineffectual, inefficient; callow, green, inexperienced, raw; unequipped, unprepared, untrained; useless, worthless; ineligible; wanting **Ant** able, capable, competent, expert, fit, qualified, skilled, skillful

in·com·plete \ˌin-kəm-ˈplēt\ *adj* ♦ : lacking a part or parts : UNFINISHED, IMPERFECT — **in·com·plete·ness** *n*

♦ deficient, fragmentary, halfway, imperfect, partial; *also* broken, damaged, impaired **Ant** complete, entire, full, intact, whole

in·com·plete·ly *adv* : in an incomplete manner or to an incomplete degree : not wholly, perfectly, or fully

in·com·pre·hen·si·ble \ˌin-ˌkäm-prē-ˈhen-sə-bəl\ *adj* ♦ : impossible to comprehend : UNINTELLIGIBLE ⟨∼ muttering⟩

♦ impenetrable, unfathomable; *also* abstruse, enigmatic, esoteric, inscrutable, recondite; cryptic, mysterious, obscure; unanswerable, unknowable; baffling, bewildering, confounding, confusing, mystifying, perplexing, puzzling **Ant** fathomable, intelligible, understandable

---

List of self-explanatory words with the prefix *in-* **(continued)**

indiscernible	ineducable	inefficacious	inelastic
inedible	ineffaceable	inefficacy	inelasticity

in·con·ceiv·able \ˌin-kən-ˈsē-və-bəl\ *adj* **1** : impossible to comprehend **2** ♦ : impossible to believe : UNBELIEVABLE

♦ fantastic, implausible, incredible, unbelievable, unconvincing, unimaginable, unthinkable — more at INCREDIBLE

in·con·gru·ous \(ˌ)in-ˈkäŋ-grü-wəs\ *adj* **1** : not consistent with or suitable to the surroundings or associations **2** ♦ : lacking harmony — **in·con·gru·i·ty** \ˌin-kən-ˈgrü-ə-tē, -ˌkän-\ *n* — **in·con·gru·ous·ly** *adv*

♦ discordant, discrepant, incompatible, inharmonious

in·con·se·quen·tial \ˌin-ˌkän-sə-ˈkwen-chəl\ *adj* **1** : ILLOGICAL; *also* : IRRELEVANT **2** ♦ : of no significance : UNIMPORTANT — **in·con·se·quence** \(ˌ)in-ˈkän-sə-ˌkwens\ *n* — **in·con·se·quen·tial·ly** *adv*

♦ frivolous, inconsiderable, insignificant, little, minor, minute, negligible, slight, trifling, trivial, unimportant — more at UNIMPORTANT

in·con·sid·er·able \ˌin-kən-ˈsi-də-rə-bəl\ *adj* ♦ : not considerable : SLIGHT, TRIVIAL

♦ inconsequential, insignificant, measly, minute, negligible, nominal, paltry, petty, slight, trifling, trivial — more at NEGLIGIBLE

in·con·sid·er·ate \ˌin-kən-ˈsi-də-rət\ *adj* ♦ : not taking heed : THOUGHTLESS; *esp* : not respecting the rights or feelings of others — **in·con·sid·er·ate·ly** *adv* — **in·con·sid·er·ate·ness** *n*

♦ discourteous, ill-bred, ill-mannered, impertinent, impolite, rude, thoughtless, uncivil, ungracious, unmannerly — more at IMPOLITE

in·con·sis·tent \ˌin-kən-ˈsis-tənt\ *adj* : lacking consistency : not compatible with facts or claims

in·con·sol·able \ˌin-kən-ˈsō-lə-bəl\ *adj* : incapable of being consoled — **in·con·sol·ably** \-blē\ *adv*

in·con·spic·u·ous \ˌin-kən-ˈspi-kyə-wəs\ *adj* : not readily noticeable — **in·con·spic·u·ous·ly** *adv*

in·con·stan·cy \-stən-sē\ *n* ♦ : the quality or state of being inconstant

♦ disloyalty, faithlessness, falseness, falsity, infidelity, perfidy, unfaithfulness — more at INFIDELITY

in·con·stant \(ˌ)in-ˈkän-stənt\ *adj* ♦ : not constant : CHANGEABLE — **in·con·stant·ly** *adv*

♦ capricious, changeable, fickle, fluid, mercurial, mutable, temperamental, uncertain, unpredictable, unsettled, unstable, unsteady, variable, volatile — more at FICKLE

in·con·test·able \ˌin-kən-ˈtes-tə-bəl\ *adj* ♦ : not contestable : INDISPUTABLE

♦ indisputable, indubitable, irrefutable, unanswerable, undeniable, unquestionable — more at IRREFUTABLE

in·con·test·ably \-ˈtes-tə-blē\ *adv* ♦ : in an incontestable manner or to an incontestable degree or level : with certainty

♦ certainly, definitely, doubtless, indeed, indisputably, really, surely, truly, undeniably, undoubtedly, unquestionably — more at INDEED

in·con·ti·nent \(ˌ)in-ˈkänt-ᵊn-ənt\ *adj* **1** : lacking self-restraint **2** : unable to retain urine or feces voluntarily — **in·con·ti·nence** \-əns\ *n*

in·con·tro·vert·ible \ˌin-ˌkän-trə-ˈvər-tə-bəl\ *adj* : not open to question : INDISPUTABLE ⟨~ evidence⟩

in·con·tro·vert·ibly \-blē\ *adv* : not open to question

¹in·con·ve·nience \ˌin-kən-ˈvē-nyəns\ *n* **1** ♦ : something that is inconvenient **2** : the quality or state of being inconvenient

♦ aggravation, annoyance, bother, exasperation, frustration, hassle, headache, irritant, nuisance, peeve, pest, problem, thorn — more at ANNOYANCE

²inconvenience *vb* -nienced; -niencing ♦ : to subject to inconvenience

♦ discommode, disoblige, disturb, trouble; *also* burden, encumber, saddle, weigh; hamper, hamstring, hinder, hobble, impede; aggravate, anger, annoy, bother, bug, exasperate, gall, get, nettle, peeve, pique, put out, rile, vex; grate, inflame, provoke; agitate, perturb, upset *Ant* accommodate, oblige

in·con·ve·nient \ˌin-kən-ˈvē-nyənt\ *adj* **1** ♦ : not convenient **2** ♦ : causing trouble or annoyance — **in·con·ve·nient·ly** *adv*

♦ [1] inaccessible, unapproachable, unattainable, unavailable, unobtainable, unreachable, untouchable — more at INACCESSIBLE ♦ [2] awkward; *also* bothersome, burdensome, onerous, troublesome; annoying, irritating *Ant* convenient

in·cor·po·rate \in-ˈkȯr-pə-ˌrāt\ *vb* -rat·ed; -rat·ing **1** ♦ : to unite closely or so as to form one body **2** : to form, form into, or become a corporation **3** : to give material form to : EMBODY — **in·cor·po·ra·tion** \-ˌkȯr-pə-ˈrā-shən\ *n*

♦ assimilate, commingle, integrate, intermingle, merge

in·cor·po·re·al \ˌin-kȯr-ˈpōr-ē-əl\ *adj* ♦ : having no material body or form

♦ bodiless, immaterial, insubstantial, nonmaterial, nonphysical, spiritual, unsubstantial — more at IMMATERIAL

in·cor·rect \ˌin-kə-ˈrekt\ *adj* **1** : marked by fault or defect : INACCURATE **2** ♦ : not true : WRONG **3** ♦ : not according with appropriate standards : UNBECOMING, IMPROPER

♦ [2] erroneous, false, inaccurate, inexact, invalid, off, unsound, untrue, wrong — more at FALSE ♦ [3] improper, inappropriate, inapt, infelicitous, unbecoming, unfit, unseemly, unsuitable, wrong — more at INAPPROPRIATE

in·cor·rect·ly *adv* ♦ : in an incorrect manner

♦ amiss, erroneously, faultily, improperly, inaptly, mistakenly, wrongly

in·cor·rect·ness *n* ♦ : the quality or state of being incorrect

♦ impropriety, indecency — more at IMPROPRIETY

in·cor·ri·gi·ble \(ˌ)in-ˈkȯr-ə-jə-bəl\ *adj* ♦ : incapable of being corrected, amended, or reformed — **in·cor·ri·gi·bil·i·ty** \(ˌ)in-ˌkȯr-ə-jə-ˈbi-lə-tē\ *n* — **in·cor·ri·gi·bly** \-ˈkȯr-ə-jə-blē\ *adv*

♦ hopeless, incurable, irredeemable, irremediable, unrecoverable, unredeemable — more at HOPELESS

in·cor·rupt·ible \ˌin-kə-ˈrəp-tə-bəl\ *adj* **1** : not subject to decay or dissolution **2** : incapable of being bribed or morally corrupted — **in·cor·rupt·ibil·i·ty** \-ˌrəp-tə-ˈbi-lə-tē\ *n* — **in·cor·rupt·ibly** \-ˈrəp-tə-blē\ *adv*

incr *abbr* increase; increased

¹in·crease \in-ˈkrēs, ˈin-ˌkrēs\ *vb* **in·creased; in·creas·ing** [ME *encresen*, fr. AF *encreistre*, fr. L. *increscere*, fr. *crescere* to grow] **1** ♦ : to become greater : GROW **2** : to multiply by the production of young ⟨rabbits ~ rapidly⟩ **3** ♦ : to make greater — **in·creas·ing·ly** \-ˈkrē-siŋ-lē\ *adv*

♦ [1] accumulate, appreciate, balloon, build, burgeon, enlarge, escalate, expand, grow, mount, multiply, mushroom, proliferate, rise, snowball, swell, wax; *also* rocket, skyrocket; heighten, intensify; blow up, distend, inflate; crest, peak, surge *Ant* contract, decrease, diminish, lessen, wane ♦ [3] add, aggrandize, amplify, augment, boost, compound, enlarge, escalate, expand, extend, multiply, raise, swell, up; *also* skyrocket; blow up, dilate, distend, inflate; elongate, lengthen, prolong, protract; enhance, heighten, intensify, magnify; complement, supplement; beef (up), reinforce, strengthen; maximize; accumulate, amass, collect; parlay *Ant* abate, contract, decrease, diminish, lessen, lower, reduce, subtract (from)

List of self-explanatory words with the prefix *in-* (continued)

inequitable	ineradicable	inexpedient	infeasible
inequity	inerrant	inextinguishable	injudicious

²**in·crease** \'in-ˌkrēs, in-'krēs\ *n* **1** ♦ : addition or enlargement in size, extent, or quantity : GROWTH **2** ♦ : something that is added to an original stock or amount (as by growth)

♦ accretion, addition, augmentation, boost, expansion, gain, growth, increment, plus, proliferation, raise, rise, supplement; *also* accumulation; complement; appendix, continuation, extension, uptrend, upturn; jump *Ant* abatement, decrease, lessening, lowering, reduction

in·cred·i·ble \(ˌ)in-'kre-də-bəl\ *adj* ♦ : too extraordinary and improbable to be believed; *also* : hard to believe — **in·cred·i·bil·i·ty** \(ˌ)in-ˌkre-də-'bi-lə-tē\ *n*

♦ fantastic, implausible, inconceivable, unbelievable, unconvincing, unimaginable, unthinkable; *also* doubtful, dubious, fishy, flimsy, questionable, suspect, unlikely, unreasonable; absurd, outlandish, preposterous, ridiculous *Ant* believable, conceivable, convincing, credible, imaginable, plausible

in·cred·i·bly \(ˌ)in-'kre-də-blē\ *adv* ♦ : in an incredible manner : to an incredible extent : EXTREMELY

♦ extremely, greatly, highly, hugely, mightily, mighty, mortally, most, much, real, right, so, very — more at VERY

in·cred·u·lous \-'kre-jə-ləs\ *adj* **1** ♦ : unwilling to admit or accept what is offered as true : SKEPTICAL **2** : expressing disbelief — **in·cre·du·li·ty** \ˌin-kri-'dü-lə-tē, -'dyü-\ *n* — **in·cred·u·lous·ly** *adv*

♦ distrustful, leery, mistrustful, skeptical, suspicious — more at SKEPTICAL

in·cre·ment \'iŋ-krə-mənt, 'in-\ *n* **1** : the action or process of increasing esp. in quantity or value : ENLARGEMENT; *also* : QUANTITY **2** ♦ : something gained or added; *esp* : one of a series of regular consecutive additions

♦ accretion, addition, augmentation, boost, expansion, gain, increase, plus, proliferation, raise, rise, supplement — more at INCREASE

in·cre·men·tal \ˌiŋ-krə-'ment-ᵊl, ˌin-\ *adj* : of, relating to, being, or occurring in esp. small increments — **in·cre·men·tal·ly** *adv*

in·crim·i·nate \in-'kri-mə-ˌnāt\ *vb* **-nat·ed; -nat·ing** ♦ : to charge with or prove involvement in a crime or fault : ACCUSE — **in·crim·i·na·tion** \-ˌkri-mə-'nā-shən\ *n* — **in·crim·i·na·to·ry** \-'kri-mə-nə-ˌtōr-ē\ *adj*

♦ accuse, charge, indict — more at ACCUSE

incrust *var of* ENCRUST

in·crus·ta·tion \ˌin-ˌkrəs-'tā-shən\ *also* **en·crus·ta·tion** \ˌin-, ˌen-\ *n* **1** : CRUST; *also* : an accumulation (as of habits, opinions, or customs) resembling a crust **2** : the act of encrusting : the state of being encrusted

in·cu·bate \'iŋ-kyu̇-ˌbāt, 'in-\ *vb* **-bat·ed; -bat·ing** ♦ : to sit on (eggs) to hatch by the warmth of the body; *also* : to keep (as an embryo) under conditions favorable for development — **in·cu·ba·tion** \ˌiŋ-kyu̇-'bā-shən, ˌin-\ *n*

♦ brood, hatch, set, sit — more at SET

in·cu·ba·tor \'iŋ-kyu̇-ˌbāt-ər, 'in-\ *n* : one that incubates; *esp* : an apparatus providing suitable conditions (as of warmth and moisture) for incubating something (as a premature baby)

in·cu·bus \'iŋ-kyə-bəs, 'in-\ *n, pl* **-bi** \-ˌbī\, **-bē** *also* **-bus·es** [ME, fr. LL, fr. L *incubare* to lie on] **1** : a spirit supposed to work evil on persons in their sleep **2** : NIGHTMARE 1 **3** : one that oppresses like a nightmare

in·cul·cate \in-'kəl-ˌkāt, 'in-(ˌ)kəl-\ *vb* **-cat·ed; -cat·ing** [L *inculcare*, lit., to tread on, fr. *calcare* to trample, fr. *calx* heel] ♦ : to teach and impress by frequent repetitions or admonitions — **in·cul·ca·tion** \ˌin-(ˌ)kəl-'kā-shən\ *n*

♦ imbue, infuse, ingrain, invest, steep, suffuse — more at INFUSE

in·cul·pa·ble \(ˌ)in-'kəl-pə-bəl\ *adj* : free from guilt : INNOCENT

in·cul·pate \in-'kəl-ˌpāt, 'in-(ˌ)kəl-\ *vb* **-pat·ed; -pat·ing** : INCRIMINATE

in·cum·ben·cy \in-'kəm-bən-sē\ *n, pl* **-cies** **1** : something that is incumbent **2** : the quality or state of being incumbent **3** : the office or period of office of an incumbent

¹**in·cum·bent** \in-'kəm-bənt\ *n* : the holder of an office or position

²**incumbent** *adj* **1** ♦ : imposed as a duty **2** : occupying a specified office **3** : lying or resting on something else

♦ compulsory, imperative, involuntary, mandatory, necessary, nonelective, obligatory, peremptory — more at MANDATORY

in·cu·nab·u·lum \ˌin-kyə-'na-byə-ləm, ˌiŋ-\ *n, pl* **-la** \-lə\ [NL, fr. L *incunabula*, pl., bands holding the baby in a cradle, fr. *cunae* cradle] : a book printed before 1501

in·cur \in-'kər\ *vb* **in·curred; in·cur·ring** : to become liable or subject to : bring down upon oneself

in·cur·able \(ˌ)in-'kyu̇r-ə-bəl\ *adj* **1** ♦ : not curable **2** ♦ : not likely to be changed — **incurable** *n* — **in·cur·ably** \(ˌ)in-'kyu̇r-ə-blē\ *adv*

♦ [1, 2] hopeless, incorrigible, irredeemable, irremediable, unrecoverable, unredeemable — more at HOPELESS

in·cu·ri·ous \(ˌ)in-'kyu̇r-ē-əs\ *adj* : lacking a normal or usual curiosity

in·cur·sion \in-'kər-zhən\ *n* **1** ♦ : a sudden hostile invasion : RAID **2** : an entering in or into (as an activity)

♦ descent, foray, invasion, irruption, raid — more at RAID

in·cus \'iŋ-kəs\ *n, pl* **in·cu·des** \iŋ-'kyü-(ˌ)dēz\ [NL, fr. L, anvil] : the middle bone of a chain of three small bones in the middle ear of a mammal

ind *abbr* **1** independent **2** index **3** industrial; industry

Ind *abbr* **1** Indian **2** Indiana

in·debt·ed \in-'de-təd\ *adj* **1** ♦ : owing gratitude or recognition to another **2** ♦ : owing money — **in·debt·ed·ness** *n*

♦ [1, 2] beholden, obligated, obliged — more at BEHOLDEN

in·de·cen·cy \(ˌ)in-'dēs-ᵊn-sē\ *n* ♦ : the quality or state of being indecent

♦ impropriety, incorrectness — more at IMPROPRIETY

in·de·cent \(ˌ)in-'dēs-ᵊnt\ *adj* ♦ : not decent; *esp* : morally offensive — **in·de·cent·ly** *adv*

♦ bawdy, coarse, crude, dirty, filthy, foul, gross, lascivious, lewd, nasty, obscene, pornographic, ribald, smutty, unprintable, vulgar, wanton — more at OBSCENE

in·de·ci·sion \ˌin-di-'si-zhən\ *n* ♦ : a wavering between two or more possible courses of action : IRRESOLUTION

♦ hesitancy, hesitation, irresolution, vacillation — more at HESITATION

in·de·ci·sive \ˌin-di-'sī-siv\ *adj* **1** : leading to no conclusion or definite result **2** : marked by or prone to indecision **3** : INDEFINITE — **in·de·ci·sive·ly** *adv* — **in·de·ci·sive·ness** *n*

in·de·co·rous \(ˌ)in-'de-kə-rəs, ˌin-di-'kōr-əs\ *adj* ♦ : not decorous — **in·de·co·rous·ly** *adv* — **in·de·co·rous·ness** *n*

♦ improper, inappropriate, inapt, infelicitous, unbecoming, unfit, unseemly, unsuitable, wrong — more at INAPPROPRIATE

in·deed \in-'dēd\ *adv* **1** ♦ : without any question — often used interjectionally to express irony, disbelief, or surprise **2** ♦ : in reality **3** : all things considered

♦ [1] certainly, definitely, doubtless, incontestably, indisputably, really, surely, truly, undeniably, undoubtedly, unquestionably; *also* conceivably, likely, perhaps, possibly, probably; clearly, obviously, unmistakably
♦ [2] even, nay, truly, verily, yea — more at EVEN

List of self-explanatory words with the prefix *in-* (continued)

inoffensive	insensitive	insignificance	insusceptible
insanitary	insensitivity	insolvable	

indef *abbr* indefinite

in·de·fat·i·ga·ble \ˌin-di-ˈfa-ti-gə-bəl\ *adj* ♦ : incapable of being fatigued : UNTIRING

♦ inexhaustible, tireless, unflagging, untiring — more at TIRELESS

in·de·fat·i·ga·bly \-blē\ *adv* : in an indefatigable manner

in·de·fea·si·ble \-ˈfē-zə-bəl\ *adj* : not capable of being annulled or voided — **in·de·fea·si·bly** \-blē\ *adv*

in·de·fen·si·ble \-ˈfen-sə-bəl\ *adj* 1 : incapable of being maintained as right or valid 2 ♦ : incapable of being justified or excused : INEXCUSABLE 3 : incapable of being protected against physical attack

♦ inexcusable, unforgivable, unjustifiable, unpardonable, unwarrantable — more at INEXCUSABLE

in·de·fin·able \-ˈfī-nə-bəl\ *adj* : incapable of being precisely described or analyzed — **in·de·fin·ably** \-blē\ *adv*

in·def·i·nite \(ˌ)in-ˈde-fə-nət\ *adj* 1 : not defining or identifying ⟨an is an ∼ article⟩ 2 ♦ : not precise : VAGUE 3 ♦ : having no fixed limit — **in·def·i·nite·ly** *adv* — **in·def·i·nite·ness** *n*

♦ [2] bleary, dim, faint, foggy, fuzzy, hazy, indistinct, indistinguishable, murky, nebulous, obscure, opaque, shadowy, unclear, undefined, undetermined, vague — more at FAINT ♦ [3] boundless, endless, illimitable, immeasurable, infinite, limitless, measureless, unbounded, unfathomable, unlimited — more at INFINITE

in·del·i·ble \in-ˈde-lə-bəl\ *adj* [ME, fr. ML *indelibilis*, alter. of L *indelebilis*, fr. *delēre* to delete, destroy] 1 : not capable of being removed or erased 2 : making marks that cannot be erased 3 : LASTING, UNFORGETTABLE ⟨an ∼ performance⟩ — **in·del·i·bly** \in-ˈde-lə-blē\ *adv*

in·del·i·ca·cy \in-ˈde-lə-kə-sē\ *n* 1 ♦ : the quality or state of being indelicate 2 : something that is indelicate

♦ coarseness, grossness, lowness, rudeness, vulgarity — more at VULGARITY

in·del·i·cate \(ˌ)in-ˈde-li-kət\ *adj* : not delicate; *esp* : IMPROPER, COARSE, TACTLESS

in·dem·ni·fi·ca·tion \-ˌdem-nə-fə-ˈkā-shən\ *n* 1 : the action of indemnifying; *also* : the condition of being indemnified 2 : something that indemnifies

in·dem·ni·fy \in-ˈdem-nə-ˌfī\ *vb* **-fied; -fy·ing** [L *indemnis* unharmed, fr. *in-* not + *damnum* damage] 1 : to secure against hurt, loss, or damage 2 ♦ : to make compensation to for hurt, loss, or damage

♦ compensate, recompense, recoup, remunerate, requite — more at COMPENSATE

in·dem·ni·ty \in-ˈdem-nə-tē\ *n, pl* **-ties** 1 : security against hurt, loss, or damage; *also* : exemption from incurred penalties or liabilities 2 ♦ : something that indemnifies

♦ compensation, damages, quittance, recompense, redress, remuneration, reparation, requital, restitution, satisfaction — more at COMPENSATION

¹**in·dent** \in-ˈdent\ *vb* [ME, fr. AF *endenter*, fr. *dent* tooth, fr. L *dent-, dens*] 1 : to notch the edge of 2 : INDENTURE 3 : to set (as a line of a paragraph) in from the margin

²**indent** *vb* 1 : to force inward so as to form a depression 2 : to form a dent in

in·den·ta·tion \ˌin-ˌden-ˈtā-shən\ *n* 1 ♦ : a V-shaped cut usu. on an edge or a surface : NOTCH; *also* : a usu. deep recess (as in a coastline) 2 : the action of indenting : the condition of being indented 3 ♦ : a depression or hollow made by a blow or by pressure : DENT 4 : INDENTION 2

♦ [1] chip, hack, nick, notch — more at NOTCH
♦ [3] cavity, concavity, dent, depression, hole, hollow, pit, recess — more at HOLE

in·den·tion \in-ˈden-chən\ *n* 1 : INDENTATION 2 2 : the blank space produced by indenting

¹**in·den·ture** \in-ˈden-chər\ *n* 1 : a written certificate or agreement; *esp* : a contract binding one person (as an apprentice) to work for another for a given period of time — usu. used in pl. 2 : INDENTATION 1 3 : DENT

²**indenture** *vb* **in·den·tured; in·den·tur·ing** : to bind (as an apprentice) by indentures

in·de·pen·dence \ˌin-də-ˈpen-dəns\ *n* ♦ : the quality or state of being independent : FREEDOM

♦ autonomy, freedom, liberty, self-government, sovereignty — more at FREEDOM

Independence Day *n* : July 4 observed as a legal holiday in commemoration of the adoption of the Declaration of Independence in 1776

in·de·pen·dent \ˌin-də-ˈpen-dənt\ *adj* 1 ♦ : not subject to control by others : SELF-GOVERNING; *also* : not affiliated with a larger controlling unit 2 ♦ : not requiring or relying on something else or somebody else ⟨an ∼ conclusion⟩ ⟨∼ of her parents⟩ 3 : not easily influenced : showing self-reliance and personal freedom ⟨an ∼ mind⟩ 4 : not committed to a political party ⟨an ∼ voter⟩ 5 : MAIN ⟨an ∼ clause⟩ — **independent** *n*

♦ [1] autonomous, free, self-governing, separate, sovereign — more at FREE ♦ [2] self-reliant, self-sufficient, self-supporting — more at SELF-SUFFICIENT

in·de·pen·dent·ly *adv* ♦ : in an independent manner : without dependence on another

♦ alone, singly, solely, unaided, unassisted — more at ALONE

independent variable *n* : a variable whose value is not determined by that of any other variable in a function

in·de·scrib·able \ˌin-di-ˈskrī-bə-bəl\ *adj* 1 ♦ : that cannot be described 2 : being too intense or great for description — **in·de·scrib·ably** \-blē\ *adv*

♦ ineffable, inexpressible, nameless, unspeakable, unutterable; *also* inconceivable, incredible, unbelievable, unimaginable, unthinkable; featureless, nondescript *Ant* communicable, definable

in·de·ter·mi·nate \ˌin-di-ˈtər-mə-nət\ *adj* 1 : VAGUE; *also* : not known in advance 2 : not limited in advance; *also* : not leading to an end or result — **in·de·ter·mi·na·cy** \-nə-sē\ *n* — **in·de·ter·mi·nate·ly** *adv*

¹**in·dex** \ˈin-ˌdeks\ *n, pl* **in·dex·es** *or* **in·di·ces** \-də-ˌsēz\ 1 ♦ : a device (as the pointer on a scale) that serves to indicate a value or quantity 2 : SIGN, INDICATION ⟨an ∼ of character⟩ 3 : a guide for facilitating references; *esp* : an alphabetical list of items treated in a printed work with the page number where each item may be found 4 : a list of restricted or prohibited material 5 *pl usu* **indices** : a number or symbol or expression (as an exponent) associated with another to indicate a mathematical operation or use or position in an arrangement or expansion 6 : a character ☞ used to direct attention (as to a note) 7 : INDEX NUMBER

♦ indicator, needle, pointer — more at POINTER

²**index** *vb* 1 ♦ : to provide with or put into an index 2 : to serve as an index of 3 : to regulate by indexation

♦ catalog, enroll, enter, inscribe, list, put down, record, register, schedule, slate — more at LIST

in·dex·ation \ˌin-ˌdek-ˈsā-shən\ *n* : a system of economic control in which a body of variables (as wages and interest) rise or fall at the same rate as an index of the cost of living

index finger *n* : the finger next to the thumb

in·dex·ing *n* : INDEXATION

index number *n* : a number used to indicate change in magnitude (as of cost) as compared with the magnitude at some specified time usu. taken as 100

index of refraction : REFRACTIVE INDEX

in·dia ink \ˈin-dē-ə-\ *n, often cap 1st I* 1 : a solid black pigment used in drawing 2 : a fluid made from india ink

In·di·an \ˈin-dē-ən\ *n* 1 : a native or inhabitant of India or of the East Indies 2 : a person of Indian descent 3 : AMERICAN INDIAN — **Indian** *adj*

Indian corn *n* 1 : CORN 2 2 : corn having hard kernels of various colors (as reddish-brown or purple) used esp. for ornament

Indian meal *n* : CORNMEAL

Indian paintbrush *n* : any of a genus of herbaceous plants related to the snapdragon that have brightly colored bracts

Indian pipe *n* : a waxy white leafless saprophytic herb of Asia and the U.S.

Indian summer *n* : a period of mild weather in late autumn or early winter

In·dia paper \'in-dē-ə-\ *n* **1** : a thin absorbent paper used esp. for taking impressions (as of steel engravings) **2** : a thin tough opaque printing paper

indic *abbr* indicative

in·di·cate \'in-də-ˌkāt\ *vb* **-cat·ed; -cat·ing 1** : to point out or to **2** ♦ : to show indirectly **3** : to state briefly

♦ allude, hint, imply, infer, insinuate, intimate, suggest — more at HINT

in·di·ca·tion \ˌin-də-'kā-shən\ *n* **1** ♦ : something that serves to indicate; *also* : something that is indicated as advisable or necessary **2** : the action of indicating

♦ clue, cue, hint, inkling, intimation, lead, suggestion — more at HINT

¹**in·dic·a·tive** \in-'di-kə-tiv\ *adj* **1** : of, relating to, or being a verb form that represents an act or state as a fact ⟨~ mood⟩ **2** ♦ : serving to indicate ⟨actions ~ of fear⟩

♦ denotative, significant, telltale; *also* alluding, allusive, referring; characteristic, symptomatic; demonstrative, exhibiting, expressive; symbolic; connoting, implying, insinuating, suggestive

²**indicative** *n* **1** : the indicative mood of a language **2** : a form in the indicative mood

in·di·ca·tor \'in-də-ˌkā-tər\ *n* ♦ : one that indicates; *esp* : an index hand (as on a dial)

♦ hand, index, needle, pointer — more at POINTER

in·di·cia \in-'di-shə, -shē-ə\ *n pl* **1** : distinctive marks **2** : postal markings often imprinted on mail or mailing labels

in·dict \in-'dīt\ *vb* [alter. of earlier *indite*, fr. ME, fr. AF to write, point out, indict, ultim. fr. L *indicere* to make known formally, fr. *dicere* to say] **1** ♦ : to charge with a fault or offense **2** : to charge with a crime by the finding of a jury — **in·dict·able** *adj*

♦ accuse, charge, incriminate — more at ACCUSE

in·dict·ment \-mənt\ *n* ♦ : the action or the legal process of indicting

♦ charge, complaint, count, rap — more at CHARGE

in·die \'in-dē\ *n* **1** : one that is independent; *esp* : an unaffiliated record or motion-picture production company **2** : something produced by an indie — **indie** *adj*

in·dif·fer·ence \-frəns, -fə-rəns\ *n* ♦ : the quality, state, or fact of being indifferent; *also* : absence of compulsion to or toward one thing or another

♦ apathy, disinterestedness, disregard, insouciance, nonchalance; *also* halfheartedness; carelessness, heedlessness, recklessness, unawareness; lethargy, listlessness; calmness, detachment, dispassion; callousness, hardness, insensitivity; impassivity, phlegm; aloofness, coldness *Ant* concern, interest, regard

in·dif·fer·ent \in-'di-frənt, -fə-rənt\ *adj* **1** : UNBIASED, UNPREJUDICED **2** : of no importance one way or the other **3** ♦ : marked by no special liking for or dislike of something **4** : being neither excessive nor inadequate **5** ♦ : being neither good nor bad : PASSABLE, MEDIOCRE **6** : being neither right nor wrong — **in·dif·fer·ent·ly** *adv*

♦ [3] apathetic, casual, disinterested, insouciant, nonchalant, perfunctory, unconcerned, uncurious, uninterested; *also* halfhearted, lukewarm; aloof, cold, numb, remote, unemotional; calm, detached, dispassionate; careless, heedless, mindless; impassive, phlegmatic, stoic, stolid; lethargic, listless; unimpressed *Ant* concerned, interested ♦ [5] common, fair, mediocre, medium, middling, ordinary, passable, run-of-the-mill, second-rate, so-so — more at MEDIOCRE

in·di·gence \-jəns\ *n* ♦ : a level of poverty in which real hardship and deprivation are suffered and comforts of life are wholly lacking

♦ beggary, destitution, impecuniousness, impoverishment, need, pauperism, penury, poverty, want — more at POVERTY

in·dig·e·nous \in-'di-jə-nəs\ *adj* ♦ : produced, growing, or living naturally in a particular region

♦ aboriginal, born, endemic, native — more at NATIVE

in·di·gent \'in-di-jənt\ *adj* ♦ : suffering from indigence : NEEDY

♦ broke, destitute, impecunious, needy, penniless, penurious, poor, poverty-stricken — more at POOR

in·di·gest·ible \ˌin-dī-'jes-tə-bəl, -də-\ *adj* : not readily digested

in·di·ges·tion \-'jes-chən\ *n* : inadequate or difficult digestion : DYSPEPSIA

in·dig·nant \in-'dig-nənt\ *adj* : filled with or marked by indignation — **in·dig·nant·ly** *adv*

in·dig·na·tion \ˌin-dig-'nā-shən\ *n* ♦ : anger aroused by something unjust, unworthy, or mean

♦ anger, furor, fury, ire, outrage, rage, spleen, wrath, wrathfulness — more at ANGER

in·dig·ni·ty \in-'dig-nə-tē\ *n, pl* **-ties** ♦ : an offense against personal dignity or self-respect; *also* : humiliating treatment

♦ affront, barb, dart, dig, insult, name, offense, outrage, put-down, sarcasm, slight, slur, wound — more at INSULT

in·di·go \'in-di-ˌgō\ *n, pl* **-gos** *or* **-goes** [It dial., fr. L *indicum*, fr. Gk *indikon*, fr. *indikos* Indic, fr. *Indos* India] **1** : a blue dye obtained from plants or synthesized **2** : a deep reddish blue color

in·di·rect \ˌin-də-'rekt, -dī-\ *adj* **1** : not straight ⟨an ~ route⟩ **2** ♦ : not straightforward and open ⟨~ methods⟩ **3** : not having a plainly seen connection ⟨an ~ cause⟩ **4** : not directly to the point ⟨an ~ answer⟩ — **in·di·rec·tion** \-'rek-shən\ *n* — **in·di·rect·ly** *adv* — **in·di·rect·ness** *n*

♦ circuitous, circular, roundabout; *also* crooked, serpentine, sinuous, tortuous, twisting, winding; meandering, rambling, wandering; long-winded, prolix, verbose; deceitful, deceptive, devious, dishonest, insidious, misleading, sneaky, underhand, underhanded; calculating, crafty, cunning, subtle, tricky *Ant* direct, straight, straightforward

in·dis·creet \ˌin-di-'skrēt\ *adj* ♦ : not discreet : IMPRUDENT — **in·dis·creet·ly** *adv*

♦ ill-advised, imprudent, tactless, unwise; *also* dumb, idiotic, moronic, stupid; inconsiderate, thoughtless; ill-mannered, improper, inappropriate, indecorous, unbecoming, uncivil, unseemly; foolish, harebrained, nonsensical, preposterous, senseless, silly *Ant* advisable, discreet, judicious, prudent, tactful, wise

in·dis·cre·tion \ˌin-di-'skre-shən\ *n* **1** : IMPRUDENCE **2** ♦ : something marked by lack of discretion; *esp* : an act deviating from accepted morality

♦ familiarity, gaffe, impropriety — more at IMPROPRIETY

in·dis·crim·i·nate \ˌin-di-'skri-mə-nət\ *adj* **1** : not careful in making choices **2** : HAPHAZARD, RANDOM ⟨an ~ application of a law⟩ **3** : UNRESTRAINED **4** : MOTLEY — **in·dis·crim·i·nate·ly** *adv*

in·dis·pens·able \ˌin-di-'spen-sə-bəl\ *adj* ♦ : absolutely essential : REQUISITE — **in·dis·pens·abil·i·ty** \-ˌspen-sə-'bi-lə-tē\ *n* — **indispensable** *n* — **in·dis·pens·ably** \-'spen-sə-blē\ *adv*

♦ essential, imperative, integral, necessary, needful, requisite, vital — more at ESSENTIAL

in·dis·posed \-'spōzd\ *adj* **1** ♦ : slightly ill **2** ♦ : having an active feeling of reluctance or dislike : AVERSE

♦ [1] bad, down, ill, peaked, punk, sick, unhealthy, unsound, unwell — more at SICK ♦ [2] afraid, dubious, hesitant, reluctant — more at HESITANT

in·dis·po·si·tion \(ˌ)in-ˌdis-pə-'zi-shən\ *n* : the condition of being indisposed: as **a** : slight aversion **b** : a usu. slight illness

in·dis·put·able \ˌin-di-'spyü-tə-bəl, (ˌ)in-'dis-pyə-\ *adj* ♦ : not disputable : UNQUESTIONABLE ⟨∼ proof⟩

♦ incontestable, indubitable, irrefutable, unanswerable, undeniable, unquestionable — more at IRREFUTABLE

in·dis·put·ably \-blē\ *adv* ♦ : not open to question

♦ certainly, definitely, doubtless, incontestably, indeed, really, surely, truly, undeniably, undoubtedly, unquestionably — more at INDEED

in·dis·sol·u·ble \ˌin-di-'säl-yə-bəl\ *adj* : not capable of being dissolved, undone, or broken : PERMANENT

in·dis·tinct \ˌin-di-'stiŋkt\ *adj* **1** : not sharply outlined or separable : BLURRED, FAINT, DIM **2** ♦ : not readily distinguishable — **in·dis·tinct·ly** *adv* — **in·dis·tinct·ness** *n*

♦ bleary, dim, faint, foggy, fuzzy, hazy, indefinite, indistinguishable, murky, nebulous, obscure, opaque, shadowy, unclear, undefined, undetermined, vague — more at FAINT

in·dis·tin·guish·able \ˌin-di-'stiŋ-gwi-shə-bəl, -'stiŋ-wi-\ *adj* : not distinguishable: as **a** : indeterminate in shape or structure **b** ♦ : not clearly recognizable or understandable **c** ♦ : lacking identifying or individualizing qualities

♦ [b] impalpable, imperceptible, inappreciable — more at IMPERCEPTIBLE ♦ [c] duplicate, equal, even, identical, same — more at SAME

in·dite \in-'dīt\ *vb* **in·dit·ed; in·dit·ing** : COMPOSE ⟨∼ a poem⟩; *also* : to put in writing ⟨∼ a letter⟩

in·di·um \'in-dē-əm\ *n* : a malleable silvery metallic chemical element

indiv *abbr* individual

¹**in·di·vid·u·al** \ˌin-də-'vi-jə-wəl\ *adj* **1** ♦ : of, relating to, or associated with an individual ⟨∼ traits⟩ **2** : being an individual : existing as an indivisible whole **3** : intended for one person **4** : SEPARATE ⟨∼ copies⟩ **5** ♦ : having marked individuality ⟨an ∼ style⟩ — **in·di·vid·u·al·ly** *adv*

♦ [1] particular, peculiar, personal, private, separate, singular, unique; *also* characteristic, distinctive, intimate; identifying, idiosyncratic, special, specific; independent, nonconformist, self-sufficient; custom, customized, specialized *Ant* general, generic, public, popular, shared, universal ♦ [5] different, respective, separate — more at SEPARATE

²**individual** *n* **1** ♦ : a single member of a category : a particular person, animal, or thing **2** ♦ : a single human being ⟨a disagreeable ∼⟩

♦ [1] being, entity, object, substance, thing — more at ENTITY ♦ [2] being, body, creature, human, man, mortal, person — more at HUMAN

in·di·vid·u·al·ise *chiefly Brit var of* INDIVIDUALIZE

in·di·vid·u·al·ism \ˌin-də-'vi-jə-wə-ˌli-zəm\ *n* **1** : a doctrine that the interests of the individual are primary **2** : a doctrine holding that the individual has political or economic rights with which the state must not interfere **3** : INDIVIDUALITY

in·di·vid·u·al·ist \-list\ *n* **1** ♦ : one that pursues a markedly independent course in thought or action **2** : one that advocates or practices individualism — **individualist** *or* **in·di·vid·u·al·is·tic** \-ˌvi-jə-wə-'lis-tik\ *adj*

♦ bohemian, deviant, loner, maverick, nonconformist — more at NONCONFORMIST

in·di·vid·u·al·i·ty \-ˌvi-jə-'wa-lə-tē\ *n, pl* **-ties** **1** ♦ : the sum of qualities that characterize and distinguish an individ-

ual from all others; *also* : PERSONALITY **2** : separate or distinct existence **3** : INDIVIDUAL, PERSON

♦ character, identity, personality, self-identity; *also* distinctiveness, oneness, peculiarity, singleness, singularity, uniqueness; disposition, humor, nature, temper, temperament; independence

in·di·vid·u·al·ize \-'vi-jə-wə-ˌlīz\ *vb* **-ized; -iz·ing** **1** : to make individual in character **2** : to treat or notice individually : PARTICULARIZE **3** : to adapt to the needs of an individual

individual retirement account *n* : IRA

in·di·vid·u·ate \ˌin-də-'vi-jə-ˌwāt\ *vb* **-at·ed; -at·ing** : to give individuality to : form into an individual — **in·di·vid·u·a·tion** \-ˌvi-jə-'wā-shən\ *n*

in·di·vis·i·ble \ˌin-də-'vi-zə-bəl\ *adj* : impossible to divide or separate — **in·di·vis·i·bil·i·ty** \-ˌvi-zə-'bi-lə-tē\ *n* — **in·di·vis·i·bly** *adv*

In·do–Ar·y·an \ˌin-dō-'er-ē-ən\ *n* : a branch of the Indo-European language family that includes Hindi and other languages of south Asia

in·doc·tri·nate \in-'däk-trə-ˌnāt\ *vb* **-nat·ed; -nat·ing** **1** ♦ : to instruct esp. in fundamentals or rudiments : TEACH **2** : to teach the beliefs and doctrines of a particular group — **in·doc·tri·na·tion** \(ˌ)in-ˌdäk-trə-'nā-shən\ *n* — **in·doc·tri·na·tor** *n*

♦ educate, instruct, school, teach, train, tutor — more at TEACH

In·do–Eu·ro·pe·an \ˌin-dō-ˌyùr-ə-'pē-ən\ *adj* : of, relating to, or constituting a family of languages comprising those spoken in most of Europe and in the parts of the world colonized by Europeans since 1500 and also in Persia, the subcontinent of India, and some other parts of Asia

in·do·lence \-ləns\ *n* ♦ : inclination to laziness

♦ idleness, inertia, laziness, sloth — more at LAZINESS

in·do·lent \'in-də-lənt\ *adj* [LL *indolens* insensitive to pain, fr. L *dolēre* to feel pain] **1** : slow to develop or heal ⟨∼ ulcers⟩ **2** ♦ : averse to activity, effort, or movement : LAZY — **in·do·lent·ly** *adv*

♦ idle, lazy, shiftless, slothful — more at LAZY

in·dom·i·ta·ble \in-'dä-mə-tə-bəl\ *adj* ♦ : incapable of being subdued : UNCONQUERABLE ⟨∼ courage⟩ — **in·dom·i·ta·bly** \-blē\ *adv*

♦ impregnable, insurmountable, invincible, invulnerable, unbeatable, unconquerable — more at INVINCIBLE

In·do·ne·sian \ˌin-də-'nē-zhən\ *n* : a native or inhabitant of the Republic of Indonesia — **Indonesian** *adj*

in·door \'in-ˌdór\ *adj* **1** : of or relating to the inside of a building **2** : living, located, or carried on within a building

in·doors \in-'dórz\ *adv* : in or into a building

indorse, indorsement *var of* ENDORSE, ENDORSEMENT

in·du·bi·ta·ble \(ˌ)in-'dü-bə-tə-bəl, -'dyü-\ *adj* ♦ : too evident to be doubted : UNQUESTIONABLE ⟨∼ truths⟩ — **in·du·bi·ta·bly** \-blē\ *adv*

♦ incontestable, indisputable, irrefutable, unanswerable, undeniable, unquestionable — more at IRREFUTABLE

in·duce \in-'düs, -'dyüs\ *vb* **in·duced; in·duc·ing** **1** ♦ : to move by persuasion or influence : PERSUADE **2** : to serve as the cause of : BRING ABOUT **3** : to produce (as an electric current) by induction **4** : to determine by induction; *esp* : to infer from particulars — **in·duc·er** *n*

♦ argue, convince, get, move, persuade, prevail, satisfy, talk, win — more at PERSUADE

in·duce·ment \-mənt\ *n* **1** : something that induces : MOTIVE **2** ♦ : the act or process of inducing

♦ convincing, persuasion — more at PERSUASION

in·duct \in-'dəkt\ *vb* **1** ♦ : to place in office **2** ♦ : to admit as a member **3** : to enroll for military training or service — **in·duct·ee** \-ˌdək-'tē\ *n*

♦ [1, 2] baptize, inaugurate, initiate, install, invest — more at INSTALL

in·duc·tance \in-'dək-təns\ *n* : a property of an electric circuit by which a varying current produces an electromotive force in that circuit or in a nearby circuit; *also* : the measure of this property

in·duc·tion \in-'dək-shən\ *n* 1 ♦ : the act or process of inducting; *also* : INITIATION 2 : the formality by which a civilian is inducted into military service 3 : inference of a generalized conclusion from particular instances; *also* : a conclusion so reached 4 : the act of causing or bringing on or about 5 : the process by which an electric current, an electric charge, or magnetism is produced in a body by the proximity of an electric or magnetic field

♦ inaugural, inauguration, installation, investiture — more at INSTALLATION

in·duc·tive \in-'dək-tiv\ *adj* : of, relating to, or employing induction

in·duc·tor \in-'dək-tər\ *n* : an electrical component that acts upon another or is itself acted upon by induction

in·dulge \in-'dəlj\ *vb* **in·dulged; in·dulg·ing** 1 ♦ : to give free rein to : GRATIFY 2 : HUMOR 3 : to gratify one's taste or desire for ⟨∼ in alcohol⟩

♦ cater to, gratify, humor (*or* humour); *also* bask, luxuriate, revel, wallow; coddle, mollycoddle, pamper, spoil; sate, satiate, satisfy

in·dul·gence \in-'dəl-jəns\ *n* 1 : remission of temporal punishment due in Roman Catholic doctrine for sins whose eternal punishment has been remitted by reception of the sacrament of penance 2 : the act of indulging : the state of being indulgent 3 : an indulgent act 4 ♦ : the thing indulged in 5 : SELF-INDULGENCE

♦ amenity, comfort, extra, frill, luxury, superfluity — more at LUXURY

in·dul·gent \in-'dəl-jənt\ *adj* ♦ : indulging or characterized by indulgence — **in·dul·gent·ly** *adv*

♦ accommodating, friendly, obliging — more at AC-COMMODATING

in·du·rat·ed \'in-dyu̇-,rā-təd, -du̇-\ *adj* : physically or emotionally hardened — **in·du·ra·tion** \,in-dyu̇-'rā-shən, -du̇-\ *n*

in·dus·tri·al \in-'dəs-trē-əl\ *adj* 1 : of or relating to industry; *also* : HEAVY-DUTY 2 : characterized by highly developed industries — **in·dus·tri·al·ly** *adv*

in·dus·tri·al·ise *chiefly Brit var of* INDUSTRIALIZE

in·dus·tri·al·ist \-ə-list\ *n* : a person owning or engaged in the management of an industry

in·dus·tri·al·ize \in-'dəs-trē-ə-,līz\ *vb* **-ized; -iz·ing** : to make or become industrial — **in·dus·tri·al·i·za·tion** \-,dəs-trē-ə-lə-'zā-shən\ *n*

in·dus·tri·ous \in-'dəs-trē-əs\ *adj* : constantly, regularly, or habitually active or occupied : DILIGENT, BUSY

in·dus·tri·ous·ly *adv* : in an industrious manner

in·dus·tri·ous·ness *n* : the quality or state of being industrious

in·dus·try \'in-(,)dəs-trē\ *n, pl* **-tries** 1 ♦ : steady or habitual effort : DILIGENCE 2 : a department or branch of a craft, art, business, or manufacture; *esp* : one that employs a large personnel and capital 3 : a distinct group of productive enterprises 4 : manufacturing activity as a whole

♦ assiduity, diligence — more at DILIGENCE

in·dwell \(,)in-'dwel\ *vb* : to exist within as an activating spirit or force

In·dy car \'in-dē-\ *n* : a single-seat, open-cockpit racing car with the engine in the rear

¹**in·ebri·ate** \i-'nē-brē-,āt\ *vb* **-at·ed; -at·ing** : to make drunk : INTOXICATE — **in·ebri·a·tion** \-,nē-brē-'ā-shən\ *n*

²**in·ebri·ate** \-ət\ *n* : one that is drunk; *esp* : DRUNKARD

♦ drunk, drunkard, soak, souse, tippler — more at DRUNK

in·ef·fa·ble \(,)in-'e-fə-bəl\ *adj* 1 ♦ : incapable of being expressed in words : INDESCRIBABLE ⟨∼ joy⟩ 2 : UN-SPEAKABLE ⟨∼ disgust⟩ 3 : not to be uttered : TABOO — **in·ef·fa·bly** \-blē\ *adv*

♦ indescribable, inexpressible, nameless, unspeakable, unutterable — more at INDESCRIBABLE

in·ef·fec·tive \,i-nə-'fek-tiv\ *adj* 1 : not producing an intended effect : INEFFECTUAL 2 : incapable of performing efficiently — **in·ef·fec·tive·ly** *adv* — **in·ef·fec·tive·ness** *n*

in·ef·fec·tu·al \-'fek-chə-wəl\ *adj* : INEFFECTIVE — **in·ef·fec·tu·al·ly** *adv*

in·ef·fi·cient \,i-nə-'fi-shənt\ *adj* 1 : not producing the desired effect 2 : wasteful of time or energy 3 : INCAPABLE, INCOMPETENT — **in·ef·fi·cien·cy** \-'fi-shən-sē\ *n* — **in·ef·fi·cient·ly** *adv*

in·el·e·gant \(,)i-'ne-li-gənt\ *adj* ♦ : lacking in refinement, grace, or good taste — **in·el·e·gance** \-gəns\ *n* — **in·el·e·gant·ly** *adv*

♦ awkward, clumsy, gauche, graceless, stiff, stilted, uncomfortable, uneasy, ungraceful, wooden — more at AWKWARD ♦ dowdy, tacky, tasteless, trashy, unfashionable, unstylish — more at TACKY

in·el·i·gi·ble \(,)i-'ne-lə-jə-bəl\ *adj* : not qualified for an office or position — **in·el·i·gi·bil·i·ty** \(,)i-,ne-lə-jə-'bi-lə-tē\ *n*

in·eluc·ta·ble \,i-ni-'lək-tə-bəl\ *adj* : not to be avoided, changed, or resisted — **in·eluc·ta·bly** \-blē\ *adv*

in·ept \i-'nept\ *adj* 1 ♦ : lacking in fitness or aptitude : UNFIT 2 : FOOLISH 3 ♦ : inappropriate to the time or circumstances 4 ♦ : generally incompetent : BUNGLING — **in·ept·ly** *adv* — **in·ept·ness** *n*

♦ [1, 4] incapable, incompetent, inexpert, unfit, unqualified, unskilled, unskillful — more at INCOMPE-TENT ♦ [3] improper, inappropriate, inapt, infelicitous, unbecoming, unfit, unseemly, unsuitable, wrong — more at INAPPROPRIATE

in·ep·ti·tude \(,)i-'nep-ti-,tüd, -,tyüd\ *n* ♦ : the quality or state of being inept; *esp* : INCOMPETENCE

♦ impotence, inability, inadequacy, incapability, incompetence — more at INABILITY

in·equal·i·ty \,i-ni-'kwä-lə-tē\ *n* 1 : the quality of being unequal or uneven; *esp* : UNEVENNESS, DISPARITY 2 : an instance of being unequal

in·ert \i-'nərt\ *adj* [L *inert-, iners* unskilled, idle, fr. *art-, ars* skill] 1 ♦ : powerless to move 2 ♦ : averse to activity or exertion : SLUGGISH 3 : lacking in active properties ⟨chemically ∼⟩ — **in·ert·ly** *adv*

♦ [1] dead, dormant, fallow, free, idle, inactive, inoperative, latent, off, vacant — more at INACTIVE ♦ [2] dull, inactive, lethargic, quiescent, sleepy, sluggish, torpid — more at INACTIVE

in·er·tia \i-'nər-shə, -shē-ə\ *n* 1 : a property of matter whereby it remains at rest or continues in uniform motion unless acted upon by some outside force 2 ♦ : indisposition to motion, exertion, or change — **in·er·tial** \-shəl\ *adj*

♦ idleness, indolence, laziness, sloth — more at LAZI-NESS

in·ert·ness *n* ♦ : the quality or state of being inert : lack of activity

♦ dormancy, idleness, inaction, inactivity, quiescence — more at INACTION

in·es·cap·able \,i-nə-'skā-pə-bəl\ *adj* : incapable of being escaped : INEVITABLE

in·es·cap·ably \-blē\ *adv* : in an inevitable way

in·es·ti·ma·ble \(,)i-'nes-tə-mə-bəl\ *adj* 1 : incapable of being estimated or computed ⟨∼ errors⟩ 2 : too valuable or excellent to be fully appreciated — **in·es·ti·ma·bly** \-blē\ *adv*

in·ev·i·ta·ble \i-'ne-və-tə-bəl\ *adj* ♦ : incapable of being avoided or evaded : bound to happen ⟨the ∼ result⟩ — **in·ev·i·ta·bil·i·ty** \(,)i-,ne-və-tə-'bi-lə-tē\ *n*

♦ certain, necessary, sure, unavoidable; *also* decided, definite, settled; likely, possible, probable; destined, fated, foreordained, predestined, preordained; inexorable, relentless, unremitting *Ant* avoidable, uncertain, unsure

in·ev·i·ta·bly \-blē\ *adv* **1** : in an inevitable way **2** ♦ : as is to be expected

♦ necessarily, needs, perforce, unavoidably — more at NEEDS

in·ex·act \ˌi-nig-ˈzakt\ *adj* **1** ♦ : not precisely correct or true : INACCURATE **2** : not rigorous and careful — **in·ex·act·ly** *adv* — **in·ex·act·ness** *n*

♦ erroneous, false, inaccurate, incorrect, invalid, off, unsound, untrue, wrong — more at FALSE ♦ imprecise, inaccurate, loose; *also* approximate; erroneous, false, incorrect, off, wrong; general, indefinable, indefinite, indeterminate, indistinct, undefined, undetermined, unsettled, vague; faulty, mistaken; specious; distorted, fallacious, misleading; doubtful, dubious, questionable, uncertain; inconclusive, indecisive, debatable, disputable; unconfirmed, unsubstantiated, unsupported *Ant* accurate, dead, exact, precise

in·ex·cus·able \ˌi-nik-ˈskyü-zə-bəl\ *adj* ♦ : being without excuse or justification — **in·ex·cus·ably** \-blē\ *adv*

♦ indefensible, unforgivable, unjustifiable, unpardonable, unwarrantable; *also* insufferable, insupportable, intolerable, unbearable, unendurable; abominable, atrocious, heinous, monstrous, outrageous, scandalous, shocking; egregious, flagrant, glaring, gross, rank; unacceptable, untenable; black, evil, iniquitous, vicious, wicked; base, contemptible, deplorable, despicable, dirty, execrable, ignoble, vile, reprobate, wretched; cruel, nasty; blamable, blameworthy, censurable, reprehensible; banned, barred, condemned, disallowed, forbidden, interdicted, outlawed, prohibited, proscribed *Ant* defensible, excusable, forgivable, justifiable, pardonable

in·ex·haust·ible \ˌi-nig-ˈzȯ-stə-bəl\ *adj* **1** : incapable of being used up ⟨an ~ supply⟩ **2** ♦ : incapable of being wearied or worn out : UNTIRING — **in·ex·haust·ibly** \-blē\ *adv*

♦ indefatigable, tireless, unflagging, untiring — more at TIRELESS

in·ex·o·ra·ble \(ˌ)i-ˈnek-sə-rə-bəl\ *adj* : not to be moved by entreaty : RELENTLESS — **in·ex·o·ra·bly** *adv*

in·ex·pen·sive \ˌi-nik-ˈspen(t)-siv\ *adj* : reasonable in price

in·ex·pe·ri·ence \ˌi-nik-ˈspir-ē-əns\ *n* : lack of experience or of knowledge gained by experience

in·ex·pe·ri·enced \-ənst\ *adj* ♦ : lacking practical experience

♦ amateur, amateurish, inexpert, nonprofessional, unprofessional, unskilled, unskillful — more at AMATEURISH

in·ex·pert \(ˌ)i-ˈnek-ˌspərt\ *adj* ♦ : not expert : UNSKILLED — **in·ex·pert·ly** *adv*

♦ amateur, amateurish, inexperienced, nonprofessional, unprofessional, unskilled, unskillful — more at AMATEURISH

in·ex·pi·a·ble \(ˌ)i-ˈnek-spē-ə-bəl\ *adj* : not capable of being atoned for

in·ex·pli·ca·ble \ˌi-nik-ˈspli-kə-bəl, (ˌ)i-ˈnek-(ˌ)spli-\ *adj* : incapable of being explained or accounted for ⟨an ~ mistake⟩ — **in·ex·pli·ca·bly** \-blē\ *adv*

in·ex·press·ible \-ˈspre-sə-bəl\ *adj* ♦ : not capable of being expressed ⟨~ joy⟩ — **in·ex·press·ibly** \-blē\ *adv*

♦ indescribable, ineffable, nameless, unspeakable, unutterable — more at INDESCRIBABLE

in·ex·pres·sive \-ˈspre-siv\ *adj* ♦ : lacking expression or meaning

♦ blank, deadpan, expressionless, impassive, stolid, vacant — more at BLANK

in ex·tre·mis \ˌin-ik-ˈstrā-məs, -ˈstrē-\ *adv* : in extreme circumstances; *esp* : at the point of death

in·ex·tri·ca·ble \ˌi-nik-ˈstri-kə-bəl, (ˌ)i-ˈnek-(ˌ)stri-\ *adj* **1** : forming a maze or tangle from which it is impossible to get free **2** : incapable of being disentangled or untied — **in·ex·tri·ca·bly** \-blē\ *adv*

inf *abbr* **1** infantry **2** infinitive

in·fal·li·ble \(ˌ)in-ˈfa-lə-bəl\ *adj* **1** : incapable of error : UNERRING **2** ♦ : not liable to mislead, deceive, or disappoint : SURE, CERTAIN ⟨an ~ remedy⟩ — **in·fal·li·bil·i·ty** \(ˌ)in-ˌfa-lə-ˈbi-lə-tē\ *n* — **in·fal·li·bly** \(ˌ)in-ˈfa-lə-blē\ *adv*

♦ certain, sure, unfailing; *also* dependable, reliable, surefire; deadly, unerring *Ant* fallible

in·fa·mous \ˈin-fə-məs\ *adj* **1** ♦ : having a reputation of the worst kind **2** ♦ : causing or bringing infamy : DISGRACEFUL — **in·fa·mous·ly** *adv*

♦ [1, 2] discreditable, disgraceful, dishonorable (*or* dishonourable), disreputable, ignominious, notorious, shameful — more at DISREPUTABLE

in·fa·my \-mē\ *n, pl* **-mies** **1** : evil reputation brought about by something grossly criminal, shocking, or brutal **2** : an extreme and publicly known criminal or evil act **3** ♦ : the state of being infamous

♦ discredit, disgrace, dishonor (*or* dishonour), disrepute, ignominy, odium, opprobrium, reproach, shame — more at DISGRACE

in·fan·cy \ˈin-fən-sē\ *n, pl* **-cies** **1** : early childhood **2** : a beginning or early period of existence

in·fant \ˈin-fənt\ *n* [ME *enfaunt*, fr. AF *enfant*, fr. L *infant-*, *infans*, adj., incapable of speech, young, fr. *fant-*, *fans*, prp. of *fari* to speak] ♦ : a child in the first period of life : BABY; *also* : a person who is a legal minor

♦ baby, child, newborn — more at BABY

in·fan·ti·cide \in-ˈfan-tə-ˌsīd\ *n* : the killing of an infant

in·fan·tile \ˈin-fən-ˌtīl, -tᵊl, -ˌtēl\ *adj* ♦ : of or relating to infants; *also* : CHILDISH

♦ adolescent, babyish, childish, immature, juvenile, kiddish — more at CHILDISH

infantile paralysis *n* : POLIOMYELITIS

in·fan·try \ˈin-fən-trē\ *n, pl* **-tries** [MF & It; MF *infanterie*, fr. It *infanteria*, fr. *infante* boy, foot soldier] : soldiers trained, armed, and equipped to fight on foot — **in·fan·try·man** \-mən\ *n*

in·farct \ˈin-ˌfärkt\ *n* [L *infarctus*, pp. of *infarcire* to stuff] : an area of dead tissue (as of the heart wall) caused by blocking of local blood circulation — **in·farc·tion** \in-ˈfärk-shən\ *n*

in·fat·u·ate \in-ˈfa-chə-ˌwāt\ *vb* **-at·ed; -at·ing** : to inspire with a foolish or extravagant love or admiration — **in·fat·u·a·tion** \-ˌfa-chə-ˈwā-shən\ *n*

in·fect \in-ˈfekt\ *vb* **1** : to contaminate with disease-producing matter **2** : to communicate a pathogen or disease to **3** : to cause to share one's feelings

in·fec·tion \in-ˈfek-shən\ *n* **1** : a disease or condition caused by a germ or parasite; *also* : such a germ or parasite **2** : an act or process of infecting — **in·fec·tive** \-ˈfek-tiv\ *adj*

in·fec·tious \-shəs\ *adj* **1** : capable of causing infection; *also* : communicable by infection **2** ♦ : spreading or capable of spreading rapidly to others

♦ catching, contagious — more at CONTAGIOUS

infectious mononucleosis *n* : an acute infectious disease characterized by fever, swelling of lymph glands, and increased numbers of lymph cells in the blood

in·fe·lic·i·tous \ˌin-fi-ˈli-sə-təs\ *adj* ♦ : not appropriate in application or expression — **in·fe·lic·i·ty** \-sə-tē\ *n*

♦ improper, inappropriate, inapt, unbecoming, unfit, unseemly, unsuitable, wrong — more at INAPPROPRIATE

in·fer \in-ˈfər\ *vb* **in·ferred; in·fer·ring** **1** ♦ : to derive as a conclusion from facts or premises **2** : GUESS, SURMISE **3** : to lead to as a conclusion or consequence **4** ♦ : to convey indirectly and by allusion rather than explicitly : HINT, SUGGEST

♦ [1] conclude, deduce, extrapolate, gather, judge, reason, understand; *also* conjecture, guess, speculate, surmise; construe, interpret; contemplate, rationalize, think; ascertain, dope (out), find out ♦ [4] allude, hint, imply, indicate, insinuate, intimate, suggest — more at HINT

¹in·fe·ri·or \in-ˈfir-ē-ər\ *adj* **1** : situated lower down **2** ♦ : of low or lower degree or rank **3** ♦ : of lesser quality **4** ♦ : of little or less importance, value, or merit ⟨an ∼ opponent⟩ — **in·fe·ri·or·i·ty** \(ˌ)in-ˌfir-ē-ˈór-ə-tē\ *n*

♦ [2] common, humble, ignoble, low, lowly, mean, plebeian, vulgar — more at IGNOBLE ♦ [3] cheap, cut-rate, junky, lousy, mediocre, shoddy, sleazy, trashy — more at CHEAP ♦ [4] junior, less, lesser, lower, minor, subordinate, under — more at LESSER ♦ [4] mean, minor, secondary, second-rate; *also* junior, lesser, lower, petty, subordinate, under; average, common, fair, middling, ordinary; amiss, bad, defective, unsatisfactory, wrong; deficient, inadequate, insufficient, unacceptable; littler; jerkwater *Ant* superior

²inferior *n* ♦ : a person or thing inferior to another (as in worth, status, or importance)

♦ junior, subordinate, underling — more at UNDERLING

in·fer·nal \in-ˈfərn-ᵊl\ *adj* **1** : of or relating to hell **2** : HELLISH, FIENDISH ⟨∼ schemes⟩ **3** : DAMNABLE ⟨an ∼ pest⟩ — **in·fer·nal·ly** *adv*

in·fer·no \in-ˈfər-nō\ *n, pl* **-nos** [It, hell, fr. LL *infernus*, fr. L, lower] ♦ : a place or a state that resembles or suggests hell; *also* : intense heat

♦ conflagration, fire, holocaust — more at FIRE

in·fer·tile \(ˌ)in-ˈfərt-ᵊl\ *adj* ♦ : not fertile or productive : BARREN — **in·fer·til·i·ty** \ˌin-fər-ˈti-lə-tē\ *n*

♦ barren, impotent, sterile, unproductive — more at STERILE

in·fest \in-ˈfest\ *vb* : to trouble by spreading or swarming in or over; *also* : to live in or on as a parasite — **in·fes·ta·tion** \ˌin-ˌfes-ˈtā-shən\ *n*

in·fi·del \ˈin-fəd-ᵊl, -fə-ˌdel\ *n* **1** : one who is not a Christian or opposes Christianity **2** : an unbeliever esp. with respect to a particular religion

in·fi·del·i·ty \ˌin-fə-ˈde-lə-tē, -fī-\ *n, pl* **-ties** **1** : lack of belief in a religion **2** ♦ : unfaithfulness to a moral obligation : DISLOYALTY **3** ♦ : marital unfaithfulness or an instance of it

♦ [2, 3] betrayal, disloyalty, double cross, treachery, treason — more at BETRAYAL ♦ [3] disloyalty, faithlessness, falseness, falsity, inconstancy, perfidy, unfaithfulness; *also* adultery; betrayal, double-dealing, duplicity, treachery, treason; deceit, deception, lying *Ant* allegiance, constancy, devotion, faith, faithfulness, fealty, fidelity, loyalty

in·field \ˈin-ˌfēld\ *n* : the part of a baseball field inside the baselines — **in·field·er** *n*

in·fight·ing \ˈin-ˌfīt-iŋ\ *n* **1** : fighting at close quarters **2** : dissension or rivalry among members of a group

in·fil·trate \in-ˈfil-ˌtrāt, ˈin-(ˌ)fil-\ *vb* **-trat·ed; -trat·ing** **1** : to enter or filter into or through something **2** ♦ : to pass into or through by or as if by filtering or permeating — **in·fil·tra·tion** \ˌin-(ˌ)fil-ˈtrā-shən\ *n* — **in·fil·tra·tor** *n*

♦ insinuate, slip, sneak, work, worm — more at INSINUATE

in·fi·nite \ˈin-fə-nət\ *adj* **1** ♦ : extending indefinitely : LIMITLESS, ENDLESS ⟨∼ space⟩ ⟨∼ patience⟩ **2** : VAST, IMMENSE; *also* : INEXHAUSTIBLE ⟨∼ wealth⟩ **3** : greater than any preassigned finite value however large ⟨∼ number of positive integers⟩; *also* : extending to infinity ⟨∼ plane surface⟩ — **infinite** *n* — **in·fi·nite·ly** *adv*

♦ boundless, endless, illimitable, immeasurable, indefinite, limitless, measureless, unbounded, unfathomable, unlimited; *also* abysmal, bottomless; countless, incalculable, inestimable, innumerable, unmeasured; inexhaustible; far-flung, immense, vast *Ant* bounded, circumscribed, confined, definite, finite, limited, restricted

in·fin·i·tes·i·mal \(ˌ)in-ˌfi-nə-ˈte-sə-məl\ *adj* ♦ : immeasurably or incalculably small — **in·fin·i·tes·i·mal·ly** *adv*

♦ atomic, microscopic, miniature, minute, teeny, tiny, wee — more at TINY

in·fin·i·tive \in-ˈfi-nə-tiv\ *n* : a verb form having the characteristics of both verb and noun and in English usu. being used with *to*

in·fin·i·tude \in-ˈfi-nə-ˌtüd, -ˌtyüd\ *n* **1** : the quality or state of being infinite **2** : something that is infinite esp. in extent

in·fin·i·ty \in-ˈfi-nə-tē\ *n, pl* **-ties** **1** : the quality of being infinite **2** : unlimited extent of time, space, or quantity **3** : an indefinitely great number or amount

in·firm \in-ˈfərm\ *adj* **1** ♦ : deficient in vitality; *esp* : feeble from age **2** : weak of mind, will, or character : IRRESOLUTE **3** : not solid or stable : INSECURE

♦ delicate, faint, feeble, frail, wasted, weak — more at WEAK

in·fir·ma·ry \in-ˈfər-mə-rē\ *n, pl* **-ries** : a place for the care of the infirm or sick

in·fir·mi·ty \in-ˈfər-mə-tē\ *n, pl* **-ties** **1** ♦ : the condition of being feeble : FEEBLENESS **2** ♦ : a disease or disorder of the animal body : AILMENT **3** : a personal failing : FOIBLE

♦ [1] debility, delicacy, enfeeblement, faintness, feebleness, frailty, languor, lowness, weakness — more at WEAKNESS ♦ [2] ailment, bug, complaint, complication, condition, disease, disorder, fever, illness, malady, sickness, trouble

infl *abbr* influenced

in fla·gran·te de·lic·to \ˌin-flə-ˈgrän-tē-di-ˈlik-tō, -ˈgran-\ *adv* **1** : in the very act of committing a misdeed **2** : in the midst of sexual activity

in·flame \in-ˈflām\ *vb* **in·flamed; in·flam·ing** **1** ♦ : to set on fire : KINDLE **2** ♦ : to excite to excessive or uncontrollable action or feeling; *also* : INTENSIFY **3** : to affect or become affected with inflammation

♦ [1] burn, fire, ignite, kindle, light — more at BURN ♦ [2] anger, antagonize, enrage, incense, infuriate, intensify, madden, outrage, rankle, rile, roil — more at ANGER

in·flam·ma·ble \in-ˈfla-mə-bəl\ *adj* **1** ♦ : capable of being easily ignited and of burning quickly : FLAMMABLE **2** : easily inflamed, excited, or angered : IRASCIBLE

♦ combustible, flammable, ignitable — more at COMBUSTIBLE

in·flam·ma·tion \ˌin-flə-ˈmā-shən\ *n* : a bodily response to injury in which an affected area becomes red, hot, and painful and congested with blood

in·flam·ma·to·ry \in-ˈfla-mə-ˌtȯr-ē\ *adj* **1** : tending to excite the senses or to arouse anger, disorder, or tumult : SEDITIOUS **2** : causing or accompanied by inflammation ⟨an ∼ disease⟩

in·flate \in-ˈflāt\ *vb* **in·flat·ed; in·flat·ing** **1** : to swell with air or gas ⟨∼ a balloon⟩ **2** : to puff up : ELATE **3** : to expand or increase abnormally ⟨∼ prices⟩ — **in·flat·able** *adj*

in·fla·tion \in-ˈflā-shən\ *n* **1** : an act of inflating : the state of being inflated **2** : empty pretentiousness : POMPOSITY **3** : a continuing rise in the general price level usu. attributed to an increase in the volume of money and credit

in·fla·tion·ary \-shə-ˌner-ē\ *adj* : of, characterized by, or productive of inflation

in·flect \in-ˈflekt\ *vb* **1** : to turn from a direct line or course : CURVE **2** : to vary a word by inflection **3** : to change or vary the pitch of the voice

in·flec·tion \in-ˈflek-shən\ *n* **1** : the act or result of curving or bending **2** : a change in pitch or loudness of the voice **3** : the change of form that words undergo to mark case, gender, number, tense, person, mood, or voice — **in·flec·tion·al** \-shə-nəl\ *adj*

in·flex·i·bil·i·ty \-ˌflek-sə-ˈbi-lə-tē\ *n* ♦ : the quality or state of being inflexible

♦ hardness, harshness, rigidity, severity, sternness, strictness — more at SEVERITY

in·flex·i·ble \(ˌ)in-ˈflek-sə-bəl\ adj 1 ♦ : rigidly firm in will or purpose : UNYIELDING 2 ♦ : not readily bent : RIGID 3 ♦ : incapable of change — in·flex·i·bly \-ˈflek-sə-blē\ adv

♦ [1, 2] adamant, hard, immovable, implacable, pat, rigid, steadfast, unbending, uncompromising, unflinching, unrelenting, unyielding; also grim, severe, stern, strict; determined, firm; dogged, intractable, obdurate, obstinate, relentless, stubborn, tenacious; confirmed, inveterate, unregenerate; demanding, exacting Ant acquiescent, agreeable, amenable, compliant, flexible, pliant, pliable ♦ [3] fast, fixed, hard-and-fast, immutable, unalterable, unchangeable; also constant, determinate, established, set, settled, stable, steadfast, steady, unaltered, unchanging, unvarying; immovable, unmovable Ant changeable, flexible, mutable, variable

in·flex·ion \in-ˈflek-shən\ chiefly Brit var of INFLECTION
in·flict \in-ˈflikt\ vb : AFFLICT; also : to give by or as if by striking ⟨~ pain⟩ — in·flic·tion \-ˈflik-shən\ n
in·flo·res·cence \ˌin-flə-ˈres-ᵊns\ n : the manner of development and arrangement of flowers on a stem; also : a flowering stem with its appendages : a flower cluster
in·flow \ˈin-ˌflō\ n : a flowing in
¹in·flu·ence \ˈin-ˌflü-əns\ n 1 ♦ : the act or power of producing an effect without apparent force or direct authority 2 ♦ : the power or capacity of causing an effect in indirect or intangible ways ⟨under the ~ of liquor⟩ 3 : a person or thing that exerts influence — in·flu·enc·er n

♦ [1] authority, clout, pull, sway, weight; also command, dominance, dominion, mastery, predominance, scepter, sovereignty, supremacy; consequence, eminence, importance, moment; impact, impression, mark ♦ [2] effect, impact, mark, repercussion, sway — more at EFFECT

²influence vb -enced; -enc·ing 1 ♦ : to affect or alter by influence : SWAY 2 : to have an effect on the condition or development of : MODIFY

♦ affect, impact, impress, move, strike, sway, tell, touch — more at AFFECT

in·flu·en·tial \ˌin-flü-ˈen-chəl\ adj ♦ : exerting or possessing influence; also : having authority or ascendancy

♦ important, mighty, potent, powerful, significant, strong — more at IMPORTANT ♦ authoritative, forceful, weighty; also controlling, dominating, masterful; dominant, predominant, sovereign, supreme; eminent, important, momentous

in·flu·en·za \ˌin-flü-ˈen-zə\ n [It., lit., influence, fr. ML influentia; fr. the belief that epidemics were due to the influence of the stars] : an acute and highly contagious virus disease marked by fever, prostration, aches and pains, and respiratory inflammation; also : any of various feverish usu. virus diseases typically with respiratory symptoms
in·flux \ˈin-ˌfləks\ n : a coming in
in·fo \ˈin-(ˌ)fō\ n : INFORMATION
in·fold \in-ˈfōld\ vb 1 : ENFOLD 2 : to fold inward or toward one another
in·fo·mer·cial \ˈin-fō-ˌmər-shəl\ n : a television program that is an extended advertisement often including a discussion or demonstration
in·form \in-ˈfȯrm\ vb 1 ♦ : to communicate knowledge to : TELL 2 : to give information or knowledge 3 ♦ : to act as an informer

♦ [1] acquaint, advise, apprise, brief, clue, enlighten, familiarize, fill in, instruct, tell, wise — more at ENLIGHTEN ♦ [3] snitch, squeal, talk, tell — more at SQUEAL

in·for·mal \(ˌ)in-ˈfȯr-məl\ adj 1 ♦ : conducted or carried out without formality or ceremony ⟨an ~ party⟩ 2 ♦ : characteristic of or appropriate to ordinary, casual, or familiar use ⟨~ clothes⟩ — in·for·mal·i·ty \ˌin-fȯr-ˈma-lə-tē, -fər-\ n — in·for·mal·ly \(ˌ)in-ˈfȯr-mə-lē\ adv

♦ [1] irregular, unceremonious, unconventional, unorthodox; also unauthorized, unofficial; casual, easygoing, lax, loose, relaxed Ant ceremonial, ceremonious,

conventional, formal, orthodox, regular, routine ♦ [2] casual, everyday, workaday — more at CASUAL

in·for·mant \in-ˈfȯr-mənt\ n : a person who gives information : INFORMER
in·for·ma·tion \ˌin-fər-ˈmā-shən\ n 1 : the communication or reception of knowledge or intelligence 2 : knowledge obtained from investigation, study, or instruction : FACTS, DATA
in·for·ma·tion·al \-shə-nəl\ adj : relating to or giving information
information superhighway n : INTERNET
information technology n : technology involving computer systems and networks for the processing and distribution of data
in·for·ma·tive \in-ˈfȯr-mə-tiv\ adj ♦ : imparting knowledge : INSTRUCTIVE

♦ educational, instructive; also comprehensive, detailed, full; enlightening, explanatory, illuminating; chatty, gossipy, newsy; availing, beneficial, constructive, helpful, profitable; practical, serviceable, usable, useful, worthwhile Ant uninstructive

in·formed \in-ˈfȯrmd\ adj 1 ♦ : having or based on information 2 ♦ : having an education : KNOWLEDGEABLE

♦ [1] good, hard, just, levelheaded, logical, rational, reasonable, reasoned, sensible, sober, solid, valid, wellfounded — more at GOOD ♦ [2] abreast, conversant, familiar, knowledgeable, up, up-to-date, versed — more at FAMILIAR

informed consent n : consent to a medical procedure by someone who understands what is involved
in·form·er \-ˈfȯr-mər\ n ♦ : one that informs; esp : a person who informs against others for illegalities esp. for financial gain

♦ betrayer, blabbermouth, rat, snitch, stool pigeon, tattler, tattletale; also collaborator; gossip; snoop, spy

in·fo·tain·ment \ˌin-fō-ˈtān-mənt\ n : a television program that presents information (as news) in a manner intended to be entertaining
in·frac·tion \in-ˈfrak-shən\ n [ME, fr. ML infractio, fr. L, subduing, fr. infringere to break, crush] ♦ : the act of infringing : VIOLATION

♦ breach, infringement, offense, transgression, trespass, violation — more at BREACH

in·fra dig \ˌin-frə-ˈdig\ adj [short for L infra dignitatem] : being beneath one's dignity
in·fra·red \ˌin-frə-ˈred\ adj : being, relating to, or using radiation having wavelengths longer than those of red light — infrared n
in·fra·struc·ture \ˈin-frə-ˌstrək-chər\ n 1 : the underlying foundation or basic framework (as of a system or organization) 2 : the system of public works of a country, state, or region; also : the resources (as buildings or equipment) required for an activity
in·fre·quent \(ˌ)in-ˈfrē-kwənt\ adj 1 ♦ : seldom happening : RARE 2 : placed or occurring at wide intervals in space or time

♦ occasional, rare, sporadic; also scarce, scattered, uncommon, unique, unusual; choppy, discontinuous, erratic, fitful, intermittent, irregular, spasmodic, spotty, unsteady Ant frequent

in·fre·quent·ly \-lē\ adv ♦ : in an infrequent manner

♦ little, rarely, seldom — more at SELDOM

in·fringe \in-ˈfrinj\ vb in·fringed; in·fring·ing 1 : to encroach upon in a way that violates law or the rights of another : VIOLATE, TRANSGRESS ⟨~ a patent⟩ 2 : ENCROACH, TRESPASS
in·fringe·ment n ♦ : the act of infringing; also : an encroachment or trespass on a right or privilege

♦ breach, infraction, offense, transgression, trespass, violation — more at BREACH

in·fu·ri·ate \in-ˈfyu̇r-ē-ˌāt\ vb -at·ed; -at·ing ♦ : to make furious : ENRAGE — in·fu·ri·at·ing·ly adv

♦ anger, antagonize, enrage, incense, inflame, madden, outrage, rankle, rile, roil — more at ANGER

in·fuse \in-ˈfyüz\ *vb* **in·fused; in·fus·ing** 1 ♦ : to instill a principle or quality in 2 : INSPIRE, ANIMATE 3 : to steep (as tea) without boiling — **in·fu·sion** \-ˈfyü-zhən\ *n*

♦ imbue, inculcate, ingrain, invest, steep, suffuse; *also* animate, enliven, invigorate; implant, instill, plant; impregnate, permeate, pervade, saturate; deluge, drown, fill, flood, inundate, overwhelm, submerge

¹**-ing** \iŋ\ *n suffix* 1 : action or process ⟨sleep*ing*⟩ : instance of an action or process ⟨a meet*ing*⟩ 2 : product or result of an action or process ⟨an engrav*ing*⟩ ⟨earn*ings*⟩ 3 : something used in an action or process ⟨a bed cover*ing*⟩ 4 : something connected with, consisting of, or used in making (a specified thing) ⟨scaffold*ing*⟩ 5 : something related to (a specified concept) ⟨off*ing*⟩

²**-ing** *n suffix* : one of a (specified) kind

³**-ing** *vb suffix or adj suffix* — used to form the present participle ⟨sail*ing*⟩ and sometimes to form an adjective resembling a present participle but not derived from a verb ⟨swashbuckl*ing*⟩

in·ga·ther \ˈin-ˌga-thər\ *vb* : to gather in : ASSEMBLE

in·ge·nious \in-ˈjēn-yəs\ *adj* 1 ♦ : marked by special aptitude at discovering, inventing, or contriving 2 ♦ : marked by originality, resourcefulness, and cleverness in conception or execution — **in·ge·nious·ly** *adv*

♦ [1, 2] creative, imaginative, innovative, inventive, original — more at CREATIVE ♦ [2] artful, clever, creative, imaginative — more at CLEVER

in·ge·nious·ness *n* : the power or quality of ready invention

in·ge·nue *or* **in·gé·nue** \ˈan-jə-ˌnü, ˈän-; ˈaⁿ-zhə-, ˈäⁿ-\ *n* : a naive girl or young woman; *esp* : an actress portraying such a person

in·ge·nu·i·ty \ˌin-jə-ˈnü-ə-tē, -ˈnyü-\ *n, pl* **-ties** ♦ : skill or cleverness in planning or inventing : INVENTIVENESS

♦ creativity, invention, inventiveness, originality — more at CREATIVITY

in·gen·u·ous \in-ˈjen-yə-wəs\ *adj* [L *ingenuus* native, freeborn, fr. *gignere* to beget] 1 : STRAIGHTFORWARD, FRANK 2 ♦ : showing innocent or childlike simplicity and candidness : NAIVE

♦ green, innocent, naive, simple, unknowing, unsophisticated, unwary, unworldly — more at NAIVE

in·gen·u·ous·ly *adv* ♦ : in an ingenuous manner

♦ artlessly, naively, naturally, unaffectedly — more at NATURALLY

in·gen·u·ous·ness *n* ♦ : the quality of being ingenuous : absence of guile, reserve, or disguise

♦ artlessness, greenness, innocence, naïveté, naturalness, simplicity, unworldliness — more at NAÏVETÉ

in·gest \in-ˈjest\ *vb* : to take in for or as if for digestion — **in·ges·tion** \-ˈjes-chən\ *n*

in·gle·nook \ˈiŋ-gəl-ˌnuk\ *n* : a nook by a large open fireplace; *also* : a bench occupying this nook

in·glo·ri·ous \(ˌ)in-ˈglȯr-ē-əs\ *adj* 1 : SHAMEFUL 2 : not glorious : lacking fame or honor — **in·glo·ri·ous·ly** *adv*

in·got \ˈiŋ-gət\ *n* : a mass of metal cast in a form convenient for storage or transportation

¹**in·grain** \(ˌ)in-ˈgrān\ *vb* ♦ : to work indelibly into the natural texture or mental or moral constitution

♦ imbue, inculcate, infuse, invest, steep, suffuse — more at INFUSE

²**in·grain** \ˈin-ˌgrān\ *adj* 1 : made of fiber that is dyed before being spun into yarn 2 : made of yarn that is dyed before being woven or knitted 3 : INNATE — **in·grain** *n*

in·grained *adj* 1 : worked into the grain or fiber 2 ♦ : forming a part of the essence or inmost being

♦ essential, inborn, inherent, innate, integral, intrinsic, natural — more at INHERENT

in·grate \ˈin-ˌgrāt\ *n* : an ungrateful person

in·gra·ti·ate \in-ˈgrā-shē-ˌāt\ *vb* **-at·ed; -at·ing** : to gain favor by deliberate effort

in·gra·ti·at·ing *adj* 1 ♦ : capable of winning favor ⟨an ∼ smile⟩ 2 : FLATTERING ⟨an ∼ manner⟩

♦ endearing, winning, winsome; *also* adorable, charming, likable, lovable; affecting, poignant, touching; adulatory, deferential, groveling, kowtowing, obsequious, servile, sycophantic; drooling, slobbering; soapy, sugary, unctuous

in·grat·i·tude \(ˌ)in-ˈgra-tə-ˌtüd, -ˌtyüd\ *n* : lack of gratitude : UNGRATEFULNESS

in·gre·di·ent \in-ˈgrē-dē-ənt\ *n* ♦ : one of the substances that make up a mixture or compound : CONSTITUENT

♦ component, constituent, element, factor, member — more at ELEMENT

in·gress \ˈin-ˌgres\ *n* ♦ : a means or place of entry : ENTRANCE, ACCESS — **in·gres·sion** \in-ˈgre-shən\ *n*

♦ access, admission, doorway, entrance, entrée, entry, gateway — more at ENTRANCE

in·grow·ing \ˈin-ˌgrō-iŋ\ *adj* : growing or tending inward

in·grown \-ˌgrōn\ *adj* : grown in; *esp* : having the free tip or edge embedded in the flesh ⟨∼ toenail⟩

in·gui·nal \ˈiŋ-gwən-ᵊl\ *adj* : of, relating to, or situated in or near the region of the groin

in·hab·it \in-ˈha-bət\ *vb* : to live or dwell in — **in·hab·it·able** *adj*

in·hab·i·tant \in-ˈha-bə-tənt\ *n* ♦ : a permanent resident in a place

♦ denizen, dweller, occupant, resident; *also* aborigine, native; citizen, national, subject; colonist, émigré, migrant, newcomer, settler; burgher, townie, villager **Ant** transient

in·hal·ant \in-ˈhā-lənt\ *n* : something (as a medicine) that is inhaled

in·ha·la·tor \ˈin-hə-ˌlā-tər\ *n* : a device that provides a mixture of carbon dioxide and oxygen for breathing

in·hale \in-ˈhāl\ *vb* **in·haled; in·hal·ing** : to breathe in — **in·ha·la·tion** \ˌin-hə-ˈlā-shən\ *n*

in·hal·er \in-ˈhā-lər\ *n* : a device by means of which medicinal material is inhaled

in·har·mo·ni·ous \-här-ˈmō-nē-əs\ *adj* 1 ♦ : not harmonious 2 ♦ : not fitting or congenial

♦ discordant, discrepant, incompatible, incongruous

in·here \in-ˈhir\ *vb* **in·hered; in·her·ing** : to be inherent

in·her·ent \in-ˈhir-ənt, -ˈher-\ *adj* ♦ : established as an essential part of something : INTRINSIC

♦ essential, inborn, ingrained, innate, integral, intrinsic, natural; *also* basic, constitutional, elemental, fundamental; congenital, hereditary, inherited, inmost, inner, interior; internal; characteristic, distinctive, peculiar; normal, regular, typical **Ant** adventitious, extraneous, extrinsic

in·her·ent·ly \-lē\ *adv* ♦ : in an inherent manner

♦ constitutionally, innately, intrinsically, naturally — more at NATURALLY

in·her·it \in-ˈher-ət\ *vb* 1 : to receive esp. from one's ancestors 2 : to receive by genetic transmission — **in·her·i·tor** \-ə-tər\ *n*

in·her·it·able \-ə-tə-bəl\ *adj* 1 : capable of being inherited 2 : capable of taking by inheritance

in·her·i·tance \-ə-təns\ *n* 1 : the act of inheriting 2 ♦ : something that is or may be passed on to another generation

♦ bequest, birthright, heritage, legacy; *also* heirloom; bestowal, gift, offering, present

inherited *adj* ♦ : being something received by inheritance

♦ genetic, hereditary, heritable, inborn — more at HEREDITARY

in·hib·it \in-ˈhi-bət\ *vb* 1 : PROHIBIT, FORBID 2 ♦ : to hold in check ⟨∼ed by fear⟩

♦ bridle, check, constrain, contain, control, curb, govern, regulate, rein, restrain, tame — more at CONTROL

in·hi·bi·tion \ˌin-hə-ˈbi-shən\ *n* 1 : something that forbids or restricts 2 ♦ : a usu. inner check on free activity, expression, or functioning

♦ repression, restraint, self-control, self-restraint, suppression

in·hos·pi·ta·ble \ˌin-(ˌ)hä-ˈspi-tə-bəl, (ˌ)in-ˈhäs-(ˌ)pi-\ *adj*
1 ♦ : not showing hospitality : not friendly or receptive
2 : providing no shelter or sustenance

♦ antagonistic, hostile, inimical, jaundiced, negative, unfriendly, unsympathetic — more at HOSTILE

in–house \ˈin-ˌhaus, -ˈhaus\ *adj* : existing, originating, or carried on within a group or organization

in·hu·man \(ˌ)in-ˈhyü-mən, -ˈyü-\ *adj* **1** ♦ : lacking pity, kindness, or mercy **2** : not engaging the human personality or emotions **3** ♦ : not worthy of or conforming to the needs of human beings ⟨∼ conditions⟩ **4** : of or suggesting a nonhuman class of beings — **in·hu·man·ly** *adv* — **in·hu·man·ness** *n*

♦ [1] callous, hard, heartless, inhumane, pitiless, soulless, unfeeling, unsympathetic — more at HARD
♦ [3] bitter, brutal, burdensome, cruel, excruciating, grievous, grim, hard, harsh, heavy, murderous, onerous, oppressive, rough, rugged, severe, stiff, tough, trying — more at HARSH

in·hu·mane \ˌin-hyü-ˈmān, -yü-\ *adj* ♦ : not humane : not devoted or sympathetic to humans or human needs

♦ barbarous, brutal, cruel, heartless, sadistic, savage, vicious, wanton — more at CRUEL

in·hu·man·i·ty \-ˈma-nə-tē\ *n, pl* **-ties** **1** ♦ : the quality or state of being cruel or barbarous **2** : a cruel or barbarous act

♦ barbarity, brutality, cruelty, sadism, savagery, viciousness, wantonness — more at CRUELTY

in·im·i·cal \i-ˈni-mi-kəl\ *adj* **1** : being adverse often by reason of hostility **2** ♦ : having the disposition of an enemy : HOSTILE, UNFRIENDLY — **in·im·i·cal·ly** *adv*

♦ antagonistic, hostile, inhospitable, jaundiced, negative, unfriendly, unsympathetic — more at HOSTILE

in·im·i·ta·ble \(ˌ)i-ˈni-mə-tə-bəl\ *adj* ♦ : not capable of being imitated

♦ incomparable, matchless, nonpareil, only, peerless, unequaled, unmatched, unparalleled, unrivaled, unsurpassed — more at ONLY

in·iq·ui·tous \i-ˈni-kwə-təs\ *adj* ♦ : characterized by iniquity

♦ bad, black, evil, immoral, nefarious, rotten, sinful, unethical, unsavory, vicious, vile, villainous, wicked, wrong

in·iq·ui·ty \i-ˈni-kwə-tē\ *n, pl* **-ties** [ME *iniquite*, fr. AF *iniquité*, fr. L *iniquitas*, fr. *iniquus* uneven, fr. *aequus* equal] **1** : gross injustice : WICKEDNESS **2** ♦ : a wicked act

♦ corruption, debauchery, depravity, immorality, licentiousness, sin, vice — more at VICE

¹ini·tial \i-ˈni-shəl\ *adj* **1** : of or relating to the beginning : INCIPIENT **2** ♦ : placed at the beginning : FIRST

♦ first, inaugural, maiden, original, pioneer, premier — more at FIRST

²initial *n* : the first letter of a word or name
³initial *vb* **-tialed** *or* **-tialled; -tial·ing** *or* **-tial·ling** : to affix an initial to

ini·tial·ly *adv* ♦ : in the first place : at the beginning

♦ firstly, originally, primarily — more at ORIGINALLY

¹ini·ti·ate \i-ˈni-shē-ˌāt\ *vb* **-at·ed; -at·ing** **1** ♦ : set going : START, BEGIN **2** ♦ : to induct into membership by or as if by special ceremonies **3** ♦ : to instruct in the rudiments or principles of something

♦ [1] begin, constitute, establish, found, inaugurate, innovate, institute, introduce, launch, pioneer, set up, start — more at FOUND ♦ [2] baptize, inaugurate, induct, install, invest — more at INSTALL ♦ [3] acquaint, familiarize, introduce, orient — more at ACQUAINT

²ini·ti·ate \i-ˈni-shē-ət\ *n* **1** : a person who is undergoing or has passed an initiation **2** : a person who is instructed or adept in some special field

ini·ti·a·tion \-ˌni-shē-ˈā-shən\ *n* **1** : the act or an instance of initiating **2** : the process of being initiated; *specif* : the rites, ceremonies, ordeals, or instructions with which one is made a member of a sect or society or is invested with a particular function or status

ini·tia·tive \i-ˈni-shə-tiv\ *n* **1** : an introductory step **2** ♦ : self-reliant enterprise ⟨showed great ∼⟩ **3** : a process by which laws may be introduced or enacted directly by vote of the people

♦ aggressiveness, ambition, drive, enterprise, go, hustle — more at ENTERPRISE

ini·tia·to·ry \i-ˈni-shē-ə-ˌtōr-ē\ *adj* **1** : INTRODUCTORY **2** : tending or serving to initiate ⟨∼ rites⟩

in·ject \in-ˈjekt\ *vb* **1** : to force into something ⟨∼ serum with a needle⟩ **2** ♦ : to introduce as an element into some situation or subject ⟨∼ a note of suspicion⟩ — **in·jec·tion** \-ˈjek-shən\ *n*

♦ fit, insert, insinuate, interject, interpose, introduce — more at INSERT

in·junc·tion \in-ˈjəŋk-shən\ *n* **1** : ORDER, ADMONITION **2** : a court writ whereby one is required to do or to refrain from doing a specified act

in·jure \ˈin-jər\ *vb* **in·jured; in·jur·ing** **1** : to do an injustice to : WRONG **2** ♦ : to inflict bodily hurt on : HURT; *also* : to impair the soundness of

♦ damage, harm, hurt, wound; *also* batter, bruise, contuse, gash, gore, lacerate, scald, scar, tear; cripple, lame, maim, mangle, mutilate; afflict, torment, torture; lay up; blemish, impair, mar, scrape, spoil

in·ju·ri·ous \in-ˈjūr-ē-əs\ *adj* ♦ : inflicting or tending to inflict injury

♦ adverse, bad, baleful, baneful, damaging, deleterious, detrimental, evil, harmful, hurtful, ill, mischievous, noxious, pernicious, prejudicial — more at HARMFUL

in·ju·ry \ˈin-jə-rē\ *n, pl* **-ries** **1** ♦ : an act that damages or hurts **2** : hurt, damage, or loss sustained

♦ damage, detriment, harm, hurt; *also* disservice, injustice, outrage, wrong; affront, dart, indignity, insult, offense; crippling, mayhem, mutilation; defacement, disability, disfigurement; abrasion, bruise, bump, contusion, scald, scar, scrape, scratch, sear

in·jus·tice \(ˌ)in-ˈjəs-təs\ *n* **1** ♦ : violation of a person's rights : UNFAIRNESS **2** ♦ : an unjust act or deed : WRONG

♦ [1, 2] disservice, injury, raw deal, wrong — more at DISSERVICE

¹ink \ˈiŋk\ *n* [ME *enke*, fr. AF *encre, enke*, fr. LL *encaustum*, fr. L *encaustus* burned in, fr. Gk *enkaustos*, fr. *enkaiein* to burn in] : a usu. liquid and colored material for writing and printing — **inky** *adj*

²ink *vb* : to put ink on; *esp* : SIGN

ink·blot test \ˈiŋk-ˌblät-\ *n* : any of several psychological tests based on the interpretation of irregular figures

ink·horn \-ˌhorn\ *n* : a small bottle (as of horn) for holding ink

in–kind \ˈin-ˈkīnd\ *adj* : consisting of something (as goods) other than money

ink–jet *n* : a computer printer that sprays electrically charged droplets of ink onto paper — **inkjet** *adj*

in·kling \ˈiŋ-kliŋ\ *n* **1** ♦ : a slight indication or suggestion : HINT, INTIMATION **2** : a vague idea

♦ clue, cue, hint, indication, intimation, lead, suggestion — more at HINT

ink·stand \ˈiŋk-ˌstand\ *n* : INKWELL; *also* : a pen and ink stand

ink·well \-ˌwel\ *n* : a container for ink

in·laid \ˈin-ˈlād\ *adj* : decorated with material set into a surface

¹in·land \ˈin-ˌland, -lənd\ *adj* **1** *chiefly Brit* : not foreign : DOMESTIC ⟨∼ revenue⟩ **2** : of or relating to the interior of a country

²inland *n* : the interior of a country

³inland *adv* : into or toward the interior

in–law \ˈin-ˌlo\ *n* : a relative by marriage

¹in·lay \ˌin-ˈlā, ˈin-ˌlā\ vb in·laid \-ˈlād\; in·lay·ing : to set (a material) into a surface or ground material esp. for decoration

²in·lay \ˈin-ˌlā\ n 1 : inlaid work 2 : a shaped filling cemented into a tooth

in·let \ˈin-ˌlet, -lət\ n 1 ♦ : a small or narrow bay 2 : an opening for intake esp. of a fluid

♦ bay, bight, cove, estuary, fjord, gulf — more at GULF

in–line skate n : a roller skate whose four wheels are set in a straight line

in·mate \ˈin-ˌmāt\ n : any of a group occupying a single place of residence; esp : a person confined (as in a hospital or prison)

in me·di·as res \in-ˌmā-dē-əs-ˈrās\ adv [L, lit., into the midst of things] : in or into the middle of a narrative or plot

in me·mo·ri·am \ˌin-mə-ˈmōr-ē-əm\ prep [L] : in memory of

in·most \ˈin-ˌmōst\ adj : deepest within : INNERMOST

inn \ˈin\ n ♦ : an establishment for the lodging and entertaining of travelers : HOTEL, TAVERN

♦ hospice, hotel, lodge, public house, tavern — more at HOTEL

in·nards \ˈi-nərdz\ n pl [alter. of inwards] 1 : the internal organs of a human being or animal; esp : VISCERA 2 : the internal parts of a structure or mechanism

in·nate \i-ˈnāt\ adj 1 : existing in, belonging to, or determined by factors present in an individual from birth : NATIVE 2 ♦ : belonging to the essential nature of something : INHERENT, INTRINSIC ⟨the ∼ defects of the plan⟩

♦ essential, inborn, ingrained, inherent, integral, intrinsic, natural — more at INHERENT

in·nate·ly adv ♦ : in an innate manner

♦ constitutionally, inherently, intrinsically, naturally — more at NATURALLY

in·ner \ˈi-nər\ adj 1 ♦ : located farther in ⟨the ∼ bark⟩ 2 : near a center esp. of influence ⟨the ∼ circle⟩ 3 ♦ : of or relating to the mind or spirit

♦ [1] inside, interior, internal, inward; also inmost, innermost; central, mid, middle Ant exterior, external, outer, outside, outward ♦ [3] cerebral, intellectual, mental, psychological — more at MENTAL

inner city n : the usu. older, poorer, and more densely populated section of a city — inner–city adj

in·ner–di·rect·ed \ˌi-nər-də-ˈrek-təd, -ˌ)dī-\ adj : directed in thought and action by one's own scale of values as opposed to external norms

inner ear n : the part of the ear that is most important for hearing, is located in a cavity in the temporal bone, and contains sense organs of hearing and of awareness of position in space

in·ner·most \ˈi-nər-ˌmōst\ adj : farthest inward : INMOST

in·ner·sole \ˈi-nər-ˈsōl\ n : INSOLE

in·ner·spring \ˈi-nər-ˈspriŋ\ adj : having coil springs inside a padded casing

inner tube n : an airtight rubber tube inside a tire to hold air under pressure

in·ning \ˈi-niŋ\ n 1 sing or pl : a division of a cricket match 2 : a baseball team's turn at bat; also : a division of a baseball game consisting of a turn at bat for each team

inn·keep·er \ˈin-ˈkē-pər\ n 1 : a proprietor of an inn 2 : a hotel manager

in·no·cence \ˈi-nə-səns\ n 1 ♦ : freedom from guilt or sin through being unacquainted with evil : BLAMELESSNESS; also : freedom from legal guilt 2 ♦ : freedom from guile or cunning : SIMPLICITY; also : IGNORANCE

♦ [1] decency, goodness, honesty, integrity, righteousness Ant blameworthiness, culpability, guilt, guiltiness ♦ [2] artlessness, greenness, ignorance, ingenuousness, naïveté, naturalness, simplicity, unworldliness — more at NAÏVETÉ

¹in·no·cent \-sənt\ adj [ME, fr. AF, fr. L innocens, fr. nocens wicked, fr. nocēre to harm] 1 ♦ : free from guilt or sin : BLAMELESS 2 ♦ : harmless in effect or intention; also : CANDID 3 : free from legal guilt or fault : LAWFUL 4 ♦ : lacking or reflecting a lack of sophistication, guile, or self-consciousness : INGENUOUS 5 : UNAWARE

♦ [1] blameless, clear, faultless, guiltless, impeccable, irreproachable; also absolved, acquitted, cleared, exonerated, vindicated; ethical, moral, righteous, upright, virtuous Ant guilty ♦ [2] candid, harmless, innocuous, safe, white — more at HARMLESS ♦ [4] green, ingenuous, naive, simple, unknowing, unsophisticated, unwary, unworldly — more at NAIVE

²innocent n ♦ : an innocent one

♦ angel, dove, lamb, sheep — more at LAMB

in·no·cent·ly \-lē\ adv : in an innocent manner

in·noc·u·ous \i-ˈnä-kyə-wəs\ adj 1 ♦ : producing no injury : HARMLESS 2 : not offensive; also : INSIPID

♦ harmless, innocent, safe, white — more at HARMLESS

in·nom·i·nate \i-ˈnä-mə-nət\ adj : having no name; also : ANONYMOUS

in·no·vate \ˈi-nə-ˌvāt\ vb -vat·ed; -vat·ing ♦ : to introduce as or as if new; also : to make changes

♦ constitute, establish, found, inaugurate, initiate, institute, introduce, launch, pioneer, set up, start — more at FOUND

in·no·va·tion \ˌi-nə-ˈvā-shən\ n 1 : the introduction of something new 2 ♦ : a new idea, method, or device

♦ coinage, concoction, contrivance, creation, invention, wrinkle — more at INVENTION

in·no·va·tive \-ˌvā-tiv\ adj ♦ : characterized by, tending to, or introducing innovations

♦ creative, imaginative, ingenious, inventive, original — more at CREATIVE

in·no·va·tor \-ˌvā-tər\ n ♦ : one that innovates

♦ designer, developer, inventor, originator — more at INVENTOR

in·nu·en·do \ˌin-yə-ˈwen-dō\ n, pl -dos or -does [L, by nodding, fr. innuere to nod to, make a sign to, fr. nuere to nod] : HINT, INSINUATION; esp : a veiled reflection on character or reputation

in·nu·mer·a·ble \i-ˈnü-mə-rə-bəl, -ˈnyü-\ adj ♦ : too many to be numbered

♦ countless, numberless, uncountable, unnumbered, untold — more at COUNTLESS

¹in·oc·u·late \i-ˈnä-kyə-ˌlāt\ vb -lat·ed; -lat·ing [ME, to insert a bud in a plant, fr. L inoculare, fr. oculus eye, bud] : to introduce something into: as a : to introduce a serum or antibody into (an organism) to treat or prevent a disease b : to introduce information to — in·oc·u·la·tion \-ˌnä-kyə-ˈlā-shən\ n

in·op·er·a·ble \ˌ)i-ˈnä-pə-rə-bəl\ adj 1 : not suitable for surgery 2 ♦ : not operable

♦ inoperative, nonfunctional; also broken; off; deactivated, ineffective, ineffectual, nonproductive, unproductive, unusable, unworkable, useless Ant functional, functioning, operable, operating, operational, operative, running, working ♦ impractical, unusable, unworkable, useless — more at IMPRACTICAL

in·op·er·a·tive \-ˈnä-pə-rə-tiv, -ˈnä-pə-ˌrā-\ adj ♦ : not functioning

♦ dead, dormant, fallow, free, idle, inactive, inert, latent, off, vacant — more at INACTIVE

in·op·por·tune \ˌ)i-ˌnä-pər-ˈtün, -ˈtyün\ adj : not opportune : INCONVENIENT

in·op·por·tune·ly \-lē\ adv : in an inopportune manner

in·or·di·nate \i-ˈnȯrd-ᵊn-ət\ adj ♦ : exceeding reasonable limits : IMMODERATE ⟨an ∼ curiosity⟩

♦ devilish, excessive, exorbitant, extravagant, extreme, immoderate, lavish, overmuch, overweening, steep, stiff, towering, unconscionable — more at EXCESSIVE

in·or·di·nate·ly adv ♦ : to an excessive or unreasonable degree

♦ devilishly, excessively, monstrously, overly, overmuch, too — more at TOO

in·or·gan·ic \ˌi-ˌnȯr-'ga-nik\ *adj* : being or composed of matter of other than plant or animal origin : MINERAL

in·pa·tient \'in-ˌpā-shənt\ *n* : a hospital patient who receives lodging and food as well as treatment

in·put \'in-ˌpu̇t\ *n* **1** : something put in **2** : power or energy put into a machine or system **3** : information fed into a computer or data processing system **4** ♦ : recommendation with regard to a course of action : ADVICE — **input** *vb*

♦ advice, counsel, guidance — more at ADVICE

in·quest \'in-ˌkwest\ *n* **1** : an official inquiry or examination esp. before a jury **2** : a systematic investigation : INQUIRY, INVESTIGATION

in·qui·e·tude \(ˌ)in-'kwī-ə-ˌtüd, -ˌtyüd\ *n* : UNEASINESS, RESTLESSNESS

in·quire \in-'kwīr\ *vb* **in·quired; in·quir·ing 1** ♦ : to ask or ask about **2** ♦ : to make investigation or inquiry : INVESTIGATE — often used with *into* — **in·quir·er** *n* — **in·quir·ing·ly** *adv*

♦ *usu* inquire of [1] ask, query, question, quiz — more at ASK ♦ *usu* inquire into [2] delve, dig, explore, go, investigate, look, probe, research — more at EXPLORE

in·qui·ry \'in-ˌkwīr-ē, in-'kwīr-ē; 'in-kwə-rē, 'iŋ-\ *n, pl* **-ries 1** ♦ : a request for information; *also* : RESEARCH **2** ♦ : a systematic investigation of a matter of public interest

♦ [1] query, question, request — more at QUESTION
♦ [2] examination, exploration, investigation, probe, research, study; *also* quest; audit, check; checkup; diagnosis, inspection; hearing, interrogation, trial; feeler, query, question; poll, questionnaire; challenge, cross-examination, grilling, quiz

in·qui·si·tion \ˌin-kwə-'zi-shən, ˌiŋ-\ *n* **1** : a judicial or official inquiry usu. before a jury **2** *cap* : a former Roman Catholic tribunal for the discovery and punishment of heresy **3** : a severe questioning **4** : the act of inquiring — **in·quis·i·tor** \in-'kwi-zə-tər\ *n* — **in·quis·i·to·ri·al** \-ˌkwi-zə-'tȯr-ē-əl\ *adj*

in·quis·i·tive \in-'kwi-zə-tiv\ *adj* **1** : given to examination or investigation ⟨an ~ mind⟩ **2** ♦ : unduly curious — **in·quis·i·tive·ly** *adv*

♦ curious, nosy, prying — more at CURIOUS

in·quis·i·tive·ness *n* : the quality or state of being inquisitive

in re \in-'rā, -'rē\ *prep* : in the matter of

INRI *abbr* [L *Iesus Nazarenus Rex Iudaeorum*] Jesus of Nazareth, King of the Jews

in·road \'in-ˌrōd\ *n* **1** : a sudden hostile incursion : INVASION, RAID **2** : an advance made usu. at the expense of another

in·rush \'in-ˌrəsh\ *n* : a crowding or flooding in

ins *abbr* **1** inches **2** insurance

INS *abbr* Immigration and Naturalization Service

in·sa·lu·bri·ous \ˌin-sə-'lü-brē-əs\ *adj* : UNWHOLESOME, NOXIOUS ⟨~ air⟩

ins and outs *n pl* **1** : characteristic peculiarities **2** : RAMIFICATIONS

in·sane \(ˌ)in-'sān\ *adj* **1** ♦ : exhibiting serious and debilitating mental disorder; *also* : used by or for the insane **2** ♦ : ridiculously unreasonable, unsound, or incongruous : ABSURD — **in·sane·ly** *adv*

♦ [1] crazy, cuckoo, deranged, loco, lunatic, mad, nuts, nutty, screwy, unsound, wacky; *also* off; aberrant, delusional, disordered; eccentric, odd, queer, strange; foolish, senseless, witless; irrational, unreasonable; berserk, delirious; depressed; distraught, frantic, frenzied, hysterical *Ant* balanced, sane, sound ♦ [2] absurd, bizarre, crazy, fanciful, fantastic, foolish, nonsensical, preposterous, unreal, wild — more at FANTASTIC

in·san·i·ty \in-'sa-nə-tē\ *n* **1** ♦ : a deranged state of the mind usu. occurring as a specific disorder (as schizophrenia) **2** ♦ : extreme folly or unreasonableness; *also* : something utterly foolish or unreasonable

♦ [1] aberration, dementia, derangement, lunacy, madness, mania; *also* irrationality, unreasonableness; delirium, frenzy, hysteria; neurosis, psychosis, schizophrenia; delusion, hallucination, obsession, phobia; abnormality, unsoundness *Ant* mind, sanity ♦ [2] absurdity, asininity, balminess, craziness, daftness, fatuity, folly, foolishness, inanity, lunacy, madness, silliness, simplicity, zaniness

in·sa·tia·ble \(ˌ)in-'sā-shə-bəl\ *adj* : incapable of being satisfied — **in·sa·tia·bil·i·ty** \(ˌ)in-ˌsā-shə-'bi-lə-tē\ *n* — **in·sa·tia·bly** *adv*

in·sa·tiate \(ˌ)in-'sā-shē-ət, -shət\ *adj* : INSATIABLE — **in·sa·tiate·ly** *adv*

in·scribe \in-'skrīb\ *vb* **1** : to write, engrave, or print as a lasting record **2** ♦ : to enter on a list : ENROLL **3** ♦ : to write, engrave, or print characters upon **4** : to dedicate to someone **5** : to draw within a figure so as to touch in as many places as possible — **in·scrip·tion** \-'skrip-shən\ *n*

♦ [2] catalog, enroll, enter, index, list, put down, record, register, schedule, slate — more at LIST ♦ [3] engrave, etch, grave — more at ENGRAVE

in·scru·ta·ble \in-'skrü-tə-bəl\ *adj* ♦ : not readily comprehensible : MYSTERIOUS — **in·scru·ta·bly** \-blē\ *adv*

♦ cryptic, darkling, deep, enigmatic, impenetrable, mysterious, mystic, occult, uncanny — more at MYSTERIOUS

in·seam \'in-ˌsēm\ *n* : the seam on the inside of the leg of a pair of pants; *also* : the length of this seam

in·sect \'in-ˌsekt\ *n* [L *insectum*, fr. *insectus*, pp. of *insecare* to cut into, fr. *secare* to cut] : any of a class of small usu. winged arthropod animals (as flies, bees, beetles, and moths) with usu. three pairs of legs as adults

in·sec·ti·cide \in-'sek-tə-ˌsīd\ *n* : an agent for destroying insects — **in·sec·ti·cid·al** \(ˌ)in-ˌsek-tə-'sīd-əl\ *adj*

in·sec·tiv·o·rous \ˌin-ˌsek-'ti-və-rəs\ *adj* : feeding on insects

in·se·cure \ˌin-si-'kyu̇r\ *adj* **1** : UNCERTAIN **2** : not protected : UNSAFE **3** ♦ : not firmly fastened or fixed : LOOSE **4** : not highly stable; *also* : lacking assurance : ANXIOUS, FEARFUL — **in·se·cure·ly** *adv*

♦ lax, loose, relaxed, slack — more at LOOSE

in·se·cu·ri·ty \-'kyu̇r-ə-tē\ *n* ♦ : the quality or state of being insecure

♦ instability, precariousness, shakiness, unsteadiness — more at INSTABILITY

in·sem·i·nate \in-'se-mə-ˌnāt\ *vb* **-nat·ed; -nat·ing** : to introduce semen into the genital tract of (a female) — **in·sem·i·na·tion** \-ˌse-mə-'nā-shən\ *n*

in·sen·sate \(ˌ)in-'sen-ˌsāt, -sət\ *adj* **1** : lacking sense or understanding; *also* : FOOLISH **2** : INANIMATE **3** : lacking humane feeling : INHUMAN ⟨~ rage⟩

in·sen·si·bil·i·ty \-ˌsen-sə-'bi-lə-tē\ *n* : the quality or state of being insensible: as **a** : lack of mental or emotional feeling or response **b** : an unconscious or comatose state

in·sen·si·ble \(ˌ)in-'sen-sə-bəl\ *adj* **1** : not perceptible by a sense or by the mind : IMPERCEPTIBLE; *also* : SLIGHT, GRADUAL **2** : INANIMATE **3** : not knowing or perceiving : UNCONSCIOUS **4** : lacking sensory perception or ability to react ⟨~ to pain⟩ **5** : APATHETIC, INDIFFERENT; *also* : UNAWARE ⟨~ of their danger⟩ **6** : MEANINGLESS **7** : lacking delicacy or refinement — **in·sen·si·bly** \-'sen-sə-blē\ *adv*

in·sen·tient \(ˌ)in-'sen-chē-ənt\ *adj* : lacking perception, consciousness, or animation — **in·sen·tience** \-chē-əns\ *n*

in·sep·a·ra·bil·i·ty \-ˌse-prə-'bi-lə-tē, -pə-rə-\ *n* : the quality or state of being inseparable

in·sep·a·ra·ble \(ˌ)in-'se-prə-bəl, -pə-rə-\ *adj* **1** : incapable of being separated or disjoined **2** : very close or intimate — **inseparable** *n* — **in·sep·a·ra·bly** \-'se-prə-blē, -pə-rə-\ *adv*

¹in·sert \in-'sərt\ *vb* **1** : to put or thrust in ⟨~ a key in a lock⟩ ⟨~ a comma⟩ **2** ♦ : to put or introduce into the body of something : INTERPOLATE **3** : to set in (as a piece of fabric) and make fast

♦ fit, inject, insinuate, interject, interpose, introduce; *also* inlay, inset, install, weave, work (in); cram, sandwich, shove, thrust, wedge; add, append, attach

²in·sert \'in-ˌsərt\ n : something that is inserted or is for insertion; *esp* : written or printed material inserted (as between the leaves of a book)

in·ser·tion \in-'sər-shən\ n 1 : something that is inserted 2 : the act or process of inserting

in·set \'in-ˌset\ vb inset *or* in·set·ted; in·set·ting : to set in : INSERT — inset n

¹in·shore \'in-'shōr\ adj 1 : situated, living, or carried on near shore 2 : moving toward shore

²inshore adv : to or toward shore

¹in·side \in-'sīd, 'in-ˌsīd\ n 1 : an inner side or surface : INTERIOR 2 : inward nature, thoughts, or feeling 3 *pl* : VISCERA, ENTRAILS 4 : a position of power, trust, or familiarity

²inside adv 1 : on the inner side 2 : in or into the interior

³inside prep 1 : in or into the inside of 2 : WITHIN ⟨~ an hour⟩

⁴inside adj 1 ♦ : of, relating to, or being on or near the inside 2 ♦ : relating or known to a select group

♦ [1] inner, interior, internal, inward — more at INNER ♦ [2] confidential, hushed, intimate, private, secret — more at PRIVATE

inside of prep : INSIDE

inside out adv 1 : in such a manner that the inner surface becomes the outer ⟨turned the shirt *inside out*⟩ 2 : in a state of disarray or reorganization ⟨turned her life *inside out*⟩

in·sid·er \in-'sī-dər\ n : a person who is in a position of power or has access to confidential information

in·sid·i·ous \in-'si-dē-əs\ adj [L insidiosus, fr. insidiae ambush, fr. *insidēre* to sit in, sit on, fr. *sedēre* to sit] 1 : SLY, TREACHEROUS 2 : SEDUCTIVE 3 : having a gradual and cumulative effect : SUBTLE — in·sid·i·ous·ly adv — in·sid·i·ous·ness n

in·sight \'in-ˌsīt\ n ♦ : the power, act, or result of seeing into a situation

♦ discernment, perception, sagacity, sapience, wisdom — more at WISDOM

in·sight·ful \'in-ˌsīt-fəl, in-'sīt-\ adj ♦ : exhibiting or characterized by insight

♦ discerning, perceptive, sagacious, sage, sapient, wise — more at WISE

in·sig·nia \in-'sig-nē-ə\ *also* in·sig·ne \-(ˌ)nē\ n, pl **-nia** *or* **-ni·as** : a distinguishing mark esp. of authority or honor : BADGE

in·sig·nif·i·cant \-kənt\ adj : not significant as: **a** ♦ : lacking meaning or import **b** ♦ : not worth considering

♦ frivolous, inconsequential, inconsiderable, little, minor, minute, negligible, slight, small, trifling, trivial, unimportant — more at UNIMPORTANT

in·sin·cere \ˌin-sin-'sir\ adj ♦ : not sincere : HYPOCRITICAL — in·sin·cere·ly adv

♦ artificial, double-dealing, feigned, hypocritical, left-handed, mealy, mealymouthed, two-faced, unctuous; *also* empty, hollow, meaningless; deceitful, devious, dishonest, untruthful; facile, glib, superficial; bogus, counterfeit, fake, false, phony, sham; facetious, jocular **Ant** genuine, heartfelt, honest, sincere, unfeigned

in·sin·cer·i·ty \-'ser-ə-tē\ n ♦ : the quality or state of being insincere

♦ cant, dissimulation, hypocrisy, piety — more at HYPOCRISY

in·sin·u·ate \in-'sin-yə-ˌwāt\ vb **-at·ed; -at·ing** [L insinuare, fr. *sinuare* to bend, curve, fr. *sinus* curve] 1 ♦ : to introduce gradually or in a subtle, indirect, or artful way 2 ♦ : to imply in a subtle or devious way — in·sin·u·a·tion \(ˌ)in-ˌsin-yə-'wā-shən\ n

♦ [1] infiltrate, insert, interpose, introduce, slip, sneak, work, worm ♦ [2] allude, hint, imply, indicate, infer, intimate, suggest — more at HINT

in·sin·u·at·ing adj 1 : winning favor and confidence by imperceptible degrees 2 : tending gradually to cause doubt, distrust, or change of outlook

in·sip·id \in-'si-pəd\ adj 1 ♦ : lacking taste or savor 2 ♦ : lacking in qualities that interest, stimulate, or challenge : FLAT — in·si·pid·i·ty \ˌin-sə-'pi-də-tē\ n

♦ [1] flat, flavorless (*or* flavourless), tasteless; *also* bland, dilute, thin, watery, weak; plain, unflavored **Ant** flavorful, savory, tasty ♦ [2] banal, flat, wishy-washy — more at WISHY-WASHY

in·sist \in-'sist\ vb [MF *or* L; MF insister, fr. L insistere to stand upon, persist, fr. *sistere* to take a stand] ♦ : to take a resolute stand

♦ affirm, allege, assert, aver, avouch, avow, claim, contend, declare, maintain, profess, protest, warrant — more at CLAIM ✦ *usu* insist on call, claim, clamor (*or* clamour), command, demand, enjoin, exact, press, quest, stipulate (for) — more at DEMAND

in·sis·tence \'in-'sis-təns\ n : the act of insisting; *also* : an insistent attitude or quality : URGENCY

in·sis·tent \in-'sis-tənt\ adj ♦ : disposed to insist — in·sis·tent·ly adv

♦ dogged, patient, persevering, persistent, pertinacious, tenacious — more at PERSISTENT

in si·tu \in-'sī-tü, -'sē-\ adv *or* adj [L, in position] : in the natural or original position

in·so·far as \ˌin-sə-'fär-\ conj : to the extent or degree that

insol *abbr* insoluble

in·so·la·tion \ˌin-(ˌ)sō-'lā-shən\ n : solar radiation that has been received

in·sole \'in-ˌsōl\ n 1 : an inside sole of a shoe 2 : a loose strip placed inside a shoe for warmth or comfort

in·so·lence \-ləns\ n 1 : the quality or state of being insolent 2 ♦ : an instance of insolent conduct or treatment

♦ back talk, cheek, impertinence, impudence, sauce — more at BACK TALK ♦ brazenness, discourtesy, disrespect, impertinence, impudence, incivility, rudeness — more at DISCOURTESY

in·so·lent \'in-sə-lənt\ adj ♦ : contemptuous, rude, disrespectful, or bold in behavior or language

♦ bold, brash, fresh, impertinent, impudent, nervy, sassy, saucy — more at NERVY

in·sol·u·ble \(ˌ)in-'säl-yə-bəl\ adj 1 ♦ : having or admitting of no solution or explanation 2 : difficult or impossible to dissolve — in·sol·u·bil·i·ty \-ˌsäl-yə-'bi-lə-tē\ n

♦ hopeless, impossible, unattainable, unsolvable — more at IMPOSSIBLE

in·sol·vent \(ˌ)in-'säl-vənt\ adj 1 : unable or insufficient to pay all debts ⟨an ~ estate⟩ 2 : IMPOVERISHED, DEFICIENT — in·sol·ven·cy \-vən-sē\ n

in·som·nia \in-'säm-nē-ə\ n : prolonged and usu. abnormal sleeplessness — in·som·ni·ac \-nē-ˌak\ n

in·so·much as \ˌin-sə-'məch-\ conj : INASMUCH AS

insomuch that conj : to such a degree that : SO

in·sou·ci·ance \in-'sü-sē-əns, aⁿ-süs-'yäⁿs\ n [F] ♦ : lighthearted unconcern ⟨youthful ~⟩

♦ apathy, disinterestedness, disregard, indifference, nonchalance — more at INDIFFERENCE

in·sou·ci·ant \in-'sü-sē-ənt, aⁿ-süs-'yäⁿ\ adj ♦ : exhibiting or characterized by insouciance

♦ carefree, careless, cavalier, easygoing, gay, happy-go-lucky, lighthearted, nonchalant, unconcerned

insp *abbr* inspector

in·spect \in-'spekt\ vb ♦ : to view closely and critically : EXAMINE — in·spec·tor \-tər\ n

♦ audit, check, examine, review, scan, scrutinize, survey; *also* notice, observe, watch; peruse, pore (over); analyze, dissect; delve (into), explore, investigate, probe, research, study; categorize, classify

in·spec·tion \-'spek-shən\ n 1 : the act of inspecting 2 ♦ : a checking or testing of an individual against established standards

♦ audit, check, checkup, examination, review, scan, scrutiny, survey; *also* analysis, dissection; exploration, investigation, probe, research, study; inquisition, interrogation; perusal; observation, surveillance, watch

inspector general *n* : the head of a system of inspection (as of an army)

in·spi·ra·tion \ˌin-spə-ˈrā-shən\ *n* 1 : the act or power of moving the intellect or emotions 2 : INHALATION 3 : the quality or state of being inspired; *also* : something that is inspired 4 : an inspiring agent or influence — **in·spi·ra·tion·al** \-shə-nəl\ *adj*

in·spire \in-ˈspīr\ *vb* **in·spired**; **in·spir·ing** 1 : to influence, move, or guide by divine or supernatural inspiration 2 ♦ : to exert an animating, enlivening, or exalting influence upon; *also* : AFFECT 3 : to communicate to an agent supernaturally; *also* : to bring out or about 4 : INHALE 5 : INCITE 6 : to spread by indirect means — **in·spir·er** *n*

♦ buoy (up), cheer, comfort, embolden, encourage, hearten, steel — more at ENCOURAGE

in·spir·it \in-ˈspir-ət\ *vb* : ENCOURAGE, HEARTEN

inst *abbr* 1 instant 2 institute; institution; institutional

in·sta·bil·i·ty \ˌin-stə-ˈbi-lə-tē\ *n* ♦ : lack of steadiness; *esp* : lack of emotional or mental stability

♦ insecurity, precariousness, shakiness, unsteadiness; *also* unsoundness; inconstancy, mutability **Ant** fixedness, security, stability, steadiness

in·stall *or* **in·stal** \in-ˈstȯl\ *vb* **in·stalled**; **in·stall·ing** 1 ♦ : to place formally in office : induct into an office, rank, or order 2 ♦ : to establish in an indicated place, condition, or status 3 : to set up for use or service

♦ [1] baptize, inaugurate, induct, initiate, invest; *also* swear in; accept, admit, receive, take in; enlist, enroll ♦ [2] ensconce, lodge, perch, roost, settle — more at ENSCONCE

in·stal·la·tion \ˌin-stə-ˈlā-shən\ *n* 1 ♦ : the act of installing : the state of being installed 2 ♦ : a military camp, fort, or base

♦ [1] inaugural, inauguration, induction, investiture; *also* enlistment, enrollment; promotion ♦ [2] complex, establishment, facility — more at FACILITY

¹**in·stall·ment** *also* **in·stal·ment** \in-ˈstȯl-mənt\ *n* : INSTALLATION

²**installment** *also* **instalment** *n* 1 : one of the parts into which a debt or sum is divided for payment 2 : one of several parts presented at intervals

¹**in·stance** \ˈin-stəns\ *n* 1 : INSTIGATION, REQUEST 2 ♦ : an individual illustrative of a category or brought forward in support or disproof of a generalization : EXAMPLE ⟨for ∼⟩ 3 : an event or step that is part of a process or series

♦ case, example, exemplar, illustration, representative, sample, specimen — more at EXAMPLE

²**instance** *vb* **in·stanced**; **in·stanc·ing** 1 ♦ : to mention as a case or example 2 ♦ : to explain by reference to examples

♦ [1] advert (to), cite, mention, name, note, notice, quote, refer (to), specify, touch (*on* or *upon*) — more at MENTION ♦ [2] demonstrate, exemplify, illustrate — more at ILLUSTRATE

¹**in·stant** \ˈin-stənt\ *n* 1 ♦ : an immeasurably small space of time : MOMENT ⟨the ∼ we met⟩ 2 : the present or current month

♦ flash, jiffy, minute, moment, second, shake, trice, twinkle, twinkling, wink; *also* microsecond, nanosecond; snatch, spurt

²**instant** *adj* 1 : calling for immediate attention : URGENT 2 : PRESENT, CURRENT 3 : occurring, acting, or accomplished without loss or interval of time : IMMEDIATE ⟨∼ relief⟩ 4 : premixed or precooked for easy final preparation ⟨∼ cake mix⟩; *also* : immediately soluble in water ⟨∼ coffee⟩

in·stan·ta·neous \ˌin-stən-ˈtā-nē-əs\ *adj* ♦ : done or occurring in an instant or without delay — **in·stan·ta·neous·ly** *adv*

♦ immediate, instant, straightaway; *also* summary; fast, prompt, quick, rapid, speedy, swift

in·stan·ter \in-ˈstan-tər\ *adv* : at once

in·stan·ti·ate \in-ˈstan-chē-ˌāt\ *vb* **-at·ed**; **-at·ing** : to represent (an abstraction) by a concrete example — **in·stan·ti·a·tion** \-ˌstan-chē-ˈā-shən\ *n*

in·stant·ly \ˈin-stənt-lē\ *adv* ♦ : at once : IMMEDIATELY

♦ directly, forthwith, immediately, now, promptly, pronto, right away, right now — more at IMMEDIATELY

instant messaging *n* : a means or system for transmitting electronic messages instantly — **instant message** *n* or *vb*

in·state \in-ˈstāt\ *vb* : to establish in a rank or office : INSTALL

in·stead \in-ˈsted\ *adv* 1 : as a substitute or equivalent 2 : as an alternative : RATHER

instead of *prep* : as a substitute for or alternative to

in·step \ˈin-ˌstep\ *n* : the arched part of the human foot in front of the ankle joint; *esp* : its upper surface

in·sti·gate \ˈin-stə-ˌgāt\ *vb* **-gat·ed**; **-gat·ing** ♦ : to goad or urge forward : PROVOKE, INCITE ⟨∼ a revolt⟩

♦ abet, ferment, foment, incite, provoke, raise, stir, whip — more at INCITE

in·sti·ga·tion \ˌin-stə-ˈgā-shən\ *n* 1 : an act of instigating or the state of being instigated 2 ♦ : something that instigates

♦ boost, encouragement, goad, impetus, impulse, incentive, incitement, momentum, motivation, provocation, spur, stimulus, yeast — more at IMPULSE

in·sti·ga·tor \ˈin-stə-ˌgā-tər\ *n* : one that instigates

in·stil *chiefly Brit var of* INSTILL

in·still \in-ˈstil\ *vb* **in·stilled**; **in·still·ing** 1 : to cause to enter drop by drop 2 : to impart gradually

¹**in·stinct** \ˈin-ˌstiŋkt\ *n* 1 : a natural aptitude 2 : a largely inheritable and unalterable tendency of an organism to make a complex and specific response to environmental stimuli without involving reason; *also* : behavior originating below the conscious level

²**instinct** \in-ˈstiŋkt, ˈin-ˌstiŋkt\ *adj* : IMBUED, INFUSED

in·stinc·tive \in-ˈstiŋk-tiv\ *adj* 1 : of, relating to, or being instinct 2 : prompted by natural instinct or propensity : arising spontaneously — **in·stinc·tive·ly** *adv*

in·stinc·tu·al \in-ˈstiŋk-chə-wəl\ *adj* : of, relating to, or based on instinct

¹**in·sti·tute** \ˈin-stə-ˌtüt, -ˌtyüt\ *vb* **-tut·ed**; **-tut·ing** 1 : to establish in a position or office 2 : ORGANIZE 3 ♦ : to bring about the beginning of : INAUGURATE, INITIATE

♦ constitute, establish, found, inaugurate, initiate, innovate, introduce, launch, pioneer, set up, start — more at FOUND

²**institute** *n* 1 : an elementary principle recognized as authoritative; *also*, *pl* : a collection of such principles and precepts 2 ♦ : an organization for the promotion of a cause : ASSOCIATION 3 : an educational institution 4 : a brief course of instruction on a particular field

♦ association, brotherhood, club, college, congress, council, fellowship, fraternity, guild, institution, league, order, organization, society — more at ASSOCIATION

in·sti·tu·tion \ˌin-stə-ˈtü-shən, -ˈtyü-\ *n* 1 : an act of originating, setting up, or founding 2 : an established practice, law, or custom 3 ♦ : a society or corporation esp. of a public character ⟨a charitable ∼⟩ 4 : ASYLUM 3 — **in·sti·tu·tion·al** \-ˈtü-shə-nəl, -ˈtyü-\ *adj* — **in·sti·tu·tion·al·ize** \-nə-ˌlīz\ *vb* — **in·sti·tu·tion·al·ly** *adv*

♦ establishment, foundation, institute; *also* body, collective, group; corporation, enterprise; charity, philanthropy; think tank

instr *abbr* 1 instructor 2 instrument; instrumental

in·struct \in-ˈstrəkt\ *vb* [ME, fr. L *instructus*, pp. of *instruere*, fr. *struere* to build] 1 ♦ : to give knowledge to : TEACH 2 ♦ : to provide with authoritative information or advice : INFORM 3 ♦ : to give an order or a command to

♦ [1] educate, indoctrinate, school, teach, train, tutor — more at TEACH ♦ [2] acquaint, advise, apprise, brief, clue, enlighten, familiarize, fill in, inform, tell, wise — more at ENLIGHTEN ♦ [3] bid, boss, charge, command, direct, enjoin, order, tell — more at COMMAND

in·struc·tion \in-'strək-shən\ *n* **1** : LESSON, PRECEPT **2** ♦ : a direction calling for compliance : COMMAND, ORDER **3** *pl* : DIRECTIONS **4** ♦ : the action, practice, or profession of a teacher

♦ [2] behest, charge, command, commandment, decree, dictate, direction, directive, edict, order, word — more at COMMAND ♦ [4] education, teaching, training, tutelage — more at EDUCATION

in·struc·tion·al \-shə-nəl\ *adj* **1** : relating to, serving for, or promoting instruction **2** : containing or conveying instruction or information

in·struc·tive \in-'strək-tiv\ *adj* ♦ : carrying a lesson

♦ educational, informative — more at INFORMATIVE

in·struc·tor \in-'strək-tər\ *n* ♦ : one that instructs; *esp* : a college teacher below professorial rank — **in·struc·tor·ship** *n*

♦ educator, pedagogue, schoolteacher, teacher — more at TEACHER

in·stru·ment \'in-strə-mənt\ *n* **1** : a device used to produce music **2** ♦ : a means by which something is done **3** ♦ : a device for doing work and esp. precision work **4** : a legal document (as a deed) **5** : a device used in navigating an airplane — **in·stru·ment** \-ˌment\ *vb*

♦ [2] agency, agent, instrumentality, machinery, means, medium, organ, vehicle — more at AGENT ♦ [3] device, implement, tool, utensil — more at IMPLEMENT

in·stru·men·tal \ˌin-strə-'ment-ᵊl\ *adj* **1** : acting as a crucial agent or means **2** : of, relating to, or done with an instrument **3** : relating to, composed for, or performed on a musical instrument

in·stru·men·tal·ist \-'men-tə-list\ *n* : a player on a musical instrument

in·stru·men·tal·i·ty \ˌin-strə-mən-'ta-lə-tē, -ˌmen-\ *n, pl* **-ties** **1** : the quality or state of being instrumental **2** ♦ : something useful or helpful to a desired end : MEANS, AGENCY

♦ agency, agent, instrument, machinery, means, medium, organ, vehicle — more at AGENT

in·stru·men·ta·tion \ˌin-strə-mən-'tā-shən, -ˌmen-\ *n* **1** : ORCHESTRATION **2** : instruments for a particular purpose

instrument panel *n* : DASHBOARD

in·sub·or·di·nate \ˌin-sə-'bord-ᵊn-ət\ *adj* : disobedient to authority

in·sub·or·di·na·tion \-ˌbord-ᵊn-'ā-shən\ *n* ♦ : the quality or state of being insubordinate : defiance of authority

♦ defiance, disobedience, rebelliousness, recalcitrance, refractoriness, unruliness — more at DISOBEDIENCE

in·sub·stan·tial \ˌin-səb-'stan-chəl\ *adj* **1** : lacking substance or reality **2** ♦ : lacking firmness or solidity

♦ flimsy, gauzy, unsubstantial — more at FLIMSY

in·suf·fer·able \(ˌ)in-'sə-fə-rə-bəl\ *adj* ♦ : not to be endured : INTOLERABLE ⟨an ∼ bore⟩ — **in·suf·fer·ably** \-blē\ *adv*

♦ insupportable, intolerable, unbearable, unendurable, unsupportable — more at UNBEARABLE

in·suf·fi·cien·cy \-shən-sē\ *n* : the quality or state of being insufficient: as **a** : lack of mental or moral fitness **b** ♦ : lack of adequate supply

♦ dearth, deficiency, deficit, failure, famine, inadequacy, lack, paucity, poverty, scantiness, scarcity, shortage, want — more at DEFICIENCY

in·suf·fi·cient \ˌin-sə-'fi-shənt\ *adj* ♦ : not sufficient — **in·suf·fi·cient·ly** *adv*

♦ deficient, inadequate, scarce, short, shy, wanting — more at SHORT

in·su·lar \'in-sə-lər, -syə-\ *adj* **1** : of, relating to, or forming an island **2** : dwelling or situated on an island **3** ♦ : being, having, or reflecting a narrow provincial viewpoint

: NARROW-MINDED — **in·su·lar·i·ty** \ˌin-sə-'lar-ə-tē, -syə-\ *n*

♦ little, narrow, narrow-minded, parochial, petty, provincial, sectarian, small — more at NARROW

in·su·late \'in-sə-ˌlāt\ *vb* **-lat·ed; -lat·ing** [L *insula* island] **1** ♦ : to place in a detached situation : ISOLATE **2** : to separate a conductor of electricity, heat, or sound from other conducting bodies by means of a nonconductor — **in·su·la·tor** \'in-sə-ˌlā-tər\ *n*

♦ cut off, isolate, seclude, segregate, separate, sequester — more at ISOLATE

in·su·la·tion \ˌin-sə-'lā-shən\ *n* **1 a** : the action of insulating **b** ♦ : the state of being insulated **2** : material used in insulating

♦ isolation, seclusion, segregation, sequestration, solitude — more at ISOLATION

in·su·lin \'in-sə-lən\ *n* : a pancreatic hormone essential esp. for the metabolism of carbohydrates and the regulation of glucose in the blood

¹in·sult \in-'səlt\ *vb* [MF or L; MF *insulter*, fr. L *insultare*, lit., to spring upon, fr. *saltare* to leap] ♦ : to treat with insolence or contempt : AFFRONT — **in·sult·ing·ly** *adv*

♦ affront, offend, outrage, slight, wound; *also* cut, snub; displease, distress, disturb, hurt, pain, trouble, upset; jeer, mock, ridicule, sneer (at), taunt; defame, disparage, libel, malign, revile, slander, slur, smear; oppress, persecute, torment, torture

²in·sult \'in-ˌsəlt\ *n* ♦ : a gross indignity

♦ affront, barb, dart, dig, indignity, name, offense, outrage, put-down, sarcasm, slight, slur, wound; *also* gibe, jeer, sneer, taunt; abuse, invective, vituperation; disapproval, opprobrium; disgrace, dishonor, shame; attack, criticism, slam; torment, torture

in·su·per·a·ble \(ˌ)in-'sü-pə-rə-bəl\ *adj* ♦ : incapable of being surmounted, overcome, passed over, or solved — **in·su·per·a·bly** \-blē\ *adv*

♦ impregnable, indomitable, insurmountable, invincible, invulnerable, unbeatable, unconquerable — more at INVINCIBLE

in·sup·port·able \ˌin-sə-'pōr-tə-bəl\ *adj* **1** ♦ : more than can be endured : UNENDURABLE **2** : UNJUSTIFIABLE

♦ insufferable, intolerable, unbearable, unendurable, unsupportable — more at UNBEARABLE

in·sur·able \in-'shu̇-rə-bəl\ *adj* : capable of being or proper to be insured

in·sur·ance \in-'shu̇r-əns\ *n* **1** : the business of insuring persons or property **2** : coverage by contract whereby one party agrees to guarantee another against a specified loss **3** : the sum for which something is insured **4** : a means of guaranteeing protection or safety

in·sure \in-'shu̇r\ *vb* **in·sured; in·sur·ing** **1** : to provide or obtain insurance on or for : UNDERWRITE **2** ♦ : to make certain : ENSURE

♦ assure, cinch, ensure, guarantee, guaranty, secure — more at ENSURE

in·sured \in-'shu̇rd\ *n* : a person whose life or property is insured

in·sur·er \in-'shu̇r-ər\ *n* : one that insures; *esp* : an insurance company

in·sur·gen·cy \-jən-sē\ *n* : the quality or state of being insurgent; *specif* : a condition of revolt against a government that is less than an organized revolution and that is not recognized as belligerency

¹in·sur·gent \in-'sər-jənt\ *n* **1** : a person who revolts against civil authority or an established government : REBEL **2** : a member of a political party who rebels against it — **in·sur·gence** \-jəns\ *n*

²in·sur·gent *adj* ♦ : rising in opposition to civil authority or established leadership

♦ mutinous, rebellious, revolutionary — more at REBELLIOUS

in·sur·mount·able \ˌin-sər-ˈmaůn-tə-bəl\ *adj* ♦ : incapable of being surmounted, overcome, passed over, or solved — **in·sur·mount·ably** \-blē\ *adv*

♦ impregnable, indomitable, invincible, invulnerable, unbeatable, unconquerable — more at INVINCIBLE

in·sur·rec·tion \ˌin-sə-ˈrek-shən\ *n* ♦ : an act or instance of revolting against civil authority or an established government

♦ mutiny, rebellion, revolt, revolution, uprising — more at REBELLION

in·sur·rec·tion·ist \-shə-nist\ *n* ♦ : a favorer of or participant in insurrection

♦ insurgent, mutineer, rebel, red, revolter, revolutionary — more at REBEL

int *abbr* **1** interest **2** interior **3** intermediate **4** internal **5** international **6** intransitive

in·tact \in-ˈtakt\ *adj* **1** : untouched esp. by anything that harms or diminishes **2** ♦ : being complete or entire

♦ complete, comprehensive, entire, full, grand, integral, perfect, plenary, total, whole — more at COMPLETE

in·ta·glio \in-ˈtal-yō\ *n, pl* **-glios** [It] : an engraving cut deeply into the surface of a hard material (as stone)

in·take \ˈin-ˌtāk\ *n* **1** : an opening through which fluid enters **2** : the act of taking in **3** : something taken in

in·tan·gi·ble \(ˌ)in-ˈtan-jə-bəl\ *adj* : incapable of being touched : IMPALPABLE ⟨∼ benefits⟩ — **intangible** *n* — **in·tan·gi·bly** \-blē\ *adv*

in·te·ger \ˈin-ti-jər\ *n* [L, adj., whole, entire] ♦ : a number (as 1, 2, 3, 12, 432) that is not a fraction and does not include a fraction, is the negative of such a number, or is 0

♦ digit, figure, number, numeral, whole number — more at NUMBER

in·te·gral \ˈin-ti-grəl\ *adj* **1** ♦ : essential to completeness **2** : formed as a unit with another part **3** : composed of parts that make up a whole **4** ♦ : lacking nothing essential : ENTIRE **5** ♦ : being or involved in the essential nature of a thing

♦ [1] essential, imperative, indispensable, necessary, needful, requisite, vital — more at ESSENTIAL ♦ [4] complete, comprehensive, entire, full, grand, intact, perfect, plenary, total, whole — more at COMPLETE ♦ [5] essential, inborn, ingrained, inherent, innate, intrinsic, natural — more at INHERENT

integral calculus *n* : calculus concerned esp. with advanced methods of finding lengths, areas, and volumes

in·te·grate \ˈin-tə-ˌgrāt\ *vb* **-grat·ed; -grat·ing** **1** ♦ : to form, coordinate, or blend into a functioning whole **2** ♦ : to incorporate into a larger unit **3** : to end the segregation of and bring into equal membership in society or an organization; *also* : DESEGREGATE — **in·te·gra·tion** \ˌin-tə-ˈgrā-shən\ *n*

♦ [1] assimilate, embody, incorporate — more at EMBODY ♦ [2] amalgamate, blend, combine, commingle, fuse, incorporate, intermingle, merge, mingle, mix — more at MIX

integrated circuit *n* : a group of tiny electronic components and their connections that is produced in or on a small slice of material (as silicon)

in·teg·ri·ty \in-ˈte-grə-tē\ *n* **1** ♦ : adherence to a code of values **2** : SOUNDNESS **3** : COMPLETENESS

♦ character, decency, goodness, honesty, honor (*or* honour), morality, probity, rectitude, righteousness, uprightness, virtue — more at MORALITY

in·teg·u·ment \in-ˈte-gyə-mənt\ *n* : a covering layer (as a skin or cuticle) of an organism or one of its parts

in·tel·lect \ˈin-tə-ˌlekt\ *n* **1** : the power of knowing : the capacity for knowledge **2** : the capacity for rational or intelligent thought esp. when highly developed **3** ♦ : a person with great intellectual powers

♦ brain, genius, thinker, whiz, wizard — more at GENIUS

¹**in·tel·lec·tu·al** \ˌin-tə-ˈlek-chə-wəl\ *adj* **1** ♦ : of, relating to, or performed by the intellect **2** ♦ : given to study, reflec-

tion, and speculation **3** : engaged in activity requiring the creative use of the intellect — **in·tel·lec·tu·al·ly** *adv*

♦ [1] cerebral, inner, mental, psychological — more at MENTAL ♦ [2] cerebral, erudite, learned, literate, scholarly; *also* cultivated, cultured; well-read; academic, bookish, professorial; didactic, pedantic; educated, schooled; brainy, bright, brilliant, clever, intelligent, quick-witted, smart *Ant* lowbrow, nonintellectual

²**intellectual** *n* ♦ : an intellectual person

♦ highbrow, nerd; *also* brain, genius, intellect, thinker, whiz, wizard *Ant* lowbrow, philistine

intellectual disability *n* : significant impairment in intellectual ability accompanied by deficits in skills necessary for independent daily functioning

in·tel·lec·tu·al·ism \-chə-wə-ˌli-zəm\ *n* : devotion to the exercise of intellect or to intellectual pursuits

in·tel·lec·tu·al·i·ty \ˌin-tə-ˌlek-chə-ˈwa-lə-tē\ *n* : the quality or state of being intellectual

in·tel·li·gence \in-ˈte-lə-jəns\ *n* **1** ♦ : ability to learn and understand or to deal with new or trying situations **2** : mental acuteness **3** : INFORMATION, NEWS **4** : an agency engaged in obtaining information esp. concerning an enemy or possible enemy; *also* : the information so gained

♦ brains, gray matter (*or* grey matter), intellect, reason, sense; *also* acumen, alertness, astuteness, discernment, insight, judgment, mentality, perception, perspicacity; sagacity, sapience, wisdom, wit; head, mind, skull

intelligence quotient *n* : IQ

in·tel·li·gent \in-ˈte-lə-jənt\ *adj* [L *intelligens*, fr. *intelligere* to understand, fr. *inter* between + *legere* to select] ♦ : having or showing intelligence or intellect ⟨an ∼ decision⟩ — **in·tel·li·gent·ly** *adv*

♦ alert, brainy, bright, brilliant, clever, keen, nimble, quick, quick-witted, sharp, smart; *also* apt, ingenious, resourceful; acute, astute, discerning, insightful, knowing, perceptive, perspicacious, sagacious, sapient, savvy, wise; cerebral, erudite, highbrow, knowledgeable, learned, literate, scholarly, well-read; educated, informed, schooled, skilled, trained; creative, inventive, judicious, prudent, sage, sane, sapient, sensible, sound, wise; crafty, cunning, foxy, shrewd, wily; logical, rational, reasonable *Ant* brainless, dumb, mindless, stupid, thick, unintelligent ♦ rational, reasonable, reasoning — more at RATIONAL

in·tel·li·gen·tsia \in-ˌte-lə-ˈjent-sē-ə, -ˈgent-\ *n* [Russ *intelligentsiya*, fr. L *intelligentia* intelligence] : intellectuals forming a vanguard or elite

in·tel·li·gi·ble \in-ˈte-lə-jə-bəl\ *adj* : capable of being understood or comprehended — **in·tel·li·gi·bil·i·ty** \-ˌte-lə-jə-ˈbi-lə-tē\ *n* — **in·tel·li·gi·bly** \-ˈte-lə-jə-blē\ *adv*

in·tem·per·ance \(ˌ)in-ˈtem-pə-rəns\ *n* : lack of moderation; *esp* : habitual or excessive drinking of intoxicants — **in·tem·per·ate·ness** *n*

in·tem·per·ate \-pə-rət\ *adj* ♦ : not temperate; *also* : given to excessive use of intoxicating liquors

♦ rampant, unbridled, unchecked, uncontrolled, ungoverned, unhampered, unhindered, unrestrained — more at RAMPANT

in·tend \in-ˈtend\ *vb* [ME *entenden, intenden*, fr. AF *entendre*, fr. L *intendere* to stretch out, direct, aim at, fr. *tendere* to stretch] **1** ♦ : to have in mind as a purpose or aim **2** : to design for a specified use or future

♦ aim, aspire, contemplate, design, mean, meditate, plan, propose; *also* dream, hope, wish; consider, debate, mull (over), ponder; attempt, endeavor, strive, struggle, try; plot, scheme; accomplish, achieve, effect, execute, perform

in·ten·dant \in-ˈten-dənt\ *n* : an official (as a governor) esp. under the French, Spanish, or Portuguese monarchies

¹**in·tend·ed** *adj* **1** : expected to be such in the future; *esp* : BETROTHED **2** : INTENTIONAL

²**intended** *n* ♦ : an engaged person
  ♦ betrothed — more at BETROTHED

in·tense \in-'tens\ *adj* **1** ♦ : existing in an extreme degree **2** : marked by great zeal, energy, or eagerness **3** : showing strong feeling; *also* : deeply felt
  ♦ deep, explosive, exquisite, fearful, ferocious, fierce, furious, hard, heavy, profound, terrible, vehement, vicious, violent; *also* accentuated, aggravated, concentrated, deepened; emphasized, enhanced, heightened, intensified, magnified; stressed; exhaustive, thorough; harsh, rigorous, severe *Ant* light, moderate, soft

in·tense·ly \-lē\ *adv* : in an intense manner

in·ten·si·fy \in-'ten-sə-ˌfī\ *vb* **-fied; -fy·ing** **1** ♦ : to make or become intense or more intensive **2** : to make more acute : SHARPEN — **in·ten·si·fi·ca·tion** \-ˌten-sə-fə-'kā-shən\ *n*
  ♦ amplify, beef, boost, consolidate, deepen, enhance, heighten, magnify, redouble, step up, strengthen; *also* broaden, enlarge, expand, extend, lengthen; accelerate, hasten, quicken; accentuate, emphasize, stress; augment, reinforce, supplement; maximize; enliven, jazz (up); aggravate, exacerbate *Ant* abate, moderate

in·ten·si·ty \in-'ten-sə-tē\ *n, pl* **-ties** ♦ : the quality or state of being intense; *esp* : degree of strength, energy, or force
  ♦ ardor, emotion, fervency, fervor, heat, passion, vehemence, warmth — more at ARDOR

¹**in·ten·sive** \in-'ten-siv\ *adj* **1** : marked by intensity : highly concentrated **2** : serving to give emphasis

²**intensive** *n* : an intensive word, particle, or prefix ⟨the word "very" is an ~⟩

intensive care *n* : continuous monitoring and treatment of seriously ill patients; *also* : an area of a hospital providing this treatment

in·ten·sive·ly \-lē\ *adv* : in an intensive manner

¹**in·tent** \in-'tent\ *n* **1** : the state of mind with which an act is done : VOLITION **2** ♦ : a usu. clearly formulated or planned intention : PURPOSE, AIM **3** ♦ : the thing that is conveyed or intended to be conveyed esp. by language : MEANING, SIGNIFICANCE
  ♦ [2] aim, ambition, aspiration, design, dream, end, goal, mark, meaning, object, objective, plan, pretension, purpose, thing — more at GOAL ♦ [3] denotation, drift, import, meaning, purport, sense, significance, signification — more at MEANING

²**intent** *adj* **1** : directed with keen attention ⟨an ~ gaze⟩ **2** ♦ : having the mind, attention, or will concentrated on something or some end or purpose
  ♦ bound, decisive, determined, firm, purposeful, resolute, set, single-minded — more at DETERMINED ♦ absorbed, attentive, engrossed, observant, rapt — more at ATTENTIVE

in·ten·tion \in-'ten-chən\ *n* **1** : a determination to act in a certain way **2** : what one intends to do or bring about : PURPOSE, AIM

in·ten·tion·al \in-'ten-chə-nəl\ *adj* ♦ : done by intention or design : INTENDED
  ♦ deliberate, freewill, purposeful, voluntary, willful, willing — more at DELIBERATE

in·ten·tion·al·ly *adv* ♦ : in an intentional manner : with intention
  ♦ consciously, deliberately, knowingly, purposely, willfully; *also* calculatingly; voluntarily, willingly *Ant* inadvertently, unconsciously, unintentionally, unknowingly, unwittingly

in·tent·ly *adv* : in an intent manner

in·tent·ness *n* ♦ : the quality or state of being intent
  ♦ earnest, earnestness, gravity, seriousness, sobriety, solemnity — more at EARNESTNESS

in·ter \in-'tər\ *vb* **in·terred; in·ter·ring** : BURY

in·ter·ac·tion \ˌin-tər-'ak-shən\ *n* : mutual or reciprocal action or influence — **in·ter·act** \-'akt\ *vb*

in·ter·ac·tive \-'ak-tiv\ *adj* **1** : mutually or reciprocally active **2** : allowing two-way electronic communications (as between a person and a computer) — **in·ter·ac·tive·ly** *adv*

in·ter alia \ˌin-tər-'ā-lē-ə, -'ä-\ *adv* : among other things

in·ter·atom·ic \ˌin-tər-ə-'tä-mik\ *adj* : existing or acting between atoms

in·ter·breed \-'brēd\ *vb* **-bred** \-'bred\; **-breed·ing** : to breed together

in·ter·ca·la·ry \in-'tər-kə-ˌler-ē\ *adj* **1** : INTERCALATED ⟨February 29 is an ~ day⟩ **2** : INTERPOLATED

in·ter·ca·late \-ˌlāt\ *vb* **-lat·ed; -lat·ing** **1** : to insert (as a day) in a calendar **2** : to insert between or among existing elements or layers — **in·ter·ca·la·tion** \-ˌtər-kə-'lā-shən\ *n*

in·ter·cede \ˌin-tər-'sēd\ *vb* **-ced·ed; -ced·ing** ♦ : to act between parties with a view to reconciling differences
  ♦ interpose, intervene, mediate — more at INTERVENE

¹**in·ter·cept** \ˌin-tər-'sept\ *vb* **1** : to stop or interrupt the progress or course of **2** : to include (as part of a curve or solid) between two points, curves, or surfaces **3** : to gain possession of (an opponent's pass in football) — **in·ter·cep·tion** \-'sep-shən\ *n*

²**in·ter·cept** \'in-tər-ˌsept\ *n* : INTERCEPTION; *esp* : the interception of a target by an interceptor or missile

in·ter·cep·tor \ˌin-tər-'sep-tər\ *n* : a fighter plane designed for defense against attacking bombers

in·ter·ces·sion \ˌin-tər-'se-shən\ *n* **1** : MEDIATION **2** : prayer or petition in favor of another — **in·ter·ces·so·ry** \-'se-sə-rē\ *adj*

in·ter·ces·sor \-'se-sər\ *n* ♦ : one who intercedes
  ♦ arbiter, arbitrator, broker, go-between, intermediary, mediator, middleman, peacemaker — more at MEDIATOR

¹**in·ter·change** \ˌin-tər-'chānj\ *vb* **1** : to put each in the place of the other **2** : EXCHANGE **3** : to change places mutually — **in·ter·change·able** \-'chān-jə-bəl\ *adj* — **in·ter·change·ably** \-blē\ *adv*

²**in·ter·change** \'in-tər-ˌchānj\ *n* **1** : EXCHANGE **2** : a highway junction that by separated levels permits passage between highways without crossing traffic streams

in·ter·col·le·giate \ˌin-tər-kə-'lē-jət\ *adj* : existing or carried on between colleges

in·ter·com \'in-tər-ˌkäm\ *n* : a two-way system for localized communication

in·ter·con·nect \ˌin-tər-kə-'nekt\ *vb* ♦ : to connect with one another — **in·ter·con·nec·tion** \-'nek-shən\ *n*
  ♦ chain, compound, connect, couple, hitch, hook, join, link, yoke — more at CONNECT

in·ter·con·ti·nen·tal \-ˌkänt-ᵊn-'ent-ᵊl\ *adj* **1** : extending among or carried on between continents ⟨~ trade⟩ **2** : capable of traveling between continents ⟨~ ballistic missiles⟩

in·ter·course \'in-tər-ˌkōrs\ *n* **1** ♦ : connection or dealings between persons or nations **2** ♦ : physical sexual contact between individuals that involves the genitalia of at least one person ⟨anal ~⟩; *esp* : SEXUAL INTERCOURSE
  ♦ [1] dealings, relations ♦ [2] copulation, sexual intercourse — more at SEXUAL INTERCOURSE

in·ter·de·nom·i·na·tion·al \ˌin-tər-di-ˌnä-mə-'nā-shə-nəl\ *adj* : involving different denominations

in·ter·de·part·men·tal \ˌin-tər-di-ˌpärt-'ment-ᵊl, -ˌdē-\ *adj* : carried on between or involving different departments (as of a college)

in·ter·de·pen·dent \ˌin-tər-di-'pen-dənt\ *adj* : dependent upon one another — **in·ter·de·pen·dence** \-dəns\ *n*

in·ter·dict \ˌin-tər-'dikt\ *vb* **1** ♦ : to prohibit by decree **2** : to destroy, cut off, or damage (as an enemy line of supply) **3** : INTERCEPT
  ♦ ban, bar, enjoin, forbid, outlaw, prohibit, proscribe — more at FORBID

in·ter·dic·tion \-'dik-shən\ *n* ♦ : the act of interdicting or state of being interdicted; *also* : a prohibitory decree

♦ barring, forbidding, prohibition, proscription — more at PROHIBITION

in·ter·dis·ci·plin·ary \-'di-sə-plə-ˌner-ē\ *adj* : involving two or more academic, scientific, or artistic disciplines

¹in·ter·est \'in-trəst; 'in-tə-rəst, -ˌrest\ *n* 1 ♦ : right, title, or legal share in something 2 : a charge for borrowed money that is generally a percentage of the amount borrowed; *also* : the return received by capital on its investment 3 a ♦ : a benefit resulting from some course of action : WELFARE b : SELF-INTEREST 4 : CURIOSITY, CONCERN 5 : readiness to be concerned with or moved by an object or class of objects 6 : a quality in a thing that arouses interest

♦ [1] claim, share, stake; *also* ownership, part, partnership, possession, title ♦ [3a] good, weal, welfare, well-being — more at WELFARE

²interest *vb* 1 : to persuade to participate or engage 2 ♦ : to engage the attention of

♦ absorb, busy, engage, engross, enthrall, fascinate, grip, immerse, intrigue, involve, occupy — more at ENGAGE

in·ter·est·ing *adj* ♦ : holding the attention — **in·ter·est·ing·ly** *adv*

♦ absorbing, engaging, engrossing, enthralling, fascinating, intriguing; *also* breathtaking, electric, electrifying, exciting, exhilarating, galvanizing, inspiring, rousing, stimulating, stirring, thrilling; provocative, tantalizing; emphatic, showy, striking; alluring, attractive, bewitching, captivating, charming; mesmerizing; curious, odd, unusual, weird; amazing, astounding, astonishing, eye-opening, fabulous, marvelous, surprising, wonderful, wondrous; amusing, entertaining *Ant* boring, drab, dry, dull, heavy, monotonous, tedious, uninteresting

¹in·ter·face \'in-tər-ˌfās\ *n* 1 : a surface forming a common boundary of two bodies, spaces, or phases ⟨an oil-water ∼⟩ 2 : the place at which two independent systems meet and act on or communicate with each other ⟨the man-machine ∼⟩ 3 : the means by which interaction or communication is achieved at an interface — **in·ter·fa·cial** \ˌin-tər-'fā-shəl\ *adj*

²interface *vb* **-faced; -fac·ing** 1 : to connect by means of an interface 2 : to serve as an interface

in·ter·faith \ˌin-tər-'fāth\ *adj* : involving persons of different religious faiths

in·ter·fere \ˌin-tər-'fir\ *vb* **-fered; -fer·ing** [ME *enterferen*, fr. AF *(s)entreferir* to strike one another, fr. *entre* between, among + *ferir* to strike, fr. L *ferire*] 1 ♦ : to come in collision or be in opposition : to interpose in a way that hinders or impedes 2 ♦ : to take an unwarranted active part in the affairs of others 3 : to affect one another

♦ *usu* **interfere with** [1] encumber, hamper, hinder, hold up, impede, inhibit, obstruct, tie up — more at HAMPER ♦ [2] butt in, intrude, meddle, mess, nose, obtrude, poke, pry, snoop; *also* intercede, interpose, intervene; encroach, infringe, invade, trespass; fiddle, fool, monkey, play, tamper

in·ter·fer·ence \-'fir-əns\ *n* 1 : the act or process of interfering 2 ♦ : something that interferes : OBSTRUCTION 3 : the mutual effect on meeting of two waves resulting in areas of increased and decreased amplitude 4 : the blocking of an opponent in football to make way for the ballcarrier 5 : the illegal hindering of an opponent in sports

♦ bar, block, encumbrance, hindrance, inhibition, obstacle — more at ENCUMBRANCE

in·ter·fer·om·e·ter \ˌin-tər-fə-'rä-mə-tər\ *n* : an apparatus that uses the interference of waves (as of light) for making precise measurements — **in·ter·fer·om·e·try** \-fə-'rä-mə-trē\ *n*

in·ter·fer·on \ˌin-tər-'fir-ˌän\ *n* : any of a group of antiviral proteins of low molecular weight produced usu. by animal cells in response to a virus, a parasite in the cell, or a chemical

in·ter·ga·lac·tic \ˌin-tər-gə-'lak-tik\ *adj* : relating to or situated in the spaces between galaxies

in·ter·gen·er·a·tion·al \-ˌje-nə-'rā-shə-nəl\ *adj* : existing or occurring between generations ⟨∼ conflicts⟩

in·ter·gla·cial \-'glā-shəl\ *n* : a warm period between successive glaciations

in·ter·gov·ern·men·tal \-ˌgə-vərn-'ment-ᵊl\ *adj* : existing or occurring between two governments or levels of government

¹in·ter·im \'in-tə-rəm\ *n* [L, adv., meanwhile, fr. *inter* between] ♦ : a time intervening : INTERVAL

♦ discontinuity, gap, hiatus, interlude, intermission, interruption, interval — more at GAP

²interim *adj* : done, made, appointed, or occurring for an interim

♦ impermanent, provisional, short-term, temporary — more at TEMPORARY

¹in·te·ri·or \in-'tir-ē-ər\ *adj* 1 ♦ : lying, occurring, or functioning within the limiting boundaries : INSIDE 2 : remote from the surface, border, or shore : INLAND

♦ inner, inside, internal, inward — more at INNER

²interior *n* 1 : the inland part (as of a country) 2 : INSIDE 3 : the internal affairs of a state or nation 4 : a scene or view of the interior of a building

interior decoration *n* : INTERIOR DESIGN — **interior decorator** *n*

interior design *n* : the art or practice of planning and supervising the design and execution of architectural interiors and their furnishings — **interior designer** *n*

interj *abbr* interjection

in·ter·ject \ˌin-tər-'jekt\ *vb* ♦ : to throw in between or among other things

♦ fit, inject, insert, insinuate, interpose, introduce — more at INSERT

in·ter·jec·tion \ˌin-tər-'jek-shən\ *n* ♦ : an exclamatory word or phrase (as *ouch*) — **in·ter·jec·tion·al·ly** \-shə-nə-lē\ *adv*

♦ cry, ejaculation, exclamation — more at EXCLAMATION

in·ter·lace \ˌin-tər-'lās\ *vb* ♦ : to unite by or as if by lacing together : INTERWEAVE

♦ intersperse, intertwine, interweave, lace, thread, weave, wreathe — more at THREAD

in·ter·lard \ˌin-tər-'lärd\ *vb* : to vary by inserting or interjecting something ⟨a speech ∼*ed* with anecdotes⟩

in·ter·leave \ˌin-tər-'lēv\ *vb* **-leaved; -leav·ing** : to arrange in alternate layers

in·ter·leu·kin \ˌin-tər-'lü-kən\ *n* : any of several proteins of low molecular weight that are produced by cells of the body and regulate the immune system and immune responses

¹in·ter·line \ˌin-tər-'līn\ *vb* : to insert between lines already written or printed

²interline *vb* : to provide (as a coat) with an interlining

in·ter·lin·ear \ˌin-tər-'li-nē-ər\ *adj* : inserted between lines already written or printed ⟨an ∼ translation of a text⟩

in·ter·lin·gual \ˌin-tər-'liŋ-gwəl\ *adj* : of, relating to, or existing between two or more languages

in·ter·lin·ing \'in-tər-ˌlī-niŋ\ *n* : a lining (as of a coat) between the ordinary lining and the outside fabric

in·ter·link \ˌin-tər-'liŋk\ *vb* : to link together

in·ter·lock \ˌin-tər-'läk\ *vb* 1 : to engage or interlace together : lock together : UNITE 2 : to connect so that action of one part affects action of another part — **in·ter·lock** \'in-tər-ˌläk\ *n*

in·ter·loc·u·tor \ˌin-tər-'lä-kyə-tər\ *n* : one who takes part in dialogue or conversation

in·ter·loc·u·to·ry \-ˌtōr-ē\ *adj* : made during the progress of a legal action and not final or definite ⟨an ∼ decree⟩

in·ter·lope \ˌin-tər-'lōp\ *vb* **-loped; -lop·ing** 1 : to encroach on the rights (as in trade) of others 2 : INTRUDE, INTERFERE

in·ter·lop·er *n* ♦ : one who interlopes; *esp* : one that intrudes in a place or sphere of activity

♦ busybody, intruder, kibitzer, meddler — more at BUSYBODY

in·ter·lude \'in-tər-ˌlüd\ *n* **1** : a usu. short simple play or dramatic entertainment **2** ♦ : an intervening period, space, or event **3** : a piece of music inserted between the parts of a longer composition or a religious service

♦ discontinuity, gap, hiatus, interim, intermission, interruption, interval — more at GAP

in·ter·mar·riage \ˌin-tər-'mar-ij\ *n* **1** : marriage within one's own group as required by custom **2** : marriage between members of different groups

in·ter·mar·ry \-'mar-ē\ *vb* **1** : to marry each other **2** : to marry within a group **3** : to become connected by intermarriage

¹**in·ter·me·di·ary** \ˌin-tər-'mē-dē-ˌer-ē\ *adj* **1** : being or occurring at the middle place, stage, or degree or between extremes : INTERMEDIATE **2** : acting as a mediator

²**intermediary** *n, pl* **-ar·ies** ♦ : one that mediates : MEDIATOR, GO-BETWEEN

♦ arbiter, arbitrator, broker, go-between, intercessor, mediator, middleman, peacemaker — more at MEDIATOR

¹**in·ter·me·di·ate** \ˌin-tər-'mē-dē-ət\ *adj* ♦ : being or occurring at the middle place or degree or between extremes

♦ halfway, intermediary, median, medium, middle, midmost — more at MIDDLE

²**intermediate** *n* **1** : one that is intermediate **2** : INTERMEDIARY

intermediate school *n* **1** : JUNIOR HIGH SCHOOL **2** : a school usu. comprising grades 4–6

in·ter·ment \in-'tər-mənt\ *n* ♦ : the act or ceremony of interring : BURIAL

♦ burial, entombment, sepulture — more at BURIAL

in·ter·mez·zo \ˌin-tər-'met-sō, -'med-zō\ *n, pl* **-zi** \-sē, -zē\ *or* **-zos** [It, ultim. fr. L *intermedius* intermediate] : a short movement connecting major sections of an extended musical work (as a symphony); *also* : a short independent instrumental composition

in·ter·mi·na·ble \(ˌ)in-'tər-mə-nə-bəl\ *adj* : ENDLESS; *esp* : wearisomely protracted — **in·ter·mi·na·bly** \-blē\ *adv*

in·ter·min·gle \ˌin-tər-'miŋ-gəl\ *vb* ♦ : to mingle or mix together

♦ amalgamate, blend, combine, commingle, fuse, incorporate, integrate, merge, mingle, mix — more at MIX

in·ter·mis·sion \ˌin-tər-'mi-shən\ *n* **1** ♦ : the act of intermitting : the state of being intermitted : INTERRUPTION **2** : a temporary halt esp. in a public performance

♦ discontinuity, gap, hiatus, interim, interlude, interruption, interval — more at GAP

in·ter·mit \-'mit\ *vb* **-mit·ted; -mit·ting** : DISCONTINUE; *also* : to be intermittent

in·ter·mit·tent \-'mit-ᵊnt\ *adj* ♦ : coming and going at intervals ⟨~ rain⟩ — **in·ter·mit·tent·ly** *adv*

♦ casual, choppy, discontinuous, erratic, fitful, irregular, occasional, spasmodic, sporadic, spotty, unsteady — more at FITFUL

in·ter·mix \ˌin-tər-'miks\ *vb* : to mix together : INTERMINGLE

in·ter·mix·ture \-'miks-chər\ *n* ♦ : a mass formed by mixture : a mass of ingredients mixed

♦ admixture, amalgam, blend, combination, composite, compound, fusion, mix, mixture — more at BLEND

in·ter·mo·lec·u·lar \-mə-'le-kyə-lər\ *adj* : existing or acting between molecules

¹**in·tern** \'in-ˌtərn, in-'tərn\ *vb* : to confine or impound esp. during a war

²**in·tern** *also* **in·terne** \'in-ˌtərn\ *n* : an advanced student or recent graduate (as in medicine) gaining supervised practical experience — **in·tern·ship** *n*

³**in·tern** \'in-ˌtərn\ *vb* : to work as an intern

in·ter·nal \in-'tərn-ᵊl\ *adj* **1** ♦ : existing or situated within the limits or surface of something **2** : relating to or located in the inside of the body ⟨~ pain⟩ **3** : of, relating to, or occurring within the confines of an organized structure ⟨~ affairs⟩ **4** : of, relating to, or existing within the mind **5** : INTRINSIC, INHERENT — **in·ter·nal·ly** *adv*

♦ inner, inside, interior, inward — more at INNER

internal combustion engine *n* : an engine in which the fuel is ignited within the engine cylinder

in·ter·nal·ise *chiefly Brit var of* INTERNALIZE

in·ter·nal·ize \in-'tər-nə-ˌlīz\ *vb* **-ized; -iz·ing** : to incorporate (as values) within the self through learning or socialization — **in·ter·nal·i·za·tion** \-ˌtər-nə-lə-'zā-shən\ *n*

internal medicine *n* : a branch of medicine that deals with the diagnosis and treatment of diseases not requiring surgery

¹**in·ter·na·tion·al** \ˌin-tər-'na-shə-nəl\ *adj* **1** : common to or affecting two or more nations ⟨~ trade⟩ **2** : of, relating to, or constituting a group having members in two or more nations — **in·ter·na·tion·al·ly** *adv*

²**international** *n* : one that is international; *esp* : an organization of international scope

in·ter·na·tion·al·ise *chiefly Brit var of* INTERNATIONALIZE

in·ter·na·tion·al·ism \-'na-shə-nə-ˌli-zəm\ *n* : a policy of cooperation among nations; *also* : an attitude favoring such a policy

in·ter·na·tion·al·ize \-'na-shə-nə-ˌlīz\ *vb* : to make international; *esp* : to place under international control

International System of Units *n* : a system of units based on the metric system and used by international convention esp. for scientific work

in·ter·ne·cine \ˌin-tər-'ne-ˌsēn, -'nē-ˌsīn\ *adj* [L *internecinus*, fr. *internecare* to destroy, kill, fr. *necare* to kill, fr. *nec-, nex* violent death] **1** : DEADLY; *esp* : mutually destructive **2** : of, relating to, or involving conflict within a group ⟨~ feuds⟩

in·tern·ee \(ˌ)in-ˌtər-'nē\ *n* ♦ : a person interned

♦ captive, capture, prisoner — more at CAPTIVE

In·ter·net \'in-tər-ˌnet\ *n, often not cap* : an electronic communications network that connects computer networks worldwide

Internet service provider *n* : a company that provides its customers with Internet access and related services

in·ter·nist \'in-ˌtər-nist\ *n* : a physician who specializes in internal medicine

in·tern·ment \in-'tərn-mənt\ *n* ♦ : the act of interning or the state of being interned

♦ captivity, confinement, imprisonment, incarceration; *also* bondage, enslavement, servitude; restraint, restriction; arrest, capture, entrapment; custody, detention

in·ter·nun·cio \ˌin-tər-'nən-sē-ˌō, -'nùn-\ *n* [It *internunzio*] : a papal legate of lower rank than a nuncio

in·ter·of·fice \-'ò-fəs\ *adj* : functioning or communicating between the offices of an organization

in·ter·per·son·al \-'pərs-ᵊn-əl\ *adj* : being, relating to, or involving relations between persons ⟨~ communication⟩ — **in·ter·per·son·al·ly** *adv*

in·ter·plan·e·tary \ˌin-tər-'pla-nə-ˌter-ē\ *adj* : existing, carried on, or operating between planets ⟨~ space⟩

in·ter·play \'in-tər-ˌplā\ *n* : INTERACTION

in·ter·po·late \in-'tər-pə-ˌlāt\ *vb* **-lat·ed; -lat·ing** **1** : to change (as a text) by inserting new or foreign matter **2** : to insert (as words) into a text or into a conversation **3** : to estimate values of (data or a function) between two known values **4** : to insert between other things or parts — **in·ter·po·la·tion** \-ˌtər-pə-'lā-shən\ *n*

in·ter·pose \ˌin-tər-'pōz\ *vb* **-posed; -pos·ing** **1** ♦ : to place between **2** ♦ : to thrust in : INTRUDE, INTERRUPT **3** : to inject between parts of a conversation or argument **4** : to come or be between — **in·ter·po·si·tion** \-pə-'zi-shən\ *n*

♦ [1] fit, inject, insert, insinuate, interject, introduce — more at INSERT ♦ [2] break, chime in, cut in, interrupt, intrude — more at INTERRUPT

in·ter·pret \in-'tər-prət\ *vb* **1** ♦ : to explain the meaning of; *also* : to act as an interpreter **2** : to understand according to individual belief, judgment, or interest **3** : to represent artistically — **in·ter·pret·er** *n* — **in·ter·pre·tive** \-'tər-prə-tiv\ *adj*

♦ clarify, clear (up), construe, demonstrate, elucidate, explain, explicate, expound, illuminate, illustrate, spell out — more at EXPLAIN

in·ter·pre·ta·tion \in-ˌtər-prə-'tā-shən\ *n* **1** ♦ : the act or the result of interpreting : EXPLANATION **2** : an instance of artistic interpretation in performance or adaptation

♦ clarification, construction, elucidation, explanation, explication, exposition, illumination, illustration — more at EXPLANATION

in·ter·pre·ta·tive \in-'tər-prə-ˌtā-tiv\ *adj* : designed or fitted to interpret : EXPLANATORY

in·ter·ra·cial \-'rā-shəl\ *adj* : of, involving, or designed for members of different races

in·ter·reg·num \ˌin-tə-'reg-nəm\ *n, pl* **-nums** *or* **-na** \-nə\ **1** : the time during which a throne is vacant between two successive reigns or regimes **2** : a pause in a continuous series

in·ter·re·late \ˌin-tər-ri-'lāt\ *vb* : to bring into or have a mutual relationship — **in·ter·re·lat·ed·ness** \-lā-təd-nəs\ *n* — **in·ter·re·la·tion** \-'lā-shən\ *n* — **in·ter·re·la·tion·ship** *n*

interrog *abbr* interrogative

in·ter·ro·gate \in-'ter-ə-ˌgāt\ *vb* **-gat·ed; -gat·ing** ♦ : to question esp. formally and systematically — **in·ter·ro·ga·tion** \-ˌter-ə-'gā-shən\ *n* — **in·ter·ro·ga·tor** \-'ter-ə-ˌgā-tər\ *n*

♦ ask, examine, grill, pump, query, question, quiz — more at EXAMINE

in·ter·rog·a·tive \ˌin-tə-'rä-gə-tiv\ *adj* : asking a question ⟨∼ sentence⟩ — **interrogative** *n* — **in·ter·rog·a·tive·ly** *adv*

in·ter·rog·a·to·ry \ˌin-tə-'rä-gə-ˌtōr-ē\ *adj* : INTERROGATIVE

in·ter·rupt \ˌin-tə-'rəpt\ *vb* **1** : to stop or hinder by breaking in **2** : to break the uniformity or continuity of **3** ♦ : to break in by speaking while another is speaking — **in·ter·rupt·er** *n* — **in·ter·rup·tive** \-'rəp-tiv\ *adj*

♦ break, chime in, cut in, interpose, intrude; *also* barge (in), bother; add, chip in, contribute, put in

in·ter·rup·tion \-'rəp-shən\ *n* ♦ : an act of interrupting or state of being interrupted; *also* : temporary cessation

♦ discontinuity, gap, hiatus, interim, interlude, intermission, interval — more at GAP ♦ break, breather, lull, pause — more at PAUSE

in·ter·scho·las·tic \ˌin-tər-skə-'las-tik\ *adj* : existing or carried on between schools ⟨∼ sports⟩

in·ter·sect \ˌin-tər-'sekt\ *vb* **1** : to divide by passing through or across **2** : to meet and cross (as at a point); *also* : OVERLAP

in·ter·sec·tion \-'sek-shən\ *n* ♦ : a place or area where two or more things (as streets) intersect

♦ corner, crossing, crossroad — more at CROSSROAD

in·ter·sperse \ˌin-tər-'spərs\ *vb* **-spersed; -spers·ing** **1** : to place something at intervals in or among **2** ♦ : to insert at intervals among other things — **in·ter·sper·sion** \-'spər-zhən\ *n*

♦ interlace, intertwine, interweave, lace, thread, weave, wreathe — more at THREAD

¹**in·ter·state** \ˌin-tər-'stāt\ *adj* : relating to, including, or connecting two or more states esp. of the U.S.

²**in·ter·state** \'in-tər-ˌstāt\ *n* : an interstate highway

in·ter·stel·lar \ˌin-tər-'ste-lər\ *adj* : located or taking place among the stars

in·ter·stice \in-'tər-stəs\ *n, pl* **-stic·es** \-stə-ˌsēz, -stə-səz\ ♦ : a space that intervenes between things — **in·ter·sti·tial** \ˌin-tər-'sti-shəl\ *adj*

♦ breach, break, discontinuity, gap, gulf, hiatus, hole, interval, opening, rent, rift, separation — more at GAP

in·ter·tid·al \ˌin-tər-'tīd-ᵊl\ *adj* : of, relating to, or being the area that is above low-tide mark but exposed to tidal flooding ⟨life in the ∼ mud⟩

in·ter·twine \-'twīn\ *vb* ♦ : to twine or cause to twine about one another : INTERLACE — **in·ter·twine·ment** *n*

♦ interlace, interweave, lace; *also* blend, fuse, join, link, mix

in·ter·twist \-'twist\ *vb* : INTERTWINE

in·ter·ur·ban \-'ər-bən\ *adj* : connecting cities or towns

in·ter·val \'in-tər-vəl\ *n* [ME *intervalle*, fr. AF & L; AF *entreval*, fr. L *intervallum* space between ramparts, interval, fr. *inter-* between + *vallum* rampart] **1** ♦ : a space of time between events or states : PAUSE **2** ♦ : a space between objects, units, or states **3** : the difference in pitch between two tones

♦ [1] discontinuity, gap, hiatus, interim, interlude, intermission, interruption — more at GAP ♦ [2] breach, break, discontinuity, gap, gulf, hole, opening, rent, rift, separation — more at GAP

in·ter·vene \ˌin-tər-'vēn\ *vb* **-vened; -ven·ing** **1** : to occur, fall, or come between points of time or between events **2** : to enter or appear as an unrelated feature or circumstance ⟨rain *intervened* and we postponed the trip⟩ **3** ♦ : to come in or between in order to stop, settle, or modify ⟨∼ in a quarrel⟩ **4** : to occur or lie between two things — **in·ter·ven·tion** \-'ven-chən\ *n*

♦ intercede, interpose, mediate; *also* butt in, interfere, intrude, meddle, obtrude, pry, snoop; arbitrate, moderate, negotiate; barge (in), bother; break (in), chime in, cut in; infringe, invade, trespass

in·ter·ven·tion·ism \-'ven-chə-ˌni-zəm\ *n* : interference by one country in the political affairs of another — **in·ter·ven·tion·ist** \-'ven-chə-nist\ *n or adj*

in·ter·view \'in-tər-ˌvyü\ *n* **1** : a formal consultation usu. to evaluate qualifications **2** : a meeting at which a writer or reporter obtains information from a person; *also* : the recorded or written account of such a meeting — **interview** *vb* — **in·ter·view·ee** \ˌin-tər-(ˌ)vyü-'ē\ *n* — **in·ter·view·er** *n*

in·ter·vo·cal·ic \ˌin-tər-vō-'ka-lik\ *adj* : immediately preceded and immediately followed by a vowel ⟨∼ consonants⟩

in·ter·weave \ˌin-tər-'wēv\ *vb* **-wove** \-'wōv\ *also* **-weaved; -wo·ven** \-'wō-vən\ *also* **-weaved; -weav·ing** ♦ : to weave or blend together — **interwoven** *adj*

♦ interlace, intersperse, intertwine, lace, thread, weave, wreathe — more at THREAD

in·tes·tate \in-'tes-ˌtāt, -tət\ *adj* **1** : having made no valid will ⟨died ∼⟩ **2** : not disposed of by will ⟨∼ estate⟩

in·tes·tine \in-'tes-tən\ *n* : the tubular part of the alimentary canal that extends from stomach to anus and consists of a long narrow upper part (**small intestine**) followed by a broader shorter lower part (**large intestine**) — **in·tes·ti·nal** \-tən-ᵊl\ *adj*

in·ti·fa·da \ˌin-tə-'fä-də\ *n* : an armed uprising of Palestinians against Israeli occupation of the West Bank and Gaza Strip

in·ti·ma·cy \'in-tə-mə-sē\ *n* **1** ♦ : the state of being intimate **2** : something of a personal or private nature

♦ closeness, familiarity, nearness — more at FAMILIARITY

¹**in·ti·mate** \'in-tə-ˌmāt\ *vb* **-mat·ed; -mat·ing** [LL *intimare* to put in, announce, fr. L *intimus* innermost] **1** : ANNOUNCE, NOTIFY **2** ♦ : to communicate indirectly : HINT

♦ allude, hint, imply, indicate, infer, insinuate, suggest — more at HINT

²**in·ti·mate** \'in-tə-mət\ *adj* **1** : INTRINSIC; *also* : INNERMOST **2** ♦ : marked by very close association, contact, or familiarity **3** : marked by a warm friendship ⟨∼ friends⟩ **4** : suggesting informal warmth or privacy **5** ♦ : of a very personal or private nature ⟨∼ feelings⟩ — **in·ti·mate·ly** *adv*

♦ [2] bosom, chummy, close, familiar, friendly, thick — more at FAMILIAR ♦ [5] confidential, hushed, inside, private, secret — more at PRIVATE

³**in·ti·mate** \'in-tə-mət\ *n* ♦ : an intimate friend, associate, or confidant

♦ buddy, chum, comrade, crony, familiar, friend, pal — more at FRIEND

in·ti·ma·tion \ˌin-tə-ˈmā-shən\ *n* ♦ : an indirect usu. hinted suggestion or notice; *also* : something intimated

♦ clue, cue, hint, indication, inkling, lead, suggestion — more at HINT

in·tim·i·date \in-ˈti-mə-ˌdāt\ *vb* **-dat·ed; -dat·ing** ♦ : to make timid or fearful; *esp* : to compel or deter by or as if by threats — **in·tim·i·dat·ing·ly** *adv* — **in·tim·i·da·tion** \-ˌti-mə-ˈdā-shən\ *n*

♦ browbeat, bully, cow, hector; *also* affright, alarm, frighten, horrify, scare, shock, spook, startle, terrify; menace, terrorize, threaten; badger, harass, hound; bulldoze, coerce, compel, constrain, dragoon, force, make, oblige, press, pressure; demoralize, unman, unnerve; discompose, disconcert, disquiet, distress, disturb, perturb, upset

intl *or* **intnl** *abbr* international

in·to \ˈin-tü\ *prep* **1** : to the inside of ⟨ran ∼ the house⟩ **2** : to the state, condition, or form of ⟨got ∼ trouble⟩ **3** : AGAINST ⟨ran ∼ a wall⟩

in·tol·er·a·ble \(ˌ)in-ˈtä-lə-rə-bəl\ *adj* **1** ♦ : not tolerable : UNBEARABLE **2** : EXCESSIVE — **in·tol·er·a·bly** \-blē\ *adv*

♦ insufferable, insupportable, unbearable, unendurable, unsupportable — more at UNBEARABLE

in·tol·er·ant \(ˌ)in-ˈtä-lə-rənt\ *adj* **1** : unable or unwilling to tolerate **2** ♦ : unwilling to grant equality, freedom, or other social rights : BIGOTED — **in·tol·er·ance** \-rəns\ *n*

♦ bigoted, narrow, narrow-minded, prejudiced; *also* conservative, hidebound, old-fashioned, reactionary; insular, parochial, provincial; biased, one-sided, partial, partisan *Ant* liberal, broad-minded, open-minded, tolerant, unprejudiced

in·to·na·tion \ˌin-tō-ˈnā-shən\ *n* **1** : the act of intoning and esp. of chanting **2** : something that is intoned **3** : the manner of singing, playing, or uttering tones **4** : the rise and fall in pitch of the voice in speech

in·tone \in-ˈtōn\ *vb* **in·toned; in·ton·ing** : to utter in musical or prolonged tones : CHANT ⟨∼ a prayer⟩

in to·to \in-ˈtō-tō\ *adv* [L, on the whole] : TOTALLY, ENTIRELY

in·tox·i·cant \in-ˈtäk-si-kənt\ *n* ♦ : something that intoxicates; *esp* : an alcoholic drink — **intoxicant** *adj*

♦ alcohol, booze, drink, liquor, moonshine, spirits — more at ALCOHOL

in·tox·i·cate \-sə-ˌkāt\ *vb* **-cat·ed; -cat·ing** **1** : to affect by a drug (as alcohol or cocaine) esp. to the point of physical or mental impairment **2** ♦ : to excite to enthusiasm or frenzy

♦ electrify, excite, exhilarate, galvanize, thrill, titillate, turn on — more at THRILL

in·tox·i·cat·ed \-sə-ˌkā-təd\ *adj* ♦ : affected by or as if by alcohol ⟨*intoxicated* by power⟩

♦ drunk, high, inebriate, tipsy — more at DRUNK ♦ ecstatic, elated, euphoric, rapturous, rhapsodic — more at ECSTATIC

in·tox·i·ca·tion \-ˌtäk-sə-ˈkā-shən\ *n* ♦ : the condition of being drunk; *also* : a strong excitement or elation

♦ ecstasy, elation, euphoria, exhilaration, heaven, paradise, rapture, rhapsody, transport — more at ECSTASY

in·trac·ta·ble \(ˌ)in-ˈtrak-tə-bəl\ *adj* ♦ : not easily controlled — **in·trac·ta·bil·i·ty** \(ˌ)in-ˌtrak-tə-ˈbi-lə-tē\ *n* — **in·trac·ta·bly** \(ˌ)in-ˈtrak-tə-blē\ *adv*

♦ froward, headstrong, recalcitrant, refractory, uncontrollable, unmanageable, unruly, untoward, wayward, willful — more at UNCONTROLLABLE

in·tra·mu·ral \-ˈmyùr-əl\ *adj* : being or occurring within the walls or limits (as of a city or college) ⟨∼ sports⟩

in·tra·mus·cu·lar \-ˈməs-kyə-lər\ *adj* : situated within, occurring in, or administered by entering a muscle — **in·tra·mus·cu·lar·ly** *adv*

in·tra·net \ˈin-trə-ˌnet\ *n* : a network similar to the World Wide Web but having access limited to certain authorized users

intrans *abbr* intransitive

in·tran·si·gent \-jənt\ *adj* : UNCOMPROMISING; *also* : IRRECONCILABLE — **in·tran·si·gence** \-jəns\ *n* — **intransigent** *n*

in·tran·si·tive \(ˌ)in-ˈtran-sə-tiv, -zə-\ *adj* : not transitive; *esp* : not having or containing an object ⟨an ∼ verb⟩ — **in·tran·si·tive·ly** *adv* — **in·tran·si·tive·ness** *n*

in·tra·state \ˌin-trə-ˈstāt\ *adj* : existing or occurring within a state ⟨∼ rivals⟩

in·tra·uter·ine device \-ˈyü-tə-rən-, -ˌrīn-\ *n* : a device inserted into and left in the uterus to prevent pregnancy

in·tra·ve·nous \ˌin-trə-ˈvē-nəs\ *adj* : being within or entering by way of the veins; *also* : used in or using intravenous procedures — **in·tra·ve·nous·ly** *adv*

intrench *var of* ENTRENCH

in·trep·id \in-ˈtre-pəd\ *adj* ♦ : characterized by resolute fearlessness, fortitude, and endurance ⟨∼ explorers⟩

♦ brave, courageous, dauntless, doughty, fearless, gallant, greathearted, heroic, lionhearted, manful, stalwart, stout, undaunted, valiant, valorous — more at BRAVE

in·tre·pid·i·ty \ˌin-trə-ˈpi-də-tē\ *n* : the quality or state of being intrepid : resolute bravery

in·tri·ca·cy \-tri-kə-sē\ *n* ♦ : the quality or state of being intricate; *also* : something intricate

♦ complexity, complication, difficulty — more at COMPLICATION ♦ complexity, elaborateness, sophistication — more at COMPLEXITY

in·tri·cate \ˈin-tri-kət\ *adj* [ME, fr. L *intricatus*, pp. of *intricare* to entangle, fr. *tricae* trifles, complications] **1** ♦ : having many complexly interrelated parts : COMPLICATED **2** ♦ : involving or done with precision; *also* : difficult to follow, understand, or solve — **in·tri·cate·ly** *adv*

♦ complex, complicated, convoluted, detailed, elaborate, involved, knotty, sophisticated — more at COMPLEX

¹in·trigue \in-ˈtrēg\ *vb* **in·trigued; in·trigu·ing** **1** : to accomplish by intrigue **2** ♦ : to carry on an intrigue; *esp* : PLOT, SCHEME **3** ♦ : to arouse the interest, desire, or curiosity of

♦ [2] conspire, contrive, machinate, plot, scheme — more at PLOT ♦ [3] absorb, busy, engage, engross, enthrall, fascinate, grip, immerse, interest, involve, occupy — more at ENGAGE

²in·trigue \ˈin-ˌtrēg, in-ˈtrēg\ *n* **1** ♦ : a secret scheme : PLOT **2** : a clandestine love affair

♦ conspiracy, design, machination, plot, scheme — more at PLOT

intriguing *adj* ♦ : engaging the interest to a marked degree

♦ absorbing, engaging, engrossing, enthralling, fascinating, interesting — more at INTERESTING

in·trin·sic \in-ˈtrin-zik, -sik\ *adj* ♦ : belonging to the essential nature or constitution of a thing

♦ essential, inborn, ingrained, inherent, innate, integral, natural — more at INHERENT

in·trin·si·cal·ly \in-ˈtrin-zi-k(ə-)lē, -si-\ *adv* ♦ : in an intrinsic manner : having an intrinsic quality

♦ constitutionally, inherently, innately, naturally — more at NATURALLY

introd *abbr* introduction

in·tro·duce \ˌin-trə-ˈdüs, -ˈdyüs\ *vb* **-duced; -duc·ing** **1** : to lead or bring in esp. for the first time **2** ♦ : to bring into practice or use **3** ♦ : to cause to be acquainted **4** ♦ : to present for discussion **5** ♦ : to put in : INSERT — **in·tro·duc·to·ry** \-ˈdək-tə-rē\ *adj*

♦ [2] constitute, establish, found, inaugurate, initiate, innovate, institute, launch, pioneer, set up, start — more at FOUND ♦ [3] acquaint, familiarize, initiate, orient — more at ACQUAINT ♦ [4] bring up, broach, moot, raise; *also* allude (to), cite, mention, name, refer (to); offer, propose, suggest; air, express, speak (of), talk (about), vent, ventilate; interject, interrupt; debate, discuss, thrash (out *or* over) ♦ [5] fit, inject, insert, insinuate, interject, interpose — more at INSERT

in·tro·duc·tion \-'dək-shən\ *n* **1** ♦ : something that introduces **2** : the act or process of introducing : the state of being introduced; *also* : something introduced

♦ foreword, preamble, preface, prologue; *also* beginning, commencement, initiation, opening, origin, outset, start *Ant* epilogue

in·troit \'in-,tròit, -,trō-ət\ *n* **1** *often cap* : the first part of the traditional proper of the Mass **2** : a piece of music sung or played at the beginning of a worship service

in·tro·spec·tion \-'spek-shən\ *n* : a reflective looking inward : an examination of one's own thoughts or feelings — **in·tro·spect** \,in-trə-'spekt\ *vb* — **in·tro·spec·tive** \-'spek-tiv\ *adj* — **in·tro·spec·tive·ly** *adv*

in·tro·vert \'in-trə-,vərt\ *n* : a reserved or shy person — **in·tro·ver·sion** \,in-trə-'vər-zhən\ *n* — **introvert** *adj*

in·tro·vert·ed \'in-trə-,vər-təd\ *adj* ♦ : turned in upon itself; *specif* : marked by being wholly or predominantly concerned with and interested in one's own mental life

♦ bashful, coy, demure, diffident, modest, retiring, sheepish, shy — more at SHY

in·trude \in-'trüd\ *vb* **in·trud·ed; in·trud·ing 1** ♦ : to thrust, enter, or force in or upon **2** : ENCROACH, TRESPASS — **in·tru·sion** \-'trü-zhən\ *n*

♦ break, chime in, cut in, interpose, interrupt — more at INTERRUPT ♦ butt in, interfere, meddle, mess, nose, obtrude, poke, pry, snoop — more at INTERFERE ♦ *usu* **intrude upon** bother, bug, disturb, pester — more at BOTHER

in·trud·er *n* ♦ : one that intrudes

♦ busybody, interloper, kibitzer, meddler — more at BUSYBODY

in·tru·sive \-'trü-siv\ *adj* ♦ : characterized by intrusion : intruding where one is not welcome or invited — **in·tru·sive·ness** *n*

♦ meddlesome, nosy, obtrusive, officious, presumptuous, prying; *also* bold, brazen, impertinent, impudent, insolent, rude; invading, trespassing; curious, inquisitive; annoying, harassing, pestiferous *Ant* unobtrusive

intrust *var of* ENTRUST

in·tu·it \in-'tü-ət, -'tyü-\ *vb* : to know, sense, or understand by intuition

in·tu·ition \,in-tù-'wi-shən, -tyù-\ *n* **1** ♦ : quick and ready insight **2** : the power or faculty of knowing things without conscious reasoning — **in·tu·i·tive** \in-'tü-ə-tiv, -'tyü-\ *adj* — **in·tu·i·tive·ly** *adv*

In·u·it \'i-nü-wət, 'in-yù-\ *n* [Inuit *inuit*, pl. of *inuk* person] **1** *pl* **Inuit** *or* **Inuits** : a member of the indigenous people of No. America and Greenland **2** : the language of the Inuit people

in·un·date \'i-nən-,dāt\ *vb* **-dat·ed; -dat·ing** ♦ : to cover with or as if with a flood : OVERFLOW

♦ deluge, drown, engulf, flood, overflow, overwhelm, submerge, swamp — more at FLOOD

in·un·da·tion \,i-nən-'dā-shən\ *n* ♦ : an overflowing of the land by water; *also* : an overwhelming amount or number

♦ cataclysm, cataract, deluge, flood, overflow, spate, torrent — more at FLOOD

in·ure \i-'nùr, -'nyùr\ *vb* **in·ured; in·ur·ing** [ME *enuren*, fr. *in ure* customary, fr. *putten in ure* to use, put into practice, part trans. of AF *mettre en ovre, en uevre*] **1** : to accustom to accept something undesirable ⟨*inured* to violence⟩ **2** : to become of advantage

in utero \in-'yü-tə-,rō\ *adv or adj* [L] : in the uterus : before birth

inv *abbr* **1** inventor **2** invoice

in vac·uo \in-'va-kyù-,wō\ *adv* [L] : in a vacuum

in·vade \in-'vād\ *vb* **in·vad·ed; in·vad·ing 1** ♦ : to enter in a hostile manner **2** : to encroach upon **3** : to spread through and usu. harm ⟨germs ∼ the tissues⟩ — **in·vad·er** *n*

♦ foray, overrun, raid; *also* despoil, loot, maraud, pillage, plunder, ravage, sack; conquer, crush, overcome, overpower, overwhelm, subdue, subjugate; assail, assault, attack; battle, combat, fight, war (with); encroach, infringe, trespass; besiege, blockade; occupy

¹**in·val·id** \(,)in-'va-ləd\ *adj* ♦ : being without foundation or force in fact, reason, or law — **in·va·lid·i·ty** \,in-və-'li-də-tē\ *n* — **in·val·id·ly** *adv*

♦ baseless, groundless, unfounded, unreasonable, unsubstantiated, unsupported, unwarranted — more at BASELESS ♦ null, void — more at NULL ♦ erroneous, false, inaccurate, incorrect, inexact, off, unsound, untrue, wrong — more at FALSE

²**in·val·id** \'in-və-ləd\ *adj* : being in ill health : SICKLY

³**invalid** \'in-və-ləd\ *n* : a person in usu. chronic ill health — **in·va·lid·ism** \-lə-,di-zəm\ *n*

⁴**in·va·lid** \'in-və-ləd, -,lid\ *vb* **1** : to remove from active duty by reason of sickness or disability **2** : to make sickly or disabled

in·val·i·date \(,)in-'va-lə-,dāt\ *vb* ♦ : to make invalid ⟨*invalidated* a contract⟩; *esp* : to weaken or make valueless — **in·val·i·da·tion** \in-,va-lə-'dā-shən\ *n*

♦ abolish, abrogate, annul, cancel, dissolve, negate, nullify, quash, repeal, rescind, void — more at ABOLISH

in·valu·able \-'val-yə-bəl, -yə-wə-bəl\ *adj* : valuable beyond estimation

in·vari·able \-'ver-ē-ə-bəl\ *adj* : not changing or capable of change : CONSTANT

in·vari·ably \-blē\ *adv* ♦ : on every occasion

♦ always, constantly, continually, ever, forever, incessantly, perpetually, unfailingly — more at ALWAYS

in·va·sion \in-'vā-zhən\ *n* ♦ : an act or instance of invading; *esp* : entry of an army into a country for conquest

♦ descent, foray, incursion, irruption, raid — more at RAID

in·va·sive \in-'vā-siv, -ziv\ *adj* **1** : tending to spread ⟨∼ cancer cells⟩ **2** : involving entry into the living body (as by surgery) ⟨∼ therapy⟩

in·vec·tive \in-'vek-tiv\ *n* **1** : an abusive expression or speech **2** ♦ : abusive language — **invective** *adj*

♦ abuse, fulmination, vitriol, vituperation — more at ABUSE

in·veigh \in-'vā\ *vb* : to protest or complain bitterly or vehemently : RAIL

in·vei·gle \in-'vā-gəl, -'vē-\ *vb* **in·vei·gled; in·vei·gling** [AF *enveegler, aveogler* to blind, hoodwink, fr. *avogle, enveugle* blind, fr. ML *ab oculis*, lit., lacking eyes] **1** : to win over by flattery : ENTICE **2** : to acquire by ingenuity or flattery

in·vent \in-'vent\ *vb* **1** ♦ : to think up **2** ♦ : to create or produce for the first time

♦ [1, 2] concoct, contrive, cook up, devise, fabricate, make up, manufacture, think up; *also* coin, contrive, create, design, hatch, produce; daydream, dream, fantasize; conceive, envisage, imagine, picture, visualize

in·ven·tion \in-'ven-chən\ *n* **1** ♦ : productive imagination : INVENTIVENESS **2** ♦ : a creation of the imagination; *esp* : a false conception **3** ♦ : a device, contrivance, or process originated after study and experiment **4** : the act or process of inventing

♦ [1] creativity, fancy, fantasy, imagination, inventiveness — more at IMAGINATION ♦ [2] fabrication, fantasy, fiction, figment — more at FICTION ♦ [3] coinage, concoction, contrivance, creation, innovation, wrinkle; *also* contraption, device, gadget, gizmo, novelty; design, product, work; dream, fantasy, picture, vision; conception, imagining

in·ven·tive \in-'ven-tiv\ *adj* **1** ♦ : adept or prolific at producing inventions : CREATIVE, INGENIOUS ⟨an ∼ composer⟩ **2** : characterized by invention ⟨an ∼ turn of mind⟩

♦ creative, imaginative, ingenious, innovative, original — more at CREATIVE

in·ven·tive·ness *n* ♦ : the quality or state of being inventive

♦ creativity, ingenuity, invention, originality — more at CREATIVITY

in·ven·tor \-'ven-tər\ *n* ♦ : one that invents: as **a** : one that conceives by creative imagination **b** : one that creates a new device or process

♦ designer, developer, innovator, originator; *also* author, creator, father, founder, originator; pioneer, researcher; builder, maker, producer; dreamer

¹**in·ven·to·ry** \'in-vən-ˌtōr-ē\ *n, pl* **-ries** **1** : an itemized list of current goods or assets **2** : SURVEY, SUMMARY **3** : STOCK, SUPPLY **4** : the act or process of taking an inventory

²**inventory** *vb* **-ried; -ry·ing** ♦ : to make an inventory of

♦ enumerate, itemize, list, numerate — more at LIST

¹**in·verse** \(ˌ)in-'vərs, 'in-ˌvərs\ *adj* : opposite in order, nature, or effect : REVERSED — **in·verse·ly** *adv*

²**inverse** *n* : something inverse or resulting in or from inversion : OPPOSITE

in·ver·sion \in-'vər-zhən\ *n* **1** : a reversal of position, order, or relationship; *esp* : an increase of temperature with altitude through a layer of air **2** : the act or process of inverting

in·vert \in-'vərt\ *vb* **1** : to reverse in position, order, or relationship **2** : to turn upside down or inside out **3** : to turn inward

in·ver·te·brate \(ˌ)in-'vər-tə-brət, -ˌbrāt\ *adj* **1** : lacking a backbone; *also* : of or relating to invertebrate animals **2** : lacking in strength or vitality — **invertebrate** *n*

¹**in·vest** \in-'vest\ *vb* **1** ♦ : to install formally in an office or honor **2** ♦ : to furnish with power or authority **3** : to cover completely : ENVELOP **4** : to cover with or as if with cloth or clothing : CLOTHE, ADORN **5** : to surround with troops or ships so as to prevent escape or entry : BESIEGE **6** ♦ : to endow with a quality or characteristic

♦ [1] baptize, inaugurate, induct, initiate, install — more at INSTALL ♦ [2] accredit, authorize, certify, commission, empower, enable, license, qualify — more at AUTHORIZE ♦ [6] imbue, inculcate, infuse, ingrain, steep, suffuse — more at INFUSE

²**invest** *vb* **1** : to commit (money) in order to earn a financial return **2** : to expend for future benefits or advantages **3** : to make an investment — **in·ves·tor** \-'ves-tər\ *n*

in·ves·ti·gate \in-'ves-tə-ˌgāt\ *vb* **-gat·ed; -gat·ing** [L *investigare* to track, investigate, fr. *vestigium* footprint, track] ♦ : to study by close examination and systematic inquiry — **in·ves·ti·ga·tive** \-'ves-tə-ˌgā-tiv\ *adj*

♦ delve, dig, explore, go, inquire into, look, probe, research — more at EXPLORE

in·ves·ti·ga·tion \-ˌves-tə-'gā-shən\ *n* ♦ : the action or process of investigating; *esp* : detailed examination or a searching inquiry

♦ examination, exploration, inquiry, probe, research, study — more at INQUIRY

in·ves·ti·ga·tor \-ˌgā-tər\ *n* ♦ : one that investigates; *esp* : one employed or engaged in detecting lawbreakers or in getting information that is not readily or publicly accessible

♦ detective, operative, shadow, sleuth, tail — more at DETECTIVE

in·ves·ti·ture \in-'ves-tə-ˌchùr, -chər\ *n* **1** ♦ : the act of ratifying or establishing in office **2** : something that covers or adorns

♦ inaugural, inauguration, induction, installation — more at INSTALLATION

¹**in·vest·ment** \in-'vest-mənt\ *n* **1** : an outer layer : ENVELOPE **2** : INVESTITURE 1 **3** : BLOCKADE, SIEGE

²**investment** *n* : the outlay of money for income or profit; *also* : the sum invested or the property purchased

in·vet·er·ate \in-'ve-tə-rət\ *adj* **1** ♦ : firmly established by age or long persistence **2** ♦ : confirmed in a habit

♦ [1] confirmed, deep-rooted, deep-seated, settled; *also* fixed, immutable, set; implanted, instilled; inborn, inbred,

innate, inherent, natural; accustomed, chronic, customary, habitual, regular, typical, usual; abiding, enduring, lifelong, persistent, persisting ♦ [2] chronic, confirmed, habitual — more at HABITUAL

in·vi·a·ble \(ˌ)in-'vī-ə-bəl\ *adj* : incapable of surviving

in·vid·i·ous \in-'vi-dē-əs\ *adj* **1** : tending to cause discontent, animosity, or envy ⟨an ~ comparison⟩ **2** : feeling or showing envy : ENVIOUS **3** : OBNOXIOUS — **in·vid·i·ous·ly** *adv*

in·vig·o·rate \in-'vi-gə-ˌrāt\ *vb* **-rat·ed; -rat·ing** ♦ : to give life and energy to : ANIMATE ⟨~ the economy⟩ — **in·vig·o·ra·tion** \-ˌvi-gə-'rā-shən\ *n*

♦ animate, brace, energize, enliven, fire, jazz up, liven up, pep up, quicken, stimulate, vitalize, vivify, zip (up) — more at ANIMATE

invigorating *adj* ♦ : having an enlivening effect

♦ bracing, refreshing, restorative, stimulative, tonic — more at TONIC

in·vin·ci·ble \(ˌ)in-'vin-sə-bəl\ *adj* ♦ : incapable of being conquered, overcome, or subdued — **in·vin·ci·bil·i·ty** \-ˌvin-sə-'bi-lə-tē\ *n* — **in·vin·ci·bly** \-'vin-sə-blē\ *adv*

♦ impregnable, indomitable, insurmountable, invulnerable, unbeatable, unconquerable; *also* inviolable, unassailable, untouchable; armored, defended, guarded, protected, safe, safeguarded, secure, shielded; unbeaten, unconquered, undefeated, unsubdued *Ant* vulnerable

in·vi·o·la·ble \-'vī-ə-lə-bəl\ *adj* **1** ♦ : safe from violation or profanation **2** : secure from assault or trespass : UNASSAILABLE — **in·vi·o·la·bil·i·ty** \-ˌvī-ə-lə-'bi-lə-tē\ *n*

♦ holy, sacred, sacrosanct — more at SACRED

in·vi·o·late \-'vī-ə-lət\ *adj* : not violated or profaned : PURE

in·vis·i·ble \-'vi-zə-bəl\ *adj* **1** : incapable of being seen ⟨~ to the naked eye⟩ **2** : HIDDEN **3** : IMPERCEPTIBLE, INCONSPICUOUS — **in·vis·i·bil·i·ty** \-ˌvi-zə-'bi-lə-tē\ *n* — **in·vis·i·bly** \-'vi-zə-blē\ *adv*

invisible hand *n* : a hypothetical economic force that works for the benefit of all

in·vi·ta·tion·al \ˌin-və-'tā-shə-nəl\ *adj* : limited to invited participants ⟨an ~ tournament⟩ — **invitational** *n*

in·vite \in-'vīt\ *vb* **in·vit·ed; in·vit·ing** **1** : ENTICE, TEMPT **2** : to increase the likelihood of **3** : to request the presence or participation of : ASK **4** : to request formally **5** : ENCOURAGE — **in·vi·ta·tion** \ˌin-və-'tā-shən\ *n*

in·vit·ing *adj* : ATTRACTIVE, TEMPTING

in vi·tro \in-'vē-trō, -'vī-, -'vi-\ *adv or adj* [NL, lit., in glass] : outside the living body and in an artificial environment ⟨*in vitro* fertilization⟩

in·vo·ca·tion \ˌin-və-'kā-shən\ *n* **1** : SUPPLICATION; *esp* : a prayer at the beginning of a service **2** : a formula for conjuring : INCANTATION

¹**in·voice** \'in-ˌvòis\ *n* [modif. of MF *envois*, pl. of *envoi* message] ♦ : an itemized list of goods shipped usu. specifying the price and the terms of sale : BILL

♦ account, bill, check, statement, tab — more at BILL

²**invoice** *vb* **in·voiced; in·voic·ing** : to send an invoice to or for : BILL

in·voke \in-'vōk\ *vb* **in·voked; in·vok·ing** **1** : to petition for help or support **2** : to appeal to or cite as authority ⟨~ a law⟩ **3** : to call forth by incantation : CONJURE ⟨~ spirits⟩ **4** : to make an earnest request for : SOLICIT **5** : to put into effect or operation **6** : to bring about : CAUSE

in·vol·un·tary \(ˌ)in-'vä-lən-ˌter-ē\ *adj* **1** ♦ : done contrary to or without choice **2** ♦ : dictated by authority or circumstance : COMPULSORY **3** ♦ : not controlled by the will ⟨~ contractions⟩ — **in·vol·un·tari·ly** \-ˌvä-lən-'ter-ə-lē\ *adv*

♦ [1] unintended, unintentional; *also* accidental, unplanned, unpremeditated; automatic, impulsive, instinctive, spontaneous, unprompted; inadvertent, unconscious, unknowing, unwitting *Ant* deliberate, intentional, unforced, voluntary, willful, willing

♦ [2] compulsory, imperative, incumbent, mandatory, necessary, nonelective, obligatory, peremptory — more at MANDATORY ♦ [3] automatic, mechanical, spontaneous — more at AUTOMATIC

in·vo·lute \'in-və-ˌlüt\ *adj* : INVOLVED, INTRICATE

in·vo·lu·tion \ˌin-və-'lü-shən\ *n* 1 : the act or an instance of enfolding or entangling 2 : the quality or state of being complex : COMPLEXITY, INTRICACY

in·volve \in-'välv\ *vb* **in·volved; in·volv·ing** 1 ♦ : to draw in as a participant 2 : ENVELOP 3 ♦ : to occupy (as oneself) absorbingly; *esp* : to commit oneself emotionally 4 : to relate closely : CONNECT 5 ♦ : to have as part of itself : INCLUDE 6 : ENTAIL, IMPLY ⟨the job ∼s traveling⟩ 7 : to have an effect on — **in·volve·ment** *n*

♦ [1] affect, concern, interest, touch — more at CONCERN ♦ [3] absorb, busy, engage, engross, enthrall, fascinate, grip, immerse, interest, intrigue, occupy — more at ENGAGE ♦ [5] carry, comprehend, contain, embrace, encompass, entail, include, number, take in — more at INCLUDE

in·volved \-'välvd\ *adj* ♦ : marked by extreme and often needless or excessive complexity : INTRICATE, COMPLEX ⟨an ∼ plot⟩

♦ complex, complicated, convoluted, detailed, elaborate, intricate, knotty, sophisticated — more at COMPLEX

in·vul·ner·a·ble \(ˌ)in-'vəl-nə-rə-bəl\ *adj* 1 : incapable of being wounded, injured, or damaged 2 ♦ : immune to or proof against attack — **in·vul·ner·a·bil·i·ty** \-ˌvəl-nə-rə-'bi-lə-tē\ *n* — **in·vul·ner·a·bly** \-'vəl-nə-rə-blē\ *adv*

♦ impregnable, indomitable, insurmountable, invincible, unbeatable, unconquerable — more at INVINCIBLE

¹in·ward \'in-wərd\ *adj* 1 ♦ : situated on the inside 2 : MENTAL; *also* : SPIRITUAL 3 : directed toward the interior

♦ inner, inside, interior, internal — more at INNER

²inward *or* **in·wards** \-wərdz\ *adv* 1 : toward the inside, center, or interior 2 : toward the inner being

in·ward·ly \'in-wərd-lē\ *adv* 1 : MENTALLY, SPIRITUALLY 2 : INTERNALLY ⟨bled ∼⟩ 3 : to oneself ⟨cursed ∼⟩

IOC *abbr* International Olympic Committee

io·dide \'ī-ə-ˌdīd\ *n* : a compound of iodine with another element or group

io·dine \'ī-ə-ˌdīn, -əd-ᵊn\ *n* 1 : a nonmetallic chemical element used esp. in medicine and photography 2 : a solution of iodine used as a local antiseptic

io·dise *chiefly Brit var of* IODIZE

io·dize \'ī-ə-ˌdīz\ *vb* **io·dized; io·diz·ing** : to treat with iodine or an iodide

ion \'ī-ən, 'ī-ˌän\ *n* [Gk, neut. of *iōn*, prp. of *ienai* to go; so called because in electrolysis it goes to one of the two poles] : an electrically charged particle, atom, or group of atoms — **ion·ic** \ī-'ä-nik\ *adj*

-ion *n suffix* : act, process, state, or condition ⟨valida*tion*⟩

ion·ise *chiefly Brit var of* IONIZE

ion·ize \'ī-ə-ˌnīz\ *vb* **ion·ized; ion·iz·ing** 1 : to convert wholly or partly into ions 2 : to become ionized — **ion·iz·able** \ˌī-ə-'nī-zə-bəl\ *adj* — **ion·iza·tion** \ˌī-ə-nə-'zā-shən\ *n* — **ion·iz·er** \'ī-ə-ˌnī-zər\ *n*

ion·o·sphere \ī-'ä-nə-ˌsfir\ *n* : the part of the earth's atmosphere extending from about 30 miles (50 kilometers) to the exosphere that contains ionized atmospheric gases — **ion·o·spher·ic** \ī-ˌä-nə-'sfir-ik, -'sfer-\ *adj*

IOOF *abbr* Independent Order of Odd Fellows

io·ta \ī-'ō-tə\ *n* [L, fr. Gk *iōta*] 1 : the 9th letter of the Greek alphabet — I or ι 2 : a very small quantity : JOT

IOU \ˌī-(ˌ)ō-'yü\ *n* : an acknowledgment of a debt

IP *abbr* innings pitched

IP address \'ī-ˌpē-\ *n* [Internet *protocol*] : the numeric address of a computer on the Internet

ip·e·cac \'i-pi-ˌkak\ *n* [Pg *ipecacuanha*] : an emetic and expectorant drug used esp. as a syrup in treating accidental poisoning; *also* : either of two tropical American plants or their rhizomes and roots used to make ipecac

IPO \ˌī-ˌpē-'ō\ *n, pl* **IPOs** : an initial public offering of a company's stock

ip·so fac·to \ˌip-sō-'fak-tō\ *adv* [NL, lit., by the fact itself] : by the very nature of the case

iq *abbr* [L *idem quod*] the same as

IQ \'ī-ˌkyü\ *n* : a number used to express a person's relative intelligence as determined by a standardized test

¹Ir *abbr* Irish

²Ir *symbol* iridium

IR *abbr* infrared

¹IRA \ˌī-(ˌ)är-'ā; 'ī-rə\ *n* [*individual retirement account*] : a retirement savings account in which income taxes are deferred until withdrawals are made

²IRA *abbr* Irish Republican Army

Ira·ni·an \i-'rä-nē-ən *also* -'rä-\ *n* : a native or inhabitant of Iran — **Iranian** *adj*

Iraqi \i-'rä-kē, -'ra-\ *n* : a native or inhabitant of Iraq — **Iraqi** *adj*

iras·ci·bil·i·ty \-ˌra-sə-'bi-lə-tē\ *n* : the quality or state of being irascible : proneness to anger

iras·ci·ble \i-'ra-sə-bəl\ *adj* ♦ : marked by hot temper and easily provoked anger

♦ choleric, crabby, cranky, cross, irritable, short-tempered, snappish, snappy, snippy, testy, waspish — more at IRRITABLE

irate \ī-'rāt\ *adj* 1 ♦ : roused to ire ⟨an ∼ customer⟩ 2 : arising from anger — **irate·ly** *adv*

♦ angry, boiling, enraged, furious, rabid, sore — more at ANGRY

¹ire \'īr\ *n* ♦ : intense and usu. openly displayed anger : ANGER, WRATH

♦ anger, furor, fury, indignation, outrage, rage, spleen, wrath, wrathfulness — more at ANGER

²ire *vb* **ired; iring** ♦ : to provoke to anger

♦ anger, antagonize, enrage, incense, inflame, infuriate, madden, outrage, rankle, rile, roil — more at ANGER

Ire *abbr* Ireland

ire·ful *adj* : full of ire : marked by ire; *also* : easily angered

iren·ic \ī-'re-nik\ *adj* : favoring, conducive to, or operating toward peace or conciliation ⟨∼ measures⟩

ir·i·des·cence \ˌir-ə-'des-ᵊns\ *n* : a rainbowlike play of colors — **ir·i·des·cent** \-ᵊnt\ *adj*

irid·i·um \ir-'i-dē-əm\ *n* : a hard brittle heavy metallic chemical element

iris \'ī-rəs\ *n, pl* **iris·es** *also* **iri·des** \'ī-rə-ˌdēz, 'ir-ə-\ [ME, fr. L *iris* rainbow, iris plant, fr. Gk, rainbow, iris plant, iris of the eye] 1 : the colored part around the pupil of the eye 2 : any of a large genus of plants with linear basal leaves and large showy flowers

Irish \'īr-ish\ *n* 1 **Irish** *pl* : the people of Ireland 2 : the Celtic language of Ireland — **Irish** *adj* — **Irish·man** \-mən\ *n* — **Irish·wom·an** \-ˌwu̇-mən\ *n*

Irish bull *n* : an incongruous statement (as "it was hereditary in his family to have no children")

Irish coffee *n* : hot sugared coffee with Irish whiskey and whipped cream

Irish moss *n* : the dried and bleached plants of a red alga that is a source of carrageenan; *also* : this red alga

Irish setter *n* : any of a breed of hunting dogs with a mahogany-red coat

irk \'ərk\ *vb* ♦ : to make weary, irritated, or bored : ANNOY

♦ aggravate, annoy, bother, bug, chafe, exasperate, gall, get, grate, irritate, nettle, peeve, persecute, pique, put out, rasp, rile, vex — more at IRRITATE

irk·some \'ərk-səm\ *adj* ♦ : tending to irk : ANNOYING — **irk·some·ly** *adv*

♦ aggravating, annoying, bothersome, frustrating, galling, irritating, pesty, vexatious — more at ANNOYING

¹iron \'īrn, 'ī-ərn\ *n* [ME, fr. OE *īsern, īren*] 1 : a heavy malleable magnetic metallic chemical element that rusts easily and is vital to biological processes 2 **a** : something made of metal and esp. iron **b** *pl* ♦ : something (as handcuffs)

used to bind or restrain ⟨put them in ~*s*⟩   **3** : a household device with a flat base that is heated and used for pressing cloth   **4** : STRENGTH, HARDNESS

♦ *usu* **irons** band, bond, chain, fetter, ligature, manacle, shackle — more at BOND

²**iron** *vb*   **1** : to press or smooth with or as if with a heated iron   **2** : to remove (as wrinkles) by ironing — **iron·er** *n*

¹**iron·clad** \-'klad\ *adj*   **1** : sheathed in iron armor   **2** : so firm or secure as to be unbreakable

²**iron·clad** \-,klad\ *n* : an armored naval vessel esp. of the 19th century

iron curtain *n* : a political, military, and ideological barrier that isolates an area; *esp, often cap* : one formerly isolating an area under Soviet control

iron·ic \ī-'rä-nik\ *also* **iron·i·cal** \-ni-kəl\ *adj*   **1** : of, relating to, or marked by irony   **2** : given to irony

iron·i·cal·ly \-ni-k(ə-)lē\ *adv*   **1** : in an ironic manner   **2** : it is ironic

iron·ing *n* : clothes ironed or to be ironed

iron lung *n* : a device for artificial respiration that encloses the chest in a chamber in which changes of pressure force air into and out of the lungs

iron out *vb* : to remove or lessen difficulties in or extremes of

iron oxide *n* : FERRIC OXIDE

iron·stone \'ī(-ə)rn-,stōn, 'ī-ərn-\ *n*   **1** : a hard iron-rich sedimentary rock   **2** : a hard heavy durable pottery developed in England in the 19th century

iron·ware \-,war\ *n* : articles made of iron

iron·weed \-,wēd\ *n* : any of a genus of mostly weedy plants related to the asters that have terminal heads of red, purple, or white flowers

iron·wood \-,wud\ *n* : any of numerous trees or shrubs with exceptionally hard wood; *also* : the wood

iron·work \-,wərk\ *n*   **1** : work in iron   **2** *pl* : a mill or building where iron or steel is smelted or heavy iron or steel products are made — **iron·work·er** *n*

iro·ny \'ī-rə-nē\ *n, pl* -**nies** [L *ironia*, fr. Gk *eirōnia*, fr. *eirōn* dissembler]   **1** : the use of words to express the opposite of what one really means   **2** : incongruity between the actual result of a sequence of events and the expected result

Iro·quois \'ir-ə-,kwòi\ *n, pl* **Iroquois** *same or* -,kwòiz\   **1** *pl* : an American Indian confederacy orig. of New York that consisted of the Cayuga, Mohawk, Oneida, Onondaga, and Seneca and later included the Tuscarora   **2** : a member of any of the Iroquois peoples

ir·ra·di·ate \i-'rā-dē-,āt\ *vb* -**at·ed; -at·ing**   **1** : to supply or brighten with light : ILLUMINATE   **2** : ENLIGHTEN   **3** : to treat by exposure to radiation   **4** : RADIATE — **ir·ra·di·a·tion** \-,rā-dē-'ā-shən\ *n*

¹**ir·ra·tio·nal** \(,)i-'ra-shə-nəl\ *adj*   **1** : incapable of reasoning ⟨~ beasts⟩; *also* : defective in mental power ⟨~ with fever⟩   **2** ♦ : not based on reason ⟨~ fears⟩   **3** : being or numerically equal to an irrational number — **ir·ra·tio·nal·i·ty** \(,)i-,ra-shə-'na-lə-tē\ *n* — **ir·ra·tio·nal·ly** *adv*

♦ fallacious, illogical, invalid, unreasonable, unsound, weak — more at ILLOGICAL

²**irrational** *n* : IRRATIONAL NUMBER

irrational number *n* : a real number that cannot be expressed as the quotient of two integers

ir·rec·on·cil·able   \(,)i-,re-kən-'sī-lə-bəl,   -'re-kən-,sī-\ *adj* : impossible to reconcile, adjust, or harmonize — **ir·rec·on·cil·abil·i·ty** \(,)i-,re-kən-,sī-lə-'bi-lə-tē\ *n*

ir·re·cov·er·able \,ir-i-'kə-və-rə-bəl\ *adj* : not capable of being recovered or rectified : IRREPARABLE — **ir·re·cov·er·ably** \-blē\ *adv*

ir·re·deem·able \,ir-i-'dē-mə-bəl\ *adj*   **1** : not redeemable; *esp* : not terminable by payment of the principal ⟨an ~ bond⟩   **2** : not convertible into gold or silver at the will of the holder   **3** ♦ : being beyond remedy ⟨~ villains⟩

♦ hopeless, incorrigible, incurable, irremediable, irreparable, unrecoverable, unredeemable — more at HOPELESS

ir·re·den·tism \-'den-,ti-zəm\ *n* : a principle or policy directed toward the incorporation of a territory historically or ethnically part of another into that other — **ir·re·den·tist** \-tist\ *n or adj*

ir·re·duc·ible \,ir-i-'dü-sə-bəl, -'dyü-\ *adj* : not reducible ⟨an ~ fraction⟩ — **ir·re·duc·ibly** \-blē\ *adv*

ir·re·fut·able \,ir-i-'fyü-tə-bəl, (,)i-'re-fyət-\ *adj* ♦ : impossible to refute

♦ incontestable, indisputable, indubitable, unanswerable, undeniable, unquestionable; *also* certain, definite, positive, sure; unambiguous, unequivocal; absolute, clear, conclusive, decisive; uncontested, undisputed *Ant* answerable, debatable, disputable, questionable

irreg *abbr* irregular

ir·reg·u·lar \(,)i-'re-gyə-lər\ *adj*   **1** ♦ : not regular : not natural or uniform   **2** : not conforming to the normal or usual manner of inflection ⟨~ verbs⟩   **3** : not belonging to a regular or organized army ⟨~ troops⟩ — **irregular** *n* — **ir·reg·u·lar·ly** *adv*

♦ aberrant, abnormal, anomalous, atypical, deviant, unnatural — more at DEVIANT   ♦ informal, unceremonious, unconventional, unorthodox — more at INFORMAL

ir·reg·u·lar·i·ty \i-,re-gyə-'lar-ə-tē\ *n, pl* -**ties**   **1** : something that is irregular   **2** : the quality or state of being irregular   **3** : occasional constipation

ir·rel·e·vant \(,)i-'re-lə-vənt\ *adj* ♦ : not relevant — **ir·rel·e·vance** \-vəns\ *n*

♦ extraneous, immaterial; *also* inconsequential, insignificant, unimportant; meaningless, pointless, senseless, useless; inappropriate, inapt, unsuitable

ir·re·li·gious \,ir-i-'li-jəs\ *adj* ♦ : lacking religious emotions, doctrines, or practices

♦ blasphemous, nonreligious, sacrilegious *Ant* religious

ir·re·me·di·a·ble \,ir-i-'mē-dē-ə-bəl\ *adj* ♦ : impossible to remedy or correct

♦ hopeless, incorrigible, incurable, irredeemable, unrecoverable, unredeemable — more at HOPELESS

ir·re·mov·able \,ir-i-'mü-və-bəl\ *adj* : not removable

ir·rep·a·ra·ble \(,)i-'re-pə-rə-bəl\ *adj* ♦ : impossible to make good, undo, repair, or remedy ⟨~ damage⟩

♦ irredeemable, irremediable, unrecoverable, unredeemable; *also* irreplaceable, irrevocable *Ant* redeemable, remediable, retrievable

ir·re·place·able \,ir-i-'plā-sə-bəl\ *adj* : not replaceable

ir·re·press·ible \-'pre-sə-bəl\ *adj* : impossible to repress or control ⟨~ curiosity⟩

ir·re·proach·able \-'prō-chə-bəl\ *adj* ♦ : not reproachable

♦ blameless, clear, faultless, guiltless, impeccable, innocent — more at INNOCENT

ir·re·sist·ible \,ir-i-'zis-tə-bəl\ *adj* : impossible to successfully resist ⟨an ~ craving⟩ — **ir·re·sist·ibly** \-blē\ *adv*

ir·res·o·lute \(,)i-'re-zə-,lüt\ *adj* : uncertain how to act or proceed : VACILLATING — **ir·res·o·lute·ly** \-,lüt-lē; (,)i-,re-zə-'lüt-\ *adv*

ir·res·o·lu·tion \(,)i-,re-zə-'lü-shən\ *n* ♦ : lack of resolution : a fluctuation of mind (as in doubt or between hope and fear)

♦ hesitancy, hesitation, indecision, vacillation — more at HESITATION

ir·re·spec·tive of \,ir-i-'spek-tiv-\ *prep* : without regard to

ir·re·spon·si·ble \-'spän-sə-bəl\ *adj* ♦ : not responsible ⟨an ~ choice⟩ — **ir·re·spon·si·bil·i·ty** \-,spän-sə-'bi-lə-tē\ *n* — **ir·re·spon·si·bly** \-'spän-sə-blē\ *adv*

♦ foolhardy, reckless — more at RECKLESS

ir·re·triev·able \,ir-i-'trē-və-bəl\ *adj* : not retrievable : IRRECOVERABLE

ir·rev·er·ence \(,)i-'re-və-rəns\ *n*   **1** : lack of reverence   **2** ♦ : an irreverent act or utterance

♦ blasphemy, defilement, desecration, impiety, sacrilege — more at BLASPHEMY

ir·rev·er·ent \-rənt\ *adj* : lacking proper respect or seriousness; *also* : SATIRIC — **ir·rev·er·ent·ly** *adv* ir·re·vers·ible \ˌir-i-'vər-sə-bəl\ adj : incapable of being reversed ⟨an ∼ loss⟩

ir·rev·o·ca·ble \(ˌ)i-'re-və-kə-bəl\ adj : incapable of being revoked or recalled ⟨∼ change⟩ — ir·rev·o·ca·bly \-blē\ adv

ir·ri·gate \'ir-ə-ˌgāt\ vb -gat·ed; -gat·ing ♦ : to supply (as land) with water by artificial means; also : to flush with liquid — ir·ri·ga·tion \ˌir-ə-'gā-shən\ n

♦ flush, rinse, sluice, wash — more at FLUSH

ir·ri·ta·bil·i·ty \ˌir-ə-tə-'bi-lə-tē\ n 1 : the property of living things and of protoplasm that enables reaction to stimuli 2 ♦ : the quality or state of being irritable; esp : readiness to become annoyed or angry

♦ grumpiness, peevishness

ir·ri·ta·ble \'ir-ə-tə-bəl\ adj ♦ : capable of being irritated; esp : readily or easily irritated — ir·ri·ta·bly \-blē\ adv

♦ choleric, crabby, cranky, cross, crotchety, grouchy, grumpy, irascible, peevish, perverse, petulant, short-tempered, snappish, snappy, snippy, testy, waspish; also bearish, bilious, cantankerous, disagreeable, dyspeptic, ill-humored, ill-natured, ill-tempered, ornery, surly; sensitive, sulky, thin-skinned, touchy; hot=blooded, passionate

ir·ri·tant \'ir-ə-tənt\ n ♦ : something that irritates or excites — irritant adj

♦ aggravation, annoyance, bother, exasperation, frustration, hassle, headache, inconvenience, nuisance, peeve, pest, problem, thorn — more at ANNOYANCE

ir·ri·tate \'ir-ə-ˌtāt\ vb -tat·ed; -tat·ing 1 ♦ : to excite to anger : EXASPERATE 2 ♦ : to make sore or inflamed — ir·ri·tat·ing·ly adv

♦ [1] aggravate, annoy, bother, bug, chafe, exasperate, gall, get, grate, irk, nettle, peeve, persecute, pique, put out, rasp, rile, vex; also hassle, heckle; nag; inflame, provoke, rouse; bait, harass, harry, pester; anger, enrage, incense, infuriate, madden; agitate, disturb, fret, perturb, upset; affront, insult, offend, outrage
♦ [2] abrade, chafe, gall — more at CHAFE

irritating adj ♦ : causing displeasure or annoyance

♦ aggravating, annoying, bothersome, frustrating, galling, irksome, pesty, vexatious — more at ANNOYING

ir·ri·ta·tion \ˌir-ə-'tā-shən\ n : the act of irritating : the state of being irritated; also : something that irritates

ir·rupt \(ˌ)i-'rəpt\ vb 1 : to rush in forcibly or violently 2 : to increase suddenly in numbers ⟨rabbits ∼ in cycles⟩

ir·rup·tion \i-'rəp-shən\ n ♦ : an act or instance of irrupting; esp : a sudden violent or forcible entry

♦ descent, foray, incursion, invasion, raid — more at RAID

IRS abbr Internal Revenue Service

is pres 3d sing of BE

Isa or Is abbr Isaiah

Isa·iah \ī-'zā-ə\ n 1 : a major Hebrew prophet in Judah about 740 to 701 B.C. 2 : a book of Jewish and Christian Scripture

Isa·ias \ī-'zā-əs\ n : ISAIAH

ISBN abbr International Standard Book Number

is·che·mia \is-'kē-mē-ə\ n : deficient supply of blood to a body part (as the brain) — is·che·mic \-mik\ adj

-ish \ish\ adj suffix 1 : of, relating to, or being ⟨Finnish⟩ 2 : characteristic of ⟨boyish⟩ ⟨mulish⟩ 3 : inclined or liable to ⟨bookish⟩ 4 : having a touch or trace of : somewhat ⟨purplish⟩ 5 : having the approximate age of ⟨fortyish⟩

isin·glass \'īz-ᵊn-ˌglas, 'ī-ziŋ-\ n 1 : a gelatin obtained from various fish 2 : mica esp. in thin sheets

isl abbr island

Is·lam \is-'läm, iz-, -'lam, 'is-, 'iz-\ n [Ar islām submission (to the will of God)] : the religious faith of Muslims including belief in Allah as the sole deity and in Muhammad as his prophet; also : the civilization built on this faith — Is·lam·ic \is-'lä-mik, iz-, -'la-\ adj

is·land \'ī-lənd\ n [ME iland, fr. OE īgland, fr. īg island + land]

land] 1 ♦ : a body of land smaller than a continent surrounded by water 2 : something resembling an island in its isolation

♦ cay, isle, key

is·land·er \'ī-lən-dər\ n : a native or inhabitant of an island

isle \'ī(-ə)l\ n ♦ : a small island

♦ cay, island, key

is·let \'ī-lət\ n : a small island

ism \'i-zəm\ n : a distinctive doctrine, cause, or theory

-ism \ˌi-zəm\ n suffix 1 : act : practice : process ⟨criticism⟩ 2 : manner of action or behavior characteristic of a (specified) person or thing ⟨fanaticism⟩ 3 : state : condition : property ⟨dualism⟩ 4 : abnormal state or condition ⟨alcoholism⟩ 5 : doctrine : theory : cult ⟨Buddhism⟩ 6 : adherence to a set of principles ⟨stoicism⟩ 7 : prejudice or discrimination on the basis of a (specified) attribute ⟨racism⟩ ⟨sexism⟩ 8 : characteristic or peculiar feature or trait ⟨colloquialism⟩

iso·bar \'ī-sə-ˌbär\ n : a line on a map connecting places of equal barometric pressure — iso·bar·ic \ˌī-sə-'bär-ik, -'bar-\ adj

iso·late \'ī-sə-ˌlāt\ vb -lat·ed; -lat·ing [fr. isolated set apart, fr. F isolé, fr. It isolato, fr. isola island, fr. L insula] ♦ : to place or keep by itself : separate from others

♦ cut off, insulate, seclude, segregate, separate, sequester; also quarantine; confine, immure, incarcerate, intern, jail, lock (up), restrain, restrict; detach, disengage, remove; detain, hold, keep Ant desegregate, integrate

iso·lat·ed adj 1 : occurring alone or once : UNIQUE 2 : SPORADIC ⟨∼ outbreaks⟩ 3 ♦ : placed alone or apart

♦ cloistered, covert, quiet, remote, secluded, secret — more at SECLUDED

iso·la·tion \ˌī-sə-'lā-shən\ n ♦ : the action of isolating : the condition of being isolated

♦ insulation, seclusion, segregation, sequestration, solitude; also loneliness, lonesomeness; confinement, incarceration, internment, quarantine; retirement, withdrawal

iso·la·tion·ism \ˌī-sə-'lā-shə-ˌni-zəm\ n : a policy of national isolation by abstention from international political and economic relations — iso·la·tion·ist \-shə-nist\ n or adj

iso·mer \'ī-sə-mər\ n : any of two or more chemical compounds that contain the same numbers of atoms of the same elements but differ in structural arrangement and properties — iso·mer·ic \ˌī-sə-'mer-ik\ adj — isom·er·ism \ī-'sä-mə-ˌri-zəm\ n

iso·met·rics \ˌī-sə-'me-triks\ n sing or pl : exercise involving a series of brief and intense contractions of muscles against each other or against an immovable resistance — iso·met·ric adj

iso·prene \'ī-sə-ˌprēn\ n : a hydrocarbon used esp. in making synthetic rubber

isos·ce·les \ī-'sä-sə-ˌlēz\ adj : having two equal sides ⟨an ∼ triangle⟩

iso·therm \'ī-sə-ˌthərm\ n : a line on a map connecting points having the same temperature

iso·ther·mal \ˌī-sə-'thər-məl\ adj : of, relating to, or marked by equality of temperature

iso·tope \'ī-sə-ˌtōp\ n [Gk isos equal + topos place] : any of the forms of a chemical element that differ chiefly in the number of neutrons in an atom — iso·to·pic \ˌī-sə-'tä-pik, -'tō-\ adj — iso·to·pi·cal·ly \-'tä-pi-k(ə-)lē, -'tō-\ adv

ISP abbr Internet service provider

Isr abbr Israel; Israeli

Is·rae·li \iz-'rā-lē\ n, pl Israelis also Israeli : a native or inhabitant of Israel — Israeli adj

Is·ra·el·ite \'iz-rē-ə-ˌlīt\ n : a member of the Hebrew people descended from Jacob

is·su·ance \'i-shü-wəns\ n ♦ : the act of issuing or giving out esp. officially

♦ allocation, dispensation, distribution, division — more at DISTRIBUTION

¹is·sue \'i-shü\ n [ME, exit, proceeds, fr. AF, fr. issir to

come out, go out, fr. L. *exire*, fr. *ire* to go] **1** : the action of going, coming, or flowing out : EGRESS, EMERGENCE **2** : a means or place of going out : EXIT, OUTLET **3** ♦ : the product of the reproductive processes of an animal or plant : OFFSPRING, PROGENY **4** : OUTCOME, RESULT **5** : a point of debate or controversy; *also* : the point at which an unsettled matter is ready for a decision **6** : a discharge (as of blood) from the body **7** : something coming forth from a specified source **8** : the act of officially giving out or printing : PUBLICATION; *also* : the quantity of things given out at one time

♦ offspring, posterity, progeny, seed, spawn — more at OFFSPRING

²**issue** *vb* **is·sued; is·su·ing 1** : to go, come, or flow out **2** ♦ : to come forth or cause to come forth : EMIT **3** : ACCRUE **4** : to descend from a specified parent or ancestor **5** : to result in **6** : to put forth or distribute officially **7** ♦ : to send out for sale or circulation : PUBLISH **8** : EMANATE, RESULT — **is·su·er** *n*

♦ [2] cast, discharge, emit, exhale, expel, release, shoot, vent — more at EMIT ♦ [7] get out, print, publish — more at PUBLISH

¹**-ist** \ist\ *n suffix* **1** : one that performs a (specified) action ⟨cyc*list*⟩ : one that makes or produces ⟨nove*list*⟩ **2** : one that plays a (specified) musical instrument ⟨harp*ist*⟩ **3** : one that operates a (specified) mechanical instrument or contrivance ⟨machin*ist*⟩ **4** : one that specializes in a (specified) art or science or skill ⟨geolog*ist*⟩ **5** : one that adheres to or advocates a (specified) doctrine or system or code of behavior ⟨social*ist*⟩ or that of a (specified) individual ⟨Darwin*ist*⟩

²**-ist** *adj suffix* : -ISTIC

isth·mus \'is-məs\ *n* : a narrow strip of land connecting two larger land areas

-is·tic \'is-tik\ *or* **-is·ti·cal** \'is-ti-kəl\ *adj suffix* : of, relating to, or characteristic of ⟨altru*istic*⟩

¹**it** \'it\ *pron* **1** : that one — used of a lifeless thing, a plant, a person or animal, or an abstract entity ⟨∼'s a big building⟩ ⟨∼'s a shade tree⟩ ⟨who is ∼⟩ ⟨beauty is everywhere and ∼ is a source of joy⟩ **2** — used as a subject of an impersonal verb that expresses a condition or action without reference to an agent ⟨∼ is raining⟩ **3** — used as an anticipatory subject or object ⟨∼'s good to see you⟩

²**it** \'it\ *n* : the player in a game who performs the principal action (as trying to find others in hide-and-seek)

It *abbr* Italian; Italy

ital *abbr* italic; italicized

Ital *abbr* Italian

Ital·ian \i-'tal-yən\ *n* **1** : a native or inhabitant of Italy **2** : the language of Italy — **Italian** *adj*

ital·ic \i-'ta-lik, ī-\ *adj* : relating to type in which the letters slope up toward the right (as in "*italic*") — **italic** *n*

ital·i·cise *Brit var of* ITALICIZE

ital·i·cize \i-'ta-lə-,sīz, ī-\ *vb* **-cized; -ciz·ing** : to print in italics — **ital·i·ci·za·tion** \-,ta-lə-sə-'zā-shən\ *n*

¹**itch** \'ich\ *n* **1** : an uneasy irritating skin sensation that evokes a desire to scratch the affected area **2** : a skin disorder accompanied by an itch **3** ♦ : a persistent desire — **itchy** *adj*

♦ appetite, craving, desire, drive, hankering, hunger, longing, lust, passion, thirst, urge, yearning, yen — more at DESIRE

²**itch** *vb* **1** : to have an itch; *also* : to produce an itchy sensation **2** ♦ : to have a restless desire or hankering for something — usu. used with *for*

♦ *usu* itch for ache for, crave, desire, die for, hanker for, hunger for, long for, lust (for *or* after), pine for, repine for, thirst for, want, wish for, yearn for — more at DESIRE

-ite \,īt\ *n suffix* **1** : native : resident ⟨suburban*ite*⟩ **2** : adherent : follower ⟨Lenin*ite*⟩ **3** : product ⟨metabol*ite*⟩ **4** : mineral : rock ⟨quartz*ite*⟩

item \'ī-təm\ *n* [L, likewise, also] **1** ♦ : a separate particular in a list, account, or series : ARTICLE **2** ♦ : a separate piece of news (as in a newspaper)

♦ [1] article, constituent, detail, element, feature, ingredient, particular, point ♦ [2] intelligence, news, story, tidings, word — more at NEWS

item·ise *chiefly Brit var of* ITEMIZE

item·ize \'ī-tə-,mīz\ *vb* **-ized; -iz·ing** ♦ : to set down in detail — **item·i·za·tion** \,ī-tə-mə-'zā-shən\ *n*

♦ detail, enumerate, inventory, list, numerate — more at LIST

it·er·ate \'i-tə-,rāt\ *vb* **-at·ed; -at·ing** : REITERATE, REPEAT

it·er·a·tion \,i-tə-'rā-shən\ *n* **1** : REPETITION; *esp* : a computational process in which a series of operations is repeated until a condition is met **2** : one repetition of the series of operations in iteration

itin·er·ant \ī-'ti-nə-rənt, ə-\ *adj* ♦ : traveling from place to place; *esp* : covering a circuit ⟨an ∼ preacher⟩

♦ errant, nomad, peripatetic, roaming, vagabond, vagrant; *also* drifting, footloose, meandering, rambling; sauntering, strolling, traipsing, walking

itin·er·ary \ī-'ti-nə-,rer-ē, ə-\ *n, pl* **-ar·ies 1** : the route of a journey or the proposed outline of one **2** : a travel diary **3** : GUIDEBOOK

its \'its\ *adj* : of or relating to it or itself

it·self \it-'self\ *pron* : that identical one — used reflexively, for emphasis, or in absolute constructions

-ity \ə-tē\ *n suffix* : quality : state : degree ⟨alkalin*ity*⟩

IUD \,ī-(,)yü-'dē\ *n* : INTRAUTERINE DEVICE

IV \,ī-'vē\ *n* [*intravenous*] : an apparatus used to administer a fluid (as of nutrients) intravenously; *also* : a fluid administered by IV

-ive \iv\ *adj suffix* : that performs or tends toward an (indicated) action ⟨correc*tive*⟩

ivo·ry \'ī-vrē, -və-rē\ *n, pl* **-ries** [ME *ivorie*, fr. AF *ivoire, ivurie*, fr. L *eboreus* of ivory, fr. *ebur* ivory] **1** : the hard creamy-white material composing the tusks of an elephant or walrus **2** : a pale yellow color **3** : something made of ivory or of a similar substance

ivory tower *n* **1** : an impractical lack of concern with urgent problems **2** : a place of learning

ivy \'ī-vē\ *n, pl* **ivies** : a trailing woody evergreen vine with small black berries that is related to ginseng

IWW *abbr* Industrial Workers of the World

-ize \,īz\ *vb suffix* **1** : cause to be or conform to or resemble ⟨America*nize*⟩ : cause to be formed into ⟨union*ize*⟩ **2** : subject to a (specified) action ⟨satir*ize*⟩ **3** : saturate, treat, or combine with ⟨macadam*ize*⟩ **4** : treat like ⟨idol*ize*⟩ **5** : become : become like ⟨crystall*ize*⟩ **6** : be productive in or of : engage in a (specified) activity ⟨philosoph*ize*⟩ **7** : adopt or spread the manner of activity or the teaching of ⟨Christian*ize*⟩

J

¹**j** \'jā\ *n, pl* **j's** *or* **js** \'jāz\ *often cap* : the 10th letter of the English alphabet

²**j** *abbr, often cap* **1** jack **2** journal **3** judge **4** justice

¹**jab** \'jab\ *vb* **jabbed; jab·bing** : to thrust quickly or abruptly : POKE

²**jab** *n* ♦ : a usu. short straight punch

    ♦ dab, dig, poke — more at POKE

¹**jab·ber** \'ja-bər\ *vb* ♦ : to talk rapidly, indistinctly, or unintelligibly : CHATTER

    ♦ babble, chatter, drivel, gabble, gibber, prattle, sputter — more at BABBLE

²**jabber** *n* : unintelligible or meaningless language

jab·ber·er *n* ♦ : one that jabbers

    ♦ chatterbox, magpie, talker — more at CHATTERBOX

jab·ber·wocky \'ja-bər-,wä-kē\ *n* ♦ : meaningless speech or writing

    ♦ babble, gabble, gibberish, gobbledygook, hogwash, jabber, nonsense, piffle, prattle — more at GIBBERISH

ja·bot \zha-'bō, 'ja-,bō\ *n* : a ruffle worn down the front of a dress or shirt

jac·a·ran·da \,ja-kə-'ran-də\ *n* : any of a genus of pinnate-leaved tropical American trees with clusters of showy blue flowers

¹**jack** \'jak\ *n* **1** : a mechanical device; *esp* : one used to raise a heavy body a short distance **2** : a male donkey **3** : a small target ball in lawn bowling **4** ♦ : a small national flag flown by a ship **5** : a small 6-pointed metal object used in a game (**jacks**) **6** : a playing card bearing the figure of a soldier or servant **7** : a socket into which a plug is inserted for connecting electric circuits **8 a** : an adult male human **b** : a member of a ship's crew

    ♦ banner, colors (*or* colours), ensign, flag, pennant, standard, streamer — more at FLAG

²**jack** *vb* **1** : to raise by means of a jack **2** ♦ : to raise the level of ⟨~ up prices⟩

    ♦ boost, crane, elevate, heave, heft, heighten, hike, hoist, lift, pick up, raise, up, uphold — more at RAISE

jack·al \'ja-kəl\ *n* [Turk *çakal*, fr. Pers *shaqāl*] : any of several mammals of Asia and Africa related to the wolves

jack·a·napes \'ja-kə-,nāps\ *n* **1** : MONKEY, APE **2** : an impudent or conceited person

jack·ass \'jak-,as\ *n* **1** ♦ : the domestic ass : DONKEY; *esp* : a male donkey **2** ♦ : a stupid, annoying, or detestable person

    ♦ [1] ass, donkey — more at DONKEY ♦ [2] blockhead, dolt, donkey, dope, dummy, idiot, imbecile, nitwit, numskull, simpleton — more at IDIOT

jack·boot \-,büt\ *n* **1** : a heavy military boot of glossy black leather extending above the knee **2** : a laceless military boot reaching to the calf

jack·daw \'jak-,dȯ\ *n* : a black and gray Old World crow-like bird

jack·et \'ja-kət\ *n* [ME *jaket*, fr. AF *jackés*, pl., dim. of MF *jaque* short jacket, fr. *jacques* peasant, fr. the name *Jacques* James] **1** : a garment for the upper body usu. having a front opening, collar, and sleeves **2** ♦ : an outer covering or casing ⟨a book ~⟩

    ♦ armor, capsule, case, casing, cocoon, cover, housing, husk, pod, sheath, shell — more at CASE

Jack Frost *n* : frost or frosty weather personified

jack·ham·mer \'jak-,ha-mər\ *n* : a pneumatic percussion tool for drilling rock or breaking pavement

jack–in–the–box *n, pl* **jack–in–the–boxes** *or* **jacks–in–the–box** : a toy consisting of a small box out of which a figure springs when the lid is raised

jack–in–the–pulpit *n, pl* **jack–in–the–pulpits** *also* **jacks–in–the–pulpit** : a No. American spring-flowering woodland herb having an upright club-shaped spadix arched over by a green and purple spathe

¹**jack·knife** \'jak-,nīf\ *n* **1** : a large pocketknife **2** : a dive in which the diver bends from the waist and touches the ankles before straightening out

²**jackknife** *vb* : to fold like a jackknife ⟨the trailer truck *jackknifed*⟩

jack·leg \'jak-,leg\ *adj* **1** : lacking skill or training **2** : MAKESHIFT

jack–of–all–trades *n, pl* **jacks–of–all–trades** : one who is able to do passable work at various tasks

jack–o'–lan·tern \'ja-kə-,lan-tərn\ *n* : a lantern made of a pumpkin cut to look like a human face

jack·pot \'jak-,pät\ *n* **1** : a large sum of money formed by the accumulation of stakes from previous play (as in poker) **2** : an impressive and often unexpected success or reward

jack·rab·bit \-,ra-bət\ *n* : any of several large hares of western No. America with very long ears and hind legs

Jack Russell terrier \'jak-'rə-səl-\ *n* : any of a breed of small terriers having a white coat with dark markings

jack·straw \-,strȯ\ *n* **1** *pl* : a game in which straws or thin sticks are let fall in a heap and each player in turn tries to remove them one at a time without disturbing the rest **2** : one of the straws or sticks in jackstraws

jack–tar \-'tär\ *n, often cap* ♦ : a member of a ship's crew : SAILOR

    ♦ gob, jack, mariner, sailor, seaman, swab, tar — more at SAILOR

Ja·cob's ladder \'jā-kəbz-\ *n* : any of several perennial herbs related to phlox that have pinnate leaves and blue or white bell-shaped flowers

jac·quard \'ja-,kärd\ *n, often cap* : a fabric of intricate variegated weave or pattern

¹**jade** \'jād\ *n* **1** : a broken-down, vicious, or worthless horse **2** : a disreputable woman

²**jade** *vb* **jad·ed; jad·ing** **1** : to wear out by overwork or abuse **2** ♦ : to become weary esp. through repetition or excess

    ♦ bore, tire, weary — more at BORE

³**jade** *n* [F, fr. obs. Sp (*piedra de la*) *ijada*, lit., loin stone; fr. the belief that jade cures renal colic] : a usu. green gemstone that takes a high polish

jad·ed *adj* ♦ : fatigued by overwork; *also* : made dull, apathetic, or cynical by experience or by surfeit

    ♦ beat, bushed, dead, drained, limp, prostrate, spent, tired, weary, worn-out — more at WEARY

¹**jag** \'jag\ *n* : a sharp projecting part

²**jag** *n* : SPREE

jag·ged \'ja-gəd\ *adj* ♦ : sharply notched

    ♦ broken, craggy, ragged, scraggly — more at RAGGED

jag·uar \'ja-,gwär\ *n* : a black-spotted tropical American cat that is larger and stockier than the Old World leopard

jai alai \'hī-,lī\ *n* [Sp, fr. Basque, fr. *jai* festival + *alai* merry] : a court game played by usu. two or four players with a ball and a curved wicker basket strapped to the wrist

¹**jail** \'jāl\ *n* [ME *jaiole*, fr. AF *gaiole, jaiole*, fr. LL *caveola*, dim. of L *cavea* cage] ♦ : a place of confinement for persons held in lawful custody : PRISON; *esp* : such a place for the confinement of persons awaiting trial or those convicted of minor crimes

    ♦ brig, hoosegow, jug, lockup, pen, penitentiary, prison, stockade; *also* bull pen; concentration camp, prison camp; dungeon, keep; reformatory, reform school

²**jail** *vb* ♦ : to confine in or as if in a jail

♦ commit, confine, immure, imprison — more at IM-PRISON

jail·bird \-ˌbərd\ *n* : an habitual criminal

jail·break \-ˌbrāk\ *n* : a forcible escape from jail

jail·er *also* **jail·or** \ˈjā-lər\ *n* : a keeper of a jail

jal·ap \ˈja-ləp, ˈjä-\ *n* : a powdered purgative drug from the root of a Mexican plant related to the morning glory; *also* : this root or plant

ja·la·pe·ño \ˌhä-lə-ˈpān-(ˌ)yō\ *n* : a small plump dark green chili pepper

ja·lopy \jə-ˈlä-pē\ *n, pl* **ja·lop·ies** : a dilapidated vehicle (as an automobile)

jal·ou·sie \ˈja-lə-sē\ *n* [F, lit., jealousy] : a blind, window, or door with adjustable horizontal slats or louvers

¹**jam** \ˈjam\ *vb* **jammed; jam·ming 1** ♦ : to press into a close or tight position; *also* : to become blocked or wedged **2** : to cause to become wedged so as to be unworkable; *also* : to make or become unworkable through the jamming of a movable part **3** : to push forcibly ⟨∼ on the brakes⟩ **4** : CRUSH, BRUISE **5** : to make unintelligible by sending out interfering signals or messages **6** : to take part in a jam session **7** : to fill often to excess — **jam·mer** *n*

♦ cram, crowd, ram, sandwich, squeeze, stuff, wedge — more at CROWD ♦ block, choke, clog, close (off), congest, dam, obstruct, plug (up), stop (up), stuff — more at CLOG

²**jam** *n* **1** ♦ : a crowded mass that impedes or blocks ⟨traffic ∼⟩ **2** : a difficult state of affairs

♦ backup, bottleneck, snarl

³**jam** *n* : a food made by boiling fruit and sugar to a thick consistency

Jam *abbr* Jamaica

Ja·mai·can \jə-ˈmā-kən\ *n* : a native or inhabitant of Jamaica — **Jamaican** *adj*

jamb \ˈjam\ *n* [ME *jambe*, fr. AF *jambe, gambe*, lit., leg] : an upright piece forming the side of an opening (as of a door)

jam·ba·laya \ˌjəm-bə-ˈlī-ə\ *n* [LaF] : rice cooked with ham, sausage, chicken, shrimp, or oysters and seasoned with herbs

jam·bo·ree \ˌjam-bə-ˈrē\ *n* : a large festive gathering

James \ˈjāmz\ *n* : a moral lecture addressed to early Christians and included as a book in the New Testament

jam–pack \ˈjam-ˈpak\ *vb* ♦ : to pack tightly or to excess

♦ charge, cram, fill, heap, jam, load, pack, stuff — more at FILL

jam session *n* : an impromptu performance esp. by jazz musicians

Jan *abbr* January

jan·gle \ˈjaŋ-gəl\ *vb* **jan·gled; jan·gling** : to make a harsh or discordant sound — **jangle** *n*

jan·i·tor \ˈja-nə-tər\ *n* [L, doorkeeper, fr. *janus* arch, gate] **1** ♦ : a person who has the care of a building **2** : a person who tends a door — **jan·i·to·ri·al** \ˌja-nə-ˈtōr-ē-əl\ *adj*

♦ caretaker, custodian, guardian, keeper, warden, watchman — more at CUSTODIAN

Jan·u·ary \ˈja-nyə-ˌwer-ē\ *n* [ME *Januarie*, fr. L *Januarius*, first month of the ancient Roman year, fr. *Janus*, two-faced god of gates and beginnings] : the 1st month of the year

¹**ja·pan** \jə-ˈpan\ *n* : a varnish giving a hard brilliant finish

²**japan** *vb* **ja·panned; ja·pan·ning** : to cover with a coat of japan

Jap·a·nese \ˌja-pə-ˈnēz, -ˈnēs\ *n, pl* **Japanese 1** : a native or inhabitant of Japan **2** : the language of Japan — **Japanese** *adj*

Japanese beetle *n* : a small metallic green and brown scarab beetle introduced from Japan that is a pest on the roots of grasses as a grub and on foliage and fruits as an adult

¹**jape** \ˈjāp\ *vb* **japed; jap·ing 1** : JOKE **2** : MOCK

²**jape** *n* : JEST, GIBE

¹**jar** \ˈjär\ *vb* **jarred; jar·ring 1** : to make a harsh or discor-

dant sound **2** ♦ : to have a harsh or disagreeable effect **3** : VIBRATE, SHAKE ⟨tremors *jarred* the house⟩

♦ clash, collide, conflict — more at CLASH

²**jar** *n* **1** : a state of conflict **2** : a harsh discordant sound **3** ♦ : a sudden or unexpected shake : JOLT **4** : a painful effect : SHOCK

♦ bump, collision, concussion, crash, impact, jolt, shock, smash, strike, wallop — more at IMPACT

³**jar** *n* : a widemouthed container usu. of glass or earthenware

jar·di·niere \ˌjärd-ᵊn-ˈir\ *n* : an ornamental stand for plants or flowers

jar·gon \ˈjär-gən\ *n* **1** : confused unintelligible language **2** ♦ : the special vocabulary of a particular group or activity **3** : obscure and often pretentious language

♦ argot, cant, language, lingo, slang, terminology, vocabulary — more at TERMINOLOGY

Jas *abbr* James

jas·mine \ˈjaz-mən\ *n* [MF *jasmin*, fr. Ar *yāsamīn*, fr. Pers] : any of various climbing shrubs with fragrant flowers

jas·per \ˈjas-pər\ *n* : a usu. red, yellow, or brown opaque quartz

jaun·dice \ˈjȯn-dəs\ *n* **1** : yellowish discoloration of skin, tissues, and body fluids by bile pigments; *also* : an abnormal condition marked by jaundice **2** : a state or attitude characterized by satiety, distaste, or hostility

jaun·diced \-dəst\ *adj* **1** : affected with or as if with jaundice **2** ♦ : exhibiting envy, distaste, or hostility

♦ covetous, envious, jealous, resentful — more at ENVIOUS ♦ antagonistic, hostile, inhospitable, inimical, negative, unfriendly, unsympathetic — more at HOSTILE

jaunt \ˈjȯnt\ *n* ♦ : a short trip usu. for pleasure

♦ excursion, junket, outing, sally — more at EXCURSION

jaun·ti·ly \ˈjȯn-tə-lē\ *adv* ♦ : in a light or carefree manner

♦ exuberantly, gaily, sprightly — more at GAILY

jaun·ty \ˈjȯn-tē\ *adj* **jaun·ti·er; -est** ♦ : sprightly in manner or appearance : LIVELY — **jaun·ti·ness** \-tē-nəs\ *n*

♦ active, animate, animated, brisk, energetic, lively, snappy, spirited, sprightly, springy — more at LIVELY

ja·va \ˈja-və, ˈjä-\ *n* : COFFEE

Ja·va·nese \ˌja-və-ˈnēz, ˌjä-, -ˈnēs\ *n* : a native or inhabitant of the Indonesian island of Java

jav·e·lin \ˈja-və-lən\ *n* **1** : a light spear **2** : a slender shaft thrown for distance in a track-and-field contest

¹**jaw** \ˈjȯ\ *n* **1** : either of the bony or cartilaginous structures that support the soft tissues enclosing the mouth and that usu. bear teeth **2** : the parts forming the walls of the mouth and serving to open and close it — usu. used in pl. **3** : one of a pair of movable parts for holding or crushing something — **jawed** \ˈjȯd\ *adj*

²**jaw** *vb* ♦ : to talk abusively, indignantly, or at length

♦ admonish, chide, lecture, rail (at *or* against), rate, rebuke, reprimand, scold — more at SCOLD ♦ chat, converse, gab, palaver, patter, prattle, rattle, talk, visit — more at CHAT

¹**jaw·bone** \-ˌbōn\ *n* : JAW 1

²**jawbone** *vb* : to talk forcefully and persuasively

jaw·break·er \-ˌbrā-kər\ *n* **1** : a word difficult to pronounce **2** : a round hard candy

jaw–drop·ping \ˈjȯ-ˌdra-piŋ\ *adj* : causing great surprise or astonishment

jaw·less fish \ˈjȯ-ləs-\ *n* : any of a group of primitive vertebrates (as lampreys) without jaws

jay \ˈjā\ *n* : any of various noisy brightly colored often largely blue birds smaller than the related crows

jay·bird \ˈjā-ˌbərd\ *n* : JAY

jay·vee \ˈjā-ˈvē\ *n* **1** : JUNIOR VARSITY **2** : a member of a junior varsity team

jay·walk \ˈjā-ˌwȯk\ *vb* : to cross a street carelessly without regard for traffic regulations — **jay·walk·er** *n*

¹**jazz** \ˈjaz\ *n* **1** : American music characterized by improvisation, syncopated rhythms, and contrapuntal ensemble

playing 2 ♦ : empty talk 3 : similar but unspecified things
: STUFF

♦ bunk, claptrap, drivel, gibberish, hogwash, nonsense,
piffle, prattle, rot — more at GIBBERISH

²**jazz** vb ♦ : to increase the appeal or excitement of : EN-
LIVEN ⟨∼ things up⟩

♦ usu **jazz up** animate, brace, energize, enliven, fire, invigorate, liven up, pep up, quicken, stimulate, vitalize,
vivify, zip (up) — more at ANIMATE

jazzy \ˈja-zē\ adj **jazz·i·er; -est** 1 : having the characteristics of jazz 2 ♦ : marked by unrestraint, animation, or
flashiness

♦ active, animate, animated, flashy, jaunty, lively, racy,
sharp, smart, snappy, spirited, sprightly

JCS abbr joint chiefs of staff

jct abbr junction

JD abbr 1 [L juris doctor] doctor of jurisprudence; doctor
of law 2 [L jurum doctor] doctor of laws 3 justice department 4 juvenile delinquent

jeal·ous \ˈje-ləs\ adj 1 : demanding complete devotion
2 ♦ : hostile toward a rival or of one believed to enjoy an
advantage 3 : VIGILANT — **jeal·ous·ly** adv

♦ covetous, envious, jaundiced, resentful — more at
ENVIOUS

jeal·ou·sy \-lə-sē\ n 1 ♦ : a jealous disposition, attitude, or
feeling 2 : zealous vigilance

♦ covetousness, enviousness, envy, resentment — more
at ENVY

jeans \ˈjēnz\ n pl [pl. of jean twilled cloth, short for jean
fustian, fr. ME Gene Genoa, Italy] : pants made of durable
twilled cotton cloth

jeep \ˈjēp\ n [prob. fr. g.p. (abbr. of general purpose)] : a
small four-wheel drive general-purpose motor vehicle
used in World War II

¹**jeer** \ˈjir\ vb ♦ : to speak or cry out in derision : MOCK
♦ deride, gibe, laugh, mock, ridicule, scout — more at
RIDICULE

²**jeer** n ♦ : a jeering remark or sound : TAUNT
♦ boo, catcall, hiss, hoot, raspberry, snort, taunt —
more at CATCALL

Je·ho·vah \ji-ˈhō-və\ n ♦ : the supreme or ultimate reality
♦ Almighty, deity, Supreme Being

je·hu \ˈjē-hü, -hyü\ n : a driver of a coach or cab

je·june \ji-ˈjün\ adj [L jejunus empty of food, hungry, mea-
ger] : lacking interest or significance : DULL

je·ju·num \ji-ˈjü-nəm\ n [L] : the section of the small intestine between the duodenum and the ileum — **je·ju·nal**
\-ˈjün-ᵊl\ adj

jell \ˈjel\ vb 1 ♦ : to come to the consistency of jelly
2 ♦ : to take shape

♦ [1] clot, coagulate, congeal, gel, set — more at COAG-
ULATE ♦ [2] crystallize, form, shape, solidify

¹**jel·ly** \ˈje-lē\ n, pl **jellies** 1 : a food with a soft elastic consistency due usu. to the presence of gelatin or pectin; esp
: a fruit product made by boiling sugar and the juice of a
fruit 2 : a substance resembling jelly

²**jelly** vb : to bring to or come to the consistency of jelly

jelly bean n : a bean-shaped candy

jel·ly·fish \ˈje-lē-ˌfish\ n : a marine coelenterate with a
nearly transparent jellylike body and stinging tentacles

jen·net \ˈje-nət\ n 1 : a small Spanish horse 2 : a female
donkey

jen·ny \ˈje-nē\ n, pl **jennies** : a female bird or donkey

jeop·ar·dize \-ˌdīz\ vb ♦ : to expose to danger or risk
♦ adventure, compromise, gamble with, hazard, imperil, menace, risk, venture

jeop·ar·dy \ˈje-pər-dē\ n [ME jeopardie, fr. AF juparti,
jeuparti alternative, lit., divided game] ♦ : exposure to
death, loss, or injury

♦ danger, distress, peril, risk, trouble — more at DANGER

Jer abbr Jeremiah; Jeremias

jer·e·mi·ad \ˌjer-ə-ˈmī-əd, -ˌad\ n : a prolonged lamentation
or complaint; also : a cautionary or angry harangue

Jer·e·mi·ah \ˌjer-ə-ˈmī-ə\ n : a book of Jewish and Christian
Scripture

Jer·e·mi·as \ˌjer-ə-ˈmī-əs\ n : JEREMIAH

¹**jerk** \ˈjərk\ n 1 ♦ : a short quick pull or twist : TWITCH
2 ♦ : an annoyingly stupid or foolish person — **jerk·i·ly**
\ˈjər-kə-lē\ adv

♦ [1] draw, haul, pluck, pull, tug, twitch, wrench — more
at PULL ♦ [2] beast, boor, churl, clown, creep, cretin, cur,
heel, joker, louse, lout, skunk, slob, snake; also brute,
Neanderthal, savage; rascal, rogue, scamp, villain; fool,
jackass, nitwit, nincompoop; blockhead, dolt, goon, idiot

²**jerk** vb 1 ♦ : to give a sharp quick push, pull, or twist
2 ♦ : to move in short abrupt motions

♦ [1] buck, hitch, jolt, twitch; also jounce, lurch, stagger; jiggle, shake; lug, pull, tug; pluck, tweak; grab,
snap, snatch, wrench, wrest, wring ♦ [2] fiddle, fidget,
squirm, twitch, wiggle — more at FIDGET

jer·kin \ˈjər-kən\ n : a close-fitting usu. sleeveless jacket

jerk·wa·ter \ˈjərk-ˌwȯ-tər, -ˌwä-\ adj [fr. jerkwater rural
train] : of minor importance : INSIGNIFICANT ⟨∼ towns⟩

jerky \ˈjər-kē\ adj 1 : moving along with or marked by fits
and starts 2 : lacking in sense, judgment, or discretion

jer·ry-built \ˈjer-ē-ˌbilt\ adj : built cheaply and flimsily

jer·ry-rigged \-ˌrigd\ adj ♦ : organized or constructed in a
crude or improvised manner

♦ artless, clumsy, crude, rough, rude, unrefined —
more at RUDE

jer·sey \ˈjər-zē\ n, pl **jerseys** [Jersey, one of the Channel
islands] 1 : a plain weft-knitted fabric 2 : a close-fitting
knitted shirt 3 often cap : any of a breed of small usu.
fawn-colored dairy cattle

Jersey barrier n : a concrete slab that is used with others to
block or reroute traffic or to divide a highway

Je·ru·sa·lem artichoke \jə-ˈrü-sə-ləm-\ n : a No. American
sunflower widely grown for its edible tubers that are used
as a vegetable; also : its tubers

jess \ˈjes\ n : a leg strap by which a captive bird of prey
may be controlled

jessamine var of JASMINE

¹**jest** \ˈjest\ n 1 ♦ : an act intended to provoke laughter
2 ♦ : a witty remark 3 ♦ : a frivolous mood ⟨said in ∼⟩

♦ [1, 2] crack, gag, joke, laugh, pleasantry, quip,
sally, waggery, wisecrack, witticism — more at JOKE
♦ [3] fun, game, play, sport — more at FUN

²**jest** vb ♦ : to speak or act without seriousness or in a frivolous manner; also : to make a witty remark

♦ banter, fool, fun, jive, joke, josh, kid, quip, wisecrack
— more at JOKE

jest·er \ˈjes-tər\ n ♦ : a retainer formerly kept to provide
casual entertainment; broadly : one given to jests

♦ card, comedian, comic, humorist, joker, wag, wit —
more at HUMORIST

¹**jet** \ˈjet\ n : a velvet-black coal that takes a good polish and
is often used for jewelry

²**jet** vb **jet·ted; jet·ting** ♦ : to spout or emit in a stream

♦ gush, pour, rush, spew, spout, spurt, squirt — more
at GUSH

³**jet** n 1 : a forceful rush (as of liquid or gas) through a
narrow opening; also : a nozzle for a jet of fluid 2 : a
jet-propelled airplane

⁴**jet** vb **jet·ted; jet·ting** : to travel by jet

jet lag n : a condition that is marked esp. by fatigue and
irritability and occurs following a long flight through several time zones — **jet–lagged** adj

jet·lin·er \ˈjet-ˌlī-nər\ n : a jet-propelled airliner

jet·port \-ˌpȯrt\ n : an airport designed to handle jets

jet–pro·pelled \ˌjet-prə-ˈpeld\ adj : driven by an engine (**jet
engine**) that produces propulsion (**jet propulsion**) by the
rearward discharge of a jet of fluid (as heated air and
exhaust gases)

jet·sam \ˈjet-səm\ n : jettisoned goods; *esp* : such goods washed ashore

jet set n : an international group of wealthy people who frequent fashionable resorts

jet stream n : a long narrow high-altitude current of high-speed winds blowing generally from the west

¹jet·ti·son \ˈje-tə-sən\ vb **1** : to throw (goods) overboard to lighten a ship or aircraft in distress **2 ♦** : to get rid of as superfluous or encumbering : DISCARD ⟨~ed an old computer⟩

♦ cast, discard, ditch, dump, fling, junk, lose, reject, scrap, shed, shuck, slough, throw away, throw out, unload — more at DISCARD

²jettison n : a voluntary sacrifice of cargo to lighten a ship's load in time of distress

jet·ty \ˈje-tē\ n, pl **jetties** **1** : a pier built to influence the current or to protect a harbor **2 ♦** : a landing wharf

♦ dock, float, landing, levee, pier, quay, wharf — more at DOCK

jeu d'es·prit \zhœ-des-ˈprē\ n, pl **jeux d'esprit** *same*\ [F, lit., play of the mind] : a witty comment or composition

Jew \ˈjü\ n **1** : one whose religion is Judaism **2** : ISRAELITE — **Jew·ish** adj

¹jew·el \ˈjü-əl\ n [ME *juel*, fr. AF, dim. of *ju, jeu* game, play, fr. L *jocus* game, joke] **1** : an ornament of precious metal **2 ♦** : a precious stone : GEMSTONE **3 ♦** : one that is highly esteemed

♦ [2] brilliant, gem, gemstone — more at GEM ♦ [3] boast, credit, glory, honor (*or* honour), pride, treasure — more at GLORY ♦ [3] catch, gem, pearl, plum, prize, treasure — more at PRIZE

²jewel vb **-eled** *or* **-elled; -el·ing** *or* **-el·ling** : to adorn or equip with jewels

jewel box n : a thin plastic case for a CD or DVD

jew·el·er *or* **jew·el·ler** \ˈjü-ə-lər\ n : a person who makes or deals in jewelry and related articles

jew·el·ry *or Can and Brit* **jew·el·lery** \ˈjü-əl-rē\ n : JEWELS; *esp* : objects of precious metal set with gems and worn for personal adornment

Jew·ry \ˈjur-ē, ˈjü-ər-ē, ˈjü-rē\ n : the Jewish people

jg abbr junior grade

¹jib \ˈjib\ n : a triangular sail set on a line running from the bow to the mast

²jib vb **jibbed; jib·bing** : to refuse to proceed further

¹jibe var of GIBE

²jibe \ˈjīb\ vb **jibed; jib·ing ♦** : to be in accord : AGREE

♦ accord, agree, answer, check, coincide, comport, conform, correspond, dovetail, fit, go, harmonize, square, tally — more at CHECK

ji·ca·ma \ˈhē-kə-mə\ n : an edible starchy tuber of a tropical American vine of the legume family

jif·fy \ˈji-fē\ n, pl **jiffies ♦** : a small portion or point of time : MOMENT, INSTANT ⟨I'll be ready in a ~⟩

♦ flash, instant, minute, moment, second, shake, trice, twinkle, twinkling, wink — more at INSTANT

¹jig \ˈjig\ n **1** : a lively dance in triple rhythm **2 ♦** : a crafty procedure or practice meant to deceive or defraud : TRICK ⟨the ~ is up⟩ **3** : a device used to hold work during manufacture or assembly

♦ artifice, device, dodge, gimmick, ploy, scheme, sleight, stratagem, trick, wile — more at TRICK

²jig vb **jigged; jig·ging** : to dance a jig

jig·ger \ˈji-gər\ n **1** : a measure usu. holding 1 to 2 ounces (30 to 60 milliliters) used in mixing drinks **2 ♦** : an often small mechanical or electronic device with a practical use but often thought of as a novelty

♦ contraption, contrivance, gadget, gimmick, gizmo — more at GADGET

jig·gle \ˈji-gəl\ vb **jig·gled; jig·gling ♦** : to move with quick little jerks — **jiggle** n

♦ fiddle, fidget, jerk, squirm, twitch, wiggle — more at FIDGET

jig·saw \ˈjig-ˌsȯ\ n : a machine saw with a narrow vertically reciprocating blade for cutting curved lines

jigsaw puzzle n : a puzzle consisting of small irregularly cut pieces to be fitted together to form a picture

ji·had \ji-ˈhäd, -ˈhad\ n **1** : a Muslim holy war **2** : a reforming enterprise undertaken with zeal

ji·had·ist \-ˈhä-dist, -ˈha-\ n : a Muslim who advocates or participates in a jihad

¹jilt \ˈjilt\ vb : to drop (a lover) capriciously or unfeelingly

²jilt n : one who jilts a lover

jim crow \ˈjim-ˈkrō\ n, often cap J&C : discrimination against black people esp. by legal enforcement or traditional sanctions — **jim crow** adj, often cap J&C — **jim crow·ism** \-ˈkrō-ˌi-zəm\ n, often cap J&C

¹jim–dan·dy \ˈjim-ˈdan-dē\ n ♦ : something excellent of its kind

♦ beauty, crackerjack, dandy, knockout, pip; also marvel, wonder; gem, jewel, treasure

²jim–dandy adj : fine or wonderful of its kind

jim·mies \ˈji-mēz\ n pl : tiny rod-shaped bits of usu. chocolate-flavored candy often sprinkled on ice cream

¹jim·my \ˈji-mē\ n, pl **jimmies** : a small crowbar

²jimmy vb **jim·mied; jim·my·ing ♦** : to force open with a jimmy

♦ prize, pry — more at PRY

jim·son·weed \ˈjim-sən-ˌwēd\ n, often cap : a coarse poisonous weed related to the tomato that has large trumpet-shaped white or violet flowers

¹jin·gle \ˈjiŋ-gəl\ vb **jin·gled; jin·gling ♦** : to make a light clinking or tinkling sound

♦ chink, tinkle; also clack, clang, clank; clatter, rattle; jangle, ping, ring

²jingle n **1** : a light clinking or tinkling sound **2 ♦** : a short verse or song with catchy repetition

♦ lay, lyric, song, vocal — more at SONG

jin·go·ism \ˈjiŋ-gō-ˌi-zəm\ n : extreme chauvinism or nationalism marked esp. by a belligerent foreign policy — **jin·go·ist** \-ist\ n — **jin·go·is·tic** \ˌjiŋ-gō-ˈis-tik\ adj

jin·rik·sha \jin-ˈrik-ˌshȯ\ n : RICKSHA

¹jinx \ˈjiŋks\ n : one that brings bad luck

²jinx vb : to foredoom to failure or misfortune

jit·ney \ˈjit-nē\ n, pl **jitneys** : a small bus that serves a regular route on a flexible schedule

jit·ter·bug \ˈji-tər-ˌbəg\ n : a dance in which couples two-step, balance, and twirl vigorously in standardized patterns — **jitterbug** vb

jit·ters \ˈji-tərz\ n pl ♦ : extreme nervousness

♦ shakes, shivers, willies; also cold sweat; anxiety, fear, hysteria; frazzle, nervous breakdown

jit·tery \-tə-rē\ adj **1 ♦** : suffering from the jitters **2** : marked by jittering movements

♦ excitable, flighty, fluttery, high-strung, jumpy, nervous, skittish, spooky — more at EXCITABLE ♦ aflutter, anxious, edgy, jumpy, nervous, nervy, perturbed, tense, troubled, uneasy, upset, worried — more at NERVOUS

¹jive \ˈjīv\ n **1** : swing music or dancing performed to it **2** : glib, deceptive, or foolish talk **3** : the jargon of jazz enthusiasts **4 ♦** : a special jargon of difficult or slang terms

♦ argot, cant, dialect, jargon, language, lingo, patois, patter, slang, terminology, vocabulary — more at TERMINOLOGY

²jive vb **jived; jiv·ing** **1 ♦** : to persuade with flattery or gentle urging esp. in the face of reluctance : TEASE; also : kid around **2** : to dance to or play jive

♦ chaff, josh, kid, rally, razz, rib, ride, roast, tease — more at TEASE

Jn *or* **Jno** abbr John

Jo abbr Joel

¹job \ˈjäb\ n **1** : a piece of work **2 ♦** : something that has to be done : TASK; also : a specific duty, role, or function **3 ♦** : a regular remunerative position — **job·less** adj

[2] assignment, chore, duty, stint, task — more at CHORE ♦ **[2]** assignment, charge, mission, operation, post — more at MISSION ♦ **[3]** appointment, billet, capacity, function, place, position, post, situation; *also* business, employment, occupation, profession; work; office, spot; calling, pursuit, vocation; line, racket; engagement; livelihood, living; assignment, mission, task

²**job** *vb* **jobbed; job·bing** **1** : to do occasional pieces of work for hire **2** : to hire or let by the job

Job \ˈjōb\ *n* : a book of Jewish and Christian Scripture

job action *n* : a protest action by workers to force compliance with demands

job·ber \ˈjä-bər\ *n* **1** : a person who buys goods and then sells them to other dealers : MIDDLEMAN **2** : a person who does work by the job

job·hold·er \ˈjäb-ˌhōl-dər\ *n* ♦ : one having a regular job

♦ employee, hand, hireling, worker — more at EMPLOYEE

jock \ˈjäk\ *n* [*jockstrap*] : ATHLETE; *esp* : a college athlete

¹**jock·ey** \ˈjä-kē\ *n, pl* **jockeys** : one who rides a horse esp. as a professional in a race

²**jockey** *vb* **jock·eyed; jock·ey·ing** : to maneuver or manipulate by adroit or devious means ⟨rivals ~ed for power⟩

jock·strap \ˈjäk-ˌstrap\ *n* [E slang *jock* penis] : ATHLETIC SUPPORTER

jo·cose \jō-ˈkōs\ *adj* : given to joking : MERRY ⟨~ party-goers⟩; *also* : characterized by joking

joc·u·lar \ˈjä-kyə-lər\ *adj* ♦ : marked by jesting : PLAYFUL — **joc·u·lar·i·ty** \ˌjäk-yə-ˈlar-ə-tē\ *n* — **joc·u·lar·ly** *adv*

♦ clever, facetious, humorous, playful, smart, witty — more at WITTY

jo·cund \ˈjä-kənd\ *adj* ♦ : marked by mirth or cheerfulness

♦ blithe, boon, festive, gay, gleeful, jolly, jovial, merry, mirthful, sunny — more at MERRY

jodh·pur \ˈjäd-pər\ *n* **1** *pl* : riding breeches loose above the knee and tight-fitting below **2** : an ankle-high boot fastened with a strap

Joe Blow \ˈjō-\ *n* : an average or ordinary man

Jo·el \ˈjō-əl\ *n* : a book of Jewish and Christian Scripture

Joe Six–Pack \ˈjō-\ *n* : a blue-collar worker

¹**jog** \ˈjäg\ *vb* **jogged; jog·ging** **1** : to give a slight shake or push to **2** : to go at a slow monotonous pace **3** : to run or ride at a slow trot **4** ♦ : to move up and down or about with a short heavy motion — **jog·ger** *n*

♦ bob, bobble, jounce, nod, pump, seesaw — more at NOD

²**jog** *n* **1** : a slight shake **2** : a jogging movement or pace

³**jog** *n* **1** : a projecting or retreating part of a line or surface **2** : a brief abrupt change in direction

jog·gle \ˈjä-gəl\ *vb* **jog·gled; jog·gling** : to shake slightly — **joggle** *n*

john \ˈjän\ *n* **1** : TOILET **2** : a prostitute's client

John \ˈjän\ *n* **1** : the fourth Gospel in the New Testament **2** : any of three short didactic letters addressed to early Christians and included in the New Testament

john·ny \ˈjä-nē\ *n, pl* **johnnies** : a short-sleeved gown opening in the back that is worn by hospital patients

John·ny–jump–up \ˌjä-nē-ˈjəmp-ˌəp\ *n* : any of various small-flowered cultivated pansies

joie de vi·vre \ˌzhwä-də-ˈvēvrᵊ\ *n* [F] : keen enjoyment of life

join \ˈjȯin\ *vb* **1** ♦ : to come or bring together so as to form a unit **2** : to come or bring into close association **3** ♦ : to become a member of **4** ♦ : to lie next to or in contact with : ADJOIN **5** ♦ : to take part in a collective activity

♦ **[1]** associate, coalesce, combine, conjoin, connect, couple, fuse, link, marry, unify, unite — more at UNITE ♦ **[3]** enlist, enroll, enter, sign on, sign up — more at ENTER ♦ **[4]** abut, adjoin, border (on), flank, fringe, skirt, touch, verge (on) — more at ADJOIN ♦ **[5]** collaborate, concert, cooperate, team — more at COOPERATE

join·er \ˈjȯi-nər\ *n* **1** : a worker who constructs articles by joining pieces of wood **2** : a gregarious person who joins many organizations

¹**joint** \ˈjȯint\ *n* **1** : the point of contact between bones of an animal skeleton with the parts that surround and support it **2** : a cut of meat suitable for roasting **3** ♦ : a place where two things or parts are connected **4** : a place of business or residence with its furnishings and staff : ESTABLISHMENT; *esp* : a shabby or disreputable establishment **5** : a marijuana cigarette — **joint·ed** *adj*

♦ connection, coupling, junction, juncture; *also* crux, link, tie; intersection; abutment, articulation; seam, suture; concourse, confluence, meeting; union

²**joint** *adj* **1** ♦ : acting in concert : UNITED **2** : common to two or more — **joint·ly** *adv*

♦ collective, common, communal, concerted, conjoint, mutual, public, united — more at COLLECTIVE

³**joint** *vb* **1** : to unite by or provide with a joint **2** : to separate the joints of

joist \ˈjȯist\ *n* : any of the small beams ranged parallel from wall to wall in a building to support a floor or ceiling

¹**joke** \ˈjōk\ *n* ♦ : something said or done to provoke laughter; *esp* : a brief narrative with a humorous climax

♦ crack, gag, jest, laugh, pleasantry, quip, sally, waggery, wisecrack, witticism; *also* joking, wisecracking; antic, buffoonery, caper, prank; caricature, lampoon, parody, put-on; banter, persiflage, raillery, repartee; facetiousness, humorousness; barb, humor, wit, wordplay

²**joke** *vb* **joked; jok·ing** ♦ : to make jokes — **jok·ing·ly** *adv*

♦ banter, fool, fun, jest, jive, josh, kid, quip, wisecrack; *also* chaff, mock, rally, razz, rib, ridicule, tease; caricature, lampoon, parody, satirize; amuse, divert, entertain

jok·er \ˈjō-kər\ *n* **1** ♦ : a person who jokes **2** : an extra card used in some card games **3** : a misleading part of an agreement that works to one party's disadvantage **4 a** : an adult male human **b** ♦ : an insignificant, obnoxious, or incompetent person

♦ **[1]** card, comedian, comic, humorist, jester, wag, wit — more at HUMORIST ♦ **[4b]** beast, boor, churl, clown, creep, cretin, cur, heel, jerk, louse, lout, skunk, slob, snake — more at JERK

jol·li·fi·ca·tion \ˌjä-li-fə-ˈkā-shən\ *n* ♦ : a festive celebration

♦ conviviality, festivity, gaiety, merriment, merrymaking, revelry — more at MERRYMAKING

jol·li·ty \ˈjä-lə-tē\ *n, pl* **-ties** : the quality or state of being jolly : GAIETY, MERRIMENT

jol·ly \ˈjä-lē\ *adj* **jol·li·er; -est** ♦ : full of high spirits : MERRY

♦ blithe, boon, festive, gay, gleeful, jocund, jovial, merry, mirthful, sunny — more at MERRY

¹**jolt** \ˈjōlt\ *vb* **1** : to give a quick hard knock or blow to **2** ♦ : to move with a sudden jerky motion **3** ♦ : to disturb the composure of — **jolt·er** *n*

♦ **[2]** agitate, convulse, jounce, quake, quiver, shake, shudder, vibrate, wobble — more at SHAKE ♦ **[2]** buck, hitch, jerk, twitch — more at JERK ♦ **[3]** appall, bowl, floor, shake up, shock — more at SHOCK

²**jolt** *n* **1** ♦ : an abrupt jerky blow or movement **2** ♦ : a sudden shock

♦ **[1]** bump, collision, concussion, crash, impact, jar, shock, smash, strike, wallop — more at IMPACT ♦ **[2]** bolt, bombshell, jar, surprise — more at SURPRISE

Jon *abbr* Jonah; Jonas

Jo·nah \ˈjō-nə\ *n* : a book of Jewish and Christian Scripture

Jo·nas \ˈjō-nəs\ *n* : JONAH

¹**jones** \ˈjōnz\ *n* **1** *slang* : addiction to heroin **2** *slang* : HEROIN **3** *slang* : a craving for something

²**jones** *vb, slang* : to have a craving for something

jon·gleur \zhōⁿ-ˈglər\ *n* : an itinerant medieval minstrel

jon·quil \ˈjän-kwəl\ *n* [F *jonquille*, fr. Sp *junquillo*, dim. of *junco* reed, fr. L *juncus*] : a narcissus with fragrant clustered white or yellow flowers

Jor·da·ni·an \jȯr-ˈdā-nē-ən\ *n* : a native or inhabitant of Jordan — **Jordanian** *adj*

josh \\'jäsh\\ *vb* ♦ : to tease good-naturedly; *also* : JOKE

♦ chaff, jive, kid, rally, razz, rib, ride, roast, tease — more at TEASE ♦ banter, fool, fun, jest, jive, joke, kid, quip, wisecrack — more at JOKE

Josh *abbr* Joshua

Josh·ua \\'jä-shù-ə\\ *n* : a book of Jewish and Christian Scripture

Joshua tree *n* : a tall branched yucca of the southwestern U.S.

jos·tle \\'jä-səl\\ *vb* **jos·tled; jos·tling** **1** : to come in contact or into collision **2** : to make one's way by pushing and shoving ⟨*jostled* his way onto the bus⟩

Jos·ue \\'jä-shù-ē\\ *n* : JOSHUA

¹jot \\'jät\\ *n* ♦ : the least bit : IOTA

♦ hoot, iota, lick, modicum, rap, tittle, whit; *also* ace, bit, crumb, dab, driblet, glimmer, hint, little, mite, nip, ounce, peanuts, ray, scruple, shade, shadow, shred, smidgen, snap, speck, spot, sprinkling, strain, streak, suspicion, touch, trace

²jot *vb* **jot·ted; jot·ting** ♦ : to write briefly and hurriedly

♦ *usu* jot down log, mark, note, put down, record, register, set down — more at RECORD

jot·ting \\'jä-tiŋ\\ *n* : a brief note

joule \\'jül\\ *n* : a unit of work or energy equal to the work done by a force of one newton acting through a distance of one meter

jounce \\'jaùns\\ *vb* **jounced; jounc·ing** ♦ : to move or cause to move in an up-and-down manner : JOLT — **jounce** *n*

♦ agitate, convulse, jolt, quake, quiver, shake, shudder, vibrate, wobble — more at SHAKE

jour *abbr* **1** journal **2** journeyman

¹jour·nal \\'jər-n°l\\ *n* [ME, service book containing the day hours, fr. AF *jurnal*, fr. *jurnal* daily, fr. L *diurnalis*, fr. *dies* day] **1** : a brief account of daily events **2** : a record of proceedings (as of a legislative body) **3** ♦ : a periodical (as a newspaper) dealing esp. with current events **4** : the part of a rotating axle or spindle that turns in a bearing

♦ magazine, organ, paper, review; *also* annual, bimonthly, biweekly, daily, monthly, quarterly, semimonthly, semiweekly, weekly, yearbook; broadside, extra, sheet, tabloid

²journal *vb* : to keep a personal journal : to enter or record daily thoughts, experiences, etc., in a journal

jour·nal·ese \\,jər-nə-'lēz, -'lēs\\ *n* : a style of writing held to be characteristic of newspapers

jour·nal·ism \\'jər-nə-,li-zəm\\ *n* **1** : the business of writing for, editing, or publishing periodicals (as newspapers) **2** : writing designed for or characteristic of newspapers — **jour·nal·ist** \\-list\\ *n* — **jour·nal·is·tic** \\,jər-nə-'lis-tik\\ *adj*

jour·nal·ist \\'jər-nə-,list\\ *n* **1** ♦ : a person engaged in journalism **2** : one who keeps a journal

♦ correspondent, newsman, reporter — more at REPORTER

¹jour·ney \\'jər-nē\\ *n, pl* **journeys** [ME, fr. OF *journee* day's journey, fr. *jour* day] ♦ : a traveling from one place to another

♦ expedition, passage, peregrination, trek, trip; *also* errand, excursion, flight, hop, jaunt, junket, outing, sally, tour; cruise, sail, voyage; drive, ride, spin; odyssey, pilgrimage, progress, quest, safari

²journey *vb* **jour·neyed; jour·ney·ing** ♦ : to go on a journey : TRAVEL

♦ tour, travel, trek, voyage — more at TRAVEL

jour·ney·man \\-mən\\ *n* **1** : a worker who has learned a trade and works for another person **2** : an experienced reliable worker

¹joust \\'jaùst\\ *vb* : to engage in a joust

²joust *n* : a combat on horseback between two knights with lances esp. as part of a tournament

jo·vial \\'jō-vē-əl\\ *adj* ♦ : marked by good humor ⟨a ~ mood⟩

♦ blithe, boon, festive, gay, gleeful, jocund, jolly, merry, mirthful, sunny — more at MERRY

jo·vi·al·i·ty \\,jō-vē-'a-lə-tē\\ *n* ♦ : the quality or state of being jovial

♦ cheer, cheerfulness, cheeriness, glee, hilarity, merriment, mirth — more at MIRTH

jo·vi·al·ly *adv* ♦ : in a jovial manner

♦ cheerfully, gaily, happily, heartily, merrily, mirthfully — more at GAILY

¹jowl \\'jaù(-ə)l\\ *n* : loose flesh about the lower jaw or throat

²jowl *n* **1** : the lower jaw **2** : CHEEK

joy \\'joi\\ *n* [ME, fr. AF *joie*, fr. L *gaudia*] **1** ♦ : a feeling of happiness that comes from success, good fortune, or a sense of well-being **2** ♦ : a source of happiness

♦ [1] blessedness, bliss, felicity, gladness, happiness — more at HAPPINESS ♦ [2] delectation, delight, kick, manna, pleasure, treat — more at DELIGHT

²joy *vb* : to experience great pleasure or delight : REJOICE

joy·ful \\-fəl\\ *adj* ♦ : experiencing, causing, or showing joy ⟨~ news⟩ — **joy·ful·ly** *adv*

♦ blissful, delighted, glad, happy, pleased — more at GLAD

joy·less *adj* **1** : not experiencing joy **2** : not inspiring or causing joy

joy·ous \\'joi-əs\\ *adj* : experiencing, causing, or showing joy : JOYFUL — **joy·ous·ly** *adv* — **joy·ous·ness** *n*

joy·ride \\'joi-,rīd\\ *n* : a ride for pleasure often marked by reckless driving — **joyride** *vb* — **joy·rid·er** *n* — **joy·rid·ing** *n*

joy·stick \\-,stik\\ *n* : a control device (as for a computer display) consisting of a lever capable of motion in two or more directions

JP *abbr* **1** jet propulsion **2** justice of the peace

JPEG \\'jā-,peg\\ *n* [*J*oint *P*hotographic *E*xperts *G*roup] : a computer file format for usu. high-quality digital images

Jr *abbr* junior

jt *or* **jnt** *abbr* joint

ju·bi·lant \\'jü-bə-lənt\\ *adj* [L *jubilans*, prp. of *jubilare* to rejoice] ♦ : filled with or expressing great joy or triumph : EXULTANT ⟨~ winners⟩ — **ju·bi·lant·ly** *adv*

♦ exultant, rejoicing, triumphant — more at EXULTANT

ju·bi·la·tion \\,jü-bə-'lā-shən\\ *n* : EXULTATION

ju·bi·lee \\'jü-bə-,lē, ,jü-bə-'lē\\ *n* [ME, fr. AF & LL; AF *jubilé*, fr. LL *jubilaeus*, fr. LGk *iōbēlaios*, fr. Heb *yōbhēl* ram's horn, trumpet, jubilee] **1** : a 50th anniversary **2** ♦ : a season or occasion of celebration

♦ carnival, celebration, festival, festivity, fete, fiesta, gala — more at FESTIVAL

ju·co \\'jü-,kō\\ *n, pl* **jucos** : JUNIOR COLLEGE; *also* : an athlete at a junior college

Jud *abbr* Judith

Ju·da·ic \\jü-'dā-ik\\ *also* **Ju·da·ical** \\-'dā-ə-kəl\\ *adj* : of, relating to, or characteristic of Jews or Judaism

Ju·da·ism \\'jü-də-,i-zəm, -dā-, -dē-\\ *n* : a religion developed among the ancient Hebrews and marked by belief in one God and by the moral and ceremonial laws of the Old Testament and the rabbinic tradition

Jude \\'jüd\\ *n* : a short hortatory epistle addressed to early Christians and included as a book in the New Testament

Judg *abbr* Judges

¹judge \\'jəj\\ *vb* **judged; judg·ing** **1** : to form an authoritative opinion **2** ♦ : to decide as a judge **3** ♦ : to form an estimate or evaluation about something

♦ [2] adjudicate, arbitrate, decide, determine, referee, rule, settle, umpire; *also* consider, hear, ponder, weigh; size (up); mediate, moderate, negotiate; prosecute, try; find (for *or* against) ♦ [3] calculate, call, conjecture, estimate, figure, gauge, guess, make, place, put, reckon, suppose — more at ESTIMATE ♦ [3] conclude, deduce, extrapolate, gather, infer, reason, understand — more at INFER

²judge *n* **1** ♦ : a public official authorized to decide questions brought before a court **2** ♦ : one appointed to decide in a contest or competition : UMPIRE **3** : one who gives an authoritative opinion : CRITIC — **judge·ship** *n*

♦ [1] bench, court, justice, magistrate; *also* JP, justice of the peace ♦ [2] arbiter, arbitrator, referee, umpire;

also justice, magistrate; intermediary, mediator, negotiator; go-between, peacemaker, reconciler

Judges *n* : a book of Jewish and Christian Scripture

judg·ment *or* **judge·ment** \'jəj-mənt\ *n* **1** ♦ : a decision or opinion given after judging; *esp* : a formal decision given by a court **2** *cap* : the final judging of humankind by God **3** ♦ : the process of forming an opinion by discerning and comparing **4** : the capacity for judging : DISCERNMENT

♦ [1] appraisal, assessment, estimate, estimation, evaluation — more at ESTIMATION ♦ [1] doom, finding, holding, ruling, sentence — more at SENTENCE ♦ [3] belief, conviction, eye, feeling, mind, notion, opinion, persuasion, sentiment, verdict, view — more at OPINION ♦ [3] conclusion, decision, determination, diagnosis, resolution — more at DECISION

judg·men·tal \,jəj-'men-təl\ *adj* **1** : of, relating to, or involving judgment **2** : characterized by a tendency to judge harshly — **judg·men·tal·ly** *adv*

judgment call *n* : a subjective decision, ruling, or opinion

Judgment Day *n* : the day of the final judging of all human beings by God

ju·di·ca·ture \'jü-di-kə-,chùr\ *n* **1** : the administration of justice **2** : JUDICIARY 1

ju·di·cial \jù-'di-shəl\ *adj* **1** : of or relating to the administration of justice or the judiciary **2** : ordered or enforced by a court **3** : CRITICAL — **ju·di·cial·ly** *adv*

ju·di·cia·ry \jù-'di-shē-,er-ē, -shə-rē\ *n* **1** : a system of courts of law; *also* : the judges of these courts **2** : a branch of government in which judicial power is vested — **judiciary** *adj*

ju·di·cious \jù-'di-shəs\ *adj* ♦ : having, exercising, or characterized by sound judgment — **ju·di·cious·ly** *adv*

♦ advisable, desirable, expedient, politic, prudent, tactical, wise — more at EXPEDIENT

Ju·dith \'jü-dəth\ *n* : a book of Scripture in the Roman Catholic canon of the Old Testament and in the Protestant Apocrypha

ju·do \'jü-dō\ *n* [Jp, fr. *jū* weakness, gentleness + *dō* art] : a sport derived from jujitsu that emphasizes the use of quick movement and leverage to throw an opponent — **ju·do·ist** \-ist\ *n*

ju·do·ka \'jü-dō-,kä\ *n, pl* **judoka** *or* **judokas** : one who participates in judo

¹jug \'jəg\ *n* **1** ♦ : a large deep container with a narrow mouth and a handle **2** : a place of confinement for persons held in lawful custody : JAIL, PRISON

♦ ewer, flagon, pitcher — more at PITCHER

²jug *vb* **jugged**; **jug·ging** : to confine in or as if in a jail : JAIL, IMPRISON

jug–eared \'jəg-,ird\ *adj* : having protuberant ears

jug·ger·naut \'jə-gər-,nòt\ *n* [Hindi *Jagannāth*, title of Vishnu (a Hindu god), lit., lord of the world] : a massive inexorable force or object that crushes everything in its path

jug·gle \'jə-gəl\ *vb* **jug·gled**; **jug·gling** **1** : to keep several objects in motion in the air at the same time **2** : to manipulate esp. in order to achieve a desired and often fraudulent end — **jug·gler** \'jə-glər\ *n*

jug·u·lar \'jə-gyə-lər\ *adj* : of, relating to, or situated in or on the throat or neck ⟨the ∼ veins⟩

juice \'jüs\ *n* **1** : the extractable fluid contents of cells or tissues **2** *pl* : the natural fluids of an animal body **3** : something that supplies power; *esp* : ELECTRICITY 2

juic·er \'jü-sər\ *n* : an appliance for extracting juice (as from fruit)

juice up *vb* : to give life, energy, or spirit to

juicy \'jü-sē\ *adj* **juic·i·er**; **-est** **1** ♦ : full of juice : SUCCULENT **2** : rich in interest; *also* : RACY ⟨∼ gossip⟩ — **juic·i·ly** \-sə-lē\ *adv* — **juic·i·ness** \-sē-nəs\ *n*

♦ fleshy, pulpy, succulent; *also* sappy, watery

ju·jit·su *also* **ju·jut·su** \jü-'jit-sü\ *n* [Jp *jūjutsu*, fr. *jū* weakness + *jutsu* art, skill] : an art of fighting employing holds, throws, and paralyzing blows

ju·ju \'jü-jü\ *n* : a style of African music characterized by a rapid beat, use of percussion instruments, and vocal harmonies

ju·jube \'jü-,jüb, 'jü-jù-,bē\ *n* : a fruit-flavored gumdrop or lozenge

juke·box \'jük-,bäks\ *n* : a coin-operated machine that automatically plays selected recordings

Jul *abbr* July

ju·lep \'jü-ləp\ *n* [ME, sweetened water, fr. MF, fr. Ar *julāb*, fr. Pers *gulāb*, fr. *gul* rose + *āb* water] : a drink made of bourbon, sugar, and mint served over crushed ice

Ju·ly \jù-'lī\ *n* [ME *Julie*, fr. OE *Julius*, fr. L, fr. Gaius *Julius* Caesar] : the 7th month of the year

¹jum·ble \'jəm-bəl\ *vb* **jum·bled**; **jum·bling** : to mix in a confused mass

²jumble *n* ♦ : a mass of things mingled together without order or plan; *also* : a state of confusion

♦ chaos, confusion, disarray, disorder, disorganization, havoc, hell, mess, muddle, shambles — more at CHAOS ♦ assortment, clutter, medley, mélange, miscellany, motley, muddle, variety, welter — more at MISCELLANY

¹jum·bo \'jəm-bō\ *n, pl* **jumbos** [*Jumbo*, a huge elephant exhibited by P.T. Barnum] ♦ : a very large specimen of its kind

♦ behemoth, blockbuster, colossus, giant, leviathan, mammoth, monster, titan, whale, whopper — more at GIANT

²jumbo *adj* : very large ⟨a ∼ TV screen⟩

¹jump \'jəmp\ *vb* **1** ♦ : to spring into the air : leap over **2** ♦ : to give a start **3** : to rise or increase suddenly or sharply **4** ♦ : to make a sudden attack **5** : ANTICIPATE ⟨∼ the gun⟩ **6** : to leave hurriedly and often furtively ⟨∼ town⟩ **7** : to act or move before (as a signal) — **jump bail** : to abscond after being released from custody on bail — **jump ship** **1** : to leave the company of a ship without authority **2** : to desert a cause

♦ [1] bound, hop, leap, spring, vault; *also* bounce, lope, skip; buck; caper, cavort, frolic, gambol, romp; attack, pounce; shoot, skyrocket ♦ [2] bolt, start, startle — more at START ♦ *usu* **jump on** [4] abuse, castigate, excoriate, lambaste, slam, vituperate — more at ATTACK ♦ *usu* **jump on** [4] assail, assault, attack, beset, charge, descend, pounce (on *or* upon), raid, rush, storm, strike — more at ATTACK

²jump *n* **1** ♦ : a spring into the air; *esp* : one made for height or distance in a track meet **2** : a sharp sudden increase **3** ♦ : an initial advantage ⟨got the ∼ on a rival⟩

♦ [1] bound, hop, leap, spring, vault; *also* bounce, lope, skip; caper, gambol; attack, pounce; dive, pitch, plunge ♦ [3] advantage, better, drop, edge, upper hand, vantage — more at ADVANTAGE

¹jump·er \'jəm-pər\ *n* : one that jumps

²jumper *n* **1** : a loose blouse **2** : a sleeveless one-piece dress worn usu. with a blouse **3** *pl* : a child's sleeveless coverall

jumping bean *n* : a seed of any of several Mexican shrubs that tumbles about because of the movements of a small moth larva inside it

jumping–off place *n* **1** : a remote or isolated place **2** : a place from which an enterprise is launched

jump·mas·ter \'jəmp-,mas-tər\ *n* : a person who supervises parachutists

jump–start \'jəmp-,stärt\ *vb* : to start (an engine or vehicle) by connection to an external power source

jump·suit \'jəmp-,süt\ *n* **1** : a coverall worn by parachutists in jumping **2** : a one-piece garment consisting of a blouse or shirt with attached pants or shorts

jumpy \'jəm-pē\ *adj* **jump·i·er**; **-est** ♦ : easily excited or irritated : NERVOUS, JITTERY

♦ edgy, excitable, high-strung, jittery, nervous, skittish, spooky — more at EXCITABLE

jun *abbr* junior

Jun *abbr* June

junc *abbr* junction

jun·co \'jəṅ-kō\ *n, pl* **juncos** *or* **juncoes** : any of a genus of small common pink-billed No. American finches that are largely gray with conspicuous white tail feathers

junc·tion \'jəṅk-shən\ *n* **1** ♦ : an act of joining **2** ♦ : a place or point of meeting

♦ [1] combination, connection, consolidation, coupling, unification, union — more at UNION ♦ [2] connection, coupling, joint, juncture — more at JOINT

junc·ture \'jeṅk-chər\ *n* **1** : a place where two things or parts are joined : JOINT, CONNECTION **2** : UNION **3** ♦ : a critical time or state of affairs

♦ clutch, crisis, crunch, emergency, head — more at EMERGENCY

June \'jün\ *n* [ME, fr. L *Junius*] : the 6th month of the year

jun·gle \'jəṅ-gəl\ *n* [Hindi & Urdu *jangal* forest] **1** : a thick tangled mass of tropical vegetation; *also* : a tract overgrown with vegetation **2** : a place of ruthless struggle for survival

¹**ju·nior** \'jü-nyər\ *adj* **1** : YOUNGER **2** ♦ : lower in rank **3** : of or relating to juniors

♦ inferior, less, lesser, lower, minor, subordinate, under — more at LESSER

²**junior** *n* **1** : a person who is younger or of lower rank than another **2** : a student in the next-to-last year before graduating

junior college *n* : a school that offers studies corresponding to those of the 1st two years of college

junior high school *n* : a school usu. including grades 7–9

junior varsity *n* : a team whose members lack the experience or qualifications required for the varsity

ju·ni·per \'jü-nə-pər\ *n* : any of numerous coniferous shrubs or trees with leaves like needles or scales and female cones like berries

¹**junk** \'jəṅk\ *n* **1** ♦ : old iron, glass, paper, or waste; *also* : discarded articles **2** : a shoddy product **3** *slang* : NARCOTICS; *esp* : HEROIN

♦ chaff, deadwood, dust, garbage, litter, refuse, riffraff, rubbish, scrap, trash, waste — more at GARBAGE

²**junk** *vb* : to get rid of as worthless : DISCARD, SCRAP

♦ cast, discard, ditch, dump, fling, jettison, lose, reject, scrap, shed, shuck, slough, throw away, throw out, unload — more at DISCARD

³**junk** *n* : a ship of eastern Asia with a high stern and 4-cornered sails

junk·er \'jəṅ-kər\ *n* : something (as an old automobile) ready for scrapping

Jun·ker \'yu̇ṅ-kər\ *n* [G] : a member of the Prussian landed aristocracy

jun·ket \'jəṅ-kət\ *n* **1** : a pudding of sweetened flavored milk set by rennet **2** ♦ : a pleasure trip or outing; *esp* : a trip made by an official at public expense ostensibly for public business

♦ excursion, jaunt, outing, sally — more at EXCURSION

junk food *n* : food that is high in calories but low in nutritional content

junk·ie *also* **junky** \'jəṅ-kē\ *n, pl* **junkies 1** *slang* : a narcotics peddler or addict **2** : one that derives inordinate pleasure from or is dependent on something ⟨sugar ∼⟩

junky *adj* ♦ : having the character of junk : constituting junk

♦ chaffy, empty, no-good, null, valueless, worthless — more at WORTHLESS

jun·ta \'hu̇n-tə, 'jən-, 'hən-\ *n* [Sp, fr. *junto* joined, fr. L *junctus*, pp. of *jungere* to join] : a group of persons controlling a government esp. after a revolutionary seizure of power

Ju·pi·ter \'jü-pə-tər\ *n* : the largest of the planets and the one 5th in order of distance from the sun

Ju·ras·sic \ju̇-'ra-sik\ *adj* : of, relating to, or being the period of the Mesozoic era between the Triassic and the Cretaceous that is marked esp. by the presence of dinosaurs — **Jurassic** *n*

ju·rid·i·cal \ju̇-'ri-di-kəl\ *also* **ju·rid·ic** \-dik\ *adj* **1** : of or relating to the administration of justice **2** : LEGAL — **ju·rid·i·cal·ly** \-di-k(ə-)lē\ *adv*

ju·ris·dic·tion \ju̇r-əs-'dik-shən\ *n* **1** : the power, right, or authority to interpret and apply the law **2** ♦ : the authority of a sovereign power **3** : the limits or territory within which authority may be exercised — **ju·ris·dic·tion·al** \-shə-nəl\ *adj*

♦ administration, authority, government, regime, rule — more at RULE

ju·ris·pru·dence \-'prüd-ᵊns\ *n* **1** : a system of laws **2** : the science or philosophy of law

ju·rist \'ju̇r-ist\ *n* ♦ : one having a thorough knowledge of law; *esp* : JUDGE

♦ arbiter, arbitrator, judge, referee — more at JUDGE

ju·ris·tic \ju̇-'ris-tik\ *adj* **1** : of or relating to a jurist or jurisprudence **2** : of, relating to, or recognized in law

ju·ror \'ju̇r-ər, -ȯr\ *n* : a member of a jury

¹**ju·ry** \'ju̇r-ē\ *n, pl* **juries 1** : a body of persons sworn to inquire into a matter submitted to them and to give their verdict **2** : a committee for judging and awarding prizes

²**jury** *adj* : improvised for temporary use esp. in an emergency ⟨a ∼ mast⟩

jury nullification *n* : the acquitting of a defendant by a jury in disregard of the judge's instructions and contrary to the jury's findings of fact

jury–rig \'ju̇r-ē-,rig\ *vb* : to construct or arrange in a makeshift fashion

¹**just** \'jəst\ *adj* **1** ♦ : having a basis in or conforming to fact or reason : REASONABLE ⟨∼ comment⟩ **2** ♦ : conforming to a standard of correctness ⟨∼ proportions⟩ **3** ♦ : morally or legally right ⟨a ∼ title⟩ **4** : being what is merited ⟨∼ punishment⟩ — **just·ly** *adv* — **just·ness** *n*

♦ [1] good, hard, informed, levelheaded, logical, rational, reasonable, reasoned, sensible, sober, solid, valid, well=founded — more at GOOD ♦ [2] due, right; *also* applicable, appropriate, apt, fit, fitting, meet, proper, requisite, suitable; lawful, legal; accurate, correct **Ant** undeserved, undue, unjust, unwarranted ♦ [2] disinterested, dispassionate, equal, equitable, fair, impartial, nonpartisan, objective, square, unbiased, unprejudiced — more at FAIR ♦ [3] decent, ethical, good, honest, honorable (*or* honourable), moral, principled, right, righteous, straight, upright, upstanding, virtuous — more at GOOD

²**just** \'jəst, 'jist\ *adv* **1** ♦ : in a manner or measure or to a degree or number that strictly conforms to a fact or condition : EXACTLY ⟨∼ right⟩ **2** ♦ : very recently ⟨has ∼ left⟩ **3** ♦ : by a very small margin : BARELY ⟨∼ too late⟩ **4** : DIRECTLY ⟨∼ west of here⟩ **5** ♦ : to the exclusion of all else : ONLY ⟨∼ last year⟩ **6** : QUITE ⟨∼ wonderful⟩ **7** : POSSIBLY ⟨it ∼ might work⟩

♦ [1] accurately, exactly, precisely, right, sharp, squarely — more at EXACTLY ♦ [2] freshly, late, lately, new, newly, now, only, recently — more at NEWLY ♦ [3] barely, hardly, marginally, scarcely, slightly; *also* minimally, minutely; approximately, more or less, roughly, somewhat **Ant** considerably, significantly, substantially, well ♦ [5] but, merely, only, simply

jus·tice \'jəs-təs\ *n* **1** : the administration of what is just (as by assigning merited rewards or punishments) **2** ♦ : a public official authorized to decide questions brought before a court : JUDGE **3** : the administration of law **4** : FAIRNESS; *also* : RIGHTEOUSNESS

♦ bench, court, judge, magistrate — more at JUDGE

justice of the peace : a local magistrate empowered chiefly to try minor cases, to administer oaths, and to perform marriages

jus·ti·fi·able *adj* ♦ : capable of being justified

♦ defensible, maintainable, supportable, sustainable, tenable — more at TENABLE

jus·ti·fi·ca·tion \ˌjəs-tə-fə-ˈkā-shən\ *n* ♦ : the act or an instance of justifying

♦ alibi, defense (*or* defence), excuse, plea, reason — more at EXCUSE

jus·ti·fy \ˈjəs-tə-ˌfī\ *vb* **-fied; -fy·ing** **1** ♦ : to prove or show to be just, right, or reasonable **2** : to pronounce free from guilt or blame **3** : to adjust spaces in a line of printed text so the margins are even

♦ defend, maintain, support, uphold — more at MAINTAIN ♦ account, condone, excuse, explain, rationalize

jut \ˈjət\ *vb* **jut·ted; jut·ting** : to shoot out or forward : PROJECT, PROTRUDE

jute \ˈjüt\ *n* : a strong glossy fiber from either of two tropical plants used esp. for making sacks and twine

juv *abbr* juvenile

¹ju·ve·nile \ˈjü-və-ˌnīl, -nəl\ *adj* **1** ♦ : showing incomplete development **2** ♦ : of, relating to, or characteristic of children or young people

♦ [1] adolescent, immature, young, youthful — more at YOUNG ♦ [2] adolescent, babyish, childish, immature, infantile, kiddish — more at CHILDISH

²juvenile *n* **1** ♦ : a young person; *esp* : one below the legally established age of adulthood **2** : a young animal (as a fish or a bird) or plant **3** : an actor or actress who plays youthful parts

♦ child, cub, kid, youngster, youth — more at CHILD

juvenile delinquency *n* : violation of the law or antisocial behavior by a juvenile — **juvenile delinquent** *n*

jux·ta·pose \ˈjək-stə-ˌpōz\ *vb* **-posed; -pos·ing** : to place side by side — **jux·ta·po·si·tion** \ˌjək-stə-pə-ˈzi-shən\ *n*

JV *abbr* junior varsity

¹k \ˈkā\ *n, pl* **k's** *or* **ks** \ˈkāz\ **1** *often cap* : the 11th letter of the English alphabet **2** *cap* : STRIKEOUT

²k *abbr* **1** karat **2** kitchen **3** knit **4** kosher — often enclosed in a circle

¹K *abbr* Kelvin

²K *symbol* [NL *kalium*] potassium

kab·ba·lah *also* **kab·ba·la** *or* **ka·ba·la** *or* **ca·ba·la** \kə-ˈbä-lə, ˈka-bə-lə\ *n, often cap* **1** : a medieval Jewish mysticism marked by belief in creation through emanation and a cipher method of interpreting Scripture **2** : esoteric or mysterious doctrine

kabob *var of* KEBAB

Ka·bu·ki \kə-ˈbü-kē\ *n* : traditional Japanese popular drama with highly stylized singing and dancing

kad·dish \ˈkä-dish\ *n, often cap* : a Jewish prayer recited in the daily synagogue ritual and by mourners at public services after the death of a close relative

kaf·fee·klatsch \ˈkȯ-fē-ˌklach, ˈkä-\ *n, often cap* [G] : an informal social gathering for coffee and conversation

kai·ser \ˈkī-zər\ *n* : EMPEROR; *esp* : the ruler of Germany from 1871 to 1918

Ka·lash·ni·kov \kə-ˈlash-nə-ˌkȯf\ *n* [M. T. *Kalashnikov* b1919 Soviet weapons designer] : a Soviet-designed assault rifle

kale \ˈkāl\ *n* : a hardy cabbage with curled leaves that do not form a head

ka·lei·do·scope \kə-ˈlī-də-ˌskōp\ *n* : a tube containing loose bits of colored material (as glass) and two mirrors at one end that shows many different patterns as it is turned — **ka·lei·do·scop·ic** \-ˌlī-də-ˈskä-pik\ *adj* — **ka·lei·do·scop·i·cal·ly** \-pi-k(ə-)lē\ *adv*

ka·ma·ai·na \ˌkä-mə-ˈī-nə\ *n* [Hawaiian *kama'āina*, fr. *kama* child + *'āina* land] : one who has lived in Hawaii for a long time

kame \ˈkām\ *n* [Sc, lit., comb] : a short ridge or mound of material deposited by water from a melting glacier

ka·mi·ka·ze \ˌkä-mi-ˈkä-zē\ *n* [Jp, lit., divine wind] : a member of a corps of Japanese pilots assigned to make a suicidal crash on a target; *also* : an airplane flown in such an attack

Kan *or* **Kans** *abbr* Kansas

kan·ga·roo \ˌkaŋ-gə-ˈrü\ *n, pl* **-roos** : any of various large leaping marsupial mammals of Australia and adjacent islands with powerful hind legs and a long thick tail

kangaroo court *n* : a court or an illegal self-appointed tribunal characterized by irresponsible, perverted, or irregular procedures

ka·o·lin \ˈkā-ə-lən\ *n* : a fine usu. white clay used in ceramics and refractories and for the treatment of diarrhea

ka·pok \ˈkā-ˌpäk\ *n* : silky fiber from the seeds of a tropical tree used esp. as a filling (as for life preservers)

Kap·o·si's sar·co·ma \ˈka-pə-sēz-sär-ˈkō-mə\ *n* : a neoplastic disease associated esp. with AIDS that affects esp. the skin and mucous membranes and is characterized usu. by the formation of pink to reddish-brown or bluish plaques

kap·pa \ˈka-pə\ *n* : the 10th letter of the Greek alphabet — K or κ

ka·put *also* **ka·putt** \kä-ˈpùt, kə-, -ˈpüt\ *adj* [G, fr. F *capot* not having made a trick at piquet] **1** : utterly defeated or destroyed **2** : unable to function : USELESS

kar·a·kul \ˈkar-ə-kəl\ *n* : the usu. curly glossy black coat of a very young lamb of a hardy Asian breed of sheep

kar·a·o·ke \ˌkar-ē-ˈō-kē\ *n* [Jp] : a device that plays instrumental accompaniments for songs to which the user sings along

kar·at \ˈkar-ət\ *n* : a unit for expressing proportion of gold in an alloy equal to ¹⁄₂₄ part of pure gold

ka·ra·te \kə-ˈrä-tē\ *n* [Jp, lit., empty hand] : an art of self-defense in which an attacker is disabled by crippling kicks and punches

kar·ma \ˈkär-mə\ *n, often cap* [Skt] : the force generated by a person's actions held in Hinduism and Buddhism to perpetuate reincarnation and to determine the nature of the person's next existence — **kar·mic** \-mik\ *adj*

karst \ˈkärst\ *n* [G] : an irregular limestone region with sinks, underground streams, and caverns

ka·ty·did \ˈkā-tē-ˌdid\ *n* : any of several large green tree-dwelling American grasshoppers with long antennae

kay·ak \ˈkī-ˌak\ *n* : a canoe that is made of a skin-covered frame with a small opening and propelled by a double-bladed paddle and that is associated esp. with indigenous peoples of arctic regions; *also* : a similar portable boat — **kay·ak·er** *n*

kayo \(ˌ)kā-ˈō, ˈkā-ˌō\ *n* : KNOCKOUT — **kayo** *vb*

ka·zoo \kə-ˈzü\ *n, pl* **kazoos** : a toy musical instrument consisting of a tube with a membrane sealing one end and a side hole to sing or hum into

KB *abbr* kilobyte

kc *abbr* kilocycle

KC *abbr* **1** Kansas City **2** King's Counsel **3** Knights of Columbus

kc/s *abbr* kilocycles per second

KD *abbr* knocked down

ke·bab, ke·bob \kə-'bäb, 'kä-ˌbäb\ *n* : cubes of meat cooked with vegetables usu. on a skewer

kedge \'kej\ *n* : a small anchor

¹**keel** \'kēl\ *n* **1** : the chief structural member of a ship running lengthwise along the center of its bottom **2** : something (as a bird's breastbone) like a ship's keel in form or use — **keeled** \'kēld\ *adj*

²**keel** *vb* : FAINT, SWOON — usu. used with *over*

keel·boat \'kēl-ˌbōt\ *n* : a shallow covered keeled riverboat for freight that is usu. rowed, poled, or towed

keel·haul \-ˌhȯl\ *vb* **1** : to haul under the keel of a ship as punishment **2** ♦ : to rebuke severely

 ♦ admonish, chide, lecture, rail (at *or* against), rate, rebuke, reprimand, scold — more at SCOLD

¹**keen** \'kēn\ *adj* **1** ♦ : having a fine edge or point : SHARP ⟨a ~ knife⟩ **2** ♦ : affecting one as if by cutting ⟨a ~ wind⟩ **3** ♦ : showing a quick and ardent responsiveness : ENTHUSIASTIC ⟨~ about swimming⟩ **4** ♦ : mentally alert ⟨a ~ mind⟩ **5** ♦ : extremely sensitive in perception : STRONG, ACUTE ⟨~ eyesight⟩ **6** : unusually good : WONDERFUL, EXCELLENT — **keen·ly** *adv*

 ♦ [1] cutting, edgy, ground, sharp — more at SHARP ♦ [2] biting, bitter, cutting, penetrating, piercing, raw, sharp — more at CUTTING ♦ [3] agog, anxious, ardent, athirst, avid, crazy, eager, enthusiastic, gung ho, hot, hungry, nuts, raring, solicitous, thirsty, voracious — more at EAGER ♦ [4] alert, brainy, bright, brilliant, clever, intelligent, nimble, quick, quick-witted, sharp, smart — more at INTELLIGENT ♦ [5] acute, delicate, perceptive, sensitive, sharp — more at ACUTE

²**keen** *n* ♦ : a lamentation for the dead uttered in a loud wailing voice or in a wordless cry

 ♦ groan, howl, lament, moan, plaint, wail — more at LAMENT

³**keen** *vb* **1** : to lament with a keen **2** ♦ : to make a sound suggestive of a keen

 ♦ bay, howl, wail, yowl — more at HOWL

keen·ness *n* ♦ : the quality or state of being keen

 ♦ appetite, ardor, avidity, eagerness, enthusiasm, excitement, hunger, impatience, thirst — more at EAGERNESS ♦ acuity, acuteness, delicacy, sensitiveness, sensitivity

¹**keep** \'kēp\ *vb* **kept** \'kept\; **keep·ing** **1** ♦ : to be faithful to esp. by appropriate conduct : FULFILL, OBSERVE ⟨~ a promise⟩ ⟨~ a holiday⟩ **2** : GUARD ⟨~ us from harm⟩; *also* : to take care of ⟨~ a neighbor's children⟩ **3** : MAINTAIN ⟨~ silence⟩ **4** : to have in one's service or at one's disposal ⟨~ a horse⟩ **5** : to preserve a record in ⟨~ a diary⟩ **6** : to have in stock for sale **7** ♦ : to retain in one's possession ⟨~ what you find⟩ **8** : to carry on (as a business) : CONDUCT **9** : HOLD, DETAIN ⟨~ him in jail⟩ **10** : to refrain from revealing ⟨~ a secret⟩ **11** : to continue in good condition ⟨meat will ~ in a freezer⟩ **12** ♦ : to resist an impulse or desire : ABSTAIN, REFRAIN

 ♦ [1] answer, comply, fill, fulfill, meet, redeem, satisfy — more at FULFILL ♦ [1] celebrate, commemorate, observe; *also* bless, consecrate, sanctify, solemnize; honor, laud, praise; obey, respect, revere, reverence, venerate; remember *Ant* break, transgress, violate ♦ [7] hang on, hold, reserve, retain, withhold; *also* conserve, preserve, save; enjoy, have, own, possess; conduct, control, detain, direct; bear, harbor *Ant* hand over, relinquish, surrender ♦ *usu* **keep from** [12] abstain (from), forbear, forgo, refrain — more at FORBEAR

²**keep** *n* **1** : FORTRESS **2** : the means or provisions by which one is kept — **for keeps 1** : with the provision that one keep what one has won ⟨play marbles *for keeps*⟩ **2** : PERMANENTLY

keep–away \'kēp-ə-ˌwā\ *n* : a game in which players try to keep an object from one or more other players

keep·er *n* ♦ : one that keeps; *esp* : one who cares for another or another's property

 ♦ custodian, guard, guardian, lookout, picket, sentry, warden, warder, watch, watchman — more at GUARD ♦ caretaker, custodian, guardian, janitor, warden, watchman — more at CUSTODIAN

keep·ing *n* **1** : CONFORMITY ⟨in ~ with good taste⟩ **2** ♦ : the act of one that keeps : the care, possession, or observance of something

 ♦ care, custody, guardianship, safekeeping, trust, ward — more at CUSTODY ♦ control, hands, possession — more at POSSESSION

keeping room *n* : a common room used for multiple purposes

keep·sake \'kēp-ˌsāk\ *n* ♦ : something kept or given to be kept as a memento

 ♦ memento, memorial, monument, remembrance, souvenir, token — more at MEMORIAL

keep up *vb* **1** ♦ : to persist or persevere in **2** ♦ : to keep in an existing state : MAINTAIN **3** : to keep informed **4** ♦ : to continue without interruption

 ♦ [1, 4] abide, continue, endure, hold, last, persist, run on — more at CONTINUE ♦ [2] conserve, maintain, preserve, save — more at MAINTAIN

keg \'keg\ *n* ♦ : a small cask or barrel

 ♦ barrel, cask, hogshead, pipe, puncheon — more at CASK

keg·ger \'ke-gər\ *n* : a party featuring one or more kegs of beer

keg·ler \'ke-glər\ *n* : ¹BOWLER

kelp \'kelp\ *n* : any of various coarse brown seaweeds; *also* : a mass of these or their ashes often used as fertilizer

kel·vin \'kel-vən\ *n* : a unit of temperature equal to ¹⁄₂₇₃.₁₆ of the Kelvin scale temperature of the triple point of water and equal to the Celsius degree

Kelvin *adj* : relating to, conforming to, or being a temperature scale according to which absolute zero is 0 K, the equivalent of −273.15°C

ken \'ken\ *n* **1** : range of vision : SIGHT **2** : range of understanding

ken·nel \'ken-ᵊl\ *n* : a shelter for a dog or cat; *also* : an establishment for the breeding or boarding of dogs or cats — **kennel** *vb*

ke·no \'kē-nō\ *n* : a game resembling bingo

ke·no·sis \kə-'nō-səs\ *n* : the relinquishment of divine attributes by Jesus Christ in becoming human — **ke·not·ic** \-'nä-tik\ *adj*

ken·te cloth \'ken-ˌtā-\ *n* : colorfully patterned cloth traditionally woven by hand in Ghana

Ken·tucky bluegrass \kən-'tə-kē-\ *n* : a valuable pasture and meadow grass of both Europe and America

Ken·yan \'ke-nyən, 'kē-\ *n* : a native or inhabitant of Kenya — **Kenyan** *adj*

Ke·ogh plan \'kē-(ˌ)ō-\ *n* [Eugene James *Keogh* †1989 Am. politician] : an individual retirement account for the self-employed

ke·pi \'kā-pē, 'ke-\ *n* [F] : a military cap with a round flat top and a visor

ker·a·tin \'ker-ət-ᵊn\ *n* : any of various sulfur-containing proteins that make up hair and horny tissues

kerb \'kərb\ *n, Brit* : CURB 3

ker·chief \'kər-chəf, -ˌchēf\ *n, pl* **kerchiefs** \-chəfs, -ˌchēfs\ *also* **kerchieves** \-ˌchēvz\ [ME *courchef*, fr. AF *coverchef, cuerchief,* fr. *coverir* to cover + *chef* head] **1** ♦ : a square of cloth worn by women esp. as a head covering **2** : HANDKERCHIEF

 ♦ babushka, bandanna, do-rag, mantilla — more at BANDANNA

kerf \'kərf\ *n* : a slit or notch made by a saw or cutting torch

ker·nel \'kərn-ᵊl\ *n* **1** : the inner softer part of a seed, fruit stone, or nut **2** : a whole seed of a cereal ⟨a ~ of corn⟩ **3** : a central or essential part : CORE

ker·o·sene *or* **ker·o·sine** \'ker-ə-ˌsēn, ˌker-ə-'sēn\ *n* : a flammable oil produced from petroleum and used for a fuel and as a solvent

kes·trel \\'kes-trəl\\ *n* : any of various small falcons that usu. hover in the air while searching for prey

ketch \\'kech\\ *n* : a large fore-and-aft rigged boat with two masts

ketch·up, catch·up \\'ke-chəp, 'ka-\\ *n* : a seasoned tomato puree

ket·tle \\'ket-ᵊl\\ *n* : a metallic vessel for boiling liquids

ket·tle·drum \-,drəm\ *n* : a brass, copper, or fiberglass drum with calfskin or plastic stretched across the top

¹key \\'kē\\ *n* **1** : a usu. metal instrument by which the bolt of a lock is turned; *also* : a device having the form or function of a key **2** : a means of gaining or preventing entrance, possession, or control **3** : EXPLANATION, SOLUTION **4** : one of the levers pressed by a finger in operating or playing an instrument **5** : a leading individual or principle **6** : a system of seven tones based on their relationship to a tonic; *also* : the tone or pitch of a voice **7** : a small switch for opening or closing an electric circuit ⟨a telegraph ∼⟩

²key *vb* **1** : SECURE, FASTEN **2** : to regulate the musical pitch of **3** ♦ : to bring into harmony or conformity **4** : to make nervous — usu. used with *up*

♦ accommodate, conciliate, conform, coordinate, harmonize, reconcile — more at HARMONIZE

³key *adj* ♦ : marked by or indicative of significant worth or consequence ⟨∼ issues⟩

♦ arch, cardinal, central, chief, dominant, first, foremost, grand, main, paramount, predominant, preeminent, premier, primary, principal, sovereign, supreme — more at FOREMOST ♦ critical, crucial, pivotal, vital — more at CRUCIAL

⁴key *n* ♦ : a low island or reef (as off the southern coast of Florida)

♦ cay, island, isle

⁵key *n, slang* : a kilogram esp. of marijuana or heroin

key·board \-,bōrd\ *n* **1** : a row of keys (as on a piano) **2** : an assemblage of keys for operating a machine

key chain *n* : a device used to hold keys that usu. consists of a metal ring, a short chain, and sometimes a small decoration

key club *n* : a private club serving liquor and providing entertainment

key·hole \\'kē-,hōl\\ *n* : a hole for receiving a key

¹key·note \-,nōt\ *n* **1** : the first and harmonically fundamental tone of a scale **2** : the central fact, idea, or mood

²keynote *vb* **1** : to set the keynote of **2** : to deliver the major address (as at a convention) — **key·not·er** *n*

key·punch \\'kē-,pənch\\ *n* : a machine with a keyboard used to cut holes or notches in punch cards — **keypunch** *vb* — **key·punch·er** *n*

key ring *n* : a usu. metal ring used to hold keys; *also* : KEY CHAIN

key·stone \-,stōn\ *n* **1** : the wedge-shaped piece at the crown of an arch that locks the other pieces in place **2** ♦ : something on which associated things depend for support

♦ base, basis, bedrock, cornerstone, footing, foundation, ground, groundwork, underpinning — more at CORNERSTONE

key·stroke \-,strōk\ *n* : an act or instance of depressing a key on a keyboard

key word *n* : a word that is a key; *esp, usu* **key·word** : a significant word from a title or document used esp. as an indication of the content

kg *abbr* kilogram

KGB *abbr* [Russ *Komitet gosudarstvennoĭ bezopasnosti*] (Soviet) State Security Committee

kha·ki \\'ka-kē, 'kä-\\ *n* [Hindi & Urdu *khākī* dust-colored, fr. *khāk* dust, fr. Pers] **1** : a light yellowish brown color **2** : a khaki-colored cloth; *also* : a military uniform of this cloth

khan \\'kän, 'kan\\ *n* : a Mongol leader; *esp* : a successor of Genghis Khan

khe·dive \kə-'dēv\ *n* : a ruler of Egypt from 1867 to 1914 governing as a viceroy of the sultan of Turkey

kHz *abbr* kilohertz

KIA *abbr* killed in action

kib·ble \\'ki-bəl\\ *vb* **kib·bled; kib·bling** : to grind coarsely — **kibble** *n*

kib·butz \ki-'büts, -'büts\ *n, pl* **kib·but·zim** \-,büt-'sēm, -,büt-\ [ModHeb *qibbūṣ*] : a communal farm or settlement in Israel

ki·bitz·er \\'ki-bət-sər, kə-'bit-\\ *n* ♦ : one who looks on and usu. offers unwanted advice esp. at a card game — **kib·itz** \\'ki-bəts\\ *vb*

♦ busybody, interloper, intruder, meddler — more at BUSYBODY

ki·bosh \\'kī-,bäsh\\ *n* : something that serves as a check or stop ⟨put the ∼ on his plan⟩

¹kick \\'kik\\ *vb* **1** : to strike out or hit with the foot; *also* : to score by kicking a ball **2** ♦ : to object strongly **3** : to recoil when fired — **kick·er** *n*

♦ beef, bellyache, complain, fuss, gripe, grouse, growl, grumble, moan, object, squawk, wail, whine — more at COMPLAIN

²kick *n* **1** : a blow or thrust with the foot; *esp* : a propelling of a ball with the foot **2** : the recoil of a gun **3** ♦ : a feeling or expression of objection **4** ♦ : stimulating effect esp. of pleasure

♦ [3] challenge, complaint, demur, expostulation, fuss, objection, protest, question, remonstrance — more at OBJECTION ♦ [4] bang, exhilaration, thrill, titillation — more at THRILL

kick·back \\'kik-,bak\\ *n* **1** : a sharp violent reaction **2** : a secret return of a part of a sum received

kick back *vb* ♦ : to assume a relaxed position or attitude

♦ bask, loll, lounge, relax, repose, rest — more at REST

kick·box·ing \\'kik-,bäk-siŋ\\ *n* : boxing in which boxers are permitted to kick with bare feet — **kick·box·er** \-sər\ *n*

kick in *vb* **1** ♦ : to give or supply in common with others : CONTRIBUTE **2** *slang* : DIE **3** : to begin operating or having an effect ⟨the caffeine started to *kick in*⟩

♦ chip in, contribute, pitch in — more at CONTRIBUTE

kick·off \\'kik-,of\\ *n* **1** : a kick that puts the ball in play (as in football) **2** : COMMENCEMENT

kick off *vb* **1** : to start or resume play with a placekick **2** : to begin proceedings ⟨*kick off* a campaign⟩ **3** *slang* : DIE

kick over *vb* : to begin or cause to begin to fire — used of an internal combustion engine

kick·shaw \\'kik-,sho\\ *n* [modif. of F *quelque chose* something] **1** : DELICACY **2** : TRINKET

kick·stand \\'kik-,stand\\ *n* : a swiveling metal bar attached to a 2-wheeled vehicle for holding it up when not in use

kick–start \\'kik-,stärt\\ *vb* : JUMP-START

kicky \\'ki-kē\\ *adj* : providing a kick or thrill : EXCITING; *also* : excitingly fashionable

¹kid \\'kid\\ *n* **1** : a young goat **2** : the flesh, fur, or skin of a young goat; *also* : something made of kid **3** ♦ : a young person : CHILD, YOUNGSTER

♦ child, cub, juvenile, youngster, youth — more at CHILD

²kid *vb* **kid·ded; kid·ding** **1** ♦ : to deceive as a joke : FOOL **2** ♦ : to make fun of **2** : TEASE — **kid·der** *n* — **kid·ding·ly** *adv*

♦ [1] banter, fool, fun, jest, jive, joke, josh, quip, wisecrack — more at JOKE ♦ [2] chaff, jive, josh, rally, razz, rib, ride, roast, tease — more at TEASE

kid·dish *adj* ♦ : marked by or suggestive of immaturity and lack of poise

♦ adolescent, babyish, childish, immature, infantile, juvenile — more at CHILDISH

kid·do \\'ki-dō\\ *n, pl* **kiddos** **1** — used as a familiar form of address ⟨you're okay, ∼⟩ **2** ♦ : a young person who is between infancy and adulthood : CHILD, KID

♦ child, cub, juvenile, kid, moppet, whelp, youngster, youth — more at CHILD

kid·nap \'kid-ˌnap\ vb **kid·napped** also **kid·naped** \-ˌnapt\; **kid·nap·ping** also **kid·nap·ing** \-ˌna-piŋ\ : to hold or carry a person away by unlawful force or by fraud and against one's will — **kid·nap·per** also **kid·nap·er** \-ˌna-pər\ n

kid·ney \'kid-nē\ n, pl **kidneys** : either of a pair of organs lying near the backbone that excrete waste products of the body in the form of urine

kidney bean n **1** : an edible seed of the common culti-vated bean; esp : one that is large and dark red **2** : a plant bearing kidney beans

kid·skin \'kid-ˌskin\ n : the skin of a young goat used for leather

kiel·ba·sa \kēl-'bä-sə, kil-\ n, pl **-basas** also **-ba·sy** \-'bä-sē\ [Pol kiełbasa] : a smoked sausage of Polish origin

¹kill \'kil\ vb **1** ♦ : to deprive of life **2** : to put an end to ⟨~ competition⟩; also : DEFEAT ⟨~ a proposed amend-ment⟩ **3** : USE UP ⟨~ time⟩ **4** : to mark for omission — **kill·er** n

♦ destroy, dispatch, do in, fell, slay; also annihilate, blot out, butcher, decimate, massacre, slaughter, wipe out; cut down, finish, nip, snuff; assassinate, execute, mur-der, smite **Ant** animate

²kill n **1** : an act of killing **2** : an animal or animals killed (as in a hunt); also : an aircraft, ship, or vehicle destroyed by military action

kill·deer \'kil-ˌdir\ n, pl **killdeers** or **killdeer** [imit.] : an American plover with a plaintive penetrating cry

killer app \-'ap\ n : a component (as a computer applica-tion) that in itself makes something worth having or using

killer bee n : AFRICANIZED BEE

killer whale n : a small gregarious black and white flesh-eat-ing whale with a white oval patch behind each eye

kill·ing n : a sudden notable gain or profit

killing field n : a scene of mass killing

kill·joy \'kil-ˌjȯi\ n : one who spoils the pleasures of others

kiln \'kil, 'kiln\ n [ME kilne, fr. OE cyln, fr. L culina kitchen] : a heated enclosure (as an oven) for processing a substance by burning, firing, or drying — **kiln** vb

ki·lo \'kē-lō\ n, pl **kilos** : KILOGRAM

ki·lo·byte \'ki-lə-ˌbīt, 'kē-\ n : 1024 bytes

kilo·cy·cle \'ki-lə-ˌsī-kəl\ n : KILOHERTZ

ki·lo·gram \'kē-lə-ˌgram, 'ki-\ n **1** : the basic metric unit of mass that is nearly equal to the mass of 1000 cubic centi-meters of water at its maximum density **2** : the weight of a kilogram mass under earth's gravity

ki·lo·hertz \'ki-lə-ˌhərts, 'kē-, -ˌherts\ n : 1000 hertz

kilo·li·ter \'ki-lə-ˌlē-tər\ n : a metric unit of capacity equal to 1000 liters

ki·lo·me·ter \ki-'lä-mə-tər, 'ki-lə-ˌmē-\ or Can and Brit **ki·lo·me·tre** n : a metric unit of length equal to 1000 me-ters

ki·lo·ton \'ki-lə-ˌtən, 'kē-lō-\ n **1** : 1000 tons **2** : an explo-sive force equivalent to that of 1000 tons of TNT

ki·lo·volt \-ˌvōlt\ n : 1000 volts

kilo·watt \'ki-lə-ˌwät\ n : 1000 watts

kilowatt–hour n : a unit of energy equal to that expended by one kilowatt in one hour

kilt \'kilt\ n : a knee-length pleated skirt usu. of tartan worn by men in Scotland

kil·ter \'kil-tər\ n ♦ : proper condition ⟨out of ~⟩

♦ condition, fettle, form, order, repair, shape, trim

ki·mo·no \kə-'mō-nə\ n, pl **-nos** **1** : a loose robe with wide sleeves traditionally worn with a wide sash as an outer garment by the Japanese **2** : a loose dressing gown or jacket

kin \'kin\ n **1** ♦ : an individual's relatives **2** ♦ : a person connected with another by blood or marriage : KINSMAN

♦ [1] blood, clan, family, folks, house, kindred, kin-folk, line, lineage, people, race, stock, tribe ♦ [2] kins-man, relation, relative — more at RELATIVE

ki·na·ra \kē-'nä-rə\ n : a candelabra with seven candle-sticks used during Kwanzaa

¹kind \'kīnd\ n **1** : essential quality or character **2** ♦ : a

group united by common traits or interests; also : VA-RIETY **3** : goods or commodities as distinguished from money

♦ breed, class, description, feather, ilk, like, manner, nature, order, sort, species, type, variety — more at SORT ♦ bracket, category, class, division, family, grade, group, set — more at CLASS

²kind adj **1** ♦ : of a sympathetic, forbearing, or pleasant nature **2** ♦ : arising from sympathy or forbearance ⟨~ deeds⟩

♦ [1] beneficent, benevolent, compassionate, good-hearted, humane, kindly, sympathetic, tender, tender-hearted, warmhearted — more at HUMANE ♦ [2] at-tentive, considerate, solicitous, thoughtful — more at THOUGHTFUL

kin·der·gar·ten \'kin-dər-ˌgärt-ᵊn\ n [G, lit., children's gar-den] : a school or class for children usu. from four to six years old

kin·der·gart·ner \-ˌgärt-nər\ n **1** : a kindergarten pupil **2** : a kindergarten teacher

kind·heart·ed \ˌkīnd-'här-təd\ adj : marked by a sympa-thetic nature

kin·dle \'kind-ᵊl\ vb **kin·dled**; **kin·dling** **1** ♦ : to set on fire : start burning **2** : to stir up : AROUSE **3** : ILLUMINATE, GLOW

♦ burn, fire, ignite, inflame, light — more at BURN

kind·li·ness n **1** ♦ : the quality or state of being kindly **2** : a kindly deed

♦ amity, benevolence, cordiality, fellowship, friend-liness, friendship, goodwill — more at GOODWILL ♦ charity, commiseration, compassion, feeling, heart, humanity, kindness, mercy, pity, sympathy — more at HEART

kin·dling \'kind-liŋ, 'kin-lən\ n : easily combustible mate-rial for starting a fire

¹kind·ly \'kīnd-lē\ adj **kind·li·er; -est** **1** : of an agreeable or beneficial nature **2** ♦ : of a sympathetic or generous nature

♦ beneficent, benevolent, compassionate, good-hearted, humane, kind, sympathetic, tender, tender-hearted, warmhearted — more at HUMANE

²kindly adv **1** : READILY ⟨does not take ~ to criticism⟩ **2** : SYMPATHETICALLY **3** ♦ : in a gracious manner : COURTEOUSLY

♦ courteously, nicely, thoughtfully, well — more at WELL

kind·ness n **1** ♦ : a kind deed **2** ♦ : the quality or state of being kind

♦ [1] boon, courtesy, favor (or favour), grace, indul-gence, mercy, service, turn ♦ [2] charity, commisera-tion, compassion, feeling, heart, humanity, kindliness, mercy, pity, sympathy — more at HEART

kind of adv ♦ : to a moderate degree ⟨it's kind of late to begin⟩

♦ enough, fairly, moderately, pretty, quite, rather, somewhat, sort of so-so — more at FAIRLY

¹kin·dred \'kin-drəd\ n **1** ♦ : a group of related individuals **2** : one's relatives

♦ blood, clan, family, folks, house, kin, kinfolk, line, lineage, people, race, stock, tribe

²kindred adj ♦ : of a like nature or character

♦ akin, related — more at RELATED

kine \'kīn\ archaic pl of COW

ki·ne·mat·ics \ˌki-nə-'ma-tiks\ n : a science that deals with motion apart from considerations of mass and force — **ki·ne·mat·ic** \-tik\ or **ki·ne·mat·i·cal** \-ti-kəl\ adj

kin·es·the·sia \ˌki-nəs-'thē-zhə, -zhē-ə\ or **kin·es·the·sis** \-'thē-səs\ n, pl **-the·sias** or **-the·ses** \-ˌsēz\ : a sense that perceives bodily movement, position, and weight and is mediated by nervous receptors in tendons, muscles, and joints; also : sensory experience derived from this sense — **kin·es·thet·ic** \-'the-tik\ adj

ki·net·ic \kə-'ne-tik\ *adj* : of or relating to the motion of material bodies and the forces and energy (**kinetic energy**) associated with them

ki·net·ics \-tiks\ *n sing or pl* : a science that deals with the effects of forces upon the motions of material bodies or with changes in a physical or chemical system

kin·folk \'kin-ˌfōk\ *or* **kinfolks** *n pl* ♦ : persons connected with each other by blood or affinity : RELATIVES

♦ blood, clan, family, folks, house, kin, kindred, line, lineage, people, race, stock, tribe

king \'kiŋ\ *n* 1 : a male monarch 2 ♦ : a chief among competitors ⟨home-run ∼⟩ 3 : the principal piece in the game of chess 4 : a playing card bearing the figure of a king 5 : a checker that has been crowned — **king·less** *adj* — **king·ship** *n*

♦ baron, czar, magnate, mogul, prince, tycoon — more at MAGNATE

king crab *n* 1 : HORSESHOE CRAB 2 : a large crab of the No. Pacific caught commercially for food

king·dom \'kiŋ-dəm\ *n* 1 : a country whose head is a king or queen 2 : a realm or region in which something or someone is dominant ⟨a cattle ∼⟩ 3 : one of the three primary divisions of lifeless material, plants, and animals into which natural objects are grouped; *also* : a biological category that ranks above the phylum

king·fish·er \-ˌfi-shər\ *n* : any of numerous usu. bright-colored crested birds that feed chiefly on fish

king·ly *adj* 1 : of, relating to, or befitting a king 2 ♦ : of, relating to, suggestive of, or characteristic of a monarch or monarchy

♦ monarchical, princely, queenly, regal, royal — more at MONARCHICAL

king·pin \'kiŋ-ˌpin\ *n* 1 : HEADPIN 2 ♦ : the leader in a group or undertaking

♦ boss, captain, chief, foreman, head, headman, helmsman, leader, master, taskmaster — more at BOSS

Kings *n* : either of two books of Jewish and Christian Scripture

king–size \'kiŋ-ˌsīz\ *or* **king–sized** \-ˌsīzd\ *adj* 1 : longer than the regular or standard size 2 : unusually large 3 : having dimensions of about 76 by 80 inches (1.9 by 2.0 meters) ⟨a ∼ bed⟩; *also* : of a size that fits a king-size bed

kink \'kiŋk\ *n* 1 : a short tight twist or curl 2 : a mental peculiarity : QUIRK 3 : CRAMP ⟨a ∼ in the back⟩ 4 : an imperfection likely to cause difficulties in operation

kinky *adj* ♦ : strikingly out of the ordinary

♦ bizarre, curious, far-out, funny, odd, outlandish, outré, peculiar, quaint, queer, quirky, remarkable, screwy, strange, wacky, weird, wild — more at ODD

kin·ship \'kin-ˌship\ *n* ♦ : the quality or state of being kin : RELATIONSHIP

♦ association, bearing, connection, liaison, linkage, relation, relationship — more at CONNECTION

kins·man \'kinz-mən\ *n* ♦ : a person connected with another by blood or marriage : RELATIVE; *esp* : a male relative

♦ kin, relation, relative — more at RELATIVE

kins·wom·an \-ˌwů-mən\ *n* : a female relative

ki·osk \'kē-ˌäsk\ *n* 1 : a small structure with one or more open sides 2 : a stand-alone device providing information and services on a computer screen

Ki·o·wa \'kī-ə-ˌwȯ, -ˌwä, -ˌwä\ *n, pl* **Kiowa** *or* **Kiowas** : a member of an American Indian people of Colorado, Kansas, New Mexico, Oklahoma, and Texas

kip·per \'ki-pər\ *n* : a fish (as a herring) preserved by salting and drying or smoking — **kipper** *vb*

kirk \'kərk, 'kirk\ *n, chiefly Scot* : CHURCH

kir·tle \'kərt-ᵊl\ *n* : a long gown or dress worn by women

kis·met \'kiz-ˌmet, -mət\ *n, often cap* [Turk, fr. Ar *qisma* portion, lot] : FATE

¹**kiss** \'kis\ *vb* 1 : to touch or caress with the lips as a mark of affection or greeting 2 ♦ : to touch gently or lightly

♦ brush, graze, nick, shave, skim — more at BRUSH

²**kiss** *n* 1 : a caress with the lips 2 : a gentle touch or contact 3 : a bite-size candy

kiss·er \'ki-sər\ *n* 1 : one that kisses 2 *slang* : MOUTH 3 *slang* : FACE

kit \'kit\ *n* 1 : a set of articles for personal use; *also* : a set of tools or implements or of parts to be assembled 2 : a container (as a case) for a kit

kitch·en \'ki-chən\ *n* 1 : a room with cooking facilities 2 : the staff that prepares, cooks, and serves food

kitch·en·ette \ˌki-chə-'net\ *n* : a small kitchen or an alcove containing cooking facilities

kitchen police *n* 1 : KP 2 : the work of KPs

kitch·en·ware \'ki-chən-ˌwar\ *n* : utensils and appliances for kitchen use

kite \'kīt\ *n* 1 : any of various long-winged hawks often with deeply forked tails 2 : a light frame covered with paper or cloth and designed to be flown in the air at the end of a long string

kith \'kith\ *n* [ME, fr. OE *cȳthth*, fr. *cūth* known] : familiar friends, neighbors, or relatives ⟨∼ and kin⟩

kitsch \'kich\ *n* [G] : something often of poor quality that appeals to popular or lowbrow taste — **kitschy** *adj*

kit·ten \'kit-ᵊn\ *n* : a young cat

kit·ten·ish *adj* ♦ : resembling or suggestive of a kitten; *esp* : coyly playful

♦ coquettish, coy, demure — more at COY

¹**kit·ty** \'ki-tē\ *n, pl* **kitties** ♦ : a carnivorous mammal long domesticated as a pet and for catching rats and mice : CAT; *esp* : KITTEN

♦ cat, feline, puss — more at CAT

²**kitty** *n, pl* **kitties** ♦ : a fund in a poker game made up of contributions from each pot; *also* : POOL

♦ account, budget, deposit, fund, nest egg, pool — more at FUND

kit·ty–cor·ner *also* **cat·ty–cor·ner** *or* **cat·er·cor·ner** \'ki-tē-ˌkȯr-nər, 'ka-; 'ka-tə-\ *or* **kit·ty–cor·nered** *or* **cat·ty–cor·nered** *or* **cat·er·cornered** \-nərd\ *adv or adj* : in a diagonal or oblique position

ki·wi \'kē-(ˌ)wē\ *n* 1 : any of a small genus of flightless New Zealand birds 2 : KIWIFRUIT

ki·wi·fruit \-ˌfrüt\ *n* : a brownish hairy egg-shaped fruit of a subtropical vine that has sweet bright green flesh and small edible black seeds

KJV *abbr* King James Version

KKK *abbr* Ku Klux Klan

kl *abbr* kiloliter

klatch *or* **klatsch** \'klach\ *n* [G *Klatsch* gossip] : a gathering marked by informal conversation

klep·toc·ra·cy \klep-'tä-krə-sē\ *n, pl* **-cies** : government by those who seek chiefly status and personal gain at the expense of the governed

klep·to·ma·nia \ˌklep-tə-'mā-nē-ə\ *n* : a persistent neurotic impulse to steal esp. without economic motive — **klep·to·ma·ni·ac** \-nē-ˌak\ *n*

klieg light *or* **kleig light** \'klēg-\ *n* : a very bright lamp used in making motion pictures

klutz \'kləts\ *n* [Yiddish *klots*, lit., wooden beam] : a clumsy person — **klutzy** *adj*

km *abbr* kilometer

kn *abbr* knot

knack \'nak\ *n* 1 : a clever way of doing something 2 ♦ : natural aptitude

♦ aptitude, endowment, faculty, flair, genius, gift, talent — more at TALENT

knap·sack \'nap-ˌsak\ *n* : a bag (as of canvas) strapped on the back and used esp. for carrying supplies

knave \'nāv\ *n* 1 ♦ : a tricky deceitful fellow : ROGUE 2 : JACK 6

♦ beast, devil, evildoer, fiend, no-good, reprobate, rogue, varlet, villain, wretch — more at VILLAIN

knav·ery \'nā-və-rē\ *n* ♦ : the character or actions of a rascal; *also* : a roguish or mischievous act

♦ devilishness, impishness, mischief, mischievousness, rascality, shenanigans, waggery, wickedness — more at MISCHIEF

knav·ish \'nā-vish\ *adj* ♦ : of, relating to, or characteristic of a knave

♦ devilish, impish, mischievous, rascally, roguish, sly, waggish, wicked — more at MISCHIEVOUS

knead \'nēd\ *vb* : to work and press into a mass with the hands; *also* : MASSAGE — **knead·er** *n*

knee \'nē\ *n* : the joint in the middle part of the leg — **kneed** \'nēd\ *adj*

knee·cap \'nē-ˌkap\ *n* : a thick flat triangular movable bone forming the front of the knee

knee·hole \-ˌhōl\ *n* : a space (as under a desk) for the knees

knee–jerk \'nē-ˌjərk\ *adj* : readily predictable ⟨a ∼ reaction⟩

kneel \'nēl\ *vb* **knelt** \'nelt\ *or* **kneeled; kneel·ing** : to bend the knee : fall or rest on the knees

¹**knell** \'nel\ *vb* **1** ♦ : to ring esp. for a death or disaster **2** : to summon, announce, or proclaim by a knell

♦ chime, peal, ring, toll — more at RING

²**knell** *n* **1** : a stroke of a bell esp. when tolled (as for a funeral) **2** : an indication of the end or failure of something

knew *past of* KNOW

knick·ers \'ni-kərz\ *n pl* : loose-fitting short pants gathered at the knee

knick·knack \'nik-ˌnak\ *n* ♦ : a small trivial article intended for ornament

♦ bauble, curiosity, gewgaw, novelty, tchotchke, trinket; *also* bric-a-brac, trumpery; trifle; figurine, objet d'art, ornament; souvenir

¹**knife** \'nīf\ *n, pl* **knives** \'nīvz\ **1** : a cutting instrument consisting of a sharp blade fastened to a handle **2** : a sharp cutting tool in a machine

²**knife** *vb* **knifed; knif·ing** : to stab, slash, or wound with a knife

¹**knight** \'nīt\ *n* **1** : a mounted warrior of feudal times serving a king **2** : a man honored by a sovereign for merit and in Great Britain ranking below a baronet **3** : a man devoted to the service of a lady **4** : a member of an order or society **5** : a chess piece having an L-shaped move — **knight·ly** *adj*

²**knight** *vb* : to make a knight of

knight·hood \'nīt-ˌhu̇d\ *n* **1** : the rank, dignity, or profession of a knight **2** : CHIVALRY **3** : knights as a class or body

knish \kə-'nish\ *n* [Yiddish] : a small round or square of dough stuffed with a filling (as of meat or fruit) and baked or fried

¹**knit** \'nit\ *vb* **knit** *or* **knit·ted; knit·ting 1** : to link firmly or closely **2** : WRINKLE ⟨∼ her brows⟩ **3** : to form a fabric by interlacing yarn or thread in connected loops with needles **4** : to grow together — **knit·ter** *n*

²**knit** *n* **1** : a basic knitting stitch **2** : a knitted garment or fabric

knit·wear \-ˌwar\ *n* : knitted clothing

knob \'näb\ *n* **1** : a rounded protuberance; *also* : a small rounded ornament or handle **2** : a rounded usu. isolated hill — **knobbed** \'näbd\ *adj* — **knob·by** \'nä-bē\ *adj*

¹**knock** \'näk\ *vb* **1** : to strike with a sharp blow **2** ♦ : to collide with something : BUMP **3** : to make a pounding noise; *esp* : to have engine knock **4** ♦ : to find fault with **5** ♦ : to move about without a fixed course, aim, or goal

♦ [2] bang, bash, bump, collide, crash, hit, impact, ram, slam, smash, strike, swipe, thud — more at HIT ♦ [4] blame, censure, condemn, criticize, denounce, fault, pan, reprehend — more at CRITICIZE ♦ [5] gad, gallivant, maunder, meander, mope, ramble, range, roam, rove, traipse, wander — more at WANDER

²**knock** *n* **1** : a sharp blow **2** : a pounding noise; *esp* : one caused by abnormal ignition in an automobile engine **3** ♦ : a severe misfortune or hardship

♦ adversity, misadventure, mischance, misfortune, mishap — more at MISFORTUNE

knock·down \'näk-ˌdau̇n\ *n* **1** : the action of knocking down **2** : something (as a blow) that knocks down **3** : something that can be easily assembled or disassembled

knock down *vb* **1** ♦ : to strike to the ground with or as if with as sharp blow **2** ♦ : to take apart : DISASSEMBLE **3** : to receive as income or salary : EARN **4** : to make a reduction in

♦ [1] bowl, down, drop, fell, floor, level ♦ [2] disassemble, dismantle, strike, take down — more at DISASSEMBLE

knock·er \'nä-kər\ *n* : one that knocks; *esp* : a device hinged to a door for use in knocking

knock–knee \'näk-ˌnē\ *n* : a condition in which the legs curve inward at the knees — **knock–kneed** \-ˌnēd\ *adj*

knock·off \'näk-ˌȯf\ *n* : a copy or imitation of someone or something popular

knock off *vb* **1** ♦ : to stop doing something **2** : to do quickly, carelessly, or routinely **3** : to deduct from a price **4** : KILL **5** : ROB **6** : COPY, IMITATE

♦ break, break off, cease, cut, desist, discontinue, drop, end, halt, layoff, leave off, quit, shut off, stop — more at STOP

knock·out \'näk-ˌau̇t\ *n* **1** : a blow that fells and immobilizes an opponent (as in boxing) **2** ♦ : something sensationally striking or attractive **3** ♦ : the act of knocking out; *also* : the condition of being knocked out

♦ [2] beauty, dream, enchantress, fox, goddess, queen — more at BEAUTY ♦ [2] beauty, crackerjack, dandy, jim-dandy, pip — more at JIM-DANDY ♦ [3] blackout, faint, swoon — more at FAINT

knock out *vb* **1** : to defeat by a knockout **2** : to make unconscious or inoperative **3** : to tire out : EXHAUST

knock·wurst *also* **knack·wurst** \'näk-ˌwərst, -ˌvu̇rst\ *n* : a short thick heavily seasoned sausage

knoll \'nōl\ *n* : a small round hill

¹**knot** \'nät\ *n* **1** : an interlacing (as of string) forming a lump or knob and often used for fastening or tying together **2** ♦ : something hard to solve : PROBLEM **3** ♦ : a bond of union; *esp* : the marriage bond **4** ♦ : a protuberant lump or swelling in tissue **5** : a rounded cross-grained area in lumber that is a section through the junction of a tree branch with the trunk; *also* : the woody tissue forming this junction in a tree **6** : a cluster of persons or things : GROUP **7** : an ornamental bow of ribbon **8** : one nautical mile per hour; *also* : one nautical mile

♦ [2] case, matter, problem, trouble — more at PROBLEM ♦ [3] bond, cement, ligature, link, tie — more at BOND ♦ [4] bump, lump, nodule, swelling — more at BUMP

²**knot** *vb* **knot·ted; knot·ting 1** : to tie in or with a knot **2** ♦ : to unite closely or intricately : ENTANGLE

♦ entangle, interlace, intertwine, interweave, snarl, tangle — more at ENTANGLE

knot·hole \-ˌhōl\ *n* : a hole in a board or tree trunk where a knot has come out

knot·ty *adj* ♦ : marked by or full of knots; *esp* : so full of difficulties and complications as to be likely to defy solution

♦ complex, complicated, convoluted, elaborate, intricate, involved, sophisticated — more at COMPLEX ♦ catchy, delicate, difficult, problematic, spiny, thorny, ticklish, touchy, tough, tricky — more at TRICKY

knout \'naut, 'nüt\ *n* : a whip used for flogging

know \'nō\ *vb* **knew** \'nü, 'nyü\; **known** \'nōn\; **know·ing 1** ♦ : to perceive directly : have understanding or direct cognition of; *also* : to recognize the nature of **2** : to be acquainted or familiar with **3** : to be aware of the truth of **4** ♦ : to have a practical understanding of — **know·able** *adj* — **know·er** *n* — **in the know** : possessing confidential information

♦ [1] endure, experience, feel, have, see, suffer, sustain, taste, undergo — more at EXPERIENCE ♦ [4] comprehend, grasp, understand; *also* appreciate, apprehend, fathom, perceive; have, possess

know–how \'nō-ˌhaú\ *n* ♦ : knowledge of how to do something smoothly and efficiently

♦ experience, expertise, proficiency, savvy — more at EXPERIENCE

knowing *adj* **1** : having or reflecting knowledge, intelligence, or information **2** ♦ : shrewdly and keenly alert **3** : DELIBERATE, INTENTIONAL

♦ astute, canny, hardheaded, sharp, shrewd, smart — more at SHREWD

know·ing·ly *adv* ♦ : in a knowing manner; *esp* : with awareness, deliberateness, or intention

♦ consciously, deliberately, intentionally, purposely, willfully — more at INTENTIONALLY

knowl·edge \'nä-lij\ *n* **1** : understanding gained by actual experience ⟨a ∼ of carpentry⟩ **2** : range of information ⟨to the best of my ∼⟩ **3** : clear perception of truth **4** ♦ : something learned and kept in the mind **5** ♦ : acquaintance with or understanding of a science, art, or technique

♦ [4] intelligence, lore, science, wisdom ♦ [5] education, erudition, learning, scholarship, science — more at EDUCATION

knowl·edge·able \'nä-li-jə-bəl\ *adj* ♦ : having or showing knowledge or intelligence

♦ abreast, conversant, familiar, informed, up, up-to-date, versed — more at FAMILIAR ♦ educated, erudite, learned, literate, scholarly, well-read — more at EDUCATED

know–noth·ing \'nō-ˌnə-thiŋ\ *n* ♦ : an utterly ignorant person : IGNORAMUS

♦ blockhead, dope, dummy, idiot, imbecile, jackass, moron, numskull — more at IDIOT

knuck·le \'nə-kəl\ *n* : the rounded knob at a joint and esp. at a finger joint

knuckle down *vb* : to apply oneself earnestly

knuckle under *vb* ♦ : to yield under insistence or entreaty : SUBMIT, SURRENDER

♦ blink, bow, budge, capitulate, concede, give in, quit, submit, succumb, surrender, yield — more at YIELD

knurl \'nərl\ *n* **1** : KNOB **2** : one of a series of small ridges on a metal surface to aid in gripping — **knurled** \'nərld\ *adj* — **knurly** *adj*

¹**KO** \(ˌ)kā-'ō, 'kā-ō\ *n* : KNOCKOUT

²**KO** *vb* **KO'd; KO'·ing** : to knock out in boxing

ko·ala \kō-'ä-lə\ *n* : a gray furry Australian marsupial that has large hairy ears and feeds on eucalyptus leaves

K of C *abbr* Knights of Columbus

kohl·ra·bi \kōl-'rä-bē\ *n, pl* **-bies** [G, fr. It *cavolo rapa*, lit., cabbage turnip] : a cabbage that forms no head but has a swollen fleshy edible stem

koi \'kói\ *n, pl* **koi** [Jp] : a carp bred for large size and a variety of colors and often stocked in ornamental ponds

ko·lin·sky \kə-'lin-skē\ *n, pl* **-skies** : the fur of various Asian minks

Ko·mo·do dragon \kə-'mō-dō-\ *n* [*Komodo* Island, Indonesia] : a carnivorous lizard of Indonesia that is the largest of all known lizards

kook \'kük\ *n* ♦ : one whose ideas or actions are eccentric, fantastic, or insane : SCREWBALL

♦ character, crackpot, crank, eccentric, nut, oddball, screwball, weirdo — more at ECCENTRIC

kooky *also* **kook·ie** \'kü-kē\ *adj* **kook·i·er; -est** ♦ : having the characteristics of a kook : CRAZY — **kook·i·ness** *n*

♦ absurd, crazy, cuckoo, fatuous, foolish, mad, nonsensical, nutty, senseless, silly, stupid — more at FOOLISH

Koo·te·nai *or* **Ku·te·nai** \'kü-tə-ˌnā\ *n, pl* **-nai** *or* **-nais** : a member of an American Indian people of the Rocky Mountains in both the U.S. and Canada; *also* : their language

ko·ra \'kòr-ə\ *n* : a 21-stringed African musical instrument

Ko·ran *or* **Qur·an** *also* **Qur·'an** \kə-'ran, -'rän\ *n* [Ar *qur'ān*] : a sacred book of Islam that contains revelations made to Muhammad by Allah

Ko·re·an \kə-'rē-ən\ *n* : a native or inhabitant of Korea — **Korean** *adj*

ko·sher \'kō-shər\ *adj* [Yiddish, fr. Heb *kāshēr* fit, proper] **1** : ritually fit for use according to Jewish law **2** : selling or serving kosher food

kow·tow \kaú-'taú, 'kaú-ˌtaú\ *vb* [Chin *kòutóu*, fr. *kòu* to knock + *tóu* head] **1** ♦ : to show obsequious deference **2** : to kneel and touch the forehead to the ground as a sign of homage or deep respect

♦ fawn, fuss, toady — more at FAWN

KP \ˌkā-'pē\ *n* **1** : an enlisted person detailed to help the cooks in a military mess **2** : the work of KPs

kph *abbr* kilometers per hour

Kr *symbol* krypton

kraal \'kräl, 'kròl\ *n* **1** : a native village in southern Africa **2** : an enclosure for domestic animals in southern Africa

kraut \'kraút\ *n* : SAUERKRAUT

Krem·lin \'krem-lən\ *n* : the Russian government

Krem·lin·ol·o·gist \ˌkrem-lə-'nä-lə-jist\ *n* : a specialist in the policies and practices of the former Soviet government

Kru·ger·rand \'krü-gər-ˌrand, -ˌränd\ *n* : a 1-ounce gold coin of the Republic of South Africa

kryp·ton \'krip-ˌtän\ *n* : a gaseous chemical element used esp. in electric lamps

KS *abbr* Kansas

kt *abbr* **1** karat **2** knight

ku·do \'kü-dō, 'kyü-\ *n, pl* **ku·dos** [fr. *kudos* (taken as pl.)] **1** : AWARD, HONOR **2** : COMPLIMENT, PRAISE

ku·dos \'kü-ˌdäs, 'kyü-\ *n* : fame and renown resulting from achievement

kud·zu \'kùd-zü, 'kəd-\ *n* [Jp *kuzu*] : a fast-growing weedy leguminous vine used for forage and erosion control

ku·lak \kü-'lak, kyü-, -'läk\ *n* [Russ, lit., fist] **1** : a wealthy peasant farmer in 19th century Russia **2** : a farmer characterized by Communists as too wealthy

kum·quat \'kəm-ˌkwät\ *n* : any of several small citrus fruits with sweet spongy rind and acid pulp

kung fu \ˌkəŋ-'fü, ˌkúŋ-\ *n* : a Chinese art of self-defense resembling karate

kung pao \'kəŋ-ˌpaú, 'küŋ-, 'kùŋ-\ *adj* : being stir-fried or deep-fried and served in a spicy hot sauce usu. with peanuts

kur·ta \'kər-tə\ *n* : a long loose-fitting collarless shirt

ku·rus \kə-'rüsh\ *n, pl* **kurus** : a Turkish piaster equal to ¹⁄₁₀₀ lira

Ku·waiti \kù-'wā-tē\ *n* : a native or inhabitant of Kuwait — **Kuwaiti** *adj*

kV *abbr* kilovolt

kvell \'kvel\ *vb* : to be extraordinarily proud

kvetch \'kvech, 'kfech\ *vb* : to complain habitually — **kvetch** *n*

kW *abbr* kilowatt

Kwan·zaa, Kwan·za \'kwän-zə\ *n* [Swahili *kwanza* first] : an African American cultural festival held from December 26 to January 1

kwash·i·or·kor \ˌkwä-shē-'òr-kòr, -òr-'kòr\ *n* : a disease of young children caused by deficient intake of protein

kWh *abbr* kilowatt-hour

Ky *or* **KY** *abbr* Kentucky

L

¹l \\'el\\ *n, pl* **l's** *or* **ls** \\'elz\\ *often cap* : the 12th letter of the English alphabet

²l *abbr, often cap* **1** lake **2** large **3** left **4** [L *libra*] pound **5** line **6** liter

¹La *abbr* Louisiana

²La *symbol* lanthanum

LA *abbr* **1** law agent **2** Los Angeles **3** Louisiana

lab \\'lab\\ *n* : LABORATORY

Lab *n* : LABRADOR RETRIEVER

¹la·bel \\'lā-bəl\\ *n* **1** ♦ : a slip attached to something for identification or description **2** : a descriptive or identifying word or phrase **3** : BRAND 3

   ♦ marker, tag, ticket; *also* caption, legend; brand, emblem, logo, mark, symbol; badge, decal, plaque, seal, stamp, sticker

²label *vb* **-beled** *or* **-belled; -bel·ing** *or* **-bel·ling** **1** ♦ : to affix a label to **2** ♦ : to describe or name with a label

   ♦ [1] mark, tag, ticket; *also* caption, earmark, stamp; call, designate, identify, name, tab; brand, stigmatize ♦ [2] baptize, call, christen, denominate, designate, dub, entitle, name, style, term, title — more at NAME

la·bi·al \\'lā-bē-əl\\ *adj* : of, relating to, or situated near the lips or labia

la·bia ma·jo·ra \\'lā-bē-ə-mə-'jȯr-ə\\ *n pl* : the outer fatty folds of the vulva

labia mi·no·ra \\-mə-'nȯr-ə\\ *n pl* : the inner highly vascular folds of the vulva

la·bile \\'lā-,bī(-ə)l, -bəl\\ *adj* **1** : UNSTABLE **2** : ADAPTABLE

la·bi·um \\'lā-bē-əm\\ *n, pl* **la·bia** \\-ə\\ [NL, fr. L, lip] : any of the folds at the margin of the vulva

¹la·bor *or Can and Brit* **la·bour** \\'lā-bər\\ *n* **1** ♦ : physical or mental effort; *also* : human activity that provides the goods or services in an economy **2** ♦ : the physical efforts of giving birth; *also* : the period of such labor **3** ♦ : an act or process requiring labor **4** : those who do manual labor or work for wages; *also* : labor unions or their officials

   ♦ [1] effort, exertion, expenditure, pains, sweat, trouble, while, work — more at EFFORT ♦ [2] childbirth, delivery — more at CHILDBIRTH ♦ [3] drudgery, grind, slavery, sweat, toil, travail — more at TOIL

²labor *or Can and Brit* **labour** *vb* **1** ♦ : to exert oneself physically or mentally esp. with painful or strenuous effort : WORK **2** : to move with great effort **3** : to be in the labor of giving birth **4** : to suffer from some disadvantage or distress ⟨∼ under a delusion⟩ **5** : to treat or work out laboriously

   ♦ drudge, endeavor (*or* endeavour), fag, grub, hustle, peg, plod, plug, slave, slog, strain, strive, struggle, sweat, toil, work; *also* apply (oneself), attempt, buckle (down), hammer (away), pitch in; attack, drive; essay, try; exercise, exert, overexert, overwork; eke out, grind (out), put out, scratch; trudge, wade; employ, ply, use, utilize, wield **Ant** dabble, fiddle (around), fool (around), mess (around), putter (around)

lab·o·ra·to·ry \\'la-brə-,tȯr-ē, -bə-rə-\\ *n, pl* **-ries** : a place equipped for making scientific experiments or tests

Labor Day *or Can* **Labour Day** *n* : the 1st Monday in September observed as a legal holiday in recognition of the working people

la·bored *or Can and Brit* **la·boured** \\'lā-bərd\\ *adj* : not freely or easily done ⟨∼ breathing⟩

la·bor·er *or Can and Brit* **la·bour·er** *n* : one that labors; *specif* : a person who does unskilled physical work for wages

la·bo·ri·ous \\lə-'bȯr-ē-əs\\ *adj* **1** ♦ : devoted to labor : INDUSTRIOUS **2** ♦ : requiring great effort

   ♦ [1] active, assiduous, busy, diligent, engaged, industrious, occupied, sedulous, working — more at BUSY ♦ [2] arduous, challenging, demanding, difficult, exacting, formidable, grueling, hard, onerous, rough, stiff, strenuous, tall, taxing, toilsome, tough — more at HARD

la·bo·ri·ous·ly *adv* ♦ : in a laborious manner

   ♦ determinedly, diligently, hard, hardly, mightily, slavishly, strenuously, tirelessly — more at HARD

la·bor·sav·ing *or Can and Brit* **labour–saving** \\'lā-bər-,sā-viŋ\\ *adj* ♦ : designed to replace or decrease labor

   ♦ automatic, robotic, self-acting; *also* mechanical, motorized; computerized; aiding, helping; easing, relieving

labor union *n* : an organization of workers formed to advance its members' interest in respect to wages and working conditions

la·bour *Can and Brit var of* LABOR

lab·ra·dor·ite \\'la-brə-,dȯr-,īt\\ *n* : an iridescent feldspar used in jewelry

Lab·ra·dor retriever \\'la-brə-,dȯr-\\ *n* : any of a breed of strongly built retrievers having a short dense black, yellow, or chocolate coat

la·bur·num \\lə-'bər-nəm\\ *n* : any of a genus of leguminous shrubs or trees having hanging clusters of yellow flowers

lab·y·rinth \\'la-bə-,rinth\\ *n* : a place constructed of or filled with confusing intricate passageways : MAZE

lab·y·rin·thine \\,la-bə-'rin-thən, -,thīn, -,thēn\\ *adj* : INTRICATE, INVOLVED ⟨a ∼ plot⟩ ⟨∼ hallways⟩

lac \\'lak\\ *n* : a resinous substance secreted by a scale insect and used chiefly in the form of shellac

¹lace \\'lās\\ *vb* **laced; lac·ing** **1** : TIE **2** ♦ : to adorn with or as if with lace ⟨countryside *laced* with small villages⟩ **3** ♦ : to unite by twining one with another : INTERTWINE **4** : to hit repeatedly : BEAT **5** : to add something to impart zest or savor to **6** : to criticize sharply — used with *into* ⟨*laced* into her opponents⟩

   ♦ interlace, intersperse, intertwine, interweave, thread, weave, wreathe — more at THREAD

²lace *n* [ME, fr. AF *lace, laz,* fr. L *laqueus* snare] **1** ♦ : a cord or string used for drawing together two edges **2** ♦ : an ornamental braid **3** : a fine openwork usu. figured fabric made of thread — **lacy** \\'lā-sē\\ *adj*

   ♦ [1] cable, cord, line, rope, string, wire — more at CORD ♦ [2] braid, plait — more at BRAID

lac·er·ate \\'la-sə-,rāt\\ *vb* **-at·ed; -at·ing** : to tear roughly

lac·er·a·tion \\,la-sə-'rā-shən\\ *n* ♦ : a torn and ragged wound

   ♦ gash, rent, rip, slash, slit, tear — more at GASH

lace·wing \\'lās-,wiŋ\\ *n* : any of various insects with delicate wing veins, long antennae, and often brilliant eyes

lach·ry·mal *or* **lac·ri·mal** \\'la-krə-məl\\ *adj* **1** *usu* lacrimal : of, relating to, or being glands that produce tears **2** : of, relating to, or marked by tears

lach·ry·mose \\'la-krə-,mōs\\ *adj* **1** : TEARFUL **2** : MOURNFUL

¹lack \\'lak\\ *vb* **1** : to be wanting or missing **2** : to be deficient in ⟨∼s experience⟩

²lack *n* ♦ : the fact or state of being wanting or deficient

   ♦ dearth, deficiency, deficit, failure, famine, inadequacy, insufficiency, paucity, poverty, scantiness, scarcity, shortage, want — more at DEFICIENCY ♦ absence, need, want — more at NEED

lack·a·dai·si·cal \\,la-kə-'dā-zi-kəl\\ *adj* ♦ : lacking life, spirit, or zest — **lack·a·dai·si·cal·ly** \\-k(ə-)lē\\ *adv*

   ♦ enervated, languid, languorous, limp, listless, spiritless — more at LISTLESS

lack·ey \'la-kē\ *n, pl* **lackeys** **1** ♦ : someone who does tasks or errands for another : FOOTMAN, SERVANT **2** : TOADY

♦ domestic, flunky, menial, retainer, servant, steward — more at SERVANT

lack·lus·ter *or Can and Brit* **lack·lus·tre** \'lak-ˌləs-tər\ *adj* : DULL

la·con·ic \lə-'kä-nik\ *adj* [L *laconicus* Spartan, fr. Gk *lakōnikos*; fr. the Spartan reputation for terseness of speech] ♦ : sparing of words : TERSE

♦ brief, compact, compendious, concise, crisp, epigrammatic, pithy, succinct, summary, terse — more at CONCISE

la·con·i·cal·ly \-ni-k(ə-)lē\ *adv* ♦ : in a laconic manner

♦ compactly, concisely, crisply, shortly, succinctly, summarily, tersely — more at SHORTLY

lac·quer \'la-kər\ *n* : a clear or colored usu. glossy and quick-drying surface coating — **lacquer** *vb*

lac·ri·ma·tion \ˌla-krə-'mā-shən\ *n* : secretion of tears

la·crosse \lə-'krós\ *n* [CanF *la crosse*, lit., the crooked stick] : a goal game in which players use a long-handled triangular-headed stick having a mesh pouch for catching, carrying, and throwing the ball

lac·tate \'lak-ˌtāt\ *vb* **lac·tat·ed; lac·tat·ing** : to secrete milk — **lac·ta·tion** \lak-'tā-shən\ *n*

lac·tic \'lak-tik\ *adj* **1** : of or relating to milk **2** : obtained from sour milk or whey

lactic acid *n* : a syrupy acid present in blood and muscle tissue and used esp. in food and medicine

lac·tose \'lak-ˌtōs\ *n* : a sugar present in milk

la·cu·na \lə-'kü-nə, -'kyü-\ *n, pl* **la·cu·nae** \-nē\ *also* **la·cu·nas** [L, pool, pit, gap, fr. *lacus* lake] : a blank space or missing part : GAP

lad \'lad\ *n* ♦ : a male person of any age between early boyhood and maturity : YOUTH; *also* : FELLOW

♦ boy, nipper, shaver, stripling, youth — more at BOY ♦ buck, chap, dude, fellow, gent, gentleman, guy, hombre, jack, joker, male, man — more at MAN

lad·der \'la-dər\ *n* **1** : a structure for climbing that consists of two parallel sidepieces joined at intervals by crosspieces **2** ♦ : a series of usu. ascending steps or stages

♦ graduation, scale — more at SCALE

lad·die \'la-dē\ *n* : a young lad

lad·en \'lād-ᵊn\ *adj* : LOADED, BURDENED

lad·ing \'lā-diŋ\ *n* ♦ : the goods or merchandise conveyed in a ship, airplane, or vehicle : CARGO, FREIGHT

♦ burden, cargo, freight, haul, load, payload, weight — more at LOAD

¹**la·dle** \'lād-ᵊl\ *n* : a deep-bowled long-handled spoon used in taking up and conveying liquids

²**ladle** *vb* ♦ : to take up and convey in or as if in a ladle

♦ dip, scoop, spoon — more at DIP

la·dy \'lā-dē\ *n, pl* **ladies** [ME, fr. OE *hlǣfdīge*, fr. *hlāf* bread + *-dīge* (akin to *dǣge* kneader of bread)] **1** ♦ : a woman of property, rank, or authority; *also* : a woman of superior social position or of refinement **2** : WOMAN **3** ♦ : a female partner in a marriage : WIFE

♦ [1] dame, gentlewoman, noblewoman — more at GENTLEWOMAN ♦ [3] helpmate, wife — more at WIFE

lady beetle *n* : LADYBUG

la·dy·bird \'lā-dē-ˌbərd\ *n* : LADYBUG

la·dy·bug \-ˌbəg\ *n* : any of various small nearly hemispherical and usu. brightly colored beetles that feed mostly on other insects

la·dy·fin·ger \-ˌfiŋ-gər\ *n* : a small finger-shaped sponge cake

lady–in–waiting *n, pl* **ladies–in–waiting** : a lady appointed to attend or wait on a queen or princess

la·dy·like \'lā-dē-ˌlīk\ *adj* : WELL-BRED

la·dy·ship \-ˌship\ *n* : the condition of being a lady : rank of lady

lady's slipper *n* : any of several No. American orchids with slipper-shaped flowers

¹**lag** \'lag\ *n* **1** : a slowing up or falling behind; *also* : the amount by which one lags **2** : INTERVAL

²**lag** *vb* **lagged; lag·ging** **1** ♦ : to fail to keep up : stay behind **2** ♦ : to slacken gradually

♦ [1] crawl, creep, dally, dawdle, delay, dillydally, drag, linger, loiter, poke, tarry — more at DELAY ♦ [2] decay, droop, fail, flag, go, languish, sag, waste, weaken, wilt — more at WEAKEN

la·ger \'lä-gər\ *n* : a beer brewed by slow fermentation and matured under refrigeration

lag·gard \'la-gərd\ *adj* ♦ : tending to lag — **laggard** *n* — **lag·gard·ly** *adj* — **lag·gard·ness** *n*

♦ creeping, dilatory, languid, poky, slow, sluggish, tardy — more at SLOW

lag·gard·ly *adv* ♦ : in a laggard manner

♦ slow, slowly, sluggishly, tardily — more at SLOW

la·gniappe \'lan-ˌyap\ *n* ♦ : something given free esp. with a purchase

♦ bonus, dividend, extra, perquisite, tip — more at BONUS ♦ bestowal, donation, freebie, gift, largesse, present — more at GIFT

la·goon \lə-'gün\ *n* : a shallow sound, channel, or pond near or connected to a larger body of water

laid *past and past part of* LAY

laid–back \'lād-'bak\ *adj* ♦ : having a relaxed style or character ⟨~ music⟩

♦ affable, breezy, easygoing, happy-go-lucky — more at EASYGOING

lain *past part of* ¹LIE

lair \'lar\ *n* **1** ♦ : the resting or living place of a wild animal : DEN **2** ♦ : a refuge or place for hiding

♦ [1] burrow, den, hole, lodge — more at DEN ♦ [2] concealment, covert, den, hideout, nest — more at HIDEOUT

laird \'lard\ *n, chiefly Scot* : a landed proprietor

lais·ser–faire *chiefly Brit var of* LAISSEZ-FAIRE

lais·sez–faire \ˌle-ˌsā-'far, ˌlā-, -ˌzā-\ *n* [F *laissez faire* let do] : a doctrine opposing governmental control of economic affairs beyond that necessary to maintain peace and property rights

la·ity \'lā-ə-tē\ *n* **1** : the people of a religious faith as distinct from its clergy **2** : the mass of people as distinct from those of a particular field

lake \'lāk\ *n* : an inland body of standing water of considerable size; *also* : a pool of liquid (as lava or pitch)

La·ko·ta \lə-'kō-tə\ *n, pl* **Lakota** *also* **Lakotas** : a member of a western division of the Dakota peoples; *also* : their language

¹**lam** \'lam\ *vb* **lammed; lam·ming** ♦ : to flee hastily

♦ abscond, clear out, escape, flee, fly, get out, run away, run off — more at ESCAPE

²**lam** *abbr* laminated

³**lam** *n* ♦ : sudden or hurried flight esp. from the law

♦ escape, flight, getaway, slip — more at ESCAPE

Lam *abbr* Lamentations

la·ma \'lä-mə\ *n* : a Buddhist monk of Tibet or Mongolia

la·ma·sery \'lä-mə-ˌser-ē\ *n, pl* **-ser·ies** : a monastery for lamas

¹**lamb** \'lam\ *n* **1** : a young sheep; *also* : its flesh used as food **2** ♦ : an innocent or gentle person

♦ angel, dove, innocent, sheep; *also* fledging, greenhorn, ingenue; cherub, saint; mollycoddle, sissy, weakling, wimp; dupe, pigeon, sap, sucker *Ant* wolf

²**lamb** *vb* : to bring forth a lamb

lam·baste *or* **lam·bast** \lam-'bāst, -'bast\ *vb* **1** : to assault violently : BEAT **2** ♦ : to attack verbally : EXCORIATE

♦ abuse, assail, attack, belabor, blast, castigate, excoriate, jump, slam, vituperate — more at ATTACK ♦ admonish, chide, lecture, rail (at *or* against), rate, rebuke, reprimand, scold — more at SCOLD

lamb·da \'lam-də\ *n* : the 11th letter of the Greek alphabet — Λ or λ

lam·bent \'lam-bənt\ *adj* [L *lambens*, prp. of *lambere* to lick] **1** : FLICKERING **2** ♦ : softly radiant ⟨∼ eyes⟩ **3** : marked by lightness or brilliance ⟨∼ humor⟩ — **lam·ben·cy** \-bən-sē\ *n* — **lam·bent·ly** *adv*

   ♦ beaming, bright, brilliant, effulgent, glowing, incandescent, lucent, lucid, luminous, lustrous, radiant, refulgent, shiny — more at BRIGHT

lamb·skin \'lam-,skin\ *n* : a lamb's skin or a small fine-grade sheepskin or the leather made from either

¹lame \'lām\ *adj* **lam·er; lam·est** **1** : having a body part and esp. a limb so disabled as to impair freedom of movement; *also* : marked by stiffness and soreness **2** : lacking substance : WEAK **3** : INFERIOR, PITIFUL — **lame·ly** *adv* — **lame·ness** *n*

²lame *vb* **lamed; lam·ing** ♦ : to make lame : CRIPPLE, DISABLE

   ♦ cripple, disable, maim, mutilate — more at MAIM

la·mé \lä-'mā, la-\ *n* [F] : a brocaded clothing fabric with tinsel filling threads (as of gold or silver)

lame·brain \'lām-,brān\ *n* : DOLT

lame duck *n* : an elected official continuing to hold office between an election and the inauguration of a successor — **lame–duck** *adj*

¹la·ment \lə-'ment\ *vb* **1** : to mourn aloud : WAIL **2** ♦ : to express sorrow or regret for

   ♦ bemoan, bewail, deplore, grieve, mourn, wail; *also* complain (about), cry (for), groan (about), keen, moan, weep; regret, rue; deprecate, disapprove (of) *Ant* exult (in), glory (in), rejoice (in) ♦ bemoan, deplore, regret, repent, rue — more at REGRET

²lament *n* **1** ♦ : a crying out in grief : WAIL **2** ♦ : a slow, solemn, and mournful piece of music : DIRGE, ELEGY **3** : COMPLAINT

   ♦ [1] groan, howl, keen, moan, plaint, wail; *also* grieving, mourning, weeping; regret; complaint, outcry, protest *Ant* exultation, rejoicing ♦ [2] dirge, elegy, requiem, threnody; *also* taps

lam·en·ta·ble \'la-mən-tə-bəl, lə-'men-tə-\ *adj* **1** ♦ : that is to be regretted or lamented **2** ♦ : expressing grief — **lam·en·ta·bly** \-blē\ *adv*

   ♦ [1] deplorable, distressful, grievous, heartbreaking, regrettable, unfortunate, woeful — more at REGRETTABLE ♦ [2] anguished, dolorous, mournful, plaintive, sorrowful, sorry, woeful — more at SORROWFUL

lam·en·ta·tion \,la-mən-'tā-shən\ *n* : an act or instance of lamenting

Lamentations *n* : a book of Jewish and Christian Scripture

la·mia \'lā-mē-ə\ *n* : a female demon

lam·i·na \'la-mə-nə\ *n, pl* **-nae** \-,nē\ *or* **-nas** : a thin plate or scale

¹lam·i·nate \'la-mə-,nāt\ *vb* **-nat·ed; -nat·ing** : to make by uniting layers of one or more materials — **lam·i·na·tion** \,la-mə-'nā-shən\ *n*

²lam·i·nate \-nət\ *n* : a product manufactured by laminating

lamp \'lamp\ *n* **1** : a vessel with a wick for burning a flammable liquid (as oil) to produce light **2** : a device for producing light or heat

lamp·black \-,blak\ *n* : black soot used esp. as a pigment

lamp·light·er \-,lī-tər\ *n* : one that lights a lamp

lam·poon \lam-'pün\ *n* : SATIRE; *esp* : a harsh satire directed against an individual — **lampoon** *vb*

lam·prey \'lam-prē\ *n, pl* **lampreys** : any of a family of eel-shaped jawless fishes that have well-developed eyes and a large disk-shaped sucking mouth armed with horny teeth

LAN \'lan, ,el-,ā-'en\ *n* : LOCAL AREA NETWORK

la·nai \lə-'nī\ *n* [Hawaiian *lānai*] : PORCH, VERANDA

¹lance \'lans\ *n* **1** ♦ : a spear carried by mounted soldiers **2** : any of various sharp-pointed implements; *esp* : LANCET

   ♦ pike, spear — more at SPEAR

²lance *vb* **lanced; lanc·ing** ♦ : to pierce or open with a lance ⟨∼ a boil⟩

   ♦ gore, harpoon, impale, pierce, puncture, skewer, spear, spike, stab, stick, transfix — more at IMPALE

lance corporal *n* : an enlisted person in the marine corps ranking above a private first class and below a corporal

lanc·er \'lan-sər\ *n* : a cavalryman of a unit formerly armed with lances

lan·cet \'lan-sət\ *n* : a sharp-pointed and usu. 2-edged surgical instrument

¹land \'land\ *n* **1** ♦ : the solid part of the surface of the earth; *also* : a part of the earth's surface ⟨fenced ∼⟩ ⟨marshy ∼⟩ **2** ♦ : the people of a country : NATION **3** : REALM, DOMAIN ⟨the ∼ of the living⟩ — **land·less** *adj*

   ♦ [1] belt, region, tract, zone — more at REGION ♦ [1] dirt, dust, earth, ground, soil — more at EARTH ♦ [2] commonwealth, country, nation, sovereignty, state — more at NATION

²land *vb* **1** ♦ : to set or put on shore from a ship : DISEMBARK; *also* : to touch at a place on shore **2** ♦ : to alight or cause to alight on a surface **3** ♦ : to bring to or arrive at a destination **4** ♦ : to catch and bring in ⟨∼ a fish⟩; *also* : GAIN, SECURE ⟨∼ a job⟩

   ♦ [1] disembark, dock, moor, tie up ♦ [2] alight, light, perch, roost, settle — more at ALIGHT ♦ [3] arrive, come, show up, turn up — more at COME ♦ [4] acquire, attain, capture, carry, draw, earn, gain, garner, get, make, obtain, procure, realize, secure, win — more at EARN

lan·dau \'lan-,daù\ *n* : a 4-wheeled carriage with a top divided into two sections that can be lowered, thrown back, or removed

land·ed *adj* : having an estate in land ⟨∼ gentry⟩

land·er \'lan-dər\ *n* : a space vehicle designed to land on a celestial body

land·fall \'land-,fól\ *n* : a sighting or making of land (as after a voyage); *also* : the land first sighted

land·fill \-,fil\ *n* : a low-lying area on which refuse is buried between layers of earth

land·form \-,fórm\ *n* : a natural feature of a land surface

land·hold·er \-,hōl-dər\ *n* : a holder or owner of land — **land·hold·ing** \-diŋ\ *adj or n*

land·ing \'lan-diŋ\ *n* **1** : the action of one that lands **2** ♦ : a place for discharging or taking on passengers and cargo **3** : a level part of a staircase

   ♦ dock, float, jetty, levee, pier, quay, wharf — more at DOCK

landing gear *n* : the part that supports the weight of an aircraft when it is on the ground

land·la·dy \'land-,lā-dē\ *n* : a woman who is a landlord

land·locked \-,läkt\ *adj* **1** : enclosed or nearly enclosed by land ⟨a ∼ country⟩ **2** : confined to fresh water by some barrier ⟨∼ salmon⟩

land·lord \-,lórd\ *n* **1** : the owner of property leased or rented to another **2** : a person who rents lodgings : INNKEEPER

land·lub·ber \-,lə-bər\ *n* : one who knows little of the sea or seamanship

land·mark \-,märk\ *n* **1** : an object that marks a course or boundary or serves as a guide **2** : an event that marks a turning point **3** : a structure of unusual historical and usu. aesthetic interest

land·mass \-,mas\ *n* : a large area of land

land mine *n* **1** : a mine placed on or just below the surface of the ground and designed to be exploded by the weight of someone or something passing over it **2** : a trap for the unwary

land·own·er \-,ō-nər\ *n* : an owner of land

¹land·scape \-,skāp\ *n* **1** : a picture of natural inland scenery **2** : a portion of land that can be seen in one glance

²landscape *vb* **land·scaped; land·scap·ing** : to modify (a natural landscape) by grading, clearing, or decorative planting

land·slide \-,slīd\ *n* **1** : the slipping down of a mass of rocks or earth on a steep slope; *also* : the mass of material that slides **2** : an overwhelming victory

lands·man \'landz-mən\ *n* : a person who lives on land; *esp* : LANDLUBBER

land·ward \'land-wərd\ *adv or adj* : to or toward the land
lane \'lān\ *n* 1 : a narrow passageway (as between fences) 2 : a relatively narrow way or track ⟨traffic ∼⟩
lang *abbr* language
lan·guage \'laŋ-gwij\ *n* [ME, fr. AF *langage*, fr. *langue* tongue, language, fr. L *lingua*] 1 ♦ : the words, their pronunciation, and the methods of combining them used and understood by a community 2 ♦ : form or style of verbal expression 3 ♦ : a system of signs and symbols and rules for using them that is used to carry information
   ♦ [1] argot, cant, jargon, lingo, slang, terminology, vocabulary — more at TERMINOLOGY ♦ [2] diction, phraseology, phrasing, wording — more at WORDING ♦ [3] lingo, speech, tongue, vocabulary; *also* argot, cant, dialect, idiom, jargon, parlance, patois, patter, pidgin, slang, vernacular; colloquialism; terminology
lan·guid \'laŋ-gwəd\ *adj* 1 ♦ : drooping or flagging from or as if from exhaustion : WEAK 2 ♦ : sluggish in character or disposition : LISTLESS 3 ♦ : lacking force or quickness of movement : SLOW — **lan·guid·ly** *adv* — **lan·guid·ness** *n*
   ♦ [1] delicate, effete, enervated, faint, feeble, frail, infirm, low, prostrate, slight, soft, tender, torpid, unsubstantial, wasted, weak, wimpy — more at WEAK ♦ [2] enervated, lackadaisical, languorous, limp, listless, spiritless — more at LISTLESS ♦ [3] creeping, dilatory, laggard, poky, slow, sluggish, tardy — more at SLOW
lan·guish \'laŋ-gwish\ *vb* 1 ♦ : to become languid 2 : to become dispirited : PINE 3 : to appeal for sympathy by assuming an expression of grief
   ♦ decay, droop, fail, flag, go, lag, sag, waste, weaken, wilt — more at WEAKEN
lan·guor \'laŋ-gər\ *n* 1 ♦ : a languid feeling 2 ♦ : listless indolence or inertia
   ♦ [1, 2] debility, delicacy, enfeeblement, faintness, feebleness, frailty, infirmity, lowness, weakness — more at WEAKNESS
lan·guor·ous *adj* ♦ : full of or characterized by languor — **lan·guor·ous·ly** *adv*
   ♦ enervated, lackadaisical, languid, limp, listless, spiritless — more at LISTLESS
La Ni·ña \lä-'nē-nyə\ *n* : an upwelling of unusually cold ocean water along the west coast of So. America that often follows an El Niño
lank \'laŋk\ *adj* 1 : not well filled out 2 ♦ : hanging straight and limp ⟨∼ hair⟩
   ♦ droopy, flaccid, floppy, limp, slack, yielding — more at LIMP
lanky \'laŋ-kē\ *adj* **lank·i·er; -est** ♦ : ungracefully tall and thin
   ♦ gangling, rangy, spindly; *also* angular, bony, gaunt, lank, rawboned, scrawny, skinny; lean, slender, slim, spare, thin; racy, reedy, spidery, stringy, twiggy, wiry
lan·o·lin \'lan-ᵊl-ən\ *n* : the fatty coating of sheep's wool esp. when refined for use in ointments and cosmetics
lan·ta·na \lan-'tä-nə\ *n* : any of a genus of tropical shrubs related to the vervains with showy heads of small bright flowers
lan·tern \'lan-tərn\ *n* [ME *lanterne*, fr. AF, fr. L *lanterna*, fr. Gk *lamptēr*, fr. *lampein* to shine] 1 : a usu. portable light with a protective covering 2 : the chamber in a lighthouse containing the light 3 : a projector for slides
lan·tha·num \'lan-thə-nəm\ *n* : a soft malleable metallic chemical element
lan·yard \'lan-yərd\ *n* : a piece of rope for fastening something in ships; *also* : any of various cords
Lao·tian \lā-'ō-shən, 'laù-shən\ *n* : a native or inhabitant of Laos — **Laotian** *adj*
¹**lap** \'lap\ *n* 1 : a loose panel of a garment 2 : the clothing that lies on the knees, thighs, and lower part of the trunk when one sits; *also* : the front part of the lower trunk and thighs of a seated person 3 : an environment of nurture ⟨the ∼ of luxury⟩ 4 : CHARGE, CONTROL ⟨in the ∼ of the gods⟩

²**lap** *vb* **lapped; lap·ping** 1 : FOLD 2 ♦ : to envelop entirely : WRAP 3 ♦ : to lay over or near so as to partly cover
   ♦ [2] embrace, enclose, encompass, enfold, enshroud, envelop, invest, mantle, shroud, swathe, veil, wrap — more at ENFOLD ♦ [3] overlap, overlay, overlie, overspread — more at OVERLAP
³**lap** *n* 1 : the amount by which an object overlaps another; *also* : the part of an object that overlaps another 2 ♦ : an act or instance of going over a course (as a track or swimming pool)
   ♦ leg, stage, step — more at LEG
⁴**lap** *vb* **lapped; lap·ping** 1 : to scoop up food or drink with the tip of the tongue; *also* : DEVOUR — usu. used with *up* 2 ♦ : to splash gently ⟨*lapping* waves⟩
   ♦ plash, slosh, splash, swash — more at SLOSH
⁵**lap** *n* 1 : an act or instance of lapping 2 : a gentle splashing sound
lap·a·ros·co·py \ˌla-pə-'räs-kə-pē\ *n, pl* **-pies** 1 : visual examination of the abdomen by means of an endoscope; *also* : surgery using laparoscopy — **lap·a·ro·scope** \'la-pə-rə-ˌskōp\ *n* — **lap·a·ro·scop·ic** \ˌla-pə-rə-'skä-pik\ *adj*
lap·dog \'lap-ˌdòg\ *n* : a small dog that may be held in the lap
la·pel \lə-'pel\ *n* : the fold of the front of a coat that is usu. a continuation of the collar
¹**lap·i·dary** \'la-pə-ˌder-ē\ *n, pl* **-dar·ies** : a person who cuts, polishes, or engraves precious stones
²**lapidary** *adj* 1 : of, relating to, or suitable for engraved inscriptions 2 : of or relating to precious stones or the art of cutting them
lap·in \'la-pən\ *n* : rabbit fur usu. sheared and dyed
la·pis la·zu·li \ˌla-pəs-'la-zə-lē, -zhə-\ *n* : a usu. blue semiprecious stone often having sparkling bits of pyrite
lap·pet \'la-pət\ *n* : a fold or flap on a garment
¹**lapse** \'laps\ *n* [L *lapsus*, fr. *labi* to slip] 1 ♦ : a slight error 2 ♦ : a fall from a higher to a lower state 3 : the termination of a right or privilege through failure to meet requirements 4 : a gap in the continuity of something : INTERRUPTION 5 : APOSTASY 6 : a passage of time; *also* : INTERVAL
   ♦ [1] blunder, error, fault, flub, fumble, goof, miscue, misstep, mistake, oversight, slip, stumble — more at ERROR ♦ [2] reversal, reverse, setback — more at REVERSE
²**lapse** *vb* **lapsed; laps·ing** 1 : to commit apostasy 2 : to sink or slip gradually : SUBSIDE ⟨*lapsed* into a coma⟩ 3 ♦ : to go out of existence : CEASE
   ♦ break off, break up, cease, close, conclude, die, discontinue, elapse, end, expire, finish, halt, leave off, let up, pass, quit, stop, terminate, wind up — more at CEASE
lap·top \'lap-ˌtäp\ *adj* : of a size that can be used conveniently on one's lap ⟨a ∼ computer⟩ — **laptop** *n*
lap·wing \'lap-ˌwiŋ\ *n* : an Old World crested plover
lar·board \'lär-bərd\ *n* : ⁵PORT
lar·ce·ny \'lär-sə-nē\ *n, pl* **-nies** [ME, fr. AF *larcein* theft, fr. L *latrocinium* robbery, fr. *latro* mercenary soldier] ♦ : the unlawful taking of personal property with intent to deprive the rightful owner of it permanently : THEFT — **lar·ce·nous** \-nəs\ *adj*
   ♦ robbery, theft, thievery — more at THEFT
larch \'lärch\ *n* : any of a genus of trees related to the pines that shed their needles in the fall
¹**lard** \'lärd\ *vb* 1 : to insert strips of usu. pork fat into (meat) before cooking; *also* : GREASE 2 *obs* : ENRICH
²**lard** *n* : a soft white fat obtained by rendering fatty tissue of the hog
lar·der \'lär-dər\ *n* : a place where foods (as meat) are kept
la·res and pe·na·tes \'lar-ēz . . . pə-'nä-tēz\ *n pl* 1 : household gods 2 : personal or household effects
large \'lärj\ *adj* **larg·er; larg·est** 1 : having more than usual power, capacity, or scope 2 ♦ : exceeding most other things of like kind in quantity or size — **at large** 1 : UNCONFINED 2 : as a whole

◆ big, bumper, considerable, goodly, grand, great, handsome, hefty, sizable, substantial, voluminous; *also* astronomical, cavernous, colossal, enormous, gigantic, gross, heroic, huge, immense, jumbo, major, mammoth, massive, monolithic, monstrous, monumental, prodigious, staggering, stupendous, tremendous, vast; excessive, exorbitant, extravagant, extreme, immoderate, inordinate; abundant, ample, appreciable, copious, plentiful; fat, thick; capacious, commodious, roomy, spacious *Ant* little, puny, small, undersized

large·ly \ˈlärj-lē\ *adv* ◆ : to a large extent : for the greatest part

◆ altogether, basically, chiefly, generally, mainly, mostly, overall, predominantly, primarily, principally — more at CHIEFLY

large·ness *n* ◆ : the quality or state of being large

◆ bigness, grandness, greatness; *also* enormity, grossness, healthiness, hugeness, immensity, magnitude, massiveness, vastness; extravagance, immoderacy; abundance, bountifulness, copiousness, liberality; adequacy, sufficiency *Ant* fineness, littleness, smallness

lar·gesse \lär-ˈzhes, -ˈjes\ *n* 1 : liberal giving 2 ◆ : a generous gift 3 ◆ : the quality or fact of being generous

◆ [2] bestowal, donation, freebie, gift, lagniappe, present — more at GIFT ◆ [3] bounty, generosity, liberality, philanthropy, unselfishness — more at LIBERALITY

¹**lar·go** \ˈlär-gō\ *adv or adj* [It, slow, broad, fr. L *largus* abundant] : at a very slow tempo — used as a direction in music

²**largo** *n, pl* **largos** : a largo movement

lar·i·at \ˈlar-ē-ət\ *n* [AmerSp *la reata* the lasso, fr. Sp *la* the + AmerSp *reata* lasso, fr. Sp *reatar* to tie again] : a long rope used to catch or tether livestock : LASSO

¹**lark** \ˈlärk\ *n* : any of a family of small songbirds; *esp* : SKYLARK

²**lark** *n* ◆ : something done solely for fun or adventure

◆ binge, fling, frolic, gambol, revel, rollick, romp — more at FLING

³**lark** *vb* ◆ : to engage in harmless fun or mischief — often used with *about*

◆ caper, cavort, disport, frisk, frolic, gambol, rollick, romp, sport — more at FROLIC

lark·spur \ˈlärk-ˌspər\ *n* : DELPHINIUM; *esp* : any of the widely cultivated annual delphiniums

lar·va \ˈlär-və\ *n, pl* **lar·vae** \-(ˌ)vē\ *also* **larvas** [NL, fr. L, specter, mask] : the wingless often wormlike form in which insects hatch from the egg; *also* : any young animal (as a tadpole) that is fundamentally unlike its parent — **lar·val** \-vəl\ *adj*

lar·yn·gi·tis \ˌlar-ən-ˈjī-təs\ *n* : inflammation of the larynx

lar·ynx \ˈlar-iŋks\ *n, pl* **la·ryn·ges** \lə-ˈrin-ˌjēz\ *or* **lar·ynx·es** : the upper part of the trachea containing the vocal cords. — **la·ryn·ge·al** \lə-ˈrin-jəl\ *adj*

la·sa·gna \lə-ˈzän-yə\ *n* [It] : boiled broad flat noodles baked with a sauce usu. of tomatoes, cheese, and meat

las·car \ˈlas-kər\ *n* : an Indian sailor

las·civ·i·ous \lə-ˈsi-vē-əs\ *adj* ◆ : sexually unchaste or licentious : LEWD

◆ lewd, lustful, passionate, wanton — more at LUSTFUL

las·civ·i·ous·ness *n* : the quality or state of being lascivious

la·ser \ˈlā-zər\ *n* [*l*ight *a*mplification by *s*timulated *e*mission of *r*adiation] 1 : a device that produces an intense monochromatic beam of light 2 : something thrown or directed straight with high speed or intensity ⟨threw a ∼ into the end zone⟩

laser disc *n* : OPTICAL DISK; *esp* : one containing a video recording

¹**lash** \ˈlash\ *vb* 1 : to move violently or suddenly 2 ◆ : to thrash or beat violently : WHIP 3 : to attack verbally

◆ flail, flog, hide, scourge, slash, switch, thrash, whale, whip

²**lash** *n* 1 **a** : a stroke esp. with a whip **b** ◆ : the flexible part of a whip; *also* : WHIP 2 : a stinging rebuke 3 : EYELASH

◆ scourge, switch, whip — more at WHIP

³**lash** *vb* : to bind with or as if with a line

lass \ˈlas\ *n* ◆ : a young woman : GIRL

◆ doll, girl, maid, maiden, miss — more at GIRL

lass·ie \ˈla-sē\ *n* : a young woman : LASS

las·si·tude \ˈla-sə-ˌtüd, -ˌtyüd\ *n* 1 ◆ : weakness or weariness of body or mind : FATIGUE 2 : LANGUOR

◆ burnout, collapse, exhaustion, fatigue, prostration, tiredness, weariness — more at FATIGUE

las·so \ˈla-sō, la-ˈsü\ *n, pl* **lassos** *or* **lassoes** [Sp *lazo*] : a rope or long leather thong with a noose used for catching livestock — **lasso** *vb*

¹**last** \ˈlast\ *vb* 1 ◆ : to continue in existence or operation 2 : to remain fresh or unimpaired : ENDURE 3 : to manage to continue 4 ◆ : to be enough for the needs of

◆ [1] abide, continue, endure, hold, keep up, persist, run on — more at CONTINUE ◆ [1, 4] hold, hold out, keep up, prevail, survive — more at HOLD OUT

²**last** *n* : a foot-shaped form on which a shoe is shaped or repaired

³**last** *vb* : to shape with a last

⁴**last** *adv* 1 : at the end 2 : most recently 3 : in conclusion

⁵**last** *adj* 1 ◆ : following all the rest : FINAL 2 : next before the present 3 : most up-to-date 4 : farthest from a specified quality, attitude, or likelihood ⟨the ∼ thing we want⟩ 5 : CONCLUSIVE; *also* : SUPREME — **last·ly** *adv*

◆ final, hindmost, latter, terminal, ultimate; *also* consequent, ensuing, eventual, following, succeeding; conclusive, crowning, decisive, definitive; farthest, furthest, remotest; lowermost, lowest, nethermost; endmost, extreme, outermost; penultimate *Ant* beginning, earliest, first, inaugural, initial, maiden, opening, original, primary, starting

⁶**last** *n* : something that is last — **at last** : FINALLY

last-ditch \ˈlast-ˌdich\ *adj* : made as a final effort esp. to avert disaster

last·ing \ˈlas-tiŋ\ *adj* ◆ : existing or continuing a long while : ENDURING

◆ abiding, ageless, continuing, dateless, enduring, eternal, everlasting, immortal, imperishable, perennial, perpetual, timeless, undying — more at ABIDING

last laugh *n* : an ultimate satisfaction or triumph despite previous doubt or criticism

Last Supper *n* : the supper eaten by Jesus and his disciples on the night of his betrayal

lat *abbr* latitude

Lat *abbr* Latin

¹**latch** \ˈlach\ *vb* : to catch or get hold

²**latch** *n* : a catch that holds a door or gate closed

³**latch** *vb* : to make fast with a latch

latch·et \ˈla-chət\ *n* : a strap, thong, or lace for fastening a shoe or sandal

latch·key \ˈlach-ˌkē\ *n* : a key for opening a door latch esp. from the outside

latch·string \-ˌstriŋ\ *n* : a string on a latch that may be left hanging outside the door for raising the latch

¹**late** \ˈlāt\ *adj* **lat·er; lat·est** 1 ◆ : coming or remaining after the due, usual, or proper time 2 : far advanced toward the close or end 3 ◆ : recently deceased 4 : made, appearing, or happening just previous to the present : RECENT 5 ◆ : being something or holding some position or relationship recently but not now — **late·ness** *n*

◆ [1] behind, belated, delinquent, overdue, tardy; *also* delayed, detained, postponed; dilatory, laggard, slow, sluggish *Ant* early, premature ◆ [3] breathless, dead, deceased, defunct, gone, lifeless — more at DEAD ◆ [5] erstwhile, former, old, onetime, past, sometime, whilom — more at FORMER

²**late** *adv* **lat·er; lat·est** 1 : after the usual or proper time; *also* : at or to an advanced point in time 2 : not long before the current time : RECENTLY

late·com·er \\'lāt-ˌkə-mər\ *n* : one who arrives late

la·teen \lə-'tēn\ *adj* : relating to or being a triangular sail extended by a long spar slung to a low mast

late·ly *adv* ♦ : of late

    ♦ freshly, just, late, new, newly, now, only, recently — more at NEWLY

la·ten·cy \-ᵊn-sē\ *n* ♦ : the quality or state of being latent

    ♦ abeyance, doldrums, dormancy, quiescence, suspension — more at ABEYANCE

la·tent \'lāt-ᵊnt\ *adj* ♦ : present but not visible or active

    ♦ dead, dormant, fallow, free, idle, inactive, inert, inoperative, off, vacant — more at INACTIVE

later *adv* ♦ : at some time subsequent to a given time

    ♦ after, afterward, subsequently, thereafter — more at AFTER

¹**lat·er·al** \'la-tə-rəl\ *adj* : situated on, directed toward, or coming from the side ⟨a ∼ view⟩ — **lat·er·al·ly** *adv*

²**lateral** *n* 1 : a branch from the main part 2 : a football pass thrown parallel to the line of scrimmage or away from the opponent's goal

la·tex \'lā-ˌteks\ *n*, *pl* **la·ti·ces** \'lā-tə-ˌsēz, 'la-\ *or* **la·tex·es** 1 : a milky juice produced by various plant cells (as of milkweeds, poppies, and the rubber tree) 2 : a water emulsion of a synthetic rubber or plastic used esp. in paint

lath \'lath, 'lath\ *n*, *pl* **laths** *or* **lath** : a thin narrow strip of wood used esp. as a base for plaster; *also* : a building material in sheets used for the same purpose — **lath** *vb*

lathe \'lāth\ *n* : a machine in which a piece of material is held and turned while being shaped by a tool

¹**lath·er** \'la-thər\ *n* 1 ♦ : a foam or froth formed when a detergent is agitated in water; *also* : foam from profuse sweating (as by a horse) 2 ♦ : an agitated or overwrought state : DITHER

    ♦ [1] foam, froth, head, spume — more at FOAM
    ♦ [2] dither, fluster, fret, fuss, huff, pother, stew, tizzy, twitter — more at FRET

²**lather** *vb* : to spread lather over; *also* : to form a lather

Lat·in \'lat-ᵊn\ *n* 1 : the language of ancient Rome 2 : a member of any of the peoples whose languages derive from Latin — **Latin** *adj*

La·ti·na \lə-'tē-nə\ *n* : a woman or girl who is a native or inhabitant of Latin America; *also* : a woman or girl of Latin-American origin living in the U.S.

Latin American *n* : a native or inhabitant of any of the countries of No., Central, or So. America whose official language is Spanish or Portuguese — **Latin–American** *adj*

La·ti·no \lə-'tē-nō\ *n*, *pl* **-nos** : a native or inhabitant of Latin America; *also* : a person of Latin-American origin living in the U.S. — **Latino** *adj*

lat·i·tude \'la-tə-ˌtüd, -ˌtyüd\ *n* 1 : angular distance north or south from the earth's equator measured in degrees 2 : a region marked by its latitude 3 ♦ : freedom of action or choice

    ♦ authorization, freedom, license (*or* licence), run — more at FREEDOM

lat·i·tu·di·nar·i·an \ˌla-tə-ˌtü-də-'ner-ē-ən, -ˌtyü-\ *n* : a person who is liberal in religious belief and conduct

la·trine \lə-'trēn\ *n* : a room with conveniences for washing and usu. with one or more toilets : TOILET

lat·ter \'la-tər\ *adj* 1 ♦ : more recent; *also* : FINAL 2 : of, relating to, or being the second of two things referred to

    ♦ final, hindmost, last, terminal, ultimate — more at LAST

lat·ter–day *adj* 1 : of present or recent times 2 : of a later or subsequent time

Latter–day Saint *n* : a member of a religious body founded by Joseph Smith in 1830 and accepting the Book of Mormon as divine revelation : MORMON

lat·ter·ly \'la-tər-lē\ *adv* 1 : LATER 2 : of late : RECENTLY

lat·tice \'la-təs\ *n* 1 : a framework of crossed wood or metal strips; *also* : a window, door, or gate having a lattice 2 : a regular geometrical arrangement

lat·tice·work \-ˌwərk\ *n* : LATTICE; *also* : work made of lattices

Lat·vi·an \'lat-vē-ən\ *n* 1 : a native or inhabitant of Latvia 2 : the language of the Latvians — **Latvian** *adj*

¹**laud** \'lȯd\ *n* : PRAISE, ACCLAIM

²**laud** *vb* ♦ : to express a favorable judgment of : PRAISE — **laud·ably** *adv*

    ♦ acclaim, applaud, cheer, crack up, hail, praise, salute, tout — more at ACCLAIM ♦ bless, extol, glorify, magnify, praise — more at PRAISE

laud·able *adj* ♦ : worthy of praise

    ♦ admirable, commendable, creditable, meritorious, praiseworthy — more at ADMIRABLE

lau·da·num \'lȯd-ᵊn-əm\ *n* : a tincture of opium

lau·da·to·ry \'lȯ-də-ˌtōr-ē\ *adj* : of, relating to, or expressive of praise

¹**laugh** \'laf, 'laf\ *vb* [ME, fr. OE *hliehhan*] ♦ : to show mirth, joy, or scorn with a smile and chuckle or explosive sound; *also* : to become amused or derisive — **laugh·ing·ly** *adv*

    ♦ *usu* laugh at deride, gibe, jeer, mock, ridicule, scout — more at RIDICULE

²**laugh** *n* 1 ♦ : the act of laughing 2 ♦ : a cause for derision or merriment : JOKE; *also* : an expression of scorn or mockery : JEER 3 *pl* : SPORT 1

    ♦ [1] cackle, chortle, laughter, snicker, titter; *also* crow, whoop; grin, simper, smile, smirk ♦ [2] crack, gag, jeer, jest, joke, pleasantry, quip, sally, waggery, wisecrack, witticism — more at JOKE

laugh·able *adj* ♦ : of a kind to provoke laughter or sometimes derision : amusingly ridiculous

    ♦ antic, comic, comical, droll, farcical, funny, hilarious, humorous, hysterical, ludicrous, ridiculous, riotous, risible, screaming, uproarious — more at FUNNY
    ♦ absurd, comical, derisive, farcical, ludicrous, preposterous, ridiculous, risible, silly — more at RIDICULOUS

laughing gas *n* : NITROUS OXIDE

laugh·ing·stock \'la-fiŋ-ˌstäk, 'lȧ-\ *n* ♦ : an object of ridicule

    ♦ butt, mark, mock, mockery, target; *also* chump, dupe, fall guy, fool, gull, monkey, pigeon, sap, sucker, victim

laugh·ter \'laf-tər, 'lȧf-\ *n* ♦ : the action or sound of laughing

    ♦ cackle, chortle, laugh, snicker, titter — more at LAUGH

¹**launch** \'lȯnch\ *vb* [ME, fr. OF *lancher*, fr. LL *lanceare* to wield a lance] 1 ♦ : to throw forward : HURL; *also* : to send off ⟨∼ a rocket⟩ 2 ♦ : to set afloat 3 ♦ : to set in operation : START ⟨∼ a business⟩ — **launch·er** *n*

    ♦ [1] cast, catapult, chuck, dash, fire, fling, heave, hurl, hurtle, peg, pelt, pitch, sling, throw, toss — more at THROW ♦ [3] constitute, establish, found, inaugurate, initiate, innovate, institute, introduce, pioneer, set up, start — more at FOUND ♦ [3] begin, commence, embark (on *or* upon), enter, get off, open, start, strike — more at BEGIN

²**launch** *n* ♦ : an act or instance of launching

    ♦ beginning, birth, commencement, dawn, genesis, morning, onset, outset, start, threshold — more at BEGINNING

³**launch** *n* : a small open or half-decked motorboat

launch·pad \'lȯnch-ˌpad\ *n* : a platform from which a rocket is launched

laun·der \'lȯn-dər\ *vb* 1 : to wash or wash and iron clothing and household linens 2 : to transfer (as money of an illegal origin) through an outside party to conceal the true source — **laun·der·er** *n*

laun·dress \'lȯn-drəs\ *n* : a woman who is a laundry worker

laun·dry \'lȯn-drē\ *n*, *pl* **laundries** [fr. obs. *launder* launderer, fr. AF *lavandere*, fr. ML *lavandarius*, fr. L *lavandus* needing to be washed, fr. *lavare* to wash] 1 : a place where laundering is done 2 : clothes or linens that have been or are to be laundered — **laun·dry·man** \-mən\ *n*

lau·re·ate \\'lȯr-ē-ət\\ *n* : the recipient of honor for achievement in an art or science — **lau·re·ate·ship** *n*

lau·rel \\'lȯ-rəl\\ *n* **1** : an evergreen tree or shrub of southern Europe that is related to the sassafras and cinnamon and has glossy aromatic leaves; *esp* : a small tree of southern Europe **2** : MOUNTAIN LAUREL **3 a** : a crown of laurel **b** ◆ : a recognition of achievement : HONOR — usu. used in pl.

◆ *usu* **laurels** acclaim, accolade, credit, distinction, glory, homage, honor (*or* honour) — more at GLORY

lav *abbr* lavatory

la·va \\'lä-və, 'la-\\ *n* [It] : melted rock coming from a volcano; *also* : such rock that has cooled and hardened

la·vage \\lə-'väzh\\ *n* [F] : WASHING; *esp* : the washing out (as of an organ) esp. for medicinal reasons

lav·a·to·ry \\'la-və-ˌtȯr-ē\\ *n, pl* **-ries** **1** : a fixed washbowl with running water and drainpipe **2** ◆ : a room with conveniences for washing and usu. with one or more toilets : BATHROOM

◆ bathroom, toilet — more at TOILET

lave \\'lāv\\ *vb* **laved; lav·ing** ◆ : to wash or flow along or against : WASH

◆ lap, splash, wash — more at WASH

lav·en·der \\'la-vən-dər\\ *n* **1** : a Mediterranean mint or its dried leaves and flowers used to perfume clothing and bed linen **2** : a pale purple color

¹lav·ish \\'la-vish\\ *adj* [ME *laves, lavage*, prob. fr. MF *lavasse, lavache* downpour, fr. *laver* to wash] **1** ◆ : expending or bestowing profusely **2** ◆ : expended or produced in abundance **3** ◆ : marked by excess

◆ [1] deluxe, luxuriant, luxurious, opulent, palatial, plush, sumptuous — more at LUXURIOUS ◆ [2] copious, profuse, riotous — more at PROFUSE ◆ [3] excessive, extravagant, extreme, immoderate, inordinate, overmuch — more at EXCESSIVE

²lavish *vb* ◆ : to expend or give with profusion

◆ heap, pour, rain, shower — more at RAIN ◆ blow, dissipate, fritter, misspend, run through, spend, squander, throw away, waste — more at WASTE

lav·ish·ly *adv* ◆ : in a lavish manner

◆ expensively, extravagantly, grandly, high, luxuriously, opulently, richly — more at HIGH

lav·ish·ness *n* ◆ : a lavish quality; *also* : a lavish manner or propensity

◆ extravagance, prodigality, wastefulness — more at EXTRAVAGANCE

law \\'lȯ\\ *n* **1** ◆ : a rule of conduct or action established by custom or laid down and enforced by a governing authority; *also* : the whole body of such rules **2** : the control brought about by enforcing rules **3** *cap* : the revelation of the divine will set forth in the Old Testament of Christian Scripture; *also* : the first part of the Jewish Scripture **4** : a rule or principle of construction or procedure **5** : the science that deals with laws and their interpretation and application **6** : the profession of a lawyer **7** : a rule or principle stating something that always works in the same way under the same conditions

◆ act, enactment, ordinance, statute; *also* decree, directive, edict, fiat, ruling; bylaw, regulation, rule; amendment, bill, legislation; common law, martial law; prohibition, restriction; canon, encyclical

law·break·er \\'lȯ-ˌbrā-kər\\ *n* ◆ : one who violates the law

◆ criminal, crook, culprit, felon, malefactor, offender — more at CRIMINAL

law·ful \\'lȯ-fəl\\ *adj* **1** : permitted by law **2** : RIGHTFUL — **law·ful·ly** *adv*

law·giv·er \\-ˌgi-vər\\ *n* : one that makes laws : LEGISLATOR

law·less \\'lȯ-ləs\\ *adj* **1** : having no laws **2** ◆ : not restrained or controlled by law : UNRULY, DISORDERLY ⟨a ~ mob⟩ — **law·less·ly** *adv* — **law·less·ness** *n*

◆ anarchic, disorderly, unruly; *also* defiant, insubordinate, mutinous, rebellious, refractory, riotous; undisciplined;

criminal, illegal, illegitimate, illicit, unlawful, wrongful *Ant* orderly

law·mak·er \\-ˌmā-kər\\ *n* ◆ : one that makes laws : LEGISLATOR

◆ legislator, solon — more at LEGISLATOR

law·man \\'lȯ-mən\\ *n* : a law enforcement official (as a sheriff or marshal)

¹lawn \\'lȯn\\ *n* : ground (as around a house) covered with mowed grass

²lawn *n* : a fine sheer linen or cotton fabric

lawn bowling *n* : a bowling game played on a green with wooden balls which are rolled at a jack

law·ren·ci·um \\lȯ-'ren-sē-əm\\ *n* : a short-lived radioactive element

law·suit \\'lȯ-ˌsüt\\ *n* ◆ : a suit in law

◆ action, proceeding, suit; *also* litigation; case, cause, complaint

law·yer \\'lȯ-yər\\ *n* ◆ : one who conducts lawsuits for clients or advises as to legal rights and obligations in other matters — **law·yer·ly** *adj*

◆ advocate, attorney, counsel; *also* pettifogger, shyster; district attorney, prosecutor; solicitor; jurist; lawmaker, lawgiver, legislator, solon

lax \\'laks\\ *adj* **1** ◆ : not strict ⟨~ discipline⟩ **2** ◆ : not tense, firm, or rigid — **lax·ly** *adv*

◆ [1] careless, derelict, negligent, remiss, slack — more at NEGLIGENT ◆ [1] easygoing, flexible, relaxed, unrestrained, unrestricted — more at EASYGOING ◆ [2] insecure, loose, slack — more at LOOSE

¹lax·a·tive \\'lak-sə-tiv\\ *adj* : relieving constipation

²laxative *n* : a usu. mild laxative drug

lax·i·ty \\'lak-sə-tē\\ *n* ◆ : the quality or state of being lax

◆ delinquency, dereliction, laxness, neglect, negligence, omission, remissness, slackness — more at OMISSION

lax·ness *n* ◆ : the quality or state of being lax

◆ carelessness, dereliction, heedlessness, negligence, remissness, slackness — more at NEGLIGENCE

¹lay \\'lā\\ *vb* **laid** \\'lād\\; **lay·ing** **1** : to beat or strike down **2** ◆ : to put on or set down : PLACE **3** : to produce and deposit eggs **4** : SETTLE; *also* : ALLAY **5** : SPREAD **6** ◆ : to make ready beforehand for some purpose, use, or activity : PREPARE, CONTRIVE **7** ◆ : to stake on the outcome of an issue or the performance of a contestant : WAGER **8** ◆ : to impose esp. as a duty or burden **9** ◆ : to set in order or position **10** : to bring to a specified condition ⟨*laid* waste to the land⟩ **11** : to put forward : SUBMIT

◆ [2, 9] deposit, dispose, fix, place, position, put, set, set up, stick — more at PLACE ◆ [6] contrive, fit, fix, get, prepare, ready — more at PREPARE ◆ [7] bet, gamble, go, stake, wager — more at BET ◆ [8] assess, charge, exact, fine, impose, levy, put — more at IMPOSE

²lay *n* : the way in which something lies or is laid in relation to something else

³lay *past of* **¹LIE**

⁴lay *n* **1** : a simple narrative poem **2** ◆ : a short musical composition of words and music : SONG

◆ air, melody, song, strain, tune, warble — more at MELODY

⁵lay *adj* **1** : of or relating to the laity **2** : not of a particular profession; *also* : lacking extensive knowledge of a particular subject

lay·away \\'lā-ə-ˌwā\\ *n* : a purchasing agreement by which a retailer agrees to hold merchandise secured by a deposit until the price is paid in full

lay away *vb* ◆ : to put aside for future use or delivery

◆ cache, hoard, lay up, put by, salt away, stash, stockpile, store — more at HOARD

lay down *vb* ◆ : to institute (as a law) by enactment or agreement; *also* : to assert or command dogmatically

◆ define, prescribe, specify — more at PRESCRIBE
◆ enact, legislate, make, pass — more at ENACT

lay·er \'lā-ər\ *n* **1** : one that lays **2** : one thickness, course, or fold laid or lying over or under another

lay·ette \lā-'et\ *n* [F, fr. MF, dim. of *laye* box] : an outfit of clothing and equipment for a newborn infant

lay·man \'lā-mən\ *n* : a person who is a member of the laity

lay·off \'lā-ˌȯf\ *n* **1** : a period of inactivity **2** ♦ : the act of dismissing an employee usu. temporarily

♦ discharge, dismissal; *also* closing, shutdown

lay off *vb* ♦ : to desist from

♦ *usu* lay off of discontinue, drop, give up, knock off, quit — more at QUIT

lay on *vb* : to make an attack

lay·out \'lā-ˌaůt\ *n* ♦ : the final arrangement, plan, or design of something

♦ arrangement, composition, configuration, design, form, format, makeup, pattern — more at COMPOSITION

lay out *vb* **1** ♦ : to use up or pay out **2** ♦ : to plan in detail

♦ [1] disburse, expend, give, pay, spend — more at SPEND ♦ [2] arrange, blueprint, calculate, chart, design, frame, map, plan, project, scheme — more at PLAN

lay·over \-ˌō-vər\ *n* : STOPOVER

lay·per·son \-ˌpər-sən\ *n* : a member of the laity

lay up *vb* ♦ : to store up

♦ cache, hoard, lay away, put by, salt away, stash, stockpile, store — more at HOARD

lay·wom·an \'lā-ˌwù-mən\ *n* : a woman who is a member of the laity

la·zar \'la-zər, 'lā-\ *n* : LEPER

laze \'lāz\ *vb* **lazed; laz·ing** : to pass time in idleness or relaxation

la·zi·ness \-zē-nəs\ *n* ♦ : the quality or state of being lazy

♦ idleness, indolence, inertia, sloth; *also* apathy, languor, lassitude, lethargy, listlessness, sluggishness; loafing *Ant* drive, industriousness, industry

la·zy \'lā-zē\ *adj* **la·zi·er; -est 1** ♦ : disliking activity or exertion **2** : encouraging idleness **3** : SLUGGISH **4** : DROOPY, LAX **5** : not rigorous or strict — **la·zi·ly** \-zə-lē\ *adv*

♦ idle, indolent, shiftless, slothful; *also* apathetic, languorous, lethargic, listless, sluggish, torpid *Ant* industrious

la·zy·bones \-ˌbōnz\ *n sing or pl* ♦ : a lazy individual

♦ idler, loafer, slouch, slug, sluggard; *also* bum, ne'er= do-well; dawdler, laggard, trifler; goldbrick, malingerer, shirker, slacker; lingerer, loiterer; procrastinator; quit= ter *Ant* doer, go-getter, hummer, hustler, rustler, self= starter

lazy Su·san \ˌlā-zē-'süz-ᵊn\ *n* : a revolving tray used for serving food

lb *abbr* [L *libra*] pound

lc *abbr* lowercase

LC *abbr* Library of Congress

¹LCD \ˌel-(ˌ)sē-'dē\ *n* [*l*iquid *c*rystal *d*isplay] : a display (as of the time in a digital watch) that consists of segments of a liquid crystal whose reflectivity varies with the voltage applied to them

²LCD *abbr* least common denominator; lowest common denominator

LCDR *abbr* lieutenant commander

LCM *abbr* least common multiple; lowest common multiple

LCpl *abbr* lance corporal

LCS *abbr* League Championship Series

ld *abbr* **1** load **2** lord

LD *abbr* learning disabled; learning disability

LDC *abbr* less developed country

ldg *abbr* **1** landing **2** loading

LDL \ˌel-(ˌ)dē-'el\ *n* [*l*ow-*d*ensity *l*ipoprotein] : a cholesterol-rich protein-poor lipoprotein of blood plasma correlated with increased probability of developing atherosclerosis

L–do·pa \'el-'dō-pə\ *n* : an isomer of dopa used esp. in the treatment of Parkinson's disease

LDS *abbr* Latter-day Saints

lea \'lē, 'lā\ *n* : farmland having chiefly forage plants and esp. grasses : PASTURE

leach \'lēch\ *vb* : to pass a liquid (as water) through to carry off the soluble components; *also* : to dissolve out by such means ⟨~ alkali from ashes⟩

¹lead \'lēd\ *vb* **led** \'led\; **lead·ing 1** ♦ : to guide on a way **2** : LIVE ⟨~ a quiet life⟩ **3** ♦ : to direct the operations, activity, or performance of ⟨~ an orchestra⟩ **4** : to go at the head of : be first ⟨~ a parade⟩ **5** : to begin play with; *also* : BEGIN, OPEN **6** : to tend toward a definite result ⟨study ~*ing* to a degree⟩ **7** ♦ : to lie, run, or open in a specified place or direction

♦ [1] conduct, direct, guide, marshal, pilot, route, show, steer, usher; *also* precede; accompany, attend, chaperon, convoy, escort, see; control, manage *Ant* follow, trail ♦ [3] boss, captain, command, dominate, head, spearhead; *also* control, direct, govern, handle, manage, oversee, regulate, superintend, supervise ♦ [7] extend, go, head, lie, run — more at RUN

²lead \'lēd\ *n* **1 a** : a position at the front **b** ♦ : a margin by which one leads **2** : the privilege of leading in cards; *also* : the card or suit led **3** : EXAMPLE **4** : one that leads **5** : a principal role (as in a play); *also* : one who plays such a role **6** ♦ : something serving as an indication, tip, or clue **7** : an insulated electrical conductor

♦ [1b] distance, length, remove, spread, stretch, way — more at DISTANCE ♦ [6] clue, cue, hint, indication, inkling, intimation, suggestion, tip — more at HINT

³lead \'led\ *n* **1** : a heavy malleable bluish white chemical element **2** : an article made of lead; *esp* : a weight for sounding at sea **3** : a thin strip of metal used to separate lines of type in printing **4** : a thin stick of marking substance in or for a pencil

⁴lead \'led\ *vb* **1** : to cover, line, or weight with lead **2** : to fix (glass) in position with lead **3** : to treat or mix with lead or a lead compound

lead·en \'led-ᵊn\ *adj* **1 a** : made of lead **b** ♦ : of the color of lead **2 a** : SLUGGISH **b** ♦ : lacking spirit or animation : DULL ⟨a ~ lecture⟩

♦ [1b] gray (*or* grey), pewter, silver, silvery, slate, steely — more at GRAY ♦ [2b] drab, dreary, dry, dull, flat, heavy, humdrum, monotonous, ponderous

lead·er *n* **1** ♦ : something that leads; *also* : a conduit for leading fluid from one place to another **2** ♦ : a person who leads — **lead·er·less** *adj* — **lead·er·ship** *n*

♦ [1] channel, conduit, duct, line, penstock, pipe, tube — more at PIPE ♦ [2] boss, captain, chief, foreman, head, headman, helmsman, kingpin, master, taskmaster — more at BOSS

lead·off \'lēd-ˌȯf\ *adj* ♦ : of, relating to, or being one that leads off — **leadoff** *n*

♦ first, foremost, inaugural, initial, maiden, original, pioneer, premier — more at FIRST

lead off *vb* : OPEN, BEGIN; *esp* : to bat first in an inning

lead on *vb* ♦ : to entice or induce to adopt or continue in a course or belief esp. when unwise or mistaken

♦ allure, beguile, decoy, entice, lure, seduce, tempt — more at LURE

¹leaf \'lēf\ *n, pl* **leaves** \'lēvz\ **1** : a usu. flat and green outgrowth of a plant stem that is a unit of foliage and functions esp. in photosynthesis; *also* : FOLIAGE **2** : something that is suggestive of a leaf — **leaf·less** *adj*

²leaf *vb* **1** : to produce leaves **2** : to turn the pages of a book

leaf·age \'lē-fij\ *n* ♦ : all the leaves of one or more plants : FOLIAGE

♦ flora, foliage, green, greenery, herbage, vegetation, verdure — more at GREENERY

leafed \'lēft\ *adj* : LEAVED

leaf·hop·per \'lēf-ˌhä-pər\ *n* : any of a family of small leaping insects related to the cicadas that suck the juices of plants

leaf·let \'lē-flət\ n **1** : a division of a compound leaf **2 ♦** : a usu. folded printed sheet intended for free distribution : PAMPHLET, FOLDER

♦ booklet, brochure, circular, folder, pamphlet — more at PAMPHLET

leaf mold n : a compost or layer composed chiefly of decayed leaves

leaf·stalk \'lēf-ˌstȯk\ n : PETIOLE

leafy adj **leaf·i·er; -est ♦** : furnished with or abounding in leaves

♦ green, lush, luxuriant, verdant

¹league \'lēg\ n : a unit of distance equal to about three miles (five kilometers)

²league n **1 ♦** : an association or alliance for a common purpose **2** : CLASS, CATEGORY — **leagu·er** \'lē-gər\ n

♦ association, brotherhood, club, college, congress, council, fellowship, fraternity, guild, institute, institution, order, organization, society — more at ASSOCIATION ♦ alliance, bloc, coalition, combination, combine, confederacy, confederation, federation, union — more at CONFEDERACY

³league vb **leagued; leagu·ing ♦** : to form a league

♦ ally, associate, band, club, confederate, conjoin, cooperate, federate, unite — more at ALLY

¹leak \'lēk\ vb **1** : to enter or escape through a leak **2** : to let a substance in or out through an opening **3 ♦** : to become or make known

♦ usu **leak out** come out, get out, out, spread — more at GET OUT

²leak n **1** : a crack or hole that accidentally admits a fluid or light or lets it escape; also : something that secretly or accidentally permits the admission or escape of something else **2** : LEAKAGE — **leaky** adj

leak·age \'lē-kij\ n **1** : the act of leaking **2** : the thing or amount that leaks

¹lean \'lēn\ vb **1 ♦** : to bend from a vertical position : INCLINE **2** : to cast one's weight to one side for support **3 ♦** : to rely for support **4 ♦** : to incline in opinion, taste, or desire

♦ [1] angle, cant, cock, heel, incline, list, slant, slope, tilt, tip; also bank; bend, deviate, swerve, veer; decline, descend, recline, retreat ♦ [3] count, depend, reckon, rely — more at DEPEND ♦ [4] incline, run, tend, trend; also go, gravitate; indicate, point, suggest ♦ usu **lean toward** [4] favor (or favour), like, prefer — more at PREFER

²lean adj **1 ♦** : lacking or deficient in flesh and esp. in fat **2** : lacking richness or productiveness **3** : low in fuel content — **lean·ness** n

♦ skinny, slender, slim, spare, thin — more at THIN

³lean n **♦** : the act or an instance of leaning

♦ cant, diagonal, grade, inclination, incline, pitch, slant, slope, tilt, upgrade — more at SLANT

leaning n **♦** : a definite but not decisive attraction or tendency — often used in pl.

♦ affinity, bent, devices, disposition, genius, inclination, partiality, penchant, predilection, predisposition, proclivity, propensity, talent, tendency, turn — more at INCLINATION ♦ current, drift, run, tendency, tide, trend, wind — more at TREND

leant \'lent\ chiefly Brit past of LEAN

lean–to \'lēn-ˌtü\ n, pl **lean–tos** \-ˌtüz\ : a wing or extension of a building having a roof of only one slope; also : a rough shed or shelter with a similar roof

¹leap \'lēp\ vb **leapt** \'lept, 'lēpt\ or **leaped; leap·ing ♦** : to spring free from a surface or over an obstacle : JUMP

♦ bound, hop, jump, spring, vault — more at JUMP

²leap n **♦** : an act of leaping : JUMP

♦ bound, hop, jump, spring, vault — more at JUMP

leap·frog \'lēp-ˌfrȯg, -ˌfräg\ n : a game in which a player bends down and is vaulted over by another — **leapfrog** vb

leap year n : a year containing 366 days with February 29 as the extra day

learn \'lərn\ vb **learned** \'lərnd, 'lərnt\ or Can and Brit **learnt** \'lərnt\; **learn·ing 1 a ♦** : to gain knowledge, understanding, or skill by study or experience **b** : to commit to memory : MEMORIZE ⟨∼ the poem⟩ **2 ♦** : to find out : ASCERTAIN ⟨∼ the truth⟩ — **learn·er** n

♦ [1a] get, master, pick up; also apprehend, comprehend, grasp, know, understand; absorb, assimilate, digest, imbibe; ascertain, descry, detect, determine, dig up, discern, discover, examine, find out, hear, hit (on or upon), run down, search (for), see, tumble (to), track (down), unearth; major (in), study; memorize **Ant** unlearn ♦ [2] detect, determine, dig up, discover, ferret out, find, hit on, locate, track down — more at FIND

learn·ed \'lər-nəd\ adj **♦** : characterized by or associated with learning : ERUDITE — **learn·ed·ly** adv

♦ educated, erudite, knowledgeable, literate, scholarly, well-read — more at EDUCATED

learn·ing \'lər-niŋ\ n **♦** : knowledge or skill acquired by instruction or study : ERUDITION

♦ education, erudition, knowledge, scholarship, science — more at EDUCATION

learning disability n : any of various conditions (as dyslexia) that interfere with a person's ability to learn and so result in impaired functioning (as in language) — **learning disabled** adj

learnt \'lərnt\ chiefly Can and Brit past and past part of LEARN

¹lease \'lēs\ n : a contract transferring real estate for a term of years or at will usu. for a specified rent

²lease vb **leased; leas·ing** [AF lesser, lescher to leave, hand over, lease, fr. L laxare to loosen, fr. laxus slack] **1** : to grant by lease **2 ♦** : to hold under a lease

♦ engage, hire, let, rent — more at HIRE

lease·hold \'lēs-ˌhōld\ n **1** : a tenure by lease **2** : land held by lease — **lease·hold·er** n

leash \'lēsh\ n [ME lees, leshe, fr. AF *lesche, lesse prob. fr. lesser to leave, let go] : a line for leading or restraining an animal — **leash** vb

¹least \'lēst\ adj **1** : lowest in importance or position **2 ♦** : smallest in size or degree **3** : SLIGHTEST

♦ minimal, minimum — more at MINIMAL

²least n : one that is least

³least adv : in the smallest or lowest degree

least common denominator n : the least common multiple of two or more denominators

least common multiple n : the smallest common multiple of two or more numbers

least·wise \'lēst-ˌwīz\ adv : at least

leath·er \'le-thər\ n : animal skin dressed for use — **leath·ern** \-thərn\ adj — **leath·ery** adj

leath·er·back \-ˌbak\ n : the largest existing sea turtle with a flexible leathery carapace

leath·er·neck \-ˌnek\ n : MARINE

¹leave \'lēv\ vb **left** \'left\; **leav·ing 1 ♦** : to allow or cause to remain behind **2** : to have as a remainder **3 ♦** : to give or leave by will : BEQUEATH **4** : to let stay without interference **5** : to go away : depart from **6 ♦** : to give up esp. with the intent of never again claiming a right or interest in

♦ [1] abandon, desert, forsake, quit — more at ABANDON ♦ [3] commend, commit, consign, delegate, deliver, entrust, give, hand over, pass, transfer, transmit, trust, turn over, vest — more at GIVE ♦ [6] quit, resign, retire, step down — more at QUIT

²leave n **1 ♦** : permission to do something; also : authorized absence from duty **2** : DEPARTURE

♦ break, recess, vacation — more at VACATION ♦ allowance, authorization, clearance, concurrence, consent, license (or licence), permission, sanction, sufferance — more at PERMISSION

³leave vb **leaved; leav·ing** : LEAF

leaved \'lēvd\ adj : having leaves

¹**leav·en** \'le-vən\ *n* **1** : a substance (as yeast) used to produce fermentation (as in dough) **2** : something that modifies or lightens

²**leaven** *vb* : to raise (dough) with a leaven; *also* : to permeate with a modifying or vivifying element

leav·en·ing *n* : LEAVEN

leave off *vb* ♦ : to cause to cease; *also* : to cease activity or operation

♦ break, break off, cease, cut, desist, discontinue, drop, end, halt, knock off, layoff, quit, shut off, stop — more at STOP

leaves *pl of* LEAF

leave–tak·ing \'lēv-ˌtā-kiŋ\ *n* ♦ : the act or an instance of departing : FAREWELL

♦ departure, exit, farewell, parting — more at DEPARTURE

leav·ings \'lē-viŋz\ *n pl* ♦ : a usu. small part, member, or trace remaining : REMNANT, RESIDUE

♦ balance, leftovers, odds and ends, remainder, remains, remnant, residue, rest — more at REMAINDER

Leb·a·nese \ˌle-bə-'nēz, -'nēs\ *n* : a native or inhabitant of Lebanon — **Lebanese** *adj*

lech·ery \'le-chə-rē\ *n* : inordinate indulgence in sexual activity — **lech·er** \'le-chər\ *n* — **lech·er·ous** \'le-chə-rəs\ *adj* — **lech·er·ous·ly** *adv* — **lech·er·ous·ness** *n*

lec·i·thin \'le-sə-thən\ *n* : any of several waxy phosphorus-containing substances that are common in animals and plants, form colloidal solutions in water, and have emulsifying and wetting properties

lect *abbr* lecture; lecturer

lec·tern \'lek-tərn\ *n* : a stand to support a book for a standing reader

lec·tor \-tər\ *n* : one whose chief duty is to read the lessons in a church service

¹**lec·ture** \'lek-chər\ *n* **1** : a discourse given before an audience esp. for instruction **2** : REPRIMAND — **lec·tur·er** *n* — **lec·ture·ship** *n*

²**lec·ture** *vb* **lec·tured; lec·tur·ing** **1** ♦ : to deliver a lecture or a course of lectures **2** ♦ : to reprove formally

♦ [1] declaim, descant, discourse, harangue, orate, speak, talk — more at TALK ♦ [2] rebuke, reprimand, reproach, scold

led *past and past part of* LEAD

LED \ˌel-(ˌ)ē-'dē\ *n* [*l*ight-*e*mitting *d*iode] : a semiconductor diode that emits light when a voltage is applied to it and is used esp. for electronic displays

le·der·ho·sen \'lā-dər-ˌhōz-ᵊn\ *n pl* : leather shorts often with suspenders worn esp. in Bavaria

ledge \'lej\ *n* [ME *legge* bar of a gate] **1** : a shelflike projection from a top or an edge **2** : REEF

led·ger \'le-jər\ *n* : a book containing accounts to which debits and credits are transferred in final form

lee \'lē\ *n* **1** : a protecting shelter **2** : the side (as of a ship) that is sheltered from the wind — **lee** *adj*

leech \'lēch\ *n* **1** : any of various bloodsucking segmented usu. freshwater worms that are related to the earthworms and have a sucker at each end **2** ♦ : a hanger-on who seeks gain

♦ hanger-on, parasite, sponge; *also* dependent; deadbeat, idler; flunky, henchman, lackey, satellite, stooge, sycophant, toady, yes-man; cheapskate, miser, niggard, piker, skinflint, tightwad

leek \'lēk\ *n* : an onionlike herb grown for its mildly pungent leaves and stalk

leer \'lir\ *n* : a suggestive, knowing, or malicious look — **leer** *vb*

leery \'lir-ē\ *adj* ♦ : disposed to suspect : SUSPICIOUS

♦ distrustful, incredulous, mistrustful, skeptical, suspicious — more at SKEPTICAL

lees \'lēz\ *n pl* ♦ : the sediment of a liquor (as wine) during fermentation and aging : DREGS

♦ dregs, grounds, sediment

¹**lee·ward** \'lē-wərd, 'lü-ərd\ *n* : the lee side

²**leeward** *adj* : situated away from the wind

lee·way \'lē-ˌwā\ *n* **1** : lateral movement of a ship when under way **2** : an allowable margin of freedom or variation

¹**left** \'left\ *adj* [ME, fr. OE, weak; fr. the left hand's being the weaker in most individuals] **1** : of, relating to, or being the side of the body in which the heart is mostly located; *also* : located nearer to this side than to the right **2** *often cap* : of, adhering to, or constituted by the political left — **left** *adv*

²**left** *n* **1** : the left hand; *also* : the side or part that is on or toward the left side **2** *often cap* : those professing political views marked by desire to reform the established order and usu. to give greater freedom to the common people — **left·most** \-ˌmōst\ *adj*

³**left** *past and past part of* LEAVE

left–click \'left-'klik\ *vb* : to press the leftmost button on a computer mouse or similar input device

left–hand *adj* **1** : situated on the left **2** : LEFT-HANDED

left–hand·ed \'left-'han-dəd\ *adj* **1** : using the left hand habitually or more easily than the right **2** : designed for or done with the left hand **3** ♦ : not sincere : INSINCERE, BACKHANDED ⟨a ~ compliment⟩ **4** : COUNTERCLOCKWISE — **left–handed** *adv*

♦ artificial, double-dealing, feigned, hypocritical, insincere, mealy, mealymouthed, two-faced, unctuous — more at INSINCERE

left·ism \'lef-ˌti-zəm\ *n* **1** : the principles and views of the Left **2** : advocacy of the doctrines of the Left — **left·ist** \-tist\ *n or adj*

left·over \'left-ˌō-vər\ *n* ♦ : something that remains unused or unconsumed; *esp* : leftover food served at a later meal — usu. used in pl.

♦ end, fag end, remainder, remnant, scrap — more at SCRAP ♦ *usu* **leftovers** balance, leavings, odds and ends, remainder, remains, remnant, residue, rest — more at REMAINDER

lefty \'lef-tē\ *n, pl* **left·ies** **1** : a left-handed person **2** : an advocate of leftism

¹**leg** \'leg\ *n* **1** : a limb of an animal used esp. for supporting the body and in walking; *also* : the part of the vertebrate leg between knee and foot **2** : something resembling or analogous to an animal leg ⟨table ~⟩ **3** : the part of an article of clothing that covers the leg **4** ♦ : a portion of a trip **5** *pl* : long-term appeal or interest — **leg·ged** \'le-gəd\ *adj* — **leg·less** *adj*

♦ lap, stage, step; *also* layover, stopover

²**leg** *vb* **legged; leg·ging** ♦ : to use the legs in walking or esp. in running

♦ *usu* **leg it** foot, pad, step, traipse, tread, walk — more at WALK

³**leg** *abbr* **1** legal **2** legislative; legislature

leg·a·cy \'le-gə-sē\ *n, pl* **-cies** : something that is or may be inherited : INHERITANCE; *also* : something that has come from a predecessor or the past

le·gal \'lē-gəl\ *adj* **1** : of or relating to law or lawyers **2 a** ♦ : conforming to or permitted by law or established rules : LAWFUL **b** : STATUTORY **3** : enforced in courts of law — **le·gal·i·ty** \li-'ga-lə-tē\ *n* — **le·gal·ize** \'lē-gə-ˌlīz\ *vb* — **le·gal·ly** *adv*

♦ clean, fair, sportsmanlike ♦ allowable, good, innocent, justifiable, permissible, proper, regulation, right *Ant* illegal, illegitimate, illicit, unlawful, wrongful

le·gal·ese \ˌlē-gə-'lēz\ *n* : the specialized language of the legal profession

le·gal·ism \'lē-gə-ˌli-zəm\ *n* **1** : strict, literal, or excessive conformity to the law or to a religious or moral code **2** : a legal term — **le·gal·is·tic** \ˌlē-gə-'lis-tik\ *adj*

leg·ate \'le-gət\ *n* ♦ : an official representative

♦ ambassador, delegate, emissary, envoy, minister, representative — more at AMBASSADOR

leg·a·tee \ˌle-gə-'tē\ *n* : a person to whom a legacy is bequeathed

le·ga·tion \li-'gā-shən\ *n* **1** : a diplomatic mission headed by a minister **2** : the official residence and office of a minister in a foreign country

le·ga·to \li-'gä-tō\ *adv or adj* [It, lit., tied] : in a smooth and connected manner (as of music)

leg·end \'le-jənd\ *n* [ME *legende*, fr. MF & ML; MF *legende*, fr. ML *legenda*, fr. L *legere* to read] **1 a** : a story coming down from the past; *esp* : one popularly accepted as historical though not verifiable **b** ♦ : a body of popular stories **2** : an inscription on an object; *also* : CAPTION **3** : an explanatory list of the symbols on a map or chart

   ♦ folklore, lore, myth, mythology, tradition — more at FOLKLORE

leg·end·ary \'le-jən-ˌder-ē\ *adj* **1** ♦ : of, relating to, or characteristic of a legend **2** : FAMOUS ⟨∼ actors⟩ — **leg·en·dari·ly** \-ˌder-ə-lē\ *adv*

   ♦ fabled, fabulous, mythical — more at MYTHICAL

leg·er·de·main \ˌle-jər-də-'mān\ *n* [ME, fr. MF *leger de main* light of hand] **1** : SLEIGHT OF HAND **2 a** ♦ : skill and dexterity in conjuring tricks **b** ♦ : adroitness in deception

   ♦ [2a] magic, prestidigitation ♦ [2b] artifice, chicanery, hanky-panky, subterfuge, trickery — more at TRICKERY

leg·ging *or* **leg·gin** \'le-gən, -giŋ\ *n* : a covering for the leg; *also* : TIGHTS

leg·gy \'le-gē\ *adj* **leg·gi·er; -est 1** : having unusually long legs **2** : having long and attractive legs **3** : SPINDLY — used of a plant

leg·horn \'leg-ˌhȯrn, 'le-gərn\ *n* **1** : a fine plaited straw; *also* : a hat made of this straw **2** : any of a Mediterranean breed of small hardy chickens

leg·i·ble \'le-jə-bəl\ *adj* : capable of being read : CLEAR — **leg·i·bil·i·ty** \ˌle-jə-'bi-lə-tē\ *n* — **leg·i·bly** \'le-jə-blē\ *adv*

¹le·gion \'lē-jən\ *n* **1** : a unit of the Roman army comprising 3000 to 6000 soldiers **2** ♦ : a very large number : MULTITUDE ⟨∼s of fans⟩ **3** : an association of ex-servicemen **4** ♦ : a large military force

   ♦ [2] army, crowd, crush, drove, flock, horde, host, mob, multitude, press, swarm, throng — more at CROWD ♦ [4] army, battalion, host — more at ARMY

²legion *adj* : MANY, NUMEROUS

le·gion·ary \-jə-ˌner-ē\ *n* : LEGIONNAIRE

le·gion·naire \ˌlē-jə-'nar\ *n* ♦ : a member of a legion

   ♦ fighter, man-at-arms, regular, serviceman, soldier, warrior — more at SOLDIER

Legionnaires' disease *also* **Legionnaire's disease** \-'nerz-\ *n* : a lobar pneumonia caused by a bacterium

legis *abbr* legislation; legislative; legislature

leg·is·late \'le-jəs-ˌlāt\ *vb* **-lat·ed; -lat·ing** ♦ : to make or enact laws; *also* : to bring about by legislation

   ♦ enact, lay down, make, pass — more at ENACT

leg·is·la·tion \ˌle-jəs-'lā-shən\ *n* **1** : the action of legislating **2** : laws made by a legislative body

leg·is·la·tive \'le-jəs-ˌlā-tiv\ *adj* **1** : having the power of legislating **2** : of or relating to a legislature or legislation

leg·is·la·tor \-ˌlā-tər\ *n* ♦ : one that makes laws esp. for a political unit; *esp* : a member of a legislative body

   ♦ lawmaker, solon; *also* assemblyman, assemblywoman; congressman, congresswoman; senator

leg·is·la·ture \'le-jəs-ˌlā-chər\ *n* : an organized body of persons having the authority to make laws

le·git \li-'jit\ *adj, slang* : LEGITIMATE

¹le·git·i·mate \li-'ji-tə-mət\ *adj* **1** : lawfully begotten **2** : GENUINE **3** : LAWFUL **4** : conforming to recognized principles or accepted rules or standards — **le·git·i·ma·cy** \-mə-sē\ *n* — **le·git·i·mate·ly** *adv*

²le·git·i·mate \-ˌmāt\ *vb* **-mat·ed; -mat·ing** : to make legitimate

le·git·i·mise *chiefly Brit var of* LEGITIMIZE

le·git·i·mize \li-'ji-tə-ˌmīz\ *vb* **-mized; -miz·ing** : LEGITIMATE

leg·man \'leg-ˌman\ *n* **1** : a reporter assigned usu. to

gather information **2** : an assistant who gathers information and runs errands

le·gume \'le-ˌgyüm, li-'gyüm\ *n* [F] **1** : any of a large family of plants having fruits that are dry pods and split when ripe and including important food and forage plants (as beans and clover); *also* : the part (as seeds or pods) of a legume used as food **2** : the pod of a legume — **le·gu·mi·nous** \li-'gyü-mə-nəs\ *adj*

¹lei \'lā, 'lā-ē\ *n* : a wreath or necklace usu. of flowers

lei·sure \'lē-zhər, 'le-, 'lā-\ *n* **1** ♦ : freedom provided by the cessation of activities; *also* : time free from work or duties **2** : EASE; *also* : CONVENIENCE ⟨read it at your ∼⟩

   ♦ ease, relaxation, repose, rest — more at REST

¹lei·sure·ly *adj* : characterized by slowness

²leisurely *adv* : without haste

leit·mo·tif *also* **leit·mo·tiv** \'līt-mō-ˌtēf\ *n* [G *Leitmotiv*, fr. *leiten* to lead + *Motiv* motive] : a dominant recurring theme

lem·ming \'le-miŋ\ *n* [Norw] : any of various short-tailed rodents found mostly in northern regions and noted for recurrent mass migrations

lem·on \'le-mən\ *n* **1** : an acid yellow usu. nearly oblong citrus fruit; *also* : a citrus tree that bears lemons **2** ♦ : something (as an automobile) unsatisfactory or defective — **lem·ony** *adj*

   ♦ bummer, dud, failure, fizzle, flop, loser, turkey, washout — more at FAILURE

lem·on·ade \ˌle-mə-'nād\ *n* : a beverage of lemon juice, sugar, and water

lemon curd *n* : a custard made with lemon juice, butter, sugar, and eggs

lem·on·grass \'le-mən-ˌgras\ *n* : a tropical Asian grass grown for its lemon-scented foliage used as a seasoning

le·mur \'lē-mər\ *n* : any of various arboreal primates largely of Madagascar that have large eyes, very soft woolly fur, and a long furry tail

Len·a·pe \'le-nə-pē, lə-'nä-pē\ *n, pl* **Lenape** *or* **Lenapes** : DELAWARE

lend \'lend\ *vb* **lent** \'lent\; **lend·ing 1** : to give for temporary use on condition that the same or its equivalent be returned **2** : AFFORD, FURNISH **3** : ACCOMMODATE — **lend·er** *n*

lend–lease \-'lēs\ *n* : the transfer of goods and services to an ally to aid in a common cause with payment made by a return of the items or their use in the cause or by a similar transfer of other goods and services

length \'leŋth\ *n* **1 a** : the longer or longest dimension of an object **b** ♦ : a measured distance **2** : duration or extent in time or space **3** : the length of something taken as a unit of measure **4** : a single piece of a series of pieces that may be joined together ⟨a ∼ of pipe⟩ — **at length 1** : in full **2** : FINALLY

   ♦ distance, lead, remove, spread, stretch, way — more at DISTANCE

length·en \'leŋ-thən\ *vb* ♦ : to make or become longer

   ♦ draw out, elongate, extend, prolong, protract, stretch — more at EXTEND

length·wise \'leŋth-ˌwīz\ *adv* : in the direction of the length — **lengthwise** *adj*

lengthy \'leŋ-thē\ *adj* **length·i·er; -est 1** : protracted excessively **2** ♦ : drawn out in length esp. of time : EXTENDED, LONG

   ♦ extended, far, great, long — more at LONG

le·ni·en·cy \'lē-nē-ən-sē, -nyən-sē\ *n* ♦ : the quality or state of being lenient; *also* : a lenient disposition or practice

   ♦ charity, clemency, mercy, quarter — more at MERCY

le·nient \'lē-nē-ənt, -nyənt\ *adj* : of mild and tolerant disposition or effect — **le·ni·ent·ly** *adv*

len·i·ty \'le-nə-tē\ *n* : the quality or state of being lenient : LENIENCY

lens \'lenz\ *n* [L *lent-, lens* lentil; so called fr. the shape of a convex lens] **1** : a curved piece of glass or plastic used singly or combined in an optical instrument for forming an image; *also* : a device for focusing radiation other than light **2** : a transparent body in the eye that focuses light rays on receptors at the back of the eye

Lent \'lent\ *n* : a 40-day period of penitence and fasting observed from Ash Wednesday to Easter by many churches — **Lent·en** \-ᵊn\ *adj*

len·til \'lent-ᵊl\ *n* : a Eurasian annual legume grown for its flat edible seeds and for fodder; *also* : its seed

Leo \'lē-ō\ *n* [L, lit., lion] **1** : a zodiacal constellation between Cancer and Virgo usu. pictured as a lion **2** : the 5th sign of the zodiac in astrology; *also* : one born under this sign

le·o·nine \'lē-ə-ˌnīn\ *adj* : of, relating to, or resembling a lion

leop·ard \'le-pərd\ *n* : a large usu. tawny and black-spotted cat of southern Asia and Africa

le·o·tard \'lē-ə-ˌtärd\ *n* : a close-fitting garment worn esp. by dancers and for exercise

lep·er \'le-pər\ *n* **1** : a person affected with leprosy **2** : OUTCAST

lep·re·chaun \'le-prə-ˌkän\ *n* ♦ : a mischievous elf of Irish folklore

♦ brownie, dwarf, elf, fairy, fay, gnome, hobgoblin, pixie, puck, troll

lep·ro·sy \'le-prə-sē\ *n* : a chronic bacterial disease marked esp. if not treated by slow-growing swellings with deformity and loss of sensation of affected parts — **lep·rous** \-prəs\ *adj*

lep·tin \'lep-tən\ *n* : a hormone that is produced by fat-containing cells and plays a role in body weight regulation

les·bi·an \'lez-bē-ən\ *n* [fr. the reputed homosexual group associated with the poet Sappho of Lesbos] : a woman who is a homosexual — **lesbian** *adj* — **les·bi·an·ism** \-ə-ˌni-zəm\ *n*

lése ma·jes·té *or* **lese maj·es·ty** \'lāz-ˌma-jə-stē, 'lez-, 'lēz-\ *n* [MF *lese majesté*, fr. L *laesa majestas*, lit., injured majesty] : an offense violating the dignity of a sovereign

le·sion \'lē-zhən\ *n* : an abnormal structural change in the body due to injury or disease; *esp* : one clearly marked off from healthy tissue around it

¹less \'les\ *adj, comparative of* ¹LITTLE **1** : FEWER ⟨∼ than six⟩ **2** ♦ : of lower rank, degree, or importance **3** : SMALLER; *also* : more limited in quantity

♦ inferior, junior, lesser, lower, minor, subordinate, under — more at LESSER

²less *adv, comparative of* ²LITTLE : to a lesser extent or degree

³less *n, pl* **less** **1** : a smaller portion **2** : something of less importance

⁴less *prep* : diminished by : MINUS

-less \ləs\ *adj suffix* **1** : destitute of : not having ⟨child*less*⟩ **2** : unable to be acted on or to act (in a specified way) ⟨daunt*less*⟩

les·see \le-'sē\ *n* : a tenant under a lease

les·sen \'les-ᵊn\ *vb* ♦ : to make or become less

♦ abate, decline, decrease, de-escalate, die, diminish, dwindle, ebb, fall, let up, lower, moderate, recede, reduce, relent, shrink, subside, taper, wane — more at DECREASE

less·er \'le-sər\ *adj, comparative of* ¹LITTLE ♦ : of less size, quality, or significance

♦ inferior, junior, less, lower, minor, subordinate, under; *also* little, mean, small; minute, petty; jerkwater, second-rate; secondary, subsidiary **Ant** major, more, primary, prime, senior, superior

les·son \'les-ᵊn\ *n* **1** : a passage from sacred writings read in a service of worship **2** : a reading or exercise to be studied by a pupil; *also* : something learned **3** : a period of instruction **4** : an instructive example

les·sor \'le-ˌsȯr, le-'sȯr\ *n* : one who conveys property by a lease

lest \ˌlest\ *conj* : for fear that

¹let \'let\ *n* [ME *lette*, fr. *letten* to delay, hinder, fr. OE *lettan*] **1** : something that impedes : HINDRANCE, OBSTACLE **2** : a shot or point in racket games that does not count

²let *vb* **let; let·ting** [ME *leten*, fr. OE *lǣtan*] **1** : to cause to : MAKE ⟨∼ it be known⟩ **2** : to offer or grant for rent or lease; *also* : to assign esp. after bids **3** ♦ : to give opportunity or permission to : ALLOW, PERMIT ⟨∼ me go⟩

♦ allow, enable, permit, suffer — more at ALLOW

-let \lət\ *n suffix* **1** : small one ⟨book*let*⟩ **2** : article worn on ⟨wrist*let*⟩

let·down \'let-ˌdau̇n\ *n* **1** ♦ : the state or emotion of being disappointed **2** : a slackening of effort

♦ disappointment, dismay, dissatisfaction, frustration — more at DISAPPOINTMENT

let down *vb* ♦ : to fail to meet the expectation or hope of; *also* : to cause disappointment

♦ cheat, disappoint, dissatisfy, fail — more at DISAPPOINT

le·thal \'lē-thəl\ *adj* ♦ : of, relating to, or causing death : DEADLY, FATAL ⟨∼ weapons⟩ — **le·thal·ly** *adv*

♦ baleful, deadly, deathly, fatal, fell, mortal, murderous, pestilent, vital — more at DEADLY

le·thar·gic \li-'thär-jik\ *adj* ♦ : of, relating to, or characterized by lethargy

♦ dull, inactive, inert, quiescent, sleepy, sluggish, torpid — more at INACTIVE

leth·ar·gy \'le-thər-jē\ *n* **1** : abnormal drowsiness **2** : the quality or state of being lazy or indifferent

let on *vb* **1** : REVEAL 1 **2** : PRETEND

¹let·ter \'le-tər\ *n* **1** : a symbol that stands for a speech sound and constitutes a unit of an alphabet **2** ♦ : a written or printed communication **3** *pl* : LITERATURE; *also* : LEARNING **4** : the literal meaning ⟨the ∼ of the law⟩ **5** : a single piece of type

♦ dispatch, memorandum, missive, note; *also* airmail, card, electronic mail, e-mail, junk mail, mail, postal card, postcard; communication, report; encyclical

²letter *vb* : to mark with letters : INSCRIBE — **let·ter·er** *n*

letter bomb *n* : an explosive device concealed in an envelope and mailed to the intended victim

let·ter·boxed \'le-tər-ˌbäkst\ *adj* : being a video recording formatted to display a frame size proportional to a standard theater screen

letter carrier *n* ♦ : an individual who delivers mail

♦ mailman, postman — more at POSTMAN

let·ter·head \'le-tər-ˌhed\ *n* : stationery with a printed or engraved heading; *also* : the heading itself

let·ter–per·fect \ˌle-tər-'pər-fikt\ *adj* ♦ : correct to the smallest detail

♦ absolute, faultless, flawless, ideal, impeccable, perfect, unblemished — more at PERFECT

let·ter·press \'le-tər-ˌpres\ *n* : printing done directly by impressing the paper on an inked raised surface

letters of marque \-'märk\ : a license granted to a private person by a government to fit out an armed ship to capture enemy shipping

letters patent *n pl* : a written grant from a government to a person in a form readily open for inspection by all

let·tuce \'le-təs\ *n* [ME *letuse*, fr. AF, prob. fr. pl. of *letue* lettuce plant, fr. L *lactuca*, fr. *lac* milk; fr. its milky juice] : a garden composite plant with crisp leaves used esp. in salads

let·up \'let-ˌəp\ *n* : a lessening of effort

let up *vb* ♦ : to diminish or slow down; *also* : to come to a stop

♦ cease, end, halt, quit, stop ♦ abate, decrease, die, diminish, dwindle, ebb, fall, lessen, subside, taper, wane — more at DECREASE

leu·kae·mia *chiefly Brit var of* LEUKEMIA

leu·ke·mia \lü-'kē-mē-ə\ *n* : a malignant disease characterized by an abnormal increase in the number of white blood cells in the blood-forming tissues — **leu·ke·mic** \-mik\ *adj or n*

leu·ko·cyte \\'lü-kə-ˌsīt\\ *n* : WHITE BLOOD CELL

Lev *or* **Levit** *abbr* Leviticus

¹**le·vee** \\'le-vē; lə-'vē, -'vā\\ *n* [F *lever* act of arising] : a reception held by or for a person of distinction

²**lev·ee** \\'le-vē\\ *n* ♦ : an embankment to prevent or confine flooding; *also* : a river landing place

♦ dam, dike, embankment — more at DAM ♦ dock, landing, pier — more at DOCK

¹**lev·el** \\'le-vəl\\ *n* 1 : a device for establishing a horizontal line or plane 2 : horizontal condition 3 : a horizontal position, line, or surface often taken as an index of altitude; *also* : a flat area of ground 4 ♦ : height, position, rank, or size in a scale

♦ degree, footing, place, position, rank, situation, standing, status — more at RANK

²**level** *vb* **-eled** *or* **-elled**; **-el·ing** *or* **-el·ling** 1 ♦ : to make flat or level; *also* : to come to a level 2 : to direct to or toward a specified object or goal : AIM 3 ♦ : to bring to a common level or plane : EQUALIZE 4 : RAZE 5 ♦ : to knock down — **lev·el·er** *n*

♦ [1] even, plane, smooth — more at EVEN ♦ [3] balance, equalize, equate, even — more at EQUALIZE ♦ [5] bowl, down, drop, fell, floor, knock

³**level** *adj* 1 ♦ : having a flat even surface 2 : HORIZONTAL 3 : of the same height or rank; *also* : UNIFORM 4 : steady and cool in judgment — **lev·el·ly** *adv* — **lev·el·ness** *n*

♦ even, flat, flush, plane, smooth; *also* exact, uniform; aligned, regular, true; horizontal, tabular; plumb, straight, vertical *Ant* bumpy, coarse, lumpy, rough, uneven

lev·el·head·ed \\ˌle-vəl-'he-dəd\\ *adj* ♦ : having sound judgment : SENSIBLE ⟨a ∼ decision⟩

♦ good, hard, informed, just, logical, rational, reasonable, reasoned, sensible, sober, solid, valid, wellfounded — more at GOOD

le·ver \\'le-vər, 'lē-\\ *n* 1 : a bar used for prying or dislodging something; *also* : a means for achieving one's purpose 2 : a rigid piece turning about an axis and used for transmitting and changing force and motion

lev·er·age \\'le-vrij, 'lē-, -və-rij\\ *n* : the action or mechanical effect of a lever

le·vi·a·than \\li-'vī-ə-thən\\ *n* 1 : a large sea animal 2 ♦ : something large or formidable

♦ behemoth, blockbuster, colossus, giant, jumbo, mammoth, monster, titan, whale, whopper — more at GIANT

lev·i·tate \\'le-və-ˌtāt\\ *vb* **-tat·ed**; **-tat·ing** : to rise or cause to rise in the air in seeming defiance of gravitation — **lev·i·ta·tion** \\ˌle-və-'tā-shən\\ *n*

Le·vit·i·cus \\li-'vi-tə-kəs\\ *n* : a book of Jewish and Christian Scripture

lev·i·ty \\'le-və-tē\\ *n* ♦ : lack of seriousness

♦ facetiousness, flightiness, flippancy, frivolity, lightness — more at FRIVOLITY

levo·do·pa \\ˌle-və-'dō-pə\\ *n* : L-DOPA

¹**levy** \\'le-vē\\ *n, pl* **lev·ies** 1 ♦ : the imposition or collection of an assessment; *also* : an amount levied 2 : the enlistment or conscription of men for military service; *also* : troops raised by levy

♦ assessment, duty, impost, tax — more at TAX

²**levy** *vb* **lev·ied**; **levy·ing** 1 ♦ : to impose or collect by legal authority ⟨∼ taxes⟩ 2 : to enlist for military service 3 : WAGE ⟨∼ war⟩ 4 : to seize property

♦ assess, charge, exact, fine, impose, lay, put — more at IMPOSE

lewd \\'lüd\\ *adj* [ME *lewed* vulgar, fr. OE *lǣwede* lay, ignorant] 1 ♦ : sexually unchaste 2 ♦ : abhorrent to morality or virtue : OBSCENE, VULGAR — **lewd·ly** *adv*

♦ [1] lascivious, lustful, passionate, wanton — more at LUSTFUL ♦ [2] bawdy, coarse, crude, indecent, lascivious, obscene, pornographic, ribald, smutty, unprintable, vulgar, wanton — more at OBSCENE

lewd·ness *n* ♦ : the quality or state of being lewd

♦ bawdiness, coarseness, grossness, indecency, nastiness, obscenity, ribaldry, smut, vulgarity — more at OBSCENITY

lex·i·cog·ra·phy \\ˌlek-sə-'kä-grə-fē\\ *n* 1 : the editing or making of a dictionary 2 : the principles and practices of dictionary making — **lex·i·cog·ra·pher** \\-fər\\ *n* — **lex·i·co·graph·i·cal** \\-kō-'gra-fi-kəl\\ *or* **lex·i·co·graph·ic** \\-fik\\ *adj*

lex·i·con \\'lek-sə-ˌkän\\ *n, pl* **lex·i·ca** \\-si-kə\\ *or* **lexicons** 1 : DICTIONARY 2 : the vocabulary of a language, speaker, or subject

lg *abbr* 1 large 2 long

LGBT *abbr* lesbian, gay, bisexual, and transgender

LH *abbr* 1 left hand 2 lower half

li *abbr* link

Li *symbol* lithium

LI *abbr* Long Island

li·a·bil·i·ty \\ˌlī-ə-'bi-lə-tē\\ *n, pl* **-ties** 1 ♦ : the quality or state of being liable 2 *pl* : DEBTS 3 ♦ : one that acts as a disadvantage : DISADVANTAGE

♦ [1] blame, fault, responsibility — more at RESPONSIBILITY ♦ [3] disadvantage, drawback, handicap, minus, penalty, strike — more at DISADVANTAGE

li·a·ble \\'lī-ə-bəl\\ *adj* 1 ♦ : legally obligated : RESPONSIBLE 2 : LIKELY, APT ⟨∼ to fall⟩ 3 ♦ : exposed or subject to something usu. adverse : SUSCEPTIBLE

♦ [1] accountable, answerable, responsible — more at RESPONSIBLE ♦ [3] exposed, open, sensitive, subject, susceptible, vulnerable; *also* likely, prone; uncovered, undefended, unguarded, unprotected *Ant* invulnerable, unexposed

li·ai·son \\'lē-ə-ˌzän, lē-'ā-\\ *n* [F] 1 ♦ : a close bond or connection 2 : an illicit sexual relationship 3 : communication for mutual understanding (as between parts of an armed force); *also* : one that carries on a liaison

♦ affiliation, alliance, association, collaboration, confederation, connection, cooperation, hookup, partnership, relation, relationship, union — more at ASSOCIATION

li·ar \\'lī-ər\\ *n* ♦ : a person who lies

♦ fibber, prevaricator; *also* libeler, slanderer; perjurer, gossip; charlatan, cheat, cheater, counterfeiter, cozener, deceiver, dissembler, double-dealer, fraud, hustler, mountebank, pretender

¹**lib** \\'lib\\ *n* : LIBERATION

²**lib** *abbr* 1 liberal 2 librarian; library

li·ba·tion \\lī-'bā-shən\\ *n* 1 : an act of pouring a liquid as a sacrifice (as to a god); *also* : the liquid poured 2 ♦ : a drinkable liquid : DRINK

♦ beverage, drink, quencher — more at DRINK

¹**li·bel** \\'lī-bəl\\ *n* [ME, written declaration, fr. AF, fr. L *libellus*, dim. of *liber* book] 1 : a spoken or written statement or a representation that gives an unjustly unfavorable impression of a person or thing 2 ♦ : the action or crime of publishing a libel

♦ defamation, slander, vilification — more at SLANDER

²**libel** *vb* **-beled** *or* **-belled**; **-bel·ing** *or* **-bel·ling** ♦ : to make or publish a libel — **li·bel·er** *n* — **li·bel·ist** *n*

♦ blacken, defame, malign, slander, smear, traduce, vilify — more at SLANDER

li·bel·ous *or* **li·bel·lous** \\-bə-ləs\\ *adj* ♦ : constituting or including a libel

♦ defamatory, scandalous, slanderous; *also* erroneous, false, inaccurate, incorrect, inexact, invalid, off, unsound, untrue, wrong; derogatory, disparaging, uncomplimentary, unfavorable; invidious, objectionable, maligning, traducing, vilifying; hateful, malevolent, malicious, spiteful

¹**lib·er·al** \\'li-brəl, -bə-rəl\\ *adj* [ME, fr. AF, fr. L *liberalis* suitable for a freeman, generous, fr. *liber* free] 1 : of, relating to, or based on the liberal arts 2 ♦ : given or provided in a generous and openhanded way : GENEROUS, BOUNTIFUL; *also* : generous or more than adequate

in size, scope, or capacity **3** : not literal **4 a** : not narrow in opinion or judgment : TOLERANT **b** ♦ : not orthodox **5** : not conservative — **lib·er·al·ize** \'li-brə-ˌlīz, -bə-rə-\ vb

♦ [2] abundant, ample, comfortable, generous, plentiful — more at PLENTIFUL ♦ [2] bountiful, charitable, free, generous, munificent, openhanded, unselfish, unsparing — more at GENEROUS ♦ [4b] broad-minded, nonorthodox, nontraditional, open-minded, progressive, radical, unconventional, unorthodox; also advanced, contemporary, modern; forbearing, indulgent, lenient, permissive, tolerant; extreme; impartial, objective, unbiased **Ant** conservative, conventional, old-fashioned, orthodox, traditional

²**liberal** n : a person who holds liberal views
liberal arts n pl : the studies (as language, philosophy, history, literature, or abstract science) in a college or university intended to provide chiefly general knowledge and to develop the general intellectual capacities
lib·er·al·ism \'li-brə-ˌli-zəm, -bə-rə-\ n : liberal principles and theories
lib·er·al·i·ty \ˌli-bə-'ra-lə-tē\ n ♦ : the quality or state of being liberal; also : an instance of this

♦ bounty, generosity, largesse, philanthropy, unselfishness; also beneficence, charity; kindness; gift, gratuity, lagniappe; tribute; extravagance, improvidence, lavishness, prodigality, wastefulness; spendthrift; dissipating, squandering **Ant** cheapness, closeness, meanness, miserliness, parsimony, pinching, stinginess, tightness

lib·er·al·ly adv ♦ : in a liberal manner

♦ bountifully, generously, handsomely, well — more at WELL

lib·er·ate \'li-bə-ˌrāt\ vb **-at·ed; -at·ing** **1** ♦ : to free from bondage or restraint; also : to raise to equal rights and status **2** : to free (as a gas) from combination — **lib·er·a·tor** \'li-bə-ˌrā-tər\ n

♦ discharge, emancipate, enfranchise, free, loose, loosen, manumit, release, spring, unbind, unchain, unfetter — more at FREE

lib·er·at·ed adj : freed from or opposed to traditional social and sexual attitudes or roles ⟨a ~ marriage⟩
lib·er·a·tion \ˌli-bə-'rā-shən\ n ♦ : the act of liberating : the state of being liberated

♦ emancipation, enfranchisement, manumission; also deliverance, redemption, salvation; autonomy, freedom, independence, liberty, self-government, sovereignty **Ant** enslavement

Li·be·ri·an \lī-'bir-ē-ən\ n : a native or inhabitant of Liberia — **Liberian** adj
lib·er·tar·i·an \ˌli-bər-'ter-ē-ən\ n **1** : an advocate of the doctrine of free will **2** : one who upholds the principles of unrestricted liberty
lib·er·tine \'li-bər-ˌtēn\ n ♦ : a person who leads a dissolute life

♦ decadent, degenerate, pervert, profligate — more at DEGENERATE

lib·er·ty \'li-bər-tē\ n, pl **-ties** **1** ♦ : the quality or state of being free : FREEDOM **2** : an action going beyond normal limits; esp : FAMILIARITY **3** : a short leave from naval duty

♦ autonomy, freedom, independence, self-government, sovereignty — more at FREEDOM

li·bid·i·nous \lə-'bid-ᵊn-əs\ adj **1** : LASCIVIOUS **2** : LIBIDINAL
li·bi·do \lə-'bē-dō, -'bī-\ n, pl **-dos** [NL, fr. L, desire, lust] **1** : psychic energy derived from basic biological urges **2** : sexual drive — **li·bid·i·nal** \lə-'bid-ᵊn-əl\ adj
Li·bra \'lē-brə\ n [L, lit., scales] **1** : a zodiacal constellation between Virgo and Scorpio usu. pictured as a balance scale **2** : the 7th sign of the zodiac in astrology; also : one born under this sign
li·brar·i·an \lī-'brer-ē-ən\ n : a specialist in the management of a library

li·brary \'lī-ˌbrer-ē\ n, pl **-brar·ies** **1** : a place in which books and related materials are kept for use but not for sale **2** : a collection of books
li·bret·to \lə-'bre-tō\ n, pl **-tos** or **-ti** \-tē\ [It, dim. of libro book, fr. L liber] : the text esp. of an opera — **li·bret·tist** \-tist\ n
Lib·y·an \'li-bē-ən\ n : a native or inhabitant of Libya — **Libyan** adj
lice pl of LOUSE
¹**li·cense** or chiefly Brit **li·cence** \'līs-ᵊns\ n **1** ♦ : permission to act **2** ♦ : a permission granted by authority to engage in an activity **3** : a document, plate, or tag providing proof of a license **4** : freedom used irresponsibly

♦ [1] authorization, freedom, latitude, run — more at FREEDOM ♦ [2] allowance, authorization, clearance, concurrence, consent, leave, permission, sanction, sufferance — more at PERMISSION

²**license** or chiefly Brit **licence** vb ♦ : to issue a license to

♦ accredit, authorize, certify, commission, empower, enable, invest, qualify — more at AUTHORIZE

licensed practical nurse n : a specially trained person who is licensed (as by a state) to provide routine care for the sick
li·cens·ee \ˌlīs-ᵊn-'sē\ n : a licensed person
li·cen·ti·ate \lī-'sen-chē-ət\ n : one licensed to practice a profession
li·cen·tious \lī-'sen-chəs\ adj : lacking legal or moral restraints; also : disregarding sexual restraints : LEWD, LASCIVIOUS — **li·cen·tious·ly** adv
li·cen·tious·ness n ♦ : the quality or state of being licentious

♦ corruption, debauchery, depravity, immorality, iniquity, sin, vice — more at VICE

lichee var of LITCHI
li·chen \'lī-kən\ n : any of various complex plantlike organisms made up of an alga and a fungus growing as a unit on a solid surface — **li·chen·ous** adj
lic·it \'li-sət\ adj : LAWFUL
¹**lick** \'lik\ vb **1** : to draw the tongue over; also : to flicker over like a tongue **2** : to beat soundly : THRASH; also : DEFEAT
²**lick** n **1** : a stroke of the tongue **2** ♦ : a small amount **3** : a hasty careless effort **4** : a sharp hit : BLOW **5** : a natural deposit of salt that animals lick

♦ bit, dab, little, particle, shred, touch, trace — more at PARTICLE

lick·e·ty–split \ˌli-kə-tē-'split\ adv : at great speed
lick·spit·tle \'lik-ˌspit-ᵊl\ n : a fawning subordinate : TOADY
lic·o·rice \'li-kə-rish, -rəs\ n [ME, fr. AF licoris, fr. LL liquiritia, alter. of L glycyrrhiza, fr. Gk glykyrrhiza, fr. glykys sweet + rhiza root] **1** : the dried root of a European leguminous plant; also : an extract from it used esp. as a flavoring and in medicine **2** : a candy flavored with licorice **3** : a plant yielding licorice
lid \'lid\ n **1** ♦ : a movable cover **2** : EYELID **3** : something that confines or suppresses — **lid·ded** \'li-dəd\ adj

♦ cap, cover, top — more at COVER

li·do \'lē-dō\ n, pl **lidos** : a fashionable beach resort
¹**lie** \'lī\ vb **lay** \'lā\; **lain** \'lān\; **ly·ing** \'lī-iŋ\ **1** : to be in, stay at rest in, or assume a horizontal position; also : to be in a helpless or defenseless state **2** ♦ : to have direction : EXTEND **3** : to occupy a certain relative position **4** : to have an effect esp. through mere presence

♦ [2] extend, go, head, lead, run — more at RUN
♦ [3] be, sit, stand

²**lie** n : the position in which something lies
³**lie** vb **lied; ly·ing** \'lī-iŋ\ ♦ : to tell a lie

♦ fabricate, fib, prevaricate; also forswear, perjure; equivocate, fudge, palter; beguile, cozen, deceive, delude, dupe, fool, gull, hoax, hoodwink, kid, snow, take in, trick; defame, libel, slander, traduce; falsify, misrepresent, misstate; distort, garble; dissemble, dissimulate; misguide, misinform, mislead

⁴**lie** *n* ♦ : an untrue statement made with intent to deceive

♦ fabrication, fairy tale, falsehood, falsity, fib, mendacity, prevarication, story, tale, untruth, whopper; *also* distortion, exaggeration, half-truth; ambiguity, equivocation; defamation, libel, slander; perjury; bluff, pose, pretense; humbug, jive, nonsense; fallacy, misconception, myth; misinformation, misrepresentation, misstatement; deceit, deceitfulness, dishonesty, duplicity *Ant* truth

lied \'lēt\ *n, pl* **lie·der** \'lē-dər\ [G] : a German song esp. of the 19th century

lie detector *n* : a polygraph for detecting physiological evidence of the tension that accompanies lying

lief \'lēv, 'lēf\ *adv* : GLADLY, WILLINGLY

¹**liege** \'lēj\ *adj* : LOYAL, FAITHFUL

²**liege** *n* **1** : VASSAL **2** : a feudal superior

lien \'lēn, 'lē-ən\ *n* : a legal claim on the property of another for the satisfaction of a debt or duty

lieu \'lü\ *n, archaic* : PLACE, STEAD — **in lieu of** : in the place of

lieut *abbr* lieutenant

lieu·ten·ant \lü-'te-nənt\ *n* [ME, fr. AF *lieu tenant*, fr. *liu, lieu* place + *tenant* holding, fr. *tenir* to hold, fr. L *tenēre*] **1** : a representative of another in the performance of duty **2** : FIRST LIEUTENANT; *also* : SECOND LIEUTENANT **3** : a commissioned officer in the navy ranking next below a lieutenant commander — **lieu·ten·an·cy** \-nən-sē\ *n*

lieutenant colonel *n* : a commissioned officer (as in the army) ranking next below a colonel

lieutenant commander *n* : a commissioned officer in the navy ranking next below a commander

lieutenant general *n* : a commissioned officer (as in the army) ranking next below a general

lieutenant governor *n* : a deputy or subordinate governor

lieutenant junior grade *n, pl* **lieutenants junior grade** : a commissioned officer in the navy ranking next below a lieutenant

life \'līf\ *n, pl* **lives** \'līvz\ **1** : the quality that distinguishes a vital and functional being from a dead body or inanimate matter; *also* : a state of an organism characterized esp. by capacity for metabolism, growth, reaction to stimuli, and reproduction **2** : the physical and mental experiences of an individual **3** : a written history of a person's life : BIOGRAPHY **4** ♦ : a specific phase or period ⟨adult ∼⟩ **5** : the period from birth to death; *also* : a sentence of imprisonment for the remainder of a person's life **6** ♦ : a way of living **7** : a vital or living being; *specif* : PERSON **8** ♦ : a lively or brisk quality in a person or a person's actions **9** : living beings ⟨forest ∼⟩ **10** : animate activity ⟨signs of ∼⟩ **11** : one providing interest and vigor ⟨∼ of the party⟩

♦ [4] date, duration, lifetime, run, standing, time — more at DURATION ♦ [6] civilization, culture, lifestyle, society — more at CIVILIZATION ♦ [8] dash, energy, pep, vigor (*or* vigour), vim, vitality — more at VIGOR

life·blood \'līf-,bləd\ *n* : a basic source of strength and vitality

life·boat \-,bōt\ *n* : a sturdy boat designed for use in saving lives at sea

life·guard \-,gärd\ *n* : a usu. expert swimmer employed to safeguard bathers

life·less *adj* ♦ : having no life

♦ breathless, dead, deceased, defunct, gone, late — more at DEAD

life·like *adj* ♦ : accurately representing or imitating real life

♦ natural, near, realistic — more at NATURAL

life·line \-,līn\ *n* **1** : a line to which persons may cling for safety **2** : something considered vital for survival

life·long \-,lȯŋ\ *adj* : continuing through life

life preserver *n* : a buoyant device designed to save a person from drowning

lif·er \'lī-fər\ *n* **1** : a person sentenced to life imprisonment **2** : a person who makes a career in the armed forces

life raft *n* : a raft for use by people forced into the water

life·sav·ing \'līf-,sā-viŋ\ *n* : the skill or practice of saving or protecting lives esp. of drowning persons — **life·sav·er** \-,sā-vər\ *n*

life science *n* : a branch of science (as biology, medicine, and sometimes anthropology or sociology) that deals with living organisms and life processes — usu. used in pl. — **life scientist** *n*

life span *n* : the duration of existence of an individual

life·style \'līf-,stīl\ *n* ♦ : a way of living

♦ civilization, culture, life, society — more at CIVILIZATION

life·time \-,tīm\ *n* ♦ : the duration of an individual's existence

♦ date, duration, life, run, standing, time — more at DURATION

life·work \-'wərk\ *n* : the entire or principal work of one's lifetime; *also* : a work extending over a lifetime

life·world \-,wər(-ə)ld\ *n* : the total of an individual's physical surroundings and everyday experiences

LIFO *abbr* last in, first out

¹**lift** \'lift\ *vb* **1** ♦ : to raise from a lower to a higher position : ELEVATE; *also* : RISE, ASCEND **2** : to put an end to : STOP ⟨∼ a ban⟩ **3** : to pay off ⟨∼ a mortgage⟩ — **lift·er** *n*

♦ boost, crane, elevate, heave, heft, heighten, hike, hoist, jack, pick up, raise, up, uphold — more at RAISE ♦ arise, ascend, climb, mount, rise, soar, up — more at ASCEND

²**lift** *n* **1** : LOAD **2** : the action or an instance of lifting **3** ♦ : the act of assisting or the help supplied; *also* : a ride along one's way **4** : RISE, ADVANCE **5** *chiefly Brit* : ELEVATOR **6** : an elevation of the spirits **7** : the upward force that is developed by a moving airfoil and that opposes the pull of gravity

♦ aid, assist, assistance, backing, boost, help, support — more at HELP

lift-off \'lif-,tȯf\ *n* : a vertical takeoff (as by a rocket)

lift truck *n* : a small truck for lifting and transporting loads

lig·a·ment \'li-gə-mənt\ *n* : a band of tough fibrous tissue that holds bones together or supports an organ in place

li·gate \'lī-,gāt\ *vb* **li·gat·ed; li·gat·ing** : to tie with a ligature — **li·ga·tion** \lī-'gā-shən\ *n*

lig·a·ture \'li-gə-,chur, -chər\ *n* **1** ♦ : something that binds or ties; *also* : a thread used in surgery esp. for tying blood vessels **2** : a printed or written character consisting of two or more letters or characters (as æ) united

♦ bond, cement, knot, link, tie — more at BOND

¹**light** \'līt\ *n* **1** ♦ : something that makes vision possible : electromagnetic radiation visible to the human eye; *also* : the sensation aroused by stimulation of the visual sense organs **2** : DAYLIGHT **3** ♦ : a source of light (as a candle) **4** : ENLIGHTENMENT; *also* : TRUTH **5** : public knowledge ⟨facts brought to ∼⟩ **6** : a particular aspect presented to view ⟨saw the matter in a different ∼⟩ **7** : WINDOW **8** *pl* : STANDARDS ⟨according to his ∼s⟩ **9** ♦ : a noteworthy person in a particular place or field : CELEBRITY **10** : LIGHTHOUSE, BEACON; *also* : TRAFFIC LIGHT **11** : a flame for lighting something

♦ [1] blaze, flare, fluorescence, glare, gleam, glow, illumination, incandescence, luminescence, radiance, shine; *also* flash, glimmer, glint, glitter, scintillation, shimmer, sparkle, twinkle; daylight, moonlight, sunlight; afterglow, aureole, aurora, beam, ray, shaft, streak, stream; glisten, gloss, luster, polish, reflection, sheen ♦ [3] flare ♦ [9] celebrity, figure, luminary, notable, personage, personality, somebody, standout, star, superstar, VIP — more at CELEBRITY

²**light** *adj* **1** ♦ : having light : BRIGHT **2** : not dark, intense, or swarthy in color or coloring : PALE ⟨∼ blue⟩

♦ ablaze, alight, bright — more at BRIGHT

³**light** *vb* **lit** \'lit\ *or* **light·ed; light·ing** **1** : to make or become light **2** ♦ : to cause to burn : BURN **3** : to conduct with a light **4** ♦ : to supply or brighten with light : ILLUMINATE

♦ [2] burn, fire, ignite, inflame, kindle — more at BURN ♦ [4] illuminate — more at ILLUMINATE

⁴light *adj* 1 ♦ : not heavy 2 : not serious ⟨∼ reading⟩ 3 : not abundant : SCANTY ⟨∼ rain⟩ 4 : easily disturbed ⟨a ∼ sleeper⟩ 5 a : exerting a minimum of force or pressure : GENTLE ⟨a ∼ blow⟩ b ♦ : requiring minimal effort or energy 6 ♦ : easily endurable ⟨a ∼ cold⟩; *also* : requiring little effort ⟨∼ exercise⟩ 7 ♦ : capable of moving swiftly or nimbly 8 : FRIVOLOUS 9 : DIZZY 10 : made with lower calorie content or less of some ingredient than usual ⟨∼ salad dressing⟩ 11 : producing goods for direct consumption by the consumer ⟨∼ industry⟩

♦ [1] airy, ethereal, feathery, fluffy, weightless; *also* bantam, diminutive, little, minute, small, smallish, puny, tiny, undersized, wee; flimsy, fragile, insubstantial; petite, slender, slight, slim, thin *Ant* heavy, hefty, leaden, overweight, ponderous, weighty ♦ [5b] easy, effortless, facile, fluent, fluid, painless, ready, simple, smooth, snap, soft — more at EASY ♦ [6] balmy, benign, bland, delicate, gentle, mellow, mild, soft, soothing, tender — more at GENTLE ♦ [7] agile, graceful, lissome, lithe, nimble, spry — more at GRACEFUL

⁵light *adv* 1 : LIGHTLY 2 : with little baggage ⟨travel ∼⟩
⁶light *vb* lit \'lit\ *or* light·ed; light·ing 1 ♦ : to descend from or as if from the air and come to rest : SETTLE, ALIGHT 2 : to fall unexpectedly 3 : HAPPEN ⟨∼ed on a solution⟩

♦ alight, land, perch, roost, settle — more at ALIGHT

light bulb *n* 1 : a lamp in which an electrically heated filament emits light 2 : FLUORESCENT LAMP
light–emitting diode *n* : LED
¹light·en \'lit-ᵊn\ *vb* 1 : to make light or clear : ILLUMINATE 2 : to give out flashes of lightning
²lighten *vb* 1 : to relieve of a burden 2 : GLADDEN 3 : to become lighter
lighten up *vb* : to take things less seriously
¹ligh·ter \'lī-tər\ *n* : a barge used esp. in loading or unloading ships
²light·er \'lī-tər\ *n* : one that lights; *esp* : a device for lighting
light·face \'līt-ˌfās\ *n* : a type having light thin lines — light·faced \-ˌfāst\ *adj*
light–head·ed \'līt-ˌhe-dəd\ *adj* 1 ♦ : feeling confused or dizzy 2 ♦ : lacking maturity or seriousness

♦ [1] dizzy, giddy — more at DIZZY ♦ [2] flighty, frivolous, giddy, goofy, harebrained, scatterbrained, silly — more at GIDDY

light–heart·ed \-ˌhär-təd\ *adj* ♦ : free from worry — light·heart·ed·ly *adv*

♦ carefree, careless, cavalier, easygoing, gay, happy-go-lucky, insouciant, unconcerned

light·heart·ed·ness *n* ♦ : the quality or state of being lighthearted

♦ abandon, abandonment, ease, naturalness, spontaneity, unrestraint — more at ABANDON

light·house \-ˌhaùs\ *n* : a structure with a powerful light for guiding sailors
light·ly *adv* ♦ : in a light manner

♦ easily, effortlessly, fluently, freely, handily, painlessly, readily, smoothly — more at EASILY

light meter *n* : a usu. handheld device for indicating correct photographic exposure
¹light·ness *n* ♦ : the quality or state of being illuminated

♦ brilliance, dazzle, effulgence, illumination, lucidity, luminosity, radiance, refulgence, splendor — more at BRILLIANCE

²light·ness *n* 1 ♦ : lack of seriousness and stability of character often accompanied by casual heedlessness 2 : the quality or state of being light esp. in weight

♦ facetiousness, flightiness, flippancy, frivolity, levity — more at FRIVOLITY

¹light·ning \'līt-niŋ\ *n* : the flashing of light produced by a discharge of atmospheric electricity; *also* : the discharge itself
²lightning *adj* ♦ : extremely fast

♦ breakneck, breathless, brisk, dizzy, fast, fleet, hasty, nippy, quick, rapid, rattling, snappy, speedy, swift — more at FAST

lightning bug *n* : FIREFLY
lightning rod *n* : a grounded metallic rod set up on a structure to protect it from lightning
light out *vb* : to leave in a hurry
light·proof \'līt-ˌprüf\ *adj* : impenetrable by light
lights \'līts\ *n pl* : the lungs esp. of a slaughtered animal
light·ship \'līt-ˌship\ *n* : a ship with a powerful light moored at a place dangerous to navigation
light show *n* : a kaleidoscopic display (as of colored lights)
light·some \'līt-səm\ *adj* 1 ♦ : free from care 2 : NIMBLE

♦ blithe, bright, buoyant, cheerful, cheery, chipper, gay, sunny, upbeat — more at CHEERFUL

¹light·weight \'līt-ˌwāt\ *n* 1 : one of less than average weight; *esp* : a boxer weighing not over 135 pounds 2 : one of little consequence or ability
²lightweight *adj* 1 : INCONSEQUENTIAL 2 : of less than average weight
light–year \'līt-ˌyir\ *n* 1 : an astronomical unit of distance equal to the distance that light travels in one year in a vacuum or about 5.88 trillion miles (9.46 trillion kilometers) 2 : an extremely large measure of comparison ⟨saw it ∼s ago⟩
lig·nin \'lig-nən\ *n* : a substance related to cellulose that occurs in the woody cell walls of plants and in the cementing material between them
lig·nite \'lig-ˌnīt\ *n* : brownish black soft coal
¹like \'līk\ *vb* liked; lik·ing 1 ♦ : to feel attraction toward or take pleasure in : ENJOY ⟨∼s baseball⟩ 2 ♦ : to wish to have : WANT 3 ♦ : to feel inclined : CHOOSE ⟨does as she ∼s⟩ — lik·able *or* like·able \'lī-kə-bəl\ *adj*

♦ [1] favor (*or* favour), lean, prefer — more at PREFER ♦ [1] adore, delight, dig, enjoy, fancy, groove, love, relish, revel — more at ENJOY ♦ [2, 3] choose, want, will, wish

²like *n* ♦ : favorable regard : PREFERENCE

♦ appetite, fancy, favor (*or* favour), fondness, liking, love, partiality, preference, relish, shine, taste, use — more at LIKING

³like *adj* ♦ : the same or nearly the same (as in appearance, character, or quantity) : SIMILAR

♦ akin, alike, analogous, comparable, correspondent, parallel, similar, such — more at ALIKE

⁴like *prep* 1 : similar or similarly to ⟨it's ∼ when we were kids⟩ 2 : typical of 3 : comparable to 4 : as though there would be ⟨looks ∼ rain⟩ 5 : such as ⟨a subject ∼ physics⟩
⁵like *n* 1 a : one that is similar b ♦ : a group having common traits 2 ♦ : one that is similar to another ⟨we may never see his ∼ again⟩ — and the like : ET CETERA

♦ [1b] breed, class, description, feather, ilk, kind, manner, nature, order, sort, species, type — more at SORT ♦ [2] coordinate, counterpart, equal, equivalent, fellow, match, parallel, peer, rival — more at EQUAL

⁶like *conj* : in the same way that
-like \ˌlīk\ *adj comb form* : resembling or characteristic of ⟨lady*like*⟩ ⟨life*like*⟩
like·li·hood \'lī-klē-ˌhùd\ *n* : PROBABILITY
¹like·ly \'lī-klē\ *adj* like·li·er; -est 1 ♦ : very probable 2 ♦ : offering reasonable grounds for being believed : BELIEVABLE 3 ♦ : likely to succeed or to yield good results : PROMISING ⟨a ∼ place to fish⟩

♦ [1] apt, bound, probable; *also* conceivable, earthly, imaginable, possible, potential; certain, doubtless, inescapable, inevitable, necessary, sure, unavoidable *Ant* doubtful, dubious, improbable, questionable, unlikely ♦ [2] believable, credible, plausible, probable — more at BELIEVABLE ♦ [3] auspicious, bright, encouraging, fair, golden, heartening, hopeful, promising, propitious, rosy, upbeat — more at HOPEFUL

²**likely** *adv* ♦ : in all probability

♦ doubtless, presumably, probably — more at PROBABLY

lik·en \'lī-kən\ *vb* ♦ : to represent as similar : COMPARE

♦ bracket, compare, equate — more at COMPARE

like·ness \'līk-nəs\ *n* **1** ♦ : a pictorial representation (as a painting) of a person usu. showing the face; *also* : one that resembles or corresponds to another **2** : SEMBLANCE **3** ♦ : the quality or state of being like : RESEMBLANCE

♦ [1] illustration, image, picture — more at PICTURE ♦ [3] community, correspondence, parallelism, resemblance, similarity, similitude — more at SIMILARITY

like·wise \-,wīz\ *adv* **1** ♦ : in the same manner **2** ♦ : in addition : ALSO

♦ [1] alike, also, correspondingly, similarly, so — more at ALSO ♦ [2] additionally, again, also, besides, further, furthermore, more, moreover, then, too, withal, yet

lik·ing \'lī-kiŋ\ *n* ♦ : favorable regard; *also* : TASTE

♦ appetite, fancy, favor (*or* favour), fondness, like, love, partiality, preference, relish, shine, taste, use; *also* craving, desire, longing, thirst, yen; enthusiasm, interest, passion; bias, prejudice; bent, inclination, leaning, propensity, tendency; weakness *Ant* aversion, dislike, disfavor, distaste, hatred, loathing

li·lac \'lī-lək, -,lak, -,läk\ *n* [obs. F (now *lilas*), fr. Ar *līlak*, fr. Pers *nīlak* bluish, fr. *nīl* blue, fr. Skt *nīla* dark blue] **1** : a shrub related to the olive that produces large clusters of fragrant grayish pink, purple, or white flowers **2** : a moderate purple color

lil·li·pu·tian \,li-lə-'pyü-shən\ *adj, often cap* **1** : SMALL, MINIATURE **2** : PETTY

lilt \'lilt\ *n* **1** : a cheerful lively song or tune **2** : a rhythmical swing or flow

lily \'li-lē\ *n, pl* **lil·ies** : any of a genus of tall bulbous herbs with leafy stems and usu. funnel-shaped flowers; *also* : any of various related plants

lily of the valley : a low perennial herb related to the lilies that produces a raceme of fragrant nodding bell-shaped white flowers

li·ma bean \'lī-mə-\ *n* : a bushy or tall-growing bean widely cultivated for its flat edible usu. pale green or whitish seeds; *also* : the seed

limb \'lim\ *n* **1** : one of the projecting paired appendages (as legs, arms, or wings) used by an animal esp. in moving or grasping **2** : a large branch of a tree : BOUGH — **limb·less** *adj*

¹**lim·ber** \'lim-bər\ *adj* **1** ♦ : capable of being shaped : FLEXIBLE, SUPPLE **2** : LITHE, NIMBLE

♦ flexible, lissome, lithe, pliable, supple, willowy — more at WILLOWY

²**limber** *vb* : to make or become limber

lim·bic \'lim-bik\ *adj* : of, relating to, or being a group of structures of the brain (**limbic system**) concerned esp. with emotion and motivation

¹**lim·bo** \'lim-bō\ *n, pl* **limbos** [ME, fr. ML, abl. of *limbus* limbo, fr. L, border] **1** *often cap* : an abode of souls barred from heaven through no fault of their own **2** : a place or state of confinement, oblivion, or uncertainty

²**limbo** *n, pl* **limbos** : an acrobatic dance or contest that involves passing under a horizontal pole

Lim·burg·er \'lim-,bər-gər\ *n* : a pungent semisoft surface-ripened cheese

¹**lime** \'līm\ *n* : a caustic powdery white solid that consists of calcium and oxygen, is obtained from limestone or shells, and is used in making cement and in fertilizer — **lime** *vb* — **limy** \'lī-mē\ *adj*

²**lime** *n* : a small yellowish green citrus fruit with juicy acid pulp

lime·ade \,līm-'ād, 'lī-,mād\ *n* : a beverage of lime juice, sugar, and water

lime·light \'līm-,līt\ *n* **1** : a device in which flame is di-

rected against a cylinder of lime formerly used in the theater to cast a strong white light on the stage **2** : the center of public attention

lim·er·ick \'li-mə-rik\ *n* : a light or humorous poem of 5 lines

lime·stone \'līm-,stōn\ *n* : a rock that is formed by accumulation of organic remains (as shells), is used in building, and yields lime when burned

¹**lim·it** \'li-mət\ *n* **1** ♦ : something that restrains or confines; *also* : the utmost extent **2** : BOUNDARY; *also, pl* : BOUNDS **3** : a prescribed maximum or minimum — **lim·it·less·ness** *n*

♦ bound, boundary, ceiling, confines, end, extent, limitation, line, termination; *also* extremity, fag end; border, brim, edge, margin, rim, verge; outside; bar, barrier, fence, hedge, restraint, stop, wall

²**limit** *vb* **1 a** ♦ : to set limits to **b** ♦ : to confine within set limits **2** : to reduce in quantity or extent

♦ [1a] bound, circumscribe, define, delimit, demarcate, mark, terminate; *also* control, determine, govern; delineate, describe ♦ [1b] check, circumscribe, confine, control, curb, inhibit, restrain, restrict; *also* bar, block, hinder, impede, obstruct; constrict, contract, lessen, narrow, pinch, squeeze, tighten; quell, repress, suppress; number; modify, qualify *Ant* exceed

lim·i·ta·tion \,li-mə-'tā-shən\ *n* **1** : an act or instance of limiting **2** ♦ : something that limits

♦ check, condition, constraint, curb, fetter, restraint, restriction — more at RESTRICTION

lim·it·ed *adj* **1** ♦ : confined within limits **2** : offering faster service esp. by making fewer stops ⟨a ~ train⟩

♦ definite, determinate, finite, measured, narrow, restricted; *also* modified, qualified; detailed, exact, precise, specific; confined, constricted, modest, moderate; minute, puny, small, tiny; fixed, determined, settled *Ant* boundless, endless, illimitable, immeasurable, indefinite, infinite, limitless, measureless, unbounded, undefined, unlimited, unmeasured

lim·it·less *adj* ♦ : having no limits

♦ boundless, endless, illimitable, immeasurable, indefinite, infinite, measureless, unbounded, unfathomable, unlimited — more at INFINITE

limn \'lim\ *vb* **limned; limn·ing** \'li-miŋ, 'lim-niŋ\ **1** : DRAW; *also* : PAINT **2** : DELINEATE **3** : DESCRIBE

limo \'li-(,)mō\ *n, pl* **limos** : LIMOUSINE

li·mo·nite \'lī-mə-,nīt\ *n* : a ferric oxide that is a major ore of iron — **li·mo·nit·ic** \,lī-mə-'ni-tik\ *adj*

lim·ou·sine \'li-mə-,zēn, ,li-mə-'zēn\ *n* [F] **1** : a large luxurious often chauffeur-driven sedan **2** : a large vehicle for transporting passengers to and from an airport

¹**limp** \'limp\ *vb* ♦ : to walk lamely; *also* : to proceed with difficulty

♦ flounder, lumber, plod, stumble — more at FLOUNDER

²**limp** *n* : a limping movement or gait

³**limp** *adj* **1** ♦ : having no defined shape; *also* : not stiff or rigid **2** ♦ : lacking in strength or firmness ⟨~ from fatigue⟩ — **limp·ly** *adv* — **limp·ness** *n*

♦ [1] droopy, flaccid, floppy, lank, slack, yielding; *also* flabby, mushy, semisoft, soft; delicate, flimsy, insubstantial, elastic, flexible, lax, loose, pliant, relaxed, resilient, springy, supple *Ant* inflexible, resilient, rigid, stiff, sturdy, tense; firm, hard, indurated, solid, sound, strong ♦ [2] enervated, lackadaisical, languid, languorous, listless, spiritless, weary — more at LISTLESS

lim·pet \'lim-pət\ *n* : any of numerous gastropod sea mollusks with a conical shell that clings to rocks or timbers

lim·pid \'lim-pəd\ *adj* ♦ : marked by transparency : CLEAR

♦ clear, liquid, lucent, pellucid, transparent — more at CLEAR

lin *abbr* **1** lineal **2** linear

lin·age \'lī-nij\ *n* : the number of lines of written or printed matter

linch·pin \'linch-ˌpin\ *n* : a locking pin inserted crosswise (as through the end of an axle)

lin·den \'lin-dən\ *n* : any of a genus of trees with large heart-shaped leaves and clustered yellowish flowers rich in nectar

¹**line** \'līn\ *n* 1 ♦ : a length of cord or cord-like material : ROPE, WIRE; *also* : a length of material used in measuring and leveling 2 ♦ : pipes for conveying a fluid ⟨a gas ∼⟩ 3 : a horizontal row of written or printed characters; *also* : VERSE 4 : NOTE 5 : the words making up a part in a drama — usu. used in pl. 6 a : something distinct, long, and narrow b ♦ : the course or direction of something in motion : ROUTE 7 : a state of agreement 8 ♦ : a course of conduct, action, or thought; *also* : a field of activity or interest : OCCUPATION 9 : something that bounds, restrains, or confines : LIMIT 10 ♦ : an arrangement of persons or objects of one kind in an orderly series ⟨waiting in ∼⟩ 11 : a transportation system 12 : the football players who are stationed on the line of scrimmage 13 : a long narrow mark; *also* : EQUATOR 14 : a geometric element that is the path of a moving point 15 : CONTOUR 16 : a general plan 17 : an indication based on insight or investigation 18 ♦ : a group of persons of common ancestry

♦ [1] cable, cord, lace, rope, string, wire — more at CORD ♦ [2] channel, conduit, duct, leader, penstock, pipe, tube — more at PIPE ♦ [6b] course, path, route, track, way — more at PATH ♦ [8] area, arena, discipline, domain, field, province, realm, specialty, sphere — more at FIELD ♦ [8] course, policy, procedure, program — more at COURSE ♦ [8] calling, employment, occupation, profession, trade, vocation, work — more at OCCUPATION ♦ [10] column, cue, file, queue, range, string, train; *also* echelon, rank, row, tier; progression, sequence, succession; array ♦ [18] ancestry, birth, blood, bloodline, breeding, descent, extraction, family tree, genealogy, lineage, origin, parentage, pedigree, stock, strain — more at ANCESTRY

²**line** *vb* **lined; lin·ing** 1 : to mark with a line 2 : to place or form a line along 3 : ALIGN

³**line** *vb* **lined; lin·ing** : to cover the inner surface of

lin·eage \'li-nē-ij\ *n* ♦ : lineal descent from a common progenitor; *also* : FAMILY

♦ blood, clan, family, folks, house, kin, kindred, kinfolk, line, people, race, stock, tribe ♦ ancestry, birth, bloodline, breeding, descent, extraction, family tree, genealogy, origin, parentage — more at ANCESTRY

lin·eal \'li-nē-əl\ *adj* 1 : LINEAR 2 : consisting of or being in a direct line of ancestry; *also* : HEREDITARY

lin·ea·ment \'li-nē-ə-mənt\ *n* : an outline, feature, or contour of a body and esp. of a face — usu. used in pl.

lin·ear \'li-nē-ər\ *adj* 1 : of, relating to, resembling, or having a graph that is a line and esp. a straight line : STRAIGHT 2 : composed of simply drawn lines with little attempt at pictorial representation ⟨∼ script⟩ 3 : being long and uniformly narrow

line·back·er \'līn-ˌba-kər\ *n* : a defensive football player who lines up just behind the line of scrimmage

line drive *n* : a batted baseball hit in a flatter path than a fly ball

line·man \'līn-mən\ *n* 1 : a person who sets up or repairs communication or power lines 2 : a player in the line in football

lin·en \'li-nən\ *n* 1 : cloth made of flax; *also* : thread or yarn spun from flax 2 : clothing or household articles made of linen cloth or similar fabric

line of scrimmage : an imaginary line in football parallel to the goal lines and tangent to the nose of the ball laid on the ground before a play

¹**lin·er** \'lī-nər\ *n* : a ship or airplane of a regular transportation line

²**liner** *n* : one that lines or is used as a lining — **lin·er·less** *adj*

line score *n* : a score of a baseball game giving the runs, hits, and errors made by each team

lines·man \'līnz-mən\ *n* 1 : LINEMAN 1 2 : an official who assists a referee

line·up \'lī-ˌnəp\ *n* 1 : a list of players taking part in a game (as of baseball) 2 : a line of persons arranged esp. for identification by police

ling \'liŋ\ *n* : any of various fishes related to the cod

-ling \liŋ\ *n suffix* 1 : one associated with ⟨nest*ling*⟩ 2 : young, small, or minor one ⟨duck*ling*⟩

lin·ger \'liŋ-gər\ *vb* ♦ : to be slow in parting or in quitting something : TARRY; *also* : to be slow to act — **lin·ger·er** *n*

♦ crawl, creep, dally, dawdle, delay, dillydally, drag, lag, loiter, poke, tarry — more at DELAY

lin·ge·rie \ˌlän-jə-'rā, ˌlaⁿ-zhə-, -'rē\ *n* [F, fr. MF, fr. *linge* linen, fr. L *lineus* made of linen, fr. *linum* flax, linen] : women's intimate apparel

lin·go \'liŋ-gō\ *n, pl* **lingoes** ♦ : a usu. strange or incomprehensible language

♦ argot, cant, jargon, language, slang, terminology, vocabulary — more at TERMINOLOGY

lin·gua fran·ca \ˌliŋ-gwə-'fraŋ-kə\ *n, pl* **lingua francas** *or* **lin·guae fran·cae** \-gwē-'fraŋ-ˌkē\ [It] 1 *often cap* : a common language consisting of Italian mixed with French, Spanish, Greek, and Arabic that was formerly spoken in Mediterranean ports 2 : a common or commercial tongue among speakers of different languages

lin·gual \'liŋ-gwəl\ *adj* : of, relating to, or produced by the tongue

lin·gui·ca \liŋ-'gwē-sə\ *n* : a spicy Portuguese sausage

lin·guist \'liŋ-gwist\ *n* 1 : a person skilled in languages 2 : a person who specializes in linguistics

lin·guis·tics \liŋ-'gwis-tiks\ *n* : the study of human speech including the units, nature, structure, and modification of language — **lin·guis·tic** \-tik\ *adj*

lin·i·ment \'li-nə-mənt\ *n* : a liquid preparation rubbed on the skin esp. to relieve pain

lin·ing \'lī-niŋ\ *n* : material used to line esp. an inner surface

¹**link** \'liŋk\ *n* 1 : a connecting structure; *esp* : a single ring of a chain 2 ♦ : a connecting element or factor : BOND, TIE

♦ bond, cement, knot, ligature, tie — more at BOND

²**link** *vb* ♦ : to couple or connect by or as if by a link; *also* : to become connected by or as if by a link — often used with *up* — **link·er** *n*

♦ chain, compound, connect, couple, hitch, hook, join, yoke — more at CONNECT ♦ associate, connect, correlate, identify, relate — more at ASSOCIATE ♦ *usu* link up coalesce, combine, conjoin, marry, unify, unite — more at UNITE

link·age \'liŋ-kij\ *n* 1 : the manner or style of being united 2 ♦ : the quality or state of being linked 3 : a system of links

♦ association, bearing, connection, kinship, liaison, relation, relationship — more at CONNECTION

linking verb *n* : a word or expression (as a form of *be, become, feel,* or *seem*) that links a subject with its predicate

links \'liŋks\ *n pl* : a golf course

link·up \'liŋk-ˌəp\ *n* 1 : MEETING 2 : something that serves as a linking device or factor

lin·net \'li-nət\ *n* : an Old World finch

li·no·leum \lə-'nō-lē-əm\ *n* [L *linum* flax + *oleum* oil] : a floor covering with a canvas back and a surface of hardened linseed oil and a filler

lin·seed \'lin-ˌsēd\ *n* : the seeds of flax yielding a yellowish oil (**linseed oil**) used esp. in paints and linoleum

lin·sey-wool·sey \ˌlin-zē-'wul-zē\ *n* : a coarse sturdy fabric of wool and linen or cotton

lint \'lint\ *n* 1 : linen made into a soft fleecy substance 2 ♦ : fine ravels and short fibers of yarn or fabric 3 : the fibers that surround cotton seeds and form the cotton staple

♦ down, floss, fluff, fur, fuzz, nap, pile — more at FUZZ

lin·tel \'lint-ᵊl\ *n* : a horizontal piece across the top of an opening (as of a door) that carries the weight of the structure above it

linz·er torte \'lin-sər-, -zər-\ *n, often cap L* : a baked buttery torte made with chopped almonds, sugar, and spices and filled with jam or preserves

li·on \'lī-ən\ *n, pl* **lions** : a large heavily-built cat of Africa and southern Asia with a shaggy mane in the male

li·on·ess \'lī-ə-nəs\ *n* : a female lion

li·on·heart·ed \ˌlī-ən-'här-təd\ *adj* ♦ : having or characterized by courage : BRAVE

♦ brave, courageous, dauntless, doughty, fearless, gallant, greathearted, heroic, intrepid, manful, stalwart, stout, undaunted, valiant, valorous — more at BRAVE

li·on·ise *chiefly Brit var of* LIONIZE

li·on·ize \'lī-ə-ˌnīz\ *vb* **-ized; -iz·ing** : to treat as an object of great interest or importance — **li·on·i·za·tion** \ˌlī-ə-nə-'zā-shən\ *n*

lion's den *n* : a place or state of extreme disadvantage, antagonism, or hostility

lip \'lip\ *n* **1** : either of the two fleshy folds that surround the mouth; *also* : the margin of the human lip **2** : a part or projection suggesting a lip **3** : the edge of a hollow vessel or cavity — **lipped** \'lipt\ *adj*

lip·id \'li-pəd\ *n* : any of various substances (as fats and waxes) that with proteins and carbohydrates make up the principal structural parts of living cells

lip–lock \'lip-ˌläk\ *n* : a long amorous kiss

li·po·pro·tein \ˌlī-pō-'prō-ˌtēn, ˌli-\ *n* : a protein that is a complex of protein and lipid

li·po·suc·tion \'li-pə-ˌsək-shən, 'lī-\ *n* : surgical removal of local fat deposits (as in the thighs) esp. for cosmetic purposes

lip·read·ing \'lip-ˌrē-diŋ\ *n* : the interpreting of a speaker's words by watching lip and facial movements without hearing the voice

lip service *n* : an avowal of allegiance that is not matched by action

lip·stick \'lip-ˌstik\ *n* : a waxy solid colored cosmetic in stick form for the lips — **lip·sticked** \-ˌstikt\ *adj*

liq *abbr* **1** liquid **2** liquor

liq·ue·fy *also* **liq·ui·fy** \'li-kwə-ˌfī\ *vb* **-fied; -fy·ing** ♦ : to make or become liquid — **liq·ue·fi·er** \-ˌfī-ər\ *n*

♦ deliquesce, flux, fuse, melt, run, thaw; *also* found, gutter, smelt, try; dissolve, render; soften, thin **Ant** harden, set, solidify

li·queur \li-'kər\ *n* [F] : a distilled alcoholic liquor flavored with aromatic substances and usu. sweetened

¹liq·uid \'li-kwəd\ *adj* **1** ♦ : flowing freely like water **2** : neither solid nor gaseous **3** ♦ : shining and clear ⟨large ~ eyes⟩ **4** : smooth and musical in tone; *also* : smooth and unconstrained in movement **5** : consisting of or capable of ready conversion into cash ⟨~ assets⟩ — **li·quid·i·ty** \li-'kwi-də-tē\ *n*

♦ [1] fluent, fluid, runny — more at FLUID ♦ [3] clear, limpid, lucent, pellucid, transparent — more at CLEAR

²liquid *n* : a liquid substance

liq·ui·date \'li-kwə-ˌdāt\ *vb* **-dat·ed; -dat·ing** **1** : to settle the accounts and distribute the assets of (as a business) **2** ♦ : to pay off ⟨~ a debt⟩ **3** ♦ : to get rid of; *esp* : to get rid of by force or violence and esp. by killing — **liq·ui·da·tion** \ˌli-kwə-'dā-shən\ *n*

♦ [2] clear, discharge, foot, pay, pay off, quit, recompense, settle, spring, stand — more at PAY ♦ [3] annihilate, blot out, demolish, eradicate, exterminate, obliterate, root, rub out, snuff, stamp, wipe out — more at ANNIHILATE ♦ [3] dispatch, do in, execute, murder, slay — more at MURDER

liquid crystal *n* : an organic liquid that resembles a crystal in having ordered molecular arrays

liquid crystal display *n* : LCD

liquid measure *n* : a unit or series of units for measuring liquid capacity

li·quor \'li-kər\ *n* [ME *licour*, fr. AF, fr. L *liquor*, fr. *liquēre* to be fluid] **1** : a liquid substance **2** ♦ : a distilled alcoholic beverage

♦ alcohol, booze, drink, intoxicant, moonshine, spirits — more at ALCOHOL

li·quo·rice *chiefly Brit var of* LICORICE

li·ra \'lir-ə, 'lē-rə\ *n* **1** *pl* **li·ras** : a basic monetary unit of Turkey **2** *pl* **li·re** \'lē-rā\ *also* **liras** : the former basic monetary unit of Italy

lisle \'līl\ *n* : a smooth tightly twisted thread usu. made of long-staple cotton

lisp \'lisp\ *vb* : to pronounce s and z imperfectly esp. by turning them into th and <u>th</u>; *also* : to speak childishly — **lisp** *n* — **lisp·er** *n*

lis·some *also* **lis·som** \'li-səm\ *adj* **1** ♦ : easily flexed **2** : LITHE 2 ⟨a ~ dancer⟩ **3** ♦ : quick and light in motion : NIMBLE — **lis·some·ly** *adv*

♦ [1] flexible, limber, lithe, pliable, supple, willowy — more at WILLOWY ♦ [3] agile, graceful, light, lithe, nimble, spry — more at GRACEFUL

¹list \'list\ *vb, archaic* : PLEASE; *also* : WISH

²list *vb, archaic* : LISTEN

³list *n* **1** : a simple series of words or numerals; *also* : an official roster **2** ♦ : a written record containing regular entries of items or details : CATALOG, CHECKLIST

♦ catalog, checklist, listing, menu, register, registry, roll, roster, schedule, table; *also* agenda, bibliography, compilation, directory, docket, glossary, index, inventory, manifest, payroll; calendar, chronology, timetable

⁴list *vb* ♦ : to make a list of; *also* : to include on a list — **list·ee** \li-'stē\ *n*

♦ enumerate, inventory, itemize, numerate; *also* count, mark, number; check (off), tick (off) catalog, enroll, enter, index, inscribe, put down, record, register, schedule, slate; *also* book, file, note; classify, compile, tabulate; reschedule

⁵list *vb* ♦ : to tilt to one side; *also* : to cause to list

♦ angle, cant, cock, heel, incline, lean, slant, slope, tilt, tip — more at LEAN

⁶list *n* : a leaning to one side : TILT

⁷list *n* : a band or strip of material

lis·ten \'lis-ᵊn\ *vb* **1** ♦ : to pay attention in order to hear **2** ♦ : give consideration : HEED — **lis·ten·er** *n*

♦ [1] attend, hark, hear, heed, mind **Ant** ignore, tune out ♦ [2] follow, heed, mind, note, observe, regard, watch — more at HEED

lis·ten·er·ship \'lis-ᵊn-ər-ˌship\ *n* : the audience for a radio program or recording

list·ing \'lis-tiŋ\ *n* **1** : an act or instance of making or including in a list **2** : something that is listed **3** ♦ : a simple series of words or numerals (as the names of persons or objects)

♦ catalog, checklist, list, menu, register, registry, roll, roster, schedule, table — more at LIST

list·less \'list-ləs\ *adj* ♦ : characterized by lack of interest, energy, or spirit : SPIRITLESS, LANGUID — **list·less·ly** *adv*

♦ enervated, lackadaisical, languid, languorous, limp, spiritless; *also* indolent, lazy, slothful; lethargic, logy, sleepy, sluggish, torpid; exhausted, tired, weary; feeble, frail, weak; apathetic, impassive, phlegmatic, stolid; careless, heedless, thoughtless, unwary; inactive, inert **Ant** ambitious, animated, energetic, enterprising, motivated

list·less·ness *n* ♦ : the quality or state of being listless

♦ boredom, doldrums, ennui, restlessness, tedium, tiredness, weariness — more at BOREDOM

list price *n* : the price of an item as published in a catalog, price list, or advertisement before being discounted

lists \'lists\ *n pl* : an arena for combat (as jousting)

¹lit \'lit\ *past and past part of* LIGHT

²lit *abbr* **1** liter **2** literal; literally **3** literary **4** literature

lit·a·ny \'lit-ᵊn-ē\ *n, pl* **-nies** [ME *letanie*, fr. AF & LL; AF, fr. LL *litania*, fr. LGk *litaneia*, fr. Gk, entreaty, fr. *litanos* suppliant] **1** : a prayer consisting of a series of supplications and responses said alternately by a leader and a group **2** : a lengthy list or series ⟨a ~ of complaints⟩

li·tchi *var of* LYCHEE

lite \'līt\ *adj* **1** : ⁴LIGHT 10 **2** : lacking in substance or seriousness

li·ter *or chiefly Can and Brit* **li·tre** \'lē-tər\ *n* : the basic metric unit of volume measure

lit·er·al \'li-tə-rəl\ *adj* **1** ♦ : adhering to fact or to the ordinary or usual meaning (as of a word) **2** : UNADORNED; *also* : PROSAIC **3** : VERBATIM

♦ documentary, factual, hard, historical, matter-of-fact, nonfictional, objective, true — more at FACTUAL

lit·er·al·ism \-rə-,li-zəm\ *n* **1** : adherence to the explicit substance (as of an idea) **2** : fidelity to observable fact — **lit·er·al·ist** \-list\ *n* — **lit·er·al·is·tic** \,li-tə-rə-'lis-tik\ *adj*

lit·er·al·ly \'li-tə-rə-lē, 'li-trə-\ *adv* **1** : ACTUALLY ⟨was ~ insane⟩ **2** : VIRTUALLY ⟨~ poured out new ideas⟩

lit·er·ary \'li-tə-,rer-ē\ *adj* **1 a** : of or relating to literature **b** ♦ : having a formal style characteristic of the language of literature **2** : WELL-READ

♦ bookish, erudite, learned — more at BOOKISH

lit·er·ate \'li-trət, -tə-rət\ *adj* **1** ♦ : having an education : EDUCATED; *also* : able to read and write **2** : LITERARY; *also* : POLISHED, LUCID — **lit·er·a·cy** \'li-trə-sē, -tə-rə-\ *n* — **literate** *n*

♦ educated, erudite, knowledgeable, learned, scholarly, well-read — more at EDUCATED

li·te·ra·ti \,li-tə-'rä-tē\ *n pl* **1** : the educated class **2** : persons interested in literature or the arts

lit·er·a·ture \'li-trə-,chùr, -tə-rə-, -chər\ *n* **1** : the production of written works having excellence of form or expression and dealing with ideas of permanent interest **2** : the written works produced in a particular language, country, or age

lithe \'līth, 'līth\ *adj* **1** ♦ : easily bent or flexed : SUPPLE **2 a** ♦ : characterized by effortless grace **b** : athletically slim

♦ [1] flexible, limber, lissome, pliable, supple, willowy — more at WILLOWY ♦ [2a] agile, graceful, light, lissome, nimble, spry — more at GRACEFUL

lithe·some \'līth-səm, 'līth-\ *adj* : quick and light in motion : LISSOME

lith·i·um \'li-thē-əm\ *n* : a light silver-white metallic chemical element

li·thog·ra·phy \li-'thä-grə-fē\ *n* : the process of printing from a plane surface (as a smooth stone or metal plate) on which the image to be printed is ink-receptive and the blank area ink-repellent — **lith·o·graph** \'li-thə-,graf\ *vb* — **lithograph** *n* — **li·thog·ra·pher** \li-'thä-grə-fər, 'li-thə-,gra-fər\ *n* — **lith·o·graph·ic** \,li-thə-'gra-fik\ *adj* — **lith·o·graph·i·cal·ly** \-fi-k(ə-)lē\ *adv*

li·thol·o·gy \li-'thä-lə-jē\ *n, pl* **-gies** : the study of rocks — **lith·o·log·ic** \,li-thə-'lä-jik\ *or* **lith·o·log·i·cal** \-ji-kəl\ *adj*

lith·o·sphere \'li-thə-,sfir\ *n* : the outer part of the solid earth

Lith·u·a·nian \,li-thù-'wā-nē-ən, -thyù-\ *n* **1** : a native or inhabitant of Lithuania **2** : the language of the Lithuanians — **Lithuanian** *adj*

lit·i·gant \'li-ti-gənt\ *n* : a party to a lawsuit — **litigant** *adj*

lit·i·gate \-,gāt\ *vb* **-gat·ed; -gat·ing** : to carry on a legal contest by judicial process; *also* : to contest at law — **lit·i·ga·tion** \,li-tə-'gā-shən\ *n*

li·ti·gious \lə-'ti-jəs\ *adj* **1** : CONTENTIOUS **2** : prone to engage in lawsuits **3** : of or relating to litigation — **li·ti·gious·ly** *adv* — **li·ti·gious·ness** *n*

lit·mus \'lit-məs\ *n* : a coloring matter from lichens that turns red in acid solutions and blue in alkaline

litmus test *n* : a test in which a single factor (as an attitude) is decisive

Litt D *or* **Lit D** *abbr* [ML *litterarum doctor*] : doctor of letters; doctor of literature

¹lit·ter \'li-tər\ *n* [ME, fr. AF *litere*, fr. *lit* bed, fr. L *lectus*] **1** : a covered and curtained couch with shafts that is used to carry a single passenger; *also* : a device (as a stretcher) for carrying a sick or injured person **2** : material used as bedding for animals; *also* : material used to absorb the urine and feces of animals **3** : the offspring of an animal at one birth **4** ♦ : trash, wastepaper, or garbage lying scattered about : RUBBISH; *also* : an untidy accumulation of objects

♦ chaff, deadwood, dust, garbage, junk, refuse, riffraff, rubbish, scrap, trash, waste — more at GARBAGE ♦ assortment, clutter, jumble, medley, mélange, miscellany, motley, muddle, variety, welter — more at MISCELLANY

²litter *vb* **1** : to give birth to young **2** : to strew or mark with scattered objects

lit·ter·bug \'li-tər-,bəg\ *n* : one who litters a public area

¹lit·tle \'lit-ᵊl\ *adj* **lit·tler** \'lit-ᵊl-ər\ *or* **less** \'les\ *or* **less·er** \'le-sər\; **lit·tlest** \'lit-ᵊl-əst\ *or* **least** \'lēst\ **1 a** ♦ : not big **b** : YOUNG **2** ♦ : not important **3** ♦ : illiberal in views or disposition : PETTY **3 4** : not much **5** ♦ : short in duration — **lit·tle·ness** *n*

♦ [1a] dwarf, dwarfish, fine, pocket, pygmy, slight, small, undersized — more at SMALL ♦ [2] frivolous, inconsequential, inconsiderable, insignificant, minor, minute, negligible, slight, small, trifling, trivial, unimportant — more at UNIMPORTANT ♦ [3] insular, narrow, parochial, petty, provincial, sectarian, small — more at NARROW ♦ [5] brief, short, short-lived — more at SHORT

²little *adv* **less** \'les\; **least** \'lēst\ **1** : in only a small quantity or degree : SLIGHTLY; *also* : not at all **2** ♦ : in few instances : INFREQUENTLY

♦ infrequently, rarely, seldom — more at SELDOM

³little *n* **1** : a small amount or quantity **2** : a short time or distance

Little Dipper *n* : the seven bright stars of Ursa Minor arranged in a form resembling a dipper

little finger *n* : PINKIE

little theater *n* : a small theater for low-cost dramatic productions designed for a limited audience

lit·to·ral \'li-tə-rəl, ,li-tə-'ral\ *adj* : of, relating to, or growing on or near a shore esp. of the sea — **littoral** *n*

lit·ur·gy \'li-tər-jē\ *n, pl* **-gies** : a rite or body of rites prescribed for public worship — **li·tur·gi·cal** \lə-'tər-ji-kəl\ *adj* — **li·tur·gi·cal·ly** \-k(ə-)lē\ *adv* — **lit·ur·gist** \'li-tər-jist\ *n*

liv·able *also* **live·able** \'li-və-bəl\ *adj* **1** : suitable for living in or with **2** : ENDURABLE — **liv·a·bil·i·ty** \,li-və-'bi-lə-tē\ *n*

¹live \'liv\ *vb* **lived; liv·ing 1** ♦ : to be or continue alive **2** : SUBSIST **3** ♦ : to occupy a home : RESIDE **4** : to conduct one's life **5** : to remain in human memory or record

♦ [1] be, breathe, exist, subsist — more at BE ♦ [3] abide, dwell, reside; *also* lodge, settle, stay; frequent, hang out (at), haunt; inhabit, occupy; people, populate; lease, rent, sublet, tenant

²live \'līv\ *adj* **1** ♦ : having life **2** : BURNING, GLOWING ⟨a ~ cigar⟩ **3** : connected to electric power ⟨a ~ wire⟩ **4** : charged with explosive but not yet exploded ⟨a ~ bomb⟩ **5** : of continuing interest ⟨a ~ issue⟩ **6** : of or involving the actual presence of real people ⟨~ audience⟩; *also* : broadcast directly at the time of production ⟨a ~ radio program⟩ **7** : being in play ⟨a ~ ball⟩

♦ alive, animate, living — more at ALIVE

lived-in \'livd-,in\ *adj* : of or suggesting long-term human habitation or use

live down *vb* : to live so as to wipe out the memory or effects of

live in *vb* : to live in one's place of employment — used of a servant — **live-in** \'liv-,in\ *adj*

live·li·hood \'līv-lē-,hùd\ *n* : means of support or subsistence

live·li·ness *n* ♦ : the quality or state of being lively

♦ animation, briskness, exuberance, lustiness, robustness, sprightliness, vibrancy, vitality — more at VITALITY

live·long \'liv-ˌlȯṅ\ adj [ME lef long, fr. lef dear + long long] : WHOLE, ENTIRE ⟨the ~ day⟩

live·ly \'līv-lē\ adj **live·li·er; -est** 1 ♦ : briskly alert and energetic : ANIMATED ⟨~ debate⟩ 2 : KEEN, VIVID ⟨~ interest⟩ 3 : showing activity or vigor ⟨a ~ manner⟩ 4 : quick to rebound ⟨a ~ ball⟩ 5 ♦ : full of life — **live·ly** adv

♦ [1] active, animate, animated, brisk, energetic, frisky, peppy, perky, pert, spirited, sprightly, springy, vital, vivacious; also dapper, dashing; agog, alert, awake, up, wide-awake; agile, nimble, spry; bright, buoyant, cheerful, chipper, effervescent, upbeat; eager, enthusiastic, keen; frolicsome, impish, playful; bubbly, exuberant, high-spirited; high-strung, nervous, skittish **Ant** inactive, inanimate, languid, languorous, limp, listless, spiritless ♦ [5] alive, animated, astir, busy, vibrant — more at ALIVE

liv·en \'lī-vən\ vb ♦ : to give life, action, or spirit to : ENLIVEN — often used with up; also : to become lively

♦ usu **liven up** animate, brace, energize, enliven, fire, invigorate, jazz up, pep up, quicken, stimulate, vitalize, vivify, zip (up) — more at ANIMATE

live oak n : any of several American evergreen oaks; esp : one of the southeastern U.S. that is often planted as a shade tree

¹**liv·er** \'li-vər\ n 1 : a large glandular organ of vertebrates that secretes bile and is a center of metabolic activity 2 : the liver of an animal (as a calf or chicken) eaten as food

²**liver** n : one that lives esp. in a specified way ⟨a fast ~⟩

liv·er·ish \'li-və-rish\ adj 1 : resembling liver esp. in color 2 : BILIOUS 3 : PEEVISH — **liv·er·ish·ness** adj

liv·er·mo·ri·um \ˌli-vər-'mȯr-ē-əm\ n : a short-lived artificially produced radioactive chemical element

liv·er·wort \'li-vər-ˌwərt\ n : any of a class of flowerless plants resembling the related mosses

liv·er·wurst \-ˌwərst, -ˌwu̇rst\ n [part trans. of G Leberwurst, fr. Leber liver + Wurst sausage] : a sausage consisting chiefly of liver

liv·ery \'li-və-rē\ n, pl **-er·ies** 1 : a servant's uniform; also : distinctive dress 2 : the feeding, care, and stabling of horses for pay; also : an establishment (as a stable or business) keeping horses or vehicles for hire — **liv·er·ied** \-rēd\ adj

liv·ery·man \-mən\ n : the keeper of a livery

lives pl of LIFE

live·stock \'līv-ˌstäk\ n : farm animals kept for use and profit

live wire n ♦ : an alert, active, or aggressive person

♦ go-getter, hustler, powerhouse, self-starter — more at GO-GETTER

liv·id \'li-vəd\ adj [F livide, fr. L lividus, fr. livēre to be blue] 1 : discolored by bruising 2 ♦ : deadly pale : ASHEN, PALLID 3 : REDDISH 4 : ENRAGED — **li·vid·i·ty** \li-'vi-də-tē\ n

♦ ashen, cadaverous, lurid, pale, pasty, peaked — more at PALE

¹**liv·ing** \'li-viṅ\ adj 1 ♦ : having life or existence 2 : NATURAL 3 : full of life and vigor; also : VIVID 4 ♦ : marked by present operation, transaction, movement, or use

♦ [1] alive, animate, existent, extant, live — more at EXTANT ♦ [4] active, alive, functional, on, operational, operative, running, working — more at ACTIVE

²**living** n 1 : the condition of being alive 2 : LIVELIHOOD 3 : manner of life

living room n : a room in a residence used for the common social activities of the occupants

living wage n : a wage sufficient to provide an acceptable standard of living

living will n : a document requesting that the signer not be kept alive by artificial means unless there is a reasonable expectation of recovery

livre \'lēvrᵊ\ n : the pound of Lebanon

liz·ard \'li-zərd\ n : any of a group of 4-legged reptiles with long tapering tails

Lk abbr Luke

ll abbr lines

lla·ma \'lä-mə\ n [Sp, fr. Quechua] : any of a genus of wild or domesticated So. American mammals related to the camels but smaller and without a hump

lla·no \'lä-nō\ n, pl **llanos** : an open grassy plain esp. of Latin America

LLD abbr [NL legum doctor] doctor of laws

LNG abbr liquefied natural gas

¹**load** \'lōd\ n 1 **a** ♦ : whatever is put in a ship or vehicle or airplane for conveyance : CARGO 2 : a mass of weight supported by something 3 : something that burdens the mind or spirits 4 ♦ : a large quantity — usu. used in pl. 5 : a standard, expected, or authorized burden

♦ [1b] burden, cargo, freight, haul, lading, payload, weight; also carload; ballast, deadweight; overload, surcharge; bale, pack, package, parcel, shipment; body, bulk, mass ♦ usu **loads** [4] abundance, deal, gobs, heap, lot, pile, plenty, quantity, scads — more at LOT

²**load** vb 1 **a** ♦ : to put a load in or on; also : to receive a load **b** ♦ : to fill with a load 2 : to encumber with an obligation or something heavy or disheartening 3 : to increase the weight of by adding something 4 : to supply abundantly 5 : to put a charge in (as a firearm)

♦ [1a] burden, encumber, lumber, saddle, weight; also clog, clutter, fill, heap; press, weigh; strain, tax; overburden, overload, overtax, surcharge; handicap; afflict, oppress **Ant** disencumber, unburden, unload ♦ [1b] charge, cram, fill, heap, jam, jam-pack, pack, stuff — more at FILL

load·ed adj 1 slang : HIGH 12 2 ♦ : having a large amount of money 3 : equipped with an abundance of options

♦ affluent, flush, moneyed, opulent, rich, wealthy, well-fixed, well-heeled, well-off, well-to-do — more at RICH

load·stone var of LODESTONE

¹**loaf** \'lōf\ n, pl **loaves** \'lōvz\ : a shaped or molded mass esp. of bread

²**loaf** vb ♦ : to spend time in idleness : LOUNGE

♦ dally, dawdle, dillydally, hang around, hang out, idle, loll, lounge — more at IDLE

loaf·er n 1 ♦ : one that loafs 2 : a low step-in shoe

♦ idler, lazybones, slouch, slug, sluggard — more at LAZYBONES

loam \'lōm, 'lüm\ n : SOIL; esp : a loose soil of mixed clay, sand, and silt — **loamy** adj

¹**loan** \'lōn\ n 1 : money lent at interest; also : something lent for the borrower's temporary use 2 : the grant of temporary use

²**loan** vb : LEND

loan shark n : a person who lends money at excessive rates of interest — **loan·shark·ing** \'lōn-ˌshär-kiṅ\ n

loan·word \'lōn-ˌwərd\ n : a word taken from another language and at least partly naturalized

loath \'lōth, 'lōth̲ also **loathe** \lōth̲, lōth\ adj : RELUCTANT

loathe \'lōth̲\ vb **loathed; loath·ing** ♦ : to dislike greatly

♦ abhor, abominate, despise, detest, execrate, hate — more at HATE

loath·ing \'lō-thiṅ\ n ♦ : extreme disgust

♦ disgust, distaste, nausea, repugnance, repulsion, revulsion — more at DISGUST ♦ abhorrence, abomination, execration, hate, hatred — more at HATE

loath·some \'lōth̲-səm, 'lōth-\ adj : exciting loathing : REPULSIVE

lob \'läb\ vb **lobbed; lob·bing** : to throw, hit, or propel something in a high arc — **lob** n

¹**lob·by** \'lä-bē\ n, pl **lobbies** 1 ♦ : a corridor used esp. as a passageway or waiting room 2 : a group of persons engaged in lobbying

♦ entry, foyer, hall, vestibule — more at HALL

²**lobby** *vb* **lob·bied; lob·by·ing** : to try to influence public officials and esp. legislators — **lob·by·ist** *n*

lobe \'lōb\ *n* : a curved or rounded part esp. of a bodily organ — **lo·bar** \'lō-bər\ *adj* — **lobed** \'lōbd\ *adj*

lo·be·lia \lō-'bēl-yə\ *n* : any of a genus of plants often grown for their clusters of showy flowers

lo·bot·o·my \lō-'bä-tə-mē\ *n, pl* **-mies** : surgical severance of certain nerve fibers in the brain performed esp. formerly to relieve some mental disorders

lob·ster \'läb-stər\ *n* [ME, fr. OE *loppestre*, fr. *loppe* spider] : any of a family of edible marine crustaceans with two large pincerlike claws and four other pairs of legs; *also* : SPINY LOBSTER

¹**lo·cal** \'lō-kəl\ *adj* **1** : of, relating to, or occupying a particular place **2** : serving a particular limited district; *also* : making all stops ⟨a ~ train⟩ **3** : affecting a small part of the body ⟨~ infection⟩ — **lo·cal·ly** *adv*

²**local** *n* ♦ : one that is local; *esp* : a local or particular branch, lodge, or chapter of an organization (as a labor union)

♦ affiliate, branch, chapter — more at CHAPTER

local area network *n* : a network of personal computers in a small area (as an office)

lo·cale \lō-'kal\ *n* ♦ : a place that is the setting for a particular event

♦ location, place, point, position, site, spot — more at PLACE

lo·cal·ise *chiefly Brit var of* LOCALIZE

lo·cal·i·ty \lō-'ka-lə-tē\ *n, pl* **-ties** : a particular spot, situation, or location

lo·cal·ize \'lō-kə-‚līz\ *vb* **-ized; -iz·ing** : to fix in or confine to a definite place or locality — **lo·cal·i·za·tion** \‚lō-kə-lə-'zā-shən\ *n*

lo·cate \'lō-‚kāt, lō-'kāt\ *vb* **lo·cat·ed; lo·cat·ing 1** : STATION, SETTLE **2** ♦ : to determine the site of **3** : to find or fix the place of in a sequence

♦ detect, determine, dig up, discover, ferret out, find, hit on, track down — more at FIND

lo·ca·tion \lō-'kā-shən\ *n* **1** ♦ : a position or site occupied or available for occupancy or marked by some distinguishing feature : PLACE **2** : the process of locating **3** : a place outside a studio where a motion picture is filmed

♦ locale, place, point, position, site, spot — more at PLACE

lo·ca·vore \'lō-kə-‚vȯr\ *n* [*local* + *-vore* (as in *carnivore*)] : one who eats food grown locally whenever possible

loc cit *abbr* [L *loco citato*] in the place cited

loch \'läk, 'läḵ\ *n, Scot* : LAKE; *also* : a bay or arm of the sea esp. when nearly landlocked

¹**lock** \'läk\ *n* : a tuft, strand, or ringlet of hair; *also* : a cohering bunch (as of wool or flax)

²**lock** *n* **1** : a fastening in which a bolt is operated **2** : the mechanism of a firearm by which the charge is exploded **3** : an enclosure (as in a canal) used in raising or lowering boats from level to level **4** : AIR LOCK **5** : a wrestling hold

³**lock** *vb* **1** : to fasten the lock of; *also* : to make fast with a lock **2** ♦ : to confine or exclude by means of a lock — often used with *in* or *up* **3** : INTERLOCK **4** : to make or become motionless by the interlocking of parts

♦ commit, confine, immure, imprison, jail — more at IMPRISON

lock·er \'lä-kər\ *n* **1** ♦ : a drawer, cupboard, or compartment for individual storage use **2** : an insulated compartment for storing frozen food

♦ box, caddy, case, casket, chest, trunk — more at CHEST ♦ buffet, cabinet, closet, cupboard, hutch, sideboard — more at CABINET

lock·et \'lä-kət\ *n* : a small usu. metal case for a memento worn suspended from a chain or necklace

lock·jaw \'läk-‚jȯ\ *n* : a symptom of tetanus marked by spasms of the jaw muscles and inability to open the jaws; *also* : TETANUS

lock·nut \-‚nət\ *n* **1** : a nut screwed tight on another to prevent it from slacking back **2** : a nut designed to lock itself when screwed tight

lock·out \-‚aůt\ *n* : the suspension of work by an employer during a labor dispute in order to make employees accept the terms being offered

lock·smith \-‚smith\ *n* : one who makes or repairs locks

lock·step \-‚step\ *n* : a mode of marching in step by a body of persons moving in a very close single file

lock·up \-‚əp\ *n* : JAIL; *esp* : a local jail where persons are detained prior to court hearing

lo·co \'lō-kō\ *adj* [Sp] *slang* ♦ : mentally disordered : CRAZY, FRENZIED

♦ balmy, crazy, cuckoo, deranged, frenzied, insane, lunatic, mad, maniacal, nutty, screwy, unsound, wacky — more at INSANE

lo·co·mo·tion \‚lō-kə-'mō-shən\ *n* **1** : the act or power of moving from place to place **2** : TRAVEL

¹**lo·co·mo·tive** \‚lō-kə-'mō-tiv\ *adj* : of or relating to locomotion or a locomotive

²**locomotive** *n* : a self-propelled vehicle used to move railroad cars

lo·co·mo·tor \‚lō-kə-'mō-tər\ *adj* : of or relating to locomotion or organs used in locomotion

lo·co·weed \'lō-kō-‚wēd\ *n* : any of several leguminous plants of western No. America that are poisonous to livestock

lo·cus \'lō-kəs\ *n, pl* **lo·ci** \'lō-‚sī\ [L] **1** : the place where something is situated or occurs : LOCALITY **2** : the set of all points whose location is determined by stated conditions

lo·cust \'lō-kəst\ *n* **1** : a usu. destructive migratory grasshopper **2** : CICADA **3** : any of various leguminous trees; *also* : the wood of a locust

lo·cu·tion \lō-'kyü-shən\ *n* ♦ : a particular form of expression; *also* : PHRASEOLOGY

♦ manner, mode, phraseology, style, tone, vein — more at STYLE

lode \'lōd\ *n* : an ore deposit

lode·stone \-‚stōn\ *n* **1** : an iron-containing rock with magnetic properties **2** ♦ : something that strongly attracts

♦ attraction, draw, magnet — more at MAGNET

¹**lodge** \'läj\ *vb* **lodged; lodg·ing 1** ♦ : to provide quarters for; *also* : to settle in a place **2** : CONTAIN **3** : to come to a rest and remain **4** : to deposit for safekeeping **5** : to vest (as authority) in an agent **6** : FILE ⟨~ a complaint⟩

♦ ensconce, install, perch, roost, settle — more at ENSCONCE ♦ accommodate, billet, domicile, harbor (*or* harbour), house, put up, quarter, roof, shelter, take in — more at HOUSE

²**lodge** *n* **1** ♦ : a house set apart for residence in a special season or by an employee on an estate; *also* : INN **2** ♦ : a den or lair esp. of gregarious animals **3** : the meeting place of a branch of a fraternal organization; *also* : the members of such a branch

♦ [1] cabin, camp, chalet, cottage — more at COTTAGE ♦ [1] hospice, hotel, inn, public house, tavern — more at HOTEL ♦ [2] burrow, den, hole, lair — more at DEN

lodg·er \'lä-jər\ *n* ♦ : a person who occupies a rented room in another's house

♦ boarder, renter, roomer, tenant — more at TENANT

lodg·ing \'lä-jiŋ\ *n* **1** : a place to live : DWELLING **2** ♦ : a room or suite of rooms in another's house rented as a dwelling place — usu. used in pl.

♦ flat, suite

lodg·ment *or* **lodge·ment** \'läj-mənt\ *n* **1** ♦ : a lodging place **2** : the act or manner of lodging **3** : DEPOSIT

♦ accommodation, lodging — more at ACCOMMODATION

loess \'les, 'ləs\ *n* : a usu. yellowish brown loamy deposit believed to be chiefly deposited by the wind

lo–fi \'lō-‚fī\ *n* : audio production of rough or unpolished sound quality — **lo–fi** *adj*

¹loft \'lȯft\ *n* [ME, fr. OE, air, sky, fr. ON *lopt*] **1** : AT-TIC **2** : GALLERY ⟨organ ∼⟩ **3** : an upper floor (as in a warehouse or barn) esp. when not partitioned **4** : the thickness of a fabric or insulated material (as of a sleeping bag)

²loft *vb* : to strike or throw (a ball) so that it rises high in the air

loft·i·ness \-tē-nəs\ *n* ♦ : the quality or state of being lofty
   ♦ arrogance, haughtiness, pretense, pretension, pre-tentiousness, self-importance, superiority — more at ARROGANCE

lofty \'lȯf-tē\ *adj* **loft·i·er; -est** **1** ♦ : elevated in charac-ter and spirit : NOBLE; *also* : SUPERIOR **2** ♦ : extremely proud; *also* : haughty and overbearingly arrogant **3** : ris-ing to a great height : HIGH, TALL — **loft·i·ly** \'lȯf-tə-lē\ *adv*
   ♦ [1] chivalrous, gallant, great, greathearted, high, high-minded, lordly, magnanimous, noble, sublime — more at NOBLE ♦ [1] eloquent, formal, high-flown, majestic, stately, superior, towering ♦ [2] arrogant, haughty, highfalutin, imperious, peremptory, pompous, presumptuous, pretentious, supercilious

¹log \'lȯg, 'läg\ *n* **1** : a bulky piece of a cut or fallen tree **2** : an apparatus for measuring a ship's speed **3** : the daily record of a ship's progress; *also* : a regularly kept record of performance or events

²log *vb* **logged; log·ging** **1** : to cut (trees) for lumber; *also* : to clear (land) of trees in lumbering **2** ♦ : to enter in a log; *broadly* : to make a note or record of **3** : to sail a ship or fly an airplane for (an indicated distance or period of time) **4** : to have (an indicated record) to one's credit : ACHIEVE — **log·ger** \'lȯ-gər, 'lä-\ *n*
   ♦ jot, mark, note, put down, record, register, set down — more at RECORD

³log *n* : LOGARITHM

lo·gan·ber·ry \'lō-gən-ˌber-ē\ *n* : a red-fruited upright-grow-ing dewberry; *also* : its berry

log·a·rithm \'lȯ-gə-ˌri-thəm, 'lä-\ *n* : the exponent that in-dicates the power to which a base is raised to produce a given number ⟨the ∼ of 100 to base 10 is 2 since $10^2 = 100$⟩ — **log·a·rith·mic** \ˌlȯ-gə-'rith-mik, ˌlä-\ *adj*

loge \'lōzh\ *n* **1** : a small compartment; *also* : a box in a theater **2** : a small partitioned area; *also* : the forward section of a theater mezzanine

log·ger·head \'lȯ-gər-ˌhed, 'lä-\ *n* : a large sea turtle of sub-tropical and temperate waters — **at loggerheads** : in a state of quarrelsome disagreement

log·gia \'lō-jē-ə, 'lō-jä\ *n, pl* **loggias** \'lō-jē-əz, 'lō-jäz\ : a roofed open gallery

log·ic \'lä-jik\ *n* **1** : a science that deals with the rules and tests of sound thinking and proof by reasoning **2** ♦ : sound reasoning **3** : the arrangement of circuit el-ements for arithmetical computation in a computer — **log·i·cal·ly** \-jik(ə-)lē\ *adv* — **lo·gi·cian** \lō-'ji-shən\ *n*
   ♦ reason, sense, sense; *also* cogency, coherence, ra-tionality, thought; analysis; deduction, induction

log·i·cal \-ji-kəl\ *adj* ♦ : of, relating to, involving, or being in accordance with logic
   ♦ analytic, coherent, good, rational, reasonable, sensi-ble, sober, sound, valid; *also* sane; thoughtful; scientific *Ant* incoherent, illogical, invalid, irrational, unreason-able, unsound

lo·gis·tics \lō-'jis-tiks\ *n sing or pl* : the procurement, main-tenance, and transportation of matériel, facilities, and personnel — **lo·gis·tic** \-tik\ *or* **lo·gis·ti·cal** \-ti-kəl\ *adj*

log·jam \'lȯg-ˌjam, 'läg-\ *n* **1** : a deadlocked jumble of logs in a watercourse **2** : DEADLOCK

logo \'lō-gō\ *n, pl* **log·os** \-gōz\ ♦ : an identifying symbol (as for advertising)
   ♦ emblem, hallmark, symbol, trademark — more at EMBLEM

log off *vb* : to end the connection of a computer to a net-work or system

log on *vb* : to start the connection of a computer to a net-work or system

logo·type \'lō-gə-ˌtīp, 'lä-\ *n* : LOGO

log out *vb* : LOG OFF

log·roll·ing \-ˌrō-liŋ\ *n* : the trading of votes by legislators to secure favorable action on projects of individual interest

lo·gy \'lō-gē\ *also* **log·gy** \'lȯ-gē, 'lä-\ *adj* **lo·gi·er; -est** : de-ficient in vitality : SLUGGISH

loin \'lȯin\ *n* [ME *loyne*, fr. AF *loigne*, fr. VL *lumbea*, fr. L *lumbus*] **1** : the part of the body on each side of the spinal column and between the hip and the lower ribs; *also* : a cut of meat from this part of an animal **2** *pl* : the pubic region; *also* : the organs of reproduction

loin·cloth \-ˌklȯth\ *n* : a cloth worn about the loins often as the sole article of clothing in warm climates

loi·ter \'lȯi-tər\ *vb* **1** ♦ : to delay an activity with idle stops and pauses : LINGER **2** : to hang around idly — **loi·ter·er** *n*
   ♦ crawl, creep, dally, dawdle, delay, dillydally, drag, lag, linger, poke, tarry — more at DELAY

loll \'läl\ *vb* **1** ♦ : to hang loosely or laxly : DROOP, DANGLE **2** ♦ : to act or move in a lax, lazy, or indolent manner : LOUNGE ⟨∼ing by the pool⟩
   ♦ [1] dangle, droop, flag, hang, sag, wilt — more at DROOP
   ♦ [2] bask, lounge, relax, repose, rest — more at REST

lol·la·pa·loo·za \ˌlä-lə-pə-'lü-zə\ *n* : something extraordi-narily impressive or outstanding

lol·li·pop *or* **lol·ly·pop** \'lä-li-ˌpäp\ *n* : a lump of hard candy on a stick

lol·ly·gag \'lä-lē-ˌgag\ *vb* **-gagged; -gag·ging** : DAWDLE

Lond *abbr* London

lone \'lōn\ *adj* **1** ♦ : having no company : SOLITARY ⟨a ∼ sentinel⟩ **2** ♦ : alone in a class or category : SOLE, ONLY ⟨the ∼ theater in town⟩ **3** : ISOLATED ⟨a ∼ tree⟩
   ♦ alone, only, singular, sole, solitary, special, unique — more at ONLY

lone·ly \'lōn-lē\ *adj* **lone·li·er; -est** **1** ♦ : being without company **2** : UNFREQUENTED ⟨a ∼ spot⟩ **3** : sad from being alone : LONESOME — **lone·li·ness** *n*
   ♦ alone, lone, lonesome, solitary, unaccompanied — more at ALONE

lon·er \'lō-nər\ *n* ♦ : one that avoids others; *also* : one who pursues an independent course of thought or action
   ♦ bohemian, deviant, individualist, maverick, noncon-formist — more at NONCONFORMIST

lone·some \'lōn-səm\ *adj* **1** ♦ : sad from lack of compan-ionship **2 a** : REMOTE **b** : having no company : SOLI-TARY — **lone·some·ly** *adv* — **lone·some·ness** *n*
   ♦ desolate, forlorn, lonely; *also* friendless; abandoned, deserted, forgotten, forsaken, neglected; alone, lone, solitary; only, sole

¹long \'lȯŋ\ *adj* **lon·ger** \'lȯŋ-gər\; **lon·gest** \'lȯŋ-gəst\ **1** ♦ : extending for a considerable distance; *also* : hav-ing greater height than usual : ELONGATED **2** : having a specified length **3** ♦ : extending over a considerable time; *also* : TEDIOUS **4** : containing many items in a se-ries **5** : being a syllable or speech sound of relatively great duration **6** : extending far into the future **7** : well furnished with something — used with *on* ⟨∼ on talent⟩
   ♦ [1] extended, lengthy; *also* extensive, far-reaching, outstretched; oblong, rectangular; big, considerable, hefty, hulking, jumbo, large, oversize, sizable, substan-tial, super *Ant* brief, short ♦ [3] extended, far, great, lengthy, marathon; *also* endless, everlasting, intermina-ble, persistent; overlong, prolonged, protracted; perma-nent *Ant* brief, short, short-lived, short-term

²long *adv* : for or during a long time

³long *n* : a long period of time

⁴long *vb* **longed; long·ing** \'lȯŋ-iŋ\ ♦ : to feel a strong desire or wish
   ♦ *usu* **long for** ache for, covet, crave, desire, die for, han-ker for, hunger for, lust (for *or* after), pine for, repine for, thirst for, want, wish for, yearn for — more at DESIRE

⁵long *abbr* longitude

long·boat \'loŋ-ˌbōt\ *n* : a large boat usu. carried by a merchant sailing ship

long·bow \-ˌbō\ *n* : a wooden bow drawn by hand and used esp. by medieval English archers

lon·gev·i·ty \län-'je-və-tē\ *n* [LL *longaevitas*, fr. L *longaevus* long-lived, fr. *longus* long + *aevum* age] : a long duration of individual life; *also* : length of life

long·hair \'loŋ-ˌher\ *n* **1** : a lover of classical music **2** : HIPPIE **3** : a domestic cat having long outer fur — **long·haired** \-ˌherd\ *or* **long·hair** *adj*

long·hand \-ˌhand\ *n* : writing done by hand : HANDWRITING; *also* : cursive writing

long·horn \-ˌhórn\ *n* : any of the cattle with long horns formerly common in the southwestern U.S.

long hundredweight *n, Brit* : a unit of weight equal to 112 pounds

long·ing \'loŋ-iŋ\ *n* ♦ : a strong desire esp. for something unattainable — **long·ing·ly** *adv*

♦ appetite, craving, desire, drive, hankering, hunger, itch, lust, passion, thirst, urge, yearning, yen — more at DESIRE

lon·gi·tude \'län-jə-ˌtüd, -ˌtyüd\ *n* : angular distance expressed usu. in degrees east or west from the prime meridian through Greenwich, England

lon·gi·tu·di·nal \ˌlän-jə-'tüd-ᵊn-əl, -'tyüd-\ *adj* **1** : extending lengthwise **2** : of or relating to length — **lon·gi·tu·di·nal·ly** *adv*

long–range \'loŋ-'rānj\ *adj* **1** : relating to or fit for long distances **2** : involving a long period of time

long·shore·man \'loŋ-ˌshōr-mən\ *n* : a laborer at a wharf who loads and unloads cargo

long–suf·fer·ing \-'sə-friŋ, -fə-riŋ\ *adj* ♦ : patiently enduring lasting offense or hardship

♦ forbearing, patient, stoic, tolerant, uncomplaining — more at PATIENT

long–term \'loŋ-'tərm\ *adj* **1** : extending over or involving a long period of time **2** : constituting a financial obligation based on a term usu. of more than 10 years ⟨~ bonds⟩

long·time \'loŋ-'tīm\ *adj* : of long duration ⟨~ friends⟩

long ton *n* : a British unit of weight equal to 20 long hundredweight

lon·gueur \lōⁿ-'gœr\ *n, pl* **longueurs** *same or* -'gœrz\ [F, lit., length] : a dull tedious portion (as of a book)

long–wind·ed \ˌloŋ-'win-dəd\ *adj* ♦ : tediously long in speaking or writing

♦ circuitous, diffuse, prolix, rambling, verbose, windy, wordy — more at WORDY

loo·fah \'lü-fə\ *n* : a sponge consisting of the fibrous skeleton of a gourd

¹look \'lúk\ *vb* **1** : to exercise the power of vision : SEE **2** : EXPECT **3** : to have an appearance that befits ⟨~s the part⟩ **4** ♦ : to have the appearance or likelihood of being : SEEM ⟨~s thin⟩ **5** : to direct one's attention : HEED **6** ♦ : to have a specified direction : POINT, FACE **7** : to show a tendency **8** ♦ : to express by the eyes or facial expression — **look after** : to take care of — **look for** : EXPECT

♦ [4] act, appear, make, seem, sound — more at SEEM ♦ *usu* **look toward** [6] face, front, point — more at FACE ♦ [8] air, express, give, sound, state, vent, voice — more at EXPRESS

²look *n* **1** ♦ : the action of looking : GLANCE **2** ♦ : the expression of the countenance; *also* : physical appearance — usu. used in pl. **3** ♦ : the state or form in which something appears : ASPECT

♦ [1] cast, eye, gander, glance, glimpse, peek, peep, regard, sight, view; *also* gape, gaze, glare, leer, ogle, stare; squint ♦ [2] cast, countenance, expression, face, visage; *also* frown, grimace, mouth, scowl; air, appearance, aspect, bearing, demeanor, manner, mien ♦ *usu* **looks** [2] attractiveness, beauty, comeliness, handsomeness,

loveliness, prettiness — more at BEAUTY ♦ [3] appearance, aspect, mien, presence — more at APPEARANCE

look down *vb* : to regard with contempt — used with *on* or *upon*

looking glass *n* : MIRROR

look into *vb* ♦ : to investigate, study, or analyze

♦ delve, dig, explore, go, inquire into, investigate, probe, research — more at EXPLORE

look·out \'lúk-ˌaút\ *n* **1** ♦ : a person assigned to watch (as on a ship) **2** ♦ : a careful watch **3** ♦ : a view from a particular place : VIEW **4** : a matter of concern **5** : an elevated place or structure affording a wide view for observation

♦ [1] custodian, guard, guardian, keeper, picket, sentry, warden, warder, watch, watchman — more at GUARD ♦ [2] alertness, attentiveness, vigilance, watch ♦ [3] outlook, panorama, prospect, view, vista — more at VIEW

look up *vb* **1** : IMPROVE ⟨business is *looking up*⟩ **2** : to search for in or as if in a reference work **3** : to seek out esp. for a brief visit

¹loom \'lüm\ *n* : a frame or machine for weaving together threads or yarns into cloth

²loom *vb* **1** : to come into sight in an unnaturally large, indistinct, or distorted form **2** : to appear in an impressively exaggerated form **3** : to take shape as an impending occurrence

loon \'lün\ *n* : any of several web-footed black-and-white fish-eating diving birds

loon·ie \'lü-nē\ *n* [fr. the image of a loon on the obverse of the coin] *Can* : a coin worth one Canadian dollar

loo·ny *also* **loo·ney** \'lü-nē\ *adj* **loo·ni·er; -est** : disordered in mind : CRAZY, FOOLISH

loony bin *n, now often offensive* : a psychiatric hospital

¹loop \'lüp\ *n* **1 a** : a fold or doubling of a line through which another line or hook can be passed **b** : a loop-shaped figure or course ⟨a ~ in a river⟩ **2** : a circular airplane maneuver executed in the vertical plane **3** : a continuously repeated segment of film, music, or sound

²loop *vb* ♦ : to make a loop in, on, or about

♦ circle, circumnavigate, coil, compass, encircle, girdle, orbit, ring, round — more at ENCIRCLE

loop·er \'lü-pər\ *n* : any of numerous rather small hairless moth caterpillars that move with a looping motion

loop·hole \'lüp-ˌhōl\ *n* **1** : a small opening in a wall through which firearms may be discharged **2** : a means of escape; *esp* : an ambiguity or omission that allows one to evade the intent of a law or contract

¹loose \'lüs\ *adj* **loos·er; loos·est 1** ♦ : not rigidly fastened **2** ♦ : free from restraint or obligation **3** : not dense or compact in structure **4** : not chaste : LEWD **5** ♦ : not tightly drawn or stretched : SLACK **6** ♦ : not precise or exact — **loose·ly** *adv* — **loose·ness** *n*

♦ [1, 5] insecure, lax, relaxed, slack; *also* detached, free, unattached, unbound, undone, unfastened, untied; baggy; nonrestrictive **Ant** taut, tense, tight ♦ [2] footloose, free, unbound, unconfined, unrestrained — more at FREE ♦ [6] imprecise, inaccurate, inexact — more at INEXACT

²loose *vb* **loosed; loos·ing 1** ♦ : to let loose : RELEASE; *also* : to free from restraint **2** : UNTIE **3** : DETACH **4** ♦ : to let fly : DISCHARGE **5** : RELAX, SLACKEN

♦ [1] discharge, emancipate, enfranchise, free, liberate, loosen, manumit, release, spring, unbind, unchain, unfetter — more at FREE ♦ [4] blast, discharge, fire, shoot — more at SHOOT

³loose *adv* : LOOSELY

loos·en \'lüs-ᵊn\ *vb* **1** ♦ : to release from restraint : FREE **2** ♦ : to make or become loose **3** : to relax the severity of

♦ [1] free, loose, release, uncork, unleash, unlock, unloosen — more at RELEASE ♦ [2] ease, relax, slack, slacken — more at SLACKEN

loosen up *vb* : to become less tense

¹**loot** \'lüt\ *n* [Hindi & Urdu *lūṭ*; akin to Skt *luṇṭati* he plunders] ♦ : goods taken in war or by robbery : PLUNDER — **loot·er** *n*

  ♦ booty, plunder, spoil, swag; *also* prize; catch, haul, take; windfall

²**loot** *vb* ♦ : to plunder or sack in war

  ♦ despoil, maraud, pillage, plunder, ransack, sack, strip — more at RANSACK

¹**lop** \'läp\ *vb* **lopped; lop·ping** 1 : to cut branches or twigs from 2 ♦ : to eliminate as unnecessary or undesirable — usu. used with *off*

  ♦ *usu* lop off bob, clip, crop, curtail, cut, cut back, dock, nip, prune, shave, shear, trim — more at CLIP

²**lop** *vb* **lopped; lop·ping** : to hang downward; *also* : to flop or sway loosely

¹**lope** \'lōp\ *n* : an easy bounding gait

²**lope** *vb* : to move or ride at a lope

lop·sid·ed \'läp-'sī-dəd\ *adj* 1 ♦ : leaning to one side 2 : not symmetrical — **lop·sid·ed·ly** *adv* — **lop·sid·ed·ness** *n*

  ♦ askew, awry, cockeyed, crooked, listing, slantwise, uneven — more at AWRY

lo·qua·cious \lō-'kwā-shəs\ *adj* ♦ : excessively talkative — **lo·quac·i·ty** \-'kwa-sə-tē\ *n*

  ♦ chatty, conversational, gabby, garrulous, talkative — more at TALKATIVE

¹**lord** \'lord\ *n* [ME *loverd, lord*, fr. OE *hlāford*, fr. *hlāf* loaf + *weard* keeper] 1 : one having power and authority over others; *esp* : a person from whom a feudal fee or estate is held 2 : a man of rank or high position; *esp* : a British nobleman 3 *pl, cap* : the upper house of the British parliament 4 : a person of great power in some field 5 *cap* : GOD 1

²**lord** *vb* : to act like a lord; *esp* : to put on airs — usu. used with *it*

lord chancellor *n, pl* **lords chancellor** : a British officer of state who presides over the House of Lords, serves as head of the British judiciary, and is usu. a leading member of the cabinet

lord·ly \-lē\ *adj* **lord·li·er; -est** 1 ♦ : of, relating to, or having the characteristics of a lord : DIGNIFIED; *also* : possessing or arising from a sense of high moral character 2 ♦ : exhibiting the pride and assurance associated with one of the highest birth or rank : HAUGHTY

  ♦ [1] chivalrous, dignified, gallant, great, greathearted, high, high-minded, lofty, magnanimous, noble, sublime — more at NOBLE ♦ [2] disdainful, haughty, highfalutin, lofty, prideful, proud, superior — more at PROUD

lord·ship \-,ship\ *n* 1 : the rank or dignity of a lord — used as a title 2 : the authority or territory of a lord

Lord's Supper *n* : COMMUNION

lore \'lōr\ *n* 1 ♦ : something that has been learned : KNOWLEDGE; *esp* : traditional knowledge or belief 2 ♦ : a particular body of knowledge or tradition

  ♦ [1] intelligence, knowledge, science, wisdom — more at KNOWLEDGE ♦ [2] folklore, legend, myth, mythology, tradition — more at FOLKLORE

lor·gnette \lórn-'yet\ *n* [F, fr. *lorgner* to take a sidelong look at, fr. MF, fr. *lorgne* squinting] : a pair of eyeglasses or opera glasses with a handle

lorn \'lórn\ *adj* : miserable and forlorn as if deserted : DESOLATE

lor·ry \'lór-ē\ *n, pl* **lorries** *chiefly Brit* : MOTORTRUCK

lose \'lüz\ *vb* **lost** \'lóst\; **los·ing** \'lü-ziŋ\ 1 : DESTROY 2 : to miss from a customary place : MISLAY 3 : to suffer deprivation of 4 : to fail to use : WASTE 5 : to fail to win or obtain ⟨~ the game⟩ 6 : to fail to keep or maintain ⟨~ his balance⟩ 7 : to wander from ⟨~ her way⟩ 8 ♦ : to get rid of

  ♦ cast, discard, ditch, dump, fling, jettison, junk, reject, scrap, shed, shuck, slough, throw away, throw out, unload — more at DISCARD

los·er *n* 1 : a person or thing that loses esp. consistently 2 a : a person who is incompetent or unable to succeed b ♦ : something doomed to fail or disappoint

  ♦ bummer, bust, catastrophe, debacle, dud, failure, fiasco, fizzle, flop, lemon, turkey, washout — more at FAILURE

loss \'lós\ *n* 1 ♦ : the state or fact of being destroyed : RUIN 2 : the harm resulting from losing 3 ♦ : something that is lost 4 *pl* : killed, wounded, or captured soldiers 5 ♦ : failure to win 6 : an amount by which the cost exceeds the selling price 7 ♦ : decrease in amount or degree 8 : the act of losing possession

  ♦ [1] annihilation, demolition, desolation, destruction, devastation, havoc, obliteration, ruin, wastage, wreckage — more at DESTRUCTION ♦ [3] casualty, fatality, victim — more at CASUALTY ♦ [5] defeat, rout, shellacking — more at DEFEAT ♦ [7] abatement, decline, decrease, decrement, diminution, drop, fall, reduction, shrinkage — more at DECREASE

loss leader *n* : an article sold at a loss in order to draw customers

lost \'lóst\ *adj* 1 : not used, won, or claimed 2 ♦ : no longer possessed or known 3 : ruined or destroyed physically or morally 4 : DENIED; *also* : HARDENED 5 : unable to find the way; *also* : HELPLESS 6 : ABSORBED, RAPT 7 : not appreciated or understood ⟨his jokes were ~ on me⟩

  ♦ gone, missing; *also* absent, castaway; irrecoverable, irretrievable; forgotten, unknown *Ant* owned, possessed, retained

lot \'lät\ *n* 1 : an object used in deciding something by chance; *also* : the use of lots to decide something 2 a : SHARE, PORTION b ♦ : one's way of life or worldly fate : FORTUNE 3 ♦ : a plot of land 4 ♦ : a group of individuals 5 ♦ : a considerable quantity ⟨a ~ of trouble⟩

  ♦ [2b] circumstance, destiny, doom, fate, fortune, portion — more at FATE ♦ [3] parcel, plat, plot, property, tract; *also* patch; frontage; lease; development; real estate ♦ [4] array, batch, body, bunch, cluster, crop, group, huddle, knot, parcel, party ♦ [5] abundance, barrel, bucket, bushel, chunk, deal, gobs, heap, loads, mass, mess, mountain, much, oodles, pile, plenty, profusion, quantity, reams, scads, stack, wad, wealth; *also* embarrassment, excess, overabundance, overage, overkill, overmuch, oversupply, superabundance, superfluity, surfeit, surplus; deluge, flood, overflow *Ant* bit, hint, little, pinch, smidgen, speck, spot, touch, trace

loth *var of* LOATH

lo·tion \'lō-shən\ *n* : a liquid preparation for cosmetic and external medicinal use

lot·tery \'lä-tə-rē\ *n, pl* **-ter·ies** 1 : a drawing of lots in which prizes are given to the winning names or numbers 2 : a matter determined by chance

lo·tus \'lō-təs\ *n* 1 : a fruit held in Greek legend to cause dreamy contentment and forgetfulness 2 : any of various water lilies represented esp. in ancient Egyptian and Hindu art 3 : any of several leguminous forage plants

loud \'laud\ *adj* 1 ♦ : marked by intensity or volume of sound 2 : CLAMOROUS, NOISY 3 ♦ : obtrusive or offensive in color or pattern ⟨a ~ suit⟩ — **loud** *adv* — **loud·ly** *adv* — **loud·ness** *n*

  ♦ [1] booming, clamorous (*or* clamourous), deafening, earsplitting, piercing, resounding, ringing, roaring, sonorous, stentorian, thunderous; *also* brazen, discordant, noisy, obstreperous, raucous, vociferous; grating, harsh, shrill, strident *Ant* gentle, low, soft ♦ [3] flamboyant, flashy, garish, gaudy, glitzy, ostentatious, swank, tawdry — more at GAUDY

loud-mouthed \-,mautht, -,mauthd\ *adj* : given to loud offensive talk

loud·speak·er \-,spē-kər\ *n* : a device that changes electrical signals into sound

¹**lounge** \'laůnj\ *vb* **lounged; loung·ing** ♦ : to act or move lazily or listlessly

♦ bask, loll, relax, repose, rest — more at REST ♦ dally, dawdle, dillydally, hang around, hang out, idle, loaf, loll — more at IDLE

²**lounge** *n* **1** : a room with comfortable furniture; *also* : a room (as in a theater) with lounging, smoking, and toilet facilities **2** ♦ : a long couch

♦ couch, davenport, divan, settee, sofa — more at COUCH

lour, loury *var of* LOWER, LOWERY

louse \'laůs\ *n, pl* **lice** \'lïs\ **1** : any of various small wingless usu. flattened insects parasitic on warm-blooded animals **2** : a plant pest (as an aphid) **3** *pl* **lous·es** ♦ : a contemptible person

♦ beast, boor, churl, clown, creep, cretin, cur, heel, jerk, joker, lout, skunk, slob, snake — more at JERK

lousy \'laů-zē\ *adj* **lous·i·er; -est** **1** : infested with lice **2** ♦ : miserably poor or inferior **3** : amply supplied ⟨∼ with money⟩ **4** ♦ : totally repulsive — **lous·i·ly** \-zə-lē\ *adv* — **lous·i·ness** \-zē-nəs\ *n*

♦ [2] atrocious, awful, bad, deficient, inferior, off, poor, punk, rotten, substandard, terrible, unacceptable, unsatisfactory, wanting, wretched, wrong — more at BAD ♦ [4] contemptible, despicable, nasty, pitiful, scabby, scurvy, sorry, wretched — more at CONTEMPTIBLE

lout \'laůt\ *n* ♦ : a stupid awkward fellow

♦ clod, hulk, lubber, lug, oaf — more at OAF

lout·ish *adj* ♦ : resembling or befitting a lout — **lout·ish·ly** *adv*

♦ boorish, churlish, clownish, uncouth — more at CLOWNISH

lou·ver *or* **lou·vre** \'lü-vər\ *n* **1** : an opening having parallel slanted slats to allow flow of air but to exclude rain or sun or to provide privacy; *also* : a slat in such an opening **2** : a device with movable slats for controlling the flow of air or light

lov·able \'lə-və-bəl\ *adj* ♦ : having qualities that attract affection

♦ adorable, darling, dear, endearing, precious, sweet, winning; *also* beloved, cherished, treasured; attractive, beautiful, desirable, lovely; captivating, charming, fascinating; admirable, likable, reputable, respectable; affable, agreeable, cheerful, cordial, friendly, genial, gracious, kind, pleasant; delightful, pleasing *Ant* abhorrent, abominable, detestable, hateful, odious, unlovable

¹**love** \'ləv\ *n* **1** ♦ : strong affection **2** ♦ : warm attachment ⟨∼ of the sea⟩ **3** : attraction based on sexual desire **4** ♦ : a beloved person **5** : unselfish loyal and benevolent concern for others **6** : a score of zero in tennis — **love·less** *adj*

♦ [1] appetite, fancy, favor (*or* favour), fondness, like, liking, partiality, preference, relish, shine, taste, use — more at LIKING ♦ [2] affection, attachment, devotion, fondness, passion; *also* appetite, favor, like, liking, partiality, preference, taste; craving, crush, desire, infatuation, longing, lust, yearning; ardor, eagerness, enthusiasm, fervor, zeal; esteem, regard, respect; adoration, idolatry, worship; allegiance, fealty, fidelity, loyalty *Ant* abomination, hate, hatred, loathing, rancor ♦ [4] beloved, darling, dear, flame, honey, sweet, sweetheart — more at SWEETHEART

²**love** *vb* **loved; lov·ing** **1** ♦ : to value highly : CHERISH **2** ♦ : to feel a lover's passion, devotion, or tenderness for **3** ♦ : to touch or stroke lightly in a loving or endearing manner : CARESS **4** ♦ : to like or desire actively ⟨∼s to play bridge⟩

♦ [1] appreciate, cherish, prize, treasure, value; *also* adore, delight (in), dig, enjoy, fancy, groove (on), like, relish, revel (in); admire, esteem, respect, venerate; dote (on), idolize, worship ♦ [2] adore, cherish, worship; *also* idealize, idolize; revere, reverence, venerate;

delight (in), dote (on) *Ant* abhor, abominate, despise, detest, execrate, hate, loathe ♦ [3] caress, fondle, pat, pet, stroke — more at FONDLE ♦ [4] adore, delight, dig, enjoy, fancy, groove, like, relish, revel — more at ENJOY

love affair *n* ♦ : a romantic attachment or episode between lovers

♦ affair, amour, romance — more at AFFAIR

love·bird \'ləv-,bərd\ *n* : any of various small usu. gray or green parrots that seem to show caring behavior for their mates

loved *adj* ♦ : held dear

♦ beloved, darling, dear, favorite (*or* favourite), pet, precious, special, sweet

love·li·ness *n* ♦ : the quality or state of being lovely

♦ attractiveness, beauty, comeliness, handsomeness, looks, prettiness — more at BEAUTY

love·lorn \-,lȯrn\ *adj* : deprived of love or of a lover

love·ly \'ləv-lē\ *adj* **love·li·er; -est** ♦ : delightful for beauty, harmony, or grace : BEAUTIFUL — **love·li·ly** \'ləv-lə-lē\ *adv* — **lovely** *adv*

♦ attractive, beautiful, cute, fair, gorgeous, handsome, knockout, pretty, ravishing, stunning — more at BEAUTIFUL

love·mak·ing \-,mā-kiŋ\ *n* **1** : COURTSHIP **2** : sexual activity; *esp* : COPULATION

lov·er *n* ♦ : a person in love; *also* : an ardent follower, supporter, or enthusiast (as of a religion, art form, or sport)

♦ addict, aficionado, buff, bug, devotee, enthusiast, fan, fanatic, fancier, fiend, freak, maniac, nut — more at FAN

love seat *n* : a seat or sofa for two people

love·sick \-,sik\ *adj* **1** : YEARNING ⟨a ∼ suitor⟩ **2** : expressing a lover's longing — **love·sick·ness** *n*

lov·ing \'lə-viŋ\ *adj* **1** ♦ : having affection or warm regard : AFFECTIONATE **2** : PAINSTAKING — **lov·ing·ly** *adv*

♦ affectionate, devoted, fond, tender, tenderhearted; *also* caring, compassionate, considerate, cordial, doting, forgiving, friendly, kind, warmhearted; ardent, fervent, impassioned, passionate, warm; amatory, amorous, erotic; enamored, infatuated, lovesick; mushy, romantic, sentimental; brotherly, fatherly, motherly, sisterly *Ant* unloving

¹**low** \'lō\ *vb* : MOO

²**low** *n* : MOO

³**low** *adj* **low·er** \'lō-ər\; **low·est** \'lō-əst\ **1** : not high or tall ⟨∼ wall⟩; *also* : DÉCOLLETÉ **2** : situated or passing below the normal level or surface ⟨∼ ground⟩; *also* : marking a nadir **3** ♦ : not loud ⟨∼ voice⟩ **4** : being near the equator **5 a** ♦ : humble in status **b** ♦ : lacking in cultural advancement **c** ♦ : lacking in dignity **6** ♦ : lacking strength, health, or vitality : WEAK; *also* : DEPRESSED **7** : STRICKEN, PROSTRATE **8** ♦ : less than usual in number, amount, or value; *also* : of lesser degree than average **9** : falling short of a standard **10** : UNFAVORABLE — **low** *adv*

♦ [3] dull, quiet, soft — more at SOFT ♦ [5a] common, humble, ignoble, inferior, lowly, mean, plebeian, vulgar — more at IGNOBLE ♦ [5b] crude, primitive, rude, rudimentary — more at PRIMITIVE ♦ [5b] coarse, common, crass, crude, gross, ill-bred, rough, rude, tasteless, uncouth, uncultivated, uncultured, unpolished, unrefined, vulgar — more at COARSE ♦ [5c] base, contemptible, despicable, detestable, dirty, dishonorable (*or* dishonourable), ignoble, mean, snide, sordid, vile, wretched — more at IGNOBLE ♦ [6] blue, dejected, depressed, down, downcast, glum, melancholy, sad, sorrowful, sorry, unhappy, woeful, wretched — more at SAD ♦ [6] faint, feeble, frail, infirm, unsubstantial, weak — more at WEAK ♦ [8] cheap, cut-rate, reasonable — more at CHEAP

⁴**low** *n* **1** : something that is low **2** : a region of low barometric pressure **3** : the arrangement of gears in an

automobile transmission that gives the slowest speed and greatest power

low·ball \\'lō-,ból\\ *vb* : to give a deceptively low price, cost estimate, or offer to

low beam *n* : a vehicle headlight beam with short-range focus

low blow *n* : an unprincipled attack

low·brow \\'lō-,braú\\ *adj* : having little taste or intellectual interest — **lowbrow** *n*

low–density lipoprotein *n* : LDL

low–down \\-,daún\\ *n* ♦ : pertinent and esp. guarded information

♦ dope, scoop, tip — more at DOPE

low–down \\-,daún\\ *adj* 1 : MEAN, CONTEMPTIBLE 2 : deeply emotional

low–end \\-,end\\ *adj* : of, relating to, or being the lowest-priced merchandise in a manufacturer's line

¹**low·er** \\'laú-ər\\ *vb* 1 ♦ : to look sullen : FROWN 2 : to become dark, gloomy, and threatening

♦ frown, glare, gloom, glower, scowl — more at FROWN

²**low·er** \\'lō-ər\\ *adj* 1 ♦ : relatively low (as in rank) 2 : situated beneath the earth's surface 3 : constituting the popular and more representative branch of a bicameral legislative body 4 : less advanced in the scale of evolutionary development

♦ inferior, junior, less, lesser, minor, subordinate, under — more at LESSER

³**low·er** \\'lō-ər\\ *vb* 1 ♦ : to move down : DROP; *also* : DIMINISH 2 : to let descend by its own weight; *also* : to reduce the height of 3 ♦ : to reduce or decline in value, number, or amount 4 ♦ : to bring down in quality or character : DEGRADE; *also* : HUMBLE

♦ [1] decline, descend, diminish, dip, drop, fall, plummet, plunge, sink, tumble — more at DROP ♦ [3] abate, decrease, de-escalate, diminish, downsize, dwindle, lessen, reduce ♦ [4] abase, debase, degrade, demean, discredit, disgrace, dishonor (*or* dishonour), humble, humiliate, shame, smirch, take down — more at HUMBLE

low·er·case \\,lō-ər-'kās\\ *adj* : being a letter that belongs to or conforms to the series a, b, c, etc., rather than A, B, C, etc. — **lowercase** *n*

lower class *n* : a social class occupying a position below the middle class and having the lowest status in a society — **lower–class** \\-'klas\\ *adj*

low·er·most \\'lō-ər-,mōst\\ *adj* : LOWEST

low·ery \\'laú-ə-rē\\ *adj* : GLOOMY, LOWERING ⟨a ~ sky⟩

lowest common denominator *n* 1 : LEAST COMMON DENOMINATOR 2 : something designed to appeal to a lowbrow audience; *also* : such an audience

lowest common multiple *n* : LEAST COMMON MULTIPLE

low–key \\'lō-'kē\\ *also* **low–keyed** \\-'kēd\\ *adj* : of low intensity : RESTRAINED

low·land \\'lō-lənd, -,land\\ *n* : low and usu. level country

low–lev·el \\'lō-'le-vəl\\ *adj* 1 : being of low importance or rank 2 : being or relating to nuclear waste of low concentration

low·life \\'lō-,līf\\ *n*, *pl* **low·lifes** \\-,līfs\\ *also* **low·lives** \\-,līvz\\ : a person of low social status or moral character

low·li·ness *n* ♦ : the quality or state of being lowly

♦ humbleness, humility, meekness, modesty — more at HUMILITY

low·ly \\'lō-lē\\ *adj* **low·li·er; -est** 1 ♦ : humble in manner or spirit : MEEK 2 ♦ : ranking low in some hierarchy

♦ [1] demure, humble, meek, modest, retiring, unassuming, unpretentious — more at HUMBLE ♦ [2] common, humble, ignoble, inferior, low, mean, plebeian, vulgar — more at IGNOBLE

low·ness *n* ♦ : the quality or state of being low

♦ debility, delicacy, enfeeblement, faintness, feebleness, frailty, infirmity, languor, weakness — more at WEAKNESS ♦ coarseness, grossness, indelicacy, rudeness, vulgarity — more at VULGARITY

low–rise \\'lō-'rīz\\ *adj* 1 : having few stories and not equipped with elevators ⟨a ~ building⟩ 2 : of, relating to, or characterized by low-rise buildings

low–slung \\'lō-,sləŋ\\ *adj* : relatively low to the ground or floor ⟨a ~ building⟩ ⟨~ pants⟩

low–tech \\'lō-'tek\\ *adj* : technologically simple or unsophisticated

¹**lox** \\'läks\\ *n* : liquid oxygen

²**lox** *n*, *pl* **lox** *or* **lox·es** : salmon cured in brine and sometimes smoked

loy·al \\'lói-əl\\ *adj* [MF, fr. OF *leial, leel*, fr. L *legalis* legal] 1 : faithful in allegiance to one's government 2 ♦ : faithful esp. to a cause or ideal : CONSTANT — **loy·al·ly** \\'lói-ə-lē\\ *adv*

♦ constant, devoted, faithful, fast, good, pious, staunch, steadfast, steady, true, true-blue — more at FAITHFUL

loy·al·ist \\'lói-ə-list\\ *n* : one who is or remains loyal to a political party, government, or sovereign

loy·al·ty \\'lói-əl-tē\\ *n* ♦ : the quality or state or an instance of being loyal

♦ allegiance, constancy, dedication, devotion, faith, faithfulness, fastness, fealty, fidelity, steadfastness — more at FIDELITY

loz·enge \\'lä-zənj\\ *n* 1 : a diamond-shaped figure 2 : a small flat often medicated candy

LP *abbr* low pressure

LPG *abbr* liquefied petroleum gas

LPGA *abbr* Ladies Professional Golf Association

LPN \\'el-'pē-'en\\ *n* : LICENSED PRACTICAL NURSE

Lr *symbol* Lawrencium

LSD \\,el-(,)es-'dē\\ *n* [G *Lysergsäure-Diäthylamid* lysergic acid diethylamide] : an illicit and highly potent hallucinogenic drug derived from ergot or produced synthetically

lt *abbr* light

Lt *abbr* lieutenant

LT *abbr* long ton

LTC *or* **Lt Col** *abbr* lieutenant colonel

Lt Comdr *abbr* lieutenant commander

ltd *abbr* limited

LTG *or* **Lt Gen** *abbr* lieutenant general

LTJG *abbr* lieutenant, junior grade

ltr *abbr* letter

Lu *symbol* lutetium

lu·au \\'lü-,aú\\ *n* : a Hawaiian feast

lub *abbr* lubricant; lubricating

lub·ber \\'lə-bər\\ *n* 1 ♦ : a big clumsy fellow : LOUT 2 : an unskilled seaman

♦ clod, hulk, lout, lug, oaf — more at OAF

lub·ber·ly *adj* ♦ : resembling or having the characteristics of a lubber

♦ awkward, clumsy, gawky, graceless, heavy-handed, lumpish, ungainly, unhandy — more at CLUMSY

lube \\'lüb\\ *n* : LUBRICANT; *also* : an application of a lubricant

lu·bri·cant \\'lü-bri-kənt\\ *n* : a material capable of reducing friction when applied between moving parts

lu·bri·cate \\'lü-brə-,kāt\\ *vb* **-cat·ed; -cat·ing** ♦ : to apply a lubricant to — **lu·bri·ca·tion** \\,lü-brə-'kā-shən\\ *n* — **lu·bri·ca·tor** \\'lü-brə-,kā-tər\\ *n*

♦ grease, oil, slick, wax

lu·bri·cious \\lü-'bri-shəs\\ *or* **lu·bri·cous** \\'lü-bri-kəs\\ *adj* 1 : SMOOTH, SLIPPERY 2 : LECHEROUS; *also* : SALACIOUS — **lu·bric·i·ty** \\'lü-'bri-sə-tē\\ *n*

lu·cent \\'lüs-³nt\\ *adj* 1 ♦ : glowing with light : LUMINOUS 2 ♦ : marked by clarity or translucence — **lu·cent·ly** *adv*

♦ [1] beaming, bright, brilliant, effulgent, glowing, incandescent, lambent, lucid, luminous, lustrous, radiant, refulgent, shiny — more at BRIGHT ♦ [2] clear, limpid, liquid, pellucid, transparent — more at CLEAR

lu·cerne \\lü-'sərn\\ *n*, *chiefly Brit* : ALFALFA

lu·cid \\'lü-səd\\ *adj* 1 : suffused with light : SHINING 2 ♦ : mentally sound 3 ♦ : easily understood ⟨a ~ explanation⟩ — **lu·cid·ly** *adv*

♦ [2] balanced, clearheaded, normal, right, sane, stable — more at SANE ♦ [3] apparent, broad, clear, clear-cut, distinct, evident, manifest, obvious, palpable, patent, perspicuous, plain, transparent, unambiguous, unequivocal, unmistakable — more at CLEAR

lu·cid·i·ty \lü-'si-də-tē\ *n* ♦ : clearness of thought or style

♦ clarity, explicitness, perspicuity, simplicity — more at SIMPLICITY

lu·cid·ness *n* : the quality or state of being lucid esp. in thought or style

Lu·ci·fer \'lü-sə-fər\ *n* [ME, the morning star, a fallen rebel archangel, the Devil, fr. OE, fr. L, the morning star, fr. *lucifer* light-bearing] : DEVIL, SATAN

¹luck \'lək\ *n* 1 ♦ : a force that brings good fortune or adversity : CHANCE 2 ♦ : good fortune

♦ [1] accident, chance, circumstance, hazard — more at CHANCE ♦ [2] chance, fortune; *also* break, fluke, godsend, hit, serendipity, strike, windfall; opportunity; coup, stroke *Ant* mischance, misfortune

²luck *vb* 1 : to prosper or succeed esp. through chance or good fortune — usu. used with *out* 2 : to come upon something desirable by chance — usu. used with *out, on, onto,* or *into*

luck·i·ly \'lə-kə-lē\ *adv* 1 : in a lucky manner 2 : FORTUNATELY 2

luck·less *adj* ♦ : being without luck

♦ hapless, ill-fated, ill-starred, unfortunate, unhappy, unlucky — more at UNLUCKY

lucky \'lə-kē\ *adj* **luck·i·er; -est** 1 ♦ : favored by luck : FORTUNATE 2 ♦ : happening by chance : FORTUITOUS 3 : seeming to bring good luck — **luck·i·ness** *n*

♦ [1] blessed, fortunate, happy *Ant* hapless, ill-fated, ill-starred, luckless, unfortunate, unlucky ♦ [2] fluky, fortuitous, fortunate, happy, providential — more at FORTUNATE

lu·cra·tive \'lü-krə-tiv\ *adj* ♦ : producing wealth : PROFITABLE — **lu·cra·tive·ly** *adv* — **lu·cra·tive·ness** *n*

♦ fat, gainful, profitable, remunerative — more at PROFITABLE

lu·cre \'lü-kər\ *n* [ME, fr. AF, fr. L *lucrum*] ♦ : monetary gain : PROFIT; *also* : MONEY

♦ earnings, gain, net, payoff, proceeds, profit, return — more at PROFIT ♦ cash, currency, dough, money, pelf, tender — more at MONEY

lu·cu·bra·tion \,lü-kyə-'brā-shən, -kə-\ *n* : laborious study : MEDITATION

Lud·dite \'lə-,dīt\ *n* [perh. fr. Ned *Ludd*, 18th cent. Eng. workman who destroyed a knitting frame] : one who is opposed to technological change

lu·di·crous \'lü-də-krəs\ *adj* ♦ : amusing or laughable through obvious absurdity, incongruity, exaggeration, or eccentricity : RIDICULOUS ⟨a ∼ idea⟩; *also* : meriting derisive laughter or scorn as absurdly inept, false, or foolish — **lu·di·crous·ly** *adv* — **lu·di·crous·ness** *n*

♦ antic, comic, droll, funny, hilarious, humorous, hysterical, laughable, riotous, screaming, uproarious — more at FUNNY ♦ absurd, comical, derisive, farcical, laughable, preposterous, ridiculous, risible, silly — more at RIDICULOUS

luff \'ləf\ *vb* : to turn the head of a ship toward the wind

¹lug \'ləg\ *vb* **lugged; lug·ging** 1 ♦ : to draw slowly or heavily : DRAG, PULL 2 ♦ : to carry laboriously

♦ [1] drag, draw, hale, haul, pull, tow, tug — more at PULL ♦ [2] bear, carry, cart, convey, ferry, haul, pack, tote, transport — more at CARRY

²lug *n* 1 : a projecting piece (as for fastening, support, or traction) 2 : a nut securing a wheel on an automobile 3 ♦ : a big clumsy fellow

♦ clod, hulk, lout, lubber, oaf — more at OAF

lug·gage \'lə-gij\ *n* : containers (as suitcases) for carrying personal belongings : BAGGAGE

lu·gu·bri·ous \lù-'gü-brē-əs\ *adj* ♦ : mournful often to an exaggerated degree ⟨∼ music⟩ — **lu·gu·bri·ous·ly** *adv* — **lu·gu·bri·ous·ness** *n*

♦ dolorous, funeral, mournful, plaintive, regretful, rueful, sorrowful, weeping, woeful — more at MOURNFUL

Luke \'lük\ *n* : a book of the New Testament of Christian Scripture

luke·warm \'lük-'wórm\ *adj* 1 : moderately warm : TEPID 2 : not enthusiastic — **luke·warm·ly** *adv*

¹lull \'ləl\ *vb* 1 ♦ : to make peaceful : SOOTHE, CALM 2 : to cause to relax vigilance

♦ allay, calm, compose, quiet, settle, soothe, still, tranquilize — more at CALM

²lull *n* 1 : a temporary calm (as during a storm) 2 ♦ : a temporary drop in activity

♦ break, breath, breather, interruption, pause — more at PAUSE

lul·la·by \'lə-lə-,bī\ *n, pl* **-bies** : a song to lull children to sleep

lum·ba·go \,ləm-'bā-gō\ *n* : acute or chronic pain in the lower back

lum·bar \'ləm-bər, -,bär\ *adj* : of, relating to, or constituting the loins or the vertebrae between the thoracic vertebrae and sacrum ⟨∼ region⟩

¹lum·ber \'ləm-bər\ *vb* 1 ♦ : to move heavily or clumsily 2 ♦ : to make a low heavy rolling sound

♦ [1] clump, flounder, lump, plod, scuff, scuffle, shamble, shuffle, stamp, stomp, stumble, tramp, tromp; *also* drag, flop, haul; labor; careen, lurch, stagger, sway, teeter, totter, waddle, weave, wobble *Ant* breeze, coast, glide, slide, waltz, whisk ♦ [2] growl, grumble, roll, rumble — more at RUMBLE

²lumber *n* 1 : surplus or disused articles that are stored away 2 : timber or logs esp. when dressed for use

³lumber *vb* 1 : to cut logs; *also* : to saw logs into lumber 2 ♦ : to clutter with or as if with lumber — **lum·ber·man** \-mən\ *n*

♦ burden, encumber, load, saddle, weight — more at LOAD

lum·ber·jack \-,jak\ *n* : LOGGER

lum·ber·yard \-,yärd\ *n* : a place where lumber is kept for sale

lu·mi·nary \'lü-mə-,ner-ē\ *n, pl* **-nar·ies** 1 ♦ : a very famous person 2 : a source of light; *esp* : a celestial body

♦ celebrity, figure, light, notable, personage, personality, somebody, standout, star, superstar, VIP — more at CELEBRITY

lu·mi·nes·cence \,lü-mə-'nes-°ns\ *n* ♦ : the low-temperature emission of light (as by a chemical or physiological process); *also* : such light — **lu·mi·nes·cent** \-°nt\ *adj*

♦ blaze, flare, fluorescence, glare, gleam, glow, illumination, incandescence, light, radiance, shine — more at LIGHT

lu·mi·nos·i·ty \,lü-mə-'nä-sə-tē\ *n* ♦ : the quality or state of being luminous

♦ brilliance, dazzle, effulgence, illumination, lightness, lucidity, radiance, refulgence, splendor — more at BRILLIANCE

lu·mi·nous \'lü-mə-nəs\ *adj* 1 ♦ : emitting light; *also* : LIGHTED 2 : CLEAR, INTELLIGIBLE 3 : ILLUSTRIOUS — **lu·mi·nance** \-nəns\ *n* — **lu·mi·nous·ly** *adv*

♦ beaming, bright, brilliant, effulgent, glowing, incandescent, lambent, lucent, lucid, lustrous, radiant, refulgent, shiny — more at BRIGHT

lum·mox \'lə-məks\ *n* : a clumsy person

¹lump \'ləmp\ *n* 1 ♦ : a piece or mass of indefinite size and shape 2 : AGGREGATE, TOTALITY 3 ♦ : a usu. abnormal swelling

♦ [1] blob, chunk, clod, clump, glob, gob, hunk, nub, wad; *also* bead, drop, globule; block, body, bulk; particle, piece, portion; bit, chip, crumb, morsel, scrap ♦ [3] excrescence, growth, neoplasm, tumor — more at GROWTH ♦ [3] bump, knot, nodule, swelling — more at BUMP

²**lump** *vb* **1 ♦** : to heap together in a lump **2** : to form into lumps **3** : to move noisily and clumsily

    ♦ accumulate, amass, assemble, collect, concentrate, garner, gather, group, pick up, round up, scrape — more at GATHER

³**lump** *adj* : not divided into parts ⟨a ∼ sum⟩

lump·ec·to·my \ˌləm-ˈpek-tə-mē\ *n, pl* **-mies** : excision of a breast tumor

lump·ish *adj* **♦** : lacking ease or grace (as of movement or expression)

    ♦ awkward, clumsy, gawky, graceless, heavy-handed, lubberly, ungainly, unhandy — more at CLUMSY

lumpy *adj* **♦** : filled or covered with lumps

    ♦ broken, bumpy, coarse, irregular, jagged, pebbly, ragged, rough, rugged, uneven — more at UNEVEN

lu·na·cy \ˈlü-nə-sē\ *n, pl* **-cies 1** *dated* **♦** : a deranged state of the mind : INSANITY **2 ♦** : extreme folly; *also* : a foolish act

    ♦ [1] aberration, dementia, derangement, insanity, madness, mania — more at INSANITY **♦** [2] absurdity, fatuity, folly, foolery, foolishness, idiocy, inanity, madness, stupidity

lu·nar \ˈlü-nər\ *adj* : of or relating to the moon

¹**lu·na·tic** \ˈlü-nə-ˌtik\ *adj* [ME *lunatik*, fr. AF & LL; AF *lunatik*, fr. LL *lunaticus*, fr. L *luna* moon; fr. the belief that lunacy fluctuated with the phases of the moon] **1 a** *dated* : affected with lunacy : INSANE **b** *dated* : used for insane persons **2 ♦** : extremely foolish

    ♦ absurd, crazy, cuckoo, fatuous, foolish, mad, nonsensical, nutty, senseless, silly, stupid — more at FOOLISH

²**lunatic** *n* **♦** : a person affected with lunacy; *also* : one capable of crazy actions or extravagances

    ♦ maniac, nut, psychotic; *also* madman, madwoman; deviant; paranoid, schizophrenic; character, crackpot, crank, eccentric, kook, oddball, screwball; case, patient

¹**lunch** \ˈlənch\ *n* **1** : a light meal usu. eaten in the middle of the day **2** : the food prepared for a lunch

²**lunch** *vb* : to eat lunch

lun·cheon \ˈlən-chən\ *n* : a usu. formal lunch

lun·cheon·ette \ˌlən-chə-ˈnet\ *n* : a small restaurant serving light lunches

lunch·room \ˈlənch-ˌrüm, -ˌrum\ *n* **1** : LUNCHEONETTE **2** : a room (as in a school) where lunches are sold and eaten or lunches brought from home may be eaten

lu·nette \lü-ˈnet\ *n* : something shaped like a crescent

lung \ˈləŋ\ *n* **1** : one of the usu. paired baglike breathing organs in the chest of an air-breathing vertebrate **2** : a mechanical device to promote breathing and make it easier — **lunged** \ˈləŋd\ *adj*

lunge \ˈlənj\ *n* **1** : a sudden thrust or pass (as with a sword) **2** : a sudden forward stride or leap — **lunge** *vb*

lu·pine \ˈlü-pən\ *n* : any of a genus of leguminous plants with long upright clusters of pealike flowers

lu·pus \ˈlü-pəs\ *n* [ML, fr. L, wolf] : any of several diseases characterized by skin lesions; *esp* : SYSTEMIC LUPUS ERYTHEMATOSUS

¹**lurch** \ˈlərch\ *n* : a sudden swaying or tipping movement

²**lurch** *vb* **♦** : to roll or tip abruptly; *also* : to move with a lurch

    ♦ careen, pitch, rock, roll, seesaw, sway, toss, wobble — more at ROCK **♦** careen, dodder, reel, stagger, teeter, totter — more at STAGGER

¹**lure** \ˈlur\ *n* **1 ♦** : an inducement to pleasure or gain : ENTICEMENT; *also* : APPEAL ⟨the ∼ of easy money⟩ **2** : an artificial bait for catching fish

    ♦ appeal, attraction, bait, call, decoy, enticement, incentive, inducement, persuasion, seduction, snare, spur, temptation, trap

²**lure** *vb* **lured; lur·ing ♦** : to draw on with a promise of pleasure or gain

    ♦ allure, beguile, decoy, entice, lead on, seduce, tempt; *also* persuade, inveigle, rope (in); snow; catch, ensnare, entrap, snare; captivate, charm, enchant

lu·rid \ˈlur-əd\ *adj* **1 ♦** : wan and ghostly pale in appearance **2** : shining with the red glow of fire seen through smoke or cloud **3 a ♦** : causing horror or revulsion : GRUESOME **b** : SENSATIONAL — **lu·rid·ly** *adv*

    ♦ [1] ashen, cadaverous, livid, pale, pasty, peaked — more at PALE **♦** [3a] appalling, atrocious, awful, dreadful, frightful, ghastly, grisly, gruesome, hideous, horrible, horrid, macabre, monstrous, nightmarish, shocking, terrible — more at HORRIBLE

lurk \ˈlərk\ *vb* **1 ♦** : to move furtively : SNEAK **2** : to lie concealed

    ♦ pussyfoot, skulk, slide, slink, slip, snake, sneak, steal — more at SNEAK

lus·cious \ˈlə-shəs\ *adj* **1 ♦** : having a pleasingly sweet taste or smell **2 ♦** : sensually appealing ⟨a ∼ voice⟩ — **lus·cious·ly** *adv*

    ♦ [1] agreeable, ambrosial, appetizing, delectable, delicious, delightful, enjoyable, flavorful (*or* flavourful), palatable, savory, scrumptious, tasty, toothsome, yummy — more at DELICIOUS **♦** [2] carnal, fleshly, sensual, sensuous, voluptuous — more at SENSUAL

lus·cious·ness *n* **♦** : the quality or state of being luscious

    ♦ savor, tastiness

¹**lush** \ˈləsh\ *adj* **♦** : having or covered with abundant growth ⟨∼ pastures⟩

    ♦ green, leafy, luxuriant, verdant; *also* fat, fecund, fertile, fruitful, productive, rich; dense, tangled *Ant* barren, leafless

²**lush** *n* : an habitual heavy drinker

¹**lust** \ˈləst\ *n* **1** : usu. intense or unbridled sexual desire : LASCIVIOUSNESS **2 ♦** : an intense longing

    ♦ appetite, craving, desire, drive, hankering, hunger, itch, longing, passion, thirst, urge, yearning, yen — more at DESIRE

²**lust** *vb* **♦** : to have an intense desire or need

    ♦ *usu* **lust for** *or* **lust after** ache for, covet, crave, desire, die for, hanker for, hunger for, long for, pine for, repine for, thirst for, want, wish for, yearn for — more at DESIRE

lus·ter *or* **lus·tre** \ˈləs-tər\ *n* **1 ♦** : a shine or sheen esp. from reflected light **2** : BRIGHTNESS, GLITTER **3** : GLORY, SPLENDOR

    ♦ gloss, polish, sheen, shine — more at SHINE

lus·ter·less *adj* **♦** : lacking luster

    ♦ dim, dull, flat

lust·ful *adj* **♦** : excited by lust

    ♦ lascivious, lewd, passionate, wanton; *also* prurient; dissipated, dissolute, libertine; corrupt, debauched, depraved, immoral, indecent

lust·i·ness \-tē-nəs\ *n* **♦** : the quality or state of being lusty

    ♦ animation, briskness, exuberance, liveliness, robustness, sprightliness, vibrancy, vitality — more at VITALITY

lus·tral \ˈləs-trəl\ *adj* : serving or intended to purify

lus·trous \-trəs\ *adj* **♦** : reflecting light evenly and efficiently without glitter or sparkle

    ♦ beaming, bright, brilliant, effulgent, glowing, incandescent, lambent, lucent, lucid, luminous, radiant, refulgent, shiny — more at BRIGHT **♦** glossy, polished, satiny, sleek — more at GLOSSY

lusty \ˈləs-tē\ *adj* **lust·i·er; -est 1 ♦** : full of vitality : ROBUST **2 ♦** : full of energy or activity — **lust·i·ly** \ˈləs-tə-lē\ *adv*

    ♦ [1] dynamic, energetic, flush, peppy, robust, strenuous, vigorous, vital — more at VIGOROUS **♦** [2] firm, forceful, hearty, robust, solid, stout, strong, sturdy, vigorous

lute \ˈlüt\ *n* : a stringed musical instrument with a large pear-shaped body and a fretted fingerboard — **lu·te·nist** *or* **lu·ta·nist** \ˈlüt-ᵊn-ist\ *n*

lu·te·tium *also* **lu·te·cium** \lü-ˈtē-shē-əm, -shəm\ *n* : a metallic chemical element

Lu·ther·an \ˈlü-thə-rən\ *n* : a member of a Protestant

denomination adhering to the doctrines of Martin Luther — **Lu·ther·an·ism** \-rə-ˌni-zəm\ n

lux·u·ri·ant \ˌləg-ˈzhu̇r-ē-ənt, ˌlək-ˈshu̇r-\ adj 1 ♦ : yielding or growing abundantly : LUSH, PRODUCTIVE 2 : abundantly rich and varied; also : FLORID 3 : characterized by luxury — **lux·u·ri·ance** \-ē-əns\ n — **lux·u·ri·ant·ly** adv

♦ green, leafy, lush, verdant ♦ fat, fecund, fertile, fruitful, productive, prolific, rich — more at FERTILE

lux·u·ri·ate \-ē-ˌāt\ vb **-at·ed; -at·ing** 1 : to grow profusely 2 : REVEL

lux·u·ri·ous \ˌləg-ˈzhu̇r-ē-əs, ˌlək-ˈshu̇r-\ adj ♦ : of, relating to, or marked by luxury

♦ deluxe, lavish, luxuriant, opulent, palatial, plush, sumptuous; also costly, expensive; rich; extravagant, grandiose, ostentatious, pretentious, showy; awesome, awful, beautiful, gorgeous, grand, imposing, impressive, magnificent, majestic, splendid, stately; comfortable, cozy, homey, snug **Ant** ascetic, austere, humble

lux·u·ri·ous·ly adv ♦ : in a luxurious manner

♦ expensively, extravagantly, grandly, high, lavishly, opulently, richly — more at HIGH

¹**lux·u·ry** \ˈlək-shə-rē, ˈləg-zhə-\ n, pl **-ries** 1 : great ease and comfort 2 ♦ : something adding to pleasure or comfort but not absolutely necessary

♦ amenity, comfort, extra, frill, indulgence, superfluity; also extravagance; dainty, delicacy, treat; accessory, option **Ant** basic, essential, fundamental, necessity, requirement

²**luxury** adj ♦ : of or relating to luxury or luxuries or catering to luxurious tastes

♦ deluxe, lavish, luxuriant, luxurious, opulent, palatial, plush, sumptuous — more at LUXURIOUS

lv abbr leave

Lv symbol livermorium

LWV abbr League of Women Voters

¹**-ly** \lē\ adj suffix 1 : like in appearance, manner, or nature ⟨queenly⟩ 2 : characterized by regular recurrence in (specified) units of time : every ⟨hourly⟩

²**-ly** adv suffix 1 : in a (specified) manner ⟨slowly⟩ 2 : from a (specified) point of view ⟨grammatically⟩

ly·ce·um \lī-ˈsē-əm, ˈlī-sē-\ n 1 : a hall for public lectures 2 : an association providing public lectures, concerts, and entertainments

ly·chee or **li·tchi** \ˈlē-chē\ n [Ch(Beijing) lìzhī] 1 : an oval fruit with a hard scaly outer covering, a small hard seed, and edible flesh 2 : an Asian tree bearing lychees

lye \ˈlī\ n : a corrosive alkaline substance used esp. in making soap

ly·ing \ˈlī-iŋ\ adj ♦ : marked by or containing falsehoods : UNTRUTHFUL

♦ dishonest, mendacious — more at DISHONEST

ly·ing–in \ˌlī-iŋ-ˈin\ n, pl **lyings–in** or **lying–ins** : the state during and consequent to childbirth : CONFINEMENT

Lyme disease \ˈlīm-\ n [Lyme, Connecticut, where it was first reported] : an acute inflammatory disease that is caused by a spirochete transmitted by ticks, is characterized usu. by chills and fever, and if left untreated may result in joint pain, arthritis, and cardiac and neurological disorders

lymph \ˈlimf\ n : a usu. clear fluid consisting chiefly of blood plasma and white blood cells, circulating in thin-walled tubes (**lymphatic vessels**), and bathing the body tissues — **lym·phat·ic** \lim-ˈfa-tik\ adj

lymph·ade·nop·a·thy \ˌlim-ˌfad-ᵊn-ˈä-pə-thē\ n, pl **-thies** : abnormal enlargement of the lymph nodes

lymph node n : any of the rounded masses of lymphoid tissue surrounded by a capsule

lym·pho·cyte \ˈlim-fə-ˌsīt\ n : any of the white blood cells arising from lymphoid tissue that are typically found in lymph and blood and that include the cellular mediators (as a B cell or a T cell) of immunity — **lym·pho·cyt·ic** \ˌlim-fə-ˈsi-tik\ adj

lym·phoid \ˈlim-ˌfȯid\ adj 1 : of, relating to, or being tissue (as of the lymph nodes) containing lymphocytes 2 : of, relating to, or resembling lymph

lym·pho·ma \lim-ˈfō-mə\ n, pl **-mas** or **-ma·ta** \-mə-tə\ : a usu. malignant tumor of lymphoid tissue

lynch \ˈlinch\ vb : to put to death by mob action without legal sanction or due process of law — **lynch·er** n

lynx \ˈliŋks\ n, pl **lynx** or **lynx·es** : any of several wildcats with a short tail, long legs, and usu. tufted ears

lyre \ˈlīr\ n : a stringed musical instrument of the harp class having a U-shaped frame and used by the ancient Greeks

¹**lyr·ic** \ˈlir-ik\ n 1 ♦ : a lyric poem 2 : the words of a popular song — often used in pl.

♦ poem, song, verse — more at POEM

²**lyric** adj 1 ♦ : suitable for singing : MELODIC 2 ♦ : expressing direct and usu. intense personal emotion ⟨~ poetry⟩

♦ [1] euphonious, mellifluous, mellow, melodic, melodious, musical; also dulcet, golden, sweet ♦ [2] bardic, lyrical, poetic — more at POETIC

lyr·i·cal \-i-kəl\ adj ♦ : having qualities suggestive of music or poetry : LYRIC

♦ bardic, lyric, poetic — more at POETIC

ly·ser·gic acid di·eth·yl·am·ide \lə-ˈsər-jik . . . ˌdī-ˌe-thə-ˈla-ˌmīd, lī-, -ˈla-məd\ n : LSD

LZ abbr landing zone

¹**m** \ˈem\ n, pl **m's** or **ms** \ˈemz\ often cap : the 13th letter of the English alphabet

²**m** abbr, often cap 1 Mach 2 male 3 married 4 masculine 5 medium 6 [L meridies] noon 7 meter 8 mile 9 [L mille] thousand 10 minute 11 month 12 moon

ma \ˈmä, ˈmȯ\ n ♦ : a female parent : MOTHER

♦ mom, mommy, mother

MA abbr 1 [ML magister artium] master of arts 2 Massachusetts 3 mental age

ma'am \ˈmam, after "yes" often əm\ n : MADAM

¹**Mac** abbr Machabees

²**Mac** or **Macc** abbr Maccabees

ma·ca·bre \mə-ˈkäb; -ˈkä-brə, -bər\ adj [F] 1 : having death as a subject 2 : dwelling on the gruesome 3 ♦ : tending to produce horror in a beholder

♦ appalling, atrocious, awful, dreadful, frightful, ghastly, grisly, gruesome, hideous, horrible, horrid, lurid, monstrous, nightmarish, shocking, terrible — more at HORRIBLE

mac·ad·am \mə-ˈka-dəm\ n [John L. McAdam †1836 Brit. engineer] : a roadway or pavement of small closely packed broken stone — **mac·ad·am·ize** \-də-ˌmīz\ vb

mac·a·da·mia nut \ˌma-kə-ˈdā-mē-ə\ n : a hard-shelled richly-flavored nut of any of several Australian trees

ma·caque \mə-ˈkak, -ˈkäk\ n : any of a genus of short-tailed chiefly Asian monkeys; esp : RHESUS MONKEY

mac·a·ro·ni \ˌma-kə-ˈrō-nē\ n 1 : pasta made chiefly of wheat flour and shaped in the form of slender tubes 2 pl **-nis** or **-nies** : FOP, DANDY

mac·a·roon \ˌma-kə-ˈrün\ n : a small cookie made chiefly of egg whites, sugar, and ground almonds or coconut

ma·caw \mə-ˈkȯ\ *n* : any of numerous parrots of Central and So. America

Mac·ca·bees \ˈma-kə-ˌbēz\ *n* : either of two books of Scripture in the Roman Catholic canon and the Protestant Apocrypha

¹**mace** \ˈmās\ *n* : a spice made from the fibrous coating of the nutmeg

²**mace** *n* **1** : a heavy often spiked club used as a weapon esp. in the Middle Ages **2** : an ornamental staff carried as a symbol of authority

Mac·e·do·nian \ˌma-sə-ˈdō-nyən, -nē-ən\ *n* : a native or inhabitant of Macedonia — **Macedonian** *adj*

mac·er·ate \ˈma-sə-ˌrāt\ *vb* **-at·ed; -at·ing** **1** : to cause to waste away **2** : to soften by steeping or soaking so as to separate the parts — **mac·er·a·tion** \ˌma-sə-ˈrā-shən\ *n*

Mac·Guf·fin *or* **Mc·Guf·fin** \mə-ˈgə-fən\ *n* : an object, event, or character whose main purpose is to advance the plot of a motion picture

mach *abbr* machine; machinery; machinist

Mach \ˈmäk\ *n* : a speed expressed by a Mach number

Mach·a·bees \ˈma-kə-ˌbēz\ *n* : MACCABEES

ma·chete \mə-ˈshe-tē\ *n* : a large heavy knife used for cutting sugarcane and underbrush and as a weapon

Ma·chi·a·vel·lian \ˌma-kē-ə-ˈve-lē-ən\ *adj* [Niccolò *Machiavelli*, †1527 Ital. political philosopher] ♦ : characterized by cunning, duplicity, and bad faith — **Ma·chi·a·vel·lian·ism** *n*

♦ cutthroat, immoral, unconscionable, unethical, unprincipled, unscrupulous — more at UNPRINCIPLED

mach·i·nate \ˈma-kə-ˌnāt, ˈma-shə-\ *vb* ♦ : to plan or plot esp. to do harm

♦ conspire, contrive, intrigue, plot, scheme — more at PLOT ♦ contrive, finagle, finesse, frame, maneuver (*or* manoeuvre), mastermind, negotiate, wangle

mach·i·na·tion \ˌma-kə-ˈnā-shən, ˌma-shə-\ *n* ♦ : an act of planning esp. to do harm; *esp* : PLOT

♦ conspiracy, design, intrigue, plot, scheme — more at PLOT

¹**ma·chine** \mə-ˈshēn\ *n* **1** ♦ : an automotive vehicle not operated on rails; *esp* : AUTOMOBILE **2** : a combination of mechanical parts that transmit forces, motion, and energy one to another **3** : an instrument (as a lever) for transmitting or modifying force or motion **4** : an electrical, electronic, or mechanical device for performing a task ⟨a sewing ∼⟩ **5** : a highly organized political group under the leadership of a boss or small clique

♦ automobile, car, motor vehicle — more at CAR

²**machine** *vb* **ma·chined; ma·chin·ing** : to shape or finish by machine-operated tools — **ma·chin·able** \-ˈshē-nə-bəl\ *adj*

machine gun *n* : an automatic gun capable of rapid continuous firing — **machine–gun** *vb* — **machine gunner** *n*

machine language *n* : the set of symbolic instruction codes used to represent operations and data in a machine (as a computer)

machine–readable *adj* : directly usable by a computer

ma·chin·ery \mə-ˈshē-nə-rē\ *n, pl* **-er·ies** **1** : MACHINES; *also* : the working parts of a machine **2** ♦ : the means by which something is done

♦ agency, agent, instrument, instrumentality, means, medium, organ, vehicle — more at AGENT

ma·chin·ist \mə-ˈshē-nist\ *n* : a person who makes or works on machines

ma·chis·mo \mä-ˈchēz-(ˌ)mō, -ˈchiz-\ *n* : a strong or exaggerated pride in one's masculinity

Mach number \ˈmäk-\ *n* : a number representing the ratio of the speed of a body (as an aircraft) to the speed of sound in the surrounding atmosphere

ma·cho \ˈmä-chō\ *adj* [Sp, lit., male, fr. L *masculus*] : characterized by machismo

mack·er·el \ˈma-kə-rəl\ *n, pl* **mackerel** *or* **mackerels** : a No. Atlantic food fish greenish above and silvery below

mack·i·naw \ˈma-kə-ˌnȯ\ *n* : a short heavy plaid coat

mack·in·tosh *also* **mac·in·tosh** \ˈma-kən-ˌtäsh\ *n* **1** *chiefly Brit* : RAINCOAT **2** : a lightweight waterproof fabric

mac·ra·mé *also* **mac·ra·me** \ˈma-krə-ˌmā\ *n* [ultim. fr. Ar *miqrama* coverlet] : a coarse lace or fringe made by knotting threads or cords in a geometrical pattern

¹**mac·ro** \ˈma-(ˌ)krō\ *adj* : very large; *also* : involving large quantities or being on a large scale

²**macro** *n, pl* **macros** : a single computer instruction that stands for a sequence of operations

mac·ro·bi·ot·ic \ˌma-krō-bī-ˈä-tik, -bē-\ *adj* : relating to or being a very restricted diet (as one containing chiefly whole cereals or grains)

mac·ro·cosm \ˈma-krə-ˌkä-zəm\ *n* ♦ : the great world : UNIVERSE

♦ cosmos, creation, nature, universe, world — more at UNIVERSE

ma·cron \ˈmā-ˌkrän, ˈma-\ *n* : a mark ¯ placed over a vowel (as in māk) to show that the vowel is long

mac·ro·scop·ic \ˌma-krə-ˈskä-pik\ *adj* : visible to the naked eye — **mac·ro·scop·i·cal·ly** \-pi-k(ə-)lē\ *adv*

mac·u·la \ˈma-kyə-lə\ *n, pl* **-lae** \-ˌlē, -ˌlī\ *also* **-las** : an anatomical spot distinguishable from surrounding tissues — **mac·u·lar** \-lər\ *adj*

mad \ˈmad\ *adj* **mad·der; mad·dest** **1** ♦ : disordered in mind : INSANE **2** ♦ : being rash and foolish **3** ♦ : carried away by intense anger : FURIOUS, ENRAGED ⟨∼ at myself⟩ ⟨∼ about the delay⟩ **4** ♦ : carried away by enthusiasm or desire ⟨∼ about horses⟩ ⟨∼ for the boy next door⟩ **5** : RABID **6** : marked by wild gaiety and merriment **7** ♦ : intensely excited : FRANTIC **8** ♦ : marked by intense and often chaotic activity : WILD ⟨a ∼ rush⟩

♦ [1, 2] absurd, crazy, cuckoo, fatuous, foolish, nonsensical, nutty, senseless, silly, stupid — more at FOOLISH ♦ [3] angry, boiling, enraged, furious, irate, rabid, sore, wrathful — more at ANGRY ♦ *usu* mad about [4] crazy, nuts ♦ [7, 8] delirious, feverish, fierce, frantic, frenetic, frenzied, furious, rabid, violent, wild — more at FURIOUS

Mad·a·gas·can \ˌma-də-ˈgas-kən\ *n* : a native or inhabitant of Madagascar

mad·am \ˈma-dəm\ *n* **1** *pl* **mes·dames** \mā-ˈdäm\ — used as a form of polite address to a woman **2** *pl* **madams** : the female head of a house of prostitution

ma·dame \mə-ˈdam, *before a surname also* ˈma-dəm\ *n, pl* **mes·dames** \mā-ˈdäm\ : MISTRESS — used as a title equivalent to *Mrs.* for a married woman not of English-speaking nationality

¹**mad·cap** \ˈmad-ˌkap\ *adj* ♦ : marked by capriciousness, recklessness, or foolishness — **madcap** *n*

♦ brash, foolhardy, overbold, overconfident, reckless — more at FOOLHARDY

²**madcap** *n* ♦ : one who is madcap

♦ daredevil, devil — more at DAREDEVIL

mad cow disease *n* : a fatal disease of the brain of cattle affecting the nervous system and probably caused by infected tissue in food

mad·den \ˈmad-ᵊn\ *vb* ♦ : to make mad

♦ craze, derange, unhinge — more at CRAZE ♦ anger, antagonize, enrage, incense, inflame, infuriate, outrage, rankle, rile, roil — more at ANGER

mad·den·ing *adj* ♦ : tending to infuriate or irritate — **mad·den·ing·ly** *adv*

♦ aggravating, annoying, galling, irritating; *also* grating, inflaming, provocative, provoking; bothersome, troublesome; enraging, incensing, infuriating; distressing, upsetting; offensive, outrageous

mad·der \ˈma-dər\ *n* : a Eurasian herb with yellow flowers and fleshy red roots; *also* : its root or a dye prepared from it

made *past and past part of* MAKE

Ma·dei·ra \mə-ˈdir-ə\ *n* : an amber-colored dessert wine

ma·de·moi·selle \ˌma-də-mə-ˈzel, -mwə-, mam-ˈzel\ *n, pl* **ma·de·moi·selles** \-ˈzelz\ *or* **mes·de·moi·selles** \ˌmā-də-me-ˈzel, -mwe-\ : an unmarried girl or woman — used as a title for an unmarried woman not of English-speaking nationality

made-to-measure *adj* : CUSTOM-MADE

made-up \'mā-dəp\ *adj* **1** ♦ : fancifully conceived or falsely devised **2** : marked by the use of makeup

♦ chimerical, fabulous, fanciful, fantastic, fictitious, imaginary, mythical, phantom, pretend, unreal — more at IMAGINARY

mad·house \'mad-ˌhaủs\ *n* **1** : a place for the detention and care of the insane **2** ♦ : a place of great uproar

♦ bedlam, circus, hell; *also* commotion, havoc, pandemonium, racket, ruckus, tumult, turmoil; clamor, clatter, din, hubbub, noise; chaos, confusion, disarray, disorder, maelstrom, mess, muss

mad·ly \'mad-lē\ *adv* **1** ♦ : in a mad manner **2** : to an extreme or excessive degree

♦ amok, berserk, frantically, harum-scarum, hectically, helter-skelter, pell-mell, wild, wildly — more at HELTER-SKELTER

mad·man \'mad-ˌman, -mən\ *n* : LUNATIC

mad·ness \'mad-nəs\ *n* **1** ♦ : the quality or state of being mad **2** ♦ : lack of good sense or judgment

♦ [1] aberration, dementia, derangement, insanity, lunacy, mania — more at INSANITY ♦ [2] absurdity, asininity, balminess, craziness, daftness, fatuity, folly, foolishness, inanity, insanity, lunacy, silliness, simplicity, zaniness

Ma·don·na \mə-'dä-nə\ *n* : a representation (as a picture or statue) of the Virgin Mary

ma·dras \'ma-drəs; ˌmə-'dras, -'dräs\ *n* [*Madras*, India] : a fine usu. cotton fabric with various designs (as plaid)

ma·dras·sa *or* **ma·dra·sa** \mə-'dra-sə, -'drä-\ *n* : a Muslim school, college, or university that is often part of a mosque

mad·ri·gal \'ma-dri-gəl\ *n* [It *madrigale*] **1** : a short lyrical poem in a strict poetic form **2** : an elaborate part-song esp. of the 16th and 17th centuries

mad·wom·an \'mad-ˌwủ-mən\ *n* : a woman who is insane

mael·strom \'māl-strəm\ *n* **1** : a violent whirlpool **2** : TUMULT

mae·stro \'mī-strō\ *n, pl* **maestros** *or* **mae·stri** \-ˌstrē\ [It] **1** ♦ : a master in an art **2** : an eminent composer, conductor, or teacher of music

♦ ace, adept, artist, authority, crackerjack, expert, master, scholar, shark, virtuoso, whiz, wizard — more at EXPERT

Ma·fia \'mä-fē-ə\ *n* [It] : a secret criminal society of Sicily or Italy; *also* : a similar organization elsewhere

ma·fi·o·so \ˌmä-fē-'ō-(ˌ)sō\ *n, pl* **-si** \-(ˌ)sē\ : a member of the Mafia

¹mag \'mag\ *n* : MAGAZINE

²mag *abbr* **1** magnetism **2** magneto **3** magnitude

mag·a·zine \'ma-gə-ˌzēn\ *n* [MF, fr. Old Occitan, fr. Ar *makhāzin*, pl. of *makhzan* storehouse] **1** ♦ : a storehouse esp. for military supplies **2** : a place for keeping gunpowder in a fort or ship **3** : a publication usu. containing stories, articles, or poems and issued periodically **4** : a container in a gun for holding cartridges; *also* : a chamber (as on a camera) for film

♦ armory, arsenal, depot, dump — more at ARMORY

ma·gen·ta \mə-'jen-tə\ *n* : a deep purplish red color

mag·got \'ma-gət\ *n* : the legless wormlike larva of a dipteran fly — **mag·goty** *adj*

ma·gi \'mā-jī\ *n pl, often cap* : the three wise men from the East who paid homage to the infant Jesus

¹mag·ic \'ma-jik\ *n* **1** : the use of means (as charms or spells) believed to have supernatural power over natural forces **2 a** ♦ : an extraordinary power or influence seemingly from a supernatural force **b** ♦ : something that seems to cast a spell **3** ♦ : the art of producing illusions by sleight of hand

♦ [2a] bewitchment, enchantment, necromancy, sorcery, witchcraft, wizardry; *also* abracadabra, amulet,

charm, fetish, mascot, phylactery, talisman; curse, hex, incantation, jinx, spell; augury, divining, forecasting, foreknowing, foreseeing, foretelling, fortune-telling, predicting, presaging, prognosticating, prophesying, soothsaying; hoodoo, occultism, spiritualism; augur, omen; exorcism; alchemy ♦ [2b] allure, appeal, attractiveness, captivation, charisma, charm, enchantment, fascination, glamour, magnetism — more at CHARM ♦ [3] legerdemain, prestidigitation

²magic *adj* **1** : of or relating to magic **2** ♦ : having unusually distinctive qualities resembling the supernatural

♦ magical, mystic, occult, weird — more at MYSTIC

mag·i·cal \'ma-ji-kəl\ *adj* **1** : of or relating to magic **2** ♦ : resembling magic; *also* : giving a feeling of enchantment — **mag·i·cal·ly** \-ji-k(ə-)lē\ *adv*

♦ miraculous, phenomenal, superhuman, supernatural, uncanny, unearthly — more at SUPERNATURAL

ma·gi·cian \mə-'ji-shən\ *n* ♦ : a person skilled in magic

♦ conjurer, enchanter, necromancer, sorcerer, voodoo, witch, wizard; *also* enchantress, hag, hex, sorceress, warlock; medicine man; fortune-teller, prognosticator, prophesier, prophet, soothsayer; medium; exorcist ♦ conjurer, illusionist, trickster

mag·is·te·ri·al \ˌma-jə-'stir-ē-əl\ *adj* **1** : AUTHORITATIVE ⟨a ~ attitude⟩ **2** : of or relating to a magistrate or a magistrate's office or duties

ma·gis·tral \'ma-jə-strəl\ *adj* : AUTHORITATIVE

mag·is·trate \'ma-jə-ˌstrāt\ *n* ♦ : an official entrusted with administration of the laws — **mag·is·tra·cy** \-strə-sē\ *n*

♦ bench, court, judge, justice — more at JUDGE

mag·lev \'mag-lev\ *n* **1** : the use of magnetic fields to float an object above a solid surface **2** : a train using maglev technology

mag·ma \'mag-mə\ *n* : molten rock material within the earth — **mag·mat·ic** \mag-'ma-tik\ *adj*

mag·nan·i·mous \mag-'na-nə-məs\ *adj* **1** : showing or suggesting a lofty and courageous spirit **2** ♦ : showing or suggesting nobility of feeling and generosity of mind — **mag·na·nim·i·ty** \ˌmag-nə-'ni-mə-tē\ *n* — **mag·nan·i·mous·ness** *n*

♦ chivalrous, gallant, great, greathearted, high, high-minded, lofty, lordly, noble, sublime — more at NOBLE

mag·nan·i·mous·ly \-lē\ *adv* ♦ : in a magnanimous manner

♦ gallantly, grandly, greatly, heroically, honorably (*or* honourably), nobly — more at GREATLY

mag·nate \'mag-ˌnāt\ *n* ♦ : a person of rank, influence, or distinction

♦ baron, czar, king, mogul, prince, tycoon; *also* big shot, bigwig, figure, nabob, notable, personage, VIP; celebrity, personality, star; plutocrat

mag·ne·sia \mag-'nē-shə, -zhə\ *n* [NL, fr. *magnes carneus*, a white earth, lit., flesh magnet] : a light white oxide of magnesium used as a laxative

mag·ne·sium \mag-'nē-zē-əm, -zhəm\ *n* : a silver-white light malleable metallic chemical element

mag·net \'mag-nət\ *n* **1** : LODESTONE **2** : a body that is able to attract iron **3** ♦ : something that attracts

♦ attraction, draw, lodestone; *also* capital, cynosure, mecca; allure, bait, enticement, fascination, lure, temptation; appeal, call; incentive, inducement, persuasion, spur

mag·net·ic \mag-'ne-tik\ *adj* **1** ♦ : having an unusual ability to attract ⟨a ~ leader⟩ **2** : of or relating to a magnet or magnetism **3** : magnetized or capable of being magnetized — **mag·net·i·cal·ly** \-ti-k(ə-)lē\ *adv*

♦ alluring, attractive, captivating, charming, elfin, engaging, fascinating, fetching, glamorous, seductive — more at FASCINATING

magnetic disk *n* : DISK 3

magnetic levitation *n* : MAGLEV 1

magnetic north *n* : the northerly direction in the earth's magnetic field indicated by the north-seeking pole of a compass needle

magnetic resonance imaging *n* : a noninvasive diagnostic technique that produces computerized images of internal body tissues based on electromagnetically induced activity of atoms within the body

magnetic tape *n* : a ribbon coated with a magnetic material on which information (as sound) may be stored

mag·ne·tise *chiefly Brit var of* MAGNETIZE

mag·ne·tism \'mag-nə-ˌti-zəm\ *n* **1** : the power (as of a magnet) to attract iron **2** : the science that deals with magnetic phenomena **3** ♦ : an ability to attract or charm

♦ allure, appeal, attractiveness, captivation, charisma, charm, enchantment, fascination, glamour, magic — more at CHARM

mag·ne·tite \'mag-nə-ˌtīt\ *n* : a black mineral that is an important iron ore

mag·ne·tize \'mag-nə-ˌtīz\ *vb* **-tized; -tiz·ing** **1** : to induce magnetic properties in **2** : to attract like a magnet : CHARM — **mag·ne·tiz·able** *adj* — **mag·ne·ti·za·tion** \ˌmag-nə-tə-'zā-shən\ *n* — **mag·ne·tiz·er** *n*

mag·ne·to \mag-'nē-tō\ *n, pl* **-tos** : a generator used to produce sparks in an internal combustion engine

mag·ne·tom·e·ter \ˌmag-nə-'tä-mə-tər\ *n* : an instrument for measuring the strength of a magnetic field

mag·ne·to·sphere \mag-'nē-tə-ˌsfir, -'ne-\ *n* : a region around a celestial object (as the earth) in which charged particles are trapped by its magnetic field — **mag·ne·to·spher·ic** \-ˌnē-tə-'sfir-ik, -'sfer-\ *adj*

mag·ni·fi·ca·tion \ˌmag-nə-fə-'kā-shən\ *n* **1** ♦ : the act of magnifying **2** : the amount by which an optical lens or instrument magnifies

♦ caricature, elaboration, embellishment, exaggeration, hyperbole, overstatement, padding — more at EXAGGERATION

mag·nif·i·cence \mag-'ni-fə-səns\ *n* **1** ♦ : the quality or state of being magnificent **2** : splendor of surroundings

♦ augustness, brilliance, glory, grandeur, grandness, majesty, nobility, nobleness, resplendence, splendor, stateliness; *also* marvelousness, wondrousness; lavishness, luxuriance, luxury, opulence; grandiosity, ostentation, pretentiousness; flashiness, gaudiness, ornateness, showiness; remarkableness

mag·nif·i·cent \mag-'ni-fə-sənt\ *adj* **1** ♦ : characterized by grandeur or beauty : SPLENDID **2** : EXALTED, NOBLE — **mag·nif·i·cent·ly** *adv*

♦ august, baronial, gallant, glorious, grand, grandiose, heroic, imposing, majestic, monumental, noble, proud, regal, royal, splendid, stately — more at GRAND

mag·nif·i·co \mag-'ni-fi-ˌkō\ *n, pl* **-coes** *or* **-cos** **1** : a nobleman of Venice **2** : a person of high position

mag·ni·fy \'mag-nə-ˌfī\ *vb* **-fied; -fy·ing** **1 a** : to praise highly : EXTOL, LAUD **b** ♦ : to cause to be held in greater esteem **2 a** ♦ : to increase in significance : INTENSIFY **b** ♦ : to enlarge beyond bounds or the truth : EXAGGERATE **3** : to enlarge in fact or in appearance ⟨a microscope *magnifies* an object⟩ — **mag·ni·fi·er** \'mag-nə-ˌfī-ər\ *n*

♦ [1b] aggrandize, dignify, ennoble, exalt, glorify — more at EXALT ♦ [2a] amplify, beef, boost, consolidate, deepen, enhance, heighten, intensify, redouble, step up, strengthen — more at INTENSIFY ♦ [2b] color (*or* colour), elaborate, embellish, embroider, exaggerate, pad, stretch — more at EMBROIDER

mag·nil·o·quent \mag-'ni-lə-kwənt\ *adj* : characterized by an exalted and often bombastic style or manner — **mag·nil·o·quence** \-kwəns\ *n*

mag·ni·tude \'mag-nə-ˌtüd, -ˌtyüd\ *n* **1** ♦ : greatness of size or extent **2** ♦ : spatial quality : SIZE **3** : QUANTITY **4** : a number representing the brightness of a celestial body **5** ♦ : the importance, quality, or caliber of something **6** : a number representing the intensity of an earthquake

♦ [1] enormity, hugeness, immensity, massiveness, vastness — more at IMMENSITY ♦ [2] dimension, extent, measure, measurement, proportion, size — more at SIZE ♦ [5] consequence, import, moment, significance, weight

mag·no·lia \mag-'nōl-yə\ *n* : any of a genus of usu. spring-flowering shrubs and trees with large often fragrant flowers

mag·num opus \ˌmag-nəm-'ō-pəs\ *n* [L] : the greatest achievement of an artist or writer

mag·pie \'mag-ˌpī\ *n* **1** : any of various long-tailed often black-and-white birds related to the jays **2** ♦ : a person who chatters noisily

♦ chatterbox, jabberer, talker — more at CHATTERBOX

Mag·yar \'mag-ˌyär, 'mäg-; 'mä-ˌjär\ *n* : a member of the dominant people of Hungary — **Magyar** *adj*

ma·ha·ra·ja *or* **ma·ha·ra·jah** \ˌmä-hə-'rä-jə\ *n* : a Hindu prince ranking above a raja

ma·ha·ra·ni *or* **ma·ha·ra·nee** \-'rä-nē\ *n* **1** : the wife of a maharaja **2** : a Hindu princess ranking above a rani

ma·ha·ri·shi \ˌmä-hə-'rē-shē\ *n* : a Hindu teacher of mystical knowledge

ma·hat·ma \mə-'hät-mə, -'hat-\ *n* [Skt *mahātman*, fr. *mahātma* great-souled, fr. *mahat* great + *ātman* soul] : a person revered for high-mindedness, wisdom, and selflessness

Ma·hi·can \mə-'hē-kən\ *or* **Mo·hi·can** \mō-, mə-\ *n, pl* **-can** *or* **-cans** : a member of an American Indian people of the upper Hudson River valley

ma·hog·a·ny \mə-'hä-gə-nē\ *n, pl* **-nies** : the reddish wood of any of various chiefly tropical trees that is used in furniture; *also* : a tree yielding this wood

ma·hout \mə-'haut\ *n* [Hindi & Urdu *mahāwat, mahāut*] : a keeper and driver of an elephant

maid \'mād\ *n* **1** : an unmarried girl or young woman **2** ♦ : a female servant : MAIDSERVANT

♦ domestic, girl, housemaid, maidservant; *also* attendant, chambermaid, handmaiden (or handmaid), lady-in-waiting; nursemaid

¹maid·en \'mād-ᵊn\ *n* ♦ : an unmarried girl or young woman : MAID — **maid·en·ly** *adj*

♦ doll, girl, lass, maid, miss — more at GIRL

²maiden *adj* **1** : UNMARRIED; *also* : VIRGIN **2** : of, relating to, or befitting a maiden **3** ♦ : preceding all others in time or order : FIRST ⟨~ voyage⟩

♦ first, inaugural, initial, original, pioneer, premier — more at FIRST

maid·en·hair fern \-ˌhar-\ *n* : any of a genus of ferns with delicate feathery fronds

maid·en·head \'mād-ᵊn-ˌhed\ *n* **1** : VIRGINITY **2** : HYMEN

maid·en·hood \-ˌhud\ *n* : the condition or time of being a maiden

maid–in–waiting *n, pl* **maids–in–waiting** : a young woman appointed to attend a queen or princess

maid of honor *n* : a bride's principal unmarried wedding attendant

maid·ser·vant \'mād-ˌsər-vənt\ *n* ♦ : a girl or woman who is a servant

♦ domestic, girl, housemaid, maid — more at MAID

¹mail \'māl\ *n* [ME *male* bag, fr. AF, of Gmc origin] **1** ♦ : something sent or carried in the postal system **2** : a nation's postal system — often used in pl.

♦ matter, parcel post, post, snail mail; *also* electronic mail, e-mail; dispatch, epistle, message, missive, note, postcard; airmail, special delivery; junk mail

²mail *vb* : to send by mail

³mail *n* [ME *maille* metal link, mail, fr. AF, fr. L *macula* spot, mesh] : armor made of metal links or plates

mail·box \'māl-ˌbäks\ *n* **1** : a public box for the collection of mail **2** : a private box for the delivery of mail

mail carrier *n* : LETTER CARRIER

mail·man \-ˌman\ *n* ♦ : a man who delivers mail

♦ letter carrier, postman — more at POSTMAN

maim \'mām\ *vb* ♦ : to mutilate, disfigure, or wound seriously : CRIPPLE

♦ cripple, disable, lame, mutilate; *also* dismember, hamstring, hobble; batter, bruise, bung (up), mangle, maul, rough (up); gore, lacerate, wound; disfigure, scar; break, damage, harm, hurt, impair, injure; bash, beat, belt, bludgeon, buffet, drub, hammer, lace, lambaste, lick, paste, pelt, pound, pummel, thump; bang, box, hit, punch, slap, smack, smash, sock, spank, swat, swipe, thrash, thwack, whack; flog, lash, wallop, whip; kill, murder; torment, torture

¹**main** \'mān\ *n* 1 ♦ : physical strength : FORCE ⟨with might and ~⟩ 2 : MAINLAND; *also* : HIGH SEA 3 ♦ : the chief part 4 : a principal pipe, duct, or circuit of a utility system

♦ [1] energy, force, might, muscle, potency, power, sinew, strength, vigor (*or* vigour) — more at POWER ♦ [3] body, bulk, core, generality, mass, staple, weight — more at BODY

²**main** *adj* 1 ♦ : of greatest importance or influence : CHIEF, PRINCIPAL 2 : fully exerted ⟨~ force⟩ 3 : expressing the chief predication in a complex sentence ⟨the ~ clause⟩

♦ arch, cardinal, central, chief, dominant, first, foremost, grand, key, paramount, predominant, preeminent, premier, primary, principal, sovereign, supreme — more at FOREMOST

main·frame \'mān-ˌfrām\ *n* : a large fast computer
main·land \-ˌland, -lənd\ *n* : a continuous body of land constituting the chief part of a country or continent
main·line \-ˌlīn\ *vb, slang* : to inject a narcotic drug into a vein
main line *n* : a principal highway or railroad line
main·ly \'mān-lē\ *adv* ♦ : for the most part : CHIEFLY

♦ altogether, basically, chiefly, generally, largely, mostly, overall, predominantly, primarily, principally — more at CHIEFLY

main·mast \'mān-ˌmast, -məst\ *n* : the principal mast on a sailing ship
main·sail \-ˌsāl, -səl\ *n* : the largest sail on the mainmast
main·spring \-ˌspriŋ\ *n* 1 : the chief spring in a mechanism (as of a watch) 2 : the chief motive, agent, or cause
main·stay \-ˌstā\ *n* 1 : a stay running from the head of the mainmast to the foot of the foremast 2 ♦ : a chief support

♦ buttress, dependence, pillar, reliance, standby, support — more at DEPENDENCE

main·stream \-ˌstrēm\ *n* : a prevailing current or direction of activity or influence — **mainstream** *adj*
main·tain \mān-'tān\ *vb* [ME *mainteinen*, fr. AF *maintenir*, *maynteiner*, fr. ML *manutenēre*, fr. L *manu tenēre* to hold in the hand] 1 ♦ : to keep in an existing state (as of repair) 2 ♦ : to sustain against opposition or danger 3 : to continue in : CARRY ON 4 : to provide for : SUPPORT 5 ♦ : to affirm in or as if in argument : ASSERT

♦ [1] conserve, keep up, preserve, save; *also* support, sustain; care (for), husband, manage; defend, guard, protect, safeguard, screen, shield; cure, fix, heal, remedy; mend, patch, rebuild, reconstruct ♦ [2] defend, justify, support, uphold; *also* advocate, champion, espouse; confirm, vindicate, warrant; affirm, assert, avow, claim, contend, declare, insist, proclaim, profess, state; argue, debate, discuss; emphasize, stress, underline, underscore ♦ [5] affirm, allege, argue, assert, aver, avouch, avow, claim, contend, declare, insist, profess, protest, warrant — more at CLAIM

main·tain·able \mān-'tā-nə-bəl\ *adj* ♦ : capable of being maintained — **main·tain·abil·i·ty** \-ˌtā-nə-'bi-lə-tē\ *n*

♦ defensible, justifiable, supportable, sustainable, tenable — more at TENABLE

main·te·nance \'mānt-ᵊn-əns\ *n* ♦ : the act of maintaining : the state of being maintained

♦ conservation, preservation, upkeep; *also* support, sustaining; care, guardianship; defense, guarding, protection, safeguarding, safekeeping

main·top \'mān-ˌtäp\ *n* : a platform at the head of the mainmast of a square-rigged ship
mai·son·ette \ˌmāz-ᵊn-'et\ *n* 1 : a small house 2 : an apartment often on two floors
mai tai \'mī-ˌtī\ *n* : a cocktail made with liquors and fruit juices
maî·tre d' *or* **mai·tre d'** \ˌmā-trə-'dē, ˌme-\ *n, pl* **maître d's** *or* **maitre d's** \-'dēz\ : MAÎTRE D'HÔTEL
maî·tre d'hô·tel \ˌmā-trə-dō-'tel, ˌme-\ *n, pl* **maîtres d'hô·tel** *same*\ [F, lit., master of house] 1 : MAJORDOMO 2 : HEADWAITER
maize \'māz\ *n* : CORN 2
Maj *abbr* major
ma·jes·tic \mə-'jes-tik\ *adj* ♦ : having or exhibiting majesty — **ma·jes·ti·cal·ly** \-ti-k(ə-)lē\ *adv*

♦ august, baronial, gallant, glorious, grand, grandiose, heroic, imposing, magnificent, monumental, noble, proud, regal, royal, splendid, stately — more at GRAND

maj·es·ty \'ma-jə-stē\ *n, pl* **-ties** 1 : sovereign power, authority, or dignity; *also* : the person of a sovereign — used as a title 2 ♦ : greatness or splendor of quality or character

♦ augustness, brilliance, glory, grandeur, grandness, magnificence, nobility, nobleness, resplendence, splendor, stateliness — more at MAGNIFICENCE

Maj Gen *abbr* Major General
ma·jol·i·ca \mə-'jä-li-kə\ *also* **ma·iol·i·ca** \-'yä-\ *n* : any of several faiences; *esp* : an Italian tin-glazed pottery
¹**ma·jor** \'mā-jər\ *adj* 1 ♦ : greater in number, extent, or importance ⟨a ~ poet⟩ 2 : notable or conspicuous in effect or scope ⟨a ~ improvement⟩ 3 : SERIOUS ⟨a ~ illness⟩ 4 : having half steps between the 3d and 4th and the 7th and 8th degrees ⟨~ scale⟩; *also* : based on a major scale ⟨~ key⟩ ⟨~ chord⟩

♦ big, consequential, eventful, important, material, meaningful, momentous, significant, substantial, weighty — more at IMPORTANT

²**major** *n* 1 : a commissioned officer (as in the army) ranking next below a lieutenant colonel 2 : an academic subject chosen as a field of specialization; *also* : a student specializing in such a field
³**major** *vb* : to pursue an academic major
ma·jor·do·mo \ˌmā-jər-'dō-mō\ *n, pl* **-mos** [Sp *mayordomo* or obs. It *maiordomo*, fr. ML *major domus*, lit., chief of the house] 1 : a head steward 2 : BUTLER
ma·jor·ette \ˌmā-jə-'ret\ *n* : DRUM MAJORETTE
major general *n* : a commissioned officer (as in the army) ranking next below a lieutenant general
ma·jor·i·ty \mə-'jòr-ə-tē\ *n, pl* **-ties** 1 : the age at which full civil rights are accorded; *also* : the status of one who has attained this age 2 : a number greater than half of a total; *also* : the excess of this greater number over the remainder 3 : the rank of a major
ma·jus·cule \'ma-jəs-ˌkyül, mə-'jəs-\ *n* : a large letter (as a capital)
Ma·kah \'mä-kä\ *n, pl* **Makah** *or* **Makahs** : a member of an American Indian people of the northwest coast of No. America
¹**make** \'māk\ *vb* **made** \'mād\; **mak·ing** 1 a ♦ : to cause to exist, occur, or appear b : DESTINE ⟨was *made* to be an actor⟩ 2 a ♦ : to bring into being by forming, shaping, or altering material ⟨~ a dress⟩ b : COMPOSE 3 : to formulate in the mind ⟨~ plans⟩ 4 ♦ : to put together from components ⟨house *made* of stone⟩ 5 ♦ : to compute or estimate to be 6 : to set in order : PREPARE ⟨~ a bed⟩ 7 : to cause to be or become; *also* : APPOINT 8 a : to establish by legal and authoritative act : ENACT b : EXECUTE ⟨~ a will⟩ 9 : CONCLUDE ⟨didn't know what to ~ of it⟩ 10 a ♦ : to carry out (an action indicated or implied by the object) ⟨~ war⟩ b : to perform with a

bodily movement ⟨∼ a gesture⟩ **11 ♦** : to cause to act in a certain way : COMPEL **12** : to assure the success of ⟨will ∼ us or break us⟩ **13** : to amount to in significance ⟨∼s no difference⟩ **14** : to be capable of developing or being fashioned into **15** : to reach as an end : ATTAIN; *also* : GAIN **16** : to start out : GO **17** : to have weight or effect ⟨courtesy ∼s for safer driving⟩ **18** : to act so as to be or to seem to be ⟨∼ merry⟩ **19 ♦** : to gain (as money) by working, trading, or dealing — **mak·er** *n* — **make believe** : PRETEND — **make do** : to manage with the means at hand — **make fun of** : RIDICULE, MOCK — **make good 1** : INDEMNIFY ⟨*make good* the loss⟩; *also* : to carry out successfully ⟨*make good* his promise⟩ **2** : SUCCEED — **make way 1** : to give room for passing, entering, or occupying **2** : to make progress

♦ **[1a]** bring about, cause, create, effect, effectuate, generate, induce, produce, prompt, result, work, yield ♦ **[2a]** fabricate, fashion, form, frame, manufacture, produce; *also* assemble, build, construct, erect, make up, put up, raise, rear, structure, throw up; craft, handcraft; forge, mold, shape; prefabricate; create, invent, originate; establish, father, institute, organize; concoct, contrive, cook up, design, devise, imagine, think (up); conceive, envisage, picture, visualize; refashion, remake, remanufacture ♦ **[4]** assemble, build, construct, erect, fabricate, make up, piece, put up, raise, rear, set up — more at BUILD ♦ **[5]** calculate, call, conjecture, estimate, figure, gauge, guess, judge, place, put, reckon, suppose — more at ESTIMATE ♦ **[10a]** accomplish, achieve, carry out, commit, compass, do, execute, follow through, fulfill, perform — more at PERFORM ♦ **[11]** coerce, compel, constrain, drive, force, muscle, obligate, oblige, press, pressure — more at FORCE ♦ **[19]** acquire, attain, capture, carry, draw, earn, gain, garner, get, land, obtain, procure, realize, secure, win — more at EARN

²**make** *n* **1** : the manner or style of construction; *also* : BRAND 3 **2** : MAKEUP **3** : the action of manufacturing — **on the make** : in search of wealth, social status, or sexual adventure

¹**make-be·lieve** \'māk-bə-ˌlēv\ *n* : a pretending that what is not real is real

²**make-believe** *adj* : existing only in the imagination

make-do \-ˌdü\ *adj* : MAKESHIFT

make out *vb* **1** : to draw up in writing ⟨*make out* a list⟩ **2 ♦** : to find or grasp the meaning of ⟨can you *make* that *out*⟩ **3** : to represent as being **4** : to pretend to be true **5** : DISCERN ⟨*make out* a ship in the fog⟩ **6 ♦** : to meet one's needs : GET ALONG, FARE ⟨*make out* well in life⟩ **7 ♦** : to engage in amorous kissing and caressing

♦ **[2]** appreciate, apprehend, catch, catch on (to), comprehend, get, grasp, make, perceive, see, seize, understand — more at COMPREHEND ♦ **[6]** cope, do, fare, get along, manage, shift — more at GET ALONG ♦ **[7]** kiss, pet

make over *vb* **1 ♦** : to transfer the title of (property) **2 ♦** : to make anew or in a different form — **make·over** \'mā-ˌkō-vər\ *n*

♦ **[1]** alienate, assign, cede, deed, transfer — more at TRANSFER ♦ **[2]** alter, change, convert, modify, recast, redo, refashion, remake, remodel, revamp, revise, rework, vary — more at CHANGE

¹**make·shift** \'māk-ˌshift\ *n* : a temporary expedient

²**makeshift** *adj* : serving as a temporary expedient

make·up \'mā-ˌkəp\ *n* **1 ♦** : the way in which something is put together; *also* : physical, mental, and moral constitution **2** : cosmetics esp. for the face; *also* : materials (as wigs and cosmetics) used in making up

♦ arrangement, composition, configuration, design, form, format, layout, pattern — more at COMPOSITION

make up *vb* **1 a** : to form by fitting together or assembling **b ♦** : to form the substance of : COMPOSE **2 ♦** : to compensate for (as a deficiency or omission) ⟨*make up* for lost time⟩ **3** : SETTLE ⟨*made up* my mind⟩ **4 ♦** : to

devise by thinking : INVENT, IMPROVISE **5** : to become reconciled **6** : to put on makeup (as for a play)

♦ **[1b]** compose, comprise, constitute, form — more at CONSTITUTE ♦ *usu* **make up for [2]** annul, cancel, compensate, correct, counteract, counterbalance, neutralize, offset — more at OFFSET ♦ **[4]** concoct, contrive, cook up, devise, fabricate, invent, manufacture, think up — more at INVENT

make-work \'māk-ˌwərk\ *n* : BUSYWORK

mak·ings \'mā-kiŋz\ *n pl* : the material from which something is made

Mal *abbr* Malachi

Mal·a·chi \'ma-lə-ˌkī\ *n* : a book of Jewish and Christian Scripture

Mal·a·chi·as \ˌma-lə-'kī-əs\ *n* : MALACHI

mal·a·chite \'ma-lə-ˌkīt\ *n* : a mineral that is a green carbonate of copper used for making ornamental objects

mal·adapt·ed \ˌma-lə-'dap-təd\ *adj* : poorly suited to a particular use, purpose, or situation

mal·ad·just·ed \ˌma-lə-'jəs-təd\ *adj* : poorly or inadequately adjusted (as to one's environment) — **mal·ad·just·ment** \-'jəst-mənt\ *n*

mal·adroit \ˌma-lə-'droit\ *adj* ♦ : not adroit : INEPT

♦ awkward, clumsy, inept, inexpert

mal·a·dy \'ma-lə-dē\ *n, pl* **-dies** ♦ : a disease or disorder of body or mind

♦ ailment, bug, complaint, condition, disease, disorder, fever, ill, illness, infirmity, sickness, trouble — more at DISEASE

mal·aise \mə-'lāz, ma-\ *n* [F] : a hazy feeling of not being well

mal·a·mute \'ma-lə-ˌmyüt\ *n* : a dog often used to draw sleds esp. in northern No. America

mal·a·prop·ism \'ma-lə-ˌprä-ˌpi-zəm\ *n* : a usu. humorous misuse of a word

mal·ap·ro·pos \ˌma-ˌla-prə-'pō, ma-'la-prə-ˌpō\ *adv* : in an inappropriate or inopportune way — **malapropos** *adj*

ma·lar·ia \mə-'ler-ē-ə\ *n* [It, fr. *mala aria* bad air] : a disease marked by recurring chills and fever and caused by a protozoan parasite of the blood that is transmitted by anopheles mosquitoes — **ma·lar·i·al** \-əl\ *adj*

ma·lar·key \mə-'lär-kē\ *n* : insincere or foolish talk

mal·a·thi·on \ˌma-lə-'thī-ən, -ˌän\ *n* : an insecticide with a relatively low toxicity for mammals

Ma·la·wi·an \mə-'lä-wē-ən\ *n* : a native or inhabitant of Malawi — **Malawian** *adj*

Ma·lay \mə-'lā, 'mā-ˌlā\ *n* **1** : a member of a people of the Malay Peninsula and Archipelago **2** : the language of the Malays — **Malay** *adj* — **Ma·lay·an** \mə-'lā-ən, 'mā-ˌlā-\ *n or adj*

Ma·lay·sian \mə-'lā-zhən, -shən\ *n* : a native or inhabitant of Malaysia — **Malaysian** *adj*

mal·con·tent \ˌmal-kən-'tent\ *adj* ♦ : marked by a dissatisfaction with the existing state of affairs : DISCONTENTED — **malcontent** *n*

♦ aggrieved, discontent, discontented, dissatisfied — more at DISCONTENTED

mal de mer \ˌmal-də-'mer\ *n* [F] : SEASICKNESS

¹**male** \'māl\ *adj* **1** : of, relating to, or being the sex that produces germ cells which fertilize the eggs of a female; *also* : STAMINATE **2 ♦** : of, relating to, or characteristic of boys or men — **male·ness** *n*

♦ manly, mannish, man-size, masculine, virile — more at MASCULINE

²**male** *n* ♦ : a male individual

♦ buck, chap, dude, fellow, gent, gentleman, guy, hombre, jack, joker, lad, man — more at MAN

male·dic·tion \ˌma-lə-'dik-shən\ *n* ♦ : a prayer or invocation for harm or injury to come upon one : CURSE, EXECRATION

♦ anathema, curse, execration, imprecation — more at CURSE

mal·e·fac·tion \ˌma-lə-ˈfak-shən\ *n* ♦ : an evil deed
  ♦ breach, crime, error, misdeed, misdoing, offense, sin, transgression, trespass, violation, wrongdoing — more at OFFENSE

male·fac·tor \ˈma-lə-ˌfak-tər\ *n* ♦ : one who does ill toward another; *esp* : one who commits an offense against the law
  ♦ criminal, crook, culprit, felon, lawbreaker, offender — more at CRIMINAL

ma·lef·ic \mə-ˈle-fik\ *adj* **1** : BALEFUL **2** : MALICIOUS

ma·lef·i·cent \-fə-sənt\ *adj* : working or productive of harm or evil

ma·lev·o·lence \mə-ˈle-və-ləns\ *n* : the quality or state of being malevolent

ma·lev·o·lent \mə-ˈle-və-lənt\ *adj* ♦ : having, showing, or arising from ill will, spite, or hatred
  ♦ catty, cruel, hateful, malicious, malign, malignant, mean, nasty, spiteful, virulent — more at HATEFUL

mal·fea·sance \mal-ˈfēz-ᵊns\ *n* ♦ : wrongful conduct esp. by a public official
  ♦ misbehavior, misconduct, misdoing, wrongdoing — more at MISCONDUCT

mal·for·ma·tion \ˌmal-fȯr-ˈmā-shən\ *n* : irregular or faulty formation or structure; *also* : an instance of this

mal·formed \mal-ˈfȯrmd\ *adj* ♦ : characterized by malformation
  ♦ deformed, distorted, misshapen, monstrous, shapeless; *also* defaced, disfigured; aberrant, abnormal, freakish, mutant; asymmetric, crooked, disproportionate, irregular, lopsided, unbalanced, unequal; horrible, terrible; ugly, unattractive *Ant* shapely

mal·func·tion \mal-ˈfəŋk-shən\ *vb* : to fail to operate normally — **malfunction** *n*

Ma·li·an \ˈmä-lē-ən\ *n* : a native or inhabitant of Mali — **Malian** *adj*

mal·ice \ˈma-ləs\ *n* ♦ : desire to cause injury or distress to another
  ♦ cattiness, despite, hatefulness, malignity, meanness, nastiness, spite, spleen, venom, viciousness; *also* abusiveness, cruelty; abhorrence, abomination, execration, hate, hatred, loathing; animosity, antagonism, antipathy, bitterness, enmity, grudge, hostility, ill will, jaundice, rancor, resentment; vindictiveness; aversion, disgust, distaste, horror, repugnance, repulsion, revulsion; contempt, disdain; jealousy, pique, scorn; bile, virulence, vitriol

ma·li·cious \mə-ˈli-shəs\ *adj* ♦ : given to, marked by, or arising from malice
  ♦ catty, cruel, hateful, malevolent, malign, malignant, mean, nasty, spiteful, virulent — more at HATEFUL

ma·li·cious·ly \-lē\ *adv* ♦ : in a malicious manner
  ♦ hatefully, meanly, nastily, spitefully, viciously, wickedly — more at NASTILY

¹ma·lign \mə-ˈlīn\ *adj* **1** ♦ : evil in nature, influence, or effect; *also* : MALIGNANT **2** ♦ : moved by ill will
  ♦ [1, 2] catty, cruel, hateful, malevolent, malicious, malignant, mean, nasty, spiteful, virulent — more at HATEFUL

²malign *vb* ♦ : to speak evil of : DEFAME
  ♦ blacken, defame, libel, slander, smear, traduce, vilify — more at SLANDER

ma·lig·nan·cy \mə-ˈlig-nən-sē\ *n* : the quality or state of being malignant

ma·lig·nant \mə-ˈlig-nənt\ *adj* **1** ♦ : passionately and relentlessly malevolent : MALIGN **2** : tending to produce death or deterioration ⟨a ~ tumor⟩
  ♦ catty, cruel, hateful, malevolent, malicious, malign, mean, nasty, spiteful, virulent — more at HATEFUL

ma·lig·nant·ly \-lē\ *adv* : in a malignant manner

ma·lig·ni·ty \mə-ˈlig-nə-tē\ *n* ♦ : the quality or state of being malignant
  ♦ cattiness, despite, hatefulness, malice, meanness, nastiness, spite, spleen, venom, viciousness — more at MALICE

ma·lin·ger \mə-ˈliŋ-gər\ *vb* [F *malingre* sickly] : to pretend illness so as to avoid duty — **ma·lin·ger·er** *n*

mal·i·son \ˈma-lə-sən, -zən\ *n* : CURSE

mall \ˈmȯl, ˈmal\ *n* **1** : a shaded walk : PROMENADE **2** : an urban shopping area featuring a variety of shops surrounding a concourse **3** : a usu. large enclosed suburban shopping area containing various shops

mal·lard \ˈma-lərd\ *n, pl* **mallard** *or* **mallards** : a common wild duck that is the source of domestic ducks

mal·lea·ble \ˈma-lē-ə-bəl\ *adj* **1** : capable of being extended or shaped by beating with a hammer or by the pressure of rollers **2 a** ♦ : capable of being altered or controlled by outside forces or influences **b** : having a capacity for adaptive change — **mal·le·a·bil·i·ty** \ˌma-lē-ə-ˈbi-lə-tē\ *n*
  ♦ adaptable, adjustable, changeable, elastic, flexible, fluid, variable — more at FLEXIBLE

mal·let \ˈma-lət\ *n* **1** : a tool with a large head for driving another tool or for striking a surface without marring it **2** : a long-handled hammerlike implement for striking a ball (as in croquet)

mal·le·us \ˈma-lē-əs\ *n, pl* **mal·lei** \-lē-ˌī, -lē-ˌē\ [NL, fr. L, hammer] : the outermost of the three small bones of the mammalian middle ear

mal·low \ˈma-lō\ *n* : any of a genus of herbs with lobed leaves, usu. showy flowers, and a disk-shaped fruit

malm·sey \ˈmälm-zē\ *n, often cap* : the sweetest variety of Madeira

mal·nour·ished \mal-ˈnər-isht\ *adj* : UNDERNOURISHED

mal·nu·tri·tion \ˌmal-nü-ˈtri-shən, -nyü-\ *n* : faulty and esp. inadequate nutrition

mal·oc·clu·sion \ˌma-lə-ˈklü-zhən\ *n* : faulty coming together of teeth in biting

mal·odor·ous \ˈma-ˈlō-də-rəs\ *adj* ♦ : ill-smelling — **mal·odor·ous·ly** *adv* — **mal·odor·ous·ness** *n*
  ♦ fetid, foul, fusty, musty, noisome, rank, reeky, smelly, strong; *also* putrid, rancid, stale; bad, disgusting, offensive, repulsive, revolting, vile; decayed, decaying, rotted, rotten, rotting, spoiled, spoiling; dirty, filthy, nasty, noxious; odorous *Ant* ambrosial, aromatic, fragrant, perfumed, redolent, savory, scented, sweet

mal·prac·tice \mal-ˈprak-təs\ *n* : a dereliction of professional duty or a failure of professional skill that results in injury, loss, or damage

malt \ˈmȯlt\ *n* **1** : grain and esp. barley steeped in water until it has sprouted and used in brewing and distilling **2** : liquor made with malt — **malty** *adj*

malted milk \ˈmȯl-təd-\ *n* : a powder prepared from dried milk and an extract from malt; *also* : a beverage of this powder in milk or other liquid

Mal·thu·sian \mal-ˈthü-zhən, -ˈthyü-\ *adj* : of or relating to a theory that population unless checked (as by war) tends to increase faster than its means of subsistence — **Malthusian** *n* — **Mal·thu·sian·ism** \-zhə-ˌni-zəm\ *n*

malt·ose \ˈmȯl-ˌtōs\ *n* : a sugar formed esp. from starch by the action of enzymes

mal·treat \mal-ˈtrēt\ *vb* ♦ : to treat cruelly or roughly — **mal·treat·ment** *n*
  ♦ abuse, ill-treat, manhandle, mishandle, mistreat, misuse — more at ABUSE

mal·ware \ˈmal-ˌwer\ *n* : software designed to interfere with a computer's normal functioning

ma·ma *also* **mam·ma** \ˈmä-mə\ *n* : a female parent : MOTHER

mam·bo \ˈmäm-bō\ *n, pl* **mambos** : a dance of Cuban origin related to the rumba — **mambo** *vb*

mam·mal \ˈma-məl\ *n* [NL *Mammalia*, fr. LL, neut. pl. of *mammalis* of the breast, fr. L *mamma* breast] : any of a class of warm-blooded vertebrates that includes humans and all other animals which nourish their young with milk and have the skin more or less covered with hair — **mam·ma·li·an** \mə-ˈmā-lē-ən, ma-\ *adj or n*

mam·ma·ry \ˈma-mə-rē\ *adj* : of, relating to, or being the glands (**mammary glands**) that in female mammals secrete milk

mam·mo·gram \'ma-mə-ˌgram\ *n* : an X-ray photograph of the breasts

mam·mog·ra·phy \ma-'mä-grə-fē\ *n* : X-ray examination of the breasts (as for early detection of cancer)

mam·mon \'ma-mən\ *n, often cap* : material wealth having a debasing influence

¹**mam·moth** \'ma-məth\ *n* **1** : any of a genus of large hairy extinct elephants **2** ♦ : something immense of its kind

♦ behemoth, blockbuster, colossus, giant, jumbo, leviathan, monster, titan, whale, whopper — more at GIANT

²**mammoth** *adj* : of very great size : GIGANTIC

¹**man** \'man\ *n, pl* **men** \'men\ **1 a** ♦ : a human being **b** ♦ : an adult male person **2** ♦ : the human race : HUMANKIND **3** : one possessing in high degree the qualities considered distinctive of manhood **4** : an adult male servant or employee **5** : the individual who can fulfill one's requirements ⟨he's your ∼⟩ **6** : one of the pieces with which various games (as chess) are played; *also* : one of the players on a team **7** *often cap* : white society or people ⟨having difficulty coping with the *Man*⟩ **8** ♦ : a male lover

♦ [1a] being, body, creature, human, individual, mortal, person — more at HUMAN ♦ [1b] buck, chap, dude, fellow, gent, gentleman, guy, hombre, jack, joker, lad, male; *also* master, mister, sir ♦ [2] Homo sapiens, humanity, humankind, mankind — more at MANKIND ♦ [8] beau, boyfriend, fellow, swain — more at BOYFRIEND

²**man** *vb* **manned; man·ning 1** : to supply with people ⟨∼ a fleet⟩ **2** : FORTIFY, BRACE

³**man** *abbr* manual

Man *abbr* Manitoba

man–about–town *n, pl* **men–about–town** : a worldly and socially active man

man·a·cle \'ma-ni-kəl\ *n* **1** : a shackle for the hand or wrist **2** ♦ : something used as a restraint

♦ band, bond, chain, fetter, irons, ligature, shackle — more at BOND

man·age \'ma-nij\ *vb* **man·aged; man·ag·ing 1** ♦ : to handle or direct with a degree of skill **2** : to make and keep compliant **3** : to treat with care **4** ♦ : to achieve one's purpose; *also* : get on or along **5** : to direct the career of ⟨the agent who ∼s the actor⟩ — **man·age·abil·i·ty** \ˌma-ni-jə-'bi-lə-tē\ *n* — **man·age·able** \'ma-ni-jə-bəl\ *adj* — **man·age·able·ness** *n* — **man·age·ably** \-blē\ *adv*

♦ [1] contend with, cope with, grapple with, handle, maneuver (*or* manoeuvre), negotiate, swing, treat — more at HANDLE ♦ [1] administer, carry on, conduct, control, direct, govern, guide, handle, operate, oversee, regulate, run, superintend, supervise — more at CONDUCT ♦ [4] cope, do, fare, get along, make out, shift — more at GET ALONG

managed care *n* : a health-care system that controls costs by limiting doctor's fees and by restricting the patient's choice of doctors

man·age·ment \'ma-nij-mənt\ *n* **1** ♦ : the act or art of managing : CONTROL **2** : judicious use of means to accomplish an end **3** : the group of those who manage or direct an enterprise

♦ administration, conduct, control, direction, government, guidance, operation, oversight, regulation, running, superintendence, supervision — more at CONDUCT

man·ag·er \'ma-ni-jər\ *n* ♦ : one that manages

♦ administrator, director, executive, superintendent, supervisor — more at EXECUTIVE

man·a·ge·ri·al \ˌma-nə-'jir-ē-əl\ *adj* ♦ : of, relating to, or characteristic of a manager

♦ directorial, executive, supervisory — more at EXECUTIVE

ma·ña·na \mən-'yä-nə\ *n* [Sp, lit., tomorrow] : an indefinite time in the future

man–at–arms *n, pl* **men–at–arms** ♦ : one engaged in military service : SOLDIER; *esp* : one who is heavily armed and mounted

♦ fighter, legionnaire, regular, serviceman, soldier, warrior — more at SOLDIER

man·a·tee \'ma-nə-ˌtē\ *n* : any of a genus of chiefly tropical plant-eating aquatic mammals having a rounded body, paddle-shaped flippers, and a broad, rounded tail

Man·chu·ri·an \man-'chùr-ē-ən\ *n* : a native or inhabitant of Manchuria, China — **Manchurian** *adj*

man·ci·ple \'man-sə-pəl\ *n* : a steward or purveyor esp. for a college or monastery

man·da·mus \man-'dā-məs\ *n* [L, we enjoin] : a writ issued by a superior court commanding that an official act or duty be performed

man·da·rin \'man-də-rən\ *n* **1** : a public official of high rank under the Chinese Empire **2** *cap* : the chief dialect group of China **3** : a yellow to reddish orange loose-skinned citrus fruit; *also* : a tree that bears mandarins

man·date \'man-ˌdāt\ *n* **1** : an authoritative command **2** ♦ : an authorization to act given to a representative **3** : a commission granted by the League of Nations to a member nation for governing conquered territory; *also* : a territory so governed

♦ authorization, commission, delegation, license (*or* licence) — more at COMMISSION

man·da·to·ry \'man-də-ˌtōr-ē\ *adj* **1** ♦ : containing or constituting a command : OBLIGATORY **2** : of or relating to a League of Nations mandate

♦ compulsory, imperative, incumbent, involuntary, necessary, nonelective, obligatory, peremptory; *also* essential, indispensable, needed, requisite; insistent, persistent, pressing, urgent; demanded; coercive *Ant* elective, optional, voluntary

man·di·ble \'man-də-bəl\ *n* **1** : JAW; *esp* : a lower jaw **2** : either segment of a bird's bill — **man·dib·u·lar** \man-'di-byə-lər\ *adj*

man·do·lin \ˌman-də-'lin, 'mand-ᵊl-ən\ *n* : a stringed musical instrument with a pear-shaped body and a fretted neck

man·drake \'man-ˌdrāk\ *n* **1** : an Old World herb related to the nightshades or its large forked root formerly credited with magical properties **2** : MAYAPPLE

man·drel *also* **man·dril** \'man-drəl\ *n* **1** : an axle or spindle inserted into a hole in a piece of work to support it during machining **2** : a metal bar used as a core around which material may be cast, shaped, or molded

man·drill \'man-drəl\ *n* : a large baboon of western central Africa

mane \'mān\ *n* : long heavy hair growing about the neck of some mammals (as a horse) — **maned** \'mānd\ *adj*

man·eat·er \'man-ˌē-tər\ *n* : one (as a shark or cannibal) that has or is thought to have an appetite for human flesh — **man·eat·ing** *adj*

ma·nège \ma-'nezh, mə-\ *n* : the art of horsemanship or of training horses

ma·nes \'mä-ˌnās, 'mä-ˌnēz\ *n pl, often cap* : the spirits of the dead and gods of the lower world in ancient Roman belief

¹**ma·neu·ver** *or Can and Brit* **ma·noeu·vre** \mə-'nü-vər, -'nyü-\ *n* [F *manœuvre*, fr. OF *maneuvre* work done by hand, fr. ML *manuopera*, fr. *manu operare* to work by hand] **1** : a military or naval movement; *also* : an armed forces training exercise — often used in pl. **2** : a procedure involving expert physical movement **3** : an evasive movement or shift of tactics; *also* : an action taken to gain a tactical end — **maneuver** *vb* — **ma·neu·ver·abil·i·ty** \-ˌnü-və-rə-'bi-lə-tē, -ˌnyü-\ *n* — **ma·neu·ver·able** \-'nü-və-rə-bəl, -'nyü-\ *adj*

²**maneuver** *or Can and Brit* **manoeuvre** *vb* **maneuvered** *or* **manoeuvred; maneuvering** *or* **manoeuvring** ♦ : to guide with adroitness and design; *also* : to use stratagems

♦ contend with, cope with, grapple with, handle, manage, negotiate, swing, treat — more at HANDLE ♦ contrive, finagle, finesse, frame, machinate, mastermind, negotiate, wangle

man Friday *n* : an efficient and devoted aide or employee

man·ful \'man-fəl\ *adj* ♦ : having or showing courage and resolution — **man·ful·ly** *adv*

♦ brave, courageous, dauntless, doughty, fearless, gallant, greathearted, heroic, intrepid, lionhearted, stalwart, stout, undaunted, valiant, valorous — more at BRAVE

man·ga \'mäŋ-gə\ *n* [Jp] : a Japanese comic book or graphic novel

man·ga·nese \'maŋ-gə-ˌnēz, -ˌnēs\ *n* : a metallic chemical element resembling iron but not magnetic

mange \'mānj\ *n* : any of several contagious itchy skin diseases esp. of domestic animals

man·ger \'mān-jər\ *n* : a trough or open box for livestock feed or fodder

¹**man·gle** \'maŋ-gəl\ *vb* **man·gled; man·gling** 1 : to cut, bruise, or hack with repeated blows 2 ♦ : to spoil, injure or make incoherent esp. through ineptitude ⟨a story *mangled* beyond recognition⟩ — **man·gler** *n*

♦ bobble, botch, bungle, butcher, flub, foul up, fumble, mess up, screw up — more at BOTCH

²**mangle** *n* : a machine with heated rollers for ironing laundry

man·go \'maŋ-gō\ *n, pl* **mangoes** *also* **mangos** [Pg *manga*, prob. fr. Malayalam (Dravidian language of India) *māṅṅa*] : an edible juicy yellowish-red fruit borne by a tropical evergreen tree related to the sumacs; *also* : this tree

man·grove \'man-ˌgrōv\ *n* : any of a genus of tropical maritime trees that send out many prop roots and form dense thickets important in coastal land building

mangy \'mān-jē\ *adj* 1 : affected with or resulting from mange 2 ♦ : decayed, deteriorated, or fallen into partial ruin esp. through neglect or misuse

♦ dilapidated, grungy, mean, neglected, ratty, seedy, shabby — more at SHABBY

man·han·dle \'man-ˌhand-ᵊl\ *vb* ♦ : to handle roughly

♦ maltreat, maul, mishandle, rough; *also* abuse, ill-treat, ill-use, mistreat, misuse; roughhouse, wrestle; bash, batter, beat, buffet, drub, lambaste, lick, pound, pummel, slap, thrash; harm, hurt, injure, wound; oppress, persecute, wrong; ambush, assail, attack; clobber, fight, gang up (on), hit, jump, knock; torment, torture

man·hat·tan \man-ˈhat-ᵊn\ *n, often cap* : a cocktail made of whiskey and vermouth

man·hole \'man-ˌhōl\ *n* : a hole through which a person may go esp. to gain access to an underground or enclosed structure

man·hood \-ˌhùd\ *n* 1 : the state of being a man 2 ♦ : qualities associated with men : MANLINESS 3 : MEN ⟨the nation's ~⟩

♦ manliness, masculinity, virility — more at VIRILITY

man–hour \-ˈaùr\ *n* : a unit of one hour's work by one person

man·hunt \-ˌhənt\ *n* : an organized hunt for a person and esp. for one charged with a crime

ma·nia \'mā-nē-ə, -nyə\ *n* 1 ♦ : excitement manifested by mental and physical hyperactivity, disorganized behavior, and elevated mood 2 a ♦ : excessive enthusiasm b ♦ : the object of enthusiasm

♦ [1] aberration, dementia, derangement, insanity, lunacy, madness — more at INSANITY ♦ [2b] fetish, fixation, obsession, preoccupation, prepossession — more at FIXATION

ma·ni·ac \'mā-nē-ˌak\ *n* 1 ♦ : one who is insane : LUNATIC 2 ♦ : a person characterized by an inordinate or ungovernable enthusiasm for something

♦ [1] lunatic, nut, psychotic — more at LUNATIC ♦ [2] addict, aficionado, buff, bug, devotee, enthusiast, fan, fanatic, fancier, fiend, freak, lover, nut — more at FAN

ma·ni·a·cal \mə-ˈnī-ə-kəl\ *also* **ma·ni·ac** \'mā-nē-ak\ *adj* 1 ♦ : affected with or suggestive of madness 2 : FRANTIC

♦ crazy, deranged, insane, loco, lunatic, mad — more at INSANE

man·ic \'ma-nik\ *adj* : affected with, relating to, characterized by, or resulting from mania — **manic** *n* — **man·i·cal·ly** \-ni-k(ə-)lē\ *adv*

manic depression *n* : BIPOLAR DISORDER

man·ic–de·pres·sive \ˌma-nik-di-ˈpre-siv\ *adj* : characterized by or affected with either mania or depression or alternating episodes of mania and depression (as in bipolar disorder) — **manic–depressive** *n*

¹**man·i·cure** \'ma-nə-ˌkyùr\ *n* 1 : MANICURIST 2 : a treatment for the care of the hands and nails

²**manicure** *vb* **-cured; -cur·ing** 1 : to do manicure work on 2 : to trim closely and evenly

man·i·cur·ist \-ˌkyùr-ist\ *n* : a person who gives manicure treatments

¹**man·i·fest** \'ma-nə-ˌfest\ *adj* [ME, fr. AF or L; AF *manifeste*, fr. L *manifestus*, caught in the act, flagrant, obvious, perh. fr. *manus* hand + *-festus* (akin to L in*festus* hostile)] 1 : readily perceived by the senses and esp. by the sight 2 ♦ : easily understood : OBVIOUS — **man·i·fest·ly** *adv*

♦ apparent, broad, clear, clear-cut, distinct, evident, lucid, obvious, palpable, patent, perspicuous, plain, transparent, unambiguous, unequivocal, unmistakable — more at CLEAR

²**manifest** *vb* ♦ : to make evident or certain by showing or displaying

♦ bespeak, betray, demonstrate, display, evince, expose, give away, reveal, show — more at SHOW

³**manifest** *n* : a list of passengers or an invoice of cargo for a ship or plane

man·i·fes·ta·tion \ˌma-nə-fə-ˈstā-shən\ *n* 1 : the act, process, or an instance of manifesting 2 ♦ : a perceptible, outward, or visible expression

♦ embodiment, epitome, incarnation, personification — more at EMBODIMENT

man·i·fes·to \ˌma-nə-ˈfes-tō\ *n, pl* **-tos** *or* **-toes** : a public declaration of intentions, motives, or views

¹**man·i·fold** \'ma-nə-ˌfōld\ *adj* 1 ♦ : marked by diversity or variety 2 : consisting of or operating many of one kind combined

♦ multifarious, myriad; *also* multiform, multiple, multiplex, multitudinous; heterogeneous, miscellaneous, mixed, sundry, various; different, diverse, unlike, varied

²**manifold** *n* : a pipe fitting with several lateral outlets for connecting it with other pipes

³**manifold** *vb* 1 : MULTIPLY 2 : to make a number of copies of (as a letter)

man·i·kin *also* **man·ni·kin** \'ma-ni-kən\ *n* 1 ♦ : a form representing the human figure used esp. for displaying clothes : MANNEQUIN 2 *dated, usu disparaging* : a little man : DWARF

♦ dummy, figure, form, mannequin — more at MANNEQUIN

Ma·ni·la hemp \mə-ˈni-lə-\ *n* : a tough fiber from a Philippine plant related to the banana that is used for cordage

manila paper *n, often cap M* : a tough brownish paper made orig. from Manila hemp

man·i·oc \'ma-nē-ˌäk\ *n* : CASSAVA

ma·nip·u·late \mə-ˈni-pyə-ˌlāt\ *vb* **-lat·ed; -lat·ing** 1 : to treat or operate manually or mechanically esp. with skill 2 : to manage or use skillfully 3 : to influence esp. with intent to deceive — **ma·nip·u·la·tion** \mə-ni-pyə-ˈlā-shən\ *n* — **ma·nip·u·la·tive** \-ˈni-pyə-ˌlā-tiv\ *adj* — **ma·nip·u·la·tor** \-ˌlā-tər\ *n*

ma·nip·u·la·tives \mə-ˈni-pyə-ˌlā-tivz\ *n pl* : objects that a student is instructed to use in a way that teaches or reinforces a lesson

man·kind *n* 1 \'man-ˈkīnd\ ♦ : the totality of human beings 2 \-ˌkīnd\ : men as distinguished from women

♦ Homo sapiens, humanity, humankind, man; *also* being, body, creature, fellow man, human, individual, mortal, party, person

man·li·ness \'man-lē-nəs\ *n* ♦ : the quality or state of being manly

♦ manhood, masculinity, virility — more at VIRILITY

¹**man·ly** \'man-lē\ *adj* **man·li·er; -est** **1** ♦ : having qualities generally associated with a man **2** : appropriate in character to a man

♦ male, mannish, man-size, masculine, virile — more at MASCULINE

²**manly** *adv* : in a manly manner

man–made \'man-'mād\ *adj* : made by humans rather than nature ⟨∼ systems⟩; *esp* : SYNTHETIC ⟨∼ fibers⟩

man·na \'ma-nə\ *n* **1** : food miraculously supplied to the Israelites in the wilderness **2** ♦ : a usu. sudden and unexpected source of gratification, pleasure, or gain

♦ benefit, blessing, boon, felicity, godsend, good, windfall — more at BLESSING

manned \'mand\ *adj* : carrying or performed by a person ⟨∼ spaceflight⟩

man·ne·quin \'ma-ni-kən\ *n* **1** ♦ : a form representing the human figure used esp. for displaying clothes **2** : a person employed to model clothing

♦ dummy, figure, form, manikin; *also* doll

man·ner \'ma-nər\ *n* **1** ♦ : a group united by common traits or interests : KIND, SORT **2 a** ♦ : a way of acting or proceeding ⟨worked in a brisk ∼⟩ **b** ♦ : a characteristic or customary mode of acting ⟨spoke bluntly as was his ∼⟩ **3** : a method of artistic execution **4** *pl* : social conduct; *also* : BEARING **5** *pl* ♦ : social conduct or rules of conduct as shown in the prevalent customs ⟨taught the child good ∼s⟩

♦ [1] breed, class, description, feather, ilk, kind, like, nature, order, sort, species, type — more at SORT ♦ [2a] approach, fashion, form, method, strategy, style, system, tack, tactics, technique, way — more at METHOD ♦ [2b] location, mode, phraseology, style, tone, vein — more at STYLE **manners** *pl* ♦ [5] etiquette, mores; *also* amenities, civilities, pleasantries; bearing, demeanor, deportment; courtesy, decorum, mannerliness, politeness; formalities, protocol, rules; air, attitude, carriage, poise, polish, pose, posture, presence; custom, habit, pattern, practice, trick, way, wont; convention, fashion, mode, style

man·nered \'ma-nərd\ *adj* **1** : having manners of a specified kind ⟨well-*mannered*⟩ **2** : having an artificial character ⟨a highly ∼ style⟩

man·ner·ism \'ma-nə-ˌri-zəm\ *n* **1** : ARTIFICIALITY, PRECIOSITY **2** ♦ : a peculiarity of action, bearing, or treatment

♦ crotchet, eccentricity, idiosyncrasy, oddity, peculiarity, quirk, singularity, trick — more at IDIOSYNCRASY

man·ner·li·ness \'ma-nər-lē-nəs\ *n* ♦ : the quality or state of being mannerly

♦ civility, courtesy, gentility, graciousness, politeness — more at POLITENESS

man·ner·ly \'ma-nər-lē\ *adj* ♦ : showing good manners : POLITE — **mannerly** *adv*

♦ civil, courteous, genteel, gracious, polite, well-bred — more at POLITE

man·nish \'ma-nish\ *adj* **1** ♦ : resembling or suggesting a man rather than a woman **2** ♦ : generally associated with or characteristic of a man ⟨a ∼ voice⟩ — **man·nish·ly** *adv* — **man·nish·ness** *n*

♦ male, manly, man-size, masculine, virile — more at MASCULINE

ma·no a ma·no \ˌmä-nō-ä-'mä-nō\ *adv or adj* : in direct competition or conflict

ma·noeu·vre \mə-'nü-vər, -'nyü-\ *chiefly Can and Brit var of* MANEUVER

man–of–war \ˌman-əv-'wȯr\ *n, pl* **men–of–war** \ˌmen-\ : WARSHIP

ma·nom·e·ter \mə-'nä-mə-tər\ *n* : an instrument for measur-

ing the pressure of gases and vapors — **mano·met·ric** \ˌma-nə-'me-trik\ *adj*

man·or \'ma-nər\ *n* **1 a** ♦ : the house or hall of an estate **b** : a landed estate **2** : an English estate of a feudal lord — **ma·no·ri·al** \mə-'nōr-ē-əl\ *adj* — **ma·no·ri·al·ism** \-ə-ˌli-zəm\ *n*

♦ castle, estate, hall, mansion, palace, villa — more at MANSION

man power *n* **1** : power available from or supplied by the physical effort of human beings **2** *usu* **man·pow·er** : the total supply of persons available and fitted for service

man·qué \mäⁿ-'kā\ *adj* [F, fr. pp. of *manquer* to lack, fail] : short of or frustrated in the fulfillment of one's aspirations or talents ⟨a poet ∼⟩

man·sard \'man-ˌsärd, -sərd\ *n* : a roof having two slopes on all sides with the lower slope steeper than the upper one

manse \'mans\ *n* : the residence esp. of a Presbyterian minister

man·ser·vant \'man-ˌsər-vənt\ *n, pl* **men·ser·vants** \'men-ˌsər-vənts\ : a male servant

man·sion \'man-chən\ *n* **1** ♦ : a large imposing residence **2** : a separate apartment in a large structure

♦ castle, estate, hall, manor, palace, villa; *also* showplace; abode, domicile, dwelling, habitation, hearth, home, house, pad, place; housing, nest, residency, roof; aerie, penthouse; salon, suite

man–size \'man-ˌsīz\ *or* **man–sized** \-ˌsīzd\ *adj* ♦ : suitable for or requiring a man ⟨a ∼ job⟩

♦ male, manly, mannish, masculine, virile — more at MASCULINE

man·slaugh·ter \-ˌslȯ-tər\ *n* : the unlawful killing of a human being without express or implied malice

man·ta \'man-tə\ *n* **1** : a square piece of cloth or blanket used in southwestern U.S. and Latin America as a cloak or shawl **2** : MANTA RAY

manta ray *n* : any of several extremely large rays

man·teau \man-'tō\ *n* : a loose cloak, coat, or robe

man·tel \'mant-ᵊl\ *n* : a beam, stone, or arch serving as a lintel to support the masonry above a fireplace; *also* : a shelf above a fireplace

man·tel·piece \'mant-ᵊl-ˌpēs\ *n* : the shelf of a mantel

man·til·la \man-'tē-yə, -'ti-lə\ *n* : a light scarf worn over the head and shoulders esp. by Spanish and Latin-American women

♦ babushka, bandanna, do-rag, kerchief — more at BANDANNA

man·tis \'man-təs\ *n, pl* **man·tis·es** *also* **man·tes** \-ˌtēz\ [NL, fr. Gk, lit., diviner, prophet] : any of a group of large usu. green insect-eating insects that hold their prey in forelimbs folded as if in prayer

man·tis·sa \man-'ti-sə\ *n* : the part of a logarithm to the right of the decimal point

¹**man·tle** \'mant-ᵊl\ *n* **1** : a loose sleeveless garment worn over other clothes **2** ♦ : something that covers, enfolds, or envelops **3** : a lacy sheath that gives light by incandescence when placed over a flame **4** : the portion of the earth lying between the crust and the core **5** : MANTEL

♦ cloak, curtain, hood, mask, shroud, veil — more at CLOAK

²**mantle** *vb* **man·tled; man·tling** **1** ♦ : to cover with or as if with a mantle **2** : BLUSH

♦ embrace, enclose, encompass, enfold, enshroud, envelop, invest, lap, shroud, swathe, veil, wrap — more at ENFOLD

man·tra \'man-trə\ *n* : a mystical formula of invocation or incantation (as in Hinduism)

¹**man·u·al** \'man-yə-wəl\ *adj* **1** : of, relating to, or involving the hands; *also* : worked by hand ⟨a ∼ pump⟩ **2** : requiring or using physical skill and energy ⟨∼ labor⟩ — **man·u·al·ly** *adv*

²**manual** *n* **1** ♦ : a small book; *esp* : a concise reference

book covering a particular subject : HANDBOOK   **2** : the prescribed movements in the handling of a military item and esp. a weapon during a drill or ceremony ⟨the ~ of arms⟩   **3** : a keyboard esp. of an organ   **4** : an automobile with a manual transmission

♦ handbook, primer, textbook — more at TEXTBOOK

man·u·fac·to·ry \ˌman-yə-'fak-tə-rē\ *n* : a building or set of buildings with facilities for manufacturing : FACTORY

¹**man·u·fac·ture** \ˌman-yə-'fak-chər\ *n* [MF, fr. ML *manufactura*, L *manu factus* made by hand]   **1** : something made from raw materials   **2** : the process of making wares by hand or by machinery; *also* : a productive industry using machinery

²**manufacture** *vb* **-tured; -tur·ing**   **1** ♦ : to make from raw materials by hand or by machinery; *also* : to engage in manufacture   **2** ♦ : to devise by thinking : INVENT, FABRICATE — **man·u·fac·tur·er** *n*

♦ [1] fabricate, fashion, form, frame, make, produce — more at MAKE ♦ [2] concoct, contrive, cook up, devise, fabricate, invent, make up, think up — more at INVENT

man·u·mis·sion \-'mi-shən\ *n* ♦ : the act or process of manumitting

♦ emancipation, enfranchisement, liberation — more at LIBERATION

man·u·mit \ˌman-yə-'mit\ *vb* **-mit·ted; -mit·ting** ♦ : to free from slavery

♦ discharge, emancipate, enfranchise, free, liberate, loose, loosen, release, spring, unbind, unchain, unfetter — more at FREE

¹**ma·nure** \mə-'nùr, -'nyùr\ *vb* **ma·nured; ma·nur·ing** : to fertilize land with manure

²**manure** *n* : FERTILIZER; *esp* : refuse from stables and barnyards — **ma·nu·ri·al** \-'nùr-ē-əl, -'nyùr-\ *adj*

man·u·script \'man-yə-ˌskript\ *n* [L *manu scriptus* written by hand]   **1** : a written or typed composition or document; *also* : a document submitted for publication   **2** ♦ : writing as opposed to print

♦ handwriting, penmanship, script — more at HANDWRITING

Manx \'maŋks\ *n pl* : the people of the Isle of Man — **Manx** *adj*

¹**many** \'me-nē\ *adj* **more** \'mȯr\; **most** \'mōst\ ♦ : consisting of or amounting to a large but indefinite number ⟨~ years ago⟩

♦ multiple, multitudinous, numerous; *also* countless, innumerable, numberless, uncountable, unnumbered, untold; several, some; miscellaneous, mixed, sundry, various; divers, manifold, multifarious, myriad *Ant* few

²**many** *pron* : a large number ⟨~ are called⟩

³**many** *n* : a large but indefinite number ⟨a good ~ of them⟩

many·fold \ˌme-nē-'fōld\ *adv* : by many times

many–sid·ed \-'sī-dəd\ *adj*   **1** : having many sides or aspects   **2** : VERSATILE

Mao·ism \'maù-ˌi-zəm\ *n* : the theory and practice of Communism developed in China chiefly by Mao Zedong — **Mao·ist** \'maù-ist\ *n or adj*

Mao·ri \'maù-(ə)r-ē\ *n, pl* **Maori** *or* **Maoris** : a member of a Polynesian people native to New Zealand

¹**map** \'map\ *n* [ML *mappa*, fr. L, napkin, towel]   **1** : a representation usu. on a flat surface of the whole or part of an area   **2** : a representation of the celestial sphere or part of it

²**map** *vb* **mapped; map·ping**   **1** : to make a map of   **2** ♦ : to plan in detail — often used with *out* ⟨~ out a program⟩ — **map·pa·ble** \'ma-pə-bəl\ *adj* — **map·per** *n*

♦ *usu* **map out** arrange, blueprint, calculate, chart, design, frame, lay out, plan, project, scheme — more at PLAN

MAP *abbr* modified American plan

ma·ple \'mā-pəl\ *n* : any of a genus of trees or shrubs with 2-winged dry fruit and opposite leaves; *also* : the hard light-colored wood of a maple used esp. for floors and furniture

maple sugar *n* : sugar made by boiling maple syrup

maple syrup *n* : syrup made by concentrating the sap of maple trees and esp. the sugar maple

mar \'mär\ *vb* **marred; mar·ring** ♦ : to detract from the wholeness or perfection of : SPOIL

♦ blemish, poison, spoil, stain, taint, tarnish, touch, vitiate — more at TAINT

Mar *abbr* March

ma·ra·ca \mə-'rä-kə, -'ra-\ *n* [Pg *maracá*] : a rattle usu. made from a gourd and used as a percussion instrument

mar·a·schi·no \ˌmar-ə-'skē-nō, -'shē-\ *n, often cap* : a cherry preserved in a sweet liqueur made from the juice of a bitter wild cherry

¹**mar·a·thon** \'mar-ə-ˌthän\ *n* [*Marathon*, Greece, site of a victory of Greeks over Persians in 490 B.C. the news of which was carried to Athens by a long-distance runner]   **1** : a long-distance race esp. on foot   **2** : an endurance contest

²**marathon** *adj* ♦ : belonging to, suggestive of, or suited for a marathon race or competition (as in being marked by unusual length of time)

♦ extended, far, great, lengthy, long — more at LONG

mar·a·thon·er \'mar-ə-ˌthä-nər\ *n* : a person who takes part in a marathon — **mar·a·thon·ing** *n*

ma·raud \mə-'rȯd\ *vb* ♦ : to roam about and raid in search of plunder : PILLAGE — **ma·raud·er** *n*

♦ despoil, loot, pillage, plunder, ransack, sack, strip — more at RANSACK

mar·ble \'mär-bəl\ *n*   **1** : a limestone that can be polished and used in fine building work   **2** : something resembling marble (as in coldness)   **3** : a small ball (as of glass) used in various games; *also, pl* : a children's game played with these small balls — **marble** *adj*

mar·bling \-bə-liŋ, -bliŋ\ *n* : an intermixture of fat through the lean of a cut of meat

mar·cel \mär-'sel\ *n* : a deep soft wave made in the hair by the use of a heated curling iron — **marcel** *vb*

¹**march** \'märch\ *n* : a border region : FRONTIER

²**march** *vb*   **1** ♦ : to move along in or as if in military formation   **2 a** : to walk in a direct purposeful manner   **b** ♦ : to make steady progress : ADVANCE   **3** : TRAVERSE ⟨~ed 10 miles⟩ — **march·er** *n*

♦ [1] file, pace, parade, stride; *also* perambulate, step, traipse, tread; hike, tramp; lumber, plod, stamp, stomp, stride, trudge ♦ [2b] advance, fare, forge, get along, go, proceed, progress — more at GO

³**march** *n*   **1** : the action of marching; *also* : the distance covered (as by a military unit) in a march   **2** : a regular measured stride or rhythmic step used in marching   **3** ♦ : forward movement   **4** : a piece of music with marked rhythm suitable for marching to

♦ advance, advancement, furtherance, headway, onrush, passage, process, procession, progress, progression — more at ADVANCE

March *n* [ME, fr. AF, fr. L *martius*, fr. *martius* of Mars, fr. *Mart-, Mars*, Roman god of war] : the 3d month of the year

mar·chio·ness \'mär-shə-nəs\ *n*   **1** : the wife or widow of a marquess   **2** : a woman holding the rank of a marquess in her own right

Mar·di Gras \'mär-dē-ˌgrä\ *n* [F, lit., fat Tuesday] : the Tuesday before Ash Wednesday often observed with parades and merrymaking

¹**mare** \'mar\ *n* : an adult female of the horse or a related mammal

²**ma·re** \'mär-(ˌ)ā\ *n, pl* **ma·ria** \'mär-ē-ə\ : any of several large dark areas on the surface of the moon or Mars

mar·ga·rine \'mär-jə-rən\ *n* : a food product made usu. from vegetable oils churned with skimmed milk and used as a substitute for butter

mar·ga·ri·ta \ˌmär-gə-'rē-tə\ *n* : a cocktail consisting of tequila, lime or lemon juice, and an orange-flavored liqueur

mar·gin \\'mär-jən\ n 1 : the part of a page outside the main body of printed or written matter 2 ♦ : the outside limit and adjoining surface of something : EDGE 3 : a spare amount, measure, or degree allowed for use if needed 4 : measure or degree of difference ⟨a one-vote ∼⟩

♦ border, bound, boundary, circumference, compass, confines, edge, end, fringe, perimeter, periphery, rim, skirt, verge — more at BORDER

mar·gin·al \-jə-nəl\ adj 1 : written or printed in the margin 2 : of, relating to, or situated at a margin or border 3 : close to the lower limit of quality or acceptability 4 : excluded from or existing outside the mainstream of society or a group

mar·gi·na·lia \ˌmär-jə-'nā-lē-ə\ n pl : marginal notes or embellishments

mar·gin·al·ize \'mär-jə-nᵊl-ˌīz\ vb -ized; -iz·ing : to relegate to an unimportant position within a society or group

mar·gin·al·ly \ˌmärj-nə-lē, 'mär-jə-nᵊl-ē\ adv ♦ : in a marginal manner

♦ barely, hardly, just, scarcely, slightly — more at JUST

mar·grave \'mär-ˌgräv\ n : the military governor esp. of a medieval German border province

ma·ri·a·chi \ˌmär-ē-'ä-chē, ˌmar-\ n : a Mexican street band; also : a member of or the music of such a band

mari·gold \'mar-ə-ˌgōld, 'mer-\ n : any of a genus of tropical American herbs related to the daisies that are grown for their showy usu. yellow, orange, or maroon flower heads

mar·i·jua·na also **mar·i·hua·na** \ˌmar-ə-'wä-nə, -'hwä-\ n [MexSp marihuana] : the dried leaves and flowering tops of the female hemp plant smoked usu. illegally for their intoxicating effect; also : HEMP

ma·rim·ba \mə-'rim-bə\ n : a xylophone of southern Africa and Central America; also : a modern version of it

ma·ri·na \mə-'rē-nə\ n : a dock or basin providing secure moorings for pleasure boats

mar·i·nade \ˌmer-ə-'nād\ n : a savory usu. acidic sauce in which meat, fish, or a vegetable is soaked to enrich its flavor or to tenderize it

mar·i·na·ra \ˌmar-ə-'nar-ə\ adj [It (alla) marinara, lit., in sailor style] : made with tomatoes, onions, garlic, and spices; also : served with marinara sauce

mar·i·nate \'mar-ə-ˌnāt\ vb -nat·ed; -nat·ing : to steep (as meat or fish) in a brine or pickle

¹marine \mə-'rēn\ adj 1 ♦ : of or relating to the sea or its navigation or commerce 2 : of or relating to marines

♦ maritime, oceanic, pelagic

²marine n 1 : the mercantile and naval shipping of a country 2 : any of a class of soldiers serving on shipboard or with a naval force

mar·i·ner \'mar-ə-nər\ n ♦ : a person who navigates or assists in navigating a ship : SAILOR

♦ gob, jack, jack-tar, sailor, seaman, swab, tar — more at SAILOR

mar·i·o·nette \ˌmar-ē-ə-'net, ˌmer-\ n : a puppet moved by strings or by hand

mar·i·tal \'mar-ət-ᵊl\ adj ♦ : of or relating to marriage : CONJUGAL

♦ conjugal, connubial, matrimonial, nuptial; also matched, mated; bridal; wifely; affianced, betrothed, committed, engaged, pledged, promised

mar·i·time \'mar-ə-ˌtīm\ adj 1 ♦ : of, relating to, or bordering on the sea 2 ♦ : of or relating to navigation or commerce of the sea

♦ [1] marine, oceanic, pelagic — more at MARINE
♦ [2] marine

mar·jo·ram \'mär-jə-rəm\ n : any of various fragrant mints often used as seasoning

¹mark \'märk\ n 1 : something (as a line or fixed object) designed to record position; also : the starting line or position in a track event 2 a : TARGET b : the end toward which effort is directed : GOAL, OBJECT 3 ♦ : an object of abuse or ridicule 4 : the question under discussion 5 ♦ : a stan-

dard of performance, quality, or condition ⟨not up to the ∼⟩ 6 a : a visible sign : INDICATION b ♦ : a distinguishing trait or quality : CHARACTERISTIC 7 : a written or printed symbol 8 : GRADE ⟨a ∼ of B+⟩ 9 : IMPORTANCE, DISTINCTION 10 a ♦ : a lasting impression : an enduring effect ⟨made his ∼ in the world⟩ b : a damaging impression (as a scratch, scar, or stain) left on a surface

♦ [3] butt, laughingstock, mock, mockery, target — more at LAUGHINGSTOCK ♦ [5] criterion, grade, measure, par, standard, touchstone, yardstick — more at STANDARD ♦ [6b] attribute, character, characteristic, feature, peculiarity, point, property, quality, trait — more at CHARACTERISTIC ♦ [10a] effect, impact, influence, repercussion, sway — more at EFFECT

²mark vb 1 ♦ : to set apart by a line or boundary 2 : to designate by a mark or make a mark on 3 : CHARACTERIZE ⟨the vehemence that ∼s his speeches⟩; also : SIGNALIZE ⟨this year ∼s our 50th anniversary⟩ 4 : to take notice of : OBSERVE ⟨∼ my words⟩ 5 ♦ : to label so as to indicate price or quality 6 ♦ : to make note of in writing

♦ [1] bound, circumscribe, define, delimit, demarcate, limit, terminate — more at LIMIT ♦ [5] label, tag, ticket — more at LABEL ♦ [6] jot, log, note, put down, record, register, set down — more at RECORD

³mark n : a former monetary unit of Germany

Mark \'märk\ n : a book of the New Testament of Christian Scripture

mark·down \'märk-ˌdaun\ n 1 : a lowering of price 2 : the amount by which an original price is reduced

mark down vb ♦ : to put a lower price on

♦ cheapen, depreciate, depress, write off — more at DEPRECIATE

marked \'märkt\ adj ♦ : having a distinctive or emphasized character : NOTICEABLE — **mark·ed·ly** \'mär-kəd-lē\ adv

♦ bold, catchy, conspicuous, emphatic, noticeable, prominent, pronounced, remarkable, striking — more at NOTICEABLE

mark·er \'mär-kər\ n ♦ : one that marks

♦ label, tag, ticket — more at LABEL

¹mar·ket \'mär-kət\ n 1 : a meeting together of people for trade by purchase and sale; also : a public place where such a meeting is held 2 : the rate or price offered for a commodity or security 3 : a geographical area of demand for commodities; also ♦ : extent of demand 4 : a retail establishment usu. of a specific kind

♦ call, demand, request — more at DEMAND

²market vb 1 : to go to a market to buy or sell 2 ♦ : to offer for sale : SELL — **mar·ket·able** adj

♦ deal, merchandise, put up, retail, sell, vend; also wholesale; hawk, peddle; barter, distribute, exchange, export, handle, trade, traffic (in); advertise, ballyhoo, boost, plug, promote, tout; bargain, chaffer, dicker, haggle; provide, supply; keep, stock Ant buy, purchase

mar·ket·place \'mär-kət-ˌplās\ n 1 : an open square in a town where markets are held 2 ♦ : the world of trade or economic activity

♦ business, commerce, trade, traffic — more at COMMERCE

mark·ka \'mär-ˌkä\ n, pl **mark·kaa** \'mär-ˌkä\ or **markkas** \-ˌkäz\ : the basic monetary unit of Finland from 1917 to 2001

marks·man \'märks-mən\ n ♦ : a person skillful at hitting a target — **marks·man·ship** n

♦ sharpshooter, shooter, shot; also rifleman; gunman, gunner, sniper

mark·up \'mär-ˌkəp\ n 1 : a raising of price 2 : an amount added to the cost price of an article to determine the selling price

mark up vb : to put a higher price on

markup language n : a system for marking the components and layout of a computer document

marl \'märl\ *n* : an earthy deposit rich in lime used esp. as fertilizer — **marly** \'mär-lē\ *adj*

mar·lin \'mär-lən\ *n* : any of several large oceanic sport fishes related to sailfishes

mar·line·spike *also* **mar·lin·spike** \'mär-lən-ˌspīk\ *n* : a pointed iron tool used to separate strands of rope or wire (as in splicing)

mar·ma·lade \'mär-mə-ˌlād\ *n* : a clear jelly holding in suspension pieces of fruit and fruit rind

mar·mo·re·al \mär-'mōr-ē-əl\ *adj* : of, relating to, or suggestive of marble

mar·mo·set \'mär-mə-ˌset\ *n* : any of numerous small bushy-tailed monkeys of Central and So. America

mar·mot \'mär-mət\ *n* : any of a genus of stout short-legged burrowing No. American rodents

¹**ma·roon** \mə-'rün\ *vb* **1** : to put ashore (as on a desolate island) and leave to one's fate **2 ♦** : to leave in isolation and without hope of escape

♦ abandon, desert, forsake, quit — more at ABANDON

²**maroon** *n* : a dark red color

¹**mar·quee** \mär-'kē\ *n* [modif. of F *marquise*, lit., marchioness] **1** : a large tent set up (as for an outdoor party) **2** : a usu. metal and glass canopy over an entrance (as of a theater) **3** : a sign over the entrance of a theater or arena advertising a performance

²**marquee** *adj* : having or being a great attraction : PREEMINENT ⟨~ athletes⟩

mar·quess \'mär-kwəs\ *or* **mar·quis** \'mär-kwəs, mär-'kē\ *n* **1** : a nobleman of hereditary rank in Europe and Japan **2** : a member of the British peerage ranking below a duke and above an earl

mar·que·try \'mär-kə-trē\ *n* : inlaid work of wood, shell, or ivory (as on a table or cabinet)

mar·quis \'mär-kwəs, mär-'kē\ *n* : MARQUESS

mar·quise \mär-'kēz\ *n, pl* **mar·quises** *same or* -'kē-zəz\ : MARCHIONESS

mar·riage \'mar-ij\ *n* **1 ♦** : the state of being united as spouses in a consensual and contractual relationship recognized by law **2 ♦** : a wedding ceremony and attendant festivities **3** : a close union — **mar·riage·able** *adj*

♦ [1] match, matrimony; *also* monogamy, attachment, commitment, relationship ♦ [2] espousal, wedding — more at WEDDING

married name *n* : a woman's surname acquired through marriage

mar·row \'mar-ō\ *n* : a soft vascular tissue that fills the cavities of most bones

mar·row·bone \'mar-ə-ˌbōn, 'mar-ō-\ *n* : a bone (as a shinbone) rich in marrow

mar·ry \'mar-ē\ *vb* **mar·ried; mar·ry·ing 1 a** : to join in marriage **b ♦** : to give in marriage ⟨*married* his daughter to his partner's son⟩ **2** : to take as a spouse : WED **3 ♦** : to enter into a close union **4** : ¹COMBINE, UNITE — **mar·ried** *adj or n*

♦ [1b] match; *also* commit, engage; affiance, betroth, pledge, promise ♦ [3] associate, coalesce, combine, conjoin, connect, couple, fuse, join, link, unify, unite — more at UNITE

Mars \'märz\ *n* : the planet 4th from the sun and conspicuous for its red color

marsh \'märsh\ *n* ♦ : a tract of soft wet land — **marshy** *adj*

♦ bog, fen, mire, morass, slough, swamp — more at SWAMP

¹**mar·shal** \'mär-shəl\ *n* [ME, fr. AF *mareschal*, of Gmc origin; akin to OHG *marahscalc* marshal, fr. *marah* horse + *scalc* servant] **1** : a high official in a medieval household; *also* : a person in charge of the ceremonial aspects of a gathering **2** : a general officer of the highest military rank **3** : an administrative officer (as of a U.S. judicial district) having duties similar to a sheriff's **4** : the administrative head of a city police or fire department

²**marshal** *vb* **mar·shaled** *or* **mar·shalled; mar·shal·ing** *or*

mar·shal·ling 1 ♦ : to arrange in order, rank, or position **2 ♦** : to bring together and order in an appropriate or effective way **3 ♦** : to lead with ceremony : USHER

♦ [1] arrange, array, classify, codify, dispose, draw up, order, organize, range, systematize — more at ORDER ♦ [2] mobilize, muster, rally — more at MOBILIZE ♦ [3] conduct, direct, guide, lead, pilot, route, show, steer, usher — more at LEAD

marsh gas *n* : METHANE

marsh·mal·low \'märsh-ˌme-lō, -ˌma-\ *n* : a light spongy confection made from corn syrup, sugar, albumen, and gelatin

marsh marigold *n* : a swamp herb related to the buttercups that has bright yellow flowers

mar·su·pi·al \mär-'sü-pē-əl\ *n* : any of an order of primitive mammals (as opossums, kangaroos, or wombats) that bear very immature young which are nourished in a pouch on the abdomen of the female — **marsupial** *adj*

mart \'märt\ *n* : MARKET

mar·ten \'märt-ᵊn\ *n, pl* **marten** *or* **martens** : a slender mammal that is larger than the related weasels and has soft gray or brown fur; *also* : this fur

mar·tial \'mär-shəl\ *adj* [L *martialis* of Mars, fr. *Mart-, Mars* Mars, Roman god of war] **1** : of, relating to, or suited for war or a warrior ⟨~ music⟩ **2** : of or relating to an army or military life **3** : WARLIKE

martial art *n* : any of several arts of combat (as karate and judo) practiced as sport

martial law *n* **1** : the law applied in occupied territory by the occupying military forces **2** : the established law of a country administered by military forces in an emergency when civilian law enforcement agencies are unable to maintain public order and safety

mar·tian \'mär-shən\ *adj, often cap* : of or relating to the planet Mars or its hypothetical inhabitants — **martian** *n, often cap*

mar·tin \'märt-ᵊn\ *n* : any of several swallows and esp. one of No. America with purplish blue plumage

mar·ti·net \ˌmärt-ᵊn-'et\ *n* : a strict disciplinarian

mar·tin·gale \'märt-ᵊn-ˌgāl\ *n* : a strap connecting a horse's girth to the bit or reins so as to hold down its head

mar·ti·ni \mär-'tē-nē\ *n* : a cocktail made of gin or vodka and dry vermouth

¹**mar·tyr** \'mär-tər\ *n* [ME, fr. OE, fr. LL, fr. Gk *martyr-, martys* witness] **1** : a person who dies rather than renounce a religion; *also* : a person who makes a great sacrifice for the sake of principle **2** : a great or constant sufferer

²**martyr** *vb* **1** : to put to death for adhering to a belief **2 ♦** : to inflict agonizing pain on : TORTURE

♦ afflict, agonize, bedevil, curse, harrow, persecute, plague, rack, torment, torture — more at AFFLICT

mar·tyr·dom \'mär-tər-dəm\ *n* **1** : the suffering and death of a martyr **2** : TORTURE

¹**mar·vel** \'mär-vəl\ *n* **1 ♦** : one that causes wonder or astonishment **2** : intense surprise or interest

♦ caution, flash, miracle, phenomenon, portent, prodigy, sensation, wonder — more at WONDER

²**marvel** *vb* **mar·veled** *or* **mar·velled; mar·vel·ing** *or* **mar·vel·ling** : to feel surprise, wonder, or amazed curiosity

mar·vel·ous *or* **mar·vel·lous** \'mär-və-ləs\ *adj* **1 ♦** : causing wonder **2** : of the highest kind or quality — **mar·vel·ous·ly** *adv* — **mar·vel·ous·ness** *n*

♦ [1] amazing, astonishing, astounding, awesome, eye-opening, fabulous, miraculous, portentous, prodigious, stunning, stupendous, sublime, surprising, wonderful; *also* incredible, unbelievable, unimaginable, unthinkable; extraordinary, phenomenal, rare, sensational, spectacular; outstanding, remarkable; impressive, striking ♦ [2] excellent, fabulous, fine, grand, great, sensational, splendid, superb, superior, swell, terrific, wonderful

Marx·ism \'märk-ˌsi-zəm\ *n* : the political, economic, and social principles and policies advocated by Karl Marx — **Marx·ist** \-sist\ *n or adj*

mar·zi·pan \'märt-sə-ˌpän, -ˌpan; 'mär-zə-ˌpan\ *n* [G, fr. It *marzapane*] : a confection of almond paste, sugar, and egg whites

masc *abbr* masculine

mas·cara \mas-'kar-ə\ *n* : a cosmetic esp. for darkening the eyelashes

mas·car·po·ne \ˌmas-kär-'pō-nā\ *n* : an Italian cream cheese

mas·cot \'mas-ˌkät, -kət\ *n* [F *mascotte*, fr. Occitan *mascoto*, fr. *masco* witch, fr. ML *masca*] ♦ : a person, animal, or object adopted usu. by a group to bring good luck

♦ amulet, charm, fetish, talisman — more at CHARM

¹mas·cu·line \'mas-kyə-lən\ *adj* **1 a** : MALE **b** ♦ : having qualities appropriate to or usu. associated with a man : MANLY **2** : of, relating to, or constituting the gender that includes most words or grammatical forms referring to males

♦ male, manly, mannish, man-size, virile; *also* boyish, tomboyish *Ant* effeminate, unmanly, unmasculine

²masculine *n* : a noun, pronoun, adjective, or inflectional form or class of the masculine gender; *also* : the masculine gender

mas·cu·lin·i·ty \ˌmas-kyə-'li-nə-tē\ *n* ♦ : the quality, state, or degree of being masculine

♦ manhood, manliness, virility — more at VIRILITY

¹mash \'mash\ *n* **1** : a mixture of ground feeds for livestock **2** : crushed malt or grain steeped in hot water to make wort **3** : a soft pulpy mass

²mash *vb* **1** ♦ : to reduce to a soft pulpy state **2** : CRUSH, SMASH ⟨∼ a finger⟩ — **mash·er** *n*

♦ crush, squash — more at CRUSH

MASH *abbr* mobile army surgical hospital

mash–up \'mash-ˌəp\ *n* : something created by combining elements from two or more sources

¹mask \'mask\ *n* **1** : a cover for the face usu. for disguise or protection **2** : MASQUE **3** : a figure of a head worn on the stage in antiquity **4** : a copy of a face made by means of a mold ⟨death ∼⟩ **5** ♦ : something that conceals or disguises **6** : the face of an animal **7** : a cosmetic preparation for the skin of the face that is applied moist and removed after it dries

♦ cloak, curtain, hood, mantle, shroud, veil — more at CLOAK

²mask *vb* **1** ♦ : to conceal from view or perception **2** : to cover for protection

♦ camouflage, cloak, disguise, dress up — more at DISGUISE ♦ blanket, blot out, cloak, conceal, cover, curtain, enshroud, hide, obscure, occult, screen, shroud, veil — more at HIDE

mask·er \'mas-kər\ *n* : a participant in a masquerade

mas·och·ism \'ma-sə-ˌki-zəm, 'ma-zə-\ *n* **1** : a sexual perversion characterized by pleasure in being subjected to pain or humiliation **2** : pleasure in being abused or dominated — **mas·och·ist** \-kist\ *n* — **mas·och·is·tic** \ˌma-sə-'kis-tik, ˌma-zə-\ *adj*

ma·son \'mās-ᵊn\ *n* **1** : a skilled worker who builds with stone, brick, or concrete **2** *cap* : FREEMASON

Ma·son·ic \mə-'sä-nik\ *adj* : of or relating to Freemasons or Freemasonry

ma·son·ry \'mās-ᵊn-rē\ *n, pl* **-ries** **1** : something constructed of materials used by masons **2** : the art, trade, or work of a mason **3** *cap* : FREEMASONRY

masque \'mask\ *n* **1** : MASQUERADE **2** : a short allegorical dramatic performance (as of the 17th century)

¹mas·quer·ade \ˌmas-kə-'rād\ *n* **1** : a social gathering of persons wearing masks; *also* : a costume for wear at such a gathering **2** : DISGUISE **3** ♦ : an action or appearance that is mere disguise or show

♦ act, airs, facade, front, guise, pose, pretense, put-on, semblance, show; *also* appearance, color, gloss; camouflage, cloak, disguise; affectation, deceit, deception, double-dealing, duplicity, guile, fraud; betrayal, double

cross, faithlessness, falsity, falseness, infidelity, perfidy, treachery, treason, unfaithfulness; excuse, pretext

²masquerade *vb* **-ad·ed; -ad·ing** **1** ♦ : to disguise oneself **2** : to take part in a masquerade — **mas·quer·ad·er** *n*

♦ impersonate, play, at IMPERSONATE

¹mass \'mas\ *n* **1** *cap* : a sequence of prayers and ceremonies forming the eucharistic service of the Roman Catholic Church **2** *often cap* : a celebration of the Eucharist **3** : a musical setting for parts of the Mass

²mass *n* **1** : a quantity or aggregate of matter usu. of considerable size **2** : EXPANSE, BULK; *also* : MASSIVENESS **3** ♦ : the principal part **4** : AGGREGATE, WHOLE **5** : the quantity of matter that a body possesses as measured by its inertia **6** : a large quantity, amount, or number **7** ♦ : the great body of people — usu. used in pl. — **massy** *adj*

♦ [3] body, bulk, core, generality, main, staple, weight — more at BODY *usu* **masses** *pl* ♦ [7] commoners, herd, mob, people, plebeians, populace, rank and file; *also* proletariat, rabble, riffraff, scum, trash; bourgeoisie, middle class; public *Ant* elite

³mass *vb* ♦ : to form or collect into a mass

♦ accumulate, amass, collect, conglomerate, gather, heap, pile up — more at COLLECT

Mass *abbr* Massachusetts

¹mas·sa·cre \'ma-si-kər\ *n* **1** ♦ : the killing of many persons under cruel or atrocious circumstances **2** : a wholesale slaughter

♦ butchery, carnage, slaughter; *also* bloodshed, foul play, homicide, killing, manslaughter, murder, slaying; mortality; annihilation, demolishing, destruction, devastation, extermination; genocide; assassination, execution

²massacre *vb* ♦ : to kill by massacre

♦ butcher, slaughter; *also* assassinate, execute, murder, slay; annihilate, decimate, demolish, destroy, devastate, eradicate, exterminate, waste, wipe out

¹mas·sage \mə-'säzh, -'säj\ *n* : manipulation of tissues (as by rubbing and kneading) esp. for therapeutic purposes

²massage *vb* **mas·saged; mas·sag·ing** **1** : to subject to massage **2** : to treat flatteringly; *also* : MANIPULATE, DOCTOR ⟨∼ data⟩

mas·seur \ma-'sər\ *n* : a man who practices massage

mas·seuse \-'sərz, -'süz\ *n* : a woman who practices massage

mas·sif \ma-'sēf\ *n* : a principal mountain mass

mas·sive \'ma-siv\ *adj* **1** ♦ : forming or consisting of a large mass **2** ♦ : large in structure, scope, or degree

♦ [1] heavy, hefty, ponderous, weighty — more at HEAVY ♦ [2] colossal, enormous, giant, gigantic, grand, huge, mammoth, monumental, prodigious, titanic, tremendous

mas·sive·ly \-lē\ *adv* ♦ : in a massive manner

♦ broadly, considerably, greatly, hugely, largely, monstrously, much, sizably, stupendously, tremendously, utterly, vastly — more at GREATLY

mas·sive·ness \-nəs\ *n* ♦ : the quality or state of being massive

♦ enormity, hugeness, immensity, magnitude, vastness — more at IMMENSITY

mass·less \'mas-ləs\ *adj* : having no mass ⟨∼ particles⟩

mass medium *n, pl* **mass media** : a medium of communication (as the newspapers or television) that is designed to reach the mass of the people

mass–pro·duce \ˌmas-prə-'düs, -'dyüs\ *vb* : to produce in quantity usu. by machinery — **mass production** *n*

¹mast \'mast\ *n* **1** : a long pole or spar rising from the keel or deck of a ship and supporting the yards, booms, and rigging **2** : a slender vertical structure — **mast·ed** \'mas-təd\ *adj*

²mast *n* : nuts (as acorns) accumulated on the forest floor and often serving as food for animals (as hogs)

mas·tec·to·my \ma-'stek-tə-mē\ *n, pl* **-mies** : surgical removal of the breast

¹mas·ter \\'mas-tər\ *n* **1** : a male teacher; *also* : a person holding an academic degree higher than a bachelor's but lower than a doctor's **2** ♦ : one highly skilled (as in an art or profession) **3** ♦ : one having authority or control **4** : one that conquers or masters : VICTOR **5** : the commander of a merchant ship **6** : a youth or boy too young to be called *mister* — used as a title **7** : an original from which copies are made — **master** *adj*

♦ [2] ace, adept, artist, authority, crackerjack, expert, maestro, scholar, shark, virtuoso, whiz, wizard — more at EXPERT ♦ [3] boss, captain, chief, foreman, head, headman, helmsman, kingpin, leader, taskmaster — more at BOSS

²master *vb* **1** : to become master of : OVERCOME **2** : to become skilled or proficient in **3** : to produce a master recording of (as a musical performance)

master chief petty officer *n* : a petty officer of the highest rank in the navy

mas·ter·ful \\'mas-tər-fəl\ *adj* **1** : inclined and usu. competent to act as a master **2** ♦ : having or reflecting the skill of a master **3** ♦ : suggestive of a domineering nature

♦ [2] adroit, artful, dexterous, practiced, skillful, virtuoso — more at SKILLFUL ♦ [2] accomplished, adept, consummate, crack, crackerjack, good, great, proficient, skilled — more at PROFICIENT ♦ [3] authoritarian, autocratic, bossy, despotic, dictatorial, domineering, imperious, overbearing, peremptory, tyrannical, tyrannous — more at BOSSY

mas·ter·ful·ly \-fə-lē\ *adv* ♦ : in a masterful manner

♦ ably, adeptly, capably, expertly, proficiently, skillfully, well — more at WELL

mas·ter·ful·ness \-nəs\ *n* ♦ : the quality or state of being masterful

♦ adeptness, adroitness, art, artfulness, artifice, artistry, cleverness, craft, cunning, deftness, skill — more at SKILL

master gunnery sergeant *n* : a noncommissioned officer in the marine corps ranking above a master sergeant

master key *n* : a key designed to open several different locks

mas·ter·ly \\'mas-tər-lē\ *adj* **1** ♦ : indicating thorough knowledge or superior skill ⟨~ performance⟩ **2** ♦ : having the power and skill of a master — **mas·ter·ly** *adv*

♦ accomplished, adept, consummate, crack, crackerjack, expert, good, great, master, masterful, proficient, skilled, skillful, virtuoso — more at PROFICIENT

¹mas·ter·mind \-,mīnd\ *n* : a person who provides the directing or creative intelligence for a project

²mastermind *vb* : to be the mastermind of

♦ contrive, finagle, finesse, frame, machinate, maneuver (*or* manoeuvre), negotiate, wangle

master of ceremonies : a person who acts as host for a special event or a program of entertainment (as on television)

mas·ter·piece \\'mas-tər-,pēs\ *n* : a work done with extraordinary skill

master plan *n* : an overall plan

mas·ter's \\'mas-tərz\ *n* : a master's degree

master sergeant *n* **1** : a noncommissioned officer in the army ranking next below a sergeant major **2** : a noncommissioned officer in the air force ranking next below a senior master sergeant **3** : a noncommissioned officer in the marine corps ranking next below a master gunnery sergeant

mas·ter·stroke \\'mas-tər-,strōk\ *n* : a masterly performance or move

mas·ter·work \-,wərk\ *n* : MASTERPIECE

mas·tery \\'mas-tə-rē\ *n* **1** ♦ : the authority of a master : DOMINION; *also* : SUPERIORITY **2** : possession or display of great skill or knowledge

♦ arm, authority, clutch, command, control, dominion, grip, hold, power, superiority, sway — more at POWER

mast·head \\'mast-,hed\ *n* **1** : the top of a mast **2** : the printed matter in a newspaper or periodical giving the title and details of ownership and rates of subscription or advertising

mas·tic \\'mas-tik\ *n* : a pasty material used as a coating or cement

mas·ti·cate \\'mas-tə-,kāt\ *vb* **-cat·ed; -cat·ing** : to grind or crush (food) with or as if with the teeth : CHEW — **mas·ti·ca·tion** \,mas-tə-'kā-shən\ *n*

mas·tiff \\'mas-təf\ *n* : any of a breed of large smooth-coated dogs used esp. as guard dogs

mast·odon \\'mas-tə-,dän\ *n* [NL, fr. Gk *mastos* breast + *odōn, odous* tooth] : any of numerous huge extinct mammals related to the mammoths

mas·toid \\'mas-,tȯid\ *n* : a bony prominence behind the ear — **mastoid** *adj*

mas·tur·ba·tion \,mas-tər-'bā-shən\ *n* : stimulation of the genital organs apart from sexual intercourse, usu. to orgasm, and esp. by use of one's own hand — **mas·tur·bate** \\'mas-tər-,bāt\ *vb* — **mas·tur·ba·to·ry** \\'mas-tər-bə-,tōr-ē\ *adj*

¹mat \\'mat\ *n* **1** : a piece of coarse woven or plaited fabric **2** : something made up of many intertwined strands **3** : a large thick pad used as a surface for wrestling and gymnastics

²mat *vb* **mat·ted; mat·ting** **1** : to provide with a mat **2** : to form into a tangled mass

³mat *vb* **mat·ted; mat·ting** **1** : to make (as a color) matte **2** : to provide (a picture) with a mat

⁴mat *var of* MATTE

⁵mat *or* **matt** *or* **matte** *n* : a border going around a picture between picture and frame or serving as the frame

mat·a·dor \\'ma-tə-,dȯr\ *n* [Sp, fr. *matar* to kill] : a bullfighter whose role is to kill the bull in a bullfight

¹match \\'mach\ *n* **1** ♦ : a person or thing equal or similar to another; *also* : one able to cope with another : RIVAL **2** : a suitable pairing of persons or objects **3** ♦ : a contest or game between two or more individuals **4** : a marriage union; *also* : a prospective marriage partner

♦ [1] coordinate, counterpart, equal, equivalent, fellow, like, parallel, peer, rival — more at EQUAL ♦ [1] carbon copy, counterpart, double, duplicate, duplication, facsimile, image, likeness, picture, replica, ringer, spit — more at IMAGE ♦ [3] bout, competition, contest, event, game, meet, tournament — more at GAME

²match *vb* **1** : to meet as an antagonist; *also* : PIT **2** : to provide with a worthy competitor; *also* : to set in comparison with **3** : to join or give in marriage : MARRY **4** : to combine suitably or congenially; *also* : ADAPT, SUIT **5** ♦ : to provide with a counterpart **6** ♦ : to be the counterpart of

♦ [5] equal, meet, tie ♦ [6] correspond, equal, parallel; *also* blend (with), coordinate (with), go (with), harmonize (with); complement, supplement; counterbalance, counterpoise; echo, mirror, repeat; amount (to), approach, near; measure (up), partake (of), rival, suggest

³match *n* : a short slender piece of flammable material (as wood) tipped with a combustible mixture that ignites through friction

match·book \\'mach-,bùk\ *n* : a small folder containing rows of paper matches

match·less \-ləs\ *adj* ♦ : having no equal

♦ incomparable, inimitable, nonpareil, only, peerless, unequaled, unmatched, unparalleled, unrivaled, unsurpassed — more at ONLY

match·lock \-,läk\ *n* : a musket with a slow-burning cord lowered over a hole in the breech to ignite the charge

match·mak·er \-,mā-kər\ *n* : one who arranges a match and esp. a marriage

match·wood \-,wùd\ *n* : small pieces of wood

¹mate \\'māt\ *vb* **mat·ed; mat·ing** : CHECKMATE — **mate** *n*

²mate *n* **1 a** ♦ : one that customarily associates with another : ASSOCIATE, COMPANION **b** ♦ : an assistant to a more skilled worker : HELPER **2** : a deck officer on a merchant ship ranking below the captain **3 a** ♦ : one of a pair **b** ♦ : either member of a married couple or a breeding pair of animals

♦ [1a] associate, cohort, companion, comrade, crony, fellow — more at ASSOCIATE ♦ [1b] aid, apprentice, assistant, deputy, helper, helpmate, sidekick — more at HELPER ♦ [3a] companion, half, match, twin; *also* coordinate; counterpart, equal, equivalent, like, parallel, peer, rival; carbon copy, double, duplicate, identical twin, ringer; analogue, similarity ♦ [3b] consort, partner, spouse — more at SPOUSE

³**mate** *vb* **mat·ed; mat·ing 1** : to join or fit together **2** : to come or bring together as mates **3** : COPULATE

¹**ma·te·ri·al** \mə-'tir-ē-əl\ *adj* **1** ♦ : having material existence : PHYSICAL ⟨∼ world⟩; *also* : of or relating to the body : BODILY ⟨∼ needs⟩ **2** : of or relating to matter rather than form ⟨∼ cause⟩; *also* : EMPIRICAL ⟨∼ knowledge⟩ **3** ♦ : highly important : SIGNIFICANT **4** ♦ : of a physical or worldly nature ⟨∼ progress⟩ — **ma·te·ri·al·ly** *adv*

♦ [1] bodily, concrete, physical, substantial; *also* carnal, corporal, fleshly; appreciable, detectable, discernible, noticeable, observable, palpable, perceptible, sensible, tangible; objective, phenomenal; bulky, heavy, massive, solid, weighty *Ant* immaterial, nonmaterial, nonphysical ♦ [3] big, consequential, eventful, important, major, meaningful, momentous, significant, substantial, weighty — more at IMPORTANT ♦ [3] applicable, apposite, apropos, germane, pertinent, pointed, relative, relevant — more at PERTINENT ♦ [4] carnal, earthly, fleshly, mundane, temporal, terrestrial, worldly — more at EARTHLY

²**material** *n* **1** ♦ : the elements or substance of which something is composed or made **2** : apparatus necessary for doing or making something

♦ raw material, stuff, substance

ma·te·ri·al·ise *chiefly Brit var of* MATERIALIZE

ma·te·ri·al·ism \mə-'tir-ē-ə-ˌli-zəm\ *n* **1** : a theory that everything can be explained as being or coming from matter **2** : a preoccupation with material rather than intellectual or spiritual things — **ma·te·ri·al·ist** \-list\ *n or adj* — **ma·te·ri·al·is·tic** \-ˌtir-ē-ə-'lis-tik\ *adj* — **ma·te·ri·al·is·ti·cal·ly** \-ti-k(ə-)lē\ *adv*

ma·te·ri·al·ize \mə-'tir-ē-ə-ˌlīz\ *vb* **-ized; -iz·ing 1** ♦ : to give material form to; *also* : to assume bodily form **2** ♦ : to make an often unexpected appearance **3** ♦ : to come into existence — **ma·te·ri·al·i·za·tion** \mə-ˌtir-ē-ə-lə-'zā-shən\ *n*

♦ [1] embody, epitomize, manifest, personify, substantiate — more at EMBODY ♦ [2] appear, come out, show up, turn up — more at APPEAR ♦ [2, 3] arise, begin, commence, dawn, form, originate, spring, start — more at BEGIN

ma·té·ri·el *or* **ma·te·ri·el** \mə-ˌtir-ē-'el\ *n* [F *matériel*] ♦ : equipment, apparatus, and supplies used by an organization

♦ accoutrements (*or* accouterments), apparatus, equipment, gear, outfit, paraphernalia, tackle — more at EQUIPMENT

ma·ter·nal \mə-'tərn-əl\ *adj* **1** : MOTHERLY **2** : related through or derived from or derived from a female parent ⟨our ∼ grandparents⟩ — **ma·ter·nal·ly** *adv*

¹**ma·ter·ni·ty** \mə-'tər-nə-tē\ *n, pl* **-ties 1** : the quality or state of being a mother; *also* : MOTHERLINESS **2** : a hospital facility for the care of women before and during childbirth and for newborn babies

²**maternity** *adj* **1** : designed for wear during pregnancy ⟨a ∼ dress⟩ **2** : effective for the period close to and including childbirth ⟨∼ leave⟩

¹**math** \'math\ *n* : MATHEMATICS

²**math** *abbr* mathematical; mathematician

math·e·mat·i·cal \ˌma-thə-'ma-ti-kəl\ *adj* **1** : of, relating to, or according with mathematics **2** ♦ : rigorously exact

♦ accurate, close, delicate, exact, fine, pinpoint, precise, rigorous — more at PRECISE

math·e·mat·ics \ˌma-thə-'ma-tiks\ *n* : the science of numbers and their properties, operations, and relations and with shapes in space and their structure and measurement — **math·e·mat·i·cal·ly** \-ti-k(ə-)lē\ *adv* — **math·e·ma·ti·cian** \ˌma-thə-mə-'ti-shən\ *n*

mat·i·nee *or* **mat·i·née** \ˌma-ᵊn-'ā\ *n* [F *matinée*, lit., morning, fr. OF, fr. *matin* morning, fr. L *matutinum*, fr. neut. of *matutinus* of the morning, fr. *Matuta*, goddess of morning] : a musical or dramatic performance in the daytime and esp. the afternoon

mat·ins \'mat-ᵊnz\ *n pl, often cap* **1** : special prayers said between midnight and 4 a.m. **2** : a morning service of liturgical prayer in Anglican churches

ma·tri·arch \'mā-trē-ˌärk\ *n* ♦ : a woman who rules or dominates a family, group, or state — **ma·tri·ar·chal** \ˌmā-trē-'är-kəl\ *adj* — **ma·tri·ar·chy** \'mā-trē-ˌär-kē\ *n*

♦ dame, dowager, matron; *also* grandam; headmistress, mistress; ma, mama, mom

ma·tri·cide \'ma-trə-ˌsīd, 'mā-\ *n* : the murder of a mother by her child — **ma·tri·cid·al** \ˌma-trə-'sīd-ᵊl, ˌmā-\ *adj*

ma·tric·u·late \mə-'tri-kyə-ˌlāt\ *vb* **-lat·ed; -lat·ing** ♦ : to enroll as a member of a body and esp. of a college or university — **ma·tric·u·la·tion** \-ˌtri-kyə-'lā-shən\ *n*

♦ enroll, inscribe, list, register — more at ENROLL

mat·ri·mo·nial \ˌma-trə-'mō-nē-əl\ *adj* ♦ : of or relating to matrimony — **mat·ri·mo·nial·ly** *adv*

♦ conjugal, connubial, marital, nuptial — more at MARITAL

mat·ri·mo·ny \'ma-trə-ˌmō-nē\ *n* [ME, fr. AF *matrimoignie*, fr. L *matrimonium*, fr. *mater* mother, matron] ♦ : the state of being married : MARRIAGE

♦ marriage, match — more at MARRIAGE

ma·trix \'mā-triks\ *n, pl* **ma·tri·ces** \'mā-trə-ˌsēz, 'mā-\ *or* **ma·trix·es** \'mā-trik-səz\ **1** : something within or from which something else originates, develops, or takes form **2** : a mold from which a relief surface (as a piece of type) is made

ma·tron \'mā-trən\ *n* **1** ♦ : a married woman usu. of dignified maturity or social distinction **2** : a woman supervisor (as in a school or police station) — **ma·tron·ly** *adj*

♦ dame, dowager, matriarch — more at MATRIARCH

Matt *abbr* Matthew

¹**matte** *or* **matt** *var of* ³MAT

²**matte** *also* **mat** *or* **matt** \'mat\ *adj* : not shiny : DULL

¹**mat·ter** \'ma-tər\ *n* **1** ♦ : a subject of interest or concern **2** *pl* : events or circumstances of a particular situation **3** : the subject of a discourse or writing **4** ♦ : a source of perplexity, distress, or vexation : TROUBLE ⟨what's the ∼⟩ **5** : the substance of which a physical object is composed **6** : PUS **7** : an indefinite amount or quantity ⟨a ∼ of a few days⟩ **8** : something written or printed **9** ♦ : something sent through the mail

♦ [1] content, motif, question, subject, theme, topic; *also* idea, point, purpose; issue, problem; body, bulk, burden, core, crux, fundamental, generality, gist, heart, kernel, keynote, main, marrow, mass, nub, nucleus, pith, purport, quick, staple, substance, sum; basis; bottom, essential; affair, argument, debate ♦ [1] affair, business, thing; *also* problem; crisis, crossroad, emergency, exigency, juncture, strait, zero hour; concern, trouble, worry; care, lookout, responsibility; deadlock, impasse, stalemate; corner, fix, hole, hot water, pinch, predicament, scrape, spot ♦ [4] case, knot, problem, trouble — more at PROBLEM ♦ [9] mail, parcel post, post, snail mail — more at MAIL

²**matter** *vb* ♦ : to have significance

♦ count, import, mean, signify, weigh; *also* affect, influence, sway; add up (to), amount (to)

mat·ter-of-fact \ˌma-tə-rəv-'fakt\ *adj* **1** ♦ : adhering to fact **2** : being plain, straightforward, or unemotional — **mat·ter-of-fact·ly** *adv* — **mat·ter-of-fact·ness** *n*

♦ [1] documentary, factual, hard, historical, literal, nonfictional, objective, true — more at FACTUAL

♦ [2] down-to-earth, earthy, hardheaded, practical, pragmatic, realistic — more at REALISTIC

Mat·thew \'ma-thyü\ n : a book of the New Testament of Christian Scripture

mat·tins often cap, chiefly Brit var of MATINS

mat·tock \'ma-tək\ n : a digging and grubbing tool with features of an adze and an ax or pick

mat·tress \'ma-trəs\ n 1 : a fabric case filled with resilient material used as or for a bed 2 : an inflatable airtight sack for use as a mattress

mat·u·rate \'ma-chə-ˌrāt\ vb -rat·ed; -rat·ing : MATURE

mat·u·ra·tion \ˌma-chə-'rā-shən\ n 1 ♦ : the process of maturing 2 : the emergence of personal and behavioral characteristics through growth processes — **mat·u·ra·tion·al** \-shə-nəl\ adj

♦ development, growth; also blossoming, flowering; mellowing, softening

¹**ma·ture** \mə-'tùr, -'tyùr\ adj **ma·tur·er; -est** 1 : based on slow careful consideration 2 ♦ : having attained a final or desired state 3 : of or relating to a condition of full development 4 : due for payment 5 : suitable only for adults — **ma·ture·ly** adv

♦ adult, full-blown, full-fledged, ripe; also aged, aging, old; golden, mellow Ant green, immature, juvenile, un-ripened, young, youthful

²**mature** vb **ma·tured; ma·tur·ing** ♦ : to reach or bring to maturity or completion

♦ age, develop, grow, grow up, progress, ripen; also mellow, soften; bloom, blossom, burgeon, flourish, flower; open, unfold; advance, evolve

ma·tu·ri·ty \mə-'tùr-ə-tē, -'tyùr-\ n 1 : the quality or state of being mature; esp : full development 2 : the date when a note becomes due for payment

ma·tu·ti·nal \ˌma-chù-'tīn-ᵊl; mə-'tüt-ᵊn-əl, -'tyüt-\ adj : of, relating to, or occurring in the morning : EARLY

mat·zo or **mat·zoh** \'mät-sə\ n, pl **mat·zoth** \-ˌsōt, -ˌsōth, -sōs\ or **mat·zos** or **mat·zohs** [Yiddish matse, fr. Heb maṣṣāh] : unleavened bread eaten esp. at Passover

maud·lin \'mòd-lən\ adj [alter. of Mary Magdalene; fr. her depiction as a weeping, penitent sinner] 1 : drunk enough to be silly 2 ♦ : weakly and effusively sentimental

♦ corny, mawkish, mushy, saccharine, sappy, schmaltzy, sentimental — more at CORNY

¹**maul** \'mòl\ n : a heavy hammer often with a wooden head used esp. for driving wedges

²**maul** vb 1 a : to strike repeatedly : BEAT b : MANGLE 2 ♦ : to handle roughly

♦ maltreat, manhandle, mishandle, rough — more at MANHANDLE

maun·der \'mòn-dər\ vb 1 ♦ : to wander slowly and idly 2 ♦ : to speak indistinctly or disconnectedly

♦ [1] gad, gallivant, knock, meander, mope, ramble, range, roam, rove, traipse, wander — more at WANDER

♦ [2] ramble, rattle, run on — more at RAMBLE

mau·so·le·um \ˌmò-sə-'lē-əm, ˌmò-zə-\ n, pl **-leums** or **-lea** \-'lē-ə\ [L, fr. Gk mausoleion, fr. Mausolos Mausolus †ab 353 B.C. ruler of Caria whose tomb was one of the seven wonders of the ancient world] : a large tomb; esp : a usu. stone building for entombment of the dead above ground

mauve \'mōv, 'mòv\ n : a moderate purple, violet, or lilac color

ma·ven also **ma·vin** \'mā-vən\ n [Yiddish meyvn, fr. LHeb mēbhīn] : EXPERT

mav·er·ick \'ma-vrik, -və-rik\ n [Samuel A. Maverick †1870 Am. pioneer who did not brand his calves] 1 : an unbranded range animal 2 ♦ : a person who does not conform to a generally accepted pattern of thought or action : NONCONFORMIST

♦ bohemian, deviant, individualist, loner, nonconform-ist — more at NONCONFORMIST

maw \'mò\ n 1 : STOMACH; also : the crop of a bird 2 : the throat, gullet, or jaws esp. of a voracious animal

mawk·ish \'mò-kish\ adj ♦ : sickly sentimental ⟨~ po-etry⟩ — **mawk·ish·ly** adv

♦ corny, maudlin, mushy, saccharine, sappy, schmaltzy, sentimental — more at CORNY

mawk·ish·ness \-nəs\ n ♦ : the quality or state of being mawkish

♦ mush, sentimentality — more at SENTIMENTALITY

max abbr maximum

maxi \'mak-sē\ n, pl **max·is** : a long skirt, dress, or coat

maxi- comb form 1 : extra long ⟨maxi-kilt⟩ 2 : extra large ⟨maxi-problems⟩

max·il·la \mak-'si-lə\ n, pl **max·il·lae** \-'si-(ˌ)lē\ or **maxillas** : JAW 1; esp : an upper jaw — **max·il·lary** \'mak-sə-ˌler-ē\ adj

max·im \'mak-səm\ n ♦ : a proverbial saying

♦ adage, aphorism, byword, epigram, proverb, saying — more at SAYING

max·i·mal \'mak-sə-məl\ adj : MAXIMUM — **max·i·mal·ly** adv

max·i·mise chiefly Brit var of MAXIMIZE

max·i·mize \'mak-sə-ˌmīz\ vb -mized; -miz·ing 1 : to in-crease to a maximum 2 : to make the most of 3 : to in-crease the size of a computer program's window to fill an entire screen — **max·i·mi·za·tion** \ˌmak-sə-mə-'zā-shən\ n

¹**max·i·mum** \'mak-sə-məm\ n, pl **-ma** \-mə\ or **-mums** 1 : the greatest quantity, value, or degree 2 : an upper limit al-lowed by authority 3 : the largest of a set of numbers

²**maximum** adj ♦ : greatest in quantity or highest in degree attainable or attained

♦ consummate, full, most, nth, paramount, supreme, top, ultimate, utmost — more at ULTIMATE

max out vb 1 : to push to or reach a limit or an extreme 2 : to use up all available credit on (a credit card)

may \'mā\ verbal auxiliary, past **might** \'mīt\ pres sing & pl **may** 1 : have permission or liberty to ⟨you ~ go now⟩ 2 : be in some degree likely to ⟨you ~ be right⟩ 3 — used as an auxiliary to express a wish, purpose, contin-gency, or concession

May \'mā\ n [ME, fr. OF mai, fr. L Maius, fr. Maia, Roman goddess] : the 5th month of the year

Ma·ya \'mī-ə\ n, pl **Maya** or **Mayas** : a member of a group of American Indian peoples of Yucatán, Guatemala, and adjacent areas — **Ma·yan** \'mī-ən\ n or adj

may·ap·ple \'mā-ˌa-pəl\ n : a No. American woodland herb related to the barberry that has a poisonous root, one or two large leaves, and an edible egg-shaped yellow fruit

may·be \'mā-bē, 'me-\ adv ♦ : possibly but not certainly : PERHAPS

♦ conceivably, perchance, perhaps, possibly — more at PERHAPS

May Day \'mā-ˌdā\ n : May 1 celebrated as a springtime festival and in some countries as Labor Day

may·flow·er \'mā-ˌflaù-ər\ n : any of several spring bloom-ing herbs (as the trailing arbutus or an anemone)

may·fly \'mā-flī\ n : any of an order of insects with an aquatic nymph and a short-lived fragile adult having membranous wings

may·hem \'mā-ˌhem, 'mā-əm\ n 1 : willful and perma-nent crippling, mutilation, or disfigurement of a person 2 : needless or willful damage

may·on·naise \'mā-ə-ˌnāz\ n [F] : a dressing made of egg yolks, vegetable oil, and vinegar or lemon juice

may·or \'mā-ər\ n : an official elected to act as chief exec-utive or nominal head of a city or borough — **may·or·al** \-əl\ adj — **may·or·al·ty** \-əl-tē\ n

may·pole \'mā-ˌpōl\ n, often cap : a tall flower-wreathed pole forming a center for May Day sports and dances

maze \'māz\ n : a confusing intricate network of passages — **mazy** adj

ma·zur·ka \mə-'zər-kə\ n : a Polish dance in moderate tri-ple measure

MB abbr Manitoba

MBA abbr master of business administration

mc abbr megacycle

Mc *symbol* moscovium

¹**MC** *n* : MASTER OF CEREMONIES

²**MC** *abbr* member of Congress

Mc- \mək; mə *before forms beginning with* k *or* g\ *prefix* : used to indicate a convenient, low-quality version of a specified thing ⟨*McBook*⟩

Mc·Coy \mə-ˈkȯi\ *n* : something that is neither imitation nor substitute ⟨the real ∼⟩

McGuffin *var of* MACGUFFIN

MCPO *abbr* master chief petty officer

¹**Md** *abbr* Maryland

²**Md** *symbol* mendelevium

MD *abbr* **1** [NL *medicinae doctor*] doctor of medicine **2** Maryland **3** muscular dystrophy

MDMA \ˌem-ˌdē-ˌem-ˈā\ *n* : ECSTASY 2

mdnt *abbr* midnight

mdse *abbr* merchandise

MDT *abbr* mountain daylight (saving) time

me \ˈmē\ *pron, objective case of* I

Me *abbr* Maine

ME *abbr* **1** Maine **2** mechanical engineer **3** medical examiner

¹**mead** \ˈmēd\ *n* : an alcoholic beverage brewed from water and honey, malt, and yeast

²**mead** *n, archaic* : MEADOW

mead·ow \ˈme-dō\ *n* : land in or mainly in grass; *esp* : a tract of moist low-lying usu. level grassland — **mead·ow·land** \-ˌland\ *n* — **mead·owy** \ˈme-də-wē\ *adj*

mead·ow·lark \ˈme-dō-ˌlärk\ *n* : any of several American songbirds related to the orioles that are streaked brown above and in northernmost forms have a yellow breast marked with a black crescent

mead·ow·sweet \-ˌswēt\ *n* : a No. American native or naturalized spirea

mea·ger *or* **mea·gre** \ˈmē-gər\ *adj* **1** : THIN **2 a** : lacking richness, fertility, or strength **b** ♦ : deficient in quality or quantity : POOR — **mea·ger·ly** *adv* — **mea·ger·ness** *n*

 ♦ light, niggardly, poor, scant, scanty, scarce, skimpy, slender, slim, spare, sparse, stingy; *also* deficient, inadequate, insufficient, lacking, wanting; bare, mere, minimum; slight, small; barren, infertile, sterile, unfruitful, unproductive *Ant* abundant, ample, bountiful, copious, generous, liberal, plenteous, plentiful

¹**meal** \ˈmēl\ *n* **1** : an act or the time of eating a portion of food **2** ♦ : the portion of food eaten at a meal

 ♦ board, chow, feed, mess, repast, table; *also* breakfast, buffet, dinner, lunch, luncheon, refreshments, smorgasbord, snack, supper, tea; bite, gulp, morsel, serving, taste; banquet, feast, spread; bake, barbecue, clambake, cookout, fry, luau, picnic, potluck, roast

²**meal** *n* **1** : usu. coarsely ground seeds of a cereal **2** : a product resembling seed meal

meal·time \ˈmēl-ˌtīm\ *n* : the usual time at which a meal is served

mealy \ˈmē-lē\ *adj* ♦ : not plain and straightforward

 ♦ artificial, double-dealing, feigned, hypocritical, insincere, left-handed, mealymouthed, two-faced, unctuous — more at INSINCERE

mealy·bug \ˈmē-lē-ˌbəg\ *n* : any of a family of scale insects with a white cottony or waxy covering that are destructive pests esp. of fruit trees

mealy·mouthed \ˈmē-lē-ˌmau̇thd, -ˌmau̇tht\ *adj* ♦ : not plain and straightforward ⟨a ∼ politician⟩

 ♦ artificial, double-dealing, feigned, hypocritical, insincere, left-handed, mealy, two-faced, unctuous — more at INSINCERE

¹**mean** \ˈmēn\ *vb* **meant** \ˈment\; **mean·ing** **1** ♦ : to have in the mind as a purpose **2** ♦ : to serve to convey, show, or indicate : SIGNIFY **3** ♦ : to have importance to the degree of **4** : to direct to a particular individual

 ♦ [1] aim, aspire, contemplate, design, intend, meditate, plan, propose — more at INTEND ♦ [2] denote, express, import, signify, spell; *also* connote, imply, suggest; add up (to), amount (to); hint, insinuate, intimate; embody, epitomize, personify, represent, symbolize; advert, allude (to), mention, refer (to), indicate, point (to), signal; announce, declare; elucidate, explain ♦ [3] count, import, matter, signify, weigh — more at MATTER

²**mean** *adj* **1** ♦ : lacking distinction or eminence : HUMBLE **2** : lacking acumen : DULL **3 a** ♦ : of poor shabby inferior quality or status **b** ♦ : worthy of little regard **4** ♦ : lacking dignity or honor : IGNOBLE, BASE **5** : sparing or scant in using, giving, or spending : STINGY **6** ♦ : pettily selfish or malicious **7** : VEXATIOUS **8** : very good of its kind : EXCELLENT

 ♦ [1] common, humble, ignoble, inferior, low, lowly, plebeian, vulgar — more at IGNOBLE ♦ [3a] dilapidated, grungy, neglected, ratty, seedy, shabby — more at SHABBY ♦ [3b] inferior, minor, secondary second-rate — more at INFERIOR ♦ [4] base, contemptible, despicable, detestable, dirty, dishonorable (*or* dishonourable), ignoble, low, snide, sordid, vile, wretched — more at IGNOBLE ♦ [6] catty, cruel, hateful, malevolent, malicious, malign, malignant, nasty, spiteful, virulent — more at HATEFUL

³**mean** *adj* **1** : occupying a middle position (as in space, order, or time) **2** : being a mean : AVERAGE ⟨a ∼ value⟩

⁴**mean** *n* **1** ♦ : a middle point between extremes **2** *pl* ♦ : something helpful in achieving a desired end **3** *pl* ♦ : material resources affording a secure life **4** : ARITHMETIC MEAN

 ♦ [1] medium, middle, midpoint; *also* arithmetic mean, average; median, norm, par, standard **means** *pl* ♦ [2] agency, agent, instrument, instrumentality, machinery, medium, organ, vehicle — more at AGENT **means** *pl* ♦ [3] assets, capital, fortune, opulence, riches, substance, wealth, wherewithal — more at WEALTH

¹**me·an·der** \mē-ˈan-dər\ *n* [L *maeander*, fr. Gk *maiandros*, fr. *Maiandros* (now *Menderes*), river in Asia Minor] **1** : a winding course **2** : a winding of a stream

²**meander** *vb* **1** : to follow a winding course **2** ♦ : to wander aimlessly or casually

 ♦ gad, gallivant, knock, maunder, mope, ramble, range, roam, rove, traipse, wander — more at WANDER

mean·ing *n* **1** ♦ : the thing one intends to convey esp. by language; *also* : the thing that is thus conveyed **2** ♦ : something meant or intended : AIM **3** : SIGNIFICANCE; *esp* : implication of a hidden significance **4** ♦ : the logical connotation of a word or phrase; *also* : DENOTATION

 ♦ [1, 4] denotation, drift, import, intent, purport, sense, significance, signification; *also* connotation; hint, implication, intimation, suggestion; message, tenor, theme; bottom, essence, nature, soul, stuff; acceptance, definition; burden, crux, gist; core, heart, kernel, marrow, nub, nucleus, pith, point, quick; matter, motif, motive, subject, topic ♦ [2] aim, ambition, aspiration, design, dream, end, goal, intent, mark, object, objective, plan, pretension, purpose, thing — more at GOAL

mean·ing·ful \-fəl\ *adj* ♦ : full of meaning : SIGNIFICANT — **mean·ing·ful·ly** *adv*

 ♦ eloquent, expressive, meaning, pregnant, significant, suggestive — more at EXPRESSIVE ♦ big, consequential, eventful, important, major, material, momentous, significant, substantial, weighty — more at IMPORTANT

mean·ing·less \-ləs\ *adj* ♦ : having no meaning

 ♦ empty, pointless, senseless; *also* insignificant, trivial, unimportant; absurd, asinine, balmy, brainless, crazy, daffy, daft, fatuous, foolish, half-witted, harebrained, insane, jerky, kooky, lunatic, mad, mindless, nonsensical, nutty, preposterous, sappy, silly, unintelligent, unwise, wacky, witless, zany; irrational, unreasonable; aimless, haphazard, purposeless *Ant* meaningful

mean·ly \ˈmēn-lē\ *adv* ♦ : in a mean manner

♦ hatefully, maliciously, nastily, spitefully, viciously, wickedly — more at NASTILY

mean·ness \'mēn-nəs\ n ♦ : the quality or state of being mean

♦ cattiness, despite, hatefulness, malice, malignity, nastiness, spite, spleen, venom, viciousness — more at MALICE

¹**mean·time** \'mēn-ˌtīm\ n : the intervening time
²**meantime** adv : MEANWHILE
¹**mean·while** \-ˌhwī(-ə)l\ n : MEANTIME
²**meanwhile** adv 1 : during the intervening time 2 : at the same time
meas abbr measure
mea·sles \'mē-zəlz\ n sing or pl : an acute virus disease marked by fever and an eruption of distinct circular red spots
mea·sly \'mēz-lē, -zə-lē\ adj **mea·sli·er; -est** ♦ : contemptibly small or insignificant

♦ inconsequential, inconsiderable, insignificant, minute, negligible, nominal, paltry, petty, slight, trifling, trivial — more at NEGLIGIBLE

¹**mea·sure** \'me-zhər, 'mā-\ n 1 : an adequate or moderate portion; also : a suitable limit 2 ♦ : the dimensions, capacity, or amount of something ascertained by measuring; also : an instrument for measuring 3 : a unit of measurement; also : a system of such units 4 : the act or process of measuring 5 ♦ : rhythmic structure or movement 6 : the part of a musical staff between two bars 7 ♦ : a basis or standard of comparison : CRITERION 8 ♦ : a means to an end 9 : a legislative bill 10 ♦ : the total number or quantity

♦ [2] dimension, extent, magnitude, measurement, proportion, size — more at SIZE ♦ [5] beat, cadence, meter (or metre), rhythm — more at RHYTHM ♦ [7] criterion, grade, mark, par, standard, touchstone, yardstick — more at STANDARD ♦ [8] expedient, move, shift, step; also act, deed, doing, feat, thing; procedure, proceeding, process; attempt, endeavor, essay, initiative, operation, undertaking; effort, exertion, labor, pains, trouble, work; makeshift, resort, resource, stopgap ♦ [10] amount, quantity — more at AMOUNT

²**measure** vb **mea·sured; mea·sur·ing** 1 : to mark or fix in multiples of a specific unit ⟨~ off five centimeters⟩ 2 ♦ : to ascertain the measurements of 3 : to bring into comparison or competition 4 : to serve as a means of measuring 5 : to have a specified measurement — **mea·sur·able** \'me-zhə-rə-bəl, 'mā-\ adj — **mea·sur·ably** \-blē\ adv — **mea·sur·er** n

♦ gauge, scale, span; also weigh; calibrate; lay off, mark (off); calculate, compute, figure, reckon, work out; conjecture, estimate, guess, judge, suppose; add up, sum, tally, total; ascertain, discover, dope (out), figure out, find out

measured adj 1 ♦ : marked by rhythm 2 ♦ : confined within limits 3 ♦ : characterized by or resulting from careful and thorough consideration : DELIBERATE, CALCULATED

♦ [1] cadenced, metrical, rhythmic — more at RHYTHMIC ♦ [2] definite, determinate, finite, limited, narrow, restricted — more at LIMITED ♦ [3] advised, calculated, deliberate, reasoned, studied, thoughtful, thought-out — more at DELIBERATE

mea·sure·less \-ləs\ adj 1 ♦ : having no observable limit 2 ♦ : very great ⟨had ~ energy⟩

♦ [1, 2] boundless, endless, illimitable, immeasurable, indefinite, infinite, limitless, unbounded, unfathomable, unlimited — more at INFINITE

mea·sure·ment \'me-zhər-mənt, 'mā-\ n 1 : the act or process of measuring 2 ♦ : a figure, extent, or amount obtained by measuring

♦ dimension, extent, magnitude, measure, proportion, size — more at SIZE

measure up vb 1 : to have necessary or fitting qualifications — often used with to 2 ♦ : to equal esp. in ability — used with to

♦ usu **measure up to** approach, approximate, compare, stack up — more at APPROXIMATE

meat \'mēt\ n ♦ : material taken into an organism and used for growth, repair, and vital processes and as a source of energy : FOOD; esp : solid food as distinguished from drink 2 : animal and esp. mammal flesh considered as food 3 : the edible part inside a covering (as a shell or rind) — **meaty** adj

♦ chow, fare, food, grub, provender, provisions, viands, victuals — more at FOOD

meat·ball \-ˌbȯl\ n : a small ball of chopped or ground meat
meat loaf n : a dish of ground meat seasoned and baked in the form of a loaf
mec·ca \'me-kə\ n, often cap [Mecca, Saudi Arabia, a destination of pilgrims in the Islamic world] ♦ : a center of a specified activity or interest

♦ base, center (or centre), core, cynosure, eye, focus, heart, hub, nucleus, seat — more at CENTER

mech abbr mechanical; mechanics
¹**me·chan·ic** \mi-'ka-nik\ adj : of or relating to manual work or skill
²**mechanic** n 1 : a manual worker 2 : MACHINIST; esp : one who repairs cars
me·chan·i·cal \mi-'ka-ni-kəl\ adj 1 : of or relating to machinery, manual operations, or mechanics 2 ♦ : done as if by a machine — **me·chan·i·cal·ly** \-k(ə-)lē\ adv

♦ automatic, involuntary, spontaneous — more at AUTOMATIC

mechanical drawing n : drawing done with the aid of instruments
me·chan·ics \mi-'ka-niks\ n sing or pl 1 : a branch of physics that deals with energy and forces and their effect on bodies 2 : the practical application of mechanics (as to the operation of machines) 3 : mechanical or functional details
mech·a·nism \'me-kə-ˌni-zəm\ n 1 : a piece of machinery; also : a process or technique for achieving a result 2 : mechanical operation or action 3 : the fundamental processes involved in or responsible for a natural phenomenon ⟨the visual ~⟩
mech·a·nis·tic \ˌme-kə-'nis-tik\ adj 1 : mechanically determined ⟨~ universe⟩ 2 : MECHANICAL — **mech·a·nis·ti·cal·ly** \-ti-k(ə-)lē\ adv
mech·a·nize \'me-kə-ˌnīz\ vb **-nized; -niz·ing** 1 : to make mechanical 2 : to equip with machinery esp. in order to replace human or animal labor 3 : to equip with armed and armored motor vehicles — **mech·a·ni·za·tion** \ˌme-kə-nə-'zā-shən\ n — **mech·a·niz·er** n
med abbr 1 medical; medicine 2 medieval 3 medium
MEd abbr master of education
med·al \'med-ᵊl\ n [MF medaille, fr. OIt medaglia coin worth half a denarius, medal, fr. VL *medalis half, alter. of LL medialis middle, fr. L medius] 1 : a small usu. metal object bearing a religious emblem or picture 2 : a piece of metal issued to commemorate a person or event or to award excellence or achievement
med·al·ist or **med·al·list** \'med-ᵊl-ist\ n 1 : a designer or maker of medals 2 : a recipient of a medal as an award
me·dal·lion \mə-'dal-yən\ n 1 : a large medal 2 : a tablet or panel bearing a portrait or an ornament
med·dle \'med-ᵊl\ vb **med·dled; med·dling** ♦ : to interfere without right or propriety

♦ butt in, interfere, intrude, mess, nose, obtrude, poke, pry, snoop — more at INTERFERE

med·dler \'med-ᵊl-ər\ n ♦ : one that meddles

♦ busybody, interloper, intruder, kibitzer — more at BUSYBODY

med·dle·some \'med-ᵊl-səm\ adj ♦ : inclined to meddle

♦ intrusive, nosy, obtrusive, officious, presumptuous, prying — more at INTRUSIVE

med·e·vac *also* **med·i·vac** \'me-də-ˌvak\ *n* **1** : emergency evacuation of the sick or wounded **2** : a helicopter used for medevac

me·dia \'mē-dē-ə\ *n, pl* **me·di·as** **1** : MEDIUM 4 **2** *sing or pl in constr* : MASS MEDIA

me·di·al \'mē-dē-əl\ *adj* : occurring in or extending toward the middle

¹**me·di·an** \'mē-dē-ən\ *n* **1** : a value in an ordered set of values below and above which there are an equal number of values **2** : MEDIAN STRIP

²**median** *adj* **1** ♦ : being in the middle or in an intermediate position **2** ♦ : relating to or constituting a statistical median

♦ [1] halfway, intermediary, intermediate, medium, middle, midmost — more at MIDDLE ♦ [2] average, middle, moderate, modest — more at MIDDLE

median strip *n* : a strip dividing a highway into lanes according to the direction of travel

me·di·ate \'mē-dē-ˌāt\ *vb* **-at·ed; -at·ing** **1** ♦ : to act as an intermediary; *esp* : to work with opposing sides in order to resolve (as a dispute) or bring about (as a settlement) **2** : to bring about, influence, or transmit (as a physical process or effect) by acting as an intermediate or controlling agent or mechanism — **me·di·a·tion** \ˌmē-dē-'ā-shən\ *n*

♦ intercede, interpose, intervene — more at INTERVENE

me·di·a·tor \'mē-dē-ˌā-tər\ *n* ♦ : one that mediates

♦ arbiter, arbitrator, broker, go-between, intercessor, intermediary, middleman, peacemaker; *also* moderator; negotiator; pacifier, reconciler; agent, attorney, deputy, factor, procurator, proxy; liaison; ambassador, emissary, envoy, messenger; delegate, representative; busybody, meddler; judge, referee, umpire; advisor, counselor

med·ic \'me-dik\ *n* : one engaged in medical work; *esp* : CORPSMAN

med·i·ca·ble \'me-di-kə-bəl\ *adj* : CURABLE

Med·ic·aid \'me-di-ˌkād\ *n* : a program of financial assistance for medical care designed for those unable to afford regular medical service and financed jointly by the state and federal governments

med·i·cal \'me-di-kəl\ *adj* : of or relating to the science or practice of medicine or the treatment of disease — **med·i·cal·ly** \-k(ə-)lē\ *adv*

medical examiner *n* : a public officer who performs autopsies on bodies to find the cause of death

med·i·ca·ment \mi-'di-kə-mənt, 'me-di-kə-\ *n* : a substance used in therapy

Medi·care \'me-di-ˌker\ *n* : a government program of financial assistance for medical care esp. for the aged

med·i·cate \'me-də-ˌkāt\ *vb* **-cat·ed; -cat·ing** : to treat with medicine

med·i·ca·tion \ˌme-də-'kā-shən\ *n* **1** : the act or process of medicating **2** : a substance or preparation used in treating disease : MEDICINE

me·dic·i·nal \mə-'dis-ᵊn-əl\ *adj* : tending or used to cure disease or relieve pain — **me·dic·i·nal·ly** *adv*

med·i·cine \'me-də-sən\ *n* **1** ♦ : a substance or preparation used in treating disease **2** : a science and art dealing with the prevention, alleviation, and cure of disease

♦ cure, drug, pharmaceutical, remedy, specific; *also* botanical, patent medicine, prescription; cordial, tonic; miracle drug, wonder drug; capsule, pill, tablet; injection, shot; liniment, lotion, ointment, potion, poultice, salve; syrup, tincture; antibiotic, antiseptic, serum

medicine ball *n* : a heavy stuffed leather ball used for conditioning exercises

medicine man *n* : a priestly healer or sorcerer esp. among the American Indians : SHAMAN

med·i·co \'me-di-ˌkō\ *n, pl* **-cos** : a medical practitioner or student

me·di·e·val *or* **me·di·ae·val** \ˌmē-dē-'ē-vəl, ˌme-, mē-'dē-vəl\ *adj* **1** : of, relating to, or characteristic of the Middle Ages

2 : extremely outmoded or antiquated — **me·di·e·val·ism** \-və-ˌli-zəm\ *n* — **me·di·e·val·ist** \-list\ *n*

me·di·o·cre \ˌmē-dē-'ō-kər\ *adj* [MF, fr. L *mediocris*, fr. *medius* middle + *ocris* stony mountain] ♦ : of moderate or low quality — **me·di·oc·ri·ty** \-'ä-krə-tē\ *n*

♦ common, fair, indifferent, medium, middling, ordinary, passable, run-of-the-mill, second-rate, so-so; *also* acceptable, adequate, all right, alright, decent, OK, reasonable, satisfactory, sufficient, sufficing, tolerable; moderate, modest; presentable, respectable; minimal, unexceptional; fine, good, nice

med·i·tate \'me-də-ˌtāt\ *vb* **-tat·ed; -tat·ing** **1** ♦ : to muse over : CONTEMPLATE, PONDER **2** : to plan or project in the mind : INTEND — **med·i·ta·tion** \ˌme-də-'tā-shən\ *n*

♦ chew over, cogitate, consider, contemplate, debate, deliberate, entertain, mull, ponder, question, ruminate, study, think, weigh — more at PONDER

med·i·ta·tive \'me-də-ˌtā-tiv\ *adj* **1** ♦ : marked by or conducive to meditation **2** ♦ : disposed or given to meditation — **med·i·ta·tive·ly** *adv*

♦ [1, 2] contemplative, melancholy, pensive, reflective, ruminant, thoughtful — more at CONTEMPLATIVE

Med·i·ter·ra·nean \ˌme-də-tə-'rā-nē-ən, -'rā-nyən\ *adj* : of or relating to the Mediterranean Sea or to the lands or people around it

¹**me·di·um** \'mē-dē-əm\ *n, pl* **mediums** *or* **me·dia** \-dē-ə\ [L] **1 a** : something in a middle position **b** ♦ : a middle position or degree **2** ♦ : a means of effecting or conveying something **3** : a surrounding or enveloping substance **4** : a channel or system of communication, information, or entertainment **5** : a mode of artistic expression **6** : an individual held to be a channel of communication between the earthly world and a world of spirits **7** ♦ : a condition or environment in which something may function or flourish

♦ [1b] mean, middle, midpoint — more at MEAN ♦ [2] agency, agent, instrument, instrumentality, machinery, means, organ, vehicle — more at AGENT ♦ [7] atmosphere, climate, environment, environs, milieu, setting, surroundings — more at ENVIRONMENT

²**medium** *adj* ♦ : intermediate in amount, quality, position, or degree

♦ average, intermediate, median, middle, moderate, modest — more at MIDDLE ♦ halfway, middle, midmost — more at MIDDLE ♦ common, fair, indifferent, mediocre, middling, ordinary, passable, run-of-the-mill, second-rate, so-so — more at MEDIOCRE

me·di·um·is·tic \ˌmē-dē-ə-'mis-tik\ *adj* : of, relating to, or being a spiritualistic medium

medivac *var of* MEDEVAC

med·ley \'med-lē\ *n, pl* **medleys** **1** ♦ : a diverse assortment or mixture : HODGEPODGE **2** : a musical composition made up esp. of a series of songs

♦ assortment, clutter, jumble, mélange, miscellany, motley, muddle, variety, welter — more at MISCELLANY

me·dul·la \mə-'də-lə\ *n, pl* **-las** *or* **-lae** \-(ˌ)lē, -ˌlī\ : an inner or deep anatomical part; *also* : the posterior part (**medulla ob·lon·ga·ta** \-ˌä-ˌblȯŋ-'gä-tə\) of the vertebrate brain that is continuous with the spinal cord

meed \'mēd\ *n* : a fitting return

meek \'mēk\ *adj* **1** ♦ : characterized by patience and long-suffering **2** : deficient in spirit and courage **3** : MODERATE

♦ demure, humble, lowly, modest, retiring, unassuming, unpretentious — more at HUMBLE

meek·ly \-lē\ *adv* ♦ : in a meek manner

♦ humbly, lowly, modestly, sheepishly

meek·ness \-nəs\ *n* ♦ : the quality or state of being meek

♦ humbleness, humility, lowliness, modesty — more at HUMILITY

meer·schaum \'mir-shəm, -ˌshȯm\ *n* [G, fr. *Meer* sea + *Schaum* foam] : a tobacco pipe made of a light white clayey mineral

¹meet \'mēt\ *vb* **met** \'met\; **meet·ing 1 ♦** : to come upon **2** : JOIN, INTERSECT **3** : to appear to the perception of **4** : OPPOSE, FIGHT **5 a** : to join in conversation or discussion **b ♦** : to come together : ASSEMBLE **6** : to conform to ⟨~s requirements⟩ **7 ♦** : to pay fully or fulfill the obligations of **8 a** : to contend successfully with : cope with **b ♦** : to produce or provide a counterpart or equal to : MATCH **9** : to provide for **10** : to be introduced to

♦ [1] chance, encounter, happen, stumble; *also* accost, confront; face, greet, salute; crash (into), collide (with); crisscross, cross, pass; hit (upon), light (upon), tumble (to) **♦** [5b] assemble, cluster, collect, concentrate, conglomerate, congregate, convene, forgather, gather, rendezvous — more at ASSEMBLE **♦** [7] answer, comply, fill, fulfill, keep, redeem, satisfy — more at FULFILL **♦** [8b] equal, match, tie

²meet *n* **♦** : an assembling esp. for a hunt or for competitive sports

♦ bout, competition, contest, event, game, match, tournament — more at GAME

³meet *adj* **♦** : precisely adapted to a particular situation, need, or circumstance : SUITABLE, PROPER

♦ applicable, appropriate, apt, felicitous, fit, fitting, good, happy, proper, right, suitable — more at FIT

meet·ing \'mē-tiŋ\ *n* **1 ♦** : the act or process of coming together : ASSEMBLY **2 ♦** : a point where things come together

♦ [1] assembly, conference, congress, convention, convocation, council, gathering, get-together, huddle, powwow, seminar; *also* caucus, conclave, synod; demonstration, rally; conversation, dialogue, discourse, discussion, palaver, talk; negotiation, parley; audience, interview, session **♦** [2] confluence, conjunction, convergence — more at CONVERGENCE

meet·ing·house \-ˌhau̇s\ *n* : a building for public assembly and esp. for Protestant worship

meg \'meg\ *n* : MEGABYTE

mega- *or* **meg-** *comb form* **1** : great : large ⟨*mega*hit⟩ **2** : million ⟨*mega*hertz⟩

mega·byte \'me-gə-ˌbīt\ *n* : 1024 kilobytes or 1,048,576 bytes; *also* : one million bytes

mega·cy·cle \-ˌsī-kəl\ *n* : MEGAHERTZ

mega·death \-ˌdeth\ *n* : one million deaths — used as a unit in reference to nuclear warfare

mega·hertz \'me-gə-ˌhəṙts, -ˌheṙts\ *n* : a unit of frequency equal to one million hertz

mega·lith \'me-gə-ˌlith\ *n* : a large stone used in prehistoric monuments — **mega·lith·ic** \ˌme-gə-'li-thik\ *adj*

meg·a·lo·ma·nia \ˌme-gə-lō-'mā-nē-ə, -nyə\ *n* : a mental disorder marked by feelings of personal omnipotence and grandeur — **meg·a·lo·ma·ni·ac** \-'mā-nē-ˌak\ *adj or n*

meg·a·lop·o·lis \ˌme-gə-'lä-pə-ləs\ *n* : a very large urban unit

mega·phone \'me-gə-ˌfōn\ *n* : a cone-shaped device used to intensify or direct the voice — **megaphone** *vb*

mega·pix·el \'me-gə-ˌpik-səl\ *n* : one million pixels

mega·plex \-ˌpleks\ *n* : a cineplex having usu. at least 16 movie theaters

mega·ton \-ˌtən\ *n* : an explosive force equivalent to that of one million tons of TNT

mega·vi·ta·min \-ˌvī-tə-mən\ *adj* : relating to or consisting of very large doses of vitamins — **mega·vi·ta·mins** *n pl*

meh \'me\ *interj* — used to express indifference or mild disappointment

mei·o·sis \mī-'ō-səs\ *n* : a process of cell division in gamete-producing cells in which the number of chromosomes is reduced to one half — **mei·ot·ic** \mī-'ä-tik\ *adj*

meit·ner·i·um \mīt-'nir-ē-əm, -'ner-\ *n* : an artificially produced radioactive chemical element

mel·an·cho·lia \ˌme-lən-'kō-lē-ə\ *n* : a mental condition marked by extreme depression often with delusions

mel·an·chol·ic \ˌme-lən-'kä-lik\ *adj* **1** : DEPRESSED **2** : of or relating to melancholia

¹mel·an·choly \'me-lən-ˌkä-lē\ *n, pl* **-chol·ies** [ME *malencolie*, fr. AF, fr. LL *melancholia*, fr. Gk, fr. *melan-, melas* black + *cholē* bile; so called fr. the former belief that it was caused by an excess of black bile] **♦** : depression of spirits : DEJECTION — **melancholy** *adj*

♦ blues, dejection, depression, desolation, despondency, doldrums, dumps, forlornness, gloom, heartsickness, sadness — more at SADNESS

²melancholy *adj* **1 a** : suggestive or expressive of melancholy **b ♦** : causing or tending to cause sadness or depression of mind or spirit **2 a ♦** : depressed in spirits **b** : musingly or dreamily thoughtful

♦ [1b] depressing, dismal, dreary, heartbreaking, pathetic, sad, sorry, tearful — more at SAD **♦** [2a] blue, depressed, down, downcast, glum, low, sad, unhappy

Mel·a·ne·sian \ˌme-lə-'nē-zhən\ *n* : a member of the dominant native group of the Pacific island grouping of Melanesia — **Melanesian** *adj*

mé·lange \mā-'länzh, -'länj\ *n* **♦** : a mixture esp. of incongruous elements

♦ assortment, clutter, jumble, medley, miscellany, motley, muddle, variety, welter — more at MISCELLANY

mel·a·nin \'me-lə-nən\ *n* : any of various dark brown pigments of animal or plant structures (as skin or hair)

mel·a·nism \'me-lə-ˌni-zəm\ *n* : an increased amount of black or nearly black pigmentation

mel·a·no·ma \ˌme-lə-'nō-mə\ *n, pl* **-mas** *also* **-ma·ta** \-mə-tə\ : a usu. malignant tumor containing dark pigment

¹meld \'meld\ *vb* : to show or announce for a score in a card game

²meld *n* : a card or combination of cards that is or can be melded

³meld *n* : a product of blending : BLEND, MIXTURE

me·lee \'mā-ˌlā, mā-'lā\ *n* [F *mêlée*] **♦** : a confused struggle

♦ brawl, fracas, fray, free-for-all, row — more at BRAWL

me·lio·rate \'mēl-yə-ˌrāt, 'mē-lē-ə-\ *vb* **-rat·ed; -rat·ing** : to make or grow better : AMELIORATE — **me·lio·ra·tion** \ˌmēl-yə-'rā-shən, ˌmē-lē-ə-\ *n* — **me·lio·ra·tive** \'mēl-yə-ˌrā-tiv, 'mē-lē-ə-\ *adj*

mel·lif·lu·ous \me-'li-flə-wəs, mə-\ *adj* [ME *mellyfluous*, fr. LL *mellifluus*, fr. L *mel* honey + *fluere* to flow] **♦** : sweetly flowing — **mel·lif·lu·ous·ly** *adv* — **mel·lif·lu·ous·ness** *n*

♦ euphonious, lyric, mellow, melodic, melodious, musical — more at LYRIC

¹mel·low \'me-lō\ *adj* **1** : soft and sweet because of ripeness; *also* : well aged and pleasingly mild ⟨~ wine⟩ **2** : made gentle by age or experience **3** : being rich and full but not garish or strident ⟨~ colors⟩ **4** : of soft loamy consistency ⟨~ soil⟩ — **mel·low·ness** *n*

♦ balmy, benign, bland, delicate, gentle, light, mild, soft, soothing, tender — more at GENTLE

²mellow *vb* : to make or become mellow

me·lod·ic \mə-'lä-dik\ *adj* **♦** : relating to, containing, constituting, or made up of melody — **me·lod·i·cal·ly** \-di-k(ə-)lē\ *adv*

♦ euphonious, lyric, mellifluous, mellow, melodious, musical — more at LYRIC

me·lo·di·ous \mə-'lō-dē-əs\ *adj* **♦** : pleasing to the ear ⟨a ~ sound⟩ — **me·lo·di·ous·ly** *adv* — **me·lo·di·ous·ness** *n*

♦ lyric, mellifluous, mellow, melodic, musical — more at LYRIC **♦** euphonious, harmonious, musical, symphonic, tuneful — more at HARMONIOUS

melo·dra·ma \'me-lə-ˌdrä-mə, -ˌdra-\ *n* **1** : an extravagantly theatrical play in which action and plot predominate over characterization **2** : something having a sensational or theatrical quality — **melo·dra·ma·tist** \ˌme-lə-'dra-mə-tist, -'drä-\ *n*

melo·dra·mat·ic \ˌme-lə-drə-'ma-tik\ *adj* **1 ♦** : of, relating to, or characteristic of melodrama **2** : appealing to the emotions — **melo·dra·mat·i·cal·ly** \-ti-k(ə-)lē\ *adv*

♦ dramatic, histrionic, theatrical — more at THEATRICAL

mel·o·dy \'me-lə-dē\ *n, pl* **-dies** **1** : sweet or agreeable sound **2** ♦ : a particular succession of notes : TUNE, AIR

♦ air, lay, song, strain, tune, warble; *also* descant; cadence, measure, meter, rhythm; ballad, ditty, hymn, lyric, madrigal

mel·on \'me-lən\ *n* : any of various typically sweet fruits (as a muskmelon or watermelon) of the gourd family usu. eaten raw

¹**melt** \'melt\ *vb* **1** ♦ : to change from a solid to a liquid state usu. by heat **2 a** : DISSOLVE, DISINTEGRATE **b** ♦ : to disperse or disappear or cause to disperse or disappear as if melting **3** : to make or become tender or gentle

♦ [1] deliquesce, flux, fuse, liquefy, run, thaw — more at LIQUEFY ♦ [2b] disappear, dissolve, evaporate, fade, flee, go, vanish — more at DISAPPEAR

²**melt** *n* : a melted substance

melt·down \'melt-ˌdaùn\ *n* **1** : the melting of the core of a nuclear reactor **2** : a rapid or disastrous decline or disaster

melting pot *n* : a place where different races, cultures, or individuals assimilate into a cohesive whole

melt·wa·ter \-ˌwò-tər, -ˌwä-\ *n* : water derived from the melting of ice and snow

mem *abbr* **1** member **2** memoir **3** memorial

mem·ber \'mem-bər\ *n* **1** : a part (as an arm, leg, leaf, or branch) of an animal or plant **2** : one of the individuals composing a group **3** ♦ : a constituent part of a whole

♦ component, constituent, element, factor, ingredient — more at ELEMENT ♦ part, partition, portion, section, segment — more at PART

mem·ber·ship \-ˌship\ *n* **1** : the state or status of being a member **2** : the body of members

mem·brane \'mem-ˌbrān\ *n* : a thin pliable layer esp. of animal or plant origin — **mem·bra·nous** \-brə-nəs\ *adj*

me·men·to \mə-'men-tō\ *n, pl* **-tos** *or* **-toes** [ME, fr. L, remember, imper. of *meminisse* to remember] ♦ : something that serves to warn or remind; *also* : SOUVENIR

♦ keepsake, memorial, monument, remembrance, souvenir, token — more at MEMORIAL

memo \'me-mō\ *n, pl* **mem·os** : MEMORANDUM

mem·oir \'mem-ˌwär\ *n* **1** : MEMORANDUM **2** : AUTOBIOGRAPHY — usu. used in pl. **3** : an account of something noteworthy; *also, pl* : the record of the proceedings of a learned society

mem·o·ra·bil·ia \ˌme-mə-rə-'bi-lē-ə, -'bil-yə\ *n pl* [L] : things worthy of remembrance; *also* : MEMENTOS

mem·o·ra·ble \'me-mə-rə-bəl\ *adj* : worth remembering : NOTABLE — **mem·o·ra·bil·i·ty** \ˌme-mə-rə-'bi-lə-tē\ *n* — **mem·o·ra·ble·ness** *n* — **mem·o·ra·bly** \-blē\ *adv*

mem·o·ran·dum \ˌme-mə-'ran-dəm\ *n, pl* **-dums** *or* **-da** \-də\ **1** : an informal record or written reminder **2** ♦ : an informal written note

♦ directive, letter, missive, note, notice; *also* announcement, declaration, proclamation, pronouncement; charge, command, dictate; instructions, orders, word; encyclical, epistle, mail, note

¹**me·mo·ri·al** \mə-'mōr-ē-əl\ *adj* : serving to preserve remembrance

²**memorial** *n* **1** ♦ : something designed to keep remembrance alive; *esp* : MONUMENT **2** : a statement of facts often accompanied with a petition — **me·mo·ri·al·ize** *vb*

♦ keepsake, memento, monument, remembrance, souvenir, token; *also* memorabilia; relic, vestige; cairn, landmark, marker; testimonial, tribute

Memorial Day *n* : the last Monday in May or formerly May 30 observed as a legal holiday in honor of those who died in war

mem·o·rise *chiefly Brit var of* MEMORIZE

mem·o·rize \'me-mə-ˌrīz\ *vb* **-rized; -riz·ing** ♦ : to learn by heart — **mem·o·ri·za·tion** \ˌme-mə-rə-'zā-shən\ *n* — **mem·o·riz·er** *n*

♦ learn, study; *also* recall, recollect, relive, remember, reminisce, retain; apprehend, accept, comprehend, get, grasp, understand; absorb, digest *Ant* unlearn

mem·o·ry \'me-mə-rē\ *n, pl* **-ries** **1** ♦ : the power or process of remembering **2** : the store of things remembered **3** : COMMEMORATION **4** ♦ : something remembered **5** : the time within which past events are remembered **6** : a device (as in a computer) in which information can be stored

♦ [1, 4] recall, recollection, remembrance, reminiscence; *also* flashback; memento, memorial, reminder, souvenir, token; association

men *pl of* MAN

¹**men·ace** \'me-nəs\ *n* **1** : THREAT **2 a** ♦ : one that represents a threat : DANGER **b** : NUISANCE

♦ danger, hazard, peril, pitfall, risk, threat, trouble — more at DANGER

²**menace** *vb* **men·aced; men·ac·ing** **1** ♦ : to make a show of intention to harm : THREATEN **2** ♦ : to represent or pose a threat to : ENDANGER

♦ [1] hang, hover, overhang, threaten — more at THREATEN ♦ [2] adventure, compromise, endanger, gamble with, hazard, imperil, jeopardize, risk, venture

men·ac·ing *adj* ♦ : presenting, suggesting, or constituting a menace — **men·ac·ing·ly** *adv*

♦ baleful, dire, foreboding, ominous, portentous, sinister — more at OMINOUS ♦ dangerous, grave, grievous, hazardous, parlous, perilous, risky, serious, unhealthy, unsafe, venturesome — more at DANGEROUS

mé·nage \mā-'näzh\ *n* [F] : a domestic establishment : HOUSEHOLD

ménage à trois \-ä-'trwä\ *n* : an arrangement in which three persons share sexual relations esp. while living together

me·nag·er·ie \mə-'na-jə-rē\ *n* : a collection of wild animals esp. for exhibition

¹**mend** \'mend\ *vb* **1** : to improve in manners or morals **2** ♦ : to put into good shape : REPAIR **3** ♦ : to improve in or restore to health : HEAL — **mend·er** *n*

♦ [2] doctor, fix, patch, recondition, renovate, repair, revamp; *also* overhaul, rebuild, reconstruct, refurbish, aid, cure, heal, help; condition, prepare, ready; care (for), maintain, service; rejuvenate, renew, restore; adjust, correct, modify, rectify, redress, reform, right; ameliorate, better, improve, meliorate ♦ [3] convalesce, gain, heal, rally, recover, recuperate, snap back — more at CONVALESCE

²**mend** *n* **1** : an act of mending **2** : a mended place

men·da·cious \men-'dā-shəs\ *adj* ♦ : given to deception or falsehood : UNTRUTHFUL — **men·da·cious·ly** *adv*

♦ dishonest, lying — more at DISHONEST

men·dac·i·ty \-'da-sə-tē\ *n* **1** : the quality or state of being mendacious **2** ♦ : an untrue statement made with intent to deceive : LIE

♦ fabrication, fairy tale, falsehood, falsity, fib, lie, prevarication, story, tale, untruth, whopper — more at LIE

men·de·le·vi·um \ˌmen-də-'lē-vē-əm, -'lā-\ *n* : a radioactive chemical element artificially produced

men·di·cant \'men-di-kənt\ *n* **1** : BEGGAR **2** *often cap* : FRIAR — **men·di·can·cy** \-kən-sē\ *n* — **mendicant** *adj*

men·folk \'men-ˌfōk\ *or* **men·folks** \-ˌfōks\ *n pl* **1** : men in general **2** : the men of a family or community

men·ha·den \men-'hād-ⁿn, mən-\ *n, pl* **-den** *also* **-dens** : a marine fish related to the herring that is abundant along the Atlantic coast of the U.S.

¹**me·nial** \'mē-nē-əl, -nyəl\ *adj* **1** : of or relating to servants **2** : HUMBLE; *also* : SERVILE — **me·ni·al·ly** *adv*

²**menial** *n* ♦ : a domestic servant

♦ domestic, flunky, lackey, retainer, servant, steward — more at SERVANT

men·in·gi·tis \ˌme-nən-'jī-təs\ *n, pl* **-git·i·des** \-'ji-tə-ˌdēz\ : inflammation of the membranes enclosing the brain and spinal cord; *also* : a usu. bacterial disease marked by this

me·ninx \'mē-niŋks, 'me-\ *n, pl* **me·nin·ges** \mə-'nin-(ˌ)jēz\

: any of the three membranes that envelop the brain and spinal cord — **men·in·ge·al** \\,me-nən-'jē-əl\ *adj*

me·nis·cus \mə-'nis-kəs\ *n, pl* **me·nis·ci** \-'nis-,kī, -,kē\ *also* **me·nis·cus·es** **1** : CRESCENT **2** : the curved upper surface of a column of liquid

men·o·pause \'me-nə-,pȯz\ *n* : the period of life when menstruation stops naturally — **men·o·paus·al** \,me-nə-'pȯ-zəl\ *adj*

me·no·rah \mə-'nȯr-ə\ *n* [Heb *mĕnōrāh* candlestick] : a candelabrum that is used in Jewish worship

men·ses \'men-,sēz\ *n sing or pl* : the menstrual flow

menstrual cycle *n* : the complete cycle of physiological changes from the beginning of one menstrual period to the beginning of the next

men·stru·a·tion \,men-strə-'wā-shən, men-'strā-\ *n* : a discharging of bloody matter at approximately monthly intervals from the uterus of breeding-age nonpregnant primate females; *also* : PERIOD 6 — **men·stru·al** \'men-strə-wəl\ *adj* — **men·stru·ate** \'men-strə-,wāt, -,strāt\ *vb*

men·su·ra·ble \'men-sə-rə-bəl, '-chə-\ *adj* : MEASURABLE

men·su·ra·tion \,men-sə-'rā-shən, ,men-chə-\ *n* : MEASUREMENT

-ment \mənt\ *n suffix* **1** : concrete result, object, or agent of a (specified) action ⟨embank*ment*⟩ ⟨entangle*ment*⟩ **2** : concrete means or instrument of a (specified) action ⟨entertain*ment*⟩ **3** : action : process ⟨encircle*ment*⟩ ⟨develop*ment*⟩ **4** : place of a (specified) action ⟨encamp*ment*⟩ **5** : state : condition ⟨amaze*ment*⟩

men·tal \'ment-ᵊl\ *adj* **1** ♦ : of or relating to the mind **2** ♦ : of, relating to, or affected with a disorder of the mind ⟨∼ illness⟩ — **men·tal·ly** *adv*

♦ [1] cerebral, inner, intellectual, psychological; *also* cognitive, conscious, psychic, telepathic; spiritual; alert, brainy, bright, clever, quick-witted, intelligent, rational, reasoning, smart, thinking ♦ [2] crazy, deranged, insane, mad — more at INSANE

mental age *n* : a measure of a child's mental development in terms of the number of years it takes an average child to reach the same level

mental deficiency *n* : INTELLECTUAL DISABILITY

men·tal·i·ty \men-'ta-lə-tē\ *n, pl* **-ties** **1** ♦ : mental power or capacity **2** : mode or way of thought

♦ brains, gray matter (*or* grey matter), intellect, intelligence, reason, sense — more at INTELLIGENCE

mental retardation *n, now sometimes offensive* : INTELLECTUAL DISABILITY — **mentally retarded** *adj, now sometimes offensive*

men·tee \men-'tē\ *n* : PROTÉGÉ

men·thol \'men-,thȯl, -,thōl\ *n* : an alcohol occurring esp. in mint oils that has the odor and cooling properties of peppermint — **men·tho·lat·ed** \-thə-,lā-təd\ *adj*

¹men·tion \'men-chən\ *n* **1** : a brief or casual reference **2** : a formal citation for outstanding achievement

²mention *vb* **1** ♦ : to refer to : CITE **2** : to cite for superior achievement — **not to mention** : to say nothing of

♦ advert (to), cite, instance, name, note, notice, quote, refer (to), specify, touch (*on or upon*); *also* allude (to), hint (at), imply, infer, intimate, suggest; point (out), signal, signify; denominate, designate, indicate; bring up, broach, interject, interpolate, interpose, introduce; infiltrate, insinuate, worm; announce, declare, pronounce; elucidate, explain

¹men·tor \'men-,tȯr, -tər\ *n* : a trusted counselor or guide; *also* : TUTOR, COACH

²mentor *vb* ♦ : to serve as a mentor for

♦ coach, counsel, guide, lead, pilot, shepherd, show, tutor — more at GUIDE

menu \'men-yü, 'mān-\ *n, pl* **menus** [F, fr. *menu* small, detailed, fr. OF, fr. L *minutus* minute (adj.)] **1** : a list of the dishes available (as in a restaurant) for a meal; *also* : the dishes served **2** ♦ : a list of offerings or options

♦ catalog, checklist, list, listing, register, registry, roll, roster, schedule, table — more at LIST

me·ow \mē-'au̇\ *vb* : to make the characteristic cry of a cat — **meow** *n*

mer *abbr* meridian

mer·can·tile \'mər-kən-,tēl, -,tīl\ *adj* : of or relating to merchants or trading

¹mer·ce·nary \'mərs-ᵊn-,er-ē\ *n, pl* **-nar·ies** : a person who serves merely for wages; *esp* : a soldier hired into foreign service

²mercenary *adj* **1** ♦ : serving merely for pay or gain **2** : hired for service in a foreign army

♦ acquisitive, avaricious, avid, covetous, grasping, greedy, rapacious — more at GREEDY

mer·cer \'mər-sər\ *n, Brit* : a dealer in usu. expensive fabrics

mer·cer·ise *chiefly Brit var of* MERCERIZE

mer·cer·ize \'mər-sə-,rīz\ *vb* **-ized; -iz·ing** : to treat cotton yarn or cloth with alkali so that it looks silky or takes a better dye

¹mer·chan·dise \'mər-chən-,dīz, -,dīs\ *n* ♦ : the commodities or goods that are bought and sold in business

♦ commodities, wares; *also* line; export, import; inventory, staples, stock, stuff

²mer·chan·dise \-,dīz\ *vb* **-dised; -dis·ing** ♦ : to buy and sell in business

♦ deal, market, put up, retail, sell, vend — more at MARKET

mer·chan·dis·er *n* : one that buys and sells in business

mer·chant \'mər-chənt\ *n* **1** ♦ : a buyer and seller of commodities for profit **2** : STOREKEEPER

♦ dealer, trader, trafficker; *also* businessman, businesswoman, buyer, purchaser; hawker, peddler; retailer, seller, shopkeeper, storekeeper, vendor; jobber, middleman, wholesaler; distributor, provider, supplier

mer·chant·able \'mər-chən-tə-bəl\ *adj* : acceptable to buyers : MARKETABLE

mer·chant·man \'mər-chənt-mən\ *n* : a ship used in commerce

merchant marine *n* : the commercial ships of a nation

merchant ship *n* : MERCHANTMAN

mer·ci·ful·ly \'mər-si-fə-lē\ *adv* **1** : in a merciful manner **2** : FORTUNATELY 2

mer·ci·less \'mər-si-ləs\ *adj* ♦ : having or showing no mercy — **mer·ci·less·ly** *adv*

♦ callous, hard, heartless, inhuman, inhumane, pitiless, soulless, unfeeling, unsympathetic — more at HARD

mer·cu·ri·al \,mər-'kyu̇r-ē-əl\ *adj* **1** ♦ : unpredictably changeable ⟨a ∼ personality⟩ **2** : MERCURIC — **mer·cu·ri·al·ly** *adv* — **mer·cu·ri·al·ness** *n*

♦ capricious, changeable, fickle, inconstant, unpredictable — more at FICKLE

mer·cu·ric \,mər-'kyu̇r-ik\ *adj* : of, relating to, or containing mercury

mercuric chloride *n* : a poisonous compound of mercury and chlorine used as an antiseptic and fungicide

mer·cu·ry \'mər-kyə-rē\ *n, pl* **-ries** **1** : a heavy silver-white liquid metallic chemical element used esp. in scientific instruments **2** *cap* : the planet nearest the sun

mer·cy \'mər-sē\ *n, pl* **mercies** [ME, fr. AF *merci*, fr. ML *merced-, merces*, fr. L, price paid, wages, fr. *merc-, merx* merchandise] **1** ♦ : compassion shown to an offender; *also* : imprisonment rather than death for first-degree murder **2** : a blessing resulting from divine favor or compassion; *also* : a fortunate circumstance **3** ♦ : compassionate treatment of those in distress — **mer·ci·ful** \-si-fəl\ *adj* — **mercy** *adj*

♦ [1] charity, clemency, leniency, quarter; *also* humanitarianism, philanthropy; empathy, pity, sympathy, understanding; commiseration, favor, grace; benevolence, care, compassion, gentleness, goodness, goodwill, kindliness, kindness, meekness, mildness, niceness, softness, tenderness; altruism, generosity, magnanimity, nobility; affection, devotion, love, worship ♦ [3] boon, courtesy, favor (or favour), grace, indulgence, kindness, service, turn

mercy killing n : EUTHANASIA

¹**mere** \'mir\ n : LAKE, POOL

²**mere** adj, superlative **mer·est** **1** : being nothing more than ⟨a ∼ child⟩ **2** : not diluted : PURE

mere·ly \-lē\ adv ◆ : no more than

◆ but, just, only, simply — more at JUST

mer·e·tri·cious \ˌmer-ə-'tri-shəs\ adj [L meretricius, fr. meretrix prostitute, fr. merēre to earn] : tawdrily attractive; also : SPECIOUS — **mer·e·tri·cious·ly** adv — **mer·e·tri·cious·ness** n

mer·gan·ser \(ˌ)mər-'gan-sər\ n : any of various fish-eating wild ducks with a usu. crested head and a slender bill hooked at the end and serrated along the margins

merge \'mərj\ vb **merged; merg·ing** **1** : to blend gradually **2** ◆ : to combine, unite, or coalesce into one

◆ amalgamate, blend, commingle, fuse, incorporate, integrate, intermingle, mingle, mix — more at BLEND

merg·er \'mər-jər\ n **1** : the act or process of merging **2** : absorption by a corporation of one or more others

me·rid·i·an \mə-'ri-dē-ən\ n [ME, fr. AF meridien, fr. meridien of noon, fr. L meridianus, fr. meridies noon, south, irreg. fr. medius mid + dies day] **1** ◆ : the highest point : CULMINATION **2** : any of the imaginary circles on the earth's surface passing through the north and south poles — **meridian** adj

◆ acme, apex, climax, crown, culmination, head, height, peak, pinnacle, summit, tip-top, top, zenith — more at HEIGHT

me·ringue \mə-'raŋ\ n [F] : a baked dessert topping of stiffly beaten egg whites and powdered sugar

me·ri·no \mə-'rē-nō\ n, pl **-nos** [Sp] **1** : any of a breed of sheep noted for fine soft wool **2** : a fine soft fabric or yarn of wool or wool and cotton

¹**mer·it** \'mer-ət\ n **1** : laudable or blameworthy traits or actions **2** ◆ : a praiseworthy quality; also : character or conduct deserving reward or honor **3** pl : the intrinsic nature of a legal case; also : legal significance

◆ distinction, excellence, value, virtue — more at EXCELLENCE ◆ account, valuation, value, worth — more at WORTH

²**merit** vb ◆ : to be worthy of or entitled or liable to : EARN, DESERVE

◆ deserve, earn, rate

mer·i·toc·ra·cy \ˌmer-ə-'tä-krə-sē\ n, pl **-cies** : a system in which the talented are chosen and moved ahead based on their achievement; also : leadership by the talented

mer·i·to·ri·ous \ˌmer-ə-'tōr-ē-əs\ adj ◆ : deserving honor or esteem — **mer·i·to·ri·ous·ly** adv — **mer·i·to·ri·ous·ness** n

◆ admirable, commendable, creditable, laudable, praiseworthy — more at ADMIRABLE ◆ deserving, good, worthy — more at WORTHY

mer·lin \'mər-lən\ n : a small compact falcon of the northern hemisphere

mer·lot \mer-'lō, mər-\ n : a dry red wine made from a widely grown grape; also : the grape itself

mer·maid \'mər-ˌmād\ n : a legendary sea creature with a woman's upper body and a fish's tail

mer·man \-ˌman, -mən\ n : a legendary sea creature with a man's upper body and a fish's tail

mer·ri·ly \'mer-ə-lē\ adv ◆ : in a merry manner

◆ cheerfully, gaily, happily, heartily, jovially, mirthfully — more at GAILY

mer·ri·ment \'mer-i-mənt\ n **1** ◆ : lighthearted gaiety or fun-making : HILARITY **2** ◆ : a lively celebration or party : FESTIVITY

◆ [1] cheer, cheerfulness, cheeriness, glee, hilarity, joviality, mirth — more at MIRTH ◆ [2] conviviality, festivity, gaiety, jollification, merrymaking, revelry — more at MERRYMAKING

mer·ry \'mer-ē\ adj **mer·ri·er; -est** **1** ◆ : full of gaiety

or high spirits **2** : marked by festivity **3** : BRISK ⟨a ∼ pace⟩

◆ blithe, boon, festive, gay, gleeful, jocund, jolly, jovial, mirthful, sunny; also amused, beaming, chuckling, giggling, smiling; bright, buoyant, carefree, cheerful, cheery, chipper, lighthearted, lightsome, upbeat; animated, jaunty, lively, perky, vivacious; blessed, blissful, delighted, ecstatic, elated, enraptured, entranced, euphoric, exhilarated, exuberant, exultant, gladsome, happy, high, joyful, joyous, jubilant, overjoyed, radiant, rapturous, ravished, thrilled; amusing, facetious, flippant, funny, hilarious, joking, joshing, playful, witty; careless, cavalier, easygoing, happy-go-lucky, insouciant, unconcerned; hopeful, rosy, sanguine

merry–go–round \'mer-ē-gō-ˌraund\ n **1** : a circular revolving platform with benches and figures of animals on which people sit for a ride **2** : a busy round of activities

mer·ry·mak·er \'mer-ē-ˌmā-kər\ n ◆ : one who engages in merrymaking

◆ celebrant, reveler, roisterer — more at CELEBRANT

mer·ry·mak·ing \'mer-ē-ˌmā-kiŋ\ n **1** ◆ : gay or festive activity **2** : a festive occasion

◆ conviviality, festivity, gaiety, jollification, merriment, revelry; also carousal, carouse; delight, diversion, entertainment, fun, pleasure, riot; glee, joviality, mirth, mirthfulness; carnival, celebration, party, revel; frolicking, gamboling, rollicking, romping; enjoyment, happiness, joy; binge, fling, frolic, gambol, lark, rollick, romp, spree; buffoonery, clownishness, flippancy, frivolity, jocularity, joking, joshing, levity, lightheartedness, playfulness; zaniness

me·sa \'mā-sə\ n [Sp, lit., table, fr. L mensa] ◆ : a flat-topped hill with steep sides

◆ plateau, table, tableland — more at PLATEAU

mes·cal \me-'skal, mə-\ n **1** : PEYOTE **2** **2** : a usu. colorless liquor distilled from the leaves of an agave; also : this agave

mes·ca·line \'mes-kə-lən, -ˌlēn\ n : a hallucinatory alkaloid from the peyote cactus

mes·clun \'mes-klən\ n : a mixture of young tender greens; also : a salad made with mesclun

mesdames pl of MADAM or of MADAME or of MRS.

mesdemoiselles pl of MADEMOISELLE

¹**mesh** \'mesh\ n **1** : one of the openings between the threads or cords of a net; also : one of the similar spaces in a network **2** : the fabric of a net **3** : NETWORK **4** : working contact (as of the teeth of gears) ⟨in ∼⟩ **5** ◆ : a woven, knit, or knotted material of open texture with evenly spaced holes — **meshed** \'mesht\ adj

◆ net, network — more at NET

²**mesh** vb **1** ◆ : to catch in or as if in a mesh **2** : to be in or come into mesh : ENGAGE **3** : to fit together properly

◆ enmesh, ensnare, entangle, entrap, snare, tangle, trap — more at ENTANGLE

mesh·work \'mesh-ˌwərk\ n : NETWORK

me·si·al \'mē-zē-əl, -sē-\ adj : of, relating to, or being the surface of a tooth that is closest to the middle of the front of the jaw

mes·mer·ise chiefly Brit var of MESMERIZE

mes·mer·ize \'mez-mə-ˌrīz\ vb **-ized; -iz·ing** ◆ : to dazzle or overcome by or as if by suggestion : HYPNOTIZE — **mes·mer·ic** \mez-'mer-ik\ adj — **mes·mer·ism** \'mez-mə-ˌri-zəm\ n

◆ arrest, enchant, enthrall, fascinate, grip, hypnotize — more at ENTHRALL

Me·so·lith·ic \ˌme-zə-'li-thik\ adj : of, relating to, or being a transitional period of the Stone Age between the Paleolithic and the Neolithic periods

me·so·sphere \'me-zə-ˌsfir\ n : a layer of the atmosphere between the stratosphere and the thermosphere

Me·so·zo·ic \ˌme-zə-'zō-ik, ˌmē-\ adj : of, relating to, or being the era of geologic history between the Paleozoic and the Cenozoic and extending from about 245 million years ago to about 65 million years ago — **Mesozoic** *n*

mes·quite \mə-ˈskēt, me-\ *n* : any of several spiny leguminous trees and shrubs chiefly of the southwestern U.S. with sugar-rich pods important as fodder; *also* : mesquite wood used esp. in grilling food

¹**mess** \ˈmes\ *n* [ME *mes*, fr. AF, fr. LL *missus* course at a meal, fr. *missus*, pp. of *mittere* to put, fr. L, to send] **1 a ◆** : a quantity of food **b** : enough food of a specified kind for a dish or meal ⟨a ∼ of beans⟩ **2 ◆** : a group of persons who regularly eat together; *also* : a meal eaten by such a group **3** : a place where meals are regularly served to a group **4 ◆** : a confused, dirty, or offensive state

> ◆ [1a, 2] board, chow, feed, meal, repast, table — more at MEAL ◆ [4] chaos, confusion, disarray, disorder, disorganization, eyesore, havoc, hell, jumble, muddle, shambles — more at CHAOS

²**mess** *vb* **1** : to supply with meals; *also* : to take meals with a mess **2 a ◆** : to make dirty or untidy — often used with *up* **b ◆** : to become confused or make an error : BUNGLE — usu. used with *up* **3 ◆** : to interest oneself in what is not one's concern : INTERFERE, MEDDLE **4** : PUTTER, TRIFLE **5 ◆** : to handle or play with something esp. carelessly

> ◆ *often* **mess up** [2a] confuse, disorder, jumble, mix, muddle, rumple ◆ *usu* **mess up** [2b] bobble, botch, bungle, butcher, flub, foul up, fumble, mangle, screw up — more at BOTCH ◆ [3] butt in, interfere, intrude, meddle, nose, obtrude, poke, pry, snoop — more at INTERFERE ◆ *usu* **mess with** [5] fiddle, fool, monkey, play, tamper, tinker — more at TAMPER

mes·sage \ˈme-sij\ *n* : a communication sent by one person to another — **message** *vb*

message board *n* : BULLETIN BOARD 2

mess around *vb* ◆ : to waste time

> ◆ fiddle, fool, monkey, play, potter, putter, trifle

messeigneurs *pl of* MONSEIGNEUR

mes·sen·ger \ˈmes-ᵊn-jər\ *n* ◆ : one who carries a message or does an errand

> ◆ courier, go-between, page, runner; *also* forerunner, harbinger, herald; agent, ambassador, delegate, deputy, emissary, envoy, representative; bearer, carrier, deliveryman, letter carrier, mail carrier, mailman

messenger RNA *n* : an RNA that carries the code for a particular protein from DNA in the nucleus to a ribosome in the cytoplasm and acts as a template for the formation of that protein

Mes·si·ah \mə-ˈsī-ə\ *n* **1** : the expected king and deliverer of the Jews **2** : Jesus **3** *not cap* : a professed or accepted leader of a cause — **mes·si·an·ic** \ˌme-sē-ˈa-nik\ *adj*

messieurs *pl of* MONSIEUR

mess·i·ness \ˈme-sē-nəs\ *n* ◆ : the quality or state of being messy

> ◆ chaos, confusion, disarray, disorder, disorganization, havoc, hell, jumble, mess, muddle, muss, shambles, tumble, welter — more at CHAOS

mess·mate \ˈmes-ˌmāt\ *n* : a member of a group who eat regularly together

Messrs. \ˈme-sərz\ *pl of* MR.

messy \ˈme-sē\ *adj* ◆ : marked by confusion, disorder, or dirt

> ◆ chaotic, confused, disheveled, disordered, muddled, sloppy, unkempt, untidy; *also* blackened, dingy, dirty, filthy, foul, grimy, grubby, grungy, mucky, nasty, soiled, spotted, squalid, stained, sullied, unclean, uncleanly; dowdy, frowsy, slatternly, slovenly, uncombed; wrinkled; contaminated, defiled, polluted, tainted; knotted, snarled, tangled; shabby, sleazy; neglected, neglectful, negligent **Ant** neat, ordered, orderly, tidy

mes·ti·zo \me-ˈstē-zō\ *n, pl* **-zos** [Sp] : a person of mixed blood

¹**met** *past and past part of* MEET

²**met** *abbr* metropolitan

me·tab·o·lism \mə-ˈta-bə-ˌli-zəm\ *n* : the processes by which the substance of plants and animals incidental to life is built up and broken down; *also* : the processes by which a substance is handled in the living body ⟨∼ of sugar⟩ — **met·a·bol·ic** \ˌme-tə-ˈbä-lik\ *adj* — **me·tab·o·lize** \mə-ˈta-bə-ˌlīz\ *vb*

me·tab·o·lite \-ˌlīt\ *n* **1** : a product of metabolism **2** : a substance essential to the metabolism of a particular organism or to a metabolic process

meta·car·pal \ˌme-tə-ˈkär-pəl\ *n* : any of usu. five more or less elongated bones of the part of the hand or forefoot between the wrist and the bones of the digits — **metacarpal** *adj*

meta·car·pus \-ˈkär-pəs\ *n* : the part of the hand or forefoot that contains the metacarpals

met·al \ˈmet-ᵊl\ *n* **1** : any of various opaque, fusible, ductile, and typically lustrous substances that are good conductors of electricity and heat **2** : METTLE; *also* : the material out of which a person or thing is made — **me·tal·lic** \mə-ˈta-lik\ *adj*

met·al·lur·gy \ˈmet-ᵊl-ˌər-jē\ *n* : the science and technology of metals — **met·al·lur·gi·cal** \ˌmet-ᵊl-ˈər-ji-kəl\ *adj* — **met·al·lur·gist** \ˈmet-ᵊl-ˌər-jist\ *n*

met·al·ware \ˈmet-ᵊl-ˌwar\ *n* : metal utensils for household use

met·al·work \-ˌwərk\ *n* : work and esp. artistic work made of metal — **met·al·work·er** \-ˌwər-kər\ *n* — **met·al·work·ing** *n*

meta·mor·phism \ˌme-tə-ˈmȯr-fi-zəm\ *n* : a change in the structure of rock; *esp* : a change to a more compact and more highly crystalline form produced by pressure, heat, and water — **meta·mor·phic** \-ˈmȯr-fik\ *adj*

meta·mor·phose \ˌme-tə-ˈmȯr-ˌfōz, -ˌfōs\ *vb* **1** : to change into a different physical form esp. by supernatural means **2 ◆** : to change strikingly the appearance or character of

> ◆ convert, make over, transfigure, transform — more at CONVERT

meta·mor·pho·sis \ˌme-tə-ˈmȯr-fə-səs\ *n, pl* **-pho·ses** \-ˌsēz\ **1 a** : a change of physical form, structure, or substance esp. by supernatural means **b ◆** : a striking alteration (as in appearance or character) **2** : a fundamental change in form and often habits of an animal accompanying the transformation of a larva into an adult

> ◆ changeover, conversion, transfiguration, transformation — more at CONVERSION

met·a·phor \ˈme-tə-ˌfȯr\ *n* : a figure of speech in which a word for one idea or thing is used in place of another to suggest a likeness between them (as in "the ship plows the sea") — **met·a·phor·ic** \ˌme-tə-ˈfȯr-ik\ *or* **met·a·phor·i·cal** \ˌme-tə-ˈfȯr-i-kəl\ *adj* — **met·a·phor·i·cal·ly** \-i-k(ə-)lē\ *adv*

meta·phys·i·cal \ˌme-tə-ˈfi-zi-kəl\ *adj* **1** : of or relating to metaphysics **2 ◆** : of or relating to the transcendent or to a reality beyond what is perceptible to the senses

> ◆ preternatural, superhuman, supernatural, unearthly — more at SUPERNATURAL

meta·phys·ics \ˌme-tə-ˈfi-ziks\ *n pl* [ML *Metaphysica*, title of Aristotle's treatise on the subject, fr. Gk (*ta*)*meta* (*ta*)*physika*, lit., the (works) after the physical (works); fr. its position in his collected works] : the philosophical study of the ultimate causes and underlying nature of things — **meta·phy·si·cian** \-fə-ˈzi-shən\ *n*

me·tas·ta·sis \mə-ˈtas-tə-səs\ *n, pl* **-ta·ses** \-ˌsēz\ : the spread of a health-impairing agency (as cancer cells) from the initial or primary site of disease to another part of the body; *also* : a secondary growth of a malignant tumor — **me·tas·ta·size** \-tə-ˌsīz\ *vb* — **met·a·stat·ic** \ˌme-tə-ˈsta-tik\ *adj*

meta·tar·sal \ˌme-tə-ˈtär-səl\ *n* : any of the bones of the foot between the tarsus and the bones of the digits that in humans include five elongated bones — **metatarsal** *adj*

meta·tar·sus \-ˈtär-səs\ *n* : the part of the human foot or the hind foot in quadrupeds that contains the metatarsals

¹**mete** \ˈmēt\ *vb* **met·ed; met·ing** **1** *archaic* : MEASURE **2 ◆** : to give out by measure — usu. used with *out*

♦ *usu* **mete out** administer, allocate, apportion, deal, dispense, distribute, parcel, portion, prorate — more at ADMINISTER

²**mete** *n* : BOUNDARY ⟨∼s and bounds⟩

me·te·or \'mē-tē-ər, -ˌór\ *n* 1 : a small particle of matter in the solar system directly observable only by its glow from frictional heating on falling into the earth's atmosphere 2 : the streak of light produced by a meteor

me·te·or·ic \ˌmē-tē-'ór-ik\ *adj* 1 : of, relating to, or resembling a meteor 2 : transiently brilliant ⟨a ∼ career⟩ — **me·te·or·i·cal·ly** \-i-k(ə-)lē\ *adv*

me·te·or·ite \'mē-tē-ə-ˌrīt\ *n* : a meteor that reaches the surface of the earth

me·te·or·oid \'mē-tē-ə-ˌróid\ *n* : a small particle of matter in the solar system

me·te·o·rol·o·gy \ˌmē-tē-ə-'rä-lə-jē\ *n* : a science that deals with the atmosphere and its phenomena and esp. with weather forecasting — **me·te·o·ro·log·ic** \ˌmē-tē-ˌór-ə-'lä-jik\ *or* **me·te·o·ro·log·i·cal** \-'lä-ji-kəl\ *adj* — **me·te·o·rol·o·gist** \ˌmē-tē-ə-'rä-lə-jist\ *n*

¹**me·ter** *or Can and Brit* **metre** \'mē-tər\ *n* ♦ : rhythm in verse or music

♦ beat, cadence, measure, rhythm — more at RHYTHM

²**meter** *or Can and Brit* **metre** *n* : the basic metric unit of length

³**meter** *n* : a measuring and sometimes recording instrument

⁴**meter** *vb* 1 : to measure by means of a meter 2 : to print postal indicia on by means of a postage meter ⟨∼ed mail⟩

meter–kilogram–second *or Can and Brit* **metre–kilogram–second** *adj* : of, relating to, or being a system of units based on the meter, the kilogram, and the second

meter maid *n* : a woman assigned to write tickets for parking violations

meth·a·done \'me-thə-ˌdōn\ *also* **meth·a·don** \-ˌdän\ *n* : a synthetic addictive narcotic drug used esp. as a substitute narcotic in the treatment of heroin addiction

meth·am·phet·amine \ˌme-tham-'fe-tə-ˌmēn, -thəm-, -mən\ *n* : a drug used medically in the form of its hydrochloride in the treatment of obesity and often illicitly as a stimulant

meth·ane \'me-ˌthān\ *n* : a colorless odorless flammable gas produced by decomposition of organic matter or from coal and used esp. as a fuel

meth·a·nol \'me-thə-ˌnól, -ˌnōl\ *n* : a volatile flammable poisonous liquid alcohol used esp. as a solvent and as an antifreeze

meth·aqua·lone \me-'tha-kwə-ˌlōn\ *n* : a sedative and hypnotic habit-forming drug that is not a barbiturate

meth·od \'me-thəd\ *n* [ME, prescribed treatment, fr. L *methodus*, fr. Gk *methodos*, fr. *meta* with + *hodos* way] 1 ♦ : a procedure or process for achieving an end 2 : orderly arrangement : PLAN

♦ approach, fashion, form, manner, strategy, style, system, tack, tactics, technique, way; *also* mode; blueprint, design, game, intrigue, layout, line, plan, plot, program, route, scheme; expedient, move, shift, step; practice, process, routine; project, proposal, proposition; policy

me·thod·i·cal \mə-'thä-di-kəl\ *adj* 1 ♦ : arranged, characterized by, or performed with method or order ⟨a ∼ treatment of the subject⟩ 2 : habitually proceeding according to method ⟨∼ in his daily routine⟩ — **me·thod·i·cal·ly** \-k(ə-)lē\ *adv* — **me·thod·i·cal·ness** *n*

♦ orderly, regular, systematic; *also* standardized; accurate, correct, exact, precise; detailed, specific *Ant* disorganized, haphazard, irregular, unsystematic

meth·od·ise *chiefly Brit var of* METHODIZE

Meth·od·ist \'me-thə-dist\ *n* : a member of a Protestant denomination adhering to the doctrines of John Wesley — **Meth·od·ism** \-ˌdi-zəm\ *n*

meth·od·ize \'me-thə-ˌdīz\ *vb* **-ized; -iz·ing** : SYSTEMATIZE

meth·od·ol·o·gy \ˌme-thə-'dä-lə-jē\ *n, pl* **-gies** 1 : a body of methods and rules followed in a science or discipline 2 : the study of the principles or procedures of inquiry in a particular field

meth·yl \'me-thəl\ *n* : a chemical radical consisting of carbon and hydrogen

methyl alcohol *n* : METHANOL

meth·yl·mer·cury \ˌme-thəl-'mər-kyə-rē\ *n* : any of various toxic compounds of mercury that often occur as pollutants which accumulate in animals esp. at the top of a food chain

me·tic·u·lous \mə-'ti-kyə-ləs\ *adj* [L *meticulosus* fearful, fr. *metus* fear] ♦ : extremely careful in attending to details — **me·tic·u·lous·ly** *adv* — **me·tic·u·lous·ness** *n*

♦ careful, conscientious, fussy, painstaking — more at PAINSTAKING

me·tic·u·lous·ness \mə-'ti-kyə-ləs-nəs\ *n* ♦ : the quality or state of being meticulous

♦ care, carefulness, heed, heedfulness, pains, scrupulousness — more at CARE

mé·tier \'me-ˌtyā, me-'tyā\ *n* : an area of activity in which one is expert or successful

me·tre \'mē-tər\ *Can and Brit var of* ¹METER, ²METER

met·ric \'me-trik\ *adj* 1 : of or relating to measurement; *esp* : of or relating to the metric system 2 : METRICAL 1

met·ri·cal \'me-tri-kəl\ *adj* 1 ♦ : of, relating to, or composed in meter 2 : of or relating to measure and esp. the metric system — **met·ri·cal·ly** \-k(ə-)lē\ *adv*

♦ cadenced, measured, rhythmic — more at RHYTHMIC

met·ri·ca·tion \ˌme-tri-'kā-shən\ *n* : the act or process of converting into or expressing in the metric system

met·ri·cize \'me-trə-ˌsīz\ *vb* **-cized; -ciz·ing** : to change into or express in the metric system

metric system *n* : a decimal system of weights and measures based on the meter and on the kilogram

metric ton *n* : a metric unit of weight equal to 1,000 kilograms

¹**met·ro** \'me-trō\ *n, pl* **metros** : SUBWAY

²**metro** *adj* : of, relating to, or characteristic of a metropolis and sometimes including its suburbs

met·ro·nome \'me-trə-ˌnōm\ *n* : an instrument for marking exact time by a regularly repeated tick

me·trop·o·lis \mə-'trä-pə-ləs\ *n* [ME, fr. LL, fr. Gk *mētropolis*, fr. *mētēr* mother + *polis* city] ♦ : the chief or capital city of a country, state, or region; *also* : a large important city — **met·ro·pol·i·tan** \ˌme-trə-'pä-lət-ᵊn\ *adj*

♦ city, municipality

met·tle \'met-ᵊl\ *n* 1 : SPIRIT, COURAGE 2 : quality of temperament

met·tle·some \'met-ᵊl-səm\ *adj* ♦ : full of mettle

♦ fiery, high-spirited, peppery, spirited, spunky — more at SPIRITED

MeV *abbr* million electron volts

¹**mew** \'myü\ *vb* : MEOW — **mew** *n*

²**mew** *vb* : CONFINE

mews \'myüz\ *n sing or pl, chiefly Brit* : stables usu. with living quarters built around a court; *also* : a narrow street with dwellings converted from stables

Mex *abbr* Mexican; Mexico

Mex·i·can \'mek-si-kən\ *n* : a native or inhabitant of Mexico — **Mexican** *adj*

mez·za·nine \'mez-ᵊn-ˌēn, ˌmez-ᵊn-'ēn\ *n* 1 : a low-ceilinged story between two main stories of a building 2 : the lowest balcony in a theater; *also* : the first few rows of such a balcony

mez·zo for·te \ˌmet-(ˌ)sō-'fór-ˌtā, ˌmed-(ˌ)zō-, -tē\ *adj or adv* [It] : moderately loud — used as a direction in music

mez·zo pia·no \-pē-'ä-(ˌ)nō\ *adj or adv* [It] : moderately soft — used as a direction in music

mez·zo–so·pra·no \-sə-'pra-nō, -'prä-\ *n* : a woman's voice having a range between that of the soprano and contralto; *also* : a singer having such a voice

MFA *abbr* master of fine arts

mfr *abbr* manufacture; manufacturer

mg *abbr* milligram

Mg *symbol* magnesium

MG *abbr* **1** machine gun **2** major general **3** military government

mgr *abbr* **1** manager **2** monseigneur **3** monsignor

mgt *or* **mgmt** *abbr* management

MGy Sgt *abbr* master gunnery sergeant

MHz *abbr* megahertz

mi *abbr* **1** mile; mileage **2** mill

MI *abbr* **1** Michigan **2** military intelligence

MIA \ˌem-(ˌ)ī-ˈā\ *n* [*missing in a*ction] : a member of the armed forces whose whereabouts following a combat mission are unknown

Mi·ami \mī-ˈa-mē, -mə\ *n, pl* **Mi·ami** *or* **Mi·am·is** : a member of an American Indian people orig. of Wisconsin and Indiana

mi·as·ma \mī-ˈaz-mə, mē-\ *n, pl* **-mas** *also* **-ma·ta** \-mə-tə\ **1** : a vapor from a swamp formerly believed to cause disease **2** : a harmful influence or atmosphere ⟨a ~ of smog⟩ — **mi·as·mal** \-məl\ *adj* — **mi·as·mic** \-mik\ *adj*

mic \ˈmīk\ *n* : MICROPHONE

Mic *abbr* Micah

mi·ca \ˈmī-kə\ *n* [NL, fr. L, grain, crumb] : any of various mineral silicates readily separable into thin transparent sheets

Mi·cah \ˈmī-kə\ *n* : a book of Jewish and Christian Scripture

mice *pl of* MOUSE

Mich *abbr* Michigan

Mi·che·as \ˈmī-kē-əs, mī-ˈkē-əs\ *n* : MICAH

Mic·mac \ˈmik-ˌmak\ *n, pl* **Micmac** *or* **Micmacs** : a member of an American Indian people of eastern Canada

micr- *or* **micro-** *comb form* **1** : small : minute ⟨*microc*apsule⟩ **2** : one millionth part of a specified unit ⟨*micro*second⟩

¹mi·cro \ˈmī-krō\ *adj* **1** : very small; *esp* : MICROSCOPIC **2** : involving minute quantities or variations

²micro *n, pl* **mi·cros** : MICROCOMPUTER

mi·crobe \ˈmī-ˌkrōb\ *n* : MICROORGANISM; *esp* : one causing disease — **mi·cro·bi·al** \mī-ˈkrō-bē-əl\ *adj*

mi·cro·bi·ol·o·gy \ˌmī-krō-bī-ˈä-lə-jē\ *n* : a branch of biology dealing esp. with microscopic forms of life — **mi·cro·bi·o·log·i·cal** \-ˌbī-ə-ˈlä-ji-kəl\ *adj* — **mi·cro·bi·ol·o·gist** \-bī-ˈä-lə-jist\ *n*

mi·cro·brew·ery \ˈmī-krō-ˌbrü-ə-rē\ *n* : a small brewery making specialty beer in limited quantities

mi·cro·burst \-ˌbərst\ *n* : a violent short-lived localized downdraft that creates extreme wind shears at low altitudes

mi·cro·cap·sule \ˈmī-krō-ˌkap-səl, -ˌsül\ *n* : a tiny capsule containing material (as a medicine) released when the capsule is broken, melted, or dissolved

mi·cro·chip \-ˌchip\ *n* : INTEGRATED CIRCUIT

mi·cro·cir·cuit \-ˌsər-kət\ *n* : a compact electronic circuit

mi·cro·com·put·er \-kəm-ˌpyü-tər\ *n* : a small computer that uses a microprocessor; *esp* : PERSONAL COMPUTER

mi·cro·cosm \ˈmī-krə-ˌkä-zəm\ *n* : an individual or community thought of as a miniature world or universe

mi·cro·elec·tron·ics \ˈmī-krō-i-ˌlek-ˈträ-niks\ *n* : a branch of electronics that deals with the miniaturization of electronic circuits and components — **mi·cro·elec·tron·ic** \-nik\ *adj*

mi·cro·en·cap·su·late \ˌmī-krō-in-ˈkap-sə-ˌlāt\ *vb* : to enclose (as a drug) in a microcapsule — **mi·cro·en·cap·su·la·tion** \-in-ˌkap-sə-ˈlā-shən\ *n*

mi·cro·fiber \ˈmī-krō-ˌfī-bər\ *n* : a fine usu. soft polyester fiber; *also* : a fabric made from such fibers

mi·cro·fiche \ˈmī-krō-ˌfēsh, -ˌfish\ *n, pl* **-fiche** *or* **-fiches** *same or* -ˌfē-shəz, -ˌfi-\ : a sheet of microfilm containing rows of images of pages of printed matter

mi·cro·film \-ˌfilm\ *n* : a film bearing a photographic record (as of print) on a reduced scale — **microfilm** *vb*

mi·cro·graph \ˈmī-krə-ˌgraf\ *n* : a graphic reproduction of the image of an object formed by a microscope

mi·cro·man·age \ˌmī-krō-ˈma-nij\ *vb* : to manage esp. with excessive control or attention to details — **mi·cro·man·age·ment** \-mənt\ *n* — **mi·cro·man·ag·er** \-ni-jər\ *n*

mi·cro·me·te·or·ite \ˌmī-krō-ˈmē-tē-ə-ˌrīt\ *n* : a very small particle in interplanetary space

mi·crom·e·ter \mī-ˈkrä-mə-tər\ *n* : an instrument used with a telescope or microscope for measuring minute distances

mi·cro·min·ia·tur·iza·tion \ˌmī-krō-ˌmi-nē-ə-ˌchùr-ə-ˈzā-shən, -ˌmi-ni-ˌchùr-, -chər-\ *n* : the process of producing things in a very small size and esp. in a size smaller than one considered miniature — **mi·cro·min·ia·tur·ized** \-ˈmi-nē-ə-chə-ˌrīzd, -ˈmi-ni-chə-\ *adj*

mi·cron \ˈmī-ˌkrän\ *n* : one millionth of a meter

mi·cro·or·gan·ism \ˌmī-krō-ˈȯr-gə-ˌni-zəm\ *n* : an organism (as a bacterium) too tiny to be seen by the unaided eye

mi·cro·phone \ˈmī-krə-ˌfōn\ *n* : an instrument for converting sound waves into variations of an electric current for transmitting or recording sound

mi·cro·pho·to·graph \ˌmī-krə-ˈfō-tə-ˌgraf\ *n* : PHOTOMICROGRAPH

mi·cro·pro·ces·sor \ˌmī-krō-ˈprä-ˌse-sər\ *n* : a computer processor contained on a microchip

mi·cro·scope \ˈmī-krə-ˌskōp\ *n* : an instrument for making magnified images of minute objects usu. using light — **mi·cros·co·py** \mī-ˈkräs-kə-pē\ *n*

mi·cro·scop·ic \ˌmī-krə-ˈskä-pik\ *also* **mi·cro·scop·i·cal** \-pi-kəl\ *adj* **1** : of, relating to, or involving the use of the microscope **2 a** : too tiny to be seen without the use of a microscope **b** ♦ : very small — **mi·cro·scop·i·cal·ly** \-pi-k(ə-)lē\ *adv*

♦ atomic, infinitesimal, miniature, minute, teeny, tiny, wee — more at TINY

mi·cro·sec·ond \ˈmī-krō-ˌse-kənd\ *n* : one millionth of a second

mi·cro·sur·gery \ˌmī-krō-ˈsər-jə-rē\ *n* : minute dissection or manipulation (as by a laser beam) of living structures or tissue — **mi·cro·sur·gi·cal** \-ˈsər-ji-kəl\ *adj*

mi·cro·tech·nol·o·gy \-tek-ˈnä-lə-jē\ *n* : technology on a small or microscopic scale

¹mi·cro·wave \ˈmī-krə-ˌwāv\ *n* **1** : a radio wave between one millimeter and one meter in wavelength **2** : MICROWAVE OVEN

²microwave *vb* : to heat or cook in a microwave oven — **mi·cro·wav·able** *or* **mi·cro·wave·able** \ˌmī-krə-ˈwā-və-bəl\ *adj*

microwave oven *n* : an oven in which food is cooked by the absorption of microwave energy by water molecules in the food

¹mid \ˈmid\ *adj* : occupying a middle position : MIDDLE

²mid *abbr* middle

mid·air \ˈmid-ˈar\ *n* : a point or region in the air well above the ground

mid·day \ˈmid-ˌdā, -ˈdā\ *n* ♦ : the middle part of the day

♦ noon, noontime — more at NOON

mid·den \ˈmid-ᵊn\ *n* : a refuse heap

¹mid·dle \ˈmid-ᵊl\ *adj* **1** ♦ : equally distant from the extremes **2** ♦ : being at neither extreme : INTERMEDIATE **3** *cap* : constituting an intermediate period

♦ [1, 2] central, halfway, intermediary, intermediate, median, medium, midmost; *also* equidistant; inmost, inner, innermost *Ant* extreme, farthest, furthest, outermost ♦ [1, 2] average, intermediate, moderate, modest; *also* reasonable; common, commonplace, conventional, normal, popular, regular, routine, standard, typical, usual; passable, tolerable

²middle *n* **1** ♦ : a middle part, point, or position **2** ♦ : the central portion of the human body : WAIST **3** ♦ : the position of being among or in the midst of something ⟨caught in the ~ of their conflict⟩

♦ [1] mean, medium, midpoint — more at MEAN ♦ [2] midriff, waist — more at MIDRIFF ♦ [3] deep, depth, height, midst, thick — more at THICK

middle age *n* : the period of life from about 45 to about 64 — **mid·dle–aged** \ˌmid-ᵊl-ˈājd\ *adj*

Middle Ages *n pl* : the period of European history from about A.D. 500 to about 1500

mid·dle·brow \ˈmid-ᵊl-ˌbrau̇\ *n* : a person who is moderately but not highly cultivated — **middlebrow** *adj*

middle class *n* : a social class holding a position between the upper class and the lower class — **middle–class** *adj*

middle ear *n* : a small membrane-lined cavity of the ear through which sound waves are transmitted by a chain of tiny bones

middle finger *n* : the midmost of the five digits of the hand

mid·dle·man \ˈmid-ᵊl-ˌman\ *n* **1** ♦ : an intermediary or agent between two parties **2** : one who is intermediate between the producer of goods and the retailer or consumer

♦ arbiter, arbitrator, go-between, intercessor, intermediary, mediator, peacemaker — more at MEDIATOR

middle–of–the–road *adj* : standing for or following a course of action midway between extremes; *esp* : being neither liberal nor conservative in politics — **mid·dle–of–the–road·er** \-ˈrō-dər\ *n* — **mid·dle–of–the–road·ism** \-ˈrō-ˌdi-zəm\ *n*

middle school *n* : a school usu. including grades 5 to 8 or 6 to 8

mid·dle·weight \ˈmid-ᵊl-ˌwāt\ *n* : one of average weight; *esp* : a boxer weighing not over 160 pounds

mid·dling \ˈmid-liŋ, -lən\ *adj* **1** : of middle, medium, or moderate size, degree, or quality **2** ♦ : of moderate or low quality, value, ability, or performance : MEDIOCRE

♦ common, fair, indifferent, mediocre, medium, ordinary, passable, run-of-the-mill, second-rate, so-so — more at MEDIOCRE

mid·dy \ˈmi-dē\ *n, pl* **middies** : MIDSHIPMAN

midge \ˈmij\ *n* : a very small fly : GNAT

midg·et \ˈmi-jət\ *n* **1** ♦ : something (as an animal) very small for its kind **2** *sometimes offensive* : a very small person

♦ dwarf, mite, peewee, pygmy, runt — more at DWARF

midi \ˈmi-dē\ *n* : a calf-length dress, coat, or skirt

MIDI \ˈmi-dē\ *n* [*musical instrument digital interface*] : a protocol for the transmission of digitally encoded music

mid·land \ˈmid-lənd, -ˌland\ *n* : the interior or central region of a country

mid·life \ˈmid-ˈlīf\ *n* : MIDDLE AGE

midlife crisis *n* : a period of emotional turmoil in middle age characterized esp. by a strong desire for change

mid·most \-ˌmōst\ *adj* ♦ : being in or near the exact middle — **midmost** *adv*

♦ halfway, intermediary, intermediate, median, medium, middle — more at MIDDLE

mid·night \-ˌnīt\ *n* : 12 o'clock at night

mid–ocean ridge \ˈmid-ˈō-shən-\ *n* : an elevation on an ocean floor at the boundary of diverging tectonic plates

mid·point \ˈmid-ˌpȯint, -ˈpȯint\ *n* ♦ : a point at or near the center or middle

♦ mean, medium, middle — more at MEAN ♦ center (*or* centre), core, midst — more at CENTER

mid·riff \ˈmi-ˌdrif\ *n* [ME *midrif*, fr. OE *midhrif*, fr. *midde* mid + *hrif* belly] **1** : DIAPHRAGM 1 **2** ♦ : the mid-region of the human torso

♦ middle, waist; *also* abdomen, torso, trunk

mid·sec·tion \-ˌsek-shən\ *n* : a section midway between the extremes; *esp* : MIDRIFF 2

mid·ship·man \ˈmid-ˌship-mən, (ˌ)mid-ˈship-\ *n* : a student in a naval academy

mid·ships \-ˌships\ *adv* : AMIDSHIPS

¹**midst** \ˈmidst\ *n* **1** ♦ : the interior or central part or point **2** : a position of proximity to the members of a group ⟨in our ∼⟩ **3** ♦ : the condition of being surrounded or beset

♦ [1] center (*or* centre), core, midpoint — more at CENTER ♦ [3] deep, depth, height, middle, thick — more at THICK

²**midst** *prep* ♦ : in the midst of

♦ amid, among, through — more at AMONG

mid·stream \ˈmid-ˈstrēm, -ˌstrēm\ *n* : the middle of a stream

mid·sum·mer \-ˈsə-mər, -ˌsə-\ *n* **1** : the middle of summer **2** : the summer solstice

mid·town \ˈmid-ˌtau̇n, -ˈtau̇n\ *n* : a central section of a city; *esp* : one situated between sections called *downtown* and *uptown* — **midtown** *adj*

¹**mid·way** \ˈmid-ˌwā, -ˈwā\ *adv* : in the middle of the way or distance

²**mid·way** \-ˌwā\ *n* : an avenue (as at a carnival) for concessions and amusements

mid·week \-ˌwēk\ *n* : the middle of the week — **mid·week·ly** \-ˌwē-klē, -ˈwē-\ *adj or adv*

mid·wife \ˈmid-ˌwīf\ *n* : a person who helps women in childbirth — **mid·wife·ry** \-ˌwī-fə-rē\ *n*

mid·win·ter \ˈmid-ˈwin-tər, -ˌwin-\ *n* **1** : the winter solstice **2** : the middle of winter

mid·year \-ˌyir\ *n* **1** : the middle of a year **2** : a midyear examination — **midyear** *adj*

mien \ˈmēn\ *n* **1** : air or bearing esp. as expressive of mood or personality : DEMEANOR **2** ♦ : outward aspect : APPEARANCE

♦ appearance, aspect, look, presence — more at APPEARANCE

miff \ˈmif\ *vb* : to put into an ill humor

¹**might** \ˈmīt\ *verbal auxiliary, past of* MAY — used as an auxiliary to express permission or possibility in the past, a present condition contrary to fact, less probability or possibility than *may*, or as a polite alternative to *may*, *ought*, or *should*

²**might** *n* ♦ : the power, authority, or resources of an individual or a group

♦ energy, force, main, muscle, potency, power, sinew, strength, vigor (*or* vigour) — more at POWER

might·i·ly \ˈmī-tə-lē\ *adv* **1** ♦ : in a mighty manner ⟨applauded ∼⟩ **2** ♦ : very much ⟨depressed me ∼⟩

♦ [1] energetically, firmly, forcefully, forcibly, hard, powerfully, stiffly, stoutly, strenuously, strongly, sturdily, vigorously — more at HARD ♦ [2] especially, extremely, greatly, highly, hugely, mighty, mortally, most, much, real, right, so, very — more at VERY

¹**mighty** \ˈmī-tē\ *adj* **might·i·er; -est** **1** ♦ : very strong : POWERFUL **2** : GREAT, NOTABLE — **might·i·ness** \-tē-nəs\ *n*

♦ important, influential, potent, powerful, significant, strong — more at IMPORTANT

²**mighty** *adv* : to a high degree

mi·gnon·ette \ˌmin-yə-ˈnet\ *n* : an annual garden herb with spikes of tiny fragrant flowers

mi·graine \ˈmī-ˌgrān\ *n* [ME *mygreyn*, fr. MF *migraine*, fr. LL *hemicrania* pain in one side of the head, fr. Gk *hēmikrania*, fr. *hēmi-* half + *kranion* cranium] : a condition marked by recurrent severe headache and often nausea; *also* : an attack of migraine

mi·grant \ˈmī-grənt\ *n* ♦ : one that migrates; *esp* : a person who moves in order to find work (as picking crops) — **migrant** *adj*

♦ emigrant, émigré, immigrant, settler — more at EMIGRANT

mi·grate \ˈmī-ˌgrāt\ *vb* **mi·grat·ed; mi·grat·ing** **1** : to move from one country or place to another **2** : to pass usu. periodically from one region or climate to another for feeding or breeding — **mi·gra·tion** \mī-ˈgrā-shən\ *n* — **mi·gra·to·ry** \ˈmī-grə-ˌtȯr-ē\ *adj*

mi·ka·do \mə-ˈkä-dō\ *n, pl* **-dos** : an emperor of Japan

mike \ˈmīk\ *n* : MICROPHONE

¹**mil** \ˈmil\ *n* : a unit of length equal to ¹/₁₀₀₀ inch

²**mil** *abbr* military

milch \ˈmilk, ˈmilch\ *adj* : giving milk ⟨∼ cow⟩

mild \ˈmī(-ə)ld\ *adj* **1** ♦ : gentle in nature or behavior **2** : moderate in action or effect **3** ♦ : not severe : TEMPERATE — **mild·ly** *adv* — **mild·ness** *n*

♦ [1] balmy, benign, bland, delicate, gentle, light, mellow, soft, soothing, tender — more at GENTLE
♦ [3] balmy, clement, equable, gentle, moderate, temperate — more at CLEMENT

mil·dew \'mil-ˌdü, -ˌdyü\ *n* : a superficial usu. whitish growth produced on organic matter and on plants by a fungus; *also* : a fungus producing this growth — **mildew** *vb*

mile \'mī(-ə)l\ *n* [ME, fr. OE *mīl*, fr. L *milia* miles, fr. *milia passuum*, lit., thousands of paces] **1** : a unit of length equal to 5280 ft. **2** : NAUTICAL MILE

mile·age \'mī-lij\ *n* **1** : an allowance for traveling expenses at a certain rate per mile **2** : distance in miles traveled (as in a day) **3** : the amount of service yielded (as by a tire) expressed in terms of miles of travel **4** : the average number of miles a motor vehicle will travel on a gallon of gasoline

mile·post \'mī(-ə)l-ˌpōst\ *n* : a post indicating the distance in miles from a given point

mile·stone \-ˌstōn\ *n* **1** : a stone serving as a milepost **2** : a significant point in development

mi·lieu \mēl-'yər, -'yü, -'yœ\ *n, pl* **mi·lieus** *or* **mi·lieux** *same or* -'yərz, -'yüz, -'yœz\ [F] ♦ : the physical or social setting in which something occurs or develops : ENVIRONMENT, SETTING

♦ atmosphere, climate, environment, environs, medium, setting, surroundings — more at ENVIRONMENT

mil·i·tan·cy \'mi-lə-tən-sē\ *n* ♦ : the quality or state of being militant

♦ aggression, aggressiveness, belligerence, fight, pugnacity, truculence — more at BELLIGERENCE

¹mil·i·tant \'mi-lə-tənt\ *adj* **1 a** : engaged in warfare **b** ♦ : prone to fighting **2** ♦ : aggressively active esp. in a cause — **mil·i·tance** \-təns\ *n* — **mil·i·tant·ly** *adv*

♦ [1b] aggressive, argumentative, bellicose, belligerent, combative, contentious, discordant, disputatious, pugnacious, quarrelsome, scrappy, truculent, warlike — more at BELLIGERENT ♦ [2] aggressive, ambitious, assertive, enterprising, fierce, go-getting, high-pressure, self-assertive — more at AGGRESSIVE

²militant *n* ♦ : one who is militant

♦ crusader, fanatic, partisan, zealot — more at ZEALOT

mil·i·ta·rise *chiefly Brit var of* MILITARIZE

mil·i·ta·rism \'mi-lə-tə-ˌri-zəm\ *n* **1** : predominance of the military class or its ideals **2** : a policy of aggressive military preparedness — **mil·i·ta·rist** \-rist\ *n* — **mil·i·ta·ris·tic** \ˌmi-lə-tə-'ris-tik\ *adj*

mil·i·ta·rize \'mi-lə-tə-ˌrīz\ *vb* **-rized; -riz·ing** **1** : to equip with military forces and defenses ⟨~ a region⟩ **2** : to give a military character to

¹mil·i·tary \'mi-lə-ˌter-ē\ *adj* **1** : of or relating to soldiers, arms, war, or the army **2** : performed by armed forces; *also* : supported by armed force — **mil·i·tar·i·ly** \ˌmi-lə-'ter-ə-lē\ *adv*

²military *n, pl* **military** *also* **mil·i·tar·ies** **1** ♦ : the military, naval, and air forces of a nation **2** : military persons

♦ armed forces, services, troops — more at ARMED FORCES

military police *n* : a branch of an army that exercises guard and police functions

mil·i·tate \'mi-lə-ˌtāt\ *vb* **-tat·ed; -tat·ing** : to have weight or effect

mi·li·tia \mə-'li-shə\ *n* : a part of the organized armed forces of a country liable to call only in an emergency — **mi·li·tia·man** \-mən\ *n*

¹milk \'milk\ *n* **1** : a nutritive usu. whitish fluid secreted by female mammals for feeding their young **2** : a milklike liquid (as a plant juice) — **milk·i·ness** \'mil-kē-nəs\ *n* — **milky** *adj*

²milk *vb* **1** : to draw off the milk of ⟨~ a cow⟩ **2** : to draw something from as if by milking

milk·maid \'milk-ˌmād\ *n* : DAIRYMAID

milk·man \-ˌman, -mən\ *n* : a person who sells or delivers milk

milk of magnesia : a milk-white mixture of hydroxide of magnesium and water used as an antacid and laxative

milk shake *n* : a thoroughly blended drink made of milk, a flavoring syrup, and often ice cream

milk·sop \'milk-ˌsäp\ *n* : an unmanly man

milk·weed \-ˌwēd\ *n* : any of a genus of herbs with milky juice and clustered flowers

Milky Way *n* **1** : a broad irregular band of light that stretches across the sky and is caused by the light of a very great number of faint stars **2** : MILKY WAY GALAXY

Milky Way galaxy *n* : the galaxy of which the sun is a member and which includes the stars that create the light of the Milky Way

¹mill \'mil\ *n* **1** : a building with machinery for grinding grain into flour **2** : a machine used in processing (as by grinding, stamping, cutting, or finishing) raw material **3** ♦ : a building or collection of buildings with machinery for manufacturing : FACTORY

♦ factory, plant, shop, works, workshop — more at FACTORY

²mill *vb* **1** : to process in a mill **2** : to move in a circle or in an eddying mass

³mill *n* : one tenth of a cent

mill·age \'mi-lij\ *n* : a rate (as of taxation) expressed in mills

¹mil·len·ni·al \mə-'le-nē-əl\ *adj* : of or relating to a millennium

²millennial *n* : a person born in the 1980s or 1990s — usu. used in pl.

mil·len·ni·um \mə-'le-nē-əm\ *n, pl* **-nia** \-nē-ə\ *or* **-niums** **1** : a period of 1000 years; *also* : a 1000th anniversary or its celebration **2** : the 1000 years mentioned in Revelation 20 when holiness is to prevail and Christ is to reign on earth **3** : a period of great happiness or human perfection

mill·er \'mi-lər\ *n* **1** : one that operates a mill and esp. a flour mill **2** : any of various moths having powdery wings

mil·let \'mi-lət\ *n* : any of several small-seeded cereal and forage grasses cultivated for grain or hay; *also* : the grain of a millet

milli- *comb form* : one thousandth part of

mil·li·am·pere \ˌmi-lē-'am-ˌpir\ *n* : one thousandth of an ampere

mil·liard \'mil-ˌyärd, 'mi-lē-ˌärd\ *n, Brit* : a thousand millions

mil·li·bar \'mi-lə-ˌbär\ *n* : a unit of atmospheric pressure

mil·li·gram \-ˌgram\ *n* : a metric unit of weight equal to ¹⁄₁₀₀₀ gram

mil·li·li·ter \-ˌlē-tər\ *or Can and Brit* **mil·li·li·tre** *n* : a metric unit of volume equal to ¹⁄₁₀₀₀ liter

mil·li·me·ter \'mi-lə-ˌmē-tər\ *or Can and Brit* **mil·li·me·tre** *n* : a metric unit of length equal to ¹⁄₁₀₀₀ meter

mil·li·ner \'mi-lə-nər\ *n* [irreg. fr. *Milan*, Italy; fr. the importation of women's finery from Italy in the 16th century] : a person who designs, makes, trims, or sells women's hats

mil·li·nery \'mi-lə-ˌner-ē\ *n* **1** : women's apparel for the head **2** : the business or work of a milliner

mill·ing \'mi-liŋ\ *n* : a corrugated edge on a coin

mil·lion \'mil-yən\ *n, pl* **millions** *or* **million** : a thousand thousands — **million** *adj* — **mil·lionth** \-yənth\ *adj or n*

mil·lion·aire \ˌmil-yə-'ner, 'mil-yə-ˌner\ *n* : one whose wealth is estimated at a million or more (as of dollars or pounds)

mil·li·pede \'mi-lə-ˌpēd\ *n* : any of a class of arthropods related to the centipedes and having a long segmented body with a hard covering, two pairs of legs on most segments, and no poison fangs

mil·li·sec·ond \-ˌse-kənd\ *n* : one thousandth of a second

mil·li·volt \-ˌvōlt\ *n* : one thousandth of a volt

mill·pond \'mil-ˌpänd\ *n* : a pond made by damming a stream to produce a fall of water for operating a mill

mill·race \-₁rās\ *n* : a canal in which water flows to and from a mill wheel

mill·stone \-₁stōn\ *n* : either of two round flat stones used for grinding grain

mill·stream \-₁strēm\ *n* : a stream whose flow is used to run a mill; *also* : the stream in a millrace

mill wheel *n* : a waterwheel that drives a mill

mill·wright \'mil-₁rīt\ *n* : a person who builds mills or sets up or maintains their machinery

milt \'milt\ *n* : the sperm-containing fluid of a male fish

¹**mime** \'mīm\ *n* **1** : MIMIC **2** : a story performed silently and entirely by body movements : PANTOMIME **3** ♦ : an actor in a mime

  ♦ mimic, mummer, pantomime

²**mime** *vb* ♦ : to imitate closely

  ♦ ape, copy, emulate, imitate, mimic — more at IMITATE

mim·eo·graph \'mi-mē-ə-₁graf\ *n* : a machine for making many copies by means of a stencil through which ink is pressed — **mimeograph** *vb*

mi·me·sis \mə-'mē-səs, mī-\ *n* : IMITATION, MIMICRY

mi·met·ic \-'me-tik\ *adj* **1** : marked by imitation : IMITATIVE **2** : relating to, characterized by, or exhibiting biological mimicry

¹**mim·ic** \'mi-mik\ *n* **1** ♦ : an actor in a mime **2** ♦ : one that mimics

  ♦ [1] mime, mummer, pantomime ♦ [2] imitator, impersonator, impressionist; *also* caricaturist, mocker, satirist; mime, mummer; entertainer, performer, player, trouper; parrot

²**mimic** *vb* **mim·icked** \-mikt\; **mim·ick·ing** **1** ♦ : to imitate closely **2** ♦ : to ridicule by imitation **3** : to resemble by biological mimicry

  ♦ [1] ape, copy, emulate, imitate, mime — more at IMITATE ♦ [2] burlesque, caricature, imitate, mock, parody, take off, travesty; *also* lampoon, satirize; deride, ridicule; ape, parrot; duplicate, emulate, replicate, reproduce; act, counterfeit, dissemble, fake, feign, pretend, sham, simulate; elaborate, embellish, embroider, exaggerate, magnify, pad, stretch; amplify, enhance, enlarge (upon), expand, flesh (out), overdraw, overstate; mime, pantomime; impersonate, perform, play

mim·ic·ry \'mi-mi-krē\ *n, pl* **-ries** **1** : an instance of mimicking **2** : a superficial resemblance of one organism to another or to natural objects among which it lives that gives it an advantage (as protection from predation)

mi·mo·sa \mə-'mō-sə, mī-, -zə\ *n* : any of a genus of trees, shrubs, and herbs of the legume family that occur in warm regions and have ball-shaped heads of small white or pink flowers

min *abbr* **1** minim **2** minimum **3** mining **4** minister **5** minor **6** minute

min·a·ret \₁mi-nə-'ret\ *n* [F, fr. Turk *minare*, fr. Ar *manāra* lighthouse] : a tall slender tower of a mosque from which a muezzin calls the faithful to prayer

mi·na·to·ry \'mi-nə-₁tōr-ē, 'mī-\ *adj* : THREATENING, MENACING

mince \'mins\ *vb* **minced**; **minc·ing** [ME, fr. AF *mincer*, fr. VL **minutiare*, fr. L *minutia* smallness, fr. *minutus* small, fr. pp. of *minuere* to lessen] **1** ♦ : to cut into very small pieces **2** : to restrain (words) within the bounds of decorum **3** : to walk in a prim affected manner

  ♦ chop, hash — more at CHOP

mince·meat \'mins-₁mēt\ *n* : a finely chopped mixture esp. of raisins, apples, spices, and often meat used as a filling for a pie

¹**mind** \'mīnd\ *n* **1** ♦ : the power or process of reproducing or recalling what has been learned and retained : MEMORY **2** : the part of an individual that feels, perceives, thinks, wills, and esp. reasons **3** : INTENTION, DESIRE **4** ♦ : normal mental condition **5** ♦ : a belief stronger than impression and less strong than positive knowledge : OPINION, VIEW **6** : MOOD **7** : mental qualities of a person or group **8** : intellectual ability **9** : ATTENTION ⟨pay them no ∼⟩

  ♦ [1] memory, recollection, remembrance, reminiscence ♦ [4] head, reason, sanity, wit; *also* rationality, reasonableness, sense; health, healthfulness, healthiness, wholesomeness; lucidity, lucidness, normality, soundness; wisdom *Ant* derangement, insanity, lunacy, madness, mania ♦ [5] belief, conviction, eye, feeling, judgment (*or* judgement), notion, opinion, persuasion, sentiment, verdict, view — more at OPINION

²**mind** *vb* **1** *chiefly dial* : REMEMBER **2** ♦ : to attend to closely **3** ♦ : to follow the orders or instructions of : OBEY **4** : to be concerned about; *also* : DISLIKE **5** ♦ : to be careful or cautious about ⟨∼ the step⟩ **6** ♦ : to take charge of **7** : to regard with attention

  ♦ [2] attend, hark, hear, heed, listen — more at LISTEN ♦ [2, 3] comply, follow, heed, listen, note, obey, observe, regard, watch — more at HEED ♦ [5] beware (of), guard (against), watch out (for) — more at BEWARE (OF) ♦ [6] attend, care, oversee, superintend, supervise, tend — more at TEND

mind–bend·ing \'mīnd-₁ben-diŋ\ *adj* : MIND-BLOWING

mind–blow·ing \-₁blō-iŋ\ *adj* : PSYCHEDELIC 1; *also* : MIND-BOGGLING ⟨∼ special effects⟩

mind–bog·gling \-₁bä-gə-liŋ\ *adj* : mentally or emotionally exciting or overwhelming

mind·ed \'mīn-dəd\ *adj* **1** ♦ : having inclination, disposition, or tendency : INCLINED, DISPOSED **2** : having a mind of a specified kind or concerned with a specific thing — usu. used in combination ⟨narrow-*minded*⟩

  ♦ amenable, disposed, game, glad, inclined, ready, willing — more at WILLING

mind·ful \'mīnd-fəl\ *adj* ♦ : bearing in mind : AWARE ⟨∼ of their needs⟩ — **mind·ful·ly** *adv* — **mind·ful·ness** *n*

  ♦ alive, aware, cognizant, conscious, sensible, sentient, witting — more at CONSCIOUS

mind·less \-ləs\ *adj* **1 a** : marked by a lack of mind or consciousness **b** ♦ : marked by no use of the intellect **2** ♦ : not mindful : HEEDLESS — **mind·less·ly** *adv*

  ♦ [1b] dumb, senseless, stupid, witless — more at STUPID ♦ [2] careless, heedless, unguarded, unsafe, unwary — more at CARELESS

mind·less·ness \-nəs\ *n* ♦ : the quality or state of being mindless

  ♦ dopiness, foolishness, imbecility, stupidity — more at STUPIDITY

¹**mine** \'mīn\ *pron* : that which belongs to me

²**mine** *n* **1** : an excavation in the earth from which minerals are taken; *also* : an ore deposit **2** : an underground passage beneath an enemy position **3** : an explosive device for destroying enemy personnel, vehicles, or ships **4** : a rich source of supply

³**mine** *vb* **mined**; **min·ing** **1** : to dig a mine **2** : UNDERMINE **3** : to get ore from the earth **4** : to place military mines in — **min·er** *n*

mine·field \'mīn-₁fēld\ *n* **1** : an area set with mines **2** : something resembling a minefield esp. in having many dangers

mine·lay·er \-₁lā-ər\ *n* : a naval vessel for laying underwater mines

min·er·al \'mi-nə-rəl\ *n* **1** : a crystalline substance (as diamond or quartz) of inorganic origin **2** : a naturally occurring substance (as coal, salt, or water) obtained usu. from the ground — **mineral** *adj*

min·er·al·ise *chiefly Brit var of* MINERALIZE

min·er·al·ize \'mi-nə-rə-₁līz\ *vb* **-ized**; **-iz·ing** **1** : to impregnate or supply with minerals **2** : to change into mineral form — **min·er·al·i·za·tion** \-rə-lə-'zā-shən\ *n*

min·er·al·o·gy \₁mi-nə-'rä-lə-jē, -'ra-\ *n* : a science dealing with minerals — **min·er·al·og·i·cal** \₁mi-nə-rə-'lä-ji-kəl\ *adj* — **min·er·al·o·gist** \₁mi-nə-'rä-lə-jist, -'ra-\ *n*

mineral oil *n* : an oil of mineral origin; *esp* : a refined petroleum oil used as a laxative

mineral water *n* : water infused with mineral salts or gases

min·e·stro·ne \ˌmi-nə-'strō-nē, -'strōn\ n [It, fr. *minestra*, fr. *minestrare* to serve, dish up, fr. L *ministrare*, fr. *minister* servant] : a rich thick vegetable soup

mine·sweep·er \'mīn-ˌswē-pər\ n : a warship designed for removing or neutralizing underwater mines

min·gle \'miŋ-gəl\ vb **min·gled; min·gling** 1 ♦ : to bring or combine together 2 ♦ : to come into contact : ASSOCIATE; *also* : to move about (as in a group)

    ♦ [1] amalgamate, blend, combine, commingle, fuse, incorporate, integrate, intermingle, merge, mix — more at MIX ♦ [2] associate, fraternize, hobnob, mix, socialize — more at SOCIALIZE

ming tree \'miŋ-\ n : a dwarfed usu. evergreen tree grown as bonsai; *also* : an artificial plant resembling this

mini \'mi-nē\ n, pl **min·is** : something small of its kind — **mini** adj

mini- comb form : smaller or briefer than usual, normal, or standard

¹min·ia·ture \'mi-nē-ə-ˌchùr, 'mi-ni-ˌchùr, -chər\ n [It *miniatura* art of illuminating a manuscript, fr. ML, fr. L *miniare* to color with red lead, fr. *minium* red lead] 1 : a copy on a much reduced scale; *also* : something small of its kind 2 : a small painting (as on ivory or metal) — **min·ia·tur·ist** \-ˌchùr-ist, -chər-\ n

²miniature adj ♦ : being or represented on a small scale

    ♦ atomic, infinitesimal, microscopic, minute, teeny, tiny, wee — more at TINY

min·ia·tur·ize \'mi-nē-ə-ˌchə-ˌrīz, 'mi-ni-\ vb **-ized; -iz·ing** : to design or construct in small size — **min·ia·tur·i·za·tion** \ˌmi-nē-ə-ˌchùr-ə-'zā-shən, ˌmi-ni-, -chər-\ n

mini·bar \'mi-nē-ˌbär\ n : a small refrigerator in a hotel room that is stocked with beverages and snacks

mini·bike \'mi-nē-ˌbīk\ n : a small one-passenger motorcycle

mini·bus \-ˌbəs\ n : a small bus or van

mini·com·put·er \-kəm-ˌpyü-tər\ n : a computer between a mainframe and a microcomputer in size and speed

mini·disc \'mi-nē-ˌdisk\ n : a miniature optical disk

min·im \'mi-nəm\ n : a unit of liquid measure equal to ¹/₆₀ fluid dram

min·i·mal \'mi-nə-məl\ adj 1 ♦ : relating to or being a minimum : LEAST 2 : of or relating to minimalism or minimal art — **min·i·mal·ly** adv

    ♦ least, minimum; *also* fewer, lesser, low, slight, small *Ant* full, largest, maximum, top, topmost, utmost

minimal art n : abstract art consisting primarily of simple geometric forms executed in an impersonal style — **minimal artist** n

min·i·mal·ism \'mi-nə-mə-ˌli-zəm\ n : MINIMAL ART; *also* : a style (as in music or literature) marked by extreme spareness or simplicity — **min·i·mal·ist** \-list\ n

mini·mart \'mi-nē-ˌmärt\ n : CONVENIENCE STORE

min·i·mise *chiefly Brit var of* MINIMIZE

min·i·mize \'mi-nə-ˌmīz\ vb **-mized; -miz·ing** 1 : to reduce or keep to a minimum 2 a : to underestimate intentionally b ♦ : to speak slightingly of : BELITTLE 3 : to replace (a window) on a computer display with a small button or icon which will restore the window when selected

    ♦ belittle, cry down, decry, deprecate, depreciate, diminish, discount, disparage, put down, write off — more at DECRY

¹min·i·mum \'mi-nə-məm\ n, pl **-ma** \-mə\ *or* **-mums** 1 : the least quantity assignable, admissible, or possible 2 : the least of a set of numbers 3 : the lowest degree or amount of variation (as of temperature) reached or recorded

²minimum adj ♦ : of, relating to, or constituting a minimum

    ♦ least, minimal — more at MINIMAL

min·ion \'min-yən\ n [MF *mignon* darling] 1 : a servile dependent, follower, or underling 2 ♦ : one highly favored 3 : a subordinate official

    ♦ darling, favorite (*or* favourite), pet, preference — more at FAVORITE

min·is·cule \'mi-nəs-ˌkyül\ *var of* MINUSCULE

mini·se·ries \'mi-nē-ˌsir-ēz\ n : a television story presented in sequential episodes

mini·skirt \-ˌskərt\ n : a skirt with the hemline several inches above the knee

¹min·is·ter \'mi-nə-stər\ n 1 : AGENT 2 ♦ : a member of the clergy esp. of a Protestant communion 3 : a high officer of state who heads a division of governmental activities 4 ♦ : a diplomatic representative to a foreign state

    ♦ [2] clergyman, divine, ecclesiastic, father, preacher, priest, reverend — more at CLERGYMAN ♦ [4] ambassador, delegate, emissary, envoy, legate, representative — more at AMBASSADOR

²minister vb 1 : to perform the functions of a minister of religion 2 ♦ : to give aid or service ⟨~ to the sick⟩ — **min·is·tra·tion** \ˌmi-nə-'strā-shən\ n

    ♦ *usu* minister to aid, care, mother, nurse — more at NURSE

min·is·te·ri·al \ˌmi-nə-'stir-ē-əl\ adj ♦ : of, relating to, or characteristic of a minister or the ministry

    ♦ clerical, pastoral, priestly, sacerdotal — more at CLERICAL

¹min·is·trant \'mi-nə-strənt\ adj, archaic : performing service as a minister

²ministrant n : one that ministers

min·is·try \'mi-nə-strē\ n, pl **-tries** 1 : MINISTRATION 2 : the office, duties, or functions of a minister; *also* : the period of service or office 3 : CLERGY 4 : AGENCY 5 *often cap* : the body of ministers governing a nation or state; *also* : a government department headed by a minister

mini·tow·er \'mi-nē-ˌtaù(-ə)r\ n : a computer tower of intermediate size

mini·van \'mi-nē-ˌvan\ n : a small van

mink \'miŋk\ n, pl **mink** *or* **minks** : either of two slender flesh-eating mammals resembling the related weasels; *also* : the soft lustrous typically dark brown fur of a mink

min·ke whale \'miŋ-kə-\ n : a small grayish baleen whale with a whitish underside

Minn abbr Minnesota

min·ne·sing·er \'mi-ni-ˌsiŋ-ər, -ˌziŋ-\ n [G, fr. Middle High German, fr. *minne* love + *singer* singer] : any of a class of German lyric poets and musicians of the 12th to the 14th centuries

min·now \'mi-nō\ n, pl **minnows** *also* **minnow** : any of numerous small freshwater fishes

¹mi·nor \'mī-nər\ adj 1 ♦ : inferior in importance, size, or degree 2 : not having reached majority 3 : having the third, sixth, and sometimes the seventh degrees lowered by a half step ⟨~ scale⟩; *also* : based on a minor scale ⟨~ key⟩ 4 : not serious ⟨~ illness⟩

    ♦ inferior, junior, less, lesser, lower, subordinate, under — more at LESSER ♦ frivolous, inconsequential, inconsiderable, insignificant, little, minute, negligible, slight, small, trifling, trivial, unimportant — more at UNIMPORTANT

²minor n 1 : a person who has not attained majority 2 : a subject of academic study chosen as a secondary field of specialization

³minor vb : to pursue an academic minor

mi·nor·i·ty \mə-'nòr-ə-tē, mī-\ n, pl **-ties** 1 : the period or state of being a minor 2 : the smaller in number of two groups; *esp* : a group having less than the number of votes necessary for control 3 : a part of a population differing from others (as in race); *also* : a member of a minority

mi·nox·i·dil \mə-'näk-sə-ˌdil\ n : a drug used orally to treat hypertension and topically in solution to promote hair regrowth in some forms of baldness

min·ster \'min-stər\ n : a large or important church

min·strel \'min-strəl\ n 1 : a medieval singer of verses 2 a : MUSICIAN b ♦ : one who writes poetry : POET 3 : any of a group of performers usu. with blackened faces caricaturing black performers that originated in the U.S. in the early 19th century ⟨a ~ show⟩

♦ bard, poet, versifier — more at POET

min·strel·sy \-sē\ *n* : the singing and playing of a minstrel; *also* : a body of minstrels

¹mint \'mint\ *n* **1** : any of a large family of aromatic square-stemmed herbs and shrubs; *esp* : one (as spearmint) that is fragrant and is the source of a flavoring oil **2** : a mint-flavored piece of candy — **minty** *adj*

²mint *n* **1** : a place where coins are made **2** ♦ : a vast sum — **mint** *vb* — **mint·age** \-ij\ *n* — **mint·er** *n*

♦ fortune, wad

³mint *vb* **1** : to make (as coins) out of metal **2** : CREATE; *also* : to give a certain status to ⟨newly ∼ed lawyers⟩ — **mint·age** \-ij\ *n* — **mint·er** *n*

⁴mint *adj* : unmarred as if fresh from a mint ⟨in ∼ condition⟩

min·u·end \'min-yə-ˌwend\ *n* : a number from which another is to be subtracted

min·u·et \ˌmin-yə-'wet\ *n* : a slow graceful dance

¹mi·nus \'mī-nəs\ *prep* **1** : diminished by : LESS ⟨7 ∼ 3 equals 4⟩ **2** ♦ : deprived of : WITHOUT ⟨∼ his hat⟩

♦ sans, wanting, without — more at WITHOUT

²minus *n* ♦ : a negative quantity or quality

♦ disadvantage, drawback, handicap, liability, penalty, strike — more at DISADVANTAGE

³minus *adj* **1** : algebraically negative ⟨∼ quantity⟩ **2** : having negative qualities

¹mi·nus·cule \'mi-nəs-ˌkyül\ *n* : a lowercase letter

²minuscule *adj* ♦ : very small

♦ atomic, infinitesimal, microscopic, miniature, minute, tiny, wee — more at TINY

minus sign *n* : a sign – used in mathematics to indicate subtraction or a negative quantity

¹min·ute \'mi-nət\ *n* **1** : a 60th part of an hour or of a degree : 60 seconds **2** ♦ : a short space of time **3** *pl* : the official record of the proceedings of a meeting

♦ flash, instant, jiffy, moment, second, shake, trice, twinkle, twinkling, wink — more at INSTANT

²mi·nute \mī-'nüt, mə-, -'nyüt\ *adj* **mi·nut·er; -est 1** ♦ : very small **2** ♦ : of little importance : TRIFLING **3** ♦ : marked by close attention to details — **mi·nute·ness** *n*

♦ [1] atomic, infinitesimal, microscopic, miniature, tiny, wee — more at TINY ♦ [2] frivolous, inconsequential, inconsiderable, insignificant, little, minor, negligible, slight, small, trifling, trivial, unimportant — more at UNIMPORTANT ♦ [3] circumstantial, detailed, elaborate, full, thorough — more at DETAILED

mi·nute·ly \mī-'nüt-lē, mə-, -'nyüt-\ *adv* ♦ : in a minute manner or degree

♦ completely, exhaustively, fully, roundly, thoroughly, totally — more at THOROUGHLY

min·ute·man \'mi-nət-ˌman\ *n* : a member of a group of armed men pledged to take the field at a minute's notice during and immediately before the American Revolution

mi·nu·tia \mə-'nü-shə, -'nyü-, -shē-ə\ *n, pl* **-ti·ae** \-shē-ˌē\ [L] : a minute or minor detail — usu. used in pl.

minx \'miŋks\ *n* : a pert girl

Mio·cene \'mī-ə-ˌsēn\ *adj* : of, relating to, or being the epoch of the Tertiary between the Oligocene and the Pliocene — **Miocene** *n*

mir·a·cle \'mir-i-kəl\ *n* **1** : an extraordinary event manifesting divine intervention in human affairs **2** ♦ : an unusual event, thing, or accomplishment : WONDER, MARVEL

♦ caution, flash, marvel, phenomenon, portent, prodigy, sensation, wonder — more at WONDER

miracle drug *n* : a usu. newly discovered drug that elicits a dramatic response in a patient's condition

mi·rac·u·lous \mə-'ra-kyə-ləs\ *adj* **1** ♦ : of the nature of a miracle **2** ♦ : suggesting a miracle : MARVELOUS **3** : working or able to work miracles — **mi·rac·u·lous·ly** *adv*

♦ [1] magical, phenomenal, superhuman, supernatural, uncanny, unearthly — more at SUPERNATURAL

♦ [2] amazing, astonishing, astounding, awesome, fabulous, marvelous (*or* marvellous), stunning, stupendous, sublime, surprising, wonderful — more at MARVELOUS

mi·rage \mə-'räzh\ *n* **1** : an illusion that often appears as a pool of water or a mirror in which distant objects are seen inverted, is sometimes seen at sea, in the desert, or over a hot pavement, and results from atmospheric conditions **2** : something illusory and unattainable

¹mire \'mīr\ *n* ♦ : heavy and often deep mud or slush

♦ muck, mud, ooze, slime, slop, sludge, slush — more at MUD ♦ bog, fen, marsh, morass, slough, swamp — more at SWAMP

²mire *vb* **mired; mir·ing 1** : to stick or sink in or as if in mire **2** ♦ : to cover or soil with mire

♦ befoul, begrime, besmirch, blacken, dirty, foul, grime, muddy, smirch, soil, stain — more at DIRTY

mire·poix \mir-'pwä\ *n, pl* **mirepoix** : a mixture of diced vegetables and sometimes meats used in soups, stews, and sauces

¹mir·ror \'mir-ər\ *n* **1** : a polished or smooth surface (as of glass) that forms images by reflection **2** : a true representation

²mirror *vb* **1** : to reflect in or as if in a mirror **2** : RESEMBLE

mirth \'mərth\ *n* ♦ : gladness or gaiety accompanied with laughter — **mirth·less** *adj*

♦ cheer, cheerfulness, cheeriness, glee, hilarity, joviality, merriment; *also* frivolity, levity; carnival, gaiety, jollification, jollity, reveling, revelry; brightness, buoyancy, humor; insouciance, lightheartedness, playfulness; buffoonery, clownishness, flippancy, jocularity, joking, joshing; animation, jauntiness, liveliness, vivacity; joyousness, rejoicing; frolicking, gamboling, rollicking, romping

mirth·ful \-fəl\ *adj* ♦ : full of mirth or merriment

♦ blithe, boon, festive, gay, gleeful, jocund, jolly, jovial, merry, sunny — more at MERRY

mirth·ful·ly \-fə-lē\ *adv* ♦ : in a mirthful manner

♦ cheerfully, gaily, happily, heartily, jovially, merrily — more at GAILY

mirth·ful·ness \-nəs\ *n* ♦ : the quality or state of being mirthful

♦ cheer, cheerfulness, glee, hilarity, joviality, merriment, mirth — more at MIRTH

MIRV \'mərv\ *n* [*m*ultiple *i*ndependently targeted *r*eentry *v*ehicle] : an ICBM with multiple warheads that have different targets — **MIRV** *vb*

miry \'mīr-ē\ *adj* ♦ : resembling a mire : characterized by swampy ground

♦ mucky, muddy, oozy, slimy, slushy — more at MUDDY

mis·ad·ven·ture \ˌmis-əd-'ven-chər\ *n* **1** ♦ : bad luck **2** ♦ : a piece of bad luck

♦ [1, 2] adversity, knock, mischance, misfortune, mishap — more at MISFORTUNE

mis·aligned \ˌmis-ə-'līnd\ *adj* : not properly aligned — **mis·align·ment** \-'līn-mənt\ *n*

mis·al·li·ance \ˌmis-ə-'lī-əns\ *n* : an improper or unsuitable marriage

mis·al·lo·ca·tion \ˌmi-sa-lə-'kā-shən\ *n* : faulty or improper allocation

mis·an·dry \'mi-ˌsan-drē\ *n* : a hatred of men — **mis·an·drist** \-drist\ *n or adj*

mis·an·thrope \'mis-ᵊn-ˌthrōp\ *n* : one who hates humankind — **mis·an·throp·ic** \ˌmis-ᵊn-'thrä-pik\ *adj* — **mis·an·throp·i·cal·ly** \-pi-k(ə-)lē\ *adv* — **mis·an·thro·py** \mi-'san-thrə-pē\ *n*

mis·ap·pli·ca·tion \ˌmi-ˌsa-plə-'kā-shən\ *n* : the action of misapplying

mis·ap·ply \ˌmi-sə-'plī\ *vb* ♦ : to apply wrongly

♦ abuse, misuse, pervert; *also* degrade, twist; mismanage, corrupt

mis·ap·pre·hend \ˌmi-ˌsa-pri-'hend\ *vb* ♦ : to fail to understand : MISUNDERSTAND

♦ misconstrue, misinterpret, misread, miss, mistake, misunderstand — more at MISUNDERSTAND

mis·ap·pre·hen·sion \-'hen-chən\ *n* ♦ : the act or instance of misapprehending

♦ misjudgment, mistake, misunderstanding — more at MISTAKE ♦ misconstruction, misinterpretation, misunderstanding — more at MISUNDERSTANDING

mis·ap·pro·pri·ate \ˌmi-sə-'prō-prē-ˌāt\ *vb* ♦ : to appropriate wrongly (as by embezzlement) — **mis·ap·pro·pri·a·tion** \-ˌprō-prē-'ā-shən\ *n*

♦ appropriate, filch, hook, nip, pilfer, pocket, purloin, snitch, steal, swipe, thieve — more at STEAL

mis·be·got·ten \-bi-'gät-ᵊn\ *adj* : born of parents not married to each other : ILLEGITIMATE; *also* : ill-conceived

mis·be·have \ˌmis-bi-'hāv\ *vb* : to behave improperly — **mis·be·hav·er** *n*

♦ act out, act up, carry on; *also* clown (around), cut up, fool around

mis·be·hav·ior \-'hā-vyər\ *n* ♦ : bad, improper, or rude behavior

♦ malfeasance, misconduct, misdoing, wrongdoing — more at MISCONDUCT

mis·be·lief \ˌmis-bə-'lēf\ *n* ♦ : erroneous or false belief

♦ error, fallacy, falsehood, falsity, illusion, misconception, myth, untruth — more at FALLACY

mis·be·liev·er \-bə-'lē-vər\ *n* : one who holds a false or unorthodox belief

mis·brand \mis-'brand\ *vb* : to brand falsely or in a misleading manner

misc *abbr* miscellaneous

mis·cal·cu·late \mis-'kal-kyə-ˌlāt\ *vb* ♦ : to calculate wrongly — **mis·cal·cu·la·tion** \ˌmis-ˌkal-kyə-'lā-shən\ *n*

♦ misconceive, misjudge, mistake; *also* misconstrue, misinterpret, misunderstand; overrate, overvalue; underestimate, underrate, undervalue; miscount

mis·call \mis-'kȯl\ *vb* : MISNAME

mis·car·riage \-'kar-ij\ *n* 1 : failure in the administration of justice 2 : spontaneous expulsion of a fetus before it is capable of independent life

mis·car·ry \-'kar-ē\ *vb* 1 : to have a miscarriage of a fetus 2 : to go wrong; *also* : to be unsuccessful

mis·ce·ge·na·tion \ˌmi-se-jə-'nā-shən, ˌmi-si-jə-'nā-\ *n* [L *miscēre* to mix + *genus* race] : marriage, cohabitation, or sexual intercourse between persons of different races

mis·cel·la·neous \ˌmi-sə-'lā-nē-əs\ *adj* 1 : consisting of diverse things or members 2 : having various traits; *also* : dealing with or interested in diverse subjects — **mis·cel·la·neous·ly** *adv* — **mis·cel·la·neous·ness** *n*

♦ assorted, heterogeneous, mixed, motley, varied; *also* manifold, multifarious, multiple, multiplex, myriad; disparate, divergent, diverse, sundry, various; chaotic, cluttered, confused, disarranged, disheveled, disordered, jumbled, littered, messed, messy, muddled; amalgamated, blended, combined, conglomerated, fused, incorporated, intermingled, intermixed, merged, mingled; unclassified, unsorted *Ant* homogeneous

mis·cel·la·ny \'mi-sə-ˌlā-nē\ *n, pl* **-nies** 1 ♦ : a collection of writings on various subjects 2 ♦ : a mixture of various things : HODGEPODGE

♦ [1] album, anthology, compilation — more at ANTHOLOGY ♦ [2] assortment, clutter, hash, hodgepodge, jumble, litter, medley, mélange, motley, muddle, potpourri, rummage, scramble, shuffle, tumble, variety, welter; *also* notions, odds and ends, sundries; accumulation, aggregation, conglomeration; catchall, patchwork; admixture, amalgam, blend, combination, composite, compound, fusion, intermixture, mix, mixture; chaos, confusion, disarray, disorder, mess, muddle, shambles; knot, snarl, tangle

mis·chance \mis-'chans\ *n* 1 ♦ : bad luck 2 ♦ : a piece of bad luck; *also* : an unfortunate accident

♦ adversity, knock, misadventure, misfortune, mishap — more at MISFORTUNE

mis·chief \'mis-chəf\ *n* [ME *meschief*, fr. AF, misfortune, hardship, fr. OF *meschever* to come out badly, fr. *mes-* badly + *chief* head, end] 1 : injury caused by a particular agent 2 ♦ : a source of harm or irritation; *esp* : a person who causes mischief 3 a ♦ : action that annoys b ♦ : the quality or state of being mischievous : MISCHIEVOUSNESS

♦ [2] devil, hellion, imp, monkey, rapscallion, rascal, rogue, scamp, urchin — more at SCAMP ♦ [3a, b] devilishness, impishness, knavery, mischievousness, rascality, shenanigans, waggery, wickedness; *also* naughtiness; friskiness, playfulness; chicanery, hanky-panky, trickery; high jinks, monkeyshines, skylarking, tomfoolery; antic, caper, practical joke; aggravation, annoyance, exasperation, irritation

mis·chie·vous \'mis-chə-vəs\ *adj* 1 ♦ : of a kind likely to be damaging : HARMFUL, INJURIOUS 2 : causing annoyance or minor injury 3 ♦ : irresponsibly playful ⟨∼ children⟩ — **mis·chie·vous·ly** *adv*

♦ [1] adverse, damaging, detrimental, harmful, hurtful, injurious, prejudicial — more at HARMFUL ♦ [3] devilish, impish, knavish, naughty, rascally, roguish, sly, waggish, wicked

mis·chie·vous·ness *n* ♦ : the quality or state of being mischievous

♦ devilishness, impishness, knavery, mischief, rascality, shenanigans, waggery, wickedness — more at MISCHIEF

mis·ci·ble \'mi-sə-bəl\ *adj* : capable of being mixed

mis·com·mu·ni·ca·tion \ˌmis-kə-ˌmyü-nə-'kā-shən\ *n* : failure to communicate clearly

mis·con·ceive \ˌmis-kən-'sēv\ *vb* ♦ : to interpret incorrectly

♦ miscalculate, misjudge, mistake — more at MISCALCULATE

mis·con·cep·tion \-'sep-shən\ *n* ♦ : the act or result of misconceiving

♦ error, fallacy, falsehood, falsity, illusion, myth, untruth — more at FALLACY

mis·con·duct \mis-'kän-(ˌ)dəkt\ *n* 1 : MISMANAGEMENT 2 ♦ : intentional wrongdoing 3 ♦ : improper behavior

♦ [2, 3] malfeasance, misbehavior, misdoing, wrongdoing; *also* crime, malefaction, misdeed, sin, wrong; malpractice; familiarity, gaffe, impropriety, indiscretion; blunder, error, fault, flub, fumble, goof, lapse, miscue, misstep, mistake, slip, slipup, stumble

mis·con·struc·tion \-'strək-shən\ *n* ♦ : the action of misconstruing

♦ misapprehension, misinterpretation, misunderstanding — more at MISUNDERSTANDING

mis·con·strue \ˌmis-kən-'strü\ *vb* ♦ : to interpret wrongly : MISINTERPRET

♦ misapprehend, misinterpret, misread, miss, mistake, misunderstand — more at MISUNDERSTAND

mis·count \mis-'kaúnt\ *vb* : to count incorrectly : MISCALCULATE

mis·cre·ant \'mis-krē-ənt\ *n* : one who behaves criminally or viciously — **miscreant** *adj*

mis·cue \mis-'kyü\ *n* ♦ : a wrong action or statement : MISTAKE, ERROR — **miscue** *vb*

♦ blunder, error, fault, flub, fumble, goof, lapse, misstep, mistake, oversight, slip, stumble — more at ERROR

mis·deed \mis-'dēd\ *n* ♦ : a wrong deed

♦ breach, crime, error, malefaction, misdoing, offense, sin, transgression, violation, wrongdoing — more at OFFENSE

mis·de·mean·or *or Can and Brit* **mis·de·mean·our** \ˌmis-di-'mē-nər\ *n* 1 : a crime less serious than a felony 2 : MISDEED

mis·di·rect \ˌmis-də-ˈrekt, -dī-\ *vb* : to give a wrong direction to — **mis·di·rec·tion** \-ˈrek-shən\ *n*

mis·do·ing \mis-ˈdü-iŋ\ *n* ♦ : the act or an instance of misbehaving : WRONGDOING — **mis·do** \-ˈdü\ *vb* — **mis·do·er** \-ˈdü-ər\ *n*

♦ malfeasance, misbehavior, misconduct, wrongdoing — more at MISCONDUCT

mise–en–scène \ˌmē-ˌzänⁿ-ˈsen, -ˈsän\ *n, pl* **mise–en–scènes** *same or* -ˈsenz, -ˈsänz\ [F] **1** : the arrangement of the scenery, property, and actors on a stage **2** : SETTING; *also* : ENVIRONMENT

mi·ser \ˈmī-zər\ *n* [L *miser* miserable] ♦ : a person who hoards and is stingy with money — **mi·ser·ly** *adj*

♦ cheapskate, niggard, skinflint, tightwad; *also* hoarder, saver

mis·er·a·ble \ˈmi-zə-rə-bəl, ˈmiz-rə-\ *adj* **1 a** ♦ : wretchedly deficient, meager, or of poor quality **b** ♦ : causing extreme discomfort or unhappiness **2** ♦ : being in a state of poverty or distress **3** : being likely to discredit or shame — **mis·er·a·ble·ness** *n* — **mis·er·a·bly** \-blē\ *adv*

♦ [1a] bad, cheap, inferior, mediocre, poor, rotten, second-rate, shabby, shoddy, sleazy, tacky, terrible, threadbare, wretched — more at CHEAP ♦ [1b] bleak, dark, dismal, dreary, gloomy, gray (*or* grey), somber (*or* sombre), wretched — more at GLOOMY ♦ [2] heartbreaking, pathetic, piteous, pitiful, poor, rueful, sorry, unhappy, wretched

mis·er·li·ness \ˈmī-zər-lē-nəs\ *n* : the quality or state of being a miser or like a miser

♦ cheapness, closeness, parsimony, stinginess, tightness — more at PARSIMONY

mis·ery \ˈmi-zə-rē\ *n, pl* **-er·ies 1** ♦ : suffering and want caused by poverty or affliction **2** : a cause of suffering or discomfort **3** : emotional distress

♦ affliction, agony, anguish, distress, pain, torment, torture, tribulation, woe — more at DISTRESS

mis·fea·sance \mis-ˈfēz-ᵊns\ *n* : the performance of a lawful action in an illegal or improper manner

mis·file \-ˈfī(-ə)l\ *vb* : to file in the wrong place

mis·fire \-ˈfī(-ə)r\ *vb* **1** : to fail to fire **2** : to miss an intended effect — **misfire** *n*

mis·fit \ˈmis-ˌfit, *sense 1 also* mis-ˈfit\ *n* **1** : something that fits badly **2** : a person who is poorly adjusted to a situation or environment

mis·for·tune \mis-ˈfor-chən\ *n* **1** ♦ : bad luck **2** ♦ : an unfortunate condition or event

♦ [1, 2] adversity, knock, misadventure, mischance, mishap; *also* calamity, cataclysm, catastrophe, disaster; tragedy; affliction, hardship, trial, tribulation; distress, misery, suffering, unhappiness; defeat, failure, fizzle, nonsuccess; curse, sorrow, trouble; accident, casualty, disappointment, letdown, setback; circumstance, destiny, doom, fate, lot, portion *Ant* fortune, luck

mis·giv·ing \-ˈgi-viŋ\ *n* ♦ : a feeling of doubt or suspicion esp. concerning an action or future event

♦ distrust, doubt, incertitude, mistrust, skepticism, suspicion, uncertainty — more at DOUBT ♦ compunction, qualm, scruple — more at QUALM ♦ alarm, apprehension, dread, foreboding

mis·gov·ern \-ˈgə-vərn\ *vb* ♦ : to govern badly — **mis·gov·ern·ment** *n*

♦ misconduct, mishandle, mismanage, misrule — more at MISMANAGE

mis·guid·ance \mis-ˈgīd-ᵊns\ *n* : faulty guidance

mis·guide \mis-ˈgīd\ *vb* : to lead astray

mis·guid·ed \-ˈgī-dəd\ *adj* : led or prompted by wrong or inappropriate motives or ideals — **mis·guid·ed·ly** *adv*

mis·han·dle \-ˈhand-ᵊl\ *vb* **1** ♦ : to treat roughly : MALTREAT **2** ♦ : to manage wrongly

♦ [1] abuse, ill-treat, maltreat, manhandle, mistreat, misuse — more at ABUSE ♦ [2] misconduct, misgovern, mismanage, misrule — more at MISMANAGE

mis·hap \ˈmis-ˌhap\ *n* ♦ : an unfortunate accident

♦ accident, casualty — more at ACCIDENT ♦ adversity, knock, misadventure, mischance, misfortune — more at MISFORTUNE

mish·mash \ˈmish-ˌmash, -ˌmäsh\ *n* : a mass of things mingled together : HODGEPODGE, JUMBLE

mis·in·form \ˌmis-ᵊn-ˈform\ *vb* ♦ : to give false or misleading information to — **mis·in·for·ma·tion** \ˌmi-sin-fər-ˈmā-shən\ *n*

♦ beguile, bluff, cozen, deceive, delude, dupe, fool, gull, have, hoax, hoodwink, humbug, mislead, string along, take in, trick — more at DECEIVE

mis·in·ter·pret \ˌmis-ᵊn-ˈtər-prət\ *vb* ♦ : to understand or explain wrongly

♦ color (*or* colour), distort, falsify, garble, misrepresent, misstate, pervert, twist, warp — more at GARBLE ♦ misapprehend, misconstrue, misread, miss, mistake, misunderstand — more at MISUNDERSTAND

mis·in·ter·pre·ta·tion \ˌmis-ᵊn-ˌtər-prə-ˈtā- shən\ *n* ♦ : incorrect interpretation

♦ misapprehension, misconstruction, misunderstanding — more at MISUNDERSTANDING

mis·judge \mis-ˈjəj\ *vb* **1** ♦ : to estimate wrongly **2** : to have an unjust opinion of

♦ miscalculate, misconceive, mistake — more at MISCALCULATE

mis·judg·ment \mis-ˈjəj-mənt\ *n* ♦ : incorrect or distorted judgment

♦ misapprehension, mistake, misunderstanding — more at MISTAKE

mis·la·bel \-ˈlā-bəl\ *vb* : to label incorrectly or falsely

mis·lay \mis-ˈlā\ *vb* **-laid** \-ˈlād\; **-lay·ing** : MISPLACE, LOSE

mis·lead \mis-ˈlēd\ *vb* **-led** \-ˈled\; **-lead·ing** ♦ : to lead in a wrong direction or into a mistaken action or belief — **mis·lead·ing·ly** *adv*

♦ beguile, bluff, cozen, deceive, delude, dupe, fool, gull, have, hoax, hoodwink, humbug, misinform, string along, take in, trick — more at DECEIVE

misleading *adj* ♦ : tending to mislead

♦ deceitful, deceptive, delusive, fallacious, false, specious — more at DECEPTIVE

mis·like \-ˈlīk\ *vb* : DISLIKE — **mis·like** *n*

mis·man·age \-ˈma-nij\ *vb* ♦ : to manage wrongly or incompetently — **mis·man·age·ment** *n*

♦ misconduct, misgovern, mishandle, misrule; *also* abuse, ill-treat, ill-use, maltreat, mistreat, misuse; damage, harm, hurt, violate

mis·match \-ˈmach\ *vb* : to match unsuitably or badly — **mis·match** \mis-ˈmach, ˈmis-ˌmach\ *n*

mis·name \-ˈnām\ *vb* : to name incorrectly : MISCALL

mis·no·mer \mis-ˈnō-mər\ *n* : a wrong or inappropriate name or designation

mi·so \ˈmē-sō\ *n* : a high-protein fermented food paste consisting chiefly of soybeans, salt, and usu. grain

mi·sog·y·ny \mə-ˈsä-jə-nē\ *n* [Gk *misogynia*, fr. *misein* to hate + *gynē* woman] : a hatred of women — **mi·sog·y·nist** \-nist\ *n or adj* — **mi·sog·y·nis·tic** \mə-ˌsä-jə-ˈnis-tik\ *adj*

mis·ori·ent \mi-ˈsor-ē-ˌent\ *vb* : to orient improperly or incorrectly — **mis·ori·en·ta·tion** \mi-ˌsor-ē-ən-ˈtā-shən\ *n*

mis·place \mis-ˈplās\ *vb* **1** : to put in a wrong or unremembered place **2** : to set on a wrong object ⟨~ trust⟩

mis·play \-ˈplā\ *n* : a wrong or unskillful play — **mis·play** \mis-ˈplā, ˈmis-ˌplā\ *vb*

mis·print \mis-ˈprint\ *n* : a mistake in printed matter — **mis·print** \mis-ˈprint\ *vb*

mis·pro·nounce \ˌmis-prə-ˈnauns\ *vb* : to pronounce incorrectly — **mis·pro·nun·ci·a·tion** \-prə-ˌnən-sē-ˈā-shən\ *n*

mis·quote \mis-ˈkwōt\ *vb* : to quote incorrectly — **mis·quo·ta·tion** \ˌmis-kwō-ˈtā-shən\ *n*

mis·read \-ˈrēd\ *vb* **-read** \-ˈred\; **-read·ing** \-ˈrē-diŋ\ ♦ : to read or interpret incorrectly

♦ misapprehend, misconstrue, misinterpret, miss, mistake, misunderstand — more at MISUNDERSTAND

mis·rep·re·sent \,mis-,re-pri-'zent\ *vb* ♦ : to represent falsely or unfairly ⟨∼ the facts⟩ — **mis·rep·re·sen·ta·tion** \-,zen-'tā-shən\ *n*

♦ color (*or* colour), distort, falsify, garble, misinterpret, misstate, pervert, twist, warp — more at GARBLE

¹**mis·rule** \mis-'rül\ *vb* ♦ : to rule incompetently : MISGOVERN

♦ misconduct, misgovern, mishandle, mismanage — more at MISMANAGE

²**misrule** *n* 1 : MISGOVERNMENT 2 : DISORDER

¹**miss** \'mis\ *vb* 1 : to fail to hit, reach, or contact 2 : to feel the absence of 3 : to fail to obtain 4 : AVOID ⟨just ∼ed hitting the other car⟩ 5 : OMIT 6 ♦ : to fail to understand 7 : to fail to perform or attend; *also* : MISFIRE

♦ misapprehend, misconstrue, misinterpret, misread, mistake, misunderstand — more at MISUNDERSTAND

²**miss** *n* 1 ♦ : a failure to hit or to attain a result 2 : MISFIRE

♦ default, delinquency, dereliction, failure, neglect, negligence, oversight — more at FAILURE

³**miss** *n* 1 *cap* — used as a title prefixed to the name of an unmarried woman or girl 2 ♦ : a young unmarried woman or girl

♦ doll, girl, lass, maid, maiden — more at GIRL

Miss *abbr* Mississippi

mis·sal \'mi-səl\ *n* : a book containing all that is said or sung at mass during the entire year

mis·send \mis-'send\ *vb* : to send incorrectly ⟨*missent* mail⟩

mis·shap·en \-'shā-pən\ *adj* ♦ : badly shaped : having an ugly shape

♦ deformed, distorted, malformed, monstrous, shapeless — more at MALFORMED

mis·sile \'mi-səl\ *n* [L, fr. neut. of *missilis* capable of being thrown, fr. *mittere* to let go, send] : an object (as a stone, bullet, or rocket) thrown or projected usu. so as to strike a target

miss·ing \'mi-siŋ\ *adj* ♦ : not present or available; *also* : in an unknown location

♦ absent, away, out — more at ABSENT ♦ absent, nonexistent, wanting — more at ABSENT ♦ gone, lost — more at LOST

mis·sion \'mi-shən\ *n* 1 : a group of missionaries; *also* : a place where missionaries work 2 : a group of envoys to a foreign country; *also* : a team of specialists or cultural leaders sent to a foreign country 3 ♦ : a specific task with which a person or a group is charged

♦ assignment, charge, job, operation, post; *also* burden, chore, duty, need, obligation, requirement, responsibility; labor, work; commitment, pledge, promise; appointment, designation, nomination; compulsion, constraint, restraint

¹**mis·sion·ary** \'mi-shə-,ner-ē\ *adj* : of, relating to, or engaged in missions

²**missionary** *n, pl* **-ar·ies** : a person commissioned by a church to spread its faith or carry on humanitarian work

mis·sion·er \'mi-shə-nər\ *n* : MISSIONARY

Mis·sis·sip·pi·an \,mi-sə-'si-pē-ən\ *adj* : of, relating to, or being the period of the Paleozoic era between the Devonian and the Pennsylvanian — **Mississippian** *n*

mis·sive \'mi-siv\ *n* ♦ : a written communication : LETTER

♦ dispatch, letter, memorandum, note — more at LETTER

mis·speak \mis-'spēk\ *vb* : to say imperfectly or incorrectly

mis·spell \-'spel\ *vb* : to spell incorrectly — **mis·spell·ing** *n*

mis·spend \-'spend\ *vb* **-spent** \-'spent\; **-spend·ing** ♦ : to spend wrongly : WASTE, SQUANDER ⟨my *misspent* youth⟩

♦ blow, dissipate, fritter, lavish, run through, spend, squander, throw away, waste — more at WASTE

mis·state \mis-'stāt\ *vb* ♦ : to state incorrectly — **mis·state·ment** *n*

♦ color (*or* colour), distort, falsify, garble, misinterpret, misrepresent, pervert, twist, warp — more at GARBLE

mis·step \-'step\ *n* 1 : a wrong step 2 ♦ : a mistake in judgment or action

♦ blunder, error, fault, flub, fumble, goof, lapse, miscue, mistake, oversight, slip, stumble — more at ERROR

¹**mist** \'mist\ *n* 1 : water in the form of particles suspended or falling in the air 2 : something that obscures understanding

²**mist** *vb* 1 : to be or become misty 2 : to become moist or blurred 3 ♦ : to cover with or as if with a mist

♦ becloud, befog, blur, cloud, darken, dim, fog, haze, obscure, overshadow, shroud — more at CLOUD

mis·tak·able \mə-'stā-kə-bəl\ *adj* : capable of being misunderstood or mistaken

¹**mis·take** \mi-'stāk\ *vb* **-took** \-'stúk\; **-tak·en** \-'stā-kən\; **-tak·ing** 1 : to blunder in the choice of 2 ♦ : to misunderstand the meaning or intention of : MISINTERPRET 3 ♦ : to make a wrong judgment of the character or ability of 4 : to confuse with another — **mis·tak·er** *n*

♦ [2] misapprehend, misconstrue, misinterpret, misread, miss, misunderstand — more at MISUNDERSTAND ♦ [3] miscalculate, misconceive, misjudge — more at MISCALCULATE

²**mistake** *n* 1 ♦ : a wrong judgment : MISUNDERSTANDING 2 ♦ : a wrong action or statement : ERROR

♦ [1] misapprehension, misconstruction, misinterpretation, misjudgment, misunderstanding ♦ [2] blunder, error, fault, flub, fumble, goof, lapse, miscue, misstep, oversight, slip, stumble — more at ERROR

mis·tak·en·ly \mi-'stā-kən-lē\ *adv* ♦ : in a way that is wrong in action or thought

♦ amiss, erroneously, faultily, improperly, inaptly, incorrectly, wrongly

¹**mis·ter** \'mis-tər\ *n* 1 *cap* — used sometimes instead of *Mr.* 2 : SIR — used without a name in addressing a man

²**mist·er** \'mis-tər\ *n* : a device for spraying mist

mis·tle·toe \'mi-səl-,tō\ *n* : a European parasitic green shrub that grows on trees and has yellowish flowers and waxy white berries

mis·tral \'mis-trəl, mi-'sträl\ *n* [F, fr. Occitan, fr. *mistral* masterful, fr. LL *magistralis* of a teacher, fr. L *magister* master] : a strong cold dry northerly wind of southern France

mis·treat \mis-'trēt\ *vb* ♦ : to treat badly : ABUSE — **mis·treat·ment** *n*

♦ abuse, ill-treat, maltreat, manhandle, mishandle, misuse — more at ABUSE

mis·tress \'mis-trəs\ *n* 1 : a woman who has power, authority, or ownership ⟨∼ of the house⟩ 2 : something personified as female that rules or dominates ⟨when Rome was ∼ of the world⟩ 3 : a woman other than his wife with whom a married man has sexual relations; *also, archaic* : SWEETHEART 4 — used archaically as a title prefixed to the name of a married or unmarried woman

mis·tri·al \'mis-,trī(-ə)l\ *n* : a trial that has no legal effect

¹**mis·trust** \mis-'trəst\ *n* ♦ : a lack of confidence : DISTRUST

♦ distrust, doubt, incertitude, misgiving, skepticism, suspicion, uncertainty — more at DOUBT

²**mistrust** *vb* ♦ : to have no trust or confidence in : SUSPECT

♦ distrust, doubt, question, suspect — more at DISTRUST

mis·trust·ful \-fəl\ *adj* ♦ : marked by mistrust

♦ distrustful, incredulous, leery, skeptical, suspicious — more at SKEPTICAL

mis·trust·ful·ly \-fə-lē\ *adv* ♦ : in a mistrustful manner

♦ askance, distrustfully, dubiously, suspiciously — more at ASKANCE

mis·trust·ful·ness \-nəs\ *n* : the quality or state of being mistrustful

misty \'mis-tē\ *adj* **mist·i·er; -est** **1** ♦ : obscured by or as if by mist ⟨a ~ memory⟩ **2** : TEARFUL — **mist·i·ly** \-tə-lē\ *adv* — **mist·i·ness** \-tē-nəs\ *n*

♦ cloudy, foggy, hazy, murky, smoggy, soupy — more at HAZY

mis·un·der·stand \ˌmi-ˌsən-dər-'stand\ *vb* **-stood** \-'stůd\; **-stand·ing** **1** ♦ : to fail to understand **2** ♦ : to interpret incorrectly

♦ [1, 2] misapprehend, misconstrue, misinterpret, misread, miss, mistake; *also* misconceive *Ant* apprehend, catch, comprehend, conceive, fathom, grasp, know, make out, penetrate, perceive, savvy, see, seize, take in, understand

mis·un·der·stand·ing \-'stan-diŋ\ *n* **1** ♦ : a failure to understand : MISINTERPRETATION **2** ♦ : a usu. verbal conflict between antagonists : DISAGREEMENT, QUARREL

♦ [1] misapprehension, misconstruction, misinterpretation; *also* misconception, mistake ♦ [2] altercation, argument, bicker, brawl, disagreement, dispute, fight, hassle, quarrel, row, scrap, spat, squabble, wrangle — more at ARGUMENT

mis·us·age \mis-'yü-sij\ *n* **1** : bad treatment : ABUSE **2** : wrong or improper use

¹mis·use \mis-'yüz\ *vb* **1** ♦ : to use incorrectly **2** ♦ : to treat badly : ABUSE, MISTREAT

♦ [1] abuse, misapply, pervert, profane, prostitute — more at MISAPPLY ♦ [2] abuse, ill-treat, maltreat, manhandle, mishandle, mistreat — more at ABUSE

²misuse \-'yüs\ *n* ♦ : wrong, careless, or improper use

♦ abuse, perversion; *also* mishandling, mismanagement, mismanaging; maltreatment, mistreatment; damage, destruction, ruin, spoiling, wrecking; corruption, debasement, desecration, profanation, prostitution

¹mite \'mīt\ *n* : any of numerous tiny arthropod animals related to the spiders that often live and feed on animals or plants

²mite *n* **1** ♦ : a small coin or sum of money **2** ♦ : a small amount : BIT **3** ♦ : a small object or creature

♦ [1] peanuts, pittance, shoestring, song; *also* petty cash *Ant* fortune, mint, wad ♦ [2] bit, dab, little, particle, speck, touch, trace — more at PARTICLE ♦ [3] dwarf, midget, peewee, pygmy, runt — more at DWARF

¹mi·ter *or* **mi·tre** \'mī-tər\ *n* [ME *mitre*, fr. AF, fr. L *mitra* headband, turban, fr. Gk] **1** : a headdress worn by bishops and abbots **2** : MITER JOINT

²miter *or* **mitre** *vb* **mi·tered** *or* **mi·tred; mi·ter·ing** *or* **mi·tring** \'mī-tə-riŋ\ **1** : to match or fit together in a miter joint **2** : to bevel the ends of for making a miter joint

miter joint *n* : a usu. perpendicular joint made by fitting together two parts with the ends cut at an angle

mit·i·gate \'mi-tə-ˌgāt\ *vb* **-gat·ed; -gat·ing** **1** : to make less harsh or hostile **2** ♦ : to make less severe or painful — **mit·i·ga·tion** \ˌmi-tə-'gā-shən\ *n* — **mit·i·ga·tive** \'mi-tə-ˌgā-tiv\ *adj*

♦ allay, alleviate, assuage, ease, help, mollify, palliate, relieve, soothe — more at HELP

mi·to·chon·dri·on \ˌmī-tə-'kän-drē-ən\ *n, pl* **-dria** \-drē-ə\ : any of various round or long cellular organelles that produce energy for the cell — **mi·to·chon·dri·al** \-drē-əl\ *adj*

mi·to·sis \mī-'tō-səs\ *n, pl* **-to·ses** \-ˌsēz\ : a process that takes place in the nucleus of a dividing cell and results in the formation of two new nuclei each of which has the same number of chromosomes as the parent nucleus; *also* : cell division in which mitosis occurs — **mi·tot·ic** \-'tä-tik\ *adj*

mitt \'mit\ *n* **1** : a baseball catcher's or first baseman's glove **2** *slang* : HAND

mit·ten \'mit-ᵊn\ *n* : a covering for the hand having a separate section for the thumb only

¹mix \'miks\ *vb* **1** ♦ : to combine into one mass **2** ♦ : to enter into relations : ASSOCIATE **3** : to form by mingling components **4** : to produce (a recording) by electronically combining sounds from different sources **5** : HYBRIDIZE

6 ♦ : to put in disorder : CONFUSE — often used with *up* ⟨~*es* up the facts⟩ **7** : to become involved — **mix·able** *adj* — **mix·er** *n*

♦ [1] amalgamate, blend, combine, commingle, fuse, incorporate, integrate, intermingle, merge, mingle; *also* coalesce; compound, join, link, unite *Ant* segregate, separate, sort (out) ♦ [2] associate, fraternize, hobnob, mingle, socialize — more at SOCIALIZE ♦ *usu* mix up [6] confuse, disorder, jumble, mess, muddle, scramble, shuffle

²mix *n* ♦ : a product of mixing; *esp* : a commercially prepared mixture of food ingredients

♦ admixture, amalgam, blend, combination, composite, compound, fusion, intermixture, mixture — more at BLEND

mixed \'mikst\ *adj* **1** ♦ : made up of or involving individuals or items of more than one kind **2** ♦ : deriving from two or more races or breeds

♦ [1] assorted, heterogeneous, miscellaneous, motley, varied — more at MISCELLANEOUS ♦ [2] hybrid, mongrel; *also* crossbred, crossed, interbred *Ant* full-blooded, purebred, thoroughbred

mixed number *n* : a number (as 5⅔) composed of an integer and a fraction

mixed–up \'mikst-'əp\ *adj* : CONFUSED

mix·er \'mik-sər\ *n* **1** : one that mixes; *esp* : a machine or device for mixing **2** : an event (as a dance) that encourages meeting and socializing **3** : a nonalcoholic beverage used in a cocktail

mixt *abbr* mixture

mix·ture \'miks-chər\ *n* **1** : the act or process of mixing; *also* : the state of being mixed **2** ♦ : a product of mixing

♦ admixture, amalgam, blend, combination, composite, compound, fusion, intermixture, mix — more at BLEND

mix–up \'miks-ˌəp\ *n* **1** : an instance of confusion **2** : CONFLICT, FIGHT

miz·zen *also* **miz·en** \'miz-ᵊn\ *n* **1** : a fore-and-aft sail set on the mizzenmast **2** : MIZZENMAST — **mizzen** *also* **mizen** *adj*

miz·zen·mast \-ˌmast, -məst\ *n* : the mast aft or next aft of the mainmast

mk *abbr* **1** mark **2** markka

Mk *abbr* Mark

mks *abbr* meter-kilogram-second

mkt *abbr* market

mktg *abbr* marketing

ml *abbr* milliliter

Mlle *abbr* [F] mademoiselle

Mlles *abbr* [F] mesdemoiselles

mm *abbr* millimeter

MM *abbr* [F] messieurs

Mme *abbr* [F] madame

Mmes *abbr* [F] mesdames

Mn *symbol* manganese

MN *abbr* Minnesota

mne·mon·ic \nə-'mä-nik\ *adj* : assisting or designed to assist memory; *also* : of or relating to memory

mo *abbr* month

¹Mo *abbr* **1** Missouri **2** Monday

²Mo *symbol* molybdenum

MO *abbr* **1** mail order **2** medical officer **3** Missouri **4** modus operandi **5** money order

¹moan \'mōn\ *n* ♦ : a low prolonged sound indicative of pain or grief

♦ groan, howl, keen, lament, plaint, wail — more at LAMENT

²moan *vb* **1** ♦ : to express grief, pain, or discontent **2** : to make a moan

♦ beef, bellyache, carp, complain, crab, croak, fuss, gripe, grouse, growl, grumble, kick, squawk, wail, whine — more at COMPLAIN

moat \'mōt\ *n* : a deep wide usu. water-filled trench around a castle

¹**mob** \'mäb\ *n* [L *mobile vulgus* vacillating crowd] **1** ♦ : the lower classes of a community : MASSES **2** ♦ : a disorderly crowd **3** ♦ : a criminal gang

♦ [1] commoners, herd, masses, people, plebeians, populace, rank and file — more at MASSES ♦ [2] army, crowd, crush, drove, flock, horde, host, legion, multitude, press, swarm, throng — more at CROWD ♦ [3] cabal, conspiracy, gang, ring, syndicate — more at RING

²**mob** *vb* **mobbed; mob·bing 1** : to crowd about and attack or annoy **2** ♦ : to crowd into or around ⟨shoppers *mobbed* the stores⟩

♦ crowd, flock, swarm, throng — more at CROWD

¹**mo·bile** \'mō-bəl, -ˌbīl, -ˌbēl\ *adj* **1** : capable of moving or being moved **2** : changeable in appearance, mood, or purpose; *also* : ADAPTABLE **3** : having the opportunity for or undergoing a shift in social status **4** : using vehicles for transportation ⟨∼ warfare⟩ — **mo·bil·i·ty** \mō-'bi-lə-tē\ *n*

²**mo·bile** \'mō-ˌbēl\ *n* : a construction or sculpture (as of wire and sheet metal) with parts that can be set in motion by air currents; *also* : a similar structure suspended so that it is moved by a current of air

mobile home *n* : a trailer used as a permanent dwelling

mobile phone *n* : CELL PHONE

mo·bi·lise *chiefly Brit var of* MOBILIZE

mo·bi·li·za·tion \ˌmō-bə-lə-'zā-shən\ *n* **1** ♦ : the act of mobilizing **2** : the state of being mobilized

♦ muster, rally — more at RALLY

mo·bi·lize \'mō-bə-ˌlīz\ *vb* **-lized; -liz·ing 1** : to put into movement or circulation **2** ♦ : to assemble and make ready for use or action ⟨∼ army reserves⟩ — **mo·bi·liz·er** \'mō-bə-ˌlī-zər\ *n*

♦ marshal, muster, rally; *also* arrange, line up, order, organize; call (up), convene, summon; activate *Ant* demobilize

mob·ster \'mäb-stər\ *n* ♦ : a member of a criminal gang

♦ bully, gangster, goon, hood, hoodlum, mug, punk, rowdy, ruffian, thug, tough — more at HOODLUM

moc·ca·sin \'mä-kə-sən\ *n* **1** : a soft leather heelless shoe **2** : WATER MOCCASIN

mo·cha \'mō-kə\ *n* [*Mocha*, port in Yemen] **1** : choice coffee grown in Arabia **2** : a mixture of coffee and chocolate or cocoa **3** : a dark chocolate-brown color

¹**mock** \'mäk, 'mȯk\ *vb* **1** ♦ : to treat with contempt or ridicule **2** : DELUDE **3** : DEFY **4** ♦ : to mimic in sport or derision — **mock** *n* — **mock·ing·ly** *adv*

♦ [1] deride, gibe, jeer, laugh, ridicule, scout — more at RIDICULE ♦ [4] burlesque, caricature, imitate, mimic, parody, take off, travesty — more at MIMIC

²**mock** *adj* **1** ♦ : of, relating to, or having the character of an imitation **2** ♦ : not real or genuine

♦ [1] artificial, fake, faux, imitation, sham, synthetic — more at IMITATION ♦ [2] affected, artificial, assumed, contrived, feigned, mechanical, phony, put-on, spurious, unnatural — more at ARTIFICIAL

mock·er *n* ♦ : one that mocks

♦ heckler, quiz, scoffer, taunter, tease — more at QUIZ

mock·ery \'mä-kə-rē, 'mȯ-\ *n* **1** : insulting or contemptuous action or speech **2** ♦ : a subject of laughter, derision, or sport **3** ♦ : an insincere, contemptible, or impertinent imitation

♦ [2] butt, laughingstock, mark, mock, target — more at LAUGHINGSTOCK ♦ [3] caricature, farce, joke, parody, sham, travesty; *also* burlesque, comedy; lampoon, takeoff; counterfeit, fake, feigning, pretense, simulation

mock–he·ro·ic \ˌmäk-hi-'rō-ik, ˌmȯk-\ *adj* : ridiculing or burlesquing heroic style, character, or action ⟨a ∼ poem⟩

mock·ing·bird \'mä-kiŋ-ˌbərd, 'mȯ-\ *n* : a grayish No. American songbird related to the catbirds and thrashers that mimics the calls of other birds

mock–up \'mä-ˌkəp, 'mȯ-\ *n* : a full-sized structural model built for study, testing, or display ⟨a ∼ of a car⟩

¹**mod** \'mäd\ *adj* **1** : of, relating to, or being the style of the 1960s British youth culture **2** ♦ : very fashionable

♦ contemporary, current, hot, modern, new, newfangled, red-hot, space-age, ultramodern, up-to-date — more at MODERN

²**mod** *abbr* **1** moderate **2** modern **3** modification; modified

¹**mode** \'mōd\ *n* **1 a** : a particular form or variety of something **b** : a form or manner of expression : STYLE **2** : a manner of doing something **3** : the most frequent value of a set of data **4** ♦ : a conscious state of mind or predominant emotion — **mod·al** \'mōd-ᵊl\ *adj*

♦ [1b] locution, manner, phraseology, style, tone, vein — more at STYLE ♦ [4] cheer, frame, humor (*or* humour), mood, spirit, temper — more at MOOD

²**mode** *n* ♦ : a prevailing fashion or style (as of dress or behavior)

♦ craze, fad, rage, style, trend, vogue — more at FAD

¹**mod·el** \'mäd-ᵊl\ *n* **1** : structural design **2** : a miniature representation; *also* : a pattern of something to be made **3** ♦ : an example for imitation or emulation **4** : one who poses (as for an artist or to display clothes); *also* : MANNEQUIN **5** : TYPE, DESIGN

♦ beau ideal, classic, exemplar, ideal, nonpareil, paragon — more at IDEAL

²**model** *vb* **mod·eled** *or* **mod·elled; mod·el·ing** *or* **mod·el·ling 1** : SHAPE, FASHION, CONSTRUCT **2** : to work as a fashion model

³**model** *adj* **1** ♦ : serving as or worthy of being a pattern ⟨a ∼ student⟩ **2** : being a miniature representation of something ⟨a ∼ airplane⟩

♦ classic, paradigmatic, quintessential; *also* ideal, nonpareil, special, unique; absolute, flawless, impeccable, perfect; bang-up, banner, capital, dandy, fine, first-rate, grand, great, groovy, jim-dandy, prime, superb, superior, superlative, terrific, tip-top, top, top-notch, unsurpassed, wonderful; exceptional, fancy

mo·dem \'mō-dəm, -ˌdem\ *n* : a device that converts signals produced by one type of device (as a computer) to a form compatible with another (as a telephone)

¹**mod·er·ate** \'mä-də-rət\ *adj* **1 a** : avoiding extremes **b** ♦ : having a climate that esp. lacks extremes in temperature **2** ♦ : tending toward the mean or average amount or dimension **3** : limited in scope or effect **4** : not expensive — **moderate** *n* — **mod·er·ate·ness** *n*

♦ [1b] balmy, clement, equable, gentle, mild, temperate — more at CLEMENT ♦ [2] average, intermediate, median, medium, middle, modest — more at MIDDLE

²**mod·er·ate** \'mä-də-ˌrāt\ *vb* **-at·ed; -at·ing 1** : to lessen the intensity of : TEMPER **2** : to act as a moderator **3** ♦ : to become less violent, severe, or intense — **mod·er·a·tion** \ˌmä-də-'rā-shən\ *n*

♦ abate, decline, decrease, de-escalate, die, diminish, dwindle, ebb, fall, lessen, let up, lower, recede, relent, shrink, subside, taper, wane — more at DECREASE

mod·er·ate·ly \-lē\ *adv* ♦ : in a moderate manner or to a moderate extent

♦ enough, fairly, kind of, pretty, quite, rather, somewhat, sort of, so-so, — more at FAIRLY

mod·er·a·tor \'mä-də-ˌrā-tər\ *n* **1** : MEDIATOR **2** ♦ : one who presides over an assembly, meeting, or discussion

♦ chair, chairman, president, speaker

mod·ern \'mä-dərn\ *adj* [LL *modernus*, fr. L *modo* just now, fr. *modus* measure] ♦ : of, relating to, or characteristic of the present or the immediate past : CONTEMPORARY ⟨∼ history⟩ — **modern** *n* — **mo·der·ni·ty** \mə-'dər-nə-tē\ *n* — **mod·ern·ly** *adv* — **mod·ern·ness** *n*

♦ contemporary, current, hot, mod, new, newfangled, red-hot, space-age, ultramodern, up-to-date; *also* fashionable, in, modish, stylish; last, latest; modernized, updated; futuristic, nontraditional *Ant* antiquated, archaic, dated, fusty, musty, old-fashioned, old-time, out=of-date, passé

mod·ern·ise, mod·ern·i·sa·tion *chiefly Brit var of* MODERNIZE, MODERNIZATION

mod·ern·ism \'mä-dər-,ni-zəm\ *n* : a practice, movement, or belief peculiar to modern times

mod·ern·ize \'mä-dər-,nīz\ *vb* **-ized; -iz·ing** : to make or become modern — **mod·ern·i·za·tion** \,mä-dər-nə-'zā-shən\ *n* — **mod·ern·iz·er** *n*

mod·est \'mä-dəst\ *adj* **1 a** ♦ : having a moderate estimate of oneself **b** ♦ : neither bold nor self-assertive : DIFFIDENT **2** ♦ : observing the proprieties of dress and behavior **3** ♦ : limited in size, amount, or scope

♦ [1a] demure, humble, lowly, meek, retiring, unassuming, unpretentious — more at HUMBLE ♦ [1b] bashful, coy, demure, diffident, introverted, retiring, sheepish, shy — more at SHY ♦ [2] chaste, clean, decent, immaculate, pure — more at CHASTE ♦ [3] average, intermediate, median, medium, middle, moderate — more at MIDDLE

mod·est·ly \-lē\ *adv* ♦ : in a modest manner or to a modest extent

♦ humbly, lowly, meekly, sheepishly ♦ chastely, purely, righteously, virtuously — more at PURELY

mod·es·ty \'mä-də-stē\ *n* **1** ♦ : freedom from conceit or vanity **2** ♦ : propriety in dress, speech, or conduct

♦ [1] humbleness, humility, lowliness, meekness — more at HUMILITY ♦ [2] chastity, purity — more at CHASTITY

mod·i·cum \'mä-di-kəm\ *n* ♦ : a small amount

♦ hoot, jot, lick, rap, tittle, whit — more at JOT

modif *abbr* modification

mod·i·fi·ca·tion \,mä-də-fə-'kā-shən\ *n* ♦ : the act, process, or result of modifying

♦ alteration, change, difference, revise, revision, variation — more at CHANGE

mod·i·fy \'mä-də-,fī\ *vb* **-fied; -fy·ing** **1** : MODERATE **2** : to limit the meaning of esp. in a grammatical construction **3** ♦ : to make changes in — **mod·i·fi·er** \'mä-də-,fī-ər\ *n*

♦ alter, change, make over, recast, redo, refashion, remake, remodel, revamp, revise, rework, vary — more at CHANGE

mod·ish \'mō-dish\ *adj* ♦ : conforming to the custom, fashion, or established mode : FASHIONABLE ⟨∼ decor⟩ — **mod·ish·ly** *adv*

♦ à la mode, chic, fashionable, in, popular, sharp, smart, snappy, stylish — more at STYLISH

mod·ish·ness \-nəs\ *n* ♦ : the quality or state of being modish

♦ favor, popularity, vogue — more at POPULARITY

mo·diste \mō-'dēst\ *n* : a maker of fashionable dresses and hats

mod·u·lar \'mä-jə-lər\ *adj* : constructed with standardized units ⟨∼ homes⟩

mod·u·lar·ized \'mä-jə-lə-,rīzd\ *adj* : containing or consisting of modules

mod·u·late \'mä-jə-,lāt\ *vb* **-lat·ed; -lat·ing** **1** : to tune to a key or pitch **2** : to keep in proper measure or proportion : TEMPER **3** : to vary the amplitude or frequency of a carrier wave for the transmission of information (as in radio or television) — **mod·u·la·tion** \,mä-jə-'lā-shən\ *n* — **mod·u·la·tor** \'mä-jə-,lā-tər\ *n* — **mod·u·la·to·ry** \-lə-,tōr-ē\ *adj*

mod·ule \'mä-jül\ *n* **1** : any in a series of standardized units for use together **2** : an assembly of wired electronic parts for use with other such assemblies **3** : an independent unit that constitutes a part of the total structure of a space vehicle ⟨a propulsion ∼⟩

mo·dus ope·ran·di \,mō-dəs-,ä-pə-'ran-dē, -,dī\ *n, pl* **mo·di operandi** \'mō-,dē-,ä-, 'mō-,dī-\ [NL] : a method of procedure ⟨a criminal's *modus operandi*⟩

¹mo·gul \'mō-gəl, mō-'gəl\ *n* [fr. *Mogul*, member of a Muslim dynasty ruling northern India] ♦ : an important person : MAGNATE

♦ baron, czar, king, magnate, prince, tycoon — more at MAGNATE

²mogul \'mō-gəl\ *n* : a bump in a ski run

mo·hair \'mō-,har\ *n* [modif. of obs. It *mocaiarro*, fr. Ar *mukhayyar*, lit., choice] : a fabric or yarn made wholly or in part from the long silky hair of the Angora goat; *also* : this goat hair

Mo·ham·med·an *also* **Mu·ham·mad·an** \mō-'ha-mə-dən, -'hä-, mü-\ *n* : MUSLIM

Mo·hawk \'mō-,hȯk\ *n, pl* **Mohawk** *or* **Mohawks** **1** : a member of an American Indian people of the Mohawk River valley, New York; *also* : the language of the Mohawk people **2** : a hairstyle with a narrow strip of upright hair down the center with the sides shaved

Mo·he·gan \mō-'hē-gən, mə-\ *or* **Mo·hi·can** \-'hē-kən\ *n, pl* **Mohegan** *or* **Mohegans** *or* **Mohican** *or* **Mohicans** : a member of an American Indian people of southeastern Connecticut

mo·hel \'mō-(h)el, 'mȯi(-ə)l\ *n, pl* **mohels** *also* **mo·hal·im** \,mō-hä-'lēm\ *also* **mo·hel·im** \-(h)e-'lēm\ : a person who performs Jewish circumcisions

Mohican *var of* MAHICAN

moi·e·ty \'mȯi-ə-tē\ *n, pl* **-ties** : one of two equal or approximately equal parts

moil \'mȯi(-ə)l\ *vb* : to work hard : DRUDGE — **moil** *n* — **moil·er** *n*

moi·ré \mȯ-'rā, mwä-\ *or* **moire** \same *or* 'mȯir, 'mwär\ *n* : a fabric (as silk) having a watered appearance

moist \'mȯist\ *adj* : slightly or moderately wet — **moist·ly** *adv* — **moist·ness** *n*

moist·en \'mȯis-ᵊn\ *vb* : to make or become moist — **moist·en·er** *n*

mois·ture \'mȯis-chər\ *n* : the small amount of liquid that causes dampness

mois·tur·ise *chiefly Brit var of* MOISTURIZE

mois·tur·ize \'mȯis-chə-,rīz\ *vb* **-ized; -iz·ing** : to add moisture to — **mois·tur·iz·er** *n*

mo·ji·to \mō-'hē-tō\ *n, pl* **-tos** : a cocktail made of rum, sugar, mint, lime juice, and soda water

mol *abbr* molecular; molecule

mo·lar \'mō-lər\ *n* [ME *molares*, pl., fr. L *molaris*, fr. *molaris* of a mill, fr. *mola* millstone] : any of the broad teeth adapted to grinding food and located in the back of the jaw — **molar** *adj*

mo·las·ses \mə-'la-səz\ *n* : the thick brown syrup that is separated from raw sugar in sugar manufacture

¹mold *or Can and Brit* **mould** \'mōld\ *n* : crumbly soil rich in organic matter

²mold *or Can and Brit* **mould** *n* **1** : distinctive nature or character **2** : the frame on or around which something is constructed **3** : a cavity in which something is shaped; *also* : an object so shaped **4** : MOLDING

³mold *or Can and Brit* **mould** *vb* **1** : to shape in or as if in a mold **2** : to ornament with molding — **mold·er** *n*

⁴mold *or Can and Brit* **mould** *n* : a surface growth of fungus esp. on damp or decaying matter; *also* : a fungus that produces molds — **mold·i·ness** \'mōl-dē-nəs\ *n* — **moldy** *adj*

⁵mold *or Can and Brit* **mould** *vb* : to become moldy

mold·board *or Can and Brit* **mould·board** \'mōld-,bȯrd\ *n* : a curved iron plate attached above the plowshare to lift and turn the soil

mold·er *or Can and Brit* **mould·er** \'mōl-dər\ *vb* ♦ : to crumble into small pieces

♦ break down, corrupt, decay, decompose, disintegrate, putrefy, rot, spoil — more at DECAY

mold·ing *or Can and Brit* **mould·ing** \'mōl-diŋ\ *n* **1** : an act or process of shaping in a mold; *also* : an object so shaped **2** : a decorative surface, plane, or curved strip

¹mole \'mōl\ *n* : a small often pigmented spot or protuberance on the skin

²mole *n* : any of numerous small burrowing insect-eating mammals related to the shrews and hedgehogs

³**mole** *n* : a massive breakwater or jetty

mo·lec·u·lar \mə-'le-kyə-lər\ *adj* : of, relating to, or being a molecule

molecular biology *n* : a branch of biology dealing with the ultimate physical and chemical organization of living matter and esp. with the molecular basis of inheritance and protein synthesis — **molecular biologist** *n*

molecular weight *n* : the mass of a molecule that is equal to the sum of the masses of all atoms contained in the molecule's formula

mol·e·cule \'mä-li-ˌkyül\ *n* 1 : the smallest particle of matter that is the same chemically as the whole mass 2 ♦ : a tiny bit

♦ atom, bit, crumb, fleck, flyspeck, grain, granule, morsel, mote, particle, patch, scrap, scruple, speck, tittle

mole·hill \'mōl-ˌhil\ *n* : a little ridge of earth thrown up by a mole

mole·skin \-ˌskin\ *n* 1 : the skin of the mole used as fur 2 : a heavy durable cotton fabric

mo·lest \mə-'lest\ *vb* 1 : ANNOY, DISTURB 2 : to make annoying sexual advances to; *esp* : to force physical and usu. sexual contact on — **mo·les·ta·tion** \ˌmō-ˌles-'tā-shən\ *n* — **mo·lest·er** *n*

moll \'mäl\ *n* : a gangster's girlfriend

mol·li·fy \'mä-lə-ˌfī\ *vb* **-fied; -fy·ing** 1 ♦ : to soothe in temper : APPEASE 2 : SOFTEN 3 ♦ : to reduce in intensity : ASSUAGE — **mol·li·fi·ca·tion** \ˌmä-lə-fə-'kā-shən\ *n*

♦ [1] appease, conciliate, disarm, pacify, placate, propitiate — more at PACIFY ♦ [3] allay, alleviate, assuage, ease, help, mitigate, palliate, relieve, soothe — more at HELP

mol·lusk *or* **mol·lusc** \'mä-ləsk\ *n* : any of a large phylum of usu. shelled and aquatic invertebrate animals (as snails, clams, and squids) — **mol·lus·can** *also* **mol·lus·kan** \mə-'ləs-kən\ *adj*

¹**mol·ly·cod·dle** \'mä-lē-ˌkäd-ᵊl\ *n* : a pampered man or boy

²**mollycoddle** *vb* **mol·ly·cod·dled; mol·ly·cod·dling** ♦ : to treat with an excessive or absurd degree of indulgence and attention : PAMPER

♦ baby, coddle, nurse, pamper, spoil — more at BABY

Mo·lo·tov cocktail \'mä-lə-ˌtȯf-, 'mȯ-\ *n* [Vyacheslav M. *Molotov* †1986 Soviet foreign minister] : a crude bomb made of a bottle filled usu. with gasoline and fitted with a wick (as a saturated rag) that is ignited just prior to hurling

¹**molt** *or Can and Brit* **moult** \'mōlt\ *vb* : to shed hair, feathers, outer skin, or horns periodically with the cast-off parts being replaced by new growth — **molt·er** *n*

²**molt** *or Can and Brit* **moult** *n* : the act or process of molting

mol·ten \'mōlt-ᵊn\ *adj* 1 : fused or liquefied by heat 2 : GLOWING

mo·ly \'mō-lē\ *n* : a mythical herb with black root, white flowers, and magic powers

mo·lyb·de·num \mə-'lib-də-nəm\ *n* : a metallic chemical element used in strengthening and hardening steel

mom \'mäm, 'məm\ *n* ♦ : a female parent : MOTHER

♦ ma, mommy, mother

mom–and–pop *adj* : being a small owner-operated business

mo·ment \'mō-mənt\ *n* 1 ♦ : a minute portion of time : INSTANT 2 : a time of excellence ⟨he has his ~s⟩ 3 ♦ : IMPORTANCE ⟨an event of great ~⟩ 4 ♦ : present time

♦ [1] flash, instant, jiffy, minute, second, shake, trice, twinkle, twinkling, wink — more at INSTANT ♦ [4] now, present, today — more at PRESENT

mo·men·tar·i·ly \ˌmō-mən-'ter-ə-lē\ *adv* 1 : for a moment 2 *archaic* : INSTANTLY 3 ♦ : at any moment : SOON

♦ anon, presently, shortly, soon — more at SHORTLY

mo·men·tary \'mō-mən-ˌter-ē\ *adj* 1 ♦ : continuing only a moment ⟨a ~ pause⟩ 2 : recurring at every moment — **mo·men·tar·i·ness** \-ˌter-ē-nəs\ *n*

♦ ephemeral, evanescent, flash, fleeting, fugitive, impermanent, short-lived, transient; *also* brief, short; acting, interim ***Ant*** enduring, eternal, everlasting, lasting, permanent, perpetual

mo·men·tous \mō-'men-təs\ *adj* ♦ : very important ⟨a ~ decision⟩ — **mo·men·tous·ly** *adv* — **mo·men·tous·ness** *n*

♦ big, consequential, eventful, important, major, material, meaningful, significant, substantial, weighty — more at IMPORTANT

mo·men·tum \mō-'men-təm\ *n, pl* **mo·men·ta** \-'men-tə\ *or* **momentums** 1 : a property that a moving body has due to its mass and motion 2 ♦ : something that rouses or incites to activity : IMPETUS

♦ boost, encouragement, goad, impetus, impulse, incentive, incitement, instigation, motivation, provocation, spur, stimulus, yeast — more at IMPULSE

mom·my \'mä-mē, 'mə-\ *n, pl* **mom·mies** ♦ : MOTHER

♦ ma, mom, mother

Mon *abbr* Monday

mon·arch \'mä-nərk, -ˌnärk\ *n* 1 ♦ : a person who reigns over a kingdom or an empire 2 : one holding preeminent position or power 3 : MONARCH BUTTERFLY

♦ autocrat, ruler, sovereign; *also* czar, emperor, empress, kaiser, king, lord, mogul, potentate, prince, queen, satrap, sultan; authoritarian, despot, dictator, overlord, tyrant; royalty

monarch butterfly *n* : a large orange and black migratory American butterfly whose larva feeds on milkweed

mo·nar·chi·cal \mə-'när-ki-kəl, mä-\ *also* **mon·ar·chic** *adj* ♦ : of, relating to, suggestive of, or characteristic of a monarch or monarchy

♦ kingly, princely, queenly, regal, royal; *also* aristocratic, baronial, imperial, lordly, noble, patrician

mon·ar·chist \'mä-nər-kist\ *n* : a believer in monarchical government — **mon·ar·chism** \-ˌki-zəm\ *n*

mon·ar·chy \'mä-nər-kē\ *n, pl* **-chies** : a nation or state governed by a monarch

mon·as·tery \'mä-nə-ˌster-ē\ *n, pl* **-ter·ies** ♦ : a house for persons under religious vows (as monks)

♦ abbey, cloister, friary, priory; *also* house; convent, nunnery; lamasery

mo·nas·tic \mə-'nas-tik\ *adj* : of or relating to monasteries or to monks or nuns — **monastic** *n* — **mo·nas·ti·cal·ly** \-ti-k(ə-)lē\ *adv* — **mo·nas·ti·cism** \-tə-ˌsi-zəm\ *n*

mon·au·ral \mä-'nȯr-əl\ *adj* : MONOPHONIC — **mon·au·ral·ly** *adv*

Mon·day \'mən-dē, -ˌdā\ *n* : the second day of the week

mon·e·tary \'mä-nə-ˌter-ē, 'mə-\ *adj* ♦ : of or relating to money or to the mechanisms by which it is supplied and circulated in the economy

♦ financial, fiscal, pecuniary — more at FINANCIAL

mon·ey \'mə-nē\ *n, pl* **moneys** *or* **mon·ies** \'mə-nēz\ 1 ♦ : something (as metal currency) accepted as a medium of exchange 2 : wealth reckoned in monetary terms 3 : the 1st, 2d, and 3d places in a horse or dog race

♦ cash, currency, dough, lucre, pelf, tender; *also* change, coinage, specie; paper money, scrip; banknote, cashier's check, check, draft, money order, note; bill, dollar, greenback; bankroll, capital, finances, funds; mite, pittance; bundle, fortune, mint, wad; abundance, means, opulence, riches, treasure, wealth; resources, wherewithal

mon·eyed \'mə-nēd\ *adj* 1 ♦ : having money : WEALTHY 2 : consisting in or derived from money

♦ affluent, flush, loaded, opulent, rich, wealthy, well-fixed, well-heeled, well-off, well-to-do — more at RICH

mon·ey·lend·er \'mə-nē-ˌlen-dər\ *n* : one (as a bank or pawnbroker) whose business is lending money

money market *n* : the trade in short-term negotiable financial instruments

money of account : a denominator of value or basis of exchange used in keeping accounts

money order *n* : an order purchased at a post office, bank, or telegraph office directing another office to pay a sum of money to a party named on it

mon·ger \'məŋ-gər, 'mäŋ-\ *n* 1 : DEALER 2 : one who tries to stir up or spread something

Mon·gol \'mäŋ-gəl, 'män-ˌgōl\ *n* : a member of any of several traditionally pastoral peoples of Mongolia — **Mongol** *adj*

Mon·go·lian \män-'gōl-yən, mäŋ-, -'gō-lē-ən\ *n* 1 : a native or inhabitant of Mongolia 2 : a member of the Mongoloid racial stock — **Mongolian** *adj*

Mon·gol·oid \'mäŋ-gə-ˌlóid\ *adj* : of, constituting, or characteristic of a race of humankind native to Asia and classified according to physical features — **Mongoloid** *n*

mon·goose \'män-ˌgüs, 'mäŋ-\ *n, pl* **mon·goos·es** *also* **mon·geese** \-ˌgēs\ : any of a group of small, agile Old World mammals that are related to the civet cats and feed chiefly on small animals and fruits

mon·grel \'mäŋ-grəl, 'məŋ-\ *n* ♦ : an offspring of parents of different breeds; *esp* : one of uncertain ancestry

♦ cross, hybrid — more at HYBRID

mon·i·ker \'mä-ni-kər\ *n* : NAME, NICKNAME

mo·nism \'mō-ˌni-zəm, 'mä-\ *n* : a view that reality is basically one unitary organic whole — **mo·nist** \'mō-nist, 'mä-\ *n*

mo·ni·tion \mō-'ni-shən, mə-\ *n* : WARNING, CAUTION

¹mon·i·tor \'mä-nə-tər\ *n* 1 : a student appointed to assist a teacher 2 : one that monitors; *esp* : a video display screen (as for a computer)

²monitor *vb* : to watch, check, or observe for a special purpose

mon·i·to·ry \'mä-nə-ˌtōr-ē\ *adj* : giving counsel or warning

¹monk \'məŋk\ *n* [ME, fr. OE *munuc*, fr. LL *monachus*, fr. LGk *monachos*, fr. Gk, adj., single, fr. *monos* single, alone] : a man belonging to a religious order and living in a monastery — **monk·ish** *adj*

²monk *n* : MONKEY

¹mon·key \'məŋ-kē\ *n, pl* **monkeys** 1 : a nonhuman primate mammal; *esp* : one of the smaller, longer-tailed, and usu. more arboreal primates as contrasted with the apes 2 ♦ : a person resembling a monkey in appearance or behavior

♦ devil, hellion, imp, mischief, rapscallion, rascal, rogue, scamp, urchin — more at SCAMP

²monkey *vb* **mon·keyed; mon·key·ing** 1 ♦ : to behave foolishly : FOOL — often used with *around* 2 ♦ : to try foolish or dangerous experiments : TAMPER — usu. used with *with*

♦ *usu* **monkey around** [1] act up, clown, cut up, fool, show off, skylark — more at CUT UP ♦ *usu* **monkey around** [1] fiddle, fool, mess, play, potter, putter, trifle ♦ *usu* **monkey with** [2] fiddle, fool, mess, play, tamper, tinker — more at TAMPER

monkey bars *n pl* : a framework of bars on which children can play

mon·key·shine \'mən-kē-ˌshīn\ *n* ♦ : a mischievous act; *also* : mischievous behavior — usu. used in pl.

♦ *usu* **monkeyshines** *pl* antic, caper, escapade, frolic, practical joke, prank, trick — more at PRANK ♦ *usu* **monkeyshines** *pl* foolery, high jinks, horseplay, roughhouse, shenanigans, tomfoolery — more at HORSEPLAY

monkey wrench *n* : a wrench with one fixed and one adjustable jaw at right angles to a handle

monk·fish \'məŋk-ˌfish\ *n* : either of two marine bony fishes that have a large flattened head and are used for food

monks·hood \'məŋks-ˌhùd\ *n* : any of a genus of poisonous plants related to the buttercups; *esp* : a tall Eurasian herb with white or purplish flowers

¹mono \'mä-nō\ *adj* : MONOPHONIC

²mono *n* : INFECTIOUS MONONUCLEOSIS

mono·chro·mat·ic \ˌmä-nə-krō-'ma-tik\ *adj* 1 : having or consisting of one color 2 : consisting of radiation (as light) of a single wavelength

mono·chrome \'mä-nə-ˌkrōm\ *adj* : involving or producing visual images in a single color or in varying tones of a single color ⟨∼ television⟩

mon·o·cle \'mä-ni-kəl\ *n* : an eyeglass for one eye

mono·clo·nal \ˌmä-nə-'klō-nəl\ *adj* : produced by, being, or composed of cells derived from a single cell ⟨∼ antibodies⟩

mono·cot·y·le·don \ˌmä-nə-ˌkät-əl-'ēd-ən\ *n* : any of a class or subclass of chiefly herbaceous seed plants having a single cotyledon and usu. parallel-veined leaves

mon·o·dy \'mä-nə-dē\ *n, pl* **-dies** : ELEGY, DIRGE — **mo·nod·ic** \mə-'nä-dik\ *or* **mo·nod·i·cal** \-di-kəl\ *adj* — **mon·o·dist** \'mä-nə-dist\ *n*

mo·nog·a·my \mə-'nä-gə-mē\ *n* 1 : marriage with but one person at a time 2 : the practice of having a single mate during a period of time — **mo·nog·a·mist** \-mist\ *n* — **mo·nog·a·mous** \-məs\ *adj*

mono·gram \'mä-nə-ˌgram\ *n* : a sign of identity composed of the combined initials of a name — **monogram** *vb*

mono·graph \'mä-nə-ˌgraf\ *n* : a learned treatise on a small area of learning

mono·lin·gual \ˌmä-nə-'liŋ-gwəl\ *adj* : knowing or using only one language

mono·lith \'män-əl-ˌith\ *n* 1 : a single great stone often in the form of a monument or column 2 : something large and powerful that acts as a single unified force ⟨a bureaucratic ∼⟩ — **mono·lith·ic** \ˌmän-əl-'i-thik\ *adj*

mono·logue *also* **mono·log** \'män-əl-ˌóg\ *n* 1 : a dramatic soliloquy; *also* : a long speech monopolizing conversation 2 : the routine of a stand-up comic — **mono·logu·ist** \-ˌóg-ist\ *or* **mo·no·lo·gist** \mə-'nä-lə-jist, 'män-əl-ˌó-gist\ *n*

mono·ma·nia \ˌmä-nə-'mä-nē-ə, -nyə\ *n* 1 : mental disorder limited in expression to one area of thought 2 : excessive concentration on a single object or idea — **mono·ma·ni·ac** \-nē-ˌak\ *n or adj*

mono·mer \'mä-nə-mər\ *n* : a simple chemical compound that can be polymerized

mono·nu·cle·o·sis \ˌmä-nō-ˌnü-klē-'ō-səs, -ˌnyü-\ *n* : INFECTIOUS MONONUCLEOSIS

mono·phon·ic \ˌmä-nə-'fä-nik\ *adj* : of or relating to sound recording or reproduction involving a single transmission path

mono·plane \'mä-nə-ˌplān\ *n* : an airplane with only one set of wings

mo·nop·o·ly \mə-'nä-pə-lē\ *n, pl* **-lies** [L *monopolium*, fr. Gk *monopōlion*, fr. *monos* alone, single + *pōlein* to sell] 1 : exclusive ownership (as through command of supply) 2 : a commodity controlled by one party 3 : one that has a monopoly — **mo·nop·o·list** \-list\ *n* — **mo·nop·o·lis·tic** \mə-ˌnä-pə-'lis-tik\ *adj* — **mo·nop·o·li·za·tion** \-lə-'zā-shən\ *n* — **mo·nop·o·lize** \mə-'nä-pə-ˌlīz\ *vb*

mono·rail \'mä-nə-ˌrāl\ *n* : a single rail serving as a track for a vehicle; *also* : a vehicle traveling on such a track

mono·so·di·um glu·ta·mate \ˌmä-nə-ˌsō-dē-əm-'glü-tə-ˌmāt\ *n* : a crystalline salt used to enhance the flavor of food

mono·syl·la·ble \'mä-nə-ˌsi-lə-bəl\ *n* : a word of one syllable — **mono·syl·lab·ic** \ˌmä-nə-sə-'la-bik\ *adj* — **mono·syl·lab·i·cal·ly** \-bi-k(ə-)lē\ *adv*

mono·the·ism \'mä-nə-(ˌ)thē-ˌi-zəm\ *n* : a doctrine or belief that there is only one deity — **mono·the·ist** \-ˌthē-ist\ *n* — **mono·the·is·tic** \-thē-'is-tik\ *adj*

mono·tone \'mä-nə-ˌtōn\ *n* : a succession of syllables, words, or sentences in one unvaried key or pitch

mo·not·o·nous \mə-'nät-ən-əs\ *adj* 1 : uttered or sounded in one unvarying tone 2 ♦ : tediously uniform — **mo·not·o·nous·ly** *adv* — **mo·not·o·nous·ness** *n*

♦ drab, dreary, dry, dull, flat, uninteresting, weary

mo·not·o·ny \mə-'nät-ən-ē\ *n* : tedious sameness or uniformity

mono·un·sat·u·rat·ed \ˌmä-nō-ˌən-'sa-chə-ˌrā-təd\ *adj* : containing one double or triple bond per molecule — used esp. of an oil or fatty acid

mon·ox·ide \mə-'näk-ˌsīd\ *n* : an oxide containing one atom of oxygen in a molecule

mon·sei·gneur \ˌmōⁿ-ˌsän-'yər\ *n, pl* **mes·sei·gneurs** \ˌmä-ˌsān-'yər, -'yərz\ : a French dignitary — used as a title

mon·sieur \məs-'yər, mə-'shər, *Fr* mə-'syœ\ *n, pl* **mes·sieurs**

\same or -'yərz, -'shərz\ : a Frenchman of high rank or station — used as a title equivalent to *Mister*

mon·si·gnor \män-'sē-nyər\ *n, pl* **monsignors** *or* **mon·si·gno·ri** \ˌmän-ˌsēn-'yȯr-ē\ [It *monsignore*] : a Roman Catholic prelate — used as a title

mon·soon \män-'sün\ *n* [obs. Dutch *monssoen*, fr. Pg *monção*, fr. Ar *mawsim* time, season] **1** : a periodic wind esp. in the Indian Ocean and southern Asia **2** : the season of the southwest monsoon esp. in India **3** : rainfall associated with the monsoon

¹**mon·ster** \'män-stər\ *n* **1** : an abnormally developed plant or animal **2 a** : an animal of strange or terrifying shape **b** ♦ : one unusually large of its kind **3** ♦ : an extremely ugly, wicked, or cruel person **4** : something monstrous

♦ [2b] behemoth, blockbuster, colossus, giant, jumbo, leviathan, mammoth, titan, whale, whopper — more at GIANT ♦ [3] beast, brute, devil, fiend, savage, villain

²**monster** *adj* : very large : ENORMOUS

mon·strance \'män-strəns\ *n* : a vessel in which the consecrated Host is exposed for the adoration of the faithful

mon·stros·i·ty \män-'strä-sə-tē\ *n* **1 a** : a malformation of a plant or animal **b** ♦ : something deviating from the normal : FREAK **2** ♦ : the quality or state of being monstrous **3 a** : an object of great and often frightening size, force, or complexity **b** ♦ : an excessively bad or shocking example

♦ [1b] abnormality, freak, monster — more at FREAK ♦ [2] atrociousness, atrocity, frightfulness, hideousness, horror, repulsiveness — more at HORROR ♦ [2] atrociousness, atrocity, depravity, enormity, heinousness, vileness, wickedness — more at ENORMITY ♦ [3b] eyesore, fright, horror, mess, sight — more at EYESORE

mon·strous \'män-strəs\ *adj* **1** ♦ : having extraordinary often overwhelming size **2** ♦ : extraordinarily ugly or vicious **3** ♦ : deviating greatly from the natural form or character

♦ [1] enormous, giant, gigantic, huge, mammoth, massive, monster, monumental, prodigious, tremendous, whopping — more at HUGE ♦ [2] appalling, atrocious, awful, dreadful, frightful, ghastly, grisly, gruesome, hideous, horrible, horrid, lurid, macabre, nightmarish, shocking, terrible — more at HORRIBLE ♦ [3] deformed, distorted, malformed, misshapen, shapeless — more at MALFORMED

mon·strous·ly \-lē\ *adv* ♦ : in a monstrous manner

♦ devilishly, excessively, inordinately, overly, overmuch, too — more at TOO ♦ broadly, considerably, greatly, hugely, largely, massively, much, sizably, stupendously, tremendously, utterly, vastly — more at GREATLY

Mont *abbr* Montana

mon·tage \män-'täzh\ *n* [F] **1** : a composite photograph made by combining several separate pictures **2** : an artistic composition made up of several different kinds of elements **3** : a varied mixture : JUMBLE

month \'mənth\ *n, pl* **months** \'məns, 'mənths\ : one of the 12 parts into which the year is divided — **month·ly** *adv or adj or n*

month·long \'mənth-ˌlȯŋ\ *adj* : lasting a month

mon·u·ment \'män-yə-mənt\ *n* **1** ♦ : a lasting reminder; *esp* : a structure erected in remembrance of a person or event **2** : NATIONAL MONUMENT

♦ gravestone, headstone, tombstone — more at TOMBSTONE ♦ keepsake, memento, memorial, remembrance, souvenir, token — more at MEMORIAL

mon·u·men·tal \ˌmän-yə-'ment-ᵊl\ *adj* **1** : of or relating to a monument **2 a** ♦ : having impressive bulk or size **b** : highly significant : OUTSTANDING **3** ♦ : very great ⟨a ∼ task⟩ — **mon·u·men·tal·ly** *adv*

♦ colossal, enormous, giant, gigantic, grand, heroic, huge, mammoth, massive, outsize, oversize, prodigious, titanic, tremendous, vast

moo \'mü\ *vb* : to make the natural throat noise of a cow — **moo** *n*

mooch·er \'mü-chər\ *n* ♦ : one that begs or lives off another's expense

♦ hanger-on, leech, parasite, sponge — more at LEECH

¹**mood** \'müd\ *n* **1** ♦ : a conscious state of mind or predominant emotion **2** : a prevailing attitude : DISPOSITION **3** ♦ : a distinctive atmosphere

♦ [1] cheer, frame, humor (*or* humour), mode, spirit, temper; *also* attitude, outlook, perspective, standpoint, viewpoint; emotion, feeling, heart, passion, sentiment; strain; belief, conviction, mind, opinion; expression, tone, vein; character, disposition, individuality, personality, temperament; responsiveness, sensibility, sensitiveness, sensitivity ♦ [3] air, atmosphere, aura, climate, flavor (*or* flavour), note, temper — more at AURA

²**mood** *n* : distinction of form of a verb to express whether its action or state is conceived as fact or in some other manner (as wish)

moody \'mü-dē\ *adj* **mood·i·er; -est 1** : GLOOMY **2** ♦ : subject to moods : TEMPERAMENTAL — **mood·i·ly** \-də-lē\ *adv* — **mood·i·ness** \-dē-nəs\ *n*

♦ glum, morose, sulky, sullen, surly — more at SULKY

¹**moon** \'mün\ *n* **1** : the earth's natural satellite **2** : SATELLITE **3** ♦ : an indefinite usu. extended period of time — often used in pl.

♦ aeon (*or* eon), age, cycle, eternity — more at AGE

²**moon** *vb* : to engage in idle reverie

moon·beam \'mün-ˌbēm\ *n* : a ray of light from the moon

¹**moon·light** \-ˌlīt\ *n* : the light of the moon — **moon·lit** \-ˌlit\ *adj*

²**moonlight** *vb* **moon·light·ed; moon·light·ing** : to hold a second job in addition to a regular one — **moon·light·er** *n*

moon·roof \-ˌrüf, -ˌru̇f\ *n* : a glass sunroof

moon·scape \-ˌskāp\ *n* : the surface of the moon as seen or as pictured

moon·shine \-ˌshīn\ *n* **1** : MOONLIGHT **2** : empty talk **3** ♦ : intoxicating liquor usu. illegally distilled

♦ alcohol, booze, drink, intoxicant, liquor, spirits — more at ALCOHOL

moon·stone \-ˌstōn\ *n* : a transparent or translucent feldspar of pearly luster used as a gem

moon·struck \-ˌstrək\ *adj* **1** : mentally unbalanced **2** : romantically sentimental **3** : lost in fantasy

¹**moor** \'mu̇r\ *n* **1** *chiefly Brit* : an expanse of open rolling infertile land **2** : a boggy area; *esp* : one that is peaty and dominated by grasses and sedges

²**moor** *vb* ♦ : to make fast with or as if with cables, lines, or anchors

♦ anchor, catch, clamp, fasten, fix, hitch, secure, set ♦ disembark, dock, land, tie up

Moor \'mu̇r\ *n* : one of the Arab and Berber conquerors of Spain — **Moor·ish** *adj*

moor·ing \'mu̇r-iŋ\ *n* **1** : a place where or an object to which a craft can be made fast **2** : an established practice or stabilizing influence — usu. used in pl.

moor·land \-lənd, -ˌland\ *n* : land consisting of moors

moose \'müs\ *n, pl* **moose** : a large heavy-antlered ruminant mammal related to the deer that has humped shoulders and long legs and inhabits northern forested areas

¹**moot** \'müt\ *vb* **1** : to bring up for discussion **2** ♦ : to argue about : DEBATE

♦ [1] bring up, broach, introduce, raise — more at INTRODUCE ♦ [2] argue, chew over, debate, discuss, dispute, hash, talk over — more at DISCUSS

²**moot** *adj* **1** ♦ : open to question; *also* : DISPUTED **2** : having no practical significance ⟨the issue is now ∼⟩

♦ arguable, debatable, disputable, doubtful, questionable — more at DEBATABLE

¹**mop** \'mäp\ *n* : an implement made of absorbent material fastened to a handle and used esp. for cleaning floors

²**mop** *vb* **mopped; mop·ping** : to use a mop on : clean with a mop

mope \'mōp\ *vb* **moped; mop·ing** **1** : to become dull, dejected, or listless **2** ♦ : to move slowly or aimlessly

♦ gad, gallivant, knock, maunder, meander, ramble, range, roam, rove, traipse, wander — more at WANDER

mo·ped \'mō-ˌped\ *n* : a light low-powered motorbike that can be pedaled

mop·pet \'mä-pət\ *n* [obs. E *mop* fool, child] ♦ : a young person who is between infancy and adulthood : CHILD

♦ child, cub, juvenile, kid, kiddo, whelp, youngster, youth — more at CHILD

mo·raine \mə-'rān\ *n* : an accumulation of earth and stones left by a glacier

¹mor·al \'mȯr-əl\ *adj* **1** : of or relating to principles of right and wrong ⟨a ∼ lesson⟩ **2** ♦ : conforming to a standard of right behavior; *also* : capable of right and wrong action **3** : probable but not proved ⟨a ∼ certainty⟩ **4** : perceptual or psychological rather than tangible or practical in nature or effect ⟨a ∼ victory⟩

♦ decent, ethical, good, honest, honorable (*or* honourable), just, right, righteous, straight, upright, virtuous — more at GOOD

²moral *n* **1** : the practical meaning (as of a story) `² *pl* ♦ : moral practices or teachings

♦ morals *pl* ethics, morality, principles, standards — more at ETHICS

mo·rale \mə-'ral\ *n* **1** : MORALITY **2** : the mental and emotional attitudes of an individual toward the tasks at hand; *also* : ESPRIT DE CORPS

mor·al·ise *chiefly Brit var of* MORALIZE

mor·al·ist \'mȯr-ə-list\ *n* **1** : one who leads a moral life **2** : a thinker or writer concerned with morals **3** : one concerned with regulating the morals of others — **mor·al·is·tic** \ˌmȯr-ə-'lis-tik\ *adj* — **mor·al·is·ti·cal·ly** \-ti-k(ə-)lē\ *adv*

mo·ral·i·ty \mə-'ra-lə-tē\ *n, pl* **-ties** **1** ♦ : a doctrine or system of moral conduct **2** ♦ : moral conduct : VIRTUE

♦ [1] ethics, morals, principles, standards — more at ETHICS ♦ [2] character, decency, goodness, honesty, honor (*or* honour), integrity, probity, rectitude, righteousness, uprightness, virtue; *also* high-mindedness, honor, incorruptibility; appropriateness, correctness, decorum, etiquette, fitness, propriety; ethics, morals *Ant* badness, evil, immorality, wickedness

mor·al·ize \'mȯr-ə-ˌlīz\ *vb* **-ized; -iz·ing** : to make moral reflections — **mor·al·i·za·tion** \ˌmȯr-ə-lə-'zā-shən\ *n* — **mor·al·iz·er** \'mȯr-ə-ˌlī-zər\ *n*

mor·al·ly \'mȯr-ə-lē\ *adv* : in accordance with morals : in a moral manner

mo·rass \mə-'ras\ *n* [D *moeras*, fr. OF *maresc*, of Gmc origin; akin to OE *mersc* marsh] ♦ : a tract of soft wet land : SWAMP; *also* : something that entangles, impedes, or confuses

♦ bog, fen, marsh, mire, slough, swamp — more at SWAMP

mor·a·to·ri·um \ˌmȯr-ə-'tōr-ē-əm\ *n, pl* **-ri·ums** *or* **-ria** \-ē-ə\ [ultim. fr. L *mora* delay] ♦ : a suspension of activity

♦ abeyance, doldrums, dormancy, holding pattern, latency, quiescence, suspension — more at ABEYANCE

mo·ray eel \mə-'rā-, 'mȯr-ˌā-\ *n* : any of numerous often brightly colored biting eels of warm seas

mor·bid \'mȯr-bəd\ *adj* **1** : of, relating to, or typical of disease; *also* : DISEASED, SICKLY **2** : characterized by gloomy or unwholesome ideas or feelings **3** : GRISLY, GRUESOME ⟨∼ details⟩ — **mor·bid·i·ty** \mȯr-'bi-də-tē\ *n* — **mor·bid·ly** *adv* — **mor·bid·ness** *n*

mor·dant \'mȯrd-ᵊnt\ *adj* **1** : biting or caustic in manner or style **2** : BURNING, PUNGENT — **mor·dant·ly** *adv*

♦ acrid, biting, caustic, cutting, pungent, sarcastic, satiric, scathing, sharp, tart — more at SARCASTIC

¹more \'mȯr\ *adj* **1** : GREATER **2** ♦ : existing by way of addition ⟨wanted ∼ coffee⟩

♦ additional, another, else, farther, further, other — more at ADDITIONAL

²more *adv* **1** : in addition **2** : to a greater or higher degree

³more *n* **1** : a greater quantity, number, or amount ⟨the ∼ the merrier⟩ **2** : an additional amount ⟨costs a little ∼⟩

⁴more *pron* : additional persons or things or a greater amount

mo·rel \mə-'rel\ *n* : any of several pitted edible fungi

more·over \mȯr-'ō-vər\ *adv* ♦ : in addition : FURTHER

♦ additionally, again, also, besides, further, furthermore, likewise, more, then, too, withal, yet

mo·res \'mȯr-ˌāz\ *n pl* [L, pl. of *mor-, mos* custom] **1** ♦ : the fixed morally binding customs of a group **2** : HABITS, MANNERS

♦ etiquette, manners

Mor·gan \'mȯr-gən\ *n* : any of an American breed of lightly built horses

morgue \'mȯrg\ *n* : a place where the bodies of dead persons are kept until released for burial or autopsy

mor·i·bund \'mȯr-ə-(ˌ)bənd\ *adj* : being in a dying condition

Mor·mon \'mȯr-mən\ *n* : a member of the Church of Jesus Christ of Latter-day Saints — **Mor·mon·ism** \-mə-ˌni-zəm\ *n*

morn \'mȯrn\ *n* **1** : the first appearance of light in the morning followed by sunrise **2** : MORNING

morn·ing \'mȯr-niŋ\ *n* **1 a** ♦ : the first appearance of light in the morning followed by sunrise **b** : the time from the sunrise to noon **2** ♦ : a period of first development : BEGINNING

♦ [1a] aurora, cockcrow, dawn, sunrise — more at DAWN ♦ [2] beginning, birth, commencement, dawn, genesis, launch, onset, outset, start, threshold — more at BEGINNING

morn·ing–after pill \ˌmȯr-niŋ-'af-tər-\ *n* : a contraceptive drug taken up to usu. three days after sexual intercourse

morning glory *n* : any of various twining plants related to the sweet potato that have often showy bell-shaped or funnel-shaped flowers

morning sickness *n* : nausea and vomiting that typically occur in the morning esp. during early pregnancy

morning star *n* : a bright planet (as Venus) seen in the eastern sky before or at sunrise

Mo·roc·can \mə-'rä-kən\ *n* : a native or inhabitant of Morocco

mo·roc·co \mə-'rä-kō\ *n* : a fine leather made of goatskins tanned with sumac

mo·ron \'mȯr-ˌän\ *n* **1** ♦ : a very stupid person **2** *dated, now offensive* : a person affected with mild intellectual disability — **mo·ron·ic** \mə-'rä-nik\ *adj* — **mo·ron·i·cal·ly** \-ni-k(ə-)lē\ *adv*

♦ blockhead, dolt, dope, dummy, idiot, imbecile, jackass, nitwit, numskull, simpleton — more at IDIOT

mo·rose \mə-'rōs\ *adj* [L *morosus* hard to please, exacting, fr. *mor-, mos* custom, disposition] **1** ♦ : having a sullen disposition **2** : marked by or expressive of gloom : GLOOMY — **mo·rose·ly** *adv* — **mo·rose·ness** *n*

♦ glum, moody, sulky, sullen, surly — more at SULKY

morph \'mȯrf\ *vb* : to change the form or character of : TRANSFORM

mor·pheme \'mȯr-ˌfēm\ *n* : a meaningful linguistic unit that contains no smaller meaningful parts — **mor·phe·mic** \mȯr-'fē-mik\ *adj*

mor·phia \'mȯr-fē-ə\ *n* : MORPHINE

mor·phine \'mȯr-ˌfēn\ *n* [F, fr. Gk *Morpheus*, Greek god of dreams] : an addictive drug obtained from opium and used to ease pain or induce sleep

mor·phol·o·gy \mȯr-'fä-lə-jē\ *n* **1** : a branch of biology dealing with the form and structure of organisms **2** : a study and description of word formation in a language — **mor·pho·log·i·cal** \ˌmȯr-fə-'lä-ji-kəl\ *adj* — **mor·phol·o·gist** \mȯr-'fä-lə-jist\ *n*

mor·ris \'mȯr-əs\ *n* : a vigorous English dance traditionally performed by men wearing costumes and bells

mor·row \'mär-ō\ *n* : the next day

Morse code \\'mȯrs-\\ *n* : either of two codes consisting of dots and dashes or long and short sounds used for transmitting messages

mor·sel \\'mȯr-səl\\ *n* [ME, fr. AF, dim. of *mors* bite, fr. L *morsus,* fr. *mordēre* to bite] **1 ♦** : a small piece or quantity **2** : a tasty dish **3 ♦** : a small piece of food

   ♦ [1] bit, crumb, grain, granule, particle, scrap
   ♦ [3] bite, mouthful, nibble, taste, tidbit; *also* snack; appetizer, hors d'oeuvre; bit, chew, crumb, dab, driblet, hint, lick, nubbin, nugget, pinch, scrap, shred, smidgen, speck, spot, sprinkling, suspicion, touch, trace; dash, drop; gulp, swallow, swig

¹mor·tal \\'mȯrt-ᵊl\\ *adj* **1 a ♦** : causing death : FATAL **b** : leading to eternal punishment ⟨~ sin⟩ **2** : subject to death ⟨~ man⟩ **3** : implacably hostile ⟨~ foe⟩ **4** : very great : EXTREME ⟨~ fear⟩ **5** : HUMAN ⟨~ limitations⟩ **6 ♦** : of, relating to, or connected with death — **mor·tal·i·ty** \\mȯr-'ta-lə-tē\\ *n*

   ♦ baleful, deadly, deathly, fatal, fell, lethal, murderous, pestilent, vital — more at DEADLY

²mortal *n* **♦** : a human being

   ♦ being, body, creature, human, individual, man, person — more at HUMAN

mor·tal·ly \\'mȯrt-ᵊl-ē\\ *adv* **1** : in a deadly or fatal manner ⟨~ wounded⟩ **2 ♦** : to an extreme degree ⟨~ afraid⟩

   ♦ especially, extremely, greatly, highly, hugely, mightily, mighty, most, much, real, right, so, very — more at VERY

¹mor·tar \\'mȯr-tər\\ *n* **1** : a strong bowl in which substances are pounded or crushed with a pestle **2** : a short-barreled cannon used to fire shells at high angles

²mortar *n* : a building material (as a mixture of lime and cement with sand and water) that is spread between bricks or stones to bind them together as it hardens — **mortar** *vb*

mor·tar·board \\'mȯr-tər-ˌbȯrd\\ *n* **1** : a square board for holding mortar **2** : an academic cap with a flat square top

mort·gage \\'mȯr-gij\\ *n* [ME *morgage,* fr. AF *mortgage,* fr. *mort* dead + *gage* pledge] : a transfer of rights to a piece of property usu. as security for the payment of a loan or debt that becomes void when the debt is paid — **mortgage** *vb* — **mort·gag·ee** \\ˌmȯr-gi-'jē\\ *n* — **mort·gag·or** \\ˌmȯr-gi-'jȯr\\ *n*

mor·ti·cian \\mȯr-'ti-shən\\ *n* [L *mort-, mors* death + E *-ician* (as in *physician*)] : UNDERTAKER

mor·ti·fi·ca·tion \\ˌmȯr-tə-fə-'kā-shən\\ *n* **♦** : a sense of humiliation and shame caused by something that wounds one's pride or self-respect

   ♦ abashment, confusion, discomfiture, embarrassment, fluster — more at EMBARRASSMENT

mor·ti·fy \\'mȯr-tə-ˌfī\\ *vb* **-fied; -fy·ing** **1** : to subdue (as the body) esp. by abstinence or self-inflicted pain **2 ♦** : to subject to severe and vexing embarrassment **3** : to become necrotic or gangrenous

   ♦ abash, confound, confuse, discomfit, disconcert, discountenance, embarrass, faze, fluster, rattle — more at EMBARRASS

mor·tise *also* **mor·tice** \\'mȯr-təs\\ *n* : a hole cut in a piece of wood into which another piece fits to form a joint

mor·tu·ary \\'mȯr-chə-ˌwer-ē\\ *n, pl* **-ar·ies** : a place in which dead bodies are kept until burial

mos *abbr* months

mo·sa·ic \\mō-'zā-ik\\ *n* : a surface decoration made by inlaying small pieces (as of colored glass or stone) to form figures or patterns; *also* : a design made in mosaic — **mosaic** *adj*

mos·co·vi·um \\mä-'skō-vē-əm\\ *n* : a short-lived artificially produced radioactive element

mo·sey \\'mō-zē\\ *vb* **mo·seyed; mo·sey·ing** : SAUNTER

mosh \\'mäsh\\ *vb* : to engage in rough uninhibited dancing near the stage at a rock concert

mosh pit *n* : an area in front of a stage where rough dancing takes place at a rock concert

Mos·lem \\'mäz-ləm\\ *var of* MUSLIM

mosque \\'mäsk\\ *n* : a building used for public worship by Muslims

mos·qui·to \\mə-'skē-tō\\ *n, pl* **-toes** *also* **-tos** : any of a family of dipteran flies the female of which sucks the blood of animals

mosquito net *n* : a net or screen for keeping out mosquitoes

moss \\'mȯs\\ *n* : any of a class of green plants that lack flowers but have small leafy stems and often grow in clumps — **mossy** *adj*

moss·back \\'mȯs-ˌbak\\ *n* : an extremely conservative person : FOGY

¹most \\'mōst\\ *adj* **1 ♦** : greatest in quantity, extent, or degree ⟨the ~ ability⟩ **2** : the majority of ⟨~ people⟩

   ♦ consummate, maximum, nth, paramount, supreme, top, ultimate, utmost — more at ULTIMATE

²most *adv* **1** : to the greatest or highest degree ⟨~ beautiful⟩ **2** : to a very great degree ⟨a ~ careful driver⟩

³most *n* : the greatest amount ⟨the ~ I can do⟩

⁴most *pron* : the greatest number or part ⟨~ became discouraged⟩

⁵most *adv* **♦** : very nearly but not exactly or entirely : ALMOST

   ♦ about, almost, much, near, nearly, next to, nigh, practically, some, virtually, well-nigh — more at ALMOST

-most \\ˌmōst\\ *adj suffix* : most ⟨inner*most*⟩ : most toward ⟨end*most*⟩

most·ly \\'mōst-lē\\ *adv* **♦** : for the greatest part : MAINLY

   ♦ altogether, basically, chiefly, generally, largely, mainly, overall, predominantly, primarily, principally — more at CHIEFLY

mot \\'mō\\ *n, pl* **mots** *same or* 'mōz\\ [F, word, saying, fr. LL *muttum* grunt] : a witty saying

mote \\'mōt\\ *n* **♦** : a small particle

   ♦ bit, fleck, flyspeck, molecule, particle, speck

mo·tel \\mō-'tel\\ *n* [blend of *motor* and *hotel*] : a hotel in which the rooms are accessible from the parking area

mo·tet \\mō-'tet\\ *n* : a choral work on a sacred text for several voices usu. without instrumental accompaniment

moth \\'mȯth\\ *n, pl* **moths** \\'mȯthz, 'mȯths\\ : any of various insects belonging to the same order as the butterflies but usu. night-flying and with a stouter body and smaller wings

moth·ball \\'mȯth-ˌbȯl\\ *n* **1** : a ball (as of naphthalene) used to keep moths out of clothing **2** *pl* : protective storage

¹moth·er \\'mə-thər\\ *n* **1 ♦** : a female parent **2** : the superior of a religious community of women **3** : SOURCE, ORIGIN — **moth·er·hood** \\-ˌhůd\\ *n* — **moth·er·less** *adj* — **moth·er·li·ness** \\-lē-nəs\\ *n* — **moth·er·ly** *adj*

   ♦ ma, mom, mommy; *also* matriarch, matron

²mother *vb* **1** : to give birth to; *also* : PRODUCE **2 ♦** : to care for or protect like a mother

   ♦ aid, care, minister, nurse — more at NURSE

moth·er·board \\'mə-thər-ˌbȯrd\\ *n* : the main circuit board esp. of a microcomputer

moth·er-in-law \\'mə-thər-ən-ˌlȯ\\ *n, pl* **mothers-in-law** \\'mə-thərz-\\ : the mother of one's spouse

moth·er·land \\'mə-thər-ˌland\\ *n* **1** : the land of origin of something **2 ♦** : the native land of one's ancestors

   ♦ country, fatherland, home, homeland, sod — more at COUNTRY

moth·er-of-pearl \\ˌmə-thər-əv-'pərl\\ *n* : the hard pearly matter forming the inner layer of a mollusk shell

mother ship *n* : a ship serving smaller craft

mo·tif \\mō-'tēf\\ *n* [F, motive, motif] **1 ♦** : a dominant idea or central theme (as in a work of art) **2 ♦** : a single or repeated design or color

   ♦ [1] content, matter, question, subject, theme, topic — more at MATTER **♦** [2] design, figure, motive, pattern — more at PATTERN

mo·tile \\'mōt-ᵊl, 'mō-ˌtīl\\ *adj* : capable of spontaneous movement ⟨~ cells⟩ — **mo·til·i·ty** \\mō-'ti-lə-tē\\ *n*

¹mo·tion \\'mō-shən\\ *n* **1 ♦** : an act, process, or instance of moving 2 : a proposal for action (as by a deliberative body) 3 *pl* : ACTIVITIES, MOVEMENTS — **mo·tion·less** *adj* — **mo·tion·less·ly** *adv* — **mo·tion·less·ness** *n*

♦ move, movement, moving, shift, stir, stirring — more at MOVEMENT

²**motion** *vb* ♦ : to direct or signal by a movement

♦ flag, gesture, signal, wave; *also* gesticulate, pantomime, sign; signalize; acquaint, advise, inform, relate, tell; flourish, shrug

motion picture *n* 1 : a series of pictures projected on a screen so rapidly that they produce a continuous picture in which persons and objects seem to move 2 ♦ : a representation (as of a story) by means of motion pictures

♦ film, movie, picture — more at MOVIE

motion sickness *n* : sickness induced by motion and characterized by nausea

mo·ti·vate \'mō-tə-ˌvāt\ *vb* **-vat·ed; -vat·ing** : to provide with a motive : IMPEL — **mo·ti·va·tor** \'mō-tə-ˌvā-tər\ *n*

mo·ti·va·tion \ˌmō-tə-'vā-shən\ *n* 1 a : the act or process of motivating b : the condition of being motivated 2 ♦ : a motivating force, stimulus, or influence — **mo·ti·va·tion·al** \-shə-nəl\ *adj*

♦ boost, encouragement, goad, impetus, impulse, incentive, incitement, instigation, momentum, provocation, spur, stimulus, yeast — more at IMPULSE

¹**mo·tive** \'mō-tiv, *2 also* mō-'tēv\ *n* 1 ♦ : something (as a need or desire) that causes a person to act 2 : a recurrent theme in a musical composition 3 : a dominant idea or central theme (as in a work of art) : MOTIF 4 : a single or repeated design or color : MOTIF — **mo·tive·less** *adj*

♦ grounds, reason, wherefore, why — more at REASON

²**mo·tive** \'mō-tiv\ *adj* 1 : moving to action or of or relating to motion

¹**mot·ley** \'mät-lē\ *adj* 1 ♦ : variegated in color 2 ♦ : made up of diverse often incongruous elements

♦ [1] multicolored, variegated ♦ [2] assorted, heterogeneous, miscellaneous, mixed, varied — more at MISCELLANEOUS

²**motley** *n* : a mixture of incongruous elements

¹**mo·tor** \'mō-tər\ *n* [L, fr. *movēre* to move] 1 : one that imparts motion 2 : a machine that produces motion or power for doing work 3 : a usu. 4-wheeled automotive vehicle designed for passenger transportation : AUTOMOBILE

²**motor** *vb* : to travel or transport by automobile : DRIVE — **mo·tor·ist** *n*

mo·tor·bike \'mō-tər-ˌbīk\ *n* : a small lightweight motorcycle

mo·tor·boat \-ˌbōt\ *n* : a boat propelled by a motor

mo·tor·cade \-ˌkād\ *n* ♦ : a procession of motor vehicles

♦ armada, caravan, cavalcade, fleet, train — more at FLEET

mo·tor·car \-ˌkär\ *n* : a usu. 4-wheeled automotive vehicle designed for passenger transportation : AUTOMOBILE

mo·tor·cy·cle \'mō-tər-ˌsī-kəl\ *n* : a 2-wheeled automotive vehicle — **mo·tor·cy·clist** \-k(ə-)list\ *n*

motor home *n* ♦ : a large motor vehicle equipped as living quarters

♦ camper, caravan, trailer — more at CAMPER

motor inn *n* : MOTEL

mo·tor·ise *chiefly Brit var of* MOTORIZE

mo·tor·ize \'mō-tə-ˌrīz\ *vb* **-ized; -iz·ing** 1 : to equip with a motor 2 : to equip with automobiles

mo·tor·man \'mō-tər-mən\ *n* : an operator of a motor-driven vehicle (as a streetcar or subway train)

motor scooter *n* : a low 2- or 3-wheeled automotive vehicle resembling a child's scooter but having a seat

mo·tor·truck \'mō-tər-ˌtrək\ *n* : an automotive truck

motor vehicle *n* ♦ : an automotive vehicle (as an automobile) not operated on rails

♦ automobile, car, machine — more at CAR

mot·tle \'mät-ᵊl\ *vb* **mot·tled; mot·tling** ♦ : to mark with spots of different color : BLOTCH

♦ blotch, dapple, dot, fleck, freckle, pepper, speck, spot, sprinkle, stipple — more at SPOT

mot·tled \'mä-tᵊld\ *adj* ♦ : marked with spots of different colors

♦ dappled, piebald, pied, spotted — more at PIED
♦ dappled, spotted, spotty, variegated — more at SPOTTED

mot·to \'mä-tō\ *n, pl* **mottoes** *also* **mottos** [It, fr. LL *muttum* grunt, fr. L *muttire* to mutter] 1 : a sentence, phrase, or word inscribed on something to indicate its character or use 2 : a short expression of a guiding rule of conduct

moue \'mü\ *n* : a little grimace

mould *chiefly Can and Brit var of* MOLD

moult *chiefly Can and Brit var of* MOLT

¹**mound** \'maund\ *vb* ♦ : to form into a mound

♦ heap, hill, pile, stack — more at PILE

²**mound** *n* 1 ♦ : an artificial bank or hill of earth or stones 2 ♦ : a rounded hill or natural formation 3 ♦ : a collection of things thrown one on another : HEAP, PILE; *also* : a great number or large quantity ⟨~s of work⟩ 4 : a small rounded mass

♦ [1] bank, bar, drift — more at BANK ♦ [2] elevation, eminence, height, highland, hill, prominence, rise — more at HEIGHT ♦ [3] cock, heap, hill, mountain, pile, rick, stack — more at PILE

¹**mount** \'maunt\ *n* ♦ : a high hill

♦ mountain, peak

²**mount** *vb* 1 a ♦ : to increase in amount or extent b ♦ : to move upward : RISE, ASCEND 2 : to get up on something; *esp* : to seat oneself on (as a horse) for riding 3 : to put in position ⟨~ artillery⟩ 4 : to set on something that elevates 5 : to attach to a support 6 ♦ : to prepare esp. for examination or display — **mount·able** *adj* — **mount·er** *n*

♦ [1a] accumulate, appreciate, balloon, build, burgeon, enlarge, escalate, expand, increase, multiply, mushroom, proliferate, rise, snowball, swell, wax — more at INCREASE ♦ [1b] arise, ascend, climb, lift, rise, soar, up — more at ASCEND ♦ [6] carry, give, offer, present, stage — more at PRESENT

³**mount** *n* 1 ♦ : an arrangement of structural parts that gives form or support : SUPPORT 2 : a means of conveyance; *esp* : SADDLE HORSE

♦ brace, bulwark, buttress, shore, stay, support, underpinning — more at SUPPORT

moun·tain \'maunt-ᵊn\ *n* 1 ♦ : a landmass higher than a hill 2 a ♦ : a great mass b ♦ : a vast number or quantity — **moun·tainy** \-ᵊn-ē\ *adj*

♦ [1] mount, peak; *also* mountain range, seamount; mountaintop, pinnacle, precipice, summit ♦ [2a] cock, heap, hill, mound, pile, rick, stack — more at PILE ♦ [2b] abundance, deal, gobs, heap, loads, lot, pile, plenty, quantity, scads — more at LOT

mountain ash *n* : any of various trees related to the roses that have pinnate leaves and red or orange-red fruits

mountain bike *n* : a bicycle with wide knobby tires, straight handlebars, and 18 or 21 gears that is designed to operate esp. over unpaved terrain

moun·tain·eer \ˌmaunt-ᵊn-'ir\ *n* 1 : a native or inhabitant of a mountainous region 2 : one who climbs mountains for sport

mountain goat *n* : a ruminant mammal of mountainous northwestern No. America that resembles a goat

mountain laurel *n* : a No. American evergreen shrub or small tree of the heath family with glossy leaves and clusters of rose-colored or white flowers

mountain lion *n* ♦ : a large powerful tawny brown wild American cat : COUGAR

♦ cougar, panther — more at COUGAR

moun·tain·ous \'maunt-ə-nəs, 'maunt-nəs\ *adj* 1 : containing many mountains 2 : resembling a mountain : HUGE

moun·tain·side \'maunt-ᵊn-ˌsīd\ *n* : the side of a mountain

moun·tain·top \-,täp\ *n* : the summit of a mountain

moun·te·bank \'maún-ti-,baŋk\ *n* [It *montimbanco*, fr. *montare* to mount + *in* in, on + *banco, banca* bench] ♦ : a boastful unscrupulous pretender : QUACK, CHARLATAN

♦ charlatan, fake, fraud, hoaxer, humbug, phony, pretender, quack

Mount·ie \'maún-tē\ *n* : a member of the Royal Canadian Mounted Police

mount·ing \'maún-tiŋ\ *n* : something that serves as a frame or support

mourn \'mōrn\ *vb* ♦ : to feel or express grief or sorrow — **mourn·er** *n*

♦ agonize, bleed, feel, grieve, hurt, sorrow, suffer — more at GRIEVE ♦ *usu* mourn for bemoan, bewail, deplore, grieve, lament, wail — more at LAMENT

mourn·ful \-fəl\ *adj* ♦ : expressing, feeling, or causing sorrow ⟨a ~ song⟩ — **mourn·ful·ness** *n*

♦ dolorous, funeral, lugubrious, plaintive, regretful, rueful, sorrowful, weeping, woeful; *also* elegiac, melancholy; depressed, despondent, disconsolate, inconsolable; careworn, sad, unhappy, woebegone; bawling, crying, groaning, howling, yammering; bleeding, suffering; black, bleak, cheerless, dark, darkening, desolate, dismal, dreary, gloomy, glum, gray, joyless, low, miserable, moody, morbid, morose, pessimistic, saturnine, somber, sullen, wretched ♦ blue, depressed, despondent, disconsolate, down, downcast, forlorn, gloomy, glum, low, melancholy, miserable, sad, sorrowful, sorry, unhappy

mourn·ful·ly \-fə-lē\ *adv* : in a mournful manner

mourn·ing \'mōr-niŋ\ *n* 1 : an outward sign (as black clothes) of grief for a person's death 2 : a period of time during which signs of grief are shown

mouse \'maús\ *n, pl* **mice** \'mīs\ 1 : any of numerous small rodents with pointed snout, long body, and slender tail 2 : a small manual device that controls cursor movement on a computer display

mouse pad *n* : a thin flat pad on which a computer mouse is used

mous·er \'maú-sər\ *n* : a cat proficient at catching mice

mouse·trap \'maús-,trap\ *n* 1 : a trap for catching mice 2 : a stratagem that lures one to defeat or destruction — **mousetrap** *vb*

mousse \'müs\ *n* [F, lit., froth, moss] 1 : a molded chilled dessert made with sweetened and flavored whipped cream or egg whites and gelatin 2 : a foamy preparation used in styling hair — **mousse** *vb*

moustache *chiefly Can and Brit var of* MUSTACHE

mousy *or* **mous·ey** \'maú-sē, -zē\ *adj* **mous·i·er; -est** 1 : QUIET, STEALTHY 2 ♦ : lacking in boldness or determination : TIMID 3 : grayish brown — **mous·i·ness** \'maú-sē-nəs, -zē-\ *n*

♦ fainthearted, fearful, scary, shy, skittish, timid — more at SHY

¹mouth \'maúth\ *n, pl* **mouths** \'maúthz, 'maúths\ 1 : the opening through which an animal takes in food; *also* : the cavity that encloses the tongue, lips, and teeth in the typical vertebrate 2 : something resembling a mouth (as in affording entrance) 3 : a facial expression usu. of disgust, disapproval, or pain : GRIMACE — **mouthed** \'maúthd, 'maútht\ *adj*

²mouth \'maúth\ *vb* 1 : SPEAK; *also* : DECLAIM 2 : to repeat without comprehension or sincerity ⟨~ed platitudes⟩ 3 : to form soundlessly with the lips 4 ♦ : to utter indistinctly 5 ♦ : to talk pompously — often used with *off*

♦ [4] mumble, murmur, mutter — more at MUMBLE ♦ *usu* mouth off [5] declaim, discourse, harangue, orate — more at ORATE

mouth·ful \'maúth-fəl\ *n* 1 : as much as a mouth will hold 2 ♦ : the quantity usu. taken into the mouth at one time

♦ bite, morsel, nibble, taste, tidbit — more at MORSEL

mouth harp *n* : HARMONICA

mouth·part \'maúth-,pärt\ *n* : a structure or appendage near the mouth (as of an insect) esp. when adapted for eating

mouth·piece \-,pēs\ *n* 1 : a part (as of a musical instrument) that goes in the mouth or to which the mouth is applied 2 ♦ : one that expresses or interprets another's views : SPOKESMAN

♦ speaker, spokesman, spokesperson, spokeswoman — more at SPOKESPERSON

mouth–to–mouth *adj* : of, relating to, or being a method of artificial respiration in which air from a rescuer's mouth is forced into a victim's lungs

mouth·wash \-,wósh, -,wäsh\ *n* : a usu. antiseptic liquid preparation for cleaning the mouth and teeth

mou·ton \'mü-,tän\ *n* : processed sheepskin that has been sheared or dyed to resemble beaver or seal

¹move \'müv\ *vb* **moved; mov·ing** 1 ♦ : to change or cause to change position or posture 2 ♦ : to go or cause to go from one point to another; *also* : DEPART 3 ♦ : to take or cause to take action 4 : to show marked activity 5 ♦ : to stir the emotions 6 : to make a formal request, application, or appeal 7 : to change one's residence 8 : EVACUATE 2 9 ♦ : to cause to operate or function — **mov·able** *or* **move·able** \'mü-və-bəl\ *adj*

♦ [1] budge, dislocate, displace, disturb, remove, shift, transfer; *also* bear, carry, convey, drive, haul, transmit, transport; transplant; replace, supersede, supplant; alter, make over, modify, redo, refashion, remake, remodel, revamp, revise, rework, vary ♦ [2] clear out, depart, exit, get off, go, pull, quit, sally, shove, take off — more at GO ♦ [3] affect, impact, impress, influence, strike, sway, tell, touch — more at AFFECT ♦ [3] argue, convince, get, induce, persuade, prevail, satisfy, talk, win — more at PERSUADE ♦ [5] arouse, encourage, excite, fire, incite, instigate, pique, provoke, stimulate, stir ♦ [9] activate, actuate, crank, drive, propel, run, set off, spark, start, touch off, trigger, turn on — more at ACTIVATE

²move *n* 1 : an act of moving 2 ♦ : a calculated step taken to gain an objective 3 : a change of location 4 : an agile action esp. in sports

♦ expedient, measure, shift, step — more at MEASURE

move·ment \'müv-mənt\ *n* 1 ♦ : the act or process of moving : MOVE 2 ♦ : a series of organized activities working toward an objective 3 : the moving parts of a mechanism (as of a watch) 4 : RHYTHM 5 : a section of an extended musical composition 6 : BOWEL MOVEMENT; *also* : STOOL 4

♦ [1] motion, move, moving, shift, stir, stirring; *also* dislocation, migration, relocation; locomotion, mobility, motility; fiddling, fidgeting, squirming, twitching, wriggling, writhing; flailing, flapping, waving **Ant** motionlessness ♦ [2] bandwagon, campaign, cause, crusade, drive — more at CAMPAIGN

mov·er \'mü-vər\ *n* : one that moves; *esp* : one that moves the belongings of others from one location to another

mov·ie \'mü-vē\ *n* 1 ♦ : a representation (as of a story) by means of motion pictures 2 *pl* : a showing of a motion picture 3 *pl* : the motion-picture industry

♦ [1] film, motion picture, picture; *also* animated cartoon, cartoon, docudrama, documentary, feature **movies** *pl* ♦ [3] film, screen; *also* show business

moving *adj* ♦ : stirring deeply in a way that evokes a strong emotional response

♦ affecting, emotional, impressive, poignant, stirring, touching; *also* eloquent, expressive, meaningful, significant; demonstrative, excitable, feeling, passionate, responsive, sensitive; exciting, provoking, rousing, stimulating; dramatic, histrionic, melodramatic, theatrical **Ant** unemotional, unimpressive

¹mow \'maú\ *n* : the part of a barn where hay or straw is stored

²mow \'mō\ *vb* **mowed; mowed** *or* **mown** \'mōn\; **mow·ing**

1 : to cut (as grass) with a scythe or machine   2 : to cut the standing herbage of ⟨∼ the lawn⟩ — **mow·er** n

mox·ie \'mäk-sē\ n   1 : ENERGY, PEP   2 : COURAGE, DETERMINATION

Mo·zam·bi·can \ˌmō-zəm-'bē-kən\ n : a native or inhabitant of Mozambique

moz·za·rel·la \ˌmät-sə-'re-lə\ n [It] : a moist white unsalted unripened mild cheese of a smooth rubbery texture

¹MP \'em-pē\ n   1 : a member of the military police   2 : an elected member of a parliament

²MP abbr   1 melting point   2 metropolitan police

MPEG \'em-ˌpeg\ n : any of a group of computer file formats for the compression and storage of digital video and audio data; also : a computer file (as of a movie) in an MPEG format

MP3 \'em-(ˌ)pē-'thrē\ n : a computer file format for the compression and storage of digital audio data; also : a computer file (as of a song) in the MP3 format

mpg abbr miles per gallon

mph abbr miles per hour

Mr. \'mis-tər\ n, pl **Messrs.** \'me-sərz\ — used as a conventional title of courtesy before a man's surname or his title of office

MRI \ˌem-ˌär-'ī\ n : MAGNETIC RESONANCE IMAGING

Mr. Right n : a man who would make the perfect husband

Mrs. \'mi-səz, -səs, esp Southern 'mi-zəz, -zəs\ n, pl **Mes·dames** \mā-'däm, -'dam\ — used as a conventional title of courtesy before a married woman's surname

Ms. \'miz\ n, pl **Mss.** or **Mses.** \'mi-zez\ — used as a conventional title of courtesy before a woman's surname

MS abbr   1 manuscript   2 master of science   3 military science   4 Mississippi   5 motor ship   6 multiple sclerosis

msec abbr millisecond

msg abbr message

MSG abbr   1 master sergeant   2 monosodium glutamate

msgr abbr   1 monseigneur   2 monsignor

MSgt abbr master sergeant

MSS abbr manuscripts

MST abbr mountain standard time

mt abbr mount; mountain

¹Mt abbr Matthew

²Mt symbol meitnerium

MT abbr   1 metric ton   2 Montana   3 mountain time

mtg abbr   1 meeting   2 mortgage

mtge abbr mortgage

mu \'myü, 'mü\ n : the 12th letter of the Greek alphabet — M or μ

¹much \'məch\ adj more \'mōr\; most \'mōst\ : great in quantity, amount, extent, or degree ⟨∼ money⟩

²much adv more; most   1 ♦ : to a great degree or extent ⟨∼ happier⟩   2 ♦ : almost but not quite : NEARLY ⟨looks ∼ as he did before⟩

  ♦ [1] broadly, considerably, greatly, hugely, largely, massively, monstrously, sizably, stupendously, tremendously, utterly, vastly — more at GREATLY ♦ [2] about, almost, most, near, nearly, next to, nigh, practically, some, virtually, well-nigh — more at ALMOST

³much n   1 ♦ : a great quantity, amount, extent, or degree   2 : something considerable or impressive

  ♦ abundance, deal, gobs, heap, loads, lot, pile, plenty, quantity, scads — more at LOT

mu·ci·lage \'myü-sə-lij\ n : a watery sticky solution (as of a gum) used esp. as an adhesive — **mu·ci·lag·i·nous** \ˌmyü-sə-'la-jə-nəs\ adj

muck \'mək\ n   1 : soft moist barnyard manure   2 ♦ : slimy dirt or filth   3 a : a dark richly organic soil   b : heavy often deep mud or slush : MUD, MIRE

  ♦ dirt, filth, grime, smut, soil — more at FILTH

muck·rake \-ˌrāk\ vb : to expose publicly real or apparent misconduct of a prominent individual or business — **muck·rak·er** n

mucky \'mə-kē\ adj   1 ♦ : not clean   2 ♦ : consisting of, marked by, or full of muck

  ♦ [1] dirty, filthy, grubby, grungy, muddy, unclean   ♦ [2] miry, muddy, oozy, slimy, slushy — more at MUDDY

mu·cus \'myü-kəs\ n : a slimy slippery protective secretion of membranes (**mucous membranes**) lining some body cavities — **mu·cous** \-kəs\ adj

mud \'məd\ n ♦ : soft wet earth : MIRE

  ♦ mire, muck, ooze, slime, slop, sludge, slush; also gumbo, silt; clay, dirt, gravel, humus, loam, sand, soil

¹mud·dle \'məd-ᵊl\ vb **mud·dled; mud·dling**   1 : to make muddy   2 ♦ : to confuse esp. with liquor   3 ♦ : to mix up or make a mess of   4 : to think or act in a confused way

  ♦ [2] addle, baffle, befog, befuddle, bemuse, bewilder, confound, confuse, disorient, muddy, mystify, perplex, puzzle — more at CONFUSE ♦ [3] disarray, dishevel, dislocate, disorder, disrupt, disturb, mess, mix

²muddle n   1 ♦ : a state of esp. mental confusion   2 ♦ : a confused mess

  ♦ [1] daze, fog, haze, spin — more at HAZE ♦ [1] bafflement, bewilderment, confusion, distraction, mystification, perplexity, puzzlement, whirl — more at CONFUSION ♦ [2] chaos, confusion, disarray, disorder, jumble, mess, shambles — more at CHAOS ♦ [2] assortment, clutter, jumble, medley, mélange, miscellany, motley, variety, welter — more at MISCELLANY

muddled adj ♦ : characterized by a confused state

  ♦ chaotic, confused, disordered, messy

mud·dle·head·ed \ˌməd-ᵊl-'he-dəd\ adj   1 : mentally confused   2 : INEPT

¹mud·dy \'mə-dē\ adj **mud·di·er; -est**   1 ♦ : full of or covered with mud   2 ♦ : turbid with sediment — **mud·di·ness** \-dē-nəs\ n

  ♦ [1] miry, mucky, oozy, slimy, slushy; also clayey, loamy, silty; bedraggled; dirty, filthy, foul, grimy, grubby, grungy, impure, squalid, unclean, uncleanly ♦ [2] cloudy, turbid — more at CLOUDY

²muddy vb   1 ♦ : to soil or stain with or as if with mud   2 a ♦ : to make indistinct ⟨don't ∼ the issue⟩   b : to disturb in mind or purpose : CONFUSE — **mud·di·ly** \'mə-də-lē\ adv

  ♦ [1] befoul, begrime, besmirch, blacken, dirty, foul, grime, mire, smirch, soil, stain — more at DIRTY ♦ [2a] becloud, befog, blur, cloud, confuse, fog — more at CONFUSE

mud·flat \'məd-ˌflat\ n : a level tract alternately covered and left bare by the tide

mud·guard \'məd-ˌgärd\ n : a guard over or a flap behind a wheel of a vehicle to catch or deflect mud

mud·room \-ˌrüm, -ˌrum\ n : a room in a house for removing dirty or wet footwear and clothing

mud·sling·er \-ˌsliŋ-ər\ n : one who uses invective esp. against a political opponent — **mud·sling·ing** \-ˌsliŋ-iŋ\ n

Muen·ster \'mən-stər, 'mün-, 'mùn-\ n : a semisoft bland cheese

mu·ez·zin \mü-'ez-ᵊn, myü-\ n : a Muslim crier who calls the hour of daily prayer

¹muff \'məf\ n : a warm tubular covering for the hands

²muff vb ♦ : to act or do (something) stupidly or clumsily

  ♦ bobble, botch, bungle, butcher, flub, foul up, fumble, mangle, mess up, screw up — more at BOTCH

³muff n : a bungling performance; esp : a failure to hold a ball in attempting a catch — **muff** vb

muf·fin \'mə-fən\ n : a small soft cake baked in a pan having cuplike molds

muf·fle \'mə-fəl\ vb **muf·fled; muf·fling**   1 : to wrap up so as to conceal or protect   2 : to wrap or pad with something to dull the sound of   3 : to keep down : SUPPRESS

muf·fler \'mə-flər\ n   1 : a scarf worn around the neck   2 : a device (as on a car's exhaust) to deaden noise

muf·ti \'məf-tē\ n : civilian clothes

¹mug \'məg\ n   1 : a usu. metal or earthenware cylindrical drinking cup   2 ♦ : the face or mouth of a person   3 ♦ : a usu. petty gangster, hoodlum, or ruffian

♦ [2] countenance, face, visage ♦ [3] bully, gangster, goon, hood, hoodlum, mobster, punk, rowdy, ruffian, thug, tough — more at HOODLUM

²**mug** *vb* **mugged; mug·ging** **1** : to pose or make faces esp. to attract attention or for a camera **2** : to take a photograph of : PHOTOGRAPH

³**mug** *vb* **mugged; mug·ging** : to assault usu. with intent to rob — **mug·ger** *n*

mug·gy \'mə-gē\ *adj* **mug·gi·er; -est** ♦ : being warm and humid — **mug·gi·ness** \-gē-nəs\ *n*

♦ humid, sticky, sultry — more at HUMID

mug·wump \'məg-ˌwəmp\ *n* [obs. slang *mugwump* kingpin, fr. Massachusett (Algonquian language of New England) *mugquomp* war leader] : an independent in politics

Mu·ham·mad·an \mō-'ha-mə-dən, -'hä-; mü-\ *n* : MUSLIM

mu·ja·hid·een *or* **mu·ja·hed·in** \mü-ja-hi-'dēn, -jä-\ *n pl* [Ar *mujāhidīn*, pl. of *mujāhid*, lit., person who wages jihad] : Islamic guerrilla fighters esp. in the Middle East

muk·luk \'mək-ˌlək\ *n* **1** : a boot of sealskin or reindeer skin typically worn by indigenous people of usu. arctic regions **2** : a boot with a soft leather sole worn over several pairs of socks

mu·lat·to \mü-'la-tō, myü-, -'lä-\ *n, pl* **-toes** *or* **-tos** [Sp *mulato*, fr. *mulo* mule, fr. L *mulus*] **1** *now sometimes offensive* : the first-generation offspring of a black person and a white person **2** *now sometimes offensive* : a person of mixed white and black ancestry

mul·ber·ry \'məl-ˌber-ē\ *n* : any of a genus of trees with edible berrylike fruit and leaves used as food for silkworms; *also* : the fruit

mulch \'məlch\ *n* : a protective covering (as of straw or leaves) spread on the ground esp. to reduce evaporation or control weeds — **mulch** *vb*

¹**mulct** \'məlkt\ *n* : a sum imposed as punishment for an offense : FINE, PENALTY

²**mulct** *vb* **1** : FINE **2** ♦ : to defraud esp. of money : CHEAT

♦ bleed, cheat, chisel, cozen, defraud, fleece, hustle, rook, shortchange, skin, squeeze, stick, sting, swindle, victimize — more at FLEECE

¹**mule** \'myül\ *n* **1** : a hybrid offspring of a male donkey and a female horse **2** : a very stubborn person

²**mule** *n* : a slipper whose upper does not extend around the heel of the foot

mule deer *n* : a long-eared deer of western No. America

mu·le·teer \ˌmyü-lə-'tir\ *n* : one who drives mules

mul·ish \'myü-lish\ *adj* ♦ : unreasonably and inflexibly obstinate — **mul·ish·ly** *adv*

♦ dogged, hardheaded, headstrong, obdurate, obstinate, opinionated, peevish, pertinacious, perverse, pigheaded, stubborn, unyielding, willful — more at OBSTINATE

mu·lish·ness \-nəs\ *n* ♦ : the quality or state of being mulish

♦ hardheadedness, obduracy, obstinacy, peevishness, pertinacity, self-will, stubbornness, tenacity — more at OBSTINACY

¹**mull** \'məl\ *vb* ♦ : to consider at length : PONDER, MEDITATE — often used with *over*

♦ usu **mull over** chew over, cogitate, consider, contemplate, debate, deliberate, entertain, meditate, ponder, question, ruminate, study, think, weigh — more at PONDER

²**mull** *vb* : to heat, sweeten, and flavor (as wine) with spices

mul·lein \'mə-lən\ *n* : a tall herb related to the snapdragons that has coarse woolly leaves and flowers in spikes

mul·let \'mə-lət\ *n, pl* **mullet** *or* **mullets** : any of a family of largely gray chiefly marine bony fishes including valuable food fishes

mul·li·gan stew \'mə-li-gən-\ *n* : a stew made from whatever ingredients are available

mul·li·ga·taw·ny \ˌmə-li-gə-'tò-nē\ *n* : a soup usu. of chicken stock seasoned with curry

mul·lion \'məl-yən\ *n* : a vertical strip separating windowpanes

multi- *comb form* **1** : many : multiple ⟨*multi*unit⟩ **2** : many times over ⟨*multi*millionaire⟩

mul·ti·col·ored \ˌməl-ti-'kə-lərd\ *adj* ♦ : having many colors

♦ colorful (*or* colourful), variegated — more at COLORFUL

mul·ti·cul·tur·al \ˌməl-tē-'kəl-chə-rəl, -ˌtī-\ *adj* : of, relating to, reflecting, or adapted to diverse cultures ⟨a ∼ society⟩

mul·ti·di·men·sion·al \-ti-də-'men-chə-nəl, -ˌtī-, -dī-\ *adj* : of, relating to, or having many facets or dimensions ⟨a ∼ problem⟩ ⟨∼ space⟩

mul·ti·eth·nic \-'eth-nik\ *adj* : including, involving, or made up of people of various ethnic groups

mul·ti·fac·et·ed \-'fa-sə-təd\ *adj* : having several distinct facets or aspects ⟨a ∼ concept⟩

mul·ti·fam·i·ly \-'fam-lē, -'fa-mə-\ *adj* : designed for use by several families

mul·ti·far·i·ous \ˌməl-tə-'far-ē-əs\ *adj* ♦ : having great variety ⟨∼ activities⟩ — **mul·ti·far·i·ous·ness** *n*

♦ manifold, myriad — more at MANIFOLD

mul·ti·form \'məl-ti-ˌfòrm\ *adj* : having many forms or appearances — **mul·ti·for·mi·ty** \ˌməl-ti-'fòr-mə-tē\ *n*

mul·ti·lat·er·al \ˌməl-ti-'la-tə-rəl, -ˌtī-, -'la-trəl\ *adj* : having many sides or participants ⟨∼ treaty⟩ — **mul·ti·lat·er·al·ism** \-'la-tə-rə-ˌli-zəm\ *n*

mul·ti·lay·ered \-'lā-ərd, -'lerd\ *or* **mul·ti·lay·er** \-'lā-ər, -'ler\ *adj* : having or involving several distinct layers or levels

mul·ti·lev·el \-'le-vəl\ *adj* : having several levels

mul·ti·lin·gual \-'liŋ-gwəl\ *adj* : knowing or using several languages — **mul·ti·lin·gual·ism** \-gwə-ˌli-zəm\ *n*

¹**mul·ti·me·dia** \-'mē-dē-ə\ *adj* : using, involving, or encompassing several media ⟨a ∼ advertising campaign⟩

²**multimedia** *n sing or pl* : the technique of using several media (as in art); *also* : something (as software) that uses or facilitates it

mul·ti·mil·lion·aire \ˌməl-ti-ˌmil-yə-'nar, -ˌtī-, -'mil-yə-ˌnar\ *n* : a person worth several million dollars

mul·ti·na·tion·al \-'na-shə-nəl\ *adj* **1** : of or relating to several nationalities **2** : relating to or involving several nations **3** : having divisions in several countries ⟨a ∼ corporation⟩ — **multinational** *n*

mul·ti·pack \'məl-tē-ˌpak\ *n* : a package of several individually packed items sold as a unit

¹**mul·ti·ple** \'məl-tə-pəl\ *adj* **1 a** : more than one **b** ♦ : consisting of or amounting to a large but indefinite number : MANY **2** : VARIOUS

♦ many, multitudinous, numerous — more at MANY

²**multiple** *n* : the product of a quantity by an integer ⟨35 is a ∼ of 7⟩

multiple–choice *adj* : having several answers given from which the correct one is to be chosen ⟨a ∼ question⟩

multiple personality disorder *n* : a neurosis in which the personality becomes separated into two or more parts each of which controls behavior part of the time

multiple sclerosis *n* : a disease marked by patches of hardened tissue in the brain or spinal cord and associated esp. with partial or complete paralysis and muscular tremor

mul·ti·plex \'məl-tə-ˌpleks\ *n* : CINEPLEX

mul·ti·pli·cand \ˌməl-tə-pli-'kand\ *n* : the number that is to be multiplied by another

mul·ti·pli·ca·tion \ˌməl-tə-plə-'kā-shən\ *n* **1** ♦ : the act or process of multiplying : the state of being multiplied **2** : a short method of finding the result of adding a figure the number of times indicated by another figure

♦ accumulation, addition, increase, proliferation; *also* doubling, quadrupling, tripling; growth, rise, spread; enlargement, escalation, expansion; amplification, distention, inflation; accretion, accrual, augmentation; extension, lengthening *Ant* decrease

multiplication sign *n* **1** : TIMES SIGN **2** : a centered dot indicating multiplication

mul·ti·plic·i·ty \ˌməl-tə-'pli-sə-tē\ *n, pl* **-ties** : a great number or variety

mul·ti·pli·er \'məl-tə-ˌplī-ər\ *n* : one that multiplies; *esp* : a number by which another number is multiplied

mul·ti·ply \\'məl-tə-ˌplī\ *vb* **-plied; -ply·ing** **1** ♦ : to increase in number (as by breeding) **2** : to find the product of by multiplication; *also* : to perform multiplication

♦ accumulate, appreciate, balloon, build, burgeon, enlarge, escalate, expand, increase, mount, mushroom, proliferate, rise, snowball, swell, wax — more at INCREASE ♦ add, aggrandize, amplify, augment, boost, compound, enlarge, escalate, expand, extend, increase, raise, swell, up — more at INCREASE ♦ breed, procreate, propagate, reproduce — more at PROCREATE

mul·ti·pur·pose \ˌməl-ti-'pər-pəs, -ˌtī-\ *adj* : having or serving several purposes

mul·ti·ra·cial \-'rā-shəl\ *adj* : composed of, involving, or representing various races

mul·ti·sense \-ˌsens\ *adj* : having several meanings ⟨∼ words⟩

mul·ti·sto·ry \-ˌstōr-ē\ *adj* : having several stories ⟨∼ buildings⟩

mul·ti·task·ing \'məl-tē-ˌtas-kiŋ, -ˌtī-\ *n* **1** : the concurrent performance of several jobs by a computer **2** : the performance of multiple tasks at one time — **mul·ti·task** \-ˌtask\ *vb* — **mul·ti·task·er** \-ˌtaskər\ *n*

mul·ti·tude \'məl-tə-ˌtüd, -ˌtyüd\ *n* ♦ : a great number

♦ army, crowd, crush, drove, flock, horde, host, legion, mob, press, swarm, throng — more at CROWD

mul·ti·tu·di·nous \ˌməl-tə-'tüd-ᵊn-əs, -'tyüd-\ *adj* ♦ : existing in a great multitude

♦ many, multiple, numerous — more at MANY

mul·ti·unit \ˌməl-ti-'yü-nət, -ˌtī-\ *adj* : having several units

mul·ti·vi·ta·min \-'vī-tə-mən\ *adj* : containing several vitamins and esp. all known to be essential to health — **multivitamin** *n*

¹**mum** \'məm\ *adj* ♦ : making no utterance : SILENT

♦ dumb, mute, silent, speechless, uncommunicative — more at SILENT

²**mum** *n* : CHRYSANTHEMUM

³**mum** *chiefly Can and Brit var of* MOM

¹**mum·ble** \'məm-bəl\ *vb* **mum·bled; mum·bling** ♦ : to speak in a low indistinct manner — **mum·bler** *n* — **mum·bly** *adj*

♦ mouth, murmur, mutter; *also* babble, blab, chatter, drivel, gabble, gibber, jabber, maunder, prattle, ramble; breathe, gasp, pant, whisper *Ant* speak out, speak up

²**mumble** *n* ♦ : a low confused indistinct utterance

♦ murmur, mutter; *also* undertone, whisper; babble, babbling, blab, blabbing, chatter, chattering, drivel, driveling, gabble, gabbling, jabber, jabbering, prattle, prattling, rambling

mum·ble·ty·peg \'məm-bəl-tē-ˌpeg\ *also* **mum·ble–the–peg** \'məm-bəl-thə-\ *n* : a game in which the players try to flip a knife from various positions so that the blade will stick into the ground

mum·bo jum·bo \ˌməm-bō-'jəm-bō\ *n* **1** : a complicated ritual with elaborate trappings **2** : unnecessarily involved and incomprehensible language : GIBBERISH, NONSENSE

mum·mer \'mə-mər\ *n* **1 a** ♦ : a performer in a pantomime **b** : ACTOR **2** : a person who goes merrymaking in disguise during festivals — **mum·mery** *n*

♦ mime, mimic, pantomime

¹**mum·my** \'mə-mē\ *n, pl* **mummies** [ME *mummie* powdered parts of a mummified body used as a drug, fr. AF *mumie*, fr. ML *mumia*, fr. Ar *mūmiya* bitumen, mummy, fr. Per *mūm* wax] : a body embalmed for burial in the manner of the ancient Egyptians — **mum·mi·fi·ca·tion** \ˌmə-mi-fə-'kā-shən\ *n* — **mum·mi·fy** \'mə-mi-ˌfī\ *vb*

²**mummy** *chiefly Can and Brit var of* MOMMY

mumps \'məmps\ *n sing or pl* [fr. pl. of obs. *mump* grimace] : a virus disease marked by fever and swelling esp. of the salivary glands

mun *or* **munic** *abbr* municipal

munch \'mənch\ *vb* : to eat with a chewing action; *also* : to snack on

munch·ies \'mən-chēz\ *n pl* **1** : hunger pangs **2** : light snack foods

mun·dane \ˌmən-'dān, 'mən-ˌdān\ *adj* **1** ♦ : of or relating to the world **2** ♦ : concerned with the practical details of everyday life — **mun·dane·ly** *adv*

♦ [1] earthly, temporal, terrestrial, worldly — more at EARTHLY ♦ [2] everyday, prosaic, workaday; *also* earthly, temporal, worldly; average, common, commonplace, customary, familiar, garden, normal, ordinary, plain, popular, routine, run-of-the-mill, typical, unexceptional, unremarkable, usual; frequent, habitual, regular; expected, predictable

mung bean \'məŋ-\ *n* : an erect bushy bean widely grown in warm regions for its edible seeds and as the chief source of bean sprouts; *also* : its seed

mu·nic·i·pal \myù-'ni-sə-pəl\ *adj* **1** : of, relating to, or characteristic of a municipality **2** : restricted to one locality — **mu·nic·i·pal·ly** *adv*

mu·nic·i·pal·i·ty \myù-ˌni-sə-'pa-lə-tē\ *n, pl* **-ties** ♦ : an urban political unit with corporate status and usu. powers of self-government

♦ city, metropolis

mu·nif·i·cent \myú-'ni-fə-sənt\ *adj* ♦ : liberal in giving : GENEROUS — **mu·nif·i·cence** \-səns\ *n*

♦ bountiful, charitable, free, generous, liberal, openhanded, unselfish, unsparing — more at GENEROUS

mu·ni·tion \myú-'ni-shən\ *n* : ARMAMENT, AMMUNITION

¹**mu·ral** \'myúr-əl\ *adj* **1** : of or relating to a wall **2** : applied to and made part of a wall or ceiling surface

²**mural** *n* : a mural painting — **mu·ral·ist** *n*

¹**mur·der** \'mər-dər\ *n* **1** ♦ : the crime of unlawfully killing a person esp. with premeditated malice **2** ♦ : something unusually difficult or dangerous

♦ [1] homicide — more at HOMICIDE ♦ [2] agony, hell, horror, misery, nightmare, torment, torture — more at HELL

²**murder** *vb* **1 a** : to commit a murder **b** ♦ : to kill (a human being) unlawfully and with premeditated malice; *also* : to kill brutally **2** : to put an end to **3** ♦ : to spoil by performing poorly ⟨∼ a song⟩ — **mur·der·er** *n*

♦ [1b] dispatch, do in, execute, liquidate, slay; *also* blot out, destroy, fell, kill, smite, zap; assassinate; butcher, massacre, mow (down), slaughter; annihilate, eliminate, eradicate, exterminate, wipe out ♦ [3] bobble, botch, bungle, butcher, flub, foul up, fumble, mangle, mess up, screw up — more at BOTCH

mur·der·ess \'mər-də-rəs\ *n* : a woman who murders

mur·der·ous \'mər-də-rəs\ *adj* **1** ♦ : having or appearing to have the purpose of murder ⟨∼ impulses⟩ **2** ♦ : marked by or causing murder or bloodshed ⟨∼ gunfire⟩ **3** ♦ : having the ability or power to overwhelm ⟨∼ heat⟩ **4** ♦ : characterized by extreme difficulty ⟨the exam was ∼⟩ — **mur·der·ous·ly** *adv*

♦ [1] bloodthirsty, bloody, homicidal, sanguinary, sanguine — more at BLOODTHIRSTY ♦ [2] baleful, deadly, deathly, fatal, fell, lethal, mortal, pestilent, vital — more at DEADLY ♦ [3] bitter, brutal, burdensome, cruel, excruciating, grievous, grim, hard, harsh, heavy, inhuman, onerous, oppressive, rough, rugged, severe, stiff, tough, trying — more at HARSH ♦ [4] arduous, demanding, difficult, exacting, formidable, grueling, hard, herculean, laborious, rough, stiff, strenuous, tall, toilsome, tough — more at HARD

murk \'mərk\ *n* **1** ♦ : partial or total darkness : GLOOM **2** ♦ : a murky condition of the atmosphere or a substance causing it : FOG — **murk·i·ly** \'mər-kə-lē\ *adv*

♦ [1] dark, darkness, dusk, gloaming, gloom, night, semidarkness, shade, shadows, twilight — more at DARK ♦ [2] fog, haze, smog, soup — more at HAZE

murk·i·ness \'mər-kē-nəs\ *n* ♦ : the quality or state of being murky

♦ ambiguity, darkness, obscurity, opacity — more at OBSCURITY

murky \'mər-kē\ *adj* **1** ♦ : characterized by a heavy dimness or obscurity caused by or like that caused by overhanging fog or smoke **2 ♦** : characterized by thickness and heaviness of air : FOGGY, MISTY **3 ♦** : darkly vague or obscure ⟨∼ writings⟩

♦ [1] dark, darkling, dim, dusky, gloomy, obscure, somber (*or* sombre) — more at DARK ♦ [2] cloudy, foggy, hazy, misty, smoggy, soupy — more at HAZY ♦ [3] ambiguous, cryptic, dark, darkling, deep, enigmatic, equivocal, inscrutable, mysterious, mystic, nebulous, obscure, occult — more at OBSCURE

¹**mur·mur** \'mər-mər\ *n* **1 ♦** : a muttered complaint **2 a** : a low indistinct often continuous sound **b ♦** : a soft or gentle utterance — **mur·mur·ous** *adj*

♦ [1] beef, complaint, fuss, grievance, gripe, grumble, plaint, squawk — more at COMPLAINT ♦ [2b] mumble, mutter — more at MUMBLE

²**murmur** *vb* **1** : to make a murmur ⟨traffic ∼ed in the distance⟩ **2** : to express grief, pain, or discontent
mur·mur·er *n* : one that murmurs
mus *abbr* **1** museum **2** music; musical; musician
mus·ca·tel \ˌməs-kə-'tel\ *n* : a sweet fortified wine
¹**mus·cle** \'mə-səl\ *n* [ME, fr. L *musculus*, fr. dim. of *mus* mouse] **1** : a body tissue consisting of long cells that contract when stimulated and produce motion; *also* : an organ consisting of this tissue and functioning in moving a body part **2 ♦** : effective strength : BRAWN — **mus·cled** \'mə-səld\ *adj*

♦ energy, force, main, might, potency, power, sinew, strength, vigor (*or* vigour) — more at POWER

²**muscle** *vb* **mus·cled; mus·cling** **1 ♦** : to move or force by or as if by muscular effort **2 ♦** : to make one's way by brute strength or by force

♦ [1] coerce, compel, constrain, drive, force, make, obligate, oblige, press, pressure — more at FORCE ♦ [2] bulldoze, elbow, press, push — more at PRESS

mus·cle–bound \'mə-səl-ˌbaund\ *adj* : having some of the muscles abnormally enlarged and lacking in elasticity (as from excessive exercise)
mus·cle·man \-ˌman\ *n* : a man with a muscular physique
mus·cu·lar \'məs-kyə-lər\ *adj* **1 a** : of, relating to, or constituting muscle **b** : of, relating to, or performed by the muscles **2 ♦** : having well-developed musculature **3** : of or relating to physical strength — **mus·cu·lar·i·ty** \ˌməs-kyə-'lar-ə-tē\ *n*

♦ brawny, rugged, sinewy, stalwart, stout, strong — more at STRONG

muscular dystrophy *n* : any of a group of diseases characterized by progressive wasting of muscles
mus·cu·la·ture \'məs-kyə-lə-ˌchùr\ *n* : the muscles of the body or its parts
muscu·lo·skel·e·tal \ˌməs-kyə-lō-'ske-lə-tᵊl\ *adj* : of, relating to, or involving both musculature and skeleton
¹**muse** \'myüz\ *vb* **mused; mus·ing** [ME, fr. AF *muser* to gape, idle, muse, fr. OF *mus* mouth of an animal, fr. ML *musus*] : to become absorbed in thought — **mus·ing·ly** *adv*
²**muse** *n* [fr. *Muse* any of the nine sister goddesses of learning and the arts in Greek myth, fr. ME, fr. MF, fr. L *Musa*, fr. Gk *Mousa*] : a source of inspiration
mu·se·um \myù-'zē-əm\ *n* : an institution devoted to the procurement, care, and display of objects of lasting interest or value
¹**mush** \'məsh\ *n* **1** : cornmeal boiled in water **2** : sentimental drivel **3 ♦** : mawkish amorousness

♦ mawkishness, sentimentality — more at SENTIMENTALITY

²**mush** *vb* : to travel esp. over snow with a sled drawn by dogs
¹**mush·room** \'məsh-ˌrüm, -ˌrùm\ *n* : the fleshy usu. caplike spore-bearing organ of various fungi esp. when edible; *also* : such a fungus
²**mushroom** *vb* **1** : to collect wild mushrooms **2 ♦** : to spread out : EXPAND **3** : to grow rapidly

♦ accumulate, appreciate, balloon, build, burgeon, enlarge, escalate, expand, increase, mount, multiply, proliferate, rise, snowball, swell, wax — more at INCREASE

mushy \'mə-shē\ *adj* **mush·i·er; -est** **1 ♦** : soft like mush **2 ♦** : excessively sentimental ⟨a ∼ movie⟩

♦ [1] flabby, pulpy, soft, spongy — more at SOFT ♦ [2] corny, maudlin, mawkish, saccharine, sappy, schmaltzy, sentimental — more at CORNY

mu·sic \'myü-zik\ *n* **1** : the science or art of combining tones into a composition having structure and continuity; *also* : vocal or instrumental sounds having rhythm, melody, or harmony **2** : an agreeable sound
¹**mu·si·cal** \'myü-zi-kəl\ *adj* **1** : of or relating to music or musicians **3 ♦** : having the pleasing tonal qualities of music **3** : fond of or gifted in music ⟨a ∼ family⟩ — **mu·si·cal·ly** \-k(ə-)lē\ *adv*

♦ euphonious, lyric, mellifluous, mellow, melodic, melodious — more at LYRIC ♦ harmonious, symphonic, tuneful — more at HARMONIOUS

²**musical** *n* : a film or theatrical production consisting of musical numbers and dialogue based on a unifying plot
mu·si·cale \ˌmyü-zi-'kal\ *n* : a usu. private social gathering featuring music
mu·si·cian \myù-'zi-shən\ *n* : a composer, conductor, or performer of music — **mu·si·cian·ly** *adj* — **mu·si·cian·ship** *n*
mu·si·col·o·gy \ˌmyü-zi-'kä-lə-jē\ *n* : the study of music as a field of knowledge or research — **mu·si·co·log·i·cal** \-kə-'lä-ji-kəl\ *adj* — **mu·si·col·o·gist** \-'kä-lə-jist\ *n*
musk \'məsk\ *n* : a substance obtained esp. from a small Asian deer (**musk deer**) and used as a perfume fixative — **musk·i·ness** \'məs-kē-nəs\ *n* — **musky** *adj*
mus·keg \'məs-ˌkeg\ *n* : wet spongy ground : BOG; *esp* : a mossy bog in northern No. America
mus·kel·lunge \'məs-kə-ˌlənj\ *n, pl* **muskellunge** : a large No. American pike that is a valuable sport fish
mus·ket \'məs-kət\ *n* [MF *mousquet*, fr. It *moschetto* small artillery piece, kind of small hawk, fr. dim. of *mosca* fly, fr. L *musca*] : a heavy large-caliber muzzle-loading shoulder firearm — **mus·ke·teer** \ˌməs-kə-'tir\ *n*
mus·ket·ry \'məs-kə-trē\ *n* **1** : MUSKETS **2** : MUSKETEERS **3** : musket fire
musk·mel·on \'məsk-ˌme-lən\ *n* : a small round to oval melon that has usu. a sweet edible green or orange flesh and a musky odor
musk ox *n* : a heavyset shaggy-coated wild ox of Greenland and the arctic tundra of northern No. America
musk·rat \'məs-ˌkrat\ *n, pl* **muskrat** *or* **muskrats** : a large No. American aquatic rodent with webbed feet and dark brown fur; *also* : its fur
Mus·lim \'məz-ləm\ *n* : an adherent of Islam — **Muslim** *adj*
mus·lin \'məz-lən\ *n* : a plain-woven sheer to coarse cotton fabric
¹**muss** \'məs\ *n* **♦** : a state of disorder

♦ chaos, confusion, disarray, disorder, disorganization, havoc, hell, jumble, mess, messiness, muddle, shambles, tumble, welter — more at CHAOS

²**muss** *vb* : to make untidy : DISARRANGE
mus·sel \'mə-səl\ *n* **1** : a dark edible saltwater bivalve mollusk **2** : any of various freshwater bivalve mollusks of the central U.S. having shells with a pearly lining
mussy \'mə-sē\ *adj* : characterized by clutter or muss — **muss·i·ly** \'mə-sə-lē\ *adv* — **muss·i·ness** \-sē-nəs\ *n*
¹**must** \'məst\ *vb* **♦** — used as an auxiliary esp. to express a command, requirement, obligation, or necessity

♦ have, need, ought, shall, should — more at NEED

²**must** *n* **1 ♦** : an imperative duty **2 ♦** : an indispensable item

♦ [1, 2] condition, demand, essential, necessity, need, requirement, requisite — more at ESSENTIAL

mus·tache *or chiefly Can and Brit* **mous·tache** \'məs-ˌtash, (ˌ)məs-'tash\ *n* : the hair growing on the human upper lip — **mus·tached** \-ˌtasht, -'tasht\ *adj*

mus·tang \'məs-ˌtaŋ\ *n* [MexSp *mestengo,* fr. Sp, stray, fr. *mesteño* strayed, fr. *mesta* annual roundup of cattle that disposed of strays, fr. ML *(animalia) mixta* mixed animals] : a small hardy naturalized horse of the western plains of America; *also* : BRONC

mus·tard \'məs-tərd\ *n* 1 : a pungent yellow powder of the seeds of an herb related to the cabbage and used as a condiment or in medicine 2 : a plant that yields mustard; *also* : a closely related plant — **mus·tardy** *adj*

mustard gas *n* : a poison gas used in warfare that has violent irritating and blistering effects

¹**mus·ter** \'məs-tər\ *n* 1 a ♦ : an act of assembling (as for military inspection) b : critical examination 2 ♦ : an assembled group

♦ [1a] mobilization, rally — more at RALLY ♦ [2] assemblage, assembly, conference, congregation, convocation, gathering, meeting — more at GATHERING

²**mus·ter** *vb* [ME *mustren* to show, muster, fr. AF *mustrer, monstrer,* fr. L *monstrare* to show, fr. *monstrum* evil omen, monster] 1 a ♦ : to gather or cause to gather ⟨~ an army⟩ b : to call the roll of 2 : ACCUMULATE 3 : to call forth : ROUSE ⟨~ed support⟩ 4 : to amount to : COMPRISE

♦ marshal, mobilize, rally — more at MOBILIZE ♦ assemble, call, convene, convoke, summon — more at CONVOKE

muster out *vb* : to discharge from military service

musty \'məs-tē\ *adj* **mus·ti·er; -est** 1 : impaired by damp or mildew : MOLDY 2 ♦ : tasting or smelling of damp or decay 3 ♦ : tedious from familiarity : STALE — **must·i·ly** \-tə-lē\ *adv* — **must·i·ness** \-tē-nəs\ *n*

♦ [2] fetid, foul, fusty, malodorous, noisome, rank, reeky, smelly, strong — more at MALODOROUS ♦ [3] banal, commonplace, hackneyed, stale, stereotyped, threadbare, tired, trite — more at STALE

mu·ta·ble \'myü-tə-bəl\ *adj* 1 ♦ : prone to change : FICKLE 2 : capable of or liable to mutation : VARIABLE — **mu·ta·bil·i·ty** \ˌmyü-tə-'bi-lə-tē\ *n*

♦ capricious, changeable, fickle, fluid, inconstant, mercurial, temperamental, uncertain, unpredictable, unsettled, unstable, unsteady, variable, volatile — more at FICKLE

mu·tant \'myüt-ᵊnt\ *adj* : of, relating to, or produced by mutation — **mu·tant** *n*

mu·tate \'myü-ˌtāt\ *vb* **mu·tat·ed; mu·tat·ing** ♦ : to undergo or cause to undergo mutation — **mu·ta·tive** \'myü-ˌtā-tiv, -tə-tiv\ *adj*

♦ change, fluctuate, shift, vary — more at CHANGE

mu·ta·tion \myü-'tā-shən\ *n* 1 : CHANGE 2 : an inherited physical or biochemical change in genetic material; *also* : the process of producing a mutation 3 : an individual, strain, or trait resulting from mutation — **mu·ta·tion·al** *adj*

¹**mute** \'myüt\ *adj* **mut·er; mut·est** 1 ♦ : unable to speak : DUMB 2 ♦ : characterized by absence of speech : SILENT — **mute·ly** *adv* — **mute·ness** *n*

♦ [1] dumb, inarticulate, speechless, voiceless; *also* tongue-tied; incoherent, incomprehensible; closemouthed, laconic, taciturn, uncommunicative; mum, nonspeaking, quiet, silent, wordless ♦ [2] dumb, mum, silent, speechless, uncommunicative — more at SILENT

²**mute** *n* 1 *sometimes offensive* : a person who cannot speak 2 : a device on a musical instrument that reduces, softens, or muffles the tone

³**mute** *vb* **mut·ed; mut·ing** ♦ : to muffle, reduce, or eliminate the sound of

♦ hush, quell, settle, silence, still — more at SILENCE

muted *adj* 1 ♦ : being mute : SILENT 2 ♦ : toned down : SUBDUED

♦ [1] hushed, noiseless, quiet, silent, soundless, still — more at SILENT ♦ [2] conservative, quiet, restrained, subdued, unpretentious — more at QUIET

mu·ti·late \'myüt-ᵊl-ˌāt\ *vb* **-lat·ed; -lat·ing** 1 : to cut up

or alter radically so as to make imperfect 2 ♦ : to cut off or permanently destroy a limb or essential part of : MAIM, CRIPPLE — **mu·ti·la·tion** \ˌmyüt-ᵊl-'ā-shən\ *n* — **mu·ti·la·tor** \'myüt-ᵊl-ˌā-tər\ *n*

♦ cripple, disable, lame, maim — more at MAIM

mu·ti·neer \ˌmyüt-ᵊn-'ir\ *n* ♦ : one that mutinies

♦ insurgent, insurrectionist, rebel, red, revolter, revolutionary — more at REBEL

mu·ti·nous \'myüt-ᵊn-əs\ *adj* 1 ♦ : disposed to or being in a state of mutiny 2 : of, relating to, or constituting mutiny — **mu·ti·nous·ly** *adv*

♦ insurgent, rebellious, revolutionary — more at REBELLIOUS

mu·ti·ny \'myü-tə-nē\ *n, pl* **-nies** ♦ : willful refusal to obey constituted authority; *esp* : revolt against a superior officer — **mutiny** *vb*

♦ insurrection, rebellion, revolt, revolution, uprising — more at REBELLION

mutt \'mət\ *n* : MONGREL, CUR

¹**mut·ter** \'mə-tər\ *vb* 1 ♦ : to speak indistinctly or with a low voice lips partly closed 2 ♦ : to murmur complainingly or angrily : GRUMBLE

♦ [1] mouth, mumble, murmur — more at MUMBLE ♦ [2] beef, bellyache, carp, complain, crab, croak, fuss, gripe, grouse, growl, grumble, kick, moan, murmur, repine, squawk, wail, whine — more at COMPLAIN

²**mutter** *n* ♦ : a subdued scarcely audible utterance

♦ mumble, murmur — more at MUMBLE

mut·ton \'mət-ᵊn\ *n* [ME *motoun* mutton, sheep, fr. AF *mutun* ram, sheep, mutton] : the flesh of a mature sheep used for food — **mut·tony** *adj*

mut·ton·chops \'mət-ᵊn-ˌchäps\ *n pl* : whiskers on the side of the face that are narrow at the temple and broad and round by the lower jaws

mu·tu·al \'myü-chə-wəl\ *adj* 1 : given and received in equal amount ⟨~ trust⟩ 2 : having the same feelings one for the other ⟨~ enemies⟩ 3 ♦ : shared in common : COMMON, JOINT ⟨a ~ friend⟩ — **mu·tu·al·ly** *adv*

♦ collective, common, communal, concerted, conjoint, joint, public, united — more at COLLECTIVE

mutual fund *n* : an investment company that invests money of its shareholders in a usu. diversified group of securities of other corporations

muu·muu \'mü-ˌmü\ *n* : a loose dress of Hawaiian origin

¹**muz·zle** \'mə-zəl\ *n* 1 : the nose and jaws of an animal; *also* : a covering for the muzzle to prevent biting or eating 2 : the mouth of a gun

²**muzzle** *vb* **muz·zled; muz·zling** 1 : to put a muzzle on 2 : to restrain from expression : GAG ⟨tried to ~ the press⟩

mV *abbr* millivolt

MV *abbr* motor vessel

MVP *abbr* most valuable player

MW *abbr* megawatt

my \'mī\ *adj* 1 : of or relating to me or myself 2 — used interjectionally esp. to express surprise

my·col·o·gy \mī-'kä-lə-jē\ *n* : a branch of biology dealing with fungi — **my·co·log·i·cal** \ˌmī-kə-'lä-ji-kəl\ *adj* — **my·col·o·gist** \mī-'kä-lə-jist\ *n*

my·elo·ma \ˌmī-ə-'lō-mə\ *n, pl* **-mas** *or* **-ma·ta** \-mə-tə\ : a primary tumor of the bone marrow

my·nah *or* **my·na** \'mī-nə\ *n* : any of several Asian starlings; *esp* : a dark brown slightly crested bird sometimes taught to mimic speech

my·o·pia \mī-'ō-pē-ə\ *n* : a condition in which visual images come to a focus in front of the retina resulting esp. in defective vision of distant objects — **my·o·pic** \-'ō-pik, -'ä-\ *adj* — **my·o·pi·cal·ly** \-pi-k(ə-)lē\ *adv*

¹**myr·i·ad** \'mir-ē-əd\ *n* [Gk *myriad-, myrias,* fr. *myrioi* countless, ten thousand] : an indefinitely large number

²**myriad** *adj* ♦ : consisting of a very great but indefinite number; *also* : both numerous and varied

♦ manifold, multifarious — more at MANIFOLD

myr·mi·don \'mər-mə-₁dän\ *n* : a loyal follower; *esp* : one who executes orders without protest or pity

myrrh \'mər\ *n* : a fragrant aromatic plant gum used in perfumes and formerly for incense

myr·tle \'mərt-ᵊl\ *n* : an evergreen shrub of southern Europe with shiny leaves, fragrant flowers, and black berries; *also* : PERIWINKLE

my·self \mī-'self, mə-\ *pron* : I, ME — used reflexively, for emphasis, or in absolute constructions ⟨I hurt ∼⟩ ⟨I ∼ did it⟩ ⟨∼ busy, I sent him instead⟩

mys·te·ri·ous \mis-'tir-ē-əs\ *adj* 1 ♦ : of, relating to, or constituting mystery 2 ♦ : exciting wonder, curiosity, or surprise while baffling efforts to comprehend or identify — **mys·te·ri·ous·ly** *adv* — **mys·te·ri·ous·ness** *n*

♦ [1] ambiguous, equivocal, murky, nebulous, obscure — more at OBSCURE ♦ [2] cryptic, darkling, deep, enigmatic, impenetrable, inscrutable, mystic, occult, uncanny; *also* dark, murky, obscure, shadowy, vague; ambiguous, equivocal; incomprehensible, unfathomable, unintelligible; inexplicable, unaccountable; unanswerable, unknowable; metaphysical, mystical, supernatural; abstruse, esoteric, recondite; baffling, bewildering, confounding, confusing, mystifying, perplexing, puzzling

mys·tery \'mis-tə-rē\ *n, pl* **-ter·ies** 1 : a religious truth known by revelation alone 2 ♦ : something not understood or beyond understanding 3 : enigmatic quality or character 4 : a work of fiction dealing with the solution of a mysterious crime

♦ conundrum, enigma, mystification, puzzle, puzzlement, riddle, secret; *also* brainteaser, challenge, perplexity, poser, problem

¹**mys·tic** \'mis-tik\ *adj* 1 : of or relating to mystics or mysticism 2 a : exciting wonder, curiosity, or surprise while baffling efforts to comprehend or identify : MYSTERIOUS b : MYSTIFYING 3 ♦ : having magical properties

♦ magic, magical, occult, weird; *also* bewitched, spellbound; bewitching, charming, wiling; awesome, extraordinary, marvelous, wondrous; divining, forecasting, foreknowing, foreseeing, foretelling, fortune-telling, predicting, presaging, prognosticating, prophesying, soothsaying

²**mystic** *n* : a person who follows, advocates, or experiences mysticism

mys·ti·cal \'mis-ti-kəl\ *adj* 1 : SPIRITUAL, SYMBOLIC 2 : of or relating to an intimate knowledge of or direct communion with God (as through contemplation or visions)

mys·ti·cism \'mis-tə-₁si-zəm\ *n* : the belief that direct knowledge of God or ultimate reality is attainable through immediate intuition or insight

mys·ti·fi·ca·tion \₁mis-tə-fə-'kā-shən\ *n* 1 ♦ : the quality or state of being mystified 2 ♦ : something designed to mystify

♦ [1] bafflement, bewilderment, confusion, distraction, muddle, perplexity, puzzlement, whirl — more at CONFUSION ♦ [2] conundrum, enigma, mystery, puzzle, puzzlement, riddle, secret — more at MYSTERY

mys·ti·fy \'mis-tə-₁fī\ *vb* **-fied; -fy·ing** 1 ♦ : to perplex the mind of 2 : to make mysterious

♦ addle, baffle, befog, befuddle, bemuse, bewilder, confound, confuse, disorient, muddle, muddy, perplex, puzzle — more at CONFUSE

mys·tique \mi-'stēk\ *n* [F] 1 : an air or attitude of mystery and reverence developing around something or someone 2 : the special esoteric skill essential in a calling or activity

myth \'mith\ *n* 1 : a usu. legendary narrative that presents part of the beliefs of a people or explains a practice or natural phenomenon 2 : an imaginary or unverifiable person or thing 3 ♦ : an unfounded or false notion 4 ♦ : the whole body of myths

♦ [3] error, fallacy, falsehood, falsity, illusion, misconception, untruth — more at FALLACY ♦ [4] folklore, legend, lore, mythology, tradition — more at FOLKLORE

myth·i·cal \'mi-thi-kəl\ *or* **myth·ic** *adj* 1 ♦ : based on or described in a myth esp. as contrasted with history 2 *usu* **mythical** ♦ : existing only in the imagination

♦ [1] fabled, fabulous, legendary; *also* famed, storied; fabricated, fantastic, fantastical, fictional, fictitious; fanciful; allegorical, mythological ♦ [2] chimerical, fabulous, fanciful, fantastic, fictitious, imaginary, made-up, phantom, pretend, unreal — more at IMAGINARY

my·thol·o·gy \mi-'thä-lə-jē\ *n, pl* **-gies** ♦ : a body of myths and esp. of those dealing with the gods and heroes of a people — **myth·o·log·i·cal** \₁mi-thə-'lä-ji-kəl\ *adj* — **my·thol·o·gist** \mi-'thä-lə-jist\ *n* — **my·thol·o·gize** \-₁jīz\ *vb*

♦ folklore, legend, lore, myth, tradition — more at FOLKLORE

¹**n** \'en\ *n, pl* **n's** *or* **ns** \'enz\ *often cap* 1 : the 14th letter of the English alphabet 2 : an unspecified quantity

²**n** *abbr, often cap* 1 net 2 neuter 3 noon 4 normal 5 north; northern 6 note 7 noun 8 number

N *symbol* nitrogen

-n — see -EN

Na *symbol* [NL *natrium*] sodium

NA *abbr* 1 no account 2 North America 3 not applicable 4 not available

NAACP \₁en-₁dē-bəl-₁ā-₁sē-'pē, ₁en-₁ā-₁ā-₁sē-\ *abbr* National Association for the Advancement of Colored People

nab \'nab\ *vb* **nabbed; nab·bing** 1 ♦ : to seize suddenly : SEIZE 2 ♦ : to catch or seize in arrest : ARREST

♦ [1] bag, capture, catch, collar, corral, get, grab, grapple, hook, land, seize, snare, trap — more at CATCH ♦ [2] apprehend, arrest, pick up, restrain, seize — more at ARREST

NAB *abbr* New American Bible

na·bob \'nā-₁bäb\ *n* [Hindi *navāb* & Urdu *nawāb*, provincial governor (in the Mogul empire), fr. Ar *nuwwāb*, pl. of *nā'ib* governor] ♦ : a person of great wealth or prominence

♦ big shot, celebrity, eminence, figure, immortal, light, luminary, notable, personage, personality, somebody, standout, star, superstar, VIP

na·celle \nə-'sel\ *n* : an enclosure (as for an engine) on an aircraft

na·cho \'nä-chō\ *n, pl* **nachos** [AmerSp] : a tortilla chip topped with melted cheese and often additional savory toppings

na·cre \'nā-kər\ *n* : MOTHER-OF-PEARL

na·dir \'nā-₁dir, -dər\ *n* [ME, fr. MF, fr. Ar *naḍhīr* opposite] 1 : the point of the celestial sphere that is directly opposite the zenith and directly beneath the observer 2 : the lowest point

¹**nag** \'nag\ *n* : a horse and esp. an old or decrepit horse

²**nag** *vb* **nagged; nag·ging** 1 : to find fault incessantly : COMPLAIN 2 ♦ : to irritate by constant scolding or

urging **3** : to be a continuing source of annoyance ⟨a *nagging* backache⟩

♦ henpeck, hound, needle; *also* carp (at), fuss (about *or* over); annoy, badger, bait, bother, bug, harass, harry, hassle, irk, pester, plague, ride, vex, yap (at); egg, goad, incite, prod, prompt, spur, urge; exhort, insist, press, pressure, push; cajole, coax, wheedle; beg, importune, plead

³**nag** *n* : one who nags habitually

Nah *abbr* Nahum

Na·huatl \'nä-ˌwät-ᵊl\ *n* : a group of American Indian languages of central and southern Mexico

Na·hum \'nā-həm, -əm\ *n* : a book of Jewish and Christian Scripture

NAIA *abbr* National Association of Intercollegiate Athletes

na·iad \'nā-əd, 'nī-, -ˌad\ *n, pl* **naiads** *or* **na·ia·des** \-ə-ˌdēz\ **1** : one of the nymphs in ancient mythology living in lakes, rivers, springs, and fountains **2** : an aquatic young of some insects (as a dragonfly)

¹**na·ïf** *or* **na·if** \nä-'ēf\ *adj* : NAIVE

²**naïf** *or* **naif** *n* : a naive person

¹**nail** \'nāl\ *n* **1** : a horny sheath protecting the end of each finger and toe in humans and related primates **2** : a slender pointed fastener with a head designed to be pounded in

²**nail** *vb* : to fasten with or as if with a nail — **nail·er** *n*

nail down *vb* : to settle or establish clearly and unmistakably ⟨*nailed down* the victory⟩

nain·sook \'nān-ˌsuk\ *n* [Hindi *nainsukh*, fr. *nain* eye + *sukh* delight] : a soft lightweight muslin

na·ive *or* **na·ïve** \nä-'ēv\ *adj* **na·iv·er; -est** [F *naïve*, fem. of *naïf*, fr. OF, inborn, natural, fr. L *nativus* native] **1** ♦ : marked by unaffected simplicity : ARTLESS, INGENUOUS **2** ♦ : lacking in worldly wisdom or informed judgment — **na·ive·ness** *n*

♦ [1] artless, genuine, honest, ingenuous, innocent, natural, real, simple, sincere, true, unaffected, unpretentious ♦ [2] green, ingenuous, innocent, simple, unknowing, unsophisticated, unwary, unworldly; *also* callow, dewy, inexperienced, raw; childlike, idealistic, impractical; believing, credulous, gullible, susceptible, trustful, trusting, unguarded; beguiled, duped, gulled, tricked; careless, heedless **Ant** cynical, experienced, knowing, sophisticated, worldly, worldly-wise

na·ive·ly *adv* ♦ : in a naive manner : with naivete

♦ artlessly, ingenuously, naturally, unaffectedly — more at NATURALLY

na·ive·te *or* **na·ïve·té** *also* **na·ive·té** \ˌnä-ˌē-və-'tā, nä-'ē-və-ˌtā\ *n* **1** : a naive remark or action **2** ♦ : the quality or state of being naive

♦ artlessness, greenness, ingenuousness, innocence, naturalness, simplicity, unworldliness; *also* candor, frankness, genuineness, honesty, openness, sincerity; callowness, childishness, inexperience, rawness; carelessness, heedlessness; ignorance, obliviousness, unawareness; credulity; idealism, optimism **Ant** artfulness, cynicism, sophistication, worldliness

na·ked \'nā-kəd\ *adj* **1** ♦ : having no clothes on : NUDE **2** : UNSHEATHED ⟨a ~ sword⟩ **3** ♦ : lacking a usual or natural covering (as of foliage or feathers) **4** ♦ : lacking embellishment : PLAIN, UNADORNED ⟨the ~ truth⟩ **5** : not aided by artificial means ⟨seen by the ~ eye⟩ — **na·ked·ly** *adv* — **na·ked·ness** *n*

♦ [1] bare, nude, unclad, unclothed, undressed; *also* denuded, peeled; raw, stark; unveiled **Ant** appareled, attired, clad, clothed, invested, robed, suited ♦ [3] bald, bare, exposed, open, uncovered; *also* displayed, revealed; hairless, shaven; disrobed, unclad, unclothed, undressed; skinned; unprotected **Ant** covered ♦ [4] bald, bare, plain, simple, unadorned, undecorated, unvarnished — more at PLAIN

nam·by-pam·by \ˌnam-bē-'pam-bē\ *adj* **1** ♦ : lacking in character or substance **2** : WEAK, INDECISIVE

♦ bland, flat, wishy-washy

¹**name** \'nām\ *n* **1** ♦ : a word or words by which a person or thing is known **2** ♦ : a disparaging epithet ⟨call him ~s⟩ **3** ♦ : overall quality or character as seen or judged by people in general : REPUTATION; *esp* : distinguished reputation ⟨made a ~ for herself⟩ **4** ♦ : FAMILY, CLAN ⟨was a disgrace to their ~⟩ **5** ♦ : appearance as opposed to reality ⟨a friend in ~ only⟩

♦ [1] appellation, cognomen, denotation, designation, handle, title; *also* Christian name, forename, given name; family name, maiden name, surname; epithet, nickname, sobriquet; alias, nom de plume, pen name, pseudonym; binomial, vernacular; misnomer; label, trademark ♦ [2] affront, barb, dart, dig, indignity, insult, offense, outrage, put-down, sarcasm, slight, slur, wound — more at INSULT ♦ [3] character, mark, note, report, reputation — more at REPUTATION ♦ [5] appearance, face, guise, semblance, show — more at APPEARANCE

²**name** *vb* **named; nam·ing 1** ♦ : to give a name to : CALL **2** : to mention or identify by name **3** ♦ : to assign to some purpose : APPOINT **4** ♦ : to decide on : CHOOSE **5** ♦ : to mention explicitly : SPECIFY ⟨~ a price⟩ — **name·able** *adj*

♦ [1] baptize, call, christen, denominate, designate, dub, entitle, label, style, term, title; *also* denote, specify; miscall, misname; nickname; rename ♦ [3] appoint, assign, attach, commission, constitute, designate, detail — more at APPOINT ♦ [4] choose, cull, elect, handpick, opt, pick, prefer, select, single, take — more at CHOOSE ♦ [5] advert (to), cite, instance, mention, note, notice, quote, refer (to), specify, touch (*on* or *upon*) — more at MENTION

³**name** *adj* **1** : of, relating to, or bearing a name ⟨~ tag⟩ **2** ♦ : having an established reputation ⟨~ brands⟩

♦ prestigious, reputable, reputed, respectable — more at RESPECTABLE

name day *n* : the church feast day of the saint after whom one is named

name·less \'nām-ləs\ *adj* **1** ♦ : having no name **2** : not marked with a name ⟨a ~ grave⟩ **3 a** ♦ : not known by name ⟨a ~ hero⟩ **b** ♦ : relatively unknown **4 a** ♦ : impossible to identify precisely or by name **b** : too distressing to be described ⟨~ fears⟩ — **name·less·ly** *adv*

♦ [1, 3a] anonymous, unbaptized, unchristened, unidentified, unnamed, untitled; *also* unspecified; obscure, unheard-of, unknown, unremarkable **Ant** baptized, christened, dubbed, named, termed ♦ [3b] anonymous, obscure, unknown, unsung — more at OBSCURE ♦ [4a] indescribable, ineffable, inexpressible, unspeakable, unutterable — more at INDESCRIBABLE

name·ly \-lē\ *adv* : that is to say : AS ⟨the cat family, ~, lions, tigers, and similar animals⟩

name·plate \-ˌplāt\ *n* : a plate or plaque bearing a name (as of a resident)

name·sake \-ˌsāk\ *n* : one that has the same name as another; *esp* : one named after another

Na·mib·ian \nə-'mi-bē-ən, -byən\ *n* : a native or inhabitant of Namibia — **Namibian** *adj*

nana \'na-nə\ *n* : GRANDMOTHER

nan·keen \nan-'kēn\ *n* : a durable brownish yellow cotton fabric orig. woven by hand in China

nan·ny \'na-nē\ *also* **nan·nie** *n, pl* **nan·nies** ♦ : a child's nurse or caregiver

♦ nurse, nursemaid — more at NURSE

nan·ny goat \'na-nē-\ *n* : a female domestic goat

nano·me·ter \'na-nə-ˌmē-tər\ *n* : one billionth of a meter

nano·scale \-ˌskāl\ *adj* : having dimensions measured in nanometers

nano·sec·ond \-ˌse-kənd\ *n* : one billionth of a second

nano·tech \'na-nō-ˌtek\ *n* : NANOTECHNOLOGY

nano·tech·nol·o·gy \ˌna-nō-tek-'nä-lə-jē\ *n* : the science of manipulating materials on an atomic or molecular scale esp. to build microscopic objects or devices

¹nap \'nap\ *vb* **napped; nap·ping** **1** ♦ : to sleep briefly esp. during the day : DOZE **2** : to be off guard ⟨was caught *napping*⟩

♦ catnap, doze, drowse, slumber, snooze; *also* relax, repose, rest; couch, lay, lie, roost; lull

²nap *n* ♦ : a short sleep esp. during the day

♦ catnap, doze, drowse, forty winks, siesta, snooze, wink; *also* repose, rest; slumber, bed

³nap *n* ♦ : a soft downy fibrous surface (as on yarn and cloth) — **nap·less** *adj* — **napped** \'napt\ *adj*

♦ down, floss, fluff, fur, fuzz, lint, pile — more at FUZZ

na·palm \'nā-ˌpälm, -ˌpäm\ *n* [*naph*thalene + *palm*itate, salt of a fatty acid] **1** : a thickener used in jelling gasoline (as for incendiary bombs) **2** : fuel jelled with napalm

nape \'nāp, 'nap\ *n* : the back of the neck

na·pery \'nā-pə-rē\ *n* : household linen esp. for the table

naph·tha \'naf-thə, 'nap-\ *n* : any of various liquid hydrocarbon mixtures used chiefly as solvents

naph·tha·lene \-ˌlēn\ *n* : a crystalline substance used esp. in organic synthesis and as a moth repellent

nap·kin \'nap-kən\ *n* **1** : a piece of material (as cloth) used at table to wipe the lips or fingers and protect the clothes **2** : a small cloth or towel

na·po·leon \nə-'pōl-yən, -'pō-lē-ən\ *n* : an oblong pastry with a filling of cream, custard, or jelly

Na·po·le·on·ic \nə-ˌpō-lē-'ä-nik\ *adj* : of, relating to, or characteristic of Napoleon I or his family

narc *also* **nark** \'närk\ *n, slang* : a person (as a government agent) who investigates narcotics violations

nar·cis·sism \'när-sə-ˌsi-zəm\ *n* [G *Narzissismus,* fr. *Narziss* Narcissus, beautiful youth of Greek mythology who fell in love with his own image] **1** : undue dwelling on one's own self or attainments **2** : love of or sexual desire for one's own body — **nar·cis·sist** \-sist\ *n or adj* — **nar·cis·sis·tic** \ˌnär-sə-'sis-tik\ *adj*

nar·cis·sus \när-'si-səs\ *n, pl* **nar·cis·si** \-ˌsī, -ˌsē\ *or* **nar·cis·sus·es** *or* **narcissus** : DAFFODIL; *esp* : one with short⸗ tubed flowers usu. borne separately

nar·co·lep·sy \'när-kə-ˌlep-sē\ *n, pl* **-sies** : a condition characterized by brief attacks of deep sleep — **nar·co·lep·tic** \ˌnär-kə-'lep-tik\ *adj or n*

nar·co·sis \när-'kō-səs\ *n, pl* **-co·ses** \-ˌsēz\ : a state of stupor, unconsciousness, or arrested activity produced by the influence of chemicals (as narcotics)

nar·co·ter·ror·ism \'när-kō-'ter-ər-ˌi-zəm\ *n* [ME *narkotik,* fr. MF *narcotique,* fr. *narcotique,* adj., fr. ML *narcoticus,* fr. Gk *narkōtikos,* fr. *narkoun* to benumb, fr. *narkē* numbness] : terrorism financed by profits from illegal drug trafficking

¹nar·cot·ic \när-'kä-tik\ *n* [ME *narkotik,* fr. MF *narcotique,* fr. *narcotique,* adj., fr. ML *narcoticus,* fr. Gk *narkōtikos,* fr. *narkoun* to benumb, fr. *narkē* numbness] **1** : a drug (as opium) that dulls the senses, relieves pain, and induces sleep **2** : an illegal drug (as marijuana or LSD)

²narcotic *adj* **1** ♦ : tending to calm the emotions and relieve stress ⟨the music's ∼ effect⟩ **2** : of or relating to narcotics, to their use, or to addicts ⟨∼ addiction⟩

♦ comforting, dreamy, sedative, soothing — more at SOOTHING

nar·co·tize \'när-kə-ˌtīz\ *vb* **-tized; -tiz·ing** **1** : to treat with or subject to a narcotic; *also* : to put into a state of narcosis **2** : to soothe to unconsciousness or unawareness

nard \'närd\ *n* : a fragrant ointment of the ancients

na·res \'nar-(ˌ)ēz\ *n pl* [L] : the pair of openings of the nose

Nar·ra·gan·sett \ˌnar-ə-'gan-sət\ *n, pl* **-sett** *or* **-setts** **1** : a member of an American Indian people of Rhode Island **2** : the Algonquian language of the Narragansett people

nar·rate \'när-ˌāt\ *vb* **nar·rat·ed; nar·rat·ing** ♦ : to recite the details of (as a story) : TELL — **nar·ra·tor** \'när-ˌā-tər\ *n*

♦ describe, recite, recount, rehearse, relate, report, tell — more at TELL

nar·ra·tion \na-'rā-shən\ *n* ♦ : an account of incidents or events : STORY

♦ account, chronicle, commentary, history, narrative, record, report, story — more at ACCOUNT

nar·ra·tive \'nar-ə-tiv\ *n* **1 a** : something that is narrated **b** ♦ : a fictional narrative shorter than a novel **2** ♦ : the art or practice of narrating

♦ [1b] novella, short story, story, tale — more at STORY
♦ [2] account, chronicle, history, record, report, story — more at ACCOUNT

¹nar·row \'nar-ō\ *adj* **1** ♦ : of slender or less than standard width **2** ♦ : limited in size or scope : RESTRICTED **3** ♦ : not liberal in views **4** : interpreted or interpreting strictly **5** ♦ : barely sufficient : CLOSE ⟨won by a ∼ margin⟩; *also* : barely successful ⟨a ∼ escape⟩ — **nar·row·ly** *adv* — **nar·row·ness** *n*

♦ [1] fine, skinny, slender, slim, thin; *also* attenuated, elongated, linear; close, compressed, condensed, constricted, contracted, squeezed, tight, tightened; reedy, stringy, twiggy, wispy; spare *Ant* broad, fat, wide ♦ [2] definite, determinate, finite, limited, measured, restricted — more at LIMITED ♦ [3] bigoted, intolerant, narrow-minded, prejudiced — more at INTOLERANT ♦ [3] insular, little, parochial, petty, provincial, sectarian, small; *also* inflexible, obdurate, obstinate, rigid, set, stubborn, unyielding, wrongheaded; bigoted, intolerant, narrow-minded; biased, discriminating, discriminatory, jaundiced, one-sided, partial, partisan, prejudiced; old-fashioned, reactionary, stodgy, straitlaced; dogmatic, opinionated; limited *Ant* broad-minded, catholic, cosmopolitan, liberal, open, open-minded, receptive, tolerant ♦ [5] close, neck and neck, nip and tuck, tight — more at CLOSE

²narrow *n* ♦ : a narrow passage : STRAIT — usu. used in pl.

♦ channel, sound, strait — more at CHANNEL

³narrow *vb* : to lessen in width or extent

nar·row–mind·ed \ˌnar-ō-'mīn-dəd\ *adj* ♦ : not liberal or broad-minded

♦ bigoted, intolerant, narrow, prejudiced — more at INTOLERANT

nar·whal \'när-ˌhwäl, 'när-wəl\ *n* : an arctic sea mammal about 20 feet (6 meters) long that is related to the dolphins and in the male has a long twisted ivory tusk

NAS *abbr* naval air station

NASA \'na-sə\ *abbr* National Aeronautics and Space Administration

¹na·sal \'nā-zəl\ *n* **1** : a nasal part **2** : a nasal consonant or vowel

²nasal *adj* **1** : of or relating to the nose **2** : uttered through the nose — **na·sal·ly** *adv*

na·sal·ize \'nā-zə-ˌlīz\ *vb* **-ized; -iz·ing** : to make nasal or pronounce as a nasal sound — **na·sal·i·za·tion** \ˌnā-zə-lə-'zā-shən\ *n*

na·scent \'nas-ᵊnt, 'nās-\ *adj* : coming into existence : beginning to grow or develop — **na·scence** \-ᵊns\ *n*

nas·ti·ly \'nas-tē-lē\ *adv* ♦ : in a nasty manner or condition

♦ hatefully, maliciously, meanly, spitefully, viciously, wickedly; *also* contemptuously, disdainfully, scornfully; acrimoniously, hostilely, invidiously, obnoxiously, venomously; bitterly, enviously, jealously, resentfully; callously, cruelly, mercilessly, pitilessly, ruthlessly, unfeelingly; disagreeably, ill, unkindly; ill-naturedly, inconsiderately, thoughtlessly; diabolically, fiendishly; misanthropically *Ant* benevolently, kindly

nas·ti·ness \'nas-tē-nəs\ *n* ♦ : the quality or state of being nasty

♦ cattiness, despite, hatefulness, malice, malignity, meanness, spite, spleen, venom, viciousness — more at MALICE ♦ bawdiness, coarseness, dirt, dirtiness, filth, filthiness, foulness, grossness, indecency, lewdness, obscenity, ribaldry, smut, vulgarity — more at OBSCENITY ♦ dinginess, dirtiness, filthiness, foulness, grubbiness, uncleanliness — more at DIRTINESS

nas·tur·tium \nə-'stər-shəm, na-\ *n* : either of two widely cultivated watery-stemmed herbs with showy spurred flowers and pungent seeds

nas·ty \'nas-tē\ *adj* **nas·ti·er; -est** **1** : FILTHY **2** ♦ : abhorrent to morality or virtue : INDECENT, OBSCENE **3 a** : HARMFUL, DANGEROUS ⟨took a ~ fall⟩ **b** ♦ : causing severe pain or suffering **4** ♦ : sharply unpleasant ⟨~ weather⟩ **5** ♦ : characterized by petty selfishness or malice : MEAN, ILL-NATURED ⟨a ~ temper⟩ **6** : DIFFICULT, VEXATIOUS ⟨a ~ problem⟩ **7** : UNFAIR, DIRTY ⟨a ~ trick⟩

♦ [2] bawdy, coarse, crude, dirty, filthy, foul, gross, indecent, lascivious, lewd, obscene, pornographic, ribald, smutty, unprintable, vulgar, wanton — more at OBSCENE ♦ [3b] achy, painful, sore — more at PAINFUL ♦ [4] bad, bleak, dirty, disagreeable, foul, inclement, raw, rough, squally, stormy, tempestuous, turbulent, unpleasant — more at FOUL ♦ [5] catty, cruel, hateful, malevolent, malicious, malign, malignant, mean, spiteful, virulent — more at HATEFUL

nat *abbr* **1** national **2** native **3** natural

na·tal \'nāt-ᵊl\ *adj* **1** : NATIVE **2** : of, relating to, or present at birth

na·ta·to·ri·um \,nā-tə-'tōr-ē-əm, ,na-\ *n* : a swimming pool esp. indoors

na·tion \'nā-shən\ *n* [ME *nacioun*, fr. AF *naciun*, fr. L *nation-, natio* birth, race, nation, fr. *nasci* to be born] **1** : NATIONALITY 5; *also* : a politically organized nationality **2** ♦ : a community of people composed of one or more nationalities with its own territory and government **3** : the territory of a nation **4** : a federation of tribes (as of American Indians) — **na·tion·hood** *n*

♦ commonwealth, country, land, sovereignty, state; *also* city-state; domain, dominion, empire, kingdom, realm, republic, duchy, dukedom, principality, sultanate; democracy, dictatorship, monarchy, oligarchy, sovereign, theocracy; colony, dependency, province, settlement, soil; fatherland, homeland, motherland; power, superpower

¹na·tion·al \'na-shə-nəl\ *adj* **1** ♦ : of or relating to a nation **2** : comprising or characteristic of a nationality **3** : FEDERAL **3** — **na·tion·al·ly** *adv*

♦ civil, public, state; *also* civic, federal, municipal; government, governmental; domestic, internal; democratic, republican; nationwide

²national *n* **1** : one who owes allegiance to a nation **2** : a competition that is national in scope — usu. used in pl.

National Guard *n* **1** : a militia force recruited by each state of the U.S., equipped by the federal government, and jointly maintained subject to the call of either **2** *often not cap* : a military force serving as a national constabulary and defense force

na·tion·al·ise *chiefly Brit var of* NATIONALIZE

na·tion·al·ism \'na-shə-nə-,li-zəm\ *n* : devotion to national interests, unity, and independence

na·tion·al·ist \-list\ *n* **1** : an advocate of or believer in nationalism **2** *cap* : a member of a political party or group advocating national independence or strong national government — **nationalist** *adj, often cap* — **na·tion·al·is·tic** \,na-shə-nə-'lis-tik\ *adj*

na·tion·al·i·ty \,na-shə-'na-lə-tē\ *n, pl* **-ties** **1** : national character **2** : a legal relationship involving allegiance of an individual and protection on the part of the state **3** : membership in a particular nation **4** : political independence or existence as a separate nation **5** : a people having a common origin, tradition, and language and capable of forming a state **6** : an ethnic group within a larger unit (as a nation)

na·tion·al·ize \'na-shə-nə-,līz\ *vb* **-ized; -iz·ing** **1** : to make national : make a nation of **2** : to remove from private ownership and place under government control — **na·tion·al·i·za·tion** \,na-shə-nə-lə-'zā-shən\ *n*

national monument *n* : a place of historic, scenic, or scientific interest set aside for preservation usu. by presidential proclamation

national park *n* : an area of special scenic, historical, or scientific importance set aside and maintained by a national government esp. for recreation or study

national seashore *n* : a recreational area adjacent to a seacoast and maintained by the federal government

na·tion·wide \,nā-shən-'wīd\ *adj* : extending throughout a nation

¹na·tive \'nā-tiv\ *adj* **1** : INBORN, NATURAL **2** ♦ : born in a particular place or country **3** : belonging to a person because of the place or circumstances of birth ⟨her ~ language⟩ **4** ♦ : grown, produced, or originating in a particular place : INDIGENOUS **5** ♦ : left or remaining in a natural state : being without embellishment or artificial change

♦ [2, 4] aboriginal, born, endemic, indigenous; *also* domestic, local; original ♦ [5] crude, natural, raw, undressed, unprocessed, unrefined, untreated — more at CRUDE

²native *n* : one that is native; *esp* : a person who belongs to a particular country by birth

Native American *n* : a member of any of the aboriginal peoples of the western hemisphere except often the Eskimos; *esp* : an American Indian of North America and esp. the U.S. : AMERICAN INDIAN

na·tiv·ism \'nā-ti-,vi-zəm\ *n* **1** : a policy of favoring native inhabitants over immigrants **2** : the revival or perpetuation of a native culture esp. in opposition to acculturation

na·tiv·i·ty \nə-'ti-və-tē, nā-\ *n, pl* **-ties** **1** : the process or circumstances of being born : BIRTH **2** *cap* : the birth of Christ

natl *abbr* national

NATO \'nā-(,)tō\ *abbr* North Atlantic Treaty Organization

nat·ty \'na-tē\ *adj* **nat·ti·er; -est** ♦ : trimly neat and tidy : SMART — **nat·ti·ly** \-tə-lē\ *adv* — **nat·ti·ness** \-tē-nəs\ *n*

♦ dapper, sharp, smart, spruce — more at SMART

¹nat·u·ral \'na-chə-rəl\ *adj* **1** ♦ : determined by nature : INBORN, INNATE ⟨~ ability⟩ **2** : having a specified character by nature : BORN ⟨a ~ fool⟩ **3** : not recognized as lawful offspring; *specif* : born of parents not married to each other **4** : HUMAN **5** ♦ : of or relating to nature **6** ♦ : not artificial **7** ♦ : being simple and sincere : not affected **8** ♦ : closely resembling an original : true to nature **9** : being neither sharp nor flat

♦ [1] essential, inborn, ingrained, inherent, innate, integral, intrinsic — more at INHERENT ♦ [5] uncultivated, untamed, wild — more at WILD ♦ [6] crude, native, raw, undressed, unprocessed, unrefined, untreated — more at CRUDE ♦ [7] artless, genuine, honest, ingenuous, innocent, naive, real, simple, sincere, true, unaffected, unpretentious ♦ [8] lifelike, near, realistic; *also* alike, like, living, matching; akin, analogous, approximate, comparable, resembling; accurate, close, faithful, true; convincing **Ant** unrealistic

²natural *n* **1** : one born without the usual powers of reason and understanding **2** : a character ♮ placed on a line or space of the musical staff to nullify the effect of a preceding sharp or flat **3** : one obviously suitable for a purpose **4** : AFRO

natural childbirth *n* : a system of managing childbirth in which the mother prepares to remain conscious and assist in delivery with little or no use of drugs

natural gas *n* : a combustible gaseous mixture of hydrocarbons coming from the earth's crust and used chiefly as a fuel and raw material

natural history *n* **1** : a treatise on some aspect of nature **2** : the study of natural objects esp. from an amateur or popular point of view

nat·u·ral·ise *chiefly Brit var of* NATURALIZE

nat·u·ral·ism \'na-chə-rə-,li-zəm\ *n* **1** : action or thought based only on natural desires and instincts **2** : a doctrine that denies a supernatural explanation of the origin or development of the universe and holds that scientific laws account for all of nature   **3** : realism in art and literature — **nat·u·ral·is·tic** \ˌna-chə-rə-'lis-tik\ *adj*

nat·u·ral·ist \-list\ *n*   **1** : one that advocates or practices naturalism   **2** : a student of animals or plants esp. in the field

nat·u·ral·ize \-ˌlīz\ *vb* **-ized; -iz·ing**   **1** : to become or cause to become established as if native ⟨∼ new forage crops⟩   **2** : to confer the rights of a citizen on — **nat·u·ral·i·za·tion** \ˌna-chə-rə-lə-'zā-shən\ *n*

nat·u·ral·ly \'na-chə-rə-lē, ˌna-chə-rə-\ *adv*   **1** ♦ : by nature : by natural character or ability   **2** ♦ : as might be expected   **3** ♦ : without artificial aid; *also* : without affectation   **4** : REALISTICALLY

♦ [1] constitutionally, inherently, innately, intrinsically; *also* essentially, fundamentally; instinctively, intuitively; intimately ♦ [2] commonly, generally, normally, ordinarily, typically, usually; *also* customarily, habitually, regularly, routinely; familiarly; conventionally, traditionally **Ant** abnormally, atypically, extraordinarily, uncommonly, unusually ♦ [3] artlessly, ingenuously, naively, unaffectedly; *also* genuinely, honestly, simply, truly; freely, openly; candidly, frankly, matter-of-factly; informally, unceremoniously **Ant** affectedly, artificially, hypocritically, insincerely, pretentiously, unnaturally

nat·u·ral·ness *n* ♦ : the quality or state of being natural

♦ artlessness, greenness, ingenuousness, innocence, naïveté, simplicity, unworldliness — more at NAÏVETÉ

natural science *n* : a science (as physics, chemistry, or biology) that deals with matter, energy, and their interrelations and transformations or with objectively measurable phenomena — **natural scientist** *n*

natural selection *n* : the natural process that results in the survival of individuals or groups best adjusted to their environment

na·ture \'nā-chər\ *n* [ME, fr. MF, fr. L *natura*, fr. *natus*, pp. of *nasci* to be born]   **1** ♦ : the inherent quality or basic constitution of a person or thing   **2** ♦ : a kind or class usu. distinguished by fundamental or essential characteristics   **3** ♦ : the fundamental character, disposition, or temperament of a living being usu. innate and unchangeable : TEMPERAMENT, DISPOSITION   **4** ♦ : the physical universe   **5** : one's natural instincts or way of life ⟨quirks of human ∼⟩; *also* : primitive state ⟨a return to ∼⟩   **6** ♦ : natural scenery or environment ⟨beauties of ∼⟩

♦ [1] essence, quintessence, soul, stuff, substance — more at ESSENCE ♦ [1] character, complexion, constitution, genius, personality, tone; *also* distinctiveness, distinctness, individuality, singularity, uniqueness; attribute, characteristic, earmark, feature, flavor, hallmark, mark, point, property, savor, stamp, trait; disposition, grain, sort, temper, temperament; composition, makeup; essence, soul, spirit, stuff, substance; habit, way ♦ [2] breed, class, description, feather, ilk, kind, like, manner, order, sort, species, type — more at SORT ♦ [3] disposition, grain, temper, temperament — more at DISPOSITION ♦ [4] cosmos, creation, macrocosm, universe, world — more at UNIVERSE ♦ [6] open, outdoors, wild, wilderness; *also* backwoods, bush, country, frontier, hinterland, sticks, up-country; outside, without; badland, barren, desert, waste, wasteland

naught \'nȯt, 'nät\ *n*   **1** : NOTHING   **2** ♦ : the arithmetical symbol 0 : ZERO

♦ aught, cipher, nil, nothing, zero, zip — more at ZERO

naugh·ty \'nȯ-tē, 'nä-\ *adj* **naugh·ti·er; -est**   **1** ♦ : guilty of disobedience or misbehavior   **2** : lacking in taste or propriety ⟨∼ jokes⟩ — **naugh·ti·ly** \-tə-lē\ *adv* — **naugh·ti·ness** \-tē-nəs\ *n*

♦ bad, contrary, errant, froward, mischievous; *also* defiant, disrespectful, ill-mannered, ill-natured, impolite, improper, impudent, indecorous, insolent, rude, uncouth, unmannerly; disobedient, headstrong, intractable, obstreperous, recalcitrant, refractory, transgressing,

unruly, untoward, willful; balky, restive, uncontrollable, ungovernable, wayward, wild; arch, elfish, impish, monkeying, ornery, rascally, roguish, waggish; dissolute, perverse, wrongheaded; disorderly, rowdy, ruffianly; corrupt, evil, wicked; insurgent, mutinous, rebellious; inconsiderate, selfish, thoughtless, unkind, unkindly; babyish, childish, immature, infantile, puerile **Ant** behaved, behaving, nice, orderly

nau·sea \'nȯ-zē-ə, -sē-; 'nȯ-zhə, -shə\ *n* [L, seasickness, nausea, fr. Gk *nautia, nausia*, fr. *nautēs* sailor]   **1** ♦ : sickness of the stomach with a desire to vomit   **2** ♦ : extreme disgust

♦ [1] queasiness, sickness, squeamishness; *also* qualm; airsickness, morning sickness, motion sickness, seasickness ♦ [2] aversion, disgust, distaste, loathing, repugnance, repulsion, revulsion — more at DISGUST

nau·se·ate \'nȯ-zē-ˌāt, -sē-, -zhē-, -shē-\ *vb* **-at·ed; -at·ing**   ♦ : to affect or become affected with nausea — **nau·se·at·ing·ly** *adv*

♦ disgust, repel, repulse, revolt, sicken, turn off — more at DISGUST

nauseating *adj* ♦ : causing nausea or esp. disgust

♦ distasteful, noisome, offensive, repellent, repugnant, repulsive, revolting, ugly — more at OFFENSIVE

nau·seous \'nȯ-shəs, -zē-əs\ *adj*   **1** ♦ : causing nausea or disgust   **2** ♦ : affected with nausea or disgust

♦ ill, queasy, queer, sick, squeamish; *also* green, peaked, sickly; unsettled, upset, woozy

naut *abbr* nautical

nau·ti·cal \'nȯ-ti-kəl\ *adj* : of or relating to sailors, navigation, or ships ⟨∼ terms⟩ — **nau·ti·cal·ly** \-k(ə-)lē\ *adv*

nautical mile *n* : a unit of distance equal to about 6080 feet (1852 meters)

nau·ti·lus \'nȯt-ᵊl-əs\ *n, pl* **-lus·es** *or* **-li** \-ᵊl-ˌī, -ˌē\ : any of a genus of sea mollusks related to the octopuses but having a spiral chambered shell

nav *abbr*   **1** naval   **2** navigable; navigation

Na·va·jo *also* **Na·va·ho** \'na-və-ˌhō, 'nä-\ *n, pl* **-jo** *or* **-jos** *also* **-ho** *or* **-hos** : a member of an American Indian people of northern New Mexico and Arizona; *also* : their language

na·val \'nā-vəl\ *adj* : of, relating to, or possessing a navy

naval stores *n pl* : products (as pitch, turpentine, or rosin) obtained from resinous conifers (as pines)

nave \'nāv\ *n* [ML *navis*, fr. L, ship] : the central part of a church running lengthwise

na·vel \'nā-vəl\ *n* : a depression in the middle of the abdomen that marks the point of attachment of fetus and mother

navel–gaz·ing \'nā-vəl-ˌgā-ziŋ\ *n* : useless or excessive self-contemplation

navel orange *n* : a seedless orange having a pit at the blossom end where the fruit encloses a small secondary fruit

nav·i·ga·ble \'na-vi-gə-bəl\ *adj*   **1** : capable of being navigated ⟨a ∼ river⟩   **2** : capable of being steered — **nav·i·ga·bil·i·ty** \ˌna-vi-gə-'bi-lə-tē\ *n*

nav·i·gate \'na-və-ˌgāt\ *vb* **-gat·ed; -gat·ing**   **1** : to sail on or through ⟨∼ the Atlantic Ocean⟩   **2** : to steer or direct the course of a ship or aircraft   **3** : MOVE; *esp* : WALK ⟨could hardly ∼⟩   **4** ♦ : to travel by water : SAIL — **nav·i·ga·tion** \ˌna-və-'gā-shən\ *n*

♦ boat, cruise, sail, voyage — more at SAIL

nav·i·ga·tor \'na-və-ˌgā-tər\ *n* : one that navigates or is qualified to navigate

na·vy \'nā-vē\ *n, pl* **navies**   **1** : FLEET; *also* : the warships belonging to a nation   **2** *often cap* : a nation's organization for naval warfare

navy yard *n* : a yard where naval vessels are built or repaired

na·wab \nə-'wäb\ *n* ♦ : a person of great wealth or prominence : NABOB

♦ big leaguer, big shot, bigwig, kingpin, nabob, wheel — more at BIG SHOT

¹nay \'nā\ *adv* : NO

²**nay** *n* **1** : a negative vote; *also* : a person casting such a vote **2** : refusal to satisfy a request or desire

³**nay** *conj* ♦ : not merely this but also : not only so but ⟨he was happy, ∼, ecstatic⟩

♦ even, indeed, truly, verily, yea — more at EVEN

nay·say·er \'nā-ˌsā-ər\ *n* : one who denies, refuses, or opposes something

Na·zi \'nät-sē, 'nat-\ *n* [G, fr. *Nationalsozialist*, lit., national socialist] : a member of a German fascist party controlling Germany from 1933 to 1945 under Adolf Hitler — **Nazi** *adj* — **Na·zism** \'nät-ˌsi-zəm, 'nat-\ *also* **Na·zi·ism** \-sē-ˌi-zəm\ *n*

Nb *symbol* niobium

NB *abbr* **1** New Brunswick **2** nota bene

NBA *abbr* **1** National Basketball Association **2** National Boxing Association

NBC *abbr* National Broadcasting Company

NBS *abbr* National Bureau of Standards

NC *abbr* **1** no charge **2** North Carolina

NCAA *abbr* National Collegiate Athletic Association

NCO \ˌen-ˌsē-'ō\ *n* : NONCOMMISSIONED OFFICER

nd *abbr* no date

Nd *symbol* neodymium

ND *abbr* North Dakota

N Dak *abbr* North Dakota

Ne *symbol* neon

NE *abbr* **1** Nebraska **2** New England **3** northeast

¹**Ne·an·der·thal** \nē-'an-dər-ˌthȯl, nä-'än-dər-ˌtäl\ *adj* **1** *or* **Ne·an·der·tal** \-ˌtäl\ : of, relating to, or being an extinct Old World hominid that lived from about 200,000 to 30,000 years ago **2** ♦ : suggestive of a caveman

♦ barbarous, heathen, heathenish, rude, savage, uncivil, uncivilized, uncultivated, wild — more at SAVAGE

²**Neanderthal** *or* **Neandertal** *n* ♦ : one who suggests a caveman in appearance, mentality, or behavior

♦ clod, gawk, hulk, lout, lubber, lug, oaf — more at OAF

neap tide \'nēp-\ *n* : a tide of minimum range occurring in the first and third quarters of the moon

¹**near** \'nir\ *adv* **1** ♦ : at, within, or to a short distance or time **2** : very nearly but not exactly or entirely : ALMOST

♦ around, by, close, hard, in, nearby, nigh; *also* hereabouts, thereabouts; along, alongside *Ant* far

²**near** *prep* ♦ : close to

♦ about, around, by, next to — more at AROUND

³**near** *adj* **1** : closely related or associated; *also* : INTIMATE **2** ♦ : not far away; *also* : being the closer or left-hand member of a pair **3** : barely avoided ⟨a ∼ accident⟩ **4** : DIRECT, SHORT ⟨by the ∼*est* route⟩ **5** : STINGY **6** ♦ : not real but very like ⟨∼ silk⟩ **7** : being the closer of two

♦ [2] close, immediate, nearby, nigh — more at CLOSE
♦ [6] lifelike, natural, realistic — more at NATURAL

⁴**near** *vb* **1** ♦ : to come closer in space or time : APPROACH **2** : to draw near to

♦ advance, approach, close — more at APPROACH

near beer *n* : any of various malt liquors low in alcohol

¹**near·by** \nir-'bī, 'nir-ˌbī\ *adj* ♦ : close at hand

♦ close, immediate, near, nigh — more at CLOSE

²**near·by** \nir-'bī, 'nir-ˌbī\ *adv* ♦ : close at hand

♦ around, by, close, hard, in, near, nigh — more at NEAR

near·ly *adv* **1** : in a close manner or relationship **2** ♦ : almost but not quite

♦ about, almost, most, much, near, next to, nigh, practically, some, virtually, well-nigh — more at ALMOST

near·ness *n* **1** ♦ : the quality or state of being near **2** ♦ : the state of being in a close personal relationship esp. marked by affection or love

♦ [1] closeness, contiguity, immediacy, proximity — more at PROXIMITY ♦ [2] closeness, familiarity, intimacy — more at FAMILIARITY

near·sight·ed \'nir-ˌsī-təd\ *adj* : able to see near things more clearly than distant ones : MYOPIC — **near·sight·ed·ly** *adv* — **near·sight·ed·ness** *n*

neat \'nēt\ *adj* [MF *net*, fr. L *nitidus* bright, neat, fr. *nitēre* to shine] **1** ♦ : being orderly and clean **2** ♦ : not mixed or diluted ⟨∼ brandy⟩ **3** : marked by tasteful simplicity **4** : PRECISE, SYSTEMATIC **5** : SKILLFUL, ADROIT **6** : superior in character, nature, ability, or prospects : FINE — **neat** *adv* — **neat·ly** *adv* — **neat·ness** *n*

♦ [1] crisp, orderly, shipshape, snug, tidy, trim, uncluttered; *also* dapper, natty, prim, saucy, smart, spruce; immaculate, spick-and-span, spotless; rakish, sleek, streamlined, taut; organized, straight, systematic *Ant* disheveled, disordered, disorderly, messy, mussed, mussy, slovenly, unkempt, untidy ♦ [2] absolute, fine, plain, pure, refined, straight, unadulterated, undiluted, unmixed — more at PURE

neath \'nēth\ *prep*, *dial* : BENEATH

neat·nik \'nēt-nik\ *n* : a person who is compulsively neat

neb \'neb\ *n* **1** : the beak of a bird or tortoise; *also* : NOSE, SNOUT **2** : NIB

Neb *or* **Nebr** *abbr* Nebraska

NEB *abbr* New English Bible

neb·u·la \'ne-byə-lə\ *n*, *pl* **-lae** \-ˌlē, -ˌlī\ *also* **-las** [NL, fr. L, mist, cloud] **1** : any of numerous clouds of gas or dust in interstellar space **2** : GALAXY — **neb·u·lar** \-lər\ *adj*

neb·u·liz·er \'ne-byə-ˌlī-zər\ *n* : ATOMIZER

neb·u·lous \'ne-byə-ləs\ *adj* **1** : of or relating to a nebula **2 a** ♦ : lacking clarity of feature or sharpness of outline : HAZY, INDISTINCT **b** ♦ : vaguely defined : dimly realized

♦ bleary, dim, faint, foggy, fuzzy, hazy, indefinite, indistinct, indistinguishable, murky, obscure, opaque, shadowy, unclear, undefined, undetermined, vague — more at FAINT

nec·es·sar·i·ly \ˌne-sə-'ser-ə-lē\ *adv* ♦ : of necessity

♦ inevitably, needs, perforce, unavoidably — more at NEEDS

¹**nec·es·sary** \'ne-sə-ˌser-ē\ *n*, *pl* **-sar·ies** : an indispensable item

²**necessary** *adj* **1** ♦ : of an inevitable nature : INEVITABLE, INESCAPABLE; *also* : CERTAIN **2** : PREDETERMINED **3** ♦ : containing or constituting a command : COMPULSORY **4** ♦ : positively needed : INDISPENSABLE ⟨∼ supplies⟩

♦ [1] certain, inescapable, inevitable, sure, unavoidable — more at INEVITABLE ♦ [3] compulsory, imperative, incumbent, involuntary, mandatory, nonelective, obligatory, peremptory — more at MANDATORY ♦ [4] essential, imperative, indispensable, integral, needful, requisite, vital — more at ESSENTIAL

ne·ces·si·tate \ni-'se-sə-ˌtāt\ *vb* **-tat·ed; -tat·ing** ♦ : to make necessary

♦ demand, need, require, take, want, warrant — more at NEED

ne·ces·si·tous \ni-'se-sə-təs\ *adj* **1** : NEEDY, IMPOVERISHED **2** : URGENT **3** : NECESSARY

ne·ces·si·ty \ni-'se-sə-tē\ *n*, *pl* **-ties** **1** : conditions that cannot be changed **2** ♦ : WANT, POVERTY **3** ♦ : something that is necessary ⟨water is a ∼⟩ **4** : very great need

♦ condition, demand, essential, must, need, requirement, requisite — more at ESSENTIAL

¹**neck** \'nek\ *n* **1** : the part of the body connecting the head and the trunk **2** : the part of a garment covering or near to the neck **3** : a relatively narrow part suggestive of a neck ⟨∼ of a bottle⟩ ⟨∼ of land⟩ **4** : a narrow margin esp. of victory ⟨won by a ∼⟩ — **necked** \'nekt\ *adj*

²**neck** *vb* : to kiss and caress amorously

¹**neck and neck** *adj* ♦ : being very close (as in margin or standing)

♦ close, narrow, nip and tuck, tight — more at CLOSE

²**neck and neck** *adv* : very close (as in a race)

neck·er·chief \'ne-kər-chəf, -ˌchēf\ *n, pl* **-chiefs** \-chəfs, -ˌchēfs\ *also* **-chieves** \-ˌchēvz\ : a square of cloth worn folded about the neck like a scarf

neck·lace \'ne-kləs\ *n* : an ornament worn around the neck

neck·line \'nek-ˌlīn\ *n* : the outline of the neck opening of a garment

neck·tie \-ˌtī\ *n* : a strip of cloth worn around the neck and tied in front

ne·crol·o·gy \nə-'krä-lə-jē\ *n, pl* **-gies** 1 : OBITUARY 2 : a list of the recently dead

nec·ro·man·cer \'ne-krə-ˌman-sər\ *n* ♦ : one that practices necromancy

♦ conjurer, enchanter, magician, sorcerer, voodoo, witch, wizard — more at MAGICIAN

nec·ro·man·cy \'ne-krə-ˌman-sē\ *n* 1 : the art or practice of conjuring up the spirits of the dead for purposes of magically revealing the future 2 : the use of means (as charms or spells) believed to have supernatural power over natural forces : MAGIC, SORCERY

♦ bewitchment, enchantment, magic, sorcery, witchcraft, wizardry — more at MAGIC

ne·crop·o·lis \nə-'krä-pə-ləs, ne-\ *n, pl* **-lis·es** *or* **-les** \-ˌlēz\ *or* **-leis** \-ˌlās\ *or* **-li** \-ˌlī, -ˌlē\ [LL, fr. Gk *nekropolis*, fr. *nekros* dead body + *polis* city] : CEMETERY; *esp* : a large elaborate cemetery of an ancient city

ne·cro·sis \nə-'krō-səs, ne-\ *n, pl* **ne·cro·ses** \-ˌsēz\ : usu. local death of body tissue — **ne·crot·ic** \-'krä-tik\ *adj*

nec·tar \'nek-tər\ *n* 1 : the drink of the Greek and Roman gods; *also* : any delicious drink 2 : a sweet plant secretion that is the raw material of honey

nec·tar·ine \ˌnek-tə-'rēn\ *n* : a smooth-skinned peach

née *or* **nee** \'nā\ *adj* [F, lit., born] — used to identify a woman by her maiden family name

¹**need** \'nēd\ *n* 1 : necessary duty : OBLIGATION ⟨no ~ to hurry⟩ 2 ♦ : a lack of something requisite, desirable, or useful 3 : a condition requiring supply or relief ⟨when the ~ arises⟩ 4 ♦ : lack of the means of subsistence : POVERTY 5 ♦ : a requirement for the well-being of an organism

♦ [1] burden, charge, commitment, duty, obligation, responsibility — more at OBLIGATION ♦ [2] absence, lack, want; *also* deficiency, deficit, inadequacy, insufficiency; dearth, meagerness, paucity, poverty, scantiness, scarcity, shortage; defect, minus; deprivation, privation; demand, essential, necessity, requirement, requisite ♦ [4] beggary, destitution, impecuniousness, impoverishment, indigence, pauperism, penury, poverty, want — more at POVERTY ♦ [5] condition, demand, essential, must, necessity, requirement, requisite — more at ESSENTIAL

²**need** *vb* 1 : to be in want 2 ♦ : to have cause or occasion for : REQUIRE ⟨he ~s advice⟩ 3 ♦ : to be under obligation or necessity ⟨we ~ to know the truth⟩

♦ [2] demand, necessitate, require, take, want, warrant; *also* entail, involve; ask, beg, claim, clamor (for), cry (for); lack; command, enjoin, exact, insist, press, quest, stipulate *Ant* have, hold ♦ **need to** [3] have, must, ought, shall, should; *also* will

need·ful \'nēd-fəl\ *adj* ♦ : absolutely needed : NECESSARY, REQUISITE ⟨bought only what was ~⟩

♦ essential, imperative, indispensable, integral, necessary, requisite, vital — more at ESSENTIAL

¹**nee·dle** \'nēd-ᵊl\ *n* 1 : a slender pointed usu. steel implement used in sewing 2 : a slender rod (as for knitting, controlling a small opening, or transmitting vibrations to or from a recording) ⟨a phonograph ~⟩ 3 ♦ : a slender hollow instrument by which material is introduced into or withdrawn from the body 4 ♦ : a slender indicator on a dial 5 : a needle-shaped leaf (as of a pine)

♦ [3] hypodermic syringe, syringe ♦ [4] hand, index, indicator, pointer — more at POINTER

²**needle** *vb* **nee·dled; nee·dling** 1 ♦ : to vex by repeated

sharp prods or gibes; *esp* : to incite to action by repeated gibes 2 ♦ : to disturb or annoy by persistent irritating or provoking esp. in a petty or mischievous way

♦ [1] henpeck, hound, nag — more at NAG ♦ [2] bait, bug, hassle, heckle, ride, taunt, tease — more at TEASE

nee·dle–nose pliers \'nē-dᵊl-ˌnōz-\ *n pl* : pliers with long slender jaws for grasping small or thin objects

nee·dle·point \'nē-dᵊl-ˌpȯint\ *n* 1 : lace worked with a needle over a paper pattern 2 : embroidery done on canvas across counted threads — **needlepoint** *adj*

need·less \'nēd-ləs\ *adj* : not necessary — **need·less·ly** *adv* — **need·less·ness** *n*

nee·dle·wom·an \'nēd-ᵊl-ˌwu̇-mən\ *n* : a woman who does needlework; *esp* : SEAMSTRESS

nee·dle·work \-ˌwərk\ *n* : work done with a needle; *esp* : work (as embroidery) other than plain sewing

needs \'nēdz\ *adv* ♦ : of necessity : NECESSARILY ⟨must ~ be recognized⟩

♦ inevitably, necessarily, perforce, unavoidably; *also* involuntarily *Ant* unnecessarily

needy \'nē-dē\ *adj* **need·i·er; -est** ♦ : being in want : POVERTY-STRICKEN

♦ broke, destitute, impecunious, indigent, penniless, penurious, poor, poverty-stricken — more at POOR

ne'er \'ner\ *adv* : NEVER

ne'er–do–well \'ner-dü-ˌwel\ *n* : an idle worthless person — **ne'er–do–well** *adj*

ne·far·i·ous \ni-'far-ē-əs\ *adj* [L *nefarius*, fr. *nefas* crime, fr. *ne-* not + *fas* right, divine law] ♦ : very wicked : EVIL — **ne·far·i·ous·ly** *adv*

♦ bad, black, evil, immoral, iniquitous, rotten, sinful, unethical, unsavory, vicious, vile, villainous, wicked, wrong

neg *abbr* negative

ne·gate \ni-'gāt\ *vb* **ne·gat·ed; ne·gat·ing** 1 ♦ : to deny the existence or truth of 2 ♦ : to cause to be ineffective or invalid : NULLIFY ⟨~ a contract⟩

♦ [1] contradict, deny, disallow, disavow, disclaim, gainsay, negative, reject, repudiate — more at DENY ♦ [2] abolish, abrogate, annul, cancel, dissolve, invalidate, nullify, quash, repeal, rescind, void — more at ABOLISH

ne·ga·tion \ni-'gā-shən\ *n* 1 ♦ : the action or operation of negating or making negative 2 : a negative doctrine or statement

♦ contradiction, denial, disallowance, disavowal, disclaimer, rejection, repudiation — more at DENIAL

¹**neg·a·tive** \'ne-gə-tiv\ *adj* 1 : marked by denial, prohibition, or refusal ⟨a ~ reply⟩ 2 : not positive or constructive; *esp* : not affirming the presence of what is sought or suspected to be present ⟨test results were ~⟩ 3 : less than zero ⟨a ~ number⟩ 4 : being, relating to, or charged with electricity of which the electron is the elementary unit 5 : having the light and dark parts opposite to what they were in the original photographic subject — **neg·a·tive·ly** *adv* — **neg·a·tive·ness** *n* — **neg·a·tiv·i·ty** \ˌne-gə-'ti-və-tē\ *n*

♦ adverse, counter, disadvantageous, hostile, inimical, prejudicial, unfavorable (*or* unfavourable), unfriendly, unsympathetic — more at ADVERSE

²**negative** *n* 1 : a negative word or statement 2 : a negative vote or reply; *also* : REFUSAL 3 ♦ : something that is the opposite or negation of something else 4 : the side that votes or argues for the opposition (as in a debate) 5 : a negative number 6 : a negative photographic image on transparent material

♦ antipode, antithesis, contrary, opposite, reverse — more at OPPOSITE

³**negative** *vb* **-tived; -tiv·ing** 1 : to refuse to accept or approve 2 ♦ : to vote against 3 : DISPROVE 4 : to imply the opposite or a denial of 5 ♦ : to deny the truth, reality, or validity of

♦ [2] blackball, kill, veto; *also* decline, disallow, disapprove, dismiss, refuse; blacklist *Ant* confirm, ratify
♦ [5] contradict, deny, disallow, disavow, disclaim, gainsay, negate, reject, repudiate — more at DENY

negative income tax *n* : a system of federal subsidy payments to families with incomes below a stipulated level

neg·a·tiv·ism \'ne-gə-ti-ˌvi-zəm\ *n* : an attitude of skepticism and denial of nearly everything affirmed or suggested by others

¹**ne·glect** \ni-'glekt\ *vb* [L *neglectus*, pp. of *neglegere, neclegere*, fr. *nec*- not + *legere* to gather] **1** ♦ : to give little attention or respect to : DISREGARD **2** ♦ : to leave undone or unattended to esp. through carelessness

♦ [1] disregard, forget, ignore, overlook, pass over, slight, slur; *also* fail; miss, omit; brush (aside *or* off), reject, shrug off, slough (off); disdain, pooh-pooh, scorn, scant, skimp *Ant* attend (to), heed, mind, regard, tend (to) ♦ [2] fail, forget, omit; *also* disregard, ignore, overlook, slight; slide, slip; default; skip

²**neglect** *n* **1** ♦ : an act or instance of neglecting something **2** ♦ : the condition of being neglected

♦ [1] default, delinquency, dereliction, failure, negligence, oversight — more at FAILURE ♦ [2] desolation, dilapidation, disrepair; *also* inattention, negligence, abandonment, desertion; decay, decrepitude, dereliction, deterioration, disintegration, ruin, ruination *Ant* repair

neg·lect·ed \ni-'glek-təd\ *adj* ♦ : that evidences improper or insufficient attention or care

♦ dilapidated, grungy, mean, ratty, seedy, shabby — more at SHABBY

neg·lect·ful *adj* : given to neglecting

neg·li·gee *also* **neg·li·gé** \ˌne-glə-'zhā\ *n* : a woman's long flowing dressing gown

neg·li·gence \'ne-gli-jəns\ *n* **1** ♦ : the quality or state of being negligent **2** ♦ : an act or instance of being negligent

♦ [1] carelessness, dereliction, heedlessness, laxness, remissness, slackness; *also* foolhardiness, rashness, recklessness, wildness; neglect, omission; delinquency, irresponsibility, malfeasance, malpractice, misconduct; misdirection, mishandling, mismanagement; inattention, obliviousness, shortsightedness *Ant* care, carefulness, caution, cautiousness, heedfulness ♦ [2] default, delinquency, dereliction, failure, neglect, oversight — more at FAILURE

neg·li·gent \'ne-gli-jənt\ *adj* ♦ : marked by neglect — **neg·li·gent·ly** *adv*

♦ careless, derelict, lax, remiss, slack; *also* heedless, incautious, irresponsible, reckless, wild; unguarded, unwary; forgetful, disregardful, disregarding, inattentive, oblivious, thoughtless, unmindful, unthinking; apathetic, disinterested, indifferent, unconcerned, uninterested; delinquent; loose *Ant* attentive, careful, conscientious

neg·li·gi·ble \'ne-gli-jə-bəl\ *adj* ♦ : so small or unimportant or of so little consequence as to warrant little or no attention

♦ inconsequential, inconsiderable, insignificant, measly, minute, nominal, paltry, petty, slight, trifling, trivial, unimportant; *also* inferior, mean; imperceptible, inappreciable; little, puny, tiny; hairsplitting, pettifogging *Ant* big, consequential, considerable, important, material, significant

ne·go·tiant \ni-'gō-shē-ənt\ *n* : NEGOTIATOR

ne·go·ti·ate \ni-'gō-shē-ˌāt\ *vb* **-at·ed; -at·ing** [L *negotiari* to carry on business, fr. *negotium* business, fr. *neg*- not + *otium* leisure] **1** ♦ : to confer with another so as to arrive at the settlement of some matter; *also* : to arrange for or bring about by such conferences ⟨∼ a treaty⟩ **2** : to transfer to another by delivery or endorsement in return for equivalent value ⟨∼ a check⟩ **3** : to get through,

around, or over successfully ⟨∼ a turn⟩ **4** ♦ : to deal with (some matter or affair that requires ability for its successful handling) — **ne·go·tia·ble** \-shə-bəl, -shē-ə-\ *adj* — **ne·go·ti·a·tor** \-'gō-shē-ˌā-tər\ *n*

♦ [1] arrange, concert, conclude; *also* settle; bargain, chaffer, deal, dicker, haggle, palter; agree; contract, covenant; argue, debate, discuss, hammer (out), hash (over), reason, talk, talk over, work out ♦ [4] contend with, cope with, grapple with, handle, manage, maneuver (*or* manoeuvre), swing, treat — more at HANDLE

ne·go·ti·a·tion \ni-ˌgō-sē-'ā-shən, -shē-\ *n* ♦ : the action or process of negotiating or being negotiated

♦ accommodation, compromise, concession, give-and-take — more at CONCESSION

ne·gri·tude \'ne-grə-ˌtüd, -ˌtyüd, 'nē-\ *n* : a consciousness of and pride in one's African heritage

Ne·gro \'nē-grō\ *n, pl* **Negroes** [Sp or Pg, fr. *negro* black] *dated, now sometimes offensive* : a member of a race of humankind native to Africa and classified according to physical features (as dark skin pigmentation) — **Negro** *adj, dated, now sometimes offensive* — **Ne·groid** \'nē-ˌgroid\ *n or adj, often not cap, dated, now sometimes offensive*

Neh *abbr* Nehemiah

Ne·he·mi·ah \ˌnē-ə-'mī-ə\ *n* : a book of Jewish and Christian Scripture

neigh \'nā\ *n* : a loud prolonged cry of a horse — **neigh** *vb*

¹**neigh·bor** *or Can and Brit* **neigh·bour** \'nā-bər\ *n* **1** : one living or located near another **2** : FELLOW MAN

²**neighbor** *or Can and Brit* **neigh·bour** *vb* ♦ : to be next to or near to : border on

♦ abut, adjoin, border (on), flank, fringe, join, skirt, touch, verge (on) — more at ADJOIN

neigh·bor·hood \'nā-bər-ˌhud\ *or Can and Brit* **neigh·bour·hood** \'nā-bər-ˌhud\ *n* **1** : NEARNESS **2** : a place or region near : VICINITY; *also* : a number or amount near ⟨costs in the ∼ of $10⟩ **3** : the people living near one another **4** ♦ : a section lived in by neighbors and usu. having distinguishing characteristics

♦ district, quarter, section — more at DISTRICT

neigh·bor·li·ness *or Can and Brit* **neigh·bour·li·ness** \'nā-bər-lē-nəs\ *n* ♦ : the quality or state of being neighborly

♦ amity, benevolence, cordiality, fellowship, friendliness, friendship, goodwill, kindliness — more at GOODWILL

neigh·bor·ly *or Can and Brit* **neigh·bour·ly** \'nā-bər-lē\ *adj* ♦ : befitting congenial neighbors; *esp* : FRIENDLY

♦ amicable, companionable, comradely, cordial, friendly, genial, hearty, warm, warmhearted — more at FRIENDLY

neigh·bour *Can and Brit var of* NEIGHBOUR

¹**nei·ther** \'nē-thər, 'nī-\ *pron* : neither one : not the one and not the other ⟨∼ of the two⟩

²**neither** *conj* **1** : not either ⟨∼ good nor bad⟩ **2** : NOR ⟨∼ did I⟩

³**neither** *adj* : not either ⟨∼ hand⟩

nel·son \'nel-sən\ *n* : a wrestling hold in which one applies leverage against an opponent's arm, neck, and head

nem·a·tode \'ne-mə-ˌtōd\ *n* : any of a phylum of elongated cylindrical worms parasitic in animals or plants or free-living in soil or water

nem·e·sis \'ne-mə-səs\ *n, pl* **-e·ses** \-ˌsēz\ [L *Nemesis*, goddess of divine retribution, fr. Gk] **1** ♦ : one that inflicts retribution or vengeance **2** : a formidable and usu. victorious rival **3** ♦ : an act or effect of retribution; *also* : CURSE

♦ [1] avenger, castigator, scourge; *also* revenger; righter ♦ [3] castigation, chastisement, correction, curse, desert, discipline, penalty, punishment, wrath — more at PUNISHMENT

neo·clas·sic \ˌnē-ō-'kla-sik\ *or* **neo·clas·si·cal** \-si-kəl\ *adj* : of or relating to a revival or adaptation of the classical style esp. in literature, art, or music

neo·co·lo·nial·ism \ˌnē-ō-kə-ˈlō-nē-ə-ˌli-zəm\ *n* : the economic and political policies by which a nation indirectly maintains or extends its influence over other areas or peoples — **neo·co·lo·nial** *adj* — **neo·co·lo·nial·ist** \-list\ *n or adj*

neo·con \ˈnē-ō-ˌkän\ *n* : NEOCONSERVATIVE

neo·con·ser·va·tive \-kən-ˈsər-və-tiv\ *n* : a former liberal espousing political conservatism — **neo·con·ser·va·tism** \-və-ˌti-zəm\ *n* — **neoconservative** *adj*

neo·dym·i·um \ˌnē-ō-ˈdi-mē-əm\ *n* : a silver-white to yellow metallic chemical element

neo·im·pres·sion·ism \ˌnē-ō-im-ˈpre-shə-ˌni-zəm\ *n, often cap N&I* : a late 19th century French art movement that attempted to make impressionism more precise and to use a pointillist painting technique

Neo·lith·ic \ˌnē-ə-ˈli-thik\ *adj* : of or relating to the latest period of the Stone Age characterized by polished stone implements

ne·ol·o·gism \nē-ˈä-lə-ˌji-zəm\ *n* : a new word or expression

ne·on \ˈnē-ˌän\ *n* [Gk, neut. of *neos* new] **1** : a gaseous colorless chemical element used in electric lamps **2** : a lamp in which a discharge through neon gives a reddish glow — **neon** *adj*

neo·na·tal \ˌnē-ō-ˈnāt-ᵊl\ *adj* : of, relating to, or affecting the newborn — **neo·na·tal·ly** *adv*

ne·o·nate \ˈnē-ə-ˌnāt\ *n* : a newborn child

neo·pa·gan \ˌnē-ō-ˈpā-gən\ *n* : a person who practices a contemporary form of paganism — **neo–pagan** *adj*

neo·phyte \ˈnē-ə-ˌfīt\ *n* **1** : a new convert : PROSELYTE **2** : NOVICE **3** ♦ : one that begins something; *esp* : an inexperienced person : BEGINNER

♦ beginner, fledgling, freshman, greenhorn, newcomer, novice, recruit, rookie, tenderfoot, tyro — more at BEGINNER

neo·plasm \ˈnē-ə-ˌpla-zəm\ *n* ♦ : a new growth of tissue serving no useful purpose in the body : TUMOR — **neo·plas·tic** \ˌnē-ə-ˈplas-tik\ *adj*

♦ excrescence, growth, lump, tumor — more at GROWTH

neo·prene \ˈnē-ə-ˌprēn\ *n* : a synthetic rubber used esp. for special-purpose clothing (as wet suits)

neo·trop·i·cal \ˌnē-ō-ˈträ-pi-kəl\ *adj, often cap* : of or relating to a zoogeographic region of America that extends south from the central plateau of Mexico

Ne·pali \nə-ˈpȯ-lē, -ˈpä-\ *n, pl* **Nepali** : a native or inhabitant of Nepal — **Nepali** *adj*

ne·pen·the \nə-ˈpen-thē\ *n* **1** : a potion used by the ancients to dull pain and sorrow **2** : something capable of making one forget grief or suffering

neph·ew \ˈne-fyü, *chiefly Brit* -vyü\ *n* [ME *nevew*, fr. AF *neveu*, fr. LL *nepot-, nepos*, fr. L, grandson, descendant] : a son of one's brother, sister, brother-in-law, or sister-in-law

ne·phrit·ic \ni-ˈfri-tik\ *adj* **1** : RENAL **2** : of, relating to, or affected with nephritis

ne·phri·tis \ni-ˈfrī-təs\ *n, pl* **ne·phrit·i·des** \-ˈfri-tə-ˌdēz\ : kidney inflammation

ne plus ul·tra \ˌnē-ˌpləs-ˈəl-trə\ *n* [NL, (go) no more beyond] : the highest point capable of being attained

nep·o·tism \ˈne-pə-ˌti-zəm\ *n* [F *népotisme*, fr. It *nepotismo*, fr. *nepote* nephew, fr. LL *nepot-, nepos*] : favoritism shown to a relative (as in the granting of jobs)

Nep·tune \ˈnep-ˌtün, -ˌtyün\ *n* : the planet 8th in order from the sun — **Nep·tu·ni·an** \nep-ˈtü-nē-ən, -ˈtyü-\ *adj*

nep·tu·ni·um \nep-ˈtü-nē-əm, -ˈtyü-\ *n* : a short-lived radioactive element

nerd \ˈnərd\ *n* : an unstylish or socially inept person; *esp* ♦ : one slavishly devoted to intellectual pursuits — **nerdy** *adj*

♦ highbrow, intellectual — more at INTELLECTUAL

Ne·re·id \ˈnir-ē-əd\ *n* : a sea nymph in Greek mythology

¹nerve \ˈnərv\ *n* **1** : SINEW, TENDON ⟨strain every ∼⟩ **2** : any of the strands of nervous tissue that carry nerve impulses between the brain and spinal cord and every

part of the body **3 a** ♦ : power of endurance or control : FORTITUDE **b** ♦ : the quality or state of being bold : BOLDNESS, DARING **4** *pl* : NERVOUSNESS **5** : a vein of a leaf or insect wing — **nerved** \ˈnərvd\ *adj*

♦ [3a] bravery, courage, daring, fearlessness, fortitude, gallantry, guts, hardihood, heart, heroism, stoutness, valor — more at COURAGE ♦ [3b] audacity, brass, brazenness, cheek, chutzpah, daring, effrontery, gall, presumption, sauce, sauciness, temerity — more at EFFRONTERY

²nerve *vb* **nerved; nerv·ing** ♦ : to give strength or courage to

♦ brace, forearm, fortify, psych (up), ready, steel, strengthen — more at FORTIFY

nerve cell *n* : NEURON; *also* : CELL BODY

nerve gas *n* : a chemical weapon damaging esp. to the nervous and respiratory systems

nerve impulse *n* : a physical and chemical change that moves along a process of a neuron after stimulation and carries a record of sensation or an instruction to act

nerve·less *adj* **1** ♦ : destitute of strength or courage **2** ♦ : exhibiting control or balance

♦ [1] effete, frail, soft, spineless, weak, wimpy, wishy-washy — more at WEAK ♦ [2] imperturbable, unflappable, unshakable — more at UNFLAPPABLE

nerve–rack·ing *or* **nerve–wrack·ing** \ˈnərv-ˌra-kiŋ\ *adj* : extremely trying on the nerves ⟨∼ noise⟩

ner·vous \ˈnər-vəs\ *adj* **1** : FORCIBLE, SPIRITED **2** : of, relating to, or made up of neurons or nerves **3** ♦ : easily excited or annoyed : JUMPY ⟨a ∼ horse⟩ **4** ♦ : viewing the future with anxiety or alarm ⟨a ∼ smile⟩ **5** ♦ : causing physical or mental discomfort — **ner·vous·ly** *adv*

♦ [3] excitable, flighty, fluttery, high-strung, jittery, jumpy, skittish, spooky — more at EXCITABLE ♦ [4] aflutter, anxious, edgy, jittery, jumpy, nervy, perturbed, tense, troubled, uneasy, upset, worried; *also* aggrieved, bothered, concerned, disquieted, distraught, distressed, disturbed; apprehensive, foreboding, hesitant, misgiving; fretful, fretting, stewing, vexed; qualmish; twittered, undone, unnerved, unstrung; obsessed, preoccupied, restless; fidgety, flighty, fluttery, high-strung, skittish, spooky **Ant** calm, easy, collected, cool, nerveless, relaxed ♦ [5] anxious, distressful, restless, tense, unsettling, upsetting, worrisome; *also* bothersome, troublesome; foreboding, misgiving; disheartening, discouraging, strained; restive, restless, unrestful; awkward, embarrassing **Ant** calming, comfortable, easy, peaceful, quiet, quieting, tranquil

nervous breakdown *n* : an attack of mental or emotional disorder esp. when of sufficient severity to require hospitalization

ner·vous·ness *n* ♦ : the quality or state of being nervous

♦ agitation, anxiety, apprehension, care, concern, disquiet, perturbation, uneasiness, worry — more at ANXIETY

nervous system *n* : a bodily system that in vertebrates is made up of the brain and spinal cord, nerves, ganglia, and parts of the sense organs and that receives and interprets stimuli and transmits nerve impulses

nervy \ˈnər-vē\ *adj* **nerv·i·er; -est** **1** ♦ : showing calm courage **2** ♦ : marked by impudence or presumption ⟨a ∼ salesperson⟩ **3** : marked by nervousness : NERVOUS

♦ [1] adventurous, audacious, bold, daring, enterprising, gutsy, hardy, venturesome — more at BOLD ♦ [2] arch, bold, brash, brazen, cheeky, cocky, fresh, impertinent, impudent, insolent, sassy, saucy; *also* assertive, forward, obtrusive; audacious, defiant, disrespectful; shameless, unabashed, unblushing; bluff, blunt, curt; facetious, flip, flippant, pert, smart, smart-alecky **Ant** meek, mousy, retiring, shy, timid

-ness \nəs\ *n suffix* : state : condition : quality : degree ⟨good*ness*⟩

¹nest \ˈnest\ *n* **1** : the shelter prepared by a bird for its eggs and young **2** : a place where eggs (as of insects or fish) are laid and hatched **3** ♦ : a place of rest, retreat, or lodging **4** : DEN, HANGOUT ⟨a ∼ of thieves⟩ **5** : the occupants of a nest **6** : a series of objects (as bowls or tables) fitting inside or under one another

♦ concealment, covert, den, hideout, lair — more at HIDEOUT

²nest *vb* **1** : to build or occupy a nest **2** : to fit compactly together or within one another

nest egg *n* ♦ : a fund of money accumulated as a reserve

♦ account, budget, deposit, fund, kitty, pool — more at FUND

nes·tle \'ne-səl\ *vb* **nes·tled; nes·tling** **1** ♦ : to settle snugly or comfortably **2** ♦ : to press closely and affectionately : CUDDLE **3** : to settle, shelter, or house as if in a nest

♦ cuddle, curl up, snug, snuggle — more at SNUGGLE

nest·ling \'nest-liŋ\ *n* : a bird too young to leave its nest

¹net \'net\ *n* **1** ♦ : a meshed fabric twisted, knotted, or woven together at regular intervals **2** ♦ : a device made all or partly of net and used esp. to catch birds, fish, or insects **3** ♦ : something made of net used esp. for protecting, confining, carrying, or dividing ⟨a tennis ∼⟩ **4** : an entrapping device or situation : SNARE, TRAP **5** *often cap* : INTERNET

♦ [1] mesh, network; *also* web, webbing; grille, lattice, screen, screening; filigree, lace ♦ [2, 3] entanglement, snare, web — more at WEB

²net *vb* **net·ted; net·ting** **1** : to cover or enclose with or as if with a net **2** : to catch in or as if in a net

³net *adj* : free from all charges or deductions ⟨∼ profit⟩ ⟨∼ weight⟩

⁴net *vb* **net·ted; net·ting** : to gain or produce as profit : CLEAR, YIELD ⟨his business *netted* $50,000 a year⟩

⁵net *n* ♦ : a net amount, profit, weight, or price

♦ earnings, gain, lucre, payoff, proceeds, profit, return — more at PROFIT

Neth *abbr* Netherlands

neth·er \'ne-thər\ *adj* : situated down or below ⟨the ∼ regions of the earth⟩

Neth·er·land·er \'ne-thər-,lan-dər\ *n* : a native or inhabitant of the Netherlands

neth·er·most \-,mōst\ *adj* : LOWEST

neth·er·world \-,wərld\ *n* **1** : the world of the dead **2** : UNDERWORLD

net·i·quette \'ne-ti-kət, -,ket\ *n* : etiquette governing communication on the Internet

net·roots \'net-,rüts, -,rüts\ *n pl* : the grassroots political activists who communicate via the Internet

net·ting *n* **1** : a fabric or structure of cords or wires that cross at regular intervals and are knotted or secured at the crossings : NETWORK **2** : the act or process of making a net or network

¹net·tle \'net-ᵊl\ *n* : any of a genus of coarse herbs with stinging hairs

²nettle *vb* **net·tled; net·tling** ♦ : to arouse to sharp but transitory annoyance or anger : VEX, IRRITATE

♦ aggravate, annoy, bother, bug, chafe, exasperate, gall, get, grate, irk, irritate, peeve, persecute, pique, put out, rasp, rile, vex — more at IRRITATE

net·tle·some \'net-ᵊl-səm\ *adj* : causing vexation : IRRITATING

net·work \'net-,wərk\ *n* **1** ♦ : a fabric or structure of cords or wires that cross at regular intervals and are knotted or secured at the crossings : NET **2** : a system of elements (as lines or channels) that cross in the manner of the threads in a net **3** : a group or system of related or connected parts; *esp* : a chain of radio or television stations **4** : a system of computers that are connected (as by telephone wires)

♦ mesh, net — more at NET

net·work·ing \'net-,wər-kiŋ\ *n* : the exchange of information or services among individuals, groups, or institutions

neu·ral \'nur-əl, 'nyur-\ *adj* : of, relating to, or involving a nerve or the nervous system

neu·ral·gia \nu-'ral-jə, nyu-\ *n* : acute pain that follows the course of a nerve — **neu·ral·gic** \-jik\ *adj*

neur·as·then·ia \,nur-əs-'thē-nē-ə\ *n* [NL, fr. Gk *neuron* nerve + *asthenia* weakness, fr. *asthenes* weak, fr. *a*- not + *sthenos* strength] : a psychological disorder marked esp. by fatiguing easily, lack of motivation, feelings of inadequacy, and psychosomatic symptoms — **neur·as·then·ic** \-the-nik, -'thē-\ *adj or n*

neu·ri·tis \-'rī-təs\ *n, pl* **-rit·i·des** \-'ri-tə-,dēz\ *or* **-ri·tis·es** : inflammation of a nerve — **neu·rit·ic** \-'ri-tik\ *adj or n*

neu·ro·bi·ol·o·gy \,nur-ō-bī-'ä-lə-jē\ *n* : a branch of biology that deals with the nervous system — **neu·ro·bi·o·log·i·cal** \-,bī-ə-'lä-ji-kəl\ *adj* — **neu·ro·bi·ol·o·gist** \-bī-'ä-lə-jist\ *n*

neu·rol·o·gy \nu-'rä-lə-jē, nyu-\ *n* : the scientific study of the nervous system — **neu·ro·log·i·cal** \,nur-ə-'lä-ji-kəl, ,nyur-\ *or* **neu·ro·log·ic** \-jik\ *adj* — **neu·ro·log·i·cal·ly** \-ji-k(ə-)lē\ *adv* — **neu·rol·o·gist** \nu-'rä-lə-jist, nyu-\ *n*

neu·ro·mus·cu·lar \,nur-ō-'məs-kyə-lər, ,nyur-\ *adj* : of, relating to, or affecting nerves and muscles ⟨a ∼ disease⟩

neu·ron \'nü-,rän, 'nyü-\ *n* : a cell with specialized processes that is the fundamental functional unit of nervous tissue — **neu·ro·nal** \'nur-ə-nᵊl, 'nyur-\ *adj*

neu·rone \-,rōn\ *chiefly Brit var of* NEURON

neu·ro·sci·ence \,nur-ō-'sī-əns, ,nyur-\ *n* : a branch of the life sciences that deals with the anatomy, physiology, biochemistry, or molecular biology of nerves and nervous tissue and esp. with their relation to behavior and learning — **neu·ro·sci·en·tist** \-ən-tist\ *n*

neu·ro·sis \nu-'rō-səs, nyu-\ *n, pl* **-ro·ses** \-,sēz\ : a mental and emotional disorder that is less serious than a psychosis, is not characterized by disturbance of the use of language, and is accompanied by various bodily and mental disturbances (as visceral symptoms, anxieties, or phobias)

neu·ro·sur·gery \,nur-ō-'sər-jə-rē, ,nyur-\ *n* : surgery of nervous structures (as nerves, the brain, or the spinal cord) — **neu·ro·sur·geon** \-'sər-jən\ *n*

¹neu·rot·ic \nu-'rä-tik, nyu-\ *adj* : of, relating to, being, or affected with a neurosis; *also* : NERVOUS — **neu·rot·i·cal·ly** \-ti-k(ə-)lē\ *adv*

²neurotic *n* : an emotionally unstable or neurotic person

neu·ro·trans·mit·ter \,nur-ō-trans-'mi-tər, ,nyur-, -tranz-\ *n* : a substance (as acetylcholine) that transmits nerve impulses across a synapse

neut *abbr* neuter

¹neu·ter \'nü-tər, 'nyü-\ *adj* [ME *neutre*, fr. MF & L; MF *neutre*, fr. L *neuter*, lit., neither, fr. *ne*- not + *uter* which of two] **1** : of, relating to, or constituting the gender that includes most words or grammatical forms referring to things classed as neither masculine nor feminine **2** : lacking or having imperfectly developed sex organs

²neuter *n* **1** : a noun, pronoun, adjective, or inflectional form or class of the neuter gender; *also* : the neuter gender **2** : WORKER 2; *also* : a spayed or castrated animal

³neuter *vb* : to remove the sex organs of : CASTRATE, SPAY

¹neu·tral \'nü-trəl, 'nyü-\ *n* **1** : one that is neutral **2** : a neutral color **3** : a position of disengagement (as of gears)

²neutral *adj* **1** ♦ : not favoring either side in a quarrel, contest, or war **2** : of or relating to a neutral state or power **3** : MIDDLING, INDIFFERENT **4** : having no hue : GRAY; *also* : not decided in color **5** : neither acid nor basic ⟨a ∼ solution⟩ **6** : not electrically charged

♦ disinterested, impartial, nonpartisan, unbiased; *also* autonomous, independent, sovereign; nonbelligerent; individualistic; evenhanded, fair, uninfluenced, unprejudiced, bipartisan *Ant* allied, confederate

neu·tral·ise *chiefly Brit var of* NEUTRALIZE

neu·tral·ism \'nü-trə-,li-zəm, 'nyü-\ *n* : a policy or the advocacy of neutrality esp. in international affairs

neu·tral·i·ty \nü-'tra-lə-tē, nyü-\ *n* ♦ : the quality or state of being neutral; *esp* : refusal to take part in a war between other powers

♦ detachment, disinterestedness, impartiality, objectivity — more at DETACHMENT

neu·tral·ize \'nü-trə-ˌlīz, 'nyü-\ *vb* **-ized; -iz·ing** ♦ : to make neutral; *esp* : to counteract the activity or effect of : COUNTERACT — **neu·tral·i·za·tion** \ˌnü-trə-lə-'zā-shən, ˌnyü-\ *n*

♦ annul, cancel, compensate, correct, counteract, counterbalance, make up, offset — more at OFFSET

neu·tri·no \nü-'trē-nō, nyü-\ *n, pl* **-nos** : an uncharged elementary particle held to be massless or very light

neu·tron \'nü-ˌträn, 'nyü-\ *n* : an uncharged atomic particle that is nearly equal in mass to the proton

neutron bomb *n* : a nuclear bomb designed to produce lethal neutrons but less blast and fire damage than other nuclear bombs

neutron star *n* : a dense celestial object that results from the collapse of a large star

Nev *abbr* Nevada

nev·er \'ne-vər\ *adv* **1** : not ever **2** ♦ : not in any degree, way, or condition

♦ no, none, nothing, nowise; *also* nowhere near *Ant* anyhow, anyway, anywise, at all, ever, half, however

nev·er·more \ˌne-vər-'mōr\ *adv* : never again

nev·er–nev·er land \ˌne-vər-'ne-vər-\ *n* : an ideal or imaginary place

nev·er·the·less \ˌne-vər-thə-'les\ *adv* ♦ : in spite of that : HOWEVER

♦ but, howbeit, however, nonetheless, notwithstanding, still, though, withal, yet — more at HOWEVER

ne·vus \'nē-vəs\ *n, pl* **ne·vi** \-ˌvī\ : a usu. pigmented area on the skin : MOLE

¹**new** \'nü, 'nyü\ *adj* **1** ♦ : having recently come into existence or occurred; *also* : of or characteristic of the present time : MODERN **2** ♦ : recently discovered, recognized, or learned about ⟨~ drugs⟩ **3** : not familiar : UNFAMILIAR **4** ♦ : different from the former **5** : not accustomed ⟨~ to the work⟩ **6** : beginning as a repetition of a previous act or thing ⟨a ~ year⟩ **7** : made or become fresh : REFRESHED, REGENERATED ⟨awoke a ~ person⟩ **8** : being in a position or place for the first time ⟨a ~ member⟩ **9** *cap* : having been in use after medieval times : MODERN ⟨*New* Latin⟩ — **new·ish** *adj*

♦ [1] contemporary, current, hot, mod, modern, new-fangled, red-hot, space-age, ultramodern, up-to-date — more at MODERN ♦ [1] brand-new, spick-and-span, unused; *also* clean, fresh, pristine, unspoiled; untouched; newfangled, new-fashioned; natural, raw, virgin, unprocessed, untreated *Ant* hand-me-down, second hand, used ♦ [2] fresh, novel, original, strange, unfamiliar, unknown; *also* innovative, unique; nontraditional, unconventional, untried, unused, unworn *Ant* familiar, old, time-honored, tired ♦ [4] backup, substitute; *also* alternate, alternative; different, other, separate; extra, spare; another, second; utility; successive; equivalent *Ant* original

²**new** *adv* ♦ : not long ago : NEWLY ⟨*new*-mown hay⟩

♦ freshly, just, late, lately, newly, now, only, recently — more at NEWLY

new age *adj, often cap N&A* **1** : of, relating to, or being New Age **2** : CONTEMPORARY, MODERN

New Age *n* **1** : a group of late 20th century social attitudes adapted from a variety of ancient and modern beliefs relating to spirituality, right living, and health **2** : a soft soothing form of instrumental music

new·bie \'nü-bē, 'nyü-\ *n* ♦ : one that begins something without prior experience : NEWCOMER; *esp* : a newcomer to cyberspace

♦ beginner, fledgling, freshman, greenhorn, neophyte, newcomer, novice, recruit, rookie, tenderfoot, tyro — more at BEGINNER

¹**new·born** \-ˌbórn\ *adj* **1** : recently born **2** : born anew ⟨~ hope⟩

²**newborn** *n, pl* **newborn** *or* **newborns** ♦ : a newborn individual

♦ baby, child, infant — more at BABY

new·com·er \-ˌkə-mər\ *n* **1** : one recently arrived **2** ♦ : one that begins something without prior experience : BEGINNER

♦ beginner, fledgling, freshman, greenhorn, neophyte, novice, recruit, rookie, tenderfoot, tyro — more at BEGINNER

New Deal *n* : the legislative and administrative program of President F. D. Roosevelt to promote economic recovery and social reform during the 1930s — **New Dealer** *n*

new·el \'nü-əl, 'nyü-\ *n* : a post about which the steps of a circular staircase wind; *also* : a post at the foot of a stairway or one at a landing

new·fan·gled \ˌnü-'faŋ-gəld, 'nyü-\ *adj* **1** : attracted to novelty **2** ♦ : of the newest style : NOVEL ⟨~ gadgets⟩

♦ contemporary, current, hot, mod, modern, new, novel, red-hot, space-age, ultramodern, up-to-date — more at MODERN

new–fash·ioned \-'fa-shənd\ *adj* **1** : made in a new fashion or form **2** : abreast of the times : UP-TO-DATE

new·found \-'faúnd\ *adj* : newly found

New Left *n* : a radical political movement originating in the 1960s

new·ly \'nü-lē, 'nyü-\ *adv* **1** ♦ : not long ago : LATELY, RECENTLY **2** : ANEW, AFRESH

♦ freshly, just, late, lately, new, now, only, recently; *also* latterly

new·ly·wed \-ˌwed\ *n* : a person recently married

new moon *n* : the phase of the moon with its dark side toward the earth; *also* : the thin crescent moon seen for a few days after the new moon phase

new·ness *n* ♦ : the quality or state of being new

♦ freshness, novelty, originality — more at NOVELTY

news \'nüz, 'nyüz\ *n* **1** ♦ : a report of recent events : TIDINGS **2** : material reported in a newspaper or news periodical or on a newscast

♦ intelligence, item, story, tidings, word; *also* announcement, communication, message; dope, lowdown, scoop, tidbit, tip; gossip, rumor, tale, tattle; feedback

news·boy \'nüz-ˌbói, 'nyüz-\ *n* : one who delivers or sells newspapers

news·cast \-ˌkast\ *n* : a radio or television broadcast of news — **news·cast·er** \-ˌkas-tər\ *n*

news·group \-ˌgrüp\ *n* : an Internet bulletin devoted to a certain topic

news·let·ter \-ˌle-tər\ *n* : a small newspaper containing news or information of interest chiefly to a special group

news·mag·a·zine \-ˌma-gə-ˌzēn\ *n* : a usu. weekly magazine devoted chiefly to summarizing and analyzing news

news·man \-mən, -ˌman\ *n* ♦ : a person who gathers, reports, or comments on the news : REPORTER

♦ correspondent, journalist, reporter — more at REPORTER

news·pa·per \-ˌpā-pər\ *n* : a paper that is published at regular intervals and contains news, articles of opinion, features, and advertising

news·pa·per·man \-ˌpā-pər-ˌman\ *n* : a person who owns or is employed by a newspaper

news·print \-ˌprint\ *n* : paper made chiefly from wood pulp and used mostly for newspapers

news·reel \-ˌrēl\ *n* : a short motion picture portraying current events

news·stand \-ˌstand\ *n* : a place where newspapers and periodicals are sold

news·week·ly \-ˌwēk-lē\ *n* : a weekly newspaper or newsmagazine

news·wire \-ˌwī(-ə)r\ *n* : WIRE SERVICE

news·wom·an \-ˌwù-mən\ *n* : a woman who is a reporter

news·wor·thy \-ˌwər-ˌt͟hē\ *adj* : sufficiently interesting to the general public to warrant reporting (as in a newspaper)

newsy \'nü-zē, 'nyü-\ *adj* **news·i·er; -est** **1** : filled with news; *esp* : TALKATIVE **2** ♦ : given to gossip

♦ chatty, colloquial, conversational — more at CHATTY

newt \'nüt, 'nyüt\ *n* [ME, alter. (from misdivision of *an ewte*) of *ewt, evete*, fr. OE *efete*] : any of various small chiefly aquatic salamanders

New Testament *n* : the second of the two chief divisions of the Christian Scripture

new·ton \'nüt-ᵊn, 'nyüt-\ *n* : the unit of force in the metric system equal to the force required to impart an acceleration of one meter per second per second to a mass of one kilogram

new wave *n, often cap N&W* : the latest and esp. the most outrageous style — **new–wave** *adj*

New World *n* : the western hemisphere; *esp* : the continental landmass of No. and So. America

New Year *n* **1** : NEW YEAR'S DAY; *also* : the first days of the year **2** : ROSH HASHANAH

New Year's Day *n* : January 1 observed as a legal holiday

New Zea·land·er \nü-'zē-lən-dər, nyü-\ *n* : a native or inhabitant of New Zealand

¹**next** \'nekst\ *adj* **1** : immediately preceding or following **2** ♦ : following that approaching or in progress

♦ coming, following, succeeding; *also* consecutive, sequential, successive; posterior, subsequent; immediate; second *Ant* antecedent, foregoing, precedent, preceding, previous, prior

²**next** *prep* : nearest or adjacent to

³**next** *adv* **1** : in the time, place, or order nearest or immediately succeeding **2** : on the first occasion to come

¹**next to** *prep* **1** ♦ : immediately following or adjacent to **2** : in comparison to ⟨*next to* you I'm wealthy⟩

♦ about, around, by, near — more at AROUND

²**next to** *adv* ♦ : very nearly ⟨*next to* impossible to win⟩

♦ about, almost, most, much, near, nearly, nigh, practically, some, virtually, well-nigh — more at ALMOST

Nez Percé \'nez-'pərs, *F* nā-per-sā\ *n* : a member of an American Indian people of Idaho, Washington, and Oregon; *also* : the language of the Nez Percé

NF *abbr* Newfoundland

NFC *abbr* National Football Conference

NFL *abbr* National Football League

Nfld *abbr* Newfoundland

NG *abbr* **1** National Guard **2** no good

Nh *symbol* nihonium

NH *abbr* New Hampshire

NHL *abbr* National Hockey League

Ni *symbol* nickel

ni·a·cin \'nī-ə-sən\ *n* : an organic acid of the vitamin B complex found widely in plants and animals and used esp. against pellagra

nib \'nib\ *n* **1** : POINT; *esp* : a pen point **2** : the jaws of a bird together with their horny covering

¹**nib·ble** \'ni-bəl\ *vb* **nib·bled; nib·bling** : to bite gently or bit by bit; *also* : eat in small pieces

²**nibble** *n* ♦ : a small or cautious bite; *also* : an amount of food taken with a small bite

♦ bite, morsel, mouthful, taste, tidbit — more at MORSEL

ni·cad \'nī-,kad\ *n* : a rechargeable dry cell that has a nickel cathode and a cadmium anode

Nic·a·ra·guan \,ni-kə-'rä-gwən\ *n* : a native or inhabitant of Nicaragua — **Nicaraguan** *adj*

nice \'nīs\ *adj* **nic·er; nic·est** [ME, foolish, wanton, fr. AF, silly, simple, fr. L *nescius* ignorant, fr. *nescire* to not know] **1** ♦ : showing fastidious or finicky tastes : FASTIDIOUS **2** ♦ : marked by delicate discrimination or treatment **3 a** ♦ : giving pleasure : PLEASING, AGREEABLE **b** : well-executed **4** : WELL-BRED ⟨∼ people⟩ **5** ♦ : decent or correct in character or behavior : RESPECTABLE **6** ♦ : of a sympathetic or helpful nature

♦ [1] choosy, dainty, delicate, demanding, exacting, fastidious, finicky, fussy, old-maidish, particular, picky — more at FINICKY ♦ [2] delicate, exact, fine, minute, refined, subtle — more at FINE ♦ [3a] agreeable, congenial, delectable, delicious, delightful, dreamy, felicitous, good, grateful, gratifying, palatable, pleasant, pleasurable, satisfying — more at PLEASANT ♦ [5] correct, decent, decorous, genteel, polite, proper, respectable, seemly — more at PROPER ♦ [6] affable, agreeable, amiable, genial, good-natured, gracious, sweet, well-disposed — more at AMIABLE

nice·ly *adv* ♦ : in a pleasing, satisfactory, courteous, or reasonable manner

♦ agreeably, favorably (*or* favourably), pleasantly, pleasingly, satisfyingly, well; courteously, kindly, thoughtfully, well — more at WELL

nice–nel·ly \'nīs-'ne-lē\ *adj, often cap 2d N* **1** : marked by euphemism **2** : PRUDISH — **nice nelly** *n, often cap 2d N* — **nice–nel·ly·ism** \-,i-zəm\ *n, often cap 2d N*

nice·ness *n* ♦ : the quality or state of being nice

♦ agreeableness, amenity, amiability, geniality, graciousness, pleasantness, sweetness — more at AMIABILITY

nice·ty \'nī-sə-tē\ *n, pl* **-ties** **1** : a dainty, delicate, or elegant thing ⟨enjoy the *niceties* of life⟩ **2** : a fine point or distinction ⟨*niceties* of workmanship⟩ **3** : EXACTNESS, PRECISION, ACCURACY

niche \'nich\ *n* [F] **1** ♦ : a recess in a wall esp. for a statue **2** : a place, employment, or activity for which a person or thing is best fitted **3** ♦ : the living space or role of an organism in an ecological community esp. with regard to food consumption

♦ [1] alcove, nook, recess; *also* corner, cranny, cubbyhole; cubicle; dent, indentation ♦ [3] habitat, home, range, territory — more at HOME

¹**nick** \'nik\ *n* **1** ♦ : a small notch, groove, or chip **2** : the final critical moment ⟨in the ∼ of time⟩

♦ chip, hack, indentation, notch — more at NOTCH

²**nick** *vb* : NOTCH, CHIP

nick·el \'ni-kəl\ *n* **1** : a hard silver-white metallic chemical element capable of a high polish and used in alloys **2** : the U.S. 5-cent piece made of copper and nickel; *also* : the Canadian 5-cent piece

nick·el·ode·on \,ni-kə-'lō-dē-ən\ *n* **1** : an early movie theater to which admission cost five cents **2** : JUKEBOX

nick·er \'ni-kər\ *vb* : to neigh gently : NEIGH, WHINNY — **nicker** *n*

nick·name \'nik-,nām\ *n* [ME *nekename* additional name, alter. (from misdivision of *an ekename*) of *ekename*, fr. *eke* also + *name*] **1** ♦ : a usu. descriptive name given instead of or in addition to the one belonging to a person, place, or thing **2** : a familiar form of a proper name — **nickname** *vb*

♦ alias, cognomen; *also* appellation, denomination, denotation, designation, handle, label, title; nom de plume, pen name, pseudonym

nic·o·tine \'ni-kə-,tēn\ *n* : a poisonous and addictive substance in tobacco that is used as an insecticide

nic·o·tin·ic acid \,ni-kə-'tē-nik-, -'ti-\ *n* : an organic acid of the vitamin B complex found in plants and animals and used against pellagra

niece \'nēs\ *n* : a daughter of one's brother, sister, brother-in-law, or sister-in-law

nif·ty \'nif-tē\ *adj* **nif·ti·er; -est** : very good : very attractive

Ni·ge·ri·an \nī-'jir-ē-ən\ *n* : a native or inhabitant of Nigeria — **Nigerian** *adj*

nig·gard \'ni-gərd\ *n* ♦ : a stingy person : MISER

♦ cheapskate, miser, skinflint, tightwad — more at MISER

nig·gard·ly *adj* **1** ♦ : grudgingly mean about spending or granting **2** ♦ : provided in meanly limited supply — **nig·gard·li·ness** \-lē-nəs\ *n* — **nig·gard·ly** *adv*

♦ [1] cheap, close, mean, parsimonious, penurious, spare, sparing, stingy, tight, tightfisted, uncharitable — more at STINGY ♦ [2] light, meager (or meagre), poor, scant, scanty, scarce, skimpy, slender, slim, spare, sparse, stingy — more at MEAGER

nig·gling \'ni-gə-liŋ\ adj 1 : PETTY ⟨∼ details⟩ 2 : bothersome in a petty way

¹nigh \'nī\ adv 1 ♦ : near in place, time, or relationship 2 ♦ : almost but not quite : NEARLY, ALMOST

♦ [1] around, by, close, hard, in, near, nearby — more at NEAR ♦ [2] about, almost, most, much, near, nearly, next to, practically, some, virtually, well-nigh — more at ALMOST

²nigh adj : being near in time, space, effect, or degree : CLOSE, NEAR

³nigh prep : NEAR

¹night \'nīt\ n 1 ♦ : the period between dusk and dawn 2 ♦ : the darkness of night 3 : a period of misery or unhappiness 4 : NIGHTFALL

♦ [1] dark, darkness, nighttime; also dusk, evening, gloaming, nightfall, twilight; midnight Ant day, daytime ♦ [2] dark, darkness, dusk, gloaming, gloom, murk, semidarkness, shade, shadows, twilight — more at DARK

²night adj ♦ : of, relating to, or associated with the night

♦ nighttime, nocturnal — more at NOCTURNAL

night blindness n : reduced visual capacity in faint light (as at night)

night·cap \'nīt-ˌkap\ n 1 : a cloth cap worn with nightclothes 2 : a usu. alcoholic drink taken at bedtime

night·clothes \-ˌklōthz, -ˌklōz\ n pl : garments worn in bed

night·club \-ˌkləb\ n ♦ : a place of entertainment open at night usu. serving food and liquor and providing music for dancing

♦ café, disco, discotheque; also barroom, saloon, tavern; dive, speakeasy; canteen

night crawl·er \-ˌkrȯ-lər\ n : EARTHWORM; esp : a large earthworm found on the soil surface at night

night·dress \'nīt-ˌdres\ n : a loose garment for wear in bed : NIGHTGOWN

night·fall \-ˌfȯl\ n ♦ : the coming of night

♦ dusk, evening, gloaming, sundown, sunset, twilight — more at DUSK

night·gown \-ˌgau̇n\ n : a loose garment for wear in bed

night·hawk \-ˌhȯk\ n : any of a genus of American birds related to and resembling the whip-poor-will

night·in·gale \'nīt-ᵊn-ˌgāl, 'nī-tiŋ-\ n [ME, fr. OE nihtegale, fr. niht night + galan to sing] : any of several Old World thrushes noted for the sweet usu. nocturnal song of the male

night·life \'nīt-ˌlīf\ n : the activity of pleasure-seekers at night

night·ly \'nīt-lē\ adj 1 : happening, done, or produced by night or every night 2 : of or relating to the night or every night — nightly adv

night·mare \'nīt-ˌmar\ n 1 : a frightening dream 2 ♦ : a frightening or horrible experience — nightmare adj

♦ agony, hell, horror, misery, murder, torment, torture — more at HELL

night·mar·ish adj ♦ : resembling or suggestive of a nightmare

♦ appalling, atrocious, awful, dreadful, frightful, ghastly, grisly, gruesome, hideous, horrible, horrid, lurid, macabre, monstrous, shocking, terrible — more at HORRIBLE

night rider n : a member of a secret band who ride masked at night doing violence to punish or terrorize

night·shade \'nīt-ˌshād\ n : any of a large genus of herbs, shrubs, and trees that includes poisonous forms (as the belladonna), ornamentals (as the petunias), and important food plants (as the potato and eggplant)

night·shirt \-ˌshərt\ n : a nightgown resembling a shirt

night soil n : human feces used esp. for fertilizing the soil

night·stick \'nīt-ˌstik\ n ♦ : a police officer's club

♦ bat, billy club, bludgeon, cudgel, truncheon — more at CLUB

night·time \-ˌtīm\ n ♦ : the time from dusk to dawn

♦ dark, darkness, night — more at NIGHT

night·walk·er \-ˌwȯ-kər\ n : a person who roves about at night esp. with criminal or immoral intent

ni·hil·ism \'nī-ə-ˌli-zəm, 'nē-hə-\ n 1 : a viewpoint that traditional values and beliefs are unfounded and that existence is senseless and useless 2 : ANARCHISM — **ni·hil·ist** \-list\ n or adj — **ni·hil·is·tic** \ˌnī-ə-'lis-tik, ˌnē-hə-\ adj

ni·ho·ni·um \ni-'hō-nē-əm\ n : a short-lived artificially produced radioactive chemical element

nil \'nil\ n ♦ : the arithmetical symbol 0 denoting the absence of all magnitude or quantity : ZERO, NOTHING

♦ aught, cipher, naught, nothing, zero, zip — more at ZERO

nim·ble \'nim-bəl\ adj **nim·bler; nim·blest** [ME nimel, fr. OE numol holding much, fr. niman to take] 1 ♦ : quick and light in motion : AGILE ⟨a ∼ dancer⟩ 2 ♦ : quick in understanding and learning : CLEVER ⟨a ∼ mind⟩ — **nim·bly** \-blē\ adv

♦ [1] agile, graceful, light, lissome, lithe, spry — more at GRACEFUL ♦ [2] alert, brainy, bright, brilliant, clever, intelligent, keen, quick, quick-witted, sharp, smart — more at INTELLIGENT

nim·ble·ness n ♦ : the quality or state of being nimble

♦ agility, deftness, dexterity, sleight — more at DEXTERITY

nim·bus \'nim-bəs\ n, pl **nim·bi** \-ˌbī, -bē\ or **nim·bus·es** 1 : a figure (as a disk) in an art work suggesting radiant light about the head of a divinity, saint, or sovereign 2 : a rain cloud; also : THUNDERHEAD

NIMBY \'nim-bē\ n [not in my backyard] : opposition to the placement of something undesirable (as a prison) in one's neighborhood

nim·rod \'nim-ˌräd\ n 1 : HUNTER 2 : IDIOT, JERK

nin·com·poop \'nin-kəm-ˌpüp\ n 1 : a person lacking in judgment or prudence : FOOL, SIMPLETON 2 : an unsophisticated person

nine \'nīn\ n 1 : one more than eight 2 : the 9th in a set or series 3 : something having nine units; esp : a baseball team — **nine** adj or pron — **ninth** \'nīnth\ adj or adv or n

nine days' wonder n : something that creates a short-lived sensation

nine·pins \'nīn-ˌpinz\ n : a bowling game using nine pins arranged usu. in a diamond-shaped configuration

nine·teen \'nīn-'tēn\ n : one more than 18 — **nineteen** adj or pron — **nine·teenth** \-'tēnth\ adj or n

nine·ty \'nīn-tē\ n, pl **nineties** : nine times 10 — **nine·ti·eth** \-tē-əth\ adj or n — **ninety** adj or pron

nin·ja \'nin-jə, -ˌ(ˌ)jä\ n, pl **ninja** or **ninjas** [Jp] : a person trained in ancient Japanese martial arts and employed esp. for espionage and assassinations

nin·ny \'ni-nē\ n, pl **ninnies** 1 : a person lacking in judgment or prudence : FOOL 2 : an unsophisticated person

ni·o·bi·um \nī-'ō-bē-əm\ n : a gray metallic chemical element used in alloys

¹nip \'nip\ vb **nipped; nip·ping** 1 : to catch hold of and squeeze tightly between two surfaces, edges, or points 2 : to sever by or as if by pinching sharply; also : to remove by cutting or pinching 3 : to destroy the growth, progress, or fulfillment of ⟨nipped in the bud⟩ 4 : to injure or make numb with cold : CHILL 5 : to take or appropriate without right or leave and with intent to keep or make use of wrongfully : STEAL

²nip n 1 : a sharp stinging cold 2 : a biting or pungent flavor 3 : PINCH, BITE 4 : a small portion : BIT

♦ bite, bitterness, bleakness, chill, rawness, sharpness — more at CHILL

³nip n : a small quantity of liquor : SIP

⁴nip vb **nipped; nip·ping** : to take liquor in nips : TIPPLE

nip and tuck adj or adv ♦ : so close that the lead shifts rapidly from one contestant to another

♦ close, narrow, neck and neck, tight — more at CLOSE

nip·per \'ni-pər\ *n* **1** : one that nips **2** *pl* : a gripping instrument with two handles and two jaws : PINCERS **3** ♦ : a young person esp. between infancy and youth : CHILD; *esp* : a small boy

♦ boy, child, lad, shaver, stripling, youth — more at BOY

nip·ple \'ni-pəl\ *n* : the protuberance of a mammary gland through which milk is drawn off : TEAT; *also* : something resembling a nipple

nip·py \'ni-pē\ *adj* **nip·pi·er; -est** **1** : having an intense flavor or odor : PUNGENT, SHARP **2** ♦ : noticeably cold : CHILLY **3** : brisk, quick, or nimble in movement

♦ bitter, chill, chilly, cold, cool, frosty, raw, sharp, snappy, wintry — more at COLD

nir·va·na \nir-'vä-nə\ *n, often cap* [Skt *nirvāṇa*, lit., act of extinguishing, fr. *nis-* out + *vāti* it blows] **1** : the final freeing of a soul from all that enslaves it; *esp* : the supreme happiness that according to Buddhism comes when all passion, hatred, and delusion die out and the soul is released from the necessity of further purification **2** : OBLIVION; *also* : PARADISE

ni·sei \nē-'sā, 'nē-,sā\ *n, pl* **nisei** *often cap* : a son or daughter of immigrant Japanese parents who is born and educated in America

ni·si \'nī-,sī\ *adj* [L, unless, fr. *ne-* not + *si* if] : taking effect at a specified time unless previously modified or voided ⟨a divorce decree ∼⟩

nit \'nit\ *n* **1** : the egg of a parasitic insect (as a louse); *also* : the young insect **2** : a minor shortcoming

nite *var of* NIGHT

ni·ter *or Can and Brit* **ni·tre** \'nī-tər\ *n* : POTASSIUM NITRATE

nit·pick·er *n* ♦ : one who engages in nitpicking

♦ carper, castigator, caviler, censurer, critic, faultfinder, railer, scold — more at CRITIC

nit–pick·ing \'nit-,pi-kiŋ\ *n* : minute and usu. unjustified criticism

¹ni·trate \'nī-,trāt, -trət\ *n* **1** : a salt or ester of nitric acid **2** : sodium nitrate or potassium nitrate used as a fertilizer

²ni·trate \-,trāt\ *vb* **ni·trat·ed; ni·trat·ing** : to treat or combine with nitric acid or a nitrate — **ni·tra·tion** \nī-'trā-shən\ *n*

ni·tre *Can and Brit var of* NITER

ni·tric acid \'nī-trik-\ *n* : a corrosive liquid acid used esp. in making dyes, explosives, and fertilizers

ni·tri·fi·ca·tion \,nī-trə-fə-'kā-shən\ *n* : the oxidation (as by bacteria) of ammonium salts to nitrites and then to nitrates — **ni·tri·fy·ing** \'nī-trə-fī-iŋ\ *adj*

ni·trite \'nī-,trīt\ *n* : a salt of nitrous acid

ni·tro \'nī-trō\ *n, pl* **nitros** : any of various nitrated products; *esp* : NITROGLYCERIN

ni·tro·gen \'nī-trə-jən\ *n* : a tasteless odorless gaseous chemical element constituting 78 percent of the atmosphere by volume — **ni·trog·e·nous** \nī-'trä-jə-nəs\ *adj*

nitrogen narcosis *n* : a state of euphoria and confusion caused by nitrogen forced into a diver's bloodstream from atmospheric air under pressure

ni·tro·glyc·er·in *or* **ni·tro·glyc·er·ine** \,nī-trə-'gli-sə-rən\ *n* : an oily explosive liquid used to make dynamite and in medicine to dilate blood vessels

ni·trous acid \'nī-trəs-\ *n* : an unstable nitrogen-containing acid known only in solution or in the form of its salts

nitrous oxide *n* : a colorless gas used esp. as an anesthetic in dentistry

nit·ty–grit·ty \'ni-tē-,gri-tē, ,ni-tē-'gri-tē\ *n* : what is essential and basic : specific practical details

nit·wit \'nit-,wit\ *n* ♦ : a scatterbrained or stupid person

♦ booby, fool, goose, half-wit, jackass, lunatic, nut, simpleton, turkey — more at FOOL blockhead, dope, dummy, idiot, imbecile, jackass, moron, numskull — more at IDIOT

¹nix \'niks\ *n* : NOTHING

²nix *vb* : VETO, REJECT

³nix *adv* : NO

NJ *abbr* New Jersey

NL *abbr* National League

NLRB *abbr* National Labor Relations Board

NM *abbr* **1** nautical mile **2** New Mexico

N Mex *abbr* New Mexico

NMI *abbr* no middle initial

NNE *abbr* north-northeast

NNW *abbr* north-northwest

¹no \'nō\ *adv* **1** — used to express the negative of an alternative ⟨shall we continue or ∼⟩ **2** ♦ : in no respect or degree ⟨he is ∼ better than the others⟩ **3** : not so ⟨∼, I'm not ready⟩ **4** — used with an adjective to imply a meaning opposite to the positive statement ⟨in ∼ uncertain terms⟩ **5** — used to introduce a more emphatic or explicit statement ⟨has the right, ∼, the duty to continue⟩ **6** ♦ — used as an interjection to express surprise or doubt ⟨∼—you don't say⟩ **7** — used in combination with a verb to form a compound adjective ⟨*no*-bake pie⟩

♦ [2] never, none, nothing, nowise — more at NEVER
♦ [6] indeed, well, why; *also* ha, hello, oh; fiddlesticks, pooh; there; gad, zounds

²no *adj* **1** : not any; *also* : hardly any **2** : not a ⟨she's ∼ expert⟩

³no \'nō\ *n, pl* **noes** *or* **nos** \'nōz\ **1** ♦ : an act or instance of refusing or denying by the use of the word no : REFUSAL, DENIAL **2** ♦ : a negative vote or decision; *also, pl* : persons voting in the negative

♦ blackball, denial, nay, negation, negative, refusal, veto *Ant* positive, yea, yes

⁴no *adj* **1** north; northern **2** [L *numero*, abl. of *numerus*] number

¹No *var of* NOH

²No *symbol* nobelium

No·bel·ist \nō-'be-list\ *n* : a winner of a Nobel prize

no·bel·i·um \nō-'be-lē-əm\ *n* : a radioactive metallic chemical element produced artificially

No·bel prize \nō-'bel-, 'nō-,bel-\ *n* : any of various annual prizes (as in peace, literature, or medicine) established by the will of Alfred Nobel for the encouragement of persons who work for the interests of humanity

no·bil·i·ty \nō-'bi-lə-tē\ *n* **1** ♦ : the quality or state of being noble in character, quality, or rank **2** : nobles considered as forming a class

♦ augustness, brilliance, glory, grandeur, grandness, magnificence, majesty, nobleness, resplendence, splendor, stateliness — more at MAGNIFICENCE

¹no·ble \'nō-bəl\ *adj* **no·bler; no·blest** [ME, fr. AF, fr. L *nobilis* well known, noble, fr. *noscere* to come to know] **1** ♦ : possessing outstanding qualities : ILLUSTRIOUS; *also* : FAMOUS, NOTABLE **2** ♦ : of high birth, rank, or station : ARISTOCRATIC **3** : possessing very high or excellent qualities or properties : EXCELLENT **4** ♦ : grand or impressive esp. in appearance : STATELY, IMPOSING ⟨a ∼ edifice⟩ **5** ♦ : of a superior nature esp. in character

♦ [1] distinguished, eminent, famous, illustrious, notable, noteworthy, outstanding, preeminent, prestigious, signal, star, superior — more at EMINENT ♦ [2] aristocratic, genteel, gentle, grand, highborn, patrician, wellborn; *also* high, lofty, superior; elevated, ennobled, exalted; gentlemanly, kingly, knightly, ladylike, lordly, princely, queenly, regal, royal; senior *Ant* baseborn, common, humble, ignoble, low, lowly, mean, plebeian ♦ [4] august, baronial, gallant, glorious, grand, grandiose, heroic, imposing, magnificent, majestic, monumental, proud, regal, royal, splendid, stately — more at GRAND ♦ [5] decent, ethical, honest, honorable, just, principled, respectable, righteous, upright, upstanding — more at HONORABLE ♦ [5] chivalrous, gallant, great, greathearted, high, high-minded, lofty, lordly, magnanimous, sublime; *also* ennobled, exalted, glorified; heroic, honorable, venerable, worthy; knightly, princely, regal; moving, inspiring, uplifting; august, magnificent, majestic *Ant* base, debased, degenerate, degraded, ignoble, low

²**no·ble** *n* ♦ : a person of noble rank or birth

♦ aristocrat, gentleman, grandee, patrician — more at GENTLEMAN

no·ble·man \'nō-bəl-mən\ *n* : a member of the nobility
no·ble·ness *n* ♦ : the quality or state of being noble

♦ augustness, brilliance, glory, grandeur, grandness, magnificence, majesty, nobility, resplendence, splendor, stateliness — more at MAGNIFICENCE

no·blesse oblige \nō-ˌbles-ə-'blēzh\ *n* [F, lit., nobility obligates] : the obligation of honorable, generous, and responsible behavior associated with high rank or birth
no·ble·wom·an \'nō-bəl-ˌwu̇-mən\ *n* ♦ : a woman of noble rank

♦ dame, gentlewoman, lady — more at GENTLEWOMAN

no·bly \-blē\ *adv* ♦ : with greatness of soul

♦ gallantly, grandly, greatly, heroically, honorably (*or* honourably), magnanimously — more at GREATLY

¹**no·body** \'nō-ˌbä-dē, -bə-\ *pron* : no person
²**nobody** *n, pl* **no·bod·ies** ♦ : a person of no influence or importance

♦ nonentity, nothing, whippersnapper, zero; *also* least; inferior, mediocrity, obscurity; figurehead, puppet *Ant* big shot, bigwig, eminence, figure, magnate, nabob, personage, somebody, VIP

no—brain·er \'nō-'brā-nər\ *n* : something that requires a minimum of thought
noc·tur·nal \näk-'tərn-ᵊl\ *adj* 1 ♦ : of, relating to, or occurring in the night 2 : active at night ⟨a ~ bird⟩

♦ night, nighttime; *also* late; midnight, overnight *Ant* daily, diurnal

noc·turne \'näk-ˌtərn\ *n* : a work of art dealing with night; *esp* : a dreamy pensive composition for the piano
noc·u·ous \'nä-kyə-wəs\ *adj* : HARMFUL — **noc·u·ous·ly** *adv*
nod \'näd\ *vb* **nod·ded; nod·ding** 1 : to bend the head downward or forward (as in bowing, going to sleep, or giving assent) 2 ♦ : to move up and down ⟨tulips *nodding* in the breeze⟩ 3 : to show by a nod of the head ⟨~ agreement⟩ 4 : to make a slip or error in a moment of abstraction — **nod** *n*

♦ bob, bobble, jog, jounce, pump, seesaw; *also* jerk, jiggle, shake, wiggle, wobble; oscillate, rock, sway, swing, undulate; drop, duck

nod·dle \'näd-ᵊl\ *n* : a person's head esp. as the seat of intellect : HEAD
nod·dy \'nä-dē\ *n, pl* **noddies** 1 : FOOL 2 : a stout-bodied tropical tern
node \'nōd\ *n* : a thickened, swollen, or differentiated area (as of tissue); *esp* : the part of a stem from which a leaf arises — **nod·al** \-ᵊl\ *adj*
nod·ule \'nä-jül\ *n* ♦ : a small lump or swelling — **nod·u·lar** \'nä-jə-lər\ *adj*

♦ bump, knot, lump, swelling — more at BUMP

no·el \nō-'el\ *n* [F *noël* Christmas, carol, fr. OF *Nael* (*Deu*), *Noel* Christmas, fr. L *natalis* birthday] 1 : a Christmas carol 2 *cap* : the Christmas season

♦ Christmastide, Christmastime, yuletide — more at YULETIDE

noes *pl of* NO
no—fault \'nō-'fȯlt\ *adj* 1 : of, relating to, or being a motor vehicle insurance plan under which someone involved in an accident is compensated usu. up to a stipulated limit for actual losses by that person's own insurance company regardless of who is responsible 2 : of, relating to, or being a divorce law under which neither party is held responsible for the breakup of the marriage
nog·gin \'nä-gən\ *n* 1 : a small mug or cup; *also* : a small quantity of drink 2 ♦ : a person's head

♦ head, pate, poll — more at HEAD

no—good \'nō-'gu̇d\ *adj* ♦ : having no worth, virtue, use, or chance of success — **no—good** \'nō-ˌgu̇d\ *n*

♦ chaffy, empty, junky, null, valueless, worthless — more at WORTHLESS

Noh *also* **No** \'nō\ *n, pl* **Noh** *also* **No** : classic Japanese dance-drama having a heroic theme, a chorus, and highly stylized action, costuming, and scenery
no—hit·ter \(ˌ)nō-'hi-tər\ *n* : a baseball game or part of a game in which a pitcher allows no base hits
no·how \'nō-ˌhau̇\ *adv* : in no manner
¹**noise** \'nȯiz\ *n* [ME, fr. AF, disturbance, noise, fr. L *nausea* nausea] 1 ♦ : loud, confused, or senseless shouting or outcry 2 ♦ : sound or a sound that lacks agreeable musical quality or is noticeably loud, harsh, or discordant 3 : unwanted electronic signal or disturbance — **noise·less·ly** *adv*

♦ [1] clamor (*or* clamour), howl, hubbub, hue and cry, hullabaloo, outcry, roar, tumult, uproar — more at CLAMOR ♦ [2] bluster, cacophony, clamor, din, racket, roar; *also* discord, dissonance; commotion, furor, hubbub, hullabaloo, hurly-burly, rumpus, tumult, uproar; babel; clatter, jangle; bang, blast, boom, clap, crack, crash *Ant* quiet, silence, still, stillness

²**noise** *vb* **noised; nois·ing** ♦ : to spread by rumor or report ⟨the story was *noised* about⟩

♦ *usu* **noise about** circulate, rumor, whisper — more at RUMOR

noise·less *adj* ♦ : making or causing no noise or stir : free from noise

♦ hushed, muted, quiet, silent, soundless, still — more at SILENT

noise·mak·er \'nȯiz-ˌmā-kər\ *n* : one that makes noise; *esp* : a device used to make noise at parties
noise pollution *n* : annoying or harmful noise in an environment
noi·some \'nȯi-səm\ *adj* 1 ♦ : physically harmful or destructive to living beings : UNWHOLESOME 2 ♦ : offensive to the senses (as smell); *also* : highly objectionable

♦ [1] noxious, unhealthy, unwholesome — more at UNHEALTHY ♦ [2] fetid, foul, fusty, malodorous, musty, rank, reeky, smelly, strong — more at MALODOROUS

noisy \'nȯi-zē\ *adj* **nois·i·er; -est** 1 : making loud noises 2 ♦ : full of noises : LOUD — **nois·i·ly** \-zə-lē\ *adv* — **nois·i·ness** \-zē-nəs\ *n*

♦ boisterous, clamorous, loud, raucous, resounding, uproarious; *also* resonant, sonorous; buzzing, humming; blustery, roaring, roistering, romping, rowdy; tumultuous, woolly; obstreperous, vociferous *Ant* hushed, noiseless, quiet, silent, soundless, stilled

nol·le pro·se·qui \ˌnä-lē-'prä-sə-ˌkwī\ *n* [L, to be unwilling to pursue] : an entry on the record of a legal action that the prosecutor or plaintiff will proceed no further in an action or suit or in some aspect of it
no·lo con·ten·de·re \ˌnō-lō-kən-'ten-də-rē\ *n* [L, I do not wish to contend] : a plea in a criminal prosecution that subjects the defendant to conviction but does not admit guilt or preclude denying the charges in another proceeding
nol—pros \'näl-'präs\ *vb* **nol—prossed; nol—pros·sing** : to discontinue by entering a nolle prosequi
nom *abbr* nominative
¹**no·mad** \'nō-ˌmad\ *n* 1 : a member of a people who have no fixed residence but move from place to place 2 ♦ : an individual who roams about aimlessly

♦ drifter, rambler, rover, vagabond, wanderer; *also* laggard, straggler; lingerer, loiterer, sojourner; bum, hobo, tramp; sightseer, traveler; transient, vagrant; gadabout, stroller

²**nomad** *adj* ♦ : traversing a random course

♦ errant, itinerant, peripatetic, roaming, vagabond, vagrant — more at ITINERANT

no·mad·ic \nō-'ma-dik\ *adj* : NOMAD
no—man's—land \'nō-ˌmanz-ˌland\ *n* 1 : an area of unowned, unclaimed, or uninhabited land 2 : an unoccupied area between opposing troops

nom de guerre \ˌnäm-di-ˈger\ *n, pl* **noms de guerre** *same or* ˌnämz-\ [F, lit., war name] : PSEUDONYM

nom de plume \-ˈplüm\ *n, pl* **noms de plume** *same or* ˌnämz-\ [F, pen name; prob. coined in E] : PEN NAME

no·men·cla·ture \ˈnō-mən-ˌklā-chər\ *n* **1** : NAME, DESIGNATION **2** : a system of terms used in a science or art

nom·i·nal \ˈnä-mən-ᵊl\ *adj* **1** ♦ : being something in name or form only ⟨~ head of a party⟩ **2** ♦ : lacking in significance or solid worth : TRIFLING ⟨a ~ price⟩ — **nom·i·nal·ly** *adv*

♦ [1] formal, paper, titular; *also* so-called; phantom, virtual ♦ [2] inconsequential, inconsiderable, insignificant, measly, minute, negligible, paltry, petty, slight, trifling, trivial — more at NEGLIGIBLE

nom·i·nate \ˈnä-mə-ˌnāt\ *vb* **-nat·ed; -nat·ing** : to choose as a candidate for election, appointment, or honor — **nom·i·na·tion** \ˌnä-mə-ˈnā-shən\ *n*

nom·i·na·tive \ˈnä-mə-nə-tiv\ *adj* : of, relating to, or constituting a grammatical case marking typically the subject of a verb — **nominative** *n*

nom·i·nee \ˌnä-mə-ˈnē\ *n* : a person nominated for an office, duty, or position

non- \(ˈ)nän *or* ˌnän *before stressed syllables*; ˌnän *elsewhere*\ *prefix* **1** : not : reverse of : absence of **2** : having no importance

non·age \ˈnä-nij, ˈnō-\ *n* **1** : legal minority **2** : a period of youth **3** : IMMATURITY

no·na·ge·nar·i·an \ˌnō-nə-jə-ˈner-ē-ən, ˌnä-\ *n* : a person whose age is in the nineties

non·aligned \ˌnän-ə-ˈlīnd\ *adj* : not allied with other nations

no–name \ˈnō-ˌnām\ *adj* : not having a readily recognizable name ⟨~ brands⟩

non·book \ˈnän-ˌbuk\ *n* : a book of little literary merit that is often a compilation (as of pictures or speeches)

¹nonce \ˈnäns\ *n* : the one, particular, or present occasion or purpose ⟨for the ~⟩

²nonce *adj* : occurring, used, or made only once or for a special occasion ⟨a ~ word⟩

non·cha·lance \ˌnän-shə-ˈläns\ *n* ♦ : the quality or state of being nonchalant

♦ disinterestedness, disregard, indifference, insouciance — more at INDIFFERENCE; *also* apathy

non·cha·lant \ˌnän-shə-ˈlänt\ *adj* [F, fr. OF, fr. prp. of *nonchaloir* to disregard, fr. *non-* not + *chaloir* to concern, fr. L *calēre* to be warm] ♦ : giving an effect of unconcern or indifference — **non·cha·lant·ly** *adv*

♦ casual, disinterested, indifferent, insouciant, unconcerned; *also* apathetic, incurious, perfunctory, uncurious, uninterested

non·com \ˈnän-ˌkäm\ *n* : NONCOMMISSIONED OFFICER

non·com·ba·tant \ˌnän-kəm-ˈbat-ᵊnt, nän-ˈkäm-bə-tənt\ *n* : a member (as a chaplain) of the armed forces whose duties do not include fighting; *also* : CIVILIAN — **noncombatant** *adj*

non·com·bus·ti·ble \ˌnän-kəm-ˈbəs-tə-bəl\ *adj* ♦ : not combustible : incapable of catching fire and burning when subjected to fire

♦ fireproof, nonflammable, noninflammable

non·com·mis·sioned officer \ˌnän-kə-ˈmi-shənd-\ *n* : a subordinate officer in the armed forces appointed from enlisted personnel

non·com·mit·tal \ˌnän-kə-ˈmit-ᵊl\ *adj* : indicating neither consent nor dissent

non com·pos men·tis \ˌnän-ˌkäm-pəs-ˈmen-təs\ *adj* : not of sound mind

non·con·duc·tor \ˌnän-kən-ˈdək-tər\ *n* : a substance that is a very poor conductor of heat, electricity, or sound

non·con·form·ing \ˌnän-kən-ˈfȯr-miŋ\ *adj* ♦ : not conforming : declining conformity

♦ dissident, heretical, heterodox, nonconformist, nonorthodox, unconventional, unorthodox — more at HERETICAL

non·con·form·ist \-kən-ˈfȯr-mist\ *n* **1** *often cap* : a person who does not conform to an established church and esp. the Church of England **2** ♦ : a person who does not conform to a generally accepted pattern of thought or action — **nonconformist** *adj*

♦ dissenter, dissident, heretic — more at HERETIC bohemian, deviant, individualist, loner, maverick; *also* character, codger, crackpot, crank, eccentric, freak, kook, nut, oddball, screwball, weirdo; misfit, outsider; anomaly

non·con·for·mi·ty \-ˈfȯr-mə-tē\ *n* ♦ : refusal to conform to an established or conventional creed, rule, or practice

♦ dissent, heresy, heterodoxy — more at HERESY

non·co·op·er·a·tion \ˌnän-kō-ˌä-pə-ˈrā-shən\ *n* : failure or refusal to cooperate; *esp* : refusal through civil disobedience of a people to cooperate with the government of a country

non·cred·it \(ˌ)nän-ˈkre-dət\ *adj* : not offering credit toward a degree

non·cus·to·di·al \ˌnän-kə-ˈstō-dē-əl\ *adj* : of or being a parent who does not have legal custody of a child

non·dairy \ˈnän-ˌder-ē\ *adj* : containing no milk or milk products ⟨~ whipped topping⟩

non·de·script \ˌnän-di-ˈskript\ *adj* **1** : not belonging to any particular class or kind **2** : lacking distinctive qualities

non·drink·er \-ˈdriŋ-kər\ *n* : a person who abstains from alcohol

¹none \ˈnən\ *pron* **1** : not any ⟨~ of them went⟩ **2** : not one ⟨~ of the family⟩ **3 a** : not any such thing ⟨half a loaf is better than ~⟩ **b** : not any such person

²none *adj, archaic* : not any : NO

³none *adv* **1** : by no means : not at all ⟨he got there ~

List of self-explanatory words with the prefix *non-*

nonabrasive	nonattendance	noncompetitive	nondelivery
nonabsorbent	nonbeliever	noncompliance	nondemocratic
nonacademic	nonbelligerent	noncomplying	nondenominational
nonacceptance	nonbiodegradable	nonconducting	nondepartmental
nonaccredited	nonbreakable	nonconfidence	nondestructive
nonacid	noncaloric	nonconflicting	nondevelopment
nonactivated	noncancerous	nonconformance	nondiscrimination
nonadaptive	noncandidate	nonconsensual	nondiscriminatory
nonaddictive	noncellular	nonconstructive	nondistinctive
nonadhesive	noncitizen	noncontagious	nondurable
nonadjacent	nonclerical	noncontinuous	noneconomic
nonadjustable	noncoital	noncorroding	noneducational
nonaggression	noncombat	noncorrosive	nonelastic
nonalcoholic	noncombative	noncriminal	nonelection
nonappearance	noncommercial	noncritical	nonelectric
nonaromatic	noncommunist	noncrystalline	nonelectrical
nonathletic	noncompeting	nondeductible	nonemotional

too soon⟩ **2 ♦** : in no way : to no extent ⟨∼ the worse for wear⟩

♦ hardly, no, scarcely — more at HARDLY never, no, nothing, nowise — more at NEVER

non·elec·tive \nän-i-'lek-tiv\ *adj* ♦ : not permitting a choice

♦ compulsory, imperative, incumbent, involuntary, mandatory, necessary, obligatory, peremptory — more at MANDATORY

non·en·ti·ty \nän-'en-tə-tē\ *n* **1** : something that does not exist or exists only in the imagination **2 ♦** : one of no consequence or significance

♦ nobody, nothing, shrimp, whippersnapper, zero — more at NOBODY

nones \'nōnz\ *n sing or pl* : the 7th day of March, May, July, or October or the 5th day of any other month in the ancient Roman calendar

non·es·sen·tial \nän-i-'sen-shəl\ *adj* **1** : not essential **2** : being a substance synthesized by the body in sufficient quantity to satisfy dietary needs

none·such \'nən-,səch\ *n* : one without an equal — **none·such** *adj*

none·the·less \nən-thə-'les\ *adv* ♦ : in spite of that : NEVERTHELESS

♦ but, howbeit, however, nevertheless, notwithstanding, still, though, withal, yet — more at HOWEVER

non·event \'nän-i-,vent\ *n* **1** : an event that fails to take place or to satisfy expectations **2** : a highly promoted event of little intrinsic interest

non·ex·is·tent \nän-ig-'zis-tənt\ *adj* ♦ : not having existence

♦ absent, missing, wanting — more at ABSENT

non·fat \-'fat\ *adj* : lacking fat solids : having fat solids removed ⟨∼ milk⟩

non·fic·tion·al \-'fik-shə-nəl\ *adj* ♦ : not fictional

♦ documentary, factual, hard, historical, literal, matter-of-fact, objective, true — more at FACTUAL

non·fig·u·ra·tive \'nän-'fi-gyə-rə-tiv, -'fi-gə-\ *adj* ♦ : representing or intended to represent no natural or actual object, figure, or scene

♦ abstract, metaphysical, theoretical — more at ABSTRACT

non·flam·ma·ble \-'fla-mə-bəl\ *adj* ♦ : not flammable

♦ fireproof, noncombustible, noninflammable

non·func·tion·al \-'fəŋk-shə-nəl\ *adj* ♦ : not performing or able to perform its regular function

♦ inoperable, inoperative — more at INOPERABLE

non·gono·coc·cal \nän-,gä-nə-'kä-kəl\ *adj* : not caused by a gonococcus

non·he·ro \'nän-'hē-rō\ *n* : ANTIHERO

non–Hodg·kin's lymphoma \'nän-'häj-kənz-\ *n* : any of numerous malignant lymphomas not classified as Hodgkin's disease

non·in·flam·ma·ble \nän-in-'fla-mə-bəl\ *adj* ♦ : incapable of being easily ignited and of burning very quickly

♦ fireproof, noncombustible, nonflammable

non·in·ter·ven·tion \nän-,in-tər-'ven-chən\ *n* : refusal or failure to intervene (as in the affairs of other countries)

non·is·sue \'nän-'i-shü\ *n* : an issue of little importance or concern

non·lit·er·ary \nän-'li-tə-,rer-ē\ *adj* ♦ : colloquial and informal as opposed to literary and formal

♦ colloquial, conversational, informal, vernacular, vulgar — more at COLLOQUIAL

non·ma·te·ri·al \nän-mə-'tir-ē-əl\ *adj* ♦ : not consisting of matter

♦ bodiless, immaterial, incorporeal, insubstantial, nonphysical, spiritual, unsubstantial — more at IMMATERIAL

non·met·al \'nän-'met-ᵊl\ *n* : a chemical element (as carbon) that lacks the characteristics of a metal — **non·me·tal·lic** \nän-mə-'ta-lik\ *adj*

non·mo·tile \nän-'mō-,tī(-əl\ *adj* ♦ : not exhibiting or capable of movement

♦ immobile, immovable, unbudging, unmovable — more at IMMOVABLE

non·neg·a·tive \-'ne-gə-tiv\ *adj* : not negative : being either positive or zero

non·nu·cle·ar \'nän-'nü-klē-ər\ *adj* **1** : not nuclear **2** : not having, using, or involving nuclear weapons

non·ob·jec·tive \nän-əb-'jek-tiv\ *adj* **1** : not objective **2** : representing no natural or actual object, figure, or scene ⟨∼ art⟩

non·or·tho·dox \nän-'òr-thə-,däks\ *adj* **1 ♦** : not conforming to established doctrine esp. in religion **2 ♦** : not according with, sanctioned by, or based on convention

♦ [1] dissident, heretical, heterodox, nonconforming, nonconformist, unconventional, unorthodox — more at HERETICAL ♦ [2] broad-minded, liberal, nontraditional, open-minded, progressive, radical, unconventional, unorthodox — more at LIBERAL

¹**non·pa·reil** \nän-pə-'rel\ *adj* ♦ : having no equal : PEERLESS

♦ incomparable, inimitable, matchless, only, peerless, unequaled, unmatched, unparalleled, unrivaled, unsurpassed — more at ONLY

²**nonpareil** *n* **1 ♦** : an individual of unequaled excellence : PARAGON **2** : a small flat disk of chocolate covered with white sugar pellets

♦ beau ideal, classic, exemplar, ideal, model, paragon — more at IDEAL

non·par·ti·san \'nän-'pär-tə-zən\ *adj* ♦ : not partisan; *esp* : not influenced by political party spirit or interests

---

List of self-explanatory words with the prefix *non-* (continued)

nonenforcement	nonfreezing	nonintoxicating	nonmoving
nonethical	nonfulfillment	noninvasive	nonnegotiable
non–euclidean	nonglare	nonionizing	nonobservance
nonexclusive	nongraded	nonirritating	nonoccurrence
nonexempt	nonhazardous	nonlegal	nonofficial
nonexistence	nonhereditary	nonlethal	nonoily
nonexplosive	nonhomogeneous	nonlife	nonparallel
nonfarm	nonhomologous	nonlinear	nonparasitic
nonfatal	nonhuman	nonliving	nonparticipant
nonfattening	nonidentical	nonlogical	nonparticipating
nonfederated	nonimportation	nonmagnetic	nonpathogenic
nonferrous	nonindustrial	nonmalignant	nonpaying
nonfiction	noninfectious	nonmember	nonpayment
nonfilamentous	nonintellectual	nonmembership	nonperformance
nonflowering	nonintercourse	nonmigratory	nonperishable
nonfood	noninterference	nonmilitary	nonpoisonous
	nonintoxicant	nonmoral	nonpolar

◆ disinterested, dispassionate, equal, equitable, fair, impartial, just, objective, square, unbiased, unprejudiced — more at FAIR

non·per·son \-'pərs-ᵊn\ *n* **1** : UNPERSON **2** : a person having no social or legal status

non·phys·i·cal \'nän-'fi-zi-kəl\ *adj* ◆ : not physical : incapable of being touched or perceived by touch

◆ bodiless, immaterial, incorporeal, insubstantial, nonmaterial, spiritual, unsubstantial — more at IMMATERIAL

non·plus \'nän-'pləs\ *vb* **-plussed** *also* **-plused** \-'pləst\; **-plus·sing** *also* **-plus·ing** : to cause to be at a loss as to what to say, think, or do : PUZZLE, PERPLEX

non·pre·scrip·tion \₁nän-pri-'skrip-shən\ *adj* : available for sale legally without a doctor's prescription

non·pro·fes·sion·al \'nän-prə-'fe-shə-nəl\ *adj* ◆ : not characterized by or conforming to the technical or ethical standards of a profession; *also* : not having the training or experience of a professional

◆ amateur, amateurish, inexperienced, inexpert, unprofessional, unskilled, unskillful — more at AMATEURISH

non·prof·it \'nän-'prä-fət\ *adj* : not conducted or maintained for the purpose of making a profit ⟨a ∼ organization⟩

non·pro·lif·er·a·tion \₁nän-prə-₁li-fə-'rä-shən\ *adj* : providing for the stoppage of proliferation (as of nuclear arms) ⟨a ∼ treaty⟩

non·read·er \'nän-'rē-dər\ *n* : one who does not read or has difficulty reading

non·re·li·gious \₁nän-ri-'li-jəs\ *adj* **1** ◆ : not religious : not having a religious character **2** : having no religion

◆ profane, secular, temporal — more at PROFANE

non·rep·re·sen·ta·tion·al \₁nän-₁re-pri-₁zen-'tä-shə-nəl\ *adj* : NONOBJECTIVE 2

non·res·i·dent \'nän-'re-zə-dənt\ *adj* : not living in a particular place — **non·res·i·dence** \-dəns\ *n* — **nonresident** *n*

non·re·sis·tance \₁nän-ri-'zis-təns\ *n* : the principles or practice of passive submission to authority even when unjust or oppressive

non·re·stric·tive \-ri-'strik-tiv\ *adj* **1** : not serving or tending to restrict **2** : not limiting the reference of the word or phrase modified ⟨a ∼ clause⟩

non·rig·id \nän-'ri-jəd\ *adj* : maintaining form by pressure of contained gas ⟨a ∼ airship⟩

non·sched·uled \'nän-'ske-jüld\ *adj* : licensed to carry passengers or freight by air without a regular schedule

non·sense \'nän-₁sens, -səns\ *n* **1** ◆ : foolish or meaningless words or actions **2** : things of no importance or value

◆ bunk, claptrap, drivel, fiddlesticks, folly, foolishness, fudge, hogwash, humbug, piffle, rot, silliness, slush, stupidity, trash; *also* absurdity, asininity, fatuity, foolery, idiocy, imbecility, inanity, insanity, lunacy; craziness, foolishness, madness, witlessness; monkeyshines, shenanigans, tomfoolery; gas, hot air, jazz, moonshine, rigmarole, twaddle; double-talk

non·sen·si·cal \nän-'sen-si-kəl\ *adj* ◆ : being nonsense or full of nonsense — **non·sen·si·cal·ly** \-k(ə-)lē\ *adv*

◆ absurd, crazy, cuckoo, fatuous, foolish, mad, nutty, senseless, silly, stupid — more at FOOLISH

non se·qui·tur \nän-'se-kwə-tər\ *n* [L, it does not follow] : an inference that does not follow from the premises

non·skid \'nän-'skid\ *adj* : designed to prevent skidding

non·slip \-'slip\ *adj* : designed to prevent slipping

non·spe·cif·ic \-spi-'si-fik\ *adj* ◆ : not specific

◆ all-around, bird's-eye, broad, general, overall — more at GENERAL

non·stan·dard \₁nän-'stan-dərd\ *adj* **1** : not standard **2** : not conforming to the usage characteristic of educated native speakers of a language

non·start·er \'nän-'stär-tər\ *n* **1** : one that does not start **2** : one that is not productive or effective

non·stick \-'stik\ *adj* : allowing easy removal of cooked food particles

non·stop \-'stäp\ *adj* : done or made without a stop ⟨∼ action⟩ — **nonstop** *adv*

non·suc·cess \-sək-'ses\ *n* ◆ : the failure to attain wealth, favor, or eminence

◆ collapse, crash, cropper, defeat, failure, fizzle — more at FAILURE

non·sup·port \₁nän-sə-'pōrt\ *n* : failure to support; *esp* : failure on the part of one under obligation to provide maintenance

non·threat·en·ing \-'thret-niŋ, -'thre-tᵊn-iŋ\ *adj* : not likely to cause danger or anxiety ⟨a ∼ illness⟩ ⟨a ∼ environment⟩

non·tra·di·tion·al \-trə-'di-shə-nəl\ *adj* ◆ : not traditional : not conforming to tradition

◆ broad-minded, liberal, nonorthodox, open-minded, progressive, radical, unconventional, unorthodox — more at LIBERAL

non-U \'nän-'yü\ *adj* : not characteristic of the upper classes

non·union \-'yü-nyən\ *adj* **1** : not belonging to a trade union ⟨∼ carpenters⟩ **2** : not recognizing or favoring trade unions or their members ⟨∼ employers⟩

non·us·er \-'yü-zər\ *n* : one who does not make use of something (as drugs)

non·vi·o·lence \'nän-'vī-ə-ləns\ *n* **1** : abstention from violence as a matter of principle **2** : avoidance of violence **3** : nonviolent political demonstrations — **non·vi·o·lent** \-lənt\ *adj*

non·white \₁nän-'hwīt, -'wīt\ *n* : a person whose features and esp. skin color are different from those of peoples of northwestern Europe — **nonwhite** *adj*

non·wo·ven \₁nän-'wō-vən\ *adj* : made of fibers held together by interlocking or bonding (as by chemical or thermal means) — **nonwoven** *n*

noo·dle \'nüd-ᵊl\ *n* [G *Nudel*] : a food paste made usu. with egg and shaped typically in ribbon form

---

List of self-explanatory words with the prefix *non-* (continued)

nonpolitical	nonrestricted	nonsinkable	nontransferable
nonporous	nonreturnable	nonsmoker	nontypical
nonpregnant	nonreusable	nonsmoking	nonuniform
nonproductive	nonreversible	nonsocial	nonvascular
nonprotein	nonruminant	nonspeaking	nonvenomous
nonradioactive	nonsalable	nonspecialist	nonverbal
nonrandom	nonscientific	nonsteroidal	nonveteran
nonrated	nonscientist	nonstudent	nonviable
nonreactive	nonseasonal	nonsurgical	nonvisual
nonreciprocal	nonsectarian	nontaxable	nonvocal
nonrecognition	nonsegregated	nonteaching	nonvolatile
nonrecurrent	nonselective	nontechnical	nonvoter
nonrecurring	non-self-governing	nontemporal	nonvoting
nonrefillable	nonsexist	nontenured	nonworker
nonrenewable	nonsexual	nontheistic	nonworking
nonresidential	nonshrinkable	nontoxic	nonzero

nook \'nuk\ *n* **1** : an interior angle or corner formed usu. by two walls ⟨a chimney ∼⟩ **2** : a sheltered or hidden place ⟨searched every ∼ and cranny⟩ **3** ♦ : a small often recessed section of a larger room ⟨a breakfast ∼⟩

♦ alcove, niche, recess — more at NICHE

noon \'nün\ *n* ♦ : the middle of the day : 12 o'clock in the daytime — **noon** *adj*

♦ midday, noontime

noon·day \'nün-,dā\ *n* : the middle of the day : NOON, MID-DAY

no one *pron* : no person : NOBODY

noon·tide \'nün-,tīd\ *n* : the middle of the day : NOON

noon·time \-,tīm\ *n* ♦ : the middle of the day : NOON

♦ midday, noon

noose \'nüs\ *n* : a loop with a slipknot that binds closer the more it is drawn

nope \'nōp\ *adv* : NO

nor \'nor\ *conj* : and not ⟨not for you ∼ for me⟩ — used esp. to introduce and negate the second member and each later member of a series of items preceded by *neither* ⟨neither here ∼ there⟩

Nor·dic \'nor-dik\ *adj* **1** : of or relating to the Germanic peoples of northern Europe and esp. of Scandinavia **2** : of or relating to competitive ski events involving cross-country racing, ski jumping, or biathlon — **Nordic** *n*

nor·epi·neph·rine \,nor-,e-pə-'ne-frən\ *n* : a nitrogen-containing neurotransmitter in parts of the sympathetic and central nervous systems

norm \'norm\ *n* [L *norma*, lit., carpenter's square] **1** ♦ : an authoritative standard or model; *esp* : a set standard of development or achievement usu. derived from the average or median achievement of a large group **2** : a typical or widespread practice, procedure, or custom

♦ average, normal, par, standard — more at AVERAGE

¹nor·mal \'nor-məl\ *adj* **1** ♦ : conforming to a type, standard, or regular pattern : STANDARD **2 a** : of average intelligence **b** ♦ : sound in mind and body

♦ [1] average, common, commonplace, everyday, ordinary, prosaic, regular, routine, run-of-the-mill, standard, typical, unexceptional, unremarkable, usual, workaday — more at ORDINARY ♦ [2b] balanced, clearheaded, lucid, right, sane, stable — more at SANE

²normal *n* **1** : one that is normal **2** : the usual condition, level, or quantity — **nor·mal·cy** \-sē\ *n* — **nor·mal·i·ty** \nor-'ma-lə-tē\ *n*

nor·mal·ise *chiefly Brit var of* NORMALIZE

nor·mal·ize \'nor-mə-,līz\ *vb* **-ized; -iz·ing** ♦ : to make or restore to normal — **nor·mal·i·za·tion** \,nor-mə-lə-'zā-shən\ *n*

♦ formalize, homogenize, regularize, standardize — more at STANDARDIZE

nor·mal·ly *adv* ♦ : as a general thing : often in the usual course of events

♦ commonly, generally, naturally, ordinarily, typically, usually — more at NATURALLY

Nor·man \'nor-mən\ *n* **1** : a native or inhabitant of Normandy **2** : one of the 10th century Scandinavian conquerors of Normandy **3** : one of the Norman-French conquerors of England in 1066 — **Norman** *adj*

nor·ma·tive \'nor-mə-tiv\ *adj* : of, relating to, or determining norms — **nor·ma·tive·ly** *adv* — **nor·ma·tive·ness** *n*

Norse \'nors\ *n, pl* **Norse 1** : NORWEGIAN; *also* : any of the western Scandinavian dialects or languages **2** *pl* : SCANDINAVIANS; *also* : NORWEGIANS

Norse·man \-mən\ *n* : any of the ancient Scandinavians

¹north \'north\ *adv* : to, toward, or in the north

²north *adj* **1** : situated toward or at the north **2** : coming from the north

³north *n* **1** : the direction to the left of one facing east **2** : the compass point directly opposite to south **3** *cap* : regions or countries north of a specified or implied

point — **north·er·ly** \'nor-thər-lē\ *adv or adj* — **north·ern** \-thərn\ *adj* — **North·ern·er** \-thər-nər\ *n* — **north·ern·most** \-thərn-,mōst\ *adj* — **north·ward** \'north-wərd\ *adv or adj* — **north·wards** \-wərdz\ *adv*

north·east \nor-'thēst\ *n* **1** : the general direction between north and east **2** : the compass point midway between north and east **3** *cap* : regions or countries northeast of a specified or implied point — **northeast** *adj or adv* — **north·east·er·ly** \-'thē-stər-lē\ *adv or adj* — **north·east·ern** \-stərn\ *adj*

north·east·er \-'thēs-tər\ *n* **1** : a strong northeast wind **2** : a storm with northeast winds

north·er \'nor-thər\ *n* **1** : a strong north wind **2** : a storm with north winds

northern lights *n pl* : AURORA BOREALIS

north pole *n, often cap N&P* : the northernmost point of the earth

North Star *n* : the star toward which the northern end of the earth's axis points

north·west \north-'west\ *n* **1** : the general direction between north and west **2** : the compass point midway between north and west **3** *cap* : regions or countries northwest of a specified or implied point — **northwest** *adj or adv* — **north·west·er·ly** \-'we-stər-lē\ *adv or adj* — **north·west·ern** \-'we-stərn\ *adj*

Norw *abbr* Norway; Norwegian

Nor·we·gian \nor-'wē-jən\ *n* **1** : a native or inhabitant of Norway **2** : the language of Norway — **Norwegian** *adj*

nos *abbr* numbers

¹nose \'nōz\ *n* **1** : the part of the face or head containing the nostrils and covering the front of the nasal cavity **2** : the sense of smell **3** : something (as a point, edge, or projecting front part) that resembles a nose ⟨the ∼ of a plane⟩ — **nosed** \'nōzd\ *adj*

²nose *vb* **nosed; nos·ing 1** ♦ : to detect by or as if by smell : SCENT **2** : to push or move with the nose **3** : to touch or rub with the nose : NUZZLE **4** ♦ : to search impertinently : PRY **5** : to move ahead slowly ⟨the ship *nosed* into her berth⟩

♦ [1] scent, smell, whiff — more at SMELL ♦ [4] butt in, interfere, intrude, meddle, mess, obtrude, poke, pry, snoop — more at INTERFERE

nose·bleed \'nōz-,blēd\ *n* : a bleeding from the nose

nose cone *n* : a protective cone constituting the forward end of an aerospace vehicle

nose·dive \'nōz-,dīv\ *n* **1** : a downward nose-first plunge (as of an airplane) **2** : a sudden extreme drop (as in prices)

nose·gay \'nōz-,gā\ *n* : a small bunch of flowers : POSY

nose out *vb* **1** : to discover often by prying **2** : to defeat by a narrow margin

nose·piece \-,pēs\ *n* **1** : a fitting at the lower end of a microscope tube to which the objectives are attached **2** : the bridge of a pair of eyeglasses

no–show \'nō-'shō\ *n* : a person who does not show up for an event as expected

nos·tal·gia \nä-'stal-jə\ *n* [NL, fr. Gk *nostos* return home + *algos* pain, grief] **1** : HOMESICKNESS **2** : a wistful yearning for something past or irrecoverable — **nos·tal·gic** \-jik\ *adj*

nos·tril \'näs-trəl\ *n* [ME *nosethirl*, fr. OE *nosthyrl*, fr. *nosu* nose + *thyrel* hole] **1** : either of the nares usu. with the adjoining nasal wall and passage **2** : either fleshy lateral wall of the nose

nos·trum \'näs-trəm\ *n* [L, neut. of *noster* our, ours, fr. *nos* we] : a questionable medicine or remedy

nosy *or* **nos·ey** \'nō-zē\ *adj* **nos·i·er; -est** ♦ : of prying or inquisitive disposition or quality : PRYING ⟨∼ neighbors⟩

♦ inquisitive, intrusive, meddlesome, obtrusive, officious, presumptuous, prying — more at INTRUSIVE

not \'nät\ *adv* **1** — used to make negative a group of words or a word ⟨the boys are ∼ here⟩ **2** — used to stand for the negative of a preceding group of words ⟨sometimes hard to see and sometimes ∼⟩

no·ta be·ne \ˌnō-tə-ˈbē-nē, -ˈbe-\ [L, mark well] — used to call attention to something important

no·ta·bil·i·ty \ˌnō-tə-ˈbi-lə-tē\ *n, pl* **-ties** **1** : the quality or state of being notable **2** : NOTABLE

¹no·ta·ble \ˈnō-tə-bəl\ *adj* **1** : NOTEWORTHY, REMARKABLE ⟨a ∼ achievement⟩ **2 ♦** : marked by eminence, distinction, or excellence : DISTINGUISHED ⟨two ∼ politicians made speeches⟩

♦ distinguished, eminent, illustrious, noble, noteworthy, outstanding, preeminent, prestigious, signal, star, superior — more at EMINENT

²notable *n* **♦** : a person of note

♦ celebrity, eminence, figure, light, luminary, personage, personality, somebody, standout, star, superstar, VIP — more at CELEBRITY

no·ta·bly \ˈnō-tə-blē\ *adv* **1** : in a notable manner **2** : ESPECIALLY, PARTICULARLY

no·tar·i·al \nō-ˈter-ē-əl\ *adj* : of, relating to, or done by a notary public

no·ta·rize \ˈnō-tə-ˌrīz\ *vb* **-rized; -riz·ing** : to acknowledge or make legally authentic as a notary public

no·ta·ry public \ˈnō-tə-rē-\ *n, pl* **notaries public** *or* **notary publics** : a public official who attests or certifies writings (as deeds) to make them legally authentic

no·ta·tion \nō-ˈtā-shən\ *n* **1** : a written reminder : NOTE **2** : the act, process, or method of representing data by marks, signs, figures, or characters; *also* : a system of symbols (as letters, numerals, or musical notes) used in such notation

¹notch \ˈnäch\ *n* **1 ♦** : a V-shaped hollow in an edge or surface **2 ♦** : a narrow pass between two mountains **3 ♦** : a step or stage in a process, course, or order of classification

♦ [1] chip, hack, indentation, nick; *also* punch; groove, score; slit, slot ♦ [2] canyon, defile, flume, gap, gorge, gulch, gulf, pass, ravine — more at CANYON ♦ [3] cut, degree, grade, inch, peg, phase, point, stage, step — more at DEGREE

²notch *vb* **1** : to cut or make notches in **2 ♦** : to score or record by or as if by cutting a series of notches ⟨∼ed 20 points for the team⟩

♦ achieve, attain, gain, hit, make, score, win — more at ACHIEVE

notch·back \ˈnäch-ˌbak\ *n* : an automobile with a trunk whose lid forms a distinct deck

¹note \ˈnōt\ *vb* **not·ed; not·ing** **1 ♦** : to notice or observe with care ⟨*noted* her reaction⟩; *also* : to record or preserve in writing **2 ♦** : to make special mention of

♦ [1] jot, log, mark, put down, record, register, set down — more at RECORD ♦ [1] behold, descry, discern, distinguish, espy, eye, look, notice, observe, perceive, regard, remark, see, sight, spy, view, witness — more at SEE ♦ [2] advert (to), cite, instance, mention, name, notice, quote, refer (to), remark, specify, touch (*on* or *upon*) — more at MENTION

²note *n* **1** : a musical sound **2** : a cry, call, or sound esp. of a bird **3** : a special tone in a person's words or voice ⟨a ∼ of fear⟩ **4** : a character in music used to indicate duration of a tone by its shape and pitch by its position on the staff **5 ♦** : a characteristic feature : MOOD ⟨a ∼ of optimism⟩ **6 ♦** : a written reminder : MEMORANDUM **7** : a brief and informal record; *also* : a written or printed comment or explanation **8** : a written promise to pay a debt **9** : a piece of paper money **10 ♦** : a short informal letter **11** : a formal diplomatic or official communication **12 ♦** : overall quality or character as seen or judged by people in general : REPUTATION ⟨an artist of ∼⟩ **13** : OBSERVATION, NOTICE, HEED ⟨take ∼ of the time⟩

♦ [5] air, atmosphere, aura, climate, flavor (*or* flavour), mood, temper — more at AURA ♦ [6, 10] dispatch, letter, memorandum, missive — more at LETTER ♦ [12] character, mark, name, report, reputation — more at REPUTATION

note·book \ˈnōt-ˌbůk\ *n* : a book for notes or memoranda

not·ed \ˈnō-təd\ *adj* **♦** : well known by reputation : EMINENT, CELEBRATED ⟨a ∼ violinist⟩

♦ celebrated, eminent, famed, famous, notorious, prominent, renowned, star, well-known — more at FAMOUS

note·wor·thy \ˈnōt-ˌwər-thē\ *adj* **♦** : worthy of note

♦ distinguished, eminent, illustrious, noble, notable, outstanding, preeminent, prestigious, signal, star, superior — more at EMINENT

¹noth·ing \ˈnə-thiŋ\ *pron* **1** : no thing ⟨leaves ∼ to the imagination⟩ **2** : no part **3** : one of no interest, value, or importance ⟨she's ∼ to me⟩

²nothing *adv* **♦** : not at all : in no degree

♦ never, no, none, nowise — more at NEVER

³nothing *n* **1** : something that does not exist **2 ♦** : the arithmetical symbol 0 denoting the absence of all magnitude or quantity : ZERO **3 ♦** : a person or thing of little or no value or importance

♦ [2] aught, cipher, naught, nil, zero, zip — more at ZERO ♦ [3] nobody, nonentity, whippersnapper, zero — more at NOBODY

⁴nothing *adj* : of no account : WORTHLESS

noth·ing·ness \ˈnə-thiŋ-nəs\ *n* **1** : the quality or state of being nothing **2 a** : the state or fact of having no existence **b** : utter insignificance **3** : something insignificant or valueless

¹no·tice \ˈnō-təs\ *n* **1 ♦** : warning or intimation of something : WARNING **2** : notification of the termination of an agreement or contract at a specified time **3 ♦** : consideration with a view to action : ATTENTION, HEED ⟨bring the matter to my ∼⟩ **4 ♦** : a written or printed announcement **5** : a short critical account or examination (as of a play) : REVIEW

♦ [1] admonition, alarm, alert, caution, warning — more at WARNING ♦ [3] attention, awareness, cognizance, ear, eye, heed, observance, observation — more at ATTENTION ♦ [4] announcement, directive, memorandum, notification — more at MEMORANDUM

²notice *vb* **no·ticed; no·tic·ing** **1 ♦** : to make mention of : remark on **2 ♦** : to take notice of : OBSERVE

♦ [1] advert (to), cite, instance, mention, name, note, quote, refer (to), specify, touch (*on* or *upon*) — more at MENTION ♦ [2] behold, descry, discern, distinguish, espy, eye, look, note, observe, perceive, regard, remark, see, sight, spy, view, witness — more at SEE

no·tice·able \ˈnō-tə-sə-bəl\ *adj* **1** : worthy of notice **2 ♦** : capable of being or likely to be noticed ⟨a ∼ scar⟩ — **no·tice·ably** \-blē\ *adv*

♦ bold, catchy, conspicuous, emphatic, marked, prominent, pronounced, remarkable, striking; *also* detectable, discernible, observable, perceptible, visible; outstanding, salient; distinguished, eminent, impressive, notable, noteworthy; highlighted; flagrant, glaring, screaming *Ant* inconspicuous, unemphatic, unnoticeable, unobtrusive, unremarkable

no·ti·fi·ca·tion \ˌnō-tə-fə-ˈkā-shən\ *n* **♦** : the act or an instance of notifying

♦ advertisement, announcement, bulletin, notice, release — more at ANNOUNCEMENT

no·ti·fy \ˈnō-tə-ˌfī\ *vb* **-fied; -fy·ing** **1** : to give notice of : report the occurrence of **2** : to give notice to

no·tion \ˈnō-shən\ *n* **1 ♦** : an individual's conception or impression of something known, experienced, or imagined : IDEA, CONCEPTION ⟨have a ∼ of what he means⟩ **2 ♦** : a belief held : OPINION, VIEW **3 ♦** : a personal inclination : WHIM, FANCY ⟨a sudden ∼ to go⟩ **4** *pl* **♦** : small useful articles (as pins, needles, or thread)

♦ [1] concept, idea, image, impression, picture, thought — more at IDEA ♦ [2] belief, conviction, eye, feeling, judgment (*or* judgement), mind, opinion, persuasion, sentiment, verdict, view — more at OPINION ♦ [3] caprice, fancy, freak, vagary, whim — more at WHIM

♦ **notions** [4] novelties, odds and ends, sundries; *also* bric-a-brac; hodgepodge, miscellany, variety

no·tion·al \'nō-shə-nəl\ *adj* 1 : existing in the mind only : IMAGINARY, UNREAL 2 : given to foolish or fanciful moods or ideas : WHIMSICAL

no·to·ri·ety \ˌnō-tə-'rī-ə-tē\ *n* ♦ : the quality or state of being notorious

♦ celebrity, fame, renown — more at FAME

no·to·ri·ous \nō-'tōr-ē-əs\ *adj* ♦ : generally known and talked of; *esp* : widely and unfavorably known — **no·to·ri·ous·ly** \nō-'tōr-ē-ə-slē\ *adv*

♦ celebrated, famed, famous, noted, prominent, renowned, star, well-known — more at FAMOUS discreditable, disgraceful, dishonorable (*or* dishonourable), disreputable, ignominious, infamous, shameful — more at DISREPUTABLE

¹**not·with·stand·ing** \ˌnät-with-'stan-diŋ, -with-\ *prep* ♦ : in spite of

♦ despite, regardless of, with — more at DESPITE

²**notwithstanding** *adv* ♦ : in spite of that : NEVERTHELESS

♦ but, howbeit, however, nevertheless, nonetheless, still, though, withal, yet — more at HOWEVER

³**notwithstanding** *conj* : ALTHOUGH

nou·gat \'nü-gət\ *n* [F, fr. Occitan, *nogat*, fr. Old Occitan, *nogat*, fr. *noga* nut, ultim. fr. L *nuc-, nux*] : a confection of nuts or fruit pieces in a sugar paste

nought *var of* NAUGHT

noun \'naun\ *n* : a word that is the name of a subject of discourse (as a person or place)

nour·ish \'nər-ish\ *vb* ♦ : to promote the growth or development of

♦ advance, cultivate, encourage, forward, foster, further, nurture, promote — more at FOSTER

nour·ish·ing *adj* ♦ : giving nourishment

♦ nutritious — more at NUTRITIOUS

nour·ish·ment \'nər-ish-mənt\ *n* 1 : FOOD, NUTRIENT 2 : the action or process of nourishing

nou·veau riche \ˌnü-ˌvō-'rēsh\ *n, pl* **nou·veaux riches** *same*\ [F] : a person newly rich : PARVENU

Nov *abbr* November

no·va \'nō-və\ *n, pl* **novas** *or* **no·vae** \-(ˌ)vē, -ˌvī\ [NL, fem. of L *novus* new] : a star that suddenly increases greatly in brightness and then within a few months or years grows dim again

¹**nov·el** \'nä-vəl\ *adj* 1 ♦ : having no precedent : NEW 2 : STRANGE, UNUSUAL

♦ fresh, new, original, strange, unfamiliar, unknown — more at NEW

²**novel** *n* : a long invented prose narrative dealing with human experience through a connected sequence of events — **nov·el·ist** \-və-list\ *n*

nov·el·ette \ˌnä-və-'let\ *n* : a brief novel or long short story

nov·el·ize \'nä-və-ˌlīz\ *vb* **-ized; -iz·ing** : to convert into the form of a novel — **nov·el·i·za·tion** \ˌnä-və-lə-'zā-shən\ *n*

no·vel·la \nō-'ve-lə\ *n, pl* **novellas** *or* **no·vel·le** \-'ve-lē\ ♦ : a work of fiction between a short story and a novel in length and complexity : NOVELETTE

♦ narrative, short story, story, tale — more at STORY

nov·el·ty \'nä-vəl-tē\ *n, pl* **-ties** 1 : something new or unusual 2 ♦ : the quality or state of being new : NEWNESS 3 ♦ : a small manufactured article intended mainly for personal or household adornment — usu. used in pl.

♦ [2] freshness, newness, originality; *also* strangeness, unfamiliarity; up-to-dateness; departure, divergence, innovation, offshoot, shoot ♦ [3] bauble, curiosity, gewgaw, knickknack, tchotchke, trinket — more at KNICKKNACK ♦ *usu* **novelties** [3] notions, odds and ends, sundries

No·vem·ber \nō-'vem-bər\ *n* [ME *Novembre*, fr. AF, fr. L *November* ninth month of the early Roman calendar, fr. *novem* nine] : the 11th month of the year

no·ve·na \nō-'vē-nə\ *n* : a Roman Catholic nine-day period of prayer

nov·ice \'nä-vəs\ *n* 1 : a new member of a religious order who is preparing to take the vows of religion 2 ♦ : one who is inexperienced or untrained

♦ beginner, fledgling, freshman, greenhorn, neophyte, newcomer, recruit, rookie, tenderfoot, tyro — more at BEGINNER

no·vi·ti·ate \nō-'vi-shət\ *n* 1 : the period or state of being a novice 2 : a house where novices are trained 3 : NOVICE

¹**now** \'nau\ *adv* 1 ♦ : at the present time or moment 2 ♦ : in the time immediately before the present 3 ♦ : in the time immediately to follow : IMMEDIATELY, FORTHWITH 4 — used with the sense of present time weakened or lost (as to express command, introduce an important point, or indicate a transition) ⟨~ hear this⟩ 5 : at times : SOMETIMES ⟨~ one and ~ another⟩ 6 : under the present circumstances 7 : at the time referred to

♦ [1] anymore, nowadays, presently, right now, today; *also* here **Ant** before, formerly, long, once, then ♦ [2] freshly, just, late, lately, new, newly, only, recently — more at NEWLY ♦ [3] directly, forthwith, immediately, instantly, promptly, pronto, right away, right now — more at IMMEDIATELY

²**now** *conj* ♦ : in view of the fact ⟨~ that you're here, we'll start⟩

♦ because, for, since, whereas — more at SINCE

³**now** *n* ♦ : the present time or moment : PRESENT

♦ moment, present, today — more at PRESENT

⁴**now** *adj* 1 : of or relating to the present time ⟨the ~ president⟩ 2 : excitingly new ⟨~ clothes⟩; *also* : constantly aware of what is new ⟨~ people⟩

NOW *abbr* 1 National Organization for Women 2 negotiable order of withdrawal

now·a·days \'nau-ə-ˌdāz\ *adv* ♦ : at the present time

♦ anymore, now, presently, right now, today — more at NOW

no·way \'nō-ˌwā\ *or* **no·ways** \-ˌwāz\ *adv* : NOWISE

no·where \-ˌhwer\ *adv* : not anywhere — **nowhere** *n*

nowhere near *adv* : not nearly

no·wise \'nō-ˌwīz\ *adv* ♦ : in no way

♦ never, no, none, nothing — more at NEVER

nox·ious \'näk-shəs\ *adj* ♦ : harmful esp. to health or morals

♦ noisome, unhealthy, unwholesome — more at UNHEALTHY adverse, bad, baleful, baneful, damaging, deleterious, detrimental, evil, harmful, hurtful, ill, injurious, mischievous, pernicious, prejudicial — more at HARMFUL

noz·zle \'nä-zəl\ *n* : a short tube constricted in the middle or at one end and used (as on a hose) to speed up or direct a flow of fluid

np *abbr* 1 no pagination 2 no place (of publication)

Np *symbol* neptunium

NP *abbr* notary public

NR *abbr* not rated

NRA *abbr* National Rifle Association

NS *abbr* 1 not specified 2 Nova Scotia

NSA *abbr* National Security Agency

NSC *abbr* National Security Council

NSF *abbr* 1 National Science Foundation 2 not sufficient funds

NSW *abbr* New South Wales

NT *abbr* 1 New Testament 2 Northern Territory 3 Northwest Territories

nth \'enth\ *adj* 1 : numbered with an unspecified or indefinitely large ordinal number ⟨for the ~ time⟩ 2 ♦ : of the greatest or highest degree, quantity, number, or amount : UTMOST ⟨to the ~ degree⟩

♦ consummate, maximum, most, paramount, supreme, top, ultimate, utmost — more at ULTIMATE

NTP *abbr* normal temperature and pressure

nt wt *or* **n wt** *abbr* net weight

nu \'nü, 'nyü\ *n* : the 13th letter of the Greek alphabet — N or ν

NU *abbr* name unknown

nu·ance \'nü-,äns; 'nyü-, nü-'äns, nyü-\ *n* [F] : a shade of difference : a delicate variation (as in tone or meaning)

nub \'nəb\ *n* 1 : a piece or mass of indefinite size and shape : KNOB, LUMP 2 ♦ : the main point or part : GIST ⟨the ∼ of the story⟩

♦ core, crux, gist, heart, pith, pivot — more at CRUX

nub·bin \'nə-bən\ *n* 1 : something (as an ear of corn) that is small for its kind, stunted, undeveloped, or imperfect 2 : a small usu. projecting part or bit

nu·bile \'nü-,bīl, 'nyü-, -bəl\ *adj* 1 : of marriageable condition or age : sexually mature 2 : sexually attractive — used of a young woman

nu·cle·ar \'nü-klē-ər, 'nyü-\ *adj* 1 : of, relating to, or constituting a nucleus 2 : of, relating to, or using the atomic nucleus or energy derived from it 3 : of, relating to, or being a weapon whose destructive power results from an uncontrolled nuclear reaction

nuclear family *n* : a family group that consists only of parents and children

nu·cle·ate \'nü-klē-,āt, 'nyü-\ *vb* **-at·ed; -at·ing** : to form, act as, or have a nucleus — **nu·cle·ation** \,nü-klē-'ā-shən, ,nyü-\ *n*

nu·cle·ic acid \nü-'klē-ik-, nyü-, -'klā-\ *n* : any of various complex organic acids (as DNA or RNA) found esp. in cell nuclei

nu·cle·o·tide \'nü-klē-ə-,tīd, 'nyü-\ *n* [NL, fr. L, kernel, dim. of *nuc-, nux* nut] : any of several compounds that are the basic structural units of nucleic acids

nu·cle·us \'nü-klē-əs, 'nyü-\ *n, pl* **nu·clei** \-klē-,ī\ *also* **nu·cle·us·es** [NL, fr. L, kernel, dim. of *nuc-, nux* nut] 1 : a central mass or part about which matter gathers or is collected : CORE 2 : a cell part that is characteristic of all living things except viruses, bacteria, and certain algae, that is necessary for heredity and for making proteins, that contains the chromosomes with their genes, and that is enclosed in a membrane 3 : a mass of gray matter or group of cell bodies of neurons in the central nervous system 4 : the central part of an atom that comprises nearly all of the atomic mass 5 ♦ : a basic or essential part

♦ base, center (*or* centre), core, cynosure, eye, focus, heart, hub, mecca, seat — more at CENTER

¹**nude** \'nüd, 'nyüd\ *adj* **nud·er; nud·est** 1 ♦ : devoid of a natural or conventional covering : BARE, NAKED 2 : featuring or catering to naked people — **nu·di·ty** \'nü-də-tē, 'nyü-\ *n*

♦ bare, naked, unclad, unclothed, undressed — more at NAKED

²**nude** *n* 1 : a nude human figure esp. as depicted in art 2 : the condition of being nude ⟨in the ∼⟩

nudge \'nəj\ *vb* **nudged; nudg·ing** : to touch or push gently (as with the elbow) usu. in order to seek attention — **nudge** *n*

nud·ism \'nü-,di-zəm, 'nyü-\ *n* : the practice of going nude esp. in mixed groups at specially secluded places — **nud·ist** \-dist\ *n*

nu·ga·to·ry \-gə-,tōr-ē\ *adj* 1 : INCONSEQUENTIAL, WORTHLESS 2 : having no force : INEFFECTUAL

nug·get \'nə-gət\ *n* 1 : a solid lump; *esp* : a lump of precious metal (as gold) 2 : TIDBIT

nui·sance \'nüs-ᵊns, 'nyüs-\ *n* ♦ : an annoying or troublesome person or thing

♦ annoyance, bother, gadfly, persecutor, pest, tease; *also* headache; harrier, heckler; hassle, plague; molester, tormentor, torturer aggravation, annoyance, bother, exasperation, frustration, hassle, headache, inconvenience, irritant, peeve, pest, problem, thorn — more at ANNOYANCE

nuisance tax *n* : an excise tax collected in small amounts directly from the consumer

¹**nuke** \'nük, 'nyük\ *n* 1 : a nuclear weapon 2 : a nuclear power plant

²**nuke** *vb* **nuked; nuk·ing** 1 : to attack with nuclear weapons 2 : MICROWAVE

null \'nəl\ *adj* 1 ♦ : having no legal or binding force : INVALID, VOID 2 ♦ : amounting to nothing 3 : INSIGNIFICANT — **nul·li·ty** \'nə-lə-tē\ *n*

♦ [1] invalid, void; *also* illegal; useless, worthless; ineffective, ineffectual *Ant* binding, good, valid ♦ [2] chaffy, empty, junky, no-good, valueless, worthless — more at WORTHLESS

null and void *adj* : having no force, binding power, or validity

nul·li·fy \'nə-lə-,fī\ *vb* **-fied; -fy·ing** ♦ : to make null or valueless; *also* : to declare or make legally invalid or void — **nul·li·fi·ca·tion** \,nə-lə-fə-'kā-shən\ *n*

♦ abolish, abrogate, annul, cancel, dissolve, invalidate, negate, quash, repeal, rescind, void — more at ABOLISH

num *abbr* numeral

Num *or* **Numb** *abbr* Numbers

¹**numb** \'nəm\ *adj* ♦ : lacking sensation or emotion — **numb·ly** *adv*

♦ asleep, dead, unfeeling; *also* chilled, nipped; deadened, drugged, stupefied; insensible, senseless, unconscious; inanimate, insensate *Ant* feeling, sensitive

²**numb** *vb* ♦ : to make as if dead : impair in vigor, force, activity, or sensation

♦ blunt, dampen, deaden, dull — more at DULL

¹**num·ber** \'nəm-bər\ *n* 1 : the total of individuals or units taken together 2 : an indefinite total ⟨a small ∼ of tickets remain unsold⟩ 3 : an ascertainable total ⟨the sands of the desert are without ∼⟩ 4 : a distinction of word form to denote reference to one or more than one 5 : a unit belonging to a mathematical system and subject to its laws; *also, pl* : ARITHMETIC 6 ♦ : a symbol used to represent a mathematical number; *also* : such a number used to identify or designate ⟨a phone ∼⟩ 7 : one in a series of musical or theatrical performances ⟨the best ∼ on the program⟩

♦ digit, figure, integer, numeral, whole number; *also* decimal, fraction; cipher; symbol

²**number** *vb* 1 : to indicate or name by units or groups so as to find the total number of units involved : COUNT, ENUMERATE 2 ♦ : to include with or be one of a group 3 : to restrict to a small or definite number 4 : to assign a number to 5 ♦ : to comprise in number : TOTAL

♦ [2] carry, comprehend, contain, embrace, encompass, entail, include, involve, take in — more at INCLUDE ♦ [5] add up, amount, come, sum, total — more at AMOUNT (TO)

number crunching *n* ♦ : the performance of long complex often repetitive mathematical calculations; *also* : statistical analysis

♦ arithmetic, calculation, computation, reckoning — more at CALCULATION

num·ber·less \-ləs\ *adj* ♦ : too many to be numbered : INNUMERABLE, COUNTLESS ⟨∼ stars in the sky⟩

♦ countless, innumerable, uncountable, unnumbered, untold — more at COUNTLESS

Numbers *n* : a book of Jewish and Christian Scripture

numb·ing \'nə-miŋ\ *adj* : tending to make numb ⟨a ∼ lecture⟩ ⟨a ∼ realization⟩

numb·ness *n* ♦ : reduced sensitivity to perception or emotion

♦ apathy, impassivity, phlegm, stupor — more at APATHY

numbskull *var of* NUMSKULL

nu·mer·a·cy \'nü-mə-rə-sē, 'nyü-\ *n* : the capacity for quantitative thought or expression

nu·mer·al \'nü-mə-rəl, 'nyü-\ *n* ♦ : a conventional symbol representing a number — **numeral** *adj*

♦ digit, figure, integer, number, whole number — more at NUMBER

nu·mer·ate \'nü-mə-ˌrāt, 'nyü-\ *vb* **-at·ed; -at·ing 1** : to ascertain the number of **2** ♦ : to specify one after another

♦ detail, enumerate, itemize, list, rehearse, tick (off) — more at ENUMERATE

nu·mer·a·tor \-ˌrā-tər\ *n* : the part of a fraction above the line

nu·mer·ic \nü-'mer-ik, nyü-\ *adj* : NUMERICAL; *esp* : denoting a number or a system of numbers

nu·mer·i·cal \-'mer-i-kəl\ *adj* **1** : of or relating to numbers ⟨in ~ order⟩ **2** : expressed in or involving numbers — **nu·mer·i·cal·ly** \-k(ə-)lē\ *adv*

nu·mer·ol·o·gy \ˌnü-mə-'rä-lə-jē, ˌnyü-\ *n* : the study of the occult significance of numbers — **nu·mer·ol·o·gist** \-jist\ *n*

nu·mer·ous \'nü-mə-rəs, 'nyü-\ *adj* ♦ : consisting of, including, or relating to a great number : MANY

♦ many, multiple, multitudinous — more at MANY

nu·mis·mat·ics \ˌnü-məz-'ma-tiks, ˌnyü-\ *n* : the study or collection of monetary objects — **nu·mis·mat·ic** \-tik\ *adj* — **nu·mis·ma·tist** \nü-'miz-mə-tist, nyü-\ *n*

num·skull \'nəm-ˌskəl\ *n* ♦ : a stupid person : DUNCE

♦ blockhead, dope, dummy, idiot, imbecile, jackass, moron — more at IDIOT

nun \'nən\ *n* : a woman belonging to a religious order; *esp* : one under solemn vows of poverty, chastity, and obedience

nun·cio \'nən-sē-ˌō, 'nün-\ *n, pl* **-ci·os** [It, fr. L *nuntius* messenger] : a permanent high-ranking papal representative to a civil government

nun·nery \'nə-nə-rē\ *n, pl* **-ner·ies** : a convent of nuns

¹nup·tial \'nəp-shəl\ *adj* ♦ : of or relating to marriage or a wedding ⟨~ vows⟩

♦ conjugal, connubial, marital, matrimonial — more at MARITAL

²nuptial *n* : MARRIAGE, WEDDING — usu. used in pl.

¹nurse \'nərs\ *n* [ME *norice, nurse*, fr. AF *nurice*, fr. LL *nutricia*, fr. L, fem. of *nutricius* nourishing] **1** ♦ : a girl or woman employed to take care of children **2** : a person trained to care for sick people

♦ nanny, nursemaid; *also* governess

²nurse *vb* **nursed; nurs·ing 1** : SUCKLE **2** ♦ : to take charge of and watch over **3** : TEND ⟨~ an invalid⟩ **4** ♦ : to treat with special care ⟨~ a headache⟩ **5** ♦ : to hold in one's mind or consideration ⟨~ a grudge⟩ **6** : to act or serve as a nurse

♦ [2] aid, care, minister, mother; *also* cure, heal, remedy; doctor, treat; conserve, preserve, provide (for), support; baby, coddle, mollycoddle, pamper, spoil; cater (to), humor (*or* humour), indulge ♦ [4] baby, coddle, mollycoddle, pamper, spoil — more at BABY ♦ [5] bear, cherish, entertain, harbor (*or* harbour), have, hold — more at HARBOR

nurse–maid \'nərs-ˌmād\ *n* ♦ : a girl or woman who is regularly employed to look after children : NURSE 1

♦ nanny, nurse — more at NURSE

nurse–prac·ti·tion·er \-prak-'ti-shə-nər\ *n* : a registered nurse who is qualified to assume some of the duties formerly assumed only by a physician

nurs·ery \'nər-sə-rē\ *n, pl* **-er·ies 1** : a room for children **2** : a place where children are temporarily cared for in their parents' absence **3** : a place where young plants are grown usu. for transplanting

nurs·ery·man \-mən\ *n* : a man who keeps or works in a plant nursery

nursery school *n* : a school for children under kindergarten age

nursing home *n* : a private establishment providing care for persons (as the aged or the chronically ill) who are unable to care for themselves

nurs·ling \'nərs-liŋ\ *n* **1** : one that is solicitously cared for **2** : a nursing child

¹nur·ture \'nər-chər\ *n* **1** : TRAINING, UPBRINGING; *also* : the influences that modify the expression of an individual's heredity **2** : FOOD, NOURISHMENT

²nurture *vb* **nur·tured; nur·tur·ing 1** : to care for : FEED, NOURISH **2** ♦ : to develop mentally, morally, or aesthetically esp. by instruction : EDUCATE ⟨~ students⟩ **3** ♦ : to further the development of : FOSTER ⟨~ creativity⟩

♦ [2] edify, educate, enlighten — more at ENLIGHTEN ♦ [3] advance, cultivate, encourage, forward, foster, further, nourish, promote — more at FOSTER

nut \'nət\ *n* **1** : a dry fruit or seed with a hard shell and a firm inner kernel; *also* : its kernel **2** : a metal block with a hole through it that is fastened to a bolt or screw by means of a screw thread within the hole **3** : the ridge on the upper end of the fingerboard in a stringed musical instrument over which the strings pass **4** ♦ : a foolish, eccentric, or crazy person **5** ♦ : one who is ardently attached to a cause, object, or pursuit : ENTHUSIAST

♦ [4] character, crackpot, crank, eccentric, kook, oddball, screwball, weirdo — more at ECCENTRIC ♦ [4] booby, fool, goose, half-wit, jackass, lunatic, nitwit, simpleton, turkey — more at FOOL ♦ [5] addict, aficionado, buff, bug, devotee, enthusiast, fan, fanatic, fancier, fiend, freak, lover, maniac — more at FAN

nut·crack·er \'nət-ˌkra-kər\ *n* : an instrument for cracking nuts

nut·hatch \-ˌhach\ *n* : any of various small tree-climbing chiefly insect-eating birds

nut·meg \-ˌmeg, -ˌmāg\ *n* [ME *notemuge*, ultim. fr. Old Occitan *noz muscada*, lit., musky nut] : a spice made by grinding the nutlike aromatic seed of a tropical tree; *also* : the seed or tree

nu·tria \'nü-trē-ə, 'nyü-\ *n* [Sp] **1** : the durable usu. light brown fur of a nutria **2** : a large So. American aquatic rodent with webbed hind feet

¹nu·tri·ent \'nü-trē-ənt, 'nyü-\ *adj* : furnishing nourishment : NOURISHING

²nutrient *n* : a nutritive substance or ingredient

nu·tri·ment \-trə-mənt\ *n* : NUTRIENT

nu·tri·tion \nù-'tri-shən, nyü-\ *n* : the act or process of nourishing; *esp* : the processes by which an individual takes in and utilizes food material

nu·tri·tion·al \-shə-nəl\ *adj* : of, relating to, or functioning in nutrition

nu·tri·tious \-shəs\ *adj* ♦ : giving nourishment

♦ nourishing; *also* dietary, dietetic; beneficial, healthful, healthy, restorative, salubrious, salutary, wholesome

nu·tri·tive \'nü-trə-tiv, 'nyü-\ *adj* : of or relating to nutrition

nuts \'nəts\ *adj* **1** ♦ : filled with or marked by enthusiasm **2** : mentally disordered : CRAZY, DEMENTED

♦ ardent, eager, enthusiastic, gung ho, keen ♦ *usu* nuts about crazy, mad

nut·shell \'nət-ˌshel\ *n* : the shell of a nut — **in a nutshell** : in a few words ⟨that's the story *in a nutshell*⟩

nut·ty \'nə-tē\ *adj* **nut·ti·er; -est 1** : containing or suggesting nuts ⟨a ~ flavor⟩ **2** ♦ : mentally unbalanced; *also* : lacking in seriousness : SILLY

♦ absurd, crazy, cuckoo, fatuous, foolish, mad, nonsensical, senseless, silly, stupid — more at FOOLISH

nuz·zle \'nə-zəl\ *vb* **nuz·zled; nuz·zling 1** : to root around, push, or touch with or as if with the nose **2** ♦ : to press closely and affectionately with : SNUGGLE

♦ cuddle, nestle, snug, snuggle; *also* curl up; crouch, huddle

NV *abbr* Nevada

NW *abbr* northwest

NWT *abbr* Northwest Territories

NY *abbr* New York

NYC *abbr* New York City

ny·lon \'nī-ˌlän\ *n* **1** : any of numerous strong tough elastic synthetic materials used esp. in textiles and plastics **2** *pl* : stockings made of nylon

nymph \'nimf\ *n* **1** : any of the lesser goddesses in ancient mythology represented as maidens living in the mountains, forests, meadows, and waters **2** : GIRL **3** : an immature insect resembling the adult but smaller, less differentiated, and usu. lacking wings

nym·pho·ma·nia \ˌnim-fə-'mā-nē-ə, -nyə\ *n* : excessive sexual desire by a female — **nym·pho·ma·ni·ac** \-nē-ˌak\ *n or adj*

NZ *abbr* New Zealand

¹o \'ō\ *n, pl* **o's** *or* **os** \'ōz\ *often cap* **1** : the 15th letter of the English alphabet **2** : ZERO

²o *abbr, often cap* **1** ocean **2** Ohio **3** ohm

¹O *var of* OH

²O *abbr* Ohio

³O *symbol* oxygen

o/a *abbr* on or about

oaf \'ōf\ *n* ♦ : a stupid or awkward person

    ♦ clod, gawk, hulk, lout, lubber, lug; *also* chump, loser, schlemiel, turkey; ass, blockhead, dolt, donkey, dope, dumbbell, dummy, goon, half-wit, idiot, ignoramus, imbecile, jackass, moron, nincompoop, ninny, nitwit, simpleton; beast, boor, brute, cad, churl, clown, creep, cretin, cur, heel, louse, skunk, snake, stinker, villain; booby, fool, goose, lunatic, madman, nut; scatterbrain; rascal, rogue, scamp

oaf·ish *adj* : having the qualities typical of an oaf

oak \'ōk\ *n, pl* **oaks** *or* **oak** : any of a genus of trees or shrubs related to the beech and chestnut and bearing a rounded thin-shelled nut surrounded at the base by a hardened cup; *also* : the usu. tough hard durable wood of an oak — **oak·en** \'ō-kən\ *adj*

oa·kum \'ō-kəm\ *n* [ME *okum*, fr. OE *ācumba* flax fiber, from *ā-* out + *-cumba* (akin to OE *camb* comb)] : loosely twisted hemp or jute fiber impregnated with tar and used esp. in caulking ships

oar \'ōr\ *n* : a long pole with a broad blade at one end used for propelling or steering a boat

oar·lock \'ōr-ˌläk\ *n* : a U-shaped device for holding an oar in place

oars·man \'ōrz-mən\ *n* : one who rows esp. in a racing crew

OAS *abbr* Organization of American States

oa·sis \ō-'ā-səs\ *n, pl* **oa·ses** \-ˌsēz\ : a fertile or green area in an arid region

oat \'ōt\ *n* : a cereal grass widely grown for its edible seed; *also* : this seed — **oat·en** \-ᵊn\ *adj*

oat·cake \'ōt-ˌkāk\ *n* : a thin flat oatmeal cake

oath \'ōth\ *n, pl* **oaths** \'ōthz, 'ōths\ **1** ♦ : a solemn appeal to God to witness to the truth of a statement or the sacredness of a promise **2** : an irreverent or careless use of a sacred name

    ♦ pledge, promise, troth, vow, word — more at PROMISE

oat·meal \'ōt-ˌmēl\ *n* **1** : ground or rolled oats **2** : porridge made from ground or rolled oats

Ob *or* **Obad** *abbr* Obadiah

Oba·di·ah \ˌō-bə-'dī-ə\ *n* : a book of canonical Jewish and Christian Scripture

ob·bli·ga·to \ˌä-blə-'gä-tō\ *n, pl* **-tos** *also* **-ti** \-'gä-tē\ [It] : an accompanying part usu. played by a solo instrument

ob·du·ra·cy \'äb-də-rə-sē, -dyə-\ *n* ♦ : the quality or state of being obdurate

    ♦ hardheadedness, mulishness, obstinacy, peevishness, pertinacity, self-will, stubbornness, tenacity — more at OBSTINACY

ob·du·rate \'äb-də-rət, -dyə-\ *adj* **1** ♦ : stubbornly resistant : UNYIELDING ⟨an ~ denial⟩ **2** ♦ : hardened in feelings

    ♦ [1] dogged, hardheaded, headstrong, mulish, obstinate, opinionated, peevish, pertinacious, perverse, pigheaded, stubborn, unyielding, willful — more at OBSTINATE ♦ [2] callous, hard, heartless, inhuman, inhumane, pitiless, soulless, unfeeling, unsympathetic — more at HARD

obe·di·ence \ō-'bē-dē-əns\ *n* ♦ : an act or instance of obeying

    ♦ compliance, conformity, observance, submission, subordination; *also* acquiescence; docility; capitulation, surrender, yielding; servility, subservience; inhibition, repression, restraint, suppression; control, discipline, order *Ant* disobedience, insubordination, noncompliance, rebelling, rebellion

obe·di·ent \ō-'bē-dē-ənt\ *adj* ♦ : submissive to the restraint or command of authority — **obe·di·ent·ly** *adv*

    ♦ amenable, compliant, conformable, docile, submissive, tractable; *also* acquiescent, agreeable, amiable, obliging; surrendering, yielding; obsequious, servile, slavish, subservient; decorous, disciplined, mannerly, orderly; constrained, curbed, inhibited, repressed, restrained; manageable; gentle, meek, mild *Ant* contrary, disobedient, froward, insubordinate, intractable, rebellious, recalcitrant, refractory, unruly

obei·sance \ō-'bē-səns, -'bā-\ *n* : a bow made to show respect or submission; *also* : DEFERENCE, HOMAGE

obe·lisk \'ä-bə-ˌlisk\ *n* [MF *obelisque*, fr. L *obeliscus*, fr. Gk *obeliskos*, fr. dim. of *obelos* spit, pointed pillar] : a 4-sided pillar that tapers toward the top and ends in a pyramid

obese \ō-'bēs\ *adj* [L *obesus*, fr. *ob-* against + *esus*, pp. of *edere* to eat] ♦ : excessively fat

    ♦ chubby, corpulent, fat, fleshy, full, gross, overweight, plump, portly, rotund, round — more at FAT

obe·si·ty \-'bē-sə-tē\ *n* ♦ : a condition characterized by the excessive accumulation and storage of fat in the body

    ♦ corpulence, fatness, grossness, plumpness — more at CORPULENCE

obey \ō-'bā\ *vb* **obeyed; obey·ing** **1** : to follow the commands or guidance of : behave obediently **2** ♦ : to comply with ⟨~ orders⟩

    ♦ comply, conform, follow, mind, observe; *also* defer (to), submit (to), surrender (to), yield (to); accede (to), acquiesce (to), agree (to), assent (to); attend, hear, heed, listen (to), mark, note, notice, regard, watch *Ant* disobey

ob·fus·cate \'äb-fə-ˌskāt\ *vb* **-cat·ed; -cat·ing** **1** : to make dark or obscure **2** : to make difficult to understand ⟨*obfuscating* the issue⟩ — **ob·fus·ca·tion** \ˌäb-fəs-'kā-shən\ *n*

OB–GYN *abbr* obstetrician gynecologist; obstetrics gynecology

obi \'ō-bē\ *n* [Jp] : a broad sash worn esp. with a Japanese kimono

obit \'ō-'bit, 'ō-bət\ *n* : OBITUARY

obi·ter dic·tum \ˌō-bə-tər-'dik-təm\ *n, pl* **obiter dic·ta** \-tə\ [LL, lit., something said in passing] : an incidental remark or observation

obit·u·ary \ə-'bi-chə-ˌwer-ē\ *n, pl* **-ar·ies** : a notice of a person's death usu. with a short biographical account

obj *abbr* object; objective

¹ob·ject \'äb-jikt\ *n* **1** ♦ : something that may be seen or felt; *also* : something that may be perceived or examined mentally **2** : something that arouses an emotional response (as of affection or pity) **3** ♦ : the goal or end of an effort or activity : AIM, PURPOSE **4** : a word or word group denoting that which the action of the verb is directed on or toward; *also* : a noun or noun equivalent in a prepositional phrase

♦ [1] being, entity, individual, substance, thing — more at ENTITY ♦ [3] aim, ambition, aspiration, design, dream, end, goal, intent, mark, meaning, objective, plan, pretension, purpose, thing — more at GOAL

²ob·ject \əb-'jekt\ *vb* **1** ♦ : to offer in opposition **2** ♦ : to oppose something; *also* : DISAPPROVE — **ob·jec·tor** \-'jek-tər\ *n*

♦ [1, 2] challenge, complain, criticize, demur, disapprove, dispute, kick, protest, quarrel, remonstrate; *also* cavil, quibble, inveigh (against); balk (at)

object code *n* : a computer program after translation from source code

ob·jec·ti·fy \əb-'jek-tə-ˌfī\ *vb* **-fied; -fy·ing** : to make objective

ob·jec·tion \əb-'jek-shən\ *n* **1** ♦ : the act of objecting **2** : a reason for or a feeling of disapproval

♦ challenge, complaint, demur, expostulation, fuss, kick, protest, question, remonstrance; *also* compunction, doubt, misgiving, qualm, scruple; difficulty, misunderstanding; cavil, quibble; argument, conflict, debate, dispute, dissent, hassle, quarrel, squabble; censure, criticism; defiance, disobedience, rebellion

ob·jec·tion·able \əb-'jek-shə-nə-bəl\ *adj* ♦ : arousing objection : UNDESIRABLE, OFFENSIVE — **ob·jec·tion·ably** \-blē\ *adv*

♦ censurable, obnoxious, offensive, reprehensible; *also* bawdy, coarse, crude, dirty, filthy, foul, gross, indecent, lewd, nasty, obscene, smutty, vulgar; blamable, blameworthy, lascivious, pornographic, ribald, scurrilous; debasing, perverted, profane; racy, salty, suggestive; unwanted, unwelcome; abhorrent, disgusting, loathsome, repellent, repugnant, repulsive, revolting; disagreeable, displeasing, distasteful, unpleasant; bad, execrable, lousy, miserable; atrocious, infamous; indecent, indecorous, unbecoming; earthy, unprintable; naughty, wicked *Ant* inoffensive, unobjectionable

¹ob·jec·tive \əb-'jek-tiv\ *adj* **1** : of or relating to an object or end **2** : existing outside and independent of the mind **3** : of, relating to, or constituting a grammatical case marking typically the object of a verb or preposition **4** ♦ : treating or dealing with facts without distortion by personal feelings or prejudices — **ob·jec·tive·ly** *adv* — **ob·jec·tive·ness** *n*

♦ disinterested, dispassionate, equal, equitable, fair, impartial, just, nonpartisan, square, unbiased, unprejudiced — more at FAIR

²objective *n* **1** : the lens (as in a microscope) nearest the object and forming an image of it **2** ♦ : an aim, goal, or end of action

♦ aim, ambition, aspiration, design, dream, end, goal, intent, mark, meaning, object, plan, pretension, purpose, thing — more at GOAL

ob·jec·tiv·i·ty \ˌäb-jek-'ti-və-tē\ *n* ♦ : the quality, state, or relation of being objective

♦ detachment, disinterestedness, impartiality, neutrality — more at DETACHMENT

ob·jet d'art \ˌòb-ˌzhä-'där\ *n, pl* **ob·jets d'art** *same*\ [F] : an article of artistic worth; *also* : CURIO

ob·jet trou·vé \'òb-ˌzhä-trü-'vä\ *n, pl* **objets trouvés** *same*\ [F, lit., found object] : a found natural or discarded object (as a piece of driftwood) held to have aesthetic value

ob·jur·ga·tion \ˌäb-jər-'gä-shən\ *n* : a harsh rebuke — **ob·jur·gate** \'äb-jər-ˌgāt\ *vb*

obl *abbr* **1** oblique **2** oblong

ob·late \ä-'blāt\ *adj* : flattened or depressed at the poles ⟨an ∼ spheroid⟩

ob·la·tion \ə-'blā-shən\ *n* : a religious offering

ob·li·gate \'ä-blə-ˌgāt\ *vb* **-gat·ed; -gat·ing** ♦ : to bind legally or morally

♦ coerce, compel, constrain, drive, force, make, muscle, oblige, press, pressure — more at FORCE

ob·li·gat·ed \'ä-blə-ˌgā-təd\ *adj* ♦ : bound legally or morally

♦ beholden, indebted, obliged — more at BEHOLDEN

ob·li·ga·tion \ˌä-blə-'gä-shən\ *n* **1** : an act of obligating oneself to a course of action **2** ♦ : something (as a promise or a contract) that binds one to a course of action **3** : INDEBTEDNESS; *also* : LIABILITY **4** : DUTY

♦ burden, charge, commitment, duty, need, responsibility; *also* pledge, promise; arrangement, prearrangement, setup; compact, contract, covenant, pact; payment, tribute; compulsion, constraint, must, requirement; coercion, duress, force; appointment, engagement, reservation

oblig·a·to·ry \ə-'bli-gə-ˌtòr-ē\ *adj* ♦ : binding in law or conscience

♦ compulsory, imperative, incumbent, involuntary, mandatory, necessary, nonelective, peremptory — more at MANDATORY

oblige \ə-'blīj\ *vb* **obliged; oblig·ing** [ME, fr. AF *obliger*, fr. L *obligare*, lit., to bind to, fr. *ob-* toward + *ligare* to bind] **1** ♦ : to constrain by physical, moral, or legal force or by the requirements of circumstance : FORCE, COMPEL **2** : to bind by a favor; *also* : to do a favor for or do something as a favor

♦ coerce, compel, constrain, drive, force, make, muscle, obligate, press, pressure — more at FORCE

obliged \ə-'blījd\ *adj* **1** ♦ : full of appreciation **2** ♦ : in someone's debt by a favor or service

♦ [1] appreciative, grateful, thankful — more at GRATEFUL ♦ [2] beholden, indebted, obligated — more at BEHOLDEN

oblig·ing *adj* ♦ : willing to do favors — **oblig·ing·ly** *adv*

♦ accommodating, friendly, indulgent — more at ACCOMMODATING

oblique \ō-'blēk\ *adj* **1** ♦ : neither perpendicular nor parallel : having a slant **2** : not straightforward : INDIRECT — **oblique·ness** *n* — **obliq·ui·ty** \-'bli-kwə-tē\ *n*

♦ canted, diagonal, inclined, leaning, listing, slantwise — more at DIAGONAL

oblique case *n* : a grammatical case other than the nominative or vocative

oblique·ly *adv* ♦ : in an oblique way or direction

♦ athwart, crosswise, transversely — more at CROSSWISE

oblit·er·ate \ə-'bli-tə-ˌrāt\ *vb* **-at·ed; -at·ing** [L *oblitterare*, fr. *ob* in the way of + *littera* letter] **1** : to make undecipherable by wiping out or covering over **2** : to remove from recognition or memory **3** : CANCEL **4** ♦ : to remove from existence

♦ annihilate, blot out, demolish, eradicate, exterminate, liquidate, root, rub out, snuff, stamp, wipe out — more at ANNIHILATE

oblit·er·a·tion \ə-ˌbli-tə-'rā-shən\ *n* ♦ : the state of being obliterated

♦ annihilation, demolition, desolation, destruction, devastation, havoc, loss, ruin, wastage, wreckage — more at DESTRUCTION

obliv·i·on \ə-'bli-vē-ən\ *n* **1** : the condition of being oblivious **2** : the condition or state of being forgotten

obliv·i·ous \ə-'bli-ve-əs\ *adj* **1** : lacking memory or mindful attention **2** ♦ : lacking active conscious knowledge or awareness : UNAWARE — **obliv·i·ous·ly** *adv*

♦ ignorant, unaware, unconscious, uninformed, unknowing, unwitting — more at IGNORANT

obliv·i·ous·ness *n* ♦ : the quality or state of being oblivious

♦ ignorance, unawareness — more at IGNORANCE

ob·long \'ä-ˌblȯŋ\ *adj* : deviating from a square, circular, or spherical form by elongation in one dimension — **oblong** *n*

ob·lo·quy \'ä-blə-kwē\ *n, pl* **-quies** 1 : strongly condemnatory utterance or language 2 : bad repute : DISGRACE

ob·nox·ious \äb-'näk-shəs\ *adj* 1 ♦ : odiously or disgustingly objectionable : highly offensive : REPUGNANT, OFFENSIVE 2 *archaic* : deserving of censure — **ob·nox·ious·ly** *adv* — **ob·nox·ious·ness** *n*

♦ abhorrent, abominable, appalling, awful, distasteful, dreadful, foul, nauseating, noisome, odious, offensive, repellent, repugnant, repulsive, revolting — more at OFFENSIVE

oboe \'ō-bō\ *n* [It, fr. F *hautbois*, fr. *haut* high + *bois* wood] : a woodwind instrument with a slender conical tube and a double reed mouthpiece — **obo·ist** \'ō-ˌbō-ist\ *n*

ob·scene \äb-'sēn\ *adj* 1 : disgusting to the senses : REPULSIVE 2 ♦ : deeply offensive to morality or decency; *esp* : designed to incite to lust or depravity — **ob·scene·ly** *adv*

♦ bawdy, coarse, crude, dirty, filthy, foul, gross, indecent, lascivious, lewd, nasty, pornographic, ribald, smutty, unprintable, vulgar, wanton; *also* earthy, racy, salty, suggestive; indecorous, unbecoming, debasing, perverted, profane; naughty, wicked; exceptionable, objectionable, unacceptable, undesirable, unwanted, unwelcome; abhorrent, disgusting, loathsome, offensive, repellent, repugnant, repulsive, revolting; distasteful, obnoxious, unpleasant; blamable, blameworthy, censurable, reprehensible; atrocious, infamous; abusive, scurrilous *Ant* clean, decent

ob·scen·i·ty \-'se-nə-tē\ *n* ♦ : the quality or state of being obscene

♦ bawdiness, coarseness, dirt, dirtiness, filth, filthiness, foulness, grossness, indecency, lewdness, nastiness, ribaldry, smut, vulgarity; *also* raciness, saltiness, suggestiveness; perversion, profanity; naughtiness, wickedness; offensiveness, repulsiveness; obnoxiousness, unpleasantness

ob·scu·ran·tism \äb-'skyùr-ən-ˌti-zəm, ˌäb-skyù-'ran-\ *n* 1 : opposition to the spread of knowledge 2 : deliberate vagueness or abstruseness — **ob·scu·ran·tist** \-tist\ *n or adj*

¹**ob·scure** \äb-'skyùr\ *adj* 1 ♦ : emitting or having a limited or insufficient amount of light : DIM, GLOOMY 2 ♦ : not readily understood 3 ♦ : relatively unknown; *also* : HUMBLE — **ob·scure·ly** *adv*

♦ [1] dark, darkling, dim, dusky, gloomy, murky, somber (*or* sombre) — more at DARK ♦ [2] ambiguous, cryptic, dark, darkling, deep, enigmatic, equivocal, inscrutable, murky, mysterious, mystic, nebulous, occult, unclear, vague; *also* abstruse, esoteric, recondite; bleary, cloudy, dim, faint, foggy, fuzzy, hazy, indefinite, indistinct, indistinguishable, shadowy, uncertain, undefined, undetermined; impenetrable, incomprehensible, inexplicable; eerie, uncanny, weird; impalpable, inappreciable, intangible, invisible; unanswerable, unknowable; baffling, bewildering, confounding, confusing, mystifying, perplexing, puzzling, unfathomable; difficult, complex, complicated, obtuse *Ant* clear, obvious, plain, unambiguous, unequivocal ♦ [3] anonymous, humble, nameless, unknown, unsung; *also* insignificant, minor, unimportant; undistinguished, unexceptional; unpopular; faceless *Ant* celebrated, famed, famous, noted, notorious, prominent, renowned, well-known

²**obscure** *vb* **ob·scured; ob·scur·ing** 1 ♦ : to make dark, dim, or indistinct 2 ♦ : to conceal or hide by or as if by covering

♦ [1] becloud, befog, blur, cloud, darken, dim, fog, haze, mist, overcast, overshadow, shroud — more at

CLOUD ♦ [2] blanket, blot out, cloak, conceal, cover, curtain, enshroud, hide, mask, occult, screen, shroud, veil — more at HIDE

ob·scu·ri·ty \-'skyùr-ə-tē\ *n* ♦ : the quality or state of being obscure

♦ ambiguity, darkness, murkiness, opacity; *also* cloudiness, dimness, faintness, fuzziness, haziness, indefiniteness, indistinctness, uncertainty, vagueness; impenetrability; invisibility; abstruseness; difficulty, complexity, complication, obtuseness *Ant* clarity, clearness, obviousness, plainness

ob·se·qui·ous \əb-'sē-kwē-əs\ *adj* : humbly or excessively attentive (as to a person in authority) : FAWNING, SYCOPHANTIC — **ob·se·qui·ous·ly** *adv* — **ob·se·qui·ous·ness** *n*

ob·se·quy \'äb-sə-kwē\ *n, pl* **-quies** : a funeral or burial rite — usu. used in pl.

ob·serv·able \əb-'zər-və-bəl\ *adj* 1 : NOTEWORTHY 2 ♦ : capable of being observed — **ob·serv·abil·ity** \-'bi-lə-tē\ *n*

♦ apparent, visible, visual — more at VISIBLE

ob·ser·vance \əb-'zər-vəns\ *n* 1 ♦ : a customary practice or ceremony 2 ♦ : an act or instance of following a custom, rule, or law 3 ♦ : an act or instance of watching : OBSERVATION

♦ [1] ceremonial, ceremony, form, formality, rite, ritual, solemnity — more at RITE ♦ [2] compliance, conformity, obedience, submission, subordination — more at OBEDIENCE ♦ [3] attention, awareness, cognizance, ear, eye, heed, notice, observation — more at ATTENTION

ob·ser·vant \-vənt\ *adj* 1 ♦ : paying strict attention ⟨~ spectators⟩ 2 : KEEN, PERCEPTIVE 3 : MINDFUL ⟨~ of the amenities⟩

♦ absorbed, attentive, engrossed, intent, rapt — more at ATTENTIVE

ob·ser·va·tion \ˌäb-sər-'vā-shən, -zər-\ *n* 1 ♦ : an act or instance of observing 2 : the gathering of information (as for scientific studies) by noting facts or occurrences 3 ♦ : a conclusion drawn from observing; *also* : REMARK 4 : the fact of being observed — **ob·ser·va·tion·al** \-shə-nəl\ *adj*

♦ [1] attention, awareness, cognizance, ear, eye, heed, notice, observance — more at ATTENTION ♦ [3] comment, note, reflection, remark — more at REMARK

ob·ser·va·to·ry \əb-'zər-və-ˌtōr-ē\ *n, pl* **-ries** : a place or institution equipped for observation of natural phenomena (as in astronomy)

ob·serve \əb-'zərv\ *vb* **ob·served; ob·serv·ing** 1 ♦ : to conform one's action or practice to 2 ♦ : to celebrate or solemnize (as a ceremony or festival) in a customary or accepted way : CELEBRATE 3 : to make a scientific observation of 4 ♦ : to see or sense esp. through careful attention 5 : to come to realize esp. through consideration of noted facts 6 ♦ : to utter as a remark : REMARK — **ob·serv·er** *n*

♦ [1] comply, conform, follow, mind, obey — more at OBEY ♦ [2] celebrate, commemorate, keep — more at KEEP ♦ [4] behold, descry, discern, distinguish, espy, eye, look, note, notice, perceive, regard, remark, see, sight, spy, view, witness — more at SEE ♦ [6] comment, note, opine, remark — more at REMARK

ob·sess \əb-'ses\ *vb* : to preoccupy intensely or abnormally

ob·ses·sion \äb-'se-shən\ *n* ♦ : a persistent disturbing preoccupation with an idea or feeling; *also* : an emotion or idea causing such a preoccupation — **ob·ses·sive** \-'se-siv\ *adj or n* — **ob·ses·sive·ly** *adv*

♦ fetish, fixation, mania, preoccupation, prepossession — more at FIXATION

obsessive–compulsive *adj* : relating to, characterized by, or affected with recurring obsessions and compulsions esp. as symptoms of a neurotic state

ob·sid·i·an \əb-'si-dē-ən\ *n* : a dark natural glass formed by the cooling of molten lava

ob·so·les·cent \ˌäb-sə-ˈles-ᵊnt\ *adj* : going out of use : becoming obsolete — **ob·so·les·cence** \-ᵊns\ *n*

ob·so·lete \ˌäb-sə-ˈlēt, ˈäb-sə-ˌlēt\ *adj* ♦ : no longer in use; *also* : OLD-FASHIONED

♦ antiquated, archaic, dated, old-fashioned, outdated, outmoded, outworn, passé; *also* aging, obsolescent; discarded, superannuated, worn-out; inoperable, unusable, unworkable, useless; dead, defunct, extinct; dormant, fallow, free, idle, inactive, inert, inoperative, latent; ancient, antediluvian, antique, fusty, musty, old, old-time, old-world; aged, age-old, hoary, venerable; bygone, erstwhile, former, late, past; historic, historical

ob·sta·cle \ˈäb-sti-kəl\ *n* ♦ : something that stands in the way or opposes

♦ bar, block, clog, crimp, drag, embarrassment, encumbrance, fetter, handicap, hindrance, let, stop, stumbling block; *also* catch, hitch, rub, snag; burden, weight; fetter, hobble; delay, holdup, setback; break, check, constraint, curb, rein, restraint; bond, chain, handcuff, leash, manacle, muzzle, shackle, strap, tether, tie, trammel; barricade, fence, wall; disability, disadvantage, handicap; difficulty, hardship, rigor; adversity

ob·stet·rics \əb-ˈste-triks\ *n sing or pl* : a branch of medicine that deals with birth and with its antecedents and sequels — **ob·stet·ric** \-trik\ *or* **ob·stet·ri·cal** \-tri-kəl\ *adj* — **ob·ste·tri·cian** \ˌäb-stə-ˈtri-shən\ *n*

ob·sti·na·cy \ˈäb-stə-nə-sē\ *n* ♦ : the quality or state of being obstinate

♦ hardheadedness, mulishness, obduracy, peevishness, pertinacity, self-will, stubbornness, tenacity; *also* perverseness, perversity, resistance, wrongheadedness; persistence, hardness, inflexibility, relentlessness, sternness, strictness; certainty, determination, firmness; resolve, rigidity, steadfastness; defiance, disobedience, insubordination, recalcitrance

ob·sti·nate \ˈäb-stə-nət\ *adj* ♦ : fixed and unyielding (as in an opinion or course) despite reason or persuasion : STUBBORN ⟨∼ opposition⟩ — **ob·sti·nate·ly** *adv*

♦ dogged, hardheaded, headstrong, mulish, obdurate, opinionated, peevish, pertinacious, perverse, pigheaded, stubborn, unyielding, willful; *also* hidebound, narrow-minded; resistant, wayward, wrongheaded; persistent, tenacious; adamant, adamantine, hard, inflexible, iron, relentless, rigid, stern, strict, unbending, uncompromising, unrelenting; determined, firm, inexorable, steadfast, sure; contrary, disobedient, froward, insubordinate, intractable, recalcitrant, refractory, uncooperative, ungovernable, unmanageable, unruly; defiant, insurgent, mutinous; indomitable

ob·strep·er·ous \əb-ˈstre-pə-rəs\ *adj* **1** ♦ : uncontrollably noisy **2** : stubbornly resistant to control : UNRULY — **ob·strep·er·ous·ness** *n*

♦ blatant, clamorous, vociferous — more at VOCIFEROUS

ob·struct \əb-ˈstrəkt\ *vb* **1** ♦ : to block by an obstacle **2** ♦ : to impede the passage, action, or operation of **3** : to cut off from sight — **ob·struc·tive** \-ˈstrək-tiv\ *adj* — **ob·struc·tor** \-tər\ *n*

♦ [1] block, choke, clog, close (off), congest, dam, jam, plug (up), stop (up), stuff — more at CLOG ♦ [2] delay, hamper, hinder, hold back, hold up, impede, inhibit, interfere with — more at HAMPER

ob·struc·tion \əb-ˈstrək-shən\ *n* **1** : an act of obstructing : the state of being obstructed **2** : something that obstructs : HINDRANCE

ob·struc·tion·ist \-shə-nist\ *n* : a person who hinders progress or business esp. in a legislative body — **ob·struc·tion·ism** \-shə-ˌni-zəm\ *n*

ob·tain \əb-ˈtān\ *vb* **1** ♦ : to gain or attain usu. by planning or effort **2** : to be generally recognized or established

♦ acquire, attain, capture, carry, draw, earn, gain, garner, get, land, make, procure, realize, secure, win — more at EARN

ob·tain·able *adj* ♦ : capable of being obtained

♦ accessible, acquirable, attainable, available, procurable — more at AVAILABLE

ob·trude \əb-ˈtrüd\ *vb* **ob·trud·ed; ob·trud·ing 1** : to thrust out **2** : to thrust forward without warrant or request **3** ♦ : to become unduly prominent or interfering : INTRUDE — **ob·tru·sion** \-ˈtrü-zhən\ *n* — **ob·tru·sive·ly** *adv* — **ob·tru·sive·ness** *n*

♦ butt in, interfere, intrude, meddle, mess, nose, poke, pry, snoop — more at INTERFERE

ob·tru·sive \-ˈtrü-siv\ *adj* ♦ : forward in manner or conduct

♦ intrusive, meddlesome, nosy, officious, presumptuous, prying — more at INTRUSIVE

ob·tuse \äb-ˈtüs, -ˈtyüs\ *adj* **ob·tus·er; -est 1** : exceeding 90 degrees but less than 180 degrees ⟨∼ angle⟩ **2** ♦ : not pointed or acute : BLUNT **3** ♦ : not sharp or quick of wit ⟨too ∼ to take a hint⟩ — **ob·tuse·ly** *adv*

♦ [2] blunt, dull — more at DULL ♦ [3] dense, dull, dumb, slow, stupid, thick, unintelligent

ob·tuse·ness *n* ♦ : the quality or state of being obtuse

♦ denseness, stupidity — more at STUPIDITY

obv *abbr* obverse

¹**ob·verse** \äb-ˈvərs, ˈäb-ˌvərs\ *adj* **1** : facing the observer or opponent **2** : being a counterpart or complement — **ob·verse·ly** *adv*

²**ob·verse** \ˈäb-ˌvərs, äb-ˈvərs\ *n* **1** : the side (as of a coin) bearing the principal design and lettering **2** : a front or principal surface **3** : a counterpart having the opposite orientation or force

ob·vi·ate \ˈäb-vē-ˌāt\ *vb* **-at·ed; -at·ing** ♦ : to anticipate and prevent (as a situation) or make unnecessary (as an action) — **ob·vi·a·tion** \ˌäb-vē-ˈā-shən\ *n*

♦ avert, forestall, help, preclude, prevent — more at PREVENT

ob·vi·ous \ˈäb-vē-əs\ *adj* [L *obvius*, fr. *obviam* in the way, fr. *ob* in the way of + *viam*, acc. of *via* way] ♦ : easily found, seen, or understood — **ob·vi·ous·ly** *adv* — **ob·vi·ous·ness** *n*

♦ apparent, broad, clear, clear-cut, distinct, evident, lucid, manifest, palpable, patent, perspicuous, plain, transparent, unambiguous, unequivocal, unmistakable — more at CLEAR ♦ blatant, conspicuous, egregious, flagrant, glaring, gross, patent, prominent, pronounced, rank, striking — more at EGREGIOUS

OC *abbr* officer candidate

oc·a·ri·na \ˌä-kə-ˈrē-nə\ *n* [It] : a wind instrument typically having an oval body with finger holes and a projecting mouthpiece

occas *abbr* occasionally

¹**oc·ca·sion** \ə-ˈkā-zhən\ *n* **1** ♦ : a favorable opportunity **2** ♦ : a direct or indirect cause **3** : the time of an event **4** : EXIGENCY **5** *pl* : AFFAIRS, BUSINESS **6** : a special event : CELEBRATION **7** ♦ : something that happens

♦ [1] chance, opening, opportunity, room — more at OPPORTUNITY ♦ [2] antecedent, cause, reason — more at CAUSE ♦ [7] affair, circumstance, episode, event, happening, incident, occurrence, thing — more at EVENT

²**occasion** *vb* : BRING ABOUT, CAUSE

oc·ca·sion·al \ə-ˈkā-zhə-nəl\ *adj* **1** ♦ : happening or met with now and then ⟨∼ visits⟩ **2** : used or designed for a special occasion ⟨∼ verse⟩ — **oc·ca·sion·al·ly** *adv*

♦ casual, choppy, discontinuous, erratic, fitful, intermittent, irregular, spasmodic, sporadic, spotty, unsteady — more at FITFUL ♦ infrequent, rare, sporadic — more at INFREQUENT

oc·ci·den·tal \ˌäk-sə-ˈdent-ᵊl\ *adj, often cap* [fr. *Occident* West, fr. ME, fr. AF, fr. L *occident-, occidens*, fr. prp.

of *occidere* to fall, set (of the sun)] : WESTERN — **Occi-dental** *n*

Oc·ci·tan \'äk-sə-ˌtan\ *n* [F, fr. ML *occitanus*, fr. Old Oc-citan *oc* yes (contrasted with OF *oïl* yes)] : a Romance language spoken in southern France

oc·clude \ə-'klüd\ *vb* **oc·clud·ed; oc·clud·ing 1** ♦ : to block by an obstacle : OBSTRUCT ⟨an *occluded* artery⟩ **2** : to come together with opposing surfaces in contact — used of teeth — **oc·clu·sion** \-'klü-zhən\ *n* — **oc·clu·sive** \-'klü-siv\ *adj*

♦ block, choke, clog, close (off), congest, dam, jam, ob-struct, plug (up), stop (up), stuff — more at CLOG

¹**oc·cult** \ə-'kəlt\ *adj* **1** : not revealed : SECRET **2** ♦ : not easily apprehended or understood : MYSTERIOUS **3** ♦ : of or relating to supernatural agencies, their effects, or knowledge of them ⟨the ~ arts⟩ — **oc·cult·ism** \-'kəl-ˌti-zəm\ *n* — **oc·cult·ist** \-tist\ *n*

♦ [2] cryptic, darkling, deep, enigmatic, impenetrable, inscrutable, mysterious, mystic, uncanny — more at MYSTERIOUS ♦ [3] magic, magical, mystic, weird — more at MYSTIC

²**occult** *n* : occult matters — used with *the*

oc·cu·pan·cy \'ä-kyə-pən-sē\ *n, pl* **-cies 1** : the act of oc-cupying : the state of being occupied **2** : an occupied building or part of a building

oc·cu·pant \-pənt\ *n* ♦ : one who occupies something; *esp* : RESIDENT

♦ denizen, dweller, inhabitant, resident — more at IN-HABITANT

oc·cu·pa·tion \ˌä-kyə-'pā-shən\ *n* **1** ♦ : an activity in which one engages; *esp* : VOCATION **2** : the taking pos-session of property; *also* : the taking possession of an area by a foreign military force — **oc·cu·pa·tion·al** \-shə-nəl\ *adj* — **oc·cu·pa·tion·al·ly** *adv*

♦ calling, employment, line, profession, trade, voca-tion, work; *also* racket; art, craft, handicraft; appoint-ment, assignment, berth, billet, duty, function, job, office, place, position, post, situation; business, engage-ment, livelihood, living

occupational therapy *n* : therapy by means of activity; *esp* : creative activity prescribed for its effect in promoting recovery or rehabilitation — **occupational therapist** *n*

oc·cu·pied \'ä-kyə-ˌpīd\ *adj* ♦ : engaged in activity

♦ active, assiduous, busy, diligent, engaged, laborious, sedulous, working — more at BUSY

oc·cu·py \'ä-kyə-ˌpī\ *vb* **-py·ing 1** ♦ : to engage the atten-tion or energies of **2** : to fill up (an extent in space or time) **3** ♦ : to take or hold possession of **4** : to reside in as owner or tenant — **oc·cu·pi·er** *n*

♦ [1] absorb, busy, engage, engross, enthrall, fascinate, grip, immerse, interest, intrigue, involve — more at EN-GAGE ♦ [3] command, enjoy, have, hold, own, possess, retain — more at HAVE

oc·cur \ə-'kər\ *vb* **oc·curred; oc·cur·ring** [L *occurrere*, fr. *ob-* in the way + *currere* to run] **1** : to be found or met with : APPEAR **2** ♦ : to come into existence : HAPPEN **3** : to come to mind ⟨it *occurred* to her⟩

♦ be, befall, betide, chance, come, go, happen, pass, transpire — more at HAPPEN

oc·cur·rence \ə-'kər-əns\ *n* **1** ♦ : something that takes place **2** : the action or process of occurring

♦ affair, circumstance, episode, event, happening, inci-dent, occasion, thing — more at EVENT

ocean \'ō-shən\ *n* **1** ♦ : the whole body of salt water that covers nearly three fourths of the surface of the earth **2** : any of the large bodies of water into which the great ocean is divided

♦ blue, brine, deep, sea; *also* high seas, main, waters; basin

ocean·ar·i·um \ˌō-shə-'nar-ē-əm\ *n, pl* **-iums** *or* **-ia** \-ē-ə\ : a large marine aquarium

ocean·front \'ō-shən-ˌfrənt\ *n* : a shore area on the ocean

ocean·go·ing \-ˌgō-iŋ\ *adj* : of, relating to, or suitable for travel on the ocean

oce·an·ic \ˌō-shē-'a-nik\ *adj* ♦ : of or relating to the ocean

♦ marine, maritime, pelagic — more at MARINE

ocean·og·ra·phy \ˌō-shə-'nä-grə-fē\ *n* : a science dealing with the ocean and its phenomena — **ocean·og·ra·pher** \-fər\ *n* — **ocean·o·graph·ic** \-nə-'gra-fik\ *adj*

oce·lot \'ä-sə-ˌlät, 'ō-\ *n* : a medium-sized American wild-cat ranging southward from Texas to northern Argen-tina and having a tawny yellow or gray coat with black markings

ocher *or* **ochre** \'ō-kər\ *n* : an earthy usu. red or yellow iron ore used as a pigment; *also* : the color esp. of yellow ocher

o'·clock \ə-'kläk\ *adv* : according to the clock

OCR *abbr* optical character reader; optical character rec-ognition

OCS *abbr* officer candidate school

oct *abbr* octavo

Oct *abbr* October

oc·ta·gon \'äk-tə-ˌgän\ *n* : a polygon of eight angles and eight sides — **oc·tag·o·nal** \äk-'ta-gən-ᵊl\ *adj*

oc·tane \'äk-ˌtān\ *n* : OCTANE NUMBER

octane number *n* : a number used to measure the anti-knock properties of gasoline that increases as the likeli-hood of knocking decreases

oc·tave \'äk-tiv\ *n* **1** : a musical interval embracing eight degrees; *also* : a tone or note at this interval or the whole series of notes, tones, or keys within this interval **2** : a group of eight

oc·ta·vo \äk-'tā-vō, -'tä-\ *n, pl* **-vos 1** : the size of a piece of paper cut eight from a sheet **2** : a book printed on octavo pages

oc·tet \äk-'tet\ *n* **1** : a musical composition for eight voices or eight instruments; *also* : the performers of such a composition **2** : a group or set of eight

Oc·to·ber \äk-'tō-bər\ *n* [ME *Octobre*, fr. OE *October*, fr. L, eighth month of the early Roman calendar, fr. *octo* eight] : the 10th month of the year

oc·to·ge·nar·i·an \ˌäk-tə-jə-'ner-ē-ən\ *n* : a person whose age is in the eighties

oc·to·pus \'äk-tə-pəs\ *n, pl* **-pus·es** *or* **-pi** \-ˌpī\ : any of various sea mollusks with eight long muscular arms fur-nished with suckers

oc·to·syl·lab·ic \ˌäk-tə-sə-'la-bik\ *adj* : composed of verses having eight syllables — **octosyllabic** *n*

¹**oc·u·lar** \'ä-kyə-lər\ *adj* **1** ♦ : based on what has been seen : VISUAL **2** : of or relating to the eye or the eyesight

♦ optical, visual — more at VISUAL

²**ocular** *n* : EYEPIECE

oc·u·list \'ä-kyə-list\ *n* **1** : OPHTHALMOLOGIST **2** : OP-TOMETRIST

¹**OD** \ˌō-'dē\ *n* : an overdose of a drug and esp. a narcotic

²**OD** *vb* **OD'd** *or* **ODed; OD'·ing; OD's** : to become ill or die from an OD

³**OD** *abbr* **1** doctor of optometry **2** [L *oculus dexter*] right eye **3** officer of the day **4** olive drab **5** overdraft **6** overdrawn

odd \'äd\ *adj* [ME *odde*, fr. ON *oddi* point of land, triangle, odd number] **1** : being only one of a pair or set ⟨an ~ shoe⟩ **2** : somewhat more than the number mentioned ⟨forty ~ years ago⟩ **3** : being an integer (as 1, 3, or 5) not divisible by two without leaving a remainder **4** : ad-ditional to what is usual ⟨~ jobs⟩ **5** ♦ : differing mark-edly from the usual or ordinary or accepted : STRANGE ⟨an ~ way of behaving⟩ — **odd·ness** *n*

♦ bizarre, curious, far-out, funny, kinky, outlandish, outré, peculiar, quaint, queer, quirky, remarkable, screwy, strange, wacky, weird, wild; *also* aberrant, ab-normal, atypical, extraordinary, fantastic, flaky, freak, freakish, idiosyncratic, phenomenal, singular, unique, unusual, unwonted; conspicuous, notable, noticeable, outstanding, prominent, salient, striking; atrocious, outrageous, shocking, nonconforming, nonconformist, unconventional, unorthodox; eccentric, idiosyncratic; rare, uncommon, uncustomary; baffling, bewildering, confounding, mystifying, perplexing, puzzling aberrant, abnormal, atypical, exceptional, extraordinary, freak, peculiar, phenomenal, rare, singular, uncommon, uncustomary, unique, unusual, unwonted — more at EXCEPTIONAL

odd·ball \'äd-ˌbȯl\ *n* ♦ : one that is eccentric — **oddball** *adj*

♦ character, crackpot, crank, eccentric, kook, nut, screwball, weirdo — more at ECCENTRIC

odd·i·ty \'ä-də-tē\ *n, pl* **-ties** **1** ♦ : one that is odd **2** ♦ : the quality or state of being odd

♦ [1] crotchet, eccentricity, idiosyncrasy, mannerism, peculiarity, quirk, singularity, trick — more at IDIOSYNCRASY ♦ [1, 2] curiosity, exotic, rarity — more at CURIOSITY

odd·ly \'äd-lē\ *adv* **1** : in an odd manner ⟨an ∼ shaped roof⟩ **2** : as is odd ⟨∼ enough, I agree⟩

odd·ment \'äd-mənt\ *n* : something left over : REMNANT

odds \'ädz\ *n pl* **1** ♦ : a difference by which one thing is favored over another **2** : DISAGREEMENT — usu. used with *at* **3** : the ratio between the amount to be paid for a winning bet and the amount of the bet ⟨the horse went off at ∼ of 6–1⟩

♦ chance, percentage, probability — more at PROBABILITY

odds and ends *n pl* **1** ♦ : miscellaneous things or matters **2** ♦ : miscellaneous remnants or leftovers

♦ [1] notions, novelties, sundries ♦ [2] balance, leavings, leftovers, remainder, remains, remnant, residue, rest — more at REMAINDER

odds–on \'ädz-'ȯn, -'än\ *adj* : having a better than even chance to win

ode \'ōd\ *n* : a lyric poem that expresses a noble feeling with dignity

odi·ous \'ō-dē-əs\ *adj* ♦ : causing or deserving hatred or repugnance — **odi·ous·ly** *adv* — **odi·ous·ness** *n*

♦ abhorrent, abominable, appalling, awful, distasteful, nauseating, noisome, obnoxious, offensive, repellent, repugnant, repulsive, revolting

odi·um \'ō-dē-əm\ *n* **1** : merited loathing : HATRED **2** ♦ : disrepute or infamy attached to something : DISGRACE ⟨the ∼ of defeat⟩

♦ discredit, disgrace, dishonor (*or* dishonour), disrepute, ignominy, infamy, opprobrium, reproach, shame — more at DISGRACE

odom·e·ter \ō-'dä-mə-tər\ *n* [F *odomètre,* fr. Gk *hodometron,* fr. *hodos* way, road + *metron* measure] : an instrument for measuring distance traveled (as by a vehicle)

odor *or Can and Brit* **odour** \'ō-dər\ *n* **1** ♦ : the quality of something that stimulates the sense of smell; *also* : a sensation resulting from such stimulation **2** : REPUTE, ESTIMATION — **odored** \'ō-dərd\ *adj* — **odor·less** *adj* — **odor·ous** *adj*

♦ redolence, scent, smell — more at SMELL

odor·if·er·ous \ˌō-də-'ri-fə-rəs\ *adj* : having or yielding an odor

odour *Can and Brit var of* ODOR

od·ys·sey \'ä-də-sē\ *n, pl* **-seys** [the *Odyssey,* epic poem attributed to Homer recounting the long wanderings of Odysseus] : a long wandering marked usu. by many changes of fortune

oe·cu·men·i·cal \ˌē-\ *chiefly Brit var of* ECUMENICAL

OED *abbr* Oxford English Dictionary

oe·de·ma *chiefly Brit var of* EDEMA

oe·di·pal \'e-də-pəl, 'ē-\ *adj, often cap* : of, relating to, or resulting from the Oedipus complex

Oe·di·pus complex \-pəs-\ *n* : the positive sexual feelings of a child toward the parent of the opposite sex and hostile or jealous feelings toward the parent of the same sex that may be a source of adult personality disorder when unresolved

OEO *abbr* Office of Economic Opportunity

o'er \'ȯr\ *adv or prep* **1** : across a barrier or intervening space : OVER **2** : once more **3** : in or to a higher place

OES *abbr* Order of the Eastern Star

oe·soph·a·gus *chiefly Brit var of* ESOPHAGUS

oeu·vre \'ər-vrə\ *n, pl* **oeuvres** *same*\ : a substantial body of work constituting the lifework of a writer, an artist, or a composer

of \'əv, 'äv\ *prep* **1** : FROM ⟨a man ∼ the West⟩ **2** : having as a significant background or character element ⟨a man ∼ noble birth⟩ ⟨a woman ∼ ability⟩ **3** : owing to ⟨died ∼ flu⟩ **4** : BY ⟨the plays ∼ Shakespeare⟩ **5** : having as component parts or material, contents, or members ⟨a house ∼ brick⟩ ⟨a glass ∼ water⟩ ⟨a pack ∼ wolves⟩ **6** : belonging to or included by ⟨the front ∼ the house⟩ ⟨a time ∼ life⟩ ⟨one ∼ you⟩ ⟨the best ∼ its kind⟩ ⟨the son ∼ a doctor⟩ **7** ♦ : relating to : ABOUT ⟨tales ∼ the West⟩ **8** : connected with : OVER ⟨the queen ∼ England⟩ **9** : that is : signified as ⟨the city ∼ Rome⟩ **10** — used to indicate apposition of the words it joins ⟨a huge barn ∼ a house⟩ **11** : as concerns : FOR ⟨love ∼ nature⟩ **12** — used to indicate the application of an adjective ⟨fond ∼ candy⟩ **13** ♦ : preceding in time : BEFORE ⟨quarter ∼ ten⟩

♦ [7] about, apropos of, concerning, on, regarding, respecting, toward — more at ABOUT ♦ [13] ahead of, before, ere, previous to, prior to, to — more at BEFORE

OF *abbr* outfield

¹off \'ȯf\ *adv* **1** : from a place or position ⟨drove ∼ in a new car⟩; *also* : ASIDE ⟨turned ∼ into a side road⟩ **2** : at a distance in time or space ⟨stood ∼ a few yards⟩ ⟨several years ∼⟩ **3** : so as to be unattached or removed ⟨the lid blew ∼⟩ **4** : to a state of discontinuance, exhaustion, or completion ⟨shut the radio ∼⟩ **5** : away from regular work ⟨took time ∼ for lunch⟩

²off *prep* **1** : away from ⟨just ∼ the highway⟩ ⟨take it ∼ the table⟩ **2** : to seaward of ⟨two miles ∼ the coast⟩ **3** : FROM ⟨borrowed a dollar ∼ me⟩ **4** : at the expense of ⟨lives ∼ his parents⟩ **5** : not now engaged in ⟨∼ duty⟩ **6** : abstaining from ⟨∼ liquor⟩ **7** : below the usual level of ⟨∼ his game⟩

³off *adj* **1** : more removed or distant **2** : started on the way **3** ♦ : not operating **4** ♦ : not correct **5** : small in degree : REMOTE, SLIGHT **6** : of poor quality : INFERIOR **7** : provided for ⟨well ∼⟩

♦ [3] dead, dormant, fallow, free, idle, inactive, inert, inoperative, latent, vacant — more at INACTIVE ♦ [4] erroneous, false, inaccurate, incorrect, inexact, invalid, unsound, untrue, wrong — more at FALSE

⁴off *abbr* office; officer; official

of·fal \'ȯ-fəl\ *n* [ME, fr. *of* off + *fall* fall] : the waste or by-product of a process; *esp* : the viscera and trimmings of a butchered animal removed in dressing

off and on *adv* : INTERMITTENTLY

¹off·beat \'ȯf-ˌbēt\ *n* : the unaccented part of a musical measure

²offbeat *adj* ♦ : deviating from conventional or accepted usage or conduct esp. in odd or whimsical ways

♦ curious, extraordinary, funny, odd, peculiar, queer, rare, strange, unaccustomed, uncommon, unique, unusual, weird — more at UNUSUAL

off–col·or \'ȯf-'kə-lər\ *or* **off–col·ored** \-lərd\ *adj* **1** : not having the right or standard color **2** : of doubtful propriety : verging on indecency ⟨∼ stories⟩

of·fend \ə-'fend\ *vb* **1** ♦ : to violate a law or rule : SIN, TRANSGRESS **2** : to cause discomfort or pain : HURT **3** ♦ : to cause dislike or vexation

♦ [1] err, sin, transgress, trespass; *also* breach, break, infringe, violate; backslide, lapse ♦ [3] affront, insult, outrage, slight, wound — more at INSULT

of·fend·er *n* ♦ : one that offends

♦ criminal, crook, culprit, felon, lawbreaker, malefactor — more at CRIMINAL

of·fense *or* **of·fence** \ə-'fens, *esp for 2 & 3* 'ä-ˌfens\ *n* **1** : something that outrages the senses **2** ♦ : the act of attacking : ATTACK, ASSAULT **3** : the offensive team or members of a team playing offensive positions **4 a** ♦ : the act of displeasing or affronting **b** ♦ : the state of being insulted or morally outraged **5** ♦ : a breach of a moral or social code : SIN, MISDEED **6** ♦ : an infraction of law : CRIME

♦ [2] aggression, assault, attack, charge, descent, offensive, onset, onslaught, raid, rush, strike — more at ATTACK ♦ [4a] affront, barb, dart, dig, indignity, insult, name, outrage, put-down, sarcasm, slight, slur, wound — more at INSULT ♦ [4b] dudgeon, huff, peeve, pique, resentment, umbrage — more at PIQUE ♦ [5, 6] breach, crime, error, malefaction, misdeed, misdoing, sin, transgression, trespass, violation, wrongdoing; *also* felony, misdemeanor; fault, foible, peccadillo; break, infringement; immorality, iniquity, sinfulness, vice, wickedness; criminality, illegality, lawlessness

¹of·fen·sive \ə-'fen-siv, *esp for 1 & 2* 'ä-ˌfen-\ *adj* **1** : AGGRESSIVE **2** : of or relating to an attempt to score in a game; *also* : of or relating to a team in possession of the ball or puck **3** ♦ : giving painful or unpleasant sensations : OBNOXIOUS **4** : INSULTING — **of·fen·sive·ly** *adv* — **of·fen·sive·ness** *n*

♦ awful, distasteful, foul, horrible, horrid, nauseating, noisome, objectionable, obnoxious, odious, repellent, repugnant, repulsive, shocking, ugly; *also* disagreeable, unpleasant; contemptible, despicable, detestable, hateful; unhealthy, unwholesome; execrable, lousy, miserable; atrocious, heinous, unspeakable; barbarous, unchristian, uncivilized, ungodly, unholy **Ant** inoffensive

²offensive *n* : the act of attacking with physical force or unfriendly words : ATTACK

¹of·fer \'ȯ-fər\ *vb* **of·fered; of·fer·ing** **1** : SACRIFICE **2** ♦ : to present for acceptance : TENDER; *also* : to propose as payment **3** ♦ : to set before the mind (as for discussion, imitation, or action) : PROPOSE, SUGGEST; *also* : to declare one's readiness **4** : to try or begin to exert ⟨~ resistance⟩ **5** : to place on sale **6** ♦ : to present in performance or exhibition

♦ [2] extend, give, proffer, tender; *also* pose, propose ♦ [3] advance, pose, proffer, propose, propound, suggest, vote — more at PROPOSE ♦ [6] carry, give, mount, present, stage — more at PRESENT

²offer *n* **1** ♦ : a presenting of something for acceptance : PROPOSAL **2** : BID **3** : TRY

♦ proffer, proposal, proposition, suggestion — more at PROPOSAL

of·fer·ing *n* : a sacrifice ceremonially offered as a part of worship

of·fer·to·ry \'ȯ-fər-ˌtōr-ē\ *n, pl* **-ries** : the presentation of offerings at a church service; *also* : the musical accompaniment during it

off–gas·sing \'ȯf-ˌga-siŋ\ *n* : the emission of esp. noxious gases (as from a building material)

off·hand \'ȯf-'hand\ *adj* ♦ : done or made without previous thought or preparation — **offhand** *adv*

♦ ad-lib, extemporaneous, impromptu, snap, unplanned, unpremeditated, unprepared, unrehearsed — more at EXTEMPORANEOUS

off–hour \-ˌau̇(-ə)r\ *n* : a period of time other than a rush hour; *also* : a period of time other than business hours

of·fice \'ȯ-fəs\ *n* **1** : a special duty or position; *esp* : a position of authority in government ⟨run for ~⟩ **2** : a prescribed form or service of worship; *also* : RITE **3** : an assigned or assumed duty or role **4** : a place where a business is transacted or a service is supplied **5** ♦ : a major administrative unit in some governments

♦ bureau, department, desk, division — more at DIVISION

of·fice·hold·er \'ȯ-fəs-ˌhōl-dər\ *n* ♦ : one holding a public office

♦ functionary, officer, official, public servant — more at OFFICIAL

of·fi·cer \'ȯ-fə-sər\ *n* **1** ♦ : one charged with the enforcement of law **2** : one who holds an office of trust or authority **3** : a person who holds a position of authority or command in the armed forces; *esp* : COMMISSIONED OFFICER

♦ constable, cop, police officer; *also* patrolman, policewoman; detective, inspector; marshal, sheriff, trooper; captain, lieutenant, sergeant

¹of·fi·cial \ə-'fi-shəl\ *n* ♦ : one who holds or is invested with an office : OFFICER

♦ functionary, officeholder, officer, public servant; *also* bureaucrat; administrator, commissioner, director, executive, manager, superintendent, supervisor; chair, chairman

²official *adj* **1** : of or relating to an office or to officers **2** : AUTHORIZED, AUTHORITATIVE **3** : befitting or characteristic of a person in office — **of·fi·cial·ly** *adv*

of·fi·cial·dom \ə-'fi-shəl-dəm\ *n* : officials as a class

of·fi·cial·ism \ə-'fi-shə-ˌli-zəm\ *n* : lack of flexibility and initiative combined with excessive adherence to regulations

of·fi·ci·ant \ə-'fi-shē-ənt\ *n* : one (as a priest) who officiates at a religious rite

of·fi·ci·ate \ə-'fi-shē-ˌāt\ *vb* **-at·ed; -at·ing** **1** : to perform a ceremony, function, or duty **2** : to act in an official capacity

of·fi·cious \ə-'fi-shəs\ *adj* ♦ : volunteering one's services where they are neither asked for nor needed ⟨an ~ busybody⟩ — **of·fi·cious·ly** *adv* — **of·fi·cious·ness** *n*

♦ intrusive, meddlesome, nosy, obtrusive, presumptuous, prying — more at INTRUSIVE

off·ing \'ȯ-fiŋ\ *n* : the near or foreseeable future

off–line \'ȯf-'līn\ *adj or adv* : not connected to or controlled directly by a computer

off of *prep* : OFF

off·print \'ȯf-ˌprint\ *n* : a separately printed excerpt (as from a magazine)

off–road \-'rōd\ *adj* : of, relating to, or being a vehicle designed for use away from public roads

off–sea·son \-ˌsēz-ᵊn\ *n* : a time of suspended or reduced activity

¹off·set \-ˌset\ *n* **1** : a sharp bend (as in a pipe) by which one part is turned aside out of line **2** : a printing process in which an inked impression is first made on a rubber-blanketed cylinder and then transferred to the paper **3** ♦ : something that serves to counterbalance or to compensate for something else

♦ balance, canceler, counterbalance, counterweight, equipoise

²off·set *vb* **off·set; off·set·ting** **1** : to place over against : BALANCE **2** ♦ : to compensate for **3** : to form an offset in (as a wall)

♦ annul, cancel, compensate, correct, counteract, counterbalance, make up, neutralize; *also* invalidate, negate, nullify; atone (for); outweigh, redeem; redress, relieve, remedy; override, overrule

off·shoot \'ȯf-ˌshüt\ *n* **1** ♦ : a collateral or derived branch, descendant, or member **2** : a branch of a main stem (as of a plant)

♦ derivative, outgrowth, spin-off — more at DERIVATIVE

¹off·shore \'ȯf-'shōr\ *adv* **1** : at a distance from the shore **2** : outside the country : ABROAD

²off·shore \'ȯf-ˌshōr\ *adj* **1** : moving away from the shore **2** : situated off the shore but within waters under a country's control

off·side \-'sīd\ *adv or adj* : illegally in advance of the ball or puck

off·spring \-ˌspriŋ\ *n, pl* **offspring** *also* **offsprings** ♦ : the product of the reproductive processes of an animal or plant : PROGENY

♦ issue, posterity, progeny, seed, spawn; *also* brood, hatch, litter, young; child, scion

off·stage \'óf-ˌstāj, -ˌstäj\ *adv or adj* **1** : off or away from the stage **2** : out of the public view ⟨deals made ∼⟩

off–the–record *adj* : given or made in confidence and not for publication

off–the–shelf *adj* : available as a stock item : not specially designed or made

off–the–wall *adj* : highly unusual : BIZARRE ⟨∼ humor⟩

off·track \'óf-ˌtrak\ *adv or adj* : away from a racetrack

off–white \'óf-ˌhwīt\ *n* : a yellowish or grayish white color

off year *n* **1** : a year in which no major election is held **2** : a year of diminished activity or production

oft \'óft\ *adv* : OFTEN

of·ten \'ó-fən\ *adv* ♦ : many times : FREQUENTLY

♦ constantly, continually, frequently, repeatedly; *also* always, continuously, consistently, perpetually; afresh, again, anew; commonly, ordinarily, regularly, routinely; intermittently, rarely, periodically; generally, usually *Ant* infrequently, rarely, seldom

of·ten·times \-ˌtīmz\ *or* **oft·times** \'óf-ˌtīmz, 'óft-\ *adv* : OFTEN

Og *symbol* oganesson

oga·nes·son \ˌō-gə-'ne-ˌsän, ä-\ *n* : a short-lived artificially produced radioactive chemical element

ogle \'ō-gəl\ *vb* **ogled; ogling** : to look at in a flirtatious way — **ogle** *n* — **ogler** *n*

ogre \'ō-gər\ *n* **1** : a monster of fairy tales and folklore that eats people **2** ♦ : a dreaded person or object

♦ bête noire, bogey, bugbear, hobgoblin — more at BOGEY

ogress \'ō-grəs\ *n* : a female ogre

oh \'ō\ *interj* **1** — used to express an emotion or in response to physical stimuli **2** — used in direct address

OH *abbr* Ohio

ohm \'ōm\ *n* : a unit of electrical resistance equal to the resistance of a circuit in which a potential difference of one volt produces a current of one ampere — **ohm·ic** \'ō-mik\ *adj*

ohm·me·ter \'ōm-ˌmē-tər\ *n* : an instrument for indicating resistance in ohms directly

¹oil \'óil\ *n* [ME *oile*, fr. AF, fr. L *oleum* olive oil, fr. Gk *elaion*, fr. *elaia* olive] **1** : any of numerous fatty or greasy liquid substances obtained from plants, animals, or minerals and used for fuel, food, medicines, and manufacturing **2** : PETROLEUM **3 a** : artists' colors made with oil **b** : a painting in oil artist's colors — **oil·i·ness** \'ói-lē-nəs\ *n* — **oily** \'ói-lē\ *adj*

²oil *vb* ♦ : to put oil in or on — **oil·er** *n*

♦ grease, lubricate, slick, wax — more at LUBRICATE

oil·cloth \'ói-(ə)l-ˌklóth\ *n* : cloth treated with oil or paint and used for table and shelf coverings

oil pan *n* : the lower section of a crankcase used as an oil reservoir

oil shale *n* : a rock (as shale) from which oil can be recovered

oil·skin \'ói-(ə)l-ˌskin\ *n* **1** : an oiled waterproof cloth **2** : an oilskin raincoat **3** *pl* : an oilskin coat and pants

oink \'óiŋk\ *n* : the natural noise of a hog — **oink** *vb*

oint·ment \'óint-mənt\ *n* : a salve for use on the skin

OJ *abbr* orange juice

Ojib·wa *or* **Ojib·way** \ō-'jib-ˌwā\ *n, pl* **Ojibwa** *or* **Ojibwas** *or* **Ojibway** *or* **Ojibways** **1** : a member of an American Indian people of the region around Lake Superior and westward **2** : the Algonquian language of the Ojibwa people

OJT *abbr* on-the-job training

¹OK *or* **okay** \ō-'kā\ *adv* ♦ : ALL RIGHT

♦ all right, alright, yea, yes — more at YES ♦ adequately, all right, fine, good, nicely, passably, satisfactorily, so-so, tolerably, well — more at WELL

²OK *or* **okay** *adj* ♦ : ALL RIGHT

♦ acceptable, adequate, all right, decent, fine, passable, respectable, satisfactory, tolerable — more at ADEQUATE ♦ agreeable, all right, alright, fine, good, palatable, satisfactory — more at SATISFACTORY

³OK *or* **okay** *vb* **OK'd** *or* **okayed; OK'·ing** *or* **okay·ing** **1** ♦ : to give formal or official sanction to : APPROVE, AUTHORIZE **2** ♦ : to have or express a favorable opinion of

♦ [1] approve, authorize, clear, ratify, sanction, warrant — more at APPROVE ♦ [2] accept, approve, care, countenance, favor (*or* favour), subscribe

⁴OK *or* **okay** *n* ♦ : an act or instance of approving

♦ approbation, approval, blessing, favor (*or* favour), imprimatur — more at APPROVAL

⁵OK *abbr* Oklahoma

Okla *abbr* Oklahoma

okra \'ō-krə\ *n* : a tall annual plant related to the mallows that has edible green pods; *also* : these pods

¹old \'ōld\ *adj* **1** : ANCIENT; *also* : of long standing **2** *cap* : belonging to an early period ⟨*Old* Irish⟩ **3** : having existed for a specified period of time **4** ♦ : of or relating to a past era **5** ♦ : advanced in years **6** : showing the effects of age or use **7** : no longer in use **8** ♦ : having been previously — **old·ish** \'ōl-dish\ *adj*

♦ [4] age-old, ancient, antediluvian, antique, dateless, hoary, venerable — more at ANCIENT ♦ [5] ancient, elderly, geriatric, senior — more at ELDERLY ♦ [8] erstwhile, former, late, onetime, past, sometime, whilom — more at FORMER

²old *n* : old or earlier time ⟨days of ∼⟩

old·en \'ōl-dən\ *adj* : of or relating to a bygone era

¹old–fash·ioned \'ōld-'fa-shənd\ *adj* **1** ♦ : of, relating to, or characteristic of a past era **2** ♦ : adhering to customs of a past era : CONSERVATIVE

♦ [1] antique, old-time, quaint; *also* antiquated, obsolete, historic, historical, olden, traditional; outdated, outmoded, out-of-date, outworn, passé; dated, fusty, musty; aged, age-old, ancient, antediluvian, hoary, venerable; bygone, erstwhile, former, late, past; forgotten, remote; ageless, dateless; timeless *Ant* contemporary, hot, mod, modern, newfangled, new-fashioned, ultramodern ♦ [2] conservative, orthodox, reactionary, traditional — more at CONSERVATIVE

²old–fashioned *n* : a cocktail usu. made with whiskey, bitters, sugar, a twist of lemon peel, and water or soda water

old–growth \'ōld-'grōth\ *adj* : of, relating to, or being a forest with large old trees, numerous snags and woody debris, and a multilayered canopy

old guard *n, often cap O&G* : the conservative members of an organization

old hat *adj* **1** : OLD-FASHIONED **2** : STALE, TRITE

old·ie \'ōl-dē\ *n* : something old; *esp* : a popular song from the past

old lady *n* ♦ : a female partner in a marriage

♦ helpmate, lady, wife — more at WIFE

old–line \'ōld-'līn\ *adj* **1** : ORIGINAL, ESTABLISHED ⟨an ∼ business⟩ **2** : adhering to old policies or practices

old maid *n* **1** : SPINSTER **2** : a prim fussy person

old–maid·ish \'ōld-'mā-dish\ *adj* ♦ : characteristic of an old maid

♦ choosy, dainty, delicate, demanding, exacting, fastidious, finicky, fussy, nice, particular, picky — more at FINICKY

old man *n* **1** : HUSBAND **2** : a male parent : FATHER

old–school *adj* : adhering to traditional policies or practices ⟨an ∼ politician⟩

old·ster \'ōld-stər\ *n* ♦ : an old or elderly person

♦ ancient, elder, golden-ager, senior citizen — more at SENIOR CITIZEN

Old Testament *n* : the first of the two chief divisions of the Christian Scripture

old–time \'ōld-'tīm\ *adj* **1** ♦ : of, relating to, or characteristic of an earlier period **2** : of long standing

♦ antique, old-fashioned, quaint — more at OLD-FASHIONED

old–tim·er \-'tī-mər\ *n* 1 : veteran 2 : an aging or elderly person : OLDSTER

old wives' tale *n* ♦ : an often traditional belief that is not based on fact

♦ error, fallacy, falsehood, falsity, illusion, misconception, myth, untruth — more at FALLACY

old–world \-'wərld\ *adj* : having old-fashioned charm

Old World *n* : the eastern hemisphere exclusive of Australia; *esp* : continental Europe

ole·ag·i·nous \,ō-lē-'a-jə-nəs\ *adj* : OILY

ole·an·der \'ō-lē-,an-dər\ *n* : a poisonous evergreen shrub often grown for its fragrant white to red flowers

oleo \'ō-lē-,ō\ *n, pl* **ole·os** : MARGARINE

oleo·mar·ga·rine \,ō-lē-ō-'mär-jə-rən\ *n* : MARGARINE

ol·fac·to·ry \äl-'fak-tə-rē, ōl-\ *adj* : of or relating to the sense of smell

oli·gar·chy \'ä-lə-,gär-kē, 'ō-\ *n, pl* **-chies** 1 : a government in which power is in the hands of a few 2 : a state having an oligarchy; *also* : the group holding power in such a state — **oli·garch** \-,gärk\ *n* — **oli·gar·chic** \,ä-lə-'gär-kik, ,ō-\ *or* **oli·gar·chi·cal** \-ki-kəl\ *adj*

Oli·go·cene \'ä-li-gō-,sēn, ə-'li-gə-,sēn\ *adj* : of, relating to, or being the epoch of the Tertiary between the Eocene and the Miocene — **Oligocene** *n*

olio \'ō-lē-,ō\ *n, pl* **oli·os** : HODGEPODGE, MEDLEY

ol·ive \'ä-liv\ *n* 1 : an Old World evergreen tree grown in warm regions for its fruit that is a food and the source of an edible oil (**olive oil**); *also* : the fruit 2 : a dull yellowish green color

olive drab *n* 1 : a grayish olive color 2 : an olive drab wool or cotton fabric; *also* : a uniform of this fabric

ol·iv·ine \'ä-lə-,vēn\ *n* : a usu. greenish mineral that is a complex silicate of magnesium and iron

Olym·pic Games \ō-'lim-pik-\ *n pl* : a modified revival of an ancient Greek festival consisting of international athletic contests that are held at separate winter and summer gatherings at four-year intervals

om \'ōm\ *n* : a mantra consisting of the sound "om" used in contemplating ultimate reality

Oma·ha \'ō-mə-,hä, -,hȯ\ *n, pl* **Omaha** *or* **Omahas** : a member of an American Indian people of northeastern Nebraska

om·buds·man \'äm-,bùdz-mən, äm-'bùdz-\ *n, pl* **-men** \-mən\ 1 : a government official appointed to investigate complaints made by individuals against abuses or capricious acts of public officials 2 : one that investigates reported complaints (as from students or consumers)

ome·ga \ō-'mā-gə\ *n* : the 24th and last letter of the Greek alphabet — Ω or ω

om·elet *or* **om·elette** \'äm-lət, 'ä-mə-\ *n* [F *omelette*, alter. of MF *amelette*, *alemette*, alter. of *alemelle* thin plate, ultim. fr. L *lamella*, dim. of *lamina*] : eggs beaten with milk or water, cooked without stirring until set, and folded over

omen \'ō-mən\ *n* ♦ : an event or phenomenon believed to be a sign or warning of a future occurrence

♦ augury, auspice, foreboding, portent, presage; *also* forerunner, harbinger, herald, precursor; foretaste, hint, inkling, intimation, suggestion; forewarning; forecast, foretelling, prediction, prognostication, prophecy; badge, mark, note, token

om·i·cron \'ä-mə-,krän, 'ō-\ *n* : the 15th letter of the Greek alphabet — O or o

om·i·nous \'ä-mə-nəs\ *adj* 1 ♦ : foretelling evil : THREATENING 2 : being or exhibiting an omen — **om·i·nous·ly** *adv* — **om·i·nous·ness** *n*

♦ baleful, dire, foreboding, menacing, portentous, sinister; *also* black, dark, gloomy; inauspicious, unfavorable, unpromising; ill-fated, ill-starred, unfortunate, unlucky; evil, malign, malignant

omis·si·ble \ō-'mi-sə-bəl\ *adj* : that may be omitted

omis·sion \ō-'mi-shən\ *n* 1 : something neglected or left undone 2 : the act of omitting : the state of being omitted 3 ♦ : apathy toward or neglect of duty : lack of action

♦ delinquency, dereliction, laxity, laxness, neglect, negligence, remissness, slackness; *also* carelessness, heedlessness, thoughtlessness; inadvertence, inattention, oversight

omit \ō-'mit\ *vb* **omit·ted**; **omit·ting** 1 : to leave out or leave unmentioned 2 ♦ : to fail to perform : NEGLECT

♦ fail, forget, neglect — more at NEGLECT

¹om·ni·bus \'äm-ni-(,)bəs\ *n* : BUS

²omnibus *adj* ♦ : of, relating to, or providing for many things at once (an ~ bill)

♦ compendious, complete, comprehensive, encyclopedic, full, global, inclusive, panoramic, universal — more at ENCYCLOPEDIC

om·nip·o·tent \äm-'ni-pə-tənt\ *adj* : having unlimited authority or influence : ALMIGHTY (an ~ ruler) — **om·nip·o·tence** \-tən(t)s\ *n* — **om·nip·o·tent·ly** *adv*

om·ni·pres·ent \,äm-ni-'prez-ᵊnt\ *adj* : present in all places at all times (an ~ problem) — **om·ni·pres·ence** \-ᵊns\ *n*

om·ni·scient \äm-'ni-shənt\ *adj* : having infinite awareness, understanding, and insight — **om·ni·science** \-shəns\ *n* — **om·ni·scient·ly** *adv*

om·ni·um–gath·er·um \,äm-nē-əm-'ga-thə-rəm\ *n, pl* **omnium–gatherums** : a miscellaneous collection

om·niv·o·rous \äm-'ni-və-rəs\ *adj* 1 : feeding on both animal and vegetable substances 2 : AVID (an ~ reader) — **om·niv·o·rous·ly** *adv*

¹on \'ȯn, 'än\ *prep* 1 : in or to a position over and in contact with (jumped ~ his horse) 2 : touching the surface of (shadows ~ the wall) 3 : AT, TO (~ the right were the mountains) 4 : IN, ABOARD (went ~ the train) 5 : during or at the time of (came ~ Monday) (every hour ~ the hour) 6 : through the agency of (was cut ~ a tin can) 7 : in a state or process of (~ fire) (~ the wane) 8 : connected with as a member or participant (~ a committee) (~ tour) 9 — used to indicate a basis, source, or standard of computation (has it ~ good authority) (10 cents ~ the dollar) 10 : with regard to (a monopoly ~ wheat) 11 : at or toward as an object (crept up ~ her) 12 : used as a function word to indicate the subject of study, discussion, or consideration : ABOUT, CONCERNING (a book ~ minerals)

²on *adv* 1 : in or into a position of contact with or attachment to a surface 2 ♦ : forward or at a more advanced point in space or time : FORWARD 3 : into operation

♦ ahead, along, forth, forward, onward — more at ALONG

³on *adj* ♦ : being in operation or in progress

♦ active, alive, functional, living, operational, operative, running, working — more at ACTIVE

ON *abbr* Ontario

¹once \'wəns\ *adv* [ME *ones*, fr. genitive of *on* one] 1 : one time only 2 : at any one time 3 : FORMERLY 4 : by one degree of relationship

²once *n* : one single time — **at once** 1 : at the same time 2 : IMMEDIATELY

³once *adj* : FORMER

⁴once *conj* : AS SOON AS

once–over \'wəns-,ō-vər\ *n* : a swift examination or survey

on·co·gene \'äŋ-kō-,jēn\ *n* : a gene having the potential to cause a normal cell to become cancerous

on·col·o·gy \än-'kä-lə-jē\ *n* : the study of tumors — **on·co·log·i·cal** \,äŋ-kə-'lä-ji-kəl\ *also* **on·co·log·ic** \-jik\ *adj* — **on·col·o·gist** \än-'kä-lə-jist\ *n*

on·com·ing \'ȯn-,kə-miŋ, 'än-\ *adj* ♦ : coming nearer in time or space (~ traffic)

♦ coming, forthcoming, imminent, impending, pending — more at FORTHCOMING

¹one \'wən\ *adj* 1 : being a single unit or thing (~ person went) 2 : being one in particular (early ~ morning)

3 : being the same in kind or quality ⟨members of ∼ race⟩; *also* : UNITED **4** ♦ : being not specified or fixed ⟨∼ day soon⟩

♦ anonymous, certain, some, unidentified, unnamed, unspecified — more at CERTAIN

²**one** *n* **1** : the number denoting unity **2** : the 1st in a set or series **3** : a single person or thing — **one·ness** \'wən-nəs\ *n*

³**one** *pron* **1** : a certain indefinitely indicated person or thing ⟨saw ∼ of his friends⟩ **2** : a person in general ⟨∼ never knows⟩ **3** — used in place of a first-person pronoun

Onei·da \ō-'nī-də\ *n, pl* **Oneida** *or* **Oneidas** : a member of an American Indian people orig. of New York

one—man band *n* **1** : a musician who plays several instruments during a solo performance **2** : a person who alone undertakes or is responsible for several tasks

oner·ous \'ä-nə-rəs, 'ō-\ *adj* ♦ : imposing or constituting a burden ⟨an ∼ task⟩

♦ arduous, burdensome, challenging, demanding, exacting, grueling, laborious, taxing, toilsome — more at DEMANDING

one·self \(ˌ)wən-'self\ *also* **one's self** *pron* : one's own self — usu. used reflexively or for emphasis

one·sid·ed \'wən-'sī-dəd\ *adj* **1** : having or occurring on one side only; *also* : having one side prominent or more developed **2** ♦ : of, relating to, or affecting one side of a subject : PARTIAL ⟨a ∼ interpretation⟩

♦ biased, partial, partisan, prejudiced — more at PARTIAL

one·time \-ˌtīm\ *adj* ♦ : of, relating to, or occurring in the past : FORMER

♦ erstwhile, former, late, old, past, sometime, whilom — more at FORMER

one—to—one \ˌwən-tə-'wən\ *adj* : pairing each element of a set uniquely with an element of another set

one up *adj* : being in a position of advantage ⟨was *one up* on the others⟩

one—way *adj* : moving, allowing movement, or functioning in only one direction ⟨∼ streets⟩

on·go·ing \'ȯn-ˌgō-iŋ, 'än-\ *adj* **1** ♦ : continuously moving forward **2** ♦ : being actually in process

♦ [1] afoot, proceeding; *also* functioning, happening, operating, working; afloat, alive; advancing, gaining **Ant** arrested, halted, stalled, stopped ♦ [2] current, extant, present — more at PRESENT

on·ion \'ən-yən\ *n* : the pungent edible bulb of a widely cultivated plant related to the lilies; *also* : this plant

on·ion·skin \-ˌskin\ *n* : a thin strong translucent paper of very light weight

on·line \'ȯn-'līn, 'än-\ *adj or adv* : connected to, served by, or available through a computer network (as the Internet); *also* : done while online

on·look·er \'ȯn-ˌlu̇-kər, 'än-\ *n* : SPECTATOR

¹**on·ly** \'ȯn-lē\ *adj* **1** ♦ : unquestionably the best **2** ♦ : alone in a class or category : SOLE

♦ [1] incomparable, inimitable, matchless, nonpareil, peerless, unequaled, unmatched, unparalleled, unrivaled, unsurpassed; *also* A1, bang-up, banner, capital, classic, dandy, excellent, fabulous, fine, first-rate, grand, great, groovy, jim-dandy, keen, marvelous, mean, neat, prime, superb, superior, superlative, terrific, tip-top, top-notch; better, preferred; exceptional, fancy, special ♦ [2] alone, lone, singular, sole, solitary, special, unique; *also* solo, unaccompanied, unattended; incomparable, inimitable, matchless, peerless, unequaled, unmatched, unparalleled, unrivaled, unsurpassed; distinct, distinctive, individual, separate

²**only** *adv* **1** : as a single fact or instance and nothing more or different : MERELY, JUST ⟨∼ $2⟩ **2** ♦ : to the exclusion of all else : SOLELY ⟨known ∼ to me⟩ **3** : at the very least ⟨was ∼ too true⟩ **4** : as a final result ⟨will ∼ make you sick⟩ **5** ♦ : in the immediate past

♦ [2] alone, exclusively, just, simply, solely — more at SOLELY ♦ [5] freshly, just, late, lately, new, newly, now, recently — more at NEWLY

³**only** *conj* ♦ : except that

♦ but, except, yet — more at EXCEPT

on·o·mato·poe·ia \ˌä-nə-ˌmä-tə-'pē-ə\ *n* [LL, fr. Gk *onomatopoiia*, fr. *onoma* name + *poiein* to make] **1** : formation of words in imitation of natural sounds (as *buzz* or *hiss*) **2** : the use of words whose sound suggests the sense — **on·o·mato·poe·ic** \-'pē-ik\ *or* **on·o·mato·po·et·ic** \-pō-'e-tik\ *adj* — **on·o·mato·poe·i·cal·ly** \-'pē-ə-k(ə-)lē\ *or* **on·o·mato·po·et·i·cal·ly** \-pō-'e-ti-k(ə-)lē\ *adv*

On·on·da·ga \ˌä-nən-'dȯ-gə, -'dā-, -'dä-\ *n, pl* **-ga** *or* **-gas** : a member of an American Indian people of New York and Canada

on·rush \'ȯn-ˌrəsh, 'än-\ *n* ♦ : a rushing onward — **on·rush·ing** *adj*

♦ advance, advancement, furtherance, headway, march, passage, process, procession, progress, progression — more at ADVANCE

on—screen \'ȯn-'skrēn, 'än-\ *adv or adj* : on a screen (as of a computer or television)

on·set \-ˌset\ *n* **1** : the act of attacking with physical force or unfriendly words : ATTACK **2** ♦ : the point at which something begins : BEGINNING

♦ beginning, birth, commencement, dawn, genesis, launch, morning, outset, start, threshold — more at BEGINNING

on·shore \-ˌshȯr\ *adj* **1** : moving toward the shore **2** : situated on or near the shore — **on·shore** \-'shȯr\ *adv*

on·slaught \'ȯn-ˌslȯt, 'än-\ *n* ♦ : a fierce attack; *also* : something resembling such an attack ⟨an ∼ of questions⟩

♦ aggression, assault, attack, charge, descent, offense (*or* offence), offensive, onset, raid, rush, strike — more at ATTACK

Ont *abbr* Ontario

on·to \'ȯn-tü, 'än-\ *prep* : to a position or point on

onus \'ō-nəs\ *n* **1** : BURDEN **2** : OBLIGATION **3** : BLAME

¹**on·ward** \'ȯn-wərd, 'än-\ *also* **on·wards** \-wərdz\ *adv* ♦ : toward or at a point lying ahead in space or time : FORWARD

♦ ahead, along, forth, forward, on — more at ALONG

²**onward** *adj* : directed or moving onward : FORWARD

on·yx \'ä-niks\ *n* [ME *oniche, onyx*, fr. AF & L; AF, fr. L *onyx*, fr. Gk, lit., claw, nail] : a translucent chalcedony in parallel layers of different colors

oo·dles \'üd-ᵊlz\ *n pl* ♦ : a great quantity : LOT

♦ abundance, deal, gobs, heap, loads, lot, pile, plenty, quantity, scads — more at LOT

oo·lite \'ō-ə-ˌlīt\ *n* : a rock consisting of small round grains cemented together — **oo·lit·ic** \ˌō-ə-'li-tik\ *adj*

¹**ooze** \'üz\ *n* [ME *wose*, fr. OE *wāse* mire] **1** : a soft deposit (as of mud) on the bottom of a body of water **2** ♦ : soft wet ground : MUD

♦ mire, muck, mud, slime, slop, sludge, slush — more at MUD

²**ooze** *vb* **oozed; ooz·ing 1** ♦ : to flow or leak out slowly or imperceptibly **2** ♦ : EXUDE

♦ [1, 2] bleed, exude, percolate, seep, strain, sweat, weep — more at EXUDE

³**ooze** *n* : something that oozes

oozy \'ü-zē\ *adj* ♦ : containing or composed of ooze

♦ miry, mucky, muddy, slimy, slushy — more at MUDDY

op *abbr* **1** operation; operative; operator **2** opportunity **3** opus

OP *abbr* **1** observation post **2** out of print

opac·i·ty \ō-'pa-sə-tē\ *n, pl* **-ties 1** : the quality or state of being opaque **2** ♦ : obscurity of meaning **3** : mental dullness **4** : an opaque spot in a normally transparent structure

♦ ambiguity, darkness, murkiness, obscurity — more at OBSCURITY

opal \'ō-pəl\ *n* : a mineral with iridescent colors that is used as a gem

opal·es·cent \ˌō-pə-'les-ᵊnt\ *adj* : IRIDESCENT — **opal·es·cence** \-ᵊns\ *n*

opaque \ō-'pāk\ *adj* 1 : blocking the passage of radiant energy and esp. light 2 ♦ : not easily understood 3 : OBTUSE — **opaque·ly** *adv* — **opaque·ness** *n*

♦ bleary, dim, faint, foggy, fuzzy, hazy, indefinite, indistinct, indistinguishable, murky, nebulous, obscure, shadowy, unclear, undefined, undetermined, vague — more at FAINT

op art \'äp-\ *n* : OPTICAL ART — **op artist** *n*

op cit *abbr* [L *opere citato*] in the work cited

ope \'ōp\ *vb* **oped; op·ing** *archaic* : OPEN

OPEC *abbr* Organization of Petroleum Exporting Countries

op–ed \'äp-'ed\ *n, often cap O&E* : a page of special features usu. opposite the editorial page of a newspaper

¹**open** \'ō-pən\ *adj* **open·er; open·est** 1 : not shut or shut up ⟨an ~ door⟩ 2 a : not secret or hidden b ♦ : free from reserve or pretense : FRANK 3 a : not enclosed or covered ⟨an ~ fire⟩ b ♦ : not protected or covered 4 ♦ : free to be entered or used ⟨an ~ tournament⟩ 5 ♦ : easy to get through or see ⟨~ country⟩ 6 : spread out : EXTENDED 7 ♦ : not decided ⟨an ~ question⟩ 8 a : readily accessible and cooperative; *also* : GENEROUS b : willing to hear and consider or to accept and deal with 9 : having components separated by a space in writing and printing ⟨the name *Spanish moss* is an ~ compound⟩ 10 : having openings, interruptions, or spaces ⟨an ~ mesh⟩ 11 : ready to operate ⟨stores are ~⟩ 12 : free from restraints or controls ⟨~ season⟩ — **open·ly** *adv*

♦ [2b] candid, direct, forthright, foursquare, frank, honest, outspoken, plain, straight, straightforward, unguarded, unreserved — more at FRANK ♦ [3b] bald, bare, exposed, naked, uncovered — more at NAKED ♦ [4] free-for-all, public, unrestricted; *also* collective, common, communal, shared; accessible, available, free; unregulated *Ant* closed, exclusive, private, restricted ♦ [5] clear, free, unobstructed; *also* emptied, unoccupied, vacant; exposed, revealed; gaping, wide, yawning; unbolted, unclasped, unfastened, unlatched, unsealed; unbuttoned, unclenched, unfolded, unfurled *Ant* blocked, closed, obstructed, uncleared ♦ [7] pending, undecided, undetermined, unresolved, unsettled — more at PENDING

²**open** \'ō-pən\ *vb* **opened; open·ing** 1 a : to change or move from a shut position b ♦ : to make open by clearing away obstacles 2 : to make accessible 3 : to make openings in 4 : to make or become functional ⟨~ a store⟩ 5 : REVEAL; *also* : ENLIGHTEN 6 ♦ : to enter upon : BEGIN — **open·er** *n*

♦ [1b] clear, free, unblock ♦ [6] begin, commence, embark (on *or* upon), enter, get off, launch, start, strike — more at BEGIN

³**open** *n* 1 : open and unobstructed space : OUTDOORS 2 : a contest or tournament open to all

♦ nature, outdoors, wild, wilderness — more at NATURE

open–air *adj* : of or relating to the outdoors : OUTDOOR ⟨~ theaters⟩

open arms *n pl* : an eager or warm welcome

open–hand·ed \ˌō-pən-'han-dəd\ *adj* ♦ : liberal in giving : GENEROUS — **open–hand·ed·ly** *adv*

♦ bountiful, charitable, free, generous, liberal, munificent, unselfish, unsparing — more at GENEROUS

open–heart *adj* : of, relating to, or performed on a heart temporarily relieved of circulatory function and laid open for repair of defects or damage

open–hearth *adj* : of, relating to, or being a process of making steel in a furnace that reflects the heat from the roof onto the material

open·ing *n* 1 : an act or instance of making or becoming open 2 : BEGINNING 3 ♦ : something that is open 4 ♦ : a favorable opportunity or circumstance : OCCASION; *also* : an opportunity for employment

♦ [3] breach, break, discontinuity, gap, gulf, hole, interval, rent, rift, separation — more at GAP ♦ [4] chance, occasion, opportunity, room — more at OPPORTUNITY

open mike *n* : an event in which amateurs may perform

open–mind·ed \ˌō-pən-'mīn-dəd\ *adj* ♦ : free from rigidly fixed preconceptions — **open–mind·ed·ness** *n*

♦ broad-minded, liberal, nonorthodox, nontraditional, progressive, radical, unconventional, unorthodox — more at LIBERAL ♦ broad-minded, open, receptive; *also* impartial, neutral, objective, unbiased, unprejudiced; easygoing, tolerant; calm, detached, dispassionate; amenable, compliant; impressionable, suggestible, susceptible *Ant* narrow-minded

open·ness *n* ♦ : the quality or state of being open

♦ candor (*or* candour), directness, forthrightness, frankness, plainness — more at CANDOR

open sentence *n* : a statement (as in mathematics) containing at least one blank or unknown so that when the blank is filled or a quantity substituted for the unknown the statement becomes a complete statement that is either true or false

open shop *n* : an establishment having members and nonmembers of a labor union on the payroll

open·work \'ō-pən-ˌwərk\ *n* : work so made as to show openings through its substance ⟨a railing of wrought-iron ~⟩ — **open–worked** \-ˌwərkt\ *adj*

¹**opera** *pl of* OPUS

²**op·era** \'ä-prə, -pə-rə\ *n* : a drama set to music — **op·er·at·ic** \ˌä-pə-'ra-tik\ *adj*

op·er·a·ble \'ä-pə-rə-bəl\ *adj* 1 ♦ : fit, possible, or desirable to use 2 : likely to result in a favorable outcome upon surgical treatment

♦ available, fit, functional, practicable, serviceable, usable, useful — more at USABLE

opera glasses *n pl* : small binoculars for use in a theater

op·er·ate \'ä-pə-ˌrāt\ *vb* **-at·ed; -at·ing** 1 ♦ : to perform work : FUNCTION 2 ♦ : to produce an effect 3 ♦ : to put or keep in operation; *also* : to manage the operation of 4 : to perform or subject to an operation — **op·er·a·tor** \-ˌrā-tər\ *n*

♦ [1, 2] act, function, perform, take, work — more at ACT ♦ [3] command, control, direct, drive, guide, handle, maneuver, pilot, run, steer, use, wield, work ♦ [3] administer, carry on, conduct, govern, guide, handle, manage, oversee, regulate, run, superintend, supervise — more at CONDUCT

operating system *n* : software that controls the operation of a computer

op·er·a·tion \ˌä-pə-'rā-shən\ *n* 1 : a doing or performing of practical work 2 a ♦ : an exertion of power or influence b ♦ : method or manner of functioning 3 : a surgical procedure 4 a : a process of deriving one mathematical expression from others according to a rule b : a function or correlation when conceived as a process of proceeding from one or more entities to another according to a definite rule 5 : a usu. military action or mission 6 : a usu. small business

♦ [2a] administration, conduct, control, direction, government, guidance, management, oversight, regulation, running, superintendence, supervision — more at CONDUCT ♦ [2b] course, procedure, proceeding, process — more at PROCESS ♦ [2b] application, employment, exercise, play, use — more at USE

op·er·a·tion·al \-shə-nəl\ *adj* ♦ : of or relating to operation or an operation

♦ active, alive, functional, living, on, operative, running, working — more at ACTIVE

¹op·er·a·tive \'ä-pə-rə-tiv, -ˌrā-\ *adj* **1** : producing an appropriate effect **2** : engaged in some form of operation : OPERATING ⟨an ~ force⟩ **3** : having to do with physical operations; *also* : WORKING ⟨an ~ craftsman⟩ **4** : based on or consisting of an operation ⟨~ dentistry⟩

²operative *n* **1** : OPERATOR **2 a** : a secret agent **b** ♦ : a person not a member of a police force who is licensed to do detective work

♦ detective, investigator, shadow, sleuth, tail — more at DETECTIVE

op·er·et·ta \ˌä-pə-'re-tə\ *n* [It, dim. of *opera* opera] : a light musical-dramatic work with a romantic plot, spoken dialogue, and dancing scenes

oph·thal·mic \äf-'thal-mik, äp-\ *adj* [Gk *ophthalmikos*, fr. *ophthalmos* eye] : of, relating to, or located near the eye

oph·thal·mol·o·gy \ˌäf-ˌthal-'mä-lə-jē, ˌäp-\ *n* : a branch of medicine dealing with the structure, functions, and diseases of the eye — **oph·thal·mol·o·gist** \-jist\ *n*

oph·thal·mo·scope \äf-'thal-mə-ˌskōp, äp-\ *n* : an instrument for use in viewing the interior of the eye and esp. the retina

¹opi·ate \'ō-pē-ət, -pē-ˌāt\ *n* **1** : a preparation or derivative of opium **2** : a narcotic or a substance with similar activity

²opiate *adj* : inducing sleep : NARCOTIC

♦ drowsy, hypnotic, narcotic, slumberous — more at HYPNOTIC

opine \ō-'pīn\ *vb* **opined; opin·ing** ♦ : to express an opinion

♦ comment, note, observe, remark — more at REMARK

opin·ion \ə-'pin-yən\ *n* **1** ♦ : a belief stronger than impression and less strong than positive knowledge **2** : JUDGMENT **3** ♦ : a formal statement by an expert after careful study

♦ [1] belief, conviction, eye, feeling, judgment (*or* judgement), mind, notion, persuasion, sentiment, verdict, view; *also* say; impression, perception, take; position, stand; comment, observation, reflection, remark ♦ [3] conclusion, decision, deliverance, determination, diagnosis, judgment (*or* judgement), resolution, verdict — more at DECISION

opin·ion·at·ed \ə-'pin-yə-ˌnā-təd\ *adj* ♦ : obstinately adhering to personal opinions

♦ dogged, hardheaded, headstrong, mulish, obdurate, obstinate, peevish, pertinacious, perverse, pigheaded, stubborn, unyielding, willful — more at OBSTINATE

opi·um \'ō-pē-əm\ *n* [ME, fr. L, fr. Gk *opion*, fr. dim. of *opos* sap] : an addictive narcotic drug that is the dried latex of a Eurasian poppy

opos·sum \ə-'pä-səm\ *n, pl* **opossums** *also* **opossum** : an omnivorous tree-dwelling No. American marsupial that is active chiefly at night and has a pointed snout and a prehensile tail

opp *abbr* opposite

op·po·nent \ə-'pō-nənt\ *n* ♦ : one that opposes : ADVERSARY

♦ adversary, antagonist, rival; *also* equal, match; enemy, foe; archenemy, nemesis; competitor, contestant; bane, bête noire, curse; assailant, combatant, invader

op·por·tune \ˌä-pər-'tün, -'tyün\ *adj* [ME, fr. MF *opportun*, fr. L *opportunus*, fr. *ob-* toward + *portus* port, harbor] : SUITABLE — **op·por·tune·ly** *adv*

op·por·tun·ism \ˌä-pər-'tü-ˌni-zəm, -'tyü-\ *n* : a taking advantage of opportunities or circumstances esp. with little regard for principles or ultimate consequences — **op·por·tun·ist** \-nist\ *n* — **op·por·tu·nis·tic** \-tü-'nis-tik, -tyü-\ *adj*

op·por·tu·ni·ty \ˌä-pər-'tü-nə-tē, -'tyü-\ *n, pl* **-ties** **1** ♦ : a favorable combination of circumstances, time, and place **2** : a chance for advancement

♦ chance, occasion, opening, room; *also* break; play, way; juncture, pass

op·pose \ə-'pōz\ *vb* **op·posed; op·pos·ing** **1** : to place opposite or against something (as to provide resistance or

contrast) **2** ♦ : to strive against : offer resistance to — **op·po·si·tion** \ˌä-pə-'zi-shən\ *n*

♦ buck, defy, fight, repel, resist, withstand — more at RESIST ♦ battle, combat, contend, counter, fight — more at FIGHT

¹op·po·site \'ä-pə-zət\ *adj* **1** : set over against something that is at the other end or side **2** : OPPOSED, HOSTILE; *also* : CONTRARY **3** : contrarily turned or moving **4** ♦ : diametrically different **5** : being the other of a matching or contrasting pair — **op·po·site·ly** *adv* — **op·po·site·ness** *n*

♦ antipodal, antithetical, contradictory, contrary, diametric, polar; *also* adverse, negative, unfavorable; antagonistic, antipathetic, counter, hostile; converse, inverse, reverse; disparate, dissimilar, divergent, unalike, unlike

²opposite *n* : one that is opposed or contrary

♦ antipode, antithesis, contrary, negative, reverse; *also* negation; antonym; converse, inverse

³opposite *adv* : on or to an opposite side

⁴opposite *prep* : across from and usu. facing ⟨the house ~ ours⟩

op·press \ə-'pres\ *vb* **1** : to crush by abuse of power or authority **2** ♦ : to be a burden to mentally or spiritually

♦ burden, depress, sadden — more at DEPRESS ♦ carry away, crush, devastate, floor, overcome, overpower, overwhelm, prostrate, snow under, swamp — more at OVERWHELM

op·pres·sion \ə-'pre-shən\ *n* **1** : unjust or cruel exercise of power or authority **2** : a sense of being affected as if with a heavy weight in body or mind : DEPRESSION

op·pres·sive \-'pre-siv\ *adj* ♦ : unreasonably burdensome or severe

♦ burdensome, grim, hard, harsh, heavy, onerous, rough, rugged, severe, stiff, tough, trying — more at HARSH

op·pres·sive·ly *adv* ♦ : in an oppressive manner

♦ hard, hardly, harshly, ill, roughly, severely, sternly, stiffly — more at HARDLY

op·pres·sor \-'pre-sər\ *n* ♦ : one that oppresses esp. when in a position of public authority

♦ autocrat, despot, dictator, tyrant — more at DESPOT

op·pro·bri·ous \ə-'prō-brē-əs\ *adj* ♦ : expressing or deserving opprobrium — **op·pro·bri·ous·ly** *adv*

♦ abusive, scurrilous — more at ABUSIVE

op·pro·bri·um \-brē-əm\ *n* **1** : something that brings disgrace **2** ♦ : public disgrace or ill fame that follows from conduct considered grossly wrong or vicious : INFAMY

♦ discredit, disgrace, dishonor (*or* dishonour), disrepute, ignominy, infamy, odium, reproach, shame — more at DISGRACE

¹opt \'äpt\ *vb* **1** ♦ : to make a choice **2** ♦ : to decide in favor of something — usu. used with *for*

♦ [1] choose, conclude, decide, determine, figure, resolve — more at DECIDE ♦ *usu* opt for [2] choose, cull, elect, handpick, name, pick, prefer, select, single, take — more at CHOOSE

²opt *abbr* **1** optical; optician; optics **2** option; optional

op·tic \'äp-tik\ *adj* : of or relating to vision or the eye

op·ti·cal \'äp-ti-kəl\ *adj* **1** : relating to optics **2** ♦ : of or relating to vision : OPTIC **3** : of, relating to, or using light

♦ ocular, visual — more at VISUAL

optical art *n* : nonobjective art characterized by the use of geometric patterns often for an illusory effect

optical disk *n* : a disk on which information has been recorded digitally and which is read using a laser

optical fiber *n* : a single fiber-optic strand

op·ti·cian \äp-'ti-shən\ *n* **1** : a maker of or dealer in optical items and instruments **2** : a person who makes or orders eyeglass and contact lenses to prescription and sells glasses

op·tics \'äp-tiks\ *n pl* **1** : a science that deals with the nature and properties of light **2** : the aspects of an action, policy, or decision that relate to public perceptions

op·ti·mal \'äp-tə-məl\ *adj* : most desirable or satisfactory — **op·ti·mal·ly** *adv*

op·ti·mism \'äp-tə-ˌmi-zəm\ *n* [F *optimisme*, fr. L *optimum*, n., best, fr. neut. of *optimus* best] **1** : a doctrine that this world is the best possible world **2** : an inclination to anticipate the best possible outcome of actions — **op·ti·mist** \-ˌmist\ *n* — **op·ti·mis·tic** \-ˌmis-tik\ *adj*

op·ti·mize \'äp-tə-ˌmīz\ *vb* **-mized; -miz·ing** : to make as perfect, effective, or functional as possible — **op·ti·mi·za·tion** \ˌäp-tə-mə-'zā-shən\ *n*

op·ti·mum \'äp-tə-məm\ *n, pl* **-ma** \-mə\ *also* **-mums** [L] : the amount or degree of something most favorable to an end; *also* : greatest degree attained under implied or specified conditions

op·tion \'äp-shən\ *n* **1** ♦ : the power or right to choose **2** : a right to buy or sell something at a specified price during a specified period **3** : something offered for choice **4** ♦ : an act of choosing

♦ [1] accord, choice, free will, self-determination, volition, will — more at FREE WILL ♦ [4] alternative, choice, discretion, pick, preference, way — more at CHOICE

op·tion·al \-shə-nəl\ *adj* ♦ : involving an option : not compulsory

♦ discretionary, elective, voluntary; *also* alternative, chosen; dispensable, unwanted **Ant** compulsory, mandatory, nonelective, obligatory, required

op·tom·e·try \äp-'tä-mə-trē\ *n* : the health-care profession concerned esp. with examining the eyes for defects of vision and with prescribing corrective lenses or eye exercises — **op·tom·e·trist** \-trist\ *n*

opt out *vb* : to choose not to participate

op·u·lence \'ä-pyə-ləns\ *n* **1** ♦ : abundance of valuable material possessions or resources : WEALTH **2** : ABUNDANCE

♦ assets, capital, fortune, means, riches, substance, wealth, wherewithal — more at WEALTH

op·u·lent \'ä-pyə-lənt\ *adj* **1** ♦ : exhibiting or characterized by opulence **2** : richly abundant

♦ deluxe, lavish, luxuriant, luxurious, palatial, plush, sumptuous — more at LUXURIOUS ♦ affluent, flush, loaded, moneyed, rich, wealthy, well-fixed, well-heeled, well-off, well-to-do — more at RICH

op·u·lent·ly *adv* ♦ : with opulence : in an opulent manner

♦ expensively, extravagantly, grandly, high, lavishly, luxuriously, richly — more at HIGH

opus \'ō-pəs\ *n, pl* **opera** \'ō-pə-rə, 'ä-\ *also* **opus·es** \'ō-pə-səz\ ♦ : something produced by the exercise of creative talent or expenditure of creative effort; *esp* : a musical composition

♦ composition, piece, work — more at COMPOSITION

or \'ȯr\ *conj* — used as a function word to indicate an alternative ⟨sink ∼ swim⟩

OR *abbr* **1** operating room **2** Oregon

-or \ər\ *n suffix* : one that does a (specified) thing ⟨calculat*or*⟩

or·a·cle \'ȯr-ə-kəl\ *n* **1** : one held to give divinely inspired answers or revelations **2** : an authoritative or wise utterance; *also* : a person of great authority or wisdom — **orac·u·lar** \ȯ-'ra-kyə-lər\ *adj*

¹**oral** \'ōr-əl\ *adj* **1** ♦ : uttered by the mouth or in words **2** : of, given through, or involving the mouth **3** : of, relating to, or characterized by the first stage of psychosexual development in psychoanalytic theory in which libidinal gratification is derived from intake (as of food), by sucking, and later by biting **4** : relating to or characterized by personality traits of passive dependency and aggressiveness — **oral·ly** *adv*

♦ vocal, voiced — more at VOCAL ♦ spoken, unwritten, verbal — more at VERBAL

²**oral** *n* : an oral examination — usu. used in pl.

oral sex *n* : oral stimulation of the genitals : CUNNILINGUS, FELLATIO

orang \ə-'raŋ\ *n* : ORANGUTAN

or·ange \'ȯr-inj\ *n* **1** : a juicy citrus fruit with reddish yellow rind; *also* : an evergreen tree with fragrant white flowers that bears this fruit **2** : a color between red and yellow

or·ange·ade \ˌȯr-in-'jād\ *n* : a beverage of orange juice, sugar, and water

orange hawkweed *n* : a weedy herb related to the daisies with bright orange-red flower heads

or·ange·ry \'ȯr-inj-rē\ *n, pl* **-ries** : a protected place (as a greenhouse) for raising oranges in cool climates

orang·utan \ə-'raŋ-ə-ˌtaŋ, -ˌtan\ *n* [Bazaar Malay (Malay-based pidgin), fr. Malay *orang* man + *hutan* forest] : a large reddish brown tree-living anthropoid ape of Borneo and Sumatra

orate \ȯ-'rāt\ *vb* **orat·ed; orat·ing** ♦ : to speak in a declamatory manner

♦ declaim, discourse, harangue, lecture, mouth, speak, talk; *also* rant, rave; preach; advertise, announce, broadcast, declare, proclaim, pronounce

ora·tion \ə-'rā-shən\ *n* ♦ : an elaborate discourse delivered in a formal and dignified manner

♦ address, declamation, harangue, speech, talk — more at SPEECH

or·a·tor \'ȯr-ə-tər\ *n* : one noted for skill and power as a public speaker

or·a·tor·i·cal \ˌȯr-ə-'tȯr-i-kəl\ *adj* ♦ : of, relating to, or characteristic of an orator or oratory; *also* : of or relating to an inflated style of speech or writing — **or·a·tor·i·cal·ly** \-'tȯr-i-k(ə-)lē\ *adv*

♦ bombastic, gaseous, grandiloquent, rhetorical, windy — more at RHETORICAL

or·a·to·rio \ˌȯr-ə-'tȯr-ē-ˌō\ *n, pl* **-rios** : a lengthy choral work usu. on a scriptural subject

¹**or·a·to·ry** \'ȯr-ə-ˌtȯr-ē\ *n, pl* **-ries** : a private or institutional chapel

²**oratory** *n* **1** : the art of speaking eloquently and effectively in public **2** : the substance of oratorical speech

orb \'ȯrb\ *n* ♦ : a spherical body; *also* : EYE

♦ ball, sphere — more at BALL

¹**or·bit** \'ȯr-bət\ *n* [L *orbita*, lit., path, rut] **1** : a path described by one body in its revolution about another **2** : range or sphere of activity — **or·bit·al** \-ᵊl\ *adj*

²**orbit** *vb* **1** ♦ : to revolve in an orbit around : CIRCLE **2** : to send up and make revolve in an orbit ⟨∼ a satellite⟩ — **or·bit·er** *n*

♦ circle, circumnavigate, coil, compass, encircle, girdle, loop, ring, round — more at ENCIRCLE

or·ca \'ȯr-kə\ *n* : KILLER WHALE

orch *abbr* orchestra

or·chard \'ȯr-chərd\ *n* [ME, fr. OE *ortgeard*, fr. *ort-* (fr. L *hortus* garden) + *geard* yard] : a place where fruit trees, sugar maples, or nut trees are grown; *also* : the trees of such a place — **or·chard·ist** \-chər-dist\ *n*

or·ches·tra \'ȯr-kə-strə\ *n* **1** : the front section of seats on the main floor of a theater **2** : a group of instrumentalists organized to perform ensemble music — **or·ches·tral** \ȯr-'kes-trəl\ *adj* — **or·ches·tral·ly** *adv*

or·ches·trate \'ȯr-kə-ˌstrāt\ *vb* **-trat·ed; -trat·ing** **1** : to compose or arrange for an orchestra **2** : to arrange so as to achieve a desired effect ⟨∼ a campaign⟩ — **or·ches·tra·tion** \ˌȯr-kə-'strā-shən\ *n*

or·chid \'ȯr-kəd\ *n* : any of a large family of plants having often showy flowers with three petals of which the middle one is enlarged into a lip; *also* : a flower of an orchid

ord *abbr* **1** order **2** ordnance

or·dain \ȯr-'dān\ *vb* **1** : to admit to the ministry or priesthood by the ritual of a church **2 a** ♦ : to order by fiat or by virtue of great or supreme authority : DECREE **b** ♦ : to predestine or destine : DESTINE — **or·dain·ment** *n*

♦ [2a] command, decree, dictate, direct, order ♦ [2b] destine, doom, fate, foredoom, foreordain, predestine — more at DESTINE

or·deal \ȯr-'dēl, 'ȯr-ˌdēl\ *n* ♦ : a severe trial or experience

♦ cross, gauntlet, trial — more at TRIAL

¹or·der \'ȯr-dər\ *vb* **1** ♦ : to arrange according to a particular plan **2** ♦ : to give an order to : COMMAND **3** ♦ : to place an order **4** ♦ : to issue orders

♦ [1] arrange, array, classify, codify, dispose, draw up, marshal, organize, range, systematize; *also* groom, make up, spruce (up), straighten (up), tidy (up); unscramble; align, line, line up, queue; alphabetize; file; place, set; display, lay out, map (out) *Ant* derange, disarrange, disarray, disorder, mess (up), muss (up), rumple, upset ♦ [2] command, decree, dictate, direct, ordain ♦ [3] ask, request, requisition; *also* commission, solicit; license, charter, hire ♦ [4] bid, boss, charge, command, direct, enjoin, instruct, tell — more at COMMAND

²order *n* **1 a** : a group of people formally united **b** : a badge or medal of such a group **2** : any of the several grades of the Christian ministry; *also, pl* : ORDINATION **3 a** ♦ : a rank, class, or special group of persons or things **b** ♦ : a division within a system of classification **4** : a category of biological classification ranking above the family and below the class **5** ♦ : the arrangement or sequence of objects or of events in time : ARRANGEMENT, SEQUENCE; *also* : the prevailing state of things **6** : a customary mode of procedure; *also* : the rule of law or proper authority **7** ♦ : a specific rule, regulation, or authoritative direction **8** : a style of building; *also* : an architectural column forming the unit of a style **9** ♦ : condition esp. with regard to repair **10** : a written direction to pay money or to buy or sell goods; *also* : goods bought or sold **11** ♦ : a particular sphere or aspect of a sociopolitical system

♦ [3a, 11] caste, class, estate, folk, stratum — more at CLASS ♦ [3b] bracket, category, class, division, family, grade, group, kind, set, species, type — more at CLASS ♦ [5] arrangement, array, disposal, disposition, distribution, sequence, setup; *also* continuity; precedence, priority; chain, progression, succession; series; aligning, alignment, lining up; design, layout, pattern, structure, system ♦ [7] behest, charge, command, commandment, decree, dictate, direction, directive, edict, instruction, word — more at COMMAND ♦ [9] condition, estate, fettle, form, repair, shape, trim — more at CONDITION

¹or·der·ly \'ȯr-dər-lē\ *adj* **1 a** ♦ : arranged according to some order **b** ♦ : marked by order : NEAT, TIDY **2** : well behaved ⟨an ∼ crowd⟩ — **or·der·li·ness** *n*

♦ [1a] methodical, regular, systematic — more at METHODICAL ♦ [1b] crisp, neat, shipshape, snug, tidy, trim, uncluttered — more at NEAT

²orderly *n, pl* **-lies** **1** : a soldier who attends a superior officer **2** : a hospital attendant who does general work

or·di·nal \'ȯrd-ᵊnəl\ *adj* : indicating order or rank (as sixth) in a series

ordinal number *n* : a number (as first, second, or third) that designates the place of an item in an ordered sequence — compare CARDINAL NUMBER

or·di·nance \'ȯrd-ᵊn-əns\ *n* ♦ : an authoritative decree or law; *esp* : a municipal regulation

♦ act, enactment, law, statute — more at LAW

or·di·nar·i·ly \ˌȯrd-ᵊn-'er-ə-lē\ *adv* ♦ : in an ordinary manner

♦ commonly, generally, naturally, normally, typically, usually — more at NATURALLY

or·di·nary \'ȯrd-ᵊn-ˌer-ē\ *adj* **1** ♦ : to be expected : USUAL **2** ♦ : of common quality, rank, or ability; *also* : POOR, INFERIOR — **or·di·nar·i·ness** \'ȯrd-ᵊn-ˌer-ē-nəs\ *n*

♦ [1] average, common, commonplace, everyday, normal, prosaic, routine, run-of-the-mill, standard, unexceptional, unremarkable, usual, workaday; *also* regular, typical; familiar, homely, plain, popular, vulgar; natural; customary, wonted; insignificant, trivial, unimportant; customary, frequent, habitual; expected, predictable *Ant* abnormal, exceptional, extraordinary, odd, out-of-the-way, strange, unusual ♦ [2] common,

fair, indifferent, inferior, mediocre, medium, middling, passable, poor, run-of-the-mill, second-rate, so-so — more at MEDIOCRE

or·di·nate \'ȯrd-ᵊn-ət, -ˌāt\ *n* : the vertical coordinate of a point in a plane coordinate system obtained by measuring parallel to the y-axis

or·di·na·tion \ˌȯrd-ᵊn-'ā-shən\ *n* : the act or ceremony by which a person is ordained

ord·nance \'ȯrd-nəns\ *n* **1** : military supplies **2** : CANNON, ARTILLERY

Or·do·vi·cian \ˌȯr-də-'vi-shən\ *adj* : of, relating to, or being the period of the Paleozoic era between the Cambrian and the Silurian — **Ordovician** *n*

or·dure \'ȯr-jər\ *n* : EXCREMENT

ore \'ȯr\ *n* : a naturally occurring mineral mined to obtain a substance that it contains

Ore *or* **Oreg** *abbr* Oregon

oreg·a·no \ə-'re-gə-ˌnō\ *n* : a bushy perennial mint used as a seasoning and a source of oil

org *abbr* organization; organized

or·gan \'ȯr-gən\ *n* **1** : a musical instrument having sets of pipes sounded by compressed air and controlled by keyboards; *also* : an electronic keyboard instrument that approximates the sounds of the pipe organ by electronic devices **2** : a differentiated animal or plant structure (as a heart or a leaf) made up of cells and tissues and performing some bodily function **3** : a group that performs a specialized function ⟨the various ∼s of government⟩ **4** : PERIODICAL **5** ♦ : a means exercising some function or accomplishing some end

♦ agency, agent, instrument, instrumentality, machinery, means, medium, vehicle — more at AGENT

or·gan·dy *also* **or·gan·die** \'ȯr-gən-dē\ *n, pl* **-dies** [F *organdi*] : a fine transparent muslin with a stiff finish

or·gan·elle \ˌȯr-gə-'nel\ *n* : a specialized cell part that resembles an organ in having a special function

or·gan·ic \ȯr-'ga-nik\ *adj* **1** : of, relating to, or arising in a bodily organ **2** : of, relating to, or derived from living things **3** : of, relating to, or containing carbon compounds **4** : of or relating to a branch of chemistry dealing with carbon compounds **5** : involving, producing, or dealing in foods produced without the use of laboratory-made fertilizers, growth substances, antibiotics, or pesticides **6** : ORGANIZED ⟨an ∼ whole⟩ — **or·gan·i·cal·ly** \-ni-k(ə-)lē\ *adv*

or·ga·ni·sa·tion, or·ga·nise *chiefly Brit var of* ORGANIZATION, ORGANIZE

or·gan·ism \'ȯr-gə-ˌni-zəm\ *n* : an individual living thing (as a person, animal, or plant) — **or·gan·is·mic** \ˌȯr-gə-'niz-mik\ *adj*

or·gan·ist \'ȯr-gə-nist\ *n* : a person who plays an organ

or·ga·ni·za·tion \ˌȯr-gə-nə-'zā-shən\ *n* **1** : the act or process of organizing or of being organized; *also* : the condition or manner of being organized **2** ♦ : an association of persons having a common interest : SOCIETY **3** : an administrative structure (as a business or a political party); *also* : the personnel of such a structure — **or·ga·ni·za·tion·al** \-shə-nəl\ *adj*

♦ association, brotherhood, club, college, congress, council, fellowship, fraternity, guild, institute, institution, league, order, society — more at ASSOCIATION

or·ga·nize \'ȯr-gə-ˌnīz\ *vb* **-nized; -niz·ing** **1** : to develop an organic structure **2** : to form into a complete and functioning whole **3** : to set up an administrative structure for **4** ♦ : to arrange by systematic planning and united effort **5** : to join in a union; *also* : UNIONIZE — **or·ga·niz·er** *n*

♦ arrange, array, classify, codify, dispose, draw up, marshal, order, range, systematize — more at ORDER

or·gano·chlo·rine \ȯr-ˌga-nə-'klȯr-ˌēn\ *adj* : of, relating to, or being a chlorinated hydrocarbon pesticide (as DDT) — **organochlorine** *n*

or·gano·phos·phate \-'fäs-ˌfāt\ *n* : an organophosphorus pesticide — **organophosphate** *adj*

or·gano·phos·pho·rus \-'fäs-fə-rəs\ *also* **or·gano·phos·pho-**

rous \-fäs-ˈfōr-əs\ *adj* : of, relating to, or being a phosphorus-containing organic pesticide (as malathion)

or·gan·za \òr-ˈgan-zə\ *n* : a sheer dress fabric resembling organdy and usu. made of silk, rayon, or nylon

or·gasm \ˈòr-ˌga-zəm\ *n* : the climax of sexual excitement — **or·gas·mic** \òr-ˈgaz-mik\ *adj*

or·gi·as·tic \ˌòr-jē-ˈas-tik\ *adj* : of, relating to, or marked by orgies

or·gu·lous \ˈòr-gyə-ləs, -gə-\ *adj* : PROUD

or·gy \ˈòr-jē\ *n, pl* **orgies** : a gathering marked by unrestrained indulgence (as in sexual activity, alcohol, or drugs)

ori·el \ˈōr-ē-əl\ *n* : a window built out from a wall and usu. supported by a bracket

ori·ent \ˈōr-ē-ˌent\ *vb* **1** : to set in a definite position esp. in relation to the points of the compass **2** ♦ : to acquaint with an existing situation or environment **3** : to direct toward the interests of a particular group

♦ acquaint, familiarize, initiate, introduce — more at ACQUAINT

Orient *n* **1** : EAST 3; *esp* : the countries of eastern Asia

ori·en·tal \ˌōr-ē-ˈent-ᵊl\ *adj, often cap* [fr. *Orient* East, fr. ME, fr. AF, fr. L *orient-, oriens*, fr. prp. of *oriri* to rise] : of or situated in the Orient — **Oriental** *n*

ori·en·tate \ˈōr-ē-ən-ˌtāt\ *vb* **-tat·ed; -tat·ing** **1** : to acquaint with the existing situation or environment : ORIENT **2** : to face east

ori·en·ta·tion \ˌòr-ē-ən-tā-shən\ *n* **1** : the act or state of being oriented **2** : a person's sexual identity as bisexual, heterosexual, homosexual, pansexual, etc.

or·i·fice \ˈòr-ə-fəs\ *n* ♦ : an opening (as a vent, mouth, or hole) through which something may pass : OPENING

♦ aperture, hole, opening, perforation — more at HOLE

ori·flamme \ˈòr-ə-ˌflam\ *n* : a brightly colored banner used as a standard or ensign in battle

orig *abbr* original; originally

ori·ga·mi \ˌòr-ə-ˈgä-mē\ *n* : the art or process of Japanese paper folding

ori·gin \ˈòr-ə-jən\ *n* **1** ♦ : line of descent : ANCESTRY **2** : rise, beginning, or derivation from a source; *also* : CAUSE **3** : the intersection of coordinate axes

♦ ancestry, birth, blood, bloodline, breeding, descent, extraction, family tree, genealogy, line, lineage, parentage, pedigree, stock, strain — more at ANCESTRY

¹**orig·i·nal** \ə-ˈri-jə-nəl\ *n* : something from which a copy, reproduction, or translation is made : PROTOTYPE

²**original** *adj* **1** ♦ : existing from the start : FIRST, INITIAL **2** ♦ : not copied from something else : FRESH **3** ♦ : gifted with powers of independent thought, direct insight, or constructive imagination : INVENTIVE

♦ [1] first, inaugural, initial, maiden, pioneer, premier — more at FIRST ♦ [2] fresh, new, novel, strange, unfamiliar, unknown — more at NEW ♦ [3] creative, imaginative, ingenious, innovative, inventive — more at CREATIVE

orig·i·nal·i·ty \-ˌri-jə-ˈna-lə-tē\ *n* **1** ♦ : freshness of aspect, design, or style **2** ♦ : the power of independent thought or constructive imagination

♦ [1] freshness, newness, novelty — more at NOVELTY ♦ [2] creativity, ingenuity, invention, inventiveness — more at CREATIVITY

orig·i·nal·ly \-ˈri-jən-ᵊl-ē\ *adv* ♦ : in the beginning : in the first place

♦ firstly, initially, primarily; *also* primitively

orig·i·nate \ə-ˈri-jə-ˌnāt\ *vb* **-nat·ed; -nat·ing** **1** : to give rise to : INITIATE **2** ♦ : to come into existence : BEGIN

♦ arise, begin, commence, dawn, form, materialize, spring, start — more at BEGIN

orig·i·na·tor \-ˌnā-tər\ *n* ♦ : one that originates

♦ author, creator, father, founder — more at FATHER ♦ designer, developer, innovator, inventor — more at INVENTOR

ori·ole \ˈòr-ē-ˌōl\ *n* : any of various New World birds of which the males are usu. black and yellow or black and orange

ori·son \ˈòr-ə-sən\ *n* : PRAYER

or·mo·lu \ˈòr-mə-ˌlü\ *n* : a golden or gilded brass used for decorative purposes

¹**or·na·ment** \ˈòr-nə-mənt\ *n* ♦ : something that lends grace or beauty — **or·na·men·ta·tion** \ˌòr-nə-mən-ˈtā-shən\ *n*

♦ adornment, caparison, decoration, embellishment, frill, garnish, trim — more at DECORATION

²**or·na·ment** \-ˌment\ *vb* ♦ : to provide with ornament : ADORN

♦ adorn, array, beautify, bedeck, deck, decorate, do, dress, embellish, enrich, garnish, grace, trim — more at DECORATE

or·na·men·tal \ˌòr-nə-ˈment-ᵊl\ *adj* : DECORATIVE : of, relating to, or serving as ornament

or·nate \òr-ˈnāt\ *adj* ♦ : elaborately decorated — **or·nate·ly** *adv* — **or·nate·ness** *n*

♦ florid, overwrought; *also* arabesque, baroque, rococo; extravagant, flamboyant, spectacular; flashy, garish, gaudy, glitzy, loud, ostentatious, pretentious, showy, swank, tawdry; elaborate, extreme; adorned, arrayed, beautified, bedecked, decked, decorated, embellished, enriched, garnished, ornamented, trimmed; flowery, frilly, lacy; enhanced, heightened, intensified; bossed, chased, embossed, embroidered, flounced, garlanded, gilded, laced, wreathed **Ant** austere, plain, severe, stark, unadorned

or·nery \ˈòr-nə-rē, ˈä-nə-\ *adj* ♦ : having an irritable disposition

♦ bearish, bilious, cantankerous, disagreeable, dyspeptic, ill-humored, ill-tempered, splenetic, surly — more at ILL-TEMPERED

or·ni·thol·o·gy \ˌòr-nə-ˈthä-lə-jē\ *n, pl* **-gies** : a branch of zoology dealing with birds — **or·ni·tho·log·i·cal** \-thə-ˈlä-ji-kəl\ *adj* — **or·ni·thol·o·gist** \-ˈthä-lə-jist\ *n*

oro·tund \ˈòr-ə-ˌtənd\ *adj* **1** : SONOROUS **2** : POMPOUS — **oro·tun·di·ty** \ˌòr-ə-ˈtən-di-tē\ *n*

or·phan \ˈòr-fən\ *n* : a child deprived by death of one or usu. both parents — **orphan** *vb*

or·phan·age \ˈòr-fə-nij\ *n* : an institution for the care of orphans

or·tho·don·tia \ˌòr-thə-ˈdän-chə, -chē-ə\ *n* : ORTHODONTICS

or·tho·don·tics \ˌòr-thə-ˈdän-tiks\ *n* : a branch of dentistry concerned with the correction of faults in the arrangement and placing of the teeth — **or·tho·don·tist** \-ˈdän-tist\ *n*

or·tho·dox \ˈòr-thə-ˌdäks\ *adj* [MF or LL; MF *orthodoxe*, fr. LL *orthodoxus*, fr. LGk *orthodoxos*, fr. Gk *orthos* right + *doxa* opinion] **1** ♦ : conforming to established doctrine esp. in religion **2** ♦ : according with, sanctioned by, or based on convention : CONVENTIONAL **3** *cap* : of or relating to a Christian church originating in the church of the Eastern Roman Empire — **or·tho·doxy** \-ˌdäk-sē\ *n*

♦ [1] conservative, old-fashioned, reactionary, traditional — more at CONSERVATIVE ♦ [2] ceremonial, ceremonious, conventional, formal, regular, routine — more at FORMAL

or·thog·ra·phy \òr-ˈthä-grə-fē\ *n* : SPELLING — **or·tho·graph·ic** \ˌòr-thə-ˈgra-fik\ *adj*

or·tho·pe·dics \ˌòr-thə-ˈpē-diks\ *n sing or pl* : a branch of medicine concerned with the correction or prevention of skeletal injuries or disorders — **or·tho·pe·dic** \-dik\ *adj* — **or·tho·pe·dist** \-dist\ *n*

-ory \ˌòr-ē, ə-rē\ *adj suffix* **1** : of, relating to, or characterized by ⟨anticipat*ory*⟩ **2** : serving for, producing, or maintaining ⟨illus*ory*⟩

Os *symbol* osmium

OS *abbr* **1** [L *oculus sinister*] left eye **2** ordinary seaman **3** out of stock

Osage \ō-ˈsāj\ *n, pl* **Osag·es** *or* **Osage** : a member of an American Indian people orig. of Missouri

os·cil·late \'ä-sə-ˌlāt\ *vb* **-lat·ed; -lat·ing** **1 :** to swing backward and forward like a pendulum **2 :** to move or travel back and forth between two points **3 :** VARY, FLUCTUATE — **os·cil·la·tor** \'ä-sə-ˌlā-tər\ *n* — **os·cil·la·to·ry** \'ä-sə-lə-ˌtōr-ē\ *adj*
os·cil·la·tion \ˌä-sə-'lā-shən\ *n* **:** the action or state of oscillating

♦ quivering, vibration — more at VIBRATION

os·cil·lo·scope \ä-'si-lə-ˌskōp\ *n* **:** an instrument in which variations in current or voltage appear as a visible wave form on a fluorescent screen
os·cu·late \'äs-kyə-ˌlāt\ *vb* **-lat·ed; -lat·ing :** KISS — **os·cu·la·tion** \ˌäs-kyə-'lā-shən\ *n* — **os·cu·la·to·ry** \'äs-kyə-lə-ˌtōr-ē\ *adj*
Osee \'ō-ˌzē, ō-'zā-ə\ *n* **:** HOSEA
OSHA \'ō-shə\ *abbr* Occupational Safety and Health Administration
osier \'ō-zhər\ *n* **:** any of various willows with pliable twigs used esp. in making baskets and furniture; *also* **:** a twig from an osier
os·mi·um \'äz-mē-əm\ *n* **:** a heavy hard brittle metallic chemical element used esp. as a catalyst and in alloys
os·mo·sis \äz-'mō-səs, äs-\ *n* **:** movement of a solvent through a semipermeable membrane into a solution of higher concentration that tends to equalize the concentrations of the solutions on either side of the membrane — **os·mot·ic** \-'mä-tik\ *adj*
os·prey \'äs-prē, -ˌprā\ *n, pl* **ospreys :** a large dark brown and white fish-eating hawk
os·si·fy \'ä-sə-ˌfī\ *vb* **-fied; -fy·ing :** to make or become hardened or set in one's ways ⟨an *ossified* regime⟩ — **os·si·fi·ca·tion** \ˌä-sə-fə-'kā-shən\ *n*
os·su·ary \'ä-shə-ˌwer-ē, -syə-\ *n, pl* **-ar·ies :** a depository for the bones of the dead
os·ten·si·ble \ä-'sten-sə-bəl\ *adj* ♦ **:** shown outwardly **:** APPARENT

♦ apparent, assumed, evident, reputed, seeming, supposed — more at APPARENT

os·ten·si·bly \-blē\ *adv* **1 :** in an ostensible manner **2** ♦ **:** to all outward appearances

♦ apparently, evidently, presumably, seemingly, supposedly — more at APPARENTLY

os·ten·ta·tion \ˌäs-tən-'tā-shən\ *n* ♦ **:** pretentious or excessive display — **os·ten·ta·tious·ly** *adv*

♦ flamboyance, flashiness, gaudiness, glitz, pretentiousness, showiness, swank; *also* extravaganza, pageant, parade, show; dazzle, pageantry, spectacle; adornment, decoration, dressing, embellishment, garnishment, ornamentation, trimming; extravagance, opulence, richness; loudness; meretriciousness, vulgarity *Ant* austerity, plainness, severity

os·ten·ta·tious \-shəs\ *adj* ♦ **:** marked by or fond of conspicuous or sometimes pretentious display

♦ flamboyant, flashy, garish, gaudy, glitzy, loud, swank, tawdry — more at GAUDY ♦ affected, grandiose, highfalutin, pompous, pretentious — more at PRETENTIOUS

os·teo·path \'äs-tē-ə-ˌpath\ *n* **:** a practitioner of osteopathy
os·te·op·a·thy \ˌäs-tē-'ä-pə-thē\ *n* **:** a system of treating diseases emphasizing manipulation (as of joints) but not excluding other agencies (as the use of medicine and surgery) — **os·teo·path·ic** \ˌäs-tē-ə-'pa-thik\ *adj*
os·teo·po·ro·sis \ˌäs-tē-ō-pə-'rō-səs, *n, pl* **-ro·ses** \-ˌsēz\ **:** a condition affecting esp. older women and characterized by fragile and porous bones
os·tra·cise *chiefly Brit var of* OSTRACIZE
os·tra·cize \'äs-trə-ˌsīz\ *vb* **-cized; -ciz·ing** [Gk *ostrakizein* to banish by voting with potsherds, fr. *ostrakon* shell, potsherd] **:** to exclude from a group by common consent — **os·tra·cism** \-ˌsi-zəm\ *n*
os·trich \'äs-trich, 'ós-\ *n* **:** a very large swift-footed flightless bird of Africa and Arabia
Os·we·go tea \ä-'swē-gō-\ *n* **:** a No. American mint with showy scarlet flowers

OT *abbr* **1** occupational therapy **2** Old Testament **3** overtime
¹oth·er \'ə-thər\ *adj* **1 :** being the one left; *also* **:** being the ones distinct from those first mentioned **2 :** ALTERNATE ⟨every ~ day⟩ **3** ♦ **:** not the same **:** DIFFERENT **4** ♦ **:** existing by way of addition **:** ADDITIONAL **5 :** recently past ⟨the ~ night⟩

♦ [3] different, disparate, dissimilar, distinct, distinctive, distinguishable, diverse, unalike, unlike — more at DIFFERENT ♦ [4] additional, another, else, farther, further, more — more at ADDITIONAL

²other *pron* **1 :** remaining one or ones **2 :** a different or additional one ⟨something or ~⟩
other than *prep* ♦ **:** with the exception of **:** BESIDES

♦ aside from, bar, barring, besides, but, except, except for, exclusive of, outside (of), save

oth·er·wise \'ə-thər-ˌwīz\ *adv* **1** ♦ **:** in a different way **2 :** in different circumstances **3 :** in other respects **4 :** if not **5 :** NOT — **otherwise** *adj*

♦ differently, else, other; *also* diversely, variously *Ant* likewise

oth·er·world \-ˌwərld\ *n* **:** a world beyond death or beyond present reality
oth·er·world·ly \ˌə-thər-'wərld-lē\ *adj* **:** not worldly **:** concerned with spiritual, intellectual, or imaginative matters
oti·ose \'ō-shē-ˌōs, 'ō-tē-\ *adj* **1 :** FUTILE **2 :** IDLE **3 :** USELESS
oto·lar·yn·gol·o·gy \ˌō-tō-ˌlar-ən-'gä-lə-jē\ *n* **:** a medical specialty concerned esp. with the ear, nose, and throat — **oto·lar·yn·gol·o·gist** \-jist\ *n*
oto·rhi·no·lar·yn·gol·o·gy \ˌō-tō-ˌrī-nō-ˌlar-ən-'gä-lə-jē\ *n* **:** OTOLARYNGOLOGY — **oto·rhi·no·lar·yn·gol·o·gist** \-jist\ *n*
OTS *abbr* officers' training school
Ot·ta·wa \'ä-tə-wə, -ˌwä, -ˌwó\ *n, pl* **Ottawas** *or* **Ottawa :** a member of an American Indian people of Michigan and southern Ontario
ot·ter \'ä-tər\ *n, pl* **otters** *also* **otter :** any of various web=footed fish-eating mammals with dark brown fur that are related to the weasels; *also* **:** the fur
ot·to·man \'ä-tə-mən\ *n* **:** an upholstered seat or couch usu. without a back; *also* **:** an overstuffed footstool
ou·bli·ette \ˌü-blē-'et\ *n* [F, fr. MF, fr. *oublier* to forget, ultim. fr. L *oblivisci*] **:** a dungeon with an opening at the top
ought \'ót\ *verbal auxiliary* ♦ — used to express moral obligation, advisability, natural expectation, or logical consequence ⟨you ~ to apologize⟩

♦ *usu* ought to have, must, need, shall, should — more at NEED

ounce \'aúns\ *n* [ME, fr. AF *unce*, fr. L *uncia* twelfth part, ounce, fr. *unus* one] **1 a :** a unit of avoirdupois, troy, and apothecaries' weight; *specif* **:** a unit of weight equal to ¹⁄₁₆ pound **b** ♦ **:** a small amount **2 :** FLUID OUNCE

♦ bit, little, particle, shred, speck, touch, trace — more at PARTICLE

our \är, 'aúr\ *adj* **:** of or relating to us or ourselves
ours \'aúrz, 'ärz\ *pron* **:** that which belongs to us
our·selves \är-'selvz, aúr-\ *pron* **:** our own selves — used reflexively, for emphasis, or in absolute constructions ⟨we pleased ~⟩ ⟨we'll do it ~⟩ ⟨we were tourists ~⟩
-ous \əs\ *adj suffix* **:** full of **:** abounding in **:** having **:** possessing the qualities of ⟨clamor*ous*⟩ ⟨poison*ous*⟩
oust \'aúst\ *vb* ♦ **:** to eject from or deprive of property or position

♦ banish, boot (out), bounce, cast, chase, dismiss, drum, eject, expel, rout, run off, throw out — more at EJECT ♦ depose — more at DEPOSE

oust·er \'aús-tər\ *n* **:** EXPULSION
¹out \'aút\ *adv* **1 :** in a direction away from the inside or center **2 :** beyond control **3 :** to extinction, exhaustion, or completion **4 :** in or into the open **5 :** so as to retire a batter or base runner; *also* **:** so as to be retired

²**out** *vb* ♦ : to become known ⟨the truth will ∼⟩

♦ come out, get out, leak out, spread — more at GET OUT

³**out** *prep* **1** : out through ⟨looked ∼ the window⟩ **2** : outward on or along ⟨drive ∼ the river road⟩

⁴**out** *adj* **1** : situated outside or at a distance **2** ♦ : not in : ABSENT; *also* : not being in power **3** : removed from play as a batter or base runner **4** : not being in vogue or fashion : not up-to-date

♦ absent, away, missing — more at ABSENT

⁵**out** *n* **1** : one who is out of office **2** : the retiring of a batter or base runner **3** ♦ : a way of escaping from an embarrassing or difficult situation

♦ avoidance, cop-out, escape, evasion — more at ESCAPE

out·age \'au̇-tij\ *n* : a period or instance of interruption esp. of electricity

out–and–out *adj* ♦ : being such completely at all times, in every way, or from every point of view : COMPLETE, THOROUGHGOING ⟨an ∼ fraud⟩

♦ absolute, all-out, complete, consummate, outright, thorough, thoroughgoing, total, unqualified, utter — more at ABSOLUTE

out·bid \ˌau̇t-'bid\ *vb* : to make a higher bid than

¹**out·board** \'au̇t-ˌbȯrd\ *adj* **1** : situated outboard **2** : having or using an outboard motor

²**outboard** *adv* **1** : outside a ship's hull : away from the long axis of a ship **2** : in a position closer to the wing tip of an airplane

outboard motor *n* : a small internal combustion engine with propeller attached for mounting at the stern of a small boat

out·bound \'au̇t-ˌbau̇nd\ *adj* : outward bound ⟨∼ traffic⟩

out·break \-ˌbrāk\ *n* **1** ♦ : a sudden increase in activity, incidence, or numbers **2** : INSURRECTION, REVOLT

♦ burst, flare, flare-up, flash, flurry, flutter, outburst, spurt; *also* binge, jag, spree; boost, increase, pickup, upswing, upturn; epidemic, eruption, explosion, paroxysm; deluge, flood, rush, spate, surge; commotion, furor, uproar

out·build·ing \-ˌbil-diŋ\ *n* : a building separate from but accessory to a main house

out·burst \-ˌbərst\ *n* **1 a** : ERUPTION **b** ♦ : a violent expression of feeling **2** : a surge of activity or growth

♦ agony, burst, eruption, explosion, fit, flare, flare-up, flash, flush, gale, gush, gust, paroxysm, spasm, storm; *also* blowup, grouch, rage, tantrum; ecstasy, rapture, transport; delirium, frenzy, furor

out·cast \-ˌkast\ *n* ♦ : one that is cast out by society

♦ castaway, reject; *also* untouchable; outsider; exile

out·class \au̇t-'klas\ *vb* ♦ : to be superior to in quality, degree, or performance : SURPASS

♦ beat, better, eclipse, excel, outdistance, outdo, outshine, outstrip, surpass, top, transcend — more at SURPASS

out·come \'au̇t-ˌkəm\ *n* ♦ : a final consequence : RESULT

♦ aftermath, conclusion, consequence, corollary, development, effect, issue, outgrowth, product, result, resultant, sequence, upshot — more at EFFECT

out·crop \-ˌkräp\ *n* : a coming out of bedrock to the surface of the ground; *also* : the part of a rock formation that thus appears — **outcrop** *vb*

out·cry \-ˌkrī\ *n* ♦ : a loud cry : CLAMOR

♦ clamor (*or* clamour), howl, hubbub, hue and cry, hullabaloo, noise, roar, tumult, uproar — more at CLAMOR

out·dat·ed \au̇t-'dā-təd\ *adj* ♦ : no longer current : OUTMODED

♦ antiquated, archaic, dated, obsolete, outmoded, outworn, passé — more at OBSOLETE

out·dis·tance \-'dis-təns\ *vb* ♦ : to leave behind : go ahead of

♦ beat, better, eclipse, excel, outdo, outshine, outstrip, surpass, top, transcend — more at SURPASS

out·do \-'dü\ *vb* **-did** \-'did\; **-done** \-'dən\; **-do·ing**; **-does** \-'dəz\ ♦ : to go beyond in action or performance

♦ beat, better, eclipse, excel, outdistance, outshine, outstrip, surpass, top, transcend — more at SURPASS

out·door \'au̇t-ˌdȯr, -'dȯr\ *also* **out·doors** \-ˌdȯrz, -'dȯrz\ *adj* **1** : of or relating to the outdoors **2** : performed outdoors **3** : not enclosed (as by a roof)

¹**out·doors** \'au̇t-ˌdȯrz, -'dȯrz\ *adv* : in or into the open air

²**outdoors** *n* **1** : the open air **2** ♦ : the world away from human habitation — **out·doorsy** \ˌau̇t-'dȯr-zē\ *adj*

♦ nature, open, wild, wilderness — more at NATURE

out·draw \au̇t-'drȯ\ *vb* **-drew** \-'drü\; **-drawn** \-'drȯn\; **-draw·ing** **1** : to attract a larger audience than **2** : to draw a handgun more quickly than

out·er \'au̇-tər\ *adj* **1** ♦ : of, relating to, or connected with the outside or an outer part : EXTERNAL **2** ♦ : situated farther out; *also* : being away from a center

♦ [1, 2] exterior, external, outside, outward; *also* outermost, outlying; superficial, surface *Ant* inner, inside, interior, internal, inward

outer ear *n* : the outer visible portion of the ear that collects and directs sound waves toward the eardrum

out·er·most \-ˌmōst\ *adj* ♦ : farthest out

♦ extreme, farthest, furthest, ultimate, utmost — more at EXTREME

outer space *n* : SPACE 5

out·er·wear \'au̇-tər-ˌwer\ *n* **1** : clothing for outdoor wear **2** : outer clothing as opposed to underwear

out·face \au̇t-'fās\ *vb* **1** : to cause to waver or submit **2** : DEFY

out·field \'au̇t-ˌfēld\ *n* : the part of a baseball field beyond the infield and within the foul lines; *also* : players in the outfield — **out·field·er** \-ˌfēl-dər\ *n*

out·fight \au̇t-'fīt\ *vb* : to surpass in fighting : DEFEAT

¹**out·fit** \'au̇t-ˌfit\ *n* **1** ♦ : the equipment or apparel for a special purpose or occasion **2** ♦ : a group that works as a team **3** ♦ : an organization engaged in a particular industry or activity

♦ [1] dress, garb, getup, guise; *also* apparel, attire, clothes, duds, raiment; fashion, mode, style; array, caparison, vestments ♦ [1] accoutrements (*or* accouterments), apparatus, equipment, gear, matériel, paraphernalia, tackle — more at EQUIPMENT ♦ [2] band, company, crew, gang, party, squad, team — more at GANG ♦ [3] business, company, concern, enterprise, establishment, firm, house — more at ENTERPRISE

²**outfit** *vb* **out·fit·ted**; **out·fit·ting** ♦ : to provide or supply with what is needed, useful, or desirable : EQUIP — **out·fit·ter** *n*

♦ accoutre, equip, fit, furnish, rig, supply — more at FURNISH

out·flank \au̇t-'flaŋk\ *vb* : to get around the flank of (an opposing force)

out·flow \'au̇t-ˌflō\ *n* **1** ♦ : a flowing out **2** : something that flows out

♦ gush, outpouring; *also* drain, flow; ebb; rush, stampede; emigration, flight; discharge, emanation, emission *Ant* flux, inflow, influx, inrush

out·fox \au̇t-'fäks\ *vb* ♦ : to outdo in trickery : OUTWIT

♦ fox, outmaneuver, outsmart, outwit, overreach — more at OUTWIT

out·go \'au̇t-ˌgō\ *n, pl* **outgoes** ♦ : something that goes out : OUTLAY

♦ cost, disbursement, expenditure, expense, outlay — more at EXPENSE

out·go·ing \-ˌgō-iŋ\ *adj* **1** : going out ⟨∼ tide⟩ **2** : retiring from a place or position **3** ♦ : openly friendly and responsive

♦ boon, companionable, convivial, extroverted, gregarious, sociable, social — more at CONVIVIAL

out·grow \aȯt-'grō\ *vb* **-grew** \-'grü\; **-grown** \-'grōn\; **-grow·ing** **1** : to grow faster than **2** : to grow too large for

out·growth \'aȯt-ˌgrōth\ *n* **1** ♦ : a product of growing out : OFFSHOOT **2** : something produced by a cause or necessarily following from a set of conditions : CONSEQUENCE, RESULT

     ♦ derivative, offshoot, spin-off — more at DERIVATIVE

out·guess \aȯt-'ges\ *vb* : OUTWIT

out·gun \-'gən\ *vb* : to surpass in firepower

out·house \'aȯt-ˌhaȯs\ *n* : OUTBUILDING; *esp* : an outdoor toilet

out·ing \'aȯ-tiŋ\ *n* ♦ : a brief stay or trip in the open

     ♦ excursion, jaunt, junket, sally — more at EXCURSION

out·land·ish \aȯt-'lan-dish\ *adj* **1 a** ♦ : of foreign appearance or manner **b** ♦ : strikingly out of the ordinary **2** : remote from civilization — **out·land·ish·ly** *adv*

     ♦ bizarre, curious, exotic, far-out, funny, kinky, odd, outré, peculiar, quaint, queer, quirky, remarkable, screwy, strange, wacky, weird, wild — more at ODD

out·last \-'last\ *vb* : to last longer than

¹**out·law** \'aȯt-ˌlȯ\ *n* **1** : a person excluded from the protection of the law **2** : a lawless person

²**outlaw** *vb* **1** : to deprive of the protection of the law **2** : to make illegal **3** ♦ : to place under a ban or restriction — **out·law·ry** \'aȯt-ˌlȯr-ē\ *n*

     ♦ ban, bar, enjoin, forbid, interdict, prohibit, proscribe — more at FORBID

out·lay \'aȯt-ˌlā\ *n* **1** ♦ : the act of spending **2** ♦ : something expended : EXPENDITURE

     ♦ cost, disbursement, expenditure, expense, outgo — more at EXPENSE

out·let \'aȯt-ˌlet, -lət\ *n* **1** ♦ : a place or opening through which something is let out : EXIT **2** : a means of release (as for an emotion) **3** : a market for a commodity **4** : a receptacle for the plug of an electrical device

     ♦ egress, exit, issue — more at EXIT

¹**out·line** \'aȯt-ˌlīn\ *n* **1** ♦ : a line marking the outer limits of an object or figure **2** : a drawing in which only contours are marked **3** ♦ : a condensed treatment of a particular subject : a summary of a written work : SUMMARY, SYNOPSIS **4** : PLAN

     ♦ [1] contour, figure, silhouette; *also* delineation, sketch; profile, skyline, form, cast, configuration, conformation, geometry, shape; framework, skeleton ♦ [3] abstract, digest, encapsulation, epitome, précis, recapitulation, roundup, résumé (*or* resume), sum, summary, synopsis, wrap-up — more at SUMMARY

²**outline** *vb* **1** ♦ : to draw the outline of **2** : to indicate the chief features or parts of

     ♦ define, delineate, silhouette, sketch, trace; *also* line; bound, fringe, margin, skirt; edge, hem, rim, trim; frame; circle, compass, encircle, girdle, girth, loop, ring, round, surround; chart, diagram, draw, map (out)

out·live \aȯt-'liv\ *vb* : to live longer than

out·look \'aȯt-ˌlȯk\ *n* **1 a** : a place offering a view **b** ♦ : a view from a particular place : VIEW **2** ♦ : a position from which something is considered or evaluated : STANDPOINT **3** : the prospect for the future

     ♦ [1b] lookout, panorama, prospect, view, vista — more at VIEW ♦ [2] angle, perspective, point of view, slant, standpoint, viewpoint — more at POINT OF VIEW

out·ly·ing \-ˌlī-iŋ\ *adj* : distant from a center or main body

out·ma·neu·ver \ˌaȯt-mə-'nü-vər, -'nyü-\ *vb* ♦ : to defeat by more skillful maneuvering

     ♦ fox, outfox, outsmart, outwit, overreach — more at OUTWIT

out·mod·ed \aȯt-'mō-dəd\ *adj* **1** ♦ : no longer in style **2** ♦ : no longer acceptable, current, or usable

     ♦ [1, 2] antiquated, archaic, dated, obsolete, outdated, outworn, passé — more at OBSOLETE

out·num·ber \-'nəm-bər\ *vb* : to exceed in number

out of *prep* **1** : out from within or behind ⟨walk *out of* the room⟩ ⟨look *out of* the window⟩ **2** : from a state of ⟨wake up *out of* a deep sleep⟩ **3** : beyond the limits of ⟨*out of* sight⟩ **4** : BECAUSE OF ⟨asked *out of* curiosity⟩ **5** : FROM, WITH ⟨built it *out of* scrap⟩ **6** : in or into a state of loss or not having ⟨cheated him *out of* $5000⟩ ⟨we're *out of* matches⟩ **7** : from among ⟨one *out of* four⟩ — **out of it** : SQUARE, OLD-FASHIONED

out–of–bounds *adv or adj* : outside the prescribed boundaries or limits

out–of–date *adj* : no longer in fashion or in use : OUTMODED

out–of–door *or* **out–of–doors** *adj* : of or relating to the out-doors : OUTDOOR

out–of–the–way *adj* **1** : UNUSUAL **2** : being off the beaten track

out·pa·tient \'aȯt-ˌpā-shənt\ *n* : a patient who visits a hospital or clinic for diagnosis or treatment without staying overnight

out·per·form \ˌaȯt-pər-'fȯrm\ *vb* : to perform better than

out·play \aȯt-'plā\ *vb* : to play more skillfully than

out·point \-'pȯint\ *vb* : to win more points than

out·post \'aȯt-ˌpōst\ *n* **1** : a security detachment dispatched by a main body of troops to protect it from enemy surprise; *also* : a military base established (as by treaty) in a foreign country **2** : an outlying or frontier settlement

out·pour·ing \-ˌpȯr-iŋ\ *n* ♦ : something that pours out or is poured out

     ♦ gush, outflow — more at OUTFLOW

out·pull \aȯt-'pȯl\ *vb* : OUTDRAW 1

¹**out·put** \'aȯt-ˌpȯt\ *n* **1 a** ♦ : the amount produced (as by a machine or factory) : PRODUCTION **b** ♦ : mental or artistic production **2** : the information produced by a computer

     ♦ [1a, b] affair, handiwork, produce, product, thing, work, yield — more at PRODUCT

²**output** *vb* **out·put·ted** *or* **output**; **out·put·ting** : to produce as output

¹**out·rage** \'aȯt-ˌrāj\ *n* [ME, fr. AF *utrage, outrage* insult, excess, fr. *utre, outre* beyond, fr. L *ultra*] **1** : a violent or shameful act **2** ♦ : a gross indignity : INSULT **3** ♦ : the anger or resentment aroused by an outrage

     ♦ [2] affront, barb, dart, dig, indignity, insult, name, offense, put-down, sarcasm, slight, slur, wound — more at INSULT ♦ [3] anger, furor, fury, indignation, ire, rage, spleen, wrath, wrathfulness — more at ANGER

²**outrage** *vb* **out·raged**; **out·rag·ing** **1** : RAPE **2** ♦ : to subject to violent injury or gross insult **3** ♦ : to arouse to extreme resentment

     ♦ [2] affront, insult, offend, slight, wound — more at INSULT ♦ [3] anger, antagonize, enrage, incense, inflame, infuriate, madden, rankle, rile, roil — more at ANGER

out·ra·geous \aȯt-'rā-jəs\ *adj* : extremely offensive, insulting, or shameful : SHOCKING — **out·ra·geous·ly** *adv*

out·rank \-'raŋk\ *vb* : to rank higher than

ou·tré \ü-'trā\ *adj* [F] ♦ : violating convention or propriety : BIZARRE ⟨~ creations⟩

     ♦ bizarre, curious, far-out, funny, kinky, odd, outlandish, peculiar, quaint, queer, quirky, remarkable, screwy, strange, wacky, weird, wild — more at ODD

¹**out·reach** \aȯt-'rēch\ *vb* **1** : to surpass in reach **2** : to get the better of by trickery

²**out·reach** \'aȯt-ˌrēch\ *n* **1** : the act of reaching out **2** : the extent of reach **3** : the extending of services beyond usual limits

out·rid·er \-ˌrī-dər\ *n* : a mounted attendant

out·rig·ger \-ˌri-gər\ *n* **1** : a frame attached to the side of a boat to prevent capsizing **2** : a craft equipped with an outrigger

¹**out·right** \aȯt-'rīt\ *adv* **1** : COMPLETELY **2** : INSTANTANEOUSLY

²**out·right** \'aȯt-ˌrīt\ *adj* **1** : being exactly what is stated ⟨an ~ lie⟩ **2** ♦ : given or made without reservation or encumbrance ⟨an ~ sale⟩

♦ absolute, all-out, complete, consummate, out-and-out, perfect, pure, sheer, thorough, thoroughgoing, total, utter — more at ABSOLUTE

out·run \aut-'rən\ vb **-ran** \-'ran\; **-run; -run·ning** 1 : to run faster than 2 ♦ : to go or be beyond the limit of : EXCEED

♦ exceed, overreach, overrun, overshoot, overstep, surpass, transcend — more at EXCEED

out·sell \-'sel\ vb **-sold** \-'sōld\; **-sell·ing** : to exceed in sales

out·set \'aut-ˌset\ n ♦ : a setting out : BEGINNING, START

♦ beginning, birth, commencement, dawn, genesis, launch, morning, onset, start, threshold — more at BEGINNING

out·shine \aut-'shīn\ vb **-shone** \-'shōn\ or **-shined; -shin·ing** 1 : to shine brighter than 2 ♦ : to go beyond in action or performance : SURPASS

♦ beat, better, eclipse, excel, outdistance, outdo, outstrip, surpass, top, transcend — more at SURPASS

¹**out·side** \aut-'sīd, 'aut-ˌsīd\ n 1 : a place or region beyond an enclosure or boundary 2 ♦ : an outer side or surface : EXTERIOR 3 : the utmost limit or extent

♦ exterior, face, skin, surface, veneer — more at EXTERIOR

²**outside** adj 1 ♦ : of, relating to, or being on or toward the outer side or surface : OUTER 2 : coming from without ⟨∼ influences⟩ 3 : being apart from one's regular duties ⟨∼ activities⟩ 4 ♦ : barely possible : REMOTE ⟨an ∼ chance⟩

♦ [1] exterior, external, outer, outward — more at OUTER ♦ [4] negligible, off, remote, slight, slim, small — more at REMOTE

³**outside** adv : on or to the outside

⁴**outside** prep 1 : on or to the outside of 2 ♦ : beyond the limits of 3 ♦ : with the exclusion or exception of : EXCEPT

♦ [2] beyond, without — more at BEYOND ♦ usu **outside of** [3] aside from, bar, barring, besides, but, except, save

outside of prep 1 : with the exclusion or exception of : OUTSIDE 2 : BESIDES 3 : beyond the limits or compass of

out·sid·er \aut-'sī-dər\ n : a person who does not belong to a group

out·size \'aut-ˌsīz\ also **out·sized** \-ˌsīzd\ adj ♦ : unusually large : extravagant in size or degree

♦ astronomical, enormous, giant, gigantic, grand, huge, jumbo, mammoth, massive, monumental, oversize, prodigious, titanic, tremendous, vast

out·skirts \-ˌskərts\ n pl ♦ : the outlying parts (as of a city)

♦ environs, exurbia, suburbia — more at ENVIRONS

out·smart \aut-'smärt\ vb ♦ : to get the better of : OUTWIT

♦ fox, outfox, outmaneuver, outwit, overreach — more at OUTWIT

out·source \'aut-ˌsörs\ vb **-sourced; -sourc·ing** : to obtain (goods or services) from an outside supplier

out·spend \-'spend\ vb 1 : to exceed the limits of in spending ⟨∼s his income⟩ 2 : to spend more than

out·spo·ken \aut-'spō-kən\ adj ♦ : direct and open in speech or expression — **out·spo·ken·ly** adv

♦ candid, direct, forthright, foursquare, frank, honest, open, plain, straight, straightforward, unguarded, unreserved — more at FRANK

out·spo·ken·ness \aut-'spō-kən-nəs\ n ♦ : the quality or state of being outspoken

♦ candidness, candor, directness, forthrightness, frankness, openness, plainness — more at CANDOR

out·spread \-'spred\ vb **-spread; -spread·ing** : to spread out

out·stand·ing \-'stan-diŋ\ adj 1 : PROJECTING 2 a ♦ : not paid : UNPAID b : UNRESOLVED 3 : publicly issued and sold 4 a : CONSPICUOUS b ♦ : marked by eminence and distinction : DISTINGUISHED — **out·stand·ing·ly** adv

♦ [2a] overdue, payable, unpaid, unsettled; also due, mature Ant cleared, liquidated, paid (off or up), repaid, settled ♦ [4b] distinguished, eminent, illustrious, noble, notable, noteworthy, preeminent, prestigious, signal, star, superior — more at EMINENT

out·stay \-'stā\ vb 1 : OVERSTAY 2 : to surpass in endurance

out·stretch \ˌaut-'strech\ vb : to stretch out : EXTEND

out·strip \-'strip\ vb 1 : to go faster than 2 ♦ : to get ahead of : EXCEL, SURPASS

♦ beat, better, eclipse, excel, outdistance, outdo, outshine, surpass, top, transcend — more at SURPASS

out·take \'aut-ˌtāk\ n : something taken out; esp : a take that is not used in an edited version of a film or videotape

out·vote \-'vōt\ vb : to defeat by a majority of votes

¹**out·ward** \'aut-wərd\ adj 1 : moving or directed toward the outside 2 : showing outwardly 3 ♦ : situated or lying on the outside of an enclosure or surface

♦ exterior, external, outer, outside — more at OUTER

²**outward** or **out·wards** \-wərdz\ adv : toward the outside

out·ward·ly \-wərd-lē\ adv : on the outside : EXTERNALLY

out·wear \aut-'war\ vb **-wore** \-'wōr\; **-worn** \-'wōrn\; **-wear·ing** : to wear longer than : OUTLAST

out·weigh \-'wā\ vb ♦ : to exceed in weight, value, or importance

♦ overshadow; also count, import, matter, mean, signify, weigh; dwarf; exceed, outstrip, surpass, transcend

out·wit \-'wit\ vb ♦ : to get the better of by superior cleverness

♦ fox, outfox, outmaneuver, outsmart, overreach; also outguess, second-guess; baffle, balk, circumvent, foil, frustrate, thwart; cozen, deceive, dupe, fool, gull, trick; conquer, defeat, lick, overcome; bar, block, hinder, impede, obstruct

¹**out·work** \-'wərk\ vb : to outdo in working

²**out·work** \'aut-ˌwərk\ n : a minor defensive position outside a fortified area

out·worn \aut-'wōrn\ adj ♦ : no longer useful or accepted : OUTMODED

♦ antiquated, archaic, dated, obsolete, outdated, outmoded, passé — more at OBSOLETE

ou·zo \'ü-(ˌ)zō\ n : a colorless anise-flavored unsweetened Greek liqueur

ova pl of OVUM

oval \'ō-vəl\ adj [ML ovalis, fr. LL, of an egg, fr. L ovum egg] : egg-shaped; also : broadly elliptical — **oval** n

ova·ry \'ō-və-rē\ n, pl **-ries** 1 : one of the usu. paired female reproductive organs producing eggs and in vertebrates sex hormones 2 : the part of a flower in which seeds are produced — **ovar·i·an** \ō-'var-ē-ən, -'ver-\ adj

ovate \'ō-ˌvāt\ adj : egg-shaped

ova·tion \ō-'vā-shən\ n [L ovation-, ovatio, fr. ovare to exult] ♦ : an enthusiastic popular tribute

♦ acclamation, applause — more at APPLAUSE

ov·en \'ə-vən\ n : a chamber (as in a stove) for baking, heating, or drying

oven·bird \-ˌbərd\ n : a large olive-green American warbler that builds its dome-shaped nest on the ground

¹**over** \'ō-vər\ adv 1 : across a barrier or intervening space 2 : across the brim ⟨boil ∼⟩ 3 ♦ : so as to bring the underside up or the upperside down 4 : out of a vertical position

---

List of self-explanatory words with the prefix over-

overabundant	overbid	overcareful	overcook
overachiever	overbuild	overcautious	overcrowd
overaggressive	overbuy	overcompensation	overdecorated
overambitious	overcapacity	overconfidence	overdependence
overanxious	overcapitalize	overconscientious	overdetermined

5 : beyond some quantity, limit, or norm **6** ♦ : in or to a higher place : ABOVE **7** : at an end **8** ♦ : from beginning to end : THROUGH; *also* : THOROUGHLY ⟨think it ∼⟩ **9** ♦ : for a second or successive time : AGAIN ⟨do it ∼⟩

  ♦ [3] below, down, downward — more at DOWN
  ♦ [6] above, aloft, overhead, skyward — more at ABOVE
  ♦ [8] around, round, thoroughly, through, throughout
  ♦ [9] again, anew — more at AGAIN

²over *prep* **1** : above in position, authority, or scope ⟨towered ∼ her⟩ ⟨obeyed those ∼ him⟩ **2** : more than ⟨cost ∼ $100⟩ **3** : ON, UPON ⟨a cape ∼ her shoulders⟩ **4** : along the length of ⟨∼ the road⟩ **5** : through the medium of : ON ⟨spoke ∼ TV⟩ **6** ♦ : all through ⟨showed me ∼ the house⟩ **7** ♦ : on or to the other side or beyond ⟨jump ∼ a ditch⟩ **8** : throughout the duration of : DURING ⟨∼ the past 25 years⟩ **9** : on account of ⟨trouble ∼ money⟩

  ♦ [6] about, around, round, through, throughout — more at AROUND ♦ [7] across, athwart, through — more at ACROSS

³over *adj* **1** : being higher or in a superior position **2** : REMAINING **3** ♦ : being at an end : ENDED

  ♦ complete, done, down, through, up — more at COMPLETE

over- *prefix* **1** : so as to exceed or surpass **2** : excessive, excessively

over·abun·dance \ō-vər-ə-'bən-dən(t)s\ *n* ♦ : an excessive abundance

  ♦ excess, fat, overflow, overkill, overmuch, superabundance, superfluity, surfeit, surplus — more at EXCESS

over·act \ō-vər-'akt\ *vb* : to exaggerate in acting

over·ac·tive \-'ak-tiv\ *adj* ♦ : excessively or abnormally active ⟨∼ glands⟩ ⟨an ∼ imagination⟩ — **over·ac·tiv·i·ty** \-ak-'ti-və-tē\ *n*

  ♦ agitated, feverish, frenzied, heated, hectic, overwrought — more at FEVERISH

¹over·age \ō-vər-'āj\ *adj* **1** : too old to be useful **2** : older than is normal for one's position, function, or grade

²over·age \ō-və-rij\ *n* : SURPLUS

¹over·all \ō-vər-'ȯl\ *adj* **1** ♦ : including everything ⟨∼ expenses⟩ **2** ♦ : viewed as a whole

  ♦ [1] blanket, common, general, generic, global, universal — more at GENERAL ♦ [1] all around, altogether, collectively, together — more at ALL AROUND
  ♦ [1, 2] all-around, bird's-eye, broad, general, nonspecific — more at GENERAL

²over·all \ō-vər-'ȯl\ *adv* ♦ : as a whole

  ♦ altogether, basically, chiefly, generally, largely, mainly, mostly, predominantly, primarily, principally — more at CHIEFLY

over·alls \ō-vər-ȯlz\ *n pl* : pants of strong material usu. with a piece extending up to cover the chest

over·arm \-ärm\ *adj* : done with the arm raised above the shoulder

over·awe \ō-vər-'ȯ\ *vb* : to restrain or subdue by awe

over·bal·ance \-'ba-ləns\ *vb* **1** : to exceed in weight, value, or importance : OUTWEIGH **2** : to cause to lose balance

over·bear·ing \-'bar-iŋ\ *adj* ♦ : decisively important : DOMINEERING

  ♦ authoritarian, autocratic, bossy, despotic, dictatorial, domineering, imperious, masterful, peremptory, tyrannical, tyrannous — more at BOSSY

over·bite \ō-vər-bīt\ *n* : the projection of the upper front teeth over the lower

over·blown \-'blōn\ *adj* **1** : PORTLY **2** : INFLATED, PRETENTIOUS

over·board \ō-vər-bȯrd\ *adv* **1** : over the side of a ship into the water **2** : to extremes of enthusiasm

over·bold \-'bōld\ *adj* ♦ : excessively bold or forward

  ♦ brash, foolhardy, madcap, overconfident, reckless — more at FOOLHARDY

over·bur·den \-'bər-d²n\ *vb* ♦ : to place an excessive burden on

  ♦ overcharge, overload — more at OVERLOAD

¹over·cast \ō-vər-ˌkast\ *adj* ♦ : clouded over : GLOOMY

  ♦ cloudy, dull, gloomy, hazy, heavy; *also* blackened, darkened, dim, dimmed, dulled, dusky, misty, murky, obscure, obscured, overshadowed; sunless; black, bleak, cheerless, dark, desolate, dismal, drear, dreary, funereal, gloomy, glum, gray, somber, sullen **Ant** clear, cloudless

²overcast *n* : COVERING; *esp* : a covering of clouds

over·charge \ō-vər-'chärj\ *vb* **1** ♦ : to charge too much **2** : to fill or load too full — **over·charge** \ō-vər-ˌchärj\ *n*

  ♦ gouge, soak, sting; *also* cheat, defraud, stick; clip, fleece, skin **Ant** undercharge

over·coat \ō-vər-ˌkōt\ *n* : a warm coat worn over indoor clothing

over·come \ō-vər-'kəm\ *vb* **-came** \-'kām\; **-come**; **-com·ing** **1** ♦ : to get the better of : CONQUER **2** ♦ : to make helpless or exhausted

  ♦ [1] beat, best, clobber, conquer, crush, defeat, drub, lick, master, prevail, rout, skunk, subdue, surmount, thrash, trim, triumph, trounce, wallop, whip, win — more at BEAT ♦ [2] carry away, crush, devastate, floor, oppress, overpower, overwhelm, prostrate, snow under, swamp — more at OVERWHELM

over·con·fi·dent \-'kän-fə-dənt, -ˌdent\ *adj* ♦ : marked by or reflecting overconfidence

  ♦ brash, foolhardy, madcap, overbold, reckless — more at FOOLHARDY

over·crit·i·cal \-'kri-ti-kəl\ *adj* ♦ : meticulously or excessively critical

  ♦ captious, carping, critical, hypercritical — more at CRITICAL

over·do \ō-vər-'dü\ *vb* **-did** \-'did\; **-done** \-'dən\; **-do·ing**; **-does** \-'dəz\ **1** : to do too much; *also* : to tire oneself **2** ♦ : to do in excess : EXAGGERATE **3** : to cook too long

  ♦ exaggerate, overstate, put on — more at OVERSTATE

over·dose \ō-vər-ˌdōs\ *n* : too great a dose (as of medicine); *also* : a lethal or toxic amount (as of a drug) — **over·dose** \ō-vər-'dōs\ *vb*

over·draft \ō-vər-ˌdraft, -ˌdraft\ *n* : an overdrawing of a bank account; *also* : the sum overdrawn

over·draw \ō-vər-'drȯ\ *vb* **-drew** \-'drü\; **-drawn** \-'drȯn\; **-draw·ing** **1** : to draw checks on a bank account for more than the balance **2** : to do in excess : EXAGGERATE

over·drive \ō-vər-ˌdrīv\ *n* : an automotive transmission gear that transmits to the driveshaft a speed greater than the engine speed

over·dub \ō-vər-'dəb\ *vb* : to transfer (recorded sound) onto an earlier recording for a combined effect — **over·dub** \ō-vər-ˌdəb\ *n*

over·due \-'dü, -'dyü\ *adj* **1 a** ♦ : unpaid when due **b** ♦ : not appearing or presented on time **2** : more than ready

  ♦ [1a] outstanding, payable, unpaid, unsettled — more at OUTSTANDING ♦ [1b] behind, belated, delinquent, late, tardy — more at LATE

List of self-explanatory words with the prefix *over-* (continued)

overdevelop	overemphasis	overexcited	overfeed
overdress	overemphasize	overexert	overgeneralization
overeager	overenthusiastic	overexertion	overgeneralize
overeat	overestimate	overextend	overgenerous
overeducated	overexcite	overfatigued	overgraze

over·ex·pose \ˌō-vər-ik-ˈspōz\ *vb* : to expose (as film) for more time than is needed — **over·ex·po·sure** \-ˈspō-zhər\ *n*

over·fill \-ˈfil\ *vt* : to fill to overflowing

¹**over·flow** \-ˈflō\ *vb* **1** ♦ : to cover with or as if with water : INUNDATE; *also* : to pour forth in a flood **2** : to flow over the brim or top of

♦ deluge, drown, engulf, flood, inundate, overwhelm, submerge, swamp — more at FLOOD

²**over·flow** \ˈō-vər-ˌflō\ *n* **1 a** ♦ : a flowing over : FLOOD **b** ♦ : a flowing over : SURPLUS **2** : an outlet for surplus liquid

♦ [1a] cataclysm, cataract, deluge, flood, inundation, spate, torrent — more at FLOOD ♦ [1b] excess, fat, overabundance, overkill, overmuch, superabundance, superfluity, surfeit, surplus — more at EXCESS

over·fly \ˌō-vər-ˈflī\ *vb* **-flew** \-ˈflü\; **-flown** \-ˈflōn\; **-fly·ing** : to fly over in an aircraft or spacecraft — **over·flight** \ˈō-vər-ˌflīt\ *n*

over·grow \ˌō-vər-ˈgrō\ *vb* **-grew** \-ˈgrü\; **-grow·ing** **1** : to grow over so as to cover **2** : OUTGROW **3** : to grow excessively

over·grown \-ˈgrōn\ *adj* : covered with overgrowth

over·hand \ˈō-vər-ˌhand\ *adj* : made with the hand brought down from above — **overhand** *adv* — **over·hand·ed** \-ˌhan-dəd\ *adv or adj*

¹**over·hang** \ˌō-vər-ˈhaŋ, ˌō-vər-ˈhaŋ\ *vb* **-hung** \-ˌhəŋ, -ˈhəŋ\; **-hang·ing** **1** : to project over : jut out **2** ♦ : to hang over threateningly

♦ hang, hover, menace, threaten — more at THREATEN

²**over·hang** \ˈō-vər-ˌhaŋ\ *n* ♦ : a part (as of a roof) that overhangs

♦ bulge, projection, protrusion — more at BULGE

over·haul \ˌō-vər-ˈhȯl\ *vb* **1** : to examine thoroughly and make necessary repairs and adjustments **2** : OVERTAKE

¹**over·head** \ˌō-vər-ˈhed\ *adv* ♦ : above one's head : ALOFT

♦ above, aloft, over, skyward — more at ABOVE

²**over·head** \ˈō-vər-ˌhed\ *adj* : operating or lying above ⟨~ storage bins⟩

³**over·head** \ˈō-vər-ˌhed\ *n* : business expenses not chargeable to a particular part of the work

over·hear \ˌō-vər-ˈhir\ *vb* **-heard** \-ˈhərd\; **-hear·ing** : to hear without the speaker's knowledge or intention

over·joyed \ˌō-vər-ˈjȯid\ *adj* : filled with great joy

over·kill \ˈō-vər-ˌkil\ *n* **1** : destructive capacity greatly exceeding that required for a target **2** ♦ : a large excess

♦ excess, fat, overabundance, overflow, overmuch, superabundance, superfluity, surfeit, surplus — more at EXCESS

over·land \ˈō-vər-ˌland, -lənd\ *adv or adj* : by, on, or across land

¹**over·lap** \ˌō-vər-ˈlap\ *vb* **1** ♦ : to lap over **2** : to have something in common

♦ lap, overlay, overlie, overspread; *also* shingle

²**over·lap** \ˈō-vər-ˌlap\ *n* : the condition or relationship of things that overlap

over·lay \ˌō-vər-ˈlā\ *vb* **-laid** \-ˈlād\; **-lay·ing** ♦ : to lay or spread over or across — **over·lay** \ˈō-vər-ˌlā\ *n*

♦ blanket, carpet, coat, cover, overlie, overspread — more at COVER

over·leap \ˌō-vər-ˈlēp\ *vb* **-leaped** *or* **-leapt** \-ˈlēpt, -ˈlept\; **-leap·ing** **1** : to leap over or across **2** : to defeat (oneself) by going too far

over·lie \ˌō-vər-ˈlī\ *vb* **-lay** \-ˈlā\; **-lain** \-ˈlān\; **-ly·ing** ♦ : to lie over or upon

♦ lap, overlap, overlay, overspread — more at OVERLAP

over·load \-ˈlōd\ *vb* ♦ : to load to excess

♦ overburden, overcharge; *also* stuff; burden, charge, encumber, load, lumber, saddle, weight

¹**over·look** \ˌō-vər-ˈluk\ *vb* **1** : INSPECT **2** : to look down on from above **3** : to fail to see **4** ♦ : to refuse to take notice of : IGNORE ⟨~ed his faults⟩; *also* : EXCUSE **5** : SUPERINTEND

♦ disregard, excuse, forget, ignore, neglect, pass over, slight, slur — more at NEGLECT

²**over·look** \ˈō-vər-ˌluk\ *n* : a place from which to look upon a scene below

over·lord \-ˌlȯrd\ *n* : a lord who has supremacy over other lords

over·ly \ˈō-vər-lē\ *adv* ♦ : to an excessive degree : EXCESSIVELY

♦ devilishly, excessively, inordinately, monstrously, overmuch, too — more at TOO

over·match \ˌō-vər-ˈmach\ *vb* : to be more than a match for : DEFEAT

¹**over·much** \-ˈməch\ *adj* ♦ : too much

♦ devilish, excessive, exorbitant, extravagant, extreme, immoderate, inordinate, lavish, overweening, steep, stiff, towering, unconscionable — more at EXCESSIVE

²**overmuch** *adv* ♦ : in too great a degree

♦ devilishly, excessively, inordinately, monstrously, overly, too — more at TOO

¹**over·night** \-ˈnīt\ *adv* **1** : on or during the night **2** : SUDDENLY ⟨became famous ~⟩

²**overnight** *adj* : of, lasting, or staying the night ⟨~ guests⟩

over·pass \ˈō-vər-ˌpas\ *n* **1** : a crossing (as of two highways) at different levels by means of a bridge **2** : the upper level of an overpass

over·play \ˌō-vər-ˈplā\ *vb* **1** : EXAGGERATE; *also* : to put undue emphasis on **2** : to rely too much on the strength of

over·pop·u·la·tion \ˌō-vər-ˌpä-pyə-ˈlā-shən\ *n* : the condition of having a population so dense as to cause a decline in population or in living conditions — **over·pop·u·lat·ed** \-ˈpä-pyə-ˌlā-təd\ *adj*

over·pow·er \-ˈpau̇-ər\ *vb* **1** ♦ : to overcome by superior force **2** ♦ : to affect with overwhelming intensity

♦ [1] conquer, dominate, subdue, subject, vanquish — more at CONQUER ♦ [2] carry away, crush, devastate, floor, oppress, overcome, overwhelm, prostrate, snow under, swamp — more at OVERWHELM

over·praise \-ˈprāz\ *vb* ♦ : to praise excessively

♦ blarney, flatter — more at FLATTER

over·price \ˌō-vər-ˈprīs\ *vb* : to price too high

over·print \-ˈprint\ *vb* : to print over with something additional — **over·print** \ˈō-vər-ˌprint\ *n*

over·qual·i·fied \-ˈkwä-lə-ˌfīd\ *adj* : having more education, training, or experience than a job calls for

over·reach \ˌō-vər-ˈrēch\ *vb* **1** : to defeat (oneself) by too great an effort **2** ♦ : to get the better of esp. in dealing and bargaining and typically by unscrupulous or crafty methods **3** ♦ : to reach above or beyond

♦ [2] fox, outfox, outmaneuver, outsmart, outwit — more at OUTWIT ♦ [3] exceed, overrun, overshoot, overstep, surpass — more at EXCEED

over·ride \-ˈrīd\ *vb* **-rode** \-ˈrōd\; **-rid·den** \-ˈrid-ᵊn\; **-rid·ing** **1** : to ride over or across **2** : to prevail over; *also* : to set aside ⟨~ a veto⟩

List of self-explanatory words with the prefix *over-* **(continued)**

overhasty	overindulgent	overmodest	overproduce
overheat	overinflate	overnice	overproduction
overhype	overlarge	overoptimism	overprotect
overindulge	overlearn	overoptimistic	overprotective
overindulgence	overlong	overpay	overrate

over·ripe \ˌō-və(r)-ˈrīp\ *adj* ♦ : marked by decay or decline : DECADENT — **over–ripe·ness** \-nəs\ *n*

♦ decadent, degenerate, effete — more at EFFETE

over·rule \-ˈrül\ *vb* **1** : to prevail over **2** : to rule against **3** : to set aside

¹**over·run** \-ˈrən\ *vb* **-ran** \-ˈran\; **-run·ning 1** ♦ : to defeat and occupy the positions of **2** : OVERSPREAD; *also* : INFEST **3** : to go beyond **4** : to flow over

♦ foray, invade, raid — more at INVADE

²**over·run** \ˈō-vər-ˌrən\ *n* **1** : an act or instance of overrunning; *esp* : an exceeding of estimated costs **2** : the amount by which something overruns

over·sea \ˌō-vər-ˈsē, ˈō-vər-ˌsē\ *adj or adv* : OVERSEAS

over·seas \ˌō-vər-ˈsēz, -ˌsēz\ *adv or adj* : beyond or across the sea : ABROAD

over·see \ˌō-vər-ˈsē\ *vb* **-saw** \-ˈsȯ\; **-seen** \-ˈsēn\; **-see·ing 1** : OVERLOOK **2 a** : INSPECT **b** ♦ : to have or exercise the charge and oversight of : SUPERVISE — **over·seer** \ˈō-vər-ˌsir\ *n*

♦ administer, carry on, conduct, control, direct, govern, guide, handle, manage, operate, regulate, run, superintend, supervise — more at CONDUCT

over·sell \ˌō-vər-ˈsel\ *vb* **-sold; -sel·ling** : to sell too much or too much of

over·sexed \ˌō-vər-ˈsekst\ *adj* : exhibiting excessive sexual drive or interest

over·shad·ow \-ˈsha-dō\ *vb* **1** ♦ : to cast a shadow over **2** ♦ : to exceed in importance

♦ [1] becloud, befog, blur, cloud, darken, dim, fog, haze, mist, obscure, overcast, shroud — more at CLOUD ♦ [2] outweigh — more at OUTWEIGH

over·shoe \ˈō-vər-ˌshü\ *n* : a protective outer shoe; *esp* : GALOSH

over·shoot \ˌō-vər-ˈshüt\ *vb* **-shot** \-ˈshät\; **-shoot·ing 1** : to pass swiftly beyond **2** ♦ : to shoot over or beyond **3** ♦ : to overreach (oneself) or cause (oneself) to go astray

♦ [2, 3] exceed, overreach, overrun, overstep, surpass — more at EXCEED

over·sight \ˈō-vər-ˌsīt\ *n* **1** ♦ : watchful and responsible care : SUPERVISION **2** ♦ : an inadvertent omission or error

♦ [1] administration, care, charge, conduct, control, direction, government, guidance, management, operation, regulation, running, superintendence, supervision — more at CONDUCT ♦ [2] blunder, error, fault, flub, fumble, goof, lapse, miscue, misstep, mistake, slip, stumble — more at ERROR

over·size \ˌō-vər-ˈsīz\ *or* **over·sized** \-ˈsīzd\ *adj* ♦ : of more than ordinary size

♦ big, considerable, goodly, grand, great, hefty, large, outsize, sizable, substantial

over·sleep \ˌō-vər-ˈslēp\ *vb* **-slept** \-ˈslept\; **-sleep·ing** : to sleep beyond the time for waking

over·spread \-ˈspred\ *vb* **-spread; -spread·ing** ♦ : to spread over or above

♦ blanket, carpet, coat, cover, overlay, overlie — more at COVER

over·state \-ˈstāt\ *vb* ♦ : to state in too strong terms : EXAGGERATE

♦ exaggerate, overdo, put on; *also* color, elaborate, embellish, embroider, magnify, pad, stretch; fudge, hedge; overemphasize, overplay *Ant* understate

over·state·ment *n* ♦ : the act of overstating

♦ caricature, elaboration, embellishment, exaggeration, hyperbole, magnification, padding — more at EXAGGERATION

over·stay \-ˈstā\ *vb* : to stay beyond the time or limits of

over·step \-ˈstep\ *vb* ♦ : to step over or beyond : EXCEED

♦ exceed, overreach, overrun, overshoot, surpass — more at EXCEED

over·sub·scribe \-səb-ˈskrīb\ *vb* : to subscribe for more of than is available, asked for, or offered for sale

overt \ō-ˈvərt, ˈō-ˌvərt\ *adj* [ME, fr. AF, fr. pp. of *ovrir* to open] : not secret — **overt·ly** *adv*

over·take \ˌō-vər-ˈtāk\ *vb* **-took** \-ˈtük\; **-tak·en** \-ˈtā-kən\; **-tak·ing** : to catch up with; *also* : to catch up with and pass by

over–the–counter *adj* : sold lawfully without a prescription ⟨∼ drugs⟩

over–the–hill *adj* **1** : past one's prime **2** : advanced in age

over–the–top *adj* : extremely flamboyant or outrageous

¹**over·throw** \ˌō-vər-ˈthrō\ *vb* **-threw** \-ˈthrü\; **-thrown** \-ˈthrōn\; **-throw·ing 1** : UPSET **2** : to bring down : DEFEAT ⟨∼ a government⟩ **3** : to throw over or past

²**over·throw** \ˈō-vər-ˌthrō\ *n* : an act of overthrowing or the state of being overthrown

over·time \ˈō-vər-ˌtīm\ *n* : time beyond a set limit; *esp* : working time in excess of a standard day or week — **overtime** *adv*

over·tone \-ˌtōn\ *n* **1** : one of the higher tones in a complex musical tone **2** : IMPLICATION, SUGGESTION ⟨political ∼s⟩

over·trick \ˈō-vər-ˌtrik\ *n* : a card trick won in excess of the number bid

over·ture \ˈō-vər-ˌchür, -chər\ *n* [ME, lit., opening, fr. AF, fr. VL *opertura, alter. of L apertura] **1** : an opening offer **2** : an orchestral introduction to a musical dramatic work

over·turn \ˌō-vər-ˈtərn\ *vb* **1** : to turn over : UPSET **2** : INVALIDATE

over·view \ˈō-vər-ˌvyü\ *n* : a general survey : SUMMARY

over·ween·ing \ˌō-vər-ˈwē-niŋ\ *adj* **1** ♦ : unduly confident ⟨∼ pride⟩ **2** ♦ : exceeding what is usual, proper, necessary, or normal : IMMODERATE

♦ [1] complacent, conceited, egotistic, important, pompous, prideful, proud, self-important, self-satisfied, smug, stuck-up, vain — more at CONCEITED ♦ [2] devilish, excessive, exorbitant, extravagant, extreme, immoderate, inordinate, lavish, overmuch, steep, stiff, towering, unconscionable — more at EXCESSIVE

over·weight \ˈō-vər-ˌwāt\ *adj* **1** : having weight above what is required or allowed **2** ♦ : having bodily weight greater than normal — **overweight** *n*

♦ chubby, corpulent, fat, fleshy, full, gross, obese, plump, portly, rotund, round — more at FAT

over·whelm \-ˈhwelm\ *vb* **1** : OVERTHROW **2** ♦ : to cover over completely (as by a great wave) : SUBMERGE **3** ♦ : to overcome completely (as in thought or feeling)

♦ [2] deluge, drown, engulf, flood, inundate, overflow, submerge, swamp — more at FLOOD ♦ [3] carry away, crush, devastate, floor, oppress, overcome, overpower, prostrate, snow under, swamp; *also* deluge, drown; confute, defeat, refute; demoralize, distress, disturb, rock, shatter, stagger, unman, unnerve, upset

over·whelm·ing *adj* : EXTREME, GREAT ⟨∼ joy⟩ — **over·whelm·ing·ly** *adv*

over·win·ter \-ˈwin-tər\ *vb* : to survive or pass the winter

---

List of self-explanatory words with the prefix *over-* (continued)

overreact	oversensitive	overspecialize	overtax
overreaction	oversensitiveness	overspend	overtired
overrefinement	oversimple	overstimulation	overtrain
overregulate	oversimplification	overstock	overuse
overreliance	oversimplify	oversubtle	overvalue
overrepresented	overspecialization	oversupply	overzealous

over·work \-'wərk\ *vb* **1** : to work or cause to work too hard or long **2** : to use too much — **overwork** *n*
over·wrought \ˌō-vər-'rȯt\ *adj* **1** ♦ : extremely excited **2** ♦ : elaborated to excess

  ♦ [1] agitated, feverish, frenzied, heated, hectic, overactive — more at FEVERISH ♦ [2] florid, ornate — more at ORNATE

ovi·duct \'ō-və-ˌdəkt\ *n* : a tube that serves for the passage of eggs from an ovary
ovip·a·rous \ō-'vi-pə-rəs\ *adj* : reproducing by eggs that hatch outside the parent's body
ovoid \'ō-ˌvȯid\ *or* **ovoi·dal** \ō-'vȯid-ᵊl\ *adj* : egg-shaped : OVAL
ovu·la·tion \ˌäv-yə-'lā-shən, ˌōv-\ *n* : the discharge of a mature egg from the ovary — **ovu·late** \'äv-yə-ˌlāt, 'ōv-\ *vb*
ovule \'äv-yül, 'ōv-\ *n* : any of the bodies in a plant ovary that after fertilization become seeds
ovum \'ō-vəm\ *n, pl* **ova** \-və\ : EGG 2
ow \'aü\ *interj* — used esp. to express sudden pain
owe \'ō\ *vb* **owed; ow·ing** **1** : to be under obligation to pay or render **2** : to be indebted to or for; *also* : to be in debt
owing to *prep* ♦ : because of

  ♦ because of, due to, through, with — more at BECAUSE OF

owl \'aü(-ə)l\ *n* : any of an order of chiefly nocturnal birds of prey with a large head and eyes and strong talons — **owl·ish** *adj* — **owl·ish·ly** *adv*
owl·et \'aü-lət\ *n* : a young or small owl
¹own \'ōn\ *adj* : belonging to oneself — used as an intensive after a possessive adjective ⟨her ~ car⟩
²own *vb* **1** ♦ : to have or hold as property **2** ♦ : to admit or confess frankly and fully : ACKNOWLEDGE; *also* : CONFESS — **own·er·ship** *n*

  ♦ [1] command, enjoy, have, hold, occupy, possess, retain — more at HAVE ♦ *usu* **own up** [2] acknowledge, admit, agree, allow, concede, confess, grant — more at ADMIT

³own *pron* : one or ones belonging to oneself
own·er *n* ♦ : one that owns : one that has the legal or rightful title whether the possessor or not

  ♦ holder, possessor, proprietor — more at PROPRIETOR

ox \'äks\ *n, pl* **ox·en** \'äk-sən\ *also* **ox** : any of the large domestic bovine mammals kept for milk, draft, and meat; *esp* : an adult castrated male ox

ox·blood \'äks-ˌbləd\ *n* : a moderate reddish brown
ox·bow \-ˌbō\ *n* **1** : a U-shaped collar worn by a draft ox **2** : a U-shaped bend in a river — **oxbow** *adj*
ox·ford \'äks-fərd\ *n* : a low shoe laced or tied over the instep
ox·i·dant \'äk-sə-dənt\ *n* : OXIDIZING AGENT — **oxidant** *adj*
ox·i·da·tion \ˌäk-sə-'dā-shən\ *n* : the act or process of oxidizing; *also* : the condition of being oxidized — **ox·i·da·tive** \'äk-sə-ˌdā-tiv\ *adj*
ox·ide \'äk-ˌsīd\ *n* : a compound of oxygen with another element or group
ox·i·dize \'äk-sə-ˌdīz\ *vb* **-dized; -diz·ing** : to combine with oxygen ⟨iron rusts because it is *oxidized* by exposure to the air⟩ — **ox·i·diz·er** *n*
oxidizing agent *n* : a substance (as oxygen or nitric acid) that oxidizes by taking up electrons
ox·y·gen \'äk-si-jən\ *n* [F *oxygène*, fr. Gk *oxys* acidic, lit., sharp + *-genēs* giving rise to; so called because it was once thought to be an essential element of all acids] : a colorless odorless gaseous chemical element that is found in the air, is essential to life, and is involved in combustion
ox·y·gen·ate \'äk-si-jə-ˌnāt\ *vb* **-at·ed; -at·ing** : to impregnate, combine, or supply with oxygen — **ox·y·gen·a·tion** \ˌäk-si-jə-'nā-shən\ *n*
oxygen mask *n* : a device worn over the nose and mouth through which oxygen is supplied
oxygen tent *n* : a canopy which can be placed over a bedridden person and within which a flow of oxygen can be maintained
ox·y·mo·ron \ˌäk-sē-'mȯr-ˌän\ *n* : a combination of contradictory words (as *cruel kindness*)
oys·ter \'ȯi-stər\ *n* : any of various marine mollusks with an irregular 2-valved shell that include commercially important edible shellfish and pearl producers — **oys·ter·ing** *n* — **oys·ter·man** \'ȯi-stər-mən\ *n*
oz *abbr* [obs. It *onza* (now *oncia*)] ounce; ounces
ozone \'ō-ˌzōn\ *n* **1** : a bluish gaseous reactive form of oxygen that is formed naturally in the atmosphere and is used for disinfecting, deodorizing, and bleaching **2** : pure and refreshing air
ozone layer *n* : an atmospheric layer at heights of about 25 miles (40 kilometers) with high ozone content which blocks most solar ultraviolet radiation

¹p \'pē\ *n, pl* **p's** *or* **ps** \'pēz\ *often cap* : the 16th letter of the English alphabet
²p *abbr, often cap* **1** page **2** participle **3** past **4** pawn **5** pence; penny **6** per **7** petite **8** pint **9** pressure **10** purl
P *symbol* phosphorus
pa \'pä, 'pȯ\ *n* : a man who has begotten a child : FATHER
¹Pa *abbr* **1** pascal **2** Pennsylvania
²Pa *symbol* protactinium
¹PA \ˌ(ˌ)pē-'ā\ *n* : PHYSICIAN'S ASSISTANT
²PA *abbr* **1** Pennsylvania **2** per annum **3** power of attorney **4** press agent **5** private account **6** professional association **7** public address **8** purchasing agent
pab·u·lum \'pa-byə-ləm\ *n* [L, food, fodder] : usu. soft digestible food
Pac *abbr* Pacific
PAC *abbr* political action committee
¹pace \'pās\ *n* **1** : rate of movement or progress (as in walking or working) **2** : a step in walking; *also* : a measure of length based on such a step **3** : GAIT; *esp* : a horse's gait in which the legs on the same side move together

²pace *vb* **paced; pac·ing** **1** ♦ : to go or cover at a pace or with slow steps **2** : to measure off by paces ⟨~ off a 15-yard penalty⟩ **3** : to set or regulate the pace of

  ♦ file, march, parade, stride — more at MARCH

³pace \'pā-sē, 'pä-ˌkā, -ˌchā\ *prep* : contrary to the opinion of
pace·mak·er \'pās-ˌmā-kər\ *n* **1** : one that sets the pace for another **2** : a body part (as of the heart) that serves to establish and maintain a rhythmic activity **3** : an electrical device for stimulating or steadying the heartbeat
pac·er \'pā-sər\ *n* **1** : a horse that paces **2** : PACEMAKER
pachy·derm \'pa-ki-ˌdərm\ *n* [F *pachyderme*, fr. Gk *pachydermos* thick-skinned, fr. *pachys* thick + *derma* skin] : any of various thick-skinned hoofed mammals (as an elephant)
pach·ys·an·dra \ˌpa-ki-'san-drə\ *n* : any of a genus of low perennial evergreen plants used as a ground cover
pa·cif·ic \pə-'si-fik\ *adj* **1** ♦ : tending to lessen conflict **2** : CALM, PEACEFUL

  ♦ conciliatory, propitiatory; *also* endearing, ingratiating; peaceable, peaceful; nonbelligerent, unaggressive, unassertive; calming, comforting, quieting, soothing; obliging, satisfying; affable, amiable, amicable, benevolent, gentle, kind, kindly; submissive, surrendering, yielding *Ant* antagonizing

pac·i·fi·er \'pa-sə-ˌfī-ər\ *n* : one that pacifies; *esp* : a device for a baby to chew or suck on

pac·i·fism \'pa-sə-ˌfi-zəm\ *n* : opposition to war or violence as a means of settling disputes — **pac·i·fist** \-fist\ *n or adj* — **pac·i·fis·tic** \ˌpa-sə-'fis-tik\ *adj*

pac·i·fy \'pa-sə-ˌfī\ *vb* **-fied; -fy·ing** **1** ♦ : to allay anger or agitation in **2** : SETTLE; *also* : SUBDUE — **pac·i·fi·ca·tion** \ˌpa-sə-fə-'kā-shən\ *n*

♦ appease, conciliate, disarm, mollify, placate, propitiate; *also* calm, comfort, console, content, quiet, soothe; endear (to), ingratiate; delight, gladden, gratify, please; blarney, flatter, overpraise; assuage, quench, sate, satiate, satisfy; cater (to), humor, indulge; cajole, coax, wheedle; coddle, mollycoddle, pamper, spoil *Ant* anger, enrage, incense, infuriate, madden, outrage

¹pack \'pak\ *n* **1** : a compact bundle; *also* : a flexible container for carrying a bundle esp. on the back **2** : a large amount : HEAP **3** : a set of playing cards **4** : a group or band of people or animals **5** : wet absorbent material for application to the body

²pack *vb* **1** : to stow goods in for transportation **2** ♦ : to fill in or surround so as to prevent passage of air, steam, or water **3** : to put into a protective container **4** : to load with a pack ⟨~ a mule⟩ **5** : to crowd in **6** : to make into a pack **7** : to cause to go without ceremony ⟨~ them off to school⟩ **8** ♦ : to wear or carry as equipment ⟨~ a gun⟩

♦ [2] charge, cram, fill, heap, jam, jam-pack, load — more at FILL ♦ [8] bear, carry, cart, convey, ferry, haul, lug, tote, transport — more at CARRY

³pack *vb* : to make up fraudulently so as to secure a desired result ⟨~ a jury⟩

¹pack·age \'pa-kij\ *n* **1** ♦ : a wrapped bundle : PARCEL **2** ♦ : a group of related things offered as a whole

♦ [1] bundle, pack, parcel; *also* bag, pouch, sack; box, container, crate ♦ [2] array, assemblage, bank, batch, block, bunch, clump, cluster, collection, group, huddle, knot, lot, parcel, set, suite

²package *vb* **pack·aged; pack·ag·ing** : to make into or enclose in a package

package deal *n* : an offer containing several items all or none of which must be accepted

package store *n* : a store that sells alcoholic beverages in sealed containers for consumption off the premises

packed \'pakt\ *adj* **1 a** : COMPRESSED **b** ♦ : having elements crowded or stuffed **2** ♦ : filled to capacity

♦ [1b] close, compact, crowded, dense, serried, thick, tight — more at CLOSE ♦ [2] brimful, chock-full, crowded, fat, fraught, full, loaded, replete — more at FULL

pack·er \'pa-kər\ *n* : one that packs; *esp* : a wholesale food dealer

pack·et \'pa-kət\ *n* **1** : a small bundle or package **2** : a passenger boat carrying mail and cargo on a regular schedule

pack·horse \'pak-ˌhȯrs\ *n* : a horse used to carry goods or supplies

pack·ing \'pa-kiŋ\ *n* : material used to pack something

pack·ing·house \-ˌhaus\ *n* : an establishment for processing and packing food and esp. meat and its by-products

pack rat *n* **1** : a bushy-tailed rodent of western No. America that hoards food and miscellaneous objects **2** : a person who collects or saves many esp. unneeded items

pack·sad·dle \'pak-ˌsad-ᵊl\ *n* : a saddle for supporting loads on the back of an animal

pack·thread \-ˌthred\ *n* : strong thread for tying

pact \'pakt\ *n* ♦ : an agreement or covenant between two or more parties

♦ accord, agreement, bargain, compact, contract, convention, covenant, deal, settlement, understanding — more at AGREEMENT

¹pad \'pad\ *vb* ♦ : to traverse or go on foot

♦ foot, leg, step, traipse, tread, walk — more at WALK

²pad *n* **1** ♦ : a cushioning part or thing : CUSHION **2** : the cushioned underside of the foot or toes of some mammals **3** : the floating leaf of a water plant **4** : a writing tablet **5** : LAUNCHPAD **6 a** : living quarters **b** : a piece of furniture on or in which to lie and sleep : BED

♦ buffer, bumper, cushion, fender — more at CUSHION

³pad *vb* **pad·ded; pad·ding** **1** ♦ : to furnish with a pad or padding **2** ♦ : to expand with needless or fraudulent matter

♦ color (*or* colour), elaborate, embellish, embroider, exaggerate, magnify, stretch — more at EMBROIDER

pad·ding *n* ♦ : the material with which something is padded

♦ fill, filler, filling, stuffing — more at FILLING ♦ caricature, elaboration, embellishment, exaggeration, hyperbole, magnification, overstatement — more at EXAGGERATION

¹pad·dle \'pad-ᵊl\ *vb* **pad·dled; pad·dling** : to move the hands and feet about in shallow water

²paddle *n* **1** : an implement with a flat blade used in propelling and steering a small craft (as a canoe) **2** : an implement used for stirring, mixing, or beating **3** : a broad board on the outer rim of a waterwheel or a paddle wheel

³paddle *vb* **pad·dled; pad·dling** **1** : to move on or through water by or as if by using a paddle **2** : to beat or stir with a paddle

paddle wheel *n* : a wheel with paddles around its outer edge used to move a boat

paddle wheeler *n* : a steam-driven vessel propelled by a paddle wheel

pad·dock \'pa-dək\ *n* **1** : a usu. enclosed area for pasturing or exercising animals; *esp* : one where racehorses are saddled and paraded before a race **2** : an area at a racecourse where racing cars are parked

pad·dy \'pa-dē\ *n, pl* **paddies** : wet land where rice is grown

paddy wagon *n* : an enclosed motortruck for carrying prisoners

pad·lock \'pad-ˌläk\ *n* : a removable lock with a curved piece that snaps into a catch — **padlock** *vb*

pa·dre \'pä-drā\ *n* [Sp or It or Pg, lit., father, fr. L *pater*] **1** : a Christian clergyman; *esp* : PRIEST **2** : a military chaplain

pad thai \'päd-'tī\ *n, often cap T* : a Thai dish of rice noodles stir-fried with additional ingredients

pae·an \'pē-ən\ *n* ♦ : an exultant song of praise or thanksgiving

♦ accolade, citation, commendation, encomium, eulogy, homage, panegyric, salutation, tribute — more at ENCOMIUM

pae·di·at·ric, pae·di·a·tri·cian, pae·di·at·rics *chiefly Brit var of* PEDIATRIC, PEDIATRICIAN, PEDIATRICS

pa·el·la \pä-'e-lə; -'āl-yə, -'ā-yə\ *n* : a saffron-flavored dish of rice, meat, seafood, and vegetables

pa·gan \'pā-gən\ *n* [ME, fr. LL *paganus*, fr. L, country dweller, fr. *pagus* country district] : an unconverted member of a people or nation that does not acknowledge the God of the Bible : HEATHEN — **pagan** *adj* — **pa·gan·ism** \-gə-ˌni-zəm\ *n*

¹page \'pāj\ *n* ♦ : one employed to deliver messages, assist patrons, serve as a guide, or attend to similar duties

♦ courier, go-between, messenger, runner — more at MESSENGER

²page *vb* **paged; pag·ing** **1** : to summon by repeatedly calling out the name of **2** : to send a message to via a pager

³page *n* **1** : a single leaf (as of a book); *also* : a single side of such a leaf **2** : the information at a single World Wide Web address

⁴page *vb* **paged; pag·ing** : to mark or number the pages of

pag·eant \'pa-jənt\ *n* [ME *pagyn, padgeant*, lit., scene of a play, fr. AF *pagine, pagent*, fr. ML *pagina*, perh. fr. L, page] : an elaborate spectacle, show, or procession esp. with tableaux or floats — **pag·eant·ry** \-jən-trē\ *n*

page·boy \'pāj-,bȯi\ *n* [¹*page*] : an often shoulder-length hairdo with the ends of the hair turned smoothly under

pag·er \'pā-jər\ *n* : one that pages; *esp* : a small radio receiver that alerts its user to incoming messages

pag·i·nate \'pa-jə-,nāt\ *vb* **-nat·ed; -nat·ing** : ⁴PAGE

pag·i·na·tion \,pa-jə-'nā-shən\ *n* **1** : the paging of written or printed matter **2** : the number and arrangement of pages (as of a book)

pa·go·da \pə-'gō-də\ *n* : a tower with roofs curving upward at the division of each of several stories

paid *past and past part of* PAY

pail \'pāl\ *n* : a usu. cylindrical vessel with a handle — **pail·ful** \-,fúl\ *n*

¹pain \'pān\ *n* **1** : PUNISHMENT, PENALTY **2 a** ◆ : suffering or distress of body or mind **b** ◆ : a basic bodily sensation marked by discomfort (as throbbing or aching) **3** *pl* ◆ : great care **4** : one that irks or annoys

◆ [2a] affliction, agony, anguish, distress, misery, torment, torture, tribulation, woe — more at DISTRESS ◆ [2b] ache, pang, prick, smart, sting, stitch, tingle, twinge; *also* discomfort, distress, soreness, tenderness; agony, anguish, misery, suffering, torment, torture; backache, bellyache, charley horse, colic, earache, gripe, headache, stomachache, toothache ◆ **pains** [3] care, carefulness, heed, heedfulness, scrupulousness — more at CARE ◆ **pains** [3] effort, exertion, expenditure, labor (*or* labour), sweat, trouble, while, work — more at EFFORT

²pain *vb* ◆ : to cause or experience pain

◆ ache, hurt, smart — more at HURT

pain·ful \-fəl\ *adj* ◆ : feeling or giving pain

◆ achy, nasty, sore; *also* damaging, harmful, hurtful, injurious, raw, tender; bleeding, burning, chafing, cramping, festering, nagging, pinching, pricking, prickling, smarting, stinging; inflamed, swollen; threatening, wounding *Ant* painless

pain·ful·ly \-f(ə-)lē\ *adv* : in a painful manner

pain·kill·er \'pān-,ki-lər\ *n* : something (as a drug) that relieves pain — **pain·kill·ing** *adj*

pain·less \-ləs\ *adj* ◆ : not causing pain

◆ easy, effortless, facile, fluent, fluid, light, ready, simple, smooth, snap, soft — more at EASY

pain·less·ly \-ləs-lē\ *adv* ◆ : in a painless manner

◆ easily, effortlessly, fluently, freely, handily, lightly, readily, smoothly — more at EASILY

pains·tak·ing \'pānz-,stā-kiŋ\ *adj* ◆ : taking pains : showing care — **painstaking** *n* — **pains·tak·ing·ly** *adv*

◆ careful, conscientious, fussy, meticulous; *also* assiduous, diligent, indefatigable, persevering, sedulous; exhaustive, thorough, thoroughgoing; attentive, observant, vigilant, watchful; accurate, precise; critical, demanding, discriminating, exacting, finicky, particular; cautious, chary, circumspect, gingerly, guarded, heedful, wary; deliberate, plodding, slow; studied, thoughtful; all-out, determined, dogged, intensive, tenacious, tireless, zealous *Ant* careless

¹paint \'pānt\ *vb* **1** ◆ : to apply color, pigment, or paint to **2** : to produce or portray in lines or colors on a surface; *also* : to practice the art of painting **3** : to decorate with colors **4** : to use cosmetics **5** ◆ : to describe vividly **6** : SWAB — **paint·er** *n*

◆ [1] color (*or* colour), dye, stain, tinge, tint — more at COLOR ◆ [5] delineate, depict, describe, draw, image, picture, portray, sketch — more at DESCRIBE

²paint *n* **1** : something produced by painting **2** : MAKEUP **3** : a mixture of a pigment and a liquid that forms a thin adherent coating when spread on a surface; *also* : the dry pigment used in making this mixture **4** : an applied coating of paint

paint·ball \'pānt-,bȯl\ *n* : a game in which two teams try to capture each other's flag using guns that shoot paint-filled pellets

paint·brush \'pānt-,brəsh\ *n* : a brush for applying paint

painted lady *n* : a migratory butterfly with wings mottled in brown, orange, black, and white

paint·ing \'pān-tiŋ\ *n* **1** ◆ : a work (as a picture) produced by painting **2** : the art or occupation of painting

◆ oil; *also* fresco, mural, panorama; cartoon, drawing, etching, pastel, sketch, watercolor, work; masterpiece; pièce de résistance, showpiece

¹pair \'par\ *n, pl* **pairs** *also* **pair** [ME *paire*, fr. AF, fr. L *paria* equal things, fr. neut. pl. of *par* equal] **1** ◆ : two things of a kind designed for use together **2** : something made up of two corresponding pieces 〈a ∼ of pants〉 **3** : a set of two people or animals

◆ brace, couple, duo, twain, twosome; *also* span, yoke; partnership, team; companion, complement, doublet, fellow, half, match, mate, twin; counterpart, equal, equivalent, like, parallel, peer

²pair *vb* **1** : to arrange in pairs **2** : to form a pair : MATCH **3** : to become associated with another

pais·ley \'pāz-lē\ *adj, often cap* : decorated with colorful curved abstract figures 〈a ∼ fabric〉

Pai·ute \'pī-,üt, -,yüt\ *n* : a member of an American Indian people orig. of Utah, Arizona, Nevada, and California

pa·ja·mas *chiefly Can and Brit* **py·ja·mas** \pə-'jä-məz, -'ja-\ *n pl* : a loose suit for sleeping or lounging

Pak·i·stani \,pa-ki-'sta-nē, ,pä-ki-'stä-nē\ *n* : a native or inhabitant of Pakistan — **Pakistani** *adj*

pal \'pal\ *n* ◆ : a close friend

◆ buddy, chum, comrade, crony, familiar, friend, intimate — more at FRIEND

pal·ace \'pa-ləs\ *n* [ME *palais*, fr. AF, fr. L *palatium*, fr. *Palatium*, the Palatine Hill in Rome where the emperors' residences were built] **1** : the official residence of a chief of state **2** ◆ : a large stately house : MANSION

◆ castle, estate, hall, manor, mansion, villa — more at MANSION

pal·a·din \'pa-lə-dən\ *n* **1** : a trusted military leader (as for a medieval prince) **2** ◆ : a leading champion of a cause

◆ advocate, apostle, backer, booster, champion, exponent, friend, promoter, proponent, supporter — more at EXPONENT

pa·laes·tra \pə-'les-trə\ *n, pl* **-trae** \-(,)trē\ : a school in ancient Greece or Rome for sports (as wrestling)

pa·lan·quin \,pa-lən-'kēn\ *n* : an enclosed couch for one person borne on the shoulders of men by means of poles

pal·at·abil·i·ty \,pa-lə-tə-'bi-lə-tē\ *n* ◆ : the quality or state of being palatable

◆ deliciousness, lusciousness, savor, tastiness

pal·at·able \'pa-lə-tə-bəl\ *adj* **1** ◆ : agreeable to the taste **2** ◆ : agreeable or acceptable to the mind

◆ [1, 2] agreeable, all right, alright, fine, good, OK, satisfactory — more at SATISFACTORY ◆ [2] agreeable, congenial, felicitous, good, grateful, gratifying, nice, pleasant, pleasurable, satisfying

pal·a·tal \'pa-lət-ᵊl\ *adj* **1** : of or relating to the palate **2** : pronounced with some part of the tongue near or touching the hard palate 〈the y in *yeast* and the sh in *she* are ∼ sounds〉

pal·a·tal·ize \'pa-lət-ᵊl-,īz\ *vb* **-ized; -iz·ing** : to pronounce as or change into a palatal sound — **pal·a·tal·i·za·tion** \,pa-lət-ᵊl-ə-'zā-shən\ *n*

pal·ate \'pa-lət\ *n* **1** : the roof of the mouth separating the mouth from the nasal cavity **2** : TASTE

pa·la·tial \pə-'lā-shəl\ *adj* **1** : of, relating to, or being a palace **2** ◆ : suitable to a palace

◆ deluxe, lavish, luxuriant, luxurious, opulent, plush, sumptuous — more at LUXURIOUS

pa·lat·i·nate \pə-'lat-ᵊn-ət\ *n* : the territory of a palatine

¹pal·a·tine \'pa-lə-,tīn\ *adj* **1** : possessing royal privileges; *also* : of or relating to a palatine or a palatinate **2** : of or relating to a palace : PALATIAL

²**palatine** *n* **1** : a feudal lord having sovereign power within his domains **2** : a high officer of an imperial palace

¹**pa·la·ver** \pə-'la-vər, -'lä-\ *n* [Pg *palavra* word, speech, fr. LL *parabola* parable, speech] **1** : a long parley **2** ♦ : idle talk — **palaver** *vb*

  ♦ chat, chatter, chitchat, gabfest, gossip, rap, talk — more at CHAT

²**palaver** *vb* : to talk profusely or idly

¹**pale** \'pāl\ *n* **1** : a stake or picket of a fence **2** : an enclosed place; *also* : a district or territory within certain bounds or under a particular jurisdiction **3** : LIMITS, BOUNDS ⟨conduct beyond the ∼⟩

²**pale** *vb* **paled; pal·ing** : to enclose with or as if with pales : FENCE

³**pale** *adj* **pal·er; pal·est** **1** ♦ : deficient in color or intensity : WAN ⟨a ∼ face⟩ **2** : lacking in brightness : DIM ⟨a ∼ star⟩ **3** ♦ : not dark or intense in hue ⟨a ∼ blue⟩ — **pale·ness** *n*

  ♦ [1] ashen, cadaverous, livid, lurid, pasty, peaked; *also* sallow, sick, sickly, waxen, waxy; white, whitened; deathlike; anemic, bloodless; untanned *Ant* florid, flush, rubicund, ruddy, sanguine ♦ [3] dull, light, pastel, washed-out; *also* flat, lackluster, lusterless, mat; dim, faint; dirty, muddy; achromatic, colorless, uncolored, undyed, unpainted, unstained; blanched, bleached, washed, white, whitened; gray, indistinct, neutral *Ant* dark, deep, gay, rich

⁴**pale** *vb* **paled; pal·ing** ♦ : to make or become pale

  ♦ blanch, bleach, blench, dull, fade, wash out, whiten; *also* mat; cloud, dim; discolor, tarnish *Ant* darken, deepen

pale ale *n* : a medium-colored very dry ale

pale·face \'pāl-ˌfās\ *n* : a white person

Pa·leo·cene \'pā-lē-ə-ˌsēn\ *adj* : of, relating to, or being the earliest epoch of the Tertiary — **Paleocene** *n*

pa·leo·con·ser·va·tive \ˌpā-lē-ō-kən-'sər-və-tiv\ *n* : a conservative espousing traditional principles and policies

pa·le·og·ra·phy \ˌpā-lē-'ä-grə-fē\ *n* [NL *palaeographia*, fr. Gk *palaios* ancient + *graphein* to write] : the study of ancient writings and inscriptions — **pa·le·og·ra·pher** *n*

Pa·leo·lith·ic \ˌpā-lē-ə-'li-thik\ *adj* : of or relating to the earliest period of the Stone Age characterized by rough or chipped stone implements

pa·le·on·tol·o·gy \ˌpā-lē-ˌän-'tä-lə-jē\ *n* : a science dealing with the life of past geologic periods as known from fossil remains — **pa·le·on·tol·o·gist** \-ˌän-'tä-lə-jist, -ən-\ *n*

Pa·leo·zo·ic \ˌpā-lē-ə-'zō-ik\ *adj* : of, relating to, or being the era of geologic history extending from about 570 million years ago to about 245 million years ago — **Paleozoic** *n*

pal·ette \'pa-lət\ *n* : a thin often oval board that a painter holds and mixes colors on; *also* : the colors on a palette

pal·frey \'pȯl-frē\ *n, pl* **palfreys** *archaic* : a saddle horse that is not a warhorse; *esp* : one suitable for a woman

pa·limp·sest \'pa-ləmp-ˌsest\ *n* [L *palimpsestus*, fr. Gk *palimpsēstos* scraped again] : writing material (as a parchment) used after the erasure of earlier writing

pal·in·drome \'pa-lən-ˌdrōm\ *n* : a word, verse, or sentence (as "Able was I ere I saw Elba") or a number (as 1881) that reads the same backward or forward

pal·ing \'pā-liŋ\ *n* **1** : a fence of pales **2** : material for pales **3** : PALE, PICKET

pal·i·sade \ˌpa-lə-'sād\ *n* **1** : a high fence of stakes esp. for defense **2** ♦ : a line of steep cliffs

  ♦ bluff, cliff, crag, escarpment, precipice, scarp — more at CLIFF

¹**pall** \'pȯl\ *vb* **1** : to lose in interest or attraction **2** : SATIATE, CLOY

²**pall** *n* **1** : a heavy cloth draped over a coffin **2** : something that produces a gloomy atmosphere

pal·la·di·um \pə-'lā-dē-əm\ *n* : a silver-white metallic chemical element used esp. as a catalyst and in alloys

pall·bear·er \'pȯl-ˌbar-ər\ *n* : a person who attends the coffin at a funeral

¹**pal·let** \'pa-lət\ *n* : a small, hard, or makeshift bed

²**pallet** *n* : a portable platform for transporting and storing materials

pal·li·ate \'pa-lē-ˌāt\ *vb* **-at·ed; -at·ing** **1** ♦ : to ease (as a disease) without curing **2** ♦ : to cover by excuses and apologies ⟨∼ faults⟩ — **pal·li·a·tion** \ˌpa-lē-'ā-shən\ *n* — **pal·li·a·tive** \'pa-lē-ˌā-tiv\ *adj or n*

  ♦ [1] allay, alleviate, assuage, ease, help, mitigate, mollify, relieve, soothe — more at HELP ♦ [2] excuse, gloss, whitewash; *also* varnish; apologize, atone, confess; explain, justify, rationalize; alleviate, lessen, lighten, mitigate, moderate, soften, temper; absolve, acquit, clear, exculpate, exonerate, vindicate

pal·lid \'pa-ləd\ *adj* : deficient in color : PALE, WAN

pal·lor \'pa-lər\ *n* : PALENESS

¹**palm** \'päm, 'pälm\ *n* [ME, fr. OE, fr. L *palma* palm of the hand, palm tree; fr. the resemblance of the tree's leaves to the outstretched hand] **1** : any of a family of mostly tropical trees, shrubs, or vines usu. with a tall unbranched stem topped by a crown of large leaves **2** : a symbol of victory; *also* : VICTORY

²**palm** *n* : the underpart of the hand between the fingers and the wrist

³**palm** *vb* **1** : to conceal in or with the hand ⟨∼ a card⟩ **2** : to impose by fraud

pal·mate \'pal-ˌmāt, 'päl-\ *also* **pal·mat·ed** \-ˌmā-təd\ *adj* : resembling a hand with the fingers spread

pal·met·to \pal-'me-tō\ *n, pl* **-tos** *or* **-toes** : any of several usu. small palms with fan-shaped leaves

palm·ist·ry \'pä-mə-strē, 'päl-\ *n* : the practice of reading a person's character or future from the markings on the palms — **palm·ist** \'pä-mist, 'päl-\ *n*

Palm Sunday *n* : the Sunday preceding Easter and commemorating Christ's triumphal entry into Jerusalem

palm·top \'päm-ˌtäp, 'pälm-\ *n* : a portable computer small enough to hold in the hand

palmy \'pä-mē, 'päl-\ *adj* **palm·i·er; -est** **1** : abounding in or bearing palms **2** ♦ : marked by prosperity : PROSPEROUS

  ♦ booming, golden, prosperous, roaring, successful — more at PROSPEROUS

pal·o·mi·no \ˌpa-lə-'mē-nō\ *n, pl* **-nos** [AmerSp, fr. Sp, like a dove, fr. L *palumbinus*, fr. *palumbes*, a species of dove] : a horse with a pale cream to golden coat and cream or white mane and tail

pal·pa·ble \'pal-pə-bəl\ *adj* **1** ♦ : capable of being touched or felt **2** ♦ : easily perceptible by the mind ⟨a ∼ sense of relief⟩ — **pal·pa·bly** \-blē\ *adv*

  ♦ [1, 2] appreciable, detectable, discernible, distinguishable, perceptible, sensible — more at PERCEPTIBLE ♦ [2] apparent, broad, clear, clear-cut, distinct, evident, lucid, manifest, obvious, patent, perspicuous, plain, transparent, unambiguous, unequivocal, unmistakable — more at CLEAR

pal·pate \'pal-ˌpāt\ *vb* **pal·pat·ed; pal·pat·ing** : to examine by touch esp. medically — **pal·pa·tion** \pal-'pā-shən\ *n*

pal·pi·tate \'pal-pə-ˌtāt\ *vb* **-tat·ed; -tat·ing** ♦ : to beat rapidly and strongly : THROB

  ♦ beat, pitter-patter, pulsate, pulse, throb — more at PULSATE

pal·pi·ta·tion \ˌpal-pə-'tā-shən\ *n* ♦ : a rapid pulsation

  ♦ beat, pulsation, pulse, throb — more at PULSATION

pal·sy \'pȯl-zē\ *n, pl* **palsies** **1** : PARALYSIS **2** : a condition marked by tremor — **pal·sied** \-zēd\ *adj*

pal·ter \'pȯl-tər\ *vb* **pal·tered; pal·ter·ing** **1** : to act insincerely : EQUIVOCATE **2** ♦ : to negotiate over the terms of a purchase, agreement, or contract : HAGGLE

  ♦ bargain, chaffer, deal, dicker, haggle, negotiate — more at BARGAIN

pal·try \'pȯl-trē\ *adj* **pal·tri·er; -est** **1** : TRASHY ⟨a ∼ pamphlet⟩ **2** : MEAN, DESPICABLE ⟨a ∼ trick⟩ **3** ♦ : of little worth or importance : TRIVIAL ⟨∼ excuses⟩ **4** : MEAGER, MEASLY ⟨a ∼ sum⟩

♦ inconsequential, inconsiderable, insignificant, measly, minute, negligible, nominal, petty, slight, trifling, trivial — more at NEGLIGIBLE

pam *abbr* pamphlet

pam·pas \'pam-pəz, 'päm-, -pəs\ *n pl* : wide grassy So. American plains

pam·per \'pam-pər\ *vb* ♦ : to treat with excessive attention

♦ baby, coddle, mollycoddle, nurse, spoil — more at BABY

pam·phlet \'pam-flət\ *n* [ME *pamflet* unbound booklet, fr. *Pamphilus seu De Amore* Pamphilus or On Love, popular Latin love poem of the 12th cent.] ♦ : an unbound printed publication

♦ booklet, brochure, circular, folder, leaflet; *also* advertisement, catalog; tract; paperback; guidebook, handbook, instructions, manual

pam·phle·teer \,pam-flə-'tir\ *n* : a writer of pamphlets attacking something or urging a cause

¹**pan** \'pan\ *n* 1 : a usu. broad, shallow, and open container for domestic use; *also* : something resembling such a container 2 : a basin or depression in land 3 : HARDPAN

²**pan** *vb* **panned; pan·ning** 1 : to wash earth or gravel in a pan in searching for gold 2 ♦ : to criticize severely

♦ blame, censure, condemn, criticize, denounce, fault, knock, reprehend — more at CRITICIZE

Pan *abbr* Panama

pan·a·cea \,pa-nə-'sē-ə\ *n* : a remedy for all ills or difficulties : CURE-ALL

pa·nache \pə-'nash, -'näsh\ *n* [MF *pennache*, ultim. fr. LL *pinnaculum* small wing] 1 : an ornamental tuft (as of feathers) esp. on a helmet 2 : dash or flamboyance in style and action

pan·a·ma \'pa-nə-,mä, -,mȯ\ *n, often cap* : a handmade hat braided from strips of the leaves from a tropical American tree

Pan·a·ma·ni·an \,pa-nə-'mä-nē-ən\ *n* : a native or inhabitant of Panama — **Panamanian** *adj*

pan·cake \'pan-,kāk\ *n* ♦ : a flat cake made of thin batter and fried on both sides

♦ flapjack, griddle cake; *also* crepe; waffle

pan·chro·mat·ic \,pan-krō-'ma-tik\ *adj* : sensitive to all colors of visible light ⟨~ film⟩

pan·cre·as \'paŋ-krē-əs, 'pan-\ *n* : a large compound gland of vertebrates that produces insulin and discharges enzymes into the intestine — **pan·cre·at·ic** \,paŋ-krē-'a-tik, ,pan-\ *adj*

pan·da \'pan-də\ *n* 1 : a long-tailed reddish brown Himalayan mammal related to and resembling the raccoon 2 : a large black-and-white mammal of China usu. classified with the bears

pan·dem·ic \pan-'de-mik\ *n* : a widespread outbreak of disease — **pandemic** *adj*

pan·de·mo·ni·um \,pan-də-'mō-nē-əm\ *n* ♦ : a wild uproar : TUMULT

♦ commotion, disturbance, furor, hubbub, hullabaloo, row, tumult, turmoil, uproar

¹**pan·der** \'pan-dər\ *n* 1 : a go-between in love intrigues 2 : PIMP 3 : a person who caters to or exploits others' desires or weaknesses

²**pander** *vb* : to act as a pander ⟨~ing to popular taste⟩

P & I *abbr* principal and interest

P & L *abbr* profit and loss

Pan·do·ra's box \pan-'dȯr-əz-\ *n* : a prolific source of troubles

pan·dow·dy \pan-'daù-dē\ *n, pl* **-dies** : a deep-dish apple dessert spiced, sweetened, and covered with a crust

pane \'pān\ *n* : a sheet of glass (as in a door or window)

pan·e·gy·ric \,pa-nə-'jir-ik\ *n* ♦ : a eulogistic oration or writing — **pan·e·gyr·ist** \-'jir-ist\ *n*

♦ accolade, citation, commendation, encomium, eulogy, homage, paean, salutation, tribute — more at ENCOMIUM

¹**pan·el** \'pan-ᵊl\ *n* [ME, piece of cloth, jury list on a piece of parchment, fr. AF, fr. VL *pannellus*, dim. of L *pannus* cloth, rag] 1 a : a list of persons appointed for special duty ⟨a jury ~⟩ b : a group of people taking part in a discussion or quiz program c ♦ : a formal discussion by a panel 2 : a section of something (as a wall or door) often sunk below the level of the frame; *also* : a flat piece of construction material 3 : a flat piece of wood on which a picture is painted 4 : a mount for controls or dials

♦ colloquy, conference, council, forum, parley, powwow, seminar, symposium — more at FORUM

²**panel** *vb* **-eled** *or* **-elled; -el·ing** *or* **-el·ling** : to decorate with panels

paneling *n* : decorative panels

pan·el·ist \'pan-ᵊl-ist\ *n* : a member of a discussion or quiz panel

panel truck *n* : a small motortruck with a fully enclosed body

pang \'paŋ\ *n* ♦ : a sudden sharp spasm (as of pain) or attack (as of remorse)

♦ ache, pain, prick, smart, sting, stitch, tingle, twinge — more at PAIN

¹**pan·han·dle** \'pan-,hand-ᵊl\ *n* : a narrow projection of a larger territory (as a state) ⟨the Texas ~⟩

²**panhandle** *vb* **-dled; -dling** : to ask for money on the street — **pan·han·dler** *n*

¹**pan·ic** \'pa-nik\ *n* ♦ : a sudden overpowering fright — **pan·icky** \-ni-kē\ *adj*

♦ alarm, anxiety, apprehension, dread, fear, fright, horror, terror, trepidation — more at FEAR

²**panic** *vb* **pan·icked** \-nikt\; **pan·ick·ing** ♦ : to affect or be affected with panic

♦ alarm, frighten, horrify, scare, shock, spook, startle, terrify, terrorize — more at FRIGHTEN

pan·i·cle \'pa-ni-kəl\ *n* : a branched flower cluster (as of a lilac) in which each branch from the main stem has one or more flowers

pa·ni·ni \pə-'nē-nē\ *also* **pa·ni·no** \-'nē-nō\ *n, pl* **-nini** *or* **-ninis** [It] : a usu. grilled sandwich made with Italian bread

pan·jan·drum \pan-'jan-drəm\ *n, pl* **-drums** *also* **-dra** \-drə\ : a powerful personage or pretentious official

pan·nier *also* **pan·ier** \'pan-yər\ *n* : a large basket esp. for bearing on the back

pan·o·ply \'pa-nə-plē\ *n, pl* **-plies** 1 : a full suit of armor 2 : a protective covering 3 : an impressive array

pan·ora·ma \,pa-nə-'ra-mə, -'rä-\ *n* 1 : a picture unrolled before one's eyes 2 ♦ : a complete view in every direction

♦ lookout, outlook, prospect, view, vista — more at VIEW

pan·oram·ic \,pa-nə-'ra-mik\ *adj* ♦ : of, relating to, or resembling a panorama

♦ compendious, complete, comprehensive, encyclopedic, full, global, inclusive, omnibus, universal — more at ENCYCLOPEDIC

pan out *vb* 1 ♦ : to become in maturity : TURN OUT 2 ♦ : to turn out well : SUCCEED

♦ [1] come out, prove, turn out — more at COME OUT
♦ [2] click, deliver, go over, succeed, work out — more at SUCCEED

pan·sex·u·al \,pan-'sek-shə-wəl\ *adj* : of, relating to, or characterized by sexual desire or attraction that is not limited to people of a particular gender identity or sexual orientation; *also* : not solely homosexual or heterosexual

pan·sy \'pan-zē\ *n, pl* **pansies** [ME *pancy, pensee*, fr. MF *pensée*, fr. *pensée* thought, fr. *penser* to think, fr. L *pensare* to ponder] 1 : a low-growing garden herb related to the violet; *also* : its showy flower

¹**pant** \'pant\ *vb* [ME, fr. AF *panteiser*, fr. VL **phantasiare* to have hallucinations, fr. Gk *phantasioun*, fr. *phantasia* appearance, imagination] 1 ♦ : to breathe in a labored manner 2 : to long eagerly : YEARN 3 : THROB

♦ blow, gasp, puff, wheeze — more at GASP

²**pant** *n* : a panting breath or sound

³**pant** *n* **1** ♦ : an outer garment covering each leg separately and usu. extending from the waist to the ankle — usu. used in pl. **2** *pl* : PANTIE

♦ **pants** britches, pantaloons, slacks, trousers; *also* corduroys, denims, jeans; hose, legging, pantsuit

pan·ta·loons \ˌpan-tə-ˈlünz\ *n pl* **1** : close-fitting pants of the 19th century usu. having straps passing under the instep **2** ♦ : loose-fitting usu. shorter than ankle-length trousers

♦ britches, pants, slacks, trousers — more at PANTS

pan·the·ism \ˈpan-thē-ˌi-zəm\ *n* : a doctrine that equates God with the forces and laws of the universe — **pan·the·ist** \-ist\ *n* — **pan·the·is·tic** \ˌpan-thē-ˈis-tik\ *adj*

pan·the·on \ˈpan-thē-ˌän, -ən\ *n* **1** : a temple dedicated to all the gods; *also* : the gods of a people **2** : a group of illustrious people ⟨a ∼ of great writers⟩

pan·ther \ˈpan-thər\ *n, pl* **panthers** *also* **panther** **1** : LEOPARD; *esp* : a black one **2** ♦ : a large powerful tawny brown wild American cat : COUGAR **3** : JAGUAR

♦ cougar, mountain lion — more at COUGAR

pant·ie *or* **panty** \ˈpan-tē\ *n, pl* **pant·ies** : a woman's or child's short underpants — usu. used in pl.

pan·to·mime \ˈpan-tə-ˌmīm\ *n* **1** : a play in which the actors use no words **2** : expression of something by bodily or facial movements only **3** ♦ : an actor or dancer in pantomimes — **pantomime** *vb* — **pan·to·mim·ic** \ˌpan-tə-ˈmi-mik\ *adj*

♦ mime, mimic, mummer

pan·try \ˈpan-trē\ *n, pl* **pantries** : a storage room for food or dishes

pant·suit \ˈpant-ˌsüt\ *n* : a woman's outfit consisting usu. of a long jacket and pants of the same material

panty hose *n pl* : a one-piece undergarment for women consisting of hosiery combined with a pantie

panty·waist \ˈpan-tē-ˌwāst\ *n* : SISSY

pap \ˈpap\ *n* : soft food for infants or invalids

pa·pa \ˈpä-pə\ *n* ♦ : a man who has begotten a child : FATHER

♦ daddy, father, pop — more at FATHER

pa·pa·cy \ˈpā-pə-sē\ *n, pl* **-cies** **1** : the office of pope **2** : a succession of popes **3** : the term of a pope's reign **4** *cap* : the system of government of the Roman Catholic Church

pa·pa·in \pə-ˈpā-ən, -ˈpī-ən\ *n* : an enzyme in papaya juice used esp. as a meat tenderizer and in medicine

pa·pal \ˈpā-pəl\ *adj* : of or relating to the pope or to the Roman Catholic Church

pa·pa·raz·zo \ˌpä-pə-ˈrät-(ˌ)sō\ *n, pl* **-raz·zi** \-ˈrät-(ˌ)sē\ [It, surname of such a photographer in the film *La dolce vita* (1959) by Federico Fellini] : a freelance photographer who aggressively pursues celebrities for the purpose of taking candid photographs

papaw *var of* PAWPAW

pa·pa·ya \pə-ˈpī-ə\ *n* : a tropical American tree with large yellow black-seeded edible fruit; *also* : its fruit

¹**pa·per** \ˈpā-pər\ *n* [ME *papir*, fr. AF, fr. L *papyrus* papyrus, paper, fr. Gk *papyros* papyrus] **1** : a pliable substance made usu. of vegetable matter and used to write or print on, to wrap things in, or to cover walls; *also* : a single sheet of this substance **2** ♦ : a printed or written document **3** : NEWSPAPER **4** : WALLPAPER **1 5** ♦ : a formal written composition often designed for publication and often intended to be read aloud — **paper** *vb* — **pa·pery** \ˈpā-pə-rē\ *adj*

♦ [2] blank, document, form — more at FORM ♦ [5] article, composition, essay, theme — more at ESSAY

²**paper** *adj* **1** : made of paper, cardboard, or papier-mâché **2** : of or relating to clerical work or written communication **3** : existing only in theory : NOMINAL

pa·per·back \-ˌbak\ *n* : a paper-covered book

pa·per·board \-ˌbȯrd\ *n* : CARDBOARD

pa·per·hang·er \ˈpā-pər-ˌhaŋ-ər\ *n* : one that applies wallpaper — **pa·per·hang·ing** *n*

pa·per·weight \-ˌwāt\ *n* : an object used to hold down loose papers by its weight

pa·pier–mâ·ché \ˌpā-pər-mə-ˈshā, ˌpa-ˌpyä-mə-, -ma-\ *n* [F, lit., chewed paper] : a molding material of wastepaper and additives (as glue) — **papier–mâché** *adj*

pa·pil·la \pə-ˈpi-lə\ *n, pl* **-lae** \-(ˌ)lē, -ˌlī\ [L, nipple] : a small projecting bodily part (as one of the nubs on the surface of the tongue) that resembles a tiny nipple in form — **pap·il·lary** \ˈpa-pə-ˌler-ē, pə-ˈpi-lə-rē\ *adj*

pa·poose \pa-ˈpüs, pə-\ *n* [Narragansett *papoòs*] *dated, now offensive* : a young child of American Indian parents

pa·pri·ka \pə-ˈprē-kə, pa-\ *n* [Hung] : a mild red spice made from the fruit of various cultivated sweet peppers

Pap smear \ˈpap-\ *n* : a method for the early detection of cancer esp. of the uterine cervix

Pap test *n* : PAP SMEAR

pap·ule \ˈpa-pyül\ *n* : a small solid usu. conical elevation of the skin — **pap·u·lar** \-pyə-lər\ *adj*

pa·py·rus \pə-ˈpī-rəs\ *n, pl* **-rus·es** *or* **-ri** \-(ˌ)rē, -ˌrī\ **1** : a tall grassy sedge of the Nile valley **2** : paper made from papyrus pith

¹**par** \ˈpär\ *n* **1** : a stated value (as of a security) **2** ♦ : a common level : EQUALITY **3** ♦ : an accepted standard or normal condition **4** : the score standard set for each hole of a golf course — **par** *adj*

♦ [2] equality, equivalence, parity, sameness — more at EQUIVALENCE ♦ [3] criterion, grade, mark, measure, standard, touchstone, yardstick — more at STANDARD ♦ [3] average, norm, normal, standard — more at AVERAGE

²**par** *abbr* **1** paragraph **2** parallel **3** parish

par·a·ble \ˈpar-ə-bəl\ *n* : a simple story told to illustrate a moral truth

pa·rab·o·la \pə-ˈra-bə-lə\ *n* : a plane curve formed by a point moving so that its distance from a fixed point is equal to its distance from a fixed line — **par·a·bol·ic** \ˌpar-ə-ˈbä-lik\ *adj*

para·chute \ˈpar-ə-ˌshüt\ *n* [F, fr. *para-* (as in *parasol*) + *chute* fall] : a device for slowing the descent of a person or object through the air that consists of a usu. hemispherical canopy beneath which the person or object is suspended — **parachute** *vb* — **para·chut·ist** \-ˈshü-tist\ *n*

parachute pants *n pl* : baggy casual pants of lightweight fabric

¹**pa·rade** \pə-ˈrād\ *n* **1** : a pompous display : EXHIBITION **2** : MARCH, PROCESSION; *esp* : a ceremonial formation and march **3** : a place for strolling

²**parade** *vb* **pa·rad·ed; pa·rad·ing** **1** ♦ : to march in a parade **2** : PROMENADE **3** ♦ : to exhibit ostentatiously : SHOW OFF **4** : MASQUERADE

♦ [1] file, march, pace, stride — more at MARCH ♦ [3] display, disport, exhibit, expose, flash, flaunt, show, show off, sport, strut, unveil — more at SHOW

par·a·digm \ˈpar-ə-ˌdīm, -ˌdim\ *n* **1** : MODEL, PATTERN **2** : a systematic inflection of a verb or noun showing a complete conjugation or declension

par·a·dig·mat·ic \ˌpar-ə-dig-ˈma-tik\ *adj* ♦ : serving as a pattern; *also* : deserving imitation

♦ classic, model, quintessential — more at MODEL

par·a·dise \ˈpar-ə-ˌdīs, -ˌdīz\ *n* [ME *paradis*, fr. AF, fr. LL *paradisus*, fr. Gk *paradeisos*, lit., enclosed park, of Iranian origin] **1** : HEAVEN **2** ♦ : a place or state of bliss

♦ Eden, Elysium, heaven, utopia; *also* dreamland, fairyland, promised land; bliss, euphoria, gladness, joy *Ant* hell ♦ ecstasy, elation, euphoria, exhilaration, heaven, intoxication, rapture, rhapsody, transport — more at ECSTASY

par·a·di·si·a·cal \ˌpar-ə-də-ˈsī-ə-kəl\ *or* **par·a·dis·i·ac** \-ˈdi-zē-ˌak, -sē-\ *adj* : of, relating to, or resembling paradise

par·a·dox \ˈpar-ə-ˌdäks\ *n* : a statement that seems contrary to common sense and yet is perhaps true — **par·a·dox·i·cal** \ˌpar-ə-ˈdäk-si-kəl\ *adj* — **par·a·dox·i·cal·ly** \-k(ə-)lē\ *adv*

par·af·fin \'par-ə-fən\ *n* : a waxy substance used esp. for making candles and sealing foods

para·glid·ing \'pa-rə-ˌglī-diŋ\ *n* : the sport of soaring from a slope or cliff using a modified parachute

par·a·gon \'par-ə-ˌgän, -gən\ *n* ♦ : a model of perfection

♦ beau ideal, classic, exemplar, ideal, model, nonpareil — more at IDEAL

¹**para·graph** \'par-ə-ˌgraf\ *n* : a subdivision of a written composition that deals with one point or gives the words of one speaker; *also* : a character (as ¶) marking the beginning of a paragraph

²**paragraph** *vb* : to divide into paragraphs

Par·a·guay·an \ˌpar-ə-'gwī-ən, -'gwä-\ *n* : a native or inhabitant of Paraguay — **Paraguayan** *adj*

par·a·keet \'par-ə-ˌkēt\ *n* : any of numerous usu. small slender parrots with a long graduated tail

par·a·le·gal \ˌpar-ə-'lē-gəl\ *adj* : of, relating to, or being a paraprofessional who assists a lawyer — **paralegal** *n*

Par·a·li·pom·e·non \ˌpar-ə-lə-'pä-mə-ˌnän\ *n* : CHRONICLES

par·al·lax \'par-ə-ˌlaks\ *n* : the difference in apparent direction of an object as seen from two different points

¹**par·al·lel** \'par-ə-ˌlel\ *adj* [L *parallelus*, fr. Gk *parallēlos*, fr. *para* beside + *allēlōn* of one another, fr. *allos . . . allos* one . . . another, fr. *allos* other] **1** : lying or moving in the same direction but always the same distance apart **2** ♦ : similar in essential parts

♦ akin, alike, analogous, comparable, correspondent, like, similar, such — more at ALIKE

²**parallel** *n* **1** : a parallel line, curve, or surface **2** : one of the imaginary circles on the earth's surface that parallel the equator and mark the latitude **3** ♦ : something essentially similar to another **4** ♦ : a comparable aspect : SIMILARITY

♦ [3] coordinate, counterpart, equal, equivalent, fellow, like, match, peer, rival — more at EQUAL ♦ [4] correspondence, resemblance, similarity, similitude

³**parallel** *vb* **1** : COMPARE **2** ♦ : to correspond to **3** : to extend in a parallel direction with

♦ correspond, equal, match — more at MATCH

par·al·lel·ism \'par-ə-ˌle-ˌli-zəm\ *n* **1** : the quality or state of being parallel **2** ♦ : the quality or state of being similar in essential parts

♦ community, correspondence, likeness, resemblance, similarity, similitude — more at SIMILARITY

par·al·lel·o·gram \ˌpar-ə-'le-lə-ˌgram\ *n* : a 4-sided geometric figure with opposite sides equal and parallel

par·a·lyse *chiefly Brit var of* PARALYZE

pa·ral·y·sis \pə-'ra-lə-səs\ *n, pl* **-y·ses** \-ˌsēz\ : complete or partial loss of function esp. when involving the motion or sensation in a part of the body — **par·a·lyt·ic** \ˌpar-ə-'li-tik\ *adj or n*

par·a·lyze \'par-ə-ˌlīz\ *vb* **-lyzed; -lyz·ing** **1** : to affect with paralysis **2** ♦ : to make powerless or inactive ⟨*paralyzed* by fear⟩ — **par·a·lyz·ing·ly** *adv*

♦ cripple, disable, hamstring, immobilize, incapacitate, prostrate; *also* attenuate, debilitate, enfeeble, sap, undermine, weaken; hobble, lame; maim, mutilate

par·a·me·cium \ˌpar-ə-'mē-shəm, -shē-əm, -sē-əm\ *n, pl* **-cia** \-shə, -shē-ə, -sē-ə\ *also* **-ciums** : any of a genus of slipper-shaped protozoans that move by cilia

para·med·ic \ˌpar-ə-'me-dik\ *also* **para·med·i·cal** \-di-kəl\ *n* **1** : a person who assists a physician in a paramedical capacity **2** : a specially trained medical technician licensed to provide a wide range of emergency services before or during transportation to a hospital

para·med·i·cal \ˌpar-ə-'me-di-kəl\ *also* **para·med·ic** \-'me-dik\ *adj* : concerned with supplementing the work of trained medical professionals

pa·ram·e·ter \pə-'ra-mə-tər\ *n* **1** : a quantity whose value characterizes a statistical population or a member of a system (as a family of curves) **2** : a physical property whose value determines the characteristics or behavior of a system **3** : a characteristic element : FACTOR

para·mil·i·tary \ˌpar-ə-'mi-lə-ˌter-ē\ *adj* : formed on a military pattern esp. as an auxiliary military force

par·a·mount \'par-ə-ˌmau̇nt\ *adj* ♦ : superior to all others : SUPREME

♦ arch, cardinal, central, chief, dominant, first, foremost, grand, key, main, predominant, preeminent, premier, primary, principal, sovereign, supreme — more at FOREMOST ♦ consummate, maximum, maximal, nth, supreme, top, ultimate, utmost — more at ULTIMATE

par·amour \'par-ə-ˌmu̇r\ *n* : an illicit lover

para·noia \ˌpar-ə-'nȯi-ə\ *n* : a psychosis marked by delusions and irrational suspicion usu. without hallucinations — **par·a·noid** \'par-ə-ˌnȯid\ *adj or n*

para·nor·mal \ˌpa-rə-'nȯr-məl\ *adj* : not scientifically explainable : SUPERNATURAL ⟨∼ phenomena⟩

par·a·pet \'par-ə-pət, -ˌpet\ *n* **1** : a protecting rampart **2** : a low wall or railing (as at the edge of a bridge)

par·a·pher·na·lia \ˌpar-ə-fə-'nāl-yə, -fər-\ *n sing or pl* **1** ♦ : personal belongings **2** ♦ : articles of equipment : APPARATUS

♦ [1] belongings, chattels, effects, holdings, possessions, things — more at POSSESSION ♦ [2] accoutrements (*or* accouterments), apparatus, equipment, gear, matériel, outfit, tackle — more at EQUIPMENT

¹**para·phrase** \'par-ə-ˌfrāz\ *n* ♦ : a restatement of a text giving the meaning in different words

♦ translation; *also* rehash; summary *Ant* quotation, quote

²**paraphrase** *vb* ♦ : to make a paraphrase

♦ rephrase, restate, translate; *also* summarize *Ant* quote

para·ple·gia \ˌpar-ə-'plē-jə, -jē-ə\ *n* : paralysis of the lower trunk and legs — **para·ple·gic** \-jik\ *adj or n*

para·pro·fes·sion·al \-prə-'fe-shə-nəl\ *n* : a trained aide who assists a professional — **paraprofessional** *adj*

para·psy·chol·o·gy \ˌpar-ə-sī-'kä-lə-jē\ *n* : a field of study concerned with investigating paranormal psychological phenomena (as extrasensory perception) — **para·psy·chol·o·gist** \-jist\ *n*

par·a·site \'par-ə-ˌsīt\ *n* [MF, fr. L *parasitus*, fr. Gk *parasitos*, fr. *para-* beside + *sitos* grain, food] **1** : a plant or animal living in, with, or on another organism usu. to its harm **2** ♦ : one depending on another and not making adequate return — **par·a·sit·ic** \ˌpar-ə-'si-tik\ *adj* — **par·a·sit·ism** \'par-ə-sə-ˌti-zəm, -ˌsī-ˌti-\ *n* — **par·a·sit·ize** \-sə-ˌtīz\ *vb*

♦ hanger-on, leech, sponge — more at LEECH

par·a·si·tol·o·gy \ˌpar-ə-sə-'tä-lə-jē\ *n* : a branch of biology dealing with parasites and parasitism esp. among animals — **par·a·si·tol·o·gist** \-jist\ *n*

para·sol \'par-ə-ˌsȯl\ *n* [F, fr. It *parasole*, fr. *parare* to shield + *sole* sun, fr. L *sol*] : a lightweight umbrella used as a shield against the sun

para·sym·pa·thet·ic nervous system \ˌpar-ə-ˌsim-pə-'the-tik-\ *n* : the part of the autonomic nervous system that tends to induce secretion, to increase the tone and contractility of smooth muscle, and to slow heart rate

para·thi·on \ˌpar-ə-'thī-ˌän, -ˌän\ *n* : an extremely toxic insecticide

para·thy·roid \-'thī-ˌrȯid\ *n* : PARATHYROID GLAND — **parathyroid** *adj*

parathyroid gland *n* : any of usu. four small endocrine glands adjacent to or embedded in the thyroid gland that produce a hormone (**parathyroid hormone**) concerned with calcium and phosphorus metabolism

para·tran·sit \ˌpa-rə-'tran-sət, -zət\ *n* : transportation service that provides individualized rules without fixed routes or timetables

para·troop·er \'par-ə-ˌtrü-pər\ *n* : a member of the paratroops

para·troops \-ˌtrüps\ *n pl* : troops trained to parachute from an airplane

para·ty·phoid \ˌpar-ə-ˈtī-ˌfȯid\ *n* : a bacterial food poisoning resembling typhoid fever

par·boil \ˈpär-ˌbȯil\ *vb* : to boil briefly

¹**par·cel** \ˈpär-səl\ *n* **1** ♦ : a tract or plot of land **2** ♦ : a company, collection, or group of persons, animals, or things : LOT **3** : a wrapped bundle : PACKAGE

♦ [1] field, ground, lot, plat, plot, tract — more at FIELD ♦ [2] array, assemblage, bank, batch, block, bunch, clump, cluster, collection, group, huddle, knot, lot, package, set, suite

²**parcel** *vb* **-celed** *or* **-celled; -cel·ing** *or* **-cel·ling** ♦ : to divide into portions — often used with *out*

♦ *usu.* **parcel out** administer, allocate, apportion, deal, dispense, distribute, mete, portion, prorate — more at ADMINISTER

parcel post *n* **1** ♦ : a mail service handling parcels **2** ♦ : packages handled by parcel post

♦ mail, matter, post, snail mail — more at MAIL

parch \ˈpärch\ *vb* **1** : to toast under dry heat **2** ♦ : to shrivel with heat

♦ dehydrate, dry, sear — more at DRY

parch·ment \ˈpärch-mənt\ *n* : the skin of an animal prepared for writing on; *also* : a writing on such material

pard \ˈpärd\ *n* : LEOPARD

¹**par·don** \ˈpärd-ᵊn\ *n* ♦ : excuse of an offense without penalty; *esp* : an official release from legal punishment

♦ absolution, amnesty, forgiveness, remission; *also* parole; acquittal, exoneration, vindication; exemption, immunity, impunity, indemnity; commutation, commuting, reprieve *Ant* penalty, punishment, retribution

²**pardon** *vb* ♦ : to free from penalty : EXCUSE, FORGIVE

♦ condone, disregard, excuse, gloss over, ignore, pass over, shrug off, wink at — more at EXCUSE

par·don·able \ˈpärd-ᵊn-ə-bəl\ *adj* ♦ : worthy of or subject to being pardoned : EXCUSABLE

♦ excusable, forgivable, venial — more at VENIAL

par·don·er \ˈpärd-ᵊn-ər\ *n* **1** : a medieval preacher delegated to raise money for religious works by soliciting offerings and granting indulgences **2** : one that pardons

pare \ˈpar\ *vb* **pared; par·ing** **1** : to trim off an outside, excess, or irregular part of **2** : to reduce as if by paring ⟨~ expenses⟩ — **par·er** *n*

par·e·gor·ic \ˌpar-ə-ˈgȯr-ik\ *n* : an alcoholic preparation of opium and camphor used esp. to relieve pain

par·ent \ˈpar-ənt\ *n* **1** : one that begets or brings forth offspring : FATHER, MOTHER **2** : one who brings up and cares for another **3** : SOURCE, ORIGIN — **pa·ren·tal** \pə-ˈrent-ᵊl\ *adj* — **par·ent·hood** *n*

par·ent·age \-ən-tij\ *n* ♦ : descent from parents or ancestors

♦ ancestry, birth, blood, bloodline, breeding, descent, extraction, family tree, genealogy, line, lineage, origin, pedigree, stock, strain — more at ANCESTRY

pa·ren·the·sis \pə-ˈren-thə-səs\ *n, pl* **-the·ses** \-ˌsēz\ **1** : a word, phrase, or sentence inserted in a passage to explain or modify the thought **2** : one of a pair of punctuation marks ( ) used esp. to enclose parenthetic matter — **par·en·thet·ic** \ˌpar-ən-ˈthe-tik\ *or* **par·en·thet·i·cal** \-ti-kəl\ *adj* — **par·en·thet·i·cal·ly** \-k(ə-)lē\ *adv*

pa·ren·the·size \pə-ˈren-thə-ˌsīz\ *vb* **-sized; -siz·ing** : to make a parenthesis of

par·ent·ing \ˈpar-ən-tiŋ, ˈper-\ *n* : the raising of a child by its parents

pa·re·sis \pə-ˈrē-səs, ˈpar-ə-\ *n, pl* **pa·re·ses** \-ˌsēz\ : a usu. incomplete paralysis; *also* : insanity caused by syphilitic alteration of the brain that leads to dementia and paralysis

par ex·cel·lence \ˌpär-ˌek-sə-ˈläⁿs\ *adj* [F, lit., by excellence] : being the best of a kind : PREEMINENT

par·fait \pär-ˈfā\ *n* [F, lit., something perfect] : a cold dessert made of layers of fruit, syrup, ice cream, and whipped cream

pa·ri·ah \pə-ˈrī-ə\ *n* : one that is despised or rejected : OUTCAST

pa·ri·etal \pə-ˈrī-ət-ᵊl\ *adj* **1** : of, relating to, or forming the walls of an anatomical structure **2** : of or relating to college living or its regulation

pari–mu·tu·el \ˌpar-i-ˈmyü-chə-wəl\ *n* : a betting system in which winners share the total stakes minus a percentage for the management

par·ing \ˈpar-iŋ\ *n* : a pared-off piece

pa·ri pas·su \ˌpar-i-ˈpa-sü\ *adv or adj* [L, with equal step] : at an equal rate or pace

par·ish \ˈpar-ish\ *n* **1** : a church district in the care of one pastor; *also* : the residents of such an area **2** : a local church community **3** : a civil division of the state of Louisiana : COUNTY

pa·rish·io·ner \pə-ˈri-shə-nər\ *n* : a member or resident of a parish

par·i·ty \ˈpar-ə-tē\ *n, pl* **-ties** ♦ : the quality or state of being equal or equivalent

♦ equality, equivalence, par, sameness — more at EQUIVALENCE

¹**park** \ˈpärk\ *n* **1** : a tract of ground kept as a game preserve or recreation area **2** : a place where vehicles (as automobiles) are parked **3** : an enclosed stadium used esp. for ball games **4** ♦ : a tract of land attached to a country house

♦ demesne, grounds, premises, yard

²**park** *vb* **1** : to leave a vehicle temporarily (as in a parking lot or garage) **2** : to set and leave temporarily

par·ka \ˈpär-kə\ *n* : a very warm jacket with a hood

Par·kin·son's disease \ˈpär-kən-sənz-\ *n* : a chronic progressive neurological disease chiefly of later life marked esp. by tremor and weakness of resting muscles and by a shuffling gait

Parkinson's Law *n* : an observation in office organization: work expands so as to fill the time available for its completion

par·kour \pär-ˈkur, ˈpär-ˌkur\ *n* [F, alter. of *parcours* course, route] : the sport of traversing environmental obstacles by running, climbing, or leaping rapidly

park·way \ˈpärk-ˌwā\ *n* : a broad landscaped thoroughfare

par·lance \ˈpär-ləns\ *n* **1** : SPEECH **2** : manner of speaking ⟨military ~⟩

¹**par·lay** \ˈpär-ˌlā, -lē\ *vb* : to increase or change into something of much greater value

²**parlay** *n* : a series of bets in which the original stake plus its winnings are risked on successive wagers

¹**par·ley** \ˈpär-lē\ *vb* : to speak with another : CONFER

²**parley** *n, pl* **parleys** ♦ : a conference usu. over matters in dispute

♦ argument, colloquy, conference, deliberation, discourse, discussion, give-and-take, talk — more at DISCUSSION

par·lia·ment \ˈpär-lə-mənt\ *n* [ME, fr. AF *parlement*, fr. *parler* to speak, fr. ML *parabolare*, fr. LL *parabola* speech, parable] **1** : a formal governmental conference **2** *cap* : an assembly that constitutes the supreme legislative body of a country (as the United Kingdom) — **par·lia·men·ta·ry** \ˌpär-lə-ˈmen-tə-rē\ *adj*

par·lia·men·tar·i·an \ˌpär-lə-ˌmen-ˈter-ē-ən\ *n* **1** *often cap* : an adherent of the parliament during the English Civil War **2** : an expert in parliamentary procedure

par·lor *or Can and Brit* **par·lour** \ˈpär-lər\ *n* **1** : a room for conversation or the reception of guests **2** : a place of business ⟨beauty ~⟩

par·lous \ˈpär-ləs\ *adj* ♦ : full of danger or risk — **par·lous·ly** *adv*

♦ dangerous, grave, grievous, hazardous, menacing, perilous, risky, serious, unhealthy, unsafe, venturesome — more at DANGEROUS

Par·me·san \ˈpär-mə-ˌzän, -ˌzhän, -ˌzan\ *n* : a hard dry cheese with a sharp flavor

par·mi·gia·na \ˌpär-mi-ˈjä-nə, ˌpär-mi-ˈzhän\ *or* **par·mi·gia·no** \-ˈjä-(ˌ)nō\ *adj* : made or covered with Parmesan cheese ⟨veal ~⟩

pa·ro·chi·al \pə-'rō-kē-əl\ *adj* 1 : of or relating to a church parish 2 ♦ : limited in scope : NARROW, PROVINCIAL — **pa·ro·chi·al·ism** \-ə-,li-zəm\ *n*

♦ insular, little, narrow, petty, provincial, sectarian, small — more at NARROW

parochial school *n* : a school maintained by a religious body

¹**par·o·dy** \'par-ə-dē\ *n, pl* **-dies** [L *parodia,* fr. Gk *parōidia,* fr. *para-* beside + *aidein* to sing] 1 ♦ : a humorous or satirical imitation 2 ♦ : a feeble or ridiculous imitation — **parody** *vb*

♦ [1] burlesque, caricature, spoof, takeoff; *also* lampoon, mockery, satire, travesty; comedy, farce, sketch, slapstick, squib; distortion, exaggeration; imitation, impersonation, mimicking ♦ [2] caricature, farce, joke, mockery, sham, travesty — more at MOCKERY

²**parody** *vb* 1 : to compose a parody on 2 ♦ : to imitate in the manner of a parody

♦ burlesque, caricature, imitate, mimic, mock, take off, travesty — more at MIMIC

pa·role \pə-'rōl\ *n* : a conditional release of a prisoner whose sentence has not expired — **parole** *vb* — **pa·rol·ee** \-,rō-'lē, -'rō-,lē\ *n*

par·ox·ysm \'par-ək-,si-zəm, pə-'räk-\ *n* 1 : a sudden sharp attack (as of pain or coughing) : CONVULSION 2 ♦ : a sudden violent emotion or action — **par·ox·ys·mal** \,par-ək-'siz-məl, pə-,räk-\ *adj*

♦ agony, burst, eruption, explosion, fit, flare, flare-up, flash, flush, gale, gush, gust, outburst, spasm, storm — more at OUTBURST

par·quet \'pär-,kā, pär-'kā\ *n* [F] 1 : a flooring of parquetry 2 : the lower floor of a theater; *esp* : the forward part of the orchestra

par·que·try \'pär-kə-trē\ *n, pl* **-tries** : fine woodwork inlaid in patterns

par·ri·cide \'par-ə-,sīd\ *n* 1 : one that murders a parent or a close relative 2 : the act of a parricide

par·rot \'par-ət\ *n* : any of numerous bright-colored tropical birds that have a stout hooked bill

parrot fever *n* : PSITTACOSIS

par·ry \'par-ē\ *vb* **par·ried; par·ry·ing** 1 : to ward off a weapon or blow 2 : to evade esp. by an adroit answer — **parry** *n*

parse \'pärs *also* 'pärz\ *vb* **parsed; pars·ing** : to give a grammatical description of a word or a group of words

par·sec \'pär-,sek\ *n* : a unit of measure for interstellar space equal to 3.26 light-years

par·si·mo·ni·ous \,pär-sə-'mō-nē-əs\ *adj* ♦ : exhibiting or marked by parsimony — **par·si·mo·ni·ous·ly** *adv*

♦ cheap, close, mean, niggardly, penurious, spare, sparing, stingy, tight, tightfisted, uncharitable — more at STINGY

par·si·mo·ny \'pär-sə-,mō-nē\ *n* ♦ : extreme or excessive frugality

♦ cheapness, closeness, miserliness, stinginess, tightness; *also* conserving, economizing, economy, frugality, husbandry, providence, scrimping, skimping, thrift; conservation, saving; husbanding, managing *Ant* generosity, liberality, philanthropy

pars·ley \'pär-slē\ *n* : a garden plant related to the carrot that has finely divided leaves used as a seasoning or garnish; *also* : the leaves

pars·nip \'pär-snəp\ *n* : a garden plant related to the carrot that has a long edible usu. whitish root which is cooked as a vegetable; *also* : the root

par·son \'pärs-ᵊn\ *n* [ME *persone,* fr. AF, fr. ML *persona,* lit., person, fr. L] : a member of the clergy : MINISTER

par·son·age \'pärs-ᵊn-ij\ *n* : a house provided by a church for its pastor

¹**part** \'pärt\ *n* 1 ♦ : a division or portion of a whole 2 : the melody or score for a particular voice or instrument 3 : a spare piece for a machine 4 : DUTY, FUNCTION

5 : one of the sides in a dispute 6 : ROLE; *also* : an actor's lines in a play 7 *pl* : TALENTS, ABILITY 8 : the line where one's hair divides (as in combing) 9 ♦ : something falling to one in a division or apportionment 10 ♦ : a function or course of action performed

♦ [1] member, partition, portion, section, segment; *also* component, constituent, element, factor, ingredient, moiety, parcel; cut, length; bit, fragment, particle, scrap ♦ [9] allotment, allowance, cut, portion, proportion, quota, share — more at SHARE ♦ [10] capacity, function, job, place, position, purpose, role, task, work — more at ROLE

²**part** *vb* 1 : to take leave of someone 2 ♦ : to divide or break into parts 3 : to go away : DEPART; *also* : DIE 4 : to give up possession ⟨~ed with her jewels⟩ 5 : APPORTION, SHARE

♦ break up, disconnect, disjoint, dissever, dissociate, disunite, divide, divorce, resolve, separate, sever, split, sunder, unyoke — more at SEPARATE

³**part** *abbr* 1 participial; participle 2 particular

par·take \pär-'tāk\ *vb* **-took** \-'tu̇k\; **-tak·en** \-'tā-kən\; **-tak·ing** 1 : to have a share or part 2 : to take a portion (as of food)

par·tak·er \-'tā-kər\ *n* ♦ : one that partakes

♦ participant, party, sharer — more at PARTICIPANT

par·terre \pär-'ter\ *n* [F, fr. MF, fr. *par terre* on the ground] 1 : an ornamental garden with paths between the flower beds 2 : the part of a theater floor behind the orchestra

par·the·no·gen·e·sis \,pär-thə-nō-'je-nə-səs\ *n* [NL, fr. Gk *parthenos* virgin + L *genesis* genesis] : development of a new individual from an unfertilized usu. female sex cell — **par·the·no·ge·net·ic** \-jə-'ne-tik\ *adj*

par·tial \'pär-shəl\ *adj* 1 ♦ : of or relating to a part rather than the whole 2 ♦ : favoring one party over the other : BIASED 3 ♦ : markedly fond — used with *to*

♦ [1] deficient, fragmentary, halfway, incomplete — more at INCOMPLETE ♦ [2] biased, one-sided, partisan, prejudiced; *also* jaundiced, unfriendly, unsympathetic; colored, distorted, misrepresented, warped; convinced, influenced, persuaded, predisposed, prepossessed, swayed; affected, concerned, interested *Ant* evenhanded, impartial, neutral, nonpartisan, unbiased, unprejudiced ♦ [3] fond, inclined — more at FOND

par·tial·i·ty \,pär-shē-'a-lə-tē\ *n* 1 ♦ : the quality or state of being partial 2 ♦ : a special taste or liking

♦ [1] bias, favor (*or* favour), partisanship, prejudice — more at BIAS ♦ [2] bent, devices, disposition, genius, inclination, leaning, penchant, predilection, proclivity, propensity, tendency, turn ♦ [2] appetite, fancy, favor (*or* favour), fondness, like, liking, love, preference, relish, shine, taste, use — more at LIKING

par·tial·ly \'pär-sh(ə-)lē\ *adv* ♦ : to some extent : in some degree

♦ part, partly — more at PARTLY

par·tic·i·pant \pär-'ti-sə-pənt\ *n* ♦ : one that participates — **participant** *adj*

♦ partaker, party, sharer; *also* actor; accessory, aide, assistant, helper; colleague, partner *Ant* nonparticipant

par·tic·i·pate \pär-'ti-sə-,pāt\ *vb* **-pat·ed; -pat·ing** 1 : to take part in something ⟨~ in a game⟩ 2 : SHARE — **par·tic·i·pa·tion** \-,ti-sə-'pā-shən\ *n* — **par·tic·i·pa·to·ry** \-'ti-sə-pə-,tōr-ē\ *adj*

par·tic·i·pa·tor \pär-'ti-sə-,pā-tər\ *n* : one that participates

par·ti·ci·ple \'pär-tə-,si-pəl\ *n* : a word having the characteristics of both verb and adjective — **par·ti·cip·i·al** \,pär-tə-'si-pē-əl\ *adj*

par·ti·cle \'pär-ti-kəl\ *n* 1 ♦ : a very small quantity or fragment 2 : a unit of speech (as an article, preposition, or conjunction) expressing some general aspect of meaning or some connective or limiting relation

♦ atom, fleck, grain, granule, molecule, morsel, scrap
♦ bit, crumb, dab, glimmer, hint, lick, little, mite, nip, ounce, shred, speck, spot, suspicion, touch, trace; *also* iota, jot, modicum, tittle, whit; atom, dot, fleck, flyspeck, grain, granule, molecule, morsel, mote, nubbin, patch, scrap; dash, drop, pinch; part, portion, section; bite, nibble, taste; handful, scattering, smattering; dose, shot; chip, flake, fragment, shard, shiver, sliver, smithereens, splinter; tatter; clipping, paring, shaving

par·ti·cle·board \-ˌbōrd\ *n* : a board made of very small pieces of wood bonded together

par·ti-col·or \ˌpär-tē-ˈkə-lər\ *or* **par·ti-col·ored** \-lərd\ *adj* : showing different colors or tints; *esp* : having one main color broken by patches of one or more other colors

¹**par·tic·u·lar** \pər-ˈti-kyə-lər\ *adj* **1** ♦ : of or relating to a specific person or thing ⟨the laws of a ∼ state⟩ **2** : DISTINCTIVE, SPECIAL ⟨the ∼ point of his talk⟩ **3** : SEPARATE, INDIVIDUAL ⟨each ∼ hair⟩ **4** : attentive to details **5** ♦ : hard to please ⟨∼ about her clothes⟩

♦ [1] individual, peculiar, personal, private, separate, singular, unique — more at INDIVIDUAL ♦ [5] choosy, dainty, delicate, demanding, exacting, fastidious, finicky, fussy, nice, old-maidish, picky — more at FINICKY

²**particular** *n* ♦ : an individual fact or detail

♦ detail, fact, item, point — more at FACT

par·tic·u·lar·ise *chiefly Brit var of* PARTICULARIZE
par·tic·u·lar·i·ty \pər-ˌti-kyə-ˈlar-ə-tē\ *n* : a minute detail
par·tic·u·lar·ize \pər-ˈti-kyə-lə-ˌrīz\ *vb* **-ized; -iz·ing 1** : to state in detail : SPECIFY **2** : to go into details
par·tic·u·lar·ly \-lē\ *adv* **1** : to an unusual degree **2** : in particular : SPECIFICALLY
par·tic·u·late \pər-ˈti-kyə-lət, pär-, -ˌlāt\ *adj* : relating to or existing as minute separate particles — **particulate** *n*

¹**part·ing** *n* **1** : a place or point of separation or divergence **2** ♦ : a mutual separation of two or more persons

♦ farewell, leave-taking, separation; *also* departure, egress, exit, exodus, leaving, quitting, running away; flight, withdrawal; abandonment, desertion, forsaking

²**parting** *adj* : given, taken, or done at parting ⟨a ∼ kiss⟩
¹**par·ti·san** *also* **par·ti·zan** \ˈpär-tə-zən, -sən\ *n* **1** ♦ : one that takes the part of another : ADHERENT **2** : GUERRILLA **3** ♦ : a strong or devoted supporter

♦ [1] adherent, convert, disciple, follower, pupil, votary — more at FOLLOWER ♦ [3] crusader, fanatic, militant, zealot — more at ZEALOT

²**partisan** *adj* ♦ : exhibiting, characterized by, or resulting from partisanship

♦ biased, one-sided, partial, prejudiced — more at PARTIAL

par·ti·san·ship \-ship\ *n* ♦ : the quality or state of being a partisan

♦ bias, favor (*or* favour), partiality, prejudice — more at BIAS

par·tite \ˈpär-ˌtīt\ *adj* : divided into a usu. specified number of parts
par·ti·tion \pär-ˈti-shən\ *n* **1** ♦ : the action of parting : the state of being parted **2** : something that divides or separates; *esp* : an interior dividing wall **3** ♦ : one of the parts or sections of a whole — **partition** *vb*

♦ [1] breakup, dissolution, division, schism, separation, split — more at SEPARATION ♦ [3] member, part, portion, section, segment — more at PART

par·ti·tive \ˈpär-tə-tiv\ *adj* : of, relating to, or denoting a part
part·ly \ˈpärt-lē\ *adv* ♦ : in part : in some measure or degree

♦ part, partially; *also* in part *Ant* completely, entirely, totally, wholly

part·ner \ˈpärt-nər\ *n* **1** : ASSOCIATE, COLLEAGUE **2** : either of two persons who dance together **3** : one who plays on the same team with another **4** ♦ : married person : SPOUSE **5** : one of two or more persons contractually associated as joint principals in a business

♦ consort, mate, spouse — more at SPOUSE

part·ner·ship \-ship\ *n* ♦ : a relationship usu. involving close cooperation between parties having specified and joint rights and responsibilities

♦ affiliation, alliance, association, collaboration, confederation, connection, cooperation, hookup, liaison, relation, relationship, union — more at ASSOCIATION

part of speech : a class of words (as nouns or verbs) distinguished according to the kind of idea denoted and the function performed in a sentence
par·tridge \ˈpär-trij\ *n, pl* **partridge** *or* **par·tridg·es** : any of various stout-bodied Old World game birds
part–song \ˈpärt-ˌsȯn\ *n* : a song with two or more voice parts
part–time \-ˈtīm\ *adj or adv* : involving or working less than a full or regular schedule — **part–tim·er** \-ˌtī-mər\ *n*
par·tu·ri·tion \ˌpär-tə-ˈri-shən, ˌpär-chə-, ˌpär-tyu̇-\ *n* : the action or process of giving birth to offspring : CHILDBIRTH
part·way \ˈpärt-ˈwä\ *adv* : to some extent : PARTLY
par·ty \ˈpär-tē\ *n, pl* **parties 1** : a person or group taking one side of a question; *esp* : a group of persons organized for the purpose of directing the policies of a government **2** ♦ : a person or group concerned in an action or affair : PARTICIPANT **3** ♦ : a group of persons detailed for a common task **4** ♦ : a social gathering **5** : a particular individual

♦ [2] partaker, participant, sharer — more at PARTICIPANT ♦ [3] band, company, crew, gang, group, outfit, squad, team — more at GANG ♦ [4] affair, blowout, event, fete, function, get-together; *also* ball, formal, prom; celebration, gala, occasion; orgy; benefit, clambake, housewarming, masquerade, mixer, shower, salon, soiree, stag, tea

party animal *n* : a person known for frequent attendance at parties
par·ty·go·er \ˈpär-tē-ˌgō-ər\ *n* : a person who attends a party or who attends parties frequently
par·ve·nu \ˈpär-və-ˌnü, -ˌnyü\ *n* [F, fr. pp. of *parvenir* to arrive, fr. L *pervenire*, fr. *per* through + *venire* to come] : one who has recently or suddenly risen to wealth or power but has not yet secured the social position associated with it
pas \ˈpä\ *n, pl* **pas** *same or* ˈpäz\ : a dance step or combination of steps
pas·cal \pas-ˈkal\ *n* : a unit of pressure in the metric system equal to one newton per square meter
pas·chal \ˈpas-kəl\ *adj* : of, relating to, appropriate for, or used during Passover or Easter ceremonies
pa·sha \ˈpä-shə, ˈpa-; pə-ˈshä\ *n* : a man (as formerly a governor in Turkey) of high rank
pash·mi·na \ˌpəsh-ˈmē-nə\ *n* : a fine wool from the undercoat of domestic Himalayan goats; *also* : a shawl made from this wool
¹**pass** \ˈpas\ *vb* **1** : MOVE, PROCEED **2 a** : to go away **b** ♦ : to stop existing or functioning : DIE — often used with *on* **3** : to move past, beyond, or over **4** : to allow to elapse : SPEND **5** ♦ : to go or make way through **6** : to go or allow to go unchallenged **7 a** : to undergo transfer **b** ♦ : to transfer or transmit from one to another **8** : to render a legal judgment **9** ♦ : to come into existence : OCCUR **10** ♦ : to become approved by a legislature or body empowered to sanction or reject **11** : to go or cause to go through an inspection, test, or course of study successfully **12** : to be regarded **13** : CIRCULATE **14** : VOID **2 15** : to transfer the ball or puck to another player **16** : to decline to bid or bet on one's hand in a card game **17** : to give a base on balls to — **pass·er** *n*

♦ *usu* **pass on** [2b] decease, depart, die, expire, pass away, perish, succumb — more at DIE ♦ *usu* **pass over** [5] cover, crisscross, cross, cut, follow, go, proceed, travel, traverse — more at TRAVERSE ♦ [7b] hand, hand over, reach, transfer; *also* relay; bear, carry; finger, handle, paw; cede, give, give up, release, relinquish, surrender ♦ [9] be, befall, betide, chance, come, go, happen, occur, transpire — more at HAPPEN ♦ [10] enact, lay down, legislate, make — more at ENACT

²pass *n* ♦ : a gap in a mountain range

♦ canyon, defile, flume, gap, gorge, gulch, gulf, notch, ravine — more at CANYON

³pass *n* **1** : the act or an instance of passing **2** ♦ : the state of being realized or accomplished : REALIZATION, ACCOMPLISHMENT **3** : a state of affairs **4** ♦ : a written authorization to leave, enter, or move about freely **5** : a transfer of a ball or puck from one player to another **6** : BASE ON BALLS **7** ♦ : a serious attempt : TRY **8** : a sexually inviting gesture or approach

♦ [2] accomplishment, achievement, actuality, attainment, consummation, fruition, fulfillment, realization — more at FRUITION ♦ [4] check, ticket — more at TICKET ♦ [7] attempt, bid, crack, endeavor (*or* endeavour), essay, fling, go, shot, stab, trial, try, whack — more at ATTEMPT

⁴pass *abbr* **1** passenger **2** passive

pass·able \'pa-sə-bəl\ *adj* **1** ♦ : capable of being passed or traveled on **2** ♦ : just good enough ⟨did a ~ job⟩

♦ [1, 2] acceptable, adequate, all right, decent, fine, OK, respectable, satisfactory, tolerable — more at ADEQUATE ♦ [2] common, fair, indifferent, mediocre, medium, middling, ordinary, run-of-the-mill, second-rate, so-so — more at MEDIOCRE

pass·ably \-blē\ *adv* ♦ : in a passable manner or to a passable extent

♦ adequately, all right, fine, good, nicely, OK, satisfactorily, so-so, tolerably, well — more at WELL

pas·sage \'pa-sij\ *n* **1** ♦ : a means (as a road or corridor) of passing **2** ♦ : the action or process of passing **3** ♦ : a voyage esp. by sea or air **4** : a right or permission to pass **5** : ENACTMENT **6** : a usu. brief portion or section (as of a book) **7** : a continuous movement or flow

♦ [1] approach, avenue, path, route, way; *also* bypath, byway, lane; bypass, drive, freeway, highway, road, street, thoroughfare; trace, track, trail; airway; channel, watercourse, waterway; door, doorway, gate, gateway, portal ♦ [2] expedition, journey, peregrination, trek, trip — more at JOURNEY ♦ [3] crossing, cruise, sail, voyage — more at SAIL

pas·sage·way \-,wā\ *n* : a way that allows passage

pass away *vb* **1** : to go out of existence **2** ♦ : to pass from physical life

♦ decease, depart, die, expire, pass, perish, succumb — more at DIE

pass·book \'pas-,bùk\ *n* : BANKBOOK

pas·sé \pa-'sā\ *adj* **1** : past one's prime **2** ♦ : not up-to-date : OUTMODED

♦ antiquated, archaic, dated, obsolete, outdated, outmoded, outworn — more at OBSOLETE

pas·sel \'pa-səl\ *n* : a large number ⟨a ~ of children⟩

pas·sen·ger \'pas-ªn-jər\ *n* : a traveler in a public or private conveyance

pass·er·by \'pa-sər-,bī\ *n, pl* **pass·ers·by** : one who passes by

pas·ser·ine \'pa-sə-,rīn\ *adj* : of or relating to the large order of birds comprising singing birds that perch

pas·sim \'pa-səm\ *adv* [L, fr. *passus* scattered, fr. pp. of *pandere* to spread] : here and there : THROUGHOUT

pass·ing *n* ♦ : the act of one that passes or causes to pass; *esp* : DEATH

♦ death, decease, demise, doom, end, quietus — more at DEATH

pas·sion \'pa-shən\ *n* **1** *often cap* : the sufferings of Christ between the night of the Last Supper and his death **2** ♦ : strong feeling; *also, pl* : the emotions as distinguished from reason **3** : RAGE, ANGER **4** ♦ : ardent affection : LOVE; *also* : an object of affection or enthusiasm **5** : sexual desire **6** ♦ : a strong liking or desire for or devotion to some activity, object, or concept — **pas·sion·less** *adj*

♦ [2] ardor, emotion, fervency, fervor, heat, intensity, vehemence, warmth — more at ARDOR ♦ [4] affection,

attachment, devotion, fondness, love — more at LOVE ♦ [6] appetite, craving, desire, drive, hankering, hunger, itch, longing, lust, thirst, urge, yearning, yen — more at DESIRE

pas·sion·ate \'pa-shə-nət\ *adj* **1 a** ♦ : capable of, affected by, or expressing intense feeling **b** : ENTHUSIASTIC **2** ♦ : swayed by or affected with sexual desire — **pas·sion·ate·ly** *adv*

♦ [1a] ardent, burning, charged, emotional, fervent, fiery, hot-blooded, impassioned, red-hot, vehement — more at FERVENT ♦ [2] lascivious, lewd, lustful, wanton — more at LUSTFUL

pas·sion·flow·er \'pa-shən-,flaù-ər\ *n* [fr. the fancied resemblance of parts of the flower to the instruments of Christ's crucifixion] : any of a genus of chiefly tropical woody climbing vines or erect herbs with showy flowers and pulpy often edible berries (**passion fruit**)

pas·sive \'pa-siv\ *adj* **1** : not active : acted upon **2** : asserting that the grammatical subject is subjected to or affected by the action represented by the verb ⟨~ voice⟩ **3** : making use of the sun's heat usu. without the aid of mechanical devices **4** ♦ : receiving or enduring without resistance — **passive** *n* — **pas·sive·ly** *adv* — **pas·siv·i·ty** \pa-'si-və-tē\ *n*

♦ acquiescent, resigned, tolerant, unresistant, unresisting, yielding; *also* forbearing, long-suffering, patient, uncomplaining; agreeable, amenable, compliant, complying, docile, guidable, obedient, subordinate, tractable, willing; submissive, surrendering; amiable, obliging; slavish, subservient; disciplined, manageable; apathetic, unresponsive **Ant** protesting, resistant, resisting, unyielding

pas·sive–ma·trix \-'mā-triks\ *adj* : of, relating to, or being on LCD in which pixels are controlled in groups

pass·key \'pas-,kē\ *n* : a key for opening two or more locks

pass out *vb* ♦ : to lose consciousness

♦ black out, faint, swoon — more at FAINT

Pass·over \'pas-,ō-vər\ *n* [fr. the exemption of the Israelites from the slaughter of the firstborn in Egypt (Exod 12:23–27)] : a Jewish holiday celebrated in March or April in commemoration of the Hebrews' liberation from slavery in Egypt

pass over *vb* **1** ♦ : to ignore in passing **2** ♦ : to pay no attention to the claims of

♦ [1] disregard, forget, ignore, neglect, overlook, slight, slur — more at NEGLECT ♦ [1, 2] condone, disregard, excuse, gloss over, ignore, pardon, shrug off, wink at — more at EXCUSE

pass·port \'pas-,pōrt\ *n* **1** : an official document issued by a country upon request to a citizen requesting protection during travel abroad **2** ♦ : something that secures admission, acceptance, or attainment

♦ gateway, key; *also* password; accomplishment, achievement, success; manner, means, method, system, technique, way; blueprint, design, plan, scheme, strategy

pass up *vb* : DECLINE, REJECT

pass·word \'pas-,wərd\ *n* **1** : a word or phrase that must be spoken by a person before being allowed to pass a guard **2** : a sequence of characters required for access to a computer system

¹past \'past\ *adj* **1** : AGO ⟨10 years ~⟩ **2** : just gone or elapsed ⟨the ~ month⟩ **3** ♦ : having existed or taken place in a period before the present **4** : of, relating to, or constituting a verb tense that expresses time gone by

♦ erstwhile, former, late, old, onetime, sometime, whilom — more at FORMER

²past *prep or adv* : BEYOND

³past *n* **1** : time gone by **2** ♦ : something that happened or was done in a former time **3** : the past tense; *also* : a verb form in it **4** : a secret past life

♦ history, yesteryear, yore; *also* bygone; flashback; annals, chronicle, record; memoir; antiquity

pas·ta \'päs-tə\ *n* [It]   **1** : a paste in processed form (as macaroni) or in the form of fresh dough (as ravioli)   **2** : a dish of cooked pasta

¹paste \'pāst\ *n* [ME, fr. AF, fr. LL *pasta* dough, paste]   **1** : DOUGH   **2** : a smooth food product made by evaporation or grinding ⟨tomato ~⟩   **3** : a shaped dough (as spaghetti or ravioli)   **4** : a preparation (as of flour and water) for sticking things together   **5** : a brilliant glass used for artificial gems

²paste *vb* **past·ed; past·ing**   **1** : to cause to adhere by paste : STICK   **2** : to put (something copied or cut from a computer document) into another place

³paste *vb* **past·ed; past·ing** : to strike hard at

paste·board \'pāst-ˌbōrd\ *n* : CARDBOARD

¹pas·tel \pas-'tel\ *n*   **1** : a paste made of powdered pigment; *also* : a crayon of such paste   **2** : a drawing in pastel   **3** : a pale or light color

²pastel *adj*   **1** : of or relating to a pastel   **2** ♦ : pale in color

   ♦ dull, light, pale, washed-out — more at PALE

pas·tern \'pas-tərn\ *n* : the part of a horse's foot extending from the fetlock to the top of the hoof

pas·teur·i·za·tion \ˌpas-chə-rə-'zā-shən, ˌpas-tə-\ *n* : partial sterilization of a substance (as milk) by heat or radiation — **pas·teur·ize** \'pas-chə-ˌrīz, 'pas-tə-\ *vb* — **pas·teur·iz·er** *n*

pas·tiche \pas-'tēsh\ *n* : a composition (as in literature or music) made up of selections from different works

pas·tille \pas-'tēl\ *n* : LOZENGE 2

pas·time \'pas-ˌtīm\ *n* : DIVERSION; *esp* : something that serves to make time pass agreeably

pas·tor \'pas-tər\ *n* [ME *pastour*, fr. AF, fr. L *pastor*, herdsman, fr. *pascere* to feed, pasture, nurture] : a minister or priest serving a local church or parish — **pas·tor·ate** \-tə-rət\ *n*

¹pas·to·ral \'pas-tə-rəl\ *adj*   **1** ♦ : of or relating to shepherds or to rural life   **2** : of or relating to spiritual guidance esp. of a congregation   **3** ♦ : of or relating to the pastor of a church

   ♦ [1] bucolic, country, rural, rustic — more at RURAL
   ♦ [3] clerical, ministerial, priestly, sacerdotal — more at CLERICAL

²pastoral *n* : a literary work dealing with shepherds or rural life

pas·to·rale \ˌpas-tə-'räl, -'ral\ *n* [It] : a musical composition having a pastoral theme

past participle *n* : a participle that typically expresses completed action, that is one of the principal parts of the verb, and that is used in the formation of perfect tenses in the active voice and of all tenses in the passive voice

pas·tra·mi \pə-'strä-mē\ *n* [Yiddish *pastrame*] : a highly seasoned smoked beef prepared esp. from shoulder cuts

pas·try \'pā-strē\ *n, pl* **pastries** : sweet baked goods made of dough or with a crust made of enriched dough

pas·tur·age \'pas-chə-rij\ *n* : PASTURE

¹pas·ture \'pas-chər\ *n*   **1** : plants (as grass) for the feeding esp. of grazing livestock   **2** ♦ : land or a plot of land used for grazing

   ♦ range — more at RANGE

²pasture *vb* **pas·tured; pas·tur·ing**   **1** ♦ : to feed on growing herbage : GRAZE   **2** : to use as pasture

   ♦ browse, forage, graze — more at GRAZE

pasty \'pā-stē\ *adj* **past·i·er; -est**   **1** : resembling paste   **2** ♦ : pallid and unhealthy in appearance

   ♦ ashen, cadaverous, livid, lurid, pale, peaked, sallow — more at PALE

¹pat \'pat\ *n*   **1** : a light tap esp. with the hand or a flat instrument; *also* : the sound made by it   **2** : something (as butter) shaped into a small flat usu. square individual portion

²pat *adv* : in a pat manner : PERFECTLY

³pat *vb* **pat·ted; pat·ting**   **1** : to strike lightly with a flat instrument   **2** : to flatten, smooth, or put into place or shape with a pat   **3** : to tap gently or lovingly with the hand

⁴pat *adj*   **1** : exactly suited to the occasion : APT   **2** : mem-

orized exactly   **3** ♦ : characterized by firmness or obduracy : UNYIELDING

   ♦ adamant, hard, immovable, implacable, inflexible, rigid, unbending, uncompromising, unrelenting, unyielding

PAT *abbr* point after touchdown

¹patch \'pach\ *n*   **1** : a piece used to cover a torn or worn place; *also* : one worn on a garment as an ornament or insignia   **2** : a small area distinct from that about it   **3** : a shield worn over the socket of an injured or missing eye   **4** : a small piece : SCRAP

²patch *vb*   **1** : to mend or cover with a patch   **2** : to make of fragments   **3** ♦ : to repair usu. in hasty fashion

   ♦ doctor, fix, mend, recondition, renovate, repair, revamp — more at MEND

patch·ou·li \'pa-chə-lē, pə-'chü-lē\ *n* : a heavy perfume made from the fragrant essential oil of an Asian mint; *also* : the plant itself

patch test *n* : a test for allergic sensitivity made by applying to the unbroken skin small pads soaked with the allergen to be tested

patch·work \'pach-ˌwərk\ *n* : something made of pieces of different materials, shapes, or colors

patchy \'pa-chē\ *adj* **patch·i·er; -est** : marked by or consisting of patches; *also* : irregular in appearance or quality — **patch·i·ness** \-chē-nəs\ *n*

pate \'pāt\ *n* ♦ : a person's head; *esp* : the crown of the head

   ♦ head, noggin, poll — more at HEAD

pâ·té *also* **pate** \pä-'tā\ *n* [F]   **1** : a meat or fish pie or patty   **2** : a spread of finely chopped or pureed seasoned meat

pa·tel·la \pə-'te-lə\ *n, pl* **-lae** \-'te-(ˌ)lē, -ˌlī\ *or* **-las** [L] : KNEECAP

pat·en \'pat-ᵊn\ *n*   **1** : PLATE; *esp* : one of precious metal for the eucharistic bread   **2** : a thin disk

¹pa·tent *1 & 4 are* 'pat-ᵊnt, *Brit also* 'pāt-, *2 & 3 are* 'pat-ᵊnt, 'pāt-\ *adj*   **1** : open to public inspection — used chiefly in the phrase *letters patent*   **2** : free from obstruction   **3** ♦ : readily visible or intelligible : OBVIOUS   **4** : protected by a patent — **pat·ent·ly** *adv*

   ♦ apparent, broad, clear, clear-cut, distinct, evident, lucid, manifest, obvious, palpable, perspicuous, plain, transparent, unambiguous, unequivocal, unmistakable — more at CLEAR

²pat·ent \'pat-ᵊnt, *Brit also* 'pāt-\ *n*   **1** : an official document conferring a right or privilege   **2** : a document securing to an inventor for a term of years exclusive right to his or her invention   **3** : something patented

³pat·ent *vb* : to secure by patent

pat·en·tee \ˌpat-ᵊn-'tē, *Brit also* ˌpāt-\ *n* : one to whom a grant is made or a privilege secured by patent

pat·ent medicine \'pat-ᵊnt-\ *n* : a packaged nonprescription drug protected by a trademark; *also* : any proprietary drug

pa·ter·fa·mil·i·as \ˌpā-tər-fə-'mi-lē-əs\ *n, pl* **pa·tres·fa·mil·i·as** \ˌpā-ˌtrēz-\ [L] : the father of a family : the male head of a household

pa·ter·nal \pə-'tərn-ᵊl\ *adj*   **1** : FATHERLY   **2** : related through or inherited or derived from a father — **pa·ter·nal·ly** *adv*

pa·ter·nal·ism \-ˌi-zəm\ *n* : a system under which an authority treats those under its control paternally (as by regulating their conduct and supplying their needs)

pa·ter·ni·ty \pə-'tər-nə-tē\ *n*   **1** : FATHERHOOD   **2** : descent from a father

¹path \'path, 'pàth\ *n, pl* **paths** \'pathz, 'paths, 'pàthz, 'pàths\   **1** ♦ : a trodden way   **2** ♦ : a line of travel : ROUTE — **path·less** *adj*

   ♦ [1] footpath, trace, track, trail — more at TRAIL
   ♦ [2] course, line, route, track, way; *also* circle, circuit, loop, orbit; flight path, trajectory; ascent, descent

²path *or* **pathol** *abbr* pathology

path·break·ing \'path-ˌbrā-kiŋ\ *adj* : TRAILBLAZING

pa·thet·ic \pə-'the-tik\ *adj*   **1** ♦ : evoking tenderness, pity, or sorrow   **2** : pitifully inadequate — **pa·thet·i·cal·ly** \-ti-k(ə-)lē\ *adv*

♦ depressing, dismal, dreary, heartbreaking, melancholy, sad, sorry, tearful — more at SAD

path·find·er \'path-ˌfīn-dər, 'påth-\ *n* : one that discovers a way; *esp* : one that explores untraveled regions to mark out a new route

patho·gen \'pa-thə-jən\ *n* : a specific agent (as a bacterium) causing disease — **patho·gen·ic** \ˌpa-thə-'je-nik\ *adj* — **patho·ge·nic·i·ty** \-jə-'ni-sə-tē\ *n*

pa·thog·ra·phy \pə-'thä-grə-fē\ *n* : biography focusing on a person's flaws and misfortunes

pa·thol·o·gy \pə-'thä-lə-jē\ *n, pl* **-gies** 1 : the study of the essential nature of disease 2 : the abnormality of structure and function characteristic of a disease — **path·o·log·i·cal** \ˌpa-thə-'lä-ji-kəl\ *adj* — **pa·thol·o·gist** \pə-'thä-lə-jist\ *n*

pa·thos \'pā-ˌthäs, -ˌthōs\ *n* : an element in experience or artistic representation evoking pity or compassion

path·way \'path-ˌwā, 'påth-\ *n* : PATH

pa·tience \'pā-shəns\ *n* 1 ♦ : the capacity, habit, or fact of being patient 2 *chiefly Brit* : SOLITAIRE 2

♦ forbearance, long-suffering, sufferance, tolerance; *also* acquiescence, resignation; passivity, compliance, docility, obedience, subordination, willingness; discipline, self-control; submission *Ant* impatience

¹**pa·tient** \'pā-shənt\ *adj* 1 ♦ : bearing pain or trials without complaint 2 : showing self-control : CALM 3 ♦ : steadfast despite opposition, difficulty, or adversity : PERSEVERING — **pa·tient·ly** *adv*

♦ [1] forbearing, long-suffering, stoic, tolerant, uncomplaining; *also* lenient; acquiescent, passive, resigned, unresistant, unresisting, yielding; agreeable, amenable, compliant, complying, docile, obedient, submissive, subordinate, tractable, willing; slavish, subservient; amiable, obliging; collected, composed, constrained, contained, curbed, inhibited, repressed, restrained; disciplined, self-contained; apathetic, unresponsive *Ant* complaining, fed up, impatient, protesting ♦ [3] dogged, insistent, persevering, persistent, pertinacious, tenacious — more at PERSISTENT

²**patient** *n* : one under medical care

pa·ti·na \'pa-tə-nə, pə-'tē-\ *n, pl* **pa·ti·nas** \-nəz\ *or* **pa·ti·nae** \'pa-tə-ˌnē, -ˌnī\ 1 : a green film formed on copper and bronze by exposure to moist air 2 : a superficial covering or exterior

pa·tio \'pa-tē-ˌō, 'pä-\ *n, pl* **pa·ti·os** 1 : a court or enclosure adjacent to a building : COURTYARD 2 : an often paved area near a dwelling used esp. for outdoor dining

pa·tois \'pa-ˌtwä\ *n, pl* **pa·tois** \-ˌtwäz\ [F] 1 : a dialect other than the standard dialect; *esp* : uneducated or provincial speech 2 ♦ : the characteristic special language of an occupational or social group : JARGON

♦ argot, cant, dialect, jargon, language, lingo, patter, slang, vocabulary — more at DIALECT

pa·tri·arch \'pā-trē-ˌärk\ *n* 1 : a man who is father or founder (as of a tribe) 2 : a venerable old man 3 : an ecclesiastical dignitary (as the bishop of an Eastern Orthodox see) — **pa·tri·ar·chal** \ˌpā-trē-'är-kəl\ *adj* — **pa·tri·arch·ate** \'pā-trē-ˌär-kət, -ˌkāt\ *n* — **pa·tri·ar·chy** \-ˌär-kē\ *n*

¹**pa·tri·cian** \pə-'tri-shən\ *n* : a person of high birth : ARISTOCRAT

²**patrician** *adj* ♦ : of, relating to, or characteristic of patricians

♦ aristocratic, genteel, gentle, grand, highborn, noble, wellborn — more at NOBLE

pat·ri·cide \'pa-tre-ˌsīd\ *n* 1 : one who murders his or her own father 2 : the murder of one's own father

pat·ri·mo·ny \'pa-trə-ˌmō-nē\ *n* : something (as an estate) inherited or derived esp. from one's father : HERITAGE — **pat·ri·mo·ni·al** \ˌpa-trə-'mō-nē-əl\ *adj*

pa·tri·ot \'pā-trē-ət, -ˌät\ *n* [MF *patriote* compatriot, fr. LL *patriota*, fr. Gk *patriōtēs*, fr. *patria* lineage, fr. *patr-, patēr* father] : one who loves his or her country — **pa·tri·ot·ic**

\ˌpā-trē-'ä-tik\ *adj* — **pa·tri·ot·i·cal·ly** \-ti-k(ə-)lē\ *adv* — **pa·tri·o·tism** \'pā-trē-ə-ˌti-zəm\ *n*

pa·tris·tic \pə-'tris-tik\ *adj* : of or relating to the church fathers or their writings

¹**pa·trol** \pə-'trōl\ *n* : the action of going the rounds (as of an area) for observation or the maintenance of security; *also* : a person or group performing such an action

²**patrol** *vb* **pa·trolled; pa·trol·ling** : to carry out a patrol

pa·trol·man \pə-'trōl-mən\ *n* : a police officer assigned to a beat

patrol wagon *n* : PADDY WAGON

pa·tron \'pā-trən\ *n* [ME, fr. AF, fr. ML & L; ML *patronus* patron saint, patron of a benefice, pattern, fr. L, defender, fr. *patr-, pater* father] 1 : a person chosen or named as special protector 2 ♦ : a wealthy or influential supporter ⟨~ of poets⟩; *also* : BENEFACTOR 3 ♦ : a regular client or customer

♦ [2] backer, guarantor, sponsor, surety — more at SPONSOR ♦ [3] customer, guest — more at CUSTOMER

pa·tron·age \'pa-trə-nij, 'pā-\ *n* 1 : the support or influence of a patron 2 : the trade of customers 3 : control of appointment to government jobs

pa·tron·ess \'pā-trə-nəs\ *n* : a woman who is a patron

pa·tron·ise *chiefly Brit var of* PATRONIZE

pa·tron·ize \'pā-trə-ˌnīz, 'pa-\ *vb* **-ized; -iz·ing** 1 : to be a customer of 2 : to treat condescendingly, haughtily, or coolly 3 ♦ : to act as patron of : provide aid or support for

♦ advocate, back, champion, endorse, support — more at SUPPORT

pat·ro·nym·ic \ˌpa-trə-'ni-mik\ *n* : a name derived from the name of one's father or a paternal ancestor usu. by the addition of an affix

pa·troon \pə-'trün\ *n* : the proprietor of a manorial estate esp. in New York under Dutch rule

pat·sy \'pat-sē\ *n, pl* **pat·sies** : a person who is easily duped or victimized

¹**pat·ter** \'pa-tər\ *vb* : to talk glibly or mechanically

²**patter** *n* 1 ♦ : a specialized lingo 2 : extremely rapid talk ⟨a comedian's ~⟩

♦ argot, cant, dialect, jargon, language, lingo, patois, slang, vocabulary — more at DIALECT

³**patter** *vb* : to strike, pat, or tap rapidly

⁴**patter** *n* : a quick succession of taps or pats ⟨the ~ of rain⟩

¹**pat·tern** \'pa-tərn\ *n* [ME *patron*, fr. AF, fr. ML *patronus*, fr. L, defender, fr. *patr-, pater* father] 1 : an ideal model 2 : something used as a model for making things ⟨a dressmaker's ~⟩ 3 : SAMPLE 4 ♦ : an artistic design 5 : CONFIGURATION 6 ♦ : an established mode of behavior or set of beliefs or attitudes

♦ [4] design, figure, motif, motive; *also* device; adornment, caparison, decoration, embellishment, frill, garnish, ornament, trim ♦ [6] custom, fashion, groove, habit, practice, routine, rut, treadmill, way, wont

²**pattern** *vb* : to form according to a pattern

pat·ty *also* **pat·tie** \'pa-tē\ *n, pl* **patties** 1 : a little pie 2 ♦ : a small flat cake esp. of chopped food

♦ cutlet, fritter

pau·ci·ty \'pȯ-sə-tē\ *n* ♦ : smallness of number or quantity

♦ dearth, deficiency, deficit, failure, famine, inadequacy, insufficiency, lack, poverty, scantiness, scarcity, shortage, want — more at DEFICIENCY

paunch \'pȯnch\ *n* : a usu. large belly : POTBELLY — **paunchy** *adj*

pau·per \'pȯ-pər\ *n* : a person without means of support except from charity — **pau·per·ize** \-pə-ˌrīz\ *vb*

pau·per·ism \'pȯ-pə-ˌri-zəm\ *n* ♦ : the quality or state of being a pauper

♦ beggary, destitution, impecuniousness, impoverishment, indigence, need, penury, poverty, want — more at POVERTY

¹pause \'póz\ *n* **1** ♦ : a temporary stop; *also* : a period of inaction **2** : a brief suspension of the voice **3** : a sign (as ⌢) above or below a musical note or rest to show it is to be prolonged **4** : a reason for pausing **5** : a function of an electronic device that pauses a recording

♦ break, breath, breathe, interruption, lull; *also* time-out; interim, interlude, intermission, interval, recess, respite, rest; cessation, discontinuance, ending, expiration, finishing, stopping, termination; abeyance, moratorium, surcease, suspension; discontinuity, gap, hiatus

²pause *vb* **paused; paus·ing** : to stop, rest, or linger for a time

pave \'pāv\ *vb* **paved; pav·ing** : to cover (as a road) with hard material in order to smooth or firm the surface

pave·ment \'pāv-mənt\ *n* **1** : a paved surface **2** : the material with which something is paved

pa·vil·ion \pə-'vil-yən\ *n* [ME *pavilloun, pavillioun,* fr. AF, fr. L *papilion-, papilio* butterfly] **1** : a large tent **2** : a light structure (as in a park) used for entertainment or shelter

pav·ing \'pā-viŋ\ *n* : PAVEMENT

¹paw \'pó\ *n* : the foot of a quadruped (as a dog or lion) having claws

²paw *vb* **1** : to touch or strike with a paw; *also* : to scrape with a hoof **2** : to feel or handle clumsily or rudely **3** : to flail about or grab for with the hands

pawl \'pól\ *n* : a pivoted tongue or sliding bolt designed to fall into notches on another machine part to permit motion in one direction only

¹pawn \'pón\ *n* [ME *pown,* fr. AF *peoun, paun,* fr. ML *pedon-, pedo* foot soldier, fr. LL, one with broad feet, fr. L *ped-, pes* foot] : a chess piece of the least value

²pawn *n* **1** ♦ : something deposited as security for a loan; *also* : HOSTAGE **2** : the state of being pledged

♦ gage, guarantee, guaranty, pledge, security — more at PLEDGE

³pawn *vb* : to deposit as a pledge

pawn·bro·ker \'pón-ˌbrō-kər\ *n* : one who lends money on goods pledged

Paw·nee \pó-'nē\ *n, pl* **Pawnee** *or* **Pawnees** : a member of an American Indian people orig. of Kansas and Nebraska

pawn·shop \'pón-ˌshäp\ *n* : a pawnbroker's place of business

paw·paw *also* **pa·paw** *n* **1** \pə-'pó\ : PAPAYA **2** \'pä-ˌpó, 'pó-\ : a No. American tree with green-skinned edible fruit; *also* : its fruit

¹pay \'pā\ *vb* **paid** \'pād\ *also in sense 7* **payed; pay·ing** [ME, fr. AF *paier,* fr. L *pacare* to pacify, fr. *pac-, pax* peace] **1** ♦ : to make due return to for goods or services ⟨~ the grocer⟩ **2** ♦ : to discharge indebtedness for : SETTLE ⟨~ a bill⟩ **3** : to give in forfeit ⟨~ the penalty⟩ **4** : REQUITE **5** : to give, offer, or make freely or as fitting ⟨~ attention⟩ **6** ♦ : to be profitable to : RETURN **7** : to make slack and allow to run out ⟨~ out a rope⟩ **8** ♦ : to give in return for goods or service ⟨~ good money⟩ — **pay·ee** \pā-'ē\ *n* — **pay·er** *n*

♦ [1] compensate, recompense, remunerate; *also* reimburse, repay, requite; pay off, pay up, prepay ♦ [2] clear, discharge, foot, liquidate, pay off, quit, recompense, settle, spring, stand **Ant** repudiate ♦ [6] give, return, yield — more at YIELD ♦ [8] disburse, expend, give, lay out, spend — more at SPEND

²pay *n* **1** ♦ : something paid for a purpose and esp. as a salary or wage **2** : the status of being paid by an employer : EMPLOY

♦ compensation, consideration, payment, recompense, remittance, remuneration, requital — more at PAYMENT ♦ emolument, hire, payment, salary, stipend, wage — more at WAGE

³pay *adj* **1** : containing something valuable (as gold) ⟨~ dirt⟩ **2** : equipped to receive a fee for use ⟨~ telephone⟩ **3** : requiring payment

pay·able \'pā-ə-bəl\ *adj* ♦ : that may, can, or must be paid

♦ outstanding, overdue, unpaid, unsettled — more at OUTSTANDING

pay·back \'pā-ˌbak\ *n* **1** : a return on an investment equal to the original capital outlay **2** : something given in return, compensation, or retaliation

pay·check \'pā-ˌchek\ *n* **1** : a check in payment of wages or salary **2** : WAGES, SALARY

pay·load \-ˌlōd\ *n* ♦ : the load carried by a vehicle in addition to what is necessary for its operation; *also* : the weight of such a load

♦ burden, cargo, draft, freight, haul, lading, load, weight — more at LOAD

pay·mas·ter \-ˌmas-tər\ *n* : one who distributes the payroll

pay·ment \'pā-mənt\ *n* **1** ♦ : the act of paying **2** ♦ : something paid

♦ [1] compensation, disbursement, remittance, remuneration; *also* rendering, tendering; reimbursement, repayment; paying off, paying up **Ant** nonpayment, repudiation ♦ [2] compensation, consideration, deposit, disbursement, expenditure, indemnity, outlay, pay, recompense, redress, remittance, remuneration, rent, reparation, requital, restitution, salary, settlement, stipend, wage

pay·off \-ˌóf\ *n* **1** ♦ : a valuable return : PROFIT; *also* : RETRIBUTION **2** : the climax of an incident or enterprise ⟨the ~ of a story⟩

♦ earnings, gain, lucre, net, proceeds, profit, return — more at PROFIT

pay off *vb* ♦ : to pay (a debt or a creditor) in full

♦ clear, discharge, foot, liquidate, pay, quit, recompense, settle, spring, stand — more at PAY

pay–per–view *n* : a cable television service by which customers can order access to a single airing of a TV feature

pay·roll \-ˌrōl\ *n* : a list of persons entitled to receive pay; *also* : the money to pay those on such a list

payt *abbr* payment

pay up *vb* : to pay what is due; *also* : to pay in full

pay·wall \'pā-ˌwól\ *n* : a system that prevents Internet users from accessing certain Web content without a paid subscription

Pb *symbol* [L *plumbum*] lead

PBS *abbr* Public Broadcasting Service

PBX \ˌpē-(ˌ)bē-'eks\ *n* [*p*rivate *b*ranch *ex*change] : a private telephone switchboard

¹PC \ˌpē-'sē\ *n, pl* **PCs** *or* **PC's** [*p*ersonal *c*omputer] : MICROCOMPUTER

²PC *abbr* **1** Peace Corps **2** percent; percentage **3** politically correct **4** postcard **5** [L *post cibum*] after meals **6** professional corporation

PCB \ˌpē-ˌsē-'bē\ *n* : POLYCHLORINATED BIPHENYL

PCP \ˌpē-ˌsē-'pē\ *n* : PHENCYCLIDINE

pct *abbr* percent; percentage

pd *abbr* paid

Pd *symbol* palladium

PD *abbr* **1** per diem **2** police department **3** potential difference

PDA \ˌpē-ˌdē-'ā\ *n* [*p*ersonal *d*igital *a*ssistant] : a small microprocessor device for storing and organizing personal information

PDQ \ˌpē-ˌdē-'kyü\ *adv, often not cap* [abbr. of *pretty damned quick*] : IMMEDIATELY

PDT *abbr* Pacific daylight (saving) time

PE *abbr* **1** physical education **2** printer's error **3** professional engineer

pea \'pē\ *n, pl* **peas** *also* **pease** \'pēz\ **1** : the round edible protein-rich seed borne in the pod of a widely grown leguminous vine; *also* : this vine **2** : any of various plants resembling or related to the pea

peace \'pēs\ *n* **1** ♦ : a state of calm and quiet; *esp* : public security under law **2** : freedom from disturbing thoughts or emotions **3** ♦ : a state of concord (as between persons or governments); *also* : an agreement to end hostilities — **peace·able** \'pē-sə-bəl\ *adj* — **peace·ably** \-blē\ *adv*

♦ [1] calm, calmness, hush, placidity, quiet, quietness, repose, serenity, still, stillness, tranquility — more at CALM ♦ [3] compatibility, concord, harmony — more at HARMONY

peace·ful \'pēs-fəl\ *adj* ♦ : untroubled by conflict, agitation, or commotion — **peace·ful·ly** *adv*

♦ calm, halcyon, hushed, placid, quiet, serene, still, tranquil, untroubled — more at CALM

peace·keep·ing \'pēs-ˌkē-piŋ\ *n* : the preserving of peace; *esp* : international enforcement and supervision of a truce — **peace·keep·er** *n*

peace·mak·er \-ˌmā-kər\ *n* ♦ : one who settles an argument or stops a fight

♦ arbiter, arbitrator, go-between, intercessor, intermediary, mediator, middleman — more at MEDIATOR

peace·time \-ˌtīm\ *n* : a time when a nation is not at war

peach \'pēch\ *n* [ME *peche*, fr. AF *pesche, peche*, fr. LL *persica*, fr. L (*malum*) *Persicum*, lit., Persian fruit] : a sweet juicy fuzzy-skinned fruit of a small usu. pink-flowered tree related to the cherry and plums; *also* : this tree — **peachy** *adj*

pea·cock \'pē-ˌkäk\ *n* [ME *pecok*, fr. *pe-* (fr. OE *pēa* peafowl, fr. L *pavo* peacock) + *cok* cock] : the male peafowl that can spread its long tail feathers to make a colorful display

pea·fowl \-ˌfau̇(-ə)l\ *n* : any of three very large pheasants often raised as ornamental birds

pea·hen \-ˌhen\ *n* : the female peafowl

¹peak \'pēk\ *n* **1** : a pointed or projecting part **2 a** : the top of a hill or mountain **b** ♦ : a prominent mountain usu. having a well-defined summit : MOUNTAIN **3** ♦ : the front projecting part of a cap **4** : the narrow part of a ship's bow or stern **5** ♦ : the highest level or greatest degree — **peak** *adj*

♦ [2b] mount, mountain — more at MOUNTAIN ♦ [3] bill, visor — more at VISOR ♦ [5] acme, apex, climax, crown, culmination, head, height, meridian, pinnacle, summit, tip-top, top, zenith — more at HEIGHT

²peak *vb* : to bring to or reach a maximum

¹peak·ed \'pēkt\ *adj* : having a peak : POINTED

²peaked \'pē-kəd\ *adj* ♦ : being pale and wan or emaciated; *also* : somewhat unwell

♦ ashen, cadaverous, livid, lurid, pale, pasty — more at PALE ♦ bad, down, ill, indisposed, punk, sick, unhealthy, unsound, unwell — more at SICK

¹peal \'pēl\ *n* **1** : the loud ringing of bells **2** : a set of tuned bells **3** : a loud sound or succession of sounds

²peal *vb* ♦ : to give out peals : RESOUND

♦ chime, knell, ring, toll — more at RING

pea·nut \'pē-(ˌ)nət\ *n* **1** : an annual herb related to the pea but having pods that ripen underground; *also* : this pod or one of its edible seeds **2** *pl* ♦ : a very small amount

♦ mite, pittance, shoestring, song — more at MITE

pear \'par\ *n* : the fleshy fruit of a tree related to the apple; *also* : this tree

pearl \'pərl\ *n* **1** : a small hard often lustrous body formed within the shell of some mollusks and used as a gem **2** ♦ : one that is choice or precious ⟨~s of wisdom⟩ **3** : a slightly bluish medium gray color — **pearly** \'pər-lē\ *adj*

♦ catch, gem, jewel, plum, prize, treasure — more at PRIZE

peas·ant \'pez-ᵊnt\ *n* **1** : any of a class of small landowners or laborers tilling the soil **2** : a usu. uneducated person of low social status — **peas·ant·ry** \-ᵊn-trē\ *n*

pea·shoot·er \'pē-ˌshü-tər\ *n* : a toy blowgun for shooting peas

peat \'pēt\ *n* : a dark substance formed by partial decay of plants (as mosses) in water — **peaty** *adj*

peat moss *n* : SPHAGNUM

¹peb·ble \'pe-bəl\ *n* : a small usu. round stone

²pebble *vb* **peb·bled; peb·bling** : to produce a rough surface texture in ⟨~ leather⟩

peb·bly \'pe-b(ə-)lē\ *adj* ♦ : containing or resembling pebbles

♦ broken, bumpy, coarse, irregular, jagged, lumpy, ragged, rough, rugged, uneven — more at UNEVEN

pec \'pek\ *n* : PECTORAL MUSCLE

pe·can \pi-'kän, -'kan; 'pē-ˌkan\ *n* : the smooth thin-shelled edible nut of a large American hickory; *also* : this tree

pec·ca·dil·lo \ˌpe-kə-'di-lō\ *n, pl* **-loes** *or* **-los** : a slight offense

pec·ca·ry \'pe-kə-rē\ *n, pl* **-ries** : any of several American chiefly tropical mammals resembling but smaller than the related pigs

pec·ca·vi \pe-'kä-ˌvē\ *n* [L, I have sinned, fr. *peccare* to sin] : an acknowledgment of sin

¹peck \'pek\ *n* **1** : a unit of dry capacity equal to ¼ bushel **2** : a large amount

²peck *vb* **1** : to strike or pierce with or as if with the bill **2** : to make (as a hole) by pecking **3** : to pick up with or as if with the bill

³peck *n* **1** : an impression made by pecking **2** : a quick sharp stroke

pecking order *also* **peck order** *n* : a basic pattern of social organization within a flock of poultry in which each bird pecks another lower in the scale without being pecked in return and submits to pecking by one of higher rank; *also* : a social hierarchy

pec·tin \'pek-tən\ *n* : any of various water-soluble plant substances that cause fruit jellies to set — **pec·tic** \-tik\ *adj*

pec·to·ral \'pek-tə-rəl\ *adj* : of or relating to the breast or chest

pectoral muscle *n* : either of two muscles on each side of the body which connect the front walls of the chest with the bones of the upper arm and shoulder

pe·cu·liar \pi-'kyül-yər\ *adj* [ME *peculier*, fr. L *peculiaris* of private property, special, fr. *peculium* private property, fr. *pecus* cattle] **1** ♦ : belonging exclusively to one person or group **2** ♦ : characteristic of only one person, group, or thing : DISTINCTIVE **3** ♦ : differing markedly from the usual or ordinary or accepted : ODD — **pe·cu·liar·ly** *adv*

♦ [1] individual, particular, personal, private, separate, singular, unique — more at INDIVIDUAL ♦ [2] characteristic, classic, distinct, distinctive, individual, proper, symptomatic, typical — more at CHARACTERISTIC ♦ [3] curious, extraordinary, funny, odd, queer, rare, strange, unaccustomed, uncommon, unique, unusual, weird — more at UNUSUAL

pe·cu·liar·i·ty \pi-ˌkyül-'yar-ə-tē, -ˌkyü-lē-'ar-\ *n* **1** : the quality or state of being peculiar **2** ♦ : a distinguishing characteristic **3** ♦ : an odd person, thing, event, or trait

♦ [2] attribute, character, characteristic, feature, mark, point, property, quality, trait — more at CHARACTERISTIC ♦ [3] crotchet, eccentricity, idiosyncrasy, mannerism, oddity, quirk, singularity, trick — more at IDIOSYNCRASY

pe·cu·ni·ary \pi-'kyü-nē-ˌer-ē\ *adj* ♦ : of or relating to money : MONETARY

♦ financial, fiscal, monetary — more at FINANCIAL

ped·a·gogue *also* **ped·a·gog** \'pe-də-ˌgäg\ *n* ♦ : one that teaches : TEACHER

♦ educator, instructor, schoolteacher, teacher — more at TEACHER

ped·a·go·gy \'pe-də-ˌgō-jē, -ˌgä-\ *n* : the art or profession of teaching; *esp* : EDUCATION **2** — **ped·a·gog·ic** \ˌpe-də-'gä-jik, -'gō-\ *or* **ped·a·gog·i·cal** \-ji-kəl\ *adj*

¹ped·al \'ped-ᵊl\ *n* : a lever worked by the foot

²pedal *adj* : of or relating to the foot

³ped·al \'ped-ᵊl\ *vb* **ped·aled** *also* **ped·alled; ped·al·ing** *also* **ped·al·ling** **1** : to use or work a pedal (as of a piano or bicycle) **2** : to ride a bicycle

ped·ant \'ped-ᵊnt\ *n* **1** : a person who makes a show of knowledge **2** : a formal uninspired teacher — **pe·dan·tic** \pi-'dan-tik\ *adj* — **ped·ant·ry** \'ped-ᵊn-trē\ *n*

ped·dle \'ped-ᵊl\ *vb* **ped·dled; ped·dling** : to sell or offer for sale from place to place — **ped·dler** *also* **ped·lar** \'ped-lər\ *n*

ped·er·ast \'pe-də-ˌrast\ *n* [Gk *paiderastēs*, lit., lover of boys] : a man who desires or engages in sexual activity with a boy — **ped·er·as·ty** \'pe-də-ˌras-tē\ *n*

ped·es·tal \'pe-dəst-ᵊl\ *n* **1** : the support or foot of something (as a column, statue, or vase) that is upright **2** : a position of high regard

¹pe·des·tri·an \pə-'des-trē-ən\ *adj* **1** : marked by dullness or ordinariness : ORDINARY **2** : going on foot

²pedestrian *n* : WALKER

pe·di·at·rics \ˌpē-dē-'a-triks\ *n* : a branch of medicine dealing with the development, care, and diseases of children — **pe·di·at·ric** \-trik\ *adj* — **pe·di·a·tri·cian** \ˌpē-dē-ə-'tri-shən\ *n*

pedi·cab \'pe-di-ˌkab\ *n* : a pedal-driven tricycle with seats for a driver and two passengers

ped·i·cure \'pe-di-ˌkyùr\ *n* : care of the feet, toes, and nails; *also* : a single treatment of these parts — **ped·i·cur·ist** \-ˌkyùr-ist\ *n*

ped·i·gree \'pe-də-ˌgrē\ *n* [ME *pedegru*, fr. AF *pé de grue*, lit., crane's foot; fr. the shape made by the lines of a genealogical chart] **1** : a record of a line of ancestors **2** ♦ : an ancestral line — **ped·i·greed** \-grēd\ *adj*

♦ ancestry, birth, blood, bloodline, breeding, descent, extraction, family tree, genealogy, line, lineage, origin, parentage, stock, strain — more at ANCESTRY

ped·i·ment \'pe-də-mənt\ *n* : a low triangular gablelike decoration (as over a door or window) on a building

pe·dom·e·ter \pi-'dä-mə-tər\ *n* : an instrument that measures the distance one walks

pe·do·phile \'pe-də-ˌfī(-ə)l, 'pē\ *n* : one affected with pedophilia

pe·do·phil·ia \ˌpe-də-'fi-lē-ə, ˌpē\ *n* : sexual perversion in which children are the preferred sexual object

pe·dun·cle \'pē-ˌdəŋ-kəl\ *n* : a narrow supporting stalk

¹peek \'pēk\ *vb* **1** : to look furtively **2** : to peer from a place of concealment **3** : to take a brief look : GLANCE

²peek *n* **1** : a furtive look **2** ♦ : a brief look : GLANCE

♦ cast, eye, gander, glance, glimpse, look, peep, regard, sight, view — more at LOOK

¹peel \'pēl\ *vb* [ME *pelen*, fr. AF *peler*, fr. L *pilare* to remove the hair from, fr. *pilus* hair] **1** ♦ : to strip the skin, bark, or rind from **2 a** ♦ : to strip off (as a coat) — often used with *off* **b** : to come off **3** : to lose the skin, bark, or rind

♦ [1] bark, flay, hull, husk, shell, skin; *also* denude, scale, strip; pare ♦ *usu* peel off [2a] doff, put off, remove, take off — more at REMOVE

²peel *n* : a skin or rind esp. of a fruit

peel·ing \'pē-liŋ\ *n* : a peeled-off piece or strip (as of skin or rind)

peen \'pēn\ *n* : the usu. hemispherical or wedge-shaped end of the head of a hammer opposite the face

¹peep \'pēp\ *vb* ♦ : to utter a feeble shrill sound or the slightest sound

♦ cheep, chirp, pipe, tweet, twitter — more at CHIRP

²peep *n* : a feeble shrill sound

³peep *vb* **1** : to look slyly esp. through an aperture : PEEK **2** : to begin to emerge **3** : to look at : WATCH — **peep·er** *n*

⁴peep *n* **1** : a first faint appearance **2** ♦ : a brief or furtive look

♦ cast, eye, gander, glance, glimpse, look, peek, regard, sight, view — more at LOOK

peep·hole \'pēp-ˌhōl\ *n* : a hole to peep through

¹peer \'pir\ *n* **1** ♦ : one of equal standing with another : EQUAL **2** : NOBLE — **peer·age** \-ij\ *n*

♦ coordinate, counterpart, equal, equivalent, fellow, like, match, parallel, rival — more at EQUAL

²peer *vb* **1** : to look intently or curiously **2** : to come slightly into view

peer·ess \'pir-əs\ *n* : a woman who is a peer

peer·less \'pir-ləs\ *adj* ♦ : having no equal : MATCHLESS

♦ incomparable, inimitable, matchless, unequaled, unmatched, unparalleled, unrivaled, unsurpassed

¹peeve \'pēv\ *vb* **peeved; peev·ing** ♦ : to make resentful : ANNOY

♦ aggravate, annoy, bother, bug, chafe, exasperate, gall, get, grate, irk, irritate, nettle, persecute, pique, put out, rasp, rile, vex — more at IRRITATE

²peeve *n* **1** ♦ : a feeling or mood of resentment **2** ♦ : a particular grievance

♦ [1] dudgeon, huff, offense, pique, resentment, umbrage — more at PIQUE ♦ [2] aggravation, annoyance, bother, exasperation, frustration, hassle, headache, inconvenience, irritant, nuisance, pest, problem, thorn — more at ANNOYANCE

pee·vish \'pē-vish\ *adj* **1** : querulous in temperament : FRETFUL **2** ♦ : perversely obstinate **3** ♦ : marked by ill temper — **pee·vish·ly** *adv*

♦ [2] dogged, hardheaded, headstrong, mulish, obdurate, obstinate, opinionated, pertinacious, perverse, pigheaded, stubborn, unyielding, willful — more at OBSTINATE ♦ [3] crabby, cranky, cross, crotchety, grouchy, grumpy, irritable, short-tempered, snappish, snappy, snippy, testy, waspish — more at IRRITABLE

pee·vish·ness \-nəs\ *n* ♦ : the quality or state of being peevish

♦ hardheadedness, mulishness, obduracy, obstinacy, pertinacity, self-will, stubbornness, tenacity — more at OBSTINACY ♦ biliousness, grumpiness, irritability, perverseness, perversity

pee·wee \'pē-ˌwē\ *n* ♦ : one that is diminutive or tiny

♦ dwarf, midget, mite, pygmy, runt — more at DWARF

¹peg \'peg\ *n* **1** : a small pointed piece (as of wood) used to pin down or fasten things or to fit into holes **2** : a projecting piece used as a support or boundary marker **3** : SUPPORT, PRETEXT **4** ♦ : a step or degree esp. in estimation ⟨set him down a ∼⟩ **5** : THROW

♦ cut, degree, grade, inch, notch, phase, point, stage, step — more at DEGREE

²peg *vb* **pegged; peg·ging** **1** : to put a peg into : fasten, pin down, or attach with or as if with pegs **2** : to work hard and steadily : PLUG **3** : HUSTLE **4** : to mark by pegs **5** : to hold (as prices) at a set level or rate **6** ♦ : to place in a definite category **7** : to propel through the air by a forward motion of the hand and arm : THROW **8** ♦ : to work steadily and diligently — often used with *away*

♦ [6] assort, break down, categorize, class, classify, grade, group, place, range, rank, separate, sort — more at CLASSIFY ♦ *usu* peg away [8] drudge, endeavor (*or* endeavour), fag, grub, hustle, labor (*or* labour), plod, plug, slave, slog, strain, strive, struggle, sweat, toil, work — more at LABOR

PEI *abbr* Prince Edward Island

pei·gnoir \pān-'wär, pen-\ *n* [F, lit., garment worn while combing the hair, fr. MF, fr. *peigner* to comb the hair, fr. L *pectinare*, fr. *pectin-, pecten* comb] : NEGLIGEE

¹pe·jo·ra·tive \pi-'jȯr-ə-tiv\ *n* : a pejorative word or phrase

²pejorative *adj* : having negative connotations : DISPARAGING — **pe·jo·ra·tive·ly** *adv*

peke \'pēk\ *n, often cap* : PEKINGESE

Pe·king·ese *or* **Pe·kin·ese** \ˌpē-kə-'nēz, -'nēs; -kiŋ-'ēz, -'ēs\ *n, pl* **Pekingese** *or* **Pekinese** : any of a breed of Chinese origin of small short-legged long-haired dogs

pe·koe \'pē-(ˌ)kō\ *n* : a black tea made from young tea leaves

pel·age \'pe-lij\ *n* ♦ : the hairy covering of a mammal

♦ coat, fleece, fur, hair, pile, wool

pe·lag·ic \pə-'la-jik\ *adj* ♦ : of, relating to, or living or occurring in the open sea : OCEANIC

♦ marine, maritime, oceanic — more at MARINE

pelf \'pelf\ *n* ♦ : something generally accepted as a medium of exchange : MONEY

♦ cash, currency, dough, lucre, money, tender — more at MONEY

pel·i·can \'pe-li-kən\ *n* : any of a genus of large web-footed birds having a pouched lower bill used to scoop in fish

pel·la·gra \pə-'la-grə, -'lä-\ *n* : a disease caused by a diet with too little niacin and protein and marked by a skin rash, disease of the digestive system, and mental disturbances

pel·let \'pe-lət\ *n* **1** : a little ball (as of medicine) **2** : BULLET — **pel·let·al** \-lə-təl\ *adj* — **pel·let·ize** \-ˌtīz\ *vb*

pell–mell \ˌpel-'mel\ *adv* **1** ♦ : in mingled confusion **2** ♦ : in confused haste : HEADLONG

♦ [1] amok, berserk, frantically, harum-scarum, hectically, helter-skelter, madly, wild, wildly — more at HELTER-SKELTER ♦ [2] cursorily, hastily, headlong, hurriedly, precipitately, rashly — more at HASTILY

pel·lu·cid \pə-'lü-səd\ *adj* ♦ : extremely clear : LIMPID, TRANSPARENT

♦ clear, limpid, liquid, lucent, transparent — more at CLEAR

pe·lo·ton \ˌpe-lə-'tän\ *n* : the main body of riders in a bicycle race

¹pelt \'pelt\ *n* ♦ : a skin esp. of a fur-bearing animal

♦ fur, hide, skin — more at HIDE

²pelt *vb* **1** ♦ : to strike with a succession of blows or missiles **2** : to propel through the air by a forward motion of the hand and arm : THROW **3** ♦ : to move rapidly and vigorously

♦ [1] bash, bat, batter, beat, hammer, pound, thrash, thump — more at BEAT ♦ [3] dash, fly, hasten, hurry, hustle, race, rocket, run, rush, shoot, speed, tear, zip, zoom — more at HURRY

pel·vis \'pel-vəs\ *n, pl* **pel·vis·es** \-və-səz\ *or* **pel·ves** \-ˌvēz\ : a basin-shaped part of the vertebrate skeleton consisting of the large bone of each hip and the nearby bones of the spine — **pel·vic** \-vik\ *adj*

pem·mi·can *also* **pem·i·can** \'pe-mi-kən\ *n* : dried meat pounded fine and mixed with melted fat

¹pen \'pen\ *vb* **penned; pen·ning** ♦ : to shut in or as if in a pen

♦ cage, closet, coop up, corral, encase, enclose, envelop, fence, hedge, hem, house, immure, wall — more at ENCLOSE

²pen *n* **1** ♦ : a small enclosure for animals **2** : a small place of confinement or storage

♦ cage, coop, corral, pound — more at CAGE

³pen *n* **1** : an implement for writing or drawing with ink or a similar fluid **2** : a writing instrument regarded as a means of expression **3** : STYLUS 3

⁴pen *vb* **penned; pen·ning** ♦ : to set down in writing as the author of : WRITE

♦ author, scribble, write — more at WRITE

⁵pen *n* ♦ : a state or federal prison : PENITENTIARY

♦ brig, hoosegow, jail, jug, lockup, penitentiary, prison, stockade — more at JAIL

⁶pen *abbr* peninsula

PEN *abbr* International Association of Poets, Playwrights, Editors, Essayists and Novelists

pe·nal \'pēn-ᵊl\ *adj* ♦ : of or relating to punishment

♦ corrective, disciplinary, punitive — more at PUNITIVE

pe·nal·ise *chiefly Brit var of* PENALIZE

pe·nal·ize \'pēn-ᵊl-ˌīz, 'pen-\ *vb* **-ized; -iz·ing** ♦ : to put a penalty on

♦ castigate, chasten, chastise, correct, discipline, punish — more at PUNISH

pen·al·ty \'pen-ᵊl-tē\ *n, pl* **-ties 1** ♦ : punishment for crime or offense **2** ♦ : something forfeited when a person fails to do something agreed to **3** : disadvantage, loss, or hardship due to some action

♦ [1] castigation, chastisement, correction, desert, discipline, nemesis, punishment, wrath — more at PUNISHMENT ♦ [2] damages, fine, forfeit, mulct — more at FINE

pen·ance \'pe-nəns\ *n* **1** : an act performed to show sorrow or repentance for sin **2** : a sacrament (as in the Roman Catholic Church) consisting of confession, absolution, and a penance directed by the confessor

pence \'pens\ *pl of* PENNY

pen·chant \'pen-chənt\ *n* [F, fr. prp. of *pencher* to incline, fr. VL **pendicare*, fr. L *pendere* to weigh] ♦ : a strong inclination ⟨a ~ for mathematics⟩

♦ bent, devices, disposition, genius, inclination, leaning, partiality, predilection, proclivity, propensity, tendency, turn

¹pen·cil \'pen-səl\ *n* : a writing or drawing tool consisting of or containing a slender cylinder of a solid marking substance

²pencil *vb* **-ciled** *or* **-cilled; -cil·ing** *or* **-cil·ling** : to draw or write with a pencil

pen·dant *also* **pen·dent** \'pen-dənt\ *n* ♦ : a hanging ornament

♦ charm; *also* locket

pen·dent *or* **pen·dant** \'pen-dənt\ *adj* : supported from above : SUSPENDED, OVERHANGING

¹pend·ing \'pen-diŋ\ *prep* **1** : DURING **2** : while awaiting

²pending *adj* **1** ♦ : not yet decided **2** ♦ : ready to take place : IMMINENT

♦ [1] open, undecided, undetermined, unresolved, unsettled; *also* hanging; arguable, debatable, disputable, moot, uncertain, unsure *Ant* decided, determined, resolved, settled ♦ [2] coming, forthcoming, imminent, impending, oncoming — more at FORTHCOMING

pen·du·lous \'pen-jə-ləs, -də-\ *adj* ♦ : hanging loosely

♦ droopy ♦ dependent

pen·du·lum \-ləm\ *n* : a body that swings freely from a fixed point

pe·ne·plain *also* **pe·ne·plane** \'pē-ni-ˌplān\ *n* : a large almost flat land surface shaped by erosion

pen·e·tra·ble \'pe-nə-trə-bəl\ *adj* ♦ : capable of being penetrated

♦ passable, permeable, porous; *also* absorbent *Ant* impassable, impenetrable, impermeable, impervious, nonporous

pen·e·trate \'pe-nə-ˌtrāt\ *vb* **-trat·ed; -trat·ing 1** ♦ : to enter into : PIERCE **2** : PERMEATE **3** : to see into : UNDERSTAND **4** : to affect deeply — **pen·e·tra·tion** \ˌpe-nə-'trā-shən\ *n* — **pen·e·tra·tive** \'pe-nə-ˌtrā-tiv\ *adj*

♦ access, enter, pierce, probe

pen·e·trat·ing *adj* **1** ♦ : having the power of entering, piercing, or pervading ⟨a ~ shriek⟩ ⟨a ~ wind⟩ **2** : ACUTE, DISCERNING ⟨a ~ look⟩

♦ biting, bitter, cutting, keen, piercing, raw, sharp — more at CUTTING

pen·guin \'pen-gwən, 'peŋ-\ *n* : any of various erect short-legged flightless seabirds of the southern hemisphere

pen·i·cil·lin \ˌpe-nə-'si-lən\ *n* : any of several antibiotics produced by molds or synthetically and used against various bacteria

pen·in·su·la \pə-'nin-sə-lə\ *n* [L *paeninsula*, fr. *paene* almost + *insula* island] ♦ : a long narrow portion of land extending out into the water — **pen·in·su·lar** \-lər\ *adj*

♦ arm, cape, headland, point, promontory, spit — more at CAPE

pe·nis \'pē-nəs\ *n, pl* **pe·nis·es** *also* **pe·nes** \-ˌnēz\ : a male organ of copulation that in the human male also functions as the channel by which urine leaves the body

pen·i·tence \'pe-nə-təns\ *n* ♦ : the quality or state of being penitent

♦ contrition, guilt, remorse, repentance, self-reproach, shame — more at GUILT

¹pen·i·tent \'pe-nə-tənt\ *adj* ♦ : feeling sorrow for sins or offenses : REPENTANT — **pen·i·ten·tial** \ˌpe-nə-'ten-chəl\ *adj*

♦ apologetic, contrite, regretful, remorseful, repentant, rueful, sorry — more at CONTRITE

²**penitent** *n* : a penitent person

¹**pen·i·ten·tia·ry** \,pe-nə-'ten-chə-rē\ *n, pl* **-ries** ♦ : a state or federal prison

♦ brig, hoosegow, jail, jug, lockup, pen, prison — more at JAIL

²**penitentiary** *adj* : of, relating to, or incurring confinement in a penitentiary

pen·knife \'pen-,nīf\ *n* : a small pocketknife

pen·light *also* **pen·lite** \-,līt\ *n* : a small flashlight resembling a fountain pen in size or shape

pen·man \'pen-mən\ *n* **1** : COPYIST **2** : one skilled in penmanship **3** : AUTHOR

pen·man·ship \-,ship\ *n* **1** ♦ : the art or practice of writing with the pen **2** ♦ : quality or style of handwriting

♦ handwriting, manuscript, script — more at HANDWRITING

Penn *or* **Penna** *abbr* Pennsylvania

pen name *n* : an author's pseudonym

pen·nant \'pe-nənt\ *n* **1** ♦ : a tapering flag used esp. for signaling **2** : a flag symbolic of championship

♦ banner, colors (*or* colours), ensign, flag, jack, standard, streamer — more at FLAG

pen·ne \'pe-nā\ *n* : short diagonally cut tubular pasta

pen·ni·less \'pe-ni-ləs\ *adj* ♦ : destitute of money

♦ broke, destitute, impecunious, indigent, needy, penurious, poor, poverty-stricken — more at POOR

pen·non \'pe-nən\ *n* **1** : a long narrow ribbonlike flag borne on a lance **2** : WING

Penn·syl·va·nian \,pen-səl-'vā-nyən\ *adj* **1** : of or relating to Pennsylvania or its people **2** : of, relating to, or being the period of the Paleozoic era between the Mississippian and the Permian — **Pennsylvanian** *n*

pen·ny \'pe-nē\ *n, pl* **pennies** \-nēz\ *or* **pence** \'pens\ **1** : a British monetary unit formerly equal to ¹/₁₂ shilling but now equal to ¹/₁₀₀ pound; *also* : a coin of this value **2** *pl* **pennies** : a cent of the U.S. or Canada

pen·ny–pinch·ing \'pe-nē-,pin-chiŋ\ *n* : PARSIMONY — **pen·ny–pinch·er** *n* — **penny–pinching** *adj*

pen·ny·weight \-,wāt\ *n* : a unit of troy weight equal to ¹/₂₀ troy ounce

pen·ny–wise \-,wīz\ *adj* : wise or prudent only in small matters

pe·nol·o·gy \pi-'nä-lə-jē\ *n* : a branch of criminology dealing with prisons and the treatment of offenders

¹**pen·sion** \'pen-chən\ *n* : a fixed sum paid regularly esp. to a person retired from service

²**pension** *vb* : to pay a pension to — **pen·sion·er** *n*

pen·sive \'pen-siv\ *adj* ♦ : musingly, dreamily, or sadly thoughtful — **pen·sive·ly** *adv*

♦ contemplative, meditative, melancholy, reflective, ruminant, thoughtful — more at CONTEMPLATIVE

pen·stock \'pen-,stäk\ *n* **1** : a sluice or gate for regulating a flow **2** ♦ : a pipe for carrying water

♦ channel, conduit, duct, leader, line, pipe, tube — more at PIPE

pent \'pent\ *adj* : shut up : CONFINED

pen·ta·gon \'pen-tə-,gän\ *n* : a polygon of five angles and five sides — **pen·tag·o·nal** \pen-'ta-gən-°l\ *adj*

pen·tam·e·ter \pen-'ta-mə-tər\ *n* : a line of verse containing five metrical feet

pen·tath·lon \pen-'tath-lən\ *n* : a composite athletic contest consisting of five events

Pen·te·cost \'pen-ti-,kost\ *n* : the 7th Sunday after Easter observed as a church festival commemorating the descent of the Holy Spirit on the apostles — **Pen·te·cos·tal** \,pen-ti-'käst-°l\ *adj*

Pentecostal *n* : a member of a Christian religious body that stresses expressive worship, evangelism, and spiritual gifts — **Pen·te·cos·tal·ism** \,pen-ti-'käst-°l-i-zəm\ *n*

pent·house \'pent-,haùs\ *n* [alter. of ME *pentis*, fr. AF *apentiz*, fr. *apent*, pp. of *apendre* to attach, hang against] **1** : a shed or sloping roof attached to a wall or building

2 : an apartment built on the top floor or roof of a building **3** ♦ : a smaller structure joined to a building

♦ addition, annex, extension — more at ANNEX

pen·ul·ti·mate \pi-'nəl-tə-mət\ *adj* : next to the last ⟨~ syllable⟩

pen·um·bra \pə-'nəm-brə\ *n, pl* **-brae** \-(,)brē\ *or* **-bras** : the partial shadow surrounding a complete shadow (as in an eclipse)

pe·nu·ri·ous \pə-'nùr-ē-əs, -'nyùr-\ *adj* **1** ♦ : marked by or suffering from penury **2** ♦ : given to or marked by extreme stinting frugality

♦ [1] broke, destitute, impecunious, indigent, needy, penniless, poor, poverty-stricken — more at POOR
♦ [2] cheap, close, mean, niggardly, parsimonious, spare, sparing, stingy, tight, tightfisted, uncharitable — more at STINGY

pen·u·ry \'pe-nyə-rē\ *n* **1** ♦ : extreme poverty **2** : extreme frugality

♦ beggary, destitution, impecuniousness, impoverishment, indigence, need, pauperism, poverty, want — more at POVERTY

pe·on \'pē-,än, -ən\ *n, pl* **peons** *or* **pe·o·nes** \pā-'ō-nēz\ **1** : a member of the landless laboring class in Spanish America **2** : one bound to service for payment of a debt **3** ♦ : one who does menial or tedious labor — **pe·on·age** \-ə-nij\ *n*

♦ drudge, fag, slave, toiler, worker — more at SLAVE

pe·o·ny \'pē-ə-nē\ *n, pl* **-nies** : any of a genus of chiefly Eurasian plants with large often double red, pink, or white flowers; *also* : the flower

¹**peo·ple** \'pē-pəl\ *n, pl* **people** [ME *peple*, fr. AF *peple, peuple*, fr. L *populus*] **1** *pl* : human beings making up a group or linked by a common characteristic or interest **2** *pl* ♦ : human beings — often used in compounds instead of *persons* ⟨sales*people*⟩ **3** *pl* ♦ : the mass of persons in a community : POPULACE; *also* : ELECTORATE ⟨the ~'s choice⟩ **4** *pl* **peoples** ♦ : a body of persons (as a tribe, nation, or race) united by a common culture, sense of kinship, or political organization

♦ [2] folks, humanity, humankind, persons, public, society, world; *also* crowd, masses, snob, populace, proletariat, rabble, riffraff ♦ [3] commoners, herd, masses, mob, masses, plebeians, populace, rank and file — more at MASSES ♦ [4] blood, clan, family, folks, house, kin, kindred, kinfolk, line, lineage, race, stock, tribe — more at FAMILY

²**people** *vb* **peo·pled; peo·pling** : to supply or fill with or as if with people

¹**pep** \'pep\ *n* ♦ : brisk energy or initiative

♦ dash, energy, life, vigor (*or* vigour), vim, vitality — more at VIGOR

²**pep** *vb* **pepped; pep·ping** ♦ : to put pep into : STIMULATE

♦ *usu* **pep up** animate, brace, energize, enliven, fire, invigorate, jazz up, liven up, quicken, stimulate, vitalize, vivify, zip (up) — more at ANIMATE

¹**pep·per** \'pe-pər\ *n* **1** : either of two pungent condiments from the berry (**pep·per·corn** \-,kòrn\) of an Indian climbing plant; *also* : this plant **2** : a plant related to the tomato and widely grown for its hot or mild sweet fruit; *also* : this fruit

²**pepper** *vb* **pep·pered; pep·per·ing** **1** ♦ : to sprinkle or season with or as if with pepper **2** : to shower with missiles or rapid blows

♦ dot, scatter, sow, spray, sprinkle, strew — more at SCATTER

pep·per·mint \-,mint, -mənt\ *n* : a pungent aromatic mint; *also* : candy flavored with its oil

pep·per·o·ni \,pe-pə-'rō-nē\ *n* : a highly seasoned beef and pork sausage

pepper spray *n* : a temporarily disabling aerosol that causes irritation and blinding of the eyes and inflammation of the nose, throat, and skin

pep·pery \'pe-pə-rē\ *adj* **1** : having the qualities of pepper : PUNGENT, HOT **2** : having a hot temper **3** ♦ : full of or exuding emotion or spirit : FIERY

♦ fiery, high-spirited, mettlesome, spirited, spunky — more at SPIRITED

pep·py \'pe-pē\ *adj* ♦ : full of pep

♦ active, animate, animated, brisk, energetic, frisky, gay, jaunty, jazzy, lively, perky, pert, racy, snappy, spirited, sprightly, springy, vital, vivacious — more at LIVELY

pep·sin \'pep-sən\ *n* : an enzyme of the stomach that promotes digestion by breaking down proteins; *also* : a preparation of this used medicinally

pep·tic \'pep-tik\ *adj* [L *pepticus*, fr. Gk *peptikos*, fr. *peptos* cooked, *peptein* to cook, digest] **1** : relating to or promoting digestion **2** : caused by digestive juices ⟨a ∼ ulcer⟩

Pe·quot \'pē-ˌkwät\ *n* : a member of an American Indian people of eastern Connecticut

¹per \'pər\ *prep* **1** ♦ : by means of **2** : to or for each **3** : ACCORDING TO

♦ by, through, with — more at BY

²per *adv* : for each : APIECE

³per *abbr* **1** period **2** person

¹per·ad·ven·ture \'pər-əd-ˌven-chər\ *adv, archaic* : PERHAPS

²peradventure *n* **1** : DOUBT **2** : CHANCE 4

per·am·bu·late \pə-'ram-byə-ˌlāt\ *vb* **-lat·ed; -lat·ing** : to travel over esp. on foot

per·am·bu·la·tion \pə-ˌram-byə-'lā-shən\ *n* ♦ : an act of walking about : STROLL

♦ ramble, stroll, turn, walk — more at WALK

per·am·bu·la·tor \pə-'ram-byə-ˌlā-tər\ *n, chiefly Brit* : a baby carriage

per an·num \(ˌ)pər-'a-nəm\ *adv* [ML] : in or for each year : ANNUALLY

per·cale \(ˌ)pər-'kāl, 'pər-ˌ; (ˌ)pər-'kal\ *n* : a fine woven cotton cloth

per cap·i·ta \(ˌ)pər-'ka-pə-tə\ *adv or adj* [ML, by heads] : by or for each person

per·ceive \pər-'sēv\ *vb* **per·ceived; per·ceiv·ing** **1** ♦ : to attain awareness or understanding of **2** ♦ : to become aware of through the senses — **per·ceiv·able** *adj*

♦ [1] appreciate, apprehend, catch, catch on (to), comprehend, get, grasp, make, make out, notice, see, seize, understand — more at COMPREHEND ♦ [2] feel, scent, see, sense, smell, taste — more at FEEL

¹per·cent \pər-'sent\ *adv* [*per* + L *centum* hundred] : in each hundred

²percent *n, pl* **percent** *or* **percents** **1** : one part in a hundred : HUNDREDTH **2** : PERCENTAGE

per·cent·age \pər-'sen-tij\ *n* **1** : a part of a whole expressed in hundredths **2** : the result obtained by multiplying a number by a percent **3** : ADVANTAGE, PROFIT **4** ♦ : a likelihood based on cumulative statistics : PROBABILITY; *also* : favorable odds

♦ chance, odds, probability — more at PROBABILITY

percentage point *n* : one hundredth of a whole ⟨rates rose one *percentage point* from 6.5 to 7.5 percent⟩

per·cen·tile \pər-'sen-ˌtīl\ *n* : a value on a scale of one hundred indicating the standing of a score or grade in terms of the percentage of scores or grades falling with or below it

per·cept \'pər-ˌsept\ *n* : an impression of an object obtained by use of the senses

per·cep·ti·ble \pər-'sep-tə-bəl\ *adj* ♦ : capable of being perceived — **per·cep·ti·bly** \-blē\ *adv*

♦ appreciable, detectable, discernible, distinguishable, palpable, sensible; *also* audible, observable, tangible, visible; clear, conspicuous, evident, manifest, noticeable, obvious, plain, prominent, striking; apparent, distinct, significant, straightforward *Ant* impalpable, imperceptible, inappreciable, indistinguishable, insensible

per·cep·tion \pər-'sep-shən\ *n* **1** ♦ : an act or result of perceiving **2** : awareness of one's environment through physical sensation **3** ♦ : ability to understand

♦ [1] appreciation, apprehension, comprehension, grasp, grip, understanding — more at COMPREHENSION ♦ [3] discernment, insight, sagacity, sapience, wisdom — more at WISDOM

per·cep·tive \pər-'sep-tiv\ *adj* ♦ : capable of or exhibiting keen perception — **per·cep·tive·ly** *adv*

♦ acute, delicate, keen, sensitive, sharp — more at ACUTE ♦ discerning, insightful, sagacious, sage, sapient, wise — more at WISE

per·cep·tu·al \pər-'sep-chə-wəl\ *adj* : of, relating to, or involving sensory stimulus as opposed to abstract concept ⟨∼ stimulation⟩ — **per·cep·tu·al·ly** *adv*

¹perch \'pərch\ *n* **1** : a roost for a bird **2** : a resting place or vantage point

²perch *vb* **1** ♦ : to alight, settle, or rest on a perch, a height, or a precarious spot **2** ♦ : to place on a perch, a height, or a precarious spot

♦ [1, 2] alight, land, light, roost, settle — more at ALIGHT

³perch *n, pl* **perch** *or* **perch·es** : either of two small freshwater bony fishes used for food; *also* : any of various fishes resembling or related to these

per·chance \pər-'chans\ *adv* ♦ : possibly but not certainly : PERHAPS

♦ conceivably, maybe, perhaps, possibly — more at PERHAPS

per·cip·i·ent \pər-'si-pē-ənt\ *adj* : capable of or characterized by perception — **per·cip·i·ence** \-əns\ *n*

per·co·late \'pər-kə-ˌlāt\ *vb* **-lat·ed; -lat·ing** **1** ♦ : to trickle or filter through a permeable substance **2** : to filter hot water through to extract the essence ⟨∼ coffee⟩ **3** ♦ : to spread gradually — **per·co·la·tor** \-ˌlā-tər\ *n*

♦ [1] bleed, exude, ooze, seep, strain, sweat, weep — more at EXUDE ♦ *usu* percolate into [3] permeate, suffuse, transfuse — more at PERMEATE

per con·tra \(ˌ)pər-'kän-trə\ *adv* [It, by the opposite side (of the ledger)] **1** : on the contrary **2** : by way of contrast

per·cus·sion \pər-'kə-shən\ *n* **1** : a sharp blow : IMPACT; *esp* : a blow upon a cap (**percussion cap**) designed to explode the charge in a firearm **2** : the beating or striking of a musical instrument; *also* : instruments sounded by striking, shaking, or scraping

per di·em \pər-'dē-əm, -'dī-\ *adv* [ML] : by the day — **per diem** *adj or n*

per·di·tion \pər-'di-shən\ *n* **1** : eternal damnation **2** : HELL

per·du·ra·ble \(ˌ)pər-'dùr-ə-bəl, -'dyùr-\ *adj* : very durable — **per·du·ra·bil·i·ty** \-ˌdùr-ə-'bi-lə-tē, -ˌdyùr-\ *n*

per·e·gri·na·tion \ˌper-ə-grə-'nā-shən\ *n* ♦ : a traveling about esp. on foot

♦ expedition, journey, passage, trek, trip — more at JOURNEY

per·e·grine falcon \'per-ə-grən, -ˌgrēn\ *n* : a swift nearly cosmopolitan falcon that often nests in cities and is often used in falconry

pe·remp·to·ry \pə-'remp-tə-rē\ *adj* **1** : barring a right of action or delay **2** ♦ : expressive of urgency or command : IMPERATIVE **3** ♦ : marked by arrogant self-assurance — **pe·remp·to·ri·ly** \-tə-rə-lē\ *adv*

♦ [2] compulsory, imperative, incumbent, involuntary, mandatory, necessary, nonelective, obligatory — more at MANDATORY ♦ [3] arrogant, cavalier, domineering, haughty, high-handed, high-hat, imperious, important, lofty, lordly, masterful, overbearing, overweening, pompous, presumptuous, pretentious, supercilious, superior — more at ARROGANT

¹pe·ren·ni·al \pə-'re-nē-əl\ *adj* **1** : present at all seasons of the year ⟨∼ streams⟩ **2** : continuing to live from year to year ⟨∼ plants⟩ **3** ♦ : existing or continuing a long while : ENDURING **4** : recurring regularly : PERMANENT ⟨∼ problems⟩ — **pe·ren·ni·al·ly** *adv*

♦ abiding, ageless, continuing, dateless, enduring, eternal, everlasting, immortal, imperishable, perpetual, timeless, undying — more at ABIDING

²perennial *n* : a perennial plant
perf *abbr* **1** perfect **2** perforated
¹per·fect \'pər-fikt\ *adj* **1** ♦ : being without fault or defect **2** : EXACT, PRECISE **3** ♦ : lacking in no essential detail : COMPLETE **4** : relating to or being a verb tense that expresses an action or state completed at the time of speaking or at a time spoken of **5** : being completely or exactly what is stated — **per·fect·ness** *n*

♦ [1] absolute, faultless, flawless, ideal, impeccable, letter-perfect, unblemished; *also* consummate, expert, masterly; classic, dandy, excellent, fabulous, fine, first-rate, grand, great, marvelous, prime, superb, superior, superlative, terrific, top, top-notch, unsurpassed; completed, finished, perfected, polished; complete, entire, intact, whole; unbruised, undamaged, unimpaired, uninjured, unspoiled; exceptional, fancy, special *Ant* bad, defective, faulty, imperfect ♦ [3] complete, comprehensive, entire, full, grand, intact, integral, plenary, total, whole — more at COMPLETE

²per·fect \pər-'fekt\ *vb* **1** ♦ : to bring to final form **2** ♦ : to make perfect : IMPROVE

♦ [1] complete, consummate, finalize, finish — more at FINISH ♦ [2] ameliorate, amend, better, enhance, enrich, improve, refine — more at IMPROVE

³per·fect \'pər-fikt\ *n* : the perfect tense; *also* : a verb form in it
per·fect·ible \pər-'fek-tə-bəl, 'pər-fik-\ *adj* : capable of improvement or perfection — **per·fect·ibil·i·ty** \pər-ˌfek-tə-'bi-lə-tē, ˌpər-fik-\ *n*
per·fec·tion \pər-'fek-shən\ *n* **1** : the quality or state of being perfect **2** : the highest degree of excellence **3** : the act or process of perfecting **4** ♦ : an exemplification of supreme excellence

♦ beau ideal, classic, epitome, exemplar, ideal, quintessence — more at QUINTESSENCE

per·fec·tion·ist \-shə-nist\ *n* : a person who will not accept or be content with anything less than perfection
per·fect·ly \'pər-fik(t)-lē\ *adv* **1** ♦ : in a perfect manner **2** ♦ : to a complete or adequate extent

♦ [1] faultlessly, flawlessly, ideally, impeccably; *also* excellently, fabulously, finely, grandly, greatly, marvelously, superbly, superlatively; exceptionally, fancily, specially *Ant* badly, faultily, imperfectly ♦ [2] altogether, completely, dead, entirely, fast, flat, full, fully, quite, thoroughly, well, wholly — more at FULLY

per·fec·to \pər-'fek-tō\ *n, pl* **-tos** : a cigar that is thick in the middle and tapers almost to a point at each end
per·fid·i·ous \pər-'fi-dē-əs\ *adj* ♦ : of, relating to, or characterized by perfidy — **per·fid·i·ous·ly** *adv*

♦ disloyal, faithless, false, fickle, inconstant, loose, recreant, traitorous, treacherous, unfaithful, untrue — more at FAITHLESS

per·fi·dy \'pər-fə-dē\ *n, pl* **-dies** [L *perfidia*, fr. *perfidus* faithless, fr. *per-* detrimental to + *fides* faith] ♦ : violation of faith or loyalty

♦ betrayal, disloyalty, faithlessness, falseness, falsity, inconstancy, infidelity, treachery, unfaithfulness — more at INFIDELITY

per·fo·rate \'pər-fə-ˌrāt\ *vb* **-rat·ed; -rat·ing** ♦ : to bore through : PIERCE; *esp* : to make a line of holes in to facilitate separation

♦ bore, drill, hole, pierce, punch, puncture; *also* broach, tap; poke, prick; penetrate; burrow (into), excavate, gouge, groove, hollow; break, cut, gash, notch, rend, rupture, slash, slit, split

per·fo·ra·tion \ˌpər-fə-'rā-shən\ *n* **1** : the act or process of perforating **2 a** ♦ : a hole or pattern made by or as if

by piercing or boring **b** : one of the series of holes (as between rows of postage stamps) in a sheet that serve as an aid in separation

♦ hole, pinhole, prick, punch, puncture, stab — more at PRICK

per·force \pər-'fōrs\ *adv* ♦ : of necessity

♦ inevitably, necessarily, needs, unavoidably — more at NEEDS

per·form \pər-'fȯrm\ *vb* **1** : to adhere to the terms of : FULFILL **2** ♦ : to bring to a successful issue : CARRY OUT **3** ♦ : to carry out an action or pattern of behavior : FUNCTION **4** : to do in a set manner **5** ♦ : to give a performance (of) — **per·form·er** *n*

♦ [2] accomplish, achieve, carry out, commit, compass, do, execute, follow through, fulfill, make; *also* bring about, effect, effectuate, implement; engage (in), practice; work (at); reenact, repeat; actualize, attain, realize; complete, end, finish, wind up ♦ [3] act, function, operate, take, work — more at ACT ♦ [5] act, impersonate, play, portray — more at ACT

per·for·mance \pər-'fȯr-ˌməns\ *n* **1** ♦ : the act or process of performing **2** : DEED, FEAT **3** : a public presentation

♦ accomplishment, achievement, commission, discharge, enactment, execution, fulfillment, implementation, perpetration — more at COMMISSION

¹per·fume \pər-'fyüm, 'pər-ˌfyüm\ *n* **1** ♦ : a usu. pleasant odor : FRAGRANCE **2** : a preparation used for scenting

♦ aroma, bouquet, fragrance, incense, redolence, scent, spice — more at FRAGRANCE

²perfume *vb* **per·fumed; per·fum·ing** : SCENT
per·fum·ery \ˌpər-'fyü-mə-rē\ *n, pl* **-er·ies** **1** : the art or process of making perfume **2** : PERFUMES **3** : an establishment where perfumes are made
per·func·to·ry \pər-'fəŋk-tə-rē\ *adj* **1** : done merely as a duty **2** ♦ : lacking in interest or enthusiasm — **per·func·to·ri·ly** *adv*

♦ apathetic, casual, disinterested, indifferent, insouciant, nonchalant, unconcerned, uncurious, uninterested — more at INDIFFERENT

per·go·la \'pər-gə-lə\ *n* [It] : a structure consisting of posts supporting an open roof in the form of a trellis
perh *abbr* perhaps
per·haps \pər-'haps\ *adv* ♦ : possibly but not certainly

♦ conceivably, maybe, perchance, possibly; *also* likely, probably; certainly, doubtless, surely, undoubtedly; presumably

per·i·gee \'per-ə-ˌjē\ *n* [MF, fr. NL *perigeum*, fr. Gk *perigeion*, fr. *peri* around, near + *gē* earth] : the point at which an orbiting object is nearest the body (as the earth) being orbited
peri·he·lion \ˌper-ə-'hēl-yən\ *n, pl* **-he·lia** \-'hēl-yə\ : the point in the path of a celestial body (as a planet) that is nearest to the sun
per·il \'per-əl\ *n* **1** ♦ : exposure to the risk of being injured, destroyed, or lost **2** ♦ : something that imperils

♦ danger, hazard, menace, pitfall, risk, threat, trouble — more at DANGER

per·il·ous \'pər-ə-ləs\ *adj* ♦ : full of or involving peril — **per·il·ous·ly** *adv*

♦ dangerous, grave, grievous, hazardous, menacing, parlous, risky, serious, unhealthy, unsafe, venturesome — more at DANGEROUS

pe·rim·e·ter \pə-'ri-mə-tər\ *n* **1** : the boundary of a closed plane figure; *also* : its length **2** ♦ : a line bounding or protecting an area

♦ border, bound, boundary, confines, edge, periphery

peri·na·tal \ˌper-ə-'nā-t²l\ *adj* : occurring in, concerned with, or being in the period around the time of birth ⟨∼ care⟩
¹pe·ri·od \'pir-ē-əd\ *n* [ultim. fr. Gk *periodos* circuit, period

of time, rhetorical period, fr. *peri* around + *hodos* way]
1 : SENTENCE; *also* : the full pause closing the utterance
of a sentence   **2** : END, STOP   **3** : a punctuation mark .
used esp. to mark the end of a declarative sentence or an
abbreviation   **4 ♦** : an extent of time; *esp* : one regarded
as a stage or division in a process or development   **5** : a
portion of time in which a recurring phenomenon completes one cycle and is ready to begin again   **6** : a single
cyclic occurrence of menstruation

> ♦ age, epoch, era, time

²**period** *adj* : of or relating to a particular historical period
⟨~ furniture⟩
pe·ri·od·ic \,pir-ē-'ä-dik\ *adj*   **1 ♦** : occurring at regular intervals of time   **2 ♦** : happening repeatedly from time to
time   **3** : of or relating to a sentence that has no trailing
elements following full grammatical statement of the essential idea

> ♦ [1] constant, frequent, habitual, regular, repeated,
> steady — more at REGULAR ♦ [2] continual, intermit-
> tent, recurrent

¹**pe·ri·od·i·cal** \,pir-ē-'ä-di-kəl\ *adj*   **1** : occurring or recurring at regular intervals or from time to time : PERIODIC
2 : published with a fixed interval between the issues or
numbers   **3** : of or relating to a periodical — **pe·ri·od·i·
cal·ly** \-k(ə-)lē\ *adv*
²**periodical** *n* : a periodical publication
periodic table *n* : an arrangement of chemical elements
based on their atomic structure and on their properties
peri·odon·tal \,per-ē-ō-'dänt-ᵊl\ *adj*   **1** : surrounding a
tooth   **2** : of or affecting periodontal tissues or regions
per·i·pa·tet·ic \,per-ə-pə-'te-tik\ *adj* : performed or performing while moving about : ITINERANT

> ♦ errant, itinerant, nomad, roaming, vagabond, vagrant
> — more at ITINERANT

¹**pe·riph·er·al** \pə-'ri-fə-rəl\ *adj*   **1** : of, relating to, involving,
or forming a periphery or surface part   **2 ♦** : added or
serving as a supplement

> ♦ accessory, auxiliary, supplementary — more at AUX-
> ILIARY

²**pe·riph·er·al** *n* : a device connected to a computer to provide communication or auxiliary functions
peripheral nervous system *n* : the part of the nervous system that is outside the central nervous system and comprises the spinal nerves, the cranial nerves except the one
supplying the retina, and the autonomic nervous system
pe·riph·ery \pə-'ri-fə-rē\ *n, pl* **-er·ies**   **1** : the boundary of a
rounded figure   **2 ♦** : outward bounds : border area

> ♦ border, bound, boundary, circumference, compass,
> confines, edge, end, fringe, margin, perimeter, rim,
> skirt, verge — more at BORDER

pe·riph·ra·sis \pə-'ri-frə-səs\ *n, pl* **-ra·ses** \-,sēz\ : CIRCUM-
LOCUTION
peri·scope \'per-ə-,skōp\ *n* : a tubular optical instrument
enabling an observer to see an otherwise blocked field
of view
per·ish \'per-ish\ *vb* ♦ : to become destroyed or ruined; *esp*
: to have one's life come to an end

> ♦ decease, depart, die, expire, pass, pass away, suc-
> cumb — more at DIE

per·ish·able \'per-i-shə-bəl\ *adj* : easily spoiled ⟨~ foods⟩
— **perishable** *n*
peri·stal·sis \,per-ə-'stöl-səs, -'stal-\ *n, pl* **-stal·ses** : waves
of contraction passing along the walls of a hollow mus-
cular organ (as the intestine) and forcing its contents onward — **per·i·stal·tic** \-'stöl-tik, -'stal-\ *adj*
peri·style \'per-ə-,stīl\ *n* : a row of columns surrounding a
building or court
peri·to·ne·um \,per-ə-tə-'nē-əm\ *n, pl* **-ne·ums** *or* **-nea** : the
smooth transparent serous membrane that lines the cav-
ity of the abdomen — **peri·to·ne·al** \-'nē-əl\ *adj*
peri·to·ni·tis \,per-ə-tə-'nī-təs\ *n* : inflammation of the peri-
toneum

peri·wig \'per-i-,wig\ *n* : WIG
¹**per·i·win·kle** \'per-i-,wiŋ-kəl\ *n* : a usu. blue-flowered
creeping plant cultivated as a ground cover
²**periwinkle** *n* : any of various small edible seashore snails
per·ju·ry \'pər-jə-rē\ *n* : the voluntary violation of an oath
to tell the truth : lying under oath — **per·jure** \'pər-jər\
vb — **per·jur·er** *n*
¹**perk** \'pərk\ *vb*   **1** : to thrust (as the head) up impudently
or jauntily   **2** : to regain vigor or spirit   **3** : to make trim
or brisk : FRESHEN
²**perk** *vb* : PERCOLATE
³**perk** *n* : PERQUISITE — usu. used in pl.
perky \'pər-kē\ *adj* ♦ : sprightly in manner or appearance

> ♦ active, animate, animated, brisk, energetic, frisky,
> gay, jaunty, lively, peppy, spirited, sprightly, springy

per·lite \'pər-,līt\ *n* : volcanic glass that when expanded by
heat forms a lightweight material used esp. in concrete
and plaster and for potting plants
¹**perm** \'pərm\ *n* : PERMANENT
²**perm** *vb* : to give (hair) a permanent
³**perm** *abbr* permanent
per·ma·frost \'pər-mə-,fróst\ *n* : a permanently frozen
layer below the surface in frigid regions of a planet
¹**per·ma·nent** \'pər-mə-nənt\ *adj* ♦ : continuing or enduring
without fundamental or marked change — **per·ma·nence**
\-nəns\ *n* — **per·ma·nen·cy** \-nən-sē\ *n*

> ♦ ceaseless, dateless, deathless, endless, eternal, ever-
> lasting, immortal, perpetual, undying, unending —
> more at EVERLASTING

²**permanent** *n* : a long-lasting hair wave or straightening
per·ma·nent·ly \-lē\ *adv* ♦ : in a permanent manner

> ♦ always, eternally, ever, everlastingly, forever, perpet-
> ually — more at EVER

permanent press *n* : the process of treating fabrics with
chemicals (as resin) and heat for setting the shape and for
aiding wrinkle resistance
per·me·able \'pər-mē-ə-bəl\ *adj* ♦ : having small openings that permit liquids or gases to seep through —
per·me·a·bil·i·ty \,pər-mē-ə-'bi-lə-tē\ *n*

> ♦ passable, penetrable, porous — more at PENETRABLE

per·me·ate \'pər-mē-,āt\ *vb* **-at·ed; -at·ing**   **1 ♦** : to spread
or diffuse through : PERVADE   **2** : to seep through the
pores of : PENETRATE — **per·me·ation** \,pər-mē-'ā-shən\ *n*

> ♦ percolate, suffuse, transfuse; *also* diffuse (through),
> impregnate, pass (into), penetrate; fill (up); drench, in-
> fuse, saturate, soak, steep; flood, glut

Perm·ian \'pər-mē-ən\ *adj* : of, relating to, or being the
latest period of the Paleozoic era — **Permian** *n*
per·mis·si·ble \pər-'mi-sə-bəl\ *adj* ♦ : that may be permitted : ALLOWABLE

> ♦ admissible, allowable, sufferable; *also* acceptable,
> bearable, endurable, tolerable; accredited, allowed,
> authorized, certified, endorsed, OK, permitted, sanc-
> tioned, warranted, mandatory, ordered, required *Ant*
> banned, barred, forbidden, impermissible, interdicted,
> prohibited, proscribed

per·mis·sion \pər-'mi-shən\ *n* ♦ : formal consent : AUTHO-
RIZATION

> ♦ allowance, authorization, clearance, concurrence,
> consent, leave, license (*or* licence), sanction, sufferance;
> *also* imprimatur, seal, signature, stamp; concession,
> patent, permit; acceptance, acquiescence, agreement,
> assent, OK *Ant* interdiction, prohibition, proscription

per·mis·sive \pər-'mi-siv\ *adj* : granting permission; *esp*
: INDULGENT — **per·mis·sive·ly** *adv* — **per·mis·sive·ness** *n*
¹**per·mit** \pər-'mit\ *vb* **per·mit·ted; per·mit·ting**   **1 ♦** : to
consent to : ALLOW ⟨~ access⟩   **2 ♦** : to make possible
3 ♦ : to give leave ⟨~ him to go⟩

> ♦ allow, have, let, suffer

²**per·mit** \'pər-,mit, pər-'mit\ *n* : a written permission : LI-
CENSE ⟨a fishing ~⟩
per·mu·ta·tion \,pər-myu̇-'tā-shən\ *n*   **1** : a major or fun-

damental change **2** : the act or process of changing the order of an ordered set of objects

per·ni·cious \pər-'ni-shəs\ *adj* [ME, fr. AF, fr. L *perniciosus*, fr. *pernicies* destruction, fr. *per-* through + *nec-*, *nex* violent death] ◆ : very destructive or injurious ⟨a ∼ influence⟩ — **per·ni·cious·ly** *adv*

◆ adverse, bad, baleful, baneful, damaging, deleterious, detrimental, evil, harmful, hurtful, ill, injurious, mischievous, noxious, prejudicial — more at HARMFUL

per·ora·tion \'per-ə-,rā-shən, 'pər-\ *n* : the concluding part of a speech

¹**per·ox·ide** \pə-'räk-,sīd\ *n* : an oxide containing a large proportion of oxygen; *esp* : HYDROGEN PEROXIDE

²**peroxide** *vb* **-id·ed; -id·ing** : to bleach with hydrogen peroxide

perp *abbr* **1** perpendicular **2** perpetrator

per·pen·dic·u·lar \,pər-pən-'di-kyə-lər\ *adj* **1** ◆ : standing at right angles to the plane of the horizon **2** : forming a right angle with each other or with a given line or plane — **perpendicular** *n* — **per·pen·dic·u·lar·i·ty** \-,di-kyə-'larə-tē\ *n* — **per·pen·dic·u·lar·ly** *adv*

◆ erect, standing, upright, upstanding, vertical — more at ERECT

per·pe·trate \'pər-pə-,trāt\ *vb* **-trat·ed; -trat·ing** : to carry out (as a crime) : COMMIT — **per·pe·tra·tor** \'pər-pə-,trātər\ *n*

per·pe·tra·tion \,pər-pə-'trā-shən\ *n* ◆ : the act or process of perpetrating

◆ accomplishment, achievement, commission, discharge, enactment, execution, fulfillment, implementation, performance — more at COMMISSION

per·pet·u·al \pər-'pe-chə-wəl\ *adj* **1** ◆ : continuing forever : EVERLASTING **2** : occurring continually : CONSTANT ⟨∼ annoyance⟩

◆ ceaseless, dateless, deathless, endless, eternal, everlasting, immortal, permanent, undying, unending — more at EVERLASTING

per·pet·u·al·ly \pər-'pe-chə-wə-lē\ *adv* **1** ◆ : for a limitless time **2** ◆ : at all times : CONTINUALLY

◆ [1] always, eternally, ever, everlastingly, forever, permanently — more at EVER ◆ [2] always, constantly, continually, ever, forever, incessantly, invariably, unfailingly — more at ALWAYS

per·pet·u·ate \pər-'pe-chə-,wāt\ *vb* **-at·ed; -at·ing** : to make perpetual : cause to last indefinitely ⟨∼ a belief⟩ — **perpet·u·a·tion** \-,pe-chə-'wā-shən\ *n*

per·pe·tu·i·ty \,pər-pə-'tü-ə-tē, -'tyü-\ *n, pl* **-ties** **1** : ETERNITY 1 **2** : the quality or state of being perpetual

per·plex \pər-'pleks\ *vb* ◆ : to disturb mentally; *esp* : CONFUSE

◆ addle, baffle, befog, befuddle, bemuse, bewilder, confound, confuse, disorient, muddle, muddy, mystify, puzzle — more at CONFUSE

per·plexed \-'plekst\ *adj* **1** : filled with uncertainty : PUZZLED ⟨a ∼ look⟩ **2** : full of difficulty : COMPLICATED — **per·plexed·ly** \-'plek-səd-lē\ *adv*

per·plex·i·ty \pər-'plek-sə-tē\ *n* ◆ : the state of being perplexed

◆ bafflement, bewilderment, confusion, distraction, muddle, mystification, puzzlement, whirl — more at CONFUSION

per·qui·site \'pər-kwə-zət\ *n* ◆ : a privilege or profit beyond regular pay

◆ bonus, dividend, extra, lagniappe, tip — more at BONUS

pers *abbr* person; personal

¹**per se** \(,)pər-'sā\ *adv* [L] : by, of, or in itself : as such

²**per se** *adj* : being such inherently, clearly, or as a matter of law

per·se·cute \'pər-si-,kyüt\ *vb* **-cut·ed; -cut·ing** ◆ : to pursue in such a way as to injure or afflict : HARASS; *esp* : to cause to suffer because of belief — **per·se·cu·tion** \,pərsi-'kyü-shən\ *n*

◆ afflict, agonize, bedevil, curse, harrow, martyr, plague, rack, torment, torture — more at AFFLICT
◆ aggravate, annoy, bother, bug, chafe, exasperate, gall, get, grate, irk, irritate, nettle, peeve, pique, put out, rasp, rile, vex — more at IRRITATE

per·se·cu·tor \'pər-si-,kyü-tər\ *n* ◆ : one that persecutes

◆ heckler, oppressor, taunter, tormentor, torturer — more at TORMENTOR ◆ annoyance, bother, gadfly, nuisance, pest, tease — more at NUISANCE

per·se·vere \,pər-sə-'vir\ *vb* **-vered; -ver·ing** : to persist (as in an undertaking) in spite of difficulties — **per·se·ver·ance** \-'vir-əns\ *n*

persevering *adj* ◆ : of or characterized by perseverance

◆ dogged, insistent, patient, persistent, pertinacious, tenacious — more at PERSISTENT

Per·sian \'pər-zhən\ *n* **1** : a native or inhabitant of ancient Persia **2** : a member of one of the peoples of modern Iran **3** : the language of the Persians

Persian cat *n* : any of a breed of stocky round-headed domestic cats that have a long silky coat

Persian lamb *n* : a pelt with very silky tightly curled fur that is obtained from newborn lambs which are older than those yielding broadtail

per·si·flage \'pər-si-,fläzh, 'per-\ *n* [F, fr. *persifler* to banter, fr. *per-* thoroughly + *siffler* to whistle, hiss, boo, ultim. fr. L *sibilare*] ◆ : lightly jesting or mocking talk

◆ banter, chaff, raillery, repartee — more at BANTER

per·sim·mon \pər-'si-mən\ *n* : either of two trees related to the ebony; *also* : the edible usu. orange or red plumlike fruit of a persimmon

per·sist \pər-'sist, -'zist\ *vb* **1** : to go on resolutely or stubbornly in spite of difficulties **2** ◆ : to continue to exist

◆ abide, continue, endure, hold, keep up, last, run on — more at CONTINUE

per·sis·tence \pər-'sis-təns, -'zis-\ *n* **1** ◆ : the action or fact of persisting **2** : the quality or state of being persistent — **per·sis·ten·cy** \-tən-sē\ *n*

◆ continuance, continuation, duration, endurance, subsistence — more at CONTINUATION

per·sis·tent \pər-'sis-tənt\ *adj* **1** ◆ : continuing or inclined to persist in a course **2** : continuing to exist in spite of interference or treatment ⟨a ∼ cough⟩ — **per·sis·tent·ly** *adv*

◆ dogged, insistent, patient, persevering, pertinacious, tenacious; *also* assured, certain, dedicated, determined, firm, intent, positive, resolute, resolved, sure; hardheaded, headstrong, mulish, obdurate, obstinate, opinionated, peevish, perverse, pigheaded, stubborn, unyielding; unfaltering, unhesitating, unwavering; resistant, wayward, wrongheaded; constant, devoted, faithful, good, loyal, staunch, steadfast, steady, true; indomitable, unconquerable; hard, inflexible, relentless, stern, unbending, unrelenting, unyielding

per·snick·e·ty \pər-'sni-kə-tē\ *adj* : fussy about small details

per·son \'pər-sən\ *n* [ME, fr. AF *persone*, fr. L *persona* actor's mask, character in a play, person, prob. fr. Etruscan *phersu* mask, fr. Gk *prosōpa*, pl. of *prosōpon* face, mask] **1** ◆ : a human being : INDIVIDUAL — used in combination esp. by those who prefer to avoid *man* in compounds applicable to both sexes ⟨chair*person*⟩ **2** : one of the three modes of being in the Godhead as understood by Trinitarians **3** : the body of a human being **4** : the individual personality of a human being : SELF **5** : reference of a segment of discourse to the speaker, to one spoken to, or to one spoken of esp. as indicated by certain pronouns

◆ being, body, creature, human, individual, man, mortal — more at HUMAN **persons** folks, humanity, humankind, people, public, society, world — more at PEOPLE

per·so·na \pər-'sō-nə\ *n, pl* **-nae** \-nē\ *or* **-nas** : the personality that a person projects in public

per·son·able \'pər-sə-nə-bəl\ *adj* : pleasant in person : ATTRACTIVE

per·son·age \'pər-sə-nij\ *n* ♦ : a person of rank, note, or distinction

♦ celebrity, figure, light, luminary, notable, personality, somebody, standout, star, superstar, VIP — more at CELEBRITY

¹**per·son·al** \'pər-sə-nəl\ *adj* 1 ♦ : of, relating to, or affecting a person : PRIVATE ⟨∼ correspondence⟩ 2 : done in person ⟨a ∼ inquiry⟩ 3 : relating to the person or body ⟨∼ injuries⟩ 4 : relating to an individual esp. in an offensive way ⟨resented such ∼ remarks⟩ 5 : of or relating to temporary or movable property as distinguished from real estate 6 : denoting grammatical person 7 : intended for use by one person

♦ individual, particular, peculiar, private, separate, singular, unique — more at INDIVIDUAL

²**personal** *n* 1 : a short newspaper paragraph relating to a person or group or to personal matters 2 : a short personal or private communication in the classified ads section of a newspaper

personal computer *n* : a computer with a microprocessor designed for an individual user to run esp. commercial software

personal digital assistant *n* : PDA

per·son·al·ise *chiefly Brit var of* PERSONALIZE

per·son·al·i·ty \,pər-sə-'na-lə-tē\ *n, pl* **-ties** 1 : an offensively personal remark ⟨indulges in *personalities*⟩ 2 ♦ : the collection of emotional and behavioral traits that characterize a person 3 : distinction of personal and social traits 4 ♦ : a well-known person ⟨a TV ∼⟩

♦ [2] character, identity, individuality, self-identity — more at INDIVIDUALITY ♦ [4] celebrity, figure, light, luminary, notable, personage, somebody, standout, star, superstar, VIP — more at CELEBRITY

per·son·al·ize \'pər-sə-nə-,līz\ *vb* **-ized; -iz·ing** 1 : to conceive of or represent as a person or as having human qualities or powers 2 : to make personal or individual; *esp* : to mark as belonging to a particular person

per·son·al·ly \-nə-lē\ *adv* 1 : in person 2 : as a person 3 : as far as oneself is concerned

per·son·al·ty \'pər-sə-nəl-tē\ *n, pl* **-ties** ♦ : personal property

♦ belongings, chattels, effects, holdings, paraphernalia, possessions, things — more at POSSESSION

per·so·na non gra·ta \pər-'sō-nə-,nän-'gra-tə, -'grä-\ *adj* [L] : being personally unacceptable or unwelcome

per·son·ate \'pər-sə-,nāt\ *vb* **-at·ed; -at·ing** : IMPERSONATE, REPRESENT

per·son·i·fi·ca·tion \pər-,sä-nə-fə-'kā-shən\ *n* ♦ : a visible representation of something abstract (as a quality)

♦ embodiment, epitome, incarnation, manifestation — more at EMBODIMENT

per·son·i·fy \pər-'sä-nə-,fī\ *vb* **-fied; -fy·ing** 1 ♦ : to think of or represent as a person 2 ♦ : to be the embodiment of : INCARNATE ⟨∼ the law⟩

♦ [1, 2] embody, epitomize, manifest, materialize, substantiate — more at EMBODY

per·son·nel \,pər-sə-'nel\ *n* ♦ : a body of persons employed

♦ force, help, pool, staff — more at FORCE

per·spec·tive \pər-'spek-tiv\ *n* 1 : the science of painting and drawing so that objects represented have apparent depth and distance 2 ♦ : the aspect in which a subject or its parts are mentally viewed; *esp* : a view of things (as objects or events) in their true relationship or relative importance

♦ angle, outlook, point of view, slant, standpoint, viewpoint — more at POINT OF VIEW

per·spi·ca·cious \,pər-spə-'kā-shəs\ *adj* : having or showing keen understanding or discernment ⟨a ∼ observation⟩ — **per·spi·cac·i·ty** \-'ka-sə-tē\ *n*

per·spi·cu·i·ty \,pər-spə-'kyü-ə-tē\ *n* ♦ : the quality or state of being clear to the understanding

♦ clarity, explicitness, lucidity, simplicity — more at SIMPLICITY

per·spic·u·ous \pər-'spi-kyə-wəs\ *adj* ♦ : plain to the understanding ⟨a ∼ argument⟩

♦ apparent, broad, clear, clear-cut, distinct, evident, lucid, manifest, obvious, palpable, patent, plain, transparent, unambiguous, unequivocal, unmistakable — more at CLEAR

per·spire \pər-'spīr\ *vb* **per·spired; per·spir·ing** : SWEAT — **per·spi·ra·tion** \,pər-spə-'rā-shən\ *n*

per·suade \pər-'swād\ *vb* **per·suad·ed; per·suad·ing** ♦ : to win over to a belief or course of action by argument or entreaty

♦ argue, convince, get, induce, move, prevail, satisfy, talk, win; *also* cajole, coax, exhort, urge, lead on, seduce, snow, tempt; incline, influence, move, prompt, sell, sway; attract, bring, draw, entice, interest; chew over, converse, debate, discuss, dispute, hash (over), moot; reason

per·sua·sion \pər-'swā-zhən\ *n* 1 ♦ : the act or process of persuading 2 ♦ : a system of religious beliefs; *also* : a group holding such beliefs 3 ♦ : an opinion held with complete assurance

♦ [1] convincing, inducement; *also* cajolery, coaxing, exhortation, urging; influencing, prompting, swaying ♦ [2] creed, cult, faith, religion — more at RELIGION ♦ [3] belief, conviction, eye, feeling, judgment (*or* judgement), mind, notion, opinion, sentiment, verdict, view — more at OPINION

per·sua·sive \pər-'swā-siv, -ziv\ *adj* ♦ : tending to persuade — **per·sua·sive·ly** *adv*

♦ cogent, compelling, conclusive, convincing, decisive, effective, forceful, satisfying, strong, telling — more at COGENT

per·sua·sive·ness \-nəs\ *n* ♦ : the quality or state of being persuasive

♦ cogency, effectiveness, force — more at COGENCY

pert \'pərt\ *adj* [ME, evident, attractive, saucy, short for *apert* evident, fr. AF, fr. L *apertus* open, fr. pp. of *aperire* to open] 1 ♦ : saucily free and forward 2 : stylishly trim : JAUNTY 3 : briskly alert and energetic : LIVELY

♦ facetious, flip, flippant, smart — more at FLIPPANT

per·tain \pər-'tān\ *vb* 1 : to belong to as a part, quality, or function ⟨duties ∼*ing* to the office⟩ 2 ♦ : to have reference : RELATE ⟨books ∼*ing* to birds⟩

♦ appertain, apply, bear, refer, relate — more at APPLY ♦ *usu* **pertain to** concern, cover, deal, treat — more at CONCERN

per·ti·na·cious \,pər-tə-'nā-shəs\ *adj* 1 ♦ : holding resolutely to an opinion or purpose 2 ♦ : obstinately persistent ⟨a ∼ bill collector⟩

♦ [1] dogged, hardheaded, headstrong, mulish, obdurate, obstinate, opinionated, peevish, perverse, pigheaded, stubborn, unyielding, willful — more at OBSTINATE ♦ [2] dogged, insistent, patient, persevering, persistent, tenacious — more at PERSISTENT

per·ti·nac·i·ty \,pər-tə-'na-sə-tē\ *n* ♦ : the quality or state of being pertinacious

♦ hardheadedness, mulishness, obduracy, obstinacy, peevishness, self-will, stubbornness, tenacity — more at OBSTINACY

per·ti·nence \'pərt-ᵊn-əns\ *n* ♦ : the quality or state of being pertinent

♦ applicability, bearing, connection, relevance; *also* appropriateness, aptness, fitness, suitability; importance, significance; usefulness *Ant* irrelevance

per·ti·nent \'pərt-ᵊn-ənt\ *adj* ♦ : relating to the matter under consideration

♦ applicable, apposite, apropos, germane, material, pointed, relative, relevant; *also* appropriate, apt, fit, fitting, suitable; important, meaningful, significant;

sensible, useful; admissible, allowable *Ant* extraneous, immaterial, inapplicable, irrelevant, pointless

per·turb \pər-'tərb\ *vb* ♦ : to cause to be worried or upset

♦ agitate, bother, concern, discompose, disquiet, distress, disturb, exercise, freak out, undo, unhinge, unsettle, upset, worry — more at DISTURB

per·tur·ba·tion \ˌpər-tər-'bā-shən\ *n* ♦ : the action of perturbing : the state of being perturbed

♦ agitation, anxiety, apprehension, care, concern, disquiet, nervousness, uneasiness, worry — more at ANXIETY

perturbed \pər-'tərbd\ *adj* ♦ : emotionally disturbed or agitated

♦ aflutter, anxious, edgy, jittery, jumpy, nervous, nervy, tense, troubled, uneasy, upset, worried — more at NERVOUS

per·tus·sis \pər-'tə-səs\ *n* : WHOOPING COUGH
pe·ruke \pə-'rük\ *n* : WIG
pe·ruse \pə-'rüz\ *vb* **pe·rused; pe·rus·ing** : READ; *esp* : to read over attentively or leisurely — **pe·rus·al** \-'rü-zəl\ *n*
Pe·ru·vi·an \pə-'rü-vē-ən\ *n* : a native or inhabitant of Peru
perv \'pərv\ *n, slang* : PERVERT
per·vade \pər-'vād\ *vb* **per·vad·ed; per·vad·ing** : to spread through every part of — **per·va·sive** \-'vā-siv, -ziv\ *adj*
per·verse \pər-'vərs\ *adj* **1** ♦ : turned away from what is right or good : CORRUPT **2** ♦ : obstinate in opposing what is reasonable or accepted **3** ♦ : marked by peevishness or petulance — **per·verse·ly** *adv*

♦ [1] corrupt, debauched, decadent, degenerate, dissolute, perverted, reprobate — more at CORRUPT ♦ [2] dogged, hardheaded, headstrong, mulish, obdurate, obstinate, opinionated, peevish, pertinacious, pigheaded, stubborn, unyielding, willful — more at OBSTINATE ♦ [3] choleric, crabby, cranky, cross, crotchety, grouchy, grumpy, irascible, irritable, peevish, petulant, short-tempered, snappish, snappy, snippy, testy, waspish — more at IRRITABLE

per·verse·ness \-nəs\ *n* ♦ : the quality or state of being perverse

♦ biliousness, grumpiness, irritability, peevishness, perversity

per·ver·sion \pər-'vər-zhən\ *n* **1** ♦ : the action of perverting : the condition of being perverted **2** ♦ : a perverted form of something; *esp* : aberrant sexual behavior

♦ corruption, debasement, debauchery, decadence, degeneracy, degeneration, degradation, demoralization, depravity, dissipation, dissoluteness — more at CORRUPTION

per·ver·si·ty \pər-'vər-sə-tē\ *n* ♦ : the quality or state of being perverse

♦ biliousness, grumpiness, irritability, peevishness, perverseness

¹per·vert \pər-'vərt\ *vb* **1** ♦ : to lead astray : CORRUPT ⟨~ the young⟩ **2** ♦ : to divert to a wrong purpose : MISAPPLY ⟨~ evidence⟩ **3** ♦ : to twist the meaning or sense of — **per·vert·er** *n*

♦ [1] debase, degrade, demean, demoralize, humble, subvert, warp — more at DEBASE ♦ [2] abuse, misapply, misuse, profane, prostitute — more at MISAPPLY ♦ [3] color (*or* colour), distort, falsify, garble, misinterpret, misrepresent, misstate, twist, warp — more at GARBLE

²per·vert \'pər-ˌvərt\ *n* : one that is perverted; *esp* : one given to sexual perversion

♦ decadent, degenerate, libertine, profligate — more at DEGENERATE

per·vert·ed \pər-'vər-təd\ *adj* ♦ : morally degenerate : DEPRAVED

♦ corrupt, debauched, decadent, degenerate, dissolute, perverse, reprobate — more at CORRUPT

pes·ky \'pes-kē\ *adj* **pes·ki·er; -est** : causing annoyance : TROUBLESOME
pe·so \'pā-sō\ *n, pl* **pesos** : the basic monetary unit in many Latin American countries (as Mexico or Chile)
pes·si·mism \'pe-sə-ˌmi-zəm\ *n* [F *pessimisme*, fr. L *pessimus* worst] : an inclination to take the least favorable view (as of events) or to expect the worst — **pes·si·mist** \-mist\ *n*
pes·si·mis·tic \ˌpe-sə-'mis-tik\ *adj* ♦ : of, relating to, or characterized by pessimism

♦ defeatist, despairing, hopeless; *also* cynical, fatalistic; desperate, discouraging, disheartening, inauspicious, unlikely, unpromising; bleak, cheerless, dismal, dreary, gloomy; grim; contrary, hostile, negative *Ant* hopeful, rosy, upbeat

pest \'pest\ *n* **1** : a destructive epidemic disease : PLAGUE **2** : a plant or animal detrimental to humans **3** ♦ : one that pesters : NUISANCE

♦ aggravation, annoyance, bother, exasperation, frustration, hassle, headache, inconvenience, irritant, nuisance, peeve, problem, thorn — more at ANNOYANCE

pes·ter \'pes-tər\ *vb* ♦ : to harass with petty irritations

♦ bother, bug, disturb, intrude — more at BOTHER

pes·ti·cide \'pes-tə-ˌsīd\ *n* : an agent used to destroy pests
pes·tif·er·ous \pes-'ti-fə-rəs\ *adj* **1** : PESTILENT **2** ♦ : causing vexation : ANNOYING ⟨~ vermin⟩

♦ aggravating, annoying, frustrating, galling, irksome, irritating, pesty, vexatious — more at ANNOYING

pes·ti·lence \'pes-tə-ləns\ *n* : a destructive infectious swiftly spreading disease; *esp* : BUBONIC PLAGUE
pes·ti·lent \-lənt\ *adj* **1** ♦ : dangerous to life : DEADLY **2** : PERNICIOUS, HARMFUL **3** : TROUBLESOME **4** : INFECTIOUS, CONTAGIOUS ⟨a ~ disease⟩

♦ baleful, deadly, deathly, fatal, fell, lethal, mortal, murderous, vital — more at DEADLY

pes·ti·len·tial \ˌpes-tə-'len-chəl\ *adj* **1** : causing or tending to cause pestilence : DEADLY **2** : morally harmful
pes·tle \'pes-əl, 'pest-ºl\ *n* : an implement for grinding substances in a mortar — **pestle** *vb*
pesty \'pes-tē\ *adj* ♦ : causing trouble or annoyance

♦ aggravating, annoying, bothersome, frustrating, galling, irksome, irritating, vexatious — more at ANNOYING

¹pet \'pet\ *n* **1** ♦ : a person who is treated with unusual kindness or consideration : FAVORITE, DARLING **2** : a domesticated animal kept for pleasure rather than utility

♦ darling, favorite (*or* favourite), minion, preference — more at FAVORITE

²pet *adj* **1** : kept or treated as a pet ⟨~ dog⟩ **2** : expressing fondness ⟨~ name⟩ **3** ♦ : particularly liked or favored

♦ beloved, darling, dear, favorite (*or* favourite), loved, precious, special, sweet

³pet *vb* **pet·ted; pet·ting** **1** ♦ : to stroke gently or lovingly **2** : to make a pet of : PAMPER **3** ♦ : to engage in amorous kissing and caressing

♦ [1] caress, fondle, love, pat, stroke — more at FONDLE ♦ [3] kiss, make out

⁴pet *n* ♦ : a fit of peevishness, sulkiness, or anger

♦ pout, sulk, sullenness — more at SULK

Pet *abbr* Peter
pet·al \'pet-ºl\ *n* : one of the modified leaves of a flower's corolla
pe·tard \pə-'tärd, -'tär\ *n* : a case containing an explosive to break down a door or gate or breach a wall
pe·ter \'pē-tər\ *vb* : to diminish gradually and come to an end ⟨his energy ~ed out⟩
Pe·ter \'pē-tər\ *n* : either of two books of the New Testament of the Christian Scripture
pet·i·ole \'pe-tē-ˌōl\ *n* : a slender stem that supports a leaf
pe·tite \pə-'tēt\ *adj* [F] : having a small trim figure — usu. used of a woman — **petite** *n*

pe·tit four \ˌpe-tē-ˈfōr\ *n, pl* **petits fours** *or* **petit fours** \-ˈfōrz\ [F, lit., small oven] : a small cake cut from pound or sponge cake and frosted

¹pe·ti·tion \pə-ˈti-shən\ *n* ◆ : an earnest request : ENTREATY; *esp* : a formal written request made to an authority

◆ appeal, cry, entreaty, plea, prayer, solicitation, suit, supplication — more at PLEA

²petition *vb* : to make a request to or for

pe·ti·tion·er \-sh(ə-)nər\ *n* : one that petitions

pe·trel \ˈpe-trəl\ *n* : any of numerous seabirds that fly far from land

pe·tri dish \ˈpē-trē-\ *n*   **1** : a small shallow dish used esp. for growing bacteria   **2** : something fostering development or innovation

pet·ri·fy \ˈpe-trə-ˌfī\ *vb* **-fied; -fy·ing**   **1** : to convert (organic matter) into stone or stony material   **2** : to make rigid or inactive (as from fear or awe) — **pet·ri·fac·tion** \ˌpe-trə-ˈfak-shən\ *n*

pet·ro·chem·i·cal \ˌpe-trō-ˈke-mi-kəl\ *n* : a chemical isolated or derived from petroleum or natural gas — **pet·ro·chem·is·try** \-ˈke-mə-strē\ *n*

pet·rol \ˈpe-trəl\ *n, chiefly Brit* : GASOLINE

pet·ro·la·tum \ˌpe-trə-ˈlā-təm\ *n* : PETROLEUM JELLY

pe·tro·leum \pə-ˈtrō-lē-əm\ *n* [ML, fr. Gk *petra* rock + L *oleum* oil] : an oily flammable liquid obtained from wells drilled in the ground and refined into gasoline, fuel oils, and other products

petroleum jelly *n* : a tasteless, odorless, and oily or greasy substance from petroleum that is used esp. in ointments and dressings

¹pet·ti·coat \ˈpe-tē-ˌkōt\ *n*   **1** : a skirt worn under a dress   **2** : an outer skirt

²petticoat *adj* : of, relating to, or exercised by women : FEMALE

pet·ti·fog \ˈpe-tē-ˌfòg, -ˌfäg\ *vb* **-fogged; -fog·ging**   **1** : to engage in legal trickery   **2** : to quibble over insignificant details — **pet·ti·fog·ger** *n*

pet·ti·fog·ger \ˈpe-tē-ˌfò-gər, -ˌfä-\ *n*   **1** : a lawyer whose methods are petty, underhanded, or disreputable   **2** : one given to quibbling over trifles — **pet·ti·fog·ging** \-giŋ\ *adj or n*

pet·tish \ˈpe-tish\ *adj* : querulous in temperament or mood : PEEVISH

pet·ty \ˈpe-tē\ *adj* **pet·ti·er; -est** [ME *pety* small, minor, alter. of *petit*, fr. AF, small]   **1** : having secondary rank : MINOR ⟨∼ prince⟩   **2** ◆ : of little importance : TRIFLING ⟨∼ faults⟩   **3** ◆ : marked by or reflective of narrow interests and sympathies — **pet·ti·ly** \ˈpe-tə-lē\ *adv* — **pet·ti·ness** \-tē-nəs\ *n*

◆ [2] inconsequential, inconsiderable, insignificant, measly, minute, negligible, nominal, paltry, slight, trifling, trivial — more at NEGLIGIBLE ◆ [3] insular, little, narrow, parochial, provincial, sectarian, small — more at NARROW

petty cash *n* : cash kept on hand for payment of minor items

petty officer *n* : a subordinate officer in the navy or coast guard appointed from among the enlisted personnel

petty officer first class *n* : a petty officer ranking below a chief petty officer

petty officer second class *n* : a petty officer ranking below a petty officer first class

petty officer third class *n* : a petty officer ranking below a petty officer second class

pet·u·lance \ˈpe-chə-ləns\ *n* : the quality or state of being petulant

pet·u·lant \ˈpe-chə-lənt\ *adj* ◆ : marked by capricious ill humor — **pet·u·lant·ly** *adv*

◆ choleric, crabby, cranky, cross, crotchety, grouchy, grumpy, irascible, irritable, peevish, perverse, short-tempered, snappish, snappy, snippy, testy, waspish — more at IRRITABLE

pe·tu·nia \pi-ˈtün-yə, -ˈtyün-\ *n* : any of a genus of tropical American herbs related to the potato and having bright funnel-shaped flowers

pew \ˈpyü\ *n* [ME *pewe*, fr. MF *puie* balustrade, fr. L *podia*, pl. of *podium* parapet, podium, fr. Gk *podion* base, dim. of *pod-, pous* foot] : any of the benches with backs fixed in rows in a church

pe·wee \ˈpē-(ˌ)wē\ *n* : any of various small American flycatchers

pew·ter \ˈpyü-tər\ *n*   **1** : an alloy of tin used esp. for household utensils   **2** ◆ : a bluish gray color — **pewter** *adj* — **pew·ter·er** *n*

◆ gray (*or* grey), leaden, silver, silvery, slate, steely — more at GRAY

pey·o·te \pā-ˈō-tē\ *also* **pey·otl** \-ˈōt-ᵊl\ *n*   **1** : a hallucinogenic drug derived from the peyote cactus and containing mescaline   **2** : a small cactus of the southwestern U.S. and Mexico

pf *abbr*   **1** pfennig   **2** preferred

PFC *or* **Pfc** *abbr* private first class

pfd *abbr* preferred

PFLAG *abbr* parents, families, and friends of lesbians and gays

pg *abbr* page

PG *abbr* postgraduate

PGA *abbr* Professional Golfers' Association

pH \(ˌ)pē-ˈāch\ *n* : a value used to express acidity and alkalinity; *also* : the condition represented by such a value

PH *abbr*   **1** pinch hit   **2** public health

pha·eton \ˈfā-ət-ᵊn\ *n* [F *phaéton*, fr. Gk *Phaethōn*, son of the sun god who persuaded his father to let him drive the chariot of the sun but who lost control of the horses with disastrous consequences]   **1** : a light 4-wheeled horse-drawn vehicle   **2** : an open automobile with two cross seats

phage \ˈfāj\ *n* : BACTERIOPHAGE

pha·lanx \ˈfā-ˌlaŋks\ *n, pl* **pha·lanx·es** *or* **pha·lan·ges** \fə-ˈlan-ˌjēz\   **1** : a group or body (as of troops) in compact formation   **2** *pl* **phalanges** : one of the digital bones of the hand or foot of a vertebrate

phal·a·rope \ˈfa-lə-ˌrōp\ *n, pl* **-ropes** *also* **-rope** : any of a genus of small shorebirds related to sandpipers

phal·lic \ˈfa-lik\ *adj*   **1** : of, relating to, or resembling a phallus   **2** : relating to or being the stage of psychosexual development in psychoanalytic theory during which children become interested in their own sexual organs

phal·lus \ˈfa-ləs\ *n, pl* **phal·li** \ˈfa-ˌlī\ *or* **phal·lus·es** : PENIS; *also* : a symbolic representation of the penis

Phan·er·o·zo·ic \ˌfa-nə-rə-ˈzō-ik\ *adj* : of, relating to, or being an eon of geologic history comprising the Paleozoic, Mesozoic, and Cenozoic

phan·tasm \ˈfan-ˌta-zəm\ *n*   **1** ◆ : a product of the imagination : ILLUSION   **2** ◆ : a visible disembodied spirit : GHOST

◆ [1] chimera, conceit, daydream, delusion, dream, fancy, fantasy, figment, hallucination, illusion, pipe dream, unreality, vision — more at FANTASY ◆ [2] apparition, bogey, ghost, phantom, poltergeist, shade, shadow, specter, spirit, spook, vision, wraith — more at GHOST

phan·tas·ma·go·ria \fan-ˌtaz-mə-ˈgòr-ē-ə\ *n* : a constantly shifting complex succession of things seen or imagined; *also* : a scene that constantly changes or fluctuates

phan·tas·mal \ˌfan-ˈtaz-məl\ *adj* : of, relating to, or like a phantasm

phantasy *var of* FANTASY

¹phan·tom \ˈfan-təm\ *n*   **1** ◆ : something (as a specter) that is apparent to sense but has no substantial existence   **2** : one that is something in appearance but not in reality : a mere show

◆ apparition, bogey, ghost, phantasm, poltergeist, shade, shadow, specter, spirit, spook, vision, wraith — more at GHOST

²phantom *adj* ◆ : of the nature of, suggesting, or being a phantom

♦ chimerical, fabulous, fanciful, fantastic, fictitious, imaginary, made-up, mythical, pretend, unreal — more at IMAGINARY

pha·raoh \'fer-ō, 'fā-rō\ *n, often cap* : a ruler of ancient Egypt

phar·i·sa·ical \,far-ə-'sā-ə-kəl\ *adj* : hypocritically self-righteous

phar·i·see \'far-ə-,sē\ *n* **1** *cap* : a member of an ancient Jewish sect noted for strict observance of rites and ceremonies of the traditional law **2** : a self-righteous or hypocritical person — **phar·i·sa·ic** \,far-ə-'sā-ik\ *adj*

pharm *abbr* pharmaceutical; pharmacist; pharmacy

¹phar·ma·ceu·ti·cal \,fär-mə-'sü-ti-kəl\ *adj* : of, relating to, or engaged in pharmacy or the manufacture and sale of medicinal drugs

²pharmaceutical *n* ♦ : a medicinal drug

♦ cure, drug, medicine, remedy, specific — more at MEDICINE

phar·ma·col·o·gy \,fär-mə-'kä-lə-jē\ *n* **1** : the science of drugs esp. as related to medicinal uses **2** : the reactions and properties of one or more drugs — **phar·ma·co·log·i·cal** \-kə-'lä-ji-kəl\ *also* **phar·ma·co·log·ic** \-kə-'lä-jik\ *adj* — **phar·ma·col·o·gist** \-'kä-lə-jist\ *n*

phar·ma·co·poe·ia *also* **phar·ma·co·pe·ia** \-kə-'pē-ə\ *n* **1** : a book describing drugs and medicinal preparations **2** : a stock of drugs

phar·ma·cy \'fär-mə-sē\ *n, pl* **-cies** **1** : the art, practice, or profession of preparing and dispensing medical drugs **2** : DRUGSTORE — **phar·ma·cist** \-sist\ *n*

phar·ynx \'far-iŋks\ *n, pl* **pha·ryn·ges** \fə-'rin-jēz\ *also* **phar·ynx·es** : the muscular tubular passage extending from the back of the nasal cavity and mouth to the esophagus — **pha·ryn·ge·al** \fə-'rin-jəl, ,far-ən-'jē-əl\ *adj*

phase \'fāz\ *n* **1** : a particular appearance in a recurring series of changes ⟨~s of the moon⟩ **2** ♦ : a stage or interval in a process or cycle ⟨first ~ of an experiment⟩ **3** ♦ : an aspect or part under consideration — **pha·sic** \'fā-zik\ *adj*

♦ [2] cut, degree, grade, inch, notch, peg, point, stage, step — more at DEGREE ♦ [3] angle, aspect, facet, hand, side — more at ASPECT

phase down *vb* : to reduce the size or amount of by phases
phase in *vb* : to introduce in stages
phase-out \'fā-,zaut\ *n* : a gradual stopping of operations or production
phase out *vb* : to stop production or use of in stages
PhD *abbr* [L *philosophiae doctor*] doctor of philosophy

pheas·ant \'fez-ᵊnt\ *n, pl* **pheasant** *or* **pheasants** : any of numerous long-tailed brilliantly colored game birds related to the domestic chicken

phen·cy·cli·dine \,fen-'sī-klə-,dēn\ *n* : a drug used esp. as a veterinary anesthetic and sometimes illicitly as a hallucinogenic drug

phe·no·bar·bi·tal \,fē-nō-'bär-bə-,tol\ *n* : a crystalline drug used as a hypnotic and sedative

phe·nol \'fē-,nol\ *n* : a corrosive poisonous acidic compound present in coal and wood tars and used in solution as a disinfectant

phe·nom·e·nal \fi-'nä-mən-ᵊl\ *adj* ♦ : relating to or being a phenomenon; *also* : so unusual as to be remarkable — **phe·nom·e·nal·ly** *adv*

♦ aberrant, abnormal, atypical, exceptional, extraordinary, freak, odd, peculiar, rare, singular, uncommon, uncustomary, unique, unusual, unwonted — more at EXCEPTIONAL ♦ magical, miraculous, superhuman, supernatural, uncanny, unearthly — more at SUPERNATURAL

phe·nom·e·non \fi-'nä-mə-,nän, -nən\ *n, pl* **-na** \-nə\ *or* **-nons** [LL *phaenomenon*, fr. Gk *phainomenon*, fr. neut. of *phainomenos*, prp. of *phainesthai* to appear] **1** *pl* **-na** : an observable fact or event **2** : an outward sign of the working of a law of nature **3** *pl* **-nons** ♦ : an extraordinary person or thing : PRODIGY

♦ caution, flash, marvel, miracle, portent, prodigy, sensation, wonder — more at WONDER

pher·o·mone \'fer-ə-,mōn\ *n* : a chemical substance that is produced by an animal and serves to stimulate a behavioral response in other individuals of the same species — **pher·o·mon·al** \,fer-ə-'mōn-ᵊl\ *adj*

phi \'fī\ *n* : the 21st letter of the Greek alphabet — Φ or φ

phi·al \'fī-əl\ *n* : VIAL

Phil *abbr* Philippians

phi·lan·der \fə-'lan-dər\ *vb* : to have casual or illicit sexual relations with many women — **phi·lan·der·er** *n*

phi·lan·throp·ic \,fi-lən-'thrä-pik\ *adj* ♦ : of, relating to, or characterized by philanthropy — **phil·an·throp·i·cal·ly** \-pi-k(ə-)lē\ *adv*

♦ altruistic, beneficent, benevolent, charitable, humanitarian — more at CHARITABLE

phi·lan·thro·py \fə-'lan-thrə-pē\ *n, pl* **-pies** **1** : goodwill toward all people; *esp* : effort to promote human welfare **2** ♦ : a charitable act or gift; *also* : an organization that distributes or is supported by donated funds — **phi·lan·thro·pist** \fə-'lan-thrə-pist\ *n*

♦ alms, benefaction, beneficence, charity, contribution, donation — more at CONTRIBUTION

phi·lat·e·ly \fə-'lat-ᵊl-ē\ *n* : the collection and study of postage and imprinted stamps — **phil·a·tel·ic** \,fi-lə-'te-lik\ *adj* — **phi·lat·e·list** \fə-'lat-ᵊl-ist\ *n*

Phi·le·mon \fə-'lē-mən, fī-\ *n* : a book of the New Testament of the Christian Scripture

Phi·lip·pi·ans \fə-'li-pē-ənz\ *n* : a book of the New Testament of the Christian Scripture

phi·lip·pic \fə-'li-pik\ *n* : TIRADE

phi·lis·tine \'fi-lə-,stēn; fə-'lis-tən\ *n, often cap* [*Philistine*, inhabitant of ancient Philistia (Palestine)] : a person who is smugly insensitive or indifferent to intellectual or artistic values — **philistine** *adj, often cap*

Phil·lips \'fi-ləps\ *adj* : of, relating to, or being a screw having a head with a cross slot or its corresponding screwdriver

phi·lo·den·dron \,fi-lə-'den-drən\ *n, pl* **-drons** *also* **-dra** \-drə\ [NL, fr. Gk, neut. of *philodendros* loving trees, fr. *philos* dear, friendly + *dendron* tree] : any of various plants of the arum family grown for their showy foliage

phi·lol·o·gy \fə-'lä-lə-jē\ *n* **1** : the study of literature and relevant fields **2** : LINGUISTICS; *esp* : historical and comparative linguistics — **phil·o·log·i·cal** \,fi-lə-'lä-ji-kəl\ *adj* — **phi·lol·o·gist** \fə-'lä-lə-jist\ *n*

philos *abbr* philosopher; philosophy

phi·los·o·pher \fə-'lä-sə-fər\ *n* **1** : a reflective thinker : SCHOLAR **2** : a student or specialist in philosophy **3** : a person whose philosophical perspective makes it possible to meet trouble calmly

phi·los·o·phise *chiefly Brit var of* PHILOSOPHIZE

phi·los·o·phize \fə-'lä-sə-,fīz\ *vb* **-phized; -phiz·ing** **1** : to reason like a philosopher : THEORIZE **2** : to expound a philosophy esp. superficially

phi·los·o·phy \fə-'lä-sə-fē\ *n, pl* **-phies** **1** : sciences and liberal arts exclusive of medicine, law, and theology ⟨doctor of ~⟩ **2** : a critical study of fundamental beliefs and the grounds for them **3** : a system of philosophical concepts ⟨Aristotelian ~⟩ **4** : a basic theory concerning a particular subject or sphere of activity **5** ♦ : the sum of the ideas and convictions of an individual or group ⟨her ~ of life⟩ **6** : calmness of temper and judgment — **phil·o·soph·i·cal** \,fi-lə-'sä-fi-kəl\ *also* **phil·o·soph·ic** \-fik\ *adj* — **phil·o·soph·i·cal·ly** \-k(ə-)lē\ *adv*

♦ creed, doctrine, gospel, ideology — more at CREED

phil·ter *or Can and Brit* **phil·tre** \'fil-tər\ *n* **1** : a potion, drug, or charm held to arouse sexual passion **2** : a magic potion

phish·ing \'fi-shiŋ\ *n* : a scam by which an e-mail user is fooled into revealing personal or confidential information which can be used illegally — **phish·er** \-shər\ *n*

phle·bi·tis \fli-'bī-təs\ *n* : inflammation of a vein

phle·bot·o·my \fli-'bä-tə-mē\ *n, pl* **-mies** : the opening of a vein esp. for removing or releasing blood

phlegm \'flem\ *n* [ME *fleume*, fr. AF, fr. LL *phlegma*, fr.

Gk, flame, inflammation, phlegm, fr. *phlegein* to burn]
1 : thick mucus secreted in abnormal quantity esp. in the nose and throat **2 ♦** : dull or apathetic coldness or indifference

♦ apathy, impassivity, numbness, stupor — more at APATHY

phleg·mat·ic \fleg-'ma-tik\ *adj* ♦ : having or showing a slow and stolid temperament

♦ apathetic, cold-blooded, impassive, stoic, stolid, un-emotional — more at IMPASSIVE

phlo·em \'flō-,em\ *n* : a vascular plant tissue external to the xylem that carries dissolved food material and functions in support and storage

phlox \'fläks\ *n, pl* **phlox** *or* **phlox·es** : any of a genus of American herbs that have tall stalks with showy spreading terminal clusters of flowers

pho·bia \'fō-bē-ə\ *n* : an irrational persistent fear or dread — **pho·bic** \'fō-bik\ *adj*

phoe·be \'fē-(,)bē\ *n* : a flycatcher of the eastern U.S. that has a slight crest and is grayish brown above and yellowish white below

phoe·nix \'fē-niks\ *n* : a legendary bird held to live for centuries and then to burn itself to death and rise fresh and young from its ashes

¹phone \'fōn\ *n* **1** : TELEPHONE **2** : EARPHONE

²phone *vb* **phoned; phon·ing** : to speak to or attempt to reach by telephone : TELEPHONE

phone card *n* : a prepaid card used in paying for telephone calls

pho·neme \'fō-,nēm\ *n* : one of the elementary units of speech that distinguish one utterance from another — **pho·ne·mic** \fō-'nē-mik\ *adj*

pho·net·ics \fə-'ne-tiks\ *n* : the study and systematic classification of the sounds made in spoken utterance — **pho·net·ic** \-tik\ *adj* — **pho·ne·ti·cian** \,fō-nə-'ti-shən\ *n*

pho·nic \'fä-nik\ *adj* **1** : of, relating to, or producing sound **2** : of or relating to the sounds of speech or to phonics — **pho·ni·cal·ly** \-ni-k(ə-)lē\ *adv*

pho·nics \'fä-niks\ *n* : a method of teaching people to read and pronounce words by learning the phonetic value of letters, letter groups, and esp. syllables

pho·no·graph \'fō-nə-,graf\ *n* : an instrument for reproducing sounds by means of the vibration of a needle following a spiral groove on a revolving disc

pho·nol·o·gy \fə-'nä-lə-jē\ *n* : a study and description of the sound changes in a language — **pho·no·log·i·cal** \,fō-nə-'lä-ji-kəl\ *adj* — **pho·nol·o·gist** \fə-'nä-lə-jist\ *n*

¹pho·ny *also* **pho·ney** \'fō-nē\ *adj* **pho·ni·er; -est** ♦ : not genuine or real : claiming or claimed to be what one is not

♦ bogus, counterfeit, fake, false, inauthentic, sham, spurious, unauthentic — more at COUNTERFEIT ♦ affected, artificial, assumed, contrived, feigned, put-on, unnatural — more at ARTIFICIAL

²phony *n* ♦ : one that is phony

♦ counterfeit, fake, forgery, hoax, humbug, sham — more at FAKE ♦ charlatan, fake, fraud, hoaxer, humbug, mountebank, pretender, quack

phos·phate \'fäs-,fāt\ *n* : a salt of a phosphoric acid — **phos·phat·ic** \fäs-'fa-tik\ *adj*

phos·phor \'fäs-fər\ *n* : a phosphorescent substance

phos·pho·res·cence \,fäs-fə-'res-ᵊns\ *n* **1** : luminescence caused by the absorption of radiations (as light or electrons) and continuing after these radiations stop **2** : an enduring luminescence without sensible heat — **phos·pho·res·cent** \-ᵊnt\ *adj* — **phos·pho·res·cent·ly** *adv*

phosphoric acid \fäs-'fȯr-ik-, -'fär-\ *n* : any of several oxygen-containing acids of phosphorus

phos·pho·rus \'fäs-fə-rəs\ *n* [NL, fr. Gk *phōsphoros* light-bearing, fr. *phōs* light + *pherein* to carry, bring] : a nonmetallic chemical element that has characteristics similar to nitrogen and occurs widely esp. as phosphates — **phos·phor·ic** \fäs-'fȯr-ik, -'fär-\ *adj* — **phos·pho·rous** \'fäs-fə-rəs; fäs-'fȯr-əs, -'fȯr-\ *adj*

phot- *or* **photo-** *comb form* **1** : light ⟨*photo*graphy⟩ **2** : photograph : photographic ⟨*photo*engraving⟩ **3** : photoelectric ⟨*photo*cell⟩

¹pho·to \'fō-tō\ *n, pl* **photos** : a picture or likeness obtained by photography : PHOTOGRAPH — **photo** *adj*

²photo *vb* : to take a photograph of

pho·to·cell \'fō-tə-,sel\ *n* : PHOTOELECTRIC CELL

pho·to·chem·i·cal \,fō-tō-'ke-mi-kəl\ *adj* : of, relating to, or resulting from the chemical action of radiant energy

pho·to·com·pose \-kəm-'pōz\ *vb* : to compose reading matter for reproduction by means of characters photographed on film — **pho·to·com·po·si·tion** \-,käm-pə-'zi-shən\ *n*

pho·to·copy \'fō-tə-,kä-pē\ *n* : a photographic reproduction of graphic matter — **photocopy** *vb*

pho·to·elec·tric \,fō-tō-i-'lek-trik\ *adj* : relating to an electrical effect due to the interaction of light with matter — **pho·to·elec·tri·cal·ly** \-tri-k(ə-)lē\ *adv*

photoelectric cell *n* : a device whose electrical properties are modified by the action of light

pho·to·en·grave \,fō-tō-in-'grāv\ *vb* : to make a photoengraving of

pho·to·en·grav·ing *n* : a process by which an etched printing plate is made from a photograph or drawing; *also* : a print made from such a plate

photo finish *n* : a race finish so close that a photograph of the finish is used to determine the winner

pho·tog \fə-'täg\ *n* : PHOTOGRAPHER

pho·to·ge·nic \,fō-tə-'je-nik\ *adj* : eminently suitable esp. aesthetically for being photographed

¹pho·to·graph \'fō-tə-,graf\ *n* ♦ : a picture taken by photography — **pho·tog·ra·pher** \fə-'tä-grə-fər\ *n*

♦ print, shot, snap, snapshot; *also* blowup, close-up, enlargement, still; daguerreotype, monochrome

²photograph *vb* ♦ : to take a photograph of

♦ mug, shoot, snap; *also* image, picture, retake; film, videotape

pho·tog·ra·phy \fə-'tä-grə-fē\ *n* : the art or process of producing images on a sensitive surface (as film or a CCD chip) by the action of light — **pho·to·graph·ic** \,fō-tə-'gra-fik\ *adj* — **pho·to·graph·i·cal·ly** \-fi-k(ə-)lē\ *adv*

pho·to·gra·vure \,fō-tə-grə-'vyu̇r\ *n* : a process for making prints from an intaglio plate prepared by photographic methods

pho·to·li·thog·ra·phy \,fō-tō-li-'thä-grə-fē\ *n* : the process of photographically transferring a pattern to a surface for etching (as in making an integrated circuit)

pho·tom·e·ter \fō-'tä-mə-tər\ *n* : an instrument for measuring the intensity of light — **pho·to·met·ric** \,fō-tə-'me-trik\ *adj* — **pho·tom·e·try** \fō-'tä-mə-trē\ *n*

pho·to·mi·cro·graph \,fō-tə-'mī-krə-,graf\ *n* : a photograph of a microscope image — **pho·to·mi·crog·ra·phy** \-mī-'krä-grə-fē\ *n*

pho·ton \'fō-,tän\ *n* : a quantum of electromagnetic radiation

photo op *n* : a situation or event that lends itself to the taking of pictures which favor the individuals photographed

pho·to·play \'fō-tō-,plā\ *n* : MOTION PICTURE

pho·to·sen·si·tive \,fō-tə-'sen-sə-tiv\ *adj* : sensitive or sensitized to the action of radiant energy

pho·to·shop \'fō-tō-,shäp\ *vb, often cap* : to alter a digital image with image-editing software

pho·to·sphere \'fō-tə-,sfir\ *n* : the luminous surface of a star — **pho·to·spher·ic** \,fō-tə-'sfir-ik, -'sfer-\ *adj*

pho·to·syn·the·sis \,fō-tō-'sin-thə-səs\ *n* : the process by which chlorophyll-containing plants make carbohydrates from water and from carbon dioxide in the air in the presence of light — **pho·to·syn·the·size** \-,sīz\ *vb* — **pho·to·syn·thet·ic** \-sin-'the-tik\ *adj*

phr *abbr* phrase

¹phrase \'frāz\ *n* **1** : a brief expression **2** : a group of two or more grammatically related words that form a sense unit expressing a thought

²**phrase** *vb* **phrased; phras·ing** ♦ : to express in words

♦ articulate, clothe, couch, express, formulate, put, say, state, word; *also* craft, frame; hint, imply, insinuate, intimate, suggest; paraphrase, rephrase, restate, summarize, translate; communicate, disclose, speak, tell; describe, render, write up

phrase·ol·o·gy \ˌfrā-zē-'ä-lə-jē\ *n, pl* **-gies** ♦ : a manner of phrasing : STYLE

♦ fashion, locution, manner, mode, style, tone, vein — more at STYLE

phras·ing *n* ♦ : style of expression

♦ diction, language, phraseology, wording — more at WORDING

phren·ic \'fre-nik\ *adj* : of or relating to the diaphragm ⟨~ nerves⟩

phre·nol·o·gy \fri-'nä-lə-jē\ *n* : the study of the conformation of the skull based on the belief that it indicates mental faculties and character traits

phy·lac·tery \fə-'lak-tə-rē\ *n, pl* **-ter·ies** 1 : one of two small square leather boxes containing slips inscribed with scripture passages and traditionally worn on the left arm and forehead by Jewish men during morning weekday prayers 2 : an ornament worn as a charm against evil : AMULET

phy·lum \'fī-ləm\ *n, pl* **phy·la** \-lə\ [NL, fr. Gk *phylon* tribe, race] : a major category in biological classification esp. of animals that ranks above the class and below the kingdom; *also* : a group (as of people) apparently of common origin

phys *abbr* 1 physical 2 physics

¹**phys·ic** \'fi-zik\ *n* 1 : the profession of medicine 2 : a substance or preparation used in treating disease : MEDICINE; *esp* : PURGATIVE

²**physic** *vb* **phys·icked; phys·ick·ing** : PURGE 2

¹**phys·i·cal** \'fi-zi-kəl\ *adj* 1 : of or relating to nature or the laws of nature 2 ♦ : material as opposed to mental or spiritual 3 : of, relating to, or produced by the forces and operations of physics 4 ♦ : of or relating to the body — **phys·i·cal·ly** \-k(ə-)lē\ *adv*

♦ [2] concrete, material, substantial — more at MATERIAL ♦ [4] animal, bodily, carnal, corporal, fleshly, material, somatic; *also* anatomic, physiological; sensual; sensuous, hand-to-hand *Ant* nonmaterial, nonphysical

²**physical** *n* : PHYSICAL EXAMINATION

physical education *n* : instruction in the development and care of the body ranging from simple calisthenics to training in hygiene, gymnastics, and the performance and management of athletic games

physical examination *n* : an examination of the bodily functions and condition of an individual

phys·i·cal·ize \'fi-zə-kə-ˌlīz\ *vb* **-ized; -iz·ing** : to give physical form or expression to

physical science *n* : any of the sciences (as physics and astronomy) that deal primarily with nonliving materials — **physical scientist** *n*

physical therapy *n* : the treatment of disease by physical and mechanical means (as massage, exercise, water, or heat) — **physical therapist** *n*

phy·si·cian \fə-'zi-shən\ *n* : a doctor of medicine

physician's assistant *n* : a person certified to provide basic medical care esp. under a licensed physician's supervision

phys·i·cist \'fi-zə-sist\ *n* : a scientist who specializes in physics

phys·ics \'fi-ziks\ *n* [L *physica*, pl., natural sciences, fr. Gk *physika*, fr. *physis* growth, nature, fr. *phyein* to bring forth] 1 : the science of matter and energy and their interactions 2 : the physical properties and composition of something

phys·i·og·no·my \ˌfi-zē-'äg-nə-mē\ *n, pl* **-mies** : facial appearance esp. as a reflection of inner character

phys·i·og·ra·phy \ˌfi-zē-'ä-grə-fē\ *n* : geography dealing with physical features of the earth — **phys·io·graph·ic** \ˌfi-zē-ō-'gra-fik\ *adj*

phys·i·ol·o·gy \ˌfi-zē-'ä-lə-jē\ *n* 1 : a branch of biology dealing with the functions and functioning of living matter and organisms 2 : functional processes in an organism or any of its parts — **phys·i·o·log·i·cal** \-zē-ə-'lä-ji-kəl\ *or* **phys·i·o·log·ic** \-jik\ *adj* — **phys·i·o·log·i·cal·ly** \-ji-k(ə-)lē\ *adv* — **phys·i·ol·o·gist** \-zē-'ä-lə-jist\ *n*

phys·io·ther·a·py \ˌfi-zē-ō-'ther-ə-pē\ *n* : PHYSICAL THERAPY — **phys·io·ther·a·pist** \-pist\ *n*

phy·sique \fə-'zēk\ *n* ♦ : the build of a person's body : bodily constitution

♦ build, constitution, figure, form, frame, shape; *also* anatomy, structure

phy·to·chem·i·cal \ˌfī-tō-'ke-mi-kəl\ *n* : a chemical compound occurring naturally in plants

phy·to·plank·ton \'fī-tō-ˌplaŋk-tən\ *n* : plant life of the plankton

pi \'pī\ *n, pl* **pis** \'pīz\ 1 : the 16th letter of the Greek alphabet — Π or π 2 : the symbol π denoting the ratio of the circumference of a circle to its diameter; *also* : the ratio itself equal to approximately 3.1416

PI *abbr* private investigator

pi·a·nis·si·mo \ˌpē-ə-'ni-sə-ˌmō\ *adv or adj* : very softly — used as a direction in music

pi·a·nist \pē-'a-nist, 'pē-ə-\ *n* : a person who plays the piano

¹**pi·a·no** \pē-'ä-nō\ *adv or adj* : SOFTLY — used as a direction in music

²**piano** \pē-'a-nō\ *n, pl* **pianos** [It, short for *pianoforte*, fr. *gravicembalo col piano e forte*, lit., harpsichord with soft and loud; fr. the fact that its tones could be varied in loudness] : a musical instrument having steel strings sounded by felt-covered hammers operated from a keyboard

pi·ano·forte \pē-ˌa-nō-'fȯr-ˌtā, -tē; pē-'a-nə-ˌfȯrt\ *n* : PIANO

pi·az·za \pē-'a-zə, *esp for 1* -'at-sə\ *n, pl* **piazzas** *or* **pi·az·ze** \-'at-(ˌ)sā, -'ät-\ [It, fr. L *platea* broad street] 1 : an open square esp. in an Italian town 2 : a long hall with an arched roof 3 *dial* : VERANDA, PORCH

pi·broch \'pē-ˌbräk\ *n* : a set of variations for the bagpipe

pic \'pik\ *n, pl* **pics** *or* **pix** \'piks\ 1 : PHOTOGRAPH 2 : MOTION PICTURE

pi·ca \'pī-kə\ *n* : a typewriter type with 10 characters to the inch

pi·ca·resque \ˌpi-kə-'resk, ˌpē-\ *adj* : of or relating to rogues ⟨~ fiction⟩

pic·a·yune \ˌpi-kē-'yün\ *adj* : of little value : TRIVIAL; *also* : PETTY

pic·ca·lil·li \ˌpi-kə-'li-lē\ *n* : a relish of chopped vegetables and spices

pic·co·lo \'pi-kə-ˌlō\ *n, pl* **-los** [It, short for *piccolo flauto* small flute] : a small shrill flute pitched an octave higher than the ordinary flute

¹**pick** \'pik\ *vb* 1 : to pierce or break up with a pointed instrument 2 : to remove bit by bit; *also* : to remove covering matter from 3 ♦ : to gather by plucking ⟨~ apples⟩ 4 ♦ : to select from a group : CULL, SELECT 5 : ROB ⟨~ a pocket⟩ 6 : PROVOKE ⟨~ a quarrel⟩ 7 : to dig into or pull lightly at 8 : to pluck with fingers or a pick 9 : to loosen or pull apart with a sharp point ⟨~ wool⟩ 10 : to unlock with a wire 11 : to eat sparingly — **pick·er** *n*

♦ [3] gather, harvest, reap — more at HARVEST ♦ [4] choose, cull, elect, handpick, name, opt, prefer, select, single, take — more at CHOOSE

²**pick** *n* 1 ♦ : the act or privilege of choosing 2 ♦ : the best or choicest one 3 : the part of a crop gathered at one time

♦ [1] alternative, choice, discretion, option, preference, way — more at CHOICE ♦ [2] best, choice, cream, elect, elite, fat, flower, prime — more at ELITE

³**pick** *n* 1 : a heavy wooden-handled tool pointed at one or both ends 2 : a pointed implement used for picking 3 : a small thin piece (as of plastic) used to pluck the strings of a stringed instrument

pick·a·back \'pi-gē-ˌbak, 'pi-kə-\ *var of* PIGGYBACK
pick·ax \'pik-ˌaks\ *n* : ³PICK 1
pick·er·el \'pi-kə-rəl\ *n, pl* **pickerel** *or* **pickerels** : either of two bony fishes related to the pikes; *also* : WALLEYE 2
pick·er·el·weed \-ˌwēd\ *n* : a No. American shallow-water herb that bears spikes of purplish blue flowers
¹**pick·et** \'pi-kət\ *n* **1** : a pointed stake (as for a fence) **2 a** : a detached body of soldiers on outpost duty **b** ♦ : one that watches or guards : SENTINEL **3** : a person posted by a labor union where workers are on strike; *also* : a person posted for a protest

♦ [2a, 2b] custodian, guard, guardian, keeper, lookout, sentinel, sentry, warden, warder, watch, watchman — more at GUARD

²**picket** *vb* **1** : to guard with pickets **2** : TETHER **3** : to post pickets at ⟨∼ a factory⟩ **4** : to serve as a picket
pick·ings \'pi-kiŋz, -kənz\ *n pl* **1** : gleanable or eatable fragments : SCRAPS **2** : yield for effort expended : RE-TURN
pick·le \'pi-kəl\ *n* **1** : a brine or vinegar solution for pre-serving foods; *also* : a food (as a cucumber) preserved in a pickle **2** ♦ : a difficult situation — **pickle** *vb*

♦ corner, fix, hole, jam, predicament, spot — more at PREDICAMENT

pick·lock \'pik-ˌläk\ *n* **1** : BURGLAR, THIEF **2** : a tool for picking locks
pick·pock·et \'pik-ˌpä-kət\ *n* : one who steals from pockets
pick·up \'pik-ˌəp\ *n* **1** : a hitchhiker who is given a ride **2** : a temporary chance acquaintance **3** : a picking up **4** : revival of business activity **5** : ACCELERATION **6** : the conversion of mechanical movements into electrical im-pulses in the reproduction of sound; *also* : a device for making such conversion **7** : a light truck having an en-closed cab and an open body with low sides and a tailgate
pick up *vb* **1** ♦ : to take hold of and lift **2** : IMPROVE **3** : to put in order **4** : to gather together : COLLECT **5** ♦ : to acquire by study or experience : LEARN **6** ♦ : to obtain esp. by payment **7** ♦ : to become progressively greater (as in size, amount, number, or intensity) **8** ♦ : to take into custody

♦ [1] boost, crane, elevate, heave, heft, heighten, hike, hoist, jack, lift, raise, up, uphold — more at RAISE ♦ [5] get, learn, master — more at LEARN ♦ [6] buy, purchase, take — more at BUY ♦ [7] build, gain, gather, grow — more at GAIN ♦ [8] apprehend, arrest, nab, restrain, seize — more at ARREST

picky \'pi-kē\ *adj* **pick·i·er; -est** ♦ : fastidiously selective

♦ choosy, dainty, delicate, demanding, exacting, fastid-ious, finicky, fussy, nice, old-maidish, particular, selec-tive — more at FINICKY

¹**pic·nic** \'pik-ˌnik\ *n* **1** : an outing with food usu. provided by members of the group and eaten in the open **2** ♦ : an easy task or feat

♦ breeze, child's play, cinch, pushover, snap — more at CINCH

²**picnic** *vb* **pic·nicked; pic·nick·ing** : to go on a picnic : eat in picnic fashion
pi·cot \'pē-ˌkō\ *n* : one of a series of small loops forming an edging on ribbon or lace
pic·to·ri·al \pik-'tōr-ē-əl\ *adj* **1** : of, relating to, or consist-ing of pictures **2** : suggesting or conveying visual images ⟨∼ poetry⟩
¹**pic·ture** \'pik-chər\ *n* **1** ♦ : a representation made by painting, drawing, or photography **2** : a vivid descrip-tion in words **3** : something that by its likeness vividly suggests some other thing : IMAGE **4** : a transitory visual image (as on a TV screen) **5** : a representation (as of a story) by means of motion pictures : MOVIE **6** : position with respect to conditions and circumstances : SITUA-TION **7** ♦ : a mental image

♦ [1] illustration, image, likeness; *also* delineation, depic-tion, representation; portrait; drawing, finger painting;

etching, silhouette, sketch, watercolor; caricature, cartoon, doodle; photograph, collage, montage; hiero-glyphic, ideogram ♦ [2] delineation, depiction, descrip-tion, portrait, portrayal, sketch — more at DESCRIPTION ♦ [7] concept, idea, image, impression, notion, thought — more at IDEA

²**picture** *vb* **pic·tured; pic·tur·ing** **1** ♦ : to paint or draw a picture of **2** ♦ : to describe vividly in words **3** ♦ : to form a mental image of

♦ [1] depict, image, portray, represent; *also* delineate, describe, render; outline, sketch; illustrate, show; car-icature ♦ [2] delineate, depict, describe, draw, image, paint, portray, sketch — more at DESCRIBE ♦ [3] con-ceive, dream, envisage, fancy, imagine, vision, visualize — more at IMAGINE

picture–perfect *adj* ♦ : completely flawless : PERFECT

♦ absolute, faultless, flawless, ideal, immaculate, im-peccable, irreproachable, letter-perfect, perfect, un-blemished — more at PERFECT

pic·tur·esque \ˌpik-chə-'resk\ *adj* **1** : resembling a picture ⟨a ∼ landscape⟩ **2** : CHARMING, QUAINT ⟨a ∼ charac-ter⟩ **3** : evoking mental images : GRAPHIC, VIVID ⟨a ∼ account⟩ — **pic·tur·esque·ness** *n*
picture tube *n* : a cathode-ray tube on which the picture in a television set appears
pid·dle \'pid-ᵊl\ *vb* **pid·dled; pid·dling** : to act or work idly : DAWDLE
pid·dling \'pid-ᵊl-ən, -iŋ\ *adj* : of little worth or importance : TRIVIAL, PALTRY
pid·dly \'pid-lē\ *adj* : TRIVIAL, PIDDLING
pid·gin \'pi-jən\ *n* [fr. *pidgin English*, fr. Chinese Pidgin English *pidgin* business] : a simplified speech used for communication between people with different languages
pie \'pī\ *n* : a dish consisting of a pastry crust and a filling (as of fruit or meat)
¹**pie·bald** \'pī-ˌbȯld\ *adj* ♦ : of different colors; *esp* : blotched with white and black ⟨a ∼ horse⟩

♦ dappled, mottled, pied, spotted — more at PIED

²**piebald** *n* : a piebald animal
¹**piece** \'pēs\ *n* **1** ♦ : a part of a whole : FRAGMENT **2** : one of a group, set, or mass; *also* : a single item ⟨a ∼ of news⟩ **3** : a length, weight, or size in which something is made or sold **4** : a product (as an essay) of creative work **5** : a weapon from which a shot is discharged by gunpowder : FIREARM **6** : COIN **7** ♦ : a literary, journalistic, artistic, dramatic, or musical composition

♦ [1] bit, fragment, scrap — more at FRAGMENT ♦ [7] composition, opus, work — more at COMPOSITION

²**piece** *vb* **pieced; piec·ing** **1** : to repair or complete by add-ing pieces : PATCH **2** ♦ : to join into a whole

♦ assemble, build, construct, erect, fabricate, make, make up, put up, raise, rear, set up — more at BUILD

piéce de ré·sis·tance \pē-ˌes-də-rā-ˌzē-'stäns\ *n, pl* **piéces de ré·sis·tance** *same*\ [F] **1** : the chief dish of a meal **2** : an outstanding item
piece·meal \'pēs-ˌmēl\ *adv or adj* : one piece at a time : GRADUALLY
piece·work \-ˌwərk\ *n* : work done and paid for by the piece — **piece·work·er** *n*
pie chart *n* : a circular chart that shows quantities or fre-quencies by parts of a circle shaped like pieces of pie
pied \'pīd\ *adj* ♦ : of two or more colors in blotches

♦ dappled, mottled, piebald, spotted; *also* shaded; checkered, motley, multicolored, varicolored, varie-gated; blotted, brindled, streaked; colored, colorful; dotted, peppered, sprinkled; stippled; discolored, dyed, marked, stained; flecked, streaked; bespattered, spat-tered

pied–à–terre \pē-ˌā-də-'ter\ *n, pl* **pieds–à–terre** *same*\ [F, lit., foot to the ground] : a temporary or second lodging
pier \'pir\ *n* **1** : a support for a bridge span **2** ♦ : a struc-ture built out into the water for use as a landing place or a

promenade or to protect or form a harbor **3 ♦** : an upright supporting part (as a pillar) of a building or structure

♦ [2] dock, float, jetty, landing, levee, quay, wharf — more at DOCK ♦ [3] column, pillar, post, stanchion — more at PILLAR

pierce \'pirs\ *vb* **pierced; pierc·ing 1 ♦** : to enter or thrust into sharply or painfully : STAB **2 ♦** : to make a hole in or through : PERFORATE **3 ♦** : to force or make a way into or through : PENETRATE **4** : to see through : DISCERN

♦ [1] gore, harpoon, impale, lance, puncture, skewer, spear, spike, stab, stick, transfix — more at IMPALE ♦ [2] bore, drill, hole, perforate, punch, puncture — more at PERFORATE ♦ [3] access, enter, penetrate, probe

pierc·ing *adj* **1 ♦** : marked by intensity or volume of sound **2** : PERCEPTIVE ⟨~ eyes⟩ **3 ♦** : penetratingly cold **4** : CUTTING, INCISIVE ⟨~ sarcasm⟩

♦ [1] booming, clamorous (*or* clamourous), deafening, earsplitting, loud, resounding, ringing, roaring, sonorous, stentorian, thunderous — more at LOUD ♦ [3] biting, bitter, cutting, keen, penetrating, raw, sharp — more at CUTTING

pies *pl of* PIE

pi·ety \'pī-ə-tē\ *n, pl* **pi·et·ies 1** : fidelity to natural obligations (as to parents) **2 ♦** : dutifulness in religion **3** : a pious act

♦ devotion, faith, religion — more at FAITH ♦ blessedness, devoutness, godliness, holiness, sainthood, sanctity — more at HOLINESS

pif·fle \'pi-fəl\ *n* **♦** : trivial nonsense

♦ bunk, claptrap, drivel, foolishness, hogwash, nonsense

pig \'pig\ *n* **1** : SWINE; *esp* : a young domesticated swine **2** : PORK **3** : a dirty, gluttonous, or repulsive person **4** : a crude casting of metal (as iron)

pi·geon \'pi-jən\ *n* **1** : any of numerous stout-bodied short-legged birds with smooth thick plumage **2 ♦** : an easy mark : DUPE

♦ dupe, gull, sap, sucker, tool — more at DUPE

¹pi·geon·hole \'pi-jən-,hōl\ *n* : a small open compartment (as in a desk) for keeping letters or documents

²pigeonhole *vb* **1** : to place in or as if in a pigeonhole : FILE **2** : to lay aside **3** : to assign to a usu. restrictive category

pi·geon–toed \-,tōd\ *adj* : having the toes turned in

pig·gish \'pi-gish\ *adj* **1 ♦** : having a strong desire for food or drink : GREEDY **2** : STUBBORN

♦ gluttonous, greedy, hoggish, rapacious, ravenous, voracious — more at VORACIOUS

pig·gy·back \'pi-gē-,bak\ *adv or adj* **1** : up on the back and shoulders **2** : on a railroad flatcar

pig·head·ed \'pig-'he-dəd\ *adj* **♦** : willfully or perversely unyielding : OBSTINATE, STUBBORN

♦ dogged, hardheaded, headstrong, mulish, obdurate, obstinate, opinionated, peevish, pertinacious, perverse, stubborn, unyielding, willful — more at OBSTINATE

pig latin *n, often cap L* : a jargon that is made by systematic alteration of English

pig·let \'pi-glət\ *n* : a small usu. young swine

pig·ment \'pig-mənt\ *n* **1 ♦** : coloring matter **2** : a powder mixed with a liquid to give color (as in paints) — **pig·ment·ed** \-mən-təd\ *adj*

♦ color (*or* colour), dye, stain; *also* cast, hue, shade, tinge, tint, tone

pig·men·ta·tion \,pig-mən-'tā-shən\ *n* : coloration with or deposition of pigment; *esp* : an excessive deposition of bodily pigment

pigmy *var of* PYGMY

pig·nut \'pig-,nət\ *n* : the bitter nut of any of several hickory trees; *also* : any of these trees

pig·pen \-,pen\ *n* **1** : a pen for pigs **2 ♦** : a dirty place

♦ hole, pigsty, shambles; *also* chaos, confusion, disarray, disorder, jumble, mess, muddle; dump; clutter, litter, mishmash

pig·skin \-,skin\ *n* **1** : the skin of a swine or leather made of it **2** : FOOTBALL 2

pig·sty \-,stī\ *n* **1** : a pen for pigs **2 ♦** : a dirty place

♦ hole, pigpen, shambles — more at PIGPEN

pig·tail \-,tāl\ *n* : a tight braid of hair

pi·ka \'pī-kə\ *n* : any of various small short-eared mammals related to the rabbits and occurring in rocky uplands of Asia and western No. America

¹pike \'pīk\ *n* : a sharp point or spike

²pike *n, pl* **pike** *or* **pikes** : a large slender long-snouted freshwater bony fish valued for food; *also* : any of various related fishes

³pike *n* **♦** : a long wooden shaft with a pointed steel head formerly used as a foot soldier's weapon

♦ lance, spear — more at SPEAR

⁴pike *n* : a main road; *esp* : a paved highway with a rounded surface : TURNPIKE

pik·er \'pī-kər\ *n* **1** : one who does things in a small way or on a small scale **2** : a close or miserly person : TIGHTWAD, CHEAPSKATE

pike·staff \'pīk-,staf\ *n* : the staff of a foot soldier's pike

pi·laf *also* **pi·laff** \pi-'läf, 'pē-,läf\ *or* **pi·lau** \pi-'lō, -'lȯ, 'pē-,lō, -lȯ\ *n* : a dish made of seasoned rice often with meat

pi·las·ter \pi-'las-tər, 'pī-,las-tər\ *n* : an architectural support that looks like a rectangular column and projects slightly from a wall

pil·chard \'pil-chərd\ *n* : a small European marine fish related to the herrings and often packed as a sardine

¹pile \'pīl\ *n* : a long slender column (as of wood or steel) driven into the ground to support a vertical load

²pile *n* **1 ♦** : a quantity of things heaped together **2** : PYRE **3 ♦** : a great number or quantity : LOT ⟨~s of money⟩

♦ [1] cock, heap, hill, mound, mountain, rick, stack; *also* bank, bar, drift, embankment; pyramid; barrow, cairn, pyre; accumulation, aggregate, assemblage, collection, conglomeration, gathering, grouping, hoard, jumble ♦ [3] abundance, deal, gobs, heap, loads, lot, plenty, quantity — more at LOT

³pile *vb* **piled; pil·ing 1 ♦** : to lay in a pile : STACK **2 ♦** : to heap up : ACCUMULATE — usu. used with *up* **3** : to press forward in a mass : CROWD

♦ [1] heap, hill, mound, stack; *also* bank; layer, pyramid; accumulate, amass, assemble, collect, gather, group, mass; bunch, clump, lump *Ant* unpile ♦ *usu* **pile up** [2] accumulate, collect, conglomerate, gather, heap — more at COLLECT

⁴pile *n* **1 ♦** : a coat or surface of usu. short close fine furry hairs **2 ♦** : a velvety surface produced by an extra set of filling yarns that form raised loops which are cut and sheared — **piled** \'pīld\ *adj* — **pile·less** *adj*

♦ [1] coat, fleece, fur, hair, pelage, wool ♦ [2] down, floss, fluff, fur, fuzz, lint, nap — more at FUZZ

piles \'pīlz\ *n pl* : HEMORRHOIDS

pil·fer \'pil-fər\ *vb* **♦** : to steal in small quantities

♦ appropriate, filch, hook, misappropriate, nip, pocket, purloin, snitch, steal, swipe, thieve — more at STEAL

pil·grim \'pil-grəm\ *n* [ME, fr. AF *pelerin, pilegrin*, fr. LL *pelegrinus*, alter. of L *peregrinus* foreigner, fr. *peregrinus* foreign, fr. *peregri* abroad, fr. *per* through + *ager* land] **1** : one who journeys in foreign lands : WAYFARER **2** : one who travels to a shrine or holy place as an act of devotion **3** *cap* : one of the English settlers founding Plymouth colony in 1620

pil·grim·age \-grə-mij\ *n* : a journey of a pilgrim esp. to a shrine or holy place

pil·ing \'pī-liŋ\ *n* : a structure of piles

pill \'pil\ *n* **1 ♦** : a medicine in a small rounded mass to be swallowed whole **2** : a disagreeable or tiresome person **3** *often cap* : an oral contraceptive — usu. used with *the*

♦ capsule, tablet; *also* drug, medication, pharmaceutical, specific; miracle drug, wonder drug; potion, preparation; dosage, dose, drop, sleeping pill, tranquilizer

pil·lage \'pi-lij\ *vb* **pil·laged; pil·lag·ing ♦ :** to take booty **:** LOOT — **pillage** *n* — **pil·lag·er** *n*

♦ despoil, loot, maraud, plunder, ransack, sack, strip — more at RANSACK

pil·lar \'pi-lər\ *n* **1 ♦ :** a strong upright support (as for a roof) **2 :** a column or shaft standing alone esp. as a monument **3 ♦ :** a supporting, integral, or upstanding member or part — **pil·lared** \-lərd\ *adj*

♦ [1] column, pier, post, stanchion; *also* caryatid, pedestal; flying buttress, buttress; needle, obelisk ♦ [3] buttress, dependence, mainstay, reliance, standby, support — more at DEPENDENCE

pill·box \'pil-ˌbäks\ *n* **1 :** a shallow round box for pills **2 :** a low concrete emplacement esp. for machine guns

pil·lion \'pil-yən\ *n* **1 :** a pad or cushion placed behind a saddle for an extra rider **2** *chiefly Brit* **:** a motorcycle or bicycle saddle for a passenger

¹pil·lo·ry \'pi-lə-rē\ *n, pl* **-ries :** a wooden frame for public punishment having holes in which the head and hands can be locked

²pillory *vb* **-ried; -ry·ing** **1 :** to set in a pillory **2 :** to expose to public scorn

¹pil·low \'pi-lō\ *n* **:** a case filled with springy material (as feathers) and used to support the head of a resting person

²pillow *vb* **:** to rest or place on or as if on a pillow; *also* **:** to serve as a pillow for

pil·low·case \-ˌkās\ *n* **:** a removable covering for a pillow

¹pi·lot \'pī-lət\ *n* **1 :** HELMSMAN, STEERSMAN **2 :** a person qualified and licensed to take ships into and out of a port **3 :** GUIDE, LEADER **4 ♦ :** one that flies an aircraft or spacecraft **5 :** a television show filmed or taped as a sample of a proposed series — **pi·lot·less** *adj*

♦ airman, aviator, flier; *also* ace, copilot, test pilot

²pilot *vb* **♦ :** to act as a guide to **:** lead or conduct over a usu. difficult course

♦ coach, counsel, guide, lead, mentor, shepherd, show, tutor — more at GUIDE ♦ conduct, direct, guide, lead, marshal, route, show, steer, usher — more at LEAD

³pilot *adj* **:** serving as a guiding or activating device or as a testing or trial unit ⟨a ~ light⟩ ⟨a ~ factory⟩

pi·lot·house \'pī-lət-ˌhau̇s\ *n* **:** a shelter on the upper deck of a ship for the steering gear and the helmsman

pilot whale *n* **:** either of two mostly black medium-sized whales

pil·sner *also* **pil·sen·er** \'pilz-nər, 'pil-zə-\ *n* [G, lit., of Pilsen (Plzeň), city in the Czech Republic] **1 :** a light beer with a strong flavor of hops **2 :** a tall slender footed glass for beer

pi·men·to \pə-'men-tō\ *n, pl* **pimentos** *or* **pimento** [Sp *pimienta* allspice, pepper, fr. L, pigment] **1 :** ALLSPICE **2 :** PIMIENTO

pi·mien·to \pə-'men-tō\ *n, pl* **-tos :** any of various mild red sweet pepper fruits used esp. to stuff olives and to make paprika

pimp \'pimp\ *n* **:** a criminal who lives off the earnings of and usu. exerts control over one or more prostitutes — **pimp** *vb*

pim·per·nel \'pim-pər-ˌnel, -nəl\ *n* **:** any of a genus of herbs related to the primroses

pim·ple \'pim-pəl\ *n* **:** a small inflamed swelling on the skin often containing pus — **pim·ply** \-p(ə-)lē\ *adj*

¹pin \'pin\ *n* **1 :** a piece of wood or metal used esp. for fastening things together or as a support by which one thing may be suspended from another; *esp* **:** a small pointed piece of wire with a head used for fastening clothes or attaching papers **2 :** an ornament or emblem fastened to clothing with a pin **3 :** one of the wooden pieces constituting the target (as in bowling); *also* **:** the staff of the flag marking a hole on a golf course **4 :** LEG

²pin *vb* **pinned; pin·ning** **1 :** to fasten, join, or secure with a pin **2 :** to hold fast or immobile **3 :** ATTACH, HANG ⟨*pinned* their hopes on a miracle⟩ **4 :** to assign the blame for ⟨~ a crime on someone⟩ **5 :** to define clearly **:** ESTABLISH ⟨~ down an idea⟩

PIN *abbr* personal identification number

pi·ña co·la·da \ˌpēn-yə-kō-'lä-də, ˌpē-nə-\ *n* [Sp, lit., strained pineapple] **:** a tall drink made of rum, cream of coconut, and pineapple juice mixed with ice

pin·afore \'pi-nə-ˌfȯr\ *n* **:** a sleeveless dress or apron fastened at the back

pin·ball machine \'pin-ˌbȯl-\ *n* **:** an amusement device in which a ball is maneuvered along a slanted surface among a series of targets for points

pince–nez \paⁿs-'nā\ *n, pl* **pince–nez** *same or* -'nāz\ [F, fr. *pincer* to pinch + *nez* nose] **:** eyeglasses clipped to the nose by a spring

pin·cer \'pin-sər\ *n* **1** *pl* **:** a gripping instrument with two handles and two grasping jaws **2 :** a claw (as of a lobster) resembling pincers

¹pinch \'pinch\ *vb* [ME, fr. AF *pincher, pincer*, fr. VL *pinctiare, *punctiare*, fr. L *punctum* puncture] **1 :** to squeeze between the finger and thumb or between the jaws of an instrument **2 :** to compress painfully **3 :** CONTRACT, SHRIVEL **4 :** to be miserly; *also* **:** to subject to strict economy **5 :** to confine or limit narrowly **6 :** to take (the property of another) wrongfully **:** STEAL **7 :** to take or keep in custody by authority of law **:** ARREST

²pinch *n* **1 :** a critical point **:** EMERGENCY **2 :** painful effect **3 :** an act of pinching **4 :** a very small quantity **5 :** ARREST

³pinch *adj* **:** SUBSTITUTE ⟨a ~ runner⟩

pinch–hit \ˌpinch-'hit\ *vb* **1 :** to bat in the place of another player esp. when a hit is particularly needed **2 ♦ :** to act or serve in place of another — **pinch hit** *n*

♦ cover, fill in, stand in, sub, substitute, take over — more at COVER

pinch hitter *n* **♦ :** one that pinch-hits

♦ backup, relief, replacement, reserve, stand-in, sub, substitute — more at SUBSTITUTE

pin curl *n* **:** a curl made usu. by dampening a strand of hair, coiling it, and securing it by a hairpin or clip

pin·cush·ion \'pin-ˌku̇-shən\ *n* **:** a cushion for pins not in use

¹pine \'pīn\ *n* **:** any of a genus of evergreen cone-bearing trees; *also* **:** the light durable resinous wood of a pine

²pine *vb* **pined; pin·ing** **1 :** to lose vigor or health through distress **2 ♦ :** to long for something intensely

♦ *usu* **pine for** ache for, covet, crave, desire, die (to *or* for), hanker for, hunger for, long for, lust (for *or* after), repine for, thirst for, want, wish for, yearn for — more at DESIRE

pi·ne·al \'pī-nē-əl, pī-'nē-əl\ *n* **:** PINEAL GLAND — **pineal** *adj*

pineal gland *n* **:** a small usu. conical appendage of the brain of all vertebrates with a cranium that functions primarily as an endocrine organ

pine·ap·ple \'pīn-ˌa-pəl\ *n* **:** a tropical plant bearing a large edible juicy fruit; *also* **:** its fruit

pin·feath·er \'pin-ˌfe-<u>th</u>ər\ *n* **:** a new feather just coming through the skin

ping \'piŋ\ *n* **1 :** a sharp sound like that of a bullet striking **2 :** engine knock

pin·hole \'pin-ˌhōl\ *n* **♦ :** a small hole made by, for, or as if by a pin

♦ perforation, prick, punch, puncture, stab — more at PRICK

¹pin·ion \'pin-yən\ *n* **:** the end section of a bird's wing; *also* **:** WING

²pinion *vb* **:** to restrain by binding the arms; *also* **:** SHACKLE

³pinion *n* **:** a gear with a small number of teeth designed to mesh with a larger wheel or rack

¹pink \'piŋk\ *n* **1 :** any of a genus of plants with narrow leaves often grown for their showy flowers **2 :** the highest degree ⟨the ~ of condition⟩

²pink *n* **:** a light tint of red

³pink *adj* **1 :** of the color pink **2 :** holding socialistic views — **pink·ish** *adj*

⁴pink *vb* **1** : to perforate in an ornamental pattern **2** : PIERCE, STAB **3** : to cut a saw-toothed edge on

pink-eye \'piŋk-ˌī\ *n* : an acute contagious eye inflammation

pin-kie *or* **pin-ky** \'piŋ-kē\ *n, pl* **pinkies** : the smallest finger of the hand

pin-nace \'pi-nəs\ *n* **1** : a light sailing ship **2** : a ship's boat

pin-na-cle \'pi-ni-kəl\ *n* [ME *pinacle*, fr. AF, fr. LL *pinnaculum* small wing, gable, fr. L *pinna* wing, battlement] **1** : a turret ending in a small spire **2** : a lofty peak **3** ♦ : the highest point of development or achievement : ACME

♦ acme, apex, climax, crown, culmination, head, height, meridian, peak, summit, tip-top, top, zenith — more at HEIGHT

pin-nate \'pi-ˌnāt\ *adj* : resembling a feather esp. in having similar parts arranged on each side of an axis ⟨a ∼ leaf⟩

pi-noch-le \'pē-ˌnə-kəl\ *n* : a card game played with a 48-card deck

pi-ñon *or* **pin-yon** \'pin-ˌyōn, -ˌyän\ *n, pl* **pi-ñons** *or* **pi-ño-nes** \pin-'yō-nēz\ *or* **pin-yons** [AmerSp *piñón*] : any of various small pines of western No. America with edible seeds; *also* : the edible seed of a piñon

pin-point \'pin-ˌpȯint\ *vb* ♦ : to locate, hit, or aim with great precision

♦ distinguish, identify, single — more at IDENTIFY

pin-prick \-ˌprik\ *n* **1** : a small puncture made by or as if by a pin **2** : a petty irritation or annoyance

pins and needles *n pl* : a pricking tingling sensation in a limb growing numb or recovering from numbness — **on pins and needles** : in a nervous or jumpy state of anticipation

pin-stripe \'pin-ˌstrīp\ *n* : a narrow stripe on a fabric; *also* : a suit with such stripes — **pin-striped** \-ˌstrīpt\ *adj*

pint \'pīnt\ *n* : a unit of capacity equal to ½ quart

pin-to \'pin-ˌtō\ *n, pl* **pintos** *also* **pintoes** : a spotted horse or pony

pinto bean *n* : a spotted seed produced by a kind of kidney bean and used for food

pint–size \'pīnt-ˌsīz\ *or* **pint–sized** \-ˌsīzd\ *adj* : having comparatively little size or slight dimensions : SMALL

pin-up \'pin-ˌəp\ *adj* : suitable or designed for hanging on a wall; *also* : suited (as by beauty) to be the subject of a pinup photograph

pin-wheel \-ˌhwēl, -ˌwēl\ *n* **1** : a fireworks device in the form of a revolving wheel of colored fire **2** : a toy consisting of lightweight vanes that revolve at the end of a stick

pin-worm \-ˌwərm\ *n* : a nematode worm parasitic in the human intestine

pin-yin \'pin-'yin\ *n, often cap* : a system for writing Chinese ideograms by using Roman letters to represent the sounds

¹pi-o-neer \ˌpī-ə-'nir\ *n* **1** : one that originates or helps open up a new line of thought or activity **2** ♦ : an early settler in a territory

♦ colonist, frontiersman, homesteader, settler — more at FRONTIERSMAN

²pioneer *vb* **1** : to act as a pioneer **2** : to open or prepare for others to follow; *also* : SETTLE **3** ♦ : to originate or take part in the development of

♦ constitute, establish, found, inaugurate, initiate, innovate, institute, introduce, launch, set up, start — more at FOUND

pi-ous \'pī-əs\ *adj* **1** ♦ : marked by reverence for deity : DEVOUT **2** : excessively or affectedly religious **3** : SACRED, DEVOTIONAL **4** ♦ : showing loyal reverence for a person or thing **5** : marked by sham or hypocrisy — **pi-ous-ly** *adv*

♦ [1] devout, faithful, godly, holy, religious, sainted, saintly — more at HOLY ♦ [4] constant, devoted, faithful, fast, good, loyal, staunch, steadfast, steady, true, true-blue — more at FAITHFUL

¹pip \'pip\ *n* : one of the dots used on dice and dominoes to indicate numerical value

²pip *n* **1** : a small fruit seed (as of an apple) **2** ♦ : one extraordinary of its kind

♦ beauty, crackerjack, dandy, jim-dandy, knockout — more at JIM-DANDY

¹pipe \'pīp\ *n* **1** : a tubular musical instrument played by forcing air through it **2** : BAGPIPE **3** ♦ : a tube designed to conduct something (as water, steam, or oil) **4** : a device for smoking having a tube with a bowl at one end and a mouthpiece at the other **5** : a large cask of varying capacity used esp. for wine and oil

♦ channel, conduit, duct, leader, line, penstock, tube; *also* drain, drainpipe, funnel, hydrant, main, smokestack, spout, tile, waterspout; pipeline, piping

²pipe *vb* **piped; pip-ing 1** : to play on a pipe **2 a** : to speak in a high or shrill voice **b** : to emit a shrill sound **3** ♦ : to convey by or as if by pipes — **pip-er** *n*

♦ channel, conduct, direct, funnel, siphon — more at CHANNEL

pipe down *vb* ♦ : to stop talking or making noise

♦ calm (down), cool (off *or* down), hush, quiet, settle (down) — more at QUIET ♦ clam up, hush, quiet (down), shut up — more at SHUT UP

pipe dream *n* ♦ : an illusory or fantastic hope

♦ chimera, conceit, daydream, delusion, dream, fancy, fantasy, figment, hallucination, illusion, phantasm, unreality, vision — more at FANTASY

pipe-line \'pīp-ˌlīn\ *n* **1** : a line of pipe with pumps, valves, and control devices for conveying fluids **2** : a channel for information

pi-pette *or* **pi-pet** \pī-'pet\ *n* : a device for measuring and transferring small volumes of liquid

pipe up *vb* : to speak loudly and distinctly; *also* : to express an opinion freely

pip-ing \'pī-piŋ\ *n* **1** : the music of pipes **2** : a narrow fold of material used to decorate edges or seams

piping hot *adj* : very hot

pip-pin \'pi-pən\ *n* : a crisp tart usu. yellowish apple

pip–squeak \'pip-ˌskwēk\ *n* ♦ : one that is small or insignificant

♦ nobody, nonentity, nothing, whippersnapper, zero — more at NOBODY

pi-quant \'pē-kənt\ *adj* **1** : pleasantly savory : PUNGENT ⟨a ∼ sauce⟩ **2** : engagingly provocative; *also* : having a lively charm — **pi-quan-cy** \-kən-sē\ *n*

¹pique \'pēk\ *n* [F] ♦ : a passing feeling of wounded vanity : RESENTMENT

♦ dudgeon, huff, offense, peeve, resentment, umbrage; *also* aggravation, anger, annoyance, bother, discomfort, exasperation, frustration, irritation, vexation; agitation, displeasure, distress, disturbance, indignation, ire, outrage, perturbation, upset; dander, temper; fit, pet, tantrum, tizzy; affront, insult

²pique *vb* **piqued; piqu-ing 1** ♦ : to arouse anger or resentment in : IRRITATE **2** ♦ : to arouse by a provocation or challenge

♦ [1] aggravate, annoy, bother, bug, chafe, exasperate, gall, get, grate, irk, irritate, nettle, peeve, persecute, put out, rasp, rile, vex — more at IRRITATE ♦ [2] arouse, encourage, excite, fire, incite, instigate, move, provoke, stimulate, stir

pi-qué *or* **pi-que** \pi-'kā\ *n* : a durable ribbed clothing fabric

pi-quet \pi-'kā\ *n* : a 2-handed card game played with 32 cards

pi-ra-cy \'pī-rə-sē\ *n, pl* **-cies 1** : robbery on the high seas; *also* : an act resembling such robbery **2** : the unauthorized use of another's production or invention

pi-ra-nha \pə-'rä-nə, -'rän-yə\ *n* [Pg, fr. Tupi (So. American Indian language) *pirája*, fr. pir' fish + *ája* tooth] : any of various usu. small So. American fishes with sharp teeth that include some known to attack humans and large animals

pi-rate \'pī-rət\ *n* [ME, fr. MF or L; MF, fr. L *pirata*, fr. Gk *peiratēs*, fr. *peiran* to attempt, test] ♦ : one who commits piracy — **pirate** *vb* — **pi·rat·i·cal** \pə-'ra-ti-kəl, pī-\ *adj*

♦ buccaneer, corsair, freebooter, rover; *also* looter, marauder, pillager, plunderer, raider, robber; privateer; burglar, thief; hijacker, rustler

¹**pir·ou·ette** \ˌpir-ə-'wet\ *n* [F] : a rapid whirling about of the body; *esp* : a full turn on the toe or ball of one foot in ballet

²**pirouette** *vb* ♦ : to turn in or as if in a pirouette

♦ gyrate, revolve, roll, rotate, spin, turn, twirl, wheel, whirl — more at SPIN

pis *pl of* PI

pis·ca·to·ri·al \ˌpis-kə-'tōr-ē-əl\ *adj* : of or relating to fishing

Pi·sces \'pī-sēz\ *n* [ME, fr. L, lit., fishes] **1** : a zodiacal constellation between Aquarius and Aries usu. pictured as a fish **2** : the 12th sign of the zodiac in astrology; *also* : one born under this sign

pis·mire \'pis-ˌmīr\ *n* : ANT

pis·ta·chio \pə-'sta-shē-ˌō, -'stä-\ *n, pl* **-chios** : the greenish edible seed of a small Asian tree related to the sumacs; *also* : the tree

pis·til \'pist-ᵊl\ *n* : the female reproductive organ in a flower — **pis·til·late** \'pis-tə-ˌlāt\ *adj*

pis·tol \'pist-ᵊl\ *n* : a handgun whose chamber is integral with the barrel

pis·tol–whip \-ˌhwip\ *vb* : to beat with a pistol

pis·ton \'pis-tən\ *n* : a sliding piece that receives and transmits motion and that usu. consists of a short cylinder inside a large cylinder

¹**pit** \'pit\ *n* **1** : a hole, shaft, or cavity in the ground **2** : an often sunken area designed for a particular use; *also* : an enclosed place (as for cockfights) **3** : HELL; *also, pl* : WORST ⟨it's the ∼s⟩ **4** ♦ : a natural hollow or indentation in a surface **5** : a small indented mark or scar (as from disease or corrosion) **6** : an area beside a racecourse where cars are fueled and repaired during a race

♦ [1, 4] cavity, concavity, dent, depression, hole, hollow, indentation, recess — more at HOLE

²**pit** *vb* **pit·ted**; **pit·ting** **1** : to form pits in or become marred with pits **2** : to match for fighting

³**pit** *n* : the stony seed of some fruits (as the cherry, peach, and date)

⁴**pit** *vb* **pit·ted**; **pit·ting** : to remove the pit from

pi·ta \'pē-tə\ *n* [ModGk] : a thin flat bread

pit–a–pat \ˌpi-ti-'pat\ *n* : PITTER-PATTER — **pit–a–pat** *adv or adj*

pit bull *n* : a powerful compact short-haired dog developed for fighting

¹**pitch** \'pich\ *n* **1** : a dark sticky substance left over esp. from distilling tar or petroleum **2** : resin from various conifers

²**pitch** *vb* **1** ♦ : to erect and fix firmly in place ⟨∼ a tent⟩ **2** ♦ : to throw usu. with a particular objective or toward a particular point **3** : to deliver a baseball to a batter **4** : to toss (as coins) toward a mark **5** : to set at a particular level ⟨∼ the voice low⟩ **6** : to fall headlong **7** : to have the front end (as of a ship) alternately plunge and rise **8** : to incline downward : SLOPE

♦ [1] erect, put up, raise, rear, set up — more at ERECT
♦ [2] cast, catapult, chuck, dash, fire, fling, heave, hurl, hurtle, launch, peg, pelt, sling, throw, toss — more at THROW

³**pitch** *n* **1** : the action or a manner of pitching **2** ♦ : degree of slope ⟨∼ of a roof⟩ **3** : the relative level of some quality or state ⟨a high ∼ of excitement⟩ **4** : highness or lowness of sound; *also* : a standard frequency for tuning instruments **5** : a presentation delivered to sell or promote something **6** : the delivery of a baseball to a batter; *also* : the baseball delivered

♦ cant, diagonal, grade, inclination, incline, lean, slant, slope, tilt, upgrade — more at SLANT

pitch·blende \'pich-ˌblend\ *n* : a dark mineral that is the chief source of uranium

¹**pitch·er** \'pi-chər\ *n* ♦ : a container for liquids that usu. has a lip and a handle

♦ ewer, flagon, jug; *also* carafe, decanter; canteen, cup, flask, mug, stein

²**pitcher** *n* : one that pitches esp. in a baseball game

pitcher plant *n* : any of various plants with leaves modified to resemble pitchers in which insects are trapped and digested

pitch·fork \'pich-ˌfȯrk\ *n* : a long-handled fork used esp. in pitching hay

pitch in *vb* **1** : to begin to work **2** ♦ : to contribute to a common effort

♦ chip in, contribute, kick in — more at CONTRIBUTE

pitch·man \'pich-mən\ *n* **1** : SALESMAN; *esp* : one who sells merchandise on the streets or from a concession **2** : one who does radio or TV commercials

pitch–per·fect \'pich-'pər-fikt\ *adj* : having just the right tone or style ⟨a ∼ translation⟩

pitchy \'pi-chē\ *adj* **1 a** : full of pitch **b** : of, relating to, or having the qualities of pitch **2** : extremely dark or black

pit·e·ous \'pi-tē-əs\ *adj* ♦ : arousing pity : PITIFUL — **pit·e·ous·ly** *adv*

♦ heartbreaking, miserable, pathetic, pitiful, poor, rueful, sorry, wretched

pit·fall \'pit-ˌfȯl\ *n* **1** : TRAP, SNARE; *esp* : a covered pit used for capturing animals **2** ♦ : a hidden danger or difficulty

♦ booby trap, catch, snag; *also* snare, trap, web; hazard, peril, risk; bombshell, surprise; bait, lure danger, hazard, menace, peril, risk, threat, trouble — more at DANGER

pith \'pith\ *n* **1** : loose spongy tissue esp. in the center of the stem of vascular plants **2** ♦ : the essential part : CORE

♦ core, crux, gist, heart, nub, pivot — more at CRUX

pithy \'pi-thē\ *adj* **pith·i·er**; **-est** **1** : consisting of or filled with pith **2** ♦ : having substance and point : CONCISE

♦ brief, compact, compendious, concise, crisp, epigrammatic, laconic, succinct, summary, terse — more at CONCISE

piti·able \'pi-tē-ə-bəl\ *adj* **1** : arousing or deserving pity : PITIFUL **2** : of a kind to evoke mingled pity and contempt esp. because of inadequacy

piti·ful \'pi-ti-fəl\ *adj* **1** ♦ : arousing or deserving pity ⟨a ∼ sight⟩ **2** ♦ : arousing pitying contempt (as by meanness or inadequacy) — **piti·ful·ly** *adv*

♦ [1] heartbreaking, miserable, pathetic, piteous, poor, rueful, sorry, wretched ♦ [2] contemptible, despicable, lousy, nasty, scabby, scurvy, sorry, wretched — more at CONTEMPTIBLE

piti·less \'pi-ti-ləs\ *adj* ♦ : devoid of pity : MERCILESS — **pit·i·less·ly** *adv*

♦ callous, hard, heartless, inhuman, inhumane, soulless, unfeeling, unsympathetic — more at HARD

pi·ton \'pē-ˌtän\ *n* [F] : a spike, wedge, or peg that can be driven into a rock or ice surface as a support

pit·tance \'pit-ᵊns\ *n* ♦ : a small portion, amount, or allowance

♦ mite, peanuts, shoestring, song — more at MITE

pit·ted \'pi-təd\ *adj* : marked with pits

¹**pit·ter–pat·ter** \'pi-tər-ˌpa-tər, 'pi-tē-\ *n* : a rapid succession of light taps or sounds ⟨the ∼ of rain⟩ — **pitter–patter** \ˌpi-tər-'pa-tər, ˌpi-tē-\ *adv or adj*

²**pitter–patter** \ˌpi-tər-'pa-tər, ˌpi-tē-\ *vb* ♦ : to go pitter-patter

♦ beat, palpitate, pulsate, pulse, throb — more at PULSATE

pi·tu·i·tary \pə-'tü-ə-ˌter-ē, -'tyü-\ *n, pl* **-i·tar·ies** : PITUITARY GLAND — **pituitary** *adj*

pituitary gland *n* : a small oval endocrine gland located at the base of the brain that produces various hormones that affect most basic bodily functions (as growth and reproduction)

pit viper *n* : any of various mostly New World venomous snakes with a sensory pit on each side of the head and hollow perforated fangs

¹**pity** \'pi-tē\ *n, pl* **pit·ies** [ME *pite*, fr. AF *pité*, fr. L *pietas* piety, pity, fr. *pius* pious] **1 ♦** : sympathetic sorrow : COMPASSION **2** : something to be regretted

♦ charity, commiseration, compassion, feeling, heart, humanity, kindliness, kindness, mercy, sympathy — more at HEART

²**pity** *vb* **pit·ied; pity·ing ♦** : to feel pity for

♦ bleed, commiserate, feel, sympathize; *also* care (for); grieve (for), sorrow (for); love; tolerate, understand

¹**piv·ot** \'pi-vət\ *n* **1** : a fixed pin on which something turns **2 ♦** : a person, thing, or factor having a major or central role, function, or effect — **pivot** *adj*

♦ core, crux, gist, heart, nub, pith — more at CRUX

²**pivot** *vb* **♦** : to turn on or as if on a pivot

♦ revolve, roll, rotate, spin, swing, swirl, turn, twirl, twist, wheel, whirl — more at TURN

piv·ot·al \'pi-vət-ᵊl\ *adj* **♦** : vitally important : CRITICAL

♦ critical, crucial, key, vital — more at CRUCIAL

pix *pl of* PIC

pix·el \'pik-səl, -ˌsel\ *n* : any of the small elements that together make up an image (as on a television screen)

pix·ie *also* **pixy** \'pik-sē\ *n, pl* **pix·ies** : FAIRY; *esp* **♦** : a mischievous sprite

♦ brownie, dwarf, elf, fairy, fay, gnome, hobgoblin, leprechaun, puck, troll — more at FAIRY

piz·za \'pēt-sə\ *n* [It] : an open pie made of rolled bread dough spread with a spiced mixture (as of tomatoes, cheese, and ground meat) and baked

piz·zazz *or* **pi·zazz** \pə-'zaz\ *n* **1** : GLAMOUR **2** : VITALITY

piz·ze·ria \ˌpēt-sə-'rē-ə\ *n* : an establishment where pizzas are made and sold

piz·zi·ca·to \ˌpit-si-'kä-tō\ *adv or adj* [It] : by means of plucking instead of bowing — used as a direction in music

pj's \'pē-ˌjāz\ *n pl* : PAJAMAS

pk *abbr* **1** park **2** peak **3** peck **4** pike

pkg *abbr* package

pkt *abbr* **1** packet **2** pocket

pkwy *abbr* parkway

pl *abbr* **1** place **2** plate **3** plural

¹**plac·ard** \'pla-kərd, -ˌkärd\ *n* **♦** : a notice posted in a public place : POSTER

♦ bill, poster — more at POSTER

²**plac·ard** \-ˌkärd, -kərd\ *vb* **1** : to cover with or as if with placards **2 ♦** : to announce by or as if by posting

♦ advertise, announce, blaze, broadcast, declare, enunciate, post, proclaim, promulgate, publicize, publish, sound — more at ANNOUNCE

pla·cate \'plā-ˌkāt, 'pla-\ *vb* **pla·cat·ed; pla·cat·ing ♦** : to soothe esp. by concessions : APPEASE — **pla·ca·ble** \'plak-ə-bəl, 'plā-\ *adj*

♦ appease, conciliate, disarm, mollify, pacify, propitiate — more at PACIFY

¹**place** \'plās\ *n* [ME, fr. AF, open space, fr. L *platea* broad street, fr. Gk *plateia* (*hodos*), fr. fem. of *platys* broad, flat] **1** : physical environment : SPACE **2** : an indefinite region : AREA **3 ♦** : a building or locality used for a special purpose **4** : a center of population **5** : a particular part of a surface : SPOT **6 ♦** : relative position in a scale or sequence; *also* : position at the end of a competition ⟨last ∼⟩ **7** : ACCOMMODATION; *esp* : SEAT **8** : the position of a figure within a numeral ⟨12 is a two ∼ number⟩ **9 ♦** : paid employment : JOB; *esp* : public office **10** : a public square **11** : 2d place at the finish (as of a horse race) **12 ♦** : a proper or designated niche **13 ♦** : a building, part of a building, or area occupied as a home

♦ [3] establishment, joint, salon; *also* spot, station; facility, installation ♦ [3, 12] locale, location, point, position,

site, spot *Ant* scene, region, section, sector ♦ [6] degree, footing, level, position, rank, situation, standing, station, status — more at RANK ♦ [9] appointment, billet, capacity, function, job, position, post, situation — more at JOB ♦ [12] part, purpose, role, task, work — more at ROLE ♦ [13] abode, domicile, dwelling, home, house, lodging, quarters, residence — more at HOME

²**place** *vb* **placed; plac·ing 1 ♦** : to put in a particular place : SET **2 ♦** : to distribute in an orderly manner **3** : IDENTIFY **4** : to give an order for ⟨∼ a bet⟩ **5 ♦** : to earn a given spot in a competition; *esp* : to come in 2d **6 ♦** : to judge tentatively or approximately the value, worth, or significance of : ESTIMATE

♦ [1] deposit, dispose, fix, lay, position, put, set, set up, stick; *also* rearrange, reorder; orient; establish, locate, settle; assemble, collect; carry; berth, park; affix, anchor, wedge; lay out, line up, queue, rank; set down ♦ [2] assort, break down, categorize, class, classify, grade, group, peg, range, rank, separate, sort — more at CLASSIFY ♦ [5] be, grade, rank, rate — more at RANK ♦ [6] calculate, call, conjecture, estimate, figure, gauge, guess, judge, make, put, reckon, suppose — more at ESTIMATE

pla·ce·bo \plə-'sē-bō\ *n, pl* **-bos** [L, I shall please] : an inert medication used for its psychological effect or for purposes of comparison in an experiment

place·hold·er \'plās-ˌhōl-dər\ *n* : a symbol in a mathematical or logical expression that may be replaced by the name of any element of a set

place·kick \-ˌkik\ *n* : the kicking of a ball placed or held on the ground — **placekick** *vb* — **place·kick·er** *n*

place·ment \'plās-mənt\ *n* : an act or instance of placing

place-name \-ˌnām\ *n* : the name of a geographical locality

pla·cen·ta \plə-'sen-tə\ *n, pl* **-tas** *or* **-tae** \-(ˌ)tē\ [NL, fr. L, flat cake] : the organ in most mammals by which the fetus is joined to the maternal uterus and is nourished — **pla·cen·tal** \-'sent-ᵊl\ *adj*

plac·er \'pla-sər\ *n* : a deposit of sand or gravel containing particles of valuable mineral (as gold)

plac·id \'pla-səd\ *adj* **♦** : serenely free of interruption or disturbance — **plac·id·ly** *adv*

♦ calm, collected, composed, cool, self-possessed, serene, tranquil, undisturbed, unperturbed, unshaken, untroubled, unworried — more at CALM ♦ calm, halcyon, hushed, peaceful, quiet, still — more at CALM

pla·cid·i·ty \pla-'si-də-tē\ *n* **♦** : the quality or state of being placid

♦ calm, calmness, hush, peace, quiet, quietness, repose, serenity, still, stillness, tranquility — more at CALM

plack·et \'pla-kət\ *n* : a slit in a garment

pla·gia·rise *chiefly Brit var of* PLAGIARIZE

pla·gia·rize \'plā-jə-ˌrīz\ *vb* **-rized; -riz·ing** : to present the ideas or words of another as one's own — **pla·gia·rism** \-ˌri-zəm\ *n* — **pla·gia·rist** \-rist\ *n*

¹**plague** \'plāg\ *n* **1** : a disastrous evil or influx; *also* : NUISANCE **2** : PESTILENCE; *esp* : a destructive contagious bacterial disease (as bubonic plague)

²**plague** *vb* **plagued; plagu·ing 1 ♦** : to afflict with or as if with disease or disaster **2 a** : to cause worry or distress to **b ♦** : to disturb or annoy persistently

♦ [1, 2b] afflict, agonize, bedevil, curse, harrow, martyr, persecute, rack, torment, torture — more at AFFLICT

plaid \'plad\ *n* [ScGael *plaide*] **1** : a rectangular length of tartan worn esp. over the left shoulder as part of the Scottish national costume **2** : a twilled woolen fabric with a tartan pattern **3** : a pattern of unevenly spaced repeated stripes crossing at right angles — **plaid** *adj*

¹**plain** \'plān\ *n* **♦** : an extensive area of level or rolling treeless country

♦ down, grassland, prairie, savanna, steppe, veld; *also* pampas; floodplain; bottom, bottomland, flat, lowland; plateau, table, tableland, upland

²**plain** *adj* **1** ♦ : lacking ornament ⟨a ∼ dress⟩ **2** ♦ : free of extraneous matter **3** : OPEN, UNOBSTRUCTED ⟨∼ view⟩ **4** : EVIDENT, OBVIOUS **5 a** ♦ : easily understood : CLEAR **b** ♦ : expressing oneself free of any attempt at deception or subterfuge **6** ♦ : marked by outspoken candor : CANDID, BLUNT **7** : SIMPLE ⟨∼ cooking⟩ **8** : lacking beauty or ugliness

♦ [1] bald, bare, naked, simple, unadorned, undecorated, unvarnished; *also* chaste, modest; unsophisticated; denuded, stripped; dry, laconic, terse; unpretentious; austere, bleak, severe, stark; inconspicuous, muted, restrained, subdued, toned (down), unobtrusive; conservative, quiet, understated *Ant* adorned, decorated, embellished, fancy, ornamented ♦ [2] absolute, fine, neat, pure, refined, straight, unadulterated, undiluted, unmixed — more at PURE ♦ [5a] apparent, broad, clear, clear-cut, distinct, evident, lucid, manifest, obvious, palpable, patent, perspicuous, transparent, unambiguous, unequivocal, unmistakable — more at CLEAR ♦ [5b, 6] blunt, candid, direct, forthright, foursquare, frank, honest, open, outspoken, straight, straightforward, unguarded, unreserved — more at FRANK

plain·clothes \'plān-ͺklō(th)z\ *adj* : dressed in civilian clothes while on duty — used esp. of a police officer ⟨∼ officers⟩
plain·ly \'plān-lē\ *adv* ♦ : in a plain manner

♦ directly, forthrightly, foursquare, plain, straight, straightforward

plain·ness \'plān-nəs\ *n* ♦ : the quality or state of being plain

♦ candor (*or* candour), directness, forthrightness, frankness, openness — more at CANDOR

plain·spo·ken \-'spō-kən\ *adj* : marked by honest sincere expression : FRANK
plaint \'plānt\ *n* **1** ♦ : an act or instance of lamenting : LAMENTATION, WAIL **2** ♦ : a critical protest : COMPLAINT

♦ [1] groan, howl, keen, lament, lamentation, moan, wail — more at LAMENT ♦ [2] beef, complaint, fuss, grievance, gripe, grumble, murmur, squawk — more at COMPLAINT

plain·tiff \'plān-təf\ *n* : the complaining party in a lawsuit
plain·tive \'plān-tiv\ *adj* ♦ : expressive of suffering or woe — **plain·tive·ly** *adv*

♦ dolorous, funeral, lugubrious, mournful, regretful, rueful, sorrowful, weeping, woeful — more at MOURNFUL

¹**plait** \'plāt, 'plat\ *n* **1** : PLEAT **2** ♦ : a braid esp. of hair or straw — **plait** *vb*

♦ braid, lace — more at BRAID

¹**plan** \'plan\ *n* **1** : a drawing or diagram showing the parts or details of something **2 a** ♦ : a method for accomplishing an objective **b** ♦ : the end toward which effort is directed : GOAL, AIM

♦ [2a] arrangement, blueprint, design, game, project, scheme, strategy, system; *also* collusion, conspiracy, plot; maneuver, ruse, stratagem, subterfuge, trick; means, method, tactic, technique; conception, idea, proposal; aim, intention, purpose, diagram, formula, layout, map, recipe ♦ [2b] aim, ambition, aspiration, design, dream, end, goal, intent, mark, meaning, object, objective, pretension, purpose, thing — more at GOAL

²**plan** *vb* **planned; plan·ning 1** ♦ : to form a plan of ⟨∼ a new city⟩ **2** ♦ : to have in mind : INTEND ⟨planned to go⟩ — **plan·ner** *n*

♦ [1] arrange, blueprint, calculate, chart, design, frame, lay out, map, project, scheme; *also* conspire, intrigue, machinate; draft, outline, sketch; aim, figure, intend, mean; contemplate, meditate, premeditate ♦ [2] aim, aspire, contemplate, design, intend, mean, meditate, propose — more at INTEND

¹**plane** \'plān\ *vb* **planed; plan·ing** ♦ : to smooth or level off with or as if with a plane — **plan·er** *n*

♦ even, level, smooth — more at EVEN

²**plane** *n* : PLANE TREE
³**plane** *n* : a tool for smoothing or shaping a wood surface
⁴**plane** *n* **1** : a level or flat surface **2** : a level of existence, consciousness, or development **3** : AIRPLANE
⁵**plane** *adj* **1** ♦ : having no elevations or depressions : FLAT, LEVEL **2** : dealing with flat surfaces or figures ⟨∼ geometry⟩

♦ even, flat, flush, level, smooth — more at LEVEL

⁶**plane** *vb* ♦ : to fly while keeping the wings motionless

♦ fly, glide, soar, wing — more at FLY

plane·load \'plān-ͺlōd\ *n* : a load that fills an airplane
plan·et \'pla-nət\ *n* [ME *planete*, fr. AF, fr. LL *planeta*, fr. Gk *planēt-, planēs*, lit., wanderer, fr. *planasthai* to wander] **1** : any of the large bodies in the solar system that revolve around the sun **2** ♦ : the celestial body on which we live that is third in order from the sun — **plan·e·tary** \-nə-ͺter-ē\ *adj*

♦ earth, world — more at EARTH

plan·e·tar·i·um \ͺpla-nə-'ter-ē-əm\ *n, pl* **-i·ums** *or* **-ia** \-ē-ə\ : a building or room housing a device to project images of celestial bodies
plan·e·tes·i·mal \ͺpla-nə-'tes-ə-məl\ *n* : any of numerous small solid celestial bodies which may have existed during the formation of the solar system
plan·e·toid \'pla-nə-ͺtóid\ *n* : a body resembling a planet; *esp* : ASTEROID
plane tree *n* : any of a genus of trees (as a sycamore) with large lobed leaves and globe-shaped fruit
plan·gent \'plan-jənt\ *adj* **1** : having a loud reverberating sound **2** : having an expressive esp. plaintive quality — **plan·gen·cy** \-jən-sē\ *n*
¹**plank** \'plaŋk\ *n* **1** : a heavy thick board **2** : an article in the platform of a political party
²**plank** *vb* **1** : to cover with planks **2** : to set or lay down forcibly **3** : to cook and serve on a board
plank·ing \'plaŋ-kiŋ\ *n* : a quantity or covering of planks
plank·ton \'plaŋk-tən\ *n* [G, fr. Gk, neut. of *planktos* drifting] : the passively floating or weakly swimming animal and plant life of a body of water — **plank·ton·ic** \plaŋk-'tä-nik\ *adj*
¹**plant** \'plant\ *vb* **1** ♦ : to set in the ground to grow **2** : ESTABLISH, SETTLE **3** : to stock or provide with something **4** : to place firmly or forcibly **5** : to hide or arrange with intent to deceive

♦ drill, seed, sow; *also* bed; replant, transplant; scatter; pot

²**plant** *n* **1** : any of a kingdom of living things that usu. have no locomotor ability or obvious sense organs and have cellulose cell walls and usu. capacity for indefinite growth **2 a** : the land, buildings, and machinery used in carrying on a trade or business **b** ♦ : a factory or workshop for the manufacture of a particular product

♦ factory, mill, shop, works, workshop — more at FACTORY

¹**plan·tain** \'plant-ᵊn\ *n* [ME, fr. AF, fr. L *plantagin-, plantago*, fr. *planta* sole of the foot; fr. its broad leaves] : any of a genus of weedy herbs with spikes of tiny greenish flowers
²**plan·tain** \plan-'tān, 'plan-ͺtān, 'plant-ᵊn\ *n* [Sp *plántano, plátano* plane tree, banana tree, fr. ML *plantanus* plane tree, alter. of L *platanus*] : a banana plant with starchy greenish fruit that is eaten cooked; *also* : its fruit
plan·tar \'plan-tər, -ͺtär\ *adj* : of or relating to the sole of the foot
plan·ta·tion \plan-'tä-shən\ *n* **1** : a large group of plants and esp. trees under cultivation **2** : an agricultural estate usu. worked by resident laborers
plant·er \'plan-tər\ *n* **1** ♦ : one that plants or sows; *esp* : an owner or operator of a plantation **2** : a container for plants

♦ agriculturist, cultivator, farmer, grower, tiller — more at FARMER

plant louse *n* : APHID

plaque \\'plak\\ *n* [F] **1** : an ornamental brooch **2** : a flat thin piece (as of metal) used for decoration; *also* : a commemorative tablet **3** : a bacteria-containing film on a tooth

¹**plash** \\'plash\\ *n* : SPLASH

²**plash** *vb* **1** ♦ : to cause a splashing or spattering effect **2** ♦ : to splash with a liquid or with any wet substance

♦ [1] lap, slosh, splash, swash — more at SLOSH
♦ [2] dash, spatter, splash — more at SPLASH

plas·ma \\'plaz-mə\\ *n* **1** : the fluid part of blood, lymph, or milk **2** : a gas composed of ionized particles — **plas·mat·ic** \\plaz-'ma-tik\\ *adj*

¹**plas·ter** \\'plas-tər\\ *n* **1** : a dressing consisting of a backing spread with an often medicated substance that clings to the skin ⟨adhesive ∼⟩ **2** : a paste that hardens as it dries and is used for coating walls and ceilings

²**plaster** *vb* : to cover with or as if with plaster — **plas·ter·er** *n*

plas·ter·board \\'plas-tər-ˌbȯrd\\ *n* : DRYWALL

plaster of par·is \\-'pa-rəs\\ *often cap 2d P* : a white powder made from gypsum and used as a quick-setting paste with water for casts and molds

¹**plas·tic** \\'plas-tik\\ *adj* [L *plasticus* of molding, fr. Gk *plastikos*, fr. *plassein* to mold, form] **1** : capable of being molded ⟨∼ clay⟩ **2** : characterized by or using modeling ⟨∼ arts⟩ **3** : made or consisting of a plastic — **plas·tic·i·ty** \\plas-'ti-sə-tē\\ *n*

²**plastic** *n* : a plastic substance; *esp* : a synthetic or processed material that can be formed into rigid objects or into films or filaments

plastic surgery *n* : surgery to repair, restore, or improve lost, injured, defective, or misshapen body parts — **plastic surgeon** *n*

¹**plat** \\'plat\\ *n* **1** ♦ : a small plot of ground **2** ♦ : a plan of a piece of land with actual or proposed features (as lots)

♦ [1, 2] lot, parcel, plot, property, tract — more at LOT

²**plat** *vb* **plat·ted; plat·ting** : to make a plat of

¹**plate** \\'plāt\\ *n* **1** : a flat thin piece of material **2** : domestic holloware made of or plated with gold, silver, or base metals **3** : DISH **4** : HOME PLATE **5** : the molded metal or plastic cast of a page of type to be printed from **6** : a sheet of glass or plastic coated with a chemical sensitive to light and used in photography **7** : the part of a denture that fits to the mouth; *also* : DENTURE **8** : something printed from an engraving **9** : a huge mobile segment of the earth's crust **10** ♦ : a full-page illustration often on different paper from the text pages

♦ diagram, figure, graphic, illustration — more at ILLUSTRATION

²**plate** *vb* **plat·ed; plat·ing** **1** : to overlay with metal (as gold or silver) **2** : to make a printing plate of

pla·teau \\pla-'tō\\ *n, pl* **plateaus** *or* **pla·teaux** \\-'tōz\\ [F] ♦ : a large level area of high land

♦ mesa, table, tableland; *also* butte, dome, height, highland, upland

plate glass *n* : rolled, ground, and polished sheet glass

plate·let \\'plāt-lət\\ *n* : a minute flattened body; *esp* : a minute colorless disklike body of mammalian blood that assists in blood clotting

plat·en \\'plat-ᵊn\\ *n* **1** : a flat plate; *esp* : one that exerts or receives pressure (as in a printing press) **2** : the roller of a typewriter or printer

plate tectonics *n* **1** : a theory in geology that the lithosphere is divided into plates at the boundaries of which much of earth's seismic activity occurs **2** : the process and dynamics of tectonic plate movement

plat·form \\'plat-ˌfȯrm\\ *n* **1** ♦ : a raised flooring or stage for speakers, performers, or workers **2** : a declaration of the principles on which a group of persons (as a political party) stands

♦ dais, podium, rostrum, stage, stand; *also* altar, pulpit; balcony

plat·ing \\'plā-tiŋ\\ *n* : a coating of metal plates or plate ⟨the ∼ of a ship⟩

plat·i·num \\'plat-ᵊn-əm\\ *n* : a heavy grayish white metallic chemical element

plat·i·tude \\'pla-tə-ˌtüd, -ˌtyüd\\ *n* ♦ : a flat or trite remark — **plat·i·tu·di·nous** \\-'tüd-ᵊn-əs, -ˌtyüd-\\ *adj*

♦ banality, cliché, commonplace, shibboleth — more at COMMONPLACE

pla·ton·ic love \\plə-'tä-nik-, plā-\\ *n, often cap P* : a close relationship between two persons without sexual desire

pla·toon \\plə-'tün\\ *n* [F *peloton* small detachment, lit., ball, fr. *pelote* little ball] **1** : a subdivision of a company-size military unit usu. consisting of two or more squads or sections **2** : a group of football players trained either for offense or for defense and sent into the game as a body

platoon sergeant *n* : a noncommissioned officer in the army ranking below a first sergeant

plat·ter \\'pla-tər\\ *n* **1** : a large serving plate **2** : a phonograph record

platy \\'pla-tē\\ *n, pl* **platy** *or* **plat·ys** *or* **plat·ies** : either of two small stocky usu. brilliantly colored bony fishes often kept in tropical aquariums

platy·pus \\'pla-ti-pəs\\ *n, pl* **platy·pus·es** *also* **platy·pi** \\-ˌpī\\ [NL, fr. Gk *platypous* flat-footed, fr. *platys* broad, flat + *pous* foot] : a small aquatic egg-laying marsupial mammal of Australia with webbed feet and a fleshy bill like a duck's

plau·dit \\'plȯ-dət\\ *n* : an act of applause

plau·si·ble \\'plȯ-zə-bəl\\ *adj* [L *plausibilis* worthy of applause, fr. *plausus*, pp. of *plaudere* to applaud] ♦ : seemingly worthy of belief — **plau·si·bil·i·ty** \\ˌplȯ-zə-'bi-lə-tē\\ *n* — **plau·si·bly** \\'plȯ-zə-blē\\ *adv*

♦ believable, credible, likely, probable — more at BELIEVABLE

¹**play** \\'plā\\ *n* **1** : brisk handling of something (as a weapon) **2** : the course of a game; *also* : a particular act or maneuver in a game **3** ♦ : recreational activity; *esp* : the spontaneous activity of children **4** : absence of serious or harmful intent : JEST ⟨said in ∼⟩ **5** : the act or an instance of punning **6** : GAMBLING **7** ♦ : the state of being active, operative, or relevant : OPERATION ⟨bring extra force into ∼⟩ **8** : a brisk or light movement **9** : free motion (as of part of a machine) **10** : scope for action **11** : PUBLICITY **12** : an effort to arouse liking ⟨made a ∼ for her⟩ **13** : a stage representation of a drama; *also* : a dramatic composition **14** : a function of an electronic device that causes a recording to play — **in play** : in condition or position to be played

♦ [3] dalliance, frolic, fun, relaxation, sport; *also* gamboling; romping, amusement, diversion, entertainment; delight, enjoyment, pleasure; friskiness, playfulness, wantonness; devilment, devilry, hob, impishness, mischief, mischievousness, rascality, roguishness, waggery; binge, fling, lark, revel, spree; hilarity, merrymaking, revelry; buffoonery, horseplay, tomfoolery ♦ [7] application, employment, exercise, operation, use — more at USE

²**play** *vb* **1** ♦ : to engage in recreation : FROLIC **2** ♦ : to handle or behave lightly or absentmindedly **3** : to make a pun ⟨∼ on words⟩ **4** ♦ : to take advantage ⟨∼ on fears⟩ **5** : to move or operate in a brisk or irregular manner ⟨a flashlight ∼ed over the wall⟩ **6** : to perform music ⟨∼ on a violin⟩; *also* : to perform (music) on an instrument ⟨∼ a waltz⟩ **7** : to perform music upon ⟨∼ the piano⟩; *also* : to sound in performance ⟨the organ is ∼ing⟩ **8** : to cause to emit sounds ⟨∼ a radio⟩; *also* : to cause to reproduce recorded material ⟨∼ a DVD⟩ **9 a** : to act in a dramatic medium **b** ♦ : to act in the character of ⟨∼ the hero⟩ **10** : GAMBLE **11 a** : to behave in a specified way ⟨∼ safe⟩ **b** ♦ : to feign a specified state or quality **c** : COOPERATE ⟨∼ along with him⟩ **12** : to deal with; *also* : EMPHASIZE ⟨∼ up her good qualities⟩

13 : to perform for amusement ⟨~ a trick⟩ 14 : WREAK 15 : to contend with in a game; *also* : to fill (a certain position) on a team 16 : to make wagers on ⟨~ the races⟩ 17 : WIELD, PLY 18 : to keep in action

♦ [1] dally, disport, frolic, recreate, rollick, sport; *also* gambol, romp; dabble, trifle; amuse, divert, entertain; delight, please; dabble, mess (around), putter; bum (around), dawdle, goldbrick, idle, loaf, lounge (around *or* about), relax, rest, slack (off); jest, joke, tease ♦ [2] fiddle, fool, mess, monkey, potter, putter, trifle ♦ *usu* play with [2] fiddle, fool, mess, monkey, tamper, tinker — more at TAMPER ♦ *usu* play on *or* play upon [4] abuse, capitalize, cash in, exploit, impose, use — more at EXPLOIT ♦ [9b] act, impersonate, perform, portray — more at ACT ♦ [11b] impersonate, masquerade, pose — more at IMPERSONATE

play·act·ing \\'plā-,ak-tiŋ\\ *n* 1 : performance in theatrical productions 2 : insincere or artificial behavior

play·back \\-,bak\\ *n* : an act of reproducing recorded sound or pictures — **play back** *vb*

play·bill \\-,bil\\ *n* : a poster advertising the performance of a play

play·book \\-,bük\\ *n* : a notebook containing diagrammed football plays

play·boy \\-,bȯi\\ *n* : a man whose chief interest is the pursuit of pleasure

play·date \\-,dāt\\ *n* : a usu. prearranged play session for small children

play·er \\'plā-ər\\ *n* ♦ : one that plays

♦ actor, impersonator, mummer, trouper

play·ful \\-fəl\\ *adj* ♦ : full of play : FROLICSOME — **play·ful·ly** *adv*

♦ antic, coltish, elfish, fay, frisky, frolicsome, sportive; *also* kittenish; gay, happy, lighthearted, whimsical; energetic, lively, spirited, sprightly; devilish, knavish, rascally; amusing, diverting, enjoyable, entertaining, fun, pleasurable; dabbling, frivolous, trifling; delightful, pleasant, pleasing; joking, teasing **Ant** earnest, sober

play·ful·ness \\-nəs\\ *n* ♦ : the quality or state of being playful

♦ friskiness, impishness, mischief, mischievousness; *also* devilment, devilry, hob, rascality, waggery; devilishness, knavery; energy, liveliness, sprightliness; gaiety, lightheartedness, whimsicality **Ant** earnestness, soberness

play·go·er \\-,gō-ər\\ *n* : a person who frequently attends plays

play·ground \\-,graùnd\\ *n* : an area used for games and play esp. by children

play·house \\-,haùs\\ *n* 1 : THEATER 2 : a small house for children to play in

playing card *n* : any of a set of 24 to 78 cards marked to show its rank and suit and used to play a game of cards

play·let \\'plā-lət\\ *n* : a short play

play·mate \\-,māt\\ *n* : a companion in play

play·off \\-,ȯf\\ *n* : a contest or series of contests to break a tie or determine a championship

play out *vb* : DEVELOP, UNFOLD ⟨see how things *play out*⟩

play·pen \\-,pen\\ *n* : a portable enclosure in which a young child may play

play·suit \\-,süt\\ *n* : a sports and play outfit for women and children

play·thing \\-,thiŋ\\ *n* : TOY

play up *vb* ♦ : to place emphasis on

♦ accent, accentuate, emphasize, feature, highlight, point, stress, underline, underscore — more at EMPHASIZE

play·wright \\-,rīt\\ *n* : a writer of plays

pla·za \\'pla-zə, 'plä-\\ *n* [Sp, fr. L *platea* broad street] 1 : a public square in a city or town 2 : a shopping center

PLC *abbr, Brit* public limited company

plea \\'plē\\ *n* 1 : a defendant's answer in law to a charge or indictment 2 : something alleged as an excuse 3 ♦ : an earnest entreaty : APPEAL

♦ [2] alibi, defense (*or* defence), excuse, justification, reason — more at EXCUSE ♦ [3] appeal, cry, entreaty, petition, prayer, solicitation, suit, supplication; *also* application; call, demand, insistence

plead \\'plēd\\ *vb* **plead·ed** *or* **pled** \\'pled\\; **plead·ing** 1 : to argue before a court or authority ⟨~ a case⟩ 2 : to answer to a charge or indictment ⟨~ guilty⟩ 3 ♦ : to argue for or against something ⟨~ for acquittal⟩ 4 ♦ : to appeal earnestly ⟨~s for help⟩ ⟨~s to the judge⟩ 5 : to offer as a plea (as in defense) ⟨~ed illness⟩

♦ [3] argue, assert, contend, maintain, reason — more at ARGUE ♦ *usu* plead for [4] ask, call, quest, request, seek, solicit, sue ♦ *usu* plead to [4] appeal, beg, beseech, entreat, implore, importune, petition, pray, solicit, supplicate — more at BEG

plead·er \\'plē-dər\\ *n* ♦ : one who pleads

♦ solicitor, suitor

pleas·ant \\'plez-°nt\\ *adj* 1 ♦ : giving pleasure : AGREEABLE ⟨a ~ experience⟩ 2 : marked by pleasing behavior or appearance ⟨a ~ person⟩

♦ agreeable, congenial, delicious, delightful, felicitous, good, grateful, gratifying, nice, palatable, pleasurable, satisfying; *also* alluring, attractive, desirable, inviting, tempting; calming, comforting, soothing; affable, amiable, amusing, charming, cheerful, cheery, genial, goodly, good-natured, gracious, hospitable, kindly, personable; blissful, glad, happy, joyous; elating, exhilarating, intoxicating; ecstatic, euphoric, rapturous **Ant** disagreeable, unpalatable, unpleasant, unwelcome

pleas·ant·ly \\-lē\\ *adv* ♦ : in a pleasant manner

♦ agreeably, delightfully, favorably (*or* favourably), felicitously, nicely, pleasingly, satisfyingly, splendidly, well

pleas·ant·ness \\-nəs\\ *n* ♦ : the quality or state of being pleasant

♦ agreeableness, amenity, amiability, geniality, graciousness, niceness, sweetness — more at AMIABILITY

pleas·ant·ry \\-°n-trē\\ *n, pl* **-ries** ♦ : a pleasant and casual act or speech

♦ crack, gag, jest, joke, laugh, quip, sally, waggery, wisecrack, witticism — more at JOKE

¹**please** \\'plēz\\ *vb* **pleased**; **pleas·ing** 1 ♦ : to give pleasure or satisfaction to 2 : LIKE ⟨do as you ~⟩ 3 : to be the will or pleasure of ⟨may it ~ his Majesty⟩

♦ content, delight, gladden, gratify, rejoice, satisfy, suit, warm; *also* appease, mollify, pacify, placate, soothe; assuage, quench, sate, satiate; excite, tickle, titillate; thrill; calm, comfort, soothe; cater (to), humor, indulge; coddle, mollycoddle, pamper, spoil **Ant** displease

²**please** *adv* — used as a function word to express politeness or emphasis in a request ⟨~ come in⟩

pleased \\'plēzd\\ *adj* ♦ : affected with or manifesting pleasure

♦ content, contented, glad, happy — more at CONTENT

pleas·ing *adj* : giving pleasure ⟨aesthetically ~ decor⟩
pleas·ing·ly \\-lē\\ *adv* ♦ : in a pleasing manner

♦ agreeably, delightfully, favorably (*or* favourably), felicitously, gloriously, nicely, pleasantly, satisfyingly, splendidly, well

plea·sur·able \\'ple-zhə-rə-bəl\\ *adj* ♦ : giving pleasure : PLEASANT ⟨a ~ activity⟩ — **plea·sur·ably** \\-blē\\ *adv*

♦ amusing, delightful, diverting, enjoyable, entertaining, fun, pleasant — more at FUN

plea·sure \\'ple-zhər\\ *n* 1 : DESIRE, INCLINATION ⟨await your ~⟩ 2 ♦ : a state of gratification 3 ♦ : a source of delight or joy

♦ [2] contentment, delectation, delight, enjoyment, gladness, gratification, relish, satisfaction; *also* bliss, felicity, glee, happiness, joy; amusement, diversion, entertainment; elation, exhilaration, exultation, intoxication; ecstasy, euphoria, heaven, rapture, cheer, cheerfulness, exuberance, gaiety, jollity, jubilation **Ant** discontent, displeasure, dissatisfaction ◆ [3] delight, diversion, entertainment, fun — more at FUN

¹**pleat** \'plēt\ *vb* **1** : FOLD; *esp* : to arrange in pleats **2** : BRAID

²**pleat** *n* : a fold (as in cloth) made by doubling material over on itself

plebe \'plēb\ *n* : a freshman at a military or naval academy

¹**ple·be·ian** \pli-'bē-ən\ *n* **1** : a member of the Roman plebs **2** ◆ : one of the common people

◆ *usu* plebians commoners, herd, masses, mob, people, populace, rank and file — more at MASSES

²**plebeian** *adj* **1** : of or relating to plebeians **2** ◆ : crude or coarse in manner or style : COMMON, VULGAR ⟨~ tastes⟩

◆ common, humble, ignoble, inferior, low, lowly, mean, vulgar — more at IGNOBLE

pleb·i·scite \'ple-bə-ˌsīt, -sət\ *n* : a vote of the people (as of a country) on a proposal submitted to them

plebs \'plebz\ *n, pl* **ple·bes** \'plē-bēz\ **1** : the general populace **2** : the common people of ancient Rome

plec·trum \'plek-trəm\ *n, pl* **plec·tra** \-trə\ *or* **plec·trums** [L] : ³PICK 3

¹**pledge** \'plej\ *n* [ME *plegge* security, fr. AF *plege*, fr. LL *plebium*, fr. **plebere* to pledge, prob. of Gmc origin] **1** ◆ : something given as security for the performance of an act **2** : the state of being held as a security or guaranty **3** : TOAST 3 **4** ◆ : a binding promise or agreement to do or forbear — more at VOW

◆ [1] gage, guarantee, guaranty, pawn, security; *also* bail, bond; deposit, down payment, surety, warranty; oath, promise, word; commitment, compact, contract, covenant; recognizance ◆ [4] oath, promise, troth, vow, word — more at PROMISE

²**pledge** *vb* **pledged; pledg·ing 1** : to deposit as a pledge **2** : TOAST **3** ◆ : to bind by a pledge **4** ◆ : to promise the performance of by a pledge : PROMISE

◆ [3] commit, engage, troth; *also* affiance, betroth, plight, promise, swear, vow; contract, enlist, enroll, sign on, sign up ◆ [4] covenant, promise, swear, vow — more at PROMISE

Pleis·to·cene \'plī-stə-ˌsēn\ *adj* : of, relating to, or being the earlier epoch of the Quaternary — **Pleistocene** *n*

ple·na·ry \'plē-nə-rē, 'ple-\ *adj* **1** ◆ : complete in every respect : FULL ⟨~ power⟩ **2** : including all entitled to attend ⟨~ session⟩

◆ complete, comprehensive, entire, full, grand, intact, integral, perfect, total, whole — more at COMPLETE

pleni·po·ten·tia·ry \ˌple-nə-pə-'ten-chə-rē, -'ten-chē-ˌer-ē\ *n, pl* **-ries** : a diplomatic agent having full authority — **plenipotentiary** *adj*

plen·i·tude \'ple-nə-ˌtüd, -ˌtyüd\ *n* **1** : COMPLETENESS **2** : a great sufficiency : ABUNDANCE

plen·te·ous \'plen-tē-əs\ *adj* **1** : FRUITFUL **2** : existing in plenty

plen·ti·ful \'plen-ti-fəl\ *adj* **1** : containing or yielding plenty **2** ◆ : characterized by, constituting, or existing in plenty : ABUNDANT ⟨a ~ harvest⟩ — **plen·ti·ful·ly** *adv*

◆ abundant, ample, bountiful, comfortable, generous, liberal; *also* abounding, overflowing, replete, rich, rife, teeming, wealthy; adequate, enough, sufficient; fat, fecund, fertile, fruitful, prolific; copious, galore, lavish, profuse; luxuriant *Ant* bare, minimal, scant

plen·ty \'plen-tē\ *n* ◆ : a more than adequate number or amount

◆ abundance, superabundance, wealth; *also* adequacy, competence, competency, enough, sufficiency; amplitude, liberality; excess, overflow, overkill, oversupply, superfluity, surfeit, surplus; fertility, fecundity, fruitfulness, richness; lavishness, luxuriance *Ant* deficiency, inadequacy, insufficiency abundance, deal, gobs, heap, loads, lot, pile, quantity — more at LOT

ple·num \'ple-nəm, 'plē-\ *n, pl* **-nums** *or* **-na** \-nə\ : a general assembly of all members esp. of a legislative body

pleth·o·ra \'ple-thə-rə\ *n* : an excessive quantity or fullness; *also* : PROFUSION

pleu·ri·sy \'plu̇r-ə-sē\ *n* : inflammation of the membrane that lines the chest and covers the lungs

plex·i·glass \'plek-si-ˌglas\ *n* : a transparent acrylic plastic often used in place of glass

plex·us \'plek-səs\ *n, pl* **plex·us·es** \-sə-səz\ : an interlacing network esp. of blood vessels or nerves

pli·able \'plī-ə-bəl\ *adj* **1** ◆ : supple enough to bend freely or repeatedly without breaking : FLEXIBLE **2** : yielding easily to others ⟨a ~ child⟩ — **pli·abil·i·ty** \ˌplī-ə-'bi-lə-tē\ *n*

◆ flexible, limber, lissome, lithe, supple, willowy — more at WILLOWY

pli·ant \'plī-ənt\ *adj* **1** : supple enough to bend freely or repeatedly without breaking : FLEXIBLE **2** : easily influenced ⟨a ~ senator⟩ — **pli·an·cy** \-ən-sē\ *n*

pli·ers \'plī-ərz\ *n pl* : small pincers for bending or cutting wire or handling small objects

¹**plight** \'plīt\ *vb* : to put or give in pledge : ENGAGE

²**plight** *n* : an unfortunate, difficult, or precarious situation

plinth \'plinth\ *n* : the lowest part of the base of an architectural column

Plio·cene \'plī-ə-ˌsēn\ *adj* : of, relating to, or being the latest epoch of the Tertiary — **Pliocene** *n*

PLO *abbr* Palestine Liberation Organization

plod \'pläd\ *vb* **plod·ded; plod·ding 1** ◆ : to walk heavily or slowly **2** : to work laboriously and monotonously : DRUDGE — **plod·der** *n* — **plod·ding·ly** *adv*

◆ [1] flounder, limp, lumber, stumble — more at FLOUNDER ◆ [2] drudge, endeavor (*or* endeavour), fag, grub, hustle, labor (*or* labour), peg, plug, slave, slog, strain, strive, struggle, sweat, toil, work — more at LABOR

plonk *var of* PLUNK

plop \'pläp\ *vb* **plopped; plop·ping 1** : to fall or move with a sound like that of something dropping into water **2** ◆ : to set, drop, or throw heavily — **plop** *n*

◆ flop, plump, plunk — more at FLOP

¹**plot** \'plät\ *n* **1** ◆ : a small area of ground **2** : a detailed diagram of the ground floor of a building **3** : the main story (as of a book or movie) **4** ◆ : a secret scheme : INTRIGUE

◆ [1] lot, parcel, plat, property, tract — more at LOT ◆ [4] conspiracy, design, intrigue, machination, scheme; *also* frame-up; manipulation, subterfuge, trickery; artifice, contrivance, maneuver, stratagem, trick; cabal, confederacy, ring; game, gimmick, racket; program, strategy, system; collusion, complicity, connivance, conniving

²**plot** *vb* **plot·ted; plot·ting 1** : to make a plot or plan of **2** : to mark on or as if on a chart **3** ◆ : to plan or contrive esp. secretly — **plot·ter** *n*

◆ conspire, contrive, intrigue, machinate, scheme; *also* brew, concoct, cook (up), hatch; connive; engineer, jockey, maneuver, manipulate; design, frame, lay out, map, plan, shape

plo·ver \'plə-vər, 'plō-\ *n, pl* **plover** *or* **plovers** [ME, fr. AF, fr. VL **pluviarius*, fr. L *pluvia* rain] : any of a family of shorebirds that differ from the sandpipers in having shorter stouter bills

¹**plow** *or chiefly Can and Brit* **plough** \'plau̇\ *n* **1** : an implement used to cut, lift, turn over, and partly break up soil **2** : a device (as a snowplow) operating like a plow

²**plow** *or chiefly Can and Brit* **plough** *vb* **1** : to open, break up, or work with a plow **2** : to move through like a plow ⟨a ship ~ing the waves⟩ **3** : to proceed laboriously ⟨~ed through the work⟩ — **plow·able** *adj* — **plow·er** *n*

plow·boy *or chiefly Can and Brit* **plough·boy** \'plau̇-ˌbȯi\ *n* : a boy who leads the horse drawing a plow

plow·man *or chiefly Can and Brit* **plough·man** \-mən, -ˌman\ *n* **1** : a man who guides a plow **2** : a farm laborer

plow·share *or chiefly Can and Brit* **plough·share** \-ˌsher\ *n* : a part of a plow that cuts the earth

ploy \'plȯi\ *n* ♦ : a tactic intended to embarrass or frustrate an opponent

♦ artifice, device, dodge, gimmick, jig, scheme, sleight, stratagem, trick, wile — more at TRICK

¹pluck \'plək\ *vb* **1** : to pull off or out : PICK; *also* : to pull something from **2** : to play (an instrument) by pulling the strings : TUG, TWITCH

²pluck *n* **1** ♦ : an act or instance of plucking **2** ♦ : courageous readiness to fight or continue against odds : SPIRIT, COURAGE

♦ [1] draw, haul, jerk, pull, tug, wrench — more at PULL ♦ [2] backbone, courage, fiber (*or* fibre), fortitude, grit, guts, spirit, spunk — more at FORTITUDE

plucky \'plə-kē\ *adj* **pluck·i·er; -est** : COURAGEOUS, SPIRITED

¹plug \'pləg\ *n* **1** : STOPPER; *also* : an obstructing mass **2** : a cake of tobacco **3** : a poor or worn-out horse **4** : SPARK PLUG **5** : a lure with several hooks used in fishing **6** : a device on the end of a cord for making an electrical connection **7** : a piece of favorable publicity

²plug *vb* **plugged; plug·ging 1** ♦ : to stop, make tight, or secure by inserting a plug **2** : to hit with a bullet : HIT, SHOOT **3** ♦ : to publicize insistently **4** ♦ : to work doggedly and persistently : PLOD, DRUDGE — often used with *away*

♦ [1] block, dam, fill, pack, stop, stuff — more at FILL ♦ *usu* **plug up** [1] block, choke, clog, close (off), congest, dam, jam, obstruct, stop (up), stuff — more at CLOG ♦ [3] ballyhoo, boast, promote, publicize, tout — more at PUBLICIZE ♦ *often* **plug away** [4] drudge, endeavor (*or* endeavour), fag, grub, hustle, labor (*or* labour), peg, plod, slave, slog, strain, strive, struggle, sweat, toil, work — more at LABOR

plug and play *n* : a computer feature enabling the operating system to automatically detect and configure peripherals — **plug–and–play** *adj*

plugged–in \'pləgd-'in\ *adj* : technologically or socially informed and connected

plug–in \'pləg-,in\ *n* : a small piece of software that supplements a larger program

plum \'pləm\ *n* [ME, fr. OE *plūme*, modif. of L *prunum* plum, fr. Gk *proumnon*] **1** : a smooth-skinned juicy fruit borne by trees related to the peach and cherry; *also* : a tree bearing plums **2** : a raisin when used in desserts (as puddings) **3** ♦ : something excellent; *esp* : something desirable given in return for a favor

♦ catch, gem, jewel, pearl, prize, treasure — more at PRIZE

plum·age \'plü-mij\ *n* : the feathers of a bird — **plum·aged** \-mijd\ *adj*

¹plumb \'pləm\ *n* : a weight on the end of a line (**plumb line**) used esp. by builders to show vertical direction

²plumb *adv* **1** : straight down or up : VERTICALLY **2** : COMPLETELY ⟨∼ tired out⟩ **3** : EXACTLY; *also* : IMMEDIATELY

³plumb *vb* : to sound, adjust, or test with a plumb ⟨∼ the depth of a well⟩

⁴plumb *adj* **1** : exactly vertical or true : VERTICAL **2** : COMPLETE

plumb·er \'plə-mər\ *n* : a worker who fits or repairs pipes and fixtures

plumb·ing \'plə-miŋ\ *n* : a system of pipes in a building for supplying and carrying off water

¹plume \'plüm\ *n* **1** : FEATHER; *esp* : a large, conspicuous, or showy feather **2** ♦ : a token of honor or prowess — **plumed** \'plümd\ *adj* — **plumy** \'plü-mē\ *adj*

♦ award, decoration, distinction, honor (*or* honour), prize — more at AWARD

²plume *vb* **plumed; plum·ing 1** : to provide or deck with feathers **2** ♦ : to indulge (oneself) in pride

♦ boast, brag, crow, swagger — more at BOAST

¹plum·met \'plə-mət\ *n* : PLUMB; *also* : PLUMB LINE

²plummet *vb* ♦ : to drop or plunge straight down

♦ decline, descend, dip, drop, fall, lower, plunge, sink, tumble — more at DROP

¹plump \'pləmp\ *vb* **1** ♦ : to drop or fall suddenly or heavily **2** : to favor something strongly ⟨∼*ing* for change⟩

♦ flop, plop, plunk — more at FLOP

²plump *n* : a sudden heavy fall or blow; *also* : the sound made by it

³plump *adv* **1** : straight down; *also* : straight ahead **2** : UNQUALIFIEDLY

⁴plump *adj* ♦ : having a full rounded usu. pleasing form

♦ chubby, fat, fleshy, full, overweight, portly, rotund, round — more at FAT

plump·ness \-nəs\ *n* ♦ : the quality or state of being plump

♦ corpulence, fatness, obesity — more at CORPULENCE

¹plun·der \'plən-dər\ *vb* ♦ : to take the goods of by force or wrongfully : PILLAGE — **plun·der·er** *n*

♦ despoil, loot, maraud, pillage, ransack, sack, strip — more at RANSACK

²plunder *n* ♦ : something taken by force or theft : LOOT

♦ booty, loot, spoil, swag — more at LOOT

¹plunge \'plənj\ *vb* **plunged; plung·ing 1** : IMMERSE, SUBMERGE **2** : to enter or cause to enter a state or course of action suddenly or violently ⟨∼ into war⟩ **3** ♦ : to cast oneself into or as if into water **4** : to gamble heavily and recklessly **5** ♦ : to descend suddenly

♦ [3] dive, pitch, sound — more at DIVE ♦ [5] decline, descend, dip, drop, fall, lower, plummet, sink, tumble — more at DROP

²plunge *n* ♦ : a sudden dive, leap, or rush

♦ descent, dip, dive, down, drop, fall — more at DESCENT

plung·er \'plən-jər\ *n* **1** : one that plunges **2** : a sliding piece driven by or against fluid pressure : PISTON **3** : a rubber cup on a handle pushed against an opening to free a waste outlet of an obstruction

plunk \'pləŋk\ *vb* **1** : to make or cause to make a hollow metallic sound **2** ♦ : to drop heavily or suddenly — **plunk** *n*

♦ flop, plop, plump — more at FLOP

plu·per·fect \(,)plü-'pər-fikt\ *adj* [ME *pluperfyth*, modif. of LL *plusquamperfectus*, lit., more than perfect] : of, relating to, or constituting a verb tense that denotes an action or state as completed at or before a past time spoken of — **pluperfect** *n*

plu·ral \'plůr-əl\ *adj* [ME, fr. AF & L; AF *plurel*, fr. L *pluralis*, fr. *plur-*, *plus* more] : of, relating to, or constituting a word form used to denote more than one — **pl.** *n*

plu·ral·i·ty \plů-'ra-lə-tē\ *n*, *pl* **-ties 1** : the state of being plural **2** : an excess of votes over those cast for an opposing candidate **3** : the greatest number of votes cast when not a majority

plu·ral·ize \'plůr-ə-,līz\ *vb* **-ized; -iz·ing** : to make plural or express in the plural form — **plu·ral·i·za·tion** \,plůr-ə-lə-'zā-shən\ *n*

¹plus \'pləs\ *adj* [L, more] **1** : mathematically positive **2** : having or being in addition to what is anticipated **3** : falling high in a specified range ⟨a grade of B ∼⟩

²plus *n*, *pl* **plus·es** \'plə-səz\ *also* **plus·ses 1** : a sign + (**plus sign**) used in mathematics to indicate addition or a positive quantity **2** ♦ : an added quantity; *also* : a positive quality **3** : SURPLUS

♦ accretion, addition, augmentation, boost, expansion, gain, increase, increment, proliferation, raise, rise, supplement — more at INCREASE

³plus *prep* **1** : increased by : with the addition of ⟨3 ∼ 4⟩ **2** : BESIDES

⁴plus *conj* : AND ⟨soup ∼ salad and bread⟩

¹plush \'pləsh\ *n* : a fabric with a pile longer and less dense than velvet pile — **plushy** *adj*

²plush *adj* ♦ : notably luxurious ⟨a ∼ hotel suite⟩ — **plush·ly** *adv* — **plush·ness** *n*

♦ deluxe, lavish, luxuriant, luxurious, opulent, palatial, sumptuous — more at LUXURIOUS

plus/minus sign *n* : the sign ± used to indicate a quantity taking on both a positive value and its negative or to indicate a plus or minus quantity

plus or minus *adj* : indicating a quantity whose positive and negative values bracket a range of values ⟨*plus or minus* 3 inches⟩

plus–size \'pləs-ˌsīz\ *also* **plus–sized** \-ˈsīzd\ *adj* : extra large ⟨∼ clothing⟩ ⟨∼ shoppers⟩

Plu·to \'plü-tō\ *n* : a dwarf planet whose orbit crosses the orbit of Neptune

plu·toc·ra·cy \plü-ˈtä-krə-sē\ *n, pl* **-cies** **1** : government by the wealthy **2** : a controlling class of the wealthy — **plu·to·crat** \'plü-tə-ˌkrat\ *n* — **plu·to·crat·ic** \ˌplü-tə-ˈkra-tik\ *adj*

plu·to·ni·um \plü-ˈtō-nē-əm\ *n* : a radioactive chemical element formed by the decay of neptunium

plu·vi·al \'plü-vē-əl\ *adj* **1** : of or relating to rain **2** : characterized by abundant rain

¹**ply** \'plī\ *vb* **plied; ply·ing** **1** : to use, practice, or work diligently ⟨∼ a trade⟩ **2** : to keep supplying something to ⟨*plied* them with liquor⟩ **3** : to go or travel regularly esp. by sea

²**ply** *n, pl* **plies** : one of the folds, thicknesses, or strands of which something (as plywood or yarn) is made

³**ply** *vb* **plied; ply·ing** : to twist together ⟨∼ yarns⟩

ply·wood \'plī-ˌwu̇d\ *n* : material made of thin sheets of wood glued and pressed together

pm *abbr* premium

Pm *symbol* promethium

PM *abbr* **1** paymaster **2** police magistrate **3** postmaster **4** post meridiem — often not cap. and often punctuated **5** postmortem **6** prime minister **7** provost marshal

pmk *abbr* postmark

PMS \ˌpē-ˌem-ˈes\ *n* : PREMENSTRUAL SYNDROME

pmt *abbr* payment

pneu·mat·ic \nu̇-ˈma-tik, nyu̇-\ *adj* **1** : of, relating to, or using air or wind **2** : moved by air pressure **3** : filled with compressed air — **pneu·mat·i·cal·ly** \-ti-k(ə-)lē\ *adv*

pneu·mo·coc·cus \ˌnü-mə-ˈkä-kəs, ˌnyü-\ *n, pl* **-coc·ci** \-ˈkäk-ˌsī, -ˌsē; -ˈkä-ˌkī, -ˌkē\ : a bacterium that causes pneumonia — **pneu·mo·coc·cal** \-ˈkä-kəl\ *adj*

pneu·mo·co·ni·o·sis \ˌnü-mō-ˌkō-nē-ˈō-səs, ˌnyü-\ *n* : a disease of the lungs caused by habitual inhalation of irritant mineral or metallic particles

pneu·mo·nia \nu̇-ˈmō-nyə, nyu̇-\ *n* : an inflammatory disease of the lungs

Po *symbol* polonium

PO *abbr* **1** petty officer **2** post office

¹**poach** \'pōch\ *vb* [ME *pocchen*, fr. MF *pocher*, fr. OF *poché* poached, lit., bagged, fr. *poche* bag, pouch, of Gmc origin] : to cook (as an egg or fish) in simmering liquid

²**poach** *vb* : to hunt or fish unlawfully — **poach·er** *n*

POB *abbr* post office box

po·bla·no \pō-ˈblä-nō\ *n, pl* **-nos** : a heart-shaped usu. mild chili pepper esp. when fresh and dark green

po'boy *var of* POOR BOY

pock \'päk\ *n* : a small swelling on the skin (as in smallpox); *also* : a spot suggesting this

¹**pock·et** \'pä-kət\ *n* **1** : a small bag open at the top or side inserted in a garment **2** ♦ : supply of money **3** : RECEPTACLE, CONTAINER **4** : a small isolated area or group **5** : a small body of ore — **pock·et·ful** *n*

♦ finances, funds, resources, wherewithal — more at FUND

²**pocket** *vb* **1** : to put in or as if in a pocket **2** ♦ : to take or appropriate without right or leave and with intent to keep or make use of wrongfully : STEAL **3** ♦ : to set aside : SUPPRESS

♦ [2] appropriate, filch, hook, misappropriate, nip, pilfer, purloin, snitch, steal, swipe, thieve — more at STEAL ♦ [3] choke, repress, smother, stifle, strangle, suppress, swallow — more at SUPPRESS

³**pocket** *adj* **1 a** : small enough to fit in a pocket **b** ♦ : having comparatively little size or slight dimensions : SMALL **2** : carried in or paid from one's own pocket

♦ dwarf, dwarfish, fine, little, pygmy, slight, small, undersized — more at SMALL

¹**pock·et·book** \-ˌbu̇k\ *n* **1** ♦ : a receptacle for carrying money and often other small objects **2** : financial resources

♦ bag, handbag, purse — more at PURSE

²**pocketbook** *adj* : relating to money

pocket gopher *n* : GOPHER

pock·et·knife \'pä-kət-ˌnīf\ *n* : a knife with a folding blade to be carried in the pocket

pocket veto *n* : an indirect veto of a legislative bill by an executive through retention of the bill unsigned until after adjournment of the legislature

pock·mark \'päk-ˌmärk\ *n* ♦ : a pit or scar caused by smallpox or acne; *also* : an imperfection or depression like a pockmark — **pock·marked** \-ˌmärkt\ *adj*

♦ blemish, defect, deformity, disfigurement, fault, flaw, imperfection, mark, scar — more at BLEMISH

po·co \'pō-kō, ˌpò-\ *adv* [It, little, fr. L *paucus*] : SOMEWHAT — used to qualify a direction in music ⟨∼ allegro⟩

po·co a po·co \ˌpō-kō-ä-ˈpō-kō, ˌpò-kō-ä-ˈpò-\ *adv* : little by little : GRADUALLY — used as a direction in music

pod \'päd\ *n* **1** ♦ : a dry fruit (as of a pea) that splits open when ripe **2** ♦ : an external streamlined compartment (as for a jet engine) on an airplane **3** ♦ : a compartment (as for personnel, a power unit, or an instrument) on a ship or craft

♦ [1, 2, 3] armor, capsule, case, casing, cocoon, cover, housing, husk, jacket, sheath, shell — more at CASE

POD *abbr* pay on delivery

pod·cast \'päd-ˌkast\ *n* : a program made available in digital format for download over the Internet — **podcast** *vb* — **pod·cast·er** *n*

po·di·a·try \pə-ˈdī-ə-trē, pō-\ *n* : the medical care and treatment of the human foot — **po·di·a·trist** \pə-ˈdī-ə-trist, pō-\ *n*

po·di·um \'pō-dē-əm\ *n, pl* **podiums** *or* **po·dia** \-dē-ə\ **1** ♦ : a dais esp. for an orchestral conductor **2** : LECTERN

♦ dais, platform, rostrum, stage, stand — more at PLATFORM

POE *abbr* port of entry

po·em \'pō-əm\ *n* ♦ : a composition in verse

♦ lyric, song, verse; *also* rhyme; ballad, lay; elegy, epic, epigram, haiku, jingle, lament, limerick, ode, psalm, sonnet; blank verse, free verse, minstrelsy, poesy, poetry

po·esy \'pō-ə-zē\ *n* : POETRY

po·et \'pō-ət\ *n* [ME, fr. AF *poete*, fr. L *poeta*, fr. Gk *poiētēs* maker, poet, fr. *poiein* to make] ♦ : a writer of poetry; *also* : a creative artist of great sensitivity

♦ bard, minstrel, versifier; *also* poetess; poet laureate; troubadour; rhymer

po·et·as·ter \'pō-ə-ˌtas-tər\ *n* : an inferior poet

po·et·ess \'pō-ə-təs\ *n* : a girl or woman who is a poet

po·et·ic \pō-ˈe-tik\ *or* **po·et·i·cal** \-ti-kəl\ *adj* ♦ : having or expressing the qualities of poetry

♦ bardic, lyric, lyrical; *also* metric, metrical, rhyming, rhythmic; rhapsodic; florid, flowery, grandiloquent, ornate; figurative, metaphorical, symbolic **Ant** prosaic, prose, unpoetic

poetic justice *n* : an outcome in which vice is punished and virtue rewarded usu. in a manner peculiarly or ironically appropriate

po·et·ry \'pō-ə-trē\ *n* **1** : metrical writing **2** : POEMS **3** ♦ : writing that formulates a concentrated imaginative awareness of experience in language chosen and arranged to create a specific emotional response through meaning, sound, and rhythm

♦ song, verse; *also* rhyme; blank verse, free verse **Ant** prose

po·grom \\'pō-grəm, pō-'gräm\\ *n* [Yiddish, fr. Russ., lit., devastation] : an organized massacre of helpless people and esp. of Jews

poi \\'pȯi\\ *n, pl* **poi** *or* **pois** [Hawaiian] : food prepared from the cooked corms of taro that are mashed with water to the consistency of a paste or thick liquid

poi·gnan·cy \\'pȯi-nyən-sē\\ *n* : the quality or state of being poignant

poi·gnant \\'pȯi-nyənt\\ *adj* **1** ♦ : painfully affecting the feelings ⟨~ grief⟩ **2** ♦ : deeply moving ⟨~ scene⟩

♦ [1, 2] affecting, emotional, impressive, moving, stirring, touching — more at MOVING

poin·ci·ana \\ˌpȯin-sē-'a-nə\\ *n* : any of several ornamental tropical leguminous trees or shrubs with bright orange or red flowers

poin·set·tia \\pȯin-'se-tē-ə\\ *n* : a showy tropical American spurge with usu. scarlet bracts that suggest petals and surround small yellow flowers

¹point \\'pȯint\\ *n* **1** ♦ : an individual detail : ITEM; *also* : the most important essential **2** : PURPOSE **3** : a geometric element that has position but no size **4** ♦ : a particular place : LOCALITY **5** ♦ : a particular stage or degree **6** ♦ : a sharp end : TIP **7** ♦ : a projecting piece of land **8** : a punctuation mark; *esp* : PERIOD **9** : DECIMAL POINT **10** : one of the divisions of the compass **11** : a unit of counting (as in a game score) **12** : a very small mark **13** ♦ : a distinguishing detail **14** : the quality of something spoken or written of being able to arouse interest and of being generally effective — **pointy** \\'pȯin-tē\\ *adj* — **beside the point** : IRRELEVANT — **to the point** : RELEVANT, PERTINENT

♦ [1] detail, fact, item, particular — more at ITEM ♦ [4] locale, location, place, position, site, spot — more at PLACE ♦ [5] cut, degree, grade, inch, notch, peg, phase, stage, step — more at DEGREE ♦ [6] apex, cusp, end, pike, tip; *also* prong, tine; barb, jag, prickle, snag, spike, sticker ♦ [7] arm, cape, headland, peninsula, promontory, spit — more at CAPE ♦ [13] attribute, character, characteristic, feature, mark, peculiarity, property, quality, trait — more at CHARACTERISTIC

²point *vb* **1** : to furnish with a point : SHARPEN **2** : PUNCTUATE **3** : to separate (a decimal fraction) from an integer by a decimal point — usu. used with *off* **4** : to indicate the position of esp. by extending a finger **5** ♦ : to direct attention to ⟨~ out an error⟩ — usu. used with *out* or *up* **6** : AIM, DIRECT **7** ♦ : to lie extended, aimed, or turned in a particular direction : FACE, LOOK

♦ *usu* **point up** [5] accent, accentuate, emphasize, feature, highlight, play, stress, underline, underscore — more at EMPHASIZE ♦ *usu* **point toward** [7] face, front, look — more at FACE

point–and–click *adj* : relating to or being a computer interface that allows the activation of a file by selection with a pointing device (as a mouse)

point–and–shoot *adj* : having or using preset or automatically adjusted controls ⟨a ~ camera⟩

point–blank \\'pȯint-'blaŋk\\ *adj* **1** : so close to the target that a missile fired will travel in a straight line to the mark **2** : DIRECT, BLUNT — **point–blank** *adv*

point·ed \\'pȯin-təd\\ *adj* **1** ♦ : having a point **2** ♦ : being to the point : PERTINENT **3** : aimed at a particular person or group; *also* : CONSPICUOUS, MARKED — **point·ed·ly** *adv*

♦ [1] peaked, sharp; *also* barbed, jagged, pronged, spiky *Ant* blunt ♦ [2] applicable, apposite, apropos, germane, material, pertinent, relative, relevant — more at PERTINENT

point·er \\'pȯin-tər\\ *n* **1** ♦ : one that points out : INDICATOR **2** : a large short-haired hunting dog **3** ♦ : a useful suggestion or hint : TIP

♦ [1] hand, index, indicator, needle; *also* dial, face, gauge ♦ [3] hint, lead, tip — more at TIP

poin·til·lism \\'pwan-tē-ˌyi-zəm, 'pȯint-ᵊl-ˌi-zəm\\ *n* [F *poin-*

tillisme, fr. *pointiller* to stipple, fr. *point* spot, point] : the theory or practice in painting of applying small strokes or dots of color to a surface so that from a distance they blend together — **poin·til·list** \\ˌpwan-tē-'yēst, 'pȯint-ᵊl-ist\\ *n or adj*

point·less \\-ləs\\ *adj* ♦ : devoid of meaning

♦ empty, meaningless, senseless — more at MEANINGLESS

point man *n* : a principal spokesman or advocate

point of no return : a critical point at which turning back or reversal is not possible

point of view ♦ : a position or perspective from which something is considered or evaluated

♦ angle, outlook, perspective, slant, standpoint, viewpoint; *also* interpretation, spin; belief, conviction, eye, feeling, judgment, mind, notion, opinion, perception, persuasion, sentiment, verdict, view; impression, take; wavelength; side; attitude, position, posture, stand

point spread *n* : the number of points by which a favorite is expected to defeat an underdog

¹poise \\'pȯiz\\ *n* **1** ♦ : a stably balanced state **2** : self-possessed calmness; *also* : a particular way of carrying oneself

♦ balance, equilibrium, equipoise — more at BALANCE

²poise *vb* **poised; pois·ing** **1** : BALANCE **2** ♦ : to remain suspended over a place or object

♦ drift, float, glide, hang, hover, ride, sail, waft — more at FLOAT

poi·sha \\'pȯi-shə\\ *n, pl* **poisha** : the paisa of Bangladesh

¹poi·son \\'pȯiz-ᵊn\\ *n* [ME, fr. AF *poisun* drink, potion, poison, fr. L *potion-, potio* drink] ♦ : a substance that through its chemical action can injure or kill — **poison** *adj*

♦ bane, toxin, venom; *also* cancer, contagion, disease, virus; fungicide, germicide, herbicide, insecticide

²poison *vb* **1** : to injure or kill with poison **2** ♦ : to treat or taint with poison **3** ♦ : to affect destructively ⟨~ed her mind⟩ — **poi·son·er** *n*

♦ [2] befoul, contaminate, defile, foul, pollute, taint — more at CONTAMINATE ♦ [3] blemish, mar, spoil, stain, taint, tarnish, touch, vitiate — more at TAINT

poison hemlock *n* : a large branching poisonous herb with finely divided leaves and white flowers that is related to the carrot

poison ivy *n* **1** : a usu. climbing plant related to the sumacs that has leaves composed of three shiny leaflets and produces an irritating oil causing a usu. intensely itching skin rash; *also* : any of several related plants **2** : a skin rash caused by poison ivy

poison oak *n* : any of several shrubby plants closely related to poison ivy and having similar properties

poi·son·ous \\'pȯiz-ᵊn-əs\\ *adj* ♦ : having the properties or effects of poison

♦ poison, venomous; *also* contagious, infectious; deleterious, harmful, hurtful, injurious, malignant, noxious, virulent; unhealthful, unhealthy, unwholesome; calamitous, deadly, fatal, lethal, murderous *Ant* nonpoisonous, nontoxic, nonvenomous

poison sumac *n* : a No. American swamp shrub with pinnate leaves, greenish flowers, greenish white berries, and irritating properties

¹poke \\'pōk\\ *n chiefly Southern & Midland* : BAG, SACK

²poke *vb* **poked; pok·ing** **1** : PROD; *also* : to stir up by prodding **2** : to make a prodding or jabbing movement esp. repeatedly **3** : HIT, PUNCH **4** ♦ : to thrust forward obtrusively **5** : RUMMAGE **6** ♦ : to interest oneself in what is not one's concern : MEDDLE, PRY **7** ♦ : to move or act slowly or aimlessly ⟨*poking* along toward home⟩ — **poke fun at** : RIDICULE, MOCK

♦ [4] bag, balloon, beetle, belly, billow, bulge, overhang, project, protrude, start, stick out — more at BULGE ♦ [6] butt in, interfere, intrude, meddle, mess, nose, obtrude, pry, snoop — more at INTERFERE ♦ [7] crawl, creep, dally, dawdle, delay, dillydally, drag, lag, linger, loiter, tarry — more at DELAY

³**poke** n ♦ : a quick thrust; *also* : PUNCH

♦ dab, dig, jab; *also* punch; stab, stick; push, shove; jam, jerk, jog, nudge

¹**pok·er** \ˈpō-kər\ n : a metal rod for stirring a fire

²**po·ker** \ˈpō-kər\ n : any of several card games in which the player with the highest hand at the end of the betting wins

poker face n : a face that does not reveal a person's thoughts or feelings

poke·weed \ˈpōk-ˌwēd\ n : a coarse American perennial herb with clusters of white flowers and dark purple juicy berries

poky *or* **pok·ey** \ˈpō-kē\ adj **pok·i·er; -est 1** : small and cramped **2** : SHABBY, DULL **3** ♦ : annoyingly slow

♦ creeping, dilatory, laggard, languid, slow, sluggish, tardy — more at SLOW

pol \ˈpäl\ n : POLITICIAN

po·lar \ˈpō-lər\ adj **1 a** : of or relating to a geographical pole **b** ♦ : coming from or having the characteristics (as cold) of such a region **2** : of or relating to a pole (as of a magnet) **3** ♦ : diametrically opposite

♦ [1b] arctic, bitter, chill, chilly, cold, cool, freezing, frigid, frosty, glacial, icy, nippy, raw, snappy, wintry — more at COLD ♦ [3] antipodal, antithetical, contradictory, contrary, diametric, opposite — more at OPPOSITE

polar bear n : a large creamy-white bear that inhabits arctic regions

Po·lar·is \pə-ˈlar-əs\ n : NORTH STAR

po·lar·ise *chiefly Brit var of* POLARIZE

po·lar·i·ty \pō-ˈlar-ə-tē\ n, pl **-ties** : the condition of having poles and esp. magnetic or electrical poles

po·lar·i·za·tion \ˌpō-lə-rə-ˈzā-shən\ n **1** : the action of polarizing : the state of being polarized **2** : concentration about opposing extremes

po·lar·ize \ˈpō-lə-ˌrīz\ vb **-ized; -iz·ing 1** : to cause (light waves) to vibrate in a definite way **2** : to give physical polarity to **3** : to break up into opposing groups

pol·der \ˈpōl-dər, ˈpäl-\ n [D] : a tract of low land reclaimed from the sea

¹**pole** \ˈpōl\ n : a long slender piece of wood or metal ⟨telephone ∼⟩

²**pole** vb **poled; pol·ing** : to impel or push with a pole

³**pole** n **1** : either end of an axis esp. of the earth **2** : either of the terminals of an electric device (as a battery or generator) **3** : one of two or more regions in a magnetized body at which the magnetism is concentrated — **pole·ward** \ˈpōl-wərd\ adj or adv

Pole \ˈpōl\ n : a native or inhabitant of Poland

¹**pole·ax** \ˈpō-ˌlaks\ n : a battle-ax with a short handle

²**poleax** vb : to attack or fell with or as if with a poleax

pole·cat \ˈpōl-ˌkat\ n, pl **polecats** *or* **polecat 1** : a European carnivorous mammal of which the ferret is considered a domesticated variety **2** : SKUNK

po·lem·ic \pə-ˈle-mik\ n : the art or practice of disputation — usu. used in pl. — **po·lem·i·cal** \-mi-kəl\ *also* **po·lem·ic** \-mik\ adj — **po·lem·i·cist** \-sist\ n

pole·star \ˈpōl-ˌstär\ n **1** : NORTH STAR **2** : a directing principle : GUIDE

pole vault n : a field contest in which each contestant uses a pole to vault for height over a crossbar — **pole–vault** vb — **pole–vault·er** n

¹**po·lice** \pə-ˈlēs\ vb **po·liced; po·lic·ing 1** : to control, regulate, or keep in order esp. by use of police ⟨∼ a highway⟩ **2** : to make clean and put in order

²**police** n, pl **police** [F, government, fr. OF, fr. LL *politia*, fr. Gk *politeia*, fr. *politēs* citizen, fr. *polis* city, state] **1** : the department of government that keeps public order and safety and enforces the laws; *also* : the members of this department **2** : a private organization resembling a police force; *also* : its members **3** : military personnel detailed to clean and put in order

po·lice·man \-mən\ n : a member of a police force : POLICE OFFICER

police officer n ♦ : a member of a police force

♦ constable, cop, officer — more at OFFICER

police state n : a state characterized by repressive, arbitrary, totalitarian rule by means of secret police

po·lice·wom·an \pə-ˈlēs-ˌwu̇-mən\ n : a woman who is a police officer

¹**pol·i·cy** \ˈpä-lə-sē\ n, pl **-cies** ♦ : a definite course or method of action selected to guide and determine present and future decisions

♦ course, line, procedure, program — more at COURSE

²**policy** n, pl **-cies** : a writing whereby a contract of insurance is made

pol·i·cy·hold·er \ˈpä-lə-sē-ˌhōl-dər\ n : one granted an insurance policy

po·lio \ˈpō-lē-ˌō\ n : POLIOMYELITIS — **polio** adj

po·lio·my·eli·tis \-ˌmī-ə-ˈlī-təs\ n : an acute virus disease marked by inflammation of the gray matter of the spinal cord leading usu. to paralysis

¹**pol·ish** \ˈpä-lish\ vb **1** ♦ : to make smooth and glossy usu. by rubbing **2** : to refine or improve in manners, condition, or style

♦ buff, burnish, dress, gloss, grind, rub, shine, smooth; *also* sleek, slick; coat, glaze; finish, veneer; brighten; rasp, sand, sandblast, sandpaper, scour, scrape, scrub

²**polish** n **1** ♦ : a smooth glossy surface appearance or finish **2** ♦ : enlightenment and excellence of taste acquired by intellectual and aesthetic training : CULTURE **3** : the action or process of polishing **4** : a preparation used to produce a gloss

♦ [1] gloss, luster (*or* lustre), sheen, shine — more at SHINE ♦ [2] civilization, cultivation, culture, refinement — more at CULTURE

Pol·ish \ˈpō-lish\ n : the Slavic language of the Poles — **Polish** adj

polished \ˈpä-lisht\ adj **1** ♦ : having a smooth and glossy surface produced by or as if by polishing **2** ♦ : characterized by elegance and refinement

♦ [1] glossy, lustrous, satiny, sleek — more at GLOSSY ♦ [2] civilized, cultivated, cultured, genteel, refined — more at CULTIVATED

polit abbr political; politician

po·lit·bu·ro \ˈpä-lət-ˌbyu̇r-ō, ˈpō-, pə-ˈlit-\ n [Russ *politbyuro*] : the principal policy-making committee of a Communist party

po·lite \pə-ˈlīt\ adj **po·lit·er; -est 1** ♦ : of, relating to, or having the characteristics of advanced culture ⟨∼ society⟩ **2** ♦ : marked by correct social conduct : COURTEOUS; *also* : CONSIDERATE, TACTFUL — **po·lite·ly** adv

♦ [1] correct, decent, decorous, genteel, nice, proper, respectable, seemly — more at PROPER ♦ [2] civil, considerate, courteous, genteel, gracious, mannerly, wellbred; *also* attentive, thoughtful; chivalrous, courtly, gallant; ceremonial, ceremonious; formal, suave, unctuous, urbane; elegant, refined; deferential, dutiful, respectful, submissive, yielding; acceptable, appropriate, becoming, correct, decent, decorous, fit, fitting, good, meet, proper, respectable, right, seemly, suitable; affable, cordial, friendly, genial, hospitable, sociable; felicitous, graceful; humble, meek, modest, unassertive **Ant** discourteous, impolite, inconsiderate, rude, ungracious, unmannerly

po·lite·ness \-nəs\ n ♦ : the quality or state of being polite

♦ civility, courtesy, gentility, graciousness, mannerliness; *also* attentiveness, consideration, thoughtfulness; ceremoniousness, ceremony, formality; chivalrousness, chivalry, courtliness, gallantry; breeding, manners; urbanity; elegance, refinement; deference, respect; decency, decorum, propriety, respectability; affability, cordiality, friendliness, geniality, hospitality, sociability; gracefulness; humility, meekness, modesty, shyness **Ant** discourtesy, incivility, rudeness

po·li·tesse \ˌpä-li-ˈtes\ n [F] : formal politeness

pol·i·tic \\'pä-lə-ˌtik\\ *adj* **1** : wise in promoting a policy ⟨a ∼ statesman⟩ **2** : shrewdly tactful ⟨a ∼ move⟩ **3** ♦ : suitable to the situation or circumstances

♦ advisable, desirable, expedient, judicious, prudent, tactical, wise — more at EXPEDIENT

po·lit·i·cal \\pə-'li-ti-kəl\\ *adj* **1** : of or relating to government or politics **2** : involving or charged or concerned with acts against a government or a political system ⟨∼ prisoners⟩ — **po·lit·i·cal·ly** \\-k(ə-)lē\\ *adv*

politically correct *adj* : conforming to a belief that language and practices which could offend sensibilities (as in matters of sex or race) should be eliminated

pol·i·ti·cian \\ˌpä-lə-'ti-shən\\ *n* : a person actively engaged in government or politics

pol·i·tick \\'pä-lə-ˌtik\\ *vb* : to engage in political discussion or activity

pol·i·ti·co \\pə-'li-ti-ˌkō\\ *n, pl* **-cos** *also* **-coes** : POLITICIAN

pol·i·tics \\'pä-lə-ˌtiks\\ *n sing or pl* **1** : the art or science of government, of guiding or influencing governmental policy, or of winning and holding control over a government **2** : political affairs or business; *esp* : competition between groups or individuals for power and leadership **3** : political opinions

pol·i·ty \\'pä-lə-tē\\ *n, pl* **-ties** : a politically organized unit; *also* : the form or constitution of such a unit

pol·ka \\'pōl-kə, 'pō-kə\\ *n* [Czech, fr. *Polka* Polish woman, fem. of *Polák* Pole] : a lively couple dance of Bohemian origin; *also* : music for this dance — **polka** *vb*

pol·ka dot \\'pō-kə-ˌdät\\ *n* : a dot in a pattern of regularly distributed dots — **polka–dot** *or* **polka–dot·ted** \\-ˌdä-təd\\ *adj*

¹**poll** \\'pōl\\ *n* **1** ♦ : a person's head **2** : the casting and recording of votes; *also* : the total vote cast **3** : the place where votes are cast — usu. used in pl. **4** : a questioning of persons to obtain information or opinions to be analyzed

♦ head, noggin, pate — more at HEAD

²**poll** *vb* **1** : to cut off or shorten a growth or part of : CLIP, SHEAR **2** : to receive and record the votes of **3** : to receive (as votes) in an election **4** ♦ : to question in a poll

♦ canvass, solicit, survey — more at CANVASS

pol·lack *or* **pol·lock** \\'pä-lək\\ *n, pl* **pollack** *or* **pollock** : an important No. Atlantic food fish that is related to the cods; *also* : a related food fish of the No. Pacific

pol·len \\'pä-lən\\ *n* [NL, fr. L, fine flour] : a mass of male spores of a seed plant usu. appearing as a yellow dust

pol·li·na·tion \\ˌpä-lə-'nā-shən\\ *n* : the carrying of pollen to the female part of a plant to fertilize the seed — **pol·li·nate** \\'pä-lə-ˌnāt\\ *vb* — **pol·li·na·tor** \\-ˌnā-tər\\ *n*

poll·ster \\'pōl-stər\\ *n* : one that conducts a poll or compiles data obtained by a poll

poll tax *n* : a tax of a fixed amount per person levied on adults and often linked to the right to vote

pol·lut·ant \\pə-'lüt-ᵊnt\\ *n* ♦ : something that pollutes

♦ adulterant, contaminant, defilement, impurity — more at IMPURITY

pol·lute \\pə-'lüt\\ *vb* **pol·lut·ed; pol·lut·ing** ♦ : to make impure; *esp* : to contaminate (an environment) esp. with man-made waste — **pol·lut·er** *n* — **pol·lu·tion** \\-'lü-shən\\ *n*

♦ befoul, contaminate, defile, foul, poison, taint — more at CONTAMINATE

polluted *adj* ♦ : made unclean or impure

♦ dilute, impure — more at IMPURE

pol·ly·wog *or* **pol·li·wog** \\'pä-lē-ˌwäg\\ *n* : TADPOLE

po·lo \\'pō-lō\\ *n* [Balti (Tibetan language of northern Kashmir), ball] : a game played by two teams on horseback using long-handled mallets to drive a wooden ball

po·lo·ni·um \\pə-'lō-nē-əm\\ *n* [NL, fr. ML *Polonia* Poland, birthplace of its discoverer, Mme. Curie] : a radioactive metallic chemical element

pol·ter·geist \\'pōl-tər-ˌgīst\\ *n* [G, fr. *poltern* to knock + *Geist* spirit] ♦ : a noisy usu. mischievous ghost held to be responsible for unexplained noises

♦ apparition, bogey, ghost, phantasm, phantom, shade, shadow, specter, spirit, spook, vision, wraith — more at GHOST

pol·troon \\päl-'trün\\ *n* ♦ : a spiritless coward

♦ chicken, coward, craven, dastard, recreant, sissy — more at COWARD

poly- *comb form* [Gk, fr. *polys* many] **1** : many : several ⟨*poly*syllabic⟩ **2** : polymeric ⟨*poly*ester⟩

poly·chlo·ri·nat·ed bi·phe·nyl \\ˌpä-li-ˌklōr-ə-ˌnā-təd-ˌbī-'fen-ᵊl, -'fēn-\\ *n* : any of several industrial compounds that are toxic environmental pollutants

poly·clin·ic \\ˌpä-li-'kli-nik\\ *n* : a clinic or hospital treating diseases of many sorts

poly·es·ter \\'pä-lē-ˌes-tər\\ *n* : a polymer composed of ester groups used esp. in making fibers or plastics

poly·eth·yl·ene \\ˌpä-lē-'e-thə-ˌlēn\\ *n* : a lightweight plastic resistant to chemicals and moisture and used chiefly in packaging

po·lyg·a·my \\pə-'li-gə-mē\\ *n* : marriage in which a spouse of either sex may have more than one mate at the same time — **po·lyg·a·mist** \\-mist\\ *n* — **po·lyg·a·mous** \\-məs\\ *adj*

poly·glot \\'pä-li-ˌglät\\ *adj* **1** : speaking or writing several languages **2** : containing or made up of several languages — **polyglot** *n*

poly·gon \\'pä-li-ˌgän\\ *n* : a closed plane figure bounded by straight lines — **po·lyg·o·nal** \\pə-'li-gən-ᵊl\\ *adj*

poly·graph \\'pä-li-ˌgraf\\ *n* : an instrument (as a lie detector) for recording variations of several bodily functions (as blood pressure) simultaneously — **po·lyg·ra·pher** \\pə-'li-grə-fər, 'pä-li-ˌgra-fər\\ *n*

poly·he·dron \\ˌpä-li-'hē-drən\\ *n* : a solid formed by plane faces that are polygons — **poly·he·dral** \\-drəl\\ *adj*

poly·math \\'pä-li-ˌmath\\ *n* : a person of encyclopedic learning

poly·mer \\'pä-lə-mər\\ *n* : a chemical compound formed by union of small molecules and usu. consisting of repeating structural units — **poly·mer·ic** \\ˌpä-lə-'mer-ik\\ *adj*

po·lym·er·i·za·tion \\pə-ˌli-mə-rə-'zā-shən\\ *n* : a chemical reaction in which two or more small molecules combine to form polymers — **po·lym·er·ize** \\pə-'li-mə-ˌrīz\\ *vb*

Poly·ne·sian \\ˌpä-lə-'nē-zhən\\ *n* **1** : a member of any of the indigenous peoples of Polynesia **2** : a group of Austronesian languages spoken in Polynesia — **Polynesian** *adj*

poly·no·mi·al \\ˌpä-lə-'nō-mē-əl\\ *n* : an algebraic expression having one or more terms each of which consists of a constant multiplied by one or more variables raised to a nonnegative integral power — **polynomial** *adj*

pol·yp \\'pä-ləp\\ *n* **1** : an invertebrate animal (as a coral) that is a coelenterate having a hollow cylindrical body closed at one end **2** : a growth projecting from a mucous membrane (as of the colon or vocal cords)

po·lyph·o·ny \\pə-'li-fə-nē\\ *n* : music consisting of two or more melodically independent but harmonizing voice parts — **poly·phon·ic** \\ˌpä-li-'fä-nik\\ *adj*

poly·pro·pyl·ene \\ˌpä-lē-'prō-pə-ˌlēn\\ *n* : any of various polymer plastics or fibers

poly·sty·rene \\ˌpä-li-'stīr-ˌēn\\ *n* : a rigid transparent nonconducting thermoplastic used esp. in molded products and foams

poly·syl·lab·ic \\-sə-'la-bik\\ *adj* **1** : having more than three syllables **2** : characterized by polysyllabic words

poly·syl·la·ble \\'pä-li-ˌsi-lə-bəl\\ *n* : a polysyllabic word

poly·tech·nic \\ˌpä-li-'tek-nik\\ *adj* : of, relating to, or instructing in many technical arts or applied sciences

poly·the·ism \\'pä-li-thē-ˌi-zəm\\ *n* : belief in or worship of many gods — **poly·the·ist** \\-ˌthē-ist\\ *adj or n* — **poly·the·is·tic** \\ˌpä-li-thē-'is-tik\\ *adj*

poly·un·sat·u·rat·ed \\ˌpä-lē-ˌən-'sa-chə-ˌrā-təd\\ *adj* : having many double or triple bonds in a molecule — used esp. of an oil or fatty acid

poly·ure·thane \\ˌpä-lē-'yür-ə-ˌthän\\ *n* : any of various polymers used esp. in foams and in resins (as for coatings)

poly·vi·nyl \ˌpä-li-ˈvīn-ᵊl\ *adj* : of, relating to, or being a polymerized vinyl compound, resin, or plastic — often used in combination

pome·gran·ate \ˈpä-mə-ˌgra-nət\ *n* [ME *poumgrenet*, fr. AF *pome garnette*, lit., seedy fruit] : a many-seeded reddish fruit that has an edible crimson pulp and is borne by a tropical Asian tree; *also* : the tree

¹pom·mel \ˈpə-məl, ˈpä-\ *n* 1 : the knob on the hilt of a sword 2 : the knoblike bulge at the front and top of a saddlebow

²pom·mel \ˈpə-məl\ *vb* **-meled** *or* **-melled; -mel·ing** *or* **-mel·ling** : to strike repeatedly : PUMMEL

pomp \ˈpämp\ *n* 1 : brilliant display : SPLENDOR 2 : OSTENTATION

pom·pa·dour \ˈpäm-pə-ˌdȯr\ *n* : a style of dressing the hair high over the forehead

pom·pa·no \ˈpäm-pə-ˌnō, ˈpəm-\ *n, pl* **-no** *or* **-nos** : a narrow silvery fish of coastal waters of the western Atlantic

pom–pom \ˈpäm-ˌpäm\ *n* 1 : an ornamental ball or tuft used on a cap or costume 2 : a fluffy ball flourished by cheerleaders

pom·pon \ˈpäm-ˌpän\ *n* 1 : POM-POM 2 : a chrysanthemum or dahlia with small rounded flower heads

pomp·ous \ˈpäm-pəs\ *adj* 1 ♦ : suggestive of pomp; *esp* : OSTENTATIOUS 2 ♦ : having or exhibiting self-importance ⟨~ politicians⟩ 3 : excessively elevated or ornate — **pom·pos·i·ty** \päm-ˈpä-sə-tē\ *n* — **pomp·ous·ly** *adv*

♦ [1] affected, grandiose, highfalutin, ostentatious, pretentious — more at PRETENTIOUS ♦ [2] arrogant, complacent, conceited, egotistic, important, overweening, prideful, proud, self-important, self-satisfied, smug, stuck-up, vain — more at CONCEITED

pon·cho \ˈpän-chō\ *n, pl* **ponchos** [AmerSp, fr. Mapuche (American Indian language of Chile)] 1 : a blanket with a slit in the middle for the head so that it can be worn as a garment 2 : a waterproof garment resembling a poncho

pond \ˈpänd\ *n* : a small body of water

pon·der \ˈpän-dər\ *vb* **-dered; pon·der·ing** 1 ♦ : to weigh in the mind 2 ♦ : to consider carefully

♦ [1, 2] chew over, cogitate, consider, contemplate, debate, deliberate, entertain, meditate, mull, question, ruminate, study, think, weigh; *also* muse (upon), reflect (on *or* upon); conclude, reason; second-guess, speculate

pon·der·o·sa pine \ˈpän-də-ˌrō-sə-, -zə-\ *n* : a tall pine of western No. America with long needles; *also* : its strong reddish wood

pon·der·ous \ˈpän-də-rəs\ *adj* 1 ♦ : of very great weight 2 : UNWIELDY, CLUMSY ⟨a ~ weapon⟩ 3 ♦ : oppressively dull ⟨a ~ speech⟩

♦ [1] heavy, hefty, massive, weighty — more at HEAVY ♦ [3] dull, flat, heavy, leaden, weary

pone \ˈpōn\ *n, Southern & Midland* : an oval-shaped cornmeal cake; *also* : corn bread in the form of pones

pon·iard \ˈpän-yərd\ *n* : DAGGER

pon·tiff \ˈpän-təf\ *n* : POPE — **pon·tif·i·cal** \pän-ˈti-fi-kəl\ *adj*

¹pon·tif·i·cate \pän-ˈti-fi-kət, -fə-ˌkāt\ *n* : the state, office, or term of office of a pontiff

²pon·tif·i·cate \pän-ˈti-fə-ˌkāt\ *vb* **-cat·ed; -cat·ing** : to deliver dogmatic opinions

pon·toon \pän-ˈtün\ *n* 1 : a flat-bottomed boat 2 : a boat or float used in building a floating temporary bridge 3 : a float of a seaplane

po·ny \ˈpō-nē\ *n, pl* **ponies** : a small horse

po·ny·tail \-ˌtāl\ *n* : a style of arranging hair to resemble the tail of a pony

pooch \ˈpüch\ *n* : a flesh-eating domestic mammal related to the wolves : DOG

poo·dle \ˈpüd-ᵊl\ *n* [G *Pudel*, short for *Pudelhund*, fr. *pudeln* to splash + *Hund* dog] : any of a breed of active intelligent dogs with a dense curly solid-colored coat

pooh–pooh \ˈpü-ˈpü\ *also* **pooh** \ˈpü\ *vb* 1 : to express contempt or impatience 2 : DERIDE, SCORN

¹pool \ˈpül\ *n* 1 : a small deep body of usu. fresh water 2 : a small body of standing liquid 3 : SWIMMING POOL

²pool *vb* : to form a pool

³pool *n* 1 : all the money bet on the result of a particular event 2 : any of several games of billiards played on a table having six pockets 3 : the amount contributed by the participants in a joint venture 4 : a combination between competing firms for mutual profit 5 ♦ : a readily available supply (as of resources or workers)

♦ force, help, personnel, staff — more at FORCE ♦ budget, fund, supply — more at SUPPLY

⁴pool *vb* : to combine (as resources) in a common fund or effort

¹poop \ˈpüp\ *n* : an enclosed superstructure at the stern of a ship

²poop *n, slang* : INFORMATION

poop deck *n* : a partial deck above a ship's main afterdeck

poor \ˈpu̇r\ *adj* 1 ♦ : lacking material possessions ⟨~ people⟩ 2 : less than adequate : MEAGER ⟨a ~ crop⟩ 3 : arousing pity ⟨you ~ thing⟩ 4 ♦ : inferior in quality or value 5 : producing inferior or little vegetation : UNPRODUCTIVE, BARREN ⟨~ soil⟩ 6 : fairly unsatisfactory ⟨~ prospects⟩; *also* : UNFAVORABLE ⟨a ~ opinion⟩ — **poor·ly** *adv*

♦ [1] broke, destitute, impecunious, indigent, needy, penniless, penurious, poverty-stricken; *also* deprived, disadvantaged, underprivileged; bankrupt, insolvent; low, short *Ant* affluent, flush, moneyed, opulent, rich, wealthy, well-heeled, well-off, well-to-do ♦ [4] cheap, inferior, junky, lousy, mediocre, second-rate, shoddy, sleazy

poor boy \ˈpō-ˌbȯi, ˈpȯr-\ *n* ♦ : a large sandwich on a long split roll : SUBMARINE

♦ grinder, hoagie, sub, submarine — more at SUBMARINE

poor·house \ˈpu̇r-ˌhau̇s\ *n* : a publicly supported home for needy or dependent persons

poor–mouth \-ˌmau̇th, -ˌmau̇th\ *vb* : to plead poverty as a defense or excuse

¹pop \ˈpäp\ *vb* **popped; pop·ping** 1 ♦ : to go, come, enter, or issue forth suddenly, quickly, or unexpectedly ⟨~ into bed⟩ ⟨~ in for a visit⟩ 2 : to put or thrust suddenly ⟨~ questions⟩ 3 ♦ : to burst or cause to burst with a sharp sound; *also* : to make a sharp sound 4 : to protrude from the sockets 5 : to fire at : SHOOT 6 : to hit a pop-up

♦ *usu* **pop in** [1] call, drop (by *or* in), stop (by *or* in), visit — more at CALL ♦ [3] blow up, burst, detonate, explode, go off — more at EXPLODE

²pop *n* 1 ♦ : a sharp explosive sound 2 : SHOT 3 : SODA POP

♦ bang, blast, boom, clap, crack, crash, report, slam, smash, snap, thwack, whack — more at CLAP

³pop *n* ♦ : a male parent : FATHER

♦ daddy, father, papa — more at FATHER

⁴pop *adj* 1 : POPULAR ⟨~ music⟩ 2 : of or relating to pop music ⟨a ~ singer⟩ 3 : of or relating to the popular culture disseminated through the mass media ⟨~ psychology⟩ 4 : of, relating to, or imitating pop art ⟨a ~ painter⟩

⁵pop *n* : pop music or culture; *also* : POP ART

⁶pop *abbr* population

pop art *n, often cap P & A* : art in which commonplace objects (as comic strips or soup cans) are used as subject matter — **pop artist** *n*

pop·corn \ˈpäp-ˌkȯrn\ *n* : corn whose kernels burst open into a white starchy mass when heated; *also* : the burst kernels

pope \ˈpōp\ *n, often cap* : the head of the Roman Catholic Church

pop–eyed \ˈpäp-ˌīd\ *adj* : having eyes that bulge (as from disease)

pop fly *n* : POP-UP

pop·gun \'päp-,gən\ *n* : a toy gun for shooting pellets with compressed air

pop·in·jay \'pä-pən-,jā\ *n* [ME *papejay* parrot, fr. MF *papegai, papejai*, fr. Ar *babghā'*] : a strutting supercilious person

pop·lar \'pä-plər\ *n* **1** : any of a genus of slender quick-growing trees (as a cottonwood) related to the willows **2** : the wood of a poplar

pop·lin \'pä-plən\ *n* : a strong plain-woven fabric with crosswise ribs

pop·over \'päp-,ō-vər\ *n* : a hollow muffin made from a thin batter rich in egg

pop·per \'pä-pər\ *n* : a utensil for popping corn

pop·py \'pä-pē\ *n, pl* **poppies** : any of a genus of herbs with showy flowers including one that yields opium

pop·py·cock \-,käk\ *n* : empty talk or writing : NONSENSE

pop·u·lace \'pä-pyə-ləs\ *n* **1** ♦ : the common people **2** : POPULATION

♦ commoners, herd, masses, mob, people, plebeians, rank and file — more at MASSES

pop·u·lar \'pä-pyə-lər\ *adj* **1 a** ♦ : of or relating to the general public **b** ♦ : involving participation of all the people ⟨~ government⟩ **2** ♦ : suited to the tastes of the general public ⟨~ style⟩ **3** : INEXPENSIVE ⟨~ rates⟩ **4** ♦ : frequently encountered or widely accepted ⟨~ notion⟩ **5** ♦ : commonly liked or approved ⟨a ~ teacher⟩ — **pop·u·lar·ize** \'pä-pyə-lə-,rīz\ *vb* — **pop·u·lar·ly** *adv*

♦ [1a] common, general, public, vulgar — more at GENERAL ♦ [1b] democratic, republican, self-governing — more at DEMOCRATIC ♦ [2, 5] fashionable, in, modish, vogue; *also* favorite, preferred; desirable, wanted; celebrated, famed, famous, noted, notorious, prominent, renowned, well-known; fabled, fabulous, legendary; leading, notable, outstanding, remarkable; important, significant *Ant* out, unpopular ♦ [4] conventional, current, customary, standard, stock, usual — more at CURRENT

pop·u·lar·i·ty \,pä-pyə-'lar-ə-tē\ *n* ♦ : the quality or state of being popular

♦ favor, modishness, vogue; *also* craze, fad, mode, rage, style, trend; bandwagon; fame, notoriety, prominence, renown; enthusiasm, fervor, passion *Ant* disfavor, unpopularity

pop·u·late \'pä-pyə-,lāt\ *vb* **-lat·ed; -lat·ing** **1** : to have a place in : INHABIT **2** : PEOPLE

pop·u·la·tion \,pä-pyə-'lā-shən\ *n* **1** : the people or number of people in an area **2** : the organisms inhabiting a particular locality **3** : a group of individuals or items from which samples are taken for statistical measurement

population explosion *n* : a pyramiding of numbers of a biological population; *esp* : the recent great increase in human numbers resulting from increased survival and exponential population growth

pop·u·list \'pä-pyə-list\ *n* : a believer in or advocate of the rights, wisdom, or virtues of the common people — **pop·u·lism** \-,li-zəm\ *n*

pop·u·lous \'pä-pyə-ləs\ *adj* **1** : densely populated; *also* : having a large population **2** : CROWDED — **pop·u·lous·ness** *n*

¹pop–up \'päp-,əp\ *n* : a short high fly in baseball

²pop–up *adj* : of, relating to, or having a component or device that pops up

por·ce·lain \'pōr-sə-lən\ *n* : a fine-grained translucent ceramic ware

porch \'pōrch\ *n* : a covered entrance usu. with a separate roof

por·cine \'pōr-,sīn\ *adj* : of, relating to, or suggesting swine

por·ci·ni \pór-'chē-nē\ *n, pl* **porcini** [It] : a large edible brownish mushroom

por·ci·no \pór-'chē-nō\ *n, pl* **-ni** : PORCINI

por·cu·pine \'pōr-kyə-,pīn\ *n* [ME *porke despyne*, fr. MF *porc espin*, fr. It *porcospino*, fr. L *porcus* pig + *spina* spine, prickle] : any of various mammals having stiff sharp spines mingled with their hair

¹pore \'pōr\ *vb* **pored; por·ing** **1** : to read studiously or attentively ⟨~ over a book⟩ **2** : PONDER, REFLECT

²pore *n* : a tiny hole or space (as in the skin or soil) — **pored** \'pōrd\ *adj*

pork \'pōrk\ *n* **1** : the flesh of swine dressed for use as food **2** : government funds, jobs, or favors distributed by politicians to gain political advantage

pork barrel *n* **1** : government projects or appropriations yielding rich patronage benefits **2** : PORK 2

pork·er \'pōr-kər\ *n* : HOG; *esp* : a young pig suitable for use as fresh pork

por·no·graph·ic \,pōr-nə-'gra-fik\ *adj* ♦ : of or relating to pornography

♦ bawdy, coarse, crude, dirty, filthy, foul, gross, indecent, lascivious, lewd, nasty, obscene, ribald, smutty, unprintable, vulgar, wanton — more at OBSCENE

por·nog·ra·phy \pór-'nä-grə-fē\ *n* : the depiction of erotic behavior intended to cause sexual excitement

po·rous \'pōr-əs\ *adj* **1** : full of pores **2** ♦ : permeable to fluids — **po·ros·i·ty** \pə-'rä-sə-tē\ *n*

♦ passable, penetrable, permeable — more at PENETRABLE

por·phy·ry \'pór-fə-rē\ *n, pl* **-ries** : a rock consisting of feldspar crystals embedded in a compact fine-grained base material — **por·phy·rit·ic** \,pór-fə-'ri-tik\ *adj*

por·poise \'pór-pəs\ *n* [ME *porpoys*, fr. AF *porpeis*, fr. ML *porcpiscis*, fr. L *porcus* pig + *piscis* fish] : any of a family of small gregarious blunt-snouted whales with spadelike teeth; *also* : DOLPHIN 1

por·ridge \'pór-ij\ *n* : a soft food made by boiling meal of grains or legumes in milk or water

por·rin·ger \'pór-ən-jər\ *n* : a low one-handled metal bowl

¹port \'pōrt\ *n* **1** ♦ : a place where ships may ride secure from storms : HARBOR **2** : a city with a harbor **3** : AIRPORT

♦ anchorage, harbor (*or* harbour), haven — more at HARBOR

²port *n* **1** : an inlet or outlet (as in an engine) for a fluid **2** : PORTHOLE

³port *vb* : to turn or put a helm to the left

⁴port *n* : the left side of a ship or airplane looking forward — **port** *adj*

⁵port *n* : a sweet fortified wine

portabella *or* **portabello** *var of* PORTOBELLO

por·ta·bil·i·ty \,pór-tə-'bil-ə-tē\ *n, pl* **-ties** **1** : the quality or state of being portable **2** : the ability to transfer benefits from one pension fund to another when a worker changes jobs

por·ta·ble \'pōr-tə-bəl\ *adj* : capable of being carried — **portable** *n*

¹por·tage \'pōr-tij, pór-'täzh\ *n* [ME, fr. AF, fr. *porter* to carry] : the carrying of boats and goods overland between navigable bodies of water; *also* : a route for such carrying

²portage *vb* **por·taged; por·tag·ing** : to carry gear over a portage

por·tal \'pōrt-ᵊl\ *n* **1** ♦ : the means or place of entry : DOOR; *esp* : a grand or imposing one **2** : a website serving as a guide or point of entry to the Internet

♦ door, gate, hatch — more at DOOR

portal–to–portal *adj* : of or relating to the time spent by a worker in traveling from the entrance to an employer's property to the worker's actual job site (as in a mine)

port·cul·lis \pōrt-'kə-ləs\ *n* : a grating at the gateway of a castle or fortress that can be let down to stop entrance

porte co·chere \,pōrt-kō-'sher\ *n* [F *porte cochère*, lit., coach door] : a roofed structure extending from the entrance of a building over an adjacent driveway and sheltering those getting in or out of vehicles

por·tend \pór-'tend\ *vb* **1** : to give a sign or warning of beforehand **2** : INDICATE, SIGNIFY

por·tent \'pór-,tent\ *n* **1** ♦ : something that foreshadows a coming event : OMEN **2** : one that causes wonder or astonishment : MARVEL, PRODIGY

♦ augury, auspice, foreboding, omen, presage — more at OMEN

por·ten·tous \pȯr-'ten-təs\ *adj* **1** ♦ : of, relating to, or constituting a portent **2** ♦ : eliciting amazement or wonder : PRODIGIOUS **3** : self-consciously solemn : POMPOUS

♦ [1] baleful, dire, foreboding, menacing, ominous, sinister — more at OMINOUS ♦ [2] amazing, astonishing, astounding, awesome, fabulous, marvelous (*or* marvellous), prodigious, stunning, surprising, wonderful — more at MARVELOUS

¹**por·ter** \'pȯr-tər\ *n, chiefly Brit* : DOORKEEPER
²**porter** *n* **1** : a person who carries burdens; *esp* : one employed (as at a terminal) to carry baggage **2** : an attendant in a railroad car **3** : a dark heavy ale
por·ter·house \'pȯr-tər-ˌhau̇s\ *n* : a choice beefsteak with a large tenderloin
port·fo·lio \pȯrt-'fō-lē-ˌō\ *n, pl* **-li·os** **1** : a portable case for papers or drawings **2** : the office and functions of a minister of state **3** : the securities held by an investor **4** : a set of drawings, paintings, or photographs usu. bound in a book or loose in a folder
port·hole \'pȯrt-ˌhōl\ *n* : an opening (as a window) in the side of a ship or aircraft
por·ti·co \'pȯr-ti-ˌkō\ *n, pl* **-coes** *or* **-cos** [It] : a row of columns supporting a roof around or at the entrance of a building
¹**por·tion** \'pȯr-shən\ *n* **1** ♦ : one's part or share ⟨a ∼ of food⟩ **2** : DOWRY **3** ♦ : an individual's lot, fate, or fortune **4** ♦ : a part of a whole ⟨a ∼ of the sky⟩

♦ [1] allotment, allowance, cut, part, proportion, quota, share — more at SHARE ♦ [3] circumstance, destiny, doom, fate, fortune, lot — more at FATE ♦ [4] member, part, partition, section, segment — more at PART

²**portion** *vb* **1** : to divide into portions **2** ♦ : to allot to as a portion

♦ administer, allocate, apportion, deal, dispense, distribute, mete, parcel, prorate — more at ADMINISTER

port·land cement \'pȯrt-lənd-\ *n* : a cement made by calcining and grinding a mixture of clay and limestone
port·ly \'pȯrt-lē\ *adj* **port·li·er; -est** : somewhat stout

♦ chubby, fat, fleshy, full, plump, rotund, round — more at FAT

port·man·teau \pȯrt-'man-ˌtō\ *n, pl* **-teaus** *or* **-teaux** \-ˌtōz\ [MF *portemanteau,* fr. *porter* to carry + *manteau* mantle, fr. L *mantellum*] ♦ : a large traveling bag

♦ carryall, grip, handbag, suitcase, traveling bag — more at TRAVELING BAG

por·to·bel·lo \pȯr-tə-'be-lō\ *also* **por·ta·bel·la** \-lə\ *or* **por·ta·bel·lo** \-lō\ *n, pl* **-los** *also* **-las** : a large dark mature mushroom noted for its meaty texture
port of call : an intermediate port where ships customarily stop for supplies, repairs, or transshipment of cargo
port of entry **1** : a place where foreign goods may be cleared through a customhouse **2** : a place where an alien may enter a country
por·trait \'pȯr-trət, -ˌtrāt\ *n* **1** : a picture (as a painting or photograph) of a person usu. showing the face **2** ♦ : a graphic portrayal in words

♦ delineation, depiction, description, picture, portrayal, sketch — more at DESCRIPTION

por·trait·ist \-trə-tist\ *n* : a maker of portraits
por·trai·ture \'pȯr-trə-ˌchu̇r\ *n* : the practice or art of making portraits
por·tray \pȯr-'trā\ *vb* **1** ♦ : to make a picture of : DEPICT **2** ♦ : to describe in words **3** ♦ : to play the role of

♦ [1] depict, image, picture, represent — more at PICTURE ♦ [2] characterize, delineate, depict, describe, draw, image, paint, picture, sketch — more at DESCRIBE ♦ [3] act, impersonate, perform, play — more at ACT

por·tray·al \pȯr-'trā-(ə)l\ *n* ♦ : the act or process or an instance of portraying

♦ delineation, depiction, description, picture, portrait, sketch — more at DESCRIPTION

Por·tu·guese \'pȯr-chə-ˌgēz, -ˌgēs; ˌpȯr-chə-'gēz, -'gēs\ *n, pl* **Portuguese** **1** : a native or inhabitant of Portugal **2** : the language of Portugal and Brazil — **Portuguese** *adj*
Portuguese man–of–war *n* : any of several large colonial marine invertebrate animals related to the jellyfishes and having a large sac by which the colony floats at the surface
por·tu·la·ca \ˌpȯr-chə-'la-kə\ *n* : any of a genus of succulent herbs cultivated for their showy flowers
pos *abbr* **1** position **2** positive
¹**pose** \'pōz\ *vb* **posed; pos·ing** **1** : to assume or cause to assume a posture usu. for artistic purposes **2** ♦ : to set forth : PROPOSE ⟨∼ a question⟩ **3** ♦ : to affect an attitude or character

♦ [2] advance, offer, proffer, propose, propound, suggest, vote — more at PROPOSE ♦ *usu* **pose as** [3] impersonate, masquerade, play — more at IMPERSONATE

²**pose** *n* **1** : a sustained posture; *esp* : one assumed by a model **2** ♦ : an attitude assumed for effect : PRETENSE

♦ act, airs, facade, front, guise, masquerade, pretense, put-on, semblance, show — more at MASQUERADE

¹**pos·er** \'pō-zər\ *n* : a puzzling question
²**poser** *n* : a person who poses
po·seur \pō-'zər\ *n* [F, lit., poser] : an affected or insincere person
posh \'päsh\ *adj* : FASHIONABLE
pos·it \'pä-zət\ *vb* : to assume the existence of : POSTULATE
¹**po·si·tion** \pə-'zi-shən\ *n* **1** : an arranging in order **2** : the stand taken on a question **3** ♦ : the point or area occupied by something or someone **4** : a certain arrangement of bodily parts ⟨exercise in a sitting ∼⟩ **5** ♦ : social or official rank or status **6** ♦ : an employment for which one has been hired : JOB

♦ [3] locale, location, place, point, site, spot — more at PLACE ♦ [5] degree, footing, level, place, rank, situation, standing, station, status — more at RANK ♦ [6] appointment, billet, capacity, function, job, place, post, situation — more at JOB

²**position** *vb* ♦ : to put in a certain position

♦ deposit, dispose, fix, lay, place, put, set, set up, stick — more at PLACE

¹**pos·i·tive** \'pä-zə-tiv\ *adj* **1** : expressed definitely ⟨her answer was a ∼ *no*⟩ **2** ♦ : fully assured : CONFIDENT, CERTAIN **3** : of, relating to, or constituting the degree of grammatical comparison that denotes no increase in quality, quantity, or relation **4** : not fictitious : REAL **5** : active and effective in function ⟨∼ leadership⟩ **6** : having the light and shade as existing in the original subject ⟨a ∼ photograph⟩ **7** : numerically greater than zero ⟨a ∼ number⟩ **8** : being, relating to, or charged with electricity of which the proton is the elementary unit **9** ♦ : marked by or indicating acceptance, approval, or affirmation ⟨a ∼ response⟩ — **pos·i·tive·ly** *adv*

♦ [2] assured, certain, clear, cocksure, confident, doubtless, sanguine, sure — more at CERTAIN ♦ [9] appreciative, complimentary, favorable (*or* favourable), friendly, good — more at FAVORABLE

²**positive** *n* **1** : the positive degree or a positive form in a language **2** : a positive photograph
pos·i·tive·ness \-nəs\ *n* ♦ : the quality or state of being positive

♦ assurance, certainty, certitude, confidence, conviction, sureness — more at CONFIDENCE

pos·i·tron \'pä-zə-ˌträn\ *n* : a positively charged particle having the same mass and magnitude of charge as the electron
po·so·le *or* **po·zo·le** \pō-'sō-lā\ *n* : a thick Mexican soup made with pork, hominy, garlic, and chili
poss *abbr* possessive
pos·se \'pä-sē\ *n* [ML *posse comitatus,* lit., power or authority of the county] : a body of persons organized to assist a sheriff in an emergency

pos·sess \pə-'zes\ *vb* 1 ♦ : to have as property : OWN 2 : to have as an attribute, knowledge, or skill 3 : to enter into and control firmly ⟨~ed by a devil⟩

♦ command, enjoy, have, hold, occupy, own, retain — more at HAVE

pos·ses·sion \-'ze-shən\ *n* 1 ♦ : control or occupancy of property without regard to ownership 2 : OWNERSHIP 3 ♦ : something owned : PROPERTY 4 : domination by something (as an evil spirit, a passion, or an idea) 5 : SELF-CONTROL

♦ [1] control, hands, keeping; *also* ownership, proprietorship; authority, command, dominion, mastery, power; enjoyment, repossession, retention; claiming, collaring, commandeering, confiscation, procurement ♦ **possessions** [3] belongings, chattels, effects, holdings, paraphernalia, property, things; *also* treasures, valuables; junk, stuff, appointments, fixtures, furnishings; property, tangibles; collateral

pos·ses·sive \pə-'ze-siv\ *adj* 1 : of, relating to, or constituting a grammatical case denoting ownership 2 : showing the desire to possess ⟨a ~ nature⟩ — **possessive** *n* — **pos·ses·sive·ness** *n*

pos·ses·sor \-'ze-sər\ *n* ♦ : one that possesses

♦ holder, owner, proprietor — more at PROPRIETOR

pos·si·bil·i·ty \ˌpä-sə-'bi-lə-tē\ *n* ♦ : something that is possible

♦ case, contingency, event, eventuality — more at EVENT

pos·si·ble \'pä-sə-bəl\ *adj* 1 ♦ : being within the limits of ability, capacity, or realization 2 : being something that may or may not occur ⟨~ dangers⟩ 3 : able or fitted to become ⟨a ~ site for a bridge⟩

♦ achievable, attainable, doable, feasible, practicable, realizable, viable, workable; *also* practical, reasonable, sensible; likely, probable; acceptable, believable, conceivable, creditable, plausible; available, usable *Ant* hopeless, impossible, impracticable, unattainable, unworkable

pos·si·bly \'pä-sə-blē\ *adv* 1 : in a possible manner : by any possibility ⟨it's all I can ~ do⟩ 2 ♦ : it is possible or imaginable

♦ conceivably, maybe, perchance, perhaps — more at PERHAPS

pos·sum \'pä-səm\ *n* : OPOSSUM

¹**post** \'pōst\ *n* 1 ♦ : an upright piece of timber or metal serving esp. as a support : PILLAR 2 : a pole or stake set up as a mark or indicator

♦ column, pier, pillar, stanchion — more at PILLAR

²**post** *vb* 1 : to affix to a usual place (as a wall) for public notices 2 ♦ : to publish or announce by or as if by a public notice ⟨~ grades⟩ 3 : to forbid (property) to trespassers by putting up a notice 4 : SCORE 4 ⟨~ed a 70 in the final round⟩ 5 : to publish in an online forum

♦ advertise, announce, blaze, broadcast, declare, enunciate, placard, proclaim, promulgate, publicize, publish, sound — more at ANNOUNCE

³**post** *n* 1 *obs* : COURIER 2 *chiefly Brit* ♦ : something sent through the mail; *also* : POST OFFICE

♦ mail, matter, parcel post, snail mail — more at MAIL

⁴**post** *vb* 1 : to ride or travel with haste : HURRY 2 : MAIL ⟨~ a letter⟩ 3 : to enter in a ledger 4 : INFORM ⟨kept him ~ed on new developments⟩

⁵**post** *n* 1 ♦ : the place at which a soldier is stationed; *esp* : a sentry's beat or station 2 ♦ : a station or task to which a person is assigned 3 : the place at which a body of troops is stationed : CAMP 4 ♦ : an office or position to which a person is appointed 5 : a trading settlement or station

♦ [1] position, quarter, station — more at STATION ♦ [2] assignment, charge, job, mission, operation — more at MISSION ♦ [4] appointment, billet, capacity, function, job, place, position, situation — more at JOB

⁶**post** *vb* 1 : to station in a given place 2 : to put up (as bond)

post·age \'pōs-tij\ *n* : the fee for postal service; *also* : stamps representing this fee

post·al \'pōst-ᵊl\ *adj* : of or relating to the mails or the post office

postal card *n* : POSTCARD

postal service *n* : a government agency or department handling the transmission of mail

post·card \'pōst-ˌkärd\ *n* : a card on which a message may be written for mailing without an envelope

post chaise *n* : a 4-wheeled closed carriage for two to four persons

post·con·sum·er \ˌpōst-kən-'sü-mər\ *adj* 1 : discarded by a consumer 2 : having been used and recycled for reuse in another product

post·date \ˌpōst-'dāt\ *vb* 1 : to date with a date later than that of execution ⟨~ a check⟩ 2 : to follow in time

post·doc·tor·al \-'däk-tə-rəl\ *also* **post·doc·tor·ate** \-tə-rət\ *adj* : of, relating to, or engaged in advanced academic or professional work beyond a doctor's degree

post·er \'pō-stər\ *n* ♦ : a bill or placard for posting often in a public place

♦ bill, placard; *also* billboard, sign, signboard; broadside, flier, handbill, handout, playbill; ad, advertisement, announcement, bulletin, dispatch, release

¹**pos·te·ri·or** \pō-'stir-ē-ər, pä-\ *adj* 1 ♦ : later in time 2 ♦ : situated behind

♦ [1] after, later, subsequent — more at SUBSEQUENT ♦ [2] back, hind, hindmost, rear — more at BACK

²**pos·te·ri·or** \pä-'stir-ē-ər, pō-\ *n* ♦ : the hinder bodily parts; *esp* : BUTTOCKS

♦ backside, bottom, butt, buttocks, rear, rump, seat — more at BUTTOCKS

pos·ter·i·ty \pä-'ster-ə-tē\ *n* 1 ♦ : the descendants from one ancestor 2 : all future generations

♦ issue, offspring, progeny, seed, spawn — more at OFFSPRING

pos·tern \'pōs-tərn, 'päs-\ *n* 1 : a back door or gate 2 : a private or side entrance

post exchange *n* : a store at a military post that sells to military personnel and authorized civilians

post·grad \'pōst-ˌgrad\ *adj* : POSTGRADUATE

post·grad·u·ate \(ˌ)pōst-'gra-jə-wət\ *adj* : of or relating to studies beyond the bachelor's degree — **postgraduate** *n*

post·haste \'pōst-'hāst\ *adv* ♦ : with all possible speed

♦ apace, briskly, fast, full tilt, hastily, presto, pronto, quick, quickly, rapidly, soon, speedily, swift, swiftly — more at FAST

post·hole \-ˌhōl\ *n* : a hole for a post and esp. a fence post

post·hu·mous \'päs-chə-məs\ *adj* [L *posthumus*, alter. of *postumus* last-born, posthumous, fr. superl. of *posterus* coming after] 1 : born after the death of the father 2 : published after the death of the author — **post·hu·mous·ly** *adv*

post·hyp·not·ic \ˌpōst-hip-'nä-tik\ *adj* : of, relating to, or characteristic of the period following a hypnotic trance

pos·til·ion *or* **pos·til·lion** \pō-'stil-yən\ *n* : a rider on the left-hand horse of a pair drawing a coach

Post·im·pres·sion·ism \ˌpōst-im-'pre-shə-ˌni-zəm\ *n* : a late 19th century French theory or practice of art that stresses variously volume, picture structure, or expressionism

post·lude \'pōst-ˌlüd\ *n* : an organ solo played at the end of a church service

post·man \-mən, -ˌman\ *n* ♦ : a man who delivers mail : MAILMAN

♦ letter carrier, mailman; *also* messenger; postmaster

post·mark \-ˌmärk\ *n* : an official postal marking on a piece of mail; *esp* : the mark canceling the postage stamp — **postmark** *vb*

post·mas·ter \-ˌmas-tər\ *n* : a person who has charge of a post office

postmaster general *n, pl* **postmasters general** : an official in charge of a national postal service

post·men·o·paus·al \ˌpōst-ˌme-nə-ˈpȯ-zəl\ *adj* 1 : having undergone menopause 2 : occurring or administered after menopause

post me·ri·di·em \ˌpōst-mə-ˈri-dē-əm\ *adj* [L] : being after noon

post·mis·tress \ˈpōst-ˌmis-trəs\ *n* : a woman who is a post-master

post·mod·ern \ˌpōst-ˈmä-dərn\ *adj* : of, relating to, or being any of various movements in reaction to modernism

¹**post·mor·tem** \ˌpōst-ˈmȯr-təm\ *adj* [L *post mortem* after death] 1 : done, occurring, or collected after death ⟨a ∼ examination⟩ 2 : following the event

²**postmortem** *n* 1 : an analysis or discussion of an event after it is over ⟨a ∼ of the election⟩ 2 : AUTOPSY

post·na·sal drip \ˈpōst-ˌnā-zəl-\ *n* : flow of mucous secretion from the posterior part of the nasal cavity onto the wall of the pharynx

post·na·tal \(ˌ)pōst-ˈnāt-ᵊl\ *adj* : occurring or being after birth; *esp* : of or relating to a newborn infant

post office *n* 1 : POSTAL SERVICE 2 : a local branch of a post office department

post·op·er·a·tive \(ˌ)pōst-ˈä-prə-tiv, -pə-ˌrā-\ *adj* : following or having undergone a surgical operation ⟨∼ care⟩

post·paid \ˈpōst-ˈpād\ *adj* : having the postage paid by the sender and not chargeable to the receiver

post·par·tum \(ˌ)pōst-ˈpär-təm\ *adj* [NL *post partum* after birth] : following parturition — **postpartum** *adv*

post·pone \pōst-ˈpōn\ *vb* **post·poned; post·pon·ing** ♦ : to put off to a later time — **post·pone·ment** *n*

   ♦ defer, delay, hold up, put off, shelve; *also* suspend; hesitate, pause, stay; detain, retard, slow; extend, lengthen, prolong, protract, stretch (out); wait

post road *n* : a road over which mail is carried

post·script \ˈpōst-ˌskript\ *n* : a note added esp. to a completed letter

post time *n* : the designated time for the start of a horse race

post–traumatic *adj* : occurring after or as a result of trauma ⟨∼ stress⟩

pos·tu·lant \ˈpäs-chə-lənt\ *n* : a probationary candidate for membership in a religious order

¹**pos·tu·late** \ˈpäs-chə-ˌlāt\ *vb* **-lat·ed; -lat·ing** ♦ : to assume as true

   ♦ assume, premise, presume, presuppose, suppose — more at ASSUME

²**pos·tu·late** \ˈpäs-chə-lət, -ˌlāt\ *n* ♦ : a proposition taken for granted as true esp. as a basis for a chain of reasoning

   ♦ assumption, premise, presumption, supposition — more at ASSUMPTION

¹**pos·ture** \ˈpäs-chər\ *n* 1 : the position or bearing of the body or one of its parts 2 : state or condition at a given time esp. with respect to capability in particular circumstances 3 : ATTITUDE

   ♦ footing, picture, scene, situation, status — more at SITUATION

²**posture** *vb* **pos·tured; pos·tur·ing** : to strike a pose esp. for effect

post·war \ˈpōst-ˈwȯr\ *adj* : occurring or existing after a war

po·sy \ˈpō-zē\ *n, pl* **posies** 1 : a brief sentiment : MOTTO 2 : a bunch of flowers; *also* : FLOWER

¹**pot** \ˈpät\ *n* 1 : a rounded container used chiefly for domestic purposes 2 : the total of the bets at stake at one time : RUIN ⟨go to ∼⟩ 4 : a large amount (as of money) — **pot·ful** *n*

²**pot** *vb* **pot·ted; pot·ting** 1 : to preserve or place in a pot 2 : SHOOT

³**pot** *n* : MARIJUANA

po·ta·ble \ˈpō-tə-bəl\ *adj* : suitable for drinking — **po·ta·bil·i·ty** \ˌpō-tə-ˈbi-lə-tē\ *n*

po·tage \pȯ-ˈtäzh\ *n* : a thick soup

pot·ash \ˈpät-ˌash\ *n* [sing. of *pot ashes*] : potassium or any of its various compounds esp. as used in agriculture

po·tas·si·um \pə-ˈta-sē-əm\ *n* : a silver-white soft metallic chemical element that occurs abundantly in nature

potassium bromide *n* : a crystalline salt used as a sedative and in photography

potassium carbonate *n* : a white salt used in making glass and soap

potassium nitrate *n* : a soluble salt used in making gunpowder, as a fertilizer, and in medicine

po·ta·tion \pō-ˈtā-shən\ *n* : a usu. alcoholic drink; *also* : the act of drinking

po·ta·to \pə-ˈtā-tō\ *n, pl* **-toes** : the edible starchy tuber of a plant related to the tomato; *also* : this plant

potato beetle *n* : COLORADO POTATO BEETLE

potato bug *n* : COLORADO POTATO BEETLE

potbellied pig *n* : any of an Asian breed of small pigs having a straight tail, potbelly, and black, white, or black and white coat

pot·bel·ly \ˈpät-ˌbe-lē\ *n* : a protruding abdomen — **pot·bel·lied** \-lēd\ *adj*

pot·boil·er \-ˌbȯi-lər\ *n* : a usu. inferior work of art or literature produced chiefly for profit

po·ten·cy \ˈpōt-ᵊn-sē\ *n* 1 ♦ : ability to act or produce an effect : POWER 2 ♦ : the quality or state of being potent

   ♦ [1, 2] energy, force, main, might, muscle, power, sinew, strength, vigor (*or* vigour) — more at POWER

po·tent \ˈpōt-ᵊnt\ *adj* 1 ♦ : having authority or influence : POWERFUL 2 ♦ : chemically or medicinally effective 3 : able to copulate — used esp. of the male 4 ♦ : rich in a characteristic constituent 5 ♦ : achieving or bringing about a particular result : EFFECTIVE

   ♦ [1] important, influential, mighty, powerful, significant, strong — more at IMPORTANT ♦ [4] concentrated, full, full-bodied, rich, robust, strong — more at FULL-BODIED ♦ [5] effective, effectual, efficacious, efficient, fruitful, productive — more at EFFECTIVE

po·ten·tate \ˈpōt-ᵊn-ˌtāt\ *n* : one who wields controlling power : RULER

¹**po·ten·tial** \pə-ˈten-chəl\ *adj* : existing in possibility : capable of becoming actual ⟨a ∼ champion⟩ — **po·ten·tial·ly** \-ˈten-chə-lē\ *adv*

²**potential** *n* 1 ♦ : something that can develop or become actual ⟨a ∼ for violence⟩ 2 : the work required to move a unit positive charge from infinity to a point in question; *also* : POTENTIAL DIFFERENCE

   ♦ eventuality, possibility; *also* likelihood, probability; latency

potential difference *n* : the difference in potential between two points that represents the work involved in the transfer of a unit quantity of electricity from one point to the other

potential energy *n* : the energy an object has because of its position or nature or the arrangement of its parts

po·ten·ti·al·i·ty \pə-ˌten-chē-ˈa-lə-tē\ *n* 1 : the ability to develop or come into existence 2 : something that can develop or become actual

po·ten·ti·ate \pə-ˈten-chē-ˌāt\ *vb* **-at·ed; -at·ing** : to make potent; *esp* : to augment the activity of (as a drug) synergistically — **po·ten·ti·a·tion** \-ˌten-chē-ˈā-shən\ *n*

pot·head \ˈpät-ˌhed\ *n* : a person who frequently smokes marijuana

poth·er \ˈpä-thər\ *n* 1 ♦ : a noisy disturbance 2 ♦ : mental turmoil

   ♦ [1] commotion, disturbance, furor, hubbub, turmoil ♦ [2] dither, fluster, fret, fuss, huff, lather, stew, tizzy, twitter — more at FRET

pot·herb \ˈpät-ˌərb, -ˌhərb\ *n* : an herb whose leaves or stems are boiled for greens or used to season food

pot·hole \ˈpät-ˌhōl\ *n* : a large pit or hole (as in a road surface)

pot·hook \-ˌhùk\ *n* : an S-shaped hook for hanging pots and kettles over an open fire

po·tion \'pō-shən\ *n* : a mixture of liquids (as liquor or medicine)

pot·luck \'pät-ˈlək\ *n* : the regular meal available to a guest for whom no special preparations have been made

pot·pie \-ˈpī\ *n* : pastry-covered meat and vegetables cooked in a deep dish

pot·pour·ri \ˌpō-pu̇-ˈrē\ *n* [F *pot pourri*, lit., rotten pot] **1** : a mixture of flowers, herbs, and spices used for scent **2** ♦ : a miscellaneous collection

♦ assortment, clutter, jumble, medley, mélange, miscellany, motley, muddle, variety, welter — more at MISCELLANY

pot·sherd \'pät-ˌshərd\ *n* : a pottery fragment

pot·shot \-ˌshät\ *n* **1** : a shot taken from ambush or at a random or easy target **2** : a critical remark made in a random or sporadic manner

pot sticker *n* : a crescent-shaped dumpling that is steamed and fried

pot·tage \'pä-tij\ *n* : a thick soup of vegetables and often meat

¹pot·ter \'pä-tər\ *n* : one that makes pottery

²potter *vb* ♦ : to move or act aimlessly or idly : PUTTER

♦ *usu* **potter around** fiddle, fool, mess, monkey, play, putter, trifle

pot·tery \'pä-tə-rē\ *n, pl* **-ter·ies 1** : a place where earthen pots and dishes are made **2** : the art of the potter **3** : dishes, pots, and vases made from clay

pot·ty–mouthed \'pä-tē-ˌmau̇thd, -ˌmau̇tht\ *adj* : given to the use of vulgar language

¹pouch \'pau̇ch\ *n* [ME *pouche*, fr. AF, of Gmc origin; akin to OE *pocca* bag] **1** : a small bag (as for tobacco) carried on the person **2** : a bag for storing or transporting goods ⟨mail ∼⟩ ⟨diplomatic ∼⟩ **3** : an anatomical sac; *esp* : one for carrying the young on the abdomen of a female marsupial (as a kangaroo)

²pouch *vb* : to put or form into or as if into a pouch

poult \'pōlt\ *n* : a young fowl; *esp* : a young turkey

poul·ter·er \'pōl-tər-ər\ *n* : one that deals in poultry

poul·tice \'pōl-təs\ *n* : a soft usu. heated and medicated mass spread on cloth and applied to a sore or injury — **poultice** *vb*

poul·try \'pōl-trē\ *n* : domesticated birds kept for eggs or meat — **poul·try·man** \-mən\ *n*

pounce \'pau̇ns\ *vb* **pounced; pounc·ing 1** : to spring or swoop upon and seize something **2** ♦ : to make a sudden assault or approach

♦ *usu* **pounce on** *or* **pounce upon** assail, assault, attack, beset, charge, descend, jump, raid, rush, storm, strike — more at ATTACK

¹pound \'pau̇nd\ *n, pl* **pounds** *also* **pound 1** : a unit of avoirdupois, troy, and apothecaries' weight **2** : a unit of weight equal to 16 ounces **3** : the basic monetary unit of any of several countries including Egypt and the United Kingdom

²pound *n* ♦ : a public enclosure where stray animals are kept

♦ cage, coop, corral, pen — more at CAGE

³pound *vb* **1** : to crush to a powder or pulp by beating **2 a** ♦ : to strike or beat heavily or repeatedly **b** ♦ : to produce by repeated blows **3** : DRILL 1 **4** : to move or move along heavily

♦ [2a] bash, bat, batter, beat, belt, bludgeon, club, hammer, hit, thrash, thump, wallop ♦ [2b] beat, forge, hammer — more at HAMMER

⁴pound *n* : an act or sound of pounding

pound·age \'pau̇n-dij\ *n* : POUNDS; *also* : weight in pounds

pound cake *n* : a rich cake made with a large proportion of eggs and shortening

pound–fool·ish \'pau̇nd-ˈfü-lish\ *adj* : imprudent in dealing with large sums or large matters

pour \'pōr\ *vb* **1** ♦ : to flow or cause to flow in a stream or flood **2** ♦ : to rain hard **3** ♦ : to supply freely and copiously

♦ [1] gush, jet, rush, spew, spout, spurt, squirt — more at GUSH ♦ [1] flow, roll, run, stream — more at FLOW ♦ [2] precipitate, rain, storm — more at RAIN ♦ [3] heap, lavish, rain, shower — more at RAIN

¹pout \'pau̇t\ *vb* : to show displeasure by thrusting out the lips; *also* : to look sullen

²pout *n* **1** ♦ : a protrusion of the lips expressive of displeasure **2** ♦ : a fit of pique

♦ [1] face, frown, grimace, lower, mouth, scowl — more at GRIMACE ♦ [2] pet, sulk, sullenness — more at SULK

pov·er·ty \'pä-vər-tē\ *n* [ME *poverte*, fr. AF *poverté*, fr. L *paupertat-, paupertas*, fr. *pauper* poor] **1** ♦ : lack of money or material possessions : WANT **2** : poor quality (as of soil) **3** ♦ : meagerness of supply

♦ [1] beggary, destitution, impecuniousness, impoverishment, indigence, need, pauperism, penury, want; *also* misery, woe, wretchedness; exigency, necessity; austerity, deprivation, privation; bankruptcy, insolvency; belt-tightening, pinching, straitening **Ant** affluence, opulence, richness ♦ [3] dearth, deficiency, deficit, failure, famine, inadequacy, insufficiency, lack, paucity, scantiness, scarcity, shortage, want — more at DEFICIENCY

poverty line *n* : a level of personal or family income below which one is classified as poor according to government standards

pov·er·ty–strick·en \'pä-vər-tē-ˌstri-kən\ *adj* ♦ : very poor : DESTITUTE

♦ broke, destitute, impecunious, indigent, needy, penniless, penurious, poor — more at POOR

POW \ˌpē-(ˌ)ō-ˈdə-bəl-(ˌ)yü\ *n* : PRISONER OF WAR

¹pow·der \'pau̇-dər\ *n* [ME *poudre*, fr. AF *pudre, podre*, fr. L *pulver-, pulvis* dust] **1** : dry material made up of fine particles; *also* : a usu. medicinal or cosmetic preparation in this form **2** : a solid explosive (as gunpowder)

²powder *vb* **1** : to sprinkle or cover with or as if with powder **2** ♦ : to reduce to powder

♦ atomize, crush, grind, pulverize; *also* grate; crumble, crunch; break, bust, dash, fracture, fragment; shatter, smash, splinter; mill

powder room *n* : a rest room for women

pow·dery \'pau̇-də-rē\ *adj* ♦ : resembling or consisting of powder

♦ dusty, fine, floury — more at FINE

¹pow·er \'pau̇-ər\ *n* **1** ♦ : the ability to act or produce an effect **2** ♦ : a position of ascendancy over others : AUTHORITY **3** : one that has control or authority; *esp* : a sovereign state **4** : physical might; *also* : mental or moral vigor **5** : the number of times as indicated by an exponent that a number occurs as a factor in a product ⟨5 to the third ∼ is 125⟩; *also* : the resulting product **6** : force or energy used to do work; *also* : the rate at which work is done or energy transferred **7** : MAGNIFICATION 2

♦ [1] energy, force, main, might, muscle, potency, sinew, strength, vigor (*or* vigour); *also* aptitude, capability, capacity, competence, competency; adequacy, effectiveness, usefulness **Ant** impotence, weakness ♦ [2] arm, authority, clutch, command, control, dominion, grip, hold, mastery, sway; *also* clout, influence, pull, weight; jurisdiction; direction, management; dominance, predominance, sovereignty, supremacy; prerogative, privilege, right; eminence, importance, moment **Ant** impotence

²power *vb* : to supply with power and esp. motive power

³power *adj* : operated mechanically or electrically rather than manually

pow·er·boat \-ˌbōt\ *n* : MOTORBOAT

pow·er·ful \'pau̇-ər-fəl\ *adj* ♦ : having great power, prestige, or influence

♦ important, influential, mighty, potent, significant, strong — more at IMPORTANT

pow·er·ful·ly \-fə-lē\ *adv* ♦ : in a powerful manner

♦ energetically, firmly, forcefully, forcibly, hard, mightily, stiffly, stoutly, strenuously, strongly, sturdily, vigorously — more at HARD

pow·er·house \'pau̇-ər-ˌhau̇s\ *n* **1** : POWER PLANT 1 **2** ♦ : one having great drive, energy, or ability

♦ go-getter, hustler, live wire, self-starter — more at GO-GETTER

pow·er·less \-ləs\ *adj* **1** ♦ : devoid of strength or resources **2** ♦ : lacking the authority or capacity to act

♦ [1, 2] helpless, impotent, weak; *also* incapable, incompetent, ineffective, ineffectual, inept, unfit, useless; feeble, frail, infirm, passive, spineless, supine, unaggressive *Ant* mighty, potent, powerful, puissant, strong

power plant *n* **1** : a building in which electric power is generated **2** : an engine and related parts supplying the motive power of a self-propelled vehicle

pow·wow \'pau̇-ˌwau̇\ *n* **1** : a No. American Indian ceremony (as for victory in war) **2** ♦ : a meeting for discussion : CONFERENCE

♦ assembly, conference, congress, convention, convocation, council, gathering, get-together, huddle, meeting, seminar — more at MEETING

pox \'päks\ *n, pl* **pox** *or* **pox·es** : any of various diseases (as smallpox or syphilis) marked by a rash on the skin

pozole *var of* POSOLE

pp *abbr* **1** pages **2** pianissimo

PP *abbr* **1** parcel post **2** past participle **3** postpaid **4** prepaid

ppd *abbr* **1** postpaid **2** prepaid

PPO \ˌpē-ˌpē-'ō\ *n, pl* **PPOs** [*p*referred *p*rovider *o*rganization] : a health-care organization that gives economic incentives to enrolled individuals who use certain health-care providers

PPS *abbr* [L *post postscriptum*] an additional postscript

ppt *abbr* precipitate

PQ *abbr* Province of Quebec

pr *abbr* **1** pair **2** price

Pr *symbol* praseodymium

¹PR *or* **p.r.** \'pē-'är\ *n* : PUBLIC RELATIONS

²PR *abbr* **1** payroll **2** public relations **3** Puerto Rico

prac·ti·ca·ble \'prak-ti-kə-bəl\ *adj* **1** ♦ : capable of being put into practice, done, or accomplished **2** ♦ : capable of being used — **prac·ti·ca·bil·i·ty** \ˌprak-ti-kə-'bi-lə-tē\ *n*

♦ [1] achievable, attainable, doable, feasible, possible, realizable, viable, workable — more at POSSIBLE ♦ [2] available, fit, functional, operable, serviceable, usable, useful — more at USABLE

prac·ti·cal \'prak-ti-kəl\ *adj* **1** : of, relating to, or shown in practice ⟨∼ questions⟩ **2** : VIRTUAL ⟨∼ control⟩ **3** ♦ : capable of being put to use ⟨a ∼ knowledge of French⟩ **4** ♦ : inclined to action as opposed to speculation or abstraction ⟨a ∼ person⟩ **5** : qualified by practice ⟨a good ∼ mechanic⟩ — **prac·ti·cal·i·ty** \ˌprak-ti-'ka-lə-tē\ *n*

♦ [3] applicable, functional, practicable, serviceable, usable, useful, workable, working; *also* down-to-earth, pragmatic, utilitarian; accessible, available, obtainable, reachable; all-around, handy; active, alive, busy, employed, functioning, operating, operative *Ant* impracticable, impractical, unusable, unworkable, useless ♦ [4] down-to-earth, earthy, hardheaded, matter-of-fact, pragmatic, realistic — more at REALISTIC

practical joke *n* ♦ : a prank intended to trick or embarrass someone or cause physical discomfort

♦ antic, caper, escapade, frolic, monkeyshine, prank, trick — more at PRANK

prac·ti·cal·ly \'prak-ti-k(ə-)lē\ *adv* **1** : in a practical manner **2** ♦ : very nearly but not exactly or entirely : ALMOST

♦ about, almost, most, much, near, nearly, next to, nigh, some, virtually, well-nigh — more at ALMOST

practical nurse *n* : a professional nurse without all of the qualifications of a registered nurse; *esp* : LICENSED PRACTICAL NURSE

¹prac·tice *chiefly Can and Brit* **prac·tise** \'prak-təs\ *vb* **prac·ticed** *also* **prac·tised**; **prac·tic·ing** *also* **prac·tis·ing** **1** : CARRY OUT, APPLY ⟨∼ what you preach⟩ **2** : to per-

form or work at repeatedly so as to become proficient ⟨∼ tennis strokes⟩ **3** : to do or perform customarily ⟨∼ politeness⟩ **4** : to be professionally engaged in ⟨∼ law⟩

²practice *n* **1** : actual performance or application **2** ♦ : customary action : HABIT **3** ♦ : systematic exercise for proficiency **4** : the exercise of a profession; *also* : a professional business

♦ [2] custom, fashion, habit, pattern, way, wont — more at HABIT ♦ [3] dry run, rehearsal, trial — more at REHEARSAL ♦ [3] drill, exercise, routine, training, workout — more at EXERCISE

practiced *chiefly Can and Brit* **practised** *adj* **1** ♦ : made skillful or wise through experience **2** : learned by practice

♦ adroit, artful, delicate, dexterous, expert, masterful, masterly, skillful, virtuoso — more at SKILLFUL

prac·ti·tion·er \prak-'ti-shə-nər\ *n* : one who practices a profession

prae·tor \'prē-tər\ *n* : an ancient Roman magistrate ranking below a consul — **prae·to·ri·an** \prē-'tōr-ē-ən, -'tȯr-\ *adj*

prag·mat·ic \prag-'ma-tik\ *also* **prag·mat·i·cal** \-ti-kəl\ *adj* **1** ♦ : of or relating to practical affairs **2** : concerned with the practical consequences of actions or beliefs ⟨a ∼ leader⟩ — **pragmatic** *n* — **prag·mat·i·cal·ly** \-ti-k(ə-)lē\ *adv*

♦ down-to-earth, earthy, hardheaded, matter-of-fact, practical, realistic — more at REALISTIC

prag·ma·tism \'prag-mə-ˌti-zəm\ *n* : a practical approach to problems and affairs

prai·rie \'prer-ē\ *n* [F, fr. OF *prairie*, fr. VL **prataria*, fr. L *pratum* meadow] ♦ : a broad tract of level or rolling grassland

♦ down, grassland, plain, savanna, steppe, veld — more at PLAIN

prairie dog *n* : an American burrowing black-tailed rodent related to the squirrels and living in colonies

prairie schooner *n* : a covered wagon used by pioneers in cross-country travel

praise \'prāz\ *vb* **praised**; **prais·ing** **1** ♦ : to express approval of **2** ♦ : to glorify (a divinity or a saint) esp. in song — **praise** *n*

♦ [1] acclaim, applaud, cheer, crack up, hail, laud, salute, tout — more at ACCLAIM ♦ [2] bless, extol, glorify, laud, magnify; *also* adore, deify, idolize, worship; acclaim, applaud, commend, compliment, hail, salute; celebrate, cheer, eulogize, rhapsodize; cite; flatter; crack up, recommend, tout

praise·wor·thy \-ˌwər-thē\ *adj* ♦ : worthy of praise : LAUDABLE

♦ admirable, commendable, creditable, laudable, meritorious — more at ADMIRABLE

pra·line \'prä-ˌlēn, 'prā-\ *n* [F] : a confection of nuts and sugar

pram \'pram\ *n, chiefly Brit* : PERAMBULATOR

prance \'prans\ *vb* **pranced**; **pranc·ing** **1** : to spring from the hind legs ⟨a *prancing* horse⟩ **2** : to walk or move in a spirited manner : SWAGGER; *also* : CAPER — **prance** *n* — **pranc·er** *n*

prank \'praŋk\ *n* ♦ : a playful or mildly mischievous act : TRICK

♦ antic, caper, escapade, frolic, monkeyshine, practical joke, trick; *also* skylarking; adventure, experience, game, lark, time; high jinks, horseplay, play, roughhousing, rowdiness; shenanigans, tomfoolery; joking, kidding, teasing; gambit, hoax, maneuver, ploy; deed, feat, mission, performance, stunt; caprice, conceit, fancy, vagary, whim, whimsy; deceit, deception, delusion, fooling, fraud, hoodwinking, ruse, sham, stratagem, subterfuge, trickery, wile

prank·ster \'praŋk-stər\ *n* : a person who plays pranks

pra·seo·dym·i·um \ˌprā-zē-ō-'di-mē-əm\ *n* : a yellowish white metallic chemical element

prate \'prāt\ *vb* **prat·ed; prat·ing** : to talk long and idly : chatter foolishly : PRATTLE

prat·fall \'prat-ˌföl\ *n* **1** : a fall on the buttocks **2** : a humiliating blunder

¹**prat·tle** \'prat-ᵊl\ *vb* **prat·tled; prat·tling** **1** : to talk long and idly : BABBLE **2** ♦ : to utter or make meaningless sounds suggestive of the chatter of children — **prat·tler** *n*

  ♦ babble, chatter, drivel, gabble, gibber, jabber, sputter — more at BABBLE

²**prattle** *n* ♦ : trifling or childish talk

  ♦ babble, gabble, gibberish, gobbledygook, nonsense, piffle, rot — more at GIBBERISH

prawn \'prȯn\ *n* : any of various edible shrimplike crustaceans; *also* : SHRIMP 1

pray \'prā\ *vb* **1** ♦ : to make a request to (someone) in an earnest manner : ENTREAT, IMPLORE **2** : to ask earnestly for something **3** : to address God or a god esp. with supplication

  ♦ appeal, beg, beseech, entreat, implore, importune, petition, plead, solicit, supplicate — more at BEG

prayer \'prar\ *n* **1** : a supplication or expression addressed to God or a god; *also* : a set order of words used in praying **2** ♦ : an earnest request or wish **3** : the act or practice of praying to God or a god **4** : a religious service consisting chiefly of prayers — often used in pl. **5** : something prayed for **6** : a slight chance

  ♦ appeal, cry, entreaty, petition, plea, solicitation, suit, supplication — more at PLEA

prayer book *n* : a book containing prayers and often directions for worship

prayer·ful \'prar-fəl\ *adj* **1** : DEVOUT **2** : characterized by or proceeding from an intense and serious state of mind : EARNEST — **prayer·ful·ly** *adv*

praying mantis *n* : MANTIS

PRC *abbr* People's Republic of China

preach \'prēch\ *vb* **1** : to deliver a sermon **2** : to set forth in a sermon **3** : to advocate earnestly — **preach·ment** *n*

preach·er \'prē-chər\ *n* ♦ : one that preaches

  ♦ clergyman, divine, ecclesiastic, father, minister, priest, reverend — more at CLERGYMAN

pre·ad·o·les·cence \ˌprē-ˌad-ᵊl-'es-ᵊns\ *n* : the period of human development just preceding adolescence — **pre·ad·o·les·cent** \-ᵊnt\ *adj or n*

pre·am·ble \'prē-ˌam-bəl\ *n* [ME, fr. MF *preamble*, fr. ML *preambulum*, fr. LL, neut. of *praeambulus* walking in front of, fr. L *prae* in front of + *ambulare* to walk] ♦ : an introductory part ⟨the ∼ to a constitution⟩

  ♦ foreword, introduction, preface, prologue — more at INTRODUCTION

pre·ap·prove \ˌprē-ə-'prüv\ *vb* : to approve in advance — **pre·ap·prov·al** \-'prü-vəl\ *n*

pre·ar·range \ˌprē-ə-'rānj\ *vb* : to arrange beforehand — **pre·ar·range·ment** *n*

pre·as·sign \ˌprē-ə-'sīn\ *vb* : to assign beforehand

pre·bake \ˌprē-'bāk\ *vb* : to bake in advance

prec *abbr* preceding

Pre·cam·bri·an \'prē-'kam-brē-ən, -'kām-\ *adj* : of, relating to, or being the era that is earliest in geologic history and is characterized esp. by the appearance of single-celled organisms — **Precambrian** *n*

pre·can·cel \(ˌ)prē-'kan-səl\ *vb* : to cancel (a postage stamp) in advance of use — **precancel** *n* — **pre·can·cel·la·tion** \ˌprē-ˌkan-sə-'lā-shən\ *n*

pre·can·cer·ous \(ˌ)prē-'kan-sə-rəs\ *adj* : likely to become cancerous

pre·car·i·ous \pri-'kar-ē-əs\ *adj* : dependent on uncertain conditions : dangerously insecure : UNSTABLE ⟨a ∼ foothold⟩ ⟨∼ prosperity⟩ — **pre·car·i·ous·ly** *adv*

pre·car·i·ous·ness \-nəs\ *n* ♦ : the quality or state of being precarious

  ♦ insecurity, instability, shakiness, unsteadiness — more at INSTABILITY

pre·cau·tion \pri-'kȯ-shən\ *n* : a measure taken beforehand to prevent harm or secure good — **pre·cau·tion·ary** \-shə-ˌner-ē\ *adj*

pre·cede \pri-'sēd\ *vb* **pre·ced·ed; pre·ced·ing** ♦ : to be, go, or come ahead or in front of (as in rank or time)

  ♦ antedate, forego *Ant* follow, succeed

prec·e·dence \'pre-sə-dəns, pri-'sēd-ᵊns\ *n* **1** : the act or fact of preceding **2** : consideration based on order of importance : PRIORITY

¹**prec·e·dent** \pri-'sēd-ᵊnt, 'pre-sə-dənt\ *adj* : prior in time, order, or significance

²**prec·e·dent** \'pre-sə-dənt\ *n* : something said or done that may serve to authorize or justify further words or acts of the same or a similar kind

pre·ced·ing \pri-'sē-diŋ\ *adj* ♦ : that precedes

  ♦ antecedent, anterior, foregoing, previous, prior — more at PREVIOUS

pre·cen·tor \pri-'sen-tər\ *n* : a leader of the singing of a choir or congregation

pre·cept \'prē-ˌsept\ *n* : a command or principle intended as a general rule of action or conduct

pre·cep·tor \pri-'sep-tər, 'prē-ˌsep-\ *n* : a person charged with the instruction and guidance of another : TUTOR

pre·ces·sion \prē-'se-shən\ *n* : a slow gyration of the rotation axis of a spinning body (as the earth) — **pre·cess** \prē-'ses\ *vb* — **pre·ces·sion·al** \-'se-shə-nəl\ *adj*

pre·cinct \'prē-ˌsiŋkt\ *n* **1** : an administrative subdivision (as of a city) : DISTRICT ⟨police ∼⟩ ⟨electoral ∼⟩ **2** : an enclosure bounded by the limits of a building or place — often used in pl. **3** *pl* : ENVIRONS

pre·ci·os·i·ty \ˌpre-shē-'ä-sə-tē\ *n, pl* **-ties** : fastidious refinement

pre·cious \'pre-shəs\ *adj* **1** ♦ : of great value ⟨∼ jewels⟩ **2** ♦ : greatly cherished : DEAR ⟨∼ memories⟩ **3** : AFFECTED ⟨∼ language⟩

  ♦ [1] costly, dear, expensive, high, valuable — more at COSTLY ♦ [2] beloved, darling, dear, favorite (*or* favourite), loved, pet, special, sweet ♦ [2] adorable, darling, dear, endearing, lovable, sweet, winning — more at LOVABLE

prec·i·pice \'pre-sə-pəs\ *n* ♦ : a steep cliff

  ♦ bluff, cliff, crag, escarpment, palisade, scarp — more at CLIFF

pre·cip·i·tan·cy \pri-'si-pə-tən-sē\ *n* : undue hastiness or suddenness

¹**pre·cip·i·tate** \pri-'si-pə-ˌtāt\ *vb* **-tat·ed; -tat·ing** [L *praecipitare*, fr. *praecipit-, praeceps* headlong, fr. *prae* in front of + *caput* head] **1** : to throw violently **2** : to throw down **3** : to cause to happen quickly or abruptly ⟨∼ a quarrel⟩ **4** : to cause to separate from solution or suspension **5** : to fall as rain, snow, or hail

²**pre·cip·i·tate** \pri-'si-pə-tət, -ˌtāt\ *n* ♦ : the solid matter that separates from a solution or suspension

  ♦ deposit, dregs, grounds, sediment — more at DEPOSIT

³**pre·cip·i·tate** \pri-'si-pə-tət\ *adj* **1** ♦ : showing extreme or unwise haste : RASH **2** : falling with steep descent; *also* : PRECIPITOUS — **pre·cip·i·tate·ness** *n*

  ♦ cursory, hasty, headlong, pell-mell, precipitous, rash — more at HASTY

pre·cip·i·tate·ly \-lē\ *adv* ♦ : in a precipitate manner

  ♦ cursorily, hastily, headlong, hurriedly, pell-mell, rashly — more at HASTILY

pre·cip·i·ta·tion \pri-ˌsi-pə-'tā-shən\ *n* **1** ♦ : rash haste **2** : the process of precipitating or forming a precipitate **3** : water that falls to earth esp. as rain or snow; *also* : the quantity of this water

  ♦ haste, hurry, hustle, rush — more at HURRY

pre·cip·i·tous \pri-'si-pə-təs\ *adj* **1** : showing extreme or unwise haste : PRECIPITATE **2** ♦ : having the character of a precipice : very steep ⟨a ∼ slope⟩; *also* : containing precipices ⟨∼ trails⟩

  ♦ abrupt, bold, sheer, steep — more at STEEP

pre·cip·i·tous·ly \-lē\ *adv* : in a precipitous manner

pré·cis \prā-'sē\ *n, pl* **pré·cis** \-'sēz\ [F] ♦ : a concise summary of essentials

♦ abstract, digest, encapsulation, epitome, outline, recapitulation, résumé (*or* resume), roundup, sum, summary, synopsis, wrap-up — more at SUMMARY

pre·cise \pri-'sīs\ *adj* **1** ♦ : exactly defined or stated **2** ♦ : highly accurate : EXACT **3** ♦ : conforming strictly to a standard : SCRUPULOUS ⟨a ~ teacher⟩

♦ [1] distinct, especial, express, set, special, specific — more at EXPRESS ♦ [2] accurate, correct, exact, proper, right, so, true — more at CORRECT ♦ [2, 3] accurate, close, delicate, exact, fine, mathematical, pinpoint, rigorous, scrupulous; *also* correct, right, strict, true; definite, definitive; nice, subtle; careful, fastidious, finicky *Ant* coarse, imprecise, inaccurate, inexact, rough

pre·cise·ly \-lē\ *adv* ♦ : in a precise manner

♦ accurately, exactly, just, right, sharp, squarely, strictly — more at EXACTLY

pre·cise·ness \-nəs\ *n* : the quality or state of being precise

pre·ci·sion \pri-'si-zhən\ *n* ♦ : the quality or state of being precise

♦ accuracy, closeness, delicacy, exactness, fineness, veracity; *also* correctness, rightness, strictness, truth; definiteness; nicety, subtlety; care, carefulness, fastidiousness *Ant* coarseness, impreciseness, imprecision, inaccuracy, inexactness, roughness

pre·clude \pri-'klüd\ *vb* **pre·clud·ed; pre·clud·ing** ♦ : to make impossible : PREVENT

♦ avert, forestall, help, obviate, prevent — more at PREVENT

pre·co·cious \pri-'kō-shəs\ *adj* [L *praecoc-, praecox,* lit., ripening early, fr. *prae-* ahead + *coquere* to cook] **1** ♦ : exceptionally early in development or occurrence **2** : exhibiting mature qualities at an unusually early age — **pre·coc·i·ty** \pri-'kä-sə-tē\ *n*

♦ early, premature, unseasonable, untimely — more at EARLY

pre·co·cious·ly \-lē\ *adv* ♦ : in a precocious manner

♦ beforehand, early, prematurely, unseasonably — more at EARLY

pre·con·ceive \ˌprē-kən-'sēv\ *vb* : to form an opinion of beforehand — **pre·con·cep·tion** \-'sep-shən\ *n*

pre·con·di·tion \-'di-shən\ *vb* : to put in proper or desired condition or frame of mind in advance

pre·cook \ˌprē-'kůk\ *vb* : to cook partially or entirely before final cooking or reheating

pre·cur·sor \pri-'kər-sər\ *n* **1** ♦ : one that precedes and indicates the approach of another : FORERUNNER **2** ♦ : one that precedes another in an office or process

♦ [1] angel, forerunner, harbinger, herald — more at FORERUNNER ♦ [2] ancestor, antecedent, forerunner — more at ANCESTOR

pred *abbr* predicate

pre·da·ceous *or* **pre·da·cious** \pri-'dā-shəs\ *adj* : living by preying on others : PREDATORY

pre·date \'prē-ˌdāt\ *vb* : to precede in time : ANTEDATE

pre·da·tion \pri-'dā-shən\ *n* **1** : the act of preying or plundering **2** : a mode of life in which food is primarily obtained by killing and consuming animals

pred·a·tor \'pre-də-tər\ *n* : an animal that lives by predation

pred·a·to·ry \'pre-də-ˌtōr-ē\ *adj* **1** : of or relating to plunder ⟨~ warfare⟩ **2** : disposed to exploit others **3** : preying upon other animals

pre·dawn \(')prē-'dȯn\ *adj* : of or relating to the time just before dawn

pre·de·cease \ˌprē-di-'sēs\ *vb* **-ceased; -ceas·ing** : to die before another person

pre·de·ces·sor \'pre-də-ˌse-sər, 'prē-\ *n* **1** : a previous holder of a position to which another has succeeded **2** : something that has been followed or displaced by another

pre·des·ig·nate \(ˌ)prē-'de-zig-ˌnāt\ *vb* : to designate beforehand

pre·des·ti·na·tion \ˌprē-ˌdes-tə-'nā-shən\ *n* : the act of foreordaining to an earthly lot or eternal destiny by divine decree; *also* : the state of being so foreordained — **pre·des·ti·nate** \prē-'des-tə-ˌnāt\ *vb*

pre·des·tine \prē-'des-tən\ *vb* ♦ : to settle beforehand : FOREORDAIN

♦ destine, doom, fate, foredoom, foreordain, ordain — more at DESTINE

pre·de·ter·mine \ˌprē-di-'tər-mən\ *vb* : to determine beforehand

pred·i·ca·ble \'pre-di-kə-bəl\ *adj* : capable of being predicated or affirmed

pre·dic·a·ment \pri-'di-kə-mənt\ *n* ♦ : a difficult or trying situation

♦ corner, fix, hole, jam, pickle, spot; *also* difficulty, dilemma, hot water, pinch, plight, quagmire, quandary, trouble; deadlock, halt, impasse, stalemate, standstill; clutch, crisis, crossroad, emergency, exigency, juncture, strait

¹**pred·i·cate** \'pre-di-kət\ *n* : the part of a sentence or clause that expresses what is said of the subject

²**pred·i·cate** \'pre-də-ˌkāt\ *vb* **-cat·ed; -cat·ing** **1** : AFFIRM **2** : to assert to be a quality or attribute **3** : to set or ground on something : BASE — **pred·i·ca·tion** \ˌpre-də-'kā-shən\ *n*

pre·dict \pri-'dikt\ *vb* ♦ : to declare in advance — **pre·dict·abil·i·ty** \-ˌdik-tə-'bi-lə-tē\ *n* — **pre·dict·able** \-'dik-tə-bəl\ *adj* — **pre·dict·ably** \-blē\ *adv*

♦ augur, forecast, foretell, presage, prognosticate, prophesy — more at FORETELL

pre·dic·tion \pri-'dik-shən\ *n* **1** ♦ : an act of predicting **2** : something that is predicted

♦ cast, forecast, prognostication, prophecy, soothsaying; *also* augury, omen, portent, sign; anticipation, foreknowledge; foresight; conjecture, guess, surmise

pre·di·gest \ˌprē-dī-'jest\ *vb* : to simplify for easy use; *also* : to subject to artificial or natural partial digestion

pre·di·lec·tion \ˌpre-də-'lek-shən, ˌprē-\ *n* ♦ : an established preference for something

♦ bent, devices, disposition, genius, inclination, leaning, partiality, penchant, proclivity, propensity, tendency, turn — more at INCLINATION

pre·dis·pose \ˌprē-di-'spōz\ *vb* : to incline in advance : make susceptible ⟨*predisposed* to infection⟩

pre·dis·po·si·tion \ˌprē-ˌdis-pə-'zi-shən\ *n* ♦ : a condition of being predisposed

♦ affinity, bent, devices, disposition, genius, inclination, leaning, partiality, penchant, predilection, proclivity, propensity, talent, tendency, turn — more at INCLINATION

pre·dom·i·nance \pri-'dä-mə-nəns\ *n* ♦ : the quality or state of being predominant

♦ ascendancy, dominance, dominion, preeminence, supremacy — more at SUPREMACY

pre·dom·i·nant \pri-'dä-mə-nənt\ *adj* ♦ : greater in importance, strength, influence, or authority

♦ arch, cardinal, central, chief, dominant, first, foremost, grand, key, main, paramount, preeminent, premier, primary, principal, sovereign, supreme — more at FOREMOST

pre·dom·i·nant·ly \-nənt-lē\ *adv* ♦ : for the most part : MAINLY

♦ altogether, basically, chiefly, generally, largely, mainly, mostly, overall, primarily, principally — more at CHIEFLY

pre·dom·i·nate \pri-'dä-mə-ˌnāt\ *vb* : to be superior esp. in power or numbers : PREVAIL

pre·dom·i·nate·ly \pri-'dä-mə-nət-lē\ *adv* : PREDOMINANTLY

pree·mie \'prē-mē\ *n* : a premature baby

pre·em·i·nence \prē-'e-mə-nəns\ *n* ♦ : the quality or state of being preeminent

♦ distinction, dominance, excellence, greatness, superiority, supremacy — more at EXCELLENCE

pre·em·i·nent \prē-'e-mə-nənt\ *adj* ♦ : having highest rank — **pre·em·i·nent·ly** *adv*

♦ arch, cardinal, central, chief, dominant, first, foremost, grand, key, main, paramount, predominant, premier, primary, principal, sovereign, supreme — more at FOREMOST ♦ distinguished, eminent, illustrious, noble, notable, noteworthy, outstanding, prestigious, signal, star, superior — more at EMINENT

pre·empt \prē-'empt\ *vb* **1** : to settle upon (public land) with the right to purchase before others; *also* : to take by such right **2** ♦ : to seize upon before someone else can **3** : to take the place of — **pre·emp·tion** \-'emp-shən\ *n*

♦ appropriate, arrogate, commandeer, usurp — more at APPROPRIATE

pre·emp·tive \prē-'emp-tiv\ *adj* : marked by the seizing of the initiative : initiated by oneself ⟨∼ attack⟩

preen \'prēn\ *vb* [ME *prenen*, alter. of *proynen, prunen*, fr. AF *puroindre, proindre*, fr. *pur-* thoroughly + *oindre* to anoint, rub, fr. L *unguere*] **1** : to dress or smooth up : PRIMP **2** : to groom with the bill — used of a bird **3** : to pride (oneself) for achievement

pre·ex·ist \,prē-ig-'zist\ *vb* : to exist before — **pre·ex·is·tence** \-'zis-təns\ *n* — **pre·ex·is·tent** \-tənt\ *adj*

pref *abbr* **1** preface **2** preference **3** preferred **4** prefix

¹**pre·fab** \(,)prē-'fab, 'prē-,fab\ *n* : a prefabricated structure

²**pre·fab** *adj* : produced by prefabrication ⟨a ∼ house⟩

pre·fab·ri·cate \(,)prē-'fa-brə-,kāt\ *vb* : to manufacture the parts of (a structure) beforehand for later assembly — **pre·fab·ri·ca·tion** \,prē-,fa-bri-'kā-shən\ *n*

¹**pref·ace** \'pre-fəs\ *n* ♦ : the introductory remarks of a speaker or writer — **pref·a·to·ry** \'pre-fə-,tōr-ē\ *adj*

♦ foreword, introduction, preamble, prologue — more at INTRODUCTION

²**preface** *vb* **pref·aced; pref·ac·ing** : to introduce with a preface

pre·fect \'prē-,fekt\ *n* **1** : a high official; *esp* : a chief officer or magistrate **2** : a student monitor

pre·fec·ture \'prē-,fek-chər\ *n* : the office, term, or residence of a prefect

pre·fer \pri-'fər\ *vb* **pre·ferred; pre·fer·ring** **1** : PROMOTE **2** ♦ : to like better **3** : to bring (as a charge) against a person — **pref·er·a·ble** \'pre-fə-rə-bəl\ *adj*

♦ choose, cull, elect, handpick, name, opt, pick, select, single, take — more at CHOOSE ♦ favor (*or* favour), lean, like; *also* adore, cotton (to), delight (in), dig, enjoy, fancy, groove (on), relish, revel (in); choose, cull, handpick, name, pick, select, single (out), take; prize, treasure, value

pref·er·a·bly \'pre-fə-rə-blē\ *adv* ♦ : it is preferred

♦ first, rather, readily, soon — more at RATHER

pref·er·ence \'pre-frəns, -fə-rəns\ *n* **1** ♦ : a special liking for one thing over another **2** ♦ : the power or opportunity of choosing : CHOICE **3** ♦ : one that is preferred — **pref·er·en·tial** \,pre-fə-'ren-chəl\ *adj*

♦ [1] appetite, fancy, favor (*or* favour), fondness, like, liking, love, partiality, relish, shine, taste, use — more at LIKING ♦ [2] alternative, choice, discretion, option, pick, way — more at CHOICE ♦ [3] darling, favorite (*or* favourite), pet, prize, treasure

pre·fer·ment \pri-'fər-mənt\ *n* : advancement or promotion in dignity, office, or station : PROMOTION, ADVANCEMENT

preferred provider organization *n* : PPO

pre·fig·ure \prē-'fi-gyər\ *vb* **1** : to show, suggest, or announce beforehand : FORESHADOW **2** : to imagine beforehand

♦ foreshadow, harbinger — more at FORESHADOW

¹**pre·fix** \'prē-,fiks, prē-'fiks\ *vb* : to place before ⟨∼ a title to a name⟩

²**pre·fix** \'prē-,fiks\ *n* : an affix occurring at the beginning of a word

pre·flight \,prē-'flīt\ *adj* : preparing for or preliminary to flight

pre·form \(,)prē-'fȯrm, 'prē-,fȯrm\ *vb* : to form or shape beforehand

preg·na·ble \'preg-nə-bəl\ *adj* : vulnerable to capture ⟨a ∼ fort⟩

preg·nant \'preg-nənt\ *adj* **1** : containing unborn offspring within the body **2** ♦ : rich in significance : MEANINGFUL — **preg·nan·cy** \-nən-sē\ *n*

♦ eloquent, expressive, meaning, meaningful, significant, suggestive — more at EXPRESSIVE

pre·heat \,prē-'hēt\ *vb* : to heat beforehand; *esp* : to heat (an oven) to a designated temperature before using

pre·hen·sile \prē-'hen-səl, -,sīl\ *adj* : adapted for grasping esp. by wrapping around ⟨a monkey with a ∼ tail⟩

pre·his·tor·ic \,prē-his-'tȯr-ik\ *also* **pre·his·tor·i·cal** \-i-kəl\ *adj* : of, relating to, or existing in the period before written history began

pre·judge \(,)prē-'jəj\ *vb* : to judge before full hearing or examination

¹**prej·u·dice** \'pre-jə-dəs\ *n* **1** : DAMAGE; *esp* : detriment to one's rights or claims **2** ♦ : an opinion made without adequate basis ⟨racial ∼⟩

♦ bias, favor (*or* favour), partiality, partisanship — more at BIAS

²**prejudice** *vb* **-diced; -dic·ing** **1** : to damage by a judgment or action esp. at law **2** : to cause to have prejudice

prejudiced *adj* ♦ : resulting from or having a prejudice or bias for or esp. against

♦ biased, one-sided, partial, partisan — more at PARTIAL ♦ bigoted, intolerant, narrow, narrow-minded — more at INTOLERANT

prej·u·di·cial \,pre-jə-'di-shəl\ *adj* **1** ♦ : tending to injure or impair **2** : leading to premature judgment or unwarranted opinion

♦ adverse, counter, disadvantageous, harmful, hostile, inimical, negative, unfavorable (*or* unfavourable), unfriendly, unsympathetic — more at ADVERSE

pre·kin·der·gar·ten \(')prē-'kin-dər-,gär-tᵊn\ *n* **1** : NURSERY SCHOOL **2** : a class or program preceding kindergarten

prel·ate \'pre-lət\ *n* : an ecclesiastic (as a bishop) of high rank — **prel·a·cy** \-lə-sē\ *n*

pre·launch \'prē-'lȯnch\ *adj* : preparing for or preliminary to launch

pre·lim \'prē-,lim, pri-'lim\ *n or adj* : PRELIMINARY

¹**pre·lim·i·nary** \pri-'li-mə-,ner-ē\ *n, pl* **-nar·ies** : something that precedes or introduces the main business or event

²**preliminary** *adj* : preceding the main discourse or business

pre·lude \'prel-,yüd; 'pre-,lüd, 'prā-\ *n* **1** : an introductory performance or event **2** : a musical section or movement introducing the main theme; *also* : an organ solo played at the beginning of a church service

prem *abbr* premium

pre·mar·i·tal \(,)prē-'mar-ət-ᵊl\ *adj* : existing or occurring before marriage

pre·ma·ture \,prē-mə-'tur, -'tyur, -'chur\ *adj* ♦ : happening, coming, born, or done before the usual or proper time

♦ early, precocious, unseasonable, untimely — more at EARLY

pre·ma·ture·ly \-lē\ *adv* ♦ : in a premature manner : too soon

♦ beforehand, early, precociously, unseasonably — more at EARLY

¹**pre·med** \,prē-'med\ *n* : a premedical student or course of study

²**premed** *adj* : PREMEDICAL

pre·med·i·cal \(,)prē-'me-di-kəl\ *adj* : preceding and preparing for the professional study of medicine

pre·med·i·tate \pri-'me-də-,tāt\ *vb* : to consider and plan beforehand — **pre·med·i·ta·tion** \-,me-də-'tā-shən\ *n*

pre·men·o·paus·al \(ˌ)prē-ˌme-nə-ˈpȯ-zəl\ *adj* : of, relating to, or being in the period preceding menopause

pre·men·stru·al \(ˌ)prē-ˈmen-strə-wəl\ *adj* : of, relating to, or occurring in the period just before menstruation

premenstrual syndrome *n* : a varying group of symptoms manifested by some women prior to menstruation

premie *var of* PREEMIE

¹pre·mier \pri-ˈmir, -ˈmyir, ˈprē-mē-ər\ *adj* [ME *primer, primier,* fr. AF, first, chief, fr. L *primarius* of the first rank] **1** ♦ : first in rank or importance : CHIEF **2** ♦ : earliest in time

♦ [1] chief, first, foremost, head, high, lead, preeminent, primary, prime, principal, supreme — more at HEAD ♦ [2] first, inaugural, initial, maiden, original, pioneer — more at FIRST

²premier *n* : PRIME MINISTER — **pre·mier·ship** *n*

¹pre·miere \pri-ˈmyer, -ˈmir\ *n* : a first performance

²premiere *also* **pre·mier** \same as ¹PREMIERE\ *vb* **pre·miered; pre·mier·ing** : to give or receive a first public performance

prem·ise \ˈpre-məs\ *n* **1** ♦ : a statement of fact or a supposition made or implied as a basis of argument **2** *pl* ♦ : a piece of land with the structures on it; *also* : the place of business of an enterprise

♦ [1] assumption, postulate, presumption, supposition — more at ASSUMPTION **premises** ♦ [2] demesne, grounds, park, yard

pre·mi·um \ˈprē-mē-əm\ *n* [L *praemium* booty, profit, reward, fr. *prae* before + *emere* to take, buy] **1** : a reward or recompense for a particular act : REWARD, PRIZE **2** : a sum over and above the stated value **3** : something paid over and above a fixed wage or price **4** : something given with a purchase **5** : the sum paid for a contract of insurance **6** : an unusually high value

pre·mix \ˌprē-ˈmiks\ *vb* : to mix before use

pre·mo·lar \(ˌ)prē-ˈmō-lər\ *adj* : situated in front of or preceding the molar teeth; *esp* : being or relating to those teeth of a mammal in front of the true molars and behind the canines — **premolar** *n*

pre·mo·ni·tion \ˌprē-mə-ˈni-shən, ˌpre-\ *n* **1** : previous warning **2** ♦ : anticipation of an event without conscious reason : PRESENTIMENT — **pre·mon·i·to·ry** \pri-ˈmä-nə-ˌtȯr-ē\ *adj*

♦ foreboding, presage, presentiment; *also* anticipation, foreknowledge; insight, intuition; augury, omen, portent, sign; impression, suspicion; anxiety, apprehension, care, concern, disquiet, doubt, dread, fear, misgiving, worry; foresight

pre·na·tal \ˈprē-ˈnāt-ᵊl\ *adj* : occurring, existing, or taking place before birth

pre·nup·tial \prē-ˈnəp-shəl\ *adj* : made or occurring before marriage

prenuptial agreement *n* : an agreement between a couple before marrying in which they give up future rights to each other's property in the event of divorce or death

pre·oc·cu·pa·tion \prē-ˌä-kyə-ˈpā-shən\ *n* **1** : complete absorption of the mind or interests **2** ♦ : something that causes complete absorption of the mind or interests

♦ fetish, fixation, mania, obsession, prepossession — more at FIXATION

pre·oc·cu·pied \prē-ˈä-kyə-ˌpīd\ *adj* **1** ♦ : lost in thought; *also* : absorbed in some preoccupation **2** : already occupied

♦ absent, absentminded, abstracted — more at ABSENTMINDED

pre·oc·cu·py \-ˌpī\ *vb* **1** : to occupy the attention of beforehand **2** : to take possession of before another

pre·op·er·a·tive \(ˌ)prē-ˈä-prə-tiv, -pə-ˌrā-\ *adj* : occurring before a surgical operation

pre·or·dain \ˌprē-ȯr-ˈdān\ *vb* : FOREORDAIN

pre–owned \(ˌ)prē-ˈōnd\ *adj* : SECONDHAND

prep *abbr* **1** preparatory **2** preposition

pre·pack·age \(ˌ)prē-ˈpa-kij\ *vb* : to package (as food) before offering for sale to the customer

preparatory school *n* **1** : a usu. private school preparing students primarily for college **2** *Brit* : a private elementary school preparing students primarily for British public schools

pre·pare \pri-ˈpar\ *vb* **pre·pared; pre·par·ing** **1** ♦ : to make or get ready ⟨~ dinner⟩ ⟨~ a student for college⟩ **2** ♦ : to get ready beforehand **3** : to put together : COMPOUND ⟨~ a prescription⟩ **4** ♦ : to put into written form — **prep·a·ra·tion** \ˌpre-pə-ˈrā-shən\ *n* — **pre·pa·ra·to·ry** \pri-ˈpar-ə-ˌtȯr-ē\ *adj*

♦ [1] equip, fit, qualify, ready, season — more at QUALIFY ♦ [2] fit, fix, get, lay, ready; *also* brace, fortify, steel; batten, gather, gear (up), mount, train; boot (up), prime; arrange, set, spread; arm, equip, furnish, outfit, provide, supply; incline, predispose; draft, draw (up), frame; warm (up) ♦ [4] cast, compose, craft, draft, draw, formulate, frame — more at COMPOSE

prepared *adj* **1** : made ready, fit, or suitable beforehand **2** : subjected to a special process or treatment

pre·pared·ness \pri-ˈpar-əd-nəs\ *n* : a state of adequate preparation

pre·pay \(ˌ)prē-ˈpā\ *vb* **-paid** \-ˈpād\; **-pay·ing** : to pay or pay the charge on in advance

pre·pon·der·ant \pri-ˈpän-də-rənt\ *adj* : having greater weight, force, influence, or frequency — **pre·pon·der·ance** \-rəns\ *n* — **pre·pon·der·ant·ly** *adv*

pre·pon·der·ate \pri-ˈpän-də-ˌrāt\ *vb* **-at·ed; -at·ing** [L *praeponderare,* fr. *prae-* ahead + *ponder-, pondus* weight] : to exceed in weight, force, influence, or frequency : PREDOMINATE

prep·o·si·tion \ˌpre-pə-ˈzi-shən\ *n* : a word that combines with a noun or pronoun to form a phrase — **prep·o·si·tion·al** \-ˈzi-shə-nəl\ *adj*

pre·pos·sess \ˌprē-pə-ˈzes\ *vb* **1** : to cause to be preoccupied **2** : to influence beforehand esp. favorably

pre·pos·sess·ing *adj* : tending to create a favorable impression ⟨a ~ manner⟩

pre·pos·ses·sion \-ˈze-shən\ *n* **1** : PREJUDICE **2** ♦ : an exclusive concern with one idea or object

♦ fetish, fixation, mania, obsession, preoccupation — more at FIXATION

pre·pos·ter·ous \pri-ˈpäs-tə-rəs\ *adj* ♦ : contrary to nature or reason : ABSURD

♦ absurd, bizarre, crazy, fanciful, fantastic, foolish, insane, nonsensical, unreal, wild — more at FANTASTIC ♦ absurd, comical, derisive, farcical, laughable, ludicrous, ridiculous, risible, silly — more at RIDICULOUS

prep·py *or* **prep·pie** \ˈpre-pē\ *n, pl* **preppies** **1** : a student at or a graduate of a preparatory school **2** : a person deemed to dress or behave like a preppy

pre·puce \ˈprē-ˌpyüs\ *n* : FORESKIN

pre·quel \ˈprē-kwəl\ *n* : a literary or dramatic work whose story precedes that of an earlier work

pre·re·cord·ed \(ˌ)prē-ri-ˈkȯr-dəd\ *adj* : recorded for later broadcast or play

pre·req·ui·site \prē-ˈre-kwə-zət\ *n* : something required beforehand or for the end in view — **prerequisite** *adj*

pre·rog·a·tive \pri-ˈrä-gə-tiv\ *n* ♦ : an exclusive or special right, power, or privilege

♦ birthright, right — more at RIGHT

pres *abbr* **1** present **2** president

¹pres·age \ˈpre-sij\ *n* [ME, fr. L *praesagium,* fr. *praesagus* having a foreboding, fr. *prae* before + *sagus* prophetic] **1** ♦ : something that foreshadows a future event : OMEN **2** ♦ : an intuition or feeling of what is going to happen in the future : FOREBODING

♦ [1] augury, auspice, foreboding, omen, portent — more at OMEN ♦ [2] foreboding, premonition, presentiment — more at PREMONITION

²pre·sage \ˈpre-sij, pri-ˈsāj\ *vb* **pre·saged; pre·sag·ing** **1** : to give an omen or warning of : FORESHADOW **2 ♦** : to tell beforehand : FORETELL, PREDICT

   ♦ augur, forecast, foretell, predict, prognosticate, prophesy — more at FORETELL

pres·by·o·pia \‚prez-bē-'ō-pē-ə\ *n* : a visual condition in which loss of elasticity of the lens of the eye causes defective accommodation and inability to focus sharply for near vision — **pres·by·o·pic** \-'ō-pik, -'ä-\ *adj or n*

pres·by·ter \'prez-bə-tər\ *n* [LL, elder, priest, fr. Gk *presbyteros*, compar. of *presbys* elder, old man] **1** : PRIEST, MINISTER **2** : an elder in a Presbyterian church

¹Pres·by·te·ri·an \‚prez-bə-'tir-ē-ən\ *n* : a member of a Presbyterian church

²Presbyterian *adj* **1** *often not cap* : characterized by a graded system of representative ecclesiastical bodies (as presbyteries) exercising legislative and judicial powers **2** : of or relating to a group of Protestant Christian bodies that are presbyterian in government — **Pres·by·te·ri·an·ism** \-ə-‚ni-zəm\ *n*

pres·by·tery \'prez-bə-‚ter-ē\ *n, pl* **-ter·ies 1** : the part of a church reserved for the officiating clergy **2** : a ruling body in Presbyterian churches consisting of the ministers and representative elders of a district

¹pre·school \'prē-‚skül\ *adj* : of or relating to the period in a child's life from infancy to the age of five or six — **pre·school·er** \-‚skü-lər\ *n*

²preschool *n* : NURSERY SCHOOL

pre·science \'pre-shəns, 'prē-\ *n* **1** : foreknowledge of events **2 ♦** : the act or fact of being concerned for and making preparations for the future

   ♦ foresight, forethought, providence — more at FORESIGHT

pre·scient \-shənt, -shē-ənt\ *adj* **♦** : having or marked by prescience : characterized by foresight

   ♦ farsighted, foresighted, provident — more at FORESIGHTED

pre·scribe \pri-'skrīb\ *vb* **pre·scribed; pre·scrib·ing 1 ♦** : to lay down as a guide or rule of action **2** : to direct the use of (as a medicine) as a remedy

   ♦ define, lay down, specify; *also* decree, dictate, ordain; assign, direct, fix, set, settle; arrange, order; choose, select; adjure, bid, charge, command, enjoin, instruct, tell; conduct, control, lead, manage; coerce, constrain, force; oblige, require

pre·scrip·tion \pri-'skrip-shən\ *n* **1** : the action of prescribing rules or directions **2** : a written direction for the preparation and use of a medicine; *also* : a medicine prescribed

pre·scrip·tive \pri-'skrip-tiv\ *adj* **1** : serving to prescribe ⟨∼ rules⟩ **2** : acquired by, based on, or determined by prescription or by custom

pres·ence \'prez-ᵊns\ *n* **1** : the fact or condition of being present **2** : the space immediately around a person **3** : one that is present **4 ♦** : the bearing, carriage, or air of a person; *esp* : stately bearing

   ♦ appearance, aspect, look, mien — more at APPEARANCE

¹pres·ent \'prez-ᵊnt\ *n* **♦** : something presented : GIFT

   ♦ bestowal, donation, freebie, gift, lagniappe, largesse — more at GIFT

²pre·sent \pri-'zent\ *vb* **1** : to bring into the presence or acquaintance of : INTRODUCE **2 ♦** : to bring before the public ⟨∼ a play⟩ **3** : to make a gift to **4 ♦** : to give formally **5** : to lay (as a charge) before a court for inquiry **6** : to aim or direct (as a weapon) so as to face in a particular direction — **pre·sent·able** *adj* — **pre·sent·ment** \pri-'zent-mənt\ *n*

   ♦ [2] carry, give, mount, offer, stage; *also* display, exhibit, show; preview; act, impersonate, perform, play, portray; depict, dramatize, enact, render, represent; extend, proffer, tender **♦** [4] bestow, contribute, donate, give — more at GIVE

³pres·ent \'prez-ᵊnt\ *adj* **1 ♦** : now existing or in progress ⟨∼ conditions⟩ **2** : being in view or at hand ⟨∼ at the meeting⟩ **3** : under consideration ⟨the ∼ problem⟩ **4** : of, relating to, or constituting a verb tense that expresses present time or the time of speaking

   ♦ current, extant, ongoing; *also* contemporary, mod, modern, new, newfangled, new-fashioned, now, recent, red-hot, space-age, ultramodern, up-to-date; being, breathing, existing, living **Ant** ago, past; future

⁴pres·ent \'prez-ᵊnt\ *n* **1** *pl* : the present legal document **2** : the present tense; *also* : a verb form in it **3 ♦** : the present time

   ♦ moment, now, today; *also* phase, stage, state; tonight, tomorrow **Ant** past; future

pre·sen·ta·tion \‚prē-‚zen-'tā-shən, ‚prez-ᵊn-\ *n* **1** : the act of presenting **2** : something presented

pres·ent–day \'prez-ᵊnt-'dā\ *adj* : now existing or occurring : CURRENT

pre·sen·ti·ment \pri-'zen-tə-mənt\ *n* **♦** : a feeling that something is about to happen : PREMONITION ⟨a ∼ of danger⟩

   ♦ foreboding, premonition, presage — more at PREMONITION

pres·ent·ly \'prez-ᵊnt-lē\ *adv* **1 ♦** : in the near future : SOON **2 ♦** : at the present time : NOW

   ♦ [1] anon, momentarily, shortly, soon — more at SHORTLY **♦** [2] anymore, now, nowadays, right now, today — more at NOW

present participle *n* : a participle that typically expresses present action and that in English is formed with the suffix *-ing* and is used in the formation of the progressive tenses

pres·er·va·tion \‚pre-zər-'vā-shən\ *n* **♦** : the act of preserving or the state of being preserved

   ♦ conservation, maintenance, upkeep — more at MAINTENANCE

¹pre·serve \pri-'zərv\ *vb* **pre·served; pre·serv·ing 1** : to keep safe : GUARD, PROTECT **2** : to keep from decaying; *esp* : to process food (as by canning or pickling) to prevent spoilage **3** : MAINTAIN ⟨∼ silence⟩ **4 ♦** : to keep alive, intact, in existence, or from decay — **pre·ser·va·tive** \pri-'zər-və-tiv\ *adj or n* — **pre·serv·er** *n*

   ♦ conserve, keep up, maintain, save — more at MAINTAIN

²preserve *n* **1** : preserved fruit — often used in pl. **2** : an area for the protection of natural resources (as animals)

pre·set \(‚)prē-'set\ *vb* **-set; -set·ting** : to set beforehand

pre·shrink \prē-'shriŋk\ *vb* **-shrank** \-'shraŋk\; **-shrunk** \-'shrəŋk\; **-shrink·ing** : to shrink (as a fabric) before making into a garment

pre·side \pri-'zīd\ *vb* **pre·sid·ed; pre·sid·ing** [L *praesidēre* to guard, preside over, fr. *prae* in front of + *sedēre* to sit] **1 ♦** : to exercise guidance or control **2** : to occupy the place of authority; *esp* : to act as chairman

   ♦ *usu* preside over boss, captain, command, control, govern, rule — more at GOVERN

pres·i·dent \'pre-zə-dənt\ *n* **1 ♦** : one chosen to preside ⟨∼ of the assembly⟩ **2** : the chief officer of an organization (as a corporation or society) **3** : an elected official serving as both chief of state and chief political executive; *also* : a chief of state often with only minimal political powers — **pres·i·den·cy** \-dən-sē\ *n* — **pres·i·den·tial** \‚pre-zə-'den-chəl\ *adj*

   ♦ chair, chairman, moderator, speaker

pre·si·dio \pri-'sē-dē-‚ō, -'si-\ *n, pl* **-di·os** [Sp] : a military post or fortified settlement in an area currently or orig. under Spanish control

pre·sid·i·um \pri-'si-dē-əm\ *n, pl* **-ia** \-dē-ə\ *or* **-iums** [Russ *prezidium*, fr. L *praesidium* garrison] : a permanent executive committee that acts for a larger body in a Communist country

¹pre·soak \(‚)prē-'sōk\ *vb* : to soak beforehand

²pre·soak \'prē-ˌsōk\ *n* **1** : an instance of presoaking **2** : a preparation used in presoaking clothes

pre·sort \(ˌ)prē-'sȯrt\ *vb* : to sort (mail) by zip code usu. before delivery to a post office

¹press \'pres\ *n* **1** ♦ : a crowd or crowded condition : THRONG **2** : a machine for exerting pressure **3** : CLOSET, CUPBOARD **4** : PRESSURE **5** : the properly creased condition of a freshly pressed garment **6** : PRINTING PRESS; *also* : the act or the process of printing **7** : a printing or publishing establishment **8** : the media (as newspapers and magazines) of public news and comment; *also* : persons (as reporters) employed in these media **9** : comment in newspapers and periodicals

♦ army, crowd, crush, drove, flock, horde, host, legion, mob, multitude, swarm, throng — more at CROWD

²press *vb* **1** ♦ : to bear down upon : push steadily against **2** : ASSAIL, COMPEL **3** ♦ : to squeeze out the juice or contents of ⟨~ grapes⟩ **4** : to squeeze to a desired density, shape, or smoothness; *esp* : IRON **5 a** : to try hard to persuade : URGE **b** ♦ : to move to action or reaction through pressure **6** : to follow through : PROSECUTE **7** ♦ : to crowd closely **8** ♦ : to force one's way **9** : to require haste or speed in action **10** ♦ : to insist on or request urgently — **press·er** *n*

♦ [1] bear, depress, shove, weigh; *also* compress, squash, squeeze; lean (on *or* against); drive, propel, thrust ♦ [3] crush, express, mash, squeeze; *also* pulp, puree; extract, extrude ♦ [5b] coerce, compel, constrain, drive, force, make, muscle, obligate, oblige, pressure, urge — more at FORCE ♦ [7] bunch, cluster, crowd, huddle; *also* assemble, collect, congregate, flock, gather, herd, swarm, throng ♦ [8] bulldoze, elbow, muscle, push; *also* jostle; ram, shove, thrust ♦ *often* **press for** [10] call, claim, clamor (*or* clamour), command, demand, enjoin, exact, insist, quest, stipulate (for) — more at DEMAND

press agent *n* : an agent employed to establish and maintain good public relations through publicity

press·ing *adj* ♦ : urgently important

♦ acute, critical, dire, imperative, imperious, instant, urgent — more at ACUTE

press·man \'pres-mən, -ˌman\ *n* : the operator of a press and esp. a printing press

press·room \-ˌrüm, -ˌru̇m\ *n* **1** : a room in a printing plant containing the printing presses **2** : a room for the use of reporters

¹pres·sure \'pre-shər\ *n* **1** : the burden of physical or mental distress **2** : the action of pressing; *esp* : the application of force to something by something else in direct contact with it **3** : the force exerted over a surface divided by its area **4** ♦ : the stress or urgency of matters demanding attention

♦ strain, stress, tension — more at STRESS ♦ coercion, compulsion, constraint, duress, force — more at FORCE

²pressure *vb* **pres·sured; pres·sur·ing** **1** : to apply pressure to **2** ♦ : to cause an action or reaction as a result of applied pressure

♦ coerce, compel, constrain, drive, force, make, muscle, obligate, oblige, press — more at FORCE

pressure group *n* : a group that seeks to influence governmental policy but not to elect candidates to office

pressure suit *n* : an inflatable suit for high-altitude flight or spaceflight to protect the body from low pressure

pres·sur·ise *chiefly Brit var of* PRESSURIZE

pres·sur·ize \'pre-shə-ˌrīz\ *vb* **-ized; -iz·ing** **1** : to maintain higher pressure within than without; *esp* : to maintain normal atmospheric pressure within (as an airplane cabin) during high-altitude flight or spaceflight **2** : to apply pressure to **3** : to design to withstand pressure — **pres·sur·i·za·tion** \ˌpre-shə-rə-'zā-shən\ *n*

pres·ti·dig·i·ta·tion \ˌpres-tə-ˌdi-jə-'tā-shən\ *n* ♦ : skill and dexterity in executing tricks or deception : SLEIGHT OF HAND

♦ legerdemain, magic

pres·tige \pres-'tēzh, -'tēj\ *n* [F, fr. MF, conjuror's trick, illusion, fr. LL *praestigium*, fr. L *praestigiae*, pl., conjuror's tricks, fr. *praestringere* to graze, blunt, constrict, fr. *prae-* in front of + *stringere* to bind tight] : standing or estimation in the eyes of people : REPUTATION

pres·ti·gious \pres-'ti-jəs, -'tē-\ *adj* ♦ : having prestige

♦ name, reputable, reputed, respectable — more at RESPECTABLE ♦ distinguished, eminent, illustrious, noble, notable, noteworthy, outstanding, preeminent, signal, star, superior — more at EMINENT

pres·to \'pres-tō\ *adv or adj* [It, quick, quickly] **1** ♦ : suddenly as if by magic : IMMEDIATELY **2** : at a rapid tempo — used as a direction in music

♦ apace, briskly, fast, full tilt, hastily, immediately, posthaste, pronto, quick, quickly, rapidly, soon, speedily, swift, swiftly — more at FAST

pre·stress \(ˌ)prē-'stres\ *vb* : to introduce internal stresses into (as a structural beam) to counteract later load stresses

pre·sum·ably \pri-'zü-mə-blē\ *adv* ♦ : by reasonable assumption

♦ apparently, evidently, ostensibly, seemingly, supposedly — more at APPARENTLY ♦ doubtless, likely, probably — more at PROBABLY

pre·sume \pri-'züm\ *vb* **pre·sumed; pre·sum·ing** **1** : to take upon oneself without leave or warrant : DARE **2** ♦ : to take for granted : ASSUME **3** : to act or behave with undue boldness — **pre·sum·able** \-'zü-mə-bəl\ *adj*

♦ assume, postulate, premise, presuppose, suppose — more at ASSUME

pre·sump·tion \pri-'zəmp-shən\ *n* **1** ♦ : presumptuous attitude or conduct : AUDACITY **2** : an attitude or belief dictated by probability; *also* : the grounds lending probability to a belief — **pre·sump·tive** \-tiv\ *adj*

♦ [1] audacity, brass, brazenness, cheek, chutzpah, effrontery, gall, nerve, sauce, sauciness, temerity — more at EFFRONTERY ♦ [2] assumption, postulate, premise, supposition — more at ASSUMPTION

pre·sump·tu·ous \pri-'zəmp-chə-wəs\ *adj* ♦ : overstepping due bounds (as of propriety or courtesy) : taking liberties — **pre·sump·tu·ous·ly** *adv*

♦ arrogant, cavalier, haughty, high-handed, imperious, important, overweening, pompous, pretentious, supercilious, superior ♦ bold, familiar, forward, free, immodest; *also* conceited, overweening, pompous, self-assertive, self-important, self-satisfied, smug, uppity, vain, vainglorious; cavalier, disdainful, haughty, lordly, pretentious, snobbish, stuck-up, supercilious, superior; audacious, brash, brassy, brazen, fresh, impertinent, impudent, pert, saucy; confident, self-assured, self-confident, sure; boastful, braggart, bragging; domineering, high-handed, imperious; self-centered, selfish *Ant* modest, unassuming ♦ intrusive, meddlesome, nosy, obtrusive, officious, prying — more at INTRUSIVE

pre·sup·pose \ˌprē-sə-'pōz\ *vb* **1** ♦ : to suppose beforehand **2** : to require beforehand as a necessary condition

♦ assume, postulate, premise, presume, suppose — more at ASSUME

pre·sup·po·si·tion \(ˌ)prē-ˌsə-pə-'zi-shən\ *n* : an act of presupposing or an assumption made in advance

pre·teen \'prē-'tēn\ *n* : a boy or girl not yet 13 years old — **preteen** *adj*

pre·tend \pri-'tend\ *vb* **1** : PROFESS ⟨doesn't ~ to be scientific⟩ **2** ♦ : to make believe : FEIGN ⟨~ to be angry⟩ **3** : to lay claim ⟨~ to a throne⟩

♦ affect, assume, counterfeit, fake, feign, profess, put on, sham, simulate — more at FEIGN ♦ dissemble, dissimulate, let on

pre·tend·er \pri-'ten-dər\ *n* ♦ : one that pretends

♦ charlatan, fake, fraud, hoaxer, humbug, mountebank, phony, quack

pre·tense *or* **pre·tence** \'prē-ˌtens, pri-'tens\ *n* **1** : a claim made or implied; *esp* : one not supported by fact **2** ♦ : an assumed display or attitude of superiority or dignity **3** : an inadequate or insincere attempt to attain a certain condition ⟨made a ∼ at discipline⟩ **4** : false show : PRETEXT **5** ♦ : excessive display : PRETENTIOUSNESS

♦ [2] act, airs, facade, front, guise, masquerade, pose, put-on, semblance, show — more at MASQUERADE ♦ [5] affectation, pretension, pretentiousness; *also* arrogance, complacency, conceit, egotism, pride, self-assertion, self-conceit, self-importance, self-satisfaction, smugness, vainglory, vanity; disdain, haughtiness, snobbery, snobbishness, superiority; confidence, presumption, self-assurance, self-confidence, sureness; braggadocio; aggressiveness, assertiveness, audaciousness, boldness, cheekiness, cockiness, forwardness, impudence, insolence, rudeness; grandiloquence; flashiness, gaudiness, ostentation, show, showiness

pre·ten·sion \pri-'ten-chən\ *n* **1** : an allegation of doubtful value : PRETEXT **2** ♦ : an effort to establish a claim **3** : a claim or right to attention or honor because of merit **4** ♦ : an aspiration or intention that may or may not reach fulfillment **5** : the quality or act of making usu. unjustified claims (as to excellence) **6** : an exaggerated sense of self-importance

♦ [2] call, claim, pretense, right — more at CLAIM ♦ [4] aim, ambition, aspiration, design, dream, end, goal, intent, mark, meaning, object, objective, plan, purpose, thing — more at GOAL

pre·ten·tious \pri-'ten-chəs\ *adj* **1** ♦ : making or possessing usu. unjustified claims (as to excellence) ⟨a ∼ literary style⟩ **2** : making demands on one's ability or means : AMBITIOUS ⟨too ∼ an undertaking⟩ — **pre·ten·tious·ly** *adv*

♦ affected, grandiose, highfalutin, ostentatious, pompous; *also* grandiloquent, high sounding, sententious; arrogant, complacent, conceited, egoistic, egotistic, important, overweening, prideful, proud, self-assertive, self-important, self-satisfied, smug, uppity, vain, vainglorious; cavalier, disdainful, haughty, lordly, snobbish, stuck-up, supercilious, superior; confident, self-assured, self-confident, sure; boastful, braggart, bragging; aggressive, assertive, audacious, bold, brassy, cheeky, cocky, forward, impudent, insolent, rude; flashy, flaunting, gaudy, showy *Ant* modest, unpretentious

pre·ten·tious·ness \-nəs\ *n* ♦ : the quality or state of being pretentious

♦ affectation, arrogance, haughtiness, loftiness, pretense, pretension, self-importance, superiority — more at ARROGANCE

pret·er·it *or* **pret·er·ite** \'pre-tə-rət\ *n* : a verb form expressing action in the past

pre·term \(ˌ)prē-'tərm, 'prē-ˌ\ *adj* : of, relating to, being, or brought forth by premature birth ⟨a ∼ infant⟩

pre·ter·nat·u·ral \ˌprē-tər-'na-chə-rəl\ *adj* **1** : exceeding what is natural ⟨his ∼ calm⟩ **2** ♦ : inexplicable by ordinary means — **pre·ter·nat·u·ral·ly** *adv*

♦ metaphysical, superhuman, supernatural, unearthly — more at SUPERNATURAL

pre·text \'prē-ˌtekst\ *n* : a purpose stated or assumed to cloak the real intention or state of affairs

pret·ti·fy \'pri-ti-ˌfī\ *vb* **-fied; -fy·ing** : to make pretty — **pret·ti·fi·ca·tion** \ˌpri-ti-fə-'kā-shən\ *n*

pret·ti·ness \'pri-tē-nəs\ *n* ♦ : the quality or state of being pretty

♦ attractiveness, beauty, comeliness, handsomeness, looks, loveliness — more at BEAUTY

¹**pret·ty** \'pri-tē\ *adj* **pret·ti·er; -est** [ME *praty, pretty*, fr. OE *prættig* tricky, fr. *prætt* trick] **1** ♦ : pleasing by delicacy or grace : having conventionally accepted elements of beauty ⟨∼ flowers⟩ **2** : MISERABLE, TERRIBLE ⟨a ∼ state of affairs⟩ **3** : moderately large ⟨a ∼ profit⟩ **4** : PLEASANT — **pret·ti·ly** \-tə-lē\ *adv*

♦ attractive, beautiful, cute, fair, handsome, lovely — more at BEAUTIFUL

²**pretty** *adv* ♦ : in some degree : MODERATELY

♦ enough, fairly, kind of, moderately, quite, rather, somewhat, sort of, so-so — more at FAIRLY

³**pretty** *vb* **pret·tied; pret·ty·ing** : to make pretty

pretty boy *n, usu disparaging* : a man who is notably good-looking

pret·zel \'pret-səl\ *n* [G *Brezel*, ultim. fr. L *brachiatus* having branches like arms, fr. *brachium* arm] : a brittle or chewy glazed usu. salted slender bread often shaped like a loose knot

prev *abbr* previous; previously

pre·vail \pri-'vāl\ *vb* **1** ♦ : to win mastery : TRIUMPH **2** : to be or become effective : SUCCEED **3** ♦ : to urge successfully ⟨∼ed upon her to sing⟩ **4** : to be frequent : PREDOMINATE **5** ♦ : to be or continue in use or fashion — **pre·vail·ing·ly** *adv*

♦ [1] conquer, triumph, win — more at WIN ♦ *usu* **prevail over** [1] beat, defeat, master, triumph, win ♦ *usu* **prevail on** *or* **prevail upon** [3] argue, convince, get, induce, move, persuade, satisfy, talk, win — more at PERSUADE ♦ [5] hold, hold out, keep up, last, survive — more at HOLD OUT

prev·a·lent \'pre-və-lənt\ *adj* : generally or widely existent : WIDESPREAD — **prev·a·lence** \-ləns\ *n*

pre·var·i·cate \pri-'var-ə-ˌkāt\ *vb* **-cat·ed; -cat·ing** [L *praevoricari* to act in collusion, lit., to straddle, fr. *prae* in front of + *varicare* to straddle, fr. *varus* bowlegged] ♦ : to deviate from the truth

♦ fabricate, fib, lie — more at LIE

pre·var·i·ca·tion \pri-ˌvar-ə-'kā-shən\ *n* **1** : the act or an instance of prevaricating **2** ♦ : a statement that deviates from or perverts the truth

♦ fabrication, fairy tale, falsehood, falsity, fib, lie, mendacity, story, tale, untruth, whopper — more at LIE

pre·var·i·ca·tor \pri-'var-ə-ˌkā-tər\ *n* ♦ : one who evades or perverts the truth

♦ fibber, liar — more at LIAR

pre·vent \pri-'vent\ *vb* **1** ♦ : to keep from happening or existing ⟨steps to ∼ war⟩ **2** : to hold back : HINDER, STOP ⟨∼ us from going⟩ — **pre·vent·able** *also* **pre·vent·ible** \-'ven-tə-bəl\ *adj* — **pre·ven·ta·tive** \-'ven-tə-tiv\ *adj or n* — **pre·ven·tive** \-'ven-tiv\ *adj or n*

♦ avert, forestall, help, obviate, preclude; *also* anticipate, provide; negate, neutralize, nullify; avoid, save; baffle, balk, checkmate, deter, foil, frustrate, thwart; bar, block, hamper, hinder, impede, interfere (with), retard, stall; deflect, fend (off), head (off), stave off, stop, ward (off); avoid, circumvent, dodge, elude, escape, evade; forbid, inhibit, prohibit; arrest, check, halt, stop; counteract, offset

pre·ven·tion \pri-'ven-chən\ *n* : the act of preventing or hindering

pre·ver·bal \ˌprē-'vər-bəl\ *adj* : having not yet acquired the faculty of speech

¹**pre·view** \'prē-ˌvyü\ *vb* : to see or discuss beforehand; *esp* : to view or show in advance of public presentation

²**preview** *n* **1** : an advance showing or viewing **2** *also* **pre·vue** \-ˌvyü\ : a showing of snatches from a motion picture advertised for future appearance **3** : FORETASTE

pre·vi·ous \'prē-vē-əs\ *adj* ♦ : going before

♦ antecedent, anterior, foregoing, preceding, prior; *also* advance, early, premature; earliest, first, inaugural, initial, maiden, original, pioneer; preliminary, introductory; erstwhile, former, whilom *Ant* after, ensuing, following, subsequent, succeeding

pre·vi·ous·ly \-lē\ *adv* ♦ : in time past

♦ ahead, before, beforehand — more at AHEAD

previous to *prep* ♦ : in advance of : BEFORE

♦ ahead of, before, ere, of, prior to, to — more at BEFORE

pre·vi·sion \prē-'vi-zhən\ *n* **1** : FORESIGHT, PRESCIENCE **2** : FORECAST, PREDICTION ⟨a ~ of success⟩
pre·war \'prē-'wȯr\ *adj* : occurring or existing before a war
¹**prey** \'prā\ *n, pl* **prey** *also* **preys** **1** : an animal taken for food by a predator; *also* : VICTIM **2** : the act or habit of preying
²**prey** *vb* **1** : to raid for booty **2** : to seize and devour prey **3** : to have a harmful or wearing effect
prf *abbr* proof
¹**price** \'prīs\ *n* **1** *archaic* : VALUE **2** ♦ : the amount of money paid or asked for the sale of a specified thing; *also* : the cost at which something is obtained
  ♦ charge, cost, fee, figure; *also* list price, market value, rate, tariff; carrying charge, overcharge, surcharge; deduction, discount, markdown, reduction, sale; deposit; down payment; account, check, bill, invoice, tab
²**price** *vb* **priced; pric·ing** **1** : to set a price on **2** : to ask the price of **3** : to drive by raising prices ⟨*priced* themselves out of the market⟩
price–fix·ing \'prīs-ˌfik-siŋ\ *n* : the setting of prices artificially (as by producers or government)
price·less \-ləs\ *adj* : having a value beyond any price : INVALUABLE
price support *n* : artificial maintenance of prices of a commodity at a level usu. fixed through government action
price war *n* : a period of commercial competition in which prices are repeatedly cut by the competitors
pric·ey *also* **pricy** \'prī-sē\ *adj* **pric·i·er; -est** : EXPENSIVE
¹**prick** \'prik\ *n* **1** ♦ : a mark or small wound made by a pointed instrument **2** : something sharp or pointed **3 a** : an instance of pricking **b** ♦ : a sensation of being pricked
  ♦ [1] perforation, pinhole, punch, puncture, stab; *also* gouge, groove, hollow; cut, break, gash, notch, rupture, slash, slit ♦ [3b] ache, pain, pang, smart, sting, stitch, tingle, twinge — more at PAIN
²**prick** *vb* **1** : to pierce slightly with a sharp point; *also* : to have or cause a pricking sensation **2** : to affect with anguish or remorse ⟨~s his conscience⟩ **3** : to outline with punctures ⟨~ out a pattern⟩ **4** : to stand or cause to stand erect ⟨the dog's ears ~ed up at the sound⟩
prick·er \'pri-kər\ *n* : BRIAR; *also* : THORN
¹**prick·le** \'pri-kəl\ *n* **1** : a small sharp process (as on a plant) **2** : a slight stinging pain
²**prickle** *vb* **prick·led; prick·ling** **1** : to prick lightly **2** : TINGLE
prick·ly \'pri-klē\ *adj* ♦ : full of or covered with prickles
  ♦ brambly, scratchy, thorny — more at SCRATCHY
prickly heat *n* : a red cutaneous eruption with intense itching and tingling caused by inflammation around the ducts of the sweat glands
prickly pear *n* : any of numerous cacti with usu. yellow flowers and prickly flat or rounded joints; *also* : the sweet pulpy pear-shaped edible fruit of various prickly pears
¹**pride** \'prīd\ *n* **1** ♦ : inordinate self-esteem : CONCEIT **2** ♦ : justifiable self-respect **3** : elation over an act or possession **4** : haughty behavior : DISDAIN **5** : ostentatious display **6** ♦ : a source of pride
  ♦ [1] complacence, conceit, ego, egotism, self-conceit, self-esteem, self-importance, self-satisfaction, smugness, vainglory, vanity — more at COMPLACENCE ♦ [2] ego, self-esteem, self-regard, self-respect; *also* confidence, self-assurance, self-confidence; dignity, face, honor, prestige ♦ [6] boast, credit, glory, honor (*or* honour), jewel, treasure — more at GLORY
²**pride** *vb* **prid·ed; prid·ing** : to indulge (as oneself) in pride
pride·ful \'prīd-fəl\ *adj* ♦ : full of pride
  ♦ disdainful, haughty, highfalutin, lofty, lordly, proud, superior — more at PROUD
priest \'prēst\ *n* [ME *preist*, fr. OE *prēost*, ultim. fr. LL *presbyter* elder, priest, fr. Gk *presbyteros*, fr. compar. of *presbys* old man, elder] : a person having authority to perform the sacred rites of a religion; *esp* ♦ : a member of

the Anglican, Eastern, or Roman Catholic clergy ranking below a bishop and above a deacon — **priest·hood** *n* — **priest·li·ness** *n*
  ♦ clergyman, divine, ecclesiastic, father, minister, preacher, reverend — more at CLERGYMAN
priest·ess \'prēs-təs\ *n* : a woman authorized to perform the sacred rites of a religion
priest·ly \'prēst-lē\ *adj* ♦ : of, relating to, or characteristic of a priest or the priesthood
  ♦ clerical, ministerial, pastoral, sacerdotal — more at CLERICAL
prig \'prig\ *n* : one who irritates by rigid or pointed observance of proprieties — **prig·gish** \'pri-gish\ *adj* — **prig·gish·ly** *adv*
¹**prim** \'prim\ *adj* **prim·mer; prim·mest** ♦ : stiffly formal and precise — **prim·ly** *adv* — **prim·ness** *n*
  ♦ prudish, puritanical, straitlaced — more at STRAIT-LACED
²**prim** *abbr* **1** primary **2** primitive
pri·ma·cy \'prī-mə-sē\ *n* **1** ♦ : the state of being first (as in rank) **2** : the office, rank, or character of an ecclesiastical primate
  ♦ distinction, dominance, eminence, preeminence, superiority, supremacy, transcendence — more at EMINENCE
pri·ma don·na \ˌpri-mə-'dä-nə\ *n, pl* **prima donnas** [It, lit., first lady] **1** : a principal female singer (as in an opera company) **2** : a vain undisciplined usu. uncooperative person
pri·ma fa·cie \'prī-mə-'fā-shə, -sē, -shē\ *adj or adv* [L, at first view] **1** : based on immediate impression : APPARENT **2** : SELF-EVIDENT
pri·mal \'prī-məl\ *adj* **1** ♦ : of or relating to the first period or state : PRIMITIVE **2** : first in importance
  ♦ ancient, early, primeval, primitive — more at EARLY
pri·mar·i·ly \prī-'mer-ə-lē\ *adv* **1** ♦ : for the most part **2** ♦ : in the first place : ORIGINALLY
  ♦ [1] altogether, basically, chiefly, generally, largely, mainly, mostly, overall, predominantly, principally — more at CHIEFLY ♦ [2] firstly, initially, originally — more at ORIGINALLY
¹**pri·ma·ry** \'prī-ˌmer-ē, -mə-rē\ *adj* **1** : first in order of time or development; *also* : PREPARATORY **2** ♦ : of first rank or importance; *also* : FUNDAMENTAL **3** ♦ : not derived from or dependent on something else ⟨~ sources⟩
  ♦ [2] arch, cardinal, central, chief, dominant, first, foremost, fundamental, grand, key, main, paramount, predominant, preeminent, premier, principal, sovereign, supreme — more at FOREMOST ♦ [3] direct, firsthand, immediate — more at DIRECT
²**primary** *n, pl* **-ries** : a preliminary election in which voters nominate or express a preference among candidates usu. of their own party
primary care *n* : health care provided by a medical professional with whom a patient has initial contact
primary color *n* : any of a set of colors from which all other colors may be derived
primary school *n* **1** : a school usu. including grades 1–3 and sometimes kindergarten **2** : ELEMENTARY SCHOOL
pri·mate \'prī-ˌmāt *or esp for 1* -mət\ *n* **1** *often cap* : the highest-ranking bishop of a province or nation **2** : any of an order of mammals including humans, apes, and monkeys
¹**prime** \'prīm\ *n* **1** : the earliest stage of something; *esp* : SPRINGTIME **2** ♦ : the most active, thriving, or successful stage or period (as of one's life) **3** ♦ : the best individual or part **4** : any integer other than 0, +1, or −1 that is not divisible without remainder by any integer except +1, −1, and plus or minus itself; *esp* : any such integer that is positive

♦ [2] bloom, blossom, flower, flush, heyday — more at BLOOM ♦ [3] best, choice, cream, elect, elite, fat, flower, pick — more at ELITE

²**prime** *adj* **1** ♦ : standing first (as in time, rank, significance, or quality) ⟨∼ requisite⟩ **2** : of, relating to, or being a number that is prime

♦ chief, first, foremost, head, high, lead, preeminent, premier, primary, principal, supreme — more at HEAD

³**prime** *vb* **primed; prim·ing 1** : FILL, LOAD **2** : to lay a preparatory coating upon (as in painting) **3** : to put in working condition **4** : to instruct beforehand : COACH
prime meridian *n* : the meridian of 0° longitude which runs through Greenwich, England, and from which other longitudes are reckoned east and west
prime minister *n* **1** : the chief minister of a ruler or state **2** : the chief executive of a parliamentary government
¹**prim·er** \'pri-mər\ *n* [ME, layperson's prayer book, fr. AF, fr. ML *primarium*, fr. LL, neut. of *primarius* primary] **1** : a small book for teaching children to read **2** ♦ : a small introductory book on a subject ⟨a ∼ on modern art⟩ **3** : a short informative piece of writing

♦ handbook, manual, textbook — more at TEXTBOOK

²**prim·er** \'prī-mər\ *n* **1** : one that primes **2** : a device for igniting an explosive **3** : material for priming a surface
prime rate *n* : an interest rate announced by a bank to be the lowest available to its most credit-worthy customers
prime time *n* **1** : the time period when the television or radio audience is largest; *also* : television shows aired in prime time **2** : the choicest or busiest time
pri·me·val \prī-'mē-vəl\ *adj* ♦ : of or relating to the earliest ages : PRIMITIVE

♦ ancient, early, primal, primitive — more at EARLY

¹**prim·i·tive** \'pri-mə-tiv\ *adj* **1** : ORIGINAL, PRIMARY **2** ♦ : of, relating to, or characteristic of an early stage of development **3** : ELEMENTAL, NATURAL **4** *now sometimes offensive* : of, relating to, or produced by a people or culture that is nonindustrial and often nonliterate and tribal **5** : SELF-TAUGHT; *also* : produced by a self-taught artist — **prim·i·tive·ly** *adv* — **prim·i·tive·ness** *n* — **prim·i·tiv·i·ty** \ˌpri-mə-'ti-və-tē\ *n*

♦ crude, low, rude, rudimentary; *also* basic, simple; homely, homespun, unsophisticated; early, primeval, primordial; backward, underdeveloped, undeveloped; aged, ancient, antediluvian, antiquated, antique, dated, fusty, hoary, musty, obsolete, old, old-fashioned, old-time, out-of-date, outworn, passé, past *Ant* advanced, developed, evolved ancient, early, primal, primeval — more at EARLY

²**primitive** *n* **1** : something primitive **2** : a primitive artist **3** : a member of a primitive people
prim·i·tiv·ism \'pri-mə-ti-ˌvi-zəm\ *n* **1** : belief in the superiority of a simple way of life close to nature **2** : the style of art of primitive peoples or primitive artists
pri·mo·gen·i·tor \ˌprī-mō-'je-nə-tər\ *n* : ANCESTOR, FOREFATHER
pri·mo·gen·i·ture \-'je-nə-ˌchùr\ *n* **1** : the state of being the firstborn of a family **2** : an exclusive right of inheritance belonging to the eldest son
pri·mor·di·al \prī-'mór-dē-əl\ *adj* : first created or developed : existing in its original state : PRIMEVAL
primp \'primp\ *vb* : to dress in a careful or finicky manner
prim·rose \'prim-ˌrōz\ *n* : any of a genus of perennial herbs with large leaves arranged at the base of the stem and clusters of showy flowers
prin *abbr* **1** principal **2** principle
prince \'prins\ *n* [ME, fr. AF, fr. L *princeps* leader, initiator, fr. *primus* first + *capere* to take] **1** : MONARCH, KING **2** : a male member of a royal family; *esp* : a son of the monarch **3** ♦ : a person of high standing (as in a class) ⟨a ∼ of poets⟩ — **prince·dom** \-dəm\ *n*

♦ baron, czar, king, magnate, mogul, tycoon — more at MAGNATE

prince·ling \-liŋ\ *n* : a petty prince
prince·ly \'prin(t)s-lē\ *adj* ♦ : of, relating to, or befitting a prince

♦ kingly, monarchical, queenly, regal, royal — more at MONARCHICAL

prin·cess \'prin-səs, -ˌses\ *n* **1** : a female member of a royal family **2** : the consort of a prince
¹**prin·ci·pal** \'prin-sə-pəl\ *adj* ♦ : most important

♦ arch, cardinal, central, chief, dominant, first, foremost, grand, key, main, paramount, predominant, preeminent, premier, primary, sovereign, supreme — more at FOREMOST

²**principal** *n* **1** : a leading person (as in a play) **2** : the chief officer of an educational institution **3** : the person from whom an agent's authority derives **4** : a capital sum earning interest or used as a fund
prin·ci·pal·i·ty \ˌprin-sə-'pa-lə-tē\ *n, pl* **-ties** : the position, territory, or jurisdiction of a prince
prin·ci·pal·ly \'prin-sə-p(ə-)lē\ *adv* ♦ : in the chief place or degree : CHIEFLY

♦ altogether, basically, chiefly, generally, largely, mainly, mostly, overall, predominantly, primarily — more at CHIEFLY

principal parts *n pl* : the inflected forms of a verb
prin·ci·ple \'prin-sə-pəl\ *n* **1** ♦ : a general or fundamental law, doctrine, or assumption **2** ♦ : a rule or code of conduct; *also* : devotion to such a code **3** : the laws or facts of nature underlying the working of an artificial device **4** : a primary source : ORIGIN; *also* : an underlying faculty or endowment **5** : the active part (as of a drug)

♦ principles ♦ [1] elements, essentials, rudiments — more at ELEMENT principles ♦ [2] ethics, morality, morals, standards — more at ETHICS

prin·ci·pled \-pəld\ *adj* ♦ : exhibiting, based on, or characterized by principle ⟨high-*principled*⟩

♦ decent, ethical, honest, honorable, just, moral, noble, respectable, righteous, upright, upstanding — more at HONORABLE

prink \'priŋk\ *vb* : PRIMP
¹**print** \'print\ *n* [ME *prente*, fr. AF, fr. *preint, prient*, pp. of *priendre* to press, fr. L. *premere*] **1** ♦ : a mark made by pressure **2** : something stamped with an impression **3** : printed state or form **4** : printed matter **5** ♦ : a copy made by printing **6** : cloth with a pattern applied by printing

♦ [1] impress, impression, imprint, stamp; *also* dent, hollow, indentation; mark, sign ♦ [5] photograph, shot, snap, snapshot — more at PHOTOGRAPH

²**print** *vb* **1** : to stamp (as a mark) in or on something **2** : to produce impressions of (as from type) **3** : to write in letters like those of printer's type **4** : to make (a positive picture) from a photographic negative **5** ♦ : to publish in print

♦ get out, issue, publish — more at PUBLISH

print·able \'prin-tə-bəl\ *adj* **1** : capable of being printed or of being printed from **2** : worthy or fit to be published
print·er \'prin-tər\ *n* : one that prints; *esp* : a device that produces printout
print·ing *n* **1** : reproduction in printed form **2** : the art, practice, or business of a printer **3** : IMPRESSION 5
printing press *n* : a machine that produces printed copies
print·out \'print-ˌaùt\ *n* : a printed output produced by a computer — **print out** *vb*
¹**pri·or** \'prī-ər\ *n* : the superior ranking next to the abbot or abbess of a religious house
²**prior** *adj* **1** ♦ : earlier in time or order **2** : taking precedence logically or in importance — **pri·or·i·ty** \prī-'ór-ə-tē\ *n*

♦ antecedent, anterior, foregoing, preceding, previous — more at PREVIOUS

pri·or·ess \'prī-ə-rəs\ *n* : a nun corresponding in rank to a prior

pri·or·i·tize \prī-'ȯr-ə-,tīz, 'prī-ə-rə-,tīz\ *vb* **-tized; -tiz·ing** : to list or rate in order of priority

prior to *prep* ♦ : in advance of : BEFORE

  ♦ ahead of, before, ere, of, previous to, to — more at BEFORE

pri·o·ry \'prī-ə-rē\ *n, pl* **-ries** ♦ : a religious house under a prior or prioress

  ♦ abbey, cloister, friary, monastery — more at MONASTERY

prise *chiefly Brit var of* ⁵PRIZE

prism \'pri-zəm\ *n* [LL *prisma,* fr. Gk. lit., something sawed, fr. *priein* to saw] **1** : a solid whose sides are parallelograms and whose ends are parallel and alike in shape and size **2** : a usu. 3-sided transparent object that refracts light so that it breaks up into rainbow colors — **pris·mat·ic** \priz-'ma-tik\ *adj*

pris·on \'priz-³n\ *n* ♦ : a place or state of confinement esp. for criminals

  ♦ brig, jail, lockup, pen, penitentiary — more at JAIL

pris·on·er \'priz-³n-ər\ *n* ♦ : a person deprived of liberty; *esp* : one on trial or in prison

  ♦ captive, capture, internee — more at CAPTIVE

prisoner of war : a person and esp. a member of the armed forces of a nation captured in war

pris·sy \'pri-sē\ *adj* **pris·si·er; -est** : being overly prim and precise : PRIGGISH — **pris·si·ness** \-sē-nəs\ *n*

pris·tine \'pris-,tēn, pri-'stēn\ *adj* **1** : PRIMITIVE **2** ♦ : having the purity of its original state

  ♦ brand-new, fresh, virgin — more at FRESH

prith·ee \'pri-thē\ *interj, archaic* — used to express a wish or request

pri·va·cy \'prī-və-sē\ *n, pl* **-cies** **1** : the quality or state of being apart from others **2** : SECRECY

¹**pri·vate** \'prī-vət\ *adj* **1** : belonging to or intended for a particular individual or group ⟨~ property⟩ **2** ♦ : restricted to the individual : PERSONAL ⟨~ opinion⟩ **3** : carried on by the individual independently ⟨~ study⟩ **4** : not holding public office ⟨a ~ citizen⟩ **5** : withdrawn from company or observation ⟨a ~ place⟩ **6** ♦ : not known publicly — **pri·vate·ly** *adv*

  ♦ [2] individual, particular, peculiar, personal, separate, singular, unique — more at INDIVIDUAL
  ♦ [6] confidential, hushed, inside, intimate, secret; *also* classified, top secret; unadvertised, unannounced, undisclosed, unmentioned; clandestine, collusive, conspiratorial, covert; surreptitious, undercover, underhand, underhanded; personal; concealed, hidden, closeted; repressed, silenced, stifled, suppressed *Ant* common, open, public

²**private** *n* : an enlisted person of the lowest rank in the marine corps or of one of the two lowest ranks in the army — **in private** : not openly or in public

pri·va·teer \,prī-və-'tir\ *n* : an armed private ship licensed to attack enemy shipping; *also* : a sailor on such a ship

private first class *n* : an enlisted person ranking next below a corporal in the army and next below a lance corporal in the marine corps

pri·va·tion \prī-'vā-shən\ *n* **1** : the act of depriving **2** : the state of being deprived; *esp* : lack of what is needed for existence

priv·et \'pri-vət\ *n* : a nearly evergreen shrub related to the olive and widely used for hedges

¹**priv·i·lege** \'priv-lij, 'pri-və-\ *n* [ME, fr. AF, fr. L *privilegium* law for or against a private person, fr. *privus* private + *leg-, lex* law] ♦ : a right or immunity granted as an advantage or favor esp. to some and not others

  ♦ boon, concession, honor (*or* honour); *also* courtesy; claim, entitlement, right; birthright; perquisite; exemption, immunity, waiver

²**privilege** *vb* **-leged; -leg·ing** ♦ : to grant a privilege to

  ♦ authorize, entitle, qualify — more at ENTITLE

priv·i·leged *adj* **1** : having or enjoying one or more privi-

leges ⟨~ classes⟩ **2** : not subject to disclosure in a court of law ⟨a ~ communication⟩

¹**privy** \'pri-vē\ *adj* **1** : of, relating to, or affecting a particular person exclusively : PERSONAL, PRIVATE **2** : kept from knowledge or view : SECRET **3** : admitted as one sharing in a secret ⟨~ to the conspiracy⟩ — **priv·i·ly** \'pri-və-lē\ *adv*

²**privy** *n, pl* **priv·ies** : TOILET; *esp* : OUTHOUSE

¹**prize** \'prīz\ *n* **1** ♦ : something offered or striven for in competition or in contests of chance **2** ♦ : something exceptionally desirable

  ♦ [1] award, decoration, distinction, honor (*or* honour), plume — more at AWARD ♦ [2] catch, gem, jewel, pearl, plum, treasure; *also* find, godsend, goody, valuable, windfall; booty, loot, spoil

²**prize** *adj* **1** : awarded or worthy of a prize ⟨a ~ essay⟩; *also* : awarded as a prize ⟨a ~ medal⟩ **2** : OUTSTANDING

³**prize** *vb* **prized; priz·ing** ♦ : to value highly : ESTEEM

  ♦ appreciate, cherish, love, treasure, value — more at LOVE

⁴**prize** *n* : property (as a ship) lawfully captured in time of war

⁵**prize** *or Can and Brit* **prise** *vb* **prized** *or* **prised; priz·ing** *or* **pris·ing** ♦ : to press, force, or move with or as if with a lever : PRY

  ♦ jimmy, pry — more at PRY

prize·fight \'prīz-,fīt\ *n* : a professional boxing match — **prize·fight·ing** *n*

prize·fight·er \-'fī-tər\ *n* ♦ : one who participates in a prizefight

  ♦ boxer, fighter, pugilist — more at BOXER

prize·win·ner \-,wi-nər\ *n* : a winner of a prize — **prize·win·ning** *n*

¹**pro** \'prō\ *n, pl* **pros** : a favorable argument, person, or position

²**pro** *adv* : in favor : FOR

³**pro** *n or adj* : PROFESSIONAL

PRO *abbr* public relations officer

pro·ac·tive \prō-'ak-tiv\ *adj* ♦ : acting in anticipation of future problems or needs — **pro·ac·tive·ly** *adv*

  ♦ farsighted, foresighted, prescient, provident, visionary — more at FORESIGHTED

pro–am \'prō-'am\ *adj* : involving professionals competing alongside or against amateurs ⟨a ~ tournament⟩ — **pro–am** *n*

prob *abbr* **1** probable; probably **2** problem

prob·a·bil·i·ty \,prä-bə-'bi-lə-tē\ *n, pl* **-ties** **1** : the quality or state of being probable **2** : something probable **3** ♦ : a measure of how often a particular event will occur if something (as tossing a coin) is done repeatedly which results in any of a number of possible events

  ♦ chance, odds, percentage; *also* outlook, prospect; possibility, potential, potentiality

prob·a·ble \'prä-bə-bəl\ *adj* **1** ♦ : apparently or presumably true ⟨a ~ hypothesis⟩ **2** : likely to be or become true or real ⟨a ~ result⟩

  ♦ believable, credible, likely, plausible — more at BELIEVABLE

prob·a·bly \'prä-bə-blē\ *adv* ♦ : without much doubt

  ♦ doubtless, likely, presumably; *also* perchance, perhaps, possibly; conceivably, imaginably, plausibly, practically, reasonably; potentially; certainly, clearly, conclusively, decisively, definitely, indubitably, positively, surely *Ant* improbably

¹**pro·bate** \'prō-,bāt\ *n* : the judicial determination of the validity of a will

²**pro·bate** *vb* **pro·bat·ed; pro·bat·ing** : to establish (a will) by probate as genuine and valid

pro·ba·tion \prō-'bā-shən\ *n* **1** : subjection of an individual to a period of testing and trial to ascertain fitness (as for a job) **2** : the action of giving a convicted offender freedom during good behavior under the supervision of a probation officer — **pro·ba·tion·ary** \-shə-,ner-ē\ *adj*

pro·ba·tion·er \-shə-nər\ *n* **1** : a person (as a newly admitted student nurse) whose fitness is being tested during a trial period **2** : a convicted offender on probation

pro·ba·tive \'prō-bə-tiv\ *adj* **1** : serving to test or try **2** : serving to prove

¹probe \'prōb\ *n* **1** : a slender instrument for examining a cavity (as a wound) **2** : an information-gathering device sent into outer space **3** ♦ : a penetrating investigation

♦ examination, exploration, inquiry, investigation, research, study — more at INQUIRY

²probe *vb* **probed; prob·ing 1** : to examine with a probe **2** ♦ : to search into and investigate thoroughly

♦ delve, dig, explore, go, inquire into, investigate, look, research — more at EXPLORE

pro·bi·ty \'prō-bə-tē\ *n* ♦ : adherence to the highest principles and ideals : HONESTY

♦ character, decency, goodness, honesty, integrity, morality, rectitude, righteousness, uprightness, virtue — more at MORALITY

prob·lem \'prä-bləm\ *n* **1** : a question raised for consideration or solution **2** ♦ : an intricate unsettled question **3** ♦ : a source of perplexity or vexation — **problem** *adj*

♦ [2] case, knot, matter, trouble; *also* issue, question; challenge; corner, fix, hole, hot water, jam, pickle, predicament, situation; glitch, hitch, snag; conundrum, enigma, mystery, puzzle, puzzlement, riddle; brainteaser, poser *Ant* answer, solution ♦ [3] aggravation, annoyance, bother, exasperation, frustration, hassle, headache, inconvenience, irritant, nuisance, peeve, pest, thorn — more at ANNOYANCE

prob·lem·at·ic \,prä-blə-'ma-tik\ *also* **prob·lem·at·i·cal** \-ti-kəl\ *adj* **1** ♦ : difficult to solve or decide **2** ♦ : open to question or debate : QUESTIONABLE

♦ [1] catchy, delicate, difficult, knotty, spiny, thorny, ticklish, touchy, tough, tricky — more at TRICKY ♦ [2] debatable, disputable, doubtful, dubious, equivocal, fishy, questionable, shady, shaky, suspect, suspicious — more at DOUBTFUL

pro·bos·cis \prə-'bä-səs, -'bäs-kəs\ *n, pl* **-bos·cis·es** *also* **-bos·ci·des** \-'bä-sə-,dēz\ [L, fr. Gk *proboskis*, fr. *pro-* before + *boskein* to feed] : a long flexible snout (as the trunk of an elephant)

proc *abbr* proceedings

pro·caine \'prō-,kān\ *n* : a drug used esp. as a local anesthetic

pro·ce·dure \prə-'sē-jər\ *n* **1** ♦ : a particular way of doing something ⟨democratic ∼⟩ **2** ♦ : a series of steps followed in a regular order ⟨a surgical ∼⟩ — **pro·ce·dur·al** \-'sē-jə-rəl\ *adj*

♦ [1] course, line, policy, program — more at COURSE ♦ [2] course, operation, proceeding, process — more at PROCESS

pro·ceed \prō-'sēd\ *vb* **1** : to come forth : ISSUE **2** : to go on in an orderly way; *also* : CONTINUE **3** : to begin and carry on an action **4** : to take legal action **5** ♦ : to move along a course

♦ advance, fare, forge, get along, go, march, progress — more at GO ♦ *usu* **proceed along** cover, crisscross, cross, cut, follow, go, pass, travel, traverse — more at TRAVERSE

pro·ceed·ing *n* **1** : a series of steps followed in a regular definite order : PROCEDURE **2** *pl* : DOINGS **3** *pl* ♦ : legal action **4** : TRANSACTION **5** *pl* : an official record of things said or done

♦ action, lawsuit, suit — more at LAWSUIT

pro·ceeds \'prō-,sēdz\ *n pl* ♦ : the total amount or the profit arising from a business deal

♦ earnings, income, profit, return, revenue, yield — more at INCOME

¹pro·cess \'prä-,ses, 'prō-\ *n, pl* **pro·cess·es** \-,se-səz, -sə-saz, -sə-,sēz\ **1** : a forward or onward movement (as to an objective or to a goal) : ADVANCE **2** : something going on

: PROCEEDING **3** : a natural phenomenon marked by gradual changes that lead toward a particular result ⟨the ∼ of growth⟩ **4** ♦ : a series of actions or operations directed toward a particular result ⟨a manufacturing ∼⟩ **5** : legal action **6** : a mandate issued by a court; *esp* : SUMMONS **7** : a projecting part of an organism or organic structure

♦ course, operation, procedure, proceeding; *also* fashion, manner, method, mode, style, system, technique, way; approach, blueprint, design, layout, plan, plot, program, scheme, strategy; accomplishment, achievement, attainment, enterprise, performance, undertaking, work; activity, functioning, movement

²process *vb* : to subject to a special process

pro·ces·sion \prə-'se-shən\ *n* **1** : a group of individuals moving along in an orderly often ceremonial way **2** ♦ : continuous forward movement

♦ advance, advancement, furtherance, headway, march, onrush, passage, process, progress, progression — more at ADVANCE

pro·ces·sion·al \-'se-shə-nəl\ *n* **1** : music for a procession **2** : a ceremonial procession

pro·ces·sor \'prä-,se-sər, 'prō-\ *n* **1** : one that processes **2** : CPU

pro–choice \(,)prō-'chȯis\ *adj* : favoring the legalization of abortion

pro·claim \prō-'klām\ *vb* ♦ : to make known publicly : DECLARE

♦ advertise, announce, blaze, broadcast, declare, enunciate, placard, post, promulgate, publicize, publish, sound — more at ANNOUNCE

proc·la·ma·tion \,prä-klə-'mā-shən\ *n* : an official public announcement

pro·cliv·i·ty \prō-'kli-və-tē\ *n, pl* **-ties** ♦ : an inherent inclination esp. toward something objectionable

♦ bent, devices, disposition, genius, inclination, leaning, partiality, penchant, predilection, propensity, tendency, turn

pro·con·sul \-'kän-səl\ *n* **1** : a governor or military commander of an ancient Roman province **2** : an administrator in a modern colony or occupied area — **pro·con·su·lar** \-sə-lər\ *adj*

pro·cras·ti·nate \prə-'kras-tə-,nāt, prō-\ *vb* **-nat·ed; -nat·ing** [L *procrastinare*, fr. *pro-* forward + *crastinus* of tomorrow, fr. *cras* tomorrow] : to put off usu. habitually doing something that should be done — **pro·cras·ti·na·tion** \-,kras-tə-'nā-shən\ *n* — **pro·cras·ti·na·tor** \-'kras-tə-,nā-tər\ *n*

pro·cre·ate \'prō-krē-,āt\ *vb* **-at·ed; -at·ing** ♦ : to beget or bring forth offspring — **pro·cre·ation** \,prō-krē-'ā-shən\ *n* — **pro·cre·ative** \'prō-krē-,ā-tiv\ *adj* — **pro·cre·ator** \-,ā-tər\ *n*

♦ breed, multiply, propagate, reproduce; *also* bear, beget, engender, generate, get, mother, parent, produce, sire; hatch, spawn

pro·crus·te·an \prə-'krəs-tē-ən\ *adj, often cap* [fr. *Procrustes*, villain of Greek mythology who made victims fit his bed by stretching them or cutting off their legs] : marked by arbitrary often ruthless disregard of individual differences or special circumstances

proc·tor \'präk-tər\ *n* : one appointed to supervise students (as at an examination) — **proctor** *vb* — **proc·to·ri·al** \präk-'tȯr-ē-əl\ *adj*

pro·cur·able \prə-'kyu̇r-ə-bəl\ *adj* ♦ : capable of being procured

♦ accessible, acquirable, attainable, available, obtainable — more at AVAILABLE

proc·u·ra·tor \'prä-kyə-,rā-tər\ *n* **1** : one that manages another's affairs **2** : a Roman provincial administrator

pro·cure \-'kyu̇r\ *vb* **pro·cured; pro·cur·ing 1** ♦ : to get possession of : obtain by particular care and effort **2** : to obtain (someone) to be employed for sexual intercourse **3** : ACHIEVE — **pro·cure·ment** *n* — **pro·cur·er** *n*

♦ acquire, attain, capture, carry, draw, earn, gain, garner, get, land, make, obtain, realize, secure, win — more at EARN

¹prod \'präd\ *vb* **prod·ded; prod·ding** **1** : to thrust a pointed instrument into : GOAD **2** ♦ : to incite to action — **prod** *n*

♦ egg on, encourage, exhort, goad, press, prompt, urge — more at URGE

²prod *abbr* product; production

¹prod·i·gal \'prä-di-gəl\ *adj* **1** : recklessly extravagant; *also* : LUXURIANT **2** ♦ : recklessly spendthrift : WASTEFUL ⟨the ∼ prince⟩

♦ extravagant, profligate, spendthrift, thriftless, unthrifty, wasteful; *also* improvident, myopic, shortsighted; bountiful, generous, lavish, liberal, openhanded, philanthropic; careless, heedless, imprudent, incautious, injudicious, unwise; indulgent, reckless, self-indulgent *Ant* conserving, economical, economizing, frugal, scrimping, skimping, thrifty

²prodigal *n* ♦ : one who spends or gives lavishly and foolishly

♦ profligate, spendthrift, wastrel *Ant* economizer

prod·i·gal·i·ty \,prä-də-'ga-lə-tē\ *n* ♦ : reckless spending of resources

♦ extravagance, lavishness, wastefulness — more at EXTRAVAGANCE

pro·di·gious \prə-'di-jəs\ *adj* **1** ♦ : exciting wonder **2** ♦ : extraordinary in size or degree : ENORMOUS — **pro·di·gious·ly** *adv*

♦ [1] amazing, astonishing, astounding, awesome, marvelous (*or* marvellous), stunning, stupendous, surprising, wonderful — more at MARVELOUS ♦ [2] colossal, enormous, giant, gigantic, huge, mammoth, massive, tremendous, vast

prod·i·gy \'prä-də-jē\ *n, pl* **-gies** **1** ♦ : something extraordinary : WONDER **2** : a highly talented child

♦ caution, flash, marvel, miracle, phenomenon, portent, sensation, wonder — more at WONDER

¹pro·duce \prə-'düs, -'dyüs\ *vb* **pro·duced; pro·duc·ing** **1** : to present to view : EXHIBIT **2a** ♦ : to give birth or rise to **b** ♦ : to become the father of **3** : EXTEND, PROLONG **4** ♦ : to give being or form to : MAKE; *esp* : MANUFACTURE **5** : to cause to accrue ⟨∼ a profit⟩ — **pro·duc·er** *n*

♦ [2a, 4] bear, bring about, cause, create, effect, effectuate, generate, induce, make, prompt, result, work, yield — more at EFFECT ♦ [2b] beget, father, get, sire — more at FATHER ♦ [4] fabricate, fashion, form, frame, make, manufacture — more at MAKE

²pro·duce \'prä-(,)düs, 'prō- *also* -(,)dyüs\ *n* **1** : something produced : PRODUCT **2** : agricultural products and esp. fresh fruits and vegetables

prod·uct \'prä-(,)dəkt\ *n* **1** : the number resulting from multiplication **2** ♦ : something produced **3** ♦ : something resulting from or necessarily following from a set of conditions

♦ [2] affair, fruit, handiwork, output, produce, thing, work, yield; *also* article, commodity, object; goods, line, merchandise, wares; by-product, derivative, offshoot, spin-off ♦ [3] aftermath, conclusion, consequence, corollary, development, effect, issue, outcome, outgrowth, result, resultant, sequence, upshot — more at EFFECT

pro·duc·tion \prə-'dək-shən\ *n* **1** ♦ : something produced : PRODUCT **2** : the act or process of producing

pro·duc·tive \prə-'dək-tiv\ *adj* **1** ♦ : having the quality or power of producing esp. in abundance **2** ♦ : effective in bringing about — **pro·duc·tiv·i·ty** \(,)prō-,dək-'ti-və-tē, ,prä-(,)dək-\ *n*

♦ [1] fat, fecund, fertile, fruitful, luxuriant, prolific, rich — more at FERTILE ♦ [2] effective, effectual, efficacious, efficient, fruitful, potent — more at EFFECTIVE

pro·duc·tive·ness \-nəs\ *n* ♦ : the quality or state of being productive

♦ effectiveness, efficacy, efficiency — more at EFFICACY

product placement *n* : the inclusion of a product in a television program or film as a means of advertising

pro·em \'prō-,em\ *n* **1** : preliminary comment : PREFACE **2** : PRELUDE

¹prof \'präf\ *n* : PROFESSOR

²prof *abbr* professional

¹pro·fane \prō-'fān\ *vb* **pro·faned; pro·fan·ing** **1** ♦ : to treat (something sacred) with irreverence or contempt **2** ♦ : to debase by an unworthy use — **prof·a·na·tion** \,prä-fə-'nā-shən\ *n*

♦ [1] defile, desecrate, violate — more at DESECRATE ♦ [2] debase, degrade, demean, demoralize, humble, subvert, warp — more at DEBASE

²profane *adj* [ME *prophane*, fr. MF, fr. L *profanus*, fr. *pro-* before + *fanum* temple] **1** ♦ : not concerned with religion : SECULAR **2** : not holy because unconsecrated, impure, or defiled **3** ♦ : serving to debase what is holy : IRREVERENT ⟨∼ language⟩ **4** : OBSCENE, VULGAR — **pro·fane·ly** *adv* — **pro·fane·ness** *n*

♦ [1] nonreligious, secular, temporal; *also* atheistic, godless, irreligious, pagan; lay, nonclerical; nondenominational, nonsectarian; earthly, mundane, terrestrial, worldly; material, physical, substantial; bodily, carnal, corporal, fleshly; blasphemous, impious, irreverent, sacrilegious; unconsecrated, unhallowed *Ant* religious, sacred ♦ [3] blasphemous, irreverent, sacrilegious

pro·fan·i·ty \prō-'fa-nə-tē\ *n, pl* **-ties** **1** : the quality or state of being profane **2** : the use of profane language **3** : profane language

pro·fess \prə-'fes\ *vb* **1** ♦ : to declare or admit openly : AFFIRM **2** ♦ : to declare in words only : PRETEND **3** : to confess one's faith in **4** : to practice or claim to be versed in (a calling or occupation) — **pro·fess·ed·ly** \-'fe-səd-lē\ *adv*

♦ [1] affirm, allege, assert, aver, avouch, avow, claim, contend, declare, insist, maintain, protest, warrant — more at CLAIM ♦ [2] affect, assume, counterfeit, fake, feign, pretend, put on, sham, simulate — more at FEIGN

pro·fes·sion \prə-'fe-shən\ *n* **1** ♦ : an open declaration or avowal of a belief or opinion **2** ♦ : a calling requiring specialized knowledge and often long academic preparation **3** : the whole body of persons engaged in a calling

♦ [1] affirmation, assertion, avowal, claim, declaration, protestation — more at PROTESTATION ♦ [2] calling, employment, line, occupation, trade, vocation, work — more at OCCUPATION

¹pro·fes·sion·al \prə-'fe-shə-nəl\ *adj* **1** : of, relating to, or characteristic of a profession **2** : engaged in one of the professions **3** : participating for gain in an activity often engaged in by amateurs — **pro·fes·sion·al·ly** *adv*

²professional *n* : one that engages in an activity professionally

pro·fes·sion·al·ism \-nə-,li-zəm\ *n* **1** : the conduct, aims, or qualities that characterize or mark a profession or a professional person **2** : the following of a profession (as athletics) for gain or livelihood

pro·fes·sion·al·ize \-nə-,līz\ *vb* **-ized; -iz·ing** : to give a professional nature to

pro·fes·sor \prə-'fe-sər\ *n* : a teacher at a university or college; *esp* : a faculty member of the highest academic rank — **pro·fes·so·ri·al** \,prō-fə-'sōr-ē-əl, ,prä-\ *adj* — **pro·fes·sor·ship** *n*

¹prof·fer \'prä-fər\ *vb* **prof·fered; prof·fer·ing** ♦ : to present for acceptance : OFFER

♦ advance, offer, pose, propose, propound, suggest, vote — more at PROPOSE

²proffer *n* ♦ : something proposed for acceptance

♦ offer, proposal, proposition, suggestion — more at PROPOSAL

pro·fi·cien·cy \prə-'fi-shən-sē\ *n* ♦ : the quality or state of being proficient

♦ experience, expertise, know-how, savvy — more at EXPERIENCE

pro·fi·cient \prə-'fi-shənt\ *adj* ♦ : well advanced in an art, occupation, or branch of knowledge — **proficient** *n*

♦ accomplished, adept, consummate, crack, crackerjack, expert, good, great, master, masterful, masterly, skilled, skillful, virtuoso; *also* adroit, clever, deft, dexterous, handy; gifted, talented; experienced, polished, practiced, seasoned, veteran; effective, effectual, efficient, workmanlike; able, capable, competent, fit, qualified; educated, knowledgeable, schooled, taught, trained, tutored, versed; all-around, well-rounded *Ant* amateur, amateurish, inexpert, unpolished, unprofessional, unskilled, unskillful

pro·fi·cient·ly \-lē\ *adv* ♦ : in a proficient manner

♦ ably, adeptly, capably, expertly, masterfully, skillfully, well — more at WELL

¹**pro·file** \'prō-ˌfīl\ *n* [It *profilo*, fr. *profilare* to draw in outline, fr. *pro-* forward (fr. L) + *filare* to spin, fr. LL, fr. L *filum* thread] **1** : a representation of something in outline; *esp* : a human head seen in side view **2** : a concise biographical sketch **3** : degree or level of public exposure ⟨keep a low ∼⟩

²**profile** *vb* **pro·filed; pro·fil·ing** : to write or draw a profile of **profiling** *n* : the act of suspecting or targeting a person solely on the basis of observed characteristics or behavior ⟨racial ∼⟩

¹**prof·it** \'prä-fət\ *n* **1** ♦ : a valuable return **2** ♦ : the excess of the selling price of goods over their cost

♦ [1] earnings, income, proceeds, return, revenue, yield — more at INCOME ♦ [2] earnings, gain, lucre, net, payoff, proceeds, return; *also* gross; compensation, emolument, income, pay, payment, remittal, requital, salary, wages

²**profit** *vb* **1** ♦ : to be of use : BENEFIT **2** : to derive benefit : GAIN ⟨∼ed from his mistakes⟩

♦ avail, benefit, serve — more at BENEFIT

prof·it·able \'prä-fə-tə-bəl\ *adj* ♦ : affording profits : yielding advantageous returns or results — **prof·it·ably** \-blē\ *adv*

♦ advantageous, beneficial, favorable (*or* favourable), helpful, salutary — more at BENEFICIAL ♦ fat, gainful, lucrative, remunerative; *also* advantageous, beneficial, rewarding, useful, worthwhile *Ant* unprofitable

prof·i·teer \ˌprä-fə-'tir\ *n* : one who makes what is considered an unreasonable profit — **profiteer** *vb*

prof·it·less \'prä-fət-ləs\ *adj* ♦ : having no profit

♦ fruitless, futile, ineffective, unproductive, unsuccessful — more at FUTILE

prof·li·ga·cy \'prä-fli-gə-sē\ *n* ♦ : the quality or state of being profligate

♦ corruption, debauchery, depravity, immorality, iniquity, licentiousness, sin, vice — more at VICE

¹**prof·li·gate** \'prä-fli-gət, -flə-ˌgāt\ *adj* **1** : completely given up to dissipation and licentiousness **2** ♦ : wildly extravagant — **prof·li·gate·ly** *adv*

♦ extravagant, prodigal, spendthrift, thriftless, unthrifty, wasteful — more at PRODIGAL

²**profligate** *n* ♦ : a profligate person

♦ decadent, degenerate, libertine, pervert — more at DEGENERATE ♦ prodigal, spendthrift, wastrel — more at PRODIGAL

pro for·ma \(ˌ)prō-'fȯr-mə\ *adj* : done or existing as a matter of form

pro·found \prə-'fau̇nd, prō-\ *adj* **1** ♦ : marked by intellectual depth or insight ⟨a ∼ thought⟩ **2** : coming from or reaching to a depth ⟨a ∼ sigh⟩ **3** : deeply felt : INTENSE ⟨∼ sympathy⟩ **4** ♦ : all encompassing : THOROUGH — **pro·found·ly** *adv*

♦ [1] abstruse, deep, esoteric; *also* erudite, learned, scholarly; academic, pedantic; complex, complicated, hard;

darkling, enigmatic, inscrutable, mysterious, mystic, uncanny; impenetrable, incomprehensible, unfathomable, unintelligible; ambiguous, cryptic; unanswerable, unknowable; baffling, bewildering, confounding, confusing, mystifying, perplexing, puzzling *Ant* shallow ♦ [4] absolute, complete, thorough, thoroughgoing, total, utter — more at ABSOLUTE

pro·fuse \-'fyüs, prō-\ *adj* ♦ : pouring forth liberally — **pro·fuse·ly** *adv*

♦ copious, extravagant, lavish, luxuriant, riotous; *also* abounding, abundant, ample, bounteous, bountiful, liberal, plenteous, plentiful; fat, fecund, fertile; free, liberal, munificent, openhanded, unsparing, unstinting; excessive, immoderate; adequate, complete, enough, sufficient *Ant* dribbling, trickling

pro·fu·sion \prə-'fyü-zhən\ *n* ♦ : great quantity

♦ abundance, deal, gobs, heap, loads, lot, pile, plenty, quantity, scads — more at LOT

prog *abbr* program

pro·gen·i·tor \prō-'je-nə-tər\ *n* **1** : a direct ancestor : FOREFATHER **2** : ORIGINATOR, PRECURSOR

prog·e·ny \'prä-jə-nē\ *n, pl* **-nies** ♦ : offspring of a person, animal, or plant

♦ issue, offspring, posterity, seed, spawn — more at OFFSPRING

pro·ges·ter·one \prō-'jes-tə-ˌrōn\ *n* : a female hormone that causes the uterus to undergo changes so as to provide a suitable environment for a fertilized egg

prog·na·thous \'präg-nə-thəs\ *adj* : having the lower jaw projecting beyond the upper part of the face

prog·no·sis \präg-'nō-səs\ *n, pl* **-no·ses** \-ˌsēz\ **1** : the prospect of recovery from disease **2** : a prophecy, estimate, or prediction of a future happening or condition : FORECAST

¹**prog·nos·tic** \präg-'näs-tik\ *n* **1** : PORTENT **2** : PROPHECY

²**prognostic** *adj* : of, relating to, or serving as ground for prognostication or a prognosis

prog·nos·ti·cate \präg-'näs-tə-ˌkāt\ *vb* **-cat·ed; -cat·ing** ♦ : to foretell from signs or symptoms

♦ augur, forecast, foretell, predict, presage, prophesy — more at FORETELL

prog·nos·ti·ca·tion \präg-ˌnäs-tə-'kā-shən\ *n* ♦ : an act, the fact, or the power of prognosticating

♦ cast, forecast, prediction, prophecy, soothsaying — more at PREDICTION

prog·nos·ti·ca·tor \präg-'näs-tə-ˌkā-tər\ *n* ♦ : one that prognosticates

♦ augur, diviner, forecaster, fortune-teller, futurist, prophet, seer, soothsayer — more at PROPHET

¹**pro·gram** *also* **programme** \'prō-ˌgram, -grəm\ *n* [F *programme* agenda, public notice, fr. Gk *programma*, fr. *prographein* to write in advance, fr. *pro-* before + *graphein* to write] **1** ♦ : a brief outline of the order to be pursued or the subjects included (as in a public entertainment); *also* : PERFORMANCE **2** ♦ : a plan of procedure **3** : coded instructions for a computer — **pro·gram·mat·ic** \ˌprō-grə-'ma-tik\ *adj*

♦ [1] agenda, calendar, docket, schedule, timetable; *also* card, exercises; arrangement, order, organization ♦ [2] course, line, policy, procedure — more at COURSE ♦ [2] blueprint, scheme, strategy, system; *also* guideline, plan, policy; arrangement, layout, setup; diagram, draft, plot; conception, design, idea, intention, proposal; means, technique, way

²**program** *also* **programme** *vb* **-grammed** *or* **-gramed; -gram·ming** *or* **-gram·ing** **1** : to arrange or furnish a program of or for **2** : to enter in a program **3** : to provide (as a computer) with a program — **pro·gram·ma·bil·i·ty** \(ˌ)prō-ˌgra-mə-'bi-lə-tē\ *n* — **pro·gram·ma·ble** \'prō-ˌgra-mə-bəl\ *adj* — **pro·gram·mer** *also* **pro·gram·er** \'prō-ˌgra-mər, -grə-\ *n*

programmed instruction *n* : instruction through information given in small steps with each requiring a correct response by the learner before going on to the next step

pro·gram·ming *also* **pro·gram·ing** *n* **1** : the planning, scheduling, or performing of a program **2** : the process of instructing or learning by means of an instruction program **3** : the process of preparing an instruction program

¹prog·ress \\'prä-grəs, -₁gres\\ *n* **1** ♦ : a forward movement : ADVANCE **2** ♦ : the action or process of advancing or improving by marked stages or degrees

♦ [1] advance, advancement, furtherance, headway, march, onrush, passage, process, procession, progression — more at ADVANCE ♦ [2] development, elaboration, evolution, expansion, growth, progression — more at DEVELOPMENT

²pro·gress \\prə-'gres\\ *vb* **1** ♦ : to move forward : PROCEED **2** ♦ : to develop to a higher, better, or more advanced stage

♦ [1] advance, fare, forge, get along, go, march, proceed — more at GO ♦ [2] age, develop, grow, grow up, mature, ripen — more at MATURE

pro·gres·sion \\prə-'gre-shən\\ *n* **1** ♦ : an act of progressing **2** ♦ : a continuous and connected series

♦ [1] advance, advancement, furtherance, headway, march, onrush, passage, process, procession, progress — more at ADVANCE ♦ [2] chain, sequence, string, train — more at CHAIN

¹pro·gres·sive \\prə-'gre-siv\\ *adj* **1** ♦ : of, relating to, or characterized by progress ⟨a ~ city⟩ **2** : moving forward or onward : ADVANCING **3** : increasing in extent or severity ⟨a ~ disease⟩ **4** *often cap* : of or relating to political Progressives **5** : of, relating to, or constituting a verb form that expresses action in progress at the time of speaking or a time spoken of **6** ♦ : making use of or interested in new ideas, findings, or opportunities — **pro·gres·sive·ly** *adv*

♦ [1] advanced, high, refined — more at ADVANCED ♦ [6] broad-minded, liberal, nonorthodox, nontraditional, open-minded, radical, unconventional, unorthodox — more at LIBERAL

²progressive *n* **1** : one that is progressive **2** : a person believing in moderate political change and social improvement by government action; *esp, cap* : a member of a Progressive Party in the U.S.

pro·hib·it \\prō-'hi-bət\\ *vb* **1** ♦ : to forbid by authority **2** : to prevent from doing something

♦ ban, bar, enjoin, forbid, interdict, outlaw, proscribe — more at FORBID

pro·hi·bi·tion \\₁prō-ə-'bi-shən\\ *n* **1** ♦ : the act of prohibiting **2** : the forbidding by law of the sale or manufacture of alcoholic beverages **3** ♦ : an order to restrain or stop — **pro·hi·bi·tion·ist** \\-'bi-shə-nist\\ *n* — **pro·hib·i·tive** \\prō-'hi-bə-tiv\\ *adj* — **pro·hib·i·tive·ly** *adv* — **pro·hib·i·to·ry** \\-'hi-bə-₁tōr-ē\\ *adj*

♦ [1] barring, forbidding, interdiction, proscription; *also* bidding, charging, decreeing, dictation, direction, instruction; deterrence, discouragement, dissuading; repression, suppression; coercion, compulsion, constraint, force ♦ [3] ban, embargo, interdict, interdiction, proscription, veto; *also* taboo; injunction; constraint, inhibition, limitation, restraint, restriction; deterrent, discouragement; repression, suppression; prevention; denial, disallowance, negation, refusal, rejection; objection, protest **Ant** prescription

¹proj·ect \\'prä-₁jekt, -jikt\\ *n* **1** ♦ : a specific plan or design : SCHEME **2** : a planned undertaking ⟨a research ~⟩

♦ arrangement, blueprint, design, game, plan, scheme, strategy, system — more at PLAN

²pro·ject \\prə-'jekt\\ *vb* **1** ♦ : to devise in the mind : DESIGN **2** : to throw forward **3** : to jut out : PROTRUDE **4** : to cause (light or shadow) to fall into space or (an image) to fall on a surface ⟨~ a beam of light⟩ **5** : to attribute (a thought, feeling, or personal characteristic) to a person, group, or object

♦ arrange, blueprint, calculate, chart, design, frame, lay out, map, plan, scheme — more at PLAN

pro·jec·tile \\prə-'jekt-²l, -'jek-₁tīl\\ *n* **1** : a body hurled or projected by external force; *esp* : a missile for a firearm **2** : a self-propelling weapon

pro·jec·tion \\prə-'jek-shən\\ *n* ♦ : a part that juts out

♦ bulge, overhang, protrusion — more at BULGE

pro·jec·tion·ist \\prə-'jek-shə-nist\\ *n* : one that operates a motion-picture projector or television equipment

pro·jec·tor \\-'jek-tər\\ *n* : one that projects; *esp* : a device for projecting pictures on a screen

pro·lapse \\'prō-₁laps, 'prō-₁\\ *n* : the falling down or slipping of a body part from its usual position

pro·le·gom·e·non \\₁prō-li-'gä-mə-₁nän, -nən\\ *n, pl* **-e·na** \\-nə\\ : prefatory remarks

pro·le·tar·i·an \\₁prō-lə-'ter-ē-ən\\ *n* [L *proletarius* belonging to the lowest class of citizens, fr. *proles* progeny, fr. *pro-* forth + *-oles* (akin to *alere* to nourish)] : a member of the proletariat — **proletarian** *adj*

pro·le·tar·i·at \\-ē-ət\\ *n* : the laboring class; *esp* : industrial workers who sell their labor to live

pro–life \\(₁)prō-'līf\\ *n* : ANTIABORTION

pro·lif·er·ate \\prə-'li-fə-₁rāt\\ *vb* **-at·ed; -at·ing** ♦ : to grow or increase by rapid production of new units (as cells or offspring)

♦ accumulate, appreciate, balloon, build, burgeon, enlarge, escalate, expand, increase, mount, multiply, mushroom, rise, snowball, swell, wax — more at INCREASE

pro·lif·er·a·tion \\prə-₁li-fə-'rā-shən\\ *n* **1** : rapid and repeated production of new parts or of buds or offspring **2** ♦ : the act, process, or result of increasing by or as if by proliferation

♦ accretion, addition, augmentation, boost, expansion, gain, increase, increment, plus, raise, rise, supplement — more at INCREASE ♦ accumulation, multiplication — more at MULTIPLICATION

pro·lif·ic \\prə-'li-fik\\ *adj* **1** ♦ : producing young or fruit abundantly **2** ♦ : marked by abundant inventiveness or productivity ⟨a ~ writer⟩ — **pro·lif·i·cal·ly** \\-fik(ə-)lē\\ *adv*

♦ [1, 2] fecund, fertile, fruitful, luxuriant, productive, rich — more at FERTILE

pro·lix \\prō-'liks, 'prō-₁liks\\ *adj* ♦ : marked by or using an excess of words : VERBOSE

♦ circuitous, diffuse, long-winded, rambling, verbose, windy, wordy — more at WORDY

pro·lix·i·ty \\prō-'lik-sə-tē\\ *n* ♦ : the quality or state of being prolix

♦ circumlocution, redundancy, verbiage, wordiness — more at VERBIAGE

pro·logue *also* **pro·log** \\'prō-₁lòg, -₁läg\\ *n* ♦ : the preface or introduction to a literary or dramatic work : PREFACE

♦ foreword, introduction, preamble, preface — more at INTRODUCTION

pro·long \\prə-'lòŋ\\ *vb* **1** ♦ : to lengthen in time ⟨~ a meeting⟩ **2** ♦ : to lengthen in extent or range

♦ [1, 2] draw out, elongate, extend, lengthen, protract, stretch — more at EXTEND

pro·lon·ga·tion \\₁prō-₁lòŋ-'gā-shən\\ *n* ♦ : an act or instance of prolonging

♦ elongation, extension — more at EXTENSION

prom \\'präm\\ *n* ♦ : a formal dance given by a high school or college class

♦ ball, dance, formal — more at DANCE

¹prom·e·nade \\₁prä-mə-'nād, -'näd\\ *vb* **-nad·ed; -nad·ing** **1** : to take a promenade **2** : to walk about in or on

²promenade *n* [F, fr. *promener* to take for a walk, fr. MF, alter. of OF *pourmener*, fr. *pour-* completely (fr. L *pro-*) + *mener* to lead, fr. LL *minare* to drive, fr. L *minari* to threaten] **1** : a place for strolling **2** : a leisurely walk for pleasure or display **3** : an opening grand march at a formal ball

pro·me·thi·um \\prə-'mē-thē-əm\\ *n* : a metallic chemical element obtained from uranium or neodymium

prom·i·nence \'prä-mə-nəns\ *n* **1** ♦ : something prominent **2** : the quality, state, or fact of being prominent or conspicuous **3** : a mass of cloudlike gas that arises from the sun's chromosphere

♦ elevation, eminence, height, highland, hill, mound, rise — more at HEIGHT

prom·i·nent \-nənt\ *adj* **1** : jutting out : PROJECTING **2** ♦ : readily noticeable : CONSPICUOUS **3** ♦ : widely and popularly known ⟨a ∼ writer⟩ — **prom·i·nent·ly** *adv*

♦ [2] bold, catchy, conspicuous, emphatic, marked, noticeable, pronounced, remarkable, striking — more at NOTICEABLE ♦ [3] celebrated, famed, famous, noted, notorious, renowned, star, well-known — more at FAMOUS

pro·mis·cu·ous \prə-'mis-kyə-wəs\ *adj* **1** : consisting of various sorts and kinds : MIXED **2** : not restricted to one class or person **3** : having a number of sexual partners — **pro·mis·cu·i·ty** \prä-mis-'kyü-ə-tē, prō-mis-\ *n* — **pro·mis·cu·ous·ly** *adv* — **pro·mis·cu·ous·ness** *n*

¹prom·ise \'prä-məs\ *n* **1** ♦ : a pledge to do or not to do something specified **2** : ground for expectation of success or improvement **3** : something promised

♦ oath, pledge, troth, vow, word; *also* appointment, arrangement, commitment, engagement; compact, contract, covenant; assurance, guarantee, guaranty; bail, bond, deposit, gage, pawn, security, token, warranty

²promise *vb* **prom·ised; prom·is·ing** **1** ♦ : to engage to do, bring about, or provide ⟨∼ help⟩ **2** : to suggest beforehand ⟨dark clouds ∼ rain⟩ **3** ♦ : to give ground for expectation ⟨it ∼s to be a good game⟩

♦ [1] covenant, pledge, swear, vow; *also* affiance, betroth, plight, troth; accede, agree, assent, consent; contract, engage, guarantee, undertake; affirm, assert, aver, avouch, avow, declare, insist, warrant ♦ [3] augur, bode — more at BODE

promised land *n* ♦ : something and esp. a place or condition believed to promise final satisfaction or realization of hopes

♦ Eden, Elysium, heaven, paradise, utopia — more at PARADISE

promising *adj* ♦ : likely to succeed or yield good results — **prom·is·ing·ly** *adv*

♦ auspicious, bright, encouraging, fair, golden, heartening, hopeful, likely, propitious, rosy, upbeat — more at HOPEFUL ♦ auspicious, bright, encouraging, favorable (*or* favourable), hopeful, propitious — more at FAVORABLE

prom·is·so·ry \'prä-mə-sōr-ē\ *adj* : containing a promise

prom·on·to·ry \'prä-mən-tōr-ē\ *n, pl* **-ries** ♦ : a point of land jutting into the sea : HEADLAND

♦ arm, cape, headland, peninsula, point, spit — more at CAPE

pro·mote \prə-'mōt\ *vb* **pro·mot·ed; pro·mot·ing** **1** ♦ : to advance in station, rank, or honor **2** ♦ : to contribute to the growth or prosperity of **3** : LAUNCH **4** ♦ : to present (merchandise) for buyer acceptance through advertising, publicity, or discounting — **pro·mo·tion·al** \-shə-nəl\ *adj*

♦ [1] advance, elevate, raise, upgrade; *also* forward, further; aggrandize, boost, heighten, improve, lift, uplift; commission, ennoble, knight; acclaim, applaud, celebrate, cite, commend, compliment, congratulate, decorate; eulogize, extol, glorify, hail, honor, laud, praise, salute *Ant* abase, degrade, demote, downgrade, lower, reduce ♦ [2] advance, cultivate, encourage, forward, foster, further, nourish, nurture — more at FOSTER ♦ [4] ballyhoo, boast, plug, publicize, tout — more at PUBLICIZE

pro·mot·er \-'mō-tər\ *n* ♦ : one that promotes; *esp* : one that assumes the financial responsibilities of a sports event

♦ advocate, apostle, backer, booster, champion, exponent, friend, proponent, supporter — more at EXPONENT

pro·mo·tion \prə-'mō-shən\ *n* ♦ : the act or fact of being raised in position or rank

♦ advancement, ascent, elevation, rise, upgrade — more at ADVANCEMENT

¹prompt \'prämpt\ *vb* **1** ♦ : to move to action **2** : to assist (one acting or reciting) by suggesting the next words **3** ♦ : to serve as the inciting cause of — **prompt·er** *n*

♦ [1] egg on, encourage, exhort, goad, press, prod, urge — more at URGE ♦ [3] bring about, cause, create, effect, effectuate, generate, induce, make, produce, result, work, yield — more at EFFECT

²prompt *adj* **1** ♦ : being ready and quick to act; *also* : being on time **2** ♦ : performed readily or immediately ⟨∼ service⟩

♦ [1, 2] immediate, punctual, quick, ready, timely; *also* apt, opportune, seasonable; early *Ant* belated, late, tardy

prompt·book \-buk\ *n* : a copy of a play with directions for performance used by a theater prompter

promp·ti·tude \'prämp-tə-tüd, -tyüd\ *n* ♦ : the quality or habit of being prompt : PROMPTNESS

♦ punctuality, timeliness; *also* aptness, quickness, readiness, willingness *Ant* tardiness

prompt·ly \'präm(p)t-lē, 'präm-plē\ *adv* ♦ : in a prompt manner

♦ directly, forthwith, immediately, instantly, now, pronto, right away, right now — more at IMMEDIATELY

prompt·ness \-nəs\ *n* : the quality or habit of being prompt

pro·mul·gate \'prä-məl-gāt; prō-'məl-\ *vb* **-gat·ed; -gat·ing** ♦ : to make known or put into force by open declaration — **prom·ul·ga·tion** \prä-məl-'gā-shən, prō-(ˌ)məl-\ *n*

♦ advertise, announce, blaze, broadcast, declare, enunciate, placard, post, proclaim, publicize, publish, sound — more at ANNOUNCE

pron *abbr* **1** pronoun **2** pronounced **3** pronunciation

prone \'prōn\ *adj* **1** ♦ : having a tendency or inclination **2** : lying face downward; *also* : lying flat or prostrate

♦ apt, given, inclined; *also* choosing, preferring; disposed, likely, predisposed, willing

prone·ness \'prōn-nəs\ *n* ♦ : the condition or fact of being prone

♦ aptness, propensity, tendency, way — more at TENDENCY

prong \'prȯŋ\ *n* : one of the sharp points of a fork : TINE; *also* : a slender projecting part (as of an antler) — **pronged** \'prȯŋd\ *adj*

prong·horn \'prȯŋ-hȯrn\ *n, pl* **pronghorn** *or* **pronghorns** : a swift horned ruminant mammal chiefly of grasslands of western No. America that resembles an antelope

pro·noun \'prō-naun\ *n* : a word used as a substitute for a noun

pro·nounce \prə-'naüns\ *vb* **pro·nounced; pro·nounc·ing** **1** : to utter officially or as an opinion ⟨∼ sentence⟩ **2** : to employ the organs of speech in order to produce ⟨∼ a word⟩; *esp* : to say or speak correctly ⟨she can't ∼ his name⟩ — **pro·nounce·able** *adj* — **pro·nun·ci·a·tion** \-ˌnən-sē-'ā-shən\ *n*

pro·nounced *adj* ♦ : strongly marked : easily recognizable

♦ bold, catchy, conspicuous, emphatic, marked, noticeable, prominent, remarkable, striking — more at NOTICEABLE

pro·nounce·ment \prə-'naüns-mənt\ *n* : a formal declaration of opinion; *also* : ANNOUNCEMENT

pron·to \'prän-tō\ *adv* [Sp, fr. L *promptus* prompt] ♦ : without delay; *also* : very quickly

♦ directly, forthwith, immediately, instantly, now, promptly, right away, right now — more at IMMEDIATELY ♦ apace, briskly, fast, full tilt, hastily, posthaste, presto, quick, quickly, rapidly, soon, speedily, swift, swiftly — more at FAST

pro·nu·clear \'prō-'nü-klē-ər, -'nyü-\ *adj* : supporting the use of nuclear-powered electric generating stations

pro·nun·ci·a·men·to \prō-ˌnən-sē-ə-'men-tō\ *n, pl* **-tos** *or* **-toes** : PROCLAMATION, MANIFESTO

¹**proof** \'prüf\ *n* [ME *prof, prove,* alter. of *preve,* fr. AF *pre-ove,* fr. LL *proba,* fr. L *probare* to test, prove, fr. *probus* good, honest] **1** ♦ : the evidence that compels acceptance by the mind of a truth or fact **2** : a process or operation that establishes validity or truth : TEST **3** : a trial impression (as from type) **4** : a trial print from a photographic negative **5** : alcoholic content (as of a beverage) indicated by a number that is twice the percent by volume of alcohol present ⟨whiskey of 90 ~ is 45% alcohol⟩

♦ attestation, confirmation, corroboration, documentation, evidence, substantiation, testament, testimony, validation, witness; *also* (the) goods; certificate, document, exhibit; demonstration, illustration; authentication, identification, manifestation, verification **Ant** disproof

²**proof** *adj* **1** : successful in resisting or repelling ⟨~ against tampering⟩ ⟨water*proof*⟩ **2** : of standard strength or quality or alcoholic content

proof·read \-ˌrēd\ *vb* : to read and mark corrections in — **proof·read·er** *n*

¹**prop** \'präp\ *n* : something that props

²**prop** *vb* **propped; prop·ping 1** ♦ : to support by placing something under or against — often used with *up* **2** ♦ : to give support or relief to — often used with *up* **3** : to support by placing against something

♦ *usu* **prop up** [1] bear, bolster, brace, buttress, carry, shore, stay, support, uphold — more at SUPPORT ♦ *usu* **prop up** [2] abet, aid, assist, back, help, support — more at HELP

³**prop** *n* : PROPERTY 4 ⟨stage ~s⟩

⁴**prop** *n* : PROPELLER

⁵**prop** *abbr* **1** property **2** proposition **3** proprietor

pro·pa·gan·da \ˌprä-pə-'gan-də, ˌprō-\ *n* [NL, fr. *Congregatio de propaganda fide* Congregation for propagating the faith, organization established by Pope Gregory XV] : the spreading of ideas or information to further or damage a cause; *also* : ideas or allegations spread for such a purpose — **pro·pa·gan·dist** \-dist\ *n*

pro·pa·gan·dize \-ˌdīz\ *vb* **-dized; -diz·ing** : to subject to or carry on propaganda

prop·a·gate \'prä-pə-ˌgāt\ *vb* **-gat·ed; -gat·ing 1** ♦ : to reproduce or cause to reproduce biologically **2** ♦ : to cause to spread — **prop·a·ga·tion** \ˌprä-pə-'gā-shən\ *n*

♦ [1] breed, multiply, procreate, reproduce — more at PROCREATE ♦ [2] broadcast, circulate, disseminate, spread, strew — more at SPREAD

pro·pane \'prō-ˌpān\ *n* : a heavy flammable gas found in petroleum and natural gas and used esp. as a fuel

pro·pel \prə-'pel\ *vb* **pro·pelled; pro·pel·ling** ♦ : to drive forward or onward

♦ drive, push, shove, thrust — more at PUSH ♦ actuate, drive, impel, move, work

pro·pel·lant *also* **pro·pel·lent** \-'pe-lənt\ *n* : something (as a fuel) that propels — **propellant** *also* **propellent** *adj*

pro·pel·ler \prə-'pe-lər\ *n* : a device consisting of a hub fitted with blades that is used to propel a vehicle (as a motorboat or an airplane)

pro·pen·si·ty \prə-'pen-sə-tē\ *n, pl* **-ties** ♦ : an often intense natural inclination or preference

♦ bent, devices, disposition, genius, inclination, leaning, partiality, penchant, predilection, proclivity, tendency, turn — more at INCLINATION

¹**prop·er** \'prä-pər\ *adj* **1** : referring to one individual only ⟨~ noun⟩ **2** : belonging characteristically to a species or individual : PECULIAR **3** : very satisfactory : EXCELLENT **4** : strictly limited to a specified thing ⟨the city ~⟩ **5** ♦ : strictly accurate : CORRECT ⟨the ~ way to proceed⟩ **6** ♦ : strictly decorous **7** ♦ : marked by suitability or rightness ⟨~ punishment⟩

♦ [5] accurate, correct, exact, precise, right, so, true — more at CORRECT ♦ [6] correct, decent, decorous, formal, genteel, nice, polite, respectable, seemly; *also* acceptable, adequate, satisfactory, tolerable; dress, dressy; dignified, elegant, gracious; priggish, prim, stuffy; apt, material, relevant; compatible, congenial, harmonious; allowed, authorized, kosher, permitted **Ant** improper, incorrect, indecent, indecorous, unbecoming, unseemly ♦ [7] applicable, appropriate, apt, felicitous, fit, fitting, good, happy, meet, right, suitable — more at FIT

²**proper** *n* : the parts of the Mass that vary according to the liturgical calendar

prop·er·ly \-lē\ *adv* ♦ : in a proper manner

♦ appropriately, correctly, fittingly, happily, rightly, suitably; *also* well; adequately, passably, satisfactorily, tolerably; decently **Ant** improperly, incongruously, incorrectly, wrongly

prop·er·tied \'prä-pər-tēd\ *adj* : owning property and esp. much property

prop·er·ty \'prä-pər-tē\ *n, pl* **-ties 1** ♦ : a quality peculiar to an individual or thing **2** ♦ : something owned; *esp* : a piece of real estate **3** : OWNERSHIP **4** : an article or object used in a play or motion picture other than painted scenery and actor's costumes

♦ [1] attribute, character, characteristic, feature, mark, peculiarity, point, quality, trait — more at CHARACTERISTIC ♦ [2] lot, parcel, plat, plot, tract — more at LOT

proph·e·cy *also* **proph·e·sy** \'prä-fə-sē\ *n, pl* **-cies** *also* **-sies 1** : an inspired utterance of a prophet **2** ♦ : a prediction of something to come

♦ cast, forecast, prediction, prognostication, soothsaying — more at PREDICTION

proph·e·si·er \'prä-fə-ˌsī-(-ə)r\ *n* : one that prophesies

proph·e·sy \-ˌsī\ *vb* **-sied; -sy·ing 1** : to speak or utter by divine inspiration **2** ♦ : to predict with assurance

♦ augur, forecast, foretell, predict, presage, prognosticate — more at FORETELL

proph·et \'prä-fət\ *n* [ME *prophete,* fr. AF, fr. L *propheta,* fr. Gk *prophētēs,* fr. *pro* for + *phanai* to speak] **1** : one who utters divinely inspired revelations **2** ♦ : one who foretells future events

♦ augur, diviner, forecaster, fortune-teller, futurist, prognosticator, seer, soothsayer; *also* mystic, oracle; astrologer

proph·et·ess \'prä-fə-təs\ *n* : a woman who is a prophet

pro·phet·ic \prə-'fe-tik\ *or* **pro·phet·i·cal** \-ti-kəl\ *adj* ♦ : of, relating to, or characteristic of a prophet or prophecy — **pro·phet·i·cal·ly** \-ti-k(ə-)lē\ *adv*

♦ foreboding, inauspicious, ominous, portentous; *also* oracular; telling **Ant** auspicious, promising, propitious, rosy

Proph·ets \'prä-fəts\ *n pl* : the second part of the canonical Jewish Scripture

¹**pro·phy·lac·tic** \ˌprō-fə-'lak-tik, ˌprä-\ *adj* **1** : preventing or guarding from the spread or occurrence of disease or infection **2** : PREVENTIVE

²**prophylactic** *n* : something prophylactic; *esp* : a device (as a condom) for preventing venereal infection or conception

pro·phy·lax·is \-'lak-səs\ *n, pl* **-lax·es** \-'lak-ˌsēz\ : measures designed to preserve health and prevent the spread of disease

pro·pin·qui·ty \prə-'piŋ-kwə-tē\ *n* **1** : KINSHIP **2** : nearness in place or time : PROXIMITY

pro·pi·ti·ate \prō-'pi-shē-ˌāt\ *vb* **-at·ed; -at·ing** ♦ : to gain or regain the favor of : APPEASE ⟨~ the angry gods⟩ — **pro·pi·ti·a·tion** \-ˌpi-shē-'ā-shən\ *n*

♦ appease, conciliate, disarm, mollify, pacify, placate — more at PACIFY

pro·pi·tia·to·ry \prō-'pi-shē-ə-ˌtōr-ē\ *adj* **1** ♦ : intended to propitiate **2** : of or relating to propitiation

♦ conciliatory, pacific — more at PACIFIC

pro·pi·tious \prə-'pi-shəs\ *adj* **1** : favorably disposed ⟨~ deities⟩ **2** ♦ : being of good omen ⟨~ circumstances⟩

♦ auspicious, bright, encouraging, fair, golden, heartening, hopeful, likely, promising, rosy, upbeat — more at HOPEFUL

prop·man \'präp-,man\ *n* : one who is in charge of stage properties

pro·po·nent \prə-'pō-nənt\ *n* ♦ : one who argues in favor of something

♦ advocate, apostle, backer, booster, champion, exponent, friend, promoter, supporter — more at EXPONENT

¹pro·por·tion \prə-'pōr-shən\ *n* **1** ♦ : harmonious relation of parts to each other or to the whole : BALANCE, SYMMETRY **2** ♦ : proper or equal share **3** : the relation of one part to another or to the whole with respect to magnitude, quantity, or degree : RATIO **4** : physical magnitude, extent, or bulk : SIZE — **in proportion** : PROPORTIONAL

♦ [1] balance, coherence, consonance, harmony, symmetry, symphony, unity — more at HARMONY ♦ [2] allotment, allowance, cut, part, portion, quota, share — more at SHARE

²proportion *vb* **-tioned; -tion·ing** **1** : to adjust (a part or thing) in size relative to other parts or things **2** : to make the parts of harmonious

pro·por·tion·al \prə-'pōr-shə-nəl\ *adj* : corresponding in size, degree, or intensity; *also* : having the same or a constant ratio — **pro·por·tion·al·ly** *adv*

pro·por·tion·ate \prə-'pōr-shə-nət\ *adj* : PROPORTIONAL — **pro·por·tion·ate·ly** *adv*

pro·pos·al \prə-'pō-zəl\ *n* **1** : an act of putting forward or stating something for consideration **2** ♦ : something that is proposed

♦ offer, proffer, proposition, suggestion; *also* feeler, overture; motion; advancement, nomination, recommendation; presentation, submission, tender; arrangement, game, layout, line, plan, plot, project, strategy, system; conception, idea, notion, thought

pro·pose \prə-'pōz\ *vb* **pro·posed; pro·pos·ing** **1** ♦ : to form or put forward a plan or intention ⟨~s to buy a house⟩ **2** : to make an offer of marriage **3** ♦ : to offer for consideration : SUGGEST ⟨~ a policy⟩ — **pro·pos·er** *n*

♦ [1] aim, aspire, contemplate, design, intend, mean, meditate, plan — more at INTEND ♦ [3] advance, offer, pose, proffer, propound, suggest, vote; *also* move; nominate, recommend; present, submit, tender; file, lay, lodge; arrange, calculate, chart, contrive, cover, frame, map, plan, plot, shape

¹prop·o·si·tion \,prä-pə-'zi-shən\ *n* **1** : something proposed for consideration : PROPOSAL **2** : a request for sexual intercourse **3** ♦ : a statement of something to be discussed, proved, or explained **4** : SITUATION, AFFAIR ⟨a tough ~⟩ — **prop·o·si·tion·al** \-'zi-shə-nəl\ *adj*

♦ conjecture, hypothesis, supposition, theory — more at THEORY

²proposition *vb* **-tioned; -tion·ing** : to make a proposal to; *esp* : to suggest sexual intercourse to

pro·pound \prə-'paùnd\ *vb* ♦ : to set forth for consideration ⟨~ a doctrine⟩

♦ advance, offer, pose, proffer, propose, suggest, vote — more at PROPOSE

pro·pri·e·tary \prə-'prī-ə-,ter-ē\ *adj* **1** : of, relating to, or characteristic of a proprietor ⟨~ rights⟩ **2** : made and sold by one with the sole right to do so ⟨~ medicines⟩

pro·pri·e·tor \prə-'prī-ə-tər\ *n* ♦ : a person who has the legal right or exclusive title to something : OWNER — **pro·pri·e·tor·ship** *n*

♦ holder, owner, possessor; *also* landowner

pro·pri·e·tress \-'prī-ə-trəs\ *n* : a woman who is a proprietor

pro·pri·e·ty \prə-'prī-ə-tē\ *n, pl* **-ties** **1** ♦ : conformity to what is socially acceptable in conduct or speech **2** *pl* : the customs of polite society

♦ decency, decorum, form — more at DECENCY

props \'präps\ *n sing or pl* **1** *slang* : DUE 1 ⟨gave him his ~⟩ **2** *slang* : RESPECT 2 ⟨earned the ~ of his peers⟩ **3** *slang* : ACKNOWLEDGMENT ⟨deserves ~ for the effort⟩

pro·pul·sion \prə-'pəl-shən\ *n* **1** : the action or process of propelling **2** : something that propels — **pro·pul·sive** \-siv\ *adj*

pro ra·ta \(,)prō-'rä-tə, -'rä-\ *adv* : in proportion to the share of each : PROPORTIONATELY

pro·rate \(,)prō-'rāt\ *vb* **pro·rat·ed; pro·rat·ing** ♦ : to divide, distribute, or assess proportionally

♦ administer, allocate, apportion, deal, dispense, distribute, mete, parcel, portion — more at ADMINISTER

pro·rogue \prə-'rōg\ *vb* **pro·rogued; pro·rogu·ing** : to suspend or end a session of (a legislative body) — **pro·ro·ga·tion** \,prō-rō-'gā-shən\ *n*

pros *pl of* PRO

pro·sa·ic \prō-'zā-ik\ *adj* **1** : lacking imagination or excitement : DULL **2** ♦ : of a kind to be expected in the normal order of events : EVERYDAY

♦ average, common, commonplace, everyday, normal, ordinary, routine, run-of-the-mill, standard, unexceptional, unremarkable, usual, workaday — more at ORDINARY

pro·sce·ni·um \prō-'sē-nē-əm\ *n* **1** : the part of a stage in front of the curtain **2** : the wall containing the arch that frames the stage

pro·scribe \prō-'skrīb\ *vb* **pro·scribed; pro·scrib·ing** **1** : to publish the name of as condemned to death with the property of the condemned forfeited to the state **2** ♦ : to condemn or forbid as harmful or unlawful

♦ ban, bar, enjoin, forbid, interdict, outlaw, prohibit — more at FORBID

pro·scrip·tion \prō-'skrip-shən\ *n* **1** ♦ : the act of proscribing : the state of being proscribed **2** ♦ : an imposed restraint or restriction

♦ [1, 2] ban, barring, embargo, forbidding, interdiction, prohibition — more at PROHIBITION

prose \'prōz\ *n* [ME, fr. AF, fr. L *prosa*, fr. fem. of *prorsus, prosus*, straightforward, being in prose, alter. of *proversus*, pp. of *provertere* to turn forward] : the ordinary language people use in speaking or writing

pros·e·cute \'prä-si-,kyüt\ *vb* **-cut·ed; -cut·ing** **1** : to follow to the end ⟨~ an investigation⟩ **2** : to seek legal punishment of ⟨~ a forger⟩ — **pros·e·cu·tion** \,prä-si-'kyü-shən\ *n* — **pros·e·cu·tor** \'prä-si-,kyü-tər\ *n*

¹pros·e·lyte \'prä-sə-,līt\ *n* : a new convert to a religion, belief, or party — **pros·e·ly·tism** \-,lī-,ti-zəm\ *n*

²proselyte *vb* **-lyt·ed; -lyt·ing** : PROSELYTIZE

pros·e·ly·tise *chiefly Brit var of* PROSELYTIZE

pros·e·ly·tize \'prä-sə-lə-,tīz\ *vb* **-tized; -tiz·ing** **1** : to induce someone to convert to one's faith **2** : to recruit someone to join one's party, institution, or cause

pros·o·dy \'prä-sə-dē, -zə-\ *n, pl* **-dies** : the study of versification and esp. of metrical structure

¹pros·pect \'prä-,spekt\ *n* **1** ♦ : an extensive view; *also* : OUTLOOK **2** : the act of looking forward **3** : a mental vision of something to come **4** : something that is awaited or expected : POSSIBILITY **5 a** : a potential buyer or customer **b** ♦ : a likely candidate — **pro·spec·tive** \prə-'spek-tiv, 'prä-,spek-\ *adj* — **pro·spec·tive·ly** *adv*

♦ [1] lookout, outlook, panorama, view, vista — more at VIEW ♦ [5b] applicant, aspirant, campaigner, candidate, contender, hopeful, seeker — more at CANDIDATE

²pros·pect \'prä-,spekt\ *vb* ♦ : to explore esp. for mineral deposits — **pros·pec·tor** \-,spek-tər, prä-'spek-\ *n*

♦ explore, hunt, probe, search — more at EXPLORE

pro·spec·tus \prə-'spek-təs\ *n* : a preliminary statement that describes an enterprise and is distributed to prospective buyers or participants

pros·per \'prä-spər\ *vb* **pros·pered; pros·per·ing** **1** ♦ : to succeed in an enterprise or activity; *esp* : to achieve economic success **2** ♦ : to become strong and flourishing

♦ [1, 2] flourish, succeed, thrive — more at SUCCEED

pros·per·i·ty \präs-'per-ə-tē\ *n* : thriving condition : SUC-CESS; *esp* : economic well-being

pros·per·ous \'präs-pə-rəs\ *adj* **1** : FAVORABLE ⟨∼ winds⟩ **2** ♦ : marked by success or economic well-being ⟨a ∼ business⟩ **3** ♦ : enjoying vigorous and healthy growth

♦ [2] palmy, successful, triumphant — more at SUC-CESSFUL ♦ [3] booming, golden, palmy, roaring, successful; *also* affluent, moneyed, opulent, rich, sub-stantial, wealthy, well-heeled, well-off, well-to-do; com-fortable *Ant* unsuccessful

pros·ta·glan·din \ˌpräs-tə-'glan-dən\ *n* : any of various ox-ygenated unsaturated fatty acids of animals that perform a variety of hormonelike actions

pros·tate \'präs-ˌtāt\ *n* [NL *prostata*, fr. Gk *prostatēs*, fr. *proïstanai* to put in front] : PROSTATE GLAND — **pros·tat·ic** \prä-'sta-tik\ *adj*

prostate gland *n* : a glandular body about the base of the male urethra that produces a secretion which is a major part of the fluid ejaculated during an orgasm

pros·ta·ti·tis \ˌpräs-tə-'tī-təs\ *n* : inflammation of the pros-tate gland

pros·the·sis \präs-'thē-səs, 'präs-thə-\ *n, pl* **-the·ses** \-ˌsēz\ : an artificial replacement for a missing body part — **pros·thet·ic** \präs-'the-tik\ *adj*

pros·thet·ics \-'the-tiks\ *n pl* : the surgical or dental spe-cialty concerned with the design, construction, and fit-ting of prostheses

¹pros·ti·tute \'präs-tə-ˌtüt, -ˌtyüt\ *vb* **-tut·ed; -tut·ing** **1** : to offer indiscriminately for sexual activity esp. for money **2** ♦ : to devote to corrupt or unworthy purposes — **pros·ti·tu·tion** \ˌpräs-tə-'tü-shən, -'tyü-\ *n*

♦ debase, degrade, demean, demoralize, humble, sub-vert, warp — more at DEBASE

²prostitute *n* : one who engages in sexual activities for money

¹pros·trate \'prä-ˌstrāt\ *adj* **1** : stretched out with face on the ground in adoration or submission **2** : lying flat **3** ♦ : completely overcome and lacking vitality ⟨∼ with a cold⟩

♦ beat, bushed, dead, drained, effete, jaded, limp, spent, tired, weak, weary, worn-out — more at WEARY

²prostrate *vb* **pros·trat·ed; pros·trat·ing** **1** : to throw or put into a prostrate position **2** ♦ : to reduce to a weak or powerless condition

♦ debilitate, enervate, enfeeble, sap, soften, tire, waste, weaken — more at WEAKEN ♦ carry away, crush, devastate, floor, oppress, overcome, overpower, over-whelm, snow under, swamp — more at OVERWHELM

pros·tra·tion \prä-'strā-shən\ *n* ♦ : complete physical or mental exhaustion

♦ burnout, collapse, exhaustion, fatigue, lassitude, tiredness, weariness — more at FATIGUE

prosy \'prō-zē\ *adj* **pros·i·er; -est** **1** : PROSAIC, ORDINARY **2** : TEDIOUS

Prot *abbr* Protestant

prot·ac·tin·i·um \ˌprō-ˌtak-'ti-nē-əm\ *n* : a metallic radioac-tive chemical element of relatively short life

pro·tag·o·nist \prō-'ta-gə-nist\ *n* **1** : the principal charac-ter in a drama or story **2** : a leader or supporter of a cause

pro·te·an \'prō-tē-ən\ *adj* ♦ : able to assume different shapes or roles

♦ adaptable, all-around, universal, versatile — more at VERSATILE

pro·tect \prə-'tekt\ *vb* ♦ : to shield from injury : GUARD

♦ cover, defend, guard, safeguard, screen, secure, shield, ward — more at DEFEND

pro·tec·tion \prə-'tek-shən\ *n* **1** : the act of protecting : the state of being protected **2** ♦ : one that protects ⟨wear a helmet as a ∼⟩ **3** : the supervision or support of one that is smaller and weaker **4** : the freeing of pro-

ducers from foreign competition in their home market by high duties on foreign competitive goods — **pro·tec·tive** \-'tek-tiv\ *adj*

♦ aegis, armor, cover, defense (*or* defence), guard, safe-guard, screen, security, shield, wall, ward — more at DEFENSE

pro·tec·tion·ist \-shə-nist\ *n* : an advocate of government economic protection for domestic producers through restrictions on foreign competitors — **pro·tec·tion·ism** \-shə-ˌni-zəm\ *n*

pro·tec·tor \prə-'tek-tər\ *n* **1** ♦ : one that protects **2** : a device used to prevent injury : GUARD **3** : REGENT 1

♦ custodian, defender, defense (*or* defence), guard, protection; *also* bodyguard, champion; keeper, look-out, sentinel, sentry, warden, warder, watch, watchdog, watchman; keeper, preserver, saver

pro·tec·tor·ate \-tə-rət\ *n* **1** : government by a protector **2** : the relationship of superior authority assumed by one state over a dependent one; *also* : the dependent political unit in such a relationship

pro·té·gé \'prō-tə-ˌzhā\ *n* [F] : one who is protected, trained, or guided by an influential person

pro·tein \'prō-ˌtēn\ *n* [F *protéine*, fr. LGk *prōteios* primary, fr. Gk *prōtos* first] : any of various complex nitrogen-con-taining substances that consist of chains of amino acids, are present in all living cells, and are an essential part of the human diet

pro tem \prō-'tem\ *adv* : PRO TEMPORE

pro tem·po·re \prō-'tem-pə-rē\ *adv* [L] : for the time being

Pro·te·ro·zo·ic \ˌprä-tə-rə-'zō-ik, ˌprō-\ *adj* : of, relating to, or being the eon of geologic history between the Archean and the Phanerozoic — **Proterozoic** *n*

¹pro·test \'prō-ˌtest\ *n* **1** : the act of protesting; *esp* : an organized public demonstration of disapproval **2** ♦ : a complaint or objection against an idea, an act, or a course of action

♦ challenge, complaint, demur, expostulation, fuss, kick, objection, question, remonstrance — more at OB-JECTION

²pro·test \prō-'test\ *vb* **1** ♦ : to assert positively : make solemn declaration of ⟨∼s his innocence⟩ **2** ♦ : to ob-ject strongly : make a protest against ⟨∼ a ruling⟩ — **pro·test·er** *or* **pro·tes·tor** \-tər\ *n*

♦ [1] affirm, allege, assert, aver, avouch, avow, claim, contend, declare, insist, maintain, profess, warrant — more at CLAIM ♦ [2] demur, kick, object, remonstrate — more at OBJECT

Prot·es·tant \'prä-təs-tənt, 3 also prə-'tes-\ *n* **1** : a mem-ber or adherent of one of the Christian churches deriving from the Reformation **2** : a Christian not of a Catholic or Orthodox church **3** *not cap* : one who makes a protest — **Prot·es·tant·ism** \'prä-təs-tən-ˌti-zəm\ *n*

pro·tes·ta·tion \ˌprä-təs-'tā-shən\ *n* **1** : the act or fact of protesting **2** ♦ : a formal declaration of dissent to or sup-port of something

♦ affirmation, assertion, avowal, claim, declaration, profession; *also* announcement, declaration, proclama-tion, pronouncement; argument, justification, rational-ization, reason; confirmation, vindication *Ant* disavowal

pro·tha·la·mi·on \ˌprō-thə-'lā-mē-ən\ *or* **pro·tha·la·mi·um** \-mē-əm\ *n, pl* **-mia** \-mē-ə\ : a song in celebration of a marriage

pro·to·col \'prō-tə-ˌkȯl\ *n* [MF *prothocole*, fr. ML *proto-collum*, fr. LGk *prōtokollon* first sheet of a papyrus roll bearing data of manufacture, fr. Gk *prōtos* first + *kollan* to glue together, fr. *kolla* glue] **1** : an original draft or record **2** : a preliminary memorandum of diplomatic ne-gotiation **3** : a code of diplomatic or military etiquette **4** : a set of conventions for formatting data in an elec-tronic communications system

pro·ton \'prō-ˌtän\ *n* [Gk *prōton*, neut. of *prōtos* first] : a positively charged atomic particle present in all atomic nuclei — **pro·ton·ic** \-'tä-nik\ *adj*

pro·to·plasm \'prō-tə-ˌpla-zəm\ *n* : the complex colloidal largely protein substance of living plant and animal cells — **pro·to·plas·mic** \ˌprō-tə-'plaz-mik\ *adj*

pro·to·type \'prō-tə-ˌtīp\ *n* : an original model : ARCHE-TYPE

pro·to·zo·an \ˌprō-tə-'zō-ən\ *n* : any of a phylum or sub-kingdom of unicellular lower invertebrate animals that include some pathogenic parasites of humans and domestic animals — **protozoan** *adj*

pro·tract \prō-'trakt\ *vb* ♦ : to prolong in time or space
  ♦ draw out, elongate, extend, lengthen, prolong, stretch — more at EXTEND

pro·trac·tor \-'trak-tər\ *n* : an instrument for drawing and measuring angles

pro·trude \prō-'trüd\ *vb* **pro·trud·ed; pro·trud·ing** ♦ : to stick out or cause to stick out : jut out
  ♦ bag, balloon, beetle, belly, billow, bulge, overhang, poke, project, start, stick out — more at BULGE

pro·tru·sion \prō-'trü-zhən\ *n* 1 : the act of protruding : the state of being protruded 2 ♦ : something that protrudes
  ♦ bulge, overhang, projection — more at BULGE

pro·tu·ber·ance \prō-'tü-bə-rəns, -'tyü-\ *n* : something that protrudes

pro·tu·ber·ant \-rənt\ *adj* : extending beyond the surrounding surface in a bulge

proud \'praùd\ *adj* 1 ♦ : having or showing excessive self-esteem : HAUGHTY 2 : highly pleased : EXULTANT 3 : having proper self-respect ⟨too ~ to beg⟩ 4 ♦ : giving reason for pride : GLORIOUS ⟨a ~ occasion⟩ 5 : SPIR-ITED ⟨a ~ steed⟩ — **proud·ly** *adv*
  ♦ [1] arrogant, disdainful, haughty, highfalutin, lofty, lordly, prideful, superior; *also* complacent, conceited, egoistic, egotistic, important, self-assertive, self-important, self-satisfied, smug, uppity, vain, vainglorious; pretentious, snobbish, stuck-up, supercilious; cavalier, overbearing, overweening, peremptory, swaggering; high-sounding, pompous; condescending, patronizing; cocky, overconfident, presumptuous; bloated, boastful, bombastic; audacious, bold, brash, brassy, cheeky, cocksure, forward, impertinent, impudent, saucy; confident, presuming, self-assured, self-confident, sure; domineering, high-handed, imperious; self-centered, selfish; dominating, magisterial, masterful *Ant* humble, lowly, modest ♦ [4] august, baronial, gallant, glorious, grand, grandiose, heroic, imposing, magnificent, majestic, monumental, noble, regal, royal, splendid, stately — more at GRAND

prov *abbr* 1 province; provincial 2 provisional

Prov *abbr* Proverbs

prov·able \'prü-və-bəl\ *adj* ♦ : capable of being proved
  ♦ demonstrable, supportable, sustainable, verifiable — more at VERIFIABLE

prove \'prüv\ *vb* **proved; proved** *or* **prov·en** \'prü-vən\; **prov·ing** 1 : to test by experiment or by a standard 2 ♦ : to establish the truth of by argument or evidence 3 : to show to be correct, valid, or genuine 4 ♦ : to turn out esp. after trial or test ⟨the car *proved* to be a good choice⟩
  ♦ [2] demonstrate, document, establish, show, substantiate, validate; *also* back (up), buttress, corroborate; evidence, evince, record, support, witness; adduce, attest, authenticate, certify, identify; confirm, sustain, verify; clinch, nail, settle; depose, testify *Ant* disprove, rebut, refute ♦ [4] come out, pan out, turn out — more at COME OUT

prov·e·nance \'prä-və-nəns\ *n* : ORIGIN, SOURCE

Pro·ven·çal \ˌprō-vän-'säl, ˌprä-vən-\ *n* 1 : a native or inhabitant of Provence 2 : OCCITAN — **Provençal** *adj*

prov·en·der \'prä-vən-dər\ *n* 1 : dry food for domestic animals : FEED 2 ♦ : food usable by people : VICTUALS
  ♦ chow, fare, food, grub, meat, provisions, viands, victuals — more at FOOD

pro·ve·nience \prə-'vē-nyəns\ *n* : ORIGIN, SOURCE

prov·erb \'prä-ˌvərb\ *n* ♦ : a pithy popular saying : ADAGE
  ♦ adage, aphorism, byword, epigram, maxim, saying — more at SAYING

pro·ver·bi·al \prə-'vər-bē-əl\ *adj* 1 : of, relating to, or resembling a proverb 2 : commonly spoken of

Proverbs *n* : a book of moral sayings in the canonical Jewish and Christian Scripture

pro·vide \prə-'vīd\ *vb* **pro·vid·ed; pro·vid·ing** [ME, fr. L *providēre*, lit., to see ahead, fr. *pro-* forward + *vidēre* to see] 1 : to take measures beforehand ⟨~ against inflation⟩ 2 : to make a proviso or stipulation 3 : to supply what is needed ⟨~ for a family⟩ 4 : EQUIP 5 ♦ : to supply for use — **pro·vid·er** *n*
  ♦ deliver, feed, furnish, give, hand, hand over, supply — more at FURNISH

pro·vid·ed *conj* : on condition that : IF

prov·i·dence \'prä-və-dəns\ *n* 1 *often cap* : divine guidance or care 2 *cap* : GOD 1 3 ♦ : the quality or state of being provident
  ♦ foresight, forethought, prescience — more at FORE-SIGHT ♦ economy, frugality, husbandry, thrift — more at ECONOMY

prov·i·dent \-dənt\ *adj* 1 ♦ : making provision for the future 2 ♦ : characterized by or reflecting economy in the use of resources : FRUGAL — **prov·i·dent·ly** *adv*
  ♦ [1] farsighted, forehanded, foresighted, prescient — more at FORESIGHTED ♦ [2] economical, frugal, sparing, thrifty — more at FRUGAL

prov·i·den·tial \ˌprä-və-'den-chəl\ *adj* 1 : of, relating to, or determined by Providence 2 ♦ : occurring by or as if by an intervention of Providence : LUCKY
  ♦ fluky, fortuitous, fortunate, happy, lucky — more at FORTUNATE

pro·vid·ing *conj* : PROVIDED

prov·ince \'prä-vəns\ *n* 1 : an administrative district or division of a country 2 *pl* : all of a country except the metropolises 3 ♦ : proper business or scope : SPHERE
  ♦ area, arena, demesne, department, discipline, domain, field, line, realm, specialty, sphere — more at FIELD

pro·vin·cial \prə-'vin-chəl\ *adj* 1 : of or relating to a province 2 ♦ : limited in outlook : NARROW ⟨~ ideas⟩ — **pro·vin·cial·ism** \-chə-ˌli-zəm\ *n*
  ♦ insular, little, narrow, parochial, petty, sectarian, small — more at NARROW

proving ground *n* : a place for scientific experimentation or testing

¹**pro·vi·sion** \prə-'vi-zhən\ *n* 1 : the act or process of providing; *also* : a measure taken beforehand 2 ♦ : a stock of needed supplies; *esp* : a stock of food — usu. used in pl. 3 : a conditional stipulation : PROVISO
  ♦ **provisions** chow, fare, food, grub, meat, provender, viands, victuals — more at FOOD

²**provision** *vb* : to supply with provisions
  ♦ board, cater, feed — more at FEED

pro·vi·sion·al \-'vi-zhə-nəl\ *adj* ♦ : provided for a temporary need — **pro·vi·sion·al·ly** *adv*
  ♦ impermanent, interim, short-term, temporary — more at TEMPORARY

pro·vi·so \prə-'vī-zō\ *n, pl* **-sos** *also* **-soes** [ME, fr. ML *proviso quod* provided that] 1 : an article or clause that introduces a condition 2 ♦ : a conditional stipulation
  ♦ condition, provision, qualification, reservation, stipulation — more at CONDITION

pro·vo·ca·teur \prō-ˌvä-kə-'tər\ *n* : one who provokes

prov·o·ca·tion \ˌprä-və-'kā-shən\ *n* 1 : the act of provoking 2 ♦ : something that provokes
  ♦ boost, encouragement, goad, impetus, impulse, incentive, momentum, motivation, spur, yeast — more at IMPULSE ♦ excitement, incitement, instigation, stimulus; *also* encouragement, goad, incentive, inducement,

jog, prod, spur; induction, inspiration, motivation; aggravation, annoyance, bother, exasperation, frustration, hassle, headache, irritant, nuisance, peeve, pest

pro·voc·a·tive \prə-'vä-kə-tiv\ *adj* ♦ : serving to provoke or excite

♦ exciting; *also* explosive, fiery, inflammatory, incendiary, triggering; inducing, inspirational, inspiring, motivating; jeering, taunting, teasing; activating, energizing, galvanizing, quickening, vitalizing; angering, enraging, maddening, upsetting; aggravating, annoying, bothersome, galling, irksome, irritating, pesky, vexatious, vexing

pro·voke \prə-'vōk\ *vb* **pro·voked; pro·vok·ing** 1 : to incite to anger : INCENSE 2 : to call forth : EVOKE ⟨a remark that *provoked* laughter⟩ 3 ♦ : to stir up on purpose ⟨~ an argument⟩ — **pro·vok·er** *n*

♦ abet, ferment, foment, incite, instigate, raise, stir, whip — more at INCITE

pro·vo·lo·ne \ˌprō-və-'lō-nē\ *n* : a usu. firm pliant often smoked Italian cheese

pro·vost \'prō-ˌvōst, 'prä-vəst\ *n* : a high official; *esp* : a high-ranking university administrative officer

pro·vost mar·shal \ˌprō-ˌvō-'mär-shəl\ *n* : an officer who supervises the military police of a command

prow \'praù\ *n* : the bow of a ship

prow·ess \'praù-əs\ *n* 1 : military valor and skill 2 : extraordinary ability

prowl \'praù(-ə)l\ *vb* : to roam about stealthily — **prowl** *n* — **prowl·er** *n*

prox·i·mal \'präk-sə-məl\ *adj* 1 : next to or nearest the point of attachment or origin; *esp* : located toward the center of the body 2 : of, relating to, or being the mesial and distal surfaces of a tooth — **prox·i·mal·ly** *adv*

prox·i·mate \'präk-sə-mət\ *adj* 1 : DIRECT ⟨the ~ cause⟩ 2 : very near

prox·im·i·ty \präk-'si-mə-tē\ *n* ♦ : the quality or state of being proximate : NEARNESS

♦ closeness, contiguity, immediacy, nearness; *also* abutment, juxtaposition *Ant* distance, remoteness

prox·i·mo \'präk-sə-ˌmō\ *adj* [L *proximo mense* in the next month] : of or occurring in the next month after the present

proxy \'präk-sē\ *n, pl* **prox·ies** [ME *proxi, procucie,* alter. of *procuracie,* fr. AF, fr. ML *procuratia,* alter. of L *procuratio* appointment of another as an agent, fr. *procurare* to take care of] 1 : the authority or power to act for another; *also* : a document giving such authorization 2 ♦ : a person authorized to act for another — **proxy** *adj*

♦ agent, attorney, commissary, delegate, deputy, envoy, factor, representative — more at AGENT

prude \'prüd\ *n* : a person who shows or affects extreme modesty — **prud·ery** \'prü-də-rē\ *n*

pru·dence \'prüd-ᵊns\ *n* ♦ : sagacity or shrewdness in the management of affairs

♦ common sense, discretion, horse sense, sagacity; *also* farsightedness, foresight, foresightedness, forethought, prescience, providence; discernment, discrimination, insight, sapience, wisdom; acumen, astuteness, keenness, penetration, perspicacity; care, caution, circumspection, precaution, premeditation *Ant* imprudence, indiscretion

pru·dent \'prüd-ᵊnt\ *adj* 1 : shrewd in the management of practical affairs 2 : CAUTIOUS, DISCREET 3 : PROVIDENT, FRUGAL 4 ♦ : marked by wisdom or judiciousness — **pru·den·tial** \prü-'den-chəl\ *adj* — **pru·dent·ly** *adv*

♦ advisable, desirable, expedient, judicious, politic, tactical, wise — more at EXPEDIENT

prud·ish \'prü-dish\ *adj* ♦ : marked by prudery — **prud·ish·ly** *adv*

♦ prim, puritanical, straitlaced — more at STRAIT-LACED

¹**prune** \'prün\ *n* : a dried plum

²**prune** *vb* **pruned; prun·ing** ♦ : to cut off unwanted parts (as of a tree)

♦ bob, clip, crop, curtail, cut, cut back, dock, lop, nip, shave, shear, trim — more at CLIP

pru·ri·ent \'prur-ē-ənt\ *adj* : LASCIVIOUS; *also* : exciting to lasciviousness — **pru·ri·ence** \-ē-əns\ *n*

¹**pry** \'prī\ *vb* **pried; pry·ing** 1 : to look closely or inquisitively 2 ♦ : to make a nosy or presumptuous inquiry

♦ butt in, interfere, intrude, meddle, mess, nose, obtrude, poke, snoop — more at INTERFERE

²**pry** *vb* **pried; pry·ing** 1 ♦ : to raise, move, or pull apart with a pry or lever 2 ♦ : to extract, detach, or open with difficulty

♦ [1] jimmy, prize; *also* elevate, hoist, lift, uplift; break, break up, detach, disengage, disjoin, divide, part, pull, separate; shift ♦ [2] extract, prize, pull, root, tear, uproot, wrest — more at EXTRACT

³**pry** *n* : a tool for prying

prying *adj* ♦ : inquisitive in an annoying, officious, or meddlesome way

♦ curious, inquisitive, nosy — more at CURIOUS ♦ intrusive, meddlesome, nosy, obtrusive, officious, presumptuous — more at INTRUSIVE

Ps *or* **Psa** *abbr* Psalms

PS *abbr* 1 [L *postscriptum*] postscript 2 public school

PSA *abbr* public service announcement

psalm \'säm, 'sälm\ *n, often cap* [ME, fr. OE *psealm,* fr. LL *psalmus,* fr. Gk *psalmos,* lit., twanging of a harp, fr. *psallein* to pluck, play a stringed instrument] ♦ : a sacred song or poem; *esp* : one of the hymns collected in the Book of Psalms — **psalm·ist** *n*

♦ anthem, canticle, carol, chorale, hymn, spiritual — more at HYMN

Psalms *n* : a book of sacred poems in canonical Jewish and Christian Scripture

Psal·ter \'sol-tər\ *n* : the Book of Psalms; *also* : a collection of the Psalms arranged for devotional use

pseud *abbr* pseudonym; pseudonymous

pseu·do \'sü-dō\ *adj* ♦ : being apparently rather than actually as stated : SPURIOUS, SHAM

pseu·do·nym \'sü-də-ˌnim\ *n* : a fictitious name — **pseu·don·y·mous** \sü-'dä-nə-məs\ *adj*

pseu·do·sci·ence \ˌsü-dō-'sī-əns\ *n* : a system of theories, assumptions, and methods erroneously regarded as scientific — **pseu·do·sci·en·tif·ic** \-ˌsī-ən-'ti-fik\ *adj*

PSG *abbr* platoon sergeant

¹**psi** \'sī, 'psī\ *n* : the 23d letter of the Greek alphabet — Ψ or ψ

²**psi** *abbr* pounds per square inch

psit·ta·co·sis \ˌsi-tə-'kō-səs\ *n* : an infectious disease of birds marked by diarrhea and wasting and transmissible to humans

pso·ri·a·sis \sə-'rī-ə-səs\ *n* : a chronic skin disease characterized by red patches covered with white scales

PST *abbr* Pacific standard time

¹**psych** *or* **psyche** \'sīk\ *vb* **psyched; psych·ing** 1 : OUTWIT, OUTGUESS; *also* : to analyze beforehand 2 : INTIMIDATE 3 ♦ : to prepare oneself psychologically ⟨get *psyched* up for the game⟩ — often used with *up*

♦ *sometimes* psych up brace, encourage, forearm, fortify, nerve, ready, steel, strengthen — more at FORTIFY

²**psych** *abbr* psychology

psy·che \'sī-kē\ *n* : SOUL, PERSONALITY; *also* : MIND

psy·che·del·ic \ˌsī-kə-'de-lik\ *adj* 1 : of, relating to, or causing abnormal psychic effects ⟨~ drugs⟩ 2 : relating to the taking of psychedelic drugs ⟨~ experience⟩ 3 : imitating, suggestive of, or reproducing the effects of psychedelic drugs ⟨~ art⟩ ⟨~ colors⟩ — **psychedelic** *n* — **psy·che·del·i·cal·ly** \-li-k(ə-)lē\ *adv*

psy·chi·a·try \sə-'kī-ə-trē, sī-\ *n* [prob. fr. F *psychiatrie,* fr. *psychiatre* psychiatrist, fr. Gk *psychē* breath, soul + *iatros* physician] : a branch of medicine dealing with mental, emotional, and behavioral disorders — **psy·chi·at·ric** \ˌsī-kē-'a-trik\ *adj* — **psy·chi·a·trist** \sə-'kī-ə-trist, sī-\ *n*

¹psy·chic \'sī-kik\ *also* psy·chi·cal \-ki-kəl\ *adj* 1 : of or relating to the psyche 2 : lying outside the sphere of physical science 3 : sensitive to nonphysical or supernatural forces — psy·chi·cal·ly \-k(ə-)lē\ *adv*

²psychic *n* : a person apparently sensitive to nonphysical forces; *also* : MEDIUM 6

psy·cho \'sī-kō\ *n, pl* psychos ♦ : a mentally disturbed person — psycho *adj*

♦ lunatic, maniac, nut, psychotic — more at LUNATIC

psy·cho·ac·tive \ˌsī-kō-'ak-tiv\ *adj* : affecting the mind or behavior

psy·cho·anal·y·sis \ˌsī-kō-ə-'na-lə-səs\ *n* : a method of dealing with psychic disorders by having the patient talk freely about personal experiences and esp. about early childhood and dreams — psy·cho·an·a·lyst \-'an-ᵊl-ist\ *n* — psy·cho·an·a·lyt·ic \-ˌan-ᵊl-'i-tik\ *adj* — psy·cho·an·a·lyze \-'an-ᵊl-ˌīz\ *vb*

psy·cho·bab·ble \'sī-kō-ˌba-bəl\ *n* : psychological jargon esp. when used in a trite or simplistic manner

psy·cho·dra·ma \ˌsī-kə-'drä-mə, -'dra-\ 1 : an extemporized dramatization designed to afford catharsis for one or more of the participants from whose life the plot is taken 2 : a dramatic event or story with psychological overtones

psy·cho·gen·ic \-'je-nik\ *adj* : originating in the mind or in mental or emotional conflict

psy·cho·graph·ics \ˌsī-kə-'gra-fiks\ *n sing or pl* : market research or statistics classifying population groups according to psychological variables

psychol *abbr* psychologist; psychology

psy·cho·log·i·cal \ˌsī-kə-'lä-ji-kəl\ *adj* 1 : of or relating to psychology 2 ♦ : of or relating to the mind — psy·cho·log·i·cal·ly \-ji-k(ə-)lē\ *adv*

♦ cerebral, inner, intellectual, mental — more at MENTAL

psy·chol·o·gy \sī-'kä-lə-jē\ *n, pl* -gies 1 : the science of mind and behavior 2 : the mental and behavioral characteristics of an individual or group — psy·chol·o·gist \sī-'kä-lə-jist\ *n*

psy·cho·path \'sī-kō-ˌpath\ *n* : a mentally ill or unstable person; *esp* : a person who engages in antisocial behavior and exhibits a pervasive disregard for the rights, feelings, and safety of others — psy·cho·path·ic \ˌsī-kə-'pa-thik\ *adj*

psy·cho·sex·u·al \ˌsī-kō-'sek-shə-wəl\ *adj* 1 : of or relating to the mental, emotional, and behavioral aspects of sexual development 2 : of or relating to the physiological psychology of sex

psy·cho·sis \sī-'kō-səs\ *n, pl* -cho·ses \-ˌsēz\ : a serious mental illness (as schizophrenia) marked by loss of or greatly lessened ability to test whether what one is thinking and feeling about the real world is really true

psy·cho·so·cial \ˌsī-kō-'sō-shəl\ *adj* 1 : involving both psychological and social aspects 2 : relating social conditions to mental health

psy·cho·so·mat·ic \ˌsī-kō-sə-'ma-tik\ *adj* : of, relating to, involving, or concerned with bodily symptoms caused by mental or emotional disturbance

psy·cho·ther·a·py \ˌsī-kō-'ther-ə-pē\ *n* : treatment of mental or emotional disorder or of related bodily ills by psychological means — psy·cho·ther·a·pist \-pist\ *n*

¹psy·chot·ic \sī-'kä-tik\ *adj* : of, relating to, marked by, or affected with psychosis ⟨∼ behavior⟩

²psychotic *n* ♦ : an individual who is psychotic

♦ lunatic, maniac, nut — more at LUNATIC

psy·cho·tro·pic \ˌsī-kə-'trō-pik\ *adj* : acting on the mind ⟨∼ drugs⟩

pt *abbr* 1 part 2 payment 3 pint 4 point 5 port

Pt *symbol* platinum

PT *abbr* 1 Pacific time 2 part-time 3 physical therapy 4 physical training

PTA *abbr* Parent-Teacher Association

ptar·mi·gan \'tär-mi-gən\ *n, pl* -gan *or* -gans : any of various grouses of northern regions with completely feathered feet

PT boat \ˌ(ˌ)pē-'tē-\ *n* [*patrol torpedo*] : a small fast patrol craft usu. armed with torpedos

pte *abbr, Brit* private

ptg *abbr* printing

PTO *abbr* 1 Parent-Teacher Organization 2 please turn over

pto·maine \'tō-ˌmān\ *n* : any of various chemical substances formed by bacteria in decaying matter (as meat) and including a few poisonous ones

PTV *abbr* public television

Pu *symbol* plutonium

¹pub \'pəb\ *n* ♦ : an establishment where alcoholic beverages are sold and consumed : TAVERN

♦ bar, barroom, café, saloon, tavern — more at BARROOM

²pub *abbr* 1 public 2 publication 3 published; publisher; publishing

pu·ber·ty \'pyü-bər-tē\ *n* : the condition of being or period of becoming first capable of reproducing sexually — pu·ber·tal \-bərt-ᵊl\ *adj*

pu·bes \'pyü-bēz\ *n, pl* pubes [NL, fr. L, manhood, body hair, pubic region] 1 : the hair that appears upon the lower middle region of the abdomen at puberty 2 : the pubic region

pu·bes·cence \pyü-'bes-ᵊns\ *n* 1 : the quality or state of being pubescent 2 : a pubescent covering or surface

pu·bes·cent \-ᵊnt\ *adj* 1 : arriving at or having reached puberty 2 : covered with fine soft short hairs

pu·bic \'pyü-bik\ *adj* : of, relating to, or situated near the pubes or the pubis

pu·bis \'pyü-bəs\ *n, pl* pu·bes \-bēz\ : the ventral and anterior of the three principal bones composing either half of the pelvis

publ *abbr* 1 publication 2 published; publisher

¹pub·lic \'pə-blik\ *adj* 1 : exposed to general view ⟨the story became ∼⟩ 2 ♦ : of, relating to, or affecting the people as a whole ⟨∼ opinion⟩ 3 : CIVIC, GOVERNMENTAL ⟨∼ expenditures⟩ 4 : of, relating to, or serving the community ⟨∼ officials⟩ 5 : not private : SOCIAL ⟨∼ morality⟩ 6 ♦ : accessible to or shared by all members of the community ⟨∼ library⟩ 7 : well known : PROMINENT ⟨∼ figures⟩ 8 ♦ : of, relating to, or affecting all the people or the whole area of a nation or state — pub·lic·ly *adv*

♦ [2] common, general, popular, vulgar — more at GENERAL ♦ [6] free-for-all, open, unrestricted — more at OPEN ♦ [6] collective, common, communal, concerted, conjoint, joint, mutual, united — more at COLLECTIVE ♦ [8] civil, national, state — more at NATIONAL

²public *n* 1 ♦ : the people as a whole 2 : a group of people having common interests

♦ folks, humanity, humankind, people, persons, society, world — more at PEOPLE

pub·li·can \'pə-bli-kən\ *n* 1 : a Jewish tax collector for the ancient Romans 2 *chiefly Brit* : the licensee of a pub

pub·li·ca·tion \ˌpə-blə-'kā-shən\ *n* 1 : the act or process of publishing 2 : a published work

public house *n* 1 ♦ : an establishment for the lodging and entertaining of travelers : INN 2 *chiefly Brit* : a licensed saloon or bar

♦ hospice, hotel, inn, lodge, tavern — more at HOTEL

pub·li·cise *chiefly Brit var of* PUBLICIZE

pub·li·cist \'pə-blə-sist\ *n* : one that publicizes; *esp* : PRESS AGENT

pub·lic·i·ty \ˌ(ˌ)pə-'bli-sə-tē\ *n* 1 : information with news value issued to gain public attention or support 2 : public attention or acclaim

pub·li·cize \'pə-blə-ˌsīz\ *vb* -cized; -ciz·ing ♦ : to bring to public attention ⟨*publicizing* the book⟩

♦ advertise, announce, blaze, broadcast, declare, enunciate, placard, post, proclaim, promulgate, publish, sound — more at ANNOUNCE ♦ ballyhoo, boast, plug, promote, tout; *also* advertise; push; acclaim, hail, laud, praise; recommend, review; announce, broadcast, publish

pub·lic–key \'pə-blik-'kē\ *n* : the publicly shared element of a code usable only to encode messages

public relations *n sing or pl* : the business of fostering public goodwill toward a person, firm, or institution; *also* : the degree of goodwill and understanding achieved

public school *n* **1** : an endowed secondary boarding school in Great Britain offering a classical curriculum and preparation for the universities or public service **2** : a free tax-supported school controlled by a local governmental authority

public servant *n* ♦ : a government official or employee

♦ functionary, officeholder, officer, official — more at OFFICIAL

public–spirited *adj* : motivated by devotion to the general or national welfare

public television *n* : television supported by public funds and private contributions rather than by commercials

public works *n pl* : works (as schools or highways) constructed with public funds for public use

pub·lish \'pə-blish\ *vb* **1** ♦ : to make generally known : announce publicly **2** ♦ : to produce or release literature, information, musical scores or sometimes recordings, or art for sale to the public — **pub·lish·er** *n*

♦ [1] advertise, announce, blaze, broadcast, declare, enunciate, placard, post, proclaim, promulgate, publicize, sound — more at ANNOUNCE ♦ [2] get out, issue, print; *also* contribute, edit, syndicate; manufacture, produce; market, distribute

¹**puck** \'pək\ *n* ♦ : a mischievous sprite — **puck·ish** *adj* — **puck·ish·ly** *adv*

♦ brownie, dwarf, elf, fairy, fay, gnome, hobgoblin, leprechaun, pixie, troll — more at FAIRY

²**puck** *n* : a disk used in ice hockey

¹**puck·er** \'pə-kər\ *vb* ♦ : to contract into folds or wrinkles

²**pucker** *n* : FOLD, WRINKLE

pud·ding \'pu̇-diŋ\ *n* : a soft, spongy, or thick creamy dessert

pud·dle \'pəd-ᵊl\ *n* : a very small pool of usu. dirty or muddy water

pu·den·dum \pyu̇-'den-dəm\ *n, pl* **-da** \-də\ [NL, fr. L *pudēre* to be ashamed] : the human external genital organs esp. of a woman

pudgy \'pə-jē\ *adj* **pudg·i·er; -est** : being short and plump : CHUBBY

pueb·lo \'pwe-blō, pü-'e-\ *n, pl* **-los** [Sp, village, lit., people, fr. L *populus*] **1** : an American Indian village of Arizona or New Mexico that consists of flat-roofed stone or adobe houses joined in groups sometimes several stories high **2** *cap* : a member of a group of American Indian peoples of the southwestern U.S.

pu·er·ile \'pyu̇-ə-rəl\ *adj* : marked by or suggestive of immaturity and lack of poise : CHILDISH, SILLY — **pu·er·il·i·ty** \ˌpyü-ə-'ri-lə-tē\ *n*

pu·er·per·al \pyü-'ər-pə-rəl\ *adj* : of, relating to, or occurring during childbirth or the period immediately following ⟨~ infection⟩ ⟨~ depression⟩

puerperal fever *n* : an abnormal condition that results from infection of the placental site following childbirth or abortion

Puer·to Ri·can \ˌpȯr-tə-'rē-kən, ˌpwer-\ *n* : a native or inhabitant of Puerto Rico — **Puerto Rican** *adj*

¹**puff** \'pəf\ *vb* **1** : to blow in short gusts **2** ♦ : to breathe hard : PANT **3** : to emit small whiffs or clouds **4** : BLUSTER, BRAG **5** : INFLATE, SWELL **6** : to make proud or conceited **7** : to praise extravagantly

♦ blow, gasp, pant, wheeze — more at GASP

²**puff** *n* **1** ♦ : a short discharge (as of air or smoke); *also* : a slight explosive sound accompanying it **2** : a light fluffy pastry **3** : a slight swelling **4** : a fluffy mass; *also* : a small pad for applying cosmetic powder **5** : a laudatory notice or review — **puffy** *adj*

♦ air, breath, breeze, waft, zephyr — more at BREEZE

puff·ball \'pəf-ˌbȯl\ *n* : any of various globe-shaped and often edible fungi

puf·fin \'pə-fən\ *n* : any of several seabirds having a short neck and a deep grooved parti-colored bill

¹**pug** \'pəg\ *n* **1** : any of a breed of small stocky short-haired dogs with a wrinkled face **2** : a close coil of hair

²**pug** *n* : ¹BOXER

pu·gi·lism \'pyü-jə-ˌli-zəm\ *n* : BOXING

pu·gi·list \'pyü-jə-list\ *n* ♦ : one that fights; *esp* : a professional boxer — **pu·gi·lis·tic** \ˌpyü-jə-'lis-tik\ *adj*

♦ boxer, fighter, prizefighter — more at BOXER

pug·na·cious \ˌpəg-'nā-shəs\ *adj* ♦ : having a quarrelsome or combative nature

♦ aggressive, argumentative, bellicose, belligerent, combative, contentious, discordant, disputatious, quarrelsome, scrappy, truculent — more at BELLIGERENT

pug·nac·i·ty \ˌpəg-'na-sə-tē\ *n* ♦ : a readiness or inclination to fight

♦ aggression, aggressiveness, belligerence, fight, truculence — more at BELLIGERENCE

puis·sance \'pwi-səns, 'pyü-ə-\ *n* : capacity for exertion or endurance : POWER, STRENGTH ⟨the ~ of the king⟩

puis·sant \'pwi-sənt, 'pyü-ə-\ *adj* : having puissance : POWERFUL

puke \'pyük\ *vb* **puked; puk·ing** ♦ : to discharge the contents of the stomach through the mouth : VOMIT — **puke** *n*

♦ barf, gag, heave, hurl, retch, spit up, throw up, vomit — more at VOMIT

puk·ka \'pə-kə\ *adj* [Hindi *pakkā* cooked, ripe, solid, fr. Skt *pakva*] : GENUINE, AUTHENTIC; *also* : FIRST-CLASS, COMPLETE

pul·chri·tude \'pəl-krə-ˌtüd, -ˌtyüd\ *n* : BEAUTY — **pul·chri·tu·di·nous** \ˌpəl-krə-'tüd-ᵊn-əs, -'tyüd-\ *adj*

¹**pull** \'pu̇l\ *vb* **1** ♦ : to exert force so as to draw (something) toward the force; *also* : MOVE ⟨~ out of a driveway⟩ **2 a** : PLUCK **b** ♦ : to take out forcibly : EXTRACT ⟨~ a tooth⟩ **3** ♦ : to strain abnormally ⟨~ a tendon⟩ **4** : to draw apart : TEAR **5** : to make (as a proof) by printing **6** : REMOVE **7** : DRAW ⟨~ a gun⟩ **8** : to carry out esp. with daring ⟨~ a robbery⟩ **9** : PERPETRATE, COMMIT **10** : ATTRACT **11** : to express strong sympathy — **pull·er** *n*

♦ [1] drag, draw, hale, haul, lug, move, tow, tug; *also* attract; jerk, yank; carry, convey, ferry, transport *Ant* drive, propel, push ♦ [2b] extract, prize, pry, root, tear, uproot, wrest — more at EXTRACT ♦ [3] rack, strain, stretch, wrench — more at STRAIN

²**pull** *n* **1** ♦ : the act or an instance of pulling **2** : the effort expended in moving **3 a** : ADVANTAGE **b** ♦ : special influence **4** : a device for pulling something or for operating by pulling **5** ♦ : a force that attracts or compels **6** : an injury from abnormal straining or stretching ⟨a muscle ~⟩

♦ [1] draw, haul, jerk, pluck, tug, wrench; *also* drag, tow; hitch, jerk, twitch; grab, snatch *Ant* push ♦ [3b, 5] authority, clout, influence, sway, weight — more at INFLUENCE

pull·back \'pu̇l-ˌbak\ *n* : an orderly withdrawal of troops

pull–down *adj* : appearing below a selected item (as a menu title) on a computer display ⟨a ~ menu⟩

pul·let \'pu̇-lət\ *n* : a young hen esp. of the domestic chicken when less than a year old

pul·ley \'pu̇-lē\ *n, pl* **pulleys** : a wheel used to transmit power by means of a belt, rope, or chain; *esp* : one with a grooved rim that forms part of a tackle for hoisting or for changing the direction of a force

Pull·man \'pu̇l-mən\ *n* : a railroad passenger car with comfortable furnishings esp. for night travel

pull off *vb* : to accomplish successfully

pull·out \'pu̇l-ˌau̇t\ *n* : PULLBACK

pull out *vb* **1** ♦ : to go away from : DEPART **2** : to take back or away : REMOVE

♦ clear out, depart, exit, get off, go, move, quit, sally, shove, take off — more at GO

pull·over \'pu̇l-ˌō-vər\ *adj* : put on by being pulled over the head ⟨∼ sweater⟩ — **pull·over** *n*

pull–up \'pu̇l-ˌəp\ *n* : CHIN-UP

pull up *vb* : to bring or come to an often abrupt halt : STOP

pul·mo·nary \'pu̇l-mə-ˌner-ē, 'pəl-\ *adj* : of, relating to, or carried on by the lungs ⟨the ∼ circulation⟩

pulp \'pəlp\ *n* **1** : the soft juicy or fleshy part of a fruit or vegetable **2** : a soft moist mass **3** : the soft sensitive tissue that fills the central cavity of a tooth **4** : a material (as from wood) used in making paper **5** : a magazine using cheap paper and often dealing with sensational material

pul·pit \'pu̇l-ˌpit\ *n* : a raised platform or high reading desk used in preaching or conducting a worship service

pulp·wood \'pəlp-ˌwu̇d\ *n* : wood used in making pulp for paper

pulpy \'pəl-pē\ *adj* ♦ : resembling or consisting of pulp
   ♦ fleshy, juicy, succulent — more at JUICY ♦ flabby, mushy, soft, spongy — more at SOFT

pul·sar \'pəl-ˌsär\ *n* : a celestial source of pulsating electromagnetic radiation (as radio waves)

pul·sate \'pəl-ˌsāt\ *vb* **pul·sat·ed; pul·sat·ing** ♦ : to expand and contract rhythmically : BEAT
   ♦ beat, palpitate, pitter-patter, pulse, throb; *also* fluctuate, oscillate, vibrate; quiver, tremble

pul·sa·tion \ˌpəl-'sā-shən\ *n* ♦ : rhythmical throbbing or vibrating
   ♦ beat, palpitation, pulse, throb; *also* fluctuation, oscillation, vibration; quiver, tremble, tremor

¹pulse \'pəls\ *n* **1** : the regular throbbing in the arteries caused by the contractions of the heart **2** : rhythmical beating, vibrating, or sounding **3** : a brief change in electrical current or voltage

²pulse *vb* ♦ : to exhibit a pulse or pulsation
   ♦ beat, palpitate, pitter-patter, pulsate, throb — more at PULSATE

pul·ver·ise *chiefly Brit var of* PULVERIZE

pul·ver·ize \'pəl-və-ˌrīz\ *vb* **-ized; -iz·ing** **1** ♦ : to reduce (as by crushing or grinding) or be reduced to very small particles **2** ♦ : to destroy by or as if by smashing into fragments : DEMOLISH
   ♦ [1] atomize, crush, grind, powder — more at POWDER ♦ [2] annihilate, blot out, demolish, desolate, destroy, devastate, do in, exterminate, extinguish, obliterate, ruin, shatter, smash, tear down, waste, wipe out, wreck — more at DESTROY

pu·ma \'pü-mə, 'pyü-\ *n, pl* **pumas** *also* **puma** [Sp, fr. Quechua] : a large powerful tawny brown wild American cat : COUGAR

pum·ice \'pə-məs\ *n* : a light porous volcanic glass used esp. for smoothing and polishing

pum·mel \'pə-məl\ *vb* **-meled** *also* **-melled; -mel·ing** *also* **-mel·ling** : to strike repeatedly : BEAT

¹pump \'pəmp\ *n* : a device for raising, transferring, or compressing fluids esp. by suction or pressure

²pump *vb* **1** : to raise (as water) with a pump **2** : to draw fluid from with a pump; *also* : to fill by means of a pump ⟨∼ up a tire⟩ **3** : to force or propel in the manner of a pump **4** ♦ : to move in a manner that resembles the action of a pump handle **5** ♦ : to question persistently — **pump·er** *n*
   ♦ [4] bob, bobble, jog, jounce, nod, seesaw — more at NOD ♦ [5] examine, grill, interrogate, query, question, quiz — more at EXAMINE

³pump *n* : a low shoe that grips the foot chiefly at the toe and heel

pumped \'pəmpt\ *adj* : filled with energetic excitement and enthusiasm

pum·per·nick·el \'pəm-pər-ˌni-kəl\ *n* : a dark rye bread

pump·kin \'pəmp-kən, 'pəŋ-kən\ *n* : the large usu. orange fruit of a vine of the gourd family that is widely used as food; *also* : this vine

pun \'pən\ *n* : the humorous use of a word in a way that suggests two or more interpretations — **pun** *vb*

¹punch \'pənch\ *vb* **1 a** : PROD, POKE **b** : to frighten or prod (as game or cattle) into moving in a desired direction : DRIVE, HERD ⟨∼ing cattle⟩ **2** ♦ : to strike with the fist **3** ♦ : to emboss, perforate, or make with a punch **4** : to operate, produce, or enter (as data) by or as if by punching — **punch·er** *n*
   ♦ [2] bang, bash, belt, clout, hit, knock, slug, strike, thump, wallop, whack ♦ [3] bore, drill, hole, perforate, pierce, puncture — more at PERFORATE

²punch *n* **1** ♦ : a quick blow with or as if with the fist **2** ♦ : effective energy or forcefulness
   ♦ [1] belt, blow, box, clout, hit, slug, smash, wallop, whack — more at BLOW ♦ [2] bounce, dash, drive, esprit, pep, snap, spirit, verve, vim, zing, zip — more at SPIRIT ♦ [2] cogency, effectiveness, force, impact, point; *also* payoff; importance, significance; appeal, attraction, charm, fascination

³punch *n* **1** : a tool for piercing, stamping, cutting, or forming **2** ♦ : a hole or notch from a perforating operation
   ♦ perforation, pinhole, prick, puncture, stab — more at PRICK

⁴punch *n* [perh. fr. Hindi *păc* five, fr. Skt *panca*; fr. the number of ingredients] : a drink usu. composed of wine or alcoholic liquor and nonalcoholic beverages; *also* : a drink composed of nonalcoholic beverages

punch card \'pənch-\ *n* : a card with holes punched in particular positions to represent data

punch–drunk \'pənch-ˌdrəŋk\ *adj* **1** : suffering from brain injury resulting from repeated head blows received in boxing **2** : DAZED, CONFUSED

pun·cheon \'pən-chən\ *n* : a large cask
   ♦ barrel, cask, hogshead, keg, pipe — more at CASK

punch line *n* : the sentence or phrase in a joke that makes the point

punch list *n* : a list of tasks to be completed at the end of a project

punchy \'pən-chē\ *adj* **punch·i·er; -est** **1** : having punch : FORCEFUL **2** : DAZED, CONFUSED **3** : VIVID, VIBRANT

punc·til·io \ˌpəŋk-'ti-lē-ˌō\ *n, pl* **-ios** **1** : a nice detail of conduct in a ceremony or in observance of a code **2** : careful observance of forms (as in social conduct)

punc·til·i·ous \ˌpəŋk-'ti-lē-əs\ *adj* ♦ : marked by precise accordance with codes or conventions
   ♦ ceremonious, correct, decorous, formal, proper, starchy — more at CEREMONIOUS

punc·tu·al \'pəŋk-chə-wəl\ *adj* ♦ : being on time : PROMPT — **punc·tu·al·ly** *adv*
   ♦ immediate, prompt, timely — more at PROMPT

punc·tu·al·i·ty \ˌpəŋk-chə-'wa-lə-tē\ *n* ♦ : the quality, state, or habit of being punctual
   ♦ promptitude, timeliness — more at PROMPTITUDE

punc·tu·ate \'pəŋk-chə-ˌwāt\ *vb* **-at·ed; -at·ing** **1** : to mark or divide (written matter) with punctuation marks **2** : to break into at intervals **3** : EMPHASIZE

punc·tu·a·tion \ˌpəŋk-chə-'wā-shən\ *n* : the act, practice, or system of inserting standardized marks in written matter to clarify the meaning and separate structural units

¹punc·ture \'pəŋk-chər\ *n* **1** : an act of puncturing **2** ♦ : a small hole or wound made by puncturing
   ♦ perforation, pinhole, prick, punch, stab — more at PRICK

²puncture *vb* **punc·tured; punc·tur·ing** **1** ♦ : to pierce with or as if with a pointed instrument or object **2** : to make useless as if by a puncture
   ♦ bore, drill, hole, perforate, pierce, punch — more at PERFORATE

pun·dit \'pən-dət\ *n* [Hindi *paṇḍit*, fr. Skt *paṇḍita*, fr.

paṇḍita learned] **1** : a learned person : TEACHER **2** : AUTHORITY, CRITIC

pun·dit·oc·ra·cy \ˌpən-dət-'ä-krə-sē\ *n, pl* **-cies** : a group of powerful and influential political commentators

pun·gen·cy \'pən-jən-sē\ *n* ♦ : the quality or state of being pungent

♦ acidity, acrimony, asperity, bite, bitterness, edge, harshness, keenness, sharpness, tartness

pun·gent \'pən-jənt\ *adj* **1** ♦ : having a sharp incisive quality : CAUSTIC ⟨a ~ editorial⟩ **2 a** : causing a sharp or irritating sensation; *esp* : ACRID ⟨~ smell of burning leaves⟩ **b** ♦ : having an intense flavor or odor — **pun·gent·ly** *adv*

♦ [1] acrid, biting, caustic, cutting, mordant, sarcastic, satiric, scathing, sharp, tart — more at SARCASTIC ♦ [2b] nippy, sharp, strong — more at SHARP

pun·ish \'pə-nish\ *vb* **1** : to impose a penalty on for a fault or crime ⟨~ an offender⟩ **2** ♦ : to inflict a penalty for ⟨~ treason with death⟩ **3** : to inflict injury on : HURT — **pun·ish·able** *adj*

♦ castigate, chasten, chastise, correct, discipline, penalize; *also* assess, charge, dock, fine, impose, levy, mulct; convict, sentence; condemn, damn, denounce; criticize, reprove; wreak *Ant* excuse, pardon, spare

pun·ish·ment *n* **1** ♦ : retributive suffering, pain, or loss : PENALTY **2** : rough treatment

♦ castigation, chastisement, correction, desert, discipline, nemesis, penalty, wrath; *also* reprisal, retaliation, retribution, revenge, vengeance; assessment, charge, fine, mulct; example, sentence; confinement, imprisonment, incarceration; damnation, denouncement; criticism, reproof

pu·ni·tive \'pyü-nə-tiv\ *adj* ♦ : inflicting, involving, or aiming at punishment

♦ corrective, disciplinary, penal; *also* retaliatory, retributive, retributory, revengeful; vengeful, wrathful

¹punk \'pəŋk\ *n* **1** : a young inexperienced person **2** ♦ : a petty hoodlum

♦ bully, gangster, goon, hood, hoodlum, mobster, mug, rowdy, ruffian, thug, tough — more at HOODLUM

²punk *adj* **1** ♦ : very poor **2** ♦ : being in poor health

♦ [1] bad, deficient, inferior, lousy, off, poor, rotten, substandard, unacceptable, unsatisfactory, wanting, wretched, wrong — more at BAD ♦ [2] bad, down, ill, indisposed, peaked, sick, unhealthy, unsound, unwell — more at SICK

³punk *n* : dry crumbly wood useful for tinder; *also* : a substance made from fungi for use as tinder

pun·ster \'pən-stər\ *n* : one who is given to punning

¹punt \'pənt\ *n* : a long narrow flat-bottomed boat with square ends

²punt *vb* : to propel (as a punt) with a pole

³punt *vb* : to kick a football or soccer ball dropped from the hands before it touches the ground

⁴punt *n* : the act or an instance of punting a ball

pu·ny \'pyü-nē\ *adj* **pu·ni·er**; **-est** [AF *puisné* younger, weakly, lit., born afterward, fr. *puis* afterward (fr. L *post* + *né* born, fr. L *natus*] : slight in power, size, or importance

pup \'pəp\ *n* : a young dog; *also* : one of the young of some other animals

pu·pa \'pyü-pə\ *n, pl* **pu·pae** \-(ˌ)pē\ *or* **pupas** [NL, fr. L *pupa* doll] : a form of some insects (as a bee, moth, or beetle) between the larva and the adult that usu. has a protective covering (as a cocoon) — **pu·pal** \-pəl\ *adj*

¹pu·pil \'pyü-pəl\ *n* **1** : a child or young person in school or in the charge of a tutor **2** ♦ : one who has been taught or influenced by a famous or distinguished person : DISCIPLE

♦ adherent, convert, disciple, follower, partisan, votary — more at FOLLOWER

²pupil *n* : the dark central opening of the iris of the eye

pup·pet \'pə-pət\ *n* [ME *popet* youth, doll, fr. MF *poupette*, ultim. fr. L *pupa* doll] **1** : a small figure of a person or animal moved by hand or by strings or wires **2** : DOLL **3** : one whose acts are controlled by an outside force or influence

pup·pe·teer \ˌpə-pə-'tir\ *n* : one who manipulates puppets

pup·py \'pə-pē\ *n, pl* **puppies** : a young domestic dog

pu·pu \'pü-ˌpü\ *n* : an Asian dish consisting of a variety of foods

pur·blind \'pər-ˌblīnd\ *adj* **1** : partly blind **2** : lacking in insight : OBTUSE

pur·chas·able \'pər-chə-sə-bəl\ *adj* **1** : capable of being purchased **2** ♦ : open to corrupt influence and esp. bribery

♦ bribable, corruptible, venal — more at VENAL

¹pur·chase \'pər-chəs\ *vb* **pur·chased**; **pur·chas·ing** ♦ : to obtain by paying money or its equivalent : BUY — **pur·chas·er** *n*

♦ buy, pick up, take — more at BUY

²purchase *n* **1** : an act or instance of purchasing **2** : something purchased **3** : a secure hold or grasp; *also* : advantageous leverage

pur·dah \'pər-də\ *n* : seclusion of women from public observation among Muslims and some Hindus esp. in India; *also* : a state of seclusion

pure \'pyùr\ *adj* **pur·er**; **pur·est** **1** ♦ : unmixed with any other matter : free from taint ⟨~ gold⟩ ⟨~ water⟩ **2** : being thus and no other : ABSOLUTE ⟨~ nonsense⟩ **3** : ABSTRACT, THEORETICAL ⟨~ mathematics⟩ **4** : free from what vitiates, weakens, or pollutes ⟨speaks a ~ French⟩ **5** : free from moral fault : INNOCENT **6** ♦ : marked by chastity : CHASTE

♦ [1] absolute, fine, neat, plain, refined, straight, unadulterated, undiluted, unmixed; *also* clarified, filtered, refined; clean, uncontaminated, undefiled, unpolluted, untainted; rendered, tried; concentrated, full-bodied, strong; uncombined *Ant* adulterated, diluted, impure, mixed ♦ [6] chaste, clean, decent, immaculate, modest — more at CHASTE

pure–blood·ed \-ˌblə-dəd\ *or* **pure–blood** \-ˌbləd\ *adj* : FULL-BLOODED — **pure·blood** *n*

pure·bred \-'bred\ *adj* ♦ : bred from members of a recognized breed, strain, or kind without crossbreeding over many generations — **pure·bred** \-ˌbred\ *n*

♦ full-blooded, thoroughbred *Ant* hybrid, mixed, mongrel

¹pu·ree \pyù-'rā, -'rē\ *n* [F *purée*, fr. MF, fr. fem. of *puré*, pp. of *purer* to purify, strain, fr. L *purare* to purify] : a paste or thick liquid suspension usu. made from finely ground cooked food; *also* : a thick soup made of pureed vegetables

²puree *vb* **pu·reed**; **pu·ree·ing** : to make a puree of

pure·ly \'pyùr-lē\ *adv* **1 a** : to a full extent : TOTALLY ⟨~ by accident⟩ **b** : WHOLLY, EXCLUSIVELY ⟨a selection based ~ on merit⟩ **2** : without admixture of anything injurious or foreign **3** : SIMPLY, MERELY ⟨read ~ for relaxation⟩ **4** ♦ : in a chaste or innocent manner

♦ chastely, modestly, righteously, virtuously; *also* decently, properly; priggishly, primly, prudishly *Ant* evilly, immorally, sinfully, wickedly

pur·ga·tion \ˌpər-'gā-shən\ *n* : the act or result of purging

¹pur·ga·tive \'pər-gə-tiv\ *adj* : purging or tending to purge

²purgative *n* : a strong laxative : CATHARTIC

pur·ga·to·ry \'pər-gə-ˌtòr-ē\ *n, pl* **-ries** **1** : an intermediate state after death for expiatory purification **2** : a place or state of temporary punishment — **pur·ga·tor·i·al** \ˌpər-gə-'tòr-ē-əl\ *adj*

¹purge \'pərj\ *vb* **purged**; **purg·ing** **1** : to cleanse or purify esp. from sin **2** : to have or cause strong and usu. repeated emptying of the bowels **3** : to get rid of ⟨the leaders had been *purged*⟩

²purge *n* **1** : something that purges; *esp* : PURGATIVE **2** : an act or result of purging; *esp* : a ridding of persons regarded as treacherous or disloyal

pu·ri·fy \\'pyùr-ə-ˌfī\\ *vb* **-fied; -fy·ing** ♦ : to make or become pure — **pu·ri·fi·ca·tion** \\ˌpyùr-ə-fə-'kā-shən\\ *n* — **pu·ri·fi·ca·to·ry** \\pyù-'ri-fi-kə-ˌtōr-ē\\ *adj* — **pu·ri·fi·er** *n*

   ♦ sanctify; *also* amend, improve, refine; heal, regenerate, restore; elevate, ennoble, uplift; absolve, acquit, clear, exonerate, vindicate ♦ clarify, clear, distill, filter — more at CLARIFY

Pu·rim \\'pùr-(ˌ)im\\ *n* : a Jewish holiday celebrated in February or March in commemoration of the deliverance of the Jews from the massacre plotted by Haman

pu·rine \\'pyùr-ˌēn\\ *n* : any of a group of bases including several (as adenine or guanine) that are constituents of DNA or RNA

pur·ism \\'pyùr-ˌi-zəm\\ *n* : rigid adherence to or insistence on purity or nicety esp. in use of words — **pur·ist** \\-ist\\ *n* — **pu·ris·tic** \\pyù-'ris-tik\\ *adj*

pu·ri·tan \\'pyùr-ət-ᵊn\\ *n* **1** *cap* : a member of a 16th and 17th century Protestant group in England and New England opposing the ceremonies and government of the Church of England **2** : one who practices or preaches a stricter or professedly purer moral code than that which prevails

pu·ri·tan·i·cal \\ˌpyùr-ə-'ta-ni-kəl\\ *adj* **1** ♦ : of, relating to, or characterized by a rigid morality **2** : of or relating to puritans, the Puritans, or puritanism — **pu·ri·tan·i·cal·ly** *adv*

   ♦ prim, prudish, straitlaced — more at STRAITLACED

pu·ri·ty \\'pyùr-ə-tē\\ *n* ♦ : the quality or state of being pure

   ♦ chastity, modesty — more at CHASTITY

¹purl \\'pərl\\ *vb* : to knit in purl stitch

²purl *n* : a stitch in knitting

³purl *n* : a gentle murmur or movement (as of purling water)

⁴purl *vb* **1** : EDDY, SWIRL **2** : to make a soft murmuring sound

pur·lieu \\'pər-lü, 'pərl-yü\\ *n* **1** : an outlying district : SUBURB **2** *pl* : the districts around a city : ENVIRONS

pur·loin \\(ˌ)pər-'lȯin, 'pər-ˌlȯin\\ *vb* ♦ : to take or make use of wrongfully and often by a breach of trust : STEAL

   ♦ appropriate, filch, hook, misappropriate, nip, pilfer, pocket, snitch, steal, swipe, thieve — more at STEAL

¹pur·ple \\'pər-pəl\\ *adj* **pur·pler; pur·plest 1** : of the color purple **2** : highly rhetorical ⟨a ~ passage⟩ **3** : PROFANE ⟨~ language⟩ — **pur·plish** *adj*

²purple *n* **1** : a bluish red color **2** : a purple robe emblematic esp. of regal rank or authority

¹pur·port \\'pər-ˌpōrt\\ *n* [ME, fr. AF, content, tenor, fr. *purporter* to carry, mean, purport, fr. *pur-* thoroughly + *porter* to carry] ♦ : meaning conveyed or implied; *also* : GIST ⟨the ~ of the letter⟩

   ♦ denotation, drift, gist, import, intent, meaning, sense, significance, signification — more at MEANING

²pur·port \\(ˌ)pər-'pōrt\\ *vb* : to convey or profess outwardly as the meaning or intention : CLAIM ⟨~s to be objective⟩ — **pur·port·ed·ly** \\-'pōr-təd-lē\\ *adv*

¹pur·pose \\'pər-pəs\\ *n* **1** ♦ : something set up as an object or end to be attained **2** : RESOLUTION, DETERMINATION — **pur·pose·less** *adj*

   ♦ aim, ambition, aspiration, design, dream, end, goal, intent, mark, meaning, object, objective, plan, pretension, thing — more at GOAL ♦ capacity, function, job, part, place, position, role, task, work — more at ROLE

²purpose *vb* **pur·posed; pur·pos·ing** : to propose as an aim to oneself

pur·pose·ful \\'pər-pəs-fəl\\ *adj* **1** : having a purpose: as **a** : MEANINGFUL ⟨~ activities⟩ **b** ♦ : done by intention or design : INTENTIONAL ⟨~ ambiguity⟩ **2** ♦ : full of determination

   ♦ [1b] deliberate, freewill, intentional, voluntary, willful, willing — more at DELIBERATE ♦ [2] bound, decisive, determined, firm, intent, resolute, set, single-minded — more at DETERMINED

pur·pose·ful·ly \\-fə-lē\\ *adv* : in a purposeful manner

pur·pose·ly *adv* ♦ : with a deliberate or express purpose

   ♦ consciously, deliberately, intentionally, knowingly, willfully — more at INTENTIONALLY

purr \\'pər\\ *n* ♦ : a low murmur typical of a contented cat — **purr** *vb*

   ♦ buzz, drone, hum, whir, whiz, zoom — more at HUM

¹purse \\'pərs\\ *n* **1** ♦ : a receptacle (as a pouch) to carry money and often other small objects **2** : RESOURCES **3** : a sum of money offered as a prize or present

   ♦ bag, handbag, pocketbook; *also* billfold, wallet; compact, vanity; poke, pouch, sack; backpack, haversack, knapsack

²purse *vb* **pursed; purs·ing** : PUCKER

purs·er \\'pər-sər\\ *n* : an official on a ship who keeps accounts and attends to the comfort of passengers

purs·lane \\'pər-slən, -ˌslān\\ *n* : a fleshy-leaved weedy trailing plant with tiny yellow flowers that is sometimes used in salads

pur·su·ance \\pər-'sü-əns\\ *n* ♦ : the act of carrying out or into effect

   ♦ accomplishment, achievement, commission, discharge, enactment, execution, fulfillment, implementation, performance, perpetration — more at COMMISSION

pur·su·ant to \\-'sü-ənt-\\ *prep* : in carrying out : ACCORDING TO

pur·sue \\pər-'sü\\ *vb* **pur·sued; pur·su·ing 1** ♦ : to follow in order to overtake or overcome **2** : to seek to accomplish ⟨~ a goal⟩ **3** : to proceed along ⟨~ a course⟩ **4** : to engage in ⟨~ a career⟩ — **pur·su·er** *n*

   ♦ chase, dog, follow, hound, shadow, tag, tail, trace, track, trail — more at FOLLOW

pur·suit \\pər-'süt\\ *n* **1** ♦ : the act of pursuing **2** : OCCUPATION, BUSINESS

   ♦ chase, following, tracing; *also* path, track, trail; search, seeking

pu·ru·lent \\'pyùr-ə-lənt, -yə-\\ *adj* : containing or accompanied by pus ⟨a ~ discharge⟩ — **pu·ru·lence** \\-ləns\\ *n*

pur·vey \\(ˌ)pər-'vā\\ *vb* **pur·veyed; pur·vey·ing** : to supply (as provisions) usu. as a business — **pur·vey·ance** \\-əns\\ *n* — **pur·vey·or** \\-ər\\ *n*

pur·view \\'pər-ˌvyü\\ *n* **1** : the range or limit esp. of authority, responsibility, or intention **2** : range of vision, understanding, or cognizance

pus \\'pəs\\ *n* : thick yellowish white fluid matter (as in a boil) formed at a place of inflammation and infection (as an abscess) and containing germs, white blood cells, and tissue debris

¹push \\'pùsh\\ *vb* [ME *possen, pusshen,* prob. fr. OF *pousser* to exert pressure, fr. L *pulsare,* fr. *pellere* to drive, strike] **1** ♦ : to press against with force in order to drive or impel **2** ♦ : to thrust forward, downward, or outward **3** : to urge on : press forward **4** : to cause to increase ⟨~ prices to record levels⟩ **5** : to urge or press the advancement, adoption, or practice of; *esp* : to make aggressive efforts to sell **6** : to engage in the illicit sale of narcotics

   ♦ [1, 2] drive, propel, shove, thrust; *also* impel; move; bear (down), compress, depress, jam, pressure, squash, squeeze, weigh (upon); bulldoze, compel, force, lean (on *or* against), muscle, ram ♦ [2] bulldoze, elbow, muscle, press — more at PRESS

²push *n* **1** : a vigorous effort : DRIVE **2** : an act of pushing : SHOVE **3** : vigorous enterprise : ENERGY

push–button *adj* **1** : operated or done by means of push buttons **2** : using or dependent on complex and more or less automatic mechanisms ⟨~ warfare⟩

push button *n* : a small button or knob that when pushed operates something esp. by closing an electric circuit

push·cart \\'pùsh-ˌkärt\\ *n* : a cart or barrow pushed by hand

push·er \\'pù-shər\\ *n* : one that pushes; *esp* : one that pushes illegal drugs

push·over \\-ˌō-vər\\ *n* **1** : an opponent easy to defeat **2** : SUCKER **3** ♦ : something easily accomplished

♦ breeze, child's play, cinch, picnic, snap — more at CINCH

push-up \-,əp\ *n* : a conditioning exercise performed in a prone position by raising and lowering the body with the straightening and bending of the arms while keeping the back straight and supporting the body on the hands and toes

pushy \'pu̇-shē\ *adj* **push·i·er; -est** : aggressive often to an objectionable degree

pu·sil·lan·i·mous \,pyü-sə-'la-nə-məs\ *adj* [LL *pusillanimis*, fr. L *pusillus* very small (dim. of *pusus* boy) + *animus* spirit] ♦ : contemptibly timid : COWARDLY — **pu·sil·la·nim·i·ty** \,pyü-sə-lə-'ni-mə-tē\ *n*

♦ chicken, cowardly, craven, dastardly, recreant, spineless, yellow — more at COWARDLY

¹puss \'pu̇s\ *n* ♦ : a domestic cat

♦ cat, feline, kitty — more at CAT

²puss *n, slang* : FACE

¹pussy \'pu̇-sē\ *n, pl* **puss·ies** : PUSS

²pus·sy \'pə-sē\ *adj* **pus·si·er; -est** : full of or resembling pus

pussy·cat \'pu̇-sē-,kat\ *n* : CAT

pussy·foot \-,fu̇t\ *vb* **1** ♦ : to tread or move warily or stealthily **2** ♦ : to refrain from committing oneself

♦ [1] lurk, skulk, slide, slink, slip, snake, sneak, steal — more at SNEAK ♦ [2] equivocate, fudge, hedge — more at EQUIVOCATE

pussy willow \'pu̇-sē-\ *n* : a willow having large silky catkins

pus·tule \'pəs-chül\ *n* : a pus-filled pimple

put \'pu̇t\ *vb* **put; put·ting** **1** ♦ : to bring into a specified position : PLACE ⟨~ the book on the table⟩ **2** : SEND, THRUST **3** : to throw with an upward pushing motion ⟨~ the shot⟩ **4** : to bring into a specified state ⟨~ the plan into effect⟩ **5** : SUBJECT ⟨~ traitors to death⟩ **6** ♦ : to establish or apply by authority : IMPOSE **7** : to set before one for decision ⟨~ the question⟩ **8** : to represent in words : EXPRESS **9** : TRANSLATE, ADAPT **10** : APPLY, ASSIGN ⟨~ them to work⟩ **11** ♦ : to give as an estimate ⟨~ the number at 20⟩ **12** : ATTACH, ATTRIBUTE ⟨~ a high value on it⟩ **13** : to take a specified course ⟨the ship ~ out to sea⟩

♦ [1] deposit, dispose, fix, lay, place, position, set, set up, stick — more at PLACE ♦ [6] assess, charge, exact, fine, impose, lay, levy — more at IMPOSE ♦ [8] articulate, clothe, couch, express, formulate, phrase, say, state, word — more at PHRASE ♦ [11] calculate, call, conjecture, estimate, figure, gauge, guess, judge, make, place, reckon, suppose — more at ESTIMATE

pu·ta·tive \'pyü-tə-tiv\ *adj* **1** : commonly accepted ⟨a ~ expert⟩ **2** : assumed to exist or to have existed

put by *vb* ♦ : to lay aside

♦ cache, hoard, lay away, lay up, salt away, stash, stockpile, store — more at HOARD

put–down \'pu̇t-,dau̇n\ *n* : an act or instance of putting down; *esp* : a humiliating remark

♦ affront, barb, dart, dig, indignity, insult, name, offense, outrage, sarcasm, slight, slur, wound — more at INSULT ♦ deprecation, depreciation, detraction, disparagement — more at DEPRECIATION

put down *vb* **1** ♦ : to bring to an end **2** ♦ : to speak slightingly of : DISPARAGE, BELITTLE **3 a** ♦ : to put in writing **b** ♦ : to enter in a list

♦ [1] clamp down, crack down, crush, quash, quell, repress, silence, snuff, squash, squelch, subdue, suppress — more at QUELL ♦ [2] belittle, cry down, decry, deprecate, depreciate, diminish, discount, disparage, minimize, write off — more at DECRY ♦ [3a] jot, log, mark, note, record, register, set down — more at RECORD ♦ [3b] catalog, enroll, enter, index, inscribe, list, record, register, schedule, slate — more at LIST

put in *vb* **1** : to come in with : INTERPOSE ⟨*put in* a good word for me⟩ **2** : to spend time at some occupation or

job ⟨*put in* eight hours at the office⟩ **3** : to put or set in the ground for growth : PLANT

put off *vb* **1** ♦ : to hold back to a later time : POSTPONE, DELAY **2** : to rid oneself of : TAKE OFF

♦ defer, delay, hold up, postpone, shelve — more at POSTPONE

¹put–on \'pu̇t-,ȯn, -,än\ *adj* : professed or avowed but not genuine : ASSUMED ⟨a ~ accent⟩

²put–on *n* **1** ♦ : a deliberate act of misleading someone **2** : PARODY, SPOOF

♦ act, airs, facade, front, guise, masquerade, pose, pretense, semblance, show — more at MASQUERADE

put on *vb* **1 a** ♦ : to dress oneself in **b** ♦ : to give a false appearance of : FEIGN **2** ♦ : to enlarge beyond bounds or the truth

♦ [1a] don, slip, throw; *also* apparel, array, attire, bedeck, bedizen, caparison, clothe, doll up, dress, garb, rig, robe, suit, trick, uniform; overdress **Ant** doff, remove, take off ♦ [1b] affect, assume, counterfeit, fake, feign, pretend, profess, sham, simulate — more at FEIGN ♦ [2] exaggerate, overdo, overstate — more at OVERSTATE

put out *vb* **1** ♦ : to cause to cease burning : EXTINGUISH **2** : to disturb or irritate esp. by repeated acts : ANNOY; *also* : INCONVENIENCE **3** : to cause to be out (as in baseball) **4** ♦ : to bring to bear esp. with sustained effort or lasting effect : EXERT

♦ [1] douse, extinguish, quench, snuff — more at EXTINGUISH ♦ [4] apply, exercise, exert, wield — more at EXERT

pu·tre·fac·tion \,pyü-trə-'fak-shən\ *n* ♦ : the decomposition of organic matter — **pu·tre·fac·tive** \-tiv\ *adj*

♦ breakdown, corruption, decay, decomposition, rot, spoilage — more at CORRUPTION

pu·tre·fy \'pyü-trə-,fī\ *vb* **-fied; -fy·ing** ♦ : to make or become putrid : ROT ⟨*putrefied* meat⟩

♦ break down, corrupt, decay, decompose, disintegrate, molder, rot, spoil — more at DECAY

pu·tres·cent \pyü-'tres-ᵊnt\ *adj* : becoming putrid : ROTTING ⟨~ carcasses⟩ — **pu·tres·cence** \-ᵊns\ *n*

pu·trid \'pyü-trəd\ *adj* **1** ♦ : being in a state of putrefaction : ROTTEN **2** : VILE, CORRUPT — **pu·trid·i·ty** \pyü-'tri-də-tē\ *n*

♦ bad, rotten — more at ROTTEN

putsch \'pu̇ch\ *n* [G] : a secretly plotted and suddenly executed attempt to overthrow a government

putt \'pət\ *n* : a golf stroke made on the green to cause the ball to roll into the hole — **putt** *vb*

put·ta·nes·ca \,pü-tä-'nes-kä\ *adj* : served with or being a pungent tomato sauce

¹put·ter \'pu̇-tər\ *n* : one that puts

²putt·er \'pə-tər\ *n* **1** : a golf club used in putting **2** : one that putts

³put·ter \'pə-tər\ *vb* **1** ♦ : to move or act aimlessly or idly **2** : TINKER

♦ *usu* **putter around** fiddle, fool, mess, monkey, play, potter, trifle

put·ty \'pə-tē\ *n, pl* **putties** [F *potée* potter's glaze, lit., potful, fr. OF, fr. *pot* pot] **1** : a doughlike cement used esp. to fasten glass in sashes **2** : one who is easily manipulated — **putty** *vb*

put up *vb* **1** : SHEATHE **2** : to prepare so as to preserve for later use **3** : to offer for public sale ⟨*put* the house *up* for auction⟩ **4** ♦ : to give food and shelter to : ACCOMMODATE **5** ♦ : to form by the fitting together of materials or parts : BUILD **6** : to engage in ⟨*put up* a struggle⟩ **7** : CONTRIBUTE, PAY — **put up with** : TOLERATE **2**

♦ [3] deal, market, merchandise, retail, sell, vend — more at MARKET ♦ [4] accommodate, billet, chamber, domicile, harbor (*or* harbour), house, lodge, quarter, roof, shelter, take in — more at HOUSE ♦ [5] assemble, build, construct, erect, fabricate, make, make up, piece, raise, rear, set up — more at BUILD

¹**puz·zle** \'pə-zəl\ *vb* **puz·zled; puz·zling 1 ♦** : to bewilder mentally : PERPLEX **2 ♦** : to solve with difficulty or ingenuity ⟨∼ out a riddle⟩ **3** : to be in a quandary ⟨∼ over what to do⟩ **4** : to attempt a solution of a puzzle ⟨∼ over a person's words⟩ — **puz·zler** *n*

　♦ [1] addle, baffle, befog, befuddle, bemuse, bewilder, confound, confuse, disorient, muddle, muddy, mystify, perplex — more at CONFUSE ♦ *usu* **puzzle out** [2] answer, break, crack, dope, figure out, resolve, riddle, solve, unravel, work, work out — more at SOLVE

²**puzzle** *n* **1 ♦** : something that puzzles **2** : a question, problem, or contrivance designed for testing ingenuity

　♦ conundrum, enigma, mystery, mystification, puzzlement, riddle, secret — more at MYSTERY

puz·zle·ment \'pə-zəl-mənt\ *n* **1 ♦** : the state of being puzzled **2** : something that puzzles

　♦ bafflement, bewilderment, confusion, distraction, muddle, mystification, perplexity, whirl — more at CONFUSION

PVC *abbr* polyvinyl chloride

pvt *abbr* private

PW *abbr* prisoner of war

pwt *abbr* pennyweight

PX *abbr* post exchange

¹**pyg·my** *also* **pig·my** \'pig-mē\ *n, pl* **-mies** [ME *pigmei*, fr. L *pygmaeus* of a pygmy, dwarfish, fr. Gk *pygmaios*, fr. *pygmē* fist, measure of length] **1** *cap* : any of a small people of equatorial Africa **2** : an unusually small person : DWARF **3 ♦** : something very small of its kind

　♦ dwarf, midget, mite, peewee, runt — more at DWARF

²**pygmy** *adj* **1** : of or relating to the Pygmies or a pygmy **2 ♦** : very small

　♦ dwarf, dwarfish, fine, little, pocket, slight, small, undersized — more at SMALL

py·ja·mas \pə-'jä-məz\ *chiefly Can and Brit var of* PAJAMAS

py·lon \'pī-,län, -lən\ *n* **1** : a usu. massive gateway; *esp* : an Egyptian one flanked by flat-topped pyramids **2** : a tower that supports wires over a long span **3** : a post or tower marking the course in an airplane race

py·or·rhea \,pī-ə-'rē-ə\ *n* : an inflammation with pus of the sockets of the teeth

¹**pyr·a·mid** \'pir-ə-,mid\ *n* **1** : a massive structure with a square base and four triangular faces meeting at a point **2** : a geometrical solid having a polygon for its base and three or more triangles for its sides that meet at a point to form the top — **py·ra·mi·dal** \pə-'ra-məd-ᵊl, ,pir-ə-'mid-\ *adj*

²**pyramid** *vb* **1** : to build up in the form of a pyramid : heap up **2** : to increase rapidly on a broadening base

pyramid scheme *n* : a usu. illegal operation in which participants pay to join and profit from payments made by subsequent participants

pyre \'pī(-ə)r\ *n* : a combustible heap for burning a dead body as a funeral rite

py·re·thrum \pī-'rē-thrəm\ *n* : an insecticide made from the dried heads of any of several Old World chrysanthemums

py·rim·i·dine \pī-'ri-mə-,dēn\ *n* : any of a group of bases including several (as cytosine, thymine, or uracil) that are constituents of DNA or RNA

py·rite \'pī-,rīt\ *n* : a mineral containing sulfur and iron that is brass-yellow in color

py·rol·y·sis \pī-'rä-lə-səs\ *n* : chemical change caused by the action of heat

py·ro·ma·nia \,pī-rō-'mā-nē-ə\ *n* : an irresistible impulse to start fires — **py·ro·ma·ni·ac** \-nē-,ak\ *n*

py·ro·tech·nics \,pī-rə-'tek-niks\ *n pl* **1** : a display of fireworks **2** : a spectacular display (as of extreme virtuosity) ⟨musical ∼⟩ — **py·ro·tech·nic** \-nik\ *also* **py·ro·tech·ni·cal** \-ni-kəl\ *adj*

Pyr·rhic \'pir-ik\ *adj* : achieved at excessive cost ⟨a ∼ victory⟩; *also* : costly to the point of outweighing expected benefits

Py·thag·o·re·an theorem \pī-,tha-gə-'rē-ən-\ *n* : a theorem in geometry: the square of the length of the hypotenuse of a right triangle equals the sum of the squares of the lengths of the other two sides

py·thon \'pī-,thän, -thən\ *n* [L, monstrous serpent killed by the god Apollo, fr. Gk *Pythōn*] : a large snake (as a boa) that squeezes and suffocates its prey; *esp* : any of the large Old World snakes that include the largest snakes living at the present time

pyx \'piks\ *n* : a small case used to carry the Eucharist to the sick

¹**q** \'kyü\ *n, pl* **q's** *or* **qs** \'kyüz\ *often cap* : the 17th letter of the English alphabet

²**q** *abbr, often cap* **1** quart **2** quarto **3** queen **4** query **5** question

QB *abbr* quarterback

QED *abbr* [L *quod erat demonstrandum*] which was to be demonstrated

qi·vi·ut \'kē-vē-,üt\ *n* [Inuit] : the wool of the undercoat of the musk ox

Qld *abbr* Queensland

QM *abbr* quartermaster

QMC *abbr* quartermaster corps

QMG *abbr* quartermaster general

qq v *abbr* [L *quae vide*] which (*pl*) see

qr *abbr* quarter

Q rating *n* [*quotient*] : a scale measuring popularity based on dividing an assessment of familiarity or recognition by an assessment of favorable opinion; *also* : position on such a scale

qt *abbr* [*quotient*] **1** quantity **2** quart

q.t. \,kyü-'tē\ *n, often cap Q&T* : QUIET — usu. used in the phrase *on the q.t.*

qto *abbr* quarto

qty *abbr* quantity

qu *or* **ques** *abbr* question

¹**quack** \'kwak\ *vb* : to make the characteristic cry of a duck

²**quack** *n* : a sound made by quacking

³**quack** *n* **1 ♦** : one making usu. showy pretenses to knowledge or ability : CHARLATAN **2** : a pretender to medical skill — **quack** *adj* — **quack·ery** \'kwa-kə-rē\ *n* — **quack·ish** *adj*

　♦ charlatan, fake, fraud, hoaxer, humbug, mountebank, phony, pretender

¹**quad** \'kwäd\ *n* : QUADRANGLE

²**quad** *n* : QUADRUPLET

³**quad** *abbr* quadrant

quad·ran·gle \'kwä-,draŋ-gəl\ *n* **1** : QUADRILATERAL **2 ♦** : a 4-sided courtyard or enclosure — **quad·ran·gu·lar** \kwä-'draŋ-gyə-lər\ *adj*

　♦ close, court, courtyard, yard — more at COURT

quad·rant \'kwä-drənt\ *n* **1** : one quarter of a circle : an arc of 90° **2** : any of the four quarters into which something is divided by two lines intersecting each other at right angles

qua·drat·ic \kwä-'dra-tik\ *adj* : having or being a term in which the variable (as *x*) is squared but containing no term in which the variable is raised to a higher power than a square ⟨a ~ equation⟩ — **quadratic** *n*

qua·dren·ni·al \kwä-'dre-nē-əl\ *adj* **1** : consisting of or lasting for four years **2** : occurring every four years

qua·dren·ni·um \-nē-əm\ *n, pl* **-ni·ums** *or* **-nia** \-nē-ə\ : a period of four years

quad·ri·ceps \'kwä-drə-ˌseps\ *n* : a muscle of the front of the thigh that is divided into four parts

¹quad·ri·lat·er·al \ˌkwä-drə-'la-tə-rəl\ *n* : a polygon of four sides

²quadrilateral *adj* : having four sides

qua·drille \kwä-'dril, kə-\ *n* : a square dance made up of five or six figures in various rhythms

quad·ri·par·tite \ˌkwä-drə-'pär-ˌtīt\ *adj* **1** : consisting of four parts **2** : shared by four parties or persons

quad·ri·ple·gia \ˌkwä-drə-'plē-jə, -jē-ə\ *n* : paralysis of both arms and both legs — **quad·ri·ple·gic** \-jik\ *adj or n*

qua·driv·i·um \kwä-'dri-vē-əm\ *n* : the four liberal arts of arithmetic, music, geometry, and astronomy in a medieval university

quad·ru·ped \'kwä-drə-ˌped\ *n* : an animal having four feet — **qua·dru·pe·dal** \kwä-'drü-pəd-ᵊl, ˌkwä-drə-'ped-\ *adj*

¹qua·dru·ple \kwä-'drü-pəl, -'drə-; 'kwä-drə-\ *vb* **qua·dru·pled; qua·dru·pling** : to make or become four times as great or as many

²quadruple *adj* : FOURFOLD

qua·dru·plet \kwä-'drə-plət, -'drü-; 'kwä-drə-\ *n* **1** : one of four offspring born at one birth **2** : a group of four of a kind

¹qua·dru·pli·cate \kwä-'drü-pli-kət\ *adj* **1** : repeated four times **2** : FOURTH

²qua·dru·pli·cate \-plə-ˌkāt\ *vb* **-cat·ed; -cat·ing** **1** : QUADRUPLE **2** : to prepare in quadruplicate — **qua·dru·pli·ca·tion** \-ˌdrü-plə-'kā-shən\ *n*

³qua·dru·pli·cate \-'drü-pli-kət\ *n* **1** : four copies all alike ⟨typed in ~⟩ **2** : one of four like things

¹quaff \'kwäf, 'kwaf\ *vb* ♦ : to drink deeply or repeatedly

♦ drink, guzzle, imbibe, sup, swig, toss — more at DRINK

²quaff *n* ♦ : a drink quaffed

♦ draft, drag, drink, nip, shot, slug, snort, swallow, swig — more at DRINK

quag·mire \'kwag-ˌmī(-ə)r, 'kwäg-\ *n* **1** : soft miry land that yields under the foot **2** ♦ : a difficult or trying situation : PREDICAMENT

♦ corner, fix, hole, jam, morass, pickle, predicament, spot — more at PREDICAMENT

qua·hog \'kō-ˌhog, 'kwo-, 'kwō-, -ˌhäg\ *n* [modif. of Narragansett *poquaûhock*] : a round thick-shelled edible No. American clam

quai \'kā\ *n* : QUAY

¹quail \'kwāl\ *n, pl* **quail** *or* **quails** [ME *quaile*, fr. AF, fr. ML *quaccula*, of imit. origin] : any of numerous small short-winged plump game birds (as a bobwhite) related to the domestic chicken

²quail *vb* [ME, to grow feeble, fr. MD *quelen*] **1** ♦ : to lose heart : COWER **2** ♦ : to recoil in dread or terror

♦ [1, 2] blench, cower, cringe, flinch, recoil, shrink, wince — more at FLINCH

quaint \'kwānt\ *adj* **1** ♦ : unusual or different in character or appearance **2** ♦ : pleasingly old-fashioned or unfamiliar — **quaint·ly** *adv* — **quaint·ness** *n*

♦ [1] bizarre, curious, odd, outré, peculiar, queer, quirky, remarkable, screwy, strange ♦ [2] antique, old-fashioned, old-time — more at OLD-FASHIONED

¹quake \'kwāk\ *vb* **quaked; quak·ing** **1** ♦ : to shake usu. from shock or instability **2** ♦ : to tremble usu. from cold or fear

♦ [1, 2] agitate, convulse, jolt, jounce, quiver, shake, shudder, vibrate, wobble — more at SHAKE

²quake *n* : a shaking or trembling; *esp* : EARTHQUAKE

Quak·er \'kwā-kər\ *n* : FRIEND 5

qual *abbr* quality

qual·i·fi·ca·tion \ˌkwä-lə-fə-'kā-shən\ *n* **1** : LIMITATION, MODIFICATION **2** ♦ : a special skill that fits a person for some work or position **3** ♦ : a condition or standard that must be complied with

♦ [2] capability, command, credentials, expertise, mastery, proficiency; *also* ability, capacity, competence, competency, facility, faculty; flair, genius, talent; forte, specialty; fitness, suitability, suitableness; makings, potentiality ♦ [3] condition, provision, proviso, reservation, stipulation — more at CONDITION

qual·i·fied \'kwä-lə-ˌfīd\ *adj* **1** ♦ : fitted for a given purpose or job **2** : limited in some way

♦ able, capable, competent, fit, good, suitable — more at COMPETENT

qual·i·fi·er \'kwä-lə-ˌfī(-ə)r\ *n* **1** : one that satisfies requirements **2** : a word or word group that limits the meaning of another word or word group

qual·i·fy \'kwä-lə-ˌfī\ *vb* **-fied; -fy·ing** **1** : to reduce from a general to a particular form : MODIFY **2** : to make less harsh **3** : to limit the meaning of (as a noun) **4** ♦ : to fit by skill or training for some purpose **5** ♦ : to give or have a legal right to do something **6** : to demonstrate the necessary ability ⟨~ for the finals⟩

♦ [4] equip, fit, prepare, ready, season; *also* accustom, adapt, adjust, condition, groom, habituate, shape, tailor, train; entitle; empower, enable ♦ [5] accredit, authorize, certify, commission, empower, enable, invest, license — more at AUTHORIZE

qual·i·ta·tive \'kwä-lə-ˌtā-tiv\ *adj* : of, relating to, or involving quality — **qual·i·ta·tive·ly** *adv*

¹qual·i·ty \'kwä-lə-tē\ *n, pl* **-ties** **1** : peculiar and essential character : NATURE **2** ♦ : degree of excellence **3** ♦ : high social status **4** ♦ : a distinguishing attribute

♦ [2] caliber (*or* calibre), class, grade, rate; *also* hallmark, standard; mark; footing, standing ♦ [3] class, rank, standing — more at RANK ♦ [4] attribute, character, characteristic, feature, mark, peculiarity, point, property, trait — more at CHARACTERISTIC

²quality *adj* : being of high quality

qualm \'kwäm, 'kwälm\ *n* **1** : a sudden attack (as of nausea) **2** ♦ : a sudden feeling of doubt, fear, or uneasiness esp. in not following one's conscience or better judgment

♦ compunction, doubt, misgiving, scruple, uneasiness; *also* conscience; distrust, mistrust, suspicion; reluctance; demur, objection, protest, guilt, regret, remorse, self-reproach, shame; contrition, penitence, repentance

qualm·ish \'kwä-mish, 'kwäl-\ *adj* **1** : feeling qualms : NAUSEATED **2** : overly scrupulous : SQUEAMISH **3** : of, relating to, or producing qualms

quan·da·ry \'kwän-drē\ *n, pl* **-ries** : a state of perplexity or doubt

quan·ti·fy \'kwän-tə-ˌfī\ *vb* **-fied; -fy·ing** : to determine, express, or measure the quantity of — **quan·ti·fi·able** \ˌkwän-tə-'fī-ə-bəl\ *adj*

quan·ti·ta·tive \'kwän-tə-ˌtā-tiv\ *adj* : of, relating to, or involving quantity — **quan·ti·ta·tive·ly** *adv*

quan·ti·ty \'kwän-tə-tē\ *n, pl* **-ties** **1** : a determinate or estimated amount : AMOUNT, NUMBER **2** ♦ : a considerable amount ⟨buys food in ~⟩

♦ abundance, deal, gobs, heap, loads, lot, pile, plenty, scads — more at LOT

quan·tize \'kwän-ˌtīz\ *vb* **quan·tized; quan·tiz·ing** : to subdivide (as energy) into small units

¹quan·tum \'kwän-təm\ *n, pl* **quan·ta** \-tə\ [L, neut. of *quantus* how much] **1** : QUANTITY, AMOUNT **2** : an elemental unit of energy

²**quantum** *adj* **1** : LARGE, SIGNIFICANT **2** : relating to or employing the principles of quantum mechanics

quantum mechanics *n sing or pl* : a theory of matter based on the concept of possession of wave properties by elementary particles — **quantum mechanical** *adj* — **quantum mechanically** *adv*

quantum theory *n* : a theory in physics based on the idea that radiant energy (as light) is composed of small separate packets of energy

quar *abbr* quarterly

quar·an·tine \'kwȯr-ən-ˌtēn\ *n* [modif. of It *quarantena*, lit., period of forty days, fr. *quaranta* forty, fr. L *quadraginta*] **1** : a period during which a ship suspected of carrying contagious disease is forbidden contact with the shore **2** : a restraint on the movements of persons or goods to prevent the spread of pests or disease **3** : a place or period of quarantine **4** : a state of enforced isolation — **quarantine** *vb*

quark \'kwȯrk, 'kwärk\ *n* : a hypothetical elementary particle that carries a fractional charge and is held to be a constituent of heavier particles (as protons and neutrons)

¹**quar·rel** \'kwȯr-əl\ *n* **1** : a ground of dispute **2** ♦ : a verbal clash

♦ altercation, argument, bicker, brawl, disagreement, dispute, fight, hassle, misunderstanding, row, scrap, spat, squabble, wrangle — more at ARGUMENT

²**quarrel** *vb* **-reled** *or* **-relled; -rel·ing** *or* **-rel·ling** **1** : to find fault **2** ♦ : to dispute angrily : WRANGLE

♦ argue, bicker, brawl, dispute, fall out, fight, hassle, row, scrap, spat, squabble, wrangle — more at ARGUE

quar·rel·some \-səm\ *adj* ♦ : apt or disposed to quarrel in an often petty manner

♦ aggressive, argumentative, bellicose, belligerent, combative, contentious, discordant, disputatious, pugnacious, scrappy, truculent — more at BELLIGERENT

¹**quar·ry** \'kwȯr-ē\ *n, pl* **quarries** [ME *querre* entrails of game given to the hounds, fr. AF *cureie, quereie*, fr. *quir, cuir* skin, hide (on which the entrails were placed), fr. L *corium*] **1** : game hunted with hawks **2** : PREY

²**quarry** *n, pl* **quarries** [ME *quarey*, alter. of *quarrere*, fr. AF, fr. VL **quadraria*, fr. LL *quadrus* hewn (lit., squared) stone, fr. L *quadrum* square] : an open excavation usu. for obtaining building stone or limestone — **quarry** *vb*

quart \'kwȯrt\ *n* **1** : a unit of liquid capacity equal to ¼ gallon **2** : a unit of dry capacity equal to 1/32 bushel

¹**quar·ter** \'kwȯr-tər\ *n* **1** : one of four equal parts **2** : a fourth of a dollar; *also* : a coin of this value **3** ♦ : a district of a city **4** *pl* ♦ : living accommodations ⟨moved into new ∼*s*⟩ **5** ♦ : merciful consideration of an opponent : MERCY ⟨gave no ∼⟩ **6** : a fourth part of the moon's period **7** ♦ : an assigned station or post

♦ [3] district, neighborhood (*or* neighbourhood), section — more at DISTRICT ♦ **quarters** [4] abode, domicile, dwelling, home, house, lodging, place, residence — more at HOME ♦ [5] charity, clemency, leniency, mercy — more at MERCY ♦ [7] position, post, station — more at STATION

²**quarter** *vb* **1** : to divide into four equal parts **2** ♦ : to provide with shelter

♦ accommodate, billet, chamber, domicile, harbor (*or* harbour), house, lodge, put up, roof, shelter, take in — more at HOUSE

¹**quar·ter·back** \-ˌbak\ *n* : a football player who calls the signals and directs the offensive play for the team

²**quarterback** *vb* **1** : to direct the offensive play of a football team **2** : LEAD, BOSS

quar·ter·deck \-ˌdek\ *n* : the stern area of a ship's upper deck

quarter horse *n* : any of a breed of compact muscular saddle horses characterized by great endurance and by high speed for short distances

¹**quar·ter·ly** \'kwȯr-tər-lē\ *adv* : at 3-month intervals

²**quarterly** *adj* : occurring, issued, or payable at 3-month intervals

³**quarterly** *n, pl* **-lies** : a periodical published four times a year

quar·ter·mas·ter \-ˌmas-tər\ *n* **1** : a petty officer who attends to a ship's helm, binnacle, and signals **2** : an army officer who provides clothing and subsistence for troops

quar·ter·staff \-ˌstaf\ *n, pl* **-staves** \-ˌstavz, -ˌstāvz\ : a long stout staff formerly used as a weapon

quar·tet *also* **quar·tette** \kwȯr-'tet\ *n* **1** : a musical composition for four instruments or voices **2** : a group of four and esp. of four musicians

quar·to \'kwȯr-tō\ *n, pl* **quartos** **1** : the size of a piece of paper cut four from a sheet **2** : a book printed on quarto pages

quartz \'kwȯrts\ *n* : a common often transparent crystalline mineral that is a form of silica

quartz·ite \'kwȯrt-ˌsīt\ *n* : a compact granular rock composed of quartz and derived from sandstone

qua·sar \'kwā-ˌzär, -ˌsär\ *n* : any of a class of extremely distant starlike celestial objects

¹**quash** \'kwäsh, 'kwȯsh\ *vb* ♦ : to suppress or extinguish summarily and completely : QUELL

♦ clamp down, crack down, crush, put down, quell, repress, silence, snuff, squash, squelch, subdue, suppress — more at QUELL

²**quash** *vb* ♦ : to set aside by judicial action

♦ abolish, abrogate, annul, cancel, dissolve, invalidate, negate, nullify, repeal, rescind, void — more at ABOLISH

qua·si \'kwā-ˌzī, -ˌsī; 'kwä-zē, -sē\ *adj* : being in some sense or degree ⟨a ∼ corporation⟩

quasi- *comb form* [L, as if, as it were, approximately, fr. *quam* as + *si* if] : in some sense or degree ⟨*quasi*-historical⟩

qua·si–gov·ern·men·tal \-gə-vərn-'men-t³l\ *adj* : supported by the government but managed privately

Qua·ter·na·ry \'kwä-tər-ˌner-ē, kwə-'tər-nə-rē\ *adj* : of, relating to, or being the geologic period from the end of the Tertiary to the present — **Quaternary** *n*

qua·train \'kwä-ˌtrān\ *n* : a unit of four lines of verse

qua·tre·foil \'ka-tər-ˌfȯil, 'ka-trə-\ *n* : a stylized figure often of a flower with four petals

qua·ver \'kwā-vər\ *vb* **1** : TREMBLE, SHAKE ⟨∼ed with fear⟩ **2** : TRILL **3** : to speak in tremulous tones — **quaver** *n*

quay \'kē, 'kwā, 'kā\ *n* ♦ : a structure built parallel to the bank of a waterway for use as a landing place : WHARF

♦ dock, float, jetty, landing, levee, pier, wharf — more at DOCK

Que *abbr* Quebec

quean \'kwēn\ *n* : PROSTITUTE

quea·si·ness \'kwē-zē-nəs\ *n* ♦ : the quality or state of being queasy

♦ nausea, sickness, squeamishness — more at NAUSEA

quea·sy \'kwē-zē\ *adj* **quea·si·er; -est** ♦ : suffering from nausea : NAUSEATED — **quea·si·ly** \-zə-lē\ *adv*

♦ ill, nauseous, queer, sick, squeamish — more at NAUSEOUS

Que·chua \'ke-chə-wə, 'kech-wə\ *n* [ME *quene*, fr. OE *cwēn* woman, wife, queen] : a family of languages spoken in Peru and adjacent countries of the So. American Andes

queen \'kwēn\ *n* **1** : the wife or widow of a king **2** : a female monarch **3** ♦ : a woman notable in rank, power, or attractiveness **4** : the most powerful piece in the game of chess **5** : a playing card bearing the figure of a queen **6** : a fertile female of a social insect (as a bee)

♦ beauty, enchantress, fox, goddess, knockout — more at BEAUTY

Queen Anne's lace \-'anz-\ *n* : a widely naturalized Eurasian herb from which the cultivated carrot originated

queen consort *n, pl* **queens consort** : the wife of a reigning king

queen·ly *adj* ♦ : of, relating to, suggestive of, or character-istic of a monarch or monarchy

♦ monarchical, regal, royal — more at MONARCHICAL

queen mother *n* : a dowager queen who is mother of the reigning sovereign

queen–size *adj* : having dimensions of approximately 60 inches by 80 inches ⟨∼ bed⟩; *also* : of a size that fits a queen-size bed

¹**queer** \'kwir\ *adj* **1** ♦ : differing from the usual or normal : PECULIAR, STRANGE **2** : COUNTERFEIT **3** ♦ : not quite well **4** *sometimes offensive* : HOMOSEXUAL; *also*, *some-times offensive* : of, relating to, or used by homosexuals — **queer·ly** *adv* — **queer·ness** *n*

♦ [1] curious, extraordinary, funny, odd, peculiar, rare, strange, unaccustomed, uncommon, unique, unusual, weird — more at UNUSUAL ♦ [3] ill, nauseous, queasy, sick, squeamish — more at NAUSEOUS

²**queer** *vb* : to spoil the effect of : DISRUPT ⟨∼ed our plans⟩
³**queer** *n* **1** *sometimes offensive* : a person who is gay, les-bian, bisexual, pansexual, or otherwise not heterosexual **2** *sometimes offensive* : a person who is not cisgender

queer theory *n* : an approach to literary and cultural study that rejects traditional categories of gender and sexuality

quell \'kwel\ *vb* **1** ♦ : to put an end to by force ⟨∼ a riot⟩ **2** ♦ : to cause to be quiet

♦ [1] clamp down, crack down, crush, put down, quash, repress, silence, snuff, squash, squelch, sub-due, suppress; *also* douse, extinguish, put out, quench; smother, stifle, strangle; annihilate, destroy, smash; exterminate, obliterate, wipe out; conquer, overcome, overwhelm, subjugate, vanquish ♦ [2] hush, mute, set-tle, silence, still — more at SILENCE

quench \'kwench\ *vb* **1** ♦ : to put out the light or fire of : PUT OUT, EXTINGUISH **2** : SUBDUE **3** ♦ : to bring (something immaterial) to an end typically by satisfy-ing, damping, cooling, or decreasing : SATISFY ⟨∼ed his thirst⟩ — **quench·able** *adj* — **quench·less** *adj*

♦ [1] douse, extinguish, put out, snuff — more at EX-TINGUISH ♦ [3] assuage, sate, satiate, satisfy

quench·er *n* ♦ : a satisfying drink

♦ beverage, drink, libation — more at DRINK

quer·u·lous \'kwer-ə-ləs, -yə-\ *adj* **1** ♦ : constantly com-plaining **2** : FRETFUL, WHINING — **quer·u·lous·ly** *adv* — **quer·u·lous·ness** *n*

♦ crabby, cranky, fussy, grouchy, grumpy, peevish, petulant — more at FUSSY

¹**que·ry** \'kwir-ē, 'kwer-\ *n, pl* **queries** ♦ : the action or an instance of asking : QUESTION

♦ call, inquiry, question, request — more at QUESTION

²**query** *vb* **1** ♦ : to ask questions about esp. in order to re-solve a doubt **2** ♦ : to ask questions of esp. with a desire for authoritative information

♦ [1] challenge, contest, dispute, question — more at CHALLENGE ♦ [2] ask, examine, grill, inquire of, inter-rogate, pump, question, quiz — more at ASK

que·sa·dil·la \ˌkā-sə-'dē-ə\ *n* : a tortilla filled with a savory mixture, folded, and usu. fried

¹**quest** \'kwest\ *n* : SEARCH
²**quest** *vb* **1** ♦ : to search for **2** ♦ : to ask for

♦ [1] cast about, forage, hunt, pursue, search (for *or* out), seek — more at SEEK ♦ [2] ask, call, plead, re-quest, seek, solicit, sue

¹**ques·tion** \'kwes-chən\ *n* **1** : an interrogative expression : QUERY **2** : a subject for debate; *also* : a proposition to be voted on **3** ♦ : an act or instance of asking : INQUIRY **4** ♦ : a subject or aspect in dispute or open for discussion **5** ♦ : a reason or argument presented in opposition : a feeling or expression of disapproval

♦ [3] call, inquiry, query, request; *also* questionnaire, survey; inquisition, interrogating, interrogation, ques-tioning ♦ [4] content, matter, motif, motive, subject,

theme, topic — more at MATTER ♦ [5] challenge, com-plaint, demur, expostulation, fuss, kick, objection, pro-test, remonstrance — more at OBJECTION

²**question** *vb* **1** ♦ : to ask questions **2** ♦ : to engage in argument : DISPUTE **3** ♦ : to subject to analysis **4** ♦ : to lack confidence in

♦ [1] ask, examine, grill, inquire of, interrogate, pump, query, quiz — more at ASK ♦ [2] challenge, contest, dispute, query — more at CHALLENGE ♦ [3] chew over, cogitate, consider, contemplate, debate, deliber-ate, entertain, meditate, mull, ponder, ruminate, study, think, weigh — more at PONDER ♦ [4] distrust, doubt, mistrust, suspect — more at DISTRUST

ques·tion·able \'kwes-chə-nə-bəl\ *adj* **1** ♦ : not certain or exact : DOUBTFUL **2** ♦ : not believed to be true, sound, or moral — **ques·tion·ably** \-blē\ *adv*

♦ [1] arguable, debatable, disputable, doubtful, dubious, equivocal, fishy, problematic, shady, shaky, suspect, sus-picious — more at DOUBTFUL ♦ [2] doubtful, dubious, flimsy, improbable, unlikely — more at IMPROBABLE

ques·tion·er *n* ♦ : one that questions

♦ disbeliever, doubter, skeptic, unbeliever — more at SKEPTIC

question mark *n* : a punctuation mark ? used esp. at the end of a sentence to indicate a direct question

ques·tion·naire \ˌkwes-chə-'nar\ *n* : a set of questions for obtaining information

quet·zal \ket-'säl, -'sal\ *n, pl* **quetzals** *or* **quet·za·les** \-'sä-läs, -'sa-\ : a Central American bird with brilliant plumage

¹**queue** \'kyü\ *n* [F, lit., tail, fr. OF *cue, coe*, fr. L *cauda, coda*] **1** : a braid of hair usu. worn hanging at the back of the head **2** ♦ : a waiting line (as of persons)

♦ column, cue, file, line, range, string, train — more at LINE

²**queue** *vb* **queued; queu·ing** *or* **queue·ing** : to line up in a queue

¹**quib·ble** \'kwi-bəl\ *n* **1** : an evasion of or shifting from the point at issue **2** : a minor objection or criticism — **quib·bler** *n*

²**quibble** *vb* ♦ : to criticize or object to something on trivial grounds

♦ carp, cavil, fuss; *also* criticize, fault; beef, bellyache, complain, crab, croak, gripe, grouse, growl, grumble, moan, squawk, wail, whine, yammer; murmur, mutter

¹**quick** \'kwik\ *adj* **1** : LIVING **2** ♦ : acting or capable of acting with speed ⟨∼ steps⟩ **3** ♦ : prompt to understand, think, or perceive : ALERT **4** : easily aroused ⟨a ∼ temper⟩ **5** : turning or bending sharply ⟨a ∼ turn in the road⟩

♦ [2] alert, expeditious, prompt, ready, willing; *also* re-ceptive, responsive; immediate, instant, instantaneous, summary; fast, rapid, speedy, swift; eager, keen, sharp; apt, clever, smart ♦ [2] brisk, fast, fleet, hasty, rapid, snappy, speedy, swift ♦ [3] alert, brainy, bright, bril-liant, clever, intelligent, keen, nimble, quick-witted, sharp, smart — more at INTELLIGENT

²**quick** *adv* ♦ : in a quick manner

♦ apace, briskly, fast, full tilt, hastily, posthaste, presto, pronto, quickly, rapidly, soon, speedily, swift, swiftly — more at FAST

³**quick** *n* **1** : a sensitive area of living flesh **2** : a vital part : HEART **3** ♦ : the inmost sensibilities

♦ core, heart, soul

quick bread *n* : a bread made with a leavening agent that permits immediate baking of the dough or batter

quick·en \'kwi-kən\ *vb* **1** : to come to life : REVIVE **2** ♦ : to cause to be enlivened : STIMULATE **3** ♦ : to in-crease in speed : HASTEN **4** : to show vitality (as by grow-ing or moving)

♦ [2] animate, brace, energize, enliven, fire, invigorate, jazz up, liven up, pep up, stimulate, vitalize, vivify, zip (up) — more at ANIMATE ♦ [3] accelerate, hasten, hurry, rush, speed (up), step up, whisk — more at HURRY

quick–freeze \'kwik-'frēz\ *vb* **-froze** \-'frōz\; **-fro·zen** \-'frōz-ᵊn\; **-freez·ing** : to freeze (food) for preservation so rapidly that the natural juices and flavor are not lost

quick·ie \'kwi-kē\ *n* : something hurriedly done or made

quick·lime \'kwik-,līm\ *n* : ¹LIME

quick·ly *adv* ♦ : in a quick manner

♦ apace, briskly, fast, full tilt, hastily, posthaste, presto, pronto, quick, rapidly, soon, speedily, swift, swiftly — more at FAST

quick·ness *n* ♦ : the quality or state of being quick

♦ celerity, fastness, fleetness, haste, hurry, rapidity, speed, swiftness, velocity — more at SPEED

quick·sand \-,sand\ *n* : a deep mass of loose sand mixed with water

quick·sil·ver \-,sil-vər\ *n* : MERCURY 1

quick·step \-,step\ *n* : a spirited march tune or dance

quick–wit·ted \'kwik-'wi-təd\ *adj* ♦ : mentally alert

♦ alert, brainy, bright, brilliant, clever, intelligent, keen, nimble, quick, sharp, smart — more at INTELLIGENT

quid \'kwid\ *n* : a lump of something chewable ⟨a ∼ of tobacco⟩

quid pro quo \,kwid-,prō-'kwō\ *n* [NL, something for something] : something given or received for something else

qui·es·cence \kwī-'es-ᵊns\ *n* ♦ : the quality or state of being quiescent

♦ abeyance, doldrums, dormancy, latency, suspension — more at ABEYANCE ♦ dormancy, idleness, inaction, inactivity, inertness — more at INACTION

qui·es·cent \kwī-'es-ᵊnt\ *adj* ♦ : being at rest : QUIET

♦ dull, inactive, inert, lethargic, quiet, sleepy, sluggish, torpid — more at INACTIVE

¹qui·et \'kwī-ət\ *n* ♦ : the quality or state of being quiet : REPOSE

♦ calm, calmness, hush, peace, placidity, quietness, repose, serenity, silence, still, stillness, tranquility — more at CALM

²quiet *adj* **1** ♦ : marked by little motion or activity : CALM **2** : GENTLE, MILD ⟨a ∼ disposition⟩ **3** : enjoyed in peace and relaxation ⟨a ∼ cup of tea⟩ **4** ♦ : free from noise or uproar **5** ♦ : not showy : MODEST ⟨∼ clothes⟩ **6** ♦ : screened or hidden from view : SECLUDED ⟨a ∼ nook⟩

♦ [1, 4] calm, hushed, noiseless, peaceful, restful, serene, silent, soundless, still, tranquil; *also* speechless, wordless; dead, motionless, quiescent; muffled, muted, quieted *Ant* boisterous, clamorous, deafening, loud, noisy, raucous, roistering, romping, rowdy, tumultuous, uproarious, woolly ♦ [5] conservative, muted, restrained, subdued, unpretentious; *also* appropriate, fit, fitting, proper, suitable; modest, plain, simple, unadorned; inconspicuous, unobtrusive; tasteful; drab, mousy; practical, sensible *Ant* flamboyant, flashy, garish, gaudy, glitzy, loud, ostentatious, swank, tawdry ♦ [6] cloistered, covert, isolated, remote, secluded, secret — more at SECLUDED

³quiet *adv* : QUIETLY

⁴quiet *vb* **1** ♦ : to cause to be quiet : CALM **2** ♦ : to become quiet — often used with *down* ⟨∼ down⟩

♦ [1] allay, calm, compose, settle, soothe, still, tranquilize — more at CALM ♦ *often* **quite down** [2] calm (down), cool (off *or* down), hush, settle (down); *also* relax, unwind *Ant* act up, carry on, cut up

qui·et·ly *adv* ♦ : in a quiet manner

♦ calmly, quiet, still — more at STILL

qui·et·ness *n* ♦ : the quality or state of being quiet

♦ calm, calmness, hush, peace, placidity, quiet, repose, serenity, silence, still, stillness, tranquility — more at CALM

qui·etude \'kwī-ə-,tüd, -,tyüd\ *n* : a quiet state : QUIETNESS, REPOSE

qui·etus \kwī-'ē-təs\ *n* [ME *quietus est*, fr. ML, he is quit,

formula of discharge from obligation] **1** ♦ : final settlement (as of a debt) **2** ♦ : removal from activity : DEATH

♦ [1] delivery, discharge, quittance, release — more at RELEASE ♦ [2] death, decease, demise, doom, end, passing — more at DEATH

quill \'kwil\ *n* : a large stiff feather; *also* : the hollow tubular part of a feather **2** : one of the hollow sharp spines of a hedgehog or porcupine **3** : a pen made from a feather

¹quilt \'kwilt\ *n* : a padded bed coverlet

²quilt *vb* **1** : to fill, pad, or line like a quilt **2** : to stitch or sew in layers with padding in between **3** : to make quilts

quince \'kwins\ *n* : a hard yellow applelike fruit; *also* : a tree related to the roses that bears this fruit

qui·nine \'kwī-,nīn\ *n* : a bitter white drug obtained from cinchona bark and used esp. in treating malaria

qui·noa \kēn-,wä, kē-'nō-ə\ *n* [Sp, fr. Quechua *kinua*] : the starchy seeds of an annual herb related to spinach which are used as food and ground into flour; *also* : this herb

quint \'kwint\ *n* : QUINTUPLET

quin·tal \'kwint-ᵊl, 'kant-\ *n* : HUNDREDWEIGHT

quin·tes·sence \kwin-'tes-ᵊns\ *n* **1** ♦ : the purest essence of something **2** ♦ : the most typical example ⟨the ∼ of self-control⟩ — **quin·tes·sen·tial·ly** *adv*

♦ [1] essence, nature, soul, stuff, substance — more at ESSENCE ♦ [2] beau ideal, classic, epitome, exemplar, ideal, perfection; *also* archetype, model, prototype; paradigm, standard; nonpareil, paragon; embodiment, incarnation, personification; acme, height, ultimate, zenith

quint·es·sen·tial \,kwin-tə-'sen-chəl\ *adj* ♦ : being a quintessence

♦ classic, model, paradigmatic — more at MODEL

quin·tet *also* **quin·tette** \kwin-'tet\ *n* **1** : a musical composition for five instruments or voices **2** : a group of five and esp. of five musicians

¹quin·tu·ple \kwin-'tü-pəl, -'tyü-, -'tə-\ *adj* **1** : having five units or members **2** : being five times as great or as many — **quintuple** *n*

²quintuple *vb* **quin·tu·pled**; **quin·tu·pling** : to make or become five times as great or as many

quin·tu·plet \kwin-'tə-plət, -'tü-, -'tyü-\ *n* **1** : a group of five of a kind **2** : one of five offspring born at one birth

¹quin·tu·pli·cate \kwin-'tü-pli-kət, -'tyü-\ *adj* **1** : repeated five times **2** : FIFTH

²quintuplicate *n* **1** : one of five like things **2** : five copies all alike ⟨typed in ∼⟩

³quin·tu·pli·cate \-plə-,kāt\ *vb* **-cat·ed**; **-cat·ing** **1** : QUINTUPLE **2** : to provide in quintuplicate

¹quip \'kwip\ *n* ♦ : a clever remark

♦ crack, gag, jest, joke, laugh, pleasantry, sally, waggery, wisecrack, witticism — more at JOKE

²quip *vb* **quipped**; **quip·ping** **1** ♦ : to make quips : GIBE **2** ♦ : to jest or gibe at

♦ [1, 2] banter, fool, fun, gibe, jest, jive, joke, josh, kid, wisecrack — more at JOKE

quire \'kwī(-ə)r\ *n* : a set of 24 or sometimes 25 sheets of paper of the same size and quality

quirk \'kwərk\ *n* ♦ : a peculiarity of action or behavior

♦ crotchet, eccentricity, idiosyncrasy, mannerism, oddity, peculiarity, singularity, trick — more at IDIOSYNCRASY

quirky *adj* ♦ : full of quirks

♦ bizarre, curious, far-out, funny, kinky, odd, outlandish, outré, peculiar, quaint, queer, remarkable, screwy, strange, wacky, weird, wild — more at ODD

quirt \'kwərt\ *n* : a riding whip with a short handle and a rawhide lash

quis·ling \'kwiz-liŋ\ *n* [Vidkun *Quisling* †1945 Norw. politician who collaborated with the Nazis] ♦ : one who helps the invaders of one's own country : one who commits treason

♦ apostate, betrayer, double-crosser, recreant, traitor, turncoat — more at TRAITOR

quit \'kwit\ *vb* **quit** *also* **quit·ted**; **quit·ting** **1** : to conduct (oneself) usu. satisfactorily esp. under stress : CONDUCT, BEHAVE ⟨∼ themselves well⟩ **2 a :** to depart from : LEAVE **b** ♦ **:** to bring to an end **3** ♦ **:** to give up for good ⟨∼ smok-ing⟩ ⟨∼ my job⟩ **4 :** to leave the company of **5** ♦ **:** to admit defeat **6 :** to make full payment of — **quit·ter** n

♦ [2b] break, break off, cease, cut, desist, discontinue, drop, end, halt, knock off, layoff, leave off, shut off, stop — more at STOP ♦ [3] leave, resign, retire, step down; *also* abandon, vacate; drop out (of) *Ant* stay (at) ♦ [3] discontinue, drop, give up, knock off, lay off; *also* break off, break up, close, conclude, end, expire, fin-ish; pause, taper off; cease, desist, leave off *Ant* carry on, continue, keep, keep up, maintain ♦ [5] blink, bow, budge, capitulate, concede, give in, knuckle under, sub-mit, succumb, surrender, yield — more at YIELD

quite \'kwīt\ *adv* **1** ♦ **:** to a complete degree : COM-PLETELY **2 :** to an extreme : POSITIVELY **3** ♦ **:** to a con-siderable extent : RATHER ⟨∼ rich⟩

♦ [1] altogether, completely, dead, entirely, fast, flat, full, fully, perfectly, thoroughly, well, wholly — more at FULLY ♦ [3] enough, fairly, kind of, moderately, pretty, rather, somewhat, sort of, so-so — more at FAIRLY

quits \'kwits\ *adj* **:** even or equal with another ⟨call it ∼⟩
quit·tance \'kwit-ᵊns\ n **1** ♦ **:** something given in return, compensation, or retaliation : REQUITAL **2** ♦ **:** discharge from a debt or an obligation

♦ [1] compensation, damages, indemnity, recompense, redress, remuneration, reparation, requital, restitution, satisfaction — more at COMPENSATION ♦ [2] delivery, discharge, quietus, release — more at RELEASE

¹quiv·er \'kwi-vər\ n **:** a case for carrying arrows
²quiver *vb* **quiv·ered; quiv·er·ing** ♦ **:** to shake with a slight trembling motion ⟨∼ed with rage⟩ — **quiv·er·ing·ly** *adv*

♦ agitate, convulse, jolt, jounce, quake, shake, shudder, vibrate, wobble — more at SHAKE

³quiver n **:** the act or action of quivering : TREMOR
quiv·er·ing \'kwi-v(ə-)riŋ\ n ♦ **:** the action or condition of one that trembles

♦ oscillation, vibration — more at VIBRATION

qui vive \kē-'vēv\ n [F *qui-vive,* fr. *qui vive?* long live who?, challenge of a French sentry] **:** ALERT ⟨on the *qui vive* for prowlers⟩
quix·ot·ic \kwik-'sä-tik\ *adj* [fr. Don *Quixote,* hero of the novel *Don Quixote de la Mancha* by Cervantes] **:** foolishly impractical esp. in the pursuit of ideals — **quix·ot·i·cal·ly** \-ti-kə-lē\ *adv*
¹quiz \'kwiz\ n, *pl* **quiz·zes** **1 :** an eccentric person **2 :** PRACTICAL JOKE **3** ♦ **:** a short oral or written test **4** ♦ **:** a person who ridicules or mocks

♦ [3] examination, test — more at EXAMINATION ♦ [4] heckler, mocker, scoffer, taunter, tease; *also* de-tractor; smart aleck, wiseacre, wise guy; satirist

²quiz *vb* **quizzed; quiz·zing** **1 :** MOCK **2 :** to look at inquis-itively **3** ♦ **:** to question closely

♦ ask, examine, grill, inquire of, interrogate, pump, query, question — more at ASK

quiz·zi·cal \'kwi-zi-kəl\ *adj* **1 :** comically quaint **2 :** mildly teasing or mocking **3 :** expressive of puzzlement, curios-ity, or disbelief ⟨gave me a ∼ look⟩
quoit \'kwāt, 'kwȯit, 'kȯit\ n **1 :** a flattened ring of iron or circle of rope used in a throwing game **2** *pl* **:** a game in which quoits are thrown at an upright pin in an attempt to ring the pin
quon·dam \'kwän-dəm, -,dam\ *adj* [L, at one time, for-merly, fr. *quom, cum* when] **:** FORMER
quo·rum \'kwȯr-əm\ n **:** the number of members required to be present for business to be legally transacted
quot *abbr* quotation
quo·ta \'kwō-tə\ n ♦ **:** a proportional part esp. when as-signed : SHARE

♦ allotment, allowance, cut, part, portion, proportion, share — more at SHARE

quot·able \'kwō-tə-bəl\ *adj* **:** fit for or worth quoting — **quot·abil·i·ty** \-'bi-lə-tē\ n
quo·ta·tion \kwō-'tā-shən\ n **1 :** the act or process of quot-ing **2 :** the price currently bid or offered for something **3 :** something that is quoted
quotation mark n **:** one of a pair of punctuation marks " " or ' ' used esp. to indicate the beginning and end of a quotation in which exact phraseology is directly cited
quote \'kwōt\ *vb* **quot·ed; quot·ing** [ML *quotare* to mark the number of, number references, fr. L *quotus* of what number or quantity, fr. *quot* how many, (as) many as] **1 a** ♦ **:** to speak or write a passage from another usu. with acknowledgment **b** ♦ **:** to repeat a passage in substantiation or illustration **2 :** to state the market price of a commodity, stock, or bond **3 :** to inform a hearer or reader that matter following is quoted — **quote** n

♦ [1a] advert (to), cite, instance, mention, name, note, notice, refer (to), specify, touch (*on* or *upon*) — more at MENTION ♦ [1b] adduce, cite, instance, mention; *also* exemplify, represent; illustrate, refer (to); document, substantiate

quoth \'kwōth\ *vb past* [ME, past of *quethen* to say, fr. OE *cwethan*] *archaic* **:** SAID — usu. used in the 1st and 3d persons with the subject following
quo·tid·i·an \kwō-'ti-dē-ən\ *adj* **1 :** DAILY **2 :** COMMON-PLACE, ORDINARY
quo·tient \'kwō-shənt\ n **:** the number obtained by dividing one number by another
Quran *also* **Qu'ran** *var of* KORAN
qv *abbr* [L *quod vide*] which see
qy *abbr* query

¹r \'är\ n, *pl* **r's** *or* **rs** \'ärz\ *often cap* **:** the 18th letter of the English alphabet
²r *abbr, often cap* **1** rabbi **2** radius **3** rare **4** Republi-can **5** rerun **6** resistance **7** right **8** river **9** roentgen **10** rook **11** run
Ra *symbol* radium
RA *abbr* **1** regular army **2** research assistant **3** Royal Academy
¹rab·bet \'ra-bət\ n **:** a groove in the edge or face of a sur-face (as a board) esp. to receive another piece

²rabbet *vb* **:** to cut a rabbet in; *also* **:** to join by means of a rabbet
rab·bi \'ra-,bī\ n [ME, fr. OE, fr. LL, fr. Gk *rhabbi,* fr. Heb *rabbī* my master, fr. *rabh* master + *-ī* my] **1 :** MASTER, TEACHER — used by Jews as a term of address **2 :** a Jew trained and ordained for professional religious leadership — **rab·bin·ic** \rə-'bi-nik\ *or* **rab·bin·i·cal** \-ni-kəl\ *adj*
rab·bin·ate \'ra-bə-nət, -,nāt\ n **1 :** the office of a rabbi **2 :** the whole body of rabbis
rab·bit \'ra-bət\ n, *pl* **rabbit** *or* **rabbits :** any of various long-

eared short-tailed burrowing mammals distinguished from the related hares by being blind, furless, and helpless at birth; *also* : the pelt of a rabbit

rabbit ears *n pl* : an indoor V-shaped television antenna

rab·ble \'ra-bəl\ *n* 1 : MOB 2 2 ♦ : the lowest class of people

♦ riffraff, scum, trash; *also* dregs; herd, masses, mob, people, populace, public, rank and file; bourgeoisie, middle class, working class *Ant* aristocracy, elite, gentry, society, upper class, upper crust

rab·ble-rous·er \'ra-bəl-ˌraủ-zər\ *n* ♦ : one that stirs up (as to hatred or violence) the masses of the people

♦ agitator, demagogue, firebrand, incendiary, inciter — more at AGITATOR

ra·bid \'ra-bəd\ *adj* 1 ♦ : extremely violent : FURIOUS 2 ♦ : being fanatical or extreme ⟨~ supporters⟩ 3 : affected with rabies — **ra·bid·ly** *adv*

♦ [1] angry, boiling, enraged, fierce, frenzied, furious, irate, mad, sore, violent — more at ANGRY ♦ [2] extreme, extremist, fanatic, radical, revolutionary, ultra — more at EXTREME

ra·bies \'rā-bēz\ *n, pl* **rabies** [NL, fr. L, madness] : an acute deadly virus disease of the nervous system transmitted by the bite of an affected animal

rac·coon \ra-'kün\ *n, pl* **raccoon** *or* **raccoons** : a gray No. American chiefly tree-dwelling mammal with a black mask, a bushy ringed tail, and nocturnal habits; *also* : its pelt

¹**race** \'rās\ *n* 1 : a strong current of running water; *also* : its channel 2 : an onward course (as of time or life) 3 : a contest of speed 4 : a contest for a desired end (as election to office)

²**race** *vb* **raced; rac·ing** 1 : to run in a race 2 ♦ : to run swiftly : RUSH 3 ♦ : to engage in a race with 4 : to drive or ride at high speed — **rac·er** *n*

♦ [2] barrel, career, course, dash, fly, hasten, hurry, hurtle, hustle, pelt, rip, rocket, run, rush, shoot, speed, tear, whirl, whisk, zip, zoom — more at HURRY ♦ [3] battle, compete, contend, fight, vie — more at COMPETE

³**race** *n* 1 ♦ : a family, tribe, people, or nation of the same stock 2 : a group of individuals within a biological species able to breed together 3 : a category of humankind that shares certain distinctive physical traits — **ra·cial** \'rā-shəl\ *adj* — **ra·cial·ly** *adv*

♦ blood, clan, family, folks, house, kin, kindred, kinfolk, line, lineage, people, stock, tribe — more at FAMILY

race·course \'rās-ˌkōrs\ *n* : a course for racing

race·horse \-ˌhȯrs\ *n* : a horse bred or kept for racing

ra·ceme \rā-'sēm\ *n* [L *racemus* bunch of grapes] : a flower cluster with flowers borne along a stem and blooming from the base toward the tip — **rac·e·mose** \'ra-sə-ˌmōs\ *adj*

race·track \'rās-ˌtrak\ *n* : a usu. oval course on which races are run

race·way \-ˌwā\ *n* 1 ♦ : a channel for a current of water 2 : RACECOURSE

♦ aqueduct, canal, channel, conduit, flume, watercourse — more at CHANNEL

ra·cial \'rā-shəl\ *adj* 1 : of, relating to, or based on a race ⟨a ~ minority⟩ 2 : existing or occurring between races ⟨~ equality⟩ — **ra·cial·ly** \-shə-lē\ *adv*

ra·cial·ism \'rā-shə-ˌli-zəm\ *n* : a theory that race determines human traits and capacities; *also* : RACISM — **ra·cial·ist** \-list\ *n* — **ra·cial·is·tic** \ˌrā-shə-'lis-tik\ *adj*

ra·cial·ize \'rā-shə-ˌlīz\ *vb* **-ized; -iz·ing** : to give a racial character to

racing form *n* : a paper giving data about racehorses for use by bettors

rac·ism \'rā-ˌsi-zəm\ *n* : a belief that some races are by nature superior to others; *also* : discrimination based on such belief — **rac·ist** \-sist\ *n*

¹**rack** \'rak\ *n* 1 : an instrument of torture on which a body is stretched 2 : a framework on or in which something may be placed (as for display or storage) 3 : a bar with teeth on one side to mesh with a pinion or worm gear

²**rack** *vb* 1 : to torture on or as if on a rack 2 ♦ : to stretch or strain by force 3 ♦ : to cause to suffer torture, pain, anguish, or ruin : TORMENT 4 : to place on or in a rack

♦ [2] pull, strain, stretch, wrench — more at STRAIN ♦ [3] afflict, agonize, bedevil, curse, harrow, martyr, persecute, plague, torment, torture — more at AFFLICT

¹**rack·et** *or* **rac·quet** \'ra-kət\ *n* [MF *raquette*, ultim. fr. ML *rasceta* wrist, carpus, fr. Ar *rusgh* wrist] : a light bat made of netting stretched in an oval open frame having a handle and used for striking a ball or shuttlecock

²**racket** *n* 1 ♦ : confused noise : DIN 2 ♦ : a fraudulent or dishonest scheme or activity ⟨a criminal ~⟩

♦ [1] bluster, cacophony, clamor (*or* clamour), din, noise, roar — more at NOISE ♦ [2] hustle, swindle

³**racket** *vb* : to make a racket

rack·e·teer \ˌra-kə-'tir\ *n* ♦ : a person who obtains money by an illegal enterprise usu. involving intimidation — **rack·e·teer·ing** *n*

♦ extortionist; *also* crook, gangster, hoodlum, mafioso, mobster; bully, ruffian, thug; cheat, cheater, chiseler, double-dealer, hustler, profiteer, shark, sharper, swindler

rack up *vb* : ACCUMULATE, GAIN

ra·con·teur \ˌra-ˌkän-'tər\ *n* : one good at telling anecdotes

rac·quet·ball \'ra-kət-ˌbȯl\ *n* : a game similar to handball that is played on a 4-walled court with a short-handled racket

racy \'rā-sē\ *adj* **rac·i·er; -est** 1 ♦ : full of zest 2 : PUNGENT, SPICY 3 ♦ : verging on impropriety or indecency : RISQUÉ, SUGGESTIVE — **rac·i·ly** \'rā-sə-lē\ *adv* — **rac·i·ness** \-sē-nəs\ *n*

♦ [1] active, animate, animated, brisk, energetic, frisky, gay, jaunty, jazzy, lively, peppy, perky, pert, snappy, spirited, sprightly, springy, vital, vivacious — more at LIVELY ♦ [3] bawdy, lewd, ribald, risqué, spicy, suggestive — more at SUGGESTIVE

rad *abbr* 1 radical 2 radio 3 radius

ra·dar \'rā-ˌdär\ *n* [radio detecting and ranging] : a device that emits radio waves for detecting and locating an object by the reflection of the radio waves and that may use this reflection to determine the object's direction and speed

radar gun *n* : a handheld device that uses radar to measure the speed of a moving object

ra·dar·scope \'rā-ˌdär-ˌskōp\ *n* : a visual display for a radar receiver

¹**ra·di·al** \'rā-dē-əl\ *adj* : arranged or having parts arranged like rays around a common center ⟨the ~ form of a starfish⟩ — **ra·di·al·ly** *adv*

²**radial** *n* : a pneumatic tire with cords laid perpendicular to the center line

radial engine *n* : an internal combustion engine with cylinders arranged radially like the spokes of a wheel

ra·di·an \'rā-dē-ən\ *n* : a unit of measure for angles that is equal to approximately 57.3 degrees

ra·di·ance \-əns\ *n* ♦ : the quality or state of being radiant

♦ brilliance, dazzle, effulgence, illumination, lightness, lucidity, luminosity, refulgence, splendor — more at BRILLIANCE ♦ blaze, flare, fluorescence, glare, gleam, glow, illumination, incandescence, light, luminescence, shine — more at LIGHT

ra·di·ant \'rā-dē-ənt\ *adj* 1 ♦ : vividly bright and shining : GLOWING 2 ♦ : beaming with happiness ⟨a ~ smile⟩ 3 : transmitted by radiation — **ra·di·ant·ly** *adv*

♦ [1] beaming, bright, brilliant, effulgent, glowing, incandescent, lambent, lucent, lucid, luminous, lustrous, refulgent, shiny — more at BRIGHT ♦ [2] aglow, beaming, glowing, sunny; *also* brilliant, dazzling, effulgent, gleaming, luminous, refulgent, shining, starry; blithe, blithesome, bright, cheerful, cheery, chipper, gay, gladsome, lightsome, merry, mirthful, upbeat; jocund, jovial, laughing, smiling; blooming, rosy

radiant energy *n* : energy traveling as electromagnetic waves

ra·di·ate \'rā-dē-ˌāt\ *vb* **-at·ed; -at·ing 1** : to send out rays : SHINE, GLOW **2** : to issue in or as if in rays ⟨light ∼*s*⟩ **3 ♦** : to spread around as from a center

♦ branch, diverge, fan; *also* diffuse, dispel, disperse, dissipate; fork, stem; divide, separate, split; scatter, splay, spread; arise, derive, emanate, flow, issue, proceed, spring *Ant* concentrate, converge, focus, funnel, meet

ra·di·a·tion \ˌrā-dē-'ā-shən\ *n* **1** : the action or process of radiating **2** : the process of emitting radiant energy in the form of waves or particles; *also* : something (as an X-ray beam) that is radiated

radiation sickness *n* : sickness that results from exposure to radiation and is commonly marked by fatigue, nausea, vomiting, loss of teeth and hair, and in more severe cases by damage to blood-forming tissue

radiation therapy *n* : RADIOTHERAPY

ra·di·a·tor \'rā-dē-ˌā-tər\ *n* : any of various devices (as a set of pipes or tubes) for transferring heat from a fluid within to an area or object outside

¹**rad·i·cal** \'ra-di-kəl\ *adj* [ME, fr. LL *radicalis*, fr. L *radic-, radix* root] **1** : FUNDAMENTAL, EXTREME, THOROUGHGOING **2** : of or relating to radicals in politics **3 ♦** : marked by a considerable departure from the usual or traditional — **rad·i·cal·ism** \-kə-ˌli-zəm\ *n* — **rad·i·cal·ly** *adv*

♦ extreme, extremist, fanatic, rabid, revolutionary, ultra — more at EXTREME ♦ broad-minded, liberal, nonorthodox, nontraditional, open-minded, progressive, unconventional, unorthodox — more at LIBERAL

²**radical** *n* **1 ♦** : a person who favors rapid and sweeping changes in laws and methods of government **2** : FREE RADICAL; *also* : a group of atoms considered as a unit in certain reactions or as a subunit of a larger molecule **3** : a mathematical expression indicating a root by means of a radical sign; *also* : RADICAL SIGN

♦ extremist, revolutionary; *also* leftist, red; progressive, reformer; anarchist, subversive; agitator, insurgent, insurrectionist, rebel; secessionist, separatist *Ant* moderate

rad·i·cal·ise *chiefly Brit var of* RADICALIZE

rad·i·cal·ize \-kə-ˌlīz\ *vb* **-ized; -iz·ing** : to make radical esp. in politics — **rad·i·cal·i·za·tion** \ˌra-di-kə-lə-lə-'zā- shən\ *n*

radical sign *n* : the sign √ placed before a mathematical expression to indicate that its root is to be taken

ra·dic·chio \ra-'di-kē-ō\ *n, pl* **–chios** : a chicory with reddish variegated leaves

radii *pl of* RADIUS

¹**ra·dio** \'rā-dē-ˌō\ *n, pl* **ra·di·os 1** : the wireless transmission or reception of signals using electromagnetic waves **2** : a radio receiving set **3** : the radio broadcasting industry — **radio** *adj*

²**radio** *vb* : to communicate or send a message to by radio

ra·dio·ac·tiv·i·ty \ˌrā-dē-ō-ˌak-'ti-və-tē\ *n* : the property that some elements or isotopes have of spontaneously emitting energetic particles by the disintegration of their atomic nuclei — **ra·dio·ac·tive** \-'ak-tiv\ *adj*

radio astronomy *n* : astronomy dealing with radio waves received from outside the earth's atmosphere

ra·dio·car·bon \ˌrā-dē-ō-'kär-bən\ *n* : CARBON 14

radio frequency *n* : an electromagnetic wave frequency intermediate between audio frequencies and infrared frequencies used esp. for communication and radar signals

ra·dio·gram \'rā-dē-ō-ˌgram\ *n* : a message transmitted by radio

ra·dio·graph \-ˌgraf\ *n* : a photograph made by some form of radiation other than light; *esp* : an X-ray photograph — **radiograph** *vb* — **ra·dio·graph·ic** \ˌrā-dē-ō-'gra-fik\ *adj* — **ra·dio·graph·i·cal·ly** \-fi-k(ə-)lē\ *adv* — **ra·di·og·ra·phy** \ˌrā-dē-'ä-grə-fē\ *n*

ra·dio·iso·tope \ˌrā-dē-ō-'ī-sə-ˌtōp\ *n* : a radioactive isotope

ra·di·ol·o·gy \ˌrā-dē-'ä-lə-jē\ *n* : the use of radiant energy (as X-rays and radium radiations) in medicine — **ra·di·ol·o·gist** \-jist\ *n*

ra·dio·man \'rā-dē-ō-ˌman\ *n* : a radio operator or technician

ra·di·om·e·ter \ˌrā-dē-'ä-mə-tər\ *n* : an instrument for measuring the intensity of radiant energy — **ra·dio·met·ric** \ˌrā-dē-ō-'me-trik\ *adj* — **ra·di·om·e·try** \-'ä-mə-trē\ *n*

ra·dio·phone \'rā-dē-ə-ˌfōn\ *n* : RADIOTELEPHONE

ra·dio·sonde \'rā-dē-ō-ˌsänd\ *n* : a small radio transmitter carried aloft (as by balloon) and used to transmit meteorological data

ra·dio·tele·phone \ˌrā-dē-ō-'te-lə-ˌfōn\ *n* : a telephone that uses radio waves wholly or partly instead of connecting wires — **ra·dio·te·le·pho·ny** \-tə-'le-fə-nē, -'te-lə-ˌfō-nē\ *n*

radio telescope *n* : a radio receiver-antenna combination used for observation in radio astronomy

ra·dio·ther·a·py \ˌrā-dē-ō-'ther-ə-pē\ *n* : the treatment of disease by means of radiation (as X-rays) — **ra·dio·ther·a·pist** \-pist\ *n*

rad·ish \'ra-dish\ *n* [ME, alter. of OE *rædic*, fr. L *radic-, radix* root, radish] : a pungent fleshy root usu. eaten raw; *also* : a plant related to the mustards that produces this root

ra·di·um \'rā-dē-əm\ *n* [NL, fr. L *radius* ray] : a very radioactive metallic chemical element that is used in the treatment of cancer

ra·di·us \'rā-dē-əs\ *n, pl* **ra·dii** \-ē-ˌī\ *also* **ra·di·us·es 1** : a straight line extending from the center of a circle or a sphere to the circumference or surface; *also* : the length of a radius **2** : the bone on the thumb side of the human forearm **3** : a circular area defined by the length of its radius

RADM *abbr* rear admiral

ra·don \'rā-ˌdän\ *n* : a heavy radioactive gaseous chemical element

RAF *abbr* Royal Air Force

raf·fia \'ra-fē-ə\ *n* : fiber used esp. for making baskets and hats that is obtained from the stalks of the leaves of a tropical African palm (**raffia palm**)

raff·ish \'ra-fish\ *adj* : jaunty or sporty esp. in a flashy or vulgar manner — **raff·ish·ly** *adv*

raff·ish·ness *n* : marked by or suggestive of flashy vulgarity or crudeness

¹**raf·fle** \'ra-fəl\ *vb* **raf·fled; raf·fling** : to dispose of by a raffle

²**raffle** *n* : a lottery in which the prize is won by one of a number of persons buying chances

¹**raft** \'raft\ *n* **1** : a number of logs or timbers fastened together to form a float **2** : a flat structure for support or transportation on water

²**raft** *vb* **1** : to travel or transport by raft **2** : to make into a raft

³**raft** *n* : a large amount or number : LOT

raf·ter \'raf-tər\ *n* : any of the parallel beams that support a roof

¹**rag** \'rag\ *n* **1 a** : a waste piece of cloth **b** *pl* : clothes usu. in poor or ragged condition **2** : a sleazy newspaper

²**rag** *n* : a composition in ragtime

ra·ga \'rä-gə\ *n* **1** : a traditional melodic pattern or mode in Indian music **2** : an improvisation based on a raga

rag·a·muf·fin \'ra-gə-ˌmə-fən\ *n* [ME *Ragamuffyn*, name for a ragged, oafish person] : a ragged dirty person

rag·bag \'rag-ˌbag\ *n* **♦** : a miscellaneous collection

♦ assortment, clutter, jumble, medley, mélange, miscellany, motley, muddle, variety, welter — more at MISCELLANY

¹**rage** \'rāj\ *n* **1 ♦** : violent and uncontrolled anger **2 ♦** : a fad pursued with intense enthusiasm : VOGUE, FASHION **3** : an intense feeling

♦ [1] anger, furor, fury, indignation, ire, outrage, spleen, wrath, wrathfulness — more at ANGER ♦ [2] craze, enthusiasm, fad, fashion, go, mode, sensation, style, trend, vogue

²**rage** *vb* **raged; rag·ing 1 ♦** : to be furiously angry **2** : to continue out of control ⟨the fire *raged*⟩ **3 ♦** : to go on a rampage

♦ [1] boil, burn, fume, seethe, steam — more at BOIL ♦ [3] fume, storm; *also* blow up, flare (up), flip; bluster, carry on, fulminate, rampage, rant, rave, take on; burn, foam, seethe, smolder, steam; chafe, fret, stew

rag·ged \'ra-gəd\ *adj* **1** ♦ : torn or worn to tatters; *also* : wearing tattered clothes **2** : done in an uneven way ⟨a ~ performance⟩ **3** ♦ : having an irregular edge or outline — **rag·ged·ly** *adv* — **rag·ged·ness** *n*

  ♦ [1] ratty, seedy, shabby, tattered, threadbare, worn-out; *also* dingy, dowdy, faded, scruffy; shredded; patchy
  ♦ [3] broken, craggy, jagged, scraggly; *also* serrate; harsh, rough, rugged; irregular, nonuniform **Ant** clean, even, smooth, unbroken

rag·lan \'ra-glən\ *n* : an overcoat with sleeves (**raglan sleeves**) sewn in with seams slanting from neck to underarm

ra·gout \ra-'gü\ *n* [F *ragoût*, fr. *ragoûter* to revive the taste, fr. MF *ragouster*, fr. *re-* + *a-* to (fr. L *ad-*) + *goust* taste, fr. L *gustus*] : a highly seasoned meat stew with vegetables

rag·pick·er \'rag-,pi-kər\ *n* : one who collects rags and refuse for a living

rag·time \-,tīm\ *n* : music in which there is more or less continuous syncopation in the melody

rag·top \'rag-,täp\ *n* : CONVERTIBLE

rag·weed \-,wēd\ *n* : any of several chiefly No. American weedy composite herbs with allergenic pollen

¹raid \'rād\ *n* ♦ : a sudden usu. surprise attack or invasion

  ♦ descent, foray, incursion, invasion, irruption; *also* pillage, plunder; aggression, assault, offense, offensive, onset, onslaught, siege, storm, strike; charge, sally, sortie; ambuscade, ambush, surprise; air raid, blitz, blitzkrieg, bombardment ♦ aggression, assault, attack, charge, descent, offense (*or* offence), offensive, onset, onslaught, rush, strike — more at ATTACK

²raid *vb* ♦ : to make a raid on — **raid·er** *n*

  ♦ foray, invade, overrun — more at INVADE ♦ assail, assault, attack, beset, charge, descend, jump, pounce (on *or* upon), rush, storm, strike — more at ATTACK

¹rail \'rāl\ *n* [ME *raile*, fr. AF *raille, reille* bar, rule, fr. L *regula* straightedge, rule, fr. *regere* to keep straight, direct] **1** : a bar extending from one support to another as a guard or barrier **2** : a bar of steel forming a track for wheeled vehicles **3** : RAILROAD

²rail *vb* : to provide with a railing

³rail *n, pl* **rail** *or* **rails** : any of numerous small wading birds often hunted as game birds

⁴rail *vb* [ME, fr. MF *railler* to mock, prob. fr. OF *reillier* to growl, mutter, fr. VL *ragulare* to bray, fr. LL *ragere* to neigh] ♦ : to revile or scold in harsh, insolent, or abusive language : SCOLD

  ♦ *usu* rail at *or* rail against admonish, chide, lecture, rate, rebuke, reprimand, scold — more at SCOLD

rail·er *n* ♦ : one that rails

  ♦ carper, castigator, caviler, censurer, critic, faultfinder, nitpicker, scold — more at CRITIC

rail·ing \'rā-liŋ\ *n* ♦ : a barrier of rails

  ♦ rail; *also* handrail; taffrail; bar

rail·lery \'rā-lə-rē\ *n, pl* **-ler·ies** ♦ : good-natured ridicule : BANTER

  ♦ banter, chaff, persiflage, repartee — more at BANTER

¹rail·road \'rāl-,rōd\ *n* ♦ : a permanent road with rails fixed to ties providing a track for cars; *also* : such a road and its assets constituting a property

  ♦ rail, road; *also* elevated railroad; monorail

²railroad *vb* **1** : to put through (as a law) too hastily **2** : to convict hastily or with insufficient or improper evidence **3** : to send by rail **4** : to work on a railroad — **rail·road·er** *n* — **rail·road·ing** *n*

rail·way \-,wā\ *n* : a permanent road with rails fixed to ties providing a track for cars : RAILROAD

rai·ment \'rā-mənt\ *n* ♦ : garments in general : CLOTHING

  ♦ apparel, attire, clothing, dress, duds, wear — more at CLOTHING

¹rain \'rān\ *n* **1** ♦ : water falling in drops from the clouds **2** ♦ : a shower of objects ⟨a ~ of bullets⟩

  ♦ [1] cloudburst, deluge, downpour, rainstorm, storm, wet; *also* precipitation, shower; thunderstorm
  ♦ [2] hail, shower, storm; *also* barrage, broadside, cannonade, fusillade, salvo, volley; flood, gush, rush, spate, torrent; eruption, outbreak, outburst

²rain *vb* **1** : to send down rain **2** ♦ : to fall as or like rain **3** ♦ : to pour down

  ♦ [2] heap, lavish, pour, shower; *also* gush, stream; flood, inundate, overflow; bombard, hail ♦ [3] pour, precipitate, storm; *also* shower; hail, squall; deluge, flood

rain·bow \-,bō\ *n* : an arc or circle of colors formed by the refraction and reflection of the sun's rays in rain, spray, or mist

rainbow trout *n* : a large stout-bodied fish of western No. America closely related to the salmons of the Pacific and usu. having red or pink stripes with black dots along its sides

rain check *n* **1** : a ticket stub good for a later performance when the scheduled one is rained out **2** : an assurance of a deferred extension of an offer

rain·coat \'rān-,kōt\ *n* : a waterproof or water-repellent coat

rain date *n* : an alternative date for an event postponed due to rain

rain·drop \-,dräp\ *n* : a drop of rain

rain·fall \-,fól\ *n* **1** : amount of precipitation measured by depth **2** : a fall of rain

rain forest *n* : a tropical woodland having an annual rainfall of at least 100 inches (254 centimeters) and marked by lofty broad-leaved evergreen trees forming a continuous canopy

rain·mak·ing \'rān-,mā-kiŋ\ *n* : the action or process of producing or attempting to produce rain by artificial means — **rain·mak·er** *n*

rain out *vb* : to interrupt or prevent by rain

rain·storm \'rān-,stórm\ *n* ♦ : a storm of or with rain

  ♦ cloudburst, deluge, downpour, rain, storm, wet — more at RAIN

rain·wa·ter \-,wò-tər, -,wä-\ *n* : water fallen as rain

rainy *adj* ♦ : marked by, abounding with, or bringing rain

  ♦ stormy, wet; *also* drizzling, misty, spitting, sprinkling

¹raise \'rāz\ *vb* **raised**; **rais·ing** **1** ♦ : to cause or help to rise : LIFT ⟨~ a window⟩ **2** : AWAKEN, AROUSE ⟨enough to ~ the dead⟩ **3** ♦ : to set upright by lifting or building : ERECT ⟨~ a monument⟩ **4** : to place higher in rank or dignity : PROMOTE ⟨was *raised* to captain⟩ **5** : END ⟨~ a siege⟩ **6** : COLLECT ⟨~ money⟩ **7 a** ♦ : to cause to grow : GROW ⟨~ cattle⟩ ⟨~ corn⟩ **b** ♦ : to bring to maturity : BRING UP ⟨~ a family⟩ **8** ♦ : to cause to arise or appear : stimulate the appearance of ⟨~ a laugh⟩ **9** ♦ : to bring to notice ⟨~ an objection⟩ **10** ♦ : to cause to rise in level or amount : INCREASE ⟨~ prices⟩; *also* : to bet more than **11** : to make light and spongy ⟨~ dough⟩ **12** : to multiply a quantity by itself a specified number of times **13** : to cause to form ⟨~ a blister⟩ — **rais·er** *n*

  ♦ [1] boost, crane, elevate, heave, heft, heighten, hike, hoist, jack, lift, pick up, up, uphold; *also* ascend, mount, rise; rear, upend **Ant** drop, lower ♦ [3] assemble, build, construct, erect, fabricate, make, make up, piece, put up, rear, set up — more at BUILD ♦ [7a] crop, cultivate, culture, grow, promote, rear, tend — more at GROW ♦ [7b] breed, bring up, foster, rear — more at BRING UP ♦ [8] elicit, evoke ♦ [9] bring up, broach, introduce, moot — more at INTRODUCE ♦ [10] add, aggrandize, amplify, augment, boost, compound, enlarge, escalate, expand, extend, increase, multiply, swell, up — more at INCREASE

²raise *n* ♦ : an increase in amount (as of a bid or bet or one's pay)

  ♦ accretion, addition, augmentation, boost, expansion, gain, increase, increment, plus, proliferation, rise, supplement — more at INCREASE

rai·sin \'rāz-ᵊn\ *n* [ME, fr. AF, grape, raisin, fr. L *racemus* cluster of grapes or berries] : a grape dried for food

rai·son d'être \ˌrā-ˌzōⁿ-'detrᵊ\ *n, pl* **rai·sons d'être** \-ˌzōⁿz-\ : reason or justification for existence

ra·ja *or* **ra·jah** \'rä-jə\ *n* [Hindi *rājā*, fr. Skt *rājan* king] : an Indian prince

¹rake \'rāk\ *n* : a long-handled garden tool having a cross-bar with prongs

²rake *vb* **raked; rak·ing** **1** : to gather, loosen, or smooth with or as if with a rake **2** : to sweep the length of (as a trench or ship) with gunfire **3** ♦ : to search through

♦ dig, dredge, hunt, ransack, rifle, rummage, scour, search — more at SEARCH

³rake *n* : inclination from either perpendicular or horizontal : SLANT

⁴rake *n* : a dissolute person : LIBERTINE

rake–off \'rāk-ˌof\ *n* : a percentage or cut taken

¹rak·ish \'rā-kish\ *adj* : DISSOLUTE — **rak·ish·ness** *n*

²rakish *adj* **1** : having a trim appearance indicative of speed ⟨a ∼ sloop⟩ **2** : JAUNTY, SPORTY ⟨∼ clothes⟩ — **rak·ish·ness** *n*

rak·ish·ly *adv* ♦ : in a rakish manner

♦ flamboyantly, flashily, gaily, jauntily — more at GAILY

¹ral·ly \'ra-lē\ *vb* **ral·lied; ral·ly·ing** **1** ♦ : to bring together for a common purpose; *also* : to bring back to order ⟨a leader ∼*ing* his forces⟩ **2** : to arouse to activity or from depression or weakness **3** ♦ : to make a comeback

♦ [1] marshal, mobilize, muster — more at MOBILIZE
♦ [3] rebound, recover, snap back — more at RECOVER

²rally *n, pl* **rallies** **1** ♦ : an act of rallying **2** ♦ : a mass meeting to arouse enthusiasm **3** : a competitive automobile event run over public roads

♦ [1] comeback, convalescence, recovery, recuperation, rehabilitation — more at CONVALESCENCE
♦ [2] mobilization, muster; *also* call-up, summons; convening

³rally *vb* **ral·lied; ral·ly·ing** : BANTER

rallying cry *n* : WAR CRY 2

¹ram \'ram\ *n* **1** : a male sheep **2** : BATTERING RAM

²ram *vb* **rammed; ram·ming** **1** : to force or drive in or through **2** ♦ : to make compact : CRAM, CROWD **3** ♦ : to strike against violently

♦ [2] cram, crowd, jam, sandwich, squeeze, stuff, wedge — more at CROWD ♦ [3] bang, bash, bump, collide, crash, hit, impact, knock, slam, smash, strike, swipe, thud — more at HIT

RAM \'ram\ *n* [*random*-*access memory*] : a computer memory that provides the main internal storage for programs and data

Ram·a·dan \'rä-mə-ˌdän\ *n* : the ninth month of the Islamic year observed as sacred with daily fasting from dawn to sunset

¹ram·ble \'ram-bəl\ *vb* **ram·bled; ram·bling** **1** ♦ : to go about aimlessly : ROAM, WANDER **2** ♦ : to talk or write in a long-winded wandering fashion

♦ gad, gallivant, knock, maunder, meander, mope, range, roam, rove, traipse, wander — more at WANDER
♦ maunder, rattle, run on; *also* deviate, digress, stray, wander; sidetrack; blab, chatter, gab, gabble, jabber, patter, prate, prattle

²ramble *n* ♦ : a leisurely excursion; *esp* : an aimless walk

♦ perambulation, stroll, turn, walk — more at WALK

ram·bler \'ram-blər\ *n* **1** ♦ : a person who rambles **2** : any of various climbing roses with large clusters of small often double flowers

♦ drifter, nomad, rover, stroller, vagabond, wanderer — more at NOMAD

ram·bling \'ram-b(ə-)liŋ\ *adj* ♦ : straying from subject to subject

♦ desultory, digressive, discursive — more at DISCURSIVE ♦ circuitous, diffuse, long-winded, prolix, verbose, windy, wordy — more at WORDY

ram·bunc·tious \ram-'bəŋk-shəs\ *adj* ♦ : marked by uncontrollable exuberance

♦ boisterous, raucous, rowdy — more at BOISTEROUS

ra·mie \'rā-mē, 'ra-\ *n* : a strong lustrous bast fiber from an Asian nettle

ram·i·fi·ca·tion \ˌra-mə-fə-'kā-shən\ *n* **1** : the act or process of branching **2** : CONSEQUENCE, OUTGROWTH

ram·i·fy \'ra-mə-ˌfī\ *vb* **-fied; -fy·ing** **1** : to branch out **2** : to separate into divisions

ramp \'ramp\ *n* : a sloping passage or roadway connecting different levels

¹ram·page \'ram-ˌpāj, (ˌ)ram-'pāj\ *vb* **ram·paged; ram·pag·ing** : to rush about wildly ⟨*rampaging* soccer fans⟩

²ram·page \'ram-ˌpāj\ *n* ♦ : a course of violent or riotous action or behavior — **ram·pa·geous** \ram-'pā-jəs\ *adj*

♦ agitation, delirium, distraction, frenzy, furor, fury, hysteria, rage, uproar — more at FRENZY

ram·pant \'ram-pənt\ *adj* ♦ : unchecked in growth or spread ⟨∼ weeds⟩ ⟨fear was ∼ in the town⟩ — **ram·pan·cy** \-pən-sē\ *n* — **ram·pant·ly** *adv*

♦ intemperate, unbridled, unchecked, uncontrolled, ungoverned, unhampered, unhindered, unrestrained; *also* uncontrollable, ungovernable; immoderate; riotous, uninhibited, wild *Ant* checked, controlled, curbed, hampered, hindered, restrained, temperate

ram·part \'ram-ˌpärt\ *n* **1** : a protective barrier **2** : a broad embankment raised as a fortification

¹ram·rod \'ram-ˌräd\ *n* **1** : a rod used to ram a charge into a muzzle-loading gun **2** : a cleaning rod for small arms **3** : BOSS, OVERSEER

²ramrod *adj* ♦ : marked by rigidity or severity

♦ austere, authoritarian, flinty, hard, harsh, heavy-handed, rigid, rigorous, severe, stern, strict — more at SEVERE

³ramrod *vb* : to direct, supervise, and control

ram·shack·le \'ram-ˌsha-kəl\ *adj* : RICKETY, TUMBLEDOWN

ran *past of* RUN

¹ranch \'ranch\ *n* [MexSp *rancho* small ranch, fr. Sp, camp, hut & Sp dial., small farm, fr. Old Spanish *ranchear(se)* to take up quarters, fr. MF *(se) ranger* to take up a position, fr. *ranger* to set in a row] **1** : an establishment for the raising and grazing of livestock (as cattle, sheep, or horses) **2** : a large farm devoted to a specialty **3** : RANCH HOUSE 2

²ranch *vb* : to live or work on a ranch — **ranch·er** *n*

ranch house *n* **1** : the main house on a ranch **2** : a one-story house typically with a low-pitched roof

ran·cho \'ran-chō, 'rän-\ *n, pl* **ranchos** : RANCH 1

ran·cid \'ran-səd\ *adj* **1** : having a rank smell or taste **2** : OBNOXIOUS — **ran·cid·i·ty** \ran-'si-də-tē\ *n*

ran·cor *or Can and Brit* **ran·cour** \'raŋ-kər\ *n* ♦ : bitter deep-seated ill will

♦ animosity, antagonism, antipathy, bitterness, enmity, gall, grudge, hostility — more at ENMITY

ran·cor·ous *adj* ♦ : deeply malevolent

♦ acrid, acrimonious, bitter, hard, resentful, sore — more at BITTER

rand \'rand, 'ränd, 'ränt\ *n, pl* **rand** : the basic monetary unit of the Republic of South Africa

R & B *abbr* rhythm and blues

R & D *abbr* research and development

ran·dom \'ran-dəm\ *adj* ♦ : lacking a definite plan, purpose, or pattern : HAPHAZARD — **ran·dom·ly** *adv* — **ran·dom·ness** *n*

♦ aimless, arbitrary, desultory, erratic, haphazard, scattered, stray; *also* accidental, casual, chance, fluky, fortuitous, inadvertent, incidental, lucky, unintended, unintentional, unplanned, unpremeditated; irregular, sporadic, spot; purposeless; unconsidered, unplanned; indiscriminate, unsystematic; undirected *Ant* methodical, nonrandom, orderly, systematic

random–access *adj* : allowing access to stored data in any order the user desires

random–access memory _n_ : RAM

ran·dom·ize \'ran-də-ˌmīz\ _vb_ **-ized; -iz·ing** : to select, assign, or arrange in a random way — **ran·dom·i·za·tion** \ˌran-də-mə-'zā-shən\ _n_

R and R _abbr_ rest and recreation; rest and recuperation

rang _past of_ RING

¹**range** \'rānj\ _n_ **1** ♦ : a series of things in a row **2** : a cooking stove having an oven and a flat top with burners **3 a** ♦ : open land where animals (as livestock) may roam and graze **b** ♦ : the region throughout which a kind of organism or ecological community naturally lives or occurs **4** : the act of ranging about : STROLL **5** : the distance a weapon will shoot or is to be shot **6** : a place where shooting is practiced **7** ♦ : the space or extent included, covered, or used : SCOPE **8** ♦ : a variation within limits

♦ [1] column, cue, file, line, queue, string, train — more at LINE ♦ [3a] pasture; _also_ ranch, station; feedlot, stockyard, yard; grassland, pampas, prairie, savanna, steppe ♦ [3b] habitat, home, niche, territory — more at HOME ♦ [7] amplitude, breadth, compass, extent, reach, realm, scope, sweep, width; _also_ gamut, spectrum, spread; domain, field, sphere; horizon, panorama ♦ [8] gamut, scale, spectrum, spread, stretch; _also_ measure, pitch, scale; amplitude, compass, extent, reach, realm, scope, sweep, width

²**range** _vb_ **ranged; rang·ing** [ME, fr. AF _renger_, fr. _renc, reng_ line, place, row, of Gmc origin] **1** ♦ : to set in a row or in proper order **2** ♦ : to set in place among others of the same kind **3** : to roam over or through : EXPLORE **4** ♦ : to roam at large or freely **5** : to correspond in direction or line **6** ♦ : to vary within limits **7** : to find the range of an object by instrument (as radar)

♦ [1] arrange, array, classify, codify, dispose, draw up, marshal, order, organize, systematize — more at ORDER ♦ [2] assort, break down, categorize, class, classify, grade, group, peg, place, rank, separate, sort — more at CLASSIFY ♦ [4] gad, gallivant, knock, maunder, meander, mope, ramble, roam, rove, traipse, wander — more at WANDER ♦ [6] go, run, vary — more at RUN

rang·er \'rān-jər\ _n_ **1** : FOREST RANGER **2** : a member of a body of troops who range over a region **3** : an expert in close-range fighting and raiding tactics

rangy \'rān-jē\ _adj_ **rang·i·er; -est** ♦ : being long-limbed and slender ⟨a ~ teenager⟩ — **rang·i·ness** \'rān-jē-nəs\ _n_

♦ gangling, lanky, spindly — more at LANKY

ra·ni _or_ **ra·nee** \rä-'nē, 'rä-ˌnē\ _n_ : a Hindu queen : a raja's wife

¹**rank** \'raŋk\ _adj_ **1** ♦ : strong and vigorous and usu. coarse in growth ⟨~ weeds⟩ **2** ♦ : unpleasantly strong-smelling **3** ♦ : shockingly conspicuous — **rank·ly** _adv_ — **rank·ness** _n_

♦ [1] lush, luxuriant, prosperous, rampant, weedy; _also_ lavish, profuse; overgrown, overrun; close, dense, thick _Ant_ sparse ♦ [2] fetid, foul, fusty, malodorous, musty, noisome, reeky, smelly, strong — more at MALODOROUS ♦ [3] blatant, conspicuous, egregious, flagrant, glaring, gross, obvious, patent, prominent, pronounced, striking — more at EGREGIOUS

²**rank** _n_ **1** : ROW **2** : a line of soldiers ranged side by side **3** _pl_ : the body of enlisted personnel ⟨rose from the ~s⟩ **4** : an orderly arrangement **5** : CLASS, DIVISION **6** ♦ : a grade of official standing (as in an army) **7** : position in a group **8** ♦ : superior position

♦ [6] degree, footing, level, place, position, situation, standing, station, status; _also_ condition, echelon, estate, order, walk; capacity, function; rating ♦ [8] class, quality, standing; _also_ gentility, gentleness, nobility, nobleness; grandness, highness, loftiness; distinction, precedence, preeminence, primacy; caste, position, station, status; preferment

³**rank** _vb_ **1** : to arrange in lines or in regular formation **2** ♦ : to determine the relative position of **3** : to rate

above (as in official standing) **4** ♦ : to take or have a relative position

♦ [2] assort, break down, categorize, class, classify, grade, group, peg, place, range, separate, sort — more at CLASSIFY ♦ [4] be, grade, place, rate; _also_ seed; count; class, classify, set, sort; install, instate

rank and file _n_ ♦ : the general membership of a body as contrasted with its leaders

♦ commoners, herd, masses, mob, people, plebeians, populace — more at MASSES

rank·ing \'raŋ-kiŋ\ _adj_ **1** : having a high position : of the highest rank **2** : being next to the chairman in seniority

ran·kle \'raŋ-kəl\ _vb_ **ran·kled; ran·kling** [ME _ranclen_ to fester, fr. AF _rancler_, fr. OF _draoncler, raoncler_, fr. _draoncle, raoncle_ festering sore, fr. ML _dracunculus_, fr. L, dim. of _draco_ serpent] ♦ : to cause anger, irritation, or bitterness

♦ anger, antagonize, enrage, incense, inflame, infuriate, madden, outrage, rile, roil — more at ANGER

ran·sack \'ran-ˌsak\ _vb_ **1** ♦ : to search thoroughly **2** ♦ : to search through and rob

♦ [1] dig, dredge, hunt, rake, rifle, rummage, scour, search — more at SEARCH ♦ [2] despoil, loot, maraud, pillage, plunder, sack, strip; _also_ burglarize; comb, hunt, rake, rifle, rummage; harry, raid; ravish

¹**ran·som** \'ran-səm\ _n_ [ME _ransoun_, fr. OF _rançun_, fr. L _redemption-, redemptio_ act of buying back, fr. _redimere_ to buy back, redeem] **1** : something paid or demanded for the freedom of a captive **2** : the act of ransoming

²**ransom** _vb_ : to free from captivity or punishment by paying a price — **ran·som·er** _n_

ran·som·ware \-ˌwar\ _n_ : malware that requires the victim to pay a ransom to access encrypted files

¹**rant** \'rant\ _vb_ **1** ♦ : to talk in a noisy, excited, or bombastic manner **2** : to scold violently ⟨~ed against his opponent⟩ — **rant·er** _n_ — **rant·ing·ly** _adv_

♦ bluster, fulminate, rave, spout; _also_ sound off, speak out, speak up; blare, blurt out, bolt; declaim, harangue, mouth, orate, pontificate; carry on, rage, storm, take on

²**rant** _n_ ♦ : a bombastic extravagant speech; _also_ : the act of ranting

♦ diatribe, harangue, tirade — more at TIRADE ♦ bluster, bombast, brag, gas, grandiloquence — more at BOMBAST

¹**rap** \'rap\ _n_ **1** : a sharp blow **2** : a sharp rebuke **3** : a negative often undeserved reputation ⟨a bum ~⟩ **4** ♦ : responsibility for or consequences of an action ⟨take the ~⟩ **5** ♦ : a criminal charge

♦ [4] blame, culpability, fault, guilt — more at BLAME ♦ [5] charge, complaint, count, indictment — more at CHARGE

²**rap** _vb_ **rapped; rap·ping** **1** : to strike sharply : KNOCK **2** : to utter sharply **3** : to criticize sharply

³**rap** _vb_ **rapped; rap·ping** **1** : to talk freely and frankly **2** : to perform rap music — **rap·per** _n_

⁴**rap** _n_ **1** : an instance or period of speech or conversation : TALK, CONVERSATION **2** : a rhythmic chanting of usu. rhymed couplets to a musical accompaniment; _also_ : a piece so performed

⁵**rap** _n_ ♦ : a minimum amount or degree

♦ hoot, jot, lick, modicum, tittle, whit — more at JOT

ra·pa·cious \rə-'pā-shəs\ _adj_ **1** ♦ : excessively greedy or covetous **2** : living on prey **3** ♦ : having a huge appetite : RAVENOUS 2 — **ra·pa·cious·ly** _adv_

♦ [1] acquisitive, avaricious, avid, covetous, grasping, greedy, mercenary — more at GREEDY ♦ [3] gluttonous, greedy, hoggish, piggish, ravenous, voracious — more at VORACIOUS

ra·pa·cious·ness _n_ ♦ : the quality or state of being rapacious

♦ acquisitiveness, avarice, avidity, covetousness, cupidity, greed — more at GREED

ra·pac·i·ty \-'pa-sə-tē\ _n_ : RAPACIOUSNESS

¹**rape** \'rāp\ _n_ : a European herb related to the mustards

that is grown as a forage crop and for its seeds (**rapeseed** \-ˌsēd\)

²**rape** *vb* **raped; rap·ing** : to commit rape on — **rap·er** *n* — **rap·ist** \'rā-pist\ *n*

³**rape** *n* **1** : a carrying away by force **2** : unlawful sexual activity and usu. sexual intercourse carried out forcibly or under threat of injury or with a person under a certain age or incapable of valid consent

¹**rap·id** \'ra-pəd\ *adj* [L *rapidus* strong-flowing, rapid, fr. *rapere* to seize, carry away] ♦ : very fast : SWIFT

 ♦ fast, fleet, quick, speedy, swift — more at FAST

²**rapid** *n* : a place in a stream where the current flows very fast usu. over obstructions — usu. used in pl.

rapid eye movement *n* : rapid conjugate movement of the eyes associated with REM sleep

ra·pid·i·ty \rə-'pi-də-tē, ra-\ *n* ♦ : the quality or state of being rapid

 ♦ celerity, fastness, fleetness, haste, hurry, quickness, speed, swiftness, velocity — more at SPEED

rap·id·ly \'ra-pəd-lē\ *adv* ♦ : in a rapid manner : at a rapid rate

 ♦ apace, briskly, fast, full tilt, hastily, posthaste, presto, pronto, quick, quickly, soon, speedily, swift, swiftly — more at FAST

rapid transit *n* : fast passenger transportation (as by subway) in cities

¹**ra·pi·er** \'rā-pē-ər\ *n* : a straight 2-edged sword with a narrow pointed blade

²**rapier** *adj* : extremely sharp or keen ⟨~ wit⟩

rap·ine \'ra-pən, -ˌpīn\ *n* : PILLAGE, PLUNDER

rap·pel \ra-'pel, ra-\ *vb* **-pelled; -pel·ling** : to descend (as from a cliff) by sliding down a rope

rap·port \ra-'pȯr\ *n* **1** : RELATION **2** : relation characterized by harmony

rap·proche·ment \ˌra-ˌprōsh-'mäⁿ, ra-'prōsh-ˌmäⁿ\ *n* : the establishment of or a state of having cordial relations

rap·scal·lion \rap-'skal-yən\ *n* **1** : RASCAL **2** ♦ : a mischievous person or animal : SCAMP

 ♦ devil, hellion, imp, mischief, monkey, rascal, rogue, scamp, urchin — more at SCAMP

rapt \'rapt\ *adj* **1** : carried away with emotion **2** ♦ : wholly absorbed : ENGROSSED — **rapt·ly** \'rapt-lē\ *adv* — **rapt·ness** *n*

 ♦ absorbed, attentive, engrossed, intent, observant — more at ATTENTIVE

rap·tor \'rap-tər, -ˌtȯr\ *n* **1** : BIRD OF PREY **2** : a usu. small-to-medium-sized predatory dinosaur

rap·ture \'rap-chər\ *n* ♦ : spiritual or emotional ecstasy — **rap·tur·ous·ly** *adv*

 ♦ ecstasy, elation, euphoria, exhilaration, heaven, intoxication, paradise, rhapsody, transport — more at ECSTASY

rapture of the deep : NITROGEN NARCOSIS

rap·tur·ous \-chə-rəs\ *adj* ♦ : feeling, expressing, or marked by rapture

 ♦ ecstatic, elated, euphoric, intoxicated, rhapsodic — more at ECSTATIC

ra·ra avis \ˌrar-ə-'ā-vəs\ *n, pl* **ra·ra avis·es** \-'ā-və-səz\ *or* **ra·rae aves** \ˌrär-ˌī-'ä-ˌwās\ [L, rare bird] : a rare person or thing : RARITY

¹**rare** \'rar\ *adj* **rar·er; rar·est 1** : not thick or dense : THIN ⟨~ air⟩ **2** ♦ : unusually fine **3** ♦ : seldom seen, encountered, or experienced — **rare·ness** *n*

 ♦ [2] choice, dainty, delicate, elegant, exquisite, select — more at CHOICE ♦ [3] aberrant, abnormal, atypical, exceptional, extraordinary, freak, odd, peculiar, phenomenal, singular, uncommon, uncustomary, unique, unusual, unwonted — more at EXCEPTIONAL ♦ [3] infrequent, occasional, sporadic — more at INFREQUENT

²**rare** *adj* **rar·er; rar·est** : cooked so that the inside is still red ⟨~ beef⟩

rare·bit \'rar-bət\ *n* : WELSH RABBIT

rar·efac·tion \ˌrar-ə-'fak-shən\ *n* **1** : the action or process of rarefying **2** : the state of being rarefied

rar·e·fy *also* **rar·i·fy** \'rar-ə-ˌfī\ *vb* **-fied; -fy·ing** : to make or become rare, thin, or less dense

rare·ly *adv* ♦ : not often

 ♦ infrequently, little, seldom — more at SELDOM

rar·ing \'rar-ən, -iŋ\ *adj* ♦ : full of enthusiasm or eagerness ⟨~ to go⟩

 ♦ agog, anxious, ardent, athirst, avid, crazy, eager, enthusiastic, gung ho, hot, hungry, keen, nuts, solicitous, thirsty, voracious — more at EAGER

rar·i·ty \'rar-ə-tē\ *n* ♦ : something rare

 ♦ curiosity, exotic, oddity — more at CURIOSITY

ras·cal \'ras-kəl\ *n* [ME *rascaile* foot soldiers, commoners, worthless person, fr. AF *rascaille*, fr. OF dial. *rasquer to scrape, clean off, ultim. fr. L *radere* to scrape, shave] **1** ♦ : a mean or dishonest person **2** ♦ : a mischievous person

 ♦ [1] beast, evildoer, fiend, no-good, reprobate, rogue, varlet, villain, wretch — more at VILLAIN ♦ [2] devil, hellion, imp, mischief, monkey, rapscallion, rogue, scamp, urchin — more at SCAMP

ras·cal·i·ty \ras-'ka-lə-tē\ *n* ♦ : the character or actions of a rascal

 ♦ devilishness, impishness, knavery, mischief, mischievousness, shenanigans, waggery, wickedness — more at MISCHIEF

ras·cal·ly \'ras-kə-lē\ *adj* ♦ : of or characteristic of a rascal

 ♦ devilish, impish, knavish, mischievous, roguish, sly, waggish, wicked — more at MISCHIEVOUS

¹**rash** \'rash\ *adj* ♦ : having or showing little regard for consequences : too hasty in decision, action, or speech — **rash·ness** *n*

 ♦ cursory, hasty, headlong, pell-mell, precipitate, precipitous — more at HASTY

²**rash** *n* : an eruption on the body

rash·er \'ra-shər\ *n* : a thin slice of bacon or ham broiled or fried; *also* : a portion consisting of several such slices

rash·ly \'rash-lē\ *adv* ♦ : in a rash manner

 ♦ cursorily, hastily, headlong, hurriedly, pell-mell, precipitately — more at HASTILY

¹**rasp** \'rasp\ *vb* **1** ♦ : to rub with or as if with a rough file **2** ♦ : to grate harshly on (as one's nerves) **3** : to speak in a grating tone

 ♦ [1] grate, grind, scrape, scratch — more at SCRAPE ♦ [2] aggravate, annoy, bother, bug, chafe, exasperate, gall, get, grate, irk, irritate, nettle, peeve, persecute, pique, put out, rile, vex — more at IRRITATE

²**rasp** *n* **1** : a coarse file with cutting points instead of ridges **2** ♦ : a rasping sound, sensation, or effect

 ♦ grind, scrape, scratch; *also* clash, jangle, jar; croak; blast, bleat, bray, screech

rasp·ber·ry \'raz-ˌber-ē, -bə-rē\ *n* **1** : any of various edible usu. black or red berries produced by some brambles; *also* : such a bramble **2** ♦ : a sound of contempt made by protruding the tongue through the lips and expelling air forcibly

 ♦ boo, catcall, hiss, hoot, jeer, snort — more at CATCALL

¹**rat** \'rat\ *n* **1** : any of numerous rodents larger than the related mice **2** : a contemptible person; *esp* ♦ : one that betrays friends or associates

 ♦ betrayer, blabbermouth, informer, snitch, stool pigeon, tattler, tattletale — more at INFORMER

²**rat** *vb* **rat·ted; rat·ting 1** : to betray or inform on one's associates **2** : to hunt or catch rats

rat cheese *n* : CHEDDAR

ratch·et \'ra-chət\ *n* : a device that consists of a bar or wheel having slanted teeth into which a pawl drops so as to allow motion in only one direction

¹**rate** \'rāt\ *vb* **rat·ed; rat·ing** ♦ : to scold violently

♦ admonish, chide, lecture, rail (at *or* against), rebuke, reprimand, scold — more at SCOLD

²**rate** *n* **1** : quantity, amount, or degree measured by some standard **2** : an amount (as of payment) measured by its relation to some other amount (as of time) **3** : a charge, payment, or price fixed according to a ratio, scale, or standard ⟨tax ∼⟩ **4** ♦ : relative condition or quality : CLASS

♦ caliber (*or* calibre), class, grade, quality — more at QUALITY

³**rate** *vb* **rat·ed; rat·ing 1** ♦ : to set an estimate on **2** ♦ : to show respect or consideration for : CONSIDER, REGARD **3** : to settle the relative rank or class of **4** ♦ : to be classed : RANK **5** ♦ : to have a right to : DESERVE ⟨the museum ∼s a visit⟩ **6** : to be of consequence — **rat·er** *n*

♦ [1] appraise, assess, estimate, evaluate, set, value — more at ESTIMATE ♦ [2] account, call, consider, count, esteem, hold, reckon, regard, take — more at CONSIDER ♦ [4] be, grade, place, rank — more at RANK ♦ [5] deserve, earn, merit

rath·er \'ra-thər, 'rä-, 'rə-\ *adv* [ME, fr. OE *hrathor*, compar. of *hrathe* quickly] **1** : more properly **2** ♦ : more readily or willingly : PREFERABLY **3** : more correctly speaking **4** : to the contrary : INSTEAD **5** ♦ : in some degree : SOMEWHAT

♦ [2] first, preferably, readily, soon; *also* alternately, either, instead; gladly; voluntarily *Ant* involuntarily, unwillingly ♦ [5] enough, fairly, kind of, moderately, pretty, quite, somewhat, sort of, so-so, — more at FAIRLY

rather than *prep* : INSTEAD OF

raths·kel·ler \'rät-,ske-lər, 'rat-\ *n* [obs. G (now *Ratskeller*), city-hall basement restaurant, fr. *Rat* council + *Keller* cellar] : a usu. basement tavern or restaurant

rat·i·fy \'ra-tə-,fī\ *vb* **-fied; -fy·ing** ♦ : to approve and accept formally — **rat·i·fi·ca·tion** \,ra-tə-fə-'kā-shən\ *n*

♦ approve, authorize, clear, OK, sanction, warrant — more at APPROVE

rat·ing \'rā-tiŋ\ *n* **1** : a classification according to grade : RANK **2** *Brit* : an enlisted person in the navy **3** : an estimate of the credit standing and business responsibility of a person or firm

ra·tio \'rā-shō, -shē-ō\ *n, pl* **ra·tios 1** : the indicated quotient of two numbers or mathematical expressions **2** : the relationship in number, quantity, or degree between two or more things

ra·ti·o·ci·na·tion \,ra-tē-,ōs-ᵊn-'ā-shən, -shē-, -,äs-\ *n* : exact thinking : REASONING — **ra·ti·o·ci·nate** \-'ōs-ᵊn-,āt, -'äs-\ *vb* — **ra·ti·o·ci·na·tive** \-'ōs-ᵊn-,ā-tiv, -'äs-\ *adj* — **ra·ti·o·ci·na·tor** \-'ōs-ᵊn-,ā-tər, -'äs-\ *n*

¹**ra·tion** \'ra-shən, 'rā-\ *n* **1** : a food allowance for one day **2** : FOOD, PROVISIONS, DIET — usu. used in pl. **3** : SHARE, ALLOTMENT

²**ration** *vb* **1** ♦ : to supply with or allot as rations **2** : to use or allot sparingly

♦ allocate, allot, allow, apportion, assign — more at ALLOT

¹**ra·tio·nal** \'ra-shə-nəl\ *adj* **1** ♦ : having reason or understanding **2** ♦ : of or relating to reason **3** : relating to, consisting of, or being one or more rational numbers **4** ♦ : of, relating to, or in accordance with the principles of rationalism — **ra·tio·nal·ly** *adv*

♦ [1] intelligent, reasonable, reasoning; *also* analytic, logical; brainy, cerebral, highbrow, intellectual; cognitive, mental; practical, sane, sensible *Ant* irrational, unintelligent, unreasonable, unreasoning, unthinking ♦ [2, 4] good, hard, informed, just, levelheaded, logical, reasonable, reasoned, sensible, sober, solid, valid, well-founded — more at GOOD

²**rational** *n* : RATIONAL NUMBER

ra·tio·nale \,ra-shə-'nal\ *n* **1** ♦ : an explanation of principles controlling belief or practice **2** : an underlying reason

♦ argument, case, defense (*or* defence), explanation, reason — more at REASON

ra·tio·nal·ise *chiefly Brit var of* RATIONALIZE

ra·tio·nal·ism \'ra-shə-nə-,li-zəm\ *n* : the practice of guiding one's actions and opinions solely by what seems reasonable — **ra·tio·nal·ist** \-list\ *n* — **rationalist** *or* **ra·tio·nal·is·tic** \,ra-shə-nə-'lis-tik\ *adj*

ra·tio·nal·i·ty \,ra-shə-'na-lə-tē\ *n, pl* **-ties** : the quality or state of being rational

ra·tio·nal·ize \'ra-shə-nə-,līz\ *vb* **-ized; -iz·ing 1** ♦ : to make (something irrational) appear rational or reasonable **2** : to provide a natural explanation of (as a myth) **3** ♦ : to justify (as one's behavior or weaknesses) esp. to oneself **4** : to find plausible but untrue reasons for conduct — **ra·tio·nal·i·za·tion** \,ra-shə-nə-lə-'zā-shən\ *n*

♦ [1, 3] account, explain — more at EXPLAIN

rational number *n* : a number that can be expressed as an integer or the quotient of an integer divided by a nonzero integer

rat race *n* : strenuous, tiresome, and usu. competitive activity or rush

rat·tan \ra-'tan, rə-\ *n* : a cane or switch made from one of the long stems of an Asian climbing palm; *also* : this palm

rat·ter \'ra-tər\ *n* : a rat-catching dog or cat

¹**rat·tle** \'rat-ᵊl\ *vb* **rat·tled; rat·tling 1** : to make or cause to make a series of clattering sounds **2** : to move with a clattering sound **3** : to say or do in a brisk lively fashion ⟨∼ off the answers⟩ **4** ♦ : to upset esp. to the point of loss of poise and composure : CONFUSE ⟨∼ a witness⟩ **5** ♦ : to chatter incessantly and aimlessly

♦ [4] abash, confound, confuse, discomfit, disconcert, discountenance, embarrass, faze, fluster, mortify — more at EMBARRASS ♦ [5] maunder, ramble, run on — more at RAMBLE

²**rattle** *n* **1** : a toy that produces a rattle when shaken **2** : a series of clattering and knocking sounds **3** : a rattling organ at the end of a rattlesnake's tail

rat·tler \'rat-lər\ *n* : RATTLESNAKE

rat·tle·snake \'rat-ᵊl-,snāk\ *n* : any of various American pit vipers with a rattle at the end of the tail

rat·tle·trap \'rat-ᵊl-,trap\ *n* : something (as an old car) rickety and full of rattles

rat·tling \'rat-liŋ\ *adj* **1** ♦ : acting or capable of acting with speed : BRISK **2** : FIRST-RATE, SPLENDID

♦ breakneck, breathless, brisk, dizzy, fast, fleet, hasty, lightning, nippy, quick, rapid, snappy, speedy, swift — more at FAST

rat·trap \'rat-,trap\ *n* **1** : a trap for rats **2** : a dilapidated building

rat·ty \'ra-tē\ *adj* **rat·ti·er; -est 1** : infested with rats **2** : of, relating to, or suggestive of rats **3** ♦ : threadbare and faded from wear : SHABBY

♦ dilapidated, grungy, mean, neglected, seedy, shabby — more at SHABBY

rau·cous \'rȯ-kəs\ *adj* **1** : HARSH, HOARSE, STRIDENT **2** ♦ : boisterously disorderly — **rau·cous·ly** *adv* — **rau·cous·ness** *n*

♦ boisterous, rambunctious, rowdy — more at BOISTEROUS

raun·chy \'rȯn-chē, 'rän-\ *adj* **raun·chi·er; -est 1** : SLOVENLY, DIRTY **2** : OBSCENE, SMUTTY — **raun·chi·ness** \-chē-nəs\ *n*

¹**rav·age** \'ra-vij\ *n* [F] : an act or result of ravaging : DEVASTATION

²**ravage** *vb* **rav·aged; rav·ag·ing** ♦ : to lay waste : DEVASTATE — **rav·ag·er** *n*

♦ destroy, devastate, ruin, scourge; *also* despoil, foray, harry, loot, maraud, pillage, plunder, sack, strip; annihilate, desolate, extirpate, obliterate, smash, waste, wipe out, wreck; decimate, mow; demolish, raze; crush, overpower, overrun, overthrow, overwhelm

¹rave \'rāv\ *vb* **raved; rav·ing** [ME *raven*] **1** : to talk wildly in or as if in delirium : STORM, RAGE **2** ♦ : to talk with extreme enthusiasm **3** ♦ : to speak out wildly

  ♦ [2] enthuse, fuss, gush, rhapsodize, slobber — more at GUSH ♦ [3] bluster, fulminate, rant, spout — more at RANT

²rave *n* **1** : an act or instance of raving **2** : an extravagantly favorable criticism

¹rav·el \'ra-vəl\ *vb* **-eled** *or* **-elled; -el·ing** *or* **-el·ling** **1** : to undo the intricacies of : UNRAVEL **2** : TANGLE, CONFUSE

²ravel *n* **1** : something tangled **2** : something raveled out; *esp* : a loose thread

¹ra·ven \'rā-vən\ *n* : a large black bird related to the crow

²raven *adj* ♦ : black and glossy like a raven's feathers

  ♦ black, ebony — more at BLACK

³rav·en \'ra-vən\ *vb* **1** : to devour greedily **2** : DESPOIL, PLUNDER **3** : PREY

rav·en·ous \'ra-və-nəs\ *adj* **1** ♦ : having a huge appetite : VORACIOUS **2** : eager for food : very hungry — **rav·en·ous·ly** *adv* — **rav·en·ous·ness** *n*

  ♦ gluttonous, greedy, hoggish, piggish, rapacious, voracious — more at VORACIOUS

ra·vine \rə-'vēn\ *n* ♦ : a small narrow steep-sided valley larger than a gully

  ♦ canyon, defile, flume, gap, gorge, gulch, gulf, notch, pass — more at CANYON

rav·i·o·li \ˌra-vē-'ō-lē\ *n, pl* **ravioli** *also* **raviolis** [It, fr. It dial., pl. of *raviolo*, lit., little turnip, dim. of *rava* turnip, fr. L *rapa*] : small cases of dough with a savory filling (as of meat or cheese)

rav·ish \'ra-vish\ *vb* **1** : to seize and take away by violence **2** ♦ : to overcome with emotion and esp. with joy or delight **3** : RAPE — **rav·ish·er** *n* — **rav·ish·ment** *n*

  ♦ carry away, enrapture, enthrall, entrance, transport — more at ENTRANCE

rav·ish·ing \'ra-vi-shin\ *adj* ♦ : unusually attractive, pleasing, or striking

  ♦ attractive, beautiful, fair, gorgeous, handsome, knockout, lovely, pretty, stunning — more at BEAUTIFUL

¹raw \'rȯ\ *adj* **raw·er** \'rȯ-ər\; **raw·est** \'rȯ-əst\ **1** : not cooked **2** ♦ : changed little from the original form : not processed ⟨~ materials⟩ **3** : having the surface abraded or irritated ⟨a ~ sore⟩ **4** ♦ : not trained or experienced ⟨~ recruits⟩ **5** : VULGAR, COARSE **6** ♦ : disagreeably cold and damp ⟨a ~ day⟩ **7** : UNFAIR ⟨~ deal⟩

  ♦ [2] crude, native, natural, undressed, unprocessed, unrefined, untreated — more at CRUDE ♦ [4] adolescent, callow, green, immature, inexperienced, juvenile — more at CALLOW ♦ [6] bitter, bleak, chill, chilly, nippy, sharp — more at CHILLY

²raw *n* : a raw place or state; *esp* : NUDITY

raw·boned \'rȯ-ˌbōnd\ *adj* **1** : LEAN, GAUNT **2** : having a heavy frame that seems to have little flesh

raw deal *n* ♦ : an instance of unfair treatment

  ♦ disservice, injury, injustice, wrong — more at DISSERVICE

raw·hide \'rȯ-ˌhīd\ *n* : the untanned skin of cattle; *also* : a whip made of this

raw material *n* ♦ : something with a potential for improvement, development, or elaboration

  ♦ material, stuff, substance

raw·ness *n* ♦ : the quality or state of being raw

  ♦ bite, bitterness, bleakness, chill, nip, sharpness — more at CHILL

¹ray \'rā\ *n* : any of an order of large flat cartilaginous fishes that have the eyes on the upper surface and the hind end of the body slender and taillike

²ray *n* [ME, fr. AF *rai*, fr. L *radius* rod, ray] **1** : any of the lines of light that appear to radiate from a bright object **2** : a thin beam of radiant energy (as light) **3** : light from a beam **4** : a thin line like a beam of light **5** : an animal or plant structure resembling a ray **6** : a tiny bit : PARTICLE ⟨a ~ of hope⟩

ray·on \'rā-ˌän\ *n* : a fiber made from cellulose; *also* : a yarn, thread, or fabric made from such fibers

raze \'rāz\ *vb* **razed; raz·ing** **1** : to scrape, cut, or shave off **2** : to destroy to the ground : DEMOLISH

ra·zor \'rā-zər\ *n* : a sharp cutting instrument used to shave off hair

ra·zor–backed \'rā-zər-ˌbakt\ *or* **ra·zor·back** \-ˌbak\ *adj* : having a sharp narrow back ⟨~ horse⟩

razor clam *n* : any of a family of marine bivalve mollusks having a long narrow curved thin shell

razor wire *n* : coiled wire fitted with sharp edges and used as an obstacle or barrier

¹razz \'raz\ *n* : RASPBERRY 2

²razz *vb* ♦ : to harass and try to disconcert with questions, challenges, or gibes : TEASE

  ♦ chaff, jive, josh, kid, rally, rib, ride, roast, tease — more at TEASE

Rb *symbol* rubidium

RBC *abbr* red blood cells

RBI \ˌär-(ˌ)bē-'ī, 'ri-bē\ *n, pl* **RBIs** *or* **RBI** [*run batted in*] : a run in baseball that is driven in by a batter

RC *abbr* **1** Red Cross **2** Roman Catholic

RCAF *abbr* Royal Canadian Air Force

RCMP *abbr* Royal Canadian Mounted Police

RCN *abbr* Royal Canadian Navy

rct *abbr* recruit

rd *abbr* **1** road **2** rod **3** round

RD *abbr* rural delivery

RDA *abbr* recommended daily allowance; recommended dietary allowance

re \'rā, 'rē\ *prep* : with regard to

Re *symbol* rhenium

re- \rē, ˌrē, 'rē\ *prefix* **1** : again : for a second time **2** : anew : in a new or different form **3** : back : backward

¹reach \'rēch\ *vb* **1** : to stretch out **2** : to touch or attempt to touch or seize **3** : to extend to **4** : to communicate with **5** : to arrive at **6** ♦ : to hand over — **reach·er** *n*

  ♦ hand, hand over, pass, transfer — more at PASS

²reach *n* **1** : an unbroken stretch of a river **2** : the act of reaching **3** : a reachable distance; *also* : ability to reach **4** ♦ : a range of knowledge or comprehension **5** ♦ : a continuous stretch or expanse

  ♦ [4] amplitude, breadth, compass, extent, range, realm, scope, sweep, width — more at RANGE ♦ [5] breadth, expanse, extent, spread, stretch — more at EXPANSE

reach·able *adj* ♦ : capable of being reached

  ♦ accessible, convenient, handy — more at CONVENIENT

re·act \rē-'akt\ *vb* **1** : to exert a return or counteracting influence **2** : to have or show a reaction **3** : to act in opposition to a force or influence **4** : to move or tend in a reverse direction **5** : to undergo chemical reaction

re·ac·tant \rē-'ak-tənt\ *n* : a chemically reacting substance

re·ac·tion \rē-'ak-shən\ *n* **1** : the act or process of reacting **2** : a counter tendency; *esp* : a tendency toward a former esp. outmoded political or social order or policy **3** ♦ : bodily, mental, or emotional response to a stimulus **4** : chemical change **5** : a process involving change in atomic nuclei

---

List of self-explanatory words with the prefix *re-*

reabsorb	reactivate	readjust	readmission
reacquire	reactivation	readjustment	readmit

♦ reply, response, take; *also* answer, return; backlash; rebound; revulsion, rise; jerk, start, twitch

¹re·ac·tion·ary \rē-'ak-shə-,ner-ē\ *adj* **1** : relating to, marked by, or favoring esp. political reaction **2** ♦ : relating to, marked by, or favoring reaction

♦ conservative, old-fashioned, orthodox, traditional — more at CONSERVATIVE

²reactionary *n* : one that is reactionary; *esp* : one tending to favor established ideas, conditions, or institutions

♦ conservative, rightist, Tory — more at CONSERVA-TIVE

re·ac·tive \rē-'ak-tiv\ *adj* : reacting or tending to react
re·ac·tor \rē-'ak-tər\ *n* **1** : one that reacts **2** : a device for the controlled release of nuclear energy

¹read \'rēd\ *vb* **read** \'red\; **read·ing** [ME *reden* to advise, interpret, read, fr. OE *rǣdan*] **1** : to understand language by interpreting written symbols for speech sounds **2** : to utter aloud written or printed words **3** : to learn by observing ⟨~ nature's signs⟩ **4** : to study by a course of reading ⟨~s law⟩ **5** : to discover the meaning of ⟨~ the clues⟩ **6** : to recognize or interpret as if by reading **7** : to attribute (a meaning) to something ⟨~ guilt in his manner⟩ **8** : INDICATE ⟨thermometer ~s 10°⟩ **9** : to consist in phrasing or meaning ⟨the two versions ~ differently⟩ — **read·abil·i·ty** \,rē-də-'bi-lə-tē\ *n* — **read·able** \'rē-də-bəl\ *adj* — **read·ably** \-blē\ *adv* — **read·er** *n*
²read \'red\ *adj* : informed by reading ⟨widely ~⟩
re·ad·dress \rē-ə-'dres\ *vb* ♦ : to deal with again

♦ reanalyze, reconceive, reconsider, reexamine, rethink, review — more at RECONSIDER

read·er·ship \'rē-dər-,ship\ *n* : the mass or a particular group of readers
read·i·ly \'re-də-lē\ *adv* **1** : in a ready manner **2** ♦ : without much difficulty

♦ easily, effortlessly, fluently, freely, handily, lightly, painlessly, smoothly — more at EASILY

read·ing \'rēd-iŋ\ *n* **1** : something read or for reading **2** : a particular version **3** : data indicated by an instrument ⟨thermometer ~⟩ **4** : a particular interpretation (as of a law) **5** : a particular performance (as of a musical work) **6** : an indication of a certain state of affairs
read–only memory *n* : ROM
read·out \'rēd-,aut\ *n* **1** : the process of removing information from an automatic device (as a computer) and displaying it in an understandable form; *also* : the information removed from such a device **2** : an electronic device that presents information in visual form
read out *vb* **1** : to read aloud **2** : to expel from an organization
¹ready \'re-dē\ *adj* **read·i·er; -est** **1** ♦ : prepared for use or action **2 a** : likely to do something indicated **b** ♦ : willingly inclined toward : prepared to do **3** ♦ : spontaneously prompt ⟨her ~ wit⟩ **4** : immediately available ⟨~ cash⟩ — **read·i·ness** \-dē-nəs\ *n* — **at the ready** : ready for immediate use

♦ [1] fit, go, set; *also* conditioned, primed; braced, fortified, steeled; qualified, trained *Ant* unprepared, unready ♦ [2b] amenable, disposed, game, glad, inclined, willing — more at WILLING ♦ [3] alert, expeditious, prompt, quick, willing — more at QUICK

²ready *vb* **read·ied; ready·ing** ♦ : to make ready

♦ equip, fit, prepare, qualify, season — more at QUALIFY ♦ brace, forearm, fortify, nerve, psych (up), steel, strengthen — more at FORTIFY

ready–made \,re-dē-'mād\ *adj* : already made up for general sale : not specially made — **ready–made** *n*

ready room *n* : a room in which pilots are briefed and await orders
re·agent \rē-'ā-jənt\ *n* : a substance that takes part in or brings about a particular chemical reaction
¹re·al \'rēl\ *adj* [ME, real, relating to things (in law), fr. AF, fr. ML & LL; ML *realis* relating to things (in law), fr. LL, real, fr. L *res* thing, fact] **1** : of or relating to fixed or immovable things (as land) ⟨~ property⟩ **2** ♦ : not artificial, fraudulent, or illusory : GENUINE **3** ♦ : occurring or existing in actuality — **re·al·ness** *n* — **for real** **1** : in earnest **2** : GENUINE

♦ [2] artless, authentic, bona fide, genuine, honest, ingenuous, innocent, naive, natural, simple, sincere, true, unaffected, unpretentious ♦ [3] actual, concrete, existent, factual, true, very — more at ACTUAL

²real *adv* : to a high degree : VERY
real estate *n* : property in buildings and land
re·al·ism \'rē-ə-,li-zəm\ *n* **1** : the disposition to face facts and to deal with them practically **2** : true and faithful portrayal of nature and of people in art or literature — **re·al·ist** \-list\ *adj or n* — **re·al·is·ti·cal·ly** \-ti-k(ə-)lē\ *adv*
re·al·is·tic \,rē-ə-'lis-tik\ *adj* **1** ♦ : of, relating to, or marked by literary or artistic realism **2** ♦ : facing reality squarely : not impractical or visionary

♦ [1] lifelike, natural, near — more at NATURAL ♦ [2] down-to-earth, earthy, hardheaded, matter-of-fact, practical, pragmatic; *also* philistine, utilitarian; logical, rational, reasonable, sane, sensible, sound; hard-boiled, unromantic, unsentimental; cynical, disillusioned *Ant* idealistic, impractical, unrealistic, utopian, visionary

re·al·i·ty \rē-'a-lə-tē\ *n, pl* **-ties** **1** ♦ : the quality or state of being real **2** : something real **3** : the totality of real things and events

♦ actuality, existence, subsistence — more at EXISTENCE

re·al·iz·able \'rē-ə-,lī-zə-bəl\ *adj* ♦ : capable of being realized

♦ achievable, attainable, doable, feasible, possible, practicable, viable, workable — more at POSSIBLE

re·al·i·za·tion \,rē-ə-lə-'zā-shən\ *n* ♦ : the action of realizing : the state of being realized

♦ accomplishment, achievement, actuality, attainment, consummation, fruition, fulfillment — more at FRUITION

re·al·ize \'rē-ə-,līz\ *vb* **-ized; -iz·ing** **1** : to make actual : ACCOMPLISH **2** : to convert into money ⟨~ assets⟩ **3** : to bring or get by sale, investment, or effort : OBTAIN, GAIN ⟨~ a profit⟩ **4** ♦ : to be aware of

♦ ascertain, catch on, discover, find out, hear, learn, see — more at DISCOVER

re·al·ly \'rē-lē, 'ri-\ *adv* **1** ♦ : in truth : in fact **2** ♦ : without any question — used as an intensifier ⟨a ~ beautiful day⟩

♦ [1] actually, frankly, genuinely, honestly, truly, truthfully, verily — more at ACTUALLY ♦ [2] certainly, definitely, doubtless, incontestably, indeed, indisputably, surely, truly, undeniably, undoubtedly, unquestionably — more at INDEED

realm \'relm\ *n* **1** : KINGDOM **2** ♦ : an area or range over or within which someone or something acts, exists, or has influence or significance : SPHERE, DOMAIN

♦ area, arena, demesne, department, discipline, domain, field, line, province, specialty, sphere — more at FIELD

real number *n* : a number that has no imaginary part ⟨the

List of self-explanatory words with the prefix re- (continued)

reaffirm	realignment	reanalysis	reannexation
reaffirmation	reallocate	reanimation	reappear
realign	reallocation	reannex	reappearance

set of all *real numbers* comprises the rationals and the irrationals⟩

re·al·po·li·tik \rā-'äl-ˌpō-li-ˌtēk\ *n, often cap* [G] : politics based on practical and material factors rather than on theoretical or ethical objectives

real time *n* : the actual time during which something takes place — **real–time** *adj*

re·al·ty \'rēl-tē\ *n* : REAL ESTATE

¹**ream** \'rēm\ *n* [ME *reme*, fr. AF, ultim. fr. Ar *rizmah*, lit., bundle] **1** : a quantity of paper that is variously 480, 500, or 516 sheets **2** ♦ : a great amount — usu. used in the pl. ⟨~s of information⟩

♦ **reams** abundance, deal, gobs, heap, loads, lot, pile, plenty, quantity, scads — more at LOT

²**ream** *vb* : to enlarge, shape, or clear with a reamer

ream·er \'rē-mər\ *n* : a tool with cutting edges that is used to enlarge or shape a hole

re·an·a·lyze \rē-'an-ᵊl-ˌīz\ *vb* ♦ : to analyze again

♦ readdress, reconceive, reconsider, reexamine, rethink, review — more at RECONSIDER

re·an·i·mate \rē-'a-nə-ˌmāt\ *vb* ♦ : to give renewed spirit and support to

♦ regenerate, reinvigorate, rejuvenate, renew, resuscitate, revitalize, revive — more at REVIVE

reap \'rēp\ *vb* **1** : to cut or clear with a scythe, sickle, or machine **2** ♦ : to gather by or as if by cutting : HARVEST ⟨~ a reward⟩ — **reap·er** *n*

♦ gather, harvest, pick — more at HARVEST

re·ap·prais·al \rē-ə-'prā-zəl\ *n* ♦ : a second or fresh appraisal

♦ reexamination, retrospection, review — more at REVIEW

¹**rear** \'rir\ *vb* **1** ♦ : to erect by building **2** : to set or raise upright **3** ♦ : to breed and raise for use or market ⟨~ livestock⟩ **4** ♦ : to bring to maturity or self-sufficiency usu. through nurturing care **5** : to lift or rise up; *esp* : to rise on the hind legs

♦ [1] assemble, build, construct, erect, fabricate, make, make up, piece, put up, raise, set up — more at BUILD ♦ [3] crop, cultivate, culture, grow, promote, raise, tend — more at GROW ♦ [4] breed, bring up, foster, raise — more at BRING UP

²**rear** *n* **1** : the unit (as of an army) or area farthest from the enemy : BACK; *also* : the position at the back of something **3** ♦ : the seat of the body

♦ backside, bottom, butt, buttocks, posterior, rump, seat — more at BUTTOCKS

³**rear** *adj* ♦ : being at the back

♦ back, hind, hindmost, posterior — more at BACK

rear admiral *n* : a commissioned officer in the navy or coast guard ranking next below a vice admiral

¹**rear·ward** \'rir-wərd\ *adj* **1** : being at or toward the rear **2** : directed toward the rear

²**rear·ward** *also* **rear·wards** \-wərdz\ *adv* : at or toward the rear

reas *abbr* reasonable

¹**rea·son** \'rēz-ᵊn\ *n* [ME *resoun*, fr. AF *raisun*, fr. L *ration-, ratio* reason, computation] **1** ♦ : a statement offered in explanation or justification **2** ♦ : a person or thing that is the occasion of an action or state : CAUSE **3** : the power to think : INTELLECT **4** ♦ : a sane or sound mind **5** ♦ : due exercise of the faculty of logical thought

♦ [1] alibi, argument, case, defense (*or* defence), excuse, explanation, justification, rationale; *also* appeal, plea; guise, pretense, pretext, rationalization ♦ [2] antecedent, cause, grounds, motive, occasion, wherefore, why ♦ [4] head, mind, sanity, wit — more at MIND ♦ [5] logic, reasoning, sense — more at LOGIC

²**reason** *vb* **1** : to talk with another to cause a change of mind **2** : to use the faculty of reason : THINK **3** ♦ : to discover or formulate by the use of reason **4** ♦ : to persuade or influence by the use of reason — **rea·son·er** *n*

♦ [3] conclude, deduce, extrapolate, gather, infer, judge, understand — more at INFER ♦ [4] argue, assert, contend, maintain, plead — more at ARGUE

rea·son·able \'rēz-ᵊn-ə-bəl\ *adj* **1** ♦ : being within the bounds of reason : not extreme **2** : reasonable in price : INEXPENSIVE **3** ♦ : able to reason : RATIONAL **4** ♦ : being in accordance with reason — **rea·son·able·ness** *n*

♦ [3] intelligent, rational, reasoning — more at RATIONAL ♦ [4] good, hard, informed, just, levelheaded, logical, rational, reasoned, sensible, sober, solid, valid, well-founded — more at GOOD

rea·son·ably \-blē\ *adv* : in a reasonable manner

rea·soned *adj* ♦ : based on or marked by reasoning

♦ advised, calculated, deliberate, measured, studied, thoughtful, thought-out — more at DELIBERATE

rea·son·ing *n* ♦ : the use of reason

♦ logic, reason, sense — more at LOGIC

re·as·sure \ˌrē-ə-'shu̇r\ *vb* **1** : to assure again **2** ♦ : to restore confidence to : free from fear — **re·as·sur·ance** \-'shu̇r-əns\ *n* — **re·as·sur·ing·ly** *adv*

♦ assure, cheer, comfort, console, solace, soothe — more at COMFORT

¹**re·bate** \'rē-ˌbāt\ *vb* **re·bat·ed; re·bat·ing** : to make or give a rebate

²**rebate** *n* : a return of part of a payment

¹**reb·el** \'re-bəl\ *adj* [ME, fr. AF, fr. L *rebellis*, fr. *re-* + *bellum* war] : of or relating to rebels

²**rebel** *n* ♦ : one that rebels against authority

♦ insurgent, insurrectionist, mutineer, red, revolter, revolutionary; *also* challenger; anarchist; extremist, malcontent, radical

³**re·bel** \ri-'bel\ *vb* **re·belled; re·bel·ling** **1** : to resist the authority of one's government **2** : to act in or show disobedience **3** : to feel or exhibit anger or revulsion

re·bel·lion \ri-'bel-yən\ *n* ♦ : resistance to authority; *esp* : defiance against a government through uprising or revolt

♦ insurrection, mutiny, revolt, revolution, uprising; *also* coup, coup d'état, overthrow; sedition, treachery, treason; sabotage, subversion

re·bel·lious \-yəs\ *adj* **1** ♦ : given to or engaged in rebellion **2** ♦ : inclined to resist authority — **re·bel·lious·ly** *adv*

♦ [1] insurgent, mutinous, revolutionary; *also* seditious, traitorous, treacherous, treasonous ♦ [1, 2] contrary, defiant, disobedient, froward, intractable, recalcitrant, refractory, unruly, untoward, wayward, willful — more at DISOBEDIENT

re·bel·lious·ness *n* ♦ : the quality or state of being rebellious

♦ defiance, disobedience, insubordination, recalcitrance, refractoriness, unruliness — more at DISOBEDIENCE

re·birth \ˌrē-'bərth\ *n* **1** : a new or second birth **2** ♦ : a return or renewal of vigor, freshness, or productivity : REVIVAL

♦ regeneration, rejuvenation, renewal, resurgence, resurrection, resuscitation, revival — more at REVIVAL

re·born \-'bȯrn\ *adj* : born again : REGENERATED, REVIVED

¹**re·bound** \ˌrē-'bau̇nd, 'rē-ˌbau̇nd\ *vb* **1** ♦ : to spring back on or as if on striking another body **2** ♦ : to recover

from a setback or frustration ⟨~ed quickly from the loss⟩

♦ [1] bounce, carom, glance, ricochet, skim, skip — more at GLANCE ♦ [2] rally, recover, snap back — more at RECOVER

²re·bound \'rē-‚baund\ n 1 : the action of rebounding 2 : a rebounding ball 3 : a reaction to setback or frustration
¹re·buff \ri-'bəf\ vb : to reject or criticize sharply
²rebuff n ♦ : an abrupt rejection of an offer or advance

♦ brush-off, cold shoulder, repulse, snub — more at COLD SHOULDER

re·build \(‚)rē-'bild\ vb -built \-'bilt\; -build·ing 1 : REPAIR, RECONSTRUCT; also : REMODEL 2 : to build again
¹re·buke \ri-'byük\ vb re·buked; re·buk·ing ♦ : to reprimand sharply

♦ censure, condemn, denounce, reprimand, reproach, reprove — more at CENSURE ♦ admonish, chide, lecture, rail (at or against), rate, reprimand, scold — more at SCOLD

²rebuke n ♦ : a sharp reprimand

♦ censure, denunciation, reprimand, reproach, reproof, stricture — more at CENSURE

re·bus \'rē-bəs\ n [L, by things, abl. pl. of res thing] : a representation of syllables or words by means of pictures; also : a riddle composed of such pictures
re·but \ri-'bət\ vb re·but·ted; re·but·ting ♦ : to refute esp. formally (as in debate) by evidence and arguments — re·but·ter n

♦ belie, confute, disprove, refute — more at DISPROVE

re·but·tal \ri-'bət-ᵊl\ n : the act of rebutting; also ♦ : argument or proof that rebuts

♦ confutation, refutation — more at CONFUTATION

rec abbr 1 receipt 2 record; recording 3 recreation
re·cal·ci·trance \ri-'kal-sə-trəns\ n ♦ : the state of being recalcitrant

♦ defiance, disobedience, insubordination, rebelliousness, refractoriness, unruliness — more at DISOBEDIENCE

re·cal·ci·trant \ri-'kal-sə-trənt\ adj [LL recalcitrant-, recalcitrans, prp. of recalcitrare to be stubbornly disobedient, fr. L, to kick back, fr. re- back, again + calcitrare to kick, fr. calc-, calx heel] 1 ♦ : stubbornly resisting authority ⟨a ~ prisoner⟩ 2 : resistant to handling or treatment

♦ contrary, defiant, disobedient, froward, intractable, rebellious, refractory, unruly, untoward, wayward, willful — more at DISOBEDIENT

¹re·call \ri-'kol\ vb 1 : to call back 2 ♦ : to bring back to mind : REMEMBER, RECOLLECT 3 ♦ : to call off usu. without expectation of conducting or performing at a later time : REVOKE, CANCEL

♦ [2] recollect, remember, reminisce, think — more at REMEMBER ♦ [3] abort, call, call off, cancel, drop, repeal, rescind, revoke — more at CANCEL

²re·call \ri-'kol, 'rē-‚kol\ n 1 : a summons to return 2 : the procedure of removing an official by popular vote 3 ♦ : remembrance of things learned or experienced 4 ♦ : the act of revoking 5 : a call by a manufacturer for the return of a product that may be defective or contaminated

♦ [3] memory, recollection, remembrance, reminiscence — more at MEMORY ♦ [4] abortion, calling, cancellation, repeal, rescission, revocation — more at CANCELLATION

re·cant \ri-'kant\ vb ♦ : to take back (something one has

said) publicly : make an open confession of error — re·can·ta·tion \‚rē-‚kan-'tā-shən\ n

♦ abjure, renounce, retract, take back, unsay, withdraw — more at ABJURE

¹re·cap \'rē-‚kap, rē-'kap\ vb re·capped; re·cap·ping : to repeat the principal stages or phases of : RECAPITULATE
²recap vb re·capped; re·cap·ping : RETREAD — re·cap \'rē-‚kap\ n
³re·cap \'rē-‚kap\ n : RECAPITULATION
re·ca·pit·u·late \‚rē-kə-'pi-chə-‚lāt\ vb -lat·ed; -lat·ing ♦ : to restate briefly : SUMMARIZE ⟨~ a news story⟩

♦ abstract, digest, encapsulate, epitomize, outline, sum up, summarize, wrap up — more at SUMMARIZE

re·ca·pit·u·la·tion \-‚pi-chə-'lā-shən\ n ♦ : a concise summary

♦ abstract, digest, encapsulation, epitome, outline, précis, résumé (or resume), roundup, sum, summary, synopsis, wrap-up — more at SUMMARY

re·cap·ture \(‚)rē-'kap-chər\ vb 1 ♦ : to capture again 2 : to experience again ⟨~ happy times⟩

♦ reclaim, recoup, recover, regain, repossess, retake, retrieve — more at RECOVER

re·cast \(‚)rē-'kast\ vb 1 : to cast again 2 ♦ : to alter the structure of : REVISE, REMODEL ⟨~ a sentence⟩

♦ alter, change, make over, modify, redo, refashion, remake, remodel, revamp, revise, rework, vary — more at CHANGE

recd abbr received
re·cede \ri-'sēd\ vb re·ced·ed; re·ced·ing 1 ♦ : to move back or away 2 : to slant backward 3 ♦ : to grow less or smaller : DIMINISH

♦ [1] back, fall back, retire, retreat, withdraw — more at RETREAT ♦ [3] abate, decline, decrease, de-escalate, die, diminish, dwindle, ebb, fall, lessen, let up, lower, moderate, relent, shrink, subside, taper, wane — more at DECREASE

¹re·ceipt \ri-'sēt\ n 1 : RECIPE 2 : the act of receiving 3 : something received — usu. used in pl. 4 : a written acknowledgment of something received
²receipt vb 1 : to give a receipt for 2 : to mark as paid
re·ceiv·able \ri-'sē-və-bəl\ adj 1 : capable of being received; esp : acceptable as legal ⟨~ certificates⟩ 2 : subject to call for payment ⟨notes ~⟩
re·ceive \ri-'sēv\ vb re·ceived; re·ceiv·ing 1 : to take in or accept (as something sent or paid) : come into possession of : GET 2 : CONTAIN, HOLD 3 : to permit to enter : GREET, WELCOME 4 : to be at home to visitors 5 : to accept as true or authoritative 6 : to be the subject of : UNDERGO, EXPERIENCE ⟨~ a shock⟩ 7 : to change incoming radio waves into sounds or pictures ⟨~ a broadcast⟩
re·ceiv·er \ri-'sē-vər\ n 1 : one that receives 2 : a person legally appointed to receive and have charge of property or money involved in a lawsuit 3 : a device for converting electromagnetic waves or signals into audio or visual form ⟨telephone ~⟩
re·ceiv·er·ship \-‚ship\ n 1 : the office or function of a receiver 2 : the condition of being in the hands of a receiver
re·cen·cy \'rēs-ᵊn-sē\ n : RECENTNESS
re·cent \'rēs-ᵊnt\ adj 1 : of the present time or time just past ⟨~ history⟩ 2 : having lately come into existence : NEW, FRESH ⟨~ buds⟩ 3 cap : HOLOCENE — re·cent·ness n
re·cent·ly adv ♦ : during a recent period of time

♦ freshly, just, late, lately, new, newly, now, only — more at NEWLY

List of self-explanatory words with the prefix re- (continued)

rearrest	reassembly	reassessment	reassume
reascend	reassert	reassign	reattach
reassemble	reassess	reassignment	reattachment

re·cep·ta·cle \ri-'sep-ti-kəl\ *n* **1** ♦ : something used to receive and hold something else : CONTAINER **2** : the enlarged end of a flower stalk upon which the parts of the flower grow **3** : an electrical fitting containing the live parts of a circuit

♦ container, holder, vessel — more at CONTAINER

re·cep·tion \ri-'sep-shən\ *n* **1** : the act of receiving **2** : a social gathering at which guests are formally welcomed

re·cep·tion·ist \ri-'sep-shə-nist\ *n* : a person employed to greet callers

re·cep·tive \ri-'sep-tiv\ *adj* **1** : able or inclined to receive **2** ♦ : open and responsive to ideas, impressions, or suggestions ⟨a ∼ audience⟩ — **re·cep·tive·ly** *adv* — **re·cep·tive·ness** *n* — **re·cep·tiv·i·ty** \ˌrē-ˌsep-'ti-və-tē\ *n*

♦ broad-minded, open, open-minded — more at OPEN-MINDED

re·cep·tor \ri-'sep-tər\ *n* **1** : one that receives stimuli : SENSE ORGAN **2** : a chemical group or molecule in the outer cell membrane or in the cell interior that has an affinity for a specific chemical group, molecule, or virus

¹**re·cess** \'rē-ˌses, ri-'ses\ *n* **1** : a secret or secluded place **2** ♦ : an indentation in a line or surface (as an alcove in a room) **3** ♦ : a suspension of business or procedure for rest or relaxation

♦ [2] alcove, niche, nook — more at NICHE ♦ [3] break, leave, vacation — more at VACATION ♦ [3] break, breath, breather, respite — more at BREAK

²**recess** *vb* **1** : to put into a recess **2** : to make a recess in **3** : to interrupt for a recess **4** : to take a recess

re·ces·sion \ri-'se-shən\ *n* **1** : the act of receding : WITHDRAWAL **2** : a departing procession (as at the end of a church service) **3** : a period of reduced economic activity

re·ces·sion·al \ri-'se-shə-nəl\ *n* **1** : a hymn or musical piece at the conclusion of a service or program **2** : RECESSION 2

¹**re·ces·sive** \ri-'se-siv\ *adj* **1** : tending to recede **2** : producing or being a bodily characteristic that is masked or not expressed when a contrasting dominant gene or trait is present ⟨∼ genes⟩ ⟨∼ traits⟩

²**recessive** *n* : a recessive characteristic or gene; *also* : an individual that has one or more recessive characteristics

re·cher·ché \rə-ˌsher-'shā, -'sher-ˌshā\ *adj* [F] **1** : CHOICE, RARE **2** : excessively refined ⟨∼ poetry⟩

re·cid·i·vism \ri-'si-də-ˌvi-zəm\ *n* : a tendency to relapse into a previous condition; *esp* : relapse into criminal behavior — **re·cid·i·vist** \-vist\ *n*

rec·i·pe \'re-sə-(ˌ)pē\ *n* [L, take, imperative of *recipere* to take, receive, fr. *re-* back + *capere* to take] **1** : a set of instructions for making something from various ingredients **2** : a method of procedure : FORMULA

re·cip·i·ent \ri-'si-pē-ənt\ *n* : one that receives

¹**re·cip·ro·cal** \ri-'si-prə-kəl\ *adj* **1** : inversely related **2** : MUTUAL, SHARED **3** : serving to reciprocate **4** : mutually corresponding — **re·cip·ro·cal·ly** *adv*

²**reciprocal** *n* **1** : something in a reciprocal relationship to another **2** : one of a pair of numbers (as ⅔ and 3/2) whose product is one

re·cip·ro·cate \-ˌkāt\ *vb* **-cat·ed; -cat·ing** **1** : to move backward and forward alternately **2** : to give and take mutually **3** : to make a return for something done or given — **re·cip·ro·ca·tion** \-ˌsi-prə-'kā-shən\ *n*

rec·i·proc·i·ty \ˌre-sə-'prä-sə-tē\ *n, pl* **-ties** **1** : the quality or state of being reciprocal **2** : mutual exchange of privileges (as trade advantages between countries)

re·cit·al \ri-'sīt-ᵊl\ *n* **1** : an act or instance of reciting : ACCOUNT **2** : a public reading or recitation ⟨a poetry ∼⟩

3 : a concert given by a musician, dancer, or dance troupe **4** : a public exhibition of skill given by music or dance pupils — **re·cit·al·ist** \-ᵊl-ist\ *n*

rec·i·ta·tion \ˌre-sə-'tā-shən\ *n* **1** : RECITING, RECITAL **2** : delivery before an audience usu. of something memorized ⟨∼ of a speech⟩ **3** : a classroom exercise in which pupils answer questions on a lesson they have studied

re·cite \ri-'sīt\ *vb* **re·cit·ed; re·cit·ing** **1** : to repeat verbatim (as something memorized) **2** ♦ : to recount in some detail : RELATE **3** : to reply to a teacher's questions on a lesson — **re·cit·er** *n*

♦ describe, narrate, recount, rehearse, relate, report, tell — more at TELL

reck·less \'re-kləs\ *adj* ♦ : lacking caution — **reck·less·ly** *adv* — **reck·less·ness** *n*

♦ brash, foolhardy, irresponsible; *also* adventurous, bold, daring, venturesome; hasty, headlong, precipitate, rash, wild; nonchalant, unconcerned, unworried; careless, heedless, inattentive, incautious; inconsiderate, thoughtless, unthinking *Ant* responsible

reck·on \'re-kən\ *vb* **1** ♦ : to arrive at or estimate by calculation : CALCULATE **2** ♦ : to regard or think of as : CONSIDER ⟨was ∼ed as the leader⟩ **3** *chiefly dial* : THINK, SUPPOSE, GUESS **4** ♦ : to accept something as certain : place reliance ⟨I ∼ on your promise to help⟩

♦ [1] calculate, call, conjecture, estimate, figure, gauge, guess, judge, make, place, put, suppose — more at ESTIMATE ♦ [2] account, call, consider, count, esteem, hold, rate, regard, take — more at CONSIDER ♦ [4] count, depend, lean, rely — more at DEPEND

reck·on·ing *n* **1** ♦ : an act or instance of reckoning **2** : a settling of accounts ⟨day of ∼⟩

♦ appraisal, assessment, estimate, estimation, evaluation, valuation — more at ESTIMATE ♦ arithmetic, calculation, computation — more at CALCULATION

re·claim \ri-'klām\ *vb* **1** ♦ : to correct or change from a pattern of wrong conduct : REFORM **2** : to change from an undesirable to a desired condition ⟨∼ marshy land⟩ **3** : to obtain from a waste product or by-product **4** ♦ : to demand or obtain the return of — **re·claim·able** *adj*

♦ [1] redeem, reform, rehabilitate — more at REFORM ♦ [4] recapture, recoup, recover, regain, repossess, retake, retrieve — more at RECOVER

rec·la·ma·tion \ˌre-klə-'mā-shən\ *n* ♦ : the act or process of reclaiming

♦ recovery, repossession, retrieval — more at RECOVERY

re·cline \ri-'klīn\ *vb* **re·clined; re·clin·ing** **1** : to lean or incline backward **2** : to lie down : REST

re·clin·er \ri-'klī-nər\ *n* : a chair with an adjustable back and footrest

re·cluse \'re-ˌklüs, ri-'klüs\ *n* ♦ : a person who leads a secluded or solitary life : HERMIT — **re·clu·sive** \ri-'klü-siv\ *adj*

♦ anchorite, hermit, solitary; *also* homebody, shut-in; monk

rec·og·nise *chiefly Brit var of* RECOGNIZE

rec·og·ni·tion \ˌre-kəg-'ni-shən\ *n* **1** : the act of recognizing : the state of being recognized : ACKNOWLEDGMENT **2** : special notice or attention

re·cog·ni·zance \ri-'käg-nə-zəns\ *n* : a promise recorded before a court or magistrate to do something (as to appear in court or to keep the peace) usu. under penalty of a money forfeiture

rec·og·nize \'re-kəg-ˌnīz\ *vb* **-nized; -niz·ing** **1** : to acknowledge (as a speaker in a meeting) as one entitled to be heard at the time **2** : to acknowledge the existence or the independence of (a country or government) **3** : to take notice of **4** : to acknowledge with appreciation **5** : to acknowledge acquaintance with **6** : to identify as previously known **7** : to perceive clearly : REALIZE — **rec·og·niz·able** \\'re-kəg-ˌnī-zə-bəl\\ *adj* — **rec·og·niz·ably** \\-blē\\ *adv*

¹**re·coil** \\ri-'kȯi(-ə)l\\ *vb* [ME *reculen, recoilen,* fr. AF *reculer, reculier,* fr. *re-* back + *cul* backside, fr. L *culus*] **1** ♦ : to draw back **2** : to spring back to or as if to a starting point
♦ blench, flinch, quail, shrink, wince — more at FLINCH

²**re·coil** \\'rē-ˌkȯil, ri-'kȯil\\ *n* : the action of recoiling (as by a gun or spring)

rec·ol·lect \\ˌre-kə-'lekt\\ *vb* ♦ : to recall to mind : REMEMBER
♦ recall, remember, reminisce, think — more at REMEMBER

rec·ol·lec·tion \\ˌre-kə-'lek-shən\\ *n* **1** ♦ : the act or power of recollecting **2** : something recollected
♦ memory, recall, remembrance, reminiscence — more at MEMORY

re·com·bi·nant \\(ˌ)rē-'käm-bə-nənt\\ *adj* **1** : relating to genetic recombination **2** : containing or produced by recombinant DNA ⟨∼ vaccines⟩

re·com·bi·nant DNA \\(ˌ)rē-'käm-bə-nənt-\\ *n* : genetically engineered DNA prepared in vitro by joining together DNA usu. from more than one species of organism

re·com·bi·na·tion \\ˌrē-ˌkäm-bə-'nā-shən\\ *n* : the formation of new combinations of genes

rec·om·mend \\ˌre-kə-'mend\\ *vb* **1** : to present as deserving of acceptance or trial **2** : to give in charge : COMMIT **3** : to make acceptable **4** : to give advice to : ADVISE, COUNSEL — **rec·om·mend·able** \\-'men-də-bəl\\ *adj*

rec·om·men·da·tion \\ˌre-kə-mən-'dā-shən\\ *n* **1** : the act of recommending **2** : something recommended **3** : something that recommends

¹**rec·om·pense** \\'re-kəm-ˌpens\\ *vb* **-pensed; -pens·ing** **1** ♦ : to give compensation to : pay for ⟨were *recompensed* for their losses⟩ **2** ♦ : to return in kind : REQUITE
♦ [1] clear, discharge, foot, liquidate, pay, pay off, quit, settle, spring, stand — more at PAY ♦ [2] compensate, indemnify, recoup, remunerate, requite — more at COMPENSATE

²**recompense** *n* ♦ : an equivalent or a return for something done, suffered, or given : COMPENSATION
♦ compensation, damages, indemnity, payment, quittance, redress, remuneration, reparation, requital, restitution, satisfaction — more at COMPENSATION

re·con·ceive \\ˌrē-kən-'sēv\\ *vb* : to form again a conception of
♦ readdress, reanalyze, reconsider, reexamine, rethink, review — more at RECONSIDER

rec·on·cile \\'re-kən-ˌsīl\\ *vb* **-ciled; -cil·ing** **1** ♦ : to cause to be friendly or harmonious again **2** : ADJUST, SETTLE ⟨∼ differences⟩ **3** : to bring to submission or acceptance — **rec·on·cil·able** *adj* — **rec·on·cile·ment** *n* — **rec·on·cil·er** *n*
♦ accommodate, conciliate, conform, coordinate, harmonize, key — more at HARMONIZE

rec·on·cil·i·a·tion \\ˌre-kən-ˌsi-lē-'ā-shən\\ *n* **1** : the action of reconciling **2** : the Roman Catholic sacrament of penance

re·con·dite \\'re-kən-ˌdīt\\ *adj* **1** : hard to understand : PROFOUND, ABSTRUSE **2** : little known : OBSCURE

re·con·di·tion \\ˌrē-kən-'di-shən\\ *vb* **1** ♦ : to restore to good condition (as by replacing parts) **2** : to condition anew

♦ doctor, fix, mend, patch, renovate, repair, revamp — more at MEND

re·con·nais·sance \\ri-'kä-nə-zəns, -səns\\ *n* [F, lit., recognition] : a preliminary survey of an area; *esp* : an exploratory military survey of enemy territory

re·con·noi·ter *or* **re·con·noi·tre** \\ˌrē-kə-'nȯi-tər, ˌre-\\ *vb* **-noi·tered** *or* **-noi·tred; -noi·ter·ing** *or* **-noi·tring** : to make a reconnaissance of : engage in reconnaissance

re·con·sid·er \\ˌrē-kən-'si-dər\\ *vb* ♦ : to consider again with a view to changing or reversing ⟨∼*ed* the decision⟩
♦ readdress, reanalyze, reconceive, reexamine, rethink, review; *also* reappraise, reassess; amend, correct, emend, rectify, reform, remedy, revise

re·con·sid·er·a·tion \\-ˌsi-də-'rā-shən\\ *n* : the action of reconsidering or state of being reconsidered

re·con·sti·tute \\ˌrē-'kän-stə-ˌtüt, -ˌtyüt\\ *vb* : to restore to a former condition by adding water ⟨∼ powdered milk⟩

re·con·struct \\ˌrē-kən-'strəkt\\ *vb* : to construct again : REBUILD

re·con·struc·tion \\ˌrē-kən-'strək-shən\\ *n* **1** : the action of reconstructing : the state of being reconstructed **2** *often cap* : the reorganization and reestablishment of the seceded states in the Union after the American Civil War **3** : something reconstructed

¹**re·cord** \\ri-'kȯrd\\ *vb* [ME, lit., to recall, fr. AF *recorder,* fr. L *recordari,* fr. *re-* back, again + *cord-, cors* heart] **1** ♦ : to set down in writing **2** : to register permanently **3** : INDICATE, READ **4** : to give evidence of **5** : to cause (as sound or visual images) to be registered (as on a disc or a magnetic tape) in a form that permits reproduction
♦ jot, log, mark, note, set down; *also* chronicle; chalk (up), score; rerecord ♦ catalog, enroll, enter, index, inscribe, list, schedule, slate — more at LIST

²**rec·ord** \\'re-kərd\\ *n* **1** : the act of being recorded **2** ♦ : a written account of proceedings **3** : known facts about a person; *also* : a collection of items of information (as in a database) treated as a unit **4** : an attested top performance **5** : something on which sound or visual images have been recorded
♦ account, chronicle, history, narrative, report, story — more at ACCOUNT

³**re·cord** \\ri-'kȯrd\\ *n* : a function of an electronic device that causes it to record

re·cord·er \\ri-'kȯr-dər\\ *n* **1** : a judge in some city courts **2** : one who records transactions officially **3** : a recording device **4** : a wind instrument with a whistle mouthpiece and eight fingerholes

re·cord·ing *n* : RECORD 5

re·cord·ist \\ri-'kȯr-dist\\ *n* : one who records sound esp. on film

¹**re·count** \\ri-'kaȯnt\\ *vb* ♦ : to relate in detail : TELL
♦ describe, narrate, recite, rehearse, relate, report, tell — more at TELL

²**re·count** \\'rē-ˌkaȯnt, (ˌ)rē-'kaȯnt\\ *vb* : to count again

³**recount** *n* : a second or fresh count

re·coup \\ri-'küp\\ *vb* **1** ♦ : to get an equivalent or compensation for : make up for something lost ⟨∼*ed* their costs⟩ **2** ♦ : to gain anew : get again
♦ [1] compensate, indemnify, recompense, remunerate, requite — more at COMPENSATE ♦ [2] recapture, reclaim, recover, regain, repossess, retake, retrieve — more at RECOVER

re·course \\'rē-ˌkȯrs, ri-'kȯrs\\ *n* **1** : a turning to someone or something for assistance or protection **2** ♦ : a source of aid : RESORT
♦ expedient, resort, resource — more at RESOURCE

List of self-explanatory words with the prefix *re-* (continued)

rebury	rechannel	recharter	reclassification
recalculate	recharge	recheck	reclassify
recalculation	rechargeable	rechristen	recoin

re·cov·er \ri-'kə-vər\ *vb* **1** ♦ : to get back again : REGAIN **2** ♦ : to regain normal health, poise, or status **3** : to make up for : RECOUP ⟨~ed all his losses⟩ **4** : RECLAIM ⟨~ land from the sea⟩ **5** : to obtain a legal judgment in one's favor — **re·cov·er·able** *adj*

♦ [1] recapture, reclaim, recoup, regain, repossess, retake, retrieve; *also* recruit, replenish; redeem, repurchase; rescue ♦ [2] convalesce, gain, heal, mend, recuperate — more at CONVALESCE ♦ [2] rally, rebound, snap back; *also* reanimate, revitalize, revive

re–cov·er \rē-'kə-vər\ *vb* : to cover again

recovering *adj* : being in the process of overcoming a shortcoming or problem ⟨a ~ alcoholic⟩

re·cov·ery \ri-'kə-və-rē\ *n* **1** ♦ : the act, process, or an instance of recovering **2** ♦ : the process of combating a disorder (as alcoholism) or a real or perceived problem

♦ [1] reclamation, repossession, retrieval; *also* recruitment, replenishment; redemption, rescue ♦ [2] comeback, convalescence, rally, recuperation, rehabilitation — more at CONVALESCENCE

¹rec·re·ant \'re-krē-ənt\ *adj* [ME, fr. AF, fr. prp. of (*se*) *recreire* to give up, yield, fr. ML (*se*) *recredere* to resign oneself (to a judgment), fr. L *re-* back + *credere* to believe] **1** ♦ : crying for mercy or yielding in a cowardly manner **2** ♦ : unfaithful to duty or allegiance

♦ [1] chicken, cowardly, craven, dastardly, pusillanimous, spineless, yellow — more at COWARDLY ♦ [2] disloyal, faithless, false, fickle, inconstant, loose, perfidious, traitorous, treacherous, unfaithful, untrue — more at FAITHLESS

²recreant *n* **1** : a cowardly wretch : COWARD **2** ♦ : one who forsakes a duty, a cause, or anyone to whom he or she owes service : DESERTER **3** ♦ : one that is unfaithful

♦ [2] defector, deserter, renegade — more at RENEGADE ♦ [3] apostate, betrayer, double-crosser, quisling, traitor, turncoat — more at TRAITOR

rec·re·ate \'re-krē-ˌāt\ *vb* **-at·ed; -at·ing** **1** ♦ : to give new life or freshness to **2** ♦ : to take recreation ⟨*recreated* at the beach⟩ — **rec·re·ative** \-ˌā-tiv\ *adj*

♦ [1] freshen, refresh, regenerate, rejuvenate, renew, restore, revitalize, revive — more at RENEW ♦ [2] dally, disport, frolic, play, rollick, sport — more at PLAY

re–cre·ate \ˌrē-krē-'āt\ *vb* : to create again — **re–cre·ation** \-'ā-shən\ *n* — **re–cre·ative** \-'ā-tiv\ *adj*

rec·re·ation \ˌre-krē-'ā-shən\ *n* : a refreshing of strength or spirits after work; *also* : a means of refreshment — **rec·re·ation·al** \-shə-nəl\ *adj*

recreational vehicle *n* ♦ : a vehicle designed for recreational use (as camping)

♦ camper, caravan, motor home, RV, trailer — more at CAMPER

re·crim·i·na·tion \ri-ˌkri-mə-'nā-shən\ *n* : a retaliatory accusation — **re·crim·i·nate** \-'kri-mə-nāt\ *vb* — **re·crim·i·na·to·ry** \-'kri-mə-nə-ˌtōr-ē\ *adj*

re·cru·des·cence \ˌrē-krü-'des-ᵊns\ *n* : a renewal or breaking out again esp. of something unhealthful or dangerous

¹re·cruit \ri-'krüt\ *vb* **1** : to form or strengthen with new members ⟨~ an army⟩ **2** : to enlist as a member of an armed service **3** : to secure the services of **4** : to seek to enroll **5** : to restore or increase in health or vigor ⟨resting to ~ his strength⟩ — **re·cruit·er** *n* — **re·cruit·ment** *n*

²recruit *n* [F *recrute, recrue* fresh growth, new levy of soldiers, fr. MF, fr. *recroistre* to grow up again, fr. L *recrescere*] ♦ : a newcomer to an activity or field; *esp* : a newly enlisted member of the armed forces

♦ beginner, fledgling, freshman, greenhorn, neophyte, newcomer, novice, rookie, tenderfoot, tyro — more at BEGINNER

rec·tal \'rekt-ᵊl\ *adj* : of or relating to the rectum — **rec·tal·ly** *adv*

rec·tan·gle \'rek-ˌtaŋ-gəl\ *n* : a 4-sided figure with four right angles; *esp* : one with adjacent sides of unequal length — **rect·an·gu·lar** \rek-'taŋ-gyə-lər\ *adj*

rec·ti·fi·er \'rek-tə-ˌfī-ər\ *n* : one that rectifies; *esp* : a device for converting alternating current into direct current

rec·ti·fy \'rek-tə-ˌfī\ *vb* **-fied; -fy·ing** ♦ : to make or set right : CORRECT — **rec·ti·fi·ca·tion** \ˌrek-tə-fə-'kā-shən\ *n*

♦ amend, correct, debug, emend, reform, remedy — more at CORRECT

rec·ti·lin·ear \ˌrek-tə-'li-nē-ər\ *adj* **1** : moving in a straight line ⟨~ motion⟩ **2** : characterized by straight lines

rec·ti·tude \'rek-tə-ˌtüd, -ˌtyüd\ *n* **1** ♦ : moral integrity **2** : correctness of procedure

♦ character, decency, goodness, honesty, honor (*or* honour), integrity, morality, probity, righteousness, uprightness, virtue — more at MORALITY

rec·to \'rek-tō\ *n, pl* **rectos** : a right-hand page

rec·tor \'rek-tər\ *n* **1** : a priest or minister in charge of a parish **2** : the head of a university or school — **rec·to·ri·al** \rek-'tōr-ē-əl\ *adj*

rec·to·ry \'rek-tə-rē\ *n, pl* **-ries** : the residence of a rector or a parish priest

rec·tum \'rek-təm\ *n, pl* **rectums** *or* **rec·ta** \-tə\ [ME, fr. ML, fr. *rectum intestinum*, lit., straight intestine] : the last part of the intestine joining the colon and anus

re·cum·bent \ri-'kəm-bənt\ *adj* : lying down : RECLINING

re·cu·per·ate \ri-'kü-pə-ˌrāt-, -'kyü-\ *vb* **-at·ed; -at·ing** ♦ : to get back (as health or strength) : RECOVER — **re·cu·per·a·tive** \-'kü-pə-ˌrā-tiv, -'kyü-\ *adj*

♦ convalesce, gain, heal, mend, rally, recover, snap back — more at CONVALESCE

re·cu·per·a·tion \-ˌkü-pə-'rā-shən, -ˌkyü-\ *n* ♦ : restoration to health or strength

♦ comeback, convalescence, rally, recovery, rehabilitation — more at CONVALESCENCE

re·cur \ri-'kər\ *vb* **re·curred; re·cur·ring** **1** : to go or come back in thought or discussion **2** : to occur or appear again esp. after an interval : occur time after time — **re·cur·rence** \-'kər-əns\ *n*

re·cur·rent \-ənt\ *adj* ♦ : returning or happening time after time

♦ continual, intermittent, periodic

re·cur·ring \ri-'kə-riŋ\ *adj* : coming or happening again

re·cy·cle \rē-'sī-kəl\ *vb* **1** : to pass again through a cycle of changes or treatment **2** : to process (as liquid body waste, glass, or cans) in order to regain materials for human use — **re·cy·cla·ble** \-k(ə-)lə-bəl\ *adj or n* — **recycle** *n*

¹red \'red\ *adj* **red·der; red·dest** **1** : of the color red **2** : endorsing radical social or political change esp. by force **3** *often cap* : of or relating to the former U.S.S.R. or its allies **4** : tending to support Republican candidates ⟨~ states⟩ — **red·ly** *adv* — **red·ness** *n*

²red *n* **1** : the color of blood or of the ruby **2** ♦ : a revolutionary in politics **3** *cap* : COMMUNIST **4** : the condition of showing a loss ⟨in the ~⟩

♦ insurgent, insurrectionist, mutineer, rebel, revolter, revolutionary — more at REBEL

re·dact \ri-'dakt\ *vb* **1** : to put in writing : FRAME ⟨~ed the proclamation⟩ **2** : EDIT **3** : to obscure or remove (text) from a document — **re·dac·tor** \-'dak-tər\ *n*

List of self-explanatory words with the prefix re- (continued)

recolonization	recombine	recommit	recomputation
recolonize	recommence	recompile	recompute
recolor	recommission	recompose	reconcentrate

re·dac·tion \-'dak-shən\ n   **1** : an act or instance of redacting   **2** : EDITION

red alga n : any of a group of reddish usu. marine algae

red blood cell n : any of the hemoglobin-containing cells that carry oxygen from the lungs to the tissues and are responsible for the red color of vertebrate blood

red·breast \'red-ˌbrest\ n : ROBIN

red–carpet adj : marked by ceremonial courtesy

red cedar n : an American juniper with scalelike leaves and fragrant close-grained red wood; also : its wood

red clover n : a European clover that has globe-shaped heads of reddish flowers and is widely cultivated for hay and forage

red·coat \'red-ˌkōt\ n : a British soldier esp. during the Revolutionary War

red·den \'red-ᵊn\ vb ♦ : to make or become red or reddish
   ♦ bloom, blush, color (or colour), crimson, flush, glow — more at BLUSH

red·dish \'re-dish\ adj : tinged with red — **red·dish·ness** n

red dwarf n : a star with lower temperature and less mass than the sun

re·deem \ri-'dēm\ vb [ME redemen, fr. AF rdemer, modif. of L redimere, fr. re-, red- back, again + emere to take, buy]   **1** : to recover (property) by discharging an obligation   **2** : to ransom, free, or rescue by paying a price   **3** : to free from the consequences of sin   **4** : to remove the obligation of by payment ⟨the government ∼s savings bonds⟩; also : to convert into something of value   **5** ♦ : to make good (a promise) by performing : FULFILL   **6** : to atone for   **7** ♦ : to change for the better — **re·deem·able** adj
   ♦ [5] answer, comply, fill, fulfill, keep, meet, satisfy — more at FULFILL ♦ [7] reclaim, reform, rehabilitate — more at REFORM

re·deem·er n ♦ : a person who redeems
   ♦ deliverer, rescuer, savior — more at SAVIOR

re·demp·tion \ri-'demp-shən\ n : the act of redeeming : the state of being redeemed — **re·demp·tive** \-tiv\ adj — **re·demp·to·ry** \-tə-rē\ adj

re·de·ploy \ˌrē-di-'plȯi\ vb   **1** : to transfer from one area or activity to another   **2** : to relocate personnel or equipment — **re·de·ploy·ment** n

red–eye \'red-ˌī\ n   **1** : cheap whiskey   **2** : a late night or overnight flight

red·fish \'red-ˌfish\ n : any of various reddish marine fishes of the Atlantic including some used for food

red fox n : a fox with orange-red to reddish brown fur

red giant n : a very large star with a relatively low surface temperature

red–hand·ed \'red-'han-dəd\ adv or adj : in the act of committing a misdeed

red·head \-ˌhed\ n : a person having red hair — **red·head·ed** \-ˌhe-dəd\ adj

red herring n : a diversion intended to distract attention from the real issue

red–hot \'red-'hät\ adj   **1** ♦ : extremely hot; esp : glowing with heat   **2** ♦ : exhibiting or marked by intense emotion, enthusiasm, or violence   **3** : very new ⟨∼ news⟩
   ♦ [1] broiling, burning, fiery, hot, scorching, sultry, torrid — more at HOT ♦ [2] ardent, burning, charged, emotional, fervent, fiery, hot-blooded, impassioned, passionate, vehement — more at FERVENT

re·dial \'rē-ˌdī(-ə)l\ n : a telephone function that automatically repeats the dialing of the last number called — **re·dial** vb

re·dis·trib·ute \ˌrē-də-'stri-byət\ vb   **1** : to alter the distribution of   **2** : to spread to other areas — **re·dis·tri·bu·tion** \(ˌ)rē-ˌdis-trə-'byü-shən\ n

re·dis·trict \ˌrē-'dis-(ˌ)trikt\ vb : to organize into new territorial and esp. political divisions

red–let·ter \'red-ˌle-tər\ adj : of special significance : MEMORABLE ⟨a ∼ day⟩

red–light district n : a district with many houses of prostitution

re·do \(ˌ)rē-'dü\ vb   **1** ♦ : to do over or again   **2** : to freshen or change a decorative scheme : REDECORATE
   ♦ alter, change, make over, modify, recast, refashion, remake, remodel, revamp, revise, rework, vary — more at CHANGE ♦ duplicate, reiterate, remake, repeat, replicate — more at REPEAT

red oak n : any of various No. American oaks with leaves usu. having spiny-tipped lobes and acorns that take two years to mature; also : the wood of a red oak

red·o·lence \'red-ᵊl-əns\ n   **1** ♦ : the quality or state of being redolent   **2** ♦ : an often pungent or agreeable odor
   ♦ [1] odor (or odour), scent, smell — more at SMELL ♦ [2] aroma, bouquet, fragrance, incense, perfume, scent, spice — more at FRAGRANCE

red·o·lent \'red-ᵊl-ənt\ adj   **1** ♦ : exuding fragrance : FRAGRANT   **2** : having a specified fragrance ⟨a room ∼ of cooked cabbage⟩   **3** : REMINISCENT, SUGGESTIVE ⟨a tavern ∼ of colonial times⟩ — **red·o·lent·ly** adv
   ♦ ambrosial, aromatic, fragrant, savory, scented, sweet — more at FRAGRANT

re·dou·ble \(ˌ)rē-'də-bəl\ vb   **1** : to make twice as great in size or amount   **2** ♦ : to make intense or more intensive : INTENSIFY
   ♦ amplify, beef, boost, consolidate, deepen, enhance, heighten, intensify, magnify, step up, strengthen — more at INTENSIFY

re·doubt \ri-'daut\ n [F redoute, fr. It ridotto, fr. ML reductus secret place, fr. L, withdrawn, fr. reducere to lead back, fr. re- back + ducere to lead] : a small usu. temporary fortification

re·doubt·able \ri-'dau-tə-bəl\ adj [ME redoutable, fr. AF, fr. reduter to dread, fr. re- back, again + duter to doubt]   ♦ : arousing dread or fear : FORMIDABLE
   ♦ dire, dreadful, fearful, fearsome, forbidding, formidable, frightful, hair-raising, scary

re·dound \ri-'daund\ vb   **1** : to have an effect   **2** : to become added or transferred : ACCRUE

red pepper n   **1** : CAYENNE PEPPER   **2** : a mature red hot pepper or sweet pepper

re·draft \rē-'draft\ vb ♦ : to prepare a revised copy or a new version of
   ♦ edit, revamp, revise, rework — more at EDIT

¹re·dress \ri-'dres\ vb   **1** : to set right : REMEDY   **2** : COMPENSATE   **3** : to remove the cause of (a grievance)   **4** : AVENGE

²redress n   **1** : relief from distress   **2** : means or possibility of seeking a remedy   **3** ♦ : compensation for loss or injury   **4** : an act or instance of redressing
   ♦ compensation, damages, indemnity, quittance, recompense, remuneration, reparation, requital, restitution, satisfaction — more at COMPENSATION

red–shift \'red-'shift\ n : displacement of the spectrum of a celestial body toward longer wavelengths; also : a measure of this displacement

red snapper n : any of various reddish fishes including several food fishes

red spider n : SPIDER MITE

red squirrel n : a common American squirrel with the upper parts chiefly red

red–tailed hawk \'red-ˌtāld-\ n : a rodent-eating No. American hawk with a rather short typically reddish tail

---

List of self-explanatory words with the prefix re- (continued)

reconception	reconfirm	reconquer	reconsecration
recondensation	reconfirmation	reconquest	recontact
recondense	reconnect	reconsecrate	recontaminate

red tape *n* [fr. the red tape formerly used to bind legal documents in England] : official routine or procedure marked by excessive complexity which results in delay or inaction

red tide *n* : seawater discolored by the presence of large numbers of dinoflagellates which produce a toxin that renders infected shellfish poisonous

re·duce \ri-'düs, -'dyüs\ *vb* **re·duced; re·duc·ing** **1** ♦ : to diminish in size, amount, extent, or number : LESSEN **2** : to bring to a specified state or condition ⟨*reduced* them to tears⟩ **3** ♦ : to put in a lower rank or grade **4** : CONQUER ⟨~ a fort⟩ **5** : to bring into a certain order or classification **6** : to correct (as a fracture) by restoration of displaced parts **7** : to lessen one's weight — **re·duc·er** *n* — **re·duc·ible** \-'dü-sə-bəl, -'dyü-\ *adj*

♦ [1] abate, decrease, de-escalate, diminish, downsize, dwindle, lessen, lower ♦ [3] break, bust, degrade, demote, downgrade — more at DEMOTE

re·duc·tion \ri-'dək-shən\ *n* **1** ♦ : the act of reducing : the state of being reduced **2** : something made by reducing **3** ♦ : the amount taken off in reducing something

♦ [1, 3] abatement, decline, decrease, decrement, diminution, drop, fall, loss, shrinkage — more at DECREASE
♦ [3] abatement, deduction, discount — more at DEDUCTION

re·dun·dan·cy \ri-'dən-dən-sē\ *n, pl* **-cies** **1** : the quality or state of being redundant : SUPERFLUITY **2** : something redundant or in excess **3** ♦ : the use of surplus words

♦ circumlocution, prolixity, verbiage, wordiness — more at VERBIAGE

re·dun·dant \-dənt\ *adj* ♦ : exceeding what is needed or normal : SUPERFLUOUS; *esp* : using more words than necessary — **re·dun·dant·ly** *adv*

♦ excess, extra, spare, superfluous, supernumerary, surplus — more at SPARE

red–winged blackbird \'red-,wiŋd-\ *n* : a No. American blackbird of which the adult male is black with a patch of bright scarlet on the wings

red·wood \'red-,wùd\ *n* : a tall coniferous timber tree esp. of coastal California; *also* : its durable wood

re-echo \rē-'e-kō\ *vb* ♦ : to continue to resound with echoes

♦ echo, resonate, resound, reverberate, sound — more at REVERBERATE

reed \'rēd\ *n* **1** : any of various tall slender grasses of wet areas; *also* : a stem or growth of reed **2** : a musical instrument made from the hollow stem of a reed **3** : an elastic tongue of cane, wood, or metal by which tones are produced in organ pipes and certain other wind instruments — **reedy** *adj*

re·ed·u·cate \(,)rē-'e-jə-,kāt\ *vb* : to train again; *esp* : to rehabilitate through education — **re·ed·u·ca·tion** *n*

¹reef \'rēf\ *n* **1** : a part of a sail taken in or let out in regulating the sail's size **2** : reduction in sail area by reefing

²reef *vb* : to reduce the area of a sail by rolling or folding part of it

³reef *n* : a ridge of rocks, sand or coral at or near the surface of the water

reef·er \'rē-fər\ *n* : a marijuana cigarette

¹reek \'rēk\ *n* **1** : a strong or disagreeable fume or odor **2** : a murky condition of the atmosphere or a substance causing it

²reek *vb* **1** : to give off or become permeated with a strong or offensive odor **2** : to give a strong impression of some constituent quality ⟨an excuse that ~ed of falsehood⟩ — **reek·er** *n*

reeky \'rē-kē\ *adj* ♦ : emitting or permeated with a reek

♦ fetid, foul, fusty, malodorous, musty, noisome, rank, smelly, strong — more at MALODOROUS

¹reel \'rēl\ *n* : a revolvable device on which something flexible (as film or tape) is wound; *also* : a quantity of something wound on such a device

²reel *vb* **1** : to wind on or as if on a reel **2** : to pull or draw (as a fish) by reeling a line — **reel·able** *adj* — **reel·er** *n*

³reel *vb* **1** ♦ : to be in a whirl : WHIRL; *also* : to be giddy **2** : to waver or fall back (as from a blow) **3** ♦ : to walk or move unsteadily

♦ [1] spin, swim, whirl ♦ [3] careen, dodder, lurch, stagger, teeter, totter — more at STAGGER

⁴reel *n* ♦ : a reeling motion

♦ gyration, pirouette, revolution, roll, rotation, spin, twirl, wheel, whirl — more at SPIN

⁵reel *n* : a lively Scottish dance or its music

reel off *vb* ♦ : to tell or recite rapidly and easily ⟨*reeled off* the right answers⟩

♦ detail, enumerate, itemize, list, numerate, recite, rehearse, tick (off) — more at ENUMERATE

re-en·try \rē-'en-trē\ *n* **1** : a second or new entry **2** : the action of reentering the earth's atmosphere from space

re-eval·u·ate \rē-i-'val-yù-,wāt\ *vb* : to determine again the significance, worth, or condition of usu. by careful appraisal and study

reeve \'rēv\ *vb* **rove** \'rōv\ *or* **reeved; reev·ing** : to pass (as a rope) through a hole in a block or cleat

re-ex·am·i·na·tion \rē-ig-,za-mə-'nā-shən\ *n* ♦ : a second or new examination

♦ reappraisal, retrospection, review — more at REVIEW

re-ex·am·ine \-ig-'za-mən\ *vb* ♦ : to subject to reexamination

♦ readdress, reanalyze, reconceive, reconsider, rethink, review — more at RECONSIDER

¹ref \'ref\ *n* : REFEREE 2

²ref *abbr* **1** reference **2** referred **3** reformed **4** refunding

re·fash·ion \rē-'fa-shən\ *vb* ♦ : to make again : make over

♦ alter, change, make over, modify, recast, redo, remake, remodel, revamp, revise, rework, vary — more at CHANGE

re·fec·tion \ri-'fek-shən\ *n* **1** : refreshment esp. after hunger or fatigue **2** : food and drink together : REPAST

re·fec·to·ry \ri-'fek-tə-rē\ *n, pl* **-ries** : a dining hall (as in a monastery or college)

re·fer \ri-'fər\ *vb* **re·ferred; re·fer·ring** [ME *referren*, fr. AF *referer, refirir*, fr. L *referre* to bring back, report, refer, fr. *re-* back + *ferre* to carry] **1** : to assign to a certain source, cause, or relationship **2** : to direct or send to some person or place (as for information or help) **3** : to submit to someone else for consideration or action **4** ♦ : to have recourse (as for information or aid) **5** ♦ : to have connection : RELATE **6** ♦ : to direct attention to or speak of : MENTION — **re·fer·able** \'re-fə-rə-bəl, ri-'fər-ə-\ *adj*

♦ *usu* refer to [4] go, resort, turn ♦ [5] appertain, apply, bear, pertain, relate — more at APPLY ♦ *usu* refer to [6] advert (to), cite, instance, mention, name, note, notice, quote, specify, touch (on or upon) — more at MENTION

¹ref·er·ee \,re-fə-'rē\ *n* **1** ♦ : a person to whom an issue esp. in law is referred for investigation or settlement **2** : an umpire in certain games

♦ arbiter, arbitrator, judge, umpire — more at JUDGE

²referee *vb* **-eed; -ee·ing** ♦ : to act as referee

List of self-explanatory words with the prefix *re-* (continued)

recontamination	recook	recrystallize	redecoration
reconvene	recopy	recut	rededicate
reconvert	recross	redecorate	rededication

♦ adjudicate, arbitrate, decide, determine, judge, rule, settle, umpire — more at JUDGE

ref·er·ence \'re-frəns, -fə-rəns\ *n* **1** : the act of referring **2** : RELATION, RESPECT **3** : ALLUSION, MENTION **4** : something that refers a reader to another passage or book **5** : consultation esp. for obtaining information ⟨books for ∼⟩ **6** : a person of whom inquiries as to character or ability can be made **7** : a written recommendation of a person for employment

ref·er·en·dum \,re-fə-'ren-dəm\ *n, pl* **-da** \-də\ *or* **-dums** : the submitting of legislative measures to the voters for approval or rejection; *also* : a vote on a measure so submitted

ref·er·ent \'re-frənt, -fə-rənt\ *n* : one that refers or is referred to; *esp* : the thing a word stands for — **referent** *adj*

re·fer·ral \ri-'fər-əl\ *n* **1** : the act or an instance of referring **2** : one that is referred

¹re·fill \,rē-'fil\ *vb* : to fill again : REPLENISH — **re·fill·able** *adj*

²re·fill \'rē-,fil\ *n* : a new or fresh supply of something

re·fi·nance \,rē-fə-'nans, (,)rē-'fī-nans\ *vb* : to renew or reorganize the financing of

re·fine \ri-'fīn\ *vb* **re·fined; re·fin·ing** **1** : to free from impurities or waste matter **2** ♦ : to improve or perfect by pruning or polishing : IMPROVE **3** : to free or become free of what is coarse or uncouth **4** : to make improvements by introducing subtle changes — **re·fin·er** *n*

♦ ameliorate, amend, better, enhance, enrich, improve, perfect — more at IMPROVE

re·fined \ri-'fīnd\ *adj* **1** ♦ : freed from impurities **2** ♦ : reflecting a meticulous, sensitive, or demanding attitude **3** ♦ : marked by subtlety of discrimination or precision of method or technique : SUBTLE

♦ [1] absolute, fine, neat, plain, pure, straight, unadulterated, undiluted, unmixed — more at PURE ♦ [2] civilized, cultivated, cultured, genteel, polished — more at CULTIVATED ♦ [3] delicate, exact, fine, minute, nice, subtle — more at FINE

re·fine·ment \ri-'fīn-mənt\ *n* **1** : the action of refining **2** ♦ : the quality or state of being refined **3** : a refined feature or method **4** ♦ : something intended to improve or perfect

♦ [2] civilization, cultivation, culture, polish — more at CULTURE ♦ [4] advance, advancement, breakthrough, enhancement, improvement — more at ADVANCE

re·fin·ery \ri-'fī-nə-rē\ *n, pl* **-er·ies** : a building and equipment for refining metals, oil, or sugar

re·flect \ri-'flekt\ *vb* [ME, fr. L *reflectere* to bend back, fr. *re-* back + *flectere* to bend] **1** : to bend or cast back (as light, heat, or sound) **2** : to give back a likeness or image of as a mirror does **3** : to bring as a result ⟨∼ed credit on him⟩ **4** : to cast reproach or blame ⟨their bad conduct ∼ed on their training⟩ **5** : PONDER, MEDITATE — **re·flec·tiv·i·ty** \(,)rē-,flek-'ti-və-tē\ *n*

re·flec·tion \-'flek-shən\ *n* ♦ : a thought, idea, or opinion formed or a remark made as a result of meditation

♦ comment, note, observation, remark — more at REMARK

re·flec·tive \-tiv\ *adj* ♦ : marked by reflection

♦ contemplative, meditative, melancholy, pensive, ruminant, thoughtful — more at CONTEMPLATIVE

re·flec·tor \ri-'flek-tər\ *n* : one that reflects; *esp* : a polished surface for reflecting radiation (as light)

¹re·flex \'rē-,fleks\ *n* **1** : an automatic and usu. inborn response to a stimulus not involving higher mental centers **2** *pl* : the power of acting or responding with enough speed ⟨an athlete with great ∼es⟩

²reflex *adj* **1** : bent or directed back **2** : of, relating to, or produced by a reflex — **re·flex·ly** *adv*

¹re·flex·ive \ri-'flek-siv\ *adj* : of or relating to an action directed back upon the doer or the grammatical subject ⟨a ∼ verb⟩ ⟨the ∼ pronoun *himself*⟩ — **re·flex·ive·ly** *adv* — **re·flex·ive·ness** *n*

²reflexive *n* : a reflexive verb or pronoun

re·flex·ol·o·gy \,rē-,flek-'sä-lə-jē\ *n* : massage in which pressure is applied to specific points on the hands or feet

re·flux \'rē-,fləks\ *n* : a flowing back

re·fo·cus \(,)rē-'fō-kəs\ *vb* **1** : to focus again **2** : to change the emphasis or direction of ⟨∼ed her life⟩

re·for·es·ta·tion \,rē-,fȯr-ə-'stā-shən\ *n* : the action of renewing forest cover by planting seeds or young trees — **re·for·est** \rē-'fȯr-əst\ *vb*

¹re·form \ri-'fȯrm\ *vb* **1** ♦ : to make better or improve by removal of faults **2** ♦ : to correct or improve one's own character or habits — **re·form·able** *adj*

♦ [1] amend, correct, debug, emend, rectify, remedy — more at CORRECT ♦ [2] reclaim, redeem, rehabilitate; *also* amend, improve; cleanse, purify, restore

²reform *n* : improvement or correction of what is corrupt or defective

re–form \,rē-'fȯrm\ *vb* : to form again

ref·or·ma·tion \,re-fər-'mā-shən\ *n* **1** : the act of reforming : the state of being reformed **2** *cap* : a 16th-century religious movement marked by the establishment of the Protestant churches

re·for·ma·tive \-'fȯr-mə-tiv\ *adj* ♦ : intended or tending to reform

♦ corrective, remedial — more at CORRECTIVE

¹re·for·ma·to·ry \ri-'fȯr-mə-,tōr-ē\ *adj* : aiming at or tending toward reformation : REFORMATIVE

²reformatory *n, pl* **-ries** : a penal institution for reforming esp. young or first offenders

re·form·er \ri-'fȯr-mər\ *n* **1** : one that works for or urges reform **2** *cap* : a leader of the Protestant Reformation

refr *abbr* refraction

re·fract \ri-'frakt\ *vb* [L *refractus*, pp. of *refringere* to break open, break up, fr. *re-* back + *frangere* to break] : to subject to refraction

re·frac·tion \ri-'frak-shən\ *n* : the bending of a ray (as of light) when it passes obliquely from one medium into another in which its speed is different — **re·frac·tive** \-tiv\ *adj*

refractive index *n* : the ratio of the speed of radiation in one medium to that in another medium

re·frac·to·ri·ness \ri-'frak-tə-rē-nəs\ *n* ♦ : the quality or state of being refractory

♦ defiance, disobedience, insubordination, rebelliousness, recalcitrance, unruliness — more at DISOBEDIENCE

re·frac·to·ry \ri-'frak-tə-rē\ *adj* **1** ♦ : resisting control or authority **2** : capable of enduring high temperature ⟨∼ bricks⟩ — **refractory** *n*

♦ contrary, defiant, disobedient, froward, headstrong, intractable, rebellious, recalcitrant, uncontrollable, unruly, untoward, wayward, willful — more at DISOBEDIENT

¹re·frain \ri-'frān\ *vb* ♦ : to hold oneself back : FORBEAR ⟨∼ from interfering⟩ — **re·frain·ment** *n*

♦ *usu* refrain from abstain (from), forbear, forgo, keep — more at FORBEAR

²refrain *n* : a phrase or verse recurring regularly in a poem or song

---

List of self-explanatory words with the prefix *re-* (continued)

redefine	redesign	redevelop	rediscount
redefinition	redetermination	redevelopment	rediscover
redeposit	redetermine	redirect	rediscovery

re·fresh \ri-'fresh\ *vb* 1 ♦ : to make or become fresh or fresher 2 ♦ : to revive by or as if by renewal of supplies ⟨∼ one's memory⟩ 3 ♦ : to freshen up : restore to a state of newness or vitality 4 : to supply or take refreshment — **re·fresh·er** *n* — **re·fresh·ing·ly** *adv*

♦ [1, 2, 3] freshen, recreate, regenerate, rejuvenate, renew, restore, revitalize, revive — more at RENEW

re·fresh·ing *adj* ♦ : serving to refresh

♦ bracing, invigorating, restorative, stimulative, tonic — more at TONIC

re·fresh·ment \-mənt\ *n* 1 : the act of refreshing : the state of being refreshed 2 : something that refreshes 3 *pl* : a light meal; *also* : assorted light foods

re·fried beans \'rē-ˌfrīd-\ *n pl* : beans cooked with seasonings, fried, then mashed and fried again

refrig *abbr* refrigerating; refrigeration

re·frig·er·ate \ri-'fri-jə-ˌrāt\ *vb* **-at·ed; -at·ing** : to make cool; *esp* : to chill or freeze (food) for preservation — **re·frig·er·ant** \-jə-rənt\ *adj or n* — **re·frig·er·a·tion** \-ˌfri-jə-'rā-shən\ *n* — **re·frig·er·a·tor** \-'fri-jə-ˌrā-tər\ *n*

ref·uge \'re-ˌfyüj\ *n* 1 ♦ : shelter or protection from danger or distress 2 ♦ : a place that provides protection

♦ [1, 2] asylum, haven, retreat, sanctuary, shelter — more at SHELTER

ref·u·gee \ˌre-fyu-'jē\ *n* ♦ : one who flees for safety esp. to a foreign country

♦ émigré, evacuee, exile, expatriate — more at ÉMIGRÉ

re·ful·gence \ri-'fül-jəns, -'fəl-\ *n* ♦ : a radiant or resplendent quality or state

♦ brilliance, dazzle, effulgence, illumination, lightness, lucidity, luminosity, radiance, splendor — more at BRILLIANCE

re·ful·gent \-jənt\ *adj* ♦ : giving out a bright light : richly radiant

♦ beaming, bright, brilliant, effulgent, glowing, incandescent, lambent, lucent, lucid, luminous, lustrous, radiant, shiny — more at BRIGHT

¹**re·fund** \ri-'fənd, 'rē-ˌfənd\ *vb* : to give or put back (money) : REPAY — **re·fund·able** *adj*

²**re·fund** \'rē-ˌfənd\ *n* 1 : the act of refunding 2 : a sum refunded

re·fur·bish \ri-'fər-bish\ *vb* : to brighten or freshen up : RENOVATE

re·fus·al \ri-'fyü-zəl\ *n* ♦ : the act of refusing or denying

♦ denial, disallowance, nay, no, rejection — more at DENIAL

¹**re·fuse** \ri-'fyüz\ *vb* **re·fused; re·fus·ing** 1 ♦ : to decline to accept : REJECT 2 ♦ : to decline to do, give, or grant

♦ [1] decline, disallow, disapprove, negative, reject, repudiate, spurn, turn down — more at DECLINE ♦ [2] decline, deny, disallow, reject, withhold — more at DENY

²**ref·use** \'re-ˌfyüs, -ˌfyüz\ *n* ♦ : rejected or worthless matter : RUBBISH, TRASH

♦ chaff, deadwood, dust, garbage, junk, litter, riffraff, rubbish, scrap, trash, waste — more at GARBAGE

ref·u·ta·tion \ˌre-fyu-'tā-shən\ *n* ♦ : the act or process of refuting; *also* : proof of falsehood or error

♦ confutation, rebuttal — more at CONFUTATION

re·fute \ri-'fyüt\ *vb* **re·fut·ed; re·fut·ing** [L *refutare* to check, suppress, refute] ♦ : to prove to be false by argument or evidence — **re·fut·er** *n*

♦ belie, confute, disprove, rebut — more at DISPROVE

¹**reg** \'reg\ *n* : REGULATION

²**reg** *abbr* 1 region 2 register; registered; registration 3 regular

re·gain \rē-'gān\ *vb* ♦ : to acquire or get possession of again

♦ recapture, reclaim, recoup, recover, repossess, retake, retrieve — more at RECOVER

re·gal \'rē-gəl\ *adj* 1 ♦ : of, relating to, or befitting a king : ROYAL 2 ♦ : of notable excellence or magnificence : STATELY, SPLENDID — **re·gal·ly** *adv*

♦ [1] kingly, monarchical, royal — more at MONARCHICAL ♦ [2] august, baronial, gallant, glorious, grand, grandiose, heroic, imposing, magnificent, majestic, monumental, noble, proud, royal, splendid, stately — more at GRAND

re·gale \ri-'gāl\ *vb* **re·galed; re·gal·ing** 1 ♦ : to entertain richly or agreeably esp. with fine food and drink 2 ♦ : to give pleasure or amusement to

♦ [1] banquet, dine, feast, junket — more at FEAST ♦ [2] amuse, disport, divert, entertain — more at AMUSE

re·ga·lia \ri-'gāl-yə\ *n pl* 1 : the emblems, symbols, or paraphernalia of royalty (as the crown and scepter) 2 : the insignia of an office or order 3 ♦ : special costume : FINERY

♦ array, best, bravery, caparison, feather, finery, frippery, full dress, gaiety — more at FINERY

¹**re·gard** \ri-'gärd\ *n* 1 : CONSIDERATION, HEED; *also* : CARE, CONCERN 2 ♦ : a quick or cursory look : GLANCE, LOOK 3 ♦ : a feeling of respect and affection : RESPECT, ESTEEM 4 *pl* ♦ : friendly greetings implying respect and esteem 5 : an aspect to be considered : PARTICULAR — **re·gard·less** *adj*

♦ [2] cast, eye, gander, glance, glimpse, look, peek, peep, sight, view — more at LOOK ♦ [3] admiration, appreciation, esteem, estimation, favor (*or* favour), respect — more at ADMIRATION **regards** ♦ [4] compliments, greetings, respects — more at COMPLIMENT

²**regard** *vb* 1 ♦ : to think of : CONSIDER 2 : to pay attention to 3 ♦ : to show respect for : HEED ⟨∼ our elders⟩ 4 ♦ : to hold in high esteem : care for 5 : to look at : gaze upon 6 *archaic* : to relate to

♦ [1] account, call, consider, count, esteem, hold, rate, reckon, take — more at CONSIDER ♦ [3] follow, heed, listen, mind, note, observe, watch — more at HEED ♦ [4] admire, appreciate, esteem, respect — more at ADMIRE

re·gard·ful *adj* ♦ : full or expressive of regard or respect

♦ deferential, dutiful, respectful — more at RESPECTFUL

re·gard·ing *prep* ♦ : with respect to : CONCERNING

♦ about, apropos of, concerning, of, on, respecting, toward — more at ABOUT

regardless of \ri-'gärd-ləs-\ *prep* ♦ : in spite of

♦ despite, notwithstanding, with — more at DESPITE

re·gat·ta \ri-'gä-tə, -'ga-\ *n* : a boat race or a series of boat races

re·gen·cy \'rē-jən-sē\ *n, pl* **-cies** 1 : the office or government of a regent or body of regents 2 : a body of regents 3 : the period during which a regent governs

re·gen·er·a·cy \ri-'je-nə-rə-sē\ *n* : the state of being regenerated

¹**re·gen·er·ate** \ri-'je-nə-rət\ *adj* 1 : formed or created again 2 : spiritually reborn or converted

²**re·gen·er·ate** \ri-'je-nə-ˌrāt\ *vb* 1 : to subject to spiritual renewal 2 : to reform completely 3 : to replace (a body part) by a new growth of tissue 4 ♦ : to give new life to : REVIVE 5 ♦ : to restore to original strength or properties — **re·gen·er·a·tive** \-'je-nə-ˌrā-tiv\ *adj* — **re·gen·er·a·tor** \-ˌrā-tər\ *n*

List of self-explanatory words with the prefix *re-* (continued)

redissolve	redraw	reelection	reemphasis
redistill	reedit	reemerge	reemphasize
redistillation	reelect	reemergence	reemploy

♦ [4] reanimate, reinvigorate, rejuvenate, renew, resuscitate, revitalize, revive — more at REVIVE

♦ [5] freshen, recreate, refresh, renew, restore

re·gen·er·a·tion \-je-nə-'rā-shən\ *n* ♦ : an act or the process of regenerating

♦ rebirth, rejuvenation, renewal, resurgence, resurrection, resuscitation, revival — more at REVIVAL

re·gent \'rē-jənt\ *n* 1 : a person who rules during the childhood, absence, or incapacity of the sovereign 2 : a member of a governing board (as of a state university) — **regent** *adj*

reg·gae \'re-ˌgā\ *n* : popular music of Jamaican origin that combines native styles with elements of rock and soul music

reg·i·cide \'re-jə-ˌsīd\ *n* 1 : one who murders a king 2 : murder of a king

re·gift \(ˌ)rē-'gift\ *vb* : to give a previously received gift to someone else

re·gime *also* **rè·gime** \rā-'zhēm, ri-\ *n* 1 : REGIMEN 2 : a form or system of government 3 ♦ : a government in power; *also* : a period of rule

♦ administration, authority, government, jurisdiction, rule — more at RULE

reg·i·men \'re-jə-mən\ *n* [ME, fr. ML, position of authority, direction, set of rules, fr. L, steering, control, fr. *regere* to direct] 1 : a systematic course of treatment or training ⟨a strict dietary ∼⟩ 2 : the continuous exercise of authority over and the performance of functions for a political unit : GOVERNMENT

¹reg·i·ment \'re-jə-mənt\ *n* : a military unit consisting usu. of a number of battalions — **reg·i·men·tal** \ˌre-jə-'men-təl\ *adj*

²reg·i·ment \'re-jə-ˌment\ *vb* : to organize rigidly so as to regulate or control; *also* : to subject to order or uniformity — **reg·i·men·ta·tion** \ˌre-jə-mən-'tā-shən\ *n*

reg·i·men·tals \ˌre-jə-'men-təlz\ *n pl* 1 : a regimental uniform 2 : military dress

re·gion \'rē-jən\ *n* [ME, fr. AF *regiun*, fr. L *region-, regio* line, direction, area, fr. *regere* to rule] ♦ : an often indefinitely defined part or area

♦ area, demesne, field, zone; *also* section; locale, locality, location, locus, place, point, position, site, spot ♦ belt, land, tract, zone; *also* district, territory

re·gion·al \'rē-jə-nəl\ *adj* 1 : affecting a particular region : LOCALIZED 2 : of, relating to, characteristic of, or serving a region — **re·gion·al·ly** *adv*

¹reg·is·ter \'re-jə-stər\ *n* 1 ♦ : a record of items or details; *also* : a book or system for keeping such a record 2 : the range of a voice or instrument 3 : a device to regulate ventilation or heating 4 : an automatic device recording a number or quantity 5 : CASH REGISTER

♦ catalog, checklist, list, listing, menu, registry, roll, roster, schedule, table — more at LIST

²register *vb* **-tered; -ter·ing** 1 ♦ : to enter in a register (as in a list of guests) 2 : to record automatically 3 : to secure special care for (mail matter) by paying additional postage 4 : to convey an impression of : EXPRESS 5 : to make or adjust so as to correspond exactly 6 ♦ : to make a record of

♦ [1] catalog, enroll, enter, index, inscribe, list, put down, record, schedule, slate — more at LIST ♦ [6] jot, log, mark, note, put down, record, set down — more at RECORD

³register *n* : one who registers or records

registered nurse *n* : a graduate trained nurse who has been licensed to practice by a state authority after passing qualifying examinations

reg·is·trant \'re-jə-strənt\ *n* : one that registers or is registered

reg·is·trar \-ˌsträr\ *n* ♦ : an official recorder or keeper of records (as at an educational institution)

♦ clerk, register, scribe — more at CLERK

reg·is·tra·tion \ˌre-jə-'strā-shən\ *n* 1 : the act of registering 2 : an entry in a register 3 : the number of persons registered : ENROLLMENT 4 : a document certifying an act of registering

reg·is·try \'re-jə-strē\ *n, pl* **-tries** 1 : ENROLLMENT, REGISTRATION 2 : a place of registration 3 ♦ : an official record book or an entry in one

♦ catalog, checklist, list, listing, menu, register, roll, roster, schedule, table — more at LIST

reg·nant \'reg-nənt\ *adj* 1 : REIGNING 2 : DOMINANT 3 : of common or widespread occurrence

¹re·gress \'rē-ˌgres\ *n* 1 : an act or the privilege of going or coming back 2 : RETROGRESSION

²re·gress \ri-'gres\ *vb* : to go or cause to go back or to a lower level — **re·gres·sive** *adj* — **re·gres·sor** \-'gre-sər\ *n*

re·gres·sion \ri-'gre-shən\ *n* : the act or an instance of regressing; *esp* : reversion to an earlier mental or behavioral level

¹re·gret \ri-'gret\ *vb* **re·gret·ted; re·gret·ting** 1 : to mourn the loss or death of 2 ♦ : to be very sorry for 3 : to experience regret — **re·gret·ter** *n*

♦ bemoan, deplore, lament, repent, rue; *also* bewail, grieve (for), mourn, sorrow (for)

²regret *n* 1 ♦ : sorrow caused by something beyond one's power to remedy 2 : an expression of sorrow 3 *pl* : a note politely declining an invitation

♦ contrition, penitence, remorse, repentance, rue

re·gret·ful \-fəl\ *adj* ♦ : full of regret

♦ apologetic, contrite, penitent, remorseful, repentant, rueful, sorry — more at CONTRITE

re·gret·ful·ly *adv* : with regret

re·gret·ta·ble \-'gre-tə-bəl\ *adj* ♦ : deserving regret

♦ deplorable, distressful, grievous, heartbreaking, lamentable, unfortunate, woeful; *also* affecting, moving, poignant, touching; awful, dire, dreadful, fearful, terrible; horrible, horrifying, intolerable, overwhelming, shocking, sickening, unbearable; miserable, pitiful, wretched; calamitous, disastrous

re·gret·ta·bly \-'gre-tə-blē\ *adv* 1 : to a regrettable extent 2 : it is to be regretted

re·group \(ˌ)rē-'grüp\ *vb* : to form into a new grouping

regt *abbr* regiment

¹reg·u·lar \'re-gyə-lər\ *adj* [ME *reguler*, fr. AF, fr. LL *regularis* regular, fr. L, of a bar, fr. *regula* rule, straightedge, fr. *regere* to keep straight, direct] 1 : belonging to a religious order 2 ♦ : made, built, or arranged according to a rule, standard, or type; *also* : even or symmetrical in form or structure 3 **a** : ORDERLY, METHODICAL ⟨∼ habits⟩ **b** ♦ : recurring, attending, or functioning at fixed, uniform, or normal intervals : not varying ⟨a ∼ pace⟩ 4 : made, selected, or conducted according to rule or custom 5 : properly qualified ⟨not a ∼ lawyer⟩ 6 : conforming to the normal or usual manner of inflection 7 : of, relating to, or constituting the permanent standing military force of a state 8 : having no restriction, exception, or qualification 9 ♦ : conforming to a type, standard, or regular pattern — **reg·u·lar·i·ty** \ˌre-gyə-'lar-ə-tē\ *n* — **reg·u·lar·ly** *adv*

♦ [2] methodical, orderly, systematic — more at METHODICAL ♦ [3b] constant, frequent, habitual, periodic, repeated, steady; *also* chronic, confirmed, inveterate; expected, usual *Ant* inconstant, infrequent,

reemployment   reenactment   reenlist   reenter
reenact   reenergize   reenlistment   reequip

irregular ♦ [9] average, characteristic, normal, representative, standard, typical — more at TYPICAL

²**regular** n 1 : one that is regular (as in attendance) 2 : a member of the regular clergy 3 : a soldier in a regular army 4 : a player on an athletic team who is usu. in the starting lineup

reg·u·lar·ize \'re-gyə-lə-ˌrīz\ vb ♦ : to make regular by conformance to law, rules, or custom

♦ formalize, homogenize, normalize, standardize — more at STANDARDIZE

reg·u·late \'re-gyə-ˌlāt\ vb -lat·ed; -lat·ing 1 ♦ : to govern or direct according to rule : CONTROL 2 : to bring under the control of law or authority 3 : to put in good order 4 : to fix or adjust the time, amount, degree, or rate of — **reg·u·la·tive** \-ˌlā-tiv\ adj — **reg·u·la·tor** \-ˌlā-tər\ n — **reg·u·la·to·ry** \-lə-ˌtōr-ē\ adj

♦ administer, carry on, conduct, control, direct, govern, guide, handle, manage, operate, oversee, run, superintend, supervise — more at CONDUCT

reg·u·la·tion \ˌre-gyə-'lā-shən\ n 1 ♦ : the act of regulating : the state of being regulated 2 : a rule dealing with details of procedure 3 : an order issued by an executive authority of a government and having the force of law

♦ administration, conduct, control, direction, government, guidance, management, operation, oversight, running, superintendence, supervision — more at CONDUCT

re·gur·gi·tate \rē-'gər-jə-ˌtāt\ vb -tat·ed; -tat·ing [ML regurgitare, fr. L re- re- + LL gurgitare to engulf, fr. L gurgit-, gurges whirlpool] : to throw or be thrown back, up, or out \∼ food\ — **re·gur·gi·ta·tion** \-ˌgər-jə-'tā-shən\ n

re·hab \'rē-ˌhab\ n 1 : REHABILITATION 2 : a rehabilitated building — **rehab** vb

re·ha·bil·i·tate \ˌrē-hə-'bi-lə-ˌtāt, ˌrē-ə-\ vb -tat·ed; -tat·ing 1 : to restore to a former capacity, rank, or right : REINSTATE 2 ♦ : to restore to good condition or health — **re·ha·bil·i·ta·tive** \-ˌtā-tiv\ adj

♦ cure, heal, mend — more at HEAL

re·ha·bil·i·ta·tion \-ˌbi-lə-lə-'tā-shən\ n ♦ : the action or process of rehabilitating or of being rehabilitated

♦ comeback, convalescence, rally, recovery, recuperation — more at CONVALESCENCE

re·hash \ˌrē-'hash\ vb : to present again in another form without real change or improvement — **rehash** n

re·hear·ing \ˌrē-'hir-iŋ\ n : a second or new hearing by the same tribunal

re·hears·al \ri-'hər-səl\ n 1 : something told again : RECITAL 2 ♦ : a private performance or practice session preparatory to a public appearance

♦ dry run, practice, trial; also dress rehearsal; preview; drill, exercise

re·hearse \ri-'hərs\ vb re·hearsed; re·hears·ing 1 : to say again : REPEAT 2 a ♦ : to recount in order : ENUMERATE b ♦ : to present an account of : RELATE 3 : to give a rehearsal of 4 : to train by rehearsal 5 : to engage in a rehearsal — **re·hears·er** n

♦ [2a] detail, enumerate, itemize, list, numerate, tick (off) — more at ENUMERATE ♦ [2b] describe, narrate, recite, recount, relate, report, tell — more at TELL

re·heat \ˌrē-'hēt\ vb : to heat again

¹**reign** \'rān\ n 1 : the authority or rule of a sovereign 2 : the time during which a sovereign rules

²**reign** vb 1 : to rule as a sovereign 2 : to be predominant or prevalent

re·im·burse \ˌrē-əm-'bərs\ vb -bursed; -burs·ing [re- re- + obs. E imburse to put in the pocket, pay, fr. ML imbursare to put into a purse, fr. L in- in + ML bursa purse, fr. LL, hide

of an ox, fr. Gk byrsa] : to pay back : make restitution — **re·im·burs·able** adj — **re·im·burse·ment** n

¹**rein** \'rān\ n 1 : a strap fastened to a bit by which a rider or driver controls an animal 2 : a restraining influence : CHECK 3 ♦ : controlling or guiding power 4 : complete freedom — usu. used in the phrase give rein to

♦ chair, head, headship, helm — more at HEAD

²**rein** vb ♦ : to check or direct by reins

♦ usu **rein in** bridle, check, constrain, contain, control, curb, govern, inhibit, regulate, restrain, tame

re·in·car·na·tion \ˌrē-(ˌ)in-(ˌ)kär-'nā-shən\ n : rebirth of the soul in a new body — **re·in·car·nate** \ˌrē-in-'kär-ˌnāt\ vb

rein·deer \'rān-ˌdir\ n [ME reindere, fr. ON hreinn reindeer + ME deer animal, deer] : CARIBOU — used esp. for one of the Old World

reindeer moss n : a gray, erect, tufted, and much-branched edible lichen of northern regions that is an important food of reindeer

re·in·fec·tion \ˌrē-in-'fek-shən\ n : infection following another infection of the same type

re·in·force \ˌrē-ən-'fōrs\ vb 1 : to strengthen with additional forces \∼ our troops\ 2 : to strengthen with new force, aid, material, or support — **re·in·force·ment** n — **re·in·forc·er** n

re·in·scribe \ˌrē-ən-'skrīb\ vb : to reestablish or rename in a new and esp. stronger form or context

re·in·state \ˌrē-in-'stāt\ vb -stat·ed; -stat·ing : to restore to a former position, condition, or capacity — **re·in·state·ment** n

re·in·vent \ˌrē-in-'vent\ vb 1 : to make as if for the first time something already invented \∼ the wheel\ 2 : to remake completely

re·in·vig·o·rate \ˌrē-in-'vi-gə-ˌrāt\ vb ♦ : to give life and energy to again

♦ reanimate, regenerate, rejuvenate, renew, resuscitate, revitalize, revive — more at REVIVE

re·it·er·ate \rē-'i-tə-ˌrāt\ vb -at·ed; -at·ing ♦ : to state or do over again or repeatedly

♦ duplicate, redo, remake, repeat, replicate — more at REPEAT

re·it·er·a·tion \-ˌi-tə-'rā-shən\ n ♦ : the action of reiterating

♦ duplication, repeat, repetition, replication — more at REPEAT

¹**re·ject** \ri-'jekt\ vb 1 ♦ : to refuse to accept, consider, use, or submit to 2 ♦ : to refuse to hear, receive, or admit 3 : to rebuff or withhold love from 4 ♦ : to throw out esp. as useless or unsatisfactory 5 : to subject (a transplanted tissue) to an attack by immune system components of the recipient organism

♦ [1] decline, disallow, disapprove, negative, refuse, repudiate, spurn, turn down — more at DECLINE ♦ [2] contradict, deny, disallow, disavow, disclaim, gainsay, negate, negative, repudiate — more at DENY ♦ [4] cast, discard, ditch, dump, fling, jettison, junk, lose, scrap, shed, shuck, slough, throw away, throw out, unload — more at DISCARD

²**re·ject** \'rē-ˌjekt\ n ♦ : a rejected person or thing

♦ castaway, outcast — more at OUTCAST ♦ cull, discard, rejection — more at CULL

re·jec·tion \ri-'jek-shən\ n 1 ♦ : the action of rejecting : the state of being rejected 2 : something rejected

♦ contradiction, denial, disallowance, disavowal, disclaimer, negation, refusal, repudiation — more at DENIAL

re·joice \ri-'jȯis\ vb re·joiced; re·joic·ing 1 ♦ : to give joy to : GLADDEN 2 ♦ : to feel joy or great delight — **re·joic·er** n

♦ [1] content, delight, gladden, gratify, please, satisfy, suit, warm — more at PLEASE ♦ [2] crow, delight, exult, glory, joy, triumph — more at EXULT

List of self-explanatory words with the prefix re- (continued)

re·joic·ing \ri-'jȯi-siŋ\ *adj* ♦ : having or expressing feelings of joy or triumph

♦ exultant, jubilant, triumphant — more at EXULTANT

re·join \(ͺ)rē-'jȯin *for 1,* ri- *for 2*\ *vb* **1** : to join again **2** ♦ : to say in answer (as to a plaintiff's plea in court) : REPLY

♦ answer, reply, respond, retort, return — more at ANSWER

re·join·der \ri-'jȯin-dər\ *n* : something said, written, or done in answer or response : REPLY; *esp* : an answer to a reply

re·ju·ve·nate \ri-'jü-və-ͺnāt\ *vb* **-nat·ed; -nat·ing** **1** ♦ : to make young or youthful again : give new vigor to **2** ♦ : to restore to an original or new state

♦ [1] reanimate, regenerate, reinvigorate, renew, resuscitate, revitalize, revive — more at REVIVE ♦ [2] freshen, recreate, refresh, renew, restore, revive — more at RENEW

re·ju·ve·na·tion \-ͺjü-və-'nā-shən\ *n* ♦ : the action of rejuvenating or the state of being rejuvenated

♦ rebirth, regeneration, renewal, resurgence, resurrection, resuscitation, revival — more at REVIVAL

re·kin·dle \rē-'kin-dᵊl\ *vb* : to kindle again : arouse again

rel *abbr* **1** relating; relative **2** religion; religious

¹re·lapse \ri-'laps, 'rē-ͺlaps\ *n* [ME, fr. ML *relapsus,* fr. L *relabi* to slide back] **1** : the act or process of backsliding or worsening **2** : a recurrence of illness after a period of improvement

²re·lapse \ri-'laps\ *vb* **re·lapsed; re·laps·ing** : to slip or fall back into a former worse state (as of illness)

re·late \ri-'lāt\ *vb* **re·lat·ed; re·lat·ing** **1** ♦ : to give an account of : TELL **2** ♦ : to show or establish logical or causal connection between **3** ♦ : to have relationship or connection **4** : to have or establish relationship ⟨the way a child ∼*s* to a teacher⟩ **5** : to respond favorably — **re·lat·able** *adj* — **re·lat·er** *or* **re·la·tor** \-'lā-tər\ *n*

♦ [1] describe, narrate, recite, recount, rehearse, report, tell — more at TELL ♦ [2] associate, connect, correlate, identify, link — more at ASSOCIATE ♦ [3] appertain, apply, bear, pertain, refer — more at APPLY

re·lat·ed *adj* **1** ♦ : connected by some understood relationship **2** : connected through membership in the same family — **re·lat·ed·ness** *n*

♦ akin, kindred; *also* associated, connected; alike, analogous, comparable, correspondent, corresponding, like, matching, parallel, resembling, similar, such, suchlike; identical, same; germane, pertinent, relevant **Ant** unrelated

re·la·tion \ri-'lā-shən\ *n* **1** : NARRATION, ACCOUNT **2** ♦ : an aspect or quality (as resemblance) that connects two or more things or parts as being or belonging or working together or as being of the same kind : CONNECTION, RELATIONSHIP **3** : connection by blood or marriage : KINSHIP; *also* : RELATIVE **4** : REFERENCE, RESPECT ⟨in ∼ to⟩ **5** : the state of being mutually interested or involved (as in social or commercial matters) **6** *pl* ♦ : commercial, professional, public, or personal business : DEALINGS **7** *pl* : SEXUAL INTERCOURSE — **re·la·tion·al** \-shə-nəl\ *adj*

♦ [2] association, bearing, connection, kinship, liaison, linkage, relationship — more at CONNECTION ♦ relations [6] dealings, intercourse; *also* interrelationship

re·la·tion·ship \-ͺship\ *n* ♦ : the state of being related or interrelated

♦ association, bearing, connection, kinship, liaison, linkage, relation — more at CONNECTION ♦ affiliation, alliance, association, collaboration, confederation, connection, cooperation, hookup, liaison, partnership, relation, union — more at ASSOCIATION

¹rel·a·tive \'re-lə-tiv\ *n* **1** : a word referring grammatically to an antecedent **2** : a thing having a relation to or a dependence upon another thing **3** ♦ : a person connected with another by blood or marriage

♦ kin, kinsman, relation; *also* in-law; kinswoman; blood, clan, family, folk, house, kindred, kinfolk, line, lineage, people, race, stock, tribe

²relative *adj* **1** : introducing a subordinate clause qualifying an expressed or implied antecedent ⟨∼ pronoun⟩; *also* : introduced by such a connective ⟨∼ clause⟩ **2** ♦ : having significant and demonstrable bearing on the matter at hand : PERTINENT **3** ♦ : not absolute or independent : COMPARATIVE **4** : expressed as the ratio of the specified quantity to the total magnitude or to the mean of all quantities involved — **rel·a·tive·ness** *n*

♦ [2] applicable, apposite, apropos, germane, material, pertinent, pointed, relevant — more at PERTINENT ♦ [3] approximate, comparative, near — more at COMPARATIVE

relative humidity *n* : the ratio of the amount of water vapor actually present in the air to the greatest amount possible at the same temperature

rel·a·tive·ly *adv* ♦ : to a relative degree or extent

♦ fairly, kind of, like, pretty, quite, rather, somewhat, sort of

rel·a·tiv·is·tic \ͺre-lə-ti-'vis-tik\ *adj* **1** : of, relating to, or characterized by relativity **2** : moving at a velocity that is a significant fraction of the speed of light so that effects predicted by the theory of relativity become evident ⟨a ∼ electron⟩ — **rel·a·tiv·is·ti·cal·ly** \-ti-k(ə-)lē\ *adv*

rel·a·tiv·i·ty \ͺre-lə-'ti-və-tē\ *n, pl* **-ties** **1** : the quality or state of being relative **2** : a theory in physics that considers mass and energy to be equivalent and that predicts changes in mass, dimension, and time which are related to speed but are noticeable esp. at speeds approaching that of light

re·lax \ri-'laks\ *vb* **1** ♦ : to make or become less firm, tense, or rigid **2** : to make less severe or strict **3** ♦ : to seek rest or recreation — **re·lax·er** *n*

♦ [1] ease, loosen, slack, slacken — more at SLACKEN ♦ [3] bask, loll, lounge, repose, rest — more at REST ♦ [3] chill out, de-stress, unwind; *also* loosen (up), unbend; repose, rest **Ant** tense (up)

¹re·lax·ant \ri-'lak-sənt\ *adj* : of, relating to, or producing relaxation

²relaxant *n* : a relaxing agent; *esp* : a drug that induces muscular relaxation

re·lax·ation \ͺrē-ͺlak-'sā-shən\ *n* **1** ♦ : the act of relaxing or state of being relaxed : a lessening of tension **2** ♦ : a relaxing or recreative state, activity, or pastime

♦ [1] ease, leisure, repose, rest — more at REST ♦ [2] dalliance, frolic, fun, play, sport — more at PLAY

re·laxed \ri-'lakst\ *adj* **1** ♦ : freed from or lacking in precision or stringency **2** ♦ : set or being at rest or at ease **3** : easy of manner

♦ [1] easygoing, flexible, lax, loose, slack, unrestrained, unrestricted — more at EASYGOING ♦ [2] comfortable, snug — more at COMFORTABLE

¹re·lay \'rē-ͺlā\ *n* [ME, set of fresh hounds, fr. *relayen* to release fresh hounds, take a fresh horse, fr. MF *relaier,* fr. *re-* again + *laier* to let go, leave] **1** : a fresh supply (as of horses) arranged beforehand to relieve others **2** : a race between teams in which each team member covers a specified part of a course **3** : an electromagnetic device in which the opening or closing of one circuit activates another device (as a switch in another circuit) **4** : the act of passing along by stages

---

List of self-explanatory words with the prefix *re- (continued)*

refix	refold	reformulate	refortify
refloat	reforge	reformulation	refound

²re·lay \'rē-ˌlā, ri-'lā\ vb re·layed; re·lay·ing 1 : to place in or provide with relays 2 : to pass along by relays 3 : to control or operate by a relay

³re·lay \(ˌ)rē-'lā\ vb -laid \-'lād\; -lay·ing : to lay again

¹re·lease \ri-'lēs\ vb re·leased; re·leas·ing 1 a ♦ : to set free from confinement or restraint b : DISMISS 2 : to relieve from something that oppresses, confines, or burdens 3 : RELINQUISH ⟨~ a claim⟩ 4 : to permit publication, performance, exhibition, or sale of; also : to make available to the public

♦ discharge, emancipate, enfranchise, free, liberate, loose, loosen, manumit, spring, unbind, unchain, unfetter — more at FREE ♦ loose, loosen, uncork, unleash, unlock, unloosen; also discharge, emancipate, enfranchise, free, liberate, manumit, spring, unbind, unchain, unfetter; air, express, vent Ant bridle, check, constrain, contain, control, curb, govern, hold in, inhibit, regulate, rein (in), restrain, tame

²release n 1 : relief or deliverance from sorrow, suffering, or trouble 2 ♦ : discharge from an obligation or responsibility 3 : an act of setting free : the state of being freed 4 : a document effecting a legal release 5 ♦ : a releasing for performance or publication; also : the matter released (as to the press) 6 : a device for holding or releasing a mechanism as required

♦ [2] delivery, discharge, quietus, quittance; also exemption, immunity, waiver ♦ [5] advertisement, announcement, bulletin, notice, notification — more at ANNOUNCEMENT

rel·e·gate \'re-lə-ˌgāt\ vb -gat·ed; -gat·ing 1 : to send into exile : BANISH 2 : to remove or dismiss to some less prominent position 3 : to assign to a particular class or sphere 4 : to submit to someone or something for appropriate action : DELEGATE — rel·e·ga·tion \ˌre-lə-shən\ n

re·lent \ri-'lent\ vb 1 ♦ : to become less stern, severe, or harsh 2 : to make slack (as by lessening tension or firmness) : SLACKEN

♦ abate, decline, decrease, de-escalate, die, diminish, dwindle, ebb, fall, lessen, let up, lower, moderate, recede, shrink, subside, taper, wane — more at DECREASE

re·lent·less \-ləs\ adj ♦ : showing or promising no abatement of severity, intensity, or pace ⟨~ pressure⟩ — re·lent·less·ly adv — re·lent·less·ness n

♦ determined, dogged, grim, implacable, unflinching, unrelenting, unyielding — more at UNYIELDING

rel·e·vance \'re-lə-vəns\ n ♦ : relation to the matter at hand; also : practical and esp. social applicability

♦ applicability, bearing, connection, pertinence — more at PERTINENCE

rel·e·van·cy \-vən-sē\ n : RELEVANCE

rel·e·vant \'re-lə-vənt\ adj ♦ : bearing on the matter at hand : PERTINENT — rel·e·vant·ly adv

♦ applicable, apposite, apropos, germane, material, pertinent, pointed, relative — more at PERTINENT

re·li·abil·i·ty \ri-ˌlī-ə-'bi-lə-tē\ n ♦ : the quality or state of being reliable

♦ dependability, solidity, sureness, trustworthiness; also infallibility

re·li·able \ri-'lī-ə-bəl\ adj ♦ : fit to be trusted or relied on : DEPENDABLE, TRUSTWORTHY — re·li·ably \-'lī-ə-blē\ adv

♦ dependable, good, responsible, safe, solid, steady, sure, tried, true, trustworthy — more at DEPENDABLE

re·li·able·ness n : the quality or state of being reliable

re·li·ance \ri-'lī-əns\ n 1 : the act of relying 2 : the state of being reliant 3 ♦ : one relied on

♦ buttress, dependence, mainstay, pillar, standby, support — more at DEPENDENCE

re·li·ant \ri-'lī-ənt\ adj : having reliance on someone or something : DEPENDENT

rel·ic \'re-lik\ n 1 : an object venerated because of its association with a saint or martyr 2 : SOUVENIR, MEMENTO 3 pl : REMAINS, RUINS 4 ♦ : a remaining trace : VESTIGE

♦ shadow, trace, vestige — more at VESTIGE

rel·ict \'re-likt\ n : WIDOW

re·lief \ri-'lēf\ n 1 ♦ : removal or lightening of something oppressive, painful, or distressing 2 : WELFARE 2 3 : military assistance to an endangered post or force 4 a : release from a post or from performance of a duty b ♦ : one that takes the place of another on duty 5 : legal remedy or redress 6 : projection of figures or ornaments from the background (as in sculpture) 7 : the elevations of a land surface

♦ [1] alleviation, comfort, ease — more at EASE
♦ [4b] backup, pinch hitter, replacement, reserve, stand-in, sub, substitute — more at SUBSTITUTE

relief pitcher n : a baseball pitcher who takes over for another during a game

re·lieve \ri-'lēv\ vb re·lieved; re·liev·ing 1 ♦ : to free partly or wholly from a burden or from distress 2 ♦ : to bring about the removal or alleviation of : MITIGATE 3 : to release from a post or duty; also : to take the place of 4 : to break the monotony of 5 : to discharge the bladder or bowels of (oneself) — re·liev·er n

♦ [1] clear, disburden, disencumber, free, rid, unburden — more at RID ♦ [2] allay, alleviate, assuage, ease, help, mitigate, mollify, palliate, soothe — more at HELP

relig abbr religion

re·li·gion \ri-'li-jən\ n 1 ♦ : the service and worship of God or the supernatural 2 : devotion to a religious faith 3 ♦ : a personal set or institutionalized system of religious beliefs, attitudes, and practices 4 : a cause, principle, or belief held to with faith and ardor — re·li·gion·ist n

♦ [1] devotion, faith, piety — more at FAITH
♦ [3] creed, cult, faith, persuasion; also church, communion, denomination, sect; belief, doctrine, dogma, theology; monotheism, theism, polytheism

¹re·li·gious \ri-'li-jəs\ adj 1 : relating or devoted to an acknowledged ultimate reality or deity 2 ♦ : of or relating to religious beliefs or observances 3 ♦ : scrupulously and conscientiously faithful 4 : FERVENT, ZEALOUS ⟨~ about football⟩ — re·li·gious·ly adv

♦ [2] devotional, sacred, spiritual; also blessed, consecrated, hallowed, holy, sacrosanct, sanctified; liturgical, ritual, sacramental Ant nonreligious, profane, secular
♦ [3] devout, faithful, godly, holy, pious, sainted, saintly — more at HOLY

²religious n, pl religious : a member of a religious order under monastic vows

re·lin·quish \ri-'liŋ-kwish, -'lin-\ vb 1 : to withdraw or retreat from : ABANDON, QUIT 2 ♦ : to yield control or possession of ⟨~ a title⟩ 3 : to let go of : RELEASE

♦ cede, deliver, give up, hand over, leave, render, surrender, turn over, yield — more at SURRENDER ♦ abdicate, abnegate, cede, renounce, resign, step down, surrender — more at ABDICATE

re·lin·quish·ment n ♦ : the act of relinquishing : a giving up

♦ capitulation, submission, surrender — more at SURRENDER

rel·i·quary \'re-lə-ˌkwer-ē\ n, pl -quar·ies : a container for religious relics

¹rel·ish \'re-lish\ n [ME reles taste, fr. OF, something left behind, release, fr. relessier to relax, release, fr. L relax-

---

List of self-explanatory words with the prefix re- (continued)

refreeze	refurnish	regild	regrade
refuel	regather	regive	regrind

are] **1** : characteristic flavor : SAVOR **2** ♦ : keen enjoyment or delight in something **3** ♦ : a strong liking : APPETITE **4** : a highly seasoned sauce (as of pickles) eaten with other food to add flavor

♦ [2] contentment, delectation, delight, enjoyment, gladness, gratification, pleasure, satisfaction — more at PLEASURE ♦ [3] appetite, fancy, favor (*or* favour), fondness, like, liking, love, partiality, preference, shine, taste, use — more at LIKING

²**relish** *vb* **1** : to add relish to **2** ♦ : to be pleased or gratified by : ENJOY **3** : to eat with pleasure — **rel·ish·able** *adj*

♦ adore, delight, dig, enjoy, fancy, groove, like, love, revel — more at ENJOY

re·live \(ˌ)rē-ˈliv\ *vb* : to live again or over again; *esp* : to experience again in the imagination

re·lo·cate \(ˌ)rē-ˈlō-ˌkāt, ˌrē-lō-ˈkāt\ *vb* **1** : to locate again **2** : to move to a new location — **re·lo·ca·tion** \ˌrē-lō-ˈkā-shən\ *n*

re·luc·tance \ri-ˈlək-tən(t)s\ *n* ♦ : the quality or state of being reluctant

♦ disinclination, hesitancy, reticence; *also* faltering, hesitation, indecision, irresolution, shilly-shallying, staggering, vacillation, wavering, wobbling; distrust, doubt, incertitude, misgiving, mistrust, mistrustfulness, skepticism, suspicion, uncertainty *Ant* inclination, willingness

re·luc·tant \ri-ˈlək-tənt\ *adj* ♦ : feeling or showing aversion, hesitation, or unwillingness ⟨~ to get involved⟩ — **re·luc·tant·ly** *adv*

♦ afraid, dubious, hesitant, indisposed — more at HESITANT

re·ly \ri-ˈlī\ *vb* **re·lied; re·ly·ing** [ME *relien* to rally, fr. AF *relier* to retie, gather, rally, fr. L *religare* to tie out of the way, fr. *re-* back + *ligare* to tie] ♦ : to place faith or confidence : DEPEND

♦ count, depend, lean, reckon — more at DEPEND

REM \ˈrem\ *n* : RAPID EYE MOVEMENT

re·main \ri-ˈmān\ *vb* **1** : to be left after others have been removed, subtracted, or destroyed **2** : to be something yet to be shown, done, or treated ⟨it ~s to be seen⟩ **3** : to stay after others have gone **4** : to continue unchanged **5** ♦ : to stay in the same place or with the same person or group

♦ abide, dwell, hang around, stay, stick around, tarry — more at STAY

re·main·der \ri-ˈmān-dər\ *n* **1** ♦ : that which is left over : a remaining group, part, or trace **2** : the number left after a subtraction **3** : the number that is left over from the dividend after division and that is less than the divisor **4** : a book sold at a reduced price by the publisher after sales have slowed

♦ end, fag end, leftover, remnant, scrap — more at SCRAP ♦ balance, leavings, leftovers, odds and ends, remains, remnant, residue, rest; *also* fragment, scrap; oddment, stub, stump; excess, surplus

re·mains \-ˈmānz\ *n pl* **1** ♦ : a remaining part or trace ⟨the ~ of a meal⟩ **2** : a dead body

♦ debris, rubble, ruins, wreck, wreckage; *also* detritus, flotsam, jetsam; garbage, refuse, trash

¹**re·make** \(ˌ)rē-ˈmāk\ *vb* **-made** \-ˈmād\; **-mak·ing** ♦ : to make anew or in a different form

♦ alter, change, make over, modify, recast, redo, refashion, remodel, revamp, revise, rework, vary — more at CHANGE ♦ duplicate, redo, reiterate, repeat, replicate — more at REPEAT

²**re·make** \ˈrē-ˌmāk\ *n* : one that is remade; *esp* : a new version of a motion picture

re·mand \ri-ˈmand\ *vb* : to order back; *esp* : to return to custody pending trial or for further detention

¹**re·mark** \ri-ˈmärk\ *n* **1** : the act of remarking : OBSERVATION, NOTICE **2** ♦ : a passing observation or comment

♦ comment, note, observation, reflection; *also* analysis, commentary, exposition; annotation; belief, conviction, eye, feeling, judgment, mind, notion, opinion, persuasion, sentiment, verdict, view

²**remark** *vb* **1** ♦ : to take notice of : OBSERVE **2** ♦ : to express as an observation or comment

♦ [1] behold, descry, discern, distinguish, espy, eye, look, note, notice, observe, perceive, regard, see, sight, spy, view, witness — more at SEE ♦ [2] comment, note, observe, opine, say; *also* articulate, express, speak, state, talk, tell, utter, verbalize, vocalize

re·mark·able \ri-ˈmär-kə-bəl\ *adj* ♦ : worthy of being or likely to be noticed esp. as being uncommon or extraordinary : NOTEWORTHY — **re·mark·able·ness** *n*

♦ bold, catchy, conspicuous, emphatic, marked, noteworthy, noticeable, prominent, pronounced, striking — more at NOTICEABLE

re·mark·ably \ri-ˈmär-kə-blē\ *adv* **1** : in a remarkable manner **2** : as is remarkable

re·me·di·able \ri-ˈmē-dē-ə-bəl\ *adj* : capable of being remedied

re·me·di·al \ri-ˈmē-dē-əl\ *adj* ♦ : intended to remedy or improve ⟨a class in ~ reading⟩

♦ corrective, reformative — more at CORRECTIVE

¹**rem·e·dy** \ˈre-mə-dē\ *n, pl* **-dies** [ME *remedie*, fr. AF, fr. L *remedium*, fr. *re-* back, again + *mederi* to heal] **1** ♦ : a medicine or treatment that cures or relieves a disease or condition **2** : something that corrects or counteracts an evil or compensates for a loss

♦ cure, drug, medicine, pharmaceutical, specific — more at MEDICINE

²**remedy** *vb* **-died; -dy·ing** ♦ : to provide or serve as a remedy for

♦ amend, correct, debug, emend, rectify, reform — more at CORRECT

re·mem·ber \ri-ˈmem-bər\ *vb* **-bered; -ber·ing** **1** ♦ : to bring to mind or think of again : RECOLLECT **2** : to keep from forgetting : keep in mind **3** : to convey greetings from **4** ♦ : COMMEMORATE

♦ recall, recollect, reminisce, think; *also* recapture, recur; educe, elicit, evoke, extract, remind; relive *Ant* forget, unlearn

re·mem·brance \-brəns\ *n* **1** ♦ : an act of remembering : RECOLLECTION **2** ♦ : the ability to remember : MEMORY **3** : the period over which one's memory extends **4** : a memory of a person, thing, or event **5** ♦ : something that serves to bring to mind : REMINDER **6** : a greeting or gift recalling or expressing friendship or affection

♦ [1, 2] memory, recall, recollection, reminiscence — more at MEMORY ♦ [5] keepsake, memento, memorial, monument, souvenir, token — more at MEMORIAL

Remembrance Day *n* : November 11 set aside in commemoration of the end of hostilities in 1918 and 1945 and observed as a legal holiday in Canada; *also* : REMEMBRANCE SUNDAY

Remembrance Sunday *n* : a Sunday that is usu. closest to November 11 and that in Great Britain is set aside in commemoration of the end of hostilities in 1918 and 1945

re·mind \ri-ˈmīnd\ *vb* : to put in mind of something : cause to remember

re·mind·er *n* : something that reminds by association

rem·i·nisce \ˌre-mə-ˈnis\ *vb* **-nisced; -nisc·ing** ♦ : to indulge in reminiscence

---

List of self-explanatory words with the prefix *re-* **(continued)**

regrow	rehandle	rehouse	reimposition
regrowth	rehear	reimpose	reincorporate

♦ *usu* **reminisce about** recall, recollect, remember, think — more at REMEMBER

rem·i·nis·cence \-'nis-²ns\ *n* **1** ♦ : a recalling or telling of a past experience **2** : an account of a memorable experience

♦ memory, recall, recollection, remembrance — more at MEMORY

rem·i·nis·cent \-²nt\ *adj* **1** : of or relating to reminiscence **2** : marked by or given to reminiscence **3** : serving to remind : SUGGESTIVE — **rem·i·nis·cent·ly** *adv*

re·miss \ri-'mis\ *adj* **1** : negligent or careless in the performance of work or duty **2** ♦ : showing neglect or inattention — **re·miss·ly** *adv*

♦ careless, derelict, lax, negligent, slack — more at NEGLIGENT

re·mis·si·ble \ri-'mi-sə-bəl\ *adj* ♦ : capable of being forgiven

♦ excusable, forgivable, pardonable, venial — more at VENIAL

re·mis·sion \ri-'mi-shən\ *n* **1** ♦ : the act or process of remitting **2** : a state or period during which something is remitted

♦ absolution, amnesty, forgiveness, pardon — more at PARDON

re·miss·ness *n* ♦ : the quality or state of being remiss

♦ carelessness, dereliction, heedlessness, laxness, neglect, negligence, slackness — more at NEGLIGENCE

re·mit \ri-'mit\ *vb* **re·mit·ted; re·mit·ting** **1** : FORGIVE, PARDON **2** : to give or gain relief from (as pain) **3** : to refer for consideration, report, or decision **4** : to refrain from exacting or enforcing (as a penalty) **5** : to send (money) in payment of a bill **6** : to abate in force or intensity **7** : to place later in order of precedence, preference, or importance

re·mit·tal \ri-'mit-²l\ *n* : the act or process of remitting : REMISSION

re·mit·tance \ri-'mit-²ns\ *n* **1** ♦ : a sum of money remitted **2** ♦ : transmittal of money (as to a distant place)

♦ [1, 2] compensation, consideration, disbursement, pay, payment, recompense, remuneration, requital — more at PAYMENT

rem·nant \'rem-nənt\ *n* **1** ♦ : a usu. small part or trace remaining **2** : an unsold or unused end of a fabric that is sold by the yard

♦ end, fag end, leftover, remainder, scrap — more at SCRAP

re·mod·el \ˌrē-'mäd-²l\ *vb* ♦ : to alter the structure of : MAKE OVER

♦ alter, change, make over, modify, recast, redo, refashion, remake, revamp, revise, rework, vary — more at CHANGE

re·mon·strance \ri-'män-strəns\ *n* ♦ : an act or instance of remonstrating

♦ challenge, complaint, demur, expostulation, fuss, kick, objection, protest, question — more at OBJECTION

re·mon·strant \-strənt\ *adj* : vigorously objecting or opposing — **remonstrant** *n* — **re·mon·strant·ly** *adv*

re·mon·strate \ri-'män-ˌstrāt\ *vb* **-strat·ed; -strat·ing** ♦ : to plead in opposition to something : speak in protest or reproof — usu. used with *with* — **re·mon·stra·tion** \ri-ˌmän-'strā-shən, ˌre-mən-\ *n* — **re·mon·stra·tor** \ri-'män-ˌstrā-tər\ *n*

♦ *usu* **remonstrate with** demur, kick, object, protest — more at OBJECT

rem·o·ra \'re-mə-rə\ *n* : any of a family of marine bony fishes with sucking organs on the head by which they cling esp. to other fishes

re·morse \ri-'mòrs\ *n* [ME, fr. AF *remors*, fr. ML *remorsus*, fr. LL, act of biting again, fr. L *remordēre* to bite again, fr. *re-* again + *mordēre* to bite] ♦ : a gnawing distress arising from a sense of guilt for past wrongs

♦ contrition, guilt, penitence, repentance, self-reproach, shame — more at GUILT

re·morse·ful *adj* ♦ : motivated or marked by remorse

♦ apologetic, contrite, guilty, penitent, regretful, repentant, rueful, sorry — more at CONTRITE

re·morse·less \-ləs\ *adj* **1** : MERCILESS **2** : PERSISTENT, RELENTLESS

¹**re·mote** \ri-'mōt\ *adj* **re·mot·er; -est** **1** ♦ : far off in place or time : not near **2** : not closely related : DISTANT **3** ♦ : located out of the way : SECLUDED ⟨a ~ village⟩ **4** : acting, acted on, or controlled indirectly or from a distance **5** ♦ : small in degree : SLIGHT ⟨a ~ chance⟩ **6** ♦ : distant or aloof in manner — **re·mote·ly** *adv* — **re·mote·ness** *n*

♦ [1] away, distant, far, far-off — more at DISTANT ♦ [3] cloistered, covert, isolated, quiet, secluded, secret — more at SECLUDED ♦ [5] negligible, off, outside, slight, slim, small *Ant* good ♦ [6] aloof, antisocial, cold, cool, detached, distant, frosty, standoffish, unsociable — more at COOL

²**remote** *n* **1** : a radio or television program or a portion of a program originating outside the studio **2** : REMOTE CONTROL 2

remote control *n* **1** : control (as by radio signal) of operation from a point at some distance removed **2** : a device or mechanism for controlling something from a distance

¹**re·mount** \(ˌ)rē-'maunt\ *vb* **1** : to mount again **2** : to furnish remounts to

²**re·mount** \'rē-ˌmaunt\ *n* : a fresh horse to replace one no longer available

re·mov·al \ri-'mü-vəl\ *n* ♦ : the act or process of removing

♦ disposal, disposition, dumping, jettison, riddance — more at DISPOSAL

¹**re·move** \ri-'müv\ *vb* **re·moved; re·mov·ing** **1** ♦ : to move from one place to another : TRANSFER **2** ♦ : to move by lifting or taking off or away **3** ♦ : to dismiss from office **4** : to get rid of : ELIMINATE **5** : to change one's residence or location **6** : to go away : DEPART **7** : to be capable of being removed — **re·mov·able** *adj* — **re·mov·er** *n*

♦ [1] budge, dislocate, displace, disturb, move, shift, transfer — more at MOVE ♦ [2] doff, peel, put off, take off; *also* husk, shed *Ant* don, put on, slip (into) ♦ [2] clear, draw, withdraw; *also* dislodge; abstract, cut, extract, pull; move, shift, transfer *Ant* place, put ♦ [3] cashier, dismiss, fire, retire, sack — more at DISMISS

²**remove** *n* **1** : a transfer from one location to another : MOVE **2** ♦ : a degree or stage of separation

♦ distance, lead, length, spread, stretch, way — more at DISTANCE

REM sleep *n* : a state of sleep that recurs cyclically several times during normal sleep and is associated with rapid eye movements and dreaming

re·mu·ner·ate \ri-'myü-nə-ˌrāt\ *vb* **-at·ed; -at·ing** ♦ : to pay an equivalent for or to : RECOMPENSE ⟨their services were *remunerated*⟩ — **re·mu·ner·a·tor** \-ˌrā-tər\ *n*

♦ compensate, indemnify, pay, recompense, recoup, requite — more at COMPENSATE

re·mu·ner·a·tion \ri-ˌmyü-nə-'rā-shən\ *n* **1** ♦ : something that remunerates : COMPENSATION, PAYMENT **2** ♦ : an act or fact of remunerating

♦ [1] compensation, consideration, disbursement, pay, payment, recompense, remittance, requital — more at

---

List of self-explanatory words with the prefix *re-* (continued)

PAYMENT ♦ [2] compensation, damages, indemnity, quittance, recompense, redress, reparation, requital, restitution, satisfaction — more at COMPENSATION

re·mu·ner·a·tive \ri-'myü-nə-rə-tiv, -ˌrā-\ *adj* ♦ : serving to remunerate : GAINFUL

♦ fat, gainful, lucrative, profitable — more at PROFITABLE

re·nais·sance \ˌre-nə-'säns, -'zäns\ *n* **1** *cap* : the cultural revival and beginnings of modern science in Europe in the 14th–17th centuries; *also* : the period of the Renaissance **2** *often cap* : a movement or period of vigorous artistic and intellectual activity **3** : REBIRTH, REVIVAL

re·nal \'rēn-ᵊl\ *adj* : of, relating to, or located in or near the kidneys

re·na·scence \ri-'nas-ᵊns, -'nās-\ *n, often cap* : RENAISSANCE

rend \'rend\ *vb* **rent** \'rent\; **rend·ing 1** : to remove by violence : WREST **2** ♦ : to tear forcibly apart

♦ rip, rive, shred, tatter, tear — more at TEAR

ren·der \'ren-dər\ *vb* **1** : to extract (as lard) by heating **2** ♦ : to give to another; *also* : YIELD **3** : to give in return **4** : to do (a service) for another ⟨∼ aid⟩ **5** : to cause to be or become : MAKE **6** : to reproduce or represent by artistic or verbal means **7** : TRANSLATE ⟨∼ into English⟩

♦ cede, deliver, give up, hand over, leave, relinquish, surrender, turn over, yield — more at SURRENDER

¹**ren·dez·vous** \'rän-di-ˌvü, -dā-\ *n, pl* **ren·dez·vous** \-ˌvüz\ [MF, fr. *rendez vous* present yourselves] **1 a** : a place appointed for a meeting; *also* : a meeting at an appointed place **b** ♦ : an agreement to meet each other or with another person or thing **2** ♦ : a place of popular resort **3** : the process of bringing two spacecraft together

♦ [1b] appointment, date, engagement, tryst — more at ENGAGEMENT ♦ [2] hangout, haunt, resort — more at HANGOUT

²**rendezvous** *vb* **-voused** \-ˌvüd\; **-vous·ing** \-ˌvü-iŋ\; **-vouses** \-ˌvüz\ ♦ : to come or bring together at a rendezvous

♦ assemble, cluster, collect, concentrate, conglomerate, congregate, convene, forgather, gather, meet — more at ASSEMBLE

ren·di·tion \ren-'di-shən\ *n* : an act or a result of rendering ⟨first ∼ of the work into English⟩

ren·e·gade \'re-ni-ˌgād\ *n* [Sp *renegado*, fr. ML *renegatus*, fr. pp. of *renegare* to deny, fr. L *re-* re- + *negare* to deny] ♦ : a deserter from one faith, cause, principle, or party for another

♦ defector, deserter, recreant; *also* betrayer, double-crosser, quisling, traitor, turncoat; chicken, coward, craven, dastard, poltroon; insurgent, insurrectionist, mutineer, rebel, red, revolter, revolutionary, revolutionist, revolutionizer *Ant* loyalist

re·nege \ri-'nig, -'neg, -'nāg\ *vb* **re·neged**; **re·neg·ing 1** ♦ : to go back on a promise or commitment **2** : to fail to follow suit when able in a card game in violation of the rules — **re·neg·er** *n*

♦ back down, cop out; *also* chicken (out); disavow, recall, recant, retract, take back, withdraw

re·new \ri-'nü, -'nyü\ *vb* **1** ♦ : to make or become new, fresh, or strong again **2** ♦ : to restore to existence : REVIVE **3** : to make or do again : REPEAT ⟨∼ a complaint⟩ **4** ♦ : to begin again : RESUME ⟨∼ed his efforts⟩ **5** : REPLACE ⟨∼ the lining of a coat⟩ **6** : to grant or obtain an extension of or on ⟨∼ a lease⟩ ⟨∼ a subscription⟩ — **re·new·er** *n*

♦ [1] freshen, recreate, refresh, regenerate, rejuvenate, restore, revitalize, revive; *also* make over, refurbish,

rehabilitate, remake, remodel, renovate; refill, replenish, resupply ♦ [1, 2] reanimate, reinvigorate, resuscitate, revive — more at REVIVE ♦ [4] continue, reopen, restart, resume — more at RESUME

re·new·able \ri-'nü-ə-bəl, -'nyü-\ *adj* **1** : capable of being renewed **2** : capable of being replaced by natural ecological cycles or sound management procedures ⟨∼ resources⟩

re·new·al \ri-'nü-əl, -'nyü-\ *n* **1** ♦ : the act of renewing : the state of being renewed **2** : something renewed

♦ rebirth, regeneration, rejuvenation, resurgence, resurrection, resuscitation, revival — more at REVIVAL

ren·net \'re-nət\ *n* **1** : the contents of the stomach of an unweaned animal (as a calf) or the lining membrane of the stomach used for curdling milk **2** : rennin or a substitute used to curdle milk

ren·nin \'re-nən\ *n* : a stomach enzyme that coagulates casein and is used commercially to curdle milk in the making of cheese

re·nounce \ri-'naůns\ *vb* **re·nounced**; **re·nounc·ing 1** ♦ : to give up, refuse, or resign usu. by formal declaration **2** ♦ : to refuse further to follow, obey, or recognize

♦ [1] abdicate, abnegate, cede, relinquish, resign, step down, surrender — more at ABDICATE ♦ [2] abjure, recant, retract, take back, unsay, withdraw — more at ABJURE

re·nounce·ment *n* ♦ : the act or practice of renouncing

♦ abnegation, renunciation, repudiation, self-denial — more at RENUNCIATION

ren·o·vate \'re-nə-ˌvāt\ *vb* **-vat·ed**; **-vat·ing 1** ♦ : to make like new again : put in good condition ⟨*renovated* the kitchen⟩ **2** : to restore to vigor or activity — **ren·o·va·tion** \ˌre-nə-'vā-shən\ *n* — **ren·o·va·tor** \'re-nə-ˌvā-tər\ *n*

♦ doctor, fix, mend, patch, recondition, repair, revamp — more at MEND

re·nown \ri-'naůn\ *n* ♦ : a state of being widely acclaimed and honored ⟨a writer of ∼⟩

♦ celebrity, fame, notoriety — more at FAME

re·nowned \-'naůnd\ *adj* ♦ : having renown

♦ celebrated, famed, famous, noted, notorious, prominent, star, well-known — more at FAMOUS

¹**rent** \'rent\ *n* **1** : money or the amount of money paid or due at intervals for the use of another's property **2** : property rented or for rent

²**rent** *vb* **1** : to give possession and use of in return for rent **2** ♦ : to take and hold under an agreement to pay rent **3** : to be for rent ⟨∼s for $100 a month⟩

♦ engage, hire, lease, let — more at HIRE

³**rent** *n* **1** ♦ : an act or instance of rending **2** : a split in a party or organized group : SCHISM **3** ♦ : an opening made by or as if by rending

♦ [1] gash, laceration, rip, slash, slit, tear — more at GASH ♦ [3] breach, break, discontinuity, gap, gulf, hole, interval, opening, rift, separation — more at GAP

¹**rent·al** \'ren-tᵊl\ *n* **1** : an amount paid or collected as rent **2** : something that is rented **3** : an act of renting

²**rental** *adj* : of or relating to rent

rent·er *n* ♦ : one that rents

♦ boarder, lodger, roomer, tenant — more at TENANT

re·nun·ci·a·tion \ri-ˌnən-sē-'ā-shən\ *n* ♦ : the act of renouncing : REPUDIATION

♦ abnegation, renouncement, repudiation, self-denial; *also* denial, refusal; relinquishment, resignation, surrender *Ant* indulgence, self-indulgence

re·open \ˌre-'ō-pən\ *vb* ♦ : to enter upon again

List of self-explanatory words with the prefix *re-* (continued)

♦ continue, renew, restart, resume — more at RESUME

¹rep \'rep\ n ♦ : one that represents another : REPRESEN-
TATIVE ⟨sales ~s⟩

♦ agent, attorney, commissary, delegate, deputy, envoy, factor, proxy, representative — more at AGENT

²rep abbr **1** repair **2** repeat **3** report; reporter **4** republic
Rep abbr Republican

re·pack·age \(ˌ)rē-'pa-kij\ vb : to package again or anew;
esp : to put into a more attractive form

¹re·pair \ri-'par\ vb [ME, fr. AF repairer to go back, return,
fr. LL repatriare to go home again, fr. L re- back + patria
native country] : to make one's way : GO ⟨~ed to the
drawing room⟩

²repair vb [ME, fr. AF reparer, fr. L reparare, fr. re- back
+ parare to prepare] **1** ♦ : to restore to good condition
: FIX **2** ♦ : to restore to a healthy state **3** : REMEDY ⟨~ a
wrong⟩ — **re·pair·er** n — **re·pair·man** \-ˌman\ n

♦ doctor, fix, mend, patch, recondition, renovate, revamp — more at MEND

³repair n **1** : a result of repairing **2** : an act of repairing
3 : condition with respect to need of repairing ⟨in bad
~⟩ **4** ♦ : the state of being in good or sound condition

♦ condition, estate, fettle, form, order, shape, trim —
more at CONDITION

rep·a·ra·tion \ˌre-pə-'rā-shən\ n **1** : the act of making
amends for a wrong **2** ♦ : amends made for a wrong
or injury; esp : money paid by a defeated nation in compensation for damages caused during hostilities — usu.
used in pl.

♦ compensation, damages, indemnity, quittance, recompense, redress, remuneration, requital, restitution,
satisfaction — more at COMPENSATION

re·par·a·tive \ri-'par-ə-tiv\ adj **1** : of, relating to, or effecting repairs **2** : serving to make amends

rep·ar·tee \ˌre-pər-'tē\ n **1** ♦ : a witty reply **2 a** ♦ : a succession of clever replies **b** : skill in making such replies

♦ [1] comeback, retort, riposte — more at RETORT
♦ [2a] banter, chaff, persiflage, raillery — more at
BANTER

re·past \ri-'past, 'rē-ˌpast\ n ♦ : a supply of food and drink
served as a meal

♦ board, chow, feed, meal, mess, table — more at MEAL

re·pa·tri·ate \rē-'pā-trē-ˌāt\ vb **-at·ed; -at·ing** : to send or
bring back to the country of origin or citizenship ⟨~
prisoners of war⟩ — **re·pa·tri·ate** \-trē-ət, -trē-ˌāt\ n —
re·pa·tri·a·tion \-ˌpā-trē-'ā-shən\ n

re·pay \rē-'pā\ vb **-paid** \-'pād\; **-pay·ing** **1** : to pay back
: REFUND **2** : to give or do in return or requital **3** : to
make a return payment to : RECOMPENSE, REQUITE —
re·pay·able adj — **re·pay·ment** n

¹re·peal \ri-'pēl\ vb [ME repelen, fr. AF repeler, lit., to call
back, fr. re- back + apeler to appeal, call] ♦ : to annul
by authoritative and esp. legislative action — **re·peal·er** n

♦ abolish, abrogate, annul, cancel, dissolve, invalidate,
negate, nullify, quash, rescind, void — more at ABOL-
ISH

²repeal n : the act or an instance of repealing

¹re·peat \ri-'pēt\ vb **1** : to say again **2** ♦ : to do again
3 : to say over from memory **4** ♦ : to say after another
— **re·peat·able** adj — **re·peat·er** n

♦ [2] duplicate, redo, reiterate, remake, replicate; also renew ♦ [4] echo, quote; also mouth; copy, imitate, mimic

²re·peat \ri-'pēt, 'rē-ˌpēt\ n **1** ♦ : the act of repeating
2 : something repeated or to be repeated (as a radio or
television program)

³re·peat \ri-'pēt\ adj : of, relating to, or being one that repeats an offense, achievement, or action

♦ duplication, reiteration, repetition, replication; also
rerun

re·peat·ed \ri-'pē-təd\ adj ♦ : done or recurring again and
again : FREQUENT ⟨~ requests⟩

♦ constant, frequent, habitual, periodic, regular, steady
— more at REGULAR

re·peat·ed·ly adv ♦ : renewed or recurring again and again

♦ constantly, continually, frequently, often — more at
OFTEN

re·pel \ri-'pel\ vb **repelled; repel·ling** **1** ♦ : to drive away
: REPULSE **2** ♦ : to fight against : RESIST **3** : to turn away
: REJECT **4** ♦ : to cause aversion in : DISGUST

♦ [1] fend, repulse, stave off; also hold off, resist,
withstand; deflect, ward (off); rebuff, snub, spurn
♦ [2] buck, defy, fight, oppose, resist, withstand —
more at RESIST ♦ [4] disgust, nauseate, repulse, revolt,
sicken, turn off — more at DISGUST

¹re·pel·lent also **re·pel·lant** \ri-'pe-lənt\ adj **1** : tending to
drive away ⟨bug-repellent spray⟩ **2** ♦ : causing disgust

♦ abhorrent, awful, distasteful, foul, nasty, nauseating,
noisome, obnoxious, obscene, odious, offensive, repugnant, repulsive, revolting

²repellent also **repellant** n : something that repels; esp : a
substance that repels insects

re·pent \ri-'pent\ vb **1** : to turn from sin and resolve to
reform one's life **2** ♦ : to feel sorry for (something done)
: REGRET ⟨~ed their decision⟩

♦ bemoan, deplore, lament, regret, rue — more at RE-
GRET

re·pen·tance \ri-'pent-ᵊns\ n ♦ : the action or process of
repenting esp. for misdeeds or moral shortcomings

♦ contrition, guilt, penitence, remorse, self-reproach,
shame — more at GUILT

re·pen·tant \-ᵊnt\ adj ♦ : experiencing repentance

♦ apologetic, contrite, guilty, penitent, regretful, remorseful, rueful, sorry — more at CONTRITE

re·per·cus·sion \ˌrē-pər-'kə-shən, ˌre-\ n **1** : REVERBERA-
TION **2** : a reciprocal action or effect **3** ♦ : a widespread,
indirect, or unforeseen effect of something done or said

♦ effect, impact, influence, mark, sway — more at EF-
FECT

rep·er·toire \'re-pər-ˌtwär\ n [F] **1** : a list of plays, operas,
pieces, or parts which a company or performer is prepared to present **2** : a list of the skills or devices possessed by a person or needed in a person's occupation

rep·er·to·ry \'re-pər-ˌtōr-ē\ n, pl **-ries** **1** : REPOSITORY
2 : REPERTOIRE **3** : a company that presents its repertoire in the course of one season at one theater

rep·e·ti·tion \ˌre-pə-'ti-shən\ n **1** ♦ : the act or an instance
of repeating **2** : the fact of being repeated

♦ duplication, reiteration, repeat, replication — more
at REPEAT

rep·e·ti·tious \-'ti-shəs\ adj : marked by repetition; esp : tediously repeating ⟨~ work⟩ — **rep·e·ti·tious·ly** adv —
rep·e·ti·tious·ness n

re·pet·i·tive \ri-'pe-ti-tiv\ adj : REPETITIOUS — **re·pet·i·
tive·ly** adv — **re·pet·i·tive·ness** n

re·phrase \-'frāz\ vb ♦ : to express again in words or in
appropriate or telling terms

♦ paraphrase, restate, translate — more at PARAPHRASE

re·pine \ri-'pīn\ vb **re·pined; re·pin·ing** **1** ♦ : to feel or
express discontent or dejection **2** ♦ : to long for something

♦ [1] beef, bellyache, complain, fuss, gripe, grouse,
grumble ♦ usu repine for [2] ache for, covet, crave, desire, die (to or for), hanker for, hunger for, long for, lust

---

List of self-explanatory words with the prefix re- (continued)

relight	reload	remap	remarry
reline	remanufacture	remarriage	rematch

(for *or* after), pine for, thirst for, want, wish for, yearn for — more at DESIRE

repl *abbr* replace; replacement

re·place \ri-'plās\ *vb* **1** : to restore to a former place or position **2** ♦ : to take the place of : SUPPLANT **3** : to put something new in the place of — **re·place·able** *adj* — **re·plac·er** *n*

♦ displace, substitute, supersede, supplant; *also* preempt, usurp

re·place·ment \ri-'plās-mənt\ *n* **1** : the act of replacing : the state of being replaced **2** ♦ : one that replaces another esp. in a job or function

♦ backup, pinch hitter, relief, reserve, stand-in, sub, substitute — more at SUBSTITUTE

¹re·play \(ˌ)rē-'plā\ *vb* : to play again or over

²re·play \'rē-ˌplā\ *n* **1** : an act or instance of replaying **2** : the playing of a tape (as a videotape)

re·plen·ish \ri-'ple-nish\ *vb* : to fill or build up again : stock or supply anew — **re·plen·ish·ment** *n*

re·plete \ri-'plēt\ *adj* **1** : fully provided **2** ♦ : fully or abundantly provided or filled : FULL; *esp* : full of food — **re·plete·ness** *n*

♦ flush, fraught, full, rife, thick

re·ple·tion \ri-'plē-shən\ *n* : the state of being replete

rep·li·ca \'re-pli-kə\ *n* [It, repetition, fr. *replicare* to repeat, fr. LL, fr. L, to fold back, fr. *re-* back + *plicare* to fold] **1** : an exact reproduction (as of a painting) executed by the original artist **2** ♦ : a copy exact in all details : DUPLICATE

♦ carbon copy, counterpart, double, duplicate, duplication, facsimile, image, likeness, match, picture, ringer, spit — more at IMAGE

¹rep·li·cate \'re-plə-ˌkāt\ *vb* **-cat·ed; -cat·ing 1** ♦ : to make a copy of : DUPLICATE **2** ♦ : to do over or again : REPEAT

♦ [1] copy, duplicate, imitate, reproduce — more at COPY ♦ [2] duplicate, redo, reiterate, remake, repeat — more at REPEAT

²rep·li·cate \-pli-kət\ *n* : one of several identical experiments or procedures

rep·li·ca·tion \ˌre-plə-'kā-shən\ *n* **1** : ANSWER, REPLY **2** ♦ : precise copying or reproduction; *also* : an act or process of this **3** ♦ : an imitation, transcript, or reproduction of an original work

♦ [2] duplication, reiteration, repeat, repetition — more at REPEAT ♦ [3] carbon copy, copy, duplicate, duplication, facsimile, imitation, replica, reproduction — more at COPY

¹re·ply \ri-'plī\ *vb* **re·plied; re·ply·ing** ♦ : to say or do in answer : RESPOND

♦ answer, rejoin, respond, retort, return — more at ANSWER

²reply *n, pl* **replies** ♦ : something said, written, or done in answer or response : RESPONSE

♦ answer, comeback, response, retort, return — more at ANSWER

repo \'rē-ˌpō\ *adj* : of, relating to, or being in the business of repossessing property (as a car)

¹re·port \ri-'pōrt\ *n* [ME, fr. AF, fr. *reporter* to bring back, report, fr. L *reportare*, fr. *re-* back + *portare* to carry] **1** : common talk : RUMOR **2** ♦ : quality of reputation **3** ♦ : a usu. detailed account or statement **4** ♦ : an explosive noise

♦ [2] character, mark, name, note, reputation — more at REPUTATION ♦ [3] account, chronicle, history, narrative, record, story — more at ACCOUNT ♦ [4] bang, blast, boom, clap, crack, crash, pop, slam, smash, snap, thwack, whack — more at CLAP

²report *vb* **1** ♦ : to give an account of : RELATE, TELL **2** : to serve as carrier of (a message) **3** : to prepare or present (as an account of an event) for a newspaper or a broadcast **4** : to make a charge of misconduct against **5** : to present oneself (as for work) **6** : to make known to the authorities ⟨~ a fire⟩ **7** : to return or present (as a matter referred to a committee) with conclusions and recommendations — **re·port·able** *adj*

♦ describe, narrate, recite, recount, rehearse, relate, tell — more at TELL

re·port·age \ri-'pōr-tij, *esp for 2* ˌre-pər-'täzh, ˌre-ˌpȯr-'\ *n* [F] **1** : the act or process of reporting news **2** : writing intended to give an account of observed or documented events

report card *n* : a periodic report on a student's grades

re·port·ed·ly \ri-'pōr-təd-lē\ *adv* : according to report

re·port·er \ri-'pōr-tər\ *n* : one that reports; *esp* : a person who gathers and reports news for a news medium — **re·por·to·ri·al** \ˌre-pər-'tōr-ē-əl\ *adj*

¹re·pose \ri-'pōz\ *vb* **re·posed; re·pos·ing 1** : to lay at rest **2** : to lie at rest **3** : to lie dead **4** ♦ : to take a rest **5** : to have as a basis or support — usu. used with *on*

♦ bask, loll, lounge, relax, rest — more at REST

²repose *n* **1** ♦ : a state of resting (as after exertion); *esp* : SLEEP **2** : eternal or heavenly rest **3** ♦ : freedom from something that disturbs or excites : CALM, PEACE **4** ♦ : cessation or absence of activity, movement, or animation **5** : composure of manner : POISE — **re·pose·ful** *adj*

♦ [1] rest, sleep, slumber — more at SLEEP ♦ [3] calm, calmness, hush, peace, placidity, quiet, quietness, serenity, still, stillness, tranquility — more at CALM ♦ [4] ease, leisure, relaxation, rest — more at REST

³repose *vb* **re·posed; re·pos·ing 1** : to place (as trust) in someone or something **2** : to place for control, management, or use

re·pos·i·to·ry \ri-'pä-zə-ˌtōr-ē\ *n, pl* **-ries 1** ♦ : a place where something is deposited or stored **2** : a person to whom something is entrusted

♦ depository, depot, magazine, storage, storehouse, warehouse — more at STOREHOUSE

re·pos·sess \ˌrē-pə-'zes\ *vb* **1** ♦ : to regain possession of **2** : to take possession of in default of the payment of installments due

♦ recapture, reclaim, recoup, recover, regain, retake, retrieve — more at RECOVER

re·pos·ses·sion \-'ze-shən\ *n* ♦ : the act or state of possessing again

♦ reclamation, recovery, retrieval — more at RECOVERY

re·post \(ˌ)rē-'pōst\ *vb* : to post again ⟨~ a message⟩

rep·re·hend \ˌre-pri-'hend\ *vb* ♦ : to express disapproval of : CENSURE — **rep·re·hen·sion** \-'hen-chən\ *n*

♦ blame, censure, condemn, criticize, denounce, fault, knock, pan — more at CRITICIZE

rep·re·hen·si·ble \-'hen-sə-bəl\ *adj* ♦ : deserving blame or censure : CULPABLE — **rep·re·hen·si·bly** \-blē\ *adv*

♦ blamable, blameworthy, censurable, culpable — more at BLAMEWORTHY ♦ censurable, objectionable, obnoxious, offensive — more at OBJECTIONABLE

rep·re·sent \ˌre-pri-'zent\ *vb* **1** ♦ : to present a picture or a likeness of : DEPICT **2** : to serve as a sign or symbol of **3** : to act the role of **4** : to stand in the place of : act or speak for; *also* : to manage the legal or business affairs of **5** : to be a member or example of : TYPIFY **6** : to serve as an elected representative of **7** ♦ : to describe as having a specified quality or character **8** : to state with the purpose of affecting judgment or action

---

List of self-explanatory words with the prefix *re-* (continued)

remelt	remix	rename	renegotiation
remigration	remold	renegotiate	renominate

♦ [1] depict, image, picture, portray — more at PIC-
TURE ♦ [7] characterize, define, depict, describe, portray — more at CHARACTERIZE

rep·re·sen·ta·tion \,re-pri-,zen-'tā-shən\ n 1 : the act of
representing 2 : one (as a picture or image) that represents something else 3 : the state of being represented
in a legislative body; *also* : the body of persons representing a constituency 4 : a usu. formal statement made to
effect a change

¹**rep·re·sen·ta·tive** \,re-pri-'zen-tə-tiv\ *adj* 1 ♦ : serving to
represent 2 : standing or acting for another 3 : founded
on the principle of representation : carried on by elected
representatives ⟨~ government⟩ — **rep·re·sen·ta·tive·ly**
adv — **rep·re·sen·ta·tive·ness** *n*

♦ average, characteristic, normal, regular, standard,
typical — more at TYPICAL

²**representative** *n* 1 ♦ : a typical example of a group, class,
or quality 2 ♦ : one that represents another; *esp* : one
representing a district in a legislative body usu. as a member of a lower house

♦ [1] case, example, exemplar, illustration, instance,
sample, specimen — more at EXAMPLE ♦ [2] ambassador, delegate, emissary, envoy, legate, minister — more
at AMBASSADOR ♦ [2] agent, attorney, commissary, delegate, deputy, envoy, factor, proxy — more at AGENT

re·press \ri-'pres\ *vb* 1 **a** : to check by or as if by pressure
: CURB **b** ♦ : to put down by force : SUBDUE 2 ♦ : to
prevent the natural or normal expression, activity, or development of : SUPPRESS 3 : to exclude from consciousness ⟨~ a painful memory⟩ — **re·pres·sive** \-'pre-siv\ *adj*

♦ [1b] clamp down, crack down, crush, put down, quash,
quell, silence, snuff, squash, squelch, subdue, suppress
— more at QUELL ♦ [2] choke, pocket, smother, stifle,
strangle, suppress, swallow — more at SUPPRESS

re·pres·sion \-'pre-shən\ *n* ♦ : the action or process of re-
pressing

♦ constraint, inhibition, restraint, self-control, self-restraint, suppression

¹**re·prieve** \ri-'prēv\ *vb* **re·prieved; re·priev·ing** 1 : to delay
the punishment or execution of 2 : to give temporary
relief to

²**reprieve** *n* 1 : the act of reprieving : the state of being re-
prieved 2 : a formal temporary suspension of a sentence
esp. of death 3 : a temporary respite

¹**rep·ri·mand** \'re-prə-,mand\ *n* ♦ : a severe or formal reproof

♦ censure, denunciation, rebuke, reproach, reproof,
stricture — more at CENSURE

²**reprimand** *vb* ♦ : to reprove severely or formally from a
position of authority

♦ censure, condemn, denounce, rebuke, reproach, reprove — more at CENSURE ♦ admonish, chide, lecture,
rail (at *or* against), rate, rebuke, scold — more at SCOLD

¹**re·print** \,(,)rē-'print\ *vb* : to print again

²**re·print** \'rē-,print\ *n* : a reproduction of printed matter

re·pri·sal \ri-'prī-zəl\ *n* ♦ : an act in retaliation for something done by another

♦ requital, retaliation, retribution, revenge, vengeance
— more at REVENGE

re·prise \ri-'prēz\ *n* : a recurrence, renewal, or resumption
of an action; *also* : a musical repetition

¹**re·proach** \ri-'prōch\ *n* 1 ♦ : an expression of disapproval
2 : the condition of one fallen from grace or honor : DIS-
GRACE 3 : the act of reproaching : REBUKE 4 : a cause
or occasion of blame or disgrace — **re·proach·ful** \-fəl\
adj — **re·proach·ful·ly** *adv* — **re·proach·ful·ness** *n*

♦ censure, denunciation, rebuke, reprimand, reproof,
stricture — more at CENSURE

²**reproach** *vb* 1 ♦ : to express disappointment in or displeasure with (a person) for conduct that is blameworthy or
in need of amendment : REBUKE 2 : to cast discredit on
— **re·proach·able** *adj*

♦ admonish, chide, lecture, rail (at *or* against), rate, rebuke, reprimand, scold — more at SCOLD ♦ censure,
condemn, denounce, rebuke, reprimand, reprove —
more at CENSURE

¹**rep·ro·bate** \'re-prə-,bāt\ *n* 1 : a person foreordained to
damnation 2 : a thoroughly bad person : SCOUNDREL

²**reprobate** *adj* ♦ : of, relating to, or having the characteristics of a reprobate

♦ corrupt, debauched, decadent, degenerate, dissolute,
perverse, perverted — more at CORRUPT

rep·ro·ba·tion \,re-prə-'bā-shən\ *n* : strong disapproval
: CONDEMNATION

re·pro·duce \,rē-prə-'düs, -'dyüs\ *vb* 1 ♦ : to produce again
or anew 2 ♦ : to produce offspring — **re·pro·duc·ible**
\-'dü-sə-bəl, -'dyü-\ *adj* — **re·pro·duc·tive** \-'dək-tiv\ *adj*

♦ [1] copy, duplicate, imitate, replicate — more at
COPY ♦ [2] breed, multiply, procreate, propagate —
more at PROCREATE

re·pro·duc·tion \-'dək-shən\ *n* ♦ : something reproduced

♦ carbon copy, copy, duplicate, duplication, facsimile,
imitation, replica, replication — more at COPY

re·proof \ri-'prüf\ *n* ♦ : blame or censure for a fault

♦ censure, denunciation, rebuke, reprimand, reproach,
stricture — more at CENSURE

re·prove \ri-'prüv\ *vb* **re·proved; re·prov·ing** 1 ♦ : to administer a rebuke to 2 ♦ : to express disapproval of —
re·prov·er *n*

♦ [1] admonish, chide, rebuke, reprimand, reproach
♦ [2] censure, condemn, denounce — more at CEN-
SURE

rept *abbr* report

rep·tile \'rep-təl, -,tīl\ *n* [ME *reptil*, fr. MF or LL; MF *reptile*, fr. LL *reptile*, fr. L *repere* to crawl] : any of a large
class of air-breathing scaly vertebrates including snakes,
lizards, alligators, turtles, and extinct related forms (as
dinosaurs) — **rep·til·i·an** \rep-'ti-lē-ən\ *adj or n*

re·pub·lic \ri-'pə-blik\ *n* [F *république*, fr. MF *republique*,
fr. L *respublica*, fr. *res* thing, wealth + *publica*, fem. of
publicus public] 1 : a government having a chief of state
who is not a monarch and is usu. a president; *also* : a
nation or other political unit having such a government
2 : a government in which supreme power is held by the
citizens entitled to vote and is exercised by elected officers and representatives governing according to law;
also : a nation or other political unit having such a form
of government 3 : a constituent political and territorial unit of the former nations of Czechoslovakia, the
U.S.S.R., or Yugoslavia

¹**re·pub·li·can** \-bli-kən\ *adj* 1 ♦ : of, relating to, or resembling a republic 2 : favoring or supporting a republic
3 *cap* : of, relating to, or constituting one of the two major political parties in the U.S. evolving in the mid-19th
century — **re·pub·li·can·ism** *n, often cap*

♦ democratic, popular, self-governing — more at DEM-
OCRATIC

²**republican** *n* 1 : one that favors or supports a republican
form of government 2 *cap* : a member of a republican
party and esp. of the Republican party of the U.S.

re·pu·di·ate \ri-'pyü-dē-,āt\ *vb* **-at·ed; -at·ing** [L *repudiare*
to cast off, divorce, fr. *repudium* rejection of a prospec-

List of self-explanatory words with the prefix *re-* (continued)

| renomination | reoccupy | reorder | reorganize |
| renumber | reoccur | reorganization | reorient |

tive spouse, divorce] **1 ♦** : to give up or renounce as one's own \-\ DISOWN **2 ♦** : to refuse to have anything to do with : refuse to acknowledge, accept, or pay ⟨∼ a charge⟩ ⟨∼ a debt⟩ **3 ♦** : to reject as untrue or unjust — **re·pu·di·a·tor** \-'pyü-dē-,ā-tər\ n

♦ [1, 2] disavow, disclaim, disown — more at DISCLAIM ♦ [2, 3] decline, deny, disallow, disapprove, negative, refuse, reject, spurn, turn down — more at DECLINE

re·pu·di·a·tion \-,pyü-dē-'ā-shən\ n ♦ : the act of repudiating : the state of being repudiated

♦ contradiction, denial, disallowance, disavowal, disclaimer, negation, rejection — more at DENIAL

re·pug·nance \ri-'pəg-nəns\ n **1** : the quality or fact of being contradictory or inconsistent **2 ♦** : strong dislike, distaste, or antagonism

♦ aversion, disgust, distaste, loathing, nausea, repulsion, revulsion — more at DISGUST

re·pug·nant \-nənt\ adj **1** : marked by repugnance **2 ♦** : contrary to a person's tastes or principles : exciting distaste or aversion — **re·pug·nant·ly** adv

♦ distasteful, foul, nasty, nauseating, noisome, obnoxious, obscene, odious, offensive, repellent, repulsive, revolting

[1]re·pulse \ri-'pəls\ vb **re·pulsed; re·puls·ing 1 ♦** : to drive or beat back : REPEL **2** : to repel by discourtesy or denial : REBUFF **3 ♦** : to cause a feeling of repulsion in : DISGUST

♦ [1] fend, repel, stave off — more at REPEL ♦ [3] disgust, nauseate, repel, revolt, sicken, turn off — more at DISGUST

[2]repulse n **1 ♦** : an abrupt rejection of an offer or advance : REBUFF **2** : the action of repelling an attacker : the fact of being repelled

♦ brush-off, cold shoulder, rebuff, snub — more at COLD SHOULDER

re·pul·sion \ri-'pəl-shən\ n **1** : the action of repulsing : the state of being repulsed **2** : the force with which bodies, particles, or like forces repel one another **3 ♦** : a feeling of aversion

♦ aversion, disgust, distaste, loathing, nausea, repugnance, revulsion — more at DISGUST

re·pul·sive \-siv\ adj **1** : serving or tending to repel or reject **2 ♦** : arousing aversion or disgust — **re·pul·sive·ly** adv

♦ abhorrent, distasteful, horrible, horrid, nasty, nauseating, noisome, obnoxious, offensive, repellent, repugnant, revolting

re·pul·sive·ness n ♦ : the quality or state of being repulsive

♦ atrociousness, atrocity, frightfulness, hideousness, horror, monstrosity — more at HORROR

re·pur·pose \(,)rē-'pər-pəs\ vb : to give a new purpose or use to

rep·u·ta·ble \'re-pyə-tə-bəl\ adj ♦ : having a good reputation ⟨a ∼ lawyer⟩ — **rep·u·ta·bly** \-blē\ adv

♦ name, prestigious, reputed, respectable — more at RESPECTABLE

rep·u·ta·tion \,re-pyù-'tā-shən\ n **1 ♦** : overall quality or character as seen or judged by people in general **2** : place in public esteem or regard

♦ character, mark, name, note, report; also credit, honor; celebrity, fame, notoriety, renown

[1]re·pute \ri-'pyüt\ vb **re·put·ed; re·put·ing** : BELIEVE, CONSIDER

[2]repute n **1** : the character or status commonly ascribed to one : REPUTATION **2** : the state of being favorably known or spoken of

re·put·ed \ri-'pyü-təd\ adj **1 ♦** : having a good repute : REPUTABLE **2 ♦** : according to reputation : SUPPOSED — **re·put·ed·ly** adv

♦ [1] name, prestigious, reputable, respectable — more at RESPECTABLE ♦ [2] apparent, assumed, evident, ostensible, seeming, supposed — more at APPARENT

req abbr **1** request **2** require; required **3** requisition

[1]re·quest \ri-'kwest\ n **1 ♦** : an act or instance of asking for something **2** : a thing asked for **3** : the condition of being requested ⟨available on ∼⟩

♦ call, inquiry, query, question — more at QUESTION

[2]request vb **1** : to make a request to or of **2 ♦** : to ask for — **re·quest·er** n

♦ ask, call, order, requisition — more at ORDER

re·qui·em \'re-kwē-əm, 'rā-\ n [ME, fr. L (first word of the requiem mass), acc. of requies rest, fr. quies quiet, rest] **1** : a mass for a dead person; also : a musical setting for this **2 ♦** : a musical service or hymn in honor of the dead **3** : something that resembles a solemn chant in honor of the dead

♦ dirge, elegy, lament, threnody — more at LAMENT

re·quire \ri-'kwīr\ vb **re·quired; re·quir·ing 1 ♦** : to demand as necessary or essential **2** : COMMAND, ORDER

♦ demand, necessitate, need, take, want, warrant — more at NEED

re·quire·ment \-mənt\ n **1** : something (as a condition or quality) required ⟨entrance ∼s⟩ **2 ♦** : something wanted or needed : NECESSITY

♦ condition, demand, essential, must, necessity, need, requisite — more at ESSENTIAL

[1]req·ui·site \'re-kwə-zət\ adj ♦ : of the utmost importance : NECESSARY

♦ essential, imperative, indispensable, integral, necessary, needful, vital — more at ESSENTIAL

[2]requisite n : something that is required or necessary

[1]req·ui·si·tion \,re-kwə-'zi-shən\ n **1** : formal application or demand (as for supplies) **2** : the state of being in demand or use

[2]requisition vb ♦ : to make a requisition for

♦ ask, order, request — more at ORDER

re·quit·al \ri-'kwīt-ᵊl\ n **1 ♦** : something given in return, compensation, or retaliation **2 ♦** : the act or action of requiting : the state of being requited

♦ [1] compensation, damages, indemnity, payment, quittance, recompense, redress, remuneration, reparation, restitution, satisfaction — more at COMPENSATION ♦ [2] reprisal, retaliation, retribution, revenge, vengeance — more at REVENGE

re·quite \ri-'kwīt\ vb **re·quit·ed; re·quit·ing 1** : to make return for : REPAY **2 ♦** : to make retaliation for : AVENGE **3 ♦** : to make return to

♦ [2] avenge, retaliate, revenge — more at AVENGE ♦ [3] compensate, indemnify, recompense, recoup, remunerate — more at COMPENSATE

rere·dos \'rer-ə-,däs\ n : a usu. ornamental wood or stone screen or partition wall behind an altar

re·run \'rē-,rən, (,)rē-'rən\ n **1** : the act or an instance of running again or anew **2** : a show or program that is shown again — **re·run** \(,)rē-'rən\ vb

res abbr **1** research **2** reservation; reserve **3** reservoir **4** residence; resident **5** resolution

re·sale \'rē-,sāl, (,)rē-'sāl\ n : the act of selling again usu. to a new party — **re·sal·able** \(,)rē-'sā-lə-bəl\ adj

re·scind \ri-'sind\ vb ♦ : to destroy the force, effectiveness, or validity of : REPEAL

♦ abolish, abrogate, annul, cancel, dissolve, invalidate, negate, nullify, quash, repeal, void — more at ABOLISH

re·scis·sion \-'si-zhən\ n ♦ : an act of rescinding

List of self-explanatory words with the prefix *re-* (continued)

reorientation	repaint	repeople	replant
repack	repass	rephotograph	repopulate

♦ abortion, calling, cancellation, recall, repeal, revocation — more at CANCELLATION

re·script \'rē-ˌskript\ *n* : an official or authoritative order or decree

¹**res·cue** \'res-kyü\ *vb* **res·cued; res·cu·ing** [ME *rescouen, rescuen,* fr. AF *rescure,* fr. *re-* back, again + *escure* to shake off, fr. L *excutere*] ♦ : to free from danger, harm, or confinement

♦ deliver, save — more at SAVE

²**rescue** *n* ♦ : an act of rescuing

♦ deliverance, salvation — more at SALVATION

res·cu·er *n* ♦ : one that rescues

♦ deliverer, redeemer, savior — more at SAVIOR

¹**re·search** \ri-'sərch, 'rē-ˌsərch\ *n* 1 : careful or diligent search 2 ♦ : studious inquiry or examination aimed at the discovery and interpretation of new knowledge 3 : the collecting of information about a particular subject — **re·search·er** *n*

♦ examination, exploration, inquiry, investigation, probe, study — more at INQUIRY

²**research** *vb* ♦ : to search or investigate exhaustively

♦ delve, dig, explore, go, inquire into, investigate, look, probe — more at EXPLORE

re·sec·tion \ri-'sek-shən\ *n* : the surgical removal of part of an organ or structure

re·sem·blance \ri-'zem-bləns\ *n* ♦ : the quality or state of resembling; *also* : a point of likeness

♦ community, correspondence, likeness, parallelism, similarity, similitude — more at SIMILARITY

re·sem·ble \ri-'zem-bəl\ *vb* **-bled; -bling** : to be like or similar to

re·sent \ri-'zent\ *vb* : to feel or exhibit annoyance or indignation at ⟨∼ed his interference⟩

re·sent·ful \-fəl\ *adj* ♦ : full of resentment : inclined to resent — **re·sent·ful·ly** *adv*

♦ acrid, acrimonious, bitter, hard, rancorous, sore — more at BITTER ♦ covetous, envious, jaundiced, jealous — more at ENVIOUS

re·sent·ment *n* ♦ : a feeling of indignant displeasure or ill will at something regarded as a wrong, insult, or injury

♦ dudgeon, huff, offense, peeve, pique, umbrage — more at PIQUE

re·ser·pine \ri-'sər-ˌpēn, -pən\ *n* : a drug used in treating high blood pressure and nervous tension

res·er·va·tion \ˌre-zər-'vā-shən\ *n* 1 : an act of reserving 2 : something (as a room in a hotel) arranged for in advance 3 : something reserved; *esp* : a tract of public land set aside for special use 4 ♦ : a limiting condition

♦ condition, provision, proviso, qualification, stipulation — more at CONDITION

¹**re·serve** \ri-'zərv\ *vb* **re·served; re·serv·ing** 1 ♦ : to store for future or special use 2 ♦ : to hold back for oneself 3 ♦ : to set aside or arrange to have set aside or held for special use

♦ [1] accumulate, cache, garner, hoard, lay up, stash, stockpile, store ♦ [2] hang on, hold, keep, retain, withhold — more at KEEP ♦ [3] allocate, consecrate, dedicate, devote, earmark, save — more at DEVOTE

²**reserve** *n* ♦ : something reserved : STORE 2 : a military force withheld from action for later use — usu. used in pl. 3 : the military forces of a country not part of the regular services; *also* : RESERVIST 4 : a tract set apart : RESERVATION 5 : an act of reserving 6 ♦ : restraint or caution in one's words or bearing 7 : money or its equivalent kept in hand or set apart to meet liabilities 8 ♦ : a person or thing that takes the place or function of another

♦ [1] cache, deposit, hoard, store — more at STORE ♦ [6] constraint, restraint, self-control; *also* aloofness, distance; bashfulness, modesty, shyness; reticence, silence, taciturnity; inhibition ♦ [8] backup, pinch hitter, relief, replacement, stand-in, sub, substitute — more at SUBSTITUTE

re·served \ri-'zərvd\ *adj* 1 ♦ : restrained in words and actions 2 : set aside for future or special use — **re·serv·ed·ly** \-'zər-vəd-lē\ *adv* — **re·serv·ed·ness** \-vəd-nəs\ *n*

♦ closemouthed, laconic, reticent, silent, taciturn, uncommunicative — more at SILENT

re·serv·ist \ri-'zər-vist\ *n* : a member of a military reserve

res·er·voir \'re-zə-ˌvwär, -zər-, -ˌvwȯr\ *n* [F] : a place where something is kept in store; *esp* : an artificial lake where water is collected and kept for use

re·shuf·fle \rē-'shə-fəl\ *vb* 1 : to shuffle again 2 : to reorganize usu. by redistribution of existing elements ⟨*reshuffled* our schedules⟩ — **reshuffle** *n*

re·side \ri-'zīd\ *vb* **re·sid·ed; re·sid·ing** 1 ♦ : to make one's home : DWELL 2 : to be present as a quality or vested as a right

♦ abide, dwell, live — more at LIVE

res·i·dence \'re-zə-dəns\ *n* 1 : the act or fact of residing in a place as a dweller or in discharge of a duty or an obligation 2 ♦ : the place where one actually lives 3 : a building used as a home : DWELLING 4 : the period of living in a place

♦ abode, domicile, dwelling, home, house, lodging, quarters — more at HOME

res·i·den·cy \'re-zə-dən-sē\ *n, pl* **-cies** 1 : the residence of or the territory under a diplomatic resident 2 : a period of advanced training in a medical specialty

¹**res·i·dent** \-dənt\ *adj* 1 : RESIDING 2 : being in residence 3 : not migratory

²**resident** *n* 1 ♦ : one who resides in a place 2 : a diplomatic representative with governing powers (as in a protectorate) 3 : a physician serving a residency

♦ denizen, dweller, inhabitant, occupant — more at INHABITANT

res·i·den·tial \ˌre-zə-'den-chəl\ *adj* 1 : used as a residence or by residents 2 : occupied by or restricted to residences — **res·i·den·tial·ly** *adv*

¹**re·sid·u·al** \ri-'zi-jə-wəl\ *adj* : being a residue or remainder

²**residual** *n* 1 : a residual product or substance 2 : a payment (as to an actor or writer) for each rerun after an initial showing (as of a taped TV show)

re·sid·u·ary \ri-'zi-jə-ˌwer-ē\ *adj* : of, relating to, or constituting a residue esp. of an estate

res·i·due \'re-zə-ˌdü, -ˌdyü\ *n* ♦ : a part remaining after another part has been taken away

♦ balance, leavings, leftovers, odds and ends, remainder, remains, remnant, rest — more at REMAINDER

re·sid·u·um \ri-'zi-jə-wəm\ *n, pl* **re·sid·ua** \-jə-wə\ [L] 1 : something remaining or residual after certain deductions are made 2 : a residual product

re·sign \ri-'zīn\ *vb* [ME, fr. AF *resigner,* fr. L *resignare,* lit., to unseal, cancel, fr. *signare* to sign, seal] 1 ♦ : to give up deliberately (as one's position) esp. by a formal act 2 : to give (oneself) over (as to grief or despair) without resistance — **re·sign·ed·ly** \-'zī-nəd-lē\ *adv*

♦ abdicate, abnegate, cede, relinquish, renounce, step down, surrender — more at ABDICATE ♦ *usu* resign from leave, quit, retire, step down — more at QUIT

re–sign \ˌrē-'sīn\ *vb* : to sign again

res·ig·na·tion \ˌre-zig-'nā-shən\ *n* 1 : an act or instance of resigning; *also* : a formal notification of such an act 2 : the quality or state of being resigned

---

List of self-explanatory words with the prefix *re-* (continued)

re·signed \ri-'zīnd\ adj ♦ : being resigned to something : characterized by resignation

♦ acquiescent, passive, tolerant, unresistant, unresisting, yielding — more at PASSIVE

re·sil·ience \ri-'zil-yəns\ n 1 : the ability of a body to regain its original size and shape after being compressed, bent, or stretched 2 : an ability to recover from or adjust easily to change or misfortune

re·sil·ien·cy \-yən-sē\ n : RESILIENCE

re·sil·ient \-yənt\ adj ♦ : marked by resilience ⟨∼ athletes⟩

♦ elastic, flexible, rubbery, springy, stretch, supple — more at ELASTIC

res·in \'rez-ᵊn\ n : any of various substances obtained from the gum or sap of some trees and used esp. in varnishes, plastics, and medicine; also : a comparable synthetic product — **res·in·ous** adj

¹re·sist \ri-'zist\ vb 1 ♦ : to fight against : OPPOSE ⟨∼ aggression⟩ 2 : to withstand the force or effect of ⟨∼ disease⟩ — **re·sist·ible** \-'zis-tə-bəl\ adj — **re·sist·less** adj

♦ buck, defy, fight, oppose, repel, withstand; also battle, combat, contend (with), counter; contest, dispute; baffle, balk, foil, frustrate, thwart; check, counter, hinder, obstruct, stem Ant bow (to), capitulate (to), give in (to), submit (to), succumb (to), surrender (to), yield (to)

²resist n : something (as a coating) that resists or prevents a particular action

re·sis·tance \ri-'zis-təns\ n 1 : the act or an instance of resisting : OPPOSITION 2 : the power or capacity to resist; esp : the inherent ability of an organism to resist harmful influences (as disease or infection) 3 : the opposition offered by a body to the passage through it of a steady electric current

re·sis·tant \-tənt\ adj : giving or capable of resistance

re·sis·tor \ri-'zis-tər\ n : a device used to provide resistance to the flow of an electric current in a circuit

res·o·lute \'re-zə-ˌlüt\ adj ♦ : firmly determined in purpose — **res·o·lute·ly** adv

♦ bound, decisive, determined, firm, intent, purposeful, set, single-minded — more at DETERMINED

res·o·lute·ness n : the quality or state of being resolute

res·o·lu·tion \ˌre-zə-'lü-shən\ n 1 : the act or process of resolving 2 : the action of solving : SOLUTION 3 ♦ : the quality of being resolute : DETERMINATION 4 ♦ : a formal statement expressing the opinion, will, or intent of a body of persons 5 : a measure of the sharpness of an image or of the fineness with which a device can produce or record such an image

♦ [3] decision, decisiveness, determination, firmness, granite, resolve — more at DETERMINATION ♦ [4] conclusion, decision, judgment (or judgement), opinion, verdict

re·solv·able adj ♦ : capable of being resolved

♦ answerable, explicable, soluble, solvable — more at SOLVABLE

¹re·solve \ri-'zälv\ vb **re·solved; re·solv·ing** 1 : to break up into constituent parts 2 : to distinguish between or make visible adjacent parts of 3 ♦ : to find an answer to : SOLVE 4 ♦ : to reach a firm decision about : DECIDE 5 : to make or pass a formal resolution

♦ [3] answer, break, crack, dope, figure out, puzzle, riddle, solve, unravel, work, work out — more at SOLVE ♦ [4] choose, conclude, decide, determine, figure, opt — more at DECIDE

²resolve n 1 ♦ : fixity of purpose 2 : something resolved

♦ decision, decisiveness, determination, firmness, granite, resolution — more at DETERMINATION

res·o·nance \'re-zə-nəns\ n 1 : the quality or state of being resonant 2 : a reinforcement of sound in a vibrating body caused by waves from another body vibrating at nearly the same rate

res·o·nant \-nənt\ adj 1 : continuing to sound : RESOUNDING 2 : relating to or exhibiting resonance 3 ♦ : intensified and enriched by or as if by resonance — **res·o·nant·ly** adv

♦ golden, resounding, ringing, round, sonorous, vibrant; also deep, full, mellifluous, mellow, rich; loud, powerful, stentorian, thundering, thunderous

res·o·nate \-ˌnāt\ vb **-nat·ed; -nat·ing** 1 : to produce or exhibit resonance 2 ♦ : to produce or exhibit resonance : REVERBERATE

♦ echo, reecho, resound, reverberate, sound — more at REVERBERATE

res·o·na·tor \-ˌnā-tər\ n : something that resounds or exhibits resonance

re·sorp·tion \rē-'sȯrp-shən, -'zȯrp-\ n : the action or process of breaking down and assimilating something (as a tooth or an embryo)

¹re·sort \ri-'zȯrt\ n [ME, return, source of aid, fr. AF, fr. resortir to rebound, resort, fr. sortir to go out, leave] 1 : one looked to for help : REFUGE 2 ♦ : a turning to someone or something for help or protection : RECOURSE 3 : frequent or general visiting ⟨place of ∼⟩ 4 ♦ : a frequently visited place : HAUNT 5 : a place providing recreation esp. to vacationers

♦ [2] expedient, recourse, resource — more at RESOURCE ♦ [4] hangout, haunt, rendezvous — more at HANGOUT

²resort vb 1 ♦ : to go often or habitually 2 ♦ : to have recourse ⟨∼ed to violence⟩

♦ usu **resort to** [1] frequent, hang around, hang out, haunt, visit — more at FREQUENT ♦ usu **resort to** [2] go, refer, turn; also employ, use, utilize; depend (on), rely (on)

re·sound \ri-'zaůnd\ vb 1 : to become filled with sound : REVERBERATE 2 : to sound loudly

♦ echo, reecho, resonate, reverberate, sound — more at REVERBERATE

re·sound·ing adj 1 ♦ : producing or characterized by resonant sound : RESONANT 2 ♦ : impressively sonorous ⟨∼ name⟩ 3 ♦ : uttered with or marked by emphasis : EMPHATIC ⟨a ∼ success⟩ — **re·sound·ing·ly** adv

♦ [1, 2] golden, resonant, ringing, round, sonorous, vibrant — more at RESONANT ♦ [3] aggressive, assertive, dynamic, emphatic, energetic, forceful, strenuous, vehement, vigorous — more at EMPHATIC

re·source \'rē-ˌsȯrs, ri-'sȯrs\ n [F ressource, fr. OF ressourse relief, resource, fr. resourdre to relieve, lit., to rise again, fr. L resurgere, fr. re- again + surgere to rise] 1 : a source of supply or support — usu. used in pl. 2 pl ♦ : available funds 3 : a possibility of relief or recovery 4 : a means of spending leisure time 5 : ability to meet and handle situations 6 ♦ : something to which one has recourse in difficulty — **re·source·ful** \ri-'sȯrs-fəl\ adj — **re·source·ful·ness** n

♦ **resources** [2] finances, funds, pocket, wherewithal — more at FUND ♦ [6] expedient, recourse, resort; also hope, opportunity, possibility, relief; makeshift, replacement, stopgap, substitute

¹re·spect \ri-'spekt\ n 1 : relation to something usu. specified : REGARD ⟨in ∼ to⟩ 2 ♦ : high or special regard : ESTEEM 3 pl ♦ : an expression of respect or deference 4 : DETAIL, PARTICULAR — **re·spect·ful·ly** adv — **re·spect·ful·ness** n

♦ [2] admiration, appreciation, esteem, estimation, favor (or favour), regard — more at ADMIRATION ♦ **respects** [3] compliments, greetings, regards — more at COMPLIMENT

List of self-explanatory words with the prefix re- (continued)

rereading	reroute	rescore	reseal
rerecord	reschedule	rescreen	reseed

²**respect** *vb* **1** ♦ : to consider deserving of high regard : ESTEEM **2** : to refrain from interfering with ⟨~ her privacy⟩ **3** : to have reference to : CONCERN — **re·spect·er** *n*

♦ admire, appreciate, esteem, regard — more at ADMIRE

re·spect·able \ri-'spek-tə-bəl\ *adj* **1** ♦ : worthy of respect **2** ♦ : decent or correct in conduct **3** ♦ : fair in size, quantity, or quality : TOLERABLE **4** : fit to be seen : PRESENTABLE — **re·spect·a·bil·i·ty** \-,spek-tə-'bi-lə-tē\ *n* — **re·spect·ably** \-'spek-tə-blē\ *adv*

♦ [1] name, prestigious, reputable, reputed; *also* honorable, worthy; creditable, good, praiseworthy; celebrated, distinguished, famed, famous, honored, illustrious, notable, prominent, renowned, well-known *Ant* disreputable, loose ♦ [2] correct, decent, decorous, genteel, nice, polite, proper, seemly — more at PROPER ♦ [3] acceptable, adequate, all right, decent, fine, OK, passable, satisfactory, tolerable — more at ADEQUATE

re·spect·ful \-fəl\ *adj* ♦ : marked by or showing respect or deference

♦ deferential, dutiful, regardful; *also* reverent, reverential, venerating, worshipful; fawning, groveling, obsequious, servile, subservient, sycophantic; civil, courteous, gracious, polite *Ant* disrespectful

re·spect·ing *prep* ♦ : with regard to

♦ about, apropos of, concerning, of, on, regarding, toward — more at ABOUT

re·spec·tive \-tiv\ *adj* ♦ : not shared with another : SEPARATE ⟨returned to their ~ homes⟩

♦ different, individual, separate — more at SEPARATE

re·spec·tive·ly \-lē\ *adv* **1** : as relating to each **2** : each in the order given

res·pi·ra·tion \,res-pə-'rā-shən\ *n* **1** : an act or the process of breathing **2** : the physical and chemical processes (as breathing and oxidation) by which a living thing obtains oxygen and eliminates waste gases (as carbon dioxide) — **re·spi·ra·to·ry** \'res-pə-rə-,tōr-ē, ri-'spī-rə-\ *adj* — **re·spire** \ri-'spīr\ *vb*

res·pi·ra·tor \'res-pə-,rā-tər\ *n* **1** : a device covering the mouth and nose esp. to prevent inhaling harmful vapors **2** : a device for artificial respiration

re·spite \'res-pət\ *n* [ME *respit*, fr. AF, fr. ML *respectus*, fr. L, act of looking back] **1** : a temporary delay **2** ♦ : an interval of rest or relief

♦ break, breath, breather, recess — more at BREAK

re·splen·dence \-dəns\ *n* ♦ : the quality or state of being resplendent

♦ augustness, brilliance, glory, grandeur, grandness, magnificence, majesty, nobility, nobleness, splendor, stateliness — more at MAGNIFICENCE

re·splen·dent \ri-'splen-dənt\ *adj* : SPLENDID ⟨~ uniforms⟩ — **re·splen·dent·ly** *adv*

re·spond \ri-'spänd\ *vb* **1** ♦ : to say something in return : ANSWER, REPLY **2** : REACT ⟨~ed to a call for help⟩ **3** : to show favorable reaction ⟨~ to medication⟩ — **re·spond·er** *n*

♦ answer, rejoin, reply, retort, return — more at ANSWER

re·spon·dent \ri-'spän-dənt\ *n* : one who responds; *esp* : one who answers in various legal proceedings — **respondent** *adj*

re·sponse \ri-'späns\ *n* **1** ♦ : an act of responding **2** ♦ : something constituting a reply or a reaction

♦ [1] reaction, reply, take — more at REACTION ♦ [2] answer, comeback, reply, retort, return — more at ANSWER

re·spon·si·bil·i·ty \ri-,spän-sə-'bi-lə-tē\ *n, pl* **-ties** **1** ♦ : the quality or state of being responsible **2** ♦ : something for which one is responsible

♦ [1] blame, fault, liability; *also* accountability ♦ [2] burden, charge, commitment, duty, need, obligation — more at OBLIGATION

re·spon·si·ble \ri-'spän-sə-bəl\ *adj* **1** ♦ : liable to be called upon to answer for one's acts or decisions : ANSWERABLE **2** ♦ : able to fulfill one's obligations : TRUSTWORTHY **3** : able to choose for oneself between right and wrong **4** : involving accountability or important duties ⟨~ position⟩ — **re·spon·si·ble·ness** *n* — **re·spon·si·bly** \-blē\ *adv*

♦ [1] accountable, answerable, liable; *also* beholden, indebted, obligated, obliged *Ant* irresponsible, unaccountable ♦ [2] dependable, good, reliable, safe, solid, steady, sure, tried, true, trustworthy — more at DEPENDABLE

re·spon·sive \-siv\ *adj* **1** : RESPONDING **2** : quick to respond **3** : using responses ⟨~ readings⟩ — **re·spon·sive·ly** *adv* — **re·spon·sive·ness** *n*

¹**rest** \'rest\ *n* **1** ♦ : a bodily state characterized by minimal functional and metabolic activities : SLEEP **2** ♦ : freedom from work or activity **3** : a state of motionlessness or inactivity **4** : a place of shelter or lodging **5** : a silence in music equivalent in duration to a note of the same value; *also* : a character indicating this **6** : something used as a support — **rest·ful·ly** *adv*

♦ [1] repose, sleep, slumber — more at SLEEP ♦ [2] ease, leisure, relaxation, repose; *also* dozing, napping, resting, sleep, slumber, slumbering, snoozing; quiet, silence, stillness; calm, peace, placidity, serenity, tranquility *Ant* exertion, labor, toil, work

²**rest** *vb* **1** ♦ : to get rest by lying down; *esp* : SLEEP **2** ♦ : to cease from action or motion **3** : to give rest to : set at rest **4** : to sit or lie fixed or supported **5** : to place on or against a support **6** : to remain based or founded **7** ♦ : to cause to be firmly fixed : GROUND **8** : to remain for action : DEPEND

♦ [1] catnap, doze, nap, sleep, slumber, snooze — more at SLEEP ♦ [2] bask, loll, lounge, relax, repose; *also* bum, goldbrick, idle, loaf, slack (off) ♦ [7] base, ground — more at BASE

³**rest** *n* ♦ : something left over

♦ balance, leavings, leftovers, odds and ends, remainder, remains, remnant, residue — more at REMAINDER

re·start \(')rē-'stärt\ *vb* ♦ : to begin again an activity or undertaking

♦ continue, renew, reopen, resume — more at RESUME

re·state \(')rē-'stāt\ *vb* ♦ : to express again in words

♦ paraphrase, rephrase, translate — more at PARAPHRASE

res·tau·rant \'res-trənt, -tə-,ränt\ *n* [F, fr. prp. of *restaurer* to restore, fr. L *restaurare*] ♦ : a public eating place

♦ café, diner, grill; *also* cafeteria, coffeehouse, garden, luncheonette, lunchroom, snack bar; bar, barroom, inn, tavern

res·tau·ra·teur \,res-tə-rə-'tər\ *also* **res·tau·ran·teur** \-,rän-\ *n* : the operator or proprietor of a restaurant

rest·ful \'rest-fəl\ *adj* ♦ : marked by, affording, or suggesting rest and repose

♦ calm, hushed, peaceful, quiet, serene, still, tranquil — more at QUIET

rest home *n* : an establishment that gives care for the aged or convalescent

res·ti·tu·tion \,res-tə-'tü-shən, -'tyü-\ *n* **1** : the act of restoring : the state of being restored; *esp* : restoration of something to its rightful owner **2** ♦ : a compensating, repaying, or giving an equivalent for some injury

♦ compensation, damages, indemnity, quittance, recompense, redress, remuneration, reparation, requital, satisfaction — more at COMPENSATION

List of self-explanatory words with the prefix re- (continued)

resell	resettle	resew	resocialization
reset	resettlement	reshow	resow

res·tive \'res-tiv\ *adj* [ME *restyf*, fr. AF *restif*, fr. *rester* to stop, resist, remain, fr. L *restare*, fr. *re-* back + *stare* to stand] **1** : stubbornly resisting control : BALKY **2** : marked by impatience or uneasiness : UNEASY — **res·tive·ly** *adv*
res·tive·ness *n* : the quality or state of being restive
rest·less \'rest-ləs\ *adj* **1** ♦ : lacking or denying rest ⟨a ~ night⟩ **2** : never resting or settled : always moving ⟨the ~ sea⟩ **3** ♦ : marked by or showing unrest esp. of mind ⟨~ pacing back and forth⟩ — **rest·less·ly** *adv*

  ♦ [1] uneasy; *also* agitated, distressed, disturbed, perturbed, troubled, unsettled; aflutter, anxious, edgy, fidgety, hung up, jittery, jumpy, nervous, nervy, tense, upset, uptight, worried *Ant* restful ♦ [3] anxious, distressful, nervous, tense, unsettling, upsetting, worrisome — more at NERVOUS

rest·less·ness *n* ♦ : the quality or state of being restless

  ♦ disquiet, ferment, turmoil, uneasiness, unrest — more at UNREST

re·stor·able \ri-'stōr-ə-bəl\ *adj* : fit for restoring or reclaiming
res·to·ra·tion \,res-tə-'rā-shən\ *n* **1** : an act of restoring : the state of being restored **2** : something (as a building) that has been restored
¹re·stor·ative \ri-'stōr-ə-tiv\ *n* : something that restores esp. to consciousness or health
²restorative *adj* ♦ : of or relating to restoration; *esp* : having power to restore

  ♦ healthful, healthy, salubrious, salutary, wholesome — more at HEALTHFUL ♦ bracing, invigorating, refreshing, stimulative, tonic — more at TONIC

re·store \ri-'stōr\ *vb* **re·stored; re·stor·ing** **1** : to give back : RETURN **2** : to put back into use or service **3** ♦ : to put or bring back into a former or original state **4** : to put again in possession of something — **re·stor·er** *n*

  ♦ freshen, recreate, refresh, regenerate, rejuvenate, renew, revitalize, revive — more at RENEW

re·strain \ri-'strān\ *vb* **1** : to prevent from doing something **2** ♦ : to limit, restrict, or keep under control : CURB **3** ♦ : to place under restraint or arrest — **re·strain·able** *adj* — **re·strain·er** *n*

  ♦ [2] bridle, check, constrain, contain, control, curb, govern, inhibit, regulate, rein, tame ♦ [3] apprehend, arrest, nab, pick up, seize — more at ARREST

re·strained \ri-'strānd\ *adj* ♦ : marked by restraint — **re·strain·ed·ly** \-'strā-nəd-lē\ *adv*

  ♦ conservative, muted, quiet, subdued, unpretentious — more at QUIET

restraining order *n* : a legal order directing one person to stay away from another
re·straint \ri-'strānt\ *n* **1** : an act of restraining : the state of being restrained **2** ♦ : a restraining force, agency, or device **3** : deprivation or limitation of liberty : CONFINEMENT **4** ♦ : control over the expression of one's feelings

  ♦ [2] check, condition, constraint, curb, fetter, limitation, restriction — more at RESTRICTION ♦ [4] self-control, self-discipline, self-government, self-possession, self-restraint, will, willpower — more at WILL ♦ [4] constraint, inhibition, repression, suppression

re·strict \ri-'strikt\ *vb* **1** ♦ : to confine within bounds : LIMIT **2** : to place under restriction as to use — **re·stric·tive** *adj* — **re·stric·tive·ly** *adv*

  ♦ check, circumscribe, confine, control, curb, inhibit, limit, restrain — more at LIMIT

re·strict·ed \ri-'strik-təd\ *adj* ♦ : subject or subjected to restriction

  ♦ definite, determinate, finite, limited, measured, narrow — more at LIMITED

re·stric·tion \ri-'strik-shən\ *n* **1** ♦ : something (as a law or rule) that restricts **2** : an act of restricting : the state of being restricted

  ♦ check, condition, constraint, curb, fetter, limitation, restraint; *also* exception, qualification, reservation, proviso, stipulation, strings

rest room *n* : a room or suite of rooms that includes sinks and toilets
¹re·sult \ri-'zəlt\ *vb* [ME, fr. ML *resultare*, fr. L, to rebound, fr. *re-* re- + *saltare* to leap] **1** : to come about as an effect or consequence **2** ♦ : to have an issue or result ⟨the disease ~ed in death⟩

  ♦ *usu* result in bring about, cause, create, effect, effectuate, generate, induce, make, produce, prompt, work, yield — more at EFFECT

²result *n* **1** ♦ : something that results : EFFECT **2** : beneficial or discernible effect **3** : something obtained by calculation or investigation

  ♦ aftermath, conclusion, consequence, corollary, development, effect, issue, outcome, outgrowth, product, resultant, sequence, upshot — more at EFFECT

¹re·sul·tant \-'zəlt-³nt\ *adj* ♦ : derived from or resulting from something else

  ♦ attendant, consequent, consequential, due; *also* accompanying, coincident, concomitant

²resultant *n* : something that results
re·sume \ri-'züm\ *vb* **re·sumed; re·sum·ing** **1** : to take or assume again **2** ♦ : to return to or begin again after interruption **3** : to take back to oneself — **re·sump·tion** \-'zəmp-shən\ *n*

  ♦ continue, renew, reopen, restart; *also* resuscitate, revive

ré·su·mé *or* **re·su·me** *also* **re·su·mé** \'re-zə-,mā, ,re-zə-'mā\ *n* [F *résumé*] **1** ♦ : an abstract, abridgment, or compendium : SUMMARY **2** : a short account of one's career and qualifications usu. prepared by a job applicant

  ♦ abstract, digest, encapsulation, epitome, outline, précis, recapitulation, roundup, sum, summary, synopsis, wrap-up — more at SUMMARY

re·sur·gence \ri-'sər-jəns\ *n* ♦ : a rising again into life, activity, or prominence — **re·sur·gent** \-jənt\ *adj*

  ♦ rebirth, regeneration, rejuvenation, renewal, resurrection, resuscitation, revival — more at REVIVAL

res·ur·rect \,re-zə-'rekt\ *vb* **1** : to raise from the dead **2** : to bring to attention or use again
res·ur·rec·tion \,re-zə-'rek-shən\ *n* **1** *cap* : the rising of Christ from the dead **2** *often cap* : the rising to life of all human dead before the final judgment **3** ♦ : an act or instance of reviving : REVIVAL ⟨the ~ of her career⟩

  ♦ rebirth, regeneration, rejuvenation, renewal, resurgence, resuscitation, revival — more at REVIVAL

re·sus·ci·tate \ri-'sə-sə-,tāt\ *vb* **-tat·ed; -tat·ing** ♦ : to revive from apparent death or unconsciousness; *also* : REVITALIZE — **re·sus·ci·ta·tor** \-,tā-tər\ *n*

  ♦ reanimate, regenerate, reinvigorate, rejuvenate, renew, revitalize, revive — more at REVIVE

re·sus·ci·ta·tion \ri-,sə-sə-'tā-shən, ,rē-\ *n* ♦ : an act of resuscitating or the state of being resuscitated

  ♦ rebirth, regeneration, rejuvenation, renewal, resurgence, resurrection, revival — more at REVIVAL

ret *abbr* retired
¹re·tail \'rē-,tāl, *esp for 2 also* ri-'tāl\ *vb* **1** ♦ : to sell in small quantities directly to the ultimate consumer **2** : to tell in detail or to one person after another — **re·tail·er** *n*

  ♦ deal, market, merchandise, put up, sell, vend — more at MARKET

²re·tail \'rē-,tāl\ *n* : the sale of goods in small amounts to ultimate consumers — **retail** *adj or adv*

List of self-explanatory words with the prefix re- (continued)

respell	restatement	restrengthen	restudy
restaff	restock	restructure	restuff

re·tain \ri-'tān\ *vb* **1** ♦ : to hold in possession or use **2** ♦ : to engage (as a lawyer) by paying a fee in advance **3** : to keep in a fixed place or position

♦ [1] hang on, hold, keep, reserve, withhold — more at KEEP ♦ [2] employ, engage, hire, take on — more at EMPLOY

¹**re·tain·er** \ri-'tā-nər\ *n* **1** : one that retains **2** ♦ : a servant in a wealthy household **3** : EMPLOYEE **4** : a device that holds something (as teeth) in place

♦ domestic, flunky, lackey, menial, servant, steward — more at SERVANT

²**retainer** *n* : a fee paid to secure services (as of a lawyer)

¹**re·take** \(,)rē-'tāk\ *vb* **-took** \-'tůk\; **-tak·en** \-'tā-kən\; **-tak·ing** **1** ♦ : to take or seize again **2** : to photograph again

♦ recapture, reclaim, recoup, recover, regain, repossess, retrieve — more at RECOVER

²**re·take** \'rē-,tāk\ *n* : a second photographing of a motion-picture scene

re·tal·i·ate \ri-'ta-lē-,āt\ *vb* **-at·ed; -at·ing** ♦ : to return like for like; *esp* : to get revenge — **re·tal·ia·to·ry** \-'tal-yə-,tōr-ē\ *adj*

♦ avenge, requite, revenge — more at AVENGE

re·tal·i·a·tion \-,ta-lē-'ā-shən\ *n* ♦ : an act of retaliating

♦ reprisal, requital, retribution, revenge, vengeance — more at REVENGE

re·tard \ri-'tärd\ *vb* ♦ : to hold back : delay the progress of — **re·tar·da·tion** \,rē-tär-'dā-shən, ri-\ *n* — **re·tard·er** *n*

♦ brake, decelerate, slow — more at SLOW

re·tar·dant \ri-'tär-dᵊnt\ *adj* : serving or tending to retard — **retardant** *n*

re·tard·ed *adj, dated, now usu offensive* : slow or limited in intellectual, emotional, or academic progress

retch \'rech\ *vb* **1** : to try to vomit **2** : to throw up : VOMIT

re·ten·tion \ri-'ten-chən\ *n* **1** : the act of retaining : the state of being retained **2** : the power of retaining esp. in the mind : RETENTIVENESS

re·ten·tive \-'ten-tiv\ *adj* : having the power of retaining; *esp* : retaining knowledge easily — **re·ten·tive·ness** *n*

re·think \(,)rē-'think\ *vb* **-thought** \-'thȯt\; **-think·ing** ♦ : to think about again : RECONSIDER

♦ readdress, reanalyze, reconceive, reconsider, reexamine, review — more at RECONSIDER

ret·i·cence \'re-tə-səns\ *n* ♦ : the quality or state or an instance of being reticent

♦ disinclination, hesitancy, reluctance — more at RELUCTANCE

ret·i·cent \'re-tə-sənt\ *adj* **1** ♦ : tending not to talk or give out information **2** : RELUCTANT **3** : restrained in expression, presentation, or appearance — **ret·i·cent·ly** *adv*

♦ closemouthed, laconic, reserved, silent, taciturn, uncommunicative — more at SILENT

ret·i·na \'ret-ᵊn-ə\ *n, pl* **retinas** *or* **ret·i·nae** \-,ē\ : the sensory membrane lining the eye that receives the image formed by the lens — **ret·i·nal** \'ret-ᵊn-əl\ *adj*

ret·i·nue \'ret-ᵊn-,ü, -,yü\ *n* ♦ : the body of attendants or followers of a distinguished person

♦ cortege, following, suite, train — more at CORTEGE

re·tire \ri-'tīr\ *vb* **re·tired; re·tir·ing** **1** ♦ : to withdraw from action or danger : RETREAT **2** : to withdraw esp. for privacy **3** ♦ : to withdraw from one's occupation or position : conclude one's career **4** : to go to bed **5** : to cause to be out in baseball **6** ♦ : to cause to retire **7** : to withdraw from use or service

♦ [1] back, fall back, recede, retreat, withdraw — more at RETREAT ♦ *usu* retire from [3] leave, quit, resign, step down — more at QUIT ♦ [6] cashier, dismiss, fire, remove, sack — more at DISMISS

re·tired \ri-'tīrd\ *adj* **1** : screened or hidden from view : SECLUDED, QUIET **2** : withdrawn from active duty or from one's career

re·tir·ee \ri-,tī-'rē\ *n* : a person who has retired from a career

re·tire·ment *n* : an act of retiring : the state of being retired

re·tir·ing *adj* ♦ : sensitively diffident : SHY

♦ bashful, coy, demure, diffident, introverted, modest, reserved, shy — more at SHY

re·tool \(,)rē-'tül\ *vb* **1** : to reequip with tools **2** : to modify with usu. minor improvements ⟨∼ed the team for next year⟩

¹**re·tort** \ri-'tȯrt\ *vb* [L *retortus*, pp. of *retorquēre*, lit., to twist back, hurl back, fr. *re-* back + *torquēre* to twist] **1** ♦ : to say in reply : answer back usu. sharply **2** : to answer (an argument) by a counter argument **3** : RETALIATE

♦ answer, rejoin, reply, respond, return — more at ANSWER

²**retort** *n* ♦ : a quick, witty, or cutting reply; *esp* : one that turns back or counters the first speaker's words

♦ comeback, repartee, riposte; *also* back talk; crack, quip, sally, wisecrack, witticism; cut, insult, put-down answer, comeback, reply, response, return — more at ANSWER

³**re·tort** \ri-'tȯrt, 'rē-,tȯrt\ *n* [MF *retorte*, fr. ML *retorta*, fr. L, fem. of *retortus*, pp. of *retorquēre* to twist back; fr. its shape] : a vessel in which substances are distilled or broken up by heat

re·touch \(,)rē-'təch\ *vb* : TOUCH UP; *esp* : to change (as a photographic negative) in order to produce a more desirable appearance

re·trace \(,)rē-'trās\ *vb* : to go over again or in a reverse direction ⟨*retraced* his steps⟩

re·tract \ri-'trakt\ *vb* **1** : to draw back or in **2** ♦ : to withdraw (as a charge or promise) — **re·tract·able** *adj* — **re·trac·tion** \-'trak-shən\ *n*

♦ abjure, recant, renounce, take back, unsay, withdraw — more at ABJURE

re·trac·tile \ri-'trakt-ᵊl, -'trak-,tīl\ *adj* : capable of being drawn back or in ⟨∼ claws⟩

¹**re·tread** \(,)rē-'tred\ *vb* **re·tread·ed; re·tread·ing** : to put a new tread on (a worn tire)

²**re·tread** \'rē-,tred\ *n* **1** : a retreaded tire **2** : one pressed into service again; *also* : REMAKE

¹**re·treat** \ri-'trēt\ *n* **1** ♦ : an act of withdrawing esp. from something dangerous, difficult, or disagreeable **2** : a military signal for withdrawal; *also* : a military flag-lowering ceremony **3** ♦ : a place of privacy or safety : REFUGE **4** : a period of group withdrawal for prayer, meditation, or study

♦ [1] revulsion, withdrawal; *also* flinch, recoil, shrinking **Ant** advancement ♦ [3] asylum, harbor (*or* harbour), haven, refuge, sanctuary, shelter — more at SHELTER

²**retreat** *vb* **1** ♦ : to make a retreat **2** : to slope backward

♦ back, fall back, recede, retire, withdraw; *also* flinch, recoil, shrink; chicken (out); back down, backtrack; abandon, depart, evacuate, go, leave, quit, vacate **Ant** advance

re·trench \ri-'trench\ *vb* [obs. F *retrencher* (now *retrancher*), fr. MF *retrenchier*, fr. *re-* + *trenchier* to cut] **1** : to cut down or pare away : REDUCE, CURTAIL **2** : to cut down expenses : ECONOMIZE — **re·trench·ment** *n*

ret·ri·bu·tion \,re-trə-'byü-shən\ *n* ♦ : something administered or exacted in recompense; *esp* : PUNISHMENT — **re·trib·u·tive** \ri-'tri-byə-tiv\ *adj* — **re·trib·u·to·ry** \-byə-,tōr-ē\ *adj*

♦ punishment, reprisal, requital, retaliation, revenge, vengeance — more at REVENGE

re·triev·al \-'trē-vəl\ *n* ♦ : an act or process of retrieving

---

List of self-explanatory words with the prefix re- (continued)

restyle	resummon	resurface	resynthesis
resubmit	resupply	resurvey	resynthesize

♦ reclamation, recovery, repossession — more at RE-
COVERY

re·trieve \ri-'trēv\ *vb* **re·trieved; re·triev·ing 1** : to search
about for and bring in (killed or wounded game) **2 ♦** : to
get back again : RECOVER — **re·triev·able** *adj*

♦ recapture, reclaim, recoup, recover, regain, repossess, retake — more at RECOVER

re·triev·er \ri-'trē-vər\ *n* : one that retrieves; *esp* : a dog of
any of several breeds used esp. for retrieving game
ret·ro \'re-trō\ *adj* : relating to or being the styles and fashions of the past ⟨∼ clothing⟩
ret·ro·ac·tive \ˌre-trō-'ak-tiv\ *adj* : made effective as of a date
prior to enactment ⟨a ∼ pay raise⟩ — **ret·ro·ac·tive·ly** *adv*
ret·ro·fit \'re-trō-ˌfit, ˌre-trō-'fit\ *vb* : to furnish (as an aircraft)
with newly available equipment — **ret·ro·fit** \'re-trō-ˌfit\ *n*
¹ret·ro·grade \'re-trə-ˌgrād\ *adj* **1** : moving or tending backward **2** : tending toward or resulting in a worse condition
²retrograde *vb* **1** : RETREAT **2** : DETERIORATE, DEGEN-
ERATE
ret·ro·gres·sion \ˌre-trə-'gre-shən\ *n* : return to a former
and less complex level of development or organization
— **ret·ro·gress** \ˌre-trə-'gres\ *vb* — **ret·ro·gres·sive** \ˌre-
trə-'gre-siv\ *adj*
ret·ro–rock·et \'re-trō-ˌrä-kət\ *n* : an auxiliary rocket engine (as on a spacecraft) used to slow forward motion
ret·ro·spect \'re-trə-ˌspekt\ *n* : a review of past events
ret·ro·spec·tion \ˌre-trə-'spek-shən\ *n* ♦ : the act or process
or an instance of surveying the past

♦ reappraisal, reexamination, review — more at REVIEW

ret·ro·spec·tive \ˌre-trə-'spek-tiv\ *n* **1** : a comprehensive examination of an artist's work over many years **2** : REVIEW
4 ⟨a war ∼⟩ — **retrospective** *adj* — **ret·ro·spec·tive·ly** *adv*
ret·ro·vi·rus \'re-trō-ˌvī-rəs\ *n* : any of a group of RNA-con-
taining viruses (as HIV) that make DNA using RNA instead of the reverse
¹re·turn \ri-'tərn\ *vb* **1** : to go or come back **2** : to pass,
give, or send back to an earlier possessor **3** : to put back
to or in a former place or state **4** : to respond in words
or writing : REPLY, ANSWER **5** : to report esp. officially
6 : to elect to office **7** : to bring in (as profit) : YIELD
8 : to give or perform in return — **re·turn·er** *n*
²return *n* **1** : an act of coming or going back to or from a
former place or state **2** : RECURRENCE **3** : a report of
the results of balloting **4** : a formal statement of taxable
income **5 ♦** : the profit from labor, investment, or business **6** : the act of returning something **7** : something
that returns or is returned; *also* : a means for conveying
something (as water) back to its starting point **8 a** : something given in repayment or reciprocation **b** : something
said, written, or done in answer or response : ANSWER,
RETORT **9** : an answering play — **return** *adj*

♦ earnings, gain, income, net, payoff, proceeds, profit,
revenue, yield — more at INCOME

¹re·turn·able \ri-'tər-nə-bəl\ *adj* : capable of being returned
(as for reuse or recycling); *also* : permitted to be returned
²returnable *n* : a returnable beverage container
re·turn·ee \ri-ˌtər-'nē\ *n* : one who returns
re·tweet \(ˌ)rē-'twēt\ *vb* : to repost to the Twitter online
messaging service ⟨fans ∼ed her tweet⟩
re·union \rē-'yü-nyən\ *n* **1** : an act of reuniting : the state
of being reunited **2** : a meeting of persons after separation
¹rev \'rev\ *n* : a revolution of a motor
²rev *vb* **revved; rev·ving** : to increase the revolutions per
minute of (a motor)
³rev *abbr* **1** revenue **2** reverse **3** review; reviewed **4** revised; revision **5** revolution
Rev *abbr* **1** Revelation **2** Reverend

re·vamp \(ˌ)rē-'vamp\ *vb* **1 ♦** : to make a new, amended,
improved, or up-to-date version of : REVISE **2 ♦** : to restore to a former better state (as by cleaning, repairing,
or rebuilding)

♦ [1] alter, change, make over, modify, recast, redo, refashion, remake, remodel, revise, rework, vary — more
at CHANGE ♦ [2] doctor, fix, mend, patch, recondition,
renovate, repair — more at MEND

re·vanche \rə-'vä^nsh\ *n* [F] : REVENGE; *esp* : a usu. political
policy designed to recover lost territory or status
re·veal \ri-'vēl\ *vb* **1 ♦** : to make known **2** : to show
plainly : open up to view

♦ bare, disclose, discover, divulge, expose, show, spill,
tell, unbosom, uncloak, uncover, unmask, unveil; *also*
debunk, show up; unclothe; advertise, announce, blaze,
broadcast, declare, placard, post, proclaim, promulgate, publicize, publish, sound; betray, blab, give away,
leak, let on; inform, squeal, talk; communicate, impart,
relate; acknowledge, admit, avow, concede, confess,
own; disinter, unearth **Ant** cloak, conceal, cover (up),
enshroud, hide, mask, shroud, veil

re·veil·le \'re-və-lē\ *n* [modif. of F *réveillez*, imper. pl. of
réveiller to awaken, fr. MF *eveiller* to awaken, fr. (assumed) VL *exvigilare*, fr. L *vigilare* to keep watch, stay
awake] : a military signal sounded at about sunrise
¹rev·el \'re-vəl\ *vb* **-eled** *or* **-elled; -el·ing** *or* **-el·ling 1** : to
take part in a revel **2 ♦** : to take great pleasure or satisfaction ⟨∼ed in the quiet after everyone had gone⟩

♦ *usu* **revel in** adore, delight, dig, enjoy, fancy, groove,
like, love, relish — more at ENJOY

²revel *n* ♦ : a usu. wild party or celebration

♦ binge, fling, frolic, gambol, lark, rollick, romp —
more at FLING

rev·e·la·tion \ˌre-və-'lā-shən\ *n* **1** : an act of revealing
2 : something revealed; *esp* : an enlightening or astonishing disclosure
Revelation *n* : a book of the New Testament of Christian
Scripture
re·ve·la·to·ry \'re-və-lə-ˌtór-ē, ri-'ve-lə-\ *adj* ♦ : of or relating to revelation : serving to reveal something

♦ eloquent, expressive, meaning, meaningful, pregnant,
significant, suggestive — more at EXPRESSIVE

rev·el·er *or* **rev·el·ler** \'re-vəl-ər\ *n* ♦ : one who engages in
revelry

♦ celebrant, merrymaker, roisterer — more at CELEBRANT

rev·el·ry \'re-vəl-rē\ *n* ♦ : noisy partying or merrymaking

♦ conviviality, festivity, gaiety, jollification, merriment,
merrymaking — more at MERRYMAKING

¹re·venge \ri-'venj\ *vb* **re·venged; re·veng·ing** ♦ : to inflict
harm or injury in return for (a wrong) : AVENGE —
re·veng·er *n*

♦ avenge, requite, retaliate — more at AVENGE

²revenge *n* **1** : a desire for revenge **2 ♦** : an act or instance
of retaliation to get even **3** : an opportunity for getting
satisfaction — **re·venge·ful** *adj*

♦ reprisal, requital, retaliation, retribution, vengeance;
also counter, counterattack, counteroffensive; castigation, chastisement, correction; discipline, nemesis,
penalty, punishment, wrath; amends, compensation,
indemnification, indemnity, quittance, recompense, redress, remuneration, restitution

rev·e·nue \'re-və-ˌnü, -ˌnyü\ *n* [ME, return, revenue, fr.
AF, fr. *revenir* to return, fr. L *revenire*, fr. *re-* back + *venire* to come] **1** : investment income **2** : money collected by a government (as through taxes) **3 ♦** : the total
income produced by a given source

List of self-explanatory words with the prefix *re-* (continued)

♦ earnings, income, proceeds, profit, return, yield — more at INCOME

re·verb \ri-'vərb, 'rē-ˌvərb\ *n* : an electronically produced echo effect in recorded music; *also* : a device for producing reverb

re·ver·ber·ate \ri-'vər-bə-ˌrāt\ *vb* **-at·ed; -at·ing 1** : RE-FLECT ⟨∼ light or heat⟩ **2** ♦ : to resound in or as if in a series of echoes — **re·ver·ber·a·tion** \-ˌvər-bə-bə-'rā-shən\ *n*

♦ echo, reecho, resonate, resound, sound

re·vere \ri-'vir\ *vb* **re·vered; re·ver·ing** ♦ : to show honor and devotion to : VENERATE

♦ adore, deify, glorify, venerate, worship — more at WORSHIP

¹rev·er·ence \'re-vrəns, -və-rəns\ *n* **1** : honor or respect felt or shown **2** : a gesture (as a bow or curtsy) of respect

²reverence *vb* **-enced; -enc·ing** : to regard or treat with reverence

¹rev·er·end \'re-vrənd, -və-rənd\ *adj* **1** ♦ : worthy of reverence : REVERED **2** : being a member of the clergy — used as a title

♦ hallowed, venerable — more at VENERABLE

²reverend *n* ♦ : a member of the clergy

♦ clergyman, divine, ecclesiastic, father, minister, preacher, priest — more at CLERGYMAN

rev·er·ent \'re-vrənt, -və-rənt\ *adj* : expressing reverence — **rev·er·ent·ly** *adv*

rev·er·en·tial \ˌre-və-'ren-chəl\ *adj* : REVERENT

rev·er·ie *also* **rev·ery** \'re-və-rē\ *n, pl* **-er·ies** [F *rêverie,* fr. MF, delirium, fr. *resver, rever* to wander, be delirious] **1** : DAYDREAM **2** ♦ : the condition of being lost in thought

♦ study, trance, woolgathering; *also* contemplation, meditation, musing; absentmindedness, absorption, abstraction, preoccupation; chimera, conceit, daydream, delusion, dream, fancy, fantasy, figment, hallucination, illusion, phantasm, pipe dream, unreality, vision

re·ver·sal \ri-'vər-səl\ *n* **1** : an act or process of reversing **2** ♦ : a change (as of fortune) often for the worse

♦ lapse, reverse, setback — more at REVERSE

¹re·verse \ri-'vərs\ *adj* **1** : opposite to a previous or normal condition ⟨in ∼ order⟩ **2** : acting or working in a manner opposite the usual **3** : bringing about reverse movement ⟨∼ gear⟩ — **re·verse·ly** *adv*

²reverse *vb* **re·versed; re·vers·ing 1** ♦ : to turn upside down or completely about in position or direction **2** : to set aside or change (as a legal decision) **3** : to change to the contrary ⟨∼ a policy⟩ **4** : to go or cause to go in the opposite direction **5** : to put (as a car) in reverse — **re·vers·ible** \-'vər-sə-bəl\ *adj*

♦ flip, turn; *also* transpose; exchange, interchange, shift, switch; overturn, upset

³reverse *n* **1** ♦ : something contrary to something else : OPPOSITE **2** ♦ : an act or instance of reversing; *esp* : a change for the worse **3** : the back side of something **4** : a gear that reverses something

♦ [1] antipode, antithesis, contrary, negative, opposite — more at OPPOSITE ♦ [2] lapse, reversal, setback; *also* disappointment, frustration, letdown; comedown, decline, descent, down, downfall, fall; turnabout; recession, regression, retrogression, reversion; relapse; breakdown, collapse, crash, meltdown, ruin, undoing

reverse engineer *vb* : to disassemble or analyze in detail in order to discover concepts involved in manufacture — **reverse engineering** *n*

re·ver·sion \ri-'vər-zhən\ *n* **1** : the right of succession or future possession (as to a title or property) **2** : return toward some former or ancestral condition; *also* : a product of this — **re·ver·sion·ary** \-zhə-ˌner-ē\ *adj*

re·vert \ri-'vərt\ *vb* **1** : to come or go back ⟨∼ed to savagery⟩ **2** : to return to a proprietor or his or her heirs **3** : to return to an ancestral type

¹re·view \ri-'vyü\ *n* **1** : an act of revising **2** : a formal military inspection **3** : a general survey **4** ♦ : an act or the process of reviewing : INSPECTION **5** : a critical evaluation (as of a book) **6** : a magazine devoted to reviews and essays **7** : a renewed study of previously studied material **8** : RE-VUE **9** ♦ : a retrospective view or survey (as of one's life)

♦ [4] audit, check, checkup, examination, inspection, scan, scrutiny, survey — more at INSPECTION ♦ [9] reappraisal, reexamination, retrospection; *also* recap, recapitulation, rehash

²re·view \ri-'vyü, *1 also* 'rē-\ *vb* **1 a** ♦ : to examine or study again **b** : to reexamine judicially **2** : to hold a review of ⟨∼ troops⟩ **3** : to write a critical examination of ⟨∼ a novel⟩ **4** : to look back over ⟨∼ed her accomplishments⟩

♦ audit, check, examine, inspect, scan, scrutinize, survey — more at INSPECT ♦ readdress, reanalyze, reconceive, reconsider, reexamine, rethink — more at RECONSIDER

re·view·er \ri-'vyü-ər\ *n* : one that reviews; *esp* : a writer of critical reviews

re·vile \ri-'vī(-ə)l\ *vb* **re·viled; re·vil·ing** : to abuse verbally : rail at — **re·vile·ment** *n* — **re·vil·er** *n*

¹re·vise \ri-'vīz\ *vb* **re·vised; re·vis·ing 1** ♦ : to look over something written in order to correct or improve **2** ♦ : to make a new version of — **re·vis·able** *adj* — **re·vis·er** *or* **re·vi·sor** \-'vī-zər\ *n*

♦ [1] edit, redraft, revamp, rework — more at EDIT ♦ [2] alter, change, make over, modify, recast, redo, refashion, remake, remodel, revamp, rework, vary — more at CHANGE

²revise *n* : an act of revising

re·vi·sion \-'vi-zhən\ *n* ♦ : an act of revising

♦ alteration, change, difference, modification, revise, variation — more at CHANGE

re·vi·tal·ise *chiefly Brit var of* REVITALIZE

re·vi·tal·i·za·tion \(ˌ)rē-ˌvīt-ᵊl-ə-'zā-shən\ *n* : an act or instance of revitalizing

re·vi·tal·ize \ˌrē-'vīt-ᵊl-ˌīz\ *vb* **-ized; -iz·ing** ♦ : to give new life or vigor to

♦ reanimate, regenerate, reinvigorate, rejuvenate, renew, resuscitate, revive — more at REVIVE

re·viv·al \ri-'vī-vəl\ *n* **1** ♦ : an act of reviving : the state of being revived **2** : a new publication or presentation (as of a book or play) **3** : an evangelistic meeting or series of meetings

♦ rebirth, regeneration, rejuvenation, renewal, resurgence, resurrection, resuscitation; *also* renaissance, renascence; reactivation; rally, recovery, recuperation

re·vive \ri-'vīv\ *vb* **re·vived; re·viv·ing 1** ♦ : to bring back or return to life, consciousness, or activity : make or become fresh or strong again **2** : to bring back into use ⟨*reviving* an old custom⟩ — **re·viv·er** *n*

♦ reanimate, regenerate, reinvigorate, rejuvenate, renew, resuscitate, revitalize; *also* reactivate, restart come around, come round, come to — more at COME TO

re·viv·i·fy \rē-'vi-və-ˌfī\ *vb* : REVIVE — **re·viv·i·fi·ca·tion** \-ˌvi-və-fə-'kā-shən\ *n*

re·vo·ca·ble \'re-və-kə-bəl *also* ri-'vō-kə-bəl\ *adj* : capable of being revoked

re·vo·ca·tion \ˌre-və-'kā-shən\ *n* ♦ : an act or instance of revoking

♦ abortion, calling, cancellation, recall, repeal, rescission — more at CANCELLATION

re·voke \ri-'vōk\ *vb* **re·voked; re·vok·ing 1** ♦ : to annul by

---

List of self-explanatory words with the prefix *re-* (continued)

recalling or taking back : REPEAL, RESCIND **2** : RENEGE **2** — **re·vok·er** n

♦ abort, call, call off, cancel, drop, recall, repeal, rescind — more at CANCEL

¹re·volt \ri-'vōlt\ vb [MF revolter, fr. It rivoltare to overthrow, fr. VL *revolvitare, fr. L revolvere to revolve, roll back] **1** : to throw off allegiance to a ruler or government : REBEL **2** : to experience disgust or shock **3** ♦ : to turn or cause to turn away with disgust or abhorrence

♦ disgust, nauseate, repel, repulse, sicken, turn off — more at DISGUST

²revolt n ♦ : a renouncing of allegiance (as to a government or party); esp : a determined armed uprising : REBELLION

♦ insurrection, mutiny, rebellion, revolution, uprising — more at REBELLION

re·volt·er n ♦ : one that revolts

♦ insurgent, insurrectionist, mutineer, rebel, red, revolutionary — more at REBEL

re·volt·ing adj ♦ : extremely offensive — **re·volt·ing·ly** adv

♦ abhorrent, abominable, appalling, awful, distasteful, hideous, horrible, horrid, nasty, nauseating, noisome, offensive, repellent, repugnant, repulsive

rev·o·lu·tion \ˌre-və-'lü-shən\ n **1** : the action by a celestial body of going round in an orbit **2** ♦ : motion of any figure about a center or axis; also : one complete turn : ROTATION **3 a** : a sudden, radical, or complete change **b** ♦ : the overthrow or renunciation of one ruler or government and substitution of another by the governed

♦ [2] gyration, pirouette, reel, roll, rotation, spin, twirl, wheel, whirl — more at SPIN ♦ [3b] insurrection, mutiny, rebellion, revolt, uprising — more at REBELLION

¹rev·o·lu·tion·ary \-shə-ˌner-ē\ adj **1** ♦ : of or relating to revolution **2** : tending to or promoting revolution **3** : constituting or bringing about a major change

♦ insurgent, mutinous, rebellious — more at REBELLIOUS

²revolutionary n, pl -ar·ies ♦ : one who takes part in a revolution or who advocates revolutionary doctrines

♦ insurgent, insurrectionist, mutineer, rebel, red, revolter — more at REBEL

rev·o·lu·tion·ise chiefly Brit var of REVOLUTIONIZE
¹rev·o·lu·tion·ist \ˌre-və-'lü-shə-nist\ n : REVOLUTIONARY
²revolutionist adj : of or relating to revolution or revolutionists
rev·o·lu·tion·ize \-ˌnīz\ vb -ized; -iz·ing : to change fundamentally or completely
rev·o·lu·tion·iz·er n : one that revolutionizes
re·volve \ri-'välv\ vb re·volved; re·volv·ing **1** : to turn over in the mind : reflect upon : PONDER **2** ♦ : to move in an orbit; also : ROTATE — **re·volv·able** adj

♦ pivot, roll, rotate, spin, swing, swirl, turn, twirl, twist, wheel, whirl — more at TURN

re·volv·er \ri-'väl-vər\ n : a pistol with a revolving cylinder of several chambers
re·vue \ri-'vyü\ n : a theatrical production consisting typically of brief often satirical sketches and songs
re·vul·sion \ri-'vəl-shən\ n **1** : a strong sudden reaction or change of feeling **2** : a feeling of complete distaste or repugnance **3** ♦ : a strong pulling or drawing away

♦ [2] aversion, disgust, distaste, loathing, nausea, repugnance, repulsion — more at DISGUST ♦ [3] retreat, withdrawal — more at RETREAT

revved past and past part of REV
revving pres part of REV
¹re·ward \ri-'wȯrd\ vb **1** : to give a reward to or for **2** : RECOMPENSE
²reward n **1** : something given in return for good or evil done or received or for some service or attainment **2** : a

stimulus that is administered to an organism after a response and that increases the probability of occurrence of the response

re·ward·ing adj **1** : yielding or likely to yield a reward **2** ♦ : serving as a reward : giving pleasure as if a reward

♦ comforting, encouraging, gratifying, heartening, heartwarming, satisfying — more at HEARTWARMING

re·warm \ˌrē-'wȯrm\ vb : to make warm again ⟨∼ food⟩ ⟨∼ed herself by the fire⟩
¹re·wind \ˌrē-'wīnd\ vb -wound; -wind·ing **1** : to wind again **2** : to reverse the winding of (as film)
²re·wind \'rē-ˌwīnd\ n **1** : something that rewinds **2** : an act of rewinding **3** : a function of an electronic device that reverses a recording to a previous portion
re·work \ˌrē-'wərk\ vb **1** ♦ : to work again or anew : REVISE **2** : to reprocess for further use

♦ alter, change, edit, make over, modify, recast, redo, refashion, remake, remodel, revamp, revise, vary — more at CHANGE

¹re·write \ˌrē-'rīt\ vb -wrote; -writ·ten; -writ·ing : to make a revision of : REVISE
²re·write \'rē-ˌrīt\ n : an instance or a piece of rewriting
Rf symbol rutherfordium
RF abbr radio frequency
Rg symbol roentgenium
Rh symbol rhodium
RH abbr right hand
rhap·sod·ic \rap-'sä-dik\ adj ♦ : extravagantly emotional — **rhap·sod·i·cal·ly** \-di-k(ə-)lē\ adv

♦ ecstatic, elated, euphoric, intoxicated, rapturous — more at ECSTATIC

rhap·so·dize \'rap-sə-ˌdīz\ vb ♦ : to speak or write in a rhapsodic manner

♦ enthuse, fuss, gush, rave, slobber — more at GUSH

rhap·so·dy \'rap-sə-dē\ n, pl -dies [L rhapsodia portion of an epic poem adapted for recitation, fr. Gk rhapsōidia recitation of selections from epic poetry, ultim. fr. rhaptein to sew, stitch together + aidein to sing] **1** : an expression of extravagant praise or ecstasy **2** : a musical composition of irregular form **3** ♦ : a state or experience of being carried away by overwhelming emotion

♦ ecstasy, elation, euphoria, exhilaration, heaven, intoxication, paradise, rapture, transport — more at ECSTASY

rhea \'rē-ə\ n : either of two large flightless 3-toed So. American birds that resemble but are smaller than the African ostrich
rhe·ni·um \'rē-nē-əm\ n : a rare heavy hard metallic chemical element
rheo·stat \'rē-ə-ˌstat\ n : a resistor for regulating an electric current by means of variable resistances — **rheo·stat·ic** \ˌrē-ə-'sta-tik\ adj
rhe·sus monkey \'rē-səs-\ n : a pale brown Asian monkey often used in medical research
rhet·o·ric \'re-tə-rik\ n [ME rethorik, fr. AF rethorique, fr. L rhetorica, fr. Gk rhētorikē, lit., art of oratory, fr. rhētōr public speaker, fr. eirein to speak] **1** ♦ : the art of speaking or writing effectively **2** ♦ : insincere or grandiloquent language — **rhet·o·ri·cian** \ˌre-tə-'ri-shən\ n

♦ [1] articulateness, eloquence, poetry — more at ELOQUENCE ♦ [2] bombast, gas, grandiloquence, hot air, wind; also claptrap, drivel, gibberish, hogwash, humbug, jabberwocky, jazz, moonshine, nonsense; floweriness, grandiosity, loftiness, pomposity, pretension, pretentiousness; verbosity, wordiness

rhe·tor·i·cal \ri-'tȯr-i-kəl\ adj **1** : of, relating to, or concerned with rhetoric **2** ♦ : given to rhetoric **3** : asked merely for effect with no answer expected ⟨a ∼ question⟩

List of self-explanatory words with the prefix re- (continued)

♦ bombastic, gaseous, grandiloquent, oratorical, windy; *also* elevated, florid, flowery, grandiose, highfalutin, high-flown, high-sounding, inflated, lofty, pompous, pretentious, stilted; overdone, verbose, wordy

rheum \'rüm\ *n* : a watery discharge from the mucous membranes esp. of the eyes or nose — **rheumy** *adj*

rheu·mat·ic fever \rù-'ma-tik-\ *n* : an acute disease chiefly of children and young adults that is characterized by fever, by inflammation and pain in and around the joints, and by inflammation of the membranes surrounding the heart and the heart valves

rheu·ma·tism \'rü-mə-ˌti-zəm, 'rù-\ *n* : any of various conditions marked by stiffness, pain, or swelling in muscles or joints 2 : RHEUMATOID ARTHRITIS — **rheu·mat·ic** \rù-'ma-tik\ *adj*

rheu·ma·toid arthritis \-ˌtȯid-\ *n* : a usu. chronic progressive autoimmune disease characterized by inflammation and swelling of joint structures

rheu·ma·tol·o·gy \ˌrü-mə-'tä-lə-jē, ˌrù-\ *n* : a medical science dealing with rheumatic diseases — **rheu·ma·tol·o·gist** \-jist\ *n*

Rh factor \ˌär-'āch-\ *n* [*rh*esus monkey (in which it was first detected)] : any of one or more inherited substances in red blood cells that may cause dangerous reactions in some infants or in transfusions

rhine·stone \'rīn-ˌstōn\ *n* : a colorless imitation stone of high luster made of glass, paste, or gem quartz

rhi·no \'rī-nō\ *n, pl* **rhinos** *also* **rhino** : RHINOCEROS

rhi·noc·er·os \rī-'nä-sə-rəs\ *n, pl* **-noc·er·os·es** *also* **-noc·er·os** *or* **-noc·eri** \-'nä-sə-ˌrī\ [ME *rinoceros,* fr. AF, fr. L *rhinoceros,* fr. Gk *rhinokerōs,* fr. *rhin-, rhis* nose + *keras* horn] : any of a family of large thick-skinned mammals of Africa and Asia with one or two upright horns of keratin on the snout and three toes on each foot

rhi·zome \'rī-ˌzōm\ *n* : a fleshy, rootlike, and usu. horizontal underground plant stem that forms shoots above and roots below — **rhi·zom·a·tous** \rī-'zä-mə-təs\ *adj*

Rh–neg·a·tive \ˌär-ˌāch-'ne-gə-tiv\ *adj* : lacking Rh factors in the red blood cells

rho \'rō\ *n* : the 17th letter of the Greek alphabet — P or ρ

rho·di·um \'rō-dē-əm\ *n* : a rare hard ductile metallic chemical element

rho·do·den·dron \ˌrō-də-'den-drən\ *n* : any of a genus of shrubs or trees of the heath family with clusters of large bright flowers

rhom·boid \'räm-ˌbȯid\ *n* : a parallelogram with unequal adjacent sides and angles that are not right angles — **rhomboid** *or* **rhom·boi·dal** \räm-'bȯid-ᵊl\ *adj*

rhom·bus \'räm-bəs\ *n, pl* **rhom·bus·es** *or* **rhom·bi** \-ˌbī\ : a parallelogram having all four sides equal

Rh–pos·i·tive \ˌär-ˌāch-'pä-zə-tiv\ *adj* : containing one or more Rh factors in the red blood cells

rhu·barb \'rü-ˌbärb\ *n* [ME *rubarbe,* fr. AF *reubarbe,* fr. ML *reubarbarum,* alter. of *rha barbarum,* lit., barbarian rhubarb] : a garden plant related to the buckwheat having leaves with thick juicy edible pink and red stems

¹**rhyme** \'rīm\ *n* 1 : a composition in verse that rhymes; *also* : POETRY 2 : correspondence in terminal sounds (as of two lines of verse)

²**rhyme** *vb* **rhymed; rhym·ing** 1 : to make rhymes; *also* : to write poetry 2 : to have rhymes : be in rhyme — **rhym·er** *n*

rhythm \'ri-thəm\ *n* 1 ♦ : regular rise and fall in the flow of sound in speech 2 : a movement or activity in which some action or element recurs regularly — **rhyth·mi·cal·ly** \-k(ə-)lē\ *adv*

♦ beat, cadence, measure, meter (*or* metre); *also* accent, accentuation, emphasis, stress; lilt, movement, sway

rhythm and blues *n* : popular music based on blues and African American folk music

rhyth·mic \'rith-mik\ *or* **rhyth·mi·cal** \-mi-kəl\ *adj* ♦ : marked by or moving in pronounced rhythm

♦ cadenced, measured, metrical; *also* even, regular, steady, uniform; musical, swaying *Ant* unmeasured, unrhythmic

rhythm method *n* : birth control by refraining from sexual intercourse during the time when ovulation is most likely to occur

RI *abbr* Rhode Island

¹**rib** \'rib\ *n* 1 : any of the series of curved bones of the chest of most vertebrates that are joined to the backbone in pairs and help to support the body wall and protect the organs inside 2 : something resembling a rib in shape or function 3 : an elongated ridge (as in fabric)

²**rib** *vb* **ribbed; rib·bing** 1 : to furnish or strengthen with ribs 2 : to knit so as to form ridges

³**rib** *vb* **ribbed; rib·bing** ♦ : to poke fun at : TEASE — **rib·ber** *n*

♦ chaff, jive, josh, kid, rally, razz, ride, roast, tease — more at TEASE

rib·ald \'ri-bəld\ *adj* ♦ : coarse or indecent esp. in language ⟨∼ jokes⟩

♦ bawdy, coarse, crude, indecent, lewd, obscene, smutty, vulgar ♦ racy, risqué, spicy, suggestive — more at SUGGESTIVE

rib·ald·ry \-bəl-drē\ *n* ♦ : a ribald quality or element

♦ bawdiness, coarseness, indecency, lewdness, obscenity, smut, vulgarity — more at OBSCENITY

rib·and \'ri-bənd\ *n* : RIBBON

rib·bon \'ri-bən\ *n* 1 : a narrow fabric typically of silk or velvet used for trimming and for badges 2 : a strip of inked cloth (as in a typewriter) 3 : TATTER, SHRED ⟨torn to ∼s⟩

ri·bo·fla·vin \ˌrī-bə-'flā-vən, 'rī-bə-ˌflā-vən\ *n* : a growth-promoting vitamin of the vitamin B complex occurring esp. in milk and liver

ri·bo·nu·cle·ic acid \ˌrī-bō-nù-ˌklē-ik-, -nyù-, -ˌklā-\ *n* : RNA

ri·bose \'rī-ˌbōs\ *n* : a sugar with five carbon atoms and five oxygen atoms in each molecule that is part of RNA

ri·bo·some \'rī-bə-ˌsōm\ *n* : any of the RNA-rich cytoplasmic granules in a cell that are sites of protein synthesis — **ri·bo·som·al** \ˌrī-bə-'sō-məl\ *adj*

rice \'rīs\ *n* : the starchy seeds of an annual grass that are cooked and used for food; *also* : this widely cultivated grass of warm wet areas

rich \'rich\ *adj* 1 ♦ : possessing or controlling great wealth : WEALTHY 2 : COSTLY, VALUABLE 3 : deep and pleasing in color or tone 4 ♦ : having great plenty 5 : containing much sugar, fat, or seasoning; *also* : high in combustible content 6 : highly productive or remunerative : FRUITFUL, FERTILE — **rich·ness** *n*

♦ [1] affluent, flush, loaded, moneyed, opulent, wealthy, well-fixed, well-heeled, well-off, well-to-do; *also* comfortable, propertied, prosperous, successful; prospering, thriving; blessed, privileged *Ant* destitute, impecunious, impoverished, indigent, needy, penniless, penurious, poor, poverty-stricken ♦ [4] concentrated, full, full-bodied, potent, robust, strong — more at FULL-BODIED

rich·es \'ri-chəz\ *n pl* [ME, sing. or pl., fr. *richesse* wealth, fr. AF *richesce,* fr. *riche* rich] ♦ : things that make one rich : WEALTH

♦ assets, capital, fortune, means, opulence, substance, wealth, wherewithal — more at WEALTH

rich·ly \'rich-lē\ *adv* ♦ : in a rich manner

♦ expensively, extravagantly, grandly, high, lavishly, luxuriously, opulently — more at HIGH

Rich·ter scale \'rik-tər-\ *n* : a scale for expressing the magnitude of a seismic disturbance (as an earthquake) in terms of the energy dissipated in it

rick \'rik\ *n* : a large stack (as of hay) in the open air

♦ cock, heap, hill, mound, mountain, pile, stack — more at PILE

rick·ets \'ri-kəts\ *n* : a childhood deficiency disease marked esp. by soft deformed bones and caused by lack of vitamin D

rick·ett·sia \ri-'ket-sē-ə\ *n, pl* **-si·as** *or* **-si·ae** \-sē-ˌē\ : any of a group of usu. rod-shaped bacteria that cause various diseases (as typhus)

rick·ety \'ri-kə-tē\ *adj* **1** : affected with rickets **2** : SHAKY; *also* : in unsound physical condition

rick·shaw *also* **rick·sha** \'rik-ˌshȯ\ *n* : a small covered 2-wheeled carriage pulled by one person and used orig. in Japan

¹ric·o·chet \'ri-kə-ˌshā, *Brit also* -ˌshet\ *n* [F] : a bouncing off at an angle (as of a bullet off a wall); *also* : an object that ricochets

²ricochet *vb* **-cheted** \-ˌshād\ *also* **-chet·ted** \-ˌshe-təd\; **-chet·ing** \-ˌshā-iŋ\ *also* **-chet·ting** \-ˌshe-tiŋ\ ♦ : to skip with or as if with glancing rebounds

♦ bounce, carom, glance, rebound, skim, skip — more at GLANCE

ri·cot·ta \ri-'kä-tə, -'kȯ-\ *n* : a white unripened whey cheese of Italy that resembles cottage cheese

rid \'rid\ *vb* **rid** *also* **rid·ded; rid·ding** ♦ : to make free of something burdensome : CLEAR ⟨~ the house of mice⟩

♦ clear, disburden, disencumber, free, relieve, unburden; *also* discharge, emancipate, enfranchise, liberate, loose, loosen, manumit, release, spring, unbind, unchain, unfetter; bail (out), deliver, redeem, rescue; disengage, disentangle, extricate *Ant* burden, encumber, saddle

rid·dance \'rid-ᵊns\ *n* ♦ : an act of ridding

♦ disposal, disposition, dumping, jettison, removal — more at DISPOSAL

rid·den \'rid-ᵊn\ *adj* **1** : harassed, oppressed, or obsessed by ⟨debt-*ridden*⟩ **2** : excessively full of or supplied with ⟨slum-*ridden*⟩

¹rid·dle \'rid-ᵊl\ *n* **1** : a puzzling question to be solved or answered by guessing **2** ♦ : something or someone difficult to understand

♦ conundrum, enigma, mystery, mystification, puzzle, puzzlement, secret — more at MYSTERY

²riddle *vb* **rid·dled; rid·dling** **1** ♦ : to find the solution of : SOLVE **2** : to speak in riddles

♦ answer, break, crack, dope, figure out, puzzle, resolve, solve, unravel, work, work out — more at SOLVE

³riddle *n* : a coarse sieve

⁴riddle *vb* **rid·dled; rid·dling** **1** : to sift with a riddle **2** : to pierce with many holes **3** : PERMEATE

¹ride \'rīd\ *vb* **rode** \'rōd\; **rid·den** \'rid-ᵊn\; **rid·ing** **1** : to go on an animal's back or in a conveyance (as a boat, car, or airplane); *also* : to sit on and control so as to be carried along ⟨~ a bicycle⟩ **2** ♦ : to float or move on water ⟨~ at anchor⟩; *also* : to move like a floating object **3** : to bear along : CARRY ⟨*rode* her on their shoulders⟩ **4** : to travel over a surface ⟨the car ~s well⟩ **5** : to proceed over on horseback **6** ♦ : to torment by nagging or teasing; *also* : to poke fun at **7** : to last longer than — usu. used with *out*

♦ [2] drift, float, glide, hang, hover, poise, sail, waft — more at FLOAT ♦ [6] bait, bug, hassle, heckle, needle, taunt, tease — more at TEASE ♦ [6] chaff, jive, josh, kid, rally, razz, rib, roast, tease — more at TEASE

²ride *n* **1** : an act of riding; *esp* : a trip on horseback or by vehicle **2** : a way (as a road or path) suitable for riding **3** : a mechanical device (as a merry-go-round) for riding on **4** : a means of transportation

rid·er \'rī-dər\ *n* **1** : one that rides **2** : an addition to a document often attached on a separate piece of paper **3** : a clause dealing with an unrelated matter attached to a legislative bill during passage — **rid·er·less** *adj*

¹ridge \'rij\ *n* [ME *rigge*, fr. OE *hrycg*] **1** : a range of hills **2** : a raised line or strip **3** : the line made where two sloping surfaces (as of a roof) meet — **ridgy** *adj*

²ridge *vb* **ridged; ridg·ing** **1** : to form into a ridge **2** : to extend in ridges

¹rid·i·cule \'ri-də-ˌkyül\ *n* : the act of ridiculing : DERISION, MOCKERY

²ridicule *vb* **-culed; -cul·ing** ♦ : to laugh at or make fun of mockingly or contemptuously

♦ deride, gibe, jeer, laugh, mock, scout; *also* scoff (at), scorn, sneer (at); bad-mouth, belittle, decry, disparage,

pooh-pooh, put down; chaff, jive, josh, kid, quiz, rally, razz, rib, ride, tease; bait, bug, harass, harry, hassle, heckle, needle, pester, target, taunt, torment; ape, burlesque, caricature, imitate, lampoon, mimic, parody, parrot, satirize, take off (on), travesty

ri·dic·u·lous \rə-'di-kyə-ləs\ *adj* ♦ : arousing or deserving ridicule : ABSURD; *also* : provoking laughter — **ri·dic·u·lous·ly** *adv* — **ri·dic·u·lous·ness** *n*

♦ absurd, comical, derisive, farcical, laughable, ludicrous, preposterous, risible, silly; *also* asinine, brainless, dumb, fatuous, foolish, half-witted, harebrained, idiotic, imbecilic, inane, jerky, moronic, nonsensical, stupid, unwise, witless; balmy, cockeyed, crazy, cuckoo, daffy, daft, insane, kooky, lunatic, mad, nutty, screwball, senseless, wacky; fantastic, inconceivable, incredible, unbelievable, unreal, unreasonable antic, comic, comical, droll, farcical, funny, hilarious, humorous, hysterical, laughable, ludicrous, riotous, risible, screaming, uproarious — more at FUNNY

rid·ley \'rid-lē\ *n* : either of two relatively small sea turtles

Ries·ling \'rēz-liŋ, 'rēs-\ *n* : a sweet to very dry white wine made from a single variety of grape orig. grown in Germany

RIF *abbr* reduction in force

rife \'rīf\ *adj* ♦ : occurring in abundance — **rife** *adv* — **rife·ly** *adv*

♦ flush, fraught, replete, thick; *also* bulging, bursting, chock-full, crammed, crowded, fat, filled, full, jammed, jam-packed, loaded, packed, saturated, stuffed; clogged, congested, overflowing, surfeited; alive, animated, astir, bustling, busy, buzzing, humming, lively

riff \'rif\ *n* : a repeated phrase in jazz typically supporting a solo improvisation; *also* : a piece based on such a phrase — **riff** *vb*

riff·raff \'rif-ˌraf\ *n* [ME *riffe raffe*, fr. *rif and raf* every single one, fr. AF *rif et raf* altogether] **1** ♦ : disreputable persons : RABBLE **2** : something worth little or nothing : REFUSE

♦ rabble, scum, trash — more at RABBLE

¹ri·fle \'rī-fəl\ *vb* **ri·fled; ri·fling** ♦ : to ransack esp. with the intent to steal — **ri·fler** *n*

♦ dig, dredge, hunt, rake, ransack, rummage, scour, search — more at SEARCH

²rifle *vb* **ri·fled; ri·fling** : to cut spiral grooves into the bore of ⟨*rifled* pipe⟩ — **rifling** *n*

³rifle *n* **1** : a shoulder weapon with a rifled bore **2** *pl* : soldiers armed with rifles — **ri·fle·man** \-fəl-mən\ *n*

rift \'rift\ *n* **1** ♦ : a narrow opening or crack of considerable length and depth usu. from some breaking or parting **2** : FAULT 6 **3** : ESTRANGEMENT, SEPARATION **4** ♦ : a clear space or interval — **rift** *vb*

♦ [1] chink, cleft, crack, cranny, crevice, fissure, split — more at CRACK ♦ [4] breach, break, discontinuity, gap, gulf, hole, interval, opening, rent, separation — more at GAP

¹rig \'rig\ *vb* **rigged; rig·ging** **1** : to fit out (as a ship) with rigging **2** ♦ : to provide with clothes : CLOTHE, DRESS — usu. used with *out* **3** ♦ : to furnish with special gear : EQUIP **4** ♦ : to set up esp. as a makeshift ⟨~ up a shelter⟩

♦ *usu* rig out [2] apparel, array, attire, caparison, clothe, deck, dress, garb, invest, suit — more at CLOTHE ♦ [3] accoutre, equip, fit, furnish, outfit, supply — more at FURNISH

²rig *n* **1** : the distinctive shape, number, and arrangement of sails and masts of a ship **2** : a carriage with its horse **3** : CLOTHING, DRESS **4** : EQUIPMENT

³rig *vb* **rigged; rig·ging** **1** : to manipulate or control esp. by deceptive or dishonest means **2** : to fix in advance for a desired result — **rig·ger** *n*

rig·ging \'ri-giŋ, -gən\ *n* **1** : the ropes and chains that hold and move masts, sails, and spars of a ship **2** : a network (as in theater scenery) used for support and manipulation

¹right \\'rīt\\ *adj* **1 ♦** : morally right or justifiable : RIGHTEOUS **2 ♦** : being in accordance with what is just, good, or proper : JUST **3 ♦** : conforming to truth or fact : CORRECT **4 ♦** : adapted to a use or purpose : APPROPRIATE **5** : free from curves, bends, angles, or irregularities : STRAIGHT ⟨a ∼ line⟩ **6** : not artificial, fraudulent, or illusory : GENUINE **7** : of, relating to, or being the side of the body which is away from the side on which the heart is mostly located **8** : located nearer to the right hand; *esp* : being on the right when facing in the same direction as the observer **9** : made to be placed or worn outward ⟨∼ side of a rug⟩ **10 ♦** : being in good physical or mental health or order : NORMAL ⟨not in her ∼ mind⟩

♦ [1] decent, ethical, good, honest, honorable (*or* honourable), just, moral, straight, upright, virtuous — more at GOOD ♦ [2] due, just — more at JUST ♦ [3] accurate, correct, exact, precise, proper, so, true — more at CORRECT ♦ [4] applicable, appropriate, apt, felicitous, fit, fitting, good, happy, meet, proper, suitable — more at FIT ♦ [10] balanced, clearheaded, lucid, normal, sane, stable — more at SANE

²right *n* **1** : qualities that constitute what is correct, just, proper, or honorable **2 ♦** : something (as a power or privilege) to which one has a just or lawful claim **3** : just action or decision : the cause of justice **4** : the side or part that is on or toward the right side **5** *cap* : political conservatives **6** *often cap* : a conservative position — **right·most** \\-,mōst\\ *adj* — **right·ward** \\-wərd\\ *adj or adv*

♦ birthright, due, perquisite, prerogative, privilege

³right *adv* **1** : according to what is right ⟨live ∼⟩ **2 ♦** : in an exact manner : EXACTLY, PRECISELY ⟨∼ here and now⟩ **3 ♦** : in a direct line, course, or manner : DIRECTLY ⟨went ∼ home⟩ **4** : according to fact or truth ⟨guess ∼⟩ **5** : all the way : COMPLETELY ⟨∼ to the end⟩ **6** : IMMEDIATELY ⟨∼ after lunch⟩ **7** : to a great degree : VERY ⟨∼ nice weather⟩ **8** : on or to the right ⟨looked ∼ and left⟩

♦ [2] accurately, exactly, just, precisely, sharp, squarely — more at EXACTLY ♦ [3] dead, direct, directly, due, plump, straight — more at DIRECTLY

⁴right *vb* **1** : to relieve from wrong **2** : to adjust or restore to a proper state or position **3** : to bring or restore to an upright position **4** : to become upright — **right·er** *n*

right angle *n* : an angle whose measure is 90° : an angle whose sides are perpendicular to each other — **right–angled** \\'rīt-'aŋ-gəld\\ *or* **right–an·gle** \\-gəl\\ *adj*

right away *adv* ♦ : without delay or hesitation

♦ directly, forthwith, immediately, instantly, now, promptly, pronto, right now — more at IMMEDIATELY

right circular cone *n* : CONE 2

right–click \\'rīt-'klik\\ *vb* : to press the rightmost button on a computer mouse or a similar input device

righ·teous \\'rī-chəs\\ *adj* ♦ : acting or being in accordance with what is just, honorable, and free from guilt or wrong : UPRIGHT

♦ decent, ethical, good, honest, honorable (*or* honourable), just, moral, right, straight, upright, virtuous — more at GOOD

righ·teous·ly *adv* ♦ : in a righteous manner

♦ chastely, modestly, purely, virtuously — more at PURELY

righ·teous·ness *n* ♦ : the quality or state of being righteous

♦ character, decency, goodness, honesty, integrity, morality, probity, rectitude, uprightness, virtue — more at MORALITY

right·ful \\'rīt-fəl\\ *adj* **1 a** : acting or being in conformity with what is morally upright or good : JUST **b** : FITTING **2** : having or held by a legally just claim — **right·ful·ly** *adv* — **right·ful·ness** *n*

right–hand \\'rīt-,hand\\ *adj* **1** : situated on the right **2** : RIGHT-HANDED **3** : chiefly relied on ⟨his ∼ man⟩

right–hand·ed \\-'han-dəd\\ *adj* **1** : using the right hand habitually or better than the left **2** : designed for or done with

the right hand **3** : CLOCKWISE ⟨a ∼ twist⟩ — **right–handed** *adv* — **right–hand·ed·ly** *adv* — **right–hand·ed·ness** *n*

right·ist \\'rī-tist\\ *n, often cap* ♦ : an advocate of or adherent of the doctrines of the Right

♦ conservative, reactionary, Tory — more at CONSERVATIVE

right·ly \\'rīt-lē\\ *adv* **1** : FAIRLY, JUSTLY **2 ♦** : in the right or proper manner : PROPERLY **3** : CORRECTLY, EXACTLY

♦ appropriately, correctly, fittingly, happily, properly, suitably — more at PROPERLY

right·ness *n* ♦ : the quality or state of being right

♦ appropriateness, aptness, fitness, suitability — more at APPROPRIATENESS

right now *adv* **1 ♦** : without delay or hesitation **2 ♦** : at present

♦ [1] directly, forthwith, immediately, instantly, now, promptly, pronto, right away — more at IMMEDIATELY ♦ [2] anymore, now, nowadays, presently, today — more at NOW

right–of–way *n, pl* **rights–of–way** **1** : a legal right of passage over another person's ground **2** : the area over which a right-of-way exists **3** : the land on which a public road is built **4** : the land occupied by a railroad **5** : the land used by a public utility **6** : the right of traffic to take precedence over other traffic

right on *interj* — used to express agreement or give encouragement

right–to–life *adj* : ANTIABORTION — **right–to–lifer** *n*

right triangle *n* : a triangle having one right angle

right whale *n* : any of a family of large baleen whales having a very large head on a stocky body

rig·id \\'ri-jəd\\ *adj* **1 a ♦** : lacking flexibility **b ♦** : inflexibly exact with respect to opinions or observances **2 ♦** : strictly observed

♦ [1a] inflexible, stiff, unyielding — more at STIFF ♦ [1b] adamant, hard, immovable, implacable, pat, unbending, uncompromising, unrelenting, unyielding ♦ [2] exacting, inflexible, rigorous, strict, stringent, uncompromising; *also* close, conscientious, scrupulous, undeviating; adamant, adamantine, determined, dogged, firm, relentless, resolved, steadfast, stubborn, tenacious, unbending, unflinching; immovable, implacable, unrelenting, unyielding; austere, demanding, flinty, grim, hard, hardened, harsh, severe, stern, tough *Ant* flexible, lax, loose, relaxed

rig·id·i·ty \\rə-'ji-də-tē\\ *n* ♦ : the quality or state of being rigid

♦ hardness, harshness, inflexibility, severity, sternness, strictness — more at SEVERITY

rig·id·ly *adv* ♦ : in a rigid manner

♦ exactly, precisely, rigorously, strictly — more at STRICTLY

rig·ma·role \\'ri-gə-mə-,rōl\\ *n* [alter. of obs. *ragman roll* long list, catalog] **1** : confused or senseless talk **2** : a complex and ritualistic procedure

rig·or *or Can and Brit* **rig·our** \\'ri-gər\\ *n* **1** : the quality of being inflexible or unyielding esp. in opinion or behavior **2 ♦** : a condition that makes life difficult, challenging, or uncomfortable **3** *Can usu* **rigor** : a tremor caused by a chill **4** : strict precision : EXACTNESS ⟨scientific ∼⟩ **5** *Can usu* **rigor** : unnatural rigidity of a body part

♦ adversity, asperity, difficulty, hardness, hardship — more at DIFFICULTY

rig·or mor·tis \\,ri-gər-'mòr-təs\\ *n* [NL, stiffness of death] : temporary rigidity of muscles occurring after death

rig·or·ous *adj* ♦ : manifesting, exercising, or favoring rigor

♦ accurate, close, delicate, exact, fine, mathematical, pinpoint, precise — more at PRECISE ♦ exacting, inflexible, rigid, strict, stringent, uncompromising — more at RIGID

rig·or·ous·ly *adv* ♦ : in a rigorous manner

♦ exactly, precisely, rigidly, strictly — more at STRICT-LY

rig·our *Can and Brit var of* RIGOR

rile \'rī(-ə)l\ *vb* **riled; ril·ing** **1** ♦ : to make angry **2** : to stir or move from a state of calm or order

♦ aggravate, anger, annoy, bother, bug, chafe, exasperate, gall, get, grate, irk, irritate, nettle, peeve, persecute, pique, put out, rasp, vex — more at IRRITATE

rill \'ril\ *n* ♦ : a very small brook

♦ brook, creek, rivulet, streamlet — more at CREEK

¹rim \'rim\ *n* **1** : the outer part of a wheel **2** ♦ : an outer edge esp. of something curved : MARGIN

♦ border, bound, boundary, circumference, compass, confines, edge, end, fringe, margin, perimeter, periphery, skirt, verge — more at BORDER

²rim *vb* **rimmed; rim·ming** **1** : to serve as a rim for : BORDER **2** : to run around the rim of

¹rime \'rīm\ *n* : FROST **2** — **rimy** \'rī-mē\ *adj*

²rime *var of* RHYME

rind \'rīnd\ *n* : a usu. hard or tough outer layer ⟨lemon ~⟩

¹ring \'riŋ\ *n* **1** : a circular band worn as an ornament or token or used for holding or fastening ⟨wedding ~⟩ ⟨key ~⟩ **2** ♦ : something circular in shape ⟨smoke ~⟩ **3** : a place for contest or display ⟨boxing ~⟩; *also* : PRIZE-FIGHTING **4** : ANNUAL RING **5** ♦ : a group of people who work together for selfish or dishonest purposes ⟨a ~ of smugglers⟩ **6** ♦ : a temporary group of persons working cooperatively — **ringed** *adj* — **ring·like** \'riŋ-ˌlīk\ *adj*

♦ [2] band, circle, eye, hoop, loop, round; *also* belt, cincture, collar, girdle; wreath; coil, spiral ♦ [5] cabal, conspiracy, gang, mob, syndicate; *also* circle, clan, clique, coterie, crowd; junta, oligarchy ♦ [6] body, bunch, circle, clan, clique, community, coterie, crowd, fold, gang, lot, set — more at GANG

²ring *vb* **ringed; ring·ing** \'riŋ-iŋ\ **1** ♦ : to place or form a ring around : ENCIRCLE **2** : to throw a ring over (a mark) in a game (as quoits) **3** : to move in a ring or spirally

♦ circle, encircle, enclose, encompass, surround — more at SURROUND

³ring *vb* **rang** \'raŋ\; **rung** \'rəŋ\; **ring·ing** \'riŋ-iŋ\ **1** : to sound resonantly when struck; *also* : to feel as if filled with such sound **2** ♦ : to cause to make a clear metallic sound by striking **3** : to announce or call by or as if by striking a bell ⟨~ an alarm⟩ **4** : to repeat loudly and persistently **5** : to summon esp. by a bell ⟨~ for the butler⟩

♦ chime, knell, peal, toll; *also* clang, clank, jangle, jingle, ping, tinkle; resound, reverberate

⁴ring *n* **1** : a set of bells **2** : the clear resonant sound of vibrating metal **3** : resonant tone : SONORITY **4** : a sound or character expressive of a particular quality **5** : an act or instance of ringing; *esp* : a telephone call

¹ring·er \'riŋ-ər\ *n* **1** : one that sounds by ringing **2** : one that enters a competition under false representations **3** ♦ : one that closely resembles another

♦ carbon copy, counterpart, double, duplicate, duplication, facsimile, image, likeness, match, picture, replica, spit — more at IMAGE

²ringer *n* : one that encircles or puts a ring around

ring finger *n* : the third finger of the hand counting the index finger as the first

ring·ing *adj* ♦ : clear and full in tone

♦ golden, resonant, resounding, round, sonorous, vibrant — more at RESONANT

ring·lead·er \'riŋ-ˌlē-dər\ *n* : a leader esp. of a group of troublemakers

ring·let \-lət\ *n* : a long curl

ring·mas·ter \-ˌmas-tər\ *n* : one in charge of performances in a circus ring

ring·tone \-ˌtōn\ *n* : the sound made by a cell phone to signal an incoming call

ring up *vb* **1** : to total and record esp. by means of a cash register **2** : ACHIEVE ⟨*rang up* many triumphs⟩

ring·worm \'riŋ-ˌwərm\ *n* : any of several contagious skin diseases caused by fungi and marked by ring-shaped discolored patches

rink \'riŋk\ *n* : a level extent of ice marked off for skating or various games; *also* : a similar surface (as of wood) marked off or enclosed for a sport or game ⟨roller-skating ~⟩

¹rinse \'rins\ *vb* **rinsed; rins·ing** [ME *rincen*, AF *rincer*, alter. of OF *recincier*, fr. VL *recentiare*, fr. L *recent-, recens* fresh, recent] **1** : to wash lightly or in water only **2** ♦ : to cleanse (as of soap) with clear water **3** : to treat (hair) with a rinse — **rins·er** *n*

♦ flush, irrigate, sluice, wash — more at FLUSH

²rinse *n* **1** : an act of rinsing **2** : a liquid used for rinsing **3** : a solution that temporarily tints hair

ri·ot \'rī-ət\ *n* **1** *archaic* : disorderly behavior **2** : disturbance of the public peace; *esp* : a violent public disorder **3** : random or disorderly profusion ⟨a ~ of color⟩ **4** : one that is wildly amusing ⟨the comedy is a ~⟩ — **riot** *vb* — **ri·ot·er** *n*

ri·ot·ous *adj* ♦ : practicing or marked by license or excess; *also* : existing in abundance

♦ copious, lavish, profuse — more at PROFUSE

¹rip \'rip\ *vb* **ripped; rip·ping** **1** ♦ : to cut or tear open **2** : to saw or split (wood) with the grain **3** ♦ : to slash or slit with or as if with a sharp blade **4** ♦ : to rush headlong **5** : CRITICIZE, DISPARAGE ⟨*ripped* into the team⟩ — **rip·per** *n*

♦ [1] rend, rive, shred, tatter, tear — more at TEAR ♦ [3] cut, gash, slash, slice, slit — more at CUT ♦ [4] barrel, dash, fly, hurry, hurtle, hustle, pelt, race, rocket, run, shoot, speed, tear, zip, zoom — more at HURRY

²rip *n* ♦ : an opening made by ripping

♦ gash, laceration, rent, slash, slit, tear — more at GASH

RIP *abbr* [L *requiescat in pace*] may he rest in peace, may she rest in peace [L *requiescant in pace*] may they rest in peace

ri·par·i·an \rə-'per-ē-ən\ *adj* : of or relating to the bank of a stream, river, or lake

rip cord *n* : a cord that is pulled to release a parachute out of its container

ripe \'rīp\ *adj* **rip·er; rip·est** **1** ♦ : fully grown and developed : MATURE ⟨~ fruit⟩ **2** : fully prepared : READY — **ripe·ly** *adv* — **ripe·ness** *n*

♦ adult, full-blown, full-fledged, mature — more at MATURE

rip·en \'rī-pən\ *vb* **rip·ened; rip·en·ing** **1** ♦ : to make ripe : become ripe **2** : to bring to completeness or perfection; *also* : to age or cure (cheese) to develop characteristic flavor, odor, body, texture, and color

♦ age, develop, grow, grow up, mature, progress — more at MATURE

rip–off \'rip-ˌóf\ *n* **1** ♦ : an act of stealing : THEFT **2** : a cheap imitation

♦ grab, theft — more at THEFT

rip off *vb* ♦ : to take something away from by force : steal from

♦ burglarize, rob, steal — more at ROB

ri·poste \ri-'pōst\ *n* [F, modif. of It *risposta*, lit., answer] **1** : a fencer's return thrust after a parry **2** ♦ : a retaliatory maneuver or response; *esp* : a quick retort — **riposte** *vb*

♦ comeback, repartee, retort — more at RETORT

ripped \'ript\ *adj* : having high muscle definition

rip·ple \'ri-pəl\ *vb* **rip·pled; rip·pling** **1** : to become lightly ruffled on the surface **2** : to make a sound like that of rippling water **3** ♦ : to flow in small waves — **ripple** *n*

♦ dribble, gurgle, lap, plash, slosh, splash, trickle, wash — more at GURGLE

rip·saw \'rip-ˌsó\ *n* : a coarse-toothed saw used to cut wood in the direction of the grain

rip·stop \-ˌstäp\ *adj* : being a fabric woven in such a way that small tears do not spread ⟨∼ nylon⟩ — **ripstop** *n*

¹**rise** \ˈrīz\ *vb* **rose** \ˈrōz\; **ris·en** \ˈriz-ᵊn\; **ris·ing** **1** : to get up from sitting, kneeling, or lying **2** : to get up from sleep or from one's bed **3** : to return from death **4** : to take up arms **5** : to end a session : ADJOURN **6** : to appear above the horizon **7** ♦ : to move upward : ASCEND **8** : to extend above other objects **9** : to attain a higher level or rank **10** ♦ : to increase in quantity, intensity, or pitch **11** : to come into being : HAPPEN, BEGIN, ORIGINATE

♦ [7] arise, ascend, climb, lift, mount, soar, up — more at ASCEND ♦ [10] accumulate, appreciate, balloon, build, burgeon, enlarge, escalate, expand, increase, mount, multiply, mushroom, proliferate, snowball, swell, wax — more at INCREASE

²**rise** *n* **1** ♦ : a spot higher than surrounding ground **2** : an upward slope **3** ♦ : an act of rising : a state of being risen **4** : BEGINNING, ORIGIN **5** : the elevation of one point above another **6** ♦ : an increase in amount, number, or volume **7** : an angry reaction

♦ [1] elevation, eminence, height, highland, hill, mound, prominence — more at HEIGHT ♦ [3] advancement, ascent, elevation, promotion, upgrade — more at ADVANCEMENT ♦ [6] accretion, addition, augmentation, boost, expansion, gain, increase, increment, plus, proliferation, raise, supplement — more at INCREASE

ris·er \ˈrī-zər\ *n* **1** : one that rises **2** : the upright part between stair treads

ris·i·bil·i·ty \ˌri-zə-ˈbi-lə-tē\ *n, pl* **-ties** : the ability or inclination to laugh — often used in pl.

ris·i·ble \ˈri-zə-bəl\ *adj* **1** : able or inclined to laugh **2** ♦ : arousing laughter; *esp* : amusingly ridiculous

♦ antic, comic, comical, droll, farcical, funny, hilarious, humorous, hysterical, laughable, ludicrous, ridiculous, riotous, screaming, uproarious — more at FUNNY

¹**risk** \ˈrisk\ *n* **1** ♦ : exposure to possible loss or injury : DANGER ⟨health ∼s⟩ **2** ♦ : someone or something that creates or suggests a hazard — **risk·i·ness** \ˈris-kē-nəs\ *n*

♦ [1, 2] danger, hazard, menace, peril, pitfall, threat, trouble — more at DANGER

²**risk** *vb* **1** ♦ : to expose to danger ⟨∼ed his life⟩ **2** ♦ : to incur the danger of

♦ [1] adventure, compromise, gamble with, hazard, imperil, jeopardize, menace, venture ♦ [2] chance, gamble, hazard, venture; *also* brave, challenge, dare, defy, face; compromise, endanger, imperil, jeopardize, menace; expose, subject; bet (on), wager

risky *adj* ♦ : attended with risk or danger

♦ dangerous, grave, grievous, hazardous, menacing, parlous, perilous, serious, unhealthy, unsafe, venturesome — more at DANGEROUS

ri·sot·to \ri-ˈsȯ-tō, -ˈzȯ-\ *n, pl* **-tos** : rice cooked usu. in meat or seafood stock and seasoned

ris·qué \ris-ˈkā\ *adj* [F] : verging on impropriety or indecency

♦ bawdy, lewd, ribald, spicy, suggestive — more at SUGGESTIVE

ri·tard \ri-ˈtärd\ *adv or adj* : with a gradual slackening in tempo — used as a direction in music

rite \ˈrīt\ *n* **1** : a set form for conducting a ceremony **2** : the liturgy of a church **3** ♦ : a ceremonial act or action

♦ ceremonial, ceremony, form, formality, observance, ritual, solemnity; *also* amenities, civility, decorum, etiquette, graces, proprieties; convention, custom, habit, manners, mores, practice, standard, tradition, way; celebration, service

¹**rit·u·al** \ˈri-chə-wəl\ *n* **1** : the established form esp. for a religious ceremony **2** : a system of rites **3** : a ceremonial act or action **4** : an act or series of acts regularly repeated in a precise manner — **rit·u·al·ism** \-wə-ˌli-zəm\ *n* — **rit·u·al·is·tic** \ˌri-chə-wə-ˈlis-tik\ *adj* — **rit·u·al·is·ti·cal·ly** \-ti-k(ə-)lē\ *adv* — **rit·u·al·ly** *adv*

²**ritual** *adj* ♦ : of, relating to, or employed in rites or a ritual

♦ ceremonial, ceremonious, formal

ritzy \ˈrit-sē\ *adj* **ritz·i·er; -est** : showily elegant : POSH

riv *abbr* river

¹**ri·val** \ˈrī-vəl\ *n* [MF or L; MF, fr. L *rivalis* one using the same stream as another, rival in love, fr. *rivalis* of a stream, fr. *rivus* stream] **1** ♦ : one of two or more trying to get what only one can have **2** ♦ : one striving for competitive advantage **3** ♦ : one that equals another esp. in desired qualities : MATCH, PEER

♦ [1] challenger, competition, competitor, contender, contestant — more at COMPETITOR ♦ [2] adversary, antagonist, opponent — more at OPPONENT ♦ [3] coordinate, counterpart, equal, equivalent, fellow, like, match, parallel, peer — more at EQUAL

²**rival** *adj* : COMPETING

³**rival** *vb* **-valed** *or* **-valled; -val·ing** *or* **-val·ling** **1** : to be in competition with **2** : to try to equal or excel **3** : to have qualities that approach or equal another's

ri·val·ry \ˈrī-vəl-rē\ *n, pl* **-ries** ♦ : the act of competing : the state of being a rival

♦ battle, combat, conflict, confrontation, contest, duel, face-off, struggle, tug-of-war, warfare — more at CONTEST

rive \ˈrīv\ *vb* **rived** \ˈrīvd\; **riv·en** \ˈri-vən\ *also* **rived; riv·ing** **1** ♦ : to wrench open or tear apart or to pieces : REND **2** : SHATTER

♦ rend, rip, shred, tatter, tear — more at TEAR

riv·er \ˈri-vər\ *n* **1** : a natural stream larger than a brook **2** : a large stream or flow

riv·er·bank \-ˌbaŋk\ *n* : the bank of a river

riv·er·bed \-ˌbed\ *n* : the channel occupied by a river

riv·er·boat \-ˌbōt\ *n* : a boat for use on a river

riv·er·front \-ˌfrənt\ *n* : the land or area along a river

riv·er·side \-ˌsīd\ *n* : the side or bank of a river

¹**riv·et** \ˈri-vət\ *n* : a metal bolt with a head at one end used to join parts by being put through holes in them and then being flattened on the plain end to make another head

²**rivet** *vb* **1** : to fasten with or as if with a rivet **2** ♦ : to fix and hold (as the attention) — **riv·et·er** *n*

♦ concentrate, fasten, focus, train — more at CONCENTRATE

riv·u·let \ˈri-vyə-lət, -və-\ *n* ♦ : a small stream

♦ brook, creek, rill, streamlet — more at CREEK

rm *abbr* room

Rn *symbol* radon

¹**RN** \ˌär-ˈen\ *n* : REGISTERED NURSE

²**RN** *abbr* Royal Navy

RNA \ˌär-(ˌ)en-ˈā\ *n* : any of various nucleic acids (as messenger RNA) that are found esp. in the cytoplasm of cells, have ribose as the 5-carbon sugar, and are associated with the control of cellular chemical activities

rnd *abbr* round

¹**roach** \ˈrōch\ *n, pl* **roach** *also* **roach·es** : any of various bony fishes related to the carp; *also* : any of several sunfishes

²**roach** *n* **1** : COCKROACH **2** : the butt of a marijuana cigarette

road \ˈrōd\ *n* [ME *rode*, fr. OE *rād* ride, journey] **1** : ROADSTEAD — often used in pl. **2** ♦ : an open way for vehicles, persons, and animals : HIGHWAY **3** : a way to a conclusion or end ⟨the ∼ to success⟩ **4** : a series of scheduled visits (as games or performances) in several locations or the travel necessary to make these visits ⟨the team is on the ∼⟩ **5** : RAILROAD

♦ artery, highway, pike, route, thoroughfare, trace, turnpike, way — more at WAY

road·bed \ˈrōd-ˌbed\ *n* **1** : the foundation of a road or railroad **2** : the part of the surface of a road on which vehicles travel

road·block \-ˌbläk\ *n* **1** : a barricade on the road ⟨a police ∼⟩ **2** : an obstruction to progress

road·ie \ˈrō-dē\ *n* : a person who works for traveling entertainers

road·kill \\'rōd-ˌkil\\ *n* : the remains of an animal that has been killed on a road by a motor vehicle

road·run·ner \\-ˌrə-nər\\ *n* : a largely terrestrial bird of the southwestern U.S. and Mexico that is a speedy runner

road·side \\'rōd-ˌsīd\\ *n* : the strip of land along a road — **roadside** *adj*

road·stead \\-ˌsted\\ *n* : an anchorage for ships usu. less sheltered than a harbor

road·ster \\'rōd-stər\\ *n* **1** : a driving horse **2** : an open automobile that seats two

road·way \\-ˌwā\\ *n* **1** : an open way for vehicles, persons, and animals : ROAD **2** : ROADBED

road·work \\-ˌwərk\\ *n* **1** : work done in constructing or repairing roads **2** : conditioning for an athletic contest (as a boxing match) consisting mainly of long runs

roam \\'rōm\\ *vb* **1** ♦ : to go from place to place without purpose or direction : WANDER **2** : to range or wander over or about **3** : to use a cell phone outside one's local calling area

  ♦ gad, gallivant, knock, maunder, meander, mope, ramble, range, rove, traipse, wander — more at WANDER

roaming *adj* ♦ : being one that roams; *also* : involving cell phone use beyond one's local calling area

  ♦ errant, itinerant, nomad, peripatetic, vagabond, vagrant — more at ITINERANT

¹roan \\'rōn\\ *adj* : of dark color (as black, red, or brown) sprinkled with white ⟨a ∼ horse⟩

²roan *n* : an animal (as a horse) with a roan coat; *also* : its color

¹roar \\'rōr\\ *vb* **1** ♦ : to utter a full loud prolonged sound **2** : to make a loud confused sound (as of wind or waves) — **roar·er** *n*

  ♦ bellow, boom, growl, thunder; *also* grumble, roll, rumble; blare, blast, peal, scream, screech, shriek, squall; cry, holler, hoot, shout, whoop, yell; caterwaul, howl, wail, yowl

²roar *n* ♦ : a sound of roaring

  ♦ clamor (*or* clamour), howl, hubbub, hue and cry, hullabaloo, noise, outcry, tumult, uproar — more at CLAMOR ♦ bluster, cacophony, clamor, din, noise, racket — more at NOISE

roar·ing \\'rō-riŋ\\ *adj* **1** ♦ : making or characterized by a noise like a roar **2** ♦ : marked by prosperity or bustle esp. of a temporary nature

  ♦ [1] booming, clamorous (*or* clamourous), deafening, earsplitting, loud, piercing, resounding, ringing, sonorous, stentorian, thunderous — more at LOUD ♦ [2] booming, golden, palmy, prosperous, successful — more at PROSPEROUS

¹roast \\'rōst\\ *vb* **1** : to cook by exposure to dry heat or an open flame **2** ♦ : to criticize severely or kiddingly

  ♦ chaff, jive, josh, kid, rally, razz, rib, ride, tease — more at TEASE

²roast *n* **1** : a piece of meat suitable for roasting **2** : an outing at which food is roasted ⟨corn ∼⟩ **3** : severe criticism or kidding

³roast *adj* : ROASTED

roast·er \\'rō-stər\\ *n* **1** : one that roasts **2** : a device for roasting **3** : something suitable for roasting

rob \\'räb\\ *vb* **robbed**; **rob·bing** **1** ♦ : to steal from **2** : to deprive of something due or expected **3** : to commit robbery — **rob·ber** *n*

  ♦ burglarize, rip off, steal; *also* despoil, loot, pillage, plunder, sack, spoil, strip; bleed, break in, cheat, chisel, cozen, defraud, exploit, fleece, mulct, rook, squeeze, stick, swindle; hold up, mug, stick up

robber fly *n* : any of a family of predaceous flies resembling bumblebees

rob·bery \\'rä-bə-rē\\ *n, pl* **-ber·ies** ♦ : the act or practice of robbing; *esp* : theft of something from a person by use of violence or threat

  ♦ larceny, theft, thievery — more at THEFT

¹robe \\'rōb\\ *n* **1** : a long flowing outer garment; *esp* : one used for ceremonial occasions **2** : a wrap or covering for the lower body (as for sitting outdoors)

²robe *vb* **robed**; **rob·ing** **1** : to clothe with or as if with a robe **2** : to dress or cover with clothing : DRESS

rob·in \\'rä-bən\\ *n* **1** : a small chiefly European thrush with a somewhat orange face and breast **2** : a large No. American thrush with a grayish back, a streaked throat, and a chiefly dull reddish breast

ro·bo·call \\'rō-bō-ˌkȯl\\ *n* : a telephone call from an automated source that delivers a message to a large number of people

ro·bot \\'rō-ˌbät, -bət\\ *n* [Czech, fr. *robota* compulsory labor] **1** : a machine that looks and acts like a human being **2** : an efficient but insensitive person **3** : a device that automatically performs esp. repetitive tasks **4** : something guided by automatic controls

ro·bot·ic \\rō-'bä-tik\\ *adj* ♦ : of or relating to mechanical robots

  ♦ automatic, laborsaving (*or* laboursaving), self-acting — more at LABORSAVING

ro·bot·ics \\rō-'bä-tiks\\ *n* : technology dealing with the design, construction, and operation of robots

ro·bust \\rō-'bəst, 'rō-(ˌ)bəst\\ *adj* [L *robustus* oaken, strong, fr. *robur* oak, strength] **1** ♦ : strong and vigorously healthy; *also* : having or showing vigor, strength, or firmness **2** : capable of performing without failure under a wide range of conditions **3** ♦ : imparting to the palate the general impression of substantial weight and rich texture — **ro·bust·ly** *adv*

  ♦ [1] able-bodied, chipper, fit, hale, healthy, hearty, sound, well, whole, wholesome — more at HEALTHY ♦ [1] firm, forceful, hearty, lusty, solid, stout, strong, sturdy, vigorous ♦ [3] concentrated, full, full-bodied, potent, rich, strong — more at FULL-BODIED

ro·bust·ness *n* ♦ : the quality or state of being robust

  ♦ fitness, health, heartiness, soundness, wellness, wholeness, wholesomeness — more at HEALTH

ROC *abbr* Republic of China (Taiwan)

¹rock \\'räk\\ *vb* **1** ♦ : to move back and forth in or as if in a cradle **2** ♦ : to sway or cause to sway back and forth **3** : to arouse to excitement (as with rock music) ⟨∼ed the crowd⟩ **4** *slang* : to be extremely enjoyable or effective ⟨this car ∼s⟩

  ♦ [1, 2] careen, lurch, pitch, roll, seesaw, sway, toss, wobble; *also* blunder, dodder, falter, flounder, halt, hitch, hobble, jerk, reel, stagger, stumble, teeter, toddle, totter, tumble, waddle, weave; oscillate, undulate, wag, waggle

²rock *n* **1** : a rocking movement **2** : popular music usu. played on electric instruments and characterized by a strong beat and much repetition

³rock *n* **1** : a mass of stony material; *also* : broken pieces of stone **2** : solid mineral deposits **3** : something like a rock in firmness **4** : GEM; *esp* : DIAMOND — **rock** *adj* — **rock·like** *adj* — **rocky** *adj*

rock and roll *n* : ²ROCK 2

rock·bound \\'räk-ˌbaund\\ *adj* : fringed or covered with rocks

rock·er \\'rä-kər\\ *n* **1** : one of the curved pieces on which something (as a chair or cradle) rocks **2** : a chair that rocks on rockers **3** : a device that works with a rocking motion **4** : a rock performer, song, or enthusiast

¹rock·et \\'rä-kət\\ *n* [It *rocchetta*, lit., small distaff] **1** : a firework that is propelled through the air by the discharge of gases produced by a burning substance **2** : a jet engine that operates on the same principle as a firework rocket but carries the oxygen needed for burning its fuel **3** : a rocket-propelled bomb or missile

²rocket *vb* **1** : to convey by means of a rocket **2** ♦ : to rise up rapidly, spectacularly, and with force **3** : to travel rapidly in or as if in a rocket

  ♦ shoot, skyrocket, soar, zoom — more at SKYROCKET

rock·et·ry \'rä-kə-trē\ *n* : the study or use of rockets

rocket ship *n* : a rocket-propelled spacecraft

rock·fall \'räk-ˌfȯl\ *n* : a mass of falling or fallen rocks

rock·fish \-ˌfish\ *n* : any of various bony fishes that live among rocks or on rocky bottoms

rock salt *n* : common salt in rocklike masses or large crystals

Rocky Mountain sheep *n* : BIGHORN

ro·co·co \rə-'kō-kō\ *adj* [F, irreg. fr. *rocaille* style of ornament, lit., stone debris] : of or relating to an artistic style esp. of the 18th century marked by fanciful curved forms and elaborate ornamentation — **rococo** *n*

rod \'räd\ *n* **1** : a straight slender stick **2 a** : a stick or bundle of twigs used in punishing a person **b** : PUNISHMENT **3** : a staff borne to show rank **4** : a unit of length equal to 5½ yards **5** : any of the rod-shaped receptor cells of the retina that are sensitive to faint light **6** *slang* : HANDGUN

rode *past of* RIDE

ro·dent \'rōd-ᵊnt\ *n* [ultim. fr. L *rodent-, rodens*, prp. of *rodere* to gnaw] : any of an order of relatively small mammals (as mice, squirrels, and beavers) with sharp front teeth used for gnawing

ro·deo \'rō-dē-ˌō, rə-'dā-ō\ *n, pl* **ro·de·os** [Sp, fr. *rodear* to surround, fr. *rueda* wheel, fr. L *rota*] **1** : ROUNDUP 1 **2** : a public performance featuring cowboy skills (as riding and roping)

¹roe \'rō\ *n, pl* **roe** *or* **roes** : DOE

²roe *n* : the eggs of a fish esp. while bound together in a mass

roe·buck \'rō-ˌbək\ *n, pl* **roebuck** *or* **roebucks** : a male roe deer

roe deer *n* : either of two small nimble European or Asian deers

roent·gen \'rent-gən, 'rənt-, -jən\ *n* : the international unit of measurement for X-rays and gamma rays

roent·gen·i·um \rent-'ge-nē-əm, rənt-, -'je-\ *n* : a short-lived radioactive chemical element

rog·er \'rä-jər\ *interj* — used esp. in radio and signaling to indicate that a message has been received and understood

rogue \'rōg\ *n* **1** : a dishonest person : SCOUNDREL **2** ♦ : a mischievous person : SCAMP — **rogu·ery** \'rō-gə-rē\ *n*

♦ devil, hellion, imp, mischief, monkey, rapscallion, rascal, scamp, urchin — more at SCAMP

rogu·ish *adj* ♦ : of, relating to, or having the characteristics of a rogue — **rogu·ish·ly** *adv* — **rogu·ish·ness** *n*

♦ devilish, impish, knavish, mischievous, rascally, sly, waggish, wicked — more at MISCHIEVOUS

roil \'rȯil, *for 2 also* 'rīl\ *vb* **1** : to make cloudy or muddy by stirring up **2** ♦ : to provoke to anger **3** ♦ : to move turbulently : be in a state of turbulence or agitation — **roily** \'rȯi-lē\ *adj*

♦ [2] anger, antagonize, enrage, incense, inflame, infuriate, madden, outrage, rankle, rile — more at ANGER
♦ [3] boil, churn, seethe — more at SEETHE

rois·ter \'rȯi-stər\ *vb* **rois·tered; rois·ter·ing** : to engage in noisy revelry : CAROUSE — **rois·ter·ous** \-stə-rəs\ *adj*

rois·ter·er *n* ♦ : one that roisters

♦ celebrant, merrymaker, reveler — more at CELEBRANT

ROK *abbr* Republic of Korea (South Korea)

role *also* **rôle** \'rōl\ *n* **1** : an assigned or assumed character; *also* : a part played (as by an actor) **2** ♦ : a function or part performed esp. in a particular operation or process : FUNCTION

♦ capacity, function, job, part, place, position, purpose, task, work; *also* affair, business, concern, involvement, participation; niche, office, post, situation; calling, occupation, pursuit, vocation; activity, assignment, charge, commission, duty, mission, responsibility, service, use

role model *n* : a person whose behavior in a particular role is imitated by others

¹roll \'rōl\ *n* [ME *rolle* scroll, fr. AF, fr. ML *rolla*, alter. of

rotula, fr. L, dim. of *rota* wheel] **1** : a document containing an official record **2** ♦ : an official list of names **3** : bread baked in a small rounded mass **4** : something that rolls : ROLLER

♦ catalog, checklist, list, listing, menu, register, registry, roster, schedule, table — more at LIST

²roll *vb* **1** ♦ : to move by causing to tumble or swivel **2** : to press with a roller **3** : to move on wheels **4** ♦ : to sound with a full reverberating tone **5** : to make a continuous beating sound (as on a drum) **6** : to utter with a trill **7** : to move onward as if by completing a revolution ⟨years ∼ed by⟩ **8** ♦ : to flow or seem to flow in a continuous stream or with a rising and falling motion ⟨the river ∼ed on⟩ **9** ♦ : to swing or sway from side to side **10** ♦ : to shape or become shaped in rounded form **11** : to move by or as if by turning a crank ⟨∼ down the window⟩

♦ [1] pivot, revolve, rotate, spin, swing, swirl, turn, twirl, twist, wheel, whirl — more at TURN ♦ [4] growl, grumble, lumber, rumble — more at RUMBLE ♦ [8] bowl, breeze, coast, drift, flow, glide, run, sail, skim, slide, slip, stream, sweep, whisk — more at FLOW ♦ [9] careen, lurch, pitch, rock, seesaw, sway, toss, wobble — more at ROCK ♦ [10] agglomerate, ball, conglomerate, round, wad — more at WAD

³roll *n* **1** : a sound produced by rapid strokes on a drum **2** : a heavy reverberating sound **3** : a rolling movement or action **4** : a swaying movement (as of a ship) **5** : a somersault made in contact with the ground

roll·back \'rōl-ˌbak\ *n* : the act or an instance of rolling back

roll back *vb* **1** : to reduce (as a commodity price) on a national scale **2** : to cause to withdraw : push back

roll bar *n* : an overhead metal bar on an automobile designed to protect riders in case the automobile overturns

roll call *n* : the act or an instance of calling off a list of names (as of soldiers); *also* : a time for a roll call

roll·er \'rō-lər\ *n* **1** : a revolving cylinder used for moving, pressing, shaping, applying, or smoothing something **2** : a rod on which something is rolled up **3** : a long heavy ocean wave

roll·er coast·er \'rō-lər-ˌkō-stər\ *n* : an amusement ride consisting of an elevated railway having sharp curves and steep slopes

roller skate *n* : a skate with wheels instead of a runner — **roller–skate** *vb* — **roller skater** *n*

rol·lick \'rä-lik\ *vb* ♦ : to move or behave in a carefree joyous manner : FROLIC

♦ caper, cavort, disport, frisk, frolic, gambol, lark, romp, sport — more at FROLIC

rol·lick·ing *adj* : full of fun and good spirits

roly–poly \ˌrō-lē-'pō-lē\ *adj* : being short and pudgy : ROTUND

Rom *abbr* **1** Roman **2** Romance **3** Romania; Romanian **4** Romans

ROM \'räm\ *n* [read-only *memory*] : a computer memory that contains special-purpose information (as a program) which cannot be altered

ro·maine \rō-'mān\ *n* [F, lit., Roman] : a garden lettuce with a tall loose head of long crisp leaves

¹Ro·man \'rō-mən\ *n* **1** : a native or resident of Rome **2** *not cap* : roman letters or type

²Roman *adj* **1** : of or relating to Rome or the Romans and esp. the ancient Romans **2** *not cap* : relating to type in which the letters are upright (as in this definition) **3** : of or relating to the Roman Catholic Church

Roman candle *n* : a cylindrical firework that discharges balls of fire

Roman Catholic *adj* : of, relating to, or being a Christian church led by the pope and having a liturgy centered in the Mass — **Roman Catholicism** *n*

¹ro·mance \rō-'mans, 'rō-ˌmans\ *n* [ME *romauns*, fr. AF *romanz* French, something written in French, tale in verse, fr. ML *Romanice* in a vernacular language, ultim. fr. L *Romanus* Roman] **1** : a medieval tale of knightly adventure **2** : a prose narrative dealing with heroic or mysterious events set in a remote time or place **3** : a love story **4** ♦ : a romantic attachment or episode between lovers — **ro·manc·er** *n*

♦ affair, amour, love affair — more at AFFAIR

²romance *vb* **ro·manced; ro·manc·ing** **1** : to exaggerate or invent detail or incident **2** : to have romantic fancies **3** : to carry on a romantic episode with

Ro·mance \rō-ˈmans, ˈrō-ˌmans\ *adj* : of or relating to any of several languages developed from Latin

Ro·ma·nian \rù-ˈmä-nē-ən, rō-, -nyən\ *also* **Ru·ma·nian** \rù-\ *n* **1** : a native or inhabitant of Romania **2** : the language of the Romanians

Roman numeral *n* : a numeral in a system of notation that is based on the ancient Roman system

Ro·ma·no \rō-ˈmä-nō\ *n* : a hard Italian cheese that is sharper than Parmesan

Ro·mans \ˈrō-mənz\ *n* : a book of the New Testament of Christian Scripture

¹ro·man·tic \rō-ˈman-tik\ *n* ♦ : a romantic person; *esp* : a romantic writer, composer, or artist

♦ dreamer, idealist, utopian, visionary — more at IDEALIST

²romantic *adj* **1** : IMAGINARY **2** : VISIONARY **3** : having an imaginative or emotional appeal **4** : of, relating to, or having the characteristics of romanticism — **ro·man·ti·cal·ly** \-ti-k(ə-)lē\ *adv*

ro·man·ti·cism \rō-ˈman-tə-ˌsi-zəm\ *n, often cap* : a literary movement (as in early 19th-century England) marked esp. by emphasis on the imagination and the emotions and by the use of autobiographical material

ro·man·ti·cist \-sist\ *n* : a romantic person, trait, or component

ro·man·ti·cize \-ˈman-tə-ˌsīz\ *vb* **-cized; -ciz·ing** **1** : to make romantic **2** : to have romantic ideas

¹romp \ˈrämp\ *vb* **1** ♦ : to play actively and noisily **2** : to win a contest easily

♦ caper, cavort, disport, frisk, frolic, gambol, lark, rollick, sport — more at FROLIC

²romp *n* ♦ : high-spirited, carefree, and boisterous play

♦ binge, fling, frolic, gambol, lark, revel, rollick — more at FLING

romp·er \ˈräm-pər\ *n* **1** : one that romps **2** : a jumpsuit usu. for infants — usu. used in pl.

rood \ˈrüd\ *n* : CROSS, CRUCIFIX

¹roof \ˈrüf, ˈrùf\ *n, pl* **roofs** \ˈrüfs, ˈrùfs; ˈrüvz, ˈrùvz\ **1** : the upper covering part of a building **2** ♦ : something suggesting a roof of a building **3** ♦ : the roof of a dwelling conventionally designating the home itself — **roofed** \ˈrüft, ˈrùft\ *adj* — **roof·ing** *n* — **roof·less** *adj*

♦ [2] canopy, ceiling, tent — more at CANOPY
♦ [3] abode, domicile, dwelling, home, house, lodging, quarters, residence — more at HOME

²roof *vb* **1** : to cover with a roof **2** : to provide with shelter or a home

roof·top \-ˌtäp\ *n* : a roof esp. of a house

¹rook \ˈrùk\ *n* : a crow that nests in usu. treetop colonies

²rook *vb* ♦ : to defraud by cheating or swindling

♦ bleed, cheat, chisel, cozen, defraud, fleece, hustle, mulct, shortchange, skin, squeeze, stick, sting, swindle, victimize — more at FLEECE

³rook *n* : a chess piece that can move parallel to the sides of the board across any number of unoccupied squares

rook·ery \ˈrù-kə-rē\ *n, pl* **-er·ies** : a breeding ground or haunt of gregarious birds or mammals; *also* : a colony of such birds or mammals

rook·ie \ˈrù-kē\ *n* **1** ♦ : one that begins something : BEGINNER **2** : a first-year player in a professional sport

♦ beginner, fledgling, freshman, greenhorn, neophyte, newcomer, novice, recruit, tenderfoot, tyro — more at BEGINNER

¹room \ˈrüm, ˈrùm\ *n* **1** ♦ : an extent of space occupied by or sufficient or available for something **2 a** ♦ : a partitioned part of a building : CHAMBER **b** : the people in a room **3** ♦ : a suitable or fit occasion or opportunity : OPPORTUNITY ⟨~ to develop his talents⟩ — **room·ful** *n*

♦ [1] place, space, way; *also* capacity, range, scope; clearance, freedom, latitude, leeway, play ♦ [2a] cell, chamber, closet; *also* accommodation, berth, booth, cabin, compartment, cubicle ♦ [3] chance, occasion, opening, opportunity — more at OPPORTUNITY

²room *vb* : to occupy lodgings : LODGE

room·er *n* ♦ : one who occupies a rented room in another's house

♦ boarder, lodger, renter, tenant — more at TENANT

room·ette \rü-ˈmet, rù-\ *n* : a small private room on a railroad sleeping car

room·ie \ˈrü-mē, ˈrù-\ *n* : ROOMMATE

room·mate \ˈrüm-ˌmāt, ˈrùm-\ *n* : one of two or more persons sharing the same room or dwelling

roomy *adj* ♦ : having ample room

♦ ample, capacious, commodious, spacious — more at SPACIOUS

¹roost \ˈrüst\ *n* : a support on which or a place where birds perch

²roost *vb* ♦ : to settle on or as if on a roost

♦ alight, land, light, perch, settle — more at ALIGHT
♦ ensconce, install, lodge, perch, settle — more at ENSCONCE

roost·er \ˈrüs-tər, ˈrùs-\ *n* : an adult male domestic chicken : COCK

¹root \ˈrüt, ˈrùt\ *n* **1** : the leafless usu. underground part of a seed plant that functions in absorption, aeration, and storage or as a means of anchorage; *also* : an underground plant part esp. when fleshy and edible **2** : something (as the basal part of a tooth or hair) resembling a root **3** : SOURCE, ORIGIN **4** : the essential core : HEART ⟨get to the ~ of the matter⟩ **5** : a number that when taken as a factor an indicated number of times gives a specified number **6** : the lower part — **root·less** *adj* — **root·like** *adj*

²root *vb* **1** : to form roots **2** ♦ : to fix or become fixed by or as if by roots : ESTABLISH **3** ♦ : to remove altogether by or as if by pulling out by the roots — usu. used with *out*

♦ [2] embed, entrench, establish, fix, implant, ingrain, lodge — more at ENTRENCH ♦ *usu* **root out** [3] extract, prize, pry, pull, tear, uproot, wrest — more at EXTRACT

³root *vb* **1** : to turn up or dig with the snout ⟨pigs ~*ing*⟩ **2** : to poke or dig around (as in search of something)

⁴root \ˈrüt\ *vb* **1** : to applaud or encourage noisily : CHEER **2** : to wish success or lend support to — **root·er** *n*

root beer *n* : a sweetened carbonated beverage flavored with extracts of roots and herbs

root canal *n* : a dental operation to save a tooth by removing the pulp in the root of the tooth and filling the cavity with a protective substance

root·let \ˈrüt-lət, ˈrùt-\ *n* : a small root

root·stock \-ˌstäk\ *n* : an underground part of a plant that resembles a rhizome

¹rope \ˈrōp\ *n* **1** ♦ : a large strong cord made of strands of fiber **2** : a hangman's noose **3** : a thick string (as of pearls) made by twisting or braiding

♦ cable, cord, lace, line, string, wire — more at CORD

²rope *vb* **roped; rop·ing** **1** : to bind, tie, or fasten together with a rope **2** : to separate or divide by means of a rope **3** : LASSO

Ror·schach test \ˈrȯr-ˌshäk-\ *n* : a psychological test in which a subject interprets ink-blot designs in terms that reveal intellectual and emotional factors

ro·sa·ry \ˈrō-zə-rē\ *n, pl* **-ries** **1** *often cap* : a Roman Catholic devotion consisting of meditation on sacred mysteries during recitation of Hail Marys **2** : a string of beads used in praying

¹rose *past of* RISE

²rose \ˈrōz\ *n* **1** : any of a genus of usu. prickly often climbing shrubs with divided leaves and bright often fragrant flowers; *also* : one of these flowers **2** : something resembling a rose in form **3** : a moderate purplish red color — **rose** *adj*

ro·sé \rō-ˈzā\ *n* [F] : a light pink wine

ro·se·ate \ˈrō-zē-ət, -zē-ˌāt\ *adj* **1** : resembling a rose esp. in color **2** : overly optimistic ⟨a ∼ view of the future⟩

rose·bud \ˈrōz-ˌbəd\ *n* : the flower of a rose when it is at most partly open

rose·bush \-ˌbùsh\ *n* : a shrubby rose

rose·mary \ˈrōz-ˌmer-ē\ *n, pl* **-mar·ies** [ME *rosmarine*, fr. AF *rosmarin*, fr. L *rosmarinus*, fr. *ros* dew + *marinus* of the sea, fr. *mare* sea] : a fragrant shrubby Mediterranean mint; *also* : its leaves used as a seasoning

ro·sette \rō-ˈzet\ *n* [F] **1** : a usu. small badge or ornament of ribbon gathered in the shape of a rose **2** : a circular ornament filled with representations of leaves

rose·wa·ter \ˈrōz-ˌwò-tər, -ˌwä-\ *n* : a watery solution of the fragrant constituents of the rose used as a perfume

rose·wood \-ˌwùd\ *n* : any of various tropical trees with dark red wood streaked with black; *also* : this wood

Rosh Ha·sha·nah \ˌräsh-hə-ˈshä-nə, ˌrōsh-, -ˈshò-\ *n* [Heb *rōsh hashshānāh*, lit., beginning of the year] : the Jewish New Year observed as a religious holiday in September or October

ros·in \ˈräz-ᵊn\ *n* : a brittle resin obtained esp. from pine trees and used esp. in varnishes and on violin bows

ros·ter \ˈräs-tər\ *n* **1** : a list of personnel; *also* : the persons listed on a roster **2** ♦ : an itemized list

  ♦ catalog, checklist, list, listing, menu, register, registry, roll, schedule, table — more at LIST

ros·trum \ˈräs-trəm\ *n, pl* **rostrums** *or* **ros·tra** \-trə\ [L *Rostra*, pl., a platform for speakers in the Roman Forum decorated with the beaks of captured ships, fr. pl. of *rostrum* beak, ship's beak, fr. *rodere* to gnaw] ♦ : a stage or platform for public speaking

  ♦ dais, platform, podium, stage, stand — more at PLATFORM

rosy \ˈrō-zē\ *adj* **ros·i·er; -est** **1** ♦ : of the color rose **2** ♦ : having or promoting optimism : HOPEFUL — **ros·i·ly** \ˈrō-zə-lē\ *adv* — **ros·i·ness** \-zē-nəs\ *n*

  ♦ [1] florid, flush, glowing, ruddy, sanguine — more at RUDDY ♦ [2] auspicious, bright, encouraging, fair, golden, heartening, hopeful, likely, promising, propitious, upbeat — more at HOPEFUL

¹rot \ˈrät\ *vb* **rot·ted; rot·ting** **1** ♦ : to undergo decomposition : DECAY **2** ♦ : to go to ruin

  ♦ [1] break down, corrupt, decay, decompose, disintegrate, molder, putrefy, spoil — more at DECAY ♦ [2] decay, decline, degenerate, descend, deteriorate, ebb, sink, worsen — more at DETERIORATE

²rot *n* **1** ♦ : the process of rotting : DECAY **2** : any of various diseases of plants or animals in which tissue breaks down **3** ♦ : language, conduct, or an idea that is absurd or contrary to good sense : NONSENSE; *also* : words or language having no meaning or conveying no intelligible ideas

  ♦ [1] breakdown, corruption, decay, decomposition, putrefaction, spoilage — more at CORRUPTION ♦ [3] bunk, claptrap, drivel, fiddlesticks, folly, foolishness, fudge, hogwash, humbug, nonsense, piffle, silliness, slush, stupidity, trash — more at NONSENSE

¹ro·ta·ry \ˈrō-tə-rē\ *adj* **1** : turning on an axis like a wheel **2** : having a rotating part

²rotary *n, pl* **-ries** **1** : a rotary machine **2** : a one-way circular road junction

ro·tate \ˈrō-ˌtāt\ *vb* **ro·tat·ed; ro·tat·ing** **1** ♦ : to turn or cause to turn about an axis or a center : REVOLVE **2** : to alternate in a series — **ro·ta·tor** \ˈrō-ˌtā-tər\ *n* — **ro·ta·to·ry** \ˈrō-tə-ˌtōr-ē\ *adj*

  ♦ pivot, revolve, roll, spin, swing, swirl, turn, twirl, twist, wheel, whirl — more at TURN

ro·ta·tion \rō-ˈtā-shən\ *n* ♦ : the action or process of rotating on or as if on an axis or center

  ♦ gyration, pirouette, reel, revolution, roll, spin, twirl, wheel, whirl — more at SPIN

ROTC *abbr* Reserve Officers' Training Corps

rote \ˈrōt\ *n* **1** : repetition from memory often without attention to meaning **2** ♦ : fixed routine or repetition — **rote** *adj*

  ♦ groove, pattern, routine, rut, treadmill — more at ROUTINE

ro·tis·ser·ie \rō-ˈti-sə-rē\ *n* [F] **1** : a restaurant specializing in broiled and barbecued meats **2** : an appliance fitted with a spit on which food is rotated before or over a source of heat

ro·tor \ˈrō-tər\ *n* **1** : a part that rotates; *esp* : the rotating part of an electrical machine **2** : a system of rotating horizontal blades for supporting a helicopter

ro·to·till·er \ˈrō-tō-ˌti-lər\ *n* : an engine-powered machine with rotating blades used to lift and turn over soil

rot·ten \ˈrät-ᵊn\ *adj* **1** ♦ : having rotted **2** ♦ : morally corrupt **3** ♦ : extremely unpleasant or inferior **4** ♦ : of very poor quality — **rot·ten·ness** *n*

  ♦ [1] bad, putrid; *also* curdled, fermented, rancid, sour, soured, turned; contaminated, defiled, fouled, polluted, tainted; corroded, crumbled, degenerated; decaying, moldering, moldy, putrefying, rotting ♦ [2] bad, black, evil, immoral, iniquitous, nefarious, sinful, unethical, unsavory, vicious, vile, villainous, wicked, wrong — more at BAD ♦ [3] bad, disagreeable, distasteful, nasty, sour, uncongenial, unlovely, unpleasant, unwelcome — more at UNPLEASANT ♦ [3, 4] bad, deficient, inferior, lousy, off, poor, punk, substandard, unacceptable, unsatisfactory, wanting, wretched, wrong — more at BAD ♦ [4] cheap, junky, lousy, mediocre, second-rate, shoddy, sleazy, trashy

rot·ten·stone \ˈrät-ᵊn-ˌstōn\ *n* : a decomposed siliceous limestone used for polishing

rott·wei·ler \ˈrät-ˌwī-lər\ *n, often cap* : any of a breed of tall powerful black-and-tan short-haired dogs

ro·tund \rō-ˈtənd\ *adj* **1** : rounded out **2** ♦ : notably plump

  ♦ chubby, fat, plump, portly, round — more at FAT

ro·tun·da \rō-ˈtən-də\ *n* **1** : a round building; *esp* : one covered by a dome **2** : a large round room

ro·tun·di·ty \-ˈtən-də-tē\ *n* : the quality or state of being rotund

roué \rù-ˈā\ *n* [F, lit., broken on the wheel, fr. pp. of *rouer* to break on the wheel, fr. ML *rotare*, fr. L, to rotate; fr. the feeling that such a person deserves this punishment] : a man devoted to a life of sensual pleasure : RAKE

rouge \ˈrüzh, ˈrüj\ *n* [F, lit., red] : a cosmetic used to give a red color to cheeks and lips — **rouge** *vb*

¹rough \ˈrəf\ *adj* **rough·er; rough·est** **1** ♦ : uneven in surface : not smooth **2** : covered with or made up of coarse and often shaggy hair : SHAGGY **3** : not calm : TURBULENT **4** ♦ : marked by harshness or violence **5** ♦ : presenting a challenge : DIFFICULT **6** : coarse or rugged in character or appearance **7** ♦ : marked by lack of refinement **8** : not brought to an end or to the desired final state : CRUDE **9** : done or made hastily or tentatively ⟨∼ estimates⟩

  ♦ [1] broken, bumpy, coarse, irregular, jagged, lumpy, pebbly, ragged, rugged, uneven — more at UNEVEN ♦ [4] bitter, brutal, burdensome, cruel, excruciating, grievous, grim, hard, harsh, heavy, inhuman, murderous, onerous, oppressive, rugged, severe, stiff, tough, trying — more at HARSH ♦ [5] arduous, demanding, difficult, exacting, formidable, grueling, hard, herculean, laborious, strenuous, tall, toilsome, tough — more at HARD ♦ [7] coarse, common, crass, crude, gross, ill-bred, low, rude, tasteless, uncouth, uncultivated, uncultured, unpolished, unrefined, vulgar — more at COARSE

²**rough** *n* **1** : uneven ground covered with high grass esp. along a golf fairway **2** : a crude, unfinished, or preliminary state; *also* : something in such a state **3** : ROWDY, TOUGH

³**rough** *vb* **1** : ROUGHEN **2** ♦ : to subject to abuse : MANHANDLE — usu. used with *up* **3** : to make or shape roughly esp. in a preliminary way — **rough·er** *n*

♦ *usu* **rough up** maltreat, manhandle, maul, mishandle — more at MANHANDLE

rough·age \ˈrə-fij\ *n* : FIBER 2; *also* : food containing much indigestible material acting as fiber

rough–and–ready \ˌrə-fən-ˈre-dē\ *adj* : rude or unpolished in nature, method, or manner but effective in action or use ⟨a ~ solution⟩

rough–and–tum·ble \-ˈtəm-bəl\ *n* : rough unrestrained fighting or struggling — **rough–and–tumble** *adj*

rough·en \ˈrə-fən\ *vb* **rough·ened; rough·en·ing** : to make or become rough

rough–hewn \ˈrəf-ˈhyün\ *adj* **1** : being rough and unfinished ⟨~ beams⟩ **2** : lacking smooth manners or social grace — **rough–hew** \-ˈhyü\ *vb*

¹**rough·house** \ˈrəf-ˌhaůs\ *vb* **rough·housed; rough·hous·ing** : to participate in rough noisy behavior

²**roughhouse** *n* ♦ : violence or rough boisterous play

♦ foolery, high jinks, horseplay, monkeyshines, shenanigans, tomfoolery — more at HORSEPLAY

rough·ly *adv* ♦ : in a rough manner

♦ hard, hardly, harshly, ill, oppressively, severely, sternly, stiffly — more at HARDLY

rough·neck \ˈrəf-ˌnek\ *n* **1** : a rough or uncouth person : ROWDY **2** : a worker on a crew drilling oil wells

rough·ness *n* : the quality or state of being rough

rough·shod \ˈrəf-ˌshäd\ *adv* : in a roughly forceful manner ⟨rode ~ over the opposition⟩

rou·lette \rü-ˈlet\ *n* [F, lit., small wheel] **1** : a gambling game in which a whirling wheel is used **2** : a wheel or disk with teeth around the outside

¹**round** \ˈraůnd\ *adj* **1** ♦ : having every part of the surface or circumference the same distance from the center **2** : CYLINDRICAL **3** : COMPLETE, FULL **4 a** : approximately correct **b** ♦ : exact only to a specific decimal or place ⟨~ numbers⟩ **5** : liberal or ample in size or amount **6** : BLUNT, OUTSPOKEN **7** : moving in or forming a circle **8** : having curves rather than angles **9** ♦ : well filled out **10** ♦ : having full or unimpeded resonance or tone — **round·ish** *adj* — **round·ness** *n*

♦ [1] circular, global; *also* annular, disklike, ringlike; curved, spiral; balled, rotund, rounded, roundish ♦ [4b] even, exact, flat, precise — more at EVEN ♦ [9] fat, full, plump, portly, rotund — more at FAT ♦ [10] golden, resonant, resounding, ringing, sonorous, vibrant — more at RESONANT

²**round** *adv* **1** : from beginning to end : AROUND **2** ♦ : in the reverse or opposite direction **3** ♦ : in all or various directions from a fixed point

♦ [2] about, around, back — more at AROUND ♦ [3] about, around, over, through, throughout — more at AROUND

³**round** *n* **1** ♦ : something round (as a circle, globe, or ring) **2** : a curved or rounded part (as a rung of a ladder) **3** : an indirect path or course; *also* : a regularly covered route (as of a security guard) **4** : a series or cycle of recurring actions or events **5** : one shot fired by a soldier or a gun; *also* : ammunition for one shot **6** : a period of time or a unit of play in a game or contest **7** : a cut of meat (as beef) esp. between the rump and the lower leg — **in the round 1** : FREESTANDING **2** : with a center stage surrounded by an audience ⟨theater *in the round*⟩

♦ band, circle, eye, hoop, loop, ring — more at RING

⁴**round** *vb* **1** ♦ : to make or become round **2** ♦ : to go or

pass around or part way around **3** ♦ : to bring to completion or perfection : FINISH — often used with *out* or *off* **4** : to become plump or shapely **5** : to express as a round number — often used with *off* **6** ♦ : to follow a winding course : BEND

♦ [1] agglomerate, ball, conglomerate, roll, wad — more at WAD ♦ [2] circle, circumnavigate, coil, compass, encircle, girdle, loop, orbit, ring — more at ENCIRCLE ♦ *usu* **round off** *or* **round out** [3] close, conclude, end, finish, terminate, wind up, wrap up — more at CLOSE ♦ [6] arc, arch, bend, bow, crook, curve, hook, sweep, swerve, wheel — more at CURVE

⁵**round** *prep* : AROUND

¹**round·about** \ˈraůn-də-ˌbaůt\ *adj* ♦ : having a circular or winding course : INDIRECT ⟨a ~ explanation⟩

♦ circuitous, circular, indirect — more at INDIRECT

²**roundabout** *n* **1** *Brit* : MERRY-GO-ROUND **2** : ROTARY 2

roun·de·lay \ˈraůn-də-ˌlā\ *n* **1** : a simple song with a refrain **2** : a poem with a recurring refrain

round·house \ˈraůnd-ˌhaůs\ *n* **1** : a circular building for housing and repairing locomotives **2** : a blow with the hand made with a wide swing

round·ly \ˈraůnd-lē\ *adv* **1 a** ♦ : in a complete manner **b** : WIDELY **2** : in a blunt way **3** : with vigor

♦ completely, exhaustively, fully, minutely, thoroughly, totally — more at THOROUGHLY

round–rob·in \ˈraůnd-ˌrä-bən\ *n* : a tournament in which each contestant meets every other contestant in turn

round–shoul·dered \-ˌshōl-dərd\ *adj* : having the shoulders stooping or rounded

round–trip *n* : a trip to a place and back

round–up \ˈraůn-ˌdəp\ *n* **1** : the gathering together of cattle on the range by riding around them and driving them in; *also* : the ranch hands and horses engaged in a roundup **2** : a gathering in of scattered persons or things **3** ♦ : a summary of information : SUMMARY ⟨news ~⟩

♦ abstract, digest, encapsulation, epitome, outline, précis, recapitulation, résumé (*or* resume), sum, summary, synopsis, wrap-up — more at SUMMARY

round up *vb* ♦ : to gather in or bring together from various quarters

♦ accumulate, amass, assemble, collect, concentrate, garner, gather, group, lump, pick up, scrape — more at GATHER

round·worm \-ˌwərm\ *n* : NEMATODE

rouse \ˈraůz\ *vb* **roused; rous·ing** **1** : to excite to activity : stir up **2** ♦ : to wake from sleep — **rous·er** *n*

♦ arouse, awake, wake

rous·ing \ˈraů-ziŋ\ *adj* ♦ : giving rise to excitement

♦ breathtaking, electric, exciting, exhilarating, stirring, thrilling — more at EXCITING

roust·about \ˈraůs-tə-ˌbaůt\ *n* : one who does heavy unskilled labor (as on a dock or in an oil field)

¹**rout** \ˈraůt\ *n* **1** : MOB 1, 2 **2** : DISTURBANCE **3** : a fashionable gathering

²**rout** *vb* **1** : RUMMAGE **2** : to gouge out **3** ♦ : to expel by force ⟨~ed out of their homes⟩

♦ banish, boot (out), bounce, cast, chase, dismiss, drum, eject, expel, oust, run off, throw out — more at EJECT

³**rout** *n* **1** : a state of wild confusion or disorderly retreat **2** ♦ : a disastrous defeat

♦ defeat, loss, shellacking — more at DEFEAT

⁴**rout** *vb* **1** ♦ : to put to flight **2** ♦ : to defeat decisively

♦ [1] banish, boot (out), bounce, cast, chase, dismiss, drum, eject, expel, oust, run off, throw out — more at EJECT ♦ [2] beat, best, clobber, conquer, crush, defeat, drub, lick, master, overcome, prevail, skunk, subdue, surmount, thrash, trim, triumph, trounce, wallop, whip, win — more at BEAT

¹**route** \ˈrüt, ˈraůt\ *n* [ME, fr. AF *rute*, fr. VL **rupta (via)*,

lit., broken way] **1** ♦ : a traveled way   **2** : CHANNEL   **3** ♦ : a line of travel

♦ [1] artery, avenue, highway, road, thoroughfare, way — more at WAY   ♦ [3] course, line, path, track, way — more at PATH

²**route** *vb* **rout·ed; rout·ing** : to send by a selected route : DI-RECT

¹**rout·er** \'raú-tər\ *n* : a machine with a revolving spindle and cutter for shaping a surface (as of wood)

²**rout·er** \'rü-tər, 'raú-\ *n* : a device that sends data from one place to another within a computer network or between computer networks

¹**rou·tine** \rü-'tēn\ *n* [F, fr. MF, fr. *route* traveled way] **1** ♦ : a regular course of procedure   **2** : an often repeated speech or formula   **3** : a part fully worked out ⟨a comedy ∼⟩   **4** : a set of computer instructions that will perform a certain task — **rou·tin·ize** \-'tē-ˌnīz\ *vb*

♦ groove, pattern, rote, rut, treadmill; *also* custom, fashion, habit, practice, wont; approach, manner, method, procedure, strategy, style, tack, way drill, exercise, practice, training, workout — more at EXERCISE

²**routine** *adj* **1** ♦ : of a commonplace or repetitious character   **2** ♦ : of, relating to, or being in accordance with established procedure — **rou·tine·ly** *adv*

♦ [1] average, common, commonplace, everyday, normal, ordinary, prosaic, run-of-the-mill, standard, unexceptional, unremarkable, usual, workaday — more at ORDINARY   ♦ [2] ceremonial, ceremonious, conventional, formal, orthodox, regular — more at FORMAL

¹**rove** \'rōv\ *vb* **roved; rov·ing** ♦ : to wander over or through

♦ gad, gallivant, knock, maunder, meander, mope, ramble, range, roam, traipse, wander — more at WANDER

²**rove** *past and past part of* REEVE

¹**rov·er** *n* ♦ : one that wanders

♦ drifter, nomad, rambler, stroller, vagabond, wanderer — more at NOMAD

²**rov·er** *n* ♦ : one who commits or practices piracy

♦ buccaneer, corsair, freebooter, pirate — more at PIRATE

¹**row** \'rō\ *vb* **1** ♦ : to propel a boat with oars   **2** : to transport in a rowboat   **3** : to pull an oar in a crew — **row·er** \'rō-ər\ *n*

♦ scull; *also* canoe; pole, punt

²**row** *n* : an act or instance of rowing

³**row** *n* **1** : a number of objects in an orderly sequence   **2** : a thoroughfare for travel or transportation from place to place : WAY

⁴**row** \'raú\ *n* **1** ♦ : a noisy quarrel   **2** ♦ : a noisy disturbance

♦ [1] altercation, argument, bicker, brawl, disagreement, dispute, fight, quarrel, scrap, spat, squabble, wrangle — more at ARGUMENT   ♦ [2] commotion, disturbance, furor, hullabaloo, pandemonium, tumult, turmoil, uproar — more at COMMOTION

⁵**row** \'raú\ *vb* ♦ : to engage in a row

♦ argue, bicker, brawl, dispute, fall out, fight, hassle, quarrel, scrap, spat, squabble, wrangle — more at ARGUE

row·boat \'rō-ˌbōt\ *n* : a small boat designed to be rowed

¹**row·dy** \'raú-dē\ *adj* **row·di·er; -est** ♦ : coarse or boisterous in behavior — **row·di·ness** \'raú-dē-nəs\ *n* — **row·dy·ish** *adj* — **row·dy·ism** *n*

♦ boisterous, rambunctious, raucous — more at BOISTEROUS

²**rowdy** *n* ♦ : a rowdy person

♦ bully, hoodlum, punk, ruffian, thug, tough — more at HOODLUM

row·el \'raú-əl\ *n* : a small pointed wheel on a rider's spur — **rowel** *vb*

¹**roy·al** \'rói-əl\ *adj* [ME *roial*, fr. AF *real, roial*, fr. L *regalis*, fr. *reg-, rex* king] **1** : of or relating to a sovereign : REGAL   **2** ♦ : fit for a king or queen ⟨a ∼ welcome⟩   **3** ♦ : of superior size, magnitude, or quality — **roy·al·ly** *adv*

♦ [2] kingly, monarchical, princely, queenly, regal — more at MONARCHICAL   ♦ [3] august, baronial, gallant, glorious, grand, grandiose, heroic, imposing, magnificent, majestic, monumental, noble, proud, regal, splendid, stately — more at GRAND

²**royal** *n* : a person of royal blood

royal flush *n* : a straight flush having an ace as the highest card

roy·al·ist \'rói-ə-list\ *n* : an adherent of a king or of monarchical government

roy·al·ty \'rói-əl-tē\ *n, pl* **-ties** **1** : the state of being royal   **2** : royal persons   **3** : a share of a product or profit (as of a mine or oil well) claimed by the owner for allowing another person to use the property   **4** : a payment made to an author or composer for each copy of a work sold or to an inventor for each article sold under a patent

RP *abbr* **1** relief pitcher   **2** Republic of the Philippines

rpm *abbr* revolutions per minute

rps *abbr* revolutions per second

rpt *abbr* **1** repeat   **2** report

RR *abbr* **1** railroad   **2** rural route

RS *abbr* **1** recording secretary   **2** revised statutes   **3** Royal Society

RSV *abbr* Revised Standard Version

RSVP *abbr* [F *répondez s'il vous plaît*] please reply

rt *abbr* **1** right   **2** route

RT *abbr* round-trip

rte *abbr* route

Ru *symbol* ruthenium

¹**rub** \'rəb\ *vb* **rubbed; rub·bing** **1** : to use pressure and friction on a body or object   **2** ♦ : to fret or chafe with friction   **3** ♦ : to scour, polish, erase, or smear by pressure and friction

♦ [2] abrade, chafe, erode, fray, fret, gall, wear — more at ABRADE   ♦ [3] buff, file, grind, hone, rasp, sand — more at GRIND   ♦ [3] buff, burnish, dress, gloss, grind, polish, shine, smooth — more at POLISH

²**rub** *n* **1** : DIFFICULTY, OBSTRUCTION   **2** ♦ : something grating to the feelings

♦ aggravation, annoyance, bother, bugbear, exasperation, frustration, hassle, headache, inconvenience, irritant, nuisance, peeve, pest, problem, ruffle, thorn, vexation — more at ANNOYANCE

¹**rub·ber** \'rə-bər\ *n* **1** : one that rubs   **2** : ERASER   **3** : a flexible waterproof elastic substance made from the milky juice of various tropical plants or made synthetically; *also* : something made of this material   **4** : CONDOM — **rubber** *adj* — **rub·ber·ize** \'rə-bə-ˌrīz\ *vb*

²**rubber** *n* **1** : a contest that consists of an odd number of games and is won by the side that takes a majority   **2** : an extra game played to decide a tie

¹**rub·ber·neck** \-ˌnek\ *n* **1** : an idly or overly inquisitive person   **2** : a person on a guided tour

²**rubberneck** *vb* ♦ : to look about, stare, or listen with excessive curiosity — **rub·ber·neck·er** *n*

♦ gape, gawk, gaze, goggle, peer, stare — more at GAPE

rub·bery *adj* ♦ : resembling rubber (as in elasticity, consistency, or texture)

♦ elastic, flexible, resilient, springy, stretch, supple — more at ELASTIC

rub·bish \'rə-bish\ *n* **1** ♦ : useless waste or rejected matter : TRASH   **2** : something worthless or nonsensical

♦ chaff, deadwood, dust, garbage, junk, litter, refuse, riffraff, scrap, trash, waste — more at GARBAGE

rub·ble \'rə-bəl\ *n* ♦ : broken fragments esp. of a destroyed building

♦ debris, remains, ruins, wreck, wreckage — more at REMAINS

ru·bel·la \rü-'be-lə\ *n* : GERMAN MEASLES

ru·bi·cund \'rü-bi-(ˌ)kənd\ *adj* : having a healthy reddish color : RED, RUDDY ⟨∼ faces⟩

ru·bid·i·um \rü-'bi-dē-əm\ *n* : a soft silvery metallic chemical element

ru·ble \'rü-bəl\ *n* : the basic monetary unit of Russia

rub out *vb* ♦ : to destroy completely

♦ annihilate, blot out, demolish, eradicate, exterminate, liquidate, obliterate, root, snuff, stamp, wipe out — more at ANNIHILATE

ru·bric \'rü-brik\ *n* [ME *rubrike* red ocher, heading in red letters of part of a book, fr. AF, fr. L *rubrica*, fr. *ruber* red] **1** : a heading of a part of a book or manuscript **2** : a rule esp. for the conduct of a religious service

ru·by \'rü-bē\ *n, pl* **rubies** : a clear red precious stone — **ruby** *adj*

ru·by-throat·ed hummingbird \'rü-bē-,thrō-təd-\ *n* : a bright green and whitish hummingbird of eastern No. America with a red throat in the male

ruck·us \'rə-kəs\ *n* : a noisy disturbance or quarrel : ROW

rud·der \'rə-dər\ *n* : a movable flat piece attached to the rear of a ship or aircraft for steering

rud·dy \'rə-dē\ *adj* **rud·di·er; -est 1** : REDDISH **2** ♦ : of a healthy reddish complexion ⟨the boy's ∼ cheeks⟩ — **rud·di·ness** \'rə-dē-nəs\ *n*

♦ florid, flush, glowing, rosy, sanguine; *also* bronzed, brown, tanned; flushed, pink, pinkish, warm; cherubic

rude \'rüd\ *adj* **rud·er; rud·est 1** ♦ : roughly made : CRUDE **2** : not developed : PRIMITIVE **3** ♦ : lacking refinement or delicacy **4** : marked by or suggestive of lack of training or skill : UNSKILLED **5** ♦ : not being in a cultural or civilized state — **rude·ly** *adv*

♦ [1] artless, clumsy, crude, rough, unrefined; *also* defective, faulty, imperfect; imprecise, inexact; inartistic, undressed, unfinished, unpolished; amateur, amateurish, inexpert, unprofessional, unskilled, unskillful; primitive, rudimentary ♦ [3] coarse, common, crass, crude, gross, ill-bred, low, rough, tasteless, uncouth, uncultivated, uncultured, unpolished, unrefined, vulgar — more at COARSE ♦ [3] discourteous, ill-bred, ill-mannered, impertinent, impolite, inconsiderate, thoughtless, uncivil, ungracious, unmannerly — more at IMPOLITE ♦ [5] barbarous, heathen, heathenish, Neanderthal, savage, uncivilized, wild — more at SAVAGE

rude·ness *n* **1** ♦ : the quality or state of being rude **2** ♦ : a rude action

♦ [1] coarseness, grossness, indelicacy, lowness, vulgarity — more at VULGARITY ♦ [2] brazenness, discourtesy, disrespect, impertinence, impudence, incivility, insolence — more at DISCOURTESY

ru·di·ment \'rü-də-mənt\ *n* **1** ♦ : an elementary principle or basic skill — usu. used in pl. **2** : something not fully developed — usu. used in pl.

♦ rudiments elements, essentials, principles — more at ELEMENT

ru·di·men·ta·ry \,rü-də-'men-tə-rē\ *adj* **1** ♦ : consisting in basic principles **2** ♦ : of a primitive kind

♦ [1] basic, elemental, elementary, essential, fundamental, underlying — more at ELEMENTARY ♦ [2] crude, low, primitive, rude — more at PRIMITIVE

¹rue \'rü\ *n* ♦ : deep distress, sadness, or regret — **rue·ful·ness** *n*

♦ contrition, penitence, regret, remorse, repentance

²rue *vb* **rued; ru·ing** ♦ : to feel regret, remorse, or penitence for ⟨∼ing the decision⟩

♦ bemoan, deplore, lament, regret, repent — more at REGRET

³rue *n* : a European strong-scented woody herb with bitter-tasting leaves

rue·ful \-fəl\ *adj* **1** ♦ : expressing sorrow **2** ♦ : full of sorrow **3** ♦ : exciting pity or sympathy

♦ [1] dolorous, funeral, lugubrious, mournful, plaintive, regretful, sorrowful, weeping, woeful — more at MOURNFUL ♦ [2] apologetic, contrite, penitent,

regretful, remorseful, repentant, sorry — more at CONTRITE ♦ [3] heartbreaking, miserable, pathetic, piteous, pitiful, poor, sorry, wretched

rue·ful·ly *adv* : in a rueful manner

ruff \'rəf\ *n* **1** : a large round pleated collar worn in the 16th and 17th centuries **2** : a fringe of long hair or feathers around the neck of an animal — **ruffed** \'rəft\ *adj*

ruf·fi·an \'rə-fē-ən\ *n* ♦ : a brutal person — **ruf·fi·an·ly** *adj*

♦ bully, gangster, goon, hood, hoodlum, mobster, mug, punk, rowdy, thug, tough — more at HOODLUM

¹ruf·fle \'rə-fəl\ *vb* **ruf·fled; ruf·fling 1** : to roughen the surface of **2** ♦ : to excite to anger : IRRITATE, VEX **3** : to erect (as hair or feathers) in or like a ruff **4** : to flip through (as pages) **5** : to draw into or provide with plaits or folds

♦ aggravate, annoy, bother, bug, chafe, exasperate, gall, get, grate, irk, irritate, nettle, peeve, persecute, pique, put out, rasp, rile, spite, vex — more at IRRITATE

²ruffle *n* **1** ♦ : a strip of fabric gathered or pleated on one edge **2** : RUFF **3** : RIPPLE — **ruf·fly** \'rə-fə-lē, -flē\ *adj*

♦ flounce, frill, furbelow; *also* border, edging, fringe, trim; pleat, ruff; bunting, skirting

RU-486 \'är-,yü-,fōr-,ā-tē-'siks\ *n* : a drug taken orally to induce abortion esp. early in pregnancy

rug \'rəg\ *n* **1** : a covering for the legs, lap, and feet **2** : a piece of heavy fabric usu. with a nap or pile used as a floor covering

rug·by \'rəg-bē\ *n, often cap* [*Rugby* School, Rugby, England, where it was first played] : a football game in which play is continuous and interference and forward passing are not permitted

rug·ged \'rə-gəd\ *adj* **1** ♦ : having a rough uneven surface **2** : TURBULENT, STORMY **3** : austere or stern in aspect, conduct, or character : STERN **4** ♦ : strongly built or constituted : STURDY **5** ♦ : presenting a severe test of ability, stamina, or resolution — **rug·ged·ize** \'rə-gə-,dīz\ *vb* — **rug·ged·ly** *adv* — **rug·ged·ness** *n*

♦ [1] broken, bumpy, coarse, irregular, jagged, lumpy, pebbly, ragged, rough, uneven — more at UNEVEN ♦ [4] hard, hard-bitten, hardy, stout, strong, sturdy, tough, vigorous — more at HARDY ♦ [5] bitter, brutal, burdensome, cruel, excruciating, grievous, grim, hard, harsh, heavy, inhuman, murderous, onerous, oppressive, rough, severe, stiff, tough, trying — more at HARSH

¹ru·in \'rü-ən\ *n* **1** ♦ : complete collapse or destruction **2** ♦ : the remains of something destroyed — usu. used in pl. **3** : a cause of destruction **4** : the action of destroying

♦ [1] annihilation, demolition, desolation, destruction, devastation, havoc, loss, obliteration, wastage, wreckage — more at DESTRUCTION **ruins** ♦ [2] debris, remains, rubble, wreck, wreckage — more at REMAINS

²ruin *vb* **1** ♦ : to reduce to ruins : DESTROY **2** ♦ : to damage beyond repair **3** : BANKRUPT

♦ [1] destroy, devastate, ravage, scourge — more at RAVAGE ♦ [2] annihilate, blot out, demolish, desolate, destroy, devastate, do in, exterminate, extinguish, obliterate, pulverize, shatter, smash, tear down, waste, wipe out, wreck — more at DESTROY

ru·in·ation \,rü-ə-'nā-shən\ *n* : the state of being ruined : RUIN, DESTRUCTION

ru·in·ous \'rü-ə-nəs\ *adj* **1** : RUINED, DILAPIDATED **2** ♦ : causing ruin ⟨∼ conflicts⟩ — **ru·in·ous·ly** *adv*

♦ calamitous, catastrophic, destructive, devastating, disastrous, fatal, fateful, unfortunate — more at FATAL

¹rule \'rül\ *n* [ME *reule*, fr. AF, fr. L *regula* straightedge, rule, fr. *regere* to keep straight, direct] **1** ♦ : a guide or principle for governing action : REGULATION **2** : the usual way of doing something **3** ♦ : the exercise of authority or control : GOVERNMENT **4** : RULER **2**

♦ [1] regulation; *also* code, constitution; act, law, ordinance, statute; command, decree, dictate, directive, edict, fiat, order; axiom, fundamental, maxim, precept;

moral, principle, value; prohibition, restriction; convention, custom, habit, manners, mores, practice, tradition, way; blueprint, canon, formula, guide, guideline, recipe, standard ♦ [3] administration, authority, government, jurisdiction, regime; *also* reign; dominion, power, sovereignty, supremacy, sway; command, leadership; direction, management, regulation, superintendence, supervision; dictatorship, domination, mastery, oppression, subjugation, tyranny

²**rule** *vb* **ruled; rul·ing 1** ♦ : to exert control, direction, or influence on; *also* : GOVERN **2** : to be supreme or outstanding in **3** ♦ : to give or state as a considered decision **4** : to mark on paper with or as if with a ruler

♦ [1] boss, captain, command, control, govern, preside — more at GOVERN ♦ *usu* **rule on** [3] adjudicate, arbitrate, decide, determine, judge, referee, settle, umpire — more at JUDGE

rule out *vb* ♦ : to remove from consideration

♦ ban, bar, debar, eliminate, except, exclude — more at EXCLUDE

rul·er \'rü-lər\ *n* **1** ♦ : one that rules **2** : a straight strip of material (as wood or metal) marked off in units and used for measuring or as a straightedge

♦ autocrat, monarch, sovereign — more at MONARCH

ruling *n* ♦ : an official or authoritative decision, decree, statement, or interpretation (as by a judge on a point of law)

♦ doom, finding, holding, judgment (*or* judgement), sentence — more at SENTENCE ♦ decree, directive, edict, fiat — more at EDICT

rum \'rəm\ *n* **1** : an alcoholic liquor made from sugarcane products (as molasses) **2** : alcoholic liquor

Ru·ma·nian *var of* ROMANIAN

rum·ba \'rəm-bə, 'rum-\ *n* : a dance of Cuban origin marked by strong rhythmic movements

¹**rum·ble** \'rəm-bəl\ *vb* **rum·bled; rum·bling 1** ♦ : to make a low heavy rolling sound **2** : to move along with such a sound — **rum·bler** *n*

♦ growl, grumble, lumber, roll; *also* boom, drum, thunder

²**rumble** *n* **1** : a low heavy rolling sound **2** : a street fight esp. among gangs

rumble seat *n* : a folding seat in the back of an automobile that is not covered by the top

rum·bling \'rəm-blin\ *n* **1** : RUMBLE **2** : widespread talk or complaints — usu. used in pl.

ru·men \'rü-mən\ *n, pl* **ru·mi·na** \-mə-nə\ *or* **rumens** : the large first compartment of the stomach of a ruminant (as a cow)

¹**ru·mi·nant** \'rü-mə-nənt\ *n* : a ruminant mammal

²**ruminant** *adj* **1** : chewing the cud; *also* : of or relating to a group of hoofed mammals (as cattle, deer, and camels) that chew the cud and have a complex 3- or 4-chambered stomach **2** ♦ : given to or engaged in contemplation : MEDITATIVE

♦ contemplative, meditative, pensive, reflective, thoughtful — more at CONTEMPLATIVE

ru·mi·nate \'rü-mə-ˌnāt\ *vb* **-nat·ed; -nat·ing** [L *ruminari* to chew the cud, muse upon, fr. *rumin-, rumen* first stomach chamber of a ruminant] **1** ♦ : to engage in contemplation : to spend time in thought on **2** : to chew the cud — **ru·mi·na·tion** \ˌrü-mə-'nā-shən\ *n*

♦ chew over, cogitate, consider, contemplate, debate, deliberate, entertain, meditate, mull, ponder, question, study, think, weigh — more at PONDER

¹**rum·mage** \'rə-mij\ *vb* **rum·maged; rum·mag·ing** ♦ : to search thoroughly — **rum·mag·er** *n*

♦ dig, dredge, hunt, rake, ransack, rifle, scour, search — more at SEARCH

²**rummage** *n* **1** ♦ : a miscellaneous collection **2** : an act of rummaging

♦ assortment, clutter, jumble, medley, mélange, miscellany, motley, muddle, variety, welter — more at MISCELLANY

rummage sale *n* : a usu. informal sale of miscellaneous goods

rum·my \'rə-mē\ *n* : any of several card games for two or more players

¹**ru·mor** *or Can and Brit* **ru·mour** \'rü-mər\ *n* **1** : common talk **2** : a statement or report current but not authenticated

²**rumor** *or Can and Brit* **rumour** *vb* ♦ : to tell or spread by rumor

♦ circulate, noise, whisper; *also* blab, gossip; disclose, divulge, report, reveal, tell; hint, imply, insinuate, intimate; spread

rump \'rəmp\ *n* **1** : the rear part of an animal; *also* : a cut of meat (as beef) behind the upper sirloin **2** : a small or inferior remnant (as of a group) **3** : the upper rounded part of the hindquarters of a quadruped mammal

♦ backside, bottom, butt, buttocks, posterior, rear, seat — more at BUTTOCKS

rum·ple \'rəm-pəl\ *vb* **rum·pled; rum·pling 1** ♦ : to become or cause to become marked with or contracted into irregular folds : WRINKLE **2** ♦ : to make unkempt : MUSS — **rumple** *n* — **rum·ply** \'rəm-pə-lē\ *adj*

♦ [1] crease, crinkle, furrow, wrinkle — more at WRINKLE ♦ [2] dishevel, disorder, muddle, muss, tumble, upset — more at DISORDER

rum·pus \'rəm-pəs\ *n* : a usu. noisy commotion : RUCKUS

rumpus room *n* : a room usu. in the basement of a home that is used for games, parties, and recreation

¹**run** \'rən\ *vb* **ran** \'ran\; **run; run·ning 1** ♦ : to go faster than a walk **2** ♦ : to take to flight : FLEE **3** : to go without restraint ⟨let chickens ∼ loose⟩ **4** : to go rapidly or hurriedly : HASTEN, RUSH **5** : to make a quick or casual trip or visit **6** : to contend in a race; *esp* : to enter an election **7** : to put forward as a candidate for office **8** : to move on or as if on wheels : pass or slide freely **9** : to go back and forth : PLY **10 a** : to move in large numbers esp. to a spawning ground ⟨shad are *running*⟩ **b** : to drive (livestock) esp. to a grazing place **11** : FUNCTION, OPERATE ⟨left the motor *running*⟩ **12** : to continue in force ⟨two years to ∼⟩ **13 a** ♦ : to flow rapidly or under pressure : MELT **b** : DISCHARGE 7 ⟨my nose is *running*⟩ **14** : to tend to produce or to recur ⟨family ∼s to blonds⟩ **15** ♦ : to take a certain direction **16** : to be worded or written **17** : to be current ⟨rumors *running* wild⟩ **18** ♦ : to cause to produce a flow **19** : TRACE ⟨∼ down a rumor⟩ **20** : to perform or bring about by running **21** : to cause to pass ⟨∼ a wire from the antenna⟩ **22** : to cause to collide **23** : SMUGGLE **24** ♦ : to direct the business or activities of : MANAGE ⟨∼ a business⟩ **25** : INCUR ⟨∼ a risk⟩ **26** : to permit to accumulate before settling ⟨∼ up a bill⟩ **27** : PRINT, PUBLISH **28** ♦ : to exist or occur in a continuous range of variation

♦ [1] dash, gallop, jog, scamper, sprint, trip; *also* bound, canter, leap, lope, skip, spring; foot (it), hoof (it), leg (it); nip, race, scuttle, step (along) ♦ [2] bolt, break, flee, fly, retreat, run away, run off; *also* abscond, clear out, decamp, elope, escape, light out, retreat, scram, skip (out) ♦ [13a] flow, liquefy, melt, pour, roll, stream, thaw — more at FLOW ♦ [15] extend, go, head, lead, lie; *also* cross, cut, pass; follow, span, traverse ♦ [18] activate, actuate, crank, drive, move, propel, set off, spark, start, touch off, trigger, turn on — more at ACTIVATE ♦ [24] administer, carry on, conduct, control, direct, govern, guide, handle, manage, operate, oversee, regulate, superintend, supervise — more at CONDUCT ♦ [28] go, range, vary; *also* alternate, move, shift; change, mutate; extend, reach, stretch, sweep

²**run** *n* **1** : an act or the action of running **2** : a migration of fish; *also* : the migrating fish **3** : a score in baseball **4** : BROOK, CREEK **5** ♦ : a continuous series esp. of similar things : a period of existence ⟨the play's long ∼⟩ **6** : persistent heavy demands from depositors, creditors, or customers **7** : the quantity of work turned out in a

continuous operation; *also* : a period of operation (as of a machine) **8** : the usual or normal kind ⟨the ordinary ~ of students⟩ **9** : the distance covered in continuous travel or sailing **10** : a regular course or trip **11** ♦ : freedom of movement in a place or area ⟨has the ~ of the house⟩ **12** : an enclosure for animals **13** : an inclined course (as for skiing) **14** : a lengthwise ravel (as in a stocking) **15** : general tendency or direction — **run·less** *adj*

♦ **[5]** date, duration, life, lifetime, standing, time — more at DURATION ♦ **[11]** authorization, freedom, latitude, license (*or* licence) — more at FREEDOM

run·about \'rə-nə-ˌbaủt\ *n* : a light wagon, automobile, or motorboat

run·around \'rə-nə-ˌrauṅd\ *n* : evasive or delaying action esp. in response to a request

¹**run·away** \'rə-nə-ˌwā\ *n* **1** : one that runs away : FUGITIVE **2** : the act of running away out of control; *also* : something (as a horse) that is running out of control

²**runaway** *adj* **1** : FUGITIVE **2** : won by a long lead; *also* : extremely successful **3** : subject to uncontrolled changes ⟨~ inflation⟩ **4** : operating out of control ⟨a ~ locomotive⟩

run away *vb* ♦ : to leave quickly in order to avoid or escape something

♦ abscond, clear out, escape, flee, fly, get out, lam, run off — more at ESCAPE

run-down \'rən-ˌdauṅ\ *n* : an item-by-item report or review : SUMMARY

run-down \'rən-'dauṅ\ *adj* **1** : EXHAUSTED, WORN-OUT ⟨that ~ feeling⟩ **2** : being in poor repair ⟨a ~ farm⟩

run down *vb* **1** : to collide with and knock down **2** : to chase until exhausted or captured **3** ♦ : to find by search **4** : DISPARAGE **5** : to cease to operate for lack of motive power **6** : to decline in physical condition

♦ detect, determine, dig up, discover, ferret out, hit on, locate, track down — more at FIND

rune \'rün\ *n* **1** : any of the characters of any of several alphabets formerly used by the Germanic peoples **2** : MYSTERY, MAGIC **3** : a poem esp. in Finnish or Old Norse — **ru·nic** \'rü-nik\ *adj*

¹**rung** *past part of* RING

²**rung** \'rən\ *n* **1** : a rounded crosspiece between the legs of a chair **2** : one of the crosspieces of a ladder

run-in \'rən-ˌin\ *n* **1** ♦ : a noisy heated angry dispute **2** : something run in

♦ brush, encounter, hassle, scrape, skirmish — more at ENCOUNTER

run in *vb* **1** : to insert as additional matter **2** : to arrest esp. for a minor offense **3** : to pay a casual visit

run·nel \'rən-°l\ *n* : BROOK, STREAMLET

run·ner \'rə-nər\ *n* **1** : one that runs **2** : BASE RUNNER **3** : BALLCARRIER **4** : a thin piece or part on which something (as a sled or an ice skate) slides **5** : the support of a drawer or a sliding door **6** : a horizontal branch from the base of a plant that produces new plants **7** : a plant producing runners **8** : a long narrow carpet **9** : a narrow decorative cloth cover for a table or dresser top **10** ♦ : one who bears a message or does an errand

♦ courier, go-between, messenger, page — more at MESSENGER

run·ner–up \'rə-nər-ˌəp\ *n, pl* **runners–up** *also* **runner-ups** : the competitor in a contest who finishes second

¹**run·ning** *adj* **1** : FLOWING **2** : FLUID, RUNNY **3** : CONTINUOUS, INCESSANT **4** : measured in a straight line ⟨cost per ~ foot⟩ **5** : of or relating to an act of running **6** : made or trained for running ⟨~ horse⟩ ⟨~ shoes⟩ **7** ♦ : carrying on a function or being in action

♦ active, alive, functional, living, on, operational, operative, working — more at ACTIVE

²**running** *adv* : in succession

running light *n* : any of the lights carried by a vehicle (as a ship) at night

run·ny \'rə-nē\ *adj* ♦ : having a tendency to run ⟨a ~ dough⟩ ⟨a ~ nose⟩

♦ fluent, fluid, liquid — more at FLUID

run·off \'rən-ˌȯf\ *n* : a final contest (as an election) to decide a previous indecisive contest

run off *vb* **1** ♦ : to drive off (as trespassers) **2** ♦ : to run away

♦ **[1]** banish, boot (out), bounce, cast, chase, dismiss, drum, eject, expel, oust, rout, throw out — more at EJECT ♦ **[2]** bolt, break, flee, fly, retreat, run, run away — more at RUN

run–of–the–mill *adj* ♦ : not outstanding ⟨a ~ performance⟩

♦ average, common, commonplace, everyday, normal, ordinary, prosaic, routine, standard, unexceptional, unremarkable, usual, workaday — more at ORDINARY

run on *vb* **1** ♦ : to talk at length **2** : to continue (matter in type) without a break or a new paragraph **3** : to place or add (as an entry in a dictionary) at the end of a paragraphed item **4** ♦ : to keep going — **run-on** \'rən-ˌȯn, -ˌän\ *n*

♦ **[1]** maunder, ramble, rattle — more at RAMBLE ♦ **[4]** abide, continue, endure, hold, keep up, last, persist — more at CONTINUE

run out *vb* : to use up or exhaust a supply ⟨ran out of gas⟩

runt \'rənt\ *n* **1** : an animal unusually small of its kind **2** *usu disparaging* : a person of small stature — **runty** *adj*

♦ dwarf, midget, mite, peewee, pygmy — more at DWARF

run through *vb* ♦ : to spend or consume wastefully

♦ blow, dissipate, fritter, lavish, misspend, spend, squander, throw away, waste — more at WASTE

run·way \'rən-ˌwā\ *n* **1** : a beaten path made by animals; *also* : a passage for animals **2** : a paved strip of ground for the landing and takeoff of aircraft **3** : a narrow platform from a stage into an auditorium **4** : a support (as a track) on which something runs

ru·pee \rü-'pē, 'rü-ˌpē\ *n* : the basic monetary unit of several countries on the Indian subcontinent (as India and Pakistan)

¹**rup·ture** \'rəp-chər\ *n* : a breaking or tearing apart; *also* : HERNIA

²**rupture** *vb* **rup·tured; rup·tur·ing** : to cause or undergo rupture

ru·ral \'rủr-əl\ *adj* ♦ : of or relating to the country, country people, or agriculture

♦ bucolic, country, pastoral, rustic; *also* countrified, provincial; agrarian, agricultural *Ant* urban

ruse \'rüs, 'rüz\ *n* : a wily subterfuge : TRICK, ARTIFICE

¹**rush** \'rəsh\ *n* : any of various often tufted and hollow-stemmed grasslike marsh plants — **rushy** *adj*

²**rush** *vb* [ME *russhen*, fr. AF *reuser, ruser, russher* to drive back, repulse, fr. L *recusare* to oppose] **1** ♦ : to move forward or act with too great haste or eagerness or without preparation **2** : to perform in a short time or at high speed **3** ♦ : to run toward or against in attack : CHARGE **4** ♦ : to urge to an unnatural or extreme speed — **rush·er** *n*

♦ **[1]** dash, fly, hasten, hurry, pelt, race, rip, rocket, run, shoot, speed, whirl, whisk, zip, zoom — more at HURRY ♦ **[3]** assail, assault, attack, beset, charge, descend, jump, pounce (on *or* upon), raid, storm, strike — more at ATTACK ♦ **[4]** accelerate, hasten, hurry, quicken, speed (up), step up, whisk — more at HURRY

³**rush** *n* **1** ♦ : a violent forward motion **2** : unusual demand or activity **3** : a crowding of people to one place **4** : a running play in football **5** : a sudden feeling of pleasure **6** ♦ : a burst of activity, productivity, or speed

♦ **[1]** aggression, assault, attack, charge, descent, offense (*or* offence), offensive, onset, onslaught, raid, strike — more at ATTACK ♦ **[6]** haste, hurry, hustle, precipitation — more at HURRY

⁴**rush** *adj* : requiring or marked by special speed or urgency ⟨~ orders⟩

rush hour *n* : a time when the amount of traffic or business is at a peak

rusk \'rəsk\ *n* : a sweet or plain bread baked, sliced, and baked again until dry and crisp

rus·set \'rə-sət\ *n* **1** : a coarse reddish brown cloth **2** : a reddish brown **3** : a baking potato — **russet** *adj*

Rus·sian \'rə-shən\ *n* **1** : a native or inhabitant of Russia **2** : a Slavic language of the Russian people — **Russian** *adj*

rust \'rəst\ *n* **1** : a reddish coating formed on iron when it is exposed to esp. moist air **2** : any of numerous plant diseases characterized by usu. reddish spots; *also* : a fungus causing rust **3** : a strong reddish brown — **rust** *vb* — **rusty** *adj*

¹**rus·tic** \'rəs-tik\ *adj* ♦ : of, relating to, or suitable for the country or country people ⟨a ∼ inn⟩ — **rus·ti·cal·ly** \-ti-k(ə-)lē\ *adv* — **rus·tic·i·ty** \,rəs-'ti-sə-tē\ *n*

♦ bucolic, country, pastoral, rural — more at RURAL

²**rustic** *n* ♦ : a rustic person

♦ bumpkin, clodhopper, hick, yokel — more at HICK

rus·ti·cate \'rəs-ti-,kāt\ *vb* **-cat·ed; -cat·ing** : to go into or reside in the country — **rus·ti·ca·tion** \,rəs-ti-'kā-shən\ *n*

¹**rus·tle** \'rə-səl\ *vb* **rus·tled; rus·tling** **1** : to make or cause a rustle **2** : to cause to rustle ⟨∼ a newspaper⟩ **3 a** : to act or move with energy or speed **b** : to procure in this way **4** : to forage food **5** : to steal cattle from the range

²**rustle** *n* : a quick series of small sounds ⟨∼ of leaves⟩

rus·tler *n* : one that rustles: as **a** : an alert energetic driving person **b** : a cattle thief

¹**rut** \'rət\ *n* : state or period of sexual excitement esp. in male deer — **rut** *vb*

²**rut** *n* **1** : a track worn by wheels or by habitual passage of something **2** ♦ : a usual or fixed routine

♦ groove, pattern, rote, routine, treadmill — more at ROUTINE

ru·ta·ba·ga \,rü-tə-'bā-gə, ,rù-\ *n* : a turnip with a large yellowish root

Ruth \'rüth\ *n* : a book of Jewish and Christian Scripture

ru·the·ni·um \rü-'thē-nē-əm\ *n* : a hard brittle metallic chemical element

ruth·er·ford·ium \,rə-thər-'fòr-dē-əm\ *n* : an artificially produced radioactive chemical element

ruth·less \'rüth-ləs\ *adj* [fr. *ruth* compassion, pity, fr. ME *ruthe*, fr. *ruen* to rue, fr. OE *hrēowan*] ♦ : having no pity : MERCILESS — **ruth·less·ly** *adv* — **ruth·less·ness** *n*

♦ callous, hard, heartless, inhuman, inhumane, pitiless, soulless, unfeeling, unsympathetic — more at HARD

¹**RV** \,är-'vē\ *n* ♦ : a vehicle designed for recreational use (as camping) : RECREATIONAL VEHICLE

♦ camper, caravan, motor home, recreational vehicle, trailer — more at CAMPER

²**RV** *abbr* Revised Version

R–value \'är-,val-yü\ *n* : a measure of resistance to the flow of heat through a substance (as insulation)

RW *abbr* **1** right worshipful **2** right worthy

rwy *or* **ry** *abbr* railway

Rx \,är-'eks\ *n* : PRESCRIPTION 2

-ry \rē\ *n suffix* : -ERY ⟨bigot*ry*⟩

rye \'rī\ *n* **1** : a hardy annual grass grown for grain or as a cover crop; *also* : its seed **2** : a whiskey distilled from a rye mash

¹**s** \'es\ *n, pl* **s's** *or* **ss** \'e-səz\ *often cap* : the 19th letter of the English alphabet

²**s** *abbr, often cap* **1** saint **2** second **3** senate **4** series **5** shilling **6** singular **7** small **8** son **9** south; southern

¹**-s** \s *after sounds* f, k, k̲, p, t, th; əz *after sounds* ch, j, s, sh, z, zh; z *after other sounds*\ *n pl suffix* — used to form the pl. of most nouns that do not end in *s, z, sh,* or *ch* or in *y* following a consonant ⟨head*s*⟩ ⟨book*s*⟩ ⟨boy*s*⟩ ⟨belief*s*⟩, to form the pl. of proper nouns that end in *y* following a consonant ⟨Mary*s*⟩, and with or without a preceding apostrophe to form the pl. of abbreviations, numbers, letters, and symbols used as nouns ⟨MC*s*⟩ ⟨4*s*⟩ ⟨#*s*⟩ ⟨B'*s*⟩

²**-s** *adv suffix* — used to form adverbs denoting usual or repeated action or state ⟨works night*s*⟩

³**-s** *vb suffix* — used to form the third person singular present of most verbs that do not end in *s, z, sh,* or *ch* or in *y* following a consonant ⟨fall*s*⟩ ⟨take*s*⟩ ⟨play*s*⟩

S *symbol* sulfur

SA *abbr* **1** Salvation Army **2** seaman apprentice **3** sex appeal **4** [L *sine anno* without year] without date **5** South Africa **6** South America **7** subject to approval

Sab·bath \'sa-bəth\ *n* [ME *sabat*, fr. OF & OE, fr. L *sabbatum*, fr. Gk *sabbaton*, fr. Heb *shabbāth*, lit., rest] **1** : the 7th day of the week observed as a day of worship by Jews and some Christians **2** : Sunday observed among Christians as a day of worship

sab·bat·i·cal \sə-'ba-ti-kəl\ *n* : a leave often with pay granted (as to a college professor) usu. every 7th year for rest, travel, or research

sa·ber *or* **sa·bre** \'sā-bər\ *n* [F *sabre*] : a cavalry sword with a curved blade and thick back

saber saw *n* : a portable electric saw with a pointed reciprocating blade; *esp* : JIGSAW

sa·ble \'sā-bəl\ *n, pl* **sables** **1** : the color black **2** *pl* : mourning garments **3** : a dark brown mammal chiefly of northern Asia related to the weasels; *also* : its fur or pelt

¹**sab·o·tage** \'sa-bə-,täzh\ *n* [F] **1** : deliberate destruction of an employer's property or hindering of production by workers **2** : destructive or hampering action by enemy agents or sympathizers in time of war

²**sabotage** *vb* **-taged; -tag·ing** : to practice sabotage on : WRECK

sab·o·teur \,sa-bə-'tər\ *n* : a person who practices sabotage

sac \'sak\ *n* : a pouch in an animal or plant often containing a fluid

SAC *abbr* Strategic Air Command

sac·cha·rin \'sa-kə-rən\ *n* : a white crystalline compound used as an artificial calorie-free sweetener

sac·cha·rine \'sa-kə-rən\ *adj* ♦ : nauseatingly sweet ⟨∼ poetry⟩

♦ corny, maudlin, mawkish, mushy, sappy, schmaltzy, sentimental — more at CORNY

sac·er·do·tal \,sa-sər-'dōt-ᵊl, -kər-\ *adj* ♦ : of or relating to priests or a priesthood : PRIESTLY

♦ clerical, ministerial, pastoral, priestly — more at CLERICAL

sac·er·do·tal·ism \-ᵊl-,i-zəm\ *n* : a religious belief emphasizing the powers of priests as essential mediators between God and humankind

sa·chem \'sā-chəm\ *n* [Narragansett *sâchim*] : a No. American Indian chief

sa·chet \sa-'shā\ *n* [MF, fr. OF, dim. of *sac* bag] : a small bag filled with perfumed powder for scenting clothes

¹**sack** \'sak\ *n*   1 : a usu. rectangular-shaped bag (as of paper or burlap)   2 : a loose jacket or short coat   3 ♦ : a place for sleeping ⟨hit the ∼⟩

♦ bed, bunk, pad

²**sack** *vb* ♦ : to dismiss esp. summarily : FIRE

♦ cashier, dismiss, fire, remove, retire — more at DISMISS

³**sack** *n* [modif. of MF *sec* dry, fr. L *siccus*] : a white wine popular in England in the 16th and 17th centuries

⁴**sack** *vb* ♦ : to plunder a captured town

♦ despoil, loot, maraud, pillage, plunder, ransack, strip — more at RANSACK

sack·cloth \-,klȯth\ *n* : a rough garment worn as a sign of penitence

sac·ra·ment \'sa-krə-mənt\ *n*   1 : a formal religious act or rite; *esp* : one (as baptism or the Eucharist) held to have been instituted by Christ   2 : the elements of the Eucharist — **sac·ra·men·tal** \,sa-krə-'ment-ºl\ *adj*

sa·cred \'sā-krəd\ *adj*   1 ♦ : set apart for the service or worship of deity   2 : devoted exclusively to one service or use   3 ♦ : worthy of veneration or reverence   4 ♦ : of or relating to religion : RELIGIOUS — **sa·cred·ly** *adv* — **sa·cred·ness** *n*

♦ [1] blessed, hallowed, holy, sacrosanct, sanctified — more at HOLY ♦ [3] holy, inviolable, sacrosanct; *also* inviolate, pure; privileged, protected, shielded; exempt, immune ♦ [4] devotional, religious, spiritual — more at RELIGIOUS

sacred cow *n* : one that is often unreasonably immune from criticism

¹**sac·ri·fice** \'sa-krə-,fīs\ *n*   1 : the offering of something precious to deity   2 ♦ : something offered in sacrifice   3 : LOSS, DEPRIVATION   4 : a bunt allowing a base runner to advance while the batter is put out; *also* : a fly ball allowing a runner to score after the catch — **sac·ri·fi·cial** \,sa-krə-'fi-shəl\ *adj* — **sac·ri·fi·cial·ly** *adv*

♦ victim; *also* holocaust; contribution, donation

²**sac·ri·fice** *vb* -ficed; -fic·ing   1 ♦ : to offer up or kill as a sacrifice   2 : to accept the loss or destruction of for an end, cause, or ideal   3 : to make a sacrifice in baseball

♦ offer; *also* consecrate, dedicate, devote; give, surrender, yield

sac·ri·lege \'sa-krə-lij\ *n* [ME, fr. OF, fr. L *sacrilegium*, fr. *sacrilegus* one who steals sacred things, fr. *sacr-*, *sacer* sacred + *legere* to gather, steal]   1 ♦ : violation of something consecrated to God   2 ♦ : gross irreverence toward a hallowed person, place, or thing

♦ [1, 2] blasphemy, defilement, desecration, impiety, irreverence — more at BLASPHEMY

sac·ri·le·gious \,sa-krə-'li-jəs, -'lē-\ *adj* ♦ : committing sacrilege : characterized by or involving sacrilege — **sac·ri·le·gious·ly** *adv*

♦ blasphemous, irreverent, profane

sac·ris·tan \'sa-krə-stən\ *n*   1 : a church officer in charge of the sacristy   2 : SEXTON

sac·ris·ty \'sa-krə-stē\ *n, pl* -ties : VESTRY

sac·ro·il·i·ac \,sa-krō-'i-lē-,ak\ *n* : the joint between the upper part of the hipbone and the sacrum

sac·ro·sanct \'sa-krō-,saŋkt\ *adj*   1 ♦ : most sacred or holy   2 ♦ : treated as if holy : immune from criticism

♦ [1] blessed, hallowed, holy, sacred, sanctified — more at HOLY ♦ [2] holy, inviolable, sacred — more at SACRED

sa·crum \'sā-krəm, 'sa-\ *n, pl* **sa·cra** \'sa-krə, 'sā-\ : the part of the vertebral column that is directly connected with or forms a part of the pelvis and in humans consists of five fused vertebrae

sad \'sad\ *adj* **sad·der; sad·dest**   1 ♦ : affected with or expressive of grief or unhappiness : DOWNCAST   2 ♦ : causing sorrow   3 : DULL, SOMBER

♦ [1] bad, blue, dejected, depressed, disconsolate, down, downcast, droopy, forlorn, gloomy, glum, low, melancholy, miserable, mournful, sorrowful, sorry, unhappy, woeful, wretched; *also* aggrieved, distressed, troubled; despairing, hopeless; disappointed, discouraged, disheartened, dispirited; suicidal; dolorous, lugubrious, plaintive, tearful; regretful, rueful; grieving, wailing, weeping; black, bleak, cheerless, dark, darkening, depressing, desolate, dismal, drear, dreary, funereal, gray, morbid, morose, murky, saturnine, somber, sullen *Ant* cheerful, chipper, glad, happy, joyful, joyous, sunny, upbeat ♦ [2] depressing, dismal, dreary, heartbreaking, melancholy, pathetic, sorry, tearful; *also* discomforting, discomposing, disquieting, distressing, perturbing; affecting, moving, poignant, touching; discouraging, disheartening, dispiriting *Ant* cheering, cheery, glad, happy

sad·den \'sad-ºn\ *vb* ♦ : to make or become sad

♦ burden, depress, oppress — more at DEPRESS

¹**sad·dle** \'sad-ºl\ *n* : a usu. padded leather-covered seat (as for a rider on horseback)

²**saddle** *vb* **sad·dled; sad·dling**   1 : to put a saddle on   2 ♦ : to place a burden or encumbrance upon : BURDEN

♦ burden, encumber, load, lumber, weight — more at LOAD

sad·dle·bow \'sad-ºl-,bō\ *n* : the arch in the front of a saddle

saddle horse *n* : a horse suited for or trained for riding

Sad·du·cee \'sa-jə-,sē, 'sa-dyə-\ *n* : a member of an ancient Jewish sect consisting of a ruling class of priests and rejecting certain doctrines — **Sad·du·ce·an** \,sa-jə-'sē-ən, ,sa-dyə-\ *adj*

sa·dism \'sā-,di-zəm, 'sa-\ *n*   1 : a sexual perversion in which gratification is obtained by inflicting physical or mental pain on others   2 ♦ : delight in physical or mental cruelty; *also* : excessive cruelty — **sa·dist** \'sā-dist, 'sa-\ *n*

♦ barbarity, brutality, cruelty, inhumanity, savagery, viciousness, wantonness — more at CRUELTY

sa·dis·tic \sə-'dis-tik\ *adj* ♦ : of or characterized by sadism — **sa·dis·ti·cal·ly** \-ti-k(ə-)lē\ *adv*

♦ barbarous, brutal, cruel, heartless, inhumane, savage, vicious, wanton — more at CRUEL

sad·ly *adv* ♦ : in a sad manner or way

♦ agonizingly, bitterly, grievously, hard, hardly, sorrowfully, unhappily, woefully, wretchedly — more at HARD

sad·ness *n* ♦ : the quality or state of being sad : an instance (as a mood or an appearance) of being sad

♦ blues, dejection, depression, desolation, despondency, doldrums, dumps, forlornness, gloom, heartsickness, melancholy; *also* melancholia, self-pity; anguish, dolor, grief, sorrow; mournfulness; agony, distress, pain; misery, woe, wretchedness; discouragement; moodiness; despair, desperation, hopelessness; boredom, ennui, tedium *Ant* elation, euphoria, exuberance, gladness, happiness, joy, joyousness, jubilation

SAE *abbr*   1 self-addressed envelope   2 Society of Automotive Engineers   3 stamped addressed envelope

sa·fa·ri \sə-'fär-ē, -'far-\ *n* [Swahili, trip, fr. Ar *safarī* of a trip]   1 : a hunting expedition esp. in eastern Africa   2 : JOURNEY, TRIP

¹**safe** \'sāf\ *adj* **saf·er; saf·est**   1 ♦ : free from harm or risk   2 ♦ : secure from danger or loss   3 : affording safety   4 ♦ : not likely to take risks; *also* : RELIABLE   5 ♦ : not threatening danger — **safe·ly** *adv*

♦ [1, 2] all right, alright, secure; *also* hale, healthy, intact, sound, well, whole; uninjured, unscathed *Ant* endangered, imperiled, insecure, liable, threatened, unsafe, vulnerable ♦ [4] dependable, good, reliable, responsible, solid, steady, sure, tried, true, trustworthy — more at DEPENDABLE ♦ [5] harmless, innocent, innocuous, white — more at HARMLESS

²**safe** *n* : a container for keeping articles (as valuables) safe

safe–con·duct \-'kän-(,)dəkt\ *n* : a pass permitting a person to go through enemy lines

¹**safe·guard** \-,gärd\ *n* ♦ : a measure or device for preventing accident

♦ aegis, armor (*or* armour), cover, defense (*or* defence), guard, protection, screen, security, shield, wall, ward — more at DEFENSE

²**safeguard** *vb* ♦ : to provide a safeguard for : PROTECT

♦ cover, defend, guard, protect, screen, secure, shield, ward — more at DEFEND

safe·keep·ing \'sāf-'kē-piŋ\ *n* ♦ : a keeping or being kept in safety

♦ care, custody, guardianship, keeping, trust, ward — more at CUSTODY

safe sex *n* : sexual activity and esp. sexual intercourse in which various measures (as the use of latex condoms) are taken to avoid disease (as AIDS) transmitted by sexual contact

safe·ty \'sāf-tē\ *n, pl* **safeties** **1** : freedom from danger : SECURITY **2** : a protective device **3** : a football play in which the ball is downed by the offensive team behind its own goal line **4** : a defensive football back in the deepest position — **safety** *adj*

safety glass *n* : shatter-resistant material formed of two sheets of glass with a sheet of clear plastic between them

safety match *n* : a match that ignites only when struck on a special surface

saf·flow·er \'sa-,flaù-ər\ *n* : a widely grown Old World herb related to the daisies that has large orange or red flower heads yielding a dyestuff and seeds rich in edible oil

saf·fron \'sa-frən\ *n* : a deep orange powder from the flower of a crocus used to color and flavor foods

¹**sag** \'sag\ *vb* **sagged; sag·ging** **1** : to droop or settle from or as if from pressure **2** ♦ : to lose firmness or vigor

♦ decay, droop, fail, flag, go, lag, languish, waste, weaken, wilt — more at WEAKEN

²**sag** *n* **1** : a sagging part **2** ♦ : an instance or amount of sagging

♦ droop, slack, slackness; *also* laxity, laxness, looseness

sa·ga \'sä-gə\ *n* [ON] : a narrative of heroic deeds; *esp* : one recorded in Iceland in the 12th and 13th centuries

sa·ga·cious \sə-'gā-shəs\ *adj* ♦ : of keen mind

♦ discerning, insightful, perceptive, sage, sapient, wise — more at WISE

sa·gac·i·ty \-'ga-sə-tē\ *n* ♦ : the quality of being sagacious

♦ discernment, insight, perception, sapience, wisdom — more at WISDOM

sag·a·more \'sa-gə-,mōr\ *n* : a subordinate No. American Indian chief

¹**sage** \'sāj\ *adj* [ME, fr. AF, fr. VL *sapius*, fr. L *sapere* to taste, have good taste, be wise] ♦ : wise through reflection and experience; *also* : proceeding from or characterized by wisdom, prudence, and good judgment — **sage·ly** *adv*

♦ discerning, insightful, perceptive, sagacious, sapient, wise — more at WISE

²**sage** *n* : one who is distinguished for wisdom

³**sage** *n* [ME, fr. AF *sage, salge*, fr. L *salvia*, fr. *salvus* healthy; fr. its use as a medicinal herb] **1** : a perennial mint with aromatic leaves used in flavoring; *also* : its leaves **2** : SAGEBRUSH

sage·brush \'sāj-,brəsh\ *n* : any of several low shrubby No. American composite plants; *esp* : one of the western U.S. with a sagelike odor

Sag·it·tar·i·us \,sa-jə-'ter-ē-əs\ *n* [L, lit., archer] **1** : a zodiacal constellation between Scorpio and Capricorn usu. pictured as a centaur archer **2** : the 9th sign of the zodiac in astrology; *also* : one born under this sign

sa·go \'sā-gō\ *n, pl* **sagos** : a dry granulated starch esp. from the pith of various tropical palms (**sago palm**)

sa·gua·ro \sə-'wär-ə, -'gwär-, -ō\ *n, pl* **-ros** [MexSp] : a tall columnar usu. sparsely-branched cactus of dry areas

of the southwestern U.S. and Mexico that may attain a height of up to 50 feet (16 meters)

said *past and past part of* SAY

¹**sail** \'sāl\ *n* **1** : a piece of fabric by means of which the wind is used to propel a ship **2** : a sailing ship **3** : something resembling a sail **4** ♦ : a trip on a sailboat

♦ crossing, cruise, passage, voyage

²**sail** *vb* **1** ♦ : to travel on a sailing ship **2** : to pass over in a ship **3** : to manage or direct the course of a ship **4** ♦ : to move with ease, grace, nonchalance, or without resistance **5** ♦ : to travel on water; *also* : to move through the air

♦ [1] boat, cruise, navigate, voyage; *also* yacht; coast; log ♦ [4] bowl, breeze, coast, drift, flow, glide, roll, skim, slide, slip, stream, sweep, whisk — more at FLOW ♦ [5] drift, float, glide, hang, hover, poise, ride, waft — more at FLOAT

sail·board \'sāl-,bōrd\ *n* : a modified surfboard having a mast and sailed by a standing person

sail·boat \-,bōt\ *n* : a boat propelled primarily by sail

sail·cloth \-,klòth\ *n* : a heavy canvas used for sails, tents, or upholstery

sail·fish \-,fish\ *n* : any of a genus of large marine bony fishes with a large dorsal fin that are related to marlins

sail·ing *n* : the sport of handling or riding in a sailboat

sail·or \'sā-lər\ *n* ♦ : one that sails; *esp* : a member of a ship's crew

♦ gob, jack, jack-tar, mariner, seaman, swab, tar; *also* crewman, deckhand

sail·plane \'sāl-,plān\ *n* : a glider designed to rise in an upward air current

saint \'sānt, *before a name* (,)sānt *or* sənt\ *n* **1** : one officially recognized as preeminent for holiness **2** : one of the spirits of the departed in heaven **3** : a holy or godly person

Saint Ber·nard \-bər-'närd\ *n* : any of a Swiss alpine breed of tall powerful working dogs used esp. formerly in aiding lost travelers

saint·ed \-'sān-təd\ *adj* ♦ : relating to, resembling, or befitting a saint; *esp* : marked by or showing reverence for deity and devotion to divine worship

♦ devout, faithful, godly, holy, pious, religious, saintly — more at HOLY

saint·hood \-,hùd\ *n* ♦ : the quality or state of being a saint

♦ blessedness, devoutness, godliness, holiness, piety, sanctity — more at HOLINESS

Saint–John's–wort \'sānt-'jänz-,wərt, -,wòrt\ *n* **1** : any of a genus of herbs and shrubs with showy yellow flowers **2** : the dried aerial parts of a Saint-John's-wort used esp. in herbal remedies

saint·li·ness \-lē-nəs\ *n* : the quality or state of being saintly

saint·ly \'sānt-lē\ *adj* ♦ : relating to, resembling, or befitting a saint ⟨~ zeal⟩

♦ devout, faithful, godly, holy, pious, religious, sainted — more at HOLY

Saint Val·en·tine's Day \-'va-lən-,tīnz-\ *n* : VALENTINE'S DAY

¹**sake** \'sāk\ *n* **1** : END, PURPOSE **2** : personal or social welfare, safety, or well-being

²**sa·ke** *or* **sa·ki** \'sä-kē\ *n* : a Japanese alcoholic beverage of fermented rice

sa·laam \sə-'läm\ *n* [Ar *salām*, lit., peace] **1** : a salutation or ceremonial greeting in the East **2** : an obeisance performed by bowing very low and placing the right palm on the forehead — **salaam** *vb*

sa·la·cious \sə-'lā-shəs\ *adj* **1** : arousing sexual desire or imagination **2** : LUSTFUL — **sa·la·cious·ly** *adv* — **sa·la·cious·ness** *n*

sal·ad \'sa-ləd\ *n* : a cold dish (as of lettuce, vegetables, fish, eggs, or fruit) served with dressing

sal·a·man·der \'sa-lə-,man-dər\ *n* : any of numerous amphibians that look like lizards but have scaleless usu. smooth moist skin

sa·la·mi \sə-'lä-mē\ *n* [It] : a highly seasoned sausage of pork and beef

sal·a·ry \'sa-lə-rē\ *n, pl* **-ries** [ME *salarie,* fr. L *salarium* pension, salary, fr. neut. of *salarius* of salt, fr. *sal* salt] ♦ : payment made at regular intervals for services

♦ emolument, hire, pay, payment, stipend, wage — more at WAGE

sale \'sāl\ *n* 1 ♦ : transfer of ownership of property from one person to another in return for money 2 : ready market : DEMAND 3 : AUCTION 4 : a selling of goods at bargain prices — **sal·able** *or* **sale·able** \'sā-lə-bəl\ *adj*

♦ deal, trade, transaction; *also* auction; haggle, negotiation; bargain, buy; purchase; clearance; fair; garage sale, rummage sale, yard sale

sales·girl \'sālz-ˌgərl\ *n* : SALESWOMAN

sales·man \-mən\ *n* : one who sells in a given territory, in a store, or by telephone — **sales·man·ship** *n*

sales·per·son \-ˌpər-sən\ *n* : a salesman or saleswoman

sales·wom·an \-ˌwu̇-mən\ *n* : a woman who sells in a given territory, in a store, or by telephone

sal·i·cyl·ic acid \ˌsa-lə-ˌsi-lik-\ *n* : a crystalline organic acid used in making aspirin and other medicinal preparations (as skin lotions)

¹sa·lient \'sāl-yənt, 'sā-lē-ənt\ *adj* : jutting forward beyond a line; *also* : PROMINENT ⟨a ~ feature⟩

²salient *n* : a projecting part in a line of defense

¹sa·line \'sā-ˌlēn, -ˌlīn\ *adj* ♦ : consisting of or containing salt : SALTY — **sa·lin·i·ty** \sā-'li-nə-tē, sə-\ *n*

♦ briny, salty — more at SALTY

²saline *n* 1 : a metallic salt esp. with a purgative action 2 : a saline solution

sa·li·va \sə-'lī-və\ *n* ♦ : a liquid secreted into the mouth that helps digestion — **sal·i·vary** \'sa-lə-ˌver-ē\ *adj*

♦ slobber, spit; *also* foam, froth; expectoration, sputum

sal·i·vate \'sa-lə-ˌvāt\ *vb* **-vat·ed; -vat·ing** ♦ : to produce saliva esp. in excess — **sal·i·va·tion** \ˌsa-lə-'vā-shən\ *n*

♦ dribble, drivel, drool, slaver, slobber — more at DROOL

sal·low \'sa-lō\ *adj* ♦ : of a yellowish sickly color ⟨a ~ face⟩

♦ cadaverous, green, lurid, pale, pasty, peaked, sickly — more at SICKLY

¹sal·ly \'sa-lē\ *n, pl* **sallies** 1 : a rushing attack on besiegers by troops of a besieged place 2 ♦ : a witty remark or retort 3 ♦ : a brief excursion

♦ [2] crack, gag, jest, joke, laugh, pleasantry, quip, waggery, wisecrack, witticism — more at JOKE ♦ [3] excursion, jaunt, junket, outing — more at EXCURSION

²sally *vb* **sal·lied; sal·ly·ing** 1 : to leap out or burst forth suddenly 2 ♦ : to start out on a course or a journey — often used with *forth*

♦ *usu* **sally forth** clear out, depart, exit, get off, go, move, pull, quit, shove, take off — more at GO

salm·on \'sa-mən\ *n, pl* **salmon** *also* **salmons** 1 : any of several bony fishes with pinkish flesh that are used for food and are related to the trouts 2 : a strong yellowish pink color

sal·mo·nel·la \ˌsal-mə-'ne-lə\ *n, pl* **-nel·lae** \-'ne-(ˌ)lē, -ˌlī\ *or* **-nellas** *or* **-nella** : any of a genus of rod-shaped bacteria that cause various illnesses (as food poisoning)

sa·lon \sə-'län, 'sa-ˌlän, sa-'lōⁿ\ *n* [F] 1 : an elegant drawing room 2 ♦ : a fashionable shop ⟨beauty ~⟩

♦ establishment, place — more at PLACE

sa·loon \sə-'lün\ *n* 1 : a large public cabin on a ship 2 ♦ : a place where liquors are sold and drunk : BARROOM 3 *Brit* : SEDAN 2

♦ bar, barroom, café, pub, public house, tavern — more at BARROOM

sal·sa \'sȯl-sə, 'säl-\ *n* : a spicy sauce of tomatoes, onions, and hot peppers

¹salt \'sȯlt\ *n* 1 : a white crystalline substance that consists of sodium and chlorine and is used in seasoning foods 2 : a saltlike cathartic substance (as Epsom salts) 3 : a compound formed usu. by action of an acid on metal 4 : one that sails : SAILOR — **salt·i·ness** \'sȯl-tē-nəs\ *n*

²salt *vb* : to preserve, season, or feed with salt

³salt *adj* : preserved or treated with salt; *also* : SALTY

SALT *abbr* Strategic Arms Limitation Talks

salt away *vb* ♦ : to lay away safely

♦ cache, hoard, lay away, lay up, put by, stash, stockpile, store — more at HOARD

salt·box \'sȯlt-ˌbäks\ *n* : a frame dwelling with two stories in front and one behind and a long sloping roof

salt·cel·lar \-ˌse-lər\ *n* : a small container for holding salt at the table

sal·tine \sȯl-'tēn\ *n* : a thin crisp cracker sprinkled with salt

salt lick *n* : LICK 5

salt·pe·ter \'sȯlt-'pē-tər\ *n* [ME *salt petre,* alter. of *salpetre,* fr. MF, fr. ML *sal petrae,* lit., salt of the rock] 1 : POTASSIUM NITRATE 2 : SODIUM NITRATE

salt·wa·ter \-ˌwȯ-tər, -ˌwä-\ *adj* : of, relating to, or living in salt water

salty \'sȯl-tē\ *adj* **salt·i·er; -est** 1 ♦ : of, seasoned with, or containing salt 2 : suggesting the sea or nautical life 3 ♦ : marked by uncultivated vulgarity

♦ [1] briny, saline; *also* brackish ♦ [3] racy, spicy, suggestive

sa·lu·bri·ous \sə-'lü-brē-əs\ *adj* ♦ : favorable to health

♦ healthful, healthy, restorative, salutary, wholesome — more at HEALTHFUL

sal·u·tary \'sal-yə-ˌter-ē\ *adj* ♦ : health-giving; *also* : BENEFICIAL

♦ advantageous, beneficial, favorable (*or* favourable), helpful, profitable — more at BENEFICIAL ♦ healthful, healthy, restorative, salubrious, wholesome — more at HEALTHFUL

sal·u·ta·tion \ˌsal-yə-'tā-shən\ *n* ♦ : an expression of greeting, goodwill, or courtesy usu. by word or gesture; *also* : a speech of honor or praise

♦ greeting, hello, salute — more at HELLO ♦ accolade, citation, commendation, encomium, eulogy, homage, paean, panegyric, tribute — more at ENCOMIUM

sa·lu·ta·to·ri·an \sə-ˌlü-tə-'tōr-ē-ən\ *n* : the student having the 2d highest rank in a graduating class who delivers the salutatory address

sa·lu·ta·to·ry \sə-'lü-tə-ˌtōr-ē\ *adj* : relating to or being the welcoming oration delivered at an academic commencement

¹sa·lute \sə-'lüt\ *vb* **sa·lut·ed; sa·lut·ing** 1 : GREET 2 : to honor by special ceremonies 3 : to show respect to (a superior officer) by a formal position of hand, rifle, or sword 4 ♦ : to express commendation of

♦ acclaim, applaud, cheer, crack up, hail, laud, praise, tout — more at ACCLAIM

²salute *n* 1 : an expression of greeting, goodwill, or courtesy by word, gesture, or ceremony : GREETING 2 : the formal position assumed in saluting a superior

¹sal·vage \'sal-vij\ *n* 1 : money paid for saving a ship, its cargo, or passengers when the ship is wrecked or in danger 2 : the saving of a ship 3 : the saving of possessions in danger of being lost 4 : things saved from loss or destruction (as by a wreck or fire)

²salvage *vb* **sal·vaged; sal·vag·ing** : to rescue from destruction

sal·va·tion \sal-'vā-shən\ *n* 1 : the saving of a person from sin or its consequences esp. in the life after death 2 ♦ : the saving from danger, difficulty, or evil 3 : something that saves ⟨tourism became the island's ~⟩

♦ deliverance, rescue; *also* ransom, recovery, redemption; extrication

¹salve \'sav, 'sav\ *n* 1 : a medicinal substance applied to the skin 2 : a soothing influence

²**salve** *vb* **salved; salv·ing** : EASE, SOOTHE

sal·ver \'sal-vər\ *n* [F *salve*, fr. Sp *salva* sampling of food to detect poison, tray, fr. *salvar* to save, sample food to detect poison, fr. LL *salvare* to save, fr. L *salvus* safe] : a small serving tray

sal·vo \'sal-vō\ *n, pl* **salvos** *or* **salvoes** ♦ : a simultaneous discharge of guns; *also* : something suggestive of a salvo

♦ barrage, bombardment, cannonade, fusillade, hail, shower, storm, volley — more at BARRAGE

Sam *or* **Saml** *abbr* Samuel

SAM \'sam, ,es-,ā-'em\ *n* [*s*urface-to-*a*ir *m*issile] : a guided missile for use against aircraft by ground units

Sa·mar·i·tan \sə-'mer-ə-tən\ *n* **1** : a native or inhabitant of Samaria **2** : a person who is generous in helping those in distress

sa·mar·i·um \sə-'mer-ē-əm\ *n* : a silvery-white lustrous rare metallic chemical element

¹**same** \'sām\ *adj* **1** ♦ : being the one referred to : not different **2** ♦ : resembling in every relevant respect

♦ [1] identical, selfsame, very *Ant* another, different, other ♦ [2] duplicate, equal, even, identical, indistinguishable; *also* akin, alike, analogous, comparable, correspondent, corresponding, equivalent, like, matching, parallel, similar, such, suchlike, tantamount *Ant* different, dissimilar, distinguishable, other, unalike, unlike

²**same** *pron* : the same one or ones

³**same** *adv* : in the same manner

same·ness *n* ♦ : the quality or state of being the same; *also* : tedious similarity

♦ equality, equivalence, par, parity — more at EQUIVALENCE

same–sex \'sām-'seks\ *adj* : of, relating to, or involving members of the same sex

Sa·mi *also* **Saa·mi** \'sä-mē\ *n, pl* **Sami** *or* **Samis** *also* **Saami** *or* **Saamis** : a member of a people of northern Scandinavia, Finland, and the Kola Peninsula of Russia

Sa·mo·an \sə-'mō-ən\ *n* : a native or inhabitant of Samoa — **Samoan** *adj*

sa·mo·sa \sə-'mō-sə\ *n* : a small triangular pastry filled with spiced meat or vegetables and fried

sam·o·var \'sa-mə-,vär\ *n* [Russ, fr. *samo-* self + *varit'* to boil] : an urn with a spigot at the base used esp. in Russia to boil water for tea

sam·pan \'sam-,pan\ *n* : a flat-bottomed skiff of eastern Asia usu. propelled by two short oars

¹**sam·ple** \'sam-pəl\ *n* ♦ : a representative piece, item, or set of individuals that shows the quality or nature of the whole from which it was taken : EXAMPLE

♦ case, example, exemplar, illustration, instance, representative, specimen — more at EXAMPLE

²**sample** *vb* **sam·pled; sam·pling** : to judge the quality of by a sample

sam·pler \'sam-plər\ *n* **1** : a piece of needlework; *esp* : one testing skill in embroidering **2** : a collection of various examples of something ⟨a chocolate ∼⟩

Sam·u·el \'sam-yə-wəl\ *n* : either of two books of Jewish and Christian Scripture

sam·u·rai \'sa-mə-,rī, 'sam-yə-\ *n, pl* **samurai** : a military retainer of a Japanese feudal lord who adhered to strict principles of honor and duty

san·a·to·ri·um \,sa-nə-'tōr-ē-əm\ *n, pl* **-ri·ums** *or* **-ria** \-ē-ə\ **1** : a health resort **2** : an establishment for the care esp. of convalescents or the chronically ill

sanc·ti·fi·ca·tion \,saŋk-tə-fə-'kā-shən\ *n* ♦ : an act of sanctifying; *also* : the state of being sanctified

♦ blessing, consecration — more at CONSECRATION

sanc·ti·fied *adj* ♦ : made holy : made free of sin; *also* : set apart to sacred duty or use

♦ blessed, hallowed, holy, sacred, sacrosanct — more at HOLY

sanc·ti·fy \'saŋk-tə-,fī\ *vb* **-fied; -fy·ing** **1** ♦ : to make holy : CONSECRATE **2** ♦ : to free from sin

♦ [1] bless, consecrate, hallow — more at BLESS
♦ [2] purify

sanc·ti·mo·nious \,saŋk-tə-'mō-nē-əs\ *adj* : hypocritically pious ⟨∼ politicians⟩ — **sanc·ti·mo·nious·ly** *adv*

¹**sanc·tion** \'saŋk-shən\ *n* **1** ♦ : authoritative approval **2** : a measure (as a threat or fine) designed to enforce a law or standard ⟨economic ∼s⟩

♦ allowance, authorization, clearance, concurrence, consent, leave, license (*or* licence), permission, sufferance — more at PERMISSION

²**sanction** *vb* ♦ : to give approval to : RATIFY

♦ approve, authorize, clear, OK, ratify, warrant — more at APPROVE

sanc·ti·ty \'saŋk-tə-tē\ *n, pl* **-ties** **1** ♦ : holiness of life and character **2** : GODLINESS **2** : SACREDNESS

♦ blessedness, devoutness, godliness, holiness, piety, sainthood — more at HOLINESS

sanc·tu·ary \'saŋk-chə-,wer-ē\ *n, pl* **-ar·ies** **1** : a consecrated place (as the part of a church in which the altar is placed) **2** ♦ : a place of refuge ⟨bird ∼⟩

♦ asylum, haven, refuge, retreat, shelter

sanc·tum \'saŋk-təm\ *n, pl* **sanctums** *also* **sanc·ta** \-tə\ : a private office or study : DEN ⟨an editor's ∼⟩

¹**sand** \'sand\ *n* **1** : loose particles of hard broken rock **2** : a yellowish-gray color

²**sand** *vb* **1** : to cover or fill with sand **2** ♦ : to scour, smooth, or polish with an abrasive (as sandpaper) — **sand·er** *n*

♦ buff, file, grind, hone, rasp, rub — more at GRIND

san·dal \'sand-°l\ *n* : a shoe consisting of a sole strapped to the foot; *also* : a low or open slipper or rubber overshoe

san·dal·wood \-,wùd\ *n* : the fragrant yellowish heartwood of a parasitic tree of southern Asia that is much used in ornamental carving and cabinetwork; *also* : the tree

sand·bag \'sand-,bag\ *n* : a bag filled with sand and used in fortifications, as ballast, or as a weapon

sand·bank \-,baŋk\ *n* : a deposit of sand (as in a bar or shoal)

sand·bar \-,bär\ *n* : a ridge of sand formed in water by tides or currents

sand·blast \-,blast\ *vb* : to treat with a stream of sand blown (as for cleaning stone) by compressed air — **sand·blast·er** *n*

sand dollar *n* : any of numerous flat circular sea urchins living chiefly on sandy bottoms in shallow water

S & H *abbr* shipping and handling

sand·hog \'sand-,hóg, -,häg\ *n* : a laborer who builds underwater tunnels

sand·lot \-,lät\ *n* : a vacant lot esp. when used for the unorganized sports of children — **sand·lot** *adj* — **sand·lot·ter** *n*

sand·man \-,man\ *n* : the genie of folklore who makes children sleepy

sand·pa·per \-,pā-pər\ *n* : paper with abrasive (as sand) glued on one side used in smoothing and polishing surfaces — **sandpaper** *vb*

sand·pip·er \-,pī-pər\ *n* : any of various shorebirds with a soft-tipped bill longer than that of the related plovers

sand·stone \-,stōn\ *n* : rock made of sand united by a natural cement

sand·storm \-,stórm\ *n* : a windstorm that drives clouds of sand

sand trap *n* : a hazard on a golf course consisting of a hollow containing sand

¹**sand·wich** \'sand-wich\ *n* [after John Montagu, 4th Earl of *Sandwich* †1792 Eng. diplomat] **1** : two or more slices of bread with a layer (as of meat or cheese) spread between them **2** : something resembling a sandwich

²**sandwich** *vb* ♦ : to squeeze or crowd in

♦ cram, crowd, jam, ram, squeeze, stuff, wedge — more at CROWD

sandy *adj* **sand·i·er; -est** **1** : consisting of or containing sand **2** ♦ : of the color sand

♦ blond, fair, flaxen, golden, straw — more at BLOND

sane \'sān\ *adj* **san·er; san·est** 1 ♦ : mentally sound and healthy 2 : proceeding from a sound mind : SENSIBLE, RATIONAL — **sane·ly** *adv*

♦ balanced, clearheaded, lucid, normal, right, stable; *also* clear, logical, rational, reasonable; judicious, levelheaded, sensible, wise; healthy, sound *Ant* crazed, crazy, demented, deranged, insane, lunatic, mad, maniacal, mental, unbalanced, unsound

sang *past of* SING

sang-froid \'sä-'frwä\ *n* [F *sang-froid*, lit., cold blood] : self-possession or an imperturbable state esp. under strain

san·gui·nary \'saŋ-gwə-,ner-ē\ *adj* ♦ : willing or anxious to shed blood; *also* : marked by bloodshed ⟨∼ battle⟩

♦ bloodthirsty, bloody, homicidal, murderous, sanguine — more at BLOODTHIRSTY

san·guine \'saŋ-gwən\ *adj* 1 ♦ : having a healthy reddish color : RUDDY 2 ♦ : anticipating the best ⟨a ∼ disposition⟩ 3 : willing or anxious to shed blood

♦ [1] florid, flush, glowing, rosy, ruddy — more at RUDDY ♦ [2] assured, certain, clear, cocksure, confident, doubtless, positive, sure — more at CERTAIN

sanit *abbr* sanitary; sanitation

san·i·tar·i·an \,sa-nə-'ter-ē-ən\ *n* : a specialist in sanitation and public health

san·i·tar·i·um \,sa-nə-'ter-ē-əm\ *n, pl* **-i·ums** *or* **-ia** \-ē-ə\ : SANATORIUM

san·i·tary \'sa-nə-,ter-ē\ *adj* 1 : of or relating to health : HYGIENIC 2 ♦ : free from filth or infective matter

♦ aseptic, hygienic, sterile; *also* antibacterial, antibiotic, antiseptic, germicidal; clean, immaculate, spick-and-span, spotless, stainless, unsoiled, unsullied; beneficial, healthful, healthy, restorative, salubrious, salutary, wholesome *Ant* unhygienic, unsanitary

sanitary napkin *n* : a disposable absorbent pad used to absorb uterine flow (as during menstruation)

san·i·ta·tion \,sa-nə-'tā-shən\ *n* : the act or process of making sanitary; *also* : protection of health by maintenance of sanitary conditions

san·i·tize \'sa-nə-,tīz\ *vb* **-tized; -tiz·ing** 1 : to make sanitary 2 : to make more acceptable by removing unpleasant features

san·i·ty \'sa-nə-tē\ *n* ♦ : soundness of mind

♦ head, mind, reason, wit — more at MIND

sank *past of* SINK

sans \'sanz\ *prep* ♦ : deprived or destitute of : WITHOUT

♦ minus, wanting, without — more at WITHOUT

San·skrit \'san-,skrit\ *n* : an ancient language that is the classical language of India and of Hinduism — **Sanskrit** *adj*

San·ta Ana \,san-tə-'a-nə\ *n* [*Santa Ana* Mountains in southern Calif.] : a hot dry wind from the north, northeast, or east in southern California

¹**sap** \'sap\ *n* **1 a** : a vital fluid; *esp* : a watery fluid that circulates through a vascular plant **b** ♦ : bodily health and vigor **2** ♦ : a foolish gullible person — **sap·less** *adj*

♦ [1b] dash, energy, life, pep, vigor (*or* vigour), vim, vitality — more at VIGOR ♦ [2] dupe, gull, pigeon, sucker, tool — more at DUPE

²**sap** *vb* **sapped; sap·ping** 1 : UNDERMINE 2 ♦ : to weaken gradually

♦ debilitate, enervate, enfeeble, prostrate, soften, tire, waste, weaken — more at WEAKEN

sa·pi·ence \,sā-pē-əns\ *n* ♦ : keen and farsighted judgment : profound knowledge

♦ discernment, insight, perception, sagacity, wisdom — more at WISDOM

sa·pi·ent \'sā-pē-ənt, 'sa-\ *adj* ♦ : possessing or expressing great intelligence : WISE

♦ discerning, insightful, perceptive, sagacious, sage, wise — more at WISE

sap·ling \'sa-pliŋ\ *n* : a young tree

sap·phire \'sa-,fīr\ *n* : a hard transparent usu. rich blue gem

sap·py \'sa-pē\ *adj* **sap·pi·er; -est** 1 : full of sap 2 ♦ : overly sentimental 3 : lacking in good sense : SILLY, FOOLISH

♦ corny, maudlin, mawkish, mushy, saccharine, schmaltzy, sentimental — more at CORNY

sap·ro·phyte \'sa-prə-,fīt\ *n* : a living thing and esp. a plant living on dead or decaying organic matter — **sap·ro·phyt·ic** \,sa-prə-'fi-tik\ *adj*

sap·suck·er \'sap-,se-kər\ *n* : any of a genus of No. American woodpeckers

sap·wood \-,wud\ *n* : the younger active and usu. lighter and softer outer layer of wood (as of a tree trunk)

sar·casm \'sär-,ka-zəm\ *n* 1 ♦ : a cutting or contemptuous remark 2 : ironic criticism or reproach

♦ affront, barb, dart, dig, indignity, insult, name, offense, outrage, put-down, slight, slur, wound — more at INSULT

sar·cas·tic \sär-'kas-tik\ *adj* ♦ : having the character of sarcasm; *also* : given to the use of sarcasm — **sar·cas·ti·cal·ly** \-ti-k(ə-)lē\ *adv*

♦ acrid, biting, caustic, cutting, mordant, pungent, satiric, scathing, sharp, tart; *also* acid, acidic, cross, sour; incisive, trenchant; cynical, dry, ironic, wry; facetious, flippant, tongue-in-cheek; acrimonious, bitter, resentful; harsh, rough, severe, stringent; concise, crisp, curt, pithy, succinct, terse; backhanded, insincere

sar·co·ma \sär-'kō-mə\ *n, pl* **-mas** *also* **-ma·ta** \-mə-tə\ : a malignant tumor esp. of connective tissue, bone, cartilage, or striated muscle

sar·coph·a·gus \sär-'kä-fə-gəs\ *n, pl* **-gi** \-,gī, -,jī\ *also* **-gus·es** [L *sarcophagus* (*lapis*) limestone used for coffins, fr. Gk (*lithos*) *sarkophagos*, lit., flesh-eating stone, fr. *sark-, sarx* flesh + *phagein* to eat] : a large stone coffin

sar·dine \sär-'dēn\ *n, pl* **sardines** *also* **sardine** : a young or small fish preserved for use as food

sar·don·ic \sär-'dä-nik\ *adj* : disdainfully or skeptically humorous : derisively mocking : SARCASTIC — **sar·don·i·cal·ly** \-ni-k(ə-)lē\ *adv*

sa·ri *also* **sa·ree** \'sär-ē\ *n* [Hindi *sāṛī*] : a garment worn by women in southern Asia that consists of a long cloth draped around the body and head or shoulder

sa·rin \'sär-ən, zä-'rēn\ *n* : an extremely toxic chemical weapon used as a lethal nerve gas

sa·rong \sə-'rȯŋ, -'räŋ\ *n* : a loose garment wrapped around the body and worn by men and women of the Malay Archipelago and the Pacific islands

sar·sa·pa·ril·la \,sas-ə-pə-'ri-lə, ,särs-\ *n* **1** : the dried roots of a tropical American smilax used esp. for flavoring; *also* : the plant **2** : a sweetened carbonated beverage flavored with sassafras and an oil from a birch

sar·to·ri·al \sär-'tōr-ē-əl\ *adj* : of or relating to a tailor or tailored clothes — **sar·to·ri·al·ly** *adv*

SASE *abbr* self-addressed stamped envelope

¹**sash** \'sash\ *n* ♦ : a broad band worn around the waist or over the shoulder

♦ belt, cincture, cummerbund, girdle — more at BELT

²**sash** *n, pl* **sash** *also* **sash·es** : a frame for panes of glass in a door or window; *also* : the movable part of a window

sa·shay \sa-'shā\ *vb* 1 : WALK, GLIDE, GO 2 : to strut or move about in an ostentatious manner 3 : to proceed in a diagonal or sideways manner

Sask *abbr* Saskatchewan

Sas·quatch \'sas-,kwach, -,kwäch\ *n* [Halkomelem (American Indian language of British Columbia) *sésq̓əc*] : a large hairy humanlike creature reported to exist in the northwestern U.S. and western Canada

sas·sa·fras \'sa-sə-,fras\ *n* [Sp *sasafrás*] : an aromatic No. American tree related to the laurel; *also* : its carcinogenic dried root bark

sassy \'sa-sē\ *adj* **sass·i·er; -est** ♦ : marked by contemptuous or cocky boldness or disregard of others : SAUCY

♦ arch, bold, brash, brazen, cheeky, cocky, fresh, impertinent, impudent, insolent, nervy, saucy — more at NERVY

¹sat *past and past part of* SIT

²sat *abbr* **1** satellite **2** saturated

Sat *abbr* Saturday

Sa·tan \'sāt-ⁿn\ *n* : DEVIL

sa·tan·ic \sə-'ta-nik, sā-\ *adj* **1** ♦ : of or characteristic of Satan **2** ♦ : extremely malicious or wicked — **sa·tan·i·cal·ly** \-ni-k(ə-)lē\ *adv*

♦ [1, 2] demonic, devilish, diabolical, fiendish — more at FIENDISH

satch·el \'sa-chəl\ *n* : SUITCASE

sate \'sāt\ *vb* **sat·ed; sat·ing** ♦ : to satisfy to the full; *also* : GLUT

♦ assuage, quench, satiate, satisfy ♦ glut, gorge, stuff, surfeit — more at GORGE

sated *adj* ♦ : filled to the point of excess

♦ full, satiate, satiated — more at FULL

sa·teen \sa-'tēn, sə-\ *n* : a cotton cloth finished to resemble satin

sat·el·lite \'sat-ⁿl-ˌīt\ *n* [MF, fr. L *satelles* attendant] **1** : an obsequious follower of a distinguished person : TOADY **2** : a celestial body that orbits a larger body **3** : a manufactured object that orbits a celestial body

satellite dish *n* : a microwave dish for receiving usu. television transmissions from an orbiting satellite

sa·ti·ate \'sā-shē-ˌāt\ *vb* **-at·ed; -at·ing** ♦ : to satisfy fully or to excess

♦ assuage, quench, sate, satisfy

satiated *adj* ♦ : filled to satiety

♦ full, sated, satiate — more at FULL

sa·ti·ety \sə-'tī-ə-tē\ *n* : fullness to the point of excess

sat·in \'sat-ⁿn\ *n* : a fabric (as of silk) with a glossy surface

sat·in·wood \'sat-ⁿn-ˌwùd\ *n* : a hard yellowish brown wood of satiny luster; *also* : a tree yielding this wood

sat·iny *adj* ♦ : having or resembling the soft texture or lustrous smoothness of satin

♦ glossy, lustrous, polished, sleek — more at GLOSSY ♦ cottony, downy, silken, soft, velvety — more at SOFT

sat·ire \'sa-ˌtīr\ *n* : biting wit, irony, or sarcasm used to expose vice or folly; *also* : a literary work having these qualities — **sat·i·rist** \'sa-tə-rist\ *n* — **sat·i·rize** \-tə-ˌrīz\ *vb*

sa·tir·ic \sə-'tir-ik\ *or* **sa·tir·i·cal** \-i-kəl\ *adj* ♦ : of, relating to, or constituting satire; *also* : manifesting or given to satire — **sa·tir·i·cal·ly** *adv*

♦ acrid, biting, caustic, cutting, mordant, pungent, sarcastic, scathing, sharp, tart — more at SARCASTIC

sat·is·fac·tion \ˌsa-təs-'fak-shən\ *n* **1** : payment through penance of punishment incurred by sin **2** ♦ : the quality or state of being satisfied : GRATIFICATION **3** : reparation for an insult **4** ♦ : settlement of a claim

♦ [2] contentment, delectation, delight, enjoyment, gladness, gratification, pleasure, relish — more at PLEASURE ♦ [4] compensation, damages, indemnity, quittance, recompense, redress, remuneration, reparation, requital, restitution — more at COMPENSATION

sat·is·fac·to·ri·ly \-'fak-tə-rə-lē\ *adv* ♦ : in a satisfactory manner

♦ adequately, all right, fine, good, nicely, OK, passably, so-so, tolerably, well — more at WELL ♦ adequately, enough — more at ENOUGH

sat·is·fac·to·ry \-'fak-tə-rē\ *adj* ♦ : giving satisfaction; *also* : ADEQUATE

♦ agreeable, all right, alright, fine, good, OK, palatable; *also* delectable, delicious, delightful, dreamy, felicitous, gratifying, nice, pleasant, pleasing, scrumptious, welcome; acceptable, adequate, decent, passable, tolerable

Ant disagreeable, unsatisfactory ♦ acceptable, adequate, all right, decent, fine, OK, passable, respectable, tolerable — more at ADEQUATE

sat·is·fy \'sa-təs-ˌfī\ *vb* **-fied; -fy·ing** **1** : to answer or discharge (a claim) in full **2** ♦ : to make happy : GRATIFY **3** : to pay what is due to **4** ♦ : to bring (as by argument) to belief, consent, or a course of action : CONVINCE **5** ♦ : to meet the requirements of

♦ [2] content, delight, gladden, gratify, please, rejoice, suit, warm — more at PLEASE ♦ [4] argue, convince, get, induce, move, persuade, prevail, talk, win — more at PERSUADE ♦ [5] answer, comply, fill, fulfill, keep, meet, redeem — more at FULFILL

satisfying *adj* ♦ : giving satisfaction

♦ agreeable, congenial, delectable, delicious, delightful, dreamy, felicitous, good, grateful, gratifying, nice, palatable, pleasant, pleasurable ♦ cogent, compelling, conclusive, convincing, decisive, effective, forceful, persuasive, strong, telling — more at COGENT

sat·is·fy·ing·ly *adv* ♦ : in a pleasant way

♦ agreeably, delightfully, favorably (*or* favourably), felicitously, gloriously, nicely, pleasantly, pleasingly, splendidly, well

sa·trap \'sā-ˌtrap, 'sa-\ *n* [ME, fr. L *satrapes*, fr. Gk *satrapēs*, fr. OPer *khshathrapāvan*, lit., protector of the dominion] : a petty prince : a subordinate ruler

sat·u·rate \'sa-chə-ˌrāt\ *vb* **-rat·ed; -rat·ing** **1** ♦ : to soak thoroughly **2** : to treat or charge with something to the point where no more can be absorbed, dissolved, or retained — **sat·u·ra·ble** \'sa-chə-rə-bəl\ *adj* — **sat·u·ra·tion** \ˌsa-chə-'rā-shən\ *n*

♦ drench, drown, impregnate, soak, sop, souse, steep — more at SOAK

saturated *adj* **1** ♦ : full of moisture : made thoroughly wet **2** : being a solution that is unable to absorb or dissolve any more of a solute at a given temperature and pressure **3** *of a color* : having high saturation **4** : having no double or triple bonds between carbon atoms ⟨∼ fats⟩

♦ sodden, soggy, waterlogged, watery, wet — more at WET

Sat·ur·day \'sa-tər-dē, -ˌdā\ *n* : the 7th day of the week

Saturday night special *n* : a cheap easily concealed handgun

Sat·urn \'sa-tərn\ *n* : the planet 6th in order from the sun

sat·ur·nine \'sa-tər-ˌnīn\ *adj* : cold and steady in mood; *also* : of a gloomy or surly disposition : SULLEN

sa·tyr \'sā-tər\ *n* **1** *often cap* : a woodland deity in Greek mythology having certain characteristics of a horse or goat **2** : a lecherous man

¹sauce \'sòs, *3 usu* 'sas\ *n* **1** : a fluid dressing or topping for food **2** : stewed fruit **3** ♦ : pert or impudent language or actions

♦ back talk, cheek, impertinence, impudence, insolence — more at BACK TALK

²sauce \'sòs, *2 usu* 'sas\ *vb* **sauced; sauc·ing** **1** : to put sauce on; *also* : to add zest to **2** : to be impudent to

sauce·pan \'sòs-ˌpan\ *n* : a small deep cooking pan with a handle

sau·cer \'sò-sər\ *n* : a rounded shallow dish for use under a cup

sauc·i·ness \-sē-nəs\ *n* ♦ : the quality or state of being saucy

♦ audacity, brass, brazenness, cheek, chutzpah, effrontery, gall, nerve, presumption, sauce, temerity — more at EFFRONTERY

saucy \'sa-sē, 'sò-\ *adj* **sauc·i·er; -est** ♦ : impertinently bold and impudent — **sauc·i·ly** \-sə-lē\ *adv*

♦ arch, bold, brash, brazen, cheeky, cocky, fresh, impertinent, impudent, insolent, nervy, sassy — more at NERVY

Sau·di \'saù-dē, 'sò-; sä-'ü-dē\ *n* : SAUDI ARABIAN — **Saudi** *adj*

Saudi Arabian *n* : a native or inhabitant of Saudi Arabia — **Saudi Arabian** *adj*

sau·er·kraut \\'saů-ər-ˌkraůt\\ *n* [G, fr. *sauer* sour + *Kraut* greens] : finely cut cabbage fermented in brine

Sauk \\'sók\\ *or* **Sac** \\'sak, 'sók\\ *n*, *pl* **Sauk** *or* **Sauks** *or* **Sac** *or* **Sacs** : a member of an American Indian people formerly living in what is now Wisconsin

sau·na \\'só-nə, 'saů-nə\\ *n* **1** : a Finnish steam bath in which the steam is provided by water thrown on hot stones **2** : a dry heat bath; *also* : a room or cabinet used for such a bath

saun·ter \\'són-tər, 'sän-\\ *vb* : STROLL

sau·ro·pod \\'sór-ə-ˌpäd\\ *n* : any of a suborder of plant-eating dinosaurs (as a brontosaurus) with a long neck and tail and a small head — **sauropod** *adj*

sau·sage \\'só-sij\\ *n* [ME *sausige*, fr. AF *sauseche*, fr. LL *salsicia*, fr. L *salsus* salted] : minced and highly seasoned meat (as pork) usu. enclosed in a tubular casing

S Aust *abbr* South Australia

sau·té \\só-'tā, só-\\ *vb* **sau·téed** *or* **sau·téd**; **sau·té·ing** [F] : to fry lightly in a little fat — **sauté** *n*

sau·terne \\só-'tərn, só-\\ *n*, *often cap* : a usu. semisweet American white wine

¹sav·age \\'sa-vij\\ *adj* [ME, fr. AF *salvage, savage*, fr. LL *salvaticus*, alter. of L *silvaticus* of the woods, wild, fr. *silva* forest] **1** ♦ : not domesticated or under human control : WILD, UNTAMED **2** ♦ : lacking complex or advanced culture : UNCIVILIZED **3** ♦ : lacking the restraints normal to civilized human beings : FIERCE — **sav·age·ly** *adv*

♦ [1] feral, unbroken, undomesticated, untamed, wild — more at WILD ♦ [2] barbarous, heathen, heathenish, Neanderthal, rude, uncivil, uncivilized, uncultivated, wild; *also* coarse, crude, primitive, rough; uncouth, uncultured **Ant** civilized ♦ [3] barbarous, brutal, cruel, heartless, inhumane, sadistic, vicious, wanton — more at CRUEL ♦ [3] fell, ferocious, fierce, grim, vicious — more at FIERCE

²savage *n* **1** : a member of a primitive human society **2** ♦ : a rude, unmannerly, or brutal person

♦ beast, brute, devil, fiend, monster, villain

sav·age·ness *n* : the quality or state of being savage

sav·age·ry \\-rē\\ *n* **1 a** : the quality of being savage **b** ♦ : an act of cruelty or violence **2** : an uncivilized state

♦ barbarity, brutality, cruelty, inhumanity, sadism, viciousness, wantonness — more at CRUELTY

sa·van·na *also* **sa·van·nah** \\sə-'va-nə\\ *n* [Sp *zavana*] ♦ : grassland containing scattered trees

♦ down, grassland, plain, prairie, steppe, veld — more at PLAIN

sa·vant \\sa-'vänt, sə-, 'sa-vənt\\ *n* **1** : a learned person : SCHOLAR **2** : a person affected with a developmental disorder who exhibits exceptional skill in some limited field

¹save \\'sāv\\ *vb* **saved; sav·ing** **1** : to redeem from sin **2** ♦ : to rescue from danger **3** ♦ : to preserve or guard from destruction or loss; *also* : to store (data) in a computer or on a storage device **4** ♦ : to put aside as a store or reserve

♦ [2] deliver, rescue; *also* salvage; emancipate, free, liberate, manumit, release; disentangle, extricate; recover **Ant** compromise, endanger, imperil, jeopardize ♦ [3] economize, scrimp, skimp — more at ECONOMIZE ♦ [3] conserve, keep up, maintain, preserve — more at MAINTAIN ♦ [4] allocate, consecrate, dedicate, devote, earmark, reserve — more at DEVOTE

²save *n* : a play that prevents an opponent from scoring or winning

³save *prep* ♦ : other than : EXCEPT

♦ aside from, bar, barring, besides, but, except, outside (of)

⁴save *conj* : BUT

sav·er *n* : one that saves

savings and loan association *n* : a cooperative association that holds savings of members in the form of dividend-bearing shares and that invests chiefly in mortgage loans

savings bank *n* : a bank that holds funds of individual depositors in interest-bearing accounts and makes long-term investments (as mortgage loans)

savings bond *n* : a registered U.S. bond issued in denominations of $50 to $10,000

sav·ior *or* **sav·iour** \\'sāv-yər\\ *n* **1** ♦ : one who saves **2** *cap* : Jesus Christ

♦ deliverer, redeemer, rescuer; *also* custodian, defender, guard, guardian, keeper, lookout, protector, sentinel, sentry, warden, warder, watch, watchman

sa·voir faire \\ˌsav-ˌwär-'far\\ *n* [F *savoir-faire*, lit., knowing how to do] : sureness in social behavior

¹sa·vor *also* **sa·vour** \\'sā-vər\\ *n* **1** : the taste and odor of something **2** ♦ : a special flavor or quality affecting taste

♦ deliciousness, lusciousness, tastiness — more at DELICIOUSNESS

²savor *also* **savour** *vb* **1** : to have a specified taste, smell, or quality **2** : to taste with pleasure **3** ♦ : to give flavor to

♦ flavor (*or* flavour), season, spice — more at SEASON

¹sa·vory *or chiefly Can and Brit* **sa·voury** \\'sā-və-rē\\ *adj* ♦ : having savor: as **a** : pleasing to the sense of taste esp. by reason of effective seasoning **b** : pungently flavorful without sweetness

♦ ambrosial, appetizing, delectable, delicious, flavorful (*or* flavourful), luscious, palatable, scrumptious, tasty, toothsome, yummy — more at DELICIOUS

²sa·vo·ry *n*, *pl* **-ries** : either of two aromatic mints used in cooking

¹sav·vy \\'sa-vē\\ *vb* **sav·vied; sav·vy·ing** ♦ : to recognize the meaning of : UNDERSTAND, COMPREHEND

♦ appreciate, apprehend, catch, catch on (to), comprehend, dig, discern, get, grasp, make, make out, perceive, see, seize, understand — more at COMPREHEND

²savvy *n* ♦ : practical know-how ⟨political ∼⟩ — **savvy** *adj*

♦ experience, expertise, know-how, proficiency — more at EXPERIENCE

¹saw *past of* SEE

²saw \\'só\\ *n* : a cutting tool with a blade having a line of teeth along its edge

³saw *vb* **sawed** \\'sód\\; **sawed** *or* **sawn** \\'són\\; **saw·ing** : to cut or shape with or as if with a saw

⁴saw *n* : a common saying : MAXIM

saw·dust \\'só-(ˌ)dəst\\ *n* : fine particles made by a saw in cutting

saw·fly \\-ˌflī\\ *n* : any of numerous insects belonging to the same order as bees and wasps and including many whose larvae are plant-feeding pests

saw·horse \\-ˌhórs\\ *n* : a rack on which wood is rested while being sawed by hand

saw·mill \\-ˌmil\\ *n* : a mill for sawing logs

saw palmetto *n* : any of several shrubby palms with spiny-toothed petioles

saw·yer \\'só-yər\\ *n* : a person who saws timber

sax \\'saks\\ *n* : SAXOPHONE

sax·i·frage \\'sak-sə-frij, -ˌfrāj\\ *n* [ME, fr. AF, fr. LL *saxifraga*, fr. L, fem. of *saxifragus*, breaking rocks] : any of a genus of plants with showy flowers and usu. with leaves growing in tufts close to the ground

sax·o·phone \\'sak-sə-ˌfōn\\ *n* : a musical instrument having a conical metal tube with a reed mouthpiece and finger keys — **sax·o·phon·ist** \\-ˌfō-nist\\ *n*

¹say \\'sā\\ *vb* **said** \\'sed\\; **say·ing; says** \\'sez\\ **1** ♦ : to express in words ⟨∼ what you mean⟩ **2** : to state as opinion or belief **3** : PRONOUNCE; *also* : RECITE, REPEAT ⟨∼ your prayers⟩ **4** : INDICATE ⟨the clock ∼s noon⟩

♦ articulate, clothe, couch, express, formulate, phrase, put, state, word — more at PHRASE ♦ articulate, speak, state, talk, tell, utter, verbalize, vocalize; *also* air, discuss, express, give, look, sound, state, vent, ventilate, voice; advertise, announce, blaze, broadcast, declare, enunciate, proclaim, publicize, publish; affirm, allege, assert, aver, avouch, avow; breathe, drawl, gasp, mouth, murmur, shout, splutter, spout, whisper; couch, formulate, phrase, put, word; comment, remark

²say *n, pl* **says** \'sāz\ **1** : an expression of opinion **2** : power of decision

say·ing *n* ♦ : a commonly repeated statement

♦ adage, aphorism, byword, epigram, maxim, proverb; *also* cliché, commonplace, platitude; expression, felicity; axiom, motto, precept, truism, truth; observation, reflection, remark

say–so \'sā-(ˌ)sō\ *n* : an esp. authoritative assertion or decision; *also* ♦ : the right to decide

♦ say, voice, vote

sb *abbr* substantive

Sb *symbol* [L *stibium*] antimony

SB *abbr* [NL *scientiae baccalaureus*] bachelor of science

SBA *abbr* Small Business Administration

sc *abbr* **1** scale **2** scene **3** science

Sc *symbol* scandium

SC *abbr* **1** South Carolina **2** supreme court

¹scab \'skab\ *n* **1** : scabies of domestic animals **2** : a crust of hardened blood forming over a wound **3** : a worker who replaces a striker or works under conditions not authorized by a union **4** : any of various bacterial or fungus plant diseases marked by crusted spots on stems or leaves

²scab *vb* **scabbed; scab·bing** **1** : to become covered with a scab **2** : to work as a scab

scab·bard \'ska-bərd\ *n* : a sheath for the blade of a weapon (as a sword)

scab·by *adj* **scab·bi·er; -est** **1** : covered with or full of scabs **2** ♦ : worthy of contempt

♦ contemptible, despicable, lousy, nasty, pitiful, scurvy, sorry, wretched — more at CONTEMPTIBLE

sca·bies \'skā-bēz\ *n* [L] : contagious itch or mange caused by mites living as parasites under the skin

sca·brous \'ska-brəs, 'skā-\ *adj* **1** : DIFFICULT, KNOTTY **2** : rough to the touch : SCALY, SCURFY ⟨a ∼ leaf⟩ **3** : dealing with suggestive, indecent, or scandalous themes ⟨∼ lyrics⟩; *also* : SQUALID

scad \'skad\ *n* ♦ : a large number or quantity — usu. used in pl.

♦ abundance, deal, gobs, heap, loads, lot, pile, plenty, quantity — more at LOT

scaf·fold \'ska-fəld, -ˌfōld\ *n* **1** : a raised platform for workers to sit or stand on **2** : a platform on which a criminal is executed (as by hanging)

scaf·fold·ing *n* : a system of scaffolds; *also* : materials for scaffolds

scal·a·wag *or* **scal·ly·wag** \'ska-li-ˌwag\ *n* ♦ : a mean, unprincipled, or dishonest person : RASCAL

♦ beast, evildoer, fiend, no-good, reprobate, rogue, varlet, villain, wretch — more at VILLAIN

¹scald \'skóld\ *vb* **1** : to burn with or as if with hot liquid or steam **2** : to heat to just below the boiling point

²scald *n* : a burn caused by scalding

¹scale \'skāl\ *n* **1** : either pan of a balance **2** : BALANCE — usu. used in pl. **3** : a weighing instrument

²scale *vb* **scaled; scal·ing** ♦ : to weigh in scales

♦ gauge, measure, span — more at MEASURE

³scale *n* **1** : one of the small thin plates that cover the body esp. of a fish or reptile **2** : a thin plate or flake **3** : a thin coating, layer, or incrustation **4** : SCALE INSECT — **scaled** \'skāld\ *adj* — **scale·less** \'skāl-ləs\ *adj* — **scaly** *adj*

⁴scale *vb* **scaled; scal·ing** : to strip of scales

⁵scale *n* [ME, fr. LL *scala* ladder, staircase, fr. L *scalae*, pl., stairs, rungs, ladder] **1** : something divided into regular spaces as a help in drawing or measuring **2** ♦ : a graduated series **3** : the size of a sample (as a model) in proportion to the size of the actual thing **4** : a standard of estimation or judgment **5** : a series of musical tones going up or down in pitch according to a specified scheme **6** ♦ : a distinctive relative size, extent, or degree

♦ [2] graduation, ladder; *also* arrangement, array, disposal, disposition, distribution, order, sequence, series ♦ [6] gamut, range, spectrum, spread, stretch — more at RANGE

⁶scale *vb* **scaled; scal·ing** **1** : to climb by or as if by a ladder **2** : to arrange in a graded series

scale insect *n* : any of numerous small insects with wingless scale-covered females that are related to aphids and feed on and are often pests of plants

scale·pan \'skāl-ˌpan\ *n* : ¹SCALE 1

scal·lion \'skal-yən\ *n* [ultim. fr. L *ascalonia* (*caepa*) onion of Ascalon (seaport in Palestine)] : an onion without an enlarged bulb; *also* : GREEN ONION

¹scal·lop \'skä-ləp, 'ska-\ *n* **1** : any of numerous marine bivalve mollusks with radially ridged shells; *also* : a large edible muscle of this mollusk **2** : one of a continuous series of rounded projections forming an edge

²scallop *vb* **1** : to bake in a casserole ⟨∼ed potatoes⟩ **2** : to shape, cut, or finish in scallops ⟨∼ed edges⟩

¹scalp \'skalp\ *n* : the part of the skin and flesh of the head usu. covered with hair

²scalp *vb* **1** : to remove the scalp from **2** : to resell at greatly increased prices ⟨∼ tickets⟩ — **scalp·er** *n*

scal·pel \'skal-pəl\ *n* : a small straight knife with a thin blade used esp. in surgery

scam \'skam\ *n* ♦ : a fraudulent or deceptive act or operation

♦ hustle, racket, swindle; *also* phishing; double cross, fix; rip-off; squeeze; ruse, subterfuge, trick

scamp \'skamp\ *n* ♦ : a dishonest person : RASCAL; *also* : an impish or playful young person

♦ beast, evildoer, fiend, no-good, reprobate, rogue, varlet, villain, wretch — more at VILLAIN ♦ devil, hellion, imp, mischief, monkey, rapscallion, rascal, rogue, urchin; *also* cutup, madcap; ragamuffin; brat, nuisance; juvenile delinquent; gamin, gamine

scam·per \'skam-pər\ *vb* ♦ : to run nimbly and playfully — **scamper** *n*

♦ dash, gallop, jog, run, sprint, trip — more at RUN

scam·pi \'skam-pē\ *n, pl* **scampi** [It] : a usu. large shrimp; *also* : large shrimp prepared with a garlic-flavored sauce

¹scan \'skan\ *vb* **scanned; scan·ning** **1** : to read (verses) so as to show metrical structure **2** ♦ : to examine closely **3** : to input or examine systematically in order to obtain data esp. for display or storage **4** : to make a scan of (as the human body)

♦ audit, check, examine, inspect, review, scrutinize, survey — more at INSPECT

²scan *n* **1** ♦ : the act or process of scanning **2** : a picture of the distribution of radioactive material in something; *also* : an image of a bodily part produced (as by computer) by combining radiographic data obtained from several angles or sections

♦ audit, check, checkup, examination, inspection, review, scrutiny, survey — more at INSPECTION

Scand *abbr* Scandinavia

scan·dal \'skand-ᵊl\ *n* [ME, fr. LL *scandalum* stumbling block, offense, fr. Gk *skandalon*] **1** ♦ : a circumstance or action that offends propriety or established moral conceptions or disgraces those associated with it : DISGRACE, DISHONOR **2** : malicious gossip : SLANDER — **scan·dal·ize** *vb*

♦ crime, disgrace, dishonor, reflection, reproach — more at DISGRACE

scan·dal·mon·ger \-ˌmən-gər, -ˌmäŋ-\ *n* : a person who circulates scandal

scan·dal·ous *adj* ♦ : containing defamatory information; *also* : offensive to propriety or morality — **scan·dal·ous·ly** *adv*

♦ defamatory, libelous, slanderous — more at LIBELOUS ♦ appalling, awful, distasteful, dreadful, obnoxious, obscene, odious, offensive, repellent, repugnant, shocking

Scan·di·na·vian \ˌskan-də-'nā-vē-ən\ *n* : a native or inhabitant of Scandinavia — **Scandinavian** *adj*

scan·di·um \'skan-dē-əm\ *n* : a silvery white metallic chemical element

scan·ner \'ska-nər\ *n* **1** : a radio receiver that sequentially scans a range of frequencies for a signal **2** : a device that scans an image or document esp. for use or storage on a computer

¹scant \'skant\ *adj* **1** ♦ : barely sufficient ⟨food is in ∼ supply⟩ **2** : having scarcely enough

♦ light, meager (*or* meagre), niggardly, poor, scanty, scarce, skimpy, slender, slim, spare, sparse, stingy — more at MEAGER

²scant *vb* **1** : SKIMP **2** ♦ : to provide with a meager or inadequate portion or supply : STINT

♦ skimp, spare, stint — more at SPARE

scant·i·ness \-tē-nəs\ *n* ♦ : the quality or state of being scanty

♦ dearth, deficiency, deficit, failure, famine, inadequacy, insufficiency, lack, paucity, poverty, scarcity, shortage, want — more at DEFICIENCY

scant·ling \'skant-liŋ\ *n* : a small piece of lumber (as an upright in a house)

scanty \'skan-tē\ *adj* **scant·i·er; -est** ♦ : barely sufficient : SCANT ⟨wore a ∼ outfit⟩ — **scant·i·ly** \'skan-tə-lē\ *adv*

♦ light, meager (*or* meagre), niggardly, poor, scant, scarce, skimpy, slender, slim, spare, sparse, stingy — more at MEAGER

scape·goat \'skāp-ˌgōt\ *n* : one that bears the blame for others

scape·grace \-ˌgrās\ *n* [*scape* (escape)] : an incorrigible rascal

scap·u·la \'ska-pyə-lə\ *n, pl* **-lae** \-ˌlē\ *or* **-las** [L] : SHOULDER BLADE

scap·u·lar \-lər\ *n* : a pair of small cloth squares worn on the breast and back under the clothing esp. for religious purposes

scar \'skär\ *n* ♦ : a mark left after injured tissue has healed — **scar** *vb*

♦ blemish, defect, deformity, disfigurement, fault, flaw, imperfection, mark, pockmark — more at BLEMISH

scar·ab \'skar-əb\ *n* [MF *scarabee*, fr. L *scarabaeus*] : any of a family of large stout beetles; *also* : an ornament (as a gem) representing such a beetle

scarce \'skers\ *adj* **scarc·er; scarc·est 1** ♦ : deficient in quantity or number : not plentiful **2** : intentionally absent ⟨made himself ∼ at inspection time⟩

♦ deficient, inadequate, insufficient, short, shy, wanting — more at SHORT

scarce·ly \-lē\ *adv* **1** ♦ : by a narrow margin : BARELY ⟨can ∼ see them⟩ **2** : almost not **3** : very probably not

♦ barely, hardly, just, marginally, slightly — more at JUST

scar·ci·ty \'sker-sə-tē\ *n* ♦ : the quality or state of being scarce; *esp* : want of provisions for the support of life

♦ dearth, deficiency, deficit, failure, famine, inadequacy, insufficiency, lack, paucity, poverty, scantiness, shortage, want — more at DEFICIENCY

¹scare \'sker\ *vb* **scared; scar·ing** ♦ : to frighten esp. suddenly : STARTLE

♦ alarm, frighten, horrify, panic, shock, spook, startle, terrify, terrorize — more at FRIGHTEN

²scare *n* : FRIGHT

scare·crow \'sker-ˌkrō\ *n* : a crude figure set up to scare birds away from crops

scared *adj* ♦ : thrown into or being in a state of fear, fright, or panic

♦ afraid, aghast, fearful, terrified — more at AFRAID

¹scarf \'skärf\ *n, pl* **scarves** \'skärvz\ *or* **scarfs 1** : a broad band (as of cloth) worn about the shoulders, around the neck, over the head, or about the waist **2** : a long narrow cloth cover for a table or dresser top

²scarf *vb* [alter. of earlier *scoff* eat greedily] ♦ : to eat greedily ⟨∼*ed* down his lunch⟩

♦ bolt, devour, gobble, gorge, gormandize, gulp, scoff, wolf — more at GOBBLE

scar·i·fy \'skar-ə-ˌfī\ *vb* **-fied; -fy·ing 1** : to make scratches or small cuts in ⟨∼ skin for vaccination⟩ ⟨∼ seeds to help them germinate⟩ **2** : to lacerate the feelings of **3** : to break up and loosen the surface of (as a road) — **scar·i·fi·ca·tion** \ˌskar-ə-fə-'kā-shən\ *n*

scar·let \'skär-lət\ *n* : a bright red color — **scarlet** *adj*

scarlet fever *n* : an acute contagious disease marked by fever, sore throat, and red rash and caused by certain streptococci

scarp \'skärp\ *n* ♦ : a line of cliffs produced by faulting or erosion

♦ bluff, cliff, crag, escarpment, palisade, precipice — more at CLIFF

scary \'sker-ē\ *adj* **scar·i·er; -est 1** ♦ : causing fright **2** ♦ : easily scared **3** : feeling alarm or fright

♦ [1] dire, dreadful, fearful, fearsome, forbidding, formidable, frightful, hair-raising, horrible, redoubtable, shocking, terrible, terrifying — more at FEARFUL ♦ [2] fainthearted, fearful, mousy, shy, skittish, timid — more at SHY

scath·ing \'skā-thiŋ\ *adj* ♦ : bitterly severe ⟨a ∼ condemnation⟩

♦ acrid, biting, caustic, cutting, mordant, pungent, sarcastic, satiric, sharp, tart — more at SARCASTIC

scat·o·log·i·cal \ˌska-tə-'lä-ji-kəl\ *adj* : concerned with obscene matters

scat·ter \'ska-tər\ *vb* **1** ♦ : to distribute or strew about irregularly **2** ♦ : to cause to separate widely : DISPERSE

♦ [1] dot, pepper, sow, spray, sprinkle, strew; *also* blanket, dust; stud; dapple, fleck, speckle, spot, stipple ♦ [2] clear out, disband, disperse, dissipate; *also* break up, isolate, part, segregate, separate, split up; diffuse, disseminate, diverge, spread **Ant** assemble, cluster, collect, concentrate, congregate, gather

scat·ter·brain \'ska-tər-ˌbrān\ *n* : a silly careless person

scat·ter·brained \-ˌbrānd\ *adj* ♦ : having the characteristics of a scatterbrain

♦ flighty, frivolous, giddy, goofy, harebrained, lightheaded, silly — more at GIDDY

scattered *adj* ♦ : marked by disorganized dispersion

♦ aimless, arbitrary, desultory, erratic, haphazard, random, stray — more at RANDOM

scav·enge \'ska-vənj\ *vb* **scav·enged; scav·eng·ing** : to work or function as a scavenger

scav·en·ger \'ska-vən-jər\ *n* [alter. of earlier *scavager*, fr. AF *scawageour* collector of scavage (duty imposed on nonresident street merchants), fr. *skawage* scavage, fr. MF dial. (Flanders) *escauver* to inspect, fr. MD *scouwen*] : a person or animal that collects, eats, or disposes of refuse or waste

sce·nar·io \sə-'nar-ē-ˌō\ *n, pl* **-i·os** : the plot or outline of a dramatic work; *also* : an account of a possible action

scene \'sēn\ *n* [MF, stage, fr. L *scena, scaena* stage, scene, prob. fr. Etruscan, fr. Gk *skēnē* temporary shelter, tent, building forming the background for a dramatic performance, stage] **1** : a division of one act of a play **2** : a single situation or sequence in a play or motion picture **3** : a stage setting **4** : VIEW, PROSPECT **5** : the place of an occurrence or action **6** ♦ : a display of strong feeling and esp. anger **7** : a sphere of activity ⟨the fashion ∼⟩ **8** ♦ : a critical, trying, or unusual state of affairs — **sce·nic** \'sē-nik\ *adj*

♦ [6] blowup, dudgeon, explosion, fireworks, fit, huff, tantrum — more at TANTRUM ♦ [8] footing, picture, posture, situation, status — more at SITUATION

scen·ery \'sē-nə-rē\ *n, pl* **-er·ies 1** : the painted scenes or hangings and accessories used on a theater stage **2** : a picturesque view or landscape

¹**scent** \'sent\ *n* **1** ♦ : effluvia from a substance that affect the sense of smell : ODOR, SMELL **2** : sense of smell **3** : course of pursuit : TRACK **4** : PERFUME 2 **5** ♦ : an agreeable odor — **scent·less** *adj*

♦ [1] odor (*or* odour), redolence, smell, sniff — more at SMELL ♦ [5] aroma, bouquet, fragrance, incense, perfume, redolence, spice — more at FRAGRANCE

²**scent** *vb* **1** ♦ : to perceive by the olfactory organs : SMELL **2** : to imbue or fill with odor **3** ♦ : to get or have an inkling of

♦ [1] nose, smell, sniff, whiff — more at SMELL ♦ [3] feel, perceive, see, sense, smell, taste — more at FEEL

scent·ed \'sen-təd\ *adj* ♦ : having scent

♦ ambrosial, aromatic, fragrant, redolent, savory, sweet — more at FRAGRANT

scep·ter *or Can and Brit* **scep·tre** \'sep-tər\ *n* : a staff borne by a sovereign as an emblem of authority

sceptic *chiefly Brit var of* SKEPTIC

sch *abbr* school

¹**sched·ule** \'ske-jül, *esp Brit* 'she-dyül\ *n* **1** ♦ : a list of items or details **2** ♦ : a brief usu. printed outline of the order to be followed, of the features to be presented, and the persons participating (as in a public performance) : TIMETABLE

♦ [1] catalog, checklist, list, listing, menu, register, registry, roll, roster, table — more at LIST ♦ [2] agenda, calendar, docket, program, timetable — more at PROGRAM

²**schedule** *vb* **sched·uled; sched·ul·ing** **1** ♦ : to make a schedule of; *also* : to enter on a schedule **2** : to appoint, assign, or designate for a fixed time

♦ catalog, enroll, enter, index, inscribe, list, put down, record, register, slate — more at LIST

sche·ma \'skē-mə\ *n, pl* **sche·ma·ta** \-mə-tə\ *also* **schemas** : a diagrammatic presentation or plan : OUTLINE

sche·mat·ic \ski-'ma-tik\ *adj* : of or relating to a scheme or diagram : DIAGRAMMATIC — **schematic** *n* — **sche·mat·i·cal·ly** \-ti-k(ə-)lē\ *adv*

¹**scheme** \'skēm\ *n* **1** ♦ : a plan for doing something; *esp* : a crafty plot **2** ♦ : a systematic design

♦ [1] artifice, device, dodge, gimmick, jig, ploy, sleight, stratagem, trick, wile — more at TRICK ♦ [1] conspiracy, design, intrigue, machination, plot — more at PLOT ♦ [2] blueprint, program, strategy, system — more at PROGRAM

²**scheme** *vb* **schemed; schem·ing** ♦ : to form a plot : INTRIGUE — **schem·er** *n*

♦ conspire, contrive, intrigue, machinate, plot — more at PLOT

schism \'si-zəm, 'ski-\ *n* **1** ♦ : the act or process of dividing : DIVISION; *also* : DISCORD **2** : a formal division in or separation from a religious body

♦ breakup, dissolution, division, partition, separation, split — more at SEPARATION ♦ conflict, discord, dissension, dissent, disunity, friction, strife, variance, war, warfare — more at DISCORD

schis·mat·ic \siz-'ma-tik, ski-\ *n* : one who creates or takes part in schism — **schismatic** *adj*

schist \'shist\ *n* : a metamorphic crystalline rock

schizo·phre·nia \ˌskit-sə-'frē-nē-ə\ *n* [NL, fr. Gk *schizein* to split + *phrēn* diaphragm, mind] : a psychotic mental illness that is characterized by a distorted view of the real world, by a greatly reduced ability to carry out one's daily tasks, and by abnormal ways of thinking, feeling, perceiving, and behaving — **schiz·oid** \'skit-ˌsȯid\ *adj or n* — **schizo·phren·ic** \ˌskit-sə-'fre-nik\ *adj or n*

schle·miel *also* **shle·miel** \shlə-'mēl\ *n* : an unlucky bungler : CHUMP

schlep *or* **schlepp** \'shlep\ *vb* [Yiddish *shlepn*] **1** : DRAG, HAUL **2** : to move slowly or awkwardly

schlock \'shläk\ *or* **schlocky** \'shlä-kē\ *adj* : of low quality or value — **schlock** *n*

schlub *also* **shlub** \'shləb\ *n* [Yiddish *zhlob, zhlub*] yokel, boor] *slang* : a stupid, ineffectual, or unattractive person

schmaltz *also* **schmalz** \'shmȯlts, 'shmälts\ *n* [Yiddish *shmalts*, lit., rendered fat] : sentimental or florid music or art

schmaltzy *adj* ♦ : excessively sentimental

♦ corny, maudlin, mawkish, mushy, saccharine, sappy, sentimental — more at CORNY

schmooze *or* **shmooze** \'shmüz\ *vb* ♦ : to chat informally esp. to gain favor — **schmooze** *n*

♦ chat, converse, gab, jaw, palaver, patter, prattle, rattle, talk, visit — more at CHAT

schmuck \'shmək\ *n, slang* : a stupid, foolish, or unlikeable person : JERK

schnapps \'shnaps\ *n, pl* **schnapps** : a liquor (as gin) of high alcoholic content

schnau·zer \'shnaù-sər, 'shnaù-zər\ *n* [G, fr. *Schnauze* snout] : a dog of any of three breeds that are characterized by a wiry coat, long head, pointed ears, heavy eyebrows, and long hair on the muzzle

schol·ar \'skä-lər\ *n* **1** : STUDENT, PUPIL **2** : a learned person : SAVANT **3** ♦ : a person who has done advanced study in a special field

♦ ace, adept, artist, authority, crackerjack, expert, maestro, master, shark, virtuoso, whiz, wizard — more at EXPERT

schol·ar·ly *adj* ♦ : of, characteristic of, or suitable to learned persons

♦ educated, erudite, knowledgeable, learned, literate, well-read — more at EDUCATED ♦ academic, educational, scholastic — more at ACADEMIC

schol·ar·ship \-ˌship\ *n* **1** ♦ : the qualities or learning of a scholar **2** : money awarded to a student to help pay for further education

♦ education, erudition, knowledge, learning, science — more at EDUCATION

scho·las·tic \skə-'las-tik\ *adj* : of or relating to schools, scholars, or scholarship

♦ academic, educational, scholarly — more at ACADEMIC

¹**school** \'skül\ *n* **1** : an institution for teaching and learning; *also* : the pupils in attendance **2** : a body of persons of like opinions or beliefs ⟨the radical ~⟩

²**school** *vb* ♦ : to teach or drill in a specific knowledge or skill : TRAIN

♦ educate, indoctrinate, instruct, teach, train, tutor — more at TEACH

³**school** *n* : a large number of one kind of water animal swimming and feeding together

school·boy \-ˌbȯi\ *n* : a boy attending school

school·fel·low \-ˌfe-lō\ *n* : SCHOOLMATE

school·girl \-ˌgərl\ *n* : a girl attending school

school·house \-ˌhaùs\ *n* : a building used as a school

school·marm \-ˌmärm\ *or* **school·ma'am** \-ˌmäm, -ˌmam\ *n* **1** : a woman who is a schoolteacher **2** : a person who exhibits characteristics popularly attributed to schoolteachers

school·mas·ter \-ˌmas-tər\ *n* : a man who is a schoolteacher

school·mate \-ˌmāt\ *n* : a school companion

school·mis·tress \-ˌmis-trəs\ *n* : a woman who is a schoolteacher

school·room \-ˌrüm, -ˌrùm\ *n* : CLASSROOM

school·teach·er \-ˌtē-chər\ *n* ♦ : one who teaches in a school

♦ educator, instructor, pedagogue, teacher — more at TEACHER

schoo·ner \'skü-nər\ *n* : a fore-and-aft rigged sailing ship

schtick *var of* SHTICK

schuss \'shùs, 'shüs\ *vb* [G *Schuss*, n., lit., shot] : to ski down a slope at high speed — **schuss** *n*

sci *abbr* science; scientific

sci·at·i·ca \sī-'a-ti-kə\ *n* : pain in the region of the hips or along the course of the nerve at the back of the thigh

sci·ence \'sī-əns\ *n* [ME, fr. AF, fr. L *scientia*, fr. *scient-, sciens* having knowledge, fr. prp. of *scire* to know] **1** : an area of knowledge that is an object of study; *esp* : NATURAL SCIENCE **2** ♦ : knowledge covering general truths or the operation of general laws esp. as obtained and tested through the scientific method **3** ♦ : knowledge as distinguished from ignorance or misunderstanding — **sci·en·tif·ic** \ˌsī-ən-'ti-fik\ *adj* — **sci·en·tif·i·cal·ly** \-fi-k(ə-)lē\ *adv* — **sci·en·tist** \'sī-ən-tist\ *n*

♦ [2] knowledge, lore, wisdom — more at KNOWLEDGE ♦ [3] education, erudition, knowledge, learning, scholarship — more at EDUCATION

science fiction *n* : fiction dealing principally with the impact of actual or imagined science on society or individuals

scientific method *n* : the rules and methods for the pursuit of knowledge involving the finding and stating of a problem, the collection of facts through observation and experiment, and the making and testing of ideas that need to be proven right or wrong

scim·i·tar \'si-mə-tər\ *n* : a curved sword used chiefly by Arabs and Turks

scin·til·la \sin-'ti-lə\ *n* : SPARK, TRACE

scin·til·late \'sint-ᵊl-ˌāt\ *vb* **-lat·ed; -lat·ing** **1** ♦ : to throw off as a spark or as sparkling flashes : SPARKLE, GLEAM **2** : DAZZLE, IMPRESS — **scin·til·la·tion** \ˌsint-ᵊl-'ā-shən\ *n*

♦ flame, flash, glance, gleam, glimmer, glisten, glitter, shimmer, sparkle, twinkle, wink — more at FLASH

sci·on \'sī-ən\ *n* **1** : a shoot of a plant joined to a stock in grafting **2** : DESCENDANT

scis·sors \'si-zərz\ *n pl* : a cutting instrument like shears but usu. smaller

scissors kick *n* : a swimming kick in which the legs move like scissors

scle·ro·der·ma \ˌskler-ə-'dər-mə\ *n* : a chronic disease characterized by the usu. progressive hardening and thickening of the skin

scle·ro·sis \sklə-'rō-səs\ *n* : abnormal hardening of tissue (as of an artery); *also* : a disease characterized by this — **scle·rot·ic** \-'rä-tik\ *adj*

¹scoff \'skäf\ *vb* : MOCK, JEER ⟨~ed at the idea⟩

²scoff *vb* ♦ : to eat greedily

♦ bolt, devour, gobble, gorge, gormandize, gulp, scarf, wolf — more at GOBBLE

scoff·er *n* ♦ : one that scoffs

♦ heckler, mocker, quiz, taunter, tease — more at QUIZ

scoff·law \-ˌlȯ\ *n* : a contemptuous law violator

¹scold \'skōld\ *n* ♦ : a person who scolds

♦ carper, castigator, caviler, censurer, critic, faultfinder, nitpicker, railer — more at CRITIC

²scold *vb* ♦ : to censure severely or angrily

♦ berate, castigate, chew out, dress down, flay, jaw, keelhaul, lambaste, lecture, rail (at *or* against), rate, rebuke, reprimand, reproach, score, upbraid; *also* admonish, chide, remonstrate (with), reprove; abuse, assail, attack, bad-mouth, blame, blast, censure, condemn, criticize, crucify, denounce, excoriate, fault, knock, lash, pan, reprehend, slam; belittle, disparage, mock, put down; ridicule, scoff, scorn

sconce \'skäns\ *n* : a candlestick or an electric light fixture fastened to a wall

scone \'skōn, 'skän\ *n* : a biscuit (as of oatmeal) baked on a griddle

¹scoop \'sküp\ *n* **1** ♦ : a large shovel; *also* : a utensil with a shovel-like or rounded end **2** : an act of scooping **3** ♦ : information of immediate interest

♦ [1] ladle, spoon — more at SPOON ♦ [3] dope, lowdown, tip — more at DOPE

²scoop *vb* **1** ♦ : to take out or up or empty with or as if with a scoop **2** : to make hollow **3** : to report a news item in advance of ⟨~ed the other newspapers⟩

♦ dip, ladle, spoon — more at DIP

scoot \'sküt\ *vb* ♦ : to move swiftly

♦ course, dash, fly, hasten, hurry, hustle, run, rush, shoot, speed, zip, zoom — more at HURRY

scoot·er \'skü-tər\ *n* **1** : a child's vehicle consisting of a narrow board mounted between two wheels tandem with an upright steering handle attached to the front wheel **2** : MOTOR SCOOTER

¹scope \'skōp\ *n* [It *scopo* purpose, goal, fr. Gk *skopos*] **1** : space or opportunity for action or thought **2** ♦ : extent covered : RANGE ⟨is beyond the ~ of the essay⟩

♦ amplitude, breadth, compass, extent, range, reach, realm, sweep, width — more at RANGE

²scope *n* : an instrument (as a microscope or telescope) for viewing

scorch \'skȯrch\ *vb* **1** ♦ : to burn the surface of **2** : to dry or shrivel with heat ⟨~ed lawns⟩

♦ char, sear, singe; *also* fire, ignite, inflame, kindle, light; bake, cremate, incinerate; scald

scorch·ing *adj* ♦ : that scorches

♦ broiling, burning, fiery, hot, red-hot, sultry, torrid — more at HOT

¹score \'skōr\ *n, pl* **scores** **1** *or pl* **score** : TWENTY **2** : CUT, SCRATCH, SLASH **3** : a record of points made (as in a game) **4** : DEBT **5** : REASON, GROUND **6** : the music of a composition or arrangement with different parts indicated **7** : success in obtaining something (as drugs) esp. illegally **8** ♦ : a feeling of deep-seated resentment or ill will

♦ grievance, grudge, resentment — more at GRUDGE

²score *vb* **scored; scor·ing** **1** : RECORD **2** : to keep score in a game **3** ♦ : to mark with lines, grooves, scratches, or notches **4** : to gain or tally in or as if in a game ⟨*scored* a point⟩ **5** : to assign a grade or score to ⟨~ the tests⟩ **6** : to compose a score for **7** ♦ : to be successful **8** : to scold or condemn vehemently and at length — **score·less** *adj* — **scor·er** *n*

♦ [3] groove, scribe; *also* abrade, file, graze, rasp, scarify, scratch ♦ [7] achieve, attain, hit, make, win — more at ACHIEVE

¹scorn \'skȯrn\ *n* ♦ : an emotion involving both anger and disgust : CONTEMPT — **scorn·ful·ly** *adv*

♦ contempt, despite, disdain — more at CONTEMPT

²scorn *vb* ♦ : to hold in contempt : DISDAIN

♦ disdain, high-hat, slight, sniff at, snub; *also* scout; abhor, despise, detest, hate, loathe; disapprove (of), discountenance, disfavor, frown (on *or* upon) *Ant* honor, respect ♦ despise, disregard, flout; *also* dismiss, forget, ignore, neglect, overlook, overpass, pass over, slight, slur (over)

scorn·er *n* : one that scorns

scorn·ful \-fəl\ *adj* ♦ : full of scorn

♦ contemptuous, degrading, derogatory, disdainful, uncomplimentary — more at DEROGATORY

Scor·pio \'skȯr-pē-ˌō\ *n* [L, lit., scorpion] **1** : a zodiacal constellation between Libra and Sagittarius usu. pictured as a scorpion **2** : the 8th sign of the zodiac in astrology; *also* : one born under this sign

scor·pi·on \'skȯr-pē-ən\ *n* : any of an order of arthropods related to the spiders that have a poisonous stinger at the tip of a long jointed tail

¹Scot \'skät\ *n* : a native or inhabitant of Scotland

²Scot *abbr* Scotland; Scottish

Scotch \'skäch\ *n* **1** : SCOTS **2 Scotch** *pl* : the people of Scotland **3** : a whiskey distilled in Scotland esp. from malted barley — **Scotch** *adj* — **Scotch·wom·an** \-ˌwu̇-mən\ *n*

Scotch bonnet *n* : a small roundish very hot chili pepper esp. of the Caribbean

Scotch·man \-mən\ *n* : a native or inhabitant of Scotland

Scotch pine *n* : a pine that is naturalized in the U.S. from northern Europe and Asia and is a valuable timber tree

Scotch terrier *n* : SCOTTISH TERRIER

scot–free \'skät-'frē\ *adj* : free from obligation, harm, or penalty

Scots \'skäts\ *n* : the English language of Scotland

Scots·man \'skäts-mən\ *n* : a native or inhabitant of Scotland : SCOT

Scots·wom·an \-,wů-mən\ *n* : a woman who is a Scot

Scot·tie \'skä-tē\ *n* 1 : SCOTTISH TERRIER 2 : a native or inhabitant of Scotland : SCOT

Scot·tish \'skä-tish\ *adj* : of, relating to, or characteristic of Scotland, Scots, or the Scots

Scottish terrier *n* : any of an old Scottish breed of terrier with short legs, a long head with small erect ears, a broad deep chest, and a thick rough coat

scoun·drel \'skaůn-drəl\ *n* : a disreputable person : VILLAIN

¹**scour** \'skaůr\ *vb* 1 : to rub (as with a gritty substance) in order to clean 2 : to cleanse by or as if by rubbing

²**scour** *vb* 1 : to move rapidly through : RUSH 2 ♦ : to examine thoroughly

♦ dig, dredge, hunt, rake, ransack, rifle, rummage, search — more at SEARCH

¹**scourge** \'skərj\ *n* 1 : an instrument consisting usu. of a handle and lash forming a flexible rod that is used for whipping : LASH, WHIP 2 a : PUNISHMENT b : a cause of affliction (as a plague)

²**scourge** *vb* scourged; scourg·ing 1 ♦ : to beat with or as if with a rod or whip : LASH 2 ♦ : to punish severely; *also* : to distress so severely as to cause persistent suffering or anguish

♦ [1] flog, lash, thrash, whale, whip ♦ [2] destroy, devastate, ravage, ruin — more at RAVAGE

¹**scout** \'skaůt\ *vb* [ME, fr. MF *escouter* to listen, fr. L *auscultare*] 1 : to look around : RECONNOITER 2 : to inspect or observe to get information 3 ♦ : to find by making a search

♦ *usu* **scout up** detect, determine, dig up, discover, ferret out, hit on, locate, track down — more at FIND

²**scout** *n* 1 : a person sent out to get information; *also* : a soldier, airplane, or ship sent out to reconnoiter 2 : BOY SCOUT 3 : GIRL SCOUT 4 : a human being

³**scout** *vb* ♦ : to treat with contempt or ridicule; *also* : to reject scornfully

♦ deride, gibe, jeer, laugh, mock, ridicule — more at RIDICULE

scout·mas·ter \-,mas-tər\ *n* : an adult leader of a Boy Scout troop

scow \'skaů\ *n* : a large flat-bottomed boat with square ends

¹**scowl** \'skaůl\ *vb* ♦ : to make a frowning expression of displeasure

♦ frown, glare, gloom, glower, lower — more at FROWN

²**scowl** *n* ♦ : a facial expression of displeasure

♦ face, frown, grimace, lower, mouth, pout — more at GRIMACE

SCPO *abbr* senior chief petty officer

¹**scrab·ble** \'skra-bəl\ *vb* **scrab·bled; scrab·bling** 1 : SCRAPE, SCRATCH 2 ♦ : to climb awkwardly : CLAMBER, SCRAMBLE 3 : to work hard and long 4 : SCRIBBLE — **scrab·bler** *n*

♦ clamber, climb, scramble

²**scrabble** *n* ♦ : the act or an instance of scrambling

♦ battle, fight, fray, struggle — more at STRUGGLE

scrag·gly \'skra-glē\ *adj* ♦ : irregular in form or growth; *also* : RAGGED

♦ broken, craggy, jagged, ragged — more at RAGGED

scram \'skram\ *vb* **scrammed; scram·ming** : to go away at once

¹**scram·ble** \'skram-bəl\ *vb* **scram·bled; scram·bling** 1 : to clamber clumsily around 2 : to struggle for or as if for possession of something 3 : to spread irregularly 4 ♦ : to mix together 5 : to cook (eggs) by stirring during frying

♦ confuse, disarray, disorder, jumble, mix, muddle

²**scramble** *n* 1 : the act or an instance of scrambling 2 ♦ : a disordered mass

♦ assortment, clutter, jumble, medley, mélange, miscellany, motley, muddle, variety, welter — more at MISCELLANY

¹**scrap** \'skrap\ *n* 1 ♦ : a small detached piece 2 ♦ : discarded material

♦ [1] bit, fragment, piece — more at FRAGMENT ♦ [2] chaff, deadwood, dust, garbage, junk, litter, refuse, riffraff, rubbish, trash, waste — more at GARBAGE ♦ [2] end, fag end, leftover, remainder, remnant; *also* leavings, odds and ends, remains, residual, residue, stump; balance, rest; chip, flake, fragment, piece, sliver, splinter; shred, tatter

²**scrap** *vb* **scrapped; scrap·ping** 1 : to make into scrap ⟨~ a battleship⟩ 2 ♦ : to get rid of as useless

♦ cast, discard, ditch, dump, fling, jettison, junk, lose, reject, shed, shuck, slough, throw away, throw out, unload — more at DISCARD

³**scrap** *n* ♦ : a hostile encounter : FIGHT; *also* : a verbal disagreement

♦ argument, brawl, disagreement, dispute, fight, hassle, quarrel, row, spat, squabble — more at ARGUMENT

⁴**scrap** *vb* **scrapped; scrap·ping** : to contend against in or as if in battle or physical combat : FIGHT — **scrap·per** *n*

♦ argue, bicker, brawl, dispute, fall out, fight, hassle, quarrel, row, spat, squabble, wrangle — more at ARGUE

scrap·book \'skrap-,bůk\ *n* : a blank book in which mementos are kept

¹**scrape** \'skrāp\ *vb* **scraped; scrap·ing** 1 : to remove by drawing a knife over; *also* : to clean or smooth by rubbing off the covering 2 ♦ : to damage or injure the surface of by contact with something rough 3 ♦ : to draw across a surface with a grating sound 4 ♦ : to get together (as money) in small amounts by laborious effort — often used with *up* or *together* 5 : to get along with difficulty — **scrap·er** *n*

♦ [2] abrade, graze, scratch, scuff; *also* bark, skin; chafe, fret, gall; claw, cut, lacerate; bruise, contuse ♦ [3] grate, grind, rasp, scratch; *also* rub; groan, whine ♦ [4] eke out, squeeze, wrest, wring — more at EKE OUT ♦ *usu* **scrape together** [4] accumulate, amass, assemble, collect, concentrate, garner, gather, group, lump, pick up, round up — more at GATHER

²**scrape** *n* 1 ♦ : the act or the effect of scraping 2 : a bow accompanied by a drawing back of the foot 3 ♦ : an unpleasant predicament; *also* : a noisy heated angry dispute

♦ [1] grind, rasp, scratch — more at RASP ♦ [3] brush, encounter, hassle, run-in, skirmish — more at ENCOUNTER

¹**scrap·py** \'skra-pē\ *adj* **scrap·pi·er; -est** : DISCONNECTED, FRAGMENTARY

²**scrappy** *adj* **scrap·pi·er; -est** 1 ♦ : apt or disposed to quarrel in an often petty manner : QUARRELSOME 2 : having an aggressive and determined spirit

♦ argumentative, contentious, disputatious, quarrelsome — more at ARGUMENTATIVE

¹**scratch** \'skrach\ *vb* 1 ♦ : to scrape, dig, or rub with or as if with claws or nails ⟨a dog ~*ing* at the door⟩ ⟨~*ed* my arm⟩ 2 ♦ : to draw across a surface with a grating sound ⟨~*ed* his nails across the blackboard⟩ 3 : SCRAPE 4 4 : to cancel or erase by or as if by drawing a line through 5 : to withdraw from a contest

♦ [1] abrade, graze, scrape, scuff — more at SCRAPE ♦ [2] grate, grind, rasp, scrape — more at SCRAPE

²**scratch** *n* 1 a : a mark or injury made by or as if by scratching b ♦ : a sound made by scratching 2 : the starting line in a race — **from scratch** : with no steps completed or ingredients prepared ahead of time ⟨built it *from scratch*⟩

♦ grind, rasp, scrape — more at RASP

³**scratch** *adj* **1** : made as or used for a trial attempt ⟨~ paper⟩ **2** : made or done by chance ⟨a ~ hit⟩

scratchy *adj* **scratch·i·er; -est 1** ♦ : likely to scratch **2** ♦ : making a scratching noise

♦ [1] brambly, prickly, thorny; *also* coarse, jagged, rough; irritating, itchy, stinging ♦ [2] coarse, gravelly, gruff, hoarse, husky, throaty — more at HOARSE

scrawl \ˈskrȯl\ *vb* : to write hastily and carelessly — **scrawl** *n*

scraw·ny \ˈskrȯ-nē\ *adj* **scraw·ni·er; -est** : very thin : SKINNY

¹**scream** \ˈskrēm\ *vb* ♦ : to cry out loudly and shrilly

♦ howl, shriek, shrill, squeal, yell, yelp; *also* bay, caterwaul, keen, squawk, wail, yawp (or yaup), yowl; bawl, call, cry, holler, shout, vociferate

²**scream** *n* : a loud shrill cry

scream·ing \ˈskrē-miŋ\ *adj* **1** : so striking as to attract notice as if by screaming ⟨~ headlines⟩ **2** ♦ : so funny as to provoke screams of laughter

♦ antic, comic, comical, droll, farcical, funny, hilarious, humorous, hysterical, laughable, ludicrous, ridiculous, riotous, risible, uproarious — more at FUNNY

screech \ˈskrēch\ *vb* : to utter a high shrill piercing cry : SHRIEK — **screech** *n* — **screechy** \ˈskrē-chē\ *adj*

¹**screen** \ˈskrēn\ *n* **1 a** ♦ : a device or partition used to hide, restrain, protect, or decorate ⟨a window ~⟩ **b** ♦ : something that shelters, protects, or conceals **2** : a sieve or perforated material for separating finer from coarser parts (as of sand) **3** : a surface on which an image is made to appear (as in television); *also* : the information displayed on a computer screen at one time **4** : the motion-picture industry

♦ aegis, armor, cover, defense (*or* defence), guard, protection, safeguard, security, shield, wall, ward — more at DEFENSE

²**screen** *vb* **1** ♦ : to shield with or as if with a screen **2** : to separate with or as if with a screen; *also* : to select or categorize methodically ⟨~ contestants⟩ **3** : to present (as a motion picture) on the screen

♦ cover, defend, guard, protect, safeguard, secure, shield, ward — more at DEFEND ♦ blanket, blot out, cloak, conceal, cover, curtain, enshroud, hide, mask, obscure, occult, shroud, veil — more at HIDE

screen·ing \ˈskrē-niŋ\ *n* **1** : metal or plastic mesh (as for window screens) **2** : a showing of a motion picture

screen saver *n* : a computer program that displays something (as images) on the screen of a computer that is on but not in use

¹**screw** \ˈskrü\ *n* [ME, fr. MF *escroe* female screw, nut, fr. ML *scrofa*, fr. L, sow] **1** : a machine consisting of a solid cylinder with a spiral groove around it and a corresponding hollow cylinder into which it fits **2** : a naillike metal piece with a spiral groove and a head with a slot that is inserted into solid material by rotating and is used to fasten pieces of solid material together **3** : PROPELLER

²**screw** *vb* **1** : to fasten or close by means of a screw **2** : to operate or adjust by means of a screw **3** : to move or cause to move spirally; *also* : to close or set in position by such an action **4** ♦ : to twist into strained configurations : CONTORT ⟨~ed up his face⟩

♦ contort, deform, distort, warp — more at CONTORT

screw·ball \ˈskrü-ˌbȯl\ *n* **1** : a baseball pitch breaking in a direction opposite to a curve **2** ♦ : a whimsical, eccentric, or crazy person

♦ character, crackpot, crank, eccentric, kook, nut, oddball, weirdo — more at ECCENTRIC

screw·driv·er \-ˌdrī-vər\ *n* **1** : a tool for turning screws **2** : a drink made of vodka and orange juice

screw-up \ˈskrü-ˌəp\ *n* ♦ : an avoidable and usu. serious mistake

♦ blunder, error, fault, flub, fumble, gaffe, goof, lapse, miscue, misstep, mistake, oversight, slip, stumble, trip — more at ERROR

screw up *vb* ♦ : to foul up hopelessly : BUNGLE

♦ blow, bobble, botch, bungle, butcher, flub, foul up, fumble, mangle, mess up — more at BOTCH

screw·worm \ˈskrü-ˌwərm\ *n* : an American blowfly of warm regions whose larva matures in wounds or sores of mammals and may cause disease or death; *esp* : its larva

screwy \ˈskrü-ē\ *adj* **screw·i·er; -est 1** ♦ : crazily absurd, eccentric, or unusual **2** : disordered in mind : CRAZY

♦ bizarre, curious, far-out, funny, kinky, odd, outlandish, outré, peculiar, quaint, queer, quirky, remarkable, strange, wacky, weird, wild — more at ODD

scrib·ble \ˈskri-bəl\ *vb* **scrib·bled; scrib·bling** ♦ : to write hastily or carelessly — **scribble** *n* — **scrib·bler** *n*

♦ author, pen, write — more at WRITE

scribe \ˈskrīb\ *n* **1** : a scholar of Jewish law in New Testament times **2** ♦ : a person whose business is the copying of writing **3** : JOURNALIST

♦ clerk, register, registrar — more at CLERK

scrim \ˈskrim\ *n* : a light loosely woven cotton or linen cloth

¹**scrim·mage** \ˈskri-mij\ *n* **1** : the play between two football teams beginning with the snap of the ball; *also* : practice play between two teams **2** ♦ : a confused fight

♦ battle, clash, combat, conflict, contest, fight, fracas, fray, hassle, scrap, scuffle, skirmish, struggle, tussle — more at FIGHT

²**scrimmage** *vb* **scrim·maged; scrim·mag·ing** ♦ : to take part in a scrimmage

♦ *usu* scrimmage with battle, clash, combat, fight, skirmish, war — more at FIGHT

scrimp \ˈskrimp\ *vb* ♦ : to economize greatly ⟨~ and save⟩

♦ economize, save, skimp — more at ECONOMIZE

scrim·shaw \ˈskrim-ˌshȯ\ *n* : carved or engraved articles made orig. by American whalers usu. from baleen or whale ivory — **scrimshaw** *vb*

scrip \ˈskrip\ *n* **1** : a certificate showing its holder is entitled to something (as stock or land) **2** : paper money issued for temporary use in an emergency

¹**script** \ˈskript\ *n* **1** : written matter (as lines for a play or broadcast) **2** ♦ : written characters : HANDWRITING

♦ handwriting, manuscript, penmanship — more at HANDWRITING

²**script** *abbr* scripture

scrip·ture \ˈskrip-chər\ *n* **1** *cap* : the books of the Bible — often used in pl. **2** : the sacred writings of a religion — **scrip·tur·al** \ˈskrip-chə-rəl\ *adj* — **scrip·tur·al·ly** *adv*

scriv·en·er \ˈskri-və-nər\ *n* : SCRIBE, COPYIST, WRITER

scrod \ˈskräd\ *n* [prob. fr. Brit. dial. (Cornwall) *scrawed*, pp. of *scraw, scrawl* to split, salt, and dry (young fish)] : a young fish (as a cod or haddock); *esp* : one split and boned for cooking

scrof·u·la \ˈskrȯ-fyə-lə\ *n* : tuberculosis of lymph nodes esp. in the neck

¹**scroll** \ˈskrōl\ *n* : a roll of paper or parchment for writing a document; *also* : a spiral or coiled ornamental form suggesting a loosely or partly rolled scroll

²**scroll** *vb* : to move or cause to move text or graphics up, down, or across a display screen

scroll saw *n* **1** : FRETSAW **2** : a machine saw with a narrow vertically reciprocating blade for cutting curved lines or openwork

scro·tum \ˈskrō-təm\ *n, pl* **scro·ta** \-tə\ *or* **scrotums** [L] : a pouch that in most male mammals contains the testes

scrounge \ˈskraunj\ *vb* **scrounged; scroung·ing** : to collect by or as if by foraging

¹**scrub** \ˈskrəb\ *n* **1** : a thick growth of stunted trees or shrubs; *also* : an area of land covered with scrub **2** : an inferior domestic animal **3** : a person of insignificant size or standing **4** : a player not on the first team — **scrub** *adj* — **scrub·by** *adj*

²**scrub** *vb* **scrubbed; scrub·bing 1** : to clean or wash by rubbing ⟨~ clothes⟩ ⟨~ out a spot⟩ **2** : CANCEL

³scrub *n* **1** : an act or instance of scrubbing ⟨gave the clothes a good ∼⟩ **2** *pl* : loose-fitting clothing worn by hospital staff ⟨surgical ∼s⟩

scrub·ber \'skrə-bər\ *n* : one that scrubs; *esp* : an apparatus for removing impurities esp. from gases

scruff \'skrəf\ *n* : the loose skin of the back of the neck : NAPE

scruffy \'skrə-fē\ *adj* **scruff·i·er; -est** ♦ : not in order or neat ⟨a ∼ beard⟩

 ♦ dilapidated, grungy, mean, neglected, ratty, seedy, shabby — more at SHABBY

scrump·tious \'skrəmp-shəs\ *adj* ♦ : highly pleasing; *esp* : DELICIOUS ⟨a ∼ meal⟩ — **scrump·tious·ly** *adv*

 ♦ ambrosial, appetizing, delectable, delicious, flavorful (*or* flavourful), luscious, palatable, savory, tasty, toothsome, yummy — more at DELICIOUS

scrunch·ie *or* **scrunchy** \'skrən-chē, 'skrún-\ *n* : a fabric-covered elastic for the hair

¹scru·ple \'skrü-pəl\ *n* [ME *scrupil, scriple*, fr. AF *scruble*, fr. L *scrupulus*, dim. of *scrupus* source of uneasiness, lit., sharp stone] **1** : a point of conscience or honor **2** ♦ : hesitation due to ethical considerations

 ♦ compunction, misgiving, qualm — more at QUALM

²scruple *vb* **scru·pled; scru·pling** : to be reluctant on grounds of conscience : HESITATE

³scruple *n* : a minute part or quantity

scru·pu·lous \'skrü-pyə-ləs\ *adj* **1** ♦ : having moral integrity **2** : PAINSTAKING — **scru·pu·lous·ly** *adv*

 ♦ conscientious, ethical, honest, honorable (*or* honourable), just, moral, principled — more at CONSCIENTIOUS

scru·pu·lous·ness *n* ♦ : conformity to high standards of ethics or excellence

 ♦ care, carefulness, heed, heedfulness, pains — more at CARE

scru·ti·nise *chiefly Brit var of* SCRUTINIZE

scru·ti·nize \'skrü-tə-ˌnīz\ *vb* **-nized; -niz·ing** ♦ : to examine closely

 ♦ audit, check, examine, inspect, review, scan, survey — more at INSPECT

scru·ti·ny \'skrüt-ᵊn-ē\ *n, pl* **-nies** [L *scrutinium*, fr. *scrutari* to search, examine, prob. fr. *scruta* trash] ♦ : a careful looking over

 ♦ audit, check, checkup, examination, inspection, review, scan, survey — more at INSPECTION

scu·ba \'skü-bə\ *n* [*self-contained underwater breathing apparatus*] : an apparatus for breathing while swimming underwater

scuba diver *n* : one who swims underwater with the aid of scuba gear

¹scud \'skəd\ *vb* **scud·ded; scud·ding** : to move speedily

²scud *n* : light clouds driven by the wind

¹scuff \'skəf\ *vb* **1** : to scrape the feet while walking : SHUFFLE **2** ♦ : to scratch or become scratched or worn away

 ♦ abrade, graze, scrape, scratch — more at SCRAPE

²scuff *n* **1** : a mark or injury caused by scuffing **2** : a flat-soled slipper without heel strap

¹scuf·fle \'skə-fəl\ *vb* **scuf·fled; scuf·fling 1** ♦ : to struggle confusedly at close quarters **2** : to shuffle one's feet

 ♦ grapple, tussle, wrestle — more at WRESTLE

²scuffle *n* ♦ : a rough haphazard struggle with scrambling and confusion

 ♦ battle, clash, combat, conflict, contest, fight, fracas, fray, hassle, scrap, scrimmage, skirmish, struggle, tussle — more at FIGHT

¹scull \'skəl\ *n* **1** : an oar for use in sculling; *also* : one of a pair of short oars for a single oarsman **2** : a racing shell propelled by one or two persons using sculls

²scull *vb* ♦ : to propel (a boat) by an oar over the stern

 ♦ row

scul·lery \'skə-lə-rē\ *n, pl* **-ler·ies** [ME, department of

household in charge of dishes, fr. MF *escuelerie*, fr. *escuelle* bowl, fr. L *scutella* drinking bowl] : a small room near the kitchen used for cleaning dishes, cooking utensils, and vegetables

scul·lion \'skəl-yən\ *n* [ME *sculion*, fr. MF *escouillon* dishcloth, alter. of *escouvillon*, fr. *escouve* broom, fr. L *scopae*, lit., twigs bound together] : a kitchen helper

sculpt \'skəlpt\ *vb* : to cut with care or precision : CARVE, SCULPTURE

sculp·tor \'skəlp-tər\ *n* : a person who produces works of sculpture

¹sculp·ture \'skəlp-chər\ *n* : the act, process, or art of carving or molding material (as stone, wood, or plastic); *also* : work produced this way — **sculp·tur·al** \'skəlp-chə-rəl\ *adj*

²sculpture *vb* **sculp·tured; sculp·tur·ing** : to form or alter as or as if a work of sculpture ⟨*sculptured* hedges⟩

scum \'skəm\ *n* **1** : a slimy or filmy covering on the surface of a liquid **2** : waste matter **3** ♦ : a low, vile, or worthless person or group of people : RABBLE

 ♦ rabble, riffraff, trash — more at RABBLE

scup·per \'skə-pər\ *n* [ME *skopper-*, perh. fr. AF **escopoir*, fr. *escopir* to spit out] : an opening in the side of a ship through which water on deck is drained overboard

scurf \'skərf\ *n* : thin dry scales of skin (as dandruff); *also* : a scaly deposit or covering — **scurfy** \'skər-fē\ *adj*

scur·ri·lous \'skər-ə-ləs\ *adj* ♦ : using or marked by the use of coarse or abusive language

 ♦ abusive, opprobrious — more at ABUSIVE

scur·ry \'skər-ē\ *vb* **scur·ried; scur·ry·ing** ♦ : to move in or as if in a brisk pace : SCAMPER ⟨*scurried* for cover⟩

 ♦ dash, fly, hasten, hurry, run, rush, scamper, scoot, shoot, speed

¹scur·vy \'skər-vē\ *n* : a disease caused by a lack of vitamin C and characterized by spongy gums, loosened teeth, and bleeding under the skin

²scurvy *adj* ♦ : arousing disgust or scorn : CONTEMPTIBLE — **scur·vi·ly** \'skər-və-lē\ *adv*

 ♦ contemptible, despicable, lousy, nasty, pitiful, scabby, sorry, wretched — more at CONTEMPTIBLE

scutch·eon \'skə-chən\ *n* : ESCUTCHEON

¹scut·tle \'skət-ᵊl\ *n* : a pail for carrying coal

²scuttle *n* : a small opening with a lid esp. in the deck, side, or bottom of a ship

³scuttle *vb* **scut·tled; scut·tling** : to cut a hole in the deck, side, or bottom of (a ship) in order to sink

⁴scuttle *vb* **scut·tled; scut·tling** : to move in or as if in a brisk pace : SCURRY, SCAMPER

scut·tle·butt \'skət-ᵊl-ˌbət\ *n* : GOSSIP

scythe \'sīth\ *n* : an implement for mowing (as grass or grain) by hand — **scythe** *vb*

SD *abbr* **1** South Dakota **2** special delivery

S Dak *abbr* South Dakota

SDI *abbr* Strategic Defense Initiative

Se *symbol* selenium

SE *abbr* southeast

sea \'sē\ *n* **1** : a large body of salt water **2** ♦ : the waters of the earth as distinguished from the land and air : OCEAN **3** : rough water; *also* : a large wave **4** : something likened to the sea esp. in vastness — **sea** *adj* — **at sea** : LOST, BEWILDERED

 ♦ blue, brine, deep, ocean — more at OCEAN

sea anemone *n* : any of numerous coelenterate polyps whose form, bright and varied colors, and cluster of tentacles superficially resemble a flower

sea·bird \'sē-ˌbərd\ *n* : a bird (as a gull) frequenting the open ocean

sea·board \-ˌbōrd\ *n* : SEACOAST; *also* : the land bordering a coast

sea·bor·gi·um \sē-'bȯr-gē-əm\ *n* : a short-lived radioactive chemical element produced artificially

sea·coast \-ˌkōst\ *n* : the shore of the sea

sea·far·er \-ˌfar-ər\ *n* : a person who navigates or assists in navigating a ship : SEAMAN 1

sea·far·ing \-ˌfar-iŋ\ *n* : the use of the sea for travel or transportation — **seafaring** *adj*

sea·food \-ˌfüd\ *n* : edible marine fish and shellfish

sea·go·ing \-ˌgō-iŋ\ *adj* : OCEANGOING

sea·gull \-ˌgəl\ *n* : GULL

sea horse *n* : any of a genus of small marine fishes with the head and forepart of the body sharply flexed like the head and neck of a horse

¹seal \'sēl\ *n, pl* **seals** *also* **seal** [ME *sele*, fr. OE *seolh*] **1** : any of numerous large carnivorous sea mammals occurring chiefly in cold regions and having limbs adapted for swimming **2** : the pelt of a seal

²seal *vb* : to hunt seals

³seal *n* [ME *sele, seel*, fr. AF *seal, sel*, fr. L *sigillum*, fr. dim. of *signum* sign, seal] **1** : GUARANTEE, PLEDGE **2** : a device having a raised design that can be stamped on clay or wax; *also* : the impression made by stamping with such a device **3** : something that seals or closes up ⟨safety ∼⟩

⁴seal *vb* **1** : to affix a seal to; *also* : AUTHENTICATE **2** : to fasten with or as if with a seal to prevent tampering **3** : to close or make secure against access, leakage, or passage **4** : to determine irrevocably ⟨∼ed his fate⟩

sea·lane \'sē-ˌlān\ *n* : an established sea route

seal·ant \'sē-lənt\ *n* : a sealing agent

seal·er \'sē-lər\ *n* : a coat applied to prevent subsequent coats of paint or varnish from sinking in

sea level *n* : the level of the surface of the sea esp. at its mean midway between mean high and low water

sea lion *n* : any of several large Pacific seals with small external ears

seal·skin \'sēl-ˌskin\ *n* **1** : ¹SEAL 2 **2** : a garment of sealskin

¹seam \'sēm\ *n* **1** : the line of junction of two edges and esp. of edges of fabric sewn together **2** : a layer of mineral matter **3** : WRINKLE

²seam *vb* **1** : to join by or as if by sewing **2** : to mark with lines suggesting seams

sea·man \'sē-mən\ *n* **1** ♦ : one who assists in the handling of ships : MARINER **2** : an enlisted person in the navy ranking next below a petty officer third class

♦ gob, jack, jack-tar, mariner, sailor, swab, tar — more at SAILOR

seaman apprentice *n* : an enlisted person in the navy ranking next below a seaman

seaman recruit *n* : an enlisted person of the lowest rank in the navy

sea·man·ship \'sē-mən-ˌship\ *n* : the art or skill of handling a ship

seam·less \'sēm-ləs\ *adj* : having no flaws or interruptions ⟨a ∼ transition⟩ — **seam·less·ly** *adv*

sea·mount \'sē-ˌmaunt\ *n* : an underwater mountain

seam·stress \'sēm-strəs\ *n* : a woman whose occupation is sewing

seamy \'sē-mē\ *adj* **seam·i·er; -est** **1** : UNPLEASANT **2** : DEGRADED, SORDID

sé·ance \'sā-ˌäns\ *n* [F] : a meeting to receive communications from spirits

sea·plane \'sē-ˌplān\ *n* : an airplane that can take off from and land on water

sea·port \-ˌpōrt\ *n* : a port for oceangoing ships

sear \'sir\ *vb* **1** ♦ : to make withered and dry **2 a** ♦ : to burn or scorch esp. on the surface **b** : BRAND — **sear** *n*

♦ [1] dehydrate, dry, parch — more at DRY ♦ [2a] char, scorch, singe — more at SCORCH

¹search \'sərch\ *vb* [ME *cerchen*, fr. MF *cerchier* to go about, survey, search, fr. LL *circare* to go about, fr. L *circum* round about] **1** ♦ : to look through in trying to find something **2** ♦ : to uncover, find, or come to know by inquiry or scrutiny : SEEK **3** ♦ : subject to a penetrating investigation : PROBE — **search·er** *n*

♦ [1, 3] explore, hunt, probe, prospect — more at EXPLORE ♦ *usu* **search for** *or* **search out** [2] cast about, forage, hunt, pursue, quest, seek — more at SEEK ♦ [3] dig, dredge, hunt, rake, ransack, rifle, rummage, scour; *also* audit, check (out), examine, investigate, review, scan, scrutinize, survey; ascertain, descry, detect, determine, discover, ferret (out), find, find out, get, hit (on *or* upon), learn, locate, run down, track (down); explore, skirmish, snoop, probe, prospect

²search *n* : the act of searching

search engine *n* : computer software or a website used to search data (as text or other websites) for specified information

search·light \-ˌlīt\ *n* : an apparatus for projecting a powerful beam of light; *also* : the light projected

sear·ing \'sir-iŋ\ *adj* : very sharp, harsh or intense ⟨∼ pain⟩ ⟨a ∼ review⟩

sea scallop *n* : a large scallop of the Atlantic coast of No. America that is harvested for food

sea·scape \'sē-ˌskāp\ *n* **1** : a view of the sea **2** : a picture representing a scene at or of the sea

sea·shell \'sē-ˌshel\ *n* : the shell of a marine animal and esp. a mollusk

sea·shore \-ˌshōr\ *n* : the shore of a sea

sea·sick \-ˌsik\ *adj* : nauseated by or as if by the motion of a ship — **sea·sick·ness** *n*

sea·side \'sē-ˌsīd\ *n* : SEASHORE

¹sea·son \'sē-zən\ *n* [ME *sesoun*, fr. AF *seison* natural season, appropriate time, fr. L *sation-, satio* action of sowing, fr. *serere* to sow] **1** : one of the divisions of the year (as spring or summer) **2** : a period of the year associated with a particular activity, event, or holiday ⟨the Easter ∼⟩ ⟨hunting ∼⟩ — **sea·son·al** \-zə-nəl\ *adj* — **sea·son·al·ly** *adv*

²season *vb* **1** ♦ : to make pleasant to the taste by use of salt, pepper, or spices **2** : to make (as by aging or drying) suitable for use **3** ♦ : to accustom or habituate to something (as hardship) — **sea·son·er** *n*

♦ [1] flavor (*or* flavour), savor, spice; *also* enhance, enrich, sauce; pepper, salt ♦ [3] fortify, harden, steel, strengthen, toughen — more at HARDEN

sea·son·able \'sē-zə-nə-bəl\ *adj* : occurring at a good or proper time ⟨∼ weather⟩ — **sea·son·ably** \-blē\ *adv*

seasonal affective disorder *n* : depression that recurs as the days grow shorter during the fall and winter

sea·soned *adj* **1** : made fit by use **2** ♦ : made skillful or wise through experience

♦ [2] accomplished, ace, adept, crack, experienced, expert, master, masterful, masterly, practiced, proficient, skilled, skillful, versed — more at EXPERIENCED

sea·son·ing *n* ♦ : something that seasons

♦ flavor (*or* flavour), spice; *also* sauce

¹seat \'sēt\ *n* **1** : a chair, bench, or stool for sitting on **2** ♦ : a place which serves as a capital or center **3** ♦ : the part of the body that bears the weight in sitting

♦ [2] base, center (*or* centre), core, cynosure, eye, focus, heart, hub, mecca, nucleus — more at CENTER ♦ [3] backside, bottom, butt, buttocks, posterior, rear, rump — more at BUTTOCKS

²seat *vb* **1** ♦ : to place in or on a seat **2** : to provide seats for

♦ place, put, set down, sit; *also* ensconce, settle; lay, lie, rest; recline, repose

seat belt *n* : straps designed to hold a person in a seat

SEATO \'sē-ˌtō\ *abbr* Southeast Asia Treaty Organization

seat–of–the–pants *adj* : employing or based on personal experience, judgment, and effort rather than technological aids ⟨∼ navigation⟩

sea turtle *n* : any of two families of marine turtles that have the feet modified into paddles

sea urchin *n* : any of numerous spiny marine echinoderms having thin brittle globular shells

sea·wall \'sē-ˌwòl\ *n* : an embankment to protect the shore from erosion

¹**sea·ward** \'sē-wərd\ *n* : the direction or side away from land and toward the open sea

²**seaward** *also* **sea·wards** \-wərdz\ *adv* : toward the sea

³**seaward** *adj* **1** : directed or situated toward the sea **2** : coming from the sea

sea·wa·ter \'sē-ˌwȯ-tər, -ˌwä-\ *n* : water in or from the sea

sea·way \-ˌwā\ *n* : an inland waterway that admits ocean shipping

sea·weed \-ˌwēd\ *n* : a marine alga (as a kelp); *also* : a mass of marine algae

sea·wor·thy \-ˌwər-thē\ *adj* : fit for a sea voyage ⟨a ~ ship⟩

se·ba·ceous \si-'bā-shəs\ *adj* : of, relating to, or secreting fatty material

sec *abbr* **1** second; secondary **2** secretary **3** section **4** [L *secundum*] according to

SEC *abbr* Securities and Exchange Commission

se·cede \si-'sēd\ *vb* **se·ced·ed; se·ced·ing** : to withdraw from an organized body and esp. from a political body

se·ces·sion \si-'se-shən\ *n* : the act of seceding — **se·ces·sion·ist** *n*

se·clude \si-'klüd\ *vb* **se·clud·ed; se·clud·ing** ♦ : to keep or shut away from others ⟨*secluded* herself in her room⟩

♦ cut off, insulate, isolate, segregate, separate, sequester — more at ISOLATE

secluded *adj* **1** ♦ : screened or hidden from view **2** : living in seclusion

♦ cloistered, covert, isolated, quiet, remote, secret; *also* lonely, solitary; private

se·clu·sion \si-'klü-zhən\ *n* ♦ : the act of secluding : the state of being secluded — **se·clu·sive** \-siv\ *adj*

♦ insulation, isolation, segregation, sequestration, solitude — more at ISOLATION

¹**sec·ond** \'se-kənd\ *adj* [ME, fr. AF *secund*, fr. L *secundus* second, following, favorable, fr. *sequi* to follow] **1** : being number two in a countable series **2** : next after the first **3** : ALTERNATE ⟨every ~ year⟩ — **second** *or* **sec·ond·ly** *adv*

²**second** *n* **1** : one that is second **2** : one who assists another (as in a duel) **3** : an inferior or flawed article (as of merchandise) **4** : the second forward gear in a motor vehicle

³**second** *n* [ME *secunde*, fr. ML *secunda*, fr. L, fem. of *secundus* second; fr. its being the second division of a unit into 60 parts, as a minute is the first] **1** : the 60th part of a minute of time or angular measure **2** ♦ : an instant of time

♦ flash, instant, jiffy, minute, moment, shake, trice, twinkle, twinkling, wink — more at INSTANT

⁴**second** *vb* **1** : to encourage or give support to **2** : to act as a second to **3** : to support (a motion) by adding one's voice to that of a proposer

¹**sec·ond·ary** \'se-kən-ˌder-ē\ *adj* **1** ♦ : second in rank, value, or occurrence **2** : belonging to a second or later stage of development **3** : coming after the primary or elementary ⟨~ schools⟩

♦ inferior, mean, minor, second-rate — more at INFERIOR

²**secondary** *n, pl* **-ar·ies** : the defensive backfield of a football team

secondary sex characteristic *n* : a physical characteristic that appears in members of one sex at puberty or in seasonal breeders at breeding season and is not directly concerned with reproduction

second fiddle *n* : one that plays a supporting or subservient role

sec·ond–guess \ˌse-kənd-'ges\ *vb* **1** : to think out other strategies or explanations for after the event **2** : to seek to anticipate or predict ⟨~ the stock market⟩

sec·ond·hand \-'hand\ *adj* **1** : not original **2** : not new : USED ⟨~ clothes⟩ **3** : dealing in used goods

secondhand smoke *n* : tobacco smoke that is exhaled by smokers or is given off by burning tobacco and is inhaled by persons nearby

second lieutenant *n* : a commissioned officer (as in the army) ranking next below a first lieutenant

sec·ond–rate \ˌse-kənd-'rāt\ *adj* ♦ : of second or inferior quality or value ⟨~ hotels⟩

♦ common, fair, indifferent, mediocre, medium, middling, ordinary, passable, run-of-the-mill, so-so — more at MEDIOCRE ♦ cheap, cut-rate, inferior, junky, lousy, mediocre, poor, sleazy

sec·ond–string \'se-kənd-'striŋ\ *adj* : being a substitute (as on a team)

se·cre·cy \'sē-krə-sē\ *n, pl* **-cies** **1** : the habit or practice of being secretive **2** : the condition of being hidden or concealed

¹**se·cret** \'sē-krət\ *adj* **1** : kept from knowledge or view ⟨a ~ staircase⟩ **2** ♦ : working with hidden aims or methods : COVERT, STEALTHY; *also* : engaged in detecting or spying ⟨a ~ agent⟩ **3** ♦ : kept from general knowledge — **se·cret·ly** *adv*

♦ [2] clandestine, covert, furtive, hugger-mugger, private, sneak, sneaky, stealthy, surreptitious, undercover, underground, underhanded; *also* classified, confidential, restricted, top secret, undisclosed; concealed, hidden, secreted, subterranean, unadvertised, unexposed *Ant* open, overt, public ♦ [3] confidential, hushed, inside, intimate, private — more at PRIVATE

²**secret** *n* **1** ♦ : something kept hidden or unexplained : MYSTERY **2** : something kept from the knowledge of others

♦ conundrum, enigma, mystery, mystification, puzzle, puzzlement, riddle — more at MYSTERY

sec·re·tar·i·at \ˌse-krə-'ter-ē-ət\ *n* **1** : the office of a secretary **2** : the secretarial staff in an office **3** : the administrative department of a governmental organization ⟨the UN ~⟩

sec·re·tary \'se-krə-ˌter-ē\ *n, pl* **-tar·ies** **1** : a person employed to handle records, correspondence, and routine work for another person **2** ♦ : an officer of a corporation or business who is in charge of correspondence and records **3** : an official at the head of a department of government **4** : a writing desk — **sec·re·tari·al** \ˌse-krə-'ter-ē-əl\ *adj* — **sec·re·tary·ship** \'se-krə-ˌter-ē-ˌship\ *n*

♦ clerk, register, registrar, scribe — more at CLERK

¹**se·crete** \si-'krēt\ *vb* **se·cret·ed; se·cret·ing** : to form and give off (a secretion)

²**se·crete** \si-'krēt, 'sē-krət\ *vb* **se·cret·ed; se·cret·ing** ♦ : to deposit or conceal in a hiding place : HIDE

♦ bury, cache, conceal, ensconce, hide — more at HIDE

se·cre·tion \si-'krē-shən\ *n* **1** : the process of secreting something **2** : a product of glandular activity; *esp* : one (as a hormone) useful in the organism **3** ♦ : the act of hiding something — **se·cre·to·ry** \'sē-krə-ˌtȯr-ē\ *adj*

♦ concealment — more at CONCEALMENT

se·cre·tive \'sē-krə-tiv, si-'krē-\ *adj* ♦ : tending to keep secrets or to act secretly ⟨~ about his past⟩ — **se·cre·tive·ly** *adv* — **se·cre·tive·ness** *n*

♦ close, closemouthed, dark, reticent, uncommunicative; *also* quiet, reserved, silent, taciturn; discreet, prudent; clandestine, covert, furtive, hugger-mugger, secret, sneak, sneaky, stealthy, surreptitious, undercover, underhand, underhanded *Ant* communicative, open

¹**sect** \'sekt\ *n* **1** : a dissenting religious body **2** : a religious denomination **3** : a group adhering to a distinctive doctrine or to a leader **4** ♦ : an opinionated faction (as of a party)

♦ bloc, body, coalition, combination, combine, faction, party, set, side, wing — more at FACTION

²**sect** *abbr* section; sectional

¹**sec·tar·i·an** \sek-'ter-ē-ən\ *adj* **1** : of or relating to a sect or sectarian **2** ♦ : limited in character or scope — **sec·tar·i·an·ism** *n*

♦ insular, little, narrow, parochial, petty, provincial, small — more at NARROW

²**sectarian** *n* **1** : an adherent of a sect **2** : a narrow or bigoted person

¹**sec·tion** \'sek-shən\ *n* **1** ♦ : a part cut off or separated **2** ♦ : a distinct part (as of a territorial or political area, community, or group of people) **3** : the appearance that a thing has or would have if cut straight through

♦ [1] member, part, partition, portion, segment — more at PART ♦ [2] district, neighborhood (*or* neighbourhood), quarter — more at DISTRICT

²**section** *vb* **1** : to separate or become separated into sections ⟨∼ an orange⟩ **2** : to represent in sections

sec·tion·al \'sek-shə-nəl\ *adj* **1** : of, relating to, or characteristic of a section **2** : local or regional rather than general in character **3** : divided into sections — **sec·tion·al·ism** *n*

sec·tor \'sek-tər\ *n* **1** : a part of a circle between two radii **2** : an area assigned to a military leader to defend **3** : a subdivision of society

sec·u·lar \'se-kyə-lər\ *adj* **1** ♦ : not sacred or ecclesiastical **2** : not bound by monastic vows ⟨a ∼ priest⟩

♦ nonreligious, profane, temporal — more at PROFANE

sec·u·lar·ise *chiefly Brit var of* SECULARIZE

sec·u·lar·ism \'se-kyə-lə-,ri-zəm\ *n* : indifference to or exclusion of religion — **sec·u·lar·ist** \-rist\ *n* — **secularist** *also* **sec·u·lar·is·tic** \,se-kyə-lə-'ris-tik\ *adj*

sec·u·lar·ize \'se-kyə-lə-,rīz\ *vb* **-ized; -iz·ing** **1** : to make secular **2** : to transfer from ecclesiastical to civil or lay use, possession, or control — **sec·u·lar·i·za·tion** \,se-kyə-lə-rə-'zā-shən\ *n* — **sec·u·lar·iz·er** \'se-kyə-lə-,rī-zər\ *n*

¹**se·cure** \si-'kyu̇r\ *adj* **se·cur·er; -est** [L *securus* safe, secure, fr. *se* without + *cura* care] **1** : easy in mind : free from fear **2** ♦ : free from danger or risk of loss : SAFE **3** ♦ : characterized by certainty or security — **se·cure·ly** *adv*

♦ [2] all right, alright, safe — more at SAFE ♦ [3] assured, confident, self-assured, self-confident — more at CONFIDENT

²**secure** *vb* **se·cured; se·cur·ing** **1** ♦ : to make safe : GUARD **2** : to assure payment of by giving a pledge or collateral **3** ♦ : to fasten safely ⟨∼ a door⟩ **4** ♦ : to get secure usu. lasting possession or control of : ACQUIRE ⟨∼ permission⟩

♦ [1] cover, defend, guard, protect, safeguard, screen, shield, ward — more at DEFEND ♦ [1] assure, cinch, ensure, guarantee, guaranty, insure — more at ENSURE ♦ [3] anchor, catch, clamp, fasten, fix, hitch, moor, set ♦ [4] acquire, attain, capture, carry, draw, earn, gain, garner, get, land, make, obtain, procure, realize, win — more at EARN

se·cu·ri·ty \si-'kyu̇r-ə-tē\ *n, pl* **-ties** **1** : SAFETY **2** : freedom from worry **3** ♦ : something given as pledge of payment ⟨a ∼ deposit⟩ **4** *pl* : bond or stock certificates **5** ♦ : something that secures : PROTECTION

♦ [3] gage, guarantee, guaranty, pawn, pledge — more at PLEDGE ♦ [5] aegis, armor (*or* armour), cover, defense (*or* defence), guard, protection, safeguard, screen, shield, wall, ward — more at DEFENSE

secy *abbr* secretary

se·dan \si-'dan\ *n* **1** : a covered chair borne on poles by two people **2** : an automobile seating four or more people and usu. having a permanent top

¹**se·date** \si-'dāt\ *adj* : quiet and dignified in behavior — **se·date·ly** *adv*

²**sedate** *vb* **se·dat·ed; se·dat·ing** : to dose with sedatives — **se·da·tion** \si-'dā-shən\ *n*

¹**sed·a·tive** \'se-də-tiv\ *adj* ♦ : serving or tending to relieve tension

♦ comforting, dreamy, narcotic, soothing — more at SOOTHING

²**sedative** *n* : a sedative drug

sed·en·tary \'sed-ᵊn-,ter-ē\ *adj* : characterized by or requiring much sitting

sedge \'sej\ *n* : any of a family of plants esp. of marshy areas that differ from the related grasses esp. in having solid stems — **sedgy** \'se-jē\ *adj*

sed·i·ment \'se-də-mənt\ *n* **1** ♦ : the material that settles to the bottom of a liquid **2** : material (as stones and sand) deposited by water, wind, or a glacier — **sed·i·men·ta·ry** \,se-də-'men-tə-rē\ *adj* — **sed·i·men·ta·tion** \-mən-'tā-shən, -,men-\ *n*

♦ deposit, dregs, grounds, lees, precipitate — more at DEPOSIT

se·di·tion \si-'di-shən\ *n* : the causing of discontent, insurrection, or resistance against a government — **se·di·tious** \-shəs\ *adj*

se·duce \si-'düs, -'dyüs\ *vb* **se·duced; se·duc·ing** **1** : to persuade to disobedience or disloyalty **2** ♦ : to lead astray **3** : to entice to sexual intercourse — **se·duc·er** *n*

♦ allure, beguile, decoy, entice, lead on, lure, tempt — more at LURE

se·duc·tion \si-'dək-shən\ *n* **1** : the act of seducing **2** ♦ : something that seduces **3** : something that attracts or charms

♦ enticement, lure, solicitation, temptation — more at TEMPTATION

se·duc·tive \-tiv\ *adj* ♦ : tending to seduce : having alluring or tempting qualities

♦ alluring, attractive, captivating, charming, elfin, engaging, fascinating, fetching, glamorous, magnetic — more at FASCINATING

sed·u·lous \'se-jə-ləs\ *adj* [L *sedulus*, fr. *sedulo* sincerely, diligently, fr. *se* without + *dolus* guile] ♦ : diligent in application or pursuit

♦ active, assiduous, busy, diligent, engaged, laborious, occupied, working — more at BUSY

¹**see** \'sē\ *vb* **saw** \'sȯ\; **seen** \'sēn\; **see·ing** **1** ♦ : to perceive by the eye; *also* : to have the power of sight **2** ♦ : to have experience of **3** ♦ : to perceive the meaning or importance of; *also* : to be aware of **4** : to make sure ⟨∼ that order is kept⟩ **5** : to meet with **6** : to keep company with esp. in dating **7** : ACCOMPANY, ESCORT

♦ [1] behold, descry, discern, distinguish, espy, eye, look, note, notice, observe, perceive, regard, remark, sight, spy, view, witness; *also* identify, make out, pick out; attend (to), consider, heed, mark, mind; study, watch; examine, inspect, scan, scrutinize, survey; glance (at), glimpse, peer (at) ♦ [2] endure, experience, feel, have, know, suffer, sustain, taste, undergo — more at EXPERIENCE ♦ [3] ascertain, catch on, discover, find out, hear, learn, realize — more at DISCOVER ♦ [3] appreciate, apprehend, catch, catch on (to), comprehend, get, grasp, make, make out, perceive, seize, understand — more at COMPREHEND

²**see** *n* : the authority or jurisdiction of a bishop

¹**seed** \'sēd\ *n, pl* **seed** *or* **seeds** **1** : the grains of plants used for sowing **2** : a ripened ovule of a flowering plant that may develop into a new plant; *also* : a plant structure (as a spore or small dry fruit) capable of producing a new plant **3** ♦ : offspring of animals or plants **4** : SOURCE, ORIGIN — **seed·less** *adj* — **go to seed** *or* **run to seed** **1** : to develop seed **2** : DECAY

♦ issue, offspring, posterity, progeny, spawn — more at OFFSPRING

²**seed** *vb* **1** ♦ : to sprinkle with seed : PLANT ⟨∼ land to grass⟩ **2** : to bear or shed seeds **3** : to remove seeds from — **seed·er** *n*

♦ drill, plant, sow — more at PLANT

seed·bed \-,bed\ *n* : soil or a bed of soil prepared for planting seed

seed·ling \'sēd-liŋ\ *n* **1** : a young plant grown from seed **2** : a young tree before it becomes a sapling

seed·time \'sēd-,tīm\ *n* : the season for sowing

seedy \'sē-dē\ *adj* **seed·i·er; -est** **1** : containing or full of seeds **2** ♦ : inferior in condition or quality : SHABBY

♦ ragged, ratty, shabby, tattered, threadbare, worn-out
— more at RAGGED

seek \'sēk\ *vb* **sought** \'sót\; **seek·ing 1** ♦ : to search for
2 ♦ : to try to reach or obtain **3** ♦ : to make an attempt

♦ [1] cast about, forage, hunt, pursue, quest, search (for
or out); *also* ferret (out), root (out) ♦ [2] ask, call, plead,
quest, request, solicit, sue ♦ [3] assay, attempt, endeavor
(*or* endeavour), essay, strive, try — more at ATTEMPT

seek·er *n* ♦ : one that seeks or is used in seeking

♦ applicant, aspirant, campaigner, candidate, contender, hopeful, prospect — more at CANDIDATE

seem \'sēm\ *vb* **1** : to appear to the observation or understanding **2** ♦ : to be so in appearance : APPEAR

♦ act, appear, look, make, sound; *also* dissemble, pretend; resemble, suggest; hint, imply, insinuate

seem·ing *adj* ♦ : outwardly apparent ⟨∼ indifference⟩

♦ apparent, assumed, evident, ostensible, reputed, supposed — more at APPARENT

seem·ing·ly *adv* ♦ : so far as can be seen or judged

♦ apparently, evidently, ostensibly, presumably, supposedly — more at APPARENTLY

seem·ly \'sēm-lē\ *adj* **seem·li·er; -est 1** ♦ : conventionally
proper **2** : FIT

♦ correct, decent, decorous, genteel, nice, polite,
proper, respectable — more at PROPER

seep \'sēp\ *vb* ♦ : to flow or pass slowly through fine pores
or cracks — **seep·age** \'sē-pij\ *n*

♦ bleed, exude, ooze, percolate, strain, sweat, weep —
more at EXUDE

seer \'sir\ *n* ♦ : a person who foresees or predicts events
: PROPHET

♦ augur, diviner, forecaster, fortune-teller, futurist,
prognosticator, prophet, soothsayer — more at PROPHET

seer·suck·er \'sir-ˌsə-kər\ *n* [Hindi *śīrśaker*, fr. Per *shīr-o-*
shakar, lit., milk and sugar] : a light fabric of linen, cotton, or rayon usu. striped and slightly puckered

¹see·saw \'sē-ˌsó\ *n* **1** : a contest in which each side assumes then relinquishes the lead **2** : a children's sport of
riding up and down on the ends of a plank supported in
the middle; *also* : the plank so used

²seesaw *vb* ♦ : to move backward and forward or up and
down

♦ careen, lurch, pitch, rock, roll, sway, toss, wobble —
more at ROCK ♦ bob, bobble, jog, jounce, nod, pump
— more at NOD

seethe \'sēth\ *vb* **seethed; seeth·ing** [archaic *seethe* boil]
♦ : to become violently agitated

♦ boil, burn, fume, rage, steam — more at BOIL ♦ boil,
churn, roil; *also* reel, spin, swirl, whirl; agitate, stir

seg·ment \'seg-mənt\ *n* **1** ♦ : a division of a thing : SEC-
TION **2** : a part cut off from a geometrical figure (as a
circle) by one or more points, lines, or planes — **seg-**
ment·ed \-ˌmen-təd\ *adj*

♦ member, part, partition, portion, section — more at
PART

seg·re·gate \'se-gri-ˌgāt\ *vb* **-gat·ed; -gat·ing** [L *segregare*,
fr. *se-* apart + *greg-, grex* herd, flock] **1** ♦ : to cut off
from others **2** : to separate esp. by races

♦ cut off, insulate, isolate, seclude, separate, sequester
— more at ISOLATE

seg·re·ga·tion \ˌse-gri-'gā-shən\ *n* ♦ : the act or process of
segregating : the state of being segregated

♦ insulation, isolation, seclusion, sequestration, solitude — more at ISOLATION

seg·re·ga·tion·ist \ˌse-gri-'gā-shə-nist\ *n* : one who believes
in or practices the segregation of races

¹se·gue \'se-ˌgwā, 'sā-\ *vb* **se·gued; se·gue·ing 1** : to proceed without pause from one musical number to another
2 : to make a transition without interruption from one
activity, topic, scene, or part to another

²se·gue *n* : the act or an instance of segueing

sei·gneur \sān-'yər\ *n, often cap* [MF, fr. ML *senior*, fr. L,
adj., elder] : a feudal lord

¹seine \'sān\ *n* : a large weighted fishing net

²seine *vb* **seined; sein·ing** : to fish or catch with a seine —
sein·er *n*

seis·mic \'sīz-mik, 'sīs-\ *adj* : of, relating to, resembling, or
caused by an earthquake — **seis·mi·cal·ly** \-mik(ə-)lē\ *adv*
— **seis·mic·i·ty** \sīz-'mi-sə-tē, sīs-\ *n*

seis·mo·gram \'sīz-mə-ˌgram, 'sīs-\ *n* : the record of an
earth tremor made by a seismograph

seis·mo·graph \-ˌgraf\ *n* : an apparatus to measure and
record seismic vibrations — **seis·mo·graph·ic** \ˌsīz-mə-
'gra-fik, ˌsīs-\ *adj* — **seis·mog·ra·phy** \sīz-'mä-grə-fē,
sīs-\ *n*

seis·mol·o·gy \sīz-'mä-lə-jē, sīs-\ *n* : a science that deals
with earthquakes — **seis·mo·log·i·cal** \ˌsīz-mə-'lä-ji-kəl,
ˌsīs-\ *adj* — **seis·mol·o·gist** \sīz-'mä-lə-jist, sīs-\ *n*

seis·mom·e·ter \sīz-'mä-mə-tər, sīs-\ *n* : a seismograph
measuring the actual movement of the ground

seize \'sēz\ *vb* **seized; seiz·ing 1** ♦ : to lay hold of or take
possession of by force **2** ♦ : to take prisoner : ARREST
3 ♦ : to understand fully and distinctly **4** : to attack or
overwhelm physically : AFFLICT ⟨*seized* by panic⟩

♦ [1] bag, capture, catch, collar, corral, get, grab, grapple, hook, land, nab, snare, trap — more at CATCH
♦ [2] apprehend, arrest, nab, pick up, restrain — more
at ARREST ♦ [3] appreciate, apprehend, catch, catch on
(to), comprehend, get, grasp, make, make out, perceive,
see, understand — more at COMPREHEND

sei·zure \'sē-zhər\ *n* **1** : the act of seizing : the state of
being seized **2** ♦ : a sudden attack (as of disease)

♦ attack, bout, case, fit, siege, spell — more at ATTACK

sel *abbr* select; selected; selection

sel·dom \'sel-dəm\ *adv* ♦ : in few instances : RARELY

♦ infrequently, little, rarely; *also* ne'er, never *Ant* frequently, often

¹se·lect \sə-'lekt\ *adj* **1** ♦ : chosen from a number or group
by fitness or preference; *also* : of special value or excellence : CHOICE **2** : judicious or restrictive in choice : DIS-
CRIMINATING

♦ choice, dainty, delicate, elegant, exquisite, rare —
more at CHOICE ♦ chosen, elect; *also* fashionable; exclusive; culled, screened, weeded (out), winnowed (out)

²select *vb* ♦ : to choose from a number or group : pick out

♦ choose, cull, elect, handpick, name, opt, pick, prefer,
single, take — more at CHOOSE

se·lect·ed *adj* : chosen by fitness or preference : SELECT;
specif : of a higher grade or quality than the ordinary

se·lec·tion \sə-'lek-shən\ *n* **1** ♦ : the act or process of selecting **2** : something selected : CHOICE **3** : a natural
or artificial process that tends to favor the survival and
reproduction of individuals with certain traits but not
those with others

♦ choice, election; *also* option; appointment, assignment, designation, naming, nomination

se·lec·tive \sə-'lek-tiv\ *adj* ♦ : of or relating to selection
: selecting or tending to select ⟨∼ shoppers⟩

♦ choosy, particular, picky; *also* fastidious, finicky,
fussy; discriminating, discerning, judicious *Ant* nonse-
lective

selective service *n* : a system for calling men up for military service : DRAFT

select·man \si-'lekt-ˌman, -mən\ *n* : one of a board of officials elected in towns of most New England states to
administer town affairs

se·le·ni·um \sə-'lē-nē-əm\ *n* : a photosensitive chemical
element

self \'self\ *n, pl* **selves** \'selvz\ **1** : the essential person
distinct from all other persons in identity **2** : a particular side of a person's character **3** : personal interest
: SELFISHNESS

self- *comb form* **1** : oneself : itself **2** : of oneself or itself **3** : by oneself or itself; *also* : automatic **4** : to, for, or toward oneself

self–act·ing \'self-'ak-tiŋ\ *adj* ♦ : acting or capable of acting of or by itself

♦ automatic, laborsaving (*or* laboursaving), robotic — more at LABORSAVING

self–as·ser·tive \-ə-'sər-tiv\ *adj* ♦ : given to or characterized by a forceful claim or demand to being recognized or listened to

♦ aggressive, ambitious, assertive, enterprising, fierce, go-getting, high-pressure, militant — more at AGGRESSIVE

self–as·sur·ance \-ə-'shur-ən(t)s\ *n* ♦ : confidence in oneself and in one's powers and abilities

♦ aplomb, assurance, confidence, self-confidence, self-esteem — more at CONFIDENCE

self–as·sured \-ə-'shurd\ *adj* ♦ : sure of oneself

♦ assured, confident, secure, self-confident — more at CONFIDENT

self–cen·tered \'self-'sen-tərd\ *adj* : concerned only with one's own self

self–cen·tered·ness *n* ♦ : the quality or state of being self-centered

♦ egoism, egotism, self-interest, selfishness, self-regard — more at EGOISM

self–com·posed \,self-kəm-'pōzd\ *adj* : having control over one's emotions

self–con·ceit \'self-kən-'sēt\ *n* ♦ : an exaggerated opinion of one's own qualities or abilities

♦ complacence, conceit, ego, egotism, pride, self-esteem, self-importance, self-satisfaction, smugness, vainglory, vanity — more at COMPLACENCE

self–con·fi·dence \-'kän-fə-dən(t)s, -,den(t)s\ *n* ♦ : confidence in oneself and in one's powers and abilities

♦ aplomb, assurance, confidence, self-assurance, self-esteem — more at CONFIDENCE

self–con·fi·dent \-'kän-fə-dənt, -,dent\ *adj* ♦ : confident of one's own strength or ability

♦ assured, confident, secure, self-assured — more at CONFIDENT

self–con·scious \'self-'kän-chəs\ *adj* : uncomfortably conscious of oneself as an object of observation by others — **self–con·scious·ly** *adv* — **self–con·scious·ness** *n*

self–con·tained \,self-kən-'tānd\ *adj* **1** : complete in itself **2** : showing self-control; *also* : reserved in manner

self–con·trol \'self-kən-'trōl\ *n* ♦ : restraint exercised over one's own impulses, emotions, or desires

♦ constraint, inhibition, repression, restraint, self-restraint, suppression ♦ self-discipline, self-government, self-possession, will, willpower — more at WILL

self–de·fense \'self-di-'fens\ *n* **1** : a plea of justification for the use of force or for homicide **2** : the act of defending oneself, one's property, or a close relative

self–de·ni·al \-di-'nī(-ə)l\ *n* ♦ : a restraint or limitation of one's own desires or interests

♦ abnegation, renouncement, renunciation, repudiation — more at RENUNCIATION

self–des·truct \-di-'strəkt\ *vb* : to bring about one's own ruin or destruction

self–de·ter·mi·na·tion \-di-,tər-mə-'nā-shən\ *n* **1** ♦ : free choice of one's own acts or states without external compulsion **2** : determination by the people of a territorial unit of their own future political status

♦ accord, choice, free will, option, volition, will — more at FREE WILL

self–dis·ci·pline \-'di-sə-plən\ *n* ♦ : correction or regulation of oneself for the sake of improvement

♦ restraint, self-control, self-government, self-possession, self-restraint, will, willpower — more at WILL

self–ef·fac·ing \-ə-'fā-siŋ\ *adj* : RETIRING, SHY

self–es·teem \-ə-'stēm\ *n* ♦ : a confidence and satisfaction in oneself; *also* : SELF-CONCEIT

♦ aplomb, assurance, confidence, self-assurance, self-confidence, self-regard, self-respect — more at CONFIDENCE ♦ complacence, conceit, ego, egotism, pride, self-conceit, self-importance, self-satisfaction, smugness, vainglory, vanity — more at COMPLACENCE

self–ev·i·dent \,self-'e-və-dənt\ *adj* : evident without proof or reasoning

self–fer·til·iza·tion \,self-,fərt-ᵊl-ə-'zā-shən\ *n* : fertilization of a plant or animal by its own pollen or sperm

self–ful·fill·ing \,self-fül-'fi-liŋ\ *adj* : becoming real or true by virtue of having been predicted or expected ⟨a ∼ prophecy⟩

self–gov·ern·ing \-'gə-vər-niŋ\ *adj* ♦ : having control or rule over oneself; *specif* : having self-government

♦ autonomous, free, independent, separate, sovereign — more at FREE ♦ democratic, popular, republican — more at DEMOCRATIC

self–gov·ern·ment \-'gə-vər(n)-mənt, -'gə-vᵊm-ənt\ *n* **1** ♦ : restraint exercised over one's own impulses, emotions, or desires **2** ♦ : government under the control and direction of the inhabitants of a political unit rather than by an outside authority

♦ [1] restraint, self-control, self-discipline, self-possession, self-restraint, will, willpower — more at WILL ♦ [2] autonomy, freedom, independence, liberty, sovereignty — more at FREEDOM

self–help \'self-'help\ *n* : the process of bettering oneself or coping with one's problems without the aid of others — **self–help** *adj*

self–iden·ti·ty \-ī-'den-tə-tē, -'de-nə-tē\ *n* **1** : sameness of a thing with itself **2** ♦ : total character peculiar to and distinguishing an individual from others

♦ character, identity, individuality, personality — more at INDIVIDUALITY

self–ie \'sel-fē\ *n* : a digital image of oneself taken by oneself ⟨post a ∼⟩

List of self-explanatory words with the prefix *self-*

self–abasement	self–appraisal	self–contempt	self–deprecation
self–absorbed	self–asserting	self–contradiction	self–depreciation
self–absorption	self–assertion	self–contradictory	self–described
self–acceptance	self–awareness	self–correcting	self–despair
self–accusation	self–betrayal	self–created	self–destruction
self–addressed	self–cleaning	self–criticism	self–destructive
self–adjusting	self–closing	self–cultivation	self–directed
self–administer	self–complacent	self–deceit	self–distrust
self–advancement	self–concern	self–deception	self–doubt
self–aggrandizement	self–condemned	self–defeating	self–educated
self–aggrandizing	self–confessed	self–definition	self–employed
self–analysis	self–congratulation	self–delusion	self–employment
self–anointed	self–congratulatory	self–denying	self–enhancement
self–appointed	self–constituted	self–deprecating	self–examination

self–im·por·tance \'self-im-'pȯr-t°n(t)s, -tən(t)s\ *n* ♦ : an exaggerated estimate of one's own importance; *also* : arrogant or pompous behavior

♦ arrogance, haughtiness, loftiness, pretense, pretension, pretentiousness, superiority — more at ARROGANCE ♦ complacence, conceit, ego, egotism, pride, self-conceit, self-esteem, self-satisfaction, smugness, vainglory, vanity — more at COMPLACENCE

self–important \-t°nt, -tənt\ *adj* ♦ : having or showing self-importance

♦ complacent, conceited, egotistic, important, overweening, pompous, prideful, proud, self-satisfied, smug, stuck-up, vain — more at CONCEITED

self–imposed *adj* : imposed by oneself or itself : voluntarily assumed

self–in·dul·gence \-in-'dəl-jəns\ *n* : excessive or unrestrained gratification of one's own appetites, desires, or whims

self–in·ter·est \-'in-t(ə-)rəst; -'in-tə-,rest, -,trest; -'in-tərst\ *n* ♦ : a concern for one's own advantage and well-being

♦ egoism, egotism, self-centeredness, selfishness, self-regard — more at EGOISM

self·ish \'sel-fish\ *adj* ♦ : concerned with one's own welfare excessively or without regard for others — **self·ish·ly** *adv*

♦ egocentric, egotistic, self-seeking — more at EGOCENTRIC

self·ish·ness *n* ♦ : the quality or state of being selfish

♦ egoism, egotism, self-centeredness, self-interest, self-regard — more at EGOISM

self·less \'self-ləs\ *adj* : UNSELFISH — **self·less·ness** *n*

self–made \'self-'mād\ *adj* : having achieved success or prominence by one's own efforts ⟨a ~ millionaire⟩

self–pol·li·na·tion \,self-,pä-lə-lə-'nā-shən\ *n* : pollination of a flower by its own pollen or sometimes by pollen from another flower on the same plant

self–pos·sessed \'self-pə-'zest *also* -'sest\ *adj* ♦ : having or showing self-possession : composed in mind or manner

♦ calm, collected, composed, cool, placid, serene, tranquil, undisturbed, unperturbed, unshaken, untroubled, unworried — more at CALM

self–pos·ses·sion \-pə-'ze-shən *also* -'se-\ *n* ♦ : control of one's emotions or reactions esp. when under stress

♦ aplomb, calmness, composure, coolness, equanimity, placidity, serenity, tranquility — more at EQUANIMITY restraint, self-control, self-discipline, self-government, self-restraint, will, willpower — more at WILL

self–re·gard \-ri-'gärd\ *n* ♦ : regard for or consideration of oneself or one's own interests

♦ ego, pride, self-esteem, self-respect — more at PRIDE
♦ egoism, egotism, self-centeredness, self-interest, selfishness — more at EGOISM

self–reg·u·lat·ing \'self-'re-gyə-,lā-tiŋ\ *adj* : AUTOMATIC

self–re·li·ant \-ri-'lī-ənt\ *adj* ♦ : having confidence in and exercising one's own powers or judgment

♦ independent, self-sufficient, self-supporting — more at SELF-SUFFICIENT

self–re·proach \-ri-prōch\ *n* ♦ : the act or an instance of reproaching oneself

♦ contrition, guilt, penitence, remorse, repentance, shame — more at GUILT

self–re·spect \-ri-'spekt\ *n* **1** : a proper respect for oneself as a human being **2** ♦ : regard for one's own standing or position

♦ ego, pride, self-esteem, self-regard — more at PRIDE

self–re·straint \-ri-strănt\ *n* ♦ : restraint imposed on oneself

♦ constraint, inhibition, repression, restraint, self-control, suppression ♦ self-discipline, self-government, self-possession, will, willpower — more at WILL

self–righ·teous \-'rī-chəs\ *adj* : strongly convinced of one's own righteousness — **self–righ·teous·ly** *adv*

self·same \'self-,sām\ *adj* ♦ : precisely the same : IDENTICAL

♦ identical, same, very — more at SAME

self–sat·is·fac·tion \,self-,sa-təs-'fak-shən\ *n* ♦ : a usu. smug satisfaction with oneself or one's position or achievements

♦ complacence, conceit, ego, egotism, pride, self-conceit, self-esteem, self-importance, smugness, vainglory, vanity — more at COMPLACENCE

self–sat·is·fied \'self-'sa-təs-,fīd\ *adj* ♦ : feeling or showing self-satisfaction

♦ complacent, conceited, egotistic, important, overweening, pompous, prideful, proud, self-important, smug, stuck-up, vain — more at CONCEITED

self–seal·ing \'self-'sē-liŋ\ *adj* : capable of sealing itself (as after puncture)

self–seek·ing \'self-'sē-kiŋ\ *adj* ♦ : seeking only to further one's own interests — **self–seeking** *n*

♦ ambitious, go-getting — more at AMBITIOUS ♦ egocentric, egotistic, selfish — more at EGOCENTRIC

self–start·er \-'stär-tər\ *n* ♦ : a person who has initiative

♦ go-getter, hustler, live wire, powerhouse — more at GO-GETTER

self–suf·fi·cien·cy \-sə-'fi-shən(t)-sē\ *n* : the quality or state of being self-sufficient

self–suf·fi·cient \-'fi-shənt\ *adj* ♦ : able to maintain oneself or itself without outside aid : capable of providing for one's own needs

♦ independent, self-reliant, self-supporting; *also* potent, powerful, resilient, strong *Ant* dependent, reliant

self–sup·port·ing \-sə-'pȯr-tiŋ\ *adj* ♦ : meeting one's needs by one's own efforts or output

♦ independent, self-reliant, self-sufficient — more at SELF-SUFFICIENT

self–will \'self-'wil\ *n* ♦ : stubborn or willful adherence to one's own desires or ideas : OBSTINACY

♦ hardheadedness, mulishness, obduracy, obstinacy, peevishness, pertinacity, stubbornness, tenacity — more at OBSTINACY

sell \'sel\ *vb* **sold** \'sōld\; **sell·ing** **1** : to transfer (property) in return for money or something else of value **2** ♦ : to deal in as a business **3** : to achieve satisfactory sales

---

List of self-explanatory words with the prefix self- (continued)

self–explaining	self–inflicted	self–professed	self–sacrificing
self–explanatory	self–knowledge	self–promotion	self–service
self–expression	self–limiting	self–propelled	self–serving
self–forgetful	self–love	self–propelling	self–starting
self–giving	self–lubricating	self–protection	self–styled
self–harm	self–luminous	self–realization	self–sustaining
self–hate	self–operating	self–referential	self–taught
self–hypnosis	self–perception	self–reliance	self–torment
self–image	self–perpetuating	self–renewing	self–winding
self–improvement	self–pity	self–respecting	self–worth
self–incrimination	self–portrait	self–revelation	
self–induced	self–preservation	self–rule	
self–indulgent	self–proclaimed	self–sacrifice	

⟨cars are ∼*ing* well⟩ **4 ♦** : to have a specified price — usu. used with *at* or *for*

♦ [2] deal, market, merchandise, put up, retail, vend — more at MARKET **♦** *usu* **sell for** [4] bring, cost, fetch, go — more at COST

sell·er *n* **♦** : one that offers for sale

♦ dealer, vendor — more at VENDOR

sell out *vb* **1** : to dispose of entirely by sale; *esp* : to sell one's business **2** : BETRAY — **sell·out** \'sel-ˌaut\ *n*

selt·zer \'selt-sər\ *n* [modif. of G *Selterser (Wasser)* water of Selters, fr. Nieder *Selters*, Germany] : artificially carbonated water

sel·vage *or* **sel·vedge** \'sel-vij\ *n* : the edge of a woven fabric so formed as to prevent raveling

selves *pl of* SELF

sem *abbr* **1** semicolon **2** seminar **3** seminary

se·man·tic \si-'man-tik\ *also* **se·man·ti·cal** \-ti-kəl\ *adj* : of or relating to meaning in language ⟨∼ change⟩

se·man·tics \si-'man-tiks\ *n sing or pl* : the study of meanings in language

sema·phore \'se-mə-ˌfōr\ *n* **1** : a visual signaling apparatus with movable arms **2** : signaling by handheld flags

sem·blance \'sem-bləns\ *n* **1 ♦** : outward and often deceptive appearance or show **2** : IMAGE, LIKENESS

♦ appearance, face, guise, name, show — more at APPEARANCE

se·men \'sē-mən\ *n* [NL, fr. L, seed] : a sticky whitish fluid of the male reproductive tract that contains the sperm

se·mes·ter \sə-'mes-tər\ *n* [G, fr. L *semestris* half-yearly, fr. *sex* six + *mensis* month] **1** : half a year **2** : one of the two terms into which many colleges divide the school year

semi \'se-ˌmī\ *n, pl* **sem·is** : SEMITRAILER

semi- \'se-mi, -ˌmī\ *prefix* **1** : precisely half of **2** : half in quantity or value; *also* : half of or occurring halfway through a specified period **3** : partly : incompletely **4** : partial : incomplete **5** : having some of the characteristics of

semi·au·to·mat·ic \ˌse-mē-ˌȯ-tə-'ma-tik\ *adj, of a firearm* : able to fire repeatedly but requiring release and another press of the trigger for each successive shot

semi·co·lon \'se-mi-ˌkō-lən\ *n* : a punctuation mark ; used esp. to separate major sentence elements

semi·con·duc·tor \ˌse-mi-kən-'dək-tər\ *n* : a substance whose electrical conductivity is between that of a conductor and an insulator — **semi·con·duct·ing** *adj*

semi·dark·ness \-'därk-nəs\ *n* **♦** : partial darkness

♦ dusk, gloaming, gloom, murk, shade, shadows, twilight — more at DARK

¹semi·fi·nal \ˌse-mi-'fīn-ᵊl\ *adj* : being next to the last in an elimination tournament

²semi·fi·nal \'se-mi-ˌfīn-ᵊl\ *n* : a semifinal round or match — **semi·fi·nal·ist** \-ist\ *n*

sem·i·nal \'se-mən-ᵊl\ *adj* **1** : of, relating to, or consisting of seed or semen **2** : containing or contributing the seeds of later development : CREATIVE, ORIGINAL — **sem·i·nal·ly** *adv*

sem·i·nar \'se-mə-ˌnär\ *n* **1** : a course of study pursued by a group of advanced students doing original research under a professor **2 ♦** : a meeting for giving and discussing information : CONFERENCE

♦ assembly, conference, congress, convention, convocation, council, gathering, get-together, huddle, meeting,

powwow — more at MEETING **♦** colloquy, conference, council, forum, panel, parley, powwow, symposium — more at FORUM

sem·i·nary \'se-mə-ˌner-ē\ *n, pl* **-nar·ies** [ME, seedbed, nursery, fr. L *seminarium*, fr. *semen* seed] : an educational institution; *esp* : one that gives theological training — **sem·i·nar·i·an** \ˌse-mə-'ner-ē-ən\ *n*

Sem·i·nole \'se-mə-ˌnōl\ *n, pl* **Semi·noles** *or* **Seminole** : a member of an American Indian people of Florida

semi·per·me·able \ˌse-mi-'pər-mē-ə-bəl\ *adj* : partially but not freely or wholly permeable; *esp* : permeable to some usu. small molecules but not to other usu. larger particles ⟨a ∼ membrane⟩ — **semi·per·me·abil·i·ty** \-ˌpər-mē-ə-'bi-lə-tē\ *n*

Sem·ite \'se-ˌmīt\ *n* : a member of any of a group of peoples (as the Hebrews or Arabs) of southwestern Asia — **Se·mit·ic** \sə-'mi-tik\ *adj*

semi·trail·er \'se-mi-ˌtrā-lər, -ˌmī-\ *n* : a freight trailer that when attached is supported at its forward end by the truck tractor; *also* : a semitrailer with attached tractor

sem·o·li·na \ˌse-mə-'lē-nə\ *n* : the purified hard grains produced from the milling of wheat and used esp. for pasta

sen *abbr* **1** senate; senator **2** senior

sen·ate \'se-nət\ *n* : the second of two chambers of a legislature

sen·a·tor \'se-nə-tər\ *n* : a member of a senate — **sen·a·to·ri·al** \ˌse-nə-'tōr-ē-əl\ *adj*

send \'send\ *vb* **sent** \'sent\; **send·ing** **1 ♦** : to cause to go **2** : EMIT **3** : to propel or drive esp. with force **4** : to put or bring into a certain condition — **send·er** *n*

♦ consign, dispatch, pack, ship, transfer, transmit, transport; *also* convey, deliver, hand over; advance, drop, launch, remit; address, forward; bestow, contribute, donate, give, present *Ant* accept, receive

send–off \'send-ˌȯf\ *n* : a demonstration of goodwill and enthusiasm at the start of a new venture (as a trip)

send–up \'send-ˌəp\ *n* : PARODY, TAKEOFF

Sen·e·ca \'se-ni-kə\ *n, pl* **Seneca** *or* **Senecas** : a member of an American Indian people of western New York

Sen·e·ga·lese \ˌse-ni-gə-'lēz, -'lēs\ *n, pl* **Senegalese** : a native or inhabitant of Senegal — **Senegalese** *adj*

se·nes·cence \si-'nes-ᵊns\ *n* : the state of being old; *also* : the process of becoming old — **se·nes·cent** \-ᵊnt\ *adj*

se·nile \'sē-ˌnīl, 'se-\ *adj* : OLD, AGED; *esp* : exhibiting a loss of cognitive abilities associated with old age — **se·nil·i·ty** \si-'ni-lə-tē\ *n*

¹se·nior \'sē-nyər\ *n* **1 ♦** : a person older or of higher rank than another **2** : a member of the graduating class of a high school or college

♦ better, elder, superior — more at SUPERIOR

²senior *adj* [ME, fr. L, older, elder, compar. of *senex* old] **1 ♦** : of earlier birth or greater age **2** : more advanced in dignity or rank **3** : belonging to the final year of a school or college course

♦ ancient, elderly, geriatric, old — more at ELDERLY

senior airman *n* : an enlisted person in the airforce ranking next below a staff sergeant

senior chief petty officer *n* : a petty officer in the navy or coast guard ranking next below a master chief petty officer

senior citizen *n* **♦** : an elderly person; *esp* : one who has retired

---

List of self-explanatory words with the prefix *semi-*

semiannual	semidivine	semipermanent	semisoft
semiarid	semiformal	semipolitical	semisolid
semicentennial	semigloss	semiprecious	semisweet
semicircle	semi–independent	semiprivate	semitransparent
semicircular	semiliquid	semiprofessional	semiweekly
semicivilized	semiliterate	semireligious	semiyearly
semiclassical	semimonthly	semiretired	
semiconscious	semiofficial	semiskilled	

♦ ancient, elder, golden-ager, oldster; *also* senior; graybeard, patriarch; beldam, grandam; adult, grown-up *Ant* youth, youngster

senior high school *n* : a school usu. including grades 10 to 12

se·nior·i·ty \sēn-'yòr-ə-tē\ *n* **1** : the quality or state of being senior **2** : a privileged status owing to length of continuous service

senior master sergeant *n* : a noncommissioned officer in the air force ranking next below a chief master sergeant

sen·na \'se-nə\ *n* **1** : CASSIA 2; *esp* : one used medicinally **2** : the dried leaflets or pods of a cassia used as a purgative

sen·sa·tion \sen-'sā-shən\ *n* **1 a** : awareness (as of noise or heat) or a mental process (as seeing or hearing) due to stimulation of a sense organ **b** ♦ : an indefinite bodily feeling **2** ♦ : a condition of excitement; *also* : the thing that causes this condition

♦ [1b] feel, feeling, sense; *also* impression, perception; hint, suggestion ♦ [2] craze, enthusiasm, fad, fashion, go, mode, rage, style, trend, vogue — more at FASHION ♦ [2] caution, flash, marvel, miracle, phenomenon, portent, prodigy, wonder — more at WONDER

sen·sa·tion·al \-shə-nəl\ *adj* **1** ♦ : of or relating to sensation or the senses **2** : arousing an intense and usu. superficial interest or emotional reaction **3** ♦ : exceedingly or unexpectedly excellent or great ⟨a ∼ talent⟩ — **sen·sa·tion·al·ly** *adv*

♦ [1] sensitive, sensory, sensuous — more at SENSORY ♦ [3] classic, excellent, fabulous, fine, grand, great, splendid, superb, superior, terrific, wonderful — more at EXCELLENT

sen·sa·tion·al·ise *chiefly Brit var of* SENSATIONALIZE

sen·sa·tion·al·ism \-nə-₁li-zəm\ *n* : the use or effect of sensational subject matter or treatment — **sen·sa·tion·al·ist** \-nə-list\ *adj or n* — **sen·sa·tion·al·is·tic** \-₁sā-shə-nə-'lis-tik\ *adj*

sen·sa·tion·al·ize \-nə-₁līz\ *vb* **-ized; -iz·ing** : to present in a sensational manner

¹sense \'sens\ *n* **1** ♦ : semantic content : MEANING **2** : the faculty of perceiving by means of sense organs; *also* : a bodily function or mechanism (as sight, hearing, or smell) involving the action and effect of a stimulus on a sense organ **3** ♦ : a particular sensation; *also* : a motivating or discerning awareness **4** ♦ : capacity for effective application of the powers of the mind as a basis for action or response **5** : OPINION ⟨the ∼ of the meeting⟩ — **sense·less·ly** *adv*

♦ [1] denotation, drift, import, intent, meaning, purport, significance, signification — more at MEANING ♦ [3] feel, feeling, sensation — more at SENSATION ♦ [4] common sense, horse sense, wisdom, wit — more at COMMON SENSE ♦ [4] logic, reason, reasoning — more at LOGIC

²sense *vb* **sensed; sens·ing** **1** ♦ : to be or become aware of ⟨∼ danger⟩; *also* : to perceive by the senses **2** : to detect (as radiation) automatically

♦ feel, perceive, scent, see, smell, taste — more at FEEL

sense·less *adj* ♦ : destitute of, deficient in, or contrary to sense

♦ cold, unconscious — more at UNCONSCIOUS ♦ empty, meaningless, pointless — more at MEANINGLESS ♦ dumb, fatuous, foolish, mindless, silly, stupid, unintelligent, vacuous, witless — more at STUPID

sense organ *n* : a bodily structure (as an eye or ear) that receives stimuli (as heat or light) which excite neurons to send information to the brain

sen·si·bil·i·ty \₁sen-sə-'bi-lə-tē\ *n, pl* **-ties** : delicacy of feeling : SENSITIVITY

sen·si·ble \'sen-sə-bəl\ *adj* **1** ♦ : capable of being perceived by the senses or the mind; *also* : capable of receiving sense impressions **2** ♦ : emotionally aware and responsive : CONSCIOUS **3** ♦ : having, containing, or indicative of good sense or reason : REASONABLE ⟨a ∼ decision⟩ — **sen·si·bly** \-blē\ *adv*

♦ [1] appreciable, detectable, discernible, distinguishable, palpable, perceptible — more at PERCEPTIBLE ♦ [2] alive, aware, cognizant, conscious, mindful, sentient, witting — more at CONSCIOUS ♦ [3] good, hard, informed, just, levelheaded, logical, rational, reasonable, reasoned, sober, solid, valid, well-founded — more at GOOD

sen·si·tive \'sen-sə-tiv\ *adj* **1** ♦ : subject to excitation by or responsive to stimuli **2** : having power of feeling **3** ♦ : of such a nature as to be easily affected; *also* : easily hurt or damaged **4** : TOUCHY ⟨a ∼ issue⟩

♦ [1] acute, delicate, keen, perceptive, sharp — more at ACUTE ♦ [3] delicate, fragile, frail, tender — more at TENDER ♦ [3] demonstrative, emotional, feeling, intense, passionate, sentimental, soulful

sen·si·tive·ness \'sen-sə-tiv-nəs\ *n* ♦ : the quality or state of being sensitive

♦ acuity, acuteness, delicacy, keenness, sensitivity

sensitive plant *n* : any of several mimosas with leaves that fold or droop when touched

sen·si·tiv·i·ty \₁sen-sə-'ti-və-tē\ *n* ♦ : the ability to sense and to respond to slight impressions or differences

♦ acuity, acuteness, delicacy, keenness, sensitiveness

sen·si·tize \'sen-sə-₁tīz\ *vb* **-tized; -tiz·ing** : to make or become sensitive or hypersensitive — **sen·si·ti·za·tion** \₁sen-sə-tə-'zā-shən\ *n*

sen·sor \'sen-₁sòr, -sər\ *n* : a device that responds to a physical stimulus

sen·so·ry \'sen-sə-rē\ *adj* **1** ♦ : of or relating to sensation or the senses ⟨∼ perceptions⟩ **2** : AFFERENT

♦ sensational, sensitive, sensuous; *also* afferent, receptive; sensual

sen·su·al \'sen-shə-wəl\ *adj* **1** : relating to gratification of the senses **2** ♦ : devoted to the pleasures of the senses — **sen·su·al·ist** *n* — **sen·su·al·i·ty** \₁sen-shə-'wa-lə-tē\ *n* — **sen·su·al·ly** *adv*

♦ carnal, fleshly, luscious, sensuous, voluptuous; *also* bodily, corporeal; agreeable, delectable, delicious, delightful, dreamy, gratifying, palatable, pleasant, pleasurable, pleasing, scrumptious; epicurean, luxurious, self-indulgent

sen·su·ous \'sen-shə-wəs\ *adj* **1** ♦ : relating to the senses or to things that can be perceived by the senses **2** : producing or characterized by gratification of the senses : VOLUPTUOUS — **sen·su·ous·ly** *adv* — **sen·su·ous·ness** *n*

♦ sensational, sensitive, sensory — more at SENSORY

sent *past and past part of* SEND

¹sen·tence \'sent-°ns, -°nz\ *n* [ME, fr. MF, fr. L *sententia*, lit., feeling, opinion, fr. *sentire* to feel] **1** ♦ : the punishment set by a court **2** : a grammatically self-contained speech unit that expresses an assertion, a question, a command, a wish, or an exclamation

♦ doom, finding, holding, judgment (*or* judgement), ruling; *also* verdict; injunction; decree, edict, order; dictum, pronouncement; opinion

²sentence *vb* **sen·tenced; sen·tenc·ing** : to impose a sentence on

♦ condemn, damn, doom; *also* adjudge, judge; castigate, chasten, chastise, correct, discipline, penalize, punish; conclude, decide, determine, find, opine, resolve

sen·ten·tious \sen-'ten-chəs\ *adj* : using wise sayings or proverbs; *also* : using pompous language — **sen·ten·tious·ly** *adv* — **sen·ten·tious·ness** *n*

sen·tient \'sen-chənt, -chē-ənt\ *adj* ♦ : capable of feeling : having perception

♦ alive, aware, cognizant, conscious, mindful, sensible, witting — more at CONSCIOUS

sen·ti·ment \'sen-tə-mənt\ *n* **1** ♦ : an emotional state or reaction : FEELING; *also* : thought and judgment influenced by feeling **2** ♦ : a specific view or notion

♦ [1] emotion, feeling, passion — more at FEELING

♦ [2] belief, conviction, eye, feeling, judgment (*or* judgement), mind, notion, opinion, persuasion, verdict, view — more at OPINION

sen·ti·men·tal \ˌsen-tə-ˈment-ᵊl\ *adj* **1** ♦ : influenced by tender feelings **2** ♦ : affecting the emotions — **sen·ti·men·tal·ist** *n* — **sen·ti·men·tal·ly** *adv*

♦ [1] demonstrative, emotional, feeling, intense, passionate, sensitive, soulful ♦ [2] corny, maudlin, mawkish, mushy, saccharine, sappy, schmaltzy — more at CORNY

sen·ti·men·tal·ise *chiefly Brit var of* SENTIMENTALIZE
sen·ti·men·tal·ism *n* : the disposition to favor or indulge in sentimentality; *also* : an excessively sentimental conception or statement
sen·ti·men·tal·i·ty \-ˌmen-ˈta-lə-tē, -mən-\ *n* **1** ♦ : the quality or state of being sentimental esp. to excess or in affectation **2** : a sentimental idea or its expression

♦ mawkishness, mush; *also* emotion; sentiment; corn, schmaltz

sen·ti·men·tal·ize \-ˈment-ᵊl-ˌīz\ *vb* **-ized; -iz·ing** **1** : to indulge in sentiment **2** : to look upon or imbue with sentiment — **sen·ti·men·tal·i·za·tion** \-ˌment-ᵊl-ə-ˈzā-shən\ *n*
sen·ti·nel \ˈsent-ᵊn-əl\ *n* [MF *sentinelle*, fr. It *sentinella*, fr. *sentina* vigilance, fr. *sentire* to perceive, fr. L] : one that watches or guards : SENTRY
sen·try \ˈsen-trē\ *n, pl* **sentries** ♦ : person who keeps watch : GUARD; *esp* : a soldier standing guard at a point of passage (as a gate)

♦ custodian, guard, guardian, keeper, lookout, picket, warden, warder, watch, watchman — more at GUARD

SEO *abbr* search engine optimization
sep *abbr* separate, separated
Sep *abbr* September
SEP *abbr* simplified employee pension
se·pal \ˈsē-pəl, ˈse-\ *n* : one of the modified leaves comprising a flower calyx
sep·a·ra·ble \ˈse-pə-rə-bəl\ *adj* : capable of being separated
¹sep·a·rate \ˈse-pə-ˌrāt\ *vb* **-rat·ed; -rat·ing** **1** ♦ : to set or keep apart : DISCONNECT **2** : to keep apart by something intervening **3** : to cease to be together : PART ⟨the couple decided to ∼⟩ **4** ♦ : to make a distinction between; *also* : to put in a certain place or rank according to kind, class, or nature **5** ♦ : to go in different directions

♦ [1] break up, disconnect, disjoint, dissever, dissociate, disunite, divide, divorce, part, resolve, sever, split, sunder, unyoke; *also* decompose, disassemble, dissolve; bisect, halve, quarter, segment, subdivide; break, rend, rip, rupture, tear; cut off, insulate, isolate, seclude, segregate, sequester; detach, disengage, disentangle, untie *Ant* join, link, unify, unite ♦ [1] cut off, insulate, isolate, seclude, segregate, sequester — more at ISOLATE ♦ [4] differentiate, discern, discriminate, distinguish — more at DISTINGUISH ♦ [4] assort, break down, categorize, class, classify, grade, group, peg, place, range, rank, sort — more at CLASSIFY ♦ [5] branch, diverge, divide, fork; *also* broadcast, clear out, disband, dispel, disperse, dissipate, distribute, scatter, sow; distance, recede, retreat *Ant* converge, join

²sep·a·rate \ˈse-prət, -pə-rət\ *adj* **1** : not connected **2** : divided from each other **3** : SINGLE, PARTICULAR ⟨the ∼ pieces of the puzzle⟩ **4** ♦ : existing by itself **5** ♦ : not shared with another — **sep·a·rate·ly** *adv*

♦ [4] detached, disconnected, discrete, freestanding, single, unattached, unconnected; *also* independent, self-contained; individual, private *Ant* attached, connected, joined ♦ [5] different, individual, respective; *also* disparate, dissimilar, distinct, distinctive, distinguishable, diverse, unalike, varied *Ant* same

³sep·a·rate *n* : an article of dress designed to be worn interchangeably with others to form various combinations
sep·a·ra·tion \ˌse-pə-ˈrā-shən\ *n* **1** ♦ : the act or process

of separating : the state of being separated **2** ♦ : a point, line, means, or area of division **3** : a formal separating of a married couple by agreement but without divorce

♦ [1] breakup, dissolution, division, partition, schism, split; *also* breach, rupture; decomposition, subdivision; dispersal, scattering; administration, apportionment, distribution; isolation, seclusion, segregation, sequestration *Ant* unification, union ♦ [1] demarcation, discrimination, distinction; *also* differentiation ♦ [2] breach, break, discontinuity, gap, gulf, hole, interval, opening, rent, rift — more at GAP

sep·a·ra·tist \ˈse-prə-tist, ˈse-pə-ˌrā-\ *n* : an advocate of separation (as from a political body) — **sep·a·ra·tism** \ˈse-prə-ˌti-zəm\ *n*
sep·a·ra·tive \ˈse-pə-ˌrā-tiv, ˈse-prə-tiv\ *adj* : tending toward, causing, or expressing separation ⟨∼ influences⟩
sep·a·ra·tor \ˈse-pə-ˌrā-tər\ *n* : one that separates; *esp* : a device for separating cream from milk
se·pia \ˈsē-pē-ə\ *n* : a brownish gray to dark brown color
sep·sis \ˈsep-səs\ *n, pl* **sep·ses** \ˈsep-ˌsēz\ : a toxic condition due to spread of bacteria or their toxic products in the body
Sept *abbr* September
Sep·tem·ber \sep-ˈtem-bər\ *n* [ME *Septembre*, fr. AF & OE, both fr. L *September* (seventh month), fr. *septem* seven] : the 9th month of the year having 30 days
sep·tic \ˈsep-tik\ *adj* **1** : PUTREFACTIVE **2** : relating to or involving sepsis **3** : of, relating to, or used for sewage treatment and disposal
sep·ti·ce·mia \ˌsep-tə-ˈsē-mē-ə\ *n* : BLOOD POISONING
septic tank *n* : a tank in which sewage is disintegrated by bacteria
sep·tu·a·ge·nar·i·an \ˌsep-ə-ˌtü-ə-jə-ˈner-ē-ən, -ˌtyü-\ *n* : a person whose age is in the seventies — **septuagenarian** *adj*
Sep·tu·a·gint \sep-ˈtü-ə-jənt, -ˈtyü-\ *n* : a Greek version of the Old Testament prepared in the 3d and 2d centuries B.C. by Jewish scholars
sep·tum \ˈsep-təm\ *n, pl* **sep·ta** \-tə\ : a dividing wall or membrane esp. between bodily spaces or masses of soft tissue
se·pul·chral \sə-ˈpəl-krəl\ *adj* **1** : relating to burial or the grave **2** ♦ : suited to or suggestive of a sepulchre : GLOOMY

♦ bleak, dark, dismal, dreary, gloomy, gray (*or* grey), somber (*or* sombre), wretched — more at GLOOMY

¹sep·ul·chre *or* **sep·ul·cher** \ˈse-pəl-kər\ *n* : a burial vault : TOMB
²sepulchre *or* **sepulcher** *vb* **-chred** *or* **-chered; -chring** *or* **-cher·ing** : BURY, ENTOMB
sep·ul·ture \ˈse-pəl-ˌchùr\ *n* **1** ♦ : the act or process of burying : BURIAL **2** : SEPULCHRE

♦ burial, entombment, interment — more at BURIAL

se·quel \ˈsē-kwəl\ *n* **1** : logical consequence **2** : a literary or cinematic work continuing a story begun in a preceding one
se·quence \ˈsē-kwəns\ *n* **1** ♦ : a continuous or connected series **2** ♦ : chronological order of events **3** : something produced by a cause or necessarily following from a set of conditions : RESULT, SEQUEL — **se·quen·tial·ly** *adv*

♦ [1] chain, progression, string, train — more at CHAIN ♦ [2] arrangement, array, disposal, disposition, distribution, order, setup — more at ORDER

se·quent \ˈsē-kwənt\ *adj* **1** : SUCCEEDING, CONSECUTIVE **2** : RESULTANT
se·quen·tial \si-ˈkwen-chəl\ *adj* ♦ : of, relating to, or arranged in a sequence

♦ consecutive, successive — more at CONSECUTIVE

se·ques·ter \si-ˈkwes-tər\ *vb* **1** ♦ : to set apart : SEGREGATE **2** : to place (property) in custody esp. in sequestration

♦ cut off, insulate, isolate, seclude, segregate, separate — more at ISOLATE

se·ques·trate \ˈsē-kwəs-ˌtrāt, si-ˈkwes-\ *vb* **-trat·ed; -trat·ing** : SEQUESTER

se·ques·tra·tion \ˌsē-kwəs-ˈtrā-shən, ˌse-\ *n* 1 ♦ : the act of sequestering : the state of being sequestered 2 : a deposit whereby a neutral depositary agrees to hold property in litigation and to restore it to the party to whom it is adjudged to belong

♦ insulation, isolation, seclusion, segregation, solitude — more at ISOLATION

se·quin \ˈsē-kwən\ *n* 1 : an old gold coin of Turkey and Italy 2 : a small metal or plastic plate used for ornamentation esp. on clothing — **se·quined** *or* **se·quinned** \-kwənd\ *adj*

se·quoia \si-ˈkwȯi-ə\ *n* : either of two huge California coniferous trees

ser *abbr* 1 serial 2 series 3 service

sera *pl of* SERUM

se·ra·glio \sə-ˈral-yō\ *n, pl* **-glios** [It *serraglio*] : HAREM

se·ra·pe \sə-ˈrä-pē\ *n* : a colorful woolen shawl worn over the shoulders esp. by Mexican men

ser·aph \ˈser-əf\ *n, pl* **ser·a·phim** \-ə-ˌfim, -ˌfēm\ *or* **seraphs** : one of the 6-winged angels standing in the presence of God

ser·a·phim \ˈser-ə-ˌfim, -ˌfēm\ *n pl* 1 : the highest order of angels 2 *sing*; *pl* **seraphim** : SERAPH — **se·raph·ic** \sə-ˈra-fik\ *adj*

Serb \ˈsərb\ *n* : a native or inhabitant of Serbia

Ser·bi·an \ˈsər-bē-ən\ *n* 1 : SERB 2 : a south Slavic language spoken by the Serbian people — **Serbian** *adj*

Ser·bo–Cro·a·tian \ˌsər-(ˌ)bō-krō-ˈā-shən\ *n* : the Serbian and Croatian languages together with the Slavic speech of Bosnia, Herzegovina, and Montenegro taken as a single language with regional variants

sere \ˈsir\ *adj* ♦ : being dried and withered : DRY

♦ arid, dry, thirsty — more at DRY

¹ser·e·nade \ˌser-ə-ˈnād\ *n* [F, fr. It *serenata*, fr. *sereno* clear, calm (of weather)] : music sung or played as a compliment esp. outdoors at night for a woman being courted

²serenade *vb* **-nad·ed; -nad·ing** : to entertain with or perform a serenade

ser·en·dip·i·ty \ˌser-ən-ˈdi-pə-tē\ *n* [fr. its possession by the heroes of the Persian fairy tale *The Three Princes of Serendip*] : the gift of finding valuable or agreeable things not sought for — **ser·en·dip·i·tous** \-təs\ *adj*

se·rene \sə-ˈrēn\ *adj* 1 ♦ : clear and free of storms or unpleasant change ⟨∼ skies⟩ 2 ♦ : marked by or suggestive of utter calm and unruffled repose or quiet — **se·rene·ly** *adv*

♦ [1, 2] calm, halcyon, hushed, peaceful, placid, quiet, still, tranquil, untroubled — more at CALM ♦ [2] calm, collected, composed, cool, self-possessed, undisturbed, unperturbed, unshaken, unworried — more at CALM

se·ren·i·ty \sə-ˈre-nə-tē\ *n* ♦ : the quality or state of being serene

♦ calm, calmness, hush, peace, placidity, quiet, quietness, repose, still, stillness, tranquility — more at CALM ♦ aplomb, composure, coolness, equanimity, self-possession — more at EQUANIMITY

serf \ˈsərf\ *n* : a member of a servile class bound to the land and subject to the will of the landowner — **serf·dom** \-dəm\ *n*

serge \ˈsərj\ *n* : a twilled woolen cloth

ser·geant \ˈsär-jənt\ *n* [ME, servant, attendant, sergeant, fr. AF *sergant, serjant*, fr. L *servient-, serviens*, prp. of *servire* to serve] 1 : a noncommissioned officer (as in the army) ranking next below a staff sergeant 2 : an officer in a police force

sergeant at arms : an officer of an organization who preserves order and executes commands

sergeant first class *n* : a noncommissioned officer in the army ranking next below a master sergeant

sergeant major *n, pl* **sergeants major** *or* **sergeant majors** 1 : a noncommissioned officer in the army or marine corps serving as chief administrative assistant in a headquarters 2 : a noncommissioned officer in the marine corps ranking above a first sergeant

¹se·ri·al \ˈsir-ē-əl\ *adj* 1 ♦ : appearing in successive parts or numbers ⟨a ∼ story⟩ 2 : performing a series of similar acts over a period of time ⟨a ∼ killer⟩; *also* : occurring in such a series — **se·ri·al·ly** *adv*

♦ episodic, periodic; *also* sequential; recurrent, regular

²serial *n* : a serial story or other writing — **se·ri·al·ist** \-ə-list\ *n*

se·ries \ˈsir-ēz\ *n, pl* **series** : a number of things or events arranged in order and connected by being alike in some way

seri·graph \ˈser-ə-ˌgraf\ *n* : an original silk-screen print — **se·rig·ra·pher** \sə-ˈri-grə-fər\ *n* — **se·rig·ra·phy** \-fē\ *n*

se·ri·ous \ˈsir-ē-əs\ *adj* 1 ♦ : thoughtful or subdued in appearance or manner : SOBER 2 : requiring much thought or work 3 : EARNEST, DEVOTED 4 ♦ : having important or dangerous possible consequences 5 : excessive or impressive in quantity or degree ⟨making ∼ money⟩ 6 ♦ : of or relating to a matter of importance — **se·ri·ous·ly** *adv*

♦ [1] earnest, grave, humorless (*or* humourless), severe, sober, solemn, staid, unsmiling, weighty; *also* harsh, stern, strict; dignified, distinguished, elevated *Ant* facetious, flip, flippant, humorous, jocular, joking, playful ♦ [4] dangerous, grave, grievous, hazardous, menacing, parlous, perilous, risky, unhealthy, unsafe, venturesome — more at DANGEROUS ♦ [6] grave, heavy, weighty; *also* big, consequential, eventful, important, major, material, meaningful, momentous, significant, substantial *Ant* light

se·ri·ous·ness *n* ♦ : the quality or state of being serious

♦ earnestness, gravity, intentness, sobriety, solemnity — more at EARNESTNESS

ser·mon \ˈsər-mən\ *n* [ME, fr. AF *sermun*, fr. ML *sermon-, sermo*, fr. L, speech, conversation, fr. *serere* to link together] 1 : a religious discourse esp. as part of a worship service 2 : a lecture on conduct or duty

ser·mon·ize \ˈsər-mə-ˌnīz\ *vb* **-ized; -iz·ing** : to compose or deliver a sermon 2 : to preach to or on at length

se·rol·o·gy \sə-ˈrä-lə-jē\ *n* : a science dealing with serums and esp. their reactions and properties — **se·ro·log·i·cal** \ˌsir-ə-ˈlä-ji-kəl\ *or* **se·ro·log·ic** \-jik\ *adj*

se·ro·to·nin \ˌsir-ə-ˈtō-nən, ˌser-\ *n* : a neurotransmitter that is a powerful vasoconstrictor

se·rous \ˈsir-əs\ *adj* : of, relating to, resembling, or producing serum; *esp* : of thin watery constitution

ser·pent \ˈsər-pənt\ *n* : SNAKE

¹ser·pen·tine \ˈsər-pən-ˌtēn, -ˌtīn\ *adj* 1 : SLY, CRAFTY 2 ♦ : winding or turning one way and another

♦ crooked, devious, sinuous, tortuous, winding — more at CROOKED

²ser·pen·tine \-ˌtēn\ *n* : a dull-green mineral having a mottled appearance

ser·rate \ˈser-ˌāt\ *adj* : having a saw-toothed edge ⟨a ∼ leaf⟩

ser·ried \ˈser-ēd\ *adj* ♦ : crowded or pressed together : DENSE

♦ close, compact, crowded, dense, packed, thick, tight — more at CLOSE

se·rum \ˈsir-əm\ *n, pl* **serums** *or* **se·ra** \-ə\ [L, whey, whey-like fluid] : the clear yellowish antibody-containing fluid that can be separated from blood when it clots; *also* : a preparation of animal serum containing specific antibodies and used to prevent or cure disease

serv *abbr* service

ser·vant \ˈsər-vənt\ *n* ♦ : one that serves others; *esp* : a person employed for domestic or personal work

♦ domestic, flunky, lackey, menial, retainer, steward; *also* butler, footman, groom, houseboy, man, majordomo, manservant, servitor, valet; handmaiden, housekeeper, housemaid, lady-in-waiting, maid, maidservant, wench, woman; attendant, follower *Ant* master

¹serve \ˈsərv\ *vb* **served; serv·ing** 1 : to work as a servant

2 : to render obedience and worship to (God) **3** : to comply with the commands or demands of **4** : to work through or perform a term of service (as in the army) **5** : PUT IN ⟨*served* five years in jail⟩ **6** ♦ : to be of use ⟨pine boughs *served* for a bed⟩ **7** ♦ : to provide services that benefit or help : BENEFIT **8** : to prove adequate or satisfactory for ⟨a pie that ∼s eight people⟩ **9** : to make ready and pass out ⟨∼ drinks⟩ **10** : to furnish or supply with something ⟨one power company *serving* the whole state⟩ **11** : to wait on ⟨∼ a customer⟩ **12** ♦ : to treat or act toward in a specified way ⟨∼ed as her assistant⟩ **13** : to put the ball in play (as in tennis)

♦ [6] act, function, perform, work — more at FUNC-TION ♦ [7] avail, benefit, profit — more at BENEFIT ♦ [12] act, be, deal, handle, treat, use — more at TREAT

²**serve** *n* : the act of serving a ball (as in tennis)

serv·er *n* **1** ♦ : one that serves **2** : a computer in a network that is used to provide services (as access to files) to other computers in the network

♦ waiter, waitperson, waitress

¹**ser·vice** \'sər-vəs\ *n* **1** : the occupation of a servant **2** : HELP, BENEFIT **3** : a meeting for worship; *also* : a form followed in worship or in a ceremony ⟨burial ∼⟩ **4** ♦ : the act, fact, or means of serving **5** : performance of official or professional duties **6** : SERVE **7** : a set of dishes or silverware **8 a** : a branch of public employment; *also* : the persons in it ⟨civil ∼⟩ **b** ♦ : one of a nation's organized fighting forces (as the army, navy, or air force) — often used in pl. **9** : military or naval duty **10** ♦ : contribution to the welfare of others; *also* : disposal for use

♦ [4] boon, courtesy, favor (*or* favour), grace, indulgence, kindness, mercy, turn — more at FAVOR ♦ **services** [8b] armed forces, military, troops — more at ARMED FORCES ♦ [10] account, avail, use, utility — more at USE

²**service** *vb* **ser·viced; ser·vic·ing** : to do maintenance or repair work on or for

ser·vice·able \'sər-və-sə-bəl\ *adj* ♦ : prepared for service : USEFUL

♦ applicable, functional, practicable, practical, usable, useful, workable, working — more at PRACTICAL

ser·vice·man \'sər-vəs-ˌman, -mən\ *n* **1** ♦ : a man who is a member of the armed forces **2** : a man employed to repair or maintain equipment

♦ fighter, legionnaire, man-at-arms, regular, soldier, warrior — more at SOLDIER

service mark *n* : a mark or device used to identify a service (as transportation or insurance) offered to customers

service station *n* : a retail station for servicing motor vehicles

ser·vice·wom·an \'sər-vəs-ˌwu̇-mən\ *n* : a woman who is a member of the armed forces

ser·vi·ette \ˌsər-vē-'et\ *n* [F, fr. MF, fr. *servir* to serve] *chiefly Can and Brit* : a table napkin

ser·vile \'sər-vəl, -ˌvīl\ *adj* **1** : befitting a slave or servant **2** : behaving like a slave : SUBMISSIVE — **ser·vile·ly** *adv*

ser·vil·i·ty \ˌsər-'vi-lə-tē\ *n* : a slave's condition : the state of slavery

serv·ing \'sər-viŋ\ *n* : HELPING

ser·vi·tor \'sər-və-tər\ *n* : a male servant

ser·vi·tude \'sər-və-ˌtüd, -ˌtyüd\ *n* ♦ : the condition of a slave or serf : SLAVERY, BONDAGE

♦ bondage, enslavement, slavery, thrall, yoke — more at SLAVERY

ser·vo \'sər-vō\ *n, pl* **servos** **1** : SERVOMOTOR **2** : SER-VOMECHANISM

ser·vo·mech·a·nism \'sər-vō-ˌme-kə-ˌni-zəm\ *n* : a device for automatically correcting the performance of a mechanism

ser·vo·mo·tor \-ˌmō-tər\ *n* : a mechanism that supplements a primary control

ses·a·me \'se-sə-mē\ *n* : a widely cultivated annual herb of warm regions; *also* : its seeds that yield an edible oil (**sesame oil**) and are used in flavoring

ses·qui·cen·ten·ni·al \ˌses-kwi-sen-'te-nē-əl\ *n* [L *sesqui-* one and a half, half again] : a 150th anniversary or its celebration — **sesquicentennial** *adj*

ses·qui·pe·da·lian \ˌses-kwə-pə-'dāl-yən\ *adj* **1** : having many syllables : LONG **2** : using long words

ses·sile \'se-sīl, -səl\ *adj* : permanently attached and not free to move about

ses·sion \'se-shən\ *n* **1** : a meeting or series of meetings of a body (as a court or legislature) for the transaction of business **2** : a meeting or period devoted to a particular activity

¹**set** \'set\ *vb* **set; set·ting** **1** : to cause to sit **2** : PLACE **3** ♦ : to put into a desired position, adjustment, or condition **4** : to cause to be or do **5** ♦ : to fix or decide on as a time, limit, or regulation : SETTLE **6** : to fix in a frame **7** : to fix at a certain amount **8** : WAGER, STAKE **9** ♦ : to make or become fast or rigid **10** : to adapt (as words) to something (as music) **11** ♦ : to become fixed or firm or solid **12** : to be suitable : FIT **13** ♦ : to cover and warm eggs to hatch them : BROOD **14** ♦ : to have a certain direction **15** : to pass below the horizon **16** : to defeat in bridge — **set about** : to begin to do — **set forth** : to begin a trip — **set out** : to begin a trip or undertaking — **set sail** : to begin a voyage — **set upon** : to attack usu. with violence

♦ [3] deposit, dispose, fix, lay, place, position, put, set up, stick — more at PLACE ♦ [3, 9] anchor, catch, clamp, fasten, fix, hitch, moor, secure ♦ [5] arrange, decide, fix, name, settle — more at ARRANGE ♦ [11] concrete, congeal, firm, freeze, gel, harden, jell, solidify — more at HARDEN ♦ [13] brood, hatch, incubate, sit; *also* lay, spawn; pip ♦ [14] aim, bend, cast, direct, head, level, train — more at AIM

²**set** *n* **1** : a setting or a being set **2** : DIRECTION, COURSE; *also* : TENDENCY **3** : FORM, BUILD **4** : the fit of something (as a coat) **5** : an artificial setting for the scene of a play or motion picture **6** : a group of tennis games in which one side wins at least six **7** ♦ : a group of persons or things of the same kind or having a common characteristic usu. classed together **8** : a collection of things and esp. of mathematical elements (as numbers or points) **9** : an electronic apparatus ⟨a television ∼⟩

♦ bloc, body, coalition, combination, combine, faction, party, sect, side, wing — more at FACTION ♦ circle, clan, clique, community, coterie, crowd — more at GANG ♦ array, assemblage, cluster, collection, group, package, parcel, suite

³**set** *adj* **1** ♦ : firmly resolved : INTENT **2** ♦ : fixed by authority or custom ⟨∼ a price⟩ **3** ♦ : incapable of being moved **4** : PERSISTENT **5** ♦ : being in readiness

♦ [1] bound, decisive, determined, firm, intent, purposeful, resolute, single-minded — more at DETER-MINED ♦ [2] certain, determinate, final, firm, fixed, flat, frozen, hard, hard-and-fast, settled, stable — more at FIXED ♦ [2] distinct, especial, express, precise, special, specific — more at EXPRESS ♦ [3] fast, firm, frozen, secure, snug, tight — more at TIGHT ♦ [5] fit, go, ready — more at READY

set·back \'set-ˌbak\ *n* ♦ : a temporary defeat : REVERSE

♦ lapse, reversal, reverse — more at REVERSE

set back *vb* **1** : HINDER, DELAY; *also* : REVERSE **2** : COST

set down *vb* **1** : to cause to sit down **2** ♦ : to put in writing

♦ jot, log, mark, note, put down, record, register — more at RECORD

set off *vb* **1** : to start out on a course or trip **2** ♦ : to set in motion : cause to begin

♦ activate, actuate, crank, drive, move, propel, run, spark, start, touch off, trigger, turn on — more at ACTIVATE

set·screw \'set-ˌskrü\ *n* : a screw screwed through one part tightly upon or into another part to prevent relative movement

set·tee \se-'tē\ *n* ♦ : a bench or sofa with a back and arms

♦ couch, davenport, divan, lounge, sofa — more at COUCH

set·ter \'se-tər\ *n* : a large long-coated hunting dog

set·ting \'se-tiŋ\ *n* 1 : the frame in which a gem is set 2 ♦ : the time, place, and circumstances in which something occurs or develops 3 : music written for a text (as of a poem) 4 : the eggs that a fowl sits on for hatching at one time

♦ atmosphere, climate, environment, environs, medium, milieu, surroundings — more at ENVIRONMENT

set·tle \'set-ᵊl\ *vb* **set·tled; set·tling** [ME *settlen* to seat, bring to rest, come to rest, fr. OE *setlan*, fr. *setl* seat] 1 ♦ : to place or become established in a place 2 : to establish in residence; *also* : COLONIZE 3 : to make compact 4 ♦ : to make or become quiet or orderly — often used with *down* 5 : to establish or secure permanently 6 : to direct one's efforts 7 ♦ : to fix by agreement : to reach an agreement on 8 : to conclude legally ⟨~ a lawsuit⟩ 9 ♦ : to fix or resolve conclusively ⟨~ the question⟩ 10 ♦ : to make a final disposition of ⟨~ an account⟩ 11 ♦ : to come to rest 12 : to sink gradually to a lower level 13 : to become clear by depositing sediment

♦ [1] ensconce, install, lodge, perch, roost — more at ENSCONCE ♦ [4] allay, calm, compose, quiet, soothe, still, tranquilize — more at CALM ♦ *usu* **settle down** [4] calm (down), cool (off *or* down), hush, quiet — more at QUIET ♦ [7] arrange, decide, fix, set — more at ARRANGE ♦ [9] adjudicate, arbitrate, decide, determine, judge, referee, rule, umpire — more at JUDGE ♦ [10] clear, discharge, foot, liquidate, pay, pay off, quit, recompense, spring, stand — more at PAY ♦ [11] alight, land, light, perch, roost — more at ALIGHT

settled *adj* ♦ : unlikely to change or be changed : established or decided beyond dispute or doubt

♦ confirmed, deep-rooted, deep-seated, inveterate — more at INVETERATE ♦ certain, determinate, final, firm, fixed, flat, frozen, hard, hard-and-fast, set, stable — more at FIXED

set·tle·ment \'set-ᵊl-mənt\ *n* 1 : the act or process of settling 2 : BESTOWAL ⟨a marriage ~⟩ 3 : payment or adjustment of an account 4 : COLONY 5 : a small village 6 : an institution providing various community services esp. to large city populations 7 ♦ : adjustment of doubts and differences

♦ accord, agreement, bargain, compact, contract, convention, covenant, deal, pact, understanding — more at AGREEMENT

set·tler *n* ♦ : one that settles (as a new region)

♦ colonist, frontiersman, homesteader, pioneer — more at FRONTIERSMAN ♦ emigrant, émigré, immigrant, migrant — more at EMIGRANT

set-to \'set-ˌtü\ *n, pl* **set-tos** : FIGHT

set·up \'set-ˌəp\ *n* 1 ♦ : the manner or act of arranging 2 : glass, ice, and nonalcoholic beverage for mixing served to patrons who supply their own liquor 3 : something (as a plot) that has been constructed or contrived; *also* : FRAME-UP

♦ arrangement, configuration, conformation, format, layout ♦ arrangement, array, disposal, disposition, distribution, order, sequence — more at ORDER

set up *vb* 1 ♦ : to place in position; *also* : ASSEMBLE 2 : CAUSE 3 ♦ : to bring about the beginning of : FOUND ⟨*set up* a school⟩ 4 : FRAME 5 5 ♦ : to place upright

♦ [1] assemble, deposit, dispose, fix, lay, place, position, put, set, stick — more at PLACE ♦ [3] constitute, establish, found, inaugurate, initiate, innovate, institute, introduce, launch, pioneer, start — more at FOUND ♦ [5] erect, pitch, put up, raise, rear — more at ERECT

sev·en \'se-vən\ *n* 1 : one more than six 2 : the 7th in a set or series 3 : something having seven units — **seven** *adj or pron* — **sev·enth** \-vənth\ *adj or adv or n*

sev·en·teen \ˌse-vən-'tēn\ *n* : one more than 16 — **seventeen** *adj or pron* — **sev·en·teenth** \-'tēnth\ *adj or n*

seventeen-year locust *n* : a cicada of the U.S. that has in the North a life of 17 years and in the South of 13 years of which most is spent underground as a nymph and only a few weeks as a winged adult

sev·en·ty \'se-vən-tē\ *n, pl* **-ties** : seven times 10 — **sev·en·ti·eth** \-tē-əth\ *adj or n* — **seventy** *adj or pron*

sev·er \'se-vər\ *vb* **sev·ered; sev·er·ing** ♦ : to separate into individual parts : DIVIDE; *esp* : to separate by or as if by cutting — **sev·er·ance** \'sev-rəns, 'se-və-\ *n*

♦ break up, disconnect, disjoint, dissever, dissociate, disunite, divide, divorce, part, resolve, separate, split, sunder, unyoke — more at SEPARATE

sev·er·al \'sev-rəl, 'se-və-\ *adj* [ME, fr. AF, fr. ML *separalis*, fr. L *separ* separate, fr. *separare* to separate] 1 : INDIVIDUAL, DISTINCT ⟨federal union of the ~ states⟩ 2 : consisting of an indefinite number but yet not very many ⟨ate ~ cookies⟩ — **sev·er·al·ly** *adv*

severance pay *n* : extra pay given an employee upon termination of employment

se·vere \sə-'vir\ *adj* **se·ver·er; -est** 1 ♦ : marked by strictness or sternness : AUSTERE 2 ♦ : strict in discipline 3 : causing distress and esp. physical discomfort or pain ⟨~ weather⟩ ⟨a ~ wound⟩ 4 ♦ : hard to endure ⟨~ trials⟩ 5 : of a great degree : SERIOUS ⟨~ depression⟩

♦ [1, 2] austere, authoritarian, flinty, hard, harsh, heavy-handed, ramrod, rigid, rigorous, stern, strict; *also* demanding, exacting; uncharitable, unforgiving; immovable, implacable, inflexible, unbending, uncompromising, unyielding; determined, firm, resolved, steadfast, unflinching *Ant* forbearing, indulgent, lax, lenient, tolerant ♦ [4] bitter, brutal, burdensome, cruel, excruciating, grievous, grim, hard, harsh, heavy, inhuman, murderous, onerous, oppressive, rough, rugged, stiff, tough, trying — more at HARSH

se·vere·ly *adv* ♦ : in a severe manner : with severity

♦ hard, hardly, harshly, ill, oppressively, roughly, sternly, stiffly — more at HARDLY

se·ver·i·ty \sə-'ver-ə-tē\ *n* ♦ : quality or state of being severe

♦ hardness, harshness, inflexibility, rigidity, sternness, strictness; *also* implacability, obduracy; asceticism, austerity, monasticism; determination, firmness, resolve, steadfastness; obstinacy, stubbornness *Ant* gentleness, flexibility, laxness, mildness

sew \'sō\ *vb* **sewed; sewn** \'sōn\ *or* **sewed; sew·ing** 1 : to unite or fasten by stitches 2 : to engage in sewing

sew·age \'sü-ij\ *n* : waste materials carried off by sewers

¹**sew·er** \'sō-ər\ *n* : one that sews

²**sew·er** \'sü-ər\ *n* : an artificial pipe or channel to carry off waste matter

sew·er·age \'sü-ə-rij\ *n* 1 : a system of sewers 2 : SEWAGE

sew·ing *n* 1 : the activity of one who sews 2 : material that has been or is to be sewed

sex \'seks\ *n* 1 a : either of the two major forms of individuals that occur in many species and that are designated male or female esp. on the basis of their reproductive organs b : the sum of the structural, functional, and sometimes behavioral characteristics that distinguish males and females c : the state of being male or female d : males or females considered as a group ⟨the female ~⟩ 2 a : sexual activity or behavior b : SEXUAL INTERCOURSE 3 : GENITALIA — **sexed** \'sekst\ *adj* — **sex·less** *adj*

sex·a·ge·nar·i·an \ˌsek-sə-jə-'ner-ē-ən\ *n* : a person whose age is in the sixties — **sexagenarian** *adj*

sex appeal *n* : personal appeal or physical attractiveness esp. for members of the opposite sex

sex cell *n* : an egg cell or sperm cell

sex chromosome *n* : one of usu. a pair of chromosomes that are usu. similar in one sex but different in the other sex and are concerned with the inheritance of sex

sex hormone *n* : a steroid hormone (as estrogen or testosterone) that is produced esp. by the gonads or adrenal cortex and chiefly affects the growth or function of the reproductive organs

sex·ism \'sek-ˌsi-zəm\ *n* : prejudice or discrimination based on sex; *esp* : discrimination against women — **sex·ist** \'sek-sist\ *adj or n*

sex·ol·o·gy \sek-'sä-lə-jē\ *n* : the study of sex or of the interactions of the sexes — **sex·ol·o·gist** \-jist\ *n*

sex·pot \'seks-ˌpät\ *n* : a conspicuously sexy woman

sex symbol *n* : a usu. renowned person (as an entertainer) noted and admired for conspicuous attractiveness

sex·tant \'sek-stənt\ *n* [NL *sextant-, sextans* sixth part of a circle, fr. L, sixth part, fr. *sextus* sixth] : a navigational instrument for determining latitude

sex·tet \sek-'stet\ *n* **1** : a musical composition for six voices or instruments; *also* : the performers of such a composition **2** : a group or set of six

sext·ing \'sek-stiŋ\ *n* : the sending of sexually explicit messages or images by cell phone

sex·ton \'sek-stən\ *n* : one who takes care of church property

sex·u·al \'sek-shə-wəl\ *adj* : of, relating to, or involving sex or the sexes ⟨a ∼ spore⟩ ⟨∼ relations⟩ — **sex·u·al·i·ty** \ˌsek-shə-'wa-lə-tē\ *n* — **sex·u·al·ly** \'sek-shə-wə-lē\ *adv*

sexual intercourse *n* **1** ♦ : intercourse between a male and a female in which the penis is inserted into the vagina **2** : intercourse between individuals involving genital contact other than insertion of the penis into the vagina

  ♦ copulation, intercourse; *also* fornication; safe sex; sexuality

sexually transmitted disease *n* : a disease (as syphilis, gonorrhea, AIDS, or the genital form of herpes simplex) that is caused by a microorganism or virus usu. or often transmitted by direct sexual contact

sexual relations *n pl* : physical sexual contact between individuals that involves the genitalia : SEXUAL INTERCOURSE

sexy \'sek-sē\ *adj* **sex·i·er; -est** ♦ : sexually suggestive or stimulating : EROTIC — **sex·i·ly** \-sə-lē\ *adv* — **sex·i·ness** \-sē-nəs\ *n*

  ♦ amatory, amorous, erotic — more at EROTIC

SF *abbr* **1** sacrifice fly **2** science fiction

SFC *abbr* sergeant first class

Sg *symbol* seaborgium

SG *abbr* **1** senior grade **2** sergeant **3** solicitor general **4** surgeon general

sgd *abbr* signed

Sgt *abbr* sergeant

Sgt Maj *abbr* sergeant major

sh *abbr* share

shab·by \'sha-bē\ *adj* **shab·bi·er; -est** **1** : dressed in worn clothes **2** ♦ : threadbare and faded from wear **3** : DESPICABLE, MEAN; *also* : UNFAIR ⟨∼ treatment⟩ — **shab·bi·ly** \'sha-bə-lē\ *adv* — **shab·bi·ness** \-bē-nəs\ *n*

  ♦ dilapidated, grungy, mangy, mean, neglected, ragged, ratty, scruffy, seedy, tacky, tattered, threadbare; *also* abandoned, desolate, forlorn; decrepit, worn-out; bedraggled, dingy, decaying, ramshackle

shack \'shak\ *n* ♦ : an often small and temporary dwelling of simple construction : HUT

  ♦ cabin, camp, hut, hutch, shanty; *also* lean-to, shed; cot, cottage, lodge; cabana; bungalow, chalet; hogan, wickiup, wigwam

¹shack·le \'sha-kəl\ *n* ♦ **1** : something (as a manacle or fetter) that confines the legs or arms **2** ♦ : a check on free action made as if by fetters **3** : a device for making something fast or secure

  ♦ [1] band, bond, chain, fetter, irons, ligature, manacle — more at BOND ♦ [2] bar, block, encumbrance, hindrance, inhibition, obstacle — more at ENCUMBRANCE

²shackle *vb* **shack·led; shack·ling** **1** ♦ : to bind or fasten with shackles **2** ♦ : to limit free movement or expression with restrictions or handicaps

  ♦ [1] bind, chain, enchain, fetter, handcuff, manacle, trammel ♦ [2] encumber, hamper, hinder, hold up, impede, inhibit, interfere with, obstruct, tie up — more at HAMPER

shad \'shad\ *n, pl* **shad** : any of several sea fishes related to the herrings that swim up rivers to spawn and include some important food fishes

¹shade \'shād\ *n* **1 a** : partial obscurity **b** *pl* ♦ : the shadows that gather as darkness comes on **2** : space sheltered from the light esp. of the sun **3** ♦ : a disembodied spirit : PHANTOM **4** ♦ : something that shelters from or intercepts light or heat; *also, pl* : SUNGLASSES **5** ♦ : a dark color or a variety of a color **6** : a small difference

  ♦ [1b] dark, darkness, dusk, gloaming, gloom, murk, night, semidarkness, shadows, twilight — more at DARK ♦ [3] apparition, bogey, ghost, phantasm, phantom, poltergeist, shadow, specter, spirit, spook, vision, wraith — more at GHOST ♦ [5] cast, color (*or* colour), hue, tinge, tint, tone — more at COLOR

²shade *vb* **shad·ed; shad·ing** **1** : to shelter from light and heat **2** : DARKEN, OBSCURE **3** : to mark with degrees of light or color **4** : to show slight differences esp. in color or meaning

shaded *adj* ♦ : protected from heat or light (as with shade or shadow)

  ♦ shadowy, shady — more at SHADY

shad·ing *n* : the color and lines representing darkness or shadow in a drawing or painting

¹shad·ow \'sha-dō\ *n* **1 a** : partial darkness in a space from which light rays are cut off **b** *pl* ♦ : a place or time of little or no light **2** : SHELTER **3** : shade cast upon a surface by something intercepting rays from a light ⟨the ∼ of a tree⟩ **4** : something (as a specter) apparent to sense but with no substantial existence : PHANTOM **5** : a shaded portion of a picture **6** ♦ : a small portion or degree : TRACE ⟨a ∼ of doubt⟩ **7** : a source of gloom or unhappiness **8** ♦ : one (as a spy or detective) that shadows

  ♦ shadows [1b] dark, darkness, dusk, gloaming, gloom, murk, night, semidarkness, shade, twilight — more at DARK ♦ [6] relic, trace, vestige — more at VESTIGE ♦ [8] detective, investigator, operative, sleuth, tail — more at DETECTIVE

²shadow *vb* **1** ♦ : to cast a shadow on **2** : to represent faintly or vaguely **3** ♦ : to follow and watch closely

  ♦ [1] becloud, blacken, cloud, darken, dim, obscure, overcast, overshadow ♦ [3] chase, dog, follow, hound, pursue, tag, tail, trace, track, trail — more at FOLLOW

shad·ow·box \'sha-dō-ˌbäks\ *vb* : to box with an imaginary opponent esp. for training

shad·owy *adj* **1** ♦ : faintly perceptible **2** : being in or obscured by shadow; *also* : producing or providing shade

  ♦ bleary, dim, faint, foggy, fuzzy, hazy, indefinite, indistinct, indistinguishable, murky, nebulous, obscure, opaque, unclear, undefined, undetermined, vague — more at FAINT

shady \'shā-dē\ *adj* **shad·i·er; -est** **1** ♦ : affording shade **2** ♦ : of questionable honesty or reputation

  ♦ [1] shaded, shadowy; *also* covered, sheltered; cloudy; dark, darkened, darkling, dim, dimmed, dusky, gloomy; murky, obscure, obscured, somber, sunless *Ant* sunny ♦ [2] crooked, deceptive, dishonest, fast, fraudulent, sharp, shifty, underhanded — more at DISHONEST ♦ [2] debatable, disputable, doubtful, dubious, equivocal, fishy, problematic, questionable, shaky, suspect, suspicious — more at DOUBTFUL

¹shaft \'shaft\ *n, pl* **shafts** **1** : the long handle of a spear or lance **2** : a thrusting or throwing weapon with long shaft and sharp head or blade : SPEAR, LANCE **3** *or pl* **shaves** \'shavz\ : POLE; *esp* : one of two poles between which a horse is hitched to pull a vehicle **4** : something (as a column) long and slender **5** : a bar to support a rotating piece or to transmit power by rotation **6** : an inclined opening in the ground (as for finding or mining ore) **7** : a vertical opening (as for an elevator) through the floors of a building **8** : harsh or unfair treatment — usu. used with *the* **9** : a sharply delineated beam of light shining through an opening

²**shaft** *vb* **1** : to fit with a shaft **2** : to treat unfairly or harshly

shag \'shag\ *n* : a shaggy tangled mass or covering (as of wool) : long coarse or matted fiber, nap, or pile

shag·gy \'sha-gē\ *adj* **shag·gi·er; -est** **1** ♦ : rough with or as if with long hair or wool **2** : tangled or rough in surface

♦ fleecy, furry, hairy, hirsute, rough, unshorn, woolly — more at HAIRY

shah \'shä, 'shȯ\ *n, often cap* : a sovereign of Iran

Shak *abbr* Shakespeare

¹**shake** \'shāk\ *vb* **shook** \'shůk\; **shak·en** \'shā-kən\; **shak·ing** **1** ♦ : to move or cause to move jerkily or irregularly **2** : BRANDISH, WAVE ⟨*shaking* his fist⟩ **3** : to disturb emotionally ⟨*shaken* by her death⟩ **4** : WEAKEN ⟨*shook* his faith⟩ **5** : to bring or come into a certain position, condition, or arrangement by or as if by moving jerkily **6** : to clasp (hands) in greeting or as a sign of goodwill or agreement **7** ♦ : to get away from : get rid of — **shak·able** *or* **shakeable** \'shā-kə-bəl\ *adj*

♦ [1] agitate, convulse, jolt, jounce, quake, quiver, shudder, vibrate, wobble; *also* rock, sway; quaver, shiver, tremble; dodder, waver; flicker, fluctuate, flutter, oscillate, wave; beat, palpitate, pit-a-pat, pitter-patter, pulsate, pulse, throb ♦ [7] avoid, dodge, duck, elude, escape, eschew, evade, shirk, shun — more at ESCAPE

²**shake** *n* **1** : the act or a result of shaking **2** : DEAL, TREATMENT ⟨a fair ∼⟩ **3** ♦ : a very brief period of time **4** *pl* ♦ : a condition of trembling or nervousness

♦ [3] flash, instant, jiffy, minute, moment, second, trice, twinkle, twinkling, wink — more at INSTANT ♦ **shakes** [4] jitters, shivers, willies — more at JITTERS

shake·down \'shāk-ˌdaůn\ *n* **1** : an improvised bed **2** : EXTORTION **3** : a process or period of adjustment **4** : a test (as of a new ship or airplane) under operating conditions

shake down *vb* **1** : to take up temporary quarters **2** : to occupy a makeshift bed **3** : to become accustomed esp. to new surroundings or duties **4** : to settle down **5** : to give a shakedown test to **6** : to obtain money from in a deceitful or illegal manner **7** : to bring about a reduction of

shak·er \'shā-kər\ *n* **1** : one that shakes ⟨pepper ∼⟩ **2** *cap* : a member of a religious sect founded in England in 1747

Shake·spear·ean *or* **Shake·spear·ian** \shāk-'spir-ē-ən\ *adj* : of, relating to, or having the characteristics of Shakespeare or his writings

shake–up \'shāk-ˌəp\ *n* : an extensive often drastic reorganization

shake up *vb* ♦ : to jar by or as if by a physical shock

♦ appall, bowl, floor, jolt, shock — more at SHOCK

shak·i·ness \'shā-kē-nəs\ *n* ♦ : the quality or state of being shaky

♦ insecurity, instability, precariousness, unsteadiness — more at INSTABILITY

shaky \'shā-kē\ *adj* **shak·i·er; -est** **1** ♦ : lacking in authority or reliability **2** ♦ : characterized by shaking — **shak·i·ly** \'shā-kə-lē\ *adv*

♦ [1] debatable, disputable, doubtful, dubious, equivocal, fishy, problematic, questionable, shady, suspect, suspicious — more at DOUBTFUL ♦ [2] tremulous, wobbly; *also* shivering, shivery

shale \'shāl\ *n* : a finely layered rock formed from clay, mud, or silt

shall \shəl, 'shal\ *vb, past* **should** \shəd, 'shůd\ *pres sing &*

pl **shall** ♦ — used as an auxiliary to express a command, what seems inevitable or likely in the future, simple futurity, or determination

♦ have, must, need, ought, should — more at NEED

shal·lop \'sha-ləp\ *n* : a light open boat

shal·lot \shə-'lät, 'sha-lət\ *n* [modif. of F *échalote*] **1** : a small clustered bulb that is used in seasoning and is produced by a perennial herb belonging to a subspecies of the onion; *also* : this herb **2** : GREEN ONION

¹**shal·low** \'sha-lō\ *adj* **1** : not deep **2** : not intellectually profound

²**shallow** *n* : a shallow place in a body of water — usu. used in pl.

¹**sham** \'sham\ *n* **1** : an ornamental covering for a pillow **2** ♦ : an imitation or counterfeit purporting to be genuine; *also* : cheap falseness **3** : a person who shams

♦ counterfeit, fake, forgery, hoax, humbug, phony — more at FAKE ♦ caricature, farce, joke, mockery, parody, travesty — more at MOCKERY

²**sham** *vb* **shammed; sham·ming** ♦ : to act intentionally so as to give a false impression : PRETEND — **sham·mer** *n*

♦ affect, assume, counterfeit, fake, feign, pretend, profess, put on, simulate — more at FEIGN

³**sham** *adj* ♦ : not genuine : FALSE

♦ bogus, counterfeit, fake, false, inauthentic, phony, spurious, unauthentic — more at COUNTERFEIT ♦ affected, artificial, assumed, contrived, factitious, feigned, imitation, mechanical, mock, put-on, unnatural — more at ARTIFICIAL

sha·man \'shä-mən, 'shā-\ *n* [ultim. fr. Evenki (a language of Siberia) *šamān*] : a priest or priestess who uses magic to cure the sick, to divine the hidden, and to control events

sham·ble \'sham-bəl\ *vb* **sham·bled; sham·bling** ♦ : to shuffle along — **sham·ble** *n*

♦ lumber, scuff, scuffle, shuffle, stumble, tramp, tromp — more at LUMBER

sham·bles \'sham-bəlz\ *n* **1** : a scene of great slaughter **2** ♦ : a scene or state of great destruction or disorder; *also* : MESS

♦ chaos, confusion, disarray, disorder, disorganization, havoc, hell, jumble, mess, muddle — more at CHAOS

¹**shame** \'shām\ *n* **1** ♦ : a painful sense of having done something wrong, improper, or immodest **2** ♦ : a condition of humiliating disgrace or disrepute : DISGRACE **3** : a cause of feeling shame **4** : something to be regretted ⟨it's a ∼ you'll miss the party⟩ — **shame·ful·ly** *adv*

♦ [1] contrition, guilt, penitence, remorse, repentance, self-reproach — more at GUILT ♦ [2] discredit, disgrace, dishonor (*or* dishonour), disrepute, ignominy, infamy, odium, opprobrium, reproach — more at DISGRACE

²**shame** *vb* **shamed; sham·ing** **1** ♦ : to bring shame to : DISGRACE **2** : to make ashamed

♦ abase, debase, degrade, demean, discredit, disgrace, dishonor (*or* dishonour), humble, humiliate, lower, smirch, take down — more at HUMBLE

shame·faced \'shām-ˌfāst\ *adj* ♦ : showing shame : ASHAMED — **shame·faced·ly** \-ˌfā-səd-lē, -ˌfāst-lē\ *adv*

♦ ashamed, contrite, guilty, hangdog, penitent, remorseful, repentant — more at GUILTY

shame·ful \-fəl\ *adj* ♦ : bringing shame; *also* : arousing the feeling of shame

♦ discreditable, disgraceful, dishonorable (*or* dishonourable), disreputable, ignominious, infamous, notorious — more at DISREPUTABLE

shame·less *adj* ♦ : having no shame — **shame·less·ly** *adv*

♦ unabashed, unashamed, unblushing, unembarrassed — more at UNABASHED

¹**sham·poo** \sham-'pü\ *vb* [Hindi *cāpnā*, imper. of *cāpnā* to press, shampoo] : to wash (as the hair) with soap and water or with a special preparation; *also* : to clean (as a rug) similarly

²shampoo *n, pl* **shampoos** 1 : the act or an instance of shampooing 2 : a preparation for use in shampooing

sham·rock \'sham-ˌräk\ *n* [Ir *seamróg*, dim. of *seamar* clover] : a plant of folk legend with leaves composed of three leaflets that is associated with St. Patrick and Ireland

shang·hai \shaŋ-'hī\ *vb* **shang·haied; shang·hai·ing** [*Shanghai*, China] : to force aboard a ship for service as a sailor; *also* : to trick or force into an undesirable position

Shan·gri–la \ˌshaŋ-gri-'lä\ *n* [*Shangri-La*, imaginary land depicted in the novel *Lost Horizon* (1933) by James Hilton] : a remote idyllic hideaway

shank \'shaŋk\ *n* 1 : the part of the leg between the knee and the human ankle or a corresponding part of a quadruped 2 : a cut of meat from the leg 3 : the narrow part of the sole of a shoe beneath the instep 4 : the part of a tool or instrument (as a key or anchor) connecting the functioning part with a part by which it is held or moved

shan·tung \ˌshan-'təŋ\ *n* : a fabric in plain weave having a slightly irregular surface

shan·ty \'shan-tē\ *n, pl* **shanties** [prob. fr. CanF *chantier* lumber camp, hut, fr. F, builder's yard, ways, support for barrels, fr. OF, support, fr. L *cantherius* rafter, trellis] ♦ : a small roughly built shelter or dwelling

  ♦ cabin, camp, hut, hutch, shack — more at SHACK

¹shape \'shāp\ *vb* **shaped; shap·ing** 1 : to form esp. in a particular shape 2 : DESIGN 3 ♦ : to make fit for (as a particular use or purpose) : ADAPT, ADJUST 4 : REGULATE 5 ♦ : to come to pass; *also* : to take on or approach a mature or definite form — often used with *up*

  ♦ [3] acclimate, accommodate, adapt, adjust, condition, conform, fit — more at ADAPT ♦ *usu* **shape up** [5] crystallize, form, jell, solidify

²shape *n* 1 ♦ : spatial form or contour 2 : surface configuration : FORM 3 : bodily contour apart from the head and face : FIGURE 4 : PHANTOM 5 ♦ : the condition in which someone or something exists at a particular time 6 ♦ : the appearance of the body as distinguished from that of the face — **shaped** *adj*

  ♦ [1] cast, configuration, conformation, figure, form, geometry ♦ [5] condition, estate, fettle, form, order, repair, trim — more at CONDITION ♦ [6] build, constitution, figure, form, frame, physique — more at PHYSIQUE

shape·less \'shā-pləs\ *adj* 1 ♦ : having no definite shape 2 ♦ : not shapely — **shape·less·ly** *adv* — **shape·less·ness** *n*

  ♦ [1] amorphous, formless, unformed, unshaped, unstructured — more at FORMLESS ♦ [2] deformed, distorted, malformed, misshapen, monstrous — more at MALFORMED

shape·ly \'shā-plē\ *adj* **shape·li·er; -est** : having a pleasing shape ⟨a ~ model⟩ — **shape·li·ness** *n*

shape–shift·er \'shāp-ˌshif-tər\ *n* : one that seems able to change form or identity at will

shard \'shärd\ *also* **sherd** \'shərd\ *n* : a broken piece : FRAGMENT

¹share \'shar\ *n* : PLOWSHARE

²share *n* 1 ♦ : a portion belonging to one person or group 2 ♦ : any of the equal interests into which the capital stock of a corporation is divided

  ♦ [1] allotment, allowance, cut, part, portion, proportion, quota; *also* lot, ration; commission, percentage; member, partition, section, segment ♦ [2] claim, interest, stake — more at INTEREST

³share *vb* **shared; shar·ing** 1 : APPORTION 2 : to use or enjoy with others 3 : PARTICIPATE

share·crop·per \-ˌkrä-pər\ *n* : a farmer who works another's land in return for a share of the crop — **share·crop** *vb*

share·hold·er \-ˌhōl-dər\ *n* : STOCKHOLDER

shar·er *n* ♦ : one that shares

  ♦ partaker, participant, party — more at PARTICIPANT

share·ware \'sher-ˌwer\ *n* : software available for usu. lim-

ited trial use at little or no cost but that can be upgraded for a fee

¹shark \'shärk\ *n* : any of various active, usu. predatory, and mostly large marine cartilaginous fishes

²shark *n* 1 ♦ : a greedy crafty person 2 ♦ : one who excels greatly esp. in a particular field

  ♦ [1] cheat, dodger, hoaxer, sharper, swindler, trickster — more at TRICKSTER ♦ [2] ace, adept, artist, authority, crackerjack, expert, maestro, master, scholar, virtuoso, whiz, wizard — more at EXPERT

shark·skin \-ˌskin\ *n* 1 : the hide of a shark or leather made from it 2 : a fabric woven from strands of many fine threads and having a sleek appearance and silky feel

¹sharp \'shärp\ *adj* 1 ♦ : having a thin cutting edge or fine point : not dull or blunt 2 : briskly or bitingly cold : COLD ⟨a ~ wind⟩ 3 ♦ : keen in intellect, perception, or attention 4 : BRISK, ENERGETIC 5 : IRRITABLE ⟨a ~ temper⟩ 6 ♦ : causing intense distress ⟨a ~ pain⟩ 7 : cutting in language or import : HARSH ⟨a ~ rebuke⟩ 8 ♦ : affecting the senses as if cutting or piercing ⟨a ~ sound⟩ ⟨a ~ smell⟩ 9 : not smooth or rounded ⟨~ features⟩ 10 : involving an abrupt or extreme change ⟨a ~ turn⟩ 11 : CLEAR, DISTINCT ⟨mountains in ~ relief⟩; *also* : easy to perceive ⟨a ~ contrast⟩ 12 a : higher than the true pitch b : raised by a half step 13 : being in the latest or current fashion : STYLISH ⟨a ~ dresser⟩ 14 : keen in attention to one's own interest sometimes to the point of being unethical — **sharp·ly** *adv*

  ♦ [1] cutting, edgy, ground, keen; *also* jabbing, jagged, lacerating, piercing, scratching, stabbing *Ant* blunt, blunted, dull, dulled, obtuse ♦ [1] peaked, pointed — more at POINTED ♦ [3] acute, astute, canny, hardheaded, knowing, shrewd, smart — more at SHREWD ♦ [3] alert, brainy, bright, brilliant, clever, intelligent, keen, nimble, quick, quick-witted — more at INTELLIGENT ♦ [6] acute, agonizing, biting, excruciating, smart; *also* bitter, cutting, keen, penetrating, piercing, raw, stinging; afflicting, distressing, upsetting; cruel, grievous, harsh, heartrending, hurtful, lacerating, painful, paralyzing, severe, tormenting, tortuous; insufferable, insupportable, intolerable, unacceptable, unbearable, unsupportable; appalling, awful, bad, dire, dreadful, ghastly, horrible, miserable, nasty, rotten, terrible, vile, wretched *Ant* dull ♦ [8] nippy, pungent, strong; *also* acid, acidic; acrid, bitter, harsh; piquant, spicy, tart; putrid, rancid, rank; acute, keen; animating, energizing, exciting, galvanizing, invigorating, provocative; appetizing, delectable, delicious, palatable, toothsome; flavorful, savory, tasty *Ant* bland, smooth, mild

²sharp *adv* 1 : in a sharp manner 2 ♦ : in a manner or measure or to a degree or number that strictly conforms to a fact or condition : EXACTLY ⟨left at 8 ~⟩

  ♦ accurately, exactly, just, precisely, right, squarely — more at EXACTLY

³sharp *n* 1 : a sharp edge or point 2 : a character # which indicates that a specified note is to be raised by a half step; *also* : the resulting note 3 : SHARPER

⁴sharp *vb* : to raise in pitch by a half step

shar–pei \ˌshä-'pā, ˌshär-\ *n, pl* **shar–peis** *often cap* S&P [Chin (Guangdong dial.) *sà* sand + *péi* fur] : any of a Chinese breed of dogs that have loose wrinkled skin esp. when young

sharp·en \'shär-pən\ *vb* ♦ : to make or become sharp — **sharp·en·er** *n*

  ♦ edge, grind, hone, strop, whet; *also* file *Ant* blunt, dull

sharp·er \'shär-pər\ *n* ♦ : an unduly sharp or canny person; *esp* : a cheating gambler

  ♦ cheat, dodger, hoaxer, shark, swindler, trickster — more at TRICKSTER

sharp·ie *or* **sharpy** \'shär-pē\ *n, pl* **sharp·ies** 1 : SHARPER 2 : a person who is exceptionally keen or alert

sharp·ness *n* ♦ : the quality or state of being sharp

♦ acidity, acrimony, acuteness, asperity, bite, bitterness, edge, harshness, keenness, pungency, tartness ♦ bite, bitterness, bleakness, chill, nip, rawness — more at CHILL

sharp·shoot·er \'shärp-₁shü-tər\ *n* ♦ : a good marksman — **sharp·shoot·ing** *n*

♦ marksman, shooter, shot — more at MARKSMAN

shat·ter \'sha-tər\ *vb* ♦ : to dash or burst into fragments; *also* : to cause the disruption or annihilation of — **shat·ter·proof** \'sha-tər-₁prüf\ *adj*

♦ blast, blow up, burst, demolish, destroy, explode, pop, smash — more at BLAST

¹shave \'shāv\ *vb* **shaved; shaved** *or* **shav·en** \'shā-vən\; **shav·ing** **1** : to slice in thin pieces **2** : to make bare or smooth by cutting the hair from **3** : to cut or pare off by the sliding movement of a razor **4** ♦ : to skim along or near the surface of

♦ brush, graze, kiss, nick, skim — more at BRUSH

²shave *n* **1** : any of various tools for cutting thin slices **2** : an act or process of shaving

shav·er \'shā-vər\ *n* **1** : an electric razor **2** ♦ : a male child from birth to adulthood : BOY

♦ boy, lad, nipper, stripling, youth — more at BOY

shav·ing *n* **1** : the act of one that shaves **2** : something shaved off

shawl \'shȯl\ *n* : a square or oblong piece of fabric used esp. by women as a loose covering for the head or shoulders

Shaw·nee \shȯ-'nē, shä-\ *n, pl* **Shawnee** *or* **Shawnees** : a member of an American Indian people orig. of the central Ohio valley; *also* : their language

shd *abbr* should

she \'shē\ *pron* : that female one ⟨who is ∼⟩; *also* : that one regarded as feminine ⟨∼'s a fine ship⟩

sheaf \'shēf\ *n, pl* **sheaves** \'shēvz\ **1** : a bundle of stalks and ears of grain **2** : a group of things bound together

¹shear \'shir\ *vb* **sheared; sheared** *or* **shorn** \'shȯrn\; **shear·ing** **1** ♦ : to cut the hair or wool from : CLIP **2** : to deprive by or as if by cutting **3** : to cut or break sharply

♦ bob, clip, crop, curtail, cut, cut back, dock, lop, nip, prune, shave, trim — more at CLIP

²shear *n* **1** : any of various cutting tools that consist of two blades fastened together so that the edges slide one by the other — usu. used in pl. **2** *chiefly Brit* : the act, an instance, or the result of shearing **3** : an action or stress caused by applied forces that causes two parts of a body to slide on each other

sheath \'shēth\ *n, pl* **sheaths** \'shēthz, 'shēths\ **1** ♦ : a case for a blade (as of a knife); *also* : an anatomical covering suggesting such a case **2** : a close-fitting dress usu. worn without a belt

♦ armor, capsule, case, casing, cocoon, cover, housing, husk, jacket, pod, shell — more at CASE

sheathe \'shēth\ *also* **sheath** \'shēth\ *vb* **sheathed; sheath·ing** **1** : to put into a sheath **2** : to cover with something that guards or protects

sheath·ing \'shē-thiŋ, -thiŋ\ *n* : material used to sheathe something; *esp* : the first covering of boards or of waterproof material on the outside wall of a frame house or on a timber roof

sheave \'shiv, 'shēv\ *n* : a grooved wheel or pulley (as on a pulley block)

she·bang \shi-'baŋ\ *n* : everything involved in what is under consideration ⟨sold the whole ∼⟩

¹shed \'shed\ *vb* **shed; shed·ding** **1** : to cause to flow from a cut or wound ⟨∼ blood⟩ **2** : to pour down in drops ⟨∼ tears⟩ **3** : to give out (as light) : DIFFUSE **4** : to throw off (as a natural covering) **5** ♦ : to rid oneself of temporarily or permanently as superfluous or unwanted

♦ cast, discard, ditch, dump, fling, jettison, junk, lose, reject, scrap, shuck, slough, throw away, throw out, unload — more at DISCARD

²shed *n* : a slight structure built for shelter or storage

sheen \'shēn\ *n* ♦ : a subdued luster

♦ gloss, luster (*or* lustre), polish, shine — more at SHINE

sheep \'shēp\ *n, pl* **sheep** **1** : any of various cud-chewing mammals that are stockier than the related goats and lack a beard in the male; *esp* : one raised for meat or for its wool or skin **2** ♦ : a timid or defenseless person **3** : SHEEPSKIN

♦ angel, dove, innocent, lamb — more at LAMB

sheep·dog \'shēp-₁dȯg\ *n* : a dog used to tend, drive, or guard sheep

sheep·fold \'shēp-₁fōld\ *n* : a pen or shelter for sheep

sheep·herd·er \-₁hər-dər\ *n* : a worker in charge of sheep esp. on open range — **sheep·herd·ing** *n*

sheep·ish \'shē-pish\ *adj* ♦ : resembling a sheep in meekness, stupidity, or timidity : BASHFUL; *esp* : embarrassed by consciousness of a fault

♦ bashful, coy, demure, diffident, introverted, modest, retiring, shy — more at SHY

sheep·ish·ly *adv* ♦ : in a sheepish manner

♦ humbly, lowly, meekly, modestly

sheep·skin \'shēp-₁skin\ *n* **1** : the hide of a sheep or leather prepared from it; *also* : PARCHMENT **2** : DIPLOMA

¹sheer \'shir\ *vb* ♦ : to turn from a course

♦ detour, deviate, swerve, swing, turn, turn off, veer — more at TURN

²sheer *adj* **1** ♦ : very thin or transparent **2** : carried to the utmost point or highest degree : UNQUALIFIED ⟨∼ folly⟩ **3** : very steep — **sheer** *adv*

♦ gauzy, transparent; *also* clear, limpid, liquid, lucent, pellucid; lucid, translucent; dainty, delicate, flimsy, fragile, frail; colorless, uncolored

¹sheet \'shēt\ *n* **1** : a broad piece of cloth (as for a bed); *also* : SAIL 1 **2** : a single piece of paper **3** : a broad flat surface ⟨a ∼ of ice⟩ **4** : something broad and long and relatively thin

²sheet *n* : a rope used to trim a sail

sheet·ing \'shē-tiŋ\ *n* : material in the form of sheets or suitable for forming into sheets

sheikh *or* **sheik** \'shēk, 'shāk\ *n* : an Arab chief — **sheikh·dom** *or* **sheik·dom** \-dəm\ *n*

shek·el \'she-kəl\ *or* **sheq·el** *n* : a basic monetary unit of Israel

shelf \'shelf\ *n, pl* **shelves** \'shelvz\ **1** : a thin flat usu. long and narrow structure fastened horizontally (as on a wall) above the floor to hold things **2** : something (as a sandbar) that suggests a shelf

shelf life *n* : the period of storage time during which a material will remain useful

¹shell \'shel\ *n* **1** ♦ : a hard or tough often thin outer covering of an animal (as a beetle, turtle, or mollusk) or of an egg or a seed or fruit (as a nut); *also* : something that resembles a shell ⟨a pastry ∼⟩ **2** : a light narrow racing boat propelled by oarsmen **3** : a case holding an explosive and designed to be fired from a cannon; *also* : a case holding the charge of powder and shot or bullet for small arms **4** : a plain usu. sleeveless blouse or sweater **5** ♦ : a framework or exterior structure; *esp* : a building with an unfinished interior — **shelled** \'sheld\ *adj* — **shelly** \'she-lē\ *adj*

♦ [1] armor, capsule, case, casing, cocoon, cover, housing, husk, jacket, pod, sheath — more at CASE
♦ [5] configuration, frame, framework, skeleton, structure — more at FRAME

²shell *vb* **1** ♦ : to remove from a shell or husk **2** ♦ : to throw shells at, upon, or into : BOMBARD — **shell·er** *n*

♦ [1] bark, flay, hull, husk, peel, shuck, skin — more at PEEL ♦ [2] blitz, bombard — more at BOMBARD

¹shel·lac \shə-'lak\ *n* **1** : a purified lac **2** : lac dissolved in alcohol and used as a wood filler or finish

²shellac *vb* **shel·lacked; shel·lack·ing** **1** : to coat or treat with shellac **2** : to defeat decisively

shel·lack·ing *n* ♦ : a sound drubbing

♦ defeat, loss, rout — more at DEFEAT

shell bean *n* : a bean grown esp. for its edible seeds; *also* : its edible seed

shell·fish \-ˌfish\ *n* : an invertebrate water animal (as an oyster or lobster) with a shell

shell out *vb* : PAY

shell shock *n* : COMBAT FATIGUE — **shell–shocked** \'shel-ˌshäkt\ *adj*

¹shel·ter \'shel-tər\ *n* ♦ : something that gives protection : REFUGE

♦ asylum, harbor (*or* harbour), haven, refuge, retreat, sanctuary; *also* anchorage, mooring, port; cover, screen; abode, domicile, dwelling, habitation, house, housing, lodgment, lodging, quarters, residence

²shelter *vb* **shel·tered; shel·ter·ing** ♦ : to give protection or refuge to

♦ accommodate, billet, chamber, domicile, harbor (*or* harbour), house, lodge, put up, quarter, roof, take in — more at HOUSE

shelve \'shelv\ *vb* **shelved; shelv·ing** 1 : to slope gradually 2 : to store on shelves 3 : to dismiss from service or use 4 ♦ : to put aside : DEFER ⟨~ a proposal⟩

♦ defer, delay, hold up, postpone, put off — more at POSTPONE

shelv·ing \'shel-viŋ\ *n* : material for shelves; *also* : SHELVES

she·nan·i·gan \shə-'na-ni-gən\ *n* 1 : an underhand trick 2 : questionable conduct — usu. used in pl. 3 ♦ : high-spirited or mischievous activity — usu. used in pl.

♦ shenanigans devilishness, impishness, knavery, mischief, mischievousness, rascality, waggery, wickedness — more at MISCHIEF ♦ shenanigans foolery, high jinks, horseplay, monkeyshines, roughhouse, tomfoolery — more at HORSEPLAY

¹shep·herd \'she-pərd\ *n* 1 : one who tends sheep 2 : GERMAN SHEPHERD

²shepherd *vb* ♦ : to tend as or in the manner of a shepherd

♦ coach, counsel, guide, lead, mentor, pilot, show, tutor — more at GUIDE

shep·herd·ess \'she-pər-dəs\ *n* : a woman who tends sheep

shepherd's pie *n* : a meat pie with a mashed potato crust

sheqel *n, pl* **sheqalim** *var of* SHEKEL

sher·bet \'shər-bət\ *n* [Turk *şerbet*, fr. Per *sharbat*, fr. Ar *sharbah* drink] 1 : a drink of sweetened diluted fruit juice 2 *also* **sher·bert** \-bərt\ : a frozen dessert of fruit juices, sugar, milk or water, and egg whites or gelatin

sher·iff \'sher-əf\ *n* [ME *shirreve*, fr. OE *scīrgerēfa*, lit., shire reeve (local official)] : a county officer charged with the execution of the law and the preservation of order

sher·ry \'sher-ē\ *n, pl* **sherries** [alter. of earlier *sherris* (taken as pl.), fr. *Xeres* (now *Jerez*), Spain] : a fortified wine with a nutty flavor

Shet·land pony \'shet-lənd-\ *n* : any of a breed of small stocky hardy ponies

shew \'shō\ *Brit var of* SHOW

Shia \'shē-(ˌ)ä\ *n* 1 : one of the two main branches of Islam 2 : SHIITE

shi·at·su *also* **shi·at·zu** \shē-'ät-sü\ *n* [short for Jp *shiatsuryōhō*] : a form of acupressure originating in Japan

shib·bo·leth \'shi-bə-ləth\ *n* [Heb *shibbōleth* stream; fr. the use of this word as a test to distinguish the men of Gilead from members of the tribe of Ephraim (Judges 12:5, 6)] 1 ♦ : a word or saying used by adherents of a party, sect, or belief and usu. regarded by others as empty of real meaning; *also* : a banal, trite, or stale remark 2 : language that is a criterion for distinguishing members of a group

♦ cry, slogan, watchword — more at SLOGAN ♦ banality, cliché, commonplace, platitude — more at COMMONPLACE

¹shield \'shēld\ *n* 1 : a broad piece of defensive armor carried on the arm 2 ♦ : something that protects or hides 3 : a police officer's badge

♦ aegis, armor (*or* armour), cover, defense (*or* defence), guard, protection, safeguard, screen, security, wall, ward — more at DEFENSE

²shield *vb* ♦ : to protect or hide with a shield

♦ cover, defend, guard, protect, safeguard, screen, secure, ward — more at DEFEND

¹shift \'shift\ *vb* 1 ♦ : to exchange for or replace by another 2 ♦ : to change place, position, or direction : MOVE; *also* : to change gears 3 ♦ : to assume responsibility : GET BY 4 ♦ : to go through a change

♦ [1] change, commute, exchange, substitute, swap, switch, trade — more at CHANGE ♦ [2] budge, dislocate, displace, disturb, move, remove, transfer — more at MOVE ♦ [3] cope, do, fare, get along, get by, make out, manage — more at GET ALONG ♦ [4] change, fluctuate, mutate, vary — more at CHANGE

²shift *n* 1 : SCHEME, TRICK 2 : a woman's slip or loose-fitting dress 3 ♦ : a change in direction, emphasis, or attitude 4 : a group working together alternating with other groups 5 : TRANSFER 6 : GEARSHIFT 7 ♦ : a means or device for effecting an end

♦ [3] motion, move, movement, moving, stir, stirring — more at MOVEMENT ♦ [7] expedient, measure, move, step — more at MEASURE

shift·less \'shift-ləs\ *adj* ♦ : lacking in ambition or incentive : LAZY

♦ idle, indolent, lazy, slothful — more at LAZY

shift·less·ness *n* : the quality or state of being shiftless

shifty \'shif-tē\ *adj* **shift·i·er; -est** 1 a ♦ : given to deception, evasion, or fraud b : ELUSIVE 2 : indicative of a tricky nature ⟨~ eyes⟩

♦ furtive, shady, slippery, sly, sneaky, stealthy — more at SNEAKY ♦ crooked, deceptive, dishonest, fast, fraudulent, shady, sharp, underhanded — more at DISHONEST

shih tzu \'shēd-'zü, 'shēt-'sü\ *n, pl* **shih tzus** *also* **shih tzu** *often cap* S&T : any of a breed of small short-legged dogs of Chinese origin that have a short muzzle and a long dense coat

shii·ta·ke \shē-'tä-kē\ *n* [Jp] : a dark Asian mushroom widely cultivated for its edible cap

Shi·ite \'shē-ˌīt\ *n* : a Muslim of the Shia branch of Islam

shill \'shil\ *n* : one who acts as a decoy (as for a pitchman) — **shill** *vb*

shil·le·lagh *also* **shil·la·lah** \shə-'lā-lē\ *n* [*Shillelagh*, town in Ireland] : a short heavy club : CUDGEL

shil·ling \'shi-liŋ\ *n* : a former monetary unit of the United Kingdom equal to ¹⁄₂₀ pound

shil·ly–shal·ly \'shi-lē-ˌsha-lē\ *vb* **shilly–shall·ied; shilly–shally·ing** 1 ♦ : to show hesitation or lack of decisiveness 2 : to waste time

♦ falter, hang back, hesitate, stagger, teeter, vacillate, waver, wobble — more at HESITATE

shim \'shim\ *n* : a thin often tapered piece of wood, metal, or stone used (as in leveling) to fill in space

shim·mer \'shi-mər\ *vb* ♦ : to shine waveringly or tremulously : GLIMMER — **shimmer** *n* — **shim·mery** *adj*

♦ flame, flash, glance, gleam, glimmer, glisten, scintillate, sparkle, twinkle, wink — more at FLASH

shim·my \'shi-mē\ *n, pl* **shimmies** : an abnormal vibration esp. in the front wheels of a motor vehicle — **shimmy** *vb*

¹shin \'shin\ *n* : the front part of the leg below the knee

²shin *vb* **shinned; shin·ning** : to climb (as a pole) by gripping alternately with arms or hands and legs

shin·bone \'shin-ˌbōn\ *n* : TIBIA

¹shine \'shīn\ *vb* **shone** \'shōn\ *or* **shined; shin·ing** 1 ♦ : to give or cause to give light 2 : GLEAM, GLITTER 3 : to be eminent, conspicuous, or distinguished ⟨gave her a chance to ~⟩ 4 ♦ : to make bright by polishing ⟨~ your shoes⟩

♦ [1] blaze, burn, fire, flame, gleam, glimmer, glisten, glitter, glow, radiate, shimmer; *also* blink, flare, flash, flicker, scintillate, sparkle, twinkle, wink; beat (down), glare; brighten, illuminate, illumine, irradiate, light, lighten; bedazzle, blind, daze, dazzle ◆ [4] buff, burnish, dress, gloss, grind, polish, rub, smooth — more at POLISH

²shine *n* **1** ◆ : brightness caused by the emission of light : RADIANCE **2** ◆ : brightness caused by the reflection of light : LUSTER **3** : fair weather : SUNSHINE ⟨rain or ∼⟩ **4** ◆ : positive regard for something : LIKING, FANCY ⟨took a ∼ to them⟩ **5** : a polish given to shoes

◆ [1] blaze, flare, fluorescence, glare, gleam, glow, illumination, incandescence, light, luminescence, radiance — more at LIGHT ◆ [2] gloss, luster (*or* lustre), polish, sheen; *also* glare, gleam, glimmer, glint, glisten, glow, shimmer; flicker, sparkle, twinkle ◆ [4] appetite, fancy, favor (*or* favour), fondness, like, liking, love, partiality, preference, relish, taste, use — more at LIKING

shin·er \'shī-nər\ *n* **1** : a silvery fish; *esp* : any of numerous small freshwater American fishes related to the carp **2** : BLACK EYE

¹shin·gle \'shiŋ-gəl\ *n* **1** : a small thin piece of building material used in overlapping rows for covering a roof or outside wall **2** : a small sign

²shingle *vb* **shin·gled; shin·gling** : to cover with shingles

³shingle *n* : a beach strewn with gravel; *also* : coarse gravel (as on a beach)

shin·gles \'shiŋ-gəlz\ *n* : an acute inflammation of the spinal and cranial nerves caused by reactivation of the chicken pox virus and associated with eruptions and pain along the course of the affected nerves

shin·ny \'shi-nē\ *vb* **shin·nied; shin·ny·ing** : SHIN

shin splints *n sing or pl* : a condition marked by pain and sometimes tenderness and swelling in the shin caused by repeated small injuries to muscles and associated tissue esp. from running

Shin·to \'shin-ˌtō\ *n* : the indigenous religion of Japan consisting esp. in reverence of the spirits of natural forces and imperial ancestors — **Shin·to·ism** *n* — **Shin·to·ist** *n or adj*

shiny \'shī-nē\ *adj* **shin·i·er; -est 1** ◆ : filled with light : BRIGHT **2** : having a smooth, glossy surface

◆ beaming, bright, brilliant, effulgent, glowing, incandescent, lambent, lucent, lucid, luminous, lustrous, radiant, refulgent — more at BRIGHT

¹ship \'ship\ *n* **1** : a large oceangoing boat **2** : a ship's officers and crew **3** : AIRSHIP, AIRCRAFT, SPACECRAFT

²ship *vb* **shipped; ship·ping 1** : to put or receive on board a ship for transportation **2** ◆ : to have transported by a carrier **3** : to take or draw into a boat ⟨∼ oars⟩ ⟨∼ water⟩ **4** : to engage to serve on a ship — **ship·per** *n*

◆ consign, dispatch, pack, send, transfer, transmit, transport — more at SEND

-ship \ˌship\ *n suffix* **1** : state : condition : quality ⟨friendship⟩ **2** : office : dignity : profession ⟨lordship⟩ ⟨clerkship⟩ **3** : art : skill ⟨horsemanship⟩ **4** : something showing, exhibiting, or embodying a quality or state ⟨township⟩ **5** : one entitled to a (specified) rank, title, or appellation ⟨his Lordship⟩ **6** : the body of persons engaged in a specified activity ⟨readership⟩

ship·board \'ship-ˌbōrd\ *n* : SHIP

ship·build·er \-ˌbil-dər\ *n* : one who designs or builds ships

ship·fit·ter \-ˌfi-tər\ *n* : one who constructs ships

ship·mate \-ˌmāt\ *n* : a fellow sailor

ship·ment \-mənt\ *n* **1** : the process of shipping **2** ◆ : the goods shipped

◆ cargo, freight, load, payload — more at CARGO

ship·ping *n* **1** : SHIPS; *esp* : ships in one port or belonging to one country **2** : transportation of goods

ship·shape \'ship-ˌshāp\ *adj* ◆ : exhibiting neatness or good order : TIDY

◆ crisp, neat, orderly, snug, tidy, trim, uncluttered — more at NEAT

ship·worm \-ˌwərm\ *n* : any of various wormlike marine clams that have a shell used for burrowing in wood and damaging wooden ships and wharves

¹ship·wreck \-ˌrek\ *n* **1** : a wrecked ship **2** ◆ : destruction or loss of a ship **3** : total loss or failure : RUIN

◆ wreck, wreckage; *also* beaching, grounding, stranding; foundering, sinking

²shipwreck *vb* : to cause or meet disaster at sea through destruction or foundering

ship·wright \'ship-ˌrīt\ *n* : a carpenter skilled in ship construction and repair

ship·yard \-ˌyärd\ *n* : a place where ships are built or repaired

shire \'shīr, *in place-name compounds* ˌshir, shər\ *n* : a county in Great Britain

shirk \'shərk\ *vb* ◆ : to avoid performing (duty or work) — **shirk·er** *n*

◆ avoid, dodge, duck, elude, escape, eschew, evade, shake, shun — more at ESCAPE

shirr \'shər\ *vb* **1** : to make shirring in **2** : to bake (eggs removed from the shell) until set

shirr·ing \'shər-iŋ\ *n* : a decorative gathering in cloth made by drawing up parallel lines of stitches

shirt \'shərt\ *n* **1** : a loose cloth garment usu. having a collar, sleeves, a front opening, and a tail long enough to be tucked inside pants or a skirt **2** : UNDERSHIRT — **shirt·less** *adj*

shirt·ing \'shir-tiŋ\ *n* : cloth suitable for making shirts

shish ke·bab \'shish-kə-ˌbäb\ *n* [Turk *şiş kebab1*, fr. *şiş* spit + *kebap* roast meat] : kebab cooked on skewers

shiv \'shiv\ *n, slang* : KNIFE

¹shiv·er \'shi-vər\ *vb* : TREMBLE, QUIVER

²shiver *n* ◆ : an instance of shivering; *also* : an intense shivery sensation esp. of fear — often used in pl. with *the*

◆ quiver, shudder, tremble; *also* agitation, convulsing, jolt, quake, shake, tremor, vibration, wobble; fluctuation, flutter, oscillation, wave; beat, palpitation, pulsation, pulse, throb ◆ **shivers** jitters, shakes, willies — more at JITTERS

shiv·ery *adj* : causing shivers

shlemiel *var of* SCHLEMIEL

shlub *var of* SCHLUB

shmooze *var of* SCHMOOZE

Sho·ah \'shō-ə, -ˌä\ *n* : HOLOCAUST 2

¹shoal \'shōl\ *n* **1** : SHALLOW **2** : a sandbank or bar creating a shallow

²shoal *n* : a large group (as of fish)

shoat \'shōt\ *n* : a weaned young pig

¹shock \'shäk\ *n* : a pile of sheaves of grain or cornstalks set up in a field

²shock *n* [MF *choc*, fr. *choquer* to strike against] **1** ◆ : a sharp impact or violent shake or jar **2** ◆ : a sudden violent mental or emotional disturbance **3** : a state of bodily collapse that is often marked by a drop in blood pressure and volume and that is caused esp. by crushing wounds, blood loss, or burns **4** : the effect of a charge of electricity passing through the body **5** : SHOCK ABSORBER — **shock·proof** \-ˌprüf\ *adj*

◆ [1] bump, collision, concussion, crash, impact, jar, jolt, smash, strike, wallop — more at IMPACT ◆ [2] amazement, astonishment, surprise — more at SURPRISE

³shock *vb* **1** ◆ : to strike with surprise, horror, or disgust **2** : to subject to the action of an electrical discharge

◆ appall, bowl, floor, jolt, shake up; *also* affright, alarm, dismay, frighten, horrify, panic, scare, spook, startle, terrify, terrorize; disgust, nauseate, repel, revolt, sicken, turn off; displease, offend, outrage, scandalize; amaze, astound, awe; chill, daunt, demoralize, dispirit, unman, unnerve; decompose, disconcert, disquiet, disturb, perturb, unsettle, upset; crush, overpower, overwhelm ◆ amaze, astonish, astound, dumbfound, flabbergast, startle, stun, stupefy, surprise — more at SURPRISE

⁴shock *n* : a thick bushy mass (as of hair)

shock absorber *n* : any of several devices for absorbing the energy of sudden shocks in machinery

shock·er \\'shä-kər\ *n* : one that shocks; *esp* : a sensational work of fiction or drama

shock·ing \\'shä-kiŋ\ *adj* ♦ : extremely startling and offensive — **shock·ing·ly** *adv*

♦ amazing, astonishing, astounding, eye-opening, startling, stunning, surprising — more at SURPRISING ♦ dire, dreadful, fearful, fearsome, forbidding, formidable, frightful, hair-raising, horrible, redoubtable, scary, terrible, terrifying — more at FEARFUL ♦ abhorrent, abominable, appalling, awful, distasteful, foul, hideous, horrid, nasty, nauseating, noisome, obnoxious, obscene, odious, offensive, repellent, repugnant, repulsive, revolting, scandalous, ugly — more at OFFENSIVE

shock therapy *n* : the treatment of mental disorder by induction of coma or convulsions by drugs or electricity

shock wave *n* : a wave formed by the sudden violent compression of the medium through which it travels

¹**shod·dy** \\'shä-dē\ *n* **1** : wool reclaimed from old rags; *also* : a fabric made from it **2** : inferior or imitation material

²**shoddy** *adj* **shod·di·er; -est 1** : made of shoddy **2** ♦ : poorly done or made — **shod·di·ly** \\'shä-də-lē\ *adv* — **shod·di·ness** \-dē-nəs\ *n*

♦ bad, bum, cheap, inferior, junky, lousy, mediocre, poor, sleazy — more at CHEAP

¹**shoe** \\'shü\ *n* **1** : a covering for the human foot **2** : HORSESHOE **3** : the part of a brake that presses on the wheel

²**shoe** *vb* **shod** \\'shäd\ *also* **shoed** \\'shüd\; **shoe·ing** : to put a shoe or shoes on

shoe·box \-ˌbäks\ *n* **1** : a box that shoes are sold in **2** : a very small space ⟨a ~ apartment⟩

shoe·horn \-ˌhȯrn\ *n* : a curved implement (as of horn or plastic) used in putting on a shoe

shoe·lace \\'shü-ˌlās\ *n* : a lace or string for fastening a shoe

shoe·mak·er \-ˌmā-kər\ *n* : one who makes or repairs shoes

shoe·string \-ˌstriŋ\ *n* **1** : SHOELACE **2** ♦ : a small sum of money

♦ mite, peanuts, pittance, song — more at MITE

sho·gun \\'shō-gən\ *n* [Jp *shōgun* general] : any of a line of military governors ruling Japan until the revolution of 1867–68

shone *past and past part of* SHINE

shook *past of* SHAKE

shook–up \(ˌ)shùk-'əp\ *adj* : nervously upset : AGITATED

¹**shoot** \\'shüt\ *vb* **shot** \\'shät\; **shoot·ing 1** ♦ : to drive (as an arrow or bullet) forward quickly or forcibly **2** ♦ : to hit, kill, or wound with a missile **3** ♦ : to cause a missile to be driven forth or forth from ⟨~ a gun⟩ **4** ♦ : to send forth (as a ray of light) **5** : to thrust forward or out **6** : to pass rapidly along ⟨~ the rapids⟩ **7** : to take a picture or series of pictures of : PHOTOGRAPH **8** : to move swiftly : DART **9** : to grow by or as if by sending out shoots; *also* : MATURE, DEVELOP **10** ♦ : to grow or rise rapidly — often used with *up*

♦ [1] blast, discharge, fire, loose; *also* launch, project; blaze (at), snipe (at); cast, catapult, fling, heave, hurl, pelt, pitch, sling, throw, toss ♦ [2] drill, gun, plug, pop; *also* blaze, pepper; blast (at), fire (at); overshoot; snipe (at); destroy, dispatch, do in, fell, kill, slay; annihilate, blot out, butcher, decimate, massacre, slaughter, wipe out ♦ [3] blast, discharge, fire; *also* blaze, pepper, snipe ♦ [4] cast, discharge, emit, exhale, expel, issue, release, vent — more at EMIT ♦ *usu* **shoot up** [10] rocket, skyrocket, soar, zoom — more at SKYROCKET

²**shoot** *n* **1** : a plant stem with its leaves and branches esp. when not yet mature **2** : an act of shooting **3** : a shooting match

shoot·er *n* : one that shoots: as **a** ♦ : a person who fires a missile-discharging device (as a rifle or bow) **b** : one who photographs

♦ marksman, sharpshooter, shot — more at MARKSMAN

shooting iron *n* : FIREARM

shooting star *n* : METEOR 2

shoot up *vb* : to inject a narcotic into a vein

¹**shop** \\'shäp\ *n* [ME *shoppe*, fr. OE *sceoppa* booth] **1** ♦ : a place where things are made or worked on : FACTORY, MILL **2** ♦ : a retail store ⟨dress ~⟩

♦ [1] factory, mill, plant, works, workshop — more at FACTORY ♦ [2] emporium, store; *also* market, marketplace, outlet; boutique, department store

²**shop** *vb* **shopped; shop·ping** : to visit stores for purchasing or examining goods — **shop·per** *n*

shop·keep·er \\'shäp-ˌkē-pər\ *n* : a retail merchant

shop·lift \-ˌlift\ *vb* : to steal goods on display from a store — **shop·lift·er** *n*

shopping cart *n* **1** : a cart used for holding merchandise when shopping in a store **2** : a temporary record of items selected for purchase from a website

shop·talk \-ˌtȯk\ *n* ♦ : talk about one's business or special interests

♦ argot, cant, dialect, jargon, jive, language, lingo, patois, patter, shop, slang, terminology, vocabulary — more at TERMINOLOGY

shop·worn \-ˌwȯrn\ *adj* **1** : soiled or frayed from much handling in a store **2** ♦ : stale from excessive use or familiarity

♦ banal, commonplace, hackneyed, musty, stale, stereotyped, threadbare, tired, trite — more at STALE

¹**shore** \\'shȯr\ *n* : land along the edge of a body of water — **shore·less** *adj*

²**shore** *vb* **shored; shor·ing** ♦ : to give support to : BRACE — usu. used with *up*

♦ *usu* **shore up** bear, bolster, brace, buttress, carry, prop, stay, support, uphold — more at SUPPORT

³**shore** *n* ♦ : a prop for preventing sinking or sagging

♦ brace, bulwark, buttress, mount, stay, support, underpinning — more at SUPPORT

shore·bird \-ˌbərd\ *n* : any of a suborder of birds (as the plovers and sandpipers) mostly found along the seashore

shore patrol *n* : a branch of a navy that exercises guard and police functions

shor·ing \\'shȯr-iŋ\ *n* : a group of things that shore something up

shorn *past part of* SHEAR

¹**short** \\'shȯrt\ *adj* **1** : not long or tall **2** : not great in distance **3** ♦ : brief in time **4** ♦ : not coming up to standard or to an expected amount **5** : CURT, ABRUPT **6** ♦ : insufficiently supplied **7** : made with shortening : FLAKY **8** : consisting of or relating to a sale of securities or commodities that the seller does not possess or has not contracted for at the time of the sale ⟨~ sale⟩

♦ [3] brief, little, short-lived; *also* abbreviated, abridged, curtailed, shortened; compact, condensed; abrupt, sudden; ephemeral, fleeting, momentary, transient, transitory; impermanent; compendious, concise, crisp, epigrammatic, laconic, pithy, succinct, summary, terse; short-term *Ant* extended, great, lengthy, long, marathon ♦ [4, 6] deficient, inadequate, insufficient, scarce, shy, wanting; *also* hand-to-mouth, light, meager, niggardly, poor, scant, scanty, skimpy, slender, slim, spare, sparse, stingy; bare, mere, minimum; slight, small *Ant* adequate, enough, sufficient

²**short** *adv* **1** : in an abrupt manner : ABRUPTLY **2** : at some point before a goal aimed at

³**short** *n* **1** : something shorter than normal or standard **2** *pl* : drawers or pants of less than knee length **3** : SHORT CIRCUIT

⁴**short** *vb* : SHORT-CIRCUIT

short·age \\'shȯr-tij\ *n* ♦ : the fact or state of being wanting or deficient : LACK

♦ dearth, deficiency, deficit, failure, famine, inadequacy, insufficiency, lack, paucity, poverty, scantiness, scarcity, want — more at DEFICIENCY

short·cake \\'shȯrt-ˌkāk\ *n* : a dessert consisting of short biscuit spread with sweetened fruit

short·change \-'chānj\ *vb* ♦ : to cheat esp. by giving less than the correct amount of change

♦ bleed, cheat, chisel, cozen, defraud, fleece, hustle, mulct, rook, skin, squeeze, stick, sting, swindle, victimize — more at FLEECE

short circuit *n* : a connection made between points in an electric circuit where current is not intended to flow — **short–circuit** *vb*

short·com·ing \'shòrt-ˌkə-miŋ\ *n* ♦ : an imperfection or lack that detracts from the whole : FAILING

♦ demerit, failing, fault, foible, frailty, vice, weakness — more at FAULT

¹**short·cut** \-ˌkət\ *n* **1** : a route more direct than that usu. taken **2** : a quicker way of doing something

²**shortcut** *vb* : to shorten (as a route or procedure) by use of a shortcut; *also* ♦ : to manage to get around esp. by ingenuity or stratagem : CIRCUMVENT

♦ circumvent, dodge, get around, sidestep, skirt — more at CIRCUMVENT

short·en \'shòrt-ᵊn\ *vb* ♦ : to make or become short

♦ abbreviate, abridge, curtail, cut back; *also* digest, summarize; abate, compress, constrict, contract, cut, cut down, pare, prune, trim; decrease, de-escalate, deflate, diminish, dock, dwindle, lessen, lower, moderate, modify, reduce, retrench, shrink, slash, taper *Ant* elongate, extend, lengthen, prolong, protract

short·en·ing \'shòrt-ᵊn-iŋ\ *n* : a substance (as lard or butter) that makes pastry tender and flaky

short·hand \'shòrt-ˌhand\ *n* : a method of writing rapidly by using symbols and abbreviations for letters, words, or phrases : STENOGRAPHY

short·hand·ed \ˌshòrt-'han-dəd\ *adj* : short of the needed number of people

short·horn \'shòrt-ˌhòrn\ *n, often cap* : any of a breed of red, roan, or white cattle of English origin

short hundredweight *n* : a unit of weight equal to 100 pounds in the U.S.

short–lived \'shòrt-ˌlivd, -'līvd\ *adj* ♦ : of short life or duration

♦ brief, ephemeral, evanescent, flash, fleeting, fugitive, impermanent, momentary, transient — more at MOMENTARY

short·ly \'shòrt-lē\ *adv* **1** ♦ : in a few words **2** ♦ : in a short time : SOON

♦ [1] compactly, concisely, crisply, laconically, succinctly, summarily, tersely; *also* exactly, precisely; abruptly, bluntly, brusquely, curtly ♦ [2] anon, momentarily, presently, soon; *also* directly, forthwith, immediately, instantly, now, promptly, pronto, right away, right now, straightaway

short·ness *n* ♦ : the quality or state of being short esp. in duration

♦ brevity, briefness, conciseness — more at BREVITY

short–or·der \'shòrt-ˌòr-dər\ *adj* : preparing or serving food that can be quickly cooked ⟨a ~ cook⟩

short shrift *n* **1** : a brief respite from death **2** : little consideration

short·sight·ed \'shòrt-ˌsī-təd\ *adj* **1** : NEARSIGHTED **2** : lacking foresight — **short·sight·ed·ness** *n*

short·stop \-ˌstäp\ *n* : a baseball player defending the area between second and third base

short story *n* ♦ : a short work of fiction usu. dealing with a few characters and a single event

♦ narrative, novella, story, tale — more at STORY

short–tem·pered \ˌshòrt-'tem-pərd\ *adj* ♦ : having a quick temper

♦ choleric, crabby, cranky, cross, crotchety, grouchy, grumpy, irascible, irritable, peevish, perverse, petulant, snappish, snappy, snippy, testy, waspish — more at IRRITABLE

short–term \'shòrt-ˌtərm\ *adj* **1** ♦ : occurring over or involving a relatively short period of time **2** : of or relating

to a financial transaction based on a term usu. of less than a year

♦ impermanent, interim, provisional, temporary — more at TEMPORARY

short ton *n* : a unit of weight equal to 2000 pounds in the U.S.

short·wave \'shòrt-ˌwāv\ *n* : a radio wave with a wavelength between 10 and 100 meters

Sho·sho·ne *or* **Sho·sho·ni** \shə-'shō-nē\ *n, pl* **Shoshones** *or* **Shoshoni** : a member of an American Indian people orig. ranging through California, Idaho, Nevada, Utah, and Wyoming

¹**shot** \'shät\ *n* **1** : an act of shooting **2** : a stroke or throw in some games **3** : something that is shot : MISSILE, PROJECTILE; *esp* : small pellets forming a charge for a shotgun **4** : a metal sphere that is thrown for distance in the shot put **5** : RANGE, REACH **6** ♦ : one that shoots; *esp* : MARKSMAN **7** ♦ : a single photographic exposure **8** : a single sequence of a motion picture or a television program made by one camera **9** : an injection (as of medicine) into the body **10** ♦ : a small serving of undiluted liquor **11** ♦ : the act or an instance of attempting ⟨I'll give it a ~⟩

♦ [6] marksman, sharpshooter, shooter — more at MARKSMAN ♦ [7] photograph, print, snap, snapshot — more at PHOTOGRAPH ♦ [10] draft, drag, drink, nip, quaff, slug, snort, swallow, swig — more at DRINK ♦ [11] attempt, crack, endeavor (*or* endeavour), essay, fling, go, pass, stab, trial, try, whack — more at ATTEMPT

²**shot** *past and past part of* SHOOT

shot·gun \'shät-ˌgən\ *n* : a gun with a smooth bore used to fire shot at short range

shot put *n* : a field event in which a shot is heaved for distance

should \'shùd, shəd\ *past of* SHALL ♦ — used as an auxiliary to express condition, obligation or propriety, probability, or futurity from a point of view in the past

♦ have, must, need, ought, shall — more at NEED

¹**shoul·der** \'shōl-dər\ *n* **1** : the part of the body of a person or animal where the arm or foreleg joins the body **2** : either edge of a roadway **3** : a rounded or sloping part (as of a bottle) where the neck joins the body

²**shoulder** *vb* **1** : to push or thrust with the shoulder **2** : to bear on the shoulder **3** ♦ : to take the responsibility of

♦ accept, assume, bear, take over, undertake — more at ASSUME

shoulder belt *n* : an automobile safety belt worn across the torso and over the shoulder

shoulder blade *n* : a flat triangular bone at the back of each shoulder

¹**shout** \'shaùt\ *vb* ♦ : to utter a sudden loud cry; *also* : to utter in a loud voice

♦ bawl, call, cry, holler, vociferate, yell — more at CALL

²**shout** *n* ♦ : a loud cry or call

♦ cry, holler, hoot, howl, whoop, yell, yowl; *also* scream, screech, shriek, squall, squeak, squeal, yelp; bellow, clamor, roar; caterwaul, wail

shove \'shəv\ *vb* **shoved**; **shov·ing** **1** ♦ : to push along, aside, or away **2** ♦ : to go away — usu. used with *off* — **shove** *n*

♦ [1] drive, propel, push, thrust — more at PUSH ♦ *usu* **shove off** [2] clear out, depart, exit, get off, go, move, pull, quit, sally, take off — more at GO

¹**shov·el** \'shə-vəl\ *n* **1** : a broad long-handled scoop used to lift and throw material **2** : the amount a shovel will hold

²**shovel** *vb* **-eled** *or* **-elled**; **-el·ing** *or* **-el·ling** **1** : to take up and throw with a shovel **2** : to dig or clean out with a shovel

¹**show** \'shō\ *vb* **showed** \'shōd\; **shown** \'shōn\ *or* **showed**; **show·ing** **1** ♦ : to cause or permit to be seen : EXHIBIT

⟨∼ anger⟩ **2** : CONFER, BESTOW ⟨∼ mercy⟩ **3** ♦ : to reveal by one's condition, nature, or behavior : DISCLOSE ⟨∼ed courage in battle⟩ **4** ♦ : to communicate knowledge to : INSTRUCT ⟨∼ me how⟩ **5** ♦ : to demonstrate or establish by argument or reasoning : PROVE ⟨∼s he was guilty⟩ **6** : APPEAR **7** : to be noticeable **8** : to be third in a horse race **9** ♦ : to bring by or as if by leading : USHER

♦ [1] display, disport, exhibit, expose, flash, flaunt, parade, show off, sport, strut, unveil; *also* brandish, flourish; advertise, air, broadcast, proclaim, publicize; divulge, talk (about), tell (of); bare, discover, reveal, uncloak, uncover ♦ [3] bespeak, betray, demonstrate, disclose, display, evince, expose, give away, manifest, reveal; *also* bare, unbosom, uncloak, uncover; advertise, air, broadcast, proclaim, publicize ♦ [4] coach, counsel, guide, instruct, lead, mentor, pilot, shepherd, tutor — more at GUIDE ♦ [5] demonstrate, establish, prove, substantiate — more at ESTABLISH ♦ [9] conduct, direct, guide, lead, marshal, pilot, route, steer, usher — more at LEAD

²show *n* **1** ♦ : a demonstrative display **2** ♦ : outward appearance ⟨a ∼ of resistance⟩ **3** : SPECTACLE **4** : a theatrical presentation **5** : a radio or television program **6** : third place in a horse race **7** ♦ : a large display or exhibition arranged to arouse interest or stimulate sales

♦ [1] demonstration, display, exhibition; *also* act, pretense, simulation; affectation, pose, sham; betrayal, disclosure ♦ [2] appearance, face, guise, name, pretense, semblance — more at APPEARANCE ♦ [7] display, exhibit, exhibition, exposition, fair — more at EXHIBITION

¹show·case \'shō-ˌkās\ *n* : a cabinet for displaying items (as in a store)

²showcase *vb* **show·cased; show·cas·ing** : EXHIBIT

show·down \'shō-ˌdaůn\ *n* : a decisive confrontation or contest; *esp* : the showing of poker hands to determine the winner of a pot

¹show·er \'shaů-ər\ *n* **1** : a brief fall of rain **2** : a party given by friends who bring gifts **3** : a bath in which water is showered on the person; *also* : a facility (as a stall) for such a bath **4** ♦ : something resembling a rain shower — **show·ery** *adj*

♦ hail, rain, storm — more at RAIN

²shower *vb* **1** : to rain or fall in a shower **2** : to bathe in a shower **3** ♦ : to give in abundance

♦ heap, lavish, pour, rain — more at RAIN

show·i·ness \-ē-nəs\ *n* : the quality or state of being showy

♦ flamboyance, flashiness, gaudiness, glitz, ostentation, pretentiousness, swank — more at OSTENTATION

show·man \'shō-mən\ *n* : a notably spectacular, dramatic, or effective performer — **show·man·ship** *n*

show-off \'shō-ˌóf\ *n* : one that seeks to attract attention by conspicuous behavior

show off *vb* **1** ♦ : to display proudly **2** ♦ : to act as a show-off

♦ [1] display, disport, exhibit, expose, flash, flaunt, parade, show, sport, strut, unveil — more at SHOW ♦ [2] act up, clown, cut up, fool, monkey, skylark — more at CUT UP

show·piece \'shō-ˌpēs\ *n* : an outstanding example used for exhibition

show·place \-ˌplās\ *n* : an estate or building that is a showpiece

show up *vb* **1** ♦ : to make an appearance : ARRIVE **2** ♦ : to expose or discredit esp. by revealing faults **3** ♦ : to be plainly evident

♦ [1] arrive, come, land, turn up — more at COME ♦ [2] debunk, expose, uncloak, uncover, unmask — more at EXPOSE ♦ [3] appear, come out, materialize, turn up — more at APPEAR

showy \'shō-ē\ *adj* **show·i·er; -est** ♦ : superficially impressive or striking — **show·i·ly** \'shō-ə-lē\ *adv*

♦ catchy, conspicuous, dramatic, flamboyant, striking; *also* flashy, garish, gaudy, glitzy, jazzy, loud, meretricious, swank, tawdry; emphatic, marked, noticeable, prominent, pronounced, remarkable; ostentatious, pretentious; extravagant, fancy, florid, glittery, spectacular; opulent, ornate, overdone, overwrought; absorbing, engrossing, enthralling, fascinating, interesting, riveting **Ant** inconspicuous, unobtrusive

shpt *abbr* shipment

shrap·nel \'shrap-nəl\ *n, pl* **shrapnel** [Henry *Shrapnel* †1842 Eng. artillery officer] : bomb, mine, or shell fragments

¹shred \'shred\ *n* : a narrow strip cut or torn off : a small fragment

²shred *vb* **shred·ded; shred·ding** ♦ : to cut or tear into shreds

♦ rend, rip, rive, tatter, tear — more at TEAR

shrew \'shrü\ *n* **1** : any of a family of very small mammals with short velvety fur that are related to the moles **2** ♦ : an unpleasant and bad-tempered woman

♦ fury, harpy, termagant, virago; *also* carper, castigator, caviler, censurer, critic, faultfinder, nitpicker, railer, scold; detractor; pettifogger, quibbler

shrewd \'shrüd\ *adj* ♦ : given to wily and artful ways or dealing : ASTUTE — **shrewd·ly** *adv*

♦ astute, canny, hardheaded, knowing, sharp, smart; *also* artful, cagey, crafty, cunning, devious, foxy, guileful, slick, sly, subtle, wily; perspicacious, sagacious, wise **Ant** unknowing

shrewd·ness *n* ♦ : the quality or state of being shrewd

♦ acumen, astuteness, caginess, canniness, hardheadedness, intelligence, keenness, sharpness, wit — more at ACUMEN

shrew·ish \'shrü-ish\ *adj* : having an irritable disposition : ILL-TEMPERED — **shrew·ish·ly** *adv*

¹shriek \'shrēk\ *n* : a shrill cry : SCREAM, YELL

²shriek *vb* ♦ : to utter a sharp shrill sound; *also* : to utter with a shriek

♦ howl, scream, shrill, squeal, yell, yelp — more at SCREAM

shrift \'shrift\ *n, archaic* : the act of shriving

shrike \'shrīk\ *n* : any of numerous usu. largely grayish or brownish birds that often impale their usu. insect prey upon thorns before devouring it

¹shrill \'shril\ *vb* ♦ : to make a high-pitched piercing sound

♦ howl, scream, shriek, squeal, yell, yelp — more at SCREAM

²shrill *adj* ♦ : high-pitched ⟨∼ whistle⟩ — **shril·ly** *adv*

♦ acute, sharp, squeaky, treble; *also* peeping, thin, tinny; earsplitting, penetrating, piercing, strident; squealing, whining, yelping **Ant** bass, deep, low, throaty

shrimp \'shrimp\ *n, pl* **shrimps** *or* **shrimp** **1** : any of various small marine crustaceans related to the lobsters **2** *usu disparaging* : a small or puny person or thing

shrine \'shrīn\ *n* [ME, receptacle for the relics of a saint, fr. OE *scrīn*, fr. L *scrinium* case, chest] **1** : the tomb of a saint; *also* : a place where devotion is paid to a saint or deity **2** : a place or object hallowed by its associations

¹shrink \'shriŋk\ *vb* **shrank** \'shraŋk\ *or* **shrunk** \'shrəŋk\; **shrunk** *or* **shrunk·en** \'shrəŋ-kən\; **shrink·ing** **1** ♦ : to draw back or away **2** ♦ : to become smaller or more compact **3** ♦ : to lessen in value — **shrink·able** *adj*

♦ [1] blench, flinch, quail, recoil, wince — more at FLINCH ♦ [2] compress, condense, constrict, contract — more at CONTRACT ♦ [2, 3] abate, decline, decrease, de-escalate, die, diminish, dwindle, ebb, fall, lessen, let up, lower, moderate, recede, relent, subside, taper, wane — more at DECREASE

²shrink *n* : a clinical psychiatrist or psychologist

shrink·age \'shriŋ-kij\ *n* **1** : the act of shrinking **2** ♦ : the amount lost by shrinkage

♦ abatement, decline, decrease, decrement, diminution, drop, fall, loss, reduction — more at DECREASE

shrive \'shrīv\ *vb* **shrived** *or* **shrove** \'shrōv\; **shriv·en** \'shri-vən\ *or* **shrived**; **shriv·ing** [ME, fr. OE *scrīfan* to prescribe, allot, shrive, fr. L *scribere* to write] : to administer the sacrament of reconciliation to

shriv·el \'shri-vəl\ *vb* **-eled** *or* **-elled**; **-el·ing** *or* **-el·ling** : to shrink and draw into wrinkles : DWINDLE

¹**shroud** \'shraůd\ *n* **1** ♦ : something that covers or screens **2** : a cloth placed over a dead body **3** : any of the ropes leading from the masthead of a ship to the side to support the mast

♦ cloak, curtain, hood, mantle, mask, veil — more at CLOAK

²**shroud** *vb* **1** ♦ : to veil or screen from view; *also* : to veil under another appearance (as by obscuring or disguising) **2** : to cover with a shroud

♦ blanket, blot out, cloak, conceal, cover, curtain, hide, mask, obscure, occult, screen — more at HIDE ♦ embrace, enclose, encompass, enfold, enshroud, envelop, invest, lap, mantle, swathe, veil, wrap — more at ENFOLD

shrub \'shrəb\ *n* : a low usu. several-stemmed woody plant — **shrub·by** *adj*

shrub·bery \'shrə-bə-rē\ *n, pl* **-ber·ies** : a planting or growth of shrubs

shrug \'shrəg\ *vb* **shrugged**; **shrug·ging** : to hunch (the shoulders) up to express aloofness, indifference, or uncertainty — **shrug** *n*

shrug off *vb* **1** ♦ : to brush aside : MINIMIZE **2** : to shake off **3** : to remove (a garment) by wriggling out

♦ condone, disregard, excuse, ignore, minimize, pardon, pass over, wink at — more at EXCUSE

shtick *also* **schtick** *or* **shtik** \'shtik\ *n* [Yiddish *shtik* pranks, lit., piece] **1** : a usu. comic or repetitious performance or routine **2** : one's special trait, interest, or activity

¹**shuck** \'shək\ *n* : SHELL, HUSK

²**shuck** *vb* **1** : to strip of shucks **2** ♦ : to lay aside — often used with *off*

♦ *usu* **shuck off** cast, discard, ditch, dump, fling, jettison, junk, lose, reject, scrap, shed, slough, throw away, throw out, unload — more at DISCARD

¹**shud·der** \'shə-dər\ *vb* ♦ : to tremble convulsively : QUAKE

♦ agitate, convulse, jolt, jounce, quake, quiver, shake, vibrate, wobble — more at SHAKE

²**shudder** *n* ♦ : an act of shuddering

♦ quiver, shiver, tremble — more at SHIVER

¹**shuf·fle** \'shə-fəl\ *vb* **shuf·fled**; **shuf·fling** **1** ♦ : to mix in a disorderly mass **2** : to rearrange the order of (cards in a pack) by mixing two parts of the pack together **3** : to shift from place to place **4** ♦ : to move with a sliding or dragging gait **5** : to dance in a slow lagging manner

♦ [1] confuse, derange, disarray, disorder, jumble, mess, mix, muddle, scramble, upset — more at DISORDER ♦ [4] lumber, scuff, scuffle, shamble

²**shuffle** *n* **1** : an act of shuffling (as of cards) **2** ♦ : a confusing jumble (as of papers or events)

♦ assortment, clutter, jumble, medley, mélange, miscellany, motley, muddle, variety, welter — more at MISCELLANY

shuf·fle·board \'shə-fəl-ˌbōrd\ *n* : a game in which players use long-handled cues to shove disks into scoring areas marked on a smooth surface

shun \'shən\ *vb* **shunned**; **shun·ning** ♦ : to avoid deliberately or habitually

♦ avoid, dodge, duck, elude, escape, eschew, evade, shake, shirk — more at ESCAPE

¹**shunt** \'shənt\ *vb* [ME, to turn away] : to turn off to one side; *esp* : to switch (a train) from one track to another

²**shunt** *n* **1** : a method or device for turning or thrusting aside **2** : a conductor joining two points in an electrical circuit forming an alternate path through which a portion of the current may pass

shut \'shət\ *vb* **shut**; **shut·ting** **1** : CLOSE **2** : to forbid entrance into **3** : to lock up **4** : to fold together ⟨~ a penknife⟩ **5** : to cease or suspend activity ⟨~ down an assembly line⟩

shut·down \-ˌdaůn\ *n* ♦ : a temporary cessation of activity (as in a factory)

♦ cessation, close, closure, conclusion, end, ending, expiration, finish, halt, lapse, stop, stoppage, termination — more at END

shut·in \'shət-ˌin\ *n* : an invalid confined to home, a room, or bed

shut·out \'shət-ˌaůt\ *n* : a game or contest in which one side fails to score

shut out *vb* **1** ♦ : to prevent from using or participating : EXCLUDE **2** : to prevent (an opponent) from scoring in a game or contest

♦ ban, bar, count out, debar, eliminate, except, exclude, rule out — more at EXCLUDE

shut off *vb* ♦ : to stop the operation of (as a machine); *also* : to cease operating

♦ break, break off, cease, cut, desist, discontinue, drop, end, halt, knock off, layoff, leave off, quit, stop — more at STOP

shut·ter \'shə-tər\ *n* **1** : a movable cover for a door or window : BLIND **2** : the part of a camera that opens and closes to allow light to enter

shut·ter·bug \'shə-tər-ˌbəg\ *n* : a photography enthusiast

¹**shut·tle** \'shət-ᵊl\ *n* **1** : an instrument used in weaving for passing the horizontal threads between the vertical threads **2** : a vehicle traveling back and forth over a short route ⟨a ~ bus⟩ **3** : SPACE SHUTTLE

²**shuttle** *vb* **shut·tled**; **shut·tling** : to move back and forth frequently

shut·tle·cock \'shət-ᵊl-ˌkäk\ *n* : a light conical object (as of cork or plastic) used in badminton

shut up *vb* ♦ : to cease or cause to cease talking

♦ clam up, hush, pipe down, quiet (down); *also* calm (down), cool (down), settle (down); haw, hem *Ant* speak, talk

¹**shy** \'shī\ *adj* **shi·er** *or* **shy·er** \'shī-ər\; **shi·est** *or* **shy·est** \'shī-əst\ **1** ♦ : easily frightened : TIMID **2** : WARY **3** ♦ : sensitively diffident or retiring : BASHFUL **4** ♦ : having less than the full or specified amount or number : LACKING — **shy·ly** *adv* — **shy·ness** *n*

♦ [1] fainthearted, fearful, mousy, scary, skittish, timid; *also* chicken, chickenhearted, cowardly, craven, dastardly, jittery, jumpy, pusillanimous, spineless, unheroic, yellow; anxious, apprehensive, nervous; afraid, alarmed, horrified, panicked, panicky, scared, shocked, spooked, startled, terrified, terrorized *Ant* adventuresome, adventurous, audacious, bold, daring, dashing, gutsy, hardy, venturous, venturesome ♦ [3] bashful, coy, demure, diffident, introverted, modest, retiring, sheepish; *also* antisocial, unsociable; awkward, embarrassed, self-conscious, unadventurous, unassertive, unenterprising; inhibited, reserved, uneasy, uptight *Ant* extroverted, immodest, outgoing ♦ [4] deficient, inadequate, insufficient, scarce, short, wanting — more at SHORT

²**shy** *vb* **shied**; **shy·ing** **1** : to show a dislike : RECOIL **2** : to start suddenly aside through fright ⟨the horse *shied*⟩

shy·ster \'shīs-tər\ *n* : an unscrupulous lawyer or politician

Si *symbol* silicon

SI *abbr* [F *Système International d'Unités*] International System of Units

Si·a·mese \ˌsī-ə-ˈmēz, -ˈmēs\ *n, pl* **Sia·mese** : THAI — **Sia·mese** *adj*

Siamese cat *n* : any of a breed of slender blue-eyed short-haired domestic cats of Asian origin

Siamese twin *n* [fr. Chang †1874 and Eng †1874 twins born in Siam with bodies united] : one of a pair of twins with bodies joined together at birth

Siberian husky *n* : any of a breed of thick-coated compact dogs orig. developed in Siberia to pull sleds

¹**sib·i·lant** \'si-bə-lənt\ *adj* : having, containing, or producing the sound of or a sound resembling that of the *s* or the *sh* in *sash* — **sib·i·lant·ly** *adv*

²**sibilant** *n* : a sibilant speech sound as English \s\, \z\, \sh\, \zh\, \ch (=tsh)\, or \j (=dzh)\)

sib·ling \'si-bliŋ\ *n* : a brother or sister considered irrespective of sex; *also* : one of two or more offspring having one common parent

sib·yl \'si-bəl\ *n, often cap* : PROPHETESS — **sib·yl·line** \-bə-ˌlīn, -ˌlēn\ *adj*

sic \'sik, 'sēk\ *adv* : intentionally so written — used after a printed word or passage to indicate that it exactly reproduces an original ⟨said he seed [*sic*] it all⟩

sick \'sik\ *adj* **1** ♦ : not in good health : ILL; *also* : of, relating to, or intended for use in sickness ⟨~ pay⟩ **2** ♦ : suffering from nausea : NAUSEATED **3** ♦ : having a strong distaste from an overabundance; *also* : DISGUSTED **4** : PINING **5** : MACABRE, SADISTIC ⟨~ jokes⟩

♦ [1] bad, down, ill, indisposed, peaked, punk, unhealthy, unsound, unwell; *also* nauseated, nauseous, qualmish, queasy, squeamish; airsick, carsick, seasick; dizzy, woozy *Ant* chipper, hale, healthful, healthy, sound, well, whole, wholesome ♦ [2] ill, nauseous, queasy, queer, squeamish — more at NAUSEOUS ♦ [3] fed up, jaded, tired, weary — more at WEARY ♦ [3] disgusted, squeamish; *also* angry, displeased, mad, upset

sick·bed \'sik-ˌbed\ *n* : a bed on which one lies sick

sick·en \'si-kən\ *vb* ♦ : to make or become sick — **sick·en·ing·ly** *adv*

♦ disgust, nauseate, repel, repulse, revolt, turn off — more at DISGUST ♦ *usu* **sicken with** catch, come down, contract, get, take — more at CONTRACT

sickening *adj* : causing sickness or disgust

sick·le \'si-kəl\ *n* : a cutting tool consisting of a curved metal blade with a short handle

sickle–cell anemia *n* : an inherited anemia in which red blood cells tend to become crescent-shaped and clog small blood vessels and which occurs esp. in individuals of African, Mediterranean, or southwest Asian ancestry

sick·ly \sik-lē\ *adj* **1 a** : somewhat unwell **b** ♦ : habitually ailing **2** ♦ : produced by or associated with sickness

♦ [1b] invalid, weakly; *also* bedridden; delicate, fragile, frail; dying, fading, incurable, moribund; crippled, debilitated, incapacitated, lame; decrepit, enfeebled, feeble, infirm, weak, weakened, worn-out *Ant* healthy, well ♦ [2] cadaverous, green, lurid, pale, pasty, peaked, sallow; *also* ashen, ashy, blanched, colorless, livid, white; waxen, waxy; deathlike, deathly; anemic, bloodless *Ant* florid, flush, healthy, rubicund, ruddy, sanguine

sick·ness \'sik-nəs\ *n* **1** ♦ : ill health; *also* : a specific disease **2** : a stomach distress with distaste for food and an urge to vomit : NAUSEA

♦ affection, ailment, bug, complaint, complication, condition, disease, disorder, fever, ill, illness, infirmity, malady, trouble — more at DISEASE ♦ illness, unsoundness; *also* malaise; ailment, condition, disease, disorder, malady, trouble, upset; debility, decrepitude, feebleness, infirmity, lameness *Ant* health, healthiness, soundness, wellness, wholeness, wholesomeness

side \'sīd\ *n* **1** : the right or left part of the trunk of a body **2** : a place away from a central point or line **3** : a border of an object; *esp* : one of the longer borders as contrasted with an end **4** : an outer surface of an object **5** ♦ : a position regarded as opposite to another **6** ♦ : a body of partisans or contestants — **side** *adj*

♦ [5] angle, aspect, facet, hand, phase — more at ASPECT ♦ [6] bloc, body, coalition, combination, combine, faction, party, sect, wing — more at FACTION

side·arm \-ˌärm\ *adj* : made with a sideways sweep of the arm — **sidearm** *adv*

side arm *n* : a weapon worn at the side or in the belt

side·bar \'sīd-ˌbär\ *n* : a short news story accompanying a major story and presenting related information

side·board \-ˌbȯrd\ *n* ♦ : a piece of dining-room furniture for holding articles of table service

♦ buffet, cabinet, closet, cupboard, hutch, locker — more at CABINET

side·burns \-ˌbərnz\ *n pl* : whiskers on the side of the face in front of the ears

side by side *adv* **1** : beside one another **2** : in the same place, time, or circumstance — **side–by–side** *adj*

side·car \-ˌkär\ *n* : a one-wheeled passenger car attached to the side of a motorcycle

side effect *n* : a secondary and usu. adverse effect (as of a drug)

side·kick \'sīd-ˌkik\ *n* ♦ : a person closely associated with another as a subordinate or partner

♦ aid, apprentice, assistant, deputy, helper, helpmate, mate — more at HELPER

side·line \'sīd-ˌlīn\ *n* **1** : an activity pursued in addition to one's regular occupation **2** : the space immediately outside the lines of an athletic field or court **3** : a sphere of little or no participation — usu. used in pl.

¹**side·long** \'sīd-ˌlȯŋ\ *adv* : in the direction of or along the side : OBLIQUELY

²**sidelong** *adj* : directed to one side ⟨~ look⟩

side·man \'sīd-ˌman\ *n* : a member of a jazz or swing orchestra

side·piece \-ˌpēs\ *n* : a piece forming or contained in the side of something

si·de·re·al \sī-'dir-ē-əl, sə-\ *adj* [L *sidereus,* fr. *sider-, sidas* star, constellation] **1** : of or relating to the stars **2** : measured by the apparent motion of the stars

side·sad·dle \'sīd-ˌsad-ᵊl\ *n* : a saddle for women in which the rider sits with both legs on the same side of the horse — **sidesaddle** *adv*

side·show \'sīd-ˌshō\ *n* **1** : a minor show offered in addition to a main exhibition (as of a circus) **2** : an incidental diversion

side·step \-ˌstep\ *vb* **1** : to step aside **2** ♦ : to move out of the way of; *also* : to avoid an issue or decision

♦ circumvent, dodge, skirt — more at CIRCUMVENT ♦ dodge, duck — more at DODGE

side·stroke \-ˌstrōk\ *n* : a swimming stroke which is executed on the side and in which the arms are swept backward and downward and the legs do a scissors kick

side·swipe \-ˌswīp\ *vb* : to strike with a glancing blow along the side — **sideswipe** *n*

¹**side·track** \-ˌtrak\ *n* : SIDING 1

²**sidetrack** *vb* **1** : to switch from a main railroad line to a siding **2** : to turn aside from a purpose

side·walk \'sīd-ˌwȯk\ *n* : a paved walk at the side of a road or street

side·wall \-ˌwȯl\ *n* **1** : a wall forming the side of something **2** : the side of an automobile tire

side·ways \-ˌwāz\ *adv or adj* **1** : from the side **2** : with one side to the front **3** : to, toward, or at one side

side·wind·er \-ˌwīn-dər\ *n* : a small pale-colored desert rattlesnake of the southwestern U.S.

sid·ing \'sī-diŋ\ *n* **1** : a short railroad track connected with the main track **2** : material (as boards) covering the outside of frame buildings

si·dle \'sīd-ᵊl\ *vb* **si·dled; si·dling** : to move sideways or with one side foremost

SIDS *abbr* sudden infant death syndrome

siege \'sēj\ *n* **1** : the placing of an army around or before a fortified place to force its surrender **2** ♦ : a persistent attack (as of illness)

♦ attack, bout, case, fit, seizure, spell — more at ATTACK

sie·mens \'sē-mənz, 'zē-\ *n* : a unit of conductance equivalent to one ampere per volt

si·er·ra \sē-'er-ə\ *n* [Sp, lit., saw, fr. L *serra*] : a range of mountains esp. with jagged peaks

si·es·ta \sē-'es-tə\ *n* [Sp, fr. L *sexta (hora)* noon, lit., sixth hour] ♦ : a midday rest or nap

♦ catnap, doze, drowse, forty winks, nap, snooze, wink — more at NAP

sieve \'siv\ *n* : a utensil with meshes or holes to separate finer particles from coarser or solids from liquids

sift \'sift\ *vb* 1 : to pass through a sieve 2 : to separate with or as if with a sieve 3 : to examine carefully 4 : to scatter by or as if by passing through a sieve — **sift·er** *n*

sig *abbr* signature

SIG *abbr* special interest group

sigh \'sī\ *vb* 1 : to let out a deep audible breath (as in weariness or sorrow) 2 ♦ : to long persistently, wistfully, or sadly : YEARN — often used with *for* — **sigh** *n*

♦ ache, die, hanker, hunger, itch, long, pant, pine, thirst, yearn

¹sight \'sīt\ *n* 1 : something seen or worth seeing 2 ♦ : the process or power of seeing; *esp* : the sense of which the eye is the receptor and by which qualities of appearance (as position, shape, and color) are perceived 3 : INSPECTION 4 : a device (as a small bead on a gun barrel) that aids the eye in aiming 5 : the act of looking at or beholding : VIEW, GLIMPSE 6 : the range of vision 7 ♦ : something ludicrous or disorderly in appearance — **sight·less** *adj*

♦ [2] eye, vision ♦ [7] eyesore, fright, horror, mess, monstrosity — more at EYESORE

²sight *vb* 1 ♦ : to get sight of 2 : to aim by means of a sight

♦ behold, descry, discern, distinguish, espy, eye, look, note, notice, observe, perceive, regard, remark, see, spy, view, witness — more at SEE

sight·ed \'sī-təd\ *adj* : having sight

sight·ly \-lē\ *adj* : pleasing to the sight

sight·see·ing \'sīt-ˌsē-iŋ\ *adj* : engaged in or used for seeing sights of interest

sight·seer \-ˌsē-ər\ *n* ♦ : one that visits places of interest

♦ excursionist, tourist, traveler — more at TOURIST

sig·ma \'sig-mə\ *n* : the 18th letter of the Greek alphabet — Σ or or ς

¹sign \'sīn\ *n* 1 ♦ : a gesture expressing a command, wish, or thought 2 : SYMBOL 3 : a notice publicly displayed for advertising purposes or for giving direction or warning 4 : OMEN, PORTENT 5 : TRACE, VESTIGE

♦ gesture, pantomime, signal — more at GESTURE

²sign *vb* 1 : to mark with a sign 2 : to represent by a sign 3 : to make a sign or signal 4 : to write one's name on in token of assent or obligation ⟨~ed the contract⟩ 5 : to assign legally 6 : to use sign language — **sign·er** *n*

¹sig·nal \'sig-nəl\ *n* 1 : a sign agreed on as the start of some joint action 2 ♦ : a sign giving warning or notice of something 3 : the message, sound, or image transmitted in electronic communication (as radio)

♦ gesture, pantomime, sign — more at GESTURE

²signal *vb* -naled *or* -nalled; -nal·ing *or* -nal·ling 1 ♦ : to notify by a signal 2 : to communicate by signals

♦ flag, gesture, motion, wave — more at MOTION

³signal *adj* ♦ : distinguished from the ordinary ⟨a ~ honor⟩ — **sig·nal·ly** *adv*

♦ distinguished, eminent, illustrious, noble, notable, noteworthy, outstanding, preeminent, prestigious, star, superior — more at EMINENT

sig·nal·ize \'sig-nə-ˌlīz\ *vb* -ized; -iz·ing : to point out or make conspicuous — **sig·nal·i·za·tion** \ˌsig-nə-lə-'zā-shən\ *n*

sig·nal·man \'sig-nəl-mən, -ˌman\ *n* : a person who signals or works with signals

sig·na·to·ry \'sig-nə-ˌtōr-ē\ *n, pl* -ries : a person or government that signs jointly with others — **signatory** *adj*

¹sig·na·ture \'sig-nə-ˌchur\ *n* 1 : the name of a person written by himself or herself 2 : the sign placed after the clef to indicate the key or the meter of a piece of music

²signature *adj* : closely and distinctly associated and identified with someone or something ⟨her ~ style⟩

sign·board \'sīn-ˌbōrd\ *n* : a board bearing a sign or notice

sig·net \'sig-nət\ *n* : a small intaglio seal (as in a ring)

sig·nif·i·cance \sig-'ni-fi-kəns\ *n* 1 ♦ : something signified : MEANING 2 : SUGGESTIVENESS 3 ♦ : the quality of being important : IMPORTANCE

♦ [1] denotation, drift, import, intent, meaning, purport, sense, signification — more at MEANING ♦ [3] consequence, import, magnitude, moment, weight

sig·nif·i·cant \-kənt\ *adj* 1 ♦ : having meaning; *esp* : having a hidden or special meaning 2 ♦ : having or likely to have influence or effect : IMPORTANT 3 ♦ : of a noticeably or measurably large amount — **sig·nif·i·cant·ly** *adv*

♦ [1] big, consequential, eventful, important, major, material, meaningful, momentous, substantial, weighty — more at IMPORTANT ♦ [1] denotative, indicative, telltale — more at INDICATIVE ♦ [2] important, influential, mighty, potent, powerful, strong — more at IMPORTANT ♦ [3] considerable, good, goodly, healthy, respectable, sizable, substantial, tidy — more at CONSIDERABLE

sig·ni·fi·ca·tion \ˌsig-nə-fə-'kā-shən\ *n* 1 : the act or process of signifying by signs or other symbolic means 2 ♦ : the meaning that a term, symbol, or character regularly conveys or is intended to convey

♦ denotation, drift, import, intent, meaning, purport, sense, significance — more at MEANING

sig·ni·fy \'sig-nə-ˌfī\ *vb* -fied; -fy·ing 1 : to show by a sign 2 ♦ : to serve or intend to convey, show, or indicate : MEAN 3 ♦ : to have significance

♦ [2] denote, express, import, mean, spell — more at MEAN ♦ [3] count, import, matter, mean, weigh — more at MATTER

sign in *vb* : to make a record of arrival (as by signing a register)

sign language *n* : a formal system of hand gestures used for communication (as by the deaf)

sign off *vb* : to announce the end (as of a program or broadcast)

sign of the cross : a gesture of the hand forming a cross (as to invoke divine blessing)

sign on *vb* 1 ♦ : to engage oneself by or as if by a signature 2 : to announce the start of broadcasting for the day

♦ *usu* **sign on for** enlist, enroll, enter, join, sign up — more at ENTER

sign out *vb* : to make a record of departure (as by signing a register)

sign·post \'sīn-ˌpōst\ *n* : a post bearing a sign

sign up *vb* ♦ : to sign one's name (as to a contract) in order to obtain, do, or join something

♦ *usu* **sign up for** enlist, enroll, enter, join, sign on — more at ENTER

Sikh \'sēk\ *n* : an adherent of a religion of India marked by rejection of caste — **Sikh·ism** *n*

si·lage \'sī-lij\ *n* : fodder fermented (as in a silo) to produce a rich moist animal feed

¹si·lence \'sī-ləns\ *n* 1 : forbearance from speech or noise 2 ♦ : absence of sound or noise : STILLNESS 3 : SECRECY

♦ hush, quiet, quietness, still, stillness; *also* calm, lull, tranquility *Ant* noise, sound

²silence *vb* **si·lenced; si·lenc·ing** 1 ♦ : to reduce to silence : STILL 2 ♦ : to cause to cease hostile firing or criticism

♦ [1] hush, mute, quell, settle, still ♦ [2] clamp down, crack down, crush, put down, quash, quell, repress, snuff, squash, squelch, subdue, suppress — more at QUELL

si·lenc·er \'sī-lən-sər\ *n* : a device for muffling the noise of a gunshot

si·lent \'sī-lənt\ *adj* 1 ♦ : not speaking : MUTE; *also* : not inclined to talk 2 ♦ : free from sound or noise : STILL,

QUIET **3** : performed or borne without utterance ⟨a ~ prayer⟩ — **si·lent·ly** adv

♦ [1] dumb, mum, mute, speechless, uncommunicative; *also* inarticulate, tongue-tied; nonvocal, voiceless *Ant* communicative, speaking, talking ♦ [1] close-mouthed, laconic, reserved, reticent, taciturn, uncommunicative; *also* inhibited, introverted, restrained; sedate, self-contained, sober, staid *Ant* chatty, communicative, conversational, gabby, garrulous, loquacious, talkative, unreserved ♦ [2] hushed, muted, noiseless, quiet, soundless, still; *also* peaceful, tranquil *Ant* noisy, unquiet

silent treatment n ♦ : an act of completely ignoring a person or thing by resort to silence esp. as a means of expressing contempt or disapproval

♦ brush-off, cold shoulder, rebuff, repulse, snub — more at COLD SHOULDER

¹**sil·hou·ette** \ˌsi-lə-ˈwet\ n [F] **1** : a representation of the outlines of an object filled in with black or some other uniform color **2** ♦ : the outline of a body viewed as circumscribing a mass : OUTLINE ⟨~ of a ship⟩

♦ contour, figure, outline — more at OUTLINE

²**silhouette** vb **-ett·ed; -ett·ing** ♦ : to represent by a silhouette; *also* : to show against a light background

♦ define, delineate, outline, sketch, trace — more at OUTLINE

sil·i·ca \ˈsi-li-kə\ n : a mineral that consists of silicon and oxygen

sil·i·cate \ˈsi-lə-ˌkāt, ˈsi-li-kət\ n : a chemical salt that consists of a metal combined with silicon and oxygen

sil·i·ceous *also* **sil·i·cious** \sə-ˈli-shəs\ adj : of, relating to, or containing silica or a silicate

sil·i·con \ˈsi-li-kən, ˈsi-lə-ˌkän\ n : a nonmetallic chemical element that occurs in combination as the most abundant element next to oxygen in the earth's crust and is used esp. in alloys and semiconductors

sil·i·cone \ˈsi-lə-ˌkōn\ n : an organic silicon compound used esp. for lubricants and varnishes

sil·i·co·sis \ˌsi-lə-ˈkō-səs\ n : a lung disease caused by prolonged inhaling of silica dusts

silk \ˈsilk\ n **1** : a fine strong lustrous protein fiber produced by insect larvae usu. for their cocoons; *esp* : one from moth larvae (**silk·worms** \-ˌwərmz\) used for cloth **2** : thread or cloth made from silk

silk·en \ˈsil-kən\ adj ♦ : resembling silk (as in texture or appearance)

♦ cottony, downy, satiny, soft, velvety — more at SOFT

silk screen n : a stencil process in which coloring matter is forced through the meshes of a prepared silk or organdy screen; *also* : a print made by this process — **silk–screen** vb

silky adj : resembling silk (as in texture or appearance)

sill \ˈsil\ n : a heavy crosspiece (as of wood or stone) that forms the bottom member of a window frame or a doorway; *also* : a horizontal supporting piece at the base of a structure

sil·li·ness n ♦ : the quality or state of being silly; *also* : a silly practice

♦ absurdity, asininity, balminess, craziness, daftness, fatuity, folly, foolishness, inanity, insanity, lunacy, madness, nonsense, simplicity, zaniness

¹**sil·ly** \ˈsi-lē\ adj **sil·li·er; -est** [ME *sely, silly* happy, innocent, pitiable, feeble, fr. OE *sǣlig*, fr. *sǣl* happiness] ♦ : exhibiting or indicative of a lack of common sense or sound judgment; *also* : lacking in seriousness

♦ absurd, crazy, cuckoo, fatuous, foolish, mad, nonsensical, nutty, senseless, stupid — more at FOOLISH ♦ flighty, frivolous, giddy, goofy, harebrained, light= headed, scatterbrained — more at GIDDY

si·lo \ˈsī-lō\ n, pl silos [Sp] **1** : a trench, pit, or esp. a tall cylinder for making and storing silage **2** : an underground structure for housing a guided missile

¹**silt** \ˈsilt\ n **1** : fine earth; *esp* : particles of such soil floating in rivers, ponds, or lakes **2** : a deposit (as by a river) of silt — **silty** adj

²**silt** vb : to obstruct or cover with silt — **silt·ation** \sil-ˈtā-shən\ n

Si·lu·ri·an \sī-ˈlu̇r-ē-ən\ adj : of, relating to, or being the period of the Paleozoic era between the Ordovician and the Devonian marked by the appearance of the first land plants — **Silurian** n

¹**sil·ver** \ˈsil-vər\ n **1** : a white ductile metallic chemical element that takes a high polish and is a better conductor of heat and electricity than any other substance **2** : coin made of silver **3** ♦ : articles (as hollowware or table flatware) made of or plated with silver **4** : a grayish white color

♦ flatware, tableware — more at TABLEWARE

²**silver** adj **1** : relating to, made of, or coated with silver **2** ♦ : resembling silver (as in sheen or color) : SILVERY

♦ gray (*or* grey), leaden, pewter, silvery, slate, steely — more at GRAY

³**silver** vb **sil·vered; sil·ver·ing** : to coat with or as if with silver — **sil·ver·er** n

silver bromide n : a light-sensitive compound used esp. in photography

sil·ver·fish \ˈsil-vər-ˌfish\ n : any of various small wingless insects found in houses and sometimes injurious esp. to sized paper and starched clothes

silver iodide n : a light-sensitive compound used in photography, rainmaking, and medicine

silver maple n : a No. American maple with deeply cut leaves that are green above and silvery white below

silver nitrate n : a soluble compound used in photography and as an antiseptic

sil·ver·ware \ˈsil-vər-ˌwar\ n : eating and serving utensils (as knives, forks, and spoons) : FLATWARE

sil·very adj ♦ : resembling or having the luster of silver

♦ gray (*or* grey), leaden, pewter, silver, slate, steely — more at GRAY

sim·i·an \ˈsi-mē-ən\ n : MONKEY, APE — **simian** adj

sim·i·lar \ˈsi-mə-lər\ adj ♦ : marked by correspondence or resemblance

♦ akin, alike, analogous, comparable, correspondent, like, parallel, such — more at ALIKE

sim·i·lar·i·ty \ˌsi-mə-ˈlar-ə-tē\ n ♦ : the quality or state of being similar; *also* : a comparable aspect

♦ community, correspondence, likeness, parallel, parallelism, resemblance, similitude; *also* counterpart, equal, equivalence, parity; identity, sameness; correlation, relationship; accordance, agreement, compatibility, conformity, congruity *Ant* dissimilarity, unlikeness

sim·i·lar·ly adv ♦ : in the same or a comparable manner

♦ alike, also, correspondingly, likewise, so — more at ALSO

sim·i·le \ˈsi-mə-(ˌ)lē\ n [ME, fr. L, likeness, comparison, fr. neut. of *similis* like, similar] : a figure of speech in which two dissimilar things are compared by the use of *like* or *as* (as in "cheeks like roses")

si·mil·i·tude \sə-ˈmi-lə-ˌtüd, -ˌtyüd\ n ♦ : correspondence in kind or quality : RESEMBLANCE; *also* : a point of comparison

♦ community, correspondence, likeness, parallelism, resemblance, similarity — more at SIMILARITY

sim·mer \ˈsi-mər\ vb **sim·mered; sim·mer·ing 1** : to stew at or just below the boiling point **2** : to be on the point of bursting out with violence or emotional disturbance — **simmer** n

simmer down vb : to become calm or peaceful

si·mo·nize \ˈsī-mə-ˌnīz\ vb **-nized; -niz·ing** : to polish with or as if with wax

si·mo·ny \ˈsī-mə-nē, ˈsi-\ n [ME *symonie*, fr. LL *simonia*, fr. *Simon* Magus sorcerer of Samaria in Acts 8:9–24] : the buying or selling of a church office

sim·pa·ti·co \sim-ˈpä-ti-ˌkō, -ˈpa-\ adj : CONGENIAL, LIKABLE

sim·per \'sim-pər\ *vb* : to smile in a silly manner — **simper** *n*

sim·ple \'sim-pəl\ *adj* **sim·pler** \-pə-lər\; **sim·plest** \-pə-ləst\ [ME, fr. OF, plain, uncomplicated, artless, fr. L *simplus, simplex*, lit., single; L *simplus* fr. *sim-* one + *-plus* multiplied by; L *simplex* fr. *sim-* + *-plex* -fold\] **1** ♦ : free from dishonesty or vanity : INNOCENT **2** ♦ : free from ostentation **3** : of humble origin or modest position **4** : slow of mind : STUPID **5** ♦ : not complex : PLAIN ⟨a ∼ melody⟩ ⟨∼ directions⟩ **6** ♦ : lacking education, experience, or intelligence **7** : developing from a single ovary ⟨a ∼ fruit⟩ **8** : not limited or restricted — **sim·ple·ness** *n*

♦ [1, 2] artless, genuine, honest, ingenuous, innocent, naive, natural, real, sincere, true, unaffected, unpretentious ♦ [5] bald, bare, naked, plain, unadorned, undecorated, unvarnished — more at PLAIN ♦ [5] easy, effortless, facile, fluent, fluid, light, painless, ready, smooth, snap, soft — more at EASY ♦ [6] green, ignorant, ingenuous, innocent, naive, unknowing, unsophisticated, unwary, unworldly — more at NAIVE

simple interest *n* : interest paid or computed on the original principal only of a loan or on the amount of an account

sim·ple·ton \'sim-pəl-tən\ *n* ♦ : a person lacking in common sense : FOOL

♦ booby, fool, goose, half-wit, jackass, lunatic, nitwit, nut, turkey — more at FOOL

sim·plic·i·ty \sim-'pli-sə-tē\ *n, pl* **-ties** **1** : lack of complication : CLEARNESS **2** ♦ : freedom from pretense or guile **3** : plainness in manners or way of life **4** : lack of good sense or normal prudence and foresight : SILLINESS, FOLLY **5** ♦ : directness of expression

♦ [2] artlessness, greenness, ingenuousness, innocence, naïveté, naturalness, unworldliness — more at NAÏVETÉ ♦ [5] clarity, explicitness, lucidity, perspicuity; *also* directness, forthrightness, openness **Ant** obscurity

sim·pli·fy \'sim-plə-ˌfī\ *vb* **-fied; -fy·ing** : to make simple or simpler — **sim·pli·fi·ca·tion** \ˌsim-plə-fə-'kā-shən\ *n*

sim·plis·tic \sim-'plis-tik\ *adj* : excessively simple : tending to overlook complexities ⟨a ∼ solution⟩

sim·ply *adv* **1** : without ambiguity; *also* : without embellishment **2** ♦ : to the exclusion of all else; *also* : no more than

♦ alone, exclusively, just, only, solely — more at SOLELY

sim·u·late \'sim-yə-ˌlāt\ *vb* **-lat·ed; -lat·ing** ♦ : to give or create the effect or appearance of often with the intent to deceive; *also* : to make a simulation of — **sim·u·la·tor** \'sim-yə-ˌlā-tər\ *n*

♦ affect, assume, counterfeit, fake, feign, pretend, profess, put on, sham — more at FEIGN

sim·u·la·tion \ˌsim-yə-'lā-shən\ *n* **1** : the act or process of simulating **2** : an object that is not genuine **3** : the imitation by one system or process of the way in which another system or process works

si·mul·ta·ne·ous \ˌsī-məl-'tā-nē-əs, ˌsi-\ *adj* ♦ : occurring or operating at the same time — **si·mul·ta·ne·ous·ly** *adv* — **si·mul·ta·ne·ous·ness** *n*

♦ coeval, concurrent, contemporary, synchronous — more at CONTEMPORARY

¹sin \'sin\ *n* **1** ♦ : an offense esp. against God **2** : FAULT **3** : a weakened state of human nature in which the self is estranged from God **4** ♦ : an action that is or is felt to be highly reprehensible — **sin·less** *adj*

♦ [1] breach, crime, error, malefaction, misdeed, misdoing, offense, transgression, trespass, violation, wrongdoing — more at OFFENSE ♦ [4] crime, disgrace, pity, shame — more at CRIME ♦ [4] evil, ill, immorality, iniquity, villainy, wrong — more at EVIL

²sin *vb* **sinned; sin·ning** ♦ : to commit a sin

♦ err, offend, transgress, trespass — more at OFFEND

³sin *abbr* sine

¹since \'sins\ *adv* **1** : from a past time until now **2** : backward in time : AGO **3** : after a time in the past

²since *conj* **1** : from the time when **2** ♦ : seeing that : BECAUSE

♦ because, for, now, whereas

³since *prep* **1** : in the period after ⟨changes made ∼ the war⟩ **2** : continuously from ⟨has been here ∼ 1980⟩

sin·cere \sin-'sir\ *adj* **sin·cer·er; sin·cer·est** **1** ♦ : free from hypocrisy : HONEST **2** ♦ : marked by genuineness : GENUINE — **sin·cer·i·ty** \-'ser-ə-tē\ *n*

♦ [1, 2] artless, genuine, honest, ingenuous, innocent, naive, natural, real, simple, true, unaffected, unpretentious

sin·cere·ly *adv* : in a sincere manner

sine \'sīn\ *n* [ML *sinus*, fr. L, curve] : the trigonometric function that is the ratio between the side opposite an acute angle in a right triangle and the hypotenuse

si·ne·cure \'sī-ni-ˌkyur, 'si-\ *n* : a paying job that requires little or no work

si·ne die \ˌsī-ni-'dī-ˌē, ˌsi-nā-'dē-ˌā\ *adv* [L, without day] : INDEFINITELY

si·ne qua non \ˌsi-ni-ˌkwä-'nän, -'nōn\ *n, pl* **sine qua nons** *also* **sine qui·bus non** \-ˌkwi-(ˌ)bus-\ [LL, without which not] : something indispensable or essential

sin·ew \'sin-yü\ *n* **1** : TENDON **2** ♦ : physical strength

♦ energy, force, main, might, muscle, potency, power, strength, vigor (*or* vigour) — more at POWER

sin·ewy *adj* ♦ : having or marked by great physical power

♦ brawny, muscular, rugged, stalwart, stout, strong — more at STRONG

sin·ful \'sin-fəl\ *adj* ♦ : marked by or full of sin : WICKED — **sin·ful·ly** *adv*

♦ bad, black, evil, immoral, iniquitous, nefarious, rotten, unethical, unsavory, vicious, vile, villainous, wicked, wrong

sin·ful·ness *n* : the quality or state of being sinful

¹sing \'sin\ *vb* **sang** \'san\ *or* **sung** \'sən\; **sung; sing·ing** **1** ♦ : to produce musical tones with the voice; *also* : to utter with musical tones **2** : to make a prolonged shrill sound ⟨locusts ∼*ing*⟩ **3** : to produce harmonious sustained sounds ⟨birds ∼*ing*⟩ **4** : CHANT, INTONE **5** : to write poetry; *also* : to celebrate in song or verse **6** : to give information or evidence

♦ carol, chant, descant, vocalize; *also* belt, croon, harmonize, hum, lilt, quaver, sharp, slur, trill, troll, warble, yodel; serenade

²sing *abbr* singular

Sin·ga·por·ean \ˌsin-ə-'pōr-ē-ən\ *n* : a native or inhabitant of Singapore — **Singaporean** *adj*

singe \'sinj\ *vb* **singed; singe·ing** ♦ : to scorch lightly the outside of; *esp* : to remove the hair or down from usu. by passing over a flame

♦ char, scorch, sear — more at SCORCH

sing·er \'sin-ər\ *n* : one that sings

♦ caroler, songster, vocalist, voice; *also* hummer, warbler, yodeler; cantor; songstress

¹sin·gle \'sin-gəl\ *adj* **1** ♦ : not married **2** ♦ : being alone : being the only one **3** : having only one feature or part **4** : made for one person — **sin·gle·ness** *n*

♦ [1] unattached, unmarried, unwed; *also* fancy-free, footloose; marriageable, unpaired; separated **Ant** attached, married, wed ♦ [2] detached, disconnected, discrete, freestanding, separate, unattached, unconnected — more at SEPARATE

²single *vb* **sin·gled; sin·gling** **1** ♦ : to select or distinguish (one) from a group — usu. used with *out* **2** : to hit a single

♦ *usu* single out choose, cull, elect, handpick, name, opt, pick, prefer, select, take — more at CHOOSE ♦ *usu* single out distinguish, identify, pinpoint — more at IDENTIFY

³single *n* **1** : a separate person or thing; *also* : an unmarried person   **2** : a hit in baseball that enables the batter to reach first base   **3** *pl* : a tennis match with one player on each side

single bond *n* : a chemical bond in which one pair of electrons is shared by two atoms in a molecule

single–lens reflex *n* : a camera having a single lens that forms an image which is reflected to the viewfinder or recorded on film

sin·gle–mind·ed \ˌsiŋ-gəl-ˈmīn-dəd\ *adj* ♦ : having one driving purpose or resolve ⟨~ determination⟩ — **sin·gle–mind·ed·ly** *adv* — **sin·gle–mind·ed·ness** *n*

♦ bound, decisive, determined, firm, intent, purposeful, resolute, set — more at DETERMINED

sin·gly *adv* ♦ : without the company of others

♦ alone, independently, solely, unaided, unassisted — more at ALONE

sin·gu·lar \ˈsiŋ-gyə-lər\ *adj*   **1** : of, relating to, or constituting a word form denoting one person, thing, or instance   **2** : OUTSTANDING, EXCEPTIONAL   **3** : of unusual quality   **4** ♦ : departing from general usage or expectation : ODD   **5** ♦ : of or relating to a separate person or thing — **singular** *n* — **sin·gu·lar·ly** *adv*

♦ [4] curious, extraordinary, funny, odd, peculiar, queer, rare, strange, unaccustomed, uncommon, unique, unusual, weird — more at UNUSUAL ♦ [5] individual, particular, peculiar, personal, private, separate, unique — more at INDIVIDUAL

sin·gu·lar·i·ty \ˌsiŋ-gyə-ˈlar-ə-tē\ *n* ♦ : something that is singular; *esp* : unusual or distinctive manner or behavior

♦ crotchet, eccentricity, idiosyncrasy, mannerism, oddity, peculiarity, quirk, trick — more at IDIOSYNCRASY

sin·is·ter \ˈsi-nəs-tər\ *adj* [ME *sinistre*, fr. AF *senestre* on the left, fr. L *sinister* on the left side, inauspicious]   **1** : singularly evil or productive of evil   **2** ♦ : accompanied by or leading to disaster

♦ baleful, dire, foreboding, menacing, ominous, portentous — more at OMINOUS

¹**sink** \ˈsiŋk\ *vb* **sank** \ˈsaŋk\ *or* **sunk** \ˈsəŋk\; **sunk**; **sink·ing**   **1** : SUBMERGE   **2** ♦ : to descend lower and lower   **3** : to grow less in volume or height   **4** : to slope downward   **5** : to penetrate downward   **6** ♦ : to deteriorate in health, strength, or condition   **7** : LAPSE, DEGENERATE   **8** : to cause (a ship) to descend to the bottom   **9** : to make (a hole or shaft) by digging, boring, or cutting   **10** : INVEST — **sink·able** *adj*

♦ [2] decline, descend, dip, drop, fall, lower, plummet, plunge, tumble — more at DROP ♦ [6] decay, decline, degenerate, descend, deteriorate, ebb, rot, worsen — more at DETERIORATE

²**sink** *n*   **1** : DRAIN, SEWER   **2** : a basin connected with a drain   **3** : an extensive depression in the land surface

sink·er \ˈsiŋ-kər\ *n* : a weight for sinking a fishing line or net

sink·hole \ˈsiŋk-ˌhōl\ *n* : a hollow place in which drainage collects

sin·ner *n* ♦ : one that sins

♦ evildoer, malefactor, wrongdoer — more at EVILDOER

si·nol·o·gy \sī-ˈnä-lə-jē\ *n, often cap* : the study of the Chinese and esp. their language, history, and culture — **si·no·log·i·cal** \ˌsī-nə-ˈlä-ji-kəl\ *adj, often cap* — **si·nol·o·gist** \sī-ˈnä-lə-jist\ *n, often cap*

sin tax *n* : a tax on substances or activities considered sinful or harmful

sin·u·ous \ˈsin-yə-wəs\ *adj* ♦ : bending in and out : WINDING — **sin·u·os·i·ty** \ˌsin-yə-ˈwä-sə-tē\ *n* — **sin·u·ous·ly** *adv*

♦ crooked, devious, serpentine, tortuous, winding — more at CROOKED

si·nus \ˈsī-nəs\ *n* [ME, fr. ML, fr. L, curve, hollow]   **1** : any of several cavities of the skull usu. connecting with the nostrils   **2** : a space forming a channel (as for the passage of blood)

si·nus·itis \ˌsī-nə-ˈsī-təs\ *n* : inflammation of a sinus of the skull

Sioux \ˈsü\ *n, pl* **Sioux** *same or* ˈsüz\ [AmerF, short for *Nadouessioux*, fr. Ojibwa *na·towe·ssiw-*, prob. fr. Algonquian **a·towe-* speak another language] : DAKOTA

¹**sip** \ˈsip\ *vb* **sipped; sip·ping** : to drink in small quantities

²**sip** *n* : a small draft taken with the lips

¹**si·phon** *also* **syphon** \ˈsī-fən\ *n*   **1** : a bent tube through which a liquid can be transferred by means of air pressure up and over the edge of one container and into another container placed at a lower level   **2** *usu* **sy·phon** : a bottle that ejects soda water through a tube when a valve is opened

²**siphon** *also* **syphon** *vb* **si·phoned** *also* **sy·phoned; si·phon·ing** *also* **sy·phon·ing** ♦ : to draw off by or as if by means of a siphon

♦ channel, conduct, direct, funnel, pipe — more at CHANNEL

sip·py cup \ˈsi-pē-\ *n* : a cup having a lid with a perforated spout for a young child

sir \ˈsər\ *n* [ME *sir, sire*, fr. AF, lord, feudal superior, fr. VL **seior*, alter. of L *senior*, compar. of *senex* old, old man]   **1** : a man of rank or position — used as a title before the given name of a knight or baronet   **2** — used as a usu. respectful form of address

Si·rach \ˈsī-rak, sə-ˈräk\ *n* : a book of the Roman Catholic canon of the Old Testament

¹**sire** \ˈsīr\ *n*   **1** : FATHER; *also, archaic* : FOREFATHER   **2** *archaic* : LORD — used as a form of address and a title   **3** : the male parent of an animal (as a horse or dog)

²**sire** *vb* **sired; sir·ing** ♦ : to procreate as the father : BEGET

♦ beget, father, get, produce — more at FATHER

si·ren \ˈsī-rən\ *n*   **1** : a seductive or alluring woman   **2** : an electrically operated device for producing a loud shrill warning signal — **siren** *adj*

sir·loin \ˈsər-ˌlȯin\ *n* [alter. of earlier *surloin*, modif. of MF *surlonge*, fr. *sur* over (fr. L *super*) + *longe* loin] : a cut of beef taken from the part in front of the round

sirup *var of* SYRUP

si·sal \ˈsī-səl, -zəl\ *n* : a strong cordage fiber from an agave; *also* : this agave

sis·sy \ˈsi-sē\ *n, pl* **sissies**   **1** *disparaging* : an effeminate boy or man   **2** ♦ : a timid or cowardly person

♦ chicken, coward, craven, dastard, poltroon, recreant — more at COWARD

sis·ter \ˈsis-tər\ *n*   **1** : a female having one or both parents in common with another individual   **2** : a member of a religious order of women : NUN   **3** *chiefly Brit* : NURSE   **4** : a girl or woman regarded as a comrade — **sis·ter·ly** *adj*

sis·ter·hood \-ˌhu̇d\ *n*   **1** : the state of being a sister   **2** : a community or society of sisters   **3** : the solidarity of women based on shared conditions

sis·ter–in–law \ˈsis-tə-rən-ˌlȯ\ *n, pl* **sisters–in–law** : the sister of one's spouse; *also* : the wife of one's sibling or of one's spouse's sibling

sit \ˈsit\ *vb* **sat** \ˈsat\; **sit·ting**   **1** : to rest upon the buttocks or haunches   **2** : ROOST, PERCH   **3** : to occupy a seat   **4** : to hold a session   **5** ♦ : to cover eggs for hatching : BROOD   **6** : to pose for a portrait   **7** : to remain quiet or inactive   **8** : FIT   **9** : to cause (oneself) to be seated   **10** : to place in position   **11** : to keep one's seat on ⟨~ a horse⟩   **12** : BABYSIT   **13** ♦ : to occupy a position ⟨the house ~s on a hill⟩

♦ [5] brood, hatch, incubate, set — more at SET ♦ [13] be, lie, stand

si·tar \si-ˈtär\ *n* [Hindi & Urdu *sitār*] : an Indian lute with a long neck and a varying number of strings

sit·com \ˈsit-ˌkäm\ *n* : SITUATION COMEDY

site \ˈsīt\ *n*   **1** ♦ : the spatial location of an actual or planned structure (as a building, town, or monuments) : LOCATION   **2** : WEBSITE

♦ locale, location, place, point, position, spot — more at PLACE

sit–in \'sit-ˌin\ *n* : an act of sitting in the seats or on the floor of an establishment as a means of organized protest

sit·ter *n* **1** : one that sits **2** : a person who babysits

sit·u·at·ed \'si-chə-ˌwā-təd\ *adj* : LOCATED, PLACED

sit·u·a·tion \ˌsi-chə-'wā-shən\ *n* **1** : LOCATION, SITE **2** ♦ : position or place of employment : JOB **3** ♦ : position with respect to conditions and circumstances **4** : relative position or combination of circumstances at a certain moment

♦ [2] appointment, billet, capacity, function, job, place, position, post — more at JOB ♦ [3] footing, picture, posture, scene, status; *also* rank, standing; place, spot, state; score, status quo

situation comedy *n* : a radio or television comedy series that involves a continuing cast of characters in a succession of episodes

sit–up \'sit-ˌəp\ *n* : an exercise performed from a supine position by raising the torso to a sitting position and returning to the original position without lifting the feet

six \'siks\ *n* **1** : one more than five **2** : the 6th in a set or series **3** : something having six units — **six** *adj or pron* — **sixth** \'siksth\ *adj or adv or n*

six–gun \'siks-ˌgən\ *n* : a 6-chambered revolver

six–pack \-ˌpak\ *n* : six bottles or cans (as of beer) packaged and purchased together; *also* : the contents of a six-pack

six·pence \-pəns, *US also* -ˌpens\ *n* : the sum of six pence; *also* : an English silver coin of this value

six–shoot·er \'siks-ˌshü-tər\ *n* : SIX-GUN

six·teen \ˌsiks-'tēn\ *n* : one more than 15 — **sixteen** *adj or pron* — **six·teenth** \-'tēnth\ *adj or n*

six·ty \'siks-tē\ *n, pl* **sixties** : six times 10 — **six·ti·eth** \'siks-tē-əth\ *adj or n* — **sixty** *adj or pron*

siz·able *or* **size·able** \'sī-zə-bəl\ *adj* ♦ : quite large

♦ big, considerable, goodly, grand, great, handsome, large, significant, substantial, tidy

siz·ably \-blē\ *adv* ♦ : in a sizable manner : to a sizable degree

♦ broadly, considerably, greatly, largely, much

¹size \'sīz\ *n* [ME *sise* assize, judgment, quantity, fr. AF, short for *assise* assize] ♦ : physical extent or bulk : DIMENSION; *also* : considerable proportions — **sized** \'sīzd\ *adj*

♦ dimension, extent, magnitude, measure, measurement, proportion; *also* area; capaciousness, spaciousness; amplitude, bigness, bulk, grandness, greatness, grossness, hugeness, immensity, largeness, mass, massiveness, vastness, volume, voluminousness

²size *vb* **sized; siz·ing** **1** : to grade or classify according to size **2** : to form a judgment of ⟨∼ up the situation⟩

³size *n* : a gluey material used for filling the pores in paper, plaster, or textiles — **siz·ing** *n*

⁴size *vb* **sized; siz·ing** : to cover, stiffen, or glaze with size

¹siz·zle \'si-zəl\ *vb* **siz·zled; siz·zling** **1** : to fry or shrivel up with a hissing sound **2** ♦ : to make a hissing sound in or as if in burning or frying

♦ fizz, hiss, swish, whish, whiz

²sizzle *n* : a hissing sound (as of something frying over a fire)

SJ *abbr* Society of Jesus

SK *abbr* Saskatchewan

ska \'skä\ *n* : popular music of Jamaican origin combining traditional Caribbean rhythms and jazz

¹skate \'skāt\ *n, pl* **skates** *also* **skate** : any of a family of rays with thick broad winglike fins

²skate *n* **1** : a metal frame and runner attached to a shoe and used for gliding over ice **2** : ROLLER SKATE; *esp* : IN-LINE SKATE — **skate** *vb* — **skat·er** *n*

skate·board \'skāt-ˌbōrd\ *n* : a short board mounted on small wheels — **skateboard** *vb* — **skate·board·er** *n*

skeet \'skēt\ *n* : trapshooting in which clay targets are thrown in such a way that their angle of flight simulates that of a flushed game bird

skein \'skān\ *n* : a loosely twisted quantity of yarn or thread wound on a reel

skel·e·tal \'ske-lət-ᵊl\ *adj* **1** : of, relating to, forming, attached to, or resembling a skeleton **2** ♦ : extremely thin from lack of nourishment or from disease

♦ cadaverous, gaunt, haggard, wasted

skel·e·ton \'ske-lət-ᵊn\ *n* **1** : a usu. bony supporting framework of an animal body **2** : a bare minimum **3** ♦ : something forming a structural framework

♦ configuration, frame, framework, shell, structure — more at FRAME

skep·tic \'skep-tik\ *n* **1** : one who believes in skepticism **2** ♦ : a person disposed to skepticism esp. regarding religion

♦ disbeliever, doubter, questioner, unbeliever; *also* cynic, misanthrope, pessimist; scoffer

skep·ti·cal \-ti-kəl\ *adj* ♦ : relating to, characteristic of, or marked by skepticism — **skep·ti·cal·ly** \-k(ə-)lē\ *adv*

♦ distrustful, incredulous, leery, mistrustful, suspicious, uncertain, unsure; *also* paranoid; critical, puzzled, quizzical; careful, cautious, guarded, leery, wary, watchful; cynical, experienced, knowing, sophisticated, worldly, worldly-wise; curious, inquiring, inquisitive, nosy; undecided, undetermined, unsettled; hesitant *Ant* credulous, gullible, trustful, trusting, uncritical, unquestioning

skep·ti·cism \'skep-tə-ˌsi-zəm\ *n* **1** ♦ : a doubting state of mind **2** : a doctrine that certainty of knowledge cannot be attained **3** : doubt concerning religion

♦ distrust, doubt, incertitude, misgiving, mistrust, suspicion, uncertainty — more at DOUBT

¹sketch \'skech\ *n* [D *schets*, fr. It *schizzo*, lit., splash] **1** ♦ : a rough drawing or outline **2** ♦ : a short or light literary composition (as a story or essay); *also* : a short comedy piece — **sketchy** *adj*

♦ [1] cartoon, delineation, drawing — more at DRAWING ♦ [2] delineation, depiction, description, picture, portrait, portrayal — more at DESCRIPTION

²sketch *vb* ♦ : to make a sketch, rough draft, or outline of

♦ define, delineate, outline, silhouette, trace — more at OUTLINE ♦ delineate, depict, describe, draw, image, paint, picture, portray — more at DESCRIBE

¹skew \'skyü\ *vb* : to distort esp. from a true value or symmetrical form : TWIST, SWERVE

²skew *n* : SLANT

¹skew·er \'skyü-ər\ *n* : a long pin for holding small pieces of meat and vegetables for broiling

²skewer *vb* ♦ : to fasten or pierce with or as if with a skewer

♦ gore, harpoon, impale, lance, pierce, puncture, spear, spike, stab, stick, transfix — more at IMPALE

¹ski \'skē\ *n, pl* **skis** [Norw, fr. ON *skīth* stick of wood, ski] : one of a pair of long strips (as of wood, metal or plastic) curving upward in front that are used for gliding over snow or water

²ski *vb* **skied** \'skēd\; **ski·ing** : to glide on skis — **ski·able** \'skē-ə-bəl\ *adj* — **ski·er** *n*

¹skid \'skid\ *n* **1** : a plank for supporting something above the ground **2** : a device placed under a wheel to prevent turning **3** : a timber or rail over or on which something is slid or rolled **4** : the act of skidding **5** : a runner on the landing gear of an aircraft **6** : ²PALLET

²skid *vb* **skid·ded; skid·ding** **1** : to slide without rotating ⟨a *skidding* wheel⟩ **2** : to slide sideways on the road ⟨the car *skidded* on ice⟩ **3** : SLIDE, SLIP

skid row *n* : a district of cheap saloons frequented by vagrants and alcoholics

skiff \'skif\ *n* : a small boat

ski jump *n* : a jump made by a person wearing skis; *also* : a course or track prepared for such jumping — **ski jump** *vb* — **ski jumper** *n*

skil·ful *Can and Brit var of* SKILLFUL

ski lift *n* : a mechanical device (as a chairlift) for carrying skiers up a long slope

skill \'skil\ *n* **1** ♦ : ability to use one's knowledge effectively in doing something **2** : developed or acquired ability

♦ adeptness, adroitness, art, artfulness, artifice, artistry, cleverness, craft, cunning, deftness, masterfulness; *also* dexterity, ease, finesse, handiness; experience, expertise, expertness, know-how, proficiency; creativity, ingenuity, inventiveness, knowledge, learning; aptitude, bent, flair, gift, knack, talent *Ant* artlessness, ineptitude, ineptness

skilled \'skild\ *adj* **1** ♦ : having acquired mastery of or skill in something (as a technique or a trade) **2** : of, relating to, or requiring workers or labor with skill and training in a particular occupation, craft, or trade

♦ accomplished, adept, consummate, crack, crackerjack, expert, good, great, master, masterful, masterly, proficient, skillful, virtuoso — more at PROFICIENT

skil·let \'ski-lət\ *n* : a frying pan

skill·ful *or Can and Brit* **skil·ful** \'skil-fəl\ *adj* **1** : having or displaying skill : EXPERT **2** ♦ : accomplished with skill

♦ adroit, artful, delicate, dexterous, expert, masterful, masterly, practiced, proficient, virtuoso; *also* facile, smooth; artistic, creative, fancy, ingenious, neat; adept, clever, cunning; able, adequate, capable, competent *Ant* amateur, amateurish, artless, rude, unprofessional, unskillful

skill·ful·ly *or Can and Brit* **skil·ful·ly** *adv* ♦ : in a skillful manner

♦ ably, adeptly, capably, expertly, masterfully, proficiently, well — more at WELL

skill·ful·ness *or Can and Brit* **skil·ful·ness** *n* : the quality or state of being skillful

¹**skim** \'skim\ *vb* **skimmed; skim·ming** **1** : to take off from the top of a liquid; *also* : to remove (scum or cream) from ⟨∼ milk⟩ **2** ♦ : to read rapidly and superficially **3** ♦ : to pass swiftly over; *also* : to glide or skip along, above, or near a surface **4** : to throw in a gliding path; *also* : to throw so as to ricochet along the surface of water — **skim·mer** *n*

♦ [2] browse, dip, glance, glimpse, peek — more at GLANCE ♦ [3] bowl, breeze, coast, drift, flow, glide, roll, sail, skip, slide, slip, stream, sweep, whisk — more at FLOW

²**skim** *adj* : having the cream removed

skimp \'skimp\ *vb* ♦ : to give insufficient attention, effort, or funds; *also* : to save by skimping

♦ economize, save, scrimp — more at ECONOMIZE ♦ *usu* skimp on scant, spare, stint — more at SPARE

skimpy \'skim-pē\ *adj* **skimp·i·er; -est** ♦ : deficient in supply or execution

♦ light, meager (*or* meagre), niggardly, poor, scant, scanty, scarce, slender, slim, spare, sparse, stingy — more at MEAGER

¹**skin** \'skin\ *n* **1** ♦ : the outer limiting layer of an animal body; *also* : the usu. thin tough tissue of which this is made **2** ♦ : an outer or surface layer (as a rind or peel) — **skin·less** — **skinned** *adj*

♦ [1] fur, hide, pelt — more at HIDE ♦ [2] exterior, face, outside, surface, veneer — more at EXTERIOR

²**skin** *vb* **skinned; skin·ning** **1** ♦ : to free from skin : remove the skin of **2** ♦ : to strip of money or property

♦ [1] bark, flay, hull, husk, peel, shell ♦ [2] bleed, cheat, chisel, cozen, defraud, fleece, hustle, mulct, rook, shortchange, squeeze, stick, sting, swindle, victimize — more at FLEECE

³**skin** *adj* : devoted to showing nudes ⟨∼ magazines⟩

skin diving *n* : the sport of swimming under water with a face mask and flippers and esp. without a portable breathing device — **skin–dive** *vb* — **skin diver** *n*

skin·flint \'skin-ˌflint\ *n* ♦ : a very stingy person

♦ cheapskate, miser, niggard, tightwad — more at MISER

skin graft *n* : a piece of skin surgically removed from one area to replace skin in another area — **skin grafting** *n*

skin·head \'skin-ˌhed\ *n* : a person whose hair is cut very short

¹**skin·ny** \'ski-nē\ *adj* **skin·ni·er; -est** **1** : resembling skin **2** ♦ : very thin

♦ lean, narrow, slender, slim, spare, thin — more at THIN

²**skinny** *n* : inside information

skin·ny–dip \'ski-nē-ˌdip\ *vb* : to swim in the nude — **skin·ny–dip·per** \-ˌdi-pər\ *n*

skin·tight \'skin-'tīt\ *adj* : closely fitted to the figure

¹**skip** \'skip\ *vb* **skipped; skip·ping** **1** ♦ : to move with leaps and bounds; *also* : to bound off one point after another **2** : to leap lightly over **3** : to pass from point to point (as in reading) disregarding what is in between **4** : to pass over without notice or mention

♦ bound, hop, spring, trip; *also* caper, frisk, gambol, romp; skim, skitter; jump, leap, vault ♦ bounce, carom, glance, rebound, ricochet, skim — more at GLANCE

²**skip** *n* : a light bouncing step; *also* : a gait of alternate hops and steps

skip·jack \'skip-ˌjak\ *n* : a small sailboat with vertical sides and a bottom similar to a flat V

skip·per \'ski-pər\ *n* [ME, fr. MD *schipper*, fr. *schip* ship] : the master of a ship; *also* : the manager of a baseball team — **skipper** *vb*

¹**skir·mish** \'skər-mish\ *n* ♦ : a minor engagement in war; *also* : a minor dispute or contest

♦ brush, encounter, hassle, run-in, scrape — more at ENCOUNTER ♦ battle, clash, combat, conflict, contest, fight, fracas, fray, hassle, scrap, scrimmage, scuffle, struggle, tussle — more at FIGHT

²**skirmish** *vb* : to engage in a skirmish

¹**skirt** \'skərt\ *n* **1** : a free-hanging garment or part of a garment extending from the waist down **2** ♦ : the rim, periphery, or environs of an area

♦ border, bound, boundary, circumference, compass, confines, edge, end, fringe, margin, perimeter, periphery, rim, verge — more at BORDER

²**skirt** *vb* **1** ♦ : to pass around the outer edge of **2** ♦ : to form or run along the border or edge of : BORDER **3** ♦ : to avoid esp. because of difficulty or fear of controversy

♦ [1] bypass, circumvent, detour — more at DETOUR ♦ [2] abut, adjoin, border (on), flank, fringe, join, touch, verge (on) — more at ADJOIN ♦ [3] circumvent, dodge, sidestep — more at CIRCUMVENT

skit \'skit\ *n* : a brief dramatic sketch

ski tow *n* : SKI LIFT

skit·ter \'ski-tər\ *vb* : to glide or skip lightly or quickly : skim along a surface

skit·tish \'ski-tish\ *adj* **1** ♦ : lively or frisky in action **2** ♦ : easily frightened ⟨a ∼ horse⟩; *also* : WARY

♦ excitable, flighty, fluttery, high-strung, jittery, jumpy, nervous, spooky, wary — more at EXCITABLE

ski·wear \'skē-ˌwar\ *n* : clothing suitable for wear while skiing

skosh \'skōsh\ *n* [Jp *sukoshi*] : a small amount : BIT

skul·dug·gery *or* **skull·dug·gery** \ˌskəl-'də-gə-rē\ *n, pl* **-ger·ies** ♦ : underhanded or unscrupulous behavior

♦ artifice, chicanery, hanky-panky, legerdemain, subterfuge, trickery, wile — more at TRICKERY

skulk \'skəlk\ *vb* ♦ : to move furtively : SNEAK — **skulk·er** *n*

♦ lurk, pussyfoot, slide, slink, slip, snake, sneak, steal — more at SNEAK

skull \'skəl\ *n* : the skeleton of the head of a vertebrate that protects the brain and supports the jaws

skull and crossbones *n, pl* **skulls and crossbones** : a depiction of a human skull over crossbones usu. indicating a danger

skull·cap \'skəl-ˌkap\ n : a close-fitting brimless cap

¹**skunk** \'skəŋk\ n, pl **skunks** also **skunk** 1 : any of various black-and-white New World mammals related to the weasels that can forcibly eject an ill-smelling fluid when startled 2 ♦ : a contemptible person

♦ beast, boor, churl, clown, creep, cretin, cur, heel, jerk, joker, louse, lout, slob, snake — more at JERK

²**skunk** vb ♦ : to defeat decisively; esp : to prevent from scoring at all in a game

♦ beat, best, clobber, conquer, crush, defeat, drub, lick, master, overcome, prevail, rout, subdue, surmount, thrash, trim, triumph, trounce, wallop, whip, win — more at BEAT

skunk cabbage n : either of two No. American perennial herbs related to the arums that occur in shaded wet to swampy areas and have a fetid odor suggestive of a skunk

sky \'skī\ n, pl **skies** [ME, sky, cloud, fr. ON skȳ cloud] 1 ♦ : the upper air 2 : HEAVEN — **sky·ey** \'skī-ē\ adj

♦ blue, high; also horizon, skyline

sky·cap \-ˌkap\ n : a person employed to carry luggage at an airport

sky·div·ing \-ˌdī-viŋ\ n : the sport of jumping from an airplane and executing various body maneuvers before opening a parachute — **sky·div·er** n

sky·jack \-ˌjak\ vb : to commandeer an airplane in flight by threat of violence — **sky·jack·er** n — **sky·jack·ing** n

¹**sky·lark** \-ˌlärk\ n : a European lark noted for singing during flight

²**skylark** vb ♦ : to play and run about happily

♦ act up, clown, cut up, fool, monkey, show off — more at CUT UP

sky·light \'skī-ˌlīt\ n : a window in a roof or ceiling — **sky·light·ed** \-ˌlī-təd\ adj

sky·line \-ˌlīn\ n 1 : HORIZON 2 : an outline (as of buildings) against the sky

¹**sky·rock·et** \-ˌrä-kət\ n : ROCKET 1

²**skyrocket** vb ♦ : to rise or cause to rise or increase abruptly and rapidly

♦ rocket, shoot, soar, zoom; also accumulate, appreciate, balloon, build (up), burgeon, enlarge, escalate, expand, increase, mount, multiply, mushroom, proliferate, snowball, swell, wax; crest, peak, surge; heighten, intensify Ant plummet, plunge, slump, tumble

sky·scrap·er \-ˌskrā-pər\ n : a very tall building

sky·surf·ing \-ˌsər-fiŋ\ n : skydiving with a short modified surfboard attached to the feet — **sky·surf·er** \-fər\ n

sky·walk \-ˌwȯk\ n : an aerial walkway connecting two buildings

sky·ward \-wərd\ adv ♦ : toward the sky

♦ above, aloft, over, overhead — more at ABOVE

sky·writ·ing \-ˌrī-tiŋ\ n : writing in the sky formed by smoke emitted from an airplane — **sky·writ·er** n

slab \'slab\ n : a thick flat piece or slice

¹**slack** \'slak\ adj 1 ♦ : not using due diligence, care, or dispatch : CARELESS 2 : SLUGGISH, LISTLESS 3 ♦ : not taut : LOOSE 4 : not busy or active — **slack·ly** adv

♦ [1] careless, derelict, lax, negligent, remiss — more at NEGLIGENT ♦ [3] insecure, lax, loose, relaxed — more at LOOSE

²**slack** vb 1 ♦ : to make or become slack : LOOSEN 2 : SLAKE 2

♦ ease, loosen, relax, slacken — more at SLACKEN

³**slack** n 1 : cessation of movement or flow : LETUP 2 ♦ : a part that hangs loose without strain ⟨~ of a rope⟩ 3 ♦ : pants esp. for casual wear — usu. used in pl.

♦ [2] droop, sag, slackness — more at SAG ♦ **slacks** [3] britches, pantaloons, pants, trousers — more at PANTS

slack·en \'sla-kən\ vb ♦ : to make or become slack

♦ ease, loosen, relax, slack; also detach, free, unbind, undo, unfasten, untie Ant strain, stretch, tense, tighten

slack·er \'sla-kər\ n 1 : one that shirks work or evades military duty 2 : a young person perceived to be disaffected, apathetic, cynical, or lacking ambition

slack·ness n ♦ : the quality or state of being slack or behaving slackly; also : something that is slack

♦ carelessness, dereliction, heedlessness, laxness, negligence, remissness — more at NEGLIGENCE

slag \'slag\ n : the waste left after the melting of ores and the separation of metal from them

slain past part of SLAY

slake \'slāk, for 2 also 'slak\ vb **slaked**; **slak·ing** 1 : to relieve or satisfy with or as if with refreshing drink ⟨~ thirst⟩ 2 : to cause (lime) to crumble by mixture with water

sla·lom \'slä-ləm\ n [Norw slalam, lit., sloping track] : skiing in a zigzag course between obstacles

¹**slam** \'slam\ n : the winning of every trick or of all tricks but one in bridge

²**slam** n 1 ♦ : a heavy jarring impact : BANG 2 : harsh criticism 3 : a poetry competition

♦ bang, blast, boom, clap, crack, crash, pop, report, smash, snap, thwack, whack — more at CLAP

³**slam** vb **slammed**; **slam·ming** 1 : to shut violently and noisily 2 ♦ : to throw or strike with a loud impact 3 : to strike or beat hard 4 ♦ : to criticize harshly

♦ [2] bang, bash, bump, collide, crash, hit, impact, knock, ram, smash, strike, swipe, thud — more at HIT ♦ [4] abuse, assail, attack, belabor, blast, castigate, excoriate, jump, lambaste, vituperate — more at ATTACK

slam·mer \'sla-mər\ n : JAIL, PRISON

¹**slan·der** \'slan-dər\ vb ♦ : to utter slander against : DEFAME — **slan·der·er** n

♦ blacken, defame, libel, malign, smear, traduce, vilify; also belittle, detract, disparage; discredit, disgrace, dishonor, shame; abase, debase, degrade, humble, humiliate; disdain, scorn

²**slander** n [ME sclaundre, slaundre, fr. AF esclandre, alter. of escandle, fr. LL scandalum stumbling block, offense] ♦ : a false report maliciously uttered and tending to injure the reputation of a person

♦ defamation, libel, vilification; also aspersion, innuendo, smear; backbiting, detraction; abuse, invective, vituperation; attack, censure, criticism, denunciation; contempt, disdain, scorn; disparagement; cattiness, despite, hatefulness, malevolence, malice, malignancy, malignity, meanness, nastiness, spite, spitefulness, spleen, venom, viciousness

slan·der·ous adj ♦ : containing or constituting slander

♦ defamatory, libelous, scandalous — more at LIBELOUS

slang \'slaŋ\ n ♦ : an informal nonstandard vocabulary composed typically of invented words, arbitrarily changed words, and extravagant figures of speech — **slangy** adj

♦ argot, cant, jargon, language, lingo, terminology, vocabulary — more at TERMINOLOGY

¹**slant** \'slant\ n 1 ♦ : a sloping direction, line, or plane 2 ♦ : a particular or personal viewpoint — **slant** adj

♦ [1] cant, diagonal, grade, inclination, incline, lean, pitch, slope, tilt, upgrade; also ascent, bank, climb, rise, upgrade ♦ [2] angle, outlook, perspective, point of view, standpoint, viewpoint — more at POINT OF VIEW

²**slant** vb 1 ♦ : to turn or incline from a right line or a level : SLOPE 2 : to interpret or present in accordance with a special viewpoint or bias — **slant·ing·ly** adv

♦ angle, cant, cock, heel, incline, lean, list, slope, tilt, tip — more at LEAN

slant·wise \-ˌwīz\ adj ♦ : being at a slant : moving or directed in a slanting position or direction — **slant·wise** adv

♦ askew, awry, cockeyed, crooked, listing, lopsided, oblique, uneven — more at AWRY ♦ canted, diagonal, inclined, leaning — more at DIAGONAL

¹slap \'slap\ *vb* **slapped; slap·ping** **1** : to strike sharply with the open hand **2** : REBUFF, INSULT

²slap *n* : a quick sharp blow; *also* : a blow with the open hand

slap·stick \-ˌstik\ *n* ♦ : comedy stressing horseplay

♦ comedy, farce, humor (*or* humour) — more at COMEDY

¹slash \'slash\ *vb* **1** ♦ : to cut with sweeping strokes **2** : to cut slits in (a garment) **3** : to reduce sharply ⟨∼ed prices⟩ **4** : to hit with a stroke like that used in slashing — **slash·er** \'sla-shər\ *n*

♦ cut, gash, rip, slice, slit — more at CUT

²slash *n* **1** ♦ : a long cut or stroke made by or as if by slashing : GASH **2** : an ornamental slit in a garment **3** : a mark / used to denote "or" (as in *and/or*), "and/or" (as in *straggler/deserter*), or "per" (as in *feet/second*)

♦ gash, laceration, rent, rip, slit, tear — more at GASH

slat \'slat\ *n* : a thin narrow flat strip

¹slate \'slāt\ *n* **1** : a dense fine-grained rock that splits into thin layers **2** : a roofing tile or a writing tablet made from this rock **3** : a written or unwritten record ⟨start with a clean ∼⟩ **4** : a list of candidates for election

²slate *vb* **slat·ed; slat·ing** **1** : to cover with slate **2** ♦ : to designate for action or appointment ⟨*slated* to open soon⟩

♦ catalog, enroll, enter, index, inscribe, list, put down, record, register, schedule — more at LIST

³slate *adj* ♦ : being or having the dark purplish gray color of slate

♦ gray (*or* grey), leaden, pewter, silver, silvery, steely — more at GRAY

slath·er \'sla-thər\ *vb* : to spread with or on thickly or lavishly

slat·tern \'sla-tərn\ *n* : a slovenly woman — **slat·tern·ly** *adj*

¹slaugh·ter \'slȯ-tər\ *n* **1** : the butchering of livestock for market **2** ♦ : great destruction of lives esp. in battle

♦ butchery, carnage, massacre — more at MASSACRE

²slaughter *vb* **1** : to kill (animals) for food : BUTCHER **2** : to kill in large numbers or in a bloody way : MASSACRE

slaugh·ter·house \-ˌhau̇s\ *n* : an establishment where animals are butchered

Slav \'släv, 'slav\ *n* : a person speaking a Slavic language

¹slave \'slāv\ *n* [ME *sclave*, fr. AF or ML; AF *esclave*, fr. ML *sclavus*, fr. *Sclavus* Slav; fr. the enslavement of Slavs in central Europe in the Middle Ages] **1** ♦ : a person held in servitude as property **2** : a device (as the printer of a computer) that is directly responsive to another **3** ♦ : a toiler at hard monotonous work — **slave** *adj*

♦ [1] bondman, chattel, thrall; *also* helot, serf; attendant, domestic, drudge, lackey, menial, servant *Ant* freeman ♦ [3] drudge, fag, peon, toiler, worker; *also* workhorse; coolie, serf

²slave *vb* **slaved; slav·ing** ♦ : to work like a slave : DRUDGE

♦ drudge, labor (*or* labour), plod, plug, slog, strain, strive, struggle, sweat, toil, work — more at LABOR

¹sla·ver \'sla-vər, 'slā-\ *n* ♦ : to secrete saliva in anticipation of food : SLOBBER — **slaver** *vb*

♦ dribble, drivel, drool, salivate, slobber — more at DROOL

²slav·er \'slā-vər\ *n* : a ship or a person engaged in transporting slaves

slav·ery \'slāv-rē, 'slā-və-\ *n* **1** ♦ : wearisome drudgery **2** ♦ : the condition of being a slave **3** : the practice of owning slaves

♦ [1] drudgery, grind, labor (*or* labour), sweat, toil, travail — more at TOIL ♦ [2] bondage, enslavement, servitude, thrall, yoke; *also* peonage; serfdom; dependence, subjugation *Ant* freedom, liberty

¹Slav·ic \'slä-vik, 'slä-\ *n* : a branch of the Indo-European language family including various languages (as Russian or Polish) of eastern Europe

²Slavic *adj* : of or relating to the Slavs or their languages

slav·ish \'slā-vish\ *adj* **1** : SERVILE **2** ♦ : obeying or imitating with no freedom of judgment or choice

♦ imitative, mimic, unoriginal — more at IMITATIVE

slav·ish·ly *adv* ♦ : in a slavish manner

♦ determinedly, diligently, hard, hardly, laboriously, mightily, strenuously, tirelessly — more at HARD

slaw \'slȯ\ *n* : COLESLAW

slay \'slā\ *vb* **slew** \'slü\; **slain** \'slān\; **slay·ing** ♦ : to kill violently, wantonly, or in great numbers; *broadly* : to strike down : KILL — **slay·er** *n*

♦ destroy, dispatch, do in, fell, kill, murder — more at KILL

sleaze \'slēz\ *n* : a sleazy quality, appearance, or behavior

slea·zy \'slē-zē\ *adj* **slea·zi·er; -est** **1** ♦ : FLIMSY, SHODDY **2** ♦ : marked by low character or quality ⟨a ∼ lawyer⟩

♦ bad, bum, cheap, coarse, common, lousy, mediocre, rotten, second-rate, terrible, trashy — more at CHEAP

¹sled \'sled\ *n* : a vehicle usu. on runners adapted esp. for sliding on snow

²sled *vb* **sled·ded; sled·ding** : to ride or carry on a sled

¹sledge \'slej\ *n* : SLEDGEHAMMER

²sledge *n* : a strong heavy sled

sledge·ham·mer \'slej-ˌha-mər\ *n* : a large heavy hammer wielded with both hands — **sledgehammer** *adj or vb*

¹sleek \'slēk\ *vb* **1** : to make smooth or glossy **2** : to gloss over

²sleek *adj* **1** ♦ : having a smooth well-groomed look **2** : trim and graceful in design ⟨a ∼ car⟩

♦ glossy, lustrous, polished, satiny — more at GLOSSY

¹sleep \'slēp\ *n* **1** ♦ : the natural periodic suspension of consciousness during which bodily powers are restored **2** : a state (as death or coma) suggesting sleep

♦ repose, rest, slumber; *also* catnap, doze, drowse, forty winks, nap, siesta, snooze, wink; oversleeping; dreaming, rapid eye movement *Ant* consciousness, wakefulness

²sleep *vb* **slept** \'slept\; **sleep·ing** **1** ♦ : to rest or be in a state of sleep; *also* : to spend in sleep **2** : to have sexual intercourse — usu. used with *with* **3** : to provide sleeping space for

♦ catnap, doze, nap, rest, slumber, snooze; *also* drowse (off), nod (off); oversleep; dream, hibernate

sleep·er \'slē-pər\ *n* **1** : one that sleeps **2** : a horizontal beam to support something on or near ground level **3** : SLEEPING CAR **4** : someone or something unpromising or unnoticed that suddenly attains prominence or value

sleep·i·ness \-pē-nəs\ *n* : the quality or state of being sleepy

sleeping bag *n* : a warmly lined bag for sleeping esp. outdoors

sleeping car *n* : a railroad car with berths for sleeping

sleeping pill *n* : a drug in tablet or capsule form taken to induce sleep

sleeping sickness *n* : a serious disease of tropical Africa that is marked by fever, lethargy, confusion, and sleep disturbances and is caused by protozoans transmitted by the tsetse fly

sleep·less *adj* ♦ : not able to sleep; *also* : affording no sleep — **sleep·less·ness** *n*

♦ awake, wakeful, wide-awake — more at WAKEFUL

sleep·over \'slēp-ˌō-vər\ *n* : an overnight stay (as at another's home)

sleep·walk·er \'slēp-ˌwȯ-kər\ *n* : one that walks while or as if while asleep — **sleep·walk** \-ˌwȯk\ *vb*

sleepy \'slē-pē\ *adj* **sleep·i·er; -est** **1** ♦ : ready for sleep **2** ♦ : quietly inactive — **sleep·i·ly** \'slē-pə-lē\ *adv*

♦ [1] drowsy, slumberous; *also* asleep, dormant, dozing, resting, sleeping, slumbering; nodding, yawning **Ant** alert, awake, conscious, wakeful, wide-awake ♦ [2] dull, inactive, inert, lethargic, quiescent, sluggish, torpid — more at INACTIVE

sleet \'slēt\ *n* : frozen or partly frozen rain — **sleet** *vb* — **sleety** *adj*

sleeve \'slēv\ *n* **1** : a part of a garment covering an arm **2** : a tubular part designed to fit over another part — **sleeved** *adj* — **sleeve·less** *adj*

¹**sleigh** \'slā\ *n* : an open usu. horse-drawn vehicle on runners for use on snow or ice

²**sleigh** *vb* : to drive or travel in a sleigh

sleight \'slīt\ *n* **1** ♦ : deceitful craftiness : TRICK **2** ♦ : mental or physical skill or quickness : DEXTERITY

♦ [1] artifice, device, dodge, gimmick, jig, ploy, scheme, stratagem, trick, wile — more at TRICK ♦ [2] adroitness, agility, cleverness, craft, dexterity, finesse — more at DEXTERITY

sleight of hand 1 : a cleverly executed trick or deception esp. requiring manual dexterity **2** : skill in deception

slen·der \'slen-dər\ *adj* **1** ♦ : spare in frame or flesh : THIN; *also* : small or narrow in circumference or width in proportion to length or height **2** : WEAK, SLIGHT **3** ♦ : limited or inadequate in amount or scope : MEAGER, INADEQUATE

♦ [1] lean, narrow, skinny, slim, spare, thin — more at THIN ♦ [1] narrow, skinny, slim, thin — more at NARROW ♦ [3] meager (*or* meagre), poor, scant, scanty, scarce, skimpy, sparse, stingy — more at MEAGER

slen·der·ize \-də-ˌrīz\ *vb* **-ized; -iz·ing** : to make slender

sleuth \'slüth\ *n* [short for *sleuthhound* bloodhound, fr. ME (Sc) *sleuth hund*, fr. ME *sleuth, sloith, sloth* track of an animal or person, fr. ON *slōth*] ♦ : one employed or engaged in detecting lawbreakers or in getting information that is not readily or publicly accessible : DETECTIVE

♦ detective, investigator, operative, shadow, tail — more at DETECTIVE

¹**slew** \'slü\ *past of* SLAY

²**slew** *vb* : TURN, VEER, SKID

¹**slice** \'slīs\ *vb* **sliced; slic·ing 1** ♦ : to cut a slice from; *also* : to cut into slices **2** : to hit (a ball) so that a slice results

♦ cut, gash, rip, slash, slit — more at CUT

²**slice** *n* **1** : a thin flat piece cut from something **2** : a flight of a ball (as in golf) that curves in the direction of the dominant hand of the player hitting it

¹**slick** \'slik\ *vb* ♦ : to make smooth or sleek

♦ grease, lubricate, oil, wax — more at LUBRICATE

²**slick** *adj* **1** ♦ : very smooth : SLIPPERY **2** ♦ : characterized by subtlety or nimble wit

♦ [1] greasy, slippery, slithery; *also* brushed, buffed, burnished, glossed, ground, polished, rubbed, shined; coated, glazed, waxed; soapy, waxy; rasped, sandblasted, sanded, scoured, scraped, scrubbed ♦ [2] artful, cagey, crafty, cunning, devious, foxy, guileful, sly, subtle, wily — more at ARTFUL

³**slick** *n* **1** : a smooth patch of water covered with a film of oil **2** : a popular magazine printed on coated paper

slick·er \'sli-kər\ *n* **1** : a long loose raincoat **2** : a sly tricky person **3** : a city dweller esp. of natty appearance or sophisticated mannerisms

¹**slide** \'slīd\ *vb* **slid** \'slid\; **slid·ing** \'slī-diŋ\ **1** ♦ : to move smoothly along a surface **2** : to fall or dive toward a base in baseball **3** : to fall by a loss of support **4** ♦ : to pass unobtrusively **5** : to move or pass smoothly; *also* : to pass unnoticed ⟨let it ~ by⟩ **6** : to become worse gradually

♦ [1] bowl, breeze, coast, drift, flow, glide, roll, sail, skim, slip, stream, sweep, whisk — more at FLOW ♦ [4] lurk, pussyfoot, skulk, slink, slip, snake, sneak, steal — more at SNEAK

²**slide** *n* **1** : an act or instance of sliding **2** : something (as a cover or fastener) that operates by sliding **3** : a fall of a

mass of earth or snow down a hillside **4** : a surface on which something slides **5** : a glass plate on which a specimen is mounted for examination under a microscope **6** : a small transparent photograph that can be projected on a screen

slid·er \'slī-dər\ *n* **1** : one that slides **2** : a baseball pitch that looks like a fastball but curves slightly **3** : a small hamburger

slide rule *n* : a manual device for calculation consisting of a ruler and a movable middle piece graduated with logarithmic scales

slier *comparative of* SLY

sliest *superlative of* SLY

¹**slight** \'slīt\ *adj* **1 a** ♦ : having a slim or delicate build : SLENDER **b** ♦ : lacking in strength or substance : FRAIL **2** ♦ : deficient in weight, solidity, or importance **3** ♦ : small of its kind; *also* : small in amount

♦ [1b] delicate, effete, enervated, faint, feeble, frail, infirm, languid, low, prostrate, soft, tender, torpid, unsubstantial, wasted, weak, wimpy — more at WEAK ♦ [2] frivolous, inconsequential, inconsiderable, insignificant, little, minor, minute, negligible, small, trifling, trivial, unimportant — more at UNIMPORTANT ♦ [3] negligible, off, outside, remote, slim, small — more at REMOTE

²**slight** *vb* **1** ♦ : to treat as unimportant **2** ♦ : to ignore discourteously **3** : to perform or attend to carelessly

♦ [1] disregard, forget, ignore, neglect, overlook, pass over, slur — more at NEGLECT ♦ [1, 2] disdain, highhat, scorn, sniff at, snub — more at SCORN ♦ [2] affront, insult, offend, outrage, wound — more at INSULT

³**slight** *n* ♦ : a humiliating discourtesy

♦ affront, barb, dart, dig, indignity, insult, name, offense, outrage, put-down, sarcasm, slur, wound — more at INSULT

slight·ly *adv* ♦ : in a slight manner or degree

♦ barely, hardly, just, marginally, scarcely — more at JUST

¹**slim** \'slim\ *adj* **slim·mer; slim·mest** [D, bad, inferior, fr. MD, *slimp* crooked, bad] **1 a** ♦ : of small diameter or thickness in proportion to the height or length : THIN **b** ♦ : having a relatively small proportion of flesh : SLENDER **2** ♦ : limited or less than sufficient in degree, quantity, or extent : SCANTY, MEAGER

♦ [1a] fine, narrow, skinny, slender, thin — more at NARROW ♦ [1b] lean, skinny, slender, spare, thin — more at THIN ♦ [2] meager (*or* meagre), poor, scant, scanty, scarce, skimpy, sparse, stingy — more at MEAGER ♦ [2] negligible, off, outside, remote, slight, small — more at REMOTE

²**slim** *vb* **slimmed; slim·ming** : to make or become slender

slime \'slīm\ *n* **1** ♦ : sticky mud **2** : a slippery substance (as on the skin of a slug or catfish)

♦ mire, muck, mud, ooze, slop, sludge, slush — more at MUD

slimy *adj* **slim·i·er; -est 1** : of, relating to, or resembling slime **2** ♦ : covered with or yielding slime

♦ miry, mucky, muddy, oozy, slushy — more at MUDDY

¹**sling** \'sliŋ\ *vb* **slung** \'sləŋ\; **sling·ing 1** ♦ : to throw forcibly : FLING **2** : to hurl with or as if with a sling

♦ cast, catapult, chuck, dash, fire, fling, heave, hurl, hurtle, launch, peg, pelt, pitch, throw, toss — more at THROW

²**sling** *n* **1** : a short strap with strings attached for hurling stones or shot **2** : something (as a rope or chain) used to hoist, lower, support, or carry; *esp* : a bandage hanging from the neck to support an arm or hand

³**sling** *vb* **slung** \'sləŋ\; **sling·ing 1** : place in a sling for hoisting or lowering **2** ♦ : to suspend by or as if by a sling

♦ dangle, hang, suspend, swing — more at HANG

sling·shot \'sliŋ-ˌshät\ *n* : a forked stick with elastic bands for shooting small stones or shot

slink \\'slink\\ *vb* **slunk** \\'slənk\\ *also* **slinked** \\'slinkt\\; **slink·ing** 1 ♦ : to move stealthily or furtively 2 : to move sinuously — **slinky** *adj*

♦ lurk, pussyfoot, skulk, slide, slip, snake, sneak, steal — more at SNEAK

¹slip \\'slip\\ *vb* **slipped; slip·ping** 1 : to escape quietly or secretly 2 ♦ : to slide along or cause to slide along smoothly 3 : to make a mistake 4 : to pass unnoticed or undone 5 : to fall off from a standard or level 6 ♦ : to get speedily into or out of clothing 7 ♦ : to insert quietly or secretly 8 ♦ : to slide out of place or away from a support or one's grasp

♦ [2] bowl, breeze, coast, drift, flow, glide, roll, sail, skim, slide, stream, sweep, whisk — more at FLOW ♦ *usu* **slip on** *or* **slip into** [6] don, put on, throw — more at PUT ON ♦ [7] infiltrate, insinuate, sneak, work, worm — more at INSINUATE ♦ [8] fall, stumble, topple, trip, tumble — more at FALL

²slip *n* 1 : a ramp for repairing ships 2 : a ship's berth between two piers 3 ♦ : secret or hurried departure, escape, or evasion 4 ♦ : an unintentional and trivial mistake or fault : BLUNDER 5 ♦ : the act or an instance of slipping down or out of a place; *also* : a sudden mishap 6 : a woman's one-piece garment worn under a dress 7 : PILLOWCASE

♦ [3] escape, flight, getaway, lam — more at ESCAPE ♦ [4] blunder, error, fault, flub, fumble, goof, lapse, miscue, misstep, mistake, oversight, stumble — more at ERROR ♦ [5] fall, spill, stumble, tumble — more at FALL

³slip *n* 1 : a shoot or twig from a plant for planting or grafting 2 : a long narrow strip; *esp* : one of paper used for a record ⟨deposit ∼⟩

⁴slip *vb* **slipped; slip·ping** : to take slips from ⟨a plant⟩

slip·knot \\'slip-ˌnät\\ *n* : a knot that slips along the rope around which it is made

slipped disk *n* : a protrusion of one of the disks of cartilage between vertebrae with pressure on spinal nerves resulting esp. in low back pain

slip·per \\'sli-pər\\ *n* : a light low shoe that may be easily slipped on and off

slip·pery \\'sli-pə-rē\\ *adj* **slip·per·i·er; -est** 1 ♦ : icy, wet, smooth, or greasy enough to cause one to fall or lose one's hold 2 ♦ : not to be trusted : TRICKY ⟨a ∼ politician⟩ — **slip·per·i·ness** *n*

♦ [1] greasy, slick, slithery — more at SLICK ♦ [2] furtive, shady, shifty, sly, sneaky, stealthy, tricky — more at SNEAKY

slip·shod \\'slip-ˈshäd\\ *adj* : SLOVENLY, CARELESS ⟨∼ work⟩

slip·stream \\'slip-ˌstrēm\\ *n* : a stream (as of air) driven aft by a propeller

slip-up \\'slip-ˌəp\\ *n* 1 : a wrong action or statement proceeding from faulty judgment, inadequate knowledge, or inattention : MISTAKE 2 : ACCIDENT

¹slit \\'slit\\ *vb* **slit; slit·ting** 1 ♦ : to make a slit in : SLASH 2 : to cut off or away

♦ cut, gash, rip, slash, slice — more at CUT

²slit *n* : a long narrow cut or opening — **slit** *adj*

♦ gash, laceration, rent, rip, slash, tear — more at GASH

slith·er \\'sli-thər\\ *vb* ♦ : to slip or glide along like a snake

♦ crawl, creep, grovel, snake, worm — more at CRAWL

slith·ery *adj* ♦ : having a slippery surface, texture, or quality

♦ greasy, slick, slippery — more at SLICK

sliv·er \\'sli-vər\\ *n* : a long slender piece cut or torn off : SPLINTER

slob \\'släb\\ *n* ♦ : a slovenly or boorish person

♦ beast, boor, churl, clown, creep, cretin, cur, heel, jerk, joker, louse, lout, skunk, snake — more at JERK

¹slob·ber \\'slä-bər\\ *vb* **slob·bered; slob·ber·ing** 1 ♦ : to dribble saliva 2 ♦ : to be excessively or unrestrainedly enthusiastic or emotional

♦ [1] dribble, drivel, drool, salivate, slaver — more at DROOL ♦ [2] enthuse, fuss, gush, rave, rhapsodize — more at GUSH

²slobber *n* ♦ : saliva drooled from the mouth

♦ saliva, spit — more at SALIVA

sloe \\'slō\\ *n* : the fruit of the blackthorn

slog \\'släg\\ *vb* **slogged; slog·ging** 1 : to hit hard : BEAT 2 ♦ : to work hard and steadily

♦ drudge, labor (*or* labour), peg, plod, plug, slave, strain, strive, struggle, sweat, toil, work — more at LABOR

slo·gan \\'slō-gən\\ *n* [alter. of earlier *slogorn*, fr. ScGael *slu-agh-ghairm*, fr. *sluagh* army, host + *gairm* cry] ♦ : a word or phrase expressing the spirit or aim of a party, group, or cause

♦ cry, shibboleth, watchword; *also* tagline; expression, idiom; cliché; maxim, motto

slo-mo \\'slō-ˌmō\\ *n* : SLOW MOTION — **slo-mo** *adj*

sloop \\'slüp\\ *n* [D *sloep*] : a single-masted sailboat with a jib and a fore-and-aft mainsail

¹slop \\'släp\\ *n* 1 : thin tasteless drink or liquid food — usu. used in pl. 2 : food waste for animal feed : SWILL 3 ♦ : excreted body waste — usu. used in pl. 4 ♦ : soft mud

♦ **slops** [3] droppings, dung, waste — more at DROPPINGS ♦ [4] mire, muck, mud, ooze, slime, sludge, slush — more at MUD

²slop *vb* **slopped; slop·ping** 1 : SPILL 2 : to feed with slop ⟨∼ hogs⟩

¹slope \\'slōp\\ *vb* **sloped; slop·ing** ♦ : to lie or fall in a slant : INCLINE; *also* : to cause to incline or slant

♦ angle, cant, cock, heel, incline, lean, list, slant, tilt, tip — more at LEAN

²slope *n* 1 ♦ : upward or downward slant or degree of slant 2 : ground that forms an incline 3 : the part of a landmass draining into a particular ocean

♦ cant, diagonal, grade, inclination, incline, lean, pitch, slant, tilt, upgrade — more at SLANT

slop·py \\'slä-pē\\ *adj* **slop·pi·er; -est** 1 : wet so as to spatter easily : MUDDY, SLUSHY 2 ♦ : untidy esp. in personal appearance : SLOVENLY, MESSY; *also* : lazily slipshod 3 : excessive in emotional expression

♦ dowdy, frowsy, messy, slovenly, unkempt, untidy; *also* chaotic, cluttered, confused, disarranged, disheveled, disordered, messed, muddled, mussed, mussy, rumpled *Ant* dapper, dashing, dolled up, sharp, smart, spruce

sloppy joe \\-ˈjō\\ *n* : ground beef cooked in a thick spicy sauce and usu. served on a bun

slosh \\'släsh\\ *vb* 1 : to flounder through or splash about in or with water, mud, or slush 2 ♦ : to move with a splashing motion

♦ lap, plash, splash, swash; *also* babble, bubble, gurgle, ripple

slot \\'slät\\ *n* 1 : a long narrow opening or groove 2 : a position in a sequence

slot car *n* : an electric toy racing car that runs on a grooved track

sloth \\'slöth\\ *n, pl* **sloths** \\'slöths, 'slöthz\\ 1 ♦ : disinclination to action or labor : LAZINESS, INDOLENCE 2 : any of several slow-moving plant-eating arboreal mammals of So. and Central America

♦ idleness, indolence, inertia, laziness — more at LAZINESS

sloth·ful *adj* ♦ : inclined to sloth

♦ idle, indolent, lazy, shiftless — more at LAZY

slot machine *n* 1 : a machine whose operation is begun by dropping a coin into a slot 2 : a coin-operated gambling machine that pays off according to the matching of symbols on wheels spun by a handle

¹slouch \\'slau̇ch\\ *n* 1 ♦ : a lazy or incompetent person 2 : a loose or drooping gait or posture

♦ drone, idler, lazybones, loafer, slug, sluggard — more at LAZYBONES

²**slouch** vb : to walk, stand, or sit with a slouch : SLUMP

¹**slough** \'slü, 2 usu 'slaú\ n 1 ♦ : a wet and marshy or muddy place (as a swamp) 2 : a discouraged state of mind

♦ bog, fen, marsh, mire, morass, swamp — more at SWAMP

²**slough** \'sləf\ also **sluff** n : something that has been or may be shed or cast off

³**slough** \'sləf\ also **sluff** vb ♦ : to cast off

♦ cast, discard, ditch, dump, fling, jettison, junk, lose, reject, scrap, shed, shuck, throw away, throw out, unload — more at DISCARD

Slo·vak \'slō-,väk, -,vak\ n 1 : a member of a Slavic people of Slovakia 2 : the language of the Slovaks — **Slovak** adj — **Slo·va·ki·an** \slō-'vä-kē-ən, -'va-\ adj or n

slov·en \'slə-vən\ n [ME sloveyn slut, rascal, perh. fr. MD slof negligent] : an untidy person

Slo·vene \'slō-,vēn\ n 1 : a member of a Slavic people living largely in Slovenia 2 : the language of the Slovenes — **Slovene** adj — **Slo·ve·nian** \slō-'vē-nē-ən\ adj or n

slov·en·ly \'slə-vən-lē\ adj 1 ♦ : untidy in dress or person 2 : lazily or carelessly done : SLIPSHOD ⟨∼ thinking⟩

♦ dowdy, frowsy, sloppy, unkempt, untidy — more at SLOPPY

¹**slow** \'slō\ adj 1 a : SLUGGISH b : dull in mind : STUPID 2 ♦ : moving, flowing, or proceeding at less than the usual speed 3 : taking more than the usual time 4 : registering behind the correct time 5 : not lively : BORING

♦ creeping, dilatory, laggard, languid, poky, sluggish, tardy; also deliberate, measured; inactive, inert, lethargic, loafing, lounging; lingering, loitering, tarrying; ambling, inching, plodding, shuffling, strolling; decelerating, slowing; procrastinating, stalling **Ant** barreling, bolting, breakneck, brisk, careering, dizzy, fast, fleet, flying, hasty, hurrying, lightning, quick, racing, rapid, rocketing, running, rushing, scudding, scurrying, snappy, speeding, speedy, swift, whirling, whirlwind, whisking, zipping

²**slow** vb 1 ♦ : to make slow : hold back 2 : to go slower

♦ brake, decelerate, hinder, retard; also encumber, hamper, handicap, hobble, hold back, hold up, impede, inhibit, obstruct, tie up **Ant** accelerate, hasten, hurry, quicken, rush, speed (up), step up

³**slow** adv ♦ : in a slow manner : not quickly, fast, early, rashly, or readily

♦ laggardly, slowly, sluggishly, tardily; also carefully, cautiously, deliberately, purposefully; ploddingly **Ant** apace, briskly, fast, full tilt, hastily, quick, quickly, rapidly, speedily, swift, swiftly

slow·ly adv ♦ : in a slow manner : not quickly, fast, early, rashly, or readily

♦ laggardly, slow, sluggishly, tardily — more at SLOW

slow motion n : motion-picture action photographed so as to appear much slower than normal — **slow–motion** adj

slow·ness n : the quality or state of being slow

SLR abbr single-lens reflex

sludge \'sləj\ n ♦ : a slushy mass : OOZE; esp : solid matter produced by sewage treatment processes

♦ mire, muck, mud, ooze, slime, slop, slush — more at MUD

¹**slug** \'sləg\ n 1 : a small mass of metal; esp : BULLET 2 : a metal disk for use (as in a slot machine) in place of a coin 3 : any of numerous wormlike mollusks related to the snails 4 ♦ : a quantity of liquor drunk 5 : an habitually lazy person : SLUGGARD

♦ draft, drag, drink, nip, quaff, shot, snort, swallow, swig — more at DRINK

²**slug** vb **slugged; slug·ging** ♦ : to strike forcibly and heavily — **slug·ger** n

♦ belt, clout, hit, punch, strike, wallop

³**slug** n : a heavy blow esp. with the fist

slug·gard \'slə-gərd\ n ♦ : an habitually lazy person

♦ drone, idler, lazybones, loafer, slouch, slug — more at LAZYBONES

slug·gish \'slə-gish\ adj 1 : SLOTHFUL, LAZY 2 ♦ : slow in movement, flow, or growth ⟨a ∼ economy⟩ 3 : STAGNANT, DULL — **slug·gish·ness** n

♦ creeping, dilatory, laggard, languid, poky, slow, tardy

slug·gish·ly adv ♦ : in a sluggish manner

♦ laggardly, slow, slowly, tardily — more at SLOW

¹**sluice** \'slüs\ n [ME sluse, scluse, fr. AF escluse, fr. LL exclusa, fr. L, fem. of exclusus, pp. of excludere to exclude] 1 : an artificial passage for water with a gate for controlling the flow; also : the gate so used 2 : a channel that carries off surplus water 3 : an inclined trough or flume for washing ore or floating logs

²**sluice** vb **sluiced; sluic·ing** 1 : to draw off through a sluice 2 ♦ : to wash with running water : FLUSH

♦ flush, irrigate, rinse, wash — more at FLUSH

¹**slum** \'sləm\ n : a thickly populated area marked by poverty and dirty or deteriorated houses — **slum·my** \'slə-mē\ adj

²**slum** vb **slummed; slum·ming** : to visit slums esp. out of curiosity; also : to go somewhere or do something that might be considered beneath one's station

¹**slum·ber** \'sləm-bər\ vb **slum·bered; slum·ber·ing** 1 a ♦ : to sleep lightly : DOZE 1 b : to rest in a state of sleep 2 : to be in a sluggish or torpid state

♦ catnap, doze, drowse, nap, sleep, snooze — more at NAP

²**slumber** n ♦ : the natural periodic suspension of consciousness during which bodily powers are restored : SLEEP; also : a light sleep

♦ repose, rest, sleep — more at SLEEP

slum·ber·ous \'sləm-bə-rəs\ or **slum·brous** \-brəs\ adj 1 ♦ : feeling a strong inclination toward sleep : SLEEPY 2 : PEACEFUL, INACTIVE 3 ♦ : inducing slumber

♦ [1] drowsy, sleepy — more at SLEEPY ♦ [3] hypnotic, narcotic, opiate — more at HYPNOTIC

slum·lord \'sləm-,lord\ n : a landlord who receives unusually large profits from substandard properties

slump \'sləmp\ vb 1 : to sink down suddenly : COLLAPSE 2 : SLOUCH 3 : to decline sharply — **slump** n

slung past and past part of SLING

slunk past and past part of SLINK

¹**slur** \'slər\ vb **slurred; slur·ring** 1 ♦ : to slide or slip over without due mention or emphasis ⟨slurred over certain facts⟩ 2 : to perform two or more successive notes of different pitch in a smooth or connected way

♦ usu slur over disregard, forget, ignore, neglect, overlook, pass over, slight — more at NEGLECT

²**slur** n : a curved line connecting notes to be slurred; also : a group of slurred notes

³**slur** n ♦ : a slighting remark

♦ affront, barb, dart, dig, indignity, insult, name, offense, outrage, put-down, sarcasm, slight, wound — more at INSULT

slurp \'slərp\ vb : to eat or drink noisily — **slurp** n

slur·ry \'slər-ē\ n, pl **slur·ries** : a watery mixture of insoluble matter

slush \'sləsh\ n 1 : partly melted or watery snow 2 ♦ : soft mud 3 : silly, worthless, or cheaply sentimental material

♦ mire, muck, mud, ooze, slime, slop, sludge — more at MUD

slush fund n : an unregulated fund often for illicit purposes

slushy adj **slush·i·er; -est** ♦ : full of or covered with slush

♦ miry, mucky, muddy, oozy, slimy — more at MUDDY

slut \'slət\ n 1 dated, chiefly Brit, disparaging : a slovenly woman 2 offensive : a promiscuous woman — **slut·ty** adj, offensive

sly \'slī\ *adj* **sli·er** *or* **sly·er** \'slī-ər\; **sli·est** *or* **sly·est** \'slī-əst\ **1** ♦ : displaying cleverness : CRAFTY **2** ♦ : clever in concealing one's aims or ends **3** ♦ : lightly mischievous : ROGUISH — **sly·ly** *adv*

♦ [1] artful, cagey, crafty, cunning, devious, foxy, guileful, slick, subtle, wily — more at ARTFUL ♦ [2] furtive, shady, shifty, slippery, sneaky, stealthy — more at SNEAKY ♦ [3] devilish, impish, knavish, mischievous, rascally, roguish, waggish, wicked — more at MISCHIEVOUS

sly·ness *n* ♦ : the quality or state of being sly

♦ artfulness, artifice, caginess, canniness, craft, craftiness, cunning, guile, wiliness — more at CUNNING

sm *abbr* small

Sm *symbol* samarium

SM *abbr* **1** master of science **2** sergeant major **3** service mark **4** stage manager

¹smack \'smak\ *n* : characteristic flavor; *also* : a slight trace

²smack *vb* **1** : to have a taste **2** : to have a trace or suggestion

³smack *vb* **1** : to move (the lips) so as to make a sharp noise **2** : to kiss or slap with a loud noise

⁴smack *n* **1** : a sharp noise made by the lips **2** : a noisy slap

⁵smack *adv* : squarely and sharply

⁶smack *n* : a sailing ship used in fishing

⁷smack *n, slang* : HEROIN

smack·down \'smak-ˌdau̇n\ *n* **1** : the act of knocking down an opponent **2** : a wrestling match **3** : a decisive defeat **4** : a competition between rivals

SMaj *abbr* sergeant major

¹small \'smȯl\ *adj* **1** ♦ : little in size or amount **2** : operating on a limited scale **3** : little or close to zero (as in number or value) **4** : made up of little things **5** ♦ : of little consequence : UNIMPORTANT **6** : lacking in mental discrimination : PETTY

♦ [1] dwarf, dwarfish, fine, little, pocket, pygmy, slight, undersized; *also* petite; scrubby, stunted; inappreciable, infinitesimal, micro, microscopic, midget, miniature, minute, teeny, tiny, wee; underweight; meager, niggardly, poor, scant, scanty, scarce, skimpy, slender, slim, spare, sparse, stingy; deficient, inadequate, insufficient, lacking, wanting *Ant* big, bumper, considerable, goodly, grand, great, handsome, king-size, large, outsize, oversize, sizable, substantial, super, whacking, whopping ♦ [5] frivolous, inconsequential, inconsiderable, insignificant, little, minor, minute, negligible, slight, trifling, trivial, unimportant — more at UNIMPORTANT

²small *n* : a small part or product ⟨the ~ of the back⟩

small·ish *adj* : somewhat small : slightly below normal size

small·ness *n* **1** : the quality or state of being small **2** : something that is small

small·pox \'smȯl-ˌpäks\ *n* : a contagious virus disease of humans formerly common but now eradicated

small talk *n* : light or casual conversation

small–time \'smȯl-'tīm\ *adj* : insignificant in performance and standing : MINOR — **small–tim·er** *n*

smarmy \'smär-mē\ *adj* **smarm·i·er**; **-est** : marked by a smug, ingratiating, or false earnestness ⟨~ politeness⟩

¹smart \'smärt\ *vb* **1** ♦ : to cause or feel a stinging pain **2** : to feel or endure distress

♦ ache, hurt, pain — more at HURT

²smart *adj* **1** ♦ : making one smart ⟨a ~ blow⟩ **2** ♦ : mentally quick, perceptive, or clever **3** : marked by or full of wit : WITTY **4** : appealing to sophisticated tastes : STYLISH **5** : being a guided missile **6** : containing a microprocessor for limited computing capability ⟨~ terminal⟩ **7** ♦ : exhibiting neatness, good order, or compactness of line or structure ⟨soldiers in ~ uniforms⟩ **8** ♦ : impertinently bold, impudent, or facetious — **smart·ness** *n*

♦ [1] acute, agonizing, biting, excruciating, sharp — more at SHARP ♦ [2] alert, brainy, bright, brilliant,

clever, intelligent, keen, nimble, quick, quick-witted, sharp, shrewd — more at INTELLIGENT ♦ [7] dapper, natty, neat, spruce; *also* dressy, elegant, formal; tidy; fashionable, modish, stylish; careful, fastidious, fussy, meticulous; clean, immaculate, spotless *Ant* sloppy, slovenly ♦ [8] facetious, flip, flippant, pert — more at FLIPPANT

³smart *n* ♦ : a smarting pain; *esp* : a stinging local pain

♦ ache, pain, pang, prick, sting, stitch, tingle, twinge — more at PAIN

smart al·eck \'smärt-ˌa-lik\ *n* : a person given to obnoxious cleverness

smart card *n* : a small plastic card that has a built-in microprocessor to store and handle data

smart·en \'smär-t³n\ *vb* : to make smart or smarter — usu. used with *up*

smart·ly *adv* : in a smart manner : so as to be or seem smart

smart·phone \'smärt-ˌfōn\ *n* : a cell phone that includes additional software functions (as e-mail or an Internet browser)

¹smash \'smash\ *n* **1** : a smashing blow **2** : a hard, overhand stroke in tennis **3** ♦ : the act or sound of smashing **4** ♦ : collision of vehicles : CRASH **5** : COLLAPSE, RUIN; *esp* : BANKRUPTCY **6** ♦ : a striking success : HIT — **smash** *adj*

♦ [3] bang, blast, boom, clap, crack, crash, pop, report, slam, snap, thwack, whack — more at CLAP ♦ [4] collision, crack-up, crash, wreck — more at CRASH ♦ [6] blockbuster, hit, success, winner — more at HIT

²smash *vb* **1** ♦ : to break or be broken into pieces **2** ♦ : to move forward with force and shattering effect **3** : to destroy utterly : WRECK

♦ [1] blast, blow up, burst, demolish, explode, pop, shatter — more at BLAST ♦ [2] bang, bash, bump, collide, crash, hit, impact, knock, ram, slam, strike, swipe, thud — more at HIT

smat·ter·ing \'sma-tə-riŋ\ *n* **1** : superficial knowledge **2** ♦ : a small scattered number or amount

♦ few, handful, sprinkle, sprinkling — more at FEW

¹smear \'smir\ *n* **1** : a spot left by an oily or sticky substance **2** : material smeared on a surface (as of a microscope slide)

²smear *vb* **1** ♦ : to overspread esp. with something oily or sticky **2** : SMUDGE, SOIL **3** ♦ : to injure by slander or insults

♦ [1] daub; *also* coat, paint, plaster; grease, oil; gum, lard, pitch, tar; begrime, besmirch, blacken, dirty, foul, grime, mire, muddy, smirch, smudge, soil, stain, sully ♦ [3] blacken, defame, libel, malign, slander, traduce, vilify — more at SLANDER

¹smell \'smel\ *vb* **smelled** \'smeld\ *or* **smelt** \'smelt\; **smell·ing 1 a** ♦ : to perceive the odor of by sense organs of the nose **b** ♦ : to detect as if with the nose ⟨I ~ trouble⟩ **2** : to have or give off an odor

♦ [1a] nose, scent, sniff, whiff; *also* breathe, drink (in), inhale ♦ [1b] feel, perceive, scent, see, sense, taste — more at FEEL

²smell *n* **1** ♦ : the property of a thing that affects the olfactory organs : ODOR, SCENT **2** : the process or power of perceiving odor; *also* : the special sense by which one perceives odor **3** : an act of smelling

♦ odor (*or* odour), redolence, scent, sniff; *also* whiff; aroma, bouquet, fragrance, perfume; savor, spice, tang; acridness, foulness, rancidity, rankness, stench, stink

smelling salts *n pl* : an aromatic preparation used as a stimulant and restorative (as to relieve faintness)

smelly *adj* : having a usu. bad smell

♦ fetid, foul, fusty, malodorous, musty, noisome, rank, reeky, strong — more at MALODOROUS

¹smelt \'smelt\ *n, pl* **smelts** *or* **smelt** : any of a family of small food fishes of coastal or fresh waters that are related to the trouts and salmons

²**smelt** *vb* : to melt or fuse (ore) in order to separate the metal; *also* : REFINE

smelt·er \'smel-tər\ *n* 1 : one that smelts 2 : an establishment for smelting

smid·gen *also* **smid·geon** *or* **smid·gin** \'smi-jən\ *n* : a small amount : BIT

smi·lax \'smī-ˌlaks\ *n* 1 : any of various mostly climbing and prickly plants related to the lilies 2 : an ornamental plant related to the asparagus

¹**smile** \'smīl\ *vb* **smiled; smil·ing** 1 : to look with a smile 2 : to be favorable 3 : to express by a smile

²**smile** *n* : a change of facial expression to express amusement, pleasure, or affection

smil·ey \'smī-lē\ *adj* : exhibiting a smile : frequently smiling

smiley face *n* : a line drawing that symbolizes a smiling face

¹**smirch** \'smərch\ *vb* 1 ♦ : to make dirty or stained 2 ♦ : to bring disgrace on

♦ [1] befoul, begrime, besmirch, blacken, dirty, foul, grime, mire, muddy, soil, stain — more at DIRTY ♦ [2] abase, debase, degrade, demean, discredit, disgrace, dishonor (*or* dishonour), humble, humiliate, lower, shame, take down — more at HUMBLE

²**smirch** *n* 1 : a dirty blurred mark or blot 2 ♦ : something that tarnishes a reputation

♦ blot, brand, spot, stain, stigma, taint — more at STAIN

smirk \'smərk\ *vb* : to wear a self-conscious or conceited smile : SIMPER — **smirk** *n*

smite \'smīt\ *vb* **smote** \'smōt\; **smit·ten** \'smit-ᵊn\ *or* **smote; smit·ing** \'smī-tiŋ\ 1 : to strike heavily; *also* : to kill by striking 2 : to affect as if by a heavy blow

smith \'smith\ *n* : a worker in metals; *esp* : BLACKSMITH

smith·er·eens \ˌsmi-thə-'rēnz\ *n pl* [perh. fr. Ir *smidiríní*] : FRAGMENTS, BITS

smithy \'smi-thē\ *n, pl* **smith·ies** 1 : a smith's workshop 2 : BLACKSMITH

¹**smock** \'smäk\ *n* : a loose garment worn over other clothes as a protection

²**smock** *vb* : to gather (cloth) in regularly spaced tucks — **smock·ing** *n*

smog \'smäg, 'smog\ *n* [blend of *smoke* and *fog*] ♦ : a thick haze caused by the action of sunlight on air polluted by smoke and automobile exhaust fumes

♦ fog, haze, mist, murk, soup — more at HAZE

smog·gy *adj* **smog·gi·er; -est** ♦ : characterized by or abounding in smog

♦ cloudy, foggy, hazy, misty, murky, soupy — more at HAZY

¹**smoke** \'smōk\ *n* 1 : the gas from burning material (as coal, wood, or tobacco) in which are suspended particles of soot 2 : a mass or column of smoke 3 : something (as a cigarette) to smoke; *also* : the act of smoking — **smoke·less** *adj* — **smoky** *adj*

²**smoke** *vb* **smoked; smok·ing** 1 : to emit smoke 2 : to inhale and exhale the fumes of burning tobacco; *also* : to use in smoking ⟨~ a pipe⟩ 3 : to stupefy or drive away by smoke 4 : to discolor with smoke 5 : to cure (as meat) with smoke — **smok·er** *n*

smoke detector *n* : an alarm that sounds automatically when it detects smoke

smoke jumper *n* : a forest firefighter who parachutes to locations otherwise difficult to reach

smoke screen *n* 1 : a screen of smoke to hinder enemy observation 2 : something designed to obscure, confuse, or mislead

smoke·stack \'smōk-ˌstak\ *n* : a pipe or funnel through which smoke and gases are discharged

smol·der *or* **smoul·der** \'smōl-dər\ *vb* **smol·dered** *or* **smoul·dered; smol·der·ing** *or* **smoul·der·ing** 1 : to burn and smoke without flame 2 : to burn inwardly — **smolder** *n*

smooch \'smüch\ *vb* : to touch or caress with the lips as a mark of affection : KISS — **smooch** *n*

¹**smooth** \'smüth\ *adj* 1 ♦ : not rough or uneven 2 : not jarring or jolting 3 : BLAND, MILD 4 ♦ : fluent in speech and agreeable in manner 5 ♦ : free from difficulties or impediments — **smooth·ness** *n*

♦ [1] even, flat, flush, level, plane — more at LEVEL ♦ [4] debonair, sophisticated, suave, urbane — more at SUAVE ♦ [5] easy, effortless, facile, fluent, fluid, light, painless, ready, simple, snap, soft — more at EASY

²**smooth** *vb* 1 ♦ : to make smooth 2 ♦ : to free from trouble or difficulty

♦ [1] even, level, plane — more at EVEN ♦ [1] buff, burnish, dress, gloss, grind, polish, rub, shine — more at POLISH ♦ [2] ease, facilitate, loosen, unclog — more at EASE

smooth·ly *adv* ♦ : in a smooth manner : without difficulties

♦ easily, effortlessly, fluently, freely, handily, lightly, painlessly, readily — more at EASILY

smooth muscle *n* : muscle with no cross striations that is typical of visceral organs (as the stomach and bladder) and is not under voluntary control

smoothy *or* **smooth·ie** \'smü-thē\ *n, pl* **smooth·ies** 1 : an artfully suave person 2 *smoothie* : a creamy beverage of fruit blended with juice, milk, or yogurt

s'more \'smòr\ *n* : a dessert of marshmallow and pieces of chocolate sandwiched between graham crackers

smor·gas·bord \'smòr-gəs-ˌbòrd\ *n* [Sw *smörgasbord*, fr. *smörgas* open sandwich + *bord* table] : a luncheon or supper buffet consisting of many foods

smote *past and past part of* SMITE

¹**smoth·er** \'smə-thər\ *n* 1 : thick stifling smoke 2 : a dense cloud (as of fog or dust) 3 : a confused multitude of things

²**smother** *vb* **smoth·ered; smoth·er·ing** 1 ♦ : to be overcome by or die from lack of air 2 ♦ : to kill by depriving of air 3 ♦ : to suppress expression or knowledge of 4 : to cover thickly

♦ [1, 2] choke, stifle, strangle, suffocate; *also* garrote, throttle; asphyxiate; drown ♦ [3] choke, pocket, repress, stifle, strangle, suppress, swallow — more at SUPPRESS

SMSgt *abbr* senior master sergeant

¹**smudge** \'sməj\ *vb* **smudged; smudg·ing** : to soil or blur by rubbing or smearing

²**smudge** *n* : a dirty or blurred spot — **smudgy** *adj*

smug \'sməg\ *adj* **smug·ger; smug·gest** ♦ : conscious of one's virtue and importance : SELF-SATISFIED ⟨a ~ smile⟩ — **smug·ly** *adv*

♦ complacent, conceited, egotistic, important, overweening, pompous, prideful, proud, self-important, self-satisfied, stuck-up, vain — more at CONCEITED

smug·gle \'smə-gəl\ *vb* **smug·gled; smug·gling** 1 : to import or export secretly, illegally, or without paying the duties required by law 2 : to convey secretly — **smug·gler** \'smə-glər\ *n*

smug·ness *n* ♦ : the quality or state of being smug

♦ complacence, conceit, ego, egotism, pride, self-conceit, self-esteem, self-importance, self-satisfaction, vainglory, vanity — more at COMPLACENCE

smut \'smət\ *n* 1 : something (as soot) that smudges; *also* : SMUDGE, SPOT 2 : any of various destructive diseases of plants caused by fungi; *also* : a fungus causing smut 3 ♦ : indecent language or matter

♦ bawdiness, coarseness, dirt, dirtiness, filth, filthiness, foulness, grossness, indecency, lewdness, nastiness, obscenity, ribaldry, vulgarity — more at OBSCENITY

smut·ty *adj* **smut·ti·er; -est** ♦ : soiled or tainted with smut : not decent

♦ bawdy, coarse, crude, dirty, filthy, foul, gross, indecent, lascivious, lewd, nasty, obscene, pornographic, ribald, unprintable, vulgar, wanton — more at OBSCENE

Sn *symbol* [LL *stannum*] tin

SN *abbr* seaman

snack \'snak\ *n* : a light meal : BITE

snaf·fle \'sna-fəl\ *n* : a jointed bit for a horse's bridle

¹**snag** \'snag\ *n* **1** : a stump or piece of a tree esp. when under water **2** ♦ : an unexpected difficulty

♦ booby trap, catch, pitfall — more at PITFALL

²**snag** *vb* **snagged; snag·ging** **1** : to become caught on or as if on a snag **2** : to seize quickly : SNATCH

snail \'snāl\ *n* : any of numerous small gastropod mollusks with a spiral shell into which they can withdraw

snail mail *n* ♦ : mail delivered by a postal system

♦ mail, matter, parcel post, post — more at MAIL

snake \'snāk\ *n* **1** : any of numerous long-bodied limbless reptiles **2** ♦ : a treacherous person **3** : something that resembles a snake — **snaky** *adj*

♦ beast, boor, churl, clown, creep, cretin, cur, heel, jerk, joker, louse, lout, skunk, slob — more at JERK

snake·bite \-ˌbīt\ *n* : the bite of a snake and esp. a venomous snake

¹**snap** \'snap\ *vb* **snapped; snap·ping** **1** : to grasp or slash at something with the teeth **2** ♦ : to get or buy quickly — usu. used with *up* **3** : to utter sharp or angry words **4** : to break suddenly with a sharp sound **5** : to give a sharp cracking noise **6** : to throw with a quick motion **7** : FLASH ⟨her eyes *snapped*⟩ **8** : to put a football into play **9** ♦ : to take photographically — **snap·per** *n* — **snap·py** *adj*

♦ *usu* snap up [2] catch, collar, grab, nab, seize ♦ [9] mug, photograph, shoot — more at PHOTOGRAPH

²**snap** *n* **1** ♦ : the act or sound of snapping **2** ♦ : something very easy to do : CINCH **3 a** : a short period of cold weather **b** : a small amount **4** : a catch or fastening that closes with a click **5** : a thin brittle cookie **6** ♦ : a pleasing vigorous quality : ENERGY; *also* : smartness of movement **7** : the putting of the ball into play in football **8** : a casual photograph : SNAPSHOT

♦ [1] bang, blast, boom, clap, crack, crash, pop, report, slam, smash, thwack, whack — more at CLAP ♦ [2] breeze, child's play, cinch, picnic, pushover — more at CINCH ♦ [6] dash, energy, life, pep, vigor (*or* vigour), vim, vitality — more at VIGOR

³**snap** *adj* **1** ♦ : done, made, or carried through suddenly or without deliberation **2** ♦ : unusually easy or simple

♦ [1] ad-lib, extemporaneous, impromptu, offhand, unplanned, unpremeditated, unprepared, unrehearsed — more at EXTEMPORANEOUS ♦ [2] easy, effortless, facile, fluent, fluid, light, painless, ready, simple, smooth, soft — more at EASY

snap back *vb* ♦ : to make a quick or vigorous recovery

♦ convalesce, gain, heal, mend, rally, recover, recuperate — more at CONVALESCE

snap bean *n* : a bean grown primarily for its long pods that are cooked as a vegetable when young and tender

snap·drag·on \'snap-ˌdra-gən\ *n* : any of a genus of herbs with long spikes of showy flowers

snapping turtle *n* : either of two large American turtles with powerful jaws and a strong musky odor

snap·pish *adj* ♦ : given to curt irritable speech

♦ choleric, crabby, cranky, cross, crotchety, grouchy, grumpy, irascible, irritable, peevish, perverse, petulant, short-tempered, snappy, snippy, testy, waspish — more at IRRITABLE

snap·py *adj* **snap·pi·er; -est** **1** : given to curt irritable speech **2** ♦ : quickly made or done; *also* : marked by vigor or liveliness **3** : briskly cold **4** ♦ : having style

♦ [2] fast, hasty, quick, rapid, speedy, swift ♦ [2] active, brisk, energetic, lively, peppy, spirited, sprightly, springy, vital, vivacious — more at LIVELY ♦ [4] à la mode, chic, fashionable, in, modish, sharp, smart, stylish — more at STYLISH

snap·shot \'snap-ˌshät\ *n* ♦ : a photograph taken usu. with an inexpensive handheld camera

♦ photograph, print, shot, snap — more at PHOTOGRAPH

¹**snare** \'snar\ *n* ♦ : a trap often consisting of a noose for catching birds or mammals; *also* : something by which one is entangled, involved in difficulties, or impeded

♦ ambush, entanglement, net, trap, web — more at TRAP

²**snare** *vb* ♦ : to capture by or as if by use of a snare

♦ enmesh, ensnare, entangle, entrap, mesh, tangle, trap — more at ENTANGLE   bag, capture, catch, collar, corral, get, grab, grapple, hook, land, nab, seize, trap — more at CATCH

snark \'snärk\ *n* : SARCASM 2

¹**snarl** \'snärl\ *vb* ♦ : to cause to become knotted and intertwined

♦ entangle, interlace, intertwine, interweave, knot, tangle — more at ENTANGLE

²**snarl** *n* **1** : a tangled, twisted mass : TANGLE **2** ♦ : a tangled situation

♦ backup, bottleneck, jam

³**snarl** *vb* : to growl angrily or threateningly

⁴**snarl** *n* : an angry ill-tempered growl

¹**snatch** \'snach\ *vb* **1** : to try to grasp something suddenly **2** : to seize or take away suddenly

²**snatch** *n* **1** : a short period **2** : an act of snatching **3** : something brief or fragmentary ⟨~es of song⟩

¹**sneak** \'snēk\ *vb* **sneaked** \'snēkt\ *or* **snuck** \'snək\; **sneak·ing** ♦ : to go or act in a furtive manner; *also* : to put, bring, or take in a furtive or artful manner ⟨*snuck* past the guard⟩ — **sneak·ing·ly** *adv*

♦ lurk, pussyfoot, skulk, slide, slink, slip, snake, steal; *also* crawl, creep, edge, inch, worm; pad, tiptoe

²**sneak** *n* **1** : one who acts in a furtive or shifty manner **2** : a stealthy or furtive move or escape — **sneak** *adj*

sneak·er \'snē-kər\ *n* : a sports shoe with a pliable rubber sole

sneaky *adj* **sneak·i·er; -est** ♦ : marked by stealth, furtiveness, or shiftiness — **sneak·i·ly** \'snē-kə-lē\ *adv*

♦ furtive, shady, shifty, slippery, sly, stealthy; *also* devious, guileful, close, closemouthed, dark, reticent, secretive, clandestine, covert; deceiving, deceitful, deceptive, tricky, underhand, underhanded; crooked, dishonest, double-dealing, two-faced; lying, mendacious, untrustworthy, untruthful; insidious, perfidious, treacherous ♦ clandestine, covert, furtive, hugger-mugger, private, secret, sneak, stealthy, surreptitious, undercover, underground, underhanded — more at SECRET

sneer \'snir\ *vb* ♦ : to show scorn or contempt by curling the lip or by a jeering tone — **sneer** *n*

♦ jeer, laugh, snicker, snort; *also* catcall, disdain, hoot, insult, mock, ridicule; scorn

sneeze \'snēz\ *vb* **sneezed; sneez·ing** [ME *snesen*, alter. of *fnesen*, fr. OE *fnēosan*] : to force the breath out suddenly and violently as a reflex act — **sneeze** *n*

SNF *abbr* skilled nursing facility

snick·er \'sni-kər\ *n* ♦ : a partly suppressed laugh — **snicker** *vb*

♦ cackle, chortle, laugh, laughter, titter — more at LAUGH

snide \'snīd\ *adj* **1** ♦ : unworthy of esteem : LOW ⟨a ~ trick⟩ **2** : slyly disparaging ⟨a ~ remark⟩ — **snide·ly** *adv*

♦ base, contemptible, despicable, detestable, dirty, dishonorable (*or* dishonourable), ignoble, low, mean, sordid, vile, wretched — more at IGNOBLE

sniff \'snif\ *vb* **1** : to draw air audibly up the nose esp. for smelling **2** ♦ : to show disdain or scorn — usu. used with *at* **3** ♦ : to detect by or as if by smelling — **sniff** *n*

♦ *usu* sniff at [2] disdain, high-hat, scorn, slight, snub — more at SCORN ♦ [3] nose, scent, smell, whiff — more at SMELL

snif·fle \\'sni-fəl\\ *n* **1** *pl* : a head cold marked by nasal discharge **2** : SNUFFLE — **sniffle** *vb*

¹snip \\'snip\\ *n* **1** : a fragment snipped off **2** : a simple stroke of the scissors or shears

²snip *vb* **snipped; snip·ping** : to cut off by bits : CLIP; *also* : to remove by cutting off ⟨~ a flower⟩

¹snipe \\'snīp\\ *n, pl* **snipes** *or* **snipe** : any of several long-billed game birds esp. of marshy areas that belong to the same family as the sandpipers

²snipe *vb* **sniped; snip·ing** : to shoot at an exposed enemy from a concealed position — **snip·er** *n*

snip·py \\'sni-pē\\ *adj* **snip·pi·er; -est** **1** : having a quick temper : SNAPPISH **2** ♦ : unduly brief or curt ⟨a ~ comment⟩

♦ abrupt, bluff, blunt, brusque, curt — more at BLUNT

snips \\'snips\\ *n pl* : hand shears used esp. for cutting sheet metal ⟨tin ~⟩

¹snitch \\'snich\\ *vb* **1** ♦ : to give information (as of another's wrongdoing) to an authority : INFORM **2** ♦ : to take by stealth : PILFER — **snitch** *n*

♦ [1] inform, squeal, talk, tell — more at SQUEAL
♦ [2] appropriate, filch, hook, misappropriate, nip, pilfer, pocket, purloin, steal, swipe, thieve — more at STEAL

²snitch *n* ♦ : one that snitches : TATTLETALE

♦ betrayer, blabbermouth, informer, rat, stool pigeon, tattler, tattletale — more at INFORMER

sniv·el \\'sni-vəl\\ *vb* **-eled** *or* **-elled; -el·ing** *or* **-el·ling** **1** : to have a running nose; *also* : SNUFFLE **2** : to whine in a snuffling manner — **snivel** *n*

snob \\'snäb\\ *n* : one who seeks association with persons of higher social position and looks down on those considered inferior — **snob·bish** *adj* — **snob·bish·ly** *adv* — **snob·bish·ness** *n* — **snob·by** \\'snä-bē\\ *adj*

snob·bery \\'snä-bə-rē\\ *n, pl* **-ber·ies** : snobbish conduct

¹snoop \\'snüp\\ *vb* [D *snoepen* to buy or eat on the sly] ♦ : to pry in a furtive or meddlesome way

♦ butt in, interfere, intrude, meddle, mess, nose, obtrude, poke, pry — more at INTERFERE

²snoop *n* : a prying meddlesome person

snooty \\'snü-tē\\ *adj* **snoot·i·er; -est** : DISDAINFUL, SNOBBISH

¹snooze \\'snüz\\ *vb* **snoozed; snooz·ing** ♦ : to take a nap : DOZE

♦ catnap, doze, drowse, nap, slumber — more at NAP

²snooze *n* ♦ : a short sleep esp. during the day

♦ catnap, doze, drowse, forty winks, nap, siesta, wink — more at NAP

snore \\'snȯr\\ *vb* **snored; snor·ing** : to breathe with a rough hoarse noise while sleeping — **snore** *n*

snor·kel \\'snȯr-kəl\\ *n* [G *Schnorchel*] : a tube projecting above the water used by swimmers for breathing with the face under water — **snorkel** *vb*

¹snort \\'snȯrt\\ *vb* **1** : to force air violently and noisily through the nose ⟨his horse ~ed⟩ **2** : to inhale (a drug) through the nostrils **3** : to express scorn, anger, indignation, or surprise by a snort

²snort *n* **1** ♦ : the act or sound of snorting **2** ♦ : a drink of usu. straight liquor taken in one draft

♦ [1] boo, catcall, hiss, hoot, jeer, raspberry — more at CATCALL ♦ [2] draft, drag, drink, nip, quaff, shot, slug, swallow, swig — more at DRINK

snot \\'snät\\ *n* **1** : nasal mucus **2** : a snotty person

snot·ty \\'snä-tē\\ *adj* **snot·ti·er; -est** **1** : soiled with snot **2** : rudely or spitefully unpleasant ⟨a ~ remark⟩

snout \\'snau̇t\\ *n* **1** : a long projecting muzzle (as of a pig) **2** : a usu. large or grotesque nose

¹snow \\'snō\\ *n* **1** : crystals of ice formed from water vapor in the air **2** : a descent or shower of snow crystals

²snow *vb* **1** : to fall or cause to fall in or as snow **2** : to cover or shut in with or as if with snow **3** : deceive, persuade, or charm glibly

¹snow·ball \\'snō-ˌbȯl\\ *n* : a round mass of snow pressed into shape in the hand for throwing

²snowball *vb* **1** : to throw snowballs at **2** ♦ : to increase or expand at a rapidly accelerating rate

♦ accumulate, appreciate, balloon, build, burgeon, enlarge, escalate, expand, increase, mount, multiply, mushroom, proliferate, rise, swell, wax — more at INCREASE

snow·bank \\-ˌbaŋk\\ *n* : a mound or slope of snow

snow·belt \\-ˌbelt\\ *n, often cap* : a region that receives an appreciable amount of annual snowfall

snow·blow·er \\-ˌblō-ər\\ *n* : a machine in which a rotating spiral blade picks up and propels snow aside

snow·board \\-ˌbȯrd\\ *n* : a board like a wide ski ridden in a surfing position downhill over snow

snow·drift \\-ˌdrift\\ *n* : a bank of drifted snow

snow·drop \\-ˌdräp\\ *n* : a plant with narrow leaves and a nodding white flower that blooms early in the spring

snow·fall \\-ˌfȯl\\ *n* : a fall of snow

snow fence *n* : a fence across the path of prevailing winds to protect something (as a road) from drifting snow

snow·field \\'snō-ˌfēld\\ *n* : a mass of perennial snow at the head of a glacier

snow·mo·bile \\'snō-mō-ˌbēl\\ *n* : any of various automotive vehicles for travel on snow — **snow·mo·bil·er** \\-ˌbē-lər\\ *n* — **snow·mo·bil·ing** \\-liŋ\\ *n*

snow pea *n* : a cultivated pea with flat edible pods

snow·plow \\'snō-ˌplau̇\\ *n* **1** : a device for clearing away snow **2** : a skiing maneuver in which the heels of both skis are slid outward for slowing down or stopping

¹snow·shoe \\-ˌshü\\ *n* : a lightweight platform for the foot designed to enable a person to walk on soft snow without sinking

²snowshoe *vb* **snow·shoed; snow·shoe·ing** : to travel on snowshoes

snow·storm \\-ˌstȯrm\\ *n* : a storm of falling snow

snow thrower *n* : SNOWBLOWER

snow under *vb* ♦ : to overwhelm esp. in excess of capacity to absorb or deal with something

♦ carry away, crush, devastate, floor, oppress, overcome, overpower, overwhelm, prostrate, swamp — more at OVERWHELM

snowy \\'snō-ē\\ *adj* **snow·i·er; -est** **1** : marked by snow **2** : white as snow

¹snub \\'snəb\\ *vb* **snubbed; snub·bing** ♦ : to treat with disdain : SLIGHT

♦ disdain, high-hat, scorn, slight, sniff — more at SCORN

²snub *n* ♦ : an act or an instance of snubbing

♦ brush-off, cold shoulder, rebuff, repulse — more at COLD SHOULDER

snub–nosed \\'snəb-ˌnōzd\\ *adj* : having a nose slightly turned up at the end

snuck *past and past part of* SNEAK

¹snuff \\'snəf\\ *vb* **1** : to pinch off the charred end of (a candle) **2** ♦ : to put out (a candle) — often used with *out* **3** ♦ : to make extinct; *also* : put an end to — usu. used with *out* — **snuff·er** *n*

♦ *usu* snuff out [2] douse, extinguish, put out, quench — more at EXTINGUISH ♦ *usu* snuff out [3] annihilate, blot out, demolish, eradicate, exterminate, liquidate, obliterate, root, rub out, stamp, wipe out — more at ANNIHILATE ♦ *usu* snuff out [3] clamp down, crack down, crush, put down, quash, quell, repress, silence, squash, squelch, subdue, suppress — more at QUELL

²snuff *vb* **1** : to draw forcibly into or through the nose **2** : SMELL

³snuff *n* : SNIFF

⁴snuff *n* : pulverized tobacco

snuf·fle \\'snə-fəl\\ *vb* **snuf·fled; snuf·fling** **1** : to snuff or sniff audibly and repeatedly **2** : to breathe with a sniffing sound — **snuf·fle** *n*

snug \\'snəg\\ *adj* **snug·ger; snug·gest** **1** ♦ : fitting closely and comfortably **2** : CONCEALED **3** ♦ : exhibiting neatness, good order, or compactness of line or structure **4 ♦** : enjoying or affording warm secure shelter or cover and opportunity for ease and contentment ⟨a ~ cottage⟩ — **snug·ly** adv — **snug·ness** n

♦ [1] fast, firm, frozen, secure, set, tight — more at TIGHT ♦ [3] crisp, neat, orderly, shipshape, tidy, trim, uncluttered — more at NEAT ♦ [4] comfortable, easy, soft — more at COMFORTABLE

snug·gle \'snə-gəl\ vb **snug·gled; snug·gling ♦** : to curl up or draw close comfortably : NESTLE

♦ cuddle, curl up, nestle, snug; also huddle

¹**so** \'sō\ adv **1** : in the manner indicated **2 ♦** : in the same way **3** : THUS **4** : FINALLY **5** : to an indicated or great extent ⟨I'm ~ bored⟩ **6 ♦** : for that reason : THEREFORE **7** : to a great extent or degree : VERY

♦ [2] alike, also, correspondingly, likewise, similarly — more at ALSO ♦ [6] accordingly, consequently, ergo, hence, therefore, thus, wherefore — more at THEREFORE

²**so** conj : for that reason ⟨he wanted it, ~ he took it⟩
³**so** pron **1** : the same ⟨became chairman and remained ~⟩ **2** : approximately that ⟨a dozen or ~⟩
⁴**so** abbr south; southern
SO abbr strikeout
¹**soak** \'sōk\ vb **1** : to remain in a liquid **2 ♦** : to make or become saturated by or as if by immersion : WET **3 ♦** : to draw in by or as if by absorption **4 ♦** : to cause to pay an exorbitant amount

♦ [2] drench, drown, immerse, impregnate, saturate, sop, souse, steep, wet; also inundate, submerge; bathe, douse, wash, water; infiltrate, penetrate, permeate *Ant* wring (out) ♦ [3] absorb, drink, imbibe, sponge, suck — more at ABSORB ♦ [4] gouge, overcharge, sting — more at OVERCHARGE

²**soak** n **1** : the act of soaking **2** : the liquid in which something is soaked **3** : one who is habitually drunk : DRUNKARD
soap \'sōp\ n ♦ : a cleansing substance made usu. by action of alkali on fat — **soap** vb — **soapy** adj

♦ cleaner, detergent — more at CLEANER

soap·box \'sōp-ˌbäks\ n : an improvised platform used for delivering informal speeches
soap opera n [fr. its sponsorship by soap manufacturers] : a radio or television daytime serial drama
soap·stone \'sōp-ˌstōn\ n : a soft talc-containing stone with a soapy feel
soar \'sōr\ vb ♦ : to fly upward or at a height on or as if on wings; also : to rise or increase dramatically (as in position, value, or price)

♦ arise, ascend, climb, lift, mount, rise, up — more at ASCEND ♦ fly, glide, plane, wing — more at FLY ♦ rocket, shoot, skyrocket, zoom — more at SKYROCKET

sob \'säb\ vb **sobbed; sob·bing ♦** : to weep with convulsive heavings of the chest or contractions of the throat — **sob** n

♦ bawl, blubber, cry, weep — more at CRY

so·ba \'sō-bə\ n [Jp] : a Japanese noodle made from buckwheat flour
so·ber \'sō-bər\ adj **so·ber·er** \-bər-ər\; **so·ber·est** \-bə-rəst\ **1** : temperate in the use of liquor **2 ♦** : not drunk **3 ♦** : serious or grave in mood or disposition **4** : having a quiet tone or color — **so·ber·ly** adv — **so·ber·ness** n

♦ [2] clearheaded, dry, straight, temperate *Ant* drunk, high, inebriated, intoxicated, soused, tipsy ♦ [3] earnest, grave, humorless (or humourless), serious, severe, solemn, staid, unsmiling, weighty — more at SERIOUS

so·bri·ety \sō-'brī-ə-tē\ n ♦ : the quality or state of being sober

♦ earnestness, gravity, intentness, seriousness, solemnity — more at EARNESTNESS

so·bri·quet \'sō-bri-ˌkā, -ˌket\ n [F] : NICKNAME

soc abbr **1** social; society **2** sociology
so–called \'sō-'kȯld\ adj : commonly but often inaccurately so termed
soc·cer \'sä-kər\ n [by shortening & alter. fr. *association football*] : a game played on a field by two teams with a round inflated ball that is kicked or hit with any body part other than the hands or arms
so·cia·bil·i·ty \ˌsō-shə-'bi-lə-tē\ n : the quality or state of being sociable; also : the act or an instance of being sociable
¹**so·cia·ble** \'sō-shə-bəl\ adj **1** : liking companionship : FRIENDLY **2 ♦** : characterized by pleasant social relations — **so·cia·bly** \'sō-shə-blē\ adv

♦ affable, cordial, genial, gracious, hospitable — more at GRACIOUS

²**sociable** n : SOCIAL
¹**so·cial** \'sō-shəl\ adj **1 ♦** : marked by pleasant companionship with one's friends **2** : naturally living and breeding in organized communities ⟨~ insects⟩ **3** : of or relating to human society ⟨~ institutions⟩ **4** : of, relating to, or based on rank in a particular society ⟨~ circles⟩; also : of or relating to fashionable society — **so·cial·ly** adv

♦ boon, companionable, convivial, extroverted, gregarious, outgoing, sociable — more at CONVIVIAL

²**social** n : a social gathering
so·cial·ise chiefly Brit var of SOCIALIZE
so·cial·ism \'sō-shə-ˌli-zəm\ n : any of various social systems based on shared or government ownership and administration of the means of production and distribution of goods — **so·cial·ist** \'sō-shə-list\ n or adj — **so·cial·is·tic** \ˌsō-shə-'lis-tik\ adj
so·cial·ite \'sō-shə-ˌlīt\ n : a person prominent in fashionable society
so·cial·ize \'sō-shə-ˌlīz\ vb **-ized; -iz·ing 1** : to regulate according to the theory and practice of socialism **2** : to adapt to social needs or uses **3 ♦** : to participate actively in a social gathering — **so·cial·i·za·tion** \ˌsō-shə-lə-'zā-shən\ n

♦ associate, fraternize, hobnob, mingle, mix

social media n pl : forms of electronic communication (as websites) for sharing content (such as messages, photos, or videos) with other users
social networking n : the creation and maintenance of personal and business relationships esp. online
social science n : a science (as economics or political science) dealing with a particular aspect of human society — **social scientist** n
social work n : services, activities, or methods providing social services esp. to the economically or socially disadvantaged — **social worker** n
so·ci·e·ty \sə-'sī-ə-tē\ n, pl **-ties** [MF *societé*, fr. L *societat-, societas,* fr. *socius* companion] **1 ♦** : the fellowship existing among companions : COMPANY **2 ♦** : a voluntary association of persons for common ends **3** : a part of a community bound together by common interests and values; esp : the group or set of fashionable people **4** : people in general — **societal** adj

♦ [1] camaraderie, companionship, company, comradeship, fellowship — more at COMPANIONSHIP ♦ [2] association, brotherhood, club, college, congress, council, fellowship, fraternity, guild, institute, institution, league, order, organization — more at ASSOCIATION

so·cio·eco·nom·ic \ˌsō-sē-ō-ˌe-kə-'nä-mik, ˌsō-shē-, -ˌē-kə-\ adj : of, relating to, or involving both social and economic factors
sociol abbr sociologist; sociology
so·ci·ol·o·gy \ˌsō-sē-'ä-lə-jē, ˌsō-shē-\ n : the science of society, social institutions, and social relationships — **so·ci·o·log·i·cal** \ˌsō-sē-ə-'lä-ji-kəl, ˌsō-shē-\ adj — **so·ci·ol·o·gist** \-'ä-lə-jist\ n
so·cio·path \'sō-sē-ə-ˌpath, 'sō-sh(ē-)ə-\ n : a person exhibiting antisocial behavior : PSYCHOPATH — **so·cio·path·ic** \ˌsō-sē-ə-'pa-thik, ˌsō-sh(ē-)ə-\ adj

¹**sock** \'säk\ *n, pl* **socks** *or* **sox** \'säks\ : a stocking with a short leg

²**sock** *vb* : to hit, strike, or apply forcefully

³**sock** *n* ♦ : a vigorous blow : PUNCH

♦ bat, belt, blow, box, clout, hit, punch, slug, thump, wallop, whack — more at BLOW

sock·et \'sä-kət\ *n* : an opening or hollow that forms a holder for something

socket wrench *n* : a wrench usu. in the form of a bar and removable socket made to fit a bolt or nut

sock·eye salmon \'säk-,ī-\ *n* : a commercially important Pacific salmon

¹**sod** \'säd\ *n* **1** : TURF 1 **2** ♦ : one's native land

♦ country, fatherland, home, homeland, motherland — more at COUNTRY

²**sod** *vb* **sod·ded; sod·ding** : to cover with sod

so·da \'sō-də\ *n* **1** : SODIUM CARBONATE **2** : SODIUM BICARBONATE **3** : SODIUM **4** : SODA WATER **5** : SODA POP **6** : a sweet drink of soda water, flavoring, and often ice cream

soda pop *n* : a carbonated, sweetened, and flavored soft drink

soda water *n* : a beverage of water charged with carbon dioxide

sod·den \'säd-²n\ *adj* **1** : lacking spirit : DULLED **2** ♦ : heavy with or as if with moisture or water : SOAKED **3** : heavy or doughy from being improperly cooked ⟨~ biscuits⟩

♦ saturated, soggy, waterlogged, watery, wet — more at WET

so·di·um \'sō-dē-əm\ *n* : a soft waxy silver white metallic chemical element occurring in nature in combined form (as in salt)

sodium bicarbonate *n* : a white weakly alkaline salt used esp. in baking powders, fire extinguishers, and medicine

sodium carbonate *n* : a carbonate of sodium used esp. in washing and bleaching textiles

sodium chloride *n* : SALT 1

sodium fluoride *n* : a salt used chiefly in tiny amounts (as in fluoridation) to prevent tooth decay

sodium hydroxide *n* : a white brittle caustic substance used in making soap and rayon and in bleaching

sodium nitrate *n* : a crystalline salt used as a fertilizer and in curing meat

sodium thiosulfate *n* : a hygroscopic crystalline salt used as a photographic fixing agent

sod·omy \'sä-də-mē\ *n* : anal or oral sexual intercourse with a member of the same or opposite sex; *also* : sexual intercourse with an animal — **sod·om·ize** \'sä-də-,mīz\ *vb*

so·ev·er \sō-'e-vər\ *adv* **1** : in any degree or manner ⟨how bad ~⟩ **2** : at all : of any kind ⟨any help ~⟩

so·fa \'sō-fə\ *n* [earlier, raised carpeted floor, fr. It *sofà*, fr. Turk *sofa*, fr. Ar *ṣuffa* carpet, divan] ♦ : a couch usu. with upholstered back and arms

♦ couch, davenport, divan, lounge, settee — more at COUCH

soft \'sȯft\ *adj* **1** : not hard or rough : NONVIOLENT **2** ♦ : marked by a gentleness, kindness, or tenderness **3** : emotionally susceptible **4** : not prepared to endure hardship **5** : not containing certain salts that prevent lathering ⟨~ water⟩ **6** : occurring at such a speed as to avoid destructive impact ⟨~ landing of a spacecraft on the moon⟩ **7** : BIODEGRADABLE ⟨a ~ pesticide⟩ **8** : not alcoholic ⟨~ drinks⟩ **9** : less detrimental than a hard narcotic ⟨~ drugs⟩ **10** ♦ : demanding little work or effort **11** : lacking robust strength, stamina, or endurance **12** ♦ : lacking firmness or strength of character **13** ♦ : bringing ease, comfort, or quiet **14** ♦ : quiet in pitch or volume **15** ♦ : smooth or delicate in texture, grain, or fiber **16** ♦ : yielding to physical pressure — **soft·ly** *adv* — **soft·ness** *n*

♦ [2] balmy, benign, bland, delicate, gentle, light, mellow, mild, soothing, tender — more at GENTLE ♦ [10] easy, effortless, facile, fluent, fluid, light, painless, ready, simple, smooth, snap — more at EASY ♦ [12] effete, frail, nerveless, spineless, weak, wimpy, wishy-washy — more at WEAK ♦ [13] comfortable, easy, snug — more at COMFORTABLE ♦ [14] dull, low, quiet; *also* dead, silent, still; dreamy, peaceful, restful, soothing, tranquil; muffled, muted, softened, toned (down) *Ant* blaring, clamorous, deafening, earsplitting, loud ♦ [15] cottony, downy, satiny, silken, velvety; *also* creamy; delicate, fine, slick, smooth *Ant* coarse, harsh, rough, scratchy ♦ [16] flabby, mushy, pulpy, spongy; *also* unhardened; doughy, fleshy; droopy, flaccid, floppy, lank, limp, slack, yielding; malleable, pliable, pliant, workable *Ant* firm, hard, solid

soft·ball \'sȯft-,bȯl\ *n* : a game similar to baseball played with a ball larger and softer than a baseball; *also* : the ball used in this game

soft·bound \-,baůnd\ *adj* : not bound in hard covers ⟨~ books⟩

soft coal *n* : BITUMINOUS COAL

soft·en \'sȯ-fən\ *vb* ♦ : to make or become soft — **soft·en·er** *n*

♦ debilitate, enervate, enfeeble, prostrate, sap, tire, waste, weaken — more at WEAKEN ♦ buffer, cushion, gentle — more at CUSHION

soft palate *n* : the fold at the back of the hard palate that partially separates the mouth from the pharynx

soft·ware \'sȯft-,war\ *n* : the entire set of programs, procedures, and related documentation associated with a system; *esp* : computer programs

soft·wood \-,wůd\ *n* **1** : the wood of a coniferous tree as compared to that of a broad-leaved deciduous tree **2** : a tree yielding softwood — **softwood** *adj*

sog·gy \'sä-gē\ *adj* **sog·gi·er; -est** ♦ : heavy with water or moisture — **sog·gi·ly** \'sä-gə-lē\ *adv* — **sog·gi·ness** \-gē-nəs\ *n*

♦ saturated, sodden, waterlogged, watery, wet — more at WET

soi·gné *or* **soi·gnée** \swän-'yā\ *adj* : elegantly maintained; *esp* : WELL-GROOMED

¹**soil** \'sȯil\ *vb* **1** : CORRUPT, POLLUTE **2** ♦ : to make or become dirty **3** : STAIN, DISGRACE

♦ befoul, begrime, besmirch, blacken, dirty, foul, grime, mire, muddy, smirch, stain — more at DIRTY

²**soil** *n* **1** : STAIN, DEFILEMENT **2** ♦ : something that spoils or pollutes

♦ dirt, filth, grime, muck, smut — more at FILTH

³**soil** *n* **1** ♦ : firm land : EARTH **2** ♦ : the upper layer of earth in which plants grow **3** : COUNTRY, REGION

♦ [1] dirt, dust, earth, ground, land — more at EARTH
♦ [2] dirt, earth, ground — more at DIRT

soi·ree *or* **soi·rée** \swä-'rā\ *n* [F *soirée* evening period, evening party, fr. MF, fr. *soir* evening, fr. L *sero* at a late hour] : an evening party

¹**so·journ** \'sō-jərn, sō-'jərn\ *vb* ♦ : to dwell in a place temporarily — **so·journ·er** *n*

♦ stay, tarry, visit — more at VISIT

²**so·journ** *n* : a temporary stay

¹**sol** *n* : a fluid colloidal system

²**sol** *abbr* **1** solicitor **2** soluble **3** solution

Sol \'säl\ *n* : SUN

¹**sol·ace** \'sä-ləs\ *n* ♦ : alleviation of grief or anxiety; *also* : a source of relief or consolation

♦ cheer, comfort, consolation, relief — more at COMFORT
♦ comforting, consolation — more at CONSOLATION

²**solace** *vb* **so·laced; so·lac·ing** ♦ : to give solace to : CONSOLE

♦ assure, cheer, comfort, console, reassure, soothe — more at COMFORT

so·lar \'sō-lər\ *adj* **1** : of, derived from, or relating to the sun **2** : measured by the earth's course in relation to the sun ⟨the ~ year⟩ **3** : operated by or using the sun's light or heat ⟨~ energy⟩

solar cell *n* : a photoelectric cell used as a power source

solar collector *n* : a device for the absorption of solar radiation for the heating of water or buildings or the production of electricity

solar flare *n* : a sudden temporary outburst of energy from a small area of the sun's surface

so·lar·i·um \sō-'lar-ē-əm\ *n, pl* **-ia** \-ē-ə\ *also* **-i·ums** : a room exposed to the sun; *esp* : a room (as in a hospital) for exposure of the body to sunshine

solar plexus *n* ♦ : the general area of the stomach below the sternum

♦ abdomen, belly, gut, stomach, tummy — more at STOMACH

solar system *n* : the sun together with the group of celestial bodies that revolve around it

solar wind *n* : plasma continuously ejected from the sun's surface

sold *past and past part of* SELL

sol·der \'sä-dər, 'sȯ-\ *n* : a metallic alloy used when melted to mend or join metallic surfaces — **solder** *vb*

soldering iron *n* : a metal device for applying heat in soldering

¹**sol·dier** \'sōl-jər\ *n* [ME *soudier*, fr. MF, fr. *soulde* pay, fr. LL *solidus* a Roman coin, fr. L, solid] ♦ : a person in military service; *esp* : an enlisted person — **sol·dier·ly** *adj or adv*

♦ fighter, legionnaire, man-at-arms, regular, serviceman, warrior; *also* servicewoman; cavalier, dragoon, trooper; doughboy, footman, infantryman; commando, marine, ranger; musketeer, rifleman; archer, lancer, spearman; Federal, GI, guardsman; guerilla, irregular, partisan; combatant, noncombatant; mercenary; veteran; conscript, draftee, recruit; reservist **Ant** civilian

²**soldier** *vb* **sol·diered; sol·dier·ing** **1** : to serve as a soldier **2** : to pretend to work while actually doing nothing

sol·diery \'sōl-jə-rē\ *n* : a body of soldiers

¹**sole** \'sōl\ *n* : any of various flatfishes including some used for food

²**sole** *n* **1** : the undersurface of the foot **2** : the bottom of a shoe

³**sole** *vb* **soled; sol·ing** : to furnish (a shoe) with a sole

⁴**sole** *adj* ♦ : being the only one : ONLY; *also* : belonging exclusively or otherwise limited to one usu. specified individual, unit, or group

♦ alone, lone, only, singular, solitary, special, unique — more at ONLY

so·le·cism \'sä-lə-,si-zəm, 'sō-\ *n* **1** : a mistake in grammar **2** : a breach of etiquette

sole·ly \'sōl-lē\ *adv* **1** ♦ : without another **2** ♦ : to the exclusion of all else

♦ [1] alone, independently, singly, unaided, unassisted — more at ALONE ♦ [2] alone, exclusively, just, only, simply; *also* mainly, mostly, primarily

sol·emn \'sä-ləm\ *adj* **1** : marked by or observed with full religious ceremony **2** : FORMAL, CEREMONIOUS **3** ♦ : highly serious **4** : SOMBER, GLOOMY — **sol·emn·ly** \'sä-ləm-lē\ *adv*

♦ august, dignified, imposing, staid, stately — more at DIGNIFIED ♦ earnest, grave, humorless (*or* humourless), serious, severe, sober, staid, unsmiling, weighty — more at SERIOUS

so·lem·ni·ty \sə-'lem-nə-tē\ *n* **1** ♦ : formal or ceremonious observance of an occasion or event **2** ♦ : a solemn condition or quality

♦ [1] ceremonial, ceremony, form, formality, observance, rite, ritual — more at RITE ♦ [2] earnestness, gravity, intentness, seriousness, sobriety — more at EARNESTNESS

sol·em·nize \'sä-ləm-,nīz\ *vb* **-nized; -niz·ing** **1** : to observe or honor with solemnity **2** : to celebrate (a marriage) with religious rites — **sol·em·ni·za·tion** \,sä-ləm-nə-'zā-shən\ *n*

so·le·noid \'sō-lə-,nȯid, 'sä-\ *n* : a coil of wire usu. in cylindrical form that when carrying a current acts like a magnet

so·lic·it \sə-'li-sət\ *vb* **1** ♦ : to make petition to : ENTREAT **2** ♦ : to approach with a request or plea **3** : TEMPT, LURE **4** ♦ : to try to obtain by usu. urgent requests or pleas

♦ [1] appeal, beg, beseech, entreat, implore, importune, petition, plead, pray, supplicate — more at BEG ♦ [2] canvass, poll, survey — more at CANVASS ♦ [4] ask, call, plead, quest, request, seek, sue

so·lic·i·ta·tion \-,li-sə-'tā-shən\ *n* ♦ : the practice or act or an instance of soliciting; *also* : a moving or drawing force

♦ appeal, cry, entreaty, petition, plea, prayer, suit, supplication — more at PLEA

so·lic·i·tor \sə-'li-sə-tər\ *n* **1** ♦ : one that solicits **2** : LAWYER; *esp* : a legal official of a city or state

♦ pleader, suitor

so·lic·i·tous \sə-'li-sə-təs\ *adj* **1** : full of concern or fears : WORRIED, CONCERNED **2** : full of desire : EAGER **3** ♦ : manifesting or expressing attentive care and protectiveness — **so·lic·i·tous·ly** *adv*

♦ attentive, considerate, kind, thoughtful — more at THOUGHTFUL

so·lic·i·tude \sə-'li-sə-,tüd, -,tyüd\ *n* : the state of being concerned and anxious : ANXIETY, CONCERN

¹**sol·id** \'sä-ləd\ *adj* **1** : not hollow; *also* : written as one word without a hyphen ⟨a ∼ compound⟩ **2** : having, involving, or dealing with three dimensions or with solids ⟨∼ geometry⟩ **3** ♦ : not loose or spongy : COMPACT ⟨a ∼ mass of rock⟩; *also* : neither gaseous nor liquid : HARD, RIGID ⟨∼ ice⟩ **4** : of good substantial quality or kind ⟨∼ comfort⟩ **5** ♦ : thoroughly dependable : RELIABLE ⟨a ∼ citizen⟩; *also* : serious in purpose or character ⟨∼ reading⟩ **6** : UNANIMOUS, UNITED ⟨∼ for pay increases⟩ **7** : of one substance or character **8** ♦ : free from error, fallacy, or misapprehension — **solid** *adv* — **sol·id·ly** *adv*

♦ [3] compact, firm, hard, rigid, stiff, unyielding — more at FIRM ♦ [5] dependable, good, reliable, responsible, safe, steady, sure, tried, true, trustworthy — more at DEPENDABLE ♦ [8] good, hard, informed, just, levelheaded, logical, rational, reasonable, reasoned, sensible, sober, valid, well-founded — more at GOOD

²**solid** *n* **1** : a geometrical figure (as a cube or sphere) having three dimensions **2** : a solid substance

sol·i·dar·i·ty \,sä-lə-'dar-ə-tē\ *n* : unity based on shared interests, objectives, or standards

so·lid·i·fy \sə-'li-də-,fī\ *vb* **-fied; -fy·ing** ♦ : to make or become solid — **so·lid·i·fi·ca·tion** \-,li-də-fə-'kā-shən\ *n*

♦ concrete, congeal, firm, freeze, harden, set — more at HARDEN ♦ crystallize, form, jell, shape

so·lid·i·ty \sə-'li-də-tē\ *n* **1** ♦ : the quality or state of being solid **2** : something solid

♦ dependability, reliability, sureness, trustworthiness — more at RELIABILITY

sol·id·ness *n* : the quality or state of being solid

solid-state *adj* **1** : relating to the structure and properties of solid material **2** : using semiconductor devices rather than vacuum tubes

so·lil·o·quize \sə-'li-lə-,kwīz\ *vb* **-quized; -quiz·ing** : to talk to oneself : utter a soliloquy

so·lil·o·quy \sə-'li-lə-kwē\ *n, pl* **-quies** [LL *soliloquium*, fr. L *solus* alone + *loqui* to speak] **1** : the act of talking to oneself **2** : a dramatic monologue that represents unspoken reflections by a character

sol·i·taire \'sä-lə-,tar\ *n* **1** : a single gem (as a diamond) set alone **2** : a card game for one person

sol·i·tary \'sä-lə-,ter-ē\ *adj* **1** ♦ : being or living apart from others **2** : LONELY, SECLUDED **3** ♦ : being the only one : ONLY ⟨a ∼ example⟩

♦ [1] alone, lone, lonely, lonesome, unaccompanied — more at ALONE ♦ [3] alone, lone, only, singular, sole, special, unique — more at ONLY

sol·i·tude \'sä-lə-ˌtüd, -ˌtyüd\ *n* **1** ♦ : the state of being alone : SECLUSION ⟨worked in ∼⟩ **2** : a lonely place

♦ insulation, isolation, seclusion, segregation, sequestration — more at ISOLATION

soln *abbr* solution

¹so·lo \'sō-lō\ *n, pl* **solos** [It, fr. *solo* alone, fr. L *solus*] **1** : a piece of music for a single voice or instrument with or without accompaniment **2** : an action in which there is only one performer — **solo** *adj or vb* — **so·lo·ist** *n*

²solo *adv* : without a companion : ALONE

so·lon \'sō-lən\ *n* **1** : a wise and skillful lawgiver **2** ♦ : a member of a legislative body

♦ lawmaker, legislator — more at LEGISLATOR

sol·stice \'säl-stəs, 'sōl-\ *n* [ME, fr. OF, fr. L *solstitium*, fr. *sol* sun + *-stit-, -stes* standing] : the time of the year when the sun is farthest north of the equator (**summer solstice**) about June 22 or farthest south (**winter solstice**) about Dec. 22 — **sol·sti·tial** \säl-'sti-shəl, sōl-\ *adj*

sol·u·ble \'säl-yə-bəl\ *adj* **1** : capable of being dissolved in or as if in a liquid **2** ♦ : capable of being solved or explained — **sol·u·bil·i·ty** \ˌsäl-yə-'bi-lə-tē\ *n*

♦ answerable, explicable, resolvable, solvable — more at SOLVABLE

sol·ute \'säl-ˌyüt\ *n* : a dissolved substance

so·lu·tion \sə-'lü-shən\ *n* **1** : an action or process of solving a problem; *also* : an answer to a problem **2** : an act or the process by which one substance is homogenously mixed with another usu. liquid substance; *also* : a mixture thus formed

solv·able \'säl-və-bəl\ *adj* ♦ : susceptible of solution or of being solved, resolved, or explained

♦ answerable, explicable, resolvable, soluble; *also* decipherable; feasible, workable **Ant** inexplicable, insoluble, unsolvable

solve \'sälv\ *vb* **solved; solv·ing** ♦ : to find the answer to or a solution for

♦ answer, break, crack, dope, figure out, puzzle, resolve, riddle, unravel, work, work out; *also* clear (up), iron out, straighten (out), unscramble, untangle, untie; divine, guess; decipher, decode

sol·ven·cy \'säl-vən-sē\ *n* : the condition of being solvent

¹sol·vent \-vənt\ *adj* **1** : able or sufficient to pay all legal debts **2** : dissolving or able to dissolve

²solvent *n* : a usu. liquid substance capable of dissolving or dispersing one or more other substances

So·ma·lian \sō-'mäl-yən\ *n* : a native or inhabitant of Somalia — **Somalian** *adj*

so·mat·ic \sō-'ma-tik\ *adj* ♦ : of, relating to, or affecting the body in contrast to the mind or the sex cells and their precursors

♦ animal, bodily, carnal, corporal, fleshly, material, physical — more at PHYSICAL

som·ber *or chiefly Can and Brit* **som·bre** \'säm-bər\ *adj* **1** ♦ : so shaded as to be dark and gloomy **2** ♦ : of a serious or depressing character : GRAVE, MELANCHOLY ⟨a ∼ mood⟩ — **som·ber·ly** *adv*

♦ [1] dark, darkling, dim, dusky, gloomy, murky, obscure — more at DARK ♦ [2] bleak, dark, dismal, dreary, gloomy, gray (*or* grey), wretched — more at GLOOMY

som·bre·ro \səm-'brer-ō\ *n, pl* **-ros** [Sp, fr. *sombra* shade] : a broad-brimmed felt hat worn esp. in the Southwest and in Mexico

¹some \'səm\ *adj* **1** ♦ : one unspecified ⟨∼ man called⟩ **2** : an unspecified or indefinite number of ⟨∼ berries are ripe⟩ **3** : at least a few or a little ⟨∼ years ago⟩

♦ anonymous, certain, one, unidentified, unnamed, unspecified — more at CERTAIN

²some *pron* : a certain number or amount ⟨∼ of the berries are ripe⟩ ⟨∼ of it is missing⟩

¹-some \səm\ *adj suffix* : characterized by a (specified) thing, quality, state, or action ⟨awe*some*⟩ ⟨burden-*some*⟩

²-some *n suffix* : a group of (so many) members and esp. persons ⟨four*some*⟩

¹some·body \'səm-ˌbä-dē, -bə-\ *pron* : some person

²somebody *n* ♦ : a person of importance

♦ celebrity, figure, light, luminary, notable, personage, personality, standout, star, superstar, VIP — more at CELEBRITY

some·day \'səm-ˌdā\ *adv* ♦ : at some future time

♦ eventually, sometime, ultimately, yet — more at YET

some·how \-ˌhau̇\ *adv* : by some means

some·one \-(ˌ)wən\ *pron* : some person

som·er·sault *also* **sum·mer·sault** \'sə-mər-ˌsȯlt\ *n* [MF *sombresaut* leap, ultim. fr. L *super* over + *saltus* leap, fr. *salire* to jump] : a leap or roll in which a person turns heels over head — **somersault** *vb*

som·er·set \-ˌset\ *n or vb* : SOMERSAULT

some·thing \'səm-thiŋ\ *pron* : some undetermined or unspecified thing

some·time \-ˌtīm\ *adv* **1** ♦ : at a future time **2** : at an unknown or unnamed time

♦ eventually, someday, ultimately, yet — more at YET

some·times \-ˌtīmz\ *adv* : at times : OCCASIONALLY

¹some·what \-ˌhwät, -ˌhwət\ *pron* : SOMETHING

²somewhat *adv* ♦ : in some degree

♦ enough, fairly, kind of, moderately, pretty, quite, rather, sort of, so-so — more at FAIRLY

some·where \-ˌhwer\ *adv* : in, at, or to an unknown or unnamed place

som·nam·bu·lism \säm-'nam-byə-ˌli-zəm\ *n* : performance of motor acts (as walking) during sleep; *also* : an abnormal condition of sleep characterized by this — **som·nam·bu·list** \-list\ *n*

som·no·lent \'säm-nə-lənt\ *adj* : inclined to or heavy with sleep : SLEEPY, DROWSY — **som·no·lence** \-ləns\ *n*

son \'sən\ *n* **1** : a male offspring or descendant **2** *cap* : Jesus Christ **3** : a person deriving from a particular source (as a country, race, or school)

so·nar \'sō-ˌnär\ *n* [*so*und *n*avigation *a*nd *r*anging] : a method or device for detecting and locating submerged objects (as submarines) by sound waves

so·na·ta \sə-'nä-tə\ *n* [It] : an instrumental composition with three or four movements differing in rhythm and mood but related in key

son·a·ti·na \ˌsä-nə-'tē-nə\ *n* [It, dim. of *sonata*] : a short usu. simplified sonata

song \'sȯŋ\ *n* **1** ♦ : vocal music; *also* : a short composition of words and music **2** ♦ : poetic composition **3** : a distinctive or characteristic sound (as of a bird) **4** ♦ : a small amount ⟨sold for a ∼⟩

♦ [1] air, lay, melody, strain, tune, warble — more at MELODY ♦ [1] jingle, lay, lyric, vocal; *also* anthem, canticle, carol, chorale, hymn, noel, psalm, spiritual; dirge, lament, requiem, threnody; hallelujah, paean; aria, barcarole, blues, cantata, chantey, chorus, croon, descant, glee, lullaby, madrigal, motet, part-song, pop, rocker, round, roundelay, serenade, troll ♦ [2] poem, poetry, verse — more at POETRY ♦ [4] mite, peanuts, pittance, shoestring — more at MITE

song·bird \'sȯŋ-ˌbərd\ *n* : a bird that utters a series of musical tones

Song of Songs : a book in the Jewish Scriptures and in the Roman Catholic canon of the Old Testament and corresponding to the Song of Solomon in the Protestant canon of the Old Testament

song·ster \'sȯŋ-stər\ *n* ♦ : one that sings

♦ caroler, singer, vocalist, voice — more at SINGER

song·stress \-strəs\ *n* : a girl or woman who is a singer

son·ic \'sä-nik\ *adj* : of or relating to sound waves or the speed of sound

sonic boom *n* : an explosive sound produced by an aircraft traveling at supersonic speed son–in–law \'sən-ən-ˌlȯ\ *n, pl* sons–in–law : the husband of one's daughter or son

son·net \'sä-nət\ *n* : a poem of 14 lines usu. in iambic pentameter with a definite rhyme scheme

son of a gun *n, pl* sons of guns : an offensive or disagreeable person

so·no·rous \sə-'nȯr-əs, 'sä-nə-rəs\ *adj* 1 : giving out sound when struck 2 ♦ : loud, deep, or rich in sound 3 : high-sounding : IMPRESSIVE — so·nor·i·ty \sə-'nȯr-ə-tē\ *n*
   ♦ golden, loud, resonant, resounding, ringing, round, vibrant — more at RESONANT

soon \'sün\ *adv* 1 ♦ : before long 2 : in a prompt manner : QUICKLY 3 *archaic* : EARLY 4 ♦ : in agreement with one's choice or preference : WILLINGLY
   ♦ [1] anon, momentarily, presently, shortly — more at SHORTLY ♦ [4] first, preferably, rather, readily — more at RATHER

soot \'sut, 'sət, 'süt\ *n* : a fine black powder consisting chiefly of carbon that is formed when something burns and that colors smoke — sooty *adj*

sooth \'süth\ *n, archaic* : TRUTH

soothe \'süth\ *vb* soothed; sooth·ing 1 : to please by flattery or attention 2 ♦ : to calm down 3 : RELIEVE, ALLEVIATE ⟨~ a burn⟩ — sooth·er *n* — sooth·ing·ly *adv*
   ♦ assure, cheer, comfort, console, reassure, solace — more at COMFORT ♦ allay, alleviate, assuage, calm, ease, help, mitigate, mollify, palliate, relieve — more at HELP

soothing *adj* ♦ : tending to soothe; *also* : having a sedative effect
   ♦ comforting, dreamy, narcotic, sedative; *also* hypnotic, opiate; anesthetic, deadening, depressant

sooth·say·er \'süth-ˌsā-ər\ *n* ♦ : one who foretells events
   ♦ augur, diviner, forecaster, fortune-teller, futurist, prognosticator, prophet, seer — more at PROPHET

sooth·say·ing *n* ♦ : the act of foretelling events; *also* : something that is predicted
   ♦ cast, forecast, prediction, prognostication, prophecy — more at PREDICTION

¹sop \'säp\ *n* : a conciliatory bribe, gift, or concession

²sop *vb* sopped; sop·ping 1 : to steep or dip in or as if in a liquid 2 ♦ : to wet thoroughly : SOAK; *also* : to mop up (a liquid)
   ♦ drench, drown, impregnate, saturate, soak, souse, steep — more at SOAK

SOP *abbr* standard operating procedure; standing operating procedure

soph *abbr* sophomore

soph·ism \'sä-ˌfi-zəm\ *n* 1 : an argument correct in form but embodying a subtle fallacy 2 : SOPHISTRY

soph·ist \'sä-fist\ *n* : PHILOSOPHER; *esp* : a captious or fallacious reasoner

so·phis·tic \sä-'fis-tik, sə-\ *or* so·phis·ti·cal \-ti-kəl\ *adj* : of or characteristic of sophists or sophistry

so·phis·ti·cat·ed \sə-'fis-tə-ˌkā-təd\ *adj* 1 ♦ : highly complicated or developed : COMPLEX ⟨~ instruments⟩ 2 ♦ : made worldly-wise by wide experience 3 : intellectually appealing ⟨~ novel⟩
   ♦ [1] complex, complicated, convoluted, elaborate, intricate, involved, knotty — more at COMPLEX ♦ [2] cosmopolitan, smart, worldly, worldly-wise — more at WORLDLY-WISE ♦ [2] debonair, smooth, suave, urbane — more at SUAVE

so·phis·ti·ca·tion \-ˌfis-tə-'kā-shən\ *n* 1 : the process or result of becoming cultured, knowledgeable, or disillusioned 2 : the process or result of becoming more complex, developed, or subtle
   ♦ complexity, elaborateness, intricacy — more at COMPLEXITY

soph·ist·ry \'sä-fə-strē\ *n* : subtly deceptive reasoning or argument

soph·o·more \'säf-ˌmȯr, 'sä-fə-\ *n* : a student in the second year of high school or college

soph·o·mor·ic \ˌsäf-'mȯr-ik, ˌsä-fə-\ *adj* 1 : being overconfident of knowledge but poorly informed and immature 2 : of, relating to, or characteristic of a sophomore ⟨a ~ prank⟩

So·pho·ni·as \ˌsä-fə-'nī-əs, ˌsō-\ *n* : ZEPHANIAH

sop·o·rif·ic \ˌsä-pə-'ri-fik\ *adj* 1 : causing sleep or drowsiness 2 : LETHARGIC

sopping *adj* : wet through : SOAKING

so·pra·no \sə-'pra-nō, -'prä-\ *n, pl* -nos [It, fr. *sopra* above, fr. L *supra*] 1 : the highest singing voice; *also* : a singer with this voice 2 : the highest part in a 4-part chorus — soprano *adj*

sor·bet \sȯr-'bā\ *n* : a usu. fruit-flavored ice served for dessert or between courses as a palate refresher

sor·cer·er \-rər\ *n* ♦ : a person who practices sorcery
   ♦ conjurer, enchanter, magician, necromancer, voodoo, witch, wizard — more at MAGICIAN

sor·cer·ess \-rəs\ *n* : a woman who is a sorcerer

sor·cery \'sȯr-sə-rē\ *n* [ME *sorcerie*, fr. AF, fr. *sorcer* sorcerer, fr. ML *sortiarius*, fr. L *sort-, sors* chance, lot] ♦ : the use of magic : WITCHCRAFT
   ♦ bewitchment, enchantment, magic, necromancy, witchcraft, wizardry — more at MAGIC

sor·did \'sȯr-dəd\ *adj* 1 ♦ : marked by baseness or grossness : VILE 2 : marked by filthiness and degradation : DIRTY — sor·did·ly *adv* — sor·did·ness *n*
   ♦ base, contemptible, despicable, detestable, dirty, dishonorable (*or* dishonourable), ignoble, low, mean, snide, vile, wretched — more at IGNOBLE

¹sore \'sȯr\ *adj* sor·er; sor·est 1 ♦ : causing pain or distress ⟨a ~ bruise⟩ 2 : painfully sensitive ⟨~ muscles⟩ 3 : SEVERE, INTENSE 4 : feeling or showing anger : ANGRY — sore·ness *n*
   ♦ nasty, painful — more at PAINFUL

²sore *n* 1 : a sore spot on the body; *esp* : one (as an ulcer) with the tissues broken and usu. infected 2 : a source of pain or vexation

sore·head \'sȯr-ˌhed, 'sȯr-\ *n* : a person easily angered or discontented

sore·ly *adv* 1 : in a sore manner 2 : to a high degree

sore throat *n* : painful throat due to inflammation of the fauces and pharynx

sor·ghum \'sȯr-gəm\ *n* : a tall variable Old World tropical grass grown widely for its edible seed, for forage, or for its sweet juice which yields a syrup

so·ror·i·ty \sə-'rȯr-ə-tē\ *n, pl* -ties [ML *sororitas* sisterhood, fr. L *soror* sister] : a women's student organization formed chiefly for social purposes

¹sor·rel \'sȯr-əl\ *n* : a brownish orange to light brown color; *also* : a sorrel-colored animal (as a horse)

²sorrel *n* : any of various herbs having a sour juice

¹sor·row \'sär-ō\ *n* 1 ♦ : deep distress, sadness, or regret; *also* : resultant unhappy or unpleasant state 2 : a cause of grief or sadness 3 : a display of grief or sadness
   ♦ affliction, anguish, dolor, grief, heartache, woe; *also* agony, distress, pain, torment, suffering; blues, dejection, depression, desolateness, desolation, despondency, distress, doldrums, dumps, forlornness, gloom, gloominess, heartsickness, melancholy, miserableness, misery, oppression, sadness, unhappiness, wretchedness; regret, remorse, rue *Ant* blessedness, bliss, cheer, cheerfulness, cheeriness, delight, ecstasy, elation, euphoria, exhilaration, exuberance, exultation, gladness, glee, happiness, joy, joyousness, jubilation, pleasure, rapture

²sorrow *vb* ♦ : to feel or express sorrow
   ♦ agonize, bleed, feel, grieve, hurt, mourn, suffer — more at GRIEVE

sor·row·ful \-fəl\ *adj* 1 ♦ : full of or marked by sorrow 2 ♦ : expressive of or inducing sorrow
   ♦ [1] anguished, dolorous, lamentable, mournful, plaintive, sad, sorry, woeful; *also* funereal, gloomy, lugubrious; regretful, remorseful, repentant, rueful;

miserable, pathetic, piteous, wretched; bewailing, deploring, grieving, wailing, weeping; dejected, depressed, dispirited, downcast, downhearted, heartsick ♦ [2] dolorous, funeral, lugubrious, mournful, plaintive, regretful, rueful, weeping, woeful — more at MOURNFUL

sor·row·ful·ly \-f(ə-)lē\ *adv* ♦ : in a sorrowful manner

♦ agonizingly, bitterly, grievously, hard, hardly, sadly, unhappily, woefully, wretchedly — more at HARD

sor·ry \'sär-ē\ *adj* **sor·ri·er; -est 1** ♦ : feeling sorrow, regret, or penitence **2** : full of sorrow : MOURNFUL **3** ♦ : causing sorrow, pity, or scorn

♦ [1] apologetic, contrite, penitent, regretful, remorseful, repentant, rueful — more at CONTRITE ♦ [3] depressing, dismal, dreary, heartbreaking, melancholy, pathetic, sad, tearful — more at SAD ♦ [3] contemptible, despicable, pitiful

¹sort \'sort\ *n* **1** ♦ : a group of persons or things that have similar characteristics : CLASS **2** : WAY, MANNER **3** : QUALITY, NATURE **4** : an instance of sorting **5** : a single human being ⟨he's a good ∼⟩ — **out of sorts 1** : somewhat ill **2** : GROUCHY, IRRITABLE

♦ breed, class, description, feather, ilk, kind, like, manner, nature, order, species, type; *also* model; sample, specimen; bracket, category, division, family, grade, group, lot, persuasion, set

²sort *vb* **1** ♦ : to put in a certain place according to kind, class, or nature **2** : to be in accord — **sort·er** *n*

♦ assort, break down, categorize, class, classify, grade, group, peg, place, range, rank, separate — more at CLASSIFY

sor·tie \'sor-tē, sor-'tē\ *n* **1** : a sudden issuing of troops from a defensive position against the enemy **2** : one mission or attack by one airplane

sort of *adv* ♦ : to a moderate degree

♦ enough, fairly, kind of, moderately, pretty, quite, rather, somewhat, so-so — more at FAIRLY

SOS \͵es-(͵)ō-'es\ *n* : a call or request for help or rescue

¹so-so \'sō-'sō\ *adv* ♦ : moderately well

♦ adequately, all right, fine, good, nicely, OK, passably, satisfactorily, tolerably, well — more at WELL

²so-so *adj* ♦ : neither very good nor very bad

♦ common, fair, indifferent, mediocre, medium, middling, ordinary, passable, run-of-the-mill, second-rate — more at MEDIOCRE

sot \'sät\ *n* ♦ : an habitual drunkard — **sot·tish** *adj* — **sot·tish·ly** *adv*

♦ drunk, drunkard, inebriate, soak, souse, tippler — more at DRUNK

souf·flé \sü-'flā\ *n* [F, fr. *soufflé*, pp. of *souffler* to blow, puff up, fr. OF *sufler*, fr. L *sufflare*, fr. *sub-* up + *flare* to blow] : a spongy dish made light in baking by stiffly beaten egg whites

sough \'saů, 'səf\ *vb* : to make a moaning or sighing sound — **sough** *n*

sought *past and past part of* SEEK

¹soul \'sōl\ *n* **1** : the immaterial essence of an individual life **2** : the spiritual principle embodied in human beings or the universe **3** ♦ : an active or essential part **4** ♦ : the moral and emotional nature of human beings **5** : spiritual or moral force **6** : an individual human : PERSON ⟨a kindly ∼⟩ **7** : a strong, positive feeling (as of intense sensitivity and emotional fervor) conveyed esp. by African American performers **8** : SOUL MUSIC — **souled** \'sōld\ *adj*

♦ [3] core, heart, quick ♦ [4] essence, nature, quintessence, stuff, substance — more at ESSENCE

²soul *adj* **1** : of, relating to, or characteristic of African Americans or their culture ⟨∼ food⟩ **2** : designed for or controlled by black people ⟨∼ radio stations⟩

soul brother *n* : a black man or boy

soul·ful \'sōl-fəl\ *adj* ♦ : full of or expressing deep feeling — **soul·ful·ly** *adv*

♦ demonstrative, emotional, feeling, intense, passionate, sensitive, sentimental

soul·less \'sōl-ləs\ *adj* ♦ : having no soul or no greatness or warmth of mind or feeling

♦ callous, hard, heartless, inhuman, inhumane, pitiless, unfeeling, unsympathetic — more at HARD

soul music *n* : music that is closely related to rhythm and blues and characterized by intensity of feeling

¹sound \'saůnd\ *adj* **1** ♦ : not diseased or sickly **2** : free from flaw or defect **3** ♦ : securely or solidly fixed in place : STRONG **4** ♦ : free from error or fallacy **5** : LEGAL, VALID **6** : THOROUGH **7** : UNDISTURBED ⟨∼ sleep⟩ **8** : showing good judgment ⟨∼ reasoning⟩ — **sound·ly** *adv*

♦ [1] able-bodied, chipper, fit, hale, healthy, hearty, robust, well, whole, wholesome — more at HEALTHY ♦ [3] fast, firm, stable, stalwart, steady, strong, sturdy — more at STABLE ♦ [4] analytic, coherent, good, logical, rational, reasonable, sensible, sober, valid — more at LOGICAL

²sound *n* **1** : the sensation of hearing; *also* : mechanical energy transmitted by longitudinal pressure waves **(sound waves)** (as in air) that is the stimulus to hearing **2** : something heard : NOISE, TONE; *also* : hearing distance : EARSHOT **3** : a musical style ⟨the band's ∼⟩ — **sound·less·ly** *adv*

♦ earshot, hail, hearing

³sound *vb* **1** : to make or cause to make a sound **2** ♦ : to order or proclaim by a sound ⟨∼ the alarm⟩ **3** ♦ : to convey a certain impression : SEEM **4** : to examine the condition of by causing to give out sounds — **sound·able** \'saůn-də-bəl\ *adj*

♦ [2] air, express, give, state, vent, voice — more at EXPRESS ♦ [2] advertise, announce, blaze, broadcast, declare, enunciate, placard, post, proclaim, promulgate, publicize, publish — more at ANNOUNCE ♦ [3] act, appear, look, make, seem — more at SEEM

⁴sound *n* ♦ : a long passage of water wider than a strait often connecting two larger bodies of water

♦ channel, narrows, strait — more at CHANNEL

⁵sound *vb* **1** : to measure the depth of (water) esp. by a weighted line dropped from the surface : FATHOM **2** : PROBE **3** ♦ : to dive down suddenly ⟨the hooked fish ∼ed⟩ — **sound·ing** *n*

♦ dive, pitch, plunge — more at DIVE

sound bite *n* : a brief recorded statement broadcast esp. on a news program

sound card *n* : a circuit board in a computer system designed to produce or reproduce sound

sound·er \'saůn-dər\ *n* : one that sounds; *esp* : a device for making soundings

sound·less *adj* ♦ : making no sound

♦ hushed, muted, noiseless, quiet, silent, still — more at SILENT

sound·ness *n* ♦ : the quality or state of being sound

♦ firmness, stability, steadiness, strength, sturdiness — more at STABILITY ♦ fitness, health, heartiness, robustness, wellness, wholeness, wholesomeness — more at HEALTH

sound off *vb* ♦ : to voice one's opinions freely and vigorously

♦ speak out, speak up, spout — more at SPEAK UP

sound·proof \'saůn(d)-͵prüf\ *vb* : to insulate so as to obstruct the passage of sound — **soundproof** *adj*

sound·stage \'saůnd-͵stāj\ *n* : the part of a motion-picture studio in which a production is filmed

sound·track \'saůn(d)-͵trak\ *n* : music recorded to accompany a film, DVD, or videotape

soup \'süp\ *n* **1** : a liquid food with stock as its base and often containing pieces of solid food **2** ♦ : something (as a heavy fog) having or suggesting the consistency of soup **3** : an unfortunate predicament ⟨in the ∼⟩

♦ fog, haze, mist, murk, smog — more at HAZE

soup·çon \süp-'sōⁿ\ n [F, lit., suspicion] : a little bit : ¹TRACE 2 ⟨a ∼ of garlic⟩

soup up vb : to increase the power of — **souped–up** \'süpt-'əp\ adj

soupy \'sü-pē\ adj **soup·i·er; -est** 1 : having the consistency of soup 2 ♦ : densely foggy or cloudy

♦ cloudy, foggy, hazy, misty, murky, smoggy — more at HAZY

¹**sour** \'saur\ adj 1 ♦ : having an acid or tart taste ⟨∼ as vinegar⟩ 2 : SPOILED, PUTRID ⟨a ∼ odor⟩ 3 ♦ : not pleasant : DISAGREEABLE ⟨∼ disposition⟩; also : marked by overt hostility — **sour·ish** adj — **sour·ly** adv — **sour·ness** n

♦ [1] acid, tart, vinegary; also dry, soured, unsweetened; pungent, sharp, tangy; astringent; hyperacid ♦ [3] bad, disagreeable, distasteful, nasty, rotten, uncongenial, unlovely, unpleasant, unwelcome — more at UNPLEASANT

²**sour** vb ♦ : to become or make sour

♦ alienate, disaffect, disgruntle, estrange — more at ESTRANGE

source \'sōrs\ n 1 : ORIGIN, BEGINNING 2 : a supplier of information 3 : the beginning of a stream of water

source code n : a computer program in its original programming language and before translation (as by a compiler)

¹**souse** \'saus\ vb **soused; sous·ing** 1 : PICKLE 2 ♦ : to plunge into a liquid 3 ♦ : to wet thoroughly : DRENCH 4 : to make drunk

♦ [2] dip, douse, duck, dunk, immerse, submerge — more at DIP ♦ [3] drench, drown, impregnate, saturate, soak, sop, steep — more at SOAK

²**souse** n 1 : something (as pigs' feet) steeped in pickle 2 : a soaking in liquid 3 ♦ : an habitual drunkard

♦ drunk, inebriate, soak, sot, tippler — more at DRUNK

¹**south** \'sauth\ adv : to or toward the south; also : into a state of decline

²**south** adj 1 : situated toward or at the south 2 : coming from the south

³**south** n 1 : the direction to the right of one facing east 2 : the compass point directly opposite to north 3 cap : regions or countries south of a specified or implied point; esp : the southeastern part of the U.S. — **south·er·ly** \'sə-thər-lē\ adj or adv — **south·ern** \'sə-thərn\ adj — **South·ern·er** n — **south·ern·most** \-ˌmōst\ adj — **south·ward** \'sauth-wərd\ adv or adj — **south·wards** \-wərdz\ adv

South African n : a native or inhabitant of the Republic of South Africa — **South African** adj

south·east \sau-'thēst, naut sau-'ēst\ n 1 : the general direction between south and east 2 : the compass point midway between south and east 3 cap : regions or countries southeast of a specified or implied point — **southeast** adj or adv — **south·east·er·ly** adv or adj — **south·east·ern** \-'ēs-tərn\ adj

south·paw \'sauth-ˌpo\ n : a left-handed person; esp : a left-handed baseball pitcher — **southpaw** adj

south pole n, often cap S&P : the southernmost point of the earth

south·west \sauth-'west, naut sau-'west\ n 1 : the general direction between south and west 2 : the compass point midway between south and west 3 cap : regions or countries southwest of a specified or implied point — **southwest** adj or adv — **south·west·er·ly** adv or adj — **south·west·ern** \-'wes-tərn\ adj

sou·ve·nir \ˌsü-və-'nir\ n [F] ♦ : something serving as a reminder

♦ keepsake, memento, memorial, monument, remembrance, token — more at MEMORIAL

sou'·west·er \sau-'wes-tər\ n : a long waterproof coat worn in storms at sea; also : a waterproof hat

¹**sov·er·eign** \'sä-vrən, -və-rən\ n 1 : one possessing the supreme power and authority in a state 2 : a gold coin of the United Kingdom

♦ autocrat, monarch, ruler — more at MONARCH

²**sovereign** adj 1 : EXCELLENT, FINE 2 : supreme in power or authority 3 : having undisputed ascendancy : CHIEF 4 ♦ : having independent authority

♦ autonomous, free, independent, self-governing, separate — more at FREE

sov·er·eign·ty \-tē\ n, pl **-ties** 1 : supremacy in rule or power 2 : power to govern without external control 3 : the supreme political power in a state 4 ♦ : one that is sovereign; also : an autonomous state

♦ autonomy, freedom, independence, liberty, self-government — more at FREEDOM ♦ commonwealth, country, land, nation, state — more at NATION

so·vi·et \'sō-vē-ˌet, 'sä-, -ət\ n 1 : an elected governmental council in a Communist country 2 pl, cap : the people and esp. the leaders of the U.S.S.R. — **soviet** adj, often cap — **so·vi·et·ize** vb, often cap

¹**sow** \'sau\ n : an adult female swine

²**sow** \'sō\ vb **sowed; sown** \'sōn\ or **sowed; sow·ing** 1 ♦ : to plant seed esp. by scattering 2 : to strew with seed 3 ♦ : to scatter abroad — **sow·er** \'sō-ər\ n

♦ [1] drill, plant, seed — more at PLANT ♦ [3] dot, pepper, scatter, spray, sprinkle, strew — more at SCATTER

sow bug \'sau-\ n : WOOD LOUSE

sox pl of SOCK

soy \'soi\ n : a sauce made from soybeans fermented in brine

soy·bean \'soi-ˌbēn\ n : an Asian legume widely grown for forage and for its edible seeds that yield a valuable oil (**soybean oil**); also : its seed

sp abbr 1 special 2 species 3 specimen 4 spelling 5 spirit

Sp abbr Spain

SP abbr 1 shore patrol; shore patrolman 2 shore police 3 specialist

spa \'spä\ n [Spa, watering place in Belgium] 1 : a resort with mineral springs 2 : a health and fitness facility 3 : a hot tub with a whirlpool device

¹**space** \'spās\ n 1 ♦ : a period of time 2 ♦ : some small measurable distance, area, or volume 3 : the limitless area in which all things exist and move 4 : an empty place 5 : the region beyond the earth's atmosphere 6 : a definite place (as a seat on a train or ship)

♦ [1] bit, spell, stretch, while — more at WHILE ♦ [2] place, room, way — more at ROOM

²**space** vb **spaced; spac·ing** : to place at intervals — **spac·er** n

space–age \'spās-ˌāj\ adj ♦ : of or relating to the age of space exploration

♦ contemporary, current, hot, mod, modern, new, newfangled, red-hot, ultramodern, up-to-date — more at MODERN

space·craft \-ˌkraft\ n : a vehicle for travel beyond the earth's atmosphere

space·flight \-ˌflīt\ n : flight beyond the earth's atmosphere

space heater n : a usu. portable device for heating a relatively small space

space·man \'spās-ˌman, -mən\ n : one who travels outside the earth's atmosphere

space out vb : to become distracted or inattentive

space·ship \-ˌship\ n : a vehicle used for space travel

space shuttle n : a reusable spacecraft designed to transport people and cargo between earth and space

space station n : a large artificial satellite serving as a base (as for scientific observation)

space suit n : a suit equipped to make life in space possible for its wearer

space walk n : a period of activity outside a spacecraft by an astronaut in space — **space·walk** \'spās-ˌwok\ vb — **space·walk·er** n

spa·cious \'spā-shəs\ adj ♦ : very large in extent : ROOMY — **spa·cious·ly** adv — **spa·cious·ness** n

♦ ample, capacious, commodious, roomy; *also* broad, wide; big, bulky, considerable, generous, goodly, grand, great, handsome, hefty, hulking, king-size, large, outsize, oversize, sizable, substantial, super, voluminous; enormous, immense, vast; expansive, extended, extensive; boundless, limitless, unbounded

¹spade \'spād\ *n* : a shovel with a blade for digging — **spade·ful** *n*

²spade *vb* **spad·ed; spad·ing** : to dig with a spade — **spad·er** *n*

³spade *n* : any of a suit of playing cards marked with a black figure resembling an inverted heart with a short stem at the bottom

spa·dix \'spā-diks\ *n, pl* **spa·di·ces** \'spā-də-ˌsēz\ : a floral spike with a fleshy or succulent axis usu. enclosed in a spathe

spa·ghet·ti \spə-'ge-tē\ *n* [It, fr. pl. of *spaghetto*, dim. of *spago* cord, string] : thin solid pasta strings

spam \'spam\ *n* : unsolicited usu. commercial e-mail sent to a large number of addresses — **spam** *vb*

¹span \'span\ *n* **1** : an English unit of length equal to nine inches (about 23 centimeters) **2** : a limited portion of time **3** : the spread (as of an arch) from one support to another

²span *vb* **spanned; span·ning** **1** ♦ : to ascertain the measurements of : MEASURE **2** : to extend across

♦ gauge, measure, scale — more at MEASURE

³span *n* : a pair of animals (as mules) driven together

Span *abbr* Spanish

span·dex \'span-ˌdeks\ *n* : any of various elastic synthetic textile fibers

span·gle \'span-gəl\ *n* : a small disk of shining metal or plastic used esp. on a dress for ornament — **spangle** *vb*

Span·glish \'span-glish\ *n* : a combination of Spanish and English

Span·iard \'span-yərd\ *n* : a native or inhabitant of Spain

span·iel \'span-yəl\ *n* [ME *spaniell*, fr. MF *espaignol*, lit., Spaniard] : a dog of any of several breeds of mostly small and short-legged dogs usu. with long wavy hair and large drooping ears

Span·ish \'spa-nish\ *n* **1** : the chief language of Spain and of the countries colonized by the Spanish **2** **Spanish** *pl* : the people of Spain — **Spanish** *adj*

Spanish American *n* : a resident of the U.S. whose native language is Spanish; *also* : a native or inhabitant of one of the countries of America in which Spanish is the national language — **Spanish–American** *adj*

Spanish fly *n* : a toxic preparation of dried green European beetles that causes the skin to blister and is thought to be an aphrodisiac

Spanish moss *n* : a plant related to the pineapple that grows in pendent tufts of grayish green filaments on trees from the southern U.S. to Argentina

Spanish rice *n* : rice cooked with onions, green peppers, and tomatoes

¹spank \'spank\ *vb* : to hit on the buttocks with the open hand — **spank** *n*

²spank *n* : a blow usu. with the palm of the hand

spank·ing \'span-kin\ *adj* : being fresh and strong : BRISK ⟨~ breeze⟩ — **spanking** *adv*

span·ner \'span-ər\ *n, chiefly Brit* : WRENCH

¹spar \'spär\ *n* **1** : a stout pole **2** : a rounded wood or metal piece (as a mast, yard, boom, or gaff) for supporting sail rigging

²spar *vb* **sparred; spar·ring** : to box for practice without serious hitting; *also* : SKIRMISH, WRANGLE

¹spare \'spar\ *vb* **spared; spar·ing** **1** : to refrain from punishing or injuring : show mercy to ⟨*spared* the prisoners⟩ **2** : to exempt from something ⟨~ me the trouble⟩ **3** : to get along without ⟨can't ~ a dime⟩ **4** ♦ : to use frugally or rarely ⟨don't ~ the syrup⟩

♦ scant, skimp, stint; *also* dole (out), mete (out), portion (out), ration (out); pinch, shortchange

²spare *adj* **spar·er; spar·est** **1** : held in reserve **2** ♦ : being over and above what is needed : SUPERFLUOUS **3** ♦ : not liberal or profuse **4** ♦ : healthily lean : THIN **5** : not abundant or plentiful : SCANTY — **spare·ness** *n*

♦ [2] excess, extra, superfluous, supernumerary, surplus; *also* accessory, additional, supplemental, supplementary; extraneous, gratuitous, nonessential ♦ [3] cheap, close, mean, niggardly, parsimonious, penurious, stingy, tight, tightfisted, uncharitable — more at STINGY ♦ [4] lean, skinny, slender, slim, thin — more at THIN

³spare *n* **1** ♦ : a duplicate kept in reserve; *esp* : a spare tire **2** : the knocking down of all the bowling pins with the first two balls

♦ backup, duplicate, extra, reserve, substitute; *also* stock; copy, double, replacement

spar·ing \'spar-in\ *adj* ♦ : marked by or practicing careful restraint : FRUGAL — **spar·ing·ly** *adv*

♦ economical, frugal, provident, thrifty — more at FRUGAL

¹spark \'spärk\ *n* **1** : a small particle of a burning substance or a hot glowing particle struck from a mass (as by steel on flint) **2** : a short bright flash of electricity between two points **3** : SPARKLE **4** : a particle capable of being kindled or developed : GERM

²spark *vb* **1** : to emit or produce sparks **2** ♦ : to stir to activity : INCITE

♦ activate, actuate, crank, drive, incite, move, propel, run, set off, start, touch off, trigger, turn on — more at ACTIVATE

³spark *vb* : WOO, COURT

¹spar·kle \'spär-kəl\ *vb* **spar·kled; spar·kling** **1 a** : to throw out sparks **b** ♦ : to give off or reflect bright moving points of light : FLASH **2** : to perform brilliantly **3** : EFFERVESCE ⟨*sparkling* wine⟩ — **spar·kler** *n*

♦ flame, flash, glance, gleam, glimmer, glisten, glitter, scintillate, shimmer, twinkle, wink — more at FLASH

²sparkle *n* **1** : GLEAM **2** : ANIMATION

spark plug *n* **1** : a device that produces a spark to ignite the fuel mixture in an engine cylinder **2** : one that begins something or drives something forward

spar·row \'spar-ō\ *n* : any of several small dull-colored singing birds

sparse \'spärs\ *adj* **spars·er; spars·est** ♦ : thinly scattered : SCANTY — **sparse·ly** *adv* — **sparse·ness** *n*

♦ light, meager (*or* meagre), poor, scant, scanty, scarce, skimpy, slender, slim, sparse — more at MEAGER

spasm \'spa-zəm\ *n* **1** : a sudden involuntary and abnormal muscular contraction **2** ♦ : a sudden, violent, and temporary effort, feeling, or outburst

♦ agony, burst, eruption, explosion, fit, flare, flare-up, flash, flush, gale, gush, gust, outburst, paroxysm, storm — more at OUTBURST

spas·mod·ic \spaz-'mä-dik\ *adj* **1** : relating to or affected or characterized by spasm ⟨~ movements⟩; *also* : resembling a spasm **2** ♦ : acting or proceeding fitfully : INTERMITTENT — **spas·mod·i·cal·ly** \-di-k(ə-)lē\ *adv*

♦ casual, choppy, discontinuous, erratic, fitful, intermittent, irregular, occasional, sporadic, spotty, unsteady — more at FITFUL

spas·tic \'spas-tik\ *adj* : of, relating to, marked by, or affected with muscular spasm ⟨~ paralysis⟩ — **spastic** *n*

¹spat \'spat\ *past and past part of* SPIT

²spat *n, pl* **spat** *or* **spats** : a young bivalve mollusk (as an oyster)

³spat *n* : a gaiter covering instep and ankle

⁴spat *n* : a brief petty quarrel : DISPUTE

⁵spat *vb* **spat·ted; spat·ting** ♦ : to quarrel briefly

♦ argue, bicker, brawl, dispute, fall out, fight, hassle, quarrel, row, scrap, squabble, wrangle — more at ARGUE

spate \'spāt\ *n* ♦ : a great rise or overflowing of a stream; *also* : a sudden outburst

♦ cataclysm, cataract, deluge, flood, inundation, overflow, torrent — more at FLOOD

spathe \'spāth\ *n* : a sheathing bract or pair of bracts enclosing an inflorescence (as of the calla lily) and esp. a spadix on the same axis

spa·tial \'spā-shəl\ *adj* : of or relating to space or to the facility to perceive objects in space — **spa·tial·ly** *adv*

spat·ter \'spa-tər\ *vb* 1 ♦ : to splash with drops of liquid 2 : to sprinkle around — **spatter** *n*

♦ dash, plash, splash — more at SPLASH

spat·u·la \'spa-chə-lə\ *n* : a flexible knifelike implement for scooping, spreading, or mixing soft substances

spav·in \'spa-vən\ *n* : a bony enlargement of the hock of a horse — **spav·ined** \-vənd\ *adj*

¹**spawn** \'spȯn\ *vb* [ME, fr. OF *espandre* to spread out, expand, fr. L *expandere*, fr. *ex-* out + *pandere* to spread] 1 : to produce eggs or offspring esp. in large numbers 2 ♦ : to bring into existence : GENERATE — **spawn·er** *n*

♦ create, engender, generate, induce, make, produce — more at GENERATE

²**spawn** *n* 1 : the eggs of water animals (as fishes or oysters) that lay many small eggs 2 ♦ : offspring esp. when produced in great numbers

♦ issue, offspring, posterity, progeny, seed — more at OFFSPRING

spay \'spā\ *vb* **spayed; spay·ing** : to remove the ovaries of (a female animal)

SPCA *abbr* Society for the Prevention of Cruelty to Animals

SPCC *abbr* Society for the Prevention of Cruelty to Children

speak \'spēk\ *vb* **spoke** \'spōk\; **spo·ken** \'spō-kən\; **speak·ing** 1 : to utter words 2 ♦ : to express orally 3 : to mention in speech or writing 4 ♦ : to address an audience 5 : to use or be able to use (a language) in talking

♦ [2] articulate, say, state, talk, tell, utter, verbalize, vocalize — more at SAY ♦ [4] declaim, descant, discourse, harangue, lecture, orate, talk — more at TALK

speak·easy \'spēk-ˌē-zē\ *n, pl* **-eas·ies** : an illicit drinking place

speak·er \'spē-kər\ *n* 1 ♦ : one that speaks 2 ♦ : the presiding officer of a deliberative assembly 3 : LOUDSPEAKER

♦ [1] mouthpiece, spokesman, spokesperson, spokeswoman — more at SPOKESPERSON ♦ [2] chair, chairman, moderator, president

speak out *vb* 1 : to speak loud enough to be heard 2 ♦ : to speak boldly : express an opinion frankly

♦ sound off, speak up, spout — more at SPEAK UP

speak up *vb* 1 : to speak loudly and distinctly 2 ♦ : to express an opinion freely

♦ sound off, speak out, spout; *also* bawl, call, cry, holler, shout, sing (out), vociferate, yell; articulate, enunciate

¹**spear** \'spir\ *n* 1 ♦ : a long-shafted weapon with a sharp point for thrusting or throwing 2 : a sharp-pointed instrument with barbs used in spearing fish — **spear·man** \-mən\ *n*

♦ lance, pike; *also* dart, spike; gaff, halberd, harpoon, trident

²**spear** *vb* ♦ : to strike or pierce with or as if with a spear — **spear·er** *n*

♦ gore, harpoon, impale, lance, pierce, puncture, skewer, spike, stab, stick, transfix — more at IMPALE

³**spear** *n* : a usu. young blade, shoot, or sprout (as of asparagus)

spear·head \-ˌhed\ *vb* ♦ : to serve as a leading force, element, or influence — **spearhead** *n*

♦ boss, captain, command, dominate, head, lead — more at LEAD

spear·mint \-ˌmint\ *n* : a common highly aromatic garden mint

¹**spec** *abbr* 1 special 2 specifically 3 specialist

²**spec** \'spek\ *n* : SPECIFICATION 2 — usu. used in pl.

spe·cial \'spe-shəl\ *adj* 1 : UNCOMMON, NOTEWORTHY 2 ♦ : particularly favored 3 ♦ : readily distinguishable from others of the same category : UNIQUE 4 : EXTRA, ADDITIONAL 5 ♦ : confined to or designed for a definite field of action, purpose, or occasion — **special** *n*

♦ [2] beloved, darling, dear, favorite (*or* favourite), loved, pet, precious, sweet ♦ [3] alone, lone, only, singular, sole, solitary, unique — more at ONLY ♦ [5] distinct, especial, express, precise, set, specific — more at EXPRESS

special delivery *n* : delivery of mail by messenger for an extra fee

special effects *n pl* : visual or sound effects introduced into a motion picture, video recording, or taped television production

Special Forces *n pl* : a branch of the army composed of soldiers specially trained in guerrilla warfare

spe·cial·ise *chiefly Brit var of* SPECIALIZE

spe·cial·ist \'spe-shə-list\ *n* 1 : a person who specializes in a particular branch of learning or activity 2 : a rank in the U.S. Army corresponding to that of corporal

spe·cial·ize \'spe-shə-ˌlīz\ *vb* **-ized; -iz·ing** : to concentrate one's efforts in a special activity or field; *also* : to change in an adaptive manner — **spe·cial·i·za·tion** \ˌspe-shə-lə-'zā-shən\ *n*

spe·cial·ly \'spe-shə-lē\ *adv* 1 : in a special manner 2 : for a special purpose : in particular

spe·cial·ty \'spe-shəl-tē\ *n, pl* **-ties** 1 : a particular quality or detail 2 : a product of a special kind or of special excellence 3 ♦ : something (as a discipline) in which one specializes ⟨the doctor's ~ is dermatology⟩

♦ area, arena, demesne, department, discipline, domain, field, line, province, realm, sphere — more at FIELD

spe·cie \'spē-shē, -sē\ *n* : money in coin

spe·cies \'spē-shēz, -sēz\ *n, pl* **spe·cies** [ME, fr. L, appearance, kind, species, fr. *specere* to look] 1 ♦ : a group united by common traits or interests : KIND 2 : a category of biological classification ranking just below the genus or subgenus and comprising closely related organisms potentially able to breed with one another

♦ breed, class, description, feather, ilk, kind, like, manner, nature, order, sort, type — more at SORT ♦ bracket, category, class, division, family, grade, group, set — more at CLASS

specif *abbr* specific; specifically

¹**spe·cif·ic** \spi-'si-fik\ *adj* 1 : having a unique effect or influence or reacting in only one way or with only one thing ⟨~ antibodies⟩ ⟨~ enzymes⟩ 2 ♦ : free from ambiguity : DEFINITE 3 : of, relating to, or constituting a species 4 ♦ : constituting or falling into a specifiable category — **spe·cif·i·cal·ly** \-fi-k(ə-)lē\ *adv*

♦ [2] clear-cut, definite, definitive, explicit, express, unambiguous, unequivocal — more at EXPLICIT ♦ [4] distinct, especial, express, precise, set, special — more at EXPRESS

²**specific** *n* 1 : something specific : DETAIL, PARTICULAR — usu. used in pl. 2 ♦ : a drug or remedy having a specific mitigating effect on a disease ⟨used as a ~ against malaria⟩

♦ cure, drug, medicine, pharmaceutical, remedy — more at MEDICINE

spec·i·fi·ca·tion \ˌspe-sə-fə-'kā-shən\ *n* 1 : the act or process of specifying 2 : a description of work to be done and materials to be used (as in building) — usu. used in pl.

specific gravity *n* : the ratio of the density of a substance to the density of some substance (as water) taken as a standard when both densities are obtained by weighing in air

spec·i·fy \'spe-sə-ˌfī\ *vb* **-fied; -fy·ing** ♦ : to mention or name explicitly

♦ define, lay down, prescribe — more at PRESCRIBE
♦ advert (to), cite, instance, mention, name, note, notice, quote, refer (to), touch (*on* or *upon*) — more at MENTION

spec·i·men \'spe-sə-mən\ *n* ♦ : an item or part typical of a group or whole; *also* : a single human being

♦ case, example, exemplar, illustration, instance, representative, sample — more at EXAMPLE

spe·cious \'spē-shəs\ *adj* ♦ : seeming to be genuine, correct, or beautiful but not really so ⟨∼ reasoning⟩

♦ deceitful, deceptive, delusive, fallacious, false, misleading — more at DECEPTIVE

¹speck \'spek\ *n* **1** ♦ : a small spot or blemish **2** ♦ : a small particle

♦ [1] blotch, dapple, dot, fleck, mottle, patch, point, spot — more at SPOT ♦ [2] atom, bit, crumb, fleck, flyspeck, grain, granule, molecule, morsel, mote, particle, patch, scrap, scruple, tittle

²speck *vb* ♦ : to produce specks on or in

♦ blotch, dapple, dot, fleck, freckle, mottle, pepper, spot, sprinkle, stipple — more at SPOT

¹speck·le \'spe-kəl\ *n* : a little speck
²speckle *vb* **1** : to mark with speckles **2** : to be distributed in or on like speckles

specs \'speks\ *n pl* : a pair of lenses used to correct defects of vision : GLASSES

spec·ta·cle \'spek-ti-kəl\ *n* **1** : an unusual or impressive public display **2** *pl* ♦ : a pair of lenses used to correct defects of vision : GLASSES — **spec·ta·cled** \-kəld\ *adj*

♦ eyeglasses, glasses — more at GLASSES

spec·tac·u·lar \spek-'ta-kyə-lər\ *adj* : exciting to see : SENSATIONAL

spec·ta·tor \'spek-ˌtā-tər\ *n* : a person who looks on (as at a sports event)

spec·ter *or* **spec·tre** \'spek-tər\ *n* ♦ : a visible disembodied spirit : GHOST

♦ apparition, bogey, ghost, phantasm, phantom, poltergeist, shade, shadow, spirit, spook, vision, wraith — more at GHOST

spec·tral \'spek-trəl\ *adj* **1** : of, relating to, or resembling a specter **2** : of, relating to, or made by a spectrum

spec·tro·gram \'spek-trə-ˌgram\ *n* : a photograph, image, or diagram of a spectrum

spec·tro·graph \-ˌgraf\ *n* : an instrument for dispersing radiation into a spectrum and recording or mapping the spectrum — **spec·tro·graph·ic** \ˌspek-trə-'gra-fik\ *adj* — **spec·tro·graph·i·cal·ly** \-fi-k(ə-)lē\ *adv*

spec·trom·e·ter \spek-'trä-mə-tər\ *n* : an instrument for measuring spectra — **spec·tro·met·ric** \ˌspek-trə-'me-trik\ *adj* — **spec·trom·e·try** \spek-'trä-mə-trē\ *n*

spec·tro·scope \'spek-trə-ˌskōp\ *n* : an instrument that produces spectra esp. of visible electromagnetic radiation — **spec·tro·scop·ic** \ˌspek-trə-'skä-pik\ *adj* — **spec·tro·scop·i·cal·ly** \-pi-k(ə-)lē\ *adv* — **spec·tros·co·pist** \spek-'träs-kə-pist\ *n* — **spec·tros·co·py** \-pē\ *n*

spec·trum \'spek-trəm\ *n, pl* **spec·tra** \-trə\ *or* **spectrums** [NL, fr. L, appearance, fr. *specere* to look] **1** : a series of colors formed when a beam of white light is dispersed (as by a prism) so that its parts are arranged in the order of their wavelengths **2** : a series of radiations arranged in regular order **3** ♦ : a continuous sequence or range ⟨a wide ∼ of political opinions⟩

♦ gamut, range, scale, spread, stretch — more at RANGE

spec·u·late \'spe-kyə-ˌlāt\ *vb* **-lat·ed; -lat·ing** [L *speculari* to spy out, examine, fr. *specula* watchtower, fr. *specere* to look, look at] **1** ♦ : to think or wonder about a subject **2** : to take a business risk in hope of gain — **spec·u·la·tive·ly** *adv* — **spec·u·la·tor** \-ˌlā-tər\ *n*

♦ assume, conjecture, guess, presume, suppose, surmise, suspect — more at GUESS

spec·u·la·tion \ˌspe-kyə-'lā-shən\ *n* ♦ : an act or instance of speculating

♦ chance, enterprise, flier, gamble, venture — more at GAMBLE

spec·u·la·tive \'spe-kyə-ˌlā-tiv\ *adj* ♦ : involving, based on, or constituting intellectual speculation; *also* : theoretical rather than demonstrable

♦ conjectural, hypothetical, theoretical — more at THEORETICAL

speech \'spēch\ *n* **1** : the act of speaking **2** : TALK, CONVERSATION **3** ♦ : a public talk or lecture **4** : a variety of language identified with a region or group : LANGUAGE **5** : an individual manner of speaking **6** : the power of speaking

♦ address, declamation, harangue, oration, talk; *also* diatribe, rant, tirade; eulogy, panegyric, tribute; lecture; homily, sermon; monologue, soliloquy; pitch, presentation, spiel

speech·less *adj* ♦ : unable to speak; *also* : not speaking

♦ dumb, mum, mute, silent, uncommunicative — more at SILENT

¹speed \'spēd\ *n* **1** *archaic* : SUCCESS **2** ♦ : the act or state of moving swiftly : SWIFTNESS **3** : rate of motion or performance **4** : a transmission gear (as of a bicycle) **5** : METHAMPHETAMINE; *also* : a related drug

♦ celerity, fastness, fleetness, haste, hurry, quickness, rapidity, swiftness, velocity; *also* clip, pace, rate, tempo; drive, hustle; acceleration, rush; dispatch, expedition, promptness *Ant* slowness, sluggishness

²speed *vb* **sped** \'sped\ *or* **speed·ed; speed·ing 1** *archaic* : PROSPER; *also* : GET ALONG, FARE **2** ♦ : to go fast; *esp* : to go at an excessive or illegal speed **3** ♦ : to cause to go faster — **speed·er** *n*

♦ [2] barrel, dash, fly, hurry, hurtle, hustle, pelt, race, rip, rocket, shoot, tear, zip, zoom — more at HURRY
♦ *usu* speed up [3] accelerate, hasten, hurry, quicken, rush, step up, whisk — more at HURRY

speed·boat \-ˌbōt\ *n* : a fast motorboat
speed bump *n* : a low raised ridge across a roadway (as in a parking lot) to limit vehicle speed
speed·i·ly \'spē-də-lē\ *adv* ♦ : in a speedy manner

♦ apace, briskly, fast, full tilt, hastily, posthaste, presto, pronto, quick, quickly, rapidly, soon, swiftly — more at FAST

speed of light : a fundamental physical constant that is the speed of electromagnetic radiation propagation in a vacuum and has the value of 299,792,458 meters per second
speed·om·e·ter \spi-'dä-mə-tər\ *n* : an instrument for indicating speed
speed-up \'spēd-ˌəp\ *n* : ACCELERATION
speed·way \-ˌwā\ *n* : a racecourse for motor vehicles
speed·well \'spēd-ˌwel\ *n* : VERONICA
speedy *adj* ♦ : marked by swiftness of motion or action

♦ breakneck, breathless, brisk, dizzy, fast, fleet, hasty, lightning, nippy, quick, rapid, rattling, snappy, swift — more at FAST

¹spell \'spel\ *vb* **spelled** \'speld, 'spelt\ *or Can and Brit* **spelt** \'spelt\; **spell·ing** [ME, to signify, read by spelling out, fr. AF *espeler*, of Gmc origin] **1** : to name, write, or print in order the letters of a word **2** ♦ : to add up to : MEAN

♦ denote, express, import, mean, signify — more at MEAN

²spell *n* [ME, talk, tale, fr. OE] **1** ♦ : a magic formula : INCANTATION **2** : a compelling influence

♦ bewitchment, charm, conjuration, enchantment, incantation; *also* hex, jinx, curse; conjuring, magic, necromancy, sorcery, witchcraft, witchery, wizardry

³spell *n* **1** : one's turn at work or duty **2** : a stretch of a specified kind of weather **3** ♦ : a period of bodily or mental distress or disorder : ATTACK ⟨a dizzy ∼⟩ **4** ♦ : an indeterminate period of time

♦ [3] attack, bout, case, fit, seizure, siege — more at ATTACK ♦ [4] bit, space, stretch, while — more at WHILE

⁴spell *vb* **spelled** \'speld\; **spell·ing** : to take the place of for a time in work or duty : RELIEVE

⁵spell *vb* **spelled** \'speld\; **spell·ing** : to put under a spell

spell·bind·er \-ˌbīn-dər\ *n* : a speaker of compelling eloquence

spell·bound \-ˌbau̇nd\ *adj* : held by or as if by a spell

spell·check·er \'spel-ˌche-kər\ *n* : a computer program that identifies possible misspellings in a block of text — **spell·check** \-ˌchek\ *vb*

spell·er \'spe-lər\ *n* **1** : one who spells words **2** : a book with exercises for teaching spelling

spell out *vt* **1** ♦ : to make plain **2** : to write or print in letters and in full

♦ clarify, clear (up), construe, demonstrate, elucidate, explain, explicate, expound, illuminate, illustrate, interpret — more at EXPLAIN

spelt \'spelt\ *chiefly Can and Brit past and past part of* ¹SPELL

spe·lunk·er \spi-'lən-kər, 'spē-ˌlən-kər\ *n* [L *spelunca* cave, fr. Gk *spēlynx*] : one who makes a hobby of exploring caves — **spe·lunk·ing** *n*

spend \'spend\ *vb* **spent** \'spent\; **spend·ing 1** ♦ : to pay out : EXPEND **2** : to consume entirely : WEAR OUT, EXHAUST; *also* : to consume wastefully **3** : to cause or permit to elapse : PASS

♦ disburse, expend, give, lay out, pay; *also* lavish, rain; blow; squander, waste

spend·er *n* : one that spends money; *esp* : one that spends lavishly

spend·thrift \'spend-ˌthrift\ *n* ♦ : one who spends wastefully or recklessly

♦ prodigal, profligate, wastrel — more at PRODIGAL

spent \'spent\ *adj* ♦ : drained of energy

♦ beat, bushed, dead, drained, effete, jaded, limp, prostrate, tired, weary, worn-out — more at WEARY

sperm \'spərm\ *n, pl* **sperm** *or* **sperms 1** : SEMEN **2** : a male gamete

sper·ma·to·zo·on \(ˌ)spər-ˌma-tə-'zō-ˌän, -'zō-ən\ *n, pl* **-zoa** \-'zō-ə\ : a motile male gamete of an animal usu. with a rounded or elongated head and a long posterior flagellum

sperm cell *n* : SPERM 2

sper·mi·cide \'spər-mə-ˌsīd\ *n* : a preparation or substance used to kill sperm — **sper·mi·cid·al** \ˌspər-mə-'sī-dəl\ *adj*

sperm whale *n* : a large whale with a massive square-shaped head containing a fluid-filled cavity

spew \'spyü\ *vb* **1** : VOMIT **2** ♦ : to come in a flood or gush; *also* : emit or eject with vigor or violence

♦ gush, jet, pour, rush, spout, spurt, squirt — more at GUSH
♦ belch, disgorge, eject, erupt, expel — more at ERUPT

SPF *abbr* sun protection factor

sp gr *abbr* specific gravity

sphag·num \'sfag-nəm\ *n* : any of a genus of atypical mosses that grow in wet acid areas where their remains become compacted with other plant debris to form peat; *also* : a mass of these mosses

sphere \'sfir\ *n* [ME *spere* globe, celestial sphere, fr. AF *espere*, fr. L *sphaera*, fr. Gk *sphaira*, lit., ball] **1** ♦ : a globe-shaped body : BALL **2** : a celestial body **3** : a solid figure so shaped that every point on its surface is an equal distance from the center **4** ♦ : range of action or influence — **spher·i·cal** \'sfir-i-kəl, 'sfer-\ *adj* — **spher·i·cal·ly** \-i-k(ə-)lē\ *adv*

♦ [1] ball, orb — more at BALL ♦ [4] area, arena, demesne, department, discipline, domain, field, line, province, realm, specialty — more at FIELD

spher·oid \'sfir-ˌoid, 'sfer-\ *n* : a figure similar to a sphere but not perfectly round — **sphe·roi·dal** \sfir-'oi-dəl\ *adj*

sphinc·ter \'sfiŋk-tər\ *n* : a muscular ring that closes a bodily opening

sphinx \'sfiŋks\ *n, pl* **sphinx·es** *or* **sphin·ges** \'sfin-jēz\ **1** : a winged monster in Greek mythology having a woman's head and a lion's body and noted for killing anyone unable to answer its riddle **2** : an enigmatic or mysterious person **3** : an ancient Egyptian image having the body of a lion and the head of a man, ram, or hawk

¹spice \'spīs\ *n* **1** ♦ : any of various aromatic plant products (as pepper or nutmeg) used to season or flavor foods **2** : something that adds interest and relish **3** ♦ : a pungent or fragrant odor

♦ [1] flavor (*or* flavour), seasoning — more at SEASONING ♦ [3] aroma, bouquet, fragrance, incense, perfume, redolence, scent — more at FRAGRANCE

²spice *vb* **spiced**; **spic·ing** ♦ : to season with spices

♦ flavor (*or* flavour), savor, season — more at SEASON

spick–and–span *or* **spic–and–span** \ˌspik-ənd-'span\ *adj* **1** ♦ : quite new **2** ♦ : spotlessly clean

♦ [1] brand-new, new, unused — more at NEW ♦ [2] clean, immaculate, spotless, stainless, unsoiled, unsullied — more at CLEAN

spic·ule \'spi-kyül\ *n* : a slender pointed body esp. of calcium or silica ⟨sponge ~s⟩

spicy *adj* **1** : having the quality, flavor, or fragrance of spice **2** ♦ : verging on impropriety or indecency; *also* : somewhat scandalous or salacious

♦ bawdy, lewd, racy, ribald, suggestive — more at SUGGESTIVE

spi·der \'spī-dər\ *n* **1** : any of an order of arachnids that have a 2-part body, eight legs, and two or more pairs of abdominal organs for spinning threads of silk used esp. in making webs for catching prey **2** : a cast-iron frying pan — **spi·dery** *adj*

spider mite *n* : any of various small web-spinning mites that feed on and are pests of plants

spider plant *n* : a houseplant of the lily family having long green leaves usu. striped with white and producing tufts of small plants on long hanging stems

spi·der·web \'spī-dər-ˌweb\ *n* : the web spun by a spider

spiel \'spēl\ *vb* : to talk in a fast, smooth, and usu. colorful manner — **spiel** *n*

spig·ot \'spi-gət, -kət\ *n* ♦ : a fixture for drawing or regulating the flow of liquid esp. from a pipe

♦ cock, faucet, gate, tap, valve — more at FAUCET

¹spike \'spīk\ *n* **1** : a very large nail **2** : any of various pointed projections (as on the sole of a shoe to prevent slipping) — **spiky** *adj*

²spike *vb* **spiked**; **spik·ing 1** : to fasten with spikes **2** : to put an end to : QUASH ⟨~ a rumor⟩ **3** ♦ : to pierce with or impale on a spike **4** : to add alcoholic liquor to (a drink)

♦ gore, harpoon, impale, lance, pierce, puncture, skewer, spear, stab, stick, transfix — more at IMPALE

³spike *n* **1** : an ear of grain **2** : a long cluster of usu. stemless flowers

¹spill \'spil\ *vb* **spilled** \'spild, 'spilt\ *also* **spilt** \'spilt\; **spill·ing 1** : to cause or allow to fall, flow, or run out esp. unintentionally **2** : to cause (blood) to be lost by wounding **3** : to run out or over with resulting loss or waste **4** ♦ : to let out : DIVULGE — **spill·able** *adj*

♦ bare, disclose, discover, divulge, expose, reveal, tell, unbosom, uncloak, uncover, unmask, unveil — more at REVEAL

²spill *n* **1** ♦ : an act of spilling; *also* : a fall from a horse or vehicle or an erect position **2** : something spilled

♦ fall, slip, stumble, tumble — more at FALL

spill·way \-ˌwā\ *n* : a passage for surplus water to run over or around an obstruction (as a dam)

¹spin \'spin\ *vb* **spun** \'spən\; **spin·ning 1** : to draw out (fiber) and twist into thread; *also* : to form (thread) by such means **2** : to form thread by extruding a sticky quickly hardening fluid; *also* : to construct from such thread ⟨spiders ~ their webs⟩ **3** : to produce slowly and by degrees ⟨~ a story⟩ **4** ♦ : to revolve rapidly : TWIRL; *also* : to cause to whirl **5** : to feel as if in a whirl : WHIRL, REEL ⟨my head is *spinning*⟩ **6** : to move rapidly along **7** : to present (as information) with a particular spin — **spin·ner** *n*

♦ gyrate, pirouette, revolve, roll, rotate, turn, twirl, wheel, whirl; *also* coil, curl, curve, round, spiral, twine, twist, wind; circle, orbit

²spin *n* **1** ♦ : a rapid rotating motion **2** : an excursion in a wheeled vehicle **3** : a particular point of view, emphasis, or interpretation **4** ♦ : a state of mental confusion

♦ [1] gyration, pirouette, reel, revolution, roll, rotation, twirl, wheel, whirl; *also* circuit, circulation; coil, curl, curve, spiral, twist; circle, orbit; eddy, swirl ♦ [4] daze, fog, haze, muddle — more at HAZE

spi·na bi·fi·da \ˌspī-nə-ˈbi-fə-də\ *n* : a birth defect in which the spinal column has a fissure

spin·ach \ˈspi-nich\ *n* : a dark green herb grown for its edible leaves

spi·nal \ˈspīn-ᵊl\ *adj* : of or relating to the backbone or spinal cord — **spi·nal·ly** *adv*

spinal column *n* : the bony column in the back of a vertebrate that extends from the neck to the tail and protects the spinal cord : BACKBONE

spinal cord *n* : the thick cord of nervous tissue that extends from the brain along the back in the cavity of the backbone and carries nerve impulses to and from the brain

spinal nerve *n* : any of the paired nerves which arise from the spinal cord and pass to various parts of the body and of which there are normally 31 pairs in human beings

spin control *n* : the act or practice of attempting to manipulate the way an event is interpreted

spin·dle \ˈspind-ᵊl\ *n* **1** : a round tapering stick or rod by which fibers are twisted in spinning **2** : a turned part of a piece of furniture ⟨the ∼s of a chair⟩ **3** : a slender pin or rod which turns or on which something else turns

spin·dling \ˈspind-liŋ\ *adj* : of a disproportionately tall or long and thin appearance : SPINDLY

spin·dly \ˈspind-lē\ *adj* ♦ : being long or tall and thin and usu. weak

♦ gangling, lanky, rangy — more at LANKY

spin·drift \ˈspin-ˌdrift\ *n* : spray blown from waves

spine \ˈspīn\ *n* **1** ♦ : the bony column in the back of a vertebrate that extends from the neck to the tail and protects the spinal cord : BACKBONE **2** : a stiff sharp process esp. on a plant or animal **3** : the part of a book where the pages are attached

♦ backbone, vertebral column; *also* back, spinal cord, vertebra

spi·nel \spə-ˈnel\ *n* : a hard crystalline mineral of variable color used as a gem

spine·less \ˈspīn-ləs\ *adj* **1** : having no spines, thorns, or prickles **2** : lacking a backbone **3** ♦ : lacking courage or determination ⟨a ∼ politician⟩

♦ chicken, cowardly, craven, dastardly, pusillanimous, recreant, yellow — more at COWARDLY ♦ effete, frail, nerveless, soft, weak, wimpy, wishy-washy — more at WEAK

spin·et \ˈspi-nət\ *n* **1** : an early harpsichord having a single keyboard and only one string for each note **2** : a small upright piano

spin·na·ker \ˈspi-ni-kər\ *n* : a large triangular sail set on a long light pole

spinning jen·ny \-ˈje-nē\ *n* : an early multiple-spindle machine for spinning wool or cotton

spinning wheel *n* : a small machine for spinning thread or yarn in which a large wheel drives a single spindle

spin-off \ˈspin-ˌȯf\ *n* **1** ♦ : a usu. useful by-product **2** : something (as a TV show) derived from an earlier work — **spin off** *vb*

♦ derivative, offshoot, outgrowth — more at DERIVATIVE

spin·ster \ˈspin-stər\ *n* : an unmarried woman past the common age for marrying — **spin·ster·hood** \-ˌhu̇d\ *n*

spiny *adj* **1** ♦ : abounding with difficulties, obstacles, or annoyances **2** : covered or armed with spines

♦ catchy, delicate, difficult, knotty, problematic, thorny, ticklish, touchy, tough, tricky — more at TRICKY

spiny lobster *n* : any of several edible crustaceans differing from the related lobsters in lacking the large front claws and in having a spiny carapace

¹spi·ral \ˈspī-rəl\ *adj* ♦ : winding or coiling around a center or axis and usu. getting closer to or farther away from it — **spi·ral·ly** *adv*

♦ helical, winding; *also* curving, curling, twisting

²spiral *n* **1** : something that has a spiral form; *also* : a single turn in a spiral object **2** : a continuously spreading and accelerating increase or decrease

³spiral *vb* **-raled** *or* **-ralled; -ral·ing** *or* **-ral·ling** **1** ♦ : to move and esp. to rise or fall in a spiral course **2** : to form into a spiral

♦ coil, curl, entwine, twine, twist, wind — more at WIND

spi·rant \ˈspī-rənt\ *n* : a consonant (as \f\, \s\, \sh\) uttered with decided friction of the breath against some part of the oral passage — **spirant** *adj*

spire \ˈspī(ə)r\ *n* **1** : a slender tapering stalk (as of grass) **2** : a pointed tip (as of an antler) **3** : STEEPLE — **spiry** *adj*

spi·rea *or* **spi·raea** \spī-ˈrē-ə\ *n* : any of a genus of shrubs related to the roses with dense clusters of small usu. white or pink flowers

¹spir·it \ˈspir-ət\ *n* [ME, fr. OF or L; OF, fr. L *spiritus*, lit., breath, fr. *spirare* to blow, breathe] **1** : a life-giving force; *also* : the animating principle : SOUL **2** *cap* : HOLY SPIRIT **3** ♦ : an often malevolent being that is bodiless but can become visible : GHOST **4** : PERSON **5** ♦ : an inclination, impulse, or tendency of a specified kind : MOOD **6** ♦ : a lively or brisk quality in a person or a person's actions **7** : essential or real meaning : INTENT **8** ♦ : distilled alcoholic liquor — often used in pl. **9** : LOYALTY ⟨school ∼⟩

♦ [3] apparition, bogey, ghost, phantasm, phantom, poltergeist, shade, shadow, specter, spook, vision, wraith — more at GHOST ♦ [5] cheer, frame, humor (*or* humour), mode, mood, temper — more at MOOD ♦ [6] bounce, dash, drive, esprit, ginger, pep, punch, snap, verve, vim, zing, zip; *also* animation, briskness, jauntiness, liveliness, vivaciousness, vivacity; ardor, fervor, fire, passion, zeal; eagerness, enthusiasm; energy, vitality ♦ **spirits** [8] alcohol, booze, drink, intoxicant, liquor, moonshine — more at ALCOHOL

²spirit *vb* : to carry off secretly or mysteriously

spir·it·ed \ˈspir-ə-təd\ *adj* **1** ♦ : full of energy or animation : ANIMATED **2** : full of courage : COURAGEOUS

♦ active, animate, animated, brisk, energetic, frisky, lively, peppy, sprightly, springy, vital, vivacious — more at LIVELY ♦ fiery, high-spirited, mettlesome, peppery, spunky *Ant* spiritless

spir·it·less *adj* ♦ : lacking animation, cheerfulness, or courage

♦ enervated, lackadaisical, languid, languorous, limp, listless — more at LISTLESS

¹spir·i·tu·al \ˈspir-i-chəl, -chə-wəl\ *adj* **1** ♦ : of, relating to, consisting of, or affecting the spirit : INCORPOREAL ⟨∼ needs⟩ **2** ♦ : of or relating to sacred matters **3** : ecclesiastical rather than lay or temporal — **spir·i·tu·al·i·ty** \ˌspir-i-chə-ˈwa-lə-tē\ *n* — **spir·i·tu·al·ize** \ˈspir-i-chə-ˌlīz, -chə-wə-\ *vb* — **spir·i·tu·al·ly** *adv*

♦ [1] bodiless, immaterial, incorporeal, insubstantial, nonmaterial, nonphysical, unsubstantial — more at IMMATERIAL ♦ [2] devotional, religious, sacred — more at RELIGIOUS

²spiritual *n* ♦ : a religious song originating among African Americans of the southern U.S.

♦ anthem, canticle, carol, chorale, hymn, psalm — more at HYMN

spir·i·tu·al·ism \ˈspir-i-chə-ˌli-zəm, -chə-wə-\ *n* : a belief that spirits of the dead communicate with the living usu. through a medium — **spir·i·tu·al·ist** \-list\ *n, often cap* — **spir·i·tu·al·is·tic** \ˌspir-i-chə-ˈlis-tik, -chə-wə-\ *adj*

spir·i·tu·ous \ˈspir-i-chəs, -chə-wəs; ˈspir-ə-təs\ *adj* : containing alcohol

spi·ro·chete *also* **spi·ro·chaete** \ˈspī-rə-ˌkēt\ *n* : any of an order of spirally undulating bacteria including those causing syphilis and Lyme disease

spirt *var of* SPURT

¹spit \'spit\ *n* **1** : a thin pointed rod for holding meat over a fire **2** ♦ : a point of land that runs out into the water

♦ arm, cape, headland, peninsula, point, promontory — more at CAPE

²spit *vb* **spit·ted; spit·ting** : to pierce with or as if with a spit

³spit *vb* **spit** *or* **spat** \'spat\; **spit·ting** **1** : to eject (saliva) from the mouth **2** : to express by or as if by spitting **3** : to rain or snow lightly

⁴spit *n* **1** : a watery digestive secretion that is secreted into the mouth by salivary glands : SALIVA **2** ♦ : perfect likeness ⟨∼ and image of his father⟩

♦ carbon copy, counterpart, double, duplicate, duplication, facsimile, image, likeness, match, picture, replica, ringer — more at IMAGE

spit·ball \'spit-,bȯl\ *n* **1** : paper chewed and rolled into a ball to be thrown as a missile **2** : a baseball pitch delivered after the ball has been moistened with saliva or sweat

¹spite \'spīt\ *n* ♦ : ill will with a wish to annoy, anger, or frustrate : petty malice — **in spite of** : in defiance or contempt of : NOTWITHSTANDING

♦ cattiness, despite, hatefulness, malice, malignity, meanness, nastiness, spleen, venom, viciousness — more at MALICE

²spite *vb* **spit·ed; spit·ing** ♦ : to treat maliciously : ANNOY, OFFEND

♦ aggravate, annoy, bother, bug, chafe, exasperate, gall, get, grate, irk, irritate, nettle, peeve, persecute, pique, put out, rasp, rile, ruffle, vex — more at IRRITATE

spite·ful \-fəl\ *adj* ♦ : filled with or showing spite — **spite·ful·ness** *n*

♦ catty, cruel, hateful, malevolent, malicious, malign, malignant, mean, nasty, virulent — more at HATEFUL

spite·ful·ly *adv* ♦ : filled with or showing spite

♦ hatefully, maliciously, meanly, nastily, viciously, wickedly — more at NASTILY

spit·tle \'spit-ᵊl\ *n* : a watery digestive secretion that is secreted into the mouth by salivary glands : SALIVA

spit·tle·bug \-,bəg\ *n* : any of a family of leaping insects with froth-secreting larvae that are related to aphids

spit·toon \spi-'tün\ *n* : a receptacle for spit

spit up *vb* ♦ : to disgorge (the contents of the stomach) through the mouth

♦ gag, heave, throw up, vomit — more at VOMIT

splash \'splash\ *vb* **1** ♦ : to dash a liquid about **2** : to scatter a liquid on : SPATTER **3** : to fall, move, or strike with a splashing noise — **splash** *n*

♦ [1] lap, plash, slosh, swash — more at SLOSH
♦ [2] dash, plash, spatter; *also* drench, drown, impregnate, saturate, soak, sop, souse, steep; bathe, douse, wash, water, wet; throw; spray; slop, sprinkle; squirt

splash·down \'splash-,daun\ *n* : the landing of a manned spacecraft in the ocean — **splash down** *vb*

splashy \'spla-shē\ *adj* **splash·i·er; -est** : conspicuously showy : OSTENTATIOUS

splat·ter \'spla-tər\ *vb* : to splash with or as if with a liquid : SPATTER — **splatter** *n*

¹splay \'splā\ *vb* : to spread outward or apart — **splay** *n*

²splay *adj* **1** : spread out : turned outward **2** : AWKWARD, CLUMSY

spleen \'splēn\ *n* **1** : a vascular organ located near the stomach in most vertebrates that is concerned esp. with the filtration and storage of blood, destruction of red blood cells, and production of lymphocytes **2** ♦ : feelings of anger or ill will often suppressed

♦ anger, cattiness, despite, hatefulness, malice, malignity, meanness, nastiness, spite, venom, viciousness — more at MALICE

splen·did \'splen-dəd\ *adj* [L *splendidus*, fr. *splendēre* to

shine] **1** : SHINING, BRILLIANT **2** : SHOWY, GORGEOUS **3** ♦ : fine or imposing in appearance or impression **4** : very good of its kind : EXCELLENT

♦ august, baronial, gallant, glorious, grand, grandiose, heroic, imposing, magnificent, majestic, monumental, noble, proud, regal, royal, stately — more at GRAND

splen·did·ly *adv* ♦ : in a splendid manner

♦ agreeably, delightfully, favorably (*or* favourably), felicitously, gloriously, nicely, pleasantly, pleasingly, satisfyingly, well

splen·dor *or Can and Brit* **splen·dour** \'splen-dər\ *n* **1** ♦ : great brightness or luster : BRILLIANCE **2** ♦ : a display of magnificence

♦ [1] brilliance, dazzle, effulgence, illumination, lightness, lucidity, luminosity, radiance, refulgence — more at BRILLIANCE ♦ [2] augustness, brilliance, glory, grandeur, grandness, magnificence, majesty, nobility, nobleness, resplendence, stateliness — more at MAGNIFICENCE

sple·net·ic \spli-'ne-tik\ *adj* ♦ : marked by bad temper or spite

♦ bearish, bilious, cantankerous, disagreeable, dyspeptic, ill-humored, ill-tempered, ornery, surly — more at ILL-TEMPERED

splen·ic \'sple-nik\ *adj* : of, relating to, or located in the spleen

splice \'splīs\ *vb* **spliced; splic·ing** **1** : to unite (as two ropes) by weaving the strands together **2** : to unite (as two lengths of film) by connecting the ends together — **splice** *n*

splint \'splint\ *n* **1** : a thin strip of wood interwoven with others to make something (as a basket) **2** : material or a device used to protect and keep in place an injured body part (as a broken arm) **3** : a thin piece split or broken off lengthwise

¹splin·ter \'splin-tər\ *n* ♦ : a thin piece of something split off lengthwise : SLIVER

♦ chip, flake — more at CHIP

²splinter *vb* : to split into splinters

¹split \'split\ *vb* **split; split·ting** **1** : to divide lengthwise or along a grain or seam **2** : to burst or break in pieces **3** ♦ : to divide into parts or sections **4** : LEAVE

♦ break up, disconnect, disjoint, dissever, dissociate, disunite, divide, divorce, part, resolve, separate, sever, sunder, unyoke — more at SEPARATE

²split *n* **1** ♦ : a narrow break made by or as if by splitting **2** ♦ : the act or process of splitting

♦ [1] chink, cleft, crack, cranny, crevice, fissure, rift — more at CRACK ♦ [2] breakup, dissolution, division, partition, schism, separation — more at SEPARATION

split–lev·el \'split-'le-vəl\ *n* : a house divided so that the floor in one part is about halfway between two floors in the other

split personality *n* : SCHIZOPHRENIA; *also* : MULTIPLE PERSONALITY DISORDER

split–second \'split-'se-kənd\ *adj* **1** ♦ : occurring in a very brief time **2** : extremely precise ⟨∼ timing⟩

♦ immediate, instant, instantaneous, straightaway — more at INSTANTANEOUS

split·ting *adj* : causing a piercing sensation ⟨a ∼ headache⟩

splotch \'spläch\ *n* : a small area visibly different (as in color, finish, or material) from the surrounding area : BLOTCH

splurge \'splərj\ *vb* **splurged; splurg·ing** : to spend more than usual esp. on oneself — **splurge** *n*

splut·ter \'splə-tər\ *n* : SPUTTER — **splutter** *vb*

¹spoil \'spȯil\ *n* ♦ : plunder taken from an enemy in war or from a victim in robbery ⟨∼s of war⟩

♦ booty, loot, plunder, swag — more at LOOT

²spoil *vb* **spoiled** \'spȯild, 'spȯilt\ *or* **spoilt** \'spȯilt\; **spoil·ing**

1 : ROB, PILLAGE 2 : to damage seriously : RUIN 3 ♦ : to impair the quality or effect of 4 ♦ : to damage the disposition of by pampering; *also* : INDULGE, CODDLE 5 ♦ : to lose valuable or useful qualities usu. as a result of decay : DECAY, ROT 6 : to have an eager desire ⟨~ing for a fight⟩

♦ [3] blemish, mar, poison, stain, taint, tarnish, touch, vitiate — more at TAINT ♦ [4] baby, coddle, indulge, mollycoddle, nurse, pamper — more at BABY ♦ [5] break down, corrupt, decay, decompose, disintegrate, molder, putrefy, rot — more at DECAY

spoil·age \'spȯi-lij\ *n* ♦ : the act or process of spoiling

♦ breakdown, corruption, decay, decomposition, putrefaction, rot — more at CORRUPTION

spoil·er \'spȯi-lər\ *n* 1 : one that spoils 2 : a device (as on an airplane or automobile) used to disrupt airflow and decrease lift 3 : information about a movie or TV plot that can spoil a viewer's sense of surprise or suspense

spoil·sport \'spȯil-ˌspōrt\ *n* : one who spoils the fun of others

¹**spoke** \'spōk\ *past & archaic past part of* SPEAK

²**spoke** *n* : any of the rods extending from the hub of a wheel to the rim

spo·ken *adj* ♦ : delivered by word of mouth; *also* : characterized by speaking in (such) a manner

♦ oral, unwritten, verbal — more at VERBAL

spokes·man \'spōks-mən\ *n* ♦ : a person who speaks as the representative of another or others

♦ mouthpiece, speaker, spokesperson, spokeswoman

spokes·per·son \-ˌpər-sən\ *n* ♦ : a person who speaks as the representative of another or others : SPOKESMAN

♦ mouthpiece, speaker, spokesman, spokeswoman; *also* talker; agent, delegate, deputy, representative

spokes·wom·an \-ˌwu̇-mən\ *n* ♦ : a woman who speaks as the representative of another or others

♦ mouthpiece, speaker, spokesman, spokesperson

spo·li·a·tion \ˌspō-lē-'ā-shən\ *n* : the act of plundering : the state of being plundered

¹**sponge** \'spənj\ *n* 1 : an elastic porous water-absorbing mass of fibers that forms the skeleton of various primitive sea animals; *also* : any of a phylum of chiefly marine sea animals that are the source of natural sponges 2 : a spongelike or porous mass or material 3 ♦ : one who lives on others

♦ hanger-on, leech, parasite — more at LEECH

²**sponge** *vb* **sponged**; **spong·ing** 1 : to bathe or wipe with a sponge 2 : to live at another's expense 3 : to gather sponges 4 ♦ : to absorb with or as if with or in the manner of a sponge

♦ absorb, drink, imbibe, soak, suck — more at ABSORB

sponge cake *n* : a light cake made without shortening

spong·er *n* : one that sponges

sponge rubber *n* : a cellular rubber resembling natural sponge

spongy \'spən-jē\ *adj* 1 : resembling a sponge 2 ♦ : not firm or solid

♦ flabby, mushy, pulpy, soft — more at SOFT

spon·sor \'spän-sər\ *n* [LL, fr. L, guarantor, surety, fr. *spondēre* to promise] 1 ♦ : one who takes the responsibility for some other person or thing : SURETY 2 : GODPARENT 3 : a business firm that pays the cost of a radio or television program usu. in return for advertising time during its course — **sponsor** *vb* — **spon·sor·ship** *n*

♦ backer, guarantor, patron, surety; *also* chaperon; advocate, champion, supporter; benefactor; coach, mentor, teacher

spon·ta·ne·ity \ˌspän-tə-'nē-ə-tē, -'nā-\ *n* ♦ : the quality or state of being spontaneous

♦ abandon, abandonment, ease, lightheartedness, naturalness, unrestraint — more at ABANDON

spon·ta·ne·ous \spän-'tā-nē-əs\ *adj* [LL *spontaneus*, fr.

L *sponte* of one's free will, voluntarily] 1 ♦ : done or produced freely or naturally 2 : acting or taking place without external force or cause — **spon·ta·ne·ous·ly** *adv*

♦ automatic, involuntary, mechanical, natural — more at AUTOMATIC

spontaneous combustion *n* : a bursting into flame of material through heat produced within itself by chemical action (as oxidation)

¹**spoof** \'spüf\ *vb* 1 : DECEIVE, HOAX 2 : to make good-natured fun of ⟨the movie ~s horror films⟩ — **spoof** *n*

²**spoof** *n* ♦ : a light humorous parody

♦ burlesque, caricature, parody, takeoff — more at PARODY

¹**spook** \'spük\ *n* 1 : a disembodied soul : GHOST 2 : SPY 2

²**spook** *vb* ♦ : to make frightened or frantic : FRIGHTEN

♦ alarm, frighten, horrify, panic, scare, shock, startle, terrify, terrorize — more at FRIGHTEN

spooky *adj* 1 ♦ : relating to, resembling, or suggesting spooks 2 ♦ : easily frightened

♦ [1] creepy, eerie, haunting, uncanny, unearthly, weird — more at EERIE ♦ [2] excitable, flighty, fluttery, high-strung, jittery, jumpy, nervous, skittish — more at EXCITABLE

spool \'spül\ *n* : a cylinder on which flexible material (as thread) is wound

¹**spoon** \'spün\ *n* [ME, fr. OE *spōn* splinter, chip] 1 ♦ : an eating or cooking implement consisting of a small shallow bowl with a handle 2 : a metal piece used on a fishing line as a lure — **spoon·ful** *n*

♦ ladle, scoop; *also* skimmer

²**spoon** *vb* ♦ : to take up and usu. transfer in a spoon

♦ dip, ladle, scoop — more at DIP

spoon·bill \'spün-ˌbil\ *n* : any of several wading birds related to the ibises having a bill with a broad flat tip

spoon–feed \-ˌfēd\ *vb* **-fed** \-ˌfed\; **-feed·ing** : to feed by means of a spoon

spoor \'spu̇r, 'spȯr\ *n, pl* **spoor** *or* **spoors** : a track, a trail, a scent, or droppings esp. of a wild animal

spo·rad·ic \spə-'ra-dik\ *adj* ♦ : occurring now and then — **spo·rad·i·cal·ly** \-di-k(ə-)lē\ *adv*

♦ casual, choppy, discontinuous, erratic, fitful, intermittent, irregular, occasional, spasmodic, spotty, unsteady — more at FITFUL

spore \'spōr\ *n* : a primitive usu. one-celled often environmentally resistant dormant or reproductive body produced by plants, fungi, and some microorganisms

spork \'spȯrk\ *n* : an eating utensil that combines the bowl of a spoon with the tines of a fork

¹**sport** \'spōrt\ *vb* [ME, to divert, amuse, short for *disporten*, fr. AF *desporter*, to carry away, comfort, entertain, fr. *des-* (fr. L *dis-* apart) + *porter* to carry, fr. L *portare*] 1 ♦ : to amuse oneself : FROLIC 2 ♦ : to display or wear usu. ostentatiously : SHOW OFF

♦ [1] caper, cavort, disport, frisk, frolic, gambol, lark, play, rollick, romp — more at FROLIC ♦ [2] display, disport, exhibit, expose, flash, flaunt, parade, show, show off, strut, unveil — more at SHOW

²**sport** *n* 1 ♦ : a source of diversion 2 : physical activity engaged in for pleasure 3 : a frivolous mood or manner : JEST 4 : MOCKERY ⟨make ~ of his efforts⟩ 5 : BUTT, LAUGHINGSTOCK 6 : one who accepts results cheerfully whether favorable or not 7 : an individual exhibiting marked deviation from its normal type esp. as a result of mutation — **sporty** *adj*

♦ dalliance, frolic, fun, play, relaxation — more at PLAY

³**sport** *or* **sports** *adj* : of, relating to, or suitable for sport or casual wear ⟨~ coats⟩

sport fish *n* : a fish noted for the sport it affords anglers

sport·ive \'spȯr-tiv\ *adj* ♦ : full of gaiety : full of play

♦ antic, coltish, elfish, fay, frisky, frolicsome, playful — more at PLAYFUL

sports car *n* : a small and low car that usu. seats two people and that is made for fast driving

sports•cast \\'spȯrts-ˌkast\ *n* : a broadcast dealing with sports events — **sports•cast•er** \-ˌkas-tər\ *n*

sports•man \\'spȯrts-mən\ *n* **1** : a person who engages in sports (as in hunting or fishing) **2** : one who plays fairly and wins or loses gracefully — **sports•man•ship** *n*

sports•man•like \-ˌlīk\ *adj* ♦ : consistent with the ideals of good sportsmanship

♦ clean, fair, legal

sports medicine *n* : a field of medicine dealing with the prevention and treatment of sports-related injuries

sports•wom•an \-ˌwu̇-mən\ *n* : a woman who engages in sports

sports•writ•er \-ˌrī-tər\ *n* : one who writes about sports esp. for a newspaper — **sports•writ•ing** *n*

sport–util•ity vehicle \\'spȯrt-yü-'ti-lə-tē-\ *n* : SUV

¹spot \\'spät\ *n* **1** : a taint on character or reputation : STAIN **2** ♦ : a small part different (as in color) from the main part **3** ♦ : a particular place, area, or part : LOCA-TION **4** ♦ : a position usu. of difficulty or embarrassment **5** : a small quantity or amount — **on the spot 1** : at the place of action **2** : in difficulty or danger

♦ [2] blotch, dapple, dot, fleck, mottle, patch, point, speck; *also* birthmark, freckle, mole; blot, mark, smear, smudge, stain; spatter, splash ♦ [3] locale, location, place, point, position, site — more at PLACE ♦ [4] corner, fix, hole, jam, pickle, predicament — more at PRE-DICAMENT

²spot *vb* **spot•ted; spot•ting 1** ♦ : to mark or disfigure with spots **2** : to pick out : RECOGNIZE, IDENTIFY

♦ blotch, dapple, dot, fleck, freckle, mottle, pepper, speck, sprinkle, stipple; *also* marble; dye, stain; streak, stripe; intersperse, stud; bespatter, spatter

³spot *adj* **1** : being, done, or originating on the spot ⟨a ∼ broadcast⟩ **2** : paid upon delivery **3** : made at random or at a few key points ⟨a ∼ check⟩

spot–check \\'spät-ˌchek\ *vb* : to make a spot check of

spot•less *adj* ♦ : having no spot : free from impurity, fault, or stain — **spot•less•ly** *adv*

♦ clean, immaculate, spick-and-span, stainless, unsoiled, unsullied — more at CLEAN

spot•light \-ˌlīt\ *n* **1** : a circle of brilliant light projected upon a particular area, person, or object (as on a stage); *also* : the device that produces this light **2** : public notice — **spotlight** *vb*

spot–on \\'spät-'än\ *adj* : exactly correct ⟨a ∼ forecast⟩

spotted *adj* ♦ : having spots

♦ dappled, mottled, pied, spotty, variegated; *also* moiré, veined; motley, multicolored; piebald, roan

spotted owl *n* : a rare large dark brown dark-eyed owl of humid old growth forests and thickly wooded canyons from British Columbia to southern California and central Mexico

spot•ter \\'spä-tər\ *n* **1** : one that keeps watch : OBSERVER **2** : one that removes spots

spot•ty \\'spä-tē\ *adj* **spot•ti•er; -est 1** ♦ : uneven in quality; *also* : sparsely distributed ⟨∼ attendance⟩ **2** : marked with spots : SPOTTED

♦ casual, choppy, discontinuous, erratic, fitful, intermittent, irregular, occasional, spasmodic, sporadic, unsteady — more at FITFUL

spou•sal \\'spau̇-zəl, -səl\ *n* : MARRIAGE 2, WEDDING — usu. used in pl.

spouse \\'spau̇s\ *n* ♦ : one's partner in a marriage (as husband or wife) — **spou•sal** \\'spau̇-zəl, -səl\ *adj*

♦ consort, mate, partner; *also* husband, wife

¹spout \\'spau̇t\ *vb* **1** ♦ : to eject or issue forth forcibly and freely ⟨∼*ing* oil⟩ **2** ♦ : to speak pompously **3** ♦ : to speak or utter readily, volubly, and at length

♦ [1] gush, jet, pour, rush, spew, spurt, squirt — more at GUSH ♦ [1] belch, disgorge, eject, erupt, expel — more

at ERUPT ♦ [2, 3] bluster, fulminate, rant, rave — more at RANT ♦ *usu* **spout off** [3] sound off, speak out, speak up

²spout *n* **1** : a pipe or hole through which liquid spouts **2** : a jet of liquid; *esp* : WATERSPOUT 2

spp *abbr* species (*pl*)

¹sprain \\'sprān\ *n* : a sudden or severe twisting of a joint with stretching or tearing of ligaments; *also* : a sprained condition

²sprain *vb* : to subject to sprain

sprat \\'sprat\ *n* : a small European fish related to the herring; *also* : SARDINE

sprawl \\'sprȯl\ *vb* **1** : to lie or sit with limbs spread out awkwardly **2** : to spread out irregularly — **sprawl** *n*

¹spray \\'sprā\ *n* : a usu. flowering branch; *also* : a decorative arrangement of flowers and foliage

²spray *n* **1** : liquid flying in small drops like water blown from a wave **2** : a jet of fine vapor (as from an atomizer) **3** : an instrument (as an atomizer) for scattering fine liquid

³spray *vb* **1** ♦ : to scatter or let fall in a spray **2** : to discharge spray on or into — **spray•er** *n*

♦ dot, pepper, scatter, sow, sprinkle, strew — more at SCATTER

spray can *n* : a pressurized container from which aerosols are sprayed

spray gun *n* : a device for spraying liquids (as paint or insecticide)

¹spread \\'spred\ *vb* **spread; spread•ing 1** : to scatter over a surface **2** ♦ : to flatten out : open out **3** ♦ : to distribute over a period of time or among many persons **4** : to cover something with ⟨∼ rugs on the floor⟩ **5** : to prepare for a meal ⟨∼ a table⟩ **6** ♦ : to pass on from person to person **7** : to stretch, force, or push apart ⟨a bird ∼*ing* its wings⟩ **8** ♦ : to make widely known — **spread•er** *n*

♦ *usu* **spread out** [2] expand, extend, fan, flare, open, stretch, unfold ♦ [3] broadcast, circulate, disseminate, propagate, strew; *also* radiate; diffuse, dispense, disperse, dissipate, scatter, sow; communicate, pass (on), transmit ♦ [6, 8] communicate, convey, impart, transfer, transfuse, transmit — more at COMMUNICATE

²spread *n* **1** : the act or process of spreading **2** ♦ : a surface area : EXPANSE **3** : a prominent display in a periodical **4** : a food to be spread on bread or crackers **5** ♦ : a cloth cover for a bed **6** ♦ : distance between two points **7** ♦ : a sumptuous meal

♦ [2] breadth, expanse, extent, reach, stretch — more at EXPANSE ♦ [5] bedspread, counterpane — more at COUNTERPANE ♦ [6] distance, lead, length, remove, stretch, way — more at DISTANCE ♦ [7] banquet, dinner, feast, feed — more at FEAST

spread•sheet \\'spred-ˌshēt\ *n* : an accounting program for a computer

spree \\'sprē\ *n* : an unrestrained outburst ⟨buying ∼⟩; *also* : a drinking bout

sprig \\'sprig\ *n* : a small shoot or twig

spright•li•ness \\'sprīt-lē-nes\ *n* ♦ : the quality or state of being sprightly

♦ animation, briskness, exuberance, liveliness, lustiness, robustness, vibrancy, vitality — more at VITALITY

spright•ly \\'sprīt-lē\ *adj* **spright•li•er; -est** ♦ : marked by a gay lightness and vivacity : LIVELY

♦ active, animate, animated, brisk, energetic, frisky, gay, lively, peppy, spirited, springy, vital, vivacious — more at LIVELY

¹spring \\'spriŋ\ *vb* **sprang** \\'spraŋ\ *or* **sprung** \\'sprəŋ\; **sprung; spring•ing 1** ♦ : to move suddenly upward or forward **2** : to grow quickly ⟨weeds *sprang* up overnight⟩ **3** : to come from by birth or descent **4** : to move quickly by elastic force **5** : WARP **6** : to develop (a leak) through the seams **7** : to cause to close suddenly ⟨∼ a trap⟩ **8** : to make known suddenly ⟨∼ a surprise⟩ **9** : to make lame : STRAIN **10** ♦ : to come into being **11** ♦ : to release or cause to be released from confinement or custody **12** ♦ : to discharge indebtedness for — used with *for*

♦ [1] bound, hop, jump, leap, vault — more at JUMP ♦ [10] arise, begin, commence, dawn, form, materialize, originate, start — more at BEGIN ♦ *usu* **spring up** [10] crop, emerge, surface — more at ARISE ♦ [11] discharge, emancipate, enfranchise, free, liberate, loose, loosen, manumit, release, unbind, unchain, unfetter — more at FREE ♦ *usu* **spring for** [12] clear, discharge, foot, liquidate, pay, pay off, quit, recompense, settle, stand — more at PAY

²**spring** *n* **1** : a source of supply; *esp* : an issuing of water from the ground **2** : SOURCE, ORIGIN; *also* : MOTIVE **3** : the season between winter and summer **4** : an elastic body or device that recovers its original shape when it is released after being distorted **5** ♦ : the act or an instance of leaping up or forward **6** : RESILIENCE

♦ bound, hop, jump, leap, vault — more at JUMP

spring·board \'spriŋ-ˌbōrd\ *n* : a springy board used in jumping or vaulting or for diving
spring fever *n* : a lazy or restless feeling often associated with the onset of spring
spring tide *n* : a tide of greater-than-average range that occurs at each new moon and full moon
spring·time \'spriŋ-ˌtīm\ *n* : the season of spring
springy *adj* **1** ♦ : having an elastic quality **2** ♦ : having or showing a lively and energetic movement

♦ [1] elastic, flexible, resilient, rubbery, stretch, supple — more at ELASTIC ♦ [2] active, animate, animated, brisk, energetic, lively, spirited, sprightly

¹**sprin·kle** \'spriŋ-kəl\ *vb* **sprin·kled; sprin·kling** ♦ : to scatter in small drops or particles — **sprin·kler** *n*

♦ dot, pepper, scatter, sow, spray, strew — more at SCATTER

²**sprinkle** *n* **1** : a light rainfall **2** ♦ : a small number esp. distributed at random

♦ few, handful, smattering, sprinkling — more at FEW

sprin·kling *n* ♦ : a limited quantity or amount : SMATTERING

♦ few, handful, smattering, sprinkle — more at FEW

¹**sprint** \'sprint\ *vb* ♦ : to run at top speed esp. for a short distance — **sprint·er** *n*

♦ dash, gallop, jog, run, scamper, trip — more at RUN

²**sprint** *n* **1** : a short run at top speed **2** : a short distance race
sprite \'sprīt\ *n* **1** : GHOST, SPIRIT **2** : a small often mischievous fairy : ELF
spritz \'sprits, 'shprits\ *vb* : SPRAY ⟨∼ the plants⟩ — **spritz** *n*
sprock·et \'sprä-kət\ *n* : a toothed wheel whose teeth engage the links of a chain
¹**sprout** \'spraut\ *vb* : to send out new growth ⟨∼*ing* seeds⟩
²**sprout** *n* : a usu. young and growing plant shoot (as from a seed)
¹**spruce** \'sprüs\ *vb* **spruced; spruc·ing** : to make or become spruce
²**spruce** *adj* **spruc·er; spruc·est** ♦ : neat and smart in appearance

♦ dapper, natty, sharp, smart — more at SMART

³**spruce** *n, pl* **spruc·es** *also* **spruce** : any of a genus of evergreen pyramid-shaped trees related to the pines and having soft light wood; *also* : the wood of a spruce
sprung *past and past part of* SPRING
spry \'sprī\ *adj* **spri·er** *or* **spry·er** \'sprī-ər\; **spri·est** *or* **spry·est** \'sprī-əst\ ♦ : quick and light in motion : NIMBLE

♦ agile, graceful, light, lissome, lithe, nimble — more at GRACEFUL

spud \'spəd\ *n* **1** : a sharp narrow spade **2** : POTATO

spume \'spyüm\ *n* ♦ : frothy matter on liquids : FOAM — **spumy** \'spyü-mē\ *adj*

♦ foam, froth, head, lather — more at FOAM

spu·mo·ni *also* **spu·mo·ne** \spu̇-'mō-nē\ *n* [It *spumone*, fr. *spuma* foam] : ice cream in layers of different colors, flavors, and textures often with candied fruits and nuts
spun *past and past part of* SPIN
spun glass *n* : FIBERGLASS
spunk \'spəŋk\ *n* [fr. *spunk* tinder, fr. ScGael *spong* sponge, tinder, fr. Middle Irish *spongc*, fr. L *spongia* sponge] ♦ : vigor and strength of spirit or temperament : PLUCK

♦ backbone, fiber (*or* fibre), fortitude, grit, guts, pluck — more at FORTITUDE

spunky *adj* ♦ : full of spunk

♦ fiery, high-spirited, mettlesome, peppery, spirited — more at SPIRITED

¹**spur** \'spər\ *n* **1** : a pointed device fastened to a rider's boot and used to urge on a horse **2** ♦ : something that urges to action **3** : a stiff sharp spine (as on the leg of a cock); *also* : a hollow projecting appendage of a flower (as a columbine) **4** : a ridge extending sideways from a mountain **5** : a branch of railroad track extending from the main line — **spurred** \'spərd\ *adj* — **on the spur of the moment** : on hasty impulse

♦ boost, encouragement, goad, impetus, impulse, incentive, incitement, instigation, momentum, motivation, provocation, stimulus, yeast — more at IMPULSE

²**spur** *vb* **spurred; spur·ring** **1** : to urge a horse on with spurs **2** : INCITE
spurge \'spərj\ *n* : any of a family of herbs and woody plants with a bitter milky juice
spu·ri·ous \'spyu̇r-ē-əs\ *adj* [LL *spurius* false, fr. L, *spurius*, n., son of an unknown father] ♦ : not genuine : FALSE

♦ affected, artificial, assumed, bogus, contrived, factitious, fake, false, feigned, mechanical, mock, phony, put-on, sham, unnatural — more at ARTIFICIAL

spurn \'spərn\ *vb* **1** : to kick away or trample on **2** ♦ : to reject with disdain

♦ decline, disallow, disapprove, negative, refuse, reject, repudiate, turn down — more at DECLINE

¹**spurt** \'spərt\ *vb* ♦ : to gush out : SPOUT

♦ gush, jet, pour, rush, spew, spout, squirt — more at GUSH

²**spurt** *n* : a sudden gushing or spouting
³**spurt** *n* **1** : a sudden brief burst of effort, speed, or development **2** ♦ : a sharp increase of activity ⟨∼ in sales⟩

♦ burst, flare, flare-up, flash, flurry, flutter, outbreak, outburst — more at OUTBREAK

⁴**spurt** *vb* : to make a spurt
sput·ter \'spə-tər\ *vb* **1** : to spit small scattered particles : SPLUTTER **2** ♦ : to utter words hastily or explosively in excitement or confusion **3** : to make small popping sounds — **sputter** *n*

♦ babble, chatter, drivel, gabble, gibber, jabber, prattle — more at BABBLE

spu·tum \'spyü-təm\ *n, pl* **spu·ta** \-tə\ [L] : material (as phlegm) that is spit out or coughed up esp. during illness
¹**spy** \'spī\ *vb* **spied; spy·ing** **1** : to watch or search for information secretly : act as a spy **2** ♦ : to get a momentary or quick glimpse of : SEE

♦ behold, descry, discern, distinguish, espy, eye, look, note, notice, observe, perceive, regard, remark, see, sight, view, witness — more at SEE

²**spy** *n, pl* **spies** **1** : one who secretly watches others **2** : a secret agent who tries to get information for one country in the territory of an enemy
spy·glass \'spī-ˌglas\ *n* : a small telescope
sq *abbr* **1** squadron **2** square
squab \'skwäb\ *n, pl* **squabs** *or* **squab** : a young bird and esp. a pigeon
¹**squab·ble** \'skwä-bəl\ *n* ♦ : a noisy altercation : WRANGLE

♦ altercation, argument, bicker, brawl, disagreement, dispute, fight, hassle, misunderstanding, quarrel, row, scrap, spat, wrangle — more at ARGUMENT

²**squabble** *vb* ♦ : to quarrel noisily and usu. over petty matters

♦ argue, bicker, brawl, dispute, fall out, fight, hassle, quarrel, row, scrap, spat, wrangle — more at ARGUE

squad \'skwäd\ *n* **1** : a small organized group of military personnel **2** ♦ : a small group engaged in a common effort

♦ band, company, crew, gang, outfit, party, team — more at GANG

squad car *n* : a police car connected by two-way radio with headquarters

squad·ron \'skwä-drən\ *n* : any of several units of military organization

squal·id \'skwä-ləd\ *adj* **1** : filthy or degraded through neglect or poverty **2** : SORDID, DEBASED

squall \'skwȯl\ *n* **1** : a sudden violent gust of wind often with rain or snow **2** : a short-lived commotion

squally *adj* ♦ : marked by squalls

♦ bleak, dirty, foul, inclement, nasty, raw, rough, stormy, tempestuous, turbulent — more at FOUL

squa·lor \'skwä-lər\ *n* : the quality or state of being squalid

squan·der \'skwän-dər\ *vb* ♦ : to spend wastefully or foolishly

♦ blow, dissipate, fritter, lavish, misspend, run through, spend, throw away, waste — more at WASTE

¹**square** \'skwar\ *n* **1** : an instrument used to lay out or test right angles **2** : a rectangle with all four sides equal **3** : something square **4** : the product of a number multiplied by itself **5** : an area bounded by four streets **6** : an open area in a city where streets meet **7** : a highly conventional person

²**square** *adj* **squar·er; squar·est 1** : having four equal sides and four right angles **2** : forming a right angle ⟨cut a ∼ corner⟩ **3** : multiplied by itself : SQUARED ⟨x^2 is the symbol for x ∼⟩ **4** : being a unit of square measure equal to a square each side of which measures one unit ⟨a ∼ foot⟩ **5** : being of a specified length in each of two dimensions ⟨an area 10 feet ∼⟩ **6** : exactly adjusted **7** : marked by impartiality and honesty : JUST ⟨a ∼ deal⟩ **8** : leaving no balance ⟨make accounts ∼⟩ **9** : SUBSTANTIAL ⟨a ∼ meal⟩ **10** : highly conservative or conventional

♦ disinterested, dispassionate, equal, equitable, fair, impartial, just, nonpartisan, objective, unbiased, unprejudiced — more at FAIR

³**square** *vb* **squared; squar·ing 1** : to form with four equal sides and right angles or with flat surfaces ⟨∼ a timber⟩ **2** : to multiply (a number) by itself **3** ♦ : to agree precisely : CONFORM **4** : BALANCE, SETTLE ⟨∼ an account⟩

♦ accord, agree, answer, check, coincide, comport, conform, correspond, dovetail, fit, go, harmonize, jibe, tally — more at CHECK

square dance *n* : a dance for four couples arranged to form a square

square·ly *adv* ♦ : in a manner or measure or to a degree or number that strictly conforms to a fact or condition

♦ accurately, exactly, just, precisely, right, sharp — more at EXACTLY

square measure *n* : a unit or system of units for measuring area

square–rigged \'skwar-'rigd\ *adj* : having the chief sails extended on yards that are fastened to the masts horizontally and at their center

square–rig·ger \-ˌri-gər\ *n* : a square-rigged craft

square root *n* : either of the two numbers whose squares are equal to a given number ⟨the *square root* of 9 is +3 or −3⟩

¹**squash** \'skwäsh, 'skwȯsh\ *vb* **1** ♦ : to beat or press into a pulp or flat mass **2** ♦ : to bring to an end : QUASH

♦ [1] crush, mash — more at CRUSH ♦ [2] clamp down, crack down, crush, put down, quash, quell, repress, silence, snuff, squelch, subdue, suppress — more at QUELL

²**squash** *n* **1** : the impact of something soft and heavy; *also* : the sound of such impact **2** : a crushed mass **3** : a game played on a 4-wall court with a racket and rubber ball

³**squash** *n, pl* **squash·es** *or* **squash** : any of various fruits of plants of the gourd family that are used esp. as vegetables; *also* : a plant and esp. a vine bearing squashes

squash racquets *n* : SQUASH 3

¹**squat** \'skwät\ *vb* **squat·ted; squat·ting** [ME *squatten* to crush, crouch in hiding, fr. MF (dial. of Picardy) *esquatir, escuater,* fr. OF *es-* ex- + *quatir* to hide, fr. VL *coactire* to squeeze, alter. of L *coactare* to compel, fr. *cogere* to compel] **1** ♦ : to sit down upon the hams or heels **2** : to settle on land without right or title; *also* : to settle on public land with a view to acquiring title — **squat·ter** *n*

♦ crouch, huddle, hunch — more at CROUCH

²**squat** *n* : the act or posture of squatting

³**squat** *adj* **squat·ter; squat·test 1** : low to the ground **2** ♦ : short and thick in stature

♦ chunky, dumpy, heavyset, stocky, stout, stubby, stumpy, thickset — more at STOCKY

squawk \'skwȯk\ *n* ♦ : a harsh loud cry; *also* : a noisy protest — **squawk** *vb*

♦ beef, complaint, fuss, grievance, gripe, grumble, murmur, plaint — more at COMPLAINT

squeak \'skwēk\ *vb* **1** ♦ : to utter or speak in a weak shrill tone **2** : to make a thin high-pitched sound — **squeak** *n*

♦ cheep, peep, squeal

squeaky *adj* ♦ : of the nature of, emitting, or tending to emit squeaks

♦ acute, sharp, shrill, treble — more at SHRILL

¹**squeal** \'skwēl\ *vb* **1** ♦ : to make a shrill sound or cry **2** ♦ : to betray a secret or turn informer **3** : COMPLAIN, PROTEST

♦ [1] howl, scream, shriek, shrill, yell, yelp — more at SCREAM ♦ [2] inform, snitch, talk, tell; *also* betray, give away, turn in; blab, tattle; tip (off)

²**squeal** *n* : a shrill sharp cry or noise

squea·mish \'skwē-mish\ *adj* **1** ♦ : easily nauseated; *also* : NAUSEATED **2** ♦ : easily disgusted

♦ [1] ill, nauseous, queasy, queer, sick — more at NAUSEOUS ♦ [2] disgusted, sick — more at SICK

squea·mish·ness *n* ♦ : the quality or state of being squeamish

♦ nausea, queasiness, sickness — more at NAUSEA

squee·gee \'skwē-jē\ *n* : a blade set crosswise on a handle and used for spreading or wiping liquid on, across, or off a surface — **squeegee** *vb*

¹**squeeze** \'skwēz\ *vb* **squeezed; squeez·ing 1** ♦ : to exert pressure on the opposite sides or parts of : COMPRESS **2** ♦ : to obtain by pressure ⟨∼ juice from a lemon⟩ **3** ♦ : to force or move into a small space ⟨*squeezed* into her jeans⟩ **4** : to pass, win, or get by narrowly **5** : to get or deprive by extortion — **squeez·er** *n*

♦ [1] compact, compress, condense, constrict, contract — more at COMPRESS ♦ [2] crush, express, mash, press — more at PRESS ♦ [3] cram, crowd, jam, ram, sandwich, stuff, wedge — more at CROWD

²**squeeze** *n* **1** : an act of squeezing **2** : a quantity squeezed out **3** *slang* ♦ : a romantic partner

♦ beloved, darling, dear, flame, honey, love, sweet, sweetheart — more at SWEETHEART

squeeze bottle *n* : a flexible plastic bottle that dispenses its contents when it is squeezed

squelch \'skwelch\ *vb* **1** ♦ : to suppress completely : CRUSH **2** : to move in soft mud — **squelch** *n*

♦ clamp down, crack down, crush, put down, quash, quell, repress, silence, snuff, squash, subdue, suppress — more at QUELL

squib \'skwib\ *n* : a brief witty writing or speech

squid \'skwid\ *n, pl* **squid** *or* **squids** : any of an order of long-bodied sea mollusks having eight short arms and two longer tentacles and usu. a slender internal shell

squint \'skwint\ *vb* **1** : to look or aim obliquely **2** : to look or peer with the eyes partly closed ⟨~*ing* into the sun⟩ **3** : to be cross-eyed — **squint** *n or adj*

¹**squire** \'skwīr\ *n* [ME *squier*, fr. AF *esquier*, fr. LL *scutarius*, fr. L *scutum* shield] **1** : an armor-bearer of a knight **2** : a man who devotedly attends a lady **3** : a member of the British gentry ranking below a knight and above a gentleman; *also* : a prominent landowner **4** : a local magistrate

²**squire** *vb* **squired; squir·ing** ♦ : to attend as a squire or escort

♦ accompany, attend, convoy, escort — more at AC-COMPANY

squirm \'skwǝrm\ *vb* ♦ : to twist about like a worm : WRIGGLE

♦ fiddle, fidget, jerk, twitch, wiggle — more at FIDGET

¹**squir·rel** \'skwǝr-ǝl\ *n, pl* **squirrels** *also* **squirrel** [ME *squirel*, fr. AF *escurel, esquirel*, fr. VL **scuriolus*, dim. of **scurius*, alter. of L *sciurus*, fr. Gk *skiouros*, prob. fr. *skia* shadow + *oura* tail] : any of various rodents usu. with a long bushy tail and strong hind legs; *also* : the fur of a squirrel

²**squirrel** *vb* **-reled** *or* **-relled; -rel·ing** *or* **-rel·ling** : to store up for future use

¹**squirt** \'skwǝrt\ *vb* ♦ : to eject liquid in a thin spurt

♦ gush, jet, pour, rush, spew, spout, spurt — more at GUSH

²**squirt** *n* **1** : an instrument (as a syringe) for squirting **2** : a small forcible jet of liquid

¹**Sr** *abbr* **1** senior **2** sister

²**Sr** *symbol* strontium

SR *abbr* seaman recruit

¹**SRO** \ˌes-(ˌ)är-'ō\ *n* [*single-room occupancy*] : a house or apartment building in which low-income tenants live in single rooms

²**SRO** *abbr* standing room only

SS *abbr* **1** saints **2** Social Security **3** steamship **4** sworn statement

SSA *abbr* Social Security Administration

SSE *abbr* south-southeast

SSG *or* **SSgt** *abbr* staff sergeant

SSI *abbr* supplemental security income

SSM *abbr* staff sergeant major

SSN *abbr* Social Security Number

ssp *abbr* subspecies

SSR *abbr* Soviet Socialist Republic

SSS *abbr* Selective Service System

SST \ˌes-(ˌ)es-'tē\ *n* [*super sonic transport*] : a supersonic passenger airplane

SSW *abbr* south-southwest

st *abbr* **1** stanza **2** state **3** stitch **4** stone **5** street

St *abbr* saint

ST *abbr* **1** short ton **2** standard time

sta *abbr* station; stationary

¹**stab** \'stab\ *n* **1** ♦ : a wound produced by a pointed weapon **2** : a quick thrust **3** ♦ : a brief attempt

♦ [1] perforation, pinhole, prick, punch, puncture — more at PRICK ♦ [3] attempt, crack, endeavor (*or* endeavour), essay, fling, go, pass, shot, trial, try, whack — more at ATTEMPT

²**stab** *vb* **stabbed; stab·bing** **1** ♦ : to pierce or wound with or as if with a pointed weapon **2** : THRUST, DRIVE

♦ gore, harpoon, impale, lance, pierce, puncture, skewer, spear, spike, stick, transfix — more at IMPALE

sta·bile \'stā-ˌbēl\ *n* : an abstract sculpture or construction similar to a mobile but made to be stationary

sta·bil·i·ty \stǝ-'bi-lǝ-tē\ *n* ♦ : the quality, state, or degree of being stable : the strength to stand or endure

♦ firmness, soundness, steadiness, strength, sturdiness; *also* dependability, durability, reliability; solidity, solidness; cohesion, toughness *Ant* instability, unsoundness, unsteadiness ♦ constancy, fixedness, immutability, steadiness — more at CONSTANCY

sta·bi·lize \'stā-bǝ-ˌlīz\ *vb* **-lized; -liz·ing** **1** : to make stable **2** : to hold steady ⟨~ prices⟩ — **sta·bi·li·za·tion** \ˌstā-bǝ-lǝ-'zā-shǝn\ *n* — **sta·bi·liz·er** \'stā-bǝ-ˌlī-zǝr\ *n*

¹**sta·ble** \'stā-bǝl\ *n* : a building in which domestic animals are sheltered and fed — **sta·ble·man** \-mǝn, -ˌman\ *n*

²**stable** *vb* **sta·bled; sta·bling** : to put or keep in a stable

³**stable** *adj* **sta·bler; sta·blest** **1 a** ♦ : firmly established **b** ♦ : mentally and emotionally healthy **2** ♦ : steady in purpose : CONSTANT **3** ♦ : continuing or enduring without fundamental or marked change **4** ♦ : resistant to chemical or physical change

♦ [1a] certain, determinate, final, firm, fixed, flat, frozen, hard, hard-and-fast, set, settled — more at FIXED ♦ [1b] balanced, clearheaded, lucid, normal, right, sane — more at SANE *Ant* unsound, unstable, unsteady ♦ [2, 3] constant, stationary, steady, unchanging, unvarying — more at CONSTANT ♦ [3, 4] fast, firm, sound, stalwart, steady, strong, sturdy; *also* dependable, durable, reliable; solid; cohesive, tough

stac·ca·to \stǝ-'kä-tō\ *adj or adv* [It] : cut short so as not to sound connected ⟨~ notes⟩

¹**stack** \'stak\ *n* **1** ♦ : a large pile (as of hay or grain) **2** : an orderly pile (as of poker chips) **3** ♦ : a large quantity **4** : a vertical pipe : SMOKESTACK **5** : a rack with shelves for storing books ⟨library ~s⟩

♦ [1] cock, heap, hill, mound, mountain, pile, rick — more at PILE ♦ [3] abundance, deal, gobs, heap, loads, lot, pile, plenty, quantity, scads — more at LOT

²**stack** *vb* **1** ♦ : to pile up **2** : to arrange (cards) secretly for cheating

♦ heap, hill, mound, pile — more at PILE

stack up *vb* ♦ : to be equal or alike : MEASURE UP — usu. used with *against*; *also* : to add up

♦ *usu* **stack up against** approach, approximate, compare, measure up — more at APPROXIMATE

sta·di·um \'stā-dē-ǝm\ *n, pl* **-dia** \-dē-ǝ\ *or* **-di·ums** ♦ : a structure with tiers of seats for spectators built around a field for sports events

♦ bowl, circus, coliseum; *also* gym, gymnasium, spa; arena, hippodrome

¹**staff** \'staf\ *n, pl* **staffs** \'stafs, 'stavz\ *or* **staves** \'stavz, 'stāvz\ **1** : a pole, stick, rod, or bar used for supporting, for measuring, or as a symbol of authority; *also* : CLUB, CUDGEL **2** : something that sustains ⟨bread is the ~ of life⟩ **3** : the five horizontal lines on which music is written **4** ♦ : a body of assistants to an executive **5** : a group of officers holding no command but having duties concerned with planning and managing

♦ force, help, personnel, pool — more at FORCE

²**staff** *vb* : to supply with a staff or with workers

staff·er \'sta-fǝr\ *n* : a member of a staff (as of a newspaper)

staff sergeant *n* : a noncommissioned officer ranking in the army next below a sergeant first class, in the air force next below a technical sergeant, and in the marine corps next below a gunnery sergeant

¹**stag** \'stag\ *n, pl* **stags** *or* **stag** : an adult male of various large deer

²**stag** *adj* : restricted to or intended for men ⟨a ~ party⟩ ⟨~ movies⟩

³**stag** *adv* : unaccompanied by a date

¹**stage** \'stāj\ *n* [ME, fr. AF *estage* abode, story of a building, stage, fr. VL **staticum*, fr. L *stare* to stand] **1** ♦ : a raised platform on which an orator may speak or a play may be presented **2** ♦ : the acting profession : THEATER **3** : the scene of a notable action or event **4 a** : a station or resting place on a traveled road **b** ♦ : the distance between two stopping places on a road **5** : STAGECOACH **6** ♦ : a degree of advance in an undertaking, process, or development **7** : a propulsion unit in a rocket — **stagy** \'stā-jē\ *adj*

♦ [1] dais, platform, podium, rostrum, stand — more at PLATFORM ♦ [2] theater (*or* theatre), theatricals

♦ [4b] lap, leg, step — more at LEG ♦ [6] cut, degree, grade, inch, notch, peg, phase, point, step — more at DEGREE

²**stage** vb **staged; stag·ing** ♦ : to produce or perform on or as if on a stage ⟨~ a play⟩ — **stage·able** adj

♦ carry, give, mount, offer, present — more at PRESENT

stage·coach \'stāj-ˌkōch\ n : a horse-drawn coach that runs regularly between stations

stage manager n : one who supervises the physical aspects of a stage production

stag·fla·tion \ˌstag-'flā-shən\ n : inflation with stagnant economic activity and high unemployment

¹**stag·ger** \'sta-gər\ vb **1** ♦ : to reel from side to side : TOTTER **2** : to begin to doubt : WAVER **3** : to cause to reel or waver **4** : to arrange in overlapping or alternating positions or times ⟨~ working hours⟩ **5** : ASTONISH

♦ careen, dodder, lurch, reel, teeter, totter; also rock, sway, weave, wobble; shamble, shuffle

²**stagger** n **1** sing or pl : an abnormal condition of domestic animals associated with damage to the central nervous system and marked by lack of coordination and a reeling unsteady gait **2** : a reeling or unsteady gait or stance

stag·ger·ing·ly adv : in a staggering manner or to a staggering degree

stag·ing \'stā-jiŋ\ n **1** : SCAFFOLDING **2** : the assembling of troops and matériel in transit in a particular place

stag·nant \'stag-nənt\ adj **1** : not flowing : MOTIONLESS ⟨~ water in a pond⟩ **2** : DULL, INACTIVE ⟨~ business⟩

stag·nate \'stag-ˌnāt\ vb **stag·nat·ed; stag·nat·ing** : to be or become stagnant — **stag·na·tion** \stag-'nā-shən\ n

staid \'stād\ adj ♦ : marked by settled sedateness and often prim self-restraint

♦ august, dignified, imposing, solemn, stately — more at DIGNIFIED ♦ earnest, grave, humorless (or humourless), serious, severe, sober, solemn, unsmiling, weighty — more at SERIOUS

¹**stain** \'stān\ vb **1** ♦ : to discolor esp. with dirt : SOIL **2** ♦ : to touch or affect slightly with something bad : TAINT **3** : DISGRACE **4** ♦ : to color (as wood, paper, or cloth) by processes affecting the material itself

♦ [1] befoul, begrime, besmirch, blacken, dirty, foul, grime, mire, muddy, smirch, soil — more at DIRTY ♦ [2] blemish, mar, poison, spoil, taint, tarnish, touch, vitiate — more at TAINT ♦ [4] color (or colour), dye, paint, tinge, tint — more at COLOR

²**stain** n **1** : a small soiled or discolored area **2** ♦ : a taint of guilt : STIGMA **3** ♦ : a preparation (as a dye or pigment) used in staining

♦ [2] blot, brand, smirch, spot, stigma, taint; also discredit, disgrace, dishonor, disrepute, guilt, ignominy, infamy, odium, opprobrium, reproach, shame ♦ [3] color (or colour), dye, pigment — more at PIGMENT

stain·less adj ♦ : free from stain or stigma

♦ clean, immaculate, spick-and-span, spotless, unsoiled, unsullied — more at CLEAN

stainless steel n : steel alloyed with chromium that is highly resistant to stain, rust, and corrosion

stair \'star\ n **1** : a series of steps or flights of steps for passing from one level to another — often used in pl. **2** : one step of a stairway

stair·case \-ˌkās\ n : a flight of steps with their supporting framework, casing, and balusters

stair·way \-ˌwā\ n : one or more flights of stairs with connecting landings

stair·well \-ˌwel\ n : a vertical shaft in which stairs are located

¹**stake** \'stāk\ n **1** : a pointed piece of material (as of wood) driven into the ground as a marker or a support **2** : a post to which a person is bound for death by burning; also : execution by burning at the stake **3** : something that is ventured for gain or loss **4** : the prize in a contest **5** ♦ : an interest or share in an undertaking or enterprise

♦ claim, interest, share — more at INTEREST

²**stake** vb **staked; stak·ing 1** : to mark the limits of by or as if by stakes **2** : to tie to a stake **3** : to support or secure with stakes **4** : BET, WAGER **5** ♦ : to back financially

♦ capitalize, endow, finance, fund, subsidize, underwrite — more at FINANCE

stake·out \'stāk-ˌaút\ n : a surveillance by police (as of a suspected criminal)

sta·lac·tite \stə-'lak-ˌtīt\ n [NL stalactites, fr. Gk stalaktos dripping, fr. stalassein to let drip] : an icicle-shaped deposit hanging from the roof or sides of a cavern

sta·lag·mite \stə-'lag-ˌmīt\ n [NL stalagmites, fr. Gk stalagma drop or stalagmos dripping] : a deposit resembling an inverted stalactite rising from the floor of a cavern

stale \'stāl\ adj **stal·er; stal·est 1** : having lost good taste and quality from age ⟨~ bread⟩ **2** ♦ : used or heard so often as to be dull ⟨~ news⟩ **3** : not as strong or effective as before ⟨~ from lack of practice⟩ — **stale·ness** n

♦ banal, commonplace, hackneyed, musty, stereotyped, threadbare, tired, trite; also canned, unimaginative, uninspired, unoriginal; normal, ordinary, rote, routine, standard, stock, typical, usual; boring, drab, dreary, dry, dull, flat, heavy, humdrum, jading, leaden, monotonous, pedestrian, ponderous, prosaic, tame, tedious, tiresome, tiring, uninteresting, vapid, wearisome, weary, wearying; corny, maudlin, mawkish, mushy, saccharine, sappy, schmaltzy, sentimental, sloppy, sugary Ant fresh, new, original

stale·mate \'stāl-ˌmāt\ n ♦ : a drawn contest : DEADLOCK — **stalemate** vb

♦ deadlock, draw, halt, impasse, standoff, standstill, tie — more at IMPASSE

¹**stalk** \'stók\ n : a plant stem; also : any slender usu. upright supporting or connecting part — **stalked** \'stókt\ adj

²**stalk** vb **1** : to pursue (game) stealthily **2** ♦ : to walk stiffly or haughtily **3** : to follow (a person) obsessively — **stalk·er** n

♦ strut, swagger — more at STRUT

¹**stall** \'stól\ n **1** : a compartment in a stable or barn for one animal **2** : a booth or counter where articles may be displayed for sale **3** : a seat in a church choir; also : a church pew **4** chiefly Brit : a front orchestra seat in a theater

²**stall** vb ♦ : to bring or come to a standstill unintentionally ⟨~ an engine⟩

♦ arrest, catch, check, draw up, fetch up, halt, hold up, stay, still, stop — more at HALT ♦ break, break down, conk, crash, cut out, die, fail — more at FAIL

³**stall** n : the condition of an airfoil or aircraft in which lift is lost and the airfoil or aircraft tends to drop

⁴**stall** n [alter. of stale lure] : a ruse to deceive or delay

⁵**stall** vb : to hold off, divert, or delay by evasion or deception

stal·lion \'stal-yən\ n : a male horse

stal·wart \'stól-wərt\ adj ♦ : marked by outstanding strength and vigor of body, mind, or spirit : STRONG; also : VALIANT

♦ brave, courageous, dauntless, doughty, fearless, gallant, greathearted, heroic, intrepid, lionhearted, manful, stout, undaunted, valiant, valorous — more at BRAVE ♦ brawny, muscular, rugged, sinewy, stout, strong — more at STRONG

sta·men \'stā-mən\ n : an organ of a flower that produces pollen

stam·i·na \'sta-mə-nə\ n [L, pl. of stamen warp, thread of life spun by the Fates] : VIGOR, ENDURANCE

sta·mi·nate \'stā-mə-nət, 'sta-mə-, -ˌnāt\ adj **1** : having or producing stamens **2** : having stamens but no pistils

stam·mer \'sta-mər\ vb : to hesitate or stumble in speaking — **stammer** n — **stam·mer·er** n

¹**stamp** \'stamp; for 2 also 'stämp or 'stómp\ vb **1** : to pound or crush with a heavy instrument **2** ♦ : to strike

or beat with the bottom of the foot 3 : IMPRESS, IMPRINT
4 : to cut out or indent with a stamp or die 5 : to attach a
postage stamp to 6 ♦ : to extinguish or destroy by or as
if by stamping with the foot — used with *out* 7 : to strike
or thrust the foot forcibly or noisily downward

♦ [2] stomp, tramp, trample, tromp — more at TRAM-
PLE ♦ *usu* **stamp out** [6] annihilate, blot out, demolish,
eradicate, exterminate, liquidate, obliterate, root, rub
out, snuff, wipe out — more at ANNIHILATE

²**stamp** *n* 1 : a device or instrument for stamping 2 ♦ : the
mark made by stamping; *also* : a distinctive mark or quality 3 : the act of stamping 4 : a stamped or printed paper affixed to show that a charge has been paid ⟨postage
∼⟩ ⟨tax ∼⟩

♦ impress, impression, imprint, print — more at PRINT

¹**stam·pede** \stam-ˈpēd\ *n* : a wild headlong rush or flight
esp. of frightened animals

²**stampede** *vb* **stam·ped·ed; stam·ped·ing** 1 : to flee or
cause to flee in panic 2 : to act or cause to act together
suddenly and heedlessly

stance \ˈstans\ *n* : a way of standing

¹**stanch** \ˈstȯnch, ˈstänch, ˈstanch\ *or* **staunch**
\ˈstȯnch, ˈstänch\ *vb* : to check the flowing of (as blood); *also* : to
cease flowing or bleeding

²**stanch** *var of* ²STAUNCH

stan·chion \ˈstan-chən\ *n* ♦ : an upright bar, post, or support

♦ column, pier, pillar, post — more at PILLAR

¹**stand** \ˈstand\ *vb* **stood** \ˈstu̇d\; **stand·ing** 1 : to take or
be at rest in an upright or firm position 2 : to assume a
specified position 3 : to remain stationary or unchanged
4 : to be steadfast 5 : to act in resistance ⟨∼ against a
foe⟩ 6 : to maintain a relative position or rank 7 : to
gather slowly and remain ⟨tears *stood* in her eyes⟩ 8 : to
set upright 9 ♦ : to tolerate without flinching : EN-
DURE ⟨I won't ∼ for that⟩ 10 : to submit to ⟨∼ trial⟩
11 ♦ : to pay the cost of (a treat) : pay for — **stand pat**
: to oppose or resist change

♦ [9] abide, bear, brook, countenance, endure, meet,
stick out, stomach, support, sustain, take, tolerate —
more at BEAR ♦ [11] clear, discharge, foot, liquidate,
pay, pay off, quit, recompense, settle, spring — more
at PAY

²**stand** *n* 1 : an act of standing, staying, or resisting 2 : a
stop made to give a performance 3 : POSITION, VIEW-
POINT 4 : a place taken by a witness to testify in court
5 *pl* : tiered seats for spectators 6 ♦ : a raised platform
(as for speakers) 7 : a structure for a small retail business 8 : a structure for supporting or holding something
upright ⟨music ∼⟩ 9 : a group of plants growing in a
continuous area

♦ dais, platform, podium, rostrum, stage — more at
PLATFORM

stand–alone \ˈstan-də-ˌlōn\ *adj* : SELF-CONTAINED; *esp*
: capable of operation independent of a computer system

¹**stan·dard** \ˈstan-dərd\ *n* 1 : a figure adopted as an emblem by a people 2 ♦ : the personal flag of a ruler; *also*
: FLAG 3 ♦ : something set up as a rule for measuring
or as a model to be followed; *also* : a model of behavior
established by custom — often used in pl. 4 : an upright
support ⟨lamp ∼⟩

♦ [2] banner, colors (*or* colours), ensign, flag, jack,
pennant, streamer — more at FLAG ♦ [3] criterion,
grade, mark, measure, par, touchstone, yardstick; *also*
rule; case, example, instance ♦ **standards** [3] ethics,
morality, morals, principles — more at ETHICS

²**standard** *adj* 1 ♦ : constituting or conforming to a standard esp. as established by law or custom 2 ♦ : regularly
and widely used, available, or supplied

♦ [1] average, characteristic, normal, regular, representative, typical — more at TYPICAL ♦ [2] conventional,
current, customary, popular, stock, usual — more at
CURRENT

stan·dard–bear·er \-ˌbar-ər\ *n* : the leader of a cause

standard deviation *n* : a measure of dispersion in a set of
data

stan·dard·ise *chiefly Brit var of* STANDARDIZE

stan·dard–is·sue \ˈstan-dərd-ˈi-shü\ *adj* : STANDARD, TYPI-
CAL ⟨a ∼ blue suit⟩

stan·dard·ize \ˈstan-dər-ˌdīz\ *vb* **-ized; -iz·ing** ♦ : to make
standard or uniform — **stan·dard·i·za·tion** \ˌstan-dər-də-ˈzā-
shən\ *n*

♦ formalize, homogenize, normalize, regularize; *also*
codify, organize, systematize; average, equalize, even;
accredit, certify; control, govern, regulate; coordinate,
harmonize, integrate, reconcile, synthesize

standard of living : the necessities, comforts, and luxuries
that a person or group is accustomed to

standard time *n* : the time established by law or by general
usage over a region or country

¹**stand·by** \ˈstand-ˌbī\ *n, pl* **stand·bys** \-ˌbīz\ 1 ♦ : one that
can be relied on 2 : a substitute in reserve — **on standby**
: ready or available for immediate action or use

♦ buttress, dependence, mainstay, pillar, reliance, support — more at DEPENDENCE

²**standby** *adj* 1 : ready for use 2 : relating to airline travel
in which the passenger must wait for an available unreserved seat — **standby** *adv*

stand–in \ˈstan-ˌdin\ *n* 1 : someone employed to occupy
an actor's place while lights and camera are readied
2 ♦ : a person or thing that takes the place or function of
another : SUBSTITUTE

♦ backup, pinch hitter, relief, replacement, reserve,
sub, substitute — more at SUBSTITUTE

stand in *vb* ♦ : to act as a stand-in

♦ cover, fill in, pinch-hit, sub, substitute, take over —
more at COVER

¹**stand·ing** \ˈstan-diŋ\ *adj* 1 : ERECT 2 : not flowing : STAG-
NANT 3 : remaining at the same level or amount for an
indefinite period ⟨∼ offer⟩ 4 : PERMANENT 5 : done
from a standing position ⟨a ∼ jump⟩

²**standing** *n* 1 a ♦ : length of service b ♦ : relative position
in society or in a profession : RANK 2 : maintenance of
position or condition : DURATION

♦ [1a] date, duration, life, lifetime, run, time — more
at DURATION ♦ [1b] degree, footing, level, place, position, rank, situation, station, status — more at RANK

stand·off \ˈstan-ˌdȯf\ *n* ♦ : a state of inaction or neutralization resulting from the opposition of equally powerful
uncompromising persons or factions : TIE

♦ dead heat, draw, stalemate, tie — more at TIE

stand·off·ish \ˈstan-ˈdȯ-fish\ *adj* ♦ : somewhat cold and reserved

♦ aloof, antisocial, cold, cool, detached, distant, frosty,
remote, unsociable — more at COOL

stand·out \ˈstan-ˌdau̇t\ *n* ♦ : something conspicuously excellent

♦ celebrity, figure, light, luminary, notable, personage,
personality, somebody, star, superstar, VIP — more at
CELEBRITY

stand·pipe \ˈstand-ˌpīp\ *n* : a high vertical pipe or reservoir
for water used to produce a uniform pressure

stand·point \-ˌpȯint\ *n* ♦ : a position from which objects or
principles are judged

♦ angle, outlook, perspective, point of view, slant,
viewpoint — more at POINT OF VIEW

stand·still \-ˌstil\ *n* ♦ : a state of rest

♦ deadlock, halt, impasse, stalemate — more at IM-
PASSE

stank *past of* STINK

stand–up \ˈstan-ˌdəp\ *adj* : done or performing in a standing position ⟨a ∼ comic⟩ ⟨∼ comedy⟩

stan·za \ˈstan-zə\ *n* [It] : a group of lines forming a division
of a poem

sta·pes \'stā-ˌpēz\ *n, pl* **stapes** *or* **sta·pe·des** \'stā-pə-ˌdēz\ : the small innermost bone of the ear of mammals

staph \'staf\ *n* : STAPHYLOCOCCUS

staph·y·lo·coc·cus \ˌsta-fə-lō-'kä-kəs\ *n, pl* **-coc·ci** \-'kä-ˌkī, -'käk-ˌsī\ : any of various spherical bacteria including some pathogens of skin and mucous membranes — **staph·y·lo·coc·cal** \-'kä-kəl\ *adj*

¹**sta·ple** \'stā-pəl\ *n* : a U-shaped piece of metal or wire with sharp points to be driven into a surface or through thin layers (as paper) for attaching or holding together — **sta·ple** *vb* — **sta·pler** *n*

²**staple** *n* **1** : a chief commodity or product **2** ♦ : a chief part of something ⟨a ~ of their diet⟩ **3** : unmanufactured or raw material **4** : a textile fiber suitable for spinning into yarn

♦ body, bulk, core, generality, main, mass, weight — more at BODY

³**staple** *adj* **1** : regularly produced in large quantities **2** : PRINCIPAL, MAIN

¹**star** \'stär\ *n* **1** : a celestial body that appears as a fixed point of light; *esp* : such a body that is gaseous, self-luminous, and of great mass **2** : a planet or configuration of planets that is held in astrology to influence one's fortune — usu. used in pl. **3** *obs* : DESTINY, FORTUNE **4** : a conventional figure representing a star; *esp* : ASTERISK **5** : an actor or actress playing the leading role **6** ♦ : a brilliant performer **7** ♦ : a person who is preeminent in a particular field — **star** *adj* — **star·dom** \'stär-dəm\ *n* — **star·less** *adj* — **star·like** *adj*

♦ [6, 7] celebrity, figure, light, luminary, notable, personage, personality, somebody, standout, superstar, VIP — more at CELEBRITY

²**star** *vb* **starred; star·ring** **1** : to adorn with stars **2** : to mark with an asterisk **3** : to play the leading role

star·board \'stär-bərd\ *n* [ME *sterbord*, fr. OE *stēorbord*, fr. *stēor*- steering oar + *bord* ship's side] : the right side of a ship or airplane looking forward — **starboard** *adj*

¹**starch** \'stärch\ *vb* : to stiffen with or as if with starch

²**starch** *n* **1** : a complex carbohydrate that is stored in plants, is an important foodstuff, and is used in adhesives and sizes, in laundering, and in pharmacy **2** : a stiff formal manner **3** : resolute vigor

starchy *adj* **1** : containing, consisting of, or resembling starch **2** ♦ : characterized by punctilious respect for form

♦ ceremonious, correct, decorous, formal, proper — more at CEREMONIOUS

stare \'star\ *vb* **stared; star·ing** ♦ : to look fixedly with wide-open eyes — **stare** *n* — **star·er** *n*

♦ gape, gawk, gaze, goggle, peer, rubberneck — more at GAPE

star·fish \'stär-ˌfish\ *n* : any of a class of echinoderms that have usu. five arms arranged around a central disk and feed largely on mollusks

star fruit *n* : CARAMBOLA 1

¹**stark** \'stärk\ *adj* **1** : rigid as if in death; *also* : STRICT **2** *archaic* : STRONG, ROBUST **3** : SHEER, UTTER **4** ♦ : not productive : BARREN ⟨~ landscape⟩; *also* : being without a usual, typical, or expected attribute or accompaniment : UNADORNED ⟨~ realism⟩ **5** : sharply delineated **6** : rigidly conforming (as to a pattern or doctrine) — **stark·ly** *adv*

♦ barren, infertile, poor, unproductive, waste — more at BARREN

²**stark** *adv* : WHOLLY, ABSOLUTELY ⟨~ naked⟩

star·light \'stär-ˌlīt\ *n* : the light given by the stars

star·ling \'stär-liŋ\ *n* : a dark brown or in summer glossy greenish black European bird that is naturalized nearly worldwide and often considered a pest

star·ry *adj* ♦ : of, relating to, or consisting of stars

♦ astral, star, stellar — more at STELLAR

¹**start** \'stärt\ *vb* **1** ♦ : to give an involuntary twitch or jerk (as from surprise) **2** ♦ : to begin an activity or undertaking : BEGIN **3** ♦ : to set going **4** : to enter or cause to enter a game or contest; *also* : to be in the starting lineup **5** : to protrude or seem to protrude — **start·er** *n*

♦ [1] bolt, jump, startle; *also* jerk, twitch; flinch, recoil; bound, leap, spring; react, respond ♦ [2] arise, begin, commence, dawn, form, materialize, originate, spring — more at BEGIN ♦ [2] embark (on *or* upon), enter, get off, launch, open, strike — more at BEGIN ♦ [3] constitute, establish, found, inaugurate, initiate, innovate, institute, introduce, pioneer, set up — more at FOUND ♦ [3] activate, actuate, crank, drive, move, propel, run, set off, spark, touch off, trigger, turn on — more at ACTIVATE

²**start** *n* **1** : a sudden involuntary motion : LEAP **2** : a spasmodic and brief effort or action **3** ♦ : BEGINNING; *also* : the place of beginning

♦ beginning, birth, commencement, dawn, genesis, launch, morning, onset, outset, threshold — more at BEGINNING

star·tle \'stärt-ᵊl\ *vb* **star·tled; star·tling** **1** ♦ : to frighten or surprise suddenly : cause to start ⟨the noise *startled* us⟩ **2** ♦ : to move or jump suddenly (as in surprise or alarm)

♦ [1] amaze, astonish, astound, floor, shock, stun, surprise — more at SURPRISE ♦ [1] alarm, frighten, scare, spook — more at FRIGHTEN ♦ [2] bolt, jump, start — more at START

star·tling *adj* ♦ : causing sudden fear, surprise, or anxiety

♦ amazing, astonishing, astounding, eye-opening, shocking, stunning, surprising — more at SURPRISING

starve \'stärv\ *vb* **starved; starv·ing** [ME *sterven* to die, fr. OE *steorfan*] **1** : to die or cause to die from hunger **2** : to suffer extreme hunger or deprivation ⟨*starving* for affection⟩ **3** : to subdue by famine — **star·va·tion** \stär-'vā-shən\ *n*

starve·ling \'stärv-liŋ\ *n* : one that is thin from lack of nourishment

¹**stash** \'stash\ *vb* ♦ : to store in a secret place for future use

♦ cache, hoard, lay away, lay up, put by, salt away, stockpile, store — more at HOARD

²**stash** *n* ♦ : something stored or hidden away

♦ cache, hoard, stockpile, store — more at HOARD

sta·sis \'stā-səs, 'sta-\ *n, pl* **sta·ses** \'stā-ˌsēz, 'sta-\ **1** : a stoppage or slowing of the normal flow of a bodily fluid (as blood) **2** : a state of static balance : STAGNATION

¹**stat** \'stat\ *adv* [L *statim*] : without delay : IMMEDIATELY

²**stat** *abbr* statute

¹**state** \'stāt\ *n* [ME *stat*, fr. OF & L; OF *estat*, fr. L *status*, fr. *stare* to stand] **1** : mode or condition of being ⟨the four ~s of matter⟩ **2** : condition of mind **3** : social position **4** ♦ : a body of people occupying a territory and organized under one government; *also* : the government of such a body of people **5** : one of the constituent units of a nation having a federal government — **state·hood** \-ˌhu̇d\ *n*

♦ commonwealth, country, land, nation, sovereignty

²**state** *vb* **stat·ed; stat·ing** **1** : to set by regulation or authority **2** ♦ : to express in words

♦ clothe, couch, express, formulate, phrase, put, say, word — more at PHRASE ♦ articulate, say, speak, talk, tell, utter, verbalize, vocalize — more at SAY

state·craft \'stāt-ˌkraft\ *n* : the art of conducting state affairs

state·house \-ˌhau̇s\ *n* : the building in which a state legislature meets

state·li·ness *n* ♦ : impressiveness in scale or proportion; *also* : imposing or courtly formality

♦ class, elegance, grace, handsomeness, majesty, refinement — more at ELEGANCE ♦ augustness, brilliance, glory, grandeur, grandness, magnificence, majesty, nobility, nobleness, resplendence, splendor — more at MAGNIFICENCE

state·ly \'stāt-lē\ *adj* **state·li·er; -est** 1 ♦ : having lofty dignity 2 ♦ : impressive in size or proportions : MAJESTIC

♦ [1] august, dignified, imposing, lofty, solemn, staid — more at DIGNIFIED ♦ [2] august, baronial, gallant, glorious, grand, grandiose, heroic, imposing, magnificent, majestic, monumental, noble, proud, regal, royal, splendid — more at GRAND

state·ment \'stāt-mənt\ *n* 1 ♦ : the act or result of presenting in words 2 ♦ : a summary of a financial account

♦ [1] articulation, expression, formulation, utterance, voice — more at EXPRESSION ♦ [2] account, bill, check, invoice, tab — more at BILL

state·room \'stāt-ˌrüm, -ˌrum\ *n* : a private room on a ship or railroad car

state·side \'stāt-ˌsīd\ *adj* : of or relating to the U.S. as regarded from outside its continental limits — **stateside** *adv*

states·man \'stāts-mən\ *n* : a person engaged in fixing the policies and conducting the affairs of a government; *esp* : one wise and skilled in such matters — **states·man·like** *adj* — **states·man·ship** *n*

¹stat·ic \'sta-tik\ *adj* 1 : acting by mere weight without motion ⟨∼ pressure⟩ 2 : relating to bodies at rest or forces in equilibrium 3 ♦ : not moving : not active 4 : of or relating to stationary charges of electricity 5 : of, relating to, or caused by radio static

♦ immobile, immovable, standing, stationary, unmovable — more at STATIONARY

²static *n* : noise produced in a radio or television receiver by atmospheric or other electrical disturbances

¹sta·tion \'stā-shən\ *n* 1 ♦ : the place where a person or thing stands or is assigned to remain 2 : a regular stopping place on a transportation route 3 : a place where a fleet is assigned for duty 4 : a stock farm or ranch esp. in Australia or New Zealand 5 ♦ : social standing 6 : a complete assemblage of radio or television equipment for sending or receiving

♦ [1] position, post, quarter; *also* assignment, detail ♦ [5] degree, footing, level, place, position, rank, situation, standing, status — more at RANK

²station *vb* : to assign to a station

sta·tion·ary \'stā-shə-ˌner-ē\ *adj* 1 ♦ : fixed in a station, course, or mode 2 ♦ : unchanging in condition

♦ [1] immobile, immovable, standing, static, unmovable; *also* irremovable, nonmotile, unbudging; frozen, motionless, stagnant, still Ant mobile, movable, moving ♦ [2] constant, stable, steady, unchanging, unvarying — more at CONSTANT

stationary front *n* : the boundary between two air masses neither of which is advancing

station break *n* : a pause in a radio or television broadcast to announce the identity of the network or station

sta·tio·ner \'stā-shə-nər\ *n* : one that sells stationery

sta·tio·nery \'stā-shə-ˌner-ē\ *n* : materials (as paper, pens, or ink) for writing; *esp* : letter paper with envelopes

station wagon *n* : an automobile having a long interior, one or more folding or removable rear seats, and usu. a door at the rear

sta·tis·tic \stə-'tis-tik\ *n* 1 : a single term or datum in a collection of statistics 2 : a quantity (as the mean) that is computed from a sample

sta·tis·tics \-tiks\ *n sing or pl* [G *Statistik* study of political facts and figures, fr. NL *statisticus* of politics, fr. L *status* state] : a branch of mathematics dealing with the collection, analysis, and interpretation of masses of numerical data; *also* : a collection of such numerical data — **sta·tis·ti·cal** \-ti-kəl\ *adj* — **sta·tis·ti·cal·ly** \-ti-k(ə-)lē\ *adv* — **stat·is·ti·cian** \ˌsta-tə-'sti-shən\ *n*

stat·u·ary \'sta-chə-ˌwer-ē\ *n, pl* **-ar·ies** 1 : the art of making statues 2 : STATUES

stat·ue \'sta-chü\ *n* : a likeness (as of a person or animal) sculptured, modeled, or cast in a solid substance

stat·u·esque \ˌsta-chə-'wesk\ *adj* : tall and shapely

stat·u·ette \ˌsta-chə-'wet\ *n* : a small statue

stat·ure \'sta-chər\ *n* 1 : natural height (as of a person) 2 : quality or status gained (as by achievement)

sta·tus \'stā-təs, 'sta-\ *n* 1 : the condition of a person in the eyes of others or of the law 2 ♦ : state of affairs 3 ♦ : position or rank in relation to others

♦ [2] footing, picture, posture, scene, situation — more at SITUATION ♦ [3] degree, footing, level, place, position, rank, situation, standing, station — more at RANK

sta·tus quo \-'kwō\ *n* [L, state in which] : the existing state of affairs

stat·ute \'sta-chüt\ *n* ♦ : a law enacted by a legislative body

♦ act, enactment, law, ordinance — more at LAW

stat·u·to·ry \'sta-chə-ˌtōr-ē\ *adj* : imposed by statute : LAWFUL

statutory rape *n* : sexual intercourse with a person who is below the statutory age of consent

¹staunch \'stonch\ *var of* ¹STANCH

²staunch *adj* 1 : WATERTIGHT ⟨a ∼ ship⟩ 2 a : FIRM, STRONG b ♦ : steadfast in loyalty or principle — **staunch·ly** *adv*

♦ constant, devoted, faithful, fast, good, loyal, pious, steadfast, steady, true, true-blue — more at FAITHFUL

¹stave \'stāv\ *n* 1 : CUDGEL, STAFF 2 : any of several narrow strips of wood placed edge to edge to make something (as a barrel) 3 : STANZA

²stave *vb* **staved** *or* **stove** \'stōv\; **stav·ing** 1 : to break in the staves of; *also* : to break a hole in 2 : to drive or thrust away ⟨∼ off hunger⟩

stave off *vb* ♦ : to fend or ward off

♦ fend, repel, repulse — more at REPEL

staves *pl of* STAFF

¹stay \'stā\ *n* 1 : a strong rope or wire used to support a mast 2 : ¹GUY

²stay *vb* **stayed** \'stād\ *also* **staid** \'stād\; **stay·ing** 1 : PAUSE, WAIT 2 ♦ : to continue in a place or condition 3 : to stand firm 4 : to take up residence : LIVE, DWELL 5 : DELAY, POSTPONE 6 : to last out (as a race) 7 ♦ : to stop or delay the proceeding or advance of : CHECK 8 : to satisfy (as hunger) for a time

♦ [2] abide, dwell, hang around, remain, stick around, tarry, visit; *also* await, hang on, hold on, wait; dally, linger, loiter; keep Ant go, leave, quit ♦ [7] arrest, catch, check, draw up, fetch up, halt, hold up, stall, still, stop — more at HALT

³stay *n* 1 : STOP, HALT 2 ♦ : a residence or sojourn in a place

♦ sojourn, visit — more at VISIT

⁴stay *n* 1 ♦ : one that serves as a prop : SUPPORT 2 : CORSET — usu. used in pl.

♦ brace, bulwark, buttress, mount, shore, support, underpinning — more at SUPPORT

⁵stay *vb* ♦ : to hold up : PROP

♦ bear, bolster, brace, buttress, carry, prop, shore, support, uphold — more at SUPPORT

staying power *n* : STAMINA

stbd *abbr* starboard

std *abbr* standard

STD \ˌes-(ˌ)tē-'dē\ *n* : SEXUALLY TRANSMITTED DISEASE

Ste *abbr* [F *sainte*] saint (female)

stead \'sted\ *n* 1 ♦ : superiority of position : ADVANTAGE ⟨stood him in good ∼⟩ 2 : the place or function ordinarily occupied or carried out by another ⟨acted in her brother's ∼⟩

♦ advantage, better, drop, edge, jump, upper hand, vantage — more at ADVANTAGE

stead·fast \'sted-ˌfast\ *adj* 1 : firmly fixed in place 2 : not subject to change 3 ♦ : firm in belief, determination, or adherence : LOYAL — **stead·fast·ly** *adv*

♦ constant, devoted, faithful, fast, good, loyal, pious, staunch, steady, true, true-blue — more at FAITHFUL

stead·fast·ness *n* ♦ : the quality or state of being steadfast

♦ allegiance, constancy, dedication, devotion, faith, faithfulness, fastness, fealty, fidelity, loyalty — more at FIDELITY

steadi·ness \'ste-dē-nəs\ *n* ♦ : the quality or state of being steady

♦ firmness, soundness, stability, strength, sturdiness — more at STABILITY ♦ constancy, fixedness, immutability, stability — more at CONSTANCY

¹**steady** \'ste-dē\ *adj* **steadi·er; -est** **1** : direct or sure in movement; *also* : CALM **2** : firm in position : FIRM, FIXED **3** ♦ : showing little variation or fluctuation **4** ♦ : constant in feeling, principle, purpose, or attachment **5** ♦ : not changed, replaced, or interrupted : REGULAR **6** ♦ : capable of being depended on : RELIABLE — **steadi·ly** \-də-lē\ *adv* — **steady** *adv*

♦ [3] constant, stable, stationary, unchanging, unvarying — more at CONSTANT ♦ [3] undeviating, uniform, unwavering — more at UNIFORM ♦ [4] constant, devoted, faithful, fast, good, loyal, pious, staunch, steadfast, true, true-blue — more at FAITHFUL ♦ [5] constant, frequent, habitual, periodic, regular, repeated ♦ [6] dependable, good, reliable, responsible, safe, solid, sure, tried, true, trustworthy — more at DEPENDABLE

²**steady** *vb* **stead·ied; steady·ing** : to make or become steady

steak \'stāk\ *n* : a slice of meat and esp. beef; *also* : a slice of a large fish ⟨a tuna ∼⟩

¹**steal** \'stēl\ *vb* **stole** \'stōl\; **sto·len** \'stō-lən\; **steal·ing** **1** ♦ : to take and carry away without right or permission **2** ♦ : to come or go secretly or gradually **3** : to get for oneself slyly or by skill and daring ⟨∼ a kiss⟩ ⟨∼ the ball in basketball⟩ **4** : to gain or attempt to gain a base in baseball by running without the aid of a hit or an error

♦ [1] appropriate, filch, hook, misappropriate, nip, pilfer, pocket, purloin, snitch, swipe, thieve; *also* burglarize, fleece, rob; loot, pillage, plunder, sack; hijack; pick, rifle; poach, rustle, shoplift; collar, grab, grasp, nail, seize, snatch, take; sponge; abduct, kidnap, shanghai, spirit ♦ *usu* steal from [1] burglarize, rip off, rob — more at ROB ♦ [2] lurk, pussyfoot, skulk, slide, slink, slip, snake, sneak — more at SNEAK

²**steal** *n* **1** : an act of stealing **2** ♦ : an advantageous purchase : BARGAIN

♦ bargain, buy, deal — more at BARGAIN

stealth \'stelth\ *n* **1** : secret or unobtrusive procedure **2** : an aircraft design intended to produce a weak radar return

stealthy \'stel-thē\ *adj* **stealth·i·er; -est** ♦ : done by stealth : FURTIVE, SLY — **stealth·i·ly** \'stel-thə-lē\ *adv*

♦ furtive, shady, shifty, slippery, sly, sneaky — more at SNEAKY ♦ clandestine, covert, furtive, hugger-mugger, private, secret, sneak, sneaky, surreptitious, undercover, underground, underhanded — more at SECRET

¹**steam** \'stēm\ *n* **1** : the vapor into which water is changed when heated to the boiling point **2** : water vapor when compressed so that it supplies heat and power **3** : POWER, FORCE, ENERGY

²**steam** *vb* **1** : to pass off as vapor **2** : to emit vapor **3** : to move by or as if by the agency of steam **4** ♦ : to be angry — **steam·er** *n*

♦ boil, burn, fume, rage, seethe — more at BOIL

steam·boat \'stēm-ˌbōt\ *n* : a boat driven by steam

steam engine *n* : a reciprocating engine having a piston driven by steam

steam·fit·ter \'stēm-ˌfi-tər\ *n* : a worker who puts in or repairs equipment (as steam pipes) for heating, ventilating, or refrigerating systems

steam·punk \-ˌpəŋk\ *n* : science fiction involving historical or imagined steam-powered technology

steam·roll·er \-ˌrō-lər\ *n* : a machine for compacting roads or pavements — **steam·roll·er** *also* **steam·roll** \-ˌrōl\ *vb*

steam·ship \-ˌship\ *n* : a ship driven by steam

steamy \'stē-mē\ *adj* **1** : consisting of, characterized by, or full of steam **2** : relating to or dealing with sexual love : EROTIC

steed \'stēd\ *n* : a large solid-hoofed herbivorous mammal domesticated since prehistoric times and used as a pack or draft animal, or for riding : HORSE

¹**steel** \'stēl\ *n* **1** : iron treated with intense heat and mixed with carbon to make it hard and tough **2** : an article made of steel **3** : a quality (as hardness of mind) that suggests steel — **steel** *adj*

²**steel** *vb* ♦ : to fill with courage or determination

♦ encourage, fortify, harden, nerve, ready, season, strengthen, toughen — more at HARDEN

steel wool *n* : long fine steel shavings used esp. for cleaning and polishing

steely *adj* ♦ : resembling or suggesting steel (as in hardness, color, strength, or coldness)

♦ austere, dour, fierce, flinty, forbidding, grim, gruff, rough, rugged, severe, stark, stern — more at GRIM ♦ gray (*or* grey), leaden, pewter, silver, silvery, slate — more at GRAY

¹**steep** \'stēp\ *adj* **1** ♦ : having a very sharp slope : PRECIPITOUS **2** ♦ : too great or too high ⟨∼ prices⟩ — **steep·ly** *adv* — **steep·ness** *n*

♦ [1] abrupt, bold, precipitous, sheer; *also* perpendicular, plumb, straight, vertical; craggy, hilly, mountainous; angled, canted, cocked, heeled, inclined, listed, slanted, sloped, tilted, tipped *Ant* easy ♦ [2] excessive, extreme, immoderate, inordinate, stiff — more at EXCESSIVE

²**steep** *n* : a steep slope

³**steep** *vb* **1** ♦ : to soak in a liquid; *esp* : to extract the essence of by soaking ⟨∼ tea⟩ **2** ♦ : to saturate with or subject thoroughly to (some strong or pervading influence) ⟨∼ed in learning⟩

♦ [1] drench, drown, impregnate, saturate, soak, sop, souse — more at SOAK ♦ [2] imbue, inculcate, infuse, ingrain, invest, suffuse — more at INFUSE

stee·ple \'stē-pəl\ *n* : a tall tapering structure built on top of a church tower; *also* : a church tower

stee·ple·chase \-ˌchās\ *n* [fr. the use of church steeples as landmarks to guide the riders] : a horse race across country; *also* : a race over a course obstructed by hurdles

¹**steer** \'stir\ *n* : a male bovine animal castrated before sexual maturity and usu. raised for beef

²**steer** *vb* **1** ♦ : to direct the course of (as by a rudder or wheel) **2** : GUIDE, CONTROL **3** : to pursue a course of action **4** : to be subject to guidance or direction — **steers·man** \'stirz-mən\ *n*

♦ conduct, direct, guide, lead, marshal, pilot, route, show, usher — more at LEAD

steer·age \'stir-ij\ *n* **1** : DIRECTION, GUIDANCE **2** : a section in a passenger ship for passengers paying the lowest fares

stego·sau·rus \ˌste-gə-'sòr-əs\ *n* : any of a genus of plant-eating armored dinosaurs with a series of bony plates along the backbone

stein \'stīn\ *n* : an earthenware mug

stel·lar \'ste-lər\ *adj* **1** ♦ : of or relating to stars : resembling a star **2** : marked by eminence and distinction

♦ astral, star, starry; *also* celestial, empyrean, heavenly; astronomical, astrophysical; astronautic; starlike

¹**stem** \'stem\ *n* **1** : the main stalk of a plant; *also* : a plant part that supports another part (as a leaf or fruit) **2** : the bow of a ship **3** : a line of ancestry : STOCK **4** : that part of an inflected word which remains unchanged throughout a given inflection **5** : something resembling the stem of a plant — **stem·less** *adj* — **stemmed** \'stemd\ *adj*

²**stem** *vb* **stemmed; stem·ming** : to have a specified source : DERIVE

³**stem** *vb* **stemmed; stem·ming** : to make headway against ⟨∼ the tide⟩

⁴**stem** *vb* **stemmed; stem·ming** : to stop or check by or as if by damming

STEM \\'stem\\ *abbr* science, technology, engineering and math

stem cell *n* : an undifferentiated cell that may give rise to many different types of cell

stench \\'stench\\ *n* : STINK

sten·cil \\'sten-səl\\ *n* [prob. ultim. fr. ME *stanseld* brightly ornamented, fr. AF *estencelé* spangled, pp. of *estenceler* to sparkle, fr. *estencele* spark, fr. VL *stincilla*, alter. of L *scintilla*] : an impervious material (as metal or paper) perforated with lettering or a design through which a substance (as ink or paint) is applied to a surface to be printed — **stencil** *vb*

ste·nog·ra·phy \\stə-'nä-grə-fē\\ *n* : the art or process of writing in shorthand — **ste·nog·ra·pher** \\-fər\\ *n* — **steno·graph·ic** \\ste-nə-'gra-fik\\ *adj*

ste·no·sis \\stə-'nō-səs\\ *n, pl* **-no·ses** \\-ˌsēz\\ : a narrowing of a bodily passage or orifice

stent \\'stent\\ *n* : a short narrow tube inserted into an anatomical vessel esp. to keep a passage open

sten·to·ri·an \\sten-'tōr-ē-ən\\ *adj* ♦ : extremely loud and powerful

♦ booming, clamorous (*or* clamourous), deafening, earsplitting, loud, piercing, resounding, ringing, roaring, sonorous, thunderous — more at LOUD

¹**step** \\'step\\ *n* **1** : a rest for the foot in ascending or descending : STAIR **2** : an advance made by raising one foot and putting it down elsewhere **3** : manner of walking **4** : a small space or distance **5** : a degree, rank, or plane in a series **6** ♦ : a sequential measure leading to a result

♦ expedient, measure, move, shift — more at MEASURE ♦ cut, degree, grade, inch, notch, peg, phase, point, stage — more at DEGREE

²**step** *vb* **stepped; step·ping 1** : to advance or recede by steps **2** ♦ : to go on foot : WALK **3** : to move along briskly **4** : to press down with the foot **5** : to measure by steps **6** : to construct or arrange in or as if in steps **7** : to engage in or perform a dance

♦ foot, leg, pad, traipse, tread, walk — more at WALK

step aerobics *n sing or pl* : aerobics that involves repeatedly stepping on and off a raised platform

step·broth·er \\'step-ˌbrə-thər\\ *n* : the son of one's stepparent by a former marriage

step·child \\-ˌchīld\\ *n* : a child of one's husband or wife by a former marriage

step·daugh·ter \\-ˌdȯ-tər\\ *n* : a daughter of one's wife or husband by a former marriage

step down *vb* **1** ♦ : to give up deliberately : RETIRE, RESIGN **2** : to lower (a voltage) by means of a transformer

♦ *usu* **step down from** leave, quit, resign, retire — more at QUIT ♦ *usu* **step down from** abdicate, abnegate, cede, relinquish, renounce, resign, surrender — more at ABDICATE

step·fa·ther \\-ˌfä-thər\\ *n* : the husband of one's parent when distinct from one's natural or legal father

step·lad·der \\'step-ˌla-dər\\ *n* : a light portable set of steps in a hinged frame

step·moth·er \\-ˌmə-thər\\ *n* : the wife of one's parent when distinct from one's natural or legal mother

step·par·ent \\-ˌpar-ənt\\ *n* : a person who is a stepfather or stepmother

steppe \\'step\\ *n* [Russ *step'*] ♦ : dry level grass-covered treeless land in regions of wide temperature range esp. in southeastern Europe and Asia

♦ down, grassland, plain, prairie, savanna, veld — more at PLAIN

step·sis·ter \\'step-ˌsis-tər\\ *n* : the daughter of one's stepparent by a former marriage

step·son \\-ˌsən\\ *n* : a son of one's wife or husband by a former marriage

step up *vb* **1** : to increase (a voltage) by means of a transformer **2** ♦ : to increase, augment, or advance esp. by one or more steps **3** : to come forward — **step-up** \\'step-ˌəp\\ *n*

♦ amplify, beef, boost, consolidate, deepen, enhance, heighten, intensify, magnify, redouble, strengthen — more at INTENSIFY ♦ accelerate, hasten, hurry, quicken, rush, speed (up), whisk — more at HURRY

ster *abbr* sterling

ste·reo \\'ster-ē-ˌō, 'stir-\\ *n, pl* **ste·re·os 1** : stereophonic reproduction **2** : a stereophonic sound system — **stereo** *adj*

ste·reo·phon·ic \\ˌster-ē-ə-'fä-nik, ˌstir-\\ *adj* : of or relating to sound reproduction designed to create the effect of listening to the original — **ste·reo·phon·i·cal·ly** \\-'fä-ni-k(ə-)lē\\ *adv*

ster·e·o·scope \\'ster-ē-ə-ˌskōp, 'stir-\\ *n* [Gk *stereos* solid + *-skopion* means for viewing] : an optical instrument that blends two slightly different pictures of the same subject to give the effect of depth

ste·reo·scop·ic \\ˌster-ē-ə-'skä-pik, ˌstir-\\ *adj* **1** : of or relating to the stereoscope **2** : characterized by the seeing of objects in three dimensions ⟨~ vision⟩ — **ste·reo·scop·i·cal·ly** \\-'skä-pi-k(ə-)lē\\ *adv* — **ste·re·os·co·py** \\ˌster-ē-'äs-kə-pē, ˌstir-\\ *n*

ste·reo·type \\'ster-ē-ə-ˌtīp, 'stir-\\ *n* **1** : a metal printing plate cast from a mold made from set type **2** : something agreeing with a pattern; *esp* : an idea that many people have about a thing or a group and that may often be untrue or only partly true — **stereotype** *vb* — **ste·reo·typ·i·cal** \\ˌster-ē-ə-'ti-pi-kəl\\ *adj* — **ste·reo·typ·i·cal·ly** \\-pi-k(ə-)lē\\ *adv*

ste·reo·typed \\-ˌtīpt\\ *adj* ♦ : lacking originality or individuality

♦ banal, commonplace, hackneyed, musty, stale, threadbare, tired, trite — more at STALE

ster·ile \\'ster-əl\\ *adj* **1** ♦ : unable to bear fruit, crops, or offspring **2** ♦ : free from living things and esp. germs — **ste·ril·i·ty** \\stə-'ri-lə-tē\\ *n*

♦ [1] barren, impotent, infertile; *also* altered, neutered, castrated, emasculated, gelded; spayed; fruitless, unproductive *Ant* fat, fertile, fruitful ♦ [2] aseptic, hygienic, sanitary — more at SANITARY

ster·il·ize \\'ster-ə-ˌlīz\\ *vb* **-ized; -iz·ing** : to make sterile; *esp* : to free from germs — **ster·il·i·za·tion** \\ˌster-ə-lə-'zā-shən\\ *n* — **ster·il·iz·er** \\'ster-ə-ˌlī-zər\\ *n*

¹**ster·ling** \\'stər-liŋ\\ *n* **1** : British money **2** : sterling silver

²**sterling** *adj* **1** : of, relating to, or calculated in terms of British sterling **2** : having a fixed standard of purity represented by an alloy of 925 parts of silver with 75 parts of copper **3** : made of sterling silver **4** : eminently good : EXCELLENT

¹**stern** \\'stərn\\ *adj* **1** ♦ : having a definite hardness or severity of nature or manner : SEVERE **2** : STOUT, STURDY ⟨~ resolve⟩

♦ austere, authoritarian, flinty, hard, harsh, heavy=handed, ramrod, rigid, rigorous, severe, strict — more at SEVERE

²**stern** *n* : the rear end of a boat

stern·ly *adv* ♦ : in a stern manner

♦ hard, hardly, harshly, ill, oppressively, roughly, severely, stiffly — more at HARDLY

stern·ness *n* : the quality or state of being stern

♦ hardness, harshness, inflexibility, rigidity, severity, strictness — more at SEVERITY

ster·num \\'stər-nəm\\ *n, pl* **sternums** *or* **ster·na** \\-nə\\ : a long flat bone or cartilage at the center front of the chest connecting the ribs of the two sides

ste·roid \\'stir-ˌȯid\\ *n* : any of various compounds including numerous hormones (as anabolic steroids) and sugar derivatives — **steroid** *or* **ste·roi·dal** \\stə-'rȯid-°l\\ *adj*

stetho·scope \\'ste-thə-ˌskōp\\ *n* : an instrument used to detect and listen to sounds produced in the body

ste·ve·dore \\'stē-və-ˌdȯr\\ *n* [Sp *estibador*, fr. *estibar* to pack, fr. L *stipare* to press together] : one who works at loading and unloading ships

ste·via \'stē-vē-ə, -vyə\ *n* : a plant-derived powder used as a noncaloric sweetener

¹**stew** \'stü, 'styü\ *n* **1** : a dish of stewed meat and vegetables served in gravy **2** ♦ : a state of agitation, worry, or resentment

♦ dither, fluster, fret, fuss, huff, lather, pother, tizzy, twitter — more at FRET

²**stew** *vb* **1** : to boil slowly : SIMMER **2** ♦ : to be in a state of agitation, worry, or resentment ⟨~ed over the problem⟩

♦ bother, fear, fret, sweat, trouble, worry — more at WORRY

stew·ard \'stü-ərd, 'styü-\ *n* [ME, fr. OE *stīweard*, fr. *stī, stig* hall, sty + *weard* ward] **1** ♦ : one employed on a large estate to manage domestic concerns **2** : one who supervises the provision and distribution of food (as on a ship); *also* : an employee on a ship or airplane who serves passengers **3** : one actively concerned with the direction of the affairs of an organization

♦ domestic, flunky, lackey, menial, retainer, servant — more at SERVANT

stew·ard·ess \'stü-ər-dəs, 'styü-\ *n* : a woman who is a steward esp. on an airplane

stew·ard·ship *n* ♦ : the conducting, supervising, or managing of something; *esp* : the careful and responsible management of something entrusted to one's care

♦ administration, charge, conduct, control, direction, governance, government, guidance, management, operation, oversight, regulation, running, superintendence, supervision — more at CONDUCT

stg *abbr* sterling

¹**stick** \'stik\ *n* **1** : a cut or broken branch or twig; *also* : a long slender piece of wood **2** : ROD, STAFF **3** : something resembling a stick **4** : a dull uninteresting person **5** *pl* ♦ : remote usu. rural areas

♦ *usu* **sticks** backwoods, bush, frontier, hinterland, up-country — more at FRONTIER

²**stick** *vb* **stuck** \'stək\; **stick·ing 1** : STAB, PRICK **2** ♦ : to pierce with or as if with something pointed **3** : ATTACH, FASTEN **4** : to thrust or project in some direction or manner **5** : to be unable to proceed or move freely **6** ♦ : to hold fast by or as if by gluing : ADHERE **7** : to hold to something firmly or closely : CLING **8** : to become jammed or blocked **9** ♦ : to put or set in a specified place or position

♦ [2] gore, harpoon, impale, lance, pierce, puncture, skewer, spear, spike, stab, transfix — more at IMPALE ♦ [6] adhere, cling, hew; *also* bind, cohere, fasten, fuse, glue, unite ♦ [9] deposit, dispose, fix, lay, place, position, put, set, set up — more at PLACE

stick around *vb* ♦ : to stay or wait about

♦ abide, dwell, hang around, remain, stay, tarry — more at STAY

stick·er \'sti-kər\ *n* : one that sticks (as a bur) or causes sticking (as glue); *esp* : an adhesive label

sticker shock *n* : astonishment and dismay on being informed of a product's unexpectedly high price

stick insect *n* : any of various usu. wingless insects with a long round body resembling a stick

stick·ler \'sti-klər, -kə-lər\ *n* : one who insists on exactness or completeness

stick out *vb* **1** ♦ : to jut out **2** ♦ : to regard with acceptance or tolerance

♦ [1] bag, balloon, beetle, belly, billow, bulge, overhang, poke, project, protrude, start — more at BULGE ♦ [2] abide, bear, brook, countenance, endure, meet, stand, stomach, support, sustain, take, tolerate — more at BEAR

stick shift *n* : a manually operated automobile gearshift usu. mounted on the floor

stick-to-it-ive-ness \stik-'tü-ə-tiv-nəs\ *n* : dogged perseverance : TENACITY

stick up *vb* : to rob at gunpoint — **stick-up** \'stik-,əp\ *n*

sticky \'sti-kē\ *adj* **stick·i·er; -est 1** : having the quality of remaining attached or associated **2** ♦ : being thick or tacky like glue : VISCOUS **3** : tending to stick ⟨~ valve⟩ **4** : DIFFICULT ⟨a ~ problem⟩ **5** ♦ : containing or characterized by perceptible moisture : HUMID

♦ [2] adhesive, gelatinous, gluey, glutinous, gooey, gummy, viscid, viscous; *also* tacky; adherent, tenacious **Ant** nonadhesive ♦ [5] humid, muggy, sultry — more at HUMID

¹**stiff** \'stif\ *adj* **1** ♦ : not pliant : RIGID **2** : not limber ⟨~ joints⟩; *also* : TENSE, TAUT **3** : not flowing or working easily ⟨~ paste⟩ **4 a** : not natural and easy : FORMAL **b** ♦ : lacking in ease or grace : STILTED **5** : STRONG, FORCEFUL ⟨~ breeze⟩ **6** ♦ : inflicting physical discomfort or hardship : SEVERE **7** : extremely or excessively high ⟨paid a ~ fine⟩ — **stiff·ness** *n*

♦ [1] hard, inflexible, rigid, solid, unyielding; *also* inelastic **Ant** flexible, floppy, pliable, pliant, supple, yielding ♦ [4b] awkward, clumsy, gauche, graceless, inelegant, stilted, uncomfortable, uneasy, ungraceful, wooden — more at AWKWARD ♦ [6] bitter, brutal, burdensome, cruel, excruciating, grievous, grim, hard, harsh, heavy, inhuman, murderous, onerous, oppressive, rough, rugged, severe, tough, trying — more at HARSH

²**stiff** *vb* : to refuse to pay or tip

³**stiff** *n* ♦ : a human being : INDIVIDUAL

♦ being, body, creature, human, individual, man, mortal, person — more at HUMAN

stiff·en \'sti-fən\ *vb* : to make or become stiff — **stiff·en·er** *n*

stiff·ly *adv* : in a stiff manner

♦ hard, hardly, harshly, ill, oppressively, roughly, severely, sternly — more at HARDLY

stiff–necked \'stif-'nekt\ *adj* : STUBBORN, HAUGHTY

sti·fle \'stī-fəl\ *vb* **sti·fled; sti·fling 1** ♦ : to kill by depriving of oxygen or air; *also* : to die from lack of oxygen **2** ♦ : to keep in check by effort : SUPPRESS ⟨~ a sneeze⟩ — **sti·fling·ly** *adv*

♦ [1] choke, smother, strangle, suffocate — more at SMOTHER ♦ [2] choke, pocket, repress, smother, strangle, suppress, swallow — more at SUPPRESS

stig·ma \'stig-mə\ *n, pl* **stig·ma·ta** \stig-'mä-tə, 'stig-mə-tə\ *or* **stigmas** [L] **1** ♦ : a mark of disgrace or discredit **2** *stigmata pl* : bodily marks resembling the wounds of the crucified Jesus **3** : the upper part of the pistil of a flower that receives the pollen in fertilization — **stig·mat·ic** \stig-'ma-tik\ *adj*

♦ blot, brand, smirch, spot, stain, taint — more at STAIN

stig·ma·tize \'stig-mə-,tīz\ *vb* **-tized; -tiz·ing 1** : to mark with a stigma **2** : to characterize as disgraceful

stile \'stīl\ *n* : steps used for crossing a fence or wall

sti·let·to \stə-'le-tō\ *n, pl* **-tos** *or* **-toes** [It, dim. of *stilo* stylus, dagger] : a slender dagger

¹**still** \'stil\ *adj* **1** : MOTIONLESS **2** ♦ : making no sound

♦ hushed, muted, noiseless, quiet, silent, soundless — more at SILENT ♦ calm, peaceful, quiet, restful, serene, tranquil — more at QUIET

²**still** *vb* ♦ : to make or become still

♦ allay, calm, compose, quiet, settle, soothe, tranquilize — more at CALM ♦ hush, mute, quell, settle, silence — more at SILENCE

³**still** *adv* **1** ♦ : without motion ⟨sit ~⟩ **2** : up to and during this or that time **3** ♦ : in spite of that : NEVERTHELESS **4** : EVEN ⟨ran ~ faster⟩ **5** : BESIDES, YET

♦ [1] calmly, quiet, quietly; *also* immovably ♦ [3] but, howbeit, however, nevertheless, nonetheless, notwithstanding, though, withal, yet — more at HOWEVER

⁴**still** *n* **1** : the quality or state of being quiet : STILLNESS **2** : a static photograph esp. from a motion picture

⁵**still** *n* **1** : DISTILLERY **2** : apparatus used in distillation

still·birth \'stil-ˌbərth\ *n* : the birth of a dead fetus

still·born \-'bȯrn\ *adj* : born dead

still life *n, pl* **still lifes** : a picture of inanimate objects

still·ness *n* **1** ♦ : freedom from agitation **2** ♦ : the quality or state of being soundless

♦ [1] calm, calmness, hush, peace, placidity, quiet, quietness, repose, serenity, still, tranquility — more at CALM ♦ [2] hush, quiet, quietness, silence, still — more at SILENCE

stilt \'stilt\ *n* : one of a pair of poles for walking with each having a step or loop for the foot to elevate the wearer above the ground; *also* : a polelike support of a structure above ground or water level

stilt·ed \'stil-təd\ *adj* ♦ : not easy and natural ⟨~ language⟩

♦ awkward, clumsy, gauche, graceless, inelegant, stiff, uncomfortable, uneasy, ungraceful, wooden — more at AWKWARD

Stil·ton \'stilt-ᵊn\ *n* : a blue cheese of English origin

stim·u·lant \'sti-myə-lənt\ *n* **1** : an agent (as a drug) that temporarily increases the activity of an organism or any of its parts **2** : something that rouses or incites to activity : STIMULUS **3** : an alcoholic beverage — **stimulant** *adj*

stim·u·late \-ˌlāt\ *vb* **-lat·ed; -lat·ing** ♦ : to make active or more active — **stim·u·la·tion** \ˌsti-myə-'lā-shən\ *n*

♦ animate, brace, energize, enliven, fire, invigorate, jazz up, liven up, pep up, quicken, vitalize, vivify, zip (up) — more at ANIMATE ♦ arouse, encourage, excite, fire, incite, instigate, move, pique, provoke, stir

stim·u·la·tive \'sti-myə-ˌlā-tiv\ *adj* ♦ : having power or tending to stimulate

♦ bracing, invigorating, refreshing, restorative, tonic — more at TONIC

stim·u·lus \'sti-myə-ləs\ *n, pl* **-li** \-ˌlī\ [L] **1** ♦ : something that moves to activity **2** : an agent that directly influences the activity of a living organism or one of its parts

♦ boost, encouragement, goad, impetus, impulse, incentive, incitement, instigation, momentum, motivation, provocation, spur, yeast — more at IMPULSE

¹sting \'stiŋ\ *vb* **stung** \'stəŋ\; **sting·ing** **1** : to prick painfully esp. with a sharp or poisonous process **2** : to cause to suffer acutely

²sting *n* **1 a** : an act of stinging **b** ♦ : a wound, sore, or pain resulting from a sting **2** : a pointed often venom-bearing organ (as of a bee) : STINGER **3** : an elaborate confidence game; *esp* : one worked by undercover police to trap criminals

♦ ache, pain, pang, prick, smart, stitch, tingle, twinge — more at PAIN

sting·er \'stiŋ-ər\ *n* : one that stings; *specif* : a sharp blow or remark

stin·gi·ness \'stin-jē-nəs\ *n* ♦ : the quality or state of being stingy

♦ cheapness, closeness, miserliness, parsimony, tightness — more at PARSIMONY

stin·gy \'stin-jē\ *adj* **stin·gi·er; -est** **1** ♦ : not generous : giving or spending as little as possible **2** ♦ : meanly scanty or small

♦ [1] cheap, close, mean, niggardly, parsimonious, penurious, spare, sparing, tight, tightfisted, uncharitable; *also* careful, chary, conserving, economical, economizing, frugal, saving, scrimping, skimping, thrifty *Ant* bounteous, bountiful, charitable, generous, liberal, munificent, openhanded, unsparing, unstinting ♦ [2] light, meager (*or* meagre), niggardly, poor, scant, scanty, scarce, skimpy, slender, slim, spare, sparse — more at MEAGER

¹stink \'stiŋk\ *vb* **stank** \'staŋk\ *or* **stunk** \'stəŋk\; **stunk; stink·ing** **1** : to give forth a strong and offensive smell **2** : to be extremely bad in quality or repute

²stink *n* : a strong offensive odor

stink·bug \'stiŋk-ˌbəg\ *n* : any of various true bugs that emit a disagreeable odor

stink·er *n* : an offensive or contemptible person

¹stint \'stint\ *vb* **1** ♦ : to be sparing or frugal **2** ♦ : to cut short in amount

♦ *usu* **stint on** scant, skimp, spare — more at SPARE

²stint *n* **1** ♦ : an assigned amount of work **2** : RESTRAINT, LIMITATION **3** ♦ : a period of time spent at a particular activity

♦ [1] assignment, chore, duty, job, task — more at CHORE ♦ [3] hitch, tenure, term, tour — more at TERM

sti·pend \'stī-ˌpend, -pənd\ *n* [ME, alter. of *stipendy*, fr. L *stipendium*, fr. *stips* gift + *pendere* to weigh, pay] ♦ : a fixed sum of money paid periodically for services or to defray expenses

♦ emolument, hire, pay, payment, salary, wage — more at WAGE

stip·ple \'sti-pəl\ *vb* **stip·pled; stip·pling** **1** : to engrave by means of dots and light strokes **2** : to apply (as paint or ink) with small short touches **3** ♦ : to mark with speckles — **stipple** *n*

♦ blotch, dapple, dot, fleck, freckle, mottle, pepper, speck, spot, sprinkle — more at SPOT

stip·u·late \'sti-pyə-ˌlāt\ *vb* **-lat·ed; -lat·ing** **1** : to make an agreement **2** ♦ : to make a special demand (for something) as a condition in an agreement

♦ call, claim, clamor (*or* clamour), command, demand, enjoin, exact, insist, press, quest — more at DEMAND

stip·u·la·tion \ˌsti-pyə-'lā-shən\ *n* **1** : something stipulated **2** ♦ : a condition, requirement, or item specified in a legal instrument

♦ condition, provision, proviso, qualification, reservation — more at CONDITION

¹stir \'stər\ *vb* **stirred; stir·ring** **1** ♦ : to move slightly **2** : to disturb the quiet of **3** ♦ : to mix, dissolve, or make by continued circular movement ⟨~ eggs into cake batter⟩ **4** ♦ : to move to activity (as by pushing, beating, or prodding)

♦ [1] budge, move, shift ♦ [3] agitate, churn, swirl, whirl; *also* beat, paddle, whip, whisk; reel, shake, wheel ♦ *usu* **stir up** [4] abet, ferment, foment, incite, instigate, provoke, raise, whip — more at INCITE ♦ [4] arouse, encourage, excite, fire, incite, instigate, move, pique, provoke, stimulate

²stir *n* **1** ♦ : a state of agitation or activity **2** ♦ : an act of stirring

♦ [1] bustle, commotion, disturbance, turmoil, uproar, welter, whirl — more at COMMOTION ♦ [2] motion, move, movement, moving, shift, stirring — more at MOVEMENT

stir–fry \'stər-ˌfrī\ *vb* : to fry quickly over high heat while stirring continuously — **stir–fry** *n*

stir·ring \'stər-iŋ\ *adj* **1** : ACTIVE, BUSTLING **2** ♦ : giving rise to excitement

♦ breathtaking, electric, exciting, exhilarating, rousing, thrilling — more at EXCITING ♦ affecting, emotional, impressive, moving, poignant, touching — more at MOVING

stir·rup \'stər-əp\ *n* [ME *stirop*, fr. OE *stigrāp*, lit., mounting rope] **1** : a light frame hung from a saddle to support the rider's foot **2** : STAPES

¹stitch \'stich\ *n* **1** ♦ : a sudden sharp pain esp. in the side **2** : one of the series of loops formed by or over a needle in sewing

♦ ache, pain, pang, prick, smart, sting, tingle, twinge — more at PAIN

²stitch *vb* **1** : to fasten or join with stitches **2** : to make (as a design) with stitches **3** : SEW

stk *abbr* stock

stoat \'stōt\ *n, pl* **stoats** *also* **stoat** : the common Old and New World ermine esp. in its brown summer coat

¹stock \'stäk\ *n* **1** *archaic* : a block of wood **2** : a stupid person **3** : a wooden part of a thing serving as its support, frame, or handle **4** *pl* : a device for publicly punishing offenders consisting of a wooden frame with holes in which the feet and hands can be locked **5 ♦** : the original from which others derive; *also* : a group having a common origin **6** : FAMILY **6** : LIVESTOCK **7** : a supply of goods **8** : the ownership element in a corporation divided to give the owners an interest and usu. voting power **9** : a company of actors playing at a particular theater and presenting a series of plays **10** : liquid in which meat, fish, or vegetables have been simmered that is used as a basis for soup, gravy, or sauce

♦ ancestry, blood, clan, family, folks, house, kin, kindred, kinfolk, line, lineage, people, race, tribe — more at FAMILY

²stock *vb* : to provide with stock

³stock *adj* **1** : kept regularly for sale or use **2 ♦** : commonly used : STANDARD

♦ conventional, current, customary, popular, standard, usual — more at CURRENT

stock·ade \stä-'kād\ *n* [Sp *estacada*, fr. *estaca* stake, pale] ♦ : an enclosure (as of posts and stakes) for defense or confinement

♦ brig, hoosegow, jail, lockup, pen, penitentiary, prison — more at JAIL

stock·bro·ker \-ˌbrō-kər\ *n* : one who executes orders to buy and sell securities

stock car *n* : a racing car that is similar to a regular car

stock exchange *n* : a place where the buying and selling of securities is conducted

stock·hold·er \'stäk-ˌhōl-dər\ *n* : one who owns corporate stock

stock·i·nette *or* **stock·i·net** \ˌstä-kə-'net\ *n* : an elastic knitted fabric used esp. for infants' wear and bandages

stock·ing \'stä-kiŋ\ *n* : a close-fitting knitted covering for the foot and leg

stock market *n* **1** : STOCK EXCHANGE **2** : a market for stocks

¹stock·pile \'stäk-ˌpīl\ *n* ♦ : a reserve supply esp. of something essential

♦ cache, hoard, stash, store — more at HOARD

²stockpile *vb* ♦ : to place or store in or on a stockpile; *also* : to accumulate a stockpile of

♦ cache, hoard, lay away, lay up, put by, salt away, stash, store — more at HOARD

stocky \'stä-kē\ *adj* **stock·i·er; -est** ♦ : being short and relatively thick

♦ chunky, dumpy, heavyset, squat, stout, stubby, stumpy, thickset; *also* beefy, brawny, bulky, burly, husky, sturdy, thick, weighty; chubby, corpulent, fat, fleshy, full, gross, heavy, obese, overweight, plump, portly, pudgy, roly-poly, rotund, round; paunchy, potbellied; flabby, soft

stock·yard \'stäk-ˌyärd\ *n* : a yard for stock; *esp* : one for livestock about to be slaughtered or shipped

stodgy \'stä-jē\ *adj* **stodg·i·er; -est** **1** : not interesting : DULL **2** : extremely old-fashioned

¹sto·ic \'stō-ik\ *n* [ME, fr. L *stoicus*, fr. Gk *stōikos*, lit., of the portico, fr. *Stoa (Poikilē)* the Painted Portico, portico at Athens where the philosopher Zeno taught] : one who suffers without complaining

²stoic *or* **sto·i·cal** \-i-kəl\ *adj* ♦ : not affected by passion or feeling; *esp* : showing indifference to pain — **sto·i·cal·ly** \-i-k(ə-)lē\ *adv* — **sto·i·cism** \'stō-ə-ˌsi-zəm\ *n*

♦ forbearing, long-suffering, patient, tolerant, uncomplaining — more at PATIENT ♦ apathetic, cold-blooded, impassive, phlegmatic, stolid, unemotional — more at IMPASSIVE

stoke \'stōk\ *vb* **stoked; stok·ing** **1** : to stir up a fire **2** : to tend and supply fuel to a furnace — **stok·er** *n*

STOL *abbr* short takeoff and landing

¹stole *past of* STEAL

²stole *n* **1** : a long narrow band worn round the neck by some members of the clergy **2** : a long wide scarf or similar covering worn by women

stolen *past part of* STEAL

stol·id \'stä-ləd\ *adj* ♦ : not easily aroused or excited : showing little or no emotion ⟨a ~ face⟩ — **sto·lid·i·ty** \stä-'li-də-tē\ *n* — **stol·id·ly** *adv*

♦ apathetic, cold-blooded, impassive, phlegmatic, stoic, unemotional — more at IMPASSIVE ♦ blank, deadpan, expressionless, impassive, inexpressive, vacant — more at BLANK

sto·lon \'stō-lən, -ˌlän\ *n* : RUNNER 6

¹stom·ach \'stə-mək\ *n* **1** : a saclike digestive organ of a vertebrate into which food goes from the mouth by way of the throat and which opens below into the intestine **2** : a cavity in an invertebrate animal that is analogous to a stomach **3 ♦** : the part of the body that contains the stomach : ABDOMEN **4** : desire for food caused by hunger : APPETITE **5** : INCLINATION, DESIRE

♦ abdomen, belly, gut, solar plexus, tummy; *also* middle, midriff, waist; paunch, potbelly; thorax

²stomach *vb* ♦ : to bear without open resentment : put up with

♦ abide, bear, brook, countenance, endure, meet, stand, stick out, support, sustain, take, tolerate — more at BEAR

stom·ach·ache \-ˌāk\ *n* : pain in or in the region of the stomach

stom·ach·er \'stə-mi-kər, -chər\ *n* : the front of a bodice often appearing between the laces of an outer garment (as in 16th-century costume)

stomp \'stämp, 'stomp\ *vb* **1 ♦** : to walk with a loud heavy step usu. in anger **2** : to strike or beat forcibly with the bottom of the foot : STAMP — **stomp** *n*

♦ clump, lumber, pound, stamp, tramp, tromp — more at LUMBER

¹stone \'stōn\ *n* **1** : hardened earth or mineral matter : ROCK **2** : a small piece of rock **3** : a precious stone : GEM **4** : CALCULUS 3 **5** : a hard stony seed (as of a date) or one (as of a plum) with a stony covering **6** *pl usu* **stone** : a British unit of weight equal to 14 pounds

²stone *vb* **stoned; ston·ing** **1** : to pelt or kill with stones **2** : to remove the stones of (a fruit)

Stone Age *n* : the first known period of prehistoric human culture characterized by the use of stone tools

stoned \'stōnd\ *adj* **1** : DRUNK **2** : being under the influence of a drug

stone's throw *n* ♦ : a short distance

♦ ace, hair, inch, step — more at HAIR

stone·wall \'stōn-ˌwol\ *vb* : to refuse to comply or cooperate with

stone·washed \'stōn-ˌwosht, -ˌwäsht\ *adj* : having been washed with stones during manufacture to create a softer fabric ⟨~ jeans⟩

stony *also* **ston·ey** \'stō-nē\ *adj* ♦ : manifesting no movement or reaction

♦ callous, hard, heartless, inhuman, inhumane, pitiless, soulless, unfeeling, unsympathetic — more at HARD

stood *past and past part of* STAND

stooge \'stüj\ *n* **1** : a person who plays a subordinate or compliant role to a principal **2** : STRAIGHT MAN

stool \'stül\ *n* **1** : a seat usu. without back or arms **2** : FOOTSTOOL **3** : a seat used while urinating or defecating **4** : a discharge of fecal matter

stool pigeon *n* ♦ : a person acting as a decoy or informer; *esp* : a spy sent into a group to report (as to the police) on its activities

♦ betrayer, blabbermouth, informer, rat, snitch, tattler, tattletale — more at INFORMER

¹stoop \'stüp\ *vb* **1** : to bend forward and downward **2** : CONDESCEND **3** : to lower oneself morally ⟨~ to lying⟩

²stoop *n* **1** : an act of bending forward **2** : a bent position of head and shoulders

³stoop *n* [D *stoep*] : a porch, platform, or entrance stairway at a house door

¹stop \'stäp\ *vb* **stopped; stop·ping** **1 ♦** : to close (an opening) by filling or covering closely **2** : to cause to cease : HALT

3 ♦ : to cease to go on **4 ♦** : to bring activity or operation to an end **5 a** : STAY, TARRY **b ♦** : to make a brief call — usu. used with *by* or *in*

♦ *usu* **stop up** [1] block, choke, clog, close (off), congest, dam, fill, jam, obstruct, plug (up), stuff — more at CLOG ♦ [2] arrest, catch, check, draw up, fetch up, halt, hold up, stall, stay, still — more at HALT ♦ [3, 4] break, break off, cease, cut, desist, discontinue, drop, end, halt, knock off, lay off, leave off, quit, shut off; *also* complete, conclude, finish; close (down); deactivate; block, blockade, dam, delay, detain, hinder, hold, hold back, impede, obstruct, stem; call, suspend; arrest, brake, check, clamp down, rein (in), squash, squelch, stamp, stanch, stunt, suppress, turn back; pause, stay, suspend; abolish, abort, annul, demolish, destroy, dissolve, kill, ruin, scuttle, snuff ♦ *usu* **stop by** *or* **stop in** [5b] call, drop (by *or* in), pop (in), visit — more at CALL

²**stop** *n* **1 ♦** : a temporary or final ceasing : END, CESSATION **2** : a set of organ pipes of one tone quality; *also* : a control knob for such a set **3 ♦** : something that impedes, obstructs, or brings to a halt : OBSTRUCTION **4** : PLUG, STOPPER **5** : an act of stopping : CHECK **6** : a delay in a journey **7** : a place for stopping **8** *chiefly Brit* : any of several punctuation marks **9** : a function of an electronic device that stops a recording

♦ [1] cessation, close, closure, conclusion, end, ending, expiration, finish, halt, lapse, shutdown, stoppage, termination — more at END ♦ [3] bar, block, clog, crimp, drag, embarrassment, hindrance, let, obstacle, stumbling block — more at OBSTACLE

stop–ac·tion \ˈstäpˈak-shən\ *n* : STOP-MOTION
stop·gap \ˈstäp-ˌgap\ *n* : something that serves as a temporary expedient : MAKESHIFT
stop·light \-ˌlīt\ *n* : TRAFFIC LIGHT
stop–mo·tion \ˈstäp-ˈmō-shən\ *n* : a filming technique in which successive positions of objects are photographed to produce the appearance of movement
stop·over \ˈstäp-ˌō-vər\ *n* **1** : a stop at an intermediate point in one's journey **2** : a stopping place on a journey
stop·page \ˈstä-pij\ *n* ♦ : the act of stopping : the state of being stopped

♦ cessation, close, closure, conclusion, end, ending, expiration, finish, halt, lapse, shutdown, stop, termination — more at END

stop·per \ˈstä-pər\ *n* : something (as a cork) for sealing an opening
stop·watch \ˈstäp-ˌwäch\ *n* : a watch that can be started or stopped at will for exact timing
stor·age \ˈstōr-ij\ *n* **1 a** ♦ : space for storing **b** : cost of storing **2** : MEMORY 6 **3** : the act of storing; *esp* : the safekeeping of goods (as in a warehouse)

♦ depository, depot, magazine, repository, storehouse, warehouse — more at STOREHOUSE

storage battery *n* : a group of connected rechargeable electrochemical cells used to provide electric current
¹**store** \ˈstōr\ *vb* **stored; stor·ing 1 ♦** : to place or leave in a safe location for preservation or future use **2 ♦** : to provide esp. for a future need ⟨∼ information⟩

♦ [1, 2] cache, hoard, lay away, lay up, put by, salt away, stash, stockpile — more at HOARD

²**store** *n* **1 ♦** : something accumulated and kept for future use **2** : a large or ample quantity **3** : STOREHOUSE **4 ♦** : a retail business establishment

♦ [1] cache, deposit, hoard, reserve, stash, stock, stockpile; *also* budget, fund, nest egg, pool, reservoir, supply; accumulation, assemblage, collection, gathering ♦ [4] emporium, shop — more at SHOP

store·house \-ˌhaus\ *n* **1 ♦** : a building for storing goods or supplies **2** : an abundant source or supply

♦ depository, depot, magazine, repository, storage, warehouse; *also* cache, storeroom; bank, bin, container, locker; arsenal, dump

store·keep·er \-ˌkē-pər\ *n* : one who operates a retail store
store·room \-ˌrüm, -ˌrum\ *n* : a room for storing goods or supplies
sto·ried \ˈstōr-ēd\ *adj* : celebrated in story or history
stork \ˈstórk\ *n* : any of various large stout-billed Old World wading birds related to the herons and ibises
¹**storm** \ˈstórm\ *n* **1 ♦** : a heavy fall of rain, snow, or hail with high wind **2 ♦** : a sudden or violent outbreak or disturbance **3** : a mass attack on a defended position **4 ♦** : a heavy discharge of objects **5** : a disturbed or agitated state — **storm·i·ly** \ˈstór-mə-lē\ *adv* — **storm·i·ness** \-mē-nəs\ *n*

♦ [1] cloudburst, deluge, downpour, rain, rainstorm, wet — more at RAIN ♦ [2] cataclysm, convulsion, paroxysm, tempest, tumult, upheaval, uproar — more at CONVULSION ♦ [2] agony, burst, eruption, explosion, fit, flare, flare-up, flash, flush, gale, gush, gust, outburst, paroxysm, spasm — more at OUTBURST ♦ [4] barrage, bombardment, cannonade, fusillade, hail, salvo, shower, volley — more at BARRAGE

²**storm** *vb* **1 a** : to blow with violence **b ♦** : to rain, snow, or hail heavily **2 ♦** : to make a mass attack against **3** : to be violently angry : RAGE **4** : to rush along furiously

♦ [1b] pour, precipitate, rain — more at RAIN ♦ [2] assail, assault, attack, beset, charge, descend, jump, pounce (on *or* upon), raid, rush, strike — more at ATTACK

stormy *adj* **1 ♦** : relating to, characterized by, or indicative of a storm **2 ♦** : marked by turmoil or fury

♦ [1] bleak, dirty, foul, inclement, nasty, raw, rough, squally, tempestuous, turbulent, wild — more at FOUL ♦ [1] rainy, wet — more at RAINY ♦ [2] explosive, ferocious, fierce, furious, hot, rabid, rough, tempestuous, turbulent, violent, volcanic — more at VIOLENT

¹**sto·ry** \ˈstōr-ē\ *n, pl* **stories 1 ♦** : an account of incidents or events : NARRATIVE **2 ♦** : a statement regarding the facts of a situation : REPORT **3 ♦** : usu. short narrative of an interesting, amusing, or biographical incident : ANECDOTE **4 ♦** : a fictional narrative shorter than a novel : SHORT STORY **5** : an untrue statement made with intent to deceive : LIE, FALSEHOOD **6 ♦** : a news article or broadcast

♦ [1, 2] account, chronicle, history, narrative, record, report — more at ACCOUNT ♦ [3] anecdote, tale; *also* episode, event, happening, incident, occurrence; recital, recitation ♦ [4] narrative, novella, short story; *also* fable, parable; anecdote, joke; fairy tale, legend, myth, romance; account, annals, chronicle, history, record, report ♦ [6] intelligence, item, news, tidings, word — more at NEWS

²**story** *also* **sto·rey** \ˈstōr-ē\ *n, pl* **stories** *also* **storeys** : a floor of a building or the space between two adjacent floor levels
sto·ry·tell·er \-ˌte-lər\ *n* : a teller of stories
¹**stout** \ˈstaut\ *adj* **1 ♦** : strong of character : BRAVE **2 ♦** : not weak or uncertain : FIRM **3 ♦** : physically or materially strong **4** : STAUNCH, ENDURING **5** : SOLID **6 a** : possessing or filled with force : FORCEFUL **b** : VIOLENT **7 ♦** : bulky in body : THICKSET

♦ [1, 3] brave, hard, hard-bitten, hardy, rugged, strong, sturdy, tough, vigorous — more at HARDY ♦ [2] firm, forceful, hearty, lusty, robust, solid, strong, sturdy, vigorous ♦ [7] chunky, dumpy, heavyset, squat, stocky, stubby, stumpy, thickset — more at STOCKY

²**stout** *n* : a dark heavy ale
stout·ly *adv* ♦ : in a stout manner

♦ energetically, firmly, forcefully, forcibly, hard, mightily, powerfully, stiffly, strenuously, strongly, sturdily, vigorously — more at HARD

stout·ness *n* **1 ♦** : the quality or state of being strong physically or morally **2** : bulkiness of structure

♦ bravery, courage, daring, fearlessness, gallantry, guts, hardihood, heart, heroism, nerve, valor — more at COURAGE

¹**stove** \'stōv\ *n* : an apparatus that burns fuel or uses electricity to provide heat (as for cooking or heating)

²**stove** *past and past part of* STAVE

stow \'stō\ *vb* **1** : to put away : STORE ⟨~ baggage⟩ **2** : to pack in a compact mass

stow·away \'stō-ə-ˌwā\ *n* : one who hides on a vehicle to ride free

STP *abbr* standard temperature and pressure

strad·dle \'strad-ᵊl\ *vb* **strad·dled**; **strad·dling 1** : to stand, sit, or walk with legs spread apart **2** : to favor or seem to favor two apparently opposite sides — **straddle** *n*

strafe \'strāf\ *vb* **strafed**; **straf·ing** [G *Gott strafe England* may God punish England, propaganda slogan during World War I] : to fire upon with machine guns from a low-flying airplane

strag·gle \'stra-gəl\ *vb* **strag·gled**; **strag·gling 1** : to wander from the direct course : ROVE, STRAY **2** : to become separated from others of the same kind — **strag·gler** *n* — **strag·gly** \'stra-g(ə-)lē\ *adj*

¹**straight** \'strāt\ *adj* **1** ♦ : free from curves, bends, angles, or irregularities **2** ♦ : not wandering from the main point or proper course ⟨~ thinking⟩ **3** ♦ : exhibiting honesty and fairness : UPRIGHT **4** : having the elements in correct order **5** : free from extraneous matter : UNMIXED ⟨~ whiskey⟩ **6** : CONVENTIONAL, SQUARE; *also* : HETEROSEXUAL **7** : marked by honest sincere expression

♦ [1] right, straightforward; *also* unbent, uncurled; direct, undeviating, unswerving **Ant** crooked ♦ [2] direct, forthright, foursquare, plain, straightforward ♦ [3] decent, ethical, good, honest, honorable (*or* honourable), just, moral, right, righteous, upright, virtuous — more at GOOD

²**straight** *adv* ♦ : in a straight manner

♦ dead, direct, directly, due, plump, right — more at DIRECTLY ♦ directly, forthrightly, foursquare, plain, plainly, straightforward — more at STRAIGHTFORWARD

³**straight** *n* **1** : a straight line, course, or arrangement **2** : the part of a racetrack between the last turn and the finish **3** : a sequence of five cards in a poker hand

straight–arm \'strāt-ˌärm\ *n* : an act of warding off a person with the arm fully extended — **straight–arm** *vb*

¹**straight·away** \'strā-tə-ˌwā\ *n* : a straight stretch (as at a racetrack)

²**straight·away** \ˌstrā-tə-ˈwā\ *adv* ♦ : without delay : IMMEDIATELY

♦ immediate, instant, instantaneous — more at INSTANTANEOUS

straight·edge \'strāt-ˌej\ *n* : a piece of material with a straight edge for testing straight lines and surfaces or drawing straight lines

straight·en \'strāt-ᵊn\ *vb* : to make or become straight

straight flush *n* : a poker hand containing five cards of the same suit in sequence

straight·for·ward \strāt-ˈfȯr-wərd\ *adj* **1** ♦ : free from evasiveness or obscurity : CANDID **2** ♦ : proceeding in a straight course or manner

♦ [1] candid, direct, forthright, foursquare, frank, honest, open, outspoken, plain, straight, unguarded, unreserved — more at FRANK ♦ [2] right, straight — more at STRAIGHT ♦ [2] direct, forthright, foursquare, plain, straight; *also* aboveboard, candid, frank, honest, open, outspoken, plainspoken, unguarded, unreserved; artless, earnest, sincere; uninhibited, unrestrained; abrupt, bluff, blunt, brusque, curt, gruff, sharp; impolite, inconsiderate, rude, tactless, undiplomatic; true, truthful, veracious **Ant** circuitous, indirect, roundabout

straight man *n* : an entertainer who feeds lines to a comedian who replies with usu. humorous quips

straight·way \'strāt-ˈwā, -ˌwā\ *adv* : without delay or hesitation : IMMEDIATELY

¹**strain** \'strān\ *n* [ME *streen* progeny, lineage, fr. OE *strēon* gain, acquisition] **1** : line of descent : ANCESTRY **2** : a group (as of people or plants) of presumed common ancestry **3** : an inherited or inherent character or quality ⟨a ~ of madness in the family⟩ **4** : a slight admixture : TRACE **5** ♦ : a pleasing succession of musical tones : MELODY **6** : the general style or tone

♦ air, lay, melody, song, tune, warble — more at MELODY

²**strain** *vb* [ME, fr. MF *estraindre*, fr. L *stringere* to bind or draw tight, press together] **1** : to draw taut **2** ♦ : to exert to the utmost **3** : to strive violently **4** ♦ : to injure by improper or excessive use **5** : to filter or remove by filtering **6** : to stretch beyond a proper limit **7** : to pass through or as if through a strainer — **strain·er** *n*

♦ [2] drudge, endeavor (*or* endeavour), fag, grub, hustle, labor (*or* labour), peg, plod, plug, slave, slog, strive, struggle, sweat, toil, work — more at LABOR ♦ [4] pull, rack, stretch, wrench; *also* fray, tax, weaken; damage, harm, hurt, impair, wound

³**strain** *n* **1** ♦ : excessive tension or exertion (as of body or mind) **2** : bodily injury from excessive tension, effort, or use; *esp* : one in which muscles or ligaments are unduly stretched usu. from a wrench or twist **3** : deformation of a material body under the action of applied forces

♦ pressure, stress, tension — more at STRESS

strained *adj* : done or produced with excessive effort

¹**strait** \'strāt\ *adj* [ME, fr. AF *estreit*, fr. L *strictus* strait, strict, fr. pp. of *stringere*] **1** *archaic* : STRICT **2** *archaic* : NARROW **3** *archaic* : CONSTRICTED **4** : DIFFICULT, STRAITENED

²**strait** *n* **1** ♦ : a narrow channel connecting two bodies of water **2** *pl* : DISTRESS

♦ channel, narrows, sound — more at CHANNEL

strait·en \'strāt-ᵊn\ *vb* **1** : to hem in : CONFINE **2** : to subject to distress or difficulty ⟨~ed by misfortune⟩

strait·jack·et *also* **straight·jack·et** \'strāt-ja-kət\ *n* : a cover or garment of strong material (as canvas) used to bind the body and esp. the arms closely in restraining a violent prisoner or patient — **straitjacket** *vb*

strait·laced *or* **straight·laced** \-ˈlāst\ *adj* ♦ : strict in manners, morals, or opinion

♦ prim, prudish, puritanical; *also* priggish, staid, stuffy; genteel, proper, refined; decent, honest, moral, right, righteous, upright, virtuous

¹**strand** \'strand\ *n* ♦ : SHORE, BEACH

²**strand** *vb* **1** : to run, drift, or drive upon the shore ⟨a ~ed ship⟩ **2** : to place or leave in a helpless position

³**strand** *n* **1** : one of the fibers twisted or plaited together into a cord, rope, or cable; *also* : a cord, rope, or cable made up of such fibers **2** : a twisted or plaited ropelike mass ⟨a ~ of pearls⟩ — **strand·ed** \'stran-dəd\ *adj*

strange \'strānj\ *adj* **strang·er**; **strang·est** [ME, fr. AF *estrange*, fr. L *extraneus*, lit., external, fr. *extra* outside] **1** : of external origin, kind, or character **2** ♦ : not before known, heard, or seen **3** : DISTANT 6 **4** ♦ : not habituated : UNACCUSTOMED — **strange·ly** *adv* — **strange·ness** *n*

♦ [2] fresh, new, novel, original, unfamiliar, unknown — more at NEW ♦ [2] bizarre, curious, far-out, funny, kinky, odd, outlandish, outré, peculiar, quaint, queer, quirky, remarkable, screwy, wacky, weird, wild — more at ODD ♦ [4] curious, extraordinary, funny, odd, peculiar, queer, rare, unaccustomed, uncommon, unique, unusual, weird — more at UNUSUAL

strang·er \'strān-jər\ *n* **1** : FOREIGNER **2** : INTRUDER **3** : a person with whom one is unacquainted

stran·gle \'stran-gəl\ *vb* **stran·gled**; **stran·gling 1** ♦ : to choke to death **2** : to withhold from circulation or expression : SUPPRESS — **stran·gler** *n*

♦ choke, garrote, throttle — more at CHOKE

stran·gu·late \'stran-gyə-ˌlāt\ *vb* **-lat·ed**; **-lat·ing 1** : STRANGLE, CONSTRICT **2** : to become so constricted as to stop circulation

stran·gu·la·tion \ˌstran-gyə-ˈlā-shən\ *n* : the act or process of strangling or strangulating; *also* : the state of being strangled or strangulated

¹strap \'strap\ *n* : a narrow strip of flexible material used esp. for fastening, holding together, or wrapping

²strap *vb* **strapped; strap·ping 1** : to secure with a strap **2** : BIND, CONSTRICT **3** : to flog with a strap **4** : STROP

strap·less \-ləs\ *adj* : having no straps; *esp* : having no shoulder straps

¹strapping *adj* : LARGE, STRONG, HUSKY

²strap·ping *n* : material for a strap

strat·a·gem \'stra-tə-jəm, -ˌjem\ *n* **1** ♦ : a trick to deceive or outwit the enemy; *also* : a deceptive scheme **2** : skill in deception

   ♦ artifice, device, dodge, gimmick, jig, ploy, scheme, sleight, trick, wile — more at TRICK

strat·e·gy \'stra-tə-jē\ *n, pl* **-gies** [Gk *stratēgia* generalship, fr. *stratēgos* general, fr. *stratos* camp, army + *agein* to lead] **1** : the science and art of military command aimed at meeting the enemy under conditions advantageous to one's own force **2** ♦ : a careful plan or method esp. for achieving an end — **stra·te·gic** \strə-'tē-jik\ *adj* — **strat·e·gist** \'stra-tə-jist\ *n*

   ♦ approach, fashion, form, manner, method, style, system, tack, tactics, technique, way — more at METHOD

strat·i·fy \'stra-tə-ˌfī\ *vb* **-fied; -fy·ing** : to form or arrange in layers — **strat·i·fi·ca·tion** \ˌstra-tə-fə-'kā-shən\ *n*

stra·tig·ra·phy \strə-'ti-grə-fē\ *n* : geology that deals with rock strata — **strati·graph·ic** \ˌstra-tə-'gra-fik\ *adj*

strato·sphere \'stra-tə-ˌsfir\ *n* : the part of the earth's atmosphere between about 7 miles (11 kilometers) and 31 miles (50 kilometers) above the earth — **strato·spher·ic** \ˌstra-tə-'sfir-ik, -'sfer-\ *adj*

stra·tum \'strā-təm, 'stra-\ *n, pl* **stra·ta** \'strā-tə, 'stra-\ [NL, fr. L, spread, bed, fr. neut. of *stratus*, pp. of *sternere* to spread out] **1** : a bed, layer, or sheetlike mass (as of one kind of rock lying between layers of other kinds of rock) **2** ♦ : a level of culture; *also* : a group of people representing one stage in cultural development

   ♦ caste, class, estate, folk, order — more at CLASS

¹straw \'strȯ\ *n* **1** : stalks of grain after threshing; *also* : a single coarse dry stem (as of a grass) **2** : a thing of small worth : TRIFLE **3** : a tube (as of paper or plastic) for sucking up a beverage

²straw *adj* **1** : made of straw **2** : having no real force or validity ⟨a ~ vote⟩ **3** ♦ : of the color of straw

   ♦ blond, fair, flaxen, golden, sandy — more at BLOND

straw·ber·ry \'strȯ-ˌber-ē, -bə-rē\ *n* : an edible juicy usu. red pulpy fruit of any of several low herbs with white flowers and long slender runners; *also* : one of these herbs

straw boss *n* : a foreman of a small group of workers

straw·flow·er \'strȯ-ˌflau̇-ər\ *n* : any of several plants whose flowers can be dried with little loss of form or color

¹stray \'strā\ *n* **1** : a domestic animal wandering at large or lost **2** : WAIF

²stray *vb* **1** : to wander or roam without purpose **2** : DEVIATE ⟨~ed from the topic⟩

³stray *adj* **1** : having strayed : separated from the group or the main body **2** ♦ : occurring at random ⟨~ remarks⟩

   ♦ aimless, arbitrary, desultory, erratic, haphazard, random, scattered — more at RANDOM

¹streak \'strēk\ *n* **1** ♦ : a line or mark of a different color or texture from its background **2** : a narrow band of light; *also* : a lightning bolt **3** : a slight admixture : TRACE **4** : a brief run (as of luck); *also* : an unbroken series

   ♦ band, bar, stripe — more at STRIPE

²streak *vb* **1** : to form streaks in or on **2** : to move very swiftly

¹stream \'strēm\ *n* **1** : a body of water (as a river) flowing on the earth; *also* : any body of flowing fluid (as water or gas) **2** : a continuous procession ⟨a ~ of traffic⟩

²stream *vb* **1** ♦ : to flow in or as if in a stream **2** : to pour out streams of liquid **3** : to trail out in length **4** : to

move forward in a steady stream **5** : to transfer (digital data, such as audio or visual material) in a continuous stream esp. for processing or playback

   ♦ flow, pour, roll, run — more at FLOW ♦ bowl, breeze, coast, drift, flow, glide, roll, sail, skim, slide, slip, sweep, whisk — more at FLOW

stream·bed \'strēm-ˌbed\ *n* : the channel occupied by a stream

stream·er \'strē-mər\ *n* **1** ♦ : a long narrow ribbonlike flag **2** : a long ribbon on a dress or hat **3** : a newspaper headline that runs across the entire sheet **4** *pl* : AURORA

   ♦ banner, colors (*or* colours), ensign, flag, jack, pennant, standard — more at FLAG

stream·ing \'strē-miŋ\ *adj* : relating to or being the transfer of data (as music or videos) in a continuous stream esp. for immediate processing or playback

stream·let \'strēm-lət\ *n* ♦ : a small stream

   ♦ brook, creek, rill, rivulet — more at CREEK

stream·lined \-ˌlīnd\ *adj* **1** : made with contours to reduce resistance to motion through water or air **2** : SIMPLIFIED **3** : MODERNIZED — **stream·line** *vb*

street \'strēt\ *n* [ME *strete*, fr. OE *strǣt*, fr. LL *strata* paved road, fr. L, fem. of *stratus*, pp. of *sternere* to spread out] **1** ♦ : a thoroughfare esp. in a city, town, or village **2** : the occupants of the houses on a street

   ♦ artery, avenue, drag, drive, pass, road, route, thoroughfare, way — more at WAY

street·car \-ˌkär\ *n* : a passenger vehicle running on rails on city streets

street hockey *n* : a game resembling ice hockey played on a hard surface with hockey sticks and a small ball

street railway *n* : a company operating streetcars or buses

street·walk·er \'strēt-ˌwȯ-kər\ *n* : PROSTITUTE

strength \'streŋth\ *n* **1** ♦ : the quality of being strong : ability to do or endure **2** ♦ : power to resist force **3** : power to resist attack **4** : INTENSITY **5** : force as measured in numbers ⟨the ~ of an army⟩

   ♦ [1] energy, force, main, might, muscle, potency, power, sinew, vigor (*or* vigour) — more at POWER
   ♦ [2] firmness, soundness, stability, steadiness, sturdiness — more at STABILITY

strength·en \'streŋ-thən\ *vb* ♦ : to make or become stronger — **strength·en·er** *n*

   ♦ beef, fortify, harden, toughen; *also* anneal, temper; firm (up), tone (up); energize, invigorate, vitalize; restrengthen *Ant* debilitate, enervate, enfeeble, weaken
   ♦ amplify, beef, boost, consolidate, deepen, enhance, heighten, intensify, magnify, redouble, step up — more at INTENSIFY

stren·u·ous \'stren-yə-wəs\ *adj* **1** : vigorously active : ENERGETIC **2** ♦ : requiring energy or stamina

   ♦ arduous, demanding, difficult, exacting, formidable, grueling, hard, herculean, laborious, murderous, rough, stiff, tall, toilsome, tough — more at HARD

stren·u·ous·ly *adv* ♦ : in a strenuous manner

   ♦ energetically, firmly, forcefully, forcibly, hard, mightily, powerfully, stiffly, stoutly, strongly, sturdily, vigorously — more at HARD

strep \'strep\ *n* : STREPTOCOCCUS

strep throat *n* : an inflammatory sore throat caused by streptococci and marked by fever, prostration, and toxemia

strep·to·coc·cus \ˌstrep-tə-'kä-kəs\ *n, pl* **-coc·ci** \-'kä-ˌkī, -'käk-ˌsī, -'kä-ˌkē, -'käk-ˌsē\ : any of various spherical bacteria that usu. grow in chains and include some causing serious diseases — **strep·to·coc·cal** \-kəl\ *adj*

strep·to·my·cin \-'mīs-ᵊn\ *n* : an antibiotic produced by soil bacteria and used esp. in treating tuberculosis

¹stress \'stres\ *n* **1** : PRESSURE, STRAIN; *esp* : a force that tends to distort a body **2** ♦ : a factor that induces bodily or mental tension; *also* : a state induced by such a stress **3** ♦ : force or intensity that gives impressiveness or importance to something : EMPHASIS **4** : relative prominence of sound **5** : ACCENT; *also* : any syllable carrying the accent — **stress·ful** \'stres-fəl\ *adj*

♦ [2] pressure, strain, tension; *also* load, weight; anxiety, concern, uneasiness, worry; aggravation, anger, annoyance, exasperation, irritation, persecution, trouble ♦ [3] accent, accentuation, emphasis, weight — more at EMPHASIS

²**stress** *vb* **1** : to put pressure or strain on **2** ♦ : to put emphasis on : ACCENT

♦ accent, accentuate, emphasize, feature, highlight, play, point, underline, underscore — more at EMPHASIZE

¹**stretch** \'strech\ *vb* **1** ♦ : to spread or reach out : EXTEND **2** ♦ : to draw out in length or breadth : EXPAND — often used with *out* **3** : to make tense; *also* : to injure by improper or excessive use : STRAIN **4** ♦ : to amplify or enlarge beyond natural or proper limits : EXAGGERATE **5** : to become extended without breaking ⟨rubber ∼*es* easily⟩

♦ [1] draw out, elongate, extend, lengthen, prolong, protract — more at EXTEND ♦ *usu* **stretch out** [2] expand, extend, fan, flare, open, spread, unfold ♦ [4] color (*or* colour), elaborate, embellish, embroider, exaggerate, magnify, pad — more at EMBROIDER

²**stretch** *n* **1** : an act of extending or drawing out beyond ordinary or normal limits **2** ♦ : a continuous extent in length, area, or time **3** : the extent to which something may be stretched **4** : either of the straight sides of a racecourse

♦ distance, lead, length — more at DISTANCE ♦ breadth, expanse, extent, reach, spread — more at EXPANSE ♦ bit, space, spell, while — more at WHILE

³**stretch** *adj* : easily stretched ⟨∼ pants⟩
stretch·er \'stre-chər\ *n* **1** : one that stretches **2** : a device for carrying a sick, injured, or dead person
stretch marks *n pl* : striae on the skin (as of the abdomen) due to excessive stretching and rupture of elastic fibers (as from pregnancy)
strew \'strü\ *vb* **strewed; strewed** *or* **strewn** \'strün\; **strew·ing** **1** : to spread by scattering **2** ♦ : to cover by or as if by scattering something over or on **3** : DISSEMINATE

♦ dot, pepper, scatter, sow, spray, sprinkle — more at SCATTER

stria \'strī-ə\ *n, pl* **stri·ae** \'strī-ˌē\ **1** : STRIATION 3 **2** : a stripe or line (as in the skin)
stri·at·ed muscle \'strī-ˌā-təd-\ *n* : muscle tissue made up of long thin cells with many nuclei and alternate light and dark stripes that includes esp. the muscle of the heart and muscle that moves the vertebrate skeleton and is mostly under voluntary control
stri·a·tion \strī-'ā-shən\ *n* **1** : the state of being marked with stripes or lines **2** : arrangement of striations or striae **3** : a minute groove, scratch, or channel esp. when one of a parallel series
strick·en \'stri-kən\ *adj* **1** : afflicted by or as if by disease, misfortune, or sorrow **2** : WOUNDED ⟨was ∼ by an arrow⟩
strict \'strikt\ *adj* **1** ♦ : allowing no evasion or escape : RIGOROUS ⟨∼ discipline⟩ **2** ♦ : free from error : PRECISE

♦ [1] austere, authoritarian, flinty, hard, harsh, heavy-handed, ramrod, rigid, rigorous, severe, stern — more at SEVERE ♦ [2] accurate, authentic, exact, faithful, precise, right, true, veracious — more at FAITHFUL

strict·ly *adv* ♦ : in a strict manner

♦ exactly, precisely, rigidly, rigorously; *also* carefully, conscientiously, meticulously, scrupulously *Ant* imprecisely, inexactly, loosely

strict·ness *n* ♦ : the quality or state of being strict

♦ hardness, harshness, inflexibility, rigidity, severity, sternness — more at SEVERITY

stric·ture \'strik-chər\ *n* **1** : an abnormal narrowing of a bodily passage; *also* : the narrowed part **2** ♦ : hostile criticism : a critical remark

♦ censure, denunciation, rebuke, reprimand, reproach, reproof — more at CENSURE

¹**stride** \'strīd\ *vb* **strode** \'strōd\; **strid·den** \'strid-ᵊn\; **strid·ing** ♦ : to walk or run with long regular steps — **strid·er** *n*

♦ file, march, pace, parade — more at MARCH

²**stride** *n* **1** : a long step **2** : a stage of progress **3** : manner of striding : GAIT
stri·dent \'strīd-ᵊnt\ *adj* : harsh sounding : GRATING, SHRILL
strife \'strīf\ *n* **1** ♦ : the state or condition of distrust or enmity : CONFLICT **2** : FIGHT, STRUGGLE

♦ conflict, discord, dissension, dissent, disunity, friction, schism, variance, war, warfare — more at DISCORD

¹**strike** \'strīk\ *vb* **struck** \'strək\; **struck** *also* **strick·en** \'stri-kən\; **strik·ing** **1** : to take a course : GO ⟨*struck* off through the brush⟩ **2** ♦ : to touch or hit sharply; *also* : to deliver a blow **3** : to produce by or as if by a blow ⟨*struck* terror in the foe⟩ **4** : to lower (as a flag or sail) **5** ♦ : to collide with; *also* : to injure or destroy by collision **6** ♦ : DELETE, CANCEL **7** : to produce by impressing ⟨*struck* a medal⟩; *also* : COIN ⟨∼ a new cent⟩ **8** : to cause to sound ⟨∼ a bell⟩ **9** : to afflict suddenly : lay low ⟨*stricken* with a high fever⟩ **10** ♦ : to appear to; *also* : to appear to as remarkable : IMPRESS **11** : to reach by reckoning ⟨∼ an average⟩ **12** : to stop work in order to obtain a change in conditions of employment **13** : to cause (a match) to ignite by rubbing **14** : to come upon ⟨∼ gold⟩ **15** : TAKE ON, ASSUME ⟨∼ a pose⟩ **16** : to occur to **17** ♦ : to dismantle and take away — **strik·er** *n*

♦ [2] bash, bat, clout, crack, hit, slug, swat ♦ [2] assail, assault, attack, beset, charge, descend, jump, pounce (on *or* upon), raid, rush, storm — more at ATTACK ♦ [5] bang, bash, bump, collide, crash, hit, impact, knock, ram, slam, smash, swipe, thud — more at HIT ♦ [10] affect, impact, impress, influence, move, sway, tell, touch — more at AFFECT ♦ [17] disassemble, dismantle, knock down, take down — more at DISASSEMBLE

²**strike** *n* **1** ♦ : an act or instance of striking **2** : a sudden discovery of rich ore or oil deposits **3** : a pitched baseball that is swung at but not hit **4** : the knocking down of all the bowling pins with the 1st ball **5** ♦ : a military attack **6** ♦ : a quality or circumstance that makes achievement unusually difficult

♦ [1] bump, collision, concussion, crash, impact, jar, jolt, shock, smash, wallop — more at IMPACT ♦ [5] aggression, assault, attack, charge, descent, offense (*or* offence), offensive, onset, onslaught, raid, rush — more at ATTACK ♦ [6] disadvantage, drawback, handicap, liability, minus, penalty — more at DISADVANTAGE

strike·break·er \-ˌbrā-kər\ *n* : a person hired to replace a striking worker
strike·out \-ˌaut\ *n* : an out in baseball as a result of a batter's being charged with three strikes
strike out *vb* **1** : to enter upon a course of action **2** : to start out vigorously **3** : to make an out in baseball by a strikeout
strike up *vb* **1** : to begin or cause to begin to sing or play ⟨*strike up* the band⟩ **2** : BEGIN ⟨*strike up* a conversation⟩
strike zone *n* : the area over home plate through which a pitched baseball must pass to be called a strike
striking *adj* ♦ : attracting attention : very noticeable — **strik·ing·ly** *adv*

♦ bold, catchy, conspicuous, emphatic, marked, noticeable, prominent, pronounced, remarkable — more at NOTICEABLE

¹**string** \'strin\ *n* **1** ♦ : a line usu. composed of twisted threads **2** ♦ : a series of things arranged as if strung on a

cord **3** : a plant fiber (as a leaf vein) **4** *pl* : the stringed instruments of an orchestra

♦ [1] cable, cord, lace, line, rope, wire — more at CORD ♦ [2] column, cue, file, line, queue, range, train — more at LINE ♦ [2] chain, progression, sequence, train — more at CHAIN

²**string** *vb* **strung** \'strəŋ\; **string·ing 1** : to provide with strings ⟨~ a racket⟩ **2** : to make tense **3** : to thread on or as if on a string ⟨~ pearls⟩ **4** : to hang, tie, or fasten by a string **5** : to take the strings out of ⟨~ beans⟩ **6** : to extend like a string

string along *vb* ♦ : to cause to accept as true or valid what is false or invalid

♦ beguile, bluff, cozen, deceive, delude, dupe, fool, gull, have, hoax, hoodwink, humbug, misinform, mislead, take in, trick — more at DECEIVE

string bean *n* : a bean of one of the older varieties of kidney bean that have stringy fibers on the lines of separation of the pods; *also* : SNAP BEAN

string bikini *n* : a scanty bikini

string cheese *n* : cheese that can be pulled apart in narrow strips

stringed \'striŋd\ *adj* **1** : having strings ⟨~ instruments⟩ **2** : produced by strings

strin·gen·cy \'strin-jən-sē\ *n* **1** : STRICTNESS, SEVERITY **2** : SCARCITY ⟨~ of money⟩

strin·gent \-jənt\ *adj* ♦ : marked by rigor, strictness, or severity esp. with regard to rule or standard

♦ exacting, inflexible, rigid, rigorous, strict, uncompromising — more at RIGID

string·er \'striŋ-ər\ *n* **1** : a long horizontal member in a framed structure or a bridge **2** : a news correspondent paid by the amount of copy

stringy \'striŋ-ē\ *adj* **string·i·er; -est 1** : resembling string esp. in tough, fibrous, or disordered quality ⟨~ meat⟩ ⟨~ hair⟩ **2** : lean and sinewy in build

¹**strip** \'strip\ *vb* **stripped** \'stript\ *also* **stript; strip·ping 1** ♦ : to take the covering or clothing from **2** : to take off one's clothes **3** : to pull or tear off **4** : to make bare or clear (as by cutting or grazing) **5** : to deprive of possessions : PLUNDER — **strip·per** *n*

♦ unclothe, undress — more at UNDRESS

²**strip** *n* **1** : a long narrow flat piece **2** : AIRSTRIP

¹**stripe** \'strīp\ *vb* **striped** \'strīpt\; **strip·ing** ♦ : to mark with stripes

♦ band, bar, streak; *also* blaze

²**stripe** *n* **1** ♦ : a line or long narrow division having a different color from the background **2** : a strip of braid (as on a sleeve) indicating military rank or length of service **3** : TYPE, CHARACTER — **striped** \'strīpt, 'strī-pəd\ *adj*

♦ band, bar, streak; *also* blaze, crossbar, pinstripe

striped bass *n* : a large black-striped marine bony fish that occurs along the Atlantic and Pacific coasts of the U.S. and is an excellent food and sport fish

strip·ling \'stri-pliŋ\ *n* **1** : YOUTH **2** ♦ : an adolescent male : LAD

♦ boy, lad, nipper, shaver, youth — more at BOY

strip mall *n* : a long building or group of buildings housing several retail stores or service establishments

strip mine *n* : a mine that is worked from the earth's surface by the stripping of the topsoil — **strip–mine** *vb*

strip·tease \'strip-ˌtēz\ *n* : a burlesque act in which a performer removes clothing piece by piece — **strip·teas·er** *n*

strive \'strīv\ *vb* **strove** \'strōv\ *also* **strived** \'strīvd\; **striv·en** \'stri-vən\ *or* **strived; striv·ing** **1** ♦ : to make an effort : labor hard **2** : to struggle in opposition : CONTEND

♦ assay, attempt, endeavor (*or* endeavour), essay, seek, try — more at ATTEMPT

strobe \'strōb\ *n* **1** : STROBOSCOPE **2** : a device for high-speed intermittent illumination (as in photography)

stro·bo·scope \'strō-bə-ˌskōp\ *n* : an instrument for studying rapid motion by means of a rapidly flashing light

strode *past of* STRIDE

¹**stroke** \'strōk\ *vb* **stroked; strok·ing** **1 a** : to rub gently **b** ♦ : to touch or stroke lightly in a loving or endearing manner **2** : to flatter in a manner designed to persuade

♦ caress, fondle, love, pat, pet — more at FONDLE

²**stroke** *n* **1** : the act of striking : BLOW **2** : a sudden action or process producing an impact ⟨~ of lightning⟩; *also* : an unexpected result **3** : sudden weakening or loss of consciousness or the power to move or feel caused by rupture or obstruction (as by a clot) of a blood vessel of the brain **4** : one of a series of movements against air or water to get through or over it ⟨the ~ of a bird's wing⟩ **5** : a rower who sets the pace for a crew **6** : a vigorous effort **7** : the sound of striking (as of a clock) **8** : a single movement with or as if with a tool or implement (as a pen)

¹**stroll** \'strōl\ *vb* : to walk in a leisurely or idle manner

²**stroll** *n* ♦ : an idle and leisurely walk

♦ perambulation, ramble, turn, walk — more at WALK

stroll·er *n* ♦ : one who goes idly about

♦ drifter, nomad, rambler, rover, vagabond, wanderer — more at NOMAD

strong \'strȯŋ\ *adj* **stron·ger** \'strȯŋ-gər\; **stron·gest** \'strȯŋ-gəst\ **1** ♦ : having or marked by power **2** : HEALTHY, ROBUST **3** : of a specified number ⟨an army 10 thousand ~⟩ **4** ♦ : not mild or weak **5** : VIOLENT ⟨~ wind⟩ **6** : ZEALOUS **7** ♦ : not easily broken **8** : well established : FIRM, SOLID **9** ♦ : having an offensive or intense odor or flavor

♦ [1] brawny, muscular, powerful, rugged, sinewy, stalwart, stout; *also* forceful, mighty, potent, puissant; able-bodied, athletic, fit, trim; beefy, burly, husky, strapping; masculine, virile; hard, inured, strengthened, sturdy, tough, toughened; energetic, energized, invigorated, lusty, robust, vigorous, vitalized; hale, healthy, hearty, sound *Ant* delicate, feeble, frail, weak, wimpy ♦ [1] cogent, compelling, conclusive, convincing, decisive, effective, forceful, persuasive, satisfying, telling — more at COGENT ♦ [4] firm, forceful, hearty, lusty, robust, solid, stout, sturdy, vigorous ♦ [7] fast, firm, sound, stable, stalwart, steady, sturdy — more at STABLE ♦ [9] fetid, foul, fusty, malodorous, musty, noisome, rank, reeky, smelly — more at MALODOROUS ♦ [9] nippy, pungent, sharp — more at SHARP

strong–arm \'strȯŋ-ˌärm\ *adj* : having or using undue force ⟨~ methods⟩

strong force *n* : the physical force responsible for binding together nucleons in the atomic nucleus

strong·hold \-ˌhōld\ *n* ♦ : a fortified place : FORTRESS

♦ bastion, citadel, fastness, fort, fortification, fortress, hold — more at FORT

strong·ly *adv* ♦ : in a strong manner

♦ energetically, firmly, forcefully, forcibly, hard, mightily, powerfully, stiffly, stoutly, strenuously, sturdily, vigorously — more at HARD

strong·man \-ˌman\ *n* : one who leads or controls by force of will and character or by military strength

stron·tium \'strän-chē-əm, 'strän-tē-əm\ *n* : a soft malleable metallic chemical element

¹**strop** \'sträp\ *n* : STRAP; *esp* : one for sharpening a razor

²**strop** *vb* **stropped; strop·ping** ♦ : to sharpen a razor on a strop

♦ edge, grind, hone, sharpen, whet — more at SHARPEN

stro·phe \'strō-fē\ *n* [Gk *strophē*, lit., act of turning] : a division of a poem — **stroph·ic** \'strä-fik\ *adj*

strove *past of* STRIVE

struck *past and past part of* STRIKE

¹**struc·ture** \'strək-chər\ *n* [ME, fr. L *structura*, fr. *structus*, pp. of *struere* to heap up, build] **1** : the action of building : CONSTRUCTION **2** : something built (as a house or a dam); *also* : something made up of interdependent parts in a definite pattern of organization **3** ♦ : arrangement

or relationship of elements (as particles, parts, or organs) in a substance, body, or system — **struc·tur·al** *adj*

♦ configuration, frame, framework, shell, skeleton — more at FRAME

²**structure** *vb* **struc·tured; struc·tur·ing** : to make into a structure

stru·del \'strüd-ᵊl, 'shtrüd-\ *n* [G, lit., whirlpool] : a pastry made of a thin sheet of dough rolled up with filling and baked ⟨apple ∼⟩

¹**strug·gle** \'strə-gəl\ *vb* **strug·gled; strug·gling 1** : to make strenuous efforts against opposition : STRIVE **2** ♦ : to proceed with difficulty or with great effort

♦ drudge, endeavor (*or* endeavour), fag, grub, hustle, labor (*or* labour), peg, plod, plug, slave, slog, strain, strive, sweat, toil, work — more at LABOR

²**struggle** *n* **1** ♦ : exertion or contention for superiority : CONTEST **2** ♦ : a violent effort or exertion

♦ [1] battle, combat, conflict, confrontation, contest, duel, face-off, rivalry, tug-of-war, warfare — more at CONTEST ♦ [2] battle, effort, exertion, fight, fray, scrabble; *also* labor, pains, trouble, work; drudgery, grind, sweat, toil, travail; attempt, endeavor, essay, try

strum \'strəm\ *vb* **strummed; strum·ming** : to play on a stringed instrument by brushing the strings with the fingers ⟨∼ a guitar⟩

strum·pet \'strəm-pət\ *n* : PROSTITUTE

strung \'strəŋ\ *past and past part of* STRING

¹**strut** \'strət\ *vb* **strut·ted; strut·ting 1** ♦ : to walk with an affectedly proud gait **2** ♦ : to parade (as clothes) with a show of pride

♦ [1] stalk, swagger; *also* flounce, mince, traipse; pussyfoot, tiptoe; parade, promenade; pad, step, tread; pace, stride; lumber, lurch, pound, shamble, shuffle, stagger ♦ [2] display, disport, exhibit, expose, flash, flaunt, parade, show, show off, sport, unveil — more at SHOW

²**strut** *n* **1** : a bar or rod for resisting lengthwise pressure **2** : a haughty or pompous gait

strych·nine \'strik-,nīn, -nən, -,nēn\ *n* : a bitter poisonous plant alkaloid used as a poison (as for rats) and medicinally as a stimulant of the central nervous system

¹**stub** \'stəb\ *n* **1** : STUMP 2 **2** : a short blunt end **3** : a small part of each leaf (as of a checkbook) kept as a memorandum of the items on the detached part

²**stub** *vb* **stubbed; stub·bing** : to strike (as one's toe) against something

stub·ble \'stə-bəl\ *n* **1** : the cut stem ends of herbs and esp. grasses left in the soil after harvest **2** : a rough surface or growth resembling stubble — **stub·bly** \-b(ə-)lē\ *adj*

stub·born \'stə-bərn\ *adj* **1** : FIRM, DETERMINED **2** ♦ : done or continued in a willful, unreasonable, or persistent manner **3** : not easily controlled or remedied ⟨a ∼ cold⟩ — **stub·born·ly** *adv*

♦ dogged, hardheaded, headstrong, mulish, obdurate, obstinate, opinionated, peevish, pertinacious, perverse, pigheaded, unyielding, willful — more at OBSTINATE

stub·born·ness *n* ♦ : the quality or state of being stubborn

♦ hardheadedness, mulishness, obduracy, obstinacy, peevishness, pertinacity, self-will, tenacity — more at OBSTINACY

stub·by \'stə-bē\ *adj* ♦ : short, blunt, and thick like a stub

♦ chunky, dumpy, heavyset, squat, stocky, stout, stumpy, thickset — more at STOCKY

stuc·co \'stə-kō\ *n, pl* **stuccos** *or* **stuccoes** [It] : plaster for coating exterior walls — **stuc·coed** \'stə-kōd\ *adj*

stuck *past and past part of* STICK

stuck-up \'stək-'əp\ *adj* ♦ : having or showing an excessively high opinion of oneself : CONCEITED

♦ complacent, conceited, egotistic, important, overweening, pompous, prideful, proud, self-important, self-satisfied, smug, vain — more at CONCEITED

¹**stud** \'stəd\ *n* : a male animal and esp. a horse (**stud·horse** \-,hȯrs\) kept for breeding

²**stud** *n* **1** : one of the smaller uprights in a building to which the wall materials are fastened **2** : a removable device like a button used as a fastener or ornament ⟨shirt ∼s⟩ **3** : a projecting nail, pin, or rod

³**stud** *vb* **stud·ded; stud·ding 1** : to supply with or adorn with studs **2** : DOT

⁴**stud** *abbr* student

stud·book \'stəd-,bu̇k\ *n* : an official record of the pedigree of purebred animals (as horses or dogs)

stud·ding \'stə-diŋ\ *n* : the studs in a building or wall

stu·dent \'stüd-ᵊnt, 'styüd-\ *n* : SCHOLAR, PUPIL; *esp* : one who attends a school

stud·ied \'stə-dēd\ *adj* ♦ : carefully considered or prepared ⟨a ∼ insult⟩

♦ advised, calculated, deliberate, measured, reasoned, thoughtful, thought-out — more at DELIBERATE

stu·dio \'stü-dē-,ō, 'styü-\ *n, pl* **-dios 1** : a place where an artist works; *also* : a place for the study of an art **2** : a place where motion pictures are made **3** : a place equipped for the transmission of radio or television programs

stu·di·ous \'stü-dē-əs, 'styü-\ *adj* : devoted to study — **stu·di·ous·ly** *adv*

¹**study** \'stə-dē\ *n, pl* **stud·ies 1** : the use of the mind to gain knowledge **2** : the act or process of learning about something **3** : careful examination **4** : INTENT, PURPOSE **5** : a branch of learning **6** : a room esp. for reading and writing **7** ♦ : a state of contemplation

♦ [3] examination, exploration, inquiry, investigation, probe, research — more at INQUIRY ♦ [7] reverie, trance, woolgathering — more at REVERIE

²**study** *vb* **stud·ied; study·ing 1** : to engage in study or the study of **2** ♦ : to consider attentively or in detail

♦ chew over, cogitate, consider, contemplate, debate, deliberate, entertain, meditate, mull, ponder, question, ruminate, think, weigh — more at PONDER

¹**stuff** \'stəf\ *n* [ME, fr. AF *estuffes* goods, fr. *estuffer* to fill in (with rubble), furnish, equip, of Gmc origin] **1** : personal property **2** ♦ : raw material **3** : a finished textile fabric; *esp* : a worsted fabric **4** : writing, talk, or ideas of little or transitory worth **5** : an unspecified material substance or aggregate of matter **6** ♦ : fundamental material **7** ♦ : special knowledge or capability

♦ [2] material, raw material, substance ♦ [6] essence, nature, quintessence, soul, substance — more at ESSENCE ♦ [7] capability, credentials, qualification — more at QUALIFICATION

²**stuff** *vb* **1** ♦ : to fill by packing things in : CRAM **2** ♦ : to eat greedily : GORGE **3** : to prepare (as meat) by filling with a stuffing **4** : to fill (as a cushion) with a soft material **5** ♦ : to stop up : PLUG

♦ [1] charge, cram, fill, heap, jam, jam-pack, load, pack — more at FILL ♦ [2] glut, gorge, sate, surfeit — more at GORGE ♦ [5] block, choke, clog, close (off), congest, dam, jam, obstruct, plug (up), stop (up) — more at CLOG

stuffed shirt \'stəft-\ *n* : a smug, conceited, and usu. pompous and inflexibly conservative person

stuff·ing *n* ♦ : material used to fill tightly; *esp* : a mixture of bread crumbs and spices used to stuff food

♦ fill, filler, filling, padding — more at FILLING

stuffy \'stə-fē\ *adj* **stuff·i·er; -est 1** ♦ : lacking in vitality or interest : STODGY **2** ♦ : lacking fresh air : CLOSE; *also* : blocked up ⟨a ∼ nose⟩

♦ [1] drab, dreary, dry, dull, flat, heavy, humdrum, leaden, monotonous, ponderous, stupid, tame, uninteresting, weary ♦ [2] breathless, close; *also* unventilated; heavy, thick, oppressive *Ant* airy, breezy

stul·ti·fy \'stəl-tə-,fī\ *vb* **-fied; -fy·ing 1** : to cause to appear foolish or stupid **2** : to impair, invalidate, or make ineffective **3** : to have a dulling effect on — **stul·ti·fi·ca·tion** \,stəl-tə-fə-'kā-shən\ *n*

¹**stum·ble** \'stəm-bəl\ *vb* **stum·bled; stum·bling 1** : to blunder

morally **2 ♦ :** to trip in walking or running **3 a ♦ :** to walk unsteadily **b :** to speak or act in a blundering or clumsy manner **4 :** to happen by chance **5 ♦ :** to come unexpectedly or by chance

♦ [2] fall, slip, topple, trip, tumble — more at FALL **♦** [3a] clump, flounder, limp, lumber, scuff, scuffle, shamble, shuffle, tramp, tromp — more at LUMBER **♦** *usu* stumble on *or* stumble onto *or* stumble upon [5] chance, encounter, find, happen (on *or* upon), hit, meet — more at HAPPEN (on *or* upon)

²**stumble** *n* **♦ :** an act or instance of stumbling

♦ fall, slip, spill, tumble — more at FALL **♦** blunder, error, fault, flub, fumble, goof, lapse, miscue, misstep, mistake, oversight, slip — more at ERROR

stumbling block *n* **♦ :** an obstacle to belief, understanding, or progress

♦ bar, block, clog, crimp, drag, embarrassment, hindrance, let, obstacle, stop — more at OBSTACLE

¹**stump** \'stəmp\ *n* **1 :** the base of a bodily part (as a leg) left after the rest is removed **2 :** the part of a plant and esp. a tree remaining with the root after the trunk is cut off **3 :** a place or occasion for political public speaking

²**stump** *vb* **1 :** BAFFLE, PERPLEX **2 :** to clear (land) of stumps **3 :** to tour (a region) making political speeches **4 :** to walk clumsily and heavily **5 :** to challenge to perform an action

stumpy *adj* **♦ :** short and thick

♦ chunky, dumpy, heavyset, squat, stocky, stout, stubby, thickset — more at STOCKY

stun \'stən\ *vb* **stunned; stun·ning 1 :** to make senseless or dizzy by or as if by a blow **2 ♦ :** to overcome esp. with paralyzing astonishment or disbelief **:** STUPEFY

♦ amaze, astonish, astound, bowl, dumbfound, flabbergast, floor, shock, startle, stupefy, surprise — more at SURPRISE

stung *past and past part of* STING
stunk *past and past part of* STINK
stunned *adj* **♦ :** affected by stunning; *also* **:** caused by or as if by stunning

♦ amazed, awestruck, thunderstruck — more at THUNDERSTRUCK **♦** confused, dizzy — more at DIZZY

stun·ning *adj* **1 ♦ :** causing astonishment or disbelief **2 ♦ :** strikingly beautiful — **stun·ning·ly** *adv*

♦ [1] amazing, astonishing, astounding, eye-opening, shocking, startling, surprising — more at SURPRISING **♦** [1] awesome, fabulous, marvelous (*or* marvellous), miraculous, portentous, prodigious, stupendous, sublime, surprising, wonderful — more at MARVELOUS **♦** [2] attractive, beautiful, fair, gorgeous, handsome, knockout, lovely, pretty, ravishing — more at BEAUTIFUL

¹**stunt** \'stənt\ *vb* **:** to hinder the normal growth or progress of
²**stunt** *n* **♦ :** an unusual or spectacular feat

♦ deed, exploit, feat, trick — more at FEAT

stu·pe·fy \'stü-pə-ˌfī, 'styü-\ *vb* **-fied; -fy·ing 1 :** to make stupid, groggy, or insensible **2 ♦ :** to strike with sudden and usu. great wonder or surprise **:** ASTONISH — **stu·pe·fac·tion** \ˌstü-pə-'fak-shən, ˌstyü-\ *n*

♦ amaze, astonish, astound, bowl, dumbfound, flabbergast, floor, shock, startle, stun, surprise — more at SURPRISE

stu·pen·dous \stu̇-'pen-dəs, styü-\ *adj* **♦ :** causing astonishment esp. because of great size or height

♦ amazing, astonishing, astounding, awesome, awful, eye-opening, fabulous, marvelous (*or* marvellous), miraculous, portentous, prodigious, stunning, sublime, surprising, wonderful — more at MARVELOUS

stu·pen·dous·ly *adv* **♦ :** to a stupendous degree

♦ broadly, considerably, greatly, hugely, largely, massively, monstrously, much, sizably, tremendously, utterly, vastly — more at GREATLY

stu·pid \'stü-pəd, 'styü-\ *adj* [MF *stupide*, fr. L *stupidus*,

fr. *stupēre* to be numb, be astonished] **1 ♦ :** very dull in mind **2 ♦ :** showing or resulting from dullness of mind **3 ♦ :** lacking interest or intellectual stimulation ⟨a ∼ book⟩ — **stu·pid·ly** *adv*

♦ [1] dense, dull, dumb, fatuous, mindless, obtuse, senseless, simple, slow, thick, unintelligent, vacuous, witless; *also* feebleminded; foolish, idiotic, imbecile, imbecilic, moronic; ignorant, illiterate, lowbrow, uneducated; absurd, asinine *Ant* brainy, brilliant, clever, intelligent, quick-witted, sharp, smart **♦** [2] absurd, crazy, cuckoo, fatuous, foolish, mad, nonsensical, nutty, senseless, silly — more at FOOLISH **♦** [3] drab, dreary, monotonous, ponderous, uninteresting, weary

stu·pid·i·ty \stu̇-'pi-də-tē, styü-\ *n* **1 ♦ :** the quality or state of being stupid **2 ♦ :** a stupid idea or act

♦ [1] denseness, dopiness, fatuity, foolishness, imbecility, mindlessness, obtuseness, vacuity; *also* absurdity, asininity, balminess, craziness, daftness, folly, idiocy, inanity, insanity, lunacy, madness, silliness, simplicity, zaniness; fallacy, irrationality, unreasonableness *Ant* brightness, brilliance, cleverness, intelligence, keenness, quickness, sharpness, smartness **♦** [2] absurdity, asininity, fatuity, folly, foolery, idiocy, imbecility, inanity, insanity, lunacy — more at FOLLY

stu·por \'stü-pər, 'styü-\ *n* **1 ♦ :** a condition of greatly dulled or completely suspended sense or feeling **2 :** a state of extreme apathy or torpor often following stress or shock — **stu·por·ous** *adj*

♦ apathy, impassivity, numbness, phlegm — more at APATHY

stur·di·ly \'stər-də-lē\ *adv* **♦ :** in a sturdy manner

♦ energetically, firmly, forcefully, forcibly, hard, mightily, powerfully, stiffly, stoutly, strenuously, strongly, vigorously — more at HARD

stur·di·ness \-dē-nəs\ *n* **♦ :** the quality or state of being sturdy

♦ firmness, soundness, stability, steadiness, strength — more at STABILITY

stur·dy \'stər-dē\ *adj* **stur·di·er; -est** [ME, brave, stubborn, fr. AF *esturdi* stunned, fr. pp. of *esturdir* to stun, fr. VL *exturdire*, fr. L *ex-* + VL *turdus* simpleton, fr. L *turdus* thrush] **1 :** RESOLUTE, UNYIELDING **2 ♦ :** capable of withstanding adverse conditions **:** STRONG

♦ hard, hard-bitten, hardy, rugged, stout, strong, tough, vigorous — more at HARDY **♦** fast, firm, sound, stable, stalwart, steady, strong — more at STABLE

stur·geon \'stər-jən\ *n* **:** any of a family of large bony fishes including some whose roe are made into caviar

stut·ter \'stə-tər\ *vb* **:** to speak with involuntary disruption or blocking of sounds — **stutter** *n* — **stut·ter·er** *n*

stutter step *n* **:** a move made by a runner (as in football) done to fake a defender out of position

¹**sty** \'stī\ *n, pl* **sties 1 :** a pen for pigs **2 ♦ :** a dirty place

♦ dump, hole, pigsty, shambles — more at PIGPEN

²**sty** *or* **stye** *n, pl* **sties** *or* **styes :** an inflamed swelling of a skin gland on the edge of an eyelid

¹**style** \'stīl\ *n* **1 :** mode of address **:** TITLE **2 ♦ :** a way of speaking or writing; *esp* **:** one characteristic of an individual, period, school, or nation ⟨ornate ∼⟩ **3 ♦ :** manner or method of acting, making, or performing; *also* **:** a distinctive or characteristic manner **4 :** a slender pointed instrument or process; *esp* **:** STYLUS **5 ♦ :** a fashionable manner or mode **6 :** overall excellence, skill, or grace in performance, manner, or appearance **7 :** the custom followed in spelling, capitalization, punctuation, and typography — **sty·lis·tic** \stī-'lis-tik\ *adj*

♦ [2] fashion, locution, manner, mode, phraseology, tone, vein; *also* delivery, elocution; colloquialism, acceptation, connotation, denotation, idiom **♦** [3] approach, fashion, form, manner, method, strategy, system, tack, tactics, technique, way — more at METHOD **♦** [5] craze, fad, mode, rage, trend, vogue — more at FAD

²**style** *vb* **styled; styl·ing 1 ♦ :** to call or designate by an

identifying term : NAME   **2** : to make or design in accord with a prevailing mode ⟨∼ hair⟩

♦ baptize, call, christen, denominate, designate, dub, entitle, label, name, term, title — more at NAME

styl·ing \'stī-liŋ\ *n* : the way in which something is styled

styl·ise *chiefly Brit var of* STYLIZE

styl·ish \'stī-lish\ *adj* ♦ : conforming to current fashion — **styl·ish·ly** *adv* — **styl·ish·ness** *n*

♦ à la mode, chic, fashionable, in, modish, sharp, smart, snappy; *also* dapper, dashing, natty, spruce, rakish; posh, swank; elegant, graceful, handsome, majestic, refined, sophisticated, stately, tasteful, understated; foppish; classic, exquisite, quiet, restrained, simple; affected, grandiose, pretentious *Ant* dowdy, outmoded, unfashionable, unstylish

styl·ist \'stī-list\ *n*   **1** : one (as a writer) noted for a distinctive style   **2** : a developer or designer of styles

styl·ize \'stī-,līz, 'stī-ə-\ *vb* **styl·ized; styl·iz·ing** : to conform to a style; *esp* : to represent or design according to a pattern or style rather than according to nature or tradition — **styl·i·za·tion** \,stī-lə-'zā-shən\ *n*

sty·lus \'stī-ləs\ *n, pl* **sty·li** \'stī-,lī\ *also* **sty·lus·es** \'stī-lə-səz\ [L *stylus, stilus* spike, stylus]   **1** : a pointed implement used by the ancients for writing on wax   **2** : a phonograph needle   **3** : a pen-shaped pointing device for entering data into a computer

sty·mie \'stī-mē\ *vb* **sty·mied; sty·mie·ing** ♦ : to present an obstacle to : stand in the way of

♦ encumber, hamper, hinder, hold up, impede, inhibit, interfere with, obstruct, tie up — more at HAMPER

styp·tic \'stip-tik\ *adj* : tending to check bleeding — **styptic** *n*

suave \'swäv\ *adj* [MF, pleasant, sweet, fr. L *suavis*] ♦ : persuasively pleasing : smoothly agreeable — **suave·ly** *adv* — **sua·vi·ty** \'swä-və-tē\ *n*

♦ debonair, smooth, sophisticated, urbane; *also* glib, slick, unctuous; civilized, cultivated, cultured, graceful, poised, polished, refined; cosmopolitan, smart, worldly-wise; experienced, knowing, practiced, schooled, seasoned; amiable, appealing, attractive; assured, calm, collected, composed, confident, cool, placid, secure, serene, self-assured, self-confident, self-possessed, tranquil, undisturbed, unperturbed *Ant* boorish, churlish, clownish, loutish, uncouth

¹sub \'səb\ *n* : a person or thing that takes the place or function of another : SUBSTITUTE

²sub *n*   **1** : a naval vessel designed to operate underwater : SUBMARINE   **2** : a large sandwich on a long split roll with any of a variety of fillings : SUBMARINE

³sub *abbr*   **1** subtract   **2** suburb

⁴sub *vb* ♦ : to serve as a substitute

♦ cover, fill in, pinch-hit, stand in, substitute, take over — more at COVER

sub- \'səb\ *prefix*   **1** : under : beneath   **2** : subordinate : secondary   **3** : subordinate portion of : subdivision of   **4** : with repetition of a process described in a simple verb so as to form, stress, or deal with subordinate parts or relations   **5** : somewhat   **6** : falling nearly in the category of : bordering on

sub·al·pine \,səb-'al-,pīn\ *adj*   **1** : of or relating to the region about the foot and lower slopes of the Alps   **2** : of, relating to, or inhabiting high upland slopes esp. just below the timberline

sub·al·tern \sə-'bȯl-tərn\ *n* : SUBORDINATE; *esp* : a junior officer (as in the British army)

sub·as·sem·bly \,səb-ə-'sem-blē\ *n* : an assembled unit to be incorporated with other units in a finished product

sub·atom·ic \,səb-ə-'tä-mik\ *adj* : of or relating to the inside of the atom or to particles smaller than atoms

sub·clin·i·cal \,səb-'kli-ni-kəl\ *adj* : not detectable by the usual clinical tests ⟨a ∼ infection⟩

sub·com·pact \'səb-'käm-,pakt\ *n* : an automobile smaller than a compact

¹sub·con·scious \,səb-'kän-chəs, 'səb-\ *adj* : existing in the mind without entering conscious awareness — **sub·con·scious·ly** *adv* — **sub·con·scious·ness** *n*

²subconscious *n* : mental activities just below the threshold of consciousness

sub·con·ti·nent \,səb-'känt-ᵊn-ənt\ *n* : a major subdivision of a continent — **sub·con·ti·nen·tal** \,səb-,känt-ᵊn-'ent-ᵊl\ *adj*

sub·di·vide \,səb-də-'vīd, 'səb-də-,vīd\ *vb* : to divide the parts of into more parts; *esp* : to divide (a tract of land) into building lots — **sub·di·vi·sion** \-'vi-zhən, -,vi-\ *n*

sub·duc·tion \səb-'dək-shən\ *n* : the descent of the edge of one crustal plate beneath the edge of an adjacent plate

sub·due \səb-'dü, -'dyü\ *vb* **sub·dued; sub·du·ing**   **1** ♦ : to conquer and bring into subjection   **2** : to bring under control : CURB   **3** : to reduce the intensity of

♦ conquer, dominate, overpower, subject, vanquish — more at CONQUER

subdued *adj* ♦ : lacking in vitality, intensity, or strength

♦ conservative, muted, quiet, restrained, unpretentious — more at QUIET

subj *abbr*   **1** subject   **2** subjunctive

¹sub·ject \'səb-jikt\ *n* [ME *suget, subget,* fr. AF, fr. L *subjectus* one under authority & *subjectum* subject of a proposition, fr. *subicere* to subject, lit., to throw under, fr. *sub-* under + *jacere* to throw]   **1** : a person under the authority of another   **2** : a person subject to a sovereign   **3** : an individual that is studied or experimented on   **4** ♦ : the person or thing discussed or treated : TOPIC   **5** : a word or word group denoting that of which something is predicated

♦ content, matter, motif, motive, question, theme, topic — more at MATTER

²subject *adj*   **1** : being under the power or rule of another   **2** ♦ : suffering a particular liability or exposure : LIABLE ⟨∼ to floods⟩   **3** ♦ : dependent on some act or condition ⟨appointment ∼ to senate approval⟩

♦ *usu* **subject to** [2] exposed, liable, open, sensitive, susceptible, vulnerable — more at LIABLE ♦ *usu* **subject to** [3] conditional, contingent, dependent — more at DEPENDENT

³sub·ject \səb-'jekt\ *vb*   **1** ♦ : to bring under control : CONQUER   **2** : to make liable   **3** : to cause to undergo or endure

♦ conquer, dominate, overpower, subdue, vanquish — more at CONQUER

sub·jec·tion \-'jek-shən\ *n* ♦ : the act of subduing or subjecting

♦ conquest, domination — more at CONQUEST

sub·jec·tive \(,)səb-'jek-tiv\ *adj*   **1** : of, relating to, or constituting a subject   **2** : of, relating to, or arising within one's self or mind in contrast to what is outside : PERSONAL — **sub·jec·tive·ly** *adv* — **sub·jec·tiv·i·ty** \-,jek-'ti-və-tē\ *n*

subject matter *n* : matter presented for consideration, discussion, or study

sub·join \(,)səb-'jȯin\ *vb* : APPEND

List of self-explanatory words with the prefix *sub-*

subacute	subarctic	subbasement	subclass
subagency	subarea	subcategory	subclassify
subagent	subatmospheric	subcellular	subcommittee
subaqueous	subaverage	subchapter	subcontract

sub ju·di·ce \\(ˌ)sùb-ˈyü-di-ˌkā, ˈsəb-ˈjü-də-(ˌ)sē\ *adv* [L] : before a judge or court : not yet legally decided

sub·ju·gate \ˈsəb-ji-ˌgāt\ *vb* **-gat·ed; -gat·ing** **1** : to bring under control and governance as a subject : CONQUER **2** : ENSLAVE

sub·ju·ga·tion \ˌsəb-ji-ˈgā-shən\ *n* **1** : an act of subjugating **2** : the state of being subjugated

sub·junc·tive \səb-ˈjənk-tiv\ *adj* : of, relating to, or constituting a verb form that represents an act or state as contingent or possible or viewed emotionally (as with desire) ⟨the ∼ mood⟩ — **subjunctive** *n*

sub·lease \ˈsəb-ˈlēs, -ˌlēs\ *n* : a lease by a lessee of part or all of leased premises to another person with the original lessee retaining some right under the original lease — **sublease** *vb*

¹sub·let \ˈsəb-ˈlet\ *vb* **-let; -let·ting** : to let all or a part of (a leased property) to another; *also* : to rent (a property) from a lessee

²sublet \-ˌlet\ *n* : property and esp. housing obtained by or available through a sublease

sub·li·mate \ˈsə-blə-ˌmāt\ *vb* **-mat·ed; -mat·ing** **1** : SUBLIME **2** : to direct the expression of (as a desire or impulse) from a primitive to a more socially and culturally acceptable form — **sub·li·ma·tion** \ˌsə-blə-ˈmā-shən\ *n*

¹sub·lime \sə-ˈblīm\ *vb* **sub·limed; sub·lim·ing** : to pass or cause to pass directly from the solid to the vapor state

²sublime *adj* **1** : lofty, grand, or exalted in thought, expression, or manner : NOBLE **2** : having awe-inspiring beauty or grandeur — **sub·lime·ly** *adv* — **sub·lim·i·ty** \-ˈbli-mə-tē\ *n*

♦ [1] chivalrous, gallant, great, greathearted, high, high-minded, lofty, lordly, magnanimous, noble — more at NOBLE ♦ [2] amazing, astonishing, astounding, awesome, awful, eye-opening, fabulous, marvelous (*or* marvellous), miraculous, portentous, prodigious, stunning, stupendous, surprising, wonderful — more at MARVELOUS

sub·lim·i·nal \\(ˌ)səb-ˈli-mən-ᵊl, ˈsəb-\ *adj* [*sub-* + L *limin-, limen* threshold] **1** : inadequate to produce a sensation or mental awareness ⟨∼ stimuli⟩ **2** : existing or functioning below the threshold of consciousness ⟨the ∼ mind⟩ ⟨∼ advertising⟩

sub·ma·chine gun \ˌsəb-mə-ˈshēn-ˌgən\ *n* : an automatic firearm fired from the shoulder or hip

¹sub·ma·rine \ˈsəb-mə-ˌrēn, ˌsəb-mə-ˈrēn\ *adj* ♦ : lying, growing, worn, or operating below the surface of the water : UNDERWATER; *esp* : UNDERSEA

♦ sunken, underwater

²submarine *n* **1** : a naval vessel designed to operate underwater **2** ♦ : a large sandwich made from a long split roll with any of a variety of fillings

♦ grinder, hoagie, poor boy, sub

sub·merge \səb-ˈmərj\ *vb* **sub·merged; sub·merg·ing** **1** ♦ : to put or plunge under the surface of water **2** ♦ : to cover or overflow with water : INUNDATE — **sub·mer·gence** \-ˈmər-jəns\ *n*

♦ [1] dip, douse, duck, dunk, immerse, souse — more at DIP ♦ [2] deluge, drown, engulf, flood, inundate, overflow, overwhelm, swamp — more at FLOOD

sub·merse \səb-ˈmərs\ *vb* **sub·mersed; sub·mers·ing** : to put or go under water : SUBMERGE — **sub·mer·sion** \-ˈmər-zhən\ *n*

¹sub·mers·ible \səb-ˈmər-sə-bəl\ *adj* : capable of being submerged

²submersible *n* : something that is submersible; *esp* : a small underwater craft used for deep-sea research

sub·mi·cro·scop·ic \ˌsəb-ˌmī-krə-ˈskä-pik\ *adj* : too small to be seen in an ordinary light microscope

sub·min·ia·ture \ˌsəb-ˈmi-nē-ə-ˌchùr, ˈsəb-, -ˈmi-ni-ˌchùr, -chər\ *adj* : very small

sub·mis·sion \-ˈmi-shən\ *n* ♦ : an act of submitting to the authority or control of another

♦ compliance, conformity, obedience, observance, subordination — more at OBEDIENCE ♦ capitulation, relinquishment, surrender — more at SURRENDER

sub·mis·sive \-ˈmi-siv\ *adj* ♦ : submitting to others

♦ amenable, compliant, conformable, docile, obedient, tractable — more at OBEDIENT

sub·mit \səb-ˈmit\ *vb* **sub·mit·ted; sub·mit·ting** **1** ♦ : to commit to the discretion or decision of another or of others **2** ♦ : to yield oneself to the authority or will of another : SURRENDER **3** : to put forward as an opinion

♦ blink, bow, budge, capitulate, concede, give in, knuckle under, quit, succumb, surrender, yield — more at YIELD

sub·nor·mal \ˌsəb-ˈnòr-məl\ *adj* : falling below what is normal; *also* : having less of something and esp. intelligence than is normal — **sub·nor·mal·i·ty** \ˌsəb-nòr-ˈma-lə-tē\ *n*

sub·or·bit·al \ˌsəb-ˈòr-bət-ᵊl, ˈsəb-\ *adj* : being or involving less than one orbit

¹sub·or·di·nate \sə-ˈbòrd-ᵊn-ət\ *adj* **1** ♦ : of lower class or rank **2** : INFERIOR **3** : submissive to authority **4** : subordinated to other elements in a sentence ⟨∼ clause⟩

♦ inferior, junior, less, lesser, lower, minor, under — more at LESSER

²subordinate *n* ♦ : one that is subordinate

♦ inferior, junior, underling — more at UNDERLING

³sub·or·di·nate \sə-ˈbòrd-ᵊn-ˌāt\ *vb* **-nat·ed; -nat·ing** **1** : to place in a lower rank or class **2** : SUBDUE

sub·or·di·na·tion \-ˌbòrd-ᵊn-ˈā-shən\ *n* **1** : the act of subordinating (as by making secondary or subject) **2** ♦ : the quality or state of being subordinate to authority : obedient submission

♦ compliance, conformity, obedience, observance, submission — more at OBEDIENCE

sub·orn \sə-ˈbòrn\ *vb* **1** : to induce secretly to do an unlawful thing **2** : to induce to commit perjury — **sub·or·na·tion** \ˌsə-bòr-ˈnā-shən\ *n*

¹sub·poe·na \sə-ˈpē-nə\ *n* [ME *suppena*, fr. L *sub poena* under penalty] : a writ commanding the person named in it to attend court under penalty for failure to do so

²subpoena *vb* **-naed; -na·ing** : to summon with a subpoena

sub-Sa·ha·ran \ˌsəb-sə-ˈhar-ən\ *adj* : of, relating to, or being the part of Africa south of the Sahara

sub·scribe \səb-ˈskrīb\ *vb* **sub·scribed; sub·scrib·ing** **1** : to sign one's name to a document **2** : to give consent by or as if by signing one's name **3** : to promise to contribute by signing one's name with the amount promised **4** : to place an order by signing **5** : to receive a periodical or service regularly on order **6** ♦ : to feel favorably disposed : FAVOR — usu. used with *to* — **sub·scrib·er** *n*

♦ *usu* **subscribe to** accept, approve, care, countenance, favor (*or* favour), OK ♦ *usu* **subscribe to** accede, agree, assent, come round, consent — more at ACCEDE

sub·script \ˈsəb-ˌskript\ *n* : a symbol (as a letter or number) immediately below or below and to the right or left of another written character — **subscript** *adj*

sub·scrip·tion \səb-ˈskrip-shən\ *n* **1** : the act of subscribing : SIGNATURE **2** : a purchase by signed order

---

List of self-explanatory words with the prefix *sub-* (continued)

subcontractor	subentry	subgenre	subheading
subculture	subfamily	subgenus	subhuman
subcutaneous	subfield	subgroup	subkingdom
subdiscipline	subfreezing	subhead	sublethal

sub·se·quent \'səb-si-kwənt, -sə-ˌkwent\ *adj* ♦ : following after : SUCCEEDING

   ♦ after, later, posterior; *also* behind, belated, delayed, late, slow; eventual, last, ultimate; following *Ant* antecedent, anterior, fore, precedent, preceding, previous, prior

sub·se·quent·ly *adv* ♦ : in a subsequent manner

   ♦ after, afterward, later, thereafter — more at AFTER

sub·ser·vi·ence \səb-'sər-vē-əns\ *n* **1** : a subordinate place or condition **2** : SERVILITY — **sub·ser·vi·en·cy** \-ən-sē\ *n* — **sub·ser·vi·ent** \-ənt\ *adj*

sub·set \'səb-ˌset\ *n* : a set each of whose elements is an element of an inclusive set

sub·side \səb-'sīd\ *vb* **sub·sid·ed; sub·sid·ing** [L *subsidere*, fr. *sub-* under + *sidere* to sit down, sink] **1** : to settle to the bottom of a liquid **2** : to tend downward : DESCEND **3** : SINK, SUBMERGE **4** ♦ : to become quiet and tranquil — **sub·sid·ence** \səb-'sīd-ᵊns\, 'səb-sə-dəns\ *n*

   ♦ abate, decline, decrease, de-escalate, die, diminish, dwindle, ebb, fall, lessen, let up, lower, moderate, recede, relent, shrink, taper, wane — more at DECREASE

¹sub·sid·iary \səb-'si-dē-ˌer-ē\ *adj* **1** : furnishing aid or support **2** : of secondary importance **3** : of or relating to a subsidy

²subsidiary *n, pl* **-iar·ies** : one that is subsidiary; *esp* : a company controlled by another

sub·si·dise *chiefly Brit var of* SUBSIDIZE

sub·si·dize \'səb-sə-ˌdīz\ *vb* **-dized; -diz·ing** ♦ : to aid or furnish with a subsidy

   ♦ capitalize, endow, finance, fund, stake, underwrite — more at FINANCE

sub·si·dy \'səb-sə-dē\ *n, pl* **-dies** [ME, *subsidie*, fr. AF, fr. L *subsidium* reserve troops, support, assistance, fr. *sub-* near + *sedēre* to sit] ♦ : a gift of public money to a private person or company or to another government

   ♦ allocation, allotment, appropriation, grant — more at APPROPRIATION

sub·sist \səb-'sist\ *vb* **1** ♦ : to have existence; *also* : to continue to exist **2** : to have the means (as food and clothing) of maintaining life; *esp* : to nourish oneself

   ♦ be, breathe, exist, live — more at BE

sub·sis·tence \səb-'sis-təns\ *n* **1** ♦ : real being : EXISTENCE; *also* : the condition of remaining in existence : PERSISTENCE **2** : means of subsisting : the minimum (as of food and clothing) necessary to support life

   ♦ actuality, existence, reality — more at EXISTENCE
   ♦ continuance, continuation, duration, endurance, persistence — more at CONTINUATION

sub·son·ic \ˌsəb-'sä-nik, 'səb-\ *adj* : being or relating to a speed less than that of sound; *also* : moving at such a speed

sub·species \'səb-ˌspē-shēz, -sēz\ *n* : a subdivision of a species; *esp* : a category in biological classification ranking just below a species that designates a geographic population genetically distinct from other such populations and potentially able to breed with them where its range overlaps theirs

sub·stance \'səb-stəns\ *n* **1** ♦ : essential nature : ESSENCE ⟨divine ∼⟩; *also* : the fundamental or essential part or quality ⟨the ∼ of the speech⟩ **2** ♦ : physical material from which something is made or which has discrete existence; *also* : matter of particular or definite chemical constitution **3** ♦ : material possessions : WEALTH **4** : something (as drugs or alcohol) deemed harmful and usu. subject to legal restriction ⟨∼ abuse⟩

   ♦ [1] essence, nature, quintessence, soul, stuff — more at ESSENCE ♦ [2] being, entity, individual, object, thing — more at ENTITY ♦ [2] material, raw material, stuff ♦ [3] assets, capital, fortune, means, opulence, riches, wealth, wherewithal — more at WEALTH

substance abuse *n* : excessive use of a drug (as alcohol or cocaine) : use of a drug without medical justification

sub·stan·dard \ˌsəb-'stan-dərd\ *adj* ♦ : falling short of a standard or norm

   ♦ bad, deficient, inferior, lousy, off, poor, punk, rotten, unacceptable, unsatisfactory, wanting, wretched, wrong — more at BAD

sub·stan·tial \səb-'stan-chəl\ *adj* **1** ♦ : existing as or in substance : MATERIAL; *also* : not illusory : REAL **2** ♦ : marked by or indicative of significant worth or consequence : IMPORTANT **3** : NOURISHING, SATISFYING ⟨∼ meal⟩ **4** : having means : WELL-TO-DO **5** ♦ : large in extent or degree : CONSIDERABLE ⟨∼ profit⟩ **6** : STRONG, FIRM — **sub·stan·tial·ly** *adv*

   ♦ [1] concrete, material, physical, real — more at MATERIAL ♦ [2] big, consequential, eventful, important, major, material, meaningful, momentous, significant, weighty — more at IMPORTANT ♦ [5] considerable, good, goodly, healthy, respectable, significant, sizable, tidy — more at CONSIDERABLE

sub·stan·ti·ate \səb-'stan-chē-ˌāt\ *vb* **-at·ed; -at·ing 1** ♦ : to give substance or body to **2** ♦ : to establish by proof or competent evidence

   ♦ [1] embody, epitomize, manifest, materialize, personify — more at EMBODY ♦ [2] bear out, confirm, corroborate, prove, support, validate, verify, vindicate — more at CONFIRM

sub·stan·ti·a·tion \-ˌstan-chē-'ā-shən\ *n* ♦ : something offered as proof

   ♦ attestation, confirmation, corroboration, documentation, evidence, proof, testament, testimony, validation, witness — more at PROOF

¹sub·stan·tive \'səb-stən-tiv\ *n* : NOUN; *also* : a word or phrase used as a noun

²substantive *adj* : having substance : REAL ⟨∼ changes⟩

¹sub·sti·tute \'səb-stə-ˌtüt, -ˌtyüt\ *n* ♦ : a person or thing replacing another

   ♦ backup, pinch hitter, relief, replacement, reserve, stand-in, sub; *also* alternate, understudy; apology, makeshift, stopgap; agent, attorney, commissary, delegate, deputy, envoy, factor, procurator, proxy, representative, surrogate; assistant, second

²substitute *vb* **-tut·ed; -tut·ing 1** ♦ : to put or use in the place of another **2** ♦ : to serve as a substitute — **sub·sti·tu·tion** \ˌsəb-stə-'tü-shən, -'tyü-\ *n*

   ♦ [1] change, commute, exchange, shift, swap, switch, trade — more at CHANGE ♦ [2] cover, fill in, pinch-hit, stand in, sub, take over — more at COVER ♦ [2] displace, replace, supersede, supplant — more at REPLACE

³substitute *adj* ♦ : serving as or fitted for use as a substitute

   ♦ backup, new — more at NEW

sub·strate \'səb-ˌstrāt\ *n* **1** : the base on which a plant or animal lives **2** : a substance acted upon (as by an enzyme)

sub·stra·tum \'səb-ˌstrā-təm, -ˌstra-\ *n, pl* **-stra·ta** \-tə\ : the layer or structure (as subsoil) lying underneath

sub·struc·ture \'səb-ˌstrək-chər\ *n* : FOUNDATION, GROUNDWORK

List of self-explanatory words with the prefix *sub-* (*continued*)

subliterate	suborder	subplot	subprogram
subminimal	subparagraph	subpopulation	subregion
subminimum	subparallel	subproblem	subroutine
suboptimal	subphylum	subprofessional	subsection

sub·sume \səb-'süm\ *vb* **sub·sumed; sub·sum·ing** ♦ : to include or place within something larger or more comprehensive

♦ carry, comprehend, contain, embrace, encompass, entail, include, involve, number, take in — more at INCLUDE

sub·sur·face \'səb-ˌsər-fəs\ *n* : earth material near the surface of the ground — **subsurface** *adj*

sub·ter·fuge \'səb-tər-ˌfyüj\ *n* ♦ : deception by artifice or stratagem in order to conceal, escape, or evade; *also* : a trick or device used to deceive

♦ artifice, chicanery, hanky-panky, trickery, wile — more at TRICKERY

sub·ter·ra·nean \ˌsəb-tə-'rā-nē-ən\ *adj* **1** : lying or being underground **2** : SECRET, HIDDEN

sub·tile \'sət-ᵊl\ *adj* **sub·til·er** \'sət-lər, -ᵊl-ər\; **sub·til·est** \'sət-ləst, -ᵊl-əst\ : SUBTLE

sub·ti·tle \'səb-ˌtīt-ᵊl\ *n* **1** : a secondary or explanatory title (as of a book) **2** : printed matter projected on a motion-picture screen during or between the scenes

sub·tle \'sət-ᵊl\ *adj* **sub·tler** \'sət-ᵊl-ər\; **sub·tlest** \'sət-ᵊl-əst\ **1** : hardly noticeable ⟨∼ differences⟩ **2** : SHREWD, PERCEPTIVE **3** : adept in the use of subtlety and cunning : CLEVER, SLY **4** ♦ : cunningly made or contrived — **sub·tly** \'sət-ᵊl-ē\ *adv*

♦ delicate, exact, fine, minute, nice, refined — more at FINE

sub·tle·ty \-tē\ *n* : the quality or state of being subtle
sub·tract \səb-'trakt\ *vb* : to take away (as one part or number) from another; *also* : to perform the operation of deducting one number from another — **sub·trac·tion** \-'trak-shən\ *n*
sub·tra·hend \'səb-trə-ˌhend\ *n* : a number that is to be subtracted from another
sub·trop·i·cal \ˌsəb-'trä-pi-kəl, 'səb-\ *also* **sub·trop·ic** \-pik\ *adj* : of, relating to, or being regions bordering on the tropical zone — **sub·trop·ics** \-piks\ *n pl*
sub·urb \'sə-ˌbərb\ *n* **1** : an outlying part of a city; *also* : a small community adjacent to a city **2** *pl* : a residential area adjacent to a city — **sub·ur·ban** \sə-'bər-bən\ *adj or n* — **sub·ur·ban·ite** \sə-'bər-bə-ˌnīt\ *n*
sub·ur·bia \sə-'bər-bē-ə\ *n* **1** ♦ : the suburbs of a city **2** : suburban people or customs

♦ environs, exurbia, outskirts — more at ENVIRONS

sub·ven·tion \səb-'ven-chən\ *n* : SUBSIDY, ENDOWMENT
sub·vert \səb-'vərt\ *vb* **1** : OVERTHROW, RUIN **2** ♦ : to pervert or corrupt by an undermining of morals, allegiance, or faith ⟨∼ the rule of law⟩ — **sub·ver·sion** \-'vər-zhən\ *n* — **sub·ver·sive** \-'vər-siv\ *adj*

♦ debase, degrade, demean, demoralize, humble, warp — more at DEBASE

sub·way \'səb-ˌwā\ *n* : an underground way; *esp* : an underground electric railway
sub·woof·er \'səb-ˌwu̇-fər\ *n* : a loudspeaker responsive only to the lowest acoustic frequencies
suc·ceed \sək-'sēd\ *vb* **1** : to follow next in order or next after another; *esp* : to inherit sovereignty, rank, title, or property **2** ♦ : to attain a desired object or end : be successful

♦ click, deliver, go over, pan out, work out; *also* catch on; flourish, prosper, thrive *Ant* collapse, fail, flop, flunk, fold, wash out ♦ flourish, prosper, thrive; *also* prevail, triumph, win *Ant* fail

suc·ceed·ing *adj* ♦ : following next in order or next after another

♦ coming, following, next — more at NEXT

suc·cess \sək-'ses\ *n* **1** ♦ : favorable or desired outcome **2** : the gaining of wealth and fame **3** ♦ : one that succeeds — **suc·cess·ful·ly** *adv*

♦ [1] accomplishment, achievement, attainment, coup, triumph — more at ACCOMPLISHMENT ♦ [3] blockbuster, hit, smash, winner — more at HIT

suc·cess·ful \-fəl\ *adj* ♦ : resulting or terminating in success ⟨a ∼ outcome⟩; *also* : gaining or having gained success ⟨a ∼ writer⟩

♦ palmy, prosperous, triumphant; *also* coming, promising; booming, growing, roaring, robust *Ant* failed, unsuccessful

suc·ces·sion \sək-'se-shən\ *n* **1** : the order, act, or right of succeeding to a property, title, or throne **2** : the act or process of following in order **3** : a series of persons or things that follow one after another
suc·ces·sive \sək-'se-siv\ *adj* ♦ : following in order : CONSECUTIVE ⟨three ∼ days⟩ — **suc·ces·sive·ly** *adv*

♦ consecutive, sequential — more at CONSECUTIVE

suc·ces·sor \sək-'se-sər\ *n* : one that succeeds (as to a throne, title, estate, or office)
suc·cinct \(ˌ)sək-'siŋkt, sə-'siŋkt\ *adj* ♦ : marked by compact precise expression without wasted words : BRIEF

♦ brief, compact, compendious, concise, crisp, epigrammatic, laconic, pithy, summary, terse — more at CONCISE

suc·cinct·ly *adv* ♦ : in a succinct manner : with concise and precise brevity

♦ compactly, concisely, crisply, laconically, shortly, summarily, tersely — more at SHORTLY

suc·cinct·ness *n* ♦ : the quality or state of being succinct

♦ brevity, briefness, compactness, conciseness, crispness, terseness; *also* bluntness, curtness, shortness *Ant* prolixity, verbosity, wordiness

suc·cor *or Can and Brit* **suc·cour** \'sə-kər\ *n* [ME socour, sucurs (taken as pl.), fr. AF sucur, socors, fr. ML succursus, fr. L succurrere to run to the rescue, bring aid] : AID, HELP, RELIEF — **succor** *vb*
suc·co·tash \'sə-kə-ˌtash\ *n* [Narraganset (American Indian language of Rhode Island) msíckquatash boiled corn kernels] : beans and corn kernels cooked together
¹**suc·cu·lent** \'sə-kyə-lənt\ *adj* ♦ : full of juice : JUICY; *also* : having fleshy tissues that conserve moisture ⟨∼ plants⟩ — **suc·cu·lence** \-ləns\ *n*

♦ fleshy, juicy, pulpy — more at JUICY

²**succulent** *n* : a succulent plant (as a cactus or an aloe)
suc·cumb \sə-'kəm\ *vb* **1** ♦ : to yield to superior strength or force or overpowering appeal or desire **2** ♦ : to pass from physical life : DIE

♦ [1] blink, bow, budge, capitulate, concede, fall, give in, knuckle under, quit, submit, surrender, yield — more at YIELD ♦ [2] decease, depart, die, expire, pass, pass away, perish — more at DIE

¹**such** \'səch, 'sich\ *adj* **1** ♦ : of this or that kind **2** : having a quality just specified or to be specified

♦ akin, alike, analogous, comparable, correspondent, like, parallel, similar — more at ALIKE

²**such** *pron* **1** : such a one or ones ⟨he's a star, and acted as ∼⟩ **2** : that or those similar or related thereto ⟨boards and nails and ∼⟩
³**such** *adv* : to that degree : so
such·like \'səch-ˌlīk\ *adj* : of like kind : SIMILAR
¹**suck** \'sək\ *vb* **1** : to draw in liquid and esp. mother's milk

---

with the mouth **2** : to draw liquid from by action of the mouth ⟨~ an orange⟩ **3** ♦ : to take in or up or remove by or as if by suction **4** : to be objectionable

♦ *usu* **suck up** absorb, drink, imbibe, soak, sponge — more at ABSORB

²**suck** *n* **1** : a sucking movement or force **2** : the act of sucking

suck·er \'sə-kər\ *n* **1** : one that sucks **2** : a part of an animal's body used for sucking or for clinging **3** : any of numerous freshwater fishes with thick soft lips for sucking in food **4** : a shoot from the roots or lower part of a plant **5** ♦ : a person easily deceived **6** — used as a generalized term of reference

♦ dupe, gull, pigeon, sap, tool — more at DUPE

suck·le \'sə-kəl\ *vb* **suck·led; suck·ling** : to give or draw milk from the breast or udder; *also* : NURTURE

suck·ling \'sə-kliŋ\ *n* : a young unweaned mammal

suck–up \'sək-ˌəp\ *n* : a person who seeks to gain favor by flattery ⟨a ~ to the teacher⟩

su·crose \'sü-ˌkrōs, -ˌkrōz\ *n* : a sweet sugar obtained commercially esp. from sugarcane or sugar beets

suc·tion \'sək-shən\ *n* **1** : the act of sucking **2** : the act or process of drawing something (as liquid or dust) into a space (as in a vacuum cleaner or a pump) by partially exhausting the air in the space — **suc·tion·al** \-shə-nəl\ *adj*

suction cup *n* : a cup-shaped device in which a partial vacuum is produced when applied to a surface

Su·da·nese \ˌsüd-ᵊn-'ēz, -'ēs\ *n* : a native or inhabitant of Sudan — **Sudanese** *adj*

sud·den \'səd-ᵊn\ *adj* [ME *sodain*, fr. MF, fr. L *subitaneus*, fr. *subitus* sudden, fr. pp. of *subire* to come up] **1** ♦ : happening or coming unexpectedly ⟨~ shower⟩; *also* : changing angle or character all at once ⟨~ turn⟩ ⟨~ descent⟩ **2** : HASTY, RASH ⟨~ decision⟩ **3** : made or brought about in a short time : PROMPT ⟨~ cure⟩ — **sud·den·ness** *n*

♦ unanticipated, unexpected, unforeseen — more at UNEXPECTED

sudden infant death syndrome *n* : death due to unknown causes of an apparently healthy infant usu. before one year of age and esp. during sleep

sud·den·ly *adv* ♦ : in a sudden manner

♦ aback, unaware, unawares — more at UNAWARES

su·do·ku \sü-'dō-kü\ *n* [Jp *sūdoku*] : a puzzle in which several numbers are to be filled into a 9x9 grid of squares so that every row, every column, and every 3x3 box contains the numbers 1 through 9

suds \'sədz\ *n pl* : soapy water esp. when frothy — **sudsy** \'səd-zē\ *adj*

sue \'sü\ *vb* **sued; su·ing** [ME *sewen, siuen* to follow, strive for, petition, fr. AF *sivre, siure*, fr. VL **sequere*, fr. L *sequi* to follow] **1** ♦ : to make a request or application : PETITION, SOLICIT — usu. used with *for* or *to* **2** : to seek justice or right by bringing legal action ⟨*sued* the company⟩

♦ *usu* **sue for** ask, call, petition, plead, quest, request, seek, solicit

suede *also* **suède** \'swād\ *n* [F *gants de Suède* Swedish gloves] **1** : leather with a napped surface **2** : a fabric with a suedelike nap

su·et \'sü-ət\ *n* : the hard fat from beef and mutton that yields tallow

suff *abbr* **1** sufficient **2** suffix

suf·fer \'sə-fər\ *vb* **suf·fered; suf·fer·ing** **1** ♦ : to feel or endure pain **2** ♦ : to have experience of : UNDERGO **3** : to bear loss, damage, or injury **4** ♦ : to allow esp. by reason of indifference : PERMIT — **suf·fer·er** *n*

♦ [1] agonize, bleed, feel, grieve, hurt, mourn, sorrow — more at GRIEVE ♦ [2] endure, experience, feel, have, know, see, sustain, taste, undergo — more at EXPERIENCE ♦ [4] allow, have, permit

suf·fer·able \'sə-fə-rə-bəl\ *adj* **1** : not forbidden **2** ♦ : that can be suffered

♦ bearable, endurable, supportable, sustainable, tolerable — more at BEARABLE

suf·fer·ance \'sə-frəns, -fə-rəns\ *n* **1** ♦ : consent or approval implied by lack of interference or resistance **2** ♦ : power or ability to withstand : PATIENCE

♦ [1] allowance, authorization, clearance, concurrence, consent, leave, license (*or* licence), permission, sanction — more at PERMISSION ♦ [2] forbearance, long-suffering, patience, tolerance — more at PATIENCE

suf·fer·ing \'sə-friŋ, -fə-riŋ\ *n* : PAIN, MISERY, HARDSHIP

suf·fice \sə-'fīs\ *vb* **suf·ficed; suf·fic·ing** **1** : to satisfy a need : be sufficient **2** : to be capable or competent

suf·fi·cien·cy \sə-'fi-shən-sē\ *n* **1** : a sufficient quantity to meet one's needs **2** : the quality or state of being sufficient : ADEQUACY

suf·fi·cient \sə-'fi-shənt\ *adj* : adequate to accomplish a purpose or meet a need — **suf·fi·cient·ly** *adv*

¹**suf·fix** \'sə-ˌfiks\ *n* : an affix occurring at the end of a word

²**suf·fix** \'sə-ˌfiks, (ˌ)sə-'fiks\ *vb* : to attach as a suffix — **suf·fix·a·tion** \ˌsə-ˌfik-'sā-shən\ *n*

suf·fo·cate \'sə-fə-ˌkāt\ *vb* **-cat·ed; -cat·ing** ♦ : to deprive of oxygen : SMOTHER — **suf·fo·cat·ing·ly** *adv* — **suf·fo·ca·tion** \ˌsə-fə-'kā-shən\ *n*

♦ choke, smother, stifle, strangle — more at SMOTHER

suf·fra·gan \'sə-fri-gən\ *n* : an assistant bishop; *esp* : one not having the right of succession — **suffragan** *adj*

suf·frage \'sə-frij\ *n* [L *suffragium*] **1** : VOTE **2** ♦ : the right to vote : FRANCHISE

♦ enfranchisement, franchise, vote — more at VOTE

suf·frag·ette \ˌsə-fri-'jet\ *n* : a woman who advocates suffrage for women

suf·frag·ist \'səf-ri-jist\ *n* : one who advocates extension of suffrage esp. to women

suf·fuse \sə-'fyüz\ *vb* **suf·fused; suf·fus·ing** ♦ : to spread over or through in the manner of a fluid or light — **suf·fu·sion** \-'fyü-zhən\ *n*

♦ percolate, permeate, transfuse — more at PERMEATE ♦ imbue, inculcate, infuse, ingrain, invest, steep — more at INFUSE

¹**sug·ar** \'shu̇-gər\ *n* **1** : a sweet substance that is colorless or white when pure and is chiefly sucrose from sugarcane or sugar beets **2** : a water-soluble compound (as glucose) similar to sucrose

²**sugar** *vb* **sug·ared; sug·ar·ing** **1** : to mix, cover, or sprinkle with sugar **2** : SWEETEN ⟨~ advice with flattery⟩ **3** : to form sugar ⟨a syrup that ~s⟩ **4** : GRANULATE

sugar beet *n* : a large beet with a white root from which sugar is made

sug·ar·cane \'shu̇-gər-ˌkān\ *n* : a tall grass widely grown in warm regions for the sugar in its stalks

sugar daddy *n* **1** : a well-to-do usu. older man who supports or spends lavishly on a mistress, girlfriend, or boyfriend **2** : a generous benefactor of a cause

sugar maple *n* : a maple with a sweet sap; *esp* : one of eastern No. America with sap that is the chief source of maple syrup and maple sugar

sugar pea *n* : SNOW PEA

sug·ar·plum \'shu̇-gər-ˌpləm\ *n* : a small ball of candy

sug·ary *adj* : cloyingly sweet

sug·gest \səg-'jest, sə-\ *vb* **1** ♦ : to put (as a thought, plan, or desire) into a person's mind **2** ♦ : to remind or evoke by association of ideas

♦ [1] advise, counsel — more at ADVISE ♦ [1] advance, offer, pose, proffer, propose, propound, vote — more at PROPOSE ♦ [2] allude, hint, imply, indicate, infer, insinuate, intimate — more at HINT

sug·gest·ible \səg-ˈjes-tə-bəl, sə-\ *adj* : easily influenced by suggestion

sug·ges·tion \-ˈjes-chən\ *n* **1 a** : an act or instance of suggesting **b** ♦ : something suggested **2** ♦ : a slight indication

♦ [1b] offer, proffer, proposal, proposition — more at PROPOSAL ♦ [2] clue, cue, hint, indication, inkling, intimation, lead — more at HINT

sug·ges·tive \-ˈjes-tiv\ *adj* ♦ : tending to suggest something; *esp* : suggesting something improper or indecent — **sug·ges·tive·ly** *adv* — **sug·ges·tive·ness** *n*

♦ eloquent, expressive, meaning, meaningful, pregnant, significant — more at EXPRESSIVE ♦ bawdy, lewd, racy, ribald, risqué, spicy; *also* coarse, crude, earthy, foul, gross, salty; dirty, filthy, lascivious, nasty, obscene, pornographic, smutty, vulgar; naughty, wicked

¹sui·cide \ˈsü-ə-ˌsīd\ *n* **1** : the act of killing oneself purposely **2** : one that commits or attempts suicide — **sui·cid·al** \ˌsü-ə-ˈsīd-ᵊl\ *adj*

²suicide *adj* : being or performing a deliberate act resulting in the voluntary death of the person who does it ⟨a ∼ mission⟩ ⟨a ∼ bomber⟩

sui ge·ner·is \ˌsü-ˌī-ˈje-nə-rəs, ˌsü-ē-\ *adj* [L, of its own kind] : being in a class by itself : UNIQUE

¹suit \ˈsüt\ *n* **1** ♦ : an action in court to recover a right or claim **2 a** ♦ : an act of suing or entreating **b** : COURTSHIP **3** : a number of things used together ⟨∼ of clothes⟩ **4** : all the playing cards in a pack bearing the same symbol

♦ [1] action, lawsuit, proceeding — more at LAWSUIT ♦ [2a] appeal, cry, entreaty, petition, plea, prayer, solicitation, supplication — more at PLEA

²suit *vb* **1** ♦ : to be appropriate or fitting **2** : to be becoming to **3** ♦ : to meet the needs or desires of : PLEASE **4** ♦ : to outfit with clothes : DRESS

♦ [1] befit, do, fit, go, serve — more at DO ♦ [3] content, delight, gladden, gratify, please, rejoice, satisfy, warm — more at PLEASE ♦ [4] apparel, array, attire, caparison, clothe, deck, dress, garb, invest, rig — more at CLOTHE

suit·abil·i·ty \ˌsü-tə-ˈbi-lə-tē\ *n* ♦ : the quality or state of being suitable

♦ appropriateness, aptness, fitness, rightness — more at APPROPRIATENESS

suit·able \ˈsü-tə-bəl\ *adj* ♦ : adapted to a use or purpose

♦ able, capable, competent, fit, good, qualified — more at COMPETENT ♦ applicable, appropriate, apt, felicitous, fit, fitting, good, happy, meet, proper, right — more at FIT

suit·able·ness \ˈsü-tə-bəl-nəs\ *n* : the quality or state of being suitable

suit·ably \-tə-blē\ *adv* ♦ : in a suitable manner

♦ appropriately, correctly, fittingly, happily, properly, rightly — more at PROPERLY

suit·case \ˈsüt-ˌkās\ *n* ♦ : a portable case designed to hold a traveler's clothing and personal articles

♦ carryall, grip, handbag, portmanteau, traveling bag — more at TRAVELING BAG

suite \ˈswēt, *for 4 also* ˈsüt\ *n* **1** ♦ : a group of retainers or attendants : RETINUE **2** : a group of rooms occupied as a unit **3** : a modern instrumental composition in several movements of different character; *also* : a long orchestral concert arrangement in suite form of material drawn from a longer work **4** : a set of matched furniture for a room **5** : a group of things forming a unit or constituting a collection

♦ cortege, following, retinue, train — more at CORTEGE

suit·ing \ˈsü-tiŋ\ *n* : fabric for suits of clothes

suit·or \ˈsü-tər\ *n* **1** ♦ : one who sues or petitions **2** ♦ : one who seeks to marry a woman

♦ [1] pleader, solicitor ♦ [2] gallant, swain, wooer; *also* beau, boyfriend, fellow, man; admirer, crush, steady; beloved, darling, dear, favorite, flame, honey,

love, lover, sweet, sweetheart, valentine; date, escort; fiancé, intended

su·ki·ya·ki \skē-ˈyä-kē, ˌsü-kē-ˈyä-\ *n* : thin slices of meat, tofu, and vegetables cooked in soy sauce and sugar

sul·fa drug \ˈsəl-fə-\ *n* : any of various synthetic organic bacteria-inhibiting drugs

sul·fate *or Can and Brit* **sul·phate** \ˈsəl-ˌfāt\ *n* : a salt or ester of sulfuric acid

sul·fide *or Can and Brit* **sul·phide** \ˈsəl-ˌfīd\ *n* : a compound of sulfur

sul·fur *or chiefly Can and Brit* **sul·phur** \ˈsəl-fər\ *n* : a nonmetallic chemical element used esp. in the chemical and paper industries and in vulcanizing rubber

sulfur di·ox·ide \-dī-ˈäk-ˌsīd\ *n* : a heavy pungent toxic gas that is used esp. in bleaching, as a preservative, and as a refrigerant, and is a major air pollutant

sul·fu·ric *or Can and Brit* **sul·phu·ric** \ˌsəl-ˈfyu̇r-ik\ *adj* : of, relating to, or containing sulfur

sulfuric acid *or* **sul·phu·ric acid** \ˌsəl-ˈfyu̇r-ik-\ *n* : a heavy corrosive oily strong acid

sul·fu·rous *or chiefly Can and Brit* **sul·phu·rous** \ˈsəl-fə-rəs, -fyə-, *also esp for 1* ˌsəl-ˈfyu̇r-əs\ *adj* **1** ♦ : relating to, or containing sulfur **2** : of or relating to brimstone or the fire of hell : INFERNAL **3** : FIERY, INFLAMED ⟨∼ sermons⟩

¹sulk \ˈsəlk\ *vb* : to be or become moodily silent or irritable

²sulk *n* ♦ : a sulky mood or spell

♦ pet, pout, sullenness; *also* blues, dumps; surliness; biliousness, grumpiness, irascibility, irritability, peevishness, perverseness, perversity, petulance; cantankerousness, disagreeableness

sulk·i·ness \-kē-nəs\ *n* : SULK

¹sulky \ˈsəl-kē\ *adj* **sulk·i·er; -est** ♦ : inclined to sulk : MOROSE, MOODY ⟨a ∼ mood⟩ — **sulk·i·ly** \ˈsəl-kə-lē\ *adv*

♦ glum, moody, morose, sullen, surly; *also* dour, gloomy; choleric, crabby, cranky, cross, crotchety, grouchy, grumpy, irascible, irritable, peevish, perverse, pettish, petulant, short-tempered, snappy, snippy, testy, waspish; brooding, moping; bearish, bilious, cantankerous, disagreeable, dyspeptic, ill-humored, ill-natured, ill-tempered, ornery; sensitive, thin-skinned, temperamental, touchy

²sulky *n, pl* **sulkies** : a light 2-wheeled horse-drawn vehicle with a seat for the driver and usu. no body

sul·len \ˈsə-lən\ *adj* **1** ♦ : gloomily silent **2** : showing or causing gloom or depression : GLOOMY ⟨a ∼ sky⟩ — **sul·len·ly** *adv*

♦ glum, moody, morose, sulky, surly — more at SULKY

sul·len·ness *n* ♦ : the quality or state of being sullen

♦ pet, pout, sulk — more at SULK

sul·ly \ˈsə-lē\ *vb* **sul·lied; sul·ly·ing** : to make or become soiled, tarnished, or defiled : SOIL, SMIRCH ⟨∼ his name⟩

sulphate, sulphide, sulphur *chiefly Can and Brit var of* SULFATE, SULFIDE, SULFUR

sul·tan \ˈsəlt-ᵊn\ *n* : a sovereign esp. of a Muslim state — **sul·tan·ate** \-ˌāt\ *n*

sul·ta·na \ˌsəl-ˈta-nə\ *n* **1** : a female member of a sultan's family **2** : a pale seedless grape; *also* : a raisin of this grape

sul·try \ˈsəl-trē\ *adj* **sul·tri·er; -est** [obs. E *sulter* to swelter, alter. of E *swelter*] **1** ♦ : very hot and moist; *also* : burning hot **2** : exciting sexual desire ⟨a ∼ look⟩

♦ humid, muggy, sticky — more at HUMID ♦ broiling, burning, fiery, hot, red-hot, scorching, torrid — more at HOT

¹sum \ˈsəm\ *n* [ME *summe*, fr. AF *sume, somme*, fr. L *summa*, fr. fem. of *summus* highest] **1** : a quantity of money **2** ♦ : the whole amount **3** : GIST **4** : the result obtained by adding numbers **5** : a problem in arithmetic **6** : a summary of the chief points or thoughts

♦ aggregate, full, total, totality, whole — more at WHOLE

²**sum** *vb* **summed; sum·ming** ♦ : to find the sum of by adding or counting; *also* : to reach a sum

♦ add, foot, total — more at ADD ♦ *usu* **sum to** *or* **sum into** add up, amount, come, number, total — more at AMOUNT (TO)

su·mac *also* **su·mach** \'sü-ˌmak, 'shü-\ *n* : any of a genus of trees, shrubs, and woody vines having spikes or loose clusters of red or whitish berries

sum·mar·i·ly \(ˌ)sə-'mer-ə-lē, 'sə-mə-rə-lē\ *adv* ♦ : in a summary manner or form

♦ compactly, concisely, crisply, laconically, shortly, succinctly, tersely — more at SHORTLY

sum·ma·rise *chiefly Brit var of* SUMMARIZE

sum·ma·rize \'sə-mə-ˌrīz\ *vb* **-rized; -riz·ing** ♦ : to tell in a summary — **sum·ma·ri·za·tion** \ˌsə-mə-rə-'zā-shən\ *n*

♦ abstract, digest, encapsulate, epitomize, outline, recapitulate, sum up, wrap up; *also* abridge, condense, curtail, shorten; downsize, shrink; concentrate, consolidate; simplify, streamline

¹**sum·ma·ry** \'sə-mə-rē\ *adj* **1** ♦ : covering the main points briefly : CONCISE **2** : done without delay or formality ⟨∼ punishment⟩

♦ brief, compact, compendious, concise, crisp, epigrammatic, laconic, pithy, succinct, terse — more at CONCISE

²**summary** *n, pl* **-ries** ♦ : a concise statement of the main points

♦ abstract, digest, encapsulation, epitome, outline, précis, recapitulation, résumé (*or* resume), roundup, sum, synopsis, wrap-up; *also* abbreviation, abridgement, condensation, curtailment, shortening; brief; rundown; simplification

sum·ma·tion \(ˌ)sə-'mā-shən\ *n* **1** : a summing up **2** : a speech in court summing up the arguments in a case

sum·mer \'sə-mər\ *n* : the season of the year in a region in which the sun shines most directly : the warmest period of the year — **sum·mery** *adj*

sum·mer·house \'sə-mər-ˌhaùs\ *n* : a covered structure in a garden or park to provide a shady retreat

summersault *var of* SOMERSAULT

summer squash *n* : any of various squashes (as zucchini) used as a vegetable while immature

¹**sum·mit** \'sə-mət\ *n* **1** ♦ : the highest point **2** : a conference of highest-level officials

♦ acme, apex, climax, crown, culmination, head, height, meridian, peak, pinnacle, tip-top, top, zenith — more at HEIGHT

²**summit** *vb* **sum·mit·ted; sum·mit·ting 1** : to participate in a summit conference **2** : to climb to the summit

sum·mon \'sə-mən\ *vb* [ME *somnen, somonen,* fr. AF *somondre,* fr. VL **summonere,* alter. of L *summonēre* to remind secretly] **1** ♦ : to call to a meeting : CONVOKE **2** : to send for; *also* : to order to appear in court **3** : to evoke esp. by an act of the will ⟨∼ up courage⟩ — **sum·mon·er** *n*

♦ assemble, call, convene, convoke, muster — more at CONVOKE

sum·mons \'sə-mənz\ *n, pl* **sum·mons·es 1** : an authoritative call to appear at a designated place or to attend to a duty **2** : a warning or citation to appear in court at a specified time to answer charges

sump·tu·ous \'səmp-shə-wəs, -chə-\ *adj* ♦ : extremely costly, rich, luxurious, or magnificent : LUXURIOUS

♦ deluxe, lavish, luxuriant, luxurious, opulent, palatial, plush — more at LUXURIOUS

sum up *vb* ♦ : to tell in or reduce to a summary : SUMMARIZE

♦ abstract, digest, encapsulate, epitomize, outline, recapitulate, summarize, wrap up

¹**sun** \'sən\ *n* **1** : the shining celestial body around which the earth and other planets revolve and from which they receive light and heat **2** : a celestial body like the sun **3** : SUNSHINE — **sun·less** *adj*

²**sun** *vb* **sunned; sun·ning 1** : to expose to or as if to the rays of the sun **2** : to sun oneself

Sun *abbr* Sunday

sun·bath \'sən-ˌbath, -ˌbáth\ *n* : an exposure to sunlight or a sunlamp — **sun·bathe** \-ˌbāth\ *vb*

sun·beam \-ˌbēm\ *n* : a ray of sunlight

sun·block \'sən-ˌbläk\ *n* : a preparation used on the skin to prevent sunburn (as by blocking ultraviolet radiation)

sun·bon·net \-ˌbä-nət\ *n* : a bonnet with a wide brim to shield the face and neck from the sun

¹**sun·burn** \-ˌbərn\ *vb* **-burned** \-ˌbərnd\ *or* **-burnt** \-ˌbərnt\; **-burn·ing** : to cause or become affected with sunburn

²**sunburn** *n* : a skin inflammation caused by overexposure to ultraviolet radiation esp. from sunshine

sun·dae \'sən-(ˌ)dā, -dē\ *n* : ice cream served with topping

Sun·day \'sən-dē, -ˌdā\ *n* : the 1st day of the week : the Christian Sabbath

sun·der \'sən-dər\ *vb* ♦ : to force apart

♦ break up, disconnect, disjoint, dissever, dissociate, disunite, divide, divorce, part, resolve, separate, sever, split, unyoke — more at SEPARATE

sun·di·al \-ˌdī-(ə)l\ *n* : a device for showing the time of day from the shadow cast on a plate by an object with a straight edge

sun·down \-ˌdaùn\ *n* ♦ : the time at which the sun disappears below the horizon : SUNSET 2

♦ dusk, evening, gloaming, nightfall, sunset, twilight — more at DUSK

sun·dries \'sən-drēz\ *n pl* ♦ : various small articles or items

♦ novelties, notions, odds and ends

sun·dry \'sən-drē\ *adj* : SEVERAL, DIVERS, VARIOUS

sun·fish \'sən-ˌfish\ *n* **1** : a large marine fish with a deep flattened body **2** : any of numerous often brightly colored No. American freshwater fishes related to the perches and usu. having the body flattened from side to side

sun·flow·er \-ˌflaù-ər\ *n* : any of a genus of tall New World plants related to the daisies and often grown for the oil-rich seeds of their yellow-petaled dark-centered flowers

sung *past and past part of* SING

sun·glasses \'sən-ˌgla-səz\ *n pl* : glasses to protect the eyes from the sun

sunk *past and past part of* SINK

sunk·en \'səŋ-kən\ *adj* **1** ♦ : covered with water : SUBMERGED **2** ♦ : fallen in : HOLLOW ⟨∼ cheeks⟩ **3** : lying in a depression ⟨a ∼ garden⟩; *also* : constructed below the general floor level ⟨a ∼ living room⟩

♦ [1] submarine, underwater ♦ [2] concave, depressed, hollow — more at HOLLOW

sun·lamp \'sən-ˌlamp\ *n* : an electric lamp designed to emit radiation of wavelengths from ultraviolet to infrared

sun·light \-ˌlīt\ *n* : SUNSHINE

sun·lit \-ˌlit\ *adj* : lighted by or as if by the sun

Sun·ni \'sù-nē\ *n* **1** : one of the two main branches of Islam **2** : a Muslim of the Sunni branch of Islam

sun·ny \'sə-nē\ *adj* ♦ : full of sunshine; *also* : full of good spirits

♦ clear, cloudless, fair, sunshiny, unclouded — more at FAIR ♦ blithe, bright, buoyant, cheerful, cheery, chipper, gay, lightsome, merry, upbeat — more at CHEERFUL

sun protection factor *n* : a number that is the factor by which the time required for unprotected skin to become sunburned is increased when a sunscreen is used

sun·rise \-ˌrīz\ *n* **1** : the apparent rising of the sun above the horizon **2** ♦ : the time at which the sun rises

♦ aurora, cockcrow, dawn, morning — more at DAWN

sun·roof \-ˌrüf, -ˌrùf\ *n* : a panel in an automobile roof that can be opened

sun·screen \-ˌskrēn\ *n* : a preparation on the skin to prevent sunburn (as by absorbing ultraviolet radiation)

sun·set \-ˌset\ *n* **1** : the apparent descent of the sun below the horizon **2** ♦ : the time at which the sun sets

♦ dusk, evening, gloaming, nightfall, sundown, twilight — more at DUSK

sun·shade \'sən-ˌshād\ *n* : something (as a parasol or awning) used as a protection from the sun's rays

sun·shine \-ˌshīn\ *n* : the direct light of the sun

sun·shiny *adj* ♦ : bright with or as if with the rays of the sun

♦ clear, cloudless, fair, sunny, unclouded — more at FAIR

sun·spot \-ˌspät\ *n* : any of the dark spots that appear at times on the sun's surface

sun·stroke \-ˌstrōk\ *n* : heatstroke caused by direct exposure to the sun

sun·tan \-ˌtan\ *n* : a browning of the skin from exposure to the sun's rays

sun·up \-ˌəp\ *n* : the apparent rising of the sun above the horizon : SUNRISE

¹**sup** \'səp\ *vb* **supped; sup·ping** ♦ : to take or drink in swallows or gulps

♦ drink, guzzle, imbibe, quaff, swig, toss — more at DRINK

²**sup** *n* ♦ : a mouthful esp. of liquor or broth; *also* : a small quantity of liquid

♦ draft, swallow

³**sup** *vb* **supped; sup·ping** **1** : to eat the evening meal **2** : to make one's supper ⟨*supped* on roast beef⟩

⁴**sup** *abbr* **1** superior **2** supplement; supplementary **3** supply **4** supra

¹**su·per** \'sü-pər\ *n* : SUPERINTENDENT

²**super** *adj* **1** : very fine : EXCELLENT **2** : EXTREME, EXCESSIVE **3** : very large or powerful : HUGE

super- \ˌsü-pər\ *prefix* **1** : over and above : higher in quantity, quality, or degree than : more than **2** : in addition : extra **3** : exceeding a norm **4** : in excessive degree or intensity **5** : surpassing all or most others of its kind **6** : situated above, on, or at the top of **7** : next above or higher **8** : more inclusive than **9** : superior in status or position

su·per·abun·dance \ˌsü-pər-ə-ˈbən-dəns\ *n* ♦ : great abundance; *also* : the state or an instance of surpassing usual, proper, or specified limits

♦ abundance, plenty, wealth — more at PLENTY ♦ excess, fat, overabundance, overflow, overkill, overmuch, superfluity, surfeit, surplus — more at EXCESS

su·per·abun·dant \ˌsü-pər-ə-ˈbən-dənt\ *adj* : more than ample

su·per·an·nu·ate \ˌsü-pər-ˈan-yə-ˌwāt\ *vb* **-at·ed; -at·ing** **1** : to make out-of-date **2** : to retire and pension because of age or infirmity — **su·per·an·nu·at·ed** *adj*

su·per·an·nu·at·ed *adj* ♦ : no longer current : OUTDATED

♦ antiquated, archaic, dated, obsolete, outdated, outmoded, outworn, passé — more at OBSOLETE

su·perb \su̇-ˈpərb\ *adj* [L *superbus* excellent, proud, fr. *super* above] ♦ : marked to the highest degree by excellence, brilliance, or competence — **su·perb·ly** *adv*

♦ excellent, fabulous, fine, grand, great, sensational, splendid, superior, swell, terrific, unsurpassed, wonderful — more at EXCELLENT

su·per·charg·er \'sü-pər-ˌchär-jər\ *n* : a device for increasing the amount of air supplied to an internal combustion engine

su·per·cil·ious \ˌsü-pər-ˈsi-lē-əs\ *adj* [L *superciliosus*, fr. *supercilium* eyebrow, haughtiness] ♦ : haughtily contemptuous

♦ arrogant, cavalier, haughty, imperious, overweening, peremptory, pompous, presumptuous, pretentious, superior, uppity — more at ARROGANT

su·per·com·pu·ter \'sü-pər-kəm-ˌpyü-tər\ *n* : a large very fast mainframe

su·per·con·duc·tiv·i·ty \ˌsü-pər-ˌkän-dək-ˈti-və-tē\ *n* : a complete disappearance of electrical resistance in a substance esp. at very low temperatures — **su·per·con·duc·tive** \-kən-ˈdək-tiv\ *adj* — **su·per·con·duc·tor** \-ˈdək-tər\ *n*

su·per·con·ti·nent \'sü-pər-ˌkänt-ⁿ-ənt\ *n* : a former large continent from which other continents are held to have broken off and drifted away

su·per·ego \ˌsü-pər-ˈē-gō\ *n* : the one of the three divisions of the psyche in psychoanalytic theory that functions to reward and punish through a system of moral attitudes, conscience, and a sense of guilt

su·per·fi·cial \ˌsü-pər-ˈfi-shəl\ *adj* **1** : of or relating to the surface or appearance only **2** : not thorough : SHALLOW — **su·per·fi·ci·al·i·ty** \-ˌfi-shē-ˈa-lə-tē\ *n* — **su·per·fi·cial·ly** *adv*

su·per·flu·i·ty \ˌsü-pər-ˈflü-ə-tē\ *n* ♦ : the state or an instance of surpassing usual, proper, or specified limits

♦ amenity, comfort, extra, frill, indulgence, luxury — more at LUXURY ♦ excess, fat, overabundance, overflow, overkill, overmuch, superabundance, surfeit, surplus — more at EXCESS

su·per·flu·ous \su̇-ˈpər-flə-wəs\ *adj* ♦ : exceeding what is sufficient or necessary : SURPLUS ⟨~ details⟩

♦ excess, extra, spare, supernumerary, surplus — more at SPARE

su·per·high·way \ˌsü-pər-ˈhī-ˌwā\ *n* : a broad highway designed for high-speed traffic

su·per·hu·man \ˌsü-pər-ˈhyu-mən\ *adj* ♦ : being above the human; *also* : exceeding normal human power, size, or capability

♦ magical, miraculous, phenomenal, supernatural, uncanny, unearthly — more at SUPERNATURAL

su·per·im·pose \-im-ˈpōz\ *vb* : to lay (one thing) over or above something else

su·per·in·tend \ˌsü-pə-rin-ˈtend\ *vb* ♦ : to have or exercise the charge and oversight of

♦ administer, carry on, conduct, control, direct, govern, guide, handle, manage, operate, oversee, regulate, run, supervise — more at CONDUCT

su·per·in·ten·dence \-ˈten-dəns\ *n* ♦ : the act or function of superintending or directing

♦ administration, conduct, control, direction, government, guidance, management, operation, oversight, regulation, running, supervision — more at CONDUCT ♦ care, charge, guidance, headship, oversight, regulation, supervision — more at SUPERVISION

su·per·in·ten·den·cy \-dən-sē\ *n* **1** : the office, post, or jurisdiction of a superintendent **2** : the act or function of superintending or directing

su·per·in·ten·dent \-dənt\ *n* ♦ : one who has executive oversight and charge

♦ administrator, director, executive, manager, supervisor — more at EXECUTIVE

¹**su·pe·ri·or** \su̇-ˈpir-ē-ər\ *adj* **1** : situated higher up, over, or near the top; *also* : higher in rank or numbers **2** ♦ : of greater value or importance **3** : courageously indifferent (as to pain or misfortune) **4** : better than most others of

---

List of self-explanatory words with the prefix *super-*

superabsorbent	superclean	superhero	supernormal
superachiever	superexpensive	superhumanly	superpatriot
superagency	superfast	superindividual	superpatriotic
superblock	superfine	superliner	superpatriotism
superbomb	superheat	superman	superpremium
supercity	superheavy	supermom	superrich

its kind **5** ♦ : affecting or assuming an air of superiority : HAUGHTY

♦ [2] distinguished, eminent, illustrious, noble, notable, noteworthy, outstanding, preeminent, prestigious, signal, star — more at EMINENT ♦ [5] disdainful, haughty, highfalutin, lofty, lordly, prideful, proud — more at PROUD

²**superior** n **1** ♦ : one who is above another in rank, office, or station; *esp* : the head of a religious house or order **2** : one higher in quality or merit

♦ better, boss, chief, elder, head, leader, master, senior *Ant* inferior, subordinate, underling

su·pe·ri·or·i·ty \-ˌpir-ē-'ȯr-ə-tē\ n ♦ : the quality or state of being superior; *also* : a superior characteristic

♦ distinction, excellence, greatness, preeminence, supremacy — more at EXCELLENCE ♦ arrogance, haughtiness, loftiness, pretense, pretension, pretentiousness, self-importance — more at ARROGANCE

¹**su·per·la·tive** \sù-'pər-lə-tiv\ adj **1** : of, relating to, or constituting the degree of grammatical comparison that denotes an extreme or unsurpassed level or extent **2** : surpassing others : SUPREME — **su·per·la·tive·ly** adv
²**superlative** n **1** : the superlative degree or a superlative form in a language **2** : the utmost degree : ACME
su·per·mar·ket \'sü-pər-ˌmär-kət\ n : a self-service retail market selling foods and household merchandise
su·per·mod·el \'sü-pər-ˌmäd-ᵊl\ n : a famous and successful fashion model
su·per·mom \-ˌmäm\ n : an exemplary mother; *also* : a woman who performs traditional work of housekeeping and parenting while also having a full-time job
su·per·nal \sù-'pər-nəl\ adj **1** : being or coming from on high **2** : of heavenly or spiritual character **3** : superlatively good

♦ celestial, Elysian, empyrean, heavenly — more at CELESTIAL

su·per·nat·u·ral \ˌsü-pər-'na-chə-rəl\ adj **1** ♦ : of or relating to phenomena beyond or outside of nature **2** : relating to or attributed to a divinity, ghost, or devil — **su·per·nat·u·ral·ly** adv

♦ metaphysical, preternatural, superhuman, unearthly; *also* occult; extrasensory; celestial, divine, heavenly *Ant* natural ♦ magical, miraculous, phenomenal, superhuman, uncanny, unearthly; *also* bizarre, curious, far-out, funny, kinky, outlandish, out-of-the-way, outrageous, outré, peculiar, quaint, queer, quirky, remarkable, screwy, strange, wacky, way-out, weird, wild; baffling, bewildering, confounding, mystifying, perplexing, puzzling, shocking; aberrant, abnormal, atypical, extraordinary, fantastic, flaky, freak, freakish, idiosyncratic, rare, singular, uncommon, unique, unusual, unwonted; unconventional, uncustomary, unorthodox; conspicuous, notable, noticeable, outstanding, prominent, salient, striking

su·per·no·va \ˌsü-pər-'nō-və\ n : the explosion of a very large star
¹**su·per·nu·mer·ary** \-'nü-mə-ˌrer-ē, -'nyü-\ adj ♦ : exceeding the usual or required number : EXTRA

♦ excess, extra, spare, superfluous, surplus — more at SPARE

²**supernumerary** n, pl **-ar·ies** : an extra person or thing; *esp* : an actor hired for a nonspeaking part

su·per·pose \ˌsü-pər-'pōz\ vb **-posed; -pos·ing** : SUPERIMPOSE — **su·per·po·si·tion** \-pə-'zi-shən\ n
su·per·pow·er \'sü-pər-ˌpaù-ər\ n **1** : excessive or superior power **2** : one of a few politically and militarily dominant nations
su·per·sat·u·rat·ed \-'sa-chə-ˌrā-təd\ adj : containing an amount of a substance greater than that required for saturation
su·per·script \'sü-pər-ˌskript\ n : a symbol (as a numeral or letter) written immediately above or above and to one side of another character
su·per·sede \ˌsü-pər-'sēd\ vb **-sed·ed; -sed·ing** [ME (Sc) superceden to defer, fr. MF superceder, fr. L supersedēre to be superior to, refrain from, fr. super- above + sedēre to sit] ♦ : to take the place of : REPLACE

♦ displace, replace, substitute, supplant — more at REPLACE

su·per·son·ic \-'sä-nik\ adj **1** : ULTRASONIC **2** : being or relating to speeds from one to five times the speed of sound; *also* : capable of moving at such a speed ⟨a ~ airplane⟩
su·per·star \'sü-pər-ˌstär\ n ♦ : one that is very prominent or is a prime attraction

♦ celebrity, figure, light, luminary, notable, personage, personality, somebody, standout, star, VIP — more at CELEBRITY

su·per·sti·tion \ˌsü-pər-'sti-shən\ n **1** : beliefs or practices resulting from ignorance, fear of the unknown, or trust in magic or chance **2** : an unreasoning fear of nature, the unknown, or God resulting from superstition — **su·per·sti·tious** \-shəs\ adj
su·per·struc·ture \'sü-pər-ˌstrək-chər\ n : something built on a base or as a vertical extension
su·per·ti·tle \'sü-pər-ˌtī-tᵊl\ n : a translation of foreign-language dialogue displayed above a screen or performance
su·per·vene \ˌsü-pər-'vēn\ vb **-vened; -ven·ing** : to occur as something additional or unexpected
su·per·vise \'sü-pər-ˌvīz\ vb **-vised; -vis·ing** ♦ : to have or exercise the charge and oversight of

♦ administer, boss, captain, carry on, conduct, control, direct, govern, guide, handle, manage, operate, oversee, regulate, run, superintend — more at CONDUCT ♦ attend, care, mind, tend — more at TEND

su·per·vi·sion \ˌsü-pər-'vi-zhən\ n ♦ : the action, process, or occupation of supervising; *esp* : a critical watching and directing (as of activities or a course of action)

♦ administration, conduct, control, direction, government, management, operation, running — more at CONDUCT ♦ care, charge, guidance, headship, oversight, regulation, superintendence; *also* monitoring, observing; administration, control, direction, management, running; leadership, piloting, shepherding, steering; government, reign, rule; aegis, guardianship, protection, tutelage

su·per·vi·sor \'sü-pər-ˌvī-zər\ n ♦ : one that supervises; *esp* : an administrative officer in charge of a business, government, or school unit or operation

♦ administrator, director, executive, manager, superintendent — more at EXECUTIVE

su·per·vi·so·ry \ˌsü-pər-'vī-zə-rē\ adj ♦ : of or relating to supervision

♦ directorial, executive, managerial — more at EXECUTIVE

List of self-explanatory words with the prefix *super- (continued)*

supersalesman	supersophisticated	superstrength	superthin
supersecret	superspy	superstrong	superwoman
supersize	superstate	supersubtle	
supersized	superstore	supersystem	
supersmart	superstratum	supertanker	

su·pine \su̇-'pīn\ *adj* **1** : lying on the back or with the face upward **2** : LETHARGIC, SLUGGISH; *also* : ABJECT

supp *or* **suppl** *abbr* supplement; supplementary

sup·per \'sə-pər\ *n* : the evening meal esp. when dinner is taken at midday — **sup·per·time** \-,tīm\ *n*

sup·plant \sə-'plant\ *vb* **1** : to take the place of (another) esp. by force or trickery **2** ♦ : to take the place of esp. by reason of superior excellence or power : REPLACE

♦ displace, replace, substitute, supersede — more at REPLACE

sup·ple \'sə-pəl\ *adj* **sup·pler; sup·plest 1** : COMPLIANT, ADAPTABLE **2** ♦ : capable of bending without breaking or creasing : LIMBER

♦ flexible, limber, lissome, lithe, pliable, willowy — more at WILLOWY

¹sup·ple·ment \'sə-plə-mənt\ *n* **1** ♦ : something that supplies a want or makes an addition **2** : a continuation (as of a book) containing corrections or additional material **3** : DIETARY SUPPLEMENT

♦ accretion, addition, augmentation, boost, expansion, gain, increase, increment, plus, proliferation, raise, rise — more at INCREASE

²sup·ple·ment \'sə-plə-,ment\ *vb* : to fill up the deficiencies of : add to

sup·ple·men·tal \,sə-plə-'ment-³l\ *adj* : serving to supplement

sup·ple·men·ta·ry \-'men-tə-rē\ *adj* ♦ : added or serving as a supplement

♦ accessory, auxiliary, peripheral — more at AUXILIARY

sup·pli·ant \'sə-plē-ənt\ *n* : one who supplicates : PETITIONER

sup·pli·cant \'sə-pli-kənt\ *n* : one who supplicates : SUPPLIANT

sup·pli·cate \'sə-plə-,kāt\ *vb* **-cat·ed; -cat·ing 1** : to make a humble entreaty; *esp* : to pray to God **2** ♦ : to ask earnestly and humbly : BESEECH

♦ appeal, beg, beseech, entreat, implore, importune, petition, plead, pray, solicit — more at BEG

sup·pli·ca·tion \,sə-plə-'kā-shən\ *n* ♦ : a humble and earnest petition

♦ appeal, cry, entreaty, petition, plea, prayer, solicitation, suit — more at PLEA

¹sup·ply \sə-'plī\ *vb* **sup·plied; sup·ply·ing** [ME *supplien*, to complete, compensate for, fr. MF *soupplier* fr. L *supplēre* to fill up, supplement, supply, fr. *sub-* under, up to + *plēre* to fill] **1** : to add as a supplement **2** ♦ : to satisfy the needs of **3** ♦ : to make available for use : FURNISH, PROVIDE — **sup·pli·er** *n*

♦ [2] accoutre, equip, fit, furnish, outfit, rig — more at FURNISH ♦ [3] deliver, feed, furnish, give, hand, hand over, provide — more at FURNISH

²supply *n, pl* **supplies 1 a** ♦ : the quantity or amount (as of a commodity) needed or available **b** : PROVISIONS, STORES — usu. used in pl. **2** : the act or process of filling a want or need : PROVISION **3** : the quantities of goods or services offered for sale at a particular time or at one price

♦ budget, fund, pool; *also* reservoir, reserve, resource; cache, hoard, stockpile; refill, renewal, replacement; kitty, nest egg, pot, purse; source, well, wellspring

sup·ply–side \sə-'plī-,sīd\ *adj* : of, relating to, or being an economic theory that recommends the reduction of tax rates to expand economic activity

¹sup·port \sə-'pōrt\ *vb* **1** : to endure bravely or quietly : BEAR **2** ♦ : to take sides with : BACK **3** ♦ : to provide with food, clothing, and shelter **4** ♦ : to hold up or serve as a foundation for **5** : to uphold or defend as valid or right **6** ♦ : to provide with substantiation : CORROBORATE **7** ♦ : to give usu. supplementary help or aid to — **sup·port·ive** \-'pȯr-tiv\ *adj*

♦ [2] advocate, back, champion, endorse, patronize; *also* adopt, embrace, espouse; abet, aid, assist, prop (up), second; bolster, boost, buttress, reinforce; deliver, rescue, save ♦ [3, 7] abet, aid, assist, back, help, prop — more at HELP ♦ [4] bear, bolster, brace, buttress, carry, prop, shore, stay, uphold; *also* steady, truss, underlie ♦ [6] bear out, confirm, corroborate, substantiate, validate, verify, vindicate — more at CONFIRM

²support *n* **1** ♦ : the act of supporting : the state of being supported **2** ♦ : one that supports **3** : help given in the form of money, information, or services

♦ [1] aid, assist, assistance, backing, boost, help, lift — more at HELP ♦ [2] brace, bulwark, buttress, mount, shore, stay, underpinning; *also* column, pedestal, pilaster, pillar; arch, bracket, cantilever; crutch, mainstay, peg, post, stake, stanchion, stand, stilt, truss; base, foundation, frame ♦ [2] dependence, mainstay, pillar, reliance, standby — more at DEPENDENCE

sup·port·able *adj* ♦ : capable of being supported

♦ bearable, endurable, sufferable, sustainable, tolerable — more at BEARABLE ♦ defensible, justifiable, maintainable, sustainable, tenable — more at TENABLE

sup·port·er *n* ♦ : one that supports or acts as a support

♦ advocate, apostle, backer, booster, champion, exponent, friend, promoter, proponent — more at EXPONENT ♦ abettor, ally, backer, confederate, sympathizer — more at ALLY

support group *n* : a group of people with common experiences and concerns who provide emotional and moral support for one another

sup·pose \sə-'pōz\ *vb* **sup·posed; sup·pos·ing 1** ♦ : to assume to be true (as for the sake of argument) **2** : EXPECT ⟨I am *supposed* to go⟩ **3** ♦ : to think probable ⟨I ~ so⟩ **4** ♦ : to hold as an opinion — **sup·pos·al** *n*

♦ [1] assume, postulate, premise, presume, presuppose — more at ASSUME ♦ [3] assume, conjecture, guess, presume, speculate, surmise, suspect — more at GUESS ♦ [4] believe, consider, deem, feel, figure, guess, hold, imagine, think — more at BELIEVE

sup·posed \sə-'pōzd, -'pō-zəd\ *adj* ♦ : held as an opinion; *also* : mistakenly believed ⟨a ~ cure⟩

♦ apparent, assumed, evident, ostensible, reputed, seeming — more at APPARENT

sup·pos·ed·ly \-'pō-zəd-lē, -'pōzd-lē\ *adv* ♦ : as supposed

♦ apparently, evidently, ostensibly, presumably, seemingly — more at APPARENTLY

sup·pos·ing *conj* : if by way of hypothesis : on the assumption that

sup·po·si·tion \,sə-pə-'zi-shən\ *n* **1** ♦ : something that is supposed **2** : the act of supposing

♦ conjecture, hypothesis, proposition, theory — more at THEORY ♦ assumption, postulate, premise, presumption — more at ASSUMPTION ♦ conjecture, guess, surmise — more at CONJECTURE

sup·pos·i·to·ry \sə-'pä-zə-,tōr-ē\ *n, pl* **-ries** [ME *suppositorie*, fr. AF, fr. ML *suppositorium*, fr. LL, neut. of *suppositorius* placed beneath] : a small easily melted mass of usu. medicated material for insertion (as into the rectum)

sup·press \sə-'pres\ *vb* **1** ♦ : to put down by authority or force : SUBDUE ⟨~ a revolt⟩ **2** : to keep from being known; *also* : to stop the publication or circulation of **3** ♦ : to hold back : REPRESS ⟨~ anger⟩ ⟨~ a cough⟩ — **sup·press·ible** \-'pre-sə-bəl\ *adj* — **sup·pres·sor** \-'pre-sər\ *n*

♦ [1] clamp down, crack down, crush, put down, quash, quell, repress, silence, snuff, squash, squelch, subdue — more at QUELL ♦ [3] choke, pocket, repress, smother, stifle, strangle, swallow; *also* control, govern, handle, manage; bridle, check, curb, hold back, quell; bottle up, contain, hold in; muffle, squelch

sup·pres·sant \sə-'pres-ᵊnt\ *n* : an agent (as a drug) suppressing rather than eliminating something ⟨a cough ~⟩

sup·pres·sion \-'pre-shən\ *n* 1 : an act or instance of suppressing : the state of being suppressed 2 ♦ : the conscious intentional exclusion from consciousness of a thought or feeling

♦ constraint, inhibition, repression, restraint, self-control, self-restraint

sup·pu·rate \'sə-pyə-,rāt\ *vb* **-rat·ed; -rat·ing** : to form or give off pus — **sup·pu·ra·tion** \,sə-pyə-'rā-shən\ *n*

su·pra \'sü-prə, -,prä\ *adv* : earlier in this writing : ABOVE

su·pra·na·tion·al \,sü-prə-'na-shə-nəl, -,prä-\ *adj* : going beyond national boundaries, authority, or interests ⟨~ organizations⟩

su·prem·a·cist \su̇-'pre-mə-sist\ *n* : an advocate of group supremacy

su·prem·a·cy \su̇-'pre-mə-sē\ *n, pl* **-cies** 1 ♦ : the quality or state of being supreme 2 ♦ : supreme authority or power

♦ [1] distinction, excellence, greatness, preeminence, superiority — more at EXCELLENCE ♦ [2] ascendancy, dominance, dominion, predominance, preeminence; *also* primacy, superiority, lordship, scepter, sovereignty; arm, authority, command, clutch, control, grip, hold, mastery, sway; direction, jurisdiction, management; clout, pull, weight; eminence, importance, moment; prerogative, privilege, right

su·preme \su̇-'prēm\ *adj* [L *supremus*, superl. of *superus* upper, fr. *super* over, above] 1 ♦ : highest in rank or authority 2 ♦ : highest in degree or quality ⟨~ among poets⟩ 3 ♦ : the best or most extreme of its kind : ULTIMATE ⟨the ~ sacrifice⟩ — **su·preme·ness** *n*

♦ [1, 2] arch, cardinal, central, chief, dominant, first, foremost, grand, key, main, paramount, predominant, preeminent, premier, primary, principal, sovereign — more at FOREMOST ♦ [3] consummate, maximum, most, nth, paramount, top, ultimate, utmost — more at ULTIMATE

Supreme Being *n* ♦ : the Being perfect in power, wisdom, and goodness who is worshipped as creator and ruler of the universe

♦ Almighty, deity, Jehovah

su·preme·ly *adv* : in a supreme manner : so as to be supreme

supt *abbr* superintendent

sur·cease \'sər-,sēs\ *n* : a temporary or final ceasing : CESSATION ⟨a ~ from pain⟩

¹sur·charge \'sər-,chärj\ *vb* 1 : to fill to excess : OVERLOAD 2 : to apply a surcharge to (postage stamps) 3 : to charge too much or too fully

²surcharge *n* 1 : an extra fee or cost 2 : an excessive load or burden 3 : something officially printed on a postage stamp esp. to change its value

sur·cin·gle \'sər-,siŋ-gəl\ *n* : a band put around a horse's body to make something (as a saddle) fast

¹sure \'shu̇r\ *adj* **sur·er; sur·est** [ME, *seur, sure,* fr. AF *seur,* fr. L *securus* secure] 1 : firmly established 2 ♦ : suitable or fit to be relied on : TRUSTWORTHY, RELIABLE 3 ♦ : characterized by a lack of wavering or hesitation : CONFIDENT 4 : not to be disputed : UNDOUBTED 5 ♦ : bound to happen 6 : careful to remember or attend to something ⟨be ~ to lock the door⟩

♦ [2] dependable, good, reliable, responsible, safe, solid, steady, tried, true, trustworthy — more at DEPENDABLE ♦ [3] assured, certain, clear, cocksure, confident, doubtless, positive, sanguine — more at CERTAIN ♦ [5] certain, inevitable, necessary, unavoidable — more at INEVITABLE ♦ [5] infallible, surefire, unfailing — more at infallible

²sure *adv* : SURELY

sure·fire \'shu̇r-'fīr\ *adj* ♦ : certain to get results : DEPENDABLE

♦ infallible, sure, unfailing — more at INFALLIBLE

sure·ly \'shu̇r-lē\ *adv* 1 : in a sure manner 2 ♦ : without doubt 3 : INDEED, REALLY

♦ certainly, definitely, doubtless, incontestably, indeed, indisputably, really, truly, undeniably, undoubtedly, unquestionably — more at INDEED

sure·ness *n* ♦ : the quality or state of being sure

♦ assurance, certainty, certitude, confidence, conviction, positiveness — more at CONFIDENCE ♦ dependability, reliability, solidity, trustworthiness — more at RELIABILITY

sure·ty \'shu̇r-ə-tē\ *n, pl* **-ties** 1 : SURENESS, CERTAINTY 2 ♦ : something that makes sure : GUARANTEE 3 ♦ : one who is a guarantor for another person

♦ [2] bond, contract, covenant, guarantee, guaranty, warranty — more at GUARANTEE ♦ [3] backer, guarantor, patron, sponsor — more at SPONSOR

¹surf \'sərf\ *n* : waves that break upon the shore; *also* : the sound or foam of breaking waves

²surf *vb* 1 : to ride the surf (as on a surfboard) 2 : to scan the offerings of (as television or the Internet) for something of interest — **surf·er** *n* — **surf·ing** *n*

¹sur·face \'sər-fəs\ *n* 1 ♦ : the outside of an object or body 2 : outward aspect or appearance — **surface** *adj*

♦ exterior, face, outside, skin, veneer — more at EXTERIOR

²surface *vb* **sur·faced; sur·fac·ing** 1 : to give a surface to : make smooth 2 : to rise to the surface 3 ♦ : to come into public view

♦ arise, crop, emerge, materialize, spring — more at ARISE

surf·board \'sərf-,bȯrd\ *n* : a buoyant board used in surfing

¹sur·feit \'sər-fət\ *n* 1 ♦ : an overabundant supply : EXCESS 2 : excessive indulgence (as in food or drink) 3 : disgust caused by excess

♦ excess, fat, overabundance, overflow, overkill, overmuch, superabundance, superfluity, surplus — more at EXCESS

²surfeit *vb* ♦ : to feed, supply, or indulge to the point of surfeit

♦ glut, gorge, sate, stuff — more at GORGE

surg *abbr* surgeon; surgery; surgical

¹surge \'sərj\ *vb* **surged; surg·ing** 1 : to rise and fall actively : TOSS 2 : to move in waves 3 : to rise suddenly to an excessive or abnormal value

²surge *n* 1 : a sweeping onward like a wave of the sea ⟨a ~ of emotion⟩ 2 ♦ : a large billow 3 : a transient sudden increase of current or voltage in an electrical circuit

♦ billow, swell, wave — more at WAVE

sur·geon \'sər-jən\ *n* : a physician who specializes in surgery

sur·gery \'sər-jə-rē\ *n, pl* **-ger·ies** [ME *surgerie*, fr. AF *cirurgerie, surgerie,* fr. L *chirurgia,* fr. Gk *cheirourgia,* fr. *cheirourgos* surgeon, fr. *cheirourgos* doing by hand, fr. *cheir* hand + *ergon* work] 1 : a branch of medicine concerned with the correction of physical defects, the repair of injuries, and the treatment of disease esp. by operations 2 : a room or area where surgery is performed 3 : the work done by a surgeon

sur·gi·cal \'sər-ji-kəl\ *adj* : of, relating to, or associated with surgeons or surgery — **sur·gi·cal·ly** \-k(ə-)lē\ *adv*

sur·ly \'sər-lē\ *adj* **sur·li·er; -est** [alter. of ME *serreli* lordly, imperious, prob. fr. *sire, ser* sire] ♦ : having a rude unfriendly disposition — **sur·li·ness** \-lē-nəs\ *n*

♦ glum, moody, morose, sulky, sullen — more at SULKY ♦ bearish, bilious, cantankerous, disagreeable, dyspeptic, ill-humored, ill-tempered, ornery, splenetic — more at ILL-TEMPERED

¹sur·mise \sər-'mīz\ *vb* **sur·mised; sur·mis·ing** ♦ : to form a notion of from scanty evidence : GUESS

♦ assume, conjecture, guess, presume, speculate, suppose, suspect — more at GUESS

²surmise *n* ♦ : a thought or idea based on scanty evidence

♦ conjecture, guess, supposition — more at CONJECTURE

sur·mount \sər-'maůnt\ *vb* 1 ♦ : to prevail over : OVER-COME ⟨∼ a problem⟩ 2 : to get to or lie at the top of
♦ beat, conquer, crush, defeat, master, overcome, prevail, subdue, triumph, win — more at BEAT

sur·name \'sər-ˌnām\ *n* 1 : NICKNAME 2 : the name borne in common by members of a family

sur·pass \sər-'pas\ *vb* 1 ♦ : to be superior to in quality, degree, or performance : EXCEL 2 ♦ : to go beyond the range or powers of — **sur·pass·ing·ly** *adv*
♦ [1] beat, better, eclipse, excel, outdistance, outdo, outshine, outstrip, top, transcend; *also* exceed, outrun, overpass; best, clobber, conquer, crush, defeat, drub, lick, master, overcome, overmatch, prevail (over), rout, skunk, subdue, surmount, thrash, trim, triumph (over), trounce, wallop, whip, win (against), worst; outweigh, overshadow ♦ [2] exceed, overreach, overrun, overshoot, overstep — more at EXCEED

sur·plice \'sər-pləs\ *n* : a loose white outer vestment usu. of knee length

sur·plus \'sər-(ˌ)pləs\ *n* 1 ♦ : quantity left over : EXCESS 2 : the excess of assets over liabilities
♦ excess, fat, overabundance, overflow, overkill, overmuch, superabundance, superfluity, surfeit — more at EXCESS

¹sur·prise \sər-'prīz\ *n* 1 ♦ : an attack made without warning 2 : a taking unawares 3 ♦ : something that surprises 4 ♦ : the state of being surprised : AMAZEMENT
♦ [1] ambush, trap — more at AMBUSH ♦ [3] bolt, bombshell, jar, jolt; *also* shock, thunderclap; revelation, shocker ♦ [4] amazement, astonishment, shock, wonder; *also* awe, wonderment; startle; bewilderment, confusion, discomfiture, dismay

²surprise *vb* **sur·prised; sur·pris·ing** 1 ♦ : to come upon and attack unexpectedly 2 : to take unawares 3 ♦ : to strike with wonder or amazement esp. because unexpected : AMAZE 4 : to cause astonishment or surprise
♦ [1] ambush, waylay — more at AMBUSH ♦ [3] amaze, astonish, astound, bowl, dumbfound, flabbergast, floor, shock, startle, stun, stupefy; *also* befuddle, bewilder, confound, confuse, discomfit, disconcert, dismay, muddle, nonplus, perplex

surprising *adj* ♦ : of a nature that excites surprise
♦ amazing, astonishing, astounding, eye-opening, shocking, startling, stunning; *also* unannounced, unanticipated, unexpected, unforeseen; awesome, awful, breathtaking, fabulous, marvelous, miraculous, portentous, prodigious, staggering, stupendous, sublime, wonderful, wondrous; extraordinary, phenomenal, rare, sensational, spectacular; befuddling, bewildering, confounding, confusing, discomfiting, disconcerting, dismaying, muddling, nonplussing, perplexing; incomprehensible, inconceivable, incredible, unbelievable, unimaginable, unthinkable; singular, uncommon, unique, unusual, unwonted; conspicuous, notable, noticeable, outstanding, remarkable; impressive, striking ♦ awesome, eye-opening, fabulous, marvelous (*or* marvellous), miraculous, portentous, prodigious, stupendous, sublime, wonderful — more at MARVELOUS

sur·pris·ing·ly \-'prī-ziŋ-lē\ *adv* 1 : in a surprising manner or degree 2 : it is surprising that

sur·re·al \sə-'rē-əl, -'rēl\ *adj* 1 : having the intense irrational reality of a dream 2 : of or relating to surrealism ⟨∼ art⟩ — **sur·re·al·ly** *adv*

sur·re·al·ism \sə-'rē-ə-ˌli-zəm\ *n* : art, literature, or theater characterized by fantastic or incongruous imagery or effects produced by unnatural juxtapositions and combinations — **sur·re·al·ist** \-list\ *n or adj* — **sur·re·al·is·tic** \sə-ˌrē-ə-'lis-tik\ *adj* — **sur·re·al·is·ti·cal·ly** \-ti-k(ə-)lē\ *adv*

¹sur·ren·der \sə-'ren-dər\ *vb* 1 ♦ : to yield to the power of another : give up under compulsion 2 ♦ : to give up completely or agree to forgo esp. in favor of another : RE-LINQUISH 3 ♦ : to give (oneself) over to something (as an influence)

♦ [1] blink, bow, budge, capitulate, concede, fall, give in, knuckle under, quit, submit, succumb, yield — more at YIELD ♦ [2] cede, deliver, give up, hand over, leave, relinquish, render, turn over, yield; *also* commit, consign, entrust; waive; renounce, resign; abandon, desert, discard, forsake, shed ♦ [3] bow, give in, submit, succumb, yield

²surrender *n* ♦ : the act of giving up or yielding oneself or the possession of something to another
♦ capitulation, relinquishment, submission; *also* acceptance, acquiescence, concession; compromise; appeasement, conciliation; capture, fall

sur·rep·ti·tious \ˌsər-əp-'ti-shəs\ *adj* ♦ : done, made, or acquired by stealth : CLANDESTINE — **sur·rep·ti·tious·ly** *adv*
♦ clandestine, covert, furtive, hugger-mugger, private, secret, sneak, sneaky, stealthy, undercover, underground, underhanded — more at SECRET

sur·rey \'sər-ē\ *n, pl* **surreys** : a 2-seated horse-drawn carriage

sur·ro·ga·cy \'sər-ə-gə-sē\ *n* : SURROGATE MOTHERHOOD

sur·ro·gate \'sər-ə-ˌgāt, -gət\ *n* 1 : DEPUTY, SUBSTITUTE 2 : a law officer in some states with authority in the probate of wills, the settlement of estates, and the appointment of guardians 3 : SURROGATE MOTHER

surrogate mother *n* : a woman who becomes pregnant (as by surgical implantation of a fertilized egg) in order to carry the fetus for another woman — **surrogate motherhood** *n*

sur·round \sə-'raůnd\ *vb* 1 ♦ : to enclose on all sides : EN-CIRCLE 2 : to enclose so as to cut off retreat or escape
♦ circle, encircle, enclose, encompass, ring; *also* fence (in), hem (in), wall; besiege, entrench, invest

sur·round·ings \sə-'raůn-diŋz\ *n pl* ♦ : conditions by which one is surrounded
♦ atmosphere, climate, environment, environs, medium, milieu, setting — more at ENVIRONMENT

surround sound *n* : sound reproduction that uses three or more transmission channels

sur·tax \'sər-ˌtaks\ *n* : an additional tax over and above a normal tax

sur·tout \(ˌ)sər-'tü\ *n* [F, fr. *sur* over (fr. L *super*) + *tout* all, fr. L *totus* whole] : a man's long close-fitting overcoat

surv *abbr* survey; surveying; surveyor

sur·veil·lance \sər-'vā-ləns\ *n* [F] : close watch; *also* : SU-PERVISION

¹sur·vey \sər-'vā\ *vb* **sur·veyed; sur·vey·ing** [ME, fr. AF *surveer* to look over, fr. *sur-* over + *veer* to see, fr. L *vidēre*] 1 ♦ : to look over and examine closely 2 : to find and represent the contours, measurements, and position of a part of the earth's surface (as a tract of land) 3 : to view or study something as a whole 4 ♦ : to query (someone) in order to collect data for the analysis of some aspect of a group or area — **sur·vey·or** \-ər\ *n*
♦ [1] audit, check, examine, inspect, review, scan, scrutinize — more at INSPECT ♦ [4] canvass, poll, solicit — more at CANVASS

²sur·vey \'sər-ˌvā\ *n, pl* **surveys** ♦ : the act or an instance of surveying; *also* : something that is surveyed
♦ audit, check, checkup, examination, inspection, review, scan, scrutiny — more at INSPECTION

sur·vive \sər-'vīv\ *vb* **sur·vived; sur·viv·ing** 1 : to remain alive or exist 2 ♦ : to continue to exist or live after 3 ♦ : to continue to function or prosper — **sur·viv·al** *n* — **sur·vi·vor** \-'vī-vər\ *n*
♦ [2] ride; *also* outlast, outlive; abide, continue, endure, hang on, last, lead, persist; be, breathe, exist, live, subsist; flourish, prosper, thrive ♦ [3] hold, hold out, keep up, last, prevail — more at HOLD OUT

sus·cep·ti·bil·i·ty \sə-ˌsep-tə-'bi-lə-tē\ *n* : the quality or state of being susceptible; *esp* : lack of ability to resist some extraneous agent (as a pathogen or drug)

sus·cep·ti·ble \-'sep-tə-bəl\ *adj* 1 : of such a nature as to permit ⟨words ∼ of being misunderstood⟩ 2 ♦ : having little resistance to a stimulus or agency ⟨∼ to colds⟩ **3** ♦ : capable of being easily influenced

♦ [2] exposed, liable, open, sensitive, subject, vulnerable — more at LIABLE ♦ [3] easy, gullible, naive — more at EASY

su·shi \'sü-shē\ *n* [Jp] : cold rice formed into various shapes and garnished esp. with bits of raw fish or seafood

¹**sus·pect** \'səs-ˌpekt, sə-'spekt\ *adj* ♦ : regarded with suspicion; *also* : QUESTIONABLE ⟨his claim is ∼⟩

♦ debatable, disputable, doubtful, dubious, equivocal, fishy, problematic, questionable, shady, shaky, suspicious — more at DOUBTFUL

²**sus·pect** \'səs-ˌpekt\ *n* : one who is suspected (as of a crime)

³**sus·pect** \sə-'spekt\ *vb* **1** ♦ : to have doubts of : MISTRUST **2** : to imagine to be guilty without proof **3** ♦ : to imagine to exist or be true, likely, or probable : SURMISE

♦ [1] distrust, doubt, mistrust, question — more at DISTRUST ♦ [3] assume, conjecture, guess, presume, speculate, suppose, surmise — more at GUESS

sus·pend \sə-'spend\ *vb* **1** : to bar temporarily from a privilege, office, or function **2** : to stop temporarily : make inactive for a time **3** : to withhold (judgment) for a time **4** ♦ : to fasten to some elevated point without support from below; *esp* : to hang so as to be free except at one point **5** : to keep from falling or sinking by some invisible support

♦ dangle, hang, sling, swing — more at HANG

sus·pend·er \sə-'spen-dər\ *n* : one of two supporting straps which pass over the shoulders and to which the pants are fastened

sus·pense \sə-'spens\ *n* **1** : the state of being suspended : SUSPENSION **2** : mental uncertainty : ANXIETY **3** : excitement as to an outcome — **sus·pense·ful** *adj*

sus·pen·sion \sə-'spen-chən\ *n* **1** ♦ : the act of suspending : the state or period of being suspended **2** : the state of a substance when its particles are mixed with but undissolved in a fluid or solid; *also* : a substance in this state **3** : something suspended **4** : the system of devices supporting the upper part of a vehicle on the axles

♦ abeyance, doldrums, dormancy, latency, quiescence — more at ABEYANCE

sus·pi·cion \sə-'spi-shən\ *n* **1** ♦ : the act or an instance of suspecting something wrong without proof **2** : a barely detectable amount : TRACE

♦ distrust, doubt, incertitude, misgiving, mistrust, skepticism, uncertainty — more at DOUBT

sus·pi·cious \sə-'spi-shəs\ *adj* **1** ♦ : open to or arousing suspicion **2** ♦ : inclined to suspect **3** ♦ : showing suspicion ⟨is ∼ of strangers⟩

♦ [1] debatable, disputable, doubtful, dubious, equivocal, fishy, problematic, questionable, shady, shaky, suspect — more at DOUBTFUL ♦ [2, 3] distrustful, doubtful, dubious, mistrustful, skeptical, uncertain, undecided, unsettled, unsure — more at DOUBTFUL

sus·pi·cious·ly *adv* ♦ : with suspicion

♦ askance, distrustfully, dubiously, mistrustfully — more at ASKANCE

sus·tain \sə-'stān\ *vb* **1** : to provide with nourishment **2** : to keep going : PROLONG ⟨∼ed effort⟩ **3** : to hold up : PROP **4** ♦ : to hold up under : ENDURE **5** ♦ : to go through : SUFFER ⟨∼ a broken arm⟩ **6** : to support as true, legal, or valid ⟨the objection was ∼ed⟩ **7** : PROVE, CORROBORATE

♦ [4] abide, bear, brook, countenance, endure, meet, stand, stick out, stomach, support, take, tolerate — more at BEAR ♦ [5] endure, experience, feel, have, know, see, suffer, taste, undergo — more at EXPERIENCE

sus·tain·able \səs-'tā-nə-bəl\ *adj* ♦ : capable of being sustained

♦ defensible, justifiable, maintainable, supportable, tenable — more at TENABLE ♦ bearable, endurable, sufferable, tolerable — more at BEARABLE

sus·te·nance \'səs-tə-nəns\ *n* **1** : FOOD, NOURISHMENT **2** : a supplying with the necessities of life **3** : something that sustains or supports

su·ture \'sü-chər\ *n* **1** : material or a stitch for sewing a wound together **2** : a seam or line along which two things or parts are joined by or as if by sewing

SUV \ˌes-ˌyü-'vē\ *n* [*sport-u*tility *v*ehicle] : a vehicle similar to a station wagon but built on a light-truck chassis

su·zer·ain \'sü-zə-rən, -ˌrān\ *n* [F] **1** : a feudal lord **2** : a nation that has political control over the foreign relations of another nation — **su·zer·ain·ty** \-tē\ *n*

svc *or* **svce** *abbr* service

svelte \'sfelt\ *adj* **svelt·er; svelt·est** [F, fr. It *svelto*, fr. pp. of *svellere* to pluck out, modif. of L *evellere*, fr. *e-* out + *vellere* to pluck] ♦ : spare in frame or flesh : SLENDER

♦ lean, skinny, slender, slim, spare — more at THIN

svgs *abbr* savings

SW *abbr* **1** shortwave **2** southwest

¹**swab** \'swäb\ *n* **1** : MOP **2** : a wad of absorbent material esp. for applying medicine or for cleaning; *also* : a sample taken with a swab **3** ♦ : a member of a ship's crew : SAILOR

♦ gob, jack, jack-tar, mariner, sailor, seaman, tar — more at SAILOR

²**swab** *vb* **swabbed; swab·bing** : to use a swab on : MOP

swad·dle \'swäd-ᵊl\ *vb* **swad·dled; swad·dling** **1** : to bind (an infant) in bands of cloth **2** : to wrap up : SWATHE

swaddling clothes *n pl* : bands of cloth wrapped around an infant

swag \'swag\ *n* ♦ : stolen goods : LOOT

♦ booty, loot, plunder, spoil — more at LOOT

swag·ger \'swa-gər\ *vb* **1** ♦ : to walk with a conceited swing or strut **2** ♦ : to puff oneself up in speech : BOAST — **swagger** *n*

♦ [1] stalk, strut — more at STRUT ♦ [2] boast, brag, crow, plume — more at BOAST

swag·man \'swag-mən\ *n* : a person who has no job and wanders from place to place : VAGRANT

Swa·hi·li \swä-'hē-lē\ *n* : a language that is a trade and governmental language over much of eastern Africa and the Congo region

swain \'swān\ *n* [ME *swein* boy, servant, fr. ON *sveinn*] **1** : RUSTIC; *esp* : SHEPHERD **2** ♦ : a male admirer or suitor

♦ beau, boyfriend, fellow, man — more at BOYFRIEND ♦ gallant, suitor, wooer — more at SUITOR

SWAK *abbr* sealed with a kiss

¹**swal·low** \'swä-lō\ *n* : any of numerous small long-winged migratory birds that often have a deeply forked tail

²**swallow** *vb* **1** : to take into the stomach through the throat **2** : to envelop or take in as if by swallowing **3** ♦ : to accept or believe without question, protest, or anger **4** ♦ : to keep from expressing or showing

♦ [3] accept, believe, credit, trust — more at BELIEVE ♦ [4] choke, pocket, repress, smother, stifle, strangle, suppress — more at SUPPRESS

³**swallow** *n* **1** : an act of swallowing **2** ♦ : an amount that can be swallowed at one time

♦ draft, drag, drink, nip, quaff, shot, slug, snort, swig — more at DRINK

swal·low·tail \'swä-lō-ˌtāl\ *n* **1** : a deeply forked and tapering tail like that of a swallow **2** : TAILCOAT **3** : any of various large butterflies with the border of each hind wing usu. drawn out into a process resembling a tail — **swal·low–tailed** \-ˌtāld\ *adj*

swam *past of* SWIM

swa·mi \'swä-mē\ *n* [Hindi *svāmī*, fr. Skt *svāmin* owner, lord] : a Hindu ascetic or religious teacher

¹**swamp** \'swämp\ *n* ♦ : a spongy wetland — **swamp** *adj* **swampy** *adj*

♦ bog, fen, marsh, mire, morass, slough; *also* quagmire; muck, mud, ooze, slime, slop, sludge, slush

²swamp *vb* **1** ♦ : to fill or become filled with or as if with water **2** ♦ : to overwhelm numerically or by an excess of something

♦ [1] deluge, drown, engulf, flood, inundate, overflow, overwhelm, submerge — more at FLOOD ♦ [2] carry away, crush, devastate, floor, oppress, overcome, overpower, overwhelm, prostrate, snow under — more at OVERWHELM

swamp·land \-ˌland\ *n* : a spongy wetland : SWAMP
swan \ˈswän\ *n, pl* **swans** *also* **swan** : any of various heavy-bodied long-necked mostly pure white swimming birds related to the geese
¹swank \ˈswaŋk\ *or* **swanky** \ˈswaŋ-kē\ *adj* **swank·er** *or* **swank·i·er; -est** : showily smart and dashing; *also* : fashionably elegant ⟨a ∼ hotel⟩
²swank *n* **1** ♦ : arrogance or ostentation of dress or manner : PRETENTIOUSNESS **2** : ELEGANCE

♦ flamboyance, flashiness, gaudiness, glitz, ostentation, pretentiousness, showiness — more at OSTENTATION

swans·down \ˈswänz-ˌdaún\ *n* **1** : the very soft down of a swan used esp. for trimming **2** : a soft thick cotton flannel
swan song *n* : a farewell appearance, act, or pronouncement
¹swap \ˈswäp\ *vb* **swapped; swap·ping** ♦ : to give in trade : EXCHANGE

♦ change, commute, exchange, shift, substitute, switch, trade — more at CHANGE

²swap *n* ♦ : to give in trade

♦ barter, commutation, exchange, trade, truck — more at EXCHANGE

sward \ˈswórd\ *n* : the grassy surface of land
¹swarm \ˈswórm\ *n* **1** : a great number of honeybees leaving together from a hive with a queen to start a new colony; *also* : a hive of bees **2** ♦ : a large crowd

♦ army, crowd, crush, drove, flock, horde, host, legion, mob, multitude, press, throng — more at CROWD

²swarm *vb* **1** : to form in a swarm and depart from a hive **2** : to throng together : gather in great numbers **3** ♦ : to beset or surround in a swarm

♦ crowd, flock, mob, throng — more at CROWD

swart \ˈswórt\ *adj* : SWARTHY
swar·thy \ˈswór-t͟hē, -t͟hē\ *adj* **swar·thi·er; -est** : dark in color or complexion : dark-skinned
swash \ˈswäsh\ *vb* ♦ : to move about with a splashing sound — **swash** *n*

♦ lap, plash, slosh, splash — more at SLOSH

swash·buck·ler \-ˌbə-klər\ *n* : a swaggering or daring soldier or adventurer — **swash·buck·ling** *adj*
swas·ti·ka \ˈswäs-ti-kə\ *n* [Skt *svastika*, fr. *svasti* well-being, fr. *su-* well + *as-* to be] : a symbol or ornament in the form of a cross with the ends of the arms bent at right angles
¹swat \ˈswät\ *vb* **swat·ted; swat·ting** ♦ : to hit sharply ⟨∼ a fly⟩ ⟨∼ a ball⟩ — **swat·ter** *n*

♦ bat, clout, crack, hit, slam, strike

²swat *n* : a powerful or crushing blow
SWAT *abbr* Special Weapons and Tactics
swatch \ˈswäch\ *n* : a sample piece (as of fabric) or a collection of samples
swath \ˈswäth, ˈswóth\ *or* **swathe** \ˈswät͟h, ˈswót͟h, ˈswäth\ *n* [ME, fr. OE *swæth* footstep, trace] **1** : a row of cut grass or grain **2** : the sweep of a scythe or mowing machine or the path cut in mowing
swathe \ˈswät͟h, ˈswót͟h, ˈswäth\ *vb* **swathed; swath·ing** ♦ : to bind or wrap with or as if with a bandage

♦ embrace, enclose, encompass, enfold, enshroud, envelop, invest, lap, mantle, shroud, veil, wrap — more at ENFOLD

¹sway \ˈswā\ *n* **1** : a gentle swinging from side to side **2** ♦ : controlling influence or power

♦ authority, clout, influence, power, pull, weight — more at INFLUENCE

²sway *vb* **1** ♦ : to swing gently from side to side **2** : RULE, GOVERN **3** : to cause to swing from side to side **4 a** : BEND, SWERVE **b** : to exert a guiding or controlling influence on : INFLUENCE ⟨tried to ∼ the jury⟩

♦ careen, lurch, pitch, rock, roll, seesaw, toss, wobble — more at ROCK

sway·backed \ˈswā-ˌbakt\ *also* **sway·back** \-ˌbak\ *adj* : having an abnormally sagging back ⟨a ∼ mare⟩ — **swayback** *n*
¹swear \ˈswar\ *vb* **swore** \ˈswōr\; **sworn** \ˈswōrn\; **swear·ing** **1** ♦ : to make a solemn statement or promise under oath **2** ♦ : to assert or promise emphatically or earnestly **3** : to administer an oath to **4** : to bind by or as if by an oath **5** : to use profane or obscene language — **swear·er** *n*

♦ [1] attest, depose, testify, witness — more at TESTIFY
♦ [2] covenant, pledge, promise, vow — more at PROMISE

²swear *n* : a profane or obscene word
swear in *vb* : to induct into office by administration of an oath
¹sweat \ˈswet\ *vb* **sweat** *or* **sweat·ed; sweat·ing** **1** : to excrete salty moisture from glands of the skin : PERSPIRE **2 a** : to form drops of moisture on the surface **b** ♦ : to become exuded through pores or a porous surface **3** ♦ : to work so that one sweats : TOIL **4** : to cause to sweat **5** : to draw out or get rid of by or as if by sweating **6** : to make a person overwork **7** ♦ : to undergo anxiety or mental or emotional distress — **sweaty** *adj*

♦ [2b] bleed, exude, ooze, percolate, seep, strain, weep — more at EXUDE ♦ [3] drudge, fag, grub, labor (*or* labour), slave, toil — more at TOIL ♦ [7] bother, fear, fret, stew, trouble, worry — more at WORRY

²sweat *n* ♦ : hard work

♦ drudgery, grind, labor (*or* labour), slavery, toil, travail — more at TOIL

sweat·er \ˈswe-tər\ *n* **1** : one that sweats **2** : a knitted or crocheted jacket or pullover
sweat out *vb* ♦ : to endure or wait through the course of

♦ bear, deliver, drop, have, produce — more at BEAR

sweat·shirt \ˈswet-ˌshərt\ *n* : a loose collarless pullover usu. of heavy cotton jersey
sweat·shop \ˈswet-ˌshäp\ *n* : a shop or factory in which workers are employed for long hours at low wages and under unhealthy conditions
Swed *abbr* Sweden
swede \ˈswēd\ *n* **1** *cap* : a native or inhabitant of Sweden **2** *chiefly Brit* : RUTABAGA
Swed·ish \ˈswē-dish\ *n* **1** : the language of Sweden **2** Swedish *pl* : the people of Sweden — **Swedish** *adj*
¹sweep \ˈswēp\ *vb* **swept** \ˈswept\; **sweep·ing** **1** : to remove or clean by or as if by brushing **2** : to destroy completely; *also* : to remove or take with a single swift movement **3** : to remove from sight or consideration **4** ♦ : to move over with speed and force ⟨the tide *swept* over the shore⟩ **5** : to win an overwhelming victory in; *also* : to win all the games or contests of **6** ♦ : to move or extend in a wide curve **7** : to move swiftly, forcefully, or devastatingly — **sweep·er** *n*

♦ [4] bowl, breeze, coast, drift, flow, glide, roll, sail, skim, slide, slip, stream, whisk — more at FLOW
♦ [6] arc, arch, bend, bow, crook, curve, hook, round, swerve, wheel — more at CURVE

²sweep *n* **1** : something (as a long oar) that operates with a sweeping motion **2** : a clearing off or away **3** : a winning of all the contests or prizes in a competition **4** : a sweeping movement **5** : CURVE, BEND **6** ♦ : extent of treatment, activity, or influence : SCOPE

♦ amplitude, breadth, compass, extent, range, reach, realm, scope, width — more at RANGE

sweeping *adj* : EXTENSIVE ⟨∼ reforms⟩; *also* : indiscriminately inclusive ⟨∼ generalities⟩
sweep·ings \ˈswē-piŋz\ *n pl* : things collected by sweeping
sweep–sec·ond hand \ˈswēp-ˌse-kənd-\ *n* : a hand marking seconds on a timepiece

sweep·stakes \'swēp-ˌstāks\ also sweep·stake \-ˌstāk\ n, pl sweepstakes 1 : a race or contest in which the entire prize may go to the winner 2 : any of various lotteries

¹sweet \'swēt\ adj 1 : being or causing the one of the four basic taste sensations that is caused esp. by table sugar and is identified esp. by the taste buds at the front of the tongue; also : pleasing to the taste 2 ♦ : marked by gentle good humor or kindliness : AGREEABLE 3 ♦ : pleasing to a sense other than taste ⟨a ~ smell⟩ ⟨~ music⟩ 4 : not stale or spoiled : WHOLESOME ⟨~ milk⟩ 5 : not salted ⟨~ butter⟩ 6 ♦ : much loved — sweet·ish adj — sweet·ly adv

♦ [2] affable, agreeable, amiable, genial, good-natured, gracious, nice, well-disposed — more at AMIABLE ♦ [3] ambrosial, aromatic, fragrant, redolent, savory, scented — more at FRAGRANT ♦ [6] beloved, darling, dear, favorite (or favourite), loved, pet, precious, special ♦ [6] adorable, endearing, lovable, winning — more at LOVABLE

²sweet n 1 : something sweet 2 : a dearly loved person : DARLING

sweet·bread \'swēt-ˌbred\ n : the pancreas or thymus of an animal (as a calf or lamb) used for food

sweet·bri·ar or sweet·bri·er \-ˌbrī-ər\ n : a thorny Old World rose with fragrant white to deep pink flowers

sweet clover n : any of a genus of erect legumes widely grown for soil improvement or hay

sweet corn n : corn of a variety having soft kernels containing a high percentage of sugar

sweet·en \'swēt-ᵊn\ vb sweet·ened; sweet·en·ing : to make sweet — sweet·en·er n — sweet·en·ing n

sweet·heart \'swēt-ˌhärt\ n ♦ : one who is loved

♦ beloved, darling, dear, flame, honey, love, sweet; also beau, boyfriend, fellow, lover, man, swain; gal, girl, girlfriend, mistress; date, escort; gallant, suitor, wooer; groom, husband; fiancé, intended; admirer, crush, steady

sweet·meat \-ˌmēt\ n : CANDY 1

sweet·ness n ♦ : the quality or state of being sweet

♦ agreeableness, amenity, amiability, geniality, graciousness, niceness, pleasantness — more at AMIABILITY

sweet pea n : a garden plant of the legume family with climbing stems and fragrant flowers of many colors; also : its flower

sweet pepper n : any of various large mild thick-walled fruits of a pepper; also : a plant bearing sweet peppers

sweet potato n : a tropical vine related to the morning glory; also : its large sweet edible root

sweet–talk \'swēt-ˌtȯk\ vb : FLATTER, COAX — sweet talk n

sweet tooth n : a craving or fondness for sweet food

sweet wil·liam \ˌswēt-'wil-yəm\ n, often cap W : a widely cultivated Old World pink with small white to deep red or purple flowers often showily spotted, banded, or mottled

¹swell \'swel\ vb swelled; swelled or swol·len \'swō-lən\; swell·ing 1 ♦ : to grow big or make bigger 2 : to expand or distend abnormally or excessively ⟨a swollen joint⟩; also : BULGE 3 : to fill or be filled with emotion (as pride)

♦ accumulate, appreciate, balloon, build, burgeon, enlarge, escalate, expand, increase, mount, multiply, mushroom, proliferate, rise, snowball, wax — more at INCREASE ♦ add, aggrandize, amplify, augment, boost, compound, extend, increase, raise, up — more at INCREASE

²swell n 1 ♦ : a long crestless wave or series of waves in the open sea 2 : the condition of being protuberant 3 : a person dressed in the height of fashion; also : a person of high social position

♦ billow, surge, wave — more at WAVE

³swell adj 1 : STYLISH; also : socially prominent 2 : very good of its kind : EXCELLENT

swelled head n : an exaggerated opinion of oneself : SELF-CONCEIT

swell·ing n ♦ : something that is swollen; specif : an abnormal bodily protuberance or localized enlargement

♦ bump, knot, lump, nodule — more at BUMP

swel·ter \'swel-tər\ vb [ME sweltren, fr. swelten to die, be overcome by heat, fr. OE sweltan to die] 1 : to be faint or oppressed with the heat 2 : to become exceedingly hot — swel·ter·ing \-tə-riŋ\ adj

swept past and past part of SWEEP

swerve \'swərv\ vb swerved; swerv·ing ♦ : to move abruptly aside from a straight line or course — swerve n

♦ sheer, veer, yaw; also skew, slew; arc, arch, bend, bow, curve, crook, hook, round, sweep, wheel; circle, coil, curl, loop, spiral; turn, twist, wind; deviate, stray, wander, waver Ant straighten

¹swift \'swift\ adj 1 ♦ : moving or capable of moving with great speed 2 : occurring suddenly 3 : READY, ALERT

♦ breakneck, breathless, brisk, dizzy, fast, fleet, hasty, lightning, nippy, quick, rapid, rattling, snappy, speedy — more at FAST

²swift n : any of numerous small insect-eating birds with long narrow wings

swift·ly adv ♦ : in a swift manner : with speed

♦ apace, briskly, fast, full tilt, hastily, posthaste, presto, pronto, quick, quickly, rapidly, soon, speedily — more at FAST

swift·ness n ♦ : the quality or state of being swift; also : the fact of being swift

♦ celerity, fastness, fleetness, haste, hurry, quickness, rapidity, speed, velocity — more at SPEED

¹swig \'swig\ vb swigged; swig·ging ♦ : to drink in long drafts

♦ drink, guzzle, imbibe, quaff, sup, toss — more at DRINK

²swig n ♦ : a quantity drunk at one time

♦ draft, drag, drink, nip, quaff, shot, slug, snort, swallow — more at DRINK

¹swill \'swil\ vb 1 : to swallow greedily : GUZZLE 2 : to feed (as hogs) on swill

²swill n 1 : food for animals composed of edible refuse mixed with liquid 2 : GARBAGE 3 : a draft of liquor

¹swim \'swim\ vb swam \'swam\; swum \'swəm\; swim·ming 1 : to propel oneself along in water by natural means (as by hands and legs, by tail, or by fins) 2 : to glide smoothly along 3 : FLOAT 4 : to be covered with or as if with a liquid 5 ♦ : to be dizzy ⟨his head swam⟩ 6 : to cross or go over by swimming ⟨swam the river⟩ — swim·mer n

♦ reel, spin, whirl

²swim n 1 : an act of swimming 2 : the main current of activity ⟨in the ~⟩

swim·ming n : the action, art, or sport of swimming and diving

swimming pool n : a tank (as of concrete or plastic) designed for swimming

swim·suit \'swim-ˌsüt\ n : a suit for swimming or bathing

swim·wear \'swim-ˌwer\ n : clothing for wear while swimming or bathing

¹swin·dle \'swin-dᵊl\ vb swin·dled; swin·dling [fr. swindler, fr. G Schwindler giddy person, fr. schwindeln to be dizzy] ♦ : to take money or property from by fraud or deceit : CHEAT

♦ bleed, cheat, chisel, cozen, defraud, fleece, hustle, mulct, rook, shortchange, skin, squeeze, stick, sting, victimize — more at FLEECE

²swindle n ♦ : an act or instance of swindling

♦ hustle, racket

swin·dler n ♦ : one that swindles

♦ cheat, dodger, hoaxer, shark, sharper, trickster — more at TRICKSTER

swine \'swīn\ n, pl swine 1 : any of a family of stout short-legged hoofed mammals with bristly skin and a long flexible snout; esp : one widely raised as a meat animal 2 ♦ : a contemptible person

♦ beast, boor, churl, clown, creep, cretin, cur, heel, jerk, joker, louse, lout, scum, skunk, slob, snake — more at JERK

¹swing \'swiŋ\ vb **swung** \'swəŋ\; **swing·ing** 1 : to move or cause to move rapidly in an arc 2 : to sway or cause to sway back and forth 3 ♦ : to hang so as to move freely back and forth or in a curve 4 : to be executed by hanging 5 : to move or turn on a hinge or pivot 6 ♦ : to manage or handle successfully 7 : to march or walk with free swaying movements 8 : to have a steady pulsing rhythm; *also* : to play swing music 9 : to be lively and up-to-date; *also* : to engage freely in sex 10 ♦ : to cause to face or move in another direction — **swing·er** n — **swing·ing** adj

♦ [3] dangle, hang, sling, suspend — more at HANG
♦ [6] contend with, cope with, grapple with, handle, manage, maneuver (or manoeuvre), negotiate, treat — more at HANDLE ♦ [10] divert, swerve, turn, veer, wheel, whip — more at TURN

²swing n 1 : the act of swinging 2 : a swinging blow, movement, or rhythm 3 : the distance through which something swings : FLUCTUATION 4 : progression of an activity or process ⟨in full ∼⟩ 5 : a seat suspended by a rope or chain for swinging back and forth for pleasure 6 : jazz music played esp. by a large band and marked by a steady lively rhythm, simple harmony, and a basic melody often submerged in improvisation

³swing adj 1 : of or relating to swing music 2 : that may swing often decisively either way (as on an issue) ⟨∼ voters⟩

swin·ish \'swī-nish\ adj : of, suggesting, or characteristic of swine

¹swipe \'swīp\ n : a strong sweeping blow

²swipe vb **swiped**; **swip·ing** 1 : to strike or wipe with a sweeping motion 2 ♦ : to take or appropriate without right and with intent to keep : PILFER 3 : to slide (a card having a magnetic code) through a reading device

♦ appropriate, filch, hook, misappropriate, nip, pilfer, pocket, purloin, snitch, steal, thieve — more at STEAL

swirl \'swərl\ vb ♦ : to move or cause to move with a whirling motion — **swirl** n — **swirly** \'swər-lē\ adj

♦ pivot, revolve, roll, rotate, spin, swing, turn, twirl, twist, wheel, whirl — more at TURN

¹swish \'swish\ n 1 ♦ : a prolonged hissing sound 2 : a light sweeping or brushing sound

♦ fizz, hiss, sizzle, whish, whiz — more at HISS

²swish vb : to move, pass, swing, or whirl with the sound of a swish

Swiss \'swis\ n 1 pl **Swiss** : a native or inhabitant of Switzerland 2 : a hard cheese with large holes — **Swiss** adj

Swiss chard n : a beet having large leaves and succulent stalks often cooked as a vegetable

¹switch \'swich\ n 1 ♦ : a slender flexible whip, rod, or twig 2 : a blow with a switch 3 : a shift from one thing to another; *also* : change from the usual 4 : a device for adjusting the rails of a track so that a locomotive or train may be turned from one track to another; *also* : a railroad siding 5 : a device for making, breaking, or changing the connections in an electrical circuit 6 : a heavy strand of hair often used in addition to a person's own hair for some coiffures

♦ lash, scourge, whip

²switch vb 1 ♦ : to punish or urge on with a switch 2 : WHISK ⟨a cow ∼ing her tail⟩ 3 : to shift or turn by operating a switch 4 ♦ : to make a shift in or exchange of : CHANGE

♦ [1] flail, flog, hide, lash, scourge, slash, thrash, whale, whip — more at WHIP ♦ [4] change, commute, exchange, shift, substitute, swap, trade — more at CHANGE

switch·back \'swich-ˌbak\ n : a zigzag road, trail, or section of railroad tracks for climbing a steep hill

switch·blade \-ˌblād\ n : a pocket-knife with a spring-operated blade

switch·board \-ˌbōrd\ n : a panel for controlling the operation of a number of electric circuits; esp : one used to make and break telephone connections

switch–hit·ter \-'hi-tər\ n : a baseball player who bats either right-handed or left-handed — **switch–hit** \-'hit\ vb

switch·man \'swich-mən\ n : one who attends a railroad switch

Switz abbr Switzerland

¹swiv·el \'swi-vəl\ n : a device joining two parts so that one or both can turn freely

²swivel vb **-eled** or **-elled**; **-el·ing** or **-el·ling** : to swing or turn on or as if on a swivel

swiv·et \'swi-vət\ n : an agitated state

swiz·zle stick \'swi-zəl-\ n : a stick used to stir mixed drinks

swollen past part of SWELL

¹swoon \'swün\ vb ♦ : to undergo a temporary loss of consciousness : FAINT

♦ black out, faint, pass out — more at FAINT

²swoon n : a partial or total loss of consciousness; *also* : a state of suspended animation

♦ blackout, faint, knockout — more at FAINT

swoop \'swüp\ vb : to move with a sweep ⟨the eagle ∼ed down on its prey⟩ — **swoop** n

swoopy \'swü-pē\ adj : having lines that extend in a wide curve ⟨a ∼ silhouette⟩

swop chiefly Brit var of SWAP

sword \'sōrd\ n 1 : a weapon with a long blade for cutting or thrusting 2 : the use of force

sword·fish \-ˌfish\ n : a very large ocean fish used for food that has the upper jaw prolonged into a long swordlike beak

sword·play \-ˌplā\ n : the art or skill of wielding a sword

swords·man \'sōrdz-mən\ n : one skilled in swordplay; esp : FENCER

sword·tail \'sōrd-ˌtāl\ n : a small brightly marked Central American fish often kept in aquariums

swore past of SWEAR

sworn past part of SWEAR

swum past part of SWIM

swung past and past part of SWING

syb·a·rite \'si-bə-ˌrīt\ n : a lover of luxury : VOLUPTUARY — **syb·a·rit·ic** \ˌsi-bə-'ri-tik\ adj

syc·a·more \'si-kə-ˌmōr\ n : a large spreading tree chiefly of the eastern and central U.S. that has light brown flaky bark and small round fruits hanging on long stalks

sy·co·phant \'si-kə-fənt\ n : a servile flatterer — **sy·co·phan·tic** \ˌsi-kə-'fan-tik\ adj

syl or **syll** abbr syllable

syl·lab·i·ca·tion \sə-ˌla-bə-'kā-shən\ n : the division of words into syllables

syl·lab·i·fy \sə-'la-bə-ˌfī\ vb **-fied**; **-fy·ing** \sə-'la-bə-fə-'kā-shən\ n

syl·la·ble \'si-lə-bəl\ n [ME, fr. AF sillable, silable, fr. L syllaba, fr. Gk syllabē, fr. syllambanein to gather together, fr. syn- with + lambanein to take] : a unit of spoken language consisting of an uninterrupted utterance and forming either a whole word (as cat) or a commonly recognized division of a word (as syl in syl-la-ble); *also* : one or more letters representing such a unit — **syl·lab·ic** \sə-'la-bik\ adj

syl·la·bus \'si-lə-bəs\ n, pl **-bi** \-ˌbī\ or **-bus·es** : a summary containing the heads or main topics of a speech, book, or course of study

syl·lo·gism \'si-lə-ˌji-zəm\ n : a logical scheme of a formal argument consisting of a major and a minor premise and a conclusion which must logically be true if the premises are true — **syl·lo·gis·tic** \ˌsi-lə-'jis-tik\ adj

sylph \'silf\ n 1 : an imaginary being inhabiting the air 2 : a slender graceful woman or girl

syl·van \'sil-vən\ adj 1 : living or located in a wooded area; *also* : of, relating to, or characteristic of forest 2 : abounding in woods or trees

sym abbr 1 symbol 2 symmetrical

sym·bi·o·sis \ˌsim-ˌbī-'ō-səs, -bē-\ n, pl **-o·ses** \-ˌsēz\ : the living together in close association of two dissimilar organisms esp. when mutually beneficial — **sym·bi·ot·ic** \-'ä-tik\ adj

sym·bol \'sim-bəl\ n 1 ♦ : something that stands for

something else; *esp* : something concrete that represents or suggests another thing that cannot in itself be pictured ⟨the lion is a ~ of bravery⟩ **2** : a letter, character, or sign used in writing or printing to represent operations, quantities, elements, sounds, or other ideas — **sym·bol·ic** \sim-'bä-lik\ *also* **sym·bol·i·cal** \-li-kəl\ *adj* — **sym·bol·i·cal·ly** \-k(ə-)lē\ *adv*

♦ emblem, hallmark, logo, trademark — more at EMBLEM

sym·bol·ise *chiefly Brit var of* SYMBOLIZE
sym·bol·ism \'sim-bə-,li-zəm\ *n* : representation of abstract or intangible things by means of symbols
sym·bol·ize \'sim-bə-,līz\ *vb* **-ized; -iz·ing** **1** : to serve as a symbol of **2** : to represent by symbols — **sym·bol·i·za·tion** \,sim-bə-lə-'zā-shən\ *n*
sym·me·try \'si-mə-trē\ *n, pl* **-tries** **1** ♦ : an arrangement marked by regularity and balanced proportions **2** : correspondence in size, shape, and position of parts that are on opposite sides of a dividing line or center — **sym·met·ri·cal** \sə-'me-tri-kəl\ *or* **sym·met·ric** \sə-'me-trik\ *adj* — **sym·met·ri·cal·ly** \-k(ə-)lē\ *adv*

♦ balance, coherence, consonance, harmony, proportion, symphony, unity — more at HARMONY

sym·pa·thet·ic \,sim-pə-'the-tik\ *adj* ♦ : given to, marked by, or arising from sympathy, compassion, friendliness, and sensitivity to others' emotions — **sym·pa·thet·i·cal·ly** \,sim-pə-'the-ti-k(ə-)lē\ *adv*

♦ compassionate, humane, understanding; *also* gentle, sensitive, tender, tenderhearted, warm, warmhearted; benevolent, benignant, charitable, kind; clement, lenient, merciful; cordial, friendly, good-natured, good-tempered, gracious; affectionate, loving *Ant* callous, cold-blooded, heartless, inhuman, inhumane, unfeeling, unsympathetic ♦ beneficent, benevolent, good-hearted, humane, kind, kindly, tender, tenderhearted, warmhearted — more at HUMANE

sympathetic nervous system *n* : the part of the autonomic nervous system that is concerned esp. with the body's response to stress and that tends to decrease the tone and contractility of smooth muscle and increase blood pressure and the activity of the heart
sym·pa·thise *chiefly Brit var of* SYMPATHIZE
sym·pa·thize \'sim-pə-,thīz\ *vb* **-thized; -thiz·ing** ♦ : to feel or show sympathy

♦ *usu* sympathize with bleed, commiserate, feel, pity — more at PITY

sym·pa·thiz·er *n* ♦ : one that sympathizes : one that acts or reacts in sympathy

♦ abettor, ally, backer, confederate, supporter — more at ALLY

sym·pa·thy \'sim-pə-thē\ *n, pl* **-thies** **1** : a relationship between persons or things wherein whatever affects one similarly affects the other **2** : harmony of interests and aims **3** : FAVOR, SUPPORT **4** ♦ : the capacity for entering into and sharing the feelings or interests of another; *also* : COMPASSION **5** : an expression of sorrow for another's loss, grief, or misfortune

♦ commiseration, compassion, feeling; *also* condolence, regret; humanity, kindliness, kindness, mercy, pity; affinity, empathy, rapport, sensitivity; altruism, benevolence, benignity, charity, generosity, goodwill, humanitarianism, philanthropy *Ant* callousness ♦ charity, heart, humanity, kindliness, kindness, mercy, pity — more at HEART

sym·phon·ic \sim-'fä-nik\ *adj* ♦ : musically concordant

♦ euphonious, harmonious, melodious, musical, tuneful — more at HARMONIOUS

sym·pho·ny \'sim-fə-nē\ *n, pl* **-nies** **1** ♦ : harmony of sounds **2** : a large and complex composition for a full orchestra **3** : a large orchestra of a kind that plays symphonies

♦ balance, coherence, consonance, harmony, proportion, symmetry, unity — more at HARMONY

sym·po·sium \sim-'pō-zē-əm\ *n, pl* **-sia** \-zē-ə\ *or* **-siums**

♦ : a conference at which a particular topic is discussed by various speakers; *also* : a collection of opinions about a subject

♦ colloquy, conference, council, forum, panel, parley, powwow, seminar — more at FORUM

symp·tom \'simp-təm\ *n* [LL *symptoma*, fr. Gk *symptōma* happening, attribute, symptom, fr. *sympiptein* to happen, fr. *syn* with + *piptein* to fall] **1** : something that indicates the presence of disease or abnormality; *esp* : something (as a headache) that can be sensed only by the individual affected **2** : SIGN, INDICATION
symp·tom·at·ic \,simp-tə-'ma-tik\ *adj* ♦ : serving to indicate

♦ characteristic, classic, distinct, distinctive, individual, peculiar, proper, typical — more at CHARACTERISTIC

syn *abbr* synonym; synonymous; synonymy
syn·a·gogue *also* **syn·a·gog** \'si-nə-,gäg\ *n* [ME *synagoge*, fr. AF, fr. LL *synagoga*, fr. Gk *synagōgē* assembly, synagogue, fr. *synagein* to bring together] **1** : a Jewish congregation **2** : the house of worship of a Jewish congregation
syn·apse \'si-,naps, sə-'naps\ *n* : the point at which a nervous impulse passes from one neuron to another — **syn·ap·tic** \sə-'nap-tik\ *adj*
¹sync *also* **synch** \'siŋk\ *vb* **synced** *also* **synched** \'siŋkt\; **sync·ing** *also* **synch·ing** \'siŋ-kiŋ\ : SYNCHRONIZE
²sync *also* **synch** *n* : SYNCHRONIZATION, SYNCHRONISM — **sync** *adj*
syn·chro·ni·sa·tion, syn·chro·nise *chiefly Brit var of* SYNCHRONIZATION, SYNCHRONIZE
syn·chro·nize \'siŋ-krə-,nīz, 'sin-\ *vb* **-nized; -niz·ing** **1** : to occur or cause to occur at the same instant **2** : to represent, arrange, or tabulate according to dates or time **3** : to cause to agree in time **4** : to make synchronous in operation — **syn·chro·nism** \-,ni-zəm\ *n* — **syn·chro·ni·za·tion** \,siŋ-krə-nə-'zā-shən, ,sin-\ *n* — **syn·chro·niz·er** *n*
syn·chro·nous \'siŋ-krə-nəs, 'sin-\ *adj* **1** ♦ : happening at the same time : CONCURRENT **2** : working, moving, or occurring together at the same rate and at the proper time

♦ coeval, concurrent, contemporary, simultaneous — more at CONTEMPORARY

syn·co·pa·tion \,siŋ-kə-'pā-shən, ,sin-\ *n* : a shifting of the regular musical accent : occurrence of accented notes on the weak beat — **syn·co·pate** \'siŋ-kə-,pāt, 'sin-\ *vb*
syn·co·pe \'siŋ-kə-(,)pē, 'sin-\ *n* : the loss of one or more sounds or letters in the interior of a word (as in *fo'c'sle* for *forecastle*)
¹syn·di·cate \'sin-di-kət\ *n* **1** ♦ : a group of persons who combine to carry out a financial or industrial undertaking **2** ♦ : a loose association of racketeers **3** : a business concern that sells materials for publication in many newspapers and periodicals at the same time

♦ [1] cartel, combination, combine, trust — more at CARTEL ♦ [2] cabal, conspiracy, gang, mob, ring — more at RING

²syn·di·cate \-də-,kāt\ *vb* **-cat·ed; -cat·ing** **1** : to combine into or manage as a syndicate **2** : to publish through a syndicate — **syn·di·ca·tion** \,sin-də-'kā-shən\ *n*
syn·drome \'sin-,drōm\ *n* : a group of signs and symptoms that occur together and characterize a particular abnormality or condition
syn·er·gism \'sin-ər-,ji-zəm\ *n* : interaction of discrete agencies (as industrial firms), agents (as drugs), or conditions such that the total effect is greater than the sum of the individual effects — **syn·er·gist** \-jist\ *n* — **syn·er·gis·tic** \,si-nər-'jis-tik\ *adj* — **syn·er·gis·ti·cal·ly** \-ti-k(ə-)lē\ *adv*
syn·er·gy \'si-nər-je\ *n, pl* **-gies** : SYNERGISM
syn·fuel \'sin-,fyül\ *n* [*synthetic*] : a fuel derived esp. from a fossil fuel
syn·od \'si-nəd\ *n* : COUNCIL, ASSEMBLY; *esp* : a religious governing body — **syn·od·al** \-nəd-ᵊl, -,näd-ᵊl\ *adj* — **syn·od·ic** \-dik\ *or* **syn·od·i·cal** \sə-'nä-di-kəl\ *adj*

syn·o·nym \'si-nə-ˌnim\ *n* : one of two or more words in the same language which have the same or very nearly the same meaning — **syn·on·y·mous** \sə-'nä-nə-məs\ *adj* — **syn·on·y·my** \-mē\ *n*

syn·op·sis \sə-'näp-səs\ *n, pl* **-op·ses** \-ˌsēz\ ♦ : a condensed statement or outline (as of a treatise) : ABSTRACT

♦ abstract, digest, encapsulation, epitome, outline, précis, recapitulation, résumé (*or* resume), roundup, sum, summary, wrap-up — more at SUMMARY

syn·op·tic \sə-'näp-tik\ *also* **syn·op·ti·cal** \-ti-kəl\ *adj* : characterized by or affording a comprehensive view

syn·tax \'sin-ˌtaks\ *n* : the way in which words are put together to form phrases, clauses, or sentences — **syn·tac·tic** \sin-'tak-tik\ *or* **syn·tac·ti·cal** \-ti-kəl\ *adj*

syn·the·sis \'sin-thə-səs\ *n, pl* **-the·ses** \-ˌsēz\ : the combination of parts or elements into a whole; *esp* : the production of a substance by union of chemically simpler substances — **syn·the·size** \-ˌsīz\ *vb* — **syn·the·siz·er** *n*

syn·thet·ic \sin-'the-tik\ *adj* ♦ : produced artificially esp. by chemical means; *also* : not genuine — **synthetic** *n* — **syn·thet·i·cal·ly** \-ti-k(ə-)lē\ *adv*

♦ artificial, fake, faux, imitation, mock, sham — more at IMITATION

syph·i·lis \'si-fə-ləs\ *n* [NL, fr. *Syphilus*, hero of the poem *Syphilis sive Morbus Gallicus* (*Syphilis or the French disease*) (1530) by Girolamo Fracastoro †1553 Ital. physician] : an infectious use. venereal disease caused by a spirochete — **syph·i·lit·ic** \ˌsi-fə-'li-tik\ *adj or n*

syphon *var of* SIPHON

Sy·rah \sē-'rä\ *n* : a red wine

Syr·i·an \'sir-ē-ən\ *n* : a native or inhabitant of Syria — **Syrian** *adj*

¹sy·ringe \sə-'rinj\ *n* ♦ : a device used esp. for injecting liquids into or withdrawing them from the body

♦ hypodermic syringe, needle — more at NEEDLE

²syringe *vb* **sy·ringed; sy·ring·ing** : to flush or cleanse with or as if with a syringe

syr·up *also* **sir·up** \'sər-əp, 'sir-əp\ *n* **1** : a thick sticky solution of sugar and water often flavored or medicated **2** : the concentrated juice of a fruit or plant

syr·upy *adj* ♦ : resembling syrup in appearance or quality

♦ thick, viscid, viscous — more at THICK

syst *abbr* system

sys·tem \'sis-təm\ *n* **1** : a group of units so combined as to form a whole and to operate in unison **2** : the body as a functioning whole; *also* : a group of bodily organs (as the nervous system) that together carry on some vital function **3** ♦ : a definite scheme or method of procedure or classification **4** ♦ : regular method or order

♦ [3, 4] approach, fashion, form, manner, method, plan, strategy, style, tack, tactics, technique, way — more at METHOD

sys·tem·at·ic \ˌsis-tə-'ma-tik\ *adj* ♦ : methodical in procedure or plan — **sys·tem·at·i·cal·ly** \-k(ə-)lē\ *adv*

♦ methodical, orderly, regular — more at METHODICAL

sys·tem·a·tise *chiefly Brit var of* SYSTEMATIZE

sys·tem·a·tize \'sis-tə-mə-ˌtīz\ *vb* **-atized; -a·tiz·ing** ♦ : to make into a system : arrange methodically

♦ arrange, array, classify, codify, dispose, draw up, marshal, order, organize, range — more at ORDER

¹sys·tem·ic \sis-'te-mik\ *adj* **1** : of, relating to, or affecting the whole body ⟨∼ disease⟩ **2** : of, relating to, or being a pesticide that when absorbed into the sap or bloodstream makes the entire plant or animal toxic to a pest (as an insect or fungus)

²systemic *n* : a systemic pesticide

systemic lupus erythematosus *n* : a systemic disease esp. of women characterized by fever, skin rash, and arthritis, often by anemia, by small hemorrhages of the skin and mucous membranes, and in serious cases by involvement of various internal organs

sys·tem·ize \'sis-tə-ˌmīz\ *vb* **-ized; -iz·ing** : SYSTEMATIZE

systems analyst *n* : a person who studies a procedure or business to determine its goals or purposes and to discover the best ways to accomplish them — **systems analysis** *n*

sys·to·le \'sis-tə-(ˌ)lē\ *n* : a rhythmically recurrent contraction of the heart — **sys·tol·ic** \sis-'tä-lik\ *adj*

T

¹t \'tē\ *n, pl* **t's** *or* **ts** \'tēz\ *often cap* : the 20th letter of the English alphabet

²t *abbr, often cap* **1** metric ton **2** tablespoon **3** teaspoon **4** temperature **5** ton **6** transitive **7** troy **8** true

T *abbr* **1** toddler **2** T-shirt

Ta *symbol* tantalum

TA *abbr* teaching assistant

¹tab \'tab\ *n* **1** : a short projecting flap, loop, or tag; *also* : a small insert or addition **2** : close surveillance : WATCH ⟨keep ∼s on him⟩ **3** ♦ : a creditor's statement : BILL **4** : a key on a keyboard esp. for putting data in columns

♦ account, bill, check, invoice, statement — more at BILL

²tab *vb* **tabbed; tab·bing** : DESIGNATE

tab·by \'ta-bē\ *n, pl* **tabbies** : a usu. striped or mottled domestic cat; *also* : a female domestic cat

tab·er·na·cle \'ta-bər-ˌna-kəl\ *n* [ME, fr. OF, fr. LL *tabernaculum*, fr. L, tent, fr. *taberna* hut] **1** *often cap* : a tent sanctuary used by the Israelites during the Exodus **2** : a receptacle for the consecrated elements of the Eucharist **3** : a house of worship

¹ta·ble \'tā-bəl\ *n* **1** : a flat slab or plaque : TABLET **2** : a piece of furniture consisting of a smooth flat top fixed on legs **3** : a supply of food **4** : a group of people assembled at or as if at a table **5** ♦ : an orderly arrangement of data usu. in rows and columns **6** : a short list ⟨∼ of contents⟩ **7** : something that resembles a table esp. in having a flat surface : TABLELAND — **ta·ble·top** \-ˌtäp\ *n*

♦ [3] board, chow, feed, meal, mess, repast — more at MEAL ♦ [5] catalog, checklist, list, listing, menu, register, registry, roll, roster, schedule — more at LIST

²table *vb* **ta·bled; ta·bling 1** *Brit* : to place on the agenda **2** : to remove (a parliamentary motion) from consideration indefinitely

tab·leau \'ta-ˌblō\ *n, pl* **tab·leaux** \-ˌblōz\ *also* **tableaus** [F] : a scene or event usu. presented on a stage by silent and motionless costumed participants

ta·ble·cloth \'tā-bəl-ˌklȯth\ *n* : a covering spread over a dining table before the table is set

ta·ble·land \'tā-bəl-ˌland\ *n* ♦ : a broad level elevated area : PLATEAU

♦ mesa, plateau, table — more at PLATEAU

ta·ble·spoon \-ˌspün\ *n* **1** : a large spoon used esp. for serving **2** : a unit of measure equal to ½ fluid ounce (15 milliliters)

ta·ble·spoon·ful \-ˌfu̇l\ *n, pl* **-spoonfuls** \-ˌfu̇lz\ *also* **-spoons·ful** \-ˌspünz-ˌfu̇l\ : TABLESPOON 2

tab·let \'ta-blət\ *n* **1** : a flat slab suited for or bearing an inscription **2** : a collection of sheets of paper glued together at one edge **3 a** : a compressed or molded block of material **b** ♦ : a small mass of medicated material **4** : GRAPHICS TABLET **5** *or* **tablet computer** : a mobile computing device that has a flat rectangular form, is usu. controlled by means of a touch screen, and is typically used for accessing the Internet, watching videos, and reading e-books

♦ capsule, pill — more at PILL

table tennis *n* : a game resembling tennis played on a tabletop with wooden paddles and a small hollow plastic ball

ta·ble·ware \'tā-bəl-ˌwar\ *n* ♦ : utensils (as of china or silver) for table use

♦ flatware, silver; *also* setting; cutlery; chopstick, fork, knife, spoon, tablespoon, teaspoon

¹tab·loid \'ta-ˌblȯid\ *adj* : condensed into small scope

²tabloid *n* : a newspaper marked by small pages, condensation of the news, and usu. many photographs

¹ta·boo *also* **ta·bu** \tə-'bü, ta-\ *adj* [Tongan (a Polynesian language) *tabu*] ♦ : prohibited by a taboo

♦ forbidden, impermissible — more at IMPERMISSIBLE

²taboo *also* **tabu** *n, pl* **taboos** *also* **tabus** **1** : a prohibition against touching, saying, or doing something for fear of immediate harm from a supernatural force **2** : a prohibition imposed by social custom

ta·bor *also* **ta·bour** \'tā-bər\ *n* : a small drum used to accompany a pipe or fife played by the same person

tab·u·lar \'ta-byə-lər\ *adj* **1** : having a flat surface **2** : arranged in a table; *esp* : set up in rows and columns **3** : computed by means of a table

tab·u·late \-ˌlāt\ *vb* **-lat·ed; -lat·ing** : to put into tabular form — **tab·u·la·tion** \ˌta-byə-'lā-shən\ *n* — **tab·u·la·tor** \'ta-byə-ˌlā-tər\ *n*

TAC \'tak\ *abbr* Tactical Air Command

tach \'tak\ *n* : TACHOMETER

ta·chom·e·ter \ta-'kä-mə-tər, tə-\ *n* [ultim. fr. Gk *tachos* speed] : a device to indicate speed of rotation

tachy·car·dia \ˌta-ki-'kär-dē-ə\ *n* : relatively rapid heart action

tachy·on \'ta-kē-ˌän\ *n* : a hypothetical particle held to travel faster than light

tac·it \'ta-sət\ *adj* [F or L; F *tacite*, fr. L *tacitus* silent, fr. *tacēre* to be silent] **1** : expressed without words or speech **2** ♦ : implied or indicated but not actually expressed ⟨∼ consent⟩ — **tac·it·ly** *adv* — **tac·it·ness** *n*

♦ implicit, unexpressed, unspoken, unvoiced, wordless — more at IMPLICIT

tac·i·turn \'ta-sə-ˌtərn\ *adj* ♦ : disinclined to talk — **tac·i·tur·ni·ty** \ˌta-sə-'tər-nə-tē\ *n*

♦ closemouthed, laconic, reserved, reticent, silent, uncommunicative — more at SILENT

¹tack \'tak\ *vb* **1 a** : to fasten with tacks **b** ♦ : to add on **2** : to change the direction of (a sailing ship) from one tack to another **3** : to follow a zigzag course

♦ add, adjoin, annex, append — more at ADD

²tack *n* **1** : a small sharp nail with a broad flat head **2** : the direction toward the wind that a ship is sailing ⟨starboard ∼⟩; *also* : the run of a ship on one tack **3** : a change of course from one tack to another **4** : a zigzag course **5** ♦ : a course of action

♦ approach, fashion, form, manner, method, strategy, style, system, tactics, technique, way — more at METHOD

³tack *n* : gear for harnessing a horse

¹tack·le \'ta-kəl, *naut often* 'tā-\ *n* **1** ♦ : a set of the equipment used in a particular activity : GEAR **2** : the rigging of a ship **3** : an arrangement of ropes and pulleys for hoisting or pulling heavy objects **4** : the act or an instance of tackling; *also* : a football lineman playing between guard and end

♦ accoutrements (*or* accouterments), apparatus, equipment, gear, matériel, outfit, paraphernalia — more at EQUIPMENT

²tackle *vb* **tack·led; tack·ling** **1** : to attach and secure with or as if with tackle **2** : to seize, grapple with, or throw down with the intention of subduing or stopping **3** : to set about dealing with ⟨∼ a problem⟩ — **tack·ler** *n*

¹tacky \'ta-kē\ *adj* **tack·i·er; -est** : sticky to the touch

²tacky *adj* **tack·i·er; -est** **1** ♦ : decayed, deteriorated, or fallen into partial ruin esp. through neglect or misuse : SHABBY **2** ♦ : marked by lack of style or good taste; *also* : cheaply showy

♦ [1] dilapidated, grungy, mean, neglected, ratty, seedy, shabby — more at SHABBY ♦ [2] dowdy, inelegant, tasteless, trashy, unfashionable, unstylish; *also* inappropriate, incorrect, unbecoming, unseemly, unsuitable, wrong; outmoded, out-of-date, passé; coarse, crude, unrefined, vulgar; cheap, common, inferior, junky, lousy, second-rate, shoddy, sleazy, tawdry; gaudy, loud, ostentatious, overdone, showy *Ant* elegant, fashionable, modish, smart, stylish, tasteful

ta·co \'tä-kō\ *n, pl* **tacos** \-kōz\ [MexSp] : a usu. fried tortilla rolled up with or folded over a filling

tact \'takt\ *n* [F, sense of touch, fr. L *tactus*, fr. *tangere* to touch] : a keen sense of what to do or say to keep good relations with others — **tact·ful** \-fəl\ *adj* — **tact·ful·ly** *adv*

tac·tic \'tak-tik\ *n* : a planned action for accomplishing an end

tac·ti·cal \'tak-ti-kəl\ *adj* ♦ : of or relating to tactics; *esp* : intended for a particular purpose

♦ advisable, desirable, expedient, judicious, politic, prudent, wise — more at EXPEDIENT

tac·tics \'tak-tiks\ *n sing or pl* **1** : the science of maneuvering forces in combat **2** : the skill of using available means to accomplish an end **3** ♦ : a system or mode of procedure — **tac·ti·cian** \tak-'ti-shən\ *n*

♦ approach, fashion, form, manner, method, strategy, style, system, tack, technique, way — more at METHOD

tac·tile \'tak-ᵊl, 'tak-ˌtīl\ *adj* : of, relating to, or perceptible through the sense of touch

tact·less \'takt-ləs\ *adj* ♦ : marked by lack of tact — **tact·less·ly** *adv*

♦ ill-advised, imprudent, indiscreet, unwise — more at INDISCREET

tad·pole \'tad-ˌpōl\ *n* [ME *taddepol*, fr. *tode* toad + *polle* head] : an aquatic larva of a frog or toad that has a tail and gills

tae kwon do \'tī-'kwän-'dō\ *n* : a Korean martial art of self-defense

taf·fe·ta \'ta-fə-tə\ *n* : a crisp lustrous fabric (as of silk or rayon)

taff·rail \'taf-ˌrāl, -rəl\ *n* : the rail around a ship's stern

taf·fy \'ta-fē\ *n, pl* **taffies** : a candy usu. of molasses or brown sugar stretched until porous and light-colored

¹tag \'tag\ *n* **1** : a metal or plastic binding on an end of a shoelace **2** ♦ : a piece of hanging or attached material **3** : a hackneyed quotation or saying **4** : a descriptive or identifying epithet

♦ label, marker, ticket — more at LABEL

²tag *vb* **tagged; tag·ging** **1** ♦ : to provide or mark with or as if with a tag; *esp* : IDENTIFY **2** : to attach as an addition **3** ♦ : to follow closely and persistently ⟨∼s along everywhere we go⟩ **4** : to hold responsible for something

♦ [1] identify, label, mark, ticket — more at LABEL ♦ [3] chase, dog, follow, hound, pursue, shadow, tail, trace, track, trail — more at FOLLOW

³tag *n* : a game in which one player chases others and tries to touch one of them

⁴tag *vb* **tagged; tag·ging** **1** : to touch in or as if in a game of tag **2** : SELECT

TAG *abbr* the adjutant general

tag·line \'tag-ˌlīn\ *n* **1** : a final line (as in a play or joke) **2** : a phrase identified with an individual, group, or product

tag sale *n* : GARAGE SALE

Ta·hi·tian \tə-'hē-shən\ *n* 1 : a native or inhabitant of Tahiti 2 : the Polynesian language of the Tahitians — **Tahitian** *adj*

tai·ga \'tī-gə\ *n* [Russ *taĭga*] : a moist coniferous subarctic forest extending south from the tundra

¹tail \'tāl\ *n* 1 : the rear end or a process extending from the rear end of an animal 2 : something resembling an animal's tail 3 *pl* : full evening dress for men 4 : the back, last, lower, or inferior part of something; *esp* : the reverse of a coin 5 ♦ : one who follows or keeps watch on someone — **tailed** \'tāld\ *adj* — **tail·less** \'tāl-ləs\ *adj*

♦ detective, investigator, operative, shadow, sleuth — more at DETECTIVE

²tail *vb* ♦ : to follow for the purpose of surveillance

♦ chase, dog, follow, hound, pursue, shadow, tag, trace, track, trail — more at FOLLOW

tail·coat \-'kōt\ *n* : a coat with tails; *esp* : a man's full-dress coat with two long tapering skirts at the back

¹tail·gate \-₁gāt\ *n* : a board or gate at the back end of a vehicle that can be let down (as for loading)

²tailgate *vb* **tail·gat·ed; tail·gat·ing** 1 : to drive dangerously close behind another vehicle 2 : to hold a tailgate picnic

³tailgate *adj* : relating to or being a picnic set up on a tailgate ⟨a ∼ party⟩

tail·light \-₁līt\ *n* : a usu. red warning light mounted at the rear of a vehicle

¹tai·lor \'tā-lər\ *n* [ME *taillour*, fr. OF *tailleur*, fr. *taillier* to cut, fr. LL *taliare*, fr. L *talea* twig, cutting] : a person whose occupation is making or altering garments

²tailor *vb* 1 : to make or fashion as the work of a tailor 2 ♦ : to make or adapt to suit a special purpose

♦ acclimate, accommodate, adapt, adjust, condition, conform, fit, shape, suit — more at ADAPT

tai·lored *adj* ♦ : made by a tailor; *also* : altered or fitted as if custom-made

♦ custom, custom-made — more at CUSTOM-MADE

tail·pipe \'tāl-₁pīp\ *n* : an outlet by which engine exhaust gases are expelled from a vehicle (as an automobile)

tail·spin \'tāl-₁spin\ *n* : a rapid descent or downward spiral

tail·wind \'tāl-₁wind\ *n* : a wind blowing in the same general direction as a course of movement (as of an aircraft)

¹taint \'tānt\ *vb* 1 ♦ : to contaminate morally 2 ♦ : to affect or become affected with something bad (as for putrefaction)

♦ [1] blemish, mar, poison, spoil, stain, tarnish, touch, vitiate; *also* besmear, besmirch, blacken, cloud, dirty, discolor, smear, smirch, smudge, smut, soil, sully, tar; color, distort, twist; damage, deface, flaw, harm, hurt, impair; destroy, ruin, wreck ♦ [2] befoul, contaminate, defile, foul, poison, pollute — more at CONTAMINATE

²taint *n* ♦ : a contaminating mark or influence

♦ blot, brand, smirch, spot, stain, stigma — more at STAIN

Tai·wan·ese \₁tī-wə-'nēz, -'nēs\ *n* : a native or inhabitant of Taiwan — **Taiwanese** *adj*

¹take \'tāk\ *vb* **took** \'tůk\; **tak·en** \'tā-kən\; **tak·ing** [ME, fr. OE *tacan*, fr. ON *taka*] 1 ♦ : to get into one's hands or possession : GRASP 2 : CAPTURE; *also* : DEFEAT 3 : to obtain or secure for use 4 ♦ : to catch or attack through the effect of a sudden force or influence ⟨was *taken* with the flu⟩ 5 : CAPTIVATE, DELIGHT 6 : to bring into a relation ⟨∼ a wife⟩ 7 : REMOVE, SUBTRACT 8 ♦ : to pick out : CHOOSE 9 : ASSUME, UNDERTAKE 10 : RECEIVE, ACCEPT 11 : to use for transportation ⟨∼ a bus⟩ 12 : to become impregnated with : ABSORB ⟨∼s a dye⟩ 13 : to receive into one's body (as by swallowing) ⟨∼ a pill⟩ 14 ♦ : to submit to : ENDURE 15 : to lead, carry, or cause to go along to another place 16 : to be in need of : REQUIRE 17 : to obtain as the result of a special procedure ⟨∼ a snapshot⟩ 18 : to undertake and do, make, or perform ⟨∼ a walk⟩ 19 ♦ : to take effect : ACT 20 : to hold without crowding or inconvenience : ACCOM-

MODATE 21 ♦ : to understand or regard in a certain way ⟨I ∼ this to be your final offer⟩ ⟨do you ∼ me for a fool?⟩ — **tak·er** *n* — take advantage of 1 : to profit by 2 : EXPLOIT — **take after** : RESEMBLE — **take care** : to be careful — **take care of** : to attend to — **take effect** : to become operative — **take exception** : OBJECT — **take place** : HAPPEN — **take to** 1 : to go to 2 : to apply or devote oneself to 3 : to conceive a liking for

♦ [1] clasp, grasp, grip, hold; *also* clench, cling (to), clutch, hang on (to), hold on (to); catch, nab, seize, snatch ♦ [4] catch, come down, contract, get, sicken — more at CONTRACT ♦ [8] choose, cull, elect, handpick, name, opt, pick, prefer, select, single — more at CHOOSE ♦ [14] abide, bear, brook, countenance, endure, meet, stand, stick out, stomach, support, sustain, tolerate — more at BEAR ♦ [19] act, function, operate, perform, work — more at ACT ♦ *usu* take for [21] account, call, consider, count, esteem, hold, rate, reckon, regard — more at CONSIDER

²take *n* 1 : the number or quantity taken; *also* : PROCEEDS, RECEIPTS 2 : an act or the action of taking 3 : a television or movie scene filmed or taped at one time; *also* : a sound recording made at one time 4 : a distinct or personal point of view 5 ♦ : a visible response or reaction (as to something unexpected)

♦ reaction, reply, response — more at REACTION

take back *vb* ♦ : to make a retraction of : WITHDRAW

♦ abjure, recant, renounce, retract, unsay, withdraw — more at ABJURE

take down *vb* 1 ♦ : to take apart : DISASSEMBLE 2 ♦ : to lower the spirit or vanity of

♦ [1] disassemble, dismantle, knock down, strike — more at DISASSEMBLE ♦ [2] abase, debase, degrade, demean, discredit, disgrace, dishonor (*or* dishonour), humble, humiliate, lower, shame, smirch — more at HUMBLE

take in *vb* 1 ♦ : to give shelter to 2 ♦ : to encompass within its limits 3 : to cause to accept as true or valid what is false or invalid : DECEIVE

♦ [1] accommodate, billet, chamber, domicile, harbor (*or* harbour), house, lodge, put up, quarter, roof, shelter — more at HOUSE ♦ [2] carry, comprehend, contain, embrace, encompass, entail, include, involve, number — more at INCLUDE

take–no–prisoners *adj* ♦ : having a fierce, relentless, or merciless character

♦ callous, hard, heartless, inhuman, inhumane, pitiless, soulless, unfeeling, unsympathetic — more at HARD

take·off \'tā-₁kóf\ *n* 1 ♦ : an imitation esp. in the way of caricature 2 : an act or instance of taking off

♦ burlesque, caricature, parody, spoof — more at PARODY

take off *vb* 1 ♦ : to remove (an article of wear) from the body 2 : DEDUCT 3 ♦ : to set out : go away 4 : to begin flight

♦ [1] doff, peel, put off, remove — more at REMOVE ♦ [3] clear out, depart, exit, get off, go, move, pull, quit, sally, shove — more at GO

take on *vb* 1 ♦ : to begin to perform or deal with; *also* : to contend with as an opponent 2 ♦ : to provide occupation for : HIRE 3 : to assume or acquire as or as if one's own 4 : to make an unusual show of one's feelings esp. of grief or anger

♦ [1] battle, encounter, engage, face, meet — more at ENGAGE ♦ [2] employ, engage, hire, retain — more at EMPLOY

take out *vb* ♦ : to find release for

♦ loose, release, unleash, vent *Ant* bottle (up), repress, suppress

take over *vb* ♦ : to assume control or possession of or responsibility for — **take·over** \'tā-₁kō-vər\ *n*

♦ cover, fill in, pinch-hit, stand in, sub, substitute — more at COVER ♦ accept, assume, bear, shoulder, undertake — more at ASSUME

take up *vb* **1** : PICK UP **2** : to begin to occupy (land) **3** : to absorb or incorporate into itself ⟨plants *taking up* nutrients⟩ **4** : to begin to engage in ⟨*took up* jogging⟩ **5** : to make tighter or shorter ⟨*take up* the slack⟩ **6** ♦ : to accept or adopt as one's own ⟨*took up* the life of a farmer⟩

♦ adopt, borrow, embrace — more at ADOPT

tak·ings \'tā-kiŋz\ *n pl, chiefly Brit* : receipts esp. of money

talc \'talk\ *n* : a soft mineral with a soapy feel used esp. in making a soothing powder (**tal·cum powder** \'tal-kəm-\) for the skin

tale \'tāl\ *n* **1** : a relation of a series of events **2** : a report of a confidential matter **3** : idle talk; *esp* : harmful gossip **4** ♦ : a usu. imaginative narrative **5** ♦ : an intentionally untrue report : FALSEHOOD **6** : COUNT, TALLY

♦ [4] narrative, novella, short story, story — more at STORY ♦ [5] fabrication, fairy tale, falsehood, falsity, fib, lie, mendacity, prevarication, story, untruth, whopper — more at LIE

tal·ent \'ta-lənt\ *n* **1** : an ancient unit of weight and value **2** ♦ : the natural endowments of a person **3** : a special often creative or artistic aptitude **4** : mental power : ABILITY **5** : a person of talent — **tal·ent·ed** *adj*

♦ aptitude, endowment, faculty, flair, genius, gift, knack; *also* bent, inclination, leaning, partiality, penchant, predilection, predisposition, proclivity, propensity, turn; ear, eye, head, mind, nose; feel, hang, instinct, touch, way; capability, competence, facility, proficiency, skill; capacity, power, potential

ta·ler \'tä-lər\ *n* : any of numerous silver coins issued by German states from the 15th to the 19th centuries

tal·is·man \'ta-ləs-mən, -ləz-\ *n, pl* **-mans** [F *talisman* or Sp *talismán* or It *talismano*, fr. Ar *ṭilsam*, fr. MGk *telesma*, fr. Gk, consecration, fr. *telein* to initiate into the mysteries, complete, fr. *telos* end] ♦ : an object thought to act as a charm

♦ amulet, charm, fetish, mascot — more at CHARM

¹**talk** \'tök\ *vb* **1** : to express in speech : utter words : SPEAK **2** : DISCUSS ⟨~ business⟩ **3** ♦ : to influence or cause by talking ⟨~ed him into going⟩ **4** : to use (a language) for communicating **5** ♦ : to express, communicate, or exchange ideas or thoughts by means of spoken words : CONVERSE — often used with *to* or *with* **6 a** ♦ : to reveal secret or confidential information **b** ♦ : to relate rumor or report of an intimate nature : GOSSIP **7** ♦ : to give a talk : LECTURE **8** : to speak idly — **talk back** : to answer impertinently

♦ *usu* **talk into** [3] argue, convince, get, induce, move, persuade, prevail, satisfy, win — more at PERSUADE ♦ *usu* **talk to** [5] chat, speak; *also* accost, address, greet, hail, herald; inform, notify, tell ♦ [6a] inform, snitch, squeal, tell — more at SQUEAL ♦ [6b] blab, gossip, tattle — more at GOSSIP ♦ [7] declaim, descant, discourse, harangue, lecture, orate, speak; *also* recite, soliloquize; mouth, spout; filibuster; stump; eulogize

²**talk** *n* **1** ♦ : the act or an instance or period of talking **2** : a way of speaking **3** ♦ : a formal discussion, negotiation, or exchange of views **4** : REPORT, RUMOR **5** : the topic of comment or gossip ⟨the ~ of the town⟩ **6** ♦ : an analysis or discussion prepared for public presentation

♦ [1] chat, chatter, chitchat, gabfest, gossip, palaver, rap — more at CHAT ♦ [3] argument, colloquy, conference, deliberation, discourse, discussion, give-and-take, parley — more at DISCUSSION ♦ [6] address, declamation, harangue, oration, speech — more at SPEECH

talk·a·tive \'tö-kə-tiv\ *adj* ♦ : given to talking — **talk·a·tive·ly** *adv* — **talk·a·tive·ness** *n*

♦ chatty, conversational, gabby, garrulous, loquacious; *also* communicative, expansive; demonstrative, effusive, gushing; outspoken, unreserved, vocal; articulate,

fluent, glib, voluble; gossipy; long-winded, prolix, verbose, windy, wordy; extroverted, gregarious, outgoing, sociable *Ant* closemouthed, laconic, reserved, reticent, taciturn

talk·er \'tö-kər\ *n* ♦ : one that talks

♦ chatterbox, jabberer, magpie — more at CHATTERBOX

talk·ing-to \'tö-kiŋ-,tü\ *n* : REPRIMAND, REPROOF

talk over *vb* ♦ : to review or consider in conversation

♦ argue, chew over, debate, discuss, dispute, hash, moot — more at DISCUSS

talk radio *n* : radio programming consisting of call-in shows

tall \'töl\ *adj* **1** ♦ : high in stature; *also* : of a specified height ⟨six feet ~⟩ **2** ♦ : large or formidable in amount, extent, or degree ⟨a ~ order⟩ **3** : UNBELIEVABLE, IMPROBABLE ⟨a ~ story⟩ — **tall·ness** *n*

♦ [1] high, lofty, towering — more at HIGH ♦ [2] arduous, demanding, difficult, exacting, formidable, grueling, hard, herculean, laborious, murderous, rough, stiff, strenuous, toilsome, tough — more at HARD

tal·low \'ta-lō\ *n* : a hard white fat rendered usu. from cattle or sheep tissues and used esp. in candles

¹**tal·ly** \'ta-lē\ *n, pl* **tallies** [ME *talye*, fr. ML *talea*, fr. L, twig, cutting] **1** : a device for visibly recording or accounting esp. business transactions **2** : a recorded account **3** : a corresponding part; *also* : CORRESPONDENCE

²**tally** *vb* **tal·lied; tal·ly·ing 1** : to mark on or as if on a tally **2** : to make a count of : RECKON; *also* : SCORE **3** ♦ : to be in conformity or agreement : CORRESPOND

♦ accord, agree, answer, check, coincide, comport, conform, correspond, dovetail, fit, go, harmonize, jibe, square — more at CHECK

tal·ly·ho \,ta-lē-'hō\ *n, pl* **-hos** : a call of a huntsman at sight of the fox

Tal·mud \'täl-,mud, 'tal-məd\ *n* [Late Heb *talmūdh*, lit., instruction] : the authoritative body of Jewish tradition — **Tal·mu·dic** \tal-'mü-dik, -'myü-, -'mə-; täl-'mü-\ *adj* — **Tal·mud·ist** \'täl-,mü-dist, 'tal-mə-\ *n*

tal·on \'ta-lən\ *n* : the claw of an animal and esp. of a bird of prey

ta·lus \'tā-ləs, 'ta-\ *n* : rock debris at the base of a cliff

tam \'tam\ *n* : TAM-O'-SHANTER

ta·ma·le \tə-'mä-lē\ *n* [MexSp *tamales*, pl. of *tamal* tamale, fr. Nahuatl (American Indian language) *tamalli* steamed cornmeal dough] : ground meat seasoned with chili, rolled in cornmeal dough, wrapped in corn husks, and steamed

tam·a·rack \'ta-mə-,rak\ *n* : a larch of northern No. America; *also* : its hard resinous wood

tam·a·rin \'ta-mə-rən\ *n* : any of several small So. American monkeys related to the marmosets

tam·a·rind \'ta-mə-rənd, -,rind\ *n* [Sp & Pg *tamarindo*, fr. Ar *tamr hindī*, lit., Indian date] : a tropical tree of the legume family with hard yellowish wood and feathery leaves; *also* : its acid fruit

tam·bou·rine \,tam-bə-'rēn\ *n* : a small shallow drum with loose disks at the sides played by shaking or striking with the hand

¹**tame** \'tām\ *adj* **tam·er; tam·est 1** : reduced from a state of native wildness esp. so as to be useful to humans : DOMESTICATED **2** : made docile : SUBDUED **3** ♦ : lacking spirit or interest — **tame·ly** *adv* — **tame·ness** *n*

♦ dull, flat, uninteresting

²**tame** *vb* **tamed; tam·ing 1** : to make or become tame; *also* : to subject (land) to cultivation **2** : HUMBLE, SUBDUE **3** ♦ : to bring under control — **tam·able** *or* **tame·able** \'tā-mə-bəl\ *adj* — **tame·less** *adj* — **tam·er** *n*

♦ bridle, check, constrain, contain, control, curb, govern, inhibit, regulate, rein, restrain

tam-o'-shan·ter \'ta-mə-,shan-tər\ *n* [fr. poem *Tam o' Shanter* (1790) by Robert Burns †1796 Scot. poet] : a Scottish woolen cap with a wide flat circular crown and usu. a pom-pom in the center

tamp \'tamp\ *vb* : to drive down or in by a series of light blows

tam·per \'tam-pər\ *vb* **1** : to carry on underhand negotiations (as by bribery) ⟨∼ with a witness⟩ **2** ♦ : to interfere so as to weaken or change for the worse ⟨∼ with a document⟩ **3** ♦ : to try foolish or dangerous experiments

♦ *usu* **tamper with** [2, 3] fiddle, fool, mess, monkey, play, tinker; *also* alter, doctor, manhandle, manipulate, misuse; butt in, interfere, intrude, meddle

tam·pon \'tam-ˌpän\ *n* [F, lit., plug] : a plug (as of cotton) introduced into a body cavity usu. to absorb secretions (as from menstruation) or to arrest bleeding

¹**tan** \'tan\ *vb* **tanned**; **tan·ning** **1** : to change (hide) into leather esp. by soaking in a liquid containing tannin **2** : to make or become brown (as by exposure to the sun) **3** : to strike with a slender lithe implement (as a lash or rod) esp. as a punishment : WHIP

²**tan** *n* **1** : a brown skin color induced by sun or weather **2** : a light yellowish brown color

³**tan** *abbr* tangent

tan·a·ger \'ta-ni-jər\ *n* : any of numerous American birds that are often brightly colored

tan·bark \'tan-ˌbärk\ *n* : bark (as of oak or sumac) that is rich in tannin and used in tanning

¹**tan·dem** \'tan-dəm\ *n* [L, at last, at length (taken to mean "lengthwise"), fr. *tam* so] **1** : a 2-seated carriage with horses hitched tandem; *also* : its team **2** : a bicycle for two persons sitting one behind the other — **in tandem** : in a tandem arrangement

²**tandem** *adv* : one behind another

³**tandem** *adj* **1** : consisting of things arranged one behind the other **2** : working in conjunction with each other

tang \'taŋ\ *n* **1** : a part in a tool that connects the blade with the handle **2** : a sharp distinctive flavor; *also* : a pungent odor

¹**tan·gent** \'tan-jənt\ *adj* [L *tangent-, tangens*, prp. of *tangere* to touch] : TOUCHING; *esp* : touching a circle or sphere at only one point

²**tangent** *n* **1** : the trigonometric function that is the ratio between the side opposite and the side adjacent to an acute angle in a right triangle **2** : a tangent line, curve, or surface **3** : an abrupt change of course

tan·gen·tial \tan-'jen-chəl\ *adj* **1** : TANGENT **2** : touching lightly : INCIDENTAL ⟨∼ involvement⟩ — **tan·gen·tial·ly** *adv*

tan·ger·ine \'tan-jə-ˌrēn, ˌtan-jə-'rēn\ *n* : a deep orange loose-skinned citrus fruit; *also* : a tree that bears tangerines

¹**tan·gi·ble** \'tan-jə-bəl\ *adj* **1** : perceptible esp. by the sense of touch : PALPABLE **2** : substantially real : MATERIAL ⟨∼ rewards⟩ **3** : capable of being appraised — **tan·gi·bil·i·ty** \ˌtan-jə-'bi-lə-tē\ *n*

²**tangible** *n* : something tangible; *esp* : a tangible asset

¹**tan·gle** \'taŋ-gəl\ *vb* **tan·gled**; **tan·gling** **1 a** : to involve so as to hamper or embarrass **b** ♦ : to seize or hold in or as if in a snare or net : ENTRAP **2** ♦ : to unite or knit together in intricate confusion : ENTANGLE

♦ [1b] enmesh, ensnare, entangle, entrap, mesh, snare, trap — more at ENTANGLE ♦ [2] entangle, interlace, intertwine, interweave, knot, snarl — more at ENTANGLE

²**tangle** *n* **1** : a tangled twisted mass **2** : a confusedly complicated state : MUDDLE

tan·go \'taŋ-gō\ *n, pl* **tangos** : a dance of Latin-American origin — **tango** *vb*

tangy \'taŋ-ē\ *adj* ♦ : having or suggestive of a tang

♦ nippy, pungent, sharp, strong — more at SHARP

tank \'taŋk\ *n* **1** : a large artificial receptacle for liquids **2** : a heavily armed and armored combat vehicle that moves on tracks — **tank·ful** *n*

tan·kard \'taŋ-kərd\ *n* : a tall one-handled drinking vessel

tank·er \'taŋ-kər\ *n* : a vehicle equipped for transporting a liquid

tank top *n* : a sleeveless collarless pullover shirt with shoulder straps

tank town *n* : a small town

tan·ner \'ta-nər\ *n* : one that tans hides

tan·nery \'ta-nə-rē\ *n, pl* **-ner·ies** : a place where tanning is carried on

tan·nic acid \'ta-nik-\ *n* : TANNIN

tan·nin \'ta-nən\ *n* : any of various plant substances used esp. in tanning and dyeing, in inks, and as astringents

tan·sy \'tan-zē\ *n, pl* **tansies** [ME *tanesey*, fr. MF *tanesie*, fr. ML *athanasia*, fr. Gk, immortality, fr. *athanatos* immortal, fr. *a-* not + *thanatos* death] : a common weedy herb related to the daisies with an aromatic odor and bitter-tasting finely divided leaves

tan·ta·lise *chiefly Brit var of* TANTALIZE

tan·ta·lize \'tan-tə-ˌlīz\ *vb* **-lized**; **-liz·ing** [fr. *Tantalus*, king of Greek myth punished in Hades by having to stand up to his chin in water that receded as he bent to drink] : to tease or torment by presenting something desirable but keeping it out of reach — **tan·ta·liz·er** *n* — **tan·ta·liz·ing·ly** *adv*

tan·ta·lum \'tan-tə-ləm\ *n* : a gray-white ductile metallic chemical element

tan·ta·mount \'tan-tə-ˌmaúnt\ *adj* : equivalent in value or meaning

tan·trum \'tan-trəm\ *n* ♦ : a fit of bad temper

♦ blowup, dudgeon, explosion, fireworks, fit, huff, scene; *also* eruption, flare-up, outburst, storm, uproar; frenzy, furore, rage, rampage, uproar

Tan·za·ni·an \ˌtan-zə-'nē-ən\ *n* : a native or inhabitant of Tanzania — **Tanzanian** *adj*

Tao·ism \'taú-ˌi-zəm, 'daú-\ *n* : a Chinese mystical philosophy; *also* : a religion developed from Taoist philosophy and Buddhism — **Tao·ist** \-ist\ *adj or n*

¹**tap** \'tap\ *n* **1** ♦ : a device consisting of a spout and valve attached to the end of a pipe to control the flow of a fluid : FAUCET, COCK **2** : liquor drawn through a tap **3** : the removing of fluid from a container or cavity by tapping **4** : a tool for forming an internal screw thread **5** : a point in an electric circuit where a connection may be made

♦ cock, faucet, gate, spigot, valve — more at FAUCET

²**tap** *vb* **tapped**; **tap·ping** **1** ♦ : to release or cause to flow by piercing or by drawing a plug from a container or cavity **2** : to pierce so as to let out or draw off a fluid **3** : to draw from ⟨∼ resources⟩ **4** : to cut in on (as a telephone signal) to get information **5** : to form an internal screw thread in by means of a tap **6** : to connect (as a gas or water main) with a local supply — **tap·per** *n*

♦ bleed, drain, draw, pump, siphon — more at DRAIN

³**tap** *vb* **tapped**; **tap·ping** **1** ♦ : to rap lightly **2** : to bring about by repeated light blows **3** : SELECT; *esp* : to elect to membership

♦ beat, drum, rap; *also* bang, hammer, hit, knock, pound, thud, thump, thwack, whack; chink, clatter, clink, ping; pat, chuck, clap, flick, tip

⁴**tap** *n* **1** : a light blow or stroke; *also* : its sound **2** : a small metal plate for the sole or heel of a shoe

ta·pa \'tä-pə, 'ta-\ *n* [Sp, lit., cover, lid] : an hors d'oeuvre served with drinks esp. in Spanish bars — usu. used in pl.

¹**tape** \'tāp\ *n* **1** : a narrow flexible band or strip (as of woven fabric) **2** : MAGNETIC TAPE; *also* : CASSETTE

²**tape** *vb* **taped**; **tap·ing** **1** : to fasten or support with tape **2** : to record on magnetic tape

tape deck *n* : a device used to play back cassette tapes that usu. has to be connected to an audio system

tape measure *n* : a tape marked off in units (as inches) for measuring

¹**ta·per** \'tā-pər\ *n* **1** : a slender wax candle; *also* : a long waxed wick **2** : a gradual lessening of thickness or width in a long object

²**taper** *vb* **ta·pered**; **ta·per·ing** **1** : to make or become gradually smaller toward one end **2** : to diminish gradually

♦ abate, decline, decrease, de-escalate, die, diminish, dwindle, ebb, fall, lessen, let up, lower, moderate, recede, relent, shrink, subside, wane — more at DECREASE

tape–re·cord \ˌtā-pri-ˈkȯrd\ *vb* : to make a recording of on magnetic tape — **tape recorder** *n* — **tape recording** *n*

taper off *vb* : to diminish gradually : TAPER

tap·es·try \ˈta-pə-strē\ *n, pl* **-tries** : a heavy reversible textile that has designs or pictures woven into it and is used esp. as a wall hanging

tape·worm \ˈtāp-ˌwərm\ *n* : any of a class of long flat segmented worms parasitic esp. in vertebrate intestines

tap·i·o·ca \ˌta-pē-ˈō-kə\ *n* : a usu. granular preparation of cassava starch used esp. in puddings; *also* : a dish (as pudding) that contains tapioca

ta·pir \ˈtā-pər\ *n, pl* **tapirs** *also* **tapir** [Pg *tapir, tapira,* fr. Tupinambà (American Indian language of Brazil) *tapi*ı̄ra] : any of a genus of large herbivorous hoofed mammals of tropical America and southeastern Asia

tap·pet \ˈta-pət\ *n* : a lever or projection moved by some other piece (as a cam) or intended to move something else

tap·room \ˈtap-ˌrüm, -ˌru̇m\ *n* : BARROOM

tap·root \-ˌrüt, -ˌru̇t\ *n* : a large main root growing straight down and giving off small side roots

taps \ˈtaps\ *n sing or pl* : the last bugle call at night blown as a signal that lights are to be put out; *also* : a similar call blown at military funerals and memorial services

tap·ster \ˈtap-stər\ *n* : BARTENDER

¹tar \ˈtär\ *n* **1** : a thick dark sticky liquid distilled from organic material (as wood or coal) **2 ♦** : one that sails : SAILOR

♦ gob, jack, jack-tar, mariner, sailor, seaman, swab — more at SAILOR

²tar *vb* **tarred; tar·ring** : to cover or smear with or as if with tar

tar·an·tel·la \ˌtar-ən-ˈte-lə\ *n* : a lively folk dance of southern Italy in 6/8 time

ta·ran·tu·la \tə-ˈran-chə-lə, -tə-lə\ *n, pl* **tarantulas** *also* **ta·ran·tu·lae** \-ˈran-chə-ˌlē, -tə-ˌlē\ : any of a family of large hairy American spiders with a sharp bite that is not very poisonous to human beings

tar·di·ly \ˈtär-də-lē\ *adv* ♦ : in a tardy manner

♦ laggardly, slow, slowly, sluggishly — more at SLOW

tar·dy \ˈtär-dē\ *adj* **tar·di·er; -est** **1 ♦** : moving slowly : SLUGGISH **2 ♦** : delayed beyond the expected or proper time : LATE — **tar·di·ness** \-dē-nəs\ *n*

♦ [1] creeping, dilatory, laggard, languid, poky, slow, sluggish — more at SLOW ♦ [2] behind, belated, delinquent, late, overdue — more at LATE

¹tare \ˈtar\ *n* : a weed of grain fields

²tare *n* : a deduction from the gross weight of a substance and its container made in allowance for the weight of the container — **tare** *vb*

¹tar·get \ˈtär-gət\ *n* [ME, fr. MF *targette,* dim. of *targe* light shield, of Gmc origin] **1** : a mark to shoot at **2 ♦** : an object of ridicule or criticism **3** : a goal to be achieved

♦ butt, laughingstock, mark, mockery, victim

²target *vb* : to make a target of

tar·iff \ˈtar-əf\ *n* [It *tariffa,* fr. Ar *taʿrīf* notification] **1** : a schedule of duties imposed by a government esp. on imported goods; *also* : a duty or rate of duty imposed in such a schedule **2** : a schedule of rates or charges

tar·mac \ˈtär-ˌmak\ *n* : a surface paved with crushed stone covered with tar

tarn \ˈtärn\ *n* : a small mountain lake

tar·nish \ˈtär-nish\ *vb* **1** : to make or become dull or discolored **2 ♦** : to bring disgrace on — **tarnish** *n*

♦ blemish, mar, poison, spoil, stain, taint, touch, vitiate — more at TAINT

ta·ro \ˈtär-ō, ˈtar-\ *n, pl* **taros** : a large-leaved tropical plant related to the arums that is grown for its edible starchy corms; *also* : its corms

tar·ot \ˈtar-ō\ *n* : one of a set of usu. 78 playing cards used esp. for fortune-telling

tar·pau·lin \tär-ˈpȯ-lən, ˈtär-pə-\ *n* : a piece of material (as durable plastic) used for protecting exposed objects

tar·pon \ˈtär-pən\ *n, pl* **tarpon** or **tarpons** : a large silvery bony fish often caught for sport in the warm coastal waters of the Atlantic esp. off Florida

tar·ra·gon \ˈtar-ə-gən\ *n* : a small widely cultivated perennial wormwood with aromatic leaves used as a seasoning; *also* : its leaves

¹tar·ry \ˈtar-ē\ *vb* **tar·ried; tar·ry·ing** **1 ♦** : to be tardy : DELAY; *esp* : to be slow in leaving **2 ♦** : to stay in or at a place

♦ [1] crawl, creep, dally, dawdle, delay, dillydally, drag, lag, linger, loiter, poke — more at DELAY ♦ [2] abide, dwell, hang around, remain, stay, stick around — more at STAY

²tar·ry \ˈtär-ē\ *adj* : of, resembling, or smeared with tar

tar sand *n* : sand or sandstone that is naturally soaked with the heavy sticky portions of petroleum

tar·sus \ˈtär-səs\ *n, pl* **tar·si** \-ˌsī\ [NL] : the part of a vertebrate foot between the metatarsus and the leg; *also* : the small bones that support this part — **tar·sal** \-səl\ *adj or n*

¹tart \ˈtärt\ *adj* **1 ♦** : agreeably sharp or acid to the taste **2 ♦** : marked by a biting, acrimonious, or cutting quality : CAUSTIC ⟨∼ comments⟩ — **tart·ly** *adv*

♦ [1] acid, sour, vinegary — more at SOUR ♦ [2] acrid, biting, caustic, cutting, mordant, pungent, sarcastic, satiric, scathing, sharp — more at SARCASTIC

²tart *n* **1** : a small pie or pastry shell containing jelly, custard, or fruit **2** : PROSTITUTE

tar·tan \ˈtärt-ᵊn\ *n* : a plaid textile design of Scottish origin usu. distinctively patterned to designate a particular clan

tar·tar \ˈtär-tər\ *n* **1** : a substance in the juice of grapes deposited (as in wine casks) as a reddish crust or sediment **2** : a crust on the teeth formed from plaque hardened by calcium salts

tar·tar sauce *or* **tar·tare sauce** \ˈtär-tər-\ *n* : mayonnaise with chopped pickles, olives, or capers

tart·ness \-nəs\ *n* ♦ : the quality or state of being tart

♦ acidity, acrimony, acuteness, asperity, bite, bitterness, edge, harshness, keenness, pungency, sharpness

¹task \ˈtask\ *n* [ME *taske,* fr. MF dial. *tasque,* fr. ML *tasca* tax or service imposed by a feudal superior, fr. *taxare* to tax] **1 ♦** : a piece of assigned work **2 ♦** : the action for which a person or thing is specially fitted or used or for which a thing exists

♦ [1] assignment, chore, duty, job, stint — more at CHORE ♦ [2] capacity, function, job, part, place, position, purpose, role, work — more at ROLE

²task *vb* : to oppress with great labor

task bar *n* : a strip of icons usu. at the bottom of a computer screen showing programs that may be used by selecting their icons

task force *n* : a temporary grouping to accomplish a particular objective

task·mas·ter \ˈtask-ˌmas-tər\ *n* ♦ : one that imposes a task or burdens another with labor

♦ boss, captain, chief, foreman, head, headman, helmsman, kingpin, leader, master — more at BOSS

¹tas·sel \ˈta-səl, ˈtä-\ *n* **1** : a hanging ornament made of a bunch of cords of even length fastened at one end **2** : something suggesting a tassel; *esp* : a male flower cluster of corn

²tassel *vb* **-seled** *or* **-selled; -sel·ing** *or* **-sel·ling** : to adorn with or put forth tassels

¹taste \ˈtāst\ *vb* **tast·ed; tast·ing** **1 ♦** : to become acquainted with by experience : EXPERIENCE **2** : to try or determine the flavor of by taking a bit into the mouth **3** : to eat or drink esp. in small quantities : SAMPLE **4** : to have a specific flavor ⟨the milk ∼s sour⟩ **5 ♦** : to perceive or recognize as if by the sense of taste

♦ [1] endure, experience, feel, have, know, see, suffer, sustain, undergo — more at EXPERIENCE ♦ [5] feel, perceive, scent, see, sense, smell — more at FEEL

²taste *n* **1 ♦** : a small amount tasted **2** : BIT; *esp* : a sample of experience **3** : the special sense that perceives and identifies sweet, sour, bitter, or salty qualities and is mediated by taste buds on the tongue **4** : a quality perceptible to the sense of taste; *also* : the sensation obtained from a substance in the mouth : FLAVOR **5** ♦ : individual preference **6** : critical judgment, discernment, or appreciation; *also* : aesthetic quality — **tast·er** *n*

♦ [1] bite, morsel, mouthful, nibble, tidbit — more at MORSEL ♦ [5] appetite, fancy, favor (*or* favour), fondness, like, liking, love, partiality, preference, relish, shine, use — more at LIKING

taste bud *n* : a sense organ mediating the sensation of taste

taste·ful \'tāst-fəl\ *adj* **1** : tasty **2** ♦ : having, exhibiting, or conforming to good taste — **taste·ful·ly** *adv*

♦ elegant, graceful, handsome, majestic, refined, stately — more at ELEGANT

taste·less \-ləs\ *adj* **1 a** ♦ : having no taste ⟨∼ vegetables⟩ **b** : arousing no interest **2** ♦ : not having or exhibiting good taste ⟨a ∼ joke⟩ ⟨∼ clothes⟩ — **taste·less·ly** *adv*

♦ [1a] flat, flavorless (*or* flavourless), insipid — more at INSIPID ♦ [2] coarse, common, crass, crude, rough, rude, uncouth, vulgar — more at COARSE ♦ [2] dowdy, inelegant, tacky, trashy, unfashionable, unstylish — more at TACKY

tast·i·ness \'tā-stē-nəs\ *n* ♦ : the quality or state of being tasty

♦ lusciousness, savor

tasty \'tā-stē\ *adj* **tast·i·er; -est** ♦ : pleasing to the taste : SAVORY ⟨a very ∼ meal⟩

♦ ambrosial, appetizing, delectable, delicious, flavorful (*or* flavourful), luscious, palatable, savory, scrumptious, toothsome, yummy — more at DELICIOUS

tat \'tat\ *vb* **tat·ted; tat·ting** : to work at or make by tatting

¹**tat·ter** \'ta-tər\ *vb* ♦ : to make or become ragged

♦ rend, rip, rive, shred, tear — more at TEAR

²**tatter** *n* **1** : a part torn and left hanging **2** *pl* : tattered clothing

tat·tered \'ta-tərd\ *adj* ♦ : torn into shreds

♦ ragged, ratty, seedy, shabby, threadbare, worn-out — more at RAGGED

tat·ter·sall \'ta-tər-ˌsȯl, -səl\ *n* : a pattern of colored lines forming squares on solid background; *also* : a fabric in a tattersall pattern

tat·ting \'ta-tiŋ\ *n* : a delicate handmade lace formed usu. by looping and knotting with a single thread and a small shuttle; *also* : the act or process of making such lace

tat·tle \'tat-ᵊl\ *vb* **tat·tled; tat·tling** **1** : CHATTER, PRATE **2** ♦ : to tell secrets; *also* : to inform against another

♦ blab, gossip, talk — more at GOSSIP

tat·tler \'tat-lər, 'ta-tᵊl-ər\ *n* ♦ : one that tattles

♦ betrayer, blabbermouth, informer, rat, snitch, stool pigeon, tattletale — more at INFORMER

tat·tle·tale \'tat-ᵊl-ˌtāl\ *n* ♦ : one that tattles : INFORMER

♦ betrayer, blabbermouth, informer, rat, snitch, stool pigeon, tattler — more at INFORMER

¹**tat·too** \ta-'tü\ *n, pl* **tattoos** [alter. of earlier *taptoo*, fr. D *taptoe*, fr. the phrase *tap toe!* taps shut!] **1** : a call sounded before taps as notice to go to quarters **2** : a rapid rhythmic rapping

²**tattoo** *vb* : to mark (the skin) with tattoos

³**tattoo** *n, pl* **tattoos** [Tahitian *tatau*] : an indelible figure fixed upon the body esp. by insertion of pigment under the skin

tau \'taù, 'tȯ\ *n* : the 19th letter of the Greek alphabet — T or τ

taught *past and past part of* TEACH

¹**taunt** \'tȯnt\ *n* : a sarcastic challenge or insult

²**taunt** *vb* ♦ : to reproach or challenge in a mocking manner : jeer at ⟨the children ∼*ed* each other⟩

♦ bait, bug, hassle, heckle, needle, ride, tease — more at TEASE

taunt·er \'tȯn-tər, 'tän-\ *n* ♦ : one that taunts

♦ heckler, mocker, quiz, scoffer, tease — more at QUIZ

taupe \'tōp\ *n* : a brownish gray

Tau·rus \'tȯr-əs\ *n* [L, lit., bull] **1** : a zodiacal constellation between Aries and Gemini usu. pictured as a bull **2** : the 2d sign of the zodiac in astrology; *also* : one born under this sign

taut \'tȯt\ *adj* **1** ♦ : tightly drawn : not slack **2** : extremely nervous : TENSE **3** : TRIM, TIDY ⟨a ∼ ship⟩ — **taut·ly** *adv* — **taut·ness** *n*

♦ rigid, tense, tight; *also* firm, inflexible, stiff, tightened, unyielding **Ant** lax, loose, slack

tau·tol·o·gy \tȯ-'tä-lə-jē\ *n, pl* **-gies** : needless repetition of an idea, statement, or word; *also* : an instance of such repetition — **tau·to·log·i·cal** \ˌtȯt-ᵊl-'ä-ji-kəl\ *adj* — **tau·to·log·i·cal·ly** \-ji-k(ə-)lē\ *adv* — **tau·tol·o·gous** \tȯ-'tä-lə-gəs\ *adj* — **tau·tol·o·gous·ly** *adv*

tav·ern \'ta-vərn\ *n* [ME *taverne*, fr. AF, fr. L *taberna* hut, shop] **1** : an establishment where alcoholic liquors are sold to be drunk on the premises **2** ♦ : an establishment for the lodging and entertaining of travelers : INN

♦ [1] bar, barroom, café, pub, public house, saloon — more at BARROOM ♦ [2] hospice, hotel, inn, lodge, public house — more at HOTEL

taw \'tȯ\ *n* **1** : a marble used as a shooter **2** : the line from which players shoot at marbles

taw·dry \'tȯ-drē\ *adj* **taw·dri·er; -est** [*tawdry lace* a tie of lace for the neck, fr. *St. Audrey* (St. Etheldreda) †679 queen of Northumbria] ♦ : cheap and gaudy in appearance and quality ⟨∼ decorations⟩ — **taw·dri·ly** *adv*

♦ flamboyant, flashy, garish, gaudy, glitzy, loud, ostentatious, swank — more at GAUDY

taw·ny \'tȯ-nē\ *adj* **taw·ni·er; -est** : of a brownish orange color

¹**tax** \'taks\ *vb* **1** : to levy a tax on **2** : CHARGE, ACCUSE **3** ♦ : to put under pressure — **tax·able** \'tak-sə-bəl\ *adj* — **tax·a·tion** \tak-'sā-shən\ *n*

♦ strain, stretch, test, try

²**tax** *n* **1** ♦ : a charge usu. of money imposed by authority on persons or property for public purposes **2** : a heavy charge : STRAIN

♦ assessment, duty, impost, levy; *also* excise, income tax, poll tax, tariff, toll, tribute, withholding tax; surcharge, surtax; revenue

¹**taxi** \'tak-sē\ *n, pl* **tax·is** \-sēz\ *also* **tax·ies** : an automobile that carries passengers for a fare usu. based on the distance traveled : TAXICAB; *also* : a similarly operated boat or aircraft

²**taxi** *vb* **tax·ied; taxi·ing** *or* **taxy·ing; tax·is** *or* **tax·ies** **1** : to move along the ground or on the water under an aircraft's own power when starting or after a landing **2** : to go by taxicab

taxi·cab \'tak-sē-ˌkab\ *n* ♦ : an automobile that carries passengers for a fare usu. based on the distance traveled

♦ hack, taxi; *also* hackney; limousine; rickshaw

taxi·der·my \'tak-sə-ˌdər-mē\ *n* : the skill or occupation of preparing, stuffing, and mounting skins of animals — **taxi·der·mist** \-mist\ *n*

tax·ing \'tak-siŋ\ *adj* ♦ : involving, imposing, or constituting a burden

♦ arduous, burdensome, challenging, demanding, exacting, grueling, laborious, onerous, toilsome — more at DEMANDING

tax·on \'tak-ˌsän\ *n, pl* **taxa** \-sə\; *also* **taxons** : a taxonomic group or entity

tax·on·o·my \tak-'sä-nə-mē\ *n* : classification esp. of animals or plants according to natural relationships — **tax·o·nom·ic** \ˌtak-sə-'nä-mik\ *adj* — **tax·on·o·mist** \tak-'sä-nə-mist\ *n*

tax·pay·er \'taks-ˌpā-ər\ *n* : one who pays or is liable for a tax — **tax·pay·ing** *adj*

Tay–Sachs disease \'tā-'saks-\ *n* : a hereditary disorder caused by the absence of an enzyme needed to break down fatty material, marked by buildup of lipids in nervous tissue, and causing death in childhood

tb *abbr* tablespoon; tablespoonful

Tb *symbol* terbium

TB \ˌtē-ˈbē\ *n* : TUBERCULOSIS

TBA *abbr, often not cap* to be announced

T–bar \ˈtē-ˌbär\ *n* : a ski lift with a series of T-shaped bars

tbs *or* **tbsp** *abbr* tablespoon; tablespoonful

Tc *symbol* technetium

TC *abbr* teachers college

T cell *n* : any of several lymphocytes (as a helper T cell) specialized esp. for activity in and control of immunity and the immune response

tchotch·ke \ˈchäch-kə, -kē\ *n* [Yiddish *tshatshke*] ♦ : a small object used for decoration

 ♦ bauble, curiosity, gewgaw, knickknack, novelty, trinket — KNICKKNACK

TCP/IP \ˌtē-(ˌ)sē-ˈpē-ˌī-ˈpē\ *n* [*transmission control protocol/Internet protocol*] : a set of communications protocols used over networks and esp. the Internet

TD *abbr* 1 touchdown 2 Treasury Department

TDD *abbr* telecommunications device for the deaf

TDY *abbr* temporary duty

Te *symbol* tellurium

tea \ˈtē\ *n* [Chin (dialect of Fujian province) *dé*] 1 : the cured leaves and leaf buds of a shrub grown chiefly in China, Japan, India, and Sri Lanka; *also* : this shrub 2 : a drink made by steeping tea in boiling water 3 : refreshments usu. including tea served in late afternoon; *also* : a reception at which tea is served

teach \ˈtēch\ *vb* **taught** \ˈtȯt\; **teach·ing** 1 ♦ : to cause to know something : act as a teacher 2 : to show how ⟨~ her to swim⟩ 3 : to make to know the disagreeable consequences of an action 4 : to guide the studies of 5 : to impart the knowledge of ⟨~ math⟩ — **teach·able** *adj*

 ♦ educate, indoctrinate, instruct, school, train, tutor; *also* coach, drill, fit, ground, mentor, prepare, prime, qualify; direct, guide, lead, rear; catechize, lecture, moralize, preach; implant, inculcate, instill; homeschool; edify, enlighten; brief, familiarize, impart (to), inform, verse; initiate, introduce, show; reeducate, retrain

teach·er \ˈtē-chər\ *n* ♦ : one that teaches; *esp* : one whose occupation is to instruct

 ♦ educator, instructor, pedagogue, schoolteacher; *also* headmaster, master, schoolmaster; headmistress, schoolmarm, schoolmistress; coach, guide, guru, trainer; mentor, tutor; drillmaster; dean, don, professor; pedant; governess, homeschooler; catechist, lecturer, moralizer, preacher

teach·ing *n* 1 ♦ : the act, practice, or profession of a teacher 2 : something taught; *esp* : DOCTRINE

 ♦ education, instruction, training, tutelage — more at EDUCATION

tea·cup \ˈtē-ˌkəp\ *n* : a small cup used with a saucer for hot beverages

teak \ˈtēk\ *n* : the hard durable yellowish brown wood of a tall tropical Asian timber tree related to the vervains; *also* : this tree

tea·ket·tle \ˈtē-ˌket-ᵊl\ *n* : a covered kettle with a handle and spout for boiling water

teal \ˈtēl\ *n, pl* **teal** *or* **teals** 1 : any of various small short= necked wild ducks 2 : a dark greenish blue color

¹team \ˈtēm\ *n* [ME *teme*, fr. OE *tēam* offspring, lineage, group of draft animals] 1 : two or more draft animals harnessed to the same vehicle or implement 2 ♦ : a number of persons associated in work or activity; *esp* : a group on one side in a match

 ♦ band, company, crew, gang, outfit, party, squad — more at GANG

²team *vb* 1 : to haul with or drive a team 2 ♦ : to form a team : join forces

 ♦ collaborate, concert, cooperate, join — more at CO-OPERATE

³team *adj* : of or performed by a team; *also* : marked by devotion to teamwork ⟨a ~ player⟩

team·mate \-ˌmāt\ *n* : a fellow member of a team

team·ster \ˈtēm-stər\ *n* : one who drives a team or truck

team·work \-ˌwərk\ *n* ♦ : the work or activity of a number of persons acting in close association as members of a unit

 ♦ collaboration, cooperation, coordination; *also* fellowship, partnership; community, symbiosis; synergism; communion, oneness, solidarity, togetherness

tea·pot \ˈtē-ˌpät\ *n* : a vessel with a spout for brewing and serving tea

¹tear \ˈtir\ *n* : a drop of the salty liquid that moistens the eye and inner side of the eyelids; *also, pl* : an act of weeping or grieving

²tear \ˈtir\ *vb* : to fill with or shed tears ⟨eyes ~ing in the wind⟩

³tear \ˈtar\ *vb* **tore** \ˈtōr\; **torn** \ˈtȯrn\; **tear·ing** 1 ♦ : to separate parts of or pull apart by force : REND 2 : LACERATE 3 : to disrupt by the pull of contrary forces 4 ♦ : to remove by force : WRENCH ⟨~ down a house⟩ 5 ♦ : to move or act with violence, haste, or force

 ♦ [1] rend, rip, rive, shred, tatter; *also* break, cleave, rupture, split; cut, gash, incise, lacerate, slash; butcher, dismember, dissect, hack, mangle ♦ [4] rip, wrench, wrest; *also* grab, nab, seize, snap (up); snatch; jerk, lop (off), nip; amputate, cut (off), dissever, sever; force, pry ♦ [5] barrel, career, course, dash, fly, hasten, hurry, race, rip, rocket, run, rush, shoot, speed, whirl, whisk, zip, zoom — more at HURRY

⁴tear \ˈtar\ *n* 1 : the act of tearing 2 ♦ : a hole or flaw made by tearing : RENT

 ♦ gash, laceration, rent, rip, slash, slit — more at GASH

tear down *vb* 1 a ♦ : to cause to decompose or disintegrate **b** : VILIFY, DENIGRATE ⟨trying to *tear down* his reputation⟩ 2 : to take apart : disassemble

 ♦ demolish, desolate, destroy, devastate, do in, ruin, shatter, smash, waste, wipe out, wreck — more at DESTROY

tear·ful \ˈtir-fəl\ *adj* 1 : flowing with or accompanied by tears ⟨~ entreaties⟩ 2 ♦ : causing tears ⟨a ~ eulogy⟩ — **tear·ful·ly** *adv*

 ♦ depressing, dismal, dreary, heartbreaking, melancholy, pathetic, sad, sorry — more at SAD

tear gas \ˈtir-\ *n* : a substance that on dispersion in the atmosphere blinds the eyes with tears — **tear gas** *vb*

tear-jerk·er \ˈtir-ˌjər-kər\ *n* : an extravagantly pathetic story, song, play, movie, or broadcast

¹tease \ˈtēz\ *vb* **teased; teas·ing** 1 : to disentangle and lay parallel by combing or carding ⟨~ wool⟩ 2 : to scratch the surface of (cloth) so as to raise a nap 3 a ♦ : to disturb or annoy by persistent irritating or provoking esp. in a petty or mischievous way **b** ♦ : to make fun of : KID 4 : to comb (hair) by taking a strand and pushing the short hairs toward the scalp with the comb

 ♦ [3a] bait, bug, hassle, heckle, needle, ride, taunt; *also* haze; gibe, mock, ridicule; annoy, bother, chafe, fret, gall, get, gnaw (at), irritate, nag, nettle, pester, trouble, vex; aggravate, exasperate, goad, test, try; aggrieve, agitate, bedevil, beleaguer, discomfort, disturb, perturb; badger, dog, hound; browbeat, bully, hector; harass, harry, persecute, plague, terrorize, torment, torture ♦ [3b] chaff, jive, josh, kid, rally, razz, rib, ride, roast; *also* banter, joke, fool, fun, jest, quip, wisecrack

²tease *n* 1 : the act of teasing or state of being teased 2 ♦ : one that teases

 ♦ heckler, mocker, quiz, scoffer, taunter — more at QUIZ ♦ annoyance, bother, gadfly, nuisance, persecutor, pest — more at NUISANCE

tea·sel \ˈtē-zəl\ *n* : a prickly herb or its flower head covered with stiff hooked bracts and used to raise the nap on cloth; *also* : an artificial device used for this purpose

tea·spoon \'tē-ˌspün\ *n* **1** : a small spoon suitable for stirring beverages **2** : a unit of measure equal to ⅙ fluid ounce (5 milliliters)
tea·spoon·ful \-ˌfúl\ *n, pl* **-spoonfuls** *also* **-spoons·ful** \-ˌspünz-ˌfúl\ : TEASPOON 2
teat \'tit, 'tēt\ *n* : the protuberance through which milk is drawn from an udder or breast
tech *abbr* **1** technical; technically; technician **2** technological; technology
tech·ne·tium \tek-'nē-shē-əm\ *n* : a radioactive metallic chemical element
tech·nic \'tek-nik, tek-'nēk\ *n* : TECHNIQUE 1
tech·ni·cal \'tek-ni-kəl\ *adj* [Gk *technikos* of art, skillful, fr. *technē* art, craft, skill] **1** : having special knowledge esp. of a mechanical or scientific subject ⟨~ experts⟩ **2** : of or relating to a particular and esp. a practical or scientific subject ⟨~ training⟩ **3** : according to a strict interpretation of the rules **4** : of or relating to technique — **tech·ni·cal·ly** \-k(ə-)lē\ *adv*
tech·ni·cal·i·ty \ˌtek-nə-'ka-lə-tē\ *n, pl* **-ties** **1** : a detail meaningful only to a specialist **2** : the quality or state of being technical
technical sergeant *n* : a noncommissioned officer in the air force ranking next below a master sergeant
tech·ni·cian \tek-'ni-shən\ *n* : a person who has acquired the technique of a specialized skill or subject
tech·nique \tek-'nēk\ *n* [F] **1** : the manner in which technical details are treated or basic physical movements are used **2** : technical methods **3** ♦ : a method of accomplishing a desired aim

♦ approach, fashion, form, manner, method, strategy, style, system, tack, tactics, way — more at METHOD

tech·noc·ra·cy \tek-'nä-krə-sē\ *n* : management of society by technical experts — **tech·no·crat** \'tek-nə-ˌkrat\ *n* — **tech·no·crat·ic** \ˌtek-nə-'kra-tik\ *adj*
tech·nol·o·gy \tek-'nä-lə-jē\ *n, pl* **-gies** : ENGINEERING; *also* : a manner of accomplishing a task using technical methods or knowledge — **tech·no·log·i·cal** \ˌtek-nə-'lä-ji-kəl\ *adj*
tec·ton·ics \tek-'tä-niks\ *n sing or pl* **1** : geological structural features **2** : geology dealing esp. with the faulting and folding of a planet or moon — **tec·ton·ic** \-nik\ *adj*
ted·dy bear \'te-dē-ˌbar\ *n* [*Teddy* Roosevelt; fr. a cartoon depicting the president sparing the life of a bear cub while hunting] : a stuffed toy bear
te·dious \'tē-dē-əs\ *adj* : tiresome because of length or dullness : BORING — **te·dious·ly** *adv* — **te·dious·ness** *n*
te·di·um \'tē-dē-əm\ *n* **1** : TEDIOUSNESS **2** ♦ : the state of being weary and restless through lack of interest : BOREDOM

♦ boredom, doldrums, ennui, listlessness, restlessness, tiredness, weariness — more at BOREDOM

¹**tee** \'tē\ *n* : a small mound or peg on which a golf ball is placed to be hit at the beginning of play on a hole; *also* : the area from which the ball is hit to begin play
²**tee** *vb* **teed; tee·ing** : to place (a ball) on a tee
teem \'tēm\ *vb* ♦ : to become filled to overflowing : ABOUND

♦ abound, brim, bulge, burst, crawl, swarm — more at ABOUND

teen \'tēn\ *n* : a teenage person : TEENAGER — **teen** *adj*
teen·age \'tē-ˌnāj\ *or* **teen·aged** \-ˌnājd\ *adj* : of, being, or relating to people in their teens — **teen·ag·er** \-ˌnā-jər\ *n*
teens \'tēnz\ *n pl* : the numbers 13 to 19 inclusive; *esp* : the years 13 to 19 in a person's life
tee·ny \'tē-nē\ *adj* **tee·ni·er; -est** ♦ : very small or diminutive : TINY

♦ atomic, infinitesimal, microscopic, miniature, minute, tiny, wee — more at TINY

teepee *var of* TEPEE
tee shirt *var of* T-SHIRT
tee·ter \'tē-tər\ *vb* **1** ♦ : to move unsteadily **2** ♦ : to move backward and forward or up and down **3 a** : to shift back and forth uncertainly ⟨~ on the brink of bankruptcy⟩ **b** ♦ : to waver in mind, will, or feeling ⟨~s between conformity and individuality⟩ — **teeter** *n*

♦ [1] careen, dodder, lurch, reel, stagger, totter — more at STAGGER ♦ [2] falter, rock, seesaw, sway, totter, waver, wobble; *also* flounder, lurch, stumble, toddle; quaver, tremble; careen, reel, stagger, weave ♦ [3b] falter, hang back, hesitate, shilly-shally, vacillate — more at HESITATE

teethe \'tēth\ *vb* **teethed; teeth·ing** : to experience the rising of one's teeth through the gums : to grow teeth
teething *n* : growth of the first set of teeth through the gums with its accompanying phenomena
tee·to·tal·er *or* **tee·to·tal·ler** \'tē-ˌtō-t⁹l-ər\ *n* : a person who practices complete abstinence from alcoholic drinks — **tee·to·tal** \'tē-ˌtō-t⁹l, -ˌtō-\ *adj* — **tee·to·tal·ism** \-⁹l-ˌi-zəm\ *n*
TEFL *abbr* teaching English as a foreign language
Te·ja·no \tā-'hä-(ˌ)nō\ *n, pl* **-nos** [MexSp, fr. *Tejas* Texas] : a Texan of Hispanic descent
tek·tite \'tek-ˌtīt\ *n* : a glassy body of probably meteoric origin
tel *abbr* **1** telegram **2** telegraph **3** telephone
tele·cast \'te-li-ˌkast\ *vb* **-cast** *also* **-cast·ed; -cast·ing** : to broadcast by television — **telecast** *n* — **tele·cast·er** *n*
tel·e·com \'te-li-ˌkäm\ *n* : TELECOMMUNICATION; *also* : the telecommunications industry
tele·com·mu·ni·ca·tion \ˌte-li-kə-ˌmyü-nə-'kā-shən\ *n* : communication at a distance (as by telephone or radio)
tele·com·mute \'te-li-kə-ˌmyüt\ *vb* : to work at home by the use of an electronic linkup with a central office
tele·con·fer·ence \'te-li-ˌkän-fə-rəns\ *n* : a conference among people remote from one another held using telecommunications — **tele·con·fer·enc·ing** *n*
teleg *abbr* telegraphy
tele·gen·ic \ˌte-lə-'je-nik, -'jē-\ *adj* : markedly attractive to television viewers
tele·gram \'te-lə-ˌgram\ *n* : a message sent by telegraph
¹**tele·graph** \-ˌgraf\ *n* : an electric apparatus or system for sending messages by a code over wires — **tele·graph·ic** \ˌte-lə-'gra-fik\ *adj*
²**telegraph** *vb* : to send or communicate by or as if by telegraph — **te·leg·ra·pher** \tə-'le-grə-fər\ *n*
te·leg·ra·phy \tə-'le-grə-fē\ *n* : the use or operation of a telegraph apparatus or system
tele·mar·ket·ing \ˌte-lə-'mär-kə-tiŋ\ *n* : the marketing of goods or services by telephone — **tele·mar·ket·er** \-tər\ *n*
te·lem·e·try \tə-'le-mə-trē\ *n* : the transmission esp. by radio of measurements made by automatic instruments to a distant station — **tele·me·ter** \'te-lə-ˌmē-tər\ *n*
tel·e·no·vela \ˌte-lə-nō-'ve-lä\ *n* : a soap opera televised in or from many Latin American countries
te·lep·a·thy \tə-'le-pə-thē\ *n* : apparent communication from one mind to another by extrasensory means — **tele·path·ic** \ˌte-lə-'pa-thik\ *adj* — **tele·path·i·cal·ly** \-thi-k(ə-)lē\ *adv*
¹**tele·phone** \'te-lə-ˌfōn\ *n* : an instrument for sending and receiving sounds over long distances by electricity
²**telephone** *vb* **-phoned; -phon·ing** **1** : to send or communicate by telephone **2** : to speak to or attempt to reach by telephone — **tele·phon·er** *n*

♦ call, dial — more at CALL

te·le·pho·ny \tə-'le-fə-nē, 'te-lə-ˌfō-\ *n* : use or operation of an apparatus for transmission of sounds as electrical signals between distant points — **tel·e·phon·ic** \ˌte-lə-'fä-nik\ *adj*
tele·pho·to \ˌte-lə-'fō-tō\ *adj* : being a camera lens giving a large image of a distant object — **tele·pho·tog·ra·phy** \-fə-'tä-grə-fē\ *n*
tele·play \'te-li-ˌplā\ *n* : a story prepared for television production
tele·print·er \'te-lə-ˌprin-tər\ *n* : TELETYPEWRITER
tele·prompt·er \'te-lə-ˌprämp-tər\ *n* : a device for displaying prepared text to a speaker or performer

¹tele·scope \'te-lə-ˌskōp\ n **1** : a cylindrical instrument equipped with lenses or mirrors for viewing distant objects **2** : RADIO TELESCOPE
²telescope vb **-scoped; -scop·ing 1** : to slide or pass or cause to slide or pass one within another like the sections of a collapsible hand telescope **2** : COMPRESS, CONDENSE
tele·scop·ic \ˌte-lə-'skä-pik\ adj **1** : of or relating to a telescope **2** : seen only by a telescope **3** : able to discern objects at a distance **4** : having parts that telescope — **tele·scop·i·cal·ly** \-pi-k(ə-)lē\ adv
tele·text \'te-lə-ˌtekst\ n : a system for broadcasting text over a television signal and displaying it on a decoder-equipped television
tele·thon \'te-lə-ˌthän\ n : a long television program usu. to solicit funds for a charity
tele·type·writ·er \ˌte-lə-'tīp-ˌrī-tər\ n : a printing device resembling a typewriter used to send and receive signals over telephone lines
tele·vise \'te-lə-ˌvīz\ vb **-vised; -vis·ing** : to broadcast by television
tele·vi·sion \'te-lə-ˌvi-zhən\ n [F télévision, fr. Gk tēle far, at a distance + F vision vision] : a system for transmitting images and sound by converting them into electrical or radio waves which are converted back into images and sound by a receiver; also : a television receiving set
¹tell \'tel\ vb **told** \'tōld\; **tell·ing 1** : to indicate or name by units or groups so as to find the total number of units involved : COUNT **2** ♦ : to relate in detail : NARRATE **3** : to give utterance to : SAY **4** ♦ : to make known **5** ♦ : to report to : INFORM **6** ♦ : to give an order to : DIRECT **7** : to find out by observing **8** : to have a marked effect **9** : to serve as evidence

♦ [2] describe, narrate, recite, recount, rehearse, relate, report; also deliver, give, state, utter, voice; detail, enumerate, itemize, particularize; disclose, divulge, reveal; delineate, depict, express, render, sketch ♦ [4] bare, disclose, discover, divulge, expose, reveal, spill, unbosom, uncloak, uncover, unmask, unveil — more at REVEAL ♦ [5] acquaint, advise, apprise, brief, clue, enlighten, familiarize, fill in, inform, instruct, wise — more at ENLIGHTEN ♦ [6] bid, boss, charge, command, direct, enjoin, instruct, order — more at COMMAND

²tell n : a behavior or mannerism that reveals someone's true thoughts or emotions
tell·er \'te-lər\ n **1** : one that relates : NARRATOR **2** : one that counts **3** : a bank employee handling money received or paid out
tell·ing \'te-liŋ\ adj ♦ : producing a marked effect : EFFECTIVE

♦ cogent, compelling, conclusive, convincing, decisive, effective, forceful, persuasive, satisfying, strong — more at COGENT

tell off vb : REPRIMAND, SCOLD
¹tell·tale \'tel-ˌtāl\ n **1** : one that informs against another : INFORMER **2** : something that serves to disclose : INDICATION
²telltale adj **1** : telling what one should hold secret or in confidence **2** ♦ : disclosing or indicating something often of a private or secret nature ⟨~ crumbs on the kitchen counter⟩

♦ denotative, indicative, significant — more at INDICATIVE

tel·lu·ri·um \tə-'lúr-ē-əm\ n : a chemical element used esp. in alloys
tel·net \'tel-ˌnet\ n : a telecommunications protocol for accessing and using a remote computer via a local computer — **telnet** vb
tem·blor \'tem-blər\ n [Sp, lit., trembling] : EARTHQUAKE
te·mer·i·ty \tə-'mer-ə-tē\ n, pl **-ties** ♦ : rash or presumptuous daring

♦ audacity, brass, brazenness, cheek, chutzpah, effrontery, gall, nerve, presumption, sauce, sauciness — more at EFFRONTERY

¹temp \'temp\ n **1** : TEMPERATURE **2** : a temporary worker
²temp abbr temporary
¹tem·per \'tem-pər\ vb **1** : to dilute or soften by the addition of something else ⟨~ justice with mercy⟩ **2** : to bring (as steel) to a desired hardness by reheating and cooling **3** : to toughen (glass) by gradual heating and cooling **4** : TOUGHEN **5** : TUNE
²temper n **1** : characteristic tone : TENDENCY **2** : the hardness or toughness of a substance ⟨~ of a knife blade⟩ **3** : a characteristic frame of mind : DISPOSITION **4** : calmness of mind : COMPOSURE **5** ♦ : state of feeling or frame of mind at a particular time **6** : heat of mind or emotion **7** ♦ : main or essential nature esp. as strongly marked and serving to distinguish — **tem·pered** \'tem-pərd\ adj

♦ [5] cheer, frame, humor (or humour), mode, mood, spirit — more at MOOD ♦ [7] air, atmosphere, aura, climate, flavor (or flavour), mood, note — more at AURA

tem·pera \'tem-pə-rə\ n [It] : a painting process using an albuminous or colloidal medium as a vehicle; also : a painting done in tempera
tem·per·a·ment \'tem-prə-mənt, -pər-mənt\ n **1** ♦ : characteristic or habitual inclination or mode of emotional response : DISPOSITION ⟨nervous ~⟩ **2** : excessive sensitiveness or irritability

♦ disposition, grain, nature, temper — more at DISPOSITION

tem·per·a·men·tal \ˌtem-prə-'ment-ᵊl, -pər-'ment-\ adj **1** ♦ : marked by excessive sensitivity and impulsive mood changes ⟨a ~ child⟩ **2** ♦ : unpredictable in behavior or performance ⟨a ~ computer⟩

♦ [1, 2] capricious, changeable, fickle, fluid, inconstant, mercurial, mutable, uncertain, unpredictable, unsettled, unstable, unsteady, variable, volatile — more at FICKLE

tem·per·ance \'tem-prəns, -pə-rəns\ n : habitual moderation in the indulgence of the appetites or passions; esp : moderation in or abstinence from the use of alcoholic beverages
tem·per·ate \'tem-prət, -pə-rət\ adj **1** : not extreme or excessive : MILD **2** : moderate in indulgence of appetite or desire **3** : moderate in the use of alcoholic beverages **4** ♦ : having a moderate climate

♦ balmy, clement, equable, gentle, mild, moderate — more at CLEMENT

temperate zone n, often cap T&Z : the region between the Tropic of Cancer and the arctic circle or between the Tropic of Capricorn and the antarctic circle
tem·per·a·ture \'tem-pər-ˌchùr, -prə-ˌchùr, -chər\ n **1** : degree of hotness or coldness of something (as air, water, or the body) as shown by a thermometer **2** : FEVER 1
tem·pest \'tem-pəst\ n [ME tempeste, fr. AF, ultim. fr. L tempestas season, weather, storm, fr. tempus time] **1** : a violent storm **2** ♦ : a violent commotion or agitation

♦ cataclysm, convulsion, paroxysm, storm, tumult, upheaval, uproar

tem·pes·tu·ous \tem-'pes-chə-wəs\ adj ♦ : of, involving, or resembling a tempest : STORMY — **tem·pes·tu·ous·ly** adv — **tem·pes·tu·ous·ness** n

♦ explosive, ferocious, fierce, furious, hot, rabid, rough, stormy, turbulent, violent, volcanic — more at VIOLENT ♦ bleak, dirty, foul, inclement, nasty, raw, rough, squally — more at FOUL

tem·plate \'tem-plət\ n : a gauge, mold, or pattern that functions as a guide to the form or structure of something being made
¹tem·ple \'tem-pəl\ n **1** : a building reserved for religious practice **2** : a place devoted to a special or exalted purpose
²temple n : the flattened space on each side of the forehead esp. of humans

tem·po \'tem-pō\ *n, pl* **tem·pi** \-(ˌ)pē\ *or* **tempos** [It, lit., time] **1** : the rate of speed of a musical piece or passage **2** : rate of motion or activity : PACE

¹tem·po·ral \'tem-pə-rəl\ *adj* **1** : of, relating to, or limited by time ⟨∼ and spatial bounds⟩ **2** ♦ : of or relating to earthly life or secular concerns ⟨∼ power⟩

♦ carnal, earthly, fleshly, material, mundane, terrestrial, worldly — more at EARTHLY ♦ nonreligious, profane, secular — more at PROFANE

²temporal *adj* : of or relating to the temples or the sides of the skull

¹tem·po·rary \'tem-pə-ˌrer-ē\ *adj* ♦ : lasting for a time only — **tem·po·rar·i·ly** \ˌtem-pə-'rer-ə-lē\ *adv*

♦ impermanent, interim, provisional, short-term; *also* acting; alternate, proxy, substitute; expedient, improvised, makeshift; intermediary, intermediate, transitional; ephemeral, short-lived, transitory; conditional, contingent, limited, qualified, tentative; replaceable, terminable *Ant* long-term, permanent

²temporary *n, pl* **-rar·ies** : one serving for a limited time
tem·po·rise *chiefly Brit var of* TEMPORIZE
tem·po·rize \'tem-pə-ˌrīz\ *vb* **-rized; -riz·ing** **1** : to adapt one's actions to the time or the dominant opinion : COMPROMISE **2** : to draw out matters so as to gain time — **tem·po·riz·er** *n*

tempt \'tempt\ *vb* **1** ♦ : to entice to do wrong by promise of pleasure or gain **2** : PROVOKE **3** : to risk the dangers of **4** : to induce to do something : INCITE — **tempt·er** *n* — **tempt·ing·ly** *adv*

♦ allure, beguile, decoy, entice, lead on, lure, seduce — more at LURE

temp·ta·tion \temp-'tā-shən\ *n* **1** ♦ : the act of tempting : the state of being tempted **2** ♦ : something that tempts

♦ enticement, lure, seduction, solicitation; *also* appeal, attraction; beckoning, invitation; inducement, influence, persuasion, power, sway

tempt·ress \'temp-trəs\ *n* : a woman who tempts
ten \'ten\ *n* **1** : one more than nine **2** : the 10th in a set or series **3** : something having 10 units — **ten** *adj or pron* — **tenth** \'tenth\ *adj or adv or n*
ten·a·ble \'te-nə-bəl\ *adj* ♦ : capable of being held, maintained, or defended — **ten·a·bil·i·ty** \ˌte-nə-'bi-lə-tē\ *n*

♦ defensible, justifiable, maintainable, supportable, sustainable; *also* rational, reasonable, sensible; acceptable, admissible, allowable, exceptionable, legitimate, passable, unobjectionable, viable; provable, verifiable *Ant* indefensible, unjustifiable, insupportable, untenable

te·na·cious \tə-'nā-shəs\ *adj* **1** : not easily pulled apart : COHESIVE, TOUGH ⟨a ∼ metal⟩ **2** ♦ : holding fast ⟨∼ of his rights⟩ **3** : RETENTIVE ⟨a ∼ memory⟩ — **te·na·cious·ly** *adv*

♦ dogged, insistent, patient, persevering, persistent, pertinacious — more at PERSISTENT

te·nac·i·ty \tə-'na-sə-tē\ *n* ♦ : the quality or state of being tenacious

♦ hardheadedness, mulishness, obduracy, obstinacy, peevishness, pertinacity, self-will, stubbornness — more at OBSTINACY

ten·an·cy \'te-nən-sē\ *n, pl* **-cies** : the temporary possession or occupancy of something (as a house) that belongs to another; *also* : the period of a tenant's occupancy
ten·ant \'te-nənt\ *n* **1** ♦ : one who rents or leases (as a house) from a landlord **2** : DWELLER, OCCUPANT — **tenant** *vb* — **ten·ant·less** *adj*

♦ boarder, lodger, renter, roomer; *also* roommate; guest, visitor; occupant, resident *Ant* landlord

tenant farmer *n* : a farmer who works land owned by another and pays rent either in cash or in shares of produce
Ten Commandments *n pl* : the commandments of God given to Moses on Mount Sinai
¹tend \'tend\ *vb* **1** : to apply oneself ⟨∼ to your affairs⟩

2 ♦ : to take care of ⟨∼ a plant⟩ **3** : to manage the operations of ⟨∼ a machine⟩

♦ attend, care, mind, oversee, superintend, supervise; *also* direct, manage; guard, patrol, protect, safeguard; baby, babysit, chaperon, mother, shepherd ♦ crop, cultivate, culture, grow, promote, raise, rear — more at GROW

²tend *vb* **1** : to move or develop one's course in a particular direction **2** ♦ : to show an inclination or tendency

♦ incline, lean, run, trend — more at LEAN

ten·den·cy \'ten-dən-sē\ *n, pl* **-cies** **1** ♦ : direction or approach toward a place, object, effect, or limit : TREND **2** ♦ : a proneness to or readiness for a particular kind of thought or action : PROPENSITY ⟨a ∼ to overreact⟩

♦ [1] current, drift, leaning, run, tide, trend, wind — more at TREND ♦ [2] aptness, bent, disposition, inclination, leaning, penchant, predilection, proclivity, proneness, propensity, way

ten·den·tious \ten-'den-chəs\ *adj* : marked by a tendency in favor of a particular point of view : BIASED ⟨∼ remarks⟩ — **ten·den·tious·ly** *adv* — **ten·den·tious·ness** *n*
¹ten·der \'ten-dər\ *adj* [ME, fr. AF *tendre*, fr. L *tener*] **1** : having a soft texture : easily broken, chewed, or cut **2** ♦ : physically weak : DELICATE; *also* : IMMATURE **3** ♦ : expressing or responsive to love or sympathy ⟨a ∼ smile⟩ **4** : SENSITIVE, TOUCHY **5** ♦ : delicate or soft in quality or tone — **ten·der·ly** *adv* — **ten·der·ness** *n*

♦ [2] delicate, fragile, frail, immature, sensitive; *also* breakable, brittle; flimsy, puny, soft, weak; perishable, resistless, susceptible, unresistant, vulnerable, yielding *Ant* tough ♦ [3] beneficent, benevolent, compassionate, good-hearted, humane, kind, kindly, loving, sympathetic, tenderhearted, warmhearted — more at HUMANE ♦ [5] balmy, benign, bland, delicate, gentle, light, mellow, mild, soft, soothing — more at GENTLE

²tender *n* [AF *tendre*, fr. *tendre*, v., to stretch, hold out, offer, fr. L *tendere* to stretch, direct] **1** : an offer or proposal made for acceptance; *esp* : an offer of a bid for a contract **2** ♦ : something (as money) that may be offered in payment

♦ cash, currency, dough, lucre, money, pelf — more at MONEY

³tender *vb* ♦ : to present for acceptance

♦ extend, give, offer, proffer — more at OFFER

⁴tend·er \'ten-dər\ *n* **1** : one that tends or takes care **2** : a boat carrying passengers and freight to a larger ship **3** : a car attached to a steam locomotive for carrying fuel and water
⁵tender *n* [prob. short for *tenderloin*] : a strip of meat (as of chicken breast) often breaded
ten·der·foot \'ten-dər-ˌfut\ *n, pl* **-feet** \-ˌfēt\ *also* **-foots** \-ˌfuts\ **1** : one not hardened to frontier or rough outdoor life **2** ♦ : an inexperienced beginner

♦ beginner, fledgling, freshman, greenhorn, neophyte, newcomer, novice, recruit, rookie, tyro — more at BEGINNER

ten·der·heart·ed \ˌten-dər-'här-təd\ *adj* ♦ : easily moved to love, pity, or sorrow

♦ beneficent, benevolent, compassionate, good-hearted, humane, kind, kindly, sympathetic, tender, warmhearted — more at HUMANE

ten·der·ize \'ten-də-ˌrīz\ *vb* **-ized; -iz·ing** : to make (meat) tender — **ten·der·iz·er** \'ten-də-ˌrī-zər\ *n*
ten·der·loin \'ten-dər-ˌlȯin\ *n* **1** : a tender strip of beef or pork from near the backbone **2** : a district of a city largely devoted to vice
ten·di·ni·tis *or* **ten·don·itis** \ˌten-də-'nī-təs\ *n* : inflammation of a tendon
ten·don \'ten-dən\ *n* : a tough cord of dense white fibrous tissue uniting a muscle with another part (as a bone) — **ten·di·nous** \-də-nəs\ *adj*
ten·dril \'ten-drəl\ *n* : a slender coiling organ by which some climbing plants attach themselves to a support

ten·e·brous \'te-nə-brəs\ *adj* : shut off from the light : GLOOMY, OBSCURE

ten·e·ment \'te-nə-mənt\ *n* **1** : a house used as a dwelling **2** : a building divided into apartments for rent to families; *esp* : one meeting only minimum standards of safety and comfort **3** : a room or set of rooms fitted esp. with housekeeping facilities and usu. leased as a dwelling : APARTMENT, FLAT

te·net \'te-nət\ *n* [L, he holds, fr. *tenēre* to hold] : one of the principles or doctrines held in common by members of a group (as a church or profession)

ten·fold \'ten-,fōld, -'fōld\ *adj* : being 10 times as great or as many — **ten·fold** \-'fōld\ *adv*

ten–gallon hat *n* : a wide-brimmed hat with a large soft crown

Tenn *abbr* Tennessee

ten·nes·sine \'te-nə-,sēn\ *n* : a short-lived artificially produced radioactive element

ten·nis \'te-nəs\ *n* : a game played with a ball and racket on a court divided by a net

ten·on \'te-nən\ *n* : a projecting part in a piece of material (as wood) for insertion into a mortise to make a joint

ten·or \'te-nər\ *n* **1** : the general drift of something spoken or written **2** : the highest natural adult male voice; *also* : a singer having this voice **3** : a continuing in a course, movement, or activity ⟨the ~ of my life⟩

tenpenny nail *n* : a nail three inches (about 7.6 centimeters) long

ten·pin \'ten-,pin\ *n* : a bottle-shaped bowling pin set in groups of 10 and bowled at in a game (**tenpins**)

¹tense \'tens\ *n* [ME *tens* time, tense, fr. MF, fr. L *tempus*] : distinction of form of a verb to indicate the time of the action or state

²tense *adj* **tens·er; tens·est** [L *tensus*, fr. pp. of *tendere* to stretch] **1** ♦ : stretched tight : TAUT **2 a** ♦ : feeling or showing nervous tension ⟨a ~ smile⟩ **b** ♦ : marked by strain or suspense ⟨a ~ movie⟩ — **tense·ly** *adv* — **tense·ness** *n* — **ten·si·ty** \'ten-sə-tē\ *n*

  ♦ [1] rigid, taut, tight — more at TAUT ♦ [2a] aflutter, anxious, edgy, jittery, jumpy, nervous, nervy, perturbed, troubled, uneasy, upset, worried — more at NERVOUS ♦ [2b] anxious, distressful, nervous, restless, unsettling, upsetting, worrisome — more at NERVOUS

³tense *vb* **tensed; tens·ing** : to make or become tense — often used with *up*

ten·sile \'ten-səl, -,sīl\ *adj* : of or relating to tension ⟨~ strength⟩

ten·sion \'ten-chən\ *n* **1** : the act of straining or stretching; *also* : the condition of being strained or stretched **2** ♦ : a state of mental unrest often with signs of bodily stress **3** : a state of latent hostility or opposition

  ♦ pressure, strain, stress — more at STRESS

ten–speed \'ten-,spēd\ *n* : a bicycle with a derailleur having 10 possible combinations of gears

¹tent \'tent\ *n* **1** ♦ : a collapsible shelter of material stretched and supported by poles **2** : a canopy placed over the head and shoulders to retain vapors or oxygen given for medical reasons

  ♦ canopy, ceiling, roof — more at CANOPY

²tent *vb* **1** : to lodge in tents **2** : to cover with or as if with a tent

ten·ta·cle \'ten-ti-kəl\ *n* : any of various long flexible projections about the head or mouth (as of an insect, mollusk, or fish) — **ten·ta·cled** \-kəld\ *adj* — **ten·tac·u·lar** \ten-'ta-kyə-lər\ *adj*

ten·ta·tive \'ten-tə-tiv\ *adj* **1** ♦ : not fully worked out or developed ⟨~ plans⟩ **2** : HESITANT, UNCERTAIN ⟨a ~ smile⟩ — **ten·ta·tive·ly** *adv*

  ♦ conditional, contingent, qualified

ten·u·ous \'ten-yə-wəs\ *adj* **1** : not dense : RARE ⟨a ~ fluid⟩ **2** : not thick : SLENDER ⟨a ~ rope⟩ **3** : having little substance : FLIMSY, WEAK ⟨~ influences⟩ **4** : lacking stability : SHAKY ⟨~ reasoning⟩ — **te·nu·i·ty** \te-'nü-ə-tē, tə-, -'nyü-\ *n* — **ten·u·ous·ly** *adv* — **ten·u·ous·ness** *n*

ten·ure \'ten-yər\ *n* ♦ : the act, right, manner, or period of holding something (as a landed property, an office, or a position)

  ♦ hitch, stint, term, tour — more at TERM

ten·ured \'ten-yərd\ *adj* : having tenure ⟨~ faculty members⟩

te·o·sin·te \,tā-ō-'sin-tē\ *n* : a tall annual grass of Mexico that is closely related to and usu. considered ancestral to corn

te·pee *or* **tee·pee** \'tē-(,)pē\ *n* [Dakota *tʰípi*, fr. *tʰi-* to dwell] : an American Indian conical tent usu. of skins

tep·id \'te-pəd\ *adj* **1** : moderately warm : LUKEWARM **2** ♦ : marked by an absence of enthusiasm or conviction : HALFHEARTED

  ♦ halfhearted, uneager, unenthusiastic; *also* apathetic, disinterested, dispassionate, indifferent, neutral, uninterested; lackadaisical, languid, listless, perfunctory, undemonstrative, unemotional, unresponsive; unfeeling, unsympathetic; chill, chilly, cold, cool, frigid, frosty, glacial, icy, unfriendly, wintry *Ant* eager, enthusiastic, hearty, keen, passionate, warm, wholehearted

te·qui·la \tə-'kē-lə, tā-\ *n* : a Mexican liquor distilled from an agave's sap

ter *abbr* **1** terrace **2** territory

tera·byte \'ter-ə-,bīt\ *n* [*tera-* trillion (10¹²), fr. Gk *terat-, teras* monster] : 1024 gigabytes; *also* : one trillion bytes

ter·bi·um \'tər-bē-əm\ *n* : a metallic chemical element

ter·cen·te·na·ry \,tər-,sen-'te-nə-rē, tər-'sent-°n-,er-ē\ *n, pl* **-ries** : a 300th anniversary or its celebration — **tercentenary** *adj*

ter·cen·ten·ni·al \,tər-,sen-'te-nē-əl\ *adj or n* : TERCENTENARY

te·re·do \tə-'rē-dō, -'rā-\ *n, pl* **-dos** [L] : SHIPWORM

ter·i·ya·ki \,ter-ē-'yä-kē\ *n* [Jp] : a Japanese dish of meat or fish soaked in a soy marinade and cooked

¹term \'tərm\ *n* **1** : END, TERMINATION **2 a** : a limited or definite extent of time : DURATION **b** ♦ : the time for which something lasts ⟨~ of office⟩ ⟨lost money in the short ~⟩ **3** : a mathematical expression connected with another by a plus or minus sign; *also* : an element (as a numerator) of a fraction or proportion **4** : a word or expression that has a precise meaning in some uses or is limited to a particular subject or field **5** *pl* : PROVISIONS, CONDITIONS ⟨~s of a contract⟩ **6** *pl* : mutual relationship ⟨on good ~s⟩ **7** : AGREEMENT, CONCORD

  ♦ hitch, stint, tenure, tour; *also* shift, watch; go, turn; duration, standing, time; cycle, span, spell, stretch; life, lifetime

²term *vb* ♦ : to apply a term to : CALL

  ♦ baptize, call, christen, denominate, designate, dub, entitle, label, name, style, title — more at NAME

ter·ma·gant \'tər-mə-gənt\ *n* ♦ : an overbearing or nagging woman : SHREW

  ♦ fury, harpy, shrew, virago — more at SHREW

¹ter·mi·nal \'tər-mən-°l\ *adj* **1** ♦ : of, relating to, or forming an end, limit, or terminus **2** : FATAL 2 ⟨~ cancer⟩; *also* : being in or relating to the final stages of a fatal disease ⟨a ~ patient⟩ — **ter·mi·nal·ly** *adv*

  ♦ final, hindmost, last, latter, ultimate — more at LAST

²terminal *n* **1** : EXTREMITY, END **2** : a device at the end of a wire or on electrical equipment for making a connection **3** : either end of a transportation line (as a railroad) with its offices and freight and passenger stations; *also* : a freight or passenger station **4** : a device (as in a computer system) for data entry and display

ter·mi·nate \'tər-mə-,nāt\ *vb* **-nat·ed; -nat·ing** **1** ♦ : to bring or come to an end **2** ♦ : to serve as an ending, limit, or boundary of — **ter·mi·na·ble** \-nə-bəl\ *adj* — **ter·mi·na·tor** \'tər-mə-,nā-tər\ *n*

  ♦ [1] close, conclude, end, finish, round, wind up, wrap up — more at CLOSE ♦ [1] break off, break up, cease, die, discontinue, elapse, expire, halt, lapse, leave off, let up, pass, quit, stop — more at CEASE ♦ [2] bound, circumscribe, define, delimit, demarcate, limit, mark — more at LIMIT

ter·mi·na·tion \ˌtər-mə-'nā-shən\ *n* **1** ♦ : end in time or existence **2** ♦ : the act of terminating **3** ♦ : a limit in space or extent

♦ [1] death, demise, expiration — more at DEATH ♦ [2] cessation, close, closure, conclusion, end, ending, expiration, finish, halt, lapse, shutdown, stop, stoppage — more at END ♦ [3] bound, boundary, ceiling, confines, end, extent, limit, limitation, line — more at LIMIT

ter·mi·nol·o·gy \ˌtər-mə-'nä-lə-jē\ *n, pl* **-gies** ♦ : the technical or special terms used in a business, art, science, or special subject

♦ argot, cant, jargon, language, lingo, slang, vocabulary; *also* colloquialism, dialect, idiom, parlance, patois, pidgin, provincialism, speech, vernacular; journalese

ter·mi·nus \'tər-mə-nəs\ *n, pl* **-ni** \-ˌnī\ *or* **-nus·es** [L] **1** : final goal : END **2** : either end of a transportation line or travel route; *also* : the station or city at such a place

ter·mite \'tər-ˌmīt\ *n* : any of numerous pale soft-bodied social insects that feed on wood

tern \'tərn\ *n* : any of various chiefly marine birds with narrow wings and often a forked tail

ter·na·ry \'tər-nə-rē\ *adj* **1** : of, relating to, or proceeding by threes **2** : having three elements or parts

terr *abbr* territory

¹**ter·race** \'ter-əs\ *n* **1** : a flat roof or open platform **2** : a level area next to a building **3** : an embankment with level top **4** : a bank or ridge on a slope to conserve moisture and soil **5** : a row of houses on raised land; *also* : a street with such a row of houses **6** : a strip of park in the middle of a street

²**terrace** *vb* **ter·raced; ter·rac·ing** : to form into a terrace or supply with terraces

ter·ra–cot·ta \ˌter-ə-'kä-tə\ *n* [It *terra cotta*, lit., baked earth] : a reddish brown earthenware

terra fir·ma \-'fər-mə\ *n* [NL] ♦ : solid ground

♦ dirt, dust, earth, ground, land, soil — more at EARTH

ter·rain \tə-'rān\ *n* : the surface features of an area of land ⟨a rough ∼⟩

ter·ra in·cog·ni·ta \ˌter-ə-ˌin-ˌkäg-'nē-tə\ *n, pl* **ter·rae in·cog·ni·tae** \'ter-ˌī-ˌin-ˌkäg-'nē-tī\ [L] : an unexplored area or field of knowledge

ter·ra·pin \'ter-ə-pən\ *n* : any of various turtles of fresh or brackish water

ter·rar·i·um \tə-'rar-ē-əm\ *n, pl* **-ia** \-ē-ə\ *or* **-i·ums** : a usu. transparent enclosure for keeping or raising plants or small animals indoors

ter·res·tri·al \tə-'res-trē-əl\ *adj* **1** ♦ : of or relating to the earth or its inhabitants **2** : living or growing on land ⟨∼ plants⟩

♦ carnal, earthly, fleshly, material, mundane, temporal, worldly — more at EARTHLY

ter·ri·ble \'ter-ə-bəl\ *adj* **1** ♦ : exciting terror or alarm : DREADFUL **2** : hard to bear : DISTRESSING ⟨a ∼ situation⟩ **3** : extreme in degree : INTENSE ⟨∼ heat⟩ **4** ♦ : of very poor quality : AWFUL ⟨a ∼ play⟩ **5** ♦ : strongly repulsive

♦ [1] dire, dreadful, fearful, fearsome, forbidding, formidable, frightful, hair-raising, horrible, redoubtable, scary, shocking, terrifying — more at FEARFUL ♦ [4] atrocious, awful, cheap, execrable, lousy, punk, rotten, wretched ♦ [5] appalling, ghastly, grisly, gruesome, hideous, horrible, lurid, macabre, monstrous, nightmarish, shocking — more at HORRIBLE

ter·ri·bly \'ter-ə-blē\ *adv* : to an extreme degree : VERY

ter·ri·er \'ter-ē-ər\ *n* [ME *terryer, terrer*, fr. AF (*chen*) *terrer*, lit., earth dog, fr. *terre* earth, fr. L *terra*] : any of various usu. small energetic dogs orig. used by hunters to drive small game animals from their holes

ter·rif·ic \tə-'ri-fik\ *adj* **1** : exciting terror ⟨a ∼ explosion⟩ **2** : EXTRAORDINARY, ASTOUNDING ⟨∼ speed⟩ **3** ♦ : unusually good ⟨makes ∼ chili⟩

♦ A1, excellent, fabulous, fine, marvelous, sensational, splendid, superb, superior, wonderful — more at EXCELLENT

ter·ri·fied \'ter-ə-ˌfīd\ *adj* ♦ : filled with fear or anxiety

♦ afraid, aghast, fearful, scared — more at AFRAID

ter·ri·fy \'ter-ə-ˌfī\ *vb* **-fied; -fy·ing** ♦ : to fill with terror : FRIGHTEN

♦ alarm, frighten, horrify, panic, scare, shock, spook, startle, terrorize — more at FRIGHTEN

terrifying *adj* ♦ : causing terror or apprehension — **ter·ri·fy·ing·ly** *adv*

♦ dire, dreadful, fearful, fearsome, forbidding, formidable, frightful, hair-raising, horrible, redoubtable, scary, shocking, terrible — more at FEARFUL

ter·ri·to·ry \'ter-ə-ˌtōr-ē\ *n, pl* **-ries** **1** : a geographic area belonging to or under the jurisdiction of a governmental authority **2** : a part of the U.S. not included within any state but organized with a separate legislature **3** : REGION, DISTRICT; *also* : a region in which one feels at home **4** : a field of knowledge or interest **5** : an assigned area **6** ♦ : an area occupied and defended by one or a group of animals — **ter·ri·to·ri·al** \ˌter-ə-'tōr-ē-əl\ *adj*

♦ habitat, home, niche, range — more at HOME

ter·ror \'ter-ər\ *n* **1** ♦ : a state of intense fear : FRIGHT **2** : one that inspires fear

♦ alarm, anxiety, apprehension, dread, fear, fright, horror, panic, trepidation — more at FEAR

ter·ror·ism \'ter-ər-ˌi-zəm\ *n* : the systematic use of terror esp. as a means of coercion — **ter·ror·ist** \-ist\ *adj or n*

ter·ror·ize \'ter-ər-ˌīz\ *vb* **-ized; -iz·ing** **1** ♦ : to fill with terror : SCARE **2** : to coerce by threat or violence

♦ alarm, frighten, horrify, panic, scare, shock, spook, startle, terrify — more at FRIGHTEN

ter·ry \'ter-ē\ *n, pl* **terries** : an absorbent fabric with a loose pile of uncut loops

terse \'tərs\ *adj* **ters·er; ters·est** [L *tersus* clean, neat, fr. pp. of *tergēre* to wipe off] ♦ : effectively brief : CONCISE

♦ brief, compact, compendious, concise, crisp, epigrammatic, laconic, pithy, succinct, summary — more at CONCISE

terse·ly \-lē\ *adv* ♦ : in a terse manner

♦ compactly, concisely, crisply, laconically, shortly, succinctly, summarily — more at SHORTLY

terse·ness \-nəs\ *n* ♦ : the quality or state of being terse

♦ brevity, briefness, compactness, conciseness, crispness, succinctness — more at SUCCINCTNESS

ter·tia·ry \'tər-shē-ˌer-ē\ *adj* **1** : of third rank, importance, or value **2** *cap* : of, relating to, or being the earlier period of the Cenozoic era **3** : occurring in or being the third stage ⟨∼ medical care⟩

Tertiary *n* : the Tertiary period

TESL *abbr* teaching English as a second language

TESOL *abbr* Teachers of English to Speakers of Other Languages

¹**test** \'test\ *n* [ME, vessel in which metals were assayed, potsherd, fr. AF, pot, fr. L *testum* earthen vessel] **1** ♦ : a critical examination or evaluation **2** ♦ : a means or result of testing

♦ [1] experiment, trial — more at EXPERIMENT ♦ [2] examination, quiz — more at EXAMINATION

²**test** *vb* **1** ♦ : to put to test : TRY **2** : to undergo or score on tests

♦ strain, stretch, tax, try

³**test** *adj* : relating to or used in testing ⟨a ∼ group⟩

tes·ta·ment \'tes-tə-mənt\ *n* **1** *cap* : either of two main divisions of Christian Scripture **2** ♦ : a tangible proof or tribute : EVIDENCE **3** : CREED **4** : the legal instructions for the disposition of one's property after death : WILL — **tes·ta·men·ta·ry** \ˌtes-tə-'men-tə-rē\ *adj*

♦ attestation, confirmation, corroboration, documentation, evidence, proof, substantiation, testimony, validation, witness — more at PROOF

tes·tate \'tes-ˌtāt, -tət\ *adj* : having left a valid will

tes·ta·tor \'tes-ˌtā-tər, tes-'tā-\ *n* : a person who dies leaving a valid will

tes·ta·trix \tes-'tā-triks\ *n* : a woman who is a testator

¹tes·ter \'tēs-tər, 'tes-\ *n* : a canopy over a bed, pulpit, or altar

²test·er \'tes-tər\ *n* : one that tests

tes·ti·cle \'tes-ti-kəl\ *n* : TESTIS; *esp* : one of a mammal usu. with its enclosing structures — **tes·tic·u·lar** *adj*

tes·ti·fy \'tes-tə-ˌfī\ *vb* **-fied; -fy·ing** **1** : to make a statement based on personal knowledge or belief : bear witness **2** : to serve as evidence or proof **3** ♦ : to make a solemn declaration under oath for the purpose of establishing a fact (as in a court) **4** ♦ : to bear witness to : ATTEST

♦ [3] attest, depose, swear, witness; *also* vouch; vow, promise ♦ *usu* **testify to** [4] attest, authenticate, avouch, certify, vouch, witness — more at CERTIFY

tes·ti·mo·ni·al \ˌtes-tə-'mō-nē-əl\ *n* **1** : a statement testifying to benefits received; *also* : a character reference **2** : an expression of appreciation : TRIBUTE — **testimonial** *adj*

tes·ti·mo·ny \'tes-tə-ˌmō-nē\ *n, pl* **-nies** **1** ♦ : evidence based on observation or knowledge **2** : an outward sign : SYMBOL **3** : a solemn declaration made by a witness under oath esp. in a court

♦ attestation, confirmation, corroboration, documentation, evidence, proof, substantiation, testament, validation, witness — more at PROOF

tes·tis \'tes-təs\ *n, pl* **tes·tes** \'tes-ˌtēz\ [L, witness, testis] : a typically paired male reproductive gland that produces sperm and testosterone and that in most mammals is contained within the scrotum at sexual maturity

tes·tos·ter·one \te-'stäs-tə-ˌrōn\ *n* : a male sex hormone causing development of the male reproductive system and secondary sex characteristics

test tube *n* : a glass tube closed at one end and used esp. in chemistry and biology

tes·ty \'tes-tē\ *adj* **tes·ti·er; -est** [ME *testif*, fr. Anglo-French (the French of medieval England), headstrong, fr. OF *teste* head, fr. LL *testa* skull, fr. L, shell] ♦ : easily annoyed; *also* : marked by ill humor

♦ choleric, crabby, cranky, cross, crotchety, grouchy, grumpy, irascible, irritable, peevish, perverse, petulant, short-tempered, snappish, snappy, snippy, waspish — more at IRRITABLE

tet·a·nus \'tet-ᵊn-əs\ *n* : an infectious disease caused by bacterial poisons and marked by muscle stiffness and spasms esp. of the jaws — **tet·a·nal** \-əl\ *adj*

tetchy \'te-chē\ *adj* **tetchi·er; -est** : irritably or peevishly sensitive

¹tête-à-tête \'tāt-ə-ˌtāt\ *n* [F, lit., head to head] : a private conversation between two persons

²tête-à-tête \ˌtāt-ə-'tāt\ *adv* : in private

³tête-à-tête \'tāt-ə-ˌtāt\ *adj* : being face-to-face : PRIVATE

¹teth·er \'te-thər\ *n* **1** : something (as a rope) by which an animal is fastened **2** : the limit of one's strength or resources

²tether *vb* : to fasten or restrain by or as if by a tether

tet·ra·eth·yl lead \ˌte-trə-'e-thəl-\ *n* : a heavy oily poisonous liquid used esp. formerly as an antiknock agent in gasoline

tet·ra·he·dron \-'hē-drən\ *n, pl* **-drons** *or* **-dra** \-drə\ : a polyhedron that has four faces — **tet·ra·he·dral** \-drəl\ *adj*

tet·ra·hy·dro·can·nab·i·nol \-ˌhī-drə-kə-'na-bə-ˌnȯl, -ˌnōl\ *n* : THC

te·tram·e·ter \te-'tra-mə-tər\ *n* : a line of verse consisting of four metrical feet

Teu·ton·ic \tü-'tä-nik, tyü-\ *adj* : GERMANIC

Tex *abbr* Texas

Tex–Mex \'teks-'meks\ *adj* : characteristic of Mexican-American culture and esp. that of southern Texas

¹text \'tekst\ *n* **1** : the actual words of an author's work **2** : the main body of printed or written matter on a page **3** : a scriptural passage chosen as the subject esp. of a sermon **4** : THEME, TOPIC **5** : matter handled with a computer that is chiefly in the form of words **6** : TEXTBOOK **7** : TEXT MESSAGE — **tex·tu·al** \'teks-chə-wəl\ *adj*

²text *vb* : to communicate by text messaging — **texting** *n*

text·book \'tekst-ˌbu̇k\ *n* ♦ : a book used in the study of a subject

♦ handbook, manual, primer; *also* grammar, reader, speller; tract, treatise; dictionary, lexicon, vocabulary, wordbook; encyclopedia, reference; bible, guide, guidebook

tex·tile \'tek-ˌstīl, 'tekst-ᵊl\ *n* : CLOTH; *esp* : a woven or knit cloth

text message *n* : a short message sent electronically usu. from one cell phone to another

text messaging *n* : the sending of short text messages electronically esp. from one cell phone to another

tex·ture \'teks-chər\ *n* **1** : the visual or tactile surface characteristics and appearance of something ⟨a coarse ∼⟩ **2** : essential part **3** : basic scheme or structure : FABRIC **4** : overall structure

TGIF *abbr* thank God it's Friday

¹Th *abbr* Thursday

²Th *symbol* thorium

²-th *or* **-eth** *adj suffix* — used in forming ordinal numbers ⟨hundred*th*⟩

³-th *n suffix* **1** : act or process **2** : state or condition ⟨dear*th*⟩

Thai \'tī\ *n, pl* **Thai** *or* **Thais** **1** : a native or inhabitant of Thailand **2** : the official language of Thailand — **Thai** *adj*

thal·a·mus \'tha-lə-məs\ *n, pl* **-mi** \-ˌmī\ [NL] : a subdivision of the brain that serves as a relay station to and from the cerebral cortex and functions in arousal and the integration of sensory information

thal·as·se·mia \ˌtha-lə-'sē-mē-ə\ *n* : any of a group of inherited disorders of hemoglobin synthesis

tha·las·so·ther·a·py \thə-ˌla-sō-'ther-ə-pē\ *n* [Gk *thalassa* sea] : the use of seawater or sea products (as seaweed) for the benefit of health and beauty

thal·li·um \'tha-lē-əm\ *n* : a poisonous metallic chemical element

¹than \'thən, 'than\ *conj* **1** — used after a comparative adjective or adverb to introduce the second part of a comparison expressing inequality ⟨older ∼ I am⟩ **2** — used after *other* or a word of similar meaning to express a difference of kind, manner, or identity ⟨adults other ∼ parents⟩

²than *prep* : in comparison with ⟨older ∼ me⟩

thane \'thān\ *n* **1** : a free retainer of an Anglo-Saxon lord **2** : a Scottish feudal lord

thank \'thaŋk\ *vb* : to express gratitude to ⟨∼ed them for the present⟩

thank·ful \'thaŋk-fəl\ *adj* **1** : conscious of benefit received **2** ♦ : expressive of thanks **3** : GLAD

♦ appreciative, grateful, obliged — more at GRATEFUL

thank·ful·ly \-fə-lē\ *adv* **1** : in a thankful manner **2** : as makes one thankful

thank·ful·ness \-nəs\ *n* : the quality or state of being thankful

thank·less \'thaŋ-kləs\ *adj* **1** : UNGRATEFUL **2** : UNAPPRECIATED

thanks \'thaŋks\ *n pl* ♦ : an expression of gratitude

♦ appreciation, gratefulness, gratitude; *also* thanksgiving; indebtedness, gratification, satisfaction; acknowledgment, recognition, tribute *Ant* ingratitude, ungratefulness

thanks·giv·ing \thaŋks-'gi-viŋ\ *n* **1** : the act of giving thanks **2** : a prayer expressing gratitude **3** *cap* : THANKSGIVING DAY

Thanksgiving Day *n* : a day appointed for giving thanks for divine goodness: as **a** : the fourth Thursday in November observed as a legal holiday in the U.S. **b** : the second Monday in October observed as a legal holiday in Canada

¹**that** \ˈthat, thət\ *pron, pl* **those** \ˈthōz\ **1** : the one indicated, mentioned, or understood ⟨∼ is my house⟩ **2** : the one farther away or first mentioned ⟨this is an elm, ∼'s a maple⟩ **3** : what has been indicated or mentioned ⟨after ∼, we left⟩ **4** : the one or ones : IT, THEY ⟨*those* who wish to leave may do so⟩

²**that** \ˈthət, ˈthat\ *conj* **1** : the following, namely ⟨he said ∼ he would⟩; *also* : which is, namely ⟨there's a chance ∼ it may fail⟩ **2** : to this end or purpose ⟨shouted ∼ all might hear⟩ **3** : as to result in the following, namely ⟨so heavy ∼ it can't be moved⟩ **4** : for this reason, namely : BECAUSE ⟨we're glad ∼ you came⟩

³**that** *adj, pl* **those** **1** : being the one mentioned, indicated, or understood ⟨∼ boy⟩ ⟨*those* people⟩ **2** : being the one farther away or less immediately under discussion ⟨this chair or ∼ one⟩

⁴**that** \ˈthət, ˈthat\ *pron* **1** : WHO, WHOM, WHICH ⟨the person ∼ saw you⟩ ⟨the person ∼ you saw⟩ ⟨the money ∼ was spent⟩ **2** : in, on, or at which ⟨the way ∼ you drive⟩ ⟨the day ∼ it rained⟩

⁵**that** \ˈthat\ *adv* : to such an extent or degree ⟨I like it, but not ∼ much⟩

¹**thatch** \ˈthach\ *vb* : to cover with or as if with thatch — **thatch·er** *n*

²**thatch** *n* **1** : plant material (as straw) for use as roofing **2** : a mat of grass clippings accumulated next to the soil on a lawn **3** : a covering of or as if of thatch ⟨a ∼ of white hair⟩

thaw \ˈthȯ\ *vb* **1** ♦ : to melt or cause to melt **2** : to become so warm as to melt ice or snow **3** : to abandon aloofness or hostility — **thaw** *n*

♦ deliquesce, flux, fuse, liquefy, melt, run — more at LIQUEFY

THC \ˌtē-(ˌ)āch-ˈsē\ *n* [*tetra hydro cannabinol*] : a physiologically active chemical from hemp plant resin that is the chief intoxicant in marijuana

¹**the** \thə, *before vowel sounds usu* thē\ *definite article* **1** : that in particular **2** — used before adjectives functioning as nouns ⟨a word to ∼ wise⟩

²**the** *adv* **1** : to what extent ⟨∼ sooner, the better⟩ **2** : to that extent ⟨the sooner, ∼ better⟩

theat *abbr* theater; theatrical

the·ater *or chiefly Can and Brit* **the·atre** \ˈthē-ə-tər\ *n* [ME *theatre*, fr. MF, fr. L *theatrum*, fr. Gk *theatron*, fr. *theasthai* to view, fr. *thea* act of seeing] **1** ♦ : a building or area for dramatic performances; *also* : a building or area for showing motion pictures **2** : a place of enactment of significant events ⟨∼ of war⟩ **3** ♦ : a place (as a lecture room) resembling a theater **4** ♦ : dramatic literature or performance

♦ [1, 3] arena, hall — more at HALL ♦ [4] stage, theatricals

theater–in–the–round *n* : a theater with the stage in the center of the auditorium

the·at·ri·cal \thē-ˈa-tri-kəl\ *also* **the·at·ric** \-trik\ *adj* **1** : of or relating to the theater **2** ♦ : marked by artificiality of emotion : HISTRIONIC ⟨a ∼ gesture⟩ **3** : marked by extravagant display : SHOWY

♦ dramatic, histrionic, melodramatic; *also* overacted, overdone, sensational, staged; conspicuous, elaborate, flamboyant, grandiose, ostentatious, showy; affected, artificial, formal, mannered, pretentious, self-conscious, studied, unnatural

the·at·ri·cals \-kəlz\ *n pl* ♦ : the performance of plays

♦ stage, theater (*or* theatre)

the·at·rics \thē-ˈa-triks\ *n pl* **1** : THEATRICALS **2** : staged or contrived effects

thee \ˈthē\ *pron, archaic objective case of* THOU

theft \ˈtheft\ *n* ♦ : the act or an instance of stealing

♦ larceny, robbery, thievery; *also* burglary, housebreaking; embezzlement, embezzling, graft, misappropriation;

filching, pilfering, purloining, shoplifting; abduction, hijacking, kidnapping, shanghaiing; despoilment, despoliation, pillage, plundering, rapine; poaching, rustling, smuggling; banditry, piracy ♦ grab, rip-off; *also* burglary, holdup, mugging

thegn \ˈthān\ *n* : THANE 1

their \thər, ˈther\ *adj* : of or relating to them or themselves

theirs \ˈtherz\ *pron* : their one : their ones

the·ism \ˈthē-ˌi-zəm\ *n* : belief in the existence of a god or gods — **the·ist** \-ist\ *n or adj* — **the·is·tic** \thē-ˈis-tik\ *adj*

them \thəm, ˈthem\ *pron, objective case of* THEY

theme \ˈthēm\ *n* **1** ♦ : a subject or topic of discourse or of artistic representation **2** ♦ : a written exercise : COMPOSITION **3** : a melodic subject of a musical composition or movement — **the·mat·ic** \thi-ˈma-tik\ *adj*

♦ [1] content, matter, motif, motive, question, subject, topic — more at MATTER ♦ [2] article, composition, essay, paper — more at ESSAY

them·selves \thəm-ˈselvz, them-\ *pron pl* : THEY, THEM — used reflexively, for emphasis, or in absolute constructions ⟨they govern ∼⟩ ⟨they ∼ came⟩ ⟨∼ busy, they sent me⟩

¹**then** \ˈthen\ *adv* **1** : at that time **2** : soon after that : NEXT **3** ♦ : in addition : BESIDES **4** : in that case **5** : CONSEQUENTLY

♦ additionally, again, also, besides, further, furthermore, likewise, more, moreover, too, withal, yet

²**then** *n* : that time ⟨since ∼⟩

³**then** *adj* : existing or acting at that time ⟨the ∼ attorney general⟩

thence \ˈthens, ˈthens\ *adv* **1** : from that place **2** *archaic* : THENCEFORTH **3** : from that fact : THEREFROM

thence·forth \-ˌfȯrth\ *adv* : from that time forward : THEREAFTER

thence·for·ward \thens-ˈfȯr-wərd, thens-\ *also* **thence·for·wards** \-wərdz\ *adv* : onward from that place or time

the·oc·ra·cy \thē-ˈä-krə-sē\ *n, pl* **-cies** **1** : government by officials regarded as divinely inspired **2** : a state governed by a theocracy — **the·o·crat·ic** \ˌthē-ə-ˈkra-tik\ *adj*

theol *abbr* theological; theology

the·ol·o·gy \thē-ˈä-lə-jē\ *n, pl* **-gies** **1** : the study of religious faith, practice, and experience; *esp* : the study of God and of God's relation to the world **2** : a theory or system of theology — **the·o·lo·gian** \ˌthē-ə-ˈlō-jən\ *n* — **the·o·log·i·cal** \-ˈlä-ji-kəl\ *adj*

the·o·rem \ˈthē-ə-rəm, ˈthir-əm\ *n* **1** : a statement esp. in mathematics that has been or is to be proved **2** : an idea accepted or proposed as a demonstrable truth : PROPOSITION

the·o·ret·i·cal \ˌthē-ə-ˈre-ti-kəl\ *also* **the·o·ret·ic** \-tik\ *adj* **1** : relating to or having the character of theory **2** ♦ : existing only in theory : HYPOTHETICAL — **the·o·ret·i·cal·ly** \-ti-k(ə-)lē\ *adv*

♦ conjectural, hypothetical, speculative; *also* alleged, assumed, presumed, presupposed, proposed, supposed, unproven, untested; academic, debatable, moot; abstract, conceptual, intellectual *Ant* actual, factual, real

the·o·rise *chiefly Brit var of* THEORIZE

the·o·rize \ˈthē-ə-ˌrīz\ *vb* **-rized; -riz·ing** : to form a theory : SPECULATE — **the·o·rist** \-rist\ *n*

the·o·ry \ˈthē-ə-rē, ˈthir-ē\ *n, pl* **-ries** **1** : abstract thought **2** : the general principles of a subject **3** : a plausible or scientifically acceptable general principle offered to explain observed facts **4** ♦ : a hypothesis assumed for the sake of argument or investigation : CONJECTURE

♦ conjecture, hypothesis, proposition, supposition; *also* assumption, concession, premise, presumption, presupposition; generalization, guess, speculation, surmise; proffer, proposal, suggestion; feeling, hunch, impression, inkling, notion, suspicion; abstraction, concept, conception

the·os·o·phy \thē-ˈä-sə-fē\ *n* : belief about God and the world held to be based on mystical insight — **theo·soph·i·cal** \ˌthē-ə-ˈsä-fi-kəl\ *adj* — **the·os·o·phist** \thē-ˈä-sə-fist\ *n*

ther·a·peu·tic \ˌther-ə-ˈpyü-tik\ *adj* [Gk *therapeutikos*, fr. *therapeuein* to attend, treat, fr. *theraps* attendant] : of, relating to, or dealing with healing and esp. with remedies for diseases — **ther·a·peu·ti·cal·ly** \-ti-k(ə-)lē\ *adv*

ther·a·peu·tics \ˌther-ə-ˈpyü-tiks\ *n* : a branch of medical or dental science dealing with the use of remedies

ther·a·py \ˈther-ə-pē\ *n, pl* **-pies** : treatment of bodily, mental, or behavioral disorders — **ther·a·pist** \-pist\ *n*

¹**there** \ˈthar, ˈther\ *adv* **1** : in or at that place — often used interjectionally **2** : to or into that place ⟨went ∼ after work⟩ **3** : in that matter or respect

²**there** \ˈthar, ˈther, thər\ *pron* — used as a function word to introduce a sentence or clause ⟨∼'s a pen here⟩

³**there** \ˈthar, ˈther\ *n* **1** : that place ⟨get away from ∼⟩ **2** : that point ⟨you take it from ∼⟩

there·abouts \ˌthar-ə-ˈbaüts, ˌther-; ˈthar-ə-ˌbaüts, ˈther-\ *or* **there·about** \-ˈbaüt, -ˌbaüt\ *adv* **1** : near that place or time **2** : near that number, degree, or quantity

there·af·ter \thar-ˈaf-tər, ther-\ *adv* ♦ : after that : AFTERWARD

♦ after, afterward, later, subsequently — more at AFTER

there·at \-ˈat\ *adv* **1** : at that place **2** : at that occurrence : on that account

there·by \thar-ˈbī, ther-, ˈthar-ˌbī, ˈther-ˌbī\ *adv* **1** : by that : by that means **2** : connected with or with reference to that

there·for \thar-ˈfor, ther-\ *adv* : for or in return for that

there·fore \ˈthar-ˌfor, ˈther-\ *adv* ♦ : for that reason : CONSEQUENTLY

♦ accordingly, consequently, ergo, hence, so, thus, wherefore

there·from \thar-ˈfrəm, ther-\ *adv* : from that or it

there·in \thar-ˈin, ther-\ *adv* **1** : in or into that place, time, or thing **2** : in that respect

there·of \-ˈəv, -ˈäv\ *adv* **1** : of that or it **2** : from that : THEREFROM

there·on \-ˈon, -ˈän\ *adv* **1** : on that **2** *archaic* : THEREUPON 3

there·to \thar-ˈtü, ther-\ *adv* : to that

there·un·to \thar-ˈən-(ˌ)tü, ˌthar-ən-ˈtü, ˌther-\ *adv, archaic* : THERETO

there·upon \ˈthar-ə-ˌpon, ˈther-, -ˌpän; ˌthar-ə-ˈpon, -ˈpän, ˌther-\ *adv* **1** : on that matter **2** : for that reason : THEREFORE **3** : immediately after that : at once

there·with \thar-ˈwith, ther-, -ˈwith\ *adv* **1** : with that **2** *archaic* : THEREUPON, FORTHWITH

there·with·al \ˈthar-wi-ˌthol, ˈther-, -ˌthol\ *adv* **1** *archaic* : BESIDES **2** : THEREWITH

therm *abbr* thermometer

ther·mal \ˈthər-məl\ *adj* **1** : of, relating to, or caused by heat **2** : designed to prevent the loss of body heat ⟨∼ underwear⟩ — **ther·mal·ly** *adv*

thermal pollution *n* : the discharge of heated liquid (as waste water from a factory) into natural waters at a temperature harmful to the environment

therm·is·tor \ˈthər-ˌmis-tər\ *n* : an electrical resistor whose resistance varies sharply with temperature

ther·mo·cline \ˈthər-mə-ˌklīn\ *n* : the region in a thermally stratified body of water that separates warmer surface water from cold deep water

ther·mo·cou·ple \ˈthər-mə-ˌkə-pəl\ *n* : a device for measuring temperature by measuring the temperature-dependent potential difference created at the junction of two dissimilar metals

ther·mo·dy·nam·ics \ˌthər-mə-dī-ˈna-miks\ *n* : physics that deals with the mechanical action or relations of heat — **ther·mo·dy·nam·ic** \-mik\ *adj* — **ther·mo·dy·nam·i·cal·ly** \-mi-k(ə-)lē\ *adv*

ther·mom·e·ter \thər-ˈmä-mə-tər\ *n* [F *thermomètre*, fr. Gk *thermē* heat + *metron* measure] : an instrument for measuring temperature typically by the rise or fall of a liquid (as mercury) in a thin glass tube — **ther·mo·met·ric** \ˌthər-mə-ˈme-trik\ *adj* — **ther·mo·met·ri·cal·ly** \-tri-k(ə-)lē\ *adv*

ther·mo·nu·cle·ar \ˌthər-mō-ˈnü-klē-ər, -ˈnyü-\ *adj* **1** : of or relating to changes in the nucleus of atoms of low atomic weight (as hydrogen) that require a very high temperature (as in the hydrogen bomb) **2** : utilizing or relating to a thermonuclear bomb ⟨∼ war⟩

ther·mo·plas·tic \ˌthər-mə-ˈplas-tik\ *adj* : capable of softening when heated and of hardening again when cooled ⟨∼ resins⟩ — **thermoplastic** *n*

ther·mos \ˈthər-məs\ *n* : a cylindrical container with a vacuum between an inner and an outer wall used to keep liquids hot or cold

ther·mo·sphere \ˈthər-mə-ˌsfir\ *n* : the part of the earth's atmosphere that lies above the mesosphere and that is characterized by steadily increasing temperature with height

ther·mo·stat \ˈthər-mə-ˌstat\ *n* : a device that automatically controls temperature — **ther·mo·stat·ic** \ˌthər-mə-ˈsta-tik\ *adj* — **ther·mo·stat·i·cal·ly** \-ti-k(ə-)lē\ *adv*

the·sau·rus \thi-ˈsor-əs\ *n, pl* **-sau·ri** \-ˈsor-ˌī\ *or* **-sau·rus·es** \-ˈsor-ə-səz\ [NL, fr. L, treasure, collection, fr. Gk *thēsauros*] : a book of words and their synonyms — **the·sau·ral** \-ˈsor-əl\ *adj*

these *pl of* THIS

the·sis \ˈthē-səs\ *n, pl* **the·ses** \ˈthē-ˌsēz\ **1** ♦ : a proposition that a person advances and offers to maintain by argument **2** : an essay embodying results of original research; *esp* : one written for an academic degree

♦ argument, assertion, contention — more at CONTENTION

¹**thes·pi·an** \ˈthes-pē-ən\ *adj, often cap* [fr. *Thespis*, 6th cent. B.C. Greek poet and reputed originator of tragedy] : relating to the drama : DRAMATIC

²**thespian** *n* : ACTOR

Thess *abbr* Thessalonians

Thes·sa·lo·nians \ˌthe-sə-ˈlo-nyənz, -nē-ənz\ *n* : either of two books of the New Testament of Christian Scripture

the·ta \ˈthā-tə\ *n* : the 8th letter of the Greek alphabet — Θ or θ

thew \ˈthü, ˈthyü\ *n* : MUSCLE, SINEW — usu. used in pl.

they \ˈthā\ *pron* **1** : those individuals under discussion : the ones previously mentioned or referred to **2** : unspecified persons : PEOPLE

thi·a·mine \ˈthī-ə-mən, -ˌmēn\ *also* **thi·a·min** \-mən\ *n* : a vitamin of the vitamin B complex essential to normal metabolism and nerve function

¹**thick** \ˈthik\ *adj* **1** ♦ : having relatively great depth or extent from one surface to its opposite ⟨a ∼ plank⟩; *also* : heavily built : THICKSET **2** ♦ : close-packed with units or individuals; *also* : NUMEROUS **3** ♦ : dense or viscous in consistency ⟨∼ syrup⟩ **4** : marked by haze, fog, or mist ⟨∼ weather⟩ **5** : measuring in thickness ⟨one meter ∼⟩ **6** : imperfectly articulated : INDISTINCT ⟨∼ speech⟩ **7** : lacking sharpness or quickness of sensibility or intellect : STUPID, OBTUSE **8** ♦ : associated on close terms : INTIMATE **9** : EXCESSIVE — **thick·ly** *adv*

♦ [1] broad, fat, thickset, wide — more at WIDE ♦ [2] close, compact, crowded, dense, packed, serried, tight — more at CLOSE ♦ [2] flush, fraught, numerous, replete, rife ♦ [2] close, compact, crowded, dense, packed, serried, tight — more at CLOSE ♦ [3] syrupy, viscid, viscous; *also* creamy, heavy, slushy, thickened, turbid, undiluted; sticky, gluey, glutinous; gelatinous, gooey, gummy; concentrated, condensed *Ant* runny, soupy, thin, watery ♦ [8] bosom, chummy, close, familiar, friendly, intimate — more at FAMILIAR

²**thick** *n* **1** ♦ : the most crowded, intense, or active part **2** : the part of greatest thickness

♦ center, deep, depth, heart, height, middle, midst

thick and thin *n* : every difficulty and obstacle ⟨was loyal through *thick and thin*⟩

thick·en \ˈthi-kən\ *vb* : to make or become thick — **thick·en·er** *n*

thick·et \ˈthi-kət\ *n* ♦ : a dense growth of bushes or small trees

♦ brake, brushwood, chaparral, coppice, covert; *also* canebrake; brush, bush, scrub; bramble, jungle, tangle; grove, hedge, stand, woodlot; forest, greenwood, wildwood, wood, woodland

thick·ness \'thik-nəs\ *n* 1 : the smallest of three dimensions ⟨length, width, and ~⟩ 2 ♦ : the quality or state of being thick 3 : LAYER, SHEET ⟨a single ~ of canvas⟩
♦ consistency, viscosity — more at CONSISTENCY

thick·set \'thik-'set\ *adj* 1 : closely placed or planted 2 ♦ : having a thick body
♦ chunky, dumpy, heavyset, squat, stocky, stout, stubby, stumpy — more at STOCKY

thick–skinned \-'skind\ *adj* 1 : having a thick skin 2 ♦ : feeling no emotion or sympathy : CALLOUS 3 : not easily bothered by criticism or insult ⟨a ~ politician⟩
♦ callous, hard, heartless, inhuman, inhumane, pitiless, soulless, unfeeling, unsympathetic — more at HARD

thief \'thēf\ *n, pl* **thieves** \'thēvz\ : one that steals esp. secretly

thieve \'thēv\ *vb* **thieved; thiev·ing** ♦ : to take (the property of another) wrongfully and esp. as an habitual or regular practice : STEAL
♦ appropriate, filch, hook, misappropriate, nip, pilfer, pocket, purloin, snitch, steal, swipe — more at STEAL

thiev·ery \'thē-və-rē\ *n, pl* **-er·ies** ♦ : the act of stealing : THEFT
♦ larceny, robbery, theft — more at THEFT

thigh \'thī\ *n* : the part of the vertebrate hind or lower limb between the knee and the hip

thigh·bone \'thī-,bōn\ *n* : FEMUR

thim·ble \'thim-bəl\ *n* : a cap or guard worn on the finger to push the needle in sewing — **thim·ble·ful** *n*

¹**thin** \'thin\ *adj* **thin·ner; thin·nest** 1 ♦ : having little extent from one surface through to its opposite : not thick : SLENDER 2 : not closely set or placed : SPARSE ⟨~ hair⟩ 3 : not dense or not dense enough : more fluid or rarefied than normal ⟨~ air⟩ ⟨~ syrup⟩ 4 ♦ : lacking substance, fullness, or strength ⟨~ broth⟩ 5 : FLIMSY 6 ♦ : not well fleshed : LEAN — **thin·ly** *adv* — **thin·ness** *n*
♦ [1] fine, narrow, skinny, slender, slim — more at NARROW ♦ [4] dilute, watery, weak — more at WEAK ♦ [6] lean, skinny, slender, slim, spare; *also* angular, bony, rawboned, scrawny, sinewy; lank, lanky, rangy, reedy, spindling, spindly, twiggy, waspish, weedy, willowy, wiry; anorexic, cadaverous, emaciated, gaunt, haggard, pinched, skeletal, wasted, wizened; meager, puny, slight *Ant* chubby, corpulent, fat, gross, obese, overweight, plump, portly, rotund

²**thin** *vb* **thinned; thin·ning** ♦ : to make or become thin
♦ adulterate, dilute, water, weaken — more at ADULTERATE

thine \'thīn\ *pron, archaic* : one or the ones belonging to thee

thing \'thiŋ\ *n* 1 ♦ : a matter of concern : AFFAIR ⟨~s to do⟩ 2 *pl* : state of affairs ⟨~s are improving⟩ 3 : something that happens : EVENT ⟨the crime was a terrible ~⟩ 4 : something that is done : DEED, ACT ⟨expected great ~s of him⟩ 5 ♦ : a distinct entity : OBJECT 6 : an inanimate object distinguished from a living being 7 *pl* ♦ : movable property : EFFECTS 8 : an article of clothing 9 : DETAIL, POINT 10 : IDEA, NOTION 11 : something one likes to do : SPECIALTY ⟨doing her ~⟩ 12 : a single human being 13 a : a product of work or activity b ♦ : the end or aim of effort or activity ⟨the ~ is to get well⟩
♦ [1] affair, business, matter — more at MATTER ♦ [5] being, entity, individual, object, substance — more at ENTITY ♦ **things** [7] belongings, chattels, effects, holdings, paraphernalia, possessions — more at POSSESSION ♦ [13b] aim, ambition, aspiration, design, dream, end, goal, intent, mark, meaning, object, objective, plan, pretension, purpose — more at GOAL

think \'thiŋk\ *vb* **thought** \'thȯt\; **think·ing** 1 : to form or have in the mind 2 ♦ : to have as an opinion : BELIEVE 3 ♦ : to reflect on : PONDER 4 ♦ : to call to mind : REMEMBER 5 : REASON 6 : to form a mental picture of : IMAGINE 7 ♦ : to devise by thinking ⟨*thought* up a plan to escape⟩ — **think·er** *n*
♦ [2] believe, consider, deem, feel, figure, guess, hold, imagine, suppose — more at BELIEVE ♦ *usu* **think about** *or* **think over** ♦ [3] chew over, cogitate, consider, contemplate, debate, deliberate, entertain, meditate, mull, ponder, question, ruminate, study, weigh — more at PONDER ♦ *usu* **think of** [4] recall, recollect, remember, reminisce — more at REMEMBER ♦ *usu* **think up** [7] concoct, contrive, cook up, devise, fabricate, invent, make up, manufacture — more at INVENT

think·er \'thiŋ-kər\ *n* : one that thinks: as a : one that thinks in a specified way ⟨a slow ~⟩ b ♦ : one that has special capacity for thinking
♦ brain, genius, intellect, whiz, wizard — more at GENIUS

think tank *n* : an institute, corporation, or group organized for interdisciplinary research (as in technological or social problems)

thin·ner \'thi-nər\ *n* : a volatile liquid (as turpentine) used to thin paint

thin–skinned \'thin-'skind\ *adj* 1 : having a thin skin or rind 2 : extremely sensitive to criticism or insult

¹**third** \'thərd\ *adj* : next after the second — **third** *or* **third·ly** *adv*

²**third** *n* 1 : one of three equal parts of something 2 : one that is number three in a countable series 3 : the 3d forward gear in an automotive vehicle

third degree *n* : the subjection of a prisoner to mental or physical torture to force a confession

third dimension *n* 1 : thickness, depth, or apparent thickness or depth that confers solidity on an object 2 : a quality that confers reality — **third–dimensional** *adj*

third world *n, often cap T&W* : the aggregate of the underdeveloped nations of the world

¹**thirst** \'thərst\ *n* 1 : a feeling of dryness in the mouth and throat associated with a desire to drink; *also* : a bodily condition producing this 2 ♦ : an ardent desire ⟨a ~ for knowledge⟩
♦ appetite, craving, desire, drive, eagerness, hankering, hunger, itch, longing, lust, passion, urge, yearning, yen — more at DESIRE

²**thirst** *vb* 1 : to need drink : suffer thirst 2 ♦ : to have a strong desire
♦ *usu* **thirst for** ache for, covet, crave, desire, die (to *or* for), hanker for, hunger for, long for, lust (for *or* after), pine for, repine for, want, wish for, yearn for — more at DESIRE

thirsty \'thər-stē\ *adj* **thirst·i·er; -est** 1 a : feeling thirst b ♦ : deficient in moisture ⟨~ land⟩ 2 ♦ : having a strong desire : AVID
♦ [1b] arid, dry, sere — more at DRY ♦ [2] ardent, athirst, avid, eager, enthusiastic, keen — more at EAGER

thir·teen \,thər-'tēn\ *n* : one more than 12 — **thirteen** *adj or pron* — **thir·teenth** \-'tēnth\ *adj or n*

thir·ty \'thər-tē\ *n, pl* **thirties** : three times 10 — **thir·ti·eth** \-tē-əth\ *adj or n* — **thirty** *adj or pron*

¹**this** \'this\ *pron, pl* **these** \'thēz\ 1 : the one close or closest in time or space ⟨~ is your book⟩ 2 : what is in the present or under immediate observation or discussion ⟨~ is a mess⟩; *also* : what is happening or being done now ⟨after ~ we'll leave⟩

²**this** *adj, pl* **these** 1 : being the one near, present, just mentioned, or more immediately under observation ⟨~ book⟩ 2 : constituting the immediate past or future ⟨friends all *these* years⟩

³**this** *adv* : to such an extent or degree ⟨we need a book about ~ big⟩

this·tle \'thi-səl\ *n* : any of various tall prickly composite plants with often showy heads of tightly packed tubular flowers

this·tle·down \-ˌdaùn\ *n* : the down from the ripe flower head of a thistle

¹thith·er \'thi-thər\ *adv* : to that place

²thither *adj* : being on the farther side

thith·er·ward \-wərd\ *adv* : toward that place — THITHER

thong \'thóŋ\ *n* 1 : a strip esp. of leather or hide 2 : a sandal held on the foot by a thong between the toes 3 : a narrow strip of swimwear or underwear that passes between the thighs

tho·rax \'thōr-ˌaks\ *n, pl* **tho·rax·es** *or* **tho·ra·ces** \'thōr-ə-ˌsēz\ 1 : the part of the body of a mammal between the neck and the abdomen; *also* : its cavity containing the heart and lungs 2 : the middle of the three main divisions of the body of an insect — **tho·rac·ic** \thə-'ra-sik\ *adj*

tho·ri·um \'thōr-ē-əm\ *n* : a radioactive metallic chemical element

thorn \'thórn\ *n* 1 : a woody plant bearing sharp processes 2 : a sharp rigid plant process that is usu. a modified leafless branch 3 ♦ : something that causes distress

♦ aggravation, annoyance, bother, exasperation, frustration, hassle, headache, inconvenience, irritant, nuisance, peeve, pest, problem — more at ANNOYANCE

thorny \'thór-nē\ *adj* **thorn·i·er; -est** 1 ♦ : full of thorns 2 ♦ : full of difficulties or controversial points

♦ [1] brambly, prickly, scratchy — more at SCRATCHY
♦ [2] catchy, delicate, difficult, knotty, problematic, spiny, ticklish, touchy, tough, tricky — more at TRICKY

thor·ough \'thər-ō\ *adj* 1 ♦ : testing all possibilities or considering all elements : EXHAUSTIVE \a ~ search\ 2 : very careful : PAINSTAKING \a ~ scholar\ 3 : having full mastery 4 ♦ : marked by attention to many details \a ~ description\ 5 ♦ : complete in all respects \~ pleasure\ — **thor·ough·ness** *n*

♦ [1] all-out, clean, complete, comprehensive, exhaustive, full-scale, out-and-out, thoroughgoing, total — more at EXHAUSTIVE ♦ [4] circumstantial, detailed, elaborate, full, minute — more at DETAILED ♦ [5] absolute, all-out, complete, perfect, pure, total, utter — more at ABSOLUTE

¹thor·ough·bred \'thər-ə-ˌbred\ *adj* 1 ♦ : bred from the best blood through a long line 2 *cap* : of or relating to the Thoroughbred breed of horses 3 : marked by high-spirited grace

♦ full-blooded, purebred — more at PUREBRED

²thoroughbred *n* 1 *cap* : any of an English breed of light speedy horses kept chiefly for racing 2 : one (as a pedigreed animal) of excellent quality

thor·ough·fare \-ˌfar\ *n* ♦ : a public road or street

♦ artery, avenue, drag, drive, highway, pass, pike, road, route, row, street, trace, turnpike, way — more at WAY

thor·ough·go·ing \ˌthər-ə-'gō-iŋ\ *adj* ♦ : marked by thoroughness or zeal

♦ all-out, clean, complete, comprehensive, exhaustive, full-scale, out-and-out, thorough, total — more at EXHAUSTIVE

thor·ough·ly \ˌthər-ə-lē\ *adv* ♦ : in a thorough manner or degree

♦ altogether, completely, dead, entirely, fast, flat, full, fully, perfectly, quite, well, wholly — more at FULLY completely, exhaustively, fully, minutely, roundly, totally; *also* all-out, intensively; broadly, extensively, generally, globally, widely; conclusively, definitely, perfectly

¹thou \'thaù\ *pron, archaic* : the person addressed

²thou \'thaù\ *n, pl* **thou** : a thousand of something (as dollars)

¹though \'thō\ *conj* 1 ♦ : despite the fact that \~ the odds are hopeless, they fight on\ 2 : granting that \~ it may look bad, still, all is not lost\

♦ albeit, although, howbeit, when, while — more at ALTHOUGH

²though *adv* ♦ : in spite of that : HOWEVER \not for long, ~\

♦ but, howbeit, however, nevertheless, nonetheless, notwithstanding, still, withal, yet — more at HOWEVER

¹thought \'thòt\ *past and past part of* THINK

²thought *n* 1 : the process of thinking 2 ♦ : serious consideration 3 : reasoning power 4 : the power to imagine : CONCEPTION 5 ♦ : an individual act or product of thinking : IDEA 6 : OPINION, BELIEF

♦ [2] consideration, debate, deliberation — more at CONSIDERATION ♦ [5] concept, idea, image, impression, notion, picture — more at IDEA

thought·ful \'thòt-fəl\ *adj* 1 ♦ : absorbed in thought 2 ♦ : marked by careful thinking \a ~ essay\ 3 ♦ : considerate of others \a ~ host\ — **thought·ful·ness** *n*

♦ [1] contemplative, meditative, melancholy, pensive, reflective, ruminant — more at CONTEMPLATIVE ♦ [2] advised, calculated, deliberate, measured, reasoned, studied, thought-out — more at DELIBERATE ♦ [3] attentive, considerate, kind, solicitous; *also* brotherly, good, good-hearted, helpful, hospitable, kindhearted, kindly, neighborly, nice; caring, compassionate, sympathetic, tender; chivalrous, courteous, courtly, gallant, gracious, polite; diplomatic, tactful; deferential, dutiful, obliging, regardful, respectful; altruistic, beneficent, benevolent, benignant, humane, selfless, unselfish; charitable, generous, magnanimous *Ant* heedless, inconsiderate, thoughtless, unthinking

thought·ful·ly \-fə-lē\ *adv* ♦ : in a thoughtful manner

♦ courteously, kindly, nicely, well — more at WELL

thought·less \-ləs\ *adj* 1 : insufficiently alert : CARELESS \a ~ worker\ 2 : RECKLESS \a ~ act\ 3 ♦ : lacking concern for others : INCONSIDERATE \~ remarks\ — **thought·less·ly** *adv* — **thought·less·ness** *n*

♦ discourteous, ill-bred, ill-mannered, impertinent, impolite, inconsiderate, rude, uncivil, ungracious, unmannerly — more at IMPOLITE

thought–out *adj* ♦ : produced or arrived at through mental effort and esp. through careful and thorough consideration

♦ advised, calculated, deliberate, knowing, measured, reasoned, studied, thoughtful — more at DELIBERATE

thou·sand \'thaùz-ᵊnd\ *n, pl* **thousands** *or* **thousand** : 10 times 100 — **thousand** *adj* — **thou·sandth** \-ᵊnth\ *adj or n*

thousands place *n* : the place four to the left of the decimal point in an Arabic number

thrall \'thról\ *n* 1 ♦ : a servant slave : BONDMAN 2 ♦ : a state of servitude

♦ [1] bondman, chattel, slave — more at SLAVE
♦ [2] bondage, enslavement, servitude, slavery, yoke — more at SLAVERY

thrall·dom *or* **thral·dom** \'thról-dəm\ *n* : the state or condition of servitude

thrash \'thrash\ *vb* 1 : THRESH 1 2 ♦ : to defeat decisively or severely : BEAT 3 : to move about violently 4 : to go over again and again \~ over the matter\; *also* : to hammer out \~ out a plan\ 5 ♦ : to swing, beat, or strike in the manner of a rapidly moving flail

♦ [2] beat, best, clobber, conquer, crush, defeat, drub, lick, rout, skunk, triumph, trounce, wallop, whip, win — more at BEAT ♦ [5] flail, flog, hide, lash, scourge, slash, switch, whale, whip

¹thrash·er \'thra-shər\ *n* : one that thrashes or threshes

²thrasher *n* : any of various long-tailed American songbirds related to the mockingbird

¹thread \'thred\ *n* 1 : a thin continuous strand of spun and twisted textile fibers 2 : something resembling a textile thread 3 : the ridge or groove that winds around a screw

4 : a line of reasoning or train of thought 5 : a continuing element

²**thread** *vb* 1 : to pass a thread through the eye of (a needle) 2 : to pass (as film) through something 3 : to make one's way through or between 4 : to put together on or as if on a thread ⟨~ beads⟩ 5 : to form a screw thread on or in 6 ♦ : to interweave with or as if with threads

♦ interlace, intersperse, intertwine, interweave, lace, weave, wreathe; *also* insert, intermingle, mingle, mix; alternate, juxtapose; amalgamate, assimilate, blend, combine, commingle, embody, fuse, incorporate, integrate, merge

thread·bare \-ˌbar\ *adj* 1 ♦ : worn to the point that the threads show : having the nap worn off 2 ♦ : having no interest or freshness : TRITE ⟨a ~ excuse⟩

♦ [1] ragged, ratty, seedy, shabby, tattered, worn-out — more at RAGGED ♦ [2] banal, commonplace, hackneyed, musty, stale, stereotyped, tired, trite — more at STALE

thready \ˈthre-dē\ *adj* 1 : consisting of or bearing fibers of filaments ⟨a ~ bark⟩ 2 : lacking in fullness, body, or vigor

threat \ˈthret\ *n* 1 : an expression of intent to do harm 2 ♦ : one that threatens

♦ danger, hazard, menace, peril, pitfall, risk, trouble — more at DANGER

threat·en \ˈthret-ᵊn\ *vb* 1 : to utter threats against 2 : to give signs or warning of : PORTEND 3 ♦ : to hang over as a threat : MENACE 4 : to cause to feel insecure or anxious — **threat·en·ing·ly** *adv*

♦ hang, hover, menace, overhang; *also* endanger, hazard, imperil, jeopardize

threat·ened *adj* : having an uncertain chance of continued survival; *esp* : likely to become an endangered species

three \ˈthrē\ *n* 1 : one more than two 2 : the 3d in a set or series 3 : something having three units — **three** *adj or pron*

3–D \ˈthrē-ˈdē\ *n* : a three-dimensional form or picture

three–dimensional *adj* 1 : relating to or having three dimensions 2 : giving the illusion of varying distances ⟨a ~ picture⟩

three·fold \ˈthrē-ˌfōld, -ˈfōld\ *adj* 1 ♦ : having three parts : TRIPLE 2 : being three times as great or as many — **three·fold** \-ˈfōld\ *adv*

♦ treble, tripartite, triple — more at TRIPLE

three·pence \ˈthre-pəns, ˈthri-, ˈthrə-, *US also* ˈthrē-pens\ *n* 1 *pl* threepence *or* three·penc·es : a coin worth three pennies 2 : the sum of three British pennies

three–ring circus *n* ♦ : something wild, confusing, engrossing, or entertaining

♦ bedlam, circus, hell, madhouse — more at MADHOUSE

three·score \ˈthrē-ˈskōr\ *adj* : being three times twenty : SIXTY

three·some \ˈthrē-səm\ *n* ♦ : a group of three persons or things

♦ triad, trio, triple, triplet; *also* trilogy; triplicate; triplex

thren·o·dy \ˈthre-nə-dē\ *n, pl* **-dies** ♦ : a song of lamentation : ELEGY

♦ dirge, elegy, lament, requiem — more at LAMENT

thresh \ˈthrash, ˈthresh\ *vb* 1 : to separate (as grain from straw) mechanically 2 : THRASH — **thresh·er** *n*

thresh·old \ˈthresh-ˌhōld\ *n* 1 : the sill of a door 2 ♦ : a point or place of beginning or entering : OUTSET 3 : a point at which a physiological or psychological effect begins to be produced ⟨a high ~ for pain⟩

♦ beginning, birth, commencement, dawn, genesis, launch, morning, onset, outset, start — more at BEGINNING

threw *past of* THROW

thrice \ˈthrīs\ *adv* 1 : three times 2 : in a threefold manner or degree

thrift \ˈthrift\ *n* [ME, fr. ON, prosperity, fr. *thrīfask* to thrive] ♦ : careful management esp. of money : FRUGALITY — **thrift·i·ly** \ˈthrif-tə-lē\ *adv*

♦ economy, frugality, husbandry, providence — more at ECONOMY

thrift·less \ˈthrift-ləs\ *adj* ♦ : careless, wasteful, or incompetent in handling money or resources

♦ extravagant, prodigal, profligate, spendthrift, unthrifty, wasteful — more at PRODIGAL

thrifty \ˈthrif-tē\ *adj* **thrift·i·er; -est** ♦ : given to or marked by economy and good management

♦ economical, frugal, provident, sparing — more at FRUGAL

¹**thrill** \ˈthril\ *vb* [ME *thirlen, thrillen* to pierce, fr. OE *thyrlian,* fr. *thyrel* hole, fr. *thurh* through] 1 ♦ : to have or cause to have a sudden sharp feeling of excitement; *also* : TINGLE 1 2 : TREMBLE, VIBRATE — **thrill·er** *n*

♦ electrify, excite, exhilarate, galvanize, intoxicate, shiver, tingle, titillate, turn on; *also* arouse, incite, inspire, provoke, stimulate; bewitch, captivate, charm, delight, enchant, enthrall, hypnotize, mesmerize, rivet; interest, intrigue, tantalize

²**thrill** *n* ♦ : an instantaneous excitement

♦ bang, exhilaration, kick, titillation; *also* arousal, electrification, intoxication, stimulation; jolt, shock, surprise; delectation, delight, enjoyment, joy, lift, pleasure; amusement, diversion, entertainment, fun, treat

thrill·ing *adj* ♦ : causing an instantaneous surge of emotion — **thrill·ing·ly** *adv*

♦ breathtaking, electric, exciting, exhilarating, rousing, stirring — more at EXCITING

thrive \ˈthrīv\ *vb* **thrived** *or* **throve** \ˈthrōv\; **thrived** *also* **thriv·en** \ˈthri-vən\; **thriv·ing** 1 ♦ : to grow luxuriantly : FLOURISH 2 : to gain in wealth or possessions : PROSPER

♦ [1] burgeon, flourish, prosper; *also* luxuriate, overgrow, proliferate, shoot up; germinate, root, sprout; bloom, flower, fruit, produce, propagate, regenerate, seed ♦ [2] flourish, prosper, succeed — more at SUCCEED

throat \ˈthrōt\ *n* : the part of the neck in front of the spinal column; *also* : the passage through it to the stomach and lungs — **throat·ed** *adj*

throaty \ˈthrō-tē\ *adj* **throat·i·er; -est** 1 ♦ : uttered or produced from low in the throat ⟨a ~ voice⟩ 2 ♦ : heavy, thick, or deep as if from the throat — **throat·i·ly** \-tə-lē\ *adv* — **throat·i·ness** \-tē-nəs\ *n*

♦ [1] bass, deep, low — more at DEEP ♦ [2] coarse, gravelly, gruff, hoarse, husky, scratchy — more at HOARSE

¹**throb** \ˈthräb\ *vb* **throbbed; throb·bing** ♦ : to pulsate or pound esp. with abnormal force or rapidity : BEAT

♦ beat, palpitate, pitter-patter, pulsate, pulse — more at PULSATE

²**throb** *n* ♦ : a rhythmic pulsation or beating : BEAT, PULSE

♦ beat, palpitation, pulsation, pulse — more at PULSATION

throe \ˈthrō\ *n* 1 : a sudden spasm or pang 2 *pl* : a hard or painful struggle

throm·bo·sis \thräm-ˈbō-səs\ *n, pl* **-bo·ses** \-ˌsēz\ : the formation or presence of a clot in a blood vessel — **throm·bot·ic** \-ˈbä-tik\ *adj*

throm·bus \ˈthräm-bəs\ *n, pl* **throm·bi** \-ˌbī\ [NL, fr. Gk *thrombos* lump, clot] : a clot of blood formed within a blood vessel and remaining attached to its place of origin

throne \ˈthrōn\ *n* 1 : the chair of state of a sovereign or high dignitary 2 : royal power : SOVEREIGNTY

¹**throng** \ˈthrȯŋ\ *n* 1 ♦ : a multitude of assembled persons 2 : a crowding together of many persons

♦ army, crowd, crush, drove, flock, horde, host, legion, mob, multitude, press, swarm — more at CROWD

²**throng** *vb* **thronged; throng·ing** ♦ : to crowd together in great numbers

♦ crowd, flock, mob, swarm — more at CROWD

¹**throt·tle** \'thrät-²l\ *vb* **throt·tled; throt·tling** [ME *throtlen,* fr. *throte* throat] **1** ♦ : to compress the throat of : CHOKE **2** : SUPPRESS **3** : to reduce the speed of (an engine) by closing the throttle — **throt·tler** *n*

♦ choke, garrote, strangle — more at CHOKE

²**throttle** *n* : a valve regulating the flow of steam or fuel to an engine; *also* : the lever controlling this valve

¹**through** \'thrü\ *prep* **1** : from one end or side to the other of ⟨go ∼ the door⟩ **2** : by way of ⟨entered ∼ a skylight⟩ **3** ♦ : in the midst of ⟨a path ∼ the trees⟩ **4** ♦ : by means of ⟨succeeded ∼ hard work⟩ **5** ♦ : over the whole of ⟨rumors swept ∼ the office⟩ ⟨homes scattered ∼ the valley⟩ **6** ♦ : during the whole of ⟨∼ the night⟩ **7** : to and including ⟨Monday ∼ Friday⟩

♦ [3] amid, among, midst — more at AMONG ♦ [4] because of, due to, owing to, with — more at BECAUSE OF ♦ [5] about, around, over, round, throughout — more at AROUND ♦ [6] during, over, throughout — more at DURING

²**through** *adv* **1** ♦ : from one end or side to the other **2** : from beginning to end : to completion ⟨see it ∼⟩ **3** : to the core : THOROUGHLY ⟨he was wet ∼⟩ **4** : into the open : OUT ⟨break ∼⟩

♦ across, over

³**through** *adj* **1** : permitting free passage ⟨a ∼ street⟩ **2** : going from point of origin to destination without change or transfer ⟨a ∼ train⟩ **3** : coming from or going to points outside a local area ⟨∼ traffic⟩ **4** ♦ : arrived at completion or accomplishment : FINISHED ⟨∼ with the job⟩

♦ complete, done, down, over, up — more at COMPLETE

¹**through·out** \thrü-'aút\ *adv* **1** : in or to every part : EVERYWHERE **2** : from beginning to end

²**throughout** *prep* **1** ♦ : in or to every part of **2** ♦ : during the whole period of

♦ [1] about, around, over, round, through — more at AROUND ♦ [2] during, over, through — more at DURING

through·put \'thrü-ˌpút\ *n* : OUTPUT, PRODUCTION ⟨the ∼ of a computer⟩

throve *past of* THRIVE

¹**throw** \'thrō\ *vb* **threw** \'thrü\; **thrown** \'thrōn\; **throw·ing** [ME, to cause to twist, throw, fr. OE *thrāwan* to cause to twist] **1** ♦ : to propel through the air esp. with a forward motion of the hand and arm ⟨∼ a ball⟩ **2** : to cause to fall or fall off **3** ♦ : to put suddenly in a certain position or condition ⟨∼ into panic⟩ ⟨∼ on a coat⟩ **4** : to put on or take off hastily ⟨∼ on a coat⟩ **5** : to lose intentionally ⟨∼ a game⟩ **6** : to move (a lever) so as to connect or disconnect parts of something (as a clutch) **7** : to act as host for ⟨∼ a party⟩ — **throw·er** *n*

♦ [1] cast, catapult, chuck, dash, fire, fling, heave, hurl, hurtle, launch, peg, pelt, pitch, sling, toss; *also* bowl, flip, hook, pass, roll, shoot; eject, impel, precipitate, project, propel, rifle, thrust ♦ *usu* **throw on** [3] don, put on, slip — more at PUT ON

²**throw** *n* **1** : an act of throwing, hurling, or flinging; *also* : CAST **2** : the distance a missile may be thrown **3** : a light coverlet **4** : a woman's scarf or light wrap

throw·away \'thrō-ə-ˌwā\ *n* : something that is or is designed to be thrown away esp. after one use

throw away *vb* **1** ♦ : to get rid of as worthless or unnecessary **2** ♦ : to use in a foolish or wasteful manner

♦ [1] cast, discard, ditch, dump, fling, jettison, junk, lose, reject, scrap, shed, shuck, slough, throw out, unload — more at DISCARD ♦ [2] blow, dissipate, fritter,

lavish, misspend, run through, spend, squander, waste — more at WASTE

throw·back \-ˌbak\ *n* : reversion to an earlier type or phase; *also* : an instance or product of this

throw out *vb* **1** ♦ : to remove from a place, office, or employment usu. in a sudden or unexpected manner **2** ♦ : to get rid of as worthless or unnecessary

♦ [1] banish, boot (out), bounce, cast, chase, dismiss, drum, eject, expel, oust, rout, run off — more at EJECT ♦ [2] cast, discard, ditch, dump, fling, jettison, junk, lose, reject, scrap, shed, shuck, slough, throw away, unload — more at DISCARD

throw up *vb* **1** : to build hurriedly **2** ♦ : to discharge the contents of the stomach through the mouth : VOMIT

♦ gag, heave, spit up, vomit — more at VOMIT

thrum \'thrəm\ *vb* **thrummed; thrum·ming** : to play or pluck a stringed instrument idly : STRUM

thrush \'thrəsh\ *n* : any of numerous small or medium-sized songbirds that are mostly of a plain color often with spotted underparts

¹**thrust** \'thrəst\ *vb* **thrust; thrust·ing** **1** ♦ : to push or drive with force : SHOVE **2** : STAB, PIERCE **3** : INTERJECT **4** : to press the acceptance of upon someone

♦ drive, propel, push, shove — more at PUSH

²**thrust** *n* **1** : a lunge with a pointed weapon **2** : ATTACK **3** : the pressure of one part of a construction against another (as of an arch against an abutment) **4** : the force produced by a propeller or jet or rocket engine that drives a vehicle (as an aircraft) forward **5** : a violent push : SHOVE **6** : a prominent or essential element

thrust·er *also* **thrust·or** \'thrəs-tər\ *n* : one that thrusts; *esp* : a rocket engine

thru·way \'thrü-ˌwā\ *n* : EXPRESSWAY

¹**thud** \'thəd\ *n* **1** : a forcible stroke delivered with a part of the body or with an instrument : BLOW **2** : a dull sound

²**thud** *vb* **thud·ded; thud·ding** ♦ : to move or strike so as to make a thud

♦ bang, bash, bump, collide, crash, hit, impact, knock, ram, slam, smash, strike, swipe — more at HIT

thug \'thəg\ *n* [Hindi & Urdu *ṭhag,* lit., thief] ♦ : a brutal ruffian or assassin — **thug·gish** *adj*

♦ bully, gangster, goon, hood, hoodlum, mobster, mug, punk, rowdy, ruffian, tough — more at HOODLUM

thu·li·um \'thü-lē-əm, 'thyü-\ *n* : a rare metallic chemical element

¹**thumb** \'thəm\ *n* **1** : the short thick first digit of the human hand or a corresponding digit of a lower animal **2** : the part of a glove or mitten that covers the thumb

²**thumb** *vb* **1** : to leaf through (pages) with the thumb **2** : to wear or soil with the thumb by frequent handling **3** : to request or obtain (a ride) in a passing automobile by signaling with the thumb

thumb drive *n* : FLASH DRIVE

¹**thumb·nail** \'thəm-ˌnāl\ *n* : the nail of the thumb

²**thumbnail** *adj* : BRIEF, CONCISE ⟨a ∼ description⟩

thumb·print \-ˌprint\ *n* : an impression made by the thumb

thumb·screw \-ˌskrü\ *n* **1** : a screw with a head that may be turned by the thumb and forefinger **2** : a device of torture for squeezing the thumb

thumb·tack \-ˌtak\ *n* : a tack with a broad flat head for pressing with one's thumb into a board or wall

¹**thump** \'thəmp\ *vb* **1** : to strike with or as if with something thick or heavy so as to cause a dull sound **2** : to strike heavily or repeatedly : POUND

²**thump** *n* ♦ : a blow with or as if with something blunt or heavy; *also* : the sound made by such a blow

♦ blow, clout, hit, pound, punch, thud, thwack, wallop, whack — more at BLOW

¹**thun·der** \'thən-dər\ *n* **1** : the sound following a flash of lightning; *also* : a noise like such a sound **2** : a loud utterance or threat

²**thunder** *vb* **1** : to produce thunder **2** ♦ : to utter or emit a full loud prolonged sound : ROAR ⟨jets ∼ed overhead⟩
  ♦ bellow, boom, growl, roar — more at ROAR

thun·der·bolt \-ˌbōlt\ *n* : a flash of lightning with its accompanying thunder

thun·der·clap \-ˌklap\ *n* **1** : a crash of thunder **2** ♦ : something sharp, loud, or sudden like a clap of thunder
  ♦ bang, blast, boom, clap, crack, crash, pop, report, slam, smash, snap, thwack, whack — more at CLAP

thun·der·cloud \-ˌklau̇d\ *n* : a cloud charged with electricity and producing lightning and thunder

thun·der·head \-ˌhed\ *n* : a large cumulus or cumulonimbus cloud often appearing before a thunderstorm

thun·der·ous \ˈthən-də-rəs\ *adj* ♦ : producing thunder; *also* : making a noise like thunder — **thun·der·ous·ly** *adv*
  ♦ booming, clamorous (*or* clamourous), deafening, ear-splitting, loud, piercing, resounding, ringing, roaring, sonorous, stentorian — more at LOUD

thun·der·show·er \ˈthən-dər-ˌshau̇-ər\ *n* : a shower accompanied by thunder and lightning

thun·der·storm \-ˌstȯrm\ *n* : a storm accompanied by thunder and lightning

thun·der·struck \-ˌstrək\ *adj* ♦ : stunned as if struck by a thunderbolt
  ♦ amazed, awestruck, stunned; *also* startled, surprised; aghast, appalled, dismayed, horrified; bewildered, confused, dazed, overwhelmed; agape, awed, awesome, wide-eyed, widemouthed

Thurs *or* **Thu** *abbr* Thursday

Thurs·day \ˈthərz-dē, -ˌdā\ *n* [ME, fr. OE *thursdæg*, fr. ON *thōrsdagr*, lit., day of Thor (Norse god)] : the 5th day of the week

thus \ˈthəs\ *adv* **1** : in this or that manner **2** ♦ : to this degree or extent : SO ⟨∼ far⟩ **3** ♦ : because of this or that : HENCE
  ♦ *usu* **thus far** [2] heretofore, hitherto, so, yet — more at HITHERTO ♦ [3] accordingly, consequently, ergo, hence, so, therefore, wherefore — more at THEREFORE

¹**thwack** \ˈthwak\ *vb* : to strike with or as if with something flat or heavy

²**thwack** *n* **1** : a heavy blow : WHACK **2** ♦ : the sound of or as if of a heavy blow
  ♦ bang, blast, boom, clap, crack, crash, pop, report, slam, smash, snap, whack — more at CLAP

¹**thwart** \ˈthwȯrt\ *vb* **1** ♦ : to oppose successfully : FOIL **2** : BLOCK, DEFEAT ⟨∼ed the attack⟩
  ♦ baffle, balk, beat, checkmate, foil, frustrate — more at FRUSTRATE

²**thwart** \ˈthwȯrt, *naut often* ˈthȯrt\ *adv* : ATHWART

³**thwart** *adj* : situated or placed across something else

⁴**thwart** \ˈthwȯrt\ *n* : a seat extending across a boat

thy \ˈthī\ *adj, archaic* : of, relating to, or done by or to thee or thyself

thyme \ˈtīm, ˈthīm\ *n* [ME, fr. MF *thym*, fr. L *thymum*, fr. Gk *thymon*, prob. fr. *thyein* to make a burnt offering, sacrifice] : a garden mint with small aromatic leaves used esp. in seasoning; *also* : its leaves so used

thy·mine \ˈthī-ˌmēn\ *n* : a pyrimidine base that is one of the four bases coding genetic information in the molecular chain of DNA

thy·mus \ˈthī-məs\ *n, pl* **thy·mus·es** : a glandular organ of the neck region that is composed largely of lymphoid tissue, functions esp. in the development of the immune system, and tends to atrophy in the adult

thy·ris·tor \thī-ˈris-tər\ *n* : a semiconductor device that acts as a switch, rectifier, or voltage regulator

thy·roid \ˈthī-ˌrȯid\ *n* [NL *thyroides*, fr. Gk *thyreoeidēs* shield-shaped, thyroid, fr. *thyreos* shield shaped like a door, fr. *thyra* door] : a large 2-lobed endocrine gland that lies at the base of the neck and produces several iodine-containing hormones that affect growth, development, and metabolism — **thyroid** *also* **thy·roi·dal** \thī-ˈrȯi-dᵊl\ *adj*

thy·rox·ine *or* **thy·rox·in** \thī-ˈräk-ˌsēn, -sən\ *n* : an iodine-containing hormone that is produced by the thyroid gland, increases metabolic rate, and is used to treat thyroid disorders

thy·self \thī-ˈself\ *pron, archaic* : YOURSELF

Ti *symbol* titanium

ti·ara \tē-ˈar-ə, -ˈer-, -ˈär-\ *n* **1** : a 3-tiered crown worn by the pope **2** : a decorative headband or semicircle for formal wear by women

Ti·bet·an \tə-ˈbet-ᵊn\ *n* **1** : the language of the Tibetan people **2** : a native or inhabitant of Tibet — **Tibetan** *adj*

tib·ia \ˈti-bē-ə\ *n, pl* **-i·ae** \-bē-ˌē\ *also* **-i·as** [L] : the inner of the two bones of the vertebrate hind or lower limb between the knee and the ankle

tic \ˈtik\ *n* **1** : a local and habitual twitching of muscles esp. of the face **2** ♦ : a frequent usu. unconscious quirk of behavior or speech
  ♦ crotchet, eccentricity, idiosyncrasy, mannerism, oddity, peculiarity, quirk, singularity, trick — more at IDIOSYNCRASY

¹**tick** \ˈtik\ *n* : any of a large group of small bloodsucking arachnids

²**tick** *n* : the fabric case of a mattress or pillow; *also* : a mattress consisting of a tick and its filling

³**tick** *n* **1** : a light rhythmic audible tap or beat **2** : a small mark used to draw attention to or check something

⁴**tick** *vb* **1** : to make the sound of a tick or series of ticks **2** ♦ : to mark, count, or announce by or as if by ticking beats — often used with *off* **3** ♦ : to mark or check with a tick — usu. used with *off* **4** : to function as an operating mechanism : RUN
  ♦ *usu* **tick off** [2, 3] detail, enumerate, itemize, list, numerate, rehearse — more at ENUMERATE

⁵**tick** *n, chiefly Brit* : CREDIT; *also* : a credit account

tick·er \ˈti-kər\ *n* **1** : something (as a watch) that ticks **2** : a telegraph instrument that prints information (as stock prices) on paper tape **3** *slang* : HEART

ticker tape *n* : the paper ribbon on which a telegraphic ticker prints

¹**tick·et** \ˈti-kət\ *n* [MF *etiquet, estiquette* notice attached to something, fr. MF dial. *estiquier* to attach, fr. MD *steken* to stick] **1 a** : CERTIFICATE, LICENSE, PERMIT **b** ♦ : a certificate or token showing that a fare or admission fee has been paid **2** : a marker used for identification or classification : TAG, LABEL **3** : SLATE 4 **4** : a summons issued to a traffic offender
  ♦ check, note, pass, token

²**ticket** *vb* **1** ♦ : to attach a ticket to **2** : to furnish or serve with a ticket
  ♦ label, mark, tag — more at LABEL

tick·ing \ˈti-kiŋ\ *n* : a strong fabric used in upholstering and as a mattress covering

tick·le \ˈti-kəl\ *vb* **tick·led; tick·ling** **1** : to excite or stir up agreeably : PLEASE, AMUSE **2** : to have a tingling sensation **3** : to touch (as a body part) lightly so as to cause uneasiness, laughter, or spasmodic movements ⟨*tickled* her under the chin⟩ — **tickle** *n* — **tick·ler** *n*

tick·lish \-kə-lish\ *adj* **1** ♦ : overly sensitive : TOUCHY **2** : UNSTABLE ⟨a ∼ foothold⟩ **3** ♦ : requiring delicate handling ⟨∼ subject⟩ **4** : sensitive to tickling — **tick·lish·ly** *adv* — **tick·lish·ness** *n*
  ♦ catchy, delicate, difficult, knotty, problematic, spiny, thorny, touchy, tough, tricky — more at TRICKY

tidal wave *n* **1** : an unusually high sea wave that sometimes follows an earthquake **2** : an unusual rise of water alongshore due to strong winds

tid·bit \ˈtid-ˌbit\ *n* ♦ : a choice morsel
  ♦ bite, morsel, mouthful, nibble, taste — more at MORSEL ♦ dainty, delicacy, goody, treat — more at DELICACY

¹**tide** \ˈtīd\ *n* [ME, time, fr. OE *tīd*] **1** : the alternate rising and falling of the surface of the ocean **2** ♦ : something that fluctuates like the tides of the sea ⟨the ∼ of public opinion⟩ — **tid·al** \ˈtīd-ᵊl\ *adj*

♦ current, drift, leaning, run, tendency, trend, wind — more at TREND

²**tide** *vb* **tid·ed; tid·ing** : to carry through or help along as if by the tide ⟨a loan to ~ us over⟩

tide·land \'tīd-,land, -lənd\ *n* **1** : land overflowed during flood tide **2** : land under the ocean within a nation's territorial waters — often used in pl.

tide·wa·ter \-,wȯ-tər, -,wä-\ *n* **1** : water overflowing land at flood tide **2** : low-lying coastal land

tid·ings \'tī-diŋz\ *n pl* ♦ : previously unknown information : NEWS

♦ intelligence, item, news, story, word — more at NEWS

¹**ti·dy** \'tī-dē\ *adj* **ti·di·er; -est** **1** ♦ : well ordered and cared for : NEAT **2 a** ♦ : exceeding most other things of like kind esp. in quantity or size : LARGE ⟨a ~ sum⟩ **b** ♦ : significantly great : SUBSTANTIAL — **ti·di·ness** \'tī-dē-nəs\ *n*

♦ [1] crisp, neat, orderly, shipshape, snug, trim, uncluttered — more at NEAT ♦ [2a, b] considerable, good, goodly, healthy, large, respectable, significant, sizable, substantial — more at CONSIDERABLE

²**tidy** *vb* **ti·died; ti·dy·ing** **1** : to put in order **2** : to make things tidy

³**tidy** *n, pl* **tidies** : a decorated covering used to protect the back or arms of a chair from wear or soil

¹**tie** \'tī\ *n* **1** : a line, ribbon, or cord used for fastening, uniting, or closing **2** : a structural element (as a beam or rod) holding two pieces together **3** : one of the cross supports to which railroad rails are fastened **4** ♦ : a connecting link : BOND ⟨family ~s⟩ **5** ♦ : an equality in number (as of votes or scores); *also* : an undecided or deadlocked contest **6** : NECKTIE

♦ [4] bond, cement, knot, ligature, link — more at BOND ♦ [5] dead heat, draw, stalemate, standoff; *also* deadlock, impasse; photo finish; toss-up

²**tie** *vb* **tied; ty·ing** *or* **tie·ing** **1** ♦ : to fasten, attach, or close by means of a tie **2** : to bring together firmly : UNITE **3** : to form a knot or bow in ⟨~ a scarf⟩ **4** : to restrain from freedom of action : CONSTRAIN **5 a** : to make or have an equal score with **b** ♦ : to provide or offer something equal to

♦ [1] band, bind, gird, truss; *also* cinch, cord, rope, strap, thread, wire; lash, leash, tether; interlace, intertwine, interweave, lace; entangle, knot, snarl, tangle, twist; coil, wind *Ant* unbind, untie ♦ [5b] equal, match, meet

tie·back \'tī-,bak\ *n* : a decorative strip for draping a curtain to the side of a window

tie–dye·ing \'tī-,dī-iŋ\ *n* : a method of producing patterns in textiles by tying parts of the fabric so that they will not absorb the dye — **tie–dyed** \-,dīd\ *adj*

tie–in \'tī-,in\ *n* : CONNECTION

tier \'tir\ *n* : ROW, LAYER; *esp* : one of two or more rows arranged one above another — **tiered** \'tird\ *adj*

tie–rod \'tī-,räd\ *n* : a rod used as a connecting member or brace

tie–up \-,əp\ *n* **1** : a slowing or stopping of traffic or business **2** : the act of connecting : the state of being connected : CONNECTION

tie up *vb* **1 a** : to place or invest in such a manner as to make unavailable for other purposes ⟨their money was *tied up* in stocks⟩ **b** ♦ : to restrain from normal movement, operation, or progress ⟨traffic was *tied up* for miles⟩ **2 a** : to keep busy ⟨was *tied up* in conference all day⟩ **b** : to preempt the use of ⟨*tied up* the phone for an hour⟩

♦ encumber, hamper, hinder, hold up, impede, inhibit, interfere with, obstruct — more at HAMPER

tiff \'tif\ *n* : a petty quarrel — **tiff** *vb*

Tif·fa·ny \'ti-fə-nē\ *adj* : made of pieces of stained glass ⟨a ~ lamp⟩

ti·ger \'tī-gər\ *n* : a very large tawny black-striped Asian cat — **ti·ger·ish** *adj*

¹**tight** \'tīt\ *adj* **1** ♦ : so close in structure as to prevent passage of a liquid or gas **2** ♦ : strongly fixed or held : SECURE **3** : not slack or loose : TAUT **4** : fitting usu. too closely ⟨~ shoes⟩ **5** ♦ : set close together : COMPACT ⟨a ~ formation⟩ **6** : DIFFICULT, TRYING ⟨get in a ~ spot⟩ **7** : not liberal in giving : STINGY **8** ♦ : evenly contested : CLOSE **9** : INTOXICATED **10** : low in supply : hard to get ⟨money is ~⟩ — **tight·ly** *adv*

♦ [1] impenetrable, impervious; *also* close, compact, dense, snug, thick; airtight, hermetic, watertight; lightproof, soundproof, waterproof *Ant* penetrable, permeable ♦ [2] fast, firm, frozen, secure, set, snug; *also* bonded, cemented; anchored, clamped; embedded, entrenched, implanted; attached, bound, fastened, secured; immovable, unyielding *Ant* insecure, loose ♦ [5] close, compact, crowded, dense, packed, serried, thick — more at CLOSE ♦ [8] close, narrow, neck and neck, nip and tuck — more at CLOSE

²**tight** *adv* **1** : TIGHTLY, FIRMLY **2** : SOUNDLY ⟨sleep ~⟩

tight·en \'tīt-ᵊn\ *vb* : to make or become tight

tight·fist·ed \'tīt-'fis-təd\ *adj* ♦ : not liberal in giving : STINGY

♦ cheap, close, mean, niggardly, parsimonious, penurious, spare, sparing, stingy, tight, uncharitable — more at STINGY

tight·ness \'tīt-nəs\ *n* ♦ : the quality or state of being tight

♦ cheapness, closeness, miserliness, parsimony, stinginess — more at PARSIMONY

tight·rope \-,rōp\ *n* : a taut rope or wire for acrobats to perform on

tights \'tīts\ *n pl* : skintight garments covering the body esp. below the waist; *also, Brit* : PANTY HOSE

tight·wad \'tīt-,wäd\ *n* ♦ : a stingy person

♦ cheapskate, miser, niggard, skinflint — more at MISER

ti·gress \'tī-grəs\ *n* : a female tiger

ti·la·pia \tə-'lä-pē-ə, -'lā-\ *n, pl* **tilapia** *also* **ti·la·pi·as** : any of numerous chiefly African freshwater fishes widely raised for food

til·de \'til-də\ *n* [Sp, fr. ML *titulus* tittle] : a mark ~ placed esp. over the letter *n* (as in Spanish *señor* sir) to denote the sound \nʸ\ or over vowels (as in Portuguese *irmã* sister) to indicate nasal quality

¹**tile** \'tīl\ *n* **1** : a flat or curved piece of fired clay, stone, or concrete used for roofs, floors, or walls; *also* : a pipe of earthenware or concrete used for a drain **2** : a thin piece (as of linoleum) used for covering walls or floors — **til·ing** \'tī-liŋ\ *n*

²**tile** *vb* **tiled; til·ing** : to cover with tiles — **til·er** *n*

¹**till** \'til\ *prep or conj* : UNTIL

²**till** *vb* : to work by plowing, sowing, and raising crops : CULTIVATE — **till·able** *adj*

³**till** *n* : DRAWER; *esp* : a money drawer in a store or bank

till·age \'ti-lij\ *n* **1** : the work of tilling land **2** : cultivated land

¹**til·ler** \'ti-lər\ *n* [OE *telgor, telgra* twig, shoot] : a sprout or stalk esp. from the base or lower part of a plant

²**til·ler** \'ti-lər\ *n* ♦ : one that tills

♦ agriculturist, cultivator, farmer, grower, planter — more at FARMER

³**til·ler** \'ti-lər\ *n* [ME *tiler* stock of a crossbow, fr. AF *teiler* stock of a crossbow] : a lever used for turning a boat's rudder from side to side

¹**tilt** \'tilt\ *n* **1** : a contest in which two combatants charging usu. with lances try to unhorse each other : JOUST; *also* : a tournament of tilts **2** : a verbal contest : DISPUTE **3** ♦ : the act of tilting : the state or position of being tilted

♦ bend, cock, inclination, list, slant, tip; *also* turn, twist, veer; bow, dip, nod

²**tilt** *vb* **1** ♦ : to move or shift so as to incline : TIP **2** : to engage in or as if in combat with lances : JOUST, ATTACK

♦ angle, cant, cock, heel, incline, lean, list, slant, slope, tip — more at LEAN

tilth \'tilth\ *n* **1** : TILLAGE 2 **2** : the state of a soil esp. in relation to the suitability of its particle size and structure for growing crops

Tim *abbr* Timothy

tim·ber \'tim-bər\ *n* [ME, fr. OE, building, wood] **1** : growing trees or their wood — often used interjectionally to warn of a falling tree **2** : wood for use in making something **3** : a usu. large squared or dressed piece of wood

tim·bered \'tim-bərd\ *adj* : having walls framed by exposed timbers

tim·ber·land \'tim-bər-ˌland\ *n* ♦ : wooded land

♦ forest, woodland — more at FOREST

tim·ber·line \'tim-bər-ˌlīn\ *n* : the upper limit of tree growth in mountains or high latitudes

timber rattlesnake *n* : a widely distributed rattlesnake of the eastern U.S.

timber wolf *n* : GRAY WOLF

tim·bre *also* **tim·ber** \'tam-bər, 'tim-\ *n* [F, fr. MF, bell struck by a hammer, fr. OF, drum, fr. MGk *tymbanon* kettledrum, fr. Gk *tympanon*] : the distinctive quality given to a sound by its overtones

tim·brel \'tim-brəl\ *n* : a small hand drum or tambourine

¹time \'tīm\ *n* **1 a** : a period during which an action, process, or condition exists or continues ⟨gone a long ∼⟩ **b** : the duration of the existence of a living being (as a person or an animal) or a thing (as a star) : LIFETIME **2** : LEISURE ⟨found ∼ to read⟩ **3** : a point or period when something occurs : OCCASION ⟨the last ∼ we met⟩ **4** : a set or customary moment or hour for something to occur ⟨arrived on ∼⟩ **5** ♦ : a historical period : AGE, ERA **6** : state of affairs : CONDITIONS ⟨hard ∼s⟩ **7** : a rate of speed : TEMPO **8** : a moment, hour, day, or year as indicated by a clock or calendar ⟨what ∼ is it⟩ **9** : a system of reckoning time ⟨solar ∼⟩ **10** : one of a series of recurring instances; *also, pl* : added or accumulated quantities or examples ⟨five ∼s greater⟩ **11** ♦ : a person's experience during a particular period ⟨had a good ∼⟩ **12** : the hours or days of one's work; *also* : an hourly pay rate ⟨straight ∼⟩ **13** : TIME-OUT 1

♦ [5] age, epoch, era, period ♦ [11] adventure, experience, happening — more at ADVENTURE

²time *vb* **timed; tim·ing** **1** : to arrange or set the time of : SCHEDULE ⟨∼s his calls conveniently⟩ **2** : to set the tempo or duration of ⟨∼ a performance⟩ **3** : to cause to keep time with **4** : to determine or record the time, duration, or rate of ⟨∼ a sprinter⟩

time bomb *n* **1** : a bomb so made as to explode at a predetermined time **2** : something with a potentially dangerous delayed reaction

time clock *n* : a clock that records the time workers arrive and depart

time frame *n* : a period of time esp. with respect to some action or project

time–hon·ored \'tīm-ˌä-nərd\ *adj* : honored because of age or long usage

time·keep·er \-ˌkē-pər\ *n* **1** : a clerk who keeps records of the time worked by employees **2** : one appointed to mark and announce the time in an athletic game or contest

time·less \-ləs\ *adj* **1** : ETERNAL **2** ♦ : not limited or affected by time ⟨∼ works of art⟩ — **time·less·ly** *adv* — **time·less·ness** *n*

♦ abiding, ageless, continuing, dateless, enduring, eternal, everlasting, immortal, imperishable, lasting, perennial, perpetual, undying — more at ABIDING

time·li·ness \'tīm-lē-nəs\ *n* ♦ : the quality or state of being timely

♦ promptitude, punctuality — more at PROMPTITUDE

time·ly \'tīm-lē\ *adj* **time·li·er; -est** **1** ♦ : coming early or at the right time ⟨a ∼ arrival⟩ **2** : appropriate to the time ⟨a ∼ book⟩

♦ immediate, prompt, punctual — more at PROMPT

time–out \'tīm-ˈaut\ *n* **1** : a brief suspension of activity esp. in an athletic game **2** : a quiet period used esp. as a disciplinary measure for a child

time·piece \-ˌpēs\ *n* ♦ : a device (as a clock) to show the passage of time

♦ watch; *also* atomic clock, grandfather clock, time clock; hourglass, sundial; chronograph, stopwatch

tim·er \'tī-mər\ *n* : one that times

times \'tīmz\ *prep* : multiplied by ⟨2 ∼ 2 is 4⟩

time–shar·ing \'tīm-ˌshar-iŋ\ *n* **1** : simultaneous use of a computer by many users **2** *or* **time–share** \-ˌshar\ : joint ownership or rental of a vacation lodging by several persons with each taking turns using the place

times sign *n* : the symbol × used to indicate multiplication

time·ta·ble \'tīm-ˌtā-bəl\ *n* **1** : a table of the departure and arrival times (as of trains) **2** ♦ : a schedule showing a planned order or sequence

♦ agenda, calendar, docket, program, schedule — more at PROGRAM

time warp *n* : an anomaly, discontinuity, or suspension held to occur in the progress of time

time·worn \-ˌwōrn\ *adj* **1** : worn by time **2** : HACKNEYED, STALE

tim·id \'ti-məd\ *adj* ♦ : lacking in courage or self-confidence : FEARFUL — **ti·mid·i·ty** \tə-ˈmi-də-tē\ *n* — **tim·id·ly** *adv*

♦ fainthearted, fearful, mousy, scary, shy, skittish — more at SHY

tim·o·rous \'ti-mə-rəs\ *adj* : of a timid disposition : AFRAID ⟨a ∼ kitten⟩ — **tim·o·rous·ly** *adv* — **tim·o·rous·ness** *n*

tim·o·thy \'ti-mə-thē\ *n* : a perennial grass with long cylindrical spikes widely grown for hay in the U.S.

Tim·o·thy \'ti-mə-thē\ *n* : either of two books of the New Testament of Christian Scripture

tim·pa·ni \'tim-pə-nē\ *n sing or pl* [It] : a set of kettledrums played by one performer in an orchestra — **tim·pa·nist** \-nist\ *n*

¹tin \'tin\ *n* **1** : a soft white crystalline metallic chemical element malleable at ordinary temperatures that is used esp. in solders and alloys **2** ♦ : a container (as a can) made of metal (as tinplate)

♦ barrel, can, canister, drum — more at CAN

²tin *vb* **tinned; tin·ning** **1** : to cover or plate with tin **2** : to pack in tins

TIN *abbr* taxpayer identification number

tinct \'tiŋkt\ *n* : TINCTURE, TINGE

¹tinc·ture \'tiŋk-chər\ *n* **1** *archaic* : a substance that colors **2** : a slight admixture : TRACE **3** : an alcoholic solution of a medicinal substance

²tincture *vb* **tinc·tured; tinc·tur·ing** **1** : COLOR, TINGE **2** : AFFECT

tin·der \'tin-dər\ *n* **1** : a very flammable substance used as kindling **2** : something serving to incite or inflame

tin·der·box \'tin-dər-ˌbäks\ *n* **1** : a metal box for holding tinder and usu. flint and steel for striking a spark **2** : a highly flammable object or place

tine \'tīn\ *n* : a slender pointed part (as of a fork or an antler) : PRONG

tin·foil \'tin-ˌfȯil\ *n* : a thin metal sheeting usu. of aluminum or tin-lead alloy

¹tinge \'tinj\ *vb* **tinged; tinge·ing** *or* **ting·ing** **1** ♦ : to color slightly : TINT **2** : to affect or modify esp. with a slight odor or taste

♦ color (*or* colour), dye, paint, stain, tint — more at COLOR

²tinge *n* ♦ : a slight color, flavor, or quality

♦ cast, color (*or* colour), hue, shade, tint, tone — more at COLOR

¹tin·gle \'tiŋ-gəl\ *vb* **tin·gled; tin·gling** **1** : to feel a prickling or thrilling sensation **2** : TINKLE

²tingle *n* ♦ : a tingling sensation or condition

♦ ache, pain, pang, prick, smart, sting, stitch, twinge — more at PAIN

¹tin·ker \'tiŋ-kər\ *n* **1** : a usu. itinerant mender of household utensils **2** : an unskillful mender : BUNGLER

²**tinker** *vb* ♦ : to repair or adjust something in an unskillful or experimental manner — **tin·ker·er** *n*

　　♦ fiddle, fool, mess, monkey, play, tamper — more at TAMPER

¹**tin·kle** \'tiŋ-kəl\ *vb* **tin·kled; tin·kling** ♦ : to make or cause to make a tinkle

　　♦ chink, jingle — more at JINGLE

²**tinkle** *n* : a series of short high ringing or clinking sounds

tin·ni·tus \'ti-nə-təs, tə-'nī-təs\ *n* : a sensation of noise (as ringing or roaring) in the ears

tin·ny \'ti-nē\ *adj* **tin·ni·er; -est** **1** : abounding in or yielding tin **2** : resembling tin; *also* : LIGHT, CHEAP **3** : thin in tone ⟨a ~ voice⟩ — **tin·ni·ly** \-nə-lē\ *adv* — **tin·ni·ness** \-nē-nəs\ *n*

tin·plate \'tin-'plāt\ *n* : thin sheet iron or steel coated with tin — **tin–plate** *vb*

tin·sel \'tin-səl\ *n* [ME *tyneseyle* cloth interwoven with metallic thread, prob. fr. AF *tencelé*, pp. of *tenceler, estenceler* to sparkle] **1** : a thread, strip, or sheet of metal, paper, or plastic used to produce a glittering appearance **2** : something superficially attractive but of little worth

tin·smith \'tin-ˌsmith\ *n* : one that works with sheet metal (as tinplate)

¹**tint** \'tint\ *n* **1** ♦ : a slight or pale coloration : HUE **2** ♦ : any of various shades of a color

　　♦ cast, color (*or* colour), hue, shade, tinge, tone — more at COLOR

²**tint** *vb* ♦ : to impart a tint to : COLOR

　　♦ color (*or* colour), dye, paint, stain, tinge — more at COLOR

tin·tin·nab·u·la·tion \ˌtin-tə-ˌna-byə-'lā-shən\ *n* **1** : the ringing of bells **2** : a tinkling or jingling sound as if of bells

tin·ware \'tin-ˌwar\ *n* : articles and esp. utensils made of tinplate

ti·ny \'tī-nē\ *adj* **ti·ni·er; -est** ♦ : very small : MINUTE

　　♦ atomic, infinitesimal, microscopic, miniature, minute, wee; *also* diminutive, dwarf, little, midget, model, petite, pocket, pygmy, small, smallish; dinky, dwarfish, insignificant, pint-size, puny, scrubby, undersized **Ant** enormous, giant, gigantic, huge, immense, mammoth

¹**tip** \'tip\ *vb* **tipped; tip·ping** **1** : OVERTURN, UPSET **2** ♦ : to incline, deviate, or bend from a vertical position : LEAN; *also* : to raise and tilt forward ⟨*tipped* his hat⟩

　　♦ angle, cant, cock, heel, incline, lean, list, slant, slope, tilt — more at LEAN

²**tip** *n* ♦ : the act or an instance of tipping

　　♦ bend, cock, inclination, list, slant, tilt — more at TILT

³**tip** *vb* **tipped; tip·ping** **1** : to furnish with a tip **2** : to cover or adorn the tip of

⁴**tip** *n* **1** ♦ : the usu. pointed end of something **2** : a small piece or part serving as an end, cap, or point

　　♦ apex, cusp, end, pike, point — more at POINT

⁵**tip** *n* : a light touch or blow

⁶**tip** *vb* **tipped; tip·ping** : to strike lightly : TAP

⁷**tip** *n* ♦ : a piece of advice or expert or confidential information

　　♦ dope, lowdown, scoop — more at DOPE ♦ hint, lead, pointer; *also* advisement, assistance, counsel, guidance, recommendation, suggestion; caution, cautioning, sign, signal, telltale, tip-off, warning; brief, direction, feedback, instruction, observation; prompt, reminder, urging; answer, clue, solution

⁸**tip** *vb* **tipped; tip·ping** : to impart a piece of information about or to

⁹**tip** *vb* **tipped; tip·ping** : to give a gratuity to — **tip·per** *n*

¹⁰**tip** *n* ♦ : a gift or small sum given for a service performed or anticipated

　　♦ bonus, dividend, extra, lagniappe, perquisite — more at BONUS

tip–off \'tip-ˌof\ *n* ♦ : something that warns or serves to warn : WARNING

　　♦ caution, wake-up call, warning — more at WARNING

tip·pet \'ti-pət\ *n* : a long scarf or shoulder cape

tipping point *n* : the critical point in a situation or process beyond which a significant effect takes place

tip·ple \'ti-pəl\ *vb* **tip·pled; tip·pling** : to drink intoxicating liquor esp. habitually or excessively — **tipple** *n*

tip·pler \'ti-p(ə-)lər\ *n* ♦ : one that tipples

　　♦ drunk, inebriate, soak, sot, souse — more at DRUNK

tip·ster \'tip-stər\ *n* : a person who gives or sells tips esp. for gambling

tip·sy \'tip-sē\ *adj* **tip·si·er; -est** ♦ : unsteady or foolish from the effects of alcohol — **tip·si·ly** \-sə-lē\ *adv*

　　♦ drunk, high, inebriate, intoxicated — more at DRUNK

¹**tip·toe** \'tip-ˌtō\ *n* : the position of being balanced on the balls of the feet and toes with the heels raised; *also* : the ends of the toes

²**tiptoe** *adv or adj* : on or as if on tiptoe

³**tiptoe** *vb* **tip·toed; tip·toe·ing** : to walk or proceed on or as if on tiptoe

¹**tip–top** \'tip-'täp\ *n* ♦ : the highest point

　　♦ acme, apex, climax, crown, culmination, head, height, meridian, peak, pinnacle, summit, top, zenith — more at HEIGHT

²**tip–top** *adj* : very good of its kind : EXCELLENT

ti·rade \'tī-ˌrād\ *n* [F, shot, tirade, fr. MF, fr. It *tirata*, fr. *tirare* to draw, shoot] ♦ : a prolonged speech of abuse or condemnation

　　♦ diatribe, harangue, rant; *also* assault, attack, invective, lashing, tongue-lashing, vituperation; berating, rebuke, reprimand, reproach, reproof; abuse, castigation, censure, criticism, denunciation; deprecation, depreciation, disparagement; excoriation, execration, revilement; admonishment, admonition, lecture, sermon

tir·a·mi·su \ˌtir-ə-'mē-sü, -mē-'sü\ *n* [It *tiramisù*] : a dessert made with ladyfingers, mascarpone, and espresso

¹**tire** \'tīr\ *vb* **tired; tir·ing** **1** ♦ : to make or become weary **2** ♦ : to wear out the patience of : BORE

　　♦ [1] burn out, do in, drain, exhaust, fag, fatigue, tucker, wash out, wear, wear out, weary — more at EXHAUST
　　♦ [2] bore, jade, weary — more at BORE

²**tire** *n* **1** : a metal hoop that forms the tread of a wheel **2** : a rubber cushion usu. containing compressed air that encircles a wheel (as of a bike)

tired \'tīrd\ *adj* **1** ♦ : exhausted in strength, endurance, vigor, or freshness : WEARY, FATIGUED **2** ♦ : lacking in freshness or originality : HACKNEYED **3** ♦ : having one's patience, tolerance, or pleasure exhausted

　　♦ [1] beat, bushed, dead, drained, effete, jaded, limp, prostrate, spent, weary, worn-out — more at WEARY
　　♦ [2] banal, commonplace, hackneyed, musty, stale, stereotyped, threadbare, trite — more at STALE
　　♦ [3] fed up, jaded, sick, weary — more at WEARY

tired·ness *n* ♦ : the quality or state of being tired

　　♦ burnout, collapse, exhaustion, fatigue, lassitude, prostration, weariness — more at FATIGUE ♦ boredom, doldrums, ennui, listlessness, tedium, weariness — more at BOREDOM

tire·less \'tīr-ləs\ *adj* ♦ : not tiring : UNTIRING ⟨~ workers⟩ — **tire·less·ness** *n*

　　♦ indefatigable, inexhaustible, unflagging, untiring; *also* assiduous, conscientious, diligent, meticulous, painstaking, sedulous; determined, dogged, patient, persevering, persistent, pertinacious, plodding, relentless, steadfast, steady, stubborn, tenacious, unfailing, unfaltering, unflinching, unrelenting, unremitting, unwavering; active, busy, dynamic, energetic, feverish, spirited, vigorous; hard, industrious, intense, laborious, slavish, strenuous

tire·less·ly *adv* ♦ : in a tireless manner

　　♦ determinedly, diligently, hard, hardly, laboriously, mightily, slavishly, strenuously — more at HARD

tire·some \-səm\ *adj* : tending to bore : WEARISOME, TEDIOUS ⟨a ∼ lecture⟩ — **tire·some·ly** *adv* — **tire·some·ness** *n*

tis·sue \'ti-shü\ *n* [ME *tysshewe, tyssew*, a rich fabric, fr. AF, fr. *tistre* to weave, fr. L *texere*] **1** : a fine lightweight often sheer fabric **2** : NETWORK, WEB **3** : a soft absorbent paper **4** : a mass or layer of cells forming a basic structural material of an animal or plant

¹tit \'tit\ *n* : TEAT

²tit *n* : any of various small plump Old World songbirds related to the titmice

Tit *abbr* Titus

ti·tan \'tīt-ᵊn\ *n* **1** *cap* : one of a family of giants overthrown by the gods in Greek mythology **2** ♦ : one gigantic in size or power ⟨a media ∼⟩

♦ behemoth, blockbuster, colossus, giant, jumbo, leviathan, mammoth, monster, whale, whopper — more at GIANT

ti·tan·ic \tī-'ta-nik\ *adj* ♦ : enormous in size, force, or power

♦ colossal, enormous, giant, gigantic, huge, mammoth, massive, prodigious, tremendous

ti·ta·ni·um \tī-'tā-nē-əm\ *n* : a gray light strong metallic chemical element used esp. in alloys

titbit *var of* TIDBIT

tithe \'tīth\ *n* [ME, fr. OE *teogotha* tenth] : a 10th part paid or given esp. for the support of a church — **tithe** *vb* — **tith·er** *n*

tit·il·late \'tit-ᵊl-ˌāt\ *vb* **-lat·ed; -lat·ing 1** ♦ : to excite pleasurably **2** : TICKLE 3

♦ electrify, excite, exhilarate, galvanize, intoxicate, thrill, turn on — more at THRILL

tit·il·la·tion \ˌtit-ᵊl-'ā-shən\ *n* ♦ : the action of titillating or the state of being titillated

♦ bang, exhilaration, kick, thrill — more at THRILL

ti·tle \'tīt-ᵊl\ *n* **1** : CLAIM, RIGHT; *esp* : a legal right to the ownership of property **2** ♦ : the distinguishing name esp. of an artistic production (as a book) **3** ♦ : an appellation of honor, rank, or office **4** : CHAMPIONSHIP

♦ [2] heading — more at HEADING ♦ [3] appellation, cognomen, denotation, designation, handle, name — more at NAME

ti·tled \'tīt-ᵊld\ *adj* : having a title esp. of nobility

title page *n* : a page of a book bearing the title and usu. the names of the author and publisher

tit·mouse \'tit-ˌmaůs\ *n, pl* **tit·mice** \-ˌmīs\ : any of several small long-tailed No. American songbirds related to the chickadees

ti·tra·tion \tī-'trā-shən\ *n* : a process of finding the concentration of a solution (as of an acid) by adding small portions of a second solution of known concentration (as of a base) to a fixed amount of the first until an expected change (as in color) occurs

¹tit·ter \'ti-tər\ *vb* : to laugh in an affected or in a nervous or half-suppressed manner : GIGGLE

²titter *n* ♦ : an act or instance of tittering

♦ cackle, chortle, laugh, laughter, snicker — more at LAUGH

tit·tle \'tit-ᵊl\ *n* ♦ : a tiny piece

♦ bit, hoot, jot, lick, modicum, rap, whit — more at JOT

tit·tle-tat·tle \'tit-ᵊl-ˌtat-ᵊl\ *n* : idle talk : GOSSIP — **tittle-tattle** *vb*

tit·u·lar \'ti-chə-lər\ *adj* **1** ♦ : existing in title only : NOMINAL ⟨∼ ruler⟩ **2** : of, relating to, or bearing a title ⟨∼ role⟩

♦ formal, nominal, paper — more at NOMINAL

Ti·tus \'tī-təs\ *n* : a book of the New Testament of Christian Scripture

tiz·zy \'ti-zē\ *n, pl* **tizzies** ♦ : a highly excited and distracted state of mind

♦ dither, fluster, fret, fuss, huff, lather, pother, stew, twitter — more at FRET

tk *abbr* **1** tank **2** truck

TKO \ˌtē-ˌkā-'ō\ *n* [*technical knock out*] : the termination of a boxing match when a boxer is declared unable to continue the fight

tkt *abbr* ticket

Tl *symbol* thallium

TLC *abbr* tender loving care

T lymphocyte *n* : T CELL

Tm *symbol* thulium

TM *abbr* trademark

T-man \'tē-ˌman\ *n* : a special agent of the U.S. Treasury Department

tn *abbr* **1** ton **2** town

TN *abbr* Tennessee

tng *abbr* training

tnpk *abbr* turnpike

TNT \ˌtē-(ˌ)en-'tē\ *n* : a flammable toxic compound used as a high explosive and in chemical synthesis

¹to \tə, 'tü\ *prep* **1** : in the direction of and reaching ⟨drove ∼ town⟩ **2** : in the direction of : TOWARD **3** : ON, AGAINST ⟨apply salve ∼ a burn⟩ **4** : as far as ⟨can pay up ∼ a dollar⟩ **5** : so as to become or bring about ⟨beaten ∼ death⟩ ⟨broken ∼ pieces⟩ **6** ♦ : earlier than : BEFORE ⟨it's five minutes ∼ six⟩ **7** : UNTIL ⟨from May ∼ December⟩ **8** : fitting or being a part of : FOR ⟨key ∼ the lock⟩ **9** : with the accompaniment of ⟨sing ∼ the music⟩ **10** : in relation or comparison with ⟨similar ∼ that one⟩ ⟨won 10 ∼ 6⟩ **11** : in accordance with ⟨add salt ∼ taste⟩ **12** : within the range of ⟨∼ my knowledge⟩ **13** : contained, occurring, or included in ⟨two pints ∼ a quart⟩ **14** : as regards ⟨agreeable ∼ everyone⟩ **15** : affecting as the receiver or beneficiary ⟨whispered ∼ her⟩ ⟨gave it ∼ me⟩ **16** : for no one except ⟨a room ∼ myself⟩ **17** : into the action of ⟨we got ∼ talking⟩ **18** — used for marking the following verb as an infinitive ⟨wants ∼ go⟩ and often used by itself at the end of a clause in place of an infinitive suggested by the preceding context ⟨goes to town whenever he wants ∼⟩ ⟨can leave if you'd like ∼⟩

♦ ahead of, before, ere, of, previous to, prior to — more at BEFORE

²to \'tü\ *adv* **1** : in a direction toward ⟨run ∼ and fro⟩ **2** : into contact esp. with the frame of a door ⟨the door slammed ∼⟩ **3** : to the matter in hand ⟨fell ∼ and ate heartily⟩ **4** : to a state of consciousness or awareness ⟨came ∼ hours after the accident⟩

TO *abbr* turn over

toad \'tōd\ *n* : any of numerous tailless leaping amphibians differing typically from the related frogs in having a shorter stockier build, rough dry warty skin, and less aquatic habits

toad·stool \-ˌstül\ *n* : MUSHROOM; *esp* : one that is poisonous or inedible

¹toady \'tō-dē\ *n, pl* **toad·ies** : a person who flatters in the hope of gaining favors : SYCOPHANT

²toady *vb* **toad·ied; toady·ing** ♦ : to behave as a toady

♦ fawn, fuss, kowtow — more at FAWN

to-and-fro \ˌtü-ən-'frō\ *adj* : forward and backward — **to-and-fro** *n*

¹toast \'tōst\ *vb* **1** : to warm thoroughly **2** : to make (as bread) crisp, hot, and brown by heat **3** : to become toasted

²toast *n* **1** : sliced toasted bread **2** : someone or something in whose honor persons drink **3** : an act of drinking in honor of a toast

³toast *vb* : to propose or drink to as a toast

toast·er \'tō-stər\ *n* : an electrical appliance for toasting

toaster oven *n* : a portable electrical appliance that bakes, broils, and toasts

toast·mas·ter \'tōst-ˌmas-tər\ *n* : a person who presides at a banquet and introduces the after-dinner speakers

toast·mis·tress \-ˌmis-trəs\ *n* : a woman who acts as toastmaster

toasty \'tō-stē\ *adj* **toast·i·er; -est** : pleasantly warm

Tob *abbr* Tobit

to·bac·co \tə-ˈba-kō\ *n, pl* **-cos** [Sp *tabaco*] **1** : a tall broad-leaved herb related to the potato; *also* : its leaves prepared for smoking or chewing or as snuff **2** : manufactured tobacco products; *also* : smoking as a practice

to·bac·co·nist \tə-ˈba-kə-nist\ *n* : a dealer in tobacco

To·bi·as \tō-ˈbī-əs\ *n* : TOBIT

To·bit \ˈtō-bət\ *n* : a book in the Roman Catholic canon of the Old Testament and in the Protestant Apocrypha

¹to·bog·gan \tə-ˈbä-gən\ *n* : a long flat-bottomed light sled made of thin boards curved up at one end

²toboggan *vb* **1** : to coast on or as if on a toboggan **2** : to decline suddenly (as in value) — **to·bog·gan·er** *n*

toc·sin \ˈtäk-sən\ *n* **1** : an alarm bell **2** : a warning signal

¹to·day \tə-ˈdā\ *adv* **1** : on or for this day **2** ♦ : at the present time

    ♦ anymore, now, nowadays, presently, right now — more at NOW

²today *n* ♦ : the present day, time, or age

    ♦ moment, now, present — more at PRESENT

tod·dle \ˈtäd-ᵊl\ *vb* **tod·dled; tod·dling** : to walk with short tottering steps in the manner of a young child — **toddle** *n* — **tod·dler** *n*

tod·dy \ˈtä-dē\ *n, pl* **toddies** [Hindi & Urdu *tāṛī* juice of a palm, fr. *tāṛ* a palm, fr. Skt *tāla*] : a drink made of liquor, sugar, spices, and hot water

to–do \tə-ˈdü\ *n, pl* **to–dos** \-ˈdüz\ : excited and usu. exaggerated stir : BUSTLE, FUSS

¹toe \ˈtō\ *n* **1** : one of the jointed parts of the front end of the vertebrate foot **2** : the front part of a foot or hoof

²toe *vb* **toed; toe·ing** : to touch, reach, or drive with the toes

toe·hold \ˈtō-ˌhōld\ *n* **1** : a place of support for the toes **2** : a slight footing

toe·nail \ˈtō-ˌnāl\ *n* : a nail of a toe

tof·fee *or* **tof·fy** \ˈtȯ-fē, ˈtä-\ *n, pl* **toffees** *or* **toffies** : candy of brittle but tender texture made by boiling sugar and butter together

to·fu \ˈtō-(ˌ)fü\ *n* [Jp *tōfu*] : a soft white food product made from soybeans

tog \ˈtäg, ˈtȯg\ *vb* **togged; tog·ging** : to put togs on : DRESS

to·ga \ˈtō-gə\ *n* : the loose outer garment worn in public by citizens of ancient Rome — **to·gaed** \-gəd\ *adj*

¹to·geth·er \tə-ˈge-thər\ *adv* **1** : in or into one place or group **2** : in or into contact or association ⟨mix ∼⟩ **3** : at one time : SIMULTANEOUSLY ⟨talk and work ∼⟩ **4** : in succession ⟨for days ∼⟩ **5** : in or into harmony or coherence ⟨get ∼ on a plan⟩ **6** ♦ : as a group : JOINTLY — **to·geth·er·ness** *n*

    ♦ all around, altogether, collectively, overall — more at ALL AROUND

²together *adj* : composed in mind or manner

tog·gery \ˈtä-gə-rē, ˈtȯ-\ *n* : CLOTHING

tog·gle \ˈtä-gəl\ *vb* : to switch between two options esp. of an electronic device

tog·gle switch \ˈtä-gəl-\ *n* : an electric switch operated by pushing a projecting lever through a small arc

To·go·lese \ˌtō-gə-ˈlēz, -ˈlēs\ *n* : a native or inhabitant of Togo — **Togolese** *adj*

togs \ˈtägz, ˈtȯgz\ *n pl* : CLOTHING; *esp* : clothes for a specified use ⟨riding ∼⟩

¹toil \ˈtȯil\ *n* **1** : laborious effort **2** ♦ : long fatiguing labor : DRUDGERY — **toil·ful** \-fəl\ *adj*

    ♦ drudgery, grind, labor (*or* labour), slavery, sweat, travail; *also* effort, exertion, pains, struggle, trouble; chore, duty, job, obligation, responsibility; routine, tedium, treadmill *Ant* fun, play

²toil *vb* [ME, to argue, struggle, fr. AF *toiller* to make dirty, fight, wrangle, fr. L *tudiculare* to crush, grind, fr. *tu·di·cu·la* machine for crushing olives, dim. of *tudes* hammer] **1** ♦ : to work hard and long **2** : to proceed with great effort : PLOD

    ♦ drudge, fag, grub, labor (*or* labour), slave, sweat, travail; *also* drive, endeavor, strain, strive, struggle; hammer,

hump, hustle, peg (away), plod, plow (away), plug (away), slog

³toil *n* [ME *toile* cloth, net, fr. OF *teile*, fr. L *tela* cloth on a loom] : NET, TRAP — usu. used in pl.

toil·er *n* ♦ : one that toils

    ♦ drudge, fag, peon, slave, worker — more at SLAVE

toi·let \ˈtȯi-lət\ *n* **1** : the act or process of dressing and grooming oneself **2** ♦ : a room furnished with a fixture for flushing body waste **3** : a fixture for use in urinating and defecating; *esp* : one consisting essentially of a water-flushed bowl and seat — **toilet** *vb*

    ♦ bathroom, lavatory; *also* commode; outhouse, privy

toilet paper *n* : an absorbent paper for drying or cleaning oneself after defecation or urination

toi·let·ry \ˈtȯi-lə-trē\ *n, pl* **-ries** : an article or preparation used in cleaning or grooming oneself — usu. used in pl.

toi·lette \twä-ˈlet\ *n* **1** : TOILET 1 **2** : formal attire; *also* : a particular costume

toilet training *n* : the process of training a child to control bladder and bowel movements and to use the toilet — **toilet train** *vb*

toil·some \ˈtȯi(-ə)l-səm\ *adj* ♦ : marked by or full of toil or fatigue

    ♦ arduous, burdensome, challenging, demanding, exacting, grueling, laborious, onerous, taxing — more at DEMANDING

toil·worn \ˈtȯil-ˌwȯrn\ *adj* : showing the effects of toil

To·kay \tō-ˈkā\ *n* : naturally sweet wine from Hungary

toke \ˈtōk\ *n, slang* : a puff on a marijuana cigarette or pipe

¹to·ken \ˈtō-kən\ *n* **1** : an outward sign **2** : SYMBOL, EMBLEM **3** ♦ : something that serves as a reminder : KEEPSAKE **4** : a small part representing the whole **5** : a piece resembling a coin issued as money or for use by a particular group on specified terms

    ♦ keepsake, memento, memorial, monument, remembrance, souvenir — more at MEMORIAL

²token *adj* **1** : done or given as a token esp. in partial fulfillment of an obligation **2** : representing only a symbolic effort : MINIMAL, PERFUNCTORY

to·ken·ism \ˈtō-kə-ˌni-zəm\ *n* : the policy or practice of making only a symbolic effort (as to desegregate)

told *past and past part of* TELL

tole \ˈtōl\ *n* : sheet metal and esp. tinplate for use in domestic and ornamental wares

tol·er·a·ble \ˈtä-lə-rə-bəl\ *adj* **1** ♦ : capable of being borne or endured **2** ♦ : moderately good : PASSABLE

    ♦ [1] bearable, endurable, sufferable, supportable, sustainable — more at BEARABLE ♦ [2] acceptable, adequate, all right, decent, fine, OK, passable, respectable, satisfactory — more at ADEQUATE

tol·er·a·bly \ˈtä-lə-rə-blē\ *adv* ♦ : in a tolerable manner

    ♦ adequately, all right, fine, good, nicely, OK, passably, satisfactorily, so-so, well — more at WELL

tol·er·ance \ˈtä-lə-rəns\ *n* **1** ♦ : the act or practice of tolerating; *esp* : sympathy or indulgence for beliefs or practices differing from one's own **2** : the allowable deviation from a standard (as of size) **3** : the body's capacity to become less responsive over time to something (as a drug used repeatedly) — **tol·er·ant·ly** *adv*

    ♦ forbearance, long-suffering, patience, sufferance — more at PATIENCE

tol·er·ant \ˈtä-lə-rənt\ *adj* ♦ : inclined to tolerate; *esp* : marked by forbearance or endurance

    ♦ forbearing, long-suffering, patient, stoic, uncomplaining — more at PATIENT

tol·er·ate \ˈtä-lə-ˌrāt\ *vb* **-at·ed; -at·ing** **1** : to exhibit physiological tolerance for (as a drug) **2** ♦ : to allow to be or to be done without hindrance — **tol·er·a·tion** \ˌtä-lə-ˈrā-shən\ *n*

    ♦ abide, bear, brook, countenance, endure, meet, stand, stick out, stomach, support, sustain, take — more at BEAR

¹**toll** \'tōl\ *n* **1** : a tax paid for a privilege (as for passing over a bridge) **2** : a charge for a service (as for a long-distance telephone call) **3** : the cost in life, health, loss, or suffering

²**toll** *vb* **1** : to cause the slow regular sounding of (a bell) esp. by pulling a rope **2** : to give signal of : SOUND **3** ♦ : to sound with slow measured strokes **4** : to announce by tolling

♦ chime, knell, peal, ring — more at RING

³**toll** *n* : the sound of a tolling bell

toll·booth \'tōl-ˌbüth\ *n* : a booth where tolls are paid

toll·gate \-ˌgāt\ *n* : a point where vehicles stop to pay a toll

toll·house \-ˌhaùs\ *n* : a house or booth where tolls are paid

tol·u·ene \'täl-yə-ˌwēn\ *n* : a liquid hydrocarbon used esp. as a solvent

tom \'täm\ *n* : the male of various animals (as a cat or turkey)

¹**tom·a·hawk** \'tä-mə-ˌhòk\ *n* : a light ax used as a missile and as a hand weapon esp. by No. American Indians

²**tomahawk** *vb* : to strike or kill with a tomahawk

to·ma·til·lo \ˌtō-mə-ˈtē-(ˌ)yō\ *n, pl* **-los** : a small round usu. pale green edible fruit of a Mexican herb related to the tomato; *also* : this herb

to·ma·to \tə-ˈmā-tō, -ˈmä-\ *n, pl* **-toes** [alter. of earlier *tomate*, fr. Sp, fr. Nahuatl *tomatl*] : a usu. large, rounded, and red or yellow pulpy edible berry of a widely grown tropical herb related to the potato; *also* : this herb

tomb \'tüm\ *n* **1** : a place of burial : GRAVE **2** : a house, chamber, or vault for the dead — **tomb** *vb*

tom·boy \'täm-ˌbòi\ *n* : a girl who behaves in a manner usu. considered boyish

tom·boy·ish \-ish\ *adj* : relating to or being a tomboy

tomb·stone \'tüm-ˌstōn\ *n* ♦ : a stone marking a grave

♦ gravestone, headstone, monument; *also* cross, marker, plaque, stone, table, tablet; monolith, obelisk, pillar; memorial, shrine

tom·cat \'täm-ˌkat\ *n* : a male domestic cat

Tom Col·lins \'täm-ˈkä-lənz\ *n* : a tall iced drink with a base of gin

tome \'tōm\ *n* : BOOK; *esp* : a large or weighty one

tom·fool·ery \täm-ˈfü-lə-rē\ *n* ♦ : playful or foolish behavior

♦ foolery, high jinks, horseplay, monkeyshines, roughhouse, shenanigans — more at HORSEPLAY

tom·my gun \'tä-mē-ˌgən\ *n* : SUBMACHINE GUN — **tommygun** *vb*

to·mog·ra·phy \tō-ˈmä-grə-fē\ *n* : a method of producing a three-dimensional image of the internal structures of a solid object (as the human body or the earth) — **to·mo·graph·ic** \ˌtō-mə-ˈgra-fik\ *adj*

to·mor·row \tə-ˈmär-ō\ *adv* : on or for the day after today — **tomorrow** *n*

tom–tom \'täm-ˌtäm\ *n* : a small-headed drum beaten with the hands

ton \'tən\ *n, pl* **tons** *also* **ton** **1 a** : a unit of weight equal to 2000 pounds in the U.S. and Canada : SHORT TON **b** : LONG TON **2** : a unit equal to the volume of a long ton weight of seawater used in reckoning the displacement of ships and equal to 35 cubic feet

to·nal·i·ty \tō-ˈna-lə-tē\ *n, pl* **-ties** : tonal quality

¹**tone** \'tōn\ *n* [ME, fr. L *tonus* tension, tone, fr. Gk *tonos*, lit., act of stretching; fr. the dependence of the pitch of a musical string on its tension] **1** : vocal or musical sound; *esp* : sound quality **2** : a sound of definite pitch **3** : WHOLE STEP **4** : accent or inflection expressive of an emotion **5** : the pitch of a word often used to express differences of meaning **6** ♦ : style or manner of expression **7** ♦ : color quality; *also* : SHADE **8** : the effect in painting of light and shade together with color **9** : healthy and vigorous condition of a living body or bodily part; *also* : the state of partial contraction characteristic of normal muscle **10** ♦ : general character, quality, or trend — **ton·al** \'tōn-ᵊl\ *adj*

♦ [6] fashion, locution, manner, mode, phraseology, style, vein — more at STYLE ♦ [7] cast, color (*or* colour), hue, shade, tinge, tint — more at COLOR ♦ [10] character, complexion, constitution, genius, nature, personality — more at NATURE

²**tone** *vb* **toned; ton·ing** **1** : to give a particular intonation or inflection to **2** : to impart tone to **3** : SOFTEN, MELLOW ⟨∼ down your language⟩ **4** : to harmonize in color : BLEND

tone·arm *n* : the movable part of a record player that carries the pickup and the needle

toney *var of* TONY

tong \'täŋ, 'tòŋ\ *n* : a Chinese secret society in the U.S.

tongs \'täŋz, 'tòŋz\ *n pl* : a grasping device consisting of two pieces joined at one end by a pivot or hinged like scissors — **tong** *vb*

¹**tongue** \'təŋ\ *n* **1** : a fleshy movable process of the floor of the mouth used in tasting and in taking and swallowing food and in humans as a speech organ **2** : the flesh of a tongue (as of the ox) used as food **3** : the power of communication **4** ♦ : the words, their pronunciation, and the method of combining them used and understood by a community : LANGUAGE **5** : manner or quality of utterance; *also* : intended meaning **6** : ecstatic usu. unintelligible utterance accompanying religious excitation — usu. used in pl. **7** : something resembling an animal's tongue esp. in being elongated and fastened at one end only — **tongued** \'təŋd\ *adj* — **tongue·less** *adj*

♦ language, lingo, speech, vocabulary — more at LANGUAGE

²**tongue** *vb* **tongued; tongu·ing** **1** : to touch or lick with the tongue **2** : to articulate notes on a wind instrument

tongue–in–cheek *adj* : characterized by insincerity, irony, or whimsical exaggeration — **tongue in cheek** *adv*

tongue–lash \'təŋ-ˌlash\ *vb* : CHIDE, REPROVE — **tongue–lash·ing** \-iŋ\ *n*

tongue–tied \-ˌtīd\ *adj* : unable or disinclined to speak clearly or freely (as from shyness or a tongue impairment)

tongue twister *n* : an utterance that is difficult to articulate because of a succession of similar consonants

¹**ton·ic** \'tä-nik\ *adj* **1** ♦ : of, relating to, or producing a healthy physical or mental condition : INVIGORATING **2** : relating to or based on the 1st tone of a scale — **to·nic·i·ty** \tō-ˈni-sə-tē\ *n*

♦ bracing, invigorating, refreshing, restorative, stimulative; *also* conditioning, strengthening; animating, exhilarating, quickening, sharp; corrective, curative, curing, medicinal, rectifying, reformative, reformatory, remedial, remedying, reparative, therapeutic; beneficial, healthful, healthy, helpful, salubrious, salutary, wholesome

²**tonic** *n* **1** : something that invigorates, restores, or refreshes **2** : the 1st degree of a musical scale

tonic water *n* : a carbonated beverage flavored with a bit of quinine, lemon, and lime

¹**to·night** \tə-ˈnīt\ *adv* : on this present night or the coming night

²**tonight** *n* : the present or the coming night

ton·nage \'tə-nij\ *n* **1** : a duty on ships based on tons carried **2** : ships in terms of the number of tons registered or carried **3** : total weight in tons shipped, carried, or mined

ton·sil \'tän-səl\ *n* : either of a pair of oval masses of lymphoid tissue that lie one on each side of the throat at the back of the mouth

ton·sil·lec·to·my \ˌtän-sə-ˈlek-tə-mē\ *n, pl* **-mies** : the surgical removal of the tonsils

ton·sil·li·tis \-ˈlī-təs\ *n* : inflammation of the tonsils

ton·so·ri·al \tän-ˈsōr-ē-əl\ *adj* : of or relating to a barber or a barber's work

ton·sure \'tän-chər\ *n* [ME, fr. AF, ML *tonsura*, fr. L, act of shearing, fr. *tonsus*, pp. of *tondēre* to shear] **1** : the rite of admission to the clerical state by the clipping or shaving of the head **2** : the shaven crown or patch worn by clerics (as monks) — **tonsure** *vb*

tony *also* **ton·ey** \'tō-nē\ *adj* **ton·i·er; -est** : marked by an aristocratic manner or style

too \'tü\ *adv* **1** ♦ : in addition : ALSO **2** ♦ : to an excessive degree : EXCESSIVELY ⟨the rent is ~ high⟩ **3** : to such a degree as to be regrettable **4** : to a high degree : VERY

♦ [1] additionally, again, also, besides, further, furthermore, likewise, more, moreover, then, withal, yet ♦ [2] devilishly, excessively, inordinately, monstrously, overly, overmuch; *also* extravagantly, immoderately; extortionately, inexcusably, intolerably, unbearably, unconscionably, unreasonably; improperly; abnormally, extraordinarily, singularly, uncommonly, unusually; considerably, eminently, exceedingly, exceptionally, extensively, extra, extremely, incredibly, remarkably, significantly, substantially, super, very, whacking **Ant** inadequately, insufficiently

took *past of* TAKE

¹tool \'tül\ *n* **1** ♦ : a hand instrument that aids in accomplishing a task **2** : the cutting or shaping part in a machine; *also* : a machine for shaping machinery in any way **3** : something used in doing a job ⟨a scholar's books are his ~s⟩; *also* : a means to an end **4** ♦ : a person used by another : DUPE **5** *pl* : natural ability

♦ [1] device, implement, instrument, utensil — more at IMPLEMENT ♦ [4] dupe, gull, pigeon, sap, sucker — more at DUPE

²tool *vb* **1** : to shape, form, or finish with a tool; *esp* : to letter or decorate (as a book cover) by means of hand tools **2** : to equip a plant or industry with machines and tools for production **3** : DRIVE, RIDE ⟨~ing along at 60 miles per hour⟩

tool bar *n* : a strip of icons on a computer display providing quick access to the pictured functions

¹toot \'tüt\ *vb* **1** : to sound or cause to sound in short blasts **2** : to blow an instrument (as a horn) — **toot·er** *n*

²toot *n* : a short blast (as on a horn)

tooth \'tüth\ *n, pl* **teeth** \'tēth\ **1** : one of the hard bony structures borne esp. on the jaws of vertebrates and used for seizing and chewing food and as weapons; *also* : a hard sharp structure esp. around the mouth of an invertebrate **2** : something resembling an animal's tooth **3** : any of the projections on the edge of a wheel that fits into corresponding projections on another wheel **4** : effective means of enforcement — **toothed** \'tütht\ *adj* — **tooth·less** *adj*

tooth·ache \'tüth-ˌāk\ *n* : pain in or about a tooth

tooth·brush \-ˌbrəsh\ *n* : a brush for cleaning the teeth

tooth·paste \-ˌpāst\ *n* : a paste for cleaning the teeth

tooth·pick \-ˌpik\ *n* : a pointed instrument for removing food particles caught between the teeth

tooth powder *n* : a powder for cleaning the teeth

tooth·some \'tüth-səm\ *adj* **1** : AGREEABLE, ATTRACTIVE **2** ♦ : pleasing to the taste : DELICIOUS

♦ ambrosial, appetizing, delectable, delicious, flavorful (*or* flavourful), luscious, palatable, savory, scrumptious, tasty, yummy — more at DELICIOUS

toothy \'tü-thē\ *adj* **tooth·i·er; -est** : having or showing prominent teeth

¹top \'täp\ *n* **1** ♦ : the highest part, point, or level of something **2** : the part of a plant with edible roots lying above the ground ⟨beet ~s⟩ **3** : the upper end, edge, or surface ⟨the ~ of a page⟩ **4** ♦ : an upper piece, lid, or covering **5** : the highest degree, pitch, or rank

♦ [1] acme, apex, climax, crown, culmination, head, height, meridian, peak, pinnacle, summit, tip-top, zenith — more at HEIGHT ♦ [4] cap, cover, lid — more at COVER

²top *vb* **topped; top·ping** **1** : to remove or trim the top of : PRUNE ⟨~ a tree⟩ **2** : to cover with a top or on the top : CROWN, CAP **3** ♦ : to be superior to : SURPASS **4** : to

go over the top of **5** : to strike (a ball) above the center **6** : to make an end or conclusion ⟨~ off a meal with coffee⟩

♦ beat, better, eclipse, excel, outdistance, outdo, outshine, outstrip, surpass, transcend — more at SURPASS

³top *adj* **1** : of, relating to, or being at the top **2** : CHIEF **3** ♦ : of the highest quality, amount, or degree

♦ consummate, maximum, most, nth, paramount, supreme, ultimate, utmost — more at ULTIMATE ♦ full, maximum, utmost — more at FULL

⁴top *n* : a toy that has a tapering point on which it is made to spin

to·paz \'tō-ˌpaz\ *n* : a hard silicate of aluminum; *esp* : a yellow transparent topaz used as a gem

top·coat \'täp-ˌkōt\ *n* **1** : a lightweight overcoat **2** : a protective coating (as of paint)

top dollar *n* : the highest amount being paid for a commodity or service

top·dress \-ˌdres\ *vb* : to apply material to (as land) without working it in; *esp* : to scatter fertilizer over

top·dress·ing \-ˌdre-siŋ\ *n* : a material used to top-dress soil

top·end \'täp-'end\ *adj* : TOPFLIGHT

top·flight \'täp-'flīt\ *adj* : of, relating to, or being the highest level of excellence or rank — **top flight** *n*

top hat *n* : a tall-crowned hat usu. of beaver or silk

top·heavy \'täp-ˌhe-vē\ *adj* : having the top part too heavy for the lower part

to·pi·ary \'tō-pē-ˌer-ē\ *n, pl* **-ar·ies** : the art of training and trimming trees or shrubs with decorative shapes — **topiary** *adj*

top·ic \'tä-pik\ *n* **1** : a heading in an outlined argument **2** ♦ : the subject of a discourse or a section of it : THEME

♦ content, matter, motif, motive, question, subject, theme — more at MATTER

top·i·cal \-pi-kəl\ *adj* **1** : designed to be applied to or to work on a part (as of the body) **2** : of, relating to, or arranged by topics ⟨a ~ outline⟩ **3** : relating to current or local events — **top·i·cal·ly** \-k(ə-)lē\ *adv*

top·knot \'täp-ˌnät\ *n* **1** : an ornament (as a knot of ribbons) forming a headdress **2** : a crest of feathers or tuft of hair on the top of the head **3** : hair worn in a knot high on the head

top·less \-ləs\ *adj* **1** : wearing no clothing on the upper body **2** : featuring topless waitresses or entertainers

top·mast \'täp-ˌmast, -məst\ *n* : the 2d mast above a ship's deck

top·most \'täp-ˌmōst\ *adj* : highest of all : UPPERMOST

top·notch \-'näch\ *adj* : of the highest quality : FIRST-RATE

top-of-the-line *adj* ♦ : being or belonging to the highest or most expensive class

♦ A1, crackerjack, dandy, excellent, fine, first-rate, sensational, splendid, superb, terrific, wonderful — more at EXCELLENT

to·pog·ra·phy \tə-'pä-grə-fē\ *n* **1** : the art of showing in detail on a map or chart the physical features of a place or region **2** : the outline of the form of a place showing its relief and the position of features (as rivers, roads, or cities) — **to·pog·ra·pher** \-fər\ *n* — **top·o·graph·ic** \ˌtä-pə-'gra-fik\ *or* **top·o·graph·i·cal** \-fi-kəl\ *adj*

top·ping \'tä-piŋ\ *n* : a food served on top of another to make it look or taste better

top·ple \'tä-pəl\ *vb* **top·pled; top·pling** **1** ♦ : to fall from or as if from being top-heavy **2** : to push over : OVERTURN; *also* : OVERTHROW ⟨*toppled* the dictator⟩

♦ fall, slip, stumble, trip, tumble — more at FALL

tops \'täps\ *adj* : topmost in quality or importance ⟨~ in his field⟩

top·sail \'täp-ˌsāl, -səl\ *also* **top·s'l** \-səl\ *n* : the sail next above the lowest sail on a mast in a square-rigged ship

top secret *adj* : demanding complete secrecy among those concerned

top·side \'täp-'sīd\ *adv or adj* **1** : to or on the top or surface **2** : on deck

top·sides \-'sīdz\ *n pl* : the top portion of the outer surface of a ship on each side above the waterline

top·soil \'täp-ˌsȯil\ *n* : surface soil usu. including the organic layer in which plants have most of their roots

top·sy–tur·vy \ˌtäp-sē-'tər-vē\ *adj* ♦ : totally disordered — **topsy–turvy** *adv*

♦ chaotic, disheveled, disordered, disorderly, messy, untidy

toque \'tōk\ *n* : a woman's small hat without a brim

tor \'tȯr\ *n* : a high craggy hill

To·rah \'tȯr-ə\ *n* 1 : a scroll of the first five books of the Old Testament used in a synagogue; *also* : these five books 2 : the body of divine knowledge and law found in the Jewish Scriptures and tradition

¹**torch** \'tȯrch\ *n* 1 : a flaming light made of something that burns brightly and usu. carried in the hand 2 : something that resembles a torch in giving light, heat, or guidance 3 *chiefly Brit* : FLASHLIGHT 4 : a portable burner for producing a hot flame

²**torch** *vb* : to set fire to

torch·bear·er \'tȯrch-ˌber-ər\ *n* 1 : a person who carries a torch 2 : one in the forefront (as of a political campaign)

torch·light \-ˌlīt\ *n* : light given by torches

torch song *n* : a popular sentimental song of unrequited love

tore *past of* TEAR

to·re·ador \'tȯr-ē-ə-ˌdȯr\ *n* : BULLFIGHTER

to·re·ro \tə-'rer-ō\ *n, pl* **-ros** [Sp] : BULLFIGHTER

¹**tor·ment** \'tȯr-ˌment\ *n* 1 ♦ : extreme pain or anguish of body or mind 2 ♦ : a source of vexation or pain

♦ [1] affliction, agony, anguish, distress, misery, pain, torture, tribulation, woe — more at DISTRESS ♦ [2] agony, hell, horror, misery, murder, nightmare, torture — more at HELL

²**tor·ment** \tȯr-'ment\ *vb* 1 ♦ : to cause severe suffering of body or mind to 2 : DISTORT, TWIST

♦ afflict, agonize, bedevil, curse, harrow, martyr, persecute, plague, rack, torture — more at AFFLICT

tor·men·tor \-'men-tər\ *n* ♦ : one that torments

♦ heckler, oppressor, persecutor, taunter, torturer; *also* mocker, scoffer, scorner; accuser, troublemaker; assailant, molester; baiter, disturber, pest

torn *past part of* TEAR

tor·na·do \tȯr-'nā-dō\ *n, pl* **-does** *or* **-dos** [modif of Sp *tronada* thunderstorm, fr. *tronar* to thunder, fr. L *tonare*] : a violent destructive whirling wind accompanied by a funnel-shaped cloud that moves over a narrow path

¹**tor·pe·do** \tȯr-'pē-dō\ *n, pl* **-does** : a thin cylindrical self-propelled underwater weapon

²**torpedo** *vb* **tor·pe·doed; tor·pe·do·ing** : to hit or destroy with or as if with a torpedo

torpedo boat *n* : a small very fast boat for firing torpedoes

tor·pid \'tȯr-pəd\ *adj* 1 : having lost motion or the power of exertion : DORMANT 2 : sluggish in functioning or acting 3 ♦ : lacking vigor — **tor·pid·i·ty** \tȯr-'pi-də-tē\ *n*

♦ dull, inactive, inert, lethargic, quiescent, sleepy, sluggish — more at INACTIVE

tor·por \'tȯr-pər\ *n* 1 : DULLNESS, APATHY 2 : extreme sluggishness : STAGNATION

¹**torque** \'tȯrk\ *n* : a force that produces or tends to produce rotation or torsion

²**torque** *vb* **torqued; torqu·ing** : to impart torque to : cause to twist (as about an axis)

tor·rent \'tȯr-ənt\ *n* [F, fr. L *torrent-, torrens*, fr. *torrent-, torrens*, adj., burning, seething, rushing, fr. prp. of *torrēre* to parch, burn] 1 : a tumultuous outburst 2 ♦ : a rushing stream (as of water)

♦ cataclysm, cataract, deluge, flood, inundation, overflow, spate — more at FLOOD

tor·ren·tial \tȯ-'ren-chəl\ *adj* : relating to or resembling a torrent ⟨∼ rains⟩

tor·rid \'tȯr-əd\ *adj* 1 ♦ : parched with heat esp. of the sun : HOT 2 : ARDENT

♦ broiling, burning, fiery, hot, red-hot, scorching, sultry — more at HOT

torrid zone *n* : the region of the earth between the Tropic of Cancer and the Tropic of Capricorn

tor·sion \'tȯr-shən\ *n* 1 : a wrenching by which one part of a body is under pressure to turn about a longitudinal axis while the other part is held fast or is under pressure to turn in the opposite direction 2 : a twisting of a bodily organ or part on its own axis — **tor·sion·al** \'tȯr-shə-nəl\ *adj* — **tor·sion·al·ly** *adv*

tor·so \'tȯr-sō\ *n, pl* **torsos** *or* **tor·si** \'tȯr-ˌsē\ [It, lit., stalk] : the trunk of the human body

tort \'tȯrt\ *n* : a wrongful act which does not involve a breach of contract and for which the injured party can recover damages in a civil action

tor·til·la \tȯr-'tē-ə\ *n* : a round thin cake of unleavened cornmeal or wheat flour bread

tor·toise \'tȯr-təs\ *n* : TURTLE; *esp* : any of a family of land turtles

tor·toise·shell \-ˌshel\ *n* : the mottled horny substance of the shell of some turtles used in inlaying and in making various ornamental articles — **tortoiseshell** *adj*

tor·to·ni \tȯr-'tō-nē\ *n* : rich ice cream often made with minced almonds and chopped cherries and flavored with rum

tor·tu·ous \'tȯr-chə-wəs\ *adj* 1 ♦ : marked by twists or turns : WINDING ⟨a ∼ path⟩ 2 : DEVIOUS, TRICKY

♦ crooked, devious, serpentine, sinuous, winding — more at CROOKED

¹**tor·ture** \'tȯr-chər\ *n* 1 ♦ : anguish of body or mind 2 ♦ : the infliction of severe pain esp. to punish or coerce — **tor·tur·ous** \'tȯrch-rəs, 'tȯr-chə-\ *adj*

♦ [1] affliction, agony, anguish, distress, misery, pain, torment, tribulation, woe — more at DISTRESS ♦ [2] agony, hell, horror, misery, murder, nightmare, torment — more at HELL

²**torture** *vb* **tor·tured; tor·tur·ing** 1 ♦ : to cause intense suffering to : TORMENT 2 : to punish or coerce by inflicting severe pain 3 : TWIST, DISTORT

♦ afflict, agonize, bedevil, curse, harrow, martyr, persecute, plague, rack, torment — more at AFFLICT

tor·tur·er \'tȯr-chər-ər\ *n* ♦ : one that tortures

♦ heckler, oppressor, persecutor, taunter, tormentor — more at TORMENTOR

To·ry \'tȯr-ē\ *n, pl* **Tories** 1 : a member of a chiefly 18th century British party upholding the established church and the traditional political structure 2 : an American supporter of the British during the American Revolution 3 *often not cap* ♦ : an extreme conservative — **Tory** *adj*

♦ conservative, reactionary, rightist — more at CONSERVATIVE

¹**toss** \'tȯs, 'täs\ *vb* 1 : to fling to and fro or up and down; *also* : BANDY 2 ♦ : to throw with a quick light motion 3 : to fling or lift with a sudden motion ⟨∼ed her head angrily⟩ 4 : to move restlessly or turbulently ⟨∼es on the waves⟩ 5 ♦ : to twist and turn repeatedly 6 : FLOUNCE 7 : to accomplish readily ⟨∼ off an article⟩ 8 : to decide an issue by flipping a coin 9 ♦ : to consume by drinking ⟨∼ down a drink⟩

♦ [2] cast, catapult, chuck, dash, fire, fling, heave, hurl, hurtle, launch, peg, pelt, pitch, sling, throw — more at THROW ♦ [5] careen, lurch, pitch, rock, roll, seesaw, sway, wobble — more at ROCK ♦ *usu* **toss down** *or* **toss off** [9] drink, guzzle, imbibe, quaff, sup, swig — more at DRINK

²**toss** *n* : an act or instance of tossing; *esp* : TOSS-UP 1

toss–up \-ˌəp\ *n* 1 : a deciding by flipping a coin 2 : an even chance 3 : something that offers no clear basis for choice

¹**tot** \'tät\ *n* 1 : a small child 2 : a small drink of alcoholic liquor : SHOT

²**tot** *vb* **tot·ted; tot·ting** : to add up

³**tot** *abbr* total

¹to·tal \'tōt-ᵊl\ *adj* **1 ♦** : making up a whole : ENTIRE ⟨∼ amount⟩ **2** : being definitely what is stated : COMPLETE ⟨a ∼ failure⟩ **3 ♦** : involving a complete and unified effort esp. to achieve a desired effect

♦ [1] complete, comprehensive, entire, full, grand, intact, integral, perfect, plenary, whole — more at COMPLETE ♦ [3] all-out, clean, complete, comprehensive, exhaustive, full-scale, out-and-out, thorough, thoroughgoing — more at EXHAUSTIVE

²total *n* **1** : SUM 4 **2 ♦** : the entire amount

♦ aggregate, full, sum, totality, whole — more at WHOLE

³total *vb* **to·taled** *or* **to·talled; to·tal·ing** *or* **to·tal·ling** **1 ♦** : to add up **2 ♦** : to amount to : NUMBER **3** : to make a total wreck of (a car)

♦ [1] add, foot, sum — more at ADD ♦ [2] add up, amount, come, number, sum — more at AMOUNT (TO)

to·tal·i·tar·i·an \tō-,ta-lə-'ter-ē-ən\ *adj* : of, relating to, or advocating a political regime based on subordination of the individual to the state and strict control of all aspects of life esp. by coercive measures — **totalitarian** *n*

to·tal·i·tar·i·an·ism \tō-,ta-lə-'ter-ē-ə-,ni-zəm\ *n* **♦** : centralized control by an autocratic authority

♦ autocracy, despotism, dictatorship, tyranny — more at DESPOTISM

to·tal·i·ty \tō-'ta-lə-tē\ *n, pl* **-ties** **1 ♦** : an aggregate amount : SUM, WHOLE **2** : ENTIRETY, WHOLENESS

♦ aggregate, full, sum, total, whole — more at WHOLE

to·tal·iza·tor *or* **to·tal·isa·tor** \'tōt-ᵊl-ə-,zā-tər\ *n* : a machine for registering and indicating the number of bets and the odds on a horse or dog race

to·tal·ly \'tō-tᵊl-ē\ *adv* **♦** : in a total manner : to a total or complete degree

♦ absolutely, all, altogether, clean, completely, entirely, fully, quite, utterly, wholly — more at ALL ♦ completely, exhaustively, fully, minutely, roundly, thoroughly — more at THOROUGHLY

¹tote \'tōt\ *vb* **tot·ed; tot·ing** **♦** : to carry by hand

♦ bear, carry, cart, convey, ferry, haul, lug, pack, transport — more at CARRY

²tote *vb* **tot·ed; tot·ing** : ADD, TOTAL — usu. used with *up*

to·tem \'tō-təm\ *n* [Ojibwa *oto·te·man* his totem] : an object (as an animal or plant) serving as the emblem of a family or clan and often as a reminder of its ancestry; *also* : something usu. carved or painted to represent such an object

totem pole *n* : a pole that is carved with a series of totems and is erected before the houses of some northwest American Indians

tot·ter \'tä-tər\ *vb* **1 ♦** : to tremble or rock as if about to fall : SWAY **2 ♦** : to move unsteadily : STAGGER

♦ [1] falter, rock, seesaw, sway, teeter, waver, wobble — more at TEETER ♦ [2] careen, dodder, lurch, reel, stagger, teeter — more at STAGGER

tou·can \'tü-,kan\ *n* [F, fr. Pg *tucano*, fr. Tupinambá (American Indian language of Brazil) *tukána*] : any of a family of chiefly fruit-eating birds of tropical America with brilliant coloring and a very large bill

¹touch \'təch\ *vb* **1** : to bring a bodily part (as the hand) into contact with so as to feel **2 ♦** : to be or cause to be in contact **3** : to strike or push lightly esp. with the hand or foot **4** : DISTURB, HARM **5** : to make use of ⟨never ∼es alcohol⟩ **6** : to induce to give or lend **7** : to get to : REACH **8 ♦** : to refer to in passing : MENTION **9 ♦** : to affect the interest of : CONCERN **10 a** : to leave a mark on **b ♦** : to harm slightly by or as if by contact **11 ♦** : to move to sympathetic feeling **12** : to come close : VERGE **13 ♦** : to have a bearing : RELATE — used with *on* or *upon* **14** : to make a usu. brief or incidental stop in port

♦ [2] abut, adjoin, border (on), flank, fringe, join, skirt, verge (on) — more at ADJOIN ♦ *usu* **touch on** *or* **touch upon** [8, 13] advert (to), cite, instance, mention, name, note, notice, quote, refer (to), specify — more

at MENTION ♦ [9] affect, concern, interest, involve — more at CONCERN ♦ [10b] blemish, mar, poison, spoil, stain, taint, tarnish, vitiate — more at TAINT ♦ [11] affect, impact, impress, influence, move, strike, sway, tell — more at AFFECT

²touch *n* **1** : a light stroke or tap **2** : the act or fact of touching or being touched **3** : the sense by which pressure or traction on the skin or mucous membrane is perceived; *also* : a particular sensation conveyed by this sense **4** : mental or moral sensitiveness : TACT **5** : a small quantity : HINT ⟨a ∼ of spring in the air⟩ **6** : a manner of striking or touching esp. the keys of a keyboard instrument **7** : an improving detail ⟨add a few ∼es to the painting⟩ **8** : distinctive manner or skill ⟨the ∼ of a master⟩ **9** : the state of being in contact ⟨keep in ∼⟩

touch·down \'təch-,daún\ *n* : the act of scoring six points in American football by being lawfully in possession of the ball on, above, or behind an opponent's goal line

tou·ché \tü-'shā\ *interj* [F] — used to acknowledge a hit in fencing or the success of an argument, an accusation, or a witty point

touch football *n* : football in which touching is substituted for tackling

touch·ing *adj* **♦** : capable of stirring emotions

♦ affecting, emotional, impressive, moving, poignant, stirring — more at MOVING

touch off *vb* **1** : to describe with precision **2 ♦** : to start by or as if by touching with fire ⟨*touched off* a riot⟩

♦ activate, actuate, crank, drive, move, propel, run, set off, spark, start, trigger, turn on — more at ACTIVATE

touch screen *n* : a display screen (as on a computer) on which the user selects options by touching the screen

touch·stone \'təch-,stōn\ *n* **♦** : a test or criterion of genuineness or quality

♦ criterion, grade, mark, measure, par, standard, yardstick — more at STANDARD

touch–tone \'təch-'tōn\ *adj* : of, relating to, or being a telephone having push buttons that produce tones corresponding to numbers

touch up *vb* : to improve or perfect by small additional strokes or alterations — **touch–up** \'təch-,əp\ *n*

touchy \'tə-chē\ *adj* **touch·i·er; -est** **1** : easily offended : PEEVISH **2 ♦** : calling for tact in treatment ⟨a ∼ subject⟩

♦ catchy, delicate, difficult, knotty, problematic, spiny, thorny, ticklish, tough, tricky — more at TRICKY

¹tough \'təf\ *adj* **1** : strong or firm in texture but flexible and not brittle **2** : not easily chewed **3** : characterized by severity and determination ⟨a ∼ policy⟩ **4 ♦** : capable of enduring strain or hardship **5** : hard to influence : STUBBORN **6 ♦** : difficult to accomplish, resolve, or cope with ⟨a ∼ problem⟩ **7** : ROWDYISH — **tough·ly** *adv* — **tough·ness** *n*

♦ [4] hard, hard-bitten, hardy, rugged, stout, strong, sturdy, vigorous — more at HARDY ♦ [6] arduous, demanding, difficult, exacting, formidable, hard — more at HARD ♦ [6] catchy, delicate, difficult, knotty, problematic, spiny, thorny, ticklish, touchy, tricky — more at TRICKY

²tough *n* **♦** : a tough person : ROWDY

♦ bully, gangster, goon, hood, hoodlum, mobster, mug, punk, rowdy, ruffian, thug — more at HOODLUM

tough·en \'tə-fən\ *vb* **tough·ened; tough·en·ing** **♦** : to make or become tough

♦ beef, fortify, harden, steel, strengthen — more at STRENGTHEN ♦ fortify, harden, season, steel, strengthen — more at HARDEN

tou·pee \tü-'pā\ *n* [F *toupet* forelock] : a small wig for a bald spot

¹tour \'túr, *1 is also* 'taúr\ *n* **1 ♦** : one's turn **2** : a journey in which one returns to the starting point

♦ hitch, stint, tenure, term — more at TERM

²tour *vb* ♦ : to make a tour

♦ journey, travel, trek, voyage — more at TRAVEL

tour de force \ˌtur-də-ˈfōrs\ *n, pl* **tours de force** *same*\ [F] : a feat or display of strength, skill, or ingenuity

Tou·rette's syndrome \tu-ˈrets-\ *n* : a familial neurological disorder marked by recurrent involuntary tics and vocal sounds

tour·ism \ˈtur-ˌi-zəm\ *n* **1** : the practice of traveling for recreation **2** : promotion of touring **3** : accommodation of tourists

tour·ist \ˈtur-ist\ *n* ♦ : one that makes a tour for pleasure or culture

♦ excursionist, sightseer, traveler; *also* vacationer, vacationist; guest, visitor; transient; pilgrim, wayfarer

tourist class *n* : economy accommodations (as on a ship)

tour·ma·line \ˈtur-mə-lən, -ˌlēn\ *n* : a mineral that when transparent is valued as a gem

tour·na·ment \ˈtur-nə-mənt, ˈtər-\ *n* **1** : a medieval sport in which mounted armored knights contended with blunted lances or swords **2** ♦ : a championship series of games or athletic contests

♦ bout, competition, contest, event, game, match, meet — more at GAME

tour·ney \-nē\ *n, pl* **tourneys** : a championship series of games or athletic contests : TOURNAMENT

tour·ni·quet \ˈtur-ni-kət, ˈtər-\ *n* : a device (as a tight bandage) to check bleeding or blood flow

tou·sle \ˈtau-zəl\ *vb* **tou·sled; tou·sling** : to disorder by rough handling : DISHEVEL ⟨*tousled* his hair⟩

tout \ˈtaut, 2 *is also* ˈtüt\ *vb* **1** : to give a tip or solicit bets on a racehorse **2** ♦ : to praise or publicize loudly — **tout** *n*

♦ acclaim, applaud, cheer, crack up, hail, laud, praise, salute — more at ACCLAIM ♦ ballyhoo, crack up, glorify, plug, promote, publicize, trumpet; *also* advance, advertise, announce, boost, herald, offer

¹tow \ˈtō\ *vb* ♦ : to draw or pull along behind

♦ drag, draw, hale, haul, lug, pull, tug — more at PULL

²tow *n* **1** : an act of towing or condition of being towed **2** : something (as a barge) that is towed

³tow *n* : short or broken fiber (as of flax or hemp) used esp. for yarn, twine, or stuffing

to·ward \ˈtōrd, ˈtō-ərd, tə-ˈwórd\ *or* **to·wards** \ˈtōrdz, ˈtō-ərdz, tə-ˈwórdz\ *prep* **1** : in the direction of ⟨heading ∼ the river⟩ **2** : along a course leading to ⟨efforts ∼ reconciliation⟩ **3** ♦ : in regard to ⟨tolerance ∼ minorities⟩ **4** : so as to face ⟨turn the chair ∼ the window⟩ **5** : close upon ⟨it was getting along ∼ sundown⟩ **6** : for part payment of ⟨here's $100 ∼ your tuition⟩

♦ about, apropos of, concerning, of, on, regarding, respecting — more at ABOUT

tow·boat \ˈtō-ˌbōt\ *n* : TUGBOAT

tow·el \ˈtau-əl\ *n* : an absorbent cloth or paper for wiping or drying

tow·el·ing *or* **tow·el·ling** *n* : a cotton or linen fabric for making towels

¹tow·er \ˈtau-ər\ *n* **1** : a tall structure either isolated or built upon a larger structure ⟨an observation ∼⟩ **2** : a towering citadel **3** : a personal computer case that stands in an upright position — **tow·ered** *adj*

²tower *vb* : to reach or rise to a great height

tow·er·ing *adj* **1** ♦ : impressively high or great in size or quality ⟨∼ pines⟩ **2** : reaching high intensity ⟨a ∼ rage⟩ **3** ♦ : going beyond proper bounds : EXCESSIVE ⟨∼ ambition⟩

♦ [1] high, lofty, tall — more at HIGH ♦ [3] excessive, extreme, immoderate, inordinate, lavish, overmuch

tow·head \ˈtō-ˌhed\ *n* : a person having whitish blond hair — **tow·head·ed** \-ˌhe-dəd\ *adj*

to·whee \ˈtō-ˌhē, ˈtō-(ˌ)ē, tō-ˈhē\ *n* : a common finch of eastern No. America having the male black, white, and reddish; *also* : any of several closely related finches

to wit *adv* : NAMELY

town \ˈtaun\ *n* **1** : a compactly settled area usu. larger than a village but smaller than a city **2** : a large densely populated urban area : CITY **3** : the inhabitants of a town **4** : a New England territorial and political unit usu. containing both rural and urban areas; *also* : a New England community in which matters of local government are decided by a general assembly (**town meeting**) of qualified voters

town house *n* **1** : the city residence of a person having a country home **2** : a single-family house of two or sometimes three stories connected to another house by a common wall

town·ie *or* **towny** \ˈtau-nē\ *n, pl* **townies** ♦ : a permanent resident of a town as distinguished from a member of another group

♦ burgher — more at BURGHER

towns·folk \ˈtaunz-ˌfōk\ *n pl* : TOWNSPEOPLE

town·ship \ˈtaun-ˌship\ *n* **1** : TOWN **2** : a unit of local government in some states **3** : an unorganized subdivision of a county **4** : a division of territory in surveys of U.S. public land containing 36 square miles **5** : an area in the Republic of South Africa segregated for occupation by persons of non-European descent

towns·man \ˈtaunz-mən\ *n* **1** : a native or resident of a town or city **2** : a fellow citizen of a town

towns·peo·ple \-ˌpē-pəl\ *n pl* **1** : the inhabitants of a town or city **2** : town-bred persons

towns·wom·an \-ˌwu-mən\ *n* **1** : a woman who is a native or resident of a town or city **2** : a woman who is a fellow citizen of a town

tow·path \ˈtō-ˌpath, -ˌpåth\ *n* : a path (as along a canal) traveled esp. by draft animals towing boats

tow truck *n* : a truck equipped for towing vehicles

tox·emia \täk-ˈsē-mē-ə\ *n* : a bodily disorder associated with the presence of toxic substances in the blood

tox·ic \ˈtäk-sik\ *adj* [LL *toxicus*, fr. L *toxicum* poison, fr. Gk *toxikon* arrow poison, fr. neut. of *toxikos* of a bow, fr. *toxon* bow, arrow] : of, relating to, or caused by poison or a toxin : POISONOUS — **tox·ic·i·ty** \täk-ˈsi-sə-tē\ *n*

tox·i·col·o·gy \ˌtäk-si-ˈkä-lə-jē\ *n* : a science that deals with poisons and esp. with problems of their use and control — **tox·i·co·log·i·cal** \-kə-ˈlä-ji-kəl\ *also* **tox·i·co·log·ic** \-kə-ˈlä-jik\ *adj* — **tox·i·col·o·gist** \-ˈkä-lə-jist\ *n*

toxic shock syndrome *n* : an acute disease that is characterized by fever, diarrhea, nausea, diffuse erythema, and shock, that is associated esp. with the presence of a bacterium, and that occurs esp. in those using tampons during menstruation

tox·in \ˈtäk-sən\ *n* ♦ : a poisonous substance produced by metabolic activities of a living organism that is usu. unstable, very toxic when introduced into the tissues, and usu. capable of inducing antibodies

♦ bane, poison, venom — more at POISON

¹toy \ˈtói\ *n* **1** : something trifling **2** : a small ornament : BAUBLE **3** : something for a child to play with

²toy *vb* **1** : to deal with something lightly : TRIFLE **2** : FLIRT **3** : to amuse oneself as if with a plaything

³toy *adj* **1** : DIMINUTIVE **2** : designed for use as a toy

tp *abbr* **1** title page **2** township

tpk *or* **tpke** *abbr* turnpike

tr *abbr* **1** translated; translation; translator **2** transpose **3** troop

¹trace \ˈtrās\ *n* **1 a** ♦ : a mark (as a footprint or track) left by something that has passed **b** ♦ : a path or trail beaten by or as if by the passage of feet **2** ♦ : a minute or barely detectable amount ⟨disappeared without a ∼⟩ **3** ♦ : a sign or evidence of some past thing

♦ [1a] imprint, track, trail — more at TRACK ♦ [1b] footpath, path, track, trail — more at TRAIL ♦ [2] glimmer, hint, particle, shadow, suspicion, touch — more at PARTICLE ♦ [3] relic, shadow, vestige — more at VESTIGE

²trace *vb* **traced; trac·ing** **1** ♦ : to mark out : SKETCH

2 : to form (as letters) carefully 3 : to copy (a drawing) by marking lines on transparent paper laid over the drawing to be copied 4 ♦ : to follow the trail of : track down 5 : to study out and follow the development of — **trace·able** *adj*

♦ [1] define, delineate, outline, silhouette, sketch — more at OUTLINE ♦ [4] chase, dog, follow, hound, pursue, shadow, tag, tail, track, trail — more at FOLLOW

³**trace** *n* : either of two lines of a harness for fastening a draft animal to a vehicle

trac·er \'trā-sər\ *n* 1 : one that traces 2 : ammunition containing a chemical to mark the flight of projectiles by a trail of smoke or fire

trac·ery \'trā-sə-rē\ *n, pl* **-er·ies** : ornamental work having a design with branching or interlacing lines

tra·chea \'trā-kē-ə\ *n, pl* **-che·ae** \-kē-ē\ *also* **-che·as** *or* **-chea** : the main tube by which air passes from the larynx to the lungs of vertebrates — **tra·che·al** \-kē-əl\ *adj*

tra·che·ot·o·my \ˌtrā-kē-'ä-tə-mē\ *n, pl* **-mies** : the surgical operation of cutting into the trachea esp. through the skin

trac·ing *n* 1 ♦ : the act of one that traces 2 : something that is traced 3 : a graphic record made by an instrument for measuring vibrations or pulsations

♦ chase, following, pursuit — more at PURSUIT

¹**track** \'trak\ *n* 1 ♦ : a mark left in passing 2 ♦ : a path, trail, or road made by the passage of animals, people, or vehicles 3 : a course laid out for racing; *also* : track-and-field sports 4 : one of a series of paths along which material (as music) is recorded (as on a compact disc or magnetic tape) 5 : the course along which something moves; *esp* : a way made by two parallel lines of metal rails 6 : awareness of a fact or progression ⟨lost ∼ of time⟩ 7 : either of two endless metal belts on which a vehicle (as a bulldozer) travels

♦ [1] imprint, trace, trail; *also* footprint, footstep, path, print, step, tread; artifact, evidence, leavings, mark, relic, remainder, reminder, remnant, residual, residue, sign, spoor, telltale, token, vestige; clue, cue, hint, indication, inkling, intimation, suggestion; scent, shadow, whiff ♦ [2] footpath, path, trace, trail — more at TRAIL

²**track** *vb* 1 a ♦ : to follow the tracks or traces of : TRAIL b ♦ : to search for by following evidence until found — often used with *down* 2 : to observe the moving path of (as a missile) 3 : to make tracks on 4 : to carry (as mud) on the feet and deposit — **track·er** *n*

♦ [1a] chase, dog, follow, hound, pursue, shadow, tag, tail, trace, trail — more at FOLLOW ♦ *usu* **track down** [1b] detect, determine, dig up, discover, ferret out, hit on, locate — more at FIND

track·age \'tra-kij\ *n* : lines of railway track

track–and–field *adj* : of or relating to athletic contests held on a running track or on the adjacent field

¹**tract** \'trakt\ *n* 1 ♦ : an area without precise boundaries ⟨huge ∼s of land⟩ 2 ♦ : a defined area of land 3 : a system of body parts or organs that act together to perform some function ⟨the digestive ∼⟩

♦ [1] belt, land, region, zone — more at REGION
♦ [2] field, ground, lot, parcel, plat, plot — more at FIELD

²**tract** *n* : a pamphlet of political or religious propaganda

trac·ta·ble \'trak-tə-bəl\ *adj* ♦ : easily controlled : DOCILE

♦ amenable, compliant, conformable, docile, obedient, submissive — more at OBEDIENT

tract house *n* : any of many similar houses built on a tract of land

trac·tion \'trak-shən\ *n* 1 : the act of drawing : the state of being drawn 2 : the drawing of a vehicle by motive power; *also* : the particular form of motive power used 3 : the adhesive friction of a body on a surface on which it moves 4 : a pulling force applied to a skeletal structure (as a broken bone) by means of a special device; *also* : a

state of tension created by such a pulling force ⟨a leg in ∼⟩ — **trac·tion·al** \-sha-nəl\ *adj* — **trac·tive** \'trak-tiv\ *adj*

trac·tor \'trak-tər\ *n* 1 : an automotive vehicle used esp. for drawing farm equipment 2 : a truck for hauling a trailer

¹**trade** \'trād\ *n* 1 ♦ : one's regular business or work : OCCUPATION 2 ♦ : an occupation requiring manual or mechanical skill 3 : the persons engaged in a business or industry 4 ♦ : the business of buying and selling or bartering commodities 5 ♦ : an act of trading

♦ [1] calling, employment, line, occupation, profession, vocation, work — more at OCCUPATION ♦ [2] craft, handicraft — more at CRAFT ♦ [4] business, commerce, marketplace, traffic — more at COMMERCE ♦ [5] barter, commutation, exchange, swap, truck — more at EXCHANGE ♦ [5] deal, sale, transaction — more at SALE

²**trade** *vb* **trad·ed; trad·ing** 1 ♦ : to give in exchange for another commodity 2 : to engage in the exchange, purchase, or sale of goods 3 : to deal regularly as a customer — **trade on** : EXPLOIT ⟨*trades on* his family name⟩

♦ change, commute, exchange, shift, substitute, swap, switch — more at CHANGE

trade–in \'trād-ˌin\ *n* : an item of merchandise traded in

trade in *vb* : to turn in as part payment for a purchase

¹**trade·mark** \'trād-ˌmärk\ *n* 1 : a device (as a word or mark) that points distinctly to the origin or ownership of merchandise to which it is applied and that is legally reserved for the exclusive use of the owner 2 ♦ : something that identifies a person or thing

♦ emblem, hallmark, logo, symbol — more at EMBLEM

²**trademark** *vb* : to secure the trademark rights for

trade name *n* : a name that is given by a manufacturer or merchant to a product to distinguish it as made or sold by that manufacturer or merchant and that may be used and protected as a trademark

trad·er \'trā-dər\ *n* 1 ♦ : a person whose business is buying or selling 2 : a ship engaged in trade

♦ dealer, merchant, trafficker — more at MERCHANT

trades·man \'trādz-mən\ *n* 1 : one who runs a retail store 2 : a worker in a skilled trade : CRAFTSMAN

trades·peo·ple \-ˌpē-pəl\ *n pl* : people engaged in trade

trade union *n* : LABOR UNION

trade wind *n* : a wind blowing almost constantly in one direction

trading stamp *n* : a printed stamp given as a premium to a retail customer that when accumulated may be redeemed for merchandise

tra·di·tion \trə-'di-shən\ *n* 1 : an inherited, established, or customary pattern of thought or action 2 ♦ : the handing down of beliefs and customs by word of mouth or by example without written instruction; *also* : a belief or custom thus handed down

♦ folklore, legend, lore, myth, mythology — more at FOLKLORE

tra·di·tion·al \trə-'di-shə-nəl\ *adj* 1 : consisting of or derived from tradition ⟨∼ history⟩ 2 ♦ : based on an order, code, or practice accepted from the past ⟨∼ morality⟩ 3 ♦ : observant of or holding to such traditions ⟨a ∼ professor⟩ — **tra·di·tion·al·ly** *adv*

♦ [2] classical, conventional, customary; *also* authentic, established, fixed, historical; common, habitual, orthodox, usual; ancestral, historic, old-time, old-world; aged, age-old, ancient, hoary, old, venerable; ageless, dateless, immemorial, timeless *Ant* nontraditional, unconventional, uncustomary ♦ [3] conservative, old-fashioned, orthodox, reactionary — more at CONSERVATIVE

tra·duce \trə-'düs, -'dyüs\ *vb* **tra·duced; tra·duc·ing** ♦ : to lower the reputation of : SLANDER — **tra·duc·er** *n*

♦ blacken, defame, libel, malign, slander, smear, vilify — more at SLANDER

¹**traf·fic** \'tra-fik\ *n* 1 ♦ : the business of bartering or

buying and selling **2** : communication or dealings between individuals or groups **3** : the movement (as of vehicles) along a route; *also* : the vehicles, people, ships, or planes moving along a route **4** : the passengers or cargo carried by a transportation system

♦ business, commerce, marketplace, trade — more at COMMERCE

²**traffic** *vb* **traf·ficked; traf·fick·ing 1** : to carry on business dealings **2** : DEAL, TRADE ⟨*trafficked* in illegal drugs⟩

traffic circle *n* : ROTARY 2

traf·fick·er *n* ♦ : a buyer and seller of commodities for profit

♦ dealer, merchant, trader — more at MERCHANT

traffic light *n* : a visual signal (as a system of lights) for controlling traffic

tra·ge·di·an \trə-'jē-dē-ən\ *n* **1** : a writer of tragedies **2** : an actor who plays tragic roles

tra·ge·di·enne \trə-jē-dē-'en\ *n* [F] : an actress who plays tragic roles

trag·e·dy \'tra-jə-dē\ *n, pl* **-dies** [ME *tragedie*, fr. MF, fr. L *tragoedia*, fr. Gk *tragōidia*, fr. *tragos* goat + *aeidein* to sing] **1** : a serious drama with a sorrowful or disastrous conclusion **2** ♦ : a disastrous event : CALAMITY; *also* : MISFORTUNE **3** : tragic quality or element ⟨the ~ of life⟩

♦ calamity, cataclysm, catastrophe, debacle, disaster, misfortune — more at DISASTER

trag·ic \'tra-jik\ *also* **trag·i·cal** \-ji-kəl\ *adj* **1** : of, relating to, or expressive of tragedy **2** : appropriate to tragedy **3** ♦ : that is to be regretted or lamented : LAMENTABLE, UNFORTUNATE ⟨a ~ mistake⟩ — **trag·i·cal·ly** \-ji-k(ə-)lē\ *adv*

♦ deplorable, distressful, grievous, heartbreaking, lamentable, regrettable, unfortunate, unlucky, woeful — more at REGRETTABLE

¹**trail** \'trāl\ *vb* **1** : to hang down so as to drag along or sweep the ground **2** : to draw or drag along behind **3** : to extend over a surface in a straggling manner **4** : to lag behind **5** ♦ : to follow the track of : PURSUE **6** : DWINDLE ⟨her voice ~*ed* off⟩

♦ chase, dog, follow, hound, pursue, shadow, tag, tail, trace, track — more at FOLLOW

²**trail** *n* **1** : something that trails or is trailed ⟨a ~ of smoke⟩ **2** : a trace or mark left by something that has passed or been drawn along : TRACK ⟨a ~ of blood⟩ **3** ♦ : a beaten path; *also* : a marked path through woods

♦ footpath, path, trace, track; *also* towpath; bypath, byway, detour, passageway, walkway; detour, shortcut; course, passage, road, route, run, runway, way

trail bike *n* : a small motorcycle for off-road use

trail·blaz·er \-ˌblā-zər\ *n* : PATHFINDER, PIONEER — **trail·blaz·ing** *adj or n*

trail·er \'trā-lər\ *n* **1** : one that trails; *esp* : a creeping plant (as an ivy) **2** : a vehicle that is hauled by another (as a tractor) **3** ♦ : a vehicle equipped to serve wherever parked as a dwelling or place of business **4** : PREVIEW 2

♦ camper, caravan, motor home — more at CAMPER

trailing arbutus *n* : a creeping spring-flowering plant of the heath family with fragrant pink or white flowers

¹**train** \'trān\ *n* [ME, fr. AF, fr. *trainer* to draw, drag] **1** : a part of a gown that trails behind the wearer **2** ♦ : a group of retainers or attendants : RETINUE **3** ♦ : a moving file of persons, vehicles, or animals **4** ♦ : a connected series ⟨a ~ of thought⟩ **5** : AFTERMATH **6** ♦ : a connected line of railroad cars usu. hauled by a locomotive

♦ [2] cortege, following, retinue, suite — more at CORTEGE ♦ [3] column, cue, file, line, queue, range, string — more at LINE ♦ [4] chain, progression, sequence, string — more at CHAIN

²**train** *vb* [ME, to trail, drag, train, fr. AF *trainer*] **1** : to cause to grow as desired ⟨~ a vine on a trellis⟩ **2 a** : to form by instruction, discipline, or drill **b** ♦ : to teach

so as to make fit, qualified, or proficient **3** : to make or become prepared (as by exercise) for a test of skill **4** ♦ : to aim at an object or objective ⟨~ guns on a fort⟩ — **train·er** *n*

♦ [2b] educate, indoctrinate, instruct, school, teach, tutor — more at TEACH ♦ [4] concentrate, fasten, focus, rivet — more at CONCENTRATE ♦ [4] aim, bend, cast, direct, head, level, set — more at AIM

train·ee \trā-'nē\ *n* : one who is being trained esp. for a job

train·ing *n* **1** ♦ : the act, process, or method of one who trains **2** : the skill, knowledge, or experience gained by one who trains

♦ education, instruction, teaching, tutelage — more at EDUCATION ♦ drill, exercise, practice, routine, workout — more at EXERCISE

train·man \-mən\ *n* : a member of a train crew

traipse \'trāps\ *vb* **traipsed; traips·ing 1** ♦ : to go on foot : WALK **2** ♦ : to walk or travel about without apparent plan but with or without a purpose

♦ [1] foot, leg, pad, step, tread, walk — more at WALK ♦ [2] gad, gallivant, knock, maunder, meander, mope, ramble, range, roam, rove, wander — more at WANDER

trait \'trāt\ *n* **1** ♦ : a distinguishing quality (as of personality) : PECULIARITY **2** : an inherited characteristic

♦ attribute, character, characteristic, feature, mark, peculiarity, point, property, quality — more at CHARACTERISTIC

trai·tor \'trā-tər\ *n* [ME *traytour*, fr. AF *traitre*, fr. L *traditor*, fr. *tradere* to hand over, deliver, betray, fr. *trans-* across + *dare* to give] **1** ♦ : one who betrays another's trust or is false to an obligation **2** : one who commits treason

♦ apostate, betrayer, double-crosser, quisling, recreant, turncoat; *also* collaborator, subversive; conspirator, plotter, schemer; defector, deserter, renegade; gossip, informant, informer, rat, talker, tattler, tattletale

trai·tor·ous \'trā-tə-rəs\ *adj* **1** ♦ : guilty or capable of treason **2** : constituting treason ⟨~ activities⟩

♦ disloyal, faithless, false, fickle, inconstant, loose, perfidious, recreant, treacherous, unfaithful, untrue — more at FAITHLESS

tra·jec·to·ry \trə-'jek-tə-rē\ *n, pl* **-ries** : the curve that a body (as a planet in its orbit) describes in space

tram \'tram\ *n* **1** : a boxlike car running on rails (as in a mine) **2** *chiefly Brit* : STREETCAR **3** : an overhead cable car

¹**tram·mel** \'tra-məl\ *n* [ME *tramayle*, a kind of net, fr. MF *tremail*, fr. LL *tremaculum*, fr. L *tres* three + *macula* mesh, spot] ♦ : something impeding activity, progress, or freedom — usu. used in pl.

♦ chain, encumbrance, fetter, hindrance, interference, manacle, shackle — more at ENCUMBRANCE

²**trammel** *vb* **-meled** *or* **-melled; -mel·ing** *or* **-mel·ling 1** : to catch and hold in or as if in a net **2** ♦ : to prevent or impede the free play of : HAMPER

♦ fetter, hamper, hinder, hobble, impede, inhibit, interfere with, manacle, shackle, tie up — more at HAMPER

¹**tramp** \'tramp, *1 & 3 are also* 'trämp, 'trómp\ *vb* **1** ♦ : to walk, tread, or step heavily **2** : to walk about or through; *also* : HIKE **3** ♦ : to tread on forcibly and repeatedly

♦ [1, 3] clump, lumber, pound, stamp, stomp, trample, tromp — more at LUMBER

²**tramp** \'tramp, *5 is also* 'trämp, 'trómp\ *n* **1** ♦ : a begging or thieving vagrant **2** : a foot traveler **3** : an immoral woman; *esp* : PROSTITUTE **4** ♦ : a walking trip : HIKE **5** : the succession of sounds made by the beating of feet on a road **6** : a ship that does not follow a regular course but takes cargo to any port

♦ bum, hobo, vagabond, vagrant; *also* drifter, transient; beggar, derelict; dodger, malingerer, shirker, slacker; gamine, urchin, waif, ragamuffin

tram·ple \'tram-pəl\ *vb* **tram·pled; tram·pling 1** : to tread heavily so as to bruise, crush, or injure **2 :** to inflict injury or destruction **3 ♦ :** to press down or crush by or as if by treading — **trample** *n* — **tram·pler** *n*

♦ stamp, stomp, tramp, tromp; *also* override, run down, run over, step (on); mash, smash, squash; boot, kick

tram·po·line \ˌtram-pə-ˈlēn, ˈtram-pə-ˌlēn\ *n* [It *trampolino* springboard] **:** a resilient sheet or web (as of nylon) supported by springs in a metal frame and used as a springboard in tumbling — **tram·po·lin·ist** \-ˈlē-nist, -ˌlē-\ *n*

trance \ˈtrans\ *n* [ME, fr. AF *transe*, death, coma, rapture, fr. *transir* to depart, die, fr. L *transire* to cross, pass by, fr. *trans-* across + *ire* to go] **1 :** STUPOR, DAZE **2 :** a sleeplike state of altered consciousness (as of deep hypnosis) **3 ♦ :** a state of very deep absorption

♦ reverie, study, woolgathering — more at REVERIE

tran·quil \ˈtraŋ-kwəl, ˈtran-\ *adj* ♦ **:** free from agitation or disturbance — **tran·quil·ly** *adv*

♦ calm, hushed, peaceful, quiet, restful, serene, still — more at QUIET ♦ calm, collected, composed, cool, placid, self-possessed, serene, undisturbed, unperturbed, unshaken, untroubled, unworried — more at CALM

tran·quil·i·ty \tran-ˈkwi-lə-tē, traŋ-\ *or chiefly Brit* **tran·quil·li·ty** *n* ♦ **:** the quality or state of being tranquil

♦ calm, calmness, hush, peace, placidity, quiet, quietness, repose, serenity, still, stillness — more at CALM ♦ aplomb, calmness, composure, coolness, equanimity, placidity, self-possession, serenity — more at EQUANIMITY

tran·quil·ize *also* **tran·quil·lize** \ˈtraŋ-kwə-ˌlīz, ˈtran-\ *vb* **-ized** *also* **-lized; -iz·ing** *also* **-liz·ing** ♦ **:** to make or become tranquil; *esp* **:** to relieve of mental tension and anxiety by means of drugs

♦ allay, calm, compose, quiet, settle, soothe, still — more at CALM

tran·quil·iz·er *also* **tran·quil·liz·er** \-ˌlī-zər\ *n* **:** a drug used to relieve mental disturbance (as tension and anxiety)

¹trans \ˈtran(t)s, ˈtranz\ *adj* **:** TRANSGENDER, TRANSSEXUAL

²trans *abbr* **1** transaction **2** transitive **3** translated; translation; translator **4** transmission **5** transportation **6** transverse

trans·act \tran-ˈzakt, -ˈsakt\ *vb* **:** CARRY OUT, PERFORM; *also* **:** CONDUCT

trans·ac·tion \-ˈzak-shən, -ˈsak-\ *n* **1 :** something transacted; *esp* **:** a business deal **2 ♦ :** an act or process of transacting **3** *pl* **:** the records of the proceedings of a society or organization

♦ deal, sale, trade — more at SALE

trans·at·lan·tic \ˌtrans-ət-ˈlan-tik, ˌtranz-\ *adj* **:** crossing or extending across or situated beyond the Atlantic Ocean

trans·ax·le \trans-ˈak-səl\ *n* **:** a unit combining the transmission and differential gear of a front-wheel-drive automobile

trans·ceiv·er \tran-ˈsē-vər\ *n* **:** a radio transmitter-receiver that uses many of the same components for both transmission and reception

tran·scend \tran-ˈsend\ *vb* **1 :** to rise above the limits of **2 ♦ :** to rise above or go beyond the limits of **:** SURPASS

♦ beat, better, eclipse, excel, outdistance, outdo, outshine, outstrip, surpass, top — more at SURPASS

tran·scen·dence \tran-ˈsen-dən(t)s\ *n* ♦ **:** the quality or state of being transcendent

♦ distinction, dominance, eminence, preeminence, primacy, superiority, supremacy — more at EMINENCE

tran·scen·dent \-ˈsen-dənt\ *adj* **1 :** exceeding usual limits **:** SURPASSING **2 :** transcending material existence

tran·scen·den·tal \ˌtran-ˌsen-ˈdent-ᵊl, -sən-\ *adj* **1 :** TRANSCENDENT **2 2 :** of, relating to, or characteristic of transcendentalism; *also* **:** ABSTRUSE

tran·scen·den·tal·ism \-ˈᵊl-ˌi-zəm\ *n* **:** a philosophy holding that ultimate reality is unknowable or asserting the primacy of the spiritual over the material and empirical — **tran·scen·den·tal·ist** \-ˈᵊl-ist\ *adj or n*

trans·con·ti·nen·tal \ˌtrans-ˌkänt-ᵊn-ˈent-ᵊl\ *adj* **:** extending or going across a continent

tran·scribe \trans-ˈkrīb\ *vb* **tran·scribed; tran·scrib·ing** **1 :** to write a copy of **2 :** to make a copy of (dictated or recorded matter) in longhand or on a typewriter **3 :** to represent (speech sounds) by means of phonetic symbols; *also* **:** to make a musical transcription of

tran·script \ˈtran-ˌskript\ *n* **1 :** a written, printed, or typed copy **2 :** an official copy esp. of a student's educational record

tran·scrip·tion \tran-ˈskrip-shən\ *n* **1 :** an act or process of transcribing **2 :** COPY, TRANSCRIPT **3 :** an arrangement of a musical composition for some instrument or voice other than the original

tran·scrip·tion·ist \-shə-nist\ *n* **:** one that transcribes; *esp* **:** a typist who transcribes medical reports

trans·der·mal \trans-ˈdər-məl, ˈtranz-\ *adj* **:** relating to, being, or supplying a medication in a form for absorption through the skin ⟨∼ nicotine patch⟩

trans·duc·er \trans-ˈdü-sər, tranz-, -ˈdyü-\ *n* **:** a device that is actuated by power from one system and supplies power usu. in another form to a second system

tran·sept \ˈtran-ˌsept\ *n* **:** the part of a cruciform church that crosses at right angles to the greatest length; *also* **:** either of the projecting ends

trans fat \ˈtran(t)s-, ˈtranz-\ *n* **:** a fat containing unsaturated fatty acids (**trans–fatty acids**) that have been linked to an increase in blood cholesterol

¹trans·fer \trans-ˈfər, ˈtrans-ˌfər\ *vb* **trans·ferred; trans·fer·ring** **1 ♦ :** to pass or cause to pass from one person, place, or situation to another **2 ♦ :** to make over the possession of **3 :** to print or copy from one surface to another by contact **4 :** to change from one vehicle or transportation line to another — **trans·fer·able** \trans-ˈfər-ə-bəl\ *adj* — **trans·fer·al** \-əl\ *n*

♦ [1] consign, dispatch, move, pack, send, ship, transmit, transport — more at SEND ♦ [1] commend, commit, consign, delegate, deliver, entrust, give, hand over, leave, pass, transmit, trust, turn over, vest — more at GIVE ♦ [2] alienate, assign, cede, deed, make over; *also* bequeath, hand down, leave, pass down, will; bestow, confer, contribute, deliver, donate, grant, hand over, move, pass, present, release, relinquish, surrender, turn in, turn over, transmit, vest, yield; consign, entrust, trust; lease, lend, loan, rent

²trans·fer \ˈtrans-ˌfər\ *n* **1 :** conveyance of right, title, or interest in property from one person to another **2 :** an act or process of transferring **3 :** one that transfers or is transferred **4 :** a ticket entitling a passenger to continue a trip on another route

trans·fer·ence \trans-ˈfər-əns\ *n* **:** an act, process, or instance of transferring

trans·fig·u·ra·tion \ˌtrans-ˌfi-gyə-ˈrā-shən, -gə-\ *n* ♦ **:** a change in form or appearance

♦ changeover, conversion, metamorphosis, transformation — more at CONVERSION

trans·fig·ure \trans-ˈfi-gyər\ *vb* **-ured; -ur·ing** **1 ♦ :** to change the form or appearance of **2 :** EXALT, GLORIFY

♦ convert, make over, metamorphose, transform — more at CONVERT

trans·fix \trans-ˈfiks\ *vb* **1 ♦ :** to pierce through with or as if with a pointed weapon **2 :** to hold motionless by or as if by piercing

♦ gore, harpoon, impale, lance, pierce, puncture, skewer, spear, spike, stab, stick — more at IMPALE

trans·form \trans-ˈfȯrm\ *vb* ♦ **:** to change in structure, appearance, or character

♦ convert, make over, metamorphose, transfigure — more at CONVERT

trans·for·ma·tion \ˌtrans-fər-ˈmā-shən\ *n* ♦ **:** an act, process, or instance of transforming or being transformed

♦ changeover, conversion, metamorphosis, transfiguration — more at CONVERSION

trans·form·er \trans-'fôr-mər\ n : one that transforms; *esp* : a device for converting variations of current in one circuit into variations of voltage and current in another circuit

trans·fuse \trans-'fyüz\ vb **trans·fused; trans·fus·ing** 1 ♦ : to cause to pass from one to another 2 ♦ : to diffuse into or through 3 : to transfer (as blood) into a vein or an artery of a person or animal — **trans·fu·sion** \-'fyü-zhən\ n

♦ [1] communicate, convey, impart, spread, transfer, transmit — more at COMMUNICATE ♦ [2] percolate, permeate, suffuse — more at PERMEATE

trans·gen·der \tranz-'jen-dər\ *also* **trans·gen·dered** \-dərd\ adj : of, relating to, or being a person whose gender identity differs from the sex the person had or was identified as having at birth 〈a ∼ person〉

trans·gen·ic \tran(t)s-'je-nik\ adj : being or used to produce an organism or cell with genes introduced from another species of organism 〈∼ crops〉

trans·gress \trans-'gres, tranz-\ vb [ME, fr. MF *transgresser*, fr. L *transgressus*, pp. of *transgredi* to step beyond or across, fr. *trans-* across + *gradi* to step] 1 ♦ : to go beyond the limits set by 〈∼ the divine law〉 2 : to go beyond : EXCEED 3 ♦ : to violate a command or law : SIN — **trans·gres·sor** \-'gre-sər\ n

♦ [1] breach, break, violate — more at VIOLATE ♦ [3] err, offend, sin, trespass — more at OFFEND

trans·gres·sion \trans-'gre-shən\ n ♦ : an act, process, or instance of transgressing

♦ breach, crime, error, malefaction, misdeed, misdoing, offense, sin, trespass, violation, wrongdoing — more at OFFENSE

¹**tran·sient** \'tran-shənt; -sē-ənt, -shē-, -zē-\ adj 1 ♦ : not lasting long : SHORT-LIVED 2 : passing through a place with only a brief stay — **tran·sient·ly** adv

♦ ephemeral, evanescent, flash, fleeting, fugitive, impermanent, momentary, short-lived — more at MOMENTARY

²**transient** n : one that is transient; *esp* : a transient guest

tran·sis·tor \tran-'zis-tər, -'sis-\ n [*transfer* + *resistor*; fr. its transferring an electrical signal across a resistor] 1 : a small electronic semiconductor device used in electronic equipment 2 : a radio having transistors

tran·sis·tor·ized \-tə-ˌrīzd\ adj : having or using transistors

tran·sit \'tran-sət, -zət\ n 1 : a passing through, across, or over : PASSAGE 2 : conveyance of persons or things from one place to another 3 : usu. local transportation esp. of people by public conveyance 4 : a surveyor's instrument for measuring angles

tran·si·tion \tran-'si-shən, -'zi-\ n : passage from one state, place, stage, or subject to another : CHANGE — **tran·si·tion·al** \-'si-shə-nəl, -'zi-\ adj

tran·si·tive \'tran-sə-tiv, -zə-\ adj 1 : having or containing an object required to complete the meaning 〈a ∼ verb〉 2 : TRANSITIONAL — **tran·si·tive·ly** adv — **tran·si·tive·ness** n — **tran·si·tiv·i·ty** \ˌtran-sə-'ti-və-tē, -zə-\ n

tran·si·to·ry \'tran-sə-ˌtôr-ē, -zə-\ adj : of brief duration : SHORT-LIVED

transl abbr translated; translation

trans·late \trans-'lāt, tranz-\ vb **trans·lat·ed; trans·lat·ing** 1 : to change from one place, state, or form to another 2 : to convey to heaven without death 3 a : to turn into one's own or another language b ♦ : to express in different terms and esp. different words — **trans·lat·able** adj — **trans·la·tor** \-'lā-tər\ n

♦ paraphrase, rephrase, restate — more at PARAPHRASE

trans·la·tion \trans-'lā-shən\ n 1 ♦ : an act, process, or instance of translating 2 : the process of forming a protein molecule from information in messenger RNA

♦ paraphrase — more at PARAPHRASE

trans·lit·er·ate \trans-'li-tə-ˌrāt, tranz-\ vb **-at·ed; -at·ing** : to represent or spell in the characters of another alphabet — **trans·lit·er·a·tion** \ˌtrans-ˌli-tə-'rā-shən, ˌtranz-\ n

trans·lu·cent \trans-'lüs-ᵊnt, tranz-\ adj : not transparent but clear enough to allow light to pass through — **trans·lu·cence** \-ᵊns\ n — **trans·lu·cen·cy** \-ᵊn-sē\ n — **trans·lu·cent·ly** adv

trans·mi·grate \-'mī-ˌgrāt\ vb : to pass at death from one body or being to another — **trans·mi·gra·tion** \ˌtrans-mī-'grā-shən, ˌtranz-\ n — **trans·mi·gra·to·ry** \trans-'mī-grə-ˌtōr-ē\ adj

trans·mis·sion \-'mi-shən\ n 1 : an act or process of transmitting 2 : the passage of radio waves between transmitting stations and receiving stations 3 : the gears by which power is transmitted from the engine of an automobile to the axle that propels the vehicle 4 : something transmitted

trans·mit \-'mit\ vb **trans·mit·ted; trans·mit·ting** 1 ♦ : to transfer from one person or place to another 2 : to pass on by or as if by inheritance 3 : to cause or allow to spread abroad or to another 〈∼ a disease〉 4 : to cause (as light, electricity, or force) to pass through space or a medium 5 : to send out (radio or television signals) — **trans·mis·si·ble** \-'mi-sə-bəl\ adj — **trans·mit·tal** \-'mit-ᵊl\ n

♦ communicate, convey, impart, spread, transfer, transfuse — more at COMMUNICATE ♦ consign, dispatch, pack, send, ship, transfer, transport — more at SEND

trans·mit·ta·ble \trans-'mi-tə-bəl\ adj ♦ : capable of being transmitted

♦ catching, communicable, contagious — more at CONTAGIOUS

trans·mit·ter \-'mi-tər\ n : one that transmits; *esp* : an apparatus for transmitting telegraph, radio, or television signals

trans·mog·ri·fy \trans-'mä-grə-ˌfī, tranz-\ vb **-fied; -fy·ing** : to change or alter often with grotesque or humorous effect — **trans·mog·ri·fi·ca·tion** \-ˌmä-grə-fə-'kā-shən\ n

trans·mute \-'myüt\ vb **trans·muted; trans·mut·ing** : to change or alter in form, appearance, or nature — **trans·mu·ta·tion** \ˌtrans-myü-'tā-shən, ˌtranz-\ n

trans·na·tion·al \-'na-shə-nəl\ adj : extending beyond national boundaries

trans·oce·an·ic \ˌtrans-ˌō-shē-'a-nik, ˌtranz-\ adj 1 : lying or dwelling beyond the ocean 2 : crossing or extending across the ocean

tran·som \'tran-səm\ n 1 : a piece (as a crossbar in the frame of a window or door) that lies crosswise in a structure 2 : a window above an opening (as a door) built on and often hinged to a horizontal crossbar

tran·son·ic *also* **trans–son·ic** \trans-'sä-nik\ adj : being or relating to speeds near that of sound in air or about 741 miles (1185 kilometers) per hour

trans·pa·cif·ic \ˌtrans-pə-'si-fik\ adj : crossing, extending across, or situated beyond the Pacific Ocean

trans·par·ent \trans-'par-ənt\ adj 1 ♦ : clear enough to be seen through 2 ♦ : fine or sheer enough to be seen through 〈a ∼ fabric〉 3 ♦ : readily understood : CLEAR; *also* : easily detected 〈a ∼ lie〉 — **trans·par·en·cy** \-ən-sē\ n — **trans·par·ent·ly** adv

♦ [1] clear, limpid, liquid, lucent, pellucid — more at CLEAR ♦ [2] gauzy, sheer — more at SHEER ♦ [3] apparent, broad, clear, clear-cut, distinct, evident, lucid, manifest, obvious, palpable, patent, perspicuous, plain, unambiguous, unequivocal, unmistakable — more at CLEAR

tran·spire \trans-'pīr\ vb **tran·spired; tran·spir·ing** [MF *transpirer*, fr. ML *transpirare*, fr. *trans-* across + *spirare* to breathe] 1 : to pass or give off (as water vapor) through pores or a membrane 2 : to become known 3 ♦ : to take place : HAPPEN — **tran·spi·ra·tion** \ˌtrans-pə-'rā-shən\ n

♦ be, befall, betide, chance, come, go, happen, occur, pass — more at HAPPEN

¹**trans·plant** \trans-'plant\ vb 1 : to dig up and plant elsewhere 2 : to remove from one place and settle or introduce elsewhere : TRANSPORT 3 : to transfer (an organ

or tissue) from one part or individual to another — **trans·plan·ta·tion** \ˌtrans-ˌplan-'tā-shən\ n

²**trans·plant** \'trans-ˌplant\ n 1 : a person or thing transplanted 2 : the act or process of transplanting

trans·po·lar \trans-'pō-lər\ adj : going or extending across either of the polar regions

transponder \tran-'spän-dər\ n [*trans*mitter + re*sponder*] : a radio or radar set that upon receiving a certain signal emits a radio signal and that is used to locate and identify objects and in satellites to relay communications signals

¹**trans·port** \trans-'pōrt\ vb 1 ♦ : to convey from one place to another 2 ♦ : to carry away by strong emotion : EN-RAPTURE 3 ♦ : to send to a penal colony overseas — **trans·port·er** n

♦ [1] consign, dispatch, pack, send, ship, transfer, transmit — more at SEND ♦ [1] bear, carry, cart, convey, ferry, haul, lug, pack, tote — more at CARRY ♦ [2] carry away, enrapture, enthrall, entrance, ravish — more at ENTRANCE ♦ [3] banish, deport, displace, exile, expatriate — more at BANISH

²**trans·port** \'trans-ˌpōrt\ n 1 : an act of transporting 2 ♦ : strong or intensely pleasurable emotion ⟨∼s of joy⟩ 3 ♦ : a ship used in transporting troops or supplies; *also* : a vehicle (as a truck or plane) used to transport persons or goods

♦ [2] ecstasy, elation, euphoria, exhilaration, heaven, intoxication, paradise, rapture, rhapsody — more at ECSTASY ♦ [3] conveyance, vehicle — more at CONVEYANCE

trans·por·ta·tion \ˌtrans-pər-'tā-shən\ n 1 : an act, process, or instance of transporting or being transported 2 : means of conveyance or travel from one place to another

trans·pose \trans-'pōz\ vb **trans·posed; trans·pos·ing 1** : to change the position or sequence of ⟨∼ the letters in a word⟩ **2** : to write or perform (a musical composition) in a different key — **trans·po·si·tion** \ˌtrans-pə-'zi-shən\ n

trans·sex·u·al \(ˌ)trans-'sek-shə-wəl\ n : a person who psychologically identifies with the opposite sex and may seek to live as a member of this sex esp. by undergoing surgery to modify the external sex organs

trans·ship \tran-'ship, trans-\ vb : to transfer for further transportation from one ship or conveyance to another — **trans·ship·ment** n

tran·sub·stan·ti·a·tion \ˌtran-səb-ˌstan-chē-'ā-shən\ n : the change in the eucharistic elements from the substance of bread and wine to the substance of the body of Christ with only the appearances of bread and wine remaining

trans·verse \trans-'vərs, tranz-\ adj : lying across : set crosswise — **trans·verse** \'trans-ˌvərs, 'tranz-\ n **trans·verse·ly** adv ♦ : in a transverse direction or line

♦ athwart, crosswise, obliquely — more at CROSSWISE

trans·ves·tite \trans-'ves-ˌtīt, tranz-\ n : a person who wears clothes designed for the opposite sex — **transvestite** adj — **trans·ves·tism** \-ˌti-zəm\ n

¹**trap** \'trap\ n 1 : a device for catching animals 2 ♦ : something by which one is caught unawares; *also* : a situation from which escape is difficult or impossible 3 : a machine for throwing clay pigeons into the air; *also* : SAND TRAP 4 : a light one-horse carriage on springs 5 : a device to allow some one thing to pass through while keeping other things out ⟨a ∼ in a drainpipe⟩ 6 pl : a group of percussion instruments (as in a dance orchestra)

♦ ambush, net, snare, web; *also* entanglement, entrapment; booby trap, catch, hazard, pitfall, snag; deception, ploy, ruse, subterfuge, trick ♦ ambush, surprise — more at AMBUSH

²**trap** vb **trapped; trap·ping 1** ♦ : to catch in or as if in a trap; *also* : CONFINE **2** : to provide or set (a place) with traps **3** : to set traps for animals esp. as a business — **trap·per** n

♦ confine, enmesh, ensnare, entangle, entrap, mesh, snare, tangle — more at ENTANGLE

trap·door \'trap-'dōr\ n : a lifting or sliding door covering an opening in a floor or roof

tra·peze \tra-'pēz\ n : a gymnastic apparatus consisting of a horizontal bar suspended by two parallel ropes

trap·e·zoid \'tra-pə-ˌzȯid\ n [NL *trapezoïdes*, fr. Gk *trapezoeidēs* trapezoidal, fr. *trapeza* table, fr. *tra-* four + *peza* foot] : a 4-sided polygon with exactly two sides parallel — **trap·e·zoi·dal** \ˌtra-pə-'zȯid-ᵊl\ adj

trap·pings \'tra-piŋz\ n pl 1 : CAPARISON 1 2 : outward decoration or dress; *also* : outward sign ⟨∼ of success⟩

traps \'traps\ n pl : personal belongings : LUGGAGE

trap·shoot·ing \'trap-ˌshü-tiŋ\ n : shooting at clay pigeons sprung from a trap into the air away from the shooter

¹**trash** \'trash\ n 1 a ♦ : something of little worth : RUBBISH b ♦ : empty talk : NONSENSE 2 a : a worthless person b ♦ : such persons as a group : RIFFRAFF

♦ [1a] chaff, deadwood, dust, garbage, junk, litter, refuse, riffraff, rubbish, scrap, waste — more at GARBAGE ♦ [1b] bunk, claptrap, drivel, fiddlesticks, folly, foolishness, fudge, hogwash, humbug, nonsense, piffle, rot, silliness, slush, stupidity — more at NONSENSE ♦ [2b] rabble, riffraff, scum — more at RABBLE

²**trash** vb 1 : VANDALIZE, DESTROY 2 : ATTACK 3 : SPOIL, RUIN 4 : to criticize or disparage harshly 5 : to dispose of : DISCARD ⟨∼ed the plans⟩

trashy \'tra-shē\ adj **trash·i·er; -est** ♦ : being, resembling, or containing trash : of inferior quality

♦ dowdy, inelegant, tacky, tasteless, unfashionable, unstylish — more at TACKY ♦ cheap, common, cut-rate, inferior, junky, lousy, mediocre, miserable, poor, rotten, second-rate, shoddy, sleazy

trau·ma \'trau̇-mə, 'trȯ-\ n, pl **traumas** also **trau·ma·ta** \-mə-tə\ [Gk, wound] : a bodily or mental injury usu. caused by an external agent; *also* : a cause of trauma — **trau·mat·ic** \trə-'ma-tik, trȯ-, trau̇-\ adj

trau·ma·tize \-ˌtīz\ vb **-tized; -tiz·ing** : to inflict trauma upon

¹**tra·vail** \trə-'vāl, 'tra-ˌvāl\ n 1 ♦ : painful work or exertion : TOIL 2 : AGONY, TORMENT 3 : CHILDBIRTH, LABOR

♦ drudgery, grind, labor (*or* labour), slavery, sweat, toil — more at TOIL

²**travail** vb : to labor hard : TOIL

¹**trav·el** \'tra-vəl\ vb **-eled** or **-elled; -el·ing** or **-el·ling** [ME *travailen* to torment, labor, journey, fr. AF *travailler* strive, fr. VL *trepaliare* to torture, fr. LL *trepalium* instrument of torture] 1 ♦ : to go on or as if on a trip or tour : JOURNEY 2 : to move as if by traveling ⟨news ∼s fast⟩ 3 : ASSOCIATE 4 : to go from place to place as a sales representative 5 : to move from point to point ⟨light waves ∼ very fast⟩ 6 ♦ : to journey over or through ⟨∼ing the highways⟩

♦ [1] journey, tour, trek, voyage; *also* gallivant, hop, jaunt, knock (about), ramble, roam, rove, traipse, wander; cruise, drive, fly, jet, motor, navigate, sail ♦ [6] cover, crisscross, cross, cut, follow, go, pass, proceed, traverse — more at TRAVERSE

²**travel** n 1 : the act of traveling : PASSAGE 2 : JOURNEY, TRIP — often used in pl. 3 : the number traveling : TRAFFIC 4 : the motion of a piece of machinery and esp. when to and fro

trav·el·er \'tra-və-lər\ or **trav·el·ler** n ♦ : one that travels : one that takes a journey

♦ excursionist, sightseer, tourist — more at TOURIST

traveler's check n : a check paid for in advance that is signed when bought and signed again when cashed

traveling bag n ♦ : a portable case designed to hold a traveler's clothing and personal articles : SUITCASE

♦ carryall, grip, handbag, portmanteau, suitcase; *also* carpetbag, duffel bag, kit; backpack, haversack, knapsack; attaché case, valise; baggage, bags, luggage

trav·el·ogue or **trav·el·og** \'tra-və-ˌlȯg, -ˌläg\ n : a usu. illustrated lecture on travel

¹**tra·verse** \'tra-vərs\ n : something that crosses or lies across

²**tra·verse** \trə-'vərs, tra-'vərs, 'tra-vərs\ *vb* **tra·versed; tra·vers·ing** 1 ♦ : to go or travel across or over 2 : to move or pass along or through 3 : to extend over 4 : SWIVEL

  ♦ cover, crisscross, cross, cut, follow, go, pass, proceed, travel; *also* hike, tread, walk; ride

³**tra·verse** \'tra-ˌvərs\ *adj* : TRANSVERSE

trav·er·tine \'tra-vər-ˌtēn, -tən\ *n* : a crystalline mineral formed by deposition from spring waters

¹**trav·es·ty** \'tra-və-stē\ *vb* **-tied; -ty·ing** ♦ : to make a travesty of

  ♦ burlesque, caricature, imitate, mimic, mock, parody, take off — more at MIMIC

²**travesty** *n, pl* **-ties** [obs. E *travesty* disguised, parodied, fr. F *travesti*, pp. of *travestir* to disguise, fr. It *travestire*, fr. *tra-* across (fr. L *trans-*) + *vestire* to dress] ♦ : an imitation that makes crude fun of something; *also* : an inferior imitation

  ♦ caricature, farce, joke, mockery, parody, sham — more at MOCKERY

¹**trawl** \'trȯl\ *vb* : to fish or catch with a trawl — **trawl·er** *n*

²**trawl** *n* 1 : a large conical net dragged along the sea bottom in fishing 2 : a long heavy fishing line equipped with many hooks in series

tray \'trā\ *n* : an open receptacle with flat bottom and low rim for holding, carrying, or exhibiting articles

treach·er·ous \'tre-chə-rəs\ *adj* 1 ♦ : characterized by treachery 2 : UNTRUSTWORTHY, UNRELIABLE 3 : providing insecure footing or support — **treach·er·ous·ly** *adv*

  ♦ disloyal, faithless, false, fickle, inconstant, loose, perfidious, recreant, traitorous, unfaithful, untrue — more at FAITHLESS

treach·ery \'tre-chə-rē\ *n, pl* **-er·ies** ♦ : violation of allegiance or trust

  ♦ betrayal, disloyalty, double cross, faithlessness, falseness, falsity, infidelity, perfidy, treason, unfaithfulness — more at BETRAYAL

trea·cle \'trē-kəl\ *n* [ME *triacle* a medicinal compound, fr. AF, fr. L *theriaca*, fr. Gk *thēriakē* antidote against a poisonous bite, fr. *thērion* wild animal] *chiefly Brit* : MOLASSES — **trea·cly** \-k(ə-)lē\ *adj*

¹**tread** \'tred\ *vb* **trod** \'träd\; **trod·den** \'träd-ᵊn\ *or* **trod; tread·ing** 1 : to step or walk on or over 2 ♦ : to move on foot : WALK 3 : to beat or press with the feet — **tread water** : to stay afloat and upright in water by sustaining a walking motion

  ♦ foot, leg, pad, step, traipse, walk — more at WALK

²**tread** *n* 1 : a mark made by or as if by treading 2 : the manner or sound of stepping 3 : the part of a wheel that makes contact with a road 4 : the horizontal part of a step

trea·dle \'tred-ᵊl\ *n* : a lever device pressed by the foot to drive a machine — **treadle** *vb*

tread·mill \'tred-ˌmil\ *n* 1 : a mill worked by persons who tread on steps around the edge of a wheel or by animals that walk on an endless belt 2 : a device with an endless belt on which a person walks or runs in place 3 ♦ : a wearisome routine

  ♦ groove, pattern, rote, routine, rut — more at ROUTINE

treas *abbr* treasurer; treasury

trea·son \'trēz-ᵊn\ *n* 1 : the offense of attempting to overthrow the government of one's country or of assisting its enemies in war 2 ♦ : the betrayal of a trust — **trea·son·able** \-ᵊn-ə-bəl\ *adj* — **trea·son·ous** \-ᵊn-əs\ *adj*

  ♦ betrayal, disloyalty, double cross, faithlessness, falseness, falsity, infidelity, perfidy, treachery, unfaithfulness — more at BETRAYAL

¹**trea·sure** \'tre-zhər, 'trā-\ *n* [ME *tresor*, fr. AF, fr. L *thesaurus*, fr. Gk *thēsauros*] 1 : wealth stored up or held in reserve 2 ♦ : something of great value

  ♦ catch, gem, jewel, pearl, plum, prize — more at PRIZE

²**treasure** *vb* **trea·sured; trea·sur·ing** 1 : HOARD 2 ♦ : to keep as precious : CHERISH

  ♦ appreciate, cherish, love, prize, value — more at LOVE

trea·sur·er \'tre-zhə-rər, 'trā-\ *n* : an officer of a club, business, or government who has charge of money taken in and paid out

treasure trove \-ˌtrōv\ *n* 1 : treasure of unknown ownership found buried or hidden 2 : a valuable discovery

trea·sury \'tre-zhə-rē, 'trā-\ *n, pl* **-sur·ies** 1 : a place in which stores of wealth are kept 2 : the place where collected funds are stored and paid out 3 *cap* : a governmental department in charge of finances

¹**treat** \'trēt\ *vb* 1 : to discuss terms of accommodation or settlement 2 a ♦ : to deal with esp. in writing — usu. used with *of* b ♦ : to deal with : HANDLE 3 : to pay for the food or entertainment of 4 ♦ : to behave or act toward ⟨~ them well⟩ 5 : to regard in a specified manner ⟨~ as inferiors⟩ 6 : to give medical or surgical care to 7 : to subject to some action ⟨~ soil with lime⟩

  ♦ usu **treat of** [2a] concern, cover, deal, pertain — more at CONCERN ♦ [2b] contend with, cope with, grapple with, handle, manage, maneuver (*or* manoeuvre), negotiate, swing — more at HANDLE ♦ [4] act, be, deal, handle, serve, use; *also* consider, regard; react (to), respond (to)

²**treat** *n* 1 : an entertainment given free to those invited; *also* : food, drink, or entertainment provided at another's expense 2 ♦ : a source of joy or amusement

  ♦ delectation, delight, joy, kick, manna, pleasure — more at DELIGHT ♦ dainty, delicacy, goody, tidbit — more at DELICACY

trea·tise \'trē-təs\ *n* : a systematic written exposition or argument

treat·ment \'trēt-mənt\ *n* : the act or manner or an instance of treating someone or something; *also* : a substance or method used in treating

trea·ty \'trē-tē\ *n, pl* **treaties** ♦ : an agreement made by negotiation or diplomacy esp. between two or more states or governments

  ♦ accord, alliance, compact, convention, covenant, pact; *also* bargain, charter, contract, deal, settlement, understanding

¹**tre·ble** \'tre-bəl\ *n* 1 : the highest of the four voice parts in vocal music : SOPRANO 2 : a high-pitched or shrill voice or sound 3 : the upper half of the musical pitch range

²**treble** *adj* 1 ♦ : triple in number or amount 2 : relating to or having the range of a musical treble 3 ♦ : high-pitched : SHRILL — **tre·bly** *adv*

  ♦ [1] threefold, tripartite, triple — more at TRIPLE ♦ [3] acute, sharp, shrill, squeaky — more at SHRILL

³**treble** *vb* **tre·bled; tre·bling** : to make or become three times the size, amount, or number

¹**tree** \'trē\ *n* 1 : a woody perennial plant usu. with a single main stem and a head of branches and leaves at the top 2 : a piece of wood adapted to a particular use ⟨a shoe ~⟩ 3 : something resembling a tree ⟨a genealogical ~⟩ — **tree·less** *adj*

²**tree** *vb* **treed; tree·ing** : to drive to or up a tree ⟨~ a raccoon⟩

tree farm *n* : an area of forest land managed to ensure continuous commercial production

tree frog *n* : any of numerous usu. tree-dwelling amphibians with adhesive disks on the toes

tree line *n* : TIMBERLINE

tree of heaven : a Chinese ailanthus widely grown as an ornamental tree

tree surgery *n* : operative treatment of diseased trees esp. for control of decay — **tree surgeon** *n*

tre·foil \'trē-ˌfȯil, 'tre-\ *n* 1 : an herb (as a clover) with leaves that have three leaflets 2 : a decorative design with three leaflike parts

¹**trek** \'trek\ *vb* **trekked; trek·king** 1 *chiefly southern Africa* : to travel or migrate by ox wagon 2 ♦ : to make one's way arduously

♦ journey, tour, travel, voyage — more at TRAVEL

²**trek** *n* **1** *chiefly southern Africa* : a migration esp. of settlers by ox wagon **2** ♦ : a slow or difficult journey

♦ expedition, journey, passage, peregrination, trip — more at JOURNEY

¹**trel·lis** \'tre-ləs\ *n* [ME *trelis*, fr. AF *treleis*, fr. OF *treille* arbor, fr. L *trichila* summerhouse] : a frame of latticework used esp. to support climbing plants

²**trellis** *vb* : to provide with a trellis; *esp* : to train (as a vine) on a trellis

trem·a·tode \'tre-mə-ˌtōd\ *n* : any of a class of parasitic worms

¹**trem·ble** \'trem-bəl\ *vb* **trem·bled; trem·bling** **1** : to shake involuntarily (as with fear or cold) : SHIVER **2** : to move, sound, pass, or come to pass as if shaken or tremulous **3** : to be affected with fear or doubt

²**tremble** *n* ♦ : a spell of shaking or quivering

♦ quiver, shiver, shudder — more at SHIVER

tre·men·dous \tri-'men-dəs\ *adj* **1** : causing dread, awe, or terror : TERRIFYING **2** ♦ : unusually large, powerful, great, or excellent ⟨∼ strength⟩

♦ colossal, enormous, giant, gigantic, huge, mammoth, massive, monstrous, monumental, prodigious, titanic

tre·men·dous·ly *adv* ♦ : to a tremendous degree or extent

♦ broadly, considerably, greatly, hugely, largely, massively, monstrously, much, sizably, stupendously, utterly, vastly — more at GREATLY

trem·o·lo \'tre-mə-ˌlō\ *n, pl* **-los** [It] : a rapid fluttering of a tone or alternating tones

trem·or \'tre-mər\ *n* **1** : a trembling or shaking esp. from weakness, emotional stress, or disease **2** : a quivering motion of the earth (as during an earthquake)

trem·u·lous \'trem-yə-ləs\ *adj* **1** ♦ : marked by trembling or tremors **2** : TIMOROUS, TIMID — **trem·u·lous·ly** *adv*

♦ shaky, wobbly — more at SHAKY

¹**trench** \'trench\ *n* [ME *trenche* track cut through a wood, fr. MF, act of cutting, fr. *trenchier* to cut, prob. fr. (assumed) VL *trinicare* to cut in three, fr. L *trini* three each] **1** ♦ : a long narrow cut in the ground : DITCH; *esp* : a ditch protected by banks of earth and used to shelter soldiers **2** *pl* : a place or situation likened to warfare conducted from trenches **3** : a long narrow steep-sided depression in the ocean floor

♦ dike, ditch, gutter — more at DITCH

²**trench** *vb* **1** : to cut or dig trenches in **2** : to protect (troops) with trenches **3** : to come close : VERGE

tren·chant \'tren-chənt\ *adj* **1** : vigorously effective; *also* : CAUSTIC **2** : sharply perceptive : KEEN ⟨a ∼ wit⟩ **3** : CLEAR-CUT, DISTINCT **4** : having a fine edge or point : SHARP

tren·cher \'tren-chər\ *n* : a wooden platter for serving food

tren·cher·man \'tren-chər-mən\ *n* : a hearty eater

trench foot *n* : a painful foot disorder resembling frostbite and resulting from exposure to cold and wet

trench mouth *n* : a progressive painful bacterial infection of the mouth and adjacent parts marked by ulceration, bleeding gums, and foul breath

¹**trend** \'trend\ *vb* **1** : to have or take a general direction : TEND **2** ♦ : to show a tendency : INCLINE

♦ incline, lean, run, tend — more at LEAN

²**trend** *n* **1** : a general direction taken (as by a stream or mountain range) **2** ♦ : a prevailing tendency : DRIFT **3** ♦ : a current style or preference : VOGUE

♦ [2] current, drift, leaning, run, tendency, tide, wind; *also* curve, shift, swing, turn; custom, habit, propensity, tenor, way ♦ [3] craze, fad, mode, rage, style, vogue — more at FAD

trendy \'tren-dē\ *adj* **trend·i·er; -est** ♦ : very fashionable; *also* : marked by superficial or faddish appeal or taste

♦ à la mode, chic, cool, fashionable, in, modish, sharp, smart, snappy, stylish — more at STYLISH

trep·i·da·tion \ˌtre-pə-'dā-shən\ *n* ♦ : nervous agitation : APPREHENSION

♦ alarm, anxiety, apprehension, dread, fear, fright, horror, panic, terror — more at FEAR

¹**tres·pass** \'tres-pəs, -ˌpas\ *n* **1 a** ♦ : a violation of moral or social ethics : SIN **b** ♦ : an unwarranted infringement **2** : unlawful entry on someone else's land

♦ [1a] breach, crime, error, malefaction, misdeed, misdoing, offense, sin, transgression, violation, wrongdoing — more at OFFENSE ♦ [1b] breach, infraction, infringement, transgression, violation — more at BREACH

²**trespass** *vb* **1** ♦ : to commit an offense : ERR **2** : INTRUDE, ENCROACH; *esp* : to enter unlawfully upon the land of another — **tres·pass·er** *n*

♦ err, offend, sin, transgress — more at OFFEND

tress \'tres\ *n* : a long lock of hair — usu. used in pl.

tres·tle *also* **tres·sel** \'tre-səl\ *n* **1** : a supporting framework consisting usu. of a horizontal piece with spreading legs at each end **2** : a braced framework of timbers, piles, or steel for carrying a road or railroad over a depression

T. rex \'tē-'reks\ *n* : TYRANNOSAUR

trey \'trā\ *n, pl* **treys** : a card or the side of a die with three spots

tri·ad \'trī-ˌad, -əd\ *n* ♦ : a union or group of three usu. closely related persons or things

♦ threesome, trio, triple, triplet — more at THREESOME

tri·age \trē-'äzh, 'trē-ˌäzh\ *n* [F, sorting] : the sorting of and allocation of treatment to patients and esp. battle or disaster victims according to a system of priorities designed to maximize the number of survivors

tri·al \'trī-əl\ *n* **1** : the action or process of trying or putting to the proof : TEST **2** : the hearing and judgment of a matter in issue before a competent tribunal **3** ♦ : a source of vexation or annoyance **4** ♦ : a tryout or experiment to test quality, value, or usefulness **5** ♦ : the act or an instance of attempting — **trial** *adj*

♦ [3] cross, gauntlet, ordeal; *also* adversity, affliction, privation, tragedy, tribulation, trouble, woe; challenge, complication, difficulty, grief, hardship, rigor; annoyance, discomfort, inconvenience, nuisance ♦ [4] dry run, practice, rehearsal — more at REHEARSAL ♦ [4] experiment, test — more at EXPERIMENT ♦ [5] attempt, crack, endeavor (*or* endeavour), essay, fling, go, pass, shot, stab, try, whack — more at ATTEMPT

tri·an·gle \'trī-ˌaŋ-gəl\ *n* **1** : a polygon that has three sides **2** : something shaped like a triangle — **tri·an·gu·lar** \trī-'aŋ-gyə-lər\ *adj* — **tri·an·gu·lar·ly** *adv*

tri·an·gu·la·tion \(ˌ)trī-ˌaŋ-gyə-'lā-shən\ *n* : a method using trigonometry to find the location of a point using bearings from two fixed points a known distance apart — **tri·an·gu·late** \trī-'aŋ-gyə-ˌlāt\ *vb*

Tri·as·sic \trī-'a-sik\ *adj* : of, relating to, or being the earliest period of the Mesozoic era marked by the first appearance of the dinosaurs — **Triassic** *n*

tri·ath·lon \trī-'ath-lən, -ˌlän\ *n* : an athletic contest consisting of three phases (as swimming, bicycling, and running)

trib *abbr* tributary

tribe \'trīb\ *n* **1** ♦ : a social group comprising numerous families, clans, or generations **2** : a group of persons having a common character, occupation, or interest **3** : a group of related plants or animals ⟨the cat ∼⟩ — **trib·al** \'trī-bəl\ *adj*

♦ blood, clan, family, folks, house, kin, kindred, kinfolk, line, lineage, people, race, stock — more at FAMILY

tribes·man \'trībz-mən\ *n* : a member of a tribe

trib·u·la·tion \ˌtri-byə-'lā-shən\ *n* [ME *tribulacion*, fr. OF, fr. L *tribulatio*, fr. *tribulare* to press, oppress, fr. *tribulum* drag used in threshing] ♦ : distress or suffering resulting from oppression or persecution; *also* : a trying experience

♦ affliction, agony, anguish, distress, misery, pain, torment, torture, woe — more at DISTRESS

tri·bu·nal \trī-'byün-ᵊl, tri-\ *n* **1** : the seat of a judge **2** : a court of justice **3** : something that decides or determines ⟨the ~ of public opinion⟩

tri·bune \'tri-ˌbyün, tri-'byün\ *n* **1** : an official in ancient Rome with the function of protecting the interests of plebeian citizens from the patricians **2** : a defender of the people

¹trib·u·tary \'tri-byə-ˌter-ē\ *adj* **1** : paying tribute : SUBJECT **2** : flowing into a larger stream or a lake

²tributary *n, pl* **-tar·ies** **1** : a ruler or state that pays tribute **2** : a tributary stream

trib·ute \'tri-(ˌ)byüt, -byət\ *n* **1** : a payment by one ruler or nation to another as an act of submission or price of protection **2** : a usu. excessive tax, rental, or levy exacted by a sovereign or superior **3 a** ♦ : a gift or service showing respect, gratitude, or affection **b** ♦ : something (as material evidence or a formal attestation) that indicates the worth, virtue, or effectiveness of the one in question

♦ [3a, b] accolade, citation, commendation, encomium, eulogy, homage, paean, panegyric, salutation — more at ENCOMIUM

trice \'trīs\ *n* ♦ : a brief space of time : INSTANT, MOMENT

♦ flash, instant, jiffy, minute, moment, second, shake, twinkle, twinkling, wink — more at INSTANT

tri·ceps \'trī-ˌseps\ *n, pl* **triceps** : a large muscle along the back of the upper arm that is attached at its upper end by three main parts and acts to extend the forearm at the elbow joint

tri·cer·a·tops \(ˌ)trī-'ser-ə-ˌtäps\ *n, pl* **-tops** *also* **-tops·es** [NL, fr. Gk *tri-* three + *kerat-, keras* horn + *ōps* face] : any of a genus of large plant-eating Cretaceous dinosaurs with three horns, a bony crest on the neck, and hoofed toes

tri·chi·na \tri-'kī-nə\ *n, pl* **-nae** \-(ˌ)nē\ *also* **-nas** : a small slender nematode worm that in the larval state is parasitic in the striated muscles of flesh-eating mammals (as humans)

trich·i·no·sis \ˌtri-kə-'nō-səs\ *n* : infestation with or disease caused by trichinae and marked esp. by pain, fever, and swelling

¹trick \'trik\ *n* **1** ♦ : a crafty procedure meant to deceive **2** ♦ : a mischievous action : PRANK **3** : a childish action **4** ♦ : a deceptive or ingenious feat designed to puzzle or amuse **5** ♦ : an habitual peculiarity of behavior or manner **6** : a quick or artful way of getting a result : KNACK **7** : the cards played in one round of a card game **8** : a tour of duty : SHIFT

♦ [1] artifice, device, dodge, gimmick, jig, ploy, scheme, sleight, stratagem, wile; *also* bluff, deception, feint; fraud, hoax, swindle ♦ [2] antic, caper, escapade, frolic, monkeyshine, practical joke, prank — more at PRANK ♦ [4] deed, exploit, feat, stunt — more at FEAT ♦ [5] crotchet, eccentricity, idiosyncrasy, mannerism, oddity, peculiarity, quirk, singularity — more at IDIOSYNCRASY

²trick *vb* **1** ♦ : to deceive by cunning or artifice **2** : to dress ornately

♦ beguile, bluff, cozen, deceive, delude, dupe, fool, gull, have, hoax, hoodwink, humbug, misinform, mislead, string along, take in — more at DECEIVE

trick·ery \'tri-kə-rē\ *n* ♦ : deception by tricks and stratagems

♦ artifice, chicanery, hanky-panky, subterfuge, wile; *also* artfulness, caginess, craftiness, cunning, underhandedness, wiliness; deceit, deceitfulness, deception, dishonesty, guile; stealth

trick·le \'tri-kəl\ *vb* **trick·led; trick·ling** **1** : to run or fall in drops **2** ♦ : to flow in a thin gentle stream — **trickle** *n*

♦ dribble, gurgle, lap, plash, ripple, slosh, splash, wash — more at GURGLE

trick·ster \'trik-stər\ *n* **1** ♦ : one who tricks or cheats **2** ♦ : one skilled at illusions

♦ [1] cheat, dodger, hoaxer, shark, sharper, swindler; *also* double-crosser, double-dealer; charlatan, fake, faker, humbug, impostor, mountebank, pretender, quack; adventurer, fox, knave, prankster, rascal, rogue; slicker; plotter, schemer, sneak ♦ [2] conjurer, illusionist, magician

tricky \'tri-kē\ *adj* **trick·i·er; -est** **1** : inclined to trickery **2** ♦ : requiring skill or caution ⟨a ~ situation to handle⟩ **3** : UNRELIABLE ⟨a ~ lock⟩

♦ catchy, delicate, difficult, knotty, problematic, spiny, thorny, ticklish, touchy, tough; *also* abstract, abstruse, complex, complicated, hard, intricate, involved, recondite; stubborn, troublesome, vexatious, vexing; burdensome, demanding, discommoding, exacting, importunate, inconvenient, onerous, oppressive, painful

tri·col·or \'trī-ˌkə-lər\ *n* : a flag of three colors ⟨the French ~⟩

tri·cy·cle \'trī-(ˌ)si-kəl\ *n* : a 3-wheeled vehicle usu. propelled by pedals

tri·dent \'trīd-ᵊnt\ *n* [L *trident-, tridens*, fr. *tri-* three + *dent-, dens* tooth] : a 3-pronged spear

tried \'trīd\ *adj* ♦ : found trustworthy through testing **2** : subjected to trials

♦ dependable, good, reliable, responsible, safe, solid, steady, sure, true, trustworthy — more at DEPENDABLE

tri·en·ni·al \trī-'e-nē-əl\ *adj* **1** : occurring or being done every three years **2** : lasting for three years — **triennial** *n*

¹tri·fle \'trī-fəl\ *n* **1** ♦ : something of little value or importance **2** : a dessert of cake soaked with liqueur and served with toppings (as fruit or cream)

♦ child's play, frippery, nothing, triviality; *also* naught, nothingness, smoke, zero; molehill, peanuts, pittance, song, straw; nonsense, trivia

²trifle *vb* **tri·fled; tri·fling** **1** : to talk in a jesting or mocking manner **2** : to treat someone or something as unimportant **3** : DALLY, FLIRT **4** : to handle idly : TOY **5** : to spend or waste (as time or money) in trifling or on trifles — **tri·fler** *n*

tri·fling \'trī-fliŋ\ *adj* **1** : FRIVOLOUS **2** ♦ : lacking in significance or solid worth : TRIVIAL ⟨~ details⟩

♦ frivolous, inconsequential, inconsiderable, insignificant, little, minor, minute, negligible, slight, small, trivial, unimportant — more at UNIMPORTANT

tri·fo·cals \trī-'fō-kəlz\ *n pl* : eyeglasses with lenses having one part for close focus, one for intermediate focus, and one for distant focus

tri·fo·li·ate \trī-'fō-lē-ət\ *adj* : having three leaves or leaflets

¹trig \'trig\ *adj* : stylishly trim : SMART

²trig *n* : TRIGONOMETRY

¹trig·ger \'tri-gər\ *n* [alter. of earlier *tricker*, fr. D *trekker*, fr. MD *trecker* one that pulls, fr. *trecken* to pull] : a movable lever that activates a device when it is squeezed; *esp* : the part of a firearm lock moved by the finger to fire a gun — **trigger** *adj* — **trig·gered** *adj*

²trigger *vb* **1** : to fire by pulling a trigger **2** ♦ : to initiate, actuate, or set off as if by a trigger

♦ activate, actuate, crank, drive, move, propel, run, set off, spark, start, touch off, turn on — more at ACTIVATE

tri·glyc·er·ide *n* : any of a group of lipids that are formed from glycerol and fatty acids and are widespread in animal tissue

trig·o·nom·e·try \ˌtri-gə-'nä-mə-trē\ *n* : the branch of mathematics dealing with the properties of triangles and esp. with finding unknown angles or sides given the size or length of some angles or sides — **trig·o·no·met·ric** \-nə-'me-trik\ *also* **trig·o·no·met·ri·cal** \-tri-kəl\ *adj*

trike \'trīk\ *n* : TRICYCLE

¹trill \'tril\ *n* **1** : the alternation of two musical tones a scale degree apart **2** : WARBLE **3** : the rapid vibration of one speech organ against another (as of the tip of the tongue against the teeth)

²trill *vb* : to utter as or with a trill

tril·lion \'tril-yən\ *n* **1** : a thousand billions **2** *Brit* : a million billions — **trillion** *adj* — **tril·lionth** \-yənth\ *adj or n*

tril·li·um \'tri-lē-əm\ *n* : any of a genus of spring-blooming herbs that are related to the lilies and have an erect stem bearing a whorl of three leaves and a solitary flower

tril·o·gy \'tril-ə-jē\ *n, pl* **-gies** : a series of three dramas or literary or musical compositions that are closely related and develop one theme

¹**trim** \'trim\ *vb* **trimmed; trim·ming** [OE *trymian, trymman* to strengthen, arrange, fr. *trum* strong, firm] **1** ♦ : to put ornaments on : ADORN **2** ♦ : to defeat esp. resoundingly **3** ♦ : to make trim, neat, regular, or less bulky by or as if by cutting ⟨~ a beard⟩ ⟨~ a budget⟩ **4** : to cause (a boat) to assume a desired position in the water by arrangement of the load; *also* : to adjust (as a submarine or airplane) esp. for horizontal motion **5** : to adjust (a sail) to a desired position **6** : to change one's views for safety or expediency — **trim·ly** *adv* — **trim·ness** *n*

♦ [1] adorn, array, beautify, bedeck, deck, decorate, do, dress, embellish, enrich, garnish, grace, ornament — more at DECORATE ♦ [2] clobber, drub, rout, skunk, thrash, trounce, wallop, whip ♦ [3] bob, clip, crop, curtail, cut, cut back, dock, lop, nip, prune, shave, shear — more at CLIP

²**trim** *adj* **trim·mer; trim·mest** ♦ : showing neatness, good order, or compactness ⟨a ~ figure⟩

♦ crisp, neat, orderly, shipshape, snug, tidy, uncluttered — more at NEAT

³**trim** *n* **1** ♦ : good condition **2** ♦ : material used for ornament or trimming; *esp* : the woodwork in the finish of a house esp. around doors and windows **3** : the position of a ship or boat esp. with reference to the horizontal; *also* : the relation between the plane of a sail and the direction of a ship **4** : the position of an airplane at which it will continue in level flight with no adjustments to the controls **5** : something that is trimmed off

♦ [1] condition, fettle, form, kilter, order, repair, shape ♦ [2] adornment, caparison, decoration, embellishment, frill, garnish, ornament — more at DECORATION

tri·ma·ran \'trī-mə-ˌran, ˌtrī-mə-'ran\ *n* : a sailboat with three hulls

tri·mes·ter \trī-'mes-tər, 'trī-ˌmes-tər\ *n* **1** : a period of three or about three months (as in pregnancy) **2** : one of three terms into which an academic year is sometimes divided

trim·e·ter \'tri-mə-tər\ *n* : a line of verse consisting of three metrical feet

trim·mer \'tri-mər\ *n* : one that trims

trim·ming \'tri-miŋ\ *n* **1** : the loss of a contest : DEFEAT **2** : the action of one that trims **3** : something that trims, ornaments, or completes

tri·month·ly \trī-'mənth-lē\ *adj* : occurring every three months

trine \'trīn\ *adj* : THREEFOLD, TRIPLE

Trin·i·da·di·an \ˌtri-nə-'dā-dē-ən, -'da-\ *n* : a native or inhabitant of the island of Trinidad — **Trinidadian** *adj*

Trin·i·tar·i·an \ˌtri-nə-'ter-ē-ən\ *n* : a believer in the doctrine of the Trinity — **Trin·i·tar·i·an·ism** \-ē-ə-ˌni-zəm\ *n*

Trin·i·ty \'tri-nə-tē\ *n* **1** : the unity of Father, Son, and Holy Spirit as three persons in one Godhead **2** *not cap* : TRIAD

trin·ket \'triŋ-kət\ *n* **1** ♦ : a small ornament (as a jewel or ring) **2** : TRIFLE 1

♦ bauble, curiosity, gewgaw, knickknack, novelty, tchotchke — more at KNICKKNACK

trio \'trē-ō\ *n, pl* **tri·os** **1** : a musical composition for three voices or three instruments **2** : the performers of a trio **3** ♦ : a group or set of three

♦ threesome, triad, triple, triplet — more at THREESOME

¹**trip** \'trip\ *vb* **tripped; trip·ping** **1** ♦ : to move with light quick steps **2** ♦ : to catch the foot against something so as to stumble or cause to stumble **3** : to make a mistake : SLIP; *also* : to detect in a misstep : EXPOSE **4** : to release (as a spring or switch) by moving a catch; *also* : ACTIVATE **5** : to get high on a usu. hallucinatory drug

♦ [1] bound, hop, skip, spring — more at SKIP
♦ [2] fall, slip, stumble, topple, tumble — more at FALL

²**trip** *n* **1** ♦ : an act or instance of traveling : JOURNEY **2** : a quick light step **3** : a false step : STUMBLE; *also* : ERROR **4** : the action of tripping mechanically; *also* : a device for tripping **5** : an intense experience; *esp* : one triggered by a hallucinatory drug **6** : absorption in an attitude or state of mind ⟨an ego ~⟩

♦ expedition, journey, passage, peregrination, trek — more at JOURNEY

tri·par·tite \trī-'pär-ˌtīt\ *adj* **1** ♦ : divided into three parts **2** : having three corresponding parts or copies **3** : made between three parties ⟨a ~ treaty⟩

♦ threefold, treble, triple — more at TRIPLE

tripe \'trīp\ *n* **1** : stomach tissue esp. of a ruminant (as an ox) used as food **2** : something poor, worthless, or offensive : TRASH

¹**tri·ple** \'tri-pəl\ *vb* **tri·pled; tri·pling** **1** : to make or become three times as great or as many **2** : to hit a triple

²**triple** *n* **1** : a triple quantity **2** ♦ : a group of three **3** : a hit in baseball that lets the batter reach third base

♦ threesome, triad, trio, triplet — more at THREESOME

³**triple** *adj* **1** : being three times as great or as many **2** ♦ : having three units or members **3** : repeated three times

♦ threefold, treble, tripartite; *also* triplicate

triple bond *n* : a chemical bond in which three pairs of electrons are shared by two atoms in a molecule

triple point *n* : the condition of temperature and pressure under which the gaseous, liquid, and solid forms of a substance can exist in equilibrium

trip·let \'tri-plət\ *n* **1** : a unit of three lines of verse **2** ♦ : a group of three of a kind **3** : one of three offspring born at one birth

♦ threesome, triad, trio, triple — more at THREESOME

tri·plex \'tri-ˌpleks, 'trī-\ *adj* : having three units or members : THREEFOLD

¹**trip·li·cate** \'tri-pli-kət\ *adj* : made in three identical copies

²**trip·li·cate** \-plə-ˌkāt\ *vb* **-cat·ed; -cat·ing** **1** : TRIPLE **2** : to provide three copies of ⟨~ a document⟩

³**trip·li·cate** \-pli-kət\ *n* : three copies all alike — used with *in* ⟨typed in ~⟩

tri·ply \'tri-plē, 'tri-pə-lē\ *adv* : in a triple degree, amount, or manner

tri·pod \'trī-ˌpäd\ *n* : something (as a caldron, stool, or camera stand) that rests on three legs — **tripod** *or* **tri·po·dal** \'trī-pəd-ᵊl, 'trī-ˌpäd-\ *adj*

trip·tych \'trip-tik\ *n* : a picture or carving in three panels side by side

tri·reme \'trī-ˌrēm\ *n* : an ancient galley having three banks of oars

tri·sect \'trī-ˌsekt, trī-'sekt\ *vb* : to divide into three usu. equal parts — **tri·sec·tion** \'trī-ˌsek-shən\ *n*

trite \'trīt\ *adj* **trit·er; trit·est** [L *tritus,* fr. pp. of *terere* to rub, wear away] ♦ : used so commonly that the novelty is worn off : STALE

♦ banal, commonplace, hackneyed, musty, stale, stereotyped, threadbare, tired — more at STALE

tri·ti·um \'tri-tē-əm, 'tri-shē-\ *n* : a radioactive form of hydrogen with one proton and two neutrons in its nucleus and three times the mass of ordinary hydrogen

tri·ton \'trīt-ᵊn\ *n* : any of various large marine gastropod mollusks with a heavy elongated conical shell; *also* : the shell of a triton

trit·u·rate \'tri-chə-ˌrāt\ *vb* **-rat·ed; -rat·ing** : to rub or grind to a fine powder

¹**tri·umph** \'trī-əmf\ *n* **1** ♦ : the joy or exultation of victory or success **2** ♦ : VICTORY, CONQUEST **3** ♦ : a notable success — **tri·um·phal** \trī-'əm-fəl\ *adj*

♦ accomplishment, achievement, attainment, coup, success — more at ACCOMPLISHMENT

²**triumph** *vb* **1** ♦ : to obtain victory : PREVAIL **2** ♦ : to celebrate victory or success exultantly

♦ [1] conquer, prevail, win — more at WIN ♦ *usu* triumph over [1] beat, defeat, overcome, prevail, surmount, win ♦ [2] crow, delight, exult, glory, joy, rejoice — more at EXULT

tri·um·phant \trī-'əm-fənt\ *adj* **1** : VICTORIOUS **2** ♦ : rejoicing for or celebrating victory **3** ♦ : notably successful — **tri·um·phant·ly** *adv*

♦ [2] exultant, jubilant, rejoicing — more at EXULTANT ♦ [3] palmy, prosperous, successful — more at SUCCESSFUL

tri·um·vir \trī-'əm-vər\ *n, pl* **-virs** *also* **-vi·ri** \-və-‚rī\ : a member of a triumvirate

tri·um·vi·rate \-və-rət\ *n* : a ruling body of three persons

tri·une \'trī-‚ün, -‚yün\ *adj* : being three in one ⟨the ∼ God⟩

triv·et \'tri-vət\ *n* **1** : a 3-legged stand : TRIPOD **2** : a usu. metal stand with short feet for use under a hot dish

triv·ia \'tri-vē-ə\ *n sing or pl* : unimportant matters : obscure facts or details ⟨movie ∼⟩

triv·i·al \'tri-vē-əl\ *adj* [L *trivialis* found everywhere, commonplace, fr. *trivium* crossroads, fr. *tri-* three + *via* way] ♦ : of little importance

♦ frivolous, inconsequential, inconsiderable, insignificant, little, minor, minute, negligible, slight, small, trifling, unimportant — more at UNIMPORTANT

triv·i·al·i·ty \‚tri-vē-'a-lə-tē\ *n* **1** : the quality or state of being trivial **2** ♦ : something trivial

♦ child's play, frippery, nothing, trifle — more at TRIFLE

triv·i·um \'tri-vē-əm\ *n, pl* **triv·ia** \-vē-ə\ : the three liberal arts of grammar, rhetoric, and logic in a medieval university

tri·week·ly \trī-'wē-klē\ *adj* **1** : occurring or appearing three times a week **2** : occurring or appearing every three weeks — **triweekly** *adv*

tro·che \'trō-kē\ *n* : LOZENGE 2

tro·chee \'trō-‚kē\ *n* : a metrical foot of one accented syllable followed by one unaccented syllable — **tro·cha·ic** \trō-'kā-ik\ *adj*

trod *past and past part of* TREAD

trodden *past part of* TREAD

troi·ka \'trȯi-kə\ *n* [Russ *troĭka*, fr. *troe* three] : a group of three; *esp* : an administrative or ruling body of three

¹**troll** \'trōl\ *vb* **1** : to sing the parts of (a song) in succession **2** : to fish by trailing a lure or baited hook from a moving boat **3** : to sing or play jovially **4** : to deliberately antagonize (others) esp. online

²**troll** *n* **1** : a lure used in trolling; *also* : the line with its lure **2** : a person who trolls others esp. online

³**troll** *n* ♦ : a dwarf or giant in Scandinavian folklore inhabiting caves or hills

♦ brownie, dwarf, elf, fairy, fay, gnome, hobgoblin, leprechaun, pixie, puck — more at FAIRY

trol·ley *also* **trol·ly** \'trä-lē\ *n, pl* **trolleys** *also* **trollies** **1** : a device (as a grooved wheel on the end of a pole) to carry current from a wire to an electrically driven vehicle **2** : a streetcar powered electrically by overhead wires **3** : a wheeled carriage running on an overhead rail or track

trol·ley·bus \'trä-lē-‚bəs\ *n* : a bus powered electrically by overhead wires

trolley car *n* : TROLLEY 2

trol·lop \'trä-ləp\ *n* : a disreputable woman; *esp* : one who engages in sex promiscuously

trom·bone \träm-'bōn, 'träm-‚bōn\ *n* [It, lit., big trumpet, fr. *tromba* trumpet] : a brass wind instrument that consists of a long metal tube with two turns and a flaring end and that usu. has a movable slide to vary the pitch — **trom·bon·ist** \-'bō-nist, -‚bō-\ *n*

tromp \'trämp, 'trȯmp\ *vb* **1** : to walk, tread, or step esp. heavily : TRAMP **2** : to stamp with the foot **3** : to defeat decisively **4** ♦ : to tread on forcibly and repeatedly

♦ stamp, stomp, tramp, trample — more at TRAMPLE

trompe l'oeil \(‚)trȯmp-'lə-ē, trō⁽ᵖ⁾-'lœi\ *n* [F *trompe-l'oeil*, lit., deceives the eye] : a style of painting in which objects are depicted with photographic detail

¹**troop** \'trüp\ *n* **1** : a cavalry unit corresponding to an infantry company **2** *pl* ♦ : the combined military, naval, and air forces of a nation : ARMED FORCES **3** : a collection of people, animals, or things **4** : a unit of Girl Scouts or Boy Scouts under an adult leader

♦ **troops** armed forces, military, services — more at ARMED FORCES

²**troop** *vb* : to move or gather in crowds

troop·er \'trü-pər\ *n* **1** : an enlisted cavalryman; *also* : a cavalry horse **2** : a mounted or a state police officer

troop·ship \'trüp-‚ship\ *n* : a ship or aircraft for carrying troops

trope \'trōp\ *n* : a word or expression used in a figurative sense

tro·phy \'trō-fē\ *n, pl* **trophies** : something gained or given in conquest or victory esp. when preserved or mounted as a memorial

trop·ic \'trä-pik\ *n* [ME *tropik*, fr. L *tropicus* of the solstice, fr. Gk *tropikos*, fr. *tropē* turn] **1** : either of the two parallels of latitude approximately 23½ degrees north (**tropic of Can·cer** \-'kan-sər\) or south (**tropic of Cap·ri·corn** \-'ka-prə-‚kȯrn\) of the equator where the sun is directly overhead when it reaches its most northerly or southerly point in the sky **2** *pl, often cap* : the region lying between the tropics — **trop·i·cal** \-pi-kəl\ *or* **tropic** *adj*

tro·pism \'trō-‚pi-zəm\ *n* : an automatic movement by an organism in response to a source of stimulation; *also* : a reflex reaction involving this

tro·po·sphere \'trō-pə-‚sfir, 'trä-\ *n* : the part of the atmosphere between the earth's surface and the stratosphere in which most weather changes occur — **tro·po·spher·ic** \‚trō-pə-'sfir-ik, ‚trä-, -'sfer-\ *adj*

¹**trot** \'trät\ *n* **1** : a moderately fast gait of a 4-footed animal (as a horse) in which the legs move in diagonal pairs **2** : a human jogging gait between a walk and a run

²**trot** *vb* **trot·ted; trot·ting** **1** : to ride, drive, or go at a trot **2** : to proceed briskly : HURRY — **trot·ter** *n*

troth \'träth, 'trȯth, 'trōth\ *n* **1** : pledged faithfulness **2 a** ♦ : one's pledged word **b** ♦ : the act of promising to marry or the fact of being engaged to marry : BETROTHAL

♦ [2a] oath, pledge, promise, vow, word — more at PROMISE ♦ [2b] betrothal, engagement, espousal — more at ENGAGEMENT

trou·ba·dour \'trü-bə-‚dȯr\ *n* [F, fr. Old Occitan *trobador*, fr. *trobar* to compose] : any of a class of poet-musicians flourishing esp. in southern France and northern Italy during the 11th, 12th, and 13th centuries

¹**trou·ble** \'trə-bəl\ *vb* **trou·bled; trou·bling** **1** ♦ : to feel or cause to feel mentally or spiritually agitated **2** : to produce physical disorder in **3** ♦ : to put to inconvenience **4** : RUFFLE ⟨∼ the waters⟩ **5** : to make an effort

♦ [1] bother, fear, fret, stew, sweat, worry — more at WORRY ♦ [3] discommode, disoblige, disturb, inconvenience — more at INCONVENIENCE

²**trouble** *n* **1** : the quality or state of being troubled esp. mentally **2** : an instance of distress or annoyance **3** ♦ : a condition of physical distress or ill health : DISEASE ⟨heart ∼⟩ **4** ♦ : an effort made : EXERTION ⟨took the ∼ to phone⟩ **5** ♦ : a cause of disturbance, distress, difficulty, or danger **6** ♦ : a state or condition of distress, annoyance, danger, or difficulty

♦ [3] affection, ailment, bug, complaint, complication, condition, disease, disorder, fever, ill, illness, infirmity, malady, sickness — more at DISEASE ♦ [4] effort, exertion, expenditure, labor (*or* labour), pains, sweat, while, work — more at EFFORT ♦ [5] case, knot, matter, problem — more at PROBLEM ♦ [6] danger, distress, jeopardy, peril, risk — more at DANGER

troubled *adj* ♦ : feeling worry or concern

♦ aflutter, anxious, edgy, jittery, jumpy, nervous, nervy, perturbed, tense, uneasy, upset, worried — more at NERVOUS

trou·ble·mak·er \-ˌmā-kər\ n : a person who causes trouble

trou·ble·shoot·er \-ˌshü-tər\ n 1 : a worker employed to locate trouble and make repairs in equipment 2 : an expert in resolving disputes or problems — trou·ble·shoot vb

trou·ble·some \-səm\ adj 1 : DIFFICULT, BURDENSOME 2 ♦ : giving trouble or anxiety — trou·ble·some·ly adv

♦ unsettling, upsetting, worrisome; also daunting, demoralizing, discomfiting, disconcerting, discouraging, disheartening, dismaying, dispiriting Ant reassuring

trou·blous \'trə-bə-ləs\ adj 1 : full of trouble 2 : causing trouble : TROUBLESOME

trough \'trȯf, 'trȯth\ n, pl troughs \'trȯfs, 'trȯvz, 'trȯths, 'trȯthz\ 1 : a long shallow open boxlike container esp. for water or feed for livestock 2 : a gutter along the eaves of a house 3 : a long channel or depression (as between waves or hills) 4 : an elongated area of low barometric pressure

trounce \'traůns\ vb trounced; trounc·ing 1 : to thrash or punish severely 2 ♦ : to defeat decisively

♦ beat, clobber, drub, rout, skunk, thrash, trim, wallop, whip

troupe \'trüp\ n : COMPANY; esp : a group of performers on the stage

troup·er \'trü-pər\ n 1 ♦ : a member of a troupe 2 : a person who deals with and persists through difficulty or hardship without complaint

♦ actor, impersonator, mummer, player

trou·sers \'traů-zərz\ n pl [alter. of earlier trouse, fr. Sc-Gael triubhas] ♦ : an outer garment covering each leg separately and usu. extending from the waist to the ankle — trouser adj

♦ britches, pantaloons, pants, slacks — more at PANTS

trous·seau \'trü-sō, trü-'sō\ n, pl trousseaux \-sōz, -'sōz\ or trousseaus [F] : the personal outfit of a bride

trout \'traůt\ n, pl trout also trouts [ME, fr. OE trūht, fr. LL tructa, a fish with sharp teeth, fr. Gk trōktēs, lit., gnawer] : any of various mostly freshwater food and game fishes usu. smaller than the related salmons

trow \'trō\ vb, archaic : THINK, SUPPOSE

trow·el \'traů-əl\ n 1 : a hand tool used for spreading, shaping, or smoothing loose or plastic material (as mortar or plaster) 2 : a scoop-shaped tool used in gardening — trowel vb

troy \'troi\ adj : expressed in troy weight ⟨~ ounce⟩

troy weight n : a system of weights based on a pound of 12 ounces and an ounce of 480 grains (31 grams)

tru·ant \'trü-ənt\ n [ME, vagabond, idler, fr. AF, of Celt origin] : a student who stays out of school without permission — tru·an·cy \-ən-sē\ n — truant adj

truce \'trüs\ n 1 : ARMISTICE 2 : a respite esp. from something unpleasant

¹truck \'trək\ vb 1 : EXCHANGE, BARTER 2 : to have dealings : TRAFFIC

²truck n 1 ♦ : the act or practice of carrying on trade by bartering : BARTER 2 : small goods or merchandise; esp : vegetables grown for market 3 : DEALINGS

♦ barter, commutation, exchange, swap, trade — more at EXCHANGE

³truck n 1 : a wheeled vehicle (as a strong heavy automobile) designed for carrying heavy articles or hauling a trailer 2 : a swiveling frame with springs and one or more pairs of wheels used to carry and guide one end of a locomotive or railroad car

⁴truck vb 1 : to transport on a truck ⟨~s vegetables⟩ 2 : to be employed in driving a truck — truck·er n

truck farm n : a farm growing vegetables for market — truck farmer n

truck·le \'trə-kəl\ vb truck·led; truck·ling : to yield slavishly to the will of another : SUBMIT

truc·u·lence \'trə-kyə-ləns\ n ♦ : the quality or state of being truculent — truc·u·len·cy \-lən-sē\ n

♦ aggression, aggressiveness, belligerence, fight, militancy, pugnacity — more at BELLIGERENCE

truc·u·lent \'trə-kyə-lənt\ adj 1 : feeling or showing ferocity : SAVAGE 2 ♦ : aggressively self-assertive : PUGNACIOUS — truc·u·lent·ly adv

♦ aggressive, argumentative, bellicose, belligerent, combative, contentious, discordant, disputatious, militant, pugnacious, quarrelsome, scrappy, warlike — more at BELLIGERENT

trudge \'trəj\ vb trudged; trudg·ing : to walk or march steadily and usu. laboriously ⟨trudged through the snow⟩

¹true \'trü\ adj tru·er; tru·est 1 ♦ : faithful in allegiance 2 : free from fraud or deception 3 ♦ : agreeing with facts or reality ⟨a ~ description⟩ 4 : CONSISTENT ⟨~ to expectations⟩ 5 ♦ : properly so called ⟨~ love⟩ 6 : RIGHTFUL ⟨~ and lawful king⟩ 7 ♦ : conformable to a standard or pattern; also : placed or formed accurately

♦ [1] constant, devoted, faithful, fast, good, loyal, pious, staunch, steadfast, steady, true-blue — more at FAITHFUL ♦ [3] actual, concrete, existent, factual, real, very — more at ACTUAL ♦ [5] authentic, bona fide, genuine, real, right — more at AUTHENTIC ♦ [7] accurate, correct, exact, precise, proper, right, so — more at CORRECT

²true adv 1 : TRUTHFULLY 2 : ACCURATELY ⟨the bullet flew straight and ~⟩; also : without variation from type ⟨breed ~⟩

³true n 1 : TRUTH, REALITY — usu. used with the 2 : the state of being accurate (as in alignment) ⟨out of ~⟩

⁴true vb trued; true·ing also tru·ing : to bring or restore to a desired precision

true–blue adj ♦ : marked by unswerving loyalty

♦ constant, devoted, faithful, fast, good, loyal, pious, staunch, steadfast, steady, true — more at FAITHFUL

true bug n : BUG 2

true·heart·ed \'trü-'här-təd\ adj : FAITHFUL, LOYAL

truf·fle \'trə-fəl, 'trü-\ n 1 : the dark or light edible spore-bearing organ of any of several European fungi that grow underground; also : one of these fungi 2 : a candy made of chocolate, butter, and sugar shaped into balls and coated with cocoa

tru·ism \'trü-ˌi-zəm\ n : an undoubted or self-evident truth

tru·ly \'trü-lē\ adv 1 : in all sincerity ⟨is ~ sorry⟩ 2 ♦ : in agreement with fact 3 : ACCURATELY 4 : in a proper or suitable manner 5 ♦ : without any question : INDEED

♦ [2] actually, frankly, honestly, really, truthfully, verily — more at ACTUALLY ♦ [5] certainly, definitely, doubtless, incontestably, indeed, indisputably, really, surely, undeniably, undoubtedly, unquestionably — more at INDEED

¹trump \'trəmp\ n : TRUMPET

²trump n : a card of a designated suit any of whose cards will win over a card that is not of this suit; also : the suit itself — often used in pl.

³trump vb : to take with a trump

trumped–up \'trəmpt-ˌəp\ adj : fraudulently concocted : SPURIOUS ⟨~ charges⟩

trum·pery \'trəm-pə-rē\ n 1 : NONSENSE 2 : trivial articles : JUNK

¹trum·pet \'trəm-pət\ n 1 : a wind instrument consisting of a long curved metal tube flaring at one end and with a cup-shaped mouthpiece at the other 2 : something that resembles a trumpet or its tonal quality 3 : a funnel-shaped instrument for collecting, directing, or intensifying sound

²trumpet vb 1 : to blow a trumpet 2 ♦ : to proclaim on or as if on a trumpet — trum·pet·er n

♦ ballyhoo, crack up, glorify, tout — more at TOUT

¹trun·cate \'trən-ˌkāt, 'trən-\ adj : having the end square or blunt

²**truncate** *vb* **trun·cat·ed; trun·cat·ing** ♦ : to shorten by or as if by cutting — **trun·ca·tion** \ˌtrən-ˈkā-shən\ *n*

  ♦ abbreviate, abridge, curtail, cut back, dock, shorten — more at SHORTEN

trun·cheon \ˈtrən-chən\ *n* ♦ : a police officer's club

  ♦ bat, bludgeon, club, cudgel, staff — more at CLUB

trun·dle \ˈtrənd-ᵊl\ *vb* **trun·dled; trun·dling** : to roll along : WHEEL

trundle bed *n* : a low bed that can be stored under a higher bed

trunk \ˈtrəŋk\ *n* **1** : the main stem of a tree **2** : the body of a person or animal apart from the head and limbs **3** : the main or central part of something **4** ♦ : a box or chest used to hold usu. clothes or personal effects (as of a traveler); *also* : the enclosed luggage space in the rear of an automobile **5** : the long muscular nose of an elephant **6** *pl* : men's shorts worn chiefly for sports **7** : a usu. major channel or passage

  ♦ box, caddy, case, casket, chest, locker — more at CHEST

trunk line *n* : a transportation system handling long-distance through traffic

¹**truss** \ˈtrəs\ *vb* **1** ♦ : to secure tightly : BIND **2** : to arrange for cooking by binding close the wings or legs of (a fowl) **3** : to support, strengthen, or stiffen by or as if by a truss

  ♦ band, bind, gird, tie — more at TIE

²**truss** *n* **1** : a collection of structural parts (as beams) forming a rigid framework (as in bridge or building construction) **2** : a device worn to reduce a hernia by pressure

¹**trust** \ˈtrəst\ *n* **1** : assured reliance on the character, strength, or truth of someone or something **2** : a basis of reliance, faith, or hope **3** ♦ : confident hope **4** : financial credit **5** : a property interest held by one person for the benefit of another **6** ♦ : a combination of firms formed by a legal agreement; *esp* : one that reduces competition **7** : something entrusted to one to be cared for in the interest of another **8** ♦ : immediate charge and control exercised by a person or an authority : CUSTODY

  ♦ [3] confidence, credence, faith, stock; *also* acceptance, assurance, certainty, certitude, conviction, positiveness, sureness; credit, dependence, hope, reliance *Ant* distrust, mistrust ♦ [6] cartel, combination, combine, syndicate — more at CARTEL ♦ [8] care, custody, guardianship, keeping, safekeeping, ward — more at CUSTODY

²**trust** *vb* **1** : to place confidence : DEPEND **2** : to be confident : HOPE **3** ♦ : to commit or place in one's care or keeping : ENTRUST **4** : to permit to stay or go or to do something without fear or misgiving **5** ♦ : to rely on or on the truth of : BELIEVE **6** : to extend credit to

  ♦ [3] commend, commit, consign, delegate, deliver, entrust, give, hand over, leave, pass, transfer, transmit, turn over, vest — more at GIVE ♦ [5] accept, believe, credit, swallow — more at BELIEVE

trust·ee \ˌtrəs-ˈtē\ *n* **1** : a person to whom property is legally committed in trust **2** : a country charged with the supervision of a trust territory

trust·ee·ship \ˌtrəs-ˈtē-ˌship\ *n* **1** : the office or function of a trustee **2** : supervisory control by one or more nations over a trust territory

trust·ful \ˈtrəst-fəl\ *adj* : full of trust : CONFIDING — **trust·ful·ly** *adv* — **trust·ful·ness** *n*

trust territory *n* : a non-self-governing territory placed under a supervisory authority by the Trusteeship Council of the United Nations

trust·wor·thi·ness \-ˌwər-thē-nəs\ *n* ♦ : the quality or state of being trustworthy

  ♦ dependability, reliability, solidity, sureness — more at RELIABILITY

trust·wor·thy \-ˌwər-thē\ *adj* ♦ : worthy of confidence : DEPENDABLE ⟨a ∼ assistant⟩

  ♦ dependable, good, reliable, responsible, safe, solid, steady, sure, tried, true — more at DEPENDABLE

¹**trusty** \ˈtrəs-tē\ *adj* **trust·i·er; -est** : worthy of confidence : DEPENDABLE

²**trusty** \ˈtrəs-tē, ˌtrəs-ˈtē\ *n, pl* **trust·ies** : a trusted person; *esp* : a convict considered trustworthy and allowed special privileges

truth \ˈtrüth\ *n, pl* **truths** \ˈtrüthz, ˈtrüths\ **1** : TRUTHFULNESS, HONESTY **2** : the real state of things : FACT **3** : the body of real events or facts : ACTUALITY **4** : a true or accepted statement or proposition ⟨the ∼s of science⟩ **5** : agreement with fact or reality : CORRECTNESS

truth·er \ˈtrü-thər\ *n* : one who believes that the truth about an important subject or event is being concealed from the public by a powerful conspiracy

truth·ful \ˈtrüth-fəl\ *adj* : telling or disposed to tell the truth

truth·ful·ly \-fə-lē\ *adv* **1** ♦ : in reality : ACTUALLY ⟨∼, he didn't do it⟩ **2** : in a truthful manner ⟨"I didn't do it," she said ∼⟩

  ♦ actually, frankly, honestly, really, truly, verily — more at ACTUALLY

truth·ful·ness *n* ♦ : the quality or state of being truthful

  ♦ honesty, integrity, probity, veracity, verity — more at HONESTY

truth serum *n* : a drug held to induce a subject under questioning to talk freely

¹**try** \ˈtrī\ *vb* **tried; try·ing** [ME *trien*, fr. AF *trier* to select, sort, examine, prob. fr. LL *tritare* to grind] **1** : to examine or investigate judicially **2** : to conduct the trial of **3** : to put to test or trial **4** ♦ : to subject to strain, affliction, or annoyance **5** : to extract or clarify (as lard) by melting **6** ♦ : to make an effort to do something : ATTEMPT

  ♦ [4] strain, stretch, tax, test; *also* demand, exact, importune, press, pressure, push; aggravate, agitate, exasperate, get (to), gnaw (at), grate, harass, harry, hassle, irk, irritate, pain, pester ♦ [6] assay, attempt, endeavor (*or* endeavour), essay, seek, strive — more at ATTEMPT

²**try** *n, pl* **tries** ♦ : an experimental trial

  ♦ attempt, crack, endeavor (*or* endeavour), essay, fling, go, pass, shot, stab, trial, whack — more at ATTEMPT

try·ing *adj* ♦ : severely straining the powers of endurance

  ♦ bitter, brutal, burdensome, cruel, excruciating, grievous, grim, hard, harsh, heavy, inhuman, murderous, onerous, oppressive, rough, rugged, severe, stiff, tough — more at HARSH

try on *vb* : to put on (a garment) to test the fit and looks

try out *vb* : to compete for a position esp. on an athletic team or for a part in a play — **try·out** \ˈtrī-ˌaút\ *n*

tryp·to·phan \ˈtrip-tə-ˌfan\ *n* : a crystalline essential amino acid that is widely distributed in proteins

tryst \ˈtrist\ *n* **1** ♦ : an agreement (as between lovers) to meet **2** : an appointed meeting or meeting place — **tryst** *vb* — **tryst·er** *n*

  ♦ appointment, date, engagement, rendezvous — more at ENGAGEMENT

Ts *symbol* tennessine

TSA *abbr* Transportation Security Administration

tsar *var of* CZAR

tsarina *var of* CZARINA

tset·se fly \ˈtset-sē-, ˈtsēt-, ˈtet-, ˈtēt-, ˈset-, ˈsēt-\ *n* : any of several sub-Saharan African dipteran flies including the vector of sleeping sickness

TSgt *abbr* technical sergeant

T–shirt \ˈtē-ˌshərt\ *n* : a collarless short-sleeved or sleeveless cotton undershirt; *also* : an outer shirt of similar design — **T–shirt·ed** \-ˌshər-təd\ *adj*

tsk *a click; often read as* ˈtisk\ *interj* — used to express disapproval

tsp *abbr* teaspoon; teaspoonful

T square *n* : a ruler with a crosspiece at one end for making parallel lines

tsu·na·mi \sù-'nä-mē, tsù-\ *n* [Jp] : a tidal wave caused esp. by an underwater earthquake or volcanic eruption

TT *abbr* Trust Territories

TTY *abbr* teletypewriter

Tu *abbr* Tuesday

tub \'təb\ *n* **1** : a wide low bucketlike vessel **2** : BATHTUB; *also* : BATH **3** : the amount that a tub will hold

tu·ba \'tü-bə, 'tyü-\ *n* : a large low-pitched brass wind instrument

tub·al \'tü-bəl, 'tyü-\ *adj* : of, relating to, or involving a tube and esp. a fallopian tube

tube \'tüb, 'tyüb\ *n* **1** ◆ : any of various usu. cylindrical structures or devices; *esp* : one to convey fluids **2** : a slender hollow anatomical part (as a fallopian tube) functioning as a channel in a plant or animal body : DUCT **3** : a soft round container from which a paste is squeezed **4** : a tunnel for vehicular or rail travel **5** *Brit* : SUBWAY **6** : INNER TUBE **7** : ELECTRON TUBE **8** : TELEVISION — **tubed** \'tübd, 'tyübd\ *adj* — **tube·less** *adj*

◆ channel, conduit, duct, leader, line, penstock, pipe — more at PIPE

tu·ber \'tü-bər, 'tyü-\ *n* : a short fleshy usu. underground stem (as of a potato plant) bearing minute scalelike leaves each with a bud at its base

tu·ber·cle \'tü-bər-kəl, 'tyü-\ *n* **1** : a small knobby prominence or outgrowth esp. on an animal or plant **2** : a small abnormal lump in an organ or on the skin; *esp* : one caused by tuberculosis

tubercle bacillus *n* : a bacterium that is the cause of tuberculosis

tu·ber·cu·lar \tü-'bər-kyə-lər, tyù-\ *adj* **1** : TUBERCULOUS **2** : of, resembling, or being a tubercle

tu·ber·cu·lin \tü-'bər-kyə-lən, tyù-\ *n* : a sterile liquid extracted from the tubercle bacillus and used in the diagnosis of tuberculosis esp. in children and cattle

tu·ber·cu·lo·sis \tü-ˌbər-kyə-'lō-səs, tyù-\ *n, pl* **-lo·ses** \-ˌsēz\ : a communicable bacterial disease that affects esp. the lungs and is typically marked by fever, cough, difficulty in breathing, and formation of tubercles — **tu·ber·cu·lous** \-'bər-kyə-ləs\ *adj*

tube·rose \'tüb-ˌrōz, 'tyüb-\ *n* : a bulbous herb related to the agaves and often grown for its spike of fragrant waxy-white flowers

tu·ber·ous \'tü-bə-rəs, 'tyü-\ *adj* : of, resembling, or being a tuber

tub·ing \'tü-biŋ, 'tyü-\ *n* **1** : material in the form of a tube; *also* : a length of tube **2** : a series or system of tubes

tu·bu·lar \'tü-byə-lər, 'tyü-\ *adj* : having the form of or consisting of a tube; *also* : made with tubes

tu·bule \'tü-byül, 'tyü-\ *n* : a small tube

¹tuck \'tək\ *n* **1** : a fold stitched into cloth to shorten, decorate, or control fullness **2** : a cosmetic surgical operation for the removal of excess skin or fat ⟨a tummy ~⟩

²tuck *vb* **1** : to pull up into a fold ⟨~ed up her skirt⟩ **2** : to make tucks in **3** : to put into a snug often concealing place ⟨~ a book under the arm⟩ **4** : to secure in place by pushing the edges under ⟨~ in a blanket⟩ **5** : to cover by tucking in bedclothes

tuck·er \'tə-kər\ *vb* **tuck·ered; tuck·er·ing** ◆ : to tire extremely or completely : FATIGUE — often used with *out*

◆ *usu* **tucker out** burn out, do in, drain, exhaust, fag, fatigue, tire, wash out, wear, wear out, weary — more at EXHAUST

Tues *or* **Tue** *abbr* Tuesday

Tues·day \'tüz-dē, 'tyüz-, -dā\ *n* : the 3d day of the week

tu·fa \'tü-fə, 'tyü-\ *n* : a porous rock formed as a deposit from springs or streams

tuff \'təf\ *n* : a rock composed of volcanic detritus

¹tuft \'təft\ *n* **1** : a small cluster of long flexible outgrowths (as hairs); *also* : a bunch of soft fluffy threads cut off

short and used as ornament **2** : CLUMP, CLUSTER — **tuft·ed** *adj*

²tuft *vb* **1** : to provide or adorn with a tuft **2** : to make (as a mattress) firm by stitching at intervals and sewing on tufts — **tuft·er** *n*

¹tug \'təg\ *vb* **tugged; tug·ging** **1** ◆ : to pull hard **2** : to struggle in opposition : CONTEND **3** ◆ : to move by pulling hard : HAUL **4** : to tow with a tugboat

◆ [1, 3] drag, draw, hale, haul, lug, pull, tow — more at PULL

²tug *n* **1** : a harness trace **2** ◆ : an act of tugging : PULL **3** : a straining effort **4** : a struggle between opposing people or forces **5** : TUGBOAT

◆ draw, haul, jerk, pluck, pull, wrench — more at PULL

tug·boat \-ˌbōt\ *n* : a strongly built boat used for towing or pushing

tug–of–war \ˌtəg-əv-'wòr\ *n, pl* **tugs–of–war** **1** ◆ : a struggle for supremacy **2** : an athletic contest in which two teams pull against each other at opposite ends of a rope

◆ battle, combat, conflict, confrontation, contest, duel, face-off, rivalry, struggle, warfare — more at CONTEST

tu·ition \tù-'i-shən, tyù-\ *n* : money paid for instruction ⟨college ~⟩

tu·la·re·mia \ˌtü-lə-'rē-mē-ə, ˌtyü-\ *n* : an infectious bacterial disease esp. of wild rabbits, rodents, humans, and some domestic animals that in humans is marked by symptoms (as fever) similar to those of influenza

tu·lip \'tü-ləp, 'tyü-\ *n* [NL *tulipa*, fr. Turk *tülbent* turban] : any of a genus of Eurasian bulbous herbs related to the lilies and grown for their large showy erect cup-shaped flowers; *also* : a flower or bulb of a tulip

tulip tree *n* : a tall No. American timber tree that is related to the magnolias and has greenish tulip-shaped flowers and soft white wood

tulle \'tül\ *n* : a sheer often stiffened silk, rayon, or nylon net ⟨a veil of ~⟩

¹tum·ble \'təm-bəl\ *vb* **tum·bled; tum·bling** [ME, fr. *tumben* to dance, fr. OE *tumbian*] **1 a** ◆ : to fall or cause to fall suddenly and helplessly (as in price) : DROP **2** : to fall into ruin **3** : to perform gymnastic feats of rolling and turning **4** : to roll over and over : TOSS **5** : to issue forth hurriedly and confusedly **6** : to come to understand **7** ◆ : to throw together in a confused mass

◆ [1a] fall, slip, stumble, topple, trip — more at FALL
◆ [1b] decline, descend, dip, drop, fall, lower, plummet, plunge, sink — more at DROP ◆ [7] disorder, hash, jumble, mess, mix, muddle, rumple

²tumble *n* **1 a** ◆ : a disordered mass of objects or material **b** : a disorderly state **2** ◆ : an act or instance of tumbling

◆ [1a] assortment, clutter, jumble, medley, mélange, miscellany, motley, muddle, variety, welter — more at MISCELLANY ◆ [2] fall, slip, spill, stumble — more at FALL

tum·ble·down \'təm-bəl-'daùn\ *adj* ◆ : fallen into partial ruin or decay : DILAPIDATED ⟨a ~ shack⟩

◆ dilapidated, grungy, mean, neglected, ratty, seedy, shabby — more at SHABBY

tum·bler \'təm-blər\ *n* **1** : one that tumbles; *esp* : ACROBAT **2** : a drinking glass without foot or stem **3** : a movable obstruction in a lock that must be adjusted to a particular position (as by a key) before the bolt can be thrown

tum·ble·weed \'təm-bəl-ˌwēd\ *n* : a plant that breaks away from its roots in autumn and is driven about by the wind

tum·brel *or* **tum·bril** \'təm-brəl\ *n* **1** : CART **2** : a vehicle carrying condemned persons (as during the French Revolution) to a place of execution

tu·mid \'tü-məd, 'tyü-\ *adj* **1** : SWOLLEN, DISTENDED **2** : BOMBASTIC, TURGID

tum·my \'tə-mē\ *n, pl* **tummies** ◆ : the part of the body that contains the stomach : BELLY

◆ abdomen, belly, gut, solar plexus, stomach — more at STOMACH

tu·mor *or Can and Brit* **tu·mour** \'tü-mər, 'tyü-\ *n* ♦ : an abnormal and functionless new growth of tissue that arises from uncontrolled cellular proliferation — **tu·mor·ous** *adj*

♦ excrescence, growth, lump, neoplasm — more at GROWTH

tu·mult \'tü-,məlt, 'tyü-\ *n* **1 a** ♦ : a state of commotion, excitement, or confusion **b** ♦ : turbulent uprising **2 a** : violent agitation of mind or feelings **b** ♦ : a noisy, agitated outburst

♦ [1a] commotion, disturbance, furor, pandemonium, turmoil ♦ [1b] cataclysm, convulsion, paroxysm, storm, tempest, upheaval, uproar ♦ [2b] clamor (*or* clamour), howl, hubbub, hue and cry, hullabaloo, noise, outcry, roar, uproar — more at CLAMOR

tu·mul·tu·ous \tü-'məl-chə-wəs, tyü-, -chəs\ *adj* **1** : marked by tumult ⟨~ applause⟩ **2** : tending to incite a tumult **3** ♦ : marked by violent upheaval ⟨~ war years⟩

♦ convulsive, stormy, tempestuous, turbulent, wild — more at WILD

tun \'tən\ *n* : a large cask
tu·na \'tü-nə, 'tyü-\ *n, pl* **tuna** *or* **tunas** [Sp] : any of several mostly large marine fishes related to the mackerels and caught for food and sport; *also* : the flesh of a tuna
tun·able \'tü-nə-bəl, 'tyü-\ *adj* : capable of being tuned — **tun·abil·i·ty** \,tü-nə-'bi-lə-tē, ,tyü-\ *n*
tun·dra \'tən-drə\ *n* [Russ] : a treeless plain of arctic and subarctic regions
¹tune \'tün, 'tyün\ *n* **1** ♦ : a succession of pleasing musical tones : MELODY **2** : correct musical pitch **3** ♦ : harmonious relationship : AGREEMENT ⟨in ~ with the times⟩ **4** : general attitude ⟨changed his ~⟩ **5** : AMOUNT, EXTENT ⟨in debt to the ~ of millions⟩

♦ [1] air, lay, melody, song, strain, warble — more at MELODY ♦ [3] accord, agreement, conformity, consonance, harmony — more at CONFORMITY

²tune *vb* **tuned; tun·ing** **1** : to adjust in musical pitch **2** : to bring or come into harmony : ATTUNE **3** : to put in good working order **4** : to adjust a radio or television receiver so as to receive a broadcast **5** : to adjust the frequency of the output of (a device) to a chosen frequency — **tun·er** *n*
tune·ful \-fəl\ *adj* ♦ : having a pleasing melody : MELODIOUS — **tune·ful·ly** *adv* — **tune·ful·ness** *n*

♦ euphonious, harmonious, melodious, musical, symphonic — more at HARMONIOUS

tune·less \-ləs\ *adj* **1** : UNMELODIOUS **2** : not producing music — **tune·less·ly** *adv*
tune out *vb* : to stop paying attention to what is happening or to one's surroundings
tune–up \'tün-,əp, 'tyün-\ *n* : an adjustment to ensure efficient functioning ⟨an engine ~⟩
tung·sten \'təŋ-stən\ *n* [Sw, fr. *tung* heavy + *sten* stone] : a gray-white hard heavy ductile metallic chemical element used esp. in carbide materials, electrical components, and alloys
tu·nic \'tü-nik, 'tyü-\ *n* **1** : a usu. knee-length belted under or outer garment worn by ancient Greeks and Romans **2** : a hip-length or longer blouse or jacket
tuning fork *n* : a 2-pronged metal implement that gives a fixed tone when struck and is useful for tuning musical instruments
Tu·ni·sian \tü-'nē-zhən, tyü-, -'ni-\ *n* : a native or inhabitant of Tunisia — **Tunisian** *adj*
¹tun·nel \'tən-ᵊl\ *n* : an enclosed passage (as a tube or conduit); *esp* : one underground (as in a mine)
²tunnel *vb* **-neled** *or* **-nelled; -nel·ing** *or* **-nel·ling** : to make a tunnel through or under — **tun·nel·er** \'tən-ᵊl-ər, 'tə-nᵊl-ər\ *n*
tun·ny \'tə-nē\ *n, pl* **tunnies** *also* **tunny** : TUNA
tuque \'tük, 'tyük\ *n* [CanF] : a warm knitted cone-shaped cap
tur·ban \'tər-bən\ *n* **1** : a headdress worn esp. by Muslims and made of a cap around which is wound a long cloth **2** : a headdress resembling a turban; *esp* : a woman's close-fitting hat without a brim

tur·bid \'tər-bəd\ *adj* [L *turbidus* confused, turbid, fr. *turba* confusion, crowd] **1** ♦ : cloudy or discolored by suspended particles ⟨a ~ stream⟩ **2** : CONFUSED, MUDDLED — **tur·bid·i·ty** \,tər-'bi-də-tē\ *n*

♦ cloudy, muddy — more at CLOUDY

tur·bine \'tər-bən, -,bīn\ *n* [F, fr. L *turbin-, turbo* top, whirlwind, whirl] : an engine whose central driveshaft is fitted with curved vanes spun by the pressure of water, steam, or gas
tur·bo·fan \'tər-bō-,fan\ *n* : a jet engine having a fan driven by a turbine for supplying air for combustion
tur·bo·jet \-,jet\ *n* : an airplane powered by a jet engine (**turbojet engine**) having a turbine-driven air compressor supplying compressed air to the combustion chamber
tur·bo·prop \-,präp\ *n* : an airplane powered by a jet engine (**turboprop engine**) having a turbine-driven propeller
tur·bot \'tər-bət\ *n, pl* **turbot** *also* **turbots** : a European flatfish that is a popular food fish; *also* : any of several similar flatfishes
tur·bu·lence \'tər-byə-ləns\ *n* : the quality or state of being turbulent
tur·bu·lent \-lənt\ *adj* **1** : causing violence or disturbance **2** ♦ : marked by agitation or tumult : TEMPESTUOUS — **tur·bu·lent·ly** *adv*

♦ explosive, ferocious, fierce, furious, hot, rabid, rough, stormy, tempestuous, violent, volcanic — more at VIOLENT ♦ stormy, tempestuous, tumultuous, wild — more at WILD

tu·reen \tə-'rēn, tyū-\ *n* [F *terrine*, fr. MF, fr. fem. of *terrin* of earth] : a deep bowl from which foods (as soup) are served at table
¹turf \'tərf\ *n, pl* **turfs** \'tərfs\ *also* **turves** \'tərvz\ **1** : the upper layer of soil bound by grass and roots into a close mat; *also* : a piece of this **2** : an artificial substitute for turf (as on a playing field) **3** : a piece of peat dried for fuel **4** : a track or course for horse racing; *also* : horse racing as a sport or business
²turf *vb* : to cover with turf
tur·gid \'tər-jəd\ *adj* **1** : being in a swollen state **2** : excessively embellished in style or language : BOMBASTIC ⟨~ writing⟩ — **tur·gid·i·ty** \,tər-'ji-də-tē\ *n*
Turk \'tərk\ *n* : a native or inhabitant of Turkey
tur·key \'tər-kē\ *n, pl* **turkeys** [*Turkey*, country in western Asia and southeastern Europe; fr. confusion with the guinea fowl, supposed to be imported from Turkish territory] **1** : a large No. American bird related to the domestic chicken and widely raised for food **2** ♦ : a complete failure **3** ♦ : a stupid, foolish, or inept person

♦ [2] bummer, bust, catastrophe, debacle, dud, failure, fiasco, fizzle, flop, lemon, loser, washout — more at FAILURE ♦ [3] booby, fool, goose, half-wit, jackass, lunatic, nitwit, nut, simpleton — more at FOOL

turkey buzzard *n* : TURKEY VULTURE
turkey vulture *n* : an American vulture with a red head and whitish bill
Turk·ish \'tər-kish\ *n* : the language of Turkey — **Turkish** *adj*
tur·mer·ic \'tər-mə-rik\ *n* : a spice or dyestuff obtained from the large aromatic deep-yellow rhizome of an Indian perennial herb related to the ginger; *also* : this herb
tur·moil \'tər-,mȯil\ *n* ♦ : an extremely confused or agitated condition

♦ disquiet, ferment, restlessness, uneasiness, unrest — more at UNREST ♦ commotion, furor, pandemonium, storm, tumult, uproar

¹turn \'tərn\ *vb* **1** ♦ : to move or cause to move around an axis or center : ROTATE ⟨~ a wheel⟩ **2** : to effect a desired end by turning something ⟨~ the oven on⟩ **3** : WRENCH ⟨~ an ankle⟩ **4** : to change or cause to change position by moving through an arc of a circle ⟨~ed her chair to the fire⟩ **5** : to cause to move around a center so as to show another side of ⟨~ a page⟩ **6** : to revolve mentally : PONDER **7** : to become dizzy : REEL **8** : to reverse the sides or surfaces of ⟨∼ a pancake⟩ **9** : UPSET, DISORDER ⟨things were ∼ed topsy-turvy⟩ **10** ♦ : to set in another esp. contrary direction **11** ♦ : to change one's course or direction **12** : to go around ⟨∼ a corner⟩ **13** : to undergo change or development : BECOME ⟨my hair ∼ed gray⟩ ⟨∼ed twenty-one⟩ **14** : to direct toward or away from something; *also* : DEVOTE, APPLY **15** ♦ : to have recourse ⟨∼ to a friend for help⟩ **16** : to become or make hostile **17** : to cause to become of a specified nature or appearance ⟨∼s the leaves yellow⟩ **18** : to make or become spoiled : SOUR **19** : to pass from one state to another ⟨water ∼s to ice⟩ **20** : CONVERT, TRANSFORM **21** : TRANSLATE, PARAPHRASE **22** : to give a rounded form to; *esp* : to shape by means of a lathe **23** : to gain by passing in trade ⟨∼ a quick profit⟩ — **turn color 1** : BLUSH **2** : to become pale — **turn loose** : to set free

♦ [1] pivot, revolve, roll, rotate, spin, swing, swirl, twirl, twist, wheel, whirl; *also* screw, unscrew; twiddle; crank, reel, wind; circulate ♦ [10] divert, swerve, swing, veer, wheel, whip; *also* avert, move, rechannel, shift, shunt, sidetrack, switch, transfer; swivel, twist, whirl, zigzag; bend, curve, sway; reverse, turn back ♦ [11] detour, deviate, sheer, swerve, swing, turn off, veer; *also* tack, zigzag; double (back), turn back ♦ *usu* **turn to** [15] go, refer, resort

²**turn** *n* **1** : a turning about a center or axis : REVOLUTION, ROTATION **2** : the action or an act of giving or taking a different direction ⟨make a left ∼⟩ **3** : a change of course or tendency ⟨a ∼ for the better⟩ **4** ♦ : a place at which something turns : BEND **5** ♦ : a short walk or trip round about ⟨take a ∼ around the block⟩ **6** ♦ : an act affecting another ⟨did him a good ∼⟩ **7** : a place, time, or opportunity accorded in a scheduled order ⟨waited his ∼ in line⟩ **8** : a period of duty : SHIFT **9** : a short act esp. in a variety show **10** : a special purpose or requirement ⟨the job serves his ∼⟩ **11** : a skillful fashioning ⟨neat ∼ of phrase⟩ **12** : a single round (as of rope passed around an object) **13** ♦ : natural or special aptitude **14** : a usu. sudden and brief disorder of body or spirits; *esp* : a spell of nervous shock or faintness

♦ [4] angle, arc, arch, bend, bow, crook, curve, wind — more at BEND ♦ [5] perambulation, ramble, stroll, walk — more at WALK ♦ [6] boon, courtesy, favor (*or* favour), grace, indulgence, kindness, mercy, service — more at FAVOR ♦ [13] bent, devices, disposition, genius, inclination, leaning, partiality, penchant, predilection, proclivity, propensity, tendency — more at INCLINATION

turn·about \'tər-nə-ˌbau̇t\ *n* **1** : a reversal of direction, trend, or policy **2** : RETALIATION

turn·buck·le \'tərn-ˌbə-kəl\ *n* : a link with a screw thread at one or both ends for tightening a rod or stay

turn·coat \-ˌkōt\ *n* ♦ : one who switches to an opposing side or party : TRAITOR

♦ apostate, betrayer, double-crosser, quisling, recreant, traitor — more at TRAITOR

turn down *vb* ♦ : to decline to accept : REJECT — **turn·down** \'tərn-ˌdau̇n\ *n*

♦ decline, disallow, disapprove, negative, refuse, reject, repudiate, spurn — more at DECLINE

turn·er \'tər-nər\ *n* **1** : one that turns or is used for turning **2** : one that forms articles with a lathe

turn·ery \'tər-nə-rē\ *n, pl* **-er·ies** : the work, products, or shop of a turner

turn in *vb* **1** : to deliver up **2** : to inform on **3** : to acquit oneself of ⟨*turn in* a good job⟩ **4** : to go to bed

turn·ing *n* **1** : the act or course of one that turns **2** : a place of a change of direction

turning point *n* : a point at which a significant change occurs

tur·nip \'tər-nəp\ *n* **1** : a garden herb related to the cabbage with a thick edible usu. white root **2** : RUTABAGA **3** : the root of a turnip

turn·key \'tərn-ˌkē\ *n, pl* **turnkeys** : one who has charge of a prison's keys

turn·off \'tərn-ˌȯf\ *n* : a place for turning off esp. from an expressway

turn off *vb* **1** ♦ : to deviate from a straight course or a main road **2** : to stop the functioning or flow of **3** ♦ : to cause to lose interest; *also* : to evoke a negative feeling in

♦ [1] detour, deviate, sheer, swerve, swing, turn, veer — more at TURN ♦ [3] disgust, nauseate, repel, repulse, revolt, sicken — more at DISGUST

turn on *vb* **1** ♦ : to cause to flow, function, or operate **2** : to get high or cause to get high as a result of using a drug (as marijuana) **3** ♦ : to move pleasurably : EXCITE

♦ [1] activate, actuate, crank, drive, move, propel, run, set off, spark, start, touch off, trigger — more at ACTIVATE ♦ [3] electrify, excite, exhilarate, galvanize, intoxicate, thrill, titillate — more at THRILL

turn·out \'tərn-ˌau̇t\ *n* **1** : an act of turning out **2** : the number of people who participate or attend an event **3** : a widened place in a highway for vehicles to pass or park **4** : manner of dress **5** : net yield : OUTPUT

turn out *vb* **1** : EXPEL, EVICT **2** : PRODUCE **3** : to come forth and assemble **4** : to get out of bed **5** ♦ : to prove to be in the end **6** : to cause to stop functioning by turning a switch

♦ come out, pan out, prove — more at COME OUT

¹**turn·over** \'tər-ˌnō-vər\ *n* **1** : UPSET **2** : SHIFT, REVERSAL **3** : a filled pastry made by turning half of the crust over the other half **4** : the volume of business done **5** : movement (as of goods or people) into, through, and out of a place **6** : the number of persons hired within a period to replace those leaving or dropped **7** : an instance of a team's losing possession of the ball esp. through error

²**turnover** *adj* : capable of being turned over

turn over *vb* **1** ♦ : to turn from an upright position **2** ♦ : to take and hand over to or leave for another ⟨*turn* the job *over* to her⟩

♦ [1] flip, reverse — more at REVERSE ♦ [2] commend, commit, consign, delegate, deliver, entrust, give, hand over, leave, pass, surrender, transfer, transmit, trust, vest — more at GIVE

turn·pike \'tərn-ˌpīk\ *n* [ME *turnepike* revolving frame bearing spikes and serving as a barrier, fr. *turnen* to turn + *pike* 1] **1** : TOLLGATE; *also* : an expressway on which tolls are charged **2** ♦ : a main road

♦ highway, pike, road, route, thoroughfare, way

turn·stile \-ˌstīl\ *n* : a post with arms pivoted on the top set in a passageway so that persons can pass through only on foot one by one

turn·ta·ble \-ˌtā-bəl\ *n* : a circular platform that revolves (as for turning a locomotive or a phonograph record)

turn to *vb* : to apply oneself to work

turn up *vb* **1** ♦ : to come to light or bring to light **2** ♦ : to arrive at an appointed time or place **3** : to happen unexpectedly **4** : to raise or increase by or as if by turning a control

♦ [1] appear, come out, materialize, show up — more at APPEAR ♦ [2] arrive, come, land, show up — more at COME

tur·pen·tine \'tər-pən-ˌtīn\ *n* **1** : a mixture of oil and resin obtained from various cone-bearing trees (as pines) **2** : an oil distilled from turpentine or pine wood and used as a solvent and paint thinner

tur·pi·tude \'tər-pə-ˌtüd, -ˌtyüd\ *n* : inherent baseness : DEPRAVITY

tur·quoise *also* **tur·quois** \'tər-ˌkȯiz, -ˌkwȯiz\ *n* [ME *turkeys*, fr. AF *turkeise*, fr. fem. of *turkeis* Turkish, fr. *Turc* Turk] **1** : a blue, bluish green, or greenish gray mineral that is valued as a gem **2** : a light greenish blue color

tur·ret \'tər-ət\ *n* **1** : a little ornamental tower often at a corner of a building **2** : a low usu. revolving structure (as on a tank or warship) in which one or more guns are mounted

¹tur·tle \'tərt-ᵊl\ *n, archaic* : TURTLEDOVE

²turtle *n, pl* **turtles** *also* **turtle** : any of an order of horny=beaked land, freshwater, or sea reptiles with the trunk enclosed in a bony shell

tur·tle·dove \'tərt-ᵊl-ˌdəv\ *n* : any of several small pigeons noted for plaintive cooing

tur·tle·neck \-ˌnek\ *n* : a high close-fitting turnover collar (as on a sweater); *also* : a sweater or shirt with a turtle-neck — **tur·tle·necked** \-ˌnekt\ *adj*

turves *pl of* TURF

Tus·ca·ro·ra \ˌtəs-kə-'rōr-ə\ *n, pl* **Tuscarora** *or* **Tuscaroras** : a member of an American Indian people of No. Carolina and later of New York and Ontario

tusk \'təsk\ *n* : a long enlarged protruding tooth (as of an elephant, walrus, or boar) used esp. to dig up food or as a weapon — **tusked** \'təskt\ *adj*

tusk·er \'təs-kər\ *n* : an animal with tusks; *esp* : a male elephant with two normally developed tusks

¹tus·sle \'tə-səl\ *n* **1** ♦ : a physical struggle : SCUFFLE **2** : an intense argument, controversy, or struggle

♦ battle, clash, combat, conflict, contest, fight, fracas, fray, hassle, scrap, scrimmage, scuffle, skirmish, struggle — more at FIGHT

²tussle *vb* **tus·sled; tus·sling** ♦ : to struggle roughly

♦ grapple, scuffle, wrestle — more at WRESTLE

tus·sock \'tə-sək\ *n* : a dense tuft esp. of grass or sedge; *also* : a hummock in a marsh or bog bound together by roots — **tus·socky** *adj*

tu·te·lage \'tüt-ᵊl-ij, 'tyüt-\ *n* **1** : an act of guarding or protecting **2** : the state of being under a guardian or tutor **3** ♦ : instruction esp. of an individual

♦ education, instruction, teaching, training — more at EDUCATION

tu·te·lary \'tüt-ᵊl-ˌer-ē, 'tyüt-\ *adj* : acting as a guardian ⟨∼ deity⟩

¹tu·tor \'tü-tər, 'tyü-\ *n* **1** : a person charged with the instruction and guidance of another **2** : a private teacher

²tutor *vb* **1** : to have the guardianship of **2** ♦ : to teach or guide individually ⟨∼ed her in Latin⟩ **3** : to receive instruction esp. privately

♦ educate, indoctrinate, instruct, school, teach, train — more at TEACH ♦ coach, counsel, guide, lead, mentor, pilot, shepherd, show — more at GUIDE

tu·to·ri·al \tü-'tōr-ē-əl, tyü-\ *n* : a class conducted by a tutor for one student or a small number of students

tut·ti \'tü-tē, 'tü-, -ˌtē\ *adj or adv* [It, pl. of *tutto* all] : with all voices and instruments playing together — used as a direction in music

tut·ti-frut·ti \ˌtü-ti-'frü-tē, ˌtü-\ *n* [It, lit., all fruits] : a confection or ice cream containing chopped usu. candied fruits

tu·tu \'tü-(ˌ)tü\ *n* [F] : a short projecting skirt worn by a ballerina

tux·e·do \ˌtək-'sē-dō\ *n, pl* **-dos** *or* **-does** [*Tuxedo* Park, N.Y.] **1** : a usu. black or blackish blue jacket **2** : a semiformal evening suit for men

TV \'tē-'vē\ *n* : TELEVISION

TVA *abbr* Tennessee Valley Authority

TV dinner *n* : a frozen packaged dinner that needs only heating before serving

twad·dle \'twäd-ᵊl\ *n* ♦ : silly idle talk : DRIVEL — **twaddle** *vb*

♦ blarney, bunk, claptrap, drivel, fiddlesticks, folly, foolishness, fudge, hogwash, humbug, nonsense, piffle, rot, silliness, slush, stupidity, trash — more at NONSENSE

twain \'twān\ *n* **1** : TWO **2** ♦ : two similar or associated things : PAIR

♦ brace, couple, duo, pair, twosome — more at PAIR

¹twang \'twaŋ\ *n* **1** : a harsh quick ringing sound like that of a plucked bowstring **2** : nasal speech or resonance **3** : the characteristic speech of a region

²twang *vb* **twanged; twang·ing** **1** : to sound or cause to sound with a twang **2** : to speak with a nasal twang

tweak \'twēk\ *vb* **1** : to pinch and pull with a sudden jerk and twitch **2** : to make small adjustments to — **tweak** *n*

tweed \'twēd\ *n* **1** : a rough woolen fabric made usu. in twill weaves **2** *pl* : tweed clothing; *esp* : a tweed suit

tweedy \'twē-dē\ *adj* **tweed·i·er; -est** **1** : of or resembling tweed **2** : given to wearing tweeds **3** : suggestive of the outdoors in taste or habits **4** : ACADEMIC, SCHOLARLY

¹tween \'twēn\ *prep* : BETWEEN

²tween *n* : PRETEEN

¹tweet \'twēt\ *n* **1** : a chirping note **2** : a short message posted on the Twitter online service

²tweet *vb* **1** ♦ : to make a usu. repetitive short sharp sound **2** : to post a tweet

♦ cheep, chirp, peep, pipe, twitter — more at CHIRP

tweet·er \'twē-tər\ *n* : a small loudspeaker that reproduces sounds of high pitch

twee·zers \'twē-zərz\ *n pl* [obs. E *tweeze*, n., case for small implements, short for obs. E *etweese*, fr. pl. of obs. E *etwee*, fr. F *étui*] : a small pincerlike implement usu. held between the thumb and index finger and used for grasping something

twelve \'twelv\ *n* **1** : one more than 11 **2** : the 12th in a set or series **3** : something having 12 units — **twelfth** \'twelfth\ *adj or n* — **twelve** *adj or pron*

twelve·month \-ˌmənth\ *n* : YEAR

12-step \'twelv-ˌstep\ *adj* : of, relating to, or being a program designed esp. to help someone overcome a problem (as an addiction) by following 12 tenets

twen·ty \'twen-tē\ *n, pl* **twenties** : two times 10 — **twen·ti·eth** \-tē-əth\ *adj or n* — **twenty** *adj or pron*

twenty-twenty *or* **20/20** \ˌtwen-tē-'twen-tē\ *adj* : characterized by a visual capacity for seeing detail that is normal for the human eye ⟨∼ vision⟩

twice \'twīs\ *adv* **1** : on two occasions **2** : two times ⟨∼ two is four⟩

¹twid·dle \'twid-ᵊl\ *vb* **twid·dled; twid·dling** **1** : to be busy with trifles; *also* : to play idly with something **2** : to rotate lightly or idly

²twiddle *n* : TURN, TWIST

twig \'twig\ *n* : a small branch — **twig·gy** *adj*

twi·light \'twī-ˌlīt\ *n* **1** ♦ : the light from the sky between full night and sunrise or between sunset and full night; *also* : time of twilight **2** : a state of imperfect clarity; *also* : a period of decline

♦ dusk, evening, gloaming, nightfall, sundown, sunset — more at DUSK

twilight zone *n* **1** : TWILIGHT 2; *also* : an area just beyond ordinary legal or ethical limits **2** : a world of fantasy or unreality

twill \'twil\ *n* [ME *twyll*, fr. OE *twilic* having a double thread, part trans. of L *bilic-, bilix*, fr. *bi-* two + *licium* thread] **1** : a fabric with a twill weave **2** : a textile weave that gives an appearance of diagonal lines

twilled \'twild\ *adj* : made with a twill weave

¹twin \'twin\ *n* **1** : either of two offspring produced at a birth **2** ♦ : one of two persons or things closely related to or resembling each other

♦ companion, fellow, half, match, mate — more at MATE

²twin *vb* **twinned; twin·ning** **1** : to be coupled with another **2** : to bring forth twins

³twin *adj* **1** : born with one other or as a pair at one birth ⟨∼ brother⟩ ⟨∼ girls⟩ **2** ♦ : made up of two similar or related members or parts **3** : being one of a pair ⟨∼ city⟩

♦ binary, bipartite, double, dual, duplex — more at DOUBLE

¹twine \'twīn\ *n* **1** : a strong thread of two or three strands twisted together **2** : an act of entwining or interlacing — **twiny** *adj*

²twine *vb* **twined; twin·ing** **1** : to twist together; *also* : to form by twisting **2** : INTERLACE, WEAVE **3** : to coil about a support **4** ♦ : to stretch or move in a sinuous manner — **twin·er** *n*

♦ coil, curl, entwine, spiral, twist, wind — more at WIND

¹**twinge** \'twinj\ *vb* **twinged; twing·ing** *or* **twinge·ing** : to affect with or feel a sharp sudden pain

²**twinge** *n* ♦ : a sudden sharp stab (as of pain or distress)

♦ ache, pain, pang, prick, smart, sting, stitch, tingle — more at PAIN

¹**twin·kle** \'twiŋ-kəl\ *vb* **twin·kled; twin·kling** **1** ♦ : to shine or cause to shine with a flickering or sparkling light **2** : to appear bright with merriment **3** : to flutter or flit rapidly — **twin·kler** *n*

♦ flame, flash, glance, gleam, glimmer, glisten, glitter, scintillate, shimmer, sparkle, wink — more at FLASH

²**twinkle** *n* **1 a** : a wink of the eyelids **b** : the duration of a wink : TWINKLING **2** : an intermittent radiance **3** : a rapid flashing motion — **twin·kly** \'twiŋ-klē\ *adj*

twin·kling \'twiŋ-kliŋ\ *n* ♦ : the time required for a wink : INSTANT

♦ flash, instant, jiffy, minute, moment, second, shake, trice, twinkle, wink — more at INSTANT

¹**twirl** \'twərl\ *vb* ♦ : to turn or cause to turn rapidly ⟨~ a baton⟩ — **twirl·er** *n*

♦ pivot, revolve, roll, rotate, spin, swing, swirl, turn, twist, wheel, whirl — more at TURN

²**twirl** *n* **1** ♦ : an act of twirling : COIL, WHORL — **twirly** \'twər-lē\ *adj*

♦ gyration, pirouette, reel, revolution, roll, rotation, spin, wheel, whirl — more at SPIN

¹**twist** \'twist\ *vb* **1** : to unite by winding one thread or strand round another **2** : WREATHE, TWINE **3** ♦ : to wring or wrench so as to dislocate or distort ⟨~ed her ankle⟩ **4** : to twirl into spiral shape **5** ♦ : to subject (as a shaft) to torsion **6** ♦ : to turn from the true form or meaning **7** : to pull off or break by torsion **8** ♦ : to follow a winding course **9** ♦ : to turn around

♦ [3, 5] wrench, wrest, wring — more at WRENCH ♦ [6] color (*or* colour), distort, falsify, garble, misinterpret, misrepresent, misstate, pervert, warp — more at GARBLE ♦ [8] coil, curl, entwine, spiral, twine, wind — more at WIND ♦ [9] pivot, revolve, roll, rotate, spin, swing, swirl, turn, twirl, wheel, whirl — more at TURN

²**twist** *n* **1** : something formed by twisting or winding **2** : an act of twisting : the state of being twisted **3** : a spiral turn or curve; *also* : SPIN **4** : a turning aside **5** : ECCENTRICITY **6** : a distortion of meaning **7** : an unexpected turn or development **8** : DEVICE, TRICK **9** : a variant approach or method

twist·er \'twis-tər\ *n* **1** : one that twists; *esp* : a ball with a forward and spinning motion **2** : TORNADO; *also* : WATERSPOUT 2

¹**twit** \'twit\ *n* : a silly or foolish person

²**twit** *vb* **twit·ted; twit·ting** : to ridicule as a fault; *also* : TAUNT

¹**twitch** \'twich\ *vb* **1** ♦ : to move or pull with a sudden motion : JERK **2** ♦ : to move jerkily **3** : to have a twitch

♦ [1] fiddle, fidget, jerk, squirm, wiggle — more at FIDGET ♦ [2] buck, hitch, jerk, jolt — more at JERK

²**twitch** *n* **1** : an act or movement of twitching **2** : a brief spasmodic contraction of muscle fibers

¹**twit·ter** \'twi-tər\ *vb* **1** ♦ : to make a succession of chirping noises **2** ♦ : to talk in a chattering fashion **3** : to tremble with agitation : FLUTTER

♦ [1] cheep, chirp, peep, pipe, tweet — more at CHIRP ♦ [2] chat, converse, gab, jaw, palaver, patter, prattle, rattle, talk, visit — more at CHAT

²**twitter** *n* **1** ♦ : a slight agitation of the nerves **2** : a small tremulous intermittent noise (as made by a swallow) **3** : a light chattering

♦ dither, fluster, fret, fuss, huff, lather, pother, stew, tizzy — more at FRET

twixt \'twikst\ *prep* : BETWEEN

two \'tü\ *n, pl* **twos** **1** : one more than one **2** : the second in a set or series **3** : something having two units — **two** *adj or pron*

two cents *n* **1** : a sum or object of very small value **2** *or* **two cents worth** : an opinion offered on a topic under discussion

two–faced \'tü-'fāst\ *adj* **1** ♦ : given to or marked by duplicity : DOUBLE-DEALING **2** : having two faces

♦ artificial, double-dealing, feigned, hypocritical, insincere, left-handed, mealy, mealymouthed, unctuous — more at INSINCERE

¹**two–fold** \'tü-ˌfōld, -'fōld\ *adj* **1** : having two units or members **2** : being twice as much or as many

²**two–fold** \'tü-'fōld\ *adv* : to twice as much or as many : by two times

2,4–D \ˌtü-ˌfōr-'dē\ *n* : an irritant compound used esp. as a weed killer

2,4,5–T \-ˌfīv-'tē\ *n* : an irritant compound used esp. as an herbicide and defoliant

two·pence \'tə-pəns, *US also* 'tü-ˌpens\ *n* : the sum of two pence

two·pen·ny \'tə-pə-nē, *US also* 'tü-ˌpe-nē\ *adj* : of the value of or costing twopence

two–ply \'tü-'plī\ *adj* **1** : woven as a double cloth **2** : consisting of two strands or thicknesses ⟨~ toilet paper⟩

two·some \'tü-səm\ *n* **1** ♦ : a group of two persons or things : COUPLE **2** : a golf match between two players

♦ brace, couple, duo, pair, twain — more at PAIR

two–step \'tü-ˌstep\ *n* : a ballroom dance performed with a sliding step in march or polka time; *also* : a piece of music for this dance — **two–step** *vb*

two–time \'tü-ˌtīm\ *vb* : to betray (a spouse or lover) by secret lovemaking with another — **two–tim·er** *n*

two–way *adj* : involving two elements or allowing movement or use in two directions or manners

2WD *abbr* two-wheel drive

twp *abbr* township

TWX *abbr* teletypewriter exchange

TX *abbr* Texas

ty·coon \tī-'kün\ *n* [Jp *taikun* feudal lord] **1** ♦ : a leader (as in politics) **2** ♦ : a powerful businessperson or magnate

♦ [1, 2] baron, czar, king, magnate, mogul, prince — more at MAGNATE

tying *pres part of* TIE

tyke \'tīk\ *n* : a small child

tym·pan·ic membrane \tim-'pa-nik-\ *n* : EARDRUM

tym·pa·num \'tim-pə-nəm\ *n, pl* **-na** \-nə\ *also* **-nums** : EARDRUM; *also* : MIDDLE EAR — **tym·pan·ic** \tim-'pa-nik\ *adj*

¹**type** \'tīp\ *n* [ME, fr. LL *typus*, fr. L & Gk; L *typus* image, fr. Gk *typos* blow, impression, model, fr. *typtein* to strike, beat] **1** : a person, thing, or event that foreshadows another to come : TOKEN, SYMBOL **2** : MODEL, EXAMPLE **3** : a distinctive stamp, mark, or sign : EMBLEM **4** : rectangular blocks usu. of metal each having a face so shaped as to produce a character when printed **5** : the letters or characters printed from or as if from type **6** : general character or form common to a number of individuals and setting them off as a distinguishable class ⟨horses of draft ~⟩ **7** ♦ : a class, kind, or group set apart by common characteristics ⟨a seedless ~ of orange⟩; *also* : something distinguishable as a variety ⟨reactions of this ~⟩

♦ breed, class, description, feather, group, ilk, kind, like, manner, nature, order, sort, species — more at SORT

²**type** *vb* **typed; typ·ing** **1** : to produce a copy of; *also* : REPRESENT, TYPIFY **2** : to write with a typewriter or computer keyboard **3** ♦ : to identify as belonging to a type **4** : to cast (an actor or actress) repeatedly in the same type of role : TYPECAST

♦ assort, break down, categorize, class, classify, codify, grade, group, peg, place, range, rank, separate, sort — more at CLASSIFY

type·cast \-ˌkast\ *vb* **-cast; -cast·ing** **1** : to cast (an actor) in a part calling for characteristics possessed by the actor **2** : to cast repeatedly in the same type of role

type·face \-ˌfās\ *n* : all type of a single design

type·script \ˈtīp-ˌskript\ *n* : typewritten matter

type·set \-ˌset\ *vb* **-set; -set·ting** : to set in type : COMPOSE — **type·set·ter** *n*

type·write \-ˌrīt\ *vb* **-wrote** \-ˌrōt\; **-writ·ten** \-ˌrit-ᵊn\; **-writ·ing** : TYPE 2

type·writ·er \-ˌrī-tər\ *n* **1** : a machine for writing in characters similar to those produced by printers' type by means of types striking a ribbon to transfer ink or carbon impressions onto paper **2** : TYPIST

type·writ·ing \-ˌrī-tiŋ\ *n* : the use of a typewriter ⟨teach ∼⟩; *also* : writing produced with a typewriter

¹ty·phoid \ˈtī-ˌfòid, tī-ˈfòid\ *adj* : of, relating to, or being a communicable bacterial disease (**typhoid fever**) marked by fever, diarrhea, prostration, and intestinal inflammation

²typhoid *n* : TYPHOID FEVER

ty·phoon \tī-ˈfün\ *n* : a hurricane occurring esp. in the region of the Philippines or the China Sea

ty·phus \ˈtī-fəs\ *n* : a severe infectious disease transmitted esp. by body lice, caused by a rickettsia, and marked by high fever, stupor and delirium, intense headache, and a dark red rash

typ·i·cal \ˈti-pi-kəl\ *adj* **1** : being or having the nature of a type **2** ♦ : exhibiting the essential characteristics of a group **3** ♦ : conforming to a type — **typ·i·cal·i·ty** \ˌti-pə-ˈka-lə-tē\ *n* — **typ·i·cal·ness** *n*

♦ [2] characteristic, classic, distinct, distinctive, individual, peculiar, proper, symptomatic — more at CHARACTERISTIC ♦ [2, 3] average, characteristic, normal, regular, representative, standard; *also* common, conventional, customary, ordinary, usual, wonted; expected, familiar, habitual, predictable, routine, unexceptional, unremarkable; predominant, preponderant *Ant* aberrant, abnormal, anomalous, atypical, deviant, irregular, nontypical

typ·i·cal·ly \-pi-k(ə-)lē\ *adv* **1** : in a typical manner **2** ♦ : in typical circumstances

♦ commonly, generally, naturally, normally, ordinarily, usually. — more at NATURALLY

typ·i·fy \ˈti-pə-ˌfī\ *vb* **-fied; -fy·ing** **1** : to represent by an image, form, model, or resemblance **2** : to embody the essential or common characteristics of

typ·ist \ˈtī-pist\ *n* : a person who types esp. as a job

ty·po \ˈtī-pō\ *n, pl* **typos** : an error (as of spelling) in typed or typeset material

ty·pog·ra·pher \tī-ˈpä-grə-fər\ *n* : one who designs or arranges printing

ty·pog·ra·phy \tī-ˈpä-grə-fē\ *n* : the art of printing with type; *also* : the style, arrangement, or appearance of printed matter — **ty·po·graph·ic** \ˌtī-pə-ˈgra-fik\ *or* **ty·po·graph·i·cal** \-fi-kəl\ *adj* — **ty·po·graph·i·cal·ly** *adv*

ty·ran·ni·cal \tə-ˈra-ni-kəl, tī-\ *also* **ty·ran·nic** \-nik\ *adj* ♦ : being or characteristic of a tyrant or tyranny : DESPOTIC — **ty·ran·ni·cal·ly** \-ni-k(ə-)lē\ *adv*

♦ absolute, autocratic, despotic, dictatorial, tyrannous — more at ABSOLUTE

tyr·an·nise *chiefly Brit var of* TYRANNIZE

tyr·an·nize \ˈtir-ə-ˌnīz\ *vb* **-nized; -niz·ing** : to act as a tyrant : rule with unjust severity — **tyr·an·niz·er** *n*

ty·ran·no·saur \tə-ˈra-nə-ˌsòr\ *n* : a massive American flesh-eating dinosaur of the Cretaceous that had small forelegs and walked on its hind legs

ty·ran·no·sau·rus \tə-ˌra-nə-ˈsòr-əs\ *n* : TYRANNOSAUR

tyr·an·nous \ˈtir-ə-nəs\ *adj* ♦ : being or characteristic of a tyrant or tyranny; *esp* : unjustly severe : TYRANNICAL — **tyr·an·nous·ly** *adv*

♦ authoritarian, autocratic, bossy, despotic, dictatorial, domineering, imperious, masterful, overbearing, peremptory, tyrannical — more at BOSSY

tyr·an·ny \ˈtir-ə-nē\ *n, pl* **-nies** **1** : oppressive power **2** ♦ : the rule or authority of a tyrant : government in which absolute power is vested in a single ruler **3** : a tyrannical act

♦ autocracy, despotism, dictatorship, totalitarianism — more at DESPOTISM

ty·rant \ˈtī-rənt\ *n* **1** ♦ : an absolute ruler : DESPOT **2** ♦ : a ruler who governs oppressively or brutally **3** ♦ : one who uses authority or power harshly

♦ [1, 2, 3] autocrat, despot, dictator, oppressor — more at DESPOT

tyre *chiefly Brit var of* ²TIRE

ty·ro \ˈtī-rō\ *n, pl* **tyros** [ML, fr. L *tiro* young soldier, tyro] ♦ : a beginner in learning : NOVICE

♦ beginner, fledgling, freshman, greenhorn, neophyte, newcomer, novice, recruit, rookie, tenderfoot — more at BEGINNER

tzar *var of* CZAR

¹u \ˈyü\ *n, pl* **u's** *or* **us** \ˈyüz\ *often cap* : the 21st letter of the English alphabet

²u *abbr, often cap* unit

¹U \ˈyü\ *adj* : characteristic of the upper classes

²U *abbr* **1** [abbr. of *Union of Orthodox Hebrew Congregations*] kosher certification — often enclosed in a circle **2** university **3** unsatisfactory

³U *symbol* uranium

UAE *abbr* United Arab Emirates

UAR *abbr* United Arab Republic

UAW *abbr* United Automobile Workers

ubiq·ui·tous \yü-ˈbi-kwə-təs\ *adj* : existing or being everywhere at the same time : constantly encountered — **ubiq·ui·tous·ly** *adv* — **ubiq·ui·ty** \-kwə-tē\ *n*

U–boat \ˈyü-ˌbōt\ *n* [trans. of G *U-boot*, short for *Unterseeboot*, lit., undersea boat] : a German submarine

UC *abbr* uppercase

ud·der \ˈə-dər\ *n* : an organ (as of a cow) consisting of two or more milk glands enclosed in a large hanging sac and each provided with a nipple

UFO \ˌyü-(ˌ)ef-ˈō\ *n, pl* **UFO's** *or* **UFOs** \-ˈōz\ : an unidentified flying object; *esp* : FLYING SAUCER

Ugan·dan \ü-ˈgan-dən, yü-, -ˈgän-\ *n* : a native or inhabitant of Uganda — **Ugandan** *adj*

ug·ly \ˈə-glē\ *adj* **ug·li·er; -est** [ME, fr. ON *uggligr*, fr. *uggr* fear] **1** : FRIGHTFUL, DIRE **2** ♦ : offensive to the sight : HIDEOUS **3** : offensive or unpleasant to any sense **4** : morally objectionable : REPULSIVE **5** : likely to cause inconvenience or discomfort **6** : SURLY, QUARRELSOME ⟨an ∼ disposition⟩ — **ug·li·ness** \-glē-nəs\ *n*

♦ grotesque, hideous, unappealing, unattractive, unlovely, unsightly, vile; *also* disgusting, repugnant, repulsive, revolting; unimposing, unimpressive, unprepossessing; plain, unaesthetic, unbecoming, unshapely *Ant* attractive, beauteous, beautiful, comely, cute, fair, gorgeous, handsome, lovely, pretty, stunning, taking

UHF *abbr* ultrahigh frequency

UK *abbr* United Kingdom

ukase \yü-ˈkās, -ˈkāz\ *n* [F & Russ; F, fr. Russ *ukaz*, fr. *ukazat'* to show, order] : an edict esp. of a Russian emperor or government

Ukrai·ni·an \yü-ˈkrā-nē-ən\ *n* 1 : a native or inhabitant of Ukraine 2 : a slavic language of the Ukrainian people — **Ukrainian** *adj*

uku·le·le *also* **uke·le·le** \ˌyü-kə-ˈlā-lē\ *n* [Hawaiian *'ukulele,* fr. *'uku* flea + *lele* jumping] : a small usu. 4-stringed guitar popularized in Hawaii

ul·cer \ˈəl-sər\ *n* 1 : an open eroded sore of skin or mucous membrane often discharging pus 2 : something that festers and corrupts like an open sore — **ul·cer·ous** *adj*

ul·cer·ate \ˈəl-sə-ˌrāt\ *vb* **-at·ed; -at·ing** : to become affected with an ulcer — **ul·cer·a·tive** \ˈəl-sə-ˌrā-tiv\ *adj*

ul·cer·a·tion \ˌəl-sə-ˈrā-shən\ *n* 1 : the process of forming or state of having an ulcer 2 : ULCER 1

ul·na \ˈəl-nə\ *n* : the bone on the little-finger side of the human forearm; *also* : a corresponding bone of the forelimb of vertebrates above fishes

ul·ster \ˈəl-stər\ *n* : a long loose overcoat

ult *abbr* 1 ultimate 2 ultimo

ul·te·ri·or \ˌəl-ˈtir-ē-ər\ *adj* 1 : lying farther away : more remote 2 : situated beyond or on the farther side 3 : going beyond what is openly said or shown : HIDDEN ⟨∼ motives⟩

¹**ul·ti·mate** \ˈəl-tə-mət\ *adj* 1 ♦ : most remote in space or time : FARTHEST 2 ♦ : last in a progression : FINAL 3 ♦ : the best or most extreme of its kind 4 : arrived at as the last resort 5 : FUNDAMENTAL, ABSOLUTE, SUPREME ⟨∼ reality⟩ 6 : incapable of further analysis or division : ELEMENTAL 7 : MAXIMUM

♦ [1] extreme, outermost, utmost — more at EXTREME
♦ [2] final, hindmost, last, latter, terminal — more at LAST
♦ [3] consummate, maximum, most, nth, paramount, supreme, top, utmost; *also* unequaled, unmatched, unparalleled, unrivaled, unsurpassed; topmost, upmost, uppermost *Ant* least, minimal, minimum

²**ultimate** *n* : something ultimate

ul·ti·mate·ly *adv* ♦ : at an unspecified later time : in the end

♦ eventually, someday, sometime, yet — more at YET

ul·ti·ma·tum \ˌəl-tə-ˈmā-təm, -ˈmä-\ *n, pl* **-tums** *or* **-ta** \-tə\ : a final condition or demand whose rejection will bring about a resort to forceful action

ul·ti·mo \ˈəl-tə-ˌmō\ *adj* [L *ultimo mense* in the last month] : of or occurring in the month preceding the present

¹**ul·tra** \ˈəl-trə\ *adj* ♦ : going beyond others or beyond due limits : EXTREME

♦ extreme, extremist, fanatic, rabid, radical, revolutionary — more at EXTREME

²**ultra** *n* : EXTREMIST

ul·tra·con·ser·va·tive \-kən-ˈsər-və-tiv\ *adj* : extremely conservative

ul·tra·high frequency \-ˈhī-\ *n* : a radio frequency between 300 and 3000 megahertz

¹**ul·tra·light** \ˈəl-trə-ˌlīt\ *adj* : extremely light esp. in weight

²**ultralight** *n* : a very light recreational aircraft typically carrying only one person

ul·tra·ma·rine \ˌəl-trə-mə-ˈrēn\ *n* 1 : a deep blue pigment 2 : a very bright deep blue color

ul·tra·mi·cro·scop·ic \-ˌmī-krə-ˈskä-pik\ *adj* : too small to be seen with an ordinary microscope

ul·tra·mod·ern \-ˈmä-dərn\ *adj* ♦ : extremely or excessively modern in idea, style, or tendency

♦ contemporary, current, hot, mod, modern, new, newfangled, red-hot, space-age, up-to-date — more at MODERN

ul·tra·pure \-ˈpyu̇r\ *adj* : of the utmost purity

ul·tra·short \-ˈshȯrt\ *adj* 1 : having a wavelength below 10 meters 2 : very short in duration

ul·tra·son·ic \ˌəl-trə-ˈsä-nik\ *adj* : having a frequency too high to be heard by the human ear — **ul·tra·son·i·cal·ly** \-ni-k(ə-)lē\ *adv*

ul·tra·son·ics \-ˈsä-niks\ *n sing or pl* 1 : ultrasonic vibrations 2 : the science of ultrasonic phenomena

ul·tra·sound \-ˌsau̇nd\ *n* 1 : ultrasonic vibrations 2 : the diagnostic or therapeutic use of ultrasound and esp. a technique involving the formation of a two-dimensional image of internal body structures 3 : a diagnostic examination using ultrasound

ul·tra·vi·o·let \-ˈvī-ə-lət\ *adj* : having a wavelength shorter than those of visible light and longer than those of X-rays ⟨∼ radiation⟩; *also* : producing or employing ultraviolet radiation — **ultraviolet** *n*

ul·tra vi·res \ˈəl-trə-ˈvī-rēz\ *adv or adj* [NL, lit., beyond power] : beyond the scope of legal power or authority

ul·u·late \ˈəl-yə-ˌlāt\ *vb* **-lat·ed; -lat·ing** : HOWL, WAIL

uma·mi \ü-ˈmä-mē\ *n* [Jp, flavor] : a meaty or savory taste sensation produced esp. by monosodium glutamate

um·bel \ˈəm-bəl\ *n* : a flat-topped or rounded flower cluster in which the individual flower stalks all arise near one point on the main stem

um·ber \ˈəm-bər\ *n* : a brown earthy substance valued as a pigment either in its raw state or burnt — **umber** *adj*

umbilical cord *n* : a cord containing blood vessels that connects the navel of a fetus with the placenta of its mother

um·bi·li·cus \ˌəm-ˈbi-li-kəs, ˌəm-bə-ˈlī-\ *n, pl* **um·bi·li·ci** \ˌəm-ˈbi-lə-ˌkī; ˌəm-bə-ˈlī-ˌkī, -ˌsī\ *or* **um·bi·li·cus·es** : NAVEL — **um·bil·i·cal** \ˌəm-ˈbi-li-kəl\ *adj*

um·bra \ˈəm-brə\ *n, pl* **umbras** *or* **um·brae** \-(ˌ)brē, -ˌbrī\ 1 : a shaded area : SHADE 2 : the conical part of the shadow of a celestial body from which the sun's light is completely blocked

um·brage \ˈəm-brij\ *n* 1 : SHADE; *also* : FOLIAGE 2 ♦ : a feeling of pique or resentment at some often fancied slight or insult : OFFENSE ⟨take ∼ at a remark⟩

♦ dudgeon, huff, offense, peeve, pique, resentment — more at PIQUE

um·brel·la \ˌəm-ˈbre-lə\ *n* 1 : a collapsible shade for protection against weather consisting of fabric stretched over hinged ribs radiating from a center pole 2 : something that provides protection 3 : something that covers a range of elements

umi·ak \ˈü-mē-ˌak\ *n* : an open boat made of a wooden frame covered with skins used esp. by indigenous peoples of arctic regions

¹**um·pire** \ˈəm-ˌpīr\ *n* [ME *oumpere,* alter. of *noumpere* (the phrase *a noumpere* being understood as *an oumpere*), fr. AF *nounpier* single, odd, fr. *non* not + *per* equal, fr. L *par*] 1 ♦ : one having authority to decide finally a controversy or question between parties 2 : an official in a sport who rules on plays

♦ arbiter, arbitrator, judge, referee — more at JUDGE

²**umpire** *vb* ♦ : to supervise or decide as umpire

♦ adjudicate, arbitrate, decide, determine, judge, referee, rule, settle — more at JUDGE

ump·teen \ˈəm-ˌtēn\ *adj* : very many : indefinitely numerous — **ump·teenth** \-ˌtēnth\ *adj*

UN *abbr* United Nations

un- \ˌən, ˈən\ *prefix* 1 : not : IN-, NON- 2 : opposite of : contrary to

---

List of self-explanatory words with the prefix *un-*

unabated	unacclimatized	unadvertised	unambiguously
unabsorbed	unaccommodating	unaffiliated	unambitious
unabsorbent	unaccredited	unafraid	unanchored
unacademic	unacknowledged	unaggressive	unannounced
unaccented	unadventurous	unaltered	unanswered

un·abashed \-ə-'basht\ adj ♦ : not abashed

♦ unashamed, unblushing, unembarrassed; *also* prideful, proud; bold, brassy, brazen, impudent, insolent, saucy, shameless; unapologetic, undaunted, undeterred, undismayed; unblinking, unflinching *Ant* abashed, ashamed, embarrassed, shamefaced, sheepish

un·able \-'ā-bəl\ adj 1 : not able 2 : UNQUALIFIED, INCOMPETENT

un·abridged \-ə-'brijd\ adj 1 : not abridged ⟨an ~ edition of Shakespeare⟩ 2 : complete of its class : not based on one larger ⟨an ~ dictionary⟩

un·ac·cept·able \-ak-'sep-tə-bəl\ adj ♦ : not acceptable : not pleasing or welcome

♦ bad, deficient, inferior, lousy, off, poor, punk, rotten, substandard, unsatisfactory, wanting, wretched, wrong — more at BAD

un·ac·com·pa·nied \-ə-'kəm-pə-nēd\ adj 1 ♦ : not accompanied 2 : being without instrumental accompaniment

♦ alone, lone, lonely, lonesome, solitary — more at ALONE

un·ac·count·able \-ə-'kaùn-tə-bəl\ adj 1 : not to be accounted for : INEXPLICABLE 2 : not responsible — **un·ac·count·ably** \-blē\ adv

un·ac·count·ed \-'kaùn-təd\ adj : not accounted ⟨the loss was ~ for⟩

un·ac·cus·tomed \-ə-'kəs-təmd\ adj 1 ♦ : not customary : not usual or common 2 ♦ : not accustomed or habituated ⟨~ to noise⟩

♦ [1] curious, extraordinary, funny, odd, peculiar, queer, rare, strange, uncommon, uncustomary, unique, unusual, weird — more at UNUSUAL ♦ *usu* **unaccustomed to** [2] unadapted, unadjusted, unused — more at UNUSED

un·ac·quaint·ed \-ə-'kwān-təd\ adj ♦ : not having experience or knowledge

♦ ignorant, oblivious, unaware, unconscious, uninformed, unknowing, unwitting — more at IGNORANT

un·adapt·ed \-ə-'dap-təd\ adj ♦ : not adapted

♦ unaccustomed, unadjusted, unused — more at UNUSED

un·ad·just·ed \-ə-'jəs-təd\ adj ♦ : not adjusted

♦ unaccustomed, unadapted, unused — more at UNUSED

un·adorned \-ə-'dórnd\ adj ♦ : not adorned : lacking embellishment or decoration

♦ bald, bare, naked, plain, simple, undecorated, unvarnished — more at PLAIN

un·adul·ter·at·ed \-ə-'dəl-tə-ˌrā-təd\ adj 1 ♦ : not adulterated : PURE ⟨~ meat⟩ 2 ♦ : not modified or restricted by reservations

♦ [1] absolute, fine, neat, plain, pure, refined, straight, undiluted, unmixed — more at PURE ♦ [2] absolute, complete, outright, perfect, profound, pure, regular, sheer, simple, total, unequivocal, unqualified, utter — more at ABSOLUTE

un·aes·thet·ic \-es-'the-tik\ adj ♦ : not aesthetic

♦ grotesque, harsh — more at HARSH

un·af·fect·ed \-ə-'fek-təd\ adj 1 : not influenced or changed mentally, physically, or chemically 2 ♦ : free from affectation : GENUINE

♦ artless, genuine, honest, ingenuous, innocent, naive, natural, real, simple, sincere, true, unpretentious

un·af·fect·ed·ly adv ♦ : in an unaffected manner

♦ artlessly, ingenuously, naively, naturally — more at NATURALLY

un·aid·ed \-'ā-dəd\ adj ♦ : not aided : being without help

♦ alone, independently, singly, solely, unassisted — more at ALONE

un·alien·able \-'āl-yə-nə-bəl, -'ā-lē-ə-\ adj : INALIENABLE

un·aligned \ˌən-ə-'līnd\ adj : not associated with any one of competing international blocs ⟨~ nations⟩

un·alike \-ə-'līk\ adj ♦ : not alike or similar

♦ different, disparate, dissimilar, distinct, distinctive, distinguishable, diverse, other, unlike — more at DIFFERENT

un·al·loyed \-ə-'lóid\ adj : not mixed or qualified : PURE ⟨~ happiness⟩

un·al·ter·able \-'ól-tə-rə-bəl\ adj ♦ : not capable of being altered or changed ⟨an ~ rule⟩ — **un·al·ter·ably** \-blē\ adv

♦ fast, fixed, hard-and-fast, immutable, inflexible, unchangeable — more at INFLEXIBLE

un·am·big·u·ous \-am-'bi-gyə-wəs\ adj ♦ : not ambiguous : having or being a single clearly defined or stated meaning

♦ apparent, broad, clear, clear-cut, distinct, evident, lucid, manifest, obvious, palpable, patent, perspicuous, plain, transparent, unequivocal, unmistakable — more at CLEAR ♦ definite, definitive, explicit, express, specific — more at EXPLICIT

un–Amer·i·can \-ə-'mer-ə-kən\ adj : not characteristic of or consistent with American customs or principles

una·nim·i·ty \ˌyü-nə-'ni-mə-tē\ n ♦ : the quality or state of being unanimous

♦ accord, agreement, concurrence, consensus — more at AGREEMENT

unan·i·mous \yù-'na-nə-məs\ adj [L *unanimus*, fr. *unus* one + *animus* mind] 1 ♦ : being of one mind 2 ♦ : formed with or indicating the agreement of all — **unan·i·mous·ly** adv

♦ [1, 2] agreeable, amicable, compatible, congenial, harmonious, kindred, united — more at HARMONIOUS

un·an·swer·able \ˌən-'an-sə-rə-bəl\ adj ♦ : not answerable : not capable of being refuted

♦ incontestable, indisputable, indubitable, irrefutable, undeniable, unquestionable — more at IRREFUTABLE

un·an·tic·i·pat·ed \ˌən-an-'ti-sə-ˌpā-təd\ adj ♦ : not expected

♦ sudden, unexpected, unforeseen — more at UNEXPECTED

un·ap·peal·ing \ˌən-ə-'pē-liŋ\ adj ♦ : not appealing or attractive

♦ grotesque, hideous, ugly, unattractive, unlovely, unsightly, vile — more at UGLY

un·ap·pe·tiz·ing \ˌən-'a-pə-ˌtī-ziŋ\ adj ♦ : not appetizing

♦ distasteful, unsavory — more at DISTASTEFUL

un·ap·proach·able \ˌən-ə-'prō-chə-bəl\ adj 1 ♦ : not approachable : physically inaccessible 2 ♦ : discouraging intimacies

♦ [1, 2] inaccessible, inconvenient, unattainable, unavailable, unobtainable, unreachable, untouchable — more at INACCESSIBLE

un·arm \-'ärm\ vb : DISARM

un·armed \-'ärmd\ adj : not armed or armored

un·ashamed \-ə-'shāmd\ adj ♦ : not ashamed : being without guilt, self-consciousness, or doubt

---

List of self-explanatory words with the prefix *un-* (continued)

unapologetic	unappropriated	unartistic	unauthorized
unapparent	unapproved	unassertive	unavowed
unappeased	unarguable	unathletic	unawakened
unappreciated	unarguably	unattended	unbaked
unappreciative	unarmored	unattested	unbeloved

♦ unabashed, unblushing, unembarrassed — more at UNABASHED

un·asked \-'askt\ *adj* **1** : not being asked **2** ♦ : not requested

♦ unbidden, undesired, uninvited, unsolicited, unsought, unwanted, unwelcome — more at UNSOUGHT

un·as·sail·able \-ə-'sā-lə-bəl\ *adj* : not liable to doubt, challenge, or attack

un·as·sist·ed \-ə-'sis-təd\ *adj* ♦ : not assisted : lacking help

♦ alone, independently, singly, solely, unaided — more at ALONE

un·as·sum·ing \-ə-'sü-miŋ\ *adj* ♦ : neither bold nor self-assertive

♦ demure, humble, lowly, meek, modest, retiring, unpretentious — more at HUMBLE

un·at·tached \-ə-'tacht\ *adj* **1** ♦ : not married or engaged **2** ♦ : not joined or united

♦ [1] single, unmarried, unwed — more at SINGLE
♦ [2] detached, disconnected, discrete, freestanding, separate, single, unconnected — more at SEPARATE

un·at·tain·able \-ə-'tā-nə-bəl\ *adj* ♦ : not capable of being attained or accomplished

♦ inaccessible, inconvenient, unapproachable, unavailable, unobtainable, unreachable, untouchable — more at INACCESSIBLE ♦ hopeless, impossible, unsolvable, unworkable — more at IMPOSSIBLE

un·at·trac·tive \-ə-'trak-tiv\ *adj* ♦ : not attractive : lacking beauty, interest, or charm

♦ grotesque, hideous, ugly, unappealing, unlovely, unsightly, vile — more at UGLY

un·au·then·tic \-ȯ-'then-tik\ *adj* ♦ : not authentic

♦ bogus, counterfeit, fake, false, inauthentic, phony, sham, spurious — more at COUNTERFEIT

un·avail·able \-ə-'vā-lə-bəl\ *adj* ♦ : not available

♦ inaccessible, inconvenient, unapproachable, unattainable, unobtainable, unreachable, untouchable — more at INACCESSIBLE

un·avail·ing \-ə-'vā-liŋ\ *adj* ♦ : being of no avail — **un·avail·ing·ly** *adv*

♦ fruitless, futile, ineffective, unproductive, unsuccessful — more at FUTILE

un·avoid·able \-ə-'vȯi-də-bəl\ *adj* ♦ : not avoidable

♦ certain, inevitable, necessary, sure — more at INEVITABLE

un·avoid·ably \-blē\ *adv* ♦ : in a way or under a condition that is unavoidable

♦ inevitably, necessarily, needs, perforce — more at NEEDS

¹un·aware \-ə-'war\ *adv* : without warning : UNAWARES
²unaware *adj* ♦ : not aware

♦ ignorant, oblivious, unconscious, uninformed, unknowing, unwitting — more at IGNORANT

un·aware·ness *n* ♦ : the state or fact of being unaware

♦ ignorance, obliviousness — more at IGNORANCE

un·awares \-'warz\ *adv* **1** : without knowing or intention **2** ♦ : without warning : by surprise ⟨taken ∼⟩

♦ aback, suddenly, unaware; *also* abruptly, short

un·bal·anced \-'ba-lənst\ *adj* **1** : not in a state of balance **2** : mentally disordered **3** : not adjusted so as to make credits equal to debits

un·bap·tized \-bap-'tīzd\ *adj* **1 a** : not baptized **b** ♦ : not given a name **2** : PROFANE 2

♦ anonymous, nameless, unchristened, unidentified, unnamed, untitled — more at NAMELESS

un·bar \-'bär\ *vb* : UNBOLT, OPEN
un·bear·able \-'bar-ə-bəl\ *adj* ♦ : greater than can be borne ⟨∼ pain⟩ — **un·bear·ably** \-blē\ *adv*

♦ insufferable, insupportable, intolerable, unendurable, unsupportable; *also* unacceptable; crushing, overwhelming; harsh, painful, uncomfortable **Ant** endurable, sufferable, supportable, tolerable

un·beat·able \-'bē-tə-bəl\ *adj* ♦ : not capable of being defeated

♦ impregnable, indomitable, insurmountable, invincible, invulnerable, unconquerable — more at INVINCIBLE

un·beat·en \-'bēt-ᵊn\ *adj* **1** : not pounded, beaten, or whipped **2** : UNTRODDEN **3** : UNDEFEATED
un·be·com·ing \-bi-'kə-miŋ\ *adj* ♦ : not becoming : UNSUITABLE ⟨conduct ∼ an officer⟩ — **un·be·com·ing·ly** *adv*

♦ improper, inappropriate, inapt, infelicitous, unfit, unseemly, unsuitable, wrong — more at INAPPROPRIATE

un·be·knownst \-bi-'nōnst\ *also* **un·be·known** \-'nōn\ *adj* : happening or existing without one's knowledge
un·be·lief \-bə-'lēf\ *n* : the withholding or absence of belief : DOUBT — **un·be·liev·ing** \-'lē-viŋ\ *adj*
un·be·liev·able \-'lē-və-bəl\ *adj* ♦ : too improbable for belief; *also* : of such a superlative degree as to be hard to believe ⟨an ∼ catch for a touchdown⟩ — **un·be·liev·ably** \-blē\ *adv*

♦ fantastic, implausible, inconceivable, incredible, unconvincing, unimaginable, unthinkable — more at INCREDIBLE

un·be·liev·er \-'lē-vər\ *n* **1** ♦ : one that does not believe : an incredulous person **2** : INFIDEL

♦ disbeliever, doubter, questioner, skeptic — more at SKEPTIC

un·bend \-'bend\ *vb* -**bent** \-'bent\; -**bend·ing** **1** : to free from being bent : make or become straight **2** : UNTIE **3** : to make or become less stiff or more affable : RELAX
un·bend·ing *adj* **1** ♦ : formal and distant in manner : INFLEXIBLE **2** : not bending

♦ adamant, hard, immovable, implacable, inflexible, pat, rigid, uncompromising, unrelenting, unyielding

un·bi·ased \-'bī-əst\ *adj* ♦ : free from bias

♦ disinterested, dispassionate, equal, equitable, fair, impartial, just, nonpartisan, objective, square, unprejudiced — more at FAIR

un·bid·den \-'bid-ᵊn\ *also* **un·bid** \-'bid\ *adj* ♦ : not bidden : UNASKED

♦ unasked, undesired, uninvited, unsolicited, unsought, unwanted, unwelcome — more at UNSOUGHT

un·bind \-'bīnd\ *vb* -**bound** \-'baȯnd\; -**bind·ing** **1** ♦ : to remove bindings from : UNTIE **2** ♦ : to set free : RELEASE

♦ [1] undo, untie — more at UNTIE ♦ [2] discharge, emancipate, enfranchise, free, liberate, loose, loosen, manumit, release, spring, unchain, unfetter — more at FREE

un·blem·ished \-'ble-mishd\ *adj* ♦ : not blemished

♦ absolute, faultless, flawless, ideal, impeccable, letter-perfect, perfect — more at PERFECT

List of self-explanatory words with the prefix *un-* (continued)

unbleached	unbridgeable	uncanceled	uncaught
unblinking	unbruised	uncanonical	uncensored
unbranched	unbrushed	uncap	uncensured
unbranded	unburied	uncapitalized	unchallenged
unbreakable	unburned	uncaredñfor	unchanged

un·blessed also **un·blest** \-'blest\ adj **1** : not blessed **2** : EVIL

un·block \-'bläk\ vb ♦ : to free from being blocked
♦ clear, free

un·blush·ing \-'blə-shiŋ\ adj **1** : not blushing **2** ♦ : having no shame — **un·blush·ing·ly** adv
♦ unabashed, unashamed, unembarrassed — more at UNABASHED

un·bod·ied \-'bä-dēd\ adj **1** : having no body; also : DISEMBODIED **2** : FORMLESS

un·bolt \-'bōlt\ vb : to open or unfasten by withdrawing a bolt

un·bolt·ed \-'bōl-təd\ adj : not fastened by bolts

un·born \-'bȯrn\ adj : not yet born

un·bos·om \-'bu̇-zəm, -'bü-\ vb **1** ♦ : to give expression to : REVEAL **2** : to disclose the thoughts or feelings of oneself
♦ bare, disclose, discover, divulge, expose, reveal, spill, tell, uncloak, uncover, unmask, unveil — more at REVEAL

un·bound \-'bau̇nd\ adj ♦ : not bound
♦ footloose, free, loose, unconfined, unrestrained — more at FREE

un·bound·ed \-'bau̇n-dəd\ adj ♦ : having no bounds or limits ⟨~ enthusiasm⟩
♦ boundless, endless, illimitable, immeasurable, indefinite, infinite, limitless, measureless, unfathomable, unlimited — more at INFINITE

un·bowed \-'bau̇d\ adj **1** : not bowed down **2** : UNSUBDUED

un·bri·dled \-'brīd-°ld\ adj **1** ♦ : not restrained : UNRESTRAINED **2** : not confined by a bridle
♦ intemperate, rampant, unchecked, uncontrolled, ungoverned, unhampered, unhindered, unrestrained — more at RAMPANT

un·bro·ken \-'brō-kən\ adj **1** : not damaged **2** ♦ : not subdued or tamed **3** ♦ : not interrupted : CONTINUOUS
♦ [2] feral, savage, undomesticated, untamed, wild — more at WILD ♦ [3] ceaseless, continual, continuous, incessant, unceasing, uninterrupted — more at CONTINUOUS

un·buck·le \-'bə-kəl\ vb : to loose the buckle of : UNFASTEN ⟨~ a belt⟩

un·budg·ing \-'bə-jiŋ\ adj ♦ : not budging : resisting movement or change
♦ immobile, immovable, nonmotile, unmovable — more at IMMOVABLE

un·bur·den \-'bərd-°n\ vb **1** ♦ : to free or relieve from a burden **2** ♦ : to relieve oneself of (as cares or worries)
♦ [1] disburden, discharge, disencumber, unload — more at UNLOAD ♦ [1, 2] clear, disburden, disencumber, free, relieve, rid — more at RID

un·but·ton \-'bət-°n\ vb : to unfasten the buttons of ⟨~ your coat⟩

un·called–for \-'kȯld-ˌfȯr\ adj : not called for, needed, or wanted

un·can·ny \-'ka-nē\ adj **1** ♦ : seeming to have a supernatural character or origin : MYSTERIOUS **2** ♦ : suggesting superhuman or supernatural powers — **un·can·ni·ly** \-'kan-°l-ē\ adv
♦ [1] creepy, eerie, haunting, mysterious, spooky, unearthly, weird — more at EERIE ♦ [2] magical,

miraculous, phenomenal, superhuman, supernatural — more at SUPERNATURAL

un·cat·a·loged \-'kat-°l-ˌȯgd\ adj ♦ : not cataloged
♦ unlisted, unrecorded, unregistered — more at UNLISTED

un·ceas·ing \-'sē-siŋ\ adj ♦ : never ceasing — **un·ceas·ing·ly** adv
♦ ceaseless, continual, continuous, incessant, unbroken, uninterrupted — more at CONTINUOUS

un·cer·e·mo·ni·ous \-ˌser-ə-'mō-nē-əs\ adj **1** : acting without or lacking ordinary courtesy : ABRUPT ⟨his ~ dismissal⟩ **2** ♦ : marked by the absence of formality or ceremony — **un·cer·e·mo·ni·ous·ly** adv
♦ informal, irregular, unconventional, unorthodox — more at INFORMAL

un·cer·tain \-'sərt-°n\ adj **1** : not determined or fixed ⟨an ~ quantity⟩ **2** ♦ : subject to chance or change : not dependable ⟨~ weather⟩ **3** : not definitely known **4** ♦ : not sure ⟨~ of the truth⟩ — **un·cer·tain·ly** adv
♦ [2] capricious, changeable, fickle, fluid, inconstant, mercurial, mutable, temperamental, unpredictable, unsettled, unstable, unsteady, variable, volatile — more at FICKLE ♦ [4] distrustful, doubtful, dubious, mistrustful, skeptical, suspicious, undecided, unsettled, unsure — more at DOUBTFUL

un·cer·tain·ty \-°n-tē\ n **1** ♦ : lack of certainty : DOUBT **2** : something that is uncertain
♦ distrust, doubt, incertitude, misgiving, mistrust, skepticism, suspicion — more at DOUBT

un·chain \-'chān\ vb ♦ : to free by or as if by removing a chain
♦ discharge, emancipate, enfranchise, free, liberate, loose, loosen, manumit, release, spring, unbind, unfetter — more at FREE

un·change·able \-'chān-jə-bəl\ adj ♦ : not changeable : IMMUTABLE
♦ fast, fixed, hard-and-fast, immutable, inflexible, unalterable — more at INFLEXIBLE

un·chang·ing \-'chān-jiŋ\ adj ♦ : not changing or capable of change
♦ constant, stable, stationary, steady, unvarying — more at CONSTANT

un·charged \-'chärjd\ adj : having no electrical charge

un·char·i·ta·ble \-'char-ə-tə-bəl\ adj **1** ♦ : not charitable **2** ♦ : severe in judging others — **un·char·i·ta·ble·ness** n — **un·char·i·ta·bly** \-blē\ adv
♦ [1] cheap, close, mean, niggardly, parsimonious, penurious, spare, sparing, stingy, tight, tightfisted — more at STINGY ♦ [2] callous, hard, heartless, inhuman, inhumane, pitiless, soulless, unfeeling, unsympathetic — more at HARD

un·chart·ed \-'chär-təd\ adj **1** : not recorded on a map, chart, or plan **2** : UNKNOWN

un·chaste \-'chāst\ adj : not pure or modest in thought or action

un·chas·ti·ty \-'chas-tə-tē\ n : the quality or state of being unchaste

un·checked \-'chekt\ adj ♦ : not checked : not curbed or hindered
♦ intemperate, rampant, unbridled, uncontrolled, ungoverned, unhampered, unhindered, unrestrained — more at RAMPANT

un·chris·tened \-'kris-°nd\ adj ♦ : not named

List of self-explanatory words with the prefix un- (continued)

unchaperoned	unclaimed	uncollected	uncompensated
uncharacteristic	unclassified	uncombed	uncompleted
unchastely	uncleaned	uncombined	uncomplicated
unchasteness	uncleared	uncomely	uncompounded
unchivalrous	uncoated	uncommercial	uncomprehending

♦ anonymous, nameless, unbaptized, unidentified, unnamed, untitled — more at NAMELESS

un·chris·tian \-'kris-chən\ *adj* **1** : not of the Christian faith **2** : contrary to the Christian spirit

un·churched \-'chərcht\ *adj* : not belonging to or connected with a church

un·cial \'ən-shəl, -chəl; 'ən-sē-əl\ *adj* : relating to or written in a form of script with rounded letters used esp. in early Greek and Latin manuscripts — **uncial** *n*

un·cir·cu·lat·ed \-'sər-kyə-ˌlā-təd\ *adj* : issued for use as money but kept out of circulation

un·cir·cum·cised \ˌən-'sər-kəm-ˌsīzd\ *adj* **1** : not circumcised **2** : HEATHEN

un·civ·il \-'si-vəl\ *adj* **1** : not civilized : BARBAROUS **2** ♦ : lacking in courtesy : DISCOURTEOUS

♦ discourteous, ill-bred, ill-mannered, impertinent, impolite, inconsiderate, rude, thoughtless, ungracious, unmannerly — more at IMPOLITE

un·civ·i·lized \-'si-və-ˌlīzd\ *adj* **1** ♦ : not civilized : BARBAROUS **2** : remote from civilization : WILD

♦ barbarous, heathen, heathenish, Neanderthal, rude, savage, uncivil, uncultivated, wild — more at SAVAGE

un·clad \-'klad\ *adj* ♦ : not covered or clothed

♦ bare, naked, nude, unclothed, undressed — more at NAKED

un·clasp \-'klasp\ *vb* : to open by or as if by loosing the clasp

un·cle \'ən-kəl\ *n* [ME, fr. AF, fr. L *avunculus* mother's brother] **1** : the brother of one's father or mother **2** : the husband of one's aunt or uncle

un·clean \ˌən-'klēn\ *adj* **1** : morally or spiritually impure **2** : prohibited by ritual law for use or contact **3** ♦ : not clean or pure : DIRTY — **un·clean·ness** *n*

♦ dirty, dusty, filthy, foul, grubby, grungy, mucky, muddy, nasty, smutty, sordid — more at DIRTY

un·clean·li·ness \-'klen-lē-nəs\ *n* ♦ : the quality or state of being uncleanly

♦ dinginess, dirtiness, filthiness, foulness, grubbiness, nastiness — more at DIRTINESS

un·clean·ly \-'klen-lē\ *adj* : physically unclean
un·clean·ness \-'klēn-nəs\ *n* : UNCLEANLINESS

un·clear \-'klir\ *adj* **1** : difficult to grasp or understand **2** ♦ : confused or uncertain in statement or understanding

♦ bleary, dim, faint, foggy, fuzzy, hazy, indefinite, indistinct, indistinguishable, murky, nebulous, obscure, opaque, shadowy, undefined, undetermined, vague — more at FAINT

un·clench \-'klench\ *vb* : to open from a clenched position : RELAX

Uncle Tom \-'täm\ *n* [fr. *Uncle Tom*, faithful slave in Harriet Beecher Stowe's novel *Uncle Tom's Cabin* (1851-52)] *disparaging* : a black person who is eager to win the approval of white people

un·cloak \-'klōk\ *vb* **1** : to remove a cloak or cover from **2** ♦ : to make (something secret or hidden) publicly or generally known : to reveal the true nature of

♦ bare, disclose, discover, divulge, expose, reveal, spill, tell, unbosom, uncover, unmask, unveil — more at REVEAL

un·clog \-'kläg\ *vb* ♦ : to remove an obstruction from

♦ clear, free, open, unstop ♦ ease, facilitate, loosen, smooth — more at EASE

un·close \-'klōz\ *vb* : OPEN — **un·closed** \-'klōzd\ *adj*

un·clothe \-'klōth\ *vb* ♦ : to strip of clothes or a covering

♦ strip, undress — more at UNDRESS

un·clothed \-'klōthd\ *adj* ♦ : not clothed

♦ bare, naked, nude, unclad, undressed — more at NAKED

un·cloud·ed \-'klau̇-dəd\ *adj* ♦ : not covered by clouds : not darkened

♦ clear, cloudless, fair, sunny, sunshiny — more at FAIR

un·clut·tered \-'klə-tərd\ *adj* ♦ : not cluttered : having nothing extraneous or unnecessary

♦ crisp, neat, orderly, shipshape, snug, tidy, trim — more at NEAT

un·coil \-'kȯil\ *vb* : to release or become released from a coiled state

un·col·ored *or Can and Brit* **un·col·oured** \-'kə-lərd\ *adj* ♦ : having no color

♦ colorless (*or* colourless), unpainted, white — more at COLORLESS

un·com·fort·able \-'kəmf-tə-bəl, -'kəm-fər-tə-\ *adj* **1** ♦ : causing discomfort **2** : feeling discomfort : UNEASY — **un·com·fort·ably** \-blē\ *adv*

♦ awkward, disconcerting — more at AWKWARD

un·com·ic \-'kä-mik\ *adj* : not funny or amusing

un·com·mit·ted \-kə-'mi-təd\ *adj* : not committed; *esp* : not pledged to a particular belief, allegiance, or program

un·com·mon \ˌən-'kä-mən\ *adj* **1** ♦ : not ordinarily encountered : UNUSUAL **2** : remarkable in character, quality, or kind : EXCEPTIONAL — **un·com·mon·ly** *adv*

♦ curious, extraordinary, funny, odd, peculiar, queer, rare, strange, unaccustomed, unique, unusual, weird — more at UNUSUAL

un·com·mu·ni·ca·tive \-kə-'myü-nə-ˌkā-tiv, -ni-kə-\ *adj* ♦ : not inclined to talk or impart information

♦ closemouthed, laconic, reserved, reticent, secretive, silent, taciturn — more at SILENT

un·com·plain·ing \-kəm-'plā-niŋ\ *adj* ♦ : not complaining

♦ forbearing, long-suffering, patient, stoic, tolerant — more at PATIENT

un·com·pli·men·ta·ry \-ˌkäm-plə-'men-t(ə-)rē\ *adj* ♦ : not complimentary : detracting from the character or standing of something

♦ contemptuous, degrading, derogatory, disdainful, scornful — more at DEROGATORY

un·com·pro·mis·ing \-'käm-prə-ˌmī-ziŋ\ *adj* ♦ : not making or accepting a compromise : making no concessions

♦ adamant, hard, immovable, implacable, inflexible, pat, rigid, unbending, unrelenting, unyielding

un·con·cern \-kən-'sərn\ *n* **1** : lack of care or interest : INDIFFERENCE **2** : freedom from excessive concern

un·con·cerned \-'sərnd\ *adj* **1** ♦ : not having any part or interest **2** ♦ : not anxious or upset : free of worry — **un·con·cern·ed·ly** \-'sər-nəd-lē\ *adv*

♦ [1] apathetic, casual, disinterested, indifferent, insouciant, nonchalant, perfunctory, uncurious, uninterested — more at INDIFFERENT ♦ [2] carefree, careless, cavalier, easygoing, gay, happy-go-lucky, insouciant, lighthearted

un·con·di·tion·al \-kən-'di-shə-nəl\ *adj* : not limited in any way : ABSOLUTE — **un·con·di·tion·al·ly** *adv*

un·con·di·tioned \-'di-shənd\ *adj* **1** : not subject to conditions **2** : not acquired or learned : NATURAL ⟨∼ responses⟩ **3** : producing an unconditioned response ⟨∼ stimuli⟩

un·con·fined \-kən-'fīnd\ *adj* ♦ : not kept within limits

List of self-explanatory words with the prefix *un-* (continued)

unconcealed	unconsolidated	uncontested	uncoordinated
unconfirmed	unconstrained	uncontroversial	uncorrected
unconformable	unconsumed	unconverted	uncorroborated
unconquered	unconsummated	uncooked	uncreative
unconsecrated	uncontaminated	uncooperative	uncredited

♦ footloose, free, loose, unbound, unrestrained — more at FREE

un·con·ge·nial \-kən-ˈjē-nyəl\ adj 1 ♦ : not to one's taste 2 : not sympathetic

♦ bad, disagreeable, distasteful, nasty, rotten, sour, unlovely, unpleasant, unwelcome — more at UNPLEASANT

un·con·nect·ed \-kə-ˈnek-təd\ adj ♦ : not joined or grouped together

♦ detached, disconnected, discrete, freestanding, separate, single, unattached — more at SEPARATE

un·con·quer·able \-ˈkäŋ-kə-rə-bəl\ adj ♦ : incapable of being conquered or overcome : INDOMITABLE

♦ impregnable, indomitable, insurmountable, invincible, invulnerable, unbeatable — more at INVINCIBLE

un·con·scio·na·ble \-ˈkän-shə-nə-bəl\ adj 1 : not guided or controlled by conscience 2 ♦ : not in accordance with what is right or just 3 : exceeding what is usual, proper, necessary, or normal — **un·con·scio·na·bly** \-blē\ adv

♦ cutthroat, immoral, Machiavellian, unethical, unprincipled, unscrupulous — more at UNPRINCIPLED

¹**un·con·scious** \-ˈkän-chəs, -shəs\ adj 1 ♦ : not knowing or perceiving : not aware 2 : not done consciously or on purpose 3 ♦ : having lost consciousness 4 ♦ : of or relating to the unconscious — **un·con·scious·ly** adv — **un·con·scious·ness** n

♦ [1] ignorant, oblivious, unaware, uninformed, unknowing, unwitting — more at IGNORANT ♦ [3] cold, senseless; also semiconscious Ant conscious

²**unconscious** n : the part of one's mental life of which one is not ordinarily aware but which is often a powerful force in influencing behavior

un·con·sid·ered \-kən-ˈsi-dərd\ adj 1 : not resulting from consideration 2 : not considered or worth consideration

un·con·sti·tu·tion·al \-ˌkän-stə-ˈtü-shə-nəl, -ˈtyü-\ adj : not according to or consistent with the constitution of a state or society — **un·con·sti·tu·tion·al·i·ty** \-ˌtü-shə-ˈna-lə-tē, -ˌtyü-\ n — **un·con·sti·tu·tion·al·ly** \-ˈtü-shə-nə-lē, -ˈtyü-\ adv

un·con·trol·la·ble \ˌən-kən-ˈtrō-lə-bəl\ adj ♦ : incapable of being controlled : UNGOVERNABLE — **un·con·trol·la·bly** \-blē\ adv

♦ froward, headstrong, intractable, recalcitrant, refractory, unmanageable, unruly, untoward, wayward, willful; also contrary, incorrigible, obstinate, perverse, stubborn; undisciplined; uncontrolled, ungoverned, wild; boisterous, rambunctious, rowdy; disobedient, insubordinate, rebellious; misbehaving, naughty Ant tractable

un·con·trolled \-kən-ˈtrōld\ adj ♦ : not being under control

♦ intemperate, rampant, unbridled, unchecked, ungoverned, unhampered, unhindered, unrestrained — more at RAMPANT

un·con·ven·tion·al \-kən-ˈven-chə-nəl\ adj ♦ : not conventional : being out of the ordinary — **un·con·ven·tion·al·i·ty** \-ˌven-chə-ˈna-lə-tē\ n — **un·con·ven·tion·al·ly** \-ˈven-chə-nə-lē\ adv

♦ dissident, heretical, heterodox, nonconforming, nonconformist, nonorthodox, unorthodox — more at HERETICAL ♦ broad-minded, liberal, nontraditional, open-minded, progressive ♦ informal, irregular, unceremonious, unorthodox — more at INFORMAL

un·con·vinc·ing \-kən-ˈvin-siŋ\ adj ♦ : not convincing : not likely to be believed

♦ fantastic, implausible, inconceivable, incredible, unbelievable, unimaginable, unthinkable — more at INCREDIBLE

un·cork \-ˈkȯrk\ vb 1 : to draw a cork from 2 ♦ : to release from a sealed or pent-up state; also : to let go

♦ loose, loosen, release, unleash, unlock, unloosen — more at RELEASE

un·count·able \-ˈkaun-tə-bəl\ adj ♦ : too many to be numbered or counted : indefinitely numerous

♦ countless, innumerable, numberless, unnumbered, untold — more at COUNTLESS

un·count·ed \-ˈkaun-təd\ adj 1 : not counted 2 : too many to be numbered : INNUMERABLE

un·cou·ple \-ˈkə-pəl\ vb : to sever the connection of or between : DISCONNECT

un·couth \-ˈküth\ adj [ME, unfamiliar, fr. OE uncūth, fr. un- + cūth known] 1 : strange, awkward, and clumsy in shape or appearance 2 ♦ : vulgar in conduct or speech 3 ♦ : lacking in polish and grace

♦ [2, 3] coarse, common, crass, crude, gross, ill-bred, low, rough, rude, tasteless, uncultivated, uncultured, unpolished, unrefined, vulgar — more at COARSE

un·cov·er \-ˈkə-vər\ vb 1 ♦ : to make known 2 : to expose to view by removing some covering 3 : to take the cover from 4 : to remove the hat from; also : to take off the hat as a token of respect

♦ bare, disclose, discover, divulge, expose, reveal, spill, tell, unbosom, uncloak, unmask, unveil — more at REVEAL

un·cov·ered \-vərd\ adj ♦ : not covered

♦ bald, bare, exposed, naked, open — more at NAKED

un·crit·i·cal \-ˈkri-ti-kəl\ adj 1 : not critical : lacking in discrimination 2 : showing lack or improper use of critical standards or procedures — **un·crit·i·cal·ly** \-k(ə-)lē\ adv

un·cross \-ˈkrȯs\ vb : to change from a crossed position ⟨~ed his legs⟩

unc·tion \ˈəŋk-shən\ n 1 : the act of anointing as a rite of consecration or healing 2 : exaggerated or insincere earnestness of language or manner

unc·tu·ous \ˈəŋk-chə-wəs\ adj [ME, fr. MF or ML; MF unctueus, fr. ML unctuosus, fr. L unctus act of anointing, fr. unguere to anoint] 1 : FATTY, OILY 2 ♦ : insincerely smooth in speech and manner — **unc·tu·ous·ly** adv

♦ artificial, double-dealing, feigned, hypocritical, insincere, left-handed, mealy, mealymouthed, two-faced — more at INSINCERE ♦ adulatory, fulsome — more at FULSOME

un·cul·ti·vat·ed \ˌən-ˈkəl-tə-ˌvā-təd\ adj 1 a ♦ : lacking in education or refinement b : not civilized : BARBAROUS 2 ♦ : not put under cultivation : not tilled

♦ [1a] coarse, common, crass, crude, gross, ill-bred, low, rough, rude, tasteless, uncouth, uncultured, unpolished, unrefined, vulgar — more at COARSE ♦ [2] natural, untamed, wild — more at WILD

un·cul·tured \-ˈkəl-chərd\ adj 1 : not subjected to cultivation 2 ♦ : not improved or refined by education

♦ coarse, common, crass, crude, gross, ill-bred, low, rough, rude, tasteless, uncouth, uncultivated, unpolished, unrefined, vulgar — more at COARSE

un·cu·ri·ous \-ˈkyur-ē-əs\ adj ♦ : not curious or inquisitive : having no care or interest

♦ apathetic, casual, disinterested, indifferent, insouciant, nonchalant, perfunctory, unconcerned, uninterested — more at INDIFFERENT

List of self-explanatory words with the prefix un- (continued)

uncropped	uncurtained	undeclared	undemocratic
uncrowded	undamaged	undefeated	undenominational
uncrowned	undamped	undefiled	undependable
uncrystallized	undated	undefinable	undeserved
uncured	undecipherable	undemanding	undeserving

un·curl \-'kərl\ *vb* : to make or become straightened out from a curled or coiled position

un·cus·tom·ary \-'kəs-tə-ˌmer-ē\ *adj* ♦ : not customary

♦ aberrant, abnormal, atypical, exceptional, extraordinary, freak, odd, peculiar, phenomenal, rare, singular, uncommon, unique, unusual, unwonted — more at EXCEPTIONAL

un·cut \-'kət\ *adj* **1** : not cut down or into **2** : not shaped by cutting ⟨an ∼ diamond⟩ **3** : not having the folds of the leaves slit ⟨an ∼ book⟩ **4** : not abridged or curtailed ⟨the ∼ version of the film⟩ **5** : not diluted ⟨∼ heroin⟩

un·daunt·ed \-'dȯn-təd\ *adj* ♦ : not daunted : not discouraged or dismayed — **un·daunt·ed·ly** *adv*

♦ brave, courageous, dauntless, doughty, fearless, gallant, greathearted, heroic, intrepid, lionhearted, manful, stalwart, stout, valiant, valorous — more at BRAVE

un·de·ceive \-di-'sēv\ *vb* ♦ : to free from deception, illusion, or error

♦ disenchant, disillusion — more at DISILLUSION

un·de·cid·ed \-di-'sī-dəd\ *adj* **1** ♦ : not yet determined **2** ♦ : uncertain how to act or proceed

♦ [1] open, pending, undetermined, unresolved, unsettled — more at PENDING ♦ [2] distrustful, doubtful, dubious, mistrustful, skeptical, suspicious, uncertain, unsettled, unsure — more at DOUBTFUL

un·dec·o·rat·ed \-'de-kə-ˌrā-təd\ *adj* ♦ : not decorated : without ornament or embellishment

♦ bald, bare, naked, plain, simple, unadorned, unvarnished — more at PLAIN

un·de·fend·ed \-di-'fen-dəd\ *adj* ♦ : not guarded or protected

♦ defenseless (*or* defenceless), exposed, helpless, susceptible, unguarded, unprotected, unresistant, vulnerable — more at HELPLESS

un·de·fined \-di-'fīnd\ *adj* ♦ : not defined, determined, or distinguished

♦ bleary, dim, faint, foggy, fuzzy, hazy, indefinite, indistinct, indistinguishable, murky, nebulous, obscure, opaque, shadowy, unclear, undetermined, vague — more at FAINT

un·de·mon·stra·tive \-di-'män-strə-tiv\ *adj* : restrained in expression of feeling : RESERVED

un·de·ni·able \-di-'nī-ə-bəl\ *adj* **1** ♦ : plainly true : INCONTESTABLE **2** : unquestionably excellent or genuine

♦ incontestable, indisputable, indubitable, irrefutable, unanswerable, unquestionable — more at IRREFUTABLE

un·de·ni·ably \-blē\ *adv* ♦ : that cannot be denied

♦ certainly, definitely, doubtless, incontestably, indeed, indisputably, really, surely, truly, undoubtedly, unquestionably — more at INDEED

¹un·der \'ən-dər\ *adv* **1** ♦ : in or into a position below or beneath something **2** : below some quantity, level, or limit ⟨$10 or ∼⟩ **3** : in or into a condition of subjection, subordination, or unconsciousness ⟨the ether put him ∼⟩

♦ below, beneath — more at BELOW

²un·der \ˌən-dər, 'ən-\ *prep* **1** : lower than and overhung, surmounted, or sheltered by ⟨∼ a tree⟩ **2** : subject to the authority or guidance of ⟨served ∼ him⟩ ⟨was ∼ contract⟩ **3** : subject to the action or effect of ⟨∼ the influence of alcohol⟩ **4** : within the division or grouping of ⟨items ∼ this heading⟩ **5** : less or lower than (as in size, amount, or rank) ⟨earns ∼ $5000⟩

³under \'ən-dər\ *adj* **1** : lying below, beneath, or on the ventral side **2** : facing or protruding downward **3** ♦ : in or into a condition of subjection, subordination, or unconsciousness **4** : lower than usual, proper, or desired in amount, quality, or degree

♦ inferior, junior, less, lesser, lower, minor, subordinate — more at LESSER

un·der·achiev·er \ˌən-dər-ə-'chē-vər\ *n* : one who performs below an expected level of proficiency

un·der·act \-'akt\ *vb* : to perform feebly or with restraint

un·der·ac·tive \-'ak-tiv\ *adj* : characterized by abnormally low activity ⟨an ∼ thyroid gland⟩ — **un·der·ac·tiv·i·ty** \-ˌak-'ti-və-tē\ *n*

un·der·age \-'āj\ *adj* : of less than mature or legal age

un·der·arm \-'ärm\ *adj* **1** : UNDERHAND 2 ⟨an ∼ throw⟩ **2** : placed under or on the underside of the arms ⟨∼ seams⟩ — **underarm** *adv or n*

un·der·bel·ly \'ən-dər-ˌbe-lē\ *n* **1** ♦ : the underside of a body or mass **2** : a vulnerable area

♦ bottom, underside — more at BOTTOM

un·der·bid \ˌən-dər-'bid\ *vb* **-bid; -bid·ding 1** : to bid less than another **2** : to bid too low

un·der·body \'ən-dər-ˌbä-dē\ *n* : the lower parts of the body of a vehicle

un·der·bred \ˌən-dər-'bred\ *adj* : marked by lack of good breeding

un·der·brush \'ən-dər-ˌbrəsh\ *n* : shrubs, bushes, or small trees growing beneath large trees

un·der·car·riage \-ˌkar-ij\ *n* **1** : a supporting framework (as of an automobile) **2** : the landing gear of an airplane

un·der·charge \ˌən-dər-'chärj\ *vb* : to charge (as a person) too little — **undercharge** \'ən-dər-ˌchärj\ *n*

un·der·class \'ən-dər-ˌklas\ *n* : LOWER CLASS

un·der·class·man \ˌən-dər-'klas-mən\ *n* : a member of the freshman or sophomore class

un·der·clothes \'ən-dər-ˌklōthz\ *n pl* : UNDERWEAR

un·der·cloth·ing \-ˌklō-thiŋ\ *n* : clothing or an article of clothing worn next to the skin and under other clothing : UNDERWEAR

un·der·coat \-ˌkōt\ *n* **1** : a coat worn under another **2** : a growth of short hair or fur partly concealed by the longer and usu. coarser hairs of a mammal **3** : a coat of paint under another

un·der·coat·ing \-ˌkō-tiŋ\ *n* : a special waterproof coating applied to the underside of a vehicle

un·der·cov·er \ˌən-dər-'kə-vər\ *adj* ♦ : acting or executed in secret; *esp* : employed or engaged in secret investigation ⟨an ∼ agent⟩

♦ clandestine, covert, furtive, hugger-mugger, private, secret, sneak, sneaky, stealthy, surreptitious, underground, underhanded — more at SECRET

un·der·croft \'ən-dər-ˌkrȯft\ *n* [ME, fr. *under* + *crofte* crypt, fr. MD, fr. ML *crupta*, fr. L *crypta*] : a vaulted chamber under a church

un·der·cur·rent \-ˌkər-ənt\ *n* **1** : a current below the surface **2** : a hidden tendency of feeling or opinion

un·der·cut \ˌən-dər-'kət\ *vb* **-cut; -cut·ting 1** : to cut away the underpart of **2** : to offer to sell or to work at a lower rate than **3** : to strike (the ball) obliquely downward so as to give a backward spin or elevation to the shot — **un·der·cut** \'ən-dər-ˌkət\ *n*

un·der·de·vel·oped \ˌən-dər-di-'ve-ləpt\ *adj* **1** : not normally or adequately developed ⟨∼ muscles⟩ **2** : having a relatively low level of economic development ⟨the ∼ nations⟩

List of self-explanatory words with the prefix *un-* (continued)

undetected	undignified	undisciplined	undismayed
undeterred	undiminished	undisclosed	undisputed
undeveloped	undimmed	undiscovered	undissolved
undifferentiated	undiplomatic	undiscriminating	undistinguished
undigested	undirected	undisguised	undistributed

un·der·dog \'ən-dər-ˌdȯg\ *n* : the loser or predicted loser in a struggle

un·der·done \ˌən-dər-'dən\ *adj* : not thoroughly done or cooked : RARE

un·der·draw·ers \'ən-dər-ˌdrȯrz, -ˌdrȯ-ərz\ *n pl* : UNDERPANTS

un·der·em·pha·size \ˌən-dər-'em-fə-ˌsīz\ *vb* : to emphasize inadequately — **un·der·em·pha·sis** \-səs\ *n*

un·der·em·ployed \-im-'plȯid\ *adj* : having less than full-time or adequate employment

un·der·es·ti·mate \-'es-tə-ˌmāt\ *vb* : to set too low a value on

un·der·ex·pose \-ik-'spōz\ *vb* : to expose (a photographic plate or film) for less time than is needed — **un·der·ex·po·sure** \-'spō-zhər\ *n*

un·der·feed \ˌən-dər-'fēd\ *vb* **-fed** \-'fed\; **-feed·ing** : to feed with too little food

un·der·foot \-'fu̇t\ *adv* **1** : under the feet ⟨flowers trampled ∼⟩ **2** : close about one's feet : in the way

un·der·fur \'ən-dər-ˌfər\ *n* : an undercoat of fur esp. when thick and soft

un·der·gar·ment \-ˌgär-mənt\ *n* : a garment to be worn under another

un·der·gird \ˌən-dər-'gərd\ *vb* : to brace up : STRENGTHEN

un·der·go \ˌən-dər-'gō\ *vb* **-went** \-'went\; **-gone** \-'gȯn, -'gän\; **-go·ing** **1** : to submit to : ENDURE **2** ♦ : to go through : EXPERIENCE

   ♦ endure, experience, feel, have, know, see, suffer, sustain, taste — more at EXPERIENCE

un·der·grad \'ən-dər-ˌgrad\ *n* : UNDERGRADUATE

un·der·grad·u·ate \ˌən-dər-'gra-jə-wət, -jə-ˌwāt\ *n* : a student at a university or college who has not taken a first degree

¹un·der·ground \ˌən-dər-'grau̇nd\ *adv* **1** : beneath the surface of the earth **2** : in or into hiding or secret operation

²un·der·ground \'ən-dər-ˌgrau̇nd\ *n* **1** : a space under the surface of the ground; *esp* : SUBWAY **2** : a secret political movement or group; *esp* : an organized body working in secret to overthrow a government or an occupying power **3** : an avant-garde group or movement that operates outside the establishment

³underground \'ən-dər-ˌgrau̇nd\ *adj* **1** : being, growing, operating, or located below the surface of the ground ⟨∼ stems⟩ **2** ♦ : conducted by secret means **3** : produced or published by the underground ⟨∼ publications⟩; *also* : of or relating to the avant-garde underground

   ♦ clandestine, covert, furtive, hugger-mugger, private, secret, sneak, sneaky, stealthy, surreptitious, undercover, underhanded — more at SECRET

un·der·growth \'ən-dər-ˌgrōth\ *n* : low growth (as of herbs and shrubs) on the floor of a forest

¹un·der·hand \'ən-dər-ˌhand\ *adv* **1** : in a clandestine or secret manner **2** : with an underhand motion

²underhand *adj* **1** : marked by secrecy, chicanery, and deception : not honest and aboveboard : UNDERHANDED **2** : made with the hand kept below the level of the shoulder

¹un·der·hand·ed \ˌən-dər-'han-dəd\ *adv* : UNDERHAND

²underhanded *adj* ♦ : marked by secrecy and deception — **un·der·hand·ed·ly** *adv* — **un·der·hand·ed·ness** *n*

   ♦ clandestine, covert, furtive, hugger-mugger, private, secret, sneak, sneaky, stealthy, surreptitious, undercover, underground — more at SECRET ♦ crooked, deceptive, dishonest, fast, fraudulent, shady, sharp, shifty — more at DISHONEST

un·der·lie \-'lī\ *vb* **-lay** \-'lā\; **-lain** \-'lān\; **-ly·ing** \-'lī-iŋ\

1 : to lie or be situated under **2** : to be at the basis of : form the foundation of

un·der·line \'ən-dər-ˌlīn\ *vb* **1** : to draw a line under **2** ♦ : to put emphasis on : EMPHASIZE — **underline** *n*

   ♦ accent, accentuate, emphasize, feature, highlight, play, point, stress, underscore — more at EMPHASIZE

un·der·ling \'ən-dər-liŋ\ *n* ♦ : one who is under the orders of another : SUBORDINATE

   ♦ inferior, junior, subordinate; *also* attendant, follower, retainer; domestic, menial, steward; flunky, henchman, lackey, minion; adjutant, aid, aide, assistant, coadjutor, deputy, second; helpmate, helpmeet, mate, sidekick *Ant* senior, superior

un·der·lip \ˌən-dər-'lip\ *n* : the lower lip

un·der·ly·ing \ˌən-dər-'lī-iŋ\ *adj* **1** : lying under or below **2** ♦ : of, relating to, or forming the base or essence : FUNDAMENTAL ⟨∼ principles⟩

   ♦ basic, elemental, elementary, essential, fundamental, rudimentary — more at ELEMENTARY

un·der·mine \-'mīn\ *vb* **1** : to excavate beneath **2** : to weaken or wear away secretly or gradually ⟨∼ authority⟩

un·der·most \'ən-dər-ˌmōst\ *adj* : lowest in relative position — **undermost** *adv*

¹un·der·neath \ˌən-dər-'nēth\ *prep* **1** : directly under **2** : under subjection to

²underneath *adv* **1** : below a surface or object : BENEATH **2** : on the lower side

un·der·nour·ished \ˌən-dər-'nər-isht\ *adj* : supplied with insufficient nourishment — **un·der·nour·ish·ment** \-'nər-ish-mənt\ *n*

un·der·pants \'ən-dər-ˌpants\ *n pl* : a usu. short undergarment for the lower trunk : DRAWERS

un·der·part \-ˌpärt\ *n* : a part lying on the lower side (as of a bird or mammal)

un·der·pass \-ˌpas\ *n* : a crossing of a highway and another way (as a road) at different levels; *also* : the lower level

un·der·pay \ˌən-dər-'pā\ *vb* : to pay less than what is normal or required

un·der·pin \ˌən-dər-'pin\ *vb* : to hold up or serve as a foundation or prop for

un·der·pin·ning \'ən-dər-ˌpi-niŋ\ *n* **1** ♦ : the material and construction (as a foundation) used for support of a structure **2** ♦ : something that serves as a foundation

   ♦ [1] brace, bulwark, buttress, mount, shore, stay, support — more at SUPPORT ♦ [2] base, basis, bedrock, footing, foundation, ground, groundwork, keystone — more at BASE

un·der·play \ˌən-dər-'plā\ *vb* : to treat or handle with restraint; *esp* : to play a role with subdued force

un·der·pop·u·lat·ed \ˌən-dər-'pä-pyə-ˌlā-təd\ *adj* : having a lower than normal or desirable density of population

un·der·priv·i·leged \-'priv-lijd, -'pri-və-lijd\ *adj* : having fewer esp. economic and social privileges than others

un·der·pro·duc·tion \ˌən-dər-prə-'dək-shən\ *n* : the production of less than enough to satisfy the demand or of less than the usual supply

un·der·rate \-'rāt\ *vb* : to rate or value too low

un·der·rep·re·sent·ed \-ˌre-pri-'zen-təd\ *adj* : inadequately represented

un·der·score \'ən-dər-ˌskȯr\ *vb* **1** : to draw a line under : UNDERLINE **2** ♦ : to place emphasis on : EMPHASIZE — **underscore** *n*

   ♦ accent, accentuate, emphasize, feature, highlight, play, point, stress, underline — more at EMPHASIZE

List of self-explanatory words with the prefix un- (continued)

undogmatic	undreamed	uneaten	unemphatic
undone	undrinkable	uneconomic	unenclosed
undoubled	undulled	uneconomical	unencumbered
undramatic	undutiful	unedifying	unenforceable
undraped	uneatable	unedited	unenforced

¹**un·der·sea** \ˌən-dər-'sē\ adj : being, carried on, or used beneath the surface of the sea

²**undersea** or **un·der·seas** \-'sēz\ adv : beneath the surface of the sea

un·der·sec·re·tary \ˌən-dər-'se-krə-ˌter-ē\ n : a secretary immediately subordinate to a principal secretary ⟨~ of state⟩

un·der·sell \-'sel\ vb **-sold** \-'sōld\; **-sell·ing** : to sell articles cheaper than

un·der·sexed \-'sekst\ adj : deficient in sexual desire

un·der·shirt \'ən-dər-ˌshərt\ n : a collarless undergarment with or without sleeves

un·der·shoot \ˌən-dər-'shüt\ vb **-shot** \-'shät\; **-shoot·ing** 1 : to shoot short of or below (a target) 2 : to fall short of (a runway) in landing an airplane

un·der·shorts \'ən-dər-ˌshórts\ n pl : underpants for men or boys

un·der·shot \'ən-dər-ˌshät\ adj 1 : moved by water passing beneath ⟨an ~ waterwheel⟩ 2 : having the lower front teeth projecting beyond the upper when the mouth is closed

un·der·side \'ən-dər-ˌsīd, ˌən-dər-'sīd\ n ♦ : the side or surface lying underneath

   ♦ bottom, underbelly — more at BOTTOM

un·der·signed \'ən-dər-ˌsīnd\ n, pl **undersigned** : one whose name is signed at the end of a document

un·der·sized \ˌən-dər-'sīzd\ also **un·der·size** \-'sīz\ adj ♦ : of a size less than is common, proper, or normal

   ♦ dwarf, dwarfish, fine, little, pocket, pygmy, slight, small — more at SMALL

un·der·skirt \'ən-dər-ˌskərt\ n : a skirt worn under an outer skirt; esp : PETTICOAT

un·der·staffed \ˌən-dər-'staft\ adj : inadequately staffed

un·der·stand \ˌən-dər-'stand\ vb **-stood** \-'stúd\; **-stand·ing** 1 ♦ : to grasp the meaning of : COMPREHEND 2 ♦ : to have thorough or technical acquaintance with or expertness in ⟨~ finance⟩ 3 : to have reason to believe ⟨I ~ you are leaving tomorrow⟩ 4 : INTERPRET ⟨we ~ this to be a refusal⟩ 5 : to have a sympathetic attitude 6 : to accept as settled ⟨it is *understood* that he will pay the expenses⟩ 7 ♦ : to believe or infer something to be the case — **un·der·stand·able** \-'stan-də-bəl\ adj

   ♦ [1] appreciate, apprehend, catch, catch on (to), comprehend, get, grasp, make, make out, perceive, see, seize, tumble — more at COMPREHEND ♦ [2] comprehend, grasp, know — more at KNOW ♦ [7] conclude, deduce, extrapolate, gather, infer, judge, reason — more at INFER

un·der·stand·ably \-blē\ adv : as can be easily understood

¹**un·der·stand·ing** \ˌən-dər-'stan-diŋ\ n 1 : knowledge and ability to judge : INTELLIGENCE ⟨a person of ~⟩ 2 : agreement of opinion or feeling 3 ♦ : a mutual agreement informally or tacitly entered into 4 ♦ : a mental grasp

   ♦ [3] accord, agreement, bargain, compact, contract, convention, covenant, deal, pact, settlement — more at AGREEMENT ♦ [4] appreciation, apprehension, comprehension, grasp, grip, perception — more at COMPREHENSION

²**understanding** adj ♦ : endowed with understanding : SYMPATHETIC

   ♦ compassionate, humane, sympathetic — more at SYMPATHETIC

un·der·state \ˌən-dər-'stāt\ vb 1 : to represent as less than is the case 2 : to state with restraint esp. for effect — **un·der·state·ment** n

un·der·stood \ˌən-dər-'stúd\ adj 1 : agreed upon 2 : IMPLICIT

un·der·sto·ry \'ən-dər-ˌstōr-ē, -ˌstór-\ n : the vegetative layer between the top layer of a forest and the ground cover

un·der·study \'ən-dər-ˌstə-dē\ n : one who is prepared to act another's part or take over another's duties — **understudy** \'ən-dər-ˌstə-dē, ˌən-dər-'stə-dē\ vb

un·der·sur·face \'ən-dər-ˌsər-fəs\ n : the side or surface lying underneath : UNDERSIDE

un·der·take \ˌən-dər-'tāk\ vb **-took** \-'túk\; **-tak·en** \-'tā-kən\; **-tak·ing** 1 ♦ : to take upon oneself : set about ⟨~ a task⟩ 2 : to put oneself under obligation 3 : GUARANTEE, PROMISE

   ♦ accept, assume, bear, shoulder, take over — more at ASSUME

un·der·tak·er \'ən-dər-ˌtā-kər\ n : one whose business is to prepare the dead for burial and to arrange and manage funerals

un·der·tak·ing \'ən-dər-ˌtā-kiŋ, ˌən-dər-'tā-kiŋ; 2 is \'ən-dər-ˌtā-kiŋ only\ n 1 : the act of one who undertakes or engages in any project 2 : the business of an undertaker 3 : something undertaken 4 : PROMISE, GUARANTEE

under–the–counter adj : UNLAWFUL, ILLICIT ⟨~ sale of drugs⟩

un·der·tone \'ən-dər-ˌtōn\ n 1 : a low or subdued tone or utterance 2 : a subdued color (as seen through and modifying another color)

un·der·tow \-ˌtō\ n : the current beneath the surface that flows seaward when waves are breaking upon the shore

un·der·val·ue \ˌən-dər-'val-yü\ vb 1 : to value or estimate below the real worth 2 : to esteem lightly

un·der·wa·ter \ˌən-dər-'wó-tər, -'wä-\ adj ♦ : lying, growing, worn, or operating below the surface of the water ⟨an ~ camera⟩ — **un·der·wa·ter** adv

   ♦ submarine, sunken; also oceanic; abysmal, abyssal, deep, deep-sea

under way \-'wā\ adv 1 : into motion from a standstill 2 : in progress

un·der·wear \'ən-dər-ˌwar\ n : clothing or a garment worn next to the skin and under other clothing

un·der·weight \ˌən-dər-'wāt\ adj : weighing below what is normal, average, or necessary — **underweight** n

un·der·world \'ən-dər-ˌwərld\ n 1 : the place of departed souls : HADES 2 : the side of the world opposite to one 3 : the world of organized crime

un·der·write \'ən-dər-ˌrīt, ˌən-dər-'rīt\ vb **-wrote** \-ˌrōt, -'rōt\; **-writ·ten** \-ˌrit-ᵊn, -'rit-ᵊn\; **-writ·ing** 1 : to write under or at the end of something else 2 : to set one's name to an insurance policy and thereby become answerable for a designated loss or damage 3 : to subscribe to : agree to 4 ♦ : to guarantee financial support of — **un·der·writ·er** n

   ♦ capitalize, endow, finance, fund, stake, subsidize — more at FINANCE

un·de·sign·ing \ˌən-di-'zī-niŋ\ adj : having no artful, ulterior, or fraudulent purpose : SINCERE

un·de·sir·able \-'zī-rə-bəl\ adj : not desirable — **undesirable** n

un·de·sired \-di-'zīrd\ adj ♦ : not desired : UNWANTED

   ♦ unasked, unbidden, uninvited, unsolicited, unsought, unwanted, unwelcome — more at UNSOUGHT

un·de·ter·mined \-di-'tər-mənd\ adj 1 ♦ : not yet definitely

List of self-explanatory words with the prefix un- (continued)

unenlightened	unexamined	unexplained	unfading
unenterprising	unexcelled	unexploded	unfaltering
unenviable	unexcited	unexplored	unfashionably
unequipped	unexciting	unexposed	unfavorably
unessential	unexpired	unexpurgated	unfeasible

or authoritatively decided, settled, or fixed **2** : not bounded by definite limits or restrictions **3** : not determinate in form or character

♦ open, pending, undecided, unresolved, unsettled — more at PENDING

un·de·vi·at·ing \-'dē-vē-,ā-tiŋ\ *adj* ♦ : keeping a true course

♦ steady, unchanging, uniform, unvarying, unwavering — more at UNIFORM

un·dies \'ən-dēz\ *n pl* : UNDERWEAR; *esp* : women's underwear

un·di·lut·ed \,ən-dī-'lü-təd\ *adj* ♦ : not diluted

♦ absolute, fine, neat, plain, pure, refined, straight, unadulterated, unmixed — more at PURE

un·dis·turbed \-di-'stərbd\ *adj* ♦ : not disturbed

♦ calm, collected, composed, cool, placid, self-possessed, serene, tranquil, unperturbed, unshaken, untroubled, unworried — more at CALM

un·di·vid·ed \-də-'vī-dəd\ *adj* ♦ : not divided

♦ all, concentrated, entire, whole — more at WHOLE

un·do \-'dü\ *vb* **-did** \-'did\; **-done** \-'dən\; **-do·ing** **1** ♦ : to make or become unfastened or loosened **2** : to make null or as if not done : REVERSE **3** : to bring to ruin **4** ♦ : to disturb the composure of

♦ [1] unbind, untie — more at UNTIE ♦ [4] agitate, bother, concern, discompose, disquiet, distress, disturb, exercise, freak, perturb, unhinge, unsettle, upset, worry

un·doc·u·ment·ed \ən-'dä-kyə-,men-təd\ *adj* **1** : not supported by documentary evidence **2** : lacking documents required for legal immigration

un·do·ing *n* : a cause of ruin

un·do·mes·ti·cat·ed \-də-'mes-ti-,kā-təd\ *adj* ♦ : not domesticated

♦ feral, savage, unbroken, untamed, wild — more at WILD

un·doubt·ed \-'daù-təd\ *adj* : not doubted or called into question : CERTAIN

un·doubt·ed·ly *adv* ♦ : in an undoubted manner

♦ certainly, definitely, doubtless, incontestably, indeed, indisputably, really, surely, truly, undeniably, unquestionably — more at INDEED

¹un·dress \-'dres\ *vb* ♦ : to remove the clothes or covering of : STRIP

♦ strip, unclothe; *also* bare, denude, divest, expose, uncover, unveil; bark, flay, peel, skin *Ant* dress, gown, robe

²undress *n* **1** : informal dress; *esp* : a loose robe or dressing gown **2** : ordinary dress **3** : NUDITY

un·dressed \-'dresd\ *adj* ♦ : not dressed

♦ crude, native, natural, raw, unprocessed, unrefined, untreated — more at CRUDE ♦ bare, naked, nude, unclad, unclothed — more at NAKED

un·due \-'dü, -'dyü\ *adj* **1** : not due **2** : exceeding or violating propriety or fitness : EXCESSIVE

un·du·lant \'ən-jə-lənt, 'ən-də-, -dyə-\ *adj* : rising and falling in waves ⟨∼ hills⟩

undulant fever *n* : a human disease caused by bacteria from infected domestic animals or their products and marked by intermittent fever, chills, headache, weakness, and weight loss

un·du·late \-,lāt\ *vb* **-lat·ed**; **-lat·ing** [LL *undula* small wave, fr. L *unda* wave] **1** : to have a wavelike motion or appearance **2** : to rise and fall in pitch or volume

un·du·la·tion \,ən-jə-'lā-shən, ,ən-də-, -dyə-\ *n* **1** : wavy

or wavelike motion **2** : pulsation of sound **3** : a wavy appearance or outline — **un·du·la·to·ry** \'ən-jə-lə-,tōr-ē, 'ən-də-, -dyə-\ *adj*

un·du·ly \-'dü-lē, 'ən-, -'dyü-\ *adv* : in an undue manner : EXCESSIVELY

un·dyed \-'dīd\ *adj* : not dyed

un·dy·ing \-'dī-iŋ\ *adj* ♦ : not dying : IMMORTAL

♦ ceaseless, dateless, deathless, endless, eternal, everlasting, immortal, permanent, perpetual, unending — more at EVERLASTING

un·ea·ger \-'ē-gər\ *adj* ♦ : showing no eagerness

♦ halfhearted, tepid, unenthusiastic — more at TEPID

un·earned \-'ərnd\ *adj* : not earned by labor, service, or skill ⟨∼ income⟩

un·earth \-'ərth\ *vb* **1** : to dig up out of or as if out of the earth ⟨∼ buried treasure⟩ **2** : to bring to light : DISCOVER ⟨∼ a secret⟩

un·earth·ly \-lē\ *adj* **1** : not of or belonging to the earth **2** ♦ : departing from what is usual or normal esp. so as to appear to transcend the laws of nature

♦ magical, miraculous, phenomenal, superhuman, supernatural, uncanny — more at SUPERNATURAL ♦ creepy, eerie, haunting, spooky, uncanny, weird — more at EERIE

un·eas·i·ness \-'ē-zē-nəs\ *n* ♦ : the quality or state of being uneasy

♦ disquiet, ferment, restlessness, turmoil, unrest — more at UNREST ♦ agitation, anxiety, apprehension, care, concern, disquiet, nervousness, perturbation, worry — more at ANXIETY

un·easy \-'ē-zē\ *adj* **1** ♦ : marked by lack of ease : AWKWARD ⟨∼ among strangers⟩ **2** ♦ : disturbed by pain or worry **3** : lacking or denying rest **4** : UNSTABLE ⟨an ∼ truce⟩ — **un·eas·i·ly** \-'ē-zə-lē\ *adv*

♦ [1] awkward, clumsy, gauche, graceless, inelegant, stiff, stilted, uncomfortable, ungraceful, wooden — more at AWKWARD ♦ [2] aflutter, anxious, edgy, jittery, jumpy, nervous, nervy, perturbed, tense, troubled, upset, worried — more at NERVOUS

un·ed·u·cat·ed \-'e-jə-,kā-təd\ *adj* ♦ : not educated

♦ dark, ignorant, illiterate, simple, unlearned, untaught — more at IGNORANT

un·em·bar·rassed \-im-'bar-əsd\ *adj* ♦ : free from embarrassment

♦ unabashed, unashamed, unblushing — more at UNABASHED

un·emo·tion·al \-i-'mō-shə-nəl\ *adj* ♦ : not emotional : not easily aroused or excited

♦ apathetic, cold-blooded, impassive, phlegmatic, stoic, stolid — more at IMPASSIVE

un·em·ployed \-im-'ploid\ *adj* : not being used; *also* : having no job

un·em·ploy·ment \-'ploi-mənt\ *n* **1** : lack of employment **2** : money paid at regular intervals (as by a government agency) to an unemployed person

un·end·ing \-'en-diŋ\ *adj* ♦ : having no ending : ENDLESS

♦ ceaseless, dateless, deathless, endless, eternal, everlasting, immortal, permanent, perpetual, undying — more at EVERLASTING

un·en·dur·able \-in-'d(y)ùr-ə-bəl\ *adj* ♦ : not endurable : UNBEARABLE

♦ insufferable, insupportable, intolerable, unbearable, unsupportable — more at UNBEARABLE

List of self-explanatory words with the prefix *un-* (continued)

unfenced	unfitted	unforeseeable	unfree
unfermented	unflattering	unforgiving	unfulfilled
unfertilized	unflavored	unformulated	unfunded
unfilled	unfocused	unfortified	unfurnished
unfiltered	unfolded	unframed	unfussy

un·en·thu·si·as·tic \-in-ˌthü-zē-'as-tik\ *adj* ♦ : lacking ardor or excitement

♦ halfhearted, tepid, uneager — more at TEPID

un·equal \-'ē-kwəl\ *adj* 1 : not alike (as in size, amount, number, or value) 2 ♦ : not uniform 3 : badly balanced or matched 4 : INADEQUATE, INSUFFICIENT ⟨∼ to the task⟩ — un·equal·ly *adv*

♦ erratic, irregular, uneven, unstable, unsteady — more at UNEVEN

un·equaled *or* un·equalled \-kwəld\ *adj* ♦ : not equaled : UNPARALLELED

♦ incomparable, inimitable, matchless, nonpareil, only, peerless, unmatched, unparalleled, unrivaled, unsurpassed — more at ONLY

un·equiv·o·cal \-i-'kwi-və-kəl\ *adj* 1 ♦ : leaving no doubt 2 ♦ : not questionable — un·equiv·o·cal·ly *adv*

♦ [1] clear-cut, definite, definitive, explicit, express, specific, unambiguous — more at EXPLICIT ♦ [2] clear, distinct, evident, manifest, obvious, plain, unambiguous, unmistakable — more at CLEAR

un·err·ing \-'er-iŋ, ˌən-'ər-\ *adj* : making no errors : CERTAIN, UNFAILING — un·err·ing·ly *adv*

UNES·CO \yù-'nes-kō\ *abbr* United Nations Educational, Scientific, and Cultural Organization

un·eth·i·cal \ˌən-'e-thi-kəl\ *adj* ♦ : not conforming to approved standards of behavior, a socially accepted code, or professionally endorsed principles and practices

♦ cutthroat, immoral, Machiavellian, unconscionable, unprincipled, unscrupulous

un·even \-'ē-vən\ *adj* 1 : ODD 3 2 ♦ : not even : not level or smooth 3 ♦ : not uniform : IRREGULAR; *also* : varying in quality 4 : varying from the straight or parallel — un·even·ly *adv* — un·even·ness *n*

♦ [2] broken, bumpy, coarse, irregular, jagged, lumpy, pebbly, ragged, rough, rugged; *also* lopsided, unbalanced; inexact, irregular, unaligned; undulating, wavy; harsh, scraggly, scratchy; nonuniform *Ant* even, flat, level, plane, smooth ♦ [3] erratic, irregular, unequal, unstable, unsteady; *also* capricious, changeable, changeful, choppy, fickle, fluid, inconsistent, inconstant, mercurial, mutable, uncertain, unsettled, variable, volatile *Ant* constant, stable, steady, unchanging, unvarying

un·event·ful \-i-'vent-fəl\ *adj* : lacking interesting or noteworthy incidents — un·event·ful·ly *adv*

un·ex·am·pled \-ig-'zam-pəld\ *adj* : having no example or parallel : UNPARALLELED

un·ex·cep·tion·able \-ik-'sep-shə-nə-bəl\ *adj* : not open to exception or objection : beyond reproach

un·ex·cep·tion·al \-ik-'sep-shə-nəl\ *adj* 1 : open to no objection 2 : allowing no exception 3 ♦ : constituting no exception to the general rule

♦ average, common, commonplace, everyday, normal, ordinary, prosaic, routine, run-of-the-mill, standard, unremarkable, usual, workaday — more at ORDINARY

un·ex·pect·ed \-ik-'spek-təd\ *adj* ♦ : not expected : UNFORESEEN

♦ sudden, unanticipated, unforeseen; *also* unintended, unplanned; improbable, unlikely; startling, surprising *Ant* anticipated, expected, foreseen

un·ex·pect·ed·ly *adv* : in an unexpected manner

un·ex·pressed \-ik-'spresd\ *adj* ♦ : not expressed : not uttered in words

♦ implicit, tacit, unspoken, unvoiced, wordless — more at IMPLICIT

un·fail·ing \-'fā-liŋ\ *adj* 1 ♦ : not failing, flagging, or waning 2 : INEXHAUSTIBLE 3 : incapable of error

♦ certain, infallible, sure — more at INFALLIBLE

un·fail·ing·ly *adv* ♦ : in an unfailing manner : without fail

♦ always, constantly, continually, ever, forever, incessantly, invariably, perpetually — more at ALWAYS

un·fair \-'far\ *adj* 1 ♦ : marked by injustice, partiality, or deception 2 : not equitable in business dealings — un·fair·ly *adv* — un·fair·ness *n*

♦ dirty, foul, illegal, unsportsmanlike

un·faith·ful \-'fāth-fəl\ *adj* 1 ♦ : not observant of vows, allegiance, or duty : DISLOYAL 2 : INACCURATE, UNTRUSTWORTHY — un·faith·ful·ly *adv*

♦ disloyal, faithless, false, fickle, inconstant, loose, perfidious, recreant, traitorous, treacherous, untrue — more at FAITHLESS

un·faith·ful·ness *n* ♦ : the quality or state of being unfaithful

♦ disloyalty, faithlessness, falseness, falsity, inconstancy, infidelity, perfidy — more at INFIDELITY

un·fa·mil·iar \-fə-'mil-yər\ *adj* 1 ♦ : not well-known : STRANGE ⟨an ∼ place⟩ 2 : not well acquainted ⟨∼ with the subject⟩

♦ fresh, new, novel, original, strange, unknown — more at NEW

un·fa·mil·iar·i·ty \-ˌmi-lē-'ar-ə-tē, -'yar-\ *n* : the quality or state of being unfamiliar

un·fash·ion·able \-'fa-shə-nə-bəl\ *adj* ♦ : not in accord with or not following current fashion : not favored socially

♦ dowdy, inelegant, tacky, tasteless, trashy, unstylish — more at TACKY

un·fas·ten \-'fas-ᵊn\ *vb* : to make or become loose : UNDO

un·fath·om·able \-'fa-thə-mə-bəl\ *adj* 1 ♦ : not capable of being fathomed : IMMEASURABLE 2 ♦ : incomprehensible

♦ [1] boundless, endless, illimitable, immeasurable, indefinite, infinite, limitless, measureless, unbounded, unlimited — more at INFINITE ♦ [2] impenetrable, incomprehensible — more at INCOMPREHENSIBLE

un·fa·vor·able *or Can and Brit* un·fa·vour·able \-'fā-və-rə-bəl\ *adj* 1 : set or placed in opposition 2 ♦ : not propitious : DISADVANTAGEOUS

♦ adverse, counter, disadvantageous, hostile, inimical, negative, prejudicial, unfriendly, unsympathetic — more at ADVERSE

un·feel·ing \-'fē-liŋ\ *adj* 1 ♦ : lacking feeling 2 ♦ : devoid of kindness or sympathy — un·feel·ing·ly *adv*

♦ [1] asleep, dead, numb — more at NUMB ♦ [2] callous, hard, heartless, merciless, pitiless, stony, uncharitable, unsparing, unsympathetic — more at HARD

un·feigned \-'fānd\ *adj* : not feigned : not hypocritical : GENUINE

un·fem·i·nine \-'fe-mə-nən\ *adj* : not characteristic of, typical of, or appropriate for a woman : not feminine

un·fet·ter \-'fe-tər\ *vb* 1 : to free from fetters 2 ♦ : to loose from restraint : LIBERATE

♦ discharge, emancipate, enfranchise, free, liberate, loose, loosen, manumit, release, spring, unbind, unchain — more at FREE

un·fil·ial \-'fi-lē-əl, -'fil-yəl\ *adj* : not observing the obligations of a child to a parent : UNDUTIFUL

List of self-explanatory words with the prefix *un*- (continued)

ungentlemanly	ungraded	unhackneyed	unhealed
ungerminated	ungrammatical	unhardened	unheated
unglamorous	unground	unharmed	unheeded
unglazed	ungrudging	unharvested	unhelpful
ungracefully	unguided	unhatched	unheralded

un·fin·ished \-'fi-nisht\ *adj* **1** : not brought to an end **2** : being in a rough or unpolished state

¹un·fit \-'fit\ *adj* **1** ♦ : not fit or suitable **2** : physically or mentally unsound ⟨∼ for office⟩

♦ incapable, incompetent, inept, inexpert, unqualified, unskilled, unskillful — more at INCOMPETENT ♦ improper, inappropriate, inapt, infelicitous, unbecoming, unseemly, unsuitable, wrong — more at INAPPROPRIATE

²unfit *vb* : to make unfit : DISQUALIFY

un·fit·ness *n* : the quality or state of being unfit

un·fix \-'fiks\ *vb* **1** : to loosen from a fastening : DETACH **2** : UNSETTLE

un·flag·ging \-'fla-giŋ\ *adj* ♦ : not flagging : continuing with vigor

♦ indefatigable, inexhaustible, tireless, untiring — more at TIRELESS

un·flap·pa·ble \-'fla-pə-bəl\ *adj* ♦ : not easily upset or panicked — **un·flap·pa·bly** *adv*

♦ imperturbable, nerveless, unshakable; *also* calm, collected, composed, cool, nonchalant, placid, self-possessed, serene, tranquil, undisturbed, unperturbed, unruffled, unshaken, untroubled, unworried *Ant* shakable

un·fledged \-'flejd\ *adj* **1** : not feathered or ready for flight **2** : not fully developed : IMMATURE

un·flinch·ing \-'flin-chiŋ\ *adj* ♦ : not flinching or shrinking — **un·flinch·ing·ly** *adv*

♦ determined, dogged, grim, implacable, relentless, unrelenting, unyielding — more at UNYIELDING

un·fold \-'fōld\ *vb* **1 a** : to open the folds of : open up **2** : to lay open to view : DISCLOSE **3** ♦ : to produce or yield flowers : BLOSSOM **4** ♦ : to open the folds of : spread or straighten out

♦ [3] bloom, blossom, blow, burgeon, flower — more at BLOOM ♦ [4] expand, extend, fan, flare, open, spread, stretch

un·fol·low \-'fä-lō\ *vb* : to stop following (someone or something) on social media

un·forced \-'fōrst\ *adj* : not forced : not compelled

un·fore·seen \-fōr-'sēn\ *adj* ♦ : not foreseen : unexpected

♦ sudden, unanticipated, unexpected — more at UNEXPECTED

un·for·get·ta·ble \-fər-'ge-tə-bəl\ *adj* : incapable of being forgotten ⟨an ∼ event⟩ — **un·for·get·ta·bly** \-blē\ *adv*

un·for·giv·able \-fər-'gi-və-bəl\ *adj* : incapable of being forgiven

♦ indefensible, inexcusable, unjustifiable, unpardonable, unwarrantable — more at INEXCUSABLE

un·formed \-'fōrmd\ *adj* **1** : not regularly formed or ordered : UNDEVELOPED **2** ♦ : not formed

♦ amorphous, formless, shapeless, unshaped, unstructured — more at FORMLESS

un·for·tu·nate \-'fōr-chə-nət\ *adj* **1** ♦ : not fortunate : UNLUCKY **2** ♦ : attended with misfortune **3** : UNSUITABLE **4** ♦ : admitting of or deserving regret : fit to be deplored — **unfortunate** *n*

♦ [1] hapless, ill-fated, ill-starred, luckless, unhappy, unlucky — more at UNLUCKY ♦ [2] calamitous, catastrophic, destructive, disastrous, fatal, fateful, ruinous — more at FATAL ♦ [4] deplorable, distressful, grievous, heartbreaking, lamentable, regrettable, woeful — more at REGRETTABLE

un·for·tu·nate·ly \-nət-lē\ *adv* **1** : in an unfortunate manner **2** : it is unfortunate

un·found·ed \-'faùn-dəd\ *adj* ♦ : lacking a sound basis : GROUNDLESS

♦ baseless, groundless, invalid, unreasonable, unsubstantiated, unsupported, unwarranted — more at BASELESS

un·freeze \-'frēz\ *vb* **-froze** \-'frōz\; **-fro·zen** \-'frōz-ᵊn\; **-freez·ing** **1** : to cause to thaw **2** : to remove from a freeze ⟨∼ prices⟩

un·fre·quent·ed \-frē-'kwen-təd; ˌən-'frē-kwən-\ *adj* : seldom visited or traveled over

un·friend·ly \-'frend-lē\ *adj* **1** ♦ : not friendly or kind **2** ♦ : set or placed in opposition — **un·friend·li·ness** \-lē-nəs\ *n*

♦ [1] chill, chilly, cold, cold-blooded, cool, frigid, frosty, glacial, icy, unsympathetic, wintry — more at COLD ♦ [2] adverse, counter, disadvantageous, hostile, inimical, negative, prejudicial, unfavorable (*or* unfavourable), unsympathetic — more at ADVERSE

un·frock \-'fräk\ *vb* : DEFROCK

un·fruit·ful \-'früt-fəl\ *adj* **1** : not producing fruit or offspring : BARREN **2** : yielding no valuable result : UNPROFITABLE — **un·fruit·ful·ness** *n*

un·fun·ny \-'fə-nē\ *adj* : not funny : failing to achieve the humor intended

un·furl \-'fərl\ *vb* : to loose from a furled state : UNFOLD

un·gain·ly \-'gān-lē\ *adj* [*un-* + obs. *gainly* proper, becoming, fr. *gain* direct, handy, fr. ME *geyn*, fr. OE *gēn*, fr. ON *gegn*] **1** ♦ : lacking in smoothness or dexterity : CLUMSY **2** : hard to handle : UNWIELDY — **un·gain·li·ness** \-lē-nəs\ *n*

♦ awkward, clumsy, gawky, graceless, heavy-handed, lubberly, lumpish, unhandy — more at CLUMSY

un·gen·er·ous \-'je-nə-rəs\ *adj* : not generous or liberal : STINGY

un·gen·tle \-'jent-ᵊl\ *adj* : lacking in softness or congeniality

un·glued \-'glüd\ *adj* : UPSET, DISORDERED

un·god·ly \-'gäd-lē, -'gȯd-\ *adj* **1** : IMPIOUS, IRRELIGIOUS **2** : SINFUL, WICKED **3** : OUTRAGEOUS ⟨an ∼ hour⟩ **4** : offensive to civilized taste — **un·god·li·ness** \-lē-nəs\ *n*

un·gov·ern·able \-'gə-vər-nə-bəl\ *adj* : not capable of being governed, guided, or restrained : UNRULY

un·gov·erned \-'gə-vərnd\ *adj* ♦ : not subjected to regulation or control

♦ intemperate, rampant, unbridled, unchecked, uncontrolled, unhampered, unhindered, unrestrained — more at RAMPANT

un·grace·ful \-'grās-fəl\ *adj* ♦ : lacking in charm or felicity

♦ awkward, clumsy, gauche, graceless, inelegant, stiff, stilted, uncomfortable, uneasy, wooden — more at AWKWARD

un·gra·cious \-'grā-shəs\ *adj* **1** ♦ : not courteous : RUDE **2** : not pleasing : DISAGREEABLE

♦ discourteous, ill-bred, ill-mannered, impertinent, impolite, inconsiderate, rude, thoughtless, uncivil, unmannerly — more at IMPOLITE

un·grate·ful \-'grāt-fəl\ *adj* **1** : not thankful for favors **2** : DISAGREEABLE; *also* : THANKLESS — **un·grate·ful·ly** *adv* — **un·grate·ful·ness** *n*

un·guard·ed \-'gär-dəd\ *adj* **1** ♦ : vulnerable to attack : UNPROTECTED **2** ♦ : free from guile or wariness : DIRECT ⟨∼ remarks⟩ **3** ♦ : marked by lack of caution : having one's guard down

---

List of self-explanatory words with the prefix un- (continued)

unhesitating	unhygienic	unimpassioned	unimproved
unhistorical	unidentifiable	unimpeded	unincorporated
unhonored	unidiomatic	unimposing	uninfected
unhoused	unimaginative	unimpressed	uninfluenced
unhurt	unimpaired	unimpressive	uninformative

♦ [1] defenseless (or defenceless), exposed, helpless, susceptible, undefended, unprotected, unresistant, vulnerable — more at HELPLESS ♦ [2] candid, direct, forthright, foursquare, frank, honest, open, outspoken, plain, straight, straightforward, unreserved — more at FRANK ♦ [3] careless, heedless, mindless, unsafe, unwary — more at CARELESS

un·guent \'əŋ-gwənt, 'ən-\ n : a soothing or healing salve : OINTMENT

¹**un·gu·late** \'əŋ-gyə-lət, 'ən-, -ˌlāt\ adj [LL ungulatus, fr. L ungula hoof, fr. unguis nail, hoof] : having hoofs

²**ungulate** n : a hoofed mammal (as a cow, horse, or rhinoceros)

un·hal·lowed \ˌən-'ha-lōd\ adj 1 : not consecrated : UNHOLY 2 : IMPIOUS, PROFANE 3 : contrary to accepted standards : IMMORAL

un·ham·pered \-'ham-pərd\ adj ♦ : not held in check

♦ intemperate, rampant, unbridled, unchecked, uncontrolled, ungoverned, unhindered, unrestrained — more at RAMPANT

un·hand \-'hand\ vb : to remove the hand from : let go

un·hand·some \-'han-səm\ adj 1 : not beautiful or handsome : HOMELY 2 : UNBECOMING 3 : DISCOURTEOUS, RUDE

un·handy \-'han-dē\ adj 1 ♦ : hard to handle 2 : lacking in skill or dexterity : AWKWARD

♦ awkward, clumsy, cranky, cumbersome, ungainly, unwieldy — more at CUMBERSOME

un·hap·pi·ly \-'ha-pə-lē\ adv ♦ : in an unhappy manner : without pleasure

♦ agonizingly, bitterly, grievously, hard, hardly, sadly, sorrowfully, woefully, wretchedly — more at HARD

un·hap·pi·ness \-'ha-pē-nəs\ n : the quality or state of being unhappy

un·hap·py \-'ha-pē\ adj 1 ♦ : not fortunate : UNLUCKY 2 : not cheerful or glad : SAD 3 ♦ : not appropriate : INAPPROPRIATE

♦ [1] hapless, ill-fated, ill-starred, luckless, unfortunate, unlucky — more at UNLUCKY ♦ [3] improper, inappropriate, inapt, infelicitous, unbecoming, unfit, unseemly, unsuitable, wrong — more at INAPPROPRIATE

un·har·ness \-'här-nəs\ vb : to remove the harness from (as a horse)

un·health·ful \-'helth-fəl\ adj : detrimental to good health

un·healthy \-'hel-thē\ adj 1 ♦ : not conducive to health : UNWHOLESOME ⟨~ foods⟩ 2 ♦ : not in good health 3 ♦ : exposing to or involving danger

♦ [1] noisome, noxious, unwholesome; also unhygienic, unsanitary; poisonous, toxic; fatal, lethal, mortal Ant healthful, healthy ♦ [2] bad, down, ill, indisposed, peaked, punk, sick, unsound, unwell — more at SICK ♦ [3] dangerous, grave, grievous, hazardous, menacing, parlous, perilous, risky, serious, unsafe, venturesome — more at DANGEROUS

un·heard \-'hərd\ adj 1 : not heard 2 : not granted a hearing

unheard–of adj : previously unknown; esp : UNPRECEDENTED

un·he·ro·ic \-hi-'rō-ik\ adj : not heroic

un·hin·dered \-'hin-dərd\ adj : not hindered or restrained

♦ intemperate, rampant, unbridled, unchecked, uncontrolled, ungoverned, unhampered, unrestrained — more at RAMPANT

un·hinge \-'hinj\ vb 1 : to take from the hinges 2 ♦ : to make unstable esp. mentally ⟨unhinged by grief⟩

♦ craze, derange, madden — more at CRAZE ♦ agitate, bother, concern, discompose, disquiet, distress, disturb, exercise, freak, perturb, undo, unsettle, upset, worry

un·hitch \-'hich\ vb : UNFASTEN, LOOSE

un·ho·ly \-'hō-lē\ adj 1 : not holy : PROFANE, WICKED 2 : very unpleasant ⟨an ~ mess⟩ — **un·ho·li·ness** \-lē-nəs\ n

un·hook \-'hůk\ vb : to loose from a hook

un·horse \-'hȯrs\ vb : to dislodge from or as if from a horse

un·hur·ried \-'hər-ēd\ adj : not hurried : in a leisurely manner

uni·cam·er·al \ˌyü-ni-'ka-mə-rəl\ adj : having a single legislative house or chamber

UNI·CEF \'yü-nə-ˌsef\ abbr [United Nations International Children's Emergency Fund, its former name] United Nations Children's Fund

uni·cel·lu·lar \ˌyü-ni-'sel-yə-lər\ adj : having or consisting of a single cell

uni·corn \'yü-nə-ˌkȯrn\ n [ME unicorne, fr. AF, fr. LL unicornis, fr. L, having one horn, fr. unus one + cornu horn] : a mythical animal with one horn in the middle of the forehead

uni·cy·cle \'yü-ni-ˌsī-kəl\ n : a vehicle that has a single wheel and is usu. propelled by pedals

un·iden·ti·fied \ˌən-ī-'den-tə-ˌfīd\ adj ♦ : not identified though not necessarily unidentifiable

♦ anonymous, certain, one, some, unnamed, unspecified — more at CERTAIN

uni·di·rec·tion·al \ˌyü-ni-də-'rek-shə-nəl, -dī-\ adj : having, moving in, or responsive in a single direction

uni·fi·ca·tion \ˌyü-nə-fə-'kā-shən\ n ♦ : the act, process, or result of unifying : the state of being unified

♦ combination, connection, consolidation, coupling, junction, union — more at UNION

¹**uni·form** \'yü-nə-ˌfȯrm\ adj 1 ♦ : not varying 2 : of the same form with others ⟨~ procedures⟩ — **uni·form·ly** adv

♦ steady, unchanging, undeviating, unvarying, unwavering; also immutable, invariable, unalterable, unchangeable Ant changing, deviating, varying

²**uniform** vb : to clothe with a uniform

³**uniform** n : distinctive dress worn by members of a particular group (as an army or a police force)

uni·for·mi·ty \ˌyü-nə-'fȯr-mə-tē\ n, pl **-ties** : the state of being uniform

uni·fy \'yü-nə-ˌfī\ vb **-fied; -fy·ing** ♦ : to make into a unit or a coherent whole : UNITE

♦ associate, coalesce, combine, conjoin, connect, couple, fuse, join, link, marry, unite — more at UNITE

uni·lat·er·al \ˌyü-nə-'la-tə-rəl\ adj : of, having, affecting, or done by one side only — **uni·lat·er·al·ly** adv

un·imag·in·able \ˌən-i-'ma-jə-nə-bəl\ adj ♦ : not imaginable or comprehensible

♦ fantastic, implausible, inconceivable, incredible, unbelievable, unconvincing, unthinkable — more at INCREDIBLE

un·im·peach·able \-im-'pē-chə-bəl\ adj : not liable to accusation : BLAMELESS, IRREPROACHABLE

un·im·por·tant \-im-'pȯrt-ᵊnt\ adj ♦ : lacking in importance

♦ frivolous, inconsequential, inconsiderable, insignificant, little, minor, minute, negligible, slight, small, trifling, trivial; also paltry, petty, worthless; anonymous,

---

List of self-explanatory words with the prefix un- (continued)

uninhabitable	uninstall	unjointed	unlabeled
uninhabited	uninstructive	unjustified	unlamented
uninitiated	uninsured	unkept	unleavened
uninjured	unintentionally	unknowable	unlicensed
uninspired	uninviting	unknowledgeable	unlighted

nameless, obscure, unknown *Ant* important, major, meaningful, significant, substantial, weighty

un·in·formed \-in-ˈfȯrmd\ *adj* ♦ : not informed; *esp* : lacking in knowledge, awareness, or information

♦ ignorant, oblivious, unaware, unconscious, unknowing, unwitting — more at IGNORANT

un·in·hib·it·ed \-in-ˈhi-bə-təd\ *adj* ♦ : free from inhibition; *also* : boisterously informal — **un·in·hib·it·ed·ly** *adv*

♦ demonstrative, effusive, emotional, unreserved, unrestrained — more at DEMONSTRATIVE

un·in·struct·ed \-in-ˈstrək-təd\ *adj* : not instructed : deficient in knowledge or enlightenment

un·in·tel·li·gent \-ˈte-lə-jənt\ *adj* ♦ : lacking intelligence

♦ dense, dull, dumb, fatuous, mindless, obtuse, senseless, simple, slow, stupid, thick, vacuous, witless — more at STUPID

un·in·tel·li·gi·ble \-jə-bəl\ *adj* : not intelligible : OBSCURE ⟨an ~ voice mail⟩ — **un·in·tel·li·gi·bly** \-blē\ *adv*

un·in·tend·ed \-in-ˈten-dəd\ *adj* ♦ : not intended; *esp* : not deliberate

♦ accidental, casual, chance, fluky, fortuitous, incidental, unintentional, unplanned, unpremeditated, unwitting — more at ACCIDENTAL

un·in·ten·tion·al \-in-ˈten-chə-nəl\ *adj* ♦ : not intentional

♦ involuntary, unintended — more at INVOLUNTARY

un·in·ter·est·ed \-ˈin-trəs-təd, -tə-rəs-, -tə-ˌres-\ *adj* ♦ : not interested : not having the mind or feelings engaged or aroused

♦ apathetic, casual, disinterested, indifferent, insouciant, nonchalant, perfunctory, unconcerned, uncurious — more at INDIFFERENT

un·in·ter·est·ing \-ˈin-trəs-tiŋ, -ˈin-tə-rəs-tiŋ\ *adj* ♦ : not attracting interest or attention

♦ drab, dreary, dry, dull, flat, monotonous, weary

un·in·ter·rupt·ed \-ˌin-tə-ˈrəp-təd\ *adj* ♦ : not interrupted : CONTINUOUS

♦ ceaseless, continual, continuous, incessant, unbroken, unceasing — more at CONTINUOUS

un·in·vit·ed \-in-ˈvī-təd\ *adj* ♦ : not invited

♦ unasked, unbidden, undesired, unsolicited, unsought, unwanted, unwelcome — more at UNSOUGHT

union \ˈyü-nyən\ *n* **1** ♦ : an act or instance of uniting two or more things into one : the state of being so united **2** : a uniting in marriage **3** ♦ : something formed by a combining of parts or members; *esp* : a confederation of independent individuals (as nations or persons) for some common purpose **4** : an organization of workers (as a labor union or a trade union) formed to advance its members' interests esp. in respect to wages and working conditions **5** : a device emblematic of union used on or as a national flag; *also* : the upper inner corner of a flag **6** : a device for connecting parts (as of a machine); *esp* : a coupling for pipes

♦ [1] combination, connection, consolidation, coupling, junction, unification; *also* amalgamation, blend, commingling, compounding, fusion, intermingling, intermixture, mingling, mix, mixture; reunification, reunion *Ant* breakup, disconnection, dissolution, division, parting, partition, schism, split ♦ [1] affiliation, association, collaboration, cooperation, hookup, liaison, partnership, relation, relationship — more at ASSOCIATION ♦ [3] alliance, bloc, coalition, combination, combine, confederacy, confederation, federation, league — more at CONFEDERACY

union·ism \ˈyü-nyə-ˌni-zəm\ *n* **1** : the principle or policy of forming or adhering to a union; *esp, cap* : adherence to the policy of a firm federal union before or during the U.S. Civil War **2** : the principles or system of trade unions — **union·ist** *n*

union·ize \ˈyü-nyə-ˌnīz\ *vb* **-ized; -iz·ing** : to form into or cause to join a labor union — **union·i·za·tion** \ˌyü-nyə-nə-ˈzā-shən\ *n*

union jack *n* **1** : a flag consisting of the part of a national flag that signifies union **2** *cap U&J* : the national flag of the United Kingdom

unique \yu̇-ˈnēk\ *adj* **1** ♦ : being the only one of its kind **2** ♦ : very unusual — **unique·ly** *adv* — **unique·ness** *n*

♦ [1] alone, lone, only, singular, sole, solitary, special — more at ONLY ♦ [2] aberrant, abnormal, atypical, exceptional, extraordinary, freak, odd, peculiar, phenomenal, rare, singular, uncommon, uncustomary, unusual, unwonted — more at EXCEPTIONAL

uni·sex \ˈyü-nə-ˌseks\ *adj* : not distinguishable as male or female; *also* : suitable or designed for both males and females ⟨~ clothing⟩ — **unisex** *n*

uni·sex·u·al \ˌyü-nə-ˈsek-shə-wəl\ *adj* **1** : having only male or only female sex organs **2** : UNISEX

uni·son \ˈyü-nə-sən, -zən\ *n* [ME *unisoun*, fr. MF *unisson*, fr. ML *unisonus* having the same sound, fr. L *unus* one + *sonus* sound] **1** : sameness or identity in musical pitch **2** : the condition of being tuned or sounded at the same pitch or in octaves ⟨sing in ~⟩ **3** : harmonious agreement or union : ACCORD

unit \ˈyü-nət\ *n* **1** : the smallest whole number greater than zero : ONE **2** : a definite amount or quantity used as a standard of measurement **3** : a single thing, person, or group that is a constituent of a whole; *also* : a part of a military establishment that has a prescribed organization — **unit** *adj*

Uni·tar·i·an \ˌyü-nə-ˈter-ē-ən\ *n* : a member of a religious denomination stressing individual freedom of belief — **Uni·tar·i·an·ism** *n*

uni·tary \ˈyü-nə-ˌter-ē\ *adj* **1** : of or relating to a unit **2** : not divided — **uni·tar·i·ly** \ˌyü-nə-ˈter-ə-lē\ *adv*

unite \yu̇-ˈnīt\ *vb* **unit·ed; unit·ing** **1** ♦ : to put or join together so as to make one **2 a** : to join by a legal or moral bond **b** ♦ : to join in interest or fellowship **3** ♦ : to put together to form a single unit : CONSOLIDATE **4** : to act in concert

♦ [1] associate, coalesce, combine, conjoin, connect, couple, fuse, join, link, marry, unify; *also* mate, yoke; ally, confederate, league; chain, compound, hitch, hook; congregate, gather, meet; recombine, rejoin, reunify, reunite *Ant* break up, dissever, part, section, separate, sever, split, sunder ♦ [2b] ally, associate, band, club, confederate, conjoin, cooperate, federate, league — more at ALLY ♦ [3] center (*or* centre), centralize, compact, concentrate, consolidate, unify — more at CENTRALIZE

unit·ed \yu̇-ˈnī-təd\ *adj* **1** : made one : COMBINED **2** ♦ : relating to or produced by joint action **3** ♦ : being in agreement : HARMONIOUS

♦ [2] collective, common, communal, concerted, conjoint, joint, mutual, public — more at COLLECTIVE ♦ [3] agreeable, amicable, compatible, congenial, harmonious, kindred, unanimous — more at HARMONIOUS

unit·ize \ˈyü-nə-ˌtīz\ *vb* **-ized; -iz·ing** **1** : to form or convert into a unit **2** : to divide into units

uni·ty \ˈyü-nə-tē\ *n, pl* **-ties** **1** : the quality or state of be-

---

List of self-explanatory words with the prefix un- (continued)

unlikable	unloved	unmapped	unmeasurable
unlined	unloving	unmarked	unmeasured
unlit	unmade	unmarketable	unmentioned
unlivable	unmalicious	unmarred	unmerited
unlovable	unmanned	unmeant	unmilitary

ing or being made one : ONENESS 2 : a definite quantity or combination of quantities taken as one or for which 1 is made to stand in calculation 3 ♦ : a condition of harmony 4 : continuity without change ⟨∼ of purpose⟩ 5 : reference of all the parts of a literary or artistic composition to a single main idea 6 : totality of related parts

♦ balance, coherence, consonance, harmony, proportion, symmetry, symphony — more at HARMONY

univ *abbr* 1 universal 2 university

uni·valve \'yü-ni-ˌvalv\ *n* : a mollusk having a shell with only one piece; *esp* : GASTROPOD — **univalve** *adj*

uni·ver·sal \ˌyü-nə-'vər-səl\ *adj* 1 ♦ : including, covering, or affecting the whole without limit or exception ⟨a ∼ rule⟩ 2 : present or occurring everywhere 3 : used or for use among all ⟨a ∼ language⟩ 4 ♦ : comprehensively broad and versatile — **uni·ver·sal·ly** *adv*

♦ [1] blanket, common, general, generic, global, overall — more at GENERAL ♦ [1] compendious, complete, comprehensive, encyclopedic, full, global, inclusive, omnibus, panoramic — more at ENCYCLOPEDIC ♦ [4] adaptable, all-around, protean, versatile — more at VERSATILE

uni·ver·sal·i·ty \-vər-'sa-lə-tē\ *n* : the quality or state of being universal

uni·ver·sal·ize \-'vər-sə-ˌlīz\ *vb* **-ized; -iz·ing** : to make universal : GENERALIZE ⟨would ∼ equal rights⟩ — **uni·ver·sal·i·za·tion** \-ˌvər-sə-lə-'zā-shən\ *n*

universal joint *n* : a shaft coupling for transmitting rotation from one shaft to another not in a straight line with it

Universal Product Code *n* : a combination of a barcode and numbers by which a scanner can identify a product and usu. assign a price

uni·verse \'yü-nə-ˌvərs\ *n* [ME, fr. L *universum*, fr. neut. of *universus* entire, whole, fr. *unus* one + *versus* turned toward, fr. pp. of *vertere* to turn] : the whole body of things observed or assumed : COSMOS

♦ cosmos, creation, macrocosm, nature, world; *also* existence, reality

uni·ver·si·ty \ˌyü-nə-'vər-sə-tē\ *n, pl* **-ties** : an institution of higher learning authorized to confer degrees in various special fields (as theology, law, and medicine) as well as in the arts and sciences generally

un·just \ˌən-'jəst\ *adj* : characterized by injustice — **un·just·ly** *adv*

un·jus·ti·fi·able \-'jəs-tə-ˌfī-ə-bəl\ *adj* ♦ : not justifiable : lacking in propriety or justice

♦ indefensible, inexcusable, unforgivable, unpardonable, unwarrantable — more at INEXCUSABLE

un·kempt \-'kempt\ *adj* 1 a ♦ : lacking order or neatness b : ROUGH, UNPOLISHED 2 : not combed : DISHEVELED

♦ chaotic, confused, disheveled, disordered, messy, muddled, sloppy, untidy — more at MESSY

un·kind \-'kīnd\ *adj* : not kind or sympathetic ⟨an ∼ remark⟩ — **un·kind·ly** *adv* — **un·kind·ness** *n*

un·kind·ly \-'kīnd-lē\ *adj* : UNKIND — **un·kind·li·ness** *n*

un·know·ing \ˌən-'nō-iŋ\ *adj* ♦ : not knowing — **un·know·ing·ly** *adv*

♦ ignorant, oblivious, unaware, unconscious, uninformed, unwitting — more at IGNORANT

un·known \-'nōn\ *adj* ♦ : not known or not well-known — **unknown** *n*

♦ fresh, new, novel, original, strange, unfamiliar — more at NEW ♦ anonymous, nameless, obscure, unsung — more at OBSCURE

un·lace \-'lās\ *vb* : to loose by undoing a lace

un·lade \-'lād\ *vb* **-lad·ed; -laded** *or* **-lad·en** \-'lād-ᵊn\; **-lad·ing** : to take the load or cargo from : UNLOAD

un·la·dy·like \-'lā-dē-ˌlīk\ *adj* : lacking the behavior, manner, or style considered proper for a lady

un·latch \-'lach\ *vb* 1 : to open or loose by lifting the latch 2 : to become loosed or opened

un·law·ful \-'lò-fəl\ *adj* 1 ♦ : not lawful : ILLEGAL 2 : not morally right or conventional — **un·law·ful·ly** *adv*

♦ criminal, illegal, illegitimate, illicit, wrongful — more at ILLEGAL

un·lead·ed \-'le-dəd\ *adj* : not treated or mixed with lead or lead compounds

un·learn \-'lərn\ *vb* : to put out of one's knowledge or memory; *also* : to discard the habit of

un·learned \-'lər-nəd *for 1*; -'lərnd *for 2*\ *adj* 1 ♦ : possessing inadequate learning or education : UNEDUCATED 2 : not gained by study or training

♦ dark, ignorant, illiterate, simple, uneducated, untaught — more at IGNORANT

un·leash \-'lēsh\ *vb* ♦ : to free from or as if from a leash : let loose

♦ loose, loosen, release, uncork, unlock, unloosen — more at RELEASE

un·less \ən-'les, 'ən-ˌles\ *conj* : except on condition that ⟨won't go ∼ you do⟩

un·let·tered \ˌən-'le-tərd\ *adj* : not educated : ILLITERATE

¹**un·like** \-'līk\ *adj* 1 ♦ : not like : DIFFERENT 2 : UNEQUAL — **un·like·ness** *n*

♦ different, disparate, dissimilar, distinct, distinctive, distinguishable, diverse, other, unalike — more at DIFFERENT

²**unlike** *prep* 1 : different from ⟨she's quite ∼ her sister⟩ 2 : unusual for ⟨it's ∼ you to be late⟩ 3 : differently from ⟨behaves ∼ his brother⟩

un·like·li·hood \-'lī-klē-ˌhùd\ *n* : IMPROBABILITY

un·like·ly \-'lī-klē\ *adj* 1 ♦ : not likely : IMPROBABLE 2 : likely to fail

♦ doubtful, dubious, flimsy, improbable, questionable — more at IMPROBABLE

un·like·ness *n* ♦ : the quality or state of being unlike

♦ contrast, difference, disagreement, discrepancy, disparity, distinction, diversity — more at DIFFERENCE

un·lim·ber \-'lim-bər\ *vb* : to get ready for action

un·lim·it·ed \-'li-mə-təd\ *adj* 1 : lacking any controls 2 ♦ : having no bounds : without limits 3 ♦ : not bounded by exceptions

♦ [2] boundless, endless, illimitable, immeasurable, indefinite, infinite, limitless, measureless, unbounded, unfathomable — more at INFINITE ♦ [3] all-around, general, unqualified, unrestricted

un·list·ed \-'lis-təd\ *adj* 1 ♦ : not appearing on a list; *esp* : not appearing in a telephone book 2 : not listed on a stock exchange

♦ uncataloged, unrecorded, unregistered; *also* unwritten; unidentified, unspecified; undisclosed, unknown *Ant* cataloged, listed, recorded, registered

un·lit·er·ary \-'li-tə-ˌrer-ē\ *adj* : not literary

un·load \-'lōd\ *vb* 1 a : to take away or off : REMOVE ⟨∼ cargo from a hold⟩ b ♦ : to get rid of 2 ♦ : to take a load from ⟨∼ the ship⟩; *also* : to relieve or set free : UNBURDEN ⟨∼ one's mind of worries⟩ 3 : to draw the charge from ⟨∼ed the gun⟩ 4 : to sell in volume

---

List of self-explanatory words with the prefix un- (continued)

unmilled	unmoved	unnoticeable	unofficial
unmodified	unnameable	unnoticed	unofficially
unmolested	unnecessary	unobjectionable	unopened
unmotivated	unneeded	unobservant	unopposed
unmounted	unnewsworthy	unobserved	unorthodoxy

♦ [1b] cast, discard, ditch, dump, fling, jettison, junk, lose, reject, scrap, shed, shuck, slough, throw away, throw out — more at DISCARD ♦ [2] disburden, discharge, disencumber, unburden; *also* free, lighten, relieve; clear, empty, evacuate, vacate, void **Ant** load, pack

un·lock \-'läk\ *vb* **1** : to open or unfasten through release of a lock **2** ♦ : to free from restraints or restrictions : RELEASE ⟨∼ a flood of emotions⟩ **3** : DISCLOSE, REVEAL ⟨∼ nature's secrets⟩

♦ loose, loosen, release, uncork, unleash, unloosen — more at RELEASE

un·looked–for \-'lu̇kt-fȯr\ *adj* : not foreseen : UNEXPECTED

un·loose \-'lüs\ *vb* **1** : UNLOOSEN **2** : UNTIE

un·loos·en \-'lüs-ᵊn\ *vb* **1** ♦ : to relax the strain of; *also* : set free **2** : UNTIE

♦ loose, loosen, release, uncork, unleash, unlock — more at RELEASE

un·love·ly \-'ləv-lē\ *adj* **1** ♦ : having no charm or appeal **2** : not amiable

♦ bad, disagreeable, distasteful, nasty, rotten, sour, uncongenial, unpleasant, unwelcome — more at UNPLEASANT

un·luck·i·ly \-'lə-kə-lē\ *adv* : UNFORTUNATELY

un·lucky \-'lə-kē\ *adj* **1** ♦ : having or meeting with misfortune : ILL-FATED **2** : likely to bring misfortune : INAUSPICIOUS **3** : REGRETTABLE

♦ hapless, ill-fated, ill-starred, luckless, unfortunate, unhappy; *also* adverse, ill, inauspicious, unfavorable, unpromising, untoward; calamitous, catastrophic, disastrous; damned, tragic **Ant** fortunate, happy, lucky

un·man \-'man\ *vb* **1** ♦ : to deprive of manly courage **2** : CASTRATE

♦ demoralize, undo, unnerve — more at UNNERVE
♦ daunt, demoralize, discourage, dishearten, dismay, dispirit, unnerve — more at DISCOURAGE

un·man·age·able \-'ma-ni-jə-bəl\ *adj* ♦ : not manageable : INTRACTABLE

♦ froward, headstrong, intractable, recalcitrant, refractory, uncontrollable, unruly, untoward, wayward, willful — more at UNCONTROLLABLE

un·man·ly \-'man-lē\ *adj* **1** : not manly : COWARDLY **2** ♦ : having feminine qualities untypical of a man : EFFEMINATE

♦ effeminate, feminine, girlish, womanly — more at EFFEMINATE

un·man·ner·ly \-'ma-nər-lē\ *adj* ♦ : not mannerly : IMPOLITE — **unmannerly** *adv*

♦ discourteous, ill-bred, ill-mannered, impertinent, impolite, inconsiderate, rude, thoughtless, uncivil, ungracious — more at IMPOLITE

un·mar·ried \-'mar-ēd\ *adj* ♦ : not married

♦ single, unattached, unwed — more at SINGLE

un·mas·cu·line \-'mas-kyə-lən\ *adj* : not characteristic of, typical of, or appropriate for a man : not masculine

un·mask \-'mask\ *vb* **1** ♦ : to strip of a mask or a disguise : EXPOSE **2** : to remove one's mask

♦ bare, disclose, discover, divulge, expose, reveal, spill, tell, unbosom, uncloak, uncover, unveil — more at REVEAL

un·matched \-'macht\ *adj* **1** ♦ : not matchable **2** : not matching

♦ incomparable, inimitable, matchless, nonpareil, only, peerless, unequaled, unparalleled, unrivaled, unsurpassed — more at ONLY

un·mean·ing \-'mē-niŋ\ *adj* : having no meaning : SENSELESS

un·me·di·at·ed \-'mē-dē-ǝ̄,ā-təd\ *adj* : not mediated : not communicated or transformed by an intervening agency

un·meet \-'mēt\ *adj* : not meet or fit : UNSUITABLE, IMPROPER

un·me·lo·di·ous \-mə-'lō-dē-əs\ *adj* ♦ : not melodious

♦ discordant, dissonant, inharmonious, unmusical — more at DISSONANT

un·men·tion·able \-'men-chə-nə-bəl\ *adj* : not fit or proper to be talked about

un·mer·ci·ful \-'mər-si-fəl\ *adj* : not merciful : MERCILESS — **un·mer·ci·ful·ly** *adv*

un·mind·ful \-'mīnd-fəl\ *adj* : not conscientiously aware, attentive, or heedful : UNAWARE

un·mis·tak·able \-mə-'stā-kə-bəl\ *adj* ♦ : not capable of being mistaken or misunderstood : OBVIOUS — **un·mis·tak·ably** \-blē\ *adv*

♦ apparent, broad, clear, clear-cut, distinct, evident, lucid, manifest, obvious, palpable, patent, perspicuous, plain, transparent, unambiguous, unequivocal — more at CLEAR

un·mit·i·gat·ed \-'mi-tə-,gā-təd\ *adj* **1** : not softened or lessened **2** : being so definitely what is stated as to offer little chance of change or relief : ABSOLUTE ⟨an ∼ liar⟩

un·mixed \-'mikst\ *adj* ♦ : not mixed

♦ absolute, fine, neat, plain, pure, refined, straight, unadulterated, undiluted — more at PURE

un·moor \-'mu̇r\ *vb* : to loose from or as if from moorings

un·mor·al \-'mȯr-əl\ *adj* : having no moral perception or quality : AMORAL — **un·mo·ral·i·ty** \-mə-'ra-lə-tē\ *n*

un·mov·able \-'mü-və-bəl\ *adj* **1** ♦ : incapable of being moved : firmly fixed **2** ♦ : not moving or not intended to be moved

♦ [1, 2] immobile, immovable, nonmotile, stationary, unbudging — more at IMMOVABLE

un·mu·si·cal \-'myü-zi-kəl\ *adj* ♦ : not musical

♦ discordant, dissonant, inharmonious, unmelodious — more at DISSONANT

un·muz·zle \-'mə-zəl\ *vb* : to remove a muzzle from

un·named \-'nāmd\ *adj* ♦ : not named or identified

♦ anonymous, certain, one, some, unidentified, unspecified — more at CERTAIN

un·nat·u·ral \-'na-chə-rəl\ *adj* **1** : contrary to or acting contrary to nature or natural instincts **2** ♦ : not being in accordance with normal human feelings or behavior : ABNORMAL — **un·nat·u·ral·ly** *adv* — **un·nat·u·ral·ness** *n*

♦ aberrant, abnormal, anomalous, atypical, deviant, irregular — more at DEVIANT

un·nec·es·sar·i·ly \-ne-sə-'ser-ə-lē\ *adv* **1** : not by necessity **2** : to an unnecessary degree ⟨∼ harsh⟩

un·nerve \-'nərv\ *vb* **1** ♦ : to deprive of courage, strength, or steadiness **2** : to cause to become nervous

♦ demoralize, undo, unman; *also* debilitate, enervate, enfeeble, weaken; prostrate, sap, soften, tire, waste; frighten, scare, terrify, terrorize; daunt, discourage, dishearten, dismay, dispirit; craze, derange, madden, unhinge; discompose, disquiet, disturb, faze, perturb, unsettle, upset **Ant** nerve ♦ daunt, demoralize, discourage, dishearten, dismay, dispirit, unman — more at DISCOURAGE

un·nil·hex·i·um \,yün-ᵊl-'hek-sē-əm\ *n* [NL, fr. *unnil-* (fr. L *unus* one + *nil* zero) + Gk *hex* six + NL *-ium*] : the chemical element of atomic number 106

List of self-explanatory words with the prefix *un-* (continued)

un·nil·pen·ti·um \-'pen-tē-əm\ *n* : the chemical element of atomic number 105

un·nil·qua·di·um \-'kwä-dē-əm\ *n* : the chemical element of atomic number 104

un·num·bered \ˌən-'nəm-bərd\ *adj* **1** : not numbered or counted **2** ◆ : too many to be numbered : INNUMERABLE

◆ countless, innumerable, numberless, uncountable, untold — more at COUNTLESS

un·ob·struct·ed \-əb-'strək-təd\ *adj* ◆ : not obstructed or hindered

◆ clear, free, open — more at OPEN

un·ob·tain·able \-əb-'tā-nə-bəl\ *adj* ◆ : not obtainable

◆ inaccessible, inconvenient, unapproachable, unattainable, unavailable, unreachable, untouchable — more at INACCESSIBLE

un·ob·tru·sive \-əb-'trü-siv\ *adj* : not obtrusive or forward : INCONSPICUOUS — **un·ob·tru·sive·ly** *adv*

un·oc·cu·pied \-'ä-kyə-ˌpīd\ *adj* **1** : not busy : UNEMPLOYED **2** : not occupied : EMPTY, VACANT

un·or·ga·nized \-'ȯr-gə-ˌnīzd\ *adj* **1** : not formed or brought into an integrated or ordered whole **2** : not organized into unions ⟨∼ labor⟩

un·orig·i·nal \-ə-'ri-jə-nəl\ *adj* ◆ : not original

◆ imitative, mimic, slavish — more at IMITATIVE

un·or·tho·dox \-'ȯr-thə-ˌdäks\ *adj* ◆ : not orthodox : not in accord with approved, standardized, or conventional doctrine, method, thought, custom, or opinion

◆ broad-minded, liberal, nonorthodox, nontraditional, open-minded, progressive, radical, unconventional — more at LIBERAL ◆ informal, irregular, unceremonious, unconventional — more at INFORMAL

un·pack \-'pak\ *vb* **1** : to separate and remove things packed **2** : to open and remove the contents of

un·paid \-'pād\ *adj* **1** : not paid : serving without pay **2 a** : not presented as payment **b** ◆ : not cleared by payment **3** : not paying a salary

◆ outstanding, overdue, payable, unsettled — more at OUTSTANDING

un·paint·ed \-'pān-təd\ *adj* ◆ : not painted : not having a coat of paint

◆ colorless (*or* colourless), uncolored (*or* uncoloured), white — more at COLORLESS

un·pal·at·able \-'pa-lə-tə-bəl\ *adj* **1** : not palatable : DISTASTEFUL **2** : not pleasant : not amiable or agreeable

un·par·al·leled \-'par-ə-ˌleld\ *adj* **1** ◆ : having no parallel **2** ◆ : having no equal or match ⟨an ∼ achievement⟩

◆ [1, 2] incomparable, inimitable, matchless, nonpareil, only, peerless, unequaled, unmatched, unrivaled, unsurpassed — more at ONLY

un·par·don·able \-'pärd-ᵊn-ə-bəl\ *adj* ◆ : not worthy of pardon

◆ indefensible, inexcusable, unforgivable, unjustifiable, unwarrantable — more at INEXCUSABLE

un·par·lia·men·ta·ry \-ˌpär-lə-'men-tə-rē\ *adj* : contrary to parliamentary practice

un·peg \-'peg\ *vb* **1** : to remove a peg from **2** : to unfasten by or as if by removing a peg

un·per·son \'ən-ˌpərs-ᵊn, -ˌpərs-\ *n* : a person who usu. for political or ideological reasons is removed from recognition or consideration

un·per·turbed \ˌən-pər-'tərbd\ *adj* ◆ : not perturbed : unaffected by worry, interruption, disturbance, or disarrangement

◆ calm, collected, composed, cool, placid, self-possessed, serene, tranquil, undisturbed, unshaken, untroubled, unworried — more at CALM

un·pile \-'pīl\ *vb* : to take or disentangle from a pile

un·pin \-'pin\ *vb* : to remove a pin from : UNFASTEN

un·planned \-'pland\ *adj* **1** ◆ : not planned **2** ◆ : not expected

◆ [1] ad-lib, extemporaneous, impromptu, offhand, snap, unpremeditated, unprepared, unrehearsed — more at EXTEMPORANEOUS ◆ [2] accidental, casual, chance, fluky, fortuitous, incidental, unintended, unintentional, unpremeditated, unwitting — more at ACCIDENTAL

un·pleas·ant \-'plez-ᵊnt\ *adj* ◆ : not pleasant : DISAGREEABLE — **un·pleas·ant·ly** *adv* — **un·pleas·ant·ness** *n*

◆ bad, disagreeable, distasteful, nasty, rotten, sour, uncongenial, unlovely, unwelcome; *also* abhorrent, abominable, appalling, awful, beastly, disgusting, dreadful, foul, hideous, horrendous, horrible, horrid, invidious, loathsome, nauseating, noisome, obnoxious, obscene, odious, repellent, repugnant, repulsive, revolting, scandalous, shocking, sickening, ugly, villainous; annoying, galling, irritating, vexing **Ant** agreeable, nice, pleasant, pleasing, pleasurable, satisfying, welcome

un·pleas·ing \-'plē-ziŋ\ *adj* : not pleasing : causing discomfort, displeasure, or repugnance

un·plug \-'pləg\ *vb* **1** : UNCLOG **2** : to remove (a plug) from a receptacle; *also* : to disconnect from an electric circuit by removing a plug

un·plumbed \-'pləmd\ *adj* **1** : not tested or measured with a plumb line **2** : not thoroughly explored

un·pol·ished \-'pä-lisht\ *adj* **1** : not made smooth by polishing **2** ◆ : not marked by refinement

◆ coarse, common, crass, crude, gross, ill-bred, low, rough, rude, tasteless, uncouth, uncultivated, uncultured, unrefined, vulgar — more at COARSE

un·pop·u·lar \-'pä-pyə-lər\ *adj* : not popular : looked upon or received unfavorably — **un·pop·u·lar·i·ty** \-ˌpä-pyə-'lar-ə-tē\ *n*

un·prec·e·dent·ed \-'pre-sə-ˌden-təd\ *adj* : having no precedent : NOVEL

un·pre·dict·able \-pri-'dik-tə-bəl\ *adj* ◆ : not predictable

◆ capricious, changeable, fickle, fluid, inconstant, mercurial, mutable, temperamental, uncertain, unsettled, unstable, unsteady, variable, volatile — more at FICKLE

un·prej·u·diced \-'pre-jə-dəst\ *adj* ◆ : not prejudiced : free from undue bias

◆ disinterested, dispassionate, equal, equitable, fair, impartial, just, nonpartisan, objective, square, unbiased — more at FAIR

un·pre·med·i·tat·ed \-pri-'me-də-ˌtā-təd\ *adj* ◆ : not premeditated

◆ accidental, casual, chance, fluky, fortuitous, incidental, unintended, unintentional, unplanned, unwitting — more at ACCIDENTAL

un·pre·pared \-pri-'pard\ *adj* **1** : not prepared **2 a** ◆ : happening without preparation **b** : arriving or taking place unexpectedly or without warning

◆ ad-lib, extemporaneous, impromptu, offhand, snap, unplanned, unpremeditated, unrehearsed — more at EXTEMPORANEOUS

un·pre·tend·ing \-pri-'ten-diŋ\ *adj* : not pretending; *esp* : UNPRETENTIOUS

un·pre·ten·tious \-pri-'ten-chəs\ *adj* ◆ : not pretentious

List of self-explanatory words with the prefix *un-* (continued)

unpredictability	unprofessed	unpropitious	unpunished
unpreparedness	unprogrammed	unproven	unquenchable
unprepossessing	unpromising	unprovided	unquestioned
unpressed	unprompted	unprovoked	unraised
unprivileged	unpronounceable	unpublished	unrated

♦ artless, genuine, honest, ingenuous, innocent, naive, natural, real, simple, sincere, true, unaffected ♦ demure, humble, lowly, meek, modest, retiring, unassuming — more at HUMBLE

un·pret·ty \-ˈpri-tē\ *adj* : not pretty : lacking in beauty

un·prin·ci·pled \-ˈprin-sə-pəld\ *adj* ♦ : lacking sound or honorable principles : UNSCRUPULOUS ⟨an ∼ politician⟩

♦ cutthroat, immoral, Machiavellian, unconscionable, unethical, unscrupulous; *also* calculating, intriguing, opportunistic, scheming; merciless, pitiless, remorseless, ruthless; crooked, deceitful, dishonest; corrupt, debased, debauched, decadent, degenerate, degraded, demoralized, depraved, dissipated *Ant* ethical, moral, principled, scrupulous

un·print·able \-ˈprin-tə-bəl\ *adj* ♦ : unfit to be printed; *esp* : too obscene or offensive to be shown in print

♦ bawdy, coarse, crude, dirty, filthy, foul, gross, indecent, lascivious, lewd, nasty, obscene, pornographic, ribald, smutty, vulgar, wanton — more at OBSCENE

un·pro·cessed \-ˈprä-ˌsest, -ˈprō-\ *adj* ♦ : not processed; *esp* : not altered from an original or natural state

♦ crude, native, natural, raw, undressed, unrefined, untreated — more at CRUDE

un·pro·duc·tive \-prə-ˈdək-tiv\ *adj* ♦ : not productive

♦ barren, infertile, poor, stark, waste — more at BARREN ♦ fruitless, futile, ineffective, unsuccessful — more at FUTILE

un·pro·fes·sion·al \-prə-ˈfe-shə-nəl\ *adj* **1** : not belonging to or gainfully employed at a particular profession **2** ♦ : not characteristic of or befitting a professional

♦ amateur, amateurish, inexperienced, inexpert, nonprofessional, unskilled, unskillful — more at AMATEURISH

un·prof·it·able \-ˈprä-fə-tə-bəl\ *adj* : not profitable : USELESS

un·pro·gres·sive \-prə-ˈgre-siv\ *adj* : not progressive; *esp* : not devoted to or showing economic, social, or political progress

un·pro·tect·ed \-prə-ˈtek-təd\ *adj* ♦ : lacking protection or defense

♦ defenseless (*or* defenceless), exposed, helpless, susceptible, undefended, unguarded, unresistant, vulnerable — more at HELPLESS

un·qual·i·fied \-ˈkwä-lə-ˌfīd\ *adj* **1** ♦ : not having requisite qualifications **2** ♦ : not modified or restricted by reservations : COMPLETE — **un·qual·i·fied·ly** \-ˌfī-əd-lē\ *adv*

♦ [1] incapable, incompetent, inept, inexpert, unfit, unskilled, unskillful — more at INCOMPETENT ♦ [2] absolute, complete, outright, total, unequivocal ♦ [2] all-around, general, unlimited, unrestricted

un·ques·tion·able \-ˈkwes-chə-nə-bəl\ *adj* ♦ : not questionable : INDISPUTABLE

♦ incontestable, indisputable, indubitable, irrefutable, unanswerable, undeniable — more at IRREFUTABLE

un·ques·tion·ably \-blē\ *adv* ♦ : without any question

♦ certainly, definitely, doubtless, incontestably, indeed, indisputably, really, surely, truly, undeniably, undoubtedly — more at INDEED

un·ques·tion·ing \-chə-niŋ\ *adj* : not questioning : accepting without examination or hesitation ⟨∼ obedience⟩ — **un·ques·tion·ing·ly** *adv*

un·qui·et \-ˈkwī-ət\ *adj* **1** : not quiet : AGITATED, DISTURBED **2** : physically, emotionally, or mentally restless : UNEASY

un·quote \ˈən-ˌkwōt\ *n* — used orally to indicate the end of a direct quotation

un·rav·el \ˌən-ˈra-vəl\ *vb* **1** ♦ : to separate the threads of **2** ♦ : to resolve the intricacy, complexity, or obscurity of : clear up ⟨∼ a mystery⟩ **3** : to become unraveled

♦ [1] disentangle, untangle, untwine; *also* smooth, straighten (out); undo, unlace, untie, unwind *Ant* entangle, snarl, tangle ♦ [2] answer, break, crack, dope, figure out, puzzle, resolve, riddle, solve, work, work out — more at SOLVE

un·reach·able \-ˈrēch-ə-bəl\ *adj* ♦ : incapable of being reached

♦ inaccessible, inconvenient, unapproachable, unattainable, unavailable, unobtainable, untouchable — more at INACCESSIBLE

un·read \-ˈred\ *adj* **1** : not read; *also* : left unexamined **2** : lacking the benefits or the experience of reading

un·re·al \-ˈrēl\ *adj* ♦ : lacking in reality, substance, or genuineness

♦ chimerical, fabulous, fanciful, fantastic, fictitious, imaginary, made-up, mythical, phantom, pretend — more at IMAGINARY

un·re·al·i·ty \-rē-ˈa-lə-tē\ *n* **1 a** : the quality or state of being unreal : lack of substance or validity **b** ♦ : something unreal, insubstantial, or visionary **2** : ineptitude in dealing with reality

♦ chimera, conceit, daydream, delusion, dream, fancy, fantasy, figment, hallucination, illusion, phantasm, pipe dream, vision — more at FANTASY

un·rea·son·able \-ˈrēz-ᵊn-ə-bəl\ *adj* **1 a** ♦ : not governed by or acting according to reason **b** ♦ : not conformable to reason **2** : exceeding the bounds of reason or moderation — **un·rea·son·able·ness** *n* — **un·rea·son·ably** *adv*

♦ [1a] fallacious, illogical, invalid, irrational, unsound, weak — more at ILLOGICAL ♦ [1b] baseless, groundless, invalid, unfounded, unsubstantiated, unsupported, unwarranted — more at BASELESS

un·rea·soned \-ˈrēz-ᵊnd\ *adj* : not based on reason or reasoning

un·rea·son·ing \-ˈrēz-ᵊn-iŋ\ *adj* : not using or showing the use of reason as a guide or control

un·re·con·struct·ed \-ˌrē-kən-ˈstrək-təd\ *adj* : not reconciled to some political, economic, or social change; *esp* : holding stubbornly to a particular belief, view, place, or style

un·re·cord·ed \-ri-ˈkȯr-dəd\ *adj* **1** ♦ : not recorded **2** : not made a matter of official record

♦ uncataloged, unlisted, unregistered — more at UNLISTED

un·re·cov·er·able \-ri-ˈkə-və-rə-bəl\ *adj* **1** ♦ : incapable of being recovered, recaptured, or regained : hopelessly lost **2** : admitting of no remedy or correction

♦ irredeemable, irremediable, irreparable, unredeemable — more at IRREPARABLE

un·re·deem·able \-ri-ˈdē-mə-bəl\ *adj* **1** : admitting of no change or release **2** ♦ : insusceptible of redemption or reform : utterly and hopelessly bad **3** : not redeemable : not recoverable on payment of what is due

♦ hopeless, incorrigible, incurable, irredeemable, irremediable, unrecoverable — more at HOPELESS

un·reel \-ˈrēl\ *vb* **1** : to unwind from or as if from a reel **2** : to perform successfully

un·re·fined \-ri-ˈfīnd\ *adj* **1** ♦ : lacking moral or social

---

List of self-explanatory words with the prefix un- (continued)

unratified	unrecognizable	unrelated	unrepresentative
unreadable	unrecognized	unrelieved	unrepresented
unready	unreflecting	unremembered	unrepressed
unrealistic	unreflective	unremovable	unresponsive
unrealized	unregulated	unreported	unresponsiveness

cultivation or the graces of manners or speech   **2 ♦** : not separated from impurity or unwanted matter

♦ [1] coarse, common, crass, crude, gross, ill-bred, low, rough, rude, tasteless, uncouth, uncultivated, uncultured, unpolished, vulgar — more at COARSE ♦ [2] crude, native, natural, raw, undressed, unprocessed, untreated — more at CRUDE

un·re·gen·er·ate \-ri-'je-nə-rət\ *adj* : not regenerated or reformed
un·reg·is·tered \-'re-jə-stərd\ *adj* ♦ : not registered

♦ uncataloged, unlisted, unrecorded — more at UNLISTED

un·re·hearsed \-ri-'hərst\ *adj*   **1** : not narrated   **2 ♦** : not practiced or prepared

♦ ad-lib, extemporaneous, impromptu, offhand, snap, unplanned, unpremeditated, unprepared — more at EXTEMPORANEOUS

un·re·lent·ing \-'len-tiŋ\ *adj*   **1 ♦** : not yielding in determination ⟨∼ leader⟩   **2 ♦** : not letting up or weakening in vigor or pace — **un·re·lent·ing·ly** *adv*

♦ [1, 2] determined, dogged, grim, implacable, relentless, unflinching, unyielding — more at UNYIELDING

un·re·li·able \-ri-'lī-ə-bəl\ *adj* : not reliable or trustworthy
un·re·mark·able \-ri-'mär-kə-bəl\ *adj* ♦ : lacking interest or distinction : of a kind to be expected in the normal course of events

♦ average, common, commonplace, everyday, normal, ordinary, prosaic, routine, run-of-the-mill, standard, unexceptional, usual, workaday — more at ORDINARY

un·re·mit·ting \-'mi-tiŋ\ *adj* : not remitting : CONSTANT — **un·re·mit·ting·ly** *adv*
un·re·pen·tant \-ri-'pen-t³nt\ *adj*   **1** : not repentant   **2** : holding to a prior conviction or attitude
un·re·quit·ed \-ri-'kwī-təd\ *adj* : not reciprocated or returned in kind ⟨∼ love⟩
un·re·served \-'zərvd\ *adj*   **1** : not limited or partial ⟨∼ enthusiasm⟩   **2 ♦** : not cautious or reticent   **3** : not set aside for special use — **un·re·serv·ed·ly** \-'zər-vəd-lē\ *adv*

♦ candid, direct, forthright, foursquare, frank, honest, open, outspoken, plain, straight, straightforward, unguarded — more at FRANK

un·re·sis·tant \-ri-'zis-tənt\ *adj* ♦ : not resistant

♦ defenseless (*or* defenceless), exposed, helpless, susceptible, undefended, unguarded, unprotected, vulnerable — more at HELPLESS

un·re·sist·ing \-ri-'zis-tiŋ\ *adj* ♦ : not resistant

♦ acquiescent, passive, resigned, tolerant, unresistant, yielding — more at PASSIVE

un·re·solved \-ri-'zälvd\ *adj* ♦ : not yet determined

♦ open, pending, undecided, undetermined, unsettled — more at PENDING

un·rest \-'rest\ *n* ♦ : a disturbed or uneasy state : TURMOIL

♦ disquiet, ferment, restlessness, turmoil, uneasiness; *also* fidgets; agitation, commotion, confusion, tumult, turbulence, upheaval; anarchy, chaos, disorder **Ant** calm, ease, peace, quiet

un·rest·ful \-'rest-fəl\ *adj* : not restful : not feeling or not conducive to repose
un·re·strained \-ri-'strānd\ *adj*   **1 ♦** : not restrained   **2 ♦** : free of constraint, inhibition, or timidity

♦ [1] intemperate, rampant, unbridled, unchecked, uncontrolled, ungoverned, unhampered, unhindered — more at RAMPANT ♦ [2] demonstrative, effusive,

emotional, spontaneous, uninhibited, unreserved — more at DEMONSTRATIVE

un·re·straint \-ri-'strānt\ *n* ♦ : lack of restraint

♦ abandon, abandonment, ease, lightheartedness, naturalness, spontaneity — more at ABANDON

un·re·strict·ed \-ri-'strik-təd\ *adj* ♦ : not restricted

♦ free-for-all, open, public — more at OPEN ♦ all-around, general, unlimited, unqualified

un·rid·dle \-'rid-³l\ *vb* : to find the explanation of : SOLVE
un·right·eous \-'rī-chəs\ *adj*   **1** : not righteous : SINFUL, WICKED   **2** : UNJUST — **un·right·eous·ness** *n*
un·ripe \-'rīp\ *adj* : not ripe or fully developed : IMMATURE
un·rip·ened \-'rī-pənd\ *adj* : not ripened : not having attained maturity
un·ri·valed *or* **un·ri·valled** \-'rī-vəld\ *adj* ♦ : having no rival

♦ incomparable, inimitable, matchless, nonpareil, only, peerless, unequaled, unmatched, unparalleled, unsurpassed — more at ONLY

un·robe \-'rōb\ *vb* : DISROBE, UNDRESS
un·roll \-'rōl\ *vb*   **1** : to unwind a roll of : open out   **2** : DISPLAY, DISCLOSE   **3** : to become unrolled or spread out
un·roof \-'rüf, -'rùf\ *vb* : to strip off the roof or covering of
un·ruf·fled \-'rə-fəld\ *adj*   **1 ♦** : not agitated or upset   **2** : not ruffled : SMOOTH ⟨∼ water⟩

♦ calm, collected, composed, cool, placid, self-possessed, serene, tranquil, undisturbed, unperturbed, unshaken, untroubled, unworried — more at CALM

un·ru·li·ness \-'rü-lē-nəs\ *n* ♦ : the quality or state of being unruly

♦ defiance, disobedience, insubordination, rebelliousness, recalcitrance, refractoriness — more at DISOBEDIENCE

un·ruly \-'rü-lē\ *adj* [ME *unreuly*, fr. *un-* + *reuly* disciplined, fr. *reule* rule, fr. OF, fr. L *regula* straightedge, rule, fr. *regere* to direct] ♦ : not readily ruled, disciplined, or managed

♦ contrary, defiant, disobedient, froward, headstrong, intractable, rebellious, recalcitrant, refractory, uncontrollable, untoward, wayward, willful — more at DISOBEDIENT

un·sad·dle \-'sad-³l\ *vb*   **1** : to remove the saddle from a horse   **2** : UNHORSE
un·safe \-'sāf\ *adj* ♦ : not safe : exposed or exposing to danger

♦ dangerous, grave, grievous, hazardous, menacing, parlous, perilous, risky, serious, unhealthy, venturesome — more at DANGEROUS

un·sat·is·fac·to·ry \-ˌsa-təs-'fak-tə-rē\ *adj* ♦ : not satisfactory

♦ bad, deficient, inferior, lousy, off, poor, punk, rotten, substandard, unacceptable, wanting, wretched, wrong — more at BAD

un·sat·u·rat·ed \-'sa-chə-ˌrā-təd\ *adj*   **1** : capable of absorbing or dissolving more of something   **2** : containing double or triple bonds between carbon atoms ⟨∼ fats⟩ — **un·sat·u·rate** \-rət\ *n*
un·saved \-'sāvd\ *adj* : not saved; *esp* : not rescued from eternal punishment
un·sa·vory \-'sā-və-rē\ *adj*   **1** : TASTELESS   **2 ♦** : unpleasant to taste or smell   **3** : morally offensive

♦ distasteful, unappetizing — more at DISTASTEFUL

un·say \-'sā\ *vb* **-said** \-'sed\; **-say·ing** ♦ : to take back (something said) : RETRACT

List of self-explanatory words with the prefix *un-* (continued)

♦ abjure, recant, renounce, retract, take back, withdraw — more at ABJURE

un·scathed \-'skāthd\ *adj* : wholly unharmed : not injured

un·schooled \-'sküld\ *adj* : not schooled : UNTAUGHT

un·sci·en·tif·ic \-ˌsī-ən-'ti-fik\ *adj* : not scientific : not in accord with the principles and methods of science

un·scram·ble \-'skram-bəl\ *vb* **1** : RESOLVE, CLARIFY **2** : to restore (as a radio message) to intelligible form

un·screw \-'skrü\ *vb* **1** : to draw the screws from **2** : to loosen by turning

un·scru·pu·lous \-'skrü-pyə-ləs\ *adj* ♦ : not scrupulous : UNPRINCIPLED — **un·scru·pu·lous·ly** *adv* — **un·scru·pu·lous·ness** *n*

♦ cutthroat, immoral, Machiavellian, unconscionable, unethical, unprincipled — more at UNPRINCIPLED

un·seal \-'sēl\ *vb* : to break or remove the seal of : OPEN

un·search·able \-'sər-chə-bəl\ *adj* : not capable of being searched or explored

un·sea·son·able \-'sēz-ᵊn-ə-bəl\ *adj* ♦ : not seasonable : happening or coming at the wrong time : UNTIMELY

♦ early, precocious, premature, untimely — more at EARLY

un·sea·son·ably \-blē\ *adv* ♦ : in an unseasonable manner : at an unseasonable time

♦ beforehand, early, precociously, prematurely — more at EARLY

un·seat \-'sēt\ *vb* **1** : to throw from one's seat esp. on horseback **2** : to remove from political office

un·seem·ly \-'sēm-lē\ *adj* **1** : not according with established standards of good form or taste ⟨~ behavior⟩ **2** ♦ : not suitable — **un·seem·li·ness** *n*

♦ improper, inappropriate, inapt, infelicitous, unbecoming, unfit, unsuitable, wrong — more at INAPPROPRIATE

un·seen \-'sēn\ *adj* : not seen : INVISIBLE

un·seg·re·gat·ed \-'se-gri-ˌgā-təd\ *adj* : not segregated; *esp* : free from racial segregation

un·self·ish \-'sel-fish\ *adj* ♦ : not selfish : GENEROUS — **un·self·ish·ly** *adv*

♦ bountiful, charitable, free, generous, liberal, munificent, openhanded, unsparing — more at GENEROUS

un·self·ish·ness *n* ♦ : the quality or state of being unselfish

♦ bounty, generosity, largesse, liberality, philanthropy — more at LIBERALITY

un·set·tle \-'set-ᵊl\ *vb* **1** : to move or loosen from a settled position : DISPLACE **2** ♦ : to perturb or agitate mentally or emotionally

♦ agitate, bother, concern, discompose, disquiet, distress, disturb, exercise, freak, perturb, undo, unhinge, upset, worry

un·set·tled \-'set-ᵊld\ *adj* **1** ♦ : not settled : not fixed (as in position or character) **2** : not calm : DISTURBED **3** ♦ : not decided in mind **4** ♦ : not paid ⟨~ accounts⟩ **5** : not occupied by settlers

♦ [1] open, pending, undecided, undetermined, unresolved — more at PENDING ♦ [3] distrustful, doubtful, dubious, mistrustful, skeptical, suspicious, uncertain, undecided, unsure — more at DOUBTFUL ♦ [4] outstanding, overdue, payable, unpaid — more at OUTSTANDING

un·set·tling \-'set-ᵊ-liŋ\ *adj* ♦ : having the effect of upsetting, disturbing, or discomposing

♦ troublesome, upsetting, worrisome — more at TROUBLESOME

un·shack·le \-'sha-kəl\ *vb* : to free from shackles

un·shak·able \-'shā-kə-bəl\ *adj* ♦ : not shakable

♦ imperturbable, nerveless, unflappable — more at UNFLAPPABLE

un·shak·en \-'shā-kən\ *adj* ♦ : not shaken

♦ calm, collected, composed, cool, placid, self-possessed, serene, tranquil, undisturbed, unperturbed, untroubled, unworried — more at CALM

un·shaped \-'shāpt\ *adj* ♦ : not shaped; *esp* : not being in finished, final, or perfect form ⟨~ ideas⟩ ⟨~ timber⟩

♦ amorphous, formless, shapeless, unformed, unstructured — more at FORMLESS

un·sheathe \-'shēth\ *vb* : to draw from or as if from a sheath

un·ship \-'ship\ *vb* **1** : to remove from a ship **2** : to remove or become removed from position ⟨~ an oar⟩

un·shod \-'shäd\ *adj* : not wearing or provided with shoes

un·shorn \-'shōrn\ *adj* **1** : not cut **2** : not harvested **3** : not diminished

♦ fleecy, furry, hairy, hirsute, rough, shaggy, woolly — more at HAIRY

un·sight·ly \-'sīt-lē\ *adj* ♦ : unpleasant to the sight : UGLY

♦ grotesque, hideous, ugly, unappealing, unattractive, unlovely, vile — more at UGLY

un·skilled \-'skild\ *adj* **1 a** ♦ : not skilled **b** : not skilled in a specified branch of work **2** : not requiring skill

♦ amateur, amateurish, inexperienced, inexpert, nonprofessional, unprofessional, unskillful — more at AMATEURISH

un·skill·ful \-'skil-fəl\ *adj* ♦ : lacking in skill or proficiency — **un·skill·ful·ly** *adv*

♦ incapable, incompetent, inept, inexpert, unfit, unqualified, unskilled — more at INCOMPETENT

un·sling \-'sliŋ\ *vb* **-slung** \-'sləŋ\; **-sling·ing** : to remove from being slung

un·smil·ing \-'smī-liŋ\ *adj* ♦ : not smiling

♦ earnest, grave, humorless (*or* humourless), serious, severe, sober, solemn, staid, weighty — more at SERIOUS

un·snap \-'snap\ *vb* : to loosen or free by or as if by undoing a snap

un·snarl \-'snärl\ *vb* : to remove snarls from : UNTANGLE

un·so·cia·ble \-'sō-shə-bəl\ *adj* **1** ♦ : having or showing a disinclination for social activity **2** : not conducive to sociability

♦ aloof, antisocial, cold, cool, detached, distant, frosty, remote, standoffish — more at COOL

un·soiled \-'soild\ *adj* ♦ : not soiled or dirtied : not sullied

♦ clean, immaculate, spick-and-span, spotless, stainless, unsullied — more at CLEAN

un·so·lic·it·ed \-sə-'li-sə-təd\ *adj* ♦ : not solicited : not asked for

♦ unasked, unbidden, undesired, uninvited, unsought, unwanted, unwelcome — more at UNSOUGHT

un·solv·able \-'säl-və-bəl\ *adj* ♦ : not solvable

♦ hopeless, impossible, unattainable, unworkable — more at IMPOSSIBLE

un·so·phis·ti·cat·ed \-sə-'fis-tə-ˌkā-təd\ *adj* **1** ♦ : not worldly-wise : lacking sophistication **2** : SIMPLE

♦ green, ingenuous, innocent, naive, simple, unknowing, unwary, unworldly — more at NAIVE

un·sought \-'sot\ *adj* ♦ : not sought : not searched for or asked for ⟨~ honors⟩

List of self-explanatory words with the prefix *un-* (continued)

unself–consciously	**unsexual**	**unsigned**	**unsorted**
unsensational	**unshaded**	**unsinkable**	**unspectacular**
unsentimental	**unshapely**	**unsold**	**unspent**
unserious	**unshaven**	**unsoldierly**	**unspiritual**
unserviceable	**unsifted**	**unsolved**	**unspoiled**

♦ unasked, unbidden, undesired, uninvited, unsolicited, unwanted, unwelcome; *also* objectionable, offensive, unacceptable, undesirable; uncalled-for *Ant* desired, solicited, wanted, welcome

un·sound \-'saúnd\ *adj* **1 a** ♦ : not healthy or whole **b** ♦ : not mentally normal **2** ♦ : not valid **3** : not firmly made or fixed — **un·sound·ly** *adv*

♦ [1a] bad, down, ill, indisposed, peaked, punk, sick, unhealthy, unwell — more at SICK ♦ [1b] balmy, cracked, crazy, cuckoo, daft, deranged, insane, loco, lunatic, mad, maniacal, mental, nuts, nutty, screwy, wacky — more at INSANE ♦ [2] fallacious, illogical, invalid, irrational, unreasonable, weak — more at ILLOGICAL

un·sound·ness *n* ♦ : the quality or state of being unsound

♦ illness, sickness — more at SICKNESS

un·spar·ing \-'spar-iŋ\ *adj* **1** ♦ : not merciful or forbearing : HARD **2** ♦ : not frugal : LIBERAL

♦ [1] callous, hard, heartless, inhuman, inhumane, pitiless, soulless, unfeeling, unsympathetic — more at HARD ♦ [2] bountiful, charitable, free, generous, liberal, munificent, openhanded, unselfish — more at GENEROUS

un·speak·able \-'spē-kə-bəl\ *adj* **1** ♦ : impossible to express in words **2** : extremely bad — **un·speak·ably** \-blē\ *adv*

♦ indescribable, ineffable, inexpressible, nameless, unutterable — more at INDESCRIBABLE

un·spec·i·fied \-'spe-sə-ˌfīd\ *adj* ♦ : not specified

♦ anonymous, certain, one, some, unidentified, unnamed — more at CERTAIN

un·spo·ken \-'spō-kən\ *adj* **1** ♦ : not spoken or uttered **2** : not spoken to or addressed **3** : not speaking

♦ implicit, tacit, unexpressed, unvoiced, wordless — more at IMPLICIT

un·sports·man·like \-'spōrts-mən-ˌlīk\ *adj* ♦ : not sportsmanlike : not characteristic of or exhibiting good sportsmanship

♦ dirty, foul, illegal, unfair

un·spot·ted \-'spä-təd\ *adj* : not spotted or stained; *esp* : free from moral stain

un·sprung \-'sprəŋ\ *adj* : not sprung; *esp* : not equipped with springs

un·sta·ble \-'stā-bəl\ *adj* **1 a** ♦ : not stable : not steady in action or movement **b** : lacking steadiness : apt to move, sway, or fall **2** ♦ : wavering in purpose or intent : FICKLE; *also* : lacking effective emotional control **3** : readily changing (as by decomposing) in chemical or physical composition or in biological activity ⟨an ∼ atomic nucleus⟩

♦ [1a] erratic, irregular, unequal, uneven, unsteady — more at UNEVEN ♦ [2] capricious, changeable, fickle, inconstant, mercurial, temperamental, unpredictable, unsettled, unsteady, volatile — more at FICKLE

un·stained \-'stānd\ *adj* **1** : not stained or discolored : not spotted **2** : not morally blemished or stained

un·stead·i·ness \-'ste-dē-nəs\ *n* ♦ : the quality or state of being unsteady

♦ insecurity, instability, precariousness, shakiness — more at INSTABILITY

un·steady \-'ste-dē\ *adj* ♦ : not steady : UNSTABLE — **un·stead·i·ly** \-'sted-ᵊl-ē\ *adv*

♦ casual, choppy, discontinuous, erratic, fitful, intermittent, irregular, occasional, spasmodic, sporadic, spotty

— more at FITFUL ♦ erratic, irregular, unequal, uneven, unstable — more at UNEVEN

un·stint·ing \-'stin-tiŋ\ *adj* **1** : not restricting or holding back **2** : giving or being given freely or generously ⟨∼ praise⟩

un·stint·ing·ly \-'stin-tiŋ-lē\ *adv* ♦ : in an unstinting manner

♦ amply, bountifully, generously, handsomely, liberally, well — more at WELL

un·stop \-'stäp\ *vb* **1** ♦ : to free from any obstruction : UNCLOG **2** : to remove a stopper from

♦ clear, free, open, unclog

un·stop·pa·ble \-'stä-pə-bəl\ *adj* : incapable of being stopped

un·strap \-'strap\ *vb* : to remove or loose a strap from

un·stressed \-'strest\ *adj* : not stressed; *esp* : not bearing a stress or accent

un·struc·tured \-'strək-chərd\ *adj* ♦ : lacking structure or organization : not formally organized in a set or conventional pattern

♦ amorphous, formless, shapeless, unformed, unshaped — more at FORMLESS

un·strung \-'strəŋ\ *adj* **1** : having the strings loose or detached **2** : made weak, disordered, or unstable

un·stud·ied \-'stə-dēd\ *adj* **1** : not acquired by study **2** : NATURAL, UNFORCED ⟨moved with ∼ grace⟩

un·styl·ish \-'stī-lish\ *adj* ♦ : not stylish

♦ dowdy, inelegant, tacky, tasteless, trashy, unfashionable — more at TACKY

un·sub·stan·tial \-səb-'stan-chəl\ *adj* ♦ : not substantial : lacking substance, firmness, or strength

♦ flimsy, gauzy, insubstantial — more at FLIMSY ♦ bodiless, immaterial, incorporeal, insubstantial, nonmaterial, nonphysical, spiritual — more at IMMATERIAL

un·sub·stan·ti·at·ed \-səb-'stan-chē-ˌā-təd\ *adj* ♦ : not substantiated; *esp* : not supported or borne out by fact

♦ baseless, groundless, invalid, unfounded, unreasonable, unsupported, unwarranted — more at BASELESS

un·suc·cess·ful \-sək-'ses-fəl\ *adj* ♦ : not successful : not meeting with or producing success

♦ fruitless, futile, ineffective, unproductive — more at FUTILE

un·suit·able \-'sü-tə-bəl\ *adj* ♦ : not suitable or fitting

♦ improper, inappropriate, inapt, infelicitous, unbecoming, unfit, unseemly, wrong — more at INAPPROPRIATE

un·sul·lied \-'sə-lēd\ *adj* ♦ : not sullied or stained : spotlessly clean

♦ clean, immaculate, spick-and-span, spotless, stainless, unsoiled — more at CLEAN

un·sung \-'səŋ\ *adj* **1** : not sung **2** ♦ : not celebrated in song or verse or otherwise praised ⟨∼ heroes⟩

♦ anonymous, nameless, obscure, unknown — more at OBSCURE

un·sup·port·able \-sə-'pōr-tə-bəl\ *adj* ♦ : not supportable : hardly to be suffered or borne

♦ insufferable, insupportable, intolerable, unbearable, unendurable — more at UNBEARABLE

un·sup·port·ed \-sə-'pōr-təd\ *adj* **1 a** ♦ : not supported or verified **b** : not backed up or assisted **2** : not held up or sustained

♦ baseless, groundless, invalid, unfounded, unreasonable, unsubstantiated, unwarranted — more at BASELESS

List of self-explanatory words with the prefix *un-* (continued)

unstated	unsuited	unsweetened	untalented
unsterile	unsupervised	unsymmetrical	untanned
unsubdued	unsurprising	unsystematic	untapped
unsubtle	unsurprisingly	untactful	untarnished
unsuccessfully	unsuspected	untainted	untaxed

un·sure \-'shu̇r\ *adj* **1** ♦ : lacking confidence or assurance **2** : not having certain knowledge **3** ♦ : marked by lack of confidence, assurance, or certainty **4** : not steadfast or stable

♦ [1, 3] distrustful, doubtful, dubious, mistrustful, skeptical, suspicious, uncertain, undecided, unsettled — more at DOUBTFUL

un·sur·passed \-sər-'pasd\ *adj* ♦ : not surpassed or exceeded usu. in excellence

♦ incomparable, inimitable, matchless, nonpareil, only, peerless, unequaled, unmatched, unparalleled, unrivaled — more at ONLY

un·sus·pect·ing \-sə-'spek-tiŋ\ *adj* **1** : not suspecting : not being suspicious **2** : deficient in worldly wisdom or informed judgment

un·sus·pi·cious \-sə-'spi-shəs\ *adj* : UNSUSPECTING

un·swerv·ing \-'swer-viŋ\ *adj* **1** : not swerving or turning aside **2** : STEADY

un·sym·pa·thet·ic \-ˌsim-pə-'the-tik\ *adj* ♦ : not sympathetic : not responsive

♦ callous, hard, heartless, merciless, pitiless, stony, uncharitable, unfeeling — more at HARD ♦ chill, chilly, cold, cold-blooded, cool, frigid, frosty, glacial, icy, unfriendly, wintry — more at COLD

un·tamed \-'tāmd\ *adj* ♦ : not tamed or cultivated; *esp* : WILD

♦ feral, savage, unbroken, undomesticated, wild — more at WILD

un·tan·gle \-'taŋ-gəl\ *vb* **1** ♦ : to loose from tangles or entanglement : DISENTANGLE **2** : to straighten out : RESOLVE ⟨~ a problem⟩

♦ disentangle, unravel, untwine — more at UNRAVEL ♦ clear, disengage, disentangle, extricate, free, liberate, release — more at EXTRICATE

un·taught \-'tȯt\ *adj* **1** ♦ : not instructed or taught : IGNORANT **2** : NATURAL, SPONTANEOUS ⟨~ kindness⟩

♦ dark, ignorant, illiterate, simple, uneducated, unlearned — more at IGNORANT

un·think·able \-'thiŋ-kə-bəl\ *adj* ♦ : not to be thought of or considered as possible ⟨~ cruelty⟩

♦ fantastic, implausible, inconceivable, incredible, unbelievable, unconvincing, unimaginable — more at INCREDIBLE

un·think·ing \-'thiŋ-kiŋ\ *adj* : not thinking; *esp* : THOUGHTLESS, HEEDLESS ⟨~ remarks⟩ — **un·think·ing·ly** *adv*

un·thought \ˌən-'thȯt\ *adj* : not anticipated : UNEXPECTED — often used with *of* ⟨unthought-of development⟩

un·thrifty \-'thrif-tē\ *adj* **1** : marked by lack of thrift **2** : not thriving or prospering **3** ♦ : not given to thrift or saving

♦ extravagant, prodigal, profligate, spendthrift, thriftless, wasteful — more at PRODIGAL

un·ti·dy \-'tī-dē\ *adj* **1** : not fit **2 a** ♦ : not neat in appearance **b** : not neat in habits or procedure **3 a** ♦ : not neatly organized or carried out **b** ♦ : marked by or conducive to a lack of neatness

♦ [2a] dowdy, frowsy, sloppy, slovenly, unkempt — more at SLOPPY ♦ [3a, b] chaotic, confused, disheveled, disordered, messy — more at MESSY

un·tie \-'tī\ *vb* **-tied**; **-ty·ing** *or* **-tie·ing** **1** ♦ : to free from something that ties, fastens, or restrains : UNBIND **2** : DISENTANGLE, RESOLVE **3** : to become loosened or unbound

♦ unbind, undo; *also* unlace; disentangle, ravel, unravel, unsnarl, untangle, unwind; loose, loosen *Ant* bind, fasten, knot, lash, tie

¹un·til \-'til\ *prep* : up to the time of ⟨worked ~ 5 o'clock⟩

²until *conj* **1** : up to the time that ⟨wait ~ he calls⟩ **2** : to the point or degree that ⟨ran ~ she was breathless⟩

¹un·time·ly \-'tīm-lē\ *adv* : at an inopportune time : UNSEASONABLY; *also* : PREMATURELY

²untimely *adj* **1** ♦ : happening, arriving, existing, or performed before the proper, usual, or intended time ⟨~ death⟩ **2** : not convenient esp. in giving trouble or annoyance

♦ early, precocious, premature, unseasonable — more at EARLY

un·tir·ing \-'tī-riŋ\ *adj* ♦ : not becoming tired : INDEFATIGABLE — **un·tir·ing·ly** *adv*

♦ indefatigable, inexhaustible, tireless, unflagging — more at TIRELESS

un·ti·tled \-'tīt-ᵊld\ *adj* **1** : having no title or right **2** ♦ : not named **3** : not called by a title

♦ anonymous, nameless, unbaptized, unchristened, unidentified, unnamed — more at NAMELESS

un·to \'ən-ˌtü\ *prep* : TO

un·told \ˌən-'tōld\ *adj* **1** ♦ : not counted : NUMBERLESS **2** : not told : not revealed

♦ countless, innumerable, numberless, uncountable, unnumbered — more at COUNTLESS

¹un·touch·able \-'tə-chə-bəl\ *adj* **1 a** : forbidden to the touch **b** : exempt from criticism or control **2** ♦ : lying beyond reach **3** : disagreeable or defiling to the touch

♦ [1b] holy, inviolable, sacred, sacrosanct — more at SACRED ♦ [2] inaccessible, inconvenient, unapproachable, unattainable, unavailable, unobtainable, unreachable — more at INACCESSIBLE

²untouchable *n* : a member of the lowest social class in India having in traditional Hindu belief the quality of defiling by contact a member of a higher caste

un·touched \-'təcht\ *adj* **1** : not subjected to touching **2** : not described or dealt with **3** : not tasted **4** : being in a primeval state or condition **5** : UNAFFECTED

un·tow·ard \ˌən-'tȯrd, -'tō-ərd; ˌən-tə-'wȯrd\ *adj* **1** ♦ : difficult to manage : WILLFUL ⟨an ~ child⟩ **2** : INCONVENIENT, TROUBLESOME ⟨an ~ encounter⟩

♦ contrary, defiant, disobedient, froward, intractable, rebellious, recalcitrant, refractory, uncontrollable, unmanageable, unruly, wayward, willful — more at DISOBEDIENT

un·treat·ed \-'trē-təd\ *adj* ♦ : not subjected to treatment

♦ crude, native, natural, raw, undressed, unprocessed, unrefined — more at CRUDE

un·tried \-'trīd\ *adj* : not tested or proved by experience or trial; *also* : not tried in court

un·trou·bled \-'trə-bəld\ *adj* **1** : marked by calm : without rough motion, storminess, or agitated activity **2** ♦ : not given trouble : not made uneasy **3** ♦ : free from agitation, excitement, or disturbance

♦ [2, 3] calm, collected, composed, cool, placid, self-possessed, serene, tranquil, undisturbed, unperturbed, unshaken, unworried — more at CALM

un·true \-'trü\ *adj* **1** ♦ : not faithful : DISLOYAL **2** : not according with a standard of correctness **3** ♦ : not true : FALSE

♦ [1] disloyal, faithless, false, fickle, inconstant, loose, perfidious, recreant, traitorous, treacherous, unfaithful — more at FAITHLESS ♦ [3] erroneous, false, inaccurate, incorrect, inexact, invalid, off, unsound, wrong — more at FALSE

un·trust·wor·thy \-'trəst-ˌwər-thē\ *adj* : not to be trusted : not reliable

---

List of self-explanatory words with the prefix *un-* (continued)

unteachable	untested	untrained	untraveled
untenable	untilled	untrammeled	untraversed
untenanted	untraceable	untranslatable	untrimmed
untended	untraditional	untranslated	untrod

un·truth \ˌən-ˈtrüth, ˈən-ˌtrüth\ *n* **1** : lack of truthfulness **2** ♦ : something that is untrue; *esp* : FALSEHOOD **3** : absence of truth or accuracy

♦ fabrication, fairy tale, falsehood, falsity, fib, lie, mendacity, prevarication, story, tale, whopper — more at LIE

un·truth·ful \ˌən-ˈtrüth-fəl\ *adj* : not containing or telling the truth : FALSE

un·tune \-ˈtün, -ˈtyün\ *vb* **1** : to put out of tune **2** : DISARRANGE, DISCOMPOSE

un·tu·tored \-ˈtü-tərd, -ˈtyü-\ *adj* : having no formal learning or training : UNLEARNED

un·twine \-ˈtwīn\ *vb* ♦ : to unwind the twisted or tangled parts of : DISENTANGLE

♦ disentangle, unravel, untangle — more at UNRAVEL

un·twist \-ˈtwist\ *vb* **1** : to separate the twisted parts of : UNTWINE **2** : to become untwined

un·typ·i·cal \-ˈti-pi-kəl\ *adj* ♦ : not typical

♦ aberrant, abnormal, anomalous, atypical, deviant, irregular, unnatural — more at DEVIANT

un·us·able \-ˈyü-zə-bəl\ *adj* ♦ : not serviceable : having or being of no use

♦ impractical, inoperable, unworkable, useless — more at IMPRACTICAL

un·used \for 1 -ˈyüst, -ˈyüzd; for 2 -ˈyüzd\ *adj* **1** ♦ : not habituated : UNACCUSTOMED **2** ♦ : not used

♦ [1] unaccustomed, unadapted, unadjusted; *also* unhardened, unseasoned *Ant* acclimated, accustomed, adapted, adjusted, habituated, used ♦ [2] brand-new, new, spick-and-span — more at NEW

un·usu·al \-ˈyü-zhə-wəl\ *adj* ♦ : not usual : UNCOMMON — **un·usu·al·ly** *adv*

♦ curious, exceptional, extraordinary, funny, odd, peculiar, queer, rare, strange, unaccustomed, uncommon, unique, weird; *also* bizarre, eccentric, far-out, outlandish, outré, way-out; aberrant, abnormal, atypical, exceptional, irregular; newsworthy, notable, noteworthy, noticeable, particular, remarkable, special *Ant* common, ordinary, usual

un·ut·ter·able \-ˈə-tə-rə-bəl\ *adj* ♦ : being beyond the powers of description : INEXPRESSIBLE — **un·ut·ter·ably** \-blē\ *adv*

♦ indescribable, ineffable, inexpressible, nameless, unspeakable — more at INDESCRIBABLE

un·var·nished \-ˈvär-nisht\ *adj* **1** : not varnished **2** ♦ : not embellished : PLAIN ⟨the ~ truth⟩

♦ bald, bare, naked, plain, simple, unadorned, undecorated — more at PLAIN

un·vary·ing \-ˈver-ē-iŋ\ *adj* ♦ : not varying

♦ constant, steady, unchanging, undeviating, uniform, unwavering — more at UNIFORM

un·veil \-ˈvāl\ *vb* **1** ♦ : to expose to the public : DISCLOSE **2** : to present publicly for the first time

♦ bare, disclose, discover, divulge, expose, reveal, spill, tell, unbosom, uncloak, uncover, unmask — more at REVEAL

un·voiced \-ˈvȯist\ *adj* **1** ♦ : not verbally expressed : UNSPOKEN **2** : VOICELESS 2

♦ implicit, tacit, unexpressed, unspoken, wordless — more at IMPLICIT

un·want·ed \-ˈwȯn-təd, -ˈwän-təd\ *adj* **1** ♦ : not wanted **2** : not needed or useful **3** : detrimental in character

♦ unasked, unbidden, undesired, uninvited, unsolicited, unsought, unwelcome — more at UNSOUGHT

un·war·rant·able \-ˈwȯr-ən-tə-bəl\ *adj* ♦ : not justifiable : INEXCUSABLE — **un·war·rant·ably** \-blē\ *adv*

♦ indefensible, inexcusable, unforgivable, unjustifiable, unpardonable — more at INEXCUSABLE

un·war·rant·ed \-ˈwȯr-ən-təd, -ˈwär-\ *adj* ♦ : lacking adequate support : not justified

♦ baseless, groundless, invalid, unfounded, unreasonable, unsubstantiated, unsupported — more at BASELESS

un·wary \-ˈwar-ē\ *adj* **1** ♦ : not experienced or sophisticated **2** ♦ : careless of consequences : not prudent

♦ [1] green, ingenuous, innocent, naive, simple, unknowing, unsophisticated, unworldly — more at NAIVE ♦ [2] careless, heedless, mindless, unguarded, unsafe — more at CARELESS

un·wa·ver·ing \-ˈwā-və-riŋ\ *adj* ♦ : characterized by absence of fluctuation

♦ steady, unchanging, undeviating, uniform, unvarying — more at UNIFORM

un·weave \-ˈwēv\ *vb* **-wove** \-ˈwōv\; **-wo·ven** \-ˈwō-vən\; **-weav·ing** : DISENTANGLE, RAVEL

un·wed \-ˈwed\ *adj* ♦ : not married

♦ single, unattached, unmarried — more at SINGLE

un·wel·come \-ˈwel-kəm\ *adj* **1** ♦ : not welcome **2** ♦ : causing displeasure or resentment

♦ [1] unasked, unbidden, undesired, uninvited, unsolicited, unsought, unwanted — more at UNSOUGHT ♦ [2] bad, disagreeable, distasteful, nasty, rotten, sour, uncongenial, unlovely, unpleasant — more at UNPLEASANT

un·well \-ˈwel\ *adj* ♦ : being in poor health : SICK

♦ bad, down, ill, indisposed, peaked, punk, sick, unhealthy, unsound — more at SICK

un·whole·some \-ˈhōl-səm\ *adj* **1** ♦ : harmful to physical, mental, or moral well-being **2** : CORRUPT, UNSOUND; *also* : offensive to the senses

♦ noisome, noxious, unhealthy — more at UNHEALTHY

un·wieldy \-ˈwēl-dē\ *adj* ♦ : not easily managed, handled, or used (as because of bulk, weight, or complexity) ⟨an ~ tool⟩

♦ awkward, clumsy, cranky, cumbersome, ungainly, unhandy — more at CUMBERSOME

un·will·ing \-ˈwi-liŋ\ *adj* : not willing

un·wind \-ˈwīnd\ *vb* **-wound** \-ˈwaund\; **-wind·ing** **1** : to undo something that is wound : loose from coils **2** : to become unwound : be capable of being unwound **3** ♦ : to get rid of nervous tension or anxiety : RELAX

♦ chill out, de-stress, relax — more at RELAX

un·wise \-ˈwīz\ *adj* ♦ : not wise : lacking or not showing wisdom or good sense — **un·wise·ly** *adv*

♦ foolish, ill-advised, imprudent, indiscreet, tactless — more at INDISCREET

un·wit·ting \-ˈwi-tiŋ\ *adj* **1** ♦ : not knowing : UNAWARE **2** ♦ : not intended : INADVERTENT ⟨~ mistake⟩ — **un·wit·ting·ly** *adv*

♦ [1] ignorant, oblivious, unaware, unconscious, uninformed, unknowing — more at IGNORANT ♦ [2] accidental, casual, chance, fluky, fortuitous, inadvertent, incidental, unintended, unintentional, unplanned, unpremeditated — more at ACCIDENTAL

un·wont·ed \-ˈwȯn-təd, -ˈwōn-\ *adj* **1** ♦ : being out of the ordinary : UNUSUAL **2** : not accustomed by experience — **un·wont·ed·ly** *adv*

♦ aberrant, abnormal, atypical, exceptional, extraordinary, freak, odd, peculiar, phenomenal, rare, singular, uncommon, uncustomary, unique, unusual — more at EXCEPTIONAL

List of self-explanatory words with the prefix *un-* (continued)

untrodden	unverifiable	unvisited	unwearable
unvaried	unverified	unwashed	unwearied
unventilated	unversed	unweaned	

un·work·able \-'wər-kə-bəl\ *adj* ♦ : incapable of being put into use or effect or of being accomplished successfully

♦ impractical, inoperable, unusable, useless — more at IMPRACTICAL

un·world·li·ness \-'wərld-lē-nəs\ *n* ♦ : the quality or state of being unworldly

♦ artlessness, greenness, ingenuousness, innocence, naïveté, naturalness, simplicity — more at NAÏVETÉ

un·world·ly \-'wərld-lē\ *adj* **1** : not of this world; *esp* : SPIRITUAL **2** ♦ : deficient in worldly wisdom or informed judgment : NAIVE **3** : not swayed by worldly considerations

♦ green, ingenuous, innocent, naive, simple, unknowing, unsophisticated, unwary — more at NAIVE

un·wor·ried \-'wər-ēd\ *adj* ♦ : not worried

♦ calm, collected, composed, cool, placid, self-possessed, serene, tranquil, undisturbed, unperturbed, unshaken, untroubled — more at CALM

un·wor·thy \-'wər-thē\ *adj* **1** : BASE, DISHONORABLE **2** : not worthy **3** : not deserved ⟨he had his ∼ treatment⟩ — **un·wor·thi·ly** \-thə-lē\ *adv* — **un·wor·thi·ness** \-thē-nəs\ *n*

un·wrap \-'rap\ *vb* : to remove the wrapping from : DISCLOSE

un·writ·ten \-'rit-ᵊn\ *adj* **1** ♦ : not in writing : ORAL ⟨an ∼ law⟩ **2** : containing no writing : BLANK

♦ oral, spoken, verbal — more at VERBAL

un·yield·ing \-'yēl-diŋ\ *adj* **1** ♦ : characterized by lack of softness or flexibility **2** ♦ : characterized by firmness or obduracy ⟨∼ opposition⟩

♦ [1] compact, firm, hard, inflexible, rigid, solid, stiff — more at FIRM ♦ [2] determined, dogged, grim, implacable, obstinate, relentless, unflinching, unrelenting; *also* hardheaded, headstrong, mulish, opinionated, pertinacious, stubborn, willful

un·yoke \-'yōk\ *vb* **1** : to remove a yoke from **2** ♦ : to take apart : SEPARATE

♦ break up, disconnect, disjoint, dissever, dissociate, disunite, divide, divorce, part, resolve, separate, sever, split, sunder — more at SEPARATE

un·zip \-'zip\ *vb* : to zip open : open by means of a zipper

¹up \'əp\ *adv* **1** : in or to a higher position or level; *esp* : away from the center of the earth **2** : from beneath a surface (as ground or water) **3** : from below the horizon **4** : in or into an upright position; *esp* : out of bed **5** : with greater intensity ⟨speak ∼⟩ **6** : in or into a better or more advanced state or a state of greater intensity or activity ⟨stir ∼ a fire⟩ **7** : into existence, evidence, or knowledge ⟨the missing book turned ∼⟩ **8** : into consideration ⟨brought the matter ∼⟩ **9** : to or at bat **10** : into possession or custody ⟨gave himself ∼⟩ **11** : ENTIRELY, COMPLETELY ⟨eat it ∼⟩ **12** — used for emphasis ⟨clean ∼ a room⟩ **13** : ASIDE, BY ⟨lay ∼ supplies⟩ **14** : so as to arrive or approach ⟨ran ∼ the path⟩ **15** : in a direction opposite to down **16** : in or into parts ⟨tear ∼ paper⟩ **17** : to a stop ⟨pull ∼ at the curb⟩ **18** : for each side ⟨the score was 15 ∼⟩

²up *adj* **1** : risen above the horizon ⟨the sun is ∼⟩ **2** : being out of bed ⟨∼ by 6 o'clock⟩ **3** : relatively high ⟨prices are ∼⟩ **4** : RAISED, LIFTED ⟨windows are ∼⟩ **5** : BUILT, CONSTRUCTED ⟨the house is ∼⟩ **6** : grown above a surface ⟨the corn is ∼⟩ **7** : moving, inclining, or directed upward **8** : marked by agitation, excitement, or activity **9** : READY; *esp* : highly prepared **10** : going on : taking place ⟨find out what is ∼⟩ **11** : come to an end : ENDED ⟨the time is ∼⟩ **12** ♦ : well informed ⟨∼ on the news⟩ **13** : being ahead or in advance of an opponent ⟨one hole ∼ in a match⟩ **14** : presented for or being under consideration **15** : charged before a court ⟨∼ for robbery⟩

♦ [3] advanced, high — more at HIGH ♦ [12] abreast, conversant, familiar, informed, knowledgeable, up-to-date, versed — more at FAMILIAR

³up *prep* **1** : to, toward, or at a higher point of ⟨∼ a ladder⟩ **2** : to or toward the source of ⟨∼ the river⟩ **3** : to or toward the northern part of ⟨∼ the coast⟩ **4** : in or toward the interior of ⟨traveling ∼ the country⟩ **5** : ALONG ⟨walk ∼ the street⟩

⁴up *n* **1** : an upward course or slope **2** : a period or state of prosperity or success ⟨he had his ∼s and downs⟩ **3** : a quark with a charge of +⅔ that is one of the constituents of the proton and neutron

⁵up *vb* **upped** \'əpt\ *or in 2* **up; upped; up·ping; ups** *or in 2* **up** **1** : to rise from a lying or sitting position **2** : to act abruptly or surprisingly ⟨she ∼ and left home⟩ **3** ♦ : to move or cause to move upward ⟨*upped* the prices⟩

♦ add, aggrandize, amplify, augment, boost, compound, enlarge, escalate, expand, extend, increase, multiply, raise, swell — more at INCREASE ♦ boost, crane, elevate, heave, heft, heighten, hike, hoist, jack, lift, pick up, raise, uphold — more at RAISE

Upa·ni·shad \ü-'pän-i-ˌshäd\ *n* : one of a set of Vedic philosophical treatises

¹up·beat \'əp-ˌbēt\ *n* : an unaccented beat in a musical measure; *esp* : the last beat of the measure

²upbeat \'əp-'bēt\ *adj* ♦ : marked by or indicating optimism : CHEERFUL

♦ blithe, bright, buoyant, cheerful, cheery, chipper, gay, lightsome, sunny — more at CHEERFUL

up·braid \ˌəp-'brād\ *vb* ♦ : to criticize, reproach, or scold severely

♦ admonish, chide, lecture, rail (at *or* against), rate, rebuke, reprimand, scold — more at SCOLD

up·bring·ing \'əp-ˌbriŋ-iŋ\ *n* : the process of bringing up and training

UPC *abbr* Universal Product Code

up·chuck \'əp-ˌchək\ *vb* : VOMIT

up·com·ing \'əp-ˌkə-miŋ\ *adj* : coming up; *esp* : being in the near future : FORTHCOMING, APPROACHING

up–coun·try \'əp-ˌkən-trē\ *adj* ♦ : of, relating to, or characteristic of an inland, upland, or outlying region — **up-country** \'əp-'kən-\ *adv*

♦ backwoods, bush, frontier, hinterland, sticks — more at FRONTIER

up·date \ˌəp-'dāt\ *vb* : to bring up to date — **update** \'əp-ˌdāt\ *n*

up·draft \'əp-ˌdraft, -ˌdräft\ *n* : an upward movement of gas (as air)

up·end \ˌəp-'end\ *vb* **1** : to set, stand, or rise on end **2** : OVERTURN

up–front \'əp-ˌfrənt, ˌəp-'frənt\ *adj* **1** : HONEST, CANDID **2** : ADVANCE ⟨∼ payment⟩

up front *adv* : in advance ⟨paid *up front*⟩

¹up·grade \'əp-ˌgrād\ *n* **1** ♦ : an upward grade or slope **2** ♦ : an increase in price, value, rate, or sum : RISE

♦ [1] cant, diagonal, grade, inclination, incline, lean, pitch, slant, slope, tilt — more at SLANT ♦ [2] advancement, ascent, elevation, promotion, rise — more at ADVANCEMENT

²up·grade \'əp-ˌgrād, ˌəp-'grād\ *vb* **1** ♦ : to raise to a higher grade or position; *esp* : to advance to a job requiring a higher level of skill **2** : to improve or replace (as software or a device) for increased usefulness

♦ advance, elevate, promote, raise — more at PROMOTE

up·growth \'əp-ˌgrōth\ *n* : the process of growing upward : DEVELOPMENT; *also* : a product or result of this

up·heav·al \ˌəp-'hē-vəl\ *n* **1** : the action or an instance of uplifting esp. of part of the earth's crust **2** ♦ : a violent agitation or change

---

List of self-explanatory words with the prefix *un-* (continued)

unweathered	unwillingness	unworn	unwoven
unwillingly	unwomanly	unwounded	

♦ cataclysm, convulsion, paroxysm, storm, tempest, tumult, uproar — more at CONVULSION

¹up·hill \'əp-'hil\ *adv* : upward on a hill or incline; *also* : against difficulties

²up·hill \-,hil\ *adj* **1** : situated on elevated ground **2** : ASCENDING **3** ♦ : hard to do or make : DIFFICULT, LABORIOUS

♦ arduous, challenging, demanding, difficult, exacting, formidable, grueling, hard, herculean, laborious, murderous, rough, severe, stiff, strenuous, tall, toilsome, tough — more at HARD

up·hold \,əp-'hōld\ *vb* **-held** \-'held\; **-hold·ing** **1** ♦ : to give support to **2** ♦ : to support or defend against opposition **3 a** : to keep elevated **b** : to lift up — **up·hold·er** *n*

♦ [1] bear, bolster, brace, buttress, carry, prop, shore, stay, support — more at SUPPORT ♦ [2] defend, justify, maintain, support — more at MAINTAIN

up·hol·ster \,əp-'hōl-stər\ *vb* : to furnish with or as if with upholstery — **up·hol·ster·er** *n*

up·hol·stery \-stə-rē\ *n, pl* **-ster·ies** [ME *upholdester* upholsterer, fr. *upholden* to uphold, fr. *up* + *holden* to hold] : materials (as fabrics, padding, and springs) used to make a soft covering esp. for a seat

UPI *abbr* United Press International

up·keep \'əp-,kēp\ *n* ♦ : the act or cost of keeping up or maintaining; *also* : the state of being maintained

♦ conservation, maintenance, preservation — more at MAINTENANCE

up·land \'əp-lənd, -,land\ *n* : high land esp. at some distance from the sea — **upland** *adj*

¹up·lift \,əp-'lift\ *vb* **1** : to lift or raise up : ELEVATE **2** : to improve the condition of esp. morally, socially, or intellectually

²up·lift \'əp-,lift\ *n* **1** : a lifting up; *esp* : an upheaval of the earth's surface **2** : moral or social improvement; *also* : a movement to make such improvement

up·load \,əp-'lōd, 'əp-,lōd\ *vb* : to transfer (information) from a computer to a remote computer or other device

up·mar·ket \,əp-'mär-kət\ *adj* : appealing to wealthy consumers

up·most \'əp-,mōst\ *adj* : in or into the highest or most prominent position : UPPERMOST

up·on \ə-'pón, -'pän\ *prep* : in or in contact with an outer surface : ON

¹up·per \'ə-pər\ *adj* **1** : higher in physical position, rank, or order **2** : constituting the smaller and more restricted branch of a bicameral legislature **3** *cap* : being a later part or formation of a specific geological period **4** : being toward the interior ⟨the ∼ Amazon⟩ **5** : NORTHERN ⟨∼ Minnesota⟩

²upper *n* : one that is upper; *esp* : the parts of a shoe or boot above the sole

up·per·case \,ə-pər-'kās\ *adj* : CAPITAL 1 — **uppercase** *n*

upper class *n* : a social class occupying a position above the middle class and having the highest status in a society — **upper–class** *adj*

up·per·class·man \,ə-pər-'klas-mən\ *n* : a junior or senior in a college or high school

upper crust *n* : the highest social class or group; *esp* : the highest circle of the upper class

up·per·cut \'ə-pər-,kət\ *n* : a short swinging punch delivered (as in boxing) in an upward direction usu. with a bent arm

upper hand *n* ♦ : superiority of position or condition : ADVANTAGE

♦ advantage, better, drop, edge, jump, vantage — more at ADVANTAGE

up·per·most \'ə-pər-,mōst\ *adv* : in or into the highest or most prominent position — **uppermost** *adj*

up·pish \'ə-pish\ *adj* : putting on or marked by airs of superiority : UPPITY ⟨an ∼ sales clerk⟩

up·pi·ty \'ə-pə-tē\ *adj* ♦ : putting on or marked by airs of superiority : ARROGANT

♦ arrogant, cavalier, haughty, highfalutin, high-handed, high-hat, imperious, important, lofty, lordly, masterful, overweening, peremptory, pompous, presumptuous, pretentious, supercilious, superior — more at ARROGANT

up·raise \,əp-'rāz\ *vb* : to raise or lift up : ELEVATE

¹up·right \'əp-,rīt\ *adj* **1** ♦ : perpendicular to the plane of the horizon or to a primary axis : VERTICAL **2** : erect in carriage or posture **3** ♦ : morally correct : JUST ⟨an ∼ citizen⟩ — **upright** *adv* — **up·right·ly** *adv*

♦ [1] erect, perpendicular, standing, upstanding, vertical — more at ERECT ♦ [3] decent, ethical, good, honest, honorable (*or* honourable), just, moral, right, righteous, straight, virtuous — more at GOOD

²upright *n* **1** : the state of being upright : a vertical position **2** : something that stands upright

up·right·ness *n* ♦ : the state or quality of being upright

♦ character, decency, goodness, honesty, integrity, morality, probity, rectitude, righteousness, virtue — more at MORALITY

upright piano *n* : a piano whose strings run vertically

up·ris·ing \'əp-,rī-ziŋ\ *n* ♦ : an act or instance of rising up : INSURRECTION

♦ insurrection, mutiny, rebellion, revolt, revolution — more at REBELLION

up·riv·er \'əp-'ri-vər\ *adv or adj* : toward or at a point nearer the source of a river

up·roar \'əp-,rōr\ *n* [D *oproer*, fr. MD, fr. *op* up + *roer* motion] ♦ : a state of commotion, excitement, or violent disturbance

♦ commotion, disturbance, furor, hubbub, hullabaloo, pandemonium, tumult ♦ cataclysm, convulsion, paroxysm, storm, tempest, tumult, upheaval — more at CONVULSION

up·roar·i·ous \,əp-'rōr-ē-əs\ *adj* **1** : marked by uproar **2** ♦ : extremely funny — **up·roar·i·ous·ly** *adv*

♦ antic, comic, comical, droll, farcical, funny, hilarious, humorous, hysterical, laughable, ludicrous, ridiculous, riotous, risible, screaming — more at FUNNY

up·root \,əp-'rüt, -'rüt\ *vb* **1** ♦ : to remove by or as if by pulling up by the roots **2** : DISPLACE 1 ⟨families were ∼ed⟩

♦ extract, prize, pry, pull, root, tear, wrest — more at EXTRACT

¹up·set \,əp-'set\ *vb* **-set; -set·ting** **1** : to force or be forced out of the usual upright, level, or proper position **2** ♦ : to disturb emotionally : WORRY; *also* : to make somewhat ill **3** ♦ : to throw into disorder **4** : to defeat unexpectedly

♦ [2] agitate, bother, concern, discompose, disquiet, distress, disturb, exercise, freak, perturb, undo, unhinge, unsettle, worry ♦ [3] confuse, derange, disarray, dishevel, dislocate, disorder, disrupt, jumble, mess, mix, muddle, scramble, shuffle — more at DISORDER

²up·set \'əp-,set\ *n* **1** : an upsetting or being upset; *esp* : a minor illness **2** ♦ : a derangement of plans or ideas **3** : an unexpected defeat

♦ derangement, dislocation, disruption, disturbance; *also* convulsion, revolution, upheaval

³up·set \(,)əp-'set\ *adj* ♦ : emotionally disturbed or agitated

♦ aflutter, anxious, edgy, jittery, jumpy, nervous, nervy, perturbed, tense, troubled, uneasy, worried — more at NERVOUS

up·set·ting *adj* ♦ : producing an upset; *esp* : causing an emotional disturbance

♦ troublesome, unsettling, worrisome — more at TROUBLESOME

up·shot \'əp-,shät\ *n* ♦ : the final result

♦ aftermath, conclusion, consequence, corollary, development, effect, issue, outcome, outgrowth, product, result, resultant, sequence — more at EFFECT

¹up·side \'əp-ˌsīd\ *n* 1 : the upper side 2 : a positive aspect 3 : PROMISE 2 ⟨rookies with much ∼⟩

²up·side \ˌəp-'sīd\ *prep* : up on or against the side of ⟨knocked him ∼ the head⟩

up·side down \ˌəp-ˌsīd-'daún\ *adv* 1 : with the upper and the lower parts reversed in position 2 : in or into confusion or disorder — **upside-down** *adj*

up·si·lon \'üp-sə-ˌlän, 'yüp-, 'əp-\ *n* : the 20th letter of the Greek alphabet — Y or υ

¹up·stage \'əp-ˌstāj\ *adv or adj* : toward or at the rear of a theatrical stage

²up·stage \ˌəp-'stāj\ *vb* : to draw attention away from (as an actor)

¹up·stairs \ˌəp-'starz\ *adv* 1 : up the stairs : to or on a higher floor 2 : to or at a higher position

²up·stairs \ˌəp-'starz\ *adj* : situated above the stairs esp. on an upper floor ⟨∼ bedroom⟩

³up·stairs \'əp-ˌstarz, 'əp-ˌstarz\ *n sing or pl* : the part of a building above the ground floor

up·stand·ing \ˌəp-'stan-diŋ, 'əp-\ *adj* 1 : vertical in position : ERECT 2 ♦ : marked by integrity : HONEST ⟨∼ citizens⟩

♦ decent, ethical, honest, honorable, just, noble, principled, respectable, righteous, upright — more at HONORABLE

¹up·start \ˌəp-'stärt\ *vb* : to jump up suddenly

²up·start \'əp-ˌstärt\ *n* : one that has risen suddenly; *esp* : one that claims more personal importance than is warranted — **up·start** \-'stärt\ *adj*

up·state \'əp-'stāt\ *adj* : of, relating to, or characteristic of a part of a state away from a large city and esp. to the north — **upstate** *adv* — **upstate** *n*

up·stream \'əp-'strēm\ *adv* : at or toward the source of a stream — **upstream** *adj*

up·stroke \'əp-ˌstrōk\ *n* : an upward stroke (as of a pen)

up·surge \-ˌsərj\ *n* : a rapid or sudden rise

up·swept \'əp-ˌswept\ *adj* : swept upward ⟨∼ hairdo⟩

up·swing \'əp-ˌswiŋ\ *n* : an upward swing; *esp* : a marked increase or rise (as in activity)

up·take \'əp-ˌtāk\ *n* 1 : UNDERSTANDING, COMPREHENSION ⟨quick on the ∼⟩ 2 : an act or instance of absorbing and incorporating esp. into a living organism, tissue, or cell

up·thrust \'əp-ˌthrəst\ *n* : an upward thrust (as of the earth's crust) — **upthrust** *vb*

up·tight \'əp-'tīt\ *adj* 1 : being tense, nervous, or uneasy : NERVOUS; *also* : INDIGNANT 2 : rigidly conventional

up–to–date *adj* 1 : extending up to the present time 2 ♦ : being, having, or involving modern techniques, methods, or information — **up–to–date·ness** *n*

♦ contemporary, current, hot, mod, modern, new, newfangled, red-hot, space-age, ultramodern — more at MODERN ♦ abreast, conversant, familiar, informed, knowledgeable, up, versed — more at FAMILIAR

up·town \'əp-ˌtaún\ *n* : the upper part of a town or city; *esp* : the residential district — **up·town** \'əp-'taún\ *adj or adv*

¹up·turn \'əp-ˌtərn, ˌəp-'tərn\ *vb* 1 : to turn (as earth) up or over 2 : to turn or direct upward

²up·turn \'əp-ˌtərn\ *n* : an upward turn esp. toward better conditions or higher prices

¹up·ward \'əp-wərd\ *or* up·wards \-wərdz\ *adv* 1 : in a direction from lower to higher 2 : toward a higher or better condition 3 : toward a greater amount or higher number, degree, or rate

²upward *adj* : directed or moving toward or situated in a higher place or level : ASCENDING — **up·ward·ly** *adv*

upwards of *also* upward of *adv* : more than : in excess of ⟨they cost *upwards of* $25 each⟩

up·well \ˌəp-'wel\ *vb* : to move or flow upward

up·well·ing \-'we-liŋ\ *n* : a rising or an appearance of rising to the surface and flowing outward; *esp* : the movement of deep cold usu. nutrient-rich ocean water to the surface

up·wind \'əp-'wind\ *adv or adj* : in the direction from which the wind is blowing

ura·cil \'yúr-ə-ˌsil\ *n* : a pyrimidine base that is one of the four bases coding genetic information in the molecular chain of RNA

ura·ni·um \yu̇-'rā-nē-əm\ *n* : a silvery heavy radioactive metallic chemical element used as a source of atomic energy

Ura·nus \'yúr-ə-nəs, yu̇-'rā-\ *n* [LL, the sky personified as a god, fr. Gk *Ouranos*, fr. *ouranos* sky, heaven] : the planet 7th in order from the sun

ur·ban \'ər-bən\ *adj* : of, relating to, characteristic of, or constituting a city

ur·bane \ˌər-'bān\ *adj* [L *urbanus* urban, urbane, fr. *urbs* city] ♦ : very polite and polished in manner : SUAVE

♦ debonair, smooth, sophisticated, suave — more at SUAVE

ur·ban·ite \'ər-bə-ˌnīt\ *n* : a person who lives in a city

ur·ban·i·ty \ˌər-'ba-nə-tē\ *n, pl* -ties : the quality or state of being urbane

ur·ban·ize \'ər-bə-ˌnīz\ *vb* -ized; -iz·ing : to cause to take on urban characteristics — **ur·ban·i·za·tion** \ˌər-bə-nə-'zā-shən\ *n*

ur·chin \'ər-chən\ *n* [ME, hedgehog, fr. AF *heriçun, hirechoun*, ultim. fr. L *ericius*] ♦ : a pert or mischievous youngster

♦ devil, hellion, imp, mischief, monkey, rapscallion, rascal, rogue, scamp — more at SCAMP

Ur·du \'ur-dü, 'ər-\ *n* [Hindi & Urdu *urdū*, fr. Pers *zabāne-urdū-e-muallā* language of the Exalted Comp (the imperial bazaar in Delhi)] : a language that is the official language of Pakistan and that is widely used by Muslims in urban areas of India

urea \yu̇-'rē-ə\ *n* : a soluble nitrogenous compound that is the chief solid constituent of mammalian urine

ure·mia \yu̇-'rē-mē-ə\ *n* : accumulation in the blood of materials normally passed off in the urine resulting in a poisoned condition — **ure·mic** \-mik\ *adj*

ure·ter \'yúr-ə-tər\ *n* : a duct that carries the urine from a kidney to the bladder

ure·thra \yu̇-'rē-thrə\ *n, pl* -thras *or* -thrae \-(ˌ)thrē\ : the canal that in most mammals carries off the urine from the bladder and in the male also serves to carry semen from the body — **ure·thral** \-thrəl\ *adj*

ure·thri·tis \ˌyúr-i-'thrī-təs\ *n* : inflammation of the urethra

¹urge \'ərj\ *vb* urged; urg·ing 1 : to present, advocate, or demand earnestly 2 ♦ : to try to persuade or sway ⟨∼ a guest to stay⟩ 3 : to serve as a motive or reason for 4 ♦ : to impress or impel to some course or activity ⟨*urged* him to stay⟩ ⟨the dog *urged* the sheep onward⟩

♦ [2, 4] egg on, encourage, exhort, goad, press, prod, prompt; *also* drive, propel, spur, stimulate; hurry, hustle, push, rush; beseech, implore, importune; cajole, coax, wheedle; high-pressure, nag, needle, pressure; foment, incite, instigate, provoke, stir (up)

²urge *n* 1 : the act or process of urging 2 ♦ : a force or impulse that urges or drives

♦ appetite, craving, desire, drive, hankering, hunger, itch, longing, lust, passion, thirst, yearning, yen — more at DESIRE

ur·gent \'ər-jənt\ *adj* 1 ♦ : calling for immediate attention : PRESSING 2 : urging insistently — **ur·gen·cy** \-jən-sē\ *n* — **ur·gent·ly** *adv*

♦ acute, critical, dire, imperative, imperious, instant, pressing — more at ACUTE

uric \'yúr-ik\ *adj* : of, relating to, or found in urine

uric acid *n* : a nearly insoluble acid that is the chief nitrogenous excretory product of birds but is present in only small amounts in mammalian urine

uri·nal \'yúr-ən-ᵊl\ *n* 1 : a receptacle for urine 2 : a place for urinating

uri·nal·y·sis \ˌyúr-ə-'na-lə-səs\ *n* : chemical analysis of urine

uri·nary \'yúr-ə-ˌner-ē\ *adj* 1 : relating to, occurring in, or being organs for the formation and discharge of urine 2 : of, relating to, or for urine

urinary bladder *n* : a membranous sac in many vertebrates

that serves for the temporary retention of urine and discharges by the urethra

uri·nate \'yùr-ə-ˌnāt\ vb **-nat·ed; -nat·ing** : to release or give off urine — **uri·na·tion** \ˌyùr-ə-'nā-shən\ n

urine \'yùr-ən\ n : a waste material from the kidneys that is usu. a yellowish watery liquid in mammals but is semisolid in birds and reptiles

URL \ˌyü-(ˌ)är-'el, 'ər(-ə)l\ n [uniform (or universal) resource locator] : a series of usu. alphanumeric characters that specifies the storage location of a resource on the Internet

urn \'ərn\ n 1 : a vessel that typically has the form of a vase on a pedestal and often is used to hold the ashes of the dead 2 : a closed vessel usu. with a spout for serving a hot beverage

uro·gen·i·tal \ˌyùr-ō-'je-nət-ᵊl\ adj : of, relating to, or being the excretory and reproductive organs or functions

urol·o·gy \yù-'rä-lə-jē\ n : a branch of medical science dealing with the urinary or urogenital tract and its disorders — **uro·log·i·cal** \ˌyùr-ə-'lä-ji-kəl\ also **uro·log·ic** \-jik\ adj — **urol·o·gist** \yù-'rä-lə-jist\ n

Ur·sa Ma·jor \ˌər-sə-'mā-jər\ n [L, lit., greater bear] : the northern constellation that contains the stars which form the Big Dipper

Ursa Mi·nor \-'mī-nər\ n [L, lit., lesser bear] : the constellation including the north pole of the heavens and the stars that form the Little Dipper with the North Star at the tip of the handle

ur·sine \'ər-ˌsīn\ adj : of, relating to, or resembling a bear

ur·ti·car·ia \ˌər-tə-'kar-ē-ə\ n [NL, fr. L urtica nettle] : HIVES

Uru·guay·an \ˌùr-ə-'gwī-ən, ˌyùr-ə-'gwā-\ n : a native or inhabitant of Uruguay — **Uruguayan** adj

us \'əs\ pron, objective case of WE

US abbr United States

USA abbr 1 United States Army 2 United States of America

us·able also **use·able** \'yü-zə-bəl\ adj ♦ : suitable or fit for use — **us·abil·i·ty** \ˌyü-zə-'bi-lə-tē\ n

♦ available, fit, functional, operable, practicable, serviceable, useful; also applicable, relevant; doable, feasible; reusable **Ant** impracticable, inoperable, nonfunctional, unavailable, unusable

USAF abbr United States Air Force

us·age \'yü-sij, -zij\ n 1 : habitual or customary practice or procedure 2 : the way in which words and phrases are actually used 3 : the action or mode of using 4 : manner of treating

USB \ˌyü-(ˌ)es-'bē\ n [universal serial bus] : a standardized computer interface for attaching peripherals

USCG abbr United States Coast Guard

USDA abbr United States Department of Agriculture

¹use \'yüs\ n 1 ♦ : the act or practice of using or employing something : EMPLOYMENT, APPLICATION 2 : the fact or state of being used 3 : the way of using 4 : habitual or customary usage : USAGE, CUSTOM 5 : the privilege or benefit of using something 6 : the ability or power to use something (as a limb) 7 : the legal enjoyment of property that consists in its employment, occupation, or exercise; also : the benefit or profit esp. from property held in trust 8 ♦ : a particular service or end : UTILITY 9 : the occasion or need to employ (had no more ∼ for it) 10 ♦ : a favorable attitude : LIKING (had no ∼ for modern art)

♦ [1] application, employment, exercise, operation, play; also exertion; reuse ♦ [8] account, avail, service, utility; also advantage, benefit, gain; aid, assistance, help; applicability, appropriateness, fitness, relevance; profit, value, worth **Ant** uselessness, worthlessness ♦ [10] appetite, fancy, favor (or favour), fondness, like, liking, love, partiality, preference, relish, shine, taste — more at LIKING

²use \'yüz\ vb **used** \'yüzd; "used to" usu 'yüs-tə\; **us·ing** 1 ♦ : to put into action or service : EMPLOY 2 : to consume or take (as drugs) regularly 3 a : UTILIZE (∼ tact) b ♦ : to control or play upon by artful, unfair, or insidious means esp. to one's own advantage (used his friends

to get ahead) 4 : to expend or consume by putting to use 5 ♦ : to behave toward : TREAT (used the horse cruelly) 6 : to benefit from (house could ∼ a coat of paint) 7 — used in the past with to to indicate a former practice, fact, or state (we used to work harder)

♦ [1] apply, employ, exercise, exploit, harness, operate, utilize; also handle, manipulate, wield; direct, run, work; recycle, reuse ♦ [3b] abuse, capitalize, cash in, exploit, impose, play — more at EXPLOIT ♦ [5] act, be, deal, handle, serve, treat — more at TREAT

used \'yüzd\ adj 1 : having been used by another : SECONDHAND (∼ cars) 2 ♦ : being in the habit or custom : ACCUSTOMED (∼ to the heat)

♦ accustomed, given, wont — more at ACCUSTOMED

use·ful \'yüs-fəl\ adj ♦ : capable of being put to use; esp : serviceable for a beneficial end — **use·ful·ly** adv

♦ applicable, functional, practicable, practical, serviceable, usable, workable, working — more at PRACTICAL

use·ful·ness n : the quality of having utility and esp. practical worth or applicability

use·less \-ləs\ adj ♦ : having or being of no use — **use·less·ly** adv — **use·less·ness** n

♦ impractical, inoperable, unusable, unworkable — more at IMPRACTICAL ♦ fruitless, futile, ineffective, unproductive, unsuccessful — more at FUTILE

us·er n ♦ : one that uses; esp : a person who regularly uses alcoholic beverages or narcotics

♦ addict, doper, fiend — more at DOPER

us·er·name \'yü-zər-ˌnām\ n : a sequence of characters that identifies a user when logging onto a computer or website

USES abbr United States Employment Service

use up vb ♦ : to consume completely

♦ clean, consume, deplete, drain, exhaust, expend, spend — more at DEPLETE

¹ush·er \'ə-shər\ n [ME ussher, fr. MF ussier, fr. (assumed) VL ustiarius doorkeeper, fr. L ostium, ustium door, mouth of a river] 1 : an officer who walks before a person of rank 2 : one who escorts people to their seats (as in a church or theater)

²usher vb 1 ♦ : to conduct to a place 2 : to precede as an usher, forerunner, or harbinger 3 : INAUGURATE, INTRODUCE (∼ in a new era)

♦ conduct, direct, guide, lead, marshal, pilot, route, show, steer — more at LEAD

ush·er·ette \ˌə-shə-'ret\ n : a girl or woman who is an usher (as in a theater)

USIA abbr United States Information Agency

USMC abbr United States Marine Corps

USN abbr United States Navy

USO abbr United Service Organizations

USP abbr United States Pharmacopeia

USPS abbr United States Postal Service

USS abbr United States ship

USSR abbr Union of Soviet Socialist Republics

usu abbr usual; usually

usu·al \'yü-zhə-wəl\ adj 1 : accordant with usage, custom, or habit 2 ♦ : commonly or ordinarily used 3 ♦ : of a kind to be expected in the normal order of events : ORDINARY

♦ [2] conventional, current, customary, popular, standard, stock — more at CURRENT ♦ [3] average, common, commonplace, everyday, normal, ordinary, prosaic, routine, run-of-the-mill, standard, unexceptional, unremarkable, workaday — more at ORDINARY

usu·al·ly \'yü-zhə-wə-lē, 'yü-zhə-lē\ adv ♦ : more often than not : as a rule

♦ commonly, generally, naturally, normally, ordinarily, typically — more at NATURALLY

usu·fruct \'yü-zə-ˌfrəkt\ n [L ususfructus, fr. usus et fructus use and enjoyment] : the legal right to use and enjoy the benefits and profits of something belonging to another

usu·rer \'yü-zhər-ər\ *n* : one that lends money esp. at an exorbitant rate

usu·ri·ous \yu̇-'zhu̇r-ē-əs\ *adj* : practicing, involving, or constituting usury ⟨a ∼ rate of interest⟩

usurp \yu̇-'sərp, -'zərp\ *vb* [ME, fr. AF *usorper*, fr. L *usurpare*, to take possession of without legal claim, fr. *usu* (abl. of *usus* use) + *rapere* to seize] ♦ : to seize and hold by force or without right ⟨∼ a throne⟩ — **usur·pa·tion** \,yü-sər-'pā-shən, -zər-\ *n* — **usurp·er** \yu̇-'sər-pər, -'zər-\ *n*

♦ appropriate, arrogate, commandeer, preempt — more at APPROPRIATE

usu·ry \'yü-zhə-rē\ *n, pl* **-ries** 1 : the lending of money with an interest charge for its use 2 : an excessive rate or amount of interest charged; *esp* : interest above an established legal rate

UT *abbr* Utah

Ute \'yüt\ *n, pl* **Ute** *or* **Utes** : a member of an American Indian people orig. ranging through Utah, Colorado, Arizona, and New Mexico

uten·sil \yu̇-'ten-səl\ *n* [ME, vessels for domestic use, fr. MF *utensile*, fr. L *utensilia*, fr. neut. pl. of *utensilis* useful, fr. *uti* to use] 1 : an instrument or vessel used in a household and esp. a kitchen 2 ♦ : a useful tool

♦ device, implement, instrument, tool — more at IMPLEMENT

uter·us \'yü-tə-rəs\ *n, pl* **uter·us·es** *or* **uteri** \'yü-tə-,rī\ : the muscular organ of a female mammal in which the young develop before birth — **uter·ine** \-,rīn, -rən\ *adj*

utile \'yüt-ᵊl, 'yü-,tīl\ *adj* : USEFUL

uti·lise *chiefly Brit var of* UTILIZE

¹**util·i·tar·i·an** \yu̇-,ti-lə-'ter-ē-ən\ *n* : a person who believes in utilitarianism

²**utilitarian** *adj* 1 : of or relating to utilitarianism 2 : of or relating to utility : aiming at usefulness rather than beauty; *also* : serving a useful purpose

util·i·tar·i·an·ism \-ē-ə-,ni-zəm\ *n* : a theory that the greatest good for the greatest number should be the main consideration in making a choice of actions

¹**util·i·ty** \yu̇-'ti-lə-tē\ *n, pl* **-ties** 1 ♦ : fitness for some purpose or worth to some end : USEFULNESS 2 : something useful or designed for use 3 : a business organization performing a public service and subject to special governmental regulation 4 : a public service or a commodity (as electricity or water) provided by a public utility; *also* : equipment to provide such or a similar service

♦ account, avail, service, use — more at USE

²**utility** *adj* 1 : capable of serving esp. as a substitute in various uses or positions ⟨a ∼ outfielder⟩ 2 : being of a usable but poor quality ⟨∼ beef⟩

utility knife *n* : a knife designed for general use; *esp* : one with a retractable blade

uti·lize \'yüt-ᵊl-,īz\ *vb* **-lized; -liz·ing** ♦ : to make use of : turn to profitable use — **uti·li·za·tion** \,yüt-ᵊl-ə-'zā-shən\ *n*

♦ apply, employ, exercise, exploit, harness, operate, use — more at USE

ut·most \'ət-,mōst\ *adj* 1 ♦ : situated at the farthest or most distant point : EXTREME 2 ♦ : of the greatest or highest degree, quantity, number, or amount — **utmost** *n*

♦ [1] extreme, farthest, furthest, outermost, ultimate — more at EXTREME ♦ [2] consummate, maximum, most, nth, paramount, supreme, top, ultimate — more at ULTIMATE

uto·pia \yu̇-'tō-pē-ə\ *n* [*Utopia*, imaginary island described in Sir Thomas More's *Utopia*, fr. Gk *ou* not, no + *topos* place] 1 *often cap* ♦ : a place of ideal perfection esp. in laws, government, and social conditions 2 : an impractical scheme for social improvement

♦ Eden, Elysium, heaven, paradise — more at PARADISE

¹**uto·pi·an** \-pē-ən\ *adj, often cap* 1 : of, relating to, or resembling a utopia 2 : proposing ideal social and political schemes that are impractical 3 : VISIONARY

²**utopian** *n* 1 ♦ : a believer in the perfectibility of human society 2 : one who proposes or advocates utopian schemes

♦ dreamer, idealist, romantic, visionary — more at IDEALIST

¹**ut·ter** \'ə-tər\ *adj* [ME, remote, fr. OE *ūtera* outer, compar. adj. fr. *ūt* out, adv.] : carried to the utmost point or highest degree : ABSOLUTE ⟨∼ ruin⟩

²**utter** *vb* [ME *uttren*, fr. *utter* outside, adv., fr. OE *ūtor*, compar. of *ūt* out] 1 ♦ : to send forth as a sound : express in usu. spoken words 2 : to put (as currency) into circulation — **ut·ter·er** *n*

♦ articulate, say, speak, state, talk, tell, verbalize, vocalize — more at SAY

ut·ter·ance \'ə-tə-rəns\ *n* 1 : something uttered; *esp* : an oral or written statement 2 ♦ : the action of uttering with the voice 3 : power, style, or manner of speaking

♦ articulation, expression, formulation, statement, voice — more at EXPRESSION

ut·ter·ly *adv* ♦ : to the full extent

♦ absolutely, all, altogether, clean, completely, entirely, fully, quite, totally, wholly — more at ALL

ut·ter·most \'ə-tər-,mōst\ *adj* : existing in a very high degree : UTMOST ⟨the ∼ parts of the earth⟩ — **uttermost** *n*

U-turn \'yü-,tərn\ *n* : a turn resembling the letter U; *esp* : a 180-degree turn made by a vehicle in a road

UV *abbr* ultraviolet

uvu·la \'yü-vyə-lə\ *n, pl* **-las** *or* **-lae** \-,lē, -,lī\ : the fleshy lobe hanging at the back of the roof of the mouth — **uvu·lar** \-lər\ *adj*

UW *abbr* underwriter

ux·o·ri·ous \,ək-'sȯr-ē-əs, ,əg-'zȯr-\ *adj* : excessively devoted or submissive to a wife

¹**v** \'vē\ *n, pl* **v's** *or* **vs** \'vēz\ *often cap* : the 22d letter of the English alphabet

²**v** *abbr, often cap* 1 vector 2 velocity 3 verb 4 verse 5 versus 6 very 7 victory 8 vide 9 voice 10 voltage 11 volume 12 vowel

V *symbol* 1 vanadium 2 volt

Va *abbr* Virginia

VA *abbr* 1 Veterans Administration 2 vice admiral 3 Virginia

va·can·cy \'vā-kən-sē\ *n, pl* **-cies** 1 : a vacating esp. of an

office, position, or piece of property 2 : a vacant office, position, or tenancy; *also* : the period during which it stands vacant 3 ♦ : empty space : VOID 4 ♦ : the state of being vacant

♦ [3] blank, blankness, emptiness, vacuity, void; *also* nothingness; vacuum; bareness, barrenness, bleakness, desolateness, hollowness ♦ [4] emptiness, vacuity; *also* hollowness; blankness, vacuum, void; barrenness, bleakness, desolateness; availability, clearness, openness; depletion, dryness, exhaustion *Ant* fullness

va·cant \'vā-kənt\ *adj* **1** : not occupied ⟨∼ seat⟩ ⟨∼ room⟩ **2** ♦ : devoid of contents : EMPTY ⟨∼ space⟩ **3** ♦ : free from business or care ⟨a few ∼ hours⟩ **4** ♦ : devoid of thought, reflection, or expression ⟨a ∼ smile⟩ — **va·cant·ly** *adv*

♦ [2] bare, blank, devoid, empty, stark, void — more at EMPTY ♦ [3] dead, dormant, fallow, free, idle, inactive, inert, inoperative, latent, off — more at INACTIVE ♦ [4] blank, deadpan, expressionless, impassive, inexpressive, stolid — more at BLANK

va·cate \'vā-ˌkāt\ *vb* **va·cat·ed; va·cat·ing** **1** : to make void : ANNUL **2** ♦ : to make vacant (as an office or house); *also* : to give up the occupancy of

♦ clear, empty, evacuate, void — more at EMPTY

¹va·ca·tion \vā-'kā-shən, və-\ *n* ♦ : a period of rest from work

♦ break, leave, recess; *also* furlough, liberty; breather, relaxation, respite, rest; interim, intermission, interval; feast; honeymoon; idling, loafing, lounging

²vacation *vb* : to take or spend a vacation — **va·ca·tion·er** *n*
va·ca·tion·ist \-shə-nist\ *n* : a person taking a vacation
va·ca·tion·land \-shən-ˌland\ *n* : an area with recreational attractions and facilities for vacationists
vac·ci·nate \'vak-sə-ˌnāt\ *vb* **-nat·ed; -nat·ing** : to administer a vaccine to usu. by injection
vac·ci·na·tion \ˌvak-sə-'nā-shən\ *n* **1** : the act of vaccinating **2** : the scar left by vaccinating
vac·cine \vak-'sēn, 'vak-ˌsēn\ *n* [F *vaccin,* fr. *vaccine* cowpox, fr. NL *vaccina* (in *variolae vaccinae* cowpox), fr. L, fem. of *vaccinus* of or from cows, fr. *vacca* cow] : material (as a preparation of killed or weakened virus or bacteria) used in vaccinating to induce immunity to a disease
vac·cin·ia \vak-'si-nē-ə\ *n* : COWPOX
vac·il·late \'va-sə-ˌlāt\ *vb* **-lat·ed; -lat·ing** **1** : SWAY, TOTTER; *also* : FLUCTUATE **2** ♦ : to incline first to one course or opinion and then to another : WAVER

♦ falter, hang back, hesitate, shilly-shally, stagger, teeter, waver, wobble — more at HESITATE

vac·il·la·tion \ˌva-sə-'lā-shən\ *n* ♦ : an act or instance of vacillating

♦ hesitancy, hesitation, indecision, irresolution — more at HESITATION

va·cu·ity \va-'kyü-ə-tē\ *n, pl* **-ities** **1** ♦ : an empty space **2** ♦ : the state, fact, or quality of being vacuous **3** : something that is vacuous

♦ [1, 2] blank, blankness, emptiness, vacancy, void — more at VACANCY ♦ [2] dopiness, mindlessness, stupidity — more at STUPIDITY

vac·u·ole \'va-kyə-ˌwōl\ *n* : a usu. fluid-filled cavity esp. in the cytoplasm of an individual cell — **vac·u·o·lar** \ˌva-kyə-'wō-lər, -ˌlär\ *adj*
vac·u·ous \'va-kyə-wəs\ *adj* **1** : EMPTY, VACANT, BLANK **2** ♦ : marked by or indicative of a lack of ideas or intelligence : DULL — **vac·u·ous·ly** *adv* — **vac·u·ous·ness** *n*

♦ dense, dull, dumb, mindless, simple, slow, stupid, unintelligent, witless — more at STUPID

¹vac·u·um \'va-(ˌ)kyüm, -kyəm\ *n, pl* **vacuums** *or* **vac·ua** \-kyə-wə\ [L, fr. neut. of *vacuus* empty] **1** : a space entirely empty of matter **2** : a space from which most of the air has been removed (as by a pump) **3** : VOID, GAP **4** : VACUUM CLEANER — **vacuum** *adj*
²vacuum *vb* : to use a vacuum device (as a vacuum cleaner) on
vacuum bottle *n* : THERMOS
vacuum cleaner *n* : a household appliance for cleaning (as floors or rugs) by suction
vacuum–packed *adj* : having much of the air removed before being hermetically sealed
vacuum tube *n* : an electron tube from which most of the air has been removed
va·de me·cum \ˌvā-dē-'mē-kəm, ˌvä-dē-'mā-\ *n, pl* **vade mecums** [L, go with me] : something (as a handbook or manual) regularly carried about
VADM *abbr* vice admiral

¹vag·a·bond \'va-gə-ˌbänd\ *adj* **1** ♦ : moving from place to place without a fixed home : WANDERING **2** : of, relating to, or characteristic of a wanderer; *esp* : of, characteristic of, or leading the life of a vagrant or tramp **3** : leading an unsettled or irresponsible life

♦ errant, itinerant, nomad, peripatetic, roaming, vagrant — more at ITINERANT

²vagabond *n* **1** ♦ : one leading a vagabond life **2** ♦ : an idle beggar : TRAMP

♦ [1] drifter, nomad, rambler, rover, stroller, wanderer — more at NOMAD ♦ [2] bum, hobo, tramp, vagrant — more at TRAMP

va·ga·ry \'vā-gə-rē, və-'ger-ē\ *n, pl* **-ries** ♦ : an odd or eccentric idea or action : WHIM, CAPRICE

♦ caprice, fancy, freak, notion, whim — more at WHIM

va·gi·na \və-'jī-nə\ *n, pl* **-nae** \-(ˌ)nē\ *or* **-nas** [L, lit., sheath] : a canal that leads from the uterus to the external opening of the female sex organs — **vag·i·nal** \'va-jən-ᵊl\ *adj* — **vag·i·nal·ly** \-nᵊl-ē\ *adv*
vag·i·ni·tis \ˌva-jə-'nī-təs\ *n* : inflammation of the vagina
va·gran·cy \'vā-grən-sē\ *n, pl* **-cies** **1** : the quality or state of being vagrant; *also* : a vagrant act or notion **2** : the offense of being a vagrant
¹va·grant \'vā-grənt\ *n* ♦ : a person who has no job and wanders from place to place

♦ bum, hobo, tramp, vagabond — more at TRAMP

²vagrant *adj* **1** ♦ : of, relating to, or characteristic of a vagrant **2** : following no fixed course : RANDOM, CAPRICIOUS ⟨∼ thoughts⟩ — **va·grant·ly** *adv*

♦ errant, itinerant, nomad, peripatetic, roaming, vagabond — more at ITINERANT

vague \'vāg\ *adj* **vagu·er; vagu·est** [MF, fr. L *vagus,* lit., wandering] **1** ♦ : not clear, definite, or distinct in expression or perception **2** : not clearly felt or analyzed ⟨a ∼ unrest⟩ — **vague·ly** *adv* — **vague·ness** *n*

♦ fuzzy, indefinite, unclear; *also* ambiguous, cryptic, dark, enigmatic, equivocal, murky, nebulous, obscure, unintelligible; bleary, dim, faint, foggy, hazy, indeterminate, indistinguishable, uncertain, undefinable, undefined, undetermined; inexplicable, inscrutable, mysterious; baffling, bewildering, confounding, confusing, mystifying, perplexing, puzzling, unfathomable *Ant* clear, definite, explicit, specific ♦ bleary, dim, faint, foggy, fuzzy, hazy, indefinite, indistinct, indistinguishable, murky, nebulous, obscure, opaque, shadowy, unclear, undefined, undetermined — more at FAINT

vain \'vān\ *adj* [ME, fr. AF, empty, futile, fr. L *vanus*] **1** : of no real value : IDLE, WORTHLESS **2** ♦ : marked by a lack of effectiveness or success : UNSUCCESSFUL **3** ♦ : proud of one's looks or abilities — **vain·ly** *adv*

♦ [2] fruitless, futile, ineffective, unproductive, unsuccessful — more at FUTILE ♦ [3] complacent, conceited, egotistic, important, overweening, pompous, prideful, proud, self-important, self-satisfied, smug, stuck-up — more at CONCEITED

vain·glo·ri·ous \ˌvān-'glōr-ē-əs\ *adj* : marked by vainglory : being vain
vain·glo·ry \'vān-ˌglōr-ē\ *n* **1** ♦ : excessive or ostentatious pride esp. in one's own achievements **2** : vain display : VANITY

♦ complacence, conceit, ego, egotism, pride, self-conceit, self-esteem, self-importance, self-satisfaction, smugness, vanity — more at COMPLACENCE

val *abbr* value; valued
va·lance \'va-ləns, 'vā-\ *n* **1** : drapery hanging from an edge (as of an altar, table, or bed) **2** : a drapery or a decorative frame across the top of a window
vale \'vāl\ *n* : a low-lying country or tract usu. containing a brook or a stream : VALLEY
vale·dic·tion \ˌva-lə-'dik-shən\ *n* [L *valedicere* to say farewell, fr. *vale* farewell + *dicere* to say] : an act or utterance of leave-taking : FAREWELL

vale·dic·to·ri·an \-ˌdik-'tōr-ē-ən\ *n* : the student usu. of the highest rank in a graduating class who delivers the valedictory address at commencement

vale·dic·to·ry \-'dik-tə-rē\ *adj* : bidding farewell : delivered as a valediction ⟨a ∼ address⟩ — **valedictory** *n*

va·lence \'vā-ləns\ *n* [LL *valentia* power, capacity, fr. L *valēre* to be strong] : the combining power of an atom as shown by the number of its electrons that are lost, gained, or shared in the formation of chemical bonds

Va·len·ci·ennes \və-ˌlen-sē-'en, ˌva-lən-sē-, -'enz\ *n* : a fine handmade lace

val·en·tine \'va-lən-ˌtīn\ *n* : a sweetheart chosen or complimented on Valentine's Day; *also* : a gift or greeting given on this day

Valentine's Day *also* **Valentine Day** *n* : February 14 observed in honor of St. Valentine and as a time for exchanging valentines

¹**va·let** \'va-lət, -(ˌ)lā; va-'lā\ *n* 1 : a male servant who takes care of a man's clothes and performs personal services 2 : an attendant in a hotel or restaurant who performs personal services (as parking cars) for customers

²**valet** *vb* : to serve as a valet

val·e·tu·di·nar·i·an \ˌva-lə-ˌtüd-ᵊn-'er-ē-ən, -ˌtyüd-\ *n* : a person of a weak or sickly constitution; *esp* : one whose chief concern is his or her ill health — **val·e·tu·di·nar·i·an·ism** \-ē-ə-ˌni-zəm\ *n*

val·iant \'val-yənt\ *adj* ♦ : having or showing valor : BRAVE — **val·iant·ly** *adv*

♦ brave, courageous, dauntless, doughty, fearless, gallant, greathearted, heroic, intrepid, lionhearted, manful, stalwart, stout, undaunted, valorous — more at BRAVE

val·id \'va-ləd\ *adj* 1 : having legal force ⟨a ∼ contract⟩ 2 ♦ : founded on truth or fact : capable of being justified or defended ⟨a ∼ argument⟩ ⟨∼ reasons⟩ — **va·lid·i·ty** \və-'li-də-tē\ *n* — **val·id·ly** *adv*

♦ analytic, coherent, good, logical, rational, reasonable, sensible, sober, sound — more at LOGICAL ♦ good, hard, informed, just, levelheaded, logical, reasoned, solid, well-founded — more at GOOD

val·i·date \'va-lə-ˌdāt\ *vb* **-dat·ed; -dat·ing** 1 : to make legally valid 2 ♦ : to confirm the validity of 3 ♦ : to corroborate or support on a sound basis or authority : VERIFY

♦ [2] demonstrate, document, establish, prove, substantiate — more at PROVE ♦ [3] bear out, confirm, corroborate, substantiate, support, verify, vindicate — more at CONFIRM

val·i·da·tion \ˌva-lə-'dā-shən\ *n* ♦ : the act or an instance of validating

♦ attestation, confirmation, corroboration, documentation, evidence, proof, substantiation, testament, testimony, witness — more at PROOF

va·lise \və-'lēs\ *n* [F] : SUITCASE

val·ley \'va-lē\ *n, pl* **valleys** ♦ : a long depression between ranges of hills or mountains

♦ dale, hollow; *also* canyon, dell, depression, dingle, glen, ravine; basin, bowl

val·or *or Can and Brit* **val·our** \'va-lər\ *n* [ME *valour*, worth, worthiness, bravery, fr. AF, fr. ML *valor*, fr. L *valēre* to be strong] ♦ : personal bravery

♦ bravery, courage, daring, fearlessness, gallantry, guts, hardihood, heart, heroism, nerve, stoutness — more at COURAGE

val·o·ri·za·tion \ˌva-lə-rə-'zā-shən\ *n* : the support of commodity prices by any of various forms of government subsidy — **val·o·rize** \'va-lə-ˌrīz\ *vb*

val·or·ous \'va-lə-rəs\ *adj* ♦ : possessing or exhibiting valor

♦ brave, courageous, dauntless, doughty, fearless, gallant, greathearted, heroic, intrepid, lionhearted, manful, stalwart, stout, undaunted, valiant — more at BRAVE

val·our *chiefly Can and Brit var of* VALOR

¹**valu·able** \'val-yə-bəl, -yə-wə-bəl\ *adj* 1 : having money value 2 ♦ : having great money value 3 : of great use or service

♦ costly, dear, expensive, high, precious — more at COSTLY

²**valuable** *n* : a usu. personal possession of considerable value ⟨their ∼s were stolen⟩

val·u·ate \'val-yə-ˌwāt\ *vb* **-at·ed; -at·ing** : to place a value on : APPRAISE — **val·u·a·tor** \-ˌwā-tər\ *n*

val·u·a·tion \ˌval-yə-'wā-shən\ *n* 1 ♦ : the act or process of valuing; *esp* : appraisal of property 2 : the estimated or determined market value of a thing

♦ appraisal, assessment, estimate, estimation, evaluation, reckoning — more at ESTIMATE

¹**val·ue** \'val-yü\ *n* 1 : a fair return or equivalent in money, goods, or services for something exchanged 2 ♦ : the monetary worth of a thing; *also* : relative worth, utility, or importance ⟨nothing of ∼ to say⟩ 3 : an assigned or computed numerical quantity ⟨the ∼ of *x* in an equation⟩ 4 : relative lightness or darkness of a color : LUMINOSITY 5 : the relative length of a tone or note 6 : something (as a principle or ideal) intrinsically valuable or desirable ⟨human rather than material ∼s⟩

♦ distinction, excellence, merit, virtue — more at EXCELLENCE ♦ account, merit, valuation, worth — more at WORTH

²**value** *vb* **val·ued; valu·ing** 1 ♦ : to estimate the monetary worth of : APPRAISE 2 : to rate in usefulness, importance, or general worth 3 ♦ : to consider or rate highly : PRIZE — **val·u·er** *n*

♦ [1] appraise, assess, estimate, evaluate, rate, set — more at ESTIMATE ♦ [3] appreciate, cherish, love, prize, treasure — more at LOVE

val·ue-add·ed tax *n* : an incremental excise tax that is levied on the value added at each stage of the processing of a raw material or the production and distribution of a commodity

val·ue·less *adj* ♦ : having no value

♦ chaffy, empty, junky, no-good, null, worthless — more at WORTHLESS

valve \'valv\ *n* 1 : a structure (as in a vein) that temporarily closes a passage or that permits movement in one direction only 2 ♦ : a device by which the flow of a fluid material may be regulated by a movable part; *also* : the movable part of such a device 3 : a device in a brass wind instrument for quickly varying the tube length in order to change the fundamental tone by some definite interval 4 : one of the separate usu. hinged pieces of which the shell of some animals and esp. bivalve mollusks consists 5 : one of the pieces into which a ripe seed capsule or pod separates — **valved** \'valvd\ *adj* — **valve·less** *adj*

♦ cock, faucet, gate, spigot, tap — more at FAUCET

val·vu·lar \'val-vyə-lər\ *adj* : of, relating to, or affecting a valve esp. of the heart ⟨∼ heart disease⟩

va·moose \və-'müs, va-\ *vb* **va·moosed; va·moos·ing** [Sp *vamos* let us go] : to leave or go away quickly

¹**vamp** \'vamp\ *vb* 1 : to provide with a new vamp 2 : to patch up with a new part 3 : INVENT, IMPROVISE ⟨∼ up an excuse⟩

²**vamp** *n* 1 : the part of a boot or shoe upper covering esp. the front part of the foot 2 : a short introductory musical passage often repeated

³**vamp** *n* : a woman who uses her charm or wiles to seduce and exploit men

⁴**vamp** *vb* : to practice seductive wiles on : act like a vamp

vam·pire \'vam-ˌpīr\ *n* [F, fr. G *Vampir*, fr. Serbian *vampir*] 1 : a reanimated corpse of folklore that bites and sucks the blood of the living 2 : a person who preys on other people; *esp* : a woman who exploits and ruins her lover 3 : VAMPIRE BAT

vampire bat *n* : any of various bats of Central and South

America that feed on the blood of animals; *also* : any of several other bats that do not feed on blood but are sometimes reputed to do so

¹van \\'van\\ *n* : the forefront of an action or movement : VANGUARD

²van *n* : a usu. enclosed wagon or motortruck for moving goods or animals; *also* : a versatile enclosed box-like motor vehicle

va·na·di·um \\və-'nā-dē-əm\\ *n* : a soft grayish ductile metallic chemical element used esp. to form alloys

Van Al·len belt \\van-'a-lən-\\ *n* : a belt of intense radiation in the magnetosphere composed of charged particles trapped by earth's magnetic field

van·dal \\'vand-ᵊl\\ *n* **1** *cap* : a member of a Germanic people who sacked Rome in A.D. 455 **2** : a person who willfully mars or destroys property

van·dal·ise *chiefly Brit var of* VANDALIZE

van·dal·ism \\-,i-zəm\\ *n* : willful or malicious destruction or defacement of public or private property

van·dal·ize \\-,īz\\ *vb* **-ized; -iz·ing** : to subject to vandalism : DAMAGE

Van·dyke \\van-'dīk\\ *n* : a trim pointed beard

vane \\'vān\\ *n* [ME, fr. OE *fana* banner] **1** : a movable device attached to a high object for showing wind direction **2** : a thin flat or curved object that is rotated about an axis by a flow of fluid or that rotates to cause a fluid to flow or that redirects a flow of fluid ⟨the ∼s of a windmill⟩ **3** : a feather fastened near the back end of an arrow for stability in flight

van·guard \\'van-,gärd\\ *n* **1** : the troops moving at the front of an army **2** : the forefront of an action or movement

va·nil·la \\və-'ni-lə\\ *n* [NL, genus name, fr. Sp *vainilla* vanilla (plant and fruit), dim. of *vaina* sheath, fr. L *vagina*] : a flavoring extract made synthetically or obtained from the long beanlike pods (**vanilla beans**) of a tropical American climbing orchid; *also* : this orchid

van·ish \\'va-nish\\ *vb* ♦ : to pass from sight or existence : disappear completely — **van·ish·er** *n*

   ♦ disappear, dissolve, evaporate, fade, flee, go, melt — more at DISAPPEAR

van·i·ty \\'va-nə-tē\\ *n, pl* **-ties** **1** : something that is vain, empty, or useless **2** : the quality or fact of being useless or futile : FUTILITY **3** ♦ : undue pride in oneself or one's appearance : CONCEIT **4** : a small case for cosmetics : COMPACT

   ♦ complacence, conceit, ego, egotism, pride, self-conceit, self-esteem, self-importance, self-satisfaction, smugness, vainglory — more at COMPLACENCE

vanity plate *n* : an automobile license plate bearing distinctive letters or numbers designated by the owner

van·quish \\'vaṇ-kwish, 'van-\\ *vb* **1** ♦ : to overcome in battle or in a contest **2** : to gain mastery over (as an emotion)

   ♦ conquer, dominate, overpower, subdue, subject — more at CONQUER

van·tage \\'van-tij\\ *n* **1** ♦ : an advantage or superiority in a contest **2** : a position giving a strategic advantage or a commanding perspective

   ♦ advantage, better, drop, edge, jump, upper hand — more at ADVANTAGE

vape \\'vāp\\ *vb* **vaped; vap·ing** : to inhale vapor through the mouth from a usu. battery-operated electronic device that heats up and vaporizes a liquid or solid

va·pid \\'va-pəd, 'vā-\\ *adj* : lacking spirit, liveliness, or zest : FLAT, INSIPID — **va·pid·i·ty** \\va-'pi-də-tē\\ *n* — **vap·id·ly** *adv* — **vap·id·ness** *n*

va·por *or Can and Brit* **va·pour** \\'vā-pər\\ *n* **1** : fine separated particles (as fog or smoke) floating in the air and clouding it **2** : a substance in the gaseous state; *esp* : one that is liquid under ordinary conditions **3** : something insubstantial or fleeting **4** *pl* : a depressed or hysterical nervous condition

va·por·ing \\'vā-pə-riṇ\\ *n* : an idle, boastful, or high-flown expression or speech — usu. used in pl. ⟨political ∼s⟩

va·por·ise *chiefly Brit var of* VAPORIZE

va·por·ize \\'vā-pə-,rīz\\ *vb* **-ized; -iz·ing** : to convert into vapor — **va·por·i·za·tion** \\,vā-pə-rə-'zā-shən\\ *n*

va·por·iz·er \\-,rī-zər\\ *n* : a device that vaporizes something (as a medicated liquid)

vapor lock *n* : an interruption of flow of a fluid (as fuel in an engine) caused by the formation of vapor in the feeding system

va·por·ous \\'vā-pə-rəs\\ *adj* **1** : full of vapor : FOGGY, MISTY **2** : UNSUBSTANTIAL, VAGUE — **va·por·ous·ly** *adv* — **va·por·ous·ness** *n*

va·pour *chiefly Brit var of* VAPOR

va·que·ro \\vä-'ker-ō\\ *n, pl* **-ros** [Sp, fr. *vaca* cow, fr. L *vacca*] : a ranch hand : COWBOY

var *abbr* **1** variable **2** variant; variation **3** variety **4** various

¹var·i·able \\'ver-ē-ə-bəl\\ *adj* **1** ♦ : able or apt to vary : CHANGEABLE **2** : FICKLE **3** : not true to type : ABERRANT ⟨a ∼ wheat⟩ — **var·i·abil·i·ty** \\,ver-ē-ə-'bi-lə-tē, ,var-\\ *n* — **var·i·ably** \\-blē\\ *adv*

   ♦ adaptable, adjustable, changeable, elastic, flexible, fluid, malleable — more at FLEXIBLE

²variable *n* **1** : a quantity that may take on any of a set of values; *also* : a mathematical symbol representing a variable **2** : something that is variable

var·i·ance \\'ver-ē-əns\\ *n* **1** : variation or a degree of variation : DEVIATION **2** ♦ : the fact or state of being in disagreement **3** : a license to do something contrary to the usual rule ⟨a zoning ∼⟩ **4** : the square of the standard deviation

   ♦ conflict, discord, dissension, dissent, disunity, friction, schism, strife, war, warfare — more at DISCORD

¹var·i·ant \\'ver-ē-ənt\\ *adj* **1** : differing from others of its kind or class **2** : varying usu. slightly from the standard or type

²variant *n* **1** : one that exhibits variation from a type or norm **2** : one of two or more different spellings or pronunciations of a word

var·i·a·tion \\,ver-ē-'ā-shən\\ *n* **1** ♦ : the act, process, or an instance of varying : a change in form, position, or condition **2** : extent of change or difference **3** : divergence in the characteristics of an organism from those typical or usual for its group; *also* : one exhibiting such variation **4** : repetition of a musical theme with modifications in rhythm, tune, harmony, or key

   ♦ alteration, change, difference, modification, revise, revision — more at CHANGE

vari·col·ored \\'ver-i-,kə-lərd\\ *adj* : having various colors : VARIEGATED

var·i·cose \\'var-ə-,kōs\\ *adj* : abnormally swollen and dilated ⟨∼ veins⟩ — **var·i·cos·i·ty** \\,var-ə-'kä-sə-tē\\ *n*

var·ied \\'ver-ēd\\ *adj* **1** ♦ : having many forms or types ⟨∼ interests⟩; *also* : composed of distinct or unlike elements or qualities **2** : VARIEGATED — **var·ied·ly** *adv*

   ♦ assorted, heterogeneous, miscellaneous, mixed, motley — more at MISCELLANEOUS

var·ie·gat·ed \\'ver-ē-ə-,gā-təd\\ *adj* **1** ♦ : having patches, stripes, or marks of different colors ⟨∼ flowers⟩ **2** : VARIED **1** — **var·ie·gate** \\-,gāt\\ *vb* — **var·ie·ga·tion** \\,ver-ē-ə-'gā-shən\\ *n*

   ♦ colorful (*or* colourful), multicolored (*or* multicoloured) — more at COLORFUL

¹va·ri·etal \\və-'rī-ət-ᵊl\\ *adj* : of or relating to a variety; *esp* : of, relating to, or producing a varietal

²varietal *n* : a wine bearing the name of the principal grape from which it is made

va·ri·ety \\və-'rī-ə-tē\\ *n, pl* **-et·ies** **1** ♦ : the state of being varied or various : DIVERSITY **2** ♦ : a collection of different things : ASSORTMENT **3** : something varying from others of the same general kind **4** : any of various groups of plants or animals within a species distinguished by characteristics insufficient to separate species : SUBSPE-CIES 5 : entertainment such as is given in a stage presentation comprising a series of performances (as songs, dances, or acrobatic acts)

♦ [1] assortment, diversity; *also* disparity, dissimilarity, distinction, distinctiveness, distinctness, unlikeness ♦ [2] assortment, clutter, jumble, medley, mélange, miscellany, motley, muddle, welter — more at MISCELLANY

var·i·o·rum \ˌver-ē-ˈōr-əm\ *n* : an edition or text of a work containing notes by various persons or variant readings of the text

var·i·ous \ˈver-ē-əs\ *adj* 1 : VARICOLORED 2 : of differing kinds : MULTIFARIOUS 3 : UNLIKE ⟨animals as ∼ as the jaguar and the sloth⟩ 4 : having a number of different aspects 5 : NUMEROUS, MANY 6 : INDIVIDUAL, SEPARATE — **var·i·ous·ly** *adv*

var·let \ˈvär-lət\ *n* 1 : ATTENDANT 2 ♦ : a disreputable, unprincipled person : SCOUNDREL, KNAVE

♦ beast, evildoer, fiend, no-good, reprobate, rogue, villain, wretch — more at VILLAIN

var·mint \ˈvär-mənt\ *n* [alter. of *vermin*] 1 : an animal considered a pest; *esp* : one classed as vermin and unprotected by game law 2 : a contemptible person : RASCAL

¹var·nish \ˈvär-nish\ *n* 1 : a liquid preparation that is applied to a surface and dries into a hard glossy coating; *also* : the glaze of this coating 2 : something suggesting varnish by its gloss 3 : outside show : deceptive or superficial appearance

²varnish *vb* 1 : to cover with varnish 2 : to cover or conceal with something that gives a fair appearance : GLOSS

var·si·ty \ˈvär-sə-tē\ *n, pl* **-ties** [by shortening & alter. fr. *university*] 1 *Brit* : UNIVERSITY 2 : the principal team representing a college, school, or club

vary \ˈver-ē\ *vb* **var·ied; vary·ing** 1 ♦ : to make different in some attribute or characteristic : ALTER 2 : to make or be of different kinds : introduce or have variety : DIVERSIFY, DIFFER 3 ♦ : to exhibit or undergo change 4 : to change in bodily structure or function away from what is usual for members of a group

♦ [1] alter, change, make over, modify, recast, redo, refashion, remake, remodel, revamp, revise, rework — more at CHANGE ♦ [3] change, fluctuate, mutate, shift — more at CHANGE

vas·cu·lar \ˈvas-kyə-lər\ *adj* [NL *vascularis*, fr. L *vasculum* small vessel, dim. of *vas* vase, vessel] : of or relating to a channel or system of channels for the conveyance of a body fluid (as blood or sap); *also* : supplied with or containing such vessels and esp. blood vessels

vascular plant *n* : a plant having a specialized system for carrying fluids that includes xylem and phloem

vas def·er·ens \ˈvas-ˈde-fə-rənz\ *n, pl* **va·sa def·er·en·tia** \ˈvā-zə-ˌde-fə-ˈren-shē-ə\ : a sperm-carrying duct of the testis

vase \ˈvās, ˈvāz\ *n* : a usu. round vessel of greater depth than width used chiefly for ornament or for flowers

va·sec·to·my \və-ˈsek-tə-mē, vā-ˈzek-\ *n, pl* **-mies** : surgical excision of all or part of the vas deferens usu. to induce sterility

va·so·con·stric·tion \ˌvas-ō-kən-ˈstrik-shən, ˌvāz-\ *n* : narrowing of the interior diameter of blood vessels

va·so·con·stric·tor \-tər\ *n* : an agent (as a nerve fiber or a drug) that initiates or induces vasoconstriction

vas·sal \ˈva-səl\ *n* 1 : a person under the protection of a feudal lord to whom he owes homage and loyalty : a feudal tenant 2 : one occupying a dependent or subordinate position — **vassal** *adj*

vas·sal·age \-sə-lij\ *n* 1 : the state of being a vassal 2 : the homage and loyalty due from a vassal 3 : SERVITUDE, SUBJECTION

¹vast \ˈvast\ *adj* ♦ : very great in size, amount, degree, intensity, or esp. extent

♦ enormous, giant, gigantic, huge, massive, monumental, prodigious, tremendous, whopping — more at HUGE

²vast *n* : a great expanse : IMMENSITY

vast·ly *adv* ♦ : to a vast extent or degree

♦ broadly, considerably, greatly, hugely, largely, massively, monstrously, much, sizably, stupendously, tremendously, utterly — more at GREATLY

vast·ness *n* ♦ : the quality or state of being vast

♦ enormity, hugeness, immensity, magnitude, massiveness — more at IMMENSITY

vasty \ˈvas-tē\ *adj* : VAST

vat \ˈvat\ *n* : a large vessel (as a tub or barrel) esp. for holding liquids in manufacturing processes

VAT *abbr* value-added tax

vat·ic \ˈva-tik\ *adj* : PROPHETIC, ORACULAR

Vat·i·can \ˈva-ti-kən\ *n* 1 : the papal headquarters in Rome 2 : the papal government

vaude·ville \ˈvȯd-vəl, ˈväd-, ˈvȯd-, -ˌvil\ *n* [F, fr. MF, satirical song, alter. of *vaudevire*, fr. *vau-de-Vire* valley of Vire, town in northwest France where such songs were composed] : a stage entertainment consisting of unrelated acts (as of acrobats, comedians, dancers, or singers)

¹vault \ˈvȯlt\ *n* 1 : an arched masonry structure usu. forming a ceiling or roof; *also* : something (as the sky) resembling a vault 2 : a room or space covered by a vault esp. when underground 3 : a room or compartment for the safekeeping of valuables 4 : a burial chamber; *also* : a usu. metal or concrete case in which a casket is enclosed at burial — **vaulty** *adj*

²vault *vb* : to form or cover with a vault

³vault *vb* ♦ : to leap vigorously esp. by aid of the hands or a pole — **vault·er** *n*

♦ bound, hop, jump, leap, spring — more at JUMP

⁴vault *n* : an act of vaulting : LEAP

vault·ed \ˈvȯl-təd\ *adj* 1 : built in the form of a vault : ARCHED 2 : covered with a vault

vault·ing \-tiŋ\ *adj* : reaching for the heights ⟨∼ ambition⟩

vaunt \ˈvȯnt\ *vb* [ME, fr. AF *vanter*, fr. LL *vanitare*, ultim. fr. L *vanus* vain] : to boast of : BRAG — **vaunt** *n*

vaunt·ed \ˈvȯn-təd\ *adj* : much praised or boasted of

vb *abbr* verb; verbal

V–chip \ˈvē-ˌchip\ *n* : a computer chip in a television set used to block based on content the viewing of certain programs

VCR \ˌvē-(ˌ)sē-ˈär\ *n* [video cassette recorder] : a device that records and plays back videotapes

VD *abbr* venereal disease

VDT *abbr* video display terminal

veal \ˈvēl\ *n* : the flesh of a young calf

vec·tor \ˈvek-tər\ *n* 1 : a quantity that has magnitude and direction 2 : an organism (as a fly or tick) that transmits a pathogen

Ve·da \ˈvā-də\ *n* [Skt, lit., knowledge] : any of a class of Hindu sacred writings — **Ve·dic** \ˈvā-dik\ *adj*

Ve·dan·ta \vā-ˈdän-tə, və-, -ˈdan-\ *n* : an orthodox Hindu philosophy based on the Upanishads

vee·jay \ˈvē-jā\ *n* : an announcer of a program featuring music videos

veep \ˈvēp\ *n* : VICE PRESIDENT

veer \ˈvir\ *vb* ♦ : to shift from one direction or course to another — **veer** *n*

♦ divert, swerve, swing, turn, wheel, whip — more at TURN

veg·an \ˈvē-gən, ˈvā-; ˈve-jən, -jan\ *n* : a strict vegetarian who consumes no animal food or dairy products — **veg·an·ism** \ˈvē-gə-ˌni-zəm, ˈvā-, ˈve-\ *n*

¹veg·e·ta·ble \ˈvej-tə-bəl, ˈve-jə-\ *adj* [ME, fr. ML *vegetabilis* vegetative, fr. *vegetare* to grow, fr. L, to animate, fr. *vegetus* lively, fr. *vegēre* to enliven] 1 : of, relating to, or growing like plants ⟨the ∼ kingdom⟩ 2 : made from, obtained from, or containing plants or plant products ⟨∼ oils⟩ 3 : suggesting that of a plant (as in inertness) ⟨a ∼ existence⟩

²vegetable *n* 1 : PLANT 1 2 : a usu. herbaceous plant grown for an edible part that is usu. eaten as part of a meal; *also* : such an edible part

veg·e·tal \'ve-jət-ᵊl\ *adj* **1** : VEGETABLE **2** : VEGETATIVE

veg·e·tar·i·an \ˌve-jə-'ter-ē-ən\ *n* : one that believes in or practices living on a diet of vegetables, fruits, grains, nuts, and sometimes animal products (as milk and cheese) — **vegetarian** *adj* — **veg·e·tar·i·an·ism** \-ē-ə-ˌni-zəm\ *n*

veg·e·tate \'ve-jə-ˌtāt\ *vb* **-tat·ed; -tat·ing** : to live or grow in the manner of a plant; *esp* : to lead a dull inert life

veg·e·ta·tion \ˌve-jə-'tā-shən\ *n* **1** : the act or process of vegetating; *also* : inert existence **2** ♦ : plant life or cover (as of an area) — **veg·e·ta·tion·al** \-shə-nəl\ *adj*

 ♦ flora, foliage, green, greenery, herbage, leafage, verdure — more at GREENERY

veg·e·ta·tive \'ve-jə-ˌtā-tiv\ *adj* **1** : of or relating to nutrition and growth esp. as contrasted with reproduction **2** : of, relating to, or composed of vegetation ⟨∼ cover⟩ **3** : VEGETABLE 3

veg out \ ⟩ *vb* **vegged out; vegging out** [short for *vegetate*] : to spend time idly or passively

ve·he·mence \'vē-ə-məns\ *n* ♦ : the quality or state of being vehement

 ♦ ardor, emotion, fervency, fervor, heat, intensity, passion, warmth — more at ARDOR ♦ aggressiveness, assertiveness, emphasis, fierceness, intensity; *also* potency, power, strength; eloquence; fervency, insistence, passion, warmth; clearness, plainness *Ant* feebleness, mildness, weakness

ve·he·ment \'vē-ə-mənt\ *adj* **1** ♦ : marked by great force or energy **2** ♦ : marked by strong feeling or expression ⟨∼ opposition⟩ — **ve·he·ment·ly** *adv*

 ♦ [1] deep, explosive, exquisite, fearful, ferocious, fierce, furious, hard, heavy, intense, profound, terrible, vicious, violent — more at INTENSE ♦ [2] ardent, burning, charged, emotional, fervent, fiery, hot-blooded, impassioned, passionate, red-hot — more at FERVENT

ve·hi·cle \'vē-ə-kəl, 'vē-ˌhi-\ *n* **1** : a medium by which a thing is applied or administered ⟨linseed oil is a ∼ for pigments⟩ **2** ♦ : a medium through or by means of which something is conveyed or expressed **3** ♦ : a means of transporting persons or goods — **ve·hic·u·lar** \vē-'hi-kyə-lər\ *adj*

 ♦ [2] agency, agent, instrument, instrumentality, machinery, means, medium, organ — more at AGENT ♦ [3] conveyance, transport — more at CONVEYANCE

¹veil \'vāl\ *n* **1** : a piece of often sheer or diaphanous material used to screen or curtain something or to cover the head or face **2** : the life of a nun ⟨take the ∼⟩ **3** : something that hides or obscures like a veil

²veil *vb* ♦ : to cover with or as if with a veil

 ♦ cloak, conceal, cover, curtain, hide, mask, obscure, screen — more at HIDE

¹vein \'vān\ *n* **1** : a fissure in rock filled with mineral matter; *also* : a bed of useful mineral matter **2** : any of the tubular branching vessels that carry blood from the capillaries toward the heart **3** : any of the bundles of vascular vessels forming the framework of a leaf **4** : any of the thickened ribs that stiffen the wings of an insect **5** : something (as a wavy variegation in marble) suggesting veins **6** ♦ : a distinctive style of expression **7** : a distinctive element or quality : STRAIN **8** : MOOD, HUMOR — **veined** \'vānd\ *adj*

 ♦ fashion, locution, manner, mode, phraseology, style, tone — more at STYLE

²vein *vb* : to pattern with or as if with veins — **vein·ing** *n*

vel *abbr* velocity

ve·lar \'vē-lər\ *adj* : of or relating to a velum and esp. that of the soft palate

veld *or* **veldt** \'velt, 'felt\ *n* [Afrikaans *veld*, fr. D, field] ♦ : an open grassland esp. in southern Africa usu. with scattered shrubs or trees

 ♦ down, grassland, plain, prairie, savanna, steppe — more at PLAIN

vel·lum \'ve-ləm\ *n* [ME *velym*, fr. AF *velim, veeslin*, fr. *veelin*, adj., of a calf, fr. *veel* calf] **1** : a fine-grained lambskin, kidskin, or calfskin prepared for writing on or for binding books **2** : a strong cream-colored paper — **vellum** *adj*

ve·loc·i·pede \və-'lä-sə-ˌpēd\ *n* : an early bicycle

ve·loc·i·rap·tor \və-'lä-sə-ˌrap-tər\ *n* : any of a genus of agile flesh-eating bipedal dinosaurs of the Cretaceous having a sickle-shaped claw on each foot

ve·loc·i·ty \və-'lä-sə-tē\ *n, pl* **-ties** ♦ : quickness of motion : SPEED ⟨the ∼ of light⟩

 ♦ celerity, fastness, fleetness, haste, hurry, quickness, rapidity, speed, swiftness — more at SPEED

ve·lour *or* **ve·lours** \və-'lu̇r\ *n, pl* **velours** \-'lu̇rz\ : any of various textile fabrics with pile like that of velvet

ve·lum \'vē-ləm\ *n, pl* **ve·la** \-lə\ : a membranous body part (as the soft palate) resembling a veil

vel·vet \'vel-vət\ *n* [ME *veluet, velvet*, fr. AF, fr. *velu* shaggy, ultim. fr. L *villus* shaggy hair] **1** : a fabric having a short soft dense warp pile **2** : something resembling or suggesting velvet (as in softness or luster) **3** : the soft skin covering the growing antlers of deer — **velvet** *adj*

vel·ve·teen \ˌvel-və-'tēn\ *n* **1** : a fabric woven usu. of cotton in imitation of velvet **2** *pl* : clothes made of velveteen

vel·vety \'vel-və-tē\ *adj* ♦ : having the character of velvet as in being soft, smooth, thick, or richly hued

 ♦ cottony, downy, satiny, silken, soft — more at SOFT

Ven *abbr* venerable

ve·nal \'vēn-ᵊl\ *adj* ♦ : capable of being bought or bribed — **ve·nal·i·ty** \vi-'nal-ə-tē\ *n* — **ve·nal·ly** \'vēn-ᵊl-ē\ *adv*

 ♦ bribable, corruptible, purchasable; *also* hack, mercenary; crooked, cutthroat, dishonest, unethical, unprincipled, unscrupulous; corrupt, debased, debauched, degenerate, degraded, demoralized, depraved, dissipated, dissolute, perverse, perverted, warped; bad, evil, immoral, iniquitous, nefarious, sinful, vicious, wicked *Ant* incorruptible

ve·na·tion \ve-'nā-shən, vē-\ *n* : an arrangement or system of veins ⟨the ∼ of the hand⟩ ⟨leaf ∼⟩

vend \'vend\ *vb* ♦ : to sell esp. as a hawker or peddler — **vend·ible** *adj*

 ♦ deal, market, merchandise, put up, retail, sell — more at MARKET

vend·ee \ven-'dē\ *n* : one to whom a thing is sold : BUYER

ven·det·ta \ven-'de-tə\ *n* : a feud marked by acts of revenge

vending machine *n* : a coin-operated machine for selling merchandise

ven·dor \'ven-dər, *for 1 also* ven-'dȯr\ *n* **1** ♦ : one that vends : SELLER **2** : VENDING MACHINE

 ♦ dealer, seller; *also* auctioneer, concessionaire; bootlegger, fence, fencer, hustler, smuggler, trader; distributor, retailer; wholesaler; hawker, huckster, peddler; salesman, salesperson, saleswoman; exporter, handler; haggler *Ant* buyer, purchaser

¹ve·neer \və-'nir\ *n* [G *Furnier*, fr. *furnieren* to veneer, fr. F *fournir* to furnish] **1** : a thin usu. superficial layer of material ⟨brick ∼⟩; *esp* : a thin layer of fine wood glued over a cheaper wood **2** : superficial display : GLOSS **3** ♦ : a protective or ornamental facing (as of brick or stone)

 ♦ exterior, face, outside, skin, surface — more at EXTERIOR

²veneer *vb* : to overlay with a veneer

ven·er·a·ble \'ve-nə-rə-bəl\ *adj* **1** : deserving to be venerated — often used as a religious title **2** : made sacred by association **3 a** ♦ : calling forth respect through age, character, and attainments ⟨a ∼ jazz musician⟩ **b** ♦ : impressive by reason of age ⟨under ∼ pines⟩

 ♦ [3a] hallowed, reverend; *also* honorable, reputable, respectable; honored, respected; admirable, estimable, redoubtable; good, moral, righteous ♦ [3b] age-old, ancient, antediluvian, antique, dateless, hoary, old — more at ANCIENT

ven·er·ate \'ve-nə-ˌrāt\ vb **-at·ed; -at·ing** ♦ : to regard with reverential respect — **ven·er·a·tion** \ˌve-nə-'rā-shən\ n

♦ adore, deify, glorify, revere, worship — more at WORSHIP

ve·ne·re·al \və-'nir-ē-əl\ adj : of or relating to sexual intercourse or to diseases transmitted by it ⟨a ~ infection⟩

venereal disease n : a contagious disease (as gonorrhea or syphilis) usu. acquired by having sexual intercourse with someone who already has it

ve·ne·tian blind \və-'nē-shən-\ n : a blind having thin horizontal parallel slats that can be adjusted to admit a desired amount of light

Ven·e·zue·lan \ˌve-nə-'zwā-lən\ n : a native or inhabitant of Venezuela — **Venezuelan** adj

ven·geance \'ven-jəns\ n ♦ : punishment inflicted in retaliation for an injury or offense : REVENGE

♦ reprisal, requital, retaliation, retribution, revenge — more at REVENGE

venge·ful \'venj-fəl\ adj : filled with a desire for revenge : VINDICTIVE — **venge·ful·ly** adv

ve·nial \'vē-nē-əl\ adj ♦ : capable of being forgiven : EXCUSABLE ⟨~ sin⟩

♦ excusable, forgivable, pardonable; also justifiable, redeemable; allowable; insignificant, minor, trifling, trivial; harmless, tolerable Ant inexcusable, mortal, unforgivable, unpardonable

ve·ni·re \və-'nī-rē\ n : a panel from which a jury is drawn

ve·ni·re fa·ci·as \-'fā-shē-əs\ n [ME, fr. ML, you should cause to come] : a writ summoning persons to appear in court to serve as jurors

ve·ni·re·man \və-'nī-rē-mən, -'nir-ē-\ n : a member of a venire

ven·i·son \'ven-ə-sən, -zən\ n, pl **venisons** also **venison** [ME, fr. AF veneisun game, venison, fr. L venatio, fr. venari to hunt, pursue] : the edible flesh of a deer

ven·om \'ve-nəm\ n [ME venim, fr. AF, ultim. fr. L venenum magic charm, drug, poison] **1** ♦ : poisonous material secreted by some animals (as snakes, spiders, or bees) and transmitted usu. by biting or stinging **2** ♦ : desire to cause pain, injury, or distress to another : MALEVOLENCE

♦ [1] bane, poison, toxin — more at POISON ♦ [2] cattiness, despite, hatefulness, malice, malignity, meanness, nastiness, spite, spleen, viciousness — more at MALICE

ven·om·ous \'ve-nə-məs\ adj **1** ♦ : full of venom : POISONOUS **2** : SPITEFUL, MALEVOLENT ⟨~ comments⟩ **3** : secreting and using venom ⟨~ snakes⟩ — **ven·om·ous·ly** adv

♦ poison, poisonous — more at POISONOUS

ve·nous \'vē-nəs\ adj **1** : of, relating to, or full of veins **2** : being purplish red oxygen-deficient blood rich in carbon dioxide that is present in most veins

¹vent \'vent\ vb **1** : to provide with a vent **2** : to serve as a vent for **3** ♦ : to force out : DISCHARGE **4** ♦ : to give vigorous or emotional expression to

♦ [3] cast, discharge, emit, exhale, expel, issue, release, shoot — more at EMIT ♦ [4] loose, release, take out, unleash — more at TAKE OUT ♦ [4] air, express, give, look, sound, state, voice — more at EXPRESS

²vent n **1** : an opportunity or way of escape or passage : OUTLET **2** : an opening for the escape of a gas or liquid or for the relief of pressure

³vent n : a slit in a garment esp. in the lower part of a seam (as of a jacket or skirt)

ven·ti·late \'vent-ᵊl-ˌāt\ vb **-lat·ed; -lat·ing** **1** : to discuss freely and openly ⟨~ a question⟩ **2** : to give vigorous or emotional expression to ⟨~ one's grievances⟩ **3** : to cause fresh air to circulate through (as a room or mine) so as to replace foul air **4** : to provide with a vent or outlet — **ven·ti·la·tor** \-ᵊl-ˌā-tər\ n

ven·ti·la·tion \ˌvent-ᵊl-'ā-shən\ n **1** : the act or process of ventilating **2** : circulation of air (as in a room) **3** : a system or means of providing fresh air

ven·tral \'ven-trəl\ adj **1** : of or relating to the belly : ABDOMINAL **2** : of, relating to, or located on or near the surface of the body that in humans is the front but in most other animals is the lower surface — **ven·tral·ly** adv

ven·tri·cle \'ven-tri-kəl\ n **1** : a chamber of the heart that receives blood from the atrium of the same side and pumps it into the arteries **2** : any of the communicating cavities of the brain that are continuous with the central canal of the spinal cord — **ven·tric·u·lar** \ven-'tri-kyə-lər\ adj

ven·tril·o·quism \ven-'tri-lə-ˌkwi-zəm\ n [LL ventriloquus ventriloquist, fr. L venter belly + loqui to speak; fr. the belief that the voice is produced from the ventriloquist's stomach] : the production of the voice in such a manner that the sound appears to come from a source other than the speaker — **ven·tril·o·quist** \-kwist\ n

ven·tril·o·quy \-kwē\ n : VENTRILOQUISM

¹ven·ture \'ven-chər\ vb **ven·tured; ven·tur·ing** **1** ♦ : to expose to hazard : RISK **2** : to undertake the risks of : BRAVE **3** ♦ : to offer at the risk of rebuff, rejection, or censure ⟨~ an opinion⟩ **4** : to proceed despite danger : DARE

♦ [1] adventure, compromise, gamble with, hazard, imperil, jeopardize, menace, risk ♦ [3] chance, gamble, hazard, risk — more at RISK

²venture n **1** ♦ : an undertaking involving chance or risk; esp : a speculative business enterprise **2** : something risked in a speculative venture : STAKE

♦ chance, enterprise, flier, gamble, speculation — more at GAMBLE

ven·ture·some \'ven-chər-səm\ adj **1** ♦ : involving risk : DANGEROUS **2** ♦ : inclined to venture : BOLD — **ven·ture·some·ly** adv — **ven·ture·some·ness** n

♦ [1] dangerous, grave, grievous, hazardous, menacing, parlous, perilous, risky, serious, unhealthy, unsafe — more at DANGEROUS ♦ [2] adventurous, audacious, bold, daring, enterprising, gutsy, hardy, nervy — more at BOLD

ven·tur·ous \'ven-chə-rəs\ adj **1** : involving risk : DANGEROUS, HAZARDOUS **2** : inclined to venture : BOLD — **ven·tur·ous·ly** adv — **ven·tur·ous·ness** n

ven·ue \'ven-yü\ n [AF, alter. of vinné, visné, lit., neighborhood, neighbors, ultim. fr. L vicinitas vicinity] : the place in which the alleged events from which a legal action arises took place; also : the place from which the jury is taken and where the trial is held

Ve·nus \'vē-nəs\ n : the planet 2d in order from the sun

Venus fly·trap \-'flī-ˌtrap\ or **Ve·nus's–fly·trap** \'vē-nə-səz-'flī-ˌtrap\ n : an insect-eating plant of the Carolina coast that has the leaf tip modified into an insect trap

Ve·nu·sian \vi-'nü-zhən, -'nyü-\ adj : of or relating to the planet Venus

ve·ra·cious \və-'rā-shəs\ adj **1** : TRUTHFUL, HONEST **2** ♦ : marked by truth : ACCURATE — **ve·ra·cious·ly** adv

♦ accurate, authentic, exact, faithful, precise, right, strict, true — more at FAITHFUL

ve·rac·i·ty \və-'ra-sə-tē\ n, pl **-ties** **1** ♦ : devotion to truth : TRUTHFULNESS **2** ♦ : conformity with fact : ACCURACY **3** : something true

♦ [1] honesty, integrity, probity, truthfulness, verity — more at HONESTY ♦ [2] accuracy, closeness, delicacy, exactness, fineness, precision — more at PRECISION

ve·ran·da or **ve·ran·dah** \və-'ran-də\ n : a long open usu. roofed porch

verb \'vərb\ n : a word that is the grammatical center of a predicate and expresses an act, occurrence, or mode of being

¹ver·bal \'vər-bəl\ adj **1** : of, relating to, or consisting of words; esp : having to do with words rather than with the ideas to be conveyed **2** ♦ : expressed in usu. spoken words : ORAL ⟨a ~ contract⟩ **3** : of, relating to, or formed from a verb **4** : LITERAL, VERBATIM — **ver·bal·ly** adv

♦ oral, spoken, unwritten; also implicit, informal; articulated, verbalized; given, pronounced, said, sounded, stated, told, voiced Ant written

²**verbal** n : a word that combines characteristics of a verb with those of a noun or adjective

verbal auxiliary n : an auxiliary verb

ver·bal·ize \'vər-bə-ˌlīz\ vb **-ized; -iz·ing** 1 : to speak or write in wordy or empty fashion 2 ♦ : to express something in words : describe verbally 3 : to convert into a verb — **ver·bal·i·za·tion** \ˌvər-bə-lə-'zā-shən\ n

♦ articulate, say, speak, state, talk, tell, utter, vocalize — more at SAY

verbal noun n : a noun derived directly from a verb or verb stem and in some uses having the sense and constructions of a verb

ver·ba·tim \(ˌ)vər-'bā-təm\ adv or adj : in the same words : word for word

ver·be·na \(ˌ)vər-'bē-nə\ n : VERVAIN; esp : any of several garden vervains of hybrid origin with showy spikes of bright often fragrant flowers

ver·biage \'vər-bē-ij, -bij\ n 1 ♦ : superfluity of words usu. of little or obscure content 2 : DICTION, WORDING

♦ circumlocution, prolixity, redundancy, wordiness; also circularity; tautology; reiteration, repetition, repetitiousness; embellishment, embroidering, exaggeration, hyperbole

ver·bose \(ˌ)vər-'bōs\ adj ♦ : using more words than are needed : WORDY

♦ circuitous, diffuse, long-winded, prolix, rambling, windy, wordy — more at WORDY

ver·bos·i·ty \(ˌ)vər-'bä-sə-tē\ n : the quality or state of being verbose

ver·bo·ten \vər-'bōt-ᵊn, fər-\ adj [G] : forbidden usu. by dictate

ver·dant \'vərd-ᵊnt\ adj ♦ : green with growing plants — **ver·dant·ly** adv

♦ green, leafy, lush, luxuriant — more at LUSH

ver·dict \'vər-(ˌ)dikt\ n [ME verdit, verdict, fr. AF veirdit, fr. veir true (fr. L verus) + dit saying, dictum, fr. L dictum, fr. dicere to say] 1 : the finding or decision of a jury 2 ♦ : an opinion pronounced or felt : JUDGMENT

♦ belief, conviction, eye, feeling, judgment (or judgement), mind, notion, opinion, persuasion, sentiment, view — more at OPINION

ver·di·gris \'vər-də-ˌgrēs, -ˌgris\ n : a green or bluish deposit that forms on copper, brass, or bronze surfaces

ver·dure \'vər-jər\ n 1 : the greenness of growing vegetation 2 ♦ : a growth or expanse of vegetation

♦ flora, foliage, green, greenery, herbage, leafage, vegetation — more at GREENERY

¹**verge** \'vərj\ n [ME, fr. AF, rod, measuring rod, margin, fr. AF, rod, area of jurisdiction, fr. L virga twig, rod, line] 1 : a staff carried as an emblem of authority or office 2 ♦ : something that borders or bounds : EDGE 3 : BRINK, THRESHOLD

♦ border, bound, boundary, circumference, compass, confines, edge, end, fringe, margin, perimeter, periphery, rim, skirt — more at BORDER

²**verge** vb **verged; verg·ing** 1 ♦ : to be next to — often used with on 2 : to be on the verge

♦ often verge on abut, adjoin, border (on), flank, fringe, join, skirt, touch — more at ADJOIN

³**verge** vb **verged; verg·ing** 1 : to move or extend in some direction or toward some condition : INCLINE 2 : to be in transition or change

verg·er \'vər-jər\ n 1 chiefly Brit : an attendant who carries a verge (as before a bishop) 2 : SEXTON

ve·rid·i·cal \və-'ri-di-kəl\ adj 1 : TRUTHFUL 2 : not illusory : GENUINE

ver·i·fi·able \ˌver-ə-'fī-ə-bəl\ adj ♦ : capable of being verified

♦ demonstrable, provable, supportable, sustainable; also certifiable; excusable, justifiable; alleged, assumed, guessed, presumed, surmised, suspected Ant insupportable, unsupportable

ver·i·fy \'ver-ə-ˌfī\ vb **-fied; -fy·ing** 1 : to confirm in law by oath 2 ♦ : to establish the truth, accuracy, or reality of — **ver·i·fi·ca·tion** \ˌver-ə-fə-'kā-shən\ n

♦ bear out, confirm, corroborate, substantiate, support, validate, vindicate — more at CONFIRM

ver·i·ly \'ver-ə-lē\ adv 1 : in truth : in actual fact

♦ actually, frankly, honestly, really, truly, truthfully — more at ACTUALLY

veri·si·mil·i·tude \ˌver-ə-sə-'mi-lə-ˌtüd, -ˌtyüd\ n : the quality or state of appearing to be true or real

ver·i·ta·ble \'ver-ə-tə-bəl\ adj : ACTUAL, GENUINE, TRUE

ver·i·ta·bly \'ver-ə-tə-blē\ adv ♦ : in a way that is genuine or true

♦ actually, authentically, genuinely, really, very — more at VERY

ver·i·ty \'ver-ə-tē\ n, pl **-ties** 1 : the quality or state of being true or real : TRUTH, REALITY 2 : something (as a statement) that is true 3 ♦ : the quality or state of being truthful or honest : HONESTY

♦ honesty, integrity, probity, truthfulness, veracity — more at HONESTY

ver·meil n [MF] 1 \'vər-məl, -ˌmāl\ : VERMILION 2 \ver-'mā\ : gilded silver

ver·mi·cel·li \ˌvər-mə-'che-lē, -'se-\ n [It, fr. pl. of vermicello, dim. of verme worm] : a pasta made in thinner strings than spaghetti

ver·mic·u·lite \vər-'mi-kyə-ˌlīt\ n : any of various lightweight water-absorbent minerals derived from mica

ver·mi·form appendix \'vər-mə-ˌform-\ n : APPENDIX 2

ver·mil·ion also **ver·mil·lion** \vər-'mil-yən\ n : a bright reddish orange color; also : any of various red pigments

ver·min \'vər-mən\ n, pl **vermin** 1 : small common harmful or objectionable animals (as lice or mice) that are difficult to get rid of 2 : birds and mammals that prey on game — **ver·min·ous** adj

ver·mouth \vər-'müth\ n [F vermout, fr. G Wermut wormwood] : a dry or sweet wine flavored with herbs and often used in mixed drinks

¹**ver·nac·u·lar** \vər-'na-kyə-lər\ adj [L vernaculus native, fr. verna slave born in the master's house, native] 1 : of, relating to, or being a language or dialect native to a region or country rather than a literary, cultured, or foreign language 2 ♦ : of, relating to, or being the normal spoken form of a language 3 : applied to a plant or animal in common speech as distinguished from biological nomenclature ⟨~ names⟩

♦ colloquial, conversational, informal, nonliterary, vulgar — more at COLLOQUIAL

²**vernacular** n 1 : a vernacular language 2 : the mode of expression of a group or class 3 : a vernacular name of a plant or animal

ver·nal \'vərn-ᵊl\ adj : of, relating to, or occurring in the spring ⟨~ equinox⟩

ver·ni·er \'vər-nē-ər\ n : a short scale made to slide along the divisions of a graduated instrument to indicate parts of divisions

ve·ron·i·ca \və-'rä-ni-kə\ n : any of a genus of herbs related to the snapdragons that have small usu. bluish flowers

ver·sa·tile \'vər-sət-ᵊl\ adj 1 : turning with ease from one thing or position to another 2 ♦ : having many aptitudes — **ver·sa·til·i·ty** \ˌvər-sə-'ti-lə-tē\ n

♦ adaptable, all-around, protean, universal; also multipurpose; well-rounded; able, ace, adept, experienced, expert, masterful, skilled, skillful; adjustable, changeable, elastic, flexible, fluid, malleable, variable

¹**verse** \'vərs\ n 1 : a line of poetry; also : STANZA 2 : metrical writing distinguished from poetry esp. by its lower level of intensity 3 ♦ : writing that creates a specific emotional response through the intentional use of meaning, sound, and rhythm : POETRY 4 : a composition in verse : POEM 5 : one of the short divisions of a chapter in the Bible

♦ poetry, song — more at POETRY

²verse *vb* **versed; vers·ing** : to familiarize by experience, study, or practice ⟨well *versed* in the theater⟩

versed *adj* ♦ : acquainted or familiar from experience, study, or practice

♦ abreast, conversant, familiar, informed, knowledgeable, up, up-to-date — more at FAMILIAR

ver·si·cle \'vər-si-kəl\ *n* : a verse or sentence said or sung by a leader in public worship and followed by a response from the people

ver·si·fi·ca·tion \₁vər-sə-fə-'kā-shən\ *n*   **1** : the making of verses   **2** : metrical structure

ver·si·fi·er \'vər-sə-₁fī-ər\ *n* ♦ : one that versifies

♦ bard, minstrel, poet — more at POET

ver·si·fy \'vər-sə-₁fī\ *vb* **-fied; -fy·ing**   **1** : to write verse   **2** : to turn into verse

ver·sion \'vər-zhən\ *n*   **1** : TRANSLATION; *esp* : a translation of the Bible   **2** : an account or description from a particular point of view esp. as contrasted with another   **3** : a form or variant of a type or original

vers li·bre \₁ver-'lēbr⁰\ *n, pl* **vers li·bres** *same*\ [F] : FREE VERSE

ver·so \'vər-sō\ *n, pl* **versos** : a left-hand page

ver·sus \'vər-səs\ *prep*   **1** : AGAINST 1 ⟨the champion ∼ the challenger⟩   **2** : in contrast or as an alternative to ⟨free trade ∼ protection⟩

vert *abbr* vertical

ver·te·bra \'vər-tə-brə\ *n, pl* **-brae** \-₁brā, -(₁)brē\ *or* **-bras** [L] : one of the segments of bone or cartilage making up the backbone

ver·te·bral \(₁)vər-'tē-brəl, 'vər-tə-\ *adj* : of, relating to, or made up of vertebrae : SPINAL

vertebral column *n* ♦ : the bony column in the back of a vertebrate that is the chief support of the trunk and consists of a jointed series of vertebrae enclosing and protecting the spinal cord : BACKBONE

♦ backbone, spine — more at SPINE

¹ver·te·brate \'vər-tə-brət, -₁brāt\ *adj*   **1** : having a backbone   **2** : of or relating to the vertebrates

²vertebrate *n* : any of a large group of animals (as mammals, birds, reptiles, amphibians, or fishes) that have a backbone or in some primitive forms (as a lamprey) a flexible rod of cells and that have a tubular nervous system arranged along the back and divided into a brain and spinal cord

ver·tex \'vər-₁teks\ *n, pl* **ver·ti·ces** \'vər-tə-₁sēz\ *also* **ver·tex·es** [ME, top of the head, fr. L *vertex, vortex* whirl, whirlpool, top of the head, summit, fr. *vertere* to turn]   **1** : the point opposite to and farthest from the base of a geometrical figure   **2** : the point where the sides of an angle or three or more edges of a polyhedron (as a cube) meet   **3** : the highest point : TOP, SUMMIT

ver·ti·cal \'vər-ti-kəl\ *adj*   **1** : of, relating to, or located at the vertex : directly overhead   **2** ♦ : rising perpendicularly from a level surface : UPRIGHT — **vertical** *n* — **ver·ti·cal·i·ty** \₁vər-tə-'ka-lə-tē\ *n* — **ver·ti·cal·ly** \-k(ə-)lē\ *adv*

♦ erect, perpendicular, standing, upright, upstanding — more at ERECT

ver·tig·i·nous \(₁)vər-'ti-jə-nəs\ *adj* : marked by, affected with, or tending to cause dizziness

ver·ti·go \'vər-ti-₁gō\ *n, pl* **-goes** *or* **-gos** : DIZZINESS, GIDDINESS

vertu *var of* VIRTU

ver·vain \'vər-₁vān\ *n* : any of a genus of chiefly American herbs or low woody plants with often showy heads or spikes of tubular flowers

verve \'vərv\ *n*   **1** : liveliness of imagination   **2** ♦ : the quality or state of being lively in temper, conduct, or spirit

♦ bounce, dash, drive, esprit, pep, punch, snap, spirit, vim, zing, zip — more at SPIRIT

¹very \'ver-ē\ *adj* **veri·er; -est** [ME *verray, verry*, fr. OF *verai*,

ultim. fr. L *verax* truthful, fr. *verus* true]   **1** : EXACT, PRECISE ⟨the ∼ heart of the city⟩   **2** : exactly suitable ⟨the ∼ tool for the job⟩   **3** : ABSOLUTE, UTTER ⟨the *veriest* nonsense⟩   **4** — used as an intensive esp. to emphasize identity ⟨before my ∼ eyes⟩   **5** : MERE, BARE ⟨the ∼ idea scared him⟩   **6** ♦ : being the same one : IDENTICAL ⟨the ∼ man I saw⟩   **7** ♦ : existing in fact or reality : ACTUAL

♦ [6] identical, same, selfsame — more at SAME
♦ [7] actual, concrete, existent, factual, real, true — more at ACTUAL

²very *adv*   **1** ♦ : in actual fact   **2** ♦ : to a high degree : EXTREMELY

♦ [1] actually, authentically, genuinely, really, veritably; *also* accurately, exactly, just, precisely, right, sharp, squarely; almost, nearly, practically; literally, truly **Ant** professedly, supposedly ♦ [2] extra, extremely, greatly, highly, hugely, mightily, mighty, mortally, most, much, real, right, so; *also* completely, entirely, purely, thoroughly, totally, utterly; considerably, extensively, significantly, substantially; abundantly, plentifully **Ant** little, nominally, slightly

very high frequency *n* : a radio frequency of between 30 and 300 megahertz

ves·i·cant \'ve-si-kənt\ *n* : an agent that causes blistering — **vesicant** *adj*

ves·i·cle \'ve-si-kəl\ *n* : a membranous and usu. fluid-filled cavity in a plant or animal; *also* : BLISTER — **ve·sic·u·lar** \və-'si-kyə-lər\ *adj*

¹ves·per \'ves-pər\ *n*   **1** *cap, archaic* : EVENING STAR   **2** : a vesper bell   **3** *archaic* : EVENING, EVENTIDE

²vesper *adj* : of or relating to vespers or the evening

ves·pers \-pərz\ *n pl, often cap* : a late afternoon or evening worship service

ves·sel \'ve-səl\ *n*   **1** ♦ : a container (as a barrel, bottle, bowl, or cup) for holding something   **2** : a person held to be the recipient of a quality (as grace)   **3** ♦ : a craft bigger than a rowboat   **4** : a tube in which a body fluid (as blood or sap) is contained and circulated

♦ [1] container, holder, receptacle — more at CONTAINER ♦ [3] boat, bottom, craft — more at BOAT

¹vest \'vest\ *vb*   **1** ♦ : to place or give into the possession or discretion of some person or authority   **2** : to grant or endow with a particular authority, right, or property   **3** : to become legally vested   **4** : to clothe with or as if with a garment; *esp* : to garb in ecclesiastical vestments

♦ commend, commit, consign, delegate, deliver, entrust, give, hand over, leave, pass, transfer, transmit, trust, turn over — more at GIVE

²vest *n*   **1** : a sleeveless garment for the upper body usu. worn over a shirt   **2** *chiefly Brit* : a man's sleeveless undershirt   **3** : a front piece of a dress resembling the front of a vest

¹ves·tal \'vest-⁰l\ *adj* : CHASTE

²vestal *n* : VESTAL VIRGIN

vestal virgin *n*   **1** : a virgin consecrated to the Roman goddess Vesta and to the service of watching the sacred fire perpetually kept burning on her altar   **2** : a chaste woman

vest·ed \'ves-təd\ *adj* : fully and unconditionally guaranteed as a legal right, benefit, or privilege

vested interest *n* : an interest (as in an existing political, economic, or social arrangement) to which the holder has a strong commitment; *also* : one (as a corporation) having a vested interest

ves·ti·bule \'ves-tə-₁byül\ *n*   **1** : any of various bodily cavities forming or suggesting an entrance to some other cavity or space   **2** ♦ : a passage or room between the outer door and the interior of a building — **ves·tib·u·lar** \ve-'sti-byə-lər\ *adj*

♦ entry, foyer, hall, lobby — more at HALL

ves·tige \'ves-tij\ *n* [F, fr. L *vestigium* footprint, track, vestige] ♦ : a trace or visible sign left by something lost or vanished; *also* : a minute remaining amount — **ves·ti·gial** \ve-'sti-jē-əl, -jəl\ *adj* — **ves·ti·gial·ly** *adv*

♦ relic, shadow, trace; *also* memento, remembrance, reminder; artifact; afterimage, aftertaste; balance, oddment, remainder, remains, remnant, scrap; leavings, remains, residual, residue, rest

vest·ing \'ves-tiŋ\ *n* : the conveying to an employee of inalienable rights to share in a pension fund; *also* : the right so conveyed

vest·ment \'vest-mənt\ *n* **1** : an outer garment; *esp* : a ceremonial or official robe **2** *pl* : CLOTHING, GARB **3** : a garment or insignia worn by a cleric when officiating or assisting at a religious service

vest–pocket *adj* : very small ⟨a ∼ park⟩

ves·try \'ves-trē\ *n, pl* **vestries** **1** : a room in a church for vestments, altar linens, and sacred vessels **2** : a room used for church meetings and classes **3** : a body administering the temporal affairs of an Episcopal parish

ves·try·man \-mən\ *n* : a member of a vestry

ves·ture \'ves-chər\ *n* **1** : a covering garment **2** : CLOTHING, APPAREL

¹vet \'vet\ *n* : VETERINARIAN

²vet *adj or n* : VETERAN

³vet *vb* : to evaluate for appraisal or acceptance ⟨∼ a manuscript⟩

vetch \'vech\ *n* : any of a genus of twining leguminous herbs including some grown for fodder and green manure

¹vet·er·an \'ve-trən, -tə-rən\ *n* [L *veteranus*, fr. *veteranus* old, of long experience, fr. *veter-, vetus* old] **1** : an old soldier of long service **2** : a former member of the armed forces **3** : a person of long experience usu. in an occupation or skill

²veteran *adj* : of, relating to, or characteristic of a veteran

Veterans Day *n* : November 11 observed as a legal holiday in commemoration of the end of hostilities in 1918 and 1945

vet·er·i·nar·i·an \,ve-trə-'ner-ē-ən, ,ve-tə-rə-\ *n* : one qualified and authorized to practice veterinary medicine

¹vet·er·i·nary \'ve-trə-,ner-ē, 've-tə-rə-\ *adj* : of, relating to, or being the medical care of animals and esp. domestic animals

²veterinary *n, pl* **-nar·ies** : VETERINARIAN

¹ve·to \'vē-tō\ *n, pl* **vetoes** [L, I forbid] **1** ♦ : an authoritative prohibition **2** : a power of one part of a government to forbid the carrying out of projects attempted by another part; *esp* : a power vested in a chief executive to prevent the carrying out of measures adopted by a legislature **3** : the exercise of the power of veto

♦ ban, embargo, interdict, interdiction, prohibition, proscription — more at PROHIBITION

²veto *vb* **1** ♦ : to refuse to admit or approve **2** ♦ : to refuse assent to (a legislative bill) so as to prevent enactment or cause reconsideration — **ve·to·er** *n*

♦ [1, 2] blackball, kill, negative — more at NEGATIVE

vex \'veks\ *vb* **vexed** *also* **vext; vex·ing** **1** : to bring trouble, distress, or agitation to **2** ♦ : to annoy continually with little irritations

♦ aggravate, annoy, bother, bug, chafe, exasperate, gall, get, grate, irk, irritate, nettle, peeve, persecute, pique, put out, rasp, rile — more at IRRITATE

vex·a·tion \vek-'sā-shən\ *n* **1** ♦ : the act of vexing **2** : the quality or state of being vexed : IRRITATION **3** : a cause of trouble or annoyance

♦ aggravation, annoyance, disturbance, harassment — more at ANNOYANCE

vex·a·tious \-shəs\ *adj* **1** ♦ : causing vexation : ANNOYING **2** : full of distress or annoyance : TROUBLED — **vex·a·tious·ly** *adv* — **vex·a·tious·ness** *n*

♦ aggravating, annoying, bothersome, frustrating, galling, irksome, irritating, pesty — more at ANNOYING

vexed \'vekst\ *adj* : fully debated or discussed ⟨a ∼ question⟩

vexing *adj* : causing or likely to cause vexation

VF *abbr* **1** video frequency **2** visual field

VFD *abbr* volunteer fire department

VFW *abbr* Veterans of Foreign Wars

VG *abbr* **1** very good **2** vicar-general

VHF *abbr* very high frequency

VI *abbr* Virgin Islands

via \'vī-ə, 'vē-ə\ *prep* **1** : by way of **2** : by means of

vi·a·ble \'vī-ə-bəl\ *adj* **1** : capable of living; *esp* : sufficiently developed as to be capable of surviving outside the mother's womb ⟨a ∼ fetus⟩ **2** : capable of growing and developing ⟨∼ seeds⟩ **3** ♦ : capable of being put into practice : WORKABLE **4** : having a reasonable chance of succeeding ⟨a ∼ candidate⟩ — **vi·a·bil·i·ty** \,vī-ə-'bi-lə-tē\ *n* — **vi·a·bly** \'vī-ə-blē\ *adv*

♦ achievable, attainable, doable, feasible, possible, practicable, realizable, workable — more at POSSIBLE

via·duct \'vī-ə-,dəkt\ *n* : a long elevated roadway usu. consisting of a series of short spans supported on arches, piers, or columns

vi·al \'vī-əl\ *n* : a small vessel for liquids

vi·and \'vī-ənd\ *n* **1** : an article of food **2** ♦ : a stock of food — usu. used in pl.

♦ *usu* viands chow, fare, food, grub, meat, provender, provisions — more at FOOD

vi·at·i·cum \vī-'a-ti-kəm, vē-\ *n, pl* **-cums** *or* **-ca** \-kə\ **1** : the Christian Eucharist given to a person in danger of death **2** : an allowance esp. in money for traveling needs and expenses

vibes \'vībz\ *n pl* **1** : VIBRAPHONE **2** : VIBRATIONS

vi·bran·cy \'vī-brən-sē\ *n* ♦ : the quality or state of being vibrant

♦ animation, briskness, exuberance, liveliness, lustiness, robustness, sprightliness, vitality — more at VITALITY

vi·brant \'vī-brənt\ *adj* **1** : VIBRATING, PULSATING **2** ♦ : pulsating with vigor or activity **3** : readily set in vibration : RESPONSIVE **4** ♦ : sounding from vibration : RESONANT; *also* : intensified and enriched by or as if by resonance ⟨∼ colors⟩

♦ [2] alive, animated, astir, busy, lively — more at ALIVE
♦ [4] golden, resonant, resounding, ringing, round, sonorous — more at RESONANT

vi·bra·phone \'vī-brə-,fōn\ *n* : a percussion instrument like the xylophone but with metal bars and motor-driven resonators

vi·brate \'vī-,brāt\ *vb* **vi·brat·ed; vi·brat·ing** **1** : OSCILLATE **2** : to set in vibration **3** ♦ : to be in vibration : QUIVER **4** : WAVER, FLUCTUATE **5** : to respond sympathetically : THRILL

♦ agitate, convulse, jolt, jounce, quake, quiver, shake, shudder, wobble — more at SHAKE

vi·bra·tion \vī-'brā-shən\ *n* **1** : a rapid to-and-fro motion of the particles of an elastic body or medium (as a stretched cord) that produces sound **2** ♦ : an act of vibrating : OSCILLATION **3** : a trembling motion **4** : VACILLATION **5** : a feeling or impression that someone or something gives off — usu. used in pl. ⟨good ∼s⟩ — **vi·bra·tion·al** \-shə-nəl\ *adj*

♦ oscillation, quivering; *also* jiggle, palpitation, shake, shudder, tremor, twitch

vi·bra·to \vi-'brä-tō\ *n, pl* **-tos** [It] : a slightly tremulous effect imparted to vocal or instrumental music

vi·bra·tor \'vī-,brā-tər\ *n* : one that vibrates or causes vibration; *esp* : a vibrating electrical device used in massage or for sexual stimulation

vi·bra·to·ry \'vī-brə-,tōr-ē\ *adj* : consisting of, capable of, or causing vibration

vi·bur·num \vī-'bər-nəm\ *n* : any of a genus of widely distributed shrubs or small trees related to the honeysuckle and bearing small usu. white flowers in broad clusters

vic *abbr* vicinity

Vic *abbr* Victoria

vic·ar \\'vi-kər\\ *n* **1** : an administrative deputy **2** : a minister in charge of a church who serves under the authority of another minister — **vi·car·i·ate** \\vī-'ker-ē-ət\\ *n*

vic·ar·age \\'vi-kə-rij\\ *n* : a vicar's home

vicar–general *n, pl* **vicars–general** : an administrative deputy (as of a Roman Catholic or Anglican bishop)

vi·car·i·ous \\vī-'ker-ē-əs, -'kar-\\ *adj* [L *vicarius,* fr. *vicis* change, alternation, stead] **1** : acting for another **2** : done or suffered by one person on behalf of another or others ⟨a ∼ sacrifice⟩ **3** : sharing in someone else's experience through the use of the imagination or sympathetic feelings — **vi·car·i·ous·ly** *adv* — **vi·car·i·ous·ness** *n*

¹vice \\'vīs\\ *n* **1** ♦ : moral depravity or corruption **2** ♦ : a moral fault or failing **3** : an habitual usu. trivial fault **4** : an undesirable behavior pattern in a domestic animal

♦ [1] corruption, debauchery, depravity, immorality, iniquity, licentiousness, sin; *also* badness, blackness, evil, villainy, wickedness, wrong; atrociousness, heinousness, sinfulness, unscrupulousness, viciousness, vileness **Ant** morality, virtue ♦ [2] demerit, failing, fault, foible, frailty, shortcoming, weakness — more at FAULT

²vice *chiefly Brit var of* VISE

³vice *prep* : in the place of; *also* : rather than

vice admiral *n* : a commissioned officer in the navy or coast guard ranking above a rear admiral

vice·ge·rent \\'vīs-'jir-ənt\\ *n* : an administrative deputy of a king or magistrate — **vice·ge·ren·cy** \\-ən-sē\\ *n*

vi·cen·ni·al \\vī-'se-nē-əl\\ *adj* : occurring once every 20 years

vice presidency *n* : the office of vice president

vice president *n* **1** : an officer ranking next to a president and usu. empowered to act for the president during an absence or disability **2** : any of several of a president's deputies

vice·re·gal \\'vīs-'rē-gəl\\ *adj* : of or relating to a viceroy

vice·roy \\'vīs-,rói\\ *n* : the governor of a country or province who rules as representative of the sovereign — **vice·roy·al·ty** \\-əl-tē\\ *n*

vice ver·sa \\,vī-si-'vər-sə, 'vīs-'vər-\\ *adv* : with the order reversed

vi·chys·soise \\,vi-shē-'swäz, ,vē-\\ *n* [F] : a soup made esp. from leeks or onions and potatoes, cream, and chicken stock and usu. served cold

vic·i·nage \\'vis-ᵊn-ij\\ *n* : a neighboring or surrounding district : VICINITY

vi·cin·i·ty \\və-'si-nə-tē\\ *n, pl* **-ties** [MF *vicinité,* fr. L *vicinitas,* fr. *vicinus* neighboring, fr. *vicus* row of houses, village] **1** : NEARNESS, PROXIMITY **2** : a surrounding area : NEIGHBORHOOD

vi·cious \\'vi-shəs\\ *adj* **1** ♦ : having the quality of vice : WICKED **2** : DEFECTIVE, FAULTY; *also* : INVALID **3** : IMPURE, FOUL **4** ♦ : having a savage disposition; *also* : marked by violence or ferocity ⟨a ∼ attack⟩ **5** : MALICIOUS, SPITEFUL **6** : worsened by internal causes that augment each other ⟨∼ wage-price spiral⟩

♦ [1] bad, black, evil, immoral, iniquitous, nefarious, rotten, sinful, unethical, unsavory, vile, villainous, wicked, wrong ♦ [4] barbarous, brutal, cruel, heartless, inhumane, sadistic, savage, wanton — more at CRUEL ♦ [4] fell, ferocious, fierce, grim, savage — more at FIERCE

vi·cious·ly *adv* ♦ : in a vicious manner

♦ hatefully, maliciously, meanly, nastily, spitefully, wickedly — more at NASTILY

vi·cious·ness *n* ♦ : the quality or state of being vicious

♦ cattiness, despite, hatefulness, malice, malignity, meanness, nastiness, spite, spleen, venom — more at MALICE

vi·cis·si·tude \\və-'si-sə-,tüd, vī-, -,tyüd\\ *n* : an irregular, unexpected, or surprising change ⟨the ∼s of business⟩

vic·tim \\'vik-təm\\ *n* **1** : a living being offered as a sacrifice in a religious rite **2** ♦ : an individual injured or killed (as by disease or accident) **3** ♦ : a person cheated, fooled, or injured ⟨a ∼ of circumstances⟩

♦ [2] casualty, fatality, loss — more at CASUALTY
♦ [3] butt, mark, target — more at TARGET

vic·tim·ise *chiefly Brit var of* VICTIMIZE

vic·tim·ize \\'vik-tə-,mīz\\ *vb* **-ized; -iz·ing** ♦ : to make a victim of — **vic·tim·i·za·tion** \\,vik-tə-mə-'zā-shən\\ *n* — **vic·tim·iz·er** \\'vik-tə-,mī-zər\\ *n*

♦ bleed, cheat, chisel, cozen, defraud, fleece, hustle, mulct, rook, shortchange, skin, squeeze, stick, sting, swindle — more at FLEECE

vic·tim·less \\'vik-təm-ləs\\ *adj* : having no victim ⟨considered gambling to be a ∼ crime⟩

vic·tor \\'vik-tər\\ *n* ♦ : one that defeats an enemy or opponent : WINNER

♦ conqueror, master, winner; *also* champion, finalist; ruler **Ant** loser

vic·to·ria \\vik-'tōr-ē-ə\\ *n* : a low 4-wheeled carriage with a folding top and a raised driver's seat in front

¹Vic·to·ri·an \\vik-'tōr-ē-ən\\ *adj* **1** : of or relating to the reign of Queen Victoria of England or the art, letters, or tastes of her time **2** : typical of the standards, attitudes, or conduct of the age of Victoria esp. when considered prudish or narrow

²Victorian *n* **1** : a person and esp. an author of the Victorian period **2** : a typically large ornate house built during Queen Victoria's reign

vic·to·ri·ous \\vik-'tōr-ē-əs\\ *adj* **1** : having won a victory **2** : of, relating to, or characteristic of victory — **vic·to·ri·ous·ly** *adv*

vic·to·ry \\'vik-tə-rē\\ *n, pl* **-ries** **1** : the overcoming of an enemy or an antagonist **2** : achievement of mastery or success in a struggle or endeavor

¹vict·ual \\'vit-ᵊl\\ *n* [ME *vitaille, victuayle,* fr. AF, fr. LL *victualia,* pl., provisions, food, fr. neut. pl. of *victualis* of nourishment, fr. L *victus* nourishment, way of living, fr. *vivere* to live] **1** : food fit for humans **2** *pl* ♦ : food supplies

♦ victuals chow, fare, food, grub, meat, provender, provisions, viands — more at FOOD

²victual *vb* **-ualed** *or* **-ualled; -ual·ing** *or* **-ual·ling** **1** ♦ : to supply with food **2** : to store up provisions

♦ board, cater, provision — more at FEED

vict·ual·ler *or* **vict·ual·er** \\'vit-ᵊl-ər\\ *n* : one that supplies provisions (as to an army or a ship)

vi·cu·ña *or* **vi·cu·na** \\vi-'kün-yə, vī-; vī-'kü-nə, -'kyü-\\ *n* **1** : a So. American wild mammal related to the llama and alpaca; *also* : its wool **2** : a soft fabric woven from the wool of the vicuña; *also* : a sheep's wool imitation of this

vi·de \\'vī-dē, 'vē-,dā\\ *vb imper* [L] : SEE — used to direct a reader to another item

vi·de·li·cet \\və-'de-lə-,set, vī-; vi-'dā-li-,ket\\ *adv* [ME, fr. L, fr. *vidēre* to see + *licet* it is permitted] : that is to say : NAMELY

¹vid·eo \\'vi-dē-,ō\\ *n* **1** : TELEVISION **2** : VIDEOTAPE; *also* : a recording similar to a videotape but stored in digital form **3** : a videotaped performance ⟨music ∼s⟩

²video *adj* **1** : relating to or used in transmission or reception of the television image **2** : relating to or being images on a television screen or computer display ⟨a ∼ terminal⟩

video camera *n* : a camera that records visual images and usu. sound; *esp* : CAMCORDER

vid·eo·cas·sette \\,vi-dē-ō-kə-'set\\ *n* **1** : a case containing videotape for use with a VCR **2** : a recording (as of a movie) on a videocassette

videocassette recorder *n* : VCR

vid·eo·con·fer·enc·ing \\-'kän-f(ə-)rən-siŋ\\ *n* : the holding of a conference among people at remote locations by means of transmitted audio and video signals

vid·eo·disc *or* **vid·eo·disk** \\'vi-dē-ō-,disk\\ *n* **1** : OPTICAL DISK **2** : a recording (as of a movie) on a videodisc

video game *n* : an electronic game played on a video screen

vid·eo·gen·ic \\,vi-dē-ō-'je-nik\\ *adj* : TELEGENIC

vid·eo·phone \\'vid-ē-ə-,fōn\\ *n* : a telephone for transmitting both audio and video signals

¹**vid·eo·tape** \'vid-ē-ō-ˌtāp\ *n* : a recording of visual images and sound made on magnetic tape; *also* : the magnetic tape used for such a recording

²**videotape** *vb* : to make a videotape of

videotape recorder *n* : a device for recording and playing back videotapes

vie \'vī\ *vb* **vied; vy·ing** \'vī-iŋ\ ♦ : to compete for superiority : CONTEND — **vi·er** \'vī-ər\ *n*

♦ battle, compete, contend, fight, race — more at COMPETE

Viet·cong \vē-'et-'käŋ, ˌvē-ət-, -'kȯŋ\ *n, pl* **Vietcong** : a guerrilla member of the Vietnamese communist movement

Viet·nam·ese \vē-ˌet-nə-'mēz, ˌvē-ət-, -'mēs\ *n, pl* **Vietnamese** : a native or inhabitant of Vietnam — **Vietnamese** *adj*

¹**view** \'vyü\ *n* **1 a** ♦ : the act of seeing or examining **b** : SURVEY **2** : a way of looking at or regarding something **3** ♦ : an opinion or judgment colored by the feeling or bias of its holder ⟨stated his ∼s⟩ **4** ♦ : a sight (as of a landscape) regarded for its pictorial quality **5** : extent or range of vision ⟨within ∼⟩ **6** : OBJECT, PURPOSE ⟨done with a ∼ to promotion⟩ **7** : a picture of a scene

♦ [1a] cast, eye, gander, glance, glimpse, look, peek, peep, regard, sight — more at LOOK ♦ [3] belief, conviction, eye, feeling, judgment (*or* judgement), mind, notion, opinion, persuasion, sentiment, verdict — more at OPINION ♦ [4] lookout, outlook, panorama, prospect, vista; *also* landscape, scene, scenery; ken, sight

²**view** *vb* **1** : to look at attentively : EXAMINE **2** : to perceive by the eye : SEE **3** : to examine mentally : CONSIDER ⟨∼ a problem⟩ — **view·er** *n*

view·er·ship \'vyü-ər-ˌship\ *n* : a television audience esp. with respect to size or makeup

view·find·er \'vyü-ˌfīn-dər\ *n* : a device on a camera for showing the view to be included in the picture

view·point \-ˌpȯint\ *n* ♦ : a position or perspective from which something is considered or evaluated : POINT OF VIEW

♦ angle, outlook, perspective, point of view, slant, standpoint — more at POINT OF VIEW

vi·ges·i·mal \vī-'jes-ə-məl\ *adj* : based on the number 20

vig·il \'vi-jəl\ *n* **1** : a religious observance formerly held on the night before a religious feast **2** : the day before a religious feast observed as a day of spiritual preparation **3** : evening or nocturnal devotions or prayers — usu. used in pl. **4** : an act or a time of keeping awake when sleep is customary; *esp* : WATCH 1

vig·i·lance \'vi-jə-ləns\ *n* ♦ : the quality or state of being vigilant

♦ alertness, attentiveness, lookout, watch; *also* aliveness, awareness, consciousness, sensitivity; heedfulness, observance, observation; sleeplessness, wakefulness; care, carefulness, caution; preparation, readiness

vigilance committee *n* : a committee of vigilantes

vig·i·lant \'vi-jə-lənt\ *adj* ♦ : alertly watchful esp. to avoid danger — **vig·i·lant·ly** *adv*

♦ alert, attentive, awake, watchful, wide-awake — more at ALERT

vig·i·lan·te \ˌvi-jə-'lan-tē\ *n* : a member of a volunteer committee organized to suppress and punish crime summarily (as when the processes of law are viewed as inadequate); *also* : a self-appointed doer of justice — **vig·i·lan·tism** \-'lan-ˌti-zəm\ *n*

¹**vi·gnette** \vin-'yet\ *n* [F, fr. MF *vignete*, fr. dim. of *vigne* vine] **1** : a small decorative design **2** : a picture (as an engraving or a photograph) that shades off gradually into the surrounding ground **3** ♦ : a short descriptive literary sketch

♦ delineation, depiction, description, picture, portrait, portrayal, sketch — more at DESCRIPTION

²**vignette** *vb* **vi·gnett·ed; vi·gnett·ing 1** : to finish (as a photograph) like a vignette **2** : to describe briefly

vig·or *or Can and Brit* **vig·our** \'vi-gər\ *n* **1** ♦ : active strength or energy of body or mind **2** : INTENSITY, FORCE

♦ dash, drive, energy, ginger, hardihood, life, pep, sap, snap, vim, vitality, zing, zip; *also* animation, liveliness, sprightliness, vivacity; main, might, muscle, potency, power, puissance, strength; brawniness, fitness, hardiness, huskiness, virility; health, healthiness, soundness, wellness *Ant* lethargy, listlessness, sluggishness ♦ energy, force, main, might, muscle, potency, power, sinew, strength — more at POWER

vig·or·ous \'vi-gə-rəs\ *adj* **1** ♦ : having vigor **2** ♦ : done with force and energy ⟨a ∼ debate⟩

♦ [1] hard, hard-bitten, hardy, rugged, stout, strong, sturdy, tough — more at HARDY ♦ [1] dynamic, energetic, flush, lusty, peppy, robust, strenuous, vital; *also* animated, lively, spirited, sprightly, vivacious; energized, enlivened, invigorated, vitalized; firm, fortified, mettlesome, mighty, powerful, puissant, strong; refreshed, rejuvenated, revitalized; able-bodied, beefy, brawny, fit, fortified, hardy, husky, rugged, stalwart, stout, strapping, sturdy, tough; hale, healthy, sound; capable, competent *Ant* lethargic, listless, sluggish, torpid ♦ [2] aggressive, assertive, dynamic, emphatic, energetic, forceful, resounding, strenuous, vehement — more at EMPHATIC ♦ [2] firm, forceful, hearty, lusty, robust, solid, stout, strong, sturdy

vig·or·ous·ly *adv* ♦ : in a vigorous manner

♦ energetically, firmly, forcefully, forcibly, hard, mightily, powerfully, stiffly, stoutly, strenuously, strongly, sturdily — more at HARD

vig·or·ous·ness *n* : the quality or state of being vigorous

vig·our *chiefly Brit var of* VIGOR

Vi·king \'vī-kiŋ\ *n* [ON *vīkingr*] : any of the pirate Norsemen who raided or invaded the coasts of Europe in the 8th to 10th centuries

vile \'vīl\ *adj* **vil·er; vil·est 1** ♦ : morally despicable **2** : physically repulsive : FOUL **3** : of little worth **4** : DEGRADING, IGNOMINIOUS **5** : utterly bad or contemptible ⟨∼ weather⟩ — **vile·ly** \'vīl-lē\ *adv*

♦ bad, black, evil, immoral, iniquitous, nefarious, rotten, sinful, unethical, unsavory, vicious, villainous, wicked, wrong ♦ base, contemptible, despicable, detestable, dirty, dishonorable (*or* dishonourable), ignoble, low, mean, snide, sordid, wretched — more at IGNOBLE

vile·ness *n* ♦ : the quality or state of being vile

♦ atrociousness, atrocity, depravity, enormity, heinousness, monstrosity, wickedness — more at ENORMITY

vil·i·fi·ca·tion \ˌvi-lə-fə-'kā-shən\ *n* ♦ : an instance of vilifying : a defamatory utterance

♦ defamation, libel, slander — more at SLANDER

vil·i·fy \'vi-lə-ˌfī\ *vb* **-fied; -fy·ing** ♦ : to utter slanderous and abusive statements against : DEFAME — **vil·i·fi·er** \'vi-lə-ˌfī-ər\ *n*

♦ blacken, defame, libel, malign, slander, smear, traduce — more at SLANDER

vil·la \'vi-lə\ *n* **1** : a country estate **2** ♦ : the rural or suburban residence of a wealthy person

♦ castle, estate, hall, manor, mansion, palace — more at MANSION

vil·lage \'vi-lij\ *n* [ME, fr. AF *vilage*, fr. *vile* manorial estate, farmstead, fr. L *villa*] **1** : a settlement usu. larger than a hamlet and smaller than a town **2** : an incorporated minor municipality **3** : the people of a village

vil·lag·er \'vi-li-jər\ *n* : an inhabitant of a village

vil·lain \'vi-lən\ *n* **1** : VILLEIN **2** ♦ : an evil person : SCOUNDREL

♦ beast, devil, evildoer, fiend, heavy, knave, no-good, rapscallion, rascal, reprobate, rogue, scalawag, scamp, scoundrel, varlet, wretch; *also* blackguard; criminal, crook, culprit, felon, lawbreaker, malefactor, offender, transgressor; cad, heel; ne'er-do-well

vil·lain·ess \-lə-nəs\ *n* : a woman who is a villain

vil·lain·ous \-lə-nəs\ *adj* **1 ♦** : befitting a villain : WICKED **2** : highly objectionable : DETESTABLE — **vil·lain·ous·ness** *n*

♦ bad, black, evil, immoral, iniquitous, nefarious, rotten, sinful, unethical, unsavory, vicious, vile, wicked, wrong

vil·lain·ous·ly *adv* : in a villainous manner

vil·lainy \-lə-nē\ *n, pl* **-lain·ies** **1 ♦** : villainous conduct; *also* : a villainous act **2** : villainous character or nature

♦ bad, evil, ill, immorality, iniquity, sin, wrong — more at EVIL

vil·lein \'vi-lən, -ˌlān\ *n* **1** : a free villager of Anglo-Saxon times **2** : an unfree peasant having the status of a slave to a feudal lord

vil·lous \'vi-ləs\ *adj* : covered with fine hairs or villi

vil·lus \'vi-ləs\ *n, pl* **vil·li** \-ˌlī, -ˌ(ˌ)lē\ : a slender usu. vascular process; *esp* : one of the tiny projections of the mucous membrane of the small intestine that function in the absorption of food

vim \'vim\ *n* **♦** : robust energy and enthusiasm

♦ dash, energy, life, pep, vigor (*or* vigour), vitality — more at VIGOR

VIN *abbr* vehicle identification number

vin·ai·grette \ˌvi-ni-'gret\ *n* [F] : a sauce made typically of oil, vinegar, and seasonings

vin·ci·ble \'vin-sə-bəl\ *adj* : capable of being overcome or subdued

vin·di·cate \'vin-də-ˌkāt\ *vb* **-cat·ed; -cat·ing** **1** : AVENGE **2 ♦** : to free from allegation or blame : EXONERATE **3 ♦** : to establish by proof or competent evidence : CONFIRM **4** : to provide defense for : JUSTIFY **5** : to maintain a right to : ASSERT — **vin·di·ca·tor** \-ˌkā-tər\ *n*

♦ [2] absolve, acquit, clear, exculpate, exonerate — more at EXCULPATE **♦** [3] bear out, confirm, corroborate, substantiate, support, validate, verify — more at CONFIRM

vin·di·ca·tion \ˌvin-də-'kā-shən\ *n* **♦** : the act of vindicating or the state of being vindicated; *esp* : justification against denial or censure : DEFENSE

♦ acquittal, exculpation, exoneration — more at ACQUITTAL

vin·dic·tive \vin-'dik-tiv\ *adj* **1** : disposed to revenge **2** : intended for or involving revenge **3** : VICIOUS, SPITEFUL — **vin·dic·tive·ly** *adv* — **vin·dic·tive·ness** *n*

vine \'vīn\ *n* [ME, fr. OF *vigne*, fr. L *vinea* vine, vineyard, fr. fem. of *vineus* of wine, fr. *vinum* wine] **1** : GRAPE 2 **2** : a plant whose stem requires support and which climbs (as by tendrils) or trails along the ground; *also* : the stem of such a plant

vin·e·gar \'vi-ni-gər\ *n* [ME *vinegre*, fr. AF *vin egre*, lit., sour wine] : a sour liquid obtained by fermentation (as of cider, wine, or malt) and used to flavor or preserve foods

vin·e·gary \-gə-rē\ *adj* **1 ♦** : resembling vinegar : SOUR **2** : disagreeable in manner or disposition : CRABBED

♦ acid, sour, tart — more at SOUR

vine·yard \'vin-yərd\ *n* **1** : a field of grapevines esp. to produce grapes for wine production **2** : a sphere of activity : field of endeavor

vi·nous \'vī-nəs\ *adj* **1** : of, relating to, or made with wine ⟨~ medications⟩ **2** : showing the effects of the use of wine ⟨~ bloodshot eyes⟩

¹vin·tage \'vin-tij\ *n* **1** : a season's yield of grapes or wine **2** : WINE; *esp* : a usu. superior wine which comes from a single year **3** : the act or period of gathering grapes or making wine **4** : a period of origin ⟨clothes of 1890 ~⟩

²vintage *adj* **1** : of, relating to, or produced in a particular vintage **2** : of old, recognized, and enduring interest, importance, or quality : CLASSIC ⟨~ cars⟩ **3** : of the best and most characteristic — used with a proper noun

vint·ner \'vint-nər\ *n* : a dealer in wines

vi·nyl \'vīn-ᵊl\ *n* **1** : a chemical derived from ethylene by the removal of one hydrogen atom **2** : a polymer of a vinyl compound or a product (as a textile fiber) made from one

vinyl chloride *n* : a flammable gaseous carcinogenic compound used esp. to make vinyl resins

vi·ol \'vī-əl\ *n* : a bowed stringed instrument chiefly of the 16th and 17th centuries having a fretted neck and usu. six strings

¹vi·o·la \vī-'ō-lə, 'vī-ə-lə\ *n* : VIOLET 1; *esp* : any of various hybrid garden plants with white, yellow, purple, or variously colored flowers that resemble but are smaller than those of the related pansies

²vi·o·la \vē-'ō-lə\ *n* : an instrument of the violin family slightly larger and tuned lower than a violin — **vi·o·list** \-list\ *n*

vi·o·la·ble \'vī-ə-lə-bəl\ *adj* : capable of being violated

vi·o·late \'vī-ə-ˌlāt\ *vb* **-lat·ed; -lat·ing** **1 ♦** : to go beyond limits set or prescribed by : BREAK ⟨~ a law⟩ ⟨~ a frontier⟩ **2 ♦** : RAPE **3 ♦** : to fail to show proper respect for : DESECRATE **4** : INTERRUPT, DISTURB ⟨*violated* his privacy⟩ — **vi·o·la·tor** \-ˌlā-tər\ *n*

♦ [1] breach, break, transgress; *also* disobey, rebel; brush off, disregard, ignore, overlook, overpass, pass over, tune out, wink (at); dismiss, pooh-pooh, scorn, shrug off; defy, resist, withstand *Ant* comply (with), conform (to), follow, mind, obey, observe **♦** [3] defile, desecrate, profane — more at DESECRATE

vi·o·la·tion \ˌvī-ə-'lā-shən\ *n* **♦** : an act or instance of violating : the state of being violated

♦ breach, crime, error, infraction, malefaction, misdeed, misdoing, offense, sin, transgression, trespass, wrongdoing — more at OFFENSE

vi·o·lence \'vī-ləns, 'vī-ə-\ *n* **1** : exertion of physical force so as to injure or abuse **2** : injury by or as if by infringement or profanation **3** : intense or furious often destructive action or force **4** : vehement feeling or expression : INTENSITY **5** : jarring quality : a state of discord

vi·o·lent \-lənt\ *adj* **1 ♦** : marked by extreme force or sudden intense activity **2** : caused by or showing strong feeling ⟨~ words⟩ **3 ♦** : existing in an extreme degree : INTENSE **4** : emotionally agitated to the point of loss of self-control **5** : caused by force : not natural ⟨~ death⟩ — **vi·o·lent·ly** *adv*

♦ [1] explosive, ferocious, fierce, furious, hot, rabid, rough, stormy, tempestuous, turbulent, volcanic; *also* brutal, savage, vicious; antagonistic, hostile; aggressive, assertive, bellicose, belligerent, combative, contentious, gladiatorial, quarrelsome; frantic, frenzied, mad; destructive, ruinous *Ant* nonviolent, peaceable, peaceful **♦** [3] deep, exquisite, fearful, hard, heavy, intense, profound, terrible, vehement, vicious — more at INTENSE

vi·o·let \'vī-ə-lət\ *n* **1** : any of a genus of herbs or small shrubs usu. with heart-shaped leaves and both aerial and underground flowers; *esp* : one with small usu. solid-colored flowers **2** : a reddish blue color

vi·o·lin \ˌvī-ə-'lin\ *n* : a bowed stringed instrument with four strings that has a shallow body, a fingerboard without frets, and a curved bridge — **vi·o·lin·ist** \-'li-nist\ *n*

vi·o·lon·cel·lo \ˌvī-ə-lən-'che-lō\ *n* [It] : CELLO — **vi·o·lon·cel·list** \-list\ *n*

VIP \ˌvē-ˌī-'pē\ *n, pl* **VIPs** \-'pēz\ [*very important person*] **♦** : a person of great influence or prestige; *esp* : a high official with special privileges

♦ celebrity, figure, light, luminary, notable, personage, personality, somebody, standout, star, superstar — more at CELEBRITY

vi·per \'vī-pər\ *n* **1** : a common stout-bodied Eurasian venomous snake having a bite only rarely fatal to humans; *also* : any snake (as a pit viper) of the same family as the viper **2** : any venomous or reputedly venomous snake **3** : a vicious or treacherous person — **vi·per·ine** \-pə-ˌrīn\ *adj*

vi·ra·go \və-'rä-gō, -'rā-\ *n, pl* **-goes** *or* **-gos** [ME, fr. L, strong or heroic woman, fr. *vir* man] **1 ♦** : a loud over-bearing woman **2** : a woman of great strength and courage

  ♦ fury, harpy, shrew, termagant — more at SHREW

vi·ral \'vī-rəl\ *adj* **1** : of, relating to, or caused by a virus ⟨a ~ infection⟩ **2** : quickly and widely spread or popularized esp. by means of social media ⟨a ~ video⟩ — **vi·ral·ly** *adv*

vir·eo \'vir-ē-ˌō\ *n, pl* **-e·os** [L, a small bird, fr. *virēre* to be green] : any of various small insect-eating American songbirds mostly olive green and grayish in color

¹vir·gin \'vər-jən\ *n* **1** : an unmarried woman devoted to religion **2** : an unmarried girl or woman **3** *cap* : the mother of Jesus **4** : a person who has not had sexual intercourse

²virgin *adj* **1** : free from stain : PURE, SPOTLESS **2** : CHASTE **3** : befitting a virgin : MODEST **4 ♦** : having its original qualities unimpaired : FRESH; *esp* : not altered by human activity ⟨~ forest⟩ **5** : INITIAL, FIRST

  ♦ brand-new, fresh, pristine — more at FRESH

¹vir·gin·al \'vər-jən-ᵊl\ *adj* : of, relating to, or characteristic of a virgin or virginity — **vir·gin·al·ly** *adv*

²virginal *n* : a small rectangular spinet without legs popular in the 16th and 17th centuries

Vir·gin·ia creeper \vər-'jin-yə-\ *n* : a No. American vine related to the grapes that has leaves with five leaflets and bluish-black berries

Virginia reel *n* : an American country-dance

vir·gin·i·ty \vər-'ji-nə-tē\ *n, pl* **-ties** **1** : the quality or state of being virgin; *esp* : MAIDENHOOD **2** : the unmarried life : CELIBACY

Vir·go \'vər-ˌgō\ *n* [L, lit., virgin] **1** : a zodiacal constellation between Leo and Libra usu. pictured as a young woman **2** : the 6th sign of the zodiac in astrology; *also* : one born under this sign

vir·gule \'vər-gyül\ *n* : ²SLASH 3

vir·i·des·cent \ˌvir-ə-'des-ᵊnt\ *adj* : slightly green : GREENISH

vir·ile \'vir-əl\ *adj* **1** : having the nature, properties, or qualities of a man **2 ♦** : characteristic of or associated with men : MASCULINE **3** : MASTERFUL, FORCEFUL

  ♦ male, manly, mannish, man-size, masculine — more at MASCULINE

vi·ril·i·ty \və-'ri-lə-tē\ *n* **♦** : the quality or state of being virile

  ♦ manhood, manliness, masculinity; *also* maleness; boyishness, mannishness *Ant* femininity

vi·ri·on \'vī-rē-ˌän, 'vir-ē-\ *n* : a complete virus particle consisting of an RNA or DNA core with a protein coat

vi·rol·o·gy \vī-'rä-lə-jē\ *n* : a branch of science that deals with viruses and viral diseases — **vi·rol·o·gist** \-jist\ *n*

vir·tu \ˌvər-'tü, vir-\ *or* **ver·tu** \ˌvər-, ver-\ *n* [It *virtù*, lit., virtue] **1** : a love of or taste for objects of art **2** : objects of art (as curios and antiques)

vir·tu·al \'vər-chə-wəl\ *adj* **1** : being in essence or in effect though not formally recognized or admitted ⟨a ~ dictator⟩ **2** : being on or simulated on a computer or computer network ⟨~ shopping⟩

vir·tu·al·ly \'vər-chə-wə-lē\ *adv* **1 ♦** : almost entirely : NEARLY **2** : for all practical purposes

  ♦ about, almost, most, much, near, nearly, next to, nigh, practically, some, well-nigh — more at ALMOST

virtual reality *n* : an artificial environment that is experienced through sensory stimuli (as sights and sounds) provided by an interactive computer program; *also* : the technology used to create or access a virtual reality

vir·tue \'vər-chü\ *n* [ME *virtu*, fr. OF, fr. L *virtus* strength, manliness, virtue, fr. *vir* man] **1 ♦** : conformity to a standard of right : MORALITY **2** : a particular moral excellence **3** : manly strength or courage : VALOR **4 ♦** : a commendable quality : MERIT **5** : active power to accomplish a given effect : POTENCY, EFFICACY **6** : chastity esp. in a woman

  ♦ [1] character, decency, goodness, honesty, integrity, morality, probity, rectitude, righteousness, uprightness — more at MORALITY **♦** [4] distinction, excellence, merit, value — more at EXCELLENCE

vir·tu·os·i·ty \ˌvər-chə-'wä-sə-tē\ *n, pl* **-ties** : great technical skill in the practice of a fine art

¹vir·tu·o·so \ˌvər-chə-'wō-sō, -zō\ *n, pl* **-sos** *or* **-si** \-sē, -zē\ [It] **1** : one skilled in or having a taste for the fine arts **2 ♦** : one who excels in the technique of an art; *esp* : a highly skilled musical performer **3 ♦** : a person who has great skill at some endeavor

  ♦ [2, 3] ace, adept, artist, authority, crackerjack, expert, maestro, master, scholar, shark, whiz, wizard — more at EXPERT

²virtuoso *adj* **♦** : of, relating to, or characteristic of a virtuoso

  ♦ accomplished, adept, consummate, crack, crackerjack, expert, good, great, master, masterful, masterly, proficient, skilled, skillful — more at PROFICIENT

vir·tu·ous \'vər-chə-wəs\ *adj* **1 ♦** : having or showing virtue and esp. moral virtue **2** : CHASTE

  ♦ decent, ethical, good, honest, honorable (*or* honourable), just, moral, right, righteous, straight, upright — more at GOOD

vir·tu·ous·ly *adv* **♦** : in a virtuous manner

  ♦ chastely, modestly, purely, righteously — more at PURELY

vir·u·lence \'vir-ə-ləns, 'vir-yə-\ *n* **♦** : the quality or state of being virulent

  ♦ acidity, acrimony, asperity, bitterness, cattiness, tartness, vitriol — more at ACRIMONY

vir·u·lent \'vir-ə-lənt, 'vir-yə-\ *adj* **1** : highly infectious ⟨~ germ⟩; *also* : marked by a rapid, severe, and often deadly course ⟨a ~ disease⟩ **2** : extremely poisonous or venomous : NOXIOUS **3 ♦** : full of malice : MALIGNANT

  ♦ catty, cruel, hateful, malevolent, malicious, malign, malignant, mean, nasty, spiteful — more at HATEFUL

vir·u·lent·ly *adv* : in a virulent manner

vi·rus \'vī-rəs\ *n, pl* **vi·rus·es** [L, venom, poisonous emanation] **1** : any of a large group of submicroscopic infectious agents that have an outside coat of protein around a core of RNA or DNA, that can grow and multiply only in living cells, and that cause important diseases in human beings, lower animals, and plants; *also* : a disease caused by a virus **2** : something (as a corrupting influence) that poisons the mind or spirit **3** : a computer program that is usu. hidden within another program and that reproduces itself and inserts the copies into other programs and usu. performs a malicious action (as destroying data)

vis *abbr* **1** visibility **2** visual

¹vi·sa \'vē-zə, -sə\ *n* [F] **1** : an endorsement by the proper authorities on a passport to show that it has been examined and the bearer may proceed **2** : a signature by a superior official signifying approval of a document

²visa *vb* **vi·saed** \-zəd, -səd\; **vi·sa·ing** \-zə-iŋ, -sə-\ : to give a visa to (a passport)

vis·age \'vi-zij\ *n* **♦** : the face or countenance of a person or sometimes an animal; *also* : LOOK

  ♦ cast, countenance, expression, face, look — more at LOOK

¹vis-à-vis \ˌvēz-ə-'vē, ˌvēs-\ *prep* [F, lit., face-to-face] **1** : face-to-face with : OPPOSITE **2** : in relation to **3** : as compared with

²vis-à-vis *n, pl* **vis-à-vis** \same *or* -'vēz\ **1** : one that is face-to-face with another **2** : ESCORT **3** : COUNTERPART **4** : TÊTE-À-TÊTE

³vis-à-vis *adv* : in company : TOGETHER

viscera *pl of* VISCUS

vis·cer·al \'vi-sə-rəl\ *adj* **1** : felt in or as if in the viscera **2** : not intellectual : INSTINCTIVE **3** : of or relating to the viscera — **vis·cer·al·ly** *adv*

vis·cid \'vi-səd\ *adj* **1 ♦** : having an adhesive quality

2 : having a glutinous consistency : VISCOUS — **vis·cid·i·ty** \vi-'si-də-tē\ *n*

♦ adhesive, gelatinous, gluey, glutinous, gooey, gummy, sticky, viscous — more at STICKY

vis·cos·i·ty \vis-'kä-sə-tē\ *n, pl* **-ties** ♦ : the quality of being viscous; *esp* : the property of resistance to flow in a fluid

♦ consistency, thickness — more at CONSISTENCY

vis·count \'vī-ˌkaůnt\ *n* : a member of the British peerage ranking below an earl and above a baron

vis·count·ess \-ˌkaůn-təs\ *n* **1** : the wife or widow of a viscount **2** : a woman who holds the rank of viscount in her own right

vis·cous \'vis-kəs\ *adj* [ME *viscouse*, fr. AF *viscos*, fr. LL *viscosus* full of birdlime, viscous, fr. L *viscum* mistletoe, birdlime] **1** : having the sticky consistency of glue : VIS-CID **2** ♦ : having or characterized by viscosity

♦ syrupy, thick, viscid — more at THICK

vis·cus \'vis-kəs\ *n, pl* **vis·cera** \'vi-sə-rə\ : an internal organ of the body; *esp* : one (as the heart or liver) located in the cavity of the trunk

vise \'vīs\ *n* [ME *vys, vice* screw, fr. AF *vyz*, fr. L *vitis* vine] : a tool with two jaws for holding work that typically close by a screw or lever

vis·i·bil·i·ty \ˌvi-zə-'bi-lə-tē\ *n, pl* **-ties** **1** : the quality, condition, or degree of being visible **2** : the degree of clearness of the atmosphere

vis·i·ble \'vi-zə-bəl\ *adj* ♦ : capable of being seen 〈~ stars〉; *also* : APPARENT 〈has no ~ means of support〉 — **vis·i·bly** \-blē\ *adv*

♦ apparent, observable, visual; *also* external, outer, outward; detectable, discernible, noticeable, perceptible; clear, conspicuous, evident, manifest, obvious, plain, prominent, striking *Ant* invisible

¹vi·sion \'vi-zhən\ *n* **1** : something seen otherwise than by ordinary sight (as in a dream or trance) **2** ♦ : a vivid picture created by the imagination 〈~s of fame and fortune〉 **3** : the act or power of imagination **4** : unusual wisdom in foreseeing what is going to happen **5** ♦ : the act or power of seeing : SIGHT **6** : something seen; *esp* : a lovely sight **7** : the apparition of a person : PHANTOM

♦ [2] chimera, conceit, daydream, delusion, dream, fancy, fantasy, figment, hallucination, illusion, phantasm, pipe dream, unreality — more at FANTASY ♦ [5] eye, sight

²vision *vb* ♦ : to picture to oneself : IMAGINE

♦ conceive, dream, envisage, fancy, imagine, picture, visualize — more at IMAGINE

¹vi·sion·ary \'vi-zhə-ˌner-ē\ *adj* **1** : of the nature of a vision : ILLUSORY, UNREAL **2** : not practical : UTOPIAN **3** : seeing or likely to see visions : given to dreaming or imagining **4** ♦ : having or marked by foresight and imagination

♦ farsighted, forehanded, foresighted, prescient, proactive, provident — more at FORESIGHTED

²visionary *n, pl* **-ar·ies** **1** ♦ : one whose ideas or projects are impractical : DREAMER **2** : one who sees visions

♦ dreamer, idealist, romantic, utopian — more at IDE-ALIST

¹vis·it \'vi-zət\ *vb* **1** : to go to see in order to comfort or help **2** : to call on either as an act of courtesy or friendship **3** ♦ : to dwell with for a time as a guest **4** : to come to or upon as a reward, affliction, or punishment **5** : INFLICT **6** ♦ : to make a visit or regular or frequent visits **7** ♦ : to talk in an informal or familiar manner : CHAT — **vis·it·able** *adj*

♦ [3] sojourn, stay, tarry; *also* frequent, hang out (at); haunt; inhabit, occupy ♦ [6] call, drop (by *or* in), pop (in), stop (by *or* in) — more at CALL ♦ [7] chat, converse, gab, jaw, palaver, patter, prattle, rattle, talk — more at CHAT

²visit *n* **1** : a short stay : CALL **2** ♦ : a brief residence as a guest **3** : a journey to and stay at a place **4** : a formal or professional call (as by a doctor)

♦ sojourn, stay; *also* layover, stopover

vis·i·tant \'vi-zə-tənt\ *n* : VISITOR

vis·i·ta·tion \ˌvi-zə-'tā-shən\ *n* **1** : an instance of visiting : VISIT; *esp* : an official visit **2** : a special dispensation of divine favor or wrath; *also* : a severe trial

visiting nurse *n* : a nurse employed to visit sick persons or perform public health services in a community

vis·i·tor \'vi-zə-tər\ *n* ♦ : one that visits

♦ caller, guest

vi·sor \'vī-zər\ *n* **1** : the front piece of a helmet; *esp* : a movable upper piece **2** : VIZARD **3** ♦ : a projecting part (as on a cap) to shade the eyes — **vi·sored** \-zərd\ *adj*

♦ bill, peak; *also* shade

vis·ta \'vis-tə\ *n* **1** ♦ : a distant view through or along an avenue or opening **2** : an extensive mental view over a series of years or events

♦ lookout, outlook, panorama, prospect, view — more at VIEW

VISTA *abbr* Volunteers in Service to America

¹vi·su·al \'vi-zhə-wəl\ *adj* **1** ♦ : of, relating to, or used in vision 〈~ organs〉 **2** : perceived by vision 〈a ~ impression〉 **3** ♦ : capable of being seen : VISIBLE **4** : done by sight only 〈~ navigation〉 **5** : of or relating to instruction by means of sight 〈~ aids〉 — **vi·su·al·ly** *adv*

♦ [1] ocular, optical; *also* seeing, sighted; focusing *Ant* nonvisual ♦ [3] apparent, observable, visible — more at VISIBLE

²visual *n* : something (as a picture, chart, or film) that appeals to the sight and is used for illustration, demonstration, or promotion — usu. used in pl.

vi·su·al·ize \'vi-zhə-wə-ˌlīz\ *vb* **-ized; -iz·ing** ♦ : to make visible; *esp* : to form a mental image of — **vi·su·al·i·za·tion** \ˌvi-zhə-wə-lə-'zā-shən\ *n* — **vi·su·al·iz·er** *n*

♦ conceive, dream, envisage, fancy, imagine, picture, vision — more at IMAGINE

vi·ta \'vē-tə, 'vī-\ *n, pl* **vi·tae** \'vē-ˌtī, 'vī-tē\ [L, lit., life] : a brief autobiographical sketch

vi·tal \'vīt-ᵊl\ *adj* **1** : concerned with or necessary to the maintenance of life 〈~ organs〉 **2** ♦ : full of life and vigor **3** : of, relating to, or characteristic of life or living beings **4** ♦ : destructive to life : FATAL 〈~ wound〉 **5** ♦ : of the utmost importance — **vi·tal·ly** *adv*

♦ [2] active, animate, animated, brisk, energetic, lively, peppy, spirited, sprightly, springy, vigorous, vivacious — more at LIVELY ♦ [4] baleful, deadly, deathly, fatal, fell, lethal, mortal, murderous, pestilent — more at DEADLY ♦ [5] essential, imperative, indispensable, integral, necessary, needful, requisite — more at ES-SENTIAL ♦ [5] critical, crucial, key, pivotal — more at CRUCIAL

vi·tal·i·ty \vī-'ta-lə-tē\ *n, pl* **-ties** **1** : the property distinguishing the living from the nonliving **2** ♦ : mental and physical vigor **3** : enduring quality **4** ♦ : lively and animated character 〈the ~ of youth〉

♦ [2] dash, energy, life, pep, vigor (*or* vigour), vim — more at VIGOR ♦ [4] animation, briskness, exuberance, liveliness, lustiness, robustness, sprightliness, vibrancy; *also* buoyancy, jauntiness; brightness, cheer, cheerfulness, effervescence, vivaciousness, vivacity; eagerness, enthusiasm, keenness; friskiness, impishness, playfulness *Ant* inactivity

vi·tal·ize \'vīt-ᵊl-ˌīz\ *vb* **-ized; -iz·ing** ♦ : to impart life or vigor to : ANIMATE — **vi·tal·i·za·tion** \ˌvīt-ᵊl-ə-'zā-shən\ *n*

♦ animate, brace, energize, enliven, fire, invigorate, jazz up, liven up, pep up, quicken, stimulate, vivify, zip (up) — more at ANIMATE

vi·tals \'vīt-ᵊlz\ *n pl* **1** : vital organs (as the heart and brain) **2** : essential parts

vital signs *n pl* : the pulse rate, respiratory rate, body temperature, and often blood pressure of a person

vital statistics *n pl* : statistics dealing with births, deaths, marriages, health, and disease

vi·ta·min \'vī-tə-mən\ *n* : any of various organic substances that are essential in tiny amounts to the nutrition of most animals and some plants and are mostly obtained from foods

vitamin A *n* : any of several vitamins (as from egg yolk or fish-liver oils) required esp. for good vision

vitamin B *n*   **1** : VITAMIN B COMPLEX   **2** *or* **vitamin B₁** : THIAMINE

vitamin B complex *n* : a group of vitamins that are found widely in foods and are essential for normal function of certain enzymes and for growth

vitamin B₆ \-'bē-,siks\ *n* : any of several compounds that are considered essential to vertebrate nutrition

vitamin B₁₂ \-'bē-'twelv\ *n* : a complex cobalt-containing compound that occurs esp. in liver and is essential to normal blood formation, neural function, and growth; *also* : any of several compounds of similar action

vitamin C *n* : a vitamin found esp. in fruits and vegetables that is needed by the body to prevent scurvy

vitamin D *n* : any or all of several vitamins that are needed for normal bone and tooth structure and are found esp. in fish-liver oils, egg yolk, and milk or are produced by the body in response to ultraviolet light

vitamin E *n* : any of various oily fat-soluble liquid vitamins whose absence in the body is associated with such ailments as infertility, the breakdown of muscles, and vascular problems and which are found esp. in leaves and in seed germ oils

vitamin K *n* [Dan *k*oagulation coagulation] : any of several vitamins needed for blood to clot properly

vi·ti·ate \'vi-shē-,āt\ *vb* **-at·ed; -at·ing**   **1** ♦ : to make faulty or defective : IMPAIR   **2** : to make legally ineffective : INVALIDATE   **3** ♦ : to debase in moral or aesthetic status — **vi·ti·a·tion** \,vi-shē-'ā-shən\ *n* — **vi·ti·a·tor** \'vi-shē-,ā-tər\ *n*

  ♦ [1] blemish, break, cripple, damage, deface, disfigure, flaw, harm, hurt, injure, mar, spoil — more at DAMAGE ♦ [3] blemish, mar, poison, spoil, stain, taint, tarnish, touch — more at TAINT

vi·ti·cul·ture \'vi-tə-,kəl-chər\ *n* : the growing of grapes — **vi·ti·cul·tur·al** \,vi-tə-'kəl-chə-rəl\ *adj* — **vi·ti·cul·tur·ist** \-rist\ *n*

vit·re·ous \'vi-trē-əs\ *adj*   **1** : of, relating to, or resembling glass : GLASSY ⟨~ rocks⟩   **2** : of, relating to, or being the clear colorless transparent jelly (**vitreous humor**) behind the lens in the eyeball

vit·ri·ol \'vi-trē-əl\ *n* ♦ : something resembling acid in being caustic, corrosive, or biting — **vit·ri·ol·ic** \,vi-trē-'ä-lik\ *adj*

  ♦ acidity, acrimony, asperity, bitterness, cattiness, tartness, virulence — more at ACRIMONY ♦ abuse, fulmination, invective, vituperation — more at ABUSE

vit·tles \'vit-ᵊlz\ *n pl* : supplies of food : VICTUALS

vi·tu·per·ate \vī-'tü-pə-,rāt, və-, -'tyü-\ *vb* **-at·ed; -at·ing** ♦ : to abuse in words — **vi·tu·per·a·tive** \-'tü-pə-rə-tiv, -'tyü-, -,rā-\ *adj* — **vi·tu·per·a·tive·ly** *adv*

  ♦ abuse, assail, attack, belabor, blast, castigate, excoriate, jump, lambaste, slam — more at ATTACK

vi·tu·per·a·tion \(,)vī-tü-pə-'rā-shən, və-, -tyü-\ *n* ♦ : lengthy harsh criticism or abuse

  ♦ abuse, fulmination, invective, vitriol — more at ABUSE

vi·va \'vē-və\ *interj* [It & Sp, long live] — used to express goodwill or approval

vi·va·ce \vē-'vä-chā\ *adv or adj* [It] : in a brisk spirited manner — used as a direction in music

vi·va·cious \və-'vä-shəs, vī-\ *adj* ♦ : lively in temper, conduct, or spirit ⟨a ~ personality⟩ — **vi·va·cious·ness** *n*

  ♦ active, animate, animated, brisk, energetic, frisky, gay, jaunty, jazzy, lively, peppy, perky, pert, racy, snappy, spirited, sprightly, springy, vital — more at LIVELY

vi·va·cious·ly *adv* ♦ : in a vivacious manner

  ♦ gaily, jauntily, sprightly — more at GAILY

vi·vac·i·ty \-'va-sə-tē\ *n* : the quality or state of being vivacious

vi·va vo·ce \,vī-və-'vō-sē, ,vē-və-'vō-,chā\ *adj* [ML, with the living voice] : expressed or conducted by word of mouth : ORAL — **viva voce** *adv*

viv·id \'vi-vəd\ *adj*   **1** : having the appearance of vigorous life   **2** : BRILLIANT, INTENSE ⟨a ~ red⟩   **3** : producing a strong impression on the senses; *esp* : producing distinct mental pictures : GRAPHIC ⟨a ~ description⟩ — **viv·id·ly** *adv* — **viv·id·ness** *n*

viv·i·fy \'vi-və-,fī\ *vb* **-fied; -fy·ing**   **1** ♦ : to put life into : ANIMATE   **2** : to make vivid ⟨details that ~ a story⟩ — **viv·i·fi·ca·tion** \,vi-və-fə-'kā-shən\ *n* — **viv·i·fi·er** *n*

  ♦ animate, brace, energize, enliven, fire, invigorate, jazz up, liven up, pep up, quicken, stimulate, vitalize, zip (up) — more at ANIMATE

vi·vip·a·rous \vī-'vi-pə-rəs, və-\ *adj* : producing living young from within the body rather than from eggs — **vi·vi·par·i·ty** \,vī-və-'par-ə-tē, ,vi-\ *n*

viv·i·sec·tion \,vi-və-'sek-shən, 'vi-və-,sek-\ *n* : the cutting of or operation on a living animal; *also* : animal experimentation esp. if causing distress to the subject

vix·en \'vik-sən\ *n*   **1** : an angry and unpleasant woman   **2** : a female fox

viz *abbr* videlicet

viz·ard \'vi-zərd\ *n* : a mask for disguise or protection

vi·zier \və-'zir\ *n* : a high executive officer of many Muslim countries

VJ *abbr* veejay

vlog \'vlog, 'vläg\ *n* : a blog that contains video material — **vlog** *vb* — **vlog·ger** *n*

VOA *abbr* Voice of America

voc *abbr*   **1** vocational   **2** vocative

vocab *abbr* vocabulary

vo·ca·ble \'vō-kə-bəl\ *n* : TERM, NAME; *esp* : a word as such without regard to its meaning

vo·cab·u·lary \vō-'ka-byə-,ler-ē\ *n, pl* **-lar·ies**   **1** : a list or collection of words usu. alphabetically arranged and defined or explained : LEXICON   **2** ♦ : a stock of words in a language used by a class or individual or in relation to a subject

  ♦ argot, cant, jargon, language, lingo, slang, terminology — more at TERMINOLOGY

vocabulary entry *n* : a word (as the noun *book*), hyphenated or open compound (as the verb *cross-refer* or the noun *boric acid*), word element (as the affix *-an*), abbreviation (as *agt*), verbalized symbol (as *Na*), or term (as *master of ceremonies*) entered alphabetically in a dictionary for the purpose of definition or identification or expressly included as an inflected form (as the noun *mice* or the verb *saw*) or as a derived form (as the noun *godlessness* or the adverb *globally*) or related phrase (as *in spite of*) run on at its base word and usu. set in a type (as boldface) readily distinguishable from that of the lightface running text which defines, explains, or identifies the entry

¹vo·cal \'vō-kəl\ *adj*   **1** ♦ : uttered by the voice : ORAL   **2** : relating to, composed or produced for, or sung by the human voice ⟨~ music⟩   **3** : given to expressing oneself freely or insistently : OUTSPOKEN ⟨a ~ critic⟩   **4** : of or relating to the voice

  ♦ oral, voiced; *also* articulate, articulated, spoken; breathed, drawled, gasped, mouthed, mumbled, muttered, shouted, whispered **Ant** nonvocal

²vocal *n*   **1** : a vocal sound   **2** ♦ : a vocal composition or its performance

  ♦ jingle, lay, lyric, song — more at SONG

vocal cords *n pl* : either of two pairs of elastic folds of mucous membrane that project into the cavity of the larynx and function in the production of vocal sounds

vo·cal·ic \vō-'ka-lik\ *adj* : of, relating to, or functioning as a vowel

vo·cal·ise *chiefly Brit var of* VOCALIZE

vo·cal·ist \'vō-kə-list\ *n* ♦ : one that sings : SINGER

  ♦ caroler, singer, songster, voice — more at SINGER

vo·cal·ize \-ˌlīz\ *vb* **-ized; -iz·ing 1 ♦** : to give vocal expression to : UTTER; *esp* : SING **2** : to make voiced rather than voiceless

  ♦ articulate, say, speak, state, talk, tell, utter, verbalize — more at SAY ♦ carol, chant, descant, sing — more at SING

vo·cal·iz·er \'vō-kə-ˌlī-zər\ *n* : one that vocalizes
vo·ca·tion \vō-'kā-shən\ *n* **1** : a summons or strong inclination to a particular state or course of action ⟨religious ∼⟩ **2** : regular employment : OCCUPATION — **vo·ca·tion·al** \-shə-nəl\ *adj*

  ♦ calling, employment, line, occupation, profession, trade, work — more at OCCUPATION

vo·ca·tion·al·ism \-shə-nə-ˌli-zəm\ *n* : emphasis on vocational training in education
voc·a·tive \'vä-kə-tiv\ *adj* : of, relating to, or constituting a grammatical case marking the one addressed — **vocative** *n*
vo·cif·er·ate \vō-'si-fə-ˌrāt\ *vb* **-at·ed; -at·ing** [L *vociferari*, fr. *voc-, vox* voice + *ferre* to bear] ♦ : to cry out loudly : SHOUT — **vo·cif·er·a·tion** \-ˌsi-fə-'rā-shən\ *n*

  ♦ bawl, call, cry, holler, shout, yell — more at CALL

vo·cif·er·ous \vō-'si-fə-rəs\ *adj* ♦ : making or given to loud outcry — **vo·cif·er·ous·ly** *adv* — **vo·cif·er·ous·ness** *n*

  ♦ blatant, boisterous, clamorous, obstreperous; *also* discordant, noisy; loudmouthed, outspoken, vocal; rowdy, uproarious; cacophonous, dissonant, shrill, strident; blaring, booming, brassy, brazen

vod·ka \'väd-kə\ *n* [Russ., fr. *voda* water] : a colorless liquor distilled from a mash (as of rye or wheat)
vogue \'vōg\ *n* [MF, action of rowing, course, fashion, fr. *voguer* to sail, fr. OF, fr. OIt *vogare* to row] **1** ♦ : popular acceptance or favor : POPULARITY **2** : a period of popularity **3** ♦ : one that is in fashion at a particular time

  ♦ [1] favor, modishness, popularity — more at POPULARITY ♦ [3] craze, fad, mode, rage, style, trend — more at FAD

vogu·ish \'vō-gish\ *adj* **1** : FASHIONABLE, SMART **2** : suddenly or temporarily popular ⟨∼ expressions⟩
¹voice \'vȯis\ *n* **1** : sound produced through the mouth by vertebrates and esp. by human beings (as in speaking or singing) **2** : musical sound produced by the vocal cords : the power to produce such sound; *also* : one of the melodic parts in a vocal or instrumental composition **3** : the vocal organs as a means of tone production ⟨train the ∼⟩ **4** : sound produced by vibration of the vocal cords as heard in vowels and some consonants **5** : the power of speaking **6** : a sound suggesting a voice ⟨the ∼ of the sea⟩ **7** : an instrument or medium of expression **8** ♦ : a choice, opinion, or wish openly expressed; *also* : right of expression **9** : distinction of form of a verb to indicate the relation of the subject to the action expressed by the verb **10** : one that sings : SINGER

  ♦ articulation, expression, formulation, statement, utterance — more at EXPRESSION

²voice *vb* **voiced; voic·ing** ♦ : to give voice or expression to ⟨∼ a complaint⟩

  ♦ air, express, give, look, sound, state, vent — more at EXPRESS

voice box *n* : LARYNX
voiced \'vȯist\ *adj* **1** : having a voice ⟨soft-*voiced*⟩ **2** ♦ : uttered with voice ⟨a ∼ consonant⟩ — **voiced·ness** \'vȯist-nəs, 'vȯi-səd-nəs\ *n*

  ♦ oral, vocal — more at VOCAL

voice·less \'vȯis-ləs\ *adj* **1** : having no voice **2** : not pronounced with voice — **voice·less·ly** *adv* — **voice·less·ness** *n*

  ♦ dumb, inarticulate, mute, speechless — more at MUTE

voice mail *n* : an electronic communication system in which spoken messages are recorded for later playback to the intended recipient; *also* : such a message

voice–over *n* : the voice in a film or television program of a person who is heard but not seen or not seen talking
voice·print \'vȯis-ˌprint\ *n* : an individually distinctive pattern of voice characteristics that is spectrographically produced
¹void \'vȯid\ *adj* **1** : UNOCCUPIED, VACANT **2** ♦ : containing nothing : EMPTY **3** ♦ : being without something specified : DEVOID ⟨proposals ∼ of sense⟩ **4** : VAIN, USELESS **5** ♦ : of no legal force or effect : NULL

  ♦ [2] bare, blank, devoid, empty, stark, vacant — more at EMPTY ♦ [3] bereft, destitute, devoid — more at DEVOID ♦ [5] invalid, null — more at NULL

²void *n* **1** ♦ : empty space : EMPTINESS **2** : a feeling of want or hollowness

  ♦ blank, blankness, emptiness, vacancy, vacuity — more at VACANCY

³void *vb* **1** ♦ : to make or leave empty; *also* : VACATE **2** : DISCHARGE, EMIT ⟨∼ urine⟩ **3** ♦ : to render void : ANNUL ⟨∼ a contract⟩ — **void·able** *adj* — **void·er** *n*

  ♦ [1] clear, empty, evacuate, vacate — more at EMPTY ♦ [3] abolish, abrogate, annul, cancel, dissolve, invalidate, negate, nullify, quash, repeal, rescind — more at ABOLISH

voi·là \vwä-'lä\ *interj* [F] — used to call attention or to express satisfaction or approval
voile \'vȯil\ *n* : a sheer fabric used esp. for women's clothing and curtains
vol *abbr* **1** volume **2** volunteer
vol·a·tile \'vä-lət-ᵊl\ *adj* **1** : readily becoming a vapor at a relatively low temperature ⟨a ∼ liquid⟩ **2** ♦ : likely to change suddenly ⟨a ∼ temper⟩ — **vol·a·til·i·ty** \ˌvä-lə-'ti-lə-tē\ *n* — **vol·a·til·ize** \'vä-lət-ᵊl-ˌīz\ *vb*

  ♦ capricious, changeable, fickle, fluid, inconstant, mercurial, mutable, temperamental, uncertain, unpredictable, unsettled, unstable, unsteady, variable — more at FICKLE

vol·ca·nic \väl-'ka-nik\ *adj* **1** : of, relating to, or produced by a volcano **2** ♦ : explosively violent

  ♦ explosive, ferocious, fierce, furious, hot, rabid, rough, stormy, tempestuous, turbulent, violent — more at VIOLENT

vol·ca·nism \'väl-kə-ˌni-zəm\ *n* : volcanic action or activity
vol·ca·no \väl-'kā-nō\ *n, pl* **-noes** *or* **-nos** [It or Sp; It *vulcano*, fr. Sp *vulcán*, ultim. fr. L *Volcanus*, Roman god of fire and metalworking] : an opening in the crust of the earth, a planet, or a moon from which molten rock and steam issue; *also* : a hill or mountain composed of the ejected material
vol·ca·nol·o·gy \ˌväl-kə-'nä-lə-jē\ *n* : a branch of geology that deals with volcanic phenomena — **vol·ca·nol·o·gist** \-kə-'nä-lə-jist\ *n*
vole \'vōl\ *n* : any of various small rodents that are closely related to the lemmings and muskrats
vo·li·tion \vō-'li-shən\ *n* **1** ♦ : the act or the power of making a choice or decision : WILL **2** : a choice or decision made

  ♦ accord, choice, free will, option, self-determination, will — more at FREE WILL

vo·li·tion·al \vō-'li-shə-nəl\ *adj* : of, relating to, or of the nature of volition : possessing or exercising volition
¹vol·ley \'vä-lē\ *n, pl* **volleys 1** : a flight of missiles (as arrows) **2** : simultaneous discharge of a number of missile weapons **3** : an act of volleying **4** ♦ : a burst of many things at once ⟨a ∼ of angry letters⟩

  ♦ barrage, bombardment, cannonade, fusillade, hail, salvo, shower, storm — more at BARRAGE

²volley *vb* **vol·leyed; vol·ley·ing 1** : to discharge or become discharged in or as if in a volley **2** : to hit an object of play (as a ball) in the air before it touches the ground
vol·ley·ball \-ˌbȯl\ *n* : a game played by volleying an inflated ball over a net; *also* : the ball used in this game
volt \'vōlt\ *n* : the meter-kilogram-second unit of electrical

potential difference and electromotive force equal to the difference in potential between two points in a wire carrying a constant current of one ampere when the power dissipated between the points is equal to one watt

volt·age \'vōl-tij\ n : potential difference measured in volts

volt·a·ic \väl-'tā-ik, vōl-\ adj : of, relating to, or producing direct electric current by chemical action

volte–face \ˌvôlt-'fäs, ˌvôl-tə-\ n : a reversal in policy : ABOUT-FACE

volt·me·ter \'vōlt-ˌmē-tər\ n : an instrument for measuring in volts the difference in potential between different points of an electrical circuit

vol·u·ble \'väl-yə-bəl\ adj : fluent and smooth in speech : GLIB — **vol·u·bil·i·ty** \ˌväl-yə-'bi-lə-tē\ n — **vol·u·bly** \'väl-yə-blē\ adv

vol·ume \'väl-yəm\ n [ME, fr. AF, fr. L volumen roll, scroll, fr. volvere to roll] 1 : a series of printed sheets bound typically in book form; also : an arbitrary number of issues of a periodical 2 : space occupied as measured by cubic units ⟨the ~ of a cylinder⟩ 3 : sufficient matter to fill a book ⟨her glance spoke ~s⟩ 4 a : the total number or quantity : AMOUNT ⟨increasing ~ of business⟩ b : considerable quantity 5 : the degree of loudness of a sound

vo·lu·mi·nous \və-'lü-mə-nəs\ adj ♦ : having or marked by great volume or bulk : LARGE — **vo·lu·mi·nous·ly** adv

♦ big, grand, great, large, sizable, substantial — more at LARGE

vo·lu·mi·nous·ness n : the quality or state of being voluminous

¹**vol·un·tary** \'väl-ən-ˌter-ē\ adj 1 ♦ : done, made, or given freely and without compulsion ⟨a ~ sacrifice⟩ 2 : done on purpose : INTENTIONAL ⟨~ manslaughter⟩ 3 ♦ : of, relating to, or regulated by the will ⟨~ behavior⟩ 4 : having power of free choice 5 : provided or supported by voluntary action ⟨a ~ organization⟩ — **vol·un·tar·i·ly** \ˌvä-lən-'ter-ə-lē\ adv

♦ [1] deliberate, freewill, intentional, purposeful, willful, willing — more at DELIBERATE ♦ [3] discretionary, elective, optional — more at OPTIONAL

²**voluntary** n, pl **-tar·ies** : an organ solo played in a religious service

voluntary muscle n : muscle (as most striated muscle) under voluntary control

¹**vol·un·teer** \ˌvä-lən-'tir\ n 1 : a person who voluntarily undertakes a service or duty 2 : a plant growing spontaneously esp. from seeds lost from a previous crop

²**volunteer** vb 1 ♦ : to offer or give voluntarily 2 : to offer oneself as a volunteer

♦ bestow, contribute, donate, give, present — more at GIVE

vo·lup·tu·ary \və-'ləp-chə-ˌwer-ē\ n, pl **-ar·ies** : a person whose chief interest in life is the indulgence of sensual appetites

vo·lup·tu·ous \-chə-wəs\ adj 1 ♦ : giving sensual gratification 2 : given to or spent in enjoyment of luxury or pleasure — **vo·lup·tu·ous·ly** adv — **vo·lup·tu·ous·ness** n

♦ carnal, fleshly, luscious, sensual, sensuous — more at SENSUAL

vo·lute \və-'lüt\ n : a spiral or scroll-shaped decoration

¹**vom·it** \'vä-mət\ n : an act or instance of throwing up the contents of the stomach through the mouth; also : the matter thrown up

²**vomit** vb 1 ♦ : to throw up the contents of the stomach through the mouth 2 : to belch forth : GUSH

♦ gag, heave, spit up, throw up; also disgorge, regurgitate; eject, expel, spew

voo·doo \'vü-dü\ n, pl **voodoos** 1 : a religion that is derived from African polytheism and is practiced chiefly in Haiti 2 ♦ : a person who deals in spells and necromancy 3 : a charm used in voodoo; also : ²SPELL 1 — **voodoo** adj

♦ conjurer, enchanter, magician, necromancer, sorcerer, witch, wizard — more at MAGICIAN

voo·doo·ism \-ˌi-zəm\ n 1 : VOODOO 1 2 : the practice of witchcraft

vo·ra·cious \vȯ-'rā-shəs, və-\ adj 1 ♦ : having a huge appetite : RAVENOUS 2 ♦ : very eager ⟨a ~ reader⟩ — **vo·ra·cious·ly** adv — **vo·ra·cious·ness** n — **vo·rac·i·ty** \-'ra-sə-tē\ n

♦ [1] gluttonous, greedy, hoggish, piggish, rapacious, ravenous; also hearty, wolfish; devouring, gobbling, gorging, gormandizing, insatiable, unquenchable; empty, famished, hungry, starved, starving; malnourished, underfed, undernourished ♦ [2] ardent, avid, eager, enthusiastic, keen

vor·tex \'vȯr-ˌteks\ n, pl **vor·ti·ces** \'vȯr-tə-ˌsēz\ also **vor·tex·es** \'vȯr-ˌtek-səz\ : WHIRLPOOL; also : something resembling a whirlpool

vo·ta·ry \'vō-tə-rē\ n, pl **-ries** 1 a : ENTHUSIAST, DEVOTEE b ♦ : a devoted adherent or admirer 2 ♦ : a devout or zealous worshiper

♦ [1b, 2] adherent, convert, disciple, follower, partisan, pupil — more at FOLLOWER

¹**vote** \'vōt\ n [ME (Sc), fr. L votum vow, wish, fr. vovēre to vow] 1 : a choice or opinion of a person or body of persons expressed usu. by a ballot, spoken word, or raised hand; also : the ballot, word, or gesture used to express a choice or opinion 2 : the decision reached by voting 3 ♦ : the right or privilege of voting in political matters 4 : a group of voters with some common characteristics ⟨the big city ~⟩ — **vote·less** adj

♦ enfranchisement, franchise, suffrage; also say, voice Ant disenfranchisement

²**vote** vb **vot·ed; vot·ing** 1 : to cast a vote 2 : to elect, decide, pass, defeat, grant, or make legal by a vote 3 : to declare by general agreement 4 ♦ : to offer as a suggestion : PROPOSE 5 : to cause to vote esp. in a given way — **vot·er** n

♦ advance, offer, pose, proffer, propose, propound, suggest — more at PROPOSE

vo·tive \'vō-tiv\ adj : consisting of or expressing a vow, wish, or desire

vou abbr voucher

vouch \'vaùch\ vb 1 : to give tangible support to : PROVE 2 : to verify by examining documentary evidence 3 : to give a guarantee 4 ♦ : to supply supporting evidence or testimony; also : to give personal assurance

♦ attest, authenticate, avouch, certify, testify, witness — more at CERTIFY

vouch·er \'vaù-chər\ n 1 : an act of vouching 2 : one that vouches for another 3 : a documentary record of a business transaction 4 : a written affidavit or authorization 5 : a form indicating a credit against future purchases or expenditures

vouch·safe \vaùch-'sāf\ vb **vouch·safed; vouch·saf·ing** : to grant or give as or as if by a privilege or a special favor

¹**vow** \'vaù\ n ♦ : a solemn promise or statement; esp : one by which a person is bound to an act, service, or condition ⟨marriage ~s⟩

♦ oath, pledge, promise, troth, word — more at PROMISE

²**vow** vb 1 ♦ : to make a vow or as a vow 2 : to bind or commit by a vow — **vow·er** n

♦ covenant, pledge, promise, swear — more at PROMISE

vow·el \'vaù-əl\ n 1 : a speech sound produced without obstruction or friction in the mouth 2 : a letter representing such a sound

vox po·pu·li \'väks-'pä-pyə-ˌlī\ n [L, voice of the people] : popular sentiment

¹**voy·age** \'vȯi-ij\ n [ME, viage, veyage, fr. AF veiage, fr. LL viaticum, fr. L, traveling money, fr. neut. of viaticus of a journey, fr. via way] ♦ : a journey esp. by water from one place or country to another

♦ crossing, cruise, passage, sail — more at SAIL

²**voyage** *vb* **voy·aged**; **voy·ag·ing** ♦ : to take or make a voyage — **voy·ag·er** *n*

♦ journey, tour, travel, trek — more at TRAVEL ♦ boat, cruise, navigate, sail — more at SAIL

voya·geur \ˌvȯi-ə-ˈzhər, ˌvwä-yä-\ *n* [CanF] : a person employed by a fur company to transport goods to and from remote stations esp. in the Canadian Northwest

voy·eur \vwä-ˈyər, vȯi-ˈər\ *n* **1** : one who obtains sexual pleasure from viewing esp. covertly the nudity or sexual activity of others **2** : an observer of the sordid — **voy·eur·is·tic** \ˌvwä-(ˌ)yər-ˈis-tik, ˌvȯi-ər-\ *adj* — **voy·eur·ism** \-ˌi-zəm\ *n*

VP *abbr* **1** verb phrase **2** vice president

vs *abbr* **1** verse **2** versus

vss *abbr* **1** verses **2** versions

V/STOL *abbr* vertical or short takeoff and landing

Vt *or* **VT** *abbr* Vermont

VTOL *abbr* vertical takeoff and landing

VTR *abbr* videotape recorder

vul·ca·nize \ˈvəl-kə-ˌnīz\ *vb* **-nized**; **-niz·ing** : to treat rubber or rubberlike material chemically to give useful properties (as elasticity and strength)

Vulg *abbr* Vulgate

vul·gar \ˈvəl-gər\ *adj* [ME, fr. L *vulgaris* of the mob, vulgar, fr. *vulgus* mob, common people] **1** : of or relating to common speech : VERNACULAR **2** ♦ : of or relating to the common people : COMMON **3 a** ♦ : lacking cultivation or refinement **b** : offensive to good taste or refined feelings : OBSCENE ⟨~ language⟩ — **vul·gar·ly** *adv*

♦ [2] common, humble, ignoble, inferior, low, lowly, mean, plebeian — more at IGNOBLE ♦ [3a] coarse, common, crass, crude, gross, ill-bred, low, rough, rude, tasteless, uncouth, uncultivated, uncultured, unpolished, unrefined — more at COARSE

vul·gar·i·an \ˌvəl-ˈgar-ē-ən\ *n* : a vulgar person

vul·gar·ism \ˈvəl-gə-ˌri-zəm\ *n* **1** : VULGARITY **2** : a word or expression originated or used chiefly by illiterate persons **3** : a coarse expression : OBSCENITY

vul·gar·i·ty \ˌvəl-ˈgar-ə-tē\ *n*, *pl* **-ties 1** : something vulgar **2** ♦ : the quality or state of being vulgar

♦ bawdiness, grossness, indecency, lewdness, nastiness, obscenity, ribaldry, smut — more at OBSCENITY ♦ coarseness, grossness, indelicacy, lowness, rudeness; *also* churlishness, clownishness; insensitivity, thoughtlessness

vul·gar·ize \ˈvəl-gə-ˌrīz\ *vb* **-ized**; **-iz·ing** : to make vulgar — **vul·gar·i·za·tion** \ˌvəl-gə-rə-ˈzā-shən\ *n* — **vul·gar·iz·er** \ˈvəl-gə-ˌrī-zər\ *n*

Vul·gate \ˈvəl-ˌgāt\ *n* [ML *vulgata*, fr. LL *vulgata editio* edition in general circulation] : a Latin version of the Bible used by the Roman Catholic Church

vul·ner·a·bil·i·ty \ˌvəl-nə-rə-ˈbi-lə-tē\ *n* ♦ : the quality or state of being vulnerable

♦ exposure, liability, openness — more at EXPOSURE

vul·ner·a·ble \ˈvəl-nə-rə-bəl\ *adj* **1** ♦ : capable of being wounded : susceptible to wounds **2** ♦ : open to attack **3** : liable to increased penalties in contract bridge — **vul·ner·a·bly** \ˈvəl-nə-rə-blē\ *adv*

♦ [1] exposed, liable, open, sensitive, subject, susceptible — more at LIABLE ♦ [2] defenseless (*or* defenceless), exposed, helpless, susceptible, undefended, unguarded, unprotected, unresistant — more at HELPLESS

vul·pine \ˈvəl-ˌpīn\ *adj* : of, relating to, or resembling a fox esp. in cunning

vul·ture \ˈvəl-chər\ *n* **1** : any of various large birds (as a turkey vulture) related to the hawks, eagles, and falcons but having weaker claws and the head usu. naked and living chiefly on carrion **2** : a rapacious person

vul·va \ˈvəl-və\ *n*, *pl* **vul·vae** \-ˌvē\ [ME, fr. ML, fr. L *volva*, *vulva* womb, female genitals] : the external parts of the female genital organs — **vul·val** \ˈvəl-vəl\ *or* **vul·var** \-vər, -ˌvär\ *adj*

vv *abbr* **1** verses **2** vice versa

vying *pres part of* VIE

¹**w** \ˈdə-bəl-(ˌ)yü\ *n*, *pl* **w's** *or* **ws** *often cap* : the 23d letter of the English alphabet

²**w** *abbr*, *often cap* **1** water **2** watt **3** week **4** weight **5** west; western **6** wide; width **7** wife **8** with

W *symbol* [G *Wolfram*] tungsten

WA *abbr* **1** Washington **2** Western Australia

wacky \ˈwa-kē\ *adj* **wack·i·er**; **-est** ♦ : eccentric or irrational esp. in an amusing, absurd, or fantastic manner; *also* : CRAZY

♦ far-out, funny, odd, quirky, screwy, strange, wild — more at ODD ♦ absurd, cockeyed, crazy, cuckoo, daft, foolish, harebrained, insane, mad, nutty, preposterous, sappy, screwball, silly, zany — more at FOOLISH

¹**wad** \ˈwäd\ *n* **1** ♦ : a little mass, bundle, or tuft ⟨~s of clay⟩ **2** : a soft mass of usu. light fibrous material **3** : a pliable plug (as of felt) used to retain a powder charge (as in a cartridge) **4** ♦ : a considerable amount (as of money) **5** : a roll of paper money

♦ [1] blob, chunk, clod, clump, glob, gob, hunk, lump, nub — more at LUMP ♦ [4] fortune, mint

²**wad** *vb* **wad·ded**; **wad·ding 1** : to push a wad into ⟨~ a gun⟩ **2** ♦ : to form into a wad **3** : to hold in by a wad ⟨~ a bullet in a gun⟩ **4** : to stuff or line with a wad : PAD

♦ agglomerate, ball, conglomerate, roll, round; *also* clump, lump; bead *Ant* unroll

wad·ding \ˈwä-diŋ\ *n* **1** : WADS; *also* : material for making wads **2** : a soft mass or sheet of short loose fibers used for stuffing or padding

wad·dle \ˈwäd-ᵊl\ *vb* **wad·dled**; **wad·dling** : to walk with short steps swaying from side to side like a duck — **waddle** *n*

wade \ˈwād\ *vb* **wad·ed**; **wad·ing 1** : to step in or through a medium (as water) more resistant than air **2** : to move or go with difficulty or labor and often with determination ⟨~ through a dull book⟩ **3** : to set to work or attack with determination or vigor — used with *in* or *into* — **wad·able** *or* **wade·able** \ˈwā-də-bəl\ *adj* — **wade** *n*

wad·er \ˈwā-dər\ *n* **1** : one that wades : SHOREBIRD; *also* : WADING BIRD **3** *pl* : a waterproof garment consisting of pants with attached boots for wading

wa·di \ˈwä-dē\ *n* [Ar *wādiy*] : a streambed of southwest Asia and northern Africa that is dry except in the rainy season

wading bird *n* : any of an order of long-legged birds (as sandpipers, cranes, or herons) that wade in water in search of food

wa·fer \ˈwā-fər\ *n* **1** : a thin crisp cake or cracker **2** : a thin round piece of unleavened bread used in the Eucharist **3** : something (as a piece of candy) that resembles a wafer

¹**waf·fle** \ˈwä-fəl\ *n* : a soft but crisped cake of batter cooked in a special hinged metal utensil (**waffle iron**)

²waffle *vb* **waf·fled; waf·fling** \-f(ə)liŋ\ : to speak or write in a vague or evasive manner ⟨*waffled* on the issue⟩

¹waft \'wäft, 'waft\ *vb* ♦ : to cause to move or go lightly by or as if by the impulse of wind or waves

♦ drift, float, glide, hang, hover, poise, ride, sail — more at FLOAT

²waft *n* **1** ♦ : a slight breeze : PUFF **2** : the act of waving

♦ air, breath, breeze, puff, zephyr — more at BREEZE

¹wag \'wag\ *vb* **wagged; wag·ging 1** : to sway or swing shortly from side to side or to-and-fro ⟨the dog *wagged* his tail⟩ **2** : to move in chatter : GOSSIP ⟨scandal caused tongues to ∼⟩

²wag *n* : an act of wagging : a wagging movement

³wag *n* ♦ : a person full of sport and humor : JOKER

♦ card, comedian, comic, humorist, jester, joker, wit — more at HUMORIST

¹wage \'wāj\ *n* **1** ♦ : payment for labor or services usu. according to contract — often used in pl. **2** *pl* : an equivalent or a return for something done, suffered, or given : RECOMPENSE

♦ *usu* **wages** *pl* emolument, hire, pay, payment, salary, stipend; *also* compensation, recompense, remittance, remuneration, requital, return; check, commission, paycheck; redress, reparation, restitution; reimbursement, repayment; profit, takings, yield

²wage *vb* **waged; wag·ing 1** : to engage in : CARRY ON ⟨∼ a war⟩ **2** : to be in process of being waged

¹wa·ger \'wā-jər\ *n* **1** : something (as a sum of money) risked on an uncertain event : BET, STAKE **2** : something on which bets are laid : GAMBLE

²wager *vb* ♦ : to make a bet

♦ bet, gamble, go, lay, stake — more at BET

wa·ger·er *n* : one that makes a wager

wag·gery \'wa-gə-rē\ *n, pl* **-ger·ies 1** ♦ : playfulness and mischievous merriment **2** ♦ : something done or said in fun : JEST

♦ [1] devilishness, impishness, knavery, mischief, mischievousness, rascality, shenanigans, wickedness — more at MISCHIEF ♦ [2] crack, gag, jest, joke, laugh, pleasantry, quip, sally, wisecrack, witticism — more at JOKE

wag·gish \'wa-gish\ *adj* **1** ♦ : resembling or characteristic of a wag : MISCHIEVOUS **2** : done or made for fun : HUMOROUS

♦ devilish, impish, knavish, mischievous, rascally, roguish, sly, wicked — more at MISCHIEVOUS

¹wag·gle \'wa-gəl\ *vb* **wag·gled; wag·gling** : to move backward and forward or from side to side : WAG

²waggle *n* : a jerky motion back and forth or up and down

wag·on *chiefly Brit var of* WAGON

wag·on \'wa-gən\ *n* **1** : a 4-wheeled vehicle; *esp* : one drawn by animals and used for freight or merchandise **2** : PADDY WAGON **3** : a child's 4-wheeled cart **4** : STATION WAGON

wag·on·er \'wa-gə-nər\ *n* : the driver of a wagon

wag·on·ette \ˌwa-gə-'net\ *n* : a light wagon with two facing seats along the sides behind a cross seat in front

wa·gon-lit \ˌvà-gōⁿ-'lē\ *n, pl* **wagons–lits** *or* **wagon–lits** *same or* -'lēz\ [F, fr. *wagon* railroad car + *lit* bed] : a railroad sleeping car

wagon train *n* : a column of wagons traveling overland

wag·tail \'wag-ˌtāl\ *n* : any of various slender-bodied mostly Old World birds with a long tail that jerks up and down

wa·hi·ne \wä-'hē-nē, -ˌnä\ *n* **1** : a Polynesian woman **2** : a female surfer

wa·hoo \'wä-ˌhü\ *n, pl* **wahoos** : a large vigorous food and sport fish related to the mackerel and found in warm seas

waif \'wāf\ *n* **1** : something found without an owner and esp. by chance **2** : a stray person or animal; *esp* : a homeless child

¹wail \'wāl\ *vb* **1** ♦ : to express sorrow audibly : make a mournful outcry **2** : to make a sound suggestive of a mournful cry **3** : to express dissatisfaction in a manner suggestive of sadness : COMPLAIN

♦ bay, howl, keen, yowl — more at HOWL ♦ *usu* **wail for** bemoan, bewail, deplore, grieve, lament, mourn — more at LAMENT

²wail *n* ♦ : a usu. prolonged cry or sound expressing grief or pain

♦ groan, howl, keen, lament, moan, plaint — more at LAMENT

wail·ful \-fəl\ *adj* : SORROWFUL, MOURNFUL — **wail·ful·ly** *adv*

wain \'wān\ *n* : a usu. large heavy farm wagon

wain·scot \'wān-skət, -ˌskōt, -ˌskät\ *n* **1** : a usu. paneled wooden lining of an interior wall of a room **2** : the lower part of an interior wall when finished differently from the rest — **wainscot** *vb*

wain·scot·ing *or* **wain·scot·ting** \-ˌskō-tiŋ, -ˌskä-, -skə-\ *n* : material for a wainscot; *also* : WAINSCOT

waist \'wāst\ *n* **1** ♦ : the narrowed part of the body between the chest and hips **2** : a part resembling the human waist esp. in narrowness or central position ⟨the ∼ of a ship⟩ **3** : a garment or part of a garment (as a blouse or bodice) for the upper part of the body

♦ middle, midriff — more at MIDRIFF

waist·band \-ˌband\ *n* : a band (as on pants or a skirt) that fits around the waist

waist·coat \'wes-kət, 'wāst-ˌkōt\ *n, chiefly Brit* : VEST 1

waist·line \'wāst-ˌlīn\ *n* **1** : an arbitrary usu. imaginary line around the waist at its narrowest part; *also* : the length of this **2** : the line at which the bodice and skirt of a dress meet

¹wait \'wāt\ *vb* **1** ♦ : to remain inactive in readiness or expectation ⟨∼ for orders⟩ **2** : to delay serving (a meal) **3** : to act as attendant or servant ⟨∼ on customers⟩ **4** : to attend as a waiter : SERVE ⟨∼ tables⟩ ⟨∼ at a banquet⟩ **5** ♦ : to be ready ⟨a letter ∼*ing* for you⟩

♦ [1, 5] await, bide, hold on, stay; *also* hang around, linger, stick around; anticipate, expect

²wait *n* **1** : a position of concealment usu. with intent to attack or surprise ⟨lie in ∼⟩ **2** : an act or period of waiting

wait·er \'wā-tər\ *n* **1** : one that waits on another; *esp* ♦ : a person who waits tables **2** : TRAY

♦ server, waitperson, waitress

waiting game *n* : a strategy in which one or more participants withhold action in the hope of an opportunity for more effective action later

waiting room *n* : a room (as at a doctor's office) for the use of persons who are waiting

wait·per·son \'wāt-ˌpər-sən\ *n* ♦ : a waiter or waitress

♦ server, waiter, waitress

wait·ress \'wā-trəs\ *n* ♦ : a woman who waits tables

♦ server, waiter, waitperson

waive \'wāv\ *vb* **waived; waiv·ing** [ME *weiven* to decline, reject, give up, fr. AF *waiver, gaiver*, fr. *waif* lost, stray] **1** : to give up claim to ⟨*waived* his right to a trial⟩ **2** : POSTPONE

waiv·er \'wā-vər\ *n* **1** : the act of waiving right, claim, or privilege **2** : a document containing a declaration of a waiver

¹wake \'wāk\ *vb* **woke** \'wōk\ *also* **waked** \'wākt\; **wo·ken** \'wō-kən\ *or* **waked** *also* **woke; wak·ing 1** : to be or remain awake; *esp* : to keep watch (as over a corpse) **2** ♦ : to become awake : AWAKEN ⟨the baby *woke* up early⟩ **3** : to rouse from sleep : AWAKEN

♦ arouse, awake, rouse; *also* arise, get up, rise; watch; revive; reawaken; shift, stir

²wake *n* **1** : the state of being awake **2** : a watch held over the body of a dead person prior to burial

³wake *n* : the track left by a ship in the water; *also* : a track left behind

wake·board \'wāk-ˌbȯrd\ *n* : a short board with foot bindings on which a rider is towed by a motorboat across its wake — **wake·board·er** *n* — **wake·board·ing** *n*

wake·ful \'wāk-fəl\ *adj* ♦ : not sleeping or able to sleep : SLEEPLESS — **wake·ful·ness** *n*

♦ awake, sleepless, wide-awake; *also* aroused, awakened, roused, wakened; aware, conscious; revived **Ant** asleep, dormant, dozing, napping, resting, sleeping, slumbering

wak·en \'wā-kən\ *vb* **1** : to cause to come awake : WAKE **2** : to cease to be asleep : WAKE

wake–rob·in \'wāk-ˌrä-bən\ *n* : TRILLIUM

wake–up call *n* ♦ : something that serves to alert a person to a problem, danger, or need

♦ caution, tip-off, tocsin, warning — more at WARNING

wak·ing \'wā-kiŋ\ *adj* : passed in a conscious or alert state ⟨every ~ hour⟩

wale \'wāl\ *n* : a ridge esp. on cloth; *also* : the texture esp. of a fabric

¹**walk** \'wȯk\ *vb* [partly fr. ME *walken*, fr. OE *wealcan* to roll, toss and partly fr. ME *walkien*, fr. OE *wealcian* to roll up, muffle up] **1** ♦ : to move or cause to move on foot usu. at a natural unhurried gait ⟨~ to town⟩ ⟨~ a horse⟩ **2** : to pass over, through, or along by walking ⟨~ the streets⟩ **3** : to perform or accomplish by walking ⟨~ guard⟩ **4** : to follow a course of action or way of life ⟨~ humbly in the sight of God⟩ **5** : WALK OUT **6** : to receive a base on balls; *also* : to give a base on balls to — **walk·er** *n*

♦ foot, leg, pad, step, traipse, tread; *also* parade, promenade; march, pace, stride; hike, trek; amble, perambulate, ramble, saunter, stroll, wander; clump, stomp, stump, tramp, tromp; plod, trudge; hobble, limp; mince, prance, pussyfoot, tiptoe; stalk, strut, swagger; lumber, lurch, pound, shamble, shuffle, stagger; nip, trip, trot

²**walk** *n* **1** ♦ : a going on foot ⟨go for a ~⟩ **2** : a place, path, or course for walking **3** : distance to be walked ⟨a quarter-mile ~ from here⟩ **4** : manner of living : CONDUCT, BEHAVIOR **5** : social or economic status ⟨various ~s of life⟩ **6** : manner of walking : GAIT; *esp* : a slow 4-beat gait of a horse **7** : BASE ON BALLS

♦ perambulation, ramble, stroll, turn; *also* parade, promenade; expedition, hike, march, peregrination, travel, trek, trip; excursion, jaunt, junket, outing, tour; pilgrimage, progress, safari

walk·away \'wȯ-kə-ˌwā\ *n* : an easily won contest

walk·ie–talk·ie \ˌwȯ-kē-'tȯ-kē\ *n* : a small portable radio transmitting and receiving set

¹**walk–in** \'wȯk-ˌin\ *adj* : large enough to be walked into ⟨a ~ refrigerator⟩

²**walk–in** *n* **1** : an easy election victory **2** : one that walks in

walking papers *n pl* : DISMISSAL, DISCHARGE

walking stick *n* **1** : a stick used in walking **2** : STICK INSECT; *esp* : one of the U.S. and Canada

walk–on \'wȯk-ˌȯn, -ˌän\ *n* : a small part in a dramatic production

walk·out \-ˌau̇t\ *n* **1** : a labor strike **2** : the action of leaving a meeting or organization as an expression of disapproval

walk out *vb* **1** : to leave suddenly often as an expression of disapproval **2** : to go on strike

walk·over \-ˌō-vər\ *n* : a one-sided contest : an easy victory

walk–up \'wȯk-ˌəp\ *n* : a building or apartment house without an elevator — **walk–up** *adj*

walk·way \-ˌwā\ *n* : a passage for walking

¹**wall** \'wȯl\ *n* [ME, fr. OE *weall*, fr. L *vallum* rampart, fr. *vallus* stake, palisade] **1 a** ♦ : a structure (as of stone or brick) intended for defense or security or for enclosing something **b** ♦ : something that resembles a wall in function esp. by establishing limits or providing defense **2** : one of the upright enclosing parts of a building or room **3** : the inside surface of a cavity or container ⟨the ~ of a boiler⟩ **4** : something like a wall in appearance, function, or effect ⟨a tariff ~⟩ — **walled** \'wȯld\ *adj*

♦ [1a] barrier, fence, hedge — more at BARRIER
♦ [1b] aegis, armor, cover, defense (*or* defence), guard, protection, safeguard, screen, security, shield, ward — more at DEFENSE

²**wall** *vb* **1** ♦ : to provide, separate, or surround with or as if with a wall ⟨~ in a garden⟩ **2** : to close (an opening) with or as if with a wall ⟨~ up a door⟩

♦ *usu* **wall in** cage, closet, coop, corral, encase, enclose, envelop, fence, hedge, hem, house, immure, pen — more at ENCLOSE

wal·la·by \'wä-lə-bē\ *n, pl* **wallabies** *also* **wallaby** : any of various small or medium-sized kangaroos

wall·board \'wȯl-ˌbȯrd\ *n* : a structural material (as of wood pulp or plaster) made in large sheets and used for sheathing interior walls and ceilings

wal·let \'wä-lət\ *n* **1** : a bag or sack for carrying things on a journey **2** : a pocketbook with compartments (as for personal papers and usu. unfolded money) : BILLFOLD

wall·eye \'wȯ-ˌlī\ *n* **1** : an eye with a whitish iris or an opaque white cornea **2** : a large vigorous No. American food and sport fish related to the perches — **wall·eyed** \-ˌlīd\ *adj*

wall·flow·er \'wȯl-ˌflau̇-ər\ *n* **1** : any of several Old World herbs related to the mustards; *esp* : one with showy fragrant flowers **2** : a person who usu. from shyness or unpopularity remains alone (as at a dance)

Wal·loon \wä-'lün\ *n* : a member of a people of southern and southeastern Belgium and adjacent parts of France — **Walloon** *adj*

¹**wal·lop** \'wä-ləp\ *vb* [ME *walopen* to gallop, fr. OF *waloper*] **1** ♦ : to beat soundly : TROUNCE **2** ♦ : to hit hard and often repeatedly

♦ [1] clobber, drub, rout, skunk, thrash, trim, trounce, whip ♦ [2] bash, bat, batter, beat, belt, bludgeon, buffet, club, drub, flog, hammer, hide, lace, lambaste, lick, maul, pelt, pound, thrash, thump, whale, whip — more at BEAT

²**wallop** *n* **1** : a powerful blow or impact **2** : the ability to hit hard **3** : emotional, sensory, or psychological force : IMPACT

wal·lop·ing \'wä-lə-piŋ\ *adj* **1** : LARGE, WHOPPING ⟨a ~ storm⟩ **2** : exceptionally fine or impressive ⟨a ~ fun party⟩

¹**wal·low** \'wä-lō\ *vb* **1** : to roll oneself about sluggishly in or as if in deep mud ⟨hogs ~ing in the mire⟩ **2** : to indulge oneself excessively ⟨~ in luxury⟩ **3** : to become or remain helpless ⟨~ in ignorance⟩

²**wallow** *n* : a muddy or dust-filled area where animals wallow

wall·pa·per \'wȯl-ˌpā-pər\ *n* **1** : decorative paper for the walls of a room **2** : the background image or set of images displayed on a computer screen — **wallpaper** *vb*

wall–to–wall *adj* **1** : covering the entire floor ⟨*wall-to-wall* carpeting⟩ **2** : covering or filling one entire space or time ⟨crowds of *wall-to-wall* people⟩

wal·nut \'wȯl-(ˌ)nət\ *n* [ME *walnot*, fr. OE *wealhhnutu*, lit., foreign nut, fr. *Wealh* Welshman, foreigner + *hnutu* nut] **1** : a nut with a furrowed usu. rough shell and an adherent husk from any of a genus of trees related to the hickories; *esp* : the large edible nut of a Eurasian tree **2** : a tree that bears walnuts **3** : the usu. reddish to dark brown wood of a walnut used esp. in cabinetwork and veneers

wal·rus \'wȯl-rəs, 'wäl-\ *n, pl* **walrus** *or* **wal·rus·es** : a large mammal of arctic waters that is related to the seals and has long ivory tusks

¹**waltz** \'wȯlts\ *n* [G *Walzer*, fr. *walzen* to roll, dance] **1** : a gliding dance done to music having three beats to the measure **2** : music for or suitable for waltzing

²**waltz** *vb* **1** : to dance a waltz **2** : to move or advance easily, successfully, or conspicuously ⟨he ~ed off with the championship⟩

wam·ble \'wäm-bəl\ *vb* **wam·bled**; **wam·bling** : to progress unsteadily or with a lurching shambling gait

Wam·pa·no·ag \ˌwäm-pə-'nō-(ˌ)ag; ˌwȯm-\ *n, pl* **Wampa-**

noag *or* **Wampanoags** [Narragansett, lit., easterners] : a member of an American Indian people of parts of Rhode Island and Massachusetts

wam·pum \'wäm-pəm\ n [short for *wampumpeag*, fr. Massachuset (an Algonquian Indian language) *wampompeag*, fr. *wampan* white + *api* string + *-ag*, pl. suffix] **1** : beads made of shells strung in strands, belts, or sashes and used by No. American Indians as money and ornaments **2** : MONEY

wan \'wän\ *adj* **wan·ner; wan·nest** **1** : having a sickly, pale color suggestive of ill health : PALLID; *also* : FEEBLE **2** : DIM, FAINT **3** : LANGUID ⟨a ∼ smile⟩ — **wan·ly** *adv* — **wan·ness** *n*

wand \'wänd\ n **1** : a slender staff carried in a procession **2** : the staff of a fairy, diviner, or magician

wan·der \'wän-dər\ *vb* **1** ♦ : to move about aimlessly or without a fixed course or goal : RAMBLE **2** : to go astray in conduct or thought; *esp* : to become delirious

♦ gad, gallivant, knock, maunder, meander, mope, ramble, range, roam, rove, traipse; *also* amble, saunter, stroll; straggle, stray; prowl, tramp, travel

wan·der·er *n* ♦ : one that wanders

♦ drifter, nomad, rambler, rover, stroller, vagabond — more at NOMAD

wandering Jew *n* : either of two trailing or creeping plants cultivated for their showy and often white-striped foliage

wan·der·lust \'wän-dər-ˌləst\ n : strong longing for or impulse toward wandering

¹wane \'wän\ *vb* **waned; wan·ing** **1** ♦ : to grow gradually smaller or less ⟨the full moon ∼s to new⟩ ⟨his strength *waned*⟩ **2** : to lose power, prosperity, or influence **3** : to draw near an end ⟨summer is *waning*⟩

♦ abate, decline, decrease, de-escalate, die, diminish, dwindle, ebb, fall, lessen, let up, lower, moderate, recede, relent, shrink, subside, taper — more at DECREASE

²wane *n* : a waning (as in size or power); *also* : a period in which something is waning

wan·gle \'waŋ-gəl\ *vb* **wan·gled; wan·gling** **1** ♦ : to obtain by sly or devious means; *also* : to use trickery or questionable means to achieve an end **2** ♦ : to adjust or manipulate esp. for personal or fraudulent ends; *also* : FINAGLE

♦ [1, 2] contrive, finagle, finesse, frame, machinate, maneuver (*or* manoeuvre), mastermind, negotiate

wan·na–be *also* **wan·na·bee** \'wä-nə-ˌbē\ n : a person who wants or aspires to be someone or something else or who tries to look or act like someone else

¹want \'wont, 'wänt\ *vb* **1** : to fail to possess : LACK ⟨they ∼ the necessities of life⟩ **2** ♦ : to feel the need of ⟨∼ed a chance to rest⟩ **3** ♦ : to be in need of : REQUIRE ⟨the house ∼s painting⟩ **4** ♦ : to desire earnestly : WISH

♦ [2, 3] demand, necessitate, need, require, take, warrant — more at NEED ♦ [4] ache for, covet, crave, desire, die (to *or* for), hanker (for *or* after), hunger for, long for, lust (for *or* after), pine for, repine for, thirst for, wish for, yearn for — more at DESIRE

²want *n* **1** ♦ : a lack of a required or usual amount **2** ♦ : dire need : DESTITUTION **3** : something wanted : DESIRE **4** : personal defect : FAULT

♦ [1] dearth, deficiency, deficit, failure, famine, inadequacy, insufficiency, lack, paucity, poverty, scantiness, scarcity, shortage — more at DEFICIENCY ♦ [1] absence, lack, need — more at NEED ♦ [2] beggary, destitution, impecuniousness, impoverishment, indigence, need, pauperism, penury, poverty — more at POVERTY

¹want·ing \'won-tiŋ, 'wän-\ *adj* **1** ♦ : not present or in evidence : ABSENT **2** ♦ : falling below standards or expectations **3** ♦ : lacking in ability or capacity : DEFICIENT ⟨∼ in common sense⟩

♦ [1] absent, missing, nonexistent — more at ABSENT ♦ [2, 3] deficient, inadequate, insufficient, scarce, short, shy — more at SHORT

²wanting *prep* **1** : LESS, MINUS ⟨a month ∼ two days⟩ **2** : not having : WITHOUT ⟨a book ∼ a cover⟩

¹wan·ton \'wont-ᵊn, 'wänt-\ *adj* [ME, undisciplined, fr. *wan*-deficient, wrong + *towen*, pp. of *teen* to draw, train, discipline] **1** ♦ : having, expressing, or inciting sensual desire or imagination **2** ♦ : having no regard for justice or for other persons' feelings, rights, or safety : INHUMANE ⟨∼ cruelty⟩ **3** : having no just cause ⟨a ∼ attack⟩ — **wan·ton·ly** *adv*

♦ [1] lascivious, lewd, lustful, passionate — more at LUSTFUL ♦ [2] barbarous, brutal, cruel, heartless, inhumane, sadistic, savage, vicious — more at CRUEL

²wanton *n* : a wanton individual; *esp* : a lewd or immoral person

³wanton *vb* **1** : to be wanton : act wantonly **2** : to pass or waste wantonly

wan·ton·ness *n* ♦ : the quality or state of being wanton

♦ barbarity, brutality, cruelty, inhumanity, sadism, savagery, viciousness — more at CRUELTY

wa·pi·ti \'wä-pə-tē\ n, pl **wapiti** *or* **wapitis** : ELK 2

¹war \'wor\ n **1** ♦ : a state or period of usu. open and declared armed fighting between states or nations **2** : the art or science of warfare **3** ♦ : a state of hostility, conflict, or antagonism **4** : a struggle between opposing forces or for a particular end ⟨∼ against disease⟩ — **war·less** \-ləs\ *adj*

♦ [1] combat, conflict, warfare; *also* civil war, cold war; action, battle, engagement; belligerency; wartime **Ant** peace ♦ [3] conflict, discord, dissension, dissent, disunity, friction, schism, strife, variance, warfare — more at DISCORD

²war *vb* **warred; war·ring** ♦ : to engage in warfare : be in conflict

♦ *usu* war against battle, clash, combat, fight, scrimmage, skirmish — more at FIGHT

³war *abbr* warrant

¹war·ble \'wor-bəl\ n **1** ♦ : a melodious succession of low pleasing sounds **2** : a musical trill

♦ air, lay, melody, song, strain, tune — more at MELODY

²warble *vb* **war·bled; war·bling** **1** : to sing or utter in a trilling manner or with variations **2** : to express by or as if by warbling

³warble *n* : a swelling under the skin esp. of the back of cattle, horses, and wild mammals caused by the maggot of a fly (**warble fly**); *also* : its maggot

war·bler \'wor-blər\ n **1** : SONGSTER **2** : any of various small slender-billed chiefly Old World songbirds related to the thrushes and noted for their singing **3** : any of numerous small bright-colored insect-eating American birds with a usu. weak and unmusical song

war·bon·net \'wor-ˌbä-nət\ n : a feathered American Indian ceremonial headdress

war crime *n* : a crime (as genocide) committed during or in connection with war

war cry *n* **1** : a cry used by fighters in war **2** : a slogan used esp. to rally people to a cause

¹ward \'word\ n **1** ♦ : a guarding or being under guard or guardianship; *esp* : CUSTODY **2** : a body of guards **3** : a division of a prison **4** : a division in a hospital **5** : a division of a city for electoral or administrative purposes **6** : a person (as a child) under the protection of a guardian or a law court **7** : a person or body of persons under the protection or tutelage of a government **8** ♦ : a means of defense : PROTECTION

♦ [1] care, custody, guardianship, keeping, safekeeping, trust — more at CUSTODY ♦ [8] aegis, armor, cover, defense (*or* defence), guard, protection, safeguard, screen, security, shield, wall — more at DEFENSE

²ward *vb* : to turn aside : DEFLECT — usu. used with *off* ⟨∼ off a blow⟩

¹-ward \wərd\ *also* **-wards** \wərdz\ *adj suffix* **1** : that moves, tends, faces, or is directed toward ⟨wind*ward*⟩ **2** : that occurs or is situated in the direction of ⟨sea*ward*⟩

²ward *or* **-wards** *adv suffix* **1** : in a (specified) direction ⟨up*wards*⟩ ⟨after*ward*⟩ **2** : toward a (specified) point, position, or area ⟨sky*ward*⟩

war dance *n* : a dance performed (as by American Indians) before going to war or in celebration of victory

war·den \'wȯrd-ᵊn\ *n* **1** ♦ : one having care or charge of something : GUARDIAN **2** : the governor of a town, district, or fortress **3** : an official charged with special supervisory or enforcement duties ⟨game ⁓⟩ ⟨air raid ⁓⟩ **4** : an official in charge of the operation of a prison **5** : one of two ranking lay officers of an Episcopal parish **6** : any of various British college officials

♦ caretaker, custodian, guardian, janitor, keeper, watchman — more at CUSTODIAN

ward·er \'wȯr-dər\ *n* ♦ : one that keeps guard esp. at a tower, gate, or door : WATCHMAN

♦ custodian, guard, guardian, keeper, lookout, picket, sentry, warden, watch, watchman — more at GUARD

ward heeler \-ˌhē-lər\ *n* : a local worker for a political boss

ward·robe \'wȯr-ˌdrōb\ *n* [ME *warderobe*, fr. AF *warderobe, garderobe*, fr. *warder, garder* to guard + *robe* robe] **1** : a room or closet where clothes are kept; *also* : CLOTHES-PRESS **2** : a collection of wearing apparel ⟨his summer ⁓⟩

ward·room \-ˌdrüm, -ˌdrum\ *n* : the dining area for officers aboard a warship

ward·ship \'wȯrd-ˌship\ *n* **1** : GUARDIANSHIP **2** : the state of being under care of a guardian

ware \'war\ *n* **1** : manufactured articles or products of art or craft : GOODS ⟨glass*ware*⟩ **2** ♦ : an article of merchandise — often used in pl. ⟨a peddler hawking his ⁓s⟩ **3** : items (as dishes) of fired clay : POTTERY

♦ **wares** commodities, merchandise — more at MERCHANDISE

ware·house \-ˌhȧu̇s\ *n* ♦ : a place for the storage of merchandise or commodities : STOREHOUSE — **warehouse** *vb*

ware·house·man \-mən\ *n* — **ware·hous·er** \-ˌhȧu̇-zər, -sər\ *n*

♦ depository, depot, magazine, repository, storage, storehouse — more at STOREHOUSE

ware·room \'war-ˌrüm, -ˌrum\ *n* : a room in which goods are exhibited for sale

war·fare \'wȯr-ˌfar\ *n* **1** : military operations between enemies : WAR; *also* : an activity undertaken by one country to weaken or destroy another ⟨economic ⁓⟩ **2** ♦ : the process of struggle between competing entities : STRUGGLE, CONFLICT

♦ battle, combat, conflict, confrontation, contest, duel, face-off, rivalry, struggle, tug-of-war — more at CONTEST

war·fa·rin \'wȯr-fə-rən\ *n* : an anticoagulant compound used as a rodent poison and in medicine

war·head \'wȯr-ˌhed\ *n* : the section of a missile containing the charge

war·horse \-ˌhȯrs\ *n* **1** : a horse for use in war **2** : a veteran soldier or public person (as a politician) **3** : a musical composition that is often performed

war·like \-ˌlīk\ *adj* **1** ♦ : fond of war ⟨⁓ peoples⟩ **2** : of, relating to, or useful in war : MILITARY, MARTIAL ⟨⁓ supplies⟩ **3** ♦ : befitting or characteristic of war or of soldiers ⟨⁓ attitudes⟩

♦ [1, 3] aggressive, argumentative, bellicose, belligerent, combative, contentious, discordant, disputatious, militant, pugnacious, quarrelsome, scrappy, truculent — more at BELLIGERENT

war·lock \-ˌläk\ *n* [ME *warloghe*, fr. OE *wǣrloga* one that breaks faith, the Devil, fr. *wǣr* faith, troth + *-loga* (fr. *lēogan* to lie)] : SORCERER, WIZARD

war·lord \-ˌlȯrd\ *n* **1** : a high military leader **2** : a military commander exercising local civil power by force ⟨former Chinese ⁓s⟩

¹warm \'wȯrm\ *adj* **1** ♦ : having or giving out heat to a moderate or adequate degree ⟨⁓ milk⟩ ⟨a ⁓ stove⟩ **2** : serving to retain heat ⟨⁓ clothes⟩ **3** : feeling or inducing sensations of heat ⟨⁓ from exercise⟩ ⟨a ⁓ climb⟩ **4 a** : showing or marked by strong feeling : ARDENT ⟨⁓ support⟩ **b** : demonstratively genial, cordial, or sympathetic ⟨⁓ to the idea⟩ **5** : marked by tense excitement or hot anger ⟨a ⁓ campaign⟩ **6** : giving a pleasant impression of warmth, cheerfulness, or friendliness ⟨⁓ colors⟩ ⟨a ⁓ tone of voice⟩ **7** : marked by or tending toward injury, distress, or pain ⟨made things ⁓ for the enemy⟩ **8** : newly made : FRESH ⟨a ⁓ scent⟩ **9** : near to a goal ⟨getting ⁓ in a search⟩ — **warm·ly** *adv*

♦ [1] heated, tepid; *also* thawed; broiling, burning, fiery, hot, piping hot, red-hot, roasting, scalding, scorching, searing, sultry, sweltering, torrid; roasted, sweltering; blazing, glowing, molten, sizzling *Ant* chilled, cool, cooled ♦ [4b] amicable, companionable, comradely, cordial, friendly, genial, hearty, neighborly (*or* neighbourly), warmhearted — more at FRIENDLY
♦ [4b] affirmative, favorable, good, positive

²warm *vb* **1** : to make or become warm **2** : to give a feeling of warmth or vitality to **3** : to experience feelings of affection or pleasure ⟨she ⁓ed to her guest⟩ **4** : to reheat for eating ⟨⁓ed over the roast⟩ **5** : to make ready for operation or performance by preliminary exercise or operation ⟨⁓ up the motor⟩ **6** : to become increasingly ardent, interested, or competent ⟨the speaker ⁓ed to his topic⟩ — **warm·er** *n*

warm–blood·ed \-'blə-dəd\ *adj* **1** : able to maintain a relatively high and constant body temperature relatively independent of that of the surroundings **2** : ardent in spirit : expressing great feeling

warmed–over \'wȯrmd-ˌō-vər\ *adj* **1** : REHEATED ⟨⁓ cabbage⟩ **2** : not fresh or new ⟨⁓ ideas⟩

warm front *n* : an advancing edge of a warm air mass

warm·heart·ed \'wȯrm-'här-təd\ *adj* ♦ : marked by or indicative of ready affection, generosity, cordiality, sympathy, or compassion — **warm·heart·ed·ness** *n*

♦ beneficent, benevolent, compassionate, good-hearted, humane, kind, kindly, sympathetic, tender, tenderhearted — more at HUMANE ♦ amicable, companionable, comradely, cordial, friendly, genial, hearty, neighborly (*or* neighbourly), warm — more at FRIENDLY

warming pan *n* : a long-handled covered pan filled with live coals and formerly used to warm a bed

war·mon·ger \'wȯr-ˌməŋ-gər, -ˌmäŋ-\ *n* ♦ : one who urges or attempts to stir up war — **war·mon·ger·ing** \-g(ə-)riŋ\ *n*

♦ agitator, firebrand, militant, rabble-rouser *Ant* dove, pacifist

warmth \'wȯrmth\ *n* ♦ : the quality or state of being warm in temperature or feeling

♦ ardor, emotion, fervency, fervor, heat, intensity, passion, vehemence — more at ARDOR

warm up *vb* : to engage in exercise or practice esp. before entering a game or contest — **warm–up** \'wȯrm-ˌəp\ *n*

warn \'wȯrn\ *vb* **1** ♦ : to put on guard : CAUTION **b** : to give supportive advice to : ADMONISH **2** ♦ : to notify esp. in advance **3** : to order to go or keep away

♦ [1a, 2] alert, caution, forewarn; *also* augur, forecast, foretell, predict, presage, prognosticate, prophesy; advise, apprise, inform, notify; admonish; bode, forebode, portend

¹warn·ing \'wȯr-niŋ\ *n* **1** ♦ : the act of warning : the state of being warned **2** : something that warns or serves to warn

♦ admonition, alarm, alert, caution, notice; *also* auguring, augury, forecasting, foretelling, predicting, prediction, presaging, prognosticating, prophecy, prophesying; apprising, informing, notification, notifying; advice, counsel, guidance, recommendation, suggestion; announcement, declaration

²warning *adj* ♦ : serving as an alarm, signal, summons, or admonition ⟨a ⁓ bell⟩ — **warn·ing·ly** *adv*

♦ cautionary — more at CAUTIONARY

¹warp \'wȯrp\ *n* **1** : the lengthwise threads on a loom or in a woven fabric **2** : a twist out of a true plane or straight line ⟨a ∼ in a board⟩

²warp *vb* [ME, fr. OE *weorpan* to throw] **1** ♦ : to turn or twist out of shape; *also* : to become so twisted **2** ♦ : to falsify, misinterpret, or give a false impression of : DISTORT **3** : to lead astray

♦ [1] contort, deform, distort, screw — more at CONTORT ♦ [2] color (*or* colour), distort, falsify, garble, misinterpret, misrepresent, misstate, pervert, twist — more at GARBLE

war paint *n* : paint put on the face and body by American Indians as a sign of going to war

war·path \'wȯr-ˌpath, -ˌpȧth\ *n* : the course taken by a party of American Indians going on a hostile expedition — **on the warpath** : ready to fight or argue

warped \'wȯrpt\ *adj* : affected by warping : having become distorted or perverted

war·plane \-ˌplān\ *n* : a military airplane; *esp* : one armed for combat

warp speed *n* : the highest possible speed

¹war·rant \'wȯr-ənt, 'wär-\ *n* **1** : AUTHORIZATION; *also* : JUSTIFICATION, GROUND **2** : evidence (as a document) of authorization; *esp* : a legal writ authorizing an officer to take action (as in making an arrest, seizure, or search) **3** : a certificate of appointment issued to an officer of lower rank than a commissioned officer

²warrant *vb* **1** : to guarantee security or immunity to : SECURE **2** ♦ : to declare or maintain positively ⟨I ∼ this is so⟩ **3** : to assure (a person) of the truth of what is said **4** : to guarantee to be as it appears or as it is represented ⟨∼ goods as of the first quality⟩ **5** ♦ : to give authority or power to for doing or forbearing to do something : SANCTION **6** : to give proof of : ATTEST **7** : JUSTIFY ⟨his need ∼s the expenditure⟩

♦ [2] affirm, allege, assert, aver, avouch, avow, claim, contend, declare, insist, maintain, profess, protest — more at CLAIM ♦ [5] approve, authorize, clear, OK, ratify, sanction — more at APPROVE

warrant officer *n* **1** : an officer in the armed forces ranking next below a commissioned officer **2** : a commissioned officer ranking below an ensign in the navy or coast guard and below a second lieutenant in the marine corps

war·ran·ty \'wȯr-ən-tē, 'wär-\ *n, pl* **-ties** ♦ : an expressed or implied statement that some situation or thing is as it appears to be or is represented to be; *esp* : a usu. written guarantee of the integrity of a product and of the maker's responsibility for the repair or replacement of defective parts

♦ bond, contract, covenant, guarantee, guaranty, surety — more at GUARANTEE

war·ren \'wȯr-ən, 'wär-\ *n* **1** : an area where rabbits breed; *also* : a structure where rabbits are bred or kept **2** : a crowded tenement or district

war·rior \'wȯr-yər; 'wȯr-ē-ər, 'wär-\ *n* ♦ : a person engaged or experienced in warfare

♦ fighter, legionnaire, man-at-arms, regular, serviceman, soldier — more at SOLDIER

war·ship \'wȯr-ˌship\ *n* : a naval vessel

wart \'wȯrt\ *n* **1** : a small usu. horny projecting growth on the skin; *esp* : one caused by a virus **2** : a protuberance resembling a wart (as on a plant) — **warty** *adj*

wart·hog \'wȯrt-ˌhȯg, -ˌhäg\ *n* : a wild African hog that has large tusks and in the male two pairs of rough warty protuberances below the eyes

war·time \'wȯr-ˌtīm\ *n* : a period during which a war is in progress

wary \'war-ē\ *adj* **war·i·er; -est** ♦ : very cautious; *esp* : careful in guarding against danger or deception — **war·i·ly** \'wer-ə-lē\ *adv* — **war·i·ness** \'wer-ē-nəs\ *n*

♦ alert, careful, cautious, circumspect, considerate, gingerly, guarded, heedful, safe — more at CAREFUL

was *past 1st & 3d sing of* BE

wa·sa·bi \'wä-sə-bē; wä-'sä-\ *n* [Jp] : a condiment prepared from the ground greenish root of an Asian herb and similar in flavor and use to horseradish; *also* : the herb or its root

¹wash \'wȯsh, 'wäsh\ *vb* **1** : to clean with water and usu. soap or detergent ⟨∼ clothes⟩ ⟨∼ your hands⟩ **2** ♦ : to wet thoroughly : DRENCH **3** ♦ : to flow along the border of ⟨waves ∼ the shore⟩ **4** : to pour or flow in a stream or current **5** : to move or remove by or as if by the action of water **6** : to cover or daub lightly with a liquid (as whitewash) **7** ♦ : to run water over (as gravel or ore) in order to separate valuable matter from refuse ⟨∼ sand for gold⟩ **8** : to undergo laundering ⟨a dress that doesn't ∼ well⟩ **9** : to stand a test ⟨that story will not ∼⟩ **10** : to be worn away by water **11** : to pour, sweep, or flow in a stream or current

♦ [2] bathe, douse, drench, soak, sop, souse, water, wet — more at WET ♦ [3] lap, lave, splash; *also* gurgle, ripple, slosh ♦ [7] flush, irrigate, rinse, sluice — more at FLUSH

²wash *n* **1** : the act or process or an instance of washing or being washed **2** : articles to be washed or being washed **3** : the flow or action of a mass of water (as a wave) **4** : erosion by waves (as of the sea) **5** *West* : the dry bed of a stream **6** : worthless esp. liquid waste : REFUSE, SWILL **7** : a thin coat of paint (as watercolor) **8** : a disturbance in a fluid (as water or the air) caused by the passage of a wing or propeller

³wash *adj* : WASHABLE

Wash *abbr* Washington

wash·able \'wȯ-shə-bəl, 'wä-\ *adj* : capable of being washed without damage

wash–and–wear *adj* : of, relating to, or being a fabric or garment that needs little or no ironing after washing

wash·ba·sin \'wȯsh-ˌbās-ᵊn, 'wäsh-\ *n* : WASHBOWL

wash·board \-ˌbȯrd\ *n* : a grooved board to scrub clothes on

wash·bowl \-ˌbōl\ *n* : a large bowl for water for washing hands and face

wash·cloth \-ˌklȯth\ *n* : a cloth used for washing one's face and body

washed–out \'wȯsht-'aut, 'wäsht-\ *adj* **1** ♦ : faded in color **2** : EXHAUSTED ⟨felt ∼ after working all night⟩

♦ dull, light, pale, pastel — more at PALE

washed–up \-'əp\ *adj* : no longer successful, popular, skillful, or needed

wash·er \'wȯ-shər, 'wä-\ *n* **1** : a ring or perforated plate used around a bolt or screw to ensure tightness or relieve friction **2** : one that washes; *esp* : a machine for washing

wash·er·wom·an \-ˌwu-mən\ *n* : a woman whose occupation is washing clothes

wash·ing \'wȯ-shin, 'wä-\ *n* **1** : material obtained by washing **2** : articles washed or to be washed

washing soda *n* : SODIUM CARBONATE

Wash·ing·ton's Birthday \'wȯ-shin-tənz-, 'wä-\ *n* : the 3d Monday in February observed as a legal holiday

wash·out \'wȯsh-ˌaut, 'wäsh-\ *n* **1** : the washing away of earth (as from a road); *also* : a place where earth is washed away **2** ♦ : a complete failure

♦ bummer, bust, catastrophe, debacle, dud, failure, fiasco, fizzle, flop, lemon, loser, turkey — more at FAILURE

wash out *vb* **1** : to wash free of an extraneous substance (as dirt) **2** : to drain of color in laundering **3** : to eliminate as useless or unsatisfactory : REJECT **4** : to destroy or render useless by the force or action of water **5** : to deplete of strength or vitality : EXHAUST **6** ♦ : to fail to meet requirements or measure up to a standard

♦ collapse, fail, flop, flunk, fold — more at FAIL

wash·room \-ˌrüm, -ˌrum\ *n* : a room (as in a public building) equipped with washing and toilet facilities : BATHROOM

wash·stand \-ˌstand\ *n* **1** : a stand holding articles needed for washing face and hands **2** : LAVATORY 1

wash·tub \-ˌtəb\ *n* : a tub for washing or soaking clothes

wash·wom·an \'wȯsh-ˌwu̇-mən, 'wäsh-\ *n* : WASHERWOMAN

washy \'wȯ-shē, 'wä-\ *adj* **wash·i·er; -est** **1** : WEAK, WATERY **2** : PALLID ⟨a ~ yellow⟩ **3** : lacking in vigor, individuality, or definiteness

wasp \'wäsp, 'wȯsp\ *n* : any of numerous social or solitary winged insects related to the bees and ants with biting mouthparts and in females and workers an often formidable sting

WASP *or* **Wasp** *n* [white Anglo-Saxon Protestant] *sometimes disparaging* : an American of northern European and esp. British ancestry and of Protestant background

wasp·ish \'wäs-pish, 'wȯs-\ *adj* **1** ♦ : easily irritated : IRRITABLE **2** : resembling a wasp in form; *esp* : slightly built
♦ choleric, crabby, cranky, cross, crotchety, grouchy, grumpy, irascible, irritable, peevish, perverse, petulant, short-tempered, snappish, snappy, snippy, testy — more at IRRITABLE

wasp waist *n* : a very slender waist

¹was·sail \'wä-səl, wä-'sāl\ *n* [ME wæs hæil, washayl, fr. ON ves heill be well] **1** : an early English toast to someone's health **2** : a hot drink made with wine, beer, or cider, spices, sugar, and usu. baked apples and traditionally served at Christmas **3** : a period of riotous drinking

²wassail *vb* **1** : CAROUSE **2** : to drink to the health of — **was·sail·er** *n*

Was·ser·mann test \'wä-sər-mən-, 'vä-\ *n* : a blood test for the detection of syphilis

wast·age \'wā-stij\ *n* ♦ : loss, decrease, or destruction of something (as by use, decay, erosion, or leakage)
♦ annihilation, demolition, desolation, destruction, devastation, havoc, loss, obliteration, ruin, wreckage — more at DESTRUCTION

¹waste \'wāst\ *n* **1** ♦ : a sparsely settled or barren region : DESERT; *also* : uncultivated land **2 a** : the act or an instance of wasting : the state of being wasted **b** : useless or profitless consumption or expenditure **3** : gradual loss or decrease by use, wear, or decay **4** ♦ : material left over, rejected, or thrown away; *also* : an unwanted by-product of a manufacturing or chemical process **5** : refuse (as garbage) that accumulates about habitations **6** ♦ : material (as feces) produced but not used by a living organism
♦ [1] barren, desert, desolation, wasteland — more at WASTELAND ♦ [4] chaff, deadwood, dust, garbage, junk, litter, refuse, riffraff, rubbish, scrap, trash — more at GARBAGE ♦ [6] droppings, slops — more at DROPPINGS

²waste *vb* **wast·ed; wast·ing** **1** ♦ : to damage or destroy gradually and progressively : DEVASTATE **2** : to wear away or diminish gradually : CONSUME **3** ♦ : to spend or use carelessly or uselessly : SQUANDER **4** ♦ : to lose or cause to lose weight, strength, or energy ⟨*wasting* from fever⟩ **5** : to become diminished in bulk or substance : DWINDLE
♦ [1] annihilate, blot out, demolish, desolate, destroy, devastate, do in, exterminate, extinguish, obliterate, pulverize, ruin, shatter, smash, tear down, wipe out, wreck — more at DESTROY ♦ [3] blow, dissipate, fritter, lavish, misspend, run through, spend, squander, throw away; *also* splurge; consume, deplete, exhaust, impoverish; indulge, overindulge; disburse, expend, lay out *Ant* conserve ♦ [4] debilitate, enervate, enfeeble, prostrate, sap, soften, tire, weaken — more at WEAKEN
♦ *usu* **waste away** [4] decay, droop, fail, flag, go, lag, languish, sag, weaken, wilt — more at WEAKEN

³waste *adj* **1** : being wild and uninhabited : BARREN; *also* : UNCULTIVATED **2** : being in a ruined condition **3** : discarded as worthless after being used ⟨~ water⟩ **4** : excreted from or stored in inert form in a living organism as a by-product of vital activity ⟨~ matter from birds⟩

waste·bas·ket \'wāst-ˌbas-kət\ *n* : a receptacle for refuse

wast·ed *adj* ♦ : showing or feeling the effects of wasting
♦ cadaverous, gaunt, haggard, skeletal

waste·ful \-fəl\ *adj* ♦ : given to or marked by lack of thrift or careful use — **waste·ful·ly** *adv*
♦ extravagant, prodigal, profligate, spendthrift, thriftless, unthrifty — more at PRODIGAL

waste·ful·ness *n* ♦ : the quality of fact of being wasteful
♦ extravagance, lavishness, prodigality — more at EXTRAVAGANCE

waste·land \-ˌland, -lənd\ *n* ♦ : land that is barren or unfit for cultivation
♦ barren, desert, desolation, waste; *also* badland; bush, brush; dust bowl; hinterland, upland; open, open air, outdoors, out-of-doors; nature, wild, wilderness

waste·pa·per \-ˈpā-pər\ *n* : paper thrown away as used, not needed, or not fit for use

wast·er *n* : one that wastes

wast·rel \'wā-strəl\ *n* ♦ : one that wastes : SPENDTHRIFT
♦ prodigal, profligate, spendthrift — more at PRODIGAL

¹watch \'wäch, 'wȯch\ *vb* **1** : to be or stay awake intentionally : keep vigil ⟨~ed by the patient's bedside⟩ ⟨~ and pray⟩ **2** : to be on the lookout for danger : be on one's guard **3** : to keep guard ⟨~ outside the door⟩ **4 a** : OBSERVE ⟨~ a game⟩ **b** : to take care of **5 a** ♦ : to observe closely in order to check on action or change **b** : to keep in view so as to prevent harm or warn of danger ⟨~ a brush fire carefully⟩ **6** : to keep oneself informed about ⟨~ his progress⟩ **7** : to lie in wait for esp. so as to take advantage of ⟨~ed her opportunity⟩ **8** ♦ : to be expectant : wait for something
♦ [5a] follow, heed, listen, mind, note, observe, regard — more at HEED ♦ *usu* **watch for** [8] anticipate, await, expect, hope — more at EXPECT

²watch *n* **1** ♦ : the act of keeping awake to guard, protect, or attend; *also* : a state of alert and continuous attention **2** : a public weather alert ⟨a winter storm ~⟩ **3** : close observation **4** ♦ : a person who watches : LOOKOUT; *also* : the office or function of a sentinel or guard **5** : a period during which a part of a ship's crew is on duty; *also* : the part of a crew on duty during a watch **6** : a portable timepiece carried on the person
♦ [1] alertness, attentiveness, lookout, surveillance, vigilance — more at VIGILANCE ♦ [4] custodian, guard, guardian, keeper, lookout, picket, sentry, warden, warder, watchman — more at GUARD

watch·band \'wäch-ˌband, 'wȯch-\ *n* : the bracelet or strap of a wristwatch

watch·dog \-ˌdȯg\ *n* **1** : a dog kept to guard property **2** : one that guards or protects

watch·er \'wäch-ər, 'wȯch-\ *n* ♦ : one that watches
♦ custodian, guard, guardian, keeper, lookout, picket, sentinel, sentry, warden, warder, watch, watchman — more at GUARD

watch·ful \-fəl\ *adj* ♦ : steadily attentive and alert esp. to danger : VIGILANT — **watch·ful·ly** *adv*
♦ alert, attentive, awake, vigilant, wide-awake — more at ALERT

watch·ful·ness *n* : the act or state of being watchful

watch·mak·er \-ˌmā-kər\ *n* : a person who makes or repairs watches — **watch·mak·ing** \-ˌmā-kiŋ\ *n*

watch·man \-mən\ *n* **1** ♦ : a person assigned to watch : GUARD **2** ♦ : one who is employed to patrol property for the purpose of protecting it against theft, fire, or other damage
♦ [1, 2] custodian, guard, guardian, keeper, lookout, picket, sentry, warden, warder, watch — more at GUARD

watch night *n* : a devotional service lasting until after midnight esp. on New Year's Eve

watch out *vb* ♦ : to be vigilant or alert : be on the lookout — often used with *for*

♦ *usu* **watch out for** beware (of), guard (against), mind

watch·tow·er \'wäch-,taú-ər, 'wóch-\ *n* : a tower for a look-out

watch·word \-,wərd\ *n* **1** : a secret word used as a signal or sign of recognition **2** ♦ : a word or motto used as a slogan or rallying cry

♦ cry, shibboleth, slogan — more at SLOGAN

¹**wa·ter** \'wó-tər, 'wä-\ *n* **1** : the liquid that descends as rain and forms rivers, lakes, and seas **2** : a natural mineral water — usu. used in pl. **3** *pl* : the water occupying or flowing in a particular bed; *also* : a band of seawater bordering on and under the control of a country **4** : any of various liquids containing or resembling water; *esp* : a watery fluid (as tears, urine, or sap) formed or circulating in a living organism **5** : a specified degree of thoroughness or completeness ⟨a scoundrel of the first ∼⟩

²**water** *vb* **1 a** ♦ : to moisten, sprinkle, or soak with water **b** : to supply with or get or take water ⟨∼ horses⟩ ⟨the ship ∼*ed* at each port⟩ **2** : to treat (as cloth) so as to give a lustrous appearance in wavy lines **3** ♦ : to dilute by or as if by adding water to — often used with *down* **4** : to form or secrete water or watery matter ⟨her eyes ∼*ed*⟩ ⟨my mouth ∼*ed*⟩

♦ [1a] bathe, douse, drench, soak, sop, souse, wash, wet — more at WET ♦ *usu* **water down** [3] adulterate, dilute, thin, weaken — more at ADULTERATE

wa·ter·bed \-,bed\ *n* : a bed whose mattress is a watertight bag filled with water

wa·ter·borne \-,bōrn\ *adj* : supported, carried, or transmitted by water

water buffalo *n* : a common oxlike often domesticated Asian bovine

water chestnut *n* : a whitish crunchy vegetable used esp. in Chinese cooking that is the peeled tuber of a widely cultivated Asian sedge; *also* : the tuber or the sedge itself

water closet *n* : a compartment or room with a toilet bowl : BATHROOM; *also* : a toilet bowl along with its accessories

wa·ter·col·or \'wó-tər-,kə-lər, 'wä-\ *n* **1** : a paint whose liquid part is water **2** : the art of painting with watercolors **3** : a picture made with watercolors

wa·ter·course \-,kōrs\ *n* ♦ : a stream of water; *also* : the bed of a stream

♦ aqueduct, canal, channel, conduit, flume, raceway — more at CHANNEL

wa·ter·craft \-,kraft\ *n* : a craft for water transport : BOAT

wa·ter·cress \-,kres\ *n* : an aquatic perennial Eurasian cress that is naturalized in the U.S. and has edible leaves used esp. in salads

wa·ter·fall \-,fól\ *n* ♦ : a very steep descent of the water of a stream

♦ cascade, cataract, falls

wa·ter·fowl \'wó-tər-,faú(-ə)l, 'wä-\ *n, pl* **-fowl** *also* **-fowls** : a bird that frequents water; *esp* : a swimming bird (as a duck) hunted as game

wa·ter·front \-,frənt\ *n* : land or a section of a town fronting or abutting on a body of water

water gap *n* : a pass in a mountain ridge through which a stream runs

water glass *n* : a drinking glass

water hyacinth *n* : a showy floating aquatic plant of tropical America that often clogs waterways (as in the southern U.S.)

watering hole *n* : a place (as a bar) where people gather socially

watering place *n* : a resort that features mineral springs or bathing

water lily *n* : any of various aquatic plants with floating roundish leaves and showy solitary flowers

wa·ter·line \'wó-tər-,līn, 'wä-\ *n* : a line that marks the level of the surface of water on something (as a ship or the shore)

wa·ter·logged \-,lógd, -,lägd\ *adj* ♦ : so filled or soaked with water as to be heavy or unmanageable ⟨a ∼ boat⟩

♦ saturated, sodden, soggy, watery, wet — more at WET

wa·ter·loo \,wó-tər-'lü, ,wä-\ *n, pl* **-loos** [*Waterloo*, Belgium, scene of Napoleon's defeat in 1815] : a decisive or final defeat or setback

¹**wa·ter·mark** \'wó-tər-,märk, 'wä-\ *n* **1** : a mark indicating the height to which water has risen **2** : a marking in paper visible when the paper is held up to a light

²**watermark** *vb* : to mark (paper) with a watermark

wa·ter·mel·on \-,me-lən\ *n* : a large roundish or oblong fruit with sweet juicy usu. red pulp; *also* : a widely grown African vine related to the squashes that produces watermelons

water moccasin *n* : a venomous pit viper chiefly of the southeastern U.S. that is related to the copperhead

water ou·zel \-'ü-zəl\ *n* : DIPPER 1

water park *n* : an amusement park with a pool and wetted slides

water pipe *n* : a pipe for smoking that has a long flexible tube whereby the smoke is cooled by passing through water

water polo *n* : a team game played in a swimming pool with a ball resembling a soccer ball

wa·ter·pow·er \'wó-tər-,paú-ər, 'wä-\ *n* : the power of moving water used to run machinery

¹**wa·ter·proof** \'wó-tər-,prüf, 'wä-\ *adj* : not letting water through; *esp* : covered or treated with a material to prevent permeation by water — **wa·ter·proof·ing** *n*

²**waterproof** *n* **1** : a waterproof fabric **2** *chiefly Brit* : RAINCOAT

³**waterproof** *vb* : to make waterproof

wa·ter–re·pel·lent \,wó-tər-ri-'pe-lənt, ,wä-\ *adj* : treated with a finish that is resistant to water penetration

wa·ter–re·sis·tant \-ri-'zis-tənt\ *adj* : WATER-REPELLENT

wa·ter·shed \'wó-tər-,shed, 'wä-\ *n* **1** : a dividing ridge between two drainage areas **2** : the region or area drained by a particular body of water

wa·ter·side \-,sīd\ *n* : the land bordering a body of water

water ski *n* : a ski used on water when the wearer is towed — **wa·ter–ski** *vb* — **wa·ter–ski·er** \-,skē-ər\ *n*

water snake *n* : any of various snakes found in or near freshwater and feeding largely on aquatic animals

wa·ter·spout \'wó-tər-,spaút, 'wä-\ *n* **1** : a pipe for carrying water **2** : a funnel-shaped cloud extending from a cloud down to a spray torn up by whirling winds from an ocean or lake

water strider *n* : any of various long-legged bugs that move about swiftly on the surface of water

water table *n* : the upper limit of the portion of the ground wholly saturated with water

wa·ter·tight \,wó-tər-'tīt, ,wä-\ *adj* **1** : constructed so as to keep water out **2** : allowing no possibility for doubt or uncertainty ⟨a ∼ case against the accused⟩

wa·ter·way \'wó-tər-,wā, 'wä-\ *n* : a navigable body of water

wa·ter·wheel \-,hwēl, -,wēl\ *n* : a wheel made to turn by water flowing against it

water wings *n pl* : an air-filled device to give support to a person's body esp. when learning to swim

wa·ter·works \'wó-tər-,wərks, 'wä-\ *n pl* : a system for supplying water (as to a city)

wa·tery \'wó-tə-rē, 'wä-\ *adj* **1** ♦ : containing, full of, or giving out water ⟨∼ clouds⟩ **2** ♦ : resembling water or watery matter esp. in thin fluidity, soggy texture, paleness, or lack of flavor : THIN ⟨∼ lemonade⟩; *also* : being soft and soggy ⟨∼ turnips⟩

♦ [1] saturated, sodden, soggy, waterlogged, wet — more at WET ♦ [2] dilute, thin, weak — more at WEAK

WATS \'wäts\ *abbr* Wide-Area Telecommunications Service

watt \'wät\ *n* [James *Watt* †1819 Scottish engineer and inventor] : the metric unit of power equal to the work done at the rate of one joule per second or to the power produced by a current of one ampere across a potential difference of one volt

watt·age \'wä-tij\ *n* : amount of power expressed in watts

wat·tle \'wät-ᵊl\ *n* **1** : a framework of rods with flexible branches or reeds interlaced used esp. formerly in building; *also* : material for this framework   **2** : a naked fleshy process hanging usu. from the head or neck (as of a bird) — **wat·tled** \-ᵊld\ *adj*

W Aust *abbr* Western Australia

¹wave \'wāv\ *vb* **waved; wav·ing 1** : FLUTTER ⟨flags *waving* in the breeze⟩ **2** ♦ : to motion with the hands or with something held in them in signal or salute; *also* : to convey by waving ⟨*waved* farewell⟩ **3** : to become moved or brandished to-and-fro; *also* : BRANDISH, FLOURISH ⟨~ a sword⟩ **4** : to move before the wind with a wavelike motion ⟨fields of *waving* grain⟩ **5** : to curve up and down like a wave : UNDULATE

  ♦ flag, gesture, motion, signal — more at MOTION

²wave *n* **1** ♦ : a moving ridge or swell on the surface of water **2** : a wavelike formation or shape ⟨a ~ in the hair⟩ **3** : the action or process of making wavy or curly **4** : a waving motion; *esp* : a signal made by waving something **5** : FLOW, GUSH ⟨a ~ of anger swept over her⟩ **6** : a peak of activity ⟨a ~ of selling⟩ **7** : a disturbance that transfers energy progressively from point to point in a medium ⟨light travels in ~s⟩ ⟨a sound ~⟩ **8** : a period of hot or cold weather — **wave·like** *adj*

  ♦ billow, curl, surge, swell

wave·length \'wāv-ˌleŋth\ *n* **1** : the distance in the line of advance of a wave from any one point (as a crest) to the next corresponding point **2** : a line of thought that reveals a common understanding

wave·let \-lət\ *n* : a little wave : RIPPLE

wa·ver \'wā-vər\ *vb* **1** ♦ : to fluctuate in opinion, allegiance, or direction **2** ♦ : to weave or sway unsteadily to and fro : TOTTER; *also* : FLICKER ⟨~*ing* flames⟩ **3** : FALTER **4** : to give an unsteady sound : QUAVER — **waver** *n* — **wa·ver·er** *n* — **wa·ver·ing·ly** *adv*

  ♦ [1] falter, hang back, hesitate, shilly-shally, stagger, teeter, vacillate, wobble — more at HESITATE ♦ [2] falter, rock, seesaw, sway, teeter, totter, wobble — more at TEETER

wavy \'wā-vē\ *adj* **wav·i·er; -est** : having waves : moving in waves

¹wax \'waks\ *n* **1** : a yellowish plastic substance secreted by bees for constructing the honeycomb **2** : any of various substances like beeswax

²wax *vb* : to treat or rub with wax

³wax *vb* **1** ♦ : to increase in size, numbers, strength, volume, or duration **2** : to increase in apparent size ⟨the moon ~*es* toward the full⟩ **3** ♦ : to take on a quality or state : BECOME ⟨~*ed* indignant⟩ ⟨the party ~*ed* merry⟩

  ♦ [1] accumulate, appreciate, balloon, build, burgeon, enlarge, escalate, expand, increase, mount, multiply, mushroom, proliferate, rise, snowball, swell — more at INCREASE ♦ [3] become, come, get, go, grow, run, turn — more at BECOME

wax bean *n* : a kidney bean with pods that turn creamy yellow to bright yellow when mature enough to use as snap beans

wax·en \'wak-sən\ *adj* **1** : made of or covered with wax **2** : resembling wax (as in color or consistency)

wax museum *n* : a place where wax effigies are exhibited

wax myrtle *n* : any of a genus of shrubs or trees with aromatic leaves; *esp* : an evergreen shrub or small tree of the eastern U.S. that produces small hard berries with a thick coating of bluish-white wax used for candles

wax·wing \'waks-ˌwiŋ\ *n* : any of a genus of chiefly brown to gray singing birds with a showy crest and red waxy material on the tips of some wing feathers

wax·work \-ˌwərk\ *n* **1** : an effigy usu. of a person in wax **2** *pl* : an exhibition of wax figures

waxy \'wak-sē\ *adj* **wax·i·er; -est 1** : made of or full of wax **2** : WAXEN 2

way \'wā\ *n* **1** ♦ : a thoroughfare for travel or passage **2** : the course of travel from one place to another

: ROUTE   **3 a** ♦ : a course of action ⟨chose the easy ~⟩ **b** ♦ : opportunity, capability, or fact of doing as one pleases ⟨always had your own ~*s*⟩ **4** : a possible course : POSSIBILITY ⟨no two ~*s* about it⟩ **5** ♦ : a characteristic or habitual manner of acting ⟨this ~ of thinking⟩ ⟨a new ~ of painting⟩ **6** : FEATURE, RESPECT ⟨a good worker in many ~*s*⟩ **7** : the usual or characteristic state of affairs ⟨as is the ~ with old people⟩; *also* : individual characteristic or peculiarity ⟨used to her ~*s*⟩ **8 a** : the length of a course : DISTANCE ⟨a short ~ from here⟩ ⟨a long ~ from success⟩ **b** ♦ : room for moving, passing, or occupying — often used in the phrase *make way* **9** : progress along a course ⟨working my ~ through college⟩ **10** : a direction of motion, facing, pointing, or nonspatial advance or tendency ⟨turn this ~⟩; *also* : LOCALITY ⟨out our ~⟩ **11** : STATE, CONDITION ⟨the ~ things are⟩ **12** *pl* : an inclined structure upon which a ship is built or is supported in launching **13** : CATEGORY, KIND ⟨get what you need in the ~ of supplies⟩ **14** : motion or speed of a boat through the water — **by the way** : by way of interjection or digression — **by way of 1** : for the purpose of ⟨*by way of* illustration⟩ **2** : by the route through : VIA — **out of the way 1** : WRONG, IMPROPER **2** : SECLUDED, REMOTE

  ♦ [1] artery, avenue, drag, drive, highway, pass, pike, road, route, row, street, thoroughfare, trace, turnpike; *also* causeway; alley, alleyway, byway, catwalk, court, lane, place; approach, concourse, path, walkway; access; dead end; aisle, corridor, course, line; track, trail; channel; corduroy, tarmac; crossroad; bypass, overpass, underpass; cloverleaf, rotary ♦ [3a] approach, fashion, form, manner, method, strategy, style, system, tack, tactics, technique — more at METHOD ♦ [3b] alternative, choice, discretion, option, pick, preference — more at CHOICE ♦ [5] custom, fashion, habit, pattern, practice, trick, wont — more at HABIT ♦ [8b] place, room, space — more at ROOM

way·bill \'wā-ˌbil\ *n* : a paper that accompanies a freight shipment and gives details of goods, route, and charges

way·far·er \'wā-ˌfar-ər\ *n* : a traveler esp. on foot — **way·far·ing** \-ˌfar-iŋ\ *adj*

way·lay \'wā-ˌlā\ *vb* **-laid** \-ˌlād\; **-lay·ing** ♦ : to lie in wait for or attack from ambush

  ♦ ambush, surprise — more at AMBUSH

way–out \'wā-'au̇t\ *adj* : marked by a considerable departure from the conventional or traditional : FAR-OUT

-ways \ˌwāz\ *adv suffix* : in (such) a way, course, direction, or manner ⟨side*ways*⟩

ways and means *n pl* : methods and resources esp. for raising revenues needed by a state; *also* : a legislative committee concerned with this function

way·side \'wā-ˌsīd\ *n* : the side of or land adjacent to a road or path

way station *n* : an intermediate station on a line of travel (as a railroad)

way·ward \'wā-wərd\ *adj* [ME, short for *awayward* turned away, fr. *away*, adv. + *-ward* directed toward] **1** ♦ : following one's own capricious or wanton inclinations ⟨~ children⟩ **2** : UNPREDICTABLE, IRREGULAR ⟨a ~ act⟩

  ♦ contrary, defiant, disobedient, froward, intractable, rebellious, recalcitrant, refractory, unruly, untoward, willful — more at DISOBEDIENT

way·ward·ness *n* ♦ : the quality or state of being wayward

  ♦ contrariness, defiance, disobedience, frowardness, insubordination, intractability, rebelliousness, recalcitrance, refractoriness, unruliness — more at DISOBEDIENCE

WBC *abbr* white blood cells

WC *abbr* **1** water closet **2** without charge

WCTU *abbr* Women's Christian Temperance Union

we \'wē\ *pron* **1** — used of a group that includes the speaker or writer **2** — used for the singular *I* by a monarch, editor, or writer

weak \'wēk\ *adj* **1** ♦ : lacking strength or vigor : FEEBLE **2** : not able to sustain or resist much weight, pressure, or strain **3** ♦ : deficient in vigor of mind or character; *also* : resulting from or indicative of such deficiency ⟨a ~ policy⟩ ⟨a ~ will⟩ **4** ♦ : not supported by truth or logic ⟨a ~ argument⟩ **5** : lacking skill or proficiency; *also* : indicative of a lack of skill or aptitude **6** ♦ : lacking vigor of expression or effect **7** ♦ : of less than usual strength ⟨~ tea⟩ **8** : not having or exerting authority ⟨~ government⟩; *also* : INEFFECTIVE, IMPOTENT **9** : of, relating to, or constituting a verb or verb conjugation that forms the past tense and past participle by adding *-ed* or *-d* or *-t* — **weak·ly** *adv*

♦ [1] delicate, enervated, faint, feeble, frail, infirm, languid, low, prostrate, slight, soft, tender, torpid, unsubstantial, wasted; *also* incapacitated; paralyzed; decrepit, worn out; impotent, powerless, puny; breakable, flimsy, fragile; dizzy, groggy, rocky, unsteady, woozy; exhausted, tired, weary; damaged, harmed, hurt, impaired, injured; resistless, susceptible, unresistant, vulnerable, yielding *Ant* mighty, powerful, rugged, stalwart, stout, strong ♦ [3] effete, frail, ineffective, nerveless, soft, spineless, wimpy, wishy-washy; *also* impotent, powerless; emasculated, unnerved; pliable, submissive; corrupt, unprincipled, unscrupulous, villainous; cowardly, craven *Ant* firm, strong, tough ♦ [4] fallacious, illogical, invalid, irrational, unreasonable, unsound — more at ILLOGICAL ♦ [6] helpless, impotent, powerless — more at POWERLESS ♦ [7] dilute, thin, watery; *also* adulterated, watered (down) *Ant* full-bodied, rich, strong

weak·en \'wē-kən\ *vb* ♦ : to make or become weak

♦ adulterate, dilute, thin, water — more at ADULTERATE ♦ debilitate, enervate, enfeeble, prostrate, sap, soften, tire, waste; *also* cripple, disable, incapacitate; deplete, depress, exhaust, impoverish, unman, wash out; damage, harm, hurt, impair, injure; break down, wear out; paralyze *Ant* beef (up), fortify, recruit, strengthen ♦ decay, droop, fail, flag, go, lag, languish, sag, waste, wilt; *also* break down, wear out; yield

weak·fish \'wēk-,fish\ *n* [obs. D *weekvis*, fr. D *week* soft + *vis* fish; fr. its tender flesh] : a common marine fish of the Atlantic coast of the U.S. caught for food and sport; *also* : any of several related food fishes

weak force *n* : the physical force responsible for particle decay processes in radioactivity

weak–kneed \'wēk-'nēd\ *adj* : lacking willpower or resolution ⟨~ appeasers⟩

weak·ling \'wē-kliŋ\ *n* : a person who is physically, mentally, or morally weak

weak·ly \'wē-klē\ *adj* ♦ : not strong or robust in health

♦ invalid, sickly — more at SICKLY

weak·ness \'wēk-nəs\ *n* **1 a** ♦ : the quality or state of being weak : lack of strength or vigor **b** : an instance or period of being weak ⟨in a moment of ~ he agreed to go⟩ **2** ♦ : something that is a mark of lack of strength or resolution **3** : an object of special desire or fondness ⟨chocolate is her ~⟩

♦ [1a] debility, delicacy, enfeeblement, faintness, feebleness, frailty, infirmity, languor, lowness; *also* decay, decrepitude; breakdown, collapse, exhaustion, nervous breakdown, prostration; helplessness; tenderness; damage, harm, hurt, impairment, injury *Ant* hardihood, hardiness, robustness, strength, vigor ♦ [2] demerit, failing, fault, foible, frailty, shortcoming, vice — more at FAULT

¹weal \'wēl\ *n* ♦ : a sound, healthy, or prosperous state : WELL-BEING

♦ good, interest, welfare, well-being — more at WELFARE

²weal *n* : WELT

weald \'wēld\ *n* [The *Weald*, wooded district in England, fr. ME *Weeld* the Weald, fr. OE *weald* forest] **1** : FOREST **2** : WOLD

wealth \'welth\ *n* [ME *welthe* welfare, prosperity, fr. *wele* weal] **1** : abundance of possessions or resources **2** ♦ : abundant supply ⟨a ~ of detail⟩ **3** ♦ : all property that has a money or an exchange value; *also* : all objects or resources that have economic value

♦ [2] abundance, plenty, superabundance — more at PLENTY ♦ [3] assets, capital, fortune, means, opulence, riches, substance, wherewithal; *also* belongings, chattels, effects, holdings, paraphernalia, possessions, things; finances, money; abundance, affluence, prosperity, success; nest egg, resources, treasury

wealthy \'wel-thē\ *adj* **wealth·i·er; -est** ♦ : having wealth : RICH

♦ affluent, flush, loaded, moneyed, opulent, rich, well-fixed, well-heeled, well-off, well-to-do — more at RICH

wean \'wēn\ *vb* **1** : to accustom (a young mammal) to take food by means other than nursing **2** : to free from a source of dependence; *also* : to free from a usu. unwholesome habit or interest

weap·on \'we-pən\ *n* **1** : something (as a gun, knife, or club) used to injure, defeat, or destroy **2** : a means of contending against another — **weap·on·less** \-ləs\ *adj*

weap·on·ry \-rē\ *n* : WEAPONS

¹wear \'war\ *vb* **wore** \'wōr\; **worn** \'wōrn\; **wear·ing** **1** : to use as an article of clothing or adornment ⟨~ a coat⟩ ⟨~s earrings⟩; *also* : to carry on the person ⟨~ a gun⟩ **2** : EXHIBIT, PRESENT ⟨~ a smile⟩ **3** ♦ : to impair, diminish, or decay by use or by scraping or rubbing ⟨clothes *worn* to shreds⟩; *also* : to produce gradually by friction, rubbing, or wasting away ⟨~ a hole in the rug⟩ **4** ♦ : to exhaust or lessen the strength of : FATIGUE ⟨*worn* by care and toil⟩ **5** : to endure use : last under use or the passage of time ⟨this cloth ~s well⟩ **6** : to diminish or fail with the passage of time ⟨the day ~s on⟩ ⟨the effect of the drug *wore* off⟩ **7** : to grow or become affected in some way by attrition, use, or age ⟨the coin was *worn* thin⟩ — **wear·able** \'war-ə-bəl\ *adj* — **wear·er** *n*

♦ [3] abrade, chafe, erode, fray, fret, gall, rub — more at ABRADE ♦ [4] burn out, do in, drain, exhaust, fag, fatigue, tire, tucker, wash out, weary — more at EXHAUST

²wear *n* **1** : the act of wearing : the state of being worn ⟨clothes for everyday ~⟩ **2** : clothing usu. of a particular kind or for a special occasion or use ⟨children's ~⟩ **3** : wearing or lasting quality ⟨the coat still has lots of ~ in it⟩ **4** : the result of wearing or use : impairment due to use ⟨the suit shows ~⟩

wear and tear *n* : the loss, injury, or stress to which something is subjected in the course of use; *esp* : normal depreciation

wear down *vb* : to weary and overcome by persistent resistance or pressure

wea·ri·ness \-ē-nəs\ *n* ♦ : the quality or state of being weary

♦ burnout, collapse, exhaustion, fatigue, lassitude, prostration, tiredness — more at FATIGUE

wea·ri·some \'wir-ē-səm\ *adj* : causing weariness : TIRESOME — **wea·ri·some·ly** *adv* — **wea·ri·some·ness** *n*

wear out *vb* **1** ♦ : to exhaust or lessen the strength of : TIRE **2** : to make or become useless by wear

♦ burn out, do in, drain, exhaust, fag, fatigue, tire, tucker, wash out, wear, weary — more at EXHAUST

¹wea·ry \'wir-ē\ *adj* **wea·ri·er; -est** **1** ♦ : worn out in strength, energy, or freshness **2** : expressing or characteristic of weariness ⟨a ~ sigh⟩ **3** ♦ : having one's patience, tolerance, or pleasure exhausted ⟨~ of war⟩ **4** : causing weariness of body or spirit : TIRESOME ⟨a long, ~ drive home⟩ — **wea·ri·ly** \'wir-ə-lē\ *adv*

♦ [1] beat, bushed, dead, drained, effete, jaded, limp, prostrate, spent, tired, worn-out; *also* debilitated, enervated, enfeebled, sapped, weakened ♦ [3] fed up, jaded, sick, tired; *also* apathetic, disinterested, uninterested;

glutted, sated, satiated, surfeited; dejected, demoralized, discouraged, disheartened, dispirited *Ant* absorbed, engaged, engrossed, gripped, interested, intrigued

²weary *vb* **wea·ried; wea·ry·ing ♦ :** to become or make weary : TIRE

♦ burn out, do in, drain, exhaust, fag, fatigue, tire, tucker, wash out, wear, wear out — more at EXHAUST

¹wea·sel \'wē-zəl\ *n, pl* **weasels :** any of various small slender flesh-eating mammals related to the minks — **wea·sel·ly** *also* **wea·sely** \'wēz-lē, 'wē-zə-lē\ *adj*

²weasel *vb* **wea·seled; wea·sel·ing 1 :** to use weasel words : EQUIVOCATE **2 :** to escape from or evade a situation or obligation — often used with *out*

weasel word *n* [fr. the weasel's reputed habit of sucking the contents out of an egg while leaving the shell superficially intact] **:** a word used to avoid a direct or forthright statement or position

¹weath·er \'we-thər\ *n* **1 :** the state of the atmosphere with respect to heat or cold, wetness or dryness, calm or storm, clearness or cloudiness **2 :** a particular and esp. a disagreeable atmospheric state : RAIN, STORM

²weather *vb* **1 :** to expose to or endure the action of weather; *also :* to alter (as in color or texture) by such exposure **2 :** to bear up against successfully ⟨∼ a storm⟩ ⟨∼ troubles⟩

³weather *adj* : WINDWARD

weath·er–beat·en \'we-thər-ˌbēt-³n\ *adj* **:** worn or damaged by exposure to the weather; *also* **:** toughened or tanned by the weather ⟨∼ face⟩

weath·er·cock \-ˌkäk\ *n* **:** a weather vane shaped like a rooster

weath·er·ing \'we-thə-riŋ\ *n* **:** the action of the weather in altering the color, texture, composition, or form of exposed objects; *also* **:** alteration thus effected

weath·er·ize \'we-thə-ˌrīz\ *vb* **-ized; -iz·ing :** to make (as a house) better protected against winter weather (as by adding insulation)

weath·er·man \-ˌman\ *n* **:** one who reports and forecasts the weather : METEOROLOGIST

weath·er·per·son \-ˌpər-sən\ *n* **:** a person who reports and forecasts the weather : METEOROLOGIST

weath·er·proof \'we-thər-ˌprüf\ *adj* **:** able to withstand exposure to weather — **weatherproof** *vb*

weath·er·strip·ping \'we-thər-ˌstri-piŋ\ *n* **:** material used to seal a door or window at the edges — **weath·er–strip** *vb* — **weather strip** *n*

weather vane *n* : VANE 1

weath·er·worn \'we-thər-ˌwörn\ *adj* **:** worn by exposure to the weather

¹weave \'wēv\ *vb* **wove** \'wōv\ *or* **weaved; wo·ven** \'wō-vən\ *or* **weaved; weav·ing 1 :** to form by interlacing strands of material; *esp* **:** to make on a loom by interlacing warp and filling threads ⟨∼ cloth⟩ **2 :** to interlace (as threads) into a fabric and esp. cloth **3 :** SPIN 2 **4 :** to make as if by weaving together parts **5 ♦ :** to insert as a part : work in **6 :** to move in a winding or zigzag course esp. to avoid obstacles ⟨we *wove* our way through the crowd⟩ — **weav·er** *n*

♦ interlace, intersperse, intertwine, interweave, lace, thread, wreathe — more at THREAD

²weave *n* **:** something woven; *also* **:** a pattern or method of weaving ⟨a loose ∼⟩

¹web \'web\ *n* **1 :** a fabric on a loom or coming from a loom **2 a :** COBWEB **b ♦ :** something by which one is entangled, involved in difficulties, held fast, or impeded in one's progress ⟨caught in a ∼ of deceit⟩ **3 :** an animal or plant membrane; *esp* **:** one uniting the toes (as in many birds) **4 :** NETWORK ⟨a ∼ of highways⟩ **5 :** the series of barbs on each side of the shaft of a feather **6 :** WORLD WIDE WEB — **webbed** \'webd\ *adj*

♦ entanglement, net, snare, trap; *also* mesh; knot, snarl, tangle; labyrinth, maze

²web *vb* **webbed; web·bing 1 :** to make a web **2 :** to cover or provide with webs or a network **3 :** ENTANGLE, ENSNARE

web·bing \'we-biŋ\ *n* **:** a strong closely woven tape designed for bearing weight and used esp. for straps, harnesses, or upholstery

web·cam \'web-ˌkam\ *n* **:** a camera used in transmitting live images over the World Wide Web

web·cast \'web-ˌkast\ *n* **:** a transmission of sound and images via the World Wide Web — **webcast** *vb*

web–foot·ed \'web-ˈfu̇-təd\ *adj* **:** having webbed feet

web·i·nar \'we-bə-ˌnär\ *n* [*web* + sem*inar*] **:** a live online educational presentation during which participating viewers can submit questions and answers

web·log \'web-ˌlȯg, -ˌläg\ *n* : BLOG

web·mas·ter \'web-ˌmas-tər\ *n, often cap* **:** a person responsible for the creation or maintenance of a website

web page *n* : ³PAGE 2

web·site \'web-ˌsīt\ *or* **Web site** *n* **:** a group of World Wide Web pages made available online (as by an individual or business)

wed \'wed\ *vb* **wed·ded** *also* **wed; wed·ding 1 :** to take, give, enter into, or join in marriage : MARRY **2 :** to unite firmly

Wed *abbr* Wednesday

wed·ding \'we-diŋ\ *n* **1 ♦ :** a marriage ceremony usu. with accompanying festivities : NUPTIALS **2 :** a joining in close association **3 :** a wedding anniversary or its celebration

♦ espousal, marriage; *also* match, matrimony, wedlock; engagement, hand, pledge, promise, proposal, troth

¹wedge \'wej\ *n* **1 :** a piece of wood or metal that tapers to a thin edge and is used to split logs or rocks or to raise heavy weights **2 :** something (as an action or policy) that serves to open up a way for a breach, change, or intrusion **3 :** a wedge-shaped object or part ⟨a ∼ of pie⟩

²wedge *vb* **wedged; wedg·ing 1 :** to hold firm by or as if by driving in a wedge **2 ♦ :** to force (something) into a narrow space

♦ cram, crowd, jam, ram, sandwich, squeeze, stuff — more at CROWD

wed·lock \'wed-ˌläk\ *n* [ME *wedlok*, fr. OE *wedlāc* marriage bond, fr. *wedd* pledge + *-lāc*, suffix denoting activity] **:** the state of being married : MARRIAGE

Wednes·day \'wenz-(ˌ)dā,-dē\ *n* [ME, fr. OE *wōdensdæg*, lit., day of Woden (supreme god of the pagan Anglo-Saxons)] **:** the 4th day of the week

wee \'wē\ *adj* [ME (Sc) *we*, fr. *we*, n., little bit, fr. OE *wǣge* weight] **1 ♦ :** very small : TINY **2 :** very early ⟨∼ hours of the morning⟩

♦ atomic, infinitesimal, microscopic, miniature, minute, teeny, tiny — more at TINY

¹weed \'wēd\ *n* **1 :** a plant that tends to grow thickly where it is not wanted and to choke out more desirable plants **2 :** MARIJUANA

²weed *vb* **1 :** to clear of or remove weeds or something harmful, inferior, or superfluous ⟨∼ a garden⟩ **2 :** to get rid of ⟨∼ out the troublemakers⟩ — **weed·er** *n*

³weed *n* **:** mourning clothes — usu. used in pl. ⟨widow's ∼s⟩

weedy \'wē-dē\ *adj* **1 :** full of weeds **2 ♦ :** resembling a weed esp. in vigor of growth or spread **3 :** noticeably lean and scrawny : LANKY ⟨a ∼ young man⟩

♦ lush, luxuriant, prosperous, rampant, rank — more at RANK

week \'wēk\ *n* **1 :** seven successive days; *esp* **:** a calendar period of seven days beginning with Sunday and ending with Saturday **2 :** the working or school days of the calendar week

week·day \'wēk-ˌdā\ *n* **:** a day of the week except Sunday or sometimes except Saturday and Sunday

¹week·end \-ˌend\ *n* **:** the period between the close of one working or business or school week and the beginning of the next

²weekend *vb* **:** to spend the weekend

¹week·ly \'wē-klē\ *adj* **1 :** occurring, appearing, or done every week **2 :** computed in terms of one week — **weekly** *adv*

²weekly *n, pl* **weeklies** : a weekly publication

ween \'wēn\ *vb, archaic* : SUPPOSE 3

wee·ny \'wē-nē\ *also* **ween·sy** \'wēn-sē\ *adj* : exceptionally small

weep \'wēp\ *vb* **wept** \'wept\; **weep·ing** **1** ◆ : to express emotion and esp. sorrow by shedding tears : CRY **2** ◆ : to give off fluid slowly : OOZE — **weep·er** *n*

◆ [1] bawl, blubber, cry, sob — more at CRY ◆ [2] bleed, exude, ooze, percolate, seep, strain, sweat — more at EXUDE

weep·ing *adj* **1** ◆ : expressing or showing emotion by shedding tears **2** : having slender drooping branches

◆ dolorous, funeral, lugubrious, mournful, plaintive, regretful, rueful, sorrowful, woeful — more at MOURN-FUL

weeping willow *n* : a willow with slender drooping branches

weepy \'wē-pē\ *adj* : inclined to weep

wee·vil \'wē-vəl\ *n* : any of a large group of beetles having a long head usu. curved into a snout and including many whose larvae are destructive plant-feeding pests — **wee·vily** *or* **wee·vil·ly** \'wē-və-lē\ *adj*

weft \'weft\ *n* **1** : a filling thread or yarn in weaving **2** : WEB, FABRIC; *also* : something woven

¹weigh \'wā\ *vb* [ME *weyen*, fr. OE *wegan* to move, carry, weigh] **1** : to find the heaviness of **2** : to have weight or a specified weight **3** ◆ : to consider carefully : PONDER **4** : to merit consideration as important : COUNT ⟨evidence ∼ing against him⟩ **5** : to raise before sailing ⟨∼ anchor⟩ **6** ◆ : to press down with or as if with a heavy weight

◆ [3] chew over, cogitate, consider, contemplate, debate, deliberate, entertain, meditate, mull, ponder, question, ruminate, study, think — more at PONDER ◆ *usu* **weigh on** *or* **weigh upon** [6] bear, depress, press, shove — more at PRESS

²weigh *n* [alter. of *way*] : WAY — used in the phrase *under weigh*

¹weight \'wāt\ *n* **1** : the amount that something weighs; *also* : the standard amount that something should weigh **2** ◆ : a quantity or object weighing a usu. specified amount **3** ◆ : a unit (as a pound or kilogram) of weight or mass; *also* : a system of such units **4** : a heavy object for holding or pressing something down; *also* : a heavy object for throwing or lifting in an athletic contest **5** : a mental or emotional burden **6 a** ◆ : the relatively great importance or authority accorded something **b** ◆ : measurable influence esp. in determining the acts of others ⟨threw his ∼ around⟩ **7** : overpowering force **8** : relative thickness (as of a textile) ⟨summer-*weight* clothes⟩

◆ [2] burden, cargo, draft, freight, haul, lading, load, payload — more at LOAD ◆ [6a] consequence, import, magnitude, moment, significance ◆ [6b] authority, clout, influence, pull, sway — more at INFLUENCE

²weight *vb* **1** : to load with or as if with a weight **2** ◆ : to oppress with a burden ⟨∼ed down with cares⟩

◆ burden, encumber, load, lumber, saddle — more at LOAD

weight·less \'wāt-ləs\ *adj* ◆ : having little weight : lacking apparent gravitational pull ⟨a ∼ environment⟩ — **weight·less·ly** *adv* — **weight·less·ness** *n*

◆ airy, feathery, light — more at LIGHT

weighty \'wā-tē\ *adj* **weight·i·er; -est** **1** ◆ : of much importance or consequence : SERIOUS ⟨∼ problems⟩ **2** ◆ : expressing or characterized by seriousness or gravity ⟨a ∼ manner⟩ **3** ◆ : weighing a considerable amount : HEAVY **4** ◆ : having much force, influence, or authority ⟨∼ arguments⟩

◆ [1] grave, heavy, serious — more at SERIOUS ◆ [1, 2] big, consequential, eventful, important, major, material, meaningful, momentous, significant, substantial — more at IMPORTANT ◆ [3] heavy, hefty, massive, ponderous — more at HEAVY ◆ [4] authoritative, forceful, influential — more at INFLUENTIAL

weiner *var of* WIENER

weir \'war, 'wir\ *n* **1** : a fence set in a waterway for catching fish **2** : a dam in a stream to raise the water level or divert its flow

weird \'wird\ *adj* [ME *wird, werd* fate, destiny, fr. OE *wyrd*] **1** ◆ : caused by or suggesting magical influence : MAGICAL **2** ◆ : passing beyond natural limits : UNEARTHLY **3** ◆ : curious in nature or appearance : of strange or extraordinary character — **weird·ly** *adv* — **weird·ness** *n*

◆ [1] magic, magical, mystic, occult — more at MYSTIC ◆ [2] creepy, eerie, haunting, spooky, uncanny, unearthly — more at EERIE ◆ [3] bizarre, curious, far-out, funny, kinky, odd, outlandish, outré, peculiar, quaint, queer, quirky, remarkable, screwy, strange, unusual, wacky, wild — more at ODD

weirdo \'wir-(ˌ)dō\ *n, pl* **weird·os** ◆ : a person who is extraordinarily strange or eccentric

◆ character, crackpot, crank, eccentric, kook, nut, oddball, screwball — more at ECCENTRIC

Welch *var of* WELSH

¹wel·come \'wel-kəm\ *vb* **wel·comed; wel·com·ing** **1** : to greet cordially or courteously **2** : to accept, meet, or face with pleasure ⟨he ∼s criticism⟩

²welcome *adj* **1** : received gladly into one's presence ⟨a ∼ visitor⟩ **2** : giving pleasure : PLEASING ⟨∼ news⟩ **3** : willingly permitted or admitted ⟨all are ∼ to use the books⟩ **4** — used in the phrase "You're welcome" as a reply to an expression of thanks

³welcome *n* **1** : a cordial greeting or reception **2** : the state of being welcome ⟨overstayed their ∼⟩

¹weld \'weld\ *vb* **1** : to unite (metal or plastic parts) either by heating and allowing the parts to flow together or by hammering or pressing together **2** : to unite closely or intimately ⟨∼ed together in friendship⟩ — **weld·er** *n*

²weld *n* **1** : a welded joint **2** : union by welding

wel·fare \'wel-ˌfar\ *n* **1** ◆ : the state of doing well esp. in respect to happiness, well-being, or prosperity **2** : aid in the form of money or necessities for those in need; *also* : the agency through which the aid is given

◆ good, interest, weal, well-being; *also* prosperity, success; fitness, health, healthiness, robustness, soundness, wellness, wholeness, wholesomeness; bliss, felicity, happiness, joy; advantage, benefit, gain, sake; content, contentedness, gratification, satisfaction

welfare state *n* : a nation or state that assumes primary responsibility for the individual and social welfare of its citizens

wel·kin \'wel-kən\ *n* : SKY; *also* : AIR

¹well \'wel\ *n* **1** : a spring with its pool : FOUNTAIN; *also* : a source of supply ⟨a ∼ of information⟩ **2** : a hole sunk in the earth to obtain a natural deposit (as of water, oil, or gas) **3** : an open space (as for a staircase) extending vertically through floors of a structure **4** : something suggesting a well

²well *vb* : to rise up and flow out

³well *adv* **bet·ter** \'be-tər\; **best** \'best\ **1 a** : in a good or proper manner : RIGHTLY **b** ◆ : in a skillful or expert manner : SKILLFULLY **2** ◆ : in a satisfactory manner : SATISFACTORILY ⟨the party turned out ∼⟩ **3** ◆ : in a prosperous, affluent, or generous manner ⟨eat ∼⟩ ⟨was ∼ rewarded⟩ **4** ◆ : with reason or courtesy ⟨I cannot ∼ refuse⟩ **5** : to the full degree or extent : FULLY ⟨∼ worth the price⟩ ⟨*well*-hidden⟩ **6** : INTIMATELY, CLOSELY ⟨I know him ∼⟩ **7** : CONSIDERABLY, FAR ⟨∼ over a million⟩ ⟨∼ ahead⟩ **8** : without trouble or difficulty ⟨we could ∼ have gone⟩ **9** : EXACTLY, DEFINITELY ⟨remember it ∼⟩ **10** : with spirit and courage : with equanimity or good nature ⟨took the news ∼⟩

◆ [1b] ably, adeptly, capably, expertly, masterfully, proficiently, skillfully; *also* aptly; adroitly, deftly, dexterously *Ant* inefficiently, ineptly, inexpertly, poorly, unskillfully ◆ [2] adequately, all right, fine, good, nicely, OK, passably, satisfactorily, so-so, tolerably; *also* appropriately, correctly, decently, felicitously, fittingly, rightly, seemly, suitably **Ant** bad, badly, inadequately, intolerably, poorly ♦ [3] bounteously, generously, handsomely, liberally; *also* courteously, hospitably, kindly, nicely, reasonably, thoughtfully; affably, amiably, cheerfully, cheerily, genially, good-naturedly, graciously ♦ [4] courteously, kindly, nicely, thoughtfully; *also* pleasantly

⁴**well** *adj* **1** : PROSPEROUS; *also* : being in satisfactory condition or circumstances **2** : SATISFACTORY, PLEASING ⟨all is ∼⟩ **3** : ADVISABLE, DESIRABLE ⟨it is not ∼ to anger him⟩ **4** ♦ : free or recovered from ill health : HEALTHY **5** : FORTUNATE ⟨it is ∼ that this has happened⟩

♦ able-bodied, chipper, fit, hale, healthy, hearty, robust, sound, whole, wholesome — more at HEALTHY

well-ad·just·ed \ˌwel-ə-ˈjəs-təd\ *adj* : WELL-BALANCED 2
well-ad·vised \-əd-ˈvīzd\ *adj* **1** : PRUDENT **2** : resulting from, based on, or showing careful deliberation or wise counsel ⟨∼ plans⟩
well-ap·point·ed \-ə-ˈpȯin-təd\ *adj* : properly fitted out
well-ba·lanced \ˈwel-ˈba-lənst\ *adj* **1** : nicely or evenly balanced or arranged ⟨a ∼ meal⟩ **2** : emotionally or psychologically untroubled
well-be·ing \-ˈbē-iŋ\ *n* ♦ : the state of being happy, healthy, or prosperous

♦ good, interest, weal, welfare — more at WELFARE

well-born \-ˈbȯrn\ *adj* ♦ : born of noble or wealthy lineage

♦ aristocratic, genteel, gentle, grand, highborn, noble, patrician — more at NOBLE

well-bred \-ˈbred\ *adj* ♦ : having or indicating qualities or characteristics associated with good breeding

♦ civil, courteous, genteel, gracious, mannerly, polite — more at POLITE

well-de·fined \-di-ˈfīnd\ *adj* : having clearly distinguishable limits or boundaries
well-dis·posed \-di-ˈspōzd\ *adj* ♦ : disposed to be friendly, favorable, or sympathetic ⟨∼ to the idea⟩

♦ affable, agreeable, amiable, genial, good-natured, gracious, nice, sweet — more at AMIABLE

well-done \ˈwel-ˈdən\ *adj* **1** : rightly or properly performed **2** : cooked thoroughly
well-en·dowed \ˈwel-in-ˈdaůd\ *adj* **1** : having plenty of money or property **2** : having large breasts **3** : having a large penis
well-fa·vored \-ˈfā-vərd\ *adj* : GOOD-LOOKING, HANDSOME
well-fixed \-ˈfikst\ *adj* ♦ : financially well-off : WELL-HEELED

♦ affluent, flush, loaded, moneyed, opulent, rich, wealthy, well-heeled, well-off, well-to-do — more at RICH

well-found·ed \-ˈfaůn-dəd\ *adj* ♦ : based on good reasons

♦ good, hard, informed, just, levelheaded, logical, rational, reasonable, reasoned, sensible, sober, solid, valid — more at GOOD

well-groomed \-ˈgrümd, -ˈgrůmd\ *adj* : neatly dressed or cared for
well-ground·ed \-ˈgraůn-dəd\ *adj* **1** : having a firm foundation **2** : WELL-FOUNDED
well-head \-ˌhed\ *n* **1** : the source of a spring or a stream **2** : principal source **3** : the top of or a structure built over a well
well-heeled \-ˈhēld\ *adj* ♦ : financially well-off

♦ affluent, flush, loaded, moneyed, opulent, rich, wealthy, well-fixed, well-off, well-to-do — more at RICH

well-known \-ˈnōn\ *adj* ♦ : fully or widely known

♦ celebrated, famed, famous, noted, notorious, prominent, renowned, star — more at FAMOUS

well-mean·ing \-ˈmē-niŋ\ *adj* : having or based on good intentions
well-ness \-nəs\ *n* ♦ : good health esp. as an actively sought goal ⟨∼ clinics⟩ ⟨lifestyles that promote ∼⟩

♦ fitness, health, heartiness, robustness, soundness, wholeness, wholesomeness — more at HEALTH

well-nigh \-ˈnī\ *adv* ♦ : very nearly : ALMOST

♦ about, almost, most, much, near, nearly, next to, nigh, practically, virtually — more at ALMOST

well-off \-ˈȯf\ *adj* : being in good condition or circumstances; *esp* ♦ : having more than adequate financial resources : WELL-TO-DO

♦ affluent, flush, loaded, moneyed, opulent, rich, wealthy, well-fixed, well-heeled, well-to-do — more at RICH

well-or·dered \-ˈȯr-dərd\ *adj* : having an orderly procedure or arrangement
well-placed \-ˈplāst\ *adj* : appropriately or advantageously directed or positioned
well-read \-ˈred\ *adj* ♦ : well-informed through reading

♦ educated, erudite, knowledgeable, learned, literate, scholarly — more at EDUCATED

well-round·ed \-ˈraůn-dəd\ *adj* **1** : broadly trained, educated, and experienced **2** : COMPREHENSIVE ⟨a ∼ program of activities⟩
well-spo·ken \ˈwel-ˈspō-kən\ *adj* **1** ♦ : speaking well and esp. courteously **2** : spoken with propriety ⟨∼ words⟩

♦ articulate, eloquent, fluent — more at ARTICULATE

well-spring \-ˌspriŋ\ *n* : a source of continuous supply
well-timed \-ˈtīmd\ *adj* : TIMELY
well-to-do \ˌwel-tə-ˈdü\ *adj* ♦ : having more than adequate financial resources

♦ affluent, flush, loaded, moneyed, opulent, rich, wealthy, well-fixed, well-heeled, well-off — more at RICH

well-turned \ˈwel-ˈtərnd\ *adj* **1** : pleasingly shaped ⟨a ∼ ankle⟩ **2** : pleasingly expressed ⟨a ∼ phrase⟩
well-wish·er \ˈwel-ˌwi-shər\ *n* : an admiring supporter or fan — **well-wish·ing** *adj or n*
welsh \ˈwelsh, ˈwelch\ *also* **welch** \ˈwelch\ *vb* **1** *now sometimes offensive* : to avoid payment **2** *now sometimes offensive* : to break one's word ⟨∼ed on their promises⟩
Welsh \ˈwelsh\ *n* [ME *walisch, welisch*, adj., Welsh, fr. OE *wælisc* foreign, British, Welsh, fr. *Wealh* foreigner, Briton, Welshman] **1** Welsh *pl* : the people of Wales **2** : the Celtic language of Wales — **Welsh** *adj* — **Welsh·man** \-mən\ *n*
Welsh cor·gi \-ˈkȯr-gē\ *n* [W *corgi*, fr. *cor* dwarf + *ci* dog] : a short-legged long-backed dog with foxy head of either of two breeds of Welsh origin
Welsh rabbit *n* : melted often seasoned cheese served over toast or crackers
Welsh rare·bit \-ˈrar-bət\ *n* : WELSH RABBIT
¹**welt** \ˈwelt\ *n* **1** : the narrow strip of leather between a shoe upper and sole to which other parts are stitched **2** : a doubled edge, strip, insert, or seam for ornament or reinforcement **3** : a ridge or lump raised on the skin usu. by a blow; *also* : a heavy blow
²**welt** *vb* **1** : to furnish (as a shoe) with a welt **2** : to hit hard
¹**wel·ter** \ˈwel-tər\ *vb* **1** : WRITHE, TOSS; *also* : WALLOW **2** : to rise and fall or toss about in or with waves **3** : to become deeply sunk, soaked, or involved **4** : to be in turmoil
²**welter** *n* **1** : a state of wild disorder : TURMOIL **2** ♦ : a chaotic mass or jumble ⟨a ∼ of data⟩

♦ clutter, hash, hodgepodge, jumble, miscellany, motley, muddle, potpourri

wel·ter·weight \ˈwel-tər-ˌwāt\ *n* : a boxer weighing more than 135 but not over 147 pounds
wen \ˈwen\ *n* : an abnormal growth or a cyst protruding from a surface esp. of the skin
wench \ˈwench\ *n* [ME *wenche*, short for *wenchel* child, fr. OE *wencel*] **1** : a young woman **2** : a female servant
wend \ˈwend\ *vb* : to direct one's course : proceed on (one's way)

went *past of* GO

wept *past and past part of* WEEP

were *past 2d sing, past pl, or past subjunctive of* BE

were·wolf \'wer-ˌwu̇lf, 'wir-, 'wər-\ *n, pl* **were·wolves** \-ˌwu̇lvz\ [ME, fr. OE *werwulf*, fr. *wer* man + *wulf* wolf] : a person who in stories is transformed into a wolf or is capable of assuming a wolf's form

wes·kit \'wes-kət\ *n* : VEST 1

¹**west** \'west\ *adv* : to or toward the west

²**west** *adj* **1** : situated toward or at the west **2** : coming from the west

³**west** *n* **1** : the general direction of sunset **2** : the compass point directly opposite to east **3** *cap* : regions or countries west of a specified or implied point **4** *cap* : Europe and the Americas — **west·er·ly** \'wes-tər-lē\ *adv or adj* — **west·ward** *adv or adj* — **west·wards** *adv*

¹**west·ern** \'wes-tərn\ *adj* **1** : lying toward or coming from the west **2** *cap* : of, relating to, or characteristic of a region conventionally designated West **3** *cap* : of or relating to the Roman Catholic or Protestant segment of Christianity — **West·ern·er** *n*

²**western** *n, often cap* : a novel, story, film, or radio or television show about life in the western U.S. during the latter half of the 19th century

west·ern·ize \'wes-tər-ˌnīz\ *vb* **-ized; -iz·ing** : to give western characteristics to ⟨wanted to ~ the country⟩ — **west·ern·i·za·tion** \ˌwes-tər-nə-'zā-shən\ *n*

West Nile virus \-'nī(-ə)l-\ *n* [*West Nile* province of Uganda] : a virus that is transmitted to humans by mosquitoes and causes an illness marked by fever, headache, muscle ache, and sometimes encephalitis or meningitis; *also* : this illness

¹**wet** \'wet\ *adj* **wet·ter; wet·test** **1** ♦ : consisting of or covered or soaked with liquid (as water) **2** : having frequent rains : RAINY **3** : not dry ⟨~ paint⟩ **4** : permitting or advocating the manufacture and sale of alcoholic beverages ⟨a ~ town⟩ ⟨a ~ candidate⟩ — **wet·ly** *adv* — **wet·ness** *n*

♦ saturated, sodden, soggy, waterlogged, watery; *also* deluged, drowned, flooded, inundated, overflowed; submerged, swamped; dipped, dunked, splashed; steeped; flushed, irrigated, laved, rinsed, sluiced; clammy, damp, dank, humid, moist *Ant* arid, dry

²**wet** *n* **1** : WATER; *also* : WETNESS, MOISTURE **2** : rainy weather : RAIN **3** : an advocate of a wet liquor policy

³**wet** *vb* **wet** *or* **wet·ted; wet·ting** ♦ : to make or become wet — **wetter** *n*

♦ bathe, douse, drench, soak, sop, souse, wash, water; *also* damp, dampen, humidify, moisten; deluge, drown, flood, inundate, overflow; submerge, swamp, hydrate; splash; impregnate, saturate, steep; flush, irrigate, lave, rinse, sluice; dip, dunk *Ant* dry

wet blanket *n* ♦ : one that quenches or dampens enthusiasm or pleasure

♦ drag, killjoy, spoilsport — more at KILLJOY

weth·er \'we-thər\ *n* : a castrated male sheep or goat

wet·land \'wet-ˌland, -lənd\ *n* : land or areas (as swamps) containing much soil moisture — usu. used in pl.

wet nurse *n* : a woman who cares for and breastfeeds children not her own

wet suit *n* : a rubber suit for swimmers that acts to retain body heat by keeping a layer of water against the body as insulation

wh *abbr* **1** which **2** white

¹**whack** \'hwak\ *vb* **1** : to strike with a smart or resounding blow **2** : to cut with or as if with a whack

²**whack** *n* **1 a** : a smart or resounding blow **b** ♦ : the sound of or like that of a blow **2** : PORTION, SHARE **3** : CONDITION, STATE ⟨the machine is out of ~⟩ **4** ♦ : an opportunity or attempt to do something **5** : a single action or occasion ⟨made three pies at a ~⟩

♦ [1b] bang, blast, boom, clap, crack, crash, pop, report, slam, smash, snap, thwack — more at CLAP
♦ [4] attempt, crack, endeavor (*or* endeavour), essay, fling, go, pass, shot, stab, trial, try — more at ATTEMPT

¹**whale** \'hwāl\ *n, pl* **whales** **1** *or pl* **whale** : CETACEAN; *esp* : one (as a sperm whale or killer whale) of large size **2** ♦ : a person or thing impressive in size or quality ⟨a ~ of a story⟩

♦ behemoth, blockbuster, colossus, giant, jumbo, leviathan, mammoth, monster, titan, whopper — more at GIANT

²**whale** *vb* **whaled; whal·ing** : to fish or hunt for whales

³**whale** *vb* **whaled; whal·ing** **1** : to defeat soundly : THRASH **2** : to strike or hit vigorously

whale·boat \-ˌbōt\ *n* : a long narrow rowboat originally used by whalers

whale·bone \-ˌbōn\ *n* : BALEEN

whal·er \'hwā-lər\ *n* **1** : a person or ship that hunts whales **2** : WHALEBOAT

whale shark *n* : a shark of warm waters that is the largest known fish

wham·my \'hwa-mē\ *n, pl* **wham·mies** : JINX, HEX

wharf \'hwȯrf\ *n, pl* **wharves** \'hwȯrvz\ *also* **wharfs** ♦ : a structure alongside which ships lie to load and unload

♦ dock, float, jetty, landing, levee, pier, quay — more at DOCK

¹**what** \'hwät, 'hwət\ *pron* **1** — used to inquire about the identity or nature of a being, an object, or some matter or situation ⟨~ is he, a salesman⟩ ⟨~'s that⟩ ⟨~ happened⟩ **2** : that which ⟨I know ~ you want⟩ **3** : WHATEVER 1 ⟨take ~ you want⟩

²**what** *adv* **1** : in what respect : HOW ⟨~ does he care⟩ **2** — used with *with* to introduce a prepositional phrase that expresses cause ⟨kept busy ~ with school and work⟩

³**what** *adj* **1** — used to inquire about the identity or nature of a person, object, or matter ⟨~ books do you read⟩ **2** : how remarkable or surprising ⟨~ an idea⟩ **3** : WHATEVER

¹**what·ev·er** \hwät-'e-vər\ *pron* **1** : anything or everything that ⟨does ~ he wants to⟩ **2** : no matter what ⟨~ you do, don't cheat⟩ **3** : WHAT 1 — used as an intensive ⟨~ do you mean⟩

²**whatever** *adj* : of any kind at all ⟨no food ~⟩

³**whatever** *adv* : in any case : whatever the case may be — often used to suggest the unimportance of an issue or choice ⟨see a movie, watch TV,—~⟩

¹**what·not** \'hwät-ˌnät\ *pron* : any of various other things that might also be mentioned ⟨needles, pins, and ~⟩

²**whatnot** *n* : a light open set of shelves for small ornaments

what·so·ev·er \ˌhwät-sō-'e-vər\ *pron or adj* : WHATEVER

wheal \'hwēl\ *n* : a rapidly formed flat slightly raised itching or burning patch on the skin; *also* : WELT

wheat \'hwēt\ *n* : a cereal grain that yields a fine white flour used chiefly in breads, baked goods, and pastas; *also* : any of several widely grown grasses yielding wheat — **wheat·en** *adj*

wheat germ *n* : the vitamin-rich wheat embryo separated in milling

whee·dle \'hwēd-³l\ *vb* **whee·dled; whee·dling** **1** ♦ : to entice by flattery **2** : to gain or get by wheedling

♦ blarney, cajole, coax — more at COAX

¹**wheel** \'hwēl\ *n* **1** : a disk or circular frame that turns on a central axis **2** : a device whose main part is a wheel **3** : something resembling a wheel in shape or motion **4** ♦ : a curving or circular movement : a rotation or turn usu. about an axis or center **5** : machinery that imparts motion : moving power ⟨the ~s of government⟩ **6** : a person of importance **7** *pl, slang* : AUTOMOBILE — **wheeled** \'hwēld\ *adj* — **wheel·less** *adj*

♦ gyration, pirouette, reel, revolution, roll, rotation, spin, twirl, whirl — more at SPIN

²**wheel** *vb* **1** ♦ : to move or turn like a wheel on or as if on an axis : REVOLVE **2** ♦ : to change direction as if turning on a pivot : to cause to move as if turning on a pivot **3** : to convey or move on wheels or in a vehicle

♦ [1] gyrate, pirouette, revolve, roll, rotate, spin, turn, twirl, whirl — more at SPIN ♦ [2] divert, pivot, swerve, swing, turn, veer, whip — more at TURN

wheel·bar·row \-ˌbar-ō\ *n* : a vehicle with handles and usu. one wheel for carrying small loads

wheel·base \-ˌbās\ *n* : the distance in inches between the front and rear axles of an automotive vehicle

wheel·chair \-ˌcher\ *n* : a chair mounted on wheels esp. for the use of disabled persons

wheel·er \'hwē-lər\ *n* **1** : one that wheels **2** : WHEEL-HORSE **3** : something that has wheels — used in combination ⟨a side-*wheeler*⟩

wheel·er–deal·er \ˌhwē-lər-'dē-lər\ *n* : a shrewd operator esp. in business or politics

wheel·horse \'hwēl-ˌhȯrs\ *n* **1** : a horse in a position nearest the front wheels of a wagon **2** : a steady and effective worker esp. in a political body

wheel·house \-ˌhaủs\ *n* : PILOTHOUSE

wheel–thrown \'hwēl-ˌthrōn\ *adj* : made on a potter's wheel

wheel·wright \-ˌrīt\ *n* : a maker and repairer of wheels and wheeled vehicles

¹wheeze \'hwēz\ *vb* **wheezed; wheez·ing** ♦ : to breathe with difficulty usu. with a whistling sound

   ♦ blow, gasp, pant, puff — more at GASP

²wheeze *n* **1** : a sound of wheezing **2** : an often repeated and well-known joke **3** : a trite saying

wheezy \'hwē-zē\ *adj* **wheez·i·er; -est 1** : inclined to wheeze **2** : having a wheezing sound — **wheez·i·ly** \-zə-lē\ *adv* — **wheez·i·ness** \-zē-nəs\ *n*

whelk \'hwelk\ *n* : a large sea snail; *esp* : one much used as food in Europe

whelm \'hwelm\ *vb* : to overcome or engulf completely : OVERWHELM

¹whelp \'hwelp\ *n* **1** : any of the young of various carnivorous mammals (as a dog) **2** ♦ : a young boy or girl

   ♦ child, cub, juvenile, kid, kiddo, moppet, youngster, youth — more at CHILD

²whelp *vb* : to give birth to (whelps); *also* : bring forth young

¹when \'hwen\ *adv* **1** : at what time ⟨~ will you return⟩ **2** : at or during which time ⟨a time ~ things were better⟩

²when *conj* **1** : at or during the time that ⟨leave ~ I do⟩ **2** : every time that ⟨they all clapped ~ he sang⟩ **3** : in the event that : IF ⟨disqualified ~ you cheat⟩ **4** ♦ : in spite of the fact that : ALTHOUGH ⟨quit politics ~ he might have had a great career in it⟩

   ♦ albeit, although, howbeit, though, while — more at ALTHOUGH

³when *pron* : what or which time ⟨since ~ have you been the boss⟩

⁴when *n* : the time of a happening

whence \'hwens\ *adv or conj* : from what place, source, or cause

when·ev·er \hwe-'ne-vər, hwə-\ *conj or adv* : at whatever time

when·so·ev·er \'hwen-sō-ˌe-vər\ *conj* : at any or every time that

¹where \'hwer\ *adv* **1** : at, in, or to what place ⟨~ is it⟩ ⟨~ will we go⟩ **2** : at, in, or to what situation, position, direction, circumstances, or respect ⟨~ does this road lead⟩

²where *conj* **1** : at, in, or to what place ⟨knows ~ the house is⟩ **2** : at, in, or to what situation, position, direction, circumstances, or respect ⟨shows ~ the road leads⟩ **3** : WHEREVER ⟨goes ~ she likes⟩ **4** : at, in, or to which place ⟨the town ~ we live⟩ **5** : at, in, or to the place at, in, or to which ⟨stay ~ you are⟩ **6** : in a case, situation, or respect in which ⟨outstanding ~ endurance is called for⟩

³where *n* : PLACE, LOCATION ⟨the ~ and how of the accident⟩

¹where·abouts \-ə-ˌbaủts\ *also* **where·about** \-ˌbaủt\ *adv* : about where : near what place ⟨~ does he live⟩

²whereabouts *n sing or pl* : the place where a person or thing is ⟨his present ~ are unknown⟩

where·as \hwer-'az\ *conj* **1** : while on the contrary; *also* : ALTHOUGH **2** ♦ : in view of the fact that : SINCE

   ♦ because, for, now, since — more at SINCE

where·at \-'at\ *conj* **1** : at or toward which **2** : in consequence of which : WHEREUPON

where·by \-'bī\ *conj* : by, through, or in accordance with which ⟨the means ~ we achieved our goals⟩

¹where·fore \'hwer-ˌfȯr\ *adv* **1** : for what reason or purpose : WHY **2** ♦ : because of that : THEREFORE

   ♦ accordingly, consequently, ergo, hence, so, therefore, thus — more at THEREFORE

²wherefore *n* ♦ : an answer or statement giving an explanation : REASON

   ♦ grounds, motive, reason, why — more at REASON

¹where·in \hwer-'in\ *adv* : in what : in what respect ⟨~ was I wrong⟩

²wherein *conj* **1** : in which : WHERE ⟨the city ~ we live⟩ **2** : during which **3** : in what way : HOW ⟨showed me ~ I was wrong⟩

where·of \-'əv, -'äv\ *conj* **1** : of what ⟨knows ~ he speaks⟩ **2** : of which or whom ⟨books ~ the best are lost⟩

where·on \-'ȯn, -'än\ *conj* : on which ⟨the base ~ it rests⟩

where·so·ev·er \'hwer-sō-ˌe-vər\ *conj* : WHEREVER

where·to \'hwer-ˌtü\ *conj* : to which

where·up·on \'hwer-ə-ˌpȯn, -ˌpän\ *conj* **1** : on which **2** : closely following and in consequence of which

¹wher·ev·er \hwer-'e-vər\ *adv* : where in the world ⟨~ did he get that tie⟩

²wherever *conj* **1** : at, in, or to whatever place **2** : in any circumstance in which

where·with \'hwer-ˌwith, -ˌwith\ *conj* : with or by means of which

where·with·al \'hwer-wi-ˌthȯl, -ˌthȯl\ *n* ♦ : means or resources for purchasing or doing something; *esp* : MONEY

   ♦ finances, fund, pocket, resources — more at FUND

wher·ry \'hwer-ē\ *n, pl* **wherries** : a long light rowboat sharp at both ends

whet \'hwet\ *vb* **whet·ted; whet·ting 1** ♦ : to sharpen by rubbing on or with something abrasive (as a whetstone) **2** : to make keen : STIMULATE ⟨~ the appetite⟩

   ♦ edge, grind, hone, sharpen, strop — more at SHARPEN

wheth·er \'hwe-thər\ *conj* **1** : if it is or was true that ⟨ask ~ he is going⟩ **2** : if it is or was better ⟨uncertain ~ to go or stay⟩ **3** : whichever is or was the case, namely that ⟨~ we succeed or fail, we must try⟩ **4** : EITHER ⟨turned out well ~ by accident or design⟩

whet·stone \'hwet-ˌstōn\ *n* : a stone for sharpening blades

whey \'hwā\ *n* : the watery part of milk that separates after the milk sours and thickens

¹which \'hwich\ *adj* **1** : being what one or ones out of a group ⟨~ shirt should I wear⟩ **2** : WHICHEVER

²which *pron* **1** : which one or ones ⟨~ is yours⟩ ⟨~ are his⟩ ⟨it's in May or June, I'm not sure ~⟩ **2** : WHICHEVER ⟨we have all kinds; take ~ you like⟩ **3** — used to introduce a relative clause and to serve as a substitute therein for the noun modified by the clause ⟨the money ~ is coming to me⟩

¹which·ev·er \hwich-'e-vər\ *adj* : no matter which ⟨~ way you go⟩

²whichever *pron* : whatever one or ones

which·so·ev·er \ˌhwich-sō-'e-vər\ *pron or adj* : WHICHEVER

whick·er \'hwi-kər\ *vb* : NEIGH, WHINNY — **whicker** *n*

¹whiff \'hwif\ *n* **1** : a quick puff or slight gust (as of air) **2** : an inhalation of odor, gas, or smoke **3** : a slight trace **4** : STRIKEOUT

²whiff *vb* **1** : to expel, puff out, or blow away in or as if in whiffs **2** ♦ : to inhale an odor : STRIKE OUT 3

   ♦ nose, scent, smell, sniff — more at SMELL

Whig \'hwig\ *n* [short for *Whiggamore*, member of a Scottish group that marched to Edinburgh in 1648 to oppose the court party] **1** : a member or supporter of a British political group of the late 17th through early 19th centuries seeking to limit royal authority and increase parliamentary power **2** : an American favoring independence from Great Britain during the American Revolution **3** : a member or supporter of an American political party formed about 1834 to oppose the Democrats

¹**while** \'hwīl\ *n* **1** ♦ : a period of time ⟨stay a ∼⟩ **2** ♦ : the time and effort used : TROUBLE ⟨worth your ∼⟩

♦ **[1]** bit, space, spell, stretch; *also* flash, instant, jiffy, minute, moment, second; aeon, age, eon, eternity ♦ **[2]** effort, exertion, expenditure, labor (*or* labour), pains, sweat, trouble, work — more at EFFORT

²**while** *conj* **1** : during the time that ⟨she called ∼ you were out⟩ **2** : AS LONG AS ⟨∼ there's life there's hope⟩ **3** ♦ : in spite of the fact that : ALTHOUGH ⟨∼ he's respected, he's not liked⟩

♦ albeit, although, howbeit, though, when — more at ALTHOUGH

³**while** *vb* **whiled; whil·ing** : to cause to pass esp. pleasantly ⟨∼ away an hour⟩

¹**whi·lom** \'hwī-ləm\ *adv* [ME, lit., at times, fr. OE *hwīlum*, dat. pl. of *hwīl* time, while] *archaic* : FORMERLY

²**whilom** *adj* ♦ : at a time in the past : FORMER ⟨his ∼ friends⟩

♦ erstwhile, former, late, old, onetime, past, sometime — more at FORMER

whilst \'hwīlst\ *conj, chiefly Brit* : WHILE

whim \'hwim\ *n* ♦ : a sudden wish, desire, or change of mind

♦ caprice, fancy, freak, notion, vagary; *also* capriciousness, whimsicality; conceit; concept, conception, image, impression, picture, thought; brainstorm, inspiration

whim·per \'hwim-pər\ *vb* : to make a low whining plaintive or broken sound — **whimper** *n*

whim·si·cal \'hwim-zi-kəl\ *adj* **1** ♦ : full of whims : CAPRICIOUS **2** : resulting from or characterized by whim or caprice ⟨∼ notions⟩ — **whim·si·cal·i·ty** \,hwim-zə-'ka-lə-tē\ *n* — **whim·si·cal·ly** \'hwim-zi-k(ə-)lē\ *adv*

♦ capricious, impulsive; *also* mercurial, moody, temperamental, volatile; eccentric, flaky, quirky; arbitrary, erratic, fickle, inconstant, irregular, willful; impractical, quixotic, romantic

whim·sy *also* **whim·sey** \'hwim-zē\ *n, pl* **whim·sies** *also* **whimseys** **1** : a sudden impulsive apparently unmotivated change of mind : WHIM **2** : a fanciful or fantastic device, object, or creation esp. in writing or art ⟨decorative ∼⟩

whine \'hwīn\ *vb* **whined; whin·ing** [ME, fr. OE *hwīnan* to whiz] **1** : to utter a usu. high-pitched plaintive or distressed cry; *also* : to make a sound similar to such a cry **2** ♦ : to complain with or as if with a whine — **whine** *n* — **whiny** *also* **whin·ey** \'hwī-nē\ *adj*

♦ beef, bellyache, carp, complain, crab, croak, fuss, gripe, grouse, growl, grumble, kick, moan, murmur, mutter, repine, squawk, wail — more at COMPLAIN

whin·er *n* ♦ : one that whines

♦ bear, complainer, crab, crank, grouch, grumbler — more at GROUCH

¹**whin·ny** \'hwi-nē\ *vb* **whin·nied; whin·ny·ing** : to neigh usu. in a low or gentle manner

²**whinny** *n, pl* **whinnies** : NEIGH

¹**whip** \'hwip\ *vb* **whipped; whip·ping** **1** : to move, snatch, or jerk quickly or forcefully ⟨∼ out a gun⟩ ⟨whipped the car around and sped off⟩ **2** ♦ : to strike with a slender lithe implement (as a lash) esp. as a punishment; *also* : SPANK **3** : to drive or urge on by or as if by using a whip **4** : to bind or wrap (as a rope or rod) with cord in order to protect and strengthen; *also* : to wind or wrap around something **5** ♦ : to thoroughly overcome : DEFEAT **6** ♦ : to stir up : INCITE ⟨∼ up enthusiasm⟩ **7** : to produce in a hurry ⟨∼ up a meal⟩ **8** : to beat (as eggs or cream) into a froth **9 a** : to proceed nimbly or briskly **b** : to flap about forcefully ⟨flags *whipping* in the wind⟩ — **whip·per** *n* — **whip into shape** : to bring forcefully to a desired state or condition

♦ **[2]** beat, flog, hide, thrash ♦ **[5]** beat, best, clobber, conquer, crush, defeat, drub, lick, master, overcome, rout, skunk, subdue, trim, triumph, trounce, wallop, win — more at BEAT ♦ *usu* **whip up** **[6]** abet, ferment, foment, incite, instigate, provoke, raise, stir — more at INCITE

²**whip** *n* **1** ♦ : a flexible instrument used for whipping **2** : a stroke or cut with or as if with a whip **3** : a dessert made by whipping a portion of the ingredients ⟨prune ∼⟩ **4** : a person who handles a whip **5** : a member of a legislative body appointed by a party to enforce party discipline **6** : a whipping or thrashing motion

♦ lash, scourge, switch; *also* cat-o'-nine-tails, cowhide, crop, knout, quirt, rawhide, strap; cane, club, cudgel, flail; stripe

whip·cord \-,kȯrd\ *n* **1** : a thin tough braided cord **2** : a strong cloth with fine diagonal cords or ribs

whip hand *n* : positive control : ADVANTAGE

whip·lash \'hwip-,lash\ *n* **1** : the lash of a whip **2** : injury resulting from a sudden sharp movement of the neck and head (as of a person in a vehicle that is struck from the rear)

whip·per·snap·per \'hwi-pər-,sna-pər\ *n* ♦ : a small, insignificant, or presumptuous person

♦ nobody, nonentity, nothing, zero — more at NOBODY

whip·pet \'hwi-pət\ *n* : any of a breed of small swift slender dogs that are used for racing

whipping boy *n* : one who is receives criticism or blame instead of the ones deserving it : SCAPEGOAT

whip·poor·will \'hwi-pər-,wil\ *n* : an American insect-eating bird with dull variegated plumage whose call at nightfall and just before dawn is suggestive of its name

whip·saw \'hwip-,sȯ\ *vb* : to beset with two or more adverse conditions or situations at once

¹**whir** *also* **whirr** \'hwər\ *vb* **whirred; whir·ring** ♦ : to move, fly, or revolve with a whir

♦ buzz, drone, hum, whish, whiz, zip, zoom; *also* thrum; hiss, murmur, purr, rustle, sigh, whisper

²**whir** *also* **whirr** *n* : a continuous fluttering or vibratory sound made by something in rapid motion

¹**whirl** \'hwərl\ *vb* **1** ♦ : to move or drive in a circle or curve esp. with force or speed **2** ♦ : to turn or cause to turn rapidly in circles **3** : to turn abruptly **4** ♦ : to move or go quickly **5** ♦ : to become dizzy or giddy : REEL

♦ **[1, 2]** pivot, revolve, roll, rotate, spin, swing, swirl, turn, twirl, twist, wheel — more at TURN ♦ **[4]** breeze, career, course, dash, fly, hasten, hurry, race, rip, rocket, run, rush, shoot, speed, step, tear, zip, zoom — more at HURRY ♦ **[5]** reel, spin

²**whirl** *n* **1** ♦ : a rapid rotating or circling movement; *also* : something whirling **2** : COMMOTION, BUSTLE ⟨the social ∼⟩ **3** ♦ : a state of mental confusion **4** : TRY ⟨gave it a ∼⟩

♦ **[1]** gyration, pirouette, reel, revolution, roll, rotation, spin, twirl, wheel — more at SPIN ♦ **[3]** bafflement, bewilderment, confusion, distraction, muddle, mystification, perplexity, puzzlement — more at CONFUSION

whirl·i·gig \'hwər-li-,gig\ *n* [ME *whirlegigg*, fr. *whirlen* to whirl + *gigg* top] **1** : a child's toy having a whirling motion **2** : something that continuously whirls or changes

whirl·pool \'hwərl-,pül\ *n* : water moving rapidly in a circle so as to produce a depression in the center into which floating objects may be drawn

whirl·wind \-,wind\ *n* **1** : a small whirling windstorm **2** : a confused rush **3** : a violent or destructive force

whirly·bird \'hwər-lē-,bərd\ *n* : HELICOPTER

¹**whish** \'hwish\ *vb* **1** : to move with a whish or swishing sound **2** ♦ : to have or make a sound like that of a long \s\ or \sh\

♦ fizz, hiss, sizzle, swish

²**whish** *n* : a rushing sound : SWISH

¹**whisk** \'hwisk\ *n* **1** : a quick light sweeping or brushing

motion **2** : a usu. wire kitchen implement for beating food by hand **3** : WHISK BROOM
²whisk *vb* **1** ♦ : to move nimbly and quickly **2** ♦ : to move or convey briskly ⟨*~ed* the children off to bed⟩ **3** : to beat or whip lightly ⟨*~* eggs⟩ **4** : to brush or wipe off lightly ⟨*~* a coat⟩

♦ [1] bowl, breeze, coast, drift, flow, glide, roll, sail, skim, slide, slip, stream, sweep — more at FLOW
♦ [2] accelerate, hasten, hurry, quicken, rush, speed, step up — more at HURRY

whisk broom *n* : a small broom with a short handle used esp. as a clothes brush
whis·ker \'hwis-kər\ *n* **1** : one hair of the beard **2** *pl* : the part of the beard that grows on the sides of the face or on the chin **3** : one of the long bristles or hairs growing near the mouth of an animal (as a cat or mouse) — **whis·kered** \-kərd\ *adj*
whis·key *or* **whis·ky** \'hwis-kē\ *n, pl* **whiskeys** *or* **whiskies** [Ir *uisce beathadh* & ScGael *uisge beatha*, lit., water of life] : a liquor distilled from fermented wort (as that obtained from rye, corn, or barley mash)
¹whis·per \'hwis-pər\ *vb* **1 a** : to speak very low or under the breath **b** ♦ : to tell or utter by or as if by whispering ⟨*~* a secret⟩ **2** : to make a low rustling sound ⟨*~ing* leaves⟩ — **whis·per·er** \-pər-ər\ *n*

♦ circulate, noise, rumor — more at RUMOR

²whisper *n* **1** : something communicated by or as if by whispering : HINT, RUMOR **2** : an act or instance of whispering
whist \'hwist\ *n* : a card game played by four players in two partnerships with a deck of 52 cards
¹whis·tle \'hwi-səl\ *n* **1** : a device by which a shrill sound is produced ⟨steam *~*⟩ ⟨tin *~*⟩ **2** : a shrill clear sound made by forcing breath out or air in through the puckered lips **3** : the sound or signal produced by a whistle or as if by whistling **4** : the shrill clear note of an animal (as a bird)
²whistle *vb* **whis·tled; whis·tling** **1** : to utter a shrill clear sound by blowing or drawing air through the puckered lips **2** : to utter a shrill note or call resembling a whistle **3** : to make a shrill clear sound esp. by rapid movements ⟨the wind *whistled*⟩ **4** : to blow or sound a whistle **5** : to signal or call by a whistle **6** : to produce, utter, or express by whistling ⟨*~* a tune⟩ — **whis·tler** *n*
whis·tle–blow·er \'hwi-səl-‚blō-ər\ *n* : INFORMER
whis·tle–stop \-‚stäp\ *n* : a brief personal appearance by a political candidate orig. on the rear platform of a touring train
whit \'hwit\ *n* [prob. alter. of ME *wiht, wight* creature, thing, fr. OE *wiht*] ♦ : the smallest part or particle

♦ hoot, jot, lick, modicum, rap, tittle — more at JOT

¹white \'hwīt\ *adj* **whit·er; whit·est** **1** ♦ : free from color **2** : of the color of new snow or milk; *esp* : of the color white **3** : light or pallid in color ⟨lips *~* with fear⟩ **4** : SILVERY; *also* : made of silver **5** : of, relating to, or being a member of a group or race characterized by light-colored skin **6** : free from spot or blemish : PURE, INNOCENT **7** : BLANK 2 ⟨*~* space in printed matter⟩ **8** ♦ : not intended to cause harm ⟨a *~* lie⟩ ⟨*~* magic⟩ **9** : wearing white ⟨*~* friars⟩ **10** : marked by snow ⟨*~* Christmas⟩ **11** : consisting of a wide range of frequencies ⟨*~* light⟩ — **white·ness** \-nəs\ *n* — **whit·ish** \'hwī-tish\ *adj*

♦ [1] colorless (*or* colourless), uncolored (*or* uncoloured), unpainted — more at COLORLESS ♦ [8] harmless, innocent, innocuous, safe — more at HARMLESS

²white *n* **1** : the color of maximal lightness that characterizes objects which both reflect and transmit light : the opposite of black **2** : a white or light-colored part or thing ⟨the *~* of an egg⟩; *also, pl* : white garments **3** : the light-colored pieces in a 2-player board game; *also* : the person by whom these are played **4** : one that is or approaches the color white **5** : a person of a light-skinned race

white ant *n* : TERMITE
white blood cell *n* : any of the colorless blood cells (as lymphocytes) that do not contain hemoglobin but do have a nucleus
white–bread \'hwīt-‚bred\ *adj* : being, typical of, or having qualities (as blandness) associated with the white middle class ⟨*~* values⟩
white·cap \'hwīt-‚kap\ *n* : a wave crest breaking into white foam
white chocolate *n* : a whitish confection chiefly of cocoa butter, milk, and sugar
white–col·lar \'hwīt-'kä-lər\ *adj* : of, relating to, or constituting the class of salaried workers whose duties do not require the wearing of work clothes or protective clothing ⟨*~* jobs⟩
white dwarf *n* : a small very dense whitish star of low luminosity
white elephant *n* **1** : an Indian elephant of a pale color that is sometimes venerated in India, Sri Lanka, Thailand, and Myanmar **2** : something requiring much care and expense and giving little profit or enjoyment
white feather *n* [fr. the superstition that a white feather in the plumage of a gamecock is a mark of a poor fighter] : a mark or symbol of cowardice
white·fish \'hwīt-‚fish\ *n* : any of various freshwater food fishes related to the salmons and trouts
white flag *n* : a flag of pure white used to signify truce or surrender
white gold *n* : a pale alloy of gold resembling platinum in appearance
white goods *n pl* : white fabrics or articles (as sheets or towels) typically made of cotton or linen
White·hall \'hwīt-‚hȯl\ *n* : the British government
white hat *n* **1** : an admirable and honorable person **2** : a mark or symbol of goodness
white·head \-‚hed\ *n* : a small whitish lump in the skin due to retention of secretion in an oil gland duct
white heat *n* : a temperature higher than red heat at which a body becomes brightly incandescent
white–hot *adj* **1** : being at or radiating white heat **2** : FERVID
White House \-‚haủs\ *n* **1** : the executive department of the U.S. government **2** : a residence of the president of the U.S.
white lead *n* : a heavy white poisonous carbonate of lead used esp. formerly as a pigment in exterior paints
white matter *n* : whitish nerve tissue esp. of the brain and spinal cord that consists largely of neuron processes enclosed in a fatty material and that typically lies under the cortical gray matter
whit·en \'hwīt-ᵊn\ *vb* ♦ : to make or become white — **whit·en·er** *n*

♦ blanch, bleach, blench, dull, fade, pale, wash out — more at PALE

white pepper *n* : a spice that consists of the berry of a pepper plant ground after removal of its black husk
white pine *n* : a tall-growing pine of eastern No. America with needles in clusters of five; *also* : its wood
white sale *n* : a sale on white goods
white shark *n* : GREAT WHITE SHARK
white slave *n* : a woman or girl held unwillingly for purposes of prostitution — **white slavery** *n*
white·tail \'hwīt-‚tāl\ *n* : WHITE-TAILED DEER
white–tailed deer *n* : a No. American deer with a rather long tail white on the underside and the males of which have forward-arching antlers
white–tie \-‚tī\ *adj* : characterized by or requiring formal evening clothes consisting of usu. white tie and tailcoat for men and a formal gown for women
white·wall \'hwīt-‚wȯl\ *n* : an automobile tire having a white band on the sidewall
¹white·wash \-‚wȯsh, -‚wäsh\ *vb* **1** : to whiten with whitewash **2** ♦ : to clear of a charge of wrongdoing by of-

fering excuses, hiding facts, or conducting a perfunctory investigation **3** : SHUT OUT 2

♦ excuse, gloss, palliate — more at PALLIATE

²**whitewash** *n* **1** : a liquid mixture (as of lime and water) for whitening a surface **2** : a clearing of wrongdoing by whitewashing

white water *n* : frothy water (as in breakers, rapids, or falls)

white·wood \-ˌwu̇d\ *n* : any of various trees and esp. a tulip tree having light-colored wood; *also* : such wood

¹**whith·er** \ˈhwi-thər\ *adv* **1** : to what place **2** : to what situation, position, degree, or end ⟨∼ will this drive him⟩

²**whither** *conj* **1** : to the place at, in, or to which; *also* : to which place **2** : to whatever place

whith·er·so·ev·er \ˌhwi-thər-sō-ˈe-vər\ *conj* : to whatever place

¹**whit·ing** \ˈhwī-tiŋ\ *n, pl* whiting *also* whit·ings : any of several usu. light or silvery food fishes (as a hake) found mostly near seacoasts

²**whiting** *n* : calcium carbonate in powdered form used esp. as a pigment and in putty

whit·low \ˈhwit-ˌlō\ *n* : a deep inflammation of a finger or toe with pus formation

Whit·sun·day \ˈhwit-ˈsən-dē, -sən-ˌdā\ *n* [ME *Whitsonday*, fr. OE *hwīta sunnandæg*, lit., white Sunday; prob. fr. the custom of wearing white robes by those newly baptized at this season] : PENTECOST

whit·tle \ˈhwit-ᵊl\ *vb* whit·tled; whit·tling **1** : to pare or cut off chips from the surface of (wood) with a knife; *also* : to cut or shape by such paring **2** : to reduce as if by paring down ⟨∼ down expenses⟩

¹**whiz** *or* **whizz** \ˈhwiz\ *vb* whizzed; whiz·zing **1** ♦ : to hum, whir, or hiss like a speeding object (as an arrow or ball) passing through air **2** ♦ : fly or move swiftly with a hissing or buzzing sound

♦ [1, 2] buzz, drone, hiss, hum, whir, whish, zip, zoom — more at WHIR

²**whiz** *or* **whizz** *n, pl* **whiz·zes** ♦ : a hissing, buzzing, or whizzing sound

♦ buzz, drone, hiss, hum, purr, whir, zoom — more at HUM

³**whiz** *n, pl* **whiz·zes** ♦ : a person notably qualified or able usu. in a specified field of interest : WIZARD 2

♦ ace, adept, artist, authority, crackerjack, expert, maestro, master, scholar, shark, virtuoso, wizard — more at EXPERT ♦ brain, genius, intellect, thinker, wizard — more at GENIUS

who \ˈhü\ *pron* **1** : what or which person or persons ⟨∼ did it⟩ ⟨∼ is he⟩ ⟨∼ are they⟩ **2** : the person or persons that ⟨knows ∼ did it⟩ **3** — used to introduce a relative clause and to serve as a substitute therein for the substantive modified by the clause ⟨the man ∼ lives there is rich⟩

WHO *abbr* World Health Organization

whoa \ˈwō, ˈhwō, ˈhō\ *vb imper* — a command to an animal to stand still

who·dun·it *also* **who·dun·nit** \hü-ˈdə-nət\ *n* : a detective or mystery story

who·ev·er \hü-ˈe-vər\ *pron* : whatever person : no matter who

¹**whole** \ˈhōl\ *adj* [ME *hool* healthy, unhurt, entire, fr. OE *hāl*] **1** ♦ : being in healthy or sound condition : free from defect or damage **2** ♦ : having all its proper parts or elements ⟨∼ milk⟩ **3** : constituting the total sum of : ENTIRE ⟨owns the ∼ island⟩ **4** : each or all of the ⟨the ∼ family⟩ **5** ♦ : not scattered or divided : CONCENTRATED ⟨gave me his ∼ attention⟩ **6** : seemingly complete or total ⟨the ∼ idea is to help, not hinder⟩

♦ [1] able-bodied, chipper, fit, hale, healthy, hearty, robust, sound, well, wholesome — more at HEALTHY ♦ [2] complete, comprehensive, entire, full, grand, intact, integral, perfect, plenary, total — more at COMPLETE ♦ [5] all, concentrated, entire, undivided; *also*

absolute, complete, full, thorough, total; comprehensive, intact, integral, perfect *Ant* diffuse, divided, scattered

²**whole** *n* **1** ♦ : a complete amount or sum **2** : something whole or entire — **on the whole** **1** : in view of all the circumstances or conditions **2** : in general

♦ aggregate, full, sum, total, totality; *also* gross; completeness, entirety; bulk, mass

³**whole** *adv* : COMPLETELY, ENTIRELY ⟨a ∼ new team⟩

whole food *n* : a food eaten in its natural state with little or no artificial additives

whole·heart·ed \ˈhōl-ˈhär-təd\ *adj* : undivided in purpose, enthusiasm, will, or commitment

whole hog *adv* : to the fullest extent : COMPLETELY ⟨accepted the proposals *whole hog*⟩

whole·ness *n* ♦ : the quality or state of being whole : an unreduced or unbroken completeness or totality

♦ fitness, health, heartiness, robustness, soundness, wellness, wholesomeness — more at HEALTH

whole note *n* : a musical note equal to one measure of four beats

whole number *n* **1** : any of the set of nonnegative integers **2** ♦ : any of the natural numbers that do not include fractions : INTEGER

♦ digit, figure, integer, number, numeral — more at NUMBER

¹**whole·sale** \ˈhōl-ˌsāl\ *n* : the sale of goods in quantity usu. for resale by a retail merchant

²**wholesale** *adj* **1** : performed on a large scale without discrimination ⟨∼ slaughter⟩ **2** : of, relating to, or engaged in wholesaling — **wholesale** *adv*

³**wholesale** *vb* **whole·saled; whole·sal·ing** : to sell at wholesale — **whole·sal·er** *n*

whole·some \ˈhōl-səm\ *adj* **1** ♦ : promoting mental, spiritual, or bodily health or well-being ⟨a ∼ environment⟩ **2** ♦ : sound in body, mind, or morals : HEALTHY **3** : PRUDENT ⟨∼ respect for the law⟩

♦ [1] healthful, healthy, restorative, salubrious, salutary — more at HEALTHFUL ♦ [2] able-bodied, chipper, fit, hale, healthy, hearty, robust, sound, well, whole — more at HEALTHY

whole·some·ness *n* ♦ : the quality, fact, or state of being wholesome

♦ fitness, health, heartiness, robustness, soundness, wellness, wholeness — more at HEALTH

whole step *n* : a musical interval comprising two half steps (as C–D or F♯–G♯)

whole wheat *adj* : made of ground entire wheat kernels

whol·ly \ˈhōl-lē\ *adv* **1** ♦ : to the full or entire extent : COMPLETELY **2** : SOLELY, EXCLUSIVELY

♦ absolutely, all, altogether, clean, completely, entirely, fully, quite, totally, utterly — more at ALL

whom \ˈhüm\ *pron, objective case of* WHO

whom·ev·er \hü-ˈme-vər\ *pron, objective case of* WHOEVER

whom·so·ev·er \ˌhüm-sō-ˈe-vər\ *pron, objective case of* WHOSOEVER

¹**whoop** \ˈhwüp, ˈhwu̇p, ˈhüp, ˈhu̇p\ *vb* **1** : to shout or call loudly and vigorously **2** : to make the characteristic whoop of whooping cough **3** : to go or pass with a loud noise **4** : to utter or express with a whoop; *also* : to urge, drive, or cheer with a whoop

²**whoop** *n* **1** ♦ : a whooping sound or utterance : SHOUT **2** : a crowing intake of breath after a fit of coughing in whooping cough

♦ cry, holler, hoot, howl, shout, yell, yowl — more at SHOUT

¹**whoop·ee** \ˈhwu̇-(ˌ)pē, ˈhwü-\ *interj* — used to express exuberance

²**whoopee** *n* **1** : boisterous fun **2** : sexual play — usu. used with *make*

whooping cough *n* : an infectious bacterial disease esp. of children marked by convulsive coughing fits often followed by a shrill gasping intake of breath

whooping crane *n* : a large white nearly extinct No. American crane noted for its loud whooping call
whoop·la \'hwüp-ˌlä, 'hwup-\ *n* **1** : HOOPLA **2** : boisterous merrymaking
whop·per \'hwä-pər\ *n* **1 ♦** : something unusually large or extreme of its kind **2 ♦** : a monstrous lie

  ♦ [1] behemoth, blockbuster, colossus, giant, jumbo, leviathan, mammoth, monster, titan, whale — more at GIANT ♦ [2] fabrication, fairy tale, falsehood, falsity, fib, lie, mendacity, prevarication, story, tale, untruth — more at LIE

whop·ping \'hwä-piŋ\ *adj* ♦ : extremely large

  ♦ colossal, enormous, giant, gigantic, grand, huge, jumbo, mammoth, massive, outsize, oversize, prodigious, titanic, tremendous — more at HUGE

whore \'hōr\ *n* : a woman who practices unlawful sexual commerce : PROSTITUTE
whorl \'hwórl, 'hwərl\ *n* **1** : a group of parts (as leaves or petals) encircling an axis and esp. a plant stem **2** : something that whirls or coils around a center : COIL, SPIRAL **3** : one of the turns of a snail shell
whorled \'hwórld, 'hwərld\ *adj* : having or arranged in whorls
¹whose \'hüz\ *adj* : of or relating to whom or which esp. as possessor or possessors, agent or agents, or object or objects of an action ⟨asked ∼ bag it was⟩
²whose *pron* : whose one or ones ⟨∼ is this car⟩ ⟨∼ are those books⟩
who·so \'hü-ˌsō\ *pron* : WHOEVER
who·so·ev·er \ˌhü-sō-'e-vər\ *pron* : WHOEVER
whs *or* **whse** *abbr* warehouse
whsle *abbr* wholesale
¹why \'hwī\ *adv* : for what reason, cause, or purpose ⟨∼ did you do it?⟩
²why *conj* **1** : the cause, reason, or purpose for which ⟨that is ∼ you did it⟩ **2** : for which : on account of which ⟨knows the reason ∼ you did it⟩
³why *n, pl* **whys** ♦ : the reason or cause of something ⟨the ∼s of racial prejudice⟩

  ♦ grounds, motive, reason, wherefore — more at REASON

⁴why \'wī, 'hwī\ *interj* — used to express surprise, hesitation, approval, disapproval, or impatience ⟨∼, here's what I was looking for⟩
WI *abbr* **1** West Indies **2** Wisconsin
WIA *abbr* wounded in action
Wic·ca \'wi-kə\ *n* [prob. fr. OE *wicca* wizard] : a religion that affirms the existence of supernatural power (as magic) and of deities who inhere in nature and that ritually observes seasonal and life cycles
wick \'wik\ *n* : a loosely bound bundle of soft fibers that draws up oil, tallow, or wax to be burned in a candle, oil lamp, or stove
wick·ed \'wi-kəd\ *adj* **1 ♦** : morally bad : EVIL, SINFUL **2** : FIERCE, VICIOUS **3 a ♦** : playfully or engagingly mischievous : ROGUISH ⟨a ∼ glance⟩ **b** : showing or expressing ill will : MALICIOUS **4** : REPUGNANT, VILE ⟨a ∼ odor⟩ **5** : HARMFUL, DANGEROUS ⟨a ∼ attack⟩ **6** : impressively excellent ⟨throws a ∼ fastball⟩

  ♦ [1] bad, black, evil, immoral, iniquitous, nefarious, rotten, sinful, unethical, unsavory, vicious, vile, villainous, wrong — more at BAD ♦ [3a] devilish, impish, knavish, mischievous, rascally, roguish, sly, waggish — more at MISCHIEVOUS

wick·ed·ly *adv* ♦ : in a wicked manner

  ♦ hatefully, maliciously, meanly, nastily, spitefully, viciously — more at NASTILY

wick·ed·ness *n* ♦ : the quality or state of being wicked

  ♦ devilishness, impishness, knavery, mischief, mischievousness, rascality, shenanigans, waggery — more at MISCHIEF ♦ atrociousness, atrocity, depravity, enormity, heinousness, monstrosity, vileness — more at ENORMITY

wick·er \'wi-kər\ *n* **1** : a small pliant branch (as an osier or a withe) **2** : WICKERWORK — **wicker** *adj*
wick·er·work \-ˌwərk\ *n* : work made of osiers, twigs, or rods : basket weaving
wick·et \'wi-kət\ *n* **1** : a small gate or door; *esp* : one forming a part of or placed near a larger one **2** : a windowlike opening usu. with a grille or grate (as at a ticket office) **3** : a set of three upright rods topped by two crosspieces bowled at in cricket **4** : an arch or hoop in croquet
wick·i·up \'wi-kē-ˌəp\ *n* : a hut used by nomadic Indians of the western and southwestern U.S. with a usu. oval base and a rough frame covered with reed mats, grass, or brushwood
wid *abbr* widow, widower
¹wide \'wīd\ *adj* **wid·er; wid·est** **1 ♦** : covering a vast area **2** : measured across or at right angles to the length **3 ♦** : not narrow : BROAD; *also* : ROOMY **4** : opened to full width ⟨eyes ∼ with wonder⟩ **5** : not limited : EXTENSIVE ⟨∼ experience⟩ **6** : far from the goal, mark, or truth ⟨a ∼ guess⟩ — **wide·ly** *adv*

  ♦ [1] broad, expansive, extended, extensive, far-flung, far-reaching, widespread — more at EXTENSIVE ♦ [3] broad, commodious, expansive, extensive, roomy, spacious, thick *Ant* narrow, skinny, slender, slim, thin

²wide *adv* **wid·er; wid·est** **1** : over a great distance or extent : WIDELY ⟨searched far and ∼⟩ **2** : over a specified distance, area, or extent **3** : so as to leave a wide space between ⟨∼ apart⟩ **4** : so as to clear by a considerable distance ⟨ran ∼ around left end⟩ **5** : COMPLETELY, FULLY ⟨opened her eyes⟩
wide–awake \ˌwīd-ə-'wāk\ *adj* **1 ♦** : fully awake **2 ♦** : marked by careful watchfulness and promptness to cope with emergencies : ALERT

  ♦ [1] awake, sleepless, wakeful — more at WAKEFUL ♦ [2] alert, attentive, awake, vigilant, watchful — more at ALERT

wide–body \'wīd-ˌbä-dē\ *n* : a large jet aircraft having a wide cabin
wide–eyed \'wīd-'īd\ *adj* **1** : having the eyes wide open esp. with wonder or astonishment **2** : marked by unsophisticated or uncritical acceptance or admiration : NAIVE
wide·mouthed \-'maůthd, -'maůtht\ *adj* **1** : having one's mouth opened wide (as in awe) **2** : having a wide mouth ⟨∼ jars⟩
wid·en \'wīd-ᵊn\ *vb* : to increase in width, scope, or extent
wide·spread \'wīd-'spred\ *adj* **1** : widely scattered or prevalent **2 ♦** : widely extended or spread out

  ♦ broad, expansive, extended, extensive, far-flung, far-reaching, wide — more at EXTENSIVE

widgeon *var of* WIGEON
¹wid·ow \'wi-dō\ *n* : a woman who has lost her spouse or partner by death and has not married again — **wid·ow·hood** *n*
²widow *vb* : to cause to become a widow or widower
wid·ow·er \'wi-də-wər\ *n* : a man who has lost his spouse or partner by death and has not married again
width \'width\ *n* **1** : a distance from side to side : the measurement taken at right angles to the length : BREADTH **2 ♦** : largeness of extent or scope; *also* : FULLNESS **3** : a measured and cut piece of material ⟨a ∼ of calico⟩

  ♦ amplitude, breadth, compass, extent, range, reach, realm, scope, sweep — more at RANGE

wield \'wēld\ *vb* **1** : to use or handle esp. effectively ⟨∼ a broom⟩ **2 ♦** : to exert authority by means of ⟨∼ influence⟩ — **wield·er** *n*

  ♦ apply, exercise, exert, put out — more at EXERT

wie·ner *also* **wei·ner** \'wē-nər\ *n* [short for *wienerwurst*, fr. G, lit., Vienna sausage] : FRANKFURTER
wife \'wīf\ *n, pl* **wives** \'wīvz\ **1** *dial* : WOMAN **2** : a woman acting in a specified capacity — used in combination ⟨fish*wife*⟩ **3 ♦** : a female partner in a marriage — **wife·hood** *n* — **wife·less** *adj* — **wife·ly** *adj*

◆ consort, helpmate, lady, mate, partner, spouse

wig \'wig\ *n* [short for *periwig*, modif. of MF *perruque*, fr. It *parrucca, perrucca* hair, wig] : a manufactured covering of natural or synthetic hair for the head; *also* : TOUPEE

wi·geon *or* **wid·geon** \'wi-jən\ *n, pl* **wigeon** *or* **wigeons** *or* **widgeon** *or* **widgeons** : any of several medium-sized freshwater ducks

wig·gle \'wi-gəl\ *vb* **wig·gled; wig·gling** 1 ◆ : to move to and fro with quick jerky or shaking movements 2 : to proceed with twisting and turning movements ⟨*wiggled* his toes⟩ — **wiggle** *n*

◆ fiddle, fidget, jerk, squirm, twitch — more at FIDGET

wig·gler \'wi-glər, -gə-lər\ *n* 1 : a larva or pupa of a mosquito 2 : one that wiggles

wig·gly \'wi-glē, -gə-lē\ *adj* 1 : tending to wiggle ⟨a ~ worm⟩ 2 : WAVY ⟨~ lines⟩

wight \'wīt\ *n* : a living being : CREATURE

wig·let \'wi-glət\ *n* : a small wig used esp. to enhance a hairstyle

¹**wig·wag** \'wig-,wag\ *vb* 1 : to signal by or as if by a flag or light waved according to a code 2 : to make or cause to make a signal (as with the hand or arm)

²**wigwag** *n* : the art or practice of wigwagging

wig·wam \'wig-,wäm\ *n* : a hut of the Indians of the eastern U.S. having typically an arched framework of poles overlaid with bark, rush mats, or hides

¹**wild** \'wīld\ *adj* 1 ◆ : living in a state of nature and not ordinarily tamed ⟨~ ducks⟩ 2 ◆ : growing or produced without human aid or care ⟨~ honey⟩ ⟨~ plants⟩ 3 : WASTE, DESOLATE ⟨~ country⟩ 4 : not subjected to restraint or regulation : UNCONTROLLED, UNRULY ⟨~ passions⟩ ⟨a ~ young stallion⟩ 5 ◆ : marked by turbulent violent agitation ⟨a ~ night⟩ 6 ◆ : exceeding normal or conventional bounds in thought, design, conception, or nature ⟨~ ideas⟩ 7 : indicative of strong passion, desire, or emotion ⟨a ~ stare⟩ 8 ◆ : not acculturated to an advanced civilization : SAVAGE 9 a ◆ : deviating from the natural or expected course, goal, or practice : acting, appearing, or being in an unexpected, undesired, or unpredictable manner ⟨a ~ throw⟩ b ◆ : having no basis in known or surmised fact 10 : able to represent any playing card designated by the holder ⟨deuces ~⟩ — **wild** *adv* — **wild·ness** *n*

◆ [1] feral, savage, unbroken, undomesticated, untamed; *also* uncontrolled, unsubdued; bestial, brutal, brute; barbarous, uncivilized *Ant* broken, busted, domestic, domesticated, tame, tamed ◆ [1, 2] natural, uncultivated, untamed; *also* native; overgrown, untended; waste; undeveloped *Ant* cultivated, tamed ◆ [5] blustery, rough, stormy, tempestuous, tumultuous, turbulent, violent ◆ [6, 9a] bizarre, curious, far-out, funny, kinky, odd, outlandish, outré, peculiar, quaint, queer, quirky, remarkable, screwy, strange, wacky, weird — more at ODD ◆ [8] barbarous, heathen, heathenish, Neanderthal, rude, savage, uncivil, uncivilized, uncultivated — more at SAVAGE ◆ [9b] absurd, bizarre, crazy, fanciful, fantastic, foolish, insane, nonsensical, preposterous, unreal — more at FANTASTIC

²**wild** *adv* 1 ◆ : in a wild manner : WILDLY 2 ◆ : without regulation or control ⟨running ~⟩

◆ amok, berserk, frantically, harum-scarum, hectically, helter-skelter, madly, pell-mell, wildly — more at HELTER-SKELTER

³**wild** *n* 1 : a region or tract that is sparsely inhabited or uncultivated : WILDERNESS 2 : a natural or undomesticated state or existence

wild boar *n* : an Old World wild hog from which most domestic swine have been derived

wild card *n* 1 : an unknown or unpredictable factor 2 : one picked to fill a leftover play-off or tournament position 3 *usu* **wild·card** : a symbol (as ? or *) used in a keyword search to represent the presence of unspecified characters

wild carrot *n* : QUEEN ANNE'S LACE

¹**wild·cat** \'wīld-,kat\ *n, pl* **wildcats** 1 : any of various small or medium-sized cats (as a lynx or ocelot) 2 : a quick-tempered hard-fighting person

²**wildcat** *adj* 1 : not sound or safe ⟨~ schemes⟩ 2 : initiated by a group of workers without formal union approval ⟨~ strike⟩

³**wildcat** *vb* **wild·cat·ted; wild·cat·ting** : to drill an oil or gas well in a region not known to be productive

wil·de·beest \'wil-də-,bēst\ *n, pl* **wildebeests** *also* **wildebeest** [Afrikaans *wildebees*, fr. *wilde* wild + *bees* ox] : either of two large African antelopes with an oxlike head and horns and a horselike mane and tail

wil·der·ness \'wil-dər-nəs\ *n* [ME, fr. *wildern* wild, fr. OE *wilddēoren* of wild beasts] ◆ : an uncultivated and uninhabited region

◆ nature, open, outdoors, wild — more at NATURE

wild·fire \'wīld-,fīr\ *n* : an uncontrollable fire — **like wildfire** : very rapidly

wild·flow·er \-,flaù-(-ə)r\ *n* : the flower of a wild or uncultivated plant or the plant bearing it

wild·fowl \-,faùl\ *n* : a bird and esp. a waterfowl hunted as game

wild–goose chase *n* : the pursuit of something unattainable

wild·life \'wīld-,līf\ *n* : nonhuman living things and esp. wild animals living in their natural environment

wild·ly *adv* ◆ : in a wild manner

◆ amok, berserk, frantically, harum-scarum, hectically, helter-skelter, madly, pell-mell, wild — more at HELTER-SKELTER

wild oat *n* 1 : any of several Old World wild grasses 2 *pl* : offenses and indiscretions attributed to youthful exuberance — usu. used in the phrase *sow one's wild oats*

wild rice *n* : a No. American aquatic grass; *also* : its edible seed

wild·wood \'wīld-,wùd\ *n* : a wood unaltered or unfrequented by humans

¹**wile** \'wīl\ *n* 1 ◆ : a trick or stratagem intended to ensnare or deceive; *also* : a playful trick 2 ◆ : the use of deceitfulness and trickery

◆ [1] artifice, device, dodge, gimmick, jig, ploy, scheme, sleight, stratagem, trick — more at TRICK ◆ [2] artifice, chicanery, hanky-panky, subterfuge, trickery — more at TRICKERY

²**wile** *vb* **wiled; wil·ing** ◆ : to lure by or as if by a magic spell

◆ allure, beguile, bewitch, captivate, charm, enchant, fascinate — more at CHARM

wil·i·ness \-lē-nəs\ *n* ◆ : the quality or state of being wily

◆ artfulness, artifice, caginess, canniness, craft, craftiness, cunning, guile, slyness — more at CUNNING ◆ artifice, craft, craftiness, crookedness, cunning, deceit, deceitfulness, dishonesty, dissimulation, double-dealing, duplicity, guile — more at DECEIT

¹**will** \'wil\ *vb, past* **would** \'wùd\ *pres sing & pl* **will** 1 : WISH, DESIRE ⟨call it what you ~⟩ 2 — used as an auxiliary verb to express (1) desire, willingness, or in negative constructions refusal ⟨~ you have another⟩ ⟨he *won't* do it⟩, (2) customary or habitual action ⟨~ get angry over nothing⟩, (3) simple futurity ⟨tomorrow we ~ go shopping⟩, (4) capability or sufficiency ⟨the back seat ~ hold three⟩, (5) determination or willfulness ⟨I ~ go despite them⟩, (6) probability ⟨that ~ be the mailman⟩, (7) inevitability ⟨accidents ~ happen⟩, or (8) a command ⟨you ~ do as I say⟩

²**will** *n* 1 : wish or desire often combined with determination ⟨the ~ to win⟩ 2 : something desired; *esp* : a choice or determination of one having authority or power 3 : the act, process, or experience of willing : VOLITION 4 ◆ : the mental powers manifested as wishing, choosing, desiring, or intending 5 : a disposition to act according to principles or ends 6 ◆ : power of controlling one's own actions or emotions ⟨a leader of iron ~⟩ 7 : a legal

document in which a person declares to whom his or her possessions are to go after death

♦ **[4]** accord, choice, free will, option, self-determination, volition — more at FREE WILL ♦ **[6]** restraint, self-control, self-discipline, self-government, self-possession, self-restraint, willpower; *also* self-denial; moderation, temperance; determination, nerve; discipline, command, control, mastery; aplomb, assurance, composure, confidence, coolness, equanimity, poise, self-confidence; discretion

³**will** *vb* **1** : to dispose of by or as if by a will : BEQUEATH **2** : to determine by an act of choice **3** ♦ : to have the intention of : CHOOSE

♦ choose, like, want, wish

will·ful *or* **wil·ful** \'wil-fəl\ *adj* **1** ♦ : governed by will without regard to reason : obstinately or perversely doing what one wants without regard to others **2** ♦ : done deliberately : INTENTIONAL ⟨∼ murder⟩

♦ **[1]** contrary, defiant, disobedient, froward, intractable, rebellious, recalcitrant, refractory, uncontrollable, unruly, untoward, wayward — more at DISOBEDIENT ♦ **[1]** dogged, hardheaded, headstrong, mulish, obdurate, obstinate, opinionated, peevish, pertinacious, perverse, pigheaded, stubborn, unyielding — more at OBSTINATE ♦ **[2]** deliberate, freewill, intentional, purposeful

will·ful·ly *adv* ♦ : in a willful manner

♦ consciously, deliberately, intentionally, knowingly, purposely — more at INTENTIONALLY

wil·lies \'wi-lēz\ *n pl* ♦ : a fit of nervousness : JITTERS — used with *the*

♦ dither, jitters, shakes, shivers — more at JITTERS

will·ing \'wi-liŋ\ *adj* **1** ♦ : inclined or favorably disposed in mind : READY ⟨∼ to go⟩ **2** ♦ : prompt to act or respond ⟨∼ workers⟩ **3** ♦ : done, borne, or accepted voluntarily or without reluctance **4** : of or relating to the will

♦ **[1]** amenable, disposed, game, glad, inclined, ready; *also* predisposed; agreeable, compliant, obedient, submissive; favorable, receptive; prepared, prompt, quick, responsive, swift *Ant* disinclined, unwilling ♦ **[2]** alert, expeditious, prompt, quick, ready — more at QUICK ♦ **[3]** freewill, voluntary — more at VOLUNTARY

will·ing·ly *adv* : in a willing manner

will·ing·ness *n* ♦ : the quality or state of being willing

♦ alacrity, gameness, goodwill — more at ALACRITY

wil·li·waw \'wi-lē-ˌwȯ\ *n* ♦ : a sudden violent gust of cold land air common along mountainous coasts of high latitudes

♦ blast, blow, flurry, gust — more at GUST

will-o'-the-wisp \ˌwil-ə-thə-'wisp\ *n* **1** : a light that appears at night over marshy grounds **2** : a misleading or elusive goal or hope

wil·low \'wi-lō\ *n* **1** : any of a genus of quick-growing shrubs and trees with tough pliable shoots **2** : an object made of willow wood

wil·low·ware \-ˌwar\ *n* : dinnerware that is usu. blue and white and that is decorated with a story-telling design featuring a large willow tree by a little bridge

wil·lowy \'wi-lə-wē\ *adj* **1** ♦ : pliant, soft, and yielding in texture **2** : gracefully tall and slender

♦ flexible, limber, lissome, lithe, pliable, supple; *also* adaptable, ductile, elastic, fluid, malleable, plastic, variable, yielding; flaccid, floppy *Ant* inflexible, rigid, stiff

will·pow·er \'wil-ˌpau̇-ər\ *n* ♦ : the power to control one's actions or emotions : energetic determination

♦ restraint, self-control, self-discipline, self-government, self-possession, self-restraint, will — more at WILL

wil·ly-nil·ly \ˌwi-lē-'ni-lē\ *adv or adj* [alter. of *will I nill I or will ye nill ye* or *will he nill he*; *nill* fr. archaic *nill* to be

unwilling, fr. ME *nilen*, fr. OE *nyllan*, fr. *ne* not + *wyllan* to wish] **1** : without regard for one's choice : by compulsion ⟨they rushed us along ∼⟩ **2** ♦ : in a haphazard or spontaneous manner

♦ aimlessly, anyhow, anyway, anywise, desultorily, erratically, haphazard, haphazardly, helter-skelter, irregularly, randomly

¹**wilt** \'wilt\ *vb* **1** ♦ : to lose or cause to lose freshness and become limp esp. from lack of water : DROOP ⟨the roses were ∼*ing*⟩ **2** ♦ : to grow weak or faint : LANGUISH

♦ decay, droop, fail, flag, go, lag, languish, sag, waste, weaken — more at WEAKEN

²**wilt** *n* : any of various plant disorders marked by wilting and often shriveling

wily \'wī-lē\ *adj* **wil·i·er; -est** ♦ : full of guile : TRICKY

♦ artful, cagey, crafty, cunning, devious, foxy, guileful, slick, sly, subtle, tricky — more at ARTFUL

wimp \'wimp\ *n* : a weak, cowardly, or ineffectual person

¹**wim·ple** \'wim-pəl\ *n* : a cloth covering worn over the head and around the neck and chin by women esp. in the late medieval period and by some nuns

²**wimple** *vb* **wim·pled; wim·pling 1** : to cover with or as if with a wimple **2** : to ripple or cause to ripple

wimpy \'wim-pē\ *adj* ♦ : being a wimp

♦ effete, frail, nerveless, soft, spineless, weak, wishy-washy — more at WEAK

¹**win** \'win\ *vb* **won** \'wən\; **win·ning** [ME *winnen*, fr. OE *winnan* to struggle] **1 a** ♦ : to get possession of esp. by effort : GAIN **b** ♦ : to obtain by work : EARN **2 a** : to gain in or as if in battle or contest **b** ♦ : to be the victor in ⟨*won* the war⟩ **3** ♦ : to solicit and gain the favor of — often used with *over*; *esp* : to induce to accept oneself in marriage

♦ **[1b]** achieve, acquire, attain, capture, carry, draw, earn, gain, garner, get, land, make, obtain, procure, realize, secure — more at EARN ♦ **[2b]** conquer, prevail, triumph; *also* overcome, sweep; squeak, squeeze; contend, vie; succeed *Ant* lose ♦ *usu* **win over [3]** argue, convince, get, induce, move, persuade, prevail, satisfy, talk — more at PERSUADE

²**win** *n* : VICTORY; *esp* : 1st place at the finish (as of a horse race)

wince \'wins\ *vb* **winced; winc·ing** ♦ : to shrink back involuntarily (as from pain) : FLINCH — **wince** *n*

♦ blench, flinch, quail, recoil, shrink — more at FLINCH

winch \'winch\ *n* : a machine that has a drum on which is wound a rope or cable for hauling or hoisting — **winch** *vb*

¹**wind** \'wind\ *n* **1** : a movement of the air **2** ♦ : a prevailing force or influence : TENDENCY **3** : BREATH ⟨he had the ∼ knocked out of him⟩ **4** : gas produced in the stomach or intestines **5** ♦ : idle talk as insubstantial as air **6** : air carrying a scent (as of game) **7** : INTIMATION ⟨they got ∼ of our plans⟩ **8** *pl* : WIND INSTRUMENTS; *also* : players of wind instruments

♦ **[2]** current, drift, leaning, run, tendency, tide, trend — more at TREND ♦ **[5]** bombast, gas, grandiloquence, hot air, rhetoric — more at RHETORIC

²**wind** *vb* **1** : to get a scent of ⟨the dogs ∼*ed* the game⟩ **2** : to cause to be out of breath ⟨he was ∼*ed* from the climb⟩ **3** : to allow (as a horse) to rest so as to recover breath

³**wind** \'wīnd, 'wind\ *vb* **wind·ed** \'wīn-dəd, 'win-\ *or* **wound** \'wau̇nd\; **wind·ing** : to sound by blowing ⟨∼ a horn⟩

⁴**wind** \'wīnd\ *vb* **wound** \'wau̇nd\ *also* **wind·ed; wind·ing 1** : ENTANGLE, INVOLVE **2** : to introduce stealthily : INSINUATE **3** : to encircle or cover with something pliable : WRAP, COIL, TWINE ⟨∼ a bobbin⟩ **4** : to hoist or haul by a rope or chain and a winch **5** : to tighten the spring of; *also* : CRANK **6** : to raise to a high level (as of excitement) **7** : to cause to move in a curving line or path **8** ♦ : to have a curving course or shape ⟨a river ∼*ing* through the valley⟩ **9** : to move or lie so as to encircle

♦ bend, coil, curl, curve, entwine, spiral, twine, twist; *also* arc, arch, crook, hook, sweep, swerve, turn, veer, wheel; swirl, whirl; circle, encircle, loop, interlace, intertwine, lace; meander, weave, zigzag

⁵**wind** \'wind\ *n* ♦ : something having a curving or twisting form : TURN

♦ angle, arc, arch, bend, bow, crook, curve, turn — more at BEND

wind·age \'win-dij\ *n* : the influence of the wind in deflecting the course of a projectile through the air; *also* : the amount of such deflection

wind·bag \'wind-ˌbag\ *n* ♦ : an overly talkative person

♦ babbler, cackler, chatterbox, chatterer, conversationalist, gabbler, jabberer, magpie, prattler, talker — more at CHATTERBOX

wind·blown \-ˌblōn\ *adj* : blown by the wind; *also* : having the appearance of being blown by the wind ⟨~ hair⟩

wind·break \-ˌbrāk\ *n* : a growth of trees or shrubs serving to break the force of the wind; *also* : a shelter from the wind

wind·burned \-ˌbərnd\ *adj* : irritated and inflamed by exposure to the wind — **wind·burn** \-ˌbərn\ *n*

wind·chill \-ˌchil\ *n* : a still-air temperature that would have the same cooling effect on exposed human skin as a given combination of temperature and wind speed

windchill factor *n* : WINDCHILL

wind down *vb* **1** : to draw toward an end **2** : RELAX, UNWIND

wind·er \'wīn-dər\ *n* : one that winds

wind·fall \'wind-ˌfȯl\ *n* **1** : something (as a tree or fruit) blown down by the wind **2** ♦ : an unexpected or sudden gift, gain, or advantage ⟨won a ~ from the lottery⟩

♦ benefit, blessing, boon, felicity, godsend, good, manna — more at BLESSING

wind·flow·er \-ˌflaü-ər\ *n* : ANEMONE

¹**wind·ing** \'wīn-diŋ\ *n* : material (as wire) wound or coiled about an object

²**winding** *adj* **1** ♦ : having a pronounced curve or spiral ⟨~ stairs⟩ **2** ♦ : having a course that winds ⟨a ~ road⟩

♦ [1] helical, spiral — more at SPIRAL ♦ [2] crooked, devious, serpentine, sinuous, tortuous — more at CROOKED

wind·ing–sheet \-ˌshēt\ *n* : SHROUD

wind instrument *n* : a musical instrument (as a flute or horn) sounded by wind or esp. by the breath

wind·jam·mer \'wind-ˌja-mər\ *n* : a sailing ship; *also* : one of its crew

wind·lass \'wind-ləs\ *n* [ME *wyndlas*, alter. of *wyndase*, fr. OF *guindas, windas*, fr. ON *vindāss*, fr. *vinda* to wind + *āss* pole] : a winch used esp. on ships for hoisting or hauling

wind·mill \'wind-ˌmil\ *n* : a mill or machine worked by the wind turning sails or vanes that radiate from a central shaft

win·dow \'win-dō\ *n* [ME *windowe*, fr. ON *vindauga*, fr. *vindr* wind + *auga* eye] **1** : an opening in the wall of a building to let in light and air; *also* : the framework with fittings that closes such an opening **2** : WINDOWPANE **3** : an opening resembling or suggesting that of a window in a building **4** : an interval of time during which certain conditions or an opportunity exists **5** : a rectangular box appearing on a computer screen on which information (as files or program output) is displayed — **win·dow·less** *adj*

window box *n* : a box for growing plants in or by a window

window dressing *n* **1** : display of merchandise in a store window **2** : a showing made to create a deceptively favorable impression

win·dow·pane \'win-dō-ˌpān\ *n* : a pane in a window

win·dow–shop \-ˌshäp\ *vb* : to look at the displays in store windows without going inside the stores to make purchases — **win·dow–shop·per** *n*

win·dow·sill \-ˌsil\ *n* : the horizontal member at the bottom of a window

wind·pipe \'wind-ˌpīp\ *n* : TRACHEA

wind·proof \-'prüf\ *adj* : impervious to wind ⟨a ~ jacket⟩

wind·row \'wind-ˌrō\ *n* **1** : hay raked up into a row to dry **2** : a row of something (as dry leaves) swept up by or as if by the wind

wind shear *n* : a radical shift in wind speed and direction that occurs over a very short distance

wind·shield \'wind-ˌshēld\ *n* : a transparent screen (as of glass) in front of the occupants of a vehicle

wind sock *n* : an open-ended truncated cloth cone mounted in an elevated position to indicate wind direction

wind·storm \-ˌstȯrm\ *n* : a storm with high wind and little or no rain

wind·surf·ing \-ˌsər-fiŋ\ *n* : the sport or activity of riding a sailboard — **wind·surf** \-ˌsərf\ *vb* — **wind·surf·er** *n*

wind·swept \'wind-ˌswept\ *adj* : swept by or as if by wind ⟨~ plains⟩

wind tunnel *n* : an enclosed passage through which air is blown to investigate air flow around an object

wind·up \'wīn-ˌdəp\ *n* **1** ♦ : a concluding act or part : CONCLUSION **2** : a series of regular and distinctive motions made by a pitcher preliminary to delivering a pitch

♦ close, conclusion, consummation, end, ending, finale, finis, finish — more at FINALE

wind up *vb* **1** ♦ : to bring or come to a conclusion : END ⟨*wind up* the meeting⟩ **2** : to put in order for the purpose of bringing to an end **3** : to arrive in a place, situation, or condition at the end or as a result of a course of action ⟨*wound up* as paupers⟩ **4** : to make a pitching windup

♦ close, conclude, end, finish, round, terminate, wrap up — more at CLOSE

¹**wind·ward** \'win-dwərd\ *n* : the side or direction from which the wind is blowing

²**windward** *adj* : being in or facing the direction from which the wind is blowing

windy \'win-dē\ *adj* **wind·i·er; -est** **1** ♦ : having wind : exposed to winds ⟨a ~ day⟩ ⟨a ~ prairie⟩ **2** : STORMY **3** : FLATULENT **4** ♦ : indulging in or characterized by useless talk

♦ [1] blowy, blustery, breezy, gusty; *also* drafty; stormy, tempestuous ♦ [4] bombastic, gaseous, grandiloquent, oratorical, rhetorical — more at RHETORICAL ♦ [4] circuitous, diffuse, long-winded, prolix, rambling, verbose, wordy — more at WORDY

¹**wine** \'wīn\ *n* [ME *win*, fr. OE *wīn*, ultim. fr. L *vinum*] **1** : fermented grape juice used as a beverage **2** : the usu. fermented juice of a plant product (as fruit) used as a beverage ⟨rice ~⟩

²**wine** *vb* **wined; win·ing** : to treat to or drink wine

wine cellar *n* : a room for storing wines; *also* : a stock of wines

wine·grow·er \-ˌgrō-ər\ *n* : one that cultivates a vineyard and makes wine

wine·press \-ˌpres\ *n* : a vat in which juice is pressed from grapes

win·ery \'wī-nə-rē, 'wīn-rē\ *n, pl* **-eries** : a wine-making establishment

¹**wing** \'wiŋ\ *n* **1** : one of the movable feathered or membranous paired appendages by means of which a bird, bat, or insect flies **2** : something suggesting a wing; *esp* : an airfoil that develops the lift which supports an aircraft in flight **3** : a plant or animal appendage or part likened to a wing **4** : a turned-back or extended edge on an article of clothing **5** : a means of flight or rapid progress **6** : the act or manner of flying : FLIGHT **7** *pl* : the area at the side of the stage out of sight **8** : one of the positions or players on either side of a center position or line **9** ♦ : either of two opposing groups within an organization : FACTION **10** : a unit in military aviation consisting of two or more squadrons — **wing·less** *adj* — **on the wing** : in flight : FLYING — **under one's wing** : in one's charge or care

♦ bloc, body, coalition, combination, combine, faction, party, sect, set, side — more at FACTION

²**wing** \vb\ **1** : to fit with wings; *also* : to enable to fly easily **2** ♦ : to pass through in flight : FLY ⟨~ the air⟩ ⟨swallows ~*ing* southward⟩ **3** : to let fly : DISPATCH **4** : to wound in the wing ⟨~ a bird⟩; *also* : to wound without killing **5** : to perform without preparation : IMPROVISE ⟨~*ing* it⟩

  ♦ fly, glide, plane, soar — more at FLY

wing·ding \'wiŋ-ˌdiŋ\ *n* : a wild, lively, or lavish party

winged \'wiŋd, 'wiŋ-əd, *in compounds* 'wiŋd\ *adj* **1** : having wings esp. of a specified character **2** : soaring with or as if with wings : ELEVATED **3** : SWIFT, RAPID

wing nut *n* : a nut with winglike extensions that can be gripped with the thumb and finger

wing·span \'wiŋ-ˌspan\ *n* : the distance between the tips of a pair of wings

wing·spread \-ˌspred\ *n* : the spread of the wings; *esp* : the distance between the tips of the fully extended wings of a winged animal

¹**wink** \'wiŋk\ *vb* **1** : to close and open one eye quickly as a signal or hint **2** : to close and open the eyes quickly : BLINK **3** ♦ : to avoid seeing or noticing something — often used with *at* ⟨~ at a traffic violation⟩ **4** ♦ : to gleam or flash fitfully or intermittently : TWINKLE — **wink·er** \'wiŋ-kər\ *n*

  ♦ *usu* **wink at** [3] brush (off), condone, disregard, excuse, gloss, ignore, pardon, pass over, shrug off — more at EXCUSE ♦ [4] blink, flame, flash, glance, gleam, glimmer, glisten, glitter, scintillate, shimmer, sparkle, twinkle — more at FLASH

²**wink** *n* **1** ♦ : a brief period of sleep : NAP **2** : an act of winking; *esp* : a hint or sign given by winking **3** ♦ : an exceedingly brief period : INSTANT ⟨dries in a ~⟩

  ♦ [1] catnap, doze, drowse, forty winks, nap, siesta, snooze — more at NAP ♦ [3] flash, instant, jiffy, minute, moment, second, shake, trice, twinkle, twinkling — more at INSTANT

win·ner \'wi-nər\ *n* ♦ : one that wins or is successful

  ♦ blockbuster, hit, smash, success — more at HIT
  ♦ champ, champion, victor — more at CHAMPION

¹**win·ning** \'wi-niŋ\ *n* **1** : VICTORY **2** : something won; *esp* : money won at gambling ⟨large ~s⟩

²**winning** *adj* **1** : successful esp. in competition **2** ♦ : having an attractive, captivating, and charming nature

  ♦ adorable, darling, dear, endearing, lovable, precious, sweet — more at LOVABLE

win·now \'wi-nō\ *vb* **1** : to remove (as chaff) by a current of air; *also* : to free (as grain) from waste in this manner **2** : to sort or separate as if by winnowing

wino \'wī-nō\ *n, pl* **win·os** : one who is addicted to drinking wine

win·some \'win-səm\ *adj* [ME *winsum*, fr. OE *wynsum*, fr. *wynn* joy] **1** ♦ : generally pleasing and engaging ⟨a ~ smile⟩ **2** : CHEERFUL, LIGHTHEARTED — **win·some·ly** *adv* — **win·some·ness** *n*

  ♦ endearing, ingratiating, winning — more at INGRATIATING

¹**win·ter** \'win-tər\ *n* : the season of the year in any region in which the noonday sun shines most obliquely : the coldest period of the year

²**winter** *vb* **1** : to pass the winter ⟨~ed in Florida⟩ **2** : to feed or find food during the winter ⟨~ed on hay⟩

³**winter** *adj* : sown in autumn for harvesting in the following spring or summer ⟨~ wheat⟩

win·ter·green \'win-tər-ˌgrēn\ *n* **1** : a low evergreen plant of the heath family with white bell-shaped flowers and spicy red berries **2** : an aromatic oil or its flavor from the wintergreen

win·ter·ize \'win-tə-ˌrīz\ *vb* **-ized; -iz·ing** : to make ready for winter

win·ter–kill \'win-tər-ˌkil\ *vb* : to kill or die by exposure to winter weather

winter squash *n* : any of various hard-shelled squashes that keep well in storage

win·ter·tide \-ˌtīd\ *n* : WINTER

win·ter·time \-ˌtīm\ *n* : WINTER

win·try \'win-trē\ *also* **win·tery** \'win-tə-rē\ *adj* **win·tri·er; -est** **1** ♦ : of, relating to, or characteristic of winter ⟨~ weather⟩ **2** : lacking qualities that cheer ⟨a ~ welcome⟩

  ♦ arctic, bitter, chill, chilly, cold, cool, freezing, frigid, frosty, glacial, icy, nippy, polar, raw, snappy — more at COLD

¹**wipe** \'wīp\ *vb* **wiped; wip·ing** **1** : to clean or dry by rubbing ⟨~ dishes⟩ **2** : to remove by or as if by rubbing ⟨~ away tears⟩ **3** : to erase completely : OBLITERATE **4** : to pass or draw over a surface ⟨wiped his hand across his face⟩ — **wip·er** *n*

²**wipe** *n* **1** : an act or instance of wiping; *also* : BLOW, STRIKE, SWIPE **2** : something used for wiping ⟨disposable ~s⟩

wipe out *vb* ♦ : to destroy completely

  ♦ annihilate, blot out, demolish, destroy, eradicate, exterminate, liquidate, obliterate, root, rub out, snuff, stamp — more at ANNIHILATE

¹**wire** \'wī(-ə)r\ *n* **1** ♦ : metal in the form of a thread or slender rod; *also* : a thread or rod of metal **2** : hidden or secret influences controlling the action of a person or organization — usu. used in pl. ⟨pull ~s⟩ **3** : a line of wire for conducting electric current **4** : a telegraph or telephone wire or system **5** : TELEGRAM, CABLEGRAM **6** : the finish line of a race

  ♦ cable, cord, lace, line, rope, string — more at CORD

²**wire** *vb* **wired; wir·ing** **1** : to provide or equip with wire ⟨~ a house⟩ **2** : to bind, string, or mount with wire **3** : to send or send word to by telegraph

wired *adj* **1** : furnished with wires **2** : connected to the Internet **3** : feverishly excited

wire·hair \'wī(-ə)r-ˌhar\ *n* : a wirehaired dog or cat

wire·haired \-'hard\ *adj* : having a stiff wiry outer coat of hair

¹**wire·less** \-ləs\ *adj* **1** : having no wire or wires **2** : RADIO **3** : of or relating to data communications using radio waves

²**wireless** *n* **1** : telecommunication involving signals transmitted by radio waves; *also* : the technology used in radio telecommunication **2** *chiefly Brit* : RADIO

wire service *n* : a news agency that sends out syndicated news copy to subscribers by wire or satellite

wire·tap \-ˌtap\ *n* : the act or an instance of tapping a telephone or telegraph wire to get information; *also* : an electrical connection used for such tapping — **wiretap** *vb* — **wire·tap·per** \-ˌta-pər\ *n*

wire·worm \-ˌwərm\ *n* : any of various slender hard-coated beetle larvae esp. destructive to plant roots

wir·ing \'wīr-iŋ\ *n* : a system of wires

wiry \'wīr-ē\ *adj* **wir·i·er** \'wī-rē-ər\; **-est** **1** : made of or resembling wire **2** : slender yet strong and sinewy ⟨~ arms⟩ — **wir·i·ness** \'wī-rē-nəs\ *n*

Wis *or* **Wisc** *abbr* Wisconsin

Wisd *abbr* Wisdom

wis·dom \'wiz-dəm\ *n* [ME, fr. OE *wīsdom*, fr. *wīs* wise] **1** ♦ : accumulated philosophic or scientific learning : KNOWLEDGE; *also* : INSIGHT **2** ♦ : good sense : JUDGMENT **3** : a wise attitude or course of action

  ♦ [1] knowledge, lore, science — more at KNOWLEDGE ♦ [2] discernment, insight, judgment, perception, sagacity, sapience, sense, wit; *also* acuity, acumen, astuteness, penetration, perspicacity, sensitivity, understanding; appreciation, apprehension, comprehension, grasp; brightness, brilliance, canniness, cleverness, smartness; gray matter, intellect, intelligence, judgment, mentality, power, reason; discrimination, prudence, sanity; logic, rationality

Wisdom *n* : a book included in the Roman Catholic canon of the Old Testament and corresponding to the Wisdom of Solomon in the Protestant Apocrypha

wisdom tooth *n* : the last tooth of the full set on each side of the upper and lower jaws of humans

¹wise \'wīz\ *n* : WAY, MANNER, FASHION ⟨in no ∼⟩ ⟨in this ∼⟩

²wise *adj* **wis·er; wis·est** **1** ♦ : having wisdom : SAGE **2** : having or showing good sense or good judgment **3** ♦ : aware of what is going on : KNOWING; *also* : CRAFTY, SHREWD **4** ♦ : possessing inside information **5** : INSOLENT, FRESH ⟨a ∼ retort⟩ — **wise·ly** *adv*

♦ [1] discerning, insightful, perceptive, sagacious, sage, sapient; *also* acute, perspicacious; experienced; discriminating; brainy, brilliant, bright, clever, intelligent, keen, nimble, quick, quick-witted, smart; cerebral, erudite, knowledgeable, learned, literate, scholarly; astute, sharp, shrewd; contemplative, reflective, thoughtful *Ant* unperceptive, unwise ♦ [3, 4] aware, informed, knowing, ready *Ant* unknowing

³wise *vb* **wised; wis·ing; wis·es** ♦ : to supply with information — often used with *up*

♦ *usu* **wise up** acquaint, advise, apprise, brief, clue, enlighten, familiarize, fill in, inform, instruct, tell — more at ENLIGHTEN

-wise \ˌwīz\ *adv comb form* : in the manner or direction of ⟨slant*wise*⟩

wise·acre \'wī-ˌzā-kər\ *n* [MD *wijssegger* soothsayer] : SMART ALECK

¹wise·crack \'wīz-ˌkrak\ *n* ♦ : a clever, smart, or flippant remark

♦ crack, gag, jest, joke, laugh, pleasantry, quip, sally, waggery, witticism — more at JOKE

²wisecrack *vb* ♦ : to make a wisecrack

♦ banter, fool, fun, jest, jive, joke, josh, kid, quip — more at JOKE

wise guy *n* : SMART ALECK

¹wish \'wish\ *vb* **1** ♦ : to have a desire : long for ⟨∼ you were here⟩ ⟨∼ for a puppy⟩ **2** : to form or express a wish concerning ⟨∼ed him a happy birthday⟩ **3** : BID ⟨he ∼ed me good morning⟩ **4** : to request by expressing a desire ⟨I ∼ you to go now⟩ **5** ♦ : to have the intention of ⟨I don't ∼ to impose⟩

♦ *usu* **wish for** [1] ache for, covet, crave, desire, die (to *or* for), hanker (for *or* after), hunger for, long for, lust (for *or* after), pine for, repine for, thirst for, want, yearn for — more at DESIRE ♦ [5] choose, like, want, will

²wish *n* **1** : an act or instance of wishing or desiring : WANT; *also* : GOAL **2** : an expressed will or desire

wish·bone \-ˌbōn\ *n* : a forked bone in front of the breastbone in most birds

wish·ful \'wish-fəl\ *adj* **1** : expressive of a wish; *also* : having a wish **2** : according with wishes rather than fact ⟨∼ thinking⟩

wishy–washy \'wi-shē-ˌwȯ-shē, -ˌwä-\ *adj* ♦ : lacking in character or determination; *also* : morally feeble

♦ banal, flat, insipid; *also* unexciting, unrewarding; bland, boring, drab, dreary, dry, dull, heavy, humdrum, jading, leaden, monotonous, pedestrian, ponderous, tedious, tiresome, tiring, uninteresting, wearisome, weary, wearying; inane; innocuous, inoffensive; mild, soft, subdued, tame, weak; common, commonplace, ordinary, stale, unexceptional ♦ effete, feral, nerveless, soft, spineless, weak, wimpy — more at WEAK

wisp \'wisp\ *n* **1** : a small handful (as of hay or straw) **2** : a thin strand, strip, or fragment ⟨a ∼ of hair⟩; *also* : a thready streak ⟨a ∼ of smoke⟩ **3** : something frail, slight, or fleeting ⟨a ∼ of a smile⟩ — **wispy** *adj*

wis·te·ria \wis-'tir-ē-ə\ *also* **wis·tar·ia** \-'tir-ē-ə *also* -'ter-\ *n* : any of a genus of chiefly Asian mostly woody vines related to the peas and widely grown for their long showy clusters of blue, white, purple, or rose flowers

wist·ful \'wist-fəl\ *adj* : feeling or showing a yearning tinged with melancholy — **wist·ful·ly** *adv* — **wist·ful·ness** *n*

wit \'wit\ *n* **1** : reasoning power : INTELLIGENCE **2** ♦ : mental soundness : SANITY — usu. used in pl.

3 ♦ : resourcefulness and creative imagination; *esp* : quickness and cleverness in handling words and ideas **4 a** : a talent for making clever remarks **b** ♦ : a person noted for making witty remarks — **wit·ted** \'wi-təd\ *adj* — **at one's wit's end** : at a loss for a means of solving a problem

♦ [2] head, mind, reason, sanity — more at MIND ♦ [3] common sense, horse sense, sense, wisdom — more at COMMON SENSE ♦ [4b] card, comedian, comic, humorist, jester, joker, wag — more at HUMORIST

¹witch \'wich\ *n* **1** ♦ : a person believed to have magic power; *esp* : SORCERESS **2** ♦ : an ugly old woman : HAG **3** : a charming or alluring girl or woman **4** : an adherent of Wicca

♦ [1] conjurer, enchanter, magician, necromancer, sorcerer, voodoo, wizard — more at MAGICIAN ♦ [1] enchantress, hag, hex; *also* charmer, conjuror, enchanter, necromancer, voodoo; magician, sorcerer, warlock, wizard ♦ [2] crone, hag — more at CRONE

²witch *vb* : BEWITCH

witch·craft \'wich-ˌkraft\ *n* **1** ♦ : the power or practices of a witch : SORCERY **2** : WICCA

♦ bewitchment, enchantment, magic, necromancy, sorcery, wizardry — more at MAGIC

witch doctor *n* : a person in a primitive society who uses magic to treat sickness and to fight off evil spirits

witch·ery \'wi-chə-rē\ *n, pl* **-er·ies** **1** : the practice of witchcraft : SORCERY **2** : an irresistible fascination : CHARM

witch·grass \'wich-ˌgras\ *n* : any of several grasses that are weeds in cultivated areas

witch ha·zel \'wich-ˌhā-zəl\ *n* **1** : a shrub of eastern No. America bearing small yellow flowers in the fall **2** : a soothing alcoholic lotion made from witch hazel bark

witch–hunt \'wich-ˌhənt\ *n* **1** : a searching out and persecution of persons accused of witchcraft **2** : the searching out and deliberate harassment esp. of political opponents

witch·ing \'wi-chiŋ\ *adj* : of, relating to, or suitable for sorcery or supernatural occurrences

with \'with, 'with\ *prep* **1** : AGAINST ⟨a fight ∼ his brother⟩ **2** : FROM ⟨parting ∼ friends⟩ **3** : in mutual relation to ⟨talk ∼ a friend⟩ **4** : in the company of ⟨went there ∼ her⟩ **5** : AS REGARDS, TOWARD ⟨is patient ∼ children⟩ **6** : compared to ⟨on equal terms ∼ another⟩ **7** : in support of ⟨I'm ∼ you all the way⟩ **8** : in the presence of : CONTAINING ⟨tea ∼ sugar⟩ **9** : in the opinion of : as judged by ⟨their arguments had weight ∼ her⟩ **10 a** ♦ : by reason of : BECAUSE OF ⟨pale ∼ anger⟩ **b** : by means of ⟨hit him ∼ a club⟩ **11** : in a manner indicating ⟨work ∼ a will⟩ **12** : GIVEN, GRANTED ⟨∼ your permission I'll leave⟩ **13** : HAVING ⟨came ∼ good news⟩ ⟨stood there ∼ his mouth open⟩ **14** : at the time of : right after ⟨∼ that we left⟩ **15** ♦ : in spite of : DESPITE ⟨∼ all her cleverness, she failed⟩ **16** : in the direction of ⟨swim ∼ the tide⟩

♦ [10a] because of, due to, owing to, through — more at BECAUSE OF ♦ [15] despite, notwithstanding, regardless of — more at DESPITE

with·al \wi-'thȯl, -'thȯl\ *adv* **1** ♦ : together with this : BESIDES **2** ♦ : on the other hand : NEVERTHELESS

♦ [1] additionally, again, also, besides, further, furthermore, likewise, more, moreover, then, too, yet ♦ [2] but, howbeit, however, nevertheless, nonetheless, notwithstanding, still, though, yet — more at HOWEVER

with·draw \with-'drȯ, with-\ *vb* **-drew** \-'drü\; **-drawn** \-'drȯn\; **-draw·ing** \-'drȯ-iŋ\ **1** ♦ : to take back or away : REMOVE **2** ♦ : to call back (as from consideration); *also* : RETRACT **3** : to go away : RETREAT, LEAVE **4** : to terminate one's participation in or use of something **5** ♦ : to remove or draw out from a place or position

♦ [1] clear, draw, remove — more at REMOVE ♦ [2] abjure, cancel, renounce, retract, take back, unsay — more at ABJURE ♦ [5] back, fall back, recede, retire, retreat — more at RETREAT

with·draw·al \-'drȯ-əl\ *n* **1** ♦ : an act or instance of withdrawing **2** : the discontinuance of the use or administration of a drug and esp. an addicting drug; *also* : the period following such discontinuance marked by often painful physiological and psychological symptoms **3** : a pathological retreat from the real world (as in some schizophrenic states)

♦ retreat, revulsion — more at RETREAT

with·drawn \with-'drȯn\ *adj* **1** : ISOLATED, SECLUDED **2** ♦ : socially detached and unresponsive

♦ bashful, coy, demure, diffident, introverted, modest, retiring, sheepish, shy — more at SHY

withe \'with\ *n* : a slender flexible twig or branch

with·er \'wi-thər\ *vb* **1** : to shrivel from or as if from loss of bodily moisture and esp. sap **2** : to lose or cause to lose vitality, force, or freshness **3** : to cause to feel shriveled ⟨~ed him with a glance⟩

with·ers \'wi-thərz\ *n pl* : the ridge between the shoulder bones of a horse; *also* : the corresponding part in other 4-footed animals

with·hold \with-'hōld, with-\ *vb* **-held** \-'held\; **-hold·ing** **1 a** : to hold back **b** ♦ : keep in one's possession or control : RETAIN **2** ♦ : to refrain from granting, giving, or allowing ⟨~ permission⟩ ⟨~ names⟩

♦ [1b] hang on, hold, keep, reserve, retain — more at KEEP ♦ [2] decline, deny, disallow, refuse, reject — more at DENY

withholding tax *n* : a tax on income withheld at the source

¹with·in \wi-'thin, -'thin\ *adv* **1** : in or into the interior : INSIDE **2** : inside oneself : INWARDLY

²within *prep* **1** : inside the limits or influence of ⟨~ call⟩ **2** : in the limits or compass of ⟨~ a mile⟩ **3** : in or to the inner part of ⟨~ the room⟩

with-it \'wi-thət, -thət\ *adj* : socially or culturally up-to-date

¹with·out \wi-'thaůt, -'thaůt\ *prep* **1** : at, to, or on the outside of : OUTSIDE **2** ♦ : not having : LACKING ⟨~ hope⟩; *also* : not accompanied by or showing ⟨spoke ~ thinking⟩

♦ lacking, minus, sans, wanting

²without *adv* **1** : on the outside : EXTERNALLY **2** : with something lacking or absent ⟨has learned to do ~⟩

with·stand \with-'stand, with-\ *vb* **-stood** \-'stůd\; **-stand·ing** ♦ : to stand against : RESIST; *esp* : to oppose (as an attack) successfully

♦ buck, defy, fight, oppose, repel, resist — more at RESIST

wit·less \'wit-ləs\ *adj* ♦ : lacking wit or understanding — **wit·less·ly** *adv*

♦ absurd, asinine, balmy, cockeyed, crazy, foolish, harebrained, insane, mad, nonsensical, nutty, preposterous, sappy, screwball, senseless, silly, stupid, unwise, wacky, zany — more at FOOLISH

wit·less·ness *n* : the quality or state of being witless

¹wit·ness \'wit-nəs\ *n* [ME *witnesse*, fr. OE *witnes* knowledge, testimony, witness, fr. *wit* mind, intelligence] **1** : TESTIMONY ⟨bear ~ to the fact⟩ **2** : one that gives evidence; *esp* : one who testifies in a cause or before a court **3** : one present at a transaction so as to be able to testify that it has taken place **4** : one who has personal knowledge or experience of something **5** ♦ : something serving as evidence or proof

♦ attestation, confirmation, corroboration, documentation, evidence, proof, substantiation, testament, testimony, validation — more at PROOF

²witness *vb* **1** ♦ : to furnish evidence or proof such as to establish : TESTIFY **2** : to act as legal witness of **3** : to furnish proof of : BETOKEN **4** ♦ : to see or know by reason of personal presence : to be a witness of **5** : to be the scene of ⟨this region has ~ed many wars⟩

♦ [1] attest, authenticate, avouch, certify, testify, vouch — more at CERTIFY ♦ [4] behold, descry, discern, distinguish, espy, eye, look, note, notice, observe,

perceive, regard, remark, see, sight, spy, view — more at SEE

wit·ti·cism \'wi-tə-ˌsi-zəm\ *n* ♦ : a witty saying or phrase

♦ crack, gag, jest, joke, laugh, pleasantry, quip, sally, waggery, wisecrack — more at JOKE

wit·ting \'wi-tiŋ\ *adj* **1** ♦ : cognizant or aware of something **2** : done knowingly

♦ alive, aware, cognizant, conscious, mindful, sensible, sentient — more at CONSCIOUS

wit·ting·ly *adv* : with knowledge or awareness of what one is doing

wit·ty \'wi-tē\ *adj* **wit·ti·er**; **-est** ♦ : marked by or full of wit ⟨a ~ writer⟩ ⟨a ~ remark⟩ — **wit·ti·ly** \-tə-lē\ *adv* — **wit·ti·ness** \-tē-nəs\ *n*

♦ clever, facetious, humorous, jocular, smart; *also* cerebral, highbrow, intellectual; bantering, frivolous, joking, joshing, teasing; antic, comic, comical, droll, farcical, funny, hysterical, laughable, ludicrous, ridiculous, risible, riotous, rollicking, screaming, uproarious; amusing, diverting, entertaining; mischievous, playful, jocose, jocund, jolly, jovial, laughing, merry, mirthful, sunny; scintillating, sparkling; flip, flippant, pert; whimsical

wive \'wīv\ *vb* **wived**; **wiv·ing** : to take a wife

wives *pl of* WIFE

wiz·ard \'wi-zərd\ *n* [ME *wysard* wise man, fr. *wys* wise] **1** ♦ : one skilled in the knowledge and practice of the magic arts : MAGICIAN **2** ♦ : a very clever or skillful person ⟨a ~ at chess⟩

♦ [1] conjurer, enchanter, magician, necromancer, sorcerer, voodoo, witch — more at MAGICIAN ♦ [2] ace, adept, artist, authority, crackerjack, expert, maestro, master, scholar, shark, virtuoso, whiz — more at EXPERT ♦ [2] brain, genius, intellect, thinker — more at GENIUS

wiz·ard·ry \'wi-zər-drē\ *n, pl* **-ries** **1** ♦ : magic skill : SORCERY **2** : great skill or cleverness in an activity

♦ bewitchment, enchantment, magic, necromancy, sorcery, witchcraft — more at MAGIC

wiz·en \'wiz-ᵊn, 'wēz-\ *vb* : to become or cause to become dry, shrunken, or wrinkled

wk *abbr* **1** week **2** work

WL *abbr* wavelength

wmk *abbr* watermark

WNW *abbr* west-northwest

WO *abbr* warrant officer

w/o *abbr* without

woad \'wōd\ *n* : a European herb related to the mustards; *also* : a blue dyestuff made from its leaves

wob·ble \'wä-bəl\ *vb* **wob·bled**; **wob·bling** **1** ♦ : to move or cause to move with an irregular rocking or side-to-side motion **2** ♦ : to shake unsteadily **3** ♦ : to show indecision : WAVER — **wobble** *n*

♦ [1] falter, rock, seesaw, sway, teeter, totter, waver — more at TEETER ♦ [2] agitate, convulse, jolt, jounce, quake, quiver, shake, shudder, vibrate — more at SHAKE ♦ [3] falter, hang back, hesitate, shilly-shally, stagger, teeter, vacillate, waver — more at HESITATE

wob·bly \-bə-lē\ *adj* ♦ : inclined to shake, sway, or quaver unsteadily

♦ shaky, tremulous — more at SHAKY

woe \'wō\ *n* **1** ♦ : deep suffering from misfortune, affliction, or grief **2** : TROUBLE, MISFORTUNE ⟨economic ~s⟩

♦ affliction, agony, anguish, distress, misery, pain, torment, torture, tribulation — more at DISTRESS ♦ dolor, grief, heartache, sorrow — more at SORROW

woe·be·gone \'wō-bi-ˌgȯn\ *adj* : exhibiting woe, sorrow, or misery ⟨~ faces⟩; *also* : being in a sorry condition

♦ bad, blue, dejected, depressed, despondent, disconsolate, down, downcast, droopy, forlorn, low, melancholy, miserable, mournful, sad, sorrowful, sorry, unhappy, woeful, wretched — more at SAD

woe·ful also **wo·ful** \'wō-fəl\ adj **1** ♦ : full of woe : distressed with grief or sadness **2** : involving, bringing, or relating to woe **3** ♦ : to be regretted or lamented : DEPLORABLE

♦ [1] anguished, dolorous, lamentable, mournful, plaintive, sad, sorrowful, sorry — more at SORROWFUL
♦ [3] deplorable, distressful, grievous, heartbreaking, lamentable, regrettable, unfortunate — more at RE-GRETTABLE

woe·ful·ly adv ♦ : in a woeful manner

♦ agonizingly, bitterly, grievously, hard, hardly, sadly, sorrowfully, unhappily, wretchedly — more at HARD

wok \'wäk\ n [Chin (Guangzhou & Hong Kong dial.) wohk] : a bowl-shaped cooking utensil used esp. in stir-frying

¹**woke** past and past part of WAKE
²**woke** \'wōk\ adj **wok·er; wok·est** slang : aware of and actively attentive to important facts and issues (esp. issues of racial and social justice)

woken past part of WAKE

wold \'wōld\ n : an upland plain or stretch of rolling land without woods

¹**wolf** \'wu̇lf\ n, pl **wolves** \'wu̇lvz\ **1** : any of several large erect-eared bushy-tailed doglike predatory mammals that live and hunt in packs; esp : GRAY WOLF **2** : a fierce or destructive person — **wolf·ish** adj
²**wolf** vb ♦ : to eat greedily : DEVOUR

♦ bolt, devour, gobble, gorge, gormandize, gulp, scarf, scoff — more at GOBBLE

wolf·hound \-,hau̇nd\ n : any of several large dogs orig. used in hunting wolves

wol·fram \'wu̇l-frəm\ n : TUNGSTEN

wol·ver·ine \,wu̇l-və-'rēn\ n, pl **wolverines** also **wolverine** : a dark shaggy-coated flesh-eating mammal of northern forests and associated tundra that is related to the weasels

wom·an \'wu̇-mən\ n, pl **wom·en** \'wi-mən\ [ME, fr. OE wīfman, fr. wīf woman, wife + man human being, man] **1** ♦ : an adult female person **2** : WOMANKIND **3** : feminine nature : WOMANLINESS **4** : an adult female servant

♦ dame, female, gentlewoman, lady

wom·an·hood \'wu̇-mən-,hu̇d\ n **1** : the state of being a woman **2** : qualities associated with women **3** : WOMEN, WOMANKIND

wom·an·ish \'wu̇-mə-nish\ adj **1** : associated with or characteristic of women rather than men **2** : suggestive of a weak character : EFFEMINATE ⟨a ~ voice⟩

wom·an·ize \'wu̇-mə-,nīz\ vb : to pursue casual sexual relationships with numerous women — **wom·an·iz·er** n

wom·an·kind \'wu̇-mən-,kīnd\ n : female human beings : women esp. as distinguished from men

wom·an·like \-,līk\ adj : WOMANLY

wom·an·ly \-lē\ adj **1** ♦ : having qualities generally associated with a woman **2** : appropriate in character to a woman — **wom·an·li·ness** \-lē-nəs\ n

♦ female, feminine — more at FEMININE

woman suffrage n : possession and exercise of suffrage by women

womb \'wüm\ n **1** : UTERUS **2** : a place where something is generated

wom·bat \'wäm-,bat\ n : any of several stocky burrowing Australian marsupials that resemble small bears

wom·en·folk \'wi-mən-,fōk\ also **wom·en·folks** \-,fōks\ n pl : WOMEN

won \'wən\ past and past part of WIN

¹**won·der** \'wən-dər\ n **1** ♦ : a cause of astonishment or surprise : MARVEL **2** : the quality of exciting wonder ⟨the charm and ~ of the scene⟩ **3** ♦ : a feeling (as of awed astonishment or uncertainty) aroused by something extraordinary or affecting

♦ [1] caution, flash, marvel, miracle, phenomenon, portent, prodigy, sensation; also curiosity, sight, spectacle; apparition, appearance ♦ [3] admiration, amazement, astonishment, awe, wonderment; also dread; fear; respect, reverence, veneration; curiosity, interest; shock, surprise; disbelief, incomprehension, incredulity; bewitchment,

captivation, enchantment, fascination; animation, enlightenment, excitement, invigoration, stimulation; absorption, engagement, immersion, involvement

²**wonder** vb **1** : to feel surprise or amazement **2** : to feel curiosity or doubt

wonder drug n : MIRACLE DRUG

won·der·ful \'wən-dər-fəl\ adj **1** ♦ : exciting wonder : MARVELOUS **2** : unusually good : ADMIRABLE — **won·der·ful·ly** \-f(ə-)lē\ adv — **won·der·ful·ness** n

♦ amazing, astonishing, astounding, awesome, awful, eye-opening, fabulous, marvelous, miraculous, portentous, prodigious, stunning, stupendous, sublime, surprising — more at MARVELOUS

won·der·land \-,land, -lənd\ n **1** : an imaginary place of delicate beauty or magical charm **2** : a place that excites admiration or wonder

won·der·ment \-mənt\ n **1** ♦ : a state or feeling of wonder : ASTONISHMENT **2** : a cause of or occasion for wonder **3** : curiosity about something

♦ admiration, amazement, astonishment, awe, wonder — more at WONDER

won·drous \'wən-drəs\ adj : exciting wonder or surprise : MARVELOUS, WONDERFUL — **won·drous·ly** adv — **won·drous·ness** n

wonk \'wäŋk, 'wȯŋk\ n : one who works in a specialized usu. intellectual field ⟨computer ~s⟩

¹**wont** \'wȯnt, 'wōnt\ adj [ME woned, wont, fr. pp. of wonen to dwell, be used to, fr. OE wunian] **1** ♦ : in the habit or custom : ACCUSTOMED ⟨as we are ~ to do⟩ **2** : INCLINED, APT

♦ accustomed, given, used — more at ACCUSTOMED

²**wont** n ♦ : a usage or practice that is common : CUSTOM ⟨according to her ~⟩

♦ custom, fashion, habit, pattern, practice, trick, way — more at HABIT

won't \'wōnt\ : will not

wont·ed \'wȯn-təd, 'wōn-\ adj : ACCUSTOMED, CUSTOMARY ⟨his ~ courtesy⟩

woo \'wü\ vb **1** : to try to gain the love of : COURT **2** : SOLICIT, ENTREAT **3** ♦ : to try to gain or bring about ⟨~ public favor⟩

♦ ask, court — more at COURT

¹**wood** \'wu̇d\ n **1** : a dense growth of trees usu. larger than a grove and smaller than a forest — often used in pl. **2** : a hard fibrous substance that is basically xylem and forms the bulk of trees and shrubs beneath the bark; also : this material fit or prepared for some use (as burning or building) **3** : something made of wood **4** : the trunks or large branches of trees sawed or prepared for commercial use

²**wood** adj **1** : WOODEN **2** : suitable for holding, cutting, or working with wood **3** or **woods** \'wu̇dz\ : living or growing in woods

³**wood** vb **1** : to supply or load with wood esp. for fuel **2** : to cover with a growth of trees

wood alcohol n : METHANOL

wood·bine \'wu̇d-,bīn\ n : any of several honeysuckles; also : VIRGINIA CREEPER

wood·block \-,bläk\ n : WOODCUT

wood·chop·per \-,chä-pər\ n : one engaged esp. in chopping down trees

wood·chuck \-,chək\ n : a thickset grizzled marmot of Alaska, Canada, and the northeastern U.S.

wood·cock \'wu̇d-,käk\ n, pl **woodcocks** : a brown eastern No. American game bird with a short neck and long bill that is related to the snipe; also : a related and similar Old World bird

wood·craft \-,kraft\ n **1** : skill and practice in matters relating to the woods and esp. in how to take care of oneself in them **2** : skill in shaping or constructing articles from wood

wood·cut \-,kət\ n **1** : a relief printing surface engraved on a block of wood **2** : a print from a woodcut

wood·cut·ter \-ˌkə-tər\ *n* : a person who cuts wood

wood duck *n* : a showy crested American duck of which the male has iridescent multicolored plumage

wood·ed \'wu̇-dəd\ *adj* : covered with woods or trees ⟨∼ slopes⟩

wood·en \'wu̇d-ᵊn\ *adj* **1** : made of wood **2** ♦ : lacking in ease, grace, or flexibility : awkwardly stiff ⟨∼ acting⟩ — **wood·en·ly** *adv* — **wood·en·ness** *n*

♦ awkward, clumsy, gauche, graceless, inelegant, stiff, stilted, uncomfortable, uneasy, ungraceful — more at AWKWARD

wood·en·ware \'wu̇d-ᵊn-ˌwar\ *n* : articles made of wood for domestic use

wood·land \'wu̇d-lənd, -ˌland\ *n* ♦ : land covered with trees : FOREST — **woodland** *adj*

♦ forest, timberland — more at FOREST

wood·lot \'wu̇d-ˌlät\ *n* : a restricted area of woodland usu. privately kept to meet fuel and timber needs

wood louse *n* : any of various small flat crustaceans that live esp. in ground litter and under stones and bark

wood·man \'wu̇d-mən\ *n* : WOODSMAN

wood·note \-ˌnōt\ *n* : verbal expression that is natural and artless

wood nymph *n* : a nymph living in the woods

wood·peck·er \'wu̇d-ˌpe-kər\ *n* : any of numerous usu. brightly marked climbing birds with stiff spiny tail feathers and a chisellike bill used to drill into trees for insects

wood·pile \-ˌpīl\ *n* : a pile of wood and esp. firewood

wood·shed \-ˌshed\ *n* : a shed for storing wood and esp. firewood

woods·man \'wu̇dz-mən\ *n* : a person who frequents or works in the woods; *esp* : one skilled in woodcraft

woodsy \'wu̇d-zē\ *adj* **woods·i·er; -est** : relating to or suggestive of woods

wood·wind \'wu̇d-ˌwind\ *n* : one of a group of wind instruments including flutes, clarinets, oboes, bassoons, and sometimes saxophones

wood·work \-ˌwərk\ *n* : work made of wood; *esp* : interior fittings (as moldings or stairways) of wood

woody \'wu̇-dē\ *adj* **wood·i·er; -est 1** : abounding or overgrown with woods **2** : of or containing wood or wood fibers **3** : characteristic or suggestive of wood ⟨a ∼ flavor⟩ — **wood·i·ness** \'wu̇-dē-nəs\ *n*

woo·er *n* ♦ : one that woos : one that courts a woman or seeks to marry her

♦ gallant, suitor, swain — more at SUITOR

woof \'wu̇f\ *n* [alter. of ME *oof*, fr. OE *ōwef*, fr. *ō-* (fr. *on* on) + *wefan* to weave] **1** : WEFT 1 **2** : a woven fabric; *also* : its texture

woof·er \'wu̇-fər\ *n* : a loudspeaker that reproduces sounds of low pitch

wool \'wu̇l\ *n* **1** ♦ : the soft wavy or curly hair of some mammals and esp. the domestic sheep; *also* : something (as a textile or garment) made of wool **2** : material that resembles a mass of wool — **wooled** \'wu̇ld\ *adj*

♦ coat, fleece, fur, hair, pelage, pile

¹**wool·en** *or* **wool·len** \'wu̇-lən\ *adj* **1** : made of wool **2** : of or relating to the manufacture or sale of woolen products ⟨∼ mills⟩

²**woolen** *or* **woollen** *n* **1** : a fabric made of wool **2** : garments of woolen fabric — usu. used in pl.

wool·gath·er·ing \-ˌga-thə-riŋ\ *n* ♦ : idle daydreaming

♦ reverie, study, trance — more at REVERIE

¹**wool·ly** *also* **wooly** \'wu̇-lē\ *adj* **wool·li·er; -est 1** : of, relating to, or bearing wool **2 a** ♦ : consisting of or resembling wool **b** ♦ : thickly covered with long hair or fuzz **3** : mentally confused ⟨∼ thinking⟩ **4** : marked by a lack of order or restraint ⟨the wild and ∼ West⟩

♦ [2a, 2b] furry, fuzzy, hairy, rough, shaggy — more at HAIRY

²**wool·ly** *also* **wool·ie** *or* **wooly** \'wu̇-lē\ *n, pl* **wool·lies** : a

garment made from wool; *esp* : underclothing of knitted wool — usu. used in pl.

woolly bear *n* : any of numerous very hairy moth caterpillars

woolly mammoth *n* : a heavy-coated mammoth formerly inhabiting colder parts of the northern hemisphere

woo·zy \'wü-zē\ *adj* **woo·zi·er; -est 1** : BEFUDDLED **2** : somewhat dizzy, nauseated, or weak ⟨∼ from fatigue⟩ — **woo·zi·ness** \'wü-zē-nəs\ *n*

¹**word** \'wərd\ *n* **1** : something that is said; *esp* : a brief remark **2** ♦ : a speech sound or series of speech sounds that communicates a meaning; *also* : a graphic representation of such a sound or series of sounds **3** ♦ : an instruction, authorization, or direction for action or behavior : COMMAND **4** *often cap* : the 2d person of the Trinity; *also* : GOSPEL **5** ♦ : a report of a recent event or of new information : NEWS, INFORMATION **6** ♦ : a declaration that one will do or refrain from doing something : PROMISE **7** *pl* : QUARREL, DISPUTE **8** : a verbal signal : PASSWORD

♦ [2] expression, term ♦ [3] behest, charge, command, commandment, decree, dictate, direction, directive, edict, instruction, order — more at COMMAND ♦ [5] information, intelligence, item, news, story, tidings — more at NEWS ♦ [6] oath, pledge, promise, troth, vow — more at PROMISE

²**word** *vb* ♦ : to express in words : PHRASE

♦ articulate, clothe, couch, express, formulate, phrase, put, say, state — more at PHRASE

word·age \'wər-dij\ *n* **1** : WORDS **2** : number of words **3** : WORDING

word·book \'wərd-ˌbu̇k\ *n* : a book containing a collection of words : DICTIONARY

word for word *adv* ♦ : in the exact words : VERBATIM

♦ directly, exactly, verbatim — more at VERBATIM

word·i·ness \-dē-nəs\ *n* ♦ : the quality or state of being wordy

♦ circumlocution, prolixity, redundancy, verbiage — more at VERBIAGE

word·ing \'wər-diŋ\ *n* ♦ : verbal expression : PHRASEOLOGY

♦ diction, language, phraseology, phrasing; *also* expression, formulation, locution; enunciation, phrase, speech, style, utterance, voice

word·less *adj* **1** : not expressed or not expressible in words **2** ♦ : involving no use of words

♦ implicit, tacit, unexpressed, unspoken, unvoiced — more at IMPLICIT

word of mouth : oral communication

word·play \'wərd-ˌplā\ *n* : playful use of words

word processing *n* : the production of typewritten documents with automated and usu. computerized text-editing equipment — **word process** *vb*

word processor *n* : a keyboard-operated terminal for use in word processing; *also* : software to perform word processing

wordy \'wər-dē\ *adj* **word·i·er; -est** ♦ : using or having too many words : VERBOSE ⟨∼ sentences⟩

♦ circuitous, diffuse, long-winded, prolix, rambling, verbose, windy; *also* chatty, communicative, conversational, gabby, garrulous, loquacious, talkative, voluble; redundant, repetitious, tautological; embellished, embroidered; bombastic, grandiloquent, highfalutin **Ant** compact, concise, crisp, pithy, succinct, terse

wore *past of* WEAR

¹**work** \'wərk\ *n* **1** ♦ : activity in which one exerts strength or faculties to do or perform something : LABOR **2 a** : something that needs to be done or accomplished : TASK, JOB ⟨have ∼ to do⟩ **b** ♦ : the labor, task, or duty that affords one his accustomed means of livelihood : EMPLOYMENT ⟨out of ∼⟩ **3** : the energy used when a force is applied over a given distance **4** ♦ : something produced or accomplished by effort, exertion, or ex-

ercise of skill **5** : a fortified structure **6** *pl* : engineering structures **7** *pl* ♦ : a place where industrial labor is done : FACTORY **8** *pl* : the moving parts of a mechanism **9** ♦ : something produced by mental effort or physical labor; *esp* : an artistic production (as a book or needlework) **10** : WORKMANSHIP ⟨careless ~⟩ **11** : material in the process of manufacture **12** *pl* : everything possessed, available, or belonging ⟨the whole ~s went overboard⟩; *also* : drastic treatment ⟨gave him the ~s⟩ — **in the works** : in process of preparation

♦ [1] effort, exertion, expenditure, labor (*or* labour), pains, sweat, trouble, while — more at EFFORT ♦ [2b] calling, employment, line, occupation, profession, trade, vocation — more at OCCUPATION ♦ [4, 9] affair, fruit, handiwork, output, produce, product, thing, yield — more at PRODUCT ♦ *usu* works [7] factory, mill, plant, shop, workshop — more at FACTORY ♦ [9] composition, opus, piece — more at COMPOSITION

²**work** *adj* **1** : used for work ⟨~ elephants⟩ **2** : suitable or styled for wear while working ⟨~ clothes⟩
³**work** *vb* **worked** \'wərkt\ *or* **wrought** \'rot\; **work·ing** **1** ♦ : to bring to pass : EFFECT **2** : to fashion or create a useful or desired product through labor or exertion **3** : to prepare for use (as by kneading) **4** : to bring into a desired form by a manufacturing process ⟨~ cold steel⟩ **5** ♦ : to set or keep in operation ⟨a pump ~ed by hand⟩ **6** ♦ : to solve by reasoning or calculation ⟨~ out a problem⟩ **7** : to cause to toil or labor ⟨~ed the team hard⟩; *also* : to make use of ⟨~ a mine⟩ **8** : to pay for with labor or service ⟨~ off a debt⟩ **9** : to bring or get into some position or condition by stages ⟨the stream ~ed itself clear⟩ **10** : CONTRIVE, ARRANGE ⟨~ it so you can leave early⟩ **11** : to practice trickery or cajolery on ⟨~ed the management for a free ticket⟩ **12** : EXCITE, PROVOKE ⟨~ed himself into a rage⟩ **13** ♦ : to exert oneself physically or mentally; *esp* : to perform work regularly for wages **14** : to function according to plan or design **15** : to produce a desired effect : SUCCEED ⟨the plan ~ed⟩ **16** : to make way slowly and with difficulty ⟨he ~ed forward through the crowd⟩ **17** : to permit of being worked ⟨this wood ~s easily⟩ **18** : to be in restless motion; *also* : FERMENT 1 — **work on** **1** : AFFECT **2** : to try to influence or persuade — **work upon** : to have effect upon : operate on : INFLUENCE

♦ [1] bring about, cause, create, effect, effectuate, generate, induce, make, produce, prompt, result, yield — more at EFFECT ♦ [5] handle, operate, run — more at OPERATE ♦ [5] actuate, drive, impel, move, propel ♦ [6] answer, break, crack, dope, figure out, puzzle, resolve, riddle, solve, unravel, work out — more at SOLVE ♦ [13] drudge, endeavor, fag, grub, hustle, labor, peg, plod, plug, slave, slog, strain, strive, struggle, sweat, toil, travail — more at LABOR

work·able \'wər-kə-bəl\ *adj* **1** : capable of being worked **2** ♦ : capable of being put into successful operation : PRACTICABLE — **work·able·ness** *n*

♦ achievable, attainable, doable, feasible, possible, practicable, realizable, viable — more at POSSIBLE

work·a·day \'wər-kə-,dā\ *adj* **1** ♦ : relating to or suited for working days as distinguished from special occasions **2** ♦ : being ordinary and unexceptionable

♦ [1] casual, everyday, informal — more at CASUAL ♦ [2] average, common, commonplace, everyday, normal, ordinary, prosaic, routine, run-of-the-mill, standard, unexceptional, unremarkable, usual — more at ORDINARY

work·a·hol·ic \,wər-kə-'hó-lik, -'hä-\ *n* : a compulsive worker
work·bench \-,bench\ *n* : a bench on which work esp. of mechanics, machinists, and carpenters is performed
work·book \-,buk\ *n* **1** : a worker's manual **2** : a student's book of problems to be answered directly on the pages
work·day \'wərk-,dā\ *n* **1** : a day on which work is done

as distinguished from a day off **2** : the period of time in a day when work is performed
work·er \'wər-kər\ *n* **1** ♦ : one that works; *esp* : a person who works for wages **2** : any of the sexually undeveloped individuals of a colony of social insects (as bees, ants, or termites) that perform the work of the community

♦ drudge, fag, peon, slave, toiler — more at SLAVE ♦ employee, hand, hireling, jobholder — more at EMPLOYEE

workers' compensation *n* : a system of insurance that reimburses an employer for damages paid to an employee who was injured while working
work ethic *n* : belief in work as a moral good
work farm *n* : a farm on which persons guilty of minor law violations are confined
work·force \'wərk-,fórs\ *n* **1** ♦ : the workers engaged in a specific activity or enterprise **2** ♦ : the number of workers potentially available for any purpose

♦ [1, 2] force, help, manpower, personnel, pool, staff — more at FORCE

work·horse \'wərk-,hórs\ *n* **1** : a horse used for hard work **2** : a person who does most of the work of a group task **3** : something that is useful, durable, or dependable
work·house \-,haús\ *n* **1** *Brit* : POORHOUSE **2** : a house of correction for persons guilty of minor law violations
work in *vb* **1** : to insert or cause to penetrate by repeated or continued effort **2** ♦ : to interpose or insinuate gradually or unobtrusively

♦ infiltrate, insinuate, slip, sneak, worm — more at INSINUATE

¹**work·ing** \'wər-kiŋ\ *n* **1** : manner of functioning — usu. used in pl. **2** *pl* : an excavation made in mining or tunneling
²**working** *adj* **1** : engaged in work ⟨a ~ journalist⟩ **2** : adequate to allow work to be done ⟨a ~ majority⟩ ⟨a ~ knowledge of French⟩ **3** ♦ : adopted or assumed to help further work or activity ⟨a ~ draft⟩ **4** : spent at work ⟨~ life⟩

♦ applicable, functional, practicable, practical, serviceable, usable, useful, workable — more at PRACTICAL

work·ing·man \'wər-kiŋ-,man\ *n* : WORKER 1
work·man \'wərk-mən\ *n* **1** : WORKER 1 **2** : ARTISAN, CRAFTSMAN
work·man·like \-,līk\ *adj* : worthy of a good workman : SKILLFUL
work·man·ship \-,ship\ *n* : the art or skill of a workman : CRAFTSMANSHIP; *also* : the quality of a piece of work ⟨a vase of exquisite ~⟩
¹**work·out** \'wərk-,aút\ *n* **1** ♦ : a practice or exercise to test or improve one's fitness, ability, or performance **2** : a test or trial to determine ability or capacity or suitability

♦ drill, exercise, practice, routine, training — more at EXERCISE

work out *vb* **1 a** ♦ : to bring about esp. by resolving difficulties **b** ♦ : to create or cause by labor and exertion **2** : to expand, develop, or perfect esp. by analysis or reasoning : DEVELOP, ELABORATE **3** ♦ : to prove effective, practicable, or suitable ⟨I think this plan will *work out*⟩ **4 a** : to amount to a total or calculated figure — used with *at* **b** ♦ : to solve (as a problem) by a process of reasoning or calculation **5** : to engage in a workout

♦ [1a, b] build, carve, forge, grind, hammer ♦ [3] click, deliver, go over, pan out, succeed — more at SUCCEED ♦ [4b] calculate, compute, figure, reckon — more at CALCULATE ♦ [4b] answer, break, crack, dope, figure out, puzzle, resolve, riddle, solve, unravel, work — more at SOLVE

work·place \'wərk-,plās\ *n* : a place (as an office) where work is done
work·room \'wərk-,rüm, -,rúm\ *n* : a room used for work
work·shop \-,shäp\ *n* **1** ♦ : a shop where manufacturing or handicrafts are carried on **2** : a seminar emphasizing exchange of ideas and practical methods

♦ factory, mill, plant, shop, works — more at FACTORY

work·sta·tion \-ˌstā-shən\ *n* : an area with equipment for the performance of a specialized task; *also* : a personal computer usu. connected to a computer network

world \'wərld\ *n* [ME, fr. OE *woruld* human existence, this world, age, fr. a prehistoric compound whose first constituent is represented by OE *wer* man and whose second constituent is akin to OE *eald* old] **1** ♦ : the earth with its inhabitants and all things upon it **2** ♦ : people in general **3** : human affairs ⟨withdraw from the ~⟩ **4** ♦ : the entire system of created things : UNIVERSE, CREATION **5** : a state of existence : scene of life and action ⟨the ~ of the future⟩ **6** : a distinctive class of persons or their sphere of interest ⟨the musical ~⟩ **7** : a part or section of the earth or its inhabitants by itself **8** : a great number or quantity ⟨a ~ of troubles⟩ **9** : a celestial body

♦ [1] earth, planet — more at EARTH ♦ [2] folks, humanity, humankind, people, persons, public, society — more at PEOPLE ♦ [4] cosmos, creation, macrocosm, nature, universe — more at UNIVERSE

world–beat·er \-ˌbē-tər\ *n* : one that excels all others of its kind : CHAMPION

world–class *adj* : of the highest caliber in the world ⟨a ~ athlete⟩

world·ling \-liŋ\ *n* : a person absorbed in the concerns of the present world

world·ly \-lē\ *adj* **1** ♦ : of, relating to, or devoted to this world and its pursuits rather than to religion or spiritual affairs ⟨~ pleasures⟩ **2** : experienced or knowledgeable in things and ways of this world : WORLDLY-WISE — **world·li·ness** \-lē-nəs\ *n*

♦ carnal, earthly, fleshly, material, mundane, temporal, terrestrial — more at EARTHLY

world·ly–wise \-ˌwīz\ *adj* ♦ : possessing a practical and often shrewd understanding of human affairs

♦ cosmopolitan, smart, sophisticated, worldly; *also* suave, urbane; civilized, cultivated, cultured, polished, refined; experienced, knowing, practiced, schooled, seasoned; bored, cynical, jaded, skeptical; down-to-earth, pragmatic, realistic, sober *Ant* ingenuous, innocent, naive, unsophisticated, unworldly, wide-eyed

world·wide \'wərld-'wīd\ *adj* : extended throughout the entire world ⟨attracted ~ attention⟩ — **worldwide** *adv*

World Wide Web *n* : a part of the Internet usu. accessed through a browser and containing files connected by hyperlinks

¹worm \'wərm\ *n* **1** : any of various small long usu. naked and soft-bodied round or flat invertebrate animals (as an earthworm, nematode, tapeworm, or maggot) **2** : a human being who is an object of contempt, loathing, or pity : WRETCH **3** : something that inwardly torments or devours **4** *pl* : infestation with or disease caused by parasitic worms **5** : a spiral or wormlike thing (as the thread of a screw) — **wormy** *adj*

²worm *vb* **1** ♦ : to move or cause to move or proceed slowly and deviously or as if in the manner of a worm **2** ♦ : to insinuate or introduce (oneself) by devious or subtle means **3** : to obtain or extract by artful or insidious pleading, asking, or persuading ⟨~ed the truth out of him⟩ **4** : to treat (an animal) with a drug to destroy or expel parasitic worms

♦ [1] crawl, creep, grovel, slither, snake — more at CRAWL ♦ [2] infiltrate, insinuate, slip, sneak, work in — more at INSINUATE

worm–eat·en \'wərm-ˌēt-ᵊn\ *adj* : eaten or burrowed by worms

worm gear *n* : a mechanical linkage consisting of a short rotating screw whose threads mesh with the teeth of a gear wheel

worm·hole \'wərm-ˌhōl\ *n* : a hole or passage burrowed by a worm

worm·wood \-ˌwud\ *n* **1** : any of a genus of aromatic woody plants (as a sagebrush); *esp* : one of Europe used in absinthe **2** : something bitter or grievous : BITTERNESS

worn *past part of* WEAR

worn–out \'wōrn-'aut\ *adj* ♦ : damaged, used up, or exhausted by or as if by wear

♦ beat, bushed, dead, drained, effete, jaded, limp, prostrate, spent, tired, weary — more at WEARY ♦ ragged, ratty, seedy, shabby, tattered, threadbare — more at RAGGED

wor·ried *adj* ♦ : mentally troubled or concerned

♦ aflutter, anxious, edgy, jittery, jumpy, nervous, nervy, perturbed, tense, troubled, uneasy, upset — more at NERVOUS

wor·ri·some \'wər-ē-səm\ *adj* **1** ♦ : causing distress or worry **2** : inclined to worry or fret

♦ troublesome, unsettling, upsetting — more at TROUBLESOME

¹wor·ry \'wər-ē\ *vb* **wor·ried**; **wor·ry·ing** **1** : to shake and mangle with the teeth ⟨a terrier ~ing a rat⟩ **2** ♦ : to make anxious or upset ⟨her poor health *worries* me⟩ **3** ♦ : to feel or express great care or anxiety : FRET — **wor·ri·er** *n*

♦ [2] agitate, bother, concern, discompose, disquiet, distress, disturb, exercise, freak, perturb, undo, unhinge, unsettle, upset ♦ [3] bother, fear, fret, stew, sweat, trouble; *also* agonize; long, pine, yearn; chafe; despair

²worry *n, pl* **worries** **1** ♦ : mental distress or agitation resulting from concern usu. for something impending or anticipated : ANXIETY **2** : a cause of anxiety : TROUBLE

♦ agitation, anxiety, apprehension, care, concern, disquiet, nervousness, perturbation, uneasiness — more at ANXIETY

wor·ry·wart \'wər-ē-ˌwort\ *n* : one who is inclined to worry unduly

¹worse \'wərs\ *adj, comparative of* BAD *or of* ILL **1** : bad or evil in a greater degree : less good **2** : more unfavorable, unpleasant, or painful; *also* : SICKER

²worse *n* **1** : one that is worse **2** : a greater degree of ill or badness ⟨a turn for the ~⟩

³worse *adv, comparative of* BAD *or of* ILL : in a worse manner : to a worse extent or degree

wors·en \'wərs-ᵊn\ *vb* ♦ : to make or become worse

♦ decay, decline, degenerate, descend, deteriorate, ebb, rot, sink — more at DETERIORATE

¹wor·ship \'wər-shəp\ *n* [ME *worship* worthiness, respect, reverence paid to a divine being, fr. OE *weorthscipe* worthiness, respect, fr. *weorth* worthy, worth + *-scipe* -ship, suffix denoting quality or condition] **1** *chiefly Brit* : a person of importance — used as a title for officials **2** : reverence toward a divine being or supernatural power; *also* : the expression of such reverence **3** ♦ : extravagant respect or admiration or devotion ⟨~ of the dollar⟩

♦ adulation, deification, idolatry; *also* adoration, deference, glorification, reverence, veneration; idealization; affection, fancy, favor, fondness, like, liking, love; appreciation, esteem, regard, respect; approval

²worship *vb* **-shipped** *also* **-shiped**; **-ship·ping** *also* **-ship·ing** **1** ♦ : to honor or reverence as a divine being or supernatural power **2** ♦ : to regard with respect, honor, or devotion **3** : to perform or take part in worship — **wor·ship·er** *or* **wor·ship·per** *n*

♦ [1] adore, deify, glorify, revere, venerate; *also* admire, honor, regard, respect; dignify, exalt, magnify, extol, laud, praise; delight, gratify, please, satisfy ♦ [2] adore, canonize, deify, dote, idolize, love — more at IDOLIZE

wor·ship·ful \'wər-shəp-fəl\ *adj* **1** *archaic* : NOTABLE, DISTINGUISHED **2** *chiefly Brit* — used as a title for various persons or groups of rank or distinction **3** ♦ : giving or expressing adoration or reverence ⟨~ fans⟩

♦ adulatory; *also* glorifying, reverential, venerating; affectionate, fond, loving; appreciative, deferential, respectful; approving

¹**worst** \'wərst\ *adj, superlative of* BAD *or of* ILL   **1** : most bad, evil, ill, or corrupt   **2** : most unfavorable, unpleasant, or painful; *also* : most unsuitable, faulty, or unattractive   **3** : least skillful or efficient

²**worst** *adv, superlative of* ILL *or of* BAD *or* BADLY   **1** : to the extreme degree of badness or inferiority : in the worst manner   **2** : MOST ⟨those who need help ∼⟩

³**worst** *n* : one that is worst

⁴**worst** *vb* : to get the better of in a fight, conflict, or contest : DEFEAT

wor·sted \'wu̇s-təd, 'wər-stəd\ *n* [ME, fr. *Worsted* (now *Worstead*), England] : a smooth compact yarn from long wool fibers; *also* : a fabric made from such yarn

wort \'wərt, 'wȯrt\ *n* : a sweet liquid drained from mash and fermented to form beer and whiskey

¹**worth** \'wərth\ *n*   **1** : monetary value; *also* : the equivalent of a specified amount or figure ⟨$5 ∼ of gas⟩   **2** ♦ : the value of something measured by its qualities   **3** : MERIT, EXCELLENCE

    ♦ account, merit, valuation, value; *also* assessment, estimation, evaluation; excellence, greatness, perfection; consequence, importance, significance, weight; desirability

²**worth** *prep*   **1** : equal in value to; *also* : having possessions or income equal to   **2** : deserving of ⟨well ∼ the effort⟩

worth·less \'wərth-ləs\ *adj*   **1** ♦ : lacking use, value, or profit   **2** : LOW, DESPICABLE — **worth·less·ness** *n*

    ♦ chaffy, empty, junky, no-good, null, valueless; *also* base, cheap, inferior, lousy, second-rate; bad, defective, imperfect, substandard, unsatisfactory; deficient, inadequate, insufficient, unacceptable *Ant* useful, valuable, worthy

worth·while \'wərth-'hwīl\ *adj* : being worth the time or effort spent

¹**wor·thy** \'wər-thē\ *adj* **wor·thi·er; -est**   **1** : having worth or value   **2** ♦ : marked by personal qualities warranting honor, respect, or esteem : MERITORIOUS   **3** : having sufficient worth ⟨∼ of the honor⟩ — **wor·thi·ly** \'wər-thə-lē\ *adv* — **wor·thi·ness** \-thē-nəs\ *n*

    ♦ deserving, good, meritorious; *also* admirable, commendable, creditable, laudable, praiseworthy; invaluable, priceless; cherished, prized, treasured; choice, excellent, exceptional, fancy, primary, prime, special *Ant* no-good, undeserving, valueless, worthless

²**worthy** *n, pl* **worthies** : a worthy person

would \'wu̇d\ *past of* WILL   **1** *archaic* : wish for : WANT   **2** : strongly desire : WISH ⟨I ∼ I were young again⟩   **3** — used as an auxiliary to express (1) preference ⟨∼ rather run than fight⟩, (2) wish, desire, or intent ⟨those who ∼ forbid gambling⟩, (3) habitual action ⟨we ∼ meet often for lunch⟩, (4) a contingency or possibility ⟨if he were coming, he ∼ be here by now⟩, (5) probability ⟨∼ have won it if he hadn't tripped⟩, or (6) a request ⟨∼ you help us⟩   **4** : COULD   **5** : SHOULD

would–be \'wu̇d-'bē\ *adj, disparaging* : desiring or pretending to be ⟨a ∼ artist⟩

¹**wound** \'wünd\ *n*   **1** : an injury involving cutting or breaking of bodily tissue (as by violence, accident, or surgery)   **2** ♦ : an injury or hurt to feelings or reputation

    ♦ affront, barb, dart, dig, indignity, insult, name, offense, outrage, put-down, sarcasm, slight, slur — more at INSULT

²**wound** *vb* ♦ : to inflict a wound to or in

    ♦ damage, harm, hurt, injure — more at INJURE ♦ affront, insult, offend, outrage, slight — more at INSULT

³**wound** \'wau̇nd\ *past and past part of* WIND

wove *past of* WEAVE

woven *past part of* WEAVE

¹**wow** \'wau̇\ *n* : a striking success : HIT

²**wow** *vb* : to arouse enthusiastic approval

WP *abbr* word processing; word processor

WPM *abbr* words per minute

wpn *abbr* weapon

wrack \'rak\ *n* [ME, fr. OE *wræc* misery, punishment, something driven by the sea] : violent or total destruction

wraith \'rāth\ *n, pl* **wraiths** \'rāths, 'rāthz\   **1** ♦ : a visible appearance of a dead person : GHOST   **2** : an insubstantial appearance : SHADOW

    ♦ apparition, bogey, ghost, phantasm, phantom, poltergeist, shade, shadow, specter, spirit, spook, vision — more at GHOST

¹**wran·gle** \'raŋ-gəl\ *vb* **wran·gled; wran·gling**   **1** ♦ : to quarrel angrily or peevishly : BICKER   **2** : ARGUE ⟨they *wrangled* about money⟩   **3** : to obtain by persistent arguing   **4** : to herd and care for (livestock) on the range — **wran·gler** *n*

    ♦ argue, bicker, brawl, dispute, fall out, fight, hassle, quarrel, row, scrap, spat, squabble — more at ARGUE

²**wrangle** *n* ♦ : an angry, noisy, or prolonged dispute; *also* : CONTROVERSY

    ♦ altercation, argument, bicker, brawl, controversy, disagreement, dispute, fight, hassle, misunderstanding, quarrel, row, scrap, spat, squabble — more at ARGUMENT

¹**wrap** \'rap\ *vb* **wrapped; wrap·ping**   **1** : to cover esp. by winding or folding   **2** : to envelop and secure for transportation or storage   **3** ♦ : to enclose wholly   **4** : to coil, fold, draw, or twine about something   **5** : SURROUND, ENVELOP ⟨*wrapped* in mystery⟩   **6** : INVOLVE, ENGROSS ⟨*wrapped* up in a hobby⟩   **7** : to complete filming or recording

    ♦ embrace, enclose, encompass, enfold, enshroud, envelop, invest, lap, mantle, shroud, swathe, veil — more at ENFOLD

²**wrap** *n*   **1** : WRAPPER, WRAPPING   **2** : an article of clothing that may be wrapped around a person   **3** *pl* : SECRECY ⟨kept under ∼s⟩   **4** : completion of filming or recording   **5** : a thin piece of bread that is rolled around a filling

wrap·around \'ra-pə-ˌrau̇nd\ *n* : a garment (as a dress) adjusted to the figure by wrapping around

wrap·per \'ra-pər\ *n*   **1** : that in which something is wrapped   **2** : one that wraps   **3** : an article of clothing worn wrapped around the body

wrap·ping \'ra-piŋ\ *n* : something used to wrap an object : WRAPPER

wrap–up \'rap-ˌəp\ *n* ♦ : a concise statement of the main points : SUMMARY

    ♦ abstract, digest, encapsulation, epitome, outline, précis, recap, recapitulation, résumé (*or* resume), roundup, sum, summarization, summary, synopsis — more at SUMMARY

wrap up *vb*   **1** ♦ : to make a single comprehensive report from : SUMMARIZE   **2** ♦ : to bring to a usu. successful conclusion

    ♦ [1] abstract, digest, encapsulate, epitomize, outline, recapitulate, summarize, sum up — more at SUMMARIZE ♦ [2] close, conclude, end, finish, round, terminate, wind up — more at CLOSE

wrasse \'ras\ *n* : any of a large family of usu. brightly colored marine fishes including many food fishes

wrath \'rath\ *n*   **1** ♦ : violent anger : RAGE   **2** ♦ : condemnation esp. of a deity or sovereign; *esp* : divine punishment

    ♦ [1] anger, furor, fury, indignation, ire, outrage, rage, spleen, wrathfulness — more at ANGER ♦ [2] castigation, chastisement, correction, desert, discipline, nemesis, penalty, punishment — more at PUNISHMENT

wrath·ful \-fəl\ *adj*   **1** ♦ : filled with wrath : very angry   **2** ♦ : showing, marked by, or arising from anger ⟨a ∼ assault⟩ — **wrath·ful·ly** *adv*

    ♦ [1, 2] angry, boiling, enraged, furious, irate, mad, rabid, sore — more at ANGRY

wrath·ful·ness *n* ♦ : the quality or fact of being wrathful

    ♦ anger, furor, fury, indignation, ire, outrage, rage, spleen, wrath — more at ANGER

wreak \'rēk\ *vb* [ME *wreken*, fr. OE *wrecan* to drive, punish, avenge] **1** : to exact as a punishment : INFLICT ⟨∼ vengeance on an enemy⟩ **2** : to give free scope or rein to ⟨∼ed his wrath⟩ **3** : BRING ABOUT, CAUSE ⟨∼ havoc⟩

wreath \'rēth\ *n, pl* **wreaths** \'rēthz, 'rēths\ : a circular band of flowers or leaves usu. for decoration; *also* : something having a circular or coiling form ⟨a ∼ of smoke⟩

wreathe \'rēth\ *vb* **wreathed; wreath·ing** **1** : to shape or take on the shape of a wreath **2** : to crown, decorate, or cover with or as if with a wreath ⟨a face *wreathed* in smiles⟩ **3** ♦ : to interweave or blend together

♦ interlace, intersperse, intertwine, interweave, lace, thread, weave — more at THREAD

¹wreck \'rek\ *n* **1** : something (as goods) cast up on the land by the sea after a shipwreck **2** : the injury, destruction, or sinking of a vessel esp. by being cast on rocks or affected by the force of winds or waves : SHIPWRECK **3** ♦ : the action or an instance of crashing, breaking up, or destroying something **4** ♦ : broken remains (as of a vehicle after a crash) **5** : something disabled or in a state of ruin; *also* : an individual broken in health, strength, or spirits

♦ [3] collision, crack-up, crash, smash — more at CRASH ♦ [4] debris, remains, residue, rubble, ruins, wreckage — more at REMAINS

²wreck *vb* **1** : SHIPWRECK **2** ♦ : to ruin or damage by breaking up ⟨∼ed their marriage⟩ : involve in disaster or ruin

♦ annihilate, blot out, demolish, desolate, destroy, devastate, do in, exterminate, extinguish, obliterate, pulverize, ruin, shatter, smash, tear down, waste, wipe out — more at DESTROY

wreck·age \'re-kij\ *n* **1** ♦ : the act of wrecking : the state of being wrecked **2** ♦ : the remains of a wreck

♦ [1] annihilation, demolition, desolation, destruction, devastation, havoc, loss, obliteration, ruin, wastage — more at DESTRUCTION ♦ [2] debris, remains, residue, rubble, ruins, wreck — more at REMAINS

wreck·er \'re-kər\ *n* **1** : one that searches for or works upon the wrecks of ships **2** : TOW TRUCK **3** : one that wrecks; *esp* : one whose work is the demolition of buildings

wren \'ren\ *n* : any of a family of small mostly brown singing birds with short wings and often a tail that points upward

¹wrench \'rench\ *vb* **1** : to move with a violent twist **2** ♦ : to pull, strain, or tighten with violent twisting or force **3** ♦ : to injure or disable by a violent twisting or straining **4** ♦ : to snatch forcibly : WREST

♦ [2] twist, wrest, wring; *also* draw, dredge (up), extract, jerk, lug, pluck, pull, tug, tweak, yank; budge, dislocate, displace, disturb, remove; shift, transfer, transpose ♦ [3] pull, rack, strain, stretch — more at STRAIN ♦ [4] rip, tear, wrest — more at TEAR

²wrench *n* **1** : a forcible twisting; *also* : an injury (as to one's ankle) by twisting **2** : a tool for holding, twisting, or turning (as nuts or bolts)

¹wrest \'rest\ *vb* **1** ♦ : to pull or move by a forcible twisting movement **2** ♦ : to gain with difficulty by or as if by coercion, force, or violence ⟨∼ed the book from her hands⟩ ⟨∼ control of the government from the dictator⟩

♦ [1] extract, prize, pry, pull, root, tear, uproot — more at EXTRACT ♦ [1, 2] rip, tear, wrench — more at TEAR ♦ [2] exact, extort, wring — more at EXTORT

²wrest *n* : a forcible twist : WRENCH

¹wres·tle \'re-səl, 'ra-\ *vb* **wres·tled; wres·tling** **1** ♦ : to grapple with and try to throw down an opponent **2** ♦ : to compete against in wrestling **3** : to struggle for control (as of something difficult) ⟨∼ with a problem⟩ — **wres·tler** \'res-lər, 'ras-\ *n*

♦ [1, 2] grapple, scuffle, tussle; *also* battle, clash (with), combat, contend, fight, war (against); duel; brawl, skirmish

²wrestle *n* : the action or an instance of wrestling : STRUGGLE

wres·tling \'res-lin\ *n* : the sport in which two opponents wrestle each other

wretch \'rech\ *n* [ME *wrecche*, fr. OE *wrecca* outcast, exile] **1** : a miserable unhappy person **2** ♦ : a base, despicable, or vile person

♦ beast, devil, evildoer, fiend, heavy, knave, no-good, rapscallion, rascal, reprobate, rogue, scalawag, scamp, varlet, villain — more at VILLAIN

wretch·ed \'re-chəd\ *adj* **1** ♦ : deeply afflicted, dejected, or distressed : extremely sad and depressed **2** : characterized by or tending to produce discomfort, distress, or misery ⟨∼ living conditions⟩ **3** ♦ : having a mean or contemptible nature or appearance ⟨a ∼ trick⟩ **4** ♦ : poor in quality or ability : INFERIOR ⟨∼ workmanship⟩ — **wretch·ed·ness** *n*

♦ [1] dejected, depressed, despondent, disconsolate, heartsick, miserable, mournful, sad, sorrowful, sorry, unhappy, woebegone, woeful — more at SAD ♦ [3] contemptible, despicable, lousy, nasty, pitiful, scabby, scurvy, sorry — more at CONTEMPTIBLE ♦ [4] atrocious, awful, execrable, inferior, lousy, punk, rotten, terrible; *also* bad, deficient, off, poor, substandard, unsatisfactory, wanting; contemptible, miserable, shameful; defective, faulty; mediocre, reprehensible, second-rate; bum, useless, valueless, worthless; inadequate, insufficient, lacking; abominable, odious, vile *Ant* great, marvelous, wonderful

wretch·ed·ly *adv* ♦ : in a wretched state or manner

♦ agonizingly, bitterly, grievously, hard, hardly, sadly, sorrowfully, unhappily, woefully — more at HARD

wrig·gle \'ri-gəl\ *vb* **wrig·gled; wrig·gling** **1** : to twist or move to and fro like a worm ⟨*wriggled* in his chair⟩ ⟨∼ your toes⟩; *also* : to move along by twisting and turning ⟨a snake *wriggled* along the path⟩ **2** : to extricate oneself as if by wriggling ⟨∼ out of difficulty⟩ — **wriggle** *n*

wrig·gler *n* **1** : one that wriggles **2** : WIGGLER 1

wring \'rin\ *vb* **wrung** \'rən\; **wring·ing** \'rin-in\ **1** : to squeeze or twist esp. so as to make dry or to extract moisture or liquid ⟨∼ wet clothes⟩ **2** : to get by or as if by twisting or pressing ⟨∼ the truth out of him⟩ **3** ♦ : to twist so as to strain or sprain ⟨∼ his neck⟩ **4** : to twist together as a sign of anguish ⟨*wrung* her hands⟩ **5** : to affect painfully as if by wringing : TORMENT ⟨her plight *wrung* my heart⟩

♦ twist, wrench, wrest — more at WRENCH

wring·er \'rin-ər\ *n* : one that wrings; *esp* : a device for squeezing out liquid or moisture ⟨clothes ∼⟩

¹wrin·kle \'rin-kəl\ *n* **1** ♦ : a crease or small fold on a smooth surface (as in the skin or in cloth) **2** ♦ : a clever or new method, trick, or idea — **wrin·kly** \-k(ə-)lē\ *adj*

♦ [1] crease, crimp, crinkle, furrow; *also* corrugation, layer, loop, plait, pleat, ply, pucker, seam, tuck; crow's-foot ♦ [2] coinage, concoction, contrivance, creation, innovation, invention — more at INVENTION

²wrinkle *vb* **wrin·kled; wrin·kling** ♦ : to develop or cause to develop wrinkles

♦ crease, crinkle, furrow, rumple; *also* collapse, crumple, double, fold

wrist \'rist\ *n* : the joint or region between the hand and the arm; *also* : a corresponding part in a lower animal

wrist·band \-,band\ *n* : a band or the part of a sleeve encircling the wrist

wrist·let \-lət\ *n* : WRISTBAND; *esp* : a close-fitting knitted band attached to the top of a glove or the end of a sleeve

wrist·watch \-,wäch\ *n* : a small watch attached to a bracelet or strap to fasten about the wrist

writ \'rit\ *n* **1** : something written **2** : a written legal order signed by a court officer

write \'rīt\ *vb* **wrote** \'rōt\; **writ·ten** \'rit-ᵊn\ *also* **writ** \'rit\; **writ·ing** \'rī-tin\ [ME, fr. OE *wrītan* to scratch, draw, inscribe] **1** : to form characters, letters, or words on a surface ⟨learn to read and ∼⟩ **2** : to form the letters or the words of ⟨~ your name⟩ ⟨~ a check⟩ **3 ♦** : to put down on paper : express in writing **4** : to make up and set down for others to read ⟨~ a book⟩ ⟨~ music⟩ **5** : to write a letter to **6** : to communicate by letter : CORRESPOND

♦ author, pen, scratch, scribble; *also* cast, compose, craft, draft, draw (up), formulate, frame, prepare; recast, redraft, revise, rewrite; letter, print, type, typewrite; record, take down, transcribe; autograph, register, sign; couch, express, phrase, put, word

write–in \'rīt-ˌin\ *n* : a vote cast by writing in the name of a candidate; *also* : a candidate whose name is written in
write in *vb* : to insert (a name not listed on a ballot) in an appropriate space; *also* : to cast (a vote) in this manner
write off *vb* **1 a ♦** : to reduce the estimated value of : DEPRECIATE **b ♦** : to disparage or deny the worth of **2** : CANCEL ⟨write off a bad debt⟩

♦ [1a] cheapen, depreciate, depress, mark down — more at DEPRECIATE ♦ [1b] belittle, cry down, decry, deprecate, depreciate, diminish, discount, disparage, minimize, put down — more at DECRY

writ·er \'rī-tər\ *n* : one that writes esp. as a business or occupation : AUTHOR
writer's cramp *n* : a painful spasmodic contraction of muscles of the hand or fingers brought on by excessive writing
write–up \'rīt-ˌəp\ *n* : a written account (as in a newspaper); *esp* : a flattering article
writhe \'rīth\ *vb* **writhed; writh·ing** **1** : to twist and turn this way and that ⟨~ in pain⟩ **2** : to suffer with shame or confusion
writ·ing *n* **1** : the act of one that writes; *also* : HANDWRITING **2** : something that is written or printed **3** : a style or form of composition **4** : the occupation of a writer
Writings \'rī-tiŋz\ *n pl* : the third part of the Jewish scriptures
wrnt *abbr* warrant
¹wrong \'rȯŋ\ *n* **1 ♦** : an injurious, unfair, or unjust act **2** : a violation of the legal rights of another person **3 ♦** : something that is wrong : wrong principles, practices, or conduct ⟨know right from ~⟩ **4** : the state, position, or fact of being wrong ⟨was in the ~⟩

♦ [1] disservice, injury, injustice, raw deal — more at DISSERVICE ♦ [3] bad, evil, ill, immorality, iniquity, sin, villainy — more at EVIL

²wrong *adj* **wrong·er** \'rȯŋ-ər\; **wrong·est** \'rȯŋ-əst\ **1 ♦** : lacking in moral behavior and integrity : IMMORAL **2 ♦** : not right according to a standard or code : IMPROPER **3 ♦** : not agreeing with or conforming to facts : INCORRECT ⟨a ~ solution⟩ **4 ♦** : being at variance with what is generally acceptable or preferable : UNSATISFACTORY **5** : not fitted or qualified for a particular intention or purpose : UNSUITABLE, INAPPROPRIATE **6** : constituting a surface that is considered the back, bottom, inside, or reverse of something ⟨iron only on the ~ side of the fabric⟩

♦ [1] bad, black, evil, immoral, iniquitous, nefarious, rotten, sinful, unethical, unsavory, vicious, vile, villainous ♦ [2] graceless, improper, inapt, incongruous, incorrect, indecorous, inept, infelicitous, unbecoming, unfit, unhappy, unseemly, unsuitable ♦ [3] erroneous, false, inaccurate, incorrect, inexact, invalid, off, unsound, untrue — more at FALSE ♦ [4] bad, deficient, inferior, lousy, off, poor, punk, rotten, substandard,

unacceptable, unsatisfactory, wanting, wretched — more at BAD
³wrong *adv* **1** : in a mistaken or erroneous manner **2 ♦** : in a wrong direction, manner, or relation

♦ afield, amiss, astray, awry; *also* badly; faultily, improperly, incorrectly, mistakenly, wrongly; inadequately, insufficiently *Ant* aright, right, well

⁴wrong *vb* **wronged; wrong·ing** \'rȯŋ-iŋ\ **1** : to do wrong to : INJURE, HARM **2** : to treat unjustly : DISHONOR, MALIGN
wrong·do·er \'rȯŋ-ˌdü-ər\ *n ♦* : a person who does wrong and esp. moral wrong

♦ evildoer, malefactor, sinner — more at EVILDOER

wrong·do·ing \-ˌdü-iŋ\ *n ♦* : the act or action of doing wrong

♦ breach, crime, error, malefaction, misdeed, misdoing, offense, sin, transgression, trespass, violation — more at OFFENSE ♦ malfeasance, misbehavior, misconduct, misdoing — more at MISCONDUCT

wrong·ful \'rȯŋ-fəl\ *adj* **1** : WRONG, UNJUST **2 ♦** : having no legal sanction : UNLAWFUL ⟨~ conduct⟩ — **wrong·ful·ly** *adv* — **wrong·ful·ness** *n*

♦ criminal, illegal, illegitimate, illicit, unlawful — more at ILLEGAL

wrong·head·ed \-'he-dəd\ *adj* : stubborn in clinging to wrong opinion or principles — **wrong·head·ed·ly** *adv* — **wrong·head·ed·ness** *n*
wrong·ly *adv ♦* : in a bad, incorrect, inappropriate, or unsuitable manner

♦ amiss, erroneously, faultily, improperly, inaptly, incorrectly, mistakenly; *also* fallibly, imperfectly; extraneously, senselessly; inadequately, insufficiently; foolishly, unwisely *Ant* appropriately, aptly, correctly, fittingly, properly, right, rightly, suitably

wrote *past of* WRITE
wroth \'rȯth, 'rōth\ *adj* : filled with wrath : ANGRY
wrought \'rȯt\ *adj* [ME, fr. pp. of *worken* to work] **1** : FASHIONED, FORMED ⟨carefully ~ essays⟩ **2** : ORNAMENTED **3** : beaten into shape by tools : HAMMERED ⟨~ metals⟩ **4** : deeply stirred : EXCITED ⟨gets easily ~ up⟩
wrung *past and past part of* WRING
wry \'rī\ *adj* **wry·er** \'rī-ər\; **wry·est** \'rī-əst\ **1** : having a bent or twisted shape ⟨a ~ smile⟩; *also* : turned abnormally to one side : CONTORTED ⟨a ~ neck⟩ **2** : cleverly and often ironically humorous — **wry·ly** *adv* — **wry·ness** *n*
wry·neck \'rī-ˌnek\ *n* **1** : either of two Old World woodpeckers that differ from typical woodpeckers in having a peculiar manner of twisting the head and neck **2** : an abnormal twisting of the neck and head to one side caused by muscle spasms
WSW *abbr* west-southwest
wt *abbr* weight
wurst \'wərst, 'wu̇rst\ *n* : SAUSAGE
wu·shu \'wü-ˌshü\ *n* : Chinese martial arts
wuss \'wu̇s\ *n* : WIMP — **wussy** \'wu̇-sē\ *adj*
WV *or* **W Va** *abbr* West Virginia
WW *abbr* World War
w/w *abbr* wall-to-wall
WY *or* **Wyo** *abbr* Wyoming
WYS·I·WYG \'wi-zē-ˌwig\ *adj* [what you see is what you get] : of, relating to, or being a computer display that shows a document exactly as it will appear when printed out

¹x \'eks\ *n, pl* **x's** *or* **xs** \'ek-səz\ *often cap* **1** : the 24th letter of the English alphabet **2** : an unknown quantity

²x *vb* **x-ed** *also* **x'd** *or* **xed** \'ekst\; **x-ing** *or* **x'ing** \'ek-siŋ\ : to cancel or obliterate with a series of *x*'s — usu. used with *out*

³x *abbr* **1** ex **2** experimental **3** extra

⁴x *symbol* **1** times ⟨3 *x* 2 is 6⟩ **2** by ⟨a 3 *x* 5 index card⟩ **3** *often cap* power of magnification

Xan·a·du \'za-nə-,dü, -,dyü\ *n* [fr. *Xanadu*, locality in *Kubla Khan* (1798), poem by Eng. poet Samuel Taylor Coleridge †1834] : an idyllic, exotic, or luxurious place

Xan·thip·pe \zan-'thi-pē, -'ti-\ *or* **Xan·tip·pe** \-'ti-pē\ *n* [Gk *Xanthippē*, shrewish wife of Socrates] : an ill-tempered woman

x–ax·is \'eks-,ak-səs\ *n* : the axis of a graph or of a system of coordinates in a plane parallel to which abscissas are measured

X–C *abbr* cross-country

X chromosome *n* : a sex chromosome that usu. occurs paired in each female cell and single in each male cell in organisms (as humans) in which the male normally has two unlike sex chromosomes

Xe *symbol* xenon

xe·non \'zē-,nän, 'ze-\ *n* [Gk, neut. of *xenos* strange] : a heavy gaseous chemical element occurring in minute quantities in air

xe·no·pho·bia \,ze-nə-'fō-bē-ə, ,zē-\ *n* : fear and hatred of strangers or foreigners or of what is strange or foreign — **xe·no·phobe** \'ze-nə-,fōb, 'zē-\ *n* — **xe·no·pho·bic** \,ze-nə-'fō-bik, ,zē-\ *adj*

xe·ric \'zir-ik, 'zer-\ *adj* : characterized by or requiring only a small amount of moisture ⟨a ∼ habitat⟩

xeri·scape \'zir-ə-,skāp, 'zer-\ *n, often cap* : a landscaping method utilizing water-conserving techniques

xe·rog·ra·phy \zə-'rä-grə-fē\ *n* : a process for copying printed matter by the action of light on an electrically charged surface in which the latent image is developed with a powder — **xe·ro·graph·ic** \,zir-ə-'gra-fik\ *adj*

xe·ro·phyte \'zir-ə-,fīt\ *n* : a plant adapted for growth with a limited water supply — **xe·ro·phyt·ic** \,zir-ə-'fi-tik\ *adj*

xi \'zī, 'ksī\ *n* : the 14th letter of the Greek alphabet — Ξ or ξ

XL *abbr* **1** extra large **2** extra long

Xmas \'kris-məs *also* 'eks-məs\ *n* [*X* (symbol for *Christ*, fr. the Gk letter chi (X), initial of *Christos* Christ) + *-mas* (in *Christmas*)] : CHRISTMAS

XML \,eks-(,)em-'el\ *n* : a markup language that indicates the structural type of data

XO *abbr* executive officer

x–ra·di·a·tion \,eks-,rā-dē-'ā-shən\ *n, often cap* **1** : exposure to X-rays **2** : radiation consisting of X-rays

x–ray \'eks-,rā\ *vb, often cap* : to examine, treat, or photograph with X-rays

X–ray \'eks-,rā\ *n* **1** : a radiation with an extremely short wavelength of less than 100 angstroms that is able to penetrate through various thicknesses of solids and to act on photographic film **2** : a photograph taken with X-rays — **X–ray** *adj*

XS *abbr* extra small

xy·lem \'zī-ləm, -,lem\ *n* : a woody tissue of vascular plants that transports water and dissolved materials upward, functions in support and storage, and lies central to the phloem

xy·lo·phone \'zī-lə-,fōn\ *n* [Gk *xylon* wood + *phōnē* voice, sound] : a musical instrument consisting of a series of wooden bars graduated in length to produce the musical scale, supported on belts of straw or felt, and sounded by striking with two small wooden hammers — **xy·lo·phon·ist** \-,fō-nist\ *n*

¹y \'wī\ *n, pl* **y's** *or* **ys** \'wīz\ *often cap* : the 25th letter of the English alphabet

²y *abbr* **1** yard **2** year

¹Y \'wī\ *n* : YMCA, YWCA

²Y *symbol* yttrium

¹-y *also* **-ey** \ē\ *adj suffix* **1** : characterized by : full of ⟨dirt*y*⟩ ⟨clay*ey*⟩ **2** : having the character of : composed of ⟨ic*y*⟩ **3** : like : like that of ⟨home*y*⟩ ⟨wintr*y*⟩ ⟨stag*y*⟩ **4** : tending or inclined to ⟨sleep*y*⟩ ⟨chatt*y*⟩ **5** : giving occasion for (specified) action ⟨tear*y*⟩ **6** : performing (specified) action ⟨curl*y*⟩

²-y \ē\ *n suffix, pl* **-ies** **1** : state : condition : quality ⟨beggar*y*⟩ **2** : activity, place of business, or goods dealt with ⟨laundr*y*⟩ **3** : whole body or group ⟨soldier*y*⟩

³-y *n suffix, pl* **-ies** : instance of a (specified) action ⟨entreat*y*⟩ ⟨inquir*y*⟩

YA *abbr* young adult

¹yacht \'yät\ *n* [obs. D *jaght*, fr. Middle Low German *jacht*, short for *jachtschip*, lit., hunting ship] : a usu. large recreational watercraft; *also* : sailboat

²yacht *vb* : to race or cruise in a yacht

yacht·ing \'yä-tiŋ\ *n* : the sport of racing or cruising in a yacht

yachts·man \'yäts-mən\ *n* : a person who owns or sails a yacht

ya·hoo \'yā-hü, 'yä-\ *n, pl* **yahoos** [fr. *Yahoo*, one of a race of brutes having the form of people in Jonathan Swift's *Gulliver's Travels*] : a boorish, crass, or stupid person

Yah·weh \'yä-,wā\ *also* **Yah·veh** \-,vā\ *n* : GOD 1 — used esp. by the Hebrews

¹yak \'yak\ *n, pl* **yaks** *also* **yak** : a large long-haired wild or domesticated ox of Tibet and adjacent Asian uplands

²yak *also* **yack** \'yak\ *n* : persistent or voluble talk — **yak** *also* **yack** *vb*

yam \'yam\ *n* **1** : the edible starchy root of various twining plants used as a staple food in tropical areas; *also* : a plant that produces yams **2** : a usu. deep orange sweet potato

yam·mer \'ya-mər\ *vb* [ME *yameren*, alter. of *yomeren* to murmur, be sad, fr. OE *gēomrian*] **1** : to utter repeated cries of distress or sorrow : WHIMPER **2** : CHATTER — **yammer** *n*

¹yank \'yaŋk\ *n* : a strong sudden pull : JERK

²yank *vb* : to pull with a quick vigorous movement

Yank \'yaŋk\ *n* : YANKEE

Yan·kee \'yaŋ-kē\ *n* **1** : a native or inhabitant of New

England; *also* : a native or inhabitant of the northern U.S. **2** : AMERICAN 2

yan·qui \'yän-kē\ *n, often cap* [Sp] : a citizen of the U.S. as distinguished from a Latin American

¹yap \'yap\ *vb* **yapped; yap·ping** **1** : BARK, YELP **2** : GAB

²yap *n* **1** : a quick sharp bark **2** : CHATTER

¹yard \'yärd\ *n* [ME, fr. OE *geard* enclosure, yard] **1 ♦** : a small enclosed area open to the sky and adjacent to a building **2 ♦** : the grounds of a building **3** : the grounds surrounding a house usu. covered with grass **4** : an enclosure for livestock **5** : an area set aside for a particular business or activity **6** : a system of railroad tracks for storing cars and making up trains

♦ [1] close, court, courtyard, quadrangle — more at COURT ♦ [2] demesne, grounds, park, premises

²yard *n* [ME *yarde*, fr. OE *gierd* twig, measure, yard] **1** : a unit of length equal to three feet **2** : a long spar tapered toward the ends that supports and spreads the head of a sail — **the whole nine yards** : all of a set of circumstances, conditions, or details

yard·age \'yär-dij\ *n* : an aggregate number of yards; *also* : the length, extent, or volume of something as measured in yards

yard·arm \'yärd-,ärm\ *n* : either end of the yard of a square-rigged ship

yard·man \-mən, -,man\ *n* **1** : a person employed to do outdoor work (as mowing lawns) **2** : a person employed in or about a yard (as a lumberyard or railroad yard)

yard·mas·ter \-,mas-tər\ *n* : the person in charge of a railroad yard

yard sale *n* : GARAGE SALE

yard·stick \-,stik\ *n* **1** : a graduated measuring stick three feet long **2 ♦** : a standard for making a critical judgment : CRITERION

♦ criterion, grade, mark, measure, par, standard, touchstone — more at STANDARD

yar·mul·ke \'yä-mə-kə, 'yär-, -məl-\ *n* [Yiddish *yarmlke*] : a skullcap worn esp. by Jewish males in the synagogue and the home

yarn \'yärn\ *n* **1** : a continuous often plied strand composed of fibers or filaments and used in weaving and knitting to form cloth **2** : an entertaining narrative of adventures : STORY; *esp* : a tall tale

yar·row \'yar-ō\ *n* : a strong-scented herb related to the daisies that has white or pink flowers in flat clusters

yaw \'yò\ *vb* : to deviate erratically from a course ⟨the ship ~ed in the heavy seas⟩ — **yaw** *n*

♦ sheer, swerve, veer — more at SWERVE

yawl \'yòl\ *n* : a 2-masted sailboat with the shorter mast aft of the rudder

¹yawn \'yòn\ *vb* : to open wide; *esp* : to open the mouth wide and take a deep breath usu. as an involuntary reaction to fatigue or boredom — **yawn·er** *n*

²yawn *n* : the act of yawning

yawp *or* **yaup** \'yòp\ *vb* **1** : to make a raucous noise : SQUAWK **2** : CLAMOR, COMPLAIN — **yawp·er** *n*

yaws \'yòz\ *n pl* : a contagious tropical disease caused by a spirochete closely resembling the causative agent of syphilis and marked by skin lesions

y–ax·is \'wī-,ak-səs\ *n* : the axis of a graph or of a system of coordinates in a plane parallel to which the ordinates are measured

Yb *symbol* ytterbium

YB *abbr* yearbook

Y chromosome *n* : a sex chromosome that is characteristic of male cells in organisms (as humans) in which the male typically has two unlike sex chromosomes

yd *abbr* yard

¹ye \'yē\ *pron* : YOU 1

²ye \yē, yə, *originally same as* THE\ *definite article, archaic* : THE — used by early printers to represent the manuscript word þe (*the*)

¹yea \'yā\ *adv* **1 ♦** — used as a function word esp. to express assent or agreement esp. in oral voting **2 ♦** : not only so but : INDEED

♦ [1] all right, alright, OK, yes — more at YES ♦ [2] even, indeed, nay, truly, verily — more at EVEN

²yea *n* : an affirmative vote; *also* : a person casting such a vote

yeah \'yeə, 'yaə\ *adv* : YES

year \'yir\ *n* **1** : the period of about 365¼ solar days required for one revolution of the earth around the sun; *also* : the time in which a planet completes a revolution about the sun **2** : a cycle of 365 or 366 days beginning with January 1; *also* : a calendar year specified usu. by a number **3** *pl* : a time of special significance ⟨their glory ~s⟩ **4** *pl* : AGE ⟨advanced in ~s⟩ **5** : a period of time other than a calendar year ⟨the school ~⟩

year·book \-,bùk\ *n* **1** : a book published annually esp. as a report **2** : a school publication recording the history and activities of a graduating class

year·ling \'yir-liŋ, 'yər-lən\ *n* **1** : one that is a year old **2** : a racehorse between January of the year after the year in which it was born and the next January

year·long \'yir-'lòŋ\ *adj* : lasting through a year

¹year·ly \'yir-lē\ *adj* : ANNUAL

²yearly *adv* : every year

yearn \'yərn\ *vb* **1 ♦** : to feel a longing or craving ⟨~ing for freedom⟩ **2** : to feel tenderness or compassion

♦ *usu* **yearn for** ache for, crave, desire, die for, hanker for, hunger for, long for, lust (for *or* after), pine for, repine for, thirst for, want, wish for — more at DESIRE

yearn·ing *n* ♦ : a tender or urgent longing

♦ appetite, craving, desire, drive, hankering, hunger, itch, longing, lust, passion, thirst, urge, yen — more at DESIRE

year–round \'yir-'raùnd\ *adj* : effective, employed, or operating for the full year : not seasonal ⟨a ~ resort⟩

yeast \'yēst\ *n* **1** : a surface froth or a sediment in sugary liquids (as fruit juices) that consists largely of cells of a tiny fungus and is used in making alcoholic liquors and as a leaven in baking **2** : a commercial product containing yeast fungi in a moist or dry medium **3** : a minute one-celled fungus present and functionally active in yeast that reproduces by budding; *also* : any of several similar fungi **4** *archaic* : the foam of waves : SPUME **5 ♦** : something that causes ferment or activity

♦ boost, encouragement, goad, impetus, impulse, incentive, incitement, instigation, momentum, motivation, provocation, spur, stimulus — more at IMPULSE

yeast infection *n* : infection of the vagina with an excess growth of a normally present fungus that resembles a yeast

yeasty \'yē-stē\ *adj* **yeast·i·er; -est** **1** : of, relating to, or resembling yeast **2** : UNSETTLED **3** : full of vitality ⟨~ youths⟩; *also* : FRIVOLOUS

¹yell \'yel\ *vb* **1 ♦** : to utter a loud cry or scream **2 ♦** : to speak or call out in a loud voice : SHOUT — **yell·er** *n*

♦ [1] howl, scream, shriek, shrill, squeal, yelp — more at SCREAM ♦ [2] bawl, call, cry, holler, shout, vociferate — more at CALL

²yell *n* **1 ♦** : a loud or sudden outcry : SHOUT **2** : a cheer used esp. to encourage an athletic team (as at a college)

♦ cry, holler, hoot, shout, whoop — more at SHOUT

¹yel·low \'ye-lō\ *adj* **1** : of the color yellow **2** *sometimes offensive* : having a yellow complexion or skin **3** : SENSATIONAL ⟨~ journalism⟩ **4 ♦** : showing or marked by an utter lack of courage : COWARDLY — **yel·low·ish** \'ye-lə-wish\ *adj*

♦ chicken, cowardly, craven, dastardly, pusillanimous, recreant, spineless — more at COWARDLY

²yellow *n* **1** : a color between green and orange in the spectrum : the color of ripe lemons or sunflowers **2** : something yellow; *esp* : the yolk of an egg **3** *pl* : any of several plant diseases marked by stunted growth and yellowing of foliage

³yellow *vb* : to make or turn yellow

yellow birch *n* : a No. American birch with thin lustrous gray or yellow bark; *also* : its strong hard wood

yellow fever *n* : an acute infectious viral disease marked by prostration, jaundice, fever, and often hemorrhage and transmitted by a mosquito

yellow jack *n* : YELLOW FEVER

yellow jacket *n* : any of various small social wasps having the body barred with bright yellow

yel·low·tail \'ye-lō-ˌtāl\ *n* : any of various fishes with a yellow or yellowish tail including several valuable food fishes

yelp \'yelp\ *vb* [ME, to boast, cry out, fr. OE *gielpan* to boast, exult] : to utter a sharp quick shrill cry — **yelp** *n*
  ♦ howl, scream, shriek, shrill, squeal, yell — more at SCREAM

Ye·me·ni \'ye-mə-nē\ *n* : YEMENITE — **Yemeni** *adj*

Ye·men·ite \'ye-mə-ˌnīt\ *n* : a native or inhabitant of Yemen — **Yemenite** *adj*

¹**yen** \'yen\ *n, pl* **yen** : the basic monetary unit of Japan

²**yen** *n* [obs. E argot *yen-yen* craving for opium, fr. Chin (Guangdong dial.) *yīn-yáhn*, fr. *yīn* opium + *yáhn* craving]
  ♦ : a strong desire : LONGING ⟨a ~ to travel⟩
  ♦ appetite, craving, desire, drive, hankering, hunger, itch, longing, lust, passion, thirst, urge, yearning — more at DESIRE

yeo·man \'yō-mən\ *n* **1** : an attendant or officer in a royal or noble household **2** : a naval petty officer who performs clerical duties **3** : a person who owns and cultivates a small farm; *esp* : one of a class of English freeholders below the gentry — **yeo·man·ly** \-lē\ *adj*

yeo·man·ry \-rē\ *n* : the body of yeomen and esp. of small landed proprietors

¹**yes** \'yes\ *adv* ♦ — used as a function word esp. to express assent or agreement or to introduce a more emphatic or explicit phrase
  ♦ all right, alright, OK, yea; *also* certainly, indeed, indisputably, undoubtedly, unquestionably **Ant** nay, no

²**yes** *n* : an affirmative reply

ye·shi·va *also* **ye·shi·vah** \yə-'shē-və\ *n, pl* **yeshivas** *or* **ye·shi·voth** \-ˌshē-'vōt, -'vōth\ : a Jewish school esp. for religious instruction

yes–man \'yes-ˌman\ *n* : a person who endorses uncritically every opinion or proposal of a superior

¹**yes·ter·day** \'yes-tər-dē, -ˌdā\ *adv* **1** : on the day preceding today **2** : only a short time ago

²**yesterday** *n* **1** : the day last past **2** : time not long past

yes·ter·year \'yes-tər-ˌyir\ *n* **1** : last year **2** ♦ : the recent past
  ♦ history, past, yore — more at PAST

¹**yet** \'yet\ *adv* **1** ♦ : in addition : BESIDES; *also* : EVEN **6 2** ♦ : up to now; *also* : STILL **3** : so soon as now ⟨not time to go ~⟩ **4** ♦ : at an unspecified later time : EVENTUALLY **5** : in spite of that : NEVERTHELESS
  ♦ [1] additionally, again, also, besides, even, further, furthermore, likewise, more, moreover, then, too, withal
  ♦ [2] heretofore, hitherto, still — more at HITHERTO
  ♦ [4] eventually, someday, sometime, ultimately

²**yet** *conj* ♦ : but nevertheless : BUT
  ♦ but, except, only — more at EXCEPT

ye·ti \'ye-tē, 'yā-\ *n* [Tibetan] : ABOMINABLE SNOWMAN

yew \'yü\ *n* **1** : any of a genus of evergreen trees and shrubs with dark stiff poisonous needles and fleshy fruits **2** : the wood of a yew; *esp* : that of an Old World yew

Yid·dish \'yi-dish\ *n* [Yiddish *yidish*, short for *yidish daytsh*, lit., Jewish German] : a language derived from medieval German and spoken by Jews esp. of eastern European origin — **Yiddish** *adj*

¹**yield** \'yēld\ *vb* **1** : to give as fitting, owed, or required **2** ♦ : to surrender or relinquish to the physical control of another : GIVE UP; *esp* : to give up possession of on claim or demand **3** : to bear as a natural product **4** : to bear or bring forth as a natural result of effort or cultivation : PRODUCE **5** ♦ : to bring in : RETURN **6** ♦ : to give way (as to force, influence, or temptation) **7** : to give place
  ♦ [2] cede, deliver, give up, hand over, leave, relinquish, render, surrender, turn over — more at SURRENDER

  ♦ [5] give, pay, return; *also* produce; afford, furnish, provide, supply ♦ [6] blink, bow, budge, capitulate, concede, give in, knuckle under, quit, submit, succumb, surrender; *also* acquiesce **Ant** resist

²**yield** *n* ♦ : something yielded; *esp* : the amount or quantity produced or returned
  ♦ earnings, income, proceeds, profit, return, revenue — more at INCOME ♦ affair, fruit, handiwork, output, produce, product, thing, work — more at PRODUCT

yield·ing \'yēl-diŋ\ *adj* **1** ♦ : not rigid or stiff **2** ♦ : having a tendency to give in, surrender, or agree
  ♦ [1] droopy, flaccid, floppy, lank, limp, slack — more at LIMP ♦ [2] acquiescent, passive, resigned, tolerant, unresistant, unresisting — more at PASSIVE

yikes \'yīks\ *interj* — used to express fear or astonishment

yip \'yip\ *vb* **yipped; yip·ping** : YAP

YK *abbr* Yukon; Yukon Territory

YMCA \ˌwī-ˌem-(ˌ)sē-'ā\ *n* : Young Men's Christian Association

YMHA \ˌwī-ˌem-ˌāch-'ā\ *n* : Young Men's Hebrew Association

yo \'yō\ *interj* — used to call attention, indicate attentiveness, or express affirmation

YOB *abbr* year of birth

yo·del \'yōd-ᵊl\ *vb* **yo·deled** *or* **yo·delled; yo·del·ing** *or* **yo·del·ling** : to sing by suddenly changing from chest voice to falsetto and back; *also* : to shout or call in this manner — **yodel** *n* — **yo·del·er** *n*

yo·ga \'yō-gə\ *n* [Skt, lit., yoking, fr. *yunakti* he yokes] **1** *cap* : a Hindu theistic philosophy teaching the suppression of all activity of body, mind, and will in order that the self may realize its distinction from them and attain liberation **2** : a system of exercises for attaining bodily or mental control and well-being — **yo·gic** \-gik\ *adj, often cap*

yo·gi \'yō-gē\ *also* **yo·gin** \-gən, -ˌgin\ *n* **1** : a person who practices yoga **2** *cap* : an adherent of Yoga philosophy

yo·gurt *also* **yo·ghurt** \'yō-gərt\ *n* [Turk *yoğurt*] : a soured slightly acid often flavored semisolid food made of milk and milk solids to which cultures of bacteria have been added

¹**yoke** \'yōk\ *n, pl* **yokes 1** : a wooden bar or frame by which two draft animals (as oxen) are coupled at the heads or necks for working together; *also* : a frame fitted to a person's shoulders to carry a load in two equal portions **2** : a clamp that embraces two parts to hold or unite them in position **3** *pl usu* **yoke** : two animals yoked together **4** ♦ : an oppressive state of subjection, submission, or servitude : BONDAGE **5** : TIE, LINK ⟨the ~ of matrimony⟩ **6** : a fitted or shaped piece esp. at the shoulder of a garment
  ♦ bondage, enslavement, servitude, slavery, thrall — more at SLAVERY

²**yoke** *vb* **yoked; yok·ing 1** : to put a yoke on : couple with a yoke **2** : to attach a draft animal to ⟨~ a plow⟩ **3** ♦ : to couple, join, or associate as if by a yoke; *esp* : MARRY
  ♦ chain, compound, connect, couple, hitch, hook, join, link — more at CONNECT

yo·kel \'yō-kəl\ *n* ♦ : a naive or gullible country person
  ♦ bumpkin, clodhopper, hick, rustic — more at HICK

yolk \'yōk\ *n* **1** : the yellow rounded inner mass of the egg of a bird or reptile **2** : the stored food material of an egg that supplies nutrients (as proteins and cholesterol) to the developing embryo — **yolked** \'yōkt\ *adj*

Yom Kip·pur \ˌyōm-ki-'pu̇r, ˌyäm-, -'ki-pər\ *n* [Heb *yōm kippūr*, lit., day of atonement] : a Jewish holiday observed in September or October with fasting and prayer as a day of atonement

¹**yon** \'yän\ *adj* : YONDER

²**yon** *adv* **1** : YONDER **2** : THITHER ⟨ran hither and ~⟩

¹**yon·der** \'yän-dər\ *adv* ♦ : at or to that place
  ♦ beyond, farther, further — more at FARTHER

²yonder *adj* **1** : more distant ⟨the ∼ side of the river⟩ **2** : being at a distance within view ⟨∼ hills⟩

yore \'yōr\ *n* [ME, fr. *yore*, adv., long ago, fr. OE *gēara*, fr. *gēar* year] ♦ : time long past ⟨in days of ∼⟩

♦ history, past, yesteryear — more at PAST

York·ie \'yòr-kē\ *n* : YORKSHIRE TERRIER

York·shire terrier \'yòrk-,shir-, -shər\ *n* : any of a breed of compact toy terriers with long straight silky hair

you \'yü\ *pron* **1** : the person or persons addressed ⟨∼ are a nice person⟩ ⟨∼ are nice people⟩ **2** : ONE 2 ⟨∼ turn this knob to open it⟩

¹young \'yəŋ\ *adj* **youn·ger** \'yəŋ-gər\; **youn·gest** \'yəŋ-gəst\ **1** ♦ : being in the first or an early stage of life, growth, or development **2** : having little experience **3** : recently come into being **4** : YOUTHFUL **5** *cap* : belonging to or representing a new or revived usu. political group or movement

♦ adolescent, immature, juvenile, youthful; *also* minor, underage; embryonic; callow, green, inexperienced, puerile, raw; babyish, childish, childlike, infantile; undeveloped, unfinished, unfledged, unformed, unripe, unripened; blooming, blossoming, burgeoning, flowering **Ant** adult, mature, matured

²young *n, pl* **young** : young persons; *also* : young animals

young·ish \'yəŋ-ish\ *adj* : somewhat young

young·ling \'yəŋ-liŋ\ *n* : one that is young — **youngling** *adj*

young·ster \-stər\ *n* ♦ : a young person : CHILD

♦ child, cub, juvenile, kid, youth — more at CHILD

your \'yùr, 'yōr, yər\ *adj* : of or relating to you or yourself

yours \'yùrz, 'yōrz\ *pron* : one or the ones belonging to you

your·self \yər-'self\ *pron, pl* **yourselves** \-'selvz\ : YOU — used reflexively, for emphasis, or in absolute constructions ⟨you'll hurt ∼⟩ ⟨do it ∼⟩

youth \'yüth\ *n, pl* **youths** \'yüthz, 'yüths\ **1** : the period of life between childhood and maturity **2** ♦ : a young person; *esp* : a young male **3** : YOUTHFULNESS

♦ boy, lad, nipper, shaver, stripling — more at BOY child, cub, juvenile, kid, youngster — more at CHILD

youth·ful \'yüth-fəl\ *adj* **1** : of, relating to, or appropriate to youth **2** ♦ : being young and not yet mature **3** : FRESH, VIGOROUS — **youth·ful·ly** *adv* — **youth·ful·ness** *n*

♦ adolescent, immature, juvenile, young — more at YOUNG

youth hostel *n* : HOSTEL 2

¹yowl \'yaùl\ *vb* ♦ : to utter a loud long mournful cry : WAIL

♦ bay, howl, keen, wail — more at HOWL

²yowl *n* : a loud long mournful wail or howl

yo-yo \'yō-(,)yō\ *n, pl* **yo-yos** [prob. fr. Ilocano (a Philippine language) *yóyo*] : a thick grooved double disk with a string attached to its center that is made to fall and rise to the hand by unwinding and rewinding on the string — **yo-yo** *vb*

yr *abbr* **1** year **2** your

yrbk *abbr* yearbook

YT *abbr* Yukon Territory

yt·ter·bi·um \i-'tər-bē-əm\ *n* : a rare metallic chemical element

yt·tri·um \'i-trē-əm\ *n* : a rare metallic chemical element

yu·an \'yü-ən, yù-'än\ *n, pl* **yuan** : the basic monetary unit of China

yuc·ca \'yə-kə\ *n* : any of a genus of plants related to the agaves that grow esp. in warm dry regions and bear large clusters of white cup-shaped flowers atop a long stiff stalk

yuck *also* **yuk** \'yək\ *interj* — used to express rejection or disgust

yucky \'yə-kē\ *adj* ♦ : causing distaste or aversion : REPUGNANT; *also* : causing discomfort : UNPLEASANT

♦ bad, disagreeable, displeasing, distasteful, nasty, rotten, sour, uncongenial, unlovely, unpleasant, unpleasing, unsatisfying, unwelcome — more at UNPLEASANT

yule \'yül\ *n, often cap* : CHRISTMAS

Yule log *n* : a large log formerly put on the hearth on Christmas Eve as the foundation of the fire

yule·tide \'yül-,tīd\ *n, often cap* ♦ : CHRISTMASTIDE

♦ Christmastide, Christmastime, Noel; *also* Advent; Christmas, nativity, Xmas, yule

yum·my \'yə-mē\ *adj* **yum·mi·er; -est** ♦ : highly attractive or pleasing

♦ ambrosial, appetizing, delectable, delicious, flavorful, luscious, palatable, savory, scrumptious, tasty, toothsome — more at DELICIOUS

yup·pie \'yə-pē\ *n* [prob. fr. *young urban professional* + *-ie* (as in hip*pie*)] : a young college-educated adult employed in a well-paying profession and living and working in or near a large city — **yup·pie·dom** \-dəm\ *n*

yurt \'yùrt\ *n* : a light round tent of skins or felt stretched over a lattice framework used by pastoral peoples of inner Asia

YWCA \,wī-,də-bəl-yù-(,)sē-'ā\ *n* : Young Women's Christian Association

YWHA \-,āch-'ā\ *n* : Young Women's Hebrew Association

Z

¹z \'zē\ *n, pl* **z's** *or* **zs** *often cap* : the 26th letter of the English alphabet

²z *abbr* **1** zero **2** zone

Z *symbol* atomic number

Zach *abbr* Zacharias

Zach·a·ri·as \,za-kə-'rī-əs\ *n* : ZECHARIAH

Zair·ian \zä-'ir-ē-ən\ *n* : a native or inhabitant of Zaire — **Zairian** *adj*

Zam·bi·an \'zam-bē-ən\ *n* : a native or inhabitant of Zambia — **Zambian** *adj*

za·ni·ness \'zā-nē-nəs\ *n* ♦ : the quality or state of being absurd or foolish

♦ absurdity, asininity, balminess, craziness, daftness, foolishness, inanity, insanity, lunacy, madness, silliness

¹za·ny \'zā-nē\ *n, pl* **zanies** [It *zanni*, a traditional masked clown, fr. It dial. *Zanni*, nickname for It *Giovanni* John]

1 : a person who acts in a comical manner to amuse others : CLOWN **2** : a silly or foolish person

²zany *adj* **za·ni·er; -est** **1** : characteristic of a zany **2** ♦ : having an absurd or foolish manner or nature : CRAZY — **za·ni·ly** \'zā-nə-lē, 'zān-ºl-ē\ *adv*

♦ absurd, asinine, balmy, crazy, cuckoo, daft, fatuous, foolish, nutty, sappy, screwball, silly, wacky — more at FOOLISH

zap \'zap\ *vb* **zapped; zap·ping** **1** : to hit with or as if with a sudden powerful and usu. harmful force or energy; *esp* : DESTROY, KILL **2** : to heat or cook in a microwave oven ⟨*zapped* the soup⟩

zeal \'zēl\ *n* : eager and ardent interest in the pursuit of something : FERVOR

zeal·ot \'ze-lət\ *n* ♦ : a zealous person; *esp* : a fanatical partisan

♦ crusader, fanatic, militant, partisan; *also* activist; dreamer, visionary; cultist, disciple, follower, votary; addict, aficionado, buff, bug, devotee, enthusiast, fan, fancier, fiend, freak, lover, maniac, nut; backer, patron, promoter, supporter; booster, rooter, well-wisher; faddist

zeal·ous \'ze-ləs\ *adj* : filled with, characterized by, or due to zeal — **zeal·ous·ly** *adv* — **zeal·ous·ness** *n*

ze·bra \'zē-brə\ *n, pl* **zebras** *also* **zebra** : any of several African mammals related to the horse but conspicuously striped with black or dark brown and white or buff

ze·bu \'zē-bü, -byü\ *n* : any of various breeds of domestic oxen developed in India that have a large fleshy hump over the shoulders, a dewlap, drooping ears, and marked resistance to heat and to insect attack

Zech *abbr* Zechariah

Zech·a·ri·ah \ˌze-kə-'rī-ə\ *n* : a book of Jewish and Christian Scripture

zed \'zed\ *n, chiefly Brit* : the letter *z*

zeit·geist \'tsīt-ˌgīst, 'zīt-\ *n* [G, fr. *Zeit* time + *Geist* spirit] : the general intellectual, moral, and cultural state of an era

Zen \'zen\ *n* : a Japanese Buddhist sect that teaches self-discipline, meditation, and attainment of enlightenment through direct intuitive insight

ze·na·na \zə-'nä-nə\ *n* : HAREM

ze·nith \'zē-nəth\ *n* 1 : the point in the heavens directly overhead 2 ♦ : the highest point : ACME

♦ acme, apex, climax, crown, culmination, head, height, meridian, peak, pinnacle, summit, tip-top, top — more at HEIGHT

ze·o·lite \'zē-ə-ˌlīt\ *n* : any of various feldsparlike silicates used esp. as water softeners

Zeph *abbr* Zephaniah

Zeph·a·ni·ah \ˌze-fə-'nī-ə\ *n* : a book of canonical Jewish and Christian Scripture

zeph·yr \'ze-fər\ *n* 1 : a breeze from the west 2 ♦ : a gentle breeze

♦ air, breath, breeze, puff, waft — more at BREEZE

zep·pe·lin \'ze-plən, -pə-lən\ *n* [Count Ferdinand von *Zeppelin* †1917 Ger. airship manufacturer] : a cylindrical rigid blimplike airship

¹**ze·ro** \'zē-rō, 'zir-ō\ *n, pl* **zeros** *also* **zeroes** [ultim. fr. Ar *ṣifr*] 1 ♦ : the numerical symbol 0 2 ♦ : the number represented by the symbol 0 3 : the point at which the graduated degrees or measurements on a scale (as of a thermometer) begin 4 : the lowest point 5 ♦ : a person or thing that has no importance, influence, or independent existence

♦ [1, 2] aught, cipher, naught, nil, nothing, zip; *also* blank, void ♦ [5] nobody, nonentity, nothing, whippersnapper — more at NOBODY

²**zero** *adj* 1 : of, relating to, or being a zero 2 : having no magnitude or quantity 3 : ABSENT, LACKING; *esp* : having no modified inflectional form

³**zero** *vb* : to adjust the sights of a firearm to hit the point aimed at — usu. used with *in*

zero hour *n* 1 : the time at which an event (as a military operation) is scheduled to begin 2 : a time when a vital decision or decisive change must be made

zest \'zest\ *n* 1 : a quality of enhancing enjoyment : PIQUANCY 2 : keen enjoyment : GUSTO — **zest·ful** \-fəl\ *adj* — **zest·ful·ly** *adv* — **zest·ful·ness** *n* — **zesty** \'zes-tē\ *adj*

ze·ta \'zā-tə, 'zē-\ *n* : the 6th letter of the Greek alphabet — Z or ζ

zi·do·vu·dine \zi-'dō-vyü-ˌdēn\ *n* : AZT

¹**zig·zag** \'zig-ˌzag\ *n* : one of a series of short sharp turns, angles, or alterations in a course; *also* : something marked by such a series

²**zigzag** *adv* : in or by a zigzag path

³**zigzag** *adj* : having short sharp turns or angles

⁴**zigzag** *vb* **zig·zagged; zig·zag·ging** : to form into or proceed along a zigzag

zil·lion \'zil-yən\ *n* : a large indeterminate number

Zim·ba·bwe·an \zim-'bä-bwē-ən\ *n* : a native or inhabitant of Zimbabwe — **Zimbabwean** *adj*

zinc \'ziŋk\ *n* : a bluish-white metallic chemical element that is commonly found in minerals and is used esp. in alloys and as a protective coating for iron and steel

zinc oxide *n* : a white solid used esp. as a pigment, in compounding rubber, and in ointments and sunblocks

zine \'zēn\ *n* : a noncommercial publication usu. devoted to specialized subject matter

zin·fan·del \'zin-fən-ˌdel\ *n, often cap* : a dry red table wine made chiefly in California

zing \'ziŋ\ *n* 1 : a shrill humming noise 2 ♦ : the energy and vigor characteristic of a healthy life : VITALITY 3 ♦ : the quality of having activity, drive, and enthusiasm — **zing** *vb*

♦ [2, 3] dash, drive, energy, ginger, go, hardihood, life, pep, sap, snap, vigor (*or* vigour), vim, vitality, zip — more at VIGOR ♦ [3] bounce, esprit, punch, spirit, verve — more at SPIRIT

zing·er \'ziŋ-ər\ *n* : a pointed witty remark or retort

zin·nia \'zi-nē-ə, 'zēn-yə\ *n* : any of a genus of tropical American herbs or low shrubs related to the daisies and widely grown for their showy long-lasting flowers

Zi·on \'zī-ən\ *n* 1 : the Jewish people 2 : the Jewish homeland as a symbol of Judaism or of Jewish national aspiration 3 : HEAVEN 4 : UTOPIA

Zi·on·ism \'zī-ə-ˌni-zəm\ *n* : an international movement orig. for the establishment of a Jewish national or religious community in Palestine and later for the support of modern Israel — **Zi·on·ist** \-nist\ *adj or n*

¹**zip** \'zip\ *vb* **zipped; zip·ping** 1 ♦ : to move, act, or function with speed or vigor 2 : to travel with a sharp hissing or humming sound 3 ♦ : to add zest, interest, or life to — often used with *up*

♦ [1] barrel, career, course, dash, fly, hurry, race, rip, rocket, run, rush, shoot, speed, whirl, whisk, zoom — more at HURRY ♦ *or* **zip up** [3] brace, energize, enliven, fire, invigorate, jazz up, liven up, pep up, quicken, stimulate, vitalize, vivify — more at ANIMATE

²**zip** *n* 1 : a sudden sharp hissing sound 2 ♦ : the quality of being active, enthusiastic, or motivated : VIM

♦ bounce, dash, drive, esprit, ginger, pep, punch, snap, spirit, verve, vim, zing — more at SPIRIT

³**zip** *n* ♦ : the absence of any significant quality or amount : NOTHING, ZERO

♦ aught, cipher, naught (*also* nought), nil, nothing, oh, zero — more at ZERO

⁴**zip** *vb* **zipped; zip·ping** : to close or open with a zipper

zip code *n, often cap Z&I&P* [*z*one *i*mprovement *p*lan] : a number that identifies each postal delivery area in the U.S.

zip file *n* : a computer file in which a large amount of repeated information has been removed to make it smaller

zip line *n* : a cable suspended usu. over an incline to which a rider is harnessed

zip·per \'zi-pər\ *n* : a fastener consisting of two rows of metal or plastic teeth on strips of tape and a sliding piece that closes an opening by drawing the teeth together

zip·py \'zi-pē\ *adj* **zip·pi·er; -est** 1 : very speedy ⟨a ∼ car⟩ 2 : strikingly appealing ⟨∼ clothes⟩

zir·con \'zər-ˌkän\ *n* : a zirconium-containing mineral transparent varieties of which are used as gems

zir·co·ni·um \ˌzər-'kō-nē-əm\ *n* : a gray corrosion-resistant metallic chemical element used esp. in alloys and ceramics

zit \'zit\ *n* : PIMPLE

zith·er \'zi-thər, -thər\ *n* : a musical instrument having 30 to 40 strings played with plectrum and fingers

zi·ti \'zē-tē\ *n, pl* **ziti** [It] : medium-size tubular pasta

Zn *symbol* zinc

zo·di·ac \'zō-dē-ˌak\ *n* [ME, fr. MF *zodiaque*, fr. L *zodiacus*, fr. Gk *zōidiakos*, fr. *zōidion* carved figure, sign of the zodiac, fr. dim. of *zōion* living being, figure] **1** : an imaginary belt in the heavens that encompasses the paths of most of the planets and that is divided into 12 constellations or signs **2** : a figure representing the signs of the zodiac and their symbols — **zo·di·a·cal** \zō-'dī-ə-kəl\ *adj*

zom·bie *also* **zom·bi** \'zäm-bē\ *n* : a person who is believed to have died and been brought back to life without speech or free will

zon·al \'zōn-ᵊl\ *adj* : of, relating to, or having the form of a zone — **zon·al·ly** *adv*

¹zone \'zōn\ *n* [ME, fr. AF, fr. L *zona* belt, zone, fr. Gk *zōnē*] **1** : any of five great divisions of the earth's surface made according to latitude and temperature including the torrid zone, two temperate zones, and two frigid zones **2** : something that forms an encircling band ⟨a ∼ of tissue⟩ **3 a** ♦ : an area that is distinguished in some way from neighboring areas **b** : a section of an area or territory created for a particular purpose ⟨business ∼⟩ ⟨postal ∼⟩

♦ area, belt, land, region, tract — more at REGION

²zone *vb* **zoned; zon·ing 1** : ENCIRCLE **2** : to arrange in or mark off into zones; *esp* : to divide (as a city) into sections reserved for different purposes

zonked \'zäŋkt\ *adj* : being or acting as if under the influence of alcohol or a drug : HIGH

zoo \'zü\ *n, pl* **zoos** : a park where wild animals are kept for exhibition

zoo·ge·og·ra·phy \ˌzō-ə-jē-'ä-grə-fē\ *n* : a branch of biogeography concerned with the geographical distribution of animals — **zoo·ge·og·ra·pher** \-fər\ *n* — **zoo·geo·graph·ic** \-ˌjē-ə-'gra-fik\ *also* **zoo·geo·graph·i·cal** \-fi-kəl\ *adj*

zoo·keep·er \'zü-ˌkē-pər\ *n* : a person who cares for animals in a zoo

zool *abbr* zoological; zoology

zoological garden *n* : ZOO

zo·ol·o·gy \zō-'ä-lə-jē\ *n* : a branch of biology that deals with the classification and the properties and vital phenomena of animals — **zo·o·log·i·cal** \ˌzō-ə-'lä-ji-kəl\ *adj* — **zo·ol·o·gist** \zō-'ä-lə-jist\ *n*

¹zoom \'züm\ *vb* **1 a** ♦ : to move with a loud hum or buzz **b** : to move or increase suddenly or rapidly : ZIP **2** ♦ : to gain altitude quickly **3** : to focus a camera or microscope using a special lens that permits the apparent distance of the object to be varied

♦ [1a] buzz, drone, hum, whir, whish, whiz, zip — more at WHIR ♦ [2] rocket, shoot, skyrocket, soar — more at SKYROCKET

²zoom *n* **1** : the act or process of zooming **2** ♦ : the sound of something that zooms

♦ buzz, drone, hum, purr, whir, whiz — more at HUM

zoom lens *n* : a camera lens in which the image size can be varied continuously while the image remains in focus

zoo·mor·phic \ˌzō-ə-'mȯr-fik\ *adj* **1** : having the form of an animal **2** : of, relating to, or being the representation of a deity in the form or with the attributes of an animal

zoo·plank·ton \ˌzō-ə-'plaŋk-tən, -ˌtän\ *n* : plankton composed of animals

zoo·spore \'zō-ə-ˌspȯr\ *n* : a motile spore

zoot suit \'züt-\ *n* : a flashy suit of extreme cut typically consisting of a thigh-length jacket with wide padded shoulders and pants that are wide at the top and narrow at the bottom — **zoot-suit·er** \-ˌsü-tər\ *n*

Zo·ro·as·tri·an·ism \ˌzȯr-ə-'was-trē-ə-ˌni-zəm\ *n* : a religion founded by the Persian prophet Zoroaster — **Zo·ro·as·tri·an** \-trē-ən\ *adj or n*

zounds \'zaundz\ *interj* [euphemism for *God's wounds*] — used as a mild oath

zoy·sia \'zȯi-shə, -zhə, -sē-ə, -zē-ə\ *n* : any of a genus of creeping perennial grasses having fine wiry leaves and including some used as lawn grasses

ZPG *abbr* zero population growth

Zr *symbol* zirconium

zuc·chet·to \zü-'ke-tō, tsü-\ *n, pl* **-tos** [It] : a small round skullcap worn by Roman Catholic ecclesiastics

zuc·chi·ni \zü-'kē-nē\ *n, pl* **-ni** *or* **-nis** [It] : a smooth cylindrical usu. dark green summer squash; *also* : a plant that bears zucchini

Zu·lu \'zü-ˌlü\ *n, pl* **Zulu** *or* **Zulus** : a member of a Bantu-speaking people of South Africa; *also* : the Bantu language of the Zulus

Zu·ni \'zü-nē\ *or* **Zu·ñi** \-nyē\ *n, pl* **Zuni** *or* **Zunis** *or* **Zuñi** *or* **Zuñis** : a member of an American Indian people of western New Mexico; *also* : the language of the Zuni people

zwie·back \'swē-ˌbak, 'swī-, 'zwē-, 'zwī-, -ˌbäk\ *n* [G, lit., twice baked, fr. *zwie*- twice + *backen* to bake] : a usu. sweetened bread that is baked and then sliced and toasted until dry and crisp

Zwing·li·an \'zwiŋ-glē-ən, 'swiŋ-, -lē-; 'tsfiŋ-lē-\ *adj* : of or relating to the Swiss religious reformer Ulrich Zwingli or his teachings — **Zwinglian** *n*

zy·de·co \'zī-də-ˌkō\ *n* : popular music of southern Louisiana that combines tunes of French origin with elements of Caribbean music and the blues

zy·gote \'zī-ˌgōt\ *n* : a cell formed by the union of two sexual cells; *also* : the developing individual produced from such a cell — **zy·got·ic** \zī-'gä-tik\ *adj*

BASIC ENGLISH PUNCTUATION

The English writing system uses punctuation marks to separate groups of words for meaning and emphasis; to convey an idea of the variations of pitch, volume, pauses, and intonations of speech; and to help avoid ambiguity. English punctuation marks, together with general rules and examples of their use, follow.

APOSTROPHE '

1. Indicates the possessive case of nouns and indefinite pronouns.

   the boy's mother

   the boys' mothers

2. Marks omissions in contracted words.

   didn't

   o'clock

3. Often forms plurals of letters, figures, and words referred to as words.

   You should dot your *i*'s and cross your *t*'s.

   several *8*'s

BRACKETS [ ]

1. Set off extraneous data such as editorial additions especially within quoted material.

   wrote that the author was "trying to dazzle his readers with phrases like *jeu de mots* [play on words]"

2. Function as parentheses within parentheses.

   Bowman Act (22 Stat., ch. 4, § [or sec.] 4, p. 50)

COLON :

1. Introduces a word, clause, or phrase that explains, illustrates, amplifies, or restates what has gone before.

   The sentence was poorly constructed: it lacked both unity and coherence.

2. Introduces a series.

   Three countries were represented: England, France, and Belgium.

3. Introduces lengthy quoted material set off from the rest of a text by indentation but not by quotation marks.

   I quote from the text of Chapter One:

4. Separates data in time-telling and data in bibliographic and biblical references.

   8:30 a.m.

   New York: Smith Publishing Co.

   John 4:10

5. Follows the salutation in formal correspondence.

   Dear Sir:

   Gentlemen:

COMMA ,

1. Separates main clauses joined by a coordinating conjunction (such as *and, but, or, nor,* or *for*) and very short clauses not so joined.

    She knew very little about him, and he volunteered nothing.

    I came, I saw, I conquered.

2. Sets off an adverbial clause (or a long phrase) that precedes the main clause.

    When she found that her friends had deserted her, she sat down and cried.

3. Sets off from the rest of the sentence transitional words and expressions (such as *on the contrary* or *on the other hand*), conjunctive adverbs (such as *consequently, furthermore,* or *however*), and expressions that introduce an illustration or example (such as *namely* or *for example*).

    Your second question, on the other hand, remains open.

    She expects to travel through two countries, namely, France and England.

4. Separates words, phrases, or clauses in series and coordinate adjectives modifying a noun.

    Men, women, and children crowded into the square.

    The harsh, cold wind was strong.

5. Sets off from the rest of the sentence parenthetical elements (as nonrestrictive modifiers).

    Our guide, who wore a blue beret, was an experienced traveler.

    We visited Gettysburg, the site of the famous battle.

6. Introduces a direct quotation, terminates a direct quotation that is neither a question nor an exclamation, and encloses split quotations.

    John said, "I am leaving."

    "I am leaving," John said.

    "I am leaving," John said with determination, "even if you want me to stay."

7. Sets off words in direct address, absolute phrases, and mild interjections.

    You may go, Mary, if you wish.

    I fear the encounter, his temper being what it is.

    Ah, that's my idea of an excellent dinner.

8. Separates a question from the rest of the sentence which it ends.

    It's a fine day, isn't it?

9. Indicates the omission of a word or words, and especially a word or words used earlier in the sentence.

    Common stocks are preferred by some investors; bonds, by others.

10. Is used to avoid ambiguity.

    To Mary, Jane was someone special.

11. Is used to group numbers into units of three in separating thousands, millions, etc.

    Smithville, pop. 100,000

    But, it is generally not used in numbers of four figures, in page numbers, in dates, or in street numbers.

    3600 rpm

    the year 1973

    page 1411

    4507 Smith Street

12. Punctuates an inverted name.

    Smith, John W., Jr.

13. Separates a proper name from a following academic, honorary, governmental, or military title.

    John Smith, M.D.

14. Sets off geographical names (as state or country from city), items in dates, and addresses from the rest of a text.

> Shreveport, Louisiana, is the site of a large air base.
>
> On Sunday, June 23, 1940, he was wounded.
>
> Number 10 Downing Street, London, is a famous address.

But, when only the year or the month and year are given, the comma is usually omitted

> October 1929 brought an end to all that.

15. Follows the salutation in informal correspondence and follows the closing line of a formal or informal letter.

> Dear Mary,
>
> Affectionately,
>
> Very truly yours,

DASH —

1. Usually marks an abrupt change or break in the continuity of a sentence.

> When in 1960 the stockpile was sold off—indeed, dumped as surplus—natural-rubber sales were hard hit. —Barry Commoner

2. Introduces a summary statement after a series.

> Oil, steel, and wheat—these are the sinews of industrialization.

3. Often precedes the attribution of a quotation.

> My foot is on my native heath. . . . —Sir Walter Scott

ELLIPSIS . . . .

1. Indicates the omission of one or more words within a quoted passage.

> The head is not more native to the heart . . . than is the throne of Denmark to thy father. —Shakespeare

2. Indicates halting speech or an unfinished sentence in dialogue.

> "I'd like to . . . that is . . . if you don't mind. . . ." He faltered and then stopped speaking.

3. Indicates the omission of one or more sentences within a quoted passage or the omission of words at the end of a sentence by using four spaced dots the last of which represents the period.

> That recovering the manuscripts would be worth almost any effort is without question. . . . The monetary value of a body of Shakespeare's manuscripts would be almost incalculable —Charlton Ogburn

4. Usually indicates omission of one or more lines of poetry when ellipsis is extended the length of the line.

> Thus driven
> By the bright shadow of that lovely dream,
> . . . .
> He fled.
> —P. B. Shelley

EXCLAMATION POINT !

1. Terminates an emphatic phrase or sentence.

> Get out of here!

2. Terminates an emphatic interjection.

> Encore!

HYPHEN -

1. Marks separation or division of a word at the end of a line.

   mill-[end of line]stone

   pas-[end of line]sion

2. Is used between some prefix and word combinations, such as prefix + proper name

   pre-Renaissance

   Or, prefix ending with a vowel + word beginning often with the same vowel.

   co-opted

   re-ink

   Or, stressed prefix + word, especially when this combination is similar to a different one.

   re-cover a sofa

3. Is used in some compounds, especially those containing prepositions.

   president-elect

   sister-in-law

4. Is often used between elements of a unit modifier in attributive position in order to avoid ambiguity.

   He is a small-business man.

   She has gray-green eyes.

5. Suspends the first part of a hyphenated compound when used with another hyphenated compound.

   a six- or eight-cylinder engine

6. Is used in writing out compound numbers between 21 and 99.

   thirty-four

   one hundred twenty-eight

7. Is used between the numerator and the denominator in writing out fractions especially when they are used as modifiers.

   a two-thirds majority of the vote

8. Serves instead of the phrase "(up) to and including" between numbers and dates.

   pages 40-98

   the decade 1960-69

PARENTHESES ( )

1. Set off supplementary, parenthetical, or explanatory material when the interruption is more marked than that usually indicated by commas.

   Three old destroyers (all now out of commission) will be scrapped.

   He is hoping (as we all are) that this time he will succeed.

2. Enclose numerals which confirm a written number in a text.

   Delivery will be made in thirty (30) days.

3. Enclose numbers or letters in a series.

   We must set forth (1) our long-term goals, (2) our immediate objectives, and (3) the means at our disposal.

PERIOD .

1. Terminates sentences or sentence fragments that are neither interrogatory nor exclamatory.

   Obey the law.

   He obeyed the law.

2. Follows some abbreviations and contractions.

   Dr.

   Jr.

   etc.

   cont.

QUESTION MARK ?

1. Terminates a direct question.

   Who threw the bomb?

   "Who threw the bomb?" he asked.

2. Indicates the writer's ignorance or uncertainty.

   Omar Khayyám, Persian poet (?-?1123)

QUOTATION MARKS, DOUBLE " "

1. Enclose direct quotations in conventional usage.

   He said, "I am leaving."

2. Enclose words or phrases borrowed from others, words used in a special way, and often slang when it is introduced into formal writing.

   He called himself "emperor," but he was really just a dictator.

   He was arrested for smuggling "smack."

3. Enclose titles of short poems, short stories, articles, lectures, chapters of books, songs, short musical compositions, and radio and TV programs.

   Robert Frost's "Dust of Snow"

   Pushkin's "Queen of Spades"

   The third chapter of Treasure Island is entitled "The Black Spot."

   "America the Beautiful"

   Ravel's "Bolero"

   NBC's "Today Show"

4. Are used with other punctuation marks in the following ways:

   The period and the comma fall within the quotation marks.

   "I am leaving," he said.

   His camera was described as "waterproof," but "moisture-resistant" would have been a better description.

   The semicolon falls outside the quotation marks.

   He spoke of his "little cottage in the country"; he might have called it a mansion.

   The dash, question mark, and exclamation point fall within the quotation marks when they refer to the quoted matter; they fall outside when they refer to the whole sentence.

   He asked, "When did you leave?"

   What is the meaning of "the open door"?

   The sergeant shouted, "Halt!"

   Save us from his "mercy"!

QUOTATION MARKS, SINGLE ' '

Enclose a quotation within a quotation in conventional usage.

The witness said, "I distinctly heard him say, 'Don't be late,' and then I heard the door close."

SEMICOLON ;

1. Links main clauses not joined by coordinating conjunctions.

   Some people have the ability to write well; others do not.

2. Links main clauses joined by conjunctive adverbs (such as *consequently*, *furthermore*, or *however*).

   Speeding is illegal; furthermore, it is very dangerous.

3. Links clauses which themselves contain commas even when such clauses are joined by coordinating conjunctions.

   Mr. King, whom you met yesterday, will be our representative on the committee; but you should follow the proceedings carefully yourself, because they are vitally important to us.

VIRGULE /

1. Separates alternatives.

   . . . intended for high-heat and/or high-speed applications —F. S. Badger, Jr.

2. Separates successive divisions (such as months or years) of an extended period of time.

   the fiscal year 1972/73

   the June/July issue of the magazine

3. Serves as a dividing line between run-in lines of poetry.

   Say, sages, what's the charm on earth / Can turn death's dart aside? —Robert Burns

4. Often represents *per* in abbreviations.

   9 ft/sec

   20 km/hr